PRESENTED TO

_____

_____

FROM

_____

_____

ON

_____

_____

*Your word is a lamp to my feet
and a light for my path*

PSALM 119:105

Old Testament Chronology

Creation	Fall	Flood	Babel
?	?	?	?

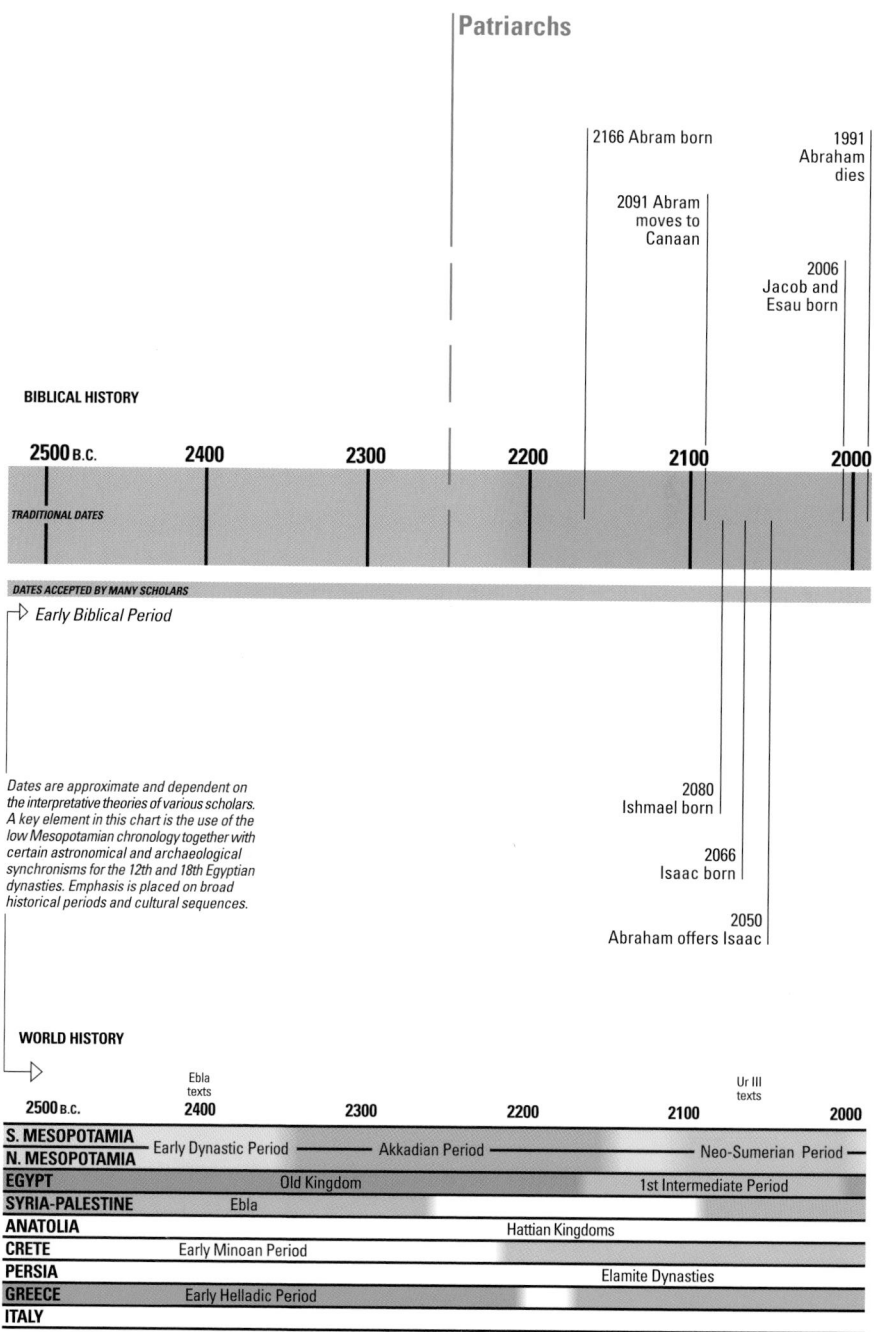

Patriarchs

2166 Abram born

1991
Abraham
dies

2091 Abram
moves to
Canaan

2006
Jacob and
Esau born

BIBLICAL HISTORY

| 2500 B.C. | 2400 | 2300 | 2200 | 2100 | 2000 |

TRADITIONAL DATES

DATES ACCEPTED BY MANY SCHOLARS

▷ *Early Biblical Period*

*Dates are approximate and dependent on
the interpretative theories of various scholars.
A key element in this chart is the use of the
low Mesopotamian chronology together with
certain astronomical and archaeological
synchronisms for the 12th and 18th Egyptian
dynasties. Emphasis is placed on broad
historical periods and cultural sequences.*

2080
Ishmael born

2066
Isaac born

2050
Abraham offers Isaac

WORLD HISTORY

▷

	Ebla texts			Ur III texts	
2500 B.C.	2400	2300	2200	2100	2000

S. MESOPOTAMIA					
S. MESOPOTAMIA **N. MESOPOTAMIA**	Early Dynastic Period ————	Akkadian Period ————		Neo-Sumerian Period —	
EGYPT	Old Kingdom			1st Intermediate Period	
SYRIA-PALESTINE	Ebla				
ANATOLIA			Hattian Kingdoms		
CRETE	Early Minoan Period				
PERSIA				Elamite Dynasties	
GREECE	Early Helladic Period				
ITALY					

Old Testament Chronology

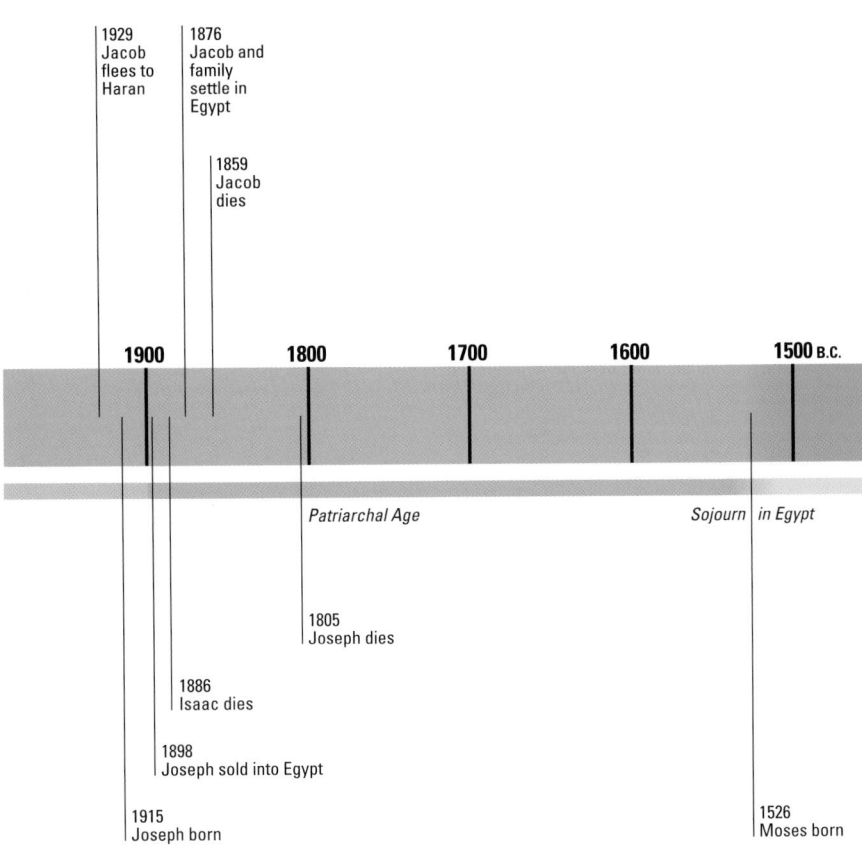

	1900	**1800**	**1700**	**1600**	**1500** B.C.

1929
Jacob
flees to
Haran

1876
Jacob and
family
settle in
Egypt

1859
Jacob
dies

Patriarchal Age

Sojourn | *in Egypt*

1805
Joseph dies

1886
Isaac dies

1898
Joseph sold into Egypt

1915
Joseph born

1526
Moses born

Cappadocian texts		Mari texts	Hammurapi texts		
1900	**1800**		**1700**	**1600**	**1500** B.C.

Isin-Larsa Period

Old Babylonian Period

Middle Kingdom

2nd Intermediate (Hyksos) Period

New Kingdom

Amorite Period

Hyksos Period

Late Canaanite Period

Hittite Old Kingdom

Middle Minoan Period

Middle Helladic Period

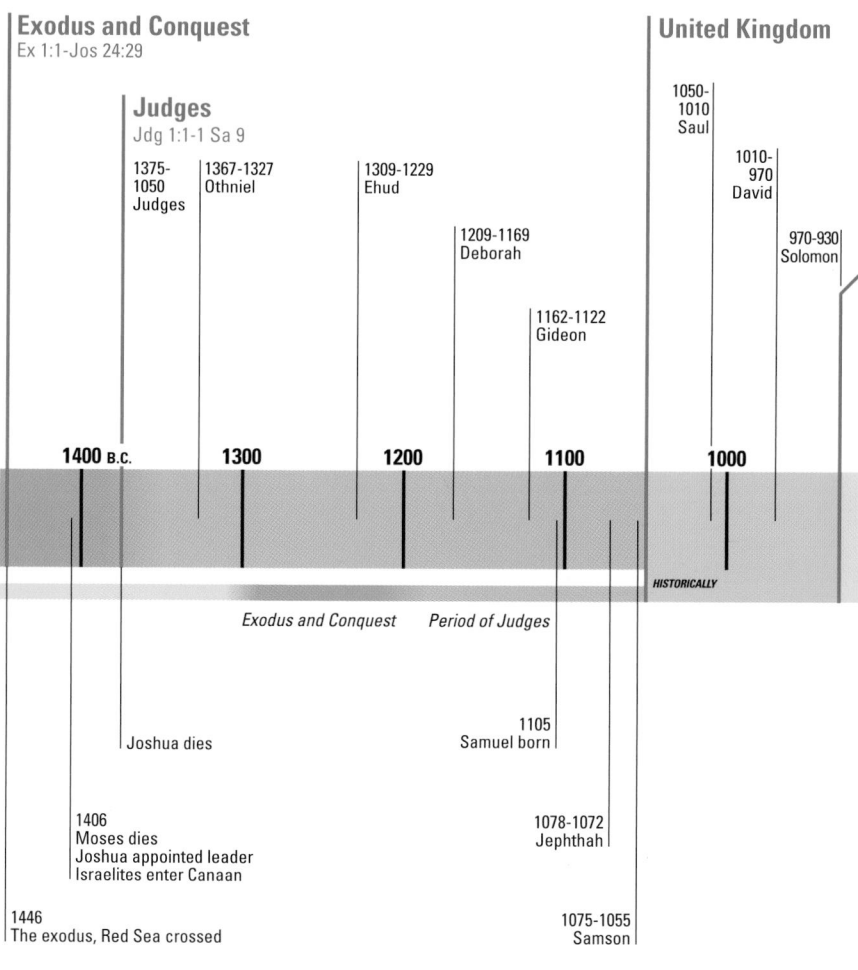

Exodus and Conquest
Ex 1:1-Jos 24:29

United Kingdom

Judges
Jdg 1:1-1 Sa 9

1050-
1010
Saul

1375-
1050
Judges

1367-1327
Othniel

1309-1229
Ehud

1010-
970
David

1209-1169
Deborah

970-930
Solomon

1162-1122
Gideon

1400 B.C.	1300	1200	1100	1000

HISTORICALLY

Exodus and Conquest   *Period of Judges*

1105
Samuel born

Joshua dies

1406
Moses dies
Joshua appointed leader
Israelites enter Canaan

1078-1072
Jephthah

1446
The exodus, Red Sea crossed

1075-1055
Samson

	Nuzi texts	Ugaritic texts					Shishak inscription
		Amarna texts	Merneptah inscription	Medinet Habu inscriptions			
1400 B.C.		**1300**	**1200**	**1100**		**1000**	
S. MESOPOTAMIA		Kassite Period					
N. MESOPOTAMIA	←—Mitannian Kingdom		Middle Assyrian Period				
EGYPT		New Kingdom					
SYRIA-PALESTINE	Late Canaanite Period			Sea Peoples			Phoenician,
ANATOLIA	Hittite Empire			Phrygian Period			
CRETE		Late Minoan Period					Dorian States
PERSIA							
GREECE	Late Helladic (Mycenean) Period					Dorian States	
ITALY							

Old Testament Chronology

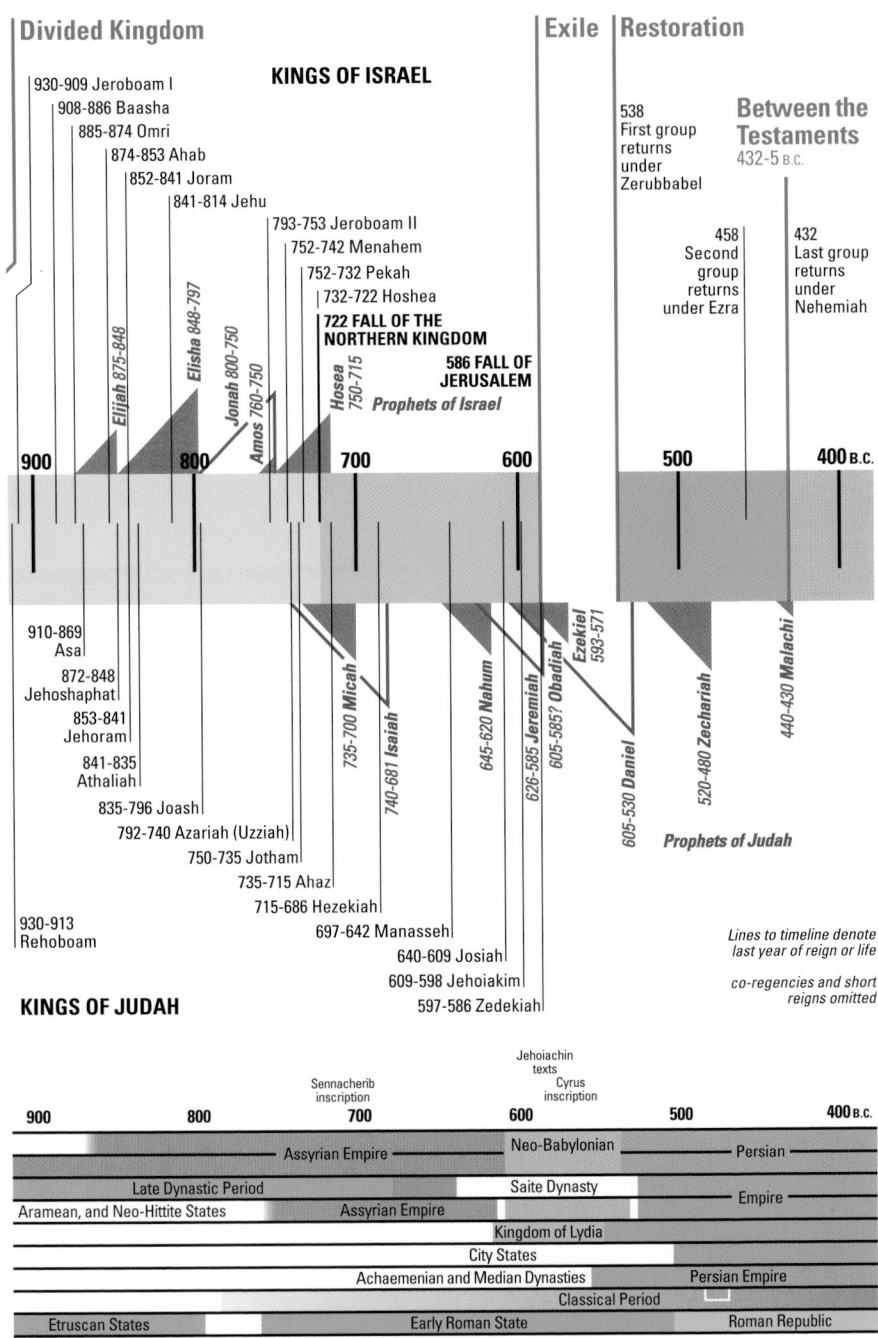

Divided Kingdom   **Exile** | **Restoration**

KINGS OF ISRAEL

930-909 Jeroboam I
908-886 Baasha
885-874 Omri
874-853 Ahab
852-841 Joram
841-814 Jehu

793-753 Jeroboam II
752-742 Menahem
752-732 Pekah
732-722 Hoshea
722 FALL OF THE NORTHERN KINGDOM
586 FALL OF JERUSALEM
Prophets of Israel

Elijah 875-848
Elisha 848-797
Jonah 800-750
Amos 760-750
Hosea 750-715

538
First group returns under Zerubbabel

Between the Testaments
432-5 B.C.

458
Second group returns under Ezra

432
Last group returns under Nehemiah

900   **800**   **700**   **600**   **500**   **400** B.C.

910-869 Asa
872-848 Jehoshaphat
853-841 Jehoram
841-835 Athaliah
835-796 Joash
792-740 Azariah (Uzziah)
750-735 Jotham
735-715 Ahaz
715-686 Hezekiah
930-913 Rehoboam
697-642 Manasseh
640-609 Josiah
609-598 Jehoiakim
597-586 Zedekiah

735-700 Micah
740-681 Isaiah
645-620 Nahum
626-585 Jeremiah
605-585? Obadiah
Ezekiel 593-571
605-530 Daniel
520-480 Zechariah
440-430 Malachi

Prophets of Judah

KINGS OF JUDAH

Lines to timeline denote
last year of reign or life

co-regencies and short
reigns omitted

Jehoiachin texts
Cyrus inscription
Sennacherib inscription

900   **800**   **700**   **600**   **500**   **400** B.C.

———— Assyrian Empire ————
Neo-Babylonian
Persian
Late Dynastic Period
Saite Dynasty
Aramean, and Neo-Hittite States | Assyrian Empire
Empire
Kingdom of Lydia
City States
Achaemenian and Median Dynasties
Persian Empire
Classical Period
Etruscan States | Early Roman State
Roman Republic

New Testament Chronology

Christ's Early Life
(Mt 1-2; Lk 1-2)

Christ's Ministry
(Mt 2-28; Mk; Lk 3-24; Jn)

6/5 B.C.
Christ born

30 Christ crucified
The ascension

29 Christ at Feast of Tabernacles
Christ at Feast of Dedication

28/29 John the Baptist dies

A.D. 7/8
Christ in temple
at age 12

27/28
John the Baptist imprisoned

26
Christ baptized

26
Christ begins
ministry

26
John the Baptist
begins ministry

| 30 B.C. | 20 | 10 | B.C. A.D. | 10 | 20 | 30 |

A.D. 6-15
Annas I

37-4 B.C.
Herod the Great

4 B.C.
Herod the
Great dies

A.D. 6
Roman
governors
begin rule

A.D. 26-36
Pontius Pilate

RULERS IN PALESTINE

| 30 B.C. | 20 | 10 | B.C. A.D. | 10 | 20 | 30 |

27 B.C. – A.D. 14
Augustus

A.D. 14
Augustus dies

ROMAN EMPERORS

©1985 The Zondervan Corporation

New Testament Chronology

The Early Church
(Acts-Revelation)

30 Pentecost

49-50 Jerusalem Council

46-48 Paul's first missionary journey

50-52 Paul's second missionary journey

35 Paul converted to Christianity

51/52 1,2 Thessalonians written

44 James martyred

53-57 Paul's third missionary journey

66/67 2 Timothy written

95 Revelation written

57 Romans written

67-68 Paul dies

90-95 John exiled on Patmos

Peter imprisoned

59-61/62 Paul imprisoned in Rome

40 **50** **60** **70** **80** **90** **A.D.100**

Lines to timeline denote end of journey or reign

47-59 Ananias

4 B.C. – A.D. 39 Herod Antipas

44 Herod Agrippa I dies

70 Jerusalem destroyed

44-100 Herod Agrippa II

37-44 Herod Agrippa I

40 **50** **60** **70** **80** **90** **A.D.100**

37-41 Caligula

41-54 Claudius

69 Galba, Otho, Vitellius

79-81 Titus

A.D. 14-37 Tiberius

54-68 Nero

69-79 Vespasian

81-96 Domitian

96-98 Nerva

ZONDERVAN

TNIV

STUDY BIBLE

ZONDERVAN

TNIV

STUDY BIBLE

EDITORS, 2006

General Editor
Kenneth L. Barker

Associate Editors
John H. Stek
Ronald Youngblood

ORIGINAL EDITORS, 1985	**REVISION EDITORS, 2002**
General Editor	**General Editor**
Kenneth L. Barker	Kenneth L. Barker
Associate Editors	**Associate Editors**
Donald W. Burdick	John H. Stek
John H. Stek	Walter W. Wessel
Walter W. Wessel	Ronald Youngblood
Ronald Youngblood	

ZONDERVAN™

GRAND RAPIDS, MICHIGAN 49530 USA

WWW.ZONDERVAN.COM

TRIBUTES

TRIBUTE TO EDWIN H. PALMER

Edwin H. Palmer, who had served so capably as Executive Secretary of the NIV Committee on Bible Translation and as coordinator of all translation work on the NIV, was appointed General Editor of the *NIV Study Bible* by Zondervan in 1979. On September 16, 1980, he departed this life to "be with Christ, which is better by far" (Philippians 1:23). Before his death, however, he had laid most of the plans for the *NIV Study Bible*, had recruited the majority of the contributors, and had done some editorial work on the first manuscripts submitted. We gratefully acknowledge his significant contribution to the earliest stages of the product of which this is a revision.

TRIBUTE TO DONALD BURDICK

Donald Burdick was one of the original Associate Editors of the 1985 edition of the *NIV Study Bible*, with special responsibility for the New Testament. He departed this life on January 4, 1996, to be "at home with the Lord" (2 Corinthians 5:8)—before work commenced on the fully revised edition in 1997. We gratefully acknowledge his outstanding work on the original *NIV Study Bible*, on which the *Zondervan TNIV Study Bible* is based.

TRIBUTE TO WALTER WESSEL

Walter Wessel was also one of the Associate Editors of the original *NIV Study Bible* (1985), as well as of the 2002 fully revised edition, with special responsibility for the New Testament. Although he was physically unable to be present at our work session in March of 2002, his handwritten proposals were available to us. Then he went home to be with his Lord on April 21, 2002. We thankfully acknowledge his substantial contributions to the *NIV Study Bible* (fully revised). "Blessed are the dead who die in the Lord . . . they will rest from their labor, for their deeds will follow them" (Revelation 14:13).

TABLE OF CONTENTS

TABLE OF CONTENTS

MAPS

CHARTS

A WORD TO THE READER

Today's New International Version (TNIV) is a revision of the New International Version (NIV). Among the many English versions of the Bible that appeared in the twentieth century, the NIV (1973, 1978, 1984) has gained the widest readership in all parts of the English-speaking world. It was a completely new translation made by over a hundred scholars working directly from the best available Hebrew, Aramaic and Greek texts. The fact that participants from the United States, Great Britain, Canada, Australia and New Zealand worked together gave the project its international scope. That they were from many denominations—including Anglican, Assemblies of God, Baptist, Brethren, Christian Reformed, Church of Christ, Evangelical Covenant, Evangelical Free, Lutheran, Mennonite, Methodist, Nazarene, Presbyterian, Wesleyan and other churches—helped to safeguard the translation from sectarian bias. Responsibility for the NIV text, and now also for the text of the TNIV, is held by a self-governing body, the Committee on Bible Translation (CBT), composed of biblical scholars from colleges, universities and seminaries. During the revision process, many of the original members of CBT have been replaced by other scholars owing to retirement and other causes, but a similar geographical and denominational mix has been maintained.

From the beginning the translators have been united in their commitment to the authority and infallibility of the Bible as God's Word in written form. For them, the Bible contains the divine answer to the deepest needs of humanity, sheds unique light on our path in a dark world and sets forth the way to our eternal well-being. Out of this deep conviction, the Committee has held to certain goals for the NIV and for the present revision: that it would be an accurate translation and one that would have clarity and literary quality and so prove suitable for public and private reading, teaching, preaching, memorizing and liturgical use. The Committee has also sought to preserve a measure of continuity with the long tradition of translating the Scriptures into English.

There is a sense in which the work of translating the Bible is never finished. This very fact has prompted the Committee to engage in an ongoing review of the text of the NIV with the assistance of many other scholars. The chief goal of this review has always been to bring the text of the NIV abreast of contemporary biblical scholarship and of shifts in English idiom and usage. Already in 1978 and again in 1984 various corrections and revisions to the NIV text were made. In the TNIV the Committee offers to the reading public the latest fruits of its review.

The first concern of the translators has continued to be the accuracy of the translation and its faithfulness to the intended meaning of the biblical writers. This has moved the translators to go beyond a formal word-for-word rendering of the original texts. Because thought patterns and syntax differ from language to language, accurate communication of the meaning of the biblical authors demands constant regard for varied contextual uses of words and idioms and for frequent modifications in sentence structures.

To achieve clarity the translators have sometimes supplied words not in the original texts but required by the context. In a few instances, where some uncertainty about such material remained, it is enclosed in corner brackets. As an aid to the reader, sectional headings have been inserted. They are not to be regarded as part of the biblical text and are not intended for oral reading. It is the Committee's hope that these headings may prove more helpful to the reader than the traditional chapter divisions (which were introduced in the thirteenth century).

For the Old Testament the standard Hebrew text, the Masoretic Text as published in the latest editions of *Biblia Hebraica*, has been used throughout. The Masoretic Text tradition contains marginal notations that offer variant readings. These have sometimes been followed instead of the text itself. Because such instances involve variants within the Masoretic tradition, they have not been indicated in the textual notes. In a few cases, words in the basic consonantal text have been divided differently than in the Masoretic

Text. Such cases are usually indicated in the textual footnotes. The Dead Sea Scrolls contain biblical texts that represent an earlier stage of the transmission of the Hebrew text. They have been consulted, as have been the Samaritan Pentateuch and the ancient scribal traditions concerning deliberate textual changes. The translators also consulted the more important early versions—the Greek Septuagint, Aquila, Symmachus and Theodotion, the Latin Vulgate, the Syriac Peshitta, the Aramaic Targums, and for the Psalms the *Juxta Hebraica* of Jerome. Readings from the Dead Sea Scrolls, the scribal traditions and these versions were occasionally followed where the Masoretic Text seemed doubtful and where accepted principles of textual criticism showed that one or more of these textual witnesses appeared to provide the correct reading. In rare cases, the translators have emended the Hebrew text where it appears to have become corrupted at an even earlier stage of its transmission. These departures from the Masoretic Text are also indicated in the textual footnotes. Sometimes the vowel indicators (which are later additions to the basic consonantal text) found in the Masoretic Text did not, in the judgment of the translators, represent the correct vowels for the original text. Accordingly, some words have been read with a different set of vowels. These instances are usually not indicated in the footnotes.

The Greek text used in translating the New Testament has been an eclectic one, based on the latest editions of the Nestle-Aland / United Bible Societies' Greek New Testament. The translators have made their choices among the variant readings in accordance with widely accepted principles of New Testament textual criticism. Footnotes call attention to places where uncertainty remains.

The New Testament authors, writing in Greek, often quote the Old Testament from its ancient Greek version, the Septuagint. This is one reason why some of the Old Testament quotations in the TNIV New Testament are not identical to the corresponding passages in the TNIV Old Testament. Such quotations in the New Testament are indicated with the footnote "(see Septuagint)."

Other footnotes in this version are of several kinds, most of which need no explanation. Those giving alternative translations begin with "Or" and generally introduce the alternative with the last word preceding it in the text, except when it is a single-word alternative. In poetry quoted in a footnote a slash mark indicates a line division.

It should be noted that references to diseases, minerals, flora and fauna, architectural details, clothing, jewelry, musical instruments and other articles cannot always be identified with precision. Also, linear measurements and measures of capacity can only be approximated (see Appendix I). The manner in which Hebrew proper names are to be represented in English has not become fully standardized. In the TNIV the spelling of many names has been revised to conform more closely to current scholarly practice and to the phonetics of the Hebrew originals. A list of such changes can be found on page 2152 in the back of this Bible. A parallel list provides the spelling of these names in the NIV. Although *Selah,* used mainly in the Psalms, is probably a musical term, its meaning is uncertain. Since it may interrupt reading and distract the reader, this word has not been kept in the English text, but every occurrence has been signaled by a footnote.

Three changes of special note in the TNIV are the frequent substitution of "Messiah" for the more traditional "Christ," the replacement of "saints" in most cases with alternative renderings, and a greater sensitivity to shifts in English idiom. A word about each is in order.

While "Messiah" (from the Hebrew) and "Christ" (from the Greek) both mean "Anointed One," what began as a title full of meaning to the early Jewish hearers of the gospel tended in the later Greek-speaking churches to become just another name for Jesus. So where the term is clearly used to designate the God-sent deliverer of Jewish expectations (primarily in the Gospels and Acts), it was judged more appropriate to use "Messiah." However, where this sense seems less prominent (primarily in the Epistles), the transliteration of the Greek word ("Christ") has been retained.

Concerning "saints," current usage (as reflected in major dictionaries of the English language) burdens it with meanings that lie outside the sense of the original-language words. The main Old Testament term that has traditionally been rendered "saints" refers to those who are faithful to God. The New Testament term primarily designates those who have become followers of the Christian Way as people consecrated to God and thus belonging to the Lord in a special sense.

Although a basic core of the English language remains relatively stable, many diverse and complex cultural forces continue to bring about subtle shifts in the meanings and/or connotations of even old, well-established words and phrases. Among the more programmatic changes in the TNIV are the removal of nearly all vocative "O"s and the elimination of most instances of the generic use of masculine nouns and pronouns. Relative to the second of these, the so-called singular "they/their/them," which has been gaining acceptance among careful writers and which actually has a venerable place in English idiom, has been employed to fill in the vocabulary gap in generic nouns and pronouns referring to human beings. Where an individual emphasis is deemed to be present, "anyone" or "everyone" or some other equivalent is generally used as the antecedent of such pronouns.

Sometimes the chapter and/or verse numbering in English translations of the Old Testament differs from that found in published Hebrew texts. This is particularly the case in the Psalms, where the traditional titles are included in the Hebrew verse numbering. Such differences are marked by asterisks (*) in the text and informative footnotes set off in a separate line (or lines) at the bottom of the page. In the New Testament, verse numbers that marked off portions of the traditional English text not supported by the best Greek manuscripts are now set alongside the immediately preceding verse numbers and placed in brackets (see, for example, Matthew 17:20[21]).

Mark 16:9–20 and John 7:53—8: 11, although long accorded virtually equal status with the rest of the Gospels in which they stand, have a very questionable—and confused—standing in the textual history of the New Testament, as noted in the bracketed annotations with which they are set off. A different typeface has now been chosen for these passages to indicate even more clearly their uncertain status.

Basic formatting of the text, such as lining the poetry, paragraphing (both prose and poetry), setting up of (administrative-like) lists, indenting letters and lengthy prayers within narratives, and the insertion of sectional headings, has been the work of the Committee. However, the choice between single-column and double-column formats has been left to the publishers. Also, the issuing of "red-letter" editions is a publisher's choice—one that the Committee does not endorse.

The Committee has again been reminded that every human effort is flawed—including this revision of the NIV. We trust, however, that many will find in it an improved representation of the Word of God, through which they hear his call to faith in our Lord Jesus Christ and to service in his kingdom. We offer this version of the Bible to him in whose name and for whose glory it has been made.

The Committee on Bible Translation

Names of the translators and editors may be secured from the International Bible Society, translation sponsors of the New International Version, 1820 Jet Stream Drive, Colorado Springs, CO 80921-3696 U.S.A.

QUICK START GUIDE

Congratulations on your purchase of the *Zondervan TNIV Study Bible*. You have in your hands a comprehensive, multi-use tool that will greatly enhance your understanding of and appreciation for God's Word.

ABOUT THE *ZONDERVAN TNIV STUDY BIBLE*

You can find out more about Today's New International Version (2005), as well as its bestselling predecessor, the New International Version (1978), in "A Word to the Reader" on page xi.

The team of evangelical scholars who brought the world the *Zondervan NIV Study Bible* in 1985 is the same team that brings you the revised and expanded system of study notes in this *Zondervan TNIV Study Bible*. Not only did this team edit the notes for these two landmark Bibles, but these editors also served as translators for both translations.

WHAT IS A STUDY BIBLE?

you may ask. A study Bible contains the full text of the Bible, along with a veritable library of study aids to help the reader more completely grasp and understand what the text is saying. These notes introduce and explain a wide variety of background information to the Biblical text, providing unparalleled insights for individuals who are ready to devote themselves to serious study of the text.

WHAT HELP DO THESE STUDY FEATURES OFFER ME?

For a full discussion of each of these features—and others—see the Introduction on page xv.

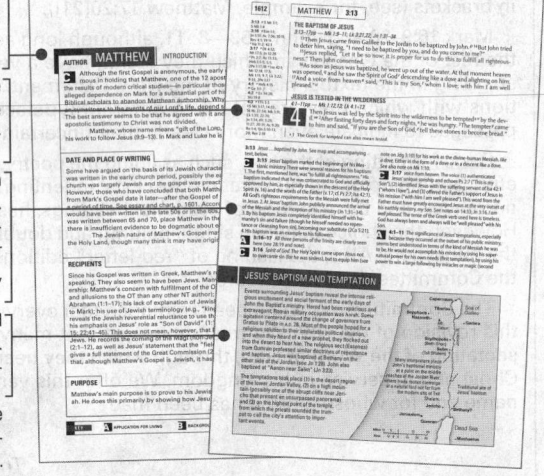

* If you want help understanding who wrote a book of the Bible, when and even why, take a few minutes to read through that book's introduction and outline.
* If you're interested in further study of a theme or concept that comes up in a verse, check the cross-references alongside to find other passages on the same theme.
* Over 20,000 bottom-of-page notes assist you in grasping what the Bible authors were saying. If you have a question as you're reading, simply glance down to the study notes to look for an explanation on that particular passage, clause, phrase or word.
* Look for the in-text maps, charts, diagrams and illustrations sprinkled throughout the Bible. They summarize and explain important information.
* The Bible's historical books often tell the same story from differing viewpoints. The four Gospels (stories of Jesus' life) are good examples. See the passages listed at the very beginning of the first Gospel, Matthew, just prior to Matthew 1:1 on page 1606. Looking up the listed passages will shed more light on the story.
* For a more in-depth study of a topic or theme (see cross-references, above), check out the more than 700-entry topical index on page 2153. Its alphabetical entries help you hone in on a subject of particular interest, allowing you to create your own study path.
* If you're a visual learner or geography lover, you'll enjoy the 16 pages of satellite-generated, full-color maps at the very end of this Bible. They're supplemented by a complete map index (page 2315).
* If you remember a specific word or words in a verse but not where it's found, the TNIV concordance on page 2319 can help. Words and names are listed alphabetically, along with their more significant verse references.

Why not go ahead and spend a few minutes trying out each of these features? If you're like most readers, certain helps will catch your interest and eventually become trusted friends as you spend time with your Bible. May God bless you as you study and come to understand the timeless truths of the Bible as priceless treasures for today.

INTRODUCTION TO THE
ZONDERVAN TNIV STUDY BIBLE

ABOUT THE *ZONDERVAN TNIV STUDY BIBLE*

Today's New International Version of the Bible (TNIV) is unsurpassed in accuracy, clarity and literary grace. The commitments that led to the completion of this version guided the General Editor and Associate Editors of the 2002 fully revised *NIV Study Bible* to adapt it to the new text of the TNIV, resulting in this *Zondervan TNIV Study Bible*. Their purpose was unchanged: to communicate the word of God to the hearts of people.

Like the TNIV itself, the *Zondervan TNIV Study Bible* is the work of a transdenominational team of Biblical scholars. All confess the authority of the Bible as God's infallible word to humanity. They have sought to clarify understanding of, develop appreciation for, and provide insight into that word.

But why a study Bible when the TNIV text itself is so clearly written? Surely there is no substitute for the reading of the text itself; nothing people write *about* God's word can be on a level with the word itself. Further, it is the Holy Spirit alone—not fallible human beings—who can open the human mind to the divine message.

However, the Spirit also uses people to explain God's word to others. It was the Spirit who led Philip to the Ethiopian eunuch's chariot, where he asked, "Do you understand what you are reading?" (Ac 8:30). "How can I," the Ethiopian replied, "unless someone explains it to me?" Philip then showed him how an Old Testament passage in Isaiah related to the good news of Jesus.

This interrelationship of the Scriptures—so essential to understanding the complete Biblical message—is a major theme of the notes in the *Zondervan TNIV Study Bible*.

Doctrinally, the *Zondervan TNIV Study Bible* reflects traditional evangelical theology. Where editors were aware of significant differences of opinion on key passages or doctrines, they tried to follow an evenhanded approach by indicating those differences (e.g., see note on Rev 20:2 about the "thousand years"). In finding solutions to problems mentioned in the book introductions, they went only as far as evidence (Biblical and non-Biblical) could carry them.

The result is a study Bible that can be used profitably by all Christians who want to be serious Bible students.

FEATURES OF THE *ZONDERVAN TNIV STUDY BIBLE*

The *Zondervan TNIV Study Bible* features the text of Today's New International Version, study notes keyed to and listed with Bible verses, introductions and outlines to books of the Bible, text notes, a cross-reference system (100,000 entries), parallel passages, a concordance (over 35,000 references), charts, maps, essays and comprehensive indexes.

The text of the TNIV, which is divided into paragraphs as well as verses, is organized into sections with headings.

STUDY NOTES

The outstanding feature of this study Bible is that it contains over 20,000 study notes, usually located on the same pages as the verses and passages they explain.

The study notes provide new information to supplement that found in the TNIV text notes. Among other things, they
1. explain important words and concepts (see note on Lev 11:44 about holiness);
2. interpret difficult verses (see notes on Mal 1:3 and Luke 14:26 for the concept of "hating" your parents);
3. draw parallels between specific people and events (see note on Ex 32:30 for the parallels between Moses and Christ as mediators);

4. describe historical and textual contexts of passages (see note on 1Co 8:1 for the practice of eating meat sacrificed to idols); and
5. demonstrate how one passage sheds light on another (see note on Ps 26:8 for how the presence of God's glory marked his presence in the tabernacle, in the temple and, finally, in Jesus Christ himself).

Some elements of style should be noted:

1. Study notes on a *passage* precede notes on individual verses within that passage.
2. When a book of the Bible is referred to within a note on that book, the book name is not repeated. For example, a reference to 2 Timothy 2:18 within the notes on 2 Timothy is written 2:18, not 2Ti 2:18.
3. In lists of references within a note, references from the book under discussion are placed first. The rest usually appear in Biblical order.
4. Certain kinds of material have been made more accessible through the use of the following symbols:

A The letter A calls attention to Scripture references containing study notes that have practical principles for personal application.

B The letter B points out references containing study notes that provide light from archaeology, history and geography. Since there is more personal application material in the study notes than background information, we have also indicated where background data can be found in certain book introductions, maps and charts.

C The letter C occurs in front of Scripture references containing study notes that provide descriptions and/or characterizations of a person or a people. It also sometimes appears in book introductions and essays.

INTRODUCTIONS TO BOOKS OF THE BIBLE

Each introduction to each book of the Bible is different. Introductions vary in length and reflect both the nature of the material itself and the strengths and interests of contributing editors.

An introduction frequently reports on a book's title, author and date of writing. It details the book's background and purpose, explores themes and theological significance and points out special problems and distinctive literary features. Where appropriate, such as in Paul's letters to the churches, it describes the original recipients of a book and the city in which they lived.

A complete outline of the book's content is provided in each introduction (except for the introduction to Psalms). For Genesis, two outlines—a literary and a thematic—are given. Pairs of books that were originally one literary work, such as 1 and 2 Samuel, 1 and 2 Kings, and 1 and 2 Chronicles, are outlined together.

TEXT NOTES

TNIV text notes are indicated by raised letters following the words or phrases they explain. They examine such things as alternative translations, meanings of Hebrew and Greek terms, Old Testament quotations and variant readings in ancient Biblical manuscripts. There are also some explanatory notes. Text notes appear at the bottom of the Bible text, above the line separating Scripture from study notes, and are preceded by their raised letters and verse numbers.

CROSS-REFERENCE SYSTEM

The cross-reference system can be used to explore concepts, as well as specific words. For example, one can either study angels as protectors (see Mt 18:10) or focus on the word "angel" (see Jn 20:12).

The TNIV cross-reference system resembles a series of interlocking chains with many links. The head, or organizing, link in each concept chain is indicated by the letter "S" (short for "See"). The appearance of a head link in a list of references usually signals another list of references that will cover a slightly different aspect of the concept or word being studied. The various chains in the cross-reference system—which is virtually inexhaustible—continually intersect and diverge.

Cross references are indicated by raised, light-italic letters. When a single word is addressed by both text notes and cross references, the TNIV text-note letter comes first. The cross references normally appear in the margin and, when necessary, continue at the bottom of the Scripture portion of the page, after the TNIV text notes.

The four lists of references are in Biblical order with one exception: If reference is made to a verse within the same chapter, that verse (indicated by "ver") is listed first. If an Old Testament verse is quoted in the New Testament, the New Testament reference is marked with an asterisk (*).

Genesis 1:1 provides a good example of the resources of the cross-reference system.

The four lists of references all relate to creation, but each takes a different perspective. Note *a* takes up the time of creation: "in the beginning." Note *b* lists three other occurrences of the word "created" in Genesis 1–2. Note *c* focuses on "the heavens" as God's creation. Because note *d* is attached to the end of the verse as well as to the word "earth," it deals with the word "earth," with the phrase "the heavens and the earth" and with creation itself (the whole verse).

1:1 *a* Ps 102:25;
Pr 8:23; Isa 40:21;
41:4,26; Jn 1:1-2
b ver 21,27; Ge 2:3
c ver 6; Ne 9:6;
Job 9:8; 37:18;
Ps 96:5; 104:2; 115:15;
—121:2; 136:5; Isa 40:22;
42:5; 51:13; Jer 10:12;
51:15 *d* Ge 14:19;
2Ki 19:15; Ne 9:6;
Job 38:4; Ps 90:2;
136:6; 146:6; Isa 37:16;
40:28; 42:5; 44:24;
45:12,18; Jer 27:5;
32:17; Ac 14:15; 17:24;
Eph 3:9; Col 1:16;
Heb 3:4; 11:3;
Rev 4:11; 10:6

THE BEGINNING

In the beginning *a* God created *b* the heavens *c* and the earth. *d* 2Now the earth was formless *e* and empty, *f* darkness was over the surface of the deep, *g* and the Spirit of God *h* was hovering *i* over the waters.

3And God said, *j* "Let there be light," and there was light. *k* 4God saw that the light was good, *l* and he separated the light from the darkness. *m* 5God called *n* the light "day," and the darkness he called "night." *o* And there was evening, and there was morning *p*—the first day.

6And God said, *q* "Let there be a vault *r* between the waters *s* to separate water from water." 7So God made the vault and separated the water under the vault from the water above it. *t* And it was so. *u* 8God called *v* the vault "sky." *w* And there was evening, and there was morning *x*—the second day.

PARALLEL PASSAGES

When two or more passages of Scripture are nearly identical or deal with the same event, this "parallel" is noted at the sectional headings for those passages. Such passages are especially common in Matthew, Mark, Luke and John, as well as in Samuel, Kings and Chronicles.

Identical or nearly identical passages are noted with *"pp."* Similar passages—those not dealing with the same event—are noted with *"Ref."*

To conserve space and avoid repetition, when a parallel passage is noted at a sectional heading, no further parallels are listed in the cross-reference system.

CONCORDANCE

The concordance is the largest ever bound with an English Bible. It was compiled and edited by John R. Kohlenberger III. By looking up key words, you can find verses for which you remember a word or two but not their location. For example, to find the verse that states that the word of God is "sharper than any double-edged sword," you could look in the concordance under either "sharper," "double-edged," or "sword."

MAPS

The *Zondervan TNIV Study Bible* includes 61 maps: 14 full-color and 48 black-and-white. The 14 full-color maps at the end of this Bible cover c. 2000 years of history.

Strategically placed throughout the text are four dozen black-and-white maps. The Contents: Maps page contains a complete list of the topics covered.

The cities of Jerusalem, Damascus, Rome, Corinth, Ephesus and Philippi have been reconstructed as they might have been in ancient times. These recreations allow Bible students to visualize David's city and, in the New Testament, the places through which Paul traveled on his missionary journeys.

CHARTS

Complementing the study notes are 40 charts, diagrams and drawings designed specifically for the *TNIV Study Bible*. Two full-color time lines, located in the front of this study Bible, pinpoint significant dates in the Old and New Testaments. Other charts, carefully placed within the text, give detailed information about ancient, non-Biblical texts; about Old Testament covenants, sacrifices and festival days; about Jewish sects; and about major archaeological finds relating to the Old and New Testaments.

ESSAYS

Five brief essays provide additional information on specific sections of the Bible: Wisdom Literature, the Minor Prophets, the Synoptic Gospels, the Pastoral Letters and the General Letters.

A sixth essay confronts the ethical question of war, and a seventh details the history, literature and social developments of the 400 years between the Old and New Testaments.

SUBJECT, NOTES AND MAP INDEXES

The subject index contains references to key Biblical information and important topics. The notes index pinpoints other references to persons, places, events and topics mentioned in the *TNIV Study Bible* notes.

Two map indexes help in locating place-names on a map.

HARMONY OF THE GOSPELS

As an additional study tool for the Gospels and the life of Christ, this study Bible contains a portion of the *TNIV Harmony of the Gospels* by Robert L. Thomas and Stanley N. Gundry.

THE DIVINE NAME YAHWEH

The editors have sometimes elected to use the divine name Yahweh (rendered "the LORD" in the TNIV) in the book introductions, study notes and essays instead of "the Lord" (or even "the LORD"). For the significance of this name, see notes on Ge 2:4; Ex 3:14–15; 6:6; Dt 28:58.

ACKNOWLEDGMENTS

1985 EDITION

My greatest debt of gratitude is owed to God for giving me the privilege of serving as General Editor of the *NIV Study Bible*. Special thanks go to the four Associate Editors: Donald W. Burdick, John H. Stek, Walter W. Wessel, and Ronald Youngblood. Without their help, it would have been impossible to complete this project in approximately seven years.

In addition, grateful acknowledgment is given to all those listed on the Contributors page. Obviously the editors and contributors have profited immensely from the labors of others. We feel deeply indebted to all the commentaries and other sources we have used in our work.

I should also thank the following individuals for rendering help in various ways (though I fear that I have inadvertently omitted a few names): Caroline Blauwkamp, David R. Douglass, Stanley N. Gundry, N. David Hill, Betty Hockenberry, Charles E. Hummel, Alan F. Johnson, Janet Johnston, Donald H. Madvig, Frances Steenwyk, and Edward Viening.

Nehemiah 8:7–8, 12 says:

> The Levites . . . instructed the people in the Law while the people were standing there. They read from the Book of the Law of God, making it clear and giving the meaning so that the people could understand what was being read . . . Then all the people went away . . . to celebrate with great joy, because they now understood the words that had been made known to them.

My associates and I will feel amply rewarded if those who use this study Bible have an experience similar to that of God's people in the time of Ezra and Nehemiah.

Kenneth L. Barker
General Editor

1995 EDITION

Since 1995 marked the 10th Anniversary of the *NIV Study Bible*, the publisher and I decided to give it a new look. We added some features, corrected a few mistakes, and made certain kinds of material more accessible through the use of symbols in the study notes. Special thanks go to Walter Wessel for his significant contribution to the study notes in the Gospel of Matthew, and to Michael Vander Klipp and other Zondervan editors for their help.

Kenneth L. Barker
General Editor

2002 EDITION

In the fully revised edition of the *NIV Study Bible*, the Associate Editors and I have added hundreds of new study notes, improved the book introductions (e.g., by paying greater attention to rhetorical, structural and other literary features) and enhanced other helps.

Special thanks go to Andrew J. Bandstra for providing additional study notes on the book of Revelation. We are also humbly grateful to God for the manner in which he has used this study Bible to bring edification and spiritual enrichment to literally millions of readers and users. It is my prayer that this will continue to be true of this fully revised edition of the *NIV Study Bible*.

Kenneth L. Barker
General Editor

TNIV STUDY BIBLE (2006)

The *TNIV Study Bible* is an adaptation of the 2002 fully revised *NIV Study Bible* to the TNIV text. My Associate Editors and I are delighted that all these helps will now be available for the TNIV. We pray that many more millions of readers and users will be similarly edified and spiritually enriched through its use. *Gloria in excelsis Deo!*

Kenneth L. Barker
General Editor

CONTRIBUTORS

General Editor: Kenneth L. Barker
Associate Editors: John H. Stek
Ronald Youngblood

1985 Edition	2002 Edition (Fully Revised)
General Editor: Kenneth L. Barker	General Editor: Kenneth L. Barker
Associate Editors: Donald W. Burdick	Associate Editors: John H. Stek
John H. Stek	Walter W. Wessel
Walter W. Wessel	Ronald Youngblood
Ronald Youngblood	

The individuals named below contributed and/or reviewed material for the *NIV Study Bible*. However, since the General Editor and the Associate Editors extensively edited the notes on most books, they alone are responsible for their final form and content.

The chief contributors of original material to the *NIV Study Bible* are listed first. Where the Associate Editors and General Editor contributed an unusually large number of notes on certain books, their names are also listed.

Genesis	Ronald Youngblood	*Isaiah*	Herbert Wolf;	*Luke*	Lewis Foster
Exodus	Ronald Youngblood;		John H. Stek	*John*	Leon Morris
	Walter C. Kaiser, Jr.	*Jeremiah*	Ronald Youngblood	*Acts*	Lewis Foster
Leviticus	R. Laird Harris;	*Lamentations*	Ronald Youngblood;	*Romans*	Walter W. Wessel
	Ronald Youngblood		John H. Stek	*1 Corinthians*	W. Harold Mare
Numbers	Ronald B. Allen;	*Ezekiel*	Mark Hillmer;	*2 Corinthians*	Philip E. Hughes
	Kenneth L. Barker		John H. Stek	*Galatians*	Robert Mounce
Deuteronomy	Earl S. Kalland;	*Daniel*	Gleason L. Archer, Jr.;	*Ephesians*	Walter L. Liefeld
	Kenneth L. Barker		Ronald Youngblood	*Philippians*	Richard B. Gaffin, Jr.
Joshua	Arthur Lewis	*Hosea*	Jack P. Lewis	*Colossians*	Gerald F. Hawthorne;
Judges	John J. Davis;	*Joel*	Jack P. Lewis		Wilber B. Wallis
	Herbert Wolf	*Amos*	Alan R. Millard;	*1,2 Thessalonians*	Leon Morris
Ruth	Marvin R. Wilson;		John H. Stek	*1,2 Timothy*	Walter W. Wessel;
	John H. Stek	*Obadiah*	John M. Zinkand		George W. Knight, III
1,2 Samuel	J. Robert Vannoy	*Jonah*	Marvin R. Wilson;	*Titus*	D. Edmond Hiebert
1,2 Kings	J. Robert Vannoy		John H. Stek	*Philemon*	John Werner
1,2 Chronicles	Raymond Dillard	*Micah*	Kenneth L. Barker;	*Hebrews*	Philip E. Hughes;
Ezra	Edwin Yamauchi;		Thomas E. McComiskey		Donald W. Burdick
	Ronald Youngblood	*Nahum*	G. Herbert Livingston;	*James*	Donald W. Burdick
Nehemiah	Edwin Yamauchi;		Kenneth L. Barker	*1,2 Peter*	Donald W. Burdick;
	Ronald Youngblood	*Habakkuk*	Roland K. Harrison;		John H. Skilton
Esther	Raymond Dillard;		William C. Williams	*1,2,3 John*	Donald W. Burdick
	Edwin Yamauchi	*Zephaniah*	Roland K. Harrison	*Jude*	Donald W. Burdick;
Job	Elmer B. Smick;	*Haggai*	Herbert Wolf		John H. Skilton
	Ronald Youngblood	*Zechariah*	Kenneth L. Barker;	*Revelation*	Robert Mounce;
Psalms	John H. Stek		Larry L. Walker		Andrew J. Bandstra
Proverbs	Herbert Wolf	*Malachi*	Herbert Wolf;	*"The Time*	David O'Brien
Ecclesiastes	Derek Kidner		John H. Stek	*between the*	
	John H. Stek	*Matthew*	Walter W. Wessel;	*Testaments"*	
Song of Songs	John H. Stek		Ralph Earle	*(essay)*	
		Mark	Walter W. Wessel;		
			William L. Lane		

ABBREVIATIONS

General		The Old Testament		The New Testament	
c.	*about, approximately*	*Genesis*	Ge	*Matthew*	Mt
cf.	*compare, confer*	*Exodus*	Ex	*Mark*	Mk
		Leviticus	Lev	*Luke*	Lk
ch., chs.	*chapter, chapters*	*Numbers*	Nu	*John*	Jn
e.g.	*for example*	*Deuteronomy*	Dt	*Acts*	Ac
		Joshua	Jos	*Romans*	Ro
etc.	*and so on*	*Judges*	Jdg	*1 Corinthians*	1Co
i.e.	*that is*	*Ruth*	Ru	*2 Corinthians*	2Co
		1 Samuel	1Sa	*Galatians*	Gal
KJV	*King James*	*2 Samuel*	2Sa	*Ephesians*	Eph
	(Authorized) Version	*1 Kings*	1Ki	*Philippians*	Php
lit.	*literally, literal*	*2 Kings*	2Ki	*Colossians*	Col
		1 Chronicles	1Ch	*1 Thessalonians*	1Th
NT	*New Testament*	*2 Chronicles*	2Ch	*2 Thessalonians*	2Th
OT	*Old Testament*	*Ezra*	Ezr	*1 Timothy*	1Ti
		Nehemiah	Neh	*2 Timothy*	2Ti
p., pp.	*page, pages*	*Esther*	Est	*Titus*	Tit
v., vv.,	*verse, verses*	*Job*	Job	*Philemon*	Phm
	(in the chapter being	*Psalms*	Ps	*Hebrews*	Heb
	commented on)	*Proverbs*	Pr	*James*	Jas
		Ecclesiastes	Ecc	*1 Peter*	1Pe
Standard abbreviations of		*Song of Songs*	SS	*2 Peter*	2Pe
month names are also some-		*Isaiah*	Isa	*1 John*	1Jn
times used, as well as a few		*Jeremiah*	Jer	*2 John*	2Jn
other common abbreviations.		*Lamentations*	La	*3 John*	3Jn
		Ezekiel	Eze	*Jude*	Jude
		Daniel	Da	*Revelation*	Rev
		Hosea	Hos		
		Joel	Joel		
		Amos	Am		
		Obadiah	Ob		
		Jonah	Jnh		
		Micah	Mic		
		Nahum	Na		
		Habakkuk	Hab		
		Zephaniah	Zep		
		Haggai	Hag		
		Zechariah	Zec		
		Malachi	Mal		

TRANSLITERATIONS

A simplified system has been used for transliterating words from ancient Biblical languages into English. The only transliterations calling for comment are these:

Transliteration	Pronunciation
'	Glottal stop
ḥ	Similar to the "ch" in the German word *Buch*
ṭ	Similar to the "t" in the verb "tear"
'	Similar to the glottal stop
ṣ	Similar to the "ts" in "hits"
ś	Similar to the "s" in "sing"

ANCIENT TEXTS RELATING TO THE OLD TESTAMENT

Major representative examples of ancient Near Eastern non-Biblical documents that provide parallels to or shed light on various OT passages.

AMARNA LETTERS
Canaanite Akkadian
14th century B.C.

Hundreds of letters, written primarily by Canaanite scribes, illuminate social, political and religious relationships between Canaan and Egypt during the reigns of Amunhotep III and Akhenaten.

AMENEMOPE'S WISDOM
Egyptian
Early 1st millennium B.C.

Thirty chapters of wisdom instruction are similar to Pr 22:17—24:22 and provide the closest external parallels to OT wisdom literature.

ATRAHASIS EPIC
Akkadian
Early 2nd millennium B.C.

A cosmological epic depicts creation and early human history, including the flood (cf. Ge 1–9).

BABYLONIAN THEODICY
Akkadian
Early 1st millennium B.C.

A sufferer and his friend dialogue with each other (cf. Job).

CYRUS CYLINDER
Akkadian
6th century B.C.

King Cyrus of Persia records the conquest of Babylon (cf. Da 5:30; 6:28) and boasts of his generous policies toward his new subjects and their gods.

DEAD SEA SCROLLS
Hebrew, Aramaic, Greek
3rd century B.C. to 1st century A.D.

Several hundred scrolls and fragments include the oldest copies of OT books and passages.

EBLA TABLETS
Sumerian, Eblaite
Mid-3rd millennium B.C.

Thousands of commercial, legal, literary and epistolary texts describe the cultural vitality and political power of a pre-patriarchal civilization in northern Syria.

ELEPHANTINE PAPYRI
Aramaic
Late 5th century B.C.

Contracts and letters document life among Jews who fled to southern Egypt after Jerusalem was destroyed in 586 B.C.

ENUMA ELISH
Akkadian
2nd millennium B.C.

Marduk, the Babylonian god of cosmic order, is elevated to the supreme position in the pantheon. The 7-tablet epic contains an account of creation (cf. Ge 1–2).

GEZER CALENDAR
Hebrew
10th century B.C.

A schoolboy from west-central Israel describes the seasons, crops and farming activity of the agricultural year.

GILGAMESH EPIC
Akkadian
Early 2nd millennium B.C.

Gilgamesh, ruler of Uruk, experiences numerous adventures, including a meeting with Utnapishtim, the only survivor of a great deluge (cf. Ge 6–9).

HAMMURAPI'S CODE
Akkadian
18th century B.C.

Together with similar law codes that preceded and followed it, the Code of Hammurapi exhibits close parallels to numerous passages in the Mosaic legislation of the OT.

HYMN TO THE ATEN
Egyptian
14th century B.C.

The poem praises the beneficence and universality of the sun in language somewhat similar to that used in Ps 104.

ISHTAR'S DESCENT
Akkadian
1st millennium B.C.

The goddess Ishtar temporarily descends to the nether world, which is pictured in terms reminiscent of OT descriptions of Sheol.

JEHOIACHIN'S RATION DOCKETS
Akkadian
Early 6th century B.C.

Brief texts from the reign of Nebuchadnezzar II refer to rations allotted to Judah's exiled king Jehoiachin and his sons (cf. 2Ki 25:27–30 and note on 25:27).

KING LISTS
Sumerian
Early 2nd millennium B.C.

The reigns of Sumerian kings before the flood are described as lasting for thousands of years, reminding us of the longevity of the preflood patriarchs in Ge 5.

LACHISH LETTERS
Hebrew
Early 6th century B.C.

Inscriptions on pottery fragments vividly portray the desperate days preceding the Babylonian siege of Jerusalem in 588–586 B.C. (cf. Jer 34:7 and note).

LAMENTATION OVER THE DESTRUCTION OF UR
Sumerian
Early 2nd millennium B.C.

The poem mourns the destruction of the city of Ur at the hands of the Elamites (cf. the OT book of Lamentations).

LUDLUL BEL NEMEQI
Akkadian
Late 2nd millennium B.C.

A suffering Babylonian nobleman describes his distress in terms faintly reminiscent of the experiences of Job.

MARI TABLETS **Akkadian** *18th century B.C.*	Letters and administrative texts provide detailed information regarding customs, language and personal names that reflect the culture of the OT patriarchs.
MERNEPTAH STELE **Egyptian** *13th century B.C.*	Pharaoh Merneptah figuratively describes his victory over various peoples in western Asia, including "Israel."
MESHA STELE (MOABITE STONE) **Moabite** *9th century B.C.*	Mesha, king of Moab (see 2Ki 3:4), rebels against a successor of Israel's king Omri.
MURASHU TABLETS **Akkadian** *5th century B.C.*	Commercial documents describe financial transactions engaged in by Murashu and Sons, a Babylonian firm that did business with Jews and other exiles.
MURSILIS'S TREATY WITH DUPPI-TESSUB **Hittite** *Mid-2nd millennium B.C.*	King Mursilis imposes a suzerainty treaty on King Duppi-Tessub. The literary outline of this and other Hittite treaties is strikingly paralleled in OT covenants established by God with his people.
NABONIDUS CHRONICLE **Akkadian** *Mid-6th century B.C.*	The account describes the absence of King Nabonidus from Babylon. His son Belshazzar is therefore the regent in charge of the kingdom (cf. Da 5:29–30).
NEBUCHADNEZZAR CHRONICLE **Akkadian** *Early 6th century B.C.*	A chronicle from the reign of Nebuchadnezzar II includes the Babylonian account of the siege of Jerusalem in 597 B.C. (see 2Ki 24:10–17).
NUZI TABLETS **Akkadian** *Mid-2nd millennium B.C.*	Adoption, birthright-sale and other legal documents graphically illustrate OT patriarchal customs current centuries earlier.
PESSIMISTIC DIALOGUE **Akkadian** *Early 1st millennium B.C.*	A master and his servant discuss the pros and cons of various activities (cf. Ecc 1–2).
RAS SHAMRA TABLETS **Ugaritic** *15th–14th century B.C.*	Canaanite deities and rulers experience adventures in epics that enrich our understanding of Canaanite mythology and religion and of OT poetry.
SARGON LEGEND **Akkadian** *1st millennium B.C.*	Sargon I (the Great), ruler of Akkad in the late 3rd millennium B.C., claims to have been rescued as an infant from a reed basket found floating in a river (cf. Ex 2).
SARGON'S DISPLAY INSCRIPTION **Akkadian** *8th century B.C.*	Sargon II takes credit for the conquest of Samaria in 722/721 B.C. and states that he captured and exiled 27,290 Israelites.
SENNACHERIB'S PRISM **Akkadian** *Early 7th century B.C.*	Sennacherib vividly describes his siege of Jerusalem in 701 B.C., making Hezekiah a prisoner in his own royal city (but cf. 2Ki 19:35–37).
SEVEN LEAN YEARS TRADITION **Egyptian** *2nd century B.C.*	Egypt experiences 7 years of low Niles and famine, which, by a contractual agreement between Pharaoh Djoser (28th century B.C.) and a god, will be followed by prosperity (cf. Ge 41).
SHALMANESER'S BLACK OBELISK **Akkadian** *9th century B.C.*	Israel's king Jehu presents tribute to Assyria's king Shalmaneser III. Additional Assyrian and Babylonian texts refer to other kings of Israel and Judah.
SHISHAK'S GEOGRAPHICAL LIST **Egyptian** *10th century B.C.*	Pharaoh Shishak lists the cities that he captured or made tributary during his campaign in Judah and Israel (cf. 1Ki 14:25–26 and note on 14:2–5).
SILOAM INSCRIPTION **Hebrew** *Late 8th century B.C.*	A Judahite workman describes the construction of an underground conduit to guarantee Jerusalem's water supply during Hezekiah's reign (cf. 2Ki 20:20; 2Ch 32:30).
SINUHE'S STORY **Egyptian** *20th-19th centuries B.C.*	An Egyptian official of the 12th dynasty goes into voluntary exile in Syria and Canaan during the OT patriarchal period.
TALE OF TWO BROTHERS **Egyptian** *13th century B.C.*	A young man rejects the amorous advances of his older brother's wife (cf. Ge 39).
WENAMUN'S JOURNEY **Egyptian** *11th century B.C.*	An official of the Temple of Amun at Thebes in Egypt is sent to Byblos in Canaan to buy lumber for the ceremonial barge of his god.

THE OLD TESTAMENT

GENESIS

TITLE

The first phrase in the Hebrew text of 1:1 is *bereshith* ("In [the] beginning"), which is also the Hebrew title of the book (books in ancient times customarily were named after their first word or two). The English title, Genesis, is Greek in origin and comes from the word *geneseos,* which appears in the pre-Christian Greek translation (Septuagint) of 2:4; 5:1. Depending on its context, the word can mean "birth," "genealogy," or "history of origin." In both its Hebrew and Greek forms, then, the traditional title of Genesis appropriately describes its content, since it is primarily a book of beginnings.

BACKGROUND

B Chs. 1–38 reflect a great deal of what we know from other sources about ancient Mesopotamian life and culture. Creation, genealogies, destructive floods, geography and mapmaking, construction techniques, migrations of peoples, sale and purchase of land, legal customs and procedures, sheepherding and cattle-raising—all these subjects and many others were matters of vital concern to the peoples of Mesopotamia during this time. They were also of interest to the individuals, families and tribes whom we read about in the first 38 chapters of Genesis. The author appears to locate Eden, humankind's first home, in or near Mesopotamia; the tower of Babel was built there; Abram was born there; Isaac took a wife from there; and Jacob lived there for 20 years. Although these patriarchs settled in Canaan, their original homeland was Mesopotamia.

The closest ancient literary parallels to Ge 1–38 also come from Mesopotamia. *Enuma elish,* the story of the god Marduk's rise to supremacy in the Babylonian pantheon, is similar in some respects (though thoroughly mythical and polytheistic) to the Ge 1 creation account. Some of the features of certain king lists from Sumer bear striking resemblance to the genealogy in Ge 5. The 11th tablet of the *Gilgamesh* epic is quite similar in outline to the flood narrative in Ge 6–8. Several of the major events of Ge 1–8 are narrated in the same order as similar events in the *Atrahasis* epic. In fact, the latter features the same basic motif of creation-alienation-flood as the Biblical account. Clay tablets found in 1974 at the ancient (c. 2500–2300 B.C.) site of Ebla (modern Tell Mardikh) in northern Syria may also contain some intriguing parallels (see chart, p. xxiii).

Two other important sets of documents demonstrate the reflection of Mesopotamia in the first 38 chapters of Genesis. From the Mari letters (see chart, p. xxiv), dating from the patriarchal period, we learn that the names of the patriarchs (including especially Abram, Jacob and Job) were typical of that time. The letters also clearly illustrate the freedom of travel that was possible between various parts of the Amorite world in which the patriarchs lived. The Nuzi tablets (see chart, p. xxiv), though a few centuries later than the patriarchal period, shed light on patriarchal customs, which tended to survive virtually intact for many centuries. The inheritance right of an adopted household member or slave (see 15:1–4), the obligation of a barren wife to furnish her husband with sons through a servant girl (see 16:2–4), strictures against expelling such a servant girl and her son (see 21:10–11), the authority of oral statements in ancient Near Eastern law, such as the deathbed bequest (see 27:1–4,22–23,33; 49:28–33)—these and other legal customs, social contracts and provisions are graphically illustrated in Mesopotamian documents.

KEY   **A** APPLICATION FOR LIVING   **B** BACKGROUND NOTES   **C** CHARACTER INFORMATION

B As Ge 1–38 is Mesopotamian in character and background, so chs. 39–50 reflect Egyptian influence—though in not quite so direct a way. Examples of such influence are: Egyptian grape cultivation (40:9–11), the riverside scene (ch. 41), Egypt as Canaan's breadbasket (ch. 42), Canaan as the source of numerous products for Egyptian consumption (ch. 43), Egyptian religious and social customs (the end of chs. 43; 46), Egyptian administrative procedures (ch. 47), Egyptian funerary practices (ch. 50) and several Egyptian words and names used throughout these chapters. The closest specific literary parallel from Egypt is the *Tale of Two Brothers*, which bears some resemblance to the story of Joseph and Potiphar's wife (ch. 39). Egyptian autobiographical narratives (such as the *Story of Sinuhe* and the *Report of Wenamun*) and certain historical legends offer more general literary parallels.

AUTHOR AND DATE OF WRITING

Historically, Jews and Christians alike have held that Moses was the author/compiler of the first five books of the OT. These books, known also as the Pentateuch (meaning "five-volumed book"), were referred to in Jewish tradition as the five fifths of the law (of Moses). The Bible itself suggests Mosaic authorship of Genesis, since Ac 15:1 refers to circumcision as "the custom taught by Moses," an allusion to Ge 17. However, a certain amount of later editorial updating does appear to be indicated (see, e.g., notes on 14:14; 36:31; 47:11).

The historical period during which Moses lived seems to be fixed with a fair degree of accuracy by 1 Kings. We are told that "the fourth year of Solomon's reign over Israel" was the same as "the four hundred and eightieth year after the Israelites came out of Egypt" (1Ki 6:1). Since the former was c. 966 B.C.—and thus the date of the exodus—was c. 1446 (assuming that the 480 in 1Ki 6:1 is to be taken literally; see Introduction to Judges: Background). The 40-year period of Israel's wanderings in the wilderness, which lasted from c. 1446 to c. 1406, would have been the most likely time for Moses to write the bulk of what is today known as the Pentateuch.

B During the last three centuries many interpreters have claimed to find in the Pentateuch four underlying sources. The presumed documents, allegedly dating from the tenth to the fifth centuries B.C., are called J (for Jahweh/Yahweh, the personal OT name for God), E (for Elohim, a generic name for God), D (for Deuteronomic) and P (for Priestly). Each of these documents is claimed to have its own characteristics and its own theology, which often contradicts that of the other documents. The Pentateuch is thus depicted as a patchwork of stories, poems and laws. However, this view is not supported by conclusive evidence, and intensive archaeological and literary research has tended to undercut many of the arguments used to challenge Mosaic authorship.

THEOLOGICAL THEME AND MESSAGE

Genesis speaks of beginnings—of the heavens and the earth, of light and darkness, of seas and skies, of land and vegetation, of sun and moon and stars, of sea and air and land animals, of human beings (made in God's own image, the climax of his creative activity), of marriage and family, of society and civilization, of sin and redemption. The list could go on and on. A key word in Genesis is "account," which also serves to divide the book into its ten major parts (see Literary Features and Literary Outline) and which includes such concepts as birth, genealogy and history.

The book of Genesis is foundational to the understanding of the rest of the Bible. Its message is rich and complex, and listing its main elements gives a succinct outline of the Biblical message as a whole. It is supremely a book that speaks about relationships, highlighting those between God and his creation, between God and humankind, and between human beings. It is thoroughly monotheistic, taking for granted that there is only one God worthy of the name and opposing the ideas that there are many gods (polytheism), that there is no god at all (atheism) and that everything is divine (pantheism). It clearly teaches that the one true God is sovereign over all that exists (i.e., his entire creation), and that he often exercises his unlimited freedom to overturn human customs, traditions and plans. It introduces us to the way in which God initiates and makes covenants with his chosen people, pledging his love and faithfulness to them and calling them to promise theirs to him. It establishes sacrifice as the substitution of life for life (ch. 22). It gives us the first hint of God's provision for redemption from the forces of evil (compare 3:15 with Ro 16:17–20) and contains the oldest and most profound statement concerning the significance of faith (15:6; see note there). More than half of Heb 11—a NT list of the faithful—refers to characters in Genesis.

LITERARY FEATURES

The message of a book is often enhanced by its literary structure and characteristics. Genesis is divided into ten main sections, each identified by the word "account" (see 2:4; 5:1; 6:9; 10:1; 11:10; 11:27; 25:12; 25:19; 36:1—repeated for emphasis at 36:9—and 37:2). The first five sections can be grouped together and, along with the introduction to the book as a whole (1:1—2:3), can be appropriately called "primeval history" (1:1—11:26). This introduction to the main story sketches the period from Adam to Abraham and tells about the ways of God with the human race as a whole. The last five sections constitute a much longer (but equally unified) account and relate the story of God's dealings with the ancestors of his chosen people Israel (Abraham, Isaac, Jacob and Joseph and their families)—a section often called "patriarchal history" (11:27—50:26). This section is in turn composed of three narrative cycles (Abraham-Isaac, 11:27—25:11; Isaac-Jacob, 25:19—35:29; 37:1; Jacob-Joseph, 37:2—50:26), interspersed by the genealogies of Ishmael (25:12–18) and Esau (ch. 36).

The narrative frequently concentrates on the life of a later son in preference to the firstborn: Seth over Cain, Shem over Japheth (but see TNIV text note on 10:21), Isaac over Ishmael, Jacob over Esau, Judah and Joseph over their brothers, and Ephraim over Manasseh. Such emphasis on divinely chosen men and their families is perhaps the most obvious literary and theological characteristic of the book of Genesis as a whole. It strikingly underscores the fact that the people of God are not the product of natural human developments but are the result of God's sovereign and gracious intrusion in human history. He brings out of the fallen human race a new humanity consecrated to himself, called and destined to be the people of his kingdom and the channel of his blessing to the whole earth.

Numbers with symbolic significance figure prominently in Genesis. The number ten, in addition to being the number of sections into which Genesis is divided, is also the number of names appearing in the genealogies of chs. 5 and 11 (see note on 5:5). The number seven also occurs frequently. The Hebrew text of 1:1 consists of exactly seven words and that of 1:2 of exactly 14 (twice seven). There are seven days of creation, seven names in the genealogy of ch. 4 (see note on 4:17–18; see also 4:15,24; 5:31), various sevens in the flood story, 70 descendants of Noah's sons (ch. 10), a sevenfold promise to Abram (12:2–3), seven years of abundance and then seven of famine in Egypt (ch. 41), and 70 descendants of Jacob (ch. 46). Other significant numbers, such as 12 and 40, are used with similar frequency.

The book of Genesis is basically prose narrative, punctuated here and there by brief poems (the longest is the so-called Blessing of Jacob in 49:2–27). Much of the prose has a lyrical quality and uses the full range of figures of speech and other devices that characterize the world's finest epic literature. Vertical and horizontal parallelism between the two sets of three days in the creation account (see note on 1:11); the ebb and flow of sin and judgment in ch. 3 (the serpent, woman and man sin successively; God questions them in reverse order; then he judges them in the original order); the powerful monotony of "and then he died" at the end of paragraphs in ch. 5; the climactic hinge effect of the phrase "But God remembered Noah" (8:1) at the midpoint of the flood story; the hourglass structure of the account of the tower of Babel in 11:1–9 (narrative in vv. 1–2,8–9; discourse in vv. 3–4,6–7; v. 5 acting as transition); the macabre pun in 40:19 (see 40:13); the alternation between brief accounts about firstborn sons and lengthy accounts about younger sons—these and numerous other literary devices add interest to the narrative and provide interpretive signals to which the reader should pay close attention.

It is no coincidence that many of the subjects and themes of the first three chapters of Genesis are reflected in the last three chapters of Revelation. We can only marvel at the superintending influence of the Lord himself, who assures us that "all Scripture is God-breathed" (2Ti 3:16) and that its writers "spoke from God as they were carried along by the Holy Spirit" (2Pe 1:21).

OUTLINES

LITERARY OUTLINE:

    I. Introduction (1:1—2:3)
   II. Body (2:4—50:26)
      A. "The account of the heavens and the earth" (2:4—4:26)
      B. "The written account of Adam's family line" (5:1—6:8)
      C. "The account of Noah" (6:9—9:29)
      D. "The account of Shem, Ham and Japheth" (10:1—11:9)
      E. "The account of Shem's family line" (11:10—26)
      F. "The account of Terah's family line" (11:27—25:11)
      G. "The account of the family line of Abraham's son Ishmael" (25:12–18)
      H. "The account of the family line of Abraham's son Isaac" (25:19—35:29)
      I. "The account of Esau's family line" (36:1—37:1)
      J. "The account of Jacob's family line" (37:2—50:26)

THEMATIC OUTLINE:

    I. Creation (1:1—2:3)
   II. Primeval History (2:4—11:26)
      A. Adam and Eve in Eden (2:4–25)
      B. The Fall and Its Consequences (ch. 3)
      C. Sin's Progression (4:1–16)
      D. The Genealogy of Cain (4:17–26)
      E. The Genealogy of Seth (ch. 5)
      F. God's Response to Human Depravity (6:1–8)
      G. The Great Flood (6:9—9:29)
        1. Preparing for the flood (6:9—7:10)
        2. Judgment and redemption (7:11—8:19)
          a. The rising of the waters (7:11–24)
          b. The receding of the waters (8:1–19)
         3. The flood's aftermath (8:20—9:29)
          a. A new promise (8:20–22)
          b. Renewed benediction and new ordinances (9:1–7)
          c. A new relationship (9:8–17)
          d. A new temptation (9:18–23)

1:1 *a* Ps 102:25;
Pr 8:23; Isa 40:21;
41:4,26; Jn 1:1-2
b ver 21,27; Ge 2:3
c ver 6; Ne 9:6;
Job 9:8; 37:18;
Ps 96:5; 104:2; 115:15;
121:2; 136:5; Isa 40:22;
42:5; 51:13; Jer 10:12;
51:15 *d* Ge 14:19;
2Ki 19:15; Ne 9:6;
Job 38:4; Ps 90:2;
136:6; 146:6; Isa 37:16;
40:28; 42:5; 44:24;
45:12,18; Jer 27:5;
32:17; Ac 14:15; 17:24;
Eph 3:9; Col 1:16;
Heb 3:4; 11:3;
Rev 4:11; 10:6
1:2 *e* Isa 23:1; 24:10;
27:10; 32:14; 34:11
f Isa 45:18; Jer 4:23
g Ge 8:2; Job 7:12;
26:8; 38:9; Ps 36:6;
42:7; 104:6; 107:24;
Pr 30:4 *h* Ge 2:7;
Job 33:4; Ps 104:30;
Isa 32:15 *i* Dt 32:11;
Isa 31:5
1:3 *j* ver 6; Ps 33:6,
9; 148:5; Heb 11:3

THE BEGINNING

1 In the beginning *a* God created *b* the heavens *c* and the earth. *d* ² Now the earth was formless *e* and empty, *f* darkness was over the surface of the deep, *g* and the Spirit of God *h* was hovering *i* over the waters.

³ And God said, *j* "Let there be light," and there was light. *k* ⁴ God saw that the light was good, *l* and he separated the light from the darkness. *m* ⁵ God called *n* the light "day," and the darkness he called "night." *o* And there was evening, and there was morning *p* —the first day.

⁶ And God said, *q* "Let there be a vault *r* between the waters *s* to separate water from water." ⁷ So God made the vault and separated the water under the vault from the water above it. *t* And it was so. *u* ⁸ God called *v* the vault "sky." *w* And there was evening, and there was morning *x* —the second day.

⁹ And God said, "Let the water under the sky be gathered to one place, *y* and let dry ground *z* appear." And it was so. *a* ¹⁰ God called *b* the dry ground "land," and the gathered waters *c* he called "seas." *d* And God saw that it was good. *e*

¹¹ Then God said, "Let the land produce vegetation: *f* seed-bearing plants and trees

1:3 *k* 2Co 4:6*; ¹* Jn 1:5-7 **1:4** *l* ver 10,12,18,21,25,31; Ps 104:31; 119:68; Jer 31:35 *m* ver 14; Ex 10:21-23; Job 26:10; 38:19; Ps 18:28; 104:20; 105:28; Isa 42:16; 45:7 **1:5** *n* ver 8,10; Ge 2:19,23 *o* Ps 74:16 *p* ver 8,13,19,23,31 **1:6** *q* S ver 3 *r* S ver 1; Isa 44:24; 2Pe 3:5 *s* ver 9; Ps 24:2; 136:6 **1:7** *t* Ge 7:11; Job 26:10; 38:8-11,16; Ps 68:33; 148:4; Pr 8:28 *u* ver 9,11,15,24 **1:8** *v* S ver 5 *w* Job 9:8; 37:18; Ps 19:1; 104:2; Isa 40:22; 44:24; 45:12; Jer 10:12; Zec 12:1 *x* S ver 5 **1:9** *y* Job 38:8-11; Ps 33:7; 104:6-9; Pr 8:29; Jer 5:22; 2Pe 3:5 *z* Ps 95:5; Jnh 1:9; Hag 2:6 *a* S ver 7 **1:10** *b* S ver 5 *c* Ps 33:7 *d* Job 38:8; Ps 90:2; 95:5 *e* S ver 4 **1:11** *f* Ps 65:9-13; 104:14

1:1—2:3 In the ancient Near East, most of the peoples had myths relating how the world came to be. Prevalent in those myths were accounts of how one of the gods triumphed over a fierce and powerful beast that represented disorder, then fashioned the ordered world that people knew, and finally was proclaimed by the other gods to be the divine "king" over the world he had created—a position ever subject to the challenge of the forces of disorder.

Over against all those pagan myths, the author of Genesis taught a radically new doctrine of creation: The one and only true God did not have to overcome a mighty cosmic champion of chaos but simply by a series of his royal creation decrees called into being the ordered world, the visible kingdom that those decrees continue to uphold and govern. The author teaches this doctrine of creation in the form of a narrative that recounts the story of God's creative acts. The author narrates those acts from the perspective of one who was an eyewitness to events in God's royal council chamber, where he issues his creative decrees. For a similar narrative perspective see Job 1:6–12; 2:1–6. (For the different narrative perspective of what follows, see note on 2:4—4:26.)

1:1 A summary statement introducing the six days of creative activity (see note on 2:1). The truth of this majestic verse was joyfully affirmed by poet (Ps 102:25) and prophet (Isa 40:21). *In the beginning God.* The Bible always assumes, and never argues, God's existence. Although everything else had a beginning, God has always been (Ps 90:2). *In the beginning.* Jn 1:1–10, which stresses the work of Christ in creation, opens with the same phrase. *God created.* "God" renders the common Hebrew noun *Elohim.* It is plural but the verb is singular, a normal usage in the OT when reference is to the one true God. This use of the plural expresses intensification rather than number and has been called the plural of majesty, or of potentiality. In the OT the Hebrew verb for "create" is used only of divine, never of human, activity. *the heavens and the earth.* "All things" (Isa 44:24). That God created everything is also taught in Ecc 11:5; Jer 10:16; Jn 1:3; Col 1:16; Heb 1:2. The positive, life-oriented teaching of v. 1 is beautifully summarized in Isa 45:18.

1:2 *earth.* The focus of this account. *formless and empty.* The phrase, which appears elsewhere only in Jer 4:23, gives structure to the rest of the chapter (see note on v. 11). God's "separating" and "gathering" on days 1–3 gave form, and his "making" and "filling" on days 4–6 removed the emptiness. *darkness ... the waters.* Completes the picture of a world awaiting God's light-giving, order-making and life-creating word. *and.* Or "but." The

awesome (and, for ancient people, fearful) picture of the original state of the visible creation is relieved by the majestic announcement that the mighty Spirit of God hovers over creation. The announcement anticipates God's creative words that follow. *Spirit of God.* He was active in creation, and his creative power continues today (see Job 33:4; Ps 104:30). *hovering over.* Like an eagle that hovers over its young when they are learning to fly (see Dt 32:11; cf. Isa 31:5).

1:3 *God said.* Merely by issuing his royal decree, God brought all things into being (Ps 33:6,9; 148:5; Heb 11:3). *Let there be light.* God's first creative word called forth light in the midst of the primeval darkness. Light is necessary for making God's creative works visible and life possible. In the OT it is also symbolic of life and blessing (see 2Sa 22:29; Job 3:20; 30:26; 33:30; Ps 49:19; 56:13; 97:11; 112:4; Isa 53:11; 58:8,10; 59:9; 60:1,3). Paul uses this word to illustrate God's re-creating work in sin-darkened hearts (2Co 4:6).

1:4 *good.* Everything God created is good (see vv. 10,12,18,21, 25); in fact, the conclusion declares it to be "very good" (v. 31). The creation, as fashioned and ordered by God, had no lingering traces of disorder and no dark and threatening forces arrayed against God or people. Even darkness and the deep were given benevolent functions in a world fashioned to bless and sustain life (see Ps 104:19–26; 127:2).

1:5 *called.* See vv. 8,10. In the ancient Near East, for a king to name people or things was an act of claiming dominion over them (see 17:5,15; 41:45; 2Ki 23:34; 24:17; Da 1:7). In this creation account, God named the great cosmic realities of day, night, sky, land and seas. He left to human beings the naming of the creatures they were given dominion over (see vv. 26,28; see also 2:19 and note). *first day.* Some say that the creation days were 24-hour days, others that they were indefinite periods.

1:6 *vault.* The atmosphere, or "sky" (v. 8), as seen from the earth. "Hard as a mirror" (Job 37:18) and "like a canopy" (Isa 40:22) are among the many pictorial phrases used to describe it.

1:7 *And it was so.* The only possible outcome, whether stated (vv. 9,11,15,24,30) or implied, to God's "Let there be" (see Ps 33:6,9 and note on 33:6).

1:9 *one place.* A picturesque way of referring to the "seas" (v. 10) that surround the dry land on all sides and into which the waters of the lakes and rivers flow. The earth was "formed out of water" (2Pe 3:5) and "founded ... on the seas" (Ps 24:2), and the waters are not to cross the boundaries set for them (Ps 104:7–9; Jer 5:22).

1:11 *God said.* This phrase is used twice on the third day (vv.

on the land that bear fruit with seed in it, according to their various kinds. *g*" And it was so. *h* 12The land produced vegetation: plants bearing seed according to their kinds *i* and trees bearing fruit with seed in it according to their kinds. And God saw that it was good. *j* 13And there was evening, and there was morning *k*—the third day.

14 And God said, "Let there be lights *l* in the vault of the sky to separate the day from the night, *m* and let them serve as signs *n* to mark seasons *o* and days and years, *p* 15and let them be lights in the vault of the sky to give light on the earth." And it was so. *q* 16God made two great lights—the greater light *r* to govern *s* the day and the lesser light to govern *t* the night. *u* He also made the stars. *v* 17God set them in the vault of the sky to give light on the earth, 18to govern the day and the night, *w* and to separate light from darkness. And God saw that it was good. *x* 19And there was evening, and there was morning *h*—the fourth day.

20 And God said, "Let the water teem with living creatures, *z* and let birds fly above the earth across the vault of the sky." *a* 21So God created *b* the great creatures of the sea *c* and every living and moving thing with which the water teems, *d* according to their kinds, and every winged bird according to its kind. *e* And God saw that it was good. *f* 22God blessed them and said, "Be fruitful and increase in number and fill the water in the seas, and let the birds increase on the earth." *g* 23And there was evening, and there was morning *h*—the fifth day.

24 And God said, "Let the land produce living creatures *i* according to their kinds: *j* livestock, creatures that move along the ground, and wild animals, each according to its kind." And it was so. *k* 25God made the wild animals *l* according to their kinds, the livestock according to their kinds, and all the creatures that move along the ground according to their kinds. *m* And God saw that it was good. *n*

26Then God said, "Let us *o* make human beings *p* in our image, *q* in our likeness, *r* so that they may rule *s* over the fish in the sea and the birds in the sky, *t* over the live-

1:24 *j* S ver 11 *k* S ver 7 **1:25** *l* Ge 7:21-22; Jer 27:5 *m* S ver 11 *n* S ver 4 **1:26** *o* Ge 3:5,22; 11:7; Ps 100:3; Isa 6:8 *p* Isa 45:18 *q* ver 27; Ge 5:3; 9:6; Ps 8:5; 82:6; 89:6; 1Co 11:7; 2Co 4:4; Col 1:15; 3:10; Jas 3:9 *r* Ac 17:28-29 *s* Ge 9:2; Ps 8:6-8 *t* Ps 8:8

1:11 *g* ver 12,21,24, 25; Ge 2:5; 6:20; 7:14; Lev 11:14,19,22; Dt 14:13,18; 1Co 15:38 *h* S ver 7
1:12 *i* S ver 11 *j* S ver 4
1:13 *k* S ver 5
1:14 *l* Ps 74:16; 136:7 *m* S ver 4 *n* Jer 10:2 *o* Ps 104:19 *p* Ge 8:22; Jer 31:35-36; 33:20,25
1:15 *q* S ver 7
1:16 *r* Dt 17:3; Job 31:26; Jer 43:13; Eze 8:16 *s* Ps 136:8 *t* Ps 136:9 *u* Job 38:33; Ps 74:16; 104:19; Jer 31:35; Jas 1:17 *v* Dt 4:19; Job 9:9; 38:7,31-32; Ps 8:3; 33:6; Ecc 12:2; Isa 40:26; Jer 8:2; Am 5:8
1:18 *w* Jer 33:20,25 *x* S ver 4
1:19 *y* S ver 5
1:20 *z* Ps 146:6 *a* Ge 2:19
1:21 *b* S ver 1 *c* Job 3:8; 7:12; Ps 74:13; 148:7; Isa 27:1; Eze 32:2 *d* Ps 104:25-26 *e* S ver 11 *f* S ver 4
1:22 *g* ver 28; Ge 8:17; 9:1,7,19; 47:27; Lev 26:9; Eze 36:11
1:23 *h* S ver 5
1:24 *i* Ge 2:19

9,11) and three times (vv. 24,26,29) on the sixth day. These two days are climactic, as the following structure of ch. 1 reveals (see note on v. 2 regarding "formless and empty").

Days of forming	Days of filling
1. "light" (v. 3)	4. "lights" (v. 14)
2. "water under the vault …water above it" (v. 7)	5. "every living and moving thing with which the water teems …every winged bird" (v. 21)
3a. "dry ground" (v. 9)	6a₁. "livestock, creatures that move along the ground, and wild animals" (v. 24)
b. "vegetation" (v. 11)	6a₂. "human beings" (v. 26)
	b. "every green plant for food" (v. 30)

Both the horizontal and vertical relationships between the days demonstrate the literary structure of the chapter and stress the orderliness and symmetry of God's creative activity. *kinds.* See vv. 12,21,24–25. Both creation and reproduction are orderly.
1:14 *serve as signs.* In the ways mentioned here, not in any astrological or other such sense (see Ps 104:19; 136:7–9).
1:16 *two great lights.* The words "sun" and "moon" seem to be avoided deliberately here, since both were used as proper names for the pagan deities associated with these heavenly bodies. They are light-givers to be appreciated, not powers to be feared, because the one true God made them (see Isa 40:26). Since the emphasis is on the greater light and lesser light, the stars seem to be mentioned almost as an afterthought. But Ps 136:9 indicates that the stars help the moon "govern the night." *govern.* The great Creator-King assigns subordinate regulating roles to certain of his creatures (see vv. 26,28).
1:17–18 The three main functions of the heavenly bodies.
B 1:21 *creatures of the sea.* The Hebrew word underlying this phrase was used in Canaanite mythology to name a

dreaded sea monster. He is often used figuratively in OT poetry to refer to one of God's most powerful opponents. He is pictured as national (Babylon, Jer 51:34; Egypt, Isa 51:9; Eze 29:3; 32:2) or cosmic (Job 7:12; Ps 74:13; Isa 27:1, though some take the latter as a reference to Egypt). In Genesis, however, the creatures of the sea are portrayed not as enemies to be feared but as part of God's good creation to be appreciated (cf. Ps 104:26 and note).
A 1:22 *Be fruitful and increase in number.* God's benediction on living things that inhabit the water and that fly in the air. By his blessing they flourish and fill both realms with life (see note on v. 28). God's rule over his created realm promotes and blesses life.
A 1:26 *us…our…our.* God speaks as the Creator-King, announcing his crowning work to the members of his heavenly court (see 3:22; 11:7; Isa 6:8; see also 1Ki 22:19–23; Job 15:8; Jer 23:18). *image…likeness.* No distinction should be made between "image" and "likeness," which are synonyms in both the OT (5:1; 9:6) and the NT (1Co 11:7; Col 3:10; Jas 3:9). Since human beings are made in God's image, they are all worthy of honor and respect; they are neither to be murdered (9:6) nor cursed (Jas 3:9). "Image" includes such characteristics as "righteousness and holiness" (Eph 4:24) and "knowledge" (Col 3:10). Believers are to be "conformed to the image" of Christ (Ro 8:29) and will someday be "like him" (1Jn 3:2). *so that they may rule.* Within the realm of his visible creation God places a creature to act as his agent in relationship to other creatures (1) to represent God's claim to kingship over his creation and (2) to bring its full potential to realization to the praise of the Creator's glory. (In the ancient Near East, kings marked their conquest of lands by setting up images of themselves in the conquered territories as a sign of their authority.) For a celebration of humanity's exalted role (under God) in the creation, see Ps 8:5–8 and notes. For the ultimate embodiment of humanity's dominion over the creation see Heb 2:5–9 and notes. *rule.* Humans are the climax of God's creative activity, and God has crowned them "with glory and honor" and made them rulers over the rest of his creation (Ps 8:5–8). Since they were created in the image of

1:27 *u* S ver 1
v Ge 2:7; Ps 103:14;
119:73 *w* S ver 26
x Ge 5:1 *y* Ge 5:2;
Mt 19:4*; Mk 10:6*;
Gal 3:28 *z* Dt 4:32
1:28 *a* Ge 33:5;
Jos 24:3; Ps 113:9;
127:3,5 *b* S Ge 17:6
c S ver 22; Ge 6:1;
Ac 17:26 *d* ver 26;
Ps 115:16 *e* Ps 8:6-8
1:29 *f* Ge 9:3;
Dt 12:15; Ps 104:14;
1Ti 4:3
1:30 *g* Ge 2:7; 7:22
h Job 38:41; Ps 78:25;
104:14,27; 111:5;
136:25; 145:15; 147:9
1:31 *i* Ps 104:24;
136:5; Pr 3:19;
Jer 10:12 *j* S ver 4;
1Ti 4:4 *k* S ver 5
2:1 *l* Dt 4:19; 17:3;
2Ki 17:16; 21:3;
Ps 104:2; Isa 44:24;
45:12; 48:13; 51:13
2:2 *m* Dt 5:14
n ver 2-3; Ex 20:11;
31:17; 34:21; Jn 5:17;
Heb 4:4*
2:3 *o* Ex 16:23;
20:10; 23:12; 31:15;
35:2; Lev 23:3;
Ne 9:14; Isa 58:13;
Jer 17:22 *p* Ps 95:11;
Heb 4:1-11 *q* S Ge 1:1
2:4 *r* Ge 5:1; 6:9;
10:1; 11:10,27; 25:12,
19; 36:1,9; 37:2
s Ge 1:1; Job 38:8-11
2:5 *t* Ge 1:11
u Job 38:28; Ps 65:9-
10; Jer 10:13
2:7 *v* Isa 29:16; 43:1,
21; 44:2 *w* S Ge 1:27
x Ge 3:19; 18:27;
Job 4:19; 10:9; 17:16;
34:15; Ps 90:3;
Ecc 3:20; 12:7
y Ge 3:23; 4:2;
Ps 103:14; Jer 18:6;
1Co 15:47 *z* S Ge 1:2;
Job 27:3; Isa 2:22

stock and all the wild animals, *a* and over all the creatures that move along the ground."

²⁷ So God created *u* human beings *v* in his own image, *w*
in the image of God *x* he created them;
male and female *y* he created them. *z*

²⁸God blessed them and said to them, *a* "Be fruitful and increase in number; *b* fill the earth *c* and subdue it. Rule over *d* the fish in the sea and the birds in the sky and over every living creature that moves on the ground. *e*"

²⁹Then God said, "I give you every seed-bearing plant on the face of the whole earth and every tree that has fruit with seed in it. They will be yours for food. *f* ³⁰And to all the beasts of the earth and all the birds in the sky and all the creatures that move on the ground—everything that has the breath of life *g* in it—I give every green plant for food. *h*" And it was so.

³¹God saw all that he had made, *i* and it was very good. *j* And there was evening, and there was morning *k*—the sixth day.

2 Thus the heavens and the earth were completed in all their vast array. *l*

²By the seventh day *m* God had finished the work he had been doing; so on the seventh day he rested from all his work. *n* ³Then God blessed the seventh day and made it holy, *o* because on it he rested *p* from all the work of creating *q* that he had done.

ADAM AND EVE

⁴This is the account *r* of the heavens and the earth when they were created, *s* when the LORD God made the earth and the heavens.

⁵Now no shrub had yet appeared on the earth *b* and no plant had yet sprung up, *t* for the LORD God had not sent rain on the earth *u* and there was no one to work the ground, ⁶but streams *c* came up from the earth and watered the whole surface of the ground. ⁷Then the LORD God formed *v* a man *d w* from the dust *x* of the ground *y* and breathed into his nostrils the breath *z* of life, *a* and the man became a living being. *b*

---

a 26 Probable reading of the original Hebrew text (see Syriac); Masoretic Text *the earth*   *b* 5 Or *land*; also in verse 6   *c* 6 Or *mist*   *d* 7 The Hebrew for *man (adam)* sounds like and may be related to the Hebrew for *ground (adamah)*; it is also the name *Adam* (see Gen. 2:20).

2:7 *a* S Ge 1:30; Isa 42:5; Ac 17:25 *b* Job 12:10; 32:8; 33:4; 34:14; Ps 104:29; Isa 57:16; Eze 37:5; 1Co 15:45*

---

the divine King, delegated sovereignty (kingship) was bestowed on them.
1:27 This highly significant verse is the first occurrence of poetry in the OT (which is about 40 percent poetry). *created.* The word is used here three times to describe the central divine act of the sixth day (see note on v. 1). *male and female.* Alike they bear the image of God, and together they share in the divine benediction that follows.

1:28 *God blessed them … fill … subdue … Rule.* Humankind goes forth from the hands of the Creator under his divine benediction—flourishing, filling the earth with their kind, and exercising dominion over the other earthly creatures (see v. 26; 2:15; Ps 8:6–8). Human culture, accordingly, is not anti-God (though fallen human beings often have turned their efforts into proud rebellion against God). Rather, it is the activity of those who bear the image of their Creator and share, as God's servants, in his kingly rule. As God's representatives in the creaturely realm, they are stewards of God's creatures. They are not to exploit, waste or despoil them, but to care for them and to use them in the service of God and humankind.

1:29–30 People and animals seem to be portrayed as originally vegetarian (see 9:3 and note).

1:31 *very good.* See note on v. 4. *the sixth day.* Perhaps to stress the finality and importance of this day, in the Hebrew text the definite article is first used here in regard to the creation days.

2:1 A summary statement concluding the six days of creative activity (see note on 1:1).

2:2 *finished … rested.* God rested on the seventh day, not because he was weary, but because nothing formless or empty remained. His creative work was completed—and it was totally effective, absolutely perfect, "very good" (1:31). It did not have to be repeated, repaired or revised, and the Creator rested to commemorate it.

2:3 *God blessed the seventh day and made it holy … rested.* Although the word "Sabbath" is not used here, the Hebrew verb translated "rested" (see v. 2) is the origin of the noun "Sabbath." Ex 20:11 quotes the first half of v. 3, but substitutes "Sabbath" for "seventh," clearly equating the two. The first record of obligatory Sabbath observance of Israel on her way from Egypt to Sinai (Ex 16), but according to Ne 9:13–14 the Sabbath was not an official covenant obligation until the giving of the law at Mount Sinai.

2:4—4:26 The beginning of human history, in distinction from the account of creation in 1:1—2:3 (see note there).

2:4 *account.* The Hebrew word for "account" occurs ten times in Genesis—at the beginning of each main section (see Introduction: Literary Features). *the heavens and the earth.* See note on 1:1. The phrase "the account of the heavens and the earth" introduces the record of what happened to God's creation. The blight of sin and rebellion brought a threefold curse that darkens the story of Adam and Eve in God's good and beautiful garden: (1) on Satan (3:14); (2) on the ground, because of Adam's sin (3:17); and (3) on Cain (4:11). *LORD God.* "LORD" (Hebrew *YHWH*, "Yahweh") is the personal and covenant name of God (see note on Ex 3:15), emphasizing his role as Israel's Redeemer and covenant Lord (see note on Ex 6:6), while "God" (Hebrew *Elohim*) is a general term. Both names occur thousands

⁸Now the LORD God had planted a garden in the east, in Eden; *c* and there he put the man he had formed. ⁹The LORD God made all kinds of trees grow out of the ground—trees *d* that were pleasing to the eye and good for food. In the middle of the garden were the tree of life *e* and the tree of the knowledge of good and evil. *f*

¹⁰A river *g* watering the garden flowed from Eden; *h* from there it was separated into four headwaters. ¹¹The name of the first is the Pishon; it winds through the entire land of Havilah, *i* where there is gold. ¹²(The gold of that land is good; aromatic resin *a j* and onyx are also there.) ¹³The name of the second river is the Gihon; it winds through the entire land of Cush. *b* ¹⁴The name of the third river is the Tigris; *k* it runs along the east side of Ashur. And the fourth river is the Euphrates. *l*

¹⁵The LORD God took the man and put him in the Garden of Eden *m* to work it and take care of it. ¹⁶And the LORD God commanded the man, "You are free to eat from any tree in the garden; *n* ¹⁷but you must not eat from the tree of the knowledge of good and evil, *o* for when you eat of it you will certainly die." *p*

¹⁸The LORD God said, "It is not good for the man to be alone. I will make a helper suitable for him." *q*

¹⁹Now the LORD God had formed out of the ground all the wild animals *r* and all the birds in the sky. *s* He brought them to the man to see what he would name them; and whatever the man called *t* each living creature, *u* that was its name. ²⁰So the man gave names to all the livestock, the birds in the sky and all the wild animals.

But for Adam *c* no suitable helper *v* was found. ²¹So the LORD God caused the man to fall into a deep sleep; *w* and while he was sleeping, he took one of the man's ribs *d* and then closed up the place with flesh. ²²Then the LORD God made a woman from the rib *e x* he had taken out of the man, and he brought her to the man.

²³The man said,

> "This is now bone of my bones
>   and flesh of my flesh; *y*
> she shall be called *z* 'woman,'
>   for she was taken out of man. *a*"

a 12 Or *good; pearls*   *b 13* Possibly southeast Mesopotamia   *c 20* Or *the man*   *d 21* Or *took part of the man's side*   *e 22* Or *part*

2:8 *c* ver 10,15; Ge 3:23,24; 4:16; 13:10; Isa 51:3; Eze 28:13; 31:9,16; 36:35; Joel 2:3
2:9 *d* Eze 31:8
e Ge 3:22,24; Pr 3:18; 11:30; S Rev 2:7
f Eze 47:12
2:10 *g* Nu 24:6; Ps 46:4; Eze 47:5
h S ver 8
2:11 *i* Ge 10:7; 25:18
2:12 *j* Nu 11:7
2:14 *k* Ge 41:1; Da 10:4 *l* Ge 15:18; 31:21; Ex 23:31; Nu 22:5; Dt 1:7; 11:24; 2Sa 8:3; 1Ki 4:21; 2Ki 23:29; 24:7; 1Ch 5:9; 18:3; 2Ch 35:20; Jer 13:4; 46:2; 51:63; S Rev 9:14
2:15 *m* S ver 8
2:16 *n* Ge 3:1-2
2:17 *o* Ge 3:11,17 *p* Ge 3:1,3; 5:5; 9:29; Dt 30:15,19; Jer 42:16; Eze 3:18; S Ro 5:12; S 6:23
2:18 *q* Pr 31:11; 1Co 11:9; 1Ti 2:13
2:19 *r* Ps 8:7 *s* S Ge 1:20 *s* S Ge 1:5 *u* Ge 1:24
2:20 *v* Ge 3:20; 4:1
2:21 *w* Ge 15:12; 1Sa 26:12; Job 33:15
2:22 *x* 1Co 11:8,9,12; 1Ti 2:13
2:23 *y* Ge 29:14; Eph 5:28-30
z S Ge 1:5 *a* 1Co 11:8

---

of times in the OT, and often, as here, they appear together—clearly indicating that they refer to the one and only God.

2:7 *formed.* The Hebrew for this verb commonly referred to the work of a potter (see Isa 45:9; Jer 18:6), who fashions vessels from clay (see Job 33:6). "Make" (1:26), "create" (1:27) and "form" are used to describe God's creation of both people and animals (v. 19; 1:21,25). *breath of life.* Humans and animals alike have the breath of life in them (see 1:30; Job 33:4). *the man became a living being.* The Hebrew phrase here translated "living being" is translated "living creatures" in 1:20,24. The words of 2:7 therefore imply that people, at least physically, have affinity with the animals. The great difference is that people are made "in the image of God" (1:27) and have an absolutely unique relation both to God as his servants and to the other creatures as God's stewards over them (Ps 8:5–8).

2:8 *in the east.* From the standpoint of the author of Genesis. The garden was thought of as being near where the Tigris and Euphrates rivers (see v. 14) meet, in what is today southern Iraq. *Eden.* A name synonymous with "paradise" and related to either (1) a Hebrew word meaning "bliss" or "delight" or (2) a Mesopotamian word meaning "a plain." Perhaps the author subtly suggests both.

2:9 *tree of life.* Signifying and giving life, without death, to those who eat its fruit (see 3:22; Rev 2:7; 22:2,14). *tree of the knowledge of good and evil.* Signifying and giving knowledge of good and evil, leading ultimately to death, to those who eat its fruit (v. 17; 3:3). "Knowledge of good and evil" refers to moral knowledge or ethical discernment (see Dt 1:39; Isa 7:15–16). Adam and Eve possessed both life and moral discernment as they came from the hand of God. Their access to the fruit of the tree of life showed that God's will and intention

for them was life. Ancient pagans believed that the gods intended for human beings always to be mortal. In eating the fruit of the tree of the knowledge of good and evil, Adam and Eve sought a creaturely source of discernment in order to be morally independent of God.

2:11 *Pishon.* Location unknown. The Hebrew word may be a common noun meaning "gusher." *Havilah.* Location unknown; perhaps mentioned again in 10:29. It is probably to be distinguished from the Havilah of 10:7 (see note there), which was in Arabia.

2:13 *Gihon.* Location unknown. The Hebrew word may be a common noun meaning "spurter." Both the Pishon and the Gihon may have been streams in Lower Mesopotamia near the Persian Gulf. The names were those current when Genesis was written.

2:14 *Ashur.* An ancient capital city of Assyria ("Assyria" and "Ashur" are related words). *Euphrates.* Often called in Hebrew simply "the River" because of its size and importance (see note on 15:18).

2:15 *work … take care.* See note on 1:28. The man is now charged to govern the earth responsibly under God's sovereignty.

2:16 *any tree.* Including the tree of life (v. 9).

2:17 *certainly die.* Despite the serpent's denial (3:4), disobeying God ultimately results in death.

2:18–25 The only full account of the creation of woman in ancient Near Eastern literature.

2:18 *not good … to be alone.* Without female companionship and a partner in reproduction, the man could not fully realize his humanity.

2:19 *name them.* His first act of dominion over the creatures around him (see note on 1:5).

2:24 *b* Mal 2:15
c Mt 19:5*; Mk 10:7-
8*; 1Co 6:16*;
Eph 5:31*
2:25 *d* Ge 3:7,10-11;
Isa 47:3; La 1:8
3:1 *e* Job 1:7; 2:2;
2Co 11:3; Rev 12:9;
20:2 *f* S Ge 2:17
3:2 *g* Ge 2:16
3:3 *h* S Ge 2:17
3:4 *i* S Jn 8:44;
2Co 11:3
3:5 *j* S Ge 1:26;
14:18,19; Ps 7:8;
Isa 14:14; Eze 28:2
3:6 *k* Jas 1:14-15;
1Jn 2:16 *l* Nu 30:7-8;
Jer 44:15,19,24
m 2Co 11:3; 1Ti 2:14
3:7 *n* Ge 2:25
o ver 21
3:8 *p* Lev 26:12;
Dt 23:14 *q* Job 13:16;
23:7; 31:33; 34:22,23;
Ps 5:5; 139:7-12;
Isa 29:15; Jer 16:17;
23:24; 49:10;
Rev 6:15-16
3:9 *r* Ge 4:9; 16:8;
18:9; 1Ki 19:9,13
3:10 *s* Ex 19:16;
20:18; Dt 5:5;
1Sa 12:18 *t* Ge 2:25
3:11 *u* Ge 2:25
v S Ge 2:17
3:12 *w* Ge 2:22
3:13 *x* Ro 7:11;
2Co 11:3; 1Ti 2:14
3:14 *y* Dt 28:15-20
z Ps 72:9; Isa 49:23;
65:25; Mic 7:17

²⁴For this reason a man will leave his father and mother and be united *b* to his wife, and they will become one flesh. *c*

²⁵The man and his wife were both naked, *d* and they felt no shame.

THE FALL

3 Now the serpent *e* was more crafty than any of the wild animals the LORD God had made. He said to the woman, "Did God really say, 'You must not eat from any tree in the garden'? *f*"

²The woman said to the serpent, "We may eat fruit from the trees in the garden, *g* ³but God did say, 'You must not eat fruit from the tree that is in the middle of the garden, and you must not touch it, or you will die.' " *h*

⁴"You will not certainly die," the serpent said to the woman. *i* ⁵"For God knows that when you eat of it your eyes will be opened, and you will be like God, *j* knowing good and evil."

⁶When the woman saw that the fruit of the tree was good for food and pleasing to the eye, and also desirable *k* for gaining wisdom, she took some and ate it. She also gave some to her husband, *l* who was with her, and he ate it. *m* ⁷Then the eyes of both of them were opened, and they realized they were naked; *n* so they sewed fig leaves together and made coverings for themselves. *o*

⁸Then the man and his wife heard the sound of the LORD God as he was walking *p* in the garden in the cool of the day, and they hid *q* from the LORD God among the trees of the garden. ⁹But the LORD God called to the man, "Where are you?" *r*

¹⁰He answered, "I heard you in the garden, and I was afraid *s* because I was naked; *t* so I hid."

¹¹And he said, "Who told you that you were naked? *u* Have you eaten from the tree that I commanded you not to eat from? *v*"

¹²The man said, "The woman you put here with me *w*—she gave me some fruit from the tree, and I ate it."

¹³Then the LORD God said to the woman, "What is this you have done?"
The woman said, "The serpent deceived me, *x* and I ate."

¹⁴So the LORD God said to the serpent, "Because you have done this,

> "Cursed *y* are you above all livestock
> and all wild animals!
> You will crawl on your belly
> and you will eat dust *z*

A **2:24** *leave his father and mother.* Instead of remaining under the protective custody of his parents, a man leaves them and, with his wife, establishes a new family unit. *united … one flesh.* The divine intention for husband and wife was monogamy. Together they were to form as inseparable a union as that between parent and child. As parents and their children are the same "flesh and blood" (see 29:14 and note), so husband and wife should be bound together as "one flesh" as long as they live—of which sexual union is an expression (cf. 1Co 6:16 and note).

A **2:25** *naked … no shame.* Freedom from shame, signifying moral innocence, would soon be lost as a result of sin (see 3:7).

C **3:1–24** The disobedience of Adam and Eve, and God's response that affects the whole course of human history (cf. Ro 5:12–21 and notes).

A C **3:1** *serpent.* The great deceiver clothed himself as a serpent, one of God's good creatures. He insinuated a falsehood and portrayed rebellion as clever, but essentially innocent, self-interest. Therefore "the devil, or Satan," is later referred to as "that ancient serpent" (Rev 12:9; 20:2). *crafty.* The Hebrew words for "crafty" and "naked" are almost identical. Though naked, the man and his wife felt no shame (2:25). The craftiness of the serpent led them to sin, and they then became ashamed of their nakedness (see v. 7). *Did God really say …?* The question and the response changed the course of human history. By causing the woman to doubt God's word, Satan brought evil into the world. Here the deceiver undertook to alienate people from God. Elsewhere he acts as an accuser, to alienate God from people (see Job 1–2; Zec 3:1 and note).

A C **3:3** *and you must not touch it.* The woman adds to God's word, distorting his directive and demonstrating that the serpent's subtle challenge was working its poison.

A **3:4** *You will not certainly die.* The blatant denial of a specific divine pronouncement (see 2:17).

C **3:5** *God knows.* Satan accuses God of having unworthy motives. In Job 1:9–11; 2:4–5 he accuses righteous Job of the same. *your eyes will be opened, and you will be like God.* The statement is only half true. Their eyes were opened, to be sure (see v. 7), but the result was quite different from what the serpent had promised. *knowing good and evil.* See note on 2:9.

A **3:6** *good for food … pleasing to the eye … desirable for gaining wisdom.* Three aspects of temptation. Cf. Lk 4:3,5,9; 1Jn 2:16.

A C **3:7** *they realized they were naked.* No longer innocent like children, they had a new awareness of themselves and of each other in their nakedness, which now produced in them a sense of shame. *they … made coverings.* Their own feeble and futile attempt to hide their shame, which only God could cover (see note on v. 21).

3:8 *garden.* Once a place of joy and of fellowship with God, it became a place of fear and of hiding from God.

3:9 *Where are you?* A rhetorical question (see 4:9).

C **3:12** *The woman you put here … gave me.* The man blames God and the woman—anyone but himself—for his sin.

C **3:13** *The serpent deceived me.* The woman blames the serpent rather than herself.

C **3:14** *Cursed.* The serpent, the woman and the man were all judged, but only the serpent and the ground were

all the days of your life.
¹⁵And I will put enmity
  between you and the woman,
  and between your offspring ᵃ ᵃ and hers; ᵇ
he will crush ᵇ your head, ᶜ
  and you will strike his heel."

¹⁶To the woman he said,

"I will make your pains in childbearing very severe;
  with pain you will give birth to children. ᵈ
Your desire will be for your husband,
  and he will rule over you. ᵉ"

¹⁷To Adam he said, "Because you listened to your wife and ate from the tree about which I commanded you, 'You must not eat of it,' ᶠ

"Cursed ᵍ is the ground ʰ because of you;
  through painful toil ⁱ you will eat of it
  all the days of your life. ʲ
¹⁸It will produce thorns and thistles ᵏ for you,
  and you will eat the plants of the field. ˡ
¹⁹By the sweat of your brow ᵐ
  you will eat your food ⁿ
until you return to the ground,
  since from it you were taken;
for dust you are
  and to dust you will return." ᵒ

²⁰Adam ᶜ named his wife Eve, ᵈ ᵖ because she would become the mother of all the living.

²¹The LORD God made garments of skin for Adam and his wife and clothed them. �q ²²And the LORD God said, "The man has now become like one of us, ʳ knowing good and evil. He must not be allowed to reach out his hand and take also from the tree of life ˢ and eat, and live forever." ²³So the LORD God banished him from the Garden of Eden ᵗ to work the ground ᵘ from which he had been taken. ²⁴After he drove them out, he placed on the east side ᵛ of the Garden of Eden ᵛ cherubim ʷ and a flaming sword ˣ flashing back and forth to guard the way to the tree of life. ʸ

ᵃ 15 Or *seed*   ᵇ 15 Or *strike*   ᶜ 20 Or *The man*   ᵈ 20 *Eve* probably means *living.*   ᵉ 24 Or *placed in front*

3:15 ᵃ Jn 8:44;
Ac 13:10; 1Jn 3:8
ᵇ Ge 16:11; Jdg 13:5;
Isa 7:14; 8:3; 9:6;
Mt 1:23; Lk 1:31;
Gal 4:4; Rev 12:17
ᶜ Ro 16:20; Heb 2:14
3:16 ᵈ Ps 48:5-6;
Isa 13:8; 21:3; 26:17;
Jer 4:31; 6:24;
Mic 4:9; 1Ti 2:15
ᵉ 1Co 11:3; Eph 5:22
3:17 ᶠ S Ge 2:17
ᵍ Ge 5:29; Nu 35:33;
Ps 106:39; Isa 24:5;
Jer 3:1; Ro 8:20-22
ʰ Ge 6:13; 8:21;
Isa 54:9 ⁱ Ge 29:32;
31:42; Ex 3:7;
Ps 66:11; 127:2;
Ecc 1:13 ʲ Ge 47:9;
Job 5:7; 7:1; 14:1;
Ecc 2:23; Jer 20:18
3:18 ᵏ Job 31:40;
Isa 5:6; Heb 6:8
ˡ Ps 104:14
3:19 ᵐ Ps 104:23
ⁿ Ge 14:18; Dt 8:3, 9;
23:4; Ru 1:6; 2:14;
2Th 3:10 ᵒ S Ge 2:7;
S Job 7:21;
S Ps 146:4; 1Co 15:47;
Heb 9:27
3:20 ᵖ S Ge 2:20;
2Co 11:3; 1Ti 2:13
3:21 �q ver 7
3:22 ʳ S Ge 1:26
ˢ S Ge 2:9; S Rev 2:7
3:23 ᵗ S Ge 2:8
ᵘ S Ge 2:7
3:24 ᵛ S Ge 2:8
ʷ Ex 25:18-22;
1Sa 4:4; 2Sa 6:2;
22:11; 1Ki 6:27; 8:6;
2Ki 19:15; 2Ch 5:8;
Ps 18:10; 80:1; 99:1;
Isa 37:16; Eze 10:1;
28:16 ˣ Job 40:19;
Ps 104:4; Isa 27:1
ʸ S Ge 2:9

cursed—the latter because of Adam (v. 17). *dust.* The symbol of death itself (v. 19) would be the serpent's food.

A **3:15** *he will crush your head, and you will strike his heel.* The antagonism between people and snakes is used to symbolize the outcome of the titanic struggle between God and the evil one, a struggle played out in the hearts and history of humankind. The offspring of the woman would eventually crush the serpent's head, a promise fulfilled in Christ's victory over Satan—a victory in which all believers will share (see Ro 16:20).

C **3:16** *pains in childbearing.* Her judgment fell on what was most uniquely hers as a woman and as a "suitable helper" (2:20) for her husband. Similarly, the man's "painful toil" (v. 17) was a judgment on him as worker of the soil. Some believe that the Hebrew root underlying "pains," "pain" and "painful toil" should perhaps be understood here in the sense of burdensome labor (see Pr 5:10, "toil"; 14:23, "hard work"). *give birth to children.* As a sign of grace in the midst of judgment, the original benediction (see 1:28 and note) is not withdrawn. *desire . . . rule.* Her sexual attraction to the man, and his headship over her, will become intimate aspects of her life in which she experiences trouble and anguish rather than unalloyed joy and blessing.

3:17–19 *you will eat.* Though he would have to work hard and long (judgment), the man would be able to produce food that would sustain life (grace).

3:18 Cultivating the ground and sowing the seed of desired crops create a situation in which certain native plants become

weeds—of which "thorns and thistles" are the most troublesome.

C **3:19** *return to the ground . . . to dust you will return.* Adam's labor would not be able to stave off death. The origin of his body (see 2:7) and the source of his food (see v. 17) became a symbol of his eventual death.

C **3:20** *named his wife.* Not an act of claiming dominion over her (see notes on 1:5; 2:19) but of memorializing her significance for him and the human race.

3:21 *clothed them.* God graciously provided Adam and Eve with more effective clothing (cf. v. 7) to cover their shame (cf. v. 10).

A **3:22** *us.* See note on 1:26. *knowing good and evil.* In a terribly perverted way, Satan's prediction (v. 5) came true. *live forever.* Sin, which always results in death (Ps 37:1–2; Pr 11:19; Eze 33:8–9; Ro 6:23; Jas 1:14–15), cuts the sinner off from God's gift of eternal life.

3:23 *banished him from the Garden . . . to work the ground.* Before Adam sinned, he had worked in a beautiful and fruitful garden (2:15). Now he would have to till undeveloped land and struggle with the curse of thorns and thistles (v. 18).

B **A** **3:24** *cherubim.* Similar to the statues of winged figures that stood guard at the entrances to palaces and temples in ancient Mesopotamia (see note on Ex 25:18). *to guard.* The sword of God's judgment stood between fallen humanity and God's garden. The reason is given in v. 22. Only through God's redemption in Christ do people have access again to the tree of life (see Rev 2:7; 22:2, 14, 19).

4:1 *z* ver 17,25
a S Ge 2:20
b Heb 11:4; 1Jn 3:12;
Jude 1:11
4:2 *c* Mt 23:35;
Lk 11:51; Heb 11:4;
12:24 *d* S Ge 2:7
4:3 *e* Lev 2:1-2;
Isa 43:23; Jer 41:5
f Nu 18:12
4:4 *g* Lev 3:16;
2Ch 29:35 *h* Ex 13:2,
12; Dt 15:19 *i* Heb 11:4
4:6 *j* Jnh 4:4
4:7 *k* Ge 44:16;
Nu 32:23; Isa 59:12
l Job 11:15; 22:27;
Ps 27:3; 46:2;
S Ro 6:16
4:8 *m* Mt 23:35;
Lk 11:51; 1Jn 3:12;
Jude 1:11
4:9 *n* S Ge 3:9
o Jn 8:44
4:10 *p* Ge 9:5;
37:20,26; Ex 21:12;
Nu 35:33; Dt 21:7,9;
2Sa 4:11; Job 16:18;
24:2; 31:38; Ps 9:12;
106:38; Heb 12:24;
Rev 6:9-10
4:11 *q* Dt 11:28;
2Ki 2:24
4:12 *r* Dt 28:15-24
s Ps 37:25; 59:15;
109:10 *t* ver 14
4:14 *u* 2Ki 17:18;
Ps 51:11; 139:7-12;
Jer 7:15; 52:3 *v* ver 12;
Dt 28:64-67
w Ge 9:6; Ex 21:12,14;
Lev 24:17; Nu 35:19,
21,27,33; 1Ki 2:32;
2Ki 11:16

CAIN AND ABEL

4 Adam[a] made love to his wife[z] Eve,[a] and she became pregnant and gave birth to Cain.[b] [b] She said, "With the help of the Lord I have brought forth[c] a man." [2]Later she gave birth to his brother Abel.[c]

Now Abel kept flocks, and Cain worked the soil.[d] [3]In the course of time Cain brought some of the fruits of the soil as an offering[e] to the Lord.[f] [4]And Abel also brought an offering—fat portions[g] from some of the firstborn of his flock.[h] The Lord looked with favor on Abel and his offering,[i] [5]but on Cain and his offering he did not look with favor. So Cain was very angry, and his face was downcast.

[6]Then the Lord said to Cain, "Why are you angry?[j] Why is your face downcast? [7]If you do what is right, will you not be accepted? But if you do not do what is right, sin is crouching at your door;[k] it desires to have you, but you must rule over it.[l]"

[8]Now Cain said to his brother Abel, "Let's go out to the field."[d] While they were in the field, Cain attacked his brother Abel and killed him.[m]

[9]Then the Lord said to Cain, "Where is your brother Abel?"[n]

"I don't know,[o]" he replied. "Am I my brother's keeper?"

[10]The Lord said, "What have you done? Listen! Your brother's blood cries out to me from the ground.[p] [11]Now you are under a curse[q] and driven from the ground, which opened its mouth to receive your brother's blood from your hand. [12]When you work the ground, it will no longer yield its crops for you.[r] You will be a restless wanderer[s] on the earth.[t]"

[13]Cain said to the Lord, "My punishment is more than I can bear. [14]Today you are driving me from the land, and I will be hidden from your presence;[u] I will be a restless wanderer on the earth,[v] and whoever finds me will kill me."[w]

[15]But the Lord said to him, "Not so[e]; anyone who kills Cain[x] will suffer vengeance[y] seven times over.[z]" Then the Lord put a mark on Cain so that no one who found him would

a 1 Or *The man*   *b* 1 *Cain* sounds like the Hebrew for *brought forth* or *acquired.*   *c* 1 Or *have acquired*   *d* 8 Samaritan Pentateuch, Septuagint, Vulgate and Syriac; Masoretic Text does not have *"Let's go out to the field."*   *e* 15 Septuagint, Vulgate and Syriac; Hebrew *Very well*

4:15 *x* Eze 9:4,6 *y* Ex 21:20 *z* ver 24; Lev 26:21; Ps 79:12

4:1–26 How human sin progressed from murder of a brother in the second generation to arrogant assertion of independence from God and claim of total self-sufficiency in the seventh generation.

A C **4:1** *With the help of the Lord.* Eve acknowledged that God is the ultimate source of life (see Ac 17:25).

C **4:2** *Abel.* The name means "breath" or "temporary" or "meaningless" (the translation of the same basic Hebrew word that is in Ecc 1:2; 12:8) and hints at the shortness of Abel's life.

A C **4:3–4** *Cain brought some of the fruits…And Abel also brought…fat portions from some of the firstborn of his flock.* The contrast is not between an offering of plant life and an offering of animal life, but between a careless, thoughtless offering and a choice, generous offering (cf. Lev 3:16 and note). Motivation and heart attitude are all-important, and God looked with favor on Abel and his offering because of Abel's faith (Heb 11:4). *firstborn.* Indicative of the recognition that all the productivity of the flock is from the Lord and all of it belongs to him.

C **4:5** *angry.* God did not look with favor on Cain and his offering, and Cain (whose motivation and attitude were bad from the outset) reacted predictably.

4:7 *sin is crouching at your door.* The Hebrew word for "crouching" is the same as an ancient Babylonian word referring to an evil demon crouching at the door of a building to threaten the people inside. Sin may thus be pictured here as just such a demon, waiting to pounce on Cain. He may already have been plotting his brother's murder. *it desires to have you.* In Hebrew, the same expression as that for "Your desire will be for [your husband]" in 3:16 (see also SS 7:10).

A C **4:8** *attacked his brother…and killed him.* The first murder was especially monstrous because it was committed with deliberate deceit ("Let's go out to the field"), against a brother (see vv. 9–11; 1Jn 3:12) and against a good

man (Mt 23:35; Heb 11:4)—a striking illustration of the awful consequences of the fall.

C **4:9** *Where…?* A rhetorical question (see 3:9). *I don't know.* An outright lie. *Am I my brother's keeper?* Demonstrating callous indifference—all too common through the whole course of human history.

C **4:10** *Your brother's blood cries out.* "Righteous Abel" (Mt 23:35), in one sense a "prophet" (Lk 11:50–51), "still speaks, even though he is dead" (Heb 11:4), for his spilled blood continues to cry out to God against all those who do violence to others. But the blood of Christ "speaks a better word" (Heb 12:24).

C **4:11** *curse.* The ground had been cursed because of human sin (3:17), and now Cain himself is cursed. Formerly he had worked the ground, and it had produced life for him (vv. 2–3). Now the ground, soaked with his brother's blood, would no longer yield its produce for him (v. 12).

4:12 *wanderer.* Estranged from other people and finding even the ground inhospitable, he became a wanderer in the land of wandering (see TNIV text note on v. 16).

A C **4:13** *My punishment is more than I can bear.* Confronted with his crime and its resulting curse, Cain responded not with remorse but with self-pity. His sin was virtually uninterrupted: impiety (v. 3), anger (v. 5), jealousy, deception and murder (v. 8), falsehood (v. 9) and self seeking (v. 13). The final result was alienation from God himself (vv. 14,16).

4:14–15 *whoever…anyone…no one.* These words seem to imply the presence of substantial numbers of people outside Cain's immediate family, but perhaps they only anticipate the future rapid growth of the race. Alternatively, Cain's reference to himself was inclusive of his whole family line, which stood under judgment with him (as did the family line of Adam). Note that Cain built a city (v. 17) and that his descendant Lamech boasted of avenging (defending) himself (vv. 23–24).

kill him. [16]So Cain went out from the LORD's presence [a] and lived in the land of Nod, [a] east of Eden. [b]

[17]Cain made love to his wife, [c] and she became pregnant and gave birth to Enoch. Cain was then building a city, [d] and he named it after his son [e] Enoch. [18]To Enoch was born Irad, and Irad was the father of Mehujael, and Mehujael was the father of Methushael, and Methushael was the father of Lamech.

[19]Lamech married [f] two women, [g] one named Adah and the other Zillah. [20]Adah gave birth to Jabal; he was the father of those who live in tents and raise livestock. [21]His brother's name was Jubal; he was the father of all who play stringed instruments [h] and pipes. [i] [22]Zillah also had a son, Tubal-Cain, who forged [j] all kinds of tools out of [b] bronze and iron. Tubal-Cain's sister was Naamah.

[23]Lamech said to his wives,

"Adah and Zillah, listen to me;
    wives of Lamech, hear my words.
I have killed [k] a man for wounding me,
    a young man for injuring me.
[24]If Cain is avenged [l] seven times, [m]
    then Lamech seventy-seven times. [n]"

[25]Adam made love to his wife [o] again, and she gave birth to a son and named him Seth, [c][p] saying, "God has granted me another child in place of Abel, since Cain killed him." [q] [26]Seth also had a son, and he named him Enosh. [r]

At that time people began to call on [d] the name of the LORD. [s]

FROM ADAM TO NOAH

5 This is the written account [t] of Adam's family line. [u]

When God created human beings, he made them in the likeness of God. [v] [2]He created them [w] male and female [x] and blessed them. And when they were created, he called them "human beings."

[3]When Adam had lived 130 years, he had a son in his own likeness, in his own image; [y] and he named him Seth. [z] [4]After Seth was born, Adam lived 800 years and had other sons and daughters. [5]Altogether, Adam lived a total of 930 years, and then he died. [a]

---

[a] 16 Nod means wandering (see verses 12 and 14).   [b] 22 Or who instructed all who work in   [c] 25 Seth probably means granted.   [d] 26 Or to proclaim

---

4:16 [a] Jude 1:11
[b] S Ge 2:8
4:17 [c] S ver 1
[d] Ps 55:9 [e] Ps 49:11
4:19 [f] Ge 6:2
[g] Ge 29:28; Dt 21:15;
Ru 4:11; 1Sa 1:2
4:21 [h] Ge 31:27;
Ex 15:20; 1Sa 16:16;
1Ch 25:3; Ps 33:2;
43:4; Isa 16:11; Da 3:5
[i] Job 21:12; 30:31;
Ps 150:4
4:22 [j] Ex 35:35;
1Sa 13:19; 2Ki 24:14
4:23 [k] Ge 9:5-6;
Ex 20:13; 21:12; 23:7;
Lev 19:18; 24:17;
Dt 27:24; 32:35
4:24 [l] Dt 32:35;
2Ki 9:7; Ps 18:47;
94:1; Isa 35:4;
Jer 51:56; Na 1:2
[m] S ver 15 [n] Mt 18:22
4:25 [o] ver 1
[p] Ge 5:3; 1Ch 1:1
[q] ver 8
4:26 [r] Ge 5:6;
1Ch 1:1; Lk 3:38
[s] Ge 12:8; 13:4; 21:33;
22:9; 26:25; 33:20;
35:1; Ex 17:15;
1Ki 18:24; Ps 116:17;
Joel 2:32; Zep 3:9;
S Ac 2:21
5:1 [t] S Ge 2:4
[u] 1Ch 1:1 [v] S Ge 1:27;
Col 3:10
5:2 [w] Ge 1:28
[x] S Ge 1:27; Mt 19:4;
Mk 10:6; Gal 3:28
5:3 [y] S Ge 1:26;
1Co 15:49
[z] S Ge 4:25; Lk 3:38
5:5 [a] S Ge 2:17;
Heb 9:27

4:15 mark. A warning sign to protect him from an avenger. For the time being, the life of the murderer is spared (but see 6:7; 9:6). For a possible parallel see Eze 9:4.
4:16 Nod. Location unknown. See TNIV text note.
4:17–18 Cain…Enoch…Irad…Mehujael…Methushael…Lamech. Together with that of Adam, these names add up to a total of seven, a number often signifying completeness (see v. 15). Each of the six names listed here is paralleled by a similar or identical name in the genealogy of Seth in ch. 5 as follows: Kenan (5:12), Enoch (5:21), Jared (5:18), Mahalalel (5:15), Methuselah (5:25), Lamech (5:28). The similarity between the two sets of names is striking and may suggest the selective nature of such genealogies (see note on 5:5). See also Introduction to 1 Chronicles: Genealogies.
4:17 city. The Hebrew for this word can refer to any permanent settlement, however small. Cain tried to redeem himself from his wandering and vulnerable state by the activity of his own hands—in the land of wandering he builds a city.
4:19 married two women. Polygamy entered history. Haughty Lamech, the seventh from Adam in the line of Cain, perhaps sought to attain the benefits of God's primeval blessing (see 1:28 and note) by his own device—multiplying his wives. Monogamy, however, was the original divine intention (see 2:23–24).
4:20–22 Jabal…Jubal…Tubal-Cain. Lamech's three sons had similar names, each derived from a Hebrew verb meaning "to bring, carry, lead," and emphasizing activity. Tubal-Cain's name was especially appropriate, since "Cain" means "metalsmith."
4:22 tools. For agriculture and construction; perhaps also for war (see 1Sa 13:19–21).

4:23 killed a man for wounding me. Violent and wanton destruction of human life by one who proclaimed his complete independence from God by taking vengeance with his own hands (see Dt 32:35 and note). Lamech proudly claimed to be master of his own destiny, thinking that he and his sons, by their own achievements, would redeem themselves from the curse on the line of Cain. This titanic claim climaxes the catalog of sins that began with Cain's unworthy offering and the murder of his brother.
4:24 seventy-seven times. Lamech's arrogant announcement of personal revenge found its counterpoint in Jesus' response to Peter's question about forgiveness in Mt 18:21–22 (see note on Mt 18:22).
4:25 again…another child. Abel was dead, and Cain was alienated, so Adam and Eve were granted a third son to carry on the family line.
4:26 Enosh. The name, like "Adam" (see TNIV text note on 2:7), means "man" or "humankind." began to call on the name of the LORD. Lamech's proud self-reliance, so characteristic of the line of Cain, is contrasted with dependence on God found in the line of Seth.
5:1 account. See note on 2:4. likeness. See note on 1:26.
5:2 male and female. See note on 1:27. blessed them. See 1:28 and note. called them. See note on 1:5.
5:3 his own likeness…his own image. See note on 1:26. As God created sinless Adam in his own perfect image, so now sinful Adam has a son in his own imperfect image.
5:5 930 years. See notes on v. 27; 6:3. Whether the large numbers describing human longevity in the early chap-

5:6 *b* S Ge 4:26;
Lk 3:38
5:9 *c* 1Ch 1:2;
Lk 3:37
5:12 *d* 1Ch 1:2;
Lk 3:37
5:15 *e* 1Ch 1:2;
Lk 3:37
5:18 *f* 1Ch 1:3;
Lk 3:37; Jude 1:14
5:21 *g* 1Ch 1:3;
Lk 3:37
5:22 *h* ver 24;
Ge 6:9; 17:1; 24:40;
48:15; 2Ki 20:3;
Ps 116:9; Mic 6:8;
Mal 2:6
5:24 *i* S ver 22
j 2Ki 2:1,11; Ps 49:15;
73:24; 89:48;
Heb 11:5
5:25 *k* 1Ch 1:3;
Lk 3:36
5:29 *l* 1Ch 1:3;
Lk 3:36 *m* S Ge 3:17;
Ro 8:20
5:32 *n* Ge 7:6,11;
8:13 *o* Lk 3:36
p Ge 6:10; 9:18; 10:1;
1Ch 1:4; Isa 65:20
6:1 *q* S Ge 1:28
6:2 *r* Job 1:6 *fn*;
2:1 *fn* *s* ver 4 *t* Dt 21:11
u S Ge 4:19
6:3 *v* Job 34:14;
Gal 5:16-17

⁶When Seth had lived 105 years, he became the father ͣ of Enosh. *b* ⁷After he became the father of Enosh, Seth lived 807 years and had other sons and daughters. ⁸Altogether, Seth lived a total of 912 years, and then he died.

⁹When Enosh had lived 90 years, he became the father of Kenan. *c* ¹⁰After he became the father of Kenan, Enosh lived 815 years and had other sons and daughters. ¹¹Altogether, Enosh lived a total of 905 years, and then he died.

¹²When Kenan had lived 70 years, he became the father of Mahalalel. *d* ¹³After he became the father of Mahalalel, Kenan lived 840 years and had other sons and daughters. ¹⁴Altogether, Kenan lived a total of 910 years, and then he died.

¹⁵When Mahalalel had lived 65 years, he became the father of Jared. *e* ¹⁶After he became the father of Jared, Mahalalel lived 830 years and had other sons and daughters. ¹⁷Altogether, Mahalalel lived a total of 895 years, and then he died.

¹⁸When Jared had lived 162 years, he became the father of Enoch. *f* ¹⁹After he became the father of Enoch, Jared lived 800 years and had other sons and daughters. ²⁰Altogether, Jared lived a total of 962 years, and then he died.

²¹When Enoch had lived 65 years, he became the father of Methuselah. *g* ²²After he became the father of Methuselah, Enoch walked faithfully with God *h* 300 years and had other sons and daughters. ²³Altogether, Enoch lived a total of 365 years. ²⁴Enoch walked faithfully with God; *i* then he was no more, because God took him away. *j*

²⁵When Methuselah had lived 187 years, he became the father of Lamech. *k* ²⁶After he became the father of Lamech, Methuselah lived 782 years and had other sons and daughters. ²⁷Altogether, Methuselah lived a total of 969 years, and then he died.

²⁸When Lamech had lived 182 years, he had a son. ²⁹He named him Noah *b l* and said, "He will comfort us in the labor and painful toil of our hands caused by the ground the LORD has cursed. *m*" ³⁰After Noah was born, Lamech lived 595 years and had other sons and daughters. ³¹Altogether, Lamech lived a total of 777 years, and then he died.

³²After Noah was 500 years old, *n* he became the father of Shem, *o* Ham and Japheth. *p*

WICKEDNESS IN THE WORLD

6 When human beings began to increase in number on the earth *q* and daughters were born to them, ²the sons of God *r* saw that these daughters *s* were beautiful, *t* and they married *u* any of them they chose. ³Then the LORD said, "My Spirit *v* will

---

ͣ 6 *Father* may mean *ancestor*; also in verses 7-26.   *b* 29 *Noah* sounds like the Hebrew for *comfort*.

---

ters of Genesis are literal or have a conventional literary function—or both—is uncertain. Some believe that several of the numbers have symbolic significance, such as Enoch's 365 (v. 23) years (365 being the number of days in a year, thus a full life) and Lamech's 777 (v. 31) years (777 being an expansion and multiple of seven, the number of completeness; cf. the "seventy-seven times" of the other Lamech in 4:24). The fact that there are exactly ten names in the Ge 5 list (as in the genealogy of 11:10–26) makes it likely that it includes gaps, the lengths of which may be summarized in the large numbers. Other ancient genealogies outside the Bible exhibit similarly large figures. For example, three kings in a Sumerian list (which also contains exactly ten names) are said to have reigned 72,000 years each—obviously exaggerated time spans. *and then he died.* Repeated as a sad refrain throughout the chapter, the only exception being Enoch (see note on v. 24). The phrase is a stark reminder of God's judgment on sin resulting from Adam's fall.

A   **5:22,24** *walked faithfully with God.* The phrase replaces the word "lived" in the other paragraphs of the chapter and reminds us that there is a difference between walking faithfully with God and merely living.

C   **5:24** *then he was no more, because God took him away.* The phrase replaces "and then he died" in the other paragraphs of the chapter. Like Elijah, who was "taken" (2Ki 2:10) to heaven, Enoch was taken away (cf. Ps 49:15; 73:24) to the presence of God without experiencing death (Heb 11:5). Lamech, the seventh from Adam in the genealogy of Cain, was evil personified. But "Enoch, the seventh from Adam" (Jude 14) in the genealogy of Seth, "was commended as one who pleased God" (Heb 11:5).

5:27 *969 years.* Only Noah and his family survived the flood. If the figures concerning life spans are literal, Methuselah died in the year of the flood (the figures in vv. 25,28 and 7:6 add up to exactly 969).

6:1–8 How the early history of humankind led to such pervasive corruption that God was moved to bring a radical judgment on his creation.

6:1 *increase in number.* See note on 1:22.

6:2 *sons of God saw . . . these daughters . . . and they married any.* See v. 4. The phrase "sons of God" here has been interpreted to refer either to angels or to human beings. In such places as Job 1:6; 2:1 it refers to angels, and probably also in Ps 29:1 (where it is translated "heavenly beings"). Some interpreters also appeal to Jude 6–7 (as well as to Jewish literature) in referring the phrase here to angels.

Others, however, maintain that intermarriage and cohabitation between angels and human beings, though commonly mentioned in ancient mythologies, are surely excluded by the very nature of the created order (ch. 1; Mk 12:25). Elsewhere, expressions equivalent to "sons of God" often refer to human beings, though in contexts quite different from the present one (see Dt 14:1; 32:5; Ps 73:15; Isa 43:6; Hos 1:10; 11:1; Lk 3:38; 1Jn 3:1–2,10). "Sons of God" (vv. 2,4) possibly refers to godly men, and "these daughters" to sinful women (significantly, they are not called "daughters of God"), probably from the wicked line of Cain. If so, the context suggests that vv. 1–2 describe the intermarriage of the Sethites ("sons of God") of ch. 5 with the Cainites ("these daughters") of ch. 4, indicating a breakdown in the separation of the two groups.

Another plausible suggestion is that the "sons of God" refers not contend with[a] human beings forever, [w] for they are mortal[b]; [x] their days will be a hundred and twenty years."

[4]The Nephilim[y] were on the earth in those days—and also afterward—when the sons of God went to the daughters of the human beings[z] and had children by them. They were the heroes of old, men of renown. [a]

[5]The Lord saw how great the wickedness of the human race had become on the earth, [b] and that every inclination of the thoughts of the human heart was only evil all the time. [c] [6]The Lord regretted[d] that he had made human beings on the earth, and his heart was deeply troubled. [7]So the Lord said, "I will wipe from the face of the earth[e] the human race I have created—and with them the animals, the birds and the creatures that move along the ground—for I regret that I have made them. [f]" [8]But Noah[g] found favor in the eyes of the Lord. [h]

NOAH AND THE FLOOD

[9]This is the account[i] of Noah and his family.

Noah was a righteous man, blameless[j] among the people of his time, [k] and he walked faithfully with God. [l] [10]Noah had three sons: Shem, [m] Ham and Japheth. [n]

[11]Now the earth was corrupt[o] in God's sight and was full of violence. [p] [12]God saw how corrupt[q] the earth had become, for all the people on earth had corrupted their ways. [r] [13]So God said to Noah, "I am going to put an end to all people, for the earth is filled with violence because of them. I am surely going to destroy[s] both them and the earth. [t] [14]So make yourself an ark of cypress[c] wood; [u] make rooms in it and coat it with pitch[v] inside and out. [15]This is how you are to build it: The ark is to be three hundred cubits long, fifty cubits wide and thirty cubits high. [d] [16]Make a roof for it, leaving below the roof an opening one cubit[e] high all around. [f] Put a door in the side of the ark and make lower, middle and

---

a 3 Or My spirit will not remain in   b 3 Or corrupt   c 14 The meaning of the Hebrew for this word is uncertain.   d 15 That is, about 450 feet long, 75 feet wide and 45 feet high or about 135 meters long, 22.5 meters wide and 13.5 meters high   e 16 That is, about 18 inches or about 45 centimeters   f 16 The meaning of the Hebrew for this clause is uncertain.

6:13 Jer 44:11 [r] ver 17; Ge 7:4,21-23; Job 34:15; Isa 5:6; 24:1-3; Jer 44:27; Eze 7:2-3   **6:14** [u] Heb 11:7; 1Pe 3:20 [v] Ex 2:3

6:3 [w] Isa 57:16;
1Pe 3:20 [x] Job 10:9;
Ps 78:39; 103:14;
Isa 40:6
6:4 [y] Nu 13:33
[z] ver 2 [a] Ge 11:4
6:5 [b] Ge 38:7;
Job 34:26; Jer 1:16;
44:5; Eze 3:19
[c] Ge 8:21; Ps 14:1-3
6:6 [d] Ex 32:14;
1Sa 15:11,35;
2Sa 24:16; 1Ch 21:15;
Isa 63:10; Jer 18:7-10;
Eph 4:30
6:7 [e] Eze 33:28;
Zep 1:2,18 [f] ver 17;
Ge 7:4,21; Dt 28:63;
29:20
6:8 [g] Eze 14:14
[h] Ge 19:19; 39:4;
Ex 33:12,13,17; 34:9;
Nu 11:15; Ru 2:2;
Lk 1:30; Ac 7:46
6:9 [i] S Ge 2:4
[j] Ge 17:1; Dt 18:13;
2Sa 22:24; Job 1:1;
4:6; 9:21; 12:4; 31:6;
Ps 15:2; 18:23; 19:13;
37:37; Pr 2:7 [k] Ge 7:1;
Ps 37:39; Jer 15:1;
Eze 14:14,20;
Da 10:11; S Lk 1:6;
Heb 11:7; 2Pe 2:5
[l] S Ge 5:22
6:10 [m] Lk 3:36
[n] S Ge 5:32
6:11 [o] Dt 31:29;
Jdg 2:19 [p] Ps 7:9;
73:6; Eze 7:23; 8:17;
28:16; Mal 2:16
6:12 [q] Ex 32:7;
Dt 4:16; 9:12,24
[r] Ps 14:1-3
6:13 [s] Dt 28:63;
2Ki 8:19; Ezr 9:14;

---

to royal figures (kings were closely associated with gods in the ancient Near East) who proudly perpetuated and aggravated the corrupt lifestyle of Lamech, son of Cain (virtually a royal figure), and established for themselves royal harems.

6:3 Two key phrases in the Hebrew of this verse are obscure: the one rendered "contend with" (see TNIV text note) and the one rendered "for they are mortal." The verse seems to announce that the period of grace between God's declaration of judgment and its arrival would be 120 years (cf. 1Pe 3:20). But if the TNIV text note reading is accepted, the verse announces that the human life span would henceforth be limited to 120 years (but see 11:10–26).

6:4 *Nephilim.* People of great size and strength (see Nu 13:31–33). The Hebrew word means "fallen ones." They were viewed by people as "the heroes of old, men of renown," but in God's eyes they were sinners ("fallen ones") ripe for judgment.

6:5 One of the Bible's most vivid descriptions of total depravity. And because human nature remained unchanged, things were no better after the flood (8:21).

6:6 *The Lord regretted ... his heart was deeply troubled.* Human sin is God's sorrow (Eph 4:30).

6:7 *I will wipe from the face of the earth the human race.* The period of grace (see v. 3 and note) was coming to an end. *animals ...birds...creatures.* Though morally innocent, the animal world, as creatures under the corrupted rule of human beings, shared in their judgment.

6:8–9 *found favor ...righteous ...blameless... walked faithfully with God.* See note on 5:22. Noah's godly life was a powerful contrast to the wicked lives of his contemporaries (see v. 5 and note; see also v. 12). This description of Noah does not imply sinless perfection.

6:9—9:29 In many legends circulating among the peoples of the ancient Near East, one of the major gods brought a devastating flood on the earth because he was

disturbed by the noisy hubbub raised by humans (see Introduction: Background). The author of Genesis also tells of a worldwide flood that destroyed all humankind except a single family. In his account, the Creator (who alone is God) was deeply grieved by the moral evil embraced and practiced by the creatures he had created in his own image and to whom he had committed the care of his creation. In his eyes they had so corrupted life in his good creation that only a radical cleansing judgment could check the rampant evil and bring humanity to account.

In his telling of the story to ancient Israel, the author of Genesis attacks the pervasive pagan notions about the gods and about humanity, as expressed in their stories of a mighty, all-destroying flood. He casts this storied flood in a radically different theological light. In the deluge (i.e., in destructive floods and other "natural" disasters) humanity had (and has) to do with the righteous Creator. For just cause, and after long forbearance, he judged (and judges) the creature created in his image and called to be his image-bearer in the creation. God's judgment on human sin represented by the flood speaks of his radical "No" to humanity's corruption of its way in the world. But that "No" is not his final word, and humanity is not at the mercy of a deity who at a whim might totally undo the creation order on which life depends. The God of the deluge has given another word, symbolized by the rainbow—a reassuring word about his enduring commitment to his creation. (See 9:8–17 and notes.)

6:9 *account.* See note on 2:4. *righteous.* See note on Ps 1:5.

6:14 *ark.* The Hebrew for this word is used elsewhere only in reference to the basket that saved the baby Moses (Ex 2:3,5). *coat it with pitch.* Moses' mother made his basket watertight in the same way (see Ex 2:3).

6:16 *roof.* Perhaps overhanging, to keep the rain from coming in. *an opening one cubit high all around.* Noah's ark probably had a series of small windows (see 8:6) encircling the entire vessel 18 inches from the top to admit light and air.

6:17 ʷPs 29:10
ˣS ver 7; S 13; 2Pe 2:5
6:18 ʸGe 9:9-16;
17:7; 19:12; Ex 6:4;
34:10,27; Dt 29:13,
14-15; Ps 25:10;
74:20; 106:45;
Isa 55:3; Jer 32:40;
Eze 16:60; Hag 2:5;
1Pe 3:20 ᶻGe 7:1,7,13
6:19 ᵃGe 7:15
6:20 ᵇGe 7:15
ᶜS Ge 1:11 ᵈGe 7:3
6:22 ᵉGe 7:5,9,16;
Ex 7:6; 39:43; 40:16,
19,21,23,25,27,29,32
7:1 ᶠS Ge 6:18;
Mt 24:38; Lk 17:26-
27; Heb 11:7;
1Pe 3:20; 2Pe 2:5
ᵍGe 6:9; Eze 14:14
7:2 ʰver 8; Ge 8:20;
Lev 10:10; 11:1-47;
Dt 14:3-20; Eze 44:23;
Hag 2:12; Ac 10:14-15
7:3 ⁱGe 6:20
7:4 ʲGe 8:2
ᵏ1Ki 13:34; Jer 28:16
ˡNu 13:25; Dt 9:9;
1Sa 17:16; 1Ki 19:8
ᵐver 12,17; Ex 24:18;
32:1; 34:28; Dt 9:9,11,
18,25; 10:10; Job 37:6,
13; Mt 4:2 ⁿS Ge 6:7,
13
7:5 ᵒS Ge 6:22
7:6 ᵖS Ge 5:32
7:7 �q S Ge 6:18
7:8 ʳS ver 2
7:9 ˢS Ge 6:22
7:10 ᵗS ver 4
7:11 ᵘS Ge 5:32
ᵛGe 8:4,14
ʷS Ge 1:7; Job 28:11;
Ps 36:6; 42:7; Pr 8:24;
Isa 51:10; Eze 26:19
ˣGe 8:2; 2Ki 7:2;
Ps 78:23; Isa 24:18;
Mal 3:10
7:12 ʸS ver 4;

upper decks. ¹⁷I am going to bring floodwaters ʷ on the earth to destroy all life under the heavens, every creature that has the breath of life in it. Everything on earth will perish. ˣ ¹⁸But I will establish my covenant with you, ʸ and you will enter the ark ᶻ—you and your sons and your wife and your sons' wives with you. ¹⁹You are to bring into the ark two of all living creatures, male and female, to keep them alive with you. ᵃ ²⁰Two ᵇ of every kind of bird, of every kind of animal and of every kind ᶜ of creature that moves along the ground will come to you to be kept alive. ᵈ ²¹You are to take every kind of food that is to be eaten and store it away as food for you and for them."

²²Noah did everything just as God commanded him. ᵉ

7 The Lᴏʀᴅ then said to Noah, "Go into the ark, you and your whole family, ᶠ because I have found you righteous ᵍ in this generation. ²Take with you seven pairs of every kind of clean ʰ animal, a male and its mate, and one pair of every kind of unclean animal, a male and its mate, ³and also seven pairs of every kind of bird, male and female, to keep their various kinds alive ⁱ throughout the earth. ⁴Seven days from now I will send rain ʲ on the earth ᵏ for forty days ˡ and forty nights, ᵐ and I will wipe from the face of the earth every living creature I have made. ⁿ"

⁵And Noah did all that the Lᴏʀᴅ commanded him. ᵒ

⁶Noah was six hundred years old ᵖ when the floodwaters came on the earth. ⁷And Noah and his sons and his wife and his sons' wives entered the ark q to escape the waters of the flood. ⁸Pairs of clean and unclean ʳ animals, of birds and of all creatures that move along the ground, ⁹male and female, came to Noah and entered the ark, as God had commanded Noah. ˢ ¹⁰And after the seven days ᵗ the floodwaters came on the earth.

¹¹In the six hundredth year of Noah's life, ᵘ on the seventeenth day of the second month ᵛ—on that day all the springs of the great deep ʷ burst forth, and the floodgates of the heavens ˣ were opened. ¹²And rain fell on the earth forty days and forty nights. ʸ

¹³On that very day Noah and his sons, ᶻ Shem, Ham and Japheth, together with his wife and the wives of his three sons, entered the ark. ᵃ ¹⁴They had with them every wild animal according to its kind, all livestock according to their kinds, every creature that moves along the ground according to its kind and every bird according to its kind, ᵇ everything with wings. ¹⁵Pairs of all creatures that have the breath of life in them came to Noah and entered the ark. ᶜ ¹⁶The animals going in were male and female of every living thing, as God had commanded Noah. ᵈ Then the Lᴏʀᴅ shut him in.

7:12 S 1Sa 12:17; S Job 28:26   **7:13** ᶻGe 8:16; 1Pe 3:20; 2Pe 2:5 ᵃS Ge 6:18   **7:14** ᵇS Ge 1:11   **7:15** ᶜver 8-9; Ge 6:19   **7:16** ᵈS Ge 6:22

6:17 *floodwaters on the earth to destroy all life under the heavens.* Some believe that the deluge was worldwide, partly because of the apparently universal terms of the text—both here and elsewhere (vv. 7,12–13; 7:4,19,21–23; 8:21; 9:11,15; cf. 2Pe 3:6 and note). Others argue that nothing in the narrative of chs. 6–9 prevents the flood from being understood as regional—destroying everything in its wake, but of relatively limited scope and universal only from the standpoint of Moses' geographic knowledge. "Earth," e.g., may be defined in the more restricted sense of "land" (see 2:5). "All life under the heavens" may mean all life within the range of Noah's perception. (See the universal language used to describe the drought and famine in the time of Joseph—41:54,57; see also note on 41:57.)

6:18 *covenant.* See note on 9:9. Noah would not be given the particulars of God's covenant with him until after the floodwaters had dried up (see 9:8–17). *enter the ark.* The story of Noah's deliverance from the flood foreshadows God's full redemption of his children (see Heb 11:7; 2Pe 2:5) and typifies baptism (see 1Pe 3:20–21). *your sons and your wife and your sons' wives with you.* God extends his loving concern to the whole family of righteous Noah—a consistent pattern in God's dealings with his people, underscoring the moral and responsible relationship of parents to their children (see 17:7–27; 18:19; Dt 30:19; Ps 78:1–7; 102:28; 103:17–18; 112:1–2; Ac 2:38–39; 16:31; 1Co 7:14).

6:19 *two of all living creatures … to keep them alive.* Most animals were doomed to die in the flood (see note on v. 7), but at least one pair of each kind was preserved to restock the earth after the waters subsided.

6:20 *kind.* See note on 1:11.

6:22 *did everything just as God commanded.* The account stresses Noah's obedience (see 7:5,9,16).

7:1 *Go into the ark.* The beginning of God's final word to Noah before the flood. God's first word to Noah after the flood begins similarly: "Come out of the ark" (8:16). *righteous.* See note on 6:8–9. Later, Noah was known as a "preacher of righteousness" (2Pe 2:5) who warned his contemporaries of coming judgment and testified to the vitality of his own faith (see Heb 11:7).

7:2 *seven pairs of every kind of clean animal … one pair of every kind of unclean animal.* The "unclean" animals would only have to reproduce themselves after the flood, but the "clean" animals would be needed also for the burnt offerings that Noah would sacrifice (see 8:20) and for food (see 9:3).

7:4 *forty days and forty nights.* A length of time often characterizing a critical period in redemptive history (see v. 12; Dt 9:11; Mt 4:1–11).

7:7 *entered the ark to escape the waters.* Noah and his family were saved, but life as usual continued for everyone else until it was too late (see Mt 24:37–39).

7:13 *Noah and his sons … together with his wife and the wives of his three sons.* "Only a few people, eight in all" (1Pe 3:20; see 2Pe 2:5), survived the flood.

7:14 *every wild animal … all livestock … every creature that moves along the ground … every bird.* Four of the five categories of animate life mentioned in 1:21–25. The fifth category—sea creatures—could remain alive outside the ark.

7:16 *God had commanded Noah … the Lᴏʀᴅ shut him in.* "God" gave the command, but in his role as redeeming "Lᴏʀᴅ" (see notes on 2:4; Ex 6:6) he closed the door of the ark behind Noah and his family. Neither divine name is mentioned in the rest of ch. 7, as the full fury of the flood was unleashed on sinful humankind.

[17]For forty days[e] the flood kept coming on the earth, and as the waters increased they lifted the ark high above the earth. [18]The waters rose and increased greatly on the earth, and the ark floated on the surface of the water. [19]They rose greatly on the earth, and all the high mountains under the entire heavens were covered. [f] [20]The waters rose and covered the mountains to a depth of more than fifteen cubits.[a, b] [g] [21]Every living thing that moved on the earth perished—birds, livestock, wild animals, all the creatures that swarm over the earth, and the entire human race. [h] [22]Everything on dry land that had the breath of life[i] in its nostrils died. [23]Every living thing on the face of the earth was wiped out; human beings and animals and the creatures that move along the ground and the birds were wiped from the earth.[j] Only Noah was left, and those with him in the ark. [k]

[24]The waters flooded the earth for a hundred and fifty days. [l]

8 But God remembered[m] Noah and all the wild animals and the livestock that were with him in the ark, and he sent a wind over the earth, [n] and the waters receded. [2]Now the springs of the deep and the floodgates of the heavens[o] had been closed, and the rain[p] had stopped falling from the sky. [3]The water receded steadily from the earth. At the end of the hundred and fifty days[q] the water had gone down, [4]and on the seventeenth day of the seventh month[r] the ark came to rest on the mountains[s] of Ararat. [t] [5]The waters continued to recede until the tenth month, and on the first day of the tenth month the tops of the mountains became visible.

[6]After forty days[u] Noah opened a window he had made in the ark [7]and sent out a raven,[v] and it kept flying back and forth until the water had dried up from the earth. [w] [8]Then he sent out a dove[x] to see if the water had receded from the surface of the ground. [9]But the dove could find nowhere to perch because there was water over all the surface of the earth; so it returned to Noah in the ark. He reached out his hand and took the dove and brought it back to himself in the ark. [10]He waited seven more days and again sent out the dove from the ark. [11]When the dove returned to him in the evening, there in its beak was a freshly plucked olive leaf! Then Noah knew that the water had receded from the earth. [y] [12]He waited seven more days and sent the dove out again, but this time it did not return to him.

[13]By the first day of the first month of Noah's six hundred and first year,[z] the water had dried up from the earth. Noah then removed the covering from the ark and saw that the surface of the ground was dry. [14]By the twenty-seventh day of the second month[a] the earth was completely dry.

[15]Then God said to Noah, [16]"Come out of the ark, you and your wife and your sons and their wives. [b] [17]Bring out every kind of living creature that is with you—the birds, the animals, and all the creatures that move along the ground—so they can multiply on the earth and be fruitful and increase in number on it." [c]

[18]So Noah came out, together with his sons and his wife and his sons' wives. [d] [19]All the animals and all the creatures that move along the ground and all the birds—everything that moves on the earth—came out of the ark, one kind after another.

---

[a] 20 That is, about 22 feet or about 6.8 meters   [b] 20 Or *rose more than fifteen cubits, and the mountains were covered*

7:17 [e]S ver 4
7:19 [f]Ps 104:6
7:20 [g]Ge 8:4-5; 2Pe 3:6
7:21 [h]S Ge 6:7,13; 2Pe 3:6
7:22 [i]S Ge 1:30
7:23 [j]Job 14:19; 21:18; 22:11,16; Ps 90:5; Isa 28:2; Mt 24:39; Lk 17:27; 1Pe 3:20; 2Pe 2:5
[k]Heb 11:7
7:24 [l]Ge 8:3; Job 12:15
8:1 [m]Ge 9:15; 19:29; 21:1; 30:22; Ex 2:24; Nu 10:9; Ru 4:13; 1Sa 1:11,19; 2Ki 20:3; 1Ch 16:15; Ne 1:8; 5:19; 13:14,22, 31; Job 14:13; Ps 105:42; 106:4; Lk 1:54,72 [n]Ex 14:21; Jos 2:10; 3:16; Job 12:15; Ps 66:6; Isa 11:15; 44:27; Na 1:4
8:2 [o]S Ge 7:11
[p]S Ge 7:4
8:3 [q]S Ge 7:24
8:4 [r]S Ge 7:11
[s]Ge 7:20 [t]2Ki 19:37; Jer 51:27
8:6 [u]Ge 7:12
8:7 [v]Lev 11:15; Dt 14:14; 1Ki 17:4,6; Job 38:41; Ps 147:9; Pr 30:17; Isa 34:11; Lk 12:24 [w]ver 11
8:8 [x]Job 30:31; Ps 55:6; 74:19; SS 2:12,14; Isa 38:14; 59:11; 60:8; Jer 48:28; Eze 7:16; Hos 7:11; 11:11; Na 2:7; Mt 3:16; 10:16; Jn 1:32
8:11 [y]ver 7
8:13 [z]S Ge 5:32
8:14 [a]S Ge 7:13
8:16 [b]S Ge 7:13
8:17 [c]S Ge 1:22
8:18 [d]1Pe 3:20; 2Pe 2:5

7:20 *covered the mountains to a depth of more than fifteen cubits.* See TNIV text note. The ark was 45 feet high (6:15; see TNIV text note there), so the water was deep enough to keep it from running aground.

7:22 *breath of life.* God's gift at creation (see 1:30; 2:7) was taken away because of sin.

8:1 So far the flood narrative has been an account of judgment; from this point on it is a story of redemption. *God remembered Noah.* Though he had not been mentioned since 7:16 or heard from for 150 days (see 7:24), God had not forgotten Noah and his family. To "remember" in the Bible is often not merely to recall people to mind but to express concern for them, to act with loving care for them. When God remembers his children, he does so "with favor" (Ne 5:19; 13:31). *wind.* The Hebrew word translated "Spirit" in 1:2 is here rendered "wind," and it introduces a series of parallels between the events of chs. 8–9 and those of ch. 1 in their literary order: Compare 8:2 with 1:7; 8:5 with 1:9; 8:7 with 1:20; 8:17 with 1:25; 9:1 with 1:28a; 9:2 with 1:28b; 9:3 with 1:30. Ch. 1 describes the original beginning, while chs. 8–9 describe a new beginning after the flood.

8:4 *mountains.* The word is plural and refers to a range of mountains. *Ararat.* The name is related to Assyrian Urartu, which became an extensive mountainous kingdom (see Jer 51:27; see also Isa 37:38), including much of the territory north of Mesopotamia and east of modern Turkey.

8:6 *window.* See note on 6:16.

8:11 *dove returned… in its beak was a freshly plucked olive leaf.* Olives do not grow at high elevations, and the fresh leaf was a sign to Noah that the water had receded from the earth. The modern symbol of peace represented by a dove carrying an olive branch in its beak has its origin in this story.

8:13 *first day of the first month of Noah's six hundred and first year.* The date formula signals humankind's new beginning after the flood.

8:14 *twenty-seventh day of the second month.* More than a year after the flood began (see 7:11).

8:16 *Come out of the ark.* See note on 7:1.

8:17 *multiply… be fruitful… increase in number.* See 1:22 and note. The animals and birds could now repopulate their former habitats.

Then Noah built an altar to the LORD *e* and, taking some of all the clean animals and *f* birds, he sacrificed burnt offerings *g* on it. ²¹The LORD smelled the pleasing aroma *h* and said in his heart: "Never again will I curse the ground *i* because of human beings, even though ª every inclination of the human heart is evil from childhood. *j* And never again will I destroy *k* all living creatures, *l* as I have done.

> ²² "As long as the earth endures,
> seedtime and harvest, *m*
> cold and heat,
> summer and winter, *n*
> day and night
> will never cease." *o*

GOD'S COVENANT WITH NOAH

9 Then God blessed Noah and his sons, saying to them, "Be fruitful and increase in number and fill the earth. *p* ²The fear and dread of you will fall on all the beasts of the earth and all the birds in the sky, on every creature that moves along the ground, and on all the fish in the sea; they are given into your hands. *q* ³Everything that lives and moves will be food for you. *r* Just as I gave you the green plants, I now give you everything. *s*

⁴"But you must not eat meat that has its lifeblood still in it. *t* ⁵And for your lifeblood I will surely demand an accounting. *u* I will demand an accounting from every animal. *v* And from each human being, too, I will demand an accounting for the life of another human being. *w*

> ⁶"Whoever sheds human blood,
> by human beings shall their blood be shed; *x*
> for in the image of God *y*
> has God made humankind.

⁷As for you, be fruitful and increase in number; multiply on the earth and increase upon it." *z*

⁸Then God said to Noah and to his sons with him: ⁹"I now establish my covenant with

---

ª 21 Or *human beings, for*

8:20 LORD. Since worship is a very personal matter, it is to God as "the LORD" (see note on 2:4) that Noah brought his sacrifice (see 4:4). *burnt offerings.* See Lev 1:3 and note.

8:21 *smelled the pleasing aroma.* A figurative way of saying that the Lord took delight in Noah's offering (cf. Eph 5:2; Php 4:18). *curse the ground.* Although the Hebrew here has a different word for "curse," the reference appears to be to the curse of 3:17. It may be that the Lord here pledged never to add curse upon curse as he had in regard to Cain (4:12). *even though every inclination of the human heart is evil.* For almost identical phraseology, see 6:5. Because of humanity's extreme wickedness, God had destroyed people (6:7) by means of a flood (6:17). Although righteous Noah and his family had been saved, he and his offspring were descendants of Adam and carried in their hearts the inheritance of sin. God graciously promises never again to deal with sin by sending such a devastating deluge (see 9:11, 15). Human history is held open for God's dealing with sin in a new and redemptive way—the way that was prepared for by God's action at Babel (see notes on 11:6, 8) and that begins to unfold with the call of Abram (12:1). *from childhood.* The phrase replaces "all the time" in 6:5 and emphasizes the truth that sin infects a person's life from conception and birth (Ps 51:5; 58:3).

8:22 Times and seasons, created by God in the beginning (see 1:14), will never cease till the end of history.

9:1–7 At this new beginning, God renewed his original benediction (1:28) and his provision for humanity's food (cf. v. 3; 1:29–30). But because sin had brought violence into the world and because God now appointed meat as a part of the human diet (v. 3), further divine provisions and stipulations are added (vv. 4–6). Yet God's benediction dominates and encloses the whole (see v. 7).

9:2 *given into your hands.* God reaffirmed that human beings would rule over all creation, including the animals (see note on 1:26).

9:3 *Everything that lives and moves will be food.* Meat would now supplement the human diet.

9:4 *you must not eat meat that has its lifeblood.* Lev 17:14 stresses the intimate relationship between blood and life by twice declaring that "the life of every creature is its blood." Life is the precious and mysterious gift of God, and people are not to seek to preserve it or increase the life-force within them by eating "life" that is "in the blood" (Lev 17:11)—as many pagan peoples throughout history have thought they could do.

9:5 *for your lifeblood … I will demand an accounting from every animal.* God himself is the great defender of human life (see 4:9–12), which is precious to him because people were created in his image (v. 6) and because they are the earthly representatives and focal point of God's kingdom. In the theocracy (kingdom of God) established at Sinai, a domestic animal that had taken human life was to be stoned to death (Ex 21:28–32).

9:6 *Whoever sheds human blood, by human beings shall their blood be shed.* In the later theocracy, those guilty of premeditated murder were to be executed (see Ex 21:12–14; Nu 35:16–32; see also Ro 13:3–4; 1Pe 2:13–14). *for in the image of God has God made humankind.* See 1:26 and note. In killing a human being, a murderer demonstrates contempt for God (see also Pr 14:31; 17:5; Jas 3:9 and notes).

9:8–17 God's first and most basic covenant with his creatures. It concerns the creation order itself and has its "sign" embedded in that creation order. Since divine judgment had seemed to undo the creation completely, sinful humanity needed God's covenanted assurance that his acts of judgment in history will not destroy the created order.

you *a* and with your descendants after you ¹⁰and with every living creature that was with you—the birds, the livestock and all the wild animals, all those that came out of the ark with you—every living creature on earth. ¹¹I establish my covenant *b* with you: *c* Never again will all life be destroyed by the waters of a flood; never again will there be a flood to destroy the earth. *d*"

¹²And God said, "This is the sign of the covenant *e* I am making between me and you and every living creature with you, a covenant for all generations to come: *f* ¹³I have set my rainbow *g* in the clouds, and it will be the sign of the covenant between me and the earth. ¹⁴Whenever I bring clouds over the earth and the rainbow *h* appears in the clouds, ¹⁵I will remember my covenant *i* between me and you and all living creatures of every kind. Never again will the waters become a flood to destroy all life. *j* ¹⁶Whenever the rainbow *k* appears in the clouds, I will see it and remember the everlasting covenant *l* between God and all living creatures of every kind on the earth."

¹⁷So God said to Noah, "This is the sign of the covenant *m* I have established between me and all life on the earth."

THE SONS OF NOAH

¹⁸The sons of Noah who came out of the ark were Shem, Ham and Japheth. *n* (Ham was the father of Canaan.) *o* ¹⁹These were the three sons of Noah, *p* and from them came the people who were scattered over the whole earth. *q*

²⁰Noah, a man of the soil, proceeded *a* to plant a vineyard. ²¹When he drank some of its wine, *r* he became drunk and lay uncovered inside his tent. ²²Ham, the father of Canaan, saw his father's nakedness *s* and told his two brothers outside. ²³But Shem and Japheth took a garment and laid it across their shoulders; then they walked in backward and covered their father's nakedness. Their faces were turned the other way so that they would not see their father's nakedness.

²⁴When Noah awoke from his wine and found out what his youngest son had done to him, ²⁵he said,

> "Cursed *t* be Canaan! *u*
> The lowest of slaves
> will he be to his brothers. *v*"

---

a 20 Or soil, was the first

Cross references

9:9 *a* ver 11; S Ge 6:18
9:11 *b* ver 16; Isa 24:5; 33:8; Hos 6:7 *c* S ver 9 *d* S Ge 8:21
9:12 *e* ver 17; Ge 17:11 *f* Ge 17:12; Ex 12:14; Lev 3:17; 6:18; 17:7; Nu 10:8
9:13 *g* ver 14; Eze 1:28; Rev 4:3; 10:1
9:14 *h* S ver 13
9:15 *i* S Ge 8:1; Ex 2:24; 6:5; 34:10; Lev 26:42,45; Dt 7:9; Ps 89:34; 103:18; 105:8; 106:45; Eze 16:60 *j* S Ge 8:21
9:16 *k* ver 13 *l* S ver 11; Ge 17:7,13, 19; 2Sa 7:13; 23:5; Ps 105:9-10; Isa 9:7; 54:10; 55:3; 59:21; 61:8; Jer 31:31-34; 32:40; 33:21; Eze 16:60; 37:26; S Heb 13:20
9:17 *m* S ver 12
9:18 *n* S Ge 5:32; Lk 3:36 *o* ver 25-27; Ge 10:6,15
9:19 *p* Ge 5:32 *q* S Ge 1:22; 10:32; 11:4,8,9
9:21 *r* Ge 19:35
9:22 *s* Hab 2:15
9:25 *t* Ge 27:12 *u* ver 18; Ex 20:5; Ps 79:8; Isa 14:21; Jer 31:29; 32:18 *v* Ge 25:23; 27:29,37, 40; 37:10; 49:8; Nu 24:18; Jos 9:23

C **9:9** *I now establish my covenant.* God sovereignly promised in this covenant to Noah, to Noah's descendants and to all other living things (as a kind of gracious reward to righteous Noah, the new father of the human race—see 6:18) never again to destroy the earth and its inhabitants until his purposes for his creation are fully realized ("as long as the earth endures," 8:22). For similar commitments by God, see his covenants with Abram (15:18–20), Phinehas (Nu 25:10–13) and David (2Sa 7). See chart, p. 20.

9:11 *Never again will all life be destroyed by the waters of a flood.* A summary of the provisions of the Lord's covenant with Noah—an eternal covenant, as seen in such words and phrases as "never again" (see also v. 15), "for all generations to come" (v. 12) and "everlasting" (v. 16).

9:12 *sign.* A covenant sign was a visible seal and reminder of covenant commitments. Circumcision would become the sign of the covenant with Abraham (see 17:11), and the Sabbath would be the sign of the covenant with Israel at Sinai (see Ex 31:16–17).

9:13 *rainbow.* Rain and the rainbow doubtless existed long before the time of Noah's flood, but after the flood the rainbow took on new meaning as the sign of the Noahic covenant. The Hebrew word is lit. "bow," as in 27:3; 48:22. The rainbow probably represents the bow with which God shoots the arrows of his lightning bolts toward the earth (Ps 18:14; 77:17; 144:6; Hab 3:9,11; for other references to God wielding a bow, see Ps 7:12; 21:12; Lam 2:4; Zec 9:13; for references to God's arrows, see also Dt 32:23,42; Job 6:4; 34:6; Ps 38:2; 64:7; Lam 3:12–13; Eze 5:16). But after a rainstorm God's bow is aimed at himself (for weapons being turned back on those wielding them, see Ps 37:15; 64:3–4,7–8; Jer 21:4). For that reason God appointed the rainbow to be the sign of his self-maledictory covenant oath (see 15:17 and note); whenever he sees it, he is reminded of his oath-bound pledge (v. 16).

9:19 *who were scattered.* The clause anticipates the list of nations in ch. 10 (see note on 11:8).

9:20 *man of the soil.* Like his father Lamech (see 5:29).

C A **9:21** *When he drank some of its wine, he became drunk.* The first person to make wine drunk to excess (cf. Pr 20:1 and note). *uncovered inside his tent.* Excessive use of wine led, among other things, to immodest behavior (see 19:30–35).

C **9:22** *father of Canaan.* Mentioned here because Ham, in acting as he did, showed himself to be the true father of Canaan (i.e., of the Canaanites; see note on 15:16). *told his two brothers.* He broadcast, rather than covered, his father's immodesty.

9:23 *faces were turned ... so that they would not see.* They wanted to avoid further disgrace to their father.

C **9:24** *from his wine.* From the drunkenness caused by the wine.

B **9:25** *Cursed be Canaan!* Some maintain that Ham's son (see vv. 18,22) was to be punished because of his father's sin (see 20:5), but Ex 20 restricts such punishment to "those who hate me." This account of Noah's cursing and blessing of his sons is addressed to Israel. Most likely it is for this reason that Canaan is here singled out from Ham's descendants as the object of Noah's curse. Israel would experience firsthand the depth of Canaanite sin (see Lev 18:2–3,6–30) and the harshness of God's judgment on it. In that judgment Noah's curse came to be fulfilled in the experience of this segment of Ham's descendants. But Ham's offspring, as listed in 10:6–13, included many of Israel's other long-term enemies (Egypt, Philistia, Assyria, Babylonia), who also experienced severe divine judgment because of their hostility to Israel and Israel's God. *lowest of slaves.* Joshua's subjection of the Gibeonites (Jos 9:27) is one of the fulfillments (see also Jos 16:10; Jdg 1:28,30,33,35; 1Ki 9:20–21).

COVENANTS	REFERENCE	TYPE	PARTICIPANT	DESCRIPTION
NOAHIC	Ge 9:8–17	Royal Grant	Made with "righteous" (6:9) Noah (and his descendants and every living thing on earth—all life that is subject to human jurisdiction)	An unconditional divine promise never to destroy all earthly life with some natural catastrophe, the covenant "sign" being the rainbow in the storm cloud
ABRAHAMIC A	Ge 15:9–21	Royal (land) Grant	Made with "righteous" (his faith was "credited to him as righteousness," v. 6) Abram (and his descendants, v. 16)	An unconditional divine promise to fulfill the grant of the land; a self-maledictory oath symbolically enacted it (v. 17)
ABRAHAMIC B	Ge 17	Suzerain-vassal	Made with Abraham as patriarchal head of his household	A conditional divine pledge to be Abraham's God and the God of his descendants (cf. "As for me," v. 4; "As for you," v. 9); the condition: total consecration to the Lord as symbolized by circumcision
SINAITIC	Ex 19–24	Suzerain-vassal	Made with Israel as the descendants of Abraham, Isaac and Jacob and as the people the Lord has redeemed from bondage to an earthly power	A conditional divine pledge to be Israel's God (as her Protector and the Guarantor of her blessed destiny); the condition: Israel's total consecration to the Lord as his people (his kingdom) who live by his rule and serve his purposes in history
PHINEHAS	Nu 25:10–13	Royal Grant	Made with the zealous priest Phinehas	An unconditional divine promise to maintain the family of Phinehas in a "lasting priesthood" (implicitly a pledge to Israel to provide her forever with a faithful priesthood)
DAVIDIC	2Sa 7:5–16	Royal Grant	Made with faithful King David after his devotion to God as Israel's king and the Lord's anointed vassal had come to special expression (v. 2)	An unconditional divine promise to establish and maintain the Davidic dynasty on the throne of Israel (implicitly a pledge to Israel) to provide her forever with a godly king like David and through that dynasty to do for her what he had done through David—bring her into rest in the promised land (1Ki 4:20–21; 5:3–4)
NEW	Jer 31:31–34	Royal Grant	Promised to rebellious Israel as she is about to be expelled from the promised land in actualization of the most severe covenant curse (Lev 26:27–39; Dt 28:36–37, 45–68)	An unconditional divine promise to unfaithful Israel to forgive her sins and establish his relationship with her on a new basis by writing his law "on their hearts"—a covenant of pure grace

Major Types of Royal Covenants/Treaties in the Ancient Near East

ROYAL GRANT (UNCONDITIONAL)
A king's grant (of land or some other benefit) to a loyal servant for faithful and exceptional service. The grant was normally perpetual and unconditional, but the servant's heirs benefited from it only as they continued their father's loyalty and service. (Cf. 1Sa 8:14; 22:7; 27:6; Est 8:1.)

PARITY
A covenant between equals, binding them to mutual friendship or at least to mutual respect for each other's spheres and interests. Participants called each other "brothers." (Cf. Ge 21:27; 26:31; 31:44–54; 1Ki 5:12; 15:19; 20:32–34; Am 1:9.)

SUZERAIN-VASSAL (CONDITIONAL)
A covenant regulating the relationship between a great king and one of his subject kings. The great king claimed absolute right of sovereignty, demanded total loyalty and service (the vassal must "love" his suzerain) and pledged protection of the subject's realm and dynasty, conditional on the vassal's faithfulness and loyalty to him. The vassal pledged absolute loyalty to his suzerain—whatever service his suzerain demanded—and exclusive reliance on the suzerain's protection. Participants called each other "lord" and "servant" or "father" and "son." (Cf. Jos 9:6,8; Eze 17:13–18; Hos 12:1.)

Commitments made in these covenants were accompanied by self-maledictory oaths (made orally, ceremonially or both). The gods were called upon to witness the covenants and implement the curses of the oaths if the covenants were violated.

²⁶He also said,

> "Praise be to the Lord, the God of Shem! ʷ
>   May Canaan be the slave ˣ of Shem.
> ²⁷ May God extend Japheth's ᵃ territory; ʸ
>   may Japheth live in the tents of Shem, ᶻ
>   and may Canaan be the slave of Japheth."

²⁸After the flood Noah lived 350 years. ²⁹Noah lived a total of 950 years, and then he died. ᵃ

THE TABLE OF NATIONS

This is the account ᵇ of Shem, Ham and Japheth, ᶜ Noah's sons, ᵈ who themselves had sons after the flood.

THE JAPHETHITES

10:2–5pp — 1Ch 1:5–7

² The sons ᵇ of Japheth:
    Gomer, ᵉ Magog, ᶠ Madai, Javan, ᵍ Tubal, ʰ Meshek ⁱ and Tiras.
³ The sons of Gomer:
    Ashkenaz, ʲ Riphath and Togarmah. ᵏ
⁴ The sons of Javan:
    Elishah, ˡ Tarshish, ᵐ the Kittites ⁿ and the Rodanites. ᶜ ⁵ (From these the maritime peoples spread out into their territories by their clans within their nations, each with its own language.) ᵒ

THE HAMITES

10:6–20pp — 1Ch 1:8–16

⁶ The sons of Ham:
    Cush, ᵖ Egypt, Put �q and Canaan. ʳ

ᵃ *27 Japheth sounds like the Hebrew for extend.*   ᵇ *2 Sons may mean descendants or successors or nations; also in verses 3, 4, 6, 7, 20-23, 29 and 31.*   ᶜ *4 Some manuscripts of the Masoretic Text and Samaritan Pentateuch (see also Septuagint and 1 Chron. 1:7); most manuscripts of the Masoretic Text Dodanites*

Noah's curse cannot be used to justify the enslavement of blacks, since most of Ham's descendants are known to be Caucasian, as the Canaanites certainly were (as shown by ancient paintings of the Canaanites discovered in Egypt).

9:26 *Praise be to the Lord.* The Lord (instead of Shem) is blessed ("praised") because he is the source of Shem's blessing. He is also the "God of Shem" (and his descendants, the Semites—which included the Israelites) in a special sense.

9:27 *live in the tents of Shem.* Share in the blessings bestowed on Shem.

9:29 *and then he died.* See note on 5:5. As the tenth and last member of the genealogy of Seth (5:3–32), Noah had an obituary that ends like those of his worthy ancestors.

10:1 *account.* See note on 2:4. The links affirmed here may not all be based on strictly physical descent, but may include geographical, historical and linguistic associations (see note on v. 5 and TNIV text notes on vv. 2,8; 11:10). See also Introduction to 1 Chronicles: Genealogies.

10:2 *sons.* See TNIV text note. *Japheth.* As the least involved in the Biblical narrative and perhaps also as the oldest of Noah's sons (see v. 21 and TNIV text note), his descendants or successors are listed first. The genealogy of Shem, the chosen line, appears last in the chapter (see vv. 21–31; see also 11:10–26). The 14 nations that came from Japheth plus the 30 from Ham and the 26 from Shem add up to 70 (the multiple of 10 and 7, both numbers signifying completeness; see note on 5:5), perhaps in anticipation of the 70 members of Jacob's family who went down to Egypt (see 46:27; Ex 1:5; see also Dt 32:8). The Japhethites lived generally north and west of Canaan in Eurasia. *Gomer.* The people of Gomer (the later Cimmerians) and related nations

(see v. 3) lived near the Black Sea (see map, p. 23). *Magog.* Possibly the father of a Scythian people who inhabited the Caucasus and adjacent regions southeast of the Black Sea. *Madai.* The later Medes. *Javan.* Ionia (southern Greece) and perhaps western Asia Minor. *Tubal, Meshek.* Not related to Tobolsk and Moscow in modern Russia. Together with Magog they are mentioned in later Assyrian inscriptions. See also Eze 38:2. Probably Tubal was in Pontus and Meshek was in the Moschian Mountains. Their movement was from eastern Asia Minor north to the Black Sea. *Tiras.* Possibly the Thrace of later times.

10:3 *Ashkenaz.* The later Scythians. All three names in this verse refer to peoples located in the upper Euphrates region.

10:4 *Elishah.* Either Alashia (an ancient name for Cyprus) or a reference to Sicily and southern Italy. *Tarshish.* Probably southern Spain. *Kittites.* A people living on Cyprus. *Rodanites.* A people whose name is perhaps reflected in Rhodes (a Greek isle).

10:5 See vv. 20,31. *territories . . . clans . . . nations . . . language.* Geographic, ethnic, political and linguistic terms, respectively. These several criteria were used to differentiate the various groups of people.

10:6 *Ham.* The Hamites named here were located in southwestern Asia and northeastern Africa. *Cush.* The upper Nile region, south of Egypt. *Egypt.* Hebrew *Mizraim,* which means "two Egypts," a reference to Upper (southern) and Lower (northern) Egypt. *Put.* Probably Libya (see note on v. 13). *Canaan.* The name possibly means "land of purple" (as does Phoenicia, the Greek name for the same general region). Canaan was a major producer and exporter of purple dye, highly prized by royalty. The territory was much later called Palestine after the Philistines (see v. 14).

9:26 ʷ Ge 14:20; Ex 18:10; Ps 7:17
ˣ 1Ki 9:21
9:27 ʸ Ge 10:2-5
ᶻ Eph 2:13-14; 3:6
9:29 ᵃ S Ge 2:17
10:1 ᵇ Ge 2:4
ᶜ S Ge 5:32 ᵈ ver 32; 1Ch 1:4
10:2 ᵉ Eze 38:2; 39:6; Rev 20:8 ᶠ Eze 27:19
ʰ Isa 66:19; Eze 27:13; 32:26 ⁱ Eze 39:1
10:3 ʲ Jer 51:27
ᵏ Eze 27:14; 38:6
10:4 ˡ Eze 27:7
ᵐ Ps 48:7; 72:10; Isa 2:16; 23:1,6,10,14; 60:9; 66:19; Jer 10:9; Eze 27:12,25; 38:13; Jnh 1:3 ⁿ Nu 24:24; Isa 23:12; Jer 2:10; Eze 27:6; Da 11:30
10:5 ᵒ Ge 9:27
10:6 ᵖ 2Ki 19:9; 2Ch 12:3; 16:8; Isa 11:11; 18:1; 20:3; 43:3; Jer 46:9; Eze 30:4,9; 38:5; Na 3:9; Zep 2:12; 3:10 ᵠ Eze 27:10; 38:5 ʳ S Ge 9:18

10:7 ᵍ Isa 43:3
ʳ S Ge 2:11
ᵘ Eze 27:22 ᵛ Ge 25:3;
1Ki 10:1; 2Ch 9:1;
Job 1:15; 6:19; 16:11;
Ps 72:10,15; Isa 60:6;
Jer 6:20; Eze 27:22;
38:13; Joel 3:8
ʷ 1Ch 1:32; Isa 21:13;
Jer 25:23-24; 49:8;
Eze 27:15,20; 38:13
10:8 ˣ Mic 5:6
10:9 ʸ 2Ch 14:9;
16:8; Isa 18:2
ᶻ Ge 25:27; 27:3
10:10 ᵃ Ge 11:9;
2Ch 36:17; Isa 13:1;
47:1; Jer 21:2; 25:12;
50:1 ᵇ Ezr 4:9
ᶜ Isa 10:9; Am 6:2
ᵈ Ge 11:2; 14:1;
Zec 5:11
10:11 ᵉ Ps 83:8;
Mic 5:6 ᶠ 2Ki 19:36;
Isa 37:37; Jnh 1:2;
3:2,3; 4:11; Na 1:1;
Zep 2:13
10:14 ᵍ Ge 21:32,
34; 26:1,8; Jos 13:2;
Jdg 3:3; Isa 14:31;
Jer 47:1,4; Am 9:7
ʰ Dt 2:23; 1Ch 1:12
10:15 ⁱ S Ge 9:18
ʲ ver 19; Jos 11:8;
Jdg 10:6; Isa 23:2,4;
Jer 25:22; 27:3; 47:4;
Eze 28:21; 32:30;
Joel 3:4; Zec 9:2
ᵏ Ex 4:22; Nu 1:20;
3:2; 18:15; 26:5; 33:4
ˡ Ge 15:20; 23:3,20;
25:10; 26:34; 27:46;
49:32; Nu 13:29;
Jos 1:4; 1Sa 26:6;
Eze 16:3
10:16 ᵐ Jdg 19:10;
1Ch 11:4; Ezr 9:1
ⁿ Ex 3:8; Nu 13:29;
21:13; 32:39; Dt 1:4;
Jos 2:10; 2Ch 8:7
ᵒ Ge 15:18-21; Dt 7:1
10:17 ᵖ Ge 34:2;
36:2; Ex 3:8; Dt 7:1;
Jdg 3:3

⁷The sons of Cush:

Seba, ˢ Havilah, ᵗ Sabtah, Raamah ᵘ and Sabteka.

The sons of Raamah:

Sheba ᵛ and Dedan. ʷ

⁸Cush was the father ᵃ of Nimrod, ˣ who became a mighty warrior on the earth. ⁹He was a mighty ʸ hunter ᶻ before the Lᴏʀᴅ; that is why it is said, "Like Nimrod, a mighty hunter before the Lᴏʀᴅ." ¹⁰The first centers of his kingdom were Babylon, ᵃ Uruk, ᵇ Akkad and Kalneh, ᶜ in ᵇ Shinar. ᶜ ᵈ ¹¹From that land he went to Assyria, ᵉ where he built Nineveh, ᶠ Rehoboth Ir, ᵈ Calah ¹²and Resen, which is between Nineveh and Calah—which is the great city.

¹³Egypt was the father of
the Ludites, Anamites, Lehabites, Naphtuhites, ¹⁴Pathrusites, Kasluhites (from whom the Philistines ᵍ came) and Caphtorites. ʰ

¹⁵Canaan ⁱ was the father of
Sidon ʲ his firstborn, ᵉ ᵏ and of the Hittites, ˡ ¹⁶Jebusites, ᵐ Amorites, ⁿ Girgashites, ᵒ ¹⁷Hivites, ᵖ Arkites, Sinites, ¹⁸Arvadites, �q Zemarites and Hamathites. ʳ

Later the Canaanite ˢ clans scattered ¹⁹and the borders of Canaan ᵗ reached from Sidon ᵘ toward Gerar ᵛ as far as Gaza, ʷ and then toward Sodom, Gomorrah, Admah and Zeboyim, ˣ as far as Lasha.

²⁰These are the sons of Ham by their clans and languages, in their territories and nations.

THE SEMITES

10:21–31pp — Ge 11:10–27; 1Ch 1:17–27

²¹Sons were also born to Shem, whose older brother was ᶠ Japheth; Shem was the ancestor of all the sons of Eber. ʸ

²²The sons of Shem:

Elam, ᶻ Ashur, ᵃ Arphaxad, ᵇ Lud and Aram. ᶜ

ᵃ **8** *Father may mean ancestor or predecessor or founder; also in verses 13, 15, 24 and 26.*   ᵇ **10** *Or Uruk and Akkad—all of them in*   ᶜ **10** *That is, Babylonia*   ᵈ **11** *Or Nineveh with its city squares*   ᵉ **15** *Or of the Sidonians, the foremost*   ᶠ **21** *Or Shem, the older brother of*

10:18 �q Eze 27:8 ʳ 1Ch 18:3 ˢ Ge 12:6; 13:7; 50:11; Ex 13:11; Nu 13:29; 14:25; 21:3; 33:40; Dt 1:7; Jdg 1:1   **10:19** ᵗ Ge 11:31; 12:1; 13:12; 17:8; 24:3; 26:34; 27:46; 28:1,6,8; 31:18; 35:6; 37:1; Lev 25:38 ᵘ S ver 15; Ge 49:13; Jos 19:28; 18:28; 2Sa 24:6 ᵛ 2Ch 14:13 ʷ Ge 14:2; Dt 29:23   **10:21** ʸ ver 24; Nu 24:24   **10:22** ᶻ Ge 14:1; Isa 11:11; 21:2; Jer 25:25; 49:34; Eze 32:24; Da 8:2 ᵃ Nu 24:22,24; Eze 27:23 ᵇ Lk 3:36 ᶜ Jdg 3:10; 1Ki 11:25; 19:15; 20:34; 22:31; 2Ki 5:1; 8:7

10:7 *sons of Cush.* The seven Cushite nations here mentioned were all in Arabia. Sheba and Dedan (or their namesakes) reappear as two of Abraham's grandsons (see 25:3). Together with Raamah they are mentioned in Eze 27:20–22.

10:8 *Cush.* Probably not the same as in v. 6. Located in Mesopotamia, the name may be related to that of the later Kassites. *Nimrod.* Possibly the Hebrew name of Sargon I, an early ruler of Akkad (see v. 10).

10:10 *Uruk.* One of the important cities in ancient Mesopotamia (see map No. 1 at the end of this study Bible).

10:12 *great city.* Possibly a reference to Calah (or even Resen), but most likely to Nineveh (see Jnh 1:2; 3:2; 4:11), either alone or including the surrounding urban areas.

10:13 *Ludites.* Perhaps the Lydians in Asia Minor (see note on v. 22). *Anamites.* Located in north Africa, west of Egypt, near Cyrene. *Lehabites.* Perhaps the Libyan desert tribes (see note on v. 6). *Naphtuhites.* People of Lower Egypt.

10:14 *Pathrusites.* The inhabitants of Upper Egypt (see note on v. 6). *Caphtorites.* Crete, known as Caphtor in ancient times, was for a while the homeland of various Philistine groups (see Jer 47:4; Am 9:7). The Philistines themselves were a vigorous Indo-European maritime people who invaded Egypt early in the 12th century B.C. After being driven out, they migrated in large numbers to southwest Canaan, later extending their influence over most of the land. The Philistines of the patriarchal period (see 21:32,34; 26:1,8,14–15,18) no doubt had earlier settled in Canaan more peacefully and in smaller numbers.

10:15 *Sidon.* An important commercial city on the northwest coast of Canaan. *Hittites.* An Indo-European-speaking people who moved into Anatolia (ancient Asia Minor, modern western Turkey) from southeast Europe in the late third millennium B.C. They came to dominate north-central Anatolia in the mid-second millennium B.C. and called themselves Hittites, a name adapted from that of the native Hatti people. They established an empire powerful enough at times to challenge both Babylonia and Egypt. The relationship, if any, between these people and the "Hittites" of Canaan mentioned in the Bible remains obscure (but see Eze 16:3 and note).

10:16 *Jebusites.* Inhabitants of Jerusalem at the time of Israel's conquest of Canaan. Jerusalem was also known as Jebus during part of its history (see Jdg 19:10–11; 1Ch 11:4). *Amorites.* The name comes from an Akkadian word meaning "westerner" (west from the Babylonian perspective). Amorites lived in the hill country of Canaan at the time of the Israelite conquest.

10:17–18 Together with the Girgashites (v. 16), these groups in Canaan for the most part inhabited small city-states.

10:19 *Sodom, Gomorrah, Admah and Zeboyim.* See 14:2,8 (see also note on 13:10); probably located east and/or southeast of the Dead Sea.

10:21 *Sons were also born to Shem.* The descendants of Shem were called Shemites (later modified to Semites). *Eber.* Though a distant descendant of Shem (see vv. 24–25; 11:14–17), Eber's importance as the ancestor of the Hebrews ("Eber" is the origin of the Hebrew word for "Hebrew") is already hinted at here.

10:22 *Elam.* The Elamites lived east of Mesopotamia. *Ashur.* An early name for Assyria (see note on 2:14) in northern Mesopota-

23 The sons of Aram:
  Uz, *d* Hul, Gether and Meshek. *a*
24 Arphaxad was the father of *b* Shelah,
  and Shelah the father of Eber. *e*
25 Two sons were born to Eber:
  One was named Peleg, *c* because in his time the earth was divided; his brother was named Joktan.
26 Joktan was the father of
  Almodad, Sheleph, Hazarmaveth, Jerah, 27Hadoram, Uzal, *f* Diklah, 28Obal, Abimael, Sheba, *g* 29Ophir, *h* Havilah and Jobab. All these were sons of Joktan.

30The region where they lived stretched from Mesha toward Sephar, in the eastern hill country.

31These are the sons of Shem by their clans and languages, in their territories and nations.

32These are the clans of Noah's sons, *i* according to their lines of descent, within their nations. From these the nations spread out over the earth *j* after the flood.

THE TOWER OF BABEL

11 Now the whole world had one language *k* and a common speech. 2As people moved eastward, *d* they found a plain in Shinar *e l* and settled there. 3They said to each other, "Come, let's make bricks *m* and bake them thorough-

---

a 23 See Septuagint and 1 Chron. 1:17; *Hebrew Mash.*   *b 24* Hebrew; Septuagint *father of Cainan, and Cainan was the father of*   *c 25* Peleg *means division.*   *d 2* Or *from the east; or in the east*   *e 2* That is, *Babylonia*

10:23 *d* Ge 22:21; Job 1:1; Jer 25:20; La 4:21
10:24 *e* S ver 21; Lk 3:35
10:27 *f* Eze 27:19
10:28 *g* 1Ki 10:1; Job 6:19; Ps 72:10,15; Isa 60:6; Eze 27:22
10:29 *h* 1Ki 9:28; 10:11; 1Ch 29:4; Job 22:24; 28:16; Ps 45:9; Isa 13:12
10:32 *i* S ver 1
j S Ge 9:19
11:1 *k* ver 6
11:2 *l* S Ge 10:10
11:3 *m* Ex 1:14; 5:7; Jer 43:9

---

mia. *Arphaxad.* See also 11:10–13; perhaps a compound form of the Hebrew word for Chaldea, in southern Mesopotamia. *Lud.* Probably the Lydians of Asia Minor (see note on v. 13). *Aram.* Located north-northeast of Canaan, the area known today as Syria (see note on Dt 26:5).
10:24 *Shelah.* See 11:12–15.
10:25 *Peleg.* See TNIV text note and 11:16–19. *earth was divided.* Perhaps resulting from the dispersion of peoples described in 11:1–9.
10:26 *Joktan.* The predecessor of numerous south Arabian kingdoms.

10:28 *Sheba.* In southwest Arabia (roughly the area of Yemen). A later queen of Sheba made a memorable visit to King Solomon in the tenth century B.C. (see 1Ki 10:1–13).
10:29 *Ophir.* The source of much of King Solomon's gold (see 1Ki 9:28; 10:11). Its location seems to have been south of Canaan, perhaps somewhere in Africa or south Arabia (but see note on 1Ki 9:28).
11:1–9 This section provides the main reason for the scattering of the peoples listed in ch. 10. The narrative is a beautiful example of inverted or hourglass structure (see Introduction: Literary Features). The author of Genesis uses the story of the flood and

TABLE OF NATIONS

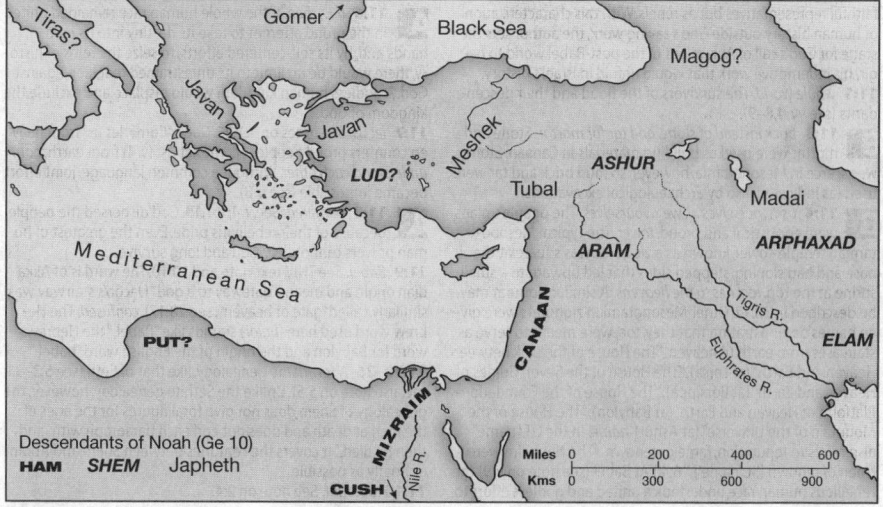

Descendants of Noah (Ge 10)
HAM *SHEM* Japheth

Tiras?
Gomer
Black Sea
Magog?
Javan
Javan
Meshek
ASHUR
Madai
LUD?
Tubal
ARPHAXAD
Mediterranean Sea
ARAM
Tigris R.
CANAAN
Euphrates R.
ELAM
PUT?
MIZRAIM
Nile R.
CUSH

Miles 0   200   400   600
Kms 0   300   600   900

11:3 *n* Isa 9:10;
Am 5:11 *o* Ge 14:10
11:4 *p* Dt 1:28; 6:10;
9:1; Job 20:6;
Jer 51:53 *q* Ge 6:4
r Dt 30:3; 1Ki 22:17;
Est 3:8; Ps 44:11;
Jer 31:10; 40:15;
Eze 6:8; Joel 3:2
s S Ge 9:19; Dt 4:27
11:5 *t* ver 7;
Ge 18:21; Ex 3:8;
19:11,18,20; Ps 18:9;
144:5
11:6 *u* S ver 1
11:7 *v* S Ge 1:26
w S ver 5 *x* Ge 42:23;
Dt 28:49; Isa 28:11;
33:19; Jer 5:15;
1Co 14:2,11
11:8 *y* S Ge 9:19;
Dt 32:8; S Lk 1:51
11:9 *z* S Ge 10:10
a Ps 55:9 *b* Ac 2:5-11
c Isa 2:10,21; 13:14;
24:1
11:10 *d* S Ge 2:4
e Lk 3:36
11:12 *f* Lk 3:35
11:14 *g* Lk 3:35
11:16 *h* Lk 3:35
11:18 *i* Lk 3:35
11:20 *j* Lk 3:35
11:22 *k* Lk 3:34

ly." They used brick instead of stone, *n* and tar *o* for mortar. ⁴Then they said, "Come, let us build ourselves a city, with a tower that reaches to the heavens, *p* so that we may make a name *q* for ourselves and not be scattered *r* over the face of the whole earth." *s*

⁵But the LORD came down *t* to see the city and the tower the people were building. ⁶The LORD said, "If as one people speaking the same language *u* they have begun to do this, then nothing they plan to do will be impossible for them. ⁷Come, let us *v* go down *w* and confuse their language so they will not understand each other." *x*

⁸So the LORD scattered them from there over all the earth, *y* and they stopped building the city. ⁹That is why it was called Babel *a z*—because there the LORD confused the language *a* of the whole world. *b* From there the LORD scattered *c* them over the face of the whole earth.

FROM SHEM TO ABRAM

11:10–27pp — Ge 10:21–31; 1Ch 1:17–27

¹⁰This is the account *d* of Shem's family line.

Two years after the flood, when Shem was 100 years old, he became the father *b* of Arphaxad. *e* ¹¹And after he became the father of Arphaxad, Shem lived 500 years and had other sons and daughters.

¹²When Arphaxad had lived 35 years, he became the father of Shelah. *f* ¹³And after he became the father of Shelah, Arphaxad lived 403 years and had other sons and daughters. *c*

¹⁴When Shelah had lived 30 years, he became the father of Eber. *g* ¹⁵And after he became the father of Eber, Shelah lived 403 years and had other sons and daughters.

¹⁶When Eber had lived 34 years, he became the father of Peleg. *h* ¹⁷And after he became the father of Peleg, Eber lived 430 years and had other sons and daughters.

¹⁸When Peleg had lived 30 years, he became the father of Reu. *i* ¹⁹And after he became the father of Reu, Peleg lived 209 years and had other sons and daughters.

²⁰When Reu had lived 32 years, he became the father of Serug. *j* ²¹And after he became the father of Serug, Reu lived 207 years and had other sons and daughters.

²²When Serug had lived 30 years, he became the father of Nahor. *k* ²³And after he became the father of Nahor, Serug lived 200 years and had other sons and daughters.

---

a 9 That is, Babylon; *Babel* sounds like the Hebrew for *confused.*   *b* 10 *Father* may mean *ancestor*; also in verses 11-25.   *c* 12,13 Hebrew; Septuagint (see also Luke 3:35, 36 and note at Gen. 10:24) *35 years, he became the father of Cainan. ¹³And after he became the father of Cainan, Arphaxad lived 430 years and had other sons and daughters, and then he died. When Cainan had lived 130 years, he became the father of Shelah. And after he became the father of Shelah, Cainan lived 330 years and had other sons and daughters*

---

the story of Babel to characterize the ways of humankind and God's responses through acts of judgment in order to thwart humanity's proud efforts to rule over the creation, not as God's faithful representatives but as rebels. With this characterization of human history outside God's saving work, the author sets the stage for God's call of Abram out of the post-Babel world to begin his redemptive work that would unfold in Israel's history.

11:1 *whole world.* The survivors of the flood and their descendants (see vv. 4,8–9).

11:3 *brick instead of stone, and tar for mortar.* Stone and mortar were used as building materials in Canaan. Stone was scarce in Mesopotamia, however, so mud brick and tar were used (as indicated also by archaeological excavations).

11:4 *us … ourselves … we … ourselves.* The people's plans were egotistical and proud. *tower.* The typical Mesopotamian temple-tower, known as a ziggurat, was square at the base and had sloping, stepped sides that led upward to a small shrine at the top. A similar ziggurat may be described in 28:12. Other Mesopotamian ziggurats were given names demonstrating that they, too, were meant to serve as staircases from earth to heaven: "The House of the Link between Heaven and Earth" (at Larsa), "The House of the Seven Guides of Heaven and Earth" (at Borsippa), "The House of the Foundation-Platform of Heaven and Earth" (at Babylon), "The House of the Mountain of the Universe" (at Ashur). *name.* In the OT, "name" also refers to reputation, fame or renown. (The Nephilim were "men of renown [lit. 'name']," 6:4.) At Babel (see note on v. 9) the rebellious human race undertook a united and godless effort to

establish for themselves, by a titanic enterprise, a world renown by which they would dominate God's creation (cf. 10:8–12; 2Sa 18:18). *scattered.* See note on v. 8.

11:6 *If … then.* If the whole human race remained united in the proud attempt to take its destiny into its own hands and, by its self-centered efforts, to seize the reins of history, there would be no limit to its unrestrained rebellion against God. A godless human kingdom would displace and exclude the kingdom of God.

11:7 *let us.* See notes on 1:1,26. God's "Come, let us" from heaven counters proud people's "Come, let us" (v. 4) from earth. *not understand each other.* Without a common language, joint effort became impossible (see v. 8).

11:8 *scattered.* See v. 4; 9:1,19. God dispersed the people because of their rebellious pride. Even the greatest of human powers cannot defy God and long survive.

11:9 *Babel.* See TNIV text note and 10:10. The word is of Akkadian origin and means "gateway to a god" (Jacob's stairway was similarly called "gate of heaven"; see 28:17). *confused.* The Hebrew word used here (*balal*) sounds like "Babel," the Hebrew word for Babylon and the origin of the English word "babel."

11:10–26 A ten-name genealogy, like that of Seth (see 5:3–31; see also note on 5:5). Unlike the Sethite genealogy, however, the genealogy of Shem does not give total figures for the ages of the men at death and does not end each paragraph with "and then he died." It covers the centuries between Shem and Abram as briefly as possible.

11:10 *account.* See note on 2:4.

²⁴When Nahor had lived 29 years, he became the father of Terah. [l] ²⁵And after he became the father of Terah, Nahor lived 119 years and had other sons and daughters.

²⁶After Terah had lived 70 years, he became the father of Abram, [m] Nahor [n] and Haran. [o]

ABRAM'S FAMILY

²⁷This is the account [p] of Terah's family line.

Terah became the father of Abram, Nahor [q] and Haran. And Haran became the father of Lot. [r] ²⁸While his father Terah was still alive, Haran died in Ur of the Chaldeans, [s] in the land of his birth. ²⁹Abram and Nahor [t] both married. The name of Abram's wife was Sarai, [u] and the name of Nahor's wife was Milkah; [v] she was the daughter of Haran, the father of both Milkah and Iskah. ³⁰Now Sarai was childless because she was not able to conceive. [w]

³¹Terah took his son Abram, his grandson Lot [x] son of Haran, and his daughter-in-law [y] Sarai, the wife of his son Abram, and together they set out from Ur of the Chaldeans [z] to go to Canaan. [a] But when they came to Harran, [b] they settled there.

³²Terah [c] lived 205 years, and he died in Harran.

THE CALL OF ABRAM

12 The LORD had said to Abram, "Go from your country, your people and your father's household [d] to the land [e] I will show you. [f]

²"I will make you into a great nation, [g]
　and I will bless you; [h]
I will make your name great,
　and you will be a blessing. [a] [i]
³I will bless those who bless you,
　and whoever curses you I will curse; [j]

---

[a] 2 Or *great,* / *and you will be seen as blessed*

12:2 2Ch 1:9; Ne 9:23; Ps 107:38; Isa 6:13; 10:22; 48:19; 51:2; 54:3; 60:22; Jer 33:22; Mic 4:7 [h] Ge 24:1,35; 25:11; 26:3; 28:4; Ex 20:24; Nu 22:12; 23:8,20; 24:9; Ps 67:6; 115:12; Isa 44:3; 61:9; 65:23; Mal 3:12 [i] Ge 22:18; Isa 19:24; Jer 4:2; Hag 2:19; Zec 8:13 **12:3** [j] Ge 27:29; Ex 23:22; Nu 24:9; Dt 30:7

11:24 [l] Lk 3:34
11:26 [m] Lk 3:34
[n] Jos 24:2 [o] 2Ki 19:12; Isa 37:12; Eze 27:23
11:27 [p] S Ge 2:4
[q] ver 29; Ge 31:53
[r] ver 31; Ge 12:4; 13:1, 5,8,12; 14:12; 19:1; Lk 17:28; 2Pe 2:7
11:28 [s] ver 31; Ge 15:7; Ne 9:7; Job 1:17; 16:11; Eze 23:23; Ac 7:4
11:29 [t] S ver 27,31; Ge 22:20,23; 24:10, 15,24; 29:5 [u] Ge 12:5, 11; 16:1; 17:15
[v] Ge 22:20
11:30 [w] Ge 16:1; 18:11; 25:21; 29:31; 30:1,22; Jdg 13:2; 1Sa 1:5; Ps 113:9; Lk 1:7,36
11:31 [x] S ver 27
[y] Ge 38:11; Lev 18:15; 20:12; Ru 1:6,22; 2:20; 4:15; 1Sa 4:19; 1Ch 2:4; Eze 22:11; Mic 7:6 [z] S ver 28
[a] S Ge 10:19
[b] S ver 29; Ge 12:4; 27:43; 28:5,10; 29:4; 2Ki 19:12; Eze 27:23
11:32 [c] Jos 24:2
12:1 [d] Ge 20:13; 24:4,27,40
[e] S Ge 10:19 [f] Ge 15:7; 26:2; Jos 24:3; Ac 7:3*; Heb 11:8
12:2 [g] Ge 13:16; 15:5; 17:2,4; 18:18; 22:17; 26:4; 28:3,14; 32:12; 35:11; 41:49; 46:3; 47:27; 48:4,16, 19; Ex 1:7; 5:5; 32:13; Dt 1:10; 10:22; 13:17; 26:5; Jos 11:4; 24:3; 2Sa 17:11; 1Ki 3:8; 4:20; 1Ch 27:23;

11:26 *Terah ... became the father of Abram, Nahor and Haran.* As in the case of Shem, Ham and Japheth, the names of the three sons may not be in chronological order by age (see 9:24; see also 10:21 and TNIV text note). Haran died while his father was still alive (see v. 28).

A C **11:27—25:11** With God's calling of Abram out of the post-Babel peoples, the story of God's ways with humankind shifts focus from universal history to the history of God's relationship with a particular person and people. Here begins the history of his saving work, in which human sin is not only judged (the flood) or restrained (Babel) but forgiven (through atonement) and overcome (through the purifying of human hearts). Throughout the rest of Scripture the unfolding of this history remains the golden thread and central theme. Its final outcome is made sure through Jesus Christ, "the son of Abraham" (Lk 3:34; see also Mt 1:1–17; Gal 3:16)—which is the core message of the NT.

The account of the God-Abram relationship found here foreshadows in many ways the God-Israel relationship, and the trials and triumphs of Abram's faith model the life of faith for his descendants.

11:27 *account.* See note on 2:4.

B **11:28** *Ur of the Chaldeans.* Possibly in northern Mesopotamia, but more likely the site on the Euphrates in southern Iraq excavated by Leonard Woolley between 1922 and 1934. Ruins and artifacts from Ur reveal a civilization and culture that reached high levels before Abram's time. King Ur-Nammu, who may have been Abram's contemporary, is famous for his law code. *Chaldeans.* See notes on Ezr 5:12; Job 1:17.

C **11:30** *Sarai was ... not able to conceive.* The sterility of Abram's wife (see 15:2–3; 17:1f) emphasized the fact that God's people would not come by natural generation from the

post-Babel peoples. God was bringing a new humanity into being, of whom Abram was father (17:5), just as Adam and Noah were fathers of the fallen human race.

11:31 *they came to Harran.* In Hebrew the name of the town is spelled differently from that of Abram's brother (v. 26). The moon-god was worshiped at both Ur and Harran, and since Terah was an idolater (see Jos 24:2), he probably felt at home in either place. Harran (an Akkadian word meaning "caravan") was a flourishing caravan city in the 19th century B.C. In the 18th century it was ruled by Amorites (see note on 10:16).

12:1 *had said.* God had spoken to Abram "while he was still in Mesopotamia, before he lived in Harran" (Ac 7:2). *Go from ... show you.* Abram must leave the settled world of the post-Babel nations and begin a pilgrimage with God to a better world of God's making (see 24:7; see also Heb 11:10 and note on 11:1–9).

12:2–3 God's promise to Abram has a sevenfold structure: (1) "I will make you into a great nation," (2) "I will bless you," (3) "I will make your name great," (4) "you will be a blessing," (5) "I will bless those who bless you," (6) "whoever curses you I will curse," and (7) "all peoples on earth will be blessed through you." God's original blessing on the whole human race (1:28) would be especially fulfilled in the lives of Abram and his offspring. In various ways and degrees, these promises were reaffirmed to Abram (v. 7; 15:5–21; 17:4–8; 18:18–19; 22:17–18), to Isaac (26:2–4), to Jacob (28:13–15; 35:11–12; 46:3) and to Moses (Ex 3:6–8; 6:2–8). The seventh promise is quoted in Ac 3:25 with reference to Peter's Jewish listeners (see Ac 3:12)—Abram's physical descendants—and in Gal 3:8 with reference to Paul's Gentile listeners—Abram's spiritual descendants.

B **12:3** *whoever curses you.* The ancient Near Eastern peoples thought that by pronouncing curses on someone they could bring down the power of the gods (or other mysteri-

12:3 *k* Ge 15:5;
18:18; 22:18; 26:4;
28:4,14; Dt 9:5;
Ps 72:17; Isa 19:25;
Ac 3:25; Gal 3:8*
12:4 *l* S Ge 11:27
m Ge 16:3,16; 17:1,17,
24; 21:5 *n* S Ge 11:31
12:5 *o* S Ge 11:29
p ver 16; Ge 13:2,6;
31:18; 46:6 *q* Ge 14:14;
15:3; 17:23; Ecc 2:7
r Ge 11:31; 16:3;
Heb 11:8
12:6 *s* Heb 11:9
t Ge 35:4; Dt 11:30;
Jos 24:26; Jdg 7:1; 9:6
u Ge 33:18; 37:12;
Jos 17:7; 20:7; 24:1;
Jdg 8:31; 21:19;
1Ki 12:1; Ps 60:6;
108:7 *v* S Ge 10:18
12:7 *w* Ge 17:1; 18:1;
26:2; 35:1; Ex 6:3;
Ac 7:2 *x* Ex 3:8;
Nu 10:29; Dt 30:5;
Heb 11:8 *y* Ge 13:15,
17; 15:18; 17:8; 23:18;
24:7; 26:3-4; 28:13;
35:12; 48:4; 50:24;
Ex 6:4,8; 13:5,11;
32:13; 33:1; Nu 11:12;
Dt 1:8; 2:31; 9:5; 11:9;
34:4; 2Ki 2:5;
1Ch 16:16; 2Ch 20:7;
Ps 105:9-11; Jer 25:5;
Eze 47:14; Ac 7:5;
Ro 4:13; Gal 3:16*
z S Ge 8:20; 13:4
12:8 *a* Ge 13:3;
28:11,19; 35:1,8,15;
Jos 7:2; 8:9; 1Sa 7:16;
1Ki 12:29; Hos 12:4;
Am 3:14; 4:4
b Ge 26:25; 33:19;
Heb 11:9

and all peoples on earth
will be blessed through you. *k* *a*

⁴So Abram went, as the LORD had told him; and Lot *l* went with him. Abram was seventy-five years old *m* when he set out from Harran. *n* ⁵He took his wife Sarai, *o* his nephew Lot, all the possessions they had accumulated *p* and the people *q* they had acquired in Harran, and they set out for the land of Canaan, *r* and they arrived there.

⁶Abram traveled through the land *s* as far as the site of the great tree of Moreh *t* at Shechem. *u* At that time the Canaanites *v* were in the land. ⁷The LORD appeared to Abram *w* and said, "To your offspring *b* I will give this land. *x* *y* So he built an altar there to the LORD, *z* who had appeared to him.

⁸From there he went on toward the hills east of Bethel *a* and pitched his tent, *b* with Bethel on the west and Ai *c* on the east. There he built an altar to the LORD and called on the name of the LORD. *d*

⁹Then Abram set out and continued toward the Negev. *e*

ABRAM IN EGYPT

12:10–20 Ref — Ge 20:1–18; 26:1–11

¹⁰Now there was a famine in the land, *f* and Abram went down to Egypt to live there for a while because the famine was severe. *g* ¹¹As he was about to enter Egypt, he said to his wife Sarai, *h* "I know what a beautiful woman *i* you are. ¹²When the Egyptians see you, they will say, 'This is his wife.' Then they will kill me but will let you live. ¹³Say you are my sister, *j* so that I will be treated well for your sake and my life will be spared because of you."

¹⁴When Abram came to Egypt, the Egyptians saw that Sarai was a very beautiful woman. *k* ¹⁵And when Pharaoh's officials saw her, they praised her to Pharaoh, and she was taken into his palace. ¹⁶He treated Abram well for her sake, and Abram acquired sheep and cattle, male and female donkeys, male and female servants, and camels. *l*

a 3 Or *earth / will use your name in blessings* (see Gen. 48:20)   *b* 7 Or *seed*

12:8 *c* Jos 7:2; 12:9; Ezr 2:28; Ne 7:32; Jer 49:3 *d* S Ge 4:26; S 8:20   **12:9** *e* Ge 13:1,3; 20:1; 24:62; Nu 13:17; 33:40; Dt 34:3; Jos 10:40   **12:10** *f* Ge 41:27,57; 42:5; 43:1; 47:4,13; Ru 1:1; 2Sa 21:1; 2Ki 8:1; Ps 105:19 *g* Ge 41:30,54,56; 47:20; Ps 105:16   **12:11** *h* S Ge 11:29 *i* ver 14; Ge 24:16; 26:7; 29:17; 39:6   **12:13** *j* Ge 20:2; 26:7   **12:14** *k* S ver 11   **12:16** *l* S ver 5; Ge 24:35; 26:14; 30:43; 32:5; 34:23; 47:17; Job 1:3; 31:25

ous powers) on that person (cf. 1Sa 17:43). They had a large conventional stock of such curses, preserved in many sources, such as the Egyptian Execration Texts, the Hittite suzerainty-vassal treaties, *kudurrus* (stone boundary markers), the Code of Hammurapi (Epilogue), etc.

A C **12:4** *Abram went, as the LORD had told him.* See Heb 11:8. Prompt obedience grounded in faith characterized this patriarch throughout his life (see 17:23; 21:14; 22:3). *Lot went with him.* See 13:1,5. Lot chose to go with his uncle Abram, seeking a better future. *seventy-five years old.* Although advanced in age at the time of his call, Abram would live for another full century (see 25:7; see also note on 5:5).

12:5 *people they had acquired.* Wealthy people in that ancient world always had servants in their employ. Some were slaves, others were servants by choice; all were considered to be members of the "household" in which they served (see 14:14; 15:3; 17:12–13; 24:2).

12:6 *site of the great tree.* Perhaps the same tree referred to in 35:4 (see also Jdg 9:6,37). *Moreh.* The name means "teacher." It suggests that the Canaanites sought directions from their gods by this tree. *Shechem.* An important city in central Canaan, founded in the patriarchal period.

C **12:7** *The LORD appeared.* The Lord at times "appeared" in some way to the patriarchs and others, but not in all his glory (see Ex 33:18–20; Jn 1:18). *altar.* The first of several Abram built (see v. 8; 13:18; 22:9). He acknowledged that the land of Canaan belonged to the Lord in a special way (see Ex 20:24; Jos 22:19).

12:8 *Bethel.* Just north of Jerusalem (see map, p. 508), it was an important town in the religious history of God's ancient people (see, e.g., 28:10–22; 35:1–8; 1Ki 12:26– 29).

12:9 *Negev.* The dry wasteland stretching southward from Beersheba (see map No. 2 at the end of this study Bible). This Hebrew word is translated "south" in 13:14.

C **12:10** *went down to Egypt … because the famine was severe.* Egypt's food supply was usually plentiful because the Nile's water supply was normally dependable. Abram's experience in this episode foreshadows Israel's later experience in Egypt, as the author of Genesis, writing after the exodus, was very much aware. The parallels are striking: a famine in the land (here; 47:4), affliction at the hands of the Egyptians (vv. 12–15; Ex 1:11–14); God's plagues on the Egyptians (v. 17; Ex 8–11); the Egyptians sending the people away as a result (vv. 19–20; Ex 12:31–32); the Egyptians letting them take with them all their possessions (v. 20; Ex 12:32); the people obtaining wealth from the Egyptians (v. 16; Ex 12:36); return to Canaan by stages through the desert (13:1–3; Exodus; Numbers; Deuteronomy; Joshua); arrival back in Canaan, where they worship the Lord (13:4; Jos 5:10; 8:30–35; 24:1–27). Abram was truly the "father" of Israel.

B C **12:11** *As he was about to enter Egypt.* Having left the promised land to find food in a time of famine (see Ru 1:1), but doing so without God's guidance or consent (see 46:3–4; 2Ki 8:1), Abram showed that he needed to learn that the God who had called him and made promises to him could and would protect him and Sarai (see v. 3) even outside the promised land (see also ch. 20). Abram's attempt to secure his own safety matches Sarai's attempt to overcome her own barrenness (see ch. 16). *beautiful.* See v. 14. She was 65 at the time (see v. 4; 17:17). The Genesis Apocryphon (one of the Dead Sea Scrolls) praises Sarai's beauty.

12:13 *Say you are my sister.* If the pharaoh were to have added Sarai to his harem while knowing that she was Abram's wife, he would have had to kill Abram first.

12:15 *Pharaoh.* See note on Ex 1:11.

B **12:16** Livestock was an important measure of wealth in ancient times (see 13:2). *male and female servants.* See note on v. 5. *camels.* Although camels were not widely used until much later (see, e.g., Jdg 6:5), archaeology has confirmed their occasional domestication as early as the patriarchal period.

[17]But the LORD inflicted [m] serious diseases on Pharaoh and his household [n] because of Abram's wife Sarai. [18]So Pharaoh summoned Abram. "What have you done to me?" [o] he said. "Why didn't you tell me she was your wife? [p] [19]Why did you say, 'She is my sister,' [q] so that I took her to be my wife? Now then, here is your wife. Take her and go!" [20]Then Pharaoh gave orders about Abram to his men, and they sent him on his way, with his wife and everything he had.

ABRAM AND LOT SEPARATE

13 So Abram went up from Egypt [r] to the Negev, [s] with his wife and everything he had, and Lot [t] went with him. [2]Abram had become very wealthy [u] in livestock [v] and in silver and gold.

[3]From the Negev [w] he went from place to place until he came to Bethel, [x] to the place between Bethel and Ai [y] where his tent had been earlier [4]and where he had first built an altar. [z] There Abram called on the name of the LORD. [a]

[5]Now Lot, [b] who was moving about with Abram, also had flocks and herds and tents. [6]But the land could not support them while they stayed together, for their possessions were so great that they were not able to stay together. [c] [7]And quarreling [d] arose between Abram's herders and the herders of Lot. The Canaanites [e] and Perizzites [f] were also living in the land [g] at that time.

[8]So Abram said to Lot, [h] "Let's not have any quarreling between you and me, [i] or between your herders and mine, for we are close relatives. [j] [9]Is not the whole land before you? Let's part company. If you go to the left, I'll go to the right; if you go to the right, I'll go to the left." [k]

[10]Lot looked around and saw that the whole plain [l] of the Jordan [m] was well watered, like the garden of the LORD, [n] like the land of Egypt, [o] toward Zoar. [p] (This was before the LORD destroyed Sodom [q] and Gomorrah.) [r] [11]So Lot chose for himself the whole plain of the Jordan and set out toward the east. The two men parted company: [12]Abram lived in the land of Canaan, [s] while Lot [t] lived among the cities of the plain [u] and pitched his tents near Sodom. [v] [13]Now the people of Sodom [w] were wicked and were sinning greatly against the LORD. [x]

[14]The LORD said to Abram after Lot had parted from him, "Look around from where you are, to the north and south, to the east and west. [y] [15]All the land that you see I will give to you and your offspring [a] forever. [z] [16]I will make your offspring like the dust of the earth, so that if anyone could count the dust, then your offspring could be counted. [a] [17]Go, walk through the length and breadth of the land, [b] for I am giving it to you." [c]

[a] 15 Or *seed*; also in verse 16

13:14 [y] Ge 28:14; 32:12; 48:16; Dt 3:27; 13:17; Isa 54:3   **13:15** [z] S Ge 12:7; Gal 3:16*   **13:16** [a] S Ge 12:2; 16:10; 17:20; 21:13,18; 25:16; Nu 23:10   **13:17** [b] ver 15; Nu 13:17-25 [c] S Ge 12:7; 15:7

Cross-reference column:

12:17 [m] 2Ki 15:5; Job 30:11; Isa 53:4,10
[n] 1Ch 16:21; Ps 105:14
12:18 [o] Ge 20:9; 26:10; 29:25; 31:26; 44:15 [p] Isa 43:27; 51:2; Eze 16:3
12:19 [q] Ge 20:5; 26:9
13:1 [r] Ge 45:25
[s] Ge 12:9
[t] S Ge 11:27
13:2 [u] S Ge 12:5; 26:13; Pr 10:22
[v] Ge 32:15; Job 1:3; 42:12
13:3 [w] S Ge 12:9
[x] S Ge 12:8 [y] Jos 7:2
13:4 [z] S Ge 12:7
[a] S Ge 4:26
13:5 [b] S Ge 11:27
13:6 [c] S Ge 12:5; 33:9; 36:7
13:7 [d] Ge 26:20,21; Nu 22:3 [e] S Ge 10:18
[f] Ge 15:20; 34:30; Ex 3:8; Jdg 1:4
[g] Ge 12:6; 34:30
13:8 [h] S Ge 11:27
[i] Pr 15:18; 20:3
[j] Ge 19:9; Ex 2:14; Nu 16:13; Ps 133:1
13:9 [k] Ge 20:15; 34:10; 47:6; Jer 40:4
13:10 [l] 1Ki 7:46; 2Ch 4:17 [m] Nu 13:29; 33:48 [n] Ge 2:8-10; Isa 51:3; Eze 31:8-9 [o] Ge 46:7 [p] Ge 14:2; 19:22,30; Dt 34:3; Isa 15:5; Jer 48:34 [q] Dt 29:23; Job 39:6; Ps 107:34; Jer 4:26 [r] Ge 14:8; 19:17-29
13:12 [s] S Ge 10:19
[t] S Ge 11:27
[u] ver 10; Ge 19:17, 29 [v] Ge 14:12
13:13 [w] Ge 19:4; Isa 1:10; 3:9
[x] Ge 18:20; 19:5; 20:6; 39:9; Nu 32:23; 1Sa 12:23; 2Sa 12:13; Ps 51:4; Eze 16:49-50; 2Pe 2:8

Study notes (bottom):

12:19 *Why did you say, 'She is my sister'?* Egyptian ethics emphasized the importance of absolute truthfulness, and Abram was put in the uncomfortable position of being exposed as a liar.
12:20 *Pharaoh gave orders.* See Ex 12:31–32.
13:1,3 *Negev.* See note on 12:9.
13:2 *had become very wealthy.* Abram left Egypt with greater wealth than he had before—even as Israel would later leave Egypt laden with wealth from the Egyptians (Ex 3:22; 12:36).
13:4 *Abram called on the name of the LORD.* As he had done earlier at the same place (12:8).
13:5–18 Lot's separation from Abram and his choice of what appeared to be the most promising portion of the land alienated him from participating in the blessings promised to Abram. Rather, he became involved in the history of Sodom and Gomorrah (see 14:12–16; 19:1–38), whereas Abram received assurances that his descendants would multiply and would inherit the whole land (vv. 15–17).
13:6 *land could not support them.* Livestock made up the greater part of their possessions, and the region around Bethel and Ai did not have enough water or pasture for such large flocks and herds (see v. 10; 26:17–22,32; 36:7).
13:7 *Perizzites.* Their identity remains obscure, but reference may be to rural inhabitants, in contrast to city dwellers.
13:9 *left...right.* That is, north...south. Abram, always generous, gave his young nephew the opportunity to

choose the land he wanted. He himself would not obtain wealth except by the Lord's blessing (see 14:22–24).
13:10 *plain.* The Hebrew for this word picturesquely describes this area as oval in shape. The precise location of the "plain" and its "cities" (v. 12) is still disputed. One plausible proposal locates them just east and southeast of the Dead Sea. *like the land of Egypt.* Because of its abundant and dependable water supply (see note on 12:10), Egypt came close to matching Eden's ideal conditions (see 2:10). *the LORD destroyed Sodom and Gomorrah.* See especially 18:16—19:29. The names of Sodom and Gomorrah became proverbial for vile wickedness and for divine judgment on sin.
13:12 *Lot...pitched his tents near Sodom.* Since the people of Sodom were known to be wicked (see v. 13), Lot was flirting with temptation by choosing to live near them. Contrast the actions of Abram (v. 18).
13:14 *Look around.* See Dt 34:1–4. Lot and Abram are a study in contrasts. The former looked selfishly and coveted (v. 10); the latter looked as God commanded and was blessed.
13:16 *like the dust of the earth.* A simile (common in the ancient Near East) for the large number of Abram's offspring (see 28:14; 2Ch 1:9; see also Nu 23:10). Similar phrases are: "as numerous as the stars in the sky" and "as the sand on the seashore" (22:17).
13:17 *walk through the length...of the land.* Either to inspect it or to claim the right to live in it while looking forward to the promised ownership (cf. Dt 32:48–49).

13:18 *d* Ge 14:13, 24;
18:1; 23:17, 19; 25:9;
49:30; 50:13
e Ge 23:2; 35:27;
37:14; Nu 13:22;
Jos 10:3, 36; Jdg 1:10;
1Sa 30:31; 2Sa 2:1, 3,
11; 1Ch 11:1
f S Ge 8:20
14:1 *g* S Ge 10:10
h ver 4, 9, 17
i S Ge 10:22
14:2 *j* S Ge 10:19
k S Ge 13:10
14:3 *l* ver 8, 10
m Nu 34:3, 12;
Dt 3:17; Jos 3:16; 12:3;
15:2, 5; 18:19
14:4 *n* S ver 1
14:5 *o* S ver 1
p Ge 15:20; Dt 2:11,
20; 3:11, 13; Jos 12:4;
13:12; 17:15; 1Ch 20:4
q Dt 2:10
14:6 *r* Ge 36:20;
Dt 2:12, 22 *s* Ge 32:3;
33:14, 16; 36:8; Dt 1:2;
2:1, 5, 22; Jos 11:17;
24:4; 1Ch 4:42;
Isa 34:5; Eze 25:8;
35:2; Am 1:6
t Ge 21:21; Nu 10:12;
12:16; 13:3, 26;
Hab 3:3
14:7 *u* Ge 16:14;
20:1; Nu 13:26; 20:1;
32:8; Dt 1:2;
Jos 10:41; Jdg 11:16;
Ps 29:8 *v* Ex 17:8;
Nu 13:29; 14:25;
24:20; Dt 25:17;
Jdg 3:13; 6:3; 10:12;
12:15; 1Sa 14:48; 15:2;
28:18; 2Sa 1:1;
1Ch 4:43; Ps 83:7
w Nu 13:29; Dt 1:4;
Jos 2:10; 13:4
x 2Ch 20:2; Eze 48:28
14:8 *y* S Ge 13:10
z Dt 29:23; Hos 11:8
a S Ge 13:10 *b* S ver 3
14:9 *c* S ver 1
d S Ge 10:22
14:10 *e* S ver 3

¹⁸So Abram went to live near the great trees of Mamre *d* at Hebron, *e* where he pitched his tents. There he built an altar to the LORD. *f*

ABRAM RESCUES LOT

14 At the time when Amraphel was king of Shinar, *a g* Arioch king of Ellasar, Kedorlaomer *h* king of Elam *i* and Tidal king of Goyim, ²these kings went to war against Bera king of Sodom, Birsha king of Gomorrah, Shinab king of Admah, Shemeber king of Zeboyim, *j* and the king of Bela (that is, Zoar). *k* ³All these latter kings joined forces in the Valley of Siddim *l* (that is, the Dead Sea Valley *m*). ⁴For twelve years they had been subject to Kedorlaomer, *n* but in the thirteenth year they rebelled.

⁵In the fourteenth year, Kedorlaomer *o* and the kings allied with him went out and defeated the Rephaites *p* in Ashteroth Karnaim, the Zuzites in Ham, the Emites *q* in Shaveh Kiriathaim ⁶and the Horites *r* in the hill country of Seir, *s* as far as El Paran *t* near the desert. ⁷Then they turned back and went to En Mishpat (that is, Kadesh), *u* and they conquered the whole territory of the Amalekites, *v* as well as the Amorites *w* who were living in Hazezon Tamar. *x*

⁸Then the king of Sodom, the king of Gomorrah, *y* the king of Admah, the king of Zeboyim *z* and the king of Bela (that is, Zoar) *a* marched out and drew up their battle lines in the Valley of Siddim *b* ⁹against Kedorlaomer *c* king of Elam, *d* Tidal king of Goyim, Amraphel king of Shinar and Arioch king of Ellasar—four kings against five. ¹⁰Now the Valley of Siddim *e* was full of tar *f* pits, and when the kings of Sodom and Gomorrah *g* fled, some of the men fell into them and the rest fled to the hills. *h* ¹¹The four kings seized all the goods *i* of Sodom and Gomorrah and all their food; then they went away. ¹²They also carried off Abram's nephew Lot *j* and his possessions, since he was living in Sodom.

¹³A man who had escaped came and reported this to Abram the Hebrew. *k* Now Abram was living near the great trees of Mamre *l* the Amorite, a brother *b* of Eshkol *m* and Aner, all of whom were allied with Abram. ¹⁴When Abram heard that his relative *n* had been taken captive, he called out the 318 trained *o* men born in his household *p* and went in pursuit as far as Dan. *q* ¹⁵During the night Abram divided his men *r* to attack them and he routed them, pursuing them as far as Hobah, north of Damascus. *s* ¹⁶He recovered *t* all the goods *u* and brought back his relative Lot and his possessions, together with the women and the other people.

^a *1* That is, Babylonia; also in verse 9   ^b *13* Or *a relative*; or *an ally*

14:10 *f* Ge 11:3 *g* ver 17, 21 *h* Ge 19:17, 30; Jos 2:16; Ps 11:1   **14:11** *i* ver 16, 21   **14:12** *j* S Ge 11:27   **14:13** *k* Ge 37:28; 39:14, 17; 40:15;
41:12; 43:32; Ex 3:18; 1Sa 4:6; 14:11 *l* ver 24; S Ge 13:18 *m* Nu 13:23; 32:9; Dt 1:24   **14:14** *n* ver 12 *o* Dt 4:9; Pr 22:6 *p* S Ge 12:5 *q* Dt 34:1;
Jdg 18:29; 1Ki 15:20   **14:15** *r* Jdg 7:16 *s* Ge 15:2; 2Sa 8:5; 1Ki 20:34; 2Ki 16:9; Isa 7:8; 8:4; 10:9; 17:1; Jer 49:23, 27; Eze 27:18; Am 1:3-5
14:16 *t* 1Sa 30:8, 18 *u* S ver 11

13:18 *great trees.* See note on 12:6. *Mamre.* A town named after one of Abram's allies (see 14:13). *Hebron.* Kiriath Arba (see note on 23:2). *altar.* See note on 12:7.

C **14:1–24** Abram's act of faith successfully challenged the foreign kings who were seeking to bring the promised land under their sphere of rule and enabled him to rescue his nephew Lot. It also won for him recognition among kings that he was a force to be reckoned with (see 12:2: "I will make your name great") and provided him with an opportunity to bear witness to his God.

14:1 *Amraphel was king of Shinar.* Not the great Babylonian king Hammurapi, as once thought. *Elam.* See note on 10:22. *Goyim.* The Hebrew word means "Gentile nations" and may be a common noun here (as in Isa 9:1).

14:3 *Dead Sea.* Lit. "Salt Sea." Its water contains an approximately five times greater concentration of chloride and bromide salts than the water in the world's oceans, making it the densest body of water on earth.

14:5 *Rephaites.* People of large stature (see Dt 3:11).

B **14:6** *Horites.* Formerly thought to be cave dwellers (the Hebrew word *hor* means "cave"), they are now commonly identified with the Hurrians, a non-Semitic people widely dispersed throughout the ancient Near East.

14:7 *En Mishpat.* Another name for Kadesh, it means "spring of judgment/justice." It is called Meribah Kadesh, "quarreling/litigation at Kadesh," in Dt 32:51 (see Nu 27:14). *Kadesh.* Located in the southwest Negev (see note on 12:9), it was later called Kadesh Barnea (see Nu 32:8). *Amalekites.* A tribal people living in the

Negev and in the Sinai peninsula. *Amorites.* See note on 10:16.

14:10 *tar pits.* Lumps of asphalt are often seen even today floating in the southern end of the Dead Sea. *hills.* The Dead Sea, the lowest body of water on earth (about 1,300 feet below sea level), is flanked by hills on both sides.

A C **14:12** *Lot … was living in Sodom.* He moved into the town and was living among its wicked people (see 2Pe 2:8). Though Lot was "righteous," he was now in danger of imitating the "depraved conduct of the lawless" (2Pe 2:7).

B C **14:13** *Hebrew.* Abram, the father of the Hebrew people, is the first Biblical character to be called a Hebrew (see "Eber" in note on 10:21). Usually an ethnic term in the Bible, it was normally used by non-Israelites in a disparaging sense (see, e.g., 39:17). Outside the Bible, people known as the Habiru/Apiru (a word probably related to the word "Hebrew") are referred to as a propertyless, dependent, immigrant (foreign) social class rather than as a specific ethnic group. Negative descriptions of them are given in the Amarna letters (clay tablets found in Egypt). *Mamre.* A town was named after him (see 13:18 and note).

B **14:14** *318 trained men born in his household.* A clear indication of Abram's great wealth. The Hebrew for "trained men" is found only here in the Bible. A related word used elsewhere in very ancient texts means "armed retainers." *Dan.* This well-known city in the north was not given the name "Dan" until the days of the judges (see Jdg 18:29). It was formerly called Laish or Leshem (see note on Jdg 18:7). Thus the designation here is most likely a later editorial updating.

¹⁷After Abram returned from defeating Kedorlaomer^v and the kings allied with him, the king of Sodom^w came out to meet him in the Valley of Shaveh (that is, the King's Valley).^x

¹⁸Then Melchizedek^y king of Salem^z brought out bread^a and wine.^b He was priest of God Most High,^c ¹⁹and he blessed Abram,^d saying,

> "Blessed be Abram by God Most High,^e
>   Creator of heaven and earth.^f
> ²⁰ And praise be to God Most High,^g
>   who delivered your enemies into your hand."

14:20 ^gS Ge 9:26; S 24:27

14:17 ^vS ver 1
^wS ver 10 ^x2Sa 18:18
14:18 ^yPs 110:4;
Heb 5:6; 7:17,21
^zPs 76:2; Heb 7:2
^aS Ge 3:19 ^bJdg 9:13;
19:19; Est 1:10;
Ps 104:15; Pr 31:6;
Ecc 10:19; SS 1:2
^cver 22; Ps 7:8,17;
Da 7:27
14:19 ^dHeb 7:6
^ever 18 ^fver 22;
S Ge 1:1; 24:3;
Jos 2:11; Ps 148:5;
Mt 11:25

14:17 *King's Valley.* Near Jerusalem (see 2Sa 18:18).

14:18 *Melchizedek king of Salem ... priest.* See Heb 7:1. In ancient times, particularly in non-Israelite circles, kingly and priestly duties were often performed by the same individual. "Melchizedek" means "My king is righteous" or "king of righteousness" (Heb 7:2). "Salem" is a shortened form of "Jerusalem" (Ps 76:2) and is related to the Hebrew word for "peace" (Heb 7:2; see Jos 10:1 and note). *bread and wine.* An ordinary meal (see Jdg 19:19), in no way related to the NT ordinance of communion. Melchizedek's interest in Abram's military success was most likely political, and his entertainment of victorious Abram with refreshment and a priestly benediction constituted a recognition that Abram was a man to be reckoned with in kingly affairs.

14:19 *God Most High, Creator of heaven and earth.* The titles "most high," "lord of heaven" and "creator of earth" were frequently applied to the chief Canaanite deity in ancient times. But Abram, by identifying Melchizedek's "God Most High" with "the LORD" (see v. 22), bore testimony to the one true God.

INTEGRATED CHRONOLOGY OF THE PATRIARCHS

ABRAHAM			
AGE 75 To Canaan*			
	Birth of		
100	**ISAAC***		
140	AGE 40 Isaac married*		
		Birth of Esau and	
160	60	**JACOB***	
175 Abraham's death*	75	AGE 15	
	100	40 Esau's marriage*	
	137	77 Jacob to Paddan Aram	Birth of
	151	91	**JOSEPH**
	157	97 Jacob's return to Canaan	AGE 6
	168	108	17 Joseph to Egypt*
	180 Isaac's death*	120	29
		121	30 Joseph enters Pharaoh's service*
		130 Jacob to Egypt*	39
		147 Jacob's death*	56
Note: The ages marked with (*) are expressly given.			110 Joseph's death*

14:20 ʰGe 28:22;
Dt 14:22; 26:12;
Lk 18:12; Heb 7:4
14:21 ⁱS ver 10
ʲS ver 11
14:22 ᵏS ver 10
ˡEx 6:8; Nu 14:30;
Dt 32:40; Ne 9:15;
Eze 20:5; Da 12:7;
Rev 10:5-6 ᵐS ver 18
ⁿS ver 19
14:23 ᵒIsa 15:3,19;
2Ki 5:16; Est 8:11;
9:10,15
14:24 ᵖS Ge 13:18
15:1 ᑫIsa 15:10;
2Sa 7:4; 1Ki 6:11;
12:22; Jer 1:13;
Eze 3:16; Da 10:1
ʳGe 46:2; Nu 12:6;
24:4; Ru 1:20;
Job 33:15.ˢGe 21:17;
26:24; 46:3; Ex 14:13;
20:20; 2Ki 6:16;
2Ch 20:15,17; Ps 27:1;
Isa 7:4; 41:10,13-14;
43:1,5; Jer 1:8;
Hag 2:5 ᵗDt 33:29;
2Sa 22:3,31; Ps 3:3;
5:12; 18:2; 28:7;
33:20; 84:11; 119:114;
144:2; Pr 2:7; 30:5
ᵘPs 18:20; 37:25;
58:11; Isa 3:10
15:2 ᵛver 8;
Isa 49:22; Jer 44:26;
Eze 5:11; 16:48
ʷAc 7:5 ˣS Ge 14:15
15:3 ʸGe 24:2,34
ᶻS Ge 12:5
15:4 ᵃGal 4:28
15:5 ᵇJob 11:8; 35:5;
Ps 8:3; 147:4;
Jer 33:22 ᶜS Ge 12:2;
S Jer 30:19; Ro 4:18*;
Heb 11:12
15:6 ᵈPs 106:31;
Ro 4:3*, 20-24*;
Gal 3:6*; Jas 2:23*
15:7 ᵉGe 12:1;
Ex 20:2; Ac 7:3;

Then Abram gave him a tenth of everything.ʰ

²¹The king of Sodomⁱ said to Abram, "Give me the people and keep the goodsʲ for yourself."

²²But Abram said to the king of Sodom, ᵏ "With raised handˡ I have sworn an oath to the Lord, God Most High, ᵐ Creator of heaven and earth, ⁿ ²³that I will accept nothing belonging to you, ᵒ not even a thread or the thong of a sandal, so that you will never be able to say, 'I made Abram rich.' ²⁴I will accept nothing but what my men have eaten and the share that belongs to the men who went with me—to Aner, Eshkol and Mamre. ᵖ Let them have their share."

GOD'S COVENANT WITH ABRAM

15

After this, the word of the Lord came to Abramᑫ in a vision:ʳ

"Do not be afraid, ˢ Abram.
    I am your shield, ᵃᵗ
    your very great reward.ᵇ ᵘ"

²But Abram said, "Sovereign Lord, ᵛ what can you give me since I remain childlessʷ and the one who will inheritᶜ my estate is Eliezer of Damascus? ˣ" ³And Abram said, "You have given me no children; so a servantʸ in my householdᶻ will be my heir."

⁴Then the word of the Lord came to him: "This man will not be your heir, but a son coming from your own body will be your heir.ᵃ" ⁵He took him outside and said, "Look up at the heavens and count the stars ᵇ—if indeed you can count them." Then he said to him, "So shall your offspringᵈ be."ᶜ

⁶Abram believed the Lord, and he credited it to him as righteousness. ᵈ

⁷He also said to him, "I am the Lord, who brought you out ᵉ of Ur of the Chaldeans ᶠ to give you this land to take possession of it." ᵍ

⁸But Abram said, "Sovereign Lord, ʰ how can I knowⁱ that I will gain possession of it?"ʲ

⁹So the Lord said to him, "Bring me a heifer, ᵏ a goat and a ram, each three years old, ˡ along with a dove and a young pigeon. ᵐ"

¹⁰Abram brought all these to him, cut them in two and arranged the halves opposite

---

ᵃ 1 Or sovereign   ᵇ 1 Or shield; / your reward will be very great   ᶜ 2 The meaning of the Hebrew for this phrase is uncertain.   ᵈ 5 Or seed

15:7 Heb 11:8 ᶠS Ge 11:28; Ac 7:4 ᵍS Ge 13:17; 17:8; 28:4; 35:12; 48:4; Ex 6:8; Dt 9:5   **15:8** ʰS ver 2 ⁱLk 1:18 ʲDt 12:20; 19:8
15:9 ᵏNu 19:2; Dt 21:3; Hos 4:16; Am 4:1 ˡ1Sa 1:24 ᵐLev 1:14; 5:7,11; 12:8

C **14:20** *Abram gave him a tenth of everything.* A tenth was a king's share (see 1Sa 8:15,17). By offering Melchizedek a tenth, Abram responded to Melchizedek's action by showing that he in turn acknowledged his kingship in Salem. At the same time, having recognized Melchizedek's blessing as a benediction from the Lord, Abram's tithe to Melchizedek constituted a declaration that he would be indebted to no king but the Lord (see v. 23 and note). Melchizedek is later spoken of as a type or prefiguration of Jesus, our "great high priest" (Heb 4:14), whose priesthood is therefore "in the order of Melchizedek, not in the order of Aaron" (Heb 7:11; see Ps 110:4).

14:22 *With raised hand.* A customary oath-taking practice in ancient times (see Dt 32:40; Rev 10:5–6).

14:23 *I will accept nothing belonging to you.* Cf. 2Ki 5:16. Abram refused to let himself become obligated to anyone but the Lord. If he had done so, this Canaanite king might later have claimed the right of kingship over Abram.

C **15:1–21** Here for the first time the Lord introduces a covenant into his relationship with Abram. In response to Abram's faltering faith, he graciously reinforces his promise with a covenant oath.

A **15:1** *I am your shield.* Whether "shield" or "sovereign" is meant (see TNIV text note), the reference is to the Lord as Abram's King. As elsewhere, "shield" stands for king (e.g., Dt 33:29; 2Sa 22:3; Ps 7:10; 84:9). *your very great reward.* Though Abram was quite rich (13:2; 14:23), God himself was Abram's greatest treasure (cf. Dt 10:9).

15:2 *Eliezer of Damascus.* A servant probably acquired by Abram on his journey southward from Harran (see 12:5). He may also be the unnamed "senior servant" of 24:2.

B **15:3–4** Ancient documents uncovered at Nuzi (see chart, p. xxiii) near Kirkuk on a branch of the Tigris River, as well as at other places, demonstrate that a childless man could adopt one of his own male servants to be heir and guardian of his estate. Abram apparently contemplated doing this with Eliezer, or perhaps had already done so.

A **15:5** *count the stars—if indeed you can.* See 22:17. More than 8,000 stars are clearly visible to the naked eye in the darkness of a Near Eastern night. *So shall your offspring be.* The promise was initially fulfilled in Egypt (see Ex 1; see also Dt 1:10; Heb 11:12). Ultimately, all who belong to Christ are Abram's offspring (see Gal 3:29).

A C **15:6** Abram is the "father of all who believe" (Ro 4:11), and this verse is the first explicit reference to faith in God's promises. It also teaches that God graciously responds to faith by crediting righteousness to one who believes (see Heb 11:7).

B **15:7** *I am the Lord, who brought you out.* Ancient royal covenants often began with (1) the self-identification of the king and (2) a brief historical prologue, as here (see Ex 20:2 and note).

15:8 *how can I know . . . ?* Cf. Lk 1:18. Abram believed God's promise of a son, but he asked for a guarantee of the promise of the land.

B **15:9–21** This expression of God's covenant with Abram was cast in the form of ancient Near Eastern royal land-grant treaties and contained a perpetual and unconditional divine promise to fulfill the grant of land to Abram and his descendants (1Ch 16:14–18; Ps 105:8–11). See chart, p. 20.

each other; *n* the birds, however, he did not cut in half. *o* ¹¹Then birds of prey came down on the carcasses, *p* but Abram drove them away.

¹²As the sun was setting, Abram fell into a deep sleep, *q* and a thick and dreadful darkness came over him. ¹³Then the LORD said to him, "Know for certain that for four hundred years *r* your descendants will be strangers in a country not their own and that they will be enslaved *s* and mistreated there. ¹⁴But I will punish the nation they serve as slaves, and afterward they will come out *t* with great possessions. *u* ¹⁵You, however, will go to your ancestors *v* in peace and be buried at a good old age. *w* ¹⁶In the fourth generation *x* your descendants will come back here, *y* for the sin of the Amorites *z* has not yet reached its full measure."

¹⁷When the sun had set and darkness had fallen, a smoking firepot with a blazing torch *a* appeared and passed between the pieces. *b* ¹⁸On that day the LORD made a covenant with Abram *c* and said, "To your descendants I give this land, *d* from the Wadi *a* of Egypt *e* to the great river, the Euphrates *f*— ¹⁹the land of the Kenites, *g* Kenizzites, Kadmonites, ²⁰Hittites, *h* Perizzites, *i* Rephaites, *j* ²¹Amorites, Canaanites, Girgashites and Jebusites." *k*

HAGAR AND ISHMAEL

16 Now Sarai, *l* Abram's wife, had borne him no children. *m* But she had an Egyptian servant *n* named Hagar; *o* ²so she said to Abram, "The LORD has kept me from having children. *p* Go, sleep with my servant; perhaps I can build a family through her." *q*

Abram agreed to what Sarai said. ³So after Abram had been living in Canaan *r* ten years, *s* Sarai his wife took her Egyptian servant Hagar and gave her to her husband to be his wife. ⁴He slept with Hagar, *t* and she conceived.

When she knew she was pregnant, she began to despise her mistress. *u* ⁵Then Sarai said to Abram, "You are responsible for the wrong I am suffering. I put my servant in your arms, and now that she knows she is pregnant, she despises me. May the LORD judge between you and me." *v*

---

a 18 Or *river*

15:20 *h* S Ge 10:15; S Dt 7:1 *i* S Ge 13:7 *j* S Ge 14:5   15:21 *k* S Ge 10:16; Jos 3:10; 24:11; Ne 9:8   16:1 *l* S Ge 11:29 *m* S Ge 11:30; Lk 1:7, 36; Gal 4:24-25 *n* Ge 21:9; 24:61; 29:24,29; 31:33; 46:18 *o* ver 3-4,8,15; Ge 21:14; 25:12   16:2 *p* Ge 29:31; 30:2 *q* Ge 19:32; 30:3-4,9-10 16:3 *r* S Ge 12:5 *s* S Ge 12:4   16:4 *t* S ver 1 *u* Ge 30:1; 1Sa 1:6   16:5 *v* Ge 31:53; Ex 5:21; Jdg 11:27; 1Sa 24:12,15; 26:10,23; Ps 50:6; 75:7

15:10 *birds … he did not cut in half.* Perhaps because they were so small (see Lev 1:17).

15:13 *four hundred years.* A round number. According to Ex 12:40 Israel spent 430 years in Egypt. *country not their own.* Egypt (see 46:3–4).

15:15 The fulfillment is recorded in 25:8.

B **15:16** *In the fourth generation.* That is, after 400 years (see v. 13). A "generation" was the age of a man when his first-born son (from a legal standpoint) was born—in Abram's case, 100 years (see 21:5). *sin of the Amorites has not yet reached its full measure.* Just how sinful many Canaanite practices is now known from archaeological artifacts and from their own epic literature, discovered at Ras Shamra (ancient Ugarit) on the north Syrian coast beginning in 1929 (see chart, p.xxiii). Their "worship" was polytheistic and included idolatry, religious prostitution, divination (cf. Dt 18:9–12) and at times even child sacrifice. God was patient in judgment, even with the wicked Canaanites.

15:17 *smoking firepot with a blazing torch.* Symbolizing the presence of God (see Ex 3:2; 14:24; 19:18; 1Ki 18:38; Ac 2:3–4). *passed between the pieces.* Of the slaughtered animals (v. 10). In ancient times the parties sometimes solemnized a covenant by walking down an aisle flanked by the pieces of slaughtered animals (see Jer 34:18–19). The practice signified a self-maledictory oath: "May it be so done to me if I do not keep my oath and pledge." Having credited Abram's faith as righteousness, God now graciously ministered to his need for assurance concerning the land. He granted Abram a promissory covenant, as he had to Noah (see 9:9 and note; see also chart, p. 20).

15:18 *made a covenant.* Lit. "cut a covenant," referring to the slaughtering of the animals (the same Hebrew verb is translated "made" and "cut" in Jer 34:18). *I give this land.* The Lord initially fulfilled this covenant through Joshua (see Jos 1:2–9; 21:43;

see also 1Ki 4:20–21). *Wadi of Egypt.* Probably the modern Wadi el-Arish in northeastern Sinai. *Euphrates.* The longest river in western Asia (about 1,700 miles). It marked the boundary between Israel and Israel's historic enemies (Assyria and Babylonia) to the east and northeast (cf. Isa 8:5–8).

15:19–21 A similar list associated with Canaan is found in 10:15–18 (see notes there). Here ten peoples are listed, the number ten signifying completeness. For other lists of the inhabitants of Canaan, see Ex 3:8,17; 13:5; 23:23; 33:2; 34:11; Nu 13:29; Dt 7:1; 20:17; Jos 3:10; 9:1; 11:3; 12:8; 24:11; Jdg 3:5; 1Ch 1:14; 2Ch 8:7; Ezr 9:1; Ne 9:8.

C **16:1–15** A failure in faith leads to a brazen attempt to provide by human means what the Lord is accused of withholding. Sarai at the beginning (v. 2) and Abram at the end ("Ishmael"; see v. 15 and TNIV text note on v. 11) express their mutual impatience with the Lord's failure as yet to overcome Sarai's barrenness.

16:1 *no children.* See note on 11:30. *Egyptian.* Perhaps Hagar was acquired while Hagar and Sarai were in Egypt (see 12:10–20).

B C **16:2** *The LORD has kept me from having children.* Some time had passed since the revelation of 15:4 (see 16:3), and Sarai impatiently implied that God was not keeping his promise. *Go, sleep with my servant.* An ancient custom, illustrated in Old Assyrian marriage contracts, the Code of Hammurapi and the Nuzi tablets (see note on 15:3–4), to ensure the birth of a male heir.

16:3 *ten years.* Abram was now 85 years old (see 12:4; 16:16).

16:4 *despise her mistress.* Peninnah acted similarly toward Hannah (see 1Sa 1:6).

16:5 *May the LORD judge between you and me.* An expression of hostility or suspicion (see 31:53; see also 31:49 and note).

15:10 *n* ver 17; Jer 34:18 *o* Lev 1:17; 5:8
15:11 *p* Dt 28:26; Jer 7:33
15:12 *q* S Ge 2:21
15:13 *r* ver 16; Ex 12:40; Nu 20:15; Ac 7:6,17; Gal 3:17 *s* Ex 1:11; 3:7; 5:6,10-14,18; 6:5; Dt 5:15; Job 3:18
15:14 *t* Ge 50:24; Ex 3:8; 6:6-8; 12:25; Nu 10:29; Jos 1:2; Ac 7:7 *u* Ex 12:32-38
15:15 *v* Ge 47:30; 49:29; Dt 31:16; 2Sa 7:12; 1Ki 1:21; Ps 49:19 *w* Ge 25:8; 35:29; Ex 23:26; Dt 34:7; Jos 14:11; Jdg 8:32; 1Ch 29:28; Job 5:26; 21:23; 42:17; Ps 91:16; Pr 3:16; 9:11; Isa 65:20
15:16 *x* S ver 13; Ex 12:40 *y* Ge 28:15; 46:4; 48:21; 50:24; Jos 13:4; Jdg 10:11; 1Ki 21:26; 2Ki 16:3; 21:11; Eze 16:3
15:17 *a* Jdg 7:16,20; 15:4,5 *b* S ver 10
15:18 *c* Ge 17:2,4,7; Ex 6:4; 34:10,27; 1Ch 16:16; Ps 105:9 *d* S Ge 12:7 *e* Nu 34:5; Jos 15:4,47; 1Ki 8:65; 2Ki 24:7; 2Ch 7:8; Isa 27:12; Jer 37:5; 46:2; La 4:17; Eze 30:22; 47:19 *f* S Ge 2:14
15:19 *g* Nu 24:21; Jdg 1:16; 4:11,17; 5:24; 1Sa 15:6; 27:10; 30:29; 1Ch 2:55

16:6 ʷJos 9:25
ˣGe 31:50
16:7 ʸver 11;
Ge 21:17; 22:11,15;
24:7, 40; 31:11; 48:16;
Ex 3:2; 14:19; 23:20,
23; 32:34; 33:2;
Nu 22:22; Jdg 2:1;
6:11; 13:3; 2Sa 24:16;
1Ki 19:5; 2Ki 1:3;
19:35; Ps 34:7;
Zec 1:11; S Ac 5:19
ᶻver 14; Ge 21:19
ᵃGe 20:1; 25:18;
Ex 15:22; 1Sa 15:7;
27:8
16:8 ᵇS ver 1
ᶜS Ge 3:9
16:10 ᵈS Ge 13:16
16:11 ᵉS ver 7;
S Ac 5:19 ᶠS Ge 3:15
ᵍGe 12:2-3; 18:19;
Ne 9:7; Isa 44:1;
Am 3:2; Mt 1:21;
Lk 1:13,31 ʰGe 17:19;
21:3; 37:25,28; 39:1;
Jdg 8:24 ⁱGe 29:32;
31:42; Ex 2:24; 3:7,9;
4:31; Nu 20:16;
Dt 26:7; 1Sa 9:16
16:12 ʲJob 6:5;
11:12; 24:5; 39:5;
Ps 104:11; Jer 2:24;
Hos 8:9 ᵏGe 25:18
16:13 ˡPs 139:1-12
ᵐGe 32:30; 33:10;
Ex 24:10; 33:20,23;
Nu 12:8; Jdg 6:22;
13:22; Isa 6:5
16:14 ⁿS ver 7
ᵒGe 24:62; 25:11
ᵖS Ge 14:7
16:15 �q S ver 1
ʳGe 21:9; Gal 4:22
ˢGe 17:18; 25:12; 28:9
16:16 ᵗS Ge 12:4
17:1 ᵘS Ge 12:4
ᵛS Ge 12:7 ʷGe 28:3;
35:11; 43:14; 48:3;
49:25; Ex 6:3;
Ru 1:20; Job 5:17; 6:4,
14; 22:21; 33:19;
36:16; Isa 13:6;
Joel 1:15; Mic 6:9

6"Your servant is in your hands, ʷ" Abram said. "Do with her whatever you think best." Then Sarai mistreated ˣ Hagar; so she fled from her.

7The angel of the Lord ʸ found Hagar near a spring ᶻ in the desert; it was the spring that is beside the road to Shur. ᵃ 8And he said, "Hagar, ᵇ servant of Sarai, where have you come from, and where are you going?" ᶜ

"I'm running away from my mistress Sarai," she answered.

9Then the angel of the Lord told her, "Go back to your mistress and submit to her." 10The angel added, "I will increase your descendants so much that they will be too numerous to count." ᵈ

11The angel of the Lord ᵉ also said to her:

"You are now pregnant
and you will give birth to a son. ᶠ
You shall name him ᵍ Ishmael, ᵃ ʰ
for the Lord has heard of your misery. ⁱ
12He will be a wild donkey ʲ of a man;
his hand will be against everyone
and everyone's hand against him,
and he will live in hostility
toward ᵇ all his brothers. ᵏ"

13She gave this name to the Lord who spoke to her: "You are the God who sees me, ˡ" for she said, "I have now seen ᶜ the One who sees me." ᵐ 14That is why the well ⁿ was called Beer Lahai Roi ᵈ; ᵒ it is still there, between Kadesh ᵖ and Bered.

15So Hagar �q bore Abram a son, ʳ and Abram gave the name Ishmael ˢ to the son she had borne. 16Abram was eighty-six years old ᵗ when Hagar bore him Ishmael.

THE COVENANT OF CIRCUMCISION

17 When Abram was ninety-nine years old, ᵘ the Lord appeared to him ᵛ and said, "I am God Almighty ᵉ; ʷ walk before me faithfully and be blameless. ˣ 2Then I will make my covenant between me and you ʸ and will greatly increase your numbers." ᶻ

3Abram fell facedown, ᵃ and God said to him, 4"As for me, this is my covenant with you: ᵇ

ᵃ 11 *Ishmael* means *God hears.*   ᵇ 12 Or *live to the east / of*   ᶜ 13 Or *seen the back of*   ᵈ 14 *Beer Lahai Roi* means *well of the Living One who sees me.*   ᵉ 1 Hebrew *El-Shaddai*

17:1 ˣS Ge 5:22; 20:5; Dt 18:13; 1Ki 3:6; 9:4; Job 1:1; Ps 15:2; 18:23; 78:72; 101:2   **17:2** ʸS Ge 15:18; S 22:16-18 ᶻS Ge 12:2
17:3 ᵃver 17; Ge 18:2; 19:1; 33:3; Ex 18:7; Nu 14:5; 7:6; Jdg 13:20; Eze 1:28; 3:23   **17:4** ᵇS Ge 15:18

16:7 *The angel of the Lord.* Since the angel of the Lord speaks for God in the first person (v. 10) and Hagar is said to name "the Lord who spoke to her: 'You are the God who sees me'" (v. 13), the angel appears to be both distinguished from the Lord (in that he is called "messenger"—the Hebrew for "angel" means "messenger") and identified with him (see also 48:16). Similar distinction and identification can be found in 19:1,21; 31:11,13; Ex 3:2,4; Jdg 2:1–5; 6:11–12,14; 13:3,6,8–11,13,15–17,20–23; Zec 3:1–6; 12:8. Traditional Christian interpretation has held that this "angel" was a preincarnate manifestation of Christ as God's Messenger-Servant. It may be, however, that, as the Lord's personal messenger who represented him and bore his credentials, the angel could speak on behalf of (and so be identified with) the One who sent him (see especially 19:21; cf. 18:2,22; 19:2). Whether this "angel" was the second person of the Trinity remains therefore uncertain (cf. Lk 2:9 and note). *Shur.* Located just east of Lower Egypt (see 25:18; 1Sa 15:7).

16:8 *I'm running away from my mistress.* Not yet knowing exactly where she was going, Hagar answered only the first of the angel's questions.

16:10 A promise reaffirmed in 17:20 and fulfilled in 25:13–16.

16:11 *Ishmael.* See TNIV text note and 17:20.

16:12 *wild donkey.* Probably the onager, which roamed the dry steppes of the Near East. Ishmael would roam the desert like a wild donkey (see Job 24:5; Hos 8:9). *hostility.* The hostility between Sarai and Hagar (see vv. 4–6) was passed on to their descendants (see 25:18).

16:13 *I have now seen the One who sees me.* See TNIV text note

and cf. Ex 33:23. To see God's face was believed to bring death (see 32:30; Ex 33:20).

16:14 *Beer Lahai Roi.* See TNIV text note. Another possible translation that fits the context equally well is: "well of the one who sees me and who lives," i.e., Hagar. *Kadesh.* See note on 14:7.

17:1–27 God's covenant with Abram renewed and expanded (see chart, p. 20). After Abram's and Sarai's attempt to obtain the promised offspring by using the womb of Sarai's servant, God appears to Abram to reaffirm his promises. But he also makes it clear that, if Abram is to receive God's covenanted benefits, he must live out "faith and obedience for his name's sake" (Ro 1:5; see also ch. 22). To that end he calls on Abram to make with him a covenanted commitment of loyal obedience.

17:1 *ninety-nine years old.* Thirteen years had passed since Ishmael's birth (see 16:16; 17:24–25). *appeared.* See note on 12:7. *I am.* See note on 15:7. *God Almighty.* The Hebrew (*El-Shaddai*) perhaps means "God, the Mountain One," either highlighting the invincible power of God or referring to the mountains as God's symbolic home (see Ps 121:1). It was the special name by which God revealed himself to the patriarchs (see Ex 6:3). *Shaddai* occurs 31 times in the book of Job and 17 times in the rest of the Bible. *walk before me faithfully and be blameless.* Perhaps equivalent to "walk with me faithfully and be blameless" (see notes on 5:22; 6:8–9).

17:2 *my covenant.* See 15:4–5. The covenant is God's; he calls it "my covenant" nine times in vv. 2–21, and he initiates (see 15:18), confirms (v. 2) and establishes (v. 7) it. *increase your numbers.* The language echoes 1:28 (Adam) and 9:7 (Noah), suggesting that

You will be the father of many nations. *c* 5No longer will you be called Abram*a*; your name will be Abraham, *b d* for I have made you a father of many nations. *e* 6I will make you very fruitful; *f* I will make nations of you, and kings will come from you. *g* 7I will establish my covenant *h i* as an everlasting covenant *j k* between me and you and your descendants after you for the generations to come, to be your God *l* and the God of your descendants after you. *m* 8The whole land of Canaan, *n* where you now reside as a foreigner, *o* I will give as an everlasting possession to you and your descendants after you; *p* and I will be their God. *q*"

9Then God said to Abraham, "As for you, you must keep my covenant, *r* you and your descendants after you for the generations to come. *s* 10This is my covenant with you and your descendants after you, the covenant you are to keep: Every male among you shall be circumcised. *t* 11You are to undergo circumcision, *u* and it will be the sign of the covenant *v* between me and you. 12For the generations to come *w* every male among you who is eight days old must be circumcised, *x* including those born in your household or bought with money from a foreigner—those who are not your offspring. 13Whether born in your household or bought with your money, they must be circumcised. *y* My covenant in your flesh is to be an everlasting covenant. *z* 14Any uncircumcised male, who has not been circumcised *a* in the flesh, will be cut off from his people; *b* he has broken my covenant. *c*"

15God also said to Abraham, "As for Sarai *d* your wife, you are no longer to call her Sarai; her name will be Sarah. *e* 16I will bless her and will surely give you a son by her. *f* I will bless her so that she will be the mother of nations; *g* kings of peoples will come from her."

17Abraham fell facedown; *h* he laughed *i* and said to himself, "Will a son be born to a man a hundred years old? *j* Will Sarah bear a child at the age of ninety?" *k* 18And Abraham said to God, "If only Ishmael *l* might live under your blessing!" *m*

---

a 5 *Abram* means *exalted father.*   *b* 5 *Abraham* probably means *father of many.*

17:11 *u* Ex 12:48; Dt 10:16 *v* S Ge 9:12; Ro 4:11   **17:12** *w* S Ge 9:12 *x* Ge 21:4; Lev 12:3; Jos 5:2; S Lk 1:59   **17:13** *y* Ex 12:44,48 *z* S Ge 9:16   **17:14** *a* ver 23 *b* Ex 4:24-26; 12:15,19; 30:33; Lev 7:20,25; 17:4; 18:29; 19:8; 20:17; Nu 9:13; 15:30; 19:13; Dt 17:12; Jos 5:2-8; Job 38:15; Ps 37:28 *c* Eze 44:7   **17:15** *d* S Ge 11:29 *e* S ver 5   **17:16** *f* S ver 6; S Isa 29:22 *g* S ver 4; Ge 24:60; Gal 4:31   **17:17** *h* S ver 3 *i* Ge 18:12; 21:6 *j* S Ge 12:4 *k* Ge 18:11,13; 21:7; 24:1,36; Jer 20:15; Lk 1:18; Ro 4:19; Gal 4:23; Heb 11:11   **17:18** *l* S Ge 16:15 *m* Ge 21:11

17:4 *c* ver 16; S Ge 12:2; 25:23
17:5 *d* ver 15; Ge 32:28; 35:10; 37:3, 13; 43:6; 46:2; 1Ki 18:31; 2Ki 17:34; 1Ch 1:34; Ne 9:7; Isa 48:1; S Jn 1:42 *e* Ro 4:17*
17:6 *f* Ge 1:28; 22:17; 26:22; 28:3; 35:11; 41:52; 47:27; 48:4; 49:22; Lev 26:9; Dt 7:13 *g* ver 16,19; Ge 18:10; 21:1; 36:31; Isa 51:2; Mt 1:6
17:7 *h* S Ge 15:18; Lev 26:9,15 *i* S Ge 6:18 *j* S Heb 13:20 *k* S Ge 9:16 *l* Ex 6:7; Lev 11:44-45; 18:2; 22:33; 25:38; 26:12, 45; Nu 15:41; Dt 4:20; 7:6,21; 29:13; 2Sa 7:24; Jer 14:9; Rev 21:7 *m* Ro 9:8; Gal 3:16
17:8 *n* S Ge 10:19 *o* Ge 23:4; 28:4; 35:27; 37:1; Ex 6:4; 1Ch 29:15 *p* S Ge 12:7; S 15:7 *q* S ver 7; Jer 31:1
17:9 *r* Ge 22:18; Ex 19:5; Dt 5:2 *s* Ge 18:19
17:10 *t* ver 23; Ge 21:4; Lev 12:3; Jos 5:2,5,7; Jn 7:22; Ac 7:8; Ro 4:11

God's original purpose for humankind, threatened by the sins of the race, will be achieved through Abraham and his descendants (see also Ex 1:7 and note). See 13:16 and note. Earlier God had covenanted to keep his promise concerning the land (ch. 15); here he broadens his covenant to include the promised offspring.

17:5 *Abram . . . Abraham.* See TNIV text notes. The first name means "Exalted Father," probably in reference to God (i.e., "[God is] Exalted Father"); the second probably means "father of many," in reference to Abraham. *your name will be.* By giving Abram a new name (see Ne 9:7) God marked him in a special way as his servant (see notes on 1:5; 2:19).

17:6 *nations . . . kings.* This promise also came to Sarah (v. 16) and was renewed to Jacob (35:11; see 48:19). It referred to the proliferation of Abraham's offspring, who, like the descendants of Noah (see ch. 10), would someday become many nations and spread over the earth. Ultimately it finds fulfillment in such passages as Ro 4:16–18; 15:8–12; Gal 3:29; Rev 7:9; 21:24.

17:7 *everlasting.* God's commitment to his covenant was forever (see vv. 13,19), but descendants of Abraham could break it (see v. 14; cf. Lk 24:5; Jer 31:32). *to be your God.* The heart of God's covenant promise, repeated over and over in the OT (see, e.g., v. 8; Jer 24:7; 31:33; Eze 34:30–31; Hos 2:23; Zec 8:8 and note). This is God's pledge to be the protector of his people and the One who provides for their well-being and guarantees their future blessing (see 15:1).

17:8 *land.* See 12:7; 15:18; Ac 7:5. *everlasting possession.* The land, though an everlasting possession given by God, could be temporarily lost because of disobedience (see Dt 28:62–63; 30:1–10).

17:9 *As for you.* Balances the "As for me" of v. 4. Having reviewed his covenanted commitment to Abraham (see 15:8–21), and having broadened it to include the promise of offspring, God now called upon Abraham to make a covenanted commitment to him—to "walk before me faithfully and be blameless" (v. 1). *keep my covenant.* Participation in the blessings of the Abrahamic covenant was conditioned on obedience (see 18:19; 22:18; 26:4–5).

17:10 *circumcised.* Circumcision was God's appointed "sign of the covenant" (v. 11), which signified Abraham's covenanted commitment to the Lord—that the Lord alone would be his God, whom he would trust and serve. It symbolized a self-maledictory oath: "If I am not loyal in faith and obedience to the Lord, may the sword of the Lord cut off me and my offspring [see v. 14] as I have cut off my foreskin" (analogous to the oath to which God had submitted himself; see note on 15:17). Thus Abraham was to place himself under the rule of the Lord as his King, consecrating himself, his offspring and all he possessed to the service of the Lord. For circumcision as signifying consecration to the Lord see Dt 10:16; 30:6; Jer 4:4; 9:25–26; Eze 44:7 and note; 44:9; cf. Ro 2:29. Other nations also practiced circumcision (see Jer 9:25–26; Eze 32:18–19), but not for the covenant reasons that Israel did.

17:11 *sign of the covenant.* See notes on 9:12; 15:17. As the covenant sign, circumcision also (see note on v. 10) marked Abraham as the one to whom God had made covenant commitment (15:7–21) in response to Abraham's faith, which he "credited . . . to him as righteousness" (15:6). Paul comments on this aspect of the covenant sign in Ro 4:11.

17:12 *eight days old.* See 21:4 and Ac 7:8 (Isaac); Lk 1:59 (John the Baptist); 2:21 (Jesus); Php 3:5 (Paul). Abraham was 99 years old when the newly initiated rite of circumcision was performed on him (see v. 24). The Arabs, who consider themselves descendants of Ishmael, are circumcised at the age of 13 (see v. 25). For them, as for other peoples, circumcision serves as a rite of transition from childhood to manhood, thus into full participation in the community.

17:14 *cut off from his people.* Removed from the covenant people by divine judgment (see note on v. 10).

17:15 *Sarai . . . Sarah.* Both names evidently mean "princess." The renaming stressed that she was to be the mother of nations and kings (see v. 16) and thus to serve the Lord's purpose (see note on v. 5).

17:16 *son.* Fulfilled in Isaac (see 21:2–3).

17:17 *laughed.* In temporary disbelief (see 18:12; cf. Ro 4:19–21). The verb is a pun on the name "Isaac," which means "he laughs" (see TNIV text notes on v. 19 and 21:3; see also 18:12–15; 21:6).

17:19 ⁿS ver 6,21;
Ge 18:14; 21:2;
1Sa 1:20 ᵒS Ge 16:11;
Mt 1:21; Lk 1:13,31
ᵖGe 26:3; 50:24;
Ex 13:11; Dt 1:8
ᵍS Ge 9:16;
S Gal 3:16
17:20 ʳS Ge 13:16
ˢGe 25:12-16
ᵗGe 25:18; 48:19
17:21 ᵘEx 34:10
ᵛS ver 19 ʷGe 18:10,
14
17:22 ˣGe 18:33;
35:13; Nu 12:9
17:23 ʸS Ge 12:5
ᶻS ver 10, S 14
17:24 ᵃS Ge 12:4
ᵇRo 4:11
17:25 ᶜGe 16:16
17:27 ᵈGe 14:14
18:1 ᵉS Ge 12:7;
Ac 7:2 ᶠS Ge 13:18
ᵍGe 19:1; 23:10,18;
34:20,24; Ru 4:1;
Ps 69:12; Heb 11:9
18:2 ʰGe 24:63
ⁱver 16,22; Ge 19:1,
10; 32:24; Jos 5:13;
Jdg 13:6-11; Hos 12:3-
4; Heb 13:2
ʲS Ge 17:3; S 43:28
18:3 ᵏGe 19:19;
39:4; Ru 2:2,10,13;
1Sa 1:18; Est 2:15
ˡGe 32:4,18,20; 33:5
18:4 ᵐGe 19:2;
24:32; 43:24;
Jdg 19:21; 2Sa 11:8;
S Lk 7:44
18:5 ⁿJdg 13:15;
19:5
18:6 ᵒGe 19:3;
2Sa 13:8
18:7 ᵖ1Sa 28:24;
Lk 15:23
18:8 ᵍIsa 7:15,22
ʳJdg 4:19; 5:25
ˢJdg 6:19
18:9 ᵗS Ge 3:9
ᵘGe 24:67; Heb 11:9
18:10 ᵛS Ge 17:21;
21:2; 2Ki 4:16
ʷS Ge 17:6; Ro 9:9*
18:11 ˣS Ge 17:17;
Lk 1:18 ʸS Ge 11:30;
Ro 4:19; Heb 11:11-12
18:12 ᶻS Ge 17:17
ᵃ1Pe 3:6
18:13 ᵇS Ge 17:17
18:14 ᶜJob 42:2;
Isa 40:29; 50:2; 51:9;
Jer 32:17,27;
S Mt 19:26; Ro 4:21

¹⁹Then God said, "Yes, but your wife Sarah will bear you a son, ⁿ and you will call him Isaac. ᵃ ᵒ I will establish my covenant with him ᵖ as an everlasting covenant ᵍ for his descendants after him. ²⁰And as for Ishmael, I have heard you: I will surely bless him; I will make him fruitful and will greatly increase his numbers. ʳ He will be the father of twelve rulers, ˢ and I will make him into a great nation. ᵗ ²¹But my covenant ᵘ I will establish with Isaac, whom Sarah will bear to you ᵛ by this time next year." ʷ ²²When he had finished speaking with Abraham, God went up from him. ˣ

²³On that very day Abraham took his son Ishmael and all those born in his household ʸ or bought with his money, every male in his household, and circumcised them, as God told him. ᶻ ²⁴Abraham was ninety-nine years old ᵃ when he was circumcised, ᵇ ²⁵and his son Ishmael ᶜ was thirteen; ²⁶Abraham and his son Ishmael were both circumcised on that same day. ²⁷And every male in Abraham's household ᵈ, including those born in his household or bought from a foreigner, was circumcised with him.

THE THREE VISITORS

18 The LORD appeared to Abraham ᵉ near the great trees of Mamre ᶠ while he was sitting at the entrance to his tent ᵍ in the heat of the day. ²Abraham looked up ʰ and saw three men ⁱ standing nearby. When he saw them, he hurried from the entrance of his tent to meet them and bowed low to the ground. ʲ

³He said, "If I have found favor in your eyes, ᵏ my lord, ᵇ do not pass your servant ˡ by. ⁴Let a little water be brought, and then you may all wash your feet ᵐ and rest under this tree. ⁵Let me get you something to eat, ⁿ so you can be refreshed and then go on your way—now that you have come to your servant."

"Very well," they answered, "do as you say."

⁶So Abraham hurried into the tent to Sarah. "Quick," he said, "get three seahs ᶜ of the finest flour and knead it and bake some bread." ᵒ

⁷Then he ran to the herd and selected a choice, tender calf ᵖ and gave it to a servant, who hurried to prepare it. ⁸He then brought some curds ᵍ and milk ʳ and the calf that had been prepared, and set these before them. ˢ While they ate, he stood near them under a tree.

⁹"Where is your wife Sarah?" ᵗ they asked him.

"There, in the tent," ᵘ he said.

¹⁰Then the LORD ᵈ said, "I will surely return to you about this time next year, ᵛ and Sarah your wife will have a son." ʷ

Now Sarah was listening at the entrance to the tent, which was behind him. ¹¹Abraham and Sarah were already very old, ˣ and Sarah was past the age of childbearing. ʸ ¹²So Sarah laughed ᶻ to herself as she thought, "After I am worn out and my lord ᵃ is old, will I now have this pleasure?"

¹³Then the LORD said to Abraham, "Why did Sarah laugh and say, 'Will I really have a child, now that I am old?' ᵇ ¹⁴Is anything too hard for the LORD? ᶜ I will return to you at the appointed time next year ᵈ and Sarah will have a son." ᵉ

ᵃ 19 *Isaac* means *he laughs.*   ᵇ 3 Or *eyes, Lord*   ᶜ 6 That is, probably about 36 pounds or about 16 kilograms   ᵈ 10 Hebrew *Then he*

18:14 ᵈS ver 10 ᵉS Ge 17:19; Ro 9:9*; Gal 4:23

17:20 *numbers.* See note on 13:16. *father of twelve rulers.* Fulfilled in 25:16.

 17:21 Paul cites the choice of Isaac (and not Ishmael) as one proof of God's sovereign right to choose to save by grace alone (see Ro 9:6–13). *by this time next year.* See 21:2.
17:22 *God went up from him.* A solemn conclusion to the conversation.

17:23 *On that very day.* Abraham was characterized by prompt obedience (see note on 12:4).
18:1–33 God appears to Abraham with two representatives (identified as "angels" in 19:1) of his heavenly council (see 1Ki 22:19–22 and note on 22:19; Jer 23:18,22 and note on 23:18). He comes to announce to Abraham what he is about to do (see note on v. 17).
18:1 *appeared.* See note on 12:7. *great trees.* See note on 12:6. *Mamre.* See note on 13:18. *heat of the day.* Early afternoon.
18:2 *three men.* Two of the "men" were angels (see 19:1; see also note on 16:7). The third was the Lord himself (see vv. 1,13,17,20,26,33; see especially v. 22). *hurried.* The story in vv. 2–8 illustrates Near Eastern hospitality in several ways:

1. Abraham gave prompt attention to the needs of his guests (vv. 2,6–7). 2. He bowed low to the ground (v. 2). 3. He politely addressed one of his guests as "my lord" and called him "your servant" (vv. 3,5), a common way of speaking when addressing a superior (see, e.g., 19:2,18–19). 4. He acted as if it would be a favor to him if they allowed him to serve them (vv. 3–5). 5. He asked that water be brought to wash their feet (see v. 4), an act of courtesy to refresh a traveler in a hot, dusty climate (see 19:2; 24:32; 43:24). 6. He prepared a lavish meal for them (vv. 5–8; a similar lavish offering was presented to a divine messenger in Jdg 6:18–19; 13:15–16). 7. He stood nearby (v. 8), assuming the posture of a servant (see v. 22), to meet their every wish. Heb 13:2 is probably a reference to vv. 2–8 and 19:1–3.
18:6 *bread.* A plural word referring to round, thin loaves.
18:10 See 17:21. Paul quotes this promise of Isaac's birth (see v. 14) in Ro 9:9 and relates it to Abraham's spiritual offspring (see Ro 9:7–8).

18:12 *laughed.* In disbelief, as also Abraham had at first (see note on 17:17).

¹⁵Sarah was afraid, so she lied and said, "I did not laugh."

But he said, "Yes, you did laugh."

ABRAHAM PLEADS FOR SODOM

¹⁶When the men *f* got up to leave, they looked down toward Sodom, and Abraham walked along with them to see them on their way. ¹⁷Then the Lord said, "Shall I hide from Abraham *g* what I am about to do? *h* ¹⁸Abraham will surely become a great and powerful nation, *i* and all nations on earth will be blessed through him. *a* ¹⁹For I have chosen him *j*, so that he will direct his children *k* and his household after him to keep the way of the Lord *l* by doing what is right and just, *m* so that the Lord will bring about for Abraham what he has promised him." *n*

²⁰Then the Lord said, "The outcry against Sodom *o* and Gomorrah is so great *p* and their sin so grievous *q* ²¹that I will go down *r* and see if what they have done is as bad as the outcry that has reached me. If not, I will know."

²²The men *s* turned away and went toward Sodom, *t* but Abraham remained standing before the Lord. *b u* ²³Then Abraham approached him and said: "Will you sweep away the righteous with the wicked? *v* ²⁴What if there are fifty righteous people in the city? Will you really sweep it away and not spare *c* the place for the sake of the fifty righteous people in it? *w* ²⁵Far be it from you to do such a thing *x*—to kill the righteous with the wicked, treating the righteous *y* and the wicked alike. *z* Far be it from you! Will not the Judge *a* of all the earth do right?" *b*

²⁶The Lord said, "If I find fifty righteous people in the city of Sodom, I will spare the whole place for their sake. *c*"

²⁷Then Abraham spoke up again: "Now that I have been so bold as to speak to the Lord, though I am nothing but dust and ashes, *d* ²⁸what if the number of the righteous is five less than fifty? Will you destroy the whole city for lack of five people?"

"If I find forty-five there," he said, "I will not destroy it."

²⁹Once again he spoke to him, "What if only forty are found there?"

He said, "For the sake of forty, I will not do it."

³⁰Then he said, "May the Lord not be angry, *e* but let me speak. What if only thirty can be found there?"

He answered, "I will not do it if I find thirty there."

³¹Abraham said, "Now that I have been so bold as to speak to the Lord, what if only twenty can be found there?"

He said, "For the sake of twenty, I will not destroy it."

³²Then he said, "May the Lord not be angry, but let me speak just once more. *f* What if only ten can be found there?"

---

a 18 Or *will use his name in blessings* (see Gen. 48:20)   *b 22* Masoretic Text; an ancient Hebrew scribal tradition *but the Lord remained standing before Abraham*   *c 24* Or *forgive*; also in verse 26

18:16 *f* S ver 2
18:17 *g* Am 3:7
h Ge 19:24; Job 1:16;
Ps 107:34
18:18 *i* S Ge 12:2;
Gal 3:8*
18:19 *j* Ge 17:9
k Dt 4:9-10; 6:7
l Jos 24:15; Eph 6:4
m Ge 22:12,18; 26:5;
2Sa 8:15; Ps 17:2;
99:4; Jer 23:5
n S Ge 16:11;
S Isa 14:1
18:20 *o* Isa 1:10;
Jer 23:14; Eze 16:46
p Ge 19:13
q S Ge 13:13
18:21 *r* S Ge 11:5
18:22 *s* S ver 2
t Ge 19:1 *u* ver 1;
Ge 19:27
18:23 *v* Ex 23:7;
Lev 4:3,22,27;
Nu 16:22; Dt 27:25;
2Sa 24:17; Ps 11:4-7;
94:21; Eze 18:4;
2Pe 2:9
18:24 *w* ver 26;
Jer 5:1
18:25 *x* Ge 44:7,17;
Dt 32:4; Job 8:3-7;
34:10 *y* Isa 5:20;
Am 5:15; Mal 2:17;
3:18 *z* Dt 1:16-17
a Jdg 11:27; Job 9:15;
Ps 7:11; 94:2;
Heb 12:23 *b* Ge 20:4;
Dt 32:4; 2Ch 19:7;
Ezr 9:15; Ne 9:33;
Job 8:3, 20; 34:10;
36:23; Ps 58:11; 75:7;
94:2; 119:137;
Isa 3:10-11; Eze 18:25;
Da 4:37; 9:14;
Mal 2:17; Ro 3:6
18:26 *c* S ver 24
18:27 *d* S Ge 2:7;
S Job 2:8
18:30 *e* ver 32;
Ge 44:18; Ex 32:22
18:32 *f* S ver 30;
Jdg 6:39

18:14 *Is anything too hard for the Lord?* The answer is no, for Sarah as well as for her descendants Mary and Elizabeth (see Lk 1:34–37). Nothing within God's will, including creation (see Jer 32:17) and redemption (see Mt 19:25–26), is impossible for him.

18:16 *Sodom.* See notes on 10:19; 13:10.

18:17 Abraham was God's friend (see v. 19; 2Ch 20:7; Jas 2:23; see also Isa 41:8). And because he was now God's covenant friend (see Job 29:4), God convened his heavenly council (see note on 1:26) at Abraham's tent. There he announced his purpose for Abraham (v. 10) and for the wicked of the plain (vv. 20–21)—redemption and judgment. He thus even gave Abraham opportunity to speak in his court and to intercede for the righteous in Sodom and Gomorrah. Accordingly, Abraham was later called a prophet (20:7). Here, in Abraham, is exemplified the great privilege of God's covenant people throughout the ages: God has revealed his purposes to them and allows their voice to be heard (in intercession) in the court of heaven itself.

18:18 *great and powerful nation ... blessed through him.* See note on 12:2–3.

18:19 *what is right and just.* See note on Ps 119:121.

18:20 *outcry.* A cry of righteous indignation (cf. the blood of Abel, 4:10) that became one of the reasons for the destruction of the cities (see 19:13). *Gomorrah.* See notes on 10:19; 13:10.

18:21 *I will go down.* The result would be judgment (as in 11:5–9), but God also comes down to redeem (as in Ex 3:8). *see.* Not a denial of God's infinite knowledge but a figurative way of stating that he as "Judge" (v. 25) does not act on the basis of mere complaints.

18:22 *Abraham remained standing before the Lord.* The text and TNIV text note both illustrate the mutual accessibility that existed between God and his servant.

18:23 The second time Abraham intervened for his relatives and for Sodom (see 14:14–16).

18:25 *Judge of all the earth.* Abraham based his plea on the justice and authority of God, confident that God would do what was right (see Dt 32:4).

18:27 *Lord.* Abraham used the title "Lord" (Adonai), not the covenantal name "Lord" (Yahweh), throughout his prayer. He was appealing to God as "Judge of all the earth." *dust and ashes.* In contrast to God's exalted position, Abraham described himself as insignificant (see Job 30:19; 42:6).

18:32 *just once more.* Abraham's questioning in vv. 23–32 did not arise from a spirit of haggling but of compassion for his relatives and of wanting to know God's ways. *ten.* Perhaps Abraham stopped at ten because he had been counting while praying: Lot, his wife, possibly two sons (see 19:12), at least two married daughters and their husbands (see 19:14 and TNIV text note), and two unmarried daughters (see 19:8).

18:32 ^{g} Jer 5:1
18:33 ^{h} Ex 31:18
^{i} S Ge 17:22 ^{j} Ge 31:55
19:1 ^{k} S Ge 18:2;
Heb 13:2 ^{l} Ge 18:22
^{m} S Ge 11:27
^{n} S Ge 18:1
^{o} S Ge 17:3; 48:12;
Ru 2:10; 1Sa 25:23;
2Sa 14:33; 2Ki 2:15
19:2 ^{p} S Ge 18:4;
Lk 7:44 ^{q} Jdg 19:15,
20
19:3 ^{r} Ge 33:11
^{s} Job 31:32 ^{t} Ex 12:39
^{u} S Ge 18:6
19:4 ^{v} S Ge 13:13
19:5 ^{w} S Ge 13:13;
Lev 18:22; Dt 23:18;
Jdg 19:22; Ro 1:24-27
19:6 ^{x} Jdg 19:23
19:8 ^{y} Jdg 19:24;
2Pe 2:7-8
19:9 ^{z} Ge 23:4
^{a} S Ge 13:8; Ac 7:27
19:10 ^{b} S Ge 18:2
19:11 ^{c} Dt 28:28-
29; 2Ki 6:18; Ac 13:11
19:12 ^{d} S Ge 6:18
19:13 ^{e} Ex 12:29;
2Sa 24:16; 2Ki 19:35;
1Ch 21:12; 2Ch 32:21
^{f} Ge 18:20
^{g} 1Ch 21:15; Ps 78:49;
Jer 21:12; 25:18;
44:22; 51:45
19:14 ^{h} Nu 16:21;
Rev 18:4 ^{i} Ex 9:21;
1Ki 13:18; Jer 5:12;
43:2; Lk 17:28
19:15 ^{j} Nu 16:26;
Job 21:18; Ps 58:9;
73:19; 90:5 ^{k} Rev 18:4
19:16 ^{l} 2Pe 2:7
^{m} Ex 34:6; Ps 33:18-
19
19:17 ^{n} 1Ki 19:3;
Jer 48:6 ^{o} ver 26
^{p} S Ge 13:12
^{q} S ver 19; S Ge 14:10;
Mt 24:16
19:19 ^{r} S Ge 6:8;
S 18:3 ^{s} Ge 24:12;
39:21; 40:14; 47:29;
Ru 1:8; 2:20; 3:10
^{t} S ver 17,30

He answered, "For the sake of ten,^{g} I will not destroy it."

^{33}When the L ORD had finished speaking^h with Abraham, he left,^{i} and Abraham returned home.^{j}

SODOM AND GOMORRAH DESTROYED

19 The two angels^k arrived at Sodom^l in the evening, and Lot^m was sitting in the gateway of the city.^{n} When he saw them, he got up to meet them and bowed down with his face to the ground.^{o} ^{2}"My lords," he said, "please turn aside to your servant's house. You can wash your feet^p and spend the night and then go on your way early in the morning."

"No," they answered, "we will spend the night in the square."^{q}

^{3}But he insisted^r so strongly that they did go with him and entered his house.^{s} He prepared a meal for them, baking bread without yeast,^{t} and they ate.^{u} ^{4}Before they had gone to bed, all the men from every part of the city of Sodom^v—both young and old—surrounded the house. ^{5}They called to Lot, "Where are the men who came to you tonight? Bring them out to us so that we can have sex with them."^{w}

^{6}Lot went outside to meet them^x and shut the door behind him ^{7}and said, "No, my friends. Don't do this wicked thing. ^{8}Look, I have two daughters who have never slept with a man. Let me bring them out to you, and you can do what you like with them. But don't do anything to these men, for they have come under the protection of my roof."^{y}

^{9}"Get out of our way," they replied. "This fellow came here as a foreigner,^{z} and now he wants to play the judge!^{a} We'll treat you worse than them." They kept bringing pressure on Lot and moved forward to break down the door.

^{10}But the men^b inside reached out and pulled Lot back into the house and shut the door. ^{11}Then they struck the men who were at the door of the house, young and old, with blindness^c so that they could not find the door.

^{12}The two men said to Lot, "Do you have anyone else here—sons-in-law, sons or daughters, or anyone else in the city who belongs to you?^{d} Get them out of here, ^{13}because we^e are going to destroy this place. The outcry to the L ORD against its people is so great^f that he has sent us to destroy it."^{g}

^{14}So Lot went out and spoke to his sons-in-law, who were pledged to marry^a his daughters. He said, "Hurry and get out of this place, because the L ORD is about to destroy the city!^{h}" But his sons-in-law thought he was joking.^{i}

^{15}With the coming of dawn, the angels urged Lot, saying, "Hurry! Take your wife and your two daughters who are here, or you will be swept away^j when the city is punished.^{k}"

^{16}When he hesitated, the men grasped his hand and the hands of his wife and of his two daughters^l and led them safely out of the city, for the L ORD was merciful to them.^{m} ^{17}As soon as they had brought them out, one of them said, "Flee for your lives!^{n} Don't look back,^{o} and don't stop anywhere in the plain!^{p} Flee to the mountains^q or you will be swept away!"

^{18}But Lot said to them, "No, my lords,^{b} please! ^{19}Your^c servant has found favor in your^c eyes,^{r} and you^c have shown great kindness^s to me in sparing my life. But I can't flee to the mountains;^{t} this disaster will overtake me, and I'll die. ^{20}Look, here is a town near

---

^{a} 14 Or *were married to* ^{b} 18 Or *No, Lord*; or *No, my lord* ^{c} 19 The Hebrew is singular.

18:33 *home.* To Mamre (see v. 1). The next morning Abraham went back to see what God had done (see 19:27).
19:1–3 See note on 18:2.
19:1 *two angels.* See notes on 16:7; 18:2. *Lot was sitting in the gateway of the city.* Lot had probably become a member of Sodom's ruling council, since a city gateway served as the administrative and judicial center where legal matters were discussed and prosecuted (see Ru 4:1–12).
19:2 *square.* An open space near the main city gateway (see 2Ch 32:6) where public gatherings were held. Important cities like Jerusalem could have two or more squares (see Ne 8:16).
19:3 *bread without yeast.* A flat bread that could be baked quickly (see 18:6; Ex 12:8,39).
19:4–9 See Jdg 19:22–25.
19:5 *have sex with them.* Homosexual practice was open and common among the men of Sodom (see Jude 7). The English word "sodomy" alludes to the perversions of the ancient city.
19:8 *under the protection of my roof.* Ancient hospitality

obliged a host to protect his guests in every situation and in every possible way.
19:9 *This fellow came here as a foreigner, and now he wants to play the judge.* Centuries later, Moses was also considered an outsider and accused of setting himself up as a judge (see Ex 2:14; Ac 7:27).
19:13 *we are going to destroy this place.* Sodom's wickedness had made it ripe for destruction (see Isa 3:9; Jer 23:14; La 4:6; Zep 2:8–9; 2Pe 2:6; Jude 7).
19:14 *his sons-in-law thought he was joking.* Lot apparently had lost his power of moral persuasion even among his family members.
19:16 *hesitated.* Perhaps because of reluctance to leave his material possessions. *his hand and the hands of his wife and of his two daughters.* The ten righteous people required to save Sodom (see 18:32) had now been reduced to four. *the L ORD was merciful to them.* Deliverance is due to divine mercy, not to human righteousness (cf. Tit 3:5 and note).

enough to run to, and it is small. Let me flee to it—it is very small, isn't it? Then my life will be spared."

²¹He said to him, "Very well, I will grant this request *u* too; I will not overthrow the town you speak of. ²²But flee there quickly, because I cannot do anything until you reach it." (That is why the town was called Zoar.*ᵃ ⱽ*)

²³By the time Lot reached Zoar, *ʷ* the sun had risen over the land. ²⁴Then the LORD rained down burning sulfur *ˣ* on Sodom and Gomorrah *ʸ*—from the LORD out of the heavens. *ᶻ* ²⁵Thus he overthrew those cities *ᵃ* and the entire plain, *ᵇ* destroying all those living in the cities—and also the vegetation in the land. *ᶜ* ²⁶But Lot's wife looked back, *ᵈ* and she became a pillar of salt. *ᵉ*

²⁷Early the next morning Abraham got up and returned to the place where he had stood before the LORD. *ᶠ* ²⁸He looked down toward Sodom and Gomorrah, toward all the land of the plain, and he saw dense smoke rising from the land, like smoke from a furnace. *ᵍ*

²⁹So when God destroyed the cities of the plain, *ʰ* he remembered *ⁱ* Abraham, and he brought Lot out of the catastrophe *ʲ* that overthrew the cities where Lot had lived. *ᵏ*

LOT AND HIS DAUGHTERS

³⁰Lot and his two daughters left Zoar *ˡ* and settled in the mountains, *ᵐ* for he was afraid to stay in Zoar. He and his two daughters lived in a cave. ³¹One day the older daughter said to the younger, "Our father is old, and there is no man around here to give us children—as is the custom all over the earth. ³²Let's get our father to drink wine and then sleep with him and preserve our family line *ⁿ* through our father." *ᵒ*

³³That night they got their father to drink wine, and the older daughter went in and slept with him. He was not aware of it when she lay down or when she got up. *ᵖ*

³⁴The next day the older daughter said to the younger, "Last night I slept with my father. Let's get him to drink wine again tonight, and you go in and sleep with him so we can preserve our family line through our father." *�q* ³⁵So they got their father to drink wine *ʳ* that night also, and the younger daughter went in and slept with him. Again he was not aware of it when she lay down or when she got up. *ˢ*

³⁶So both of Lot's daughters became pregnant by their father. *ᵗ* ³⁷The older daughter had a son, and she named him Moab*ᵇ*; *ᵘ* he is the father of the Moabites *ⱽ* of today. ³⁸The younger daughter also had a son, and she named him Ben-Ammi*ᶜ*; he is the father of the Ammonites*ᵈ ʷ* of today.

ABRAHAM AND ABIMELEK

20:1–18Ref — Ge 12:10–20; 26:1–11

20 Now Abraham moved on from there *ˣ* into the region of the Negev *ʸ* and lived between Kadesh *ᶻ* and Shur. *ᵃ* For a while *ᵇ* he stayed in Gerar, *ᶜ* ²and there Abraham said of his wife Sarah, "She is my sister. *ᵈ*" Then Abimelek *ᵉ* king of Gerar sent for Sarah and took her. *ᶠ*

³But God came to Abimelek *ᵍ* in a dream *ʰ* one night and said to him, "You are as good as dead *ⁱ* because of the woman you have taken; she is a married woman." *ʲ*

⁴Now Abimelek had not gone near her, so he said, "Lord, will you destroy an innocent

---

a 22 Zoar means small.   b 37 Moab sounds like the Hebrew for from father.   c 38 Ben-Ammi means son of my father's people.   d 38 Hebrew Bene-Ammon

20:3 Nu 12:6; Dt 13:1; Job 33:15; Da 2:1; 4:5 *ⁱ* Ex 10:7; 12:33; Ps 105:38 *ʲ* ver 7; Ge 26:11; 1Ch 16:21; Ps 105:14

19:21 *u* 1Sa 25:35; 2Sa 14:8; Job 42:9
19:22 *v* S Ge 13:10
19:23 *w* S Ge 13:10
19:24 *x* Job 18:15; Ps 11:6; Isa 30:33; 34:9; Eze 38:22 *y* Dt 29:23; Isa 1:9; 13:19; Jer 49:18; 50:40; Am 4:11 *z* S Ge 18:17; S Lev 10:2; S Mt 10:15; Lk 17:29
19:25 *a* S ver 24; Eze 26:16; Zep 3:8; Hag 2:22 *b* S Ge 13:12 *c* Ps 107:34; Isa 1:10; Jer 20:16; 23:14; La 4:6; Eze 16:48
19:26 *d* S ver 17 *e* Lk 17:32
19:27 *f* Ge 18:22
19:28 *g* Ge 15:17; Ex 19:18; Rev 9:2; 18:9
19:29 *h* S Ge 13:12 *i* S Ge 8:1 *j* 2Pe 2:7 *k* Ge 14:12; Eze 14:16
19:30 *l* ver 22; S Ge 13:10 *m* S ver 19; S Ge 14:10
19:32 *n* S Ge 16:2 *o* ver 34, 36; Ge 38:18
19:33 *p* ver 35
19:34 *q* S ver 32
19:35 *r* Ge 9:21 *s* ver 33
19:36 *t* S ver 32
19:37 *u* Ge 36:35; Ex 15:15; Nu 25:1; Isa 15:1; 25:10; Jer 25:21; 48:1; Eze 25:8; Zep 2:9 *v* Nu 22:4; 24:17; Dt 2:9; Jdg 3:28; Ru 1:4, 22; 1Sa 14:47; 22:3-4; 2Sa 8:2; 2Ki 1:1; 3:4; Ezr 9:1; Ps 108:9; Jer 48:1
19:38 *w* Nu 21:24; Dt 2:19; 23:3; Jos 12:2; Jdg 3:13; 10:6,7; 1Sa 11:1-11; 14:47; 1Ch 19:1; 2Ch 20:23; 26:8; 27:5; Ne 2:19; 4:3; Jer 25:21; 40:14; 49:1; Eze 21:28; 25:2; Am 1:13
20:1 *x* Ge 18:1 *y* S Ge 12:9 *z* S Ge 14:7 *a* S Ge 16:7 *b* Ge 26:3 *c* S Ge 26:1, 6, 17
20:2 *d* ver 12; S Ge 12:13 *e* ver 14; Ge 21:22; 26:1 *f* S Ge 12:15
20:3 *g* Nu 22:9, 20 *h* Ge 28:12; 31:10, 24; 37:5, 9; 40:5; 41:1;

19:24 *rained down burning sulfur.* Perhaps from a violent earthquake spewing up asphalt, such as is still found in this region (cf. Isa 34:9 and note).

19:26 *Lot's wife looked back, and she became a pillar of salt.* Her disobedient hesitation (see v. 17) became proverbial in later generations (see Lk 17:32). Even today, grotesque salt formations near the southern end of the Dead Sea are reminders of her folly.

19:29 *God…remembered Abraham.* See note on 8:1. *he brought Lot out of the catastrophe.* Lot's deliverance was the main concern of Abraham's prayer (18:23–32), which God now answered.

19:33 *they got their father to drink wine, and the older daughter went in and slept with him.* Though Lot's role was mainly passive, he bore the basic responsibility for what happened here and reaped the harvest of his move toward Sodom (see 13:10–12 and notes).

19:36–38 The sons born to Lot's daughters were the ancestors of the Moabites and Ammonites (see Dt 2:9,19), two nations that were to become bitter enemies of Abraham's descendants (see, e.g., 1Sa 14:47; 2Ch 20:1).

20:1–18 See 12:10–20 and notes.

20:1 *Negev.* See note on 12:9. *between Kadesh and Shur.* See notes on 14:7; 16:7. *Gerar.* Located at the edge of Philistine territory, about halfway between Gaza near the Mediterranean coast and Beersheba in the northern Negev.

20:2 *Abimelek.* Probably the father or grandfather of the later king who bore the same name (see 26:1).

20:3 *dream.* Once again God intervened to spare the mother of the promised offspring. Dreams were a frequent mode of revelation in the OT (see 28:12; 31:10–11; 37:5–9; 40:5; 41:1; Nu 12:6; Jdg 7:13; 1Ki 3:5; Da 2:3; 4:5; 7:1).

20:4 kS Ge 18:25
20:5 lS Ge 12:19
mS Ge 17:1 nPs 7:8;
25:21; 26:6; 41:12
20:6 o1Sa 25:26,34
pS Ge 13:13; Ps 41:4;
51:4
20:7 qDt 18:18;
34:10; 2Ki 3:11; 5:3;
1Ch 16:22; Ps 105:15
rver 17; Ex 8:8;
Nu 11:2; 12:13;
1Sa 7:5; 1Ki 13:6;
Job 42:8; Jer 18:20;
37:3; 42:2 sS ver 3;
S Ps 9:5
20:9 tS Ge 12:18;
34:7
20:11 uGe 42:18;
Ne 5:15; Job 31:23;
Ps 36:1; Pr 16:6
vS Ge 12:12; 31:31
20:12 wS Ge 12:13
20:13 xDt 26:5;
1Ch 16:20; Isa 30:28;
63:17 yS Ge 12:1
20:14 zS ver 2
aGe 12:16
20:15 bGe 13:9;
S 45:18
20:17 cS ver 7;
Job 42:9
20:18 dGe 12:17
21:1 e1Sa 2:21
fS Ge 8:1; S 17:16,21;
18:14; Gal 4:23;
Heb 11:11
21:2 gS Ge 17:19;
S 30:6 hGal 4:22;
Heb 11:11 iS Ge 18:10
21:3 jS Ge 16:11;
S 17:19; Jos 24:3
21:4 kGe 17:10,12;
Ac 7:8
21:5 lS Ge 12:4;
Heb 6:15
21:6 mGe 17:17;
Job 8:21; Ps 126:2;
Isa 12:6; 35:2; 44:23;
52:9; 54:1
21:7 nS Ge 17:17
21:8 o1Sa 1:23
21:9 pS Ge 16:15
qGe 39:14; Gal 4:29
21:10 rGe 39:17
sGe 25:6; Gal 4:30*

nation? k 5Did he not say to me, 'She is my sister,l and didn't she also say, 'He is my brother'? I have done this with a clear conscience m and clean hands. n"

6Then God said to him in the dream, "Yes, I know you did this with a clear conscience, and so I have kept o you from sinning against me.p That is why I did not let you touch her. 7Now return the man's wife, for he is a prophet, q and he will pray for you r and you will live. But if you do not return her, you may be sure that you and all who belong to you will die." s

8Early the next morning Abimelek summoned all his officials, and when he told them all that had happened, they were very much afraid. 9Then Abimelek called Abraham in and said, "What have you done to us? How have I wronged you that you have brought such great guilt upon me and my kingdom? You have done things to me that should never be done. t" 10And Abimelek asked Abraham, "What was your reason for doing this?"

11Abraham replied, "I said to myself, 'There is surely no fear of God u in this place, and they will kill me because of my wife.' v 12Besides, she really is my sister, w the daughter of my father though not of my mother; and she became my wife. 13And when God had me wander x from my father's household, y I said to her, 'This is how you can show your love to me: Everywhere we go, say of me, "He is my brother." ' "

14Then Abimelek z brought sheep and cattle and male and female slaves and gave them to Abraham, a and he returned Sarah his wife to him. 15And Abimelek said, "My land is before you; live wherever you like." b

16To Sarah he said, "I am giving your brother a thousand shekels a of silver. This is to cover the offense against you before all who are with you; you are completely vindicated."

17Then Abraham prayed to God, c and God healed Abimelek, his wife and his female slaves so they could have children again, 18for the LORD had kept all the women in Abimelek's household from conceiving because of Abraham's wife Sarah. d

THE BIRTH OF ISAAC

21 Now the LORD was gracious to Sarah e as he had said, and the LORD did for Sarah what he had promised. f 2Sarah became pregnant and bore a son g to Abraham in his old age, h at the very time God had promised him. i 3Abraham gave the name Isaac b j to the son Sarah bore him. 4When his son Isaac was eight days old, Abraham circumcised him, k as God commanded him. 5Abraham was a hundred years old l when his son Isaac was born to him.

6Sarah said, "God has brought me laughter, m and everyone who hears about this will laugh with me." 7And she added, "Who would have said to Abraham that Sarah would nurse children? Yet I have borne him a son in his old age." n

HAGAR AND ISHMAEL SENT AWAY

8The child grew and was weaned, o and on the day Isaac was weaned Abraham held a great feast. 9But Sarah saw that the son whom Hagar the Egyptian had borne to Abraham p was mocking, q 10and she said to Abraham, "Get rid of that slave woman r and her son, for that slave woman's son will never share in the inheritance with my son Isaac." s

---

a 16 That is, about 25 pounds or about 11.5 kilograms   b 3 Isaac means he laughs.

20:7 prophet. See notes on 18:17; Zec 1:1. Abraham was the first man to bear this title (see Ps 105:15).

A B **20:9** brought such great guilt upon me and my kingdom. Or "caused me and my kingdom to commit such a great sin." The "great sin" is adultery (see vv. 2–3,6; the same meaning for this expression is attested also in Egyptian and Canaanite texts). Everywhere else the Hebrew expression occurs in the OT it refers to idolatry (Ex 32:21,30–31; 2Ki 17:21), which is spiritual adultery (see Hos 1:2 and note). Adultery and idolatry are supreme forms of covenant infidelity.

A **20:11** fear of God. A conventional phrase equivalent to "true religion." "Fear" in this phrase has the sense of reverential trust in God and commitment to his revealed will (word); see Ps 34:8–14 and note.

C **20:12** she really is my sister, the daughter of my father though not of my mother. Abraham's half-truth was a sinful deception, not a legitimate explanation.

C **20:14–16** Abimelek's generosity was a strong contrast to Abraham's fearfulness and deception.

20:16 shekels. Though not in the Hebrew, the word is correctly supplied here as the most common unit of weight in ancient

times. Originally the shekel was only a weight, not a coin, since coinage was not invented till the seventh century B.C.

21:1 See 17:16. did for Sarah what he had promised. See Gal 4:22–23,28. The promised son through whom God will continue the covenant line (17:21) is born at last.

21:3 Isaac. See note on 17:17.

21:4 See notes on 17:10,12.

C **21:5** In fulfillment of the promise made to him (see 17:16), Abraham miraculously became a father at the age of 100 years (see 17:17).

21:6 laughter…laugh. See note on 17:17.

21:8 weaned. At age two or three, as was customary in the ancient Near East.

C **21:9** the son whom Hagar the Egyptian had borne. Ishmael, who was in his late teens at this time (see 16:15–16). mocking. Or "at play." In either case, Sarah saw Ishmael as a potential threat to Isaac's inheritance (v. 10).

21:10 Get rid of that slave woman and her son. See Gal 4:21–31. Driving them out would have had the effect of disinheriting Ishmael.

¹¹The matter distressed Abraham greatly because it concerned his son. ᵗ ¹²But God said to him, "Do not be so distressed about the boy and your servant. Listen to whatever Sarah tells you, because it is through Isaac that your offspringᵃ will be reckoned. ᵘ ¹³I will make the son of the servant into a nationᵛ also, because he is your offspring."

¹⁴Early the next morning Abraham took some food and a skin of water and gave them to Hagar. ʷ He set them on her shoulders and then sent her off with the boy. She went on her way and wandered in the Desert of Beersheba.ˣ

¹⁵When the water in the skin was gone, she put the boy under one of the bushes. ¹⁶Then she went off and sat down about a bowshot away, for she thought, "I cannot watch the boy die." And as she sat there, sheᵇ began to sob.ʸ

¹⁷God heard the boy crying,ᶻ and the angel of Godᵃ called to Hagar from heavenᵇ and said to her, "What is the matter, Hagar? Do not be afraid; ᶜ God has heard the boy crying as he lies there.ᵈ" ¹⁸Lift the boy up and take him by the hand, for I will make him into a great nation.ᵈ"

¹⁹Then God opened her eyesᵉ and she saw a well of water.ᶠ So she went and filled the skin with water and gave the boy a drink.

²⁰God was with the boyᵍ as he grew up. He lived in the desert and became an archer. ²¹While he was living in the Desert of Paran,ʰ his mother got a wife for himⁱ from Egypt.

THE TREATY AT BEERSHEBA

²²At that time Abimelekʲ and Phicol the commander of his forcesᵏ said to Abraham, "God is with you in everything you do.ˡ ²³Now swearᵐ to me here before God that you will not deal falsely with me or my children or my descendants.ⁿ Show to me and the country where you now reside as a foreigner the same kindness I have shown to you."ᵒ

²⁴Abraham said, "I swear it."

²⁵Then Abraham complained to Abimelek about a well of water that Abimelek's servants had seized.ᵖ ²⁶But Abimelek said, "I don't know who has done this. You did not tell me, and I heard about it only today."

²⁷So Abraham brought sheep and cattle and gave them to Abimelek, and the two men made a treaty.�q ²⁸Abraham set apart seven ewe lambs from the flock, ²⁹and Abimelek asked Abraham, "What is the meaning of these seven ewe lambs you have set apart by themselves?"

³⁰He replied, "Accept these seven lambs from my hand as a witnessʳ that I dug this well.ˢ"

³¹So that place was called Beersheba,ᶜ ᵗ because the two men swore an oathᵘ there.

³²After the treatyᵛ had been made at Beersheba, ʷ Abimelek and Phicol the commander of his forcesˣ returned to the land of the Philistines.ʸ ³³Abraham planted a tamarisk

---

ᵃ 12 Or *seed*   ᵇ 16 Hebrew; Septuagint *the child*   ᶜ 31 *Beersheba* can mean *well of seven* and *well of the oath.*

21:11 ᵗGe 17:18
21:12 ᵘMt 1:2;
Ro 9:7*; Heb 11:18*
21:13 ᵛver 18;
S Ge 13:16
21:14 ʷS Ge 16:1
ˣver 31,32; Ge 22:19;
26:33; 28:10; 46:1,5;
Jos 15:28; 19:2;
Jdg 20:1; 1Sa 3:20;
1Ch 4:28; Ne 11:27
21:16 ʸJer 6:26;
Am 8:10; Zec 12:10
21:17 ᶻEx 3:7;
Nu 20:16; Dt 26:7;
6:8 ᵃS Ge 16:7
ᵇGe 22:11,15
ᶜS Ge 15:1
21:18 ᵈver 13;
S Ge 17:20
21:19 ᵉNu 22:31
ᶠS Ge 16:7
21:20 ᵍGe 26:3,24;
28:15; 39:2,21,23;
Lk 1:66
21:21 ʰS Ge 14:6
ⁱGe 24:4,38; 28:2;
34:4,8; Jdg 14:2
21:22 ʲS Ge 20:2
ᵏver 23; Ge 26:26
ˡver 23; Ge 26:28;
28:15; 31:3,5,42;
39:2,3; 1Sa 3:19;
16:18; 2Ch 1:1;
Ps 46:7; Isa 7:14; 8:8,
10; 41:10; 43:5
21:23 ᵐver 31;
Ge 25:33; 26:31;
31:53; Jos 2:12;
1Ki 2:8 ⁿ1Sa 24:21
ᵒS ver 22; Jos 2:12
21:25 ᵖGe 26:15,18,
20-22
21:27 qver 31,32;
Ge 26:28,31; 31:44,53
21:30 ʳGe 31:44;
47,48,50,52;
Jos 22:27,28,34;
24:27; Isa 19:20;
Mal 2:14 ˢver 25;
Ge 26:25,32
21:31 ᵗS ver 14
ᵘS ver 23, S 27
21:32 ᵛS ver 27
ʷS ver 14 ˣS ver 22
ʸS Ge 10:14

21:11 *The matter distressed Abraham.* Both love and legal custom played a part in Abraham's anguish. He knew that the customs of his day, illustrated later in the Nuzi tablets (see chart, p. xxiii), prohibited the arbitrary expulsion of a female servant's son (whose legal status was relatively weak in any case).

21:12 *Listen to whatever Sarah tells you.* God overruled in this matter (as he had done earlier; see 15:4), promising Abraham that both Isaac and Ishmael would have numerous descendants. *it is through Isaac that your offspring will be reckoned.* See 17:19; 22:18; see also Ro 9:6–8 and Heb 11:17–19 for broader spiritual applications of this statement.

21:14 *Early the next morning.* Though Abraham would now be separated from Ishmael for the first time, he responded to God's command with prompt obedience (see note on 12:4). *Beersheba.* See note on v. 31.

21:15 *one of the bushes.* See note on v. 33.

21:17 *God heard . . . God has heard.* A pun on the name "Ishmael" (see TNIV text note on 16:11; see also 17:20).

21:21 *Desert of Paran.* Located in north central Sinai. *his mother got a wife for him from Egypt.* Parents often arranged their children's marriages (see ch. 24).

21:22 *Abimelek.* See 20:2 and note. *Phicol.* Either a family name or an official title, since it reappears over 60 years later (25:26) in a similar context (26:26).

21:23 *swear to me . . . before God . . . Show to me . . . kindness.* Phrases commonly used when making covenants or treaties (see vv. 27,32). "Kindness" as used here refers to acts of friendship (cf. v. 27; 20:14; Ps 6:4 and note). Such covenants always involved oaths.

21:27 *sheep and cattle.* Probably to be used in the treaty ceremony (see 15:10).

21:30 *as a witness.* "Witnesses" to covenant/treaty-making (or other events of continuing significance) served as disinterested (third-party) testimonies to the event they "witnessed" (see 31:44,48,52; Dt 4:26; 30:19; 31:19,26; 32:1; Jos 22:27–28; 24:27; 1Sa 6:18) and could be appealed to (see Ps 50:1 and note; Isa 1:2; Mic 6:1–2).

21:31 *Beersheba, because the two men swore an oath there.* See TNIV text note. For a similar pun on the name, see 26:33. Beersheba, an important town in the northern Negev, marked the southernmost boundary of the Israelite monarchy in later times (see, e.g., 2Sa 17:11). An ancient well there is still pointed out as "Abraham's well" (see v. 25), but its authenticity is not certain. *because.* Or "when."

21:32 *Philistines.* See note on 10:14.

21:33 *tamarisk.* A shrub or small tree that thrives in arid re-

21:33 ᶻ1Sa 22:6;
31:13 ᵃS Ge 4:26
ᵇEx 15:18; Dt 32:40;
33:27; Job 36:26;
Ps 10:16; 45:6; 90:2;
93:2; 102:24; 103:19;
146:10; Isa 40:28;
Jer 10:10; Hab 1:12;
3:6; Heb 13:8
21:34 ᶜS Ge 10:14
22:1 ᵈEx 15:25;
16:4; 20:20; Dt 8:2,
16; 13:3; Jdg 2:22; 3:1;
2Ch 32:31; Ps 66:10;
Heb 11:17; Jas 1:12-13
ᵉver 11; Ge 31:11;
46:2; 1Sa 3:4,6,8;
Isa 6:8
22:2 ᶠver 12,16;
Jn 3:16; Heb 11:17;
1Jn 4:9 ᵍ2Ch 3:1
ʰS Ge 8:20 ⁱver 9
22:3 ʲJos 8:10
22:5 ᵏEx 24:14
22:6 ˡJn 19:17
ᵐver 10; Jdg 19:29
22:7 ⁿEx 29:38-42;
Lev 1:10; Rev 13:8
22:8 ᵒver 14
ᵖver 13; S Jn 1:29
22:9 �qver 2
ʳS Ge 4:26; S 8:20
ˢLev 1:7; 1Ki 18:33
ᵗHeb 11:17-19;
Jas 2:21

tree ᶻ in Beersheba, and there he called on the name of the Lord, ᵃ the Eternal God. ᵇ ³⁴And Abraham stayed in the land of the Philistines ᶜ for a long time.

ABRAHAM TESTED

22 Some time later God tested ᵈ Abraham. He said to him, "Abraham!" "Here I am," ᵉ he replied. ²Then God said, "Take your son ᶠ, your only son, whom you love—Isaac—and go to the region of Moriah. ᵍ Sacrifice him there as a burnt offering ʰ on a mountain I will show you. ⁱ"

³Early the next morning ʲ Abraham got up and loaded his donkey. He took with him two of his servants and his son Isaac. When he had cut enough wood for the burnt offering, he set out for the place God had told him about. ⁴On the third day Abraham looked up and saw the place in the distance. ⁵He said to his servants, "Stay here with the donkey while I and the boy go over there. We will worship and then we will come back to you. ᵏ"

⁶Abraham took the wood for the burnt offering and placed it on his son Isaac, ˡ and he himself carried the fire and the knife. ᵐ As the two of them went on together, ⁷Isaac spoke up and said to his father Abraham, "Father?"

"Yes, my son?" Abraham replied.

"The fire and wood are here," Isaac said, "but where is the lamb ⁿ for the burnt offering?"

⁸Abraham answered, "God himself will provide ᵒ the lamb ᵖ for the burnt offering, my son." And the two of them went on together.

⁹When they reached the place God had told him about, q Abraham built an altar ʳ there and arranged the wood ˢ on it. He bound his son Isaac and laid him on the altar, ᵗ on top

---

gions. Its leafy branches provide welcome shade, and it is probably the unidentified bush under which Hagar put Ishmael in v. 15. *Eternal God.* Hebrew *El Olam*, a phrase unique to this passage. It is one of a series of names that include *El*, "God," as an element (see 14:19; 17:1 and notes; 33:20; 35:7).

🅰 🅲 22:1–19 The climax to the account of God's dealings with Abraham. Here we are told of God's supreme test of Abraham's faith and of his final confirmation of his covenanted promises—once again confirmed by an oath (vv. 15–18). After this, there follows only the account of how Abraham put his affairs in order with a view to the future: providing a place of burial for Sarah and himself in the promised land (ch. 23), obtaining a suitable wife for Isaac (ch. 24), and seeing to the distribution of his inheritance among his offspring (25:1–6).

This climax in many ways echoes the beginning (12:1–7) and with it frames the main body of the Abraham story. Note the striking parallels: (1) "Go from your country, your people and your father's household" (12:1); "Take your son, your only son, whom you love—Isaac ... Sacrifice him ..." (v. 2); (2) "Go ... to the land I will show you" (12:1); "go to the region of Moriah ... (to) a mountain I will show you" (v. 2); (3) having completed his "going" to the appointed land, Abram built an altar by "the great tree of Moreh" to God, who had appeared to him (12:6–7); having completed his "offering" of Isaac, Abraham sacrificed on the altar he had built in "the region of Moriah" to God who had appeared to him (v. 13); (4) before Abram left his father's household God made promises to him (12:2–3); after Abraham showed his readiness to sacrifice his son Isaac, God confirmed those promises with an oath (vv. 15-18).

🅰 22:1 *Some time later.* Isaac had grown into adolescence or young manhood, as implied also by 21:34 ("a long time"). *tested.* Not "tempted," for God does not tempt (Jas 1:13). Satan tempts us (see 1Co 7:5) in order to make us fall; God tests us in order to confirm our faith (Ex 20:20) or prove our commitment (Dt 8:2). See note on Mt 4:1. *Here I am.* Abraham answered with the response of a servant, as did Moses and Samuel when God called them by name (see Ex 3:4; 1Sa 3:4,6,8).

🅰 🅲 22:2 *your son, your only son, whom you love—Isaac.* "Isaac" follows the clause "whom you love," in order

to heighten the effect. Isaac was the "only son" of the promise (21:12; cf. Gal 4:23), and Ishmael had been sent away (21:8–21). *region of Moriah.* The author of Chronicles identifies the area as the temple mount in Jerusalem (2Ch 3:1). Today "Mount Moriah" is occupied by the Dome of the Rock, an impressive Muslim structure erected in A.D. 691. A large outcropping of rock inside the building is still pointed to as the traditional site of the intended sacrifice of Isaac. *Sacrifice him.* Abraham had committed himself by covenant to be obedient to the Lord and had consecrated his son Isaac to the Lord by circumcision. The Lord put his servant's faith and loyalty to the supreme test, thereby instructing Abraham, Isaac and their descendants as to the kind of total consecration the Lord's covenant requires. The test also foreshadowed the perfect consecration in sacrifice that another offspring of Abraham would undergo (see note on v. 16) in order to wholly consecrate Abraham and his spiritual descendants to God and to fulfill the covenant promises.

🅰 🅲 22:3 *Early the next morning.* Prompt obedience, even under such trying circumstances, characterized Abraham's response to God (see note on 12:4).

22:4 *third day.* Parts of three days were likely required for the journey from Beersheba (see v. 19) to "the region of Moriah" (Jerusalem; see v. 2 and note), a distance of about 48 miles. On the other hand, a "journey of three days" may have been a conventional expression for a short trip rather than a journey of exactly three days (see 30:36; Ex 3:18; 5:3; 8:27; 15:22; Nu 10:33; 33:8; Jos 9:16; Jnh 1:17; 3:3).

🅰 🅲 22:5 *boy.* See v. 12; see also note on v. 1. The Hebrew for this word has a wide range of meaning, from an infant (see Ex 2:6) to a young man of military age (see 1Ch 12:28). *we will come back to you.* Abraham, the man of faith and "the father of all who believe" (Ro 4:11), "reasoned that God could even raise the dead" (Heb 11:19) if that were necessary to fulfill his promise.

🅰 22:8 *God himself will provide the lamb.* The immediate fulfillment of Abraham's trusting response was the ram of v. 13, but its ultimate fulfillment is the Lamb of God (Jn 1:29,36).

🅰 🅲 22:9 *laid him on the altar, on top of the wood.* Isaac is here a type (prefiguration) of Christ (see note on v. 16).

of the wood. [10]Then he reached out his hand and took the knife [u] to slay his son. [v] [11]But the angel of the Lord [w] called out to him from heaven, [x] "Abraham! Abraham!" [y]

"Here I am," [z] he replied.

[12]"Do not lay a hand on the boy," he said. "Do not do anything to him. Now I know that you fear God, [a] because you have not withheld from me your son, your only son. [b]"

[13]Abraham looked up and there in a thicket he saw a ram [a] caught by its horns. [c] He went over and took the ram and sacrificed it as a burnt offering instead of his son. [d] [14]So Abraham called [e] that place The Lord [f] Will Provide. And to this day it is said, "On the mountain of the Lord it will be provided. [g]"

[15]The angel of the Lord [h] called to Abraham from heaven [i] a second time [16]and said, "I swear by myself, [j] declares the Lord, that because you have done this and have not withheld your son, your only son, [k] [17]I will surely bless you [l] and make your descendants [m] as numerous as the stars in the sky [n] and as the sand on the seashore. [o] Your descendants will take possession of the cities of their enemies, [p] [18]and through your offspring [b] all nations on earth will be blessed, [c] [q] because you have obeyed me." [r]

[19]Then Abraham returned to his servants, and they set off together for Beersheba. [s] And Abraham stayed in Beersheba.

NAHOR'S SONS

[20]Some time later Abraham was told, "Milkah is also a mother; she has borne sons to your brother Nahor: [t] [21]Uz [u] the firstborn, Buz [v] his brother, Kemuel (the father of Aram), [22]Kesed, Hazo, Pildash, Jidlaph and Bethuel. [w]" [23]Bethuel became the father of Rebekah. [x] Milkah bore these eight sons to Abraham's brother Nahor. [y] [24]His concubine, [z] whose name was Reumah, also had sons: Tebah, Gaham, Tahash and Maakah.

THE DEATH OF SARAH

23
Sarah lived to be a hundred and twenty-seven years old. [2]She died at Kiriath Arba [a] (that is, Hebron) [b] in the land of Canaan, and Abraham went to mourn for Sarah and to weep over her. [c]

[3]Then Abraham rose from beside his dead wife and spoke to the Hittites. [d] [d] He said, [4]"I am a foreigner and stranger [e] among you. Sell me some property for a burial site here so I can bury my dead. [f]"

---

[a] 13 Many manuscripts of the Masoretic Text, Samaritan Pentateuch, Septuagint and Syriac; most manuscripts of the Masoretic Text *a ram behind, him,*   [b] 18 Or *seed*   [c] 18 Or *and all nations on earth will use the name of your offspring in blessings* (see Gen. 48:20)   [d] 3 Or *the descendants of Heth;* also in verses 5, 7, 10, 16, 18 and 20

23:4 Lev 25:23; Ps 39:12; 105:12; 119:19; Heb 11:9,13 [f] Ge 49:30; Ac 7:16

22:10 [u] S ver 6
[v] ver 3; S Ge 18:19
22:11 [w] S Ge 16:7
[x] S Ge 21:17 [y] Ge 46:2
[z] S ver 1
22:12 [a] S Ge 18:19;
42:18; Ex 18:21;
1Sa 15:22; Job 1:1;
37:24; Pr 8:13;
Jas 2:21-22; S ver 2;
Jn 3:16; 1Jn 4:9
22:13 [c] S ver 8
[d] S Ge 8:20; Ro 8:32
22:14 [e] Ex 17:15;
Jdg 6:24 [f] Isa 30:29
[g] ver 8
22:15 [h] S Ge 16:7
[i] S Ge 21:17
22:16 [j] Ex 13:11;
32:13; 33:1; Isa 45:23;
62:8; Jer 22:5; 44:26;
49:13; 51:14; Am 6:8;
Lk 1:73; Heb 6:13
[k] S ver 2
22:17 [l] S Ge 12:2
[m] Heb 6:14*
[n] S Ge 15:5; Ex 32:13;
Dt 7:7; 28:62
[o] S Ge 12:2; S 26:24;
Hos 1:10; Ro 9:27;
Heb 11:12 [p] Ge 24:60;
Est 9:2
22:18 [x] Ge 12:3;
Ac 3:25*; Gal 3:8*
[r] S ver 10; Ge 17:2,9;
Ps 105:9
22:19 [s] Ge 21:14;
26:23; 28:10
22:20 [t] S Ge 11:29
22:21 [u] S Ge 10:23
[v] Job 32:2; Jer 25:23
22:22 [w] Ge 24:15,
47; 25:20
22:23 [x] Ge 24:15
[y] S Ge 11:29
22:24 [z] Ge 25:6;
35:22; 36:12; Jdg 8:31;
2Sa 3:7; 1Ki 2:22;
11:3; 1Ch 1:32; SS 6:8
23:2 [a] Jos 14:15;
15:13; 20:7; 21:11
[b] ver 19; S Ge 13:18
[c] Ge 24:67
23:3 [d] S Ge 10:15
23:4 [e] S Ge 17:8;
19:9; Ex 2:22;

22:11 *angel of the Lord.* See note on 16:7. The "angel of the Lord" who had seen to the safety of Abraham's son Ishmael and had spoken of Ishmael's future (16:7–12; 21:17–18) now intervenes to save Abraham's son Isaac and afterward speaks of Isaac's future (vv. 17–18). *Abraham! Abraham!* The repetition of the name indicates urgency (see 46:2; Ex 3:4; 1Sa 3:10; Ac 9:4). *Here I am.* See note on v. 1.

22:12 *fear God.* See note on 20:11. *you have not withheld from me your son, your only son.* See v. 16. Abraham's "faith was made complete by what he did" (Jas 2:21–22).

22:13 *instead of.* Substitutionary sacrifice of one life for another is here mentioned for the first time. As the ram died in Isaac's place, so also Jesus gave his life as a ransom "for" (lit. "instead of") many (Mk 10:45).

22:14 *The Lord Will Provide.* Thus Abraham memorializes the remarkable way in which God fulfilled his expectation (v. 8). The Hebrew for "will provide" is lit. "will see (to it)"; God's "seeing to it" spared Isaac, just as God's "seeing" had spared Ishmael (in Hagar's womb; see 16:13–14 and notes; cf. 21:15–21). *mountain of the Lord.* During the Israelite monarchy the mountain referred to the temple mount in Jerusalem (see Ps 24:3; Isa 2:3; 30:29; Zec 8:3).

22:16 *I swear by myself.* There is no greater name in which the Lord can take an oath (see Heb 6:13). *you . . . have not withheld your son, your only son.* Abraham's devotion is paralleled by God's love to us in Christ as reflected in Jn 3:16 and Ro 8:32, which may allude to this verse.

22:17 *descendants as numerous as the stars in the sky.* See 13:16; 15:5 and notes. *sand on the seashore.* Fulfilled, at least in part, during Solomon's reign (see 1Ki 4:20). *cities.* Lit. "gates." Taking possession of the gate of a city was tantamount to occupying the city itself (see 24:60).

22:18 *all nations on earth will be blessed.* See note on 12:2–3. *because you have obeyed me.* See note on 17:9.

22:23–24 Abraham's brother Nahor became the father of eight sons by his wife and four by his concubine (see note on 25:6). They would later become the ancestors of 12 Aramean (see v. 21) tribes, just as Abraham's son Ishmael would become the ancestor of 12 tribes (25:16) and Abraham's grandson Jacob would become the ancestor of the 12 tribes of Israel (49:28).

23:1–20 How Abraham provided a burial place for Sarah and himself in Canaan, thus in faith laying claim to Canaan as his homeland in accordance with God's promise.

23:2 *Kiriath Arba.* Means "the town of Arba" (Arba was the most prominent member of a tribe living in the Hebron area [see Jos 14:15]). It can also mean "the town of four," referring to the place where Anak (see Jos 15:13–14; 21:11) and his three sons lived (see Jdg 1:10,20). *went.* Either from Beersheba to Hebron or into the place where Sarah's body was lying.

23:3 *Hittites.* See note on 10:15. They were apparently in control of the Hebron area at this time.

23:4 *a foreigner and stranger.* The phrase was used often by the patriarchs and their descendants in reference to themselves (see 1Ch 29:15; Ps 39:12; see also Heb 11:13). On this

23:6 *g* Ge 14:14-16;
24:35
23:8 *h* Ge 25:9
23:9 *i* ver 17,19;
Ge 25:9; 47:30;
49:30; 50:13
23:10 *j* ver 18
k S Ge 18:1; Dt 22:15;
25:7; Jos 20:4;
Ru 4:11; 2Sa 15:2;
2Ki 15:35; Ps 127:5;
Pr 31:23; Jer 26:10;
36:10
23:11 *l* 2Sa 24:23
23:15 *m* Eze 45:12
23:16 *n* 2Sa 24:24;
Jer 32:9; Zec 11:12
o 2Sa 14:26
23:17 *p* S ver 9
q S Ge 13:18
23:18 *r* S Ge 12:7
s ver 10 *t* S Ge 18:1
23:19 *u* S ver 9
v S Ge 13:18;
Jos 14:13; 1Ch 29:27
w Ge 49:31
23:20 *x* Jer 32:10
y S Ge 10:15; 35:29;
47:30; 49:30; 50:5,13
24:1 *z* S Ge 17:17;
Jos 23:1 *a* Ge 12:2;
Gal 3:9 *b* ver 35
24:2 *c* S Ge 15:3
d Ge 39:4-6 *e* ver 9;
Ge 47:29
24:3 *f* Ge 47:31;
50:25 *g* ver 7
h S Ge 14:19;
S Nu 20:14 *i* Dt 7:3;
2Co 6:14-17
j S Ge 10:15-19
k ver 37
24:4 *l* S Ge 12:1;
Jdg 14:3 *m* S ver 29;
S Ge 21:21
24:5 *n* ver 39
o Heb 11:15

⁵The Hittites replied to Abraham, ⁶"Sir, listen to us. You are a mighty prince *g* among us. Bury your dead in the choicest of our tombs. None of us will refuse you his tomb for burying your dead."

⁷Then Abraham rose and bowed down before the people of the land, the Hittites. ⁸He said to them, "If you are willing to let me bury my dead, then listen to me and intercede with Ephron son of Zohar *h* on my behalf ⁹so he will sell me the cave of Machpelah, *i* which belongs to him and is at the end of his field. Ask him to sell it to me for the full price as a burial site among you."

¹⁰Ephron the Hittite was sitting among his people and he replied to Abraham in the hearing of all the Hittites *j* who had come to the gate *k* of his city. ¹¹"No, my lord," he said. "Listen to me; I give *l* you the field, and I give *a* you the cave that is in it. I give *a* it to you in the presence of my people. Bury your dead."

¹²Again Abraham bowed down before the people of the land ¹³and he said to Ephron in their hearing, "Listen to me, if you will. I will pay the price of the field. Accept it from me so I can bury my dead there."

¹⁴Ephron answered Abraham, ¹⁵"Listen to me, my lord; the land is worth four hundred shekels *b* of silver, *m* but what is that between me and you? Bury your dead."

¹⁶Abraham agreed to Ephron's terms and weighed out for him the price he had named in the hearing of the Hittites: four hundred shekels of silver, *n* according to the weight current among the merchants. *o*

¹⁷So Ephron's field in Machpelah *p* near Mamre *q*—both the field and the cave in it, and all the trees within the borders of the field—was deeded ¹⁸to Abraham as his property *r* in the presence of all the Hittites *s* who had come to the gate *t* of the city. ¹⁹Afterward Abraham buried his wife Sarah in the cave in the field of Machpelah *u* near Mamre (which is at Hebron *v*) in the land of Canaan. *w* ²⁰So the field and the cave in it were deeded *x* to Abraham by the Hittites as a burial site. *y*

ISAAC AND REBEKAH

24 Abraham was now very old, *z* and the Lord had blessed *a* him in every way. *b* ²He said to the senior servant *c* in his household, the one in charge of all that he had, *d* "Put your hand under my thigh. *e* ³I want you to swear *f* by the Lord, the God of heaven *g* and the God of earth, *h* that you will not get a wife for my son *i* from the daughters of the Canaanites, *j* among whom I am living, *k* ⁴but will go to my country and my own relatives *l* and get a wife for my son Isaac. *m*"

⁵The servant asked him, "What if the woman is unwilling to come back with me to this land? *n* Shall I then take your son back to the country you came from? *o*"

---

a 11 Or *sell*   *b 15* That is, about 10 pounds or about 4.6 kilograms

---

earth Abraham "lived in tents" (Heb 11:9), the most temporary of dwellings. But he looked forward to the more permanent home promised him, which the author of Hebrews calls "the city with foundations, whose architect and builder is God" (Heb 11:10).
23:6 *You are a mighty prince.* Probably intended as flattery.

B **23:9** *cave of Machpelah.* The tombs of several patriarchs and their wives—Abraham and Sarah, Isaac and Rebekah, Jacob and Leah (see v. 19; 25:8–10; 50:12–13)—are, according to tradition, located in a large cave deep beneath the Mosque of Abraham, a Muslim shrine in Hebron. *end of his field.* Apparently Abraham wanted to buy only a small part of the field (namely, the part where the cave was located), but Ephron insisted that he purchase the entire field (see note on v. 15).

23:10 *in the hearing of all the Hittites who had come to the gate.* The main gateway of a city was usually the place where legal matters were transacted and attested (see v. 18; see also note on 19:1).

23:11 *my lord.* Perhaps intended to flatter Abraham (see v. 15). *give.* See TNIV text note.

23:15 *four hundred shekels of silver, but what is that between me and you?* See note on 20:16. Despite Ephron's pretense of generosity, 400 shekels of silver was an exorbitant price for a field (see, e.g., Jer 32:9). Ephron was taking advantage of Abraham during a time of grief and bereavement. He knew that Abraham had to deal quickly in order to have a place to bury Sarah, so he insisted that Abraham buy the entire lot.

23:16 *weight current among the merchants.* Subject to more

variation and therefore greater dishonesty than the later royal standard (see 2Sa 14:26), which was carefully regulated and more precise.

23:17 *the field and the cave in it, and all the trees.* Ephron had held out for the sale of the entire field and its contents (see notes on vv. 9,15).

C **23:19** *buried his wife … in the land of Canaan.* In that culture, people had a strong desire to be buried "with their ancestors" (see note on 25:8) in their native land. By purchasing a burial place in Canaan, Abraham indicated his unswerving commitment to the Lord's promise. Canaan was his new homeland.

C **24:1–67** Abraham obtains a suitable wife for Isaac, relying on God who has made a covenant with him to provide an appropriate mother for his descendants who would inherit the land (see vv. 6–7).

24:2 *senior servant in his household.* Probably Eliezer of Damascus (see note on 15:2). *Put your hand under my thigh.* Near the organ of procreation, probably because this oath was related to Abraham's last will and testament and called for faithful implementation on the part of his son. Isaac must accept Abraham's and God's choice (see also 47:29 and note).

24:3 *the Lord, the God of heaven and the God of earth.* See v. 7; see also note on 1:1. For a similar majestic title used by Abraham in an oath, see 14:22.

24:4 *my country.* Mesopotamia (see note on v. 10). *get a wife for my son.* See note on 21:21.

⁶"Make sure that you do not take my son back there,"ᵖ Abraham said. ⁷"The LORD, the God of heaven,�q who brought me out of my father's household and my native landʳ and who spoke to me and promised me on oath, saying, 'To your offspringᵃˢ I will give this land'ᵗ—he will send his angel before youᵘ so that you can get a wife for my son from there. ⁸If the woman is unwilling to come back with you, then you will be released from this oathᵛ of mine. Only do not take my son back there."ʷ ⁹So the servant put his hand under the thighˣ of his masterʸ Abraham and swore an oath to him concerning this matter.

¹⁰Then the servant left, taking with him ten of his master's camelsᶻ loaded with all kinds of good thingsᵃ from his master. He set out for Aram Naharaimᵇᵇ and made his way to the town of Nahor.ᶜ ¹¹He had the camels kneel down near the welldᵈ outside the town; it was toward evening, the time the women go out to draw water.ᵉ

¹²Then he prayed, "LORD, God of my master Abraham,ᶠ make me successfulᵍ today, and show kindnessʰ to my master Abraham. ¹³See, I am standing beside this spring, and the daughters of the townspeople are coming out to draw water.ⁱ ¹⁴May it be that when I say to a girl, 'Please let down your jar that I may have a drink,' and she says, 'Drink,ʲ and I'll water your camels too'ᵏ—let her be the one you have chosen for your servant Isaac.ˡ By this I will knowᵐ that you have shown kindness to my master."

¹⁵Before he had finished praying,ⁿ Rebekahᵒ came out with her jar on her shoulder. She was the daughter of Bethuelᵖ son of Milkah,q who was the wife of Abraham's brother Nahor.ʳ ¹⁶The girl was very beautiful,ˢ a virgin;ᵗ no man had ever slept with her. She went down to the spring, filled her jar and came up again.

¹⁷The servant hurried to meet her and said, "Please give me a little water from your jar."ᵘ ¹⁸"Drink,ᵛ my lord," she said, and quickly lowered the jar to her hands and gave him a drink.

¹⁹After she had given him a drink, she said, "I'll draw water for your camelsʷ too,ˣ until they have had enough to drink." ²⁰So she quickly emptied her jar into the trough, ran back to the well to draw more water, and drew enough for all his camels.ʸ ²¹Without saying a word, the man watched her closely to learn whether or not the LORD had made his journey successful.ᶻ

²²When the camels had finished drinking, the man took out a gold nose ringᵃ weighing a bekaᶜ and two gold braceletsᵇ weighing ten shekels.ᵈ ²³Then he asked, "Whose daughter are you?ᶜ Please tell me, is there room in your father's house for us to spend the night?ᵈ"

²⁴She answered him, "I am the daughter of Bethuel, the son that Milkah bore to Nahor.ᵉ" ²⁵And she added, "We have plenty of straw and fodder,ᶠ as well as room for you to spend the night."

²⁶Then the man bowed down and worshiped the LORD,ᵍ ²⁷saying, "Praise be to the LORD,ʰ the God of my master Abraham,ⁱ who has not abandoned his kindness and faithfulnessʲ to my master. As for me, the LORD has led me on the journeyᵏ to the house of my master's relatives."ˡ

²⁸The girl ran and told her mother's household about these things.ᵐ ²⁹Now Rebekah had a brother named Laban,ⁿ and he hurried out to the man at the spring. ³⁰As soon as he had seen the nose ring, and the bracelets on his sister's arms,ᵒ and had heard Rebekah tell what the man said to her, he went out to the man and found him standing by the camels near the spring. ³¹"Come, you who are blessed by the LORD,"ᵖ he said. "Why are you standing out here? I have prepared the house and a place for the camels."

³²So the man went to the house, and the camels were unloaded. Straw and fodderq

---

ᵃ 7 Or *seed*   ᵇ 10 That is, Northwest Mesopotamia   ᶜ 22 That is, about 1/5 ounce or about 5.7 grams
ᵈ 22 That is, about 4 ounces or about 115 grams

24:28 ᵐ Ge 29:12   **24:29** ⁿ ver 4; Ge 25:20; 27:43; 28:2,5; 29:5,12,13   **24:30** ᵒ S ver 10; Eze 23:42   **24:31** ᵖ Ge 26:29; Ps 115:15
24:32 q S ver 25

24:6 ᵖ ver 8
24:7 q ver 3 ʳ Ge 12:1
ˢ Ro 4:13; Gal 3:16*
ᵗ S Ge 12:7
ᵘ S Ge 16:7
24:8 ᵛ ver 41;
Jos 2:12,17,20; 9:20
ʷ S ver 6
24:9 ˣ S ver 2
ʸ Ge 32:4; 33:8
24:10 ᶻ ver 19;
1Ki 10:2; 1Ch 12:40;
Isa 30:6 ᵃ ver 22,30,
47,53; Ge 43:11;
45:23 ᵇ Nu 23:7;
Dt 23:4; Jdg 3:8
ᶜ S Ge 11:29
24:11 ᵈ Ex 2:15
ᵉ ver 13; Ge 29:2,9-
10; Ex 2:16; 1Sa 9:11;
Jn 4:7
24:12 ᶠ ver 27,42,
48; Ge 26:24; 28:13;
31:42,53; 32:9; 43:23;
46:3; Ex 3:6,15,16;
4:5; 1Ki 18:36;
Ps 75:9; 94:7 ᵍ ver 21,
40,51,56; Ge 27:20;
Ne 1:11 ʰ S Ge 19:19;
Jos 2:12; Job 10:12
24:13 ⁱ S ver 11,43;
Ge 29:8
24:14 ʲ ver 18,46
ᵏ ver 19 ˡ ver 44
ᵐ Jos 2:12; Jdg 6:17,
37; 1Sa 14:10;
1Ki 13:3; Ps 86:17;
Isa 38:7; Jer 44:29
24:15 ⁿ ver 45
ᵒ S Ge 22:23
ᵖ S Ge 22:22
q S Ge 11:29
ʳ S Ge 11:29
24:16 ˢ S Ge 12:11
ᵗ Dt 22:15-21
24:17 ᵘ ver 45;
1Ki 17:10; Jn 4:7
24:18 ᵛ S ver 14
24:19 ʷ S ver 10
ˣ ver 14
24:20 ʸ ver 46
24:21 ᶻ S ver 12
24:22 ᵃ ver 47;
Ge 41:42; Isa 3:21;
Eze 16:11-12
ᵇ S ver 10
24:23 ᶜ ver 47
ᵈ Jdg 19:15; 20:4
24:24 ᵉ ver 29,47;
S Ge 11:29
24:25 ᶠ ver 32;
Jdg 19:19
24:26 ᵍ ver 48,52;
Ex 4:31; 12:27;
1Ch 29:20; 2Ch 20:18
24:27 ʰ Ge 14:20;
Ex 18:10; Ru 4:14;
1Sa 25:32; 2Sa 18:28;
1Ki 1:48; 8:56;
Ps 28:6; 41:13; 68:19;
106:48; Lk 1:68
ⁱ S ver 12 ʲ ver 49;
Ge 32:10; 47:29;
Jos 2:14; Ps 98:3
ᵏ ver 21 ˡ S ver 12,48;
S Ge 12:1

24:7 *To your offspring I will give this land.* Repeats the promise of 12:7. *his angel.* See note on 16:7.

B **24:10** *camels.* See note on 12:16. *Aram Naharaim.* See TNIV text note; the name means "Aram of the two rivers"—the Euphrates and the Tigris. Aram (see note on 10:22) Naharaim was the northern part of the area called later by the Greeks "Mesopotamia," meaning "between the rivers." *town of Nahor.* Nahor is the same name as that of Abraham's brother (see v. 15; 11:26). The town is mentioned in clay tablets excavated by the French beginning in 1933 at the ancient city of Mari on the Euphrates (see chart, p. xxiv). Nahor was located in the Harran (see note on 11:31) district and was ruled by an Amorite prince in the 18th century B.C.

24:11 *toward evening, the time the women go out to draw water.* After the midday heat had cooled.

24:14 *By this I will know.* Like his master Abraham, the servant asked God for a sign to validate his errand (see note on 15:8). *kindness.* See v. 27; probably a reference to God's covenant with Abraham, which had promised numerous descendants through Isaac (see 17:19; 21:12).

C **24:15** *Before he had finished praying.* God had already begun to answer. *Rebekah ... was the daughter of Bethuel son of ... the wife of Abraham's brother.* Isaac would thus be marrying his father's grandniece (see v. 48).

24:22 *beka.* Half a shekel (see Ex 38:26); see note on 20:16.

24:32 *r* S Ge 18:4
24:34 *s* S Ge 15:3
24:35 *t* S Ge 12:2
u ver 1 *v* S Ge 23:6
w S Ge 12:16
24:36 *x* S Ge 17:17
y Ge 25:5; 26:14
24:37 *z* Ge 50:5,25
a ver 3
24:38 *b* S Ge 21:21
24:39 *c* S ver 5
24:40 *d* S Ge 5:22
e S Ge 16:7 *f* S ver 12
g S Ge 12:1
24:41 *h* S ver 8
24:42 *i* S ver 12
24:43 *j* S ver 13
k Pr 30:19; Isa 7:14
l S ver 14
24:44 *m* ver 14
24:45 *n* 1Sa 1:13
o ver 15 *p* S ver 17;
Jn 4:7
24:46 *q* ver 18-19
r ver 20
24:47 *s* ver 23
t S Ge 22:22
u S ver 24 *v* S ver 22
w S ver 10; Isa 3:19;
Eze 16:11-12
24:48 *x* S ver 26
y S ver 12 *z* S ver 27
24:49 *a* S ver 27
24:50 *b* Ge 22:22
c Ps 118:23 *d* Ge 31:7,
24,29,42; 48:16
24:51 *e* S ver 12
24:52 *f* S ver 26
24:53 *g* Ge 45:22;
Ex 3:22; 12:35;
2Ki 5:5 *h* S ver 10,22
24:54 *i* ver 56,59;
Ge 30:25
24:55 *j* Jdg 19:4
24:56 *k* S ver 12
l S ver 54
24:57 *m* Jdg 19:3
24:58 *n* Ru 1:16
24:59 *o* S ver 54
p Ge 35:8
24:60 *q* Ge 27:4,19;
28:1; 31:55; 48:9,15,
20; Jos 22:6
r S Ge 17:16
s Ge 22:17; Ps 127:5;
Pr 27:11

were brought for the camels, and water for him and his men to wash their feet. *r* 33 Then food was set before him, but he said, "I will not eat until I have told you what I have to say."

"Then tell us," Laban said.

34 So he said, "I am Abraham's servant. *s* 35 The LORD has blessed *t* my master abundantly, *u* and he has become wealthy. *v* He has given him sheep and cattle, silver and gold, male and female servants, and camels and donkeys. *w* 36 My master's wife Sarah has borne him a son in her old age, *x* and he has given him everything he owns. *y* 37 And my master made me swear an oath, *z* and said, 'You must not get a wife for my son from the daughters of the Canaanites, in whose land I live, *a* 38 but go to my father's family and to my own clan, and get a wife for my son.' *b*

39 "Then I asked my master, 'What if the woman will not come back with me?' *c*

40 "He replied, 'The LORD, before whom I have walked faithfully, *d* will send his angel with you *e* and make your journey a success, *f* so that you can get a wife for my son from my own clan and from my father's family. *g* 41 Then, when you go to my clan, you will be released from my oath even if they refuse to give her to you—you will be released from my oath.' *h*

42 "When I came to the spring today, I said, 'LORD, God of my master Abraham, if you will, please grant success *i* to the journey on which I have come. 43 See, I am standing beside this spring. *j* If a young woman *k* comes out to draw water and I say to her, "Please let me drink a little water from your jar," *l* 44 and if she says to me, "Drink, and I'll draw water for your camels too," let her be the one the LORD has chosen for my master's son.' *m*

45 "Before I finished praying in my heart, *n* Rebekah came out, with her jar on her shoulder. *o* She went down to the spring and drew water, and I said to her, 'Please give me a drink.' *p*

46 "She quickly lowered her jar from her shoulder and said, 'Drink, and I'll water your camels too.' *q* So I drank, and she watered the camels also. *r*

47 "I asked her, 'Whose daughter are you?' *s*

"She said, 'The daughter of Bethuel *t* son of Nahor, whom Milkah bore to him.' *u*

"Then I put the ring in her nose *v* and the bracelets on her arms, *w* 48 and I bowed down and worshiped the LORD. *x* I praised the LORD, the God of my master Abraham, *y* who had led me on the right road to get the granddaughter of my master's brother for his son. *z* 49 Now if you will show kindness and faithfulness *a* to my master, tell me; and if not, tell me, so I may know which way to turn."

50 Laban and Bethuel *b* answered, "This is from the LORD; *c* we can say nothing to you one way or the other. *d* 51 Here is Rebekah; take her and go, and let her become the wife of your master's son, as the LORD has directed. *e*"

52 When Abraham's servant heard what they said, he bowed down to the ground before the LORD. *f* 53 Then the servant brought out gold and silver jewelry and articles of clothing *g* and gave them to Rebekah; he also gave costly gifts *h* to her brother and to her mother. 54 Then he and the men who were with him ate and drank and spent the night there.

When they got up the next morning, he said, "Send me on my way *i* to my master."

55 But her brother and her mother replied, "Let the girl remain with us ten days or so; *j* then you *a* may go."

56 But he said to them, "Do not detain me, now that the LORD has granted success *k* to my journey. Send me on my way *l* so I may go to my master."

57 Then they said, "Let's call the girl and ask her about it." *m* 58 So they called Rebekah and asked her, "Will you go with this man?"

"I will go," *n* she said.

59 So they sent their sister Rebekah on her way, *o* along with her nurse *p* and Abraham's servant and his men. 60 And they blessed *q* Rebekah and said to her,

> "Our sister, may you increase
>   to thousands upon thousands; *r*
> may your offspring possess
>   the cities of their enemies." *s*

a 55 Or *she*

24:32–33 See note on 18:2.
24:34–49 The servant explained his mission to Rebekah's family. His speech, which summarizes the narrative of the earlier part of the chapter, is an excellent example of the ancient storyteller's art, which was designed to fix the details of a story in the hearer's memory.

24:40 *before whom I have walked faithfully.* See notes on 5:22; 6:8–9; 17:1.
24:53 The rich gifts bestowed on Rebekah and her family indicated the wealth of the household into which she was being asked to marry—far from her loved ones and homeland.
24:60 See 22:17 and note.

24:61 ᵗS Ge 16:1;
30:3; 46:25
24:62 ᵘS Ge 16:14
ᵛS Ge 12:9
24:63 ʷJos 1:8;
Ps 1:2; 77:12; 119:15,
27, 48, 97, 148; 143:5;
145:5 ˣGe 18:2
24:64 ʸGe 31:17, 34;
1Sa 30:17
24:65 ᶻGe 38:14;
SS 1:7; 4:1,3; 6:7;
Isa 47:2
24:67 ᵃGe 31:33
ᵇS Ge 18:9
ᶜGe 25:20; 49:31
ᵈGe 29:18, 20; 34:3;
Jdg 16:4 ᵉGe 23:1-2
25:2 ᶠJer 25:25
ᵍGe 36:35; 37:28, 36;
Ex 2:15; Nu 22:4;
25:6, 18; 31:2;
Jos 13:21; Jdg 6:1, 3;
7:1; 8:1, 22, 24; 9:17;
1Ki 11:18; Ps 83:9;
Isa 9:4; 10:26; 60:6;
Hab 3:7 ʰJob 2:11; 8:1
25:3 ⁱS Ge 10:7
ʲS Ge 10:7
25:4 ᵏIsa 60:6
25:5 ˡS Ge 24:36
25:6 ᵐS Ge 22:24
ⁿS Ge 21:10, 14
ᵒGe 29:1; Jdg 6:3, 33;
1Ki 4:30; Job 1:3;
Eze 25:4
25:7 ᵖver 26;
Ge 12:4; 35:28; 47:9,
28; 50:22, 26;
Job 42:16
25:8 ᵠS Ge 15:15
ʳver 17; Ge 35:29;
49:29, 33; Nu 20:24;
31:2; Dt 31:14; 32:50;
34:5
25:9 ˢGe 35:29;
47:30; 49:31
ᵗS Ge 23:9
ᵘS Ge 13:18 ᵛGe 23:8
ʷGe 49:29; 50:13
25:10 ˣS Ge 10:15
25:11 ʸS Ge 12:2
ᶻS Ge 16:14
25:12 ᵃS Ge 2:4
ᵇS Ge 16:1
ᶜS Ge 17:20; 21:18
25:13 ᵈGe 28:9;
36:3 ᵉPs 120:5;
SS 1:5; Isa 21:16;
42:11; 60:7; Jer 2:10;
49:28; Eze 27:21
25:14 ᶠJos 15:52;
Isa 21:11; Ob 1:1
25:15 ᵍJob 6:19;

⁶¹Then Rebekah and her attendants ᵗ got ready and mounted their camels and went back with the man. So the servant took Rebekah and left.

⁶²Now Isaac had come from Beer Lahai Roi, ᵘ for he was living in the Negev. ᵛ ⁶³He went out to the field one evening to meditate, ᵃ ʷ and as he looked up, ˣ he saw camels approaching. ⁶⁴Rebekah also looked up and saw Isaac. She got down from her camel ʸ ⁶⁵and asked the servant, "Who is that man in the field coming to meet us?"

"He is my master," the servant answered. So she took her veil ᶻ and covered herself.

⁶⁶Then the servant told Isaac all he had done. ⁶⁷Isaac brought her into the tent ᵃ of his mother Sarah, ᵇ and he married Rebekah. ᶜ So she became his wife, and he loved her; ᵈ and Isaac was comforted after his mother's death. ᵉ

THE DEATH OF ABRAHAM

25:1–4pp — 1Ch 1:32–33

25 Abraham had taken another wife, whose name was Keturah. ²She bore him Zimran, ᶠ Jokshan, Medan, Midian, ᵍ Ishbak and Shuah. ʰ ³Jokshan was the father of Sheba ⁱ and Dedan; ʲ the descendants of Dedan were the Ashurites, the Letushites and the Leummites. ⁴The sons of Midian were Ephah, ᵏ Epher, Hanok, Abida and Eldaah. All these were descendants of Keturah.

⁵Abraham left everything he owned to Isaac. ˡ ⁶But while he was still living, he gave gifts to the sons of his concubines ᵐ and sent them away from his son Isaac ⁿ to the land of the east. ᵒ

⁷Abraham lived a hundred and seventy-five years. ᵖ ⁸Then Abraham breathed his last and died at a good old age, ᵠ an old man and full of years; and he was gathered to his people. ʳ ⁹His sons Isaac and Ishmael buried him ˢ in the cave of Machpelah ᵗ near Mamre, ᵘ in the field of Ephron ᵛ son of Zohar the Hittite, ʷ ¹⁰the field Abraham had bought from the Hittites. ᵇ ˣ There Abraham was buried with his wife Sarah. ¹¹After Abraham's death, God blessed his son Isaac, ʸ who then lived near Beer Lahai Roi. ᶻ

ISHMAEL'S SONS

25:12–16pp — 1Ch 1:29–31

¹²This is the account ᵃ of the family line of Abraham's son Ishmael, whom Sarah's servant, Hagar ᵇ the Egyptian, bore to Abraham. ᶜ

¹³These are the names of the sons of Ishmael, listed in the order of their birth: Nebaioth ᵈ the firstborn of Ishmael, Kedar, ᵉ Adbeel, Mibsam, ¹⁴Mishma, Dumah, ᶠ Massa, ¹⁵Hadad, Tema, ᵍ Jetur, ʰ Naphish and Kedemah. ¹⁶These were the sons of Ishmael, and these are the names of the twelve tribal rulers ⁱ according to their settlements and camps. ʲ ¹⁷Ishmael lived a hundred and thirty-seven years. He breathed his last and died, and he was gathered to his people. ᵏ ¹⁸His descendants ˡ settled in the area from Havilah to Shur, ᵐ

ᵃ 63 The meaning of the Hebrew for this word is uncertain.   ᵇ 10 Or *the descendants of Heth*

25:15 Isa 21:14; Jer 25:23 ʰ1Ch 5:19 **25:16** ⁱGe 17:20; ʲS Ge 13:16; Ps 83:6 **25:17** ᵏS yer 8 **25:18** ˡS Ge 17:20; 21:18 ᵐS Ge 16:7

24:62 *Beer Lahai Roi.* See note on 16:14. *Negev.* See note on 12:9.
24:65 *she took her veil and covered herself.* Apparently a sign that she was unmarried (cf. 38:14,19).
24:67 *tent.* Often used as a bridal chamber (see Ps 19:4–5).
25:1–6 Abraham's final disposition of his estate.
25:1 *had taken.* Abraham would have been 140 years old at this time if the order were chronological; hence, "had taken" instead of "took." *wife.* Elsewhere called Abraham's "concubine" (1Ch 1:32).
25:2 *She bore him.* The listing of Keturah's offspring shows that Abraham indeed became "the father of many nations" (17:4–6; see note on 17:6).
25:5 *left everything he owned to Isaac.* Isaac was the "only son" (22:2; see note there) of Abraham's wife Sarah, so he was the legal heir to Abraham's estate (cf. 21:10 and note).
25:6 *concubines.* Secondary wives, a common cultural phenomenon in the ancient Near East. Polygamy was practiced even by godly men in ancient times, though it was not the original divine intention (see note on 4:19).
25:7 *a hundred and seventy-five years.* Abraham thus lived for a full 100 years in the promised land (see 12:4 and note).

25:8 *died at a good old age.* As God had promised (see 15:15). *old man and full of years.* A phrase used also of the patriarch Job (see Job 42:17). *was gathered to his people.* Joined his ancestors and/or deceased relatives in death (see 2Ki 22:20; 2Ch 34:28).
25:9 *Isaac and Ishmael.* Isaac, as the heir of covenant and estate (see note on v. 5), is listed first.
25:11 *Beer Lahai Roi.* See note on 16:14.
25:12–18 A brief account of Ishmael's family line, showing the fulfillment of the promises made to Hagar (16:10) and Abraham (17:20) concerning their son but also noting the fulfillment of his predicted alienation from the descendants of Abraham and Sarah (16:12).
25:12 *account.* See note on 2:4.
25:13 *names of the sons of Ishmael.* Many are Arab names, giving credence to the Arab tradition that Ishmael is their ancestor.
25:16 *twelve tribal rulers.* Twelve major tribes descended from Abraham's son Ishmael (as predicted in 17:20)—as was also true of Abraham's brother Nahor (see note on 22:23–24).

25:18 ⁿGe 16:12
25:19 ᵒS Ge 2:4
25:20 ᵖver 26;
Ge 26:34; 35:28
ᑫS Ge 24:67
ʳS Ge 22:22 ᵍGe 28:2,
5,6; 30:20; 31:18;
33:18; 35:9,26; 46:15;
48:7 ˢS Ge 24:29
ᵘGe 31:20,24; Dt 26:5
25:21 ᵛS Ge 11:30
ʷGe 30:17,22;
1Sa 1:17,23; 1Ch 5:20;
2Ch 33:13; Ezr 8:23;
Ps 127:3
25:22 ˣEx 18:15;
28:30; 33:7;
Lev 24:12; Nu 9:6-8;
27:5,21; Dt 17:9;
Jdg 18:5; 1Sa 9:9;
10:22; 14:36; 22:10;
1Ki 22:8; 2Ki 3:11;
22:13; Isa 30:2;
Jer 21:2; 37:7,17;
Eze 14:7; 20:1,3
25:23 ʸS Ge 17:4
ᶻS Ge 9:25; 48:14,19;
Ro 9:11-12*
25:24 ᵃLk 1:57; 2:6
ᵇGe 38:27
25:25 ᶜ1Sa 16:12
ᵈGe 27:11 ᵉGe 27:1,
15
25:26 ᶠGe 38:29
ᵍHos 12:3 ʰGe 27:36;
32:27; Dt 23:7;
Jos 24:4; Ob 1:10,12
ⁱS ver 7,S 20
25:27 ʲS Ge 10:9
ᵏver 29; Ge 27:3,5
25:28 ˡGe 27:3,4,9,
14,19 ᵐGe 27:6; 37:3
25:29 ⁿ2Ki 4:38-40
ᵒS ver 27
25:30 ᵖver 34
ᵍGe 32:3; 36:1,8-9,
19; Nu 20:14; Dt 23:7;
Ps 137:7; Jer 25:21;
40:11; 49:7
25:31 ʳDt 21:16-17;
1Ch 5:1-2
25:33 ˢS Ge 21:23;
S 47:31 ᵗGe 27:36;
Heb 12:16
25:34 ᵘver 30

near the eastern border of Egypt, as you go toward Ashur. And they lived in hostility toward[a] all the tribes related to them. ⁿ

JACOB AND ESAU

¹⁹This is the account ᵒ of the family line of Abraham's son Isaac.

Abraham became the father of Isaac, ²⁰and Isaac was forty years old ᵖ when he married Rebekah ᑫ daughter of Bethuel ʳ the Aramean from Paddan Aram[b] ˢ and sister of Laban ᵗ the Aramean. ᵘ

²¹Isaac prayed to the LORD on behalf of his wife, because she was childless. ᵛ The LORD answered his prayer, ʷ and his wife Rebekah became pregnant. ²²The babies jostled each other within her, and she said, "Why is this happening to me?" So she went to inquire of the LORD. ˣ

²³The LORD said to her,

"Two nations ʸ are in your womb,
  and two peoples from within you will be separated;
one people will be stronger than the other,
  and the older will serve the younger. ᶻ"

²⁴When the time came for her to give birth, ᵃ there were twin boys in her womb. ᵇ ²⁵The first to come out was red, ᶜ and his whole body was like a hairy garment; ᵈ so they named him Esau. ᶜ ᵉ ²⁶After this, his brother came out, ᶠ with his hand grasping Esau's heel; ᵍ so he was named Jacob. ᵈ ʰ Isaac was sixty years old ⁱ when Rebekah gave birth to them.

²⁷The boys grew up, and Esau became a skillful hunter, ʲ a man of the open country, ᵏ while Jacob was content to stay at home among the tents. ²⁸Isaac, who had a taste for wild game, ˡ loved Esau, but Rebekah loved Jacob. ᵐ

²⁹Once when Jacob was cooking some stew, ⁿ Esau came in from the open country, ᵒ famished. ³⁰He said to Jacob, "Quick, let me have some of that red stew! ᵖ I'm famished!" (That is why he was also called Edom.ᵉ) ᑫ

³¹Jacob replied, "First sell me your birthright. ʳ"

³²"Look, I am about to die," Esau said. "What good is the birthright to me?"

³³But Jacob said, "Swear ˢ to me first." So he swore an oath to him, selling his birthright ᵗ to Jacob.

³⁴Then Jacob gave Esau some bread and some lentil stew. ᵘ He ate and drank, and then got up and left.

So Esau despised his birthright.

ᵃ 18 Or *lived to the east of*   ᵇ 20 That is, Northwest Mesopotamia   ᶜ 25 *Esau* may mean *hairy*.   ᵈ 26 *Jacob* means *he grasps the heel,* a Hebrew idiom for *he deceives.*   ᵉ 30 *Edom* means *red.*

25:18 *in hostility toward.* See note on 16:12; or possibly "to the east of" (see TNIV text notes here and on 16:12; see also 25:6).

25:19—35:29 The author now takes up the story of Jacob, which he continues until the death of Isaac. Isaac is the link between Abraham and Jacob, and his story is interwoven with theirs.

25:19 *account.* See note on 2:4.

25:20 *Paddan Aram.* See TNIV text note; means "plain of Aram," another name for Aram Naharaim (see note on 24:10).

25:21 *because she was childless.* As Sarah had been (see 11:30 and note). Rebekah was barren for 20 years (vv. 20,26). Isaac's offspring, like Abraham's, were a special gift in fulfillment of God's covenant promises.

25:22 *jostled each other.* The struggle between Jacob and Esau began in the womb (see also v. 26). *went.* Perhaps to a nearby place of worship.

25:23 *the older will serve the younger.* The ancient law of primogeniture (cf. Dt 21:15–17 and notes) provided that, under ordinary circumstances, the younger of two sons would be subservient to the older. God's election of the younger son highlights the fact that God's people are the product not of natural or worldly development but of his sovereign intervention in human affairs (see note on 11:30). Part of this verse is quoted in Ro 9:10–12 as an example of God's sovereign right to do "whatever pleases him" (Ps 115:3)—not in an arbitrary way (see Ro 9:14), but according to his own perfect will.

25:24—26 For another unusual birth of twin boys, see 38:27–30.

25:25 *red.* A pun on Edom, one of Esau's other names (see v. 30 and TNIV text note).

25:26 *his hand grasping Esau's heel.* Hostility between the Israelites (Jacob's descendants) and Edomites (Esau's descendants) became the rule rather than the exception (see, e.g., Nu 20:14–21; Ob 9–10). *Jacob.* See TNIV text note. The name became proverbial for the unsavory quality of deceptiveness (see TNIV text note on Jer 9:4).

25:31 *sell me your birthright.* In ancient times the birthright included the inheritance rights of the firstborn (see Heb 12:16). Jacob was ever the schemer, seeking by any means to gain advantage over others. But it was by God's appointment and care, not Jacob's wits, that he came into the blessing.

25:33 *Swear to me first.* A verbal oath was all that was required to make the transaction legal and forever binding.

25:34 *lentil.* A small, pea-like annual plant, the pods of which turn reddish-brown when boiled. It grows well even in bad soil and has provided an important source of nourishment in the Near East since ancient times (see 2Sa 17:28; 23:11; Eze 4:9). *Esau despised his birthright.* In so doing, he proved himself to be "godless" (Heb 12:16), since at the heart of the birthright were the covenant promises that Isaac had inherited from Abraham.

ISAAC AND ABIMELEK

26:1–11Ref — Ge 12:10–20; 20:1–18

26 Now there was a famine in the land ^{v}—besides the previous famine in Abraham's time—and Isaac went to Abimelek king of the Philistines ^{w} in Gerar. ^{x} ^{2}The LORD appeared ^{y} to Isaac and said, "Do not go down to Egypt; ^{z} live in the land where I tell you to live. ^{a} ^{3}Stay in this land for a while, ^{b} and I will be with you ^{c} and will bless you. ^{d} For to you and your descendants I will give all these lands ^{e} and will confirm the oath I swore to your father Abraham. ^{f} ^{4}I will make your descendants ^{g} as numerous as the stars in the sky ^{h} and will give them all these lands, ^{i} and through your offspring^a all nations on earth will be blessed, $^{b j}$ ^{5}because Abraham obeyed me ^{k} and did everything I required of him, keeping my commands, my decrees ^{l} and my instructions. ^{m}" ^{6}So Isaac stayed in Gerar. ^{n}

^{7}When the men of that place asked him about his wife, he said, "She is my sister, ^{o}" because he was afraid to say, "She is my wife." He thought, "The men of this place might kill me on account of Rebekah, because she is beautiful."

^{8}When Isaac had been there a long time, Abimelek king of the Philistines ^{p} looked down from a window and saw Isaac caressing his wife Rebekah. ^{9}So Abimelek summoned Isaac and said, "She is really your wife! Why did you say, 'She is my sister'? ^{q}"

Isaac answered him, "Because I thought I might lose my life on account of her."

^{10}Then Abimelek said, "What is this you have done to us? ^{r} One of the men might well have slept with your wife, and you would have brought guilt upon us."

^{11}So Abimelek gave orders to all the people: "Anyone who harms ^{s} this man or his wife shall surely be put to death." ^{t}

^{12}Isaac planted crops in that land and the same year reaped a hundredfold, ^{u} because the LORD blessed him. ^{v} ^{13}The man became rich, and his wealth continued to grow until he became very wealthy. ^{w} ^{14}He had so many flocks and herds and servants ^{x} that the Philistines envied him. ^{y} ^{15}So all the wells ^{z} that his father's servants had dug in the time of his father Abraham, the Philistines stopped up, ^{a} filling them with earth.

^{16}Then Abimelek said to Isaac, "Move away from us; ^{b} you have become too powerful for us. ^{c}"

^{17}So Isaac moved away from there and encamped in the Valley of Gerar, ^{d} where he settled. ^{18}Isaac reopened the wells ^{e} that had been dug in the time of his father Abraham, which the Philistines had stopped up after Abraham died, and he gave them the same names his father had given them.

^{19}Isaac's servants dug in the valley and discovered a well of fresh water there. ^{20}But the herders of Gerar quarreled ^{f} with those of Isaac and said, "The water is ours!" ^{g} So he named the well Esek, ^{c} because they disputed with him. ^{21}Then they dug another well, but they quarreled ^{h} over that one also; so he named it Sitnah. ^{d} ^{22}He moved on from there and

---

^{a} 4 Or *seed* ^{b} 4 Or *and all nations on earth will use the name of your offspring in blessings* (see Gen. 48:20)
^{c} 20 *Esek* means *dispute*. ^{d} 21 *Sitnah* means *opposition*.

26:1–33 The events of some of these verses (e.g., vv. 1–11) occurred before the birth of Esau and Jacob. Verses 1–11 are placed here to highlight the fact that the birthright and blessing Jacob struggled to obtain from his father (see 25:22,31–33; 27:5–29) involved the covenant inheritance of Abraham that Isaac had received.

26:1 *previous famine in Abraham's time.* See 12:10. *Abimelek.* Probably the son or grandson of the earlier king who bore the same name (see 20:2). *Philistines.* See note on 10:14. *Gerar.* See note on 20:1.

26:2 *appeared.* See note on 12:7.

Ⓐ **26:3** *I will be with you.* God's promise to be a sustainer and protector of his people is repeated often (see, e.g., v. 24; 28:15 and note; 31:3; Jos 1:5; Isa 41:10; Jer 1:8,19; Mt 28:20; Ac 18:10; see also Ge 17:7 and note). *the oath I swore to your father Abraham.* See 22:16–18.

26:4 *descendants as numerous as the stars in the sky.* See 13:16; 15:5 and notes. *through your offspring all nations on earth will be blessed.* See note on 12:2–3.

26:5 *because Abraham obeyed me.* See note on 17:9. *everything I required … commands … decrees … instructions.* Legal language describing various aspects of the divine regulations that God's

people were expected to keep (see Lev 26:14–16,46; Dt 11:1). Addressing Israel after the covenant at Sinai, the author of Genesis used language that strictly applied only to that covenant. But he emphasized to the Israelites that their father Abraham had been obedient to God's will in his time and that they must follow his example if they were to receive the covenant promises.

26:7 *because she is beautiful.* See 12:11,14.

26:8 *caressing.* The word in Hebrew (a form of the verb translated "laugh" in 17:17; 18:12–13,15; 21:6 and "mock" in 21:9) is yet another pun on Isaac's name.

26:12 *reaped a hundredfold.* Indicative of the fertility of the promised land.

Ⓐ **26:16** *you have become too powerful for us.* An indication that the covenant promises were being fulfilled. Already in the days of the patriarchs, the presence of God's people in the land was seen as a threat by the peoples of the world. As the world's people pursued their own godless living, God's people aroused their hostility. A similar complaint was voiced by an Egyptian pharaoh hundreds of years later (Ex 1:9).

26:20 *The water is ours!* In those arid regions, disputes over water rights and pasturelands were common (see 13:6 and note; 21:25; 36:7).

26:1 ^{v} S Ge 12:10;
S Dt 32:24
^{w} S Ge 10:14; Jdg 10:6
^{x} S Ge 20:1
26:2 ^{y} S Ge 12:7
^{z} Ge 46:3 ^{a} S Ge 12:1
26:3 ^{b} Ge 20:1
^{c} S Ge 21:20; 27:45;
31:3,5; 32:9; 35:3;
48:21; Ex 3:12; 33:14-
16; Nu 23:21;
Dt 31:23; Jos 1:5;
Isa 43:2; Jer 1:8,19;
Hag 1:13 ^{d} ver 12;
Gal 3:8
^{e} Ge 12:2 ^{e} S Ge 12:7;
Ac 7:5 ^{f} S Ge 17:19
26:4 ^{g} ver 24;
Ge 48:4 ^{h} S Ge 12:2;
S Nu 10:36 ^{i} S Ge 12:7
^{j} S Ge 12:3; Ac 3:25*;
Gal 3:8
26:5 ^{k} S Ge 18:19
^{l} Ps 119:80,112;
Eze 18:21 ^{m} Lev 18:4,
5,26; 19:19,37; 20:8,
22; 25:18; 26:3;
Nu 15:40; Dt 4:40;
6:2; 11:1; 1Ki 2:3
26:6 ^{n} S Ge 20:1
26:7 ^{o} S Ge 12:13
26:8 ^{p} S Ge 10:14
26:9 ^{q} S Ge 12:19
26:10 ^{r} S Ge 12:18
26:11 ^{s} 1Sa 24:6;
26:9; Ps 105:15
^{t} S Ge 20:3
26:12 ^{u} Mt 13:8
^{v} ver 3
26:13 ^{w} S Ge 13:2;
S Dt 8:18
26:14 ^{x} S Ge 12:16;
S 24:36; 32:23
^{y} Ge 37:11
26:15 ^{z} S Ge 21:30
^{a} S Ge 21:25
26:16 ^{b} ver 27;
Jdg 11:7 ^{c} Ex 1:9;
Ps 105:24-25
26:17 ^{d} S Ge 20:1
26:18 ^{e} S Ge 21:30
26:20 ^{f} S Ge 13:7
^{g} Ge 21:25
26:21 ^{h} S Ge 13:7

26:22 ⁱGe 36:37
^jPs 18:19; Isa 33:20;
54:2; Am 9:11
^kS Ge 17:6
26:23 ^lS Ge 22:19
26:24 ^mS Ge 24:12
ⁿS Ge 15:1; S Jos 8:1
^oS Ge 21:20 ^pS ver 4
^qver 4; Ge 17:7;
S 22:17; 28:14; 30:27;
39:5; Dt 13:17
26:25 ^rS Ge 8:20
^sS Ge 4:26; S Ac 2:21
^tS Ge 21:30
26:26 ^uS Ge 21:22
26:27 ^vS ver 16
26:28 ^wS Ge 21:22
^xS Ge 21:27; Jos 9:6
26:29 ^yGe 31:29,52
^zS Ge 24:31
26:30 ^aGe 31:54;
Ex 18:12; 24:11;
1Sa 20:27
26:31 ^bS Ge 21:23,
27
26:32 ^cS Ge 21:30
26:33 ^dS Ge 21:14
26:34 ^eS Ge 25:20
^fS Ge 10:15; 28:9;
36:2; Jos 3:10;
1Sa 16:6; 1Ki 10:29
26:35 ^gGe 27:46;
28:8; Job 7:16
27:1 ^hGe 48:10;
Dt 34:7; 1Sa 3:2
ⁱS Ge 25:25
27:2 ^jGe 47:29;
1Ki 2:1
27:3 ^kS Ge 25:27
27:4 ^lS Ge 25:28
^mver 10,25,31;
S Ge 24:60; 49:28;
Dt 33:1; Heb 11:20
ⁿver 7
27:5 ^oS Ge 25:27
27:6 ^pS Ge 25:27
27:7 ^qver 4
27:8 ^rver 13
27:9 ^s1Sa 16:20
^tS Ge 25:28
27:10 ^uS ver 4

dug another well, and no one quarreled over it. He named it Rehoboth,^{a i} saying, "Now the LORD has given us room^j and we will flourish^k in the land."

²³From there he went up to Beersheba.^{l 24}That night the LORD appeared to him and said, "I am the God of your father Abraham.^m Do not be afraid,ⁿ for I am with you;^o I will bless you and will increase the number of your descendants^p for the sake of my servant Abraham."^q

²⁵Isaac built an altar^r there and called on the name of the LORD.^s There he pitched his tent, and there his servants dug a well.^t

²⁶Meanwhile, Abimelek had come to him from Gerar, with Ahuzzath his personal adviser and Phicol the commander of his forces.^{u 27}Isaac asked them, "Why have you come to me, since you were hostile to me and sent me away?^v"

²⁸They answered, "We saw clearly that the LORD was with you;^w so we said, 'There ought to be a sworn agreement between us'—between you and us. Let us make a treaty^x with you ²⁹that you will do us no harm,^y just as we did not harm you but always treated you well and sent you away peacefully. And now you are blessed by the LORD."^z

³⁰Isaac then made a feast^a for them, and they ate and drank. ³¹Early the next morning the men swore an oath^b to each other. Then Isaac sent them on their way, and they went away peacefully.

³²That day Isaac's servants came and told him about the well^c they had dug. They said, "We've found water!" ³³He called it Shibah,^b and to this day the name of the town has been Beersheba.^{c d}

JACOB TAKES ESAU'S BLESSING

³⁴When Esau was forty years old,^e he married Judith daughter of Beeri the Hittite, and also Basemath daughter of Elon the Hittite.^{f 35}They were a source of grief to Isaac and Rebekah.^g

27 When Isaac was old and his eyes were so weak that he could no longer see,^h he called for Esau his older sonⁱ and said to him, "My son."

"Here I am," he answered.

²Isaac said, "I am now an old man and don't know the day of my death.^{j 3}Now then, get your equipment—your quiver and bow—and go out to the open country^k to hunt some wild game for me. ⁴Prepare me the kind of tasty food I like^l and bring it to me to eat, so that I may give you my blessing^m before I die."ⁿ

⁵Now Rebekah was listening as Isaac spoke to his son Esau. When Esau left for the open country^o to hunt game and bring it back, ⁶Rebekah said to her son Jacob,^p "Look, I overheard your father say to your brother Esau, ⁷'Bring me some game and prepare me some tasty food to eat, so that I may give you my blessing in the presence of the LORD before I die.'^{q 8}Now, my son, listen carefully and do what I tell you:^{r 9}Go out to the flock and bring me two choice young goats,^s so I can prepare some tasty food for your father, just the way he likes it.^{t 10}Then take it to your father to eat, so that he may give you his blessing^u before he dies."

---

^a 22 *Rehoboth* means *room.*   ^b 33 *Shibah* can mean *oath* or *seven.*   ^c 33 *Beersheba* can mean *well of the oath* and *well of seven.*

26:25 *built an altar.* See note on 12:7. *called on the name of the LORD.* See 4:26 and note.

26:26 *Phicol.* See note on 21:22.

26:30 *made a feast.* Covenants were often concluded with a shared meal, signifying the bond of friendship (see 31:54; Ex 24:11 and notes).

26:33 *name of the town has been Beersheba.* See note on 21:31.

26:34 *When Esau was forty years old, he married.* As had his father Isaac (see 25:20). Forty years was roughly equivalent to a generation in later times (see Nu 32:13). *Judith ... Basemath.* In addition to these two wives, Esau also married Mahalath, "sister of Nebaioth and daughter of Ishmael" (28:9). The Esau genealogy of ch. 36 also mentions three wives, but they are identified as "Adah daughter of Elon the Hittite," "Oholibamah daughter of Anah ... the Hivite" and "Basemath daughter of Ishmael and sister of Nebaioth" (36:2–3). Possibly the lists have suffered in transmission, or perhaps alternative names or nicknames are used. It is also possible that Esau married more than three wives.

26:35 *They were a source of grief.* Isaac and Rebekah were determined not to allow Jacob to make the same mistake of marrying Hittite or Canaanite women (see 27:46—28:2).

27:1–40 How Rebekah and Jacob manipulated Isaac's last will and testament.

27:1 *eyes were so weak that he could no longer see.* In ancient times, blindness and near blindness were common among elderly people (see 48:10; 1Sa 4:15). *Here I am.* See note on 22:1.

27:4 *the kind of tasty food I like.* Rebekah and Jacob took advantage of Isaac's love for a certain kind of food (see vv. 9,14). *give you my blessing before I die.* Oral statements, including deathbed bequests (see 49:28–33), had legal force in ancient Near Eastern law. *blessing.* See note on v. 36.

27:5 *listening.* Eavesdropping.

27:6 *Rebekah.* Throughout the Jacob story the author develops a wordplay on "birthright" (*bekorah*) and "blessing" (*berakah*), both of which Jacob seeks to obtain, and Rebekah (*ribqah*) does her best to further the cause of her favorite son. *said to her son Jacob.* The parental favoritism mentioned in 25:28 is about to bear its poisonous fruit.

27:8 *my son, ... do what I tell you.* Rebekah proves to be just as deceitful as Jacob, whose very name signifies deceit (see TNIV text notes on v. 36; 25:26).

[11]Jacob said to Rebekah his mother, "But my brother Esau is a hairy man[v] while I have smooth skin. [12]What if my father touches me?[w] I would appear to be tricking him and would bring down a curse[x] on myself rather than a blessing."

[13]His mother said to him, "My son, let the curse fall on me.[y] Just do what I say;[z] go and get them for me."

[14]So he went and got them and brought them to his mother, and she prepared some tasty food, just the way his father liked it.[a] [15]Then Rebekah took the best clothes[b] of Esau her older son,[c] which she had in the house, and put them on her younger son Jacob. [16]She also covered his hands and the smooth part of his neck with the goatskins.[d] [17]Then she handed to her son Jacob the tasty food and the bread she had made.

[18]He went to his father and said, "My father."

"Yes, my son," he answered. "Who is it?"[e]

[19]Jacob said to his father, "I am Esau your firstborn.[f] I have done as you told me. Please sit up and eat some of my game,[g] so that you may give me your blessing."[h]

[20]Isaac asked his son, "How did you find it so quickly, my son?"

"The LORD your God gave me success,[i]" he replied.

[21]Then Isaac said to Jacob, "Come near so I can touch you,[j] my son, to know whether you really are my son Esau or not."

[22]Jacob went close to his father Isaac,[k] who touched[l] him and said, "The voice is the voice of Jacob, but the hands are the hands of Esau." [23]He did not recognize him, for his hands were hairy like those of his brother Esau;[m] so he proceeded to bless him. [24]"Are you really my son Esau?" he asked.

"I am," he replied.

[25]Then he said, "My son, bring me some of your game to eat, so that I may give you my blessing."[n]

Jacob brought it to him and he ate; and he brought some wine and he drank. [26]Then his father Isaac said to him, "Come here, my son, and kiss me."

[27]So he went to him and kissed[o] him[p]. When Isaac caught the smell of his clothes,[q] he blessed him and said,

> "Ah, the smell of my son
> is like the smell of a field
> that the LORD has blessed.[r]
> [28]May God give you of heaven's dew[s]
> and of earth's richness[t]—
> an abundance of grain[u] and new wine.[v]
> [29]May nations serve you
> and peoples bow down to you.[w]
> Be lord over your brothers,
> and may the sons of your mother bow down to you.[x]
> May those who curse you be cursed
> and those who bless you be blessed.[y]"

[30]After Isaac finished blessing him, and Jacob had scarcely left his father's presence, his brother Esau came in from hunting. [31]He too prepared some tasty food and brought it to his father. Then he said to him, "My father, please sit up and eat some of my game, so that you may give me your blessing."[z]

[32]His father Isaac asked him, "Who are you?"[a]

"I am your son," he answered, "your firstborn, Esau.[b]"

[33]Isaac trembled violently and said, "Who was it, then, that hunted game and brought it to me?[c] I ate it just before you came and I blessed him—and indeed he will be blessed![d]"

[34]When Esau heard his father's words, he burst out with a loud and bitter cry[e] and said to his father, "Bless[f] me—me too, my father!"

27:11 vGe 25:25
27:12 wver 22
xS Ge 9:25
27:13 yMt 27:25
zS ver 8
27:14 aS Ge 25:28
27:15 bver 27;
SS 4:11 cS Ge 25:25
27:16 dver 22-23
27:18 ever 32
27:19 fver 32
gS Ge 25:28 hS ver 4
27:20 iS Ge 24:12
27:21 jver 12
27:22 kGe 45:4
lver 12
27:23 mver 16
27:25 nS ver 4
27:27 oGe 31:28,
55; 33:4; 48:10;
Ex 4:27; 18:7; Ru 1:9;
1Sa 20:41; 2Sa 14:33;
19:39 pHeb 11:20
qS ver 15 rPs 65:9-13
27:28 sDt 33:13;
2Sa 1:21; Job 18:16;
29:19; Pr 3:20;
Isa 26:19; Hos 14:5;
Hag 1:10; Zec 8:12
tver 39; Ge 49:25;
Lev 26:20; Dt 33:13
uPs 65:9; 72:16
vver 37; Nu 18:12;
Dt 7:13; 33:28;
2Ki 18:32; Ps 4:7;
Isa 36:17; Jer 31:12;
40:10
27:29 w2Sa 8:14;
Ps 68:31; 72:11;
Isa 19:21,23; 27:13;
45:14,23; 49:7,23;
60:12,14; 66:23;
Jer 12:17; Da 2:44;
Zec 14:17-18
xS Ge 9:25; S 25:23;
S 37:7 yver 33;
Ge 12:3
27:31 zS ver 4
27:32 aver 18
bver 19
27:33 cver 35
dS ver 29
27:34 eHeb 12:17
fEx 12:32

27:20 *your God.* Consistent with Jacob's language elsewhere (31:5,42; 32:9). Not until his safe return from Harran did he speak of the Lord as his own God (cf. 28:20–21; 33:18–20 and notes).

27:24 *Are you really my son Esau?* To the very end of the charade, Isaac remained suspicious.

27:29 *Be lord over your brothers.* Isaac was unwittingly blessing Jacob and thus fulfilling God's promise to Rebekah in 25:23 (see note there). *curse ... be cursed ... bless ... be blessed.* Cf. 12:2–3.

27:33 *indeed he will be blessed.* The ancient world believed that blessings and curses had a kind of magical power to accomplish what they pronounced. But Isaac, as heir and steward of God's covenant blessing, acknowledged that he had solemnly transmitted that heritage to Jacob by way of a legally binding bequest (see note on v. 4).

27:34 *loud and bitter cry.* Esau's tears "could not change what he had done" (Heb 12:17).

27:35 *g* Jer 9:4; 12:6
h ver 19, 45
27:36 *i* S Ge 25:26
j Ge 29:25; 31:20, 26; 34:13; 1Sa 28:12
k S Ge 25:33
l Heb 12:16-17
27:37 *m* S ver 28; Dt 16:13; Ezr 6:9; Isa 16:10; Jer 40:12
27:38 *n* Ge 29:11; Nu 14:1; Jdg 2:4; 21:2; Ru 1:9; 1Sa 11:4; 30:4; Heb 12:17
27:39 *o* Heb 11:20
p ver 28 *q* Ge 36:6
27:40 *r* 2Sa 8:14
s S Ge 9:25
t 2Ki 8:20-22
27:41 *u* Ge 37:4; 49:23; 50:15; 1Sa 17:28 *v* Ge 31:17; 32:11; Hos 10:14
w Ge 50:4, 10; Nu 20:29 *x* ver 42
y Ob 1:10
27:42 *z* Ge 32:3, 11; 33:4 *a* ver 41
27:43 *b* S ver 8
c S Ge 24:29
d S Ge 11:31
27:44 *e* Ge 31:38, 41
27:45 *f* S ver 35
g S Ge 26:3
27:46 *h* S Ge 10:15
i S Ge 10:15-19
j S Ge 26:35; S Job 7:7
28:1 *k* S Ge 24:60
l Ge 24:3
28:2 *m* S Ge 25:20
n S Ge 25:20
o S Ge 21:21; S 24:29
28:3 *p* S Ge 17:1
q Ge 48:16; Nu 6:24; Ru 2:4; Ps 129:8; 134:3; Jer 31:23
r S Ge 17:6 *s* S Ge 12:2
28:4 *t* S Ge 12:2, 3
u S Ge 15:7
v S Ge 17:8
28:5 *w* S Ge 11:31
x Hos 12:12
y S Ge 25:20
z S Ge 24:29
28:6 *a* S ver 1
28:8 *b* S Ge 10:15-19

³⁵But he said, "Your brother came deceitfully *g* and took your blessing." *h*

³⁶Esau said, "Isn't he rightly named Jacob*a*? *i* This is the second time he has taken advantage of *i* me: He took my birthright, *k* and now he's taken my blessing!" *l* Then he asked, "Haven't you reserved any blessing for me?"

³⁷Isaac answered Esau, "I have made him lord over you and have made all his relatives his servants, and I have sustained him with grain and new wine. *m* So what can I possibly do for you, my son?"

³⁸Esau said to his father, "Do you have only one blessing, my father? Bless me too, my father!" Then Esau wept aloud. *n*

³⁹His father Isaac answered him, *o*

"Your dwelling will be
   away from the earth's richness,
   away from the dew *p* of heaven above. *q*
⁴⁰You will live by the sword
   and you will serve *r* your brother. *s*
But when you grow restless,
   you will throw his yoke
   from off your neck. *t*"

⁴¹Esau held a grudge *u* against Jacob *v* because of the blessing his father had given him. He said to himself, "The days of mourning *w* for my father are near; then I will kill *x* my brother Jacob." *y*

⁴²When Rebekah was told what her older son Esau *z* had said, she sent for her younger son Jacob and said to him, "Your brother Esau is planning to avenge himself by killing you. *a* ⁴³Now then, my son, do what I say: *b* Flee at once to my brother Laban *c* in Harran. *d* ⁴⁴Stay with him for a while *e* until your brother's fury subsides. ⁴⁵When your brother is no longer angry with you and forgets what you did to him, *f* I'll send word for you to come back from there. *g* Why should I lose both of you in one day?"

⁴⁶Then Rebekah said to Isaac, "I'm disgusted with living because of these Hittite *h* women. If Jacob takes a wife from among the women of this land, *i* from Hittite women like these, my life will not be worth living." *j*

28 So Isaac called for Jacob and blessed *k* him. Then he commanded him: "Do not marry a Canaanite woman. *l* ²Go at once to Paddan Aram, *b* *m* to the house of your mother's father Bethuel. *n* Take a wife for yourself there, from among the daughters of Laban, your mother's brother. *o* ³May God Almighty*c* *p* bless *q* you and make you fruitful *r* and increase your numbers *s* until you become a community of peoples. ⁴May he give you and your descendants the blessing given to Abraham, *t* so that you may take possession of the land *u* where you now reside as a foreigner, *v* the land God gave to Abraham." ⁵Then Isaac sent Jacob on his way, *w* and he went to Paddan Aram, *x* to Laban son of Bethuel the Aramean, *y* the brother of Rebekah, *z* who was the mother of Jacob and Esau.

⁶Now Esau learned that Isaac had blessed Jacob and had sent him to Paddan Aram to take a wife from there, and that when he blessed him he commanded him, "Do not marry a Canaanite woman," *a* ⁷and that Jacob had obeyed his father and mother and had gone to Paddan Aram. ⁸Esau then realized how displeasing the Canaanite women *b* were to his

---

a 36 *Jacob* means *he grasps the heel*, a Hebrew idiom for *he takes advantage of* or *he deceives.*   *b* 2 That is, Northwest Mesopotamia; also in verses 5, 6 and 7   *c* 3 Hebrew *El-Shaddai*

27:36 *Isn't he rightly named Jacob?* See TNIV text notes here and on 25:26. *He took my birthright, and now he's taken my blessing!* The Hebrew for "birthright" is *bekorah*, and for "blessing" it is *berakah* (see note on v. 6). Though Esau tried to separate birthright from blessing, the former led inevitably to the latter, since both involved the inheritance of the firstborn (see Heb 12:16–17).

27:39 *away from the earth's richness, away from the dew of heaven.* Cf. v. 28. Isaac's secondary blessing of Esau could be only a parody of his primary blessing of Jacob.

27:40 See 25:23 and notes on 25:22, 26.

27:41–45 Esau's fierce hostility toward Jacob and its consequences. This account of Esau's "grudge" and the later account of the brothers' reconciliation (33:1–17) frame the story of Jacob's flight from Canaan to Paddan Aram, where he finds his wives, fathers many children and obtains great wealth

before returning to the promised land. This chain of events parallels Joseph's experiences as seen in his words to his brothers in 50:20 (see note there).

27:43 *do what I say.* Bad advice earlier (see vv. 8, 13), but sensible counsel this time.

27:44 *for a while.* Twenty years, as it turned out (see 31:38, 41).

27:45 *both of you.* Jacob and Esau. Esau would have to pay for his deed with his life (9:6; see also Ex 21:12; Lev 24:17; Nu 35:19, 21, 27, 33; 2Sa 14:6–7).

27:46 see note on 26:35.

28:2 *Paddan Aram.* See note on 25:20. *Take a wife for yourself there.* See 24:3–4.

28:3 *God Almighty.* See note on 17:1.

28:4 *the blessing given to Abraham.* For Paul's application of this phrase to Christian believers, see Gal 3:14.

28:5 See map and accompanying text, p. 57.

father Isaac; *c* *9*so he went to Ishmael *d* and married Mahalath, the sister of Nebaioth *e* and daughter of Ishmael son of Abraham, in addition to the wives he already had. *f*

JACOB'S DREAM AT BETHEL

*10*Jacob left Beersheba *g* and set out for Harran. *h* *11*When he reached a certain place, *i* he stopped for the night because the sun had set. Taking one of the stones there, he put it under his head *j* and lay down to sleep. *12*He had a dream *k* in which he saw a stairway *a* resting on the earth, with its top reaching to heaven, and the angels of God were ascending and descending on it. *l* *13*There above it *b* stood the LORD, *m* and he said: "I am the LORD, the God of your father Abraham and the God of Isaac. *n* I will give you and your descendants the land *o* on which you are lying. *p* *14*Your descendants will be like the dust of the earth, and you *q* will spread out to the west and to the east, to the north and to the south. *r* All peoples on earth will be blessed through you and your offspring. *c s* *15*I am with you *t* and will watch over you *u v* wherever you go, *w* and I will bring you back to this land. *x* I will not leave you *y* until I have done what I have promised you. *z*" *a*

*16*When Jacob awoke from his sleep, *b* he thought, "Surely the LORD is in this place, and I was not aware of it." *17*He was afraid and said, "How awesome is this place! *c* This is none other than the house of God; *d* this is the gate of heaven."

*18*Early the next morning Jacob took the stone he had placed under his head *e* and set it up as a pillar *f* and poured oil on top of it. *g* *19*He called that place Bethel, *d h* though the city used to be called Luz. *i*

*20*Then Jacob made a vow, *j* saying, "If God will be with me and will watch over me *k* on this journey I am taking and will give me food to eat and clothes to wear *l* *21*so that I return safely *m* to my father's household, *n* then the LORD *e* will be my God *o* *22*and *f* this stone that I have set up as a pillar *p* will be God's house, *q* and of all that you give me I will give you a tenth. *r*"

JACOB ARRIVES IN PADDAN ARAM

29 Then Jacob continued on his journey and came to the land of the eastern peoples. *s* *2*There he saw a well in the open country, with three flocks of sheep lying near it because the flocks were watered from that well. *t* The stone *u* over the mouth of the well was large. *3*When all the flocks were gathered there, the shepherds would roll the stone *v* away from the well's mouth and water the sheep. *w* Then they would return the stone to its place over the mouth of the well.

*4*Jacob asked the shepherds, "My brothers, where are you from?" *x*

"We're from Harran, *y*" they replied.

---

a *12* Or *ladder*   *b* *13* Or *There beside him*   *c* *14* Or *will use your name and the name of your offspring in blessings* (see Gen. 48:20)   *d* *19* *Bethel* means *house of God.*   *e* *20,21* Or *Since God . . . father's household, the LORD*   *f* *21,22* Or *household, and the LORD will be my God,* *22*then

29:1 *s* S Ge 25:6   **29:2** *t* S Ge 24:11 *u* ver 3,8,10   **29:3** *v* S ver 2 *w* ver 8   **29:4** *x* Ge 42:7; Jdg 19:17 *y* S Ge 11:31

28:8 *c* S Ge 26:35
28:9 *d* S Ge 16:15
e S Ge 25:13
f S Ge 26:34
28:10 *g* S Ge 21:14
h S Ge 11:31
28:11 *i* S Ge 12:8
j ver 18
28:12 *k* S Ge 20:3; 37:19 *l* Jn 1:51
28:13 *m* S Ge 12:7; 35:7,9; 48:3
n S Ge 24:12; 48:16; 49:25; 50:17
o S Ge 12:7 *p* Ge 46:4; 48:21
28:14 *q* Ge 26:4
r S Ge 12:2; S 13:14; S 26:24 *s* S Ge 12:3; Ac 3:25; Gal 3:8
28:15 *t* S Ge 21:20
u Ps 121:5,7-8
v ver 20 *w* ver 22; Ge 35:3 *x* ver 21; S Ge 15:16; 30:25; 31:30 *y* Dt 31:6,8; Jos 1:5; Ne 4:14; Ps 9:10 *z* Lev 26:42
a Ps 105:10
28:16 *b* 1Ki 3:15; Jer 31:26
28:17 *c* Ex 3:5; 19:21; Jos 5:15; Ps 68:24,35 *d* ver 22; Ge 32:2; 1Ch 22:1; 2Ch 3:1
28:18 *e* ver 11
f ver 22; Ge 31:13,45, 51; 35:14; Ex 24:4; Jos 24:26,27; Isa 19:19 *g* Lev 8:11; Jos 4:9
28:19 *h* S Ge 12:8
i Ge 35:6; 48:3; Jos 16:2; 18:13; Jdg 1:23,26
28:20 *j* Ge 31:13; Lev 7:16; 22:18; 23:38; 27:2,9; Nu 6:2; 15:3; Dt 12:6; Jdg 11:30; 1Sa 1:21; 2Sa 15:8 *k* S ver 15
l 1Ti 6:8
28:21 *m* Jdg 11:31
n S ver 15 *o* Ex 15:2; Dt 26:17; Jos 24:18; Ps 48:14; 118:28
28:22 *p* S ver 18; 1Sa 7:12 *q* S ver 17
r S Ge 14:20; S Nu 18:21; Lk 18:12

28:9 *in addition to the wives he already had.* See 26:34 and note.

28:10–22 God's reassuring appearance to Jacob as he is about to leave the promised land. This event and God's appearance to him at the Jabbok upon his return (32:22–32) form a frame around Jacob's stay in Paddan Aram, to which he went empty but from which he returned full.

28:11 *one of the stones . . . under his head.* In ancient times headrests (e.g., in Egypt) were often quite hard, sometimes being made of metal. People were used to sleeping on the ground.

28:12 *stairway.* Not a ladder with rungs, it was more likely a stairway such as mounted the sloping side of a ziggurat (see note on 11:4). *angels of God were ascending and descending on it.* A sign that the Lord offered to be Jacob's God. Jesus told a disciple that he would "see heaven open, and the angels of God ascending and descending on the Son of Man" (Jn 1:51). Jesus himself is the bridge between heaven and earth (see Jn 14:6), the only "mediator between God and human beings" (1Ti 2:5).

28:13 *above it stood the LORD.* Mesopotamian ziggurats were topped with a small shrine where worshipers prayed to their gods.

28:14 *like the dust of the earth.* See note on 13:16. *All peoples on earth will be blessed through you.* Repeats the blessing of 12:3.

28:15 *I am with you.* See note on 26:3. *I will not leave you.* Unlike the gods of pagan religions, in which the gods were merely local deities who gave protection only within their own territories, the one true God assured Jacob that he would always be with him wherever he went (see Dt 31:6 and note).

28:17 *house of God . . . gate of heaven.* Phrases that related Jacob's stairway to the Mesopotamian ziggurats (see notes on 11:4,9).

28:18 *pillar.* A memorial of worship or of communion between people and God, common in ancient times. *poured oil on top of it.* To consecrate it (see Ex 30:25–29).

28:21 *return safely.* Partially fulfilled in 33:18. *the LORD will be my God.* For the first time Jacob considered (conditionally: "If . . .," v. 20) acknowledging the God of Abraham and Isaac (see v. 13; 27:20) as his own. His full acknowledgment came only after his safe return from Harran (see 33:20 and note).

28:22 *this stone . . . will be God's house.* In the sense that it would memorialize Jacob's meeting with God at Bethel (see TNIV text note on v. 19). *of all that you give me I will give you a tenth.* A way of acknowledging the Lord as his God and King (see note on 14:20).

29:5 ᶻ S Ge 11:29
29:6 ᵃ Ge 30:22-24;
35:16; 46:19,22
ᵇ Ex 2:16
29:8 ᶜ S ver 2
ᵈ S Ge 24:13
29:9 ᵉ Ex 2:16
29:10 ᶠ ver 16
ᵍ S ver 2 ʰ S Ge 24:11
ⁱ ver 3; Ex 2:17
29:11 ʲ ver 13
ᵏ Ge 33:4; 42:24;
43:30; 45:2,14-15;
46:29; 50:1,17; Ru 1:9
29:12 ˡ ver 15
ᵐ S Ge 24:29
ⁿ Ge 24:28
29:13 ᵒ S Ge 24:29
ᵖ Ge 33:4; 45:14-15,
14; 48:10; Ex 4:27;
18:7; Lk 15:20
29:14 ᵍ Ge 2:23;
37:27; 2Sa 5:1;
2Sa 5:1; 19:12-13;
20:1; Ne 5:5; Isa 58:7
29:15 ʳ ver 12
ˢ Ge 30:28,32; 31:7,41
29:16 ᵗ ver 17,23,
28,30; Ge 30:9;
35:23; 47:30; 49:31;
Ru 4:11 ᵘ ver 9-10
29:17 ᵛ S ver 16
ʷ S Ge 12:11
29:18 ˣ S Ge 24:67
ʸ ver 20,27,30;
Ge 30:26; Hos 12:12
29:20 ᶻ S ver 18;
Ge 31:15 ᵃᵃ SS 8:7;
Hos 12:12
29:21 ᵇ Jdg 15:1
29:22 ᶜ Jdg 14:10;
Isa 25:6; Jn 2:1-2
29:23 ᵈ S ver 16
29:24 ᵉ Ge 30:9
ᶠ S Ge 16:1
29:25 ᵍ S Ge 12:18
ʰ S Ge 27:36
29:26 ⁱ Jdg 15:2;
1Sa 14:49; 18:17,20;
2Sa 6:23
29:27 ʲ Jdg 14:12
ᵏ S ver 18; Ge 31:41
29:28 ˡ S ver 16;
S Ge 4:19
29:29 ᵐ Ge 30:3;
35:22; 49:4;
Dt 22:30; 1Ch 5:1
ⁿ S Ge 16:1
29:30 ᵒ S ver 16
ᵖ S ver 20

⁵He said to them, "Do you know Laban, Nahor's grandson?" ᶻ
"Yes, we know him," they answered.
⁶Then Jacob asked them, "Is he well?"
"Yes, he is," they said, "and here comes his daughter Rachel ᵃ with the sheep. ᵇ"
⁷"Look," he said, "the sun is still high; it is not time for the flocks to be gathered. Water the sheep and take them back to pasture."
⁸"We can't," they replied, "until all the flocks are gathered and the stone ᶜ has been rolled away from the mouth of the well. Then we will water ᵈ the sheep."
⁹While he was still talking with them, Rachel came with her father's sheep, ᵉ for she was their shepherd. ¹⁰When Jacob saw Rachel ᶠ daughter of Laban, his mother's brother, and Laban's sheep, he went over and rolled the stone ᵍ away from the mouth of the well and watered ʰ his uncle's sheep. ⁱ ¹¹Then Jacob kissed ʲ Rachel and began to weep aloud. ᵏ ¹²He had told Rachel that he was a relative ˡ of her father and a son of Rebekah. ᵐ So she ran and told her father. ⁿ
¹³As soon as Laban ᵒ heard the news about Jacob, his sister's son, he hurried to meet him. He embraced him ᵖ and kissed him and brought him to his home, and there Jacob told him all these things. ¹⁴Then Laban said to him, "You are my own flesh and blood." ᵍ

JACOB MARRIES LEAH AND RACHEL

After Jacob had stayed with him for a whole month, ¹⁵Laban said to him, "Just because you are a relative ʳ of mine, should you work for me for nothing? Tell me what your wages ˢ should be."
¹⁶Now Laban had two daughters; the name of the older was Leah, ᵗ and the name of the younger was Rachel. ᵘ ¹⁷Leah had weak ᵃ eyes, but Rachel ᵛ had a lovely figure and was beautiful. ʷ ¹⁸Jacob was in love with Rachel ˣ and said, "I'll work for you seven years in return for your younger daughter Rachel." ʸ
¹⁹Laban said, "It's better that I give her to you than to some other man. Stay here with me." ²⁰So Jacob served seven years to get Rachel, ᶻ but they seemed like only a few days to him because of his love for her. ᵃ
²¹Then Jacob said to Laban, "Give me my wife. My time is completed, and I want to make love to her. ᵇ"
²²So Laban brought together all the people of the place and gave a feast. ᶜ ²³But when evening came, he took his daughter Leah ᵈ and brought her to Jacob, and Jacob made love to her. ²⁴And Laban gave his servant Zilpah ᵉ to his daughter as her attendant. ᶠ
²⁵When morning came, there was Leah! So Jacob said to Laban, "What is this you have done to me? ᵍ I served you for Rachel, didn't I? Why have you deceived me? ʰ"
²⁶Laban replied, "It is not our custom here to give the younger daughter in marriage before the older one. ⁱ ²⁷Finish this daughter's bridal week; ʲ then we will give you the younger one also, in return for another seven years of work. ᵏ"
²⁸And Jacob did so. He finished the week with Leah, and then Laban gave him his daughter Rachel to be his wife. ˡ ²⁹Laban gave his servant Bilhah ᵐ to his daughter Rachel as her attendant. ⁿ ³⁰Jacob made love to Rachel also, and his love for Rachel was greater than his love for Leah. ᵒ And he worked for Laban another seven years. ᵖ

ᵃ 17 Or *delicate*

29:5 *Laban, Nahor's grandson.* See 24:15,29. The Hebrew word here for "grandson" is lit. "son," which can refer to any male descendant (see TNIV text note on 10:2).
29:9 *shepherd.* The task of caring for sheep and goats in the Middle East was shared by men and women (cf. Ex 2:16–17; SS 1:8 and note).
29:10 *rolled the stone away.* A feat of unusual strength for one man, because the stone was large (see v. 2).
29:11 *weep aloud.* For joy.
29:13 *kissed him.* A common sign of affection among relatives, also between men (see 33:4; Ex 4:27; see also notes on Ro 16:16; 1Co 16:20).
29:14 *flesh and blood.* The English equivalent of a Hebrew phrase that means lit. "bone and flesh" and that stresses blood kinship (see, e.g., 2:23).
29:15 Laban's question and the author's observation in 30:43 frame the account of Jacob's receiving the fulfillment of Isaac's blessing. See also God's blessing on Jacob (28:14).

29:16 *Leah … Rachel.* The names mean "cow" and "ewe," respectively, appropriate in a herdsman's family.
29:21 *my wife.* If Jacob had said "Rachel," Laban would have had no excuse for giving him Leah.
29:22 *feast.* A wedding feast was usually seven days long (see vv. 27–28; Jdg 14:10,12).
29:23 *when evening came … Jacob made love to her.* The darkness, or perhaps a veil (see 24:65), may have concealed Leah's identity.
29:24 See v. 29; a wedding custom documented in Old Babylonian marriage contracts.
29:25 *you deceived me.* Jacob, the deceiver in name (see TNIV text notes on 25:26; 27:36) as well as in behavior (see 27:36), had himself been deceived. The one who had tried everything to obtain the benefits of the firstborn had now, against his will, received the firstborn (vv. 16,26).
29:28 *then Laban gave him his daughter Rachel.* Before Jacob worked another seven years (see v. 30).

JACOB'S CHILDREN

³¹When the LORD saw that Leah was not loved,�q he enabled her to conceive,ʳ but Rachel remained childless. ³²Leah became pregnant and gave birth to a son.ˢ She named him Reuben,ᵃᵗ for she said, "It is because the LORD has seen my misery.ᵘ Surely my husband will love me now."

³³She conceived again, and when she gave birth to a son she said, "Because the LORD heard that I am not loved,ᵛ he gave me this one too." So she named him Simeon.ᵇʷ

³⁴Again she conceived, and when she gave birth to a son she said, "Now at last my husband will become attached to me,ˣ because I have borne him three sons." So he was named Levi.ᶜʸ

³⁵She conceived again, and when she gave birth to a son she said, "This time I will praise the LORD." So she named him Judah.ᵈᶻ Then she stopped having children.ᵃ

30 When Rachel saw that she was not bearing Jacob any children,ᵇ she became jealous of her sister.ᶜ So she said to Jacob, "Give me children, or I'll die!"

²Jacob became angry with her and said, "Am I in the place of God,ᵈ who has kept you from having children?"ᵉ

³Then she said, "Here is Bilhah,ᶠ my servant.ᵍ Sleep with her so that she can bear children for me and I too can build a family through her."ʰ

⁴So she gave him her servant Bilhah as a wife.ⁱ Jacob slept with her,ʲ ⁵and she became pregnant and bore him a son. ⁶Then Rachel said, "God has vindicated me;ᵏ he has listened to my plea and given me a son."ˡ Because of this she named him Dan.ᵉᵐ

⁷Rachel's servant Bilhahⁿ conceived again and bore Jacob a second son. ⁸Then Rachel said, "I have had a great struggle with my sister, and I have won."ᵒ So she named him Naphtali.ᶠᵖ

⁹When Leahq saw that she had stopped having children,ʳ she took her servant Zilpahˢ and gave her to Jacob as a wife.ᵗ ¹⁰Leah's servant Zilpahᵘ bore Jacob a son. ¹¹Then Leah said, "What good fortune!"ᵍ So she named him Gad.ʰ

¹²Leah's servant Zilpah bore Jacob a second son. ¹³Then Leah said, "How happy I am! The women will call meʷ happy."ˣ So she named him Asher.ⁱʸ

¹⁴During wheat harvest,ᶻ Reuben went out into the fields and found some mandrake plants,ᵃ which he brought to his mother Leah. Rachel said to Leah, "Please give me some of your son's mandrakes."

¹⁵But she said to her, "Wasn't it enoughᵇ that you took away my husband? Will you take my son's mandrakes too?"

"Very well," Rachel said, "he can sleep with you tonight in return for your son's mandrakes."ᶜ

¹⁶So when Jacob came in from the fields that evening, Leah went out to meet him. "You must sleep with me," she said. "I have hired you with my son's mandrakes."ᵈ So he slept with her that night.

¹⁷God listened to Leah,ᵉ and she became pregnant and bore Jacob a fifth son. ¹⁸Then

---

ᵃ 32 *Reuben* sounds like the Hebrew for *he has seen my misery;* the name means *see, a son.*
ᵇ 33 *Simeon* probably means *one who hears.*   ᶜ 34 *Levi* sounds like and may be derived from the Hebrew for *attached.*   ᵈ 35 *Judah* sounds like and may be derived from the Hebrew for *praise.*
ᵉ 6 *Dan* here means *he has vindicated.*   ᶠ 8 *Naphtali* means *my struggle.*   ᵍ 11 Or *"A troop is coming!"*
ʰ 11 *Gad* can mean *good fortune* or *a troop.*   ⁱ 13 *Asher* means *happy.*

30:13 Jos 19:24-31; 1Ch 7:30-31   **30:14** ᶻEx 34:22; Jdg 15:1; Ru 2:23; 1Sa 6:13; 12:17 ᵃver 15,16; SS 7:13   **30:15** ᵇNu 16:9,13; Isa 7:13; Eze 34:18 ᶜGe 38:16; Eze 16:33; Hos 9:1   **30:16** ᵈS ver 14   **30:17** ᵉS Ge 25:21

29:31 ᵠver 33; Dt 21:15-17
ʳS Ge 11:30; S 16:2; Ru 4:13; 1Sa 1:19; Ps 127:3
29:32 ˢGe 30:23; Ru 4:13; 1Sa 1:20
ᵗGe 37:21; 46:8; 48:5, 14; 49:3; Ex 6:14; Nu 1:5,20; 26:5; Dt 33:6; Jos 4:12; 1Ch 5:1,3 ᵘS Ge 16:11
29:33 ᵛS ver 31
ʷGe 34:25; 46:10; 48:5; 49:5; Ex 6:15; Nu 1:6,22; 34:20; 1Ch 4:24; Eze 48:24
29:34 ˣGe 30:20; 1Sa 1:2-4 ʸGe 34:25; 46:11; 49:5-7; Ex 2:1; 6:16,19; Nu 1:47; 3:17-20; 26:57; Dt 33:8; 1Ch 6:1,16; 23:6-24,13-14
29:35 ᶻGe 35:23; 37:26; 38:1; 43:8; 44:14,18; 46:12; 49:8; 1Ch 2:3; 4:1; Isa 48:1; Mt 1:2-3 ᵃGe 30:9
30:1 ᵇS Ge 11:30; Isa Ge 30:23; 54:1
ᶜS Ge 16:4; Lev 18:18
30:2 ᵈGe 50:19; Dt 32:35; 2Ki 5:7
ᵉS Ge 16:2
30:3 ᶠver 7; S Ge 29:29
ᵍS Ge 24:61 ʰGe 16:2
30:4 ⁱver 9,18; ʲGe 16:3-4
30:6 ᵏPs 35:24; 43:1
ˡver 23; Ge 21:2; Ru 4:13; 1Sa 1:20
ᵐGe 46:23; 49:16-17; Nu 26:42-43; Jos 19:40-48; Jdg 1:34; 13:2; 18:2; Jer 4:15; 8:16; Eze 48:1
30:7 ⁿS ver 3
30:8 ᵒGe 32:28; Hos 12:3-4
ᵖGe 35:25; 46:24; 49:21; Nu 1:42; 26:48; Dt 33:23; Jdg 4:6; 5:18; 1Ch 7:13
30:9 ᵠS Ge 29:16
ʳGe 29:35 ˢGe 29:24
ᵗS ver 4
30:10 ᵘGe 46:18
30:11 ᵛGe 35:26; 46:16; 49:19; Ex 1:4; Nu 1:24; 26:18; Jos 4:12; 1Ch 5:11; 12:8; Jer 49:1
30:13 ʷPs 127:3
ˣRu 4:14; Ps 127:4-5; Lk 1:48 ʸGe 35:26; 46:17; 49:20; Nu 1:40; 26:47; Dt 33:24;

29:31–35 Leah, though unloved, nevertheless became the mother of Jacob's first four sons, including Levi (ancestor of the Aaronic priestly line) and Judah (ancestor of David and his royal line, and ultimately of Jesus).
29:32 *named him Reuben ... because the LORD has seen my misery.* See TNIV text note. Ishmael had received his name in similar circumstances (see 16:11).
30:1 *she became jealous of her sister.* As Jacob was of his older brother. *Give me children, or I'll die!* Tragically prophetic words (see 35:16–19).
30:2 *Am I in the place of God ... ?* Jacob was forever trying to secure the blessing by his own efforts. Here he has to acknowledge that the blessing of offspring could come only from God (see 31:7–13 for the blessing of flocks). Joseph later echoed these words (see 50:19).
30:3 *Sleep with her.* See v. 9; see also 16:2 and note. *for me.* Lit.

"on my knees," apparently an expression symbolic of adoption (see 48:10–16) and meaning "as though my own" (see 50:23 and TNIV text note).
30:4 *as a wife.* As a concubine (see 35:22).
30:5–12 Jacob's fifth, sixth, seventh and eighth sons were born to him through his concubines.
30:14 *give me some of your son's mandrakes.* The mandrake has fleshy, forked roots that resemble the lower part of a human body and were therefore superstitiously thought to induce pregnancy when eaten (see SS 7:13). Rachel, like Jacob (vv. 37–43), tried to obtain what she wanted by magical means.
30:16 *hired.* The Hebrew for this word is a pun on the name Issachar (see TNIV text note on v. 18).
30:17–20 Jacob's ninth and tenth sons were born through Leah, who was thus the mother of half of Jacob's 12 sons (see note on 29:31–35).

30:18 /S ver 4
ᵍGe 46:13; 49:14;
Nu 1:8,28,29; 26:25;
Dt 27:12; 33:18;
Jos 17:10; 19:17; 21:6,
28; Jdg 5:15; 10:1;
1Ch 7:1
30:20 ʰS Ge 29:34;
1Pe 3:7 ⁱGe 35:23;
46:14; 49:13; Nu 1:30;
26:27; 34:25;
Dt 33:18; Jdg 5:18
30:21 ʲGe 34:1;
46:15
30:22 ᵏS Ge 25:21
ˡS Ge 25:21
ᵐS Ge 11:30
30:23 ⁿS ver 6;
S Ge 29:32 ᵒIsa 4:1;
25:8; 45:17; 54:4;
Lk 1:25
30:24 ᵖS Ge 29:6;
32:22; 33:2,7; 35:24;
37:2; 39:1; 49:22-26;
Dt 33:13 ᵠGe 35:17;
1Sa 4:20
30:25 ʳS Ge 24:54
ˢS Ge 28:15
30:26 ᵗS Ge 29:18
30:27 ᵘGe 33:10;
50:4; Est 2:15
ᵛGe 44:5,15;
Lev 19:26; Nu 22:7;
23:23; 24:1; Jos 13:22;
2Ki 17:17; Jer 27:9
ʷver 30; S Ge 26:24;
31:38; Dt 28:11;
2Sa 6:11
30:28 ˣS Ge 29:15
30:29 ʸGe 31:6
ᶻGe 31:38-40
30:30 ᵃS ver 27
ᵇ1Ti 5:8
30:32 ᶜver 33,35,
39,40; Ge 31:8,12
ᵈS Ge 29:15
30:33 ᵉS ver 32
ᶠGe 31:39
30:35 ᵍS ver 32
ʰGe 31:1
30:36 ⁱGe 31:22;
Ex 3:18; 5:3; 8:27
30:37 ʲJer 1:11
ᵏEze 31:8 ˡver 38,41
30:38 ᵐS ver 37
ⁿEx 2:16 ᵒver 41;
Jer 2:24
30:39 ᵖver 41
ᵠS ver 32
30:40 ʳS ver 32

Leah said, "God has rewarded me for giving my servant to my husband."ᶠ So she named him Issachar.ᵃ ᵍ

¹⁹Leah conceived again and bore Jacob a sixth son. ²⁰Then Leah said, "God has presented me with a precious gift. This time my husband will treat me with honor,ʰ because I have borne him six sons." So she named him Zebulun.ᵇ ⁱ

²¹Some time later she gave birth to a daughter and named her Dinah.ʲ

²²Then God remembered Rachel;ᵏ he listened to herˡ and enabled her to conceive.ᵐ ²³She became pregnant and gave birth to a sonⁿ and said, "God has taken away my disgrace."ᵒ ²⁴She named him Joseph,ᶜ ᵖ and said, "May the Lord add to me another son."ᵠ

JACOB'S FLOCKS INCREASE

²⁵After Rachel gave birth to Joseph, Jacob said to Laban, "Send me on my wayʳ so I can go back to my own homeland. ˢ ²⁶Give me my wives and children, for whom I have served you,ᵗ and I will be on my way. You know how much work I've done for you."

²⁷But Laban said to him, "If I have found favor in your eyes,ᵘ please stay. I have learned by divinationᵛ that the Lord has blessed me because of you."ʷ ²⁸He added, "Name your wages,ˣ and I will pay them."

²⁹Jacob said to him, "You know how I have worked for youʸ and how your livestock has fared under my care.ᶻ ³⁰The little you had before I came has increased greatly, and the Lord has blessed you wherever I have been.ᵃ But now, when may I do something for my own household?ᵇ"

³¹"What shall I give you?" he asked.

"Don't give me anything," Jacob replied. "But if you will do this one thing for me, I will go on tending your flocks and watching over them: ³²Let me go through all your flocks today and remove from them every speckled or spotted sheep, every dark-colored lamb and every spotted or speckled goat.ᶜ They will be my wages.ᵈ ³³And my honesty will testify for me in the future, whenever you check on the wages you have paid me. Any goat in my possession that is not speckled or spotted, or any lamb that is not dark-colored,ᵉ will be considered stolen.ᶠ"

³⁴"Agreed," said Laban. "Let it be as you have said." ³⁵That same day he removed all the male goats that were streaked or spotted, and all the speckled or spotted female goats (all that had white on them) and all the dark-colored lambs,ᵍ and he placed them in the care of his sons.ʰ ³⁶Then he put a three-day journeyⁱ between himself and Jacob, while Jacob continued to tend the rest of Laban's flocks.

³⁷Jacob, however, took fresh-cut branches from poplar, almondʲ and plane treesᵏ and made white stripes on them by peeling the bark and exposing the white inner wood of the branches.ˡ ³⁸Then he placed the peeled branchesᵐ in all the watering troughs,ⁿ so that they would be directly in front of the flocks when they came to drink. When the flocks were in heatᵒ and came to drink, ³⁹they mated in front of the branches.ᵖ And they bore young that were streaked or speckled or spotted.ᵠ ⁴⁰Jacob set apart the young of the flock by themselves, but made the rest face the streaked and dark-colored animalsʳ that be-

---

ᵃ 18 *Issachar* sounds like the Hebrew for *reward.* ᵇ 20 *Zebulun* probably means *honor.* ᶜ 24 *Joseph* means *may he add.*

30:20 *presented…gift.* The Hebrew terms for these words are puns on the name Zebulun (see TNIV text note).
30:21 *Dinah.* See ch. 34.
30:22 *God remembered Rachel.* See note on 8:1.
30:23 *disgrace.* Barrenness was considered to be shameful, a mark of divine disfavor (see 16:2; 30:2).
30:24 *May the Lord add to me another son.* The fulfillment of Rachel's wish would bring about her death (see 35:16–19).
30:26 *I will be on my way.* Jacob had fulfilled his commitments. With his accounts squared with Laban, he asked permission to leave, taking only his family with him. Later, he will take with him also much of Laban's wealth (see 30:43—31:1).
30:27 *divination.* The attempt to discover hidden knowledge through mechanical means (see 44:5), the interpretation of omens (see Eze 21:21) or the aid of supernatural powers (see Ac 16:16). It was strictly forbidden to Israel (Lev 19:26; Dt 18:10,14) because it reflected a pagan concept of the world controlled by evil forces, and therefore obviously not under the sovereign rule of the Lord. *the Lord has blessed me be-*

cause of you. As God had promised Jacob at Bethel (28:14) and in accordance with the promise made to Abraham (see 12:2–3 and note; 22:18; see also 39:5,23; 41:41–57).
30:32 Most commonly the sheep were all white and the goats all black. So Jacob chose to identify as his wages the sheep with dark markings and the goats with white markings—on the face of it a very modest request.
30:35 *he removed.* Secretly and without telling Jacob.
30:36 *the rest of Laban's flocks.* Now made up of only pure-white sheep and all-black goats.
30:37 *poplar…white.* The Hebrew terms for these words are puns on the name Laban. As Jacob had gotten the best of Esau (whose other name, Edom, means "red"; see note on 25:25) by means of red stew (25:30), so he now tries to get the best of Laban (whose name means "white") by means of white branches. In effect, Jacob was using Laban's own tactic (deception) against him.
30:39 The scheme worked—but only because of God's intervention (see Jacob's own admission in 31:9), not because of Jacob's superstition.

longed to Laban. Thus he made separate flocks for himself and did not put them with Laban's animals. 41Whenever the stronger females were in heat,ˢ Jacob would place the branches in the troughs in front of the animals so they would mate near the branches,ᵗ 42but if the animals were weak, he would not place them there. So the weak animals went to Laban and the strong ones to Jacob.ᵘ 43In this way the man grew exceedingly prosperous and came to own large flocks, and female and male servants, and camels and donkeys.ᵛ

JACOB FLEES FROM LABAN

31 Jacob heard that Laban's sonsʷ were saying, "Jacob has taken everything our father owned and has gained all this wealth from what belonged to our father."ˣ 2And Jacob noticed that Laban's attitude toward him was not what it had been.ʸ

3Then the Lord said to Jacob, "Go backᶻ to the land of your fathers and to your relatives, and I will be with you."ᵃ

4So Jacob sent word to Rachel and Leah to come out to the fields where his flocks were. 5He said to them, "I see that your father'sᵇ attitude toward me is not what it was before,ᶜ but the God of my father has been with me.ᵈ 6You know that I've worked for your father with all my strength,ᵉ 7yet your father has cheatedᶠ me by changing my wagesᵍ ten times.ʰ However, God has not allowed him to harm me.ⁱ 8If he said, 'The speckled ones will be your wages,' then all the flocks gave birth to speckled young; and if he said, 'The streaked ones will be your wages,'ʲ then all the flocks bore streaked young. 9So God has taken away your father's livestockᵏ and has given them to me.ˡ

10"In breeding season I once had a dreamᵐ in which I looked up and saw that the male goats mating with the flock were streaked, speckled or spotted. 11The angel of Godⁿ said to me in the dream,ᵒ 'Jacob.' I answered, 'Here I am.'ᵖ 12And he said, 'Look up and see that all the male goats mating with the flock are streaked, speckled or spotted,�q for I have seen all that Laban has been doing to you.ʳ 13I am the God of Bethel,ˢ where you anointed a pillarᵗ and where you made a vowᵘ to me. Now leave this land at once and go back to your native land.ᵛ '"

14Then Rachel and Leah replied, "Do we still have any shareʷ in the inheritance of our father's estate? 15Does he not regard us as foreigners?ˣ Not only has he sold us, but he has used up what was paid for us.ʸ 16Surely all the wealth that God took away from our father belongs to us and our children.ᶻ So do whatever God has told you."

17Then Jacob put his children and his wivesᵃ on camels,ᵇ 18and he drove all his livestock ahead of him, along with all the goods he had accumulatedᶜ in Paddan Aram,ᵃ ᵈ to go to his father Isaacᵉ in the land of Canaan.ᶠ

19When Laban had gone to shear his sheep,ᵍ Rachel stole her father's household gods.ʰ

ᵃ 18 That is, Northwest Mesopotamia

30:41 ˢ S ver 38
ᵗ S ver 37
30:42 ᵘ Ge 31:1,9, 16,43
30:43 ᵛ S Ge 12:16
31:1 ʷ Ge 30:35
ˣ S Ge 30:42
31:2 ʸ ver 5
31:3 ᶻ ver 13; Ge 32:9; Dt 30:3; Isa 10:21; 35:10; Jer 30:3; 42:12
ᵃ S Ge 21:22; S 26:3
31:5 ᵇ ver 29,42,53; Ge 43:23; Da 2:23
ᶜ ver 2 ᵈ S Ge 21:22; S 26:3
31:6 ᵉ Ge 30:29
31:7 ᶠ Lev 6:2; Am 8:5 ᵍ S Ge 29:15
ʰ ver 41; Nu 14:22; Job 19:3 ⁱ ver 52; S Ge 24:50
31:8 ʲ S Ge 30:32
31:9 ᵏ Job 39:2; Eze 31:6 ˡ S Ge 30:42
31:10 ᵐ S Ge 20:3
31:11 ⁿ S Ge 16:7
ᵒ S Ge 20:3
ᵖ S Ge 22:1; S Ex 3:4
31:12 q S Ge 30:32
ʳ Ex 3:7
31:13 ˢ Ge 28:10-22
ᵗ S Ge 28:18
ᵘ S Ge 28:20 ᵛ S ver 3
31:14 ʷ 2Sa 20:1; 1Ki 12:16
31:15 ˣ Dt 15:3; 23:20; Ru 2:10; 2Sa 15:19; 1Ki 8:41; Ob 1:11 ʸ S Ge 29:20
31:16 ᶻ S Ge 30:42
31:17 ᵃ S Ge 27:41
ᵇ S Ge 24:63-64
31:18 ᶜ S Ge 12:5
ᵈ S Ge 25:20
ᵉ Ge 35:27
ᶠ S Ge 10:19
31:19 ᵍ Ge 38:12,13; 1Sa 25:2,4,7;
2Sa 13:23 ʰ ver 30,32, 34-35; Ge 35:2; Jos 24:14; Jdg 17:5; 18:14,17,24,30; 1Sa 7:3; 19:13; 2Ki 23:24; Hos 3:4

C **30:43** *the man grew exceedingly prosperous.* Over a period of six years (see 31:41). While in Harran Jacob obtained both family and wealth. His wealth came at the expense of people in Northwest Mesopotamia, just as Abram's (12:16) and later Israel's (Ex 12:36), was obtained at the expense of the Egyptians (see also Isa 60:5–17 and note on 60:5; 61:6).

C **31:1–55** Jacob's flight from Laban has a number of parallels with Israel's later flight from Egypt: (1) God's blessing of Jacob aroused the hostility of Laban and his sons, just as God's blessing of Israel aroused the hostility of Egypt's pharaoh; (2) Jacob took with him the wealth he had obtained at Laban's expense, just as the Israelites took with them the wealth they had obtained at the expense of the Egyptians; (3) in his flight Jacob crossed the great Euphrates River, just as Israel in their flight crossed the Red Sea; (4) Laban went in force to pursue Jacob, just as Egypt's pharaoh pursued Israel in force; (5) God intervened to secure Jacob against Laban's designs to keep Jacob's household under his control, just as God intervened to secure Israel against the pharaoh's design to keep the Israelites under his control.

31:1 *has taken everything.* Since Laban's sons had been caring for flocks containing the spotted and speckled animals that Laban had sorted out, Jacob could potentially lay claim to a large proportion of the flocks under their care.

31:3 *Go back to the land of your fathers.* Every sign Jacob was getting—from his wives (see vv. 14–16), from Laban (see v. 2), from Laban's sons (see v. 1) and now from God himself—told him that it was time to return to Canaan. *I will be with you.* See note on 26:3.

C **31:4** *Rachel and Leah.* At long last (see v. 14) Rachel, the younger, has been given precedence over Leah—but she will soon become a deceiver like her husband Jacob (see vv. 31,35).

31:7 *ten times.* See v. 41. "Ten" here probably signifies completeness. In effect, Jacob accused Laban of cheating him at every turn.

31:9 See note on 30:39.

31:11 *angel of God.* See note on 16:7. *Here I am.* See note on 22:1.

31:13 *Bethel, where you anointed a pillar.* See note on 28:18.

31:15 *what was paid for us.* Jacob had come empty-handed to Paddan Aram and had offered his labors instead of wealth for his wives (cf. 24:10). So what had been "paid" for them was the fruit of Jacob's labors for their father (30:27,30).

31:18 *Paddan Aram.* See note on 25:20; see also map, p. 57.

B C **31:19** *household gods.* Small portable idols, which Rachel probably stole because she thought they would bring her protection and blessing. Or perhaps she wanted to have something tangible to worship on the long journey ahead, a practice referred to much later in the writings of Josephus, a 1st-century A.D. Jewish historian. In any case, Rachel was not yet free of her pagan background (see 35:2; Jos 24:2).

31:20 ^{i} S Ge 27:36
^{j} S Ge 25:20 ^{k} ver 27
31:21 ^{l} ver 22;
Ex 2:15; 14:5;
1Ki 18:46; 19:3;
Jer 26:21 ^{m} S Ge 2:14
^{n} ver 23, 25; Ge 37:25;
Nu 26:30; 32:1;
Dt 3:10; Jos 12:2;
Jer 22:6
31:22 ^{o} S Ge 30:36
^{p} S ver 21
31:23 ^{q} ver 37
^{r} Ex 14:9 ^{s} S ver 21
31:24 ^{t} S Ge 25:20
^{u} S Ge 20:3
^{v} S Ge 24:50
31:25 ^{w} S ver 21
31:26 ^{x} S Ge 12:18
^{y} S Ge 27:36
^{z} Ge 34:29;
1Sa 30:2-3
31:27 ^{a} ver 20
^{b} Ex 15:20; Jdg 11:34;
1Sa 10:5; 2Sa 6:5;
Ps 68:25; Isa 24:8;
Jer 31:4 ^{c} S Ge 4:21
31:28 ^{d} ver 55;
S Ge 27:27; Ru 1:14;
Ac 20:37
31:29 ^{e} S ver 7;
S Ge 26:29 ^{f} S ver 5
^{g} S Ge 24:50
31:30 ^{h} S Ge 28:15;
Job 29:2 ^{i} Ge 44:8
^{j} S ver 19
31:31 ^{k} S Ge 20:11
31:32 ^{l} Ge 44:9
^{m} S ver 19
31:33 ^{n} Ge 24:67
^{o} S Ge 16:1 ^{p} ver 37
31:34 ^{q} S ver 19
^{r} S Ge 24:63-64
^{s} ver 37; Ge 44:12
31:35 ^{t} Ge 18:12;
Lev 19:3,32; Dt 21:18;
27:16; Jer 35:18
^{u} Lev 15:19-23 ^{v} ver 19
31:36 ^{w} 1Sa 19:5;
20:32 ^{x} 1Sa 23:23;
24:11
31:37 ^{y} ver 33
^{z} ver 23 ^{a} Dt 1:16; 16:18
31:38 ^{b} S Ge 27:44
^{c} S Ge 30:27
31:39 ^{d} Ge 30:33
^{e} Ex 22:13
31:40 ^{f} Ps 132:4;
2Co 11:27
31:41 ^{g} S Ge 27:44
^{h} Ge 29:30
^{i} S Ge 30:32
^{j} S Ge 29:15 ^{k} S ver 7
31:42 ^{l} S ver 5;
S Ex 3:15
^{m} S Ge 24:12 ^{n} ver 53;
Ge 46:1 ^{o} S Ge 21:22;
Ps 124:1-2 ^{p} S Ge 3:17
^{q} S Ge 24:50
31:43 ^{r} Ge 30:32, 42
31:44 ^{s} S Ge 21:27
^{t} S Ge 21:30
31:45 ^{u} S Ge 28:18

^{20}Moreover, Jacob deceived ^{i} Laban the Aramean^j by not telling him he was running away. ^{k} ^{21}So he fled ^{l} with all he had, crossed the Euphrates River, ^{m} and headed for the hill country of Gilead. ^{n}

LABAN PURSUES JACOB

^{22}On the third day^o Laban was told that Jacob had fled. ^{p} ^{23}Taking his relatives ^{q} with him^r, he pursued Jacob for seven days and caught up with him in the hill country of Gilead. ^{s} ^{24}Then God came to Laban the Aramean^t in a dream at night and said to him, ^{u} "Be careful not to say anything to Jacob, either good or bad." ^{v}

^{25}Jacob had pitched his tent in the hill country of Gilead ^{w} when Laban overtook him, and Laban and his relatives camped there too. ^{26}Then Laban said to Jacob, "What have you done? ^{x} You've deceived me, ^{y} and you've carried off my daughters like captives in war. ^{z} ^{27}Why did you run off secretly and deceive me? Why didn't you tell me, ^{a} so I could send you away with joy and singing to the music of timbrels ^{b} and harps? ^{c} ^{28}You didn't even let me kiss my grandchildren and my daughters good-by. ^{d} You have done a foolish thing. ^{29}I have the power to harm you; ^{e} but last night the God of your father^f said to me, 'Be careful not to say anything to Jacob, either good or bad.' ^{g} ^{30}Now you have gone off because you longed to return to your father's household. ^{h} But why did you steal ^{i} my gods? ^{j}"

^{31}Jacob answered Laban, "I was afraid, because I thought you would take your daughters away from me by force. ^{k} ^{32}But if you find anyone who has your gods, that one shall not live. ^{l} In the presence of our relatives, see for yourself whether there is anything of yours here with me; and if so, take it." Now Jacob did not know that Rachel had stolen the gods. ^{m}

^{33}So Laban went into Jacob's tent and into Leah's tent ^{n} and into the tent of the two female servants, ^{o} but he found nothing. ^{p} After he came out of Leah's tent, he entered Rachel's tent. ^{34}Now Rachel had taken the household gods ^{q} and put them inside her camel's saddle ^{r} and was sitting on them. Laban searched ^{s} through everything in the tent but found nothing.

^{35}Rachel said to her father, "Don't be angry, my lord, that I cannot stand up in your presence; ^{t} I'm having my period. ^{u}" So he searched but could not find the household gods. ^{v}

^{36}Jacob was angry and took Laban to task. "What is my crime?" he asked Laban. "How have I wronged ^{w} you that you hunt me down? ^{x} ^{37}Now that you have searched through all my goods, what have you found that belongs to your household? ^{y} Put it here in front of your relatives ^{z} and mine, and let them judge between the two of us. ^{a}

^{38}"I have been with you for twenty years now. ^{b} Your sheep and goats have not miscarried, ^{c} nor have I eaten rams from your flocks. ^{39}I did not bring you animals torn by wild beasts; I bore the loss myself. And you demanded payment from me for whatever was stolen ^{d} by day or night. ^{e} ^{40}This was my situation: The heat consumed me in the daytime and the cold at night, and sleep fled from my eyes. ^{f} ^{41}It was like this for the twenty years ^{g} I was in your household. I worked for you fourteen years for your two daughters ^{h} and six years for your flocks, ^{i} and you changed my wages^j ten times. ^{k} ^{42}If the God of my father, ^{l} the God of Abraham ^{m} and the Fear of Isaac, ^{n} had not been with me, ^{o} you would surely have sent me away empty-handed. But God has seen my hardship and the toil of my hands, ^{p} and last night he rebuked you. ^{q}"

^{43}Laban answered Jacob, "The women are my daughters, the children are my children, and the flocks are my flocks. ^{r} All you see is mine. Yet what can I do today about these daughters of mine, or about the children they have borne? ^{44}Come now, let's make a covenant, ^{s} you and I, and let it serve as a witness between us." ^{t}

^{45}So Jacob took a stone and set it up as a pillar. ^{u} ^{46}He said to his relatives, "Gather

---

31:21 *So he fled.* As he had fled earlier from Esau (27:42–43). Jacob's devious dealings produced only hostility from which he had to flee. *Gilead.* An area of exceptionally good grazing land southeast of the Sea of Galilee (see Nu 32:1 and note).

31:24 *not to say anything … good or bad.* Do not enter into a dispute with him; or do not press any claim against him (see also v. 29; cf. 24:50).

A C **31:26** *deceived.* Jacob's character, reflected in his name (see TNIV text notes on 25:26; 27:36), is emphasized in the narrative again and again.

31:27 *harps.* Much smaller, and with fewer strings (usually 6 to 12), than their modern counterparts.

31:32 *if you find anyone who has your gods, that one shall not*

live. Cf. 44:7–12. Though he made the offer in all innocence, Jacob almost lost his beloved Rachel. He had now been deceived even by his wife.

31:34 *inside her camel's saddle … sitting on them.* Indicating the small size and powerlessness of the household gods.

31:35 *I'm having my period.* In later times, anything a menstruating woman sat on was considered ritually unclean (Lev 15:20).

31:39 *I bore the loss.* Ancient laws (as in Ex 22:13) held that a shepherd did not have to compensate for losses to wild animals.

31:42 *Fear.* Here a surrogate for God. Or perhaps the Hebrew for this word means "Kinsman," stressing the intimacy of God's relationship to the patriarch.

31:44 See vv. 48,52; see also 21:30 and note.

some stones." So they took stones and piled them in a heap,ᵛ and they ate there by the heap. ⁴⁷Laban called it Jegar Sahadutha, and Jacob called it Galeed.ᵃ ʷ

⁴⁸Laban said, "This heapˣ is a witness between you and me today."ʸ That is why it was called Galeed. ⁴⁹It was also called Mizpah,ᵇ ᶻ because he said, "May the LORD keep watch between you and me when we are away from each other. ⁵⁰If you mistreatᵃ my daughters or if you take any wives besides my daughters, even though no one is with us, remember that God is a witnessᵇ between you and me."ᶜ

⁵¹Laban also said to Jacob, "Here is this heap,ᵈ and here is this pillarᵉ I have set up between you and me. ⁵²This heap is a witness, and this pillar is a witness,ᶠ that I will not go past this heap to your side to harm you and that you will not go past this heapᵍ and pillar to my side to harm me.ʰ ⁵³May the God of Abrahamⁱ and the God of Nahor,ʲ the God of their father, judge between us."ᵏ

So Jacob took an oathˡ in the name of the Fear of his father Isaac.ᵐ ⁵⁴He offered a sac-

ᵃ 47 The Aramaic *Jegar Sahadutha* and the Hebrew *Galeed* both mean *witness heap.*   ᵇ 49 *Mizpah* means *watchtower.*

31:46 *ate.* See note on 26:30.
31:48 For the naming of an altar under similar circumstances see Jos 22:10–12,34.
31:49 *May…other.* The so-called Mizpah benediction, which in context is in fact a denunciation or curse.
31:51 *heap…pillar…between you and me.* Boundary markers between Laban's territory and Jacob's territory. Galeed, Jacob's

name for the heap, is a pun on Gilead (see v. 47 and TNIV text note).
31:53 *God of their father.* Or possibly "gods of their father [i.e., Terah]," reflecting Laban's polytheistic background (see Jos 24:2). *Fear of his father Isaac.* See note on v. 42. Jacob had met the "God of Isaac" (28:13) at Bethel 20 years earlier.

31:46 ᵛ ver 48,51,52
31:47 ʷ S Ge 21:30
31:48 ˣ S ver 46
ʸ S Ge 21:30;
Jer 29:23; 42:5
31:49 ᶻ Jos 11:3;
Jdg 10:17; 11:29
31:50 ᵃ Ge 16:6
ᵇ Dt 31:19; Jos 24:27;
Jdg 11:10; 1Sa 12:5;
20:14,23,42;
Job 16:19; Jer 29:23;
42:5; Mic 1:2
ᶜ S Ge 21:30;
S Dt 4:26; S Jer 7:11
31:51 ᵈ S ver 46
ᵉ S Ge 28:18
31:52 ᶠ S Ge 21:30
ᵍ S ver 46 ʰ S ver 7;
S Ge 26:29
31:53 ⁱ S Ge 24:12
ʲ S Ge 11:27
ᵏ S Ge 16:5
ˡ S Ge 21:23,27
ᵐ S ver 42

JACOB'S JOURNEYS

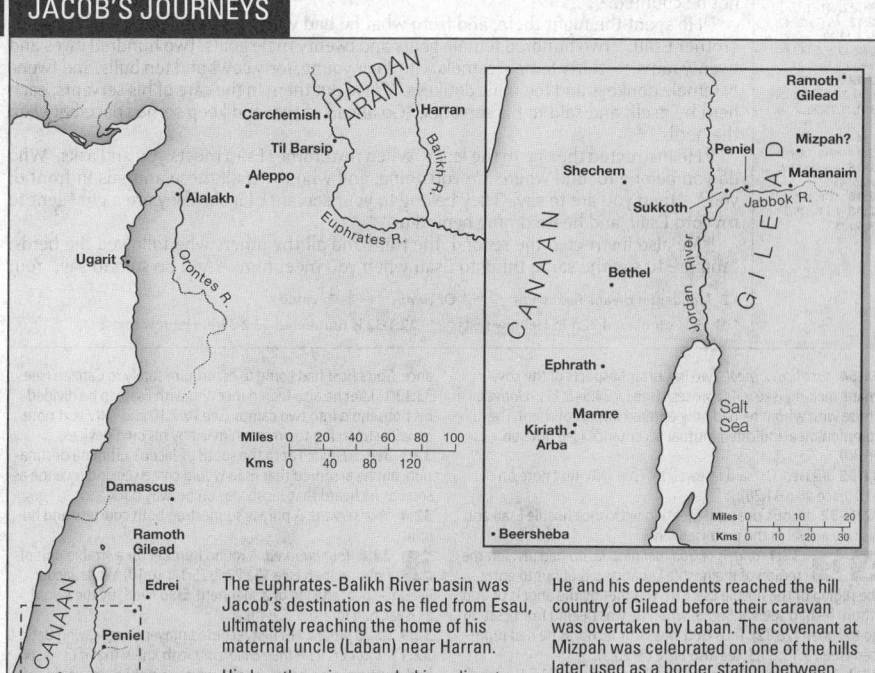

The Euphrates-Balikh River basin was Jacob's destination as he fled from Esau, ultimately reaching the home of his maternal uncle (Laban) near Harran.

His lengthy sojourn ended in a dispute with Laban and another flight—this time back to Canaan. His route likely took him toward Aleppo, then to Damascus and Edrei before reaching Peniel on the Jabbok River.

He and his dependents reached the hill country of Gilead before their caravan was overtaken by Laban. The covenant at Mizpah was celebrated on one of the hills later used as a border station between Aramean and Israelite territories.

Jacob tarried at Sukkoth, entered Canaan and proceeded to Shechem, where he erected an altar to the Lord.

31:54 *n* Ge 46:1;
Ex 24:5; Lev 3:1
o S Ge 26:30
31:55 *p* S ver 28;
Ru 1:9 *q* S Ge 24:60;
S Ex 39:43 *r* Ge 18:33
32:1 *s* S Ge 16:11;
2Ki 6:16-17;
1Ch 21:15; Ps 34:7;
35:5; 91:11; Da 6:22
32:2 *t* S Ge 28:17
u Jos 13:26,30; 21:38;
2Sa 2:8,29; 17:24;
19:32; 1Ki 2:8; 4:14;
1Ch 6:80
32:3 *v* Nu 21:21;
Jdg 11:17
w S Ge 27:41-42
x S Ge 14:6;
S Nu 24:18
y S Ge 25:30; S 36:16
32:4 *z* S Ge 24:9
a S Ge 18:3 *b* Ge 31:41
32:5 *c* S Ge 12:16
d S Ge 24:9 *e* Ge 33:8,
10,15; 34:11; 47:25,
29; 50:4; Ru 2:13
32:6 *f* Ge 33:1
32:7 *g* ver 11
h Ge 35:3; Ps 4:1;
77:2; 107:6 *i* ver 10;
Ge 33:1
32:9 *j* S Ge 24:12
k S Ge 28:13
l S Ge 26:3; 31:13
32:10 *m* S Ge 24:27
n Ge 38:18; 47:31;
Nu 17:2 *o* S ver 7
32:11 *p* S ver 7
q Ge 43:18; Ps 59:2
r S Ge 27:41
32:12 *s* S Ge 22:17;
1Ki 4:20,29
t S Ge 12:2; S 13:14;
Hos 1:10; Ro 9:27
32:13 *u* ver 13-15,
18, 20, 21; Ge 33:10;
43:11,15,25,26;
1Sa 16:20; Pr 18:16;
21:14
32:14 *v* Nu 7:88
32:15 *w* S Ge 13:2;
42:26; 45:23
32:16 *x* Ge 33:8
32:18 *y* S Ge 18:3
z S ver 13

rifice *n* there in the hill country and invited his relatives to a meal. *o* After they had eaten, they spent the night there.

*55*Early the next morning Laban kissed his grandchildren and his daughters *p* and blessed *q* them. Then he left and returned home. *r*

JACOB PREPARES TO MEET ESAU

32 *1*Jacob also went on his way, and the angels of God *s* met him. *2*When Jacob saw them, he said, "This is the camp of God!" *t* So he named that place Mahanaim. *a u*

*3*Jacob sent messengers *v* ahead of him to his brother Esau *w* in the land of Seir, *x* the country of Edom. *y* *4*He instructed them: "This is what you are to say to my lord *z* Esau: 'Your servant *a* Jacob says, I have been staying with Laban *b* and have remained there till now. *5*I have cattle and donkeys, sheep and goats, male and female servants. *c* Now I am sending this message to my lord, *d* that I may find favor in your eyes.' *e* '"

*6*When the messengers returned to Jacob, they said, "We went to your brother Esau, and now he is coming to meet you, and four hundred men are with him." *f*

*7*In great fear *g* and distress *h* Jacob divided the people who were with him into two groups, *b i* and the flocks and herds and camels as well. *8*He thought, "If Esau comes and attacks one group, *c* the group *c* that is left may escape."

*9*Then Jacob prayed, "O God of my father Abraham, *j* God of my father Isaac, *k* LORD, you who said to me, 'Go back to your country and your relatives, and I will make you prosper,' *l* *10*I am unworthy of all the kindness and faithfulness *m* you have shown your servant. I had only my staff *n* when I crossed this Jordan, but now I have become two camps. *o* *11*Save me, I pray, from the hand of my brother Esau, for I am afraid *p* he will come and attack me, *q* and also the mothers with their children. *r* *12*But you have said, 'I will surely make you prosper and will make your descendants like the sand *s* of the sea, which cannot be counted.' *t* '"

*13*He spent the night there, and from what he had with him he selected a gift *u* for his brother Esau: *14*two hundred female goats and twenty male goats, two hundred ewes and twenty rams, *v* *15*thirty female camels with their young, forty cows and ten bulls, and twenty female donkeys and ten male donkeys. *w* *16*He put them in the care of his servants, each herd by itself, and said to his servants, "Go ahead of me, and keep some space between the herds." *x*

*17*He instructed the one in the lead: "When my brother Esau meets you and asks, 'Who do you belong to, and where are you going, and who owns all these animals in front of you?' *18*then you are to say, 'They belong to your servant *y* Jacob. They are a gift *z* sent to my lord Esau, and he is coming behind us.' '"

*19*He also instructed the second, the third and all the others who followed the herds: "You are to say the same thing to Esau when you meet him. *20*And be sure to say, 'Your

---

a 2 *Mahanaim* means *two camps.*   *b* 7 Or *camps*   *c* 8 Or *camp*

* 31:55 is numbered 32:1 in Hebrew texts.   * 32:1-32 is numbered 32:2-33 in Hebrew texts.

31:54 *sacrifice … meal.* Two important aspects of the covenant-making (see v. 44) process (see Ex 24:5–8,11). *relatives.* Those with whom he had now entered into a covenant. The common meal indicated mutual acceptance (see note on 26:30).

31:55 *blessed.* Or "said farewell to" (see TNIV text note on 47:10; see also 31:28).

32:1–32 Jacob's peaceful meeting with once hostile Esau and his safe arrival in the promised land.

A C **32:1** *angels of God met him.* Jacob had just left the region of the hostile Laban and is about to enter the region of the hostile Esau. He was met by the angels of God, whom he had seen at Bethel when he was fleeing from Esau to go to Laban (28:12). Thus God was with Jacob, as he had promised (see 28:15; 31:3; see also note on 26:3).

32:2 *Mahanaim.* Located in Gilead (see note on 31:21) east of the Jordan and north of the Jabbok (see note on v. 22). Two camps (see TNIV text note) had just met in hostility and separated in peace. Two camps were again about to meet (in hostility, Jacob thought) and separate in peace. But Jacob called this crucial place "two camps" after seeing the angelic encampment, suggesting that he saw God's encampment as a divine assur-

ance. God's host had come to escort him safely to Canaan (see 33:12,15). Yet he also feared meeting with Esau, so he divided his household into two camps (see vv. 7,10 and TNIV text note on v. 7), still trying to protect himself by his own devices.

32:3 *Seir … Edom.* Far to the south of Jacob's ultimate destination, but he assumed that Esau would come seeking revenge as soon as he heard that Jacob was on his way back.

32:4 *Your servant.* A phrase suggesting both courtesy and humility.

C **32:6** *four hundred.* A round number for a sizable unit of fighting men (see 1Sa 22:2; 25:13; 30:10). While Jacob lived the peaceful life of a shepherd, Esau lived "by the sword," as Isaac had foretold (27:40).

32:9 *Jacob prayed.* His first recorded prayer since leaving Bethel.

32:11 *mothers with their children.* Jacob knew that if Esau still had revenge in his heart, Jacob's wives and children would suffer with him.

32:12 *your descendants like the sand of the sea.* A reference to God's promise in 28:14 (see 22:17 and note).

32:13 *gift.* Probably a wordplay: Out of his "two camps" (Hebrew *mahanayim,* v. 2; see vv. 7–8,10) Jacob selects a "gift" (*minhah*) for his brother.

servant [a] Jacob is coming behind us.' " For he thought, "I will pacify him with these gifts [b] I am sending on ahead; [c] later, when I see him, perhaps he will receive me." [d] 21So Jacob's gifts [e] went on ahead of him, but he himself spent the night in the camp.

JACOB WRESTLES WITH GOD

22That night Jacob got up and took his two wives, his two female servants and his eleven sons [f] and crossed the ford of the Jabbok. [g] 23After he had sent them across the stream, he sent over all his possessions. [h] 24So Jacob was left alone, [i] and a man [j] wrestled with him till daybreak. 25When the man saw that he could not overpower him, he touched the socket of Jacob's hip [k] so that his hip was wrenched as he wrestled with the man. 26Then the man said, "Let me go, for it is daybreak."

But Jacob replied, "I will not let you go unless you bless me." [l]

27The man asked him, "What is your name?"

"Jacob," [m] he answered.

28Then the man said, "Your name [n] will no longer be Jacob, but Israel, [a] [o] because you have struggled with God and with human beings and have overcome." [p]

29Jacob said, "Please tell me your name." [q]

But he replied, "Why do you ask my name?" [r] Then he blessed [s] him there.

30So Jacob called the place Peniel, [b] saying, "It is because I saw God face to face, [t] and yet my life was spared."

31The sun rose above him as he passed Peniel, [c] [u] and he was limping because of his hip. 32Therefore to this day the Israelites do not eat the tendon attached to the socket of the hip, [v] because the socket of Jacob's hip was touched near the tendon.

JACOB MEETS ESAU

33 Jacob looked up and there was Esau, coming with his four hundred men; [w] so he divided the children among Leah, Rachel and the two female servants. [x] 2He put the female servants and their children [y] in front, Leah and her children next, and Rachel and Joseph [z] in the rear. 3He himself went on ahead and bowed down to the ground [a] seven times [b] as he approached his brother.

4But Esau [c] ran to meet Jacob and embraced him; he threw his arms around his neck and kissed him. [d] And they wept. [e] 5Then Esau looked up and saw the women and children. "Who are these with you?" he asked.

Jacob answered, "They are the children God has graciously given your servant. [f]"

6Then the female servants and their children [g] approached and bowed down. [h] 7Next, Leah and her children [i] came and bowed down. [j] Last of all came Joseph and Rachel, [k] and they too bowed down.

---

[a] 28 *Israel* probably means *he struggles with God.*   [b] 30 *Peniel* means *face of God.*   [c] 31 Hebrew *Penuel*, a variant of *Peniel*

32:20 [a] S Ge 18:3
[b] S ver 13; 1Sa 9:7;
2Ki 8:8; Jer 40:5
[c] 1Sa 25:19
[d] Ge 33:10; Ex 28:38;
Lev 1:4; Mal 1:8
32:21 [e] S ver 13
32:22 [f] S Ge 30:24
[g] Nu 21:24; Dt 2:37;
3:16; Jos 12:2
32:23 [h] S Ge 26:14
32:24 [i] Da 10:8
[j] S Ge 18:2
32:25 [k] ver 32
32:26 [l] Hos 12:4
32:27 [m] S Ge 25:26
32:28 [n] Isa 1:26;
56:5; 60:14; 62:2,4,
12; 65:15 [o] S Ge 17:5
[p] S Ge 30:8
32:29 [q] Ex 3:13; 6:3;
Jdg 13:17 [r] Jdg 13:18
[s] Ge 25:11; 35:9; 48:3
32:30 [t] S Ge 16:13;
1Co 13:12
32:31 [u] Jdg 8:9
32:32 [v] ver 25
33:1 [w] S Ge 32:6
[x] S Ge 32:7
33:2 [y] ver 6
[z] S Ge 30:24
33:3 [a] ver 6,7;
S Ge 17:3; 37:7·10;
42:6; 43:26; 44:14;
48:12; 1Sa 20:41
[b] 2Ki 5:10,14
33:4 [c] S Ge 27:41-
42 [d] S Ge 29:11;
Lk 15:20 [e] S Ge 27:27
33:5 [f] S Ge 18:3;
Ge 48:9; Ps 127:3;
Isa 8:18
33:6 [g] ver 2
[h] S ver 3
33:7 [i] ver 2 [j] S ver 3
[k] S Ge 30:24

32:22 *Jabbok.* Today called the Wadi Zerqa, flowing westward into the Jordan about 20 miles north of the Dead Sea.

A C   **32:24** *left alone.* As he had been at Bethel (28:10–22). *a man.* God himself (as Jacob eventually realized; see v. 30) in the form of an angel (see Hos 12:3–4 and note on Ge 16:7). *wrestled.* God wrestled (*ye'abeq*) with Jacob (*ya'aqob*) by the Jabbok (*yabboq*)—the author delighted in wordplay. Jacob had struggled all his life to prevail, first with Esau, then with Laban. Now, as he was about to reenter Canaan, he was shown that it was with God that he must "wrestle"—not with Esau or any other human being.

32:25 *could not overpower him … touched the socket.* God came to him in such a form that Jacob could wrestle with him successfully, yet he showed Jacob that he could disable him at will.

A C   **32:26** *I will not let you go.* Jacob's persistence was soon rewarded (v. 29). *unless you bless me.* Jacob finally acknowledged that the blessing must come from God.

A C   **32:28** *Your name will no longer be Jacob.* Now that Jacob had acknowledged God as the source of blessing and was about to reenter the promised land, the Lord acknowledged Jacob as his servant by changing his name (see 17:5 and note). *Israel.* See TNIV text note. Here in Jacob/Israel, the nation of Israel got its name and characterization: the people who struggle with God (memorialized in the name Israel)

and with human beings (memorialized in the name Jacob) and overcome. God later confirmed Jacob's new name (35:10).

32:29 *Why do you ask my name?* Such a request of God is both unworthy and impossible to fulfill (see Jdg 13:17–18).

32:30 *I saw God face to face.* See note on 16:13; see also Jdg 6:22–23; 13:22. Only God's "back" (Ex 33:23) or "feet" (Ex 24:10) or "form" (Nu 12:8), in a symbolic sense, may be seen with impunity. *yet my life was spared.* If Jacob's life was spared in his encounter with God, his prayer for his life to be spared in his encounter with Esau (v. 11) will surely be granted.

32:31 *The sun rose above him.* A new day dawns in Jacob's life (see Ps 5:3 and note).

32:32 *do not eat the tendon.* Probably the sciatic muscle. Mentioned nowhere else in the Bible, this dietary prohibition is found in the later writings of Judaism. Jacob retained in his body, and Israel retained in her dietary practice, a perpetual reminder of this fateful encounter with God.

33:2 *Rachel and Joseph in the rear.* Jacob wanted to keep his favorite wife and child farthest away from potential harm.

B   **33:3** *bowed down to the ground seven times.* A sign of total submission, documented also in texts found at Tell el-Amarna in Egypt and dating to the 14th century B.C. (see chart, p. xxiii).

C   **33:4** *All Jacob's fears proved unfounded.* God had been at work and had so blessed Esau (v. 9) that he no longer held a grudge against Jacob.

33:8 /Ge 32:14-16
m S Ge 24:9; S 32:5
33:9 n ver 11;
S Ge 13:6
33:10 o S Ge 30:27;
S 32:5 p S Ge 32:13
q S Ge 16:13
r S Ge 32:20
33:11 s ISa 25:27;
30:26 t Ge 30:43
u S ver 9 v Ge 19:3
33:13 w ver 8
x Isa 40:11; Jer 31:8
33:14 y Ex 12:38
z S Ge 14:6
33:15 o S Ge 32:5
33:16 b S Ge 14:6
33:17 c Jos 13:27;
Jdg 8:5,6,8,14-16;
1Ki 7:46; 2Ch 4:17;
Ps 60:6; 108:7
33:18 d S Ge 25:20
e S Ge 12:6
33:19 f Ge 34:2;
Jdg 9:28; Ac 7:16
g Ge 34:2; Jos 24:32
h Ge 34:10,16,21;
47:27; Jn 4:5
i S Ge 12:8
33:20 j S Ge 4:26;
S 8:20
34:1 k S Ge 30:21
34:2 l S Ge 33:19
m S Ge 33:19
n S Ge 10:17
o Dt 21:14; 2Sa 13:14
34:3 p ver 26
q ver 19 r S Ge 24:67
s Ge 50:21; Isa 14:1;
40:2
34:4 t S Ge 21:21
34:5 u ver 2,13,27;
Ge 35:22; 49:4;
Dt 27:20; 33:6;
1Ch 5:1
34:6 v Jdg 14:2-5
34:7 w 1Co 5:2
x Ge 39:19; 49:6-7;
2Sa 12:5; 13:21;
Est 7:7; Pr 6:34
y Dt 22:21; Jdg 19:23;
20:6; 2Sa 13:12;
Jer 29:23 z S Ge 20:9
34:8 a S Ge 21:21;
Dt 21:11

[8]Esau asked, "What do you mean by all these flocks and herds I met?" [l]

"To find favor in your eyes, my lord," [m] he said.

[9]But Esau said, "I already have plenty, [n] my brother. Keep what you have for yourself."

[10]"No, please!" said Jacob. "If I have found favor in your eyes, [o] accept this gift [p] from me. For to see your face is like seeing the face of God, [q] now that you have received me favorably. [r] [11]Please accept the present [s] that was brought to you, for God has been gracious to me [t] and I have all I need." [u] And because Jacob insisted, [v] Esau accepted it.

[12]Then Esau said, "Let us be on our way; I'll accompany you."

[13]But Jacob said to him, "My lord [w] knows that the children are tender and that I must care for the ewes and cows that are nursing their young. [x] If they are driven hard just one day, all the animals will die. [14]So let my lord go on ahead of his servant, while I move along slowly at the pace of the flocks and herds [y] before me and the pace of the children, until I come to my lord in Seir. [z]"

[15]Esau said, "Then let me leave some of my men with you."

"But why do that?" Jacob asked. "Just let me find favor in the eyes of my lord." [a]

[16]So that day Esau started on his way back to Seir. [b] [17]Jacob, however, went to Sukkoth, [c] where he built a place for himself and made shelters for his livestock. That is why the place is called Sukkoth. [a]

[18]After Jacob came from Paddan Aram, [b] [d] he arrived safely at the [c] city of Shechem [e] in Canaan and camped within sight of the city. [19]For a hundred pieces of silver, [d] he bought from the sons of Hamor, [f] the father of Shechem, [g] the plot of ground [h] where he pitched his tent. [i] [20]There he set up an altar [j] and called it El Elohe Israel. [e]

DINAH AND THE SHECHEMITES

34 Now Dinah, [k] the daughter Leah had borne to Jacob, went out to visit the women of the land. [2]When Shechem [l] son of Hamor [m] the Hivite, [n] the ruler of that area, saw her, he took her and raped her. [o] [3]His heart was drawn to Dinah [p] daughter of Jacob; [q] he loved [r] the young woman and spoke tenderly [s] to her. [4]And Shechem said to his father Hamor, "Get me this young woman as my wife." [t]

[5]When Jacob heard that his daughter Dinah had been defiled, [u] his sons were in the fields with his livestock; so he did nothing about it until they came home.

[6]Then Shechem's father Hamor went out to talk with Jacob. [v] [7]Meanwhile, Jacob's sons had come in from the fields as soon as they heard what had happened. They were shocked [w] and furious, [x] because Shechem had done an outrageous thing in [f] Israel [y] by sleeping with Jacob's daughter—a thing that should not be done. [z]

[8]But Hamor said to them, "My son Shechem has his heart set on your daughter. Please give her to him as his wife. [a] [9]Intermarry with us; give us your daughters and take our

---

a 17 *Sukkoth* means *shelters*.   b 18 That is, Northwest Mesopotamia   c 18 Or *arrived at Shalem, a*
d 19 Hebrew *hundred kesitahs*; a kesitah was a unit of money of unknown weight and value.   e 20 *El Elohe Israel* can mean *El is the God of Israel* or *mighty is the God of Israel*.   f 7 Or *against*

C **33:9** *I already have plenty.* Esau had obtained his "plenty" while residing in "the land of Seir" (32:3; cf. 33:16) south of the promised land, just as Jacob had obtained his bounties in Paddan Aram north of the promised land. *my brother.* Esau's response was in contrast to Jacob's cautious and fearful "my lord" (v. 8).

C **33:11** *present.* The Hebrew for "present" is the same as that used for "blessing" in 27:35. The author of Genesis was conscious of the irony that Jacob now acknowledged that the blessing he had struggled for was from God. In his last attempt to express reconciliation with Esau, Jacob in a sense gave back the "blessing" he had stolen from his brother, doing so from the blessings the Lord had given him.

C **33:12** *I'll accompany you.* Resulting in another "two camps" (see 32:2 and note). Esau's proposal suggests that he had come with his 400 men to escort Jacob's vulnerable company safely home (see v. 15). Jacob declines the offer because he trusts the protection of God more than he trusts Esau and his men.

33:14 *until I come to my lord in Seir.* But Jacob, still the deceiver, had no intention of following Esau all the way to Seir.

33:18 *Paddan Aram.* See note on 25:20. *arrived safely.* The answer to Jacob's prayer 20 years earlier (see 28:21). *Shechem.* See note on 12:6. Jacob followed in the footsteps of Abraham (see 12:6). Jacob dug a well there (see Jn 4:5–6) that can still be seen today.

33:19 *pieces of silver.* See TNIV text note. The Hebrew word translated by this phrase is found only three times and always in patriarchal contexts (see Jos 24:32; Job 42:11).

33:20 *set up an altar.* See note on 12:7. *called it El Elohe Israel.* See TNIV text note. Jacob formally acknowledged the God of his ancestors as his God also (see 28:21). But he lingered at Shechem and did not return to Bethel (see 35:1), and that meant trouble (see ch. 34).

A C **34:1–31** Jacob is now confronted in the promised land with the danger of being absorbed by the native Canaanites (vv. 9,16) and then with the threat of their hostility after his sons' vengeful acts (v. 30). These were dangers the Israelites constantly faced from the peoples around them—either absorption or hostility, both of which are perpetual threats to God's people. The name of God ends ch. 33 and begins ch. 35 but is completely absent from this sordid chapter (see note on 7:16).

34:2 *Shechem.* See 33:19. He was probably named after the city.

34:4 *Get me this young woman as my wife.* See note on 21:21.

34:7 *Israel.* The clan of Israel. *a thing that should not be done.* Cf. Tamar's plea to Amnon in a similar situation (2Sa 13:12).

A **34:9** *Intermarry with us.* The Canaanites wanted to benefit from the blessings Jacob had received from the Lord (both his offspring and his possessions—vv. 21–23).

daughters for yourselves. *b* 10You can settle among us; *c* the land is open to you. *d* Live in it, trade*a* in it, *e* and acquire property in it. *f*"

11Then Shechem said to Dinah's father and brothers, "Let me find favor in your eyes, *g* and I will give you whatever you ask. 12Make the price for the bride *h* and the gift I am to bring as great as you like, and I'll pay whatever you ask me. Only give me the young woman as my wife."

13Because their sister Dinah had been defiled, *i* Jacob's sons replied deceitfully*j* as they spoke to Shechem and his father Hamor. 14They said to them, "We can't do such a thing; we can't give our sister to a man who is not circumcised. *k* That would be a disgrace to us. 15We will enter into an agreement with you on one condition *l* only: that you become like us by circumcising all your males. *m* 16Then we will give you our daughters and take your daughters for ourselves. *n* We'll settle among you and become one people with you. *o* 17But if you will not agree to be circumcised, we'll take our sister and go."

18Their proposal seemed good to Hamor and his son Shechem. 19The young man, who was the most honored*p* of all his father's family, lost no time in doing what they said, because he was delighted with Jacob's daughter. *q* 20So Hamor and his son Shechem went to the gate of their city*r* to speak to the men of their city. 21"These men are friendly toward us," they said. "Let them live in our land and trade in it; *s* the land has plenty of room for them. We can marry their daughters and they can marry ours. *t* 22But the men will agree to live with us as one people only on the condition that our males be circumcised, *u* as they themselves are. 23Won't their livestock, their property and all their other animals become ours? *v* So let us agree to their terms, and they will settle among us. *w*"

24All the men who went out of the city gate*x* agreed with Hamor and his son Shechem, and every male in the city was circumcised.

25Three days later, while all of them were still in pain, *y* two of Jacob's sons, Simeon*z* and Levi, *a* Dinah's brothers, took their swords *b* and attacked the unsuspecting city, *c* killing every male. *d* 26They put Hamor and his son Shechem to the sword *e* and took Dinah*f* from Shechem's house and left. 27The sons of Jacob came upon the dead bodies and looted the city*g* where*b* their sister had been defiled. *h* 28They seized their flocks and herds and donkeys *i* and everything else of theirs in the city and out in the fields. *j* 29They carried off all their wealth and all their women and children, *k* taking as plunder *l* everything in the houses. *m*

30Then Jacob said to Simeon and Levi, "You have brought trouble *n* on me by making me obnoxious *o* to the Canaanites and Perizzites, the people living in this land. *p* We are few in number, *q* and if they join forces against me and attack me, I and my household will be destroyed."

31But they replied, "Should he have treated our sister like a prostitute? *r*"

JACOB RETURNS TO BETHEL

35 Then God said to Jacob, "Go up to Bethel *s* and settle there, and build an altar*t* there to God, *u* who appeared to you *v* when you were fleeing from your brother Esau." *w*

2So Jacob said to his household*x* and to all who were with him, "Get rid of the foreign gods*y* you have with you, and purify yourselves and change your clothes. *z* 3Then come, let us go up to Bethel, where I will build an altar to God, *a* who answered me in the day of my distress *b* and who has been with me wherever I have gone. *c*" 4So they gave Jacob all

---

a 10 Or *move about freely*; also in verse 21   *b* 27 Or *because*

34:12 *price for the bride.* For a specific example of this marriage custom, see 24:53 and note.

34:13 *Jacob's sons replied deceitfully.* Like father, like son (see 27:24; see also note on 25:26).

34:15 Using a sacred ceremony for a sinful purpose (see vv. 24–25).

34:20 *gate of their city.* See notes on 19:1; 23:10.

34:23 The greed of the men of Shechem led to their destruction.

34:24 The Canaanites were even willing to submit to Israel's covenant rite in order to attain their purposes.

34:25 *Simeon and Levi.* Because they slaughtered the men of Shechem, their own descendants would be scattered far and wide (see note on 49:7).*Dinah's brothers.* All three children were of Leah (29:33–34; 30:21).*killing every male.* Shechem's crime,

serious as it was, hardly warranted such brutal and extensive retaliation (see vv. 27–29). Jacob's sons ran ahead of God's judgment on the Canaanites (see 15:16 and note).

34:30 *Perizzites.* See note on 13:7.

35:1–15 Whereas Abram's arrival at Shechem marked the end of his journey to Canaan—it was there that God promised to give the land to his offspring (12:6–7)—the final stage of Jacob's journey back was from Shechem to Bethel, where Jacob's pilgrimage with God had begun (28:10–22).

35:1 *God…appeared to you when you were fleeing.* See v. 7; 28:13.

35:2 *foreign gods you have with you.* See note on 31:19 (see also Jos 24:23).

35:3 *God…who has been with me.* See 28:15; see also note on 26:3.

34:9 *b* ver 16, 21; Dt 7:3; Jos 23:12
34:10 *c* ver 23; Ge 46:34; 47:6, 27
d S Ge 13:9
e Ge 42:34
f S Ge 33:19
34:11 *g* S Ge 32:5
34:12 *h* Ex 22:16; Dt 22:29; 1Sa 18:25
34:13 *i* S ver 5
j S Ge 27:36
34:14 *k* Ge 17:14; Jdg 14:3; 1Sa 31:4; Isa 52:1
34:15 *l* 1Sa 11:2
m ver 22; Ex 12:48
34:16 *n* S ver 9
o S Ge 33:19
34:19 *p* Ge 49:3; 1Ch 11:21 *q* ver 3
34:20 *r* S Ge 18:1
34:21 *s* S Ge 33:19
t S ver 9
34:22 *u* S ver 15
34:23 *v* ver 28; S Ge 12:16 *w* S ver 10
34:24 *x* S Ge 18:1
34:25 *y* Jos 5:8
z S Ge 29:33
a S Ge 29:34
b Ge 49:5; Mal 2:16
c Jdg 18:7, 10, 27; Eze 38:11 *d* Ge 49:7
34:26 *e* S ver 7; Ge 48:22 *f* ver 3
34:27 *g* 2Ki 21:14
h S ver 5
34:28 *i* Ge 43:18
j S ver 23
34:29 *k* S Ge 31:26
l Nu 14:3; 31:9, 53; Dt 2:35; Jos 7:21
m 2Ki 8:12; Isa 13:16; La 5:11; Am 1:13; Zec 14:2
34:30 *n* Ge 43:6; Ex 5:23; Nu 11:11
o Ex 5:21; 6:9; 1Sa 13:4; 27:12; 2Sa 10:6; 1Ch 19:6
p S Ge 13:7 *q* Ge 35:26; 46:27; Ex 1:5; Dt 10:22; 26:5; 1Ch 16:19; Ps 105:12
34:31 *r* ver 2
35:1 *s* S Ge 12:8
t S Ge 4:26; 8:20
u ver 3 *v* S Ge 12:7
w ver 7; Ge 27:43
35:2 *x* Ge 18:19; Jos 24:15
y S Ge 31:19; S Jos 24:14 *z* Ex 19:10, 14; Nu 8:7, 21; 19:19
35:3 *a* ver 1
b S Ge 32:7; S Jdg 2:15 *c* S Ge 26:3

35:4 *d* S Ge 24:22;
Ex 32:3; 35:22;
Jdg 8:24; Pr 25:12
e ver 8 *f* S Ge 12:6
35:5 *g* Ex 15:16;
23:27; Dt 2:25;
Jos 2:9; 1Sa 7:10;
13:7; 14:15; 2Ch 14:14;
17:10; 20:29; Ps 9:20;
Isa 19:17; Zec 14:13
h Ps 105:14
35:6 *i* S Ge 28:19
j S Ge 10:19
35:7 *k* S Ge 8:20
l Ge 28:19
m S Ge 28:13 *n* S ver 1
35:8 *o* Ge 24:59
p ver 4 *q* S Ge 12:8;
1Sa 10:3
35:9 *r* S Ge 25:20
s S Ge 28:13; S 32:29
35:10 *t* S Ge 17:5
35:11 *u* S Ge 17:1
v S Ge 12:2
w S Ge 12:2
x S Ge 17:6
35:12 *y* S Ge 28:13
z S Ge 12:7; S 15:7
35:13 *a* S Ge 17:22
35:14 *b* S Ge 28:22
c Ex 29:40; Lev 23:13;
Nu 6:15,17; 15:5;
28:7,14; 2Sa 23:16;
2Ch 29:35
d S Ge 28:18
35:15 *e* S Ge 12:8
35:16 *f* ver 19;
Ge 48:7; Ru 2:4; 4:11;
1Sa 17:12; Mic 5:2
g S Ge 29:6
35:17 *h* Ge 38:28;
Ex 1:15 *i* S Ge 30:24
35:18 *j* 1Sa 4:21;
14:3 *k* ver 24;
Ge 42:4; 43:16,29;
45:12,14; 49:27;
Nu 1:36; Dt 33:12
35:19 *l* S ver 16
m Ge 48:7; Jos 19:15;
Jdg 12:8; 17:7; 19:1,18;
Ru 1:1,19; 1Sa 17:12;
Mic 5:2
35:20 *n* Jos 4:9;
7:26; 8:28; 10:27;
1Sa 6:18 *o* 1Sa 10:2

the foreign gods they had and the rings in their ears, *d* and Jacob buried them under the oak *e* at Shechem. *f* 5 Then they set out, and the terror of God *g* fell on the towns all around them so that no one pursued them. *h*

6 Jacob and all the people with him came to Luz *i* (that is, Bethel) in the land of Canaan. *j* 7 There he built an altar, *k* and he called the place El Bethel, *a l* because it was there that God revealed himself to him *m* when he was fleeing from his brother. *n*

8 Now Deborah, Rebekah's nurse, *o* died and was buried under the oak *p* below Bethel. *q* So it was named Allon Bakuth. *b*

9 After Jacob returned from Paddan Aram, *c r* God appeared to him again and blessed him. *s* 10 God said to him, "Your name is Jacob, *d* but you will no longer be called Jacob; your name will be Israel. *e*" *t* So he named him Israel.

11 And God said to him, "I am God Almighty *f*; *u* be fruitful and increase in number. *v* A nation *w* and a community of nations will come from you, and kings will come from your body. *x* 12 The land I gave to Abraham and Isaac I also give to you, and I will give this land to your descendants after you. *y*" *z* 13 Then God went up from him *a* at the place where he had talked with him.

14 Jacob set up a stone pillar *b* at the place where God had talked with him, and he poured out a drink offering *c* on it; he also poured oil on it. *d* 15 Jacob called the place where God had talked with him Bethel. *g e*

THE DEATHS OF RACHEL AND ISAAC

35:23–26pp — 1Ch 2:1–2

16 Then they moved on from Bethel. While they were still some distance from Ephrath, *f* Rachel *g* began to give birth and had great difficulty. 17 And as she was having great difficulty in childbirth, the midwife *h* said to her, "Don't despair, for you have another son." *i* 18 As she breathed her last—for she was dying—she named her son Ben-Oni. *h j* But his father named him Benjamin. *i k*

19 So Rachel died and was buried on the way to Ephrath *l* (that is, Bethlehem *m*). 20 Over her tomb Jacob set up a pillar, and to this day *n* that pillar marks Rachel's tomb. *o*

21 Israel moved on again and pitched his tent beyond Migdal Eder. *p* 22 While Israel was living in that region, Reuben went in and slept with his father's concubine *q* Bilhah, *r* and Israel heard of it.

a 7 El Bethel means God of Bethel. *b 8 Allon Bakuth means oak of weeping.* *c 9 That is, Northwest Mesopotamia; also in verse 26* *d 10 Jacob means he grasps the heel, a Hebrew idiom for he deceives.* *e 10 Israel probably means he struggles with God.* *f 11 Hebrew El-Shaddai* *g 15 Bethel means house of God.* *h 18 Ben-Oni means son of my trouble.* *i 18 Benjamin means son of my right hand.*

35:21 *p* Jos 15:21 **35:22** *q* S Ge 22:24 *r* S Ge 29:29; S 34:5; S Lev 18:8

35:4 *rings.* Worn as amulets or charms; a pagan religious custom (cf. Hos 2:13). *oak at Shechem.* Obviously a well-known tree, perhaps the "great tree" mentioned in 12:6 (see Jos 24:26).
35:5 *terror of God.* God protected his servant.
35:7 *built an altar.* See note on 12:7.
35:8 *Deborah, Rebekah's nurse, died.* After long years of faithful service (see 24:59). *the oak.* Again probably a well-known tree (see note on v. 4), perhaps the "great tree" mentioned in 1Sa 10:3. *below.* Either "lower than" or "to the south of."
35:9 *Jacob returned.* See map, p. 57. *Paddan Aram.* See note on 25:20.
35:10 *Jacob . . . Israel.* The previous assignment of an additional name (see 32:28) is here confirmed. For similar examples compare 21:31 with 26:33 and 28:19 with 35:15.

35:11–12 This event climaxes the Isaac-Jacob cycle (see Introduction: Literary Features). Now that Jacob was at last back at Bethel, where God had begun his direct relationship with him, God confirmed to this chosen son of Isaac the covenant promises made to Abraham (17:1–8; see 28:3). His words echo his original benediction pronounced on humankind in the beginning (1:28) and renewed after the flood (9:1,7). God's blessing on the human race would be fulfilled in and through Jacob and his offspring. See also 47:27; Ex 1:7.
35:11 God identifies himself to Jacob here as "God Almighty" (El-Shaddai). At Bethel he had identified himself as "the God of your father Abraham and the God of Isaac" (28:13), but that was also as El-Shaddai (see 17:1 and note; see also 28:3; 48:3; Ex 6:3).

35:13 See note on 17:22.
35:14 See 28:18 and note. *drink offering.* A liquid poured out as a sacrifice to a deity.
35:15 See 28:19; see also note on v. 10.
35:16–29 The conclusion to the main story of Jacob's life.
35:16 *Ephrath.* The older name for Bethlehem (see v. 19) in Judah; it apparently refers to the area in which Bethlehem was located (see Ru 1:2; Mic 5:2 and notes).
35:17 *another son.* An echo of Rachel's own plea at the time of Joseph's birth (see 30:24).
35:18 *Benjamin.* See TNIV text note. The name can also mean "son of the south"—in distinction from the other sons, who were born in the north. One set of Hebrew terms for indicating direction was based on facing east, so south was on the right.

35:19 *Rachel died.* In childbirth (see note on 30:1).
35:20 *Rachel's tomb.* See 1Sa 10:2. The traditional, though not authentic, site is near Bethlehem.
35:21 *Migdal Eder.* Means "tower of the flock," doubtless referring to a watchtower built to discourage thieves from stealing sheep and other animals (see, e.g., 2Ch 26:10). The same Hebrew phrase is used figuratively in Mic 4:8, where "flock" refers to the people of Judah (see Mic 4:6–7).

35:22 Reuben's act was an arrogant and premature claim to the rights of the firstborn (see 2Sa 3:7; 12:8; 16:21; 1Ki 2:22 and notes). For this he would lose his legal status as firstborn (see 49:3–4; 1Ch 5:1; see also note on Ge 37:21).

Jacob had twelve sons:
²³ The sons of Leah:^s
Reuben the firstborn^t of Jacob,
Simeon, Levi, Judah,^u Issachar and Zebulun.^v
²⁴ The sons of Rachel:
Joseph^w and Benjamin.^x
²⁵ The sons of Rachel's servant Bilhah:^y
Dan and Naphtali.^z
²⁶ The sons of Leah's servant Zilpah:^a
Gad^b and Asher.^c
These were the sons of Jacob,^d who were born to him in Paddan Aram.^e

²⁷Jacob came home to his father Isaac^f in Mamre,^g near Kiriath Arba^h (that is, Hebron),ⁱ where Abraham and Isaac had stayed.^j ²⁸Isaac lived a hundred and eighty years.^k ²⁹Then he breathed his last and died and was gathered to his people,^l old and full of years.^m And his sons Esau and Jacob buried him.ⁿ

ESAU'S DESCENDANTS
36:10–14pp — 1Ch 1:35–37
36:20–28pp — 1Ch 1:38–42

36

¹This is the account^o of the family line of Esau (that is, Edom).^p

²Esau took his wives from the women of Canaan:^q Adah daughter of Elon the Hittite,^r and Oholibamah^s daughter of Anah^t and granddaughter of Zibeon the Hivite^u— ³also Basemath^v daughter of Ishmael and sister of Nebaioth.^w

⁴Adah bore Eliphaz to Esau, Basemath bore Reuel,^x ⁵and Oholibamah bore Jeush, Jalam and Korah.^y These were the sons of Esau, who were born to him in Canaan.

⁶Esau took his wives and sons and daughters and all the members of his household, as well as his livestock and all his other animals and all the goods he had acquired in Canaan,^z and moved to a land some distance from his brother Jacob.^a ⁷Their possessions were too great for them to remain together; the land where they were staying could not support them both because of their livestock.^b ⁸So Esau^c (that is, Edom)^d settled in the hill country of Seir.^e

⁹This is the account^f of the family line of Esau the father of the Edomites^g in the hill country of Seir.

¹⁰ These are the names of Esau's sons:
Eliphaz, the son of Esau's wife Adah, and Reuel, the son of Esau's wife Basemath.^h
¹¹ The sons of Eliphaz:ⁱ
Teman,^j Omar, Zepho, Gatam and Kenaz.^k
¹² Esau's son Eliphaz also had a concubine^l named Timna, who bore him Amalek.^m These were grandsons of Esau's wife Adah.ⁿ
¹³ The sons of Reuel:
Nahath, Zerah, Shammah and Mizzah. These were grandsons of Esau's wife Basemath.^o
¹⁴ The sons of Esau's wife Oholibamah^p daughter of Anah and granddaughter of Zibeon, whom she bore to Esau:
Jeush, Jalam and Korah.^q

35:23 ^sS Ge 29:16
^tGe 43:33; 46:8
^uS Ge 29:35
^vS Ge 30:20
35:24 ^wS Ge 30:24
^xS ver 18
35:25 ^yGe 37:2
^zS Ge 30:8
35:26 ^aGe 37:2
^bS Ge 30:11
^cS Ge 30:13
^dS Ge 34:30; 46:8;
Ex 1:1-4 ^eS Ge 25:20
35:27 ^fGe 31:18
^gS Ge 13:18
^hGe 23:2; Jos 15:54;
Jdg 1:10; Ne 11:25
ⁱS Ge 13:18
35:28 ^kS Ge 25:7,
20
35:29 ^lS Ge 25:8
^mS Ge 15:15
ⁿS Ge 23:20; S 25:9
36:1 ^oS Ge 2:4
^pS Ge 25:30
36:2 ^qGe 28:8-9
^rGe 26:34 ^sver 14,18
^tver 25; 1Ch 1:40
^uver 24; S Ge 10:17;
1Ch 1:40
36:3 ^vver 4,10,13,
17 ^wS Ge 25:13
36:4 ^xS ver 3;
1Ch 1:35
36:5 ^yver 14,18;
1Ch 1:35
36:6 ^zGe 12:5
^aGe 27:39
36:7 ^bS Ge 13:6
36:8 ^cDt 2:4
^dS Ge 25:30
^eS Ge 14:6
36:9 ^fS Ge 2:4
^gver 1,43
36:10 ^hS ver 3
36:11 ⁱver 15-16;
1Ch 1:45; Job 2:11; 4:1
^jJer 49:7,20;
Eze 25:13; Am 1:12;
Ob 1:9; Hab 3:3
^kver 15
36:12 ^lS Ge 22:24
^mEx 17:8,16;
Nu 24:20; Dt 25:17,
19; 1Sa 15:2; 27:8
ⁿver 16
36:13 ^oS ver 3
36:14 ^pS ver 2
^qS ver 5

35:26 *sons of Jacob … born to him in Paddan Aram.* Obviously a summary statement since Benjamin was born in Canaan (see vv. 16–18).
35:27 *Mamre, near Kiriath Arba (that is, Hebron).* See notes on 13:18; 23:2.
35:29 See note on 25:8. *buried him.* In the family tomb, the cave of Machpelah (49:30–31).
36:1–43 A concise account of Esau's descendants, who also belonged to the "many nations" promised to Abraham and Sarah (17:5–6,16), before the more full-blown account of Jacob's descendants (see notes on 37:2—50:26 and 37:2). Cf. the account of Ishmael's offspring in 25:12–18.
36:1 *account.* See note on 2:4. Though repeated in v. 9, the word does not mark the start of a new main section there since the information in vv. 9–43 is merely an expansion of that in vv. 1–8. *Esau (that is, Edom).* See 25:30 and TNIV text note there. Reddish

rock formations, primarily sandstone, are conspicuous in the territory of the Edomites, located south and southeast of the Dead Sea.
36:2–3 See note on 26:34.
36:7 See 13:6; 26:20 and notes.
36:8 *Seir.* Another name for Edom. The word itself is related to the Hebrew word meaning "hair," a possible meaning also for the name "Esau" (see TNIV text note on 25:25). Esau's clan must have driven away the original Horite (see v. 20) inhabitants of Seir (see 14:6 and note). The descendants of Seir are listed in vv. 20–28.
36:10–14 The same list of Esau's descendants (see 1Ch 1:35–37) is repeated in vv. 15–19 as a list of tribal chieftains.
36:11 *Eliphaz: Teman.* One of Job's friends was named Eliphaz the Temanite (Job 2:11), and Job himself was from the land of Uz (Job 1:1). Thus Job probably lived in Edom (see vv. 28,34).
36:12 *Amalek.* See note on 14:7.

36:15 ʳ ver 19, 40;
Ex 15:15 ˢ Job 2:11;
Jer 49:7; Eze 25:13;
Am 1:12; Hab 3:3
ᵗ S ver 11
36:16 ᵘ S ver 11
ᵛ Ge 32:3; Ex 15:15;
Nu 20:14; 33:37
ʷ ver 12
36:17 ˣ 1Ch 1:37
ʸ S ver 3
36:18 ᶻ S ver 2
ᵃ S ver 5
36:19 ᵇ 1Ch 1:35
ᶜ S Ge 25:30
ᵈ S ver 15
36:20 ᵉ S Ge 14:6
ᶠ ver 29
36:21 ᵍ ver 30
36:24 ʰ S ver 2
ⁱ Ge 15:19 ʲ Job 1:14
36:25 ᵏ S ver 2
ˡ S ver 2
36:29 ᵐ ver 20
36:30 ⁿ ver 21
36:31 ᵒ S Ge 17:6
36:33 ᵖ Isa 34:6;
63:1; Jer 49:13,22
36:34 ᵠ Jer 49:7;
Eze 25:13; Ob 1:9
36:35 ʳ S Ge 25:2
ˢ S Ge 19:37;
Nu 21:11; 22:1; Dt 1:5;
Jdg 3:30; Ru 1:1,6
36:37 ᵗ Ge 26:22
36:40 ᵘ S ver 15

¹⁵These were the chiefs ʳ among Esau's descendants:

The sons of Eliphaz the firstborn of Esau:

Chiefs Teman, ˢ Omar, Zepho, Kenaz, ᵗ ¹⁶Korah, ᵃ Gatam and Amalek. These were the chiefs descended from Eliphaz ᵘ in Edom; ᵛ they were grandsons of Adah. ʷ

¹⁷ The sons of Esau's son Reuel: ˣ

Chiefs Nahath, Zerah, Shammah and Mizzah. These were the chiefs descended from Reuel in Edom; they were grandsons of Esau's wife Basemath. ʸ

¹⁸ The sons of Esau's wife Oholibamah: ᶻ

Chiefs Jeush, Jalam and Korah. ᵃ These were the chiefs descended from Esau's wife Oholibamah daughter of Anah.

¹⁹These were the sons of Esau ᵇ (that is, Edom), ᶜ and these were their chiefs. ᵈ

²⁰These were the sons of Seir the Horite, ᵉ who were living in the region:

Lotan, Shobal, Zibeon, Anah, ᶠ ²¹Dishon, Ezer and Dishan. These sons of Seir in Edom were Horite chiefs. ᵍ

²² The sons of Lotan:

Hori and Homam. ᵇ Timna was Lotan's sister.

²³ The sons of Shobal:

Alvan, Manahath, Ebal, Shepho and Onam.

²⁴ The sons of Zibeon: ʰ

Aiah and Anah. This is the Anah who discovered the hot springs ᶜ ⁱ in the desert while he was grazing the donkeys ʲ of his father Zibeon.

²⁵ The children of Anah: ᵏ

Dishon and Oholibamah ˡ daughter of Anah.

²⁶ The sons of Dishon ᵈ:

Hemdan, Eshban, Ithran and Keran.

²⁷ The sons of Ezer:

Bilhan, Zaavan and Akan.

²⁸ The sons of Dishan:

Uz and Aran.

²⁹ These were the Horite chiefs:

Lotan, Shobal, Zibeon, Anah, ᵐ ³⁰Dishon, Ezer and Dishan. These were the Horite chiefs, ⁿ according to their divisions, in the land of Seir.

THE RULERS OF EDOM

36:31–43pp — 1Ch 1:43–54

³¹These were the kings who reigned in Edom before any Israelite king ᵒ reigned:

³²Bela son of Beor became king of Edom. His city was named Dinhabah.

³³When Bela died, Jobab son of Zerah from Bozrah ᵖ succeeded him as king.

³⁴When Jobab died, Husham from the land of the Temanites ᵠ succeeded him as king.

³⁵When Husham died, Hadad son of Bedad, who defeated Midian ʳ in the country of Moab, ˢ succeeded him as king. His city was named Avith.

³⁶When Hadad died, Samlah from Masrekah succeeded him as king.

³⁷When Samlah died, Shaul from Rehoboth ᵗ on the river succeeded him as king.

³⁸When Shaul died, Baal-Hanan son of Akbor succeeded him as king.

³⁹When Baal-Hanan son of Akbor died, Hadad ᵉ succeeded him as king. His city was named Pau, and his wife's name was Mehetabel daughter of Matred, the daughter of Me-Zahab.

⁴⁰These were the chiefs ᵘ descended from Esau, by name, according to their clans and regions:

Timna, Alvah, Jetheth, ⁴¹Oholibamah, Elah, Pinon, ⁴²Kenaz, Teman, Mibzar, ⁴³Magdiel and Iram. These were the chiefs of Edom, according to their settlements in the land they occupied.

ᵃ 16 Masoretic Text; Samaritan Pentateuch (see also Gen. 36:11 and 1 Chron. 1:36) does not have *Korah.*
ᵇ 22 Hebrew *Hemam,* a variant of *Homam* (see 1 Chron. 1:39)   ᶜ 24 Vulgate; Syriac *discovered water;* the meaning of the Hebrew for this word is uncertain.   ᵈ 26 Hebrew *Dishan,* a variant of *Dishon*
ᵉ 39 Many manuscripts of the Masoretic Text, Samaritan Pentateuch and Syriac (see also 1 Chron. 1:50); most manuscripts of the Masoretic Text *Hadar*

36:20–28 See note on v. 8. The same list of Seir's descendants (see 1Ch 1:38–42) is repeated in abbreviated form in vv. 29–30 as a list of tribal chieftains.
36:30 *divisions.* Tribal divisions (cf. Jos 11:23).
36:31 *before any Israelite king reigned.* Appears to presuppose the Israelite monarchy and thus to be a later editorial updating (see note on 14:14).
36:43 *This…Edomites.* A summary statement for the whole chapter (just as v. 1 is a title for the whole chapter).

This was Esau the father of the Edomites. *v*

JOSEPH'S DREAMS

37 Jacob lived in the land where his father had stayed, *w* the land of Canaan. *x*

²This is the account *y* of Jacob's family line.

Joseph, *z* a young man of seventeen, *a* was tending the flocks *b* with his brothers, the sons of Bilhah *c* and the sons of Zilpah, *d* his father's wives, and he brought their father a bad report *e* about them.

³Now Israel *f* loved Joseph more than any of his other sons, *g* because he had been born to him in his old age; *h* and he made a richly ornamented *a* robe *i* for him. *j* ⁴When his brothers saw that their father loved him more than any of them, they hated him *k* and could not speak a kind word to him.

⁵Joseph had a dream, *l* and when he told it to his brothers, *m* they hated him all the more. *n* ⁶He said to them, "Listen to this dream I had: ⁷We were binding sheaves *o* of grain out in the field when suddenly my sheaf rose and stood upright, while your sheaves gathered around mine and bowed down to it." *p*

⁸His brothers said to him, "Do you intend to reign over us? Will you actually rule us?" *q* And they hated him all the more *r* because of his dream and what he had said.

⁹Then he had another dream, *s* and he told it to his brothers. "Listen," he said, "I had another dream, and this time the sun and moon and eleven stars *t* were bowing down to me." *u*

¹⁰When he told his father as well as his brothers, *v* his father rebuked *w* him and said, "What is this dream you had? Will your mother and I and your brothers actually come and bow down to the ground before you?" *x* ¹¹His brothers were jealous of him, *y* but his father kept the matter in mind. *z*

JOSEPH SOLD BY HIS BROTHERS

¹²Now his brothers had gone to graze their father's flocks near Shechem, *a* ¹³and Israel *b* said to Joseph, "As you know, your brothers are grazing the flocks near Shechem. *c* Come, I am going to send you to them."

"Very well," he replied.

¹⁴So he said to him, "Go and see if all is well with your brothers *d* and with the flocks, and bring word back to me." Then he sent him off from the Valley of Hebron. *e*

When Joseph arrived at Shechem, ¹⁵a man found him wandering around in the fields and asked him, "What are you looking for?"

¹⁶He replied, "I'm looking for my brothers. Can you tell me where they are grazing their flocks?"

---

a 3 The meaning of the Hebrew for *richly ornamented* is uncertain; also in verses 23 and 32.

36:43 *v* S ver 9
37:1 *w* S Ge 17:8
x S Ge 10:19
37:2 *y* S Ge 2:4
z S Ge 30:24
a Ge 41:46; 2Sa 5:4
b Ge 46:32; 1Sa 16:11;
17:15; Ps 78:71;
Am 7:15 *c* Ge 35:25
d Ge 35:26 *e* 1Sa 2:24
37:3 *f* S Ge 17:5
g S Ge 25:28
h Ge 43:27; 44:20
i ver 23, 31, 32;
2Sa 13:18-19
j Ge 43:34; 45:22;
1Sa 1:4-5; Est 2:9
37:4 *k* S ver 24;
S Ge 27:41; Ac 7:9
37:5 *l* S Ge 20:3;
S 28:12 *m* ver 10
n ver 8
37:7 *o* Ru 2:7,15
p ver 9, 10; Ge 27:29;
42:6, 9; 43:26, 28;
44:14; 50:18; 2Sa 1:2;
9:6
37:8 *q* Ge 41:44;
42:10; 44:16,18;
48:22; 49:26;
Dt 33:16 *r* ver 5
37:9 *s* S ver 7;
Ge 28:12 *t* Rev 12:1
u Dt 4:19; 17:3
37:10 *v* ver 5
w Ru 2:16; Ps 9:5;
68:30; 106:9; 119:21;
Isa 17:13; 54:9;
Zec 3:2 *x* S ver 7;
S Ge 9:25; S 33:3
37:11 *y* Ge 26:14;
Ac 7:9 *z* Lk 2:19, 51
37:12 *a* S Ge 12:6
37:13 *b* S Ge 17:5
c Ge 33:19
37:14 *d* 1Sa 17:18
e S Ge 13:18

37:1 *Canaan.* Jacob made the promised land his homeland and was later buried there (49:29–30; 50:13). His son Joseph also insisted on being buried in Canaan, which he recognized as the land the Lord had promised to Israel (50:24–25).
37:2—50:26 The Jacob-Joseph cycle (see Introduction: Literary Features). It focuses mainly on Jacob's sons and how they embodied for both good and ill the family line of Abraham, Isaac and Jacob, which God had chosen to be the channel of his saving acts in history.

37:2 *account.* See note on 2:4. The word here introduces the tenth and final main section of Genesis. *Joseph.* The author immediately introduces Joseph, on whom the last cycle of the patriarchal narrative centers. In his generation he, more than any other, represented Israel—as a people who struggled with both God and human beings and overcame (see 32:28 and note) and as a source of blessing to the nations (see 12:2–3). It is, moreover, through the life of Joseph that the covenant family in Canaan becomes an emerging nation in Egypt, thus setting the stage for the exodus. The story of God's dealings with the patriarchs foreshadows the subsequent Biblical account of God's purpose with Israel. It begins with the election and calling out of Abram from the post-Babel nations and ends with Israel in Egypt (in the person of Joseph) preserving the life of the nations (see 41:57; 50:20). So God

would deliver the Israelites out of the nations (the exodus), eventually to send them on a mission of life to the nations (cf. Mt 28:18–20; Ac 1:8). *bad report about them.* Doubtless about all his brothers (as the later context indicates), not just the sons of his father's concubines.

37:3 *richly ornamented robe.* A mark of Jacob's favoritism, "the kind of garment the virgin daughters of the king wore" (2Sa 13:18).
37:5 *dream.* See note on 20:3.
37:7 *bowed down.* Joseph's dream would later come true (42:6; 43:26; 44:14).

37:8 *Will you actually rule us?* Joseph would later become the "prince among his brothers" (Dt 33:16) and receive "the rights of the firstborn" (1Ch 5:2), at least the double portion of the inheritance (see note on 25:5), since his father adopted his two sons (48:5).
37:10 *your mother.* Jacob possibly refers to Leah, since Rachel has already died (see 35:19). *bow down...before you.* An echo of Isaac's blessing of Jacob (27:29).
37:11 *kept the matter in mind.* A hint that Jacob later recalled Joseph's dreams when events brought about their fulfillment. Cf. Mary's equally sensitive response to events during Jesus' boyhood days (Lk 2:19,51).
37:12 *Shechem.* See 12:6; 33:18 and notes.

37:17 *f* 2Ki 6:13
37:18 *g* 1Sa 19:1;
2Ch 24:21; Ps 31:13,
20; 37:12,32;
S Mt 12:14; Mk 14:1;
Ac 23:12
37:19 *h* S Ge 28:12
37:20 *i* ver 22;
Jer 38:6,9 *j* ver 33;
Lev 26:6,22;
Dt 32:24; 2Ki 17:25;
Eze 34:25 *k* ver 31-33;
S Ge 4:10 *l* Ge 50:20
37:21 *m* S Ge 29:32
n Ge 42:22
37:22 *o* S ver 20
p ver 29-30
37:23 *q* ver 3
37:24 *r* S ver 4;
Ge 49:23; Jer 38:6;
41:7; Eze 22:27
37:25 *s* S Ge 16:11
t S Ge 31:21; S SS 4:1
u Jer 8:22; 22:6; 46:11
v Ge 43:11; Ex 30:23;
Ps 45:8; Pr 7:17;
SS 1:13; Mt 2:11
w ver 28; Ge 39:1;
Ps 105:17
37:26 *x* S Ge 29:35
y S Ge 4:10
37:27 *z* Ge 42:21
a S Ge 29:14
37:28 *b* S Ge 25:2
c Jer 38:13 *d* Ex 21:16
e Lev 27:5; Mt 26:15
f S Ge 16:11 *g* ver 36;
Ge 39:1; 45:4-5;
Ps 105:17; Jer 12:6;
Ac 7:9
37:29 *h* ver 34;
Ge 44:13; Nu 14:6;
Jos 7:6; 2Sa 1:11;
2Ki 2:12; 5:7; 11:14;
22:11; Job 1:20; 2:12;
Isa 36:22; 37:1;
Jer 36:24; 41:5;
Joel 2:13
37:30 *i* ver 22
37:31 *j* S ver 3
k Rev 19:13
37:32 *l* S ver 3
37:33 *m* S ver 20
n Ge 42:13,38; 44:20,
28
37:34 *o* S ver 29
p 2Sa 3:31; 1Ki 20:31;
21:27; 2Ki 6:30; 19:1,
2; Job 16:15; Ps 69:11;

¹⁷"They have moved on from here," the man answered. "I heard them say, 'Let's go to Dothan.*f*'"

So Joseph went after his brothers and found them near Dothan. ¹⁸But they saw him in the distance, and before he reached them, they plotted to kill him.*g*

¹⁹"Here comes that dreamer!*h*" they said to each other. ²⁰"Come now, let's kill him and throw him into one of these cisterns*i* and say that a ferocious animal*j* devoured him.*k* Then we'll see what comes of his dreams."*l*

²¹When Reuben*m* heard this, he tried to rescue him from their hands. "Let's not take his life," he said.*n* ²²"Don't shed any blood. Throw him into this cistern*o* here in the wilderness, but don't lay a hand on him." Reuben said this to rescue him from them and take him back to his father.*p*

²³So when Joseph came to his brothers, they stripped him of his robe—the richly ornamented robe*q* he was wearing— ²⁴and they took him and threw him into the cistern.*r* The cistern was empty; there was no water in it.

²⁵As they sat down to eat their meal, they looked up and saw a caravan of Ishmaelites*s* coming from Gilead.*t* Their camels were loaded with spices, balm*u* and myrrh,*v* and they were on their way to take them down to Egypt.*w*

²⁶Judah*x* said to his brothers, "What will we gain if we kill our brother and cover up his blood?*y* ²⁷Come, let's sell him to the Ishmaelites and not lay our hands on him; after all, he is our brother,*z* our own flesh and blood.*a*" His brothers agreed.

²⁸So when the Midianite*b* merchants came by, his brothers pulled Joseph up out of the cistern*c* and sold*d* him for twenty shekels*a* of silver*e* to the Ishmaelites,*f* who took him to Egypt.*g*

²⁹When Reuben returned to the cistern and saw that Joseph was not there, he tore his clothes.*h* ³⁰He went back to his brothers and said, "The boy isn't there! Where can I turn now?"*i*

³¹Then they got Joseph's robe,*j* slaughtered a goat and dipped the robe in the blood.*k* ³²They took the ornamented robe*l* back to their father and said, "We found this. Examine it to see whether it is your son's robe."

³³He recognized it and said, "It is my son's robe! Some ferocious animal*m* has devoured him. Joseph has surely been torn to pieces."*n*

³⁴Then Jacob tore his clothes,*o* put on sackcloth*p* and mourned for his son many days.*q* ³⁵All his sons and daughters came to comfort him,*r* but he refused to be comforted.*s* "No," he said, "in mourning will I go down to the grave*t* to my son.*u*" So his father wept for him.

³⁶Meanwhile, the Midianites*b v* sold Joseph*w* in Egypt to Potiphar, one of Pharaoh's officials, the captain of the guard.*x*

---

a 28 That is, about 8 ounces or about 230 grams   *b* 36 Samaritan Pentateuch, Septuagint, Vulgate and Syriac (see also verse 28); Masoretic Text *Medanites*

37:34 Isa 3:24; 15:3; 22:12; 32:11; 37:1; Jer 48:37; 49:3; Joel 1:13 *q* Ge 50:3,10,11; Nu 20:29; Dt 34:8   37:35 *r* Job 2:11; 15:11; 16:5; 42:11 *s* 2Sa 12:17; Ps 77:2; Jer 31:15 *t* Ge 42:38; 44:22,29,31 *u* 2Sa 12:23   37:36 *v* S Ge 25:2 *w* S ver 28 *x* Ge 39:1; 40:3; 41:10,12; Isa 22:14

37:17 *Dothan.* Located about 13 miles north of Shechem, Dothan was already an ancient city by this time.

37:19 *dreamer.* The Hebrew for this word means "master of dreams" or "dream expert" and is here used with obvious sarcasm.

37:21 *Reuben . . . tried to rescue him.* As Jacob's firstborn, he felt responsible for Joseph. He would later remind his brothers of this day (42:22). Initially Reuben's attempts to influence events seemed successful (30:14–17). But after his arrogant incest with Bilhah (see 35:22 and note) his efforts were always ineffective (see 42:37–38)—demonstrating his loss of the status of firstborn (see 49:3–4). Effective leadership passed to Judah (see vv. 26–27; 43:3–5,8–10; 44:14–34; 46:28; 49:8–12).

37:23–24 Similarly (see note on v. 21), in Egypt Joseph (though innocent of any wrongdoing) would be stripped of his position of privilege and thrown into prison—also as a result of domestic intrigue (ch. 39). His cloak also would be torn from him and shown to Potiphar, but he would be rescued (41:14).

37:25 *Ishmaelites.* Also called Midianites (v. 28; see Jdg 8:22, 24,26) and Medanites (see TNIV text note on v. 36). These various tribal groups were interrelated, since Midian and Medan, like Ishmael, were also sons of Abraham (25:2). *Gilead.* See note on 31:21. *balm.* An oil or gum with healing properties (see Jer 51:8), exuded by the fruit or stems of one or more kinds of small trees. The balm of Gilead was especially effective (see Jer 8:22; 46:11). *myrrh.* Probably to be identified with labdanum, an aromatic gum (see Ps 45:8; Pr 7:17; SS 3:6; 5:13) exuded from the leaves of the cistus rose. Its oil was used in beauty treatments (see Est 2:12), and it was sometimes mixed with wine and drunk to relieve pain (see Mk 15:23). As a gift fit for a king, myrrh was brought to Jesus after his birth (Mt 2:11) and applied to his body after his death (Jn 19:39–40).

37:28 *twenty shekels of silver.* In later times this amount was the value of a male of Joseph's age who had been dedicated to the Lord (see Lev 27:5).

37:31–33 Again a slaughtered goat figures prominently in an act of deception (see 27:5–13).

37:34 *tore his clothes, put on sackcloth.* Tearing one's clothes (see v. 29) and wearing coarse and uncomfortable sackcloth instead of ordinary clothes were both signs of mourning (see note on Rev 11:3).

37:35 *daughters.* The term can include daughters-in-law (e.g., a daughter-in-law of Jacob is mentioned in 38:2). *grave.* The Hebrew for "grave" (*Sheol*) can also refer in a more general way to the realm of the dead, the netherworld, where, it was thought, departed spirits live (see note on Dt 32:22).

37:36 *sold.* "As a slave" (Ps 105:17). The peoples of the Arabian Desert were long involved in international slave trade (cf. Am

JUDAH AND TAMAR

38 At that time, Judah *y* left his brothers and went down to stay with a man of Adullam *z* named Hirah. *a* ²There Judah met the daughter of a Canaanite man named Shua. *b* He married her and made love to her; ³she became pregnant and gave birth to a son, who was named Er. *c* ⁴She conceived again and gave birth to a son and named him Onan. *d* ⁵She gave birth to still another son and named him Shelah. *e* It was at Kezib that she gave birth to him.

⁶Judah got a wife for Er, his firstborn, and her name was Tamar. *f* ⁷But Er, Judah's firstborn, was wicked in the LORD's sight; *g* so the LORD put him to death. *h*

⁸Then Judah said to Onan, "Sleep with your brother's wife and fulfill your duty to her as a brother-in-law to raise up offspring for your brother." *i* ⁹But Onan knew that the child would not be his; so whenever he slept with his brother's wife, he spilled his semen on the ground to keep from providing offspring for his brother. ¹⁰What he did was wicked in the LORD's sight; so he put him to death also. *j*

¹¹Judah then said to his daughter-in-law *k* Tamar, *l* "Live as a widow in your father's household *m* until my son Shelah *n* grows up." *o* For he thought, "He may die too, just like his brothers." So Tamar went to live in her father's household.

¹²After a long time Judah's wife, the daughter of Shua, *p* died. When Judah had recovered from his grief, he went up to Timnah, *q* to the men who were shearing his sheep, *r* and his friend Hirah the Adullamite *s* went with him.

¹³When Tamar *t* was told, "Your father-in-law is on his way to Timnah to shear his sheep," *u* ¹⁴she took off her widow's clothes, *v* covered herself with a veil *w* to disguise herself, and then sat down *x* at the entrance to Enaim, which is on the road to Timnah. *y* For she saw that, though Shelah *z* had now grown up, she had not been given to him as his wife.

¹⁵When Judah saw her, he thought she was a prostitute, *a* for she had covered her face. ¹⁶Not realizing *b* that she was his daughter-in-law, *c* he went over to her by the roadside and said, "Come now, let me sleep with you." *d*

"And what will you give me to sleep with you?" *e* she asked.

¹⁷"I'll send you a young goat *f* from my flock," he said.

"Will you give me something as a pledge *g* until you send it?" she asked.

¹⁸He said, "What pledge should I give you?"

"Your seal *h* and its cord, and the staff *i* in your hand," she answered. So he gave them to her and slept with her, and she became pregnant by him. *j* ¹⁹After she left, she took off her veil and put on her widow's clothes *k* again.

1:6,9). *guard.* The Hebrew for this word can mean "executioners" (the captain of whom was in charge of the royal prisoners; see 40:4), or it can mean "butchers" (the captain of whom was the chief cook in the royal court; cf. 1Sa 9:23–24).

C A **38:1–30** The unsavory events of this chapter illustrate the danger that Israel as God's separated people faced if they remained among the Canaanites (see 15:16 and note). In Egypt the Israelites were kept separate because the Egyptians despised them (43:32; 46:34). While there, God's people were able to develop into a nation without losing their identity. Judah's actions contrasted with those of Joseph (ch. 39)—demonstrating the moral superiority of Joseph, to whom leadership in Israel fell in his generation (see 37:5–9). Since Judah was with his brothers when they sold Joseph to the slave traders and was with them again when they went down to Egypt to buy food, the author seems to locate the events of this chapter within a period of approximately 21 years (see chart, p. 29). Or we may suppose that Judah returned to Canaan from time to time to look after his affairs there.

38:1 *left his brothers.* Joseph was separated from his brothers by force, but Judah voluntarily separated himself to seek his fortune among the Canaanites. *Adullam.* A town southwest of Jerusalem (see 2Ch 11:5,7).

B **38:3–4** *Er . . . Onan.* The names also appear as designations of tribes in Mesopotamian documents of this time. **38:5** *Kezib.* Probably the same as Akzib (Jos 15:44), three miles west of Adullam. The "men of Kozeba" (another form of the same word) were descendants of Shelah, son of Judah (see 1Ch 4:21–22). The Hebrew root of the name means "deception" (see

Mic 1:14 and TNIV text note), a theme running throughout the story of Jacob and his sons.

38:6 *Judah got a wife for Er.* See note on 21:21.

38:8 A concise description of the custom known as "levirate marriage" (Latin *levir* means "brother-in-law"). Details of the practice are given in Dt 25:5–6 (see note there), where it is laid down as a legal obligation within Israel (cf. Mt 22:24 and note). The custom is illustrated in Ru 4:5 (see note there), though there it is extended to the nearest living relative ("family guardian," Ru 3:12; see note there and on 2:20), since neither Boaz nor the nearer kinsman was a brother-in-law.

38:9 *knew that the child would not be his.* Similarly, Ruth's nearest kinsman was fearful that if he married Ruth he would endanger his own estate (Ru 4:5–6; see note on 4:6). *spilled his semen on the ground.* A means of birth control sometimes called "onanism" (after Onan).

38:10 *What he did.* His refusal to perform his levirate duty.

38:11 *he thought, "He may die too, just like his brothers."* Thus Judah had no intention of giving Shelah to Tamar (see v. 14).

38:12 *Timnah.* Exact location unknown, but somewhere in the hill country of Judah (see Jos 15:48,57).

38:14 *sat down . . . the road.* Prostitutes (see v. 15) customarily stationed themselves by the roadside (Jer 3:2; see note there). *Enaim.* Means "two springs"; probably the same as Enam in the western foothills of Judah (see Jos 15:33–34).

B **38:18** *seal and its cord.* Probably a small cylinder seal of the type used to sign clay documents by rolling them over the clay. The owner wore it around his neck on a cord threaded through a hole drilled lengthwise through it.

38:1 *y* S Ge 29:35
z Jos 12:15; 15:35;
1Sa 22:1; 2Sa 23:13;
2Ch 11:7 *a* ver 12,20
38:2 *b* ver 12;
1Ch 2:3
38:3 *c* ver 6;
Ge 46:12; Nu 26:19
38:4 *d* ver 8,9;
Ge 46:12; Nu 26:19
38:5 *e* Nu 26:20
38:6 *f* ver 11,13
38:7 *g* S Ge 6:5
h ver 10; Ge 46:12;
Lev 10:1-2; 1Ch 2:3
38:8 *i* Dt 25:5-6;
Ru 4:5; Mt 22:24-28
38:10 *j* S ver 7;
Dt 25:7-10
38:11 *k* S Ge 11:31
l S Ge 6 *m* Ru 1:8
n ver 14,26 *o* Ru 1:13
38:12 *p* S ver 2
q ver 14; Jos 15:10,57;
19:43; Jdg 14:1,2;
2Ch 28:18
r S Ge 31:19 *s* S ver 1
38:13 *t* S ver 6
u S Ge 31:19
38:14 *v* ver 19
w S Ge 24:65 *x* Jer 3:2
y S ver 12 *z* S ver 11
38:15 *a* Jdg 11:1; 16:1
38:16 *b* Ge 42:23
c Lev 18:15; 20:12;
Ru 1:6 *d* Ge 39:7,12;
2Sa 13:11
e S Ge 30:15
38:17 *f* Jdg 15:1
g ver 20
38:18 *h* ver 25;
1Ki 21:8; Est 3:12; 8:8;
SS 8:6; Isa 49:16;
Jer 22:24; Hag 2:23;
2Co 1:22; Eph 1:13
i S Ge 32:10; S Ex 4:2
j S Ge 19:32
38:19 *k* ver 14

38:20 ᶦS ver 1
ᵐ ver 17
38:21 ⁿS Ge 19:5;
Lev 19:29; Dt 22:21;
23:17; 2Ki 23:7;
Hos 4:14
38:23 ᵒver 18
ᵖ Ex 32:25; Job 12:4;
Jer 20:7; La 3:14
38:24 �q Ge 40:10,
14; 21:9; Dt 22:21,22;
Jos 7:25; Jdg 15:6;
1Sa 31:12; Job 31:11,
28; Eze 16:38
38:25 ʳS ver 18
38:26 ˢ 1Sa 24:17
ᵗ S ver 11
38:27 ᵘ Ge 25:24
38:28 ᵛS Ge 35:17
ʷ ver 30
38:29 ˣ Ge 25:26
ʸ Ge 46:12; Nu 26:20,
21; Ru 4:12,18;
2Sa 5:20; 6:8;
1Ch 2:4; 9:4;
Isa 28:21; Mt 1:3
38:30 ᶻ ver 28
ᵃ Ge 46:12; 1Ch 2:4;
Ne 11:24
39:1 ᵇ S Ge 30:24
ᶜ S Ge 37:36
ᵈ S Ge 37:25
39:2 ᵉ S Ge 21:20,
22; Jos 1:5; 6:27;
Jdg 1:19; 1Sa 18:14;
Ac 7:9
39:3 ᶠ S Ge 21:22
ᵍ ver 23; 1Sa 18:14;
2Ki 18:7; 2Ch 20:20;
Ps 1:3; 128:2; Isa 33:6
39:4 ʰ S Ge 6:8;
S 18:3 ᶦ Ge 47:6;
1Ki 11:28; Pr 22:29
ʲ ver 8,22; Ge 40:4;
42:37
39:5 ᵏ 2Sa 6:11
ᶦ S Ge 26:24
ᵐ Dt 28:3; Ps 128:4
39:6 ⁿ Ge 24:2

²⁰Meanwhile Judah sent the young goat by his friend the Adullamite ᶦ in order to get his pledge ᵐ back from the woman, but he did not find her. ²¹He asked the men who lived there, "Where is the shrine prostitute ⁿ who was beside the road at Enaim?"

"There hasn't been any shrine prostitute here," they said.

²²So he went back to Judah and said, "I didn't find her. Besides, the men who lived there said, 'There hasn't been any shrine prostitute here.' "

²³Then Judah said, "Let her keep what she has, ᵒ or we will become a laughingstock. ᵖ After all, I did send her this young goat, but you didn't find her."

²⁴About three months later Judah was told, "Your daughter-in-law Tamar is guilty of prostitution, and as a result she is now pregnant."

Judah said, "Bring her out and have her burned to death!" q

²⁵As she was being brought out, she sent a message to her father-in-law. "I am pregnant by the man who owns these," she said. And she added, "See if you recognize whose seal and cord and staff these are." ʳ

²⁶Judah recognized them and said, "She is more righteous than I, ˢ since I wouldn't give her to my son Shelah. ᵗ" And he did not sleep with her again.

²⁷When the time came for her to give birth, there were twin boys in her womb. ᵘ ²⁸As she was giving birth, one of them put out his hand; so the midwife ᵛ took a scarlet thread and tied it on his wrist ʷ and said, "This one came out first." ²⁹But when he drew back his hand, his brother came out, ˣ and she said, "So this is how you have broken out!" And he was named Perez. ᵃ ʸ ³⁰Then his brother, who had the scarlet thread on his wrist, ᶻ came out and he was given the name Zerah. ᵇ ᵃ

JOSEPH AND POTIPHAR'S WIFE

39 Now Joseph ᵇ had been taken down to Egypt. Potiphar, an Egyptian who was one of Pharaoh's officials, the captain of the guard, ᶜ bought him from the Ishmaelites who had taken him there. ᵈ

²The LORD was with Joseph ᵉ so that he prospered, and he lived in the house of his Egyptian master. ³When his master saw that the LORD was with him ᶠ and that the LORD gave him success in everything he did, ᵍ ⁴Joseph found favor in his eyes ʰ and became his attendant. Potiphar put him in charge of his household, ᶦ and he entrusted to his care everything he owned. ʲ ⁵From the time he put him in charge of his household and of all that he owned, the LORD blessed the household ᵏ of the Egyptian because of Joseph. ᶦ The blessing of the LORD was on everything Potiphar had, both in the house and in the field. ᵐ ⁶So Potiphar left everything he had in Joseph's care; ⁿ with Joseph in charge, he did not concern himself with anything except the food he ate.

ᵃ 29 *Perez* means *breaking out.* ᵇ 30 *Zerah* can mean *scarlet* or *brightness.*

38:21 *shrine prostitute.* The Hebrew here differs from that used for "prostitute" in v. 15. Judah's friend perhaps deliberately used the more acceptable term, since ritual prostitutes enjoyed a higher social status in Canaan than did ordinary prostitutes (see note on 20:9).
38:24 *have her burned to death.* In later times, burning was the legal penalty for prostitution (see Lev 21:9).
38:27–30 For a similarly unusual birth of twin boys, see 25:24–26.
C **38:29** *Perez.* Became the head of the leading clan in Judah and the ancestor of David (see Ru 4:18–22) and ultimately of Christ (see Mt 1:1–6).
39:1–23 A continuation of the Joseph story (see 37:36)—the first stage in the movement of Israel from Canaan to Egypt.
C **39:1** *taken down to Egypt.* Joseph's experiences in Egypt, as well as those of his youth in Canaan (see note on 37:23–24), are similar to Israel's national experiences in Egypt. Initially, because of God's blessing, Joseph attains a position of honor (in Potiphar's house); he is then unjustly thrown into prison, his only crime being his attractiveness and moral integrity; and finally he is raised up among the Egyptians as the one who, because God is with him, holds their lives in his hands. Similarly, the Israelites were first received with honor in Egypt (because of Joseph); then they were subjected to cruel bondage, their only crime being God's evident blessings upon them; and finally God raised his people up in the eyes of the

Egyptians (through the ministry of Moses) as they came fearfully to recognize that these people and their God did indeed hold their lives in their hands. The author of Genesis knew the events of the exodus and shows how the history of God and the patriarchs moved forward to and foreshadowed that event (see also 15:13–16; 48:21–22; 50:24–25). *Ishmaelites.* See note on 37:25.
39:2–6 See vv. 20–23. Though Joseph's situation changed drastically, God's relationship to him remained the same.
39:2 *The LORD was with Joseph.* See note on 26:3. This fact, mentioned several times here (vv. 3,21,23), is stressed also by Stephen (Ac 7:9–10).
39:5 *the LORD blessed the household of the Egyptian because of Joseph.* As God had blessed Laban because of Jacob (30:27). The offspring of Abraham continue to be a blessing to the nations (see 12:2–3).
A C **39:6** *left everything he had in Joseph's care.* As Laban had entrusted his flocks to Jacob's care (30:31–34). Joseph had full responsibility for the welfare of Potiphar's house, as later he would have full responsibility in prison (vv. 22–23) and later still in all Egypt (41:41). Always this Israelite came to hold the welfare of his "world" in his hands—but always by the blessing and overruling of God, never by his own wits, as his father Jacob had so long attempted. In the role that he played in Israel's history and in the manner in which he lived it, Joseph was a true representative of Israel.

Now Joseph was well-built and handsome, *o* *7*and after a while his master's wife took notice of Joseph and said, "Come to bed with me!" *p*

*8*But he refused. *q* "With me in charge," he told her, "my master does not concern himself with anything in the house; everything he owns he has entrusted to my care. *r* *9*No one is greater in this house than I am. *s* My master has withheld nothing from me except you, because you are his wife. How then could I do such a wicked thing and sin against God?" *t* *10*And though she spoke to Joseph day after day, he refused *u* to go to bed with her or even be with her.

*11*One day he went into the house to attend to his duties, *v* and none of the household servants *w* was inside. *12*She caught him by his cloak *x* and said, "Come to bed with me!" *y* But he left his cloak in her hand and ran out of the house. *z*

*13*When she saw that he had left his cloak in her hand and had run out of the house, *14*she called her household servants. *a* "Look," she said to them, "this Hebrew *b* has been brought to us to make sport of us! *c* He came in here to sleep with me, but I screamed. *d* *15*When he heard me scream for help, he left his cloak beside me and ran out of the house." *e*

*16*She kept his cloak beside her until his master came home. *17*Then she told him this story: *f* "That Hebrew *g* slave *h* you brought us came to me to make sport of me. *18*But as soon as I screamed for help, he left his cloak beside me and ran out of the house."

*19*When his master heard the story his wife told him, saying, "This is how your slave treated me," he burned with anger. *i* *20*Joseph's master took him and put him in prison, *j* the place where the king's prisoners were confined.

But while Joseph was there in the prison, *21*the LORD was with him; *k* he showed him kindness *l* and granted him favor in the eyes of the prison warden. *m* *22*So the warden put Joseph in charge of all those held in the prison, and he was made responsible for all that was done there. *n* *23*The warden paid no attention to anything under Joseph's *o* care, because the LORD was with Joseph and gave him success in whatever he did. *p*

THE CUPBEARER AND THE BAKER

40 Some time later, the cupbearer *q* and the baker *r* of the king of Egypt offended their master, the king of Egypt. *2*Pharaoh was angry *s* with his two officials, *t* the chief cupbearer and the chief baker, *3*and put them in custody in the house of the captain of the guard, *u* in the same prison where Joseph was confined. *4*The captain of the guard *v* assigned them to Joseph, *w* and he attended them.

After they had been in custody *x* for some time, *5*each of the two men—the cupbearer and the baker of the king of Egypt, who were being held in prison—had a dream *y* the same night, and each dream had a meaning of its own. *z*

*6*When Joseph came to them the next morning, he saw that they were dejected. *7*So he asked Pharaoh's officials who were in custody *a* with him in his master's house, "Why do you look so sad today?" *b*

8"We both had dreams," they answered, "but there is no one to interpret them." *c*

Then Joseph said to them, "Do not interpretations belong to God? *d* Tell me your dreams."

*9*So the chief cupbearer *e* told Joseph his dream. He said to him, "In my dream I saw a vine in front of me, *10*and on the vine were three branches. As soon as it budded, it blos-

39:6 *o* S Ge 12:11;
Ex 2:2; 1Sa 9:2; 16:12;
17:42; Est 2:7; Da 1:4
39:7 *p* S Ge 38:16;
Pr 7:15-18
39:8 *q* Pr 6:23-24
r S ver 4
39:9 *s* Ge 41:33,40
t S Ge 13:13;
S Nu 22:34
39:10 *u* Est 3:4
39:11 *v* Ex 18:20;
Dt 1:18 *w* ver 14
39:12 *x* 2Sa 13:11;
Pr 7:13 *y* S Ge 38:16
z ver 15; Pr 5:8;
2Ti 2:22
39:14 *a* ver 11
b S Ge 14:13
c S Ge 21:9
d Dt 22:24,27
39:15 *e* S ver 12
39:17 *f* Ex 20:16;
23:1,7; Dt 5:20;
Ps 101:5 *g* S Ge 14:13
h Ge 21:10
39:19 *i* S Ge 34:7;
S Est 1:12
39:20 *j* Ge 40:3;
41:10; Ps 105:18
39:21 *k* S Ge 21:20
l S Ge 19:19 *m* Ex 3:21;
11:3; 12:36; Est 2:9;
Ps 106:46; Pr 16:7;
Da 1:9
39:22 *n* S ver 4
39:23 *o* S Ge 21:20;
S Nu 14:43 *p* S ver 3
40:1 *q* ver 9,13,21;
Ne 1:11 *r* ver 16,20
40:2 *s* Pr 16:14,15;
19:12 *t* Ge 41:10;
Est 2:21
40:3 *u* S Ge 37:36;
S 39:20
40:4 *v* S Ge 37:36
w S Ge 39:4 *x* ver 7;
Ge 42:17
40:5 *y* S Ge 20:3
z Ge 41:11
40:7 *a* S ver 4
b Ne 2:2
40:8 *c* Ge 41:8,15
d Ge 41:16,25,28,32;
Dt 29:29; Da 2:22,28,
47
40:9 *e* S ver 1

B **39:7** *took notice of.* Looked with desire at. The phrase is used in the same sense in Akkadian in Section 25 of the Code of Hammurapi (see chart, p. xxiii).

A **39:9** *sin against God.* All sin is against God, first and foremost (see Ps 51:4 and note).

39:10 *though she spoke to Joseph day after day, he refused.* Samson twice succumbed under similar pressure (Jdg 14:17; 16:16-17).

39:14 *this Hebrew.* See v. 17; see also note on 14:13.

39:20-23 See note on vv. 2-6.

39:20 *place where the king's prisoners were confined.* Though understandably angry (see v. 19), Potiphar put Joseph in the "house of the captain of the guard" (40:3)—certainly not the worst prison available.

C **40:1-23** God gives Joseph the interpretation of two dreams, which prepares the way for Joseph to be used by God to interpret the pharaoh's two dreams (ch. 41), leading to

the subsequent fulfillment (chs. 42-46) of Joseph's two dreams (37:5-11).

40:2 *Pharaoh.* See note on Ex 1:11. *chief cupbearer.* Would be the divinely appointed agent for introducing Joseph to the pharaoh (see 41:9-14).

40:5 *each dream had a meaning.* Throughout the ancient Near East it was believed that dreams sometimes contained disclosures about the future that a proper interpretation would bring to light (see note on 20:3). God was beginning to prepare the way for Joseph's rise in Egypt.

C **40:8** *interpretations belong to God.* Only God, who knows the future, can properly interpret dreams (see 41:16,25, 28; Da 2:28). *Tell me.* Joseph presents himself as God's agent through whom God will make known the revelation contained in their dreams—Israel is God's prophetic people through whom God's revelation comes to the nations (see 18:17 and note; 41:16,28,32).

40:10 f Isa 27:6;
35:1-2; Hos 14:7
40:12 g ver 16;
Ge 41:12,15,25;
Da 2:36; 4:19 h ver 18
40:13 i ver 19, 20;
Jos 1:11; 3:2; Ezr 8:32;
Ne 2:11 j ver 19
k S ver 1
40:14 l 1Sa 25:31;
Lk 23:42
m S Ge 19:19;
1Sa 20:14, 42; 2Sa 9:1;
1Ki 2:7 n ver 23;
Ge 41:9; Ecc 9:15
40:15 o S Ge 14:13
p Ge 13:3; 13:27
40:16 q S ver 1
r S ver 12 s Am 8:1-2
40:18 t ver 12
40:19 u ver 13
v S ver 13 w ver 22;
Dt 21:22-23; Est 2:23;
7:10 x Dt 28:26;
1Sa 17:44; 2Sa 21:10;
1Ki 14:11; 16:4; 21:24;
Eze 39:4
40:20 y S ver 13
z Mt 14:6-10
a Est 2:18; Mk 6:21
b S ver 1
40:21 c S ver 1
d 2Ki 25:27; Jer 52:31
e ver 13
40:22 f S ver 19
g Ge 41:13; Ps 105:19
40:23 h S ver 14;
S Ecc 1:11
41:1 i S Ge 20:3
j ver 17; S Ge 2:14;
Ex 1:22; 2:5; 7:15
41:2 k ver 26;
Jer 5:28 l ver 18;
Ex 2:3; Job 40:21;
Isa 19:6
41:4 m ver 7
41:5 n Jos 13:3;
2Ki 4:42; 1Ch 13:5;
Isa 23:3; Jer 2:18
41:6 o Ex 10:13;
14:21; Job 6:26; 11:2;
15:2; Ps 11:6; 48:7;
Isa 11:15; 27:8;
Jer 4:11; 18:17;
Eze 19:12; 27:26;
Hos 12:1; 13:15;
Jnh 4:8
41:7 p ver 4
41:8 q Job 7:14;
Da 2:1,3; 4:5,19
r Ex 7:11,22; Da 1:20;
2:2,27; 4:7; 5:7
s ver 24; S Ge 40:8;
Da 4:18
41:9 t S Ge 40:14
41:10 u S Ge 40:2
v S Ge 37:36; S 39:20
41:11 w S Ge 40:5
41:12 x S Ge 14:13;
39:17 y S Ge 37:36;
40:4 z S Ge 40:12
41:13 a S Ge 40:22

somed, f and its clusters ripened into grapes. ¹¹Pharaoh's cup was in my hand, and I took the grapes, squeezed them into Pharaoh's cup and put the cup in his hand."

¹²"This is what it means, g" Joseph said to him. "The three branches are three days. h ¹³Within three days i Pharaoh will lift up your head j and restore you to your position, and you will put Pharaoh's cup in his hand, just as you used to do when you were his cupbearer. k ¹⁴But when all goes well with you, remember me l and show me kindness; m mention me to Pharaoh n and get me out of this prison. ¹⁵I was forcibly carried off from the land of the Hebrews, o and even here I have done nothing to deserve being put in a dungeon." p

¹⁶When the chief baker q saw that Joseph had given a favorable interpretation, r he said to Joseph, "I too had a dream: On my head were three baskets s of bread. a ¹⁷In the top basket were all kinds of baked goods for Pharaoh, but the birds were eating them out of the basket on my head."

¹⁸"This is what it means," Joseph said. "The three baskets are three days. t ¹⁹Within three days u Pharaoh will lift off your head v and impale your body on a pole. w And the birds will eat away your flesh." x

²⁰Now the third day y was Pharaoh's birthday, z and he gave a feast for all his officials. a He lifted up the heads of the chief cupbearer and the chief baker b in the presence of his officials: ²¹He restored the chief cupbearer c to his position, d so that he once again put the cup into Pharaoh's hand e— ²²but he impaled the chief baker, f just as Joseph had said to them in his interpretation. g

²³The chief cupbearer, however, did not remember Joseph; he forgot him. h

PHARAOH'S DREAMS

41 When two full years had passed, Pharaoh had a dream: i He was standing by the Nile, j ²when out of the river there came up seven cows, sleek and fat, k and they grazed among the reeds. l ³After them, seven other cows, ugly and gaunt, came up out of the Nile and stood beside those on the riverbank. ⁴And the cows that were ugly and gaunt ate up the seven sleek, fat cows. Then Pharaoh woke up. m

⁵He fell asleep again and had a second dream: Seven heads of grain, n healthy and good, were growing on a single stalk. ⁶After them, seven other heads of grain sprouted—thin and scorched by the east wind. o ⁷The thin heads of grain swallowed up the seven healthy, full heads. Then Pharaoh woke up; p it had been a dream.

⁸In the morning his mind was troubled, q so he sent for all the magicians r and wise men of Egypt. Pharaoh told them his dreams, but no one could interpret them for him. s

⁹Then the chief cupbearer said to Pharaoh, "Today I am reminded of my shortcomings. t ¹⁰Pharaoh was once angry with his servants, u and he imprisoned me and the chief baker in the house of the captain of the guard. v ¹¹Each of us had a dream the same night, and each dream had a meaning of its own. w ¹²Now a young Hebrew x was there with us, a servant of the captain of the guard. y We told him our dreams, and he interpreted them for us, giving each man the interpretation of his dream. z ¹³And things turned out exactly as he interpreted them to us: I was restored to my position, and the other man was impaled. a"

¹⁴So Pharaoh sent for Joseph, and he was quickly brought from the dungeon. b When he had shaved c and changed his clothes, d he came before Pharaoh.

¹⁵Pharaoh said to Joseph, "I had a dream, and no one can interpret it. e But I have heard it said of you that when you hear a dream you can interpret it." f

a 16 Or three wicker baskets

41:14 b Ps 105:20 c Isa 18:2,7 d S Ge 35:2; 45:22; Ru 3:3; 2Sa 12:20   **41:15** e S Ge 40:8 f S Ge 40:12; Da 4:18; 5:16

40:13 *lift up your head and restore you to your position.* See Ps 3:3; 27:6. For this meaning of the idiom "lift up one's head," see 2Ki 25:27 and Jer 52:31, where the Hebrew for "released" in the context of freeing a prisoner means lit. "lifted up the head of."

40:14 *when all goes well with you, remember me.* Unfortunately, the cupbearer "forgot him" (v. 23) until two full years later (see 41:1,9–13).

40:15 *dungeon.* Probably hyperbole to reflect Joseph's despair (see note on 39:20). Since the same Hebrew word refers to a cistern in 37:24, the author of Genesis has established a link with Joseph's earlier experience at the hands of his brothers.

40:19 *lift off your head.* A grisly pun based on the same idiom used in v. 13 (see note there).

41:2 *out of the river there came up seven cows.* Cattle often submerged themselves up to their necks in the Nile to escape sun and insects.

41:6 *scorched by the east wind.* The Palestinian sirocco (in Egypt the khamsin), which blows in from the desert (see Hos 13:15) in late spring and early fall, often withers vegetation (see Isa 40:7; Eze 17:10 and note).

41:8 *his mind was troubled.* See 40:6–7. *magicians.* Probably priests who claimed to possess occult knowledge. *no one could interpret them.* See Da 2:10–11.

41:13 *things turned out exactly as he interpreted them.* Because his words were from the Lord (see Ps 105:19).

41:14 *Pharaoh sent for Joseph.* Effecting his permanent release from prison (see Ps 105:20). *shaved.* Egyptians were normally smooth-shaven, while Palestinians wore beards (see 2Sa 10:4; Jer 41:5 and notes).

¹⁶"I cannot do it," Joseph replied to Pharaoh, "but God will give Pharaoh the answer he desires."ᵍ

¹⁷Then Pharaoh said to Joseph, "In my dream I was standing on the bank of the Nile,ʰ ¹⁸when out of the river there came up seven cows, fat and sleek, and they grazed among the reeds.ⁱ ¹⁹After them, seven other cows came up—scrawny and very ugly and lean. I had never seen such ugly cows in all the land of Egypt. ²⁰The lean, ugly cows ate up the seven fat cows that came up first. ²¹But even after they ate them, no one could tell that they had done so; they looked just as ugly as before. Then I woke up.

²²"In my dream I saw seven heads of grain, full and good, growing on a single stalk. ²³After them, seven other heads sprouted—withered and thin and scorched by the east wind. ²⁴The thin heads of grain swallowed up the seven good heads. I told this to the magicians, but none of them could explain it to me.ʲ"

²⁵Then Joseph said to Pharaoh, "The dreams of Pharaoh are one and the same.ᵏ God has revealed to Pharaoh what he is about to do.ˡ ²⁶The seven good cowsᵐ are seven years, and the seven good heads of grain are seven years; it is one and the same dream. ²⁷The seven lean, ugly cows that came up afterward are seven years, and so are the seven worthless heads of grain scorched by the east wind: They are seven years of famine.ⁿ

²⁸"It is just as I said to Pharaoh: God has shown Pharaoh what he is about to do.ᵒ ²⁹Seven years of great abundanceᵖ are coming throughout the land of Egypt, ³⁰but seven years of famine�q will follow them. Then all the abundance in Egypt will be forgotten, and the famine will ravage the land.ʳ ³¹The abundance in the land will not be remembered, because the famine that follows it will be so severe. ³²The reason the dream was given to Pharaoh in two forms is that the matter has been firmly decidedˢ by God, and God will do it soon.ᵗ

³³"And now let Pharaoh look for a discerning and wise manᵘ and put him in charge of the land of Egypt.ᵛ ³⁴Let Pharaoh appoint commissionersʷ over the land to take a fifthˣ of the harvest of Egypt during the seven years of abundance.ʸ ³⁵They should collect all the food of these good years that are coming and store up the grain under the authority of Pharaoh, to be kept in the cities for food.ᶻ ³⁶This food should be held in reserve for the country, to be used during the seven years of famine that will come upon Egypt,ᵃ so that the country may not be ruined by the famine.

³⁷The plan seemed good to Pharaoh and to all his officials.ᵇ ³⁸So Pharaoh asked them, "Can we find anyone like this man, one in whom is the spirit of Godᵃ?"ᶜ

³⁹Then Pharaoh said to Joseph, "Since God has made all this known to you,ᵈ there is no one so discerning and wise as you.ᵉ ⁴⁰You shall be in charge of my palace,ᶠ and all my people are to submit to your orders.ᵍ Only with respect to the throne will I be greater than you.ʰ"

JOSEPH IN CHARGE OF EGYPT

⁴¹So Pharaoh said to Joseph, "I hereby put you in charge of the whole land of Egypt."ⁱ ⁴²Then Pharaoh took his signet ringʲ from his finger and put it on Joseph's finger. He dressed him in robesᵏ of fine linenˡ and put a gold chain around his neck.ᵐ ⁴³He had him ride in a chariotⁿ as his second-in-command,ᵇᵒ and people shouted before him, "Make way!ᶜ"ᵖ Thus he put him in charge of the whole land of Egypt.q

⁴⁴Then Pharaoh said to Joseph, "I am Pharaoh, but without your word no one will lift hand or foot in all Egypt."ʳ ⁴⁵Pharaoh gave Josephˢ the name Zaphenath-Paneah and

---

ᵃ 38 Or *of the gods*   ᵇ 43 Or *in the chariot of his second-in-command; or in his second chariot*
ᶜ 43 Or *Bow down*

41:16 ᵍ S Ge 40:8
41:17 ʰ S ver 1
41:18 ⁱ S ver 2
41:24 ʲ S ver 8
41:25 ᵏ S Ge 40:12
ˡ S Ge 40:8; Isa 46:11;
Da 2:45
41:26 ᵐ S ver 2
41:27 ⁿ S Ge 12:10
41:28 ᵒ S Ge 40:8
41:29 ᵖ ver 47
41:30 q ver 54;
Ge 45:6,11; 47:13;
Ps 105:16 ʳ ver 56;
S Ge 12:10
41:32 ˢ Da 2:5
ᵗ S Ge 12:10
41:33 ᵘ ver 39
ᵛ S Ge 39:9
41:34 ʷ Est 2:3
ˣ Ge 47:24,26;
1Sa 8:15 ʸ ver 48;
Ge 47:14
41:35 ᶻ ver 48
41:36 ᵃ ver 56;
Ge 42:6; 47:14
41:37 ᵇ Ge 45:16;
Est 2:4; Isa 19:11
41:38 ᶜ Nu 27:18;
Dt 34:9; Da 2:11; 4:8-
9,18; 5:11,14
41:39 ᵈ Da 2:11; 5:11
ᵉ ver 33
41:40 ᶠ 1Ki 4:6;
2Ki 15:5; Isa 22:15;
36:3 ᵍ S Ge 39:9;
Ps 105:21-22; Ac 7:10
ʰ Est 10:3
41:41 ⁱ ver 43,55;
Ge 42:6; 45:8,13,26;
Est 8:2; Jer 40:7;
Da 6:3
41:42 ʲ S Ge 24:22;
Est 3:10; 8:2,8
ᵏ 1Sa 17:38; 18:4;
1Ki 19:19; Est 6:8,11;
Da 5:29; Zec 3:4
ˡ Eze 25:4; Est 8:15;
Da 5:29 ᵐ Ps 73:6;
SS 4:9; Isa 3:18;
Eze 16:11; Da 5:7,16,
29
41:43 ⁿ Ge 46:29;
50:9; Isa 2:7; 22:18
ᵒ Est 10:3 ᵖ Est 6:9
q S ver 41
41:44 ʳ S Ge 37:8;
Est 10:2; Ps 105:22
41:45 ˢ Est 2:7

41:16 *I cannot do it ... but God will give Pharaoh the answer.* See 40:8 and note; Da 2:27–28,30; cf. 2Co 3:5.

B **41:27** *seven years of famine.* See Ac 7:11. Long famines were rare in Egypt because of the regularity of the annual overflow of the Nile, but not uncommon elsewhere (see 2Ki 8:1 and note; see also chart, p. xxiii ["Seven Lean Years Tradition"]).

41:32 Repetition of a divine revelation was often used for emphasis (see 37:5–9; Am 7:1–6,7–9; 8:1–3).

41:38 *spirit of God.* See TNIV text note. The word "spirit" should probably not be capitalized in such passages, since reference to the Holy Spirit would be out of character in statements by pagan rulers.

C **41:40** *You shall be in charge.* The pharaoh took Joseph's advice (see v. 33) and decided that Joseph himself should be "ruler over Egypt" (Ac 7:10; see also Ps 105:21). *all my people*

are to submit to your orders. More lit. "at your command all my people are to kiss (you)"—i.e., kiss your hands or feet in an act of homage and submission (see Ps 2:12 and note).

41:42 Three symbols of transfer and/or sharing of royal authority, referred to also in Est 3:10 (signet ring); Est 6:11 (robe); and Da 5:7,16,29 (gold chain).

41:43 *second-in-command.* The position was probably that of vizier, the highest executive office below that of the king himself.

C **41:45** *gave Joseph the name Zaphenath-Paneah.* As a part of assigning Joseph an official position within his royal administration (see note on 1:5). The pharaoh presumed to use this marvelously endowed servant of the Lord for his own royal purposes—as a later pharaoh would attempt to use divinely blessed Israel for the enrichment of Egypt (Ex 1). He did not recognize that Joseph served a Higher Power, whose king-

41:45 ᶠEx 2:16
ᵘEze 30:17 ᵛver 50;
Ge 46:20,27
41:46 ʷS Ge 37:2
ˣ1Sa 8:11; 16:21;
Pr 22:20; Da 1:19
41:47 ʸver 29
41:48 ᶻS ver 34
41:49 ᵃS Ge 12:2
41:50 ᵇS ver 45
41:51 ᶜGe 48:14,18,
20; 49:3 ᵈGe 46:20;
48:1; 50:23; Nu 1:34;
Dt 33:17; Jos 4:12;
17:1; 1Ch 7:14
41:52 ᵉGe 46:20;
48:1,5; 50:23;
Nu 1:32; 26:28;
Dt 33:17; Jos 14:4;
Jdg 5:14; 1Ch 7:20;
2Ch 30:1; Ps 60:7;
Jer 7:15; Ob 1:19
ᶠS Ge 17:6
41:54 ᵍS Ge 12:10
ʰAc 7:11
41:55 ⁱDt 32:24;
2Ch 20:9; Isa 51:19;
Jer 5:12; 27:8; 42:16;
44:27 ʲS ver 41;
Jn 2:5
41:56 ᵏS ver 36
ˡS Ge 12:10
ᵐS ver 30
41:57 ⁿGe 42:5;
47:15 ᵒS Ge 12:10
42:1 ᵖAc 7:12
42:2 �q Ge 43:2,4;
44:25 ʳver 19,33;
Ge 43:8; 47:19;
Ps 33:18-19
42:3 ˢver 10;
Ge 43:20
42:4 ᵗS Ge 35:18
ᵘver 38
42:5 ᵛS Ge 41:57
ʷver 13,29; Ge 31:18;
45:17 ˣS Ge 12:10;
S Dt 32:24; Ac 7:11
42:6 ʸS Ge 41:41;
S Ne 5:14
ᶻS Ge 41:36
ᵃS Ge 33:3
42:7 ᵇver 30
ᶜS Ge 29:4
42:8 ᵈGe 37:2

gave him Asenath daughter of Potiphera, priest ᶠ of On, ᵃ ᵘ to be his wife. ᵛ And Joseph went throughout the land of Egypt.

⁴⁶Joseph was thirty years old ʷ when he entered the service ˣ of Pharaoh king of Egypt. And Joseph went out from Pharaoh's presence and traveled throughout Egypt. ⁴⁷During the seven years of abundance ʸ the land produced plentifully. ⁴⁸Joseph collected all the food produced in those seven years of abundance in Egypt and stored it in the cities. ᶻ In each city he put the food grown in the fields surrounding it. ⁴⁹Joseph stored up huge quantities of grain, like the sand of the sea; ᵃ it was so much that he stopped keeping records because it was beyond measure.

⁵⁰Before the years of famine came, two sons were born to Joseph by Asenath daughter of Potiphera, priest of On. ᵇ ⁵¹Joseph named his firstborn ᶜ Manasseh ᵇ ᵈ and said, "It is because God has made me forget all my trouble and all my father's household." ⁵²The second son he named Ephraim ᶜ ᵉ and said, "It is because God has made me fruitful ᶠ in the land of my suffering."

⁵³The seven years of abundance in Egypt came to an end, ⁵⁴and the seven years of famine ᵍ began, ʰ just as Joseph had said. There was famine in all the other lands, but in the whole land of Egypt there was food. ⁵⁵When all Egypt began to feel the famine, ⁱ the people cried to Pharaoh for food. Then Pharaoh told all the Egyptians, "Go to Joseph and do what he tells you." ʲ

⁵⁶When the famine had spread over the whole country, Joseph opened all the storehouses and sold grain to the Egyptians, ᵏ for the famine ˡ was severe throughout Egypt. ᵐ ⁵⁷And all the world came to Egypt to buy grain from Joseph, ⁿ because the famine was severe everywhere. ᵒ

JOSEPH'S BROTHERS GO TO EGYPT

42 When Jacob learned that there was grain in Egypt, ᵖ he said to his sons, "Why do you just keep looking at each other?" ²He continued, "I have heard that there is grain in Egypt. Go down there and buy some for us, q so that we may live and not die." ʳ

³Then ten of Joseph's brothers went down to buy grain ˢ from Egypt. ⁴But Jacob did not send Benjamin, ᵗ Joseph's brother, with the others, because he was afraid that harm might come to him. ᵘ ⁵So Israel's sons were among those who went to buy grain, ᵛ for the famine was in the land of Canaan ʷ also. ˣ

⁶Now Joseph was the governor of the land, ʸ the person who sold grain to all its people. ᶻ So when Joseph's brothers arrived, they bowed down to him with their faces to the ground. ᵃ ⁷As soon as Joseph saw his brothers, he recognized them, but he pretended to be a stranger and spoke harshly to them. ᵇ "Where do you come from?" ᶜ he asked.

"From the land of Canaan," they replied, "to buy food."

⁸Although Joseph recognized his brothers, they did not recognize him. ᵈ ⁹Then he re-

---

ᵃ 45 That is, Heliopolis; also in verse 50   ᵇ 51 *Manasseh* sounds like and may be derived from the Hebrew for *forget.*   ᶜ 52 *Ephraim* sounds like the Hebrew for *twice fruitful.*

---

dom and redemptive purposes are being advanced. (The meaning of Joseph's Egyptian name is uncertain.) *Asenath.* The name is Egyptian and probably means "She belongs to (the goddess) Neith." *Potiphera.* Not the same person as "Potiphar" (37:36; 39:1); the name (also Egyptian) means "he whom (the sun-god) Ra has given." *On.* Located ten miles northeast of modern Cairo, it was called Heliopolis ("city of the sun") by the Greeks and was an important center for the worship of Ra, who had a temple there. Potiphera therefore bore an appropriate name.

⟨C⟩ 41:46 *thirty years old.* In just 13 years (see 37:2), Joseph had become second-in-command (v. 43) in Egypt.
41:49 *like the sand of the sea.* A simile also for the large number of offspring promised to Abraham and Jacob (see 22:17; 32:12).
41:52 *Ephraim.* The wordplay on the name (see TNIV text note) reflects the fact that God gave Joseph "two" (see v. 50) sons.

⟨C⟩ 41:57 *all the world.* The known world from the writer's perspective (the Middle East). This description of the famine in the time of Joseph echoes the author's description of the flood in the time of Noah. God saved only Noah and his family from the flood, so that Noah became the new (after Adam) father of the race. With the call of Abram out of the post-flood and post-Babel nations, God once again singled out one man, now to be the father of his special people. God promised that,

through this man and his descendants, "all peoples on earth will be blessed" (12:3). The author highlights the fact that in this new crisis hope rested with one of these descendants.
42:1—45:28 The reunion and reconciliation of Jacob's sons—but now in Egypt.
42:2–3 Stephen refers to this incident (Ac 7:12).
42:4 *did not send Benjamin, Joseph's brother.* Their mother Rachel had died (35:19), and Jacob thought Joseph also was dead (37:33). Jacob did not want to lose Benjamin, the remaining son of his beloved Rachel.
42:5 *famine was in the land of Canaan also.* As in the time of Abram (see 12:10 and note).
42:6 *they bowed down to him.* In fulfillment of Joseph's dreams (see 37:7,9; see also note on 40:1–23).

⟨C⟩ 42:8 *Joseph recognized his brothers.* Although 21 years had passed since he had last seen them (see 37:2; 41:46,53–54), they had been adults at the time and their appearance had not changed much. *they did not recognize him.* Joseph, 17 years old at the time of his enslavement (37:2), was now an adult in an unexpected position of authority, wearing Egyptian clothes and speaking to his brothers through an interpreter (see v. 23). He was, moreover, shaven in the Egyptian manner (see note on 41:14).

membered his dreams *e* about them and said to them, "You are spies! *f* You have come to see where our land is unprotected." *g*

¹⁰"No, my lord, *h*" they answered. "Your servants have come to buy food. *i* ¹¹We are all the sons of one man. Your servants *j* are honest men, *k* not spies. *l*"

¹²"No!" he said to them. "You have come to see where our land is unprotected." *m*

¹³But they replied, "Your servants *n* were twelve brothers, the sons of one man, who lives in the land of Canaan. *o* The youngest is now with our father, and one is no more." *p*

¹⁴Joseph said to them, "It is just as I told you: You are spies! *q* ¹⁵And this is how you will be tested: As surely as Pharaoh lives, *r* you will not leave this place unless your youngest brother comes here. *s* ¹⁶Send one of your number to get your brother; *t* the rest of you will be kept in prison, *u* so that your words may be tested to see if you are telling the truth. *v* If you are not, then as surely as Pharaoh lives, you are spies! *w*" ¹⁷And he put them all in custody *x* for three days.

¹⁸On the third day, Joseph said to them, "Do this and you will live, for I fear God: *y* ¹⁹If you are honest men, *z* let one of your brothers stay here in prison, *a* while the rest of you go and take grain back for your starving households. *b* ²⁰But you must bring your youngest brother to me, *c* so that your words may be verified and that you may not die." This they proceeded to do.

²¹They said to one another, "Surely we are being punished because of our brother. *d* We saw how distressed he was when he pleaded with us for his life, but we would not listen; that's why this distress *e* has come on us."

²²Reuben replied, "Didn't I tell you not to sin against the boy? *f* But you wouldn't listen! Now we must give an accounting *g* for his blood." *h* ²³They did not realize *i* that Joseph could understand them, *j* since he was using an interpreter.

²⁴He turned away from them and began to weep, *k* but then came back and spoke to them again. He had Simeon taken from them and bound before their eyes. *l*

²⁵Joseph gave orders to fill their bags with grain, *m* to put each man's silver back in his sack, *n* and to give them provisions *o* for their journey. *p* After this was done for them, ²⁶they loaded their grain on their donkeys *q* and left.

²⁷At the place where they stopped for the night one of them opened his sack to get feed for his donkey, *r* and he saw his silver in the mouth of his sack. *s* ²⁸"My silver has been returned," he said to his brothers. "Here it is in my sack."

Their hearts sank *t* and they turned to each other trembling *u* and said, "What is this that God has done to us?" *v*

²⁹When they came to their father Jacob in the land of Canaan, *w* they told him all that had happened to them. *x* They said, ³⁰"The man who is lord over the land spoke harshly to us *y* and treated us as though we were spying on the land. *z* ³¹But we said to him, 'We are honest men; we are not spies. *a* ³²We were twelve brothers, sons of one father. One is no more, and the youngest is now with our father in Canaan.' *b*

³³"Then the man who is lord over the land said to us, 'This is how I will know whether you are honest men: Leave one of your brothers here with me, and take food for your starving households and go. *c* ³⁴But bring your youngest brother to me so I will know that you are not spies but honest men. *d* Then I will give your brother back to you, *e* and you can trade *a* in the land. *f* '"

³⁵As they were emptying their sacks, there in each man's sack was his pouch of silver! *g* When they and their father saw the money pouches, they were frightened. *h* ³⁶Their father Jacob said to them, "You have deprived me of my children. Joseph is no more and Simeon is no more, *i* and now you want to take Benjamin. *j* Everything is against me! *k*"

³⁷Then Reuben said to his father, "You may put both of my sons to death if I do not bring him back to you. Entrust him to my care, *l* and I will bring him back." *m*

³⁸But Jacob said, "My son will not go down there with you; his brother is dead *n* and he

---

a 34 Or move about freely

42:9 *e* S Ge 37:7
f ver 14,16,30;
Dt 1:22; Jos 2:1; 6:22
g ver 12
42:10 *h* S Ge 37:8
i S ver 3
42:11 *j* ver 13;
Ge 44:7,9,16,19,21,
31; 46:34; 47:3
k ver 15,16,19,20,34
l ver 31
42:12 *m* ver 9
42:13 *n* S ver 11
o S ver 5; Ge 46:31;
47:1 *p* ver 24,32,36;
S Ge 37:30,33; 43:7,
29,33; 44:8; Jer 31:15
42:14 *q* S ver 9
42:15 *r* 1Sa 17:55
s S ver 11; Ge 43:3,5,
7; 44:21,23
42:16 *t* ver 15
u ver 19 *v* S ver 11
w S ver 9
42:17 *x* S Ge 40:4
42:18 *y* S Ge 20:11;
S 22:12; Lev 19:14;
25:43; 2Sa 23:3
42:19 *z* S ver 11
a ver 16 *b* S ver 2
42:20 *c* S ver 15
42:21 *d* S Ge 37:26-28
e Ge 45:5
42:22 *f* S Ge 37:21-22
g S Ge 9:5 *h* Ge 45:24
42:23 *i* Ge 38:16
j S Ge 11:7
42:24 *k* S Ge 29:11
l S ver 13; Ge 43:14,
23
42:25 *m* Ge 43:2
n ver 27,35; Ge 43:12,
18,21; 44:1,8
o Jer 40:5 *p* S Ge 45:21,
23
42:26 *q* S Ge 32:15;
44:13; 45:17;
1Sa 25:18; Isa 30:6
42:27 *r* Jdg 19:19;
Job 39:9; Isa 1:3
s S ver 25
42:28 *t* Jos 2:11; 5:1;
7:5 *u* Mk 5:33
v Ge 43:23
42:29 *w* S ver 5
x Ge 44:24
42:30 *y* ver 7
z S ver 9
42:31 *a* ver 11
42:32 *b* S ver 13
42:33 *c* S ver 2
42:34 *d* S ver 11
e S ver 24 *f* Ge 34:10
42:35 *g* S ver 25
h Ge 43:18
42:36 *i* S ver 13
j S ver 24 *k* Job 3:25;
Pr 10:24; Ro 8:31
42:37 *l* S Ge 39:4
m Ge 43:9; 44:32
42:38 *n* Ge 37:33

42:9,14,16 *You are spies!* See note on Jos 2:1–24.
42:10 *my lord…Your servants.* Unwittingly, Joseph's brothers again fulfilled his dreams and their own scornful fears (see 37:8).
42:15 *As surely as Pharaoh lives.* The most solemn oaths were pronounced in the name of the reigning monarch (as here) or of the speaker's deities (Ps 16:4; Am 8:14) or of the Lord himself (Jdg 8:19; 1Sa 14:39,45; 19:6).

42:21 *how distressed he was … distress has come on us.* The brothers realized they were beginning to reap what they had sown (see Gal 6:7).
42:22 See 37:21–22 and note on 37:21.
42:24 *He had Simeon taken.* Jacob's second son (see 29:32–33) is imprisoned instead of the firstborn Reuben, perhaps because the latter had saved Joseph's life years earlier (37:21–22).
42:37 *both of my sons.* Reuben's generous offer as security for Benjamin's safety (see note on 37:21).

42:38 °ver 4
P S Ge 37:35
q Ge 44:29,34; 48:7
43:1 r S Ge 12:10
43:2 s Ge 42:25
t S Ge 42:2
43:3 u ver 8;
Ge 44:14,18; 46:28
v S Ge 42:15
43:4 w S Ge 42:2
43:5 x S Ge 42:15;
44:26; 2Sa 3:13
43:6 y ver 8,11;
S Ge 17:5
z S Ge 34:30
43:7 a ver 27;
Ge 45:3 b S Ge 42:13;
44:19 c S Ge 42:15
43:8 d S ver 3;
S Ge 29:35 e S ver 6
f S Ge 42:2; Ps 33:18-19
43:9 g 1Sa 23:20
h Ge 44:10,17
i S Ge 42:37;
Phm 1:18-19
43:10 j Ge 45:9
43:11 k S ver 6
l S Ge 24:10
m S Ge 32:13
n S Ge 37:25;
Eze 27:17 ° Ex 30:23;
1Ki 10:2; Eze 27:22
P S Ge 37:25
43:12 q ver 15;
Ex 22:4,7; Pr 6:31
r S Ge 42:25
43:13 s ver 3
43:14 t S Ge 17:1
u Dt 13:17; Ps 25:6
v S Ge 42:24
w 2Sa 18:33; Est 4:16
43:15 x ver 12
y Ge 45:9,13
z Ge 47:2,7; Mt 2:11
43:16 a S Ge 35:18
b ver 17,24,26;
Ge 44:1,4,12;
2Sa 19:17; Isa 22:15
c ver 31; Lk 15:23
43:17 d S ver 16
43:18 e Ge 42:35
f Ge 44:14
g S Ge 42:25
h S Ge 32:11
i Ge 44:9,16,33; 50:18
j Ge 34:28
43:19 k ver 16
43:20 l S Ge 42:3
43:21 m S ver 15;
S Ge 42:25
43:23 n S Ge 24:12;
S 31:5; Ex 3:6
° Ge 42:28
P S Ge 42:25
43:24 q S ver 16
r S Ge 18:4
43:25 s S Ge 32:13
t ver 16

is the only one left. If harm comes to him °on the journey you are taking, you will bring my gray head down to the grave P in sorrow. q"

THE SECOND JOURNEY TO EGYPT

43 Now the famine was still severe in the land. r 2So when they had eaten all the grain they had brought from Egypt, s their father said to them, "Go back and buy us a little more food." t

3But Judah u said to him, "The man warned us solemnly, 'You will not see my face again unless your brother is with you.' v 4If you will send our brother along with us, we will go down and buy food for you. w 5But if you will not send him, we will not go down, because the man said to us, 'You will not see my face again unless your brother is with you.x' "

6Israel y asked, "Why did you bring this trouble z on me by telling the man you had another brother?"

7They replied, "The man questioned us closely about ourselves and our family. 'Is your father still living?' a he asked us. 'Do you have another brother?' b We simply answered his questions. How were we to know he would say, 'Bring your brother down here'?" c

8Then Judah d said to Israel e his father, "Send the boy along with me and we will go at once, so that we and you and our children may live and not die. f 9I myself will guarantee his safety; you can hold me personally responsible for him. g If I do not bring him back to you and set him here before you, I will bear the blame h before you all my life. i 10As it is, if we had not delayed, j we could have gone and returned twice."

11Then their father Israel k said to them, "If it must be, then do this: Put some of the best products l of the land in your bags and take them down to the man as a gift m—a little balm n and a little honey, some spices o and myrrh, P some pistachio nuts and almonds. 12Take double the amount q of silver with you, for you must return the silver that was put back into the mouths of your sacks. r Perhaps it was a mistake. 13Take your brother also and go back to the man at once. s 14And may God Almighty a t grant you mercy u before the man so that he will let your other brother and Benjamin come back with you. v As for me, if I am bereaved, I am bereaved." w

15So the men took the gifts and double the amount of silver, x and Benjamin also. They hurried y down to Egypt and presented themselves z to Joseph. 16When Joseph saw Benjamin a with them, he said to the steward of his house, b "Take these men to my house, slaughter an animal and prepare a meal; c they are to eat with me at noon."

17The man did as Joseph told him and took the men to Joseph's house. d 18Now the men were frightened e when they were taken to his house. f They thought, "We were brought here because of the silver that was put back into our sacks g the first time. He wants to attack us h and overpower us and seize us as slaves i and take our donkeys. j"

19So they went up to Joseph's steward k and spoke to him at the entrance to the house. 20"We beg your pardon, our lord," they said, "we came down here the first time to buy food. l 21But at the place where we stopped for the night we opened our sacks and each of us found his silver—the exact weight—in the mouth of his sack. So we have brought it back with us. m 22We have also brought additional silver with us to buy food. We don't know who put our silver in our sacks."

23"It's all right," he said. "Don't be afraid. Your God, the God of your father, n has given you treasure in your sacks; o I received your silver." Then he brought Simeon out to them. P

24The steward took the men into Joseph's house, q gave them water to wash their feet r and provided fodder for their donkeys. 25They prepared their gifts s for Joseph's arrival at noon, t because they had heard that they were to eat there.

a 14 Hebrew El-Shaddai

42:38 *grave.* See note on 37:35.

43:3 *Judah said.* From this point on, Judah became the spokesman for his brothers (see vv. 8–10; 44:14–34; 46:28). His tribe would become preeminent among the 12 (see 49:8–10), and he would be an ancestor of Jesus (see Mt 1:2–3, 16–17; Lk 3:23,33).

43:9 Judah offered himself as security for Benjamin's safety—an even more generous gesture than that of Reuben (see 42:37 and note).

43:11 *take them . . . as a gift.* A customary practice when approaching one's superior, whether political (see 1Sa 16:20), military (see 1Sa 17:18) or religious (see 2Ki 5:15). *balm . . . myrrh.*

See 37:25 and note. *honey.* Either that produced by bees, or an inferior substitute made by boiling grape or date juice down to a thick syrup. *pistachio nuts.* Mentioned only here in the Bible, they are the fruit of a small, broad-crowned tree that is native to Asia Minor, Syria (Aram) and Canaan but not to Egypt.

43:14 *God Almighty.* See notes on 17:1; 35:1. *if I am bereaved, I am bereaved.* Cf. Esther's similar phrase of resignation in Est 4:16.

43:21 The brothers' statement to Joseph's steward compressed the details (see 42:27,35).

43:23 *Your God . . . has given you treasure.* The steward spoke better than he knew.

43:24 See note on 18:2.

²⁶When Joseph came home,ᵘ they presented to him the gifts ᵛ they had brought into the house, and they bowed down before him to the ground. ʷ ²⁷He asked them how they were, and then he said, "How is your aged fatherˣ you told me about? Is he still living?"ʸ ²⁸They replied, "Your servant our fatherᶻ is still alive and well." And they bowed down,ᵃ prostrating themselves before him.ᵇ

²⁹As he looked about and saw his brother Benjamin, his own mother's son,ᶜ he asked, "Is this your youngest brother, the one you told me about?"ᵈ And he said, "God be gracious to you,ᵉ my son." ³⁰Deeply movedᶠ at the sight of his brother, Joseph hurried out and looked for a place to weep. He went into his private room and weptᵍ there.

³¹After he had washed his face, he came out and, controlling himself,ʰ said, "Serve the food."ⁱ

³²They served him by himself, the brothers by themselves, and the Egyptians who ate with him by themselves, because Egyptians could not eat with Hebrews,ʲ for that is detestable to Egyptians. ᵏ ³³The men had been seated before him in the order of their ages, from the firstbornˡ to the youngest; ᵐ and they looked at each other in astonishment. ³⁴When portions were served to them from Joseph's table, Benjamin's portion was five times as much as anyone else's.ⁿ So they feastedᵒ and drank freely with him.

A SILVER CUP IN A SACK

44 Now Joseph gave these instructions to the steward of his house:ᵖ "Fill the men's sacks with as much food as they can carry, and put each man's silver in the mouth of his sack. ᑫ ²Then put my cup,ʳ the silver one, ˢ in the mouth of the youngest one's sack, along with the silver for his grain." And he did as Joseph said.

³As morning dawned, the men were sent on their way with their donkeys. ᵗ ⁴They had not gone far from the city when Joseph said to his steward, ᵘ "Go after those men at once, and when you catch up with them, say to them, 'Why have you repaid good with evil?ᵛ ⁵Isn't this the cupʷ my master drinks from and also uses for divination?ˣ This is a wicked thing you have done.' "

⁶When he caught up with them, he repeated these words to them. ⁷But they said to him, "Why does my lord say such things? Far be it from your servantsʸ to do anything like that!ᶻ ⁸We even brought back to you from the land of Canaanᵃ the silverᵇ we found inside the mouths of our sacks. ᶜ So why would we stealᵈ silver or gold from your master's house? ⁹If any of your servantsᵉ is found to have it, he will die;ᶠ and the rest of us will become my lord's slaves.ᵍ"

¹⁰"Very well, then," he said, "let it be as you say. Whoever is found to have itʰ will become my slave;ⁱ the rest of you will be free from blame."ʲ

¹¹Each of them quickly lowered his sack to the ground and opened it. ¹²Then the stewardᵏ proceeded to search,ˡ beginning with the oldest and ending with the youngest. ᵐ And the cup was found in Benjamin's sack. ⁿ ¹³At this, they tore their clothes. ᵒ Then they all loaded their donkeysᵖ and returned to the city.

¹⁴Joseph was still in the houseᑫ when Judahʳ and his brothers came in, and they threw themselves to the ground before him. ˢ ¹⁵Joseph said to them, "What is this you have done?ᵗ Don't you know that a man like me can find things out by divination? ᵘ"

¹⁶"What can we say to my lord?ᵛ" Judahʷ replied. "What can we say? How can we prove our innocence?ˣ God has uncovered your servants'ʸ guilt. We are now my lord's slavesᶻ—we ourselves and the one who was found to have the cup. ᵃ"

43:26 ᵘ S ver 16
ᵛ S Ge 32:13; Mt 2:11
ʷ S Ge 33:3
43:27 ˣ S Ge 37:3
ʸ S ver 7
43:28 ᶻ Ge 44:24, 27,30 ᵃ Ge 18:2; Ex 18:7 ᵇ S Ge 37:7
43:29 ᶜ S Ge 35:18
ᵈ S Ge 42:13
ᵉ Nu 6:25; Ps 67:1; 119:58; Isa 30:18-19; 33:2
43:30 ᶠ Jn 11:33,38
ᵍ S Ge 29:11
43:31 ʰ Ge 45:1; Isa 30:18; 42:14;
43:32 ʲ S Ge 14:13; Gal 2:12 ᵏ Ge 46:34; Ex 8:26
43:33 ˡ S Ge 35:23
ᵐ S Ge 42:13; Ge 44:12
43:34 ⁿ S Ge 37:3; S 2Ki 25:30
ᵒ Lk 15:23
44:1 ᵖ S Ge 43:16
ᑫ S Ge 42:25
44:2 ʳ ver 5,10,12,16
ˢ ver 8
44:3 ᵗ Jdg 19:9
44:4 ᵘ S Ge 43:16
ᵛ Ps 35:12; 38:20; 109:5; Pr 17:13; Jer 18:20
44:5 ʷ S ver 2
ˣ S Ge 30:27; Dt 18:10-14
44:7 ʸ S Ge 42:11
ᶻ S Ge 18:25
44:8 ᵃ S Ge 42:13
ᵇ ver 2 ᶜ S Ge 42:25; S 43:15 ᵈ Ge 31:30
44:9 ᵉ S Ge 42:11
ᶠ Ge 31:32 ᵍ S ver 10; S Ge 43:18
44:10 ʰ S ver 2
ⁱ ver 9,17,33
ʲ S Ge 43:9
44:12 ᵏ S Ge 43:16
ˡ S Ge 31:34
ᵐ S Ge 43:33 ⁿ ver 2
44:13 ᵒ S Ge 37:29
ᵖ S Ge 42:26
44:14 ᑫ Ge 43:18
ʳ ver 16; S Ge 29:35; S 43:3 ˢ S Ge 33:3
44:15 ᵗ S Ge 12:18
ᵘ S Ge 30:27
44:16 ᵛ ver 22,24; S Ge 37:8 ʷ S ver 14 ˣ Ps 26:6; 73:13
ʸ S Ge 42:11
ᶻ S Ge 43:18 ᵃ S ver 2

43:26 *bowed down.* Additional fulfillment of Joseph's dreams (37:7,9; see also 42:6; 43:28).

43:29 *Benjamin, his own mother's son.* Joseph's special relationship to Benjamin is clear. *God be gracious to you.* Later blessings and benedictions would echo these words (see Nu 6:25; Ps 67:1).

43:30 *Joseph ... wept.* Both emotional and sensitive, he wept often (see 42:24; 45:2,14–15; 46:29).

43:32 *Egyptians could not eat with Hebrews.* The taboo was probably based on ritual or religious reasons (see Ex 8:26), unlike the Egyptian refusal to associate with shepherds (see 46:34), which was probably based on social custom.

43:34 *Benjamin's portion was five times as much.* Again reflecting his special status with Joseph (see note on v. 29; see also 45:22).

44:4 *city.* Identity unknown, though Memphis (about 13 miles south of modern Cairo) and Zoan (in the eastern delta region) have been suggested.

44:5 *divination.* See v. 15; see also note on 30:27.

44:9 *If any of your servants is found to have it, he will die.* Years earlier, Jacob had given Laban a similar rash response (see 31:32 and note).

44:10 The steward softened the penalty contained in the brothers' proposal.

44:12 *beginning with the oldest and ending with the youngest.* For a similar building up of suspense, see 31:33.

44:13 *tore their clothes.* A sign of distress and grief (see 37:29 and note on 37:34).

44:14 *threw themselves to the ground before him.* Further fulfillment of Joseph's dreams in 37:7,9 (see 42:6; 43:26,28).

44:16 *God has uncovered your servants' guilt.* Like Joseph's steward (see note on 43:23), Judah spoke better than he knew. Or perhaps he refers both to the present event and to the guilt of their sin against Joseph (see 42:21 and note).

44:17 *b* S Ge 18:25
c S ver 10 *d* S Ge 43:9
44:18 *e* S Ge 29:35
f S ver 16 *g* S Ge 18:30
44:19 *h* S Ge 42:11
i S Ge 43:7
44:20 *j* S Ge 37:3
k S Ge 37:33
l S Ge 42:13
44:21 *m* S Ge 42:11
n S Ge 42:15
44:22 *o* S ver 16
p S Ge 37:35
44:23 *q* S Ge 42:15;
S 43:5
44:24 *r* S Ge 43:28
s S ver 16 *t* Ge 42:29
44:25 *u* S Ge 42:2
44:26 *v* S Ge 43:5
44:27 *w* S Ge 43:28
x Ge 46:19
44:28 *y* S Ge 37:33
z Ge 45:26,28; 46:30;
48:11
44:29 *a* S Ge 37:35
b S Ge 42:38
44:30 *c* S Ge 43:28
d 1Sa 18:1; 2Sa 1:26
44:31 *e* S ver 22
f S Ge 42:11
g S Ge 37:35
44:32 *h* S Ge 42:37
44:33 *i* S ver 10;
S Ge 43:18 *j* Jn 15:13
44:34 *k* S Ge 42:38
l Est 8:6
45:1 *m* S Ge 43:31
n 2Sa 13:9
45:2 *o* S Ge 29:11
p ver 16; Ac 7:13
45:3 *q* S Ge 43:7
r ver 15 *s* Ge 44:20;
Job 21:6; 23:15;
Mt 17:6; Mk 6:49-50
45:4 *t* Ge 27:21-22
u Ge 37:28
45:5 *v* Ge 42:21
w Ge 42:22 *x* ver 7-8;
Ge 50:20; Job 10:12;
Ps 105:17
45:6 *y* S Ge 41:30
45:7 *z* 2Ki 19:4,30,
31; Ezr 9:8,13; Isa 1:9;
10:20,21; 11:11,16;
46:3; Jer 6:9; 42:2;
50:20; Mic 4:7; 5:7;
Zep 2:7 *a* S ver 5;
Ge 49:18; Ex 15:2;
1Sa 14:45; 2Ki 13:5;
Est 4:14; Isa 25:9;
Mic 7:7
45:8 *b* ver 5
c Jdg 17:10; 2Ki 6:21;
13:14 *d* S Ge 41:41
45:9 *e* S Ge 43:15
f Ge 43:10; Ac 7:14
45:10 *g* Ge 46:28,
34; 47:1,11,27; 50:8;
Ex 8:22; 9:26; 10:24

¹⁷But Joseph said, "Far be it from me to do such a thing! *b* Only the man who was found to have the cup will become my slave. *c* The rest of you, go back to your father in peace." *d*

¹⁸Then Judah *e* went up to him and said: "Pardon your servant, my lord, *f* let me speak a word to my lord. Do not be angry *g* with your servant, though you are equal to Pharaoh himself. ¹⁹My lord asked his servants, *h* 'Do you have a father or a brother?' *i* ²⁰And we answered, 'We have an aged father, and there is a young son born to him in his old age. *j* His brother is dead, *k* and he is the only one of his mother's sons left, and his father loves him.' *l*

²¹"Then you said to your servants, *m* 'Bring him down to me so I can see him for myself.' *n* ²²And we said to my lord, *o* 'The boy cannot leave his father; if he leaves him, his father will die.' *p* ²³But you told your servants, 'Unless your youngest brother comes down with you, you will not see my face again.' *q* ²⁴When we went back to your servant my father, *r* we told him what my lord *s* had said. *t*

²⁵"Then our father said, 'Go back and buy a little more food.' *u* ²⁶But we said, 'We cannot go down. Only if our youngest brother is with us will we go. We cannot see the man's face unless our youngest brother is with us.' *v*

²⁷"Your servant my father *w* said to us, 'You know that my wife bore me two sons. *x* ²⁸One of them went away from me, and I said, "He has surely been torn to pieces." *y* And I have not seen him since. *z* ²⁹If you take this one from me too and harm comes to him, you will bring my gray head down to the grave *a* in misery.' *b*

³⁰"So now, if the boy is not with us when I go back to your servant my father, *c* and if my father, whose life is closely bound up with the boy's life, *d* ³¹sees that the boy isn't there, he will die. *e* Your servants *f* will bring the gray head of our father down to the grave *g* in sorrow. ³²Your servant guaranteed the boy's safety to my father. I said, 'If I do not bring him back to you, I will bear the blame before you, my father, all my life!' *h*

³³"Now then, please let your servant remain here as my lord's slave *i* in place of the boy, *j* and let the boy return with his brothers. ³⁴How can I go back to my father if the boy is not with me? No! Do not let me see the misery *k* that would come on my father." *l*

JOSEPH MAKES HIMSELF KNOWN

45 Then Joseph could no longer control himself *m* before all his attendants, and he cried out, "Have everyone leave my presence!" *n* So there was no one with Joseph when he made himself known to his brothers. ²And he wept *o* so loudly that the Egyptians heard him, and Pharaoh's household heard about it. *p*

³Joseph said to his brothers, "I am Joseph! Is my father still living?" *q* But his brothers were not able to answer him, *r* because they were terrified at his presence. *s*

⁴Then Joseph said to his brothers, "Come close to me." *t* When they had done so, he said, "I am your brother Joseph, the one you sold into Egypt! *u* ⁵And now, do not be distressed *v* and do not be angry with yourselves for selling me here, *w* because it was to save lives that God sent me ahead of you. *x* ⁶For two years now there has been famine *y* in the land, and for the next five years there will be no plowing and reaping. ⁷But God sent me ahead of you to preserve for you a remnant *z* on earth and to save your lives by a great deliverance. *a a*

⁸"So then, it was not you who sent me here, but God. *b* He made me father *c* to Pharaoh, lord of his entire household and ruler of all Egypt. *d* ⁹Now hurry *e* back to my father and say to him, 'This is what your son Joseph says: God has made me lord of all Egypt. Come down to me; don't delay. *f* ¹⁰You shall live in the region of Goshen *g* and be near

a 7 Or save you as a great band of survivors

44:18 *Judah . . . said.* See note on 43:3. *lord . . . servant.* See note on 42:10. *you are equal to Pharaoh.* Words more flattering than true (see 41:40,43).

44:29,31 *grave.* See note on 37:35.

44:30 *whose life is closely bound up with the boy's life.* The Hebrew underlying this clause is later used of Jonathan's becoming "one in spirit with David" (1Sa 18:1).

44:33 *in place of the boy.* Judah's willingness to be a substitute for Benjamin helped make amends for his role in selling Joseph (see 37:26–27).

44:34 *do not let me see the misery.* Judah remembers an earlier scene (37:34–35).

45:2 *wept.* See vv. 14–15; see also 43:30 and note.

45:3 *brothers . . . were terrified.* Either because they thought they were seeing a ghost or because they were afraid of what Joseph would do to them.

45:4 *I am your brother Joseph.* See v. 3; Ac 7:13. This time Joseph emphasized his relationship to them. *you sold.* See note on 37:28.

45:5 *God sent me.* See vv. 7–9; Ac 7:9; cf. 50:20. God had a purpose to work through the brothers' jealous and cruel act (see Ac 2:23; 4:28).

45:6 Joseph was now 39 years old (see 41:46,53).

45:7 *remnant.* Although none had been lost, they had escaped a great threat to them all; so Joseph called them a remnant in the confidence that they would live to produce a great people.

45:8 *father.* A title of honor given to viziers (see note on 41:43) and other high officials (in the Apocrypha see 1 Maccabees 11:32).

45:9 *hurry back . . . don't delay.* Joseph is anxious to see Jacob as soon as possible (see v. 13).

45:10 *Goshen.* A region in the eastern part of the Nile delta, it was very fertile (see v. 18) and remains so today.

me—you, your children and grandchildren, your flocks and herds, and all you have. [h] 11I will provide for you there, [i] because five years of famine[j] are still to come. Otherwise you and your household and all who belong to you will become destitute.' [k]

12"You can see for yourselves, and so can my brother Benjamin, [l] that it is really I who am speaking to you. [m] 13Tell my father about all the honor accorded me in Egypt [n] and about everything you have seen. And bring my father down here quickly. [o]"

14Then he threw his arms around his brother Benjamin and wept, and Benjamin [p] embraced him, [q] weeping. 15And he kissed [r] all his brothers and wept over them. [s] Afterward his brothers talked with him. [t]

16When the news reached Pharaoh's palace that Joseph's brothers had come, [u] Pharaoh and all his officials [v] were pleased. [w] 17Pharaoh said to Joseph, "Tell your brothers, 'Do this: Load your animals [x] and return to the land of Canaan, [y] 18and bring your father and your families back to me. I will give you the best of the land of Egypt [z] and you can enjoy the fat of the land.' [a]

19"You are also directed to tell them, 'Do this: Take some carts [b] from Egypt for your children and your wives, and get your father and come. 20Never mind about your belongings, [c] because the best of all Egypt [d] will be yours.' "

21So the sons of Israel did this. Joseph gave them carts, [e] as Pharaoh had commanded, and he also gave them provisions for their journey. [f] 22To each of them he gave new clothing, [g] but to Benjamin he gave three hundred shekels[a] of silver and five sets of clothes. [h] 23And this is what he sent to his father: ten donkeys [i] loaded with the best things[j] of Egypt, and ten female donkeys loaded with grain and bread and other provisions for his journey. [k] 24Then he sent his brothers away, and as they were leaving he said to them, "Don't quarrel on the way!" [l]

25So they went up out of Egypt [m] and came to their father Jacob in the land of Canaan. [n] 26They told him, "Joseph is still alive! In fact, he is ruler of all Egypt." [o] Jacob was stunned; he did not believe them. [p] 27But when they told him everything Joseph had said to them, and when he saw the carts [q] Joseph had sent to carry him back, the spirit of their father Jacob revived. 28And Israel said, "I'm convinced! [r] My son Joseph is still alive. I will go and see him before I die." [s]

JACOB GOES TO EGYPT

46 So Israel [t] set out with all that was his, and when he reached Beersheba, [u] he offered sacrifices [v] to the God of his father Isaac. [w]

2And God spoke to Israel [x] in a vision at night [y] and said, "Jacob! Jacob!"

"Here I am," [z] he replied.

3"I am God, the God of your father," [a] he said. "Do not be afraid [b] to go down to Egypt, [c] for I will make you into a great nation. [e] 4I will go down to Egypt with you, and I will surely bring you back again. [f] And Joseph's own hand will close your eyes. [g]"

5Then Jacob left Beersheba, [h] and Israel's [i] sons took their father Jacob and their children and their wives in the carts[j] that Pharaoh had sent to transport him. 6So Jacob and all his offspring went to Egypt, [k] taking with them their livestock and the possessions [l] they had acquired [m] in Canaan. 7Jacob brought with him to Egypt [n] his sons and grandsons and his daughters and granddaughters—all his offspring. [o]

[a] 22 That is, about 7 1/2 pounds or about 3.5 kilograms

45:10 [h] Ge 46:6-7
45:11 [i] Ge 47:12; 50:21; [j] S Ge 41:30
[k] Ps 102:17
45:12 [l] S Ge 35:18
[m] Mk 6:50
45:13 [n] S Ge 41:41
[o] S Ge 43:15; Ac 7:14
45:14 [p] S Ge 35:18
[q] S Ge 29:13
45:15 [r] S Ge 29:11; Lk 15:20 [s] S Ge 29:11, 13; S 46:4 [t] ver 3
45:16 [u] S ver 2; Ac 7:13 [v] Ge 50:7
[w] S Ge 41:37
45:17 [x] S Ge 42:26
[y] S Ge 42:5
45:18 [z] ver 20; Ge 20:15; 46:34; 47:6, 11, 27; Jer 40:4
[a] Ezr 9:12; Ps 37:19; Isa 1:19
45:19 [b] ver 21, 27; Ge 46:5; Nu 7:3-8
45:20 [c] Ge 46:6, 32
[d] S ver 18
45:21 [e] S ver 19
45:22 [g] S Ge 24:53
[h] S Ge 37:3; S 41:14; Jdg 14:12, 13; 2Ki 5:22
45:23 [i] S Ge 42:26
[j] S Ge 24:10
[k] S Ge 42:25
45:24 [l] Ge 42:21-22
45:25 [m] Ge 13:1
[n] Ge 42:29
45:26 [o] S Ge 41:41
[p] S Ge 44:28; 1Ki 10:7
45:27 [q] S ver 19
45:28 [r] Lk 16:31
[s] S Ge 44:28
46:1 [t] ver 5
[u] S Ge 21:14
[v] S Ge 31:54
[w] S Ge 31:42
46:2 [x] S Ge 17:5
[y] S Ge 15:1 [z] S Ge 22:1
46:3 [a] S Ge 28:13
[b] S Ge 15:1 [c] Ge 26:2
[d] S Ge 12:2 [e] Ex 1:7
46:4 [f] S Ge 15:16; S 28:13 [v] ver 29; Ge 45:14-15; 50:1
46:5 [h] S Ge 21:14
[i] ver 1 [j] S Ge 45:19
46:6 [k] Nu 20:15; Dt 26:5; Jos 24:4; Ps 105:23; Isa 52:4; Ac 7:15 [l] S Ge 45:20
[m] S Ge 12:5
46:7 [n] Ge 13:10
[o] ver 6; Ge 45:10

45:12 *I...am speaking.* Not through an interpreter as before (see 42:23).

45:14 *wept.* See 43:30 and note.

45:15 *his brothers talked with him.* In intimate fellowship and friendship, rather than hostility or fear, for the first time in over 20 years (see 37:2 and note on 45:6).

45:18 *you can enjoy the fat of the land.* An echo of Isaac's blessing on Jacob (see 27:28).

45:22 *to Benjamin he gave ... five sets of clothes.* See note on 43:34. *shekels.* See note on 20:16.

A **45:24** *Don't quarrel.* Joseph wanted nothing to delay their return (see note on v. 9), and he wanted them to avoid mutual accusation and recrimination concerning the past.

46:1—47:12 Israel's (Jacob's) move to and settlement in Egypt (see 15:13 and note).

46:1 *set out.* Probably from the family estate at Hebron (see 35:27 and note). *when he reached Beersheba, he offered sacri-*

fices. Abraham and Isaac had also worshiped the Lord there (see 21:33; 26:23–25).

46:2 *God spoke to Israel in a vision at night.* See 26:24. *Jacob! Jacob!* See note on 22:11. *Here I am.* See note on 22:1.

46:3–4 As Israel and his family were about to leave Canaan, God reaffirmed his covenant promises.

46:3 *I am ... the God of your father ... Do not be afraid.* A verbatim repetition of God's statement to Isaac in 26:24. *I will make you into a great nation.* The Lord reaffirmed one aspect of his promise to Abraham (see 12:2). *there.* See Ex 1:7.

C **46:4** *I will go down to Egypt with you.* God would be with Jacob as he went south to Egypt, just as he was with him when he went north to Harran, and would again bring him back as he had done before (see 28:15 and note; see also 15:16 and note; 48:21). *will close your eyes.* A reference to Jacob's death (49:33—50:1).

46:8 ᵖ S Ge 35:26;
Ex 1:1; Nu 26:4
ᑫ S Ge 29:32
46:9 ʳ Ex 6:14;
Nu 1:20; 26:7;
1Ch 5:3 ˢ Nu 26:5;
1Ch 5:3 ᵗ Nu 26:6
46:10 ᵘ S Ge 29:33;
Nu 26:14 ᵛ Ex 6:15;
Nu 26:12 ʷ Nu 26:13
46:11 ˣ S Ge 29:34;
S Nu 3:17 ʸ Ex 6:16;
Nu 3:21; 4:38
ᶻ Ex 6:16; Nu 3:27;
1Ch 23:12 ᵃ Ex 6:19;
Nu 3:20,33; 4:29;
26:57; 1Ch 6:19
46:12 ᵇ S Ge 29:35
ᶜ S Ge 38:3
ᵈ S Ge 38:4
ᵉ S Ge 38:29
ᶠ S Ge 38:30
ᵍ S Ge 38:7; Nu 26:19
ʰ 1Ch 2:5; Mt 1:3
ⁱ Nu 26:21
46:13 ʲ S Ge 30:18
ᵏ Nu 26:23; Jdg 10:1;
1Ch 7:1 ˡ Nu 26:24
46:14 ᵐ S Ge 30:20
46:15 ⁿ S Ge 25:20;
29:31-35 ᵒ S Ge 30:21
46:16 ᵖ S Ge 30:11;
S Nu 1:25 ᑫ Nu 26:15
46:17 ʳ S Ge 30:13
46:18 ˢ Ge 30:10
ᵗ S Ge 16:1
46:19 ᵘ S Ge 29:6
ᵛ Ge 44:27
46:20 ʷ S Ge 41:51
ˣ S Ge 41:52
ʸ Nu 26:28-37
ᶻ S Ge 41:45
46:21 ᵃ Nu 26:38-
41; 1Ch 7:6-12; 8:1
ᵇ Nu 26:40; 1Ch 8:3
46:22 ᶜ S Ge 29:6
46:23 ᵈ S Ge 30:6
ᵉ Nu 26:42
46:24 ᶠ S Ge 30:8
46:25 ᵍ Ge 30:8
ʰ S Ge 24:61
46:26 ⁱ ver 5-7;
Ex 1:5; Dt 10:22
46:27 ʲ S Ge 41:45
ᵏ S Ge 34:30; Ac 7:14

⁸These are the names of the sons of Israelᵖ (Jacob and his descendants) who went to Egypt:

Reuben the firstbornᑫ of Jacob.
⁹ The sons of Reuben:ʳ
Hanok, Pallu,ˢ Hezron and Karmi.ᵗ
¹⁰ The sons of Simeon:ᵘ
Jemuel,ᵛ Jamin, Ohad, Jakin, Zoharʷ and Shaul the son of a Canaanite woman.
¹¹ The sons of Levi:ˣ
Gershon,ʸ Kohathᶻ and Merari.ᵃ
¹² The sons of Judah:ᵇ
Er,ᶜ Onan,ᵈ Shelah, Perezᵉ and Zerahᶠ (but Er and Onan had died in the land of Canaan).ᵍ
The sons of Perez:ʰ
Hezron and Hamul.ⁱ
¹³ The sons of Issachar:ʲ
Tola, Puah,ᵃᵏ Jashubᵇˡ and Shimron.
¹⁴ The sons of Zebulun:ᵐ
Sered, Elon and Jahleel.

¹⁵These were the sons Leah bore to Jacob in Paddan Aram,ᶜⁿ besides his daughter Dinah.ᵒ These sons and daughters of his were thirty-three in all.

¹⁶ The sons of Gad:ᵖ
Zephon,ᵈᑫ Haggi, Shuni, Ezbon, Eri, Arodi and Areli.
¹⁷ The sons of Asher:ʳ
Imnah, Ishvah, Ishvi and Beriah.
Their sister was Serah.
The sons of Beriah:
Heber and Malkiel.

¹⁸These were the children born to Jacob by Zilpah,ˢ whom Laban had given to his daughter Leahᵗ—sixteen in all.

¹⁹ The sons of Jacob's wife Rachel:ᵘ
Joseph and Benjamin.ᵛ ²⁰In Egypt, Manassehʷ and Ephraimˣ were born to Josephʸ by Asenath daughter of Potiphera, priest of On.ᵉᶻ
²¹ The sons of Benjamin:ᵃ
Bela, Beker, Ashbel, Gera, Naaman, Ehi, Rosh, Muppim, Huppim and Ard.ᵇ
²²These were the sons of Rachelᶜ who were born to Jacob—fourteen in all.

²³ The son of Dan:ᵈ
Hushim.ᵉ
²⁴ The sons of Naphtali:ᶠ
Jahziel, Guni, Jezer and Shillem.

²⁵These were the sons born to Jacob by Bilhah,ᵍ whom Laban had given to his daughter Rachelʰ—seven in all.

²⁶All those who went to Egypt with Jacob—those who were his direct descendants, not counting his sons' wives—numbered sixty-six persons.ⁱ ²⁷With the two sonsᶠ who had been born to Joseph in Egypt,ʲ the members of Jacob's family, which went to Egypt, were seventyᵍ in all.ᵏ

ᵃ 13 Samaritan Pentateuch and Syriac (see also 1 Chron. 7:1); Masoretic Text *Puvah*   ᵇ 13 Samaritan Pentateuch and some Septuagint manuscripts (see also Num. 26:24 and 1 Chron. 7:1); Masoretic Text *Iob*   ᶜ 15 That is, Northwest Mesopotamia   ᵈ 16 Samaritan Pentateuch and Septuagint (see also Num. 26:15); Masoretic Text *Ziphion*   ᵉ 20 That is, Heliopolis   ᶠ 27 Hebrew; Septuagint *the nine children*   ᵍ 27 Hebrew (see also Exodus 1:5 and footnote); Septuagint (see also Acts 7:14) *seventy-five*

46:8 *These are the names of the sons of Israel ... who went to Egypt.* Repeated verbatim in Ex 1:1 (see note there), where it introduces the background for the story of the exodus (predicted here in v. 4).

46:15 *Paddan Aram.* See note on 25:20. *thirty-three in all.* There are 34 names in vv. 8–15. To bring the number to 33 the name Ohad in v. 10 should probably be removed, since it does not appear in the parallel lists in Nu 26:12–13; 1Ch 4:24. The Hebrew form of "Ohad" looks very much like that of the nearby "Zohar" (see Ex 6:15), and a later scribe probably added Ohad to the text accidentally.

46:20 See note on 41:45.

46:26 *All those who went to Egypt with Jacob ... numbered sixty-six persons.* The total of 33 (see v. 15 and note), 16 (v. 18), 14 (v. 22) and 7 (v. 25) is 70 (v. 27). To arrive at 66 we must subtract Er and Onan, who "had died in the land of Canaan" (v. 12), and Manasseh and Ephraim (v. 20), who "had been born ... in Egypt" (v. 27).

46:27 *seventy.* See TNIV text note; see also Dt 10:22. Seventy is the ideal and complete number (see Introduction: Literary Features; see also notes on 5:5; 10:2) of Jacob's descendants who would have been in Egypt if Er and Onan had not died earlier (see 38:7–10). For the number 75 in Ac 7:14, see note there.

[28]Now Jacob sent Judah [l] ahead of him to Joseph to get directions to Goshen. [m] When they arrived in the region of Goshen, [29]Joseph had his chariot [n] made ready and went to Goshen to meet his father Israel. [o] As soon as Joseph appeared before him, he threw his arms around his father [a] and wept [p] for a long time. [q]

[30]Israel [r] said to Joseph, "Now I am ready to die, since I have seen for myself that you are still alive." [s]

[31]Then Joseph said to his brothers and to his father's household, "I will go up and speak to Pharaoh and will say to him, 'My brothers and my father's household, who were living in the land of Canaan, [t] have come to me. [u] [32]The men are shepherds; [v] they tend livestock, [w] and they have brought along their flocks and herds and everything they own.' [x] [33]When Pharaoh calls you in and asks, 'What is your occupation?' [y] [34]you should answer, 'Your servants [z] have tended livestock from our boyhood on, just as our fathers did.' [a] Then you will be allowed to settle [b] in the region of Goshen, [c] for all shepherds are detestable to the Egyptians. [d]"

47 Joseph went and told Pharaoh, "My father and brothers, with their flocks and herds and everything they own, have come from the land of Canaan [e] and are now in Goshen." [f] [2]He chose five of his brothers and presented them [g] before Pharaoh.

[3]Pharaoh asked the brothers, "What is your occupation?" [h]

"Your servants [i] are shepherds, [j]" they replied to Pharaoh, "just as our fathers were." [4]They also said to him, "We have come to live here for a while, [k] because the famine is severe in Canaan [l] and your servants' flocks have no pasture. [m] So now, please let your servants settle in Goshen." [n]

[5]Pharaoh said to Joseph, "Your father and your brothers have come to you, [6]and the land of Egypt is before you; settle [o] your father and your brothers in the best part of the land. [p] Let them live in Goshen. And if you know of any among them with special ability, [q] put them in charge of my own livestock. [r]"

[7]Then Joseph brought his father Jacob in and presented him [s] before Pharaoh. After Jacob blessed [b] Pharaoh, [t] [8]Pharaoh asked him, "How old are you?"

[9]And Jacob said to Pharaoh, "The years of my pilgrimage are a hundred and thirty. [u] My years have been few and difficult, [v] and they do not equal the years of the pilgrimage of my fathers. [w]" [10]Then Jacob blessed [c] Pharaoh [x] and went out from his presence.

[11]So Joseph settled his father and his brothers in Egypt and gave them property in the best part of the land, [y] the district of Rameses, [z] as Pharaoh directed. [12]Joseph also provided his father and his brothers and all his father's household with food, according to the number of their children. [a]

JOSEPH AND THE FAMINE

[13]There was no food, however, in the whole region because the famine was severe; both Egypt and Canaan wasted away because of the famine. [b] [14]Joseph collected all the money that was to be found in Egypt and Canaan in payment for the grain they were buying, [c] and he brought it to Pharaoh's palace. [d] [15]When the money of the people of Egypt and Canaan was gone, [e] all Egypt came to Joseph [f] and said, "Give us food. Why should we die before your eyes? [g] Our money is all gone."

[16]"Then bring your livestock, [h]" said Joseph. "I will sell you food in exchange for your livestock, since your money is gone. [i]" [17]So they brought their livestock to Joseph, and he gave them food in exchange for their horses, [j] their sheep and goats, their cattle and donkeys. [k] And he brought them through that year with food in exchange for all their livestock.

[18]When that year was over, they came to him the following year and said, "We cannot hide from our lord the fact that since our money is gone [l] and our livestock belongs to

---

a 29 Hebrew *around him*   b 7 Or *greeted*   c 10 Or *said farewell to*

46:28 *Jacob sent Judah ahead.* See note on 43:3.

46:29 *wept.* See 43:30 and note.

46:34 *shepherds are detestable to the Egyptians.* See note on 43:32.

47:9 *pilgrimage.* Jacob referred to the itinerant nature of patriarchal life in general and of his own in particular as he hopefully awaited the fulfillment of the promise of a land (see also Dt 26:5 and note). *they do not equal the years of ... my fathers.* Abraham lived to the age of 175 (25:7), Isaac to 180 (35:28).

47:11 *best part of the land.* See note on 45:10. *district of Rameses.* The city of Rameses is mentioned in Ex 1:11; 12:37; Nu 33:3,5. The name doubtless refers to the great Egyptian pharaoh Rameses II, who reigned centuries later (the designation here involves an editorial updating). In addition to being known as Goshen (see v. 27), the "district of Rameses" was called the "region of Zoan" in Ps 78:12,43 (see note on Ge 44:4).

47:13 *famine was severe.* After the people used up all their money to buy grain (see vv. 14–15), they traded their livestock (vv. 16–17), then their land (v. 20), then themselves (v. 21).

46:28 [l] S Ge 43:3
[m] S Ge 45:10
46:29 [n] S Ge 41:43
[o] ver 1,30;
S Ge 32:28; 47:29,31
[p] S Ge 29:11 [q] S ver 4;
Lk 15:20
46:30 [r] S ver 29
[s] S Ge 44:28
46:31 [e] S Ge 42:13
[u] S Ge 45:10
46:32 [v] Ge 47:3
[w] S Ge 37:2
[x] S Ge 45:20
46:33 [y] S Ge 47:3
Ge 47:3
46:34 [a] S Ge 42:11
Ge 47:3
[b] S Ge 34:10
[c] S Ge 45:10
[d] S Ge 43:32
47:1 [e] S Ge 42:13
[f] S Ge 46:31
47:2 [g] S Ge 43:15
47:3 [h] Ge 46:33
[i] S Ge 42:11
[j] Ge 46:32
47:4 [k] Ru 1:1
[l] S Ge 12:10
[m] 1Ki 18:5; Jer 14:5-6;
Joel 1:18 [n] Ge 46:34
47:6 [o] S Ge 34:10
[p] S Ge 13:9; S 45:18
[q] Ex 18:21,25; Dt 1:13,
15; 2Ch 19:5; Ps 15:2
[r] S Ge 39:4
47:7 [s] S Ge 43:15
[t] ver 10; 2Sa 14:22;
19:39; 1Ki 8:66
47:9 [u] S Ge 25:7
[v] S Ge 3:17; Ps 39:4;
89:47 [w] Job 8:9;
Ps 39:12
47:10 [x] S ver 7
47:11 [y] S Ge 45:10,
18 [z] Ex 1:11; 12:37;
Nu 33:3,5
47:12 [a] S Ge 45:11
47:13 [b] S Ge 12:10;
S 41:30
47:14 [c] S Ge 41:36
[d] S Ge 41:34; Ex 7:23;
8:24; Jer 43:9
47:15 [e] ver 16,18
[f] S Ge 41:57 [g] ver 19;
Ex 16:3
47:16 [h] ver 18,19
[i] ver 15
47:17 [j] Ex 14:9
[k] S Ge 12:16
47:18 [l] S ver 15

47:18 *m* S ver 16
47:19 *n* S ver 15
o S ver 16 *p* ver 21,25
q S Ge 42:2
47:20 *r* S Ge 12:10
47:21 *s* S ver 19
47:22 *t* ver 26
u Dt 14:28-29
47:23 *v* Isa 55:10;
61:11 *w* Ne 5:3
47:24 *x* S Ge 41:34
47:25 *y* S Ge 32:5
z S ver 19
47:26 *a* S Ge 41:34
b ver 22
47:27 *c* S Ge 45:10,
18 *d* S Ge 33:19
e S Ge 1:22; S 12:2;
S 17:6
47:28 *f* Ps 105:23
g S Ge 25:7
47:29 *h* S Ge 46:29
i S Ge 27:2 *j* S Ge 32:5
k S Ge 24:2
l S Ge 19:19
m S Ge 24:27;
Jdg 1:24; 2Sa 2:6
47:30 *n* S Ge 15:15
o S Ge 23:20; S 25:9;
S 29:16; 50:25;
Ex 13:19; Jos 24:32;
Ac 7:15-16
47:31 *p* Ge 21:23;
Jos 2:20; Jdg 15:12;
1Sa 24:21; 30:15
q S Ge 24:3
r S Ge 46:29
s S Ge 32:10;
Heb 11:21 *fn*; 1Ki 1:47
48:1 *t* S Ge 41:52;
Heb 11:21
48:2 *u* ver 8,9,11,14,
20
48:3 *v* S Ge 17:1
w S Ge 28:19
x S Ge 28:13; S 32:29
48:4 *y* S Ge 12:2;
S 17:6 *z* S Ge 12:7;
S 28:13 *a* S Ge 15:7
48:5 *b* S Ge 41:50-
52 *c* 1Ch 5:1
d S Ge 29:32
e S Ge 29:33

you, *m* there is nothing left for our lord except our bodies and our land. ¹⁹Why should we perish before your eyes *n*—we and our land as well? Buy us and our land in exchange for food, *o* and we with our land will be in bondage to Pharaoh. *p* Give us seed so that we may live and not die, *q* and that the land may not become desolate."

²⁰So Joseph bought all the land in Egypt for Pharaoh. The Egyptians, one and all, sold their fields, because the famine was too severe *r* for them. The land became Pharaoh's, ²¹and Joseph reduced the people to servitude, *a s* from one end of Egypt to the other. ²²However, he did not buy the land of the priests, *t* because they received a regular allotment from Pharaoh and had food enough from the allotment *u* Pharaoh gave them. That is why they did not sell their land.

²³Joseph said to the people, "Now that I have bought you and your land today for Pharaoh, here is seed *v* for you so you can plant the ground. *w* ²⁴But when the crop comes in, give a fifth *x* of it to Pharaoh. The other four-fifths you may keep as seed for the fields and as food for yourselves and your households and your children."

²⁵"You have saved our lives," they said. "May we find favor in the eyes of our lord; *y* we will be in bondage to Pharaoh." *z*

²⁶So Joseph established it as a law concerning land in Egypt—still in force today—that a fifth *a* of the produce belongs to Pharaoh. It was only the land of the priests that did not become Pharaoh's. *b*

²⁷Now the Israelites settled in Egypt in the region of Goshen. *c* They acquired property there *d* and were fruitful and increased greatly in number. *e*

²⁸Jacob lived in Egypt *f* seventeen years, and the years of his life were a hundred and forty-seven. *g* ²⁹When the time drew near for Israel *h* to die, *i* he called for his son Joseph and said to him, "If I have found favor in your eyes, *j* put your hand under my thigh *k* and promise that you will show me kindness *l* and faithfulness. *m* Do not bury me in Egypt, ³⁰but when I rest with my fathers, *n* carry me out of Egypt and bury me where they are buried." *o*

"I will do as you say," he said.

³¹"Swear to me," *p* he said. Then Joseph swore to him, *q* and Israel *r* worshiped as he leaned on the top of his staff. *b s*

MANASSEH AND EPHRAIM

48 Some time later Joseph was told, "Your father is ill." So he took his two sons Manasseh and Ephraim *t* along with him. ²When Jacob was told, "Your son Joseph has come to you," Israel *u* rallied his strength and sat up on the bed.

³Jacob said to Joseph, "God Almighty *c v* appeared to me at Luz *w* in the land of Canaan, and there he blessed me *x* ⁴and said to me, 'I am going to make you fruitful and increase your numbers. *y* I will make you a community of peoples, and I will give this land *z* as an everlasting possession to your descendants after you.' *a*

⁵"Now then, your two sons born to you in Egypt *b* before I came to you here will be reckoned as mine; Ephraim and Manasseh will be mine, *c* just as Reuben *d* and Simeon *e* are mine. ⁶Any children born to you after them will be yours; in the territory they inherit

---

a 21 Samaritan Pentateuch and Septuagint (see also Vulgate); Masoretic Text *and he moved the people into the cities* *b 31* Or *Israel bowed down at the head of his bed* *c 3* Hebrew *El-Shaddai*

47:21 The TNIV text note reading would mean that the Egyptians were to move temporarily into the cities until seed could be distributed to them for planting (see v. 23).

47:26 *a fifth of the produce belongs to Pharaoh.* The same was true "during the seven years of abundance" (41:34)—but now all the land on which the produce grew belonged to the pharaoh as well.

47:27 *Israelites . . . were fruitful and increased greatly in number.* See 35:11–12; 46:3 and notes.

47:29 *put your hand under my thigh.* See 24:2 and note. In both cases, ties of family kinship are being stressed.

47:30 *rest with my fathers.* See note on 25:8. *bury me where they are buried.* In the cave of Machpelah (see 50:12–13).

47:31 *worshiped as he leaned on the top of his staff.* Quoted in Heb 11:21. Compare 48:2 with the TNIV text note reading here.

48:1–22 How Joseph, beloved Rachel's older son, received the inheritance of the firstborn among his brothers.

48:3 *God Almighty.* See notes on 17:1; 35:11. *Luz.* The older name for Bethel (see 28:19).

48:5 *your two sons . . . will be reckoned as mine.* Jacob adopts them as his own. *Ephraim and Manasseh.* See v. 1 for the expected order, since Manasseh was Joseph's firstborn (see 41:51). Jacob mentions Ephraim first because he intends to give him the primary blessing and thus "put Ephraim ahead of Manasseh" (v. 20). *mine, just as Reuben and Simeon are mine.* Joseph's first two sons would enjoy equal status with Jacob's first two sons (35:23) and in fact would eventually supersede them. Because of an earlier sinful act (see 35:22 and note), Reuben would lose his birthright to Jacob's favorite son, Joseph (see 49:3–4; 1Ch 5:2), and thus to Joseph's sons (see 1Ch 5:1).

48:6 *children born to you after them will be yours.* They would take the place of Ephraim and Manasseh, whom Jacob had adopted. *in the territory they inherit they will be reckoned under the names of their brothers.* They would perpetuate the names of Ephraim and Manasseh for purposes of inheritance (for a similar provision see 38:8 and note; Dt 25:5–7). Joseph's territory would thus be divided between Ephraim and Manasseh, but Levi (Jacob's third son; see 35:23) would receive "no share of the land" (Jos 14:4). The total number of tribal allotments would therefore remain the same.

they will be reckoned under the names of their brothers. ⁷As I was returning from Paddan,ᵃ ᶠto my sorrowᵍ Rachel died in the land of Canaan while we were still on the way, a little distance from Ephrath. So I buried her there beside the road to Ephrath" (that is, Bethlehem).ʰ

⁸When Israelⁱ saw the sons of Joseph,ʲ he asked, "Who are these?"

⁹"They are the sons God has given me here,"ᵏ Joseph said to his father.

Then Israel said, "Bring them to me so I may blessˡ them."

¹⁰Now Israel's eyes were failing because of old age, and he could hardly see.ᵐ So Joseph brought his sons close to him, and his father kissed themⁿ and embraced them.ᵒ

¹¹Israelᵖ said to Joseph, "I never expected to see your face again,�q and now God has allowed me to see your children too."ʳ

¹²Then Joseph removed them from Israel's kneesˢ and bowed down with his face to the ground.ᵗ ¹³And Joseph took both of them, Ephraim on his right toward Israel's left hand and Manasseh on his left toward Israel's right hand,ᵘ and brought them close to him. ¹⁴But Israelᵛ reached out his right hand and put it on Ephraim's head,ʷ though he was the younger,ˣ and crossing his arms, he put his left hand on Manasseh's head, even though Manasseh was the firstborn.ʸ

¹⁵Then he blessedᶻ Joseph and said,

> "May the God before whom my fathers
>   Abraham and Isaac walked faithfully,ᵃ
> the God who has been my shepherdᵇ
>   all my life to this day,
> ¹⁶the Angelᶜ who has delivered me from all harmᵈ
>   —may he blessᵉ these boys.ᶠ
> May they be called by my name
>   and the names of my fathers Abraham and Isaac,ᵍ
> and may they increase greatly
>   on the earth."ʰ

¹⁷When Joseph saw his father placing his right handⁱ on Ephraim's headʲ he was displeased; so he took hold of his father's hand to move it from Ephraim's head to Manasseh's head. ¹⁸Joseph said to him, "No, my father, this one is the firstborn; put your right hand on his head."ᵏ

¹⁹But his father refused and said, "I know, my son, I know. He too will become a people, and he too will become great.ˡ Nevertheless, his younger brother will be greater than he,ᵐ and his descendants will become a group of nations.ⁿ" ²⁰He blessedᵒ them that dayᵖ and said,

> "In yourᵇ name will Israelq pronounce this blessing:ʳ
> 'May God make you like Ephraimˢ and Manasseh.ᵗ'"

So he put Ephraim ahead of Manasseh.

²¹Then Israel said to Joseph, "I am about to die, but God will be with youᶜ ᵘ and take

---

ᵃ 7 That is, Northwest Mesopotamia   ᵇ 20 The Hebrew is singular.   ᶜ 21 The Hebrew is plural.

48:7 *Paddan.* That is, Paddan Aram (see note on 25:20). *Rachel died.* See 35:16–19. Adopted by Joseph's father, Ephraim and Manasseh in effect took the place of other sons whom Joseph's mother, Rachel, might have borne if she had not died. *Ephrath.* See note on 35:16.
48:8 *Israel … asked, "Who are these?"* Either because he had never met them or because, being old, he could not see them clearly.
48:10 *because of old age … he could hardly see.* See note on 27:1. *kissed them and embraced them.* While they were on Jacob's knees (see v. 12), probably symbolizing adoption (see note on 30:3).
48:13–20 See note on Ac 6:6.
48:13 *Manasseh … toward Israel's right hand.* Joseph wanted Jacob to bless Manasseh, Joseph's firstborn, by placing his right hand on Manasseh's head.
48:15 *blessed.* As his father Isaac had blessed him (27:27–29). *Joseph.* Used here collectively for Ephraim and Manasseh (see TNIV text note on v. 21). *before whom … Abraham and Isaac*

walked faithfully. See notes on 5:22; 17:1. *shepherd.* Widely used in the ancient Near East as a metaphor for the king. It highlighted his care for his people. Here and in 49:24 it is used of God (see Ps 23:1 and note).
48:16 *Angel.* See note on 16:7. The angel—God himself—had earlier blessed Jacob (see 32:29; see also note on 32:24).
48:19 *his younger brother will be greater than he.* See note on 25:23. During the divided monarchy (930–722 B.C.), Ephraim's descendants were the most powerful tribe in the north. "Ephraim" was often used to refer to the northern kingdom as a whole (see, e.g., Isa 7:2,5,8–9; Hos 9:13; 12:1,8).
48:20 *he put Ephraim ahead of Manasseh.* Jacob, the younger son who struggled with Esau for the birthright and blessing and who preferred the younger sister (Rachel) above the older (Leah), now advanced Joseph's younger son ahead of the older.
48:21 *Joseph.* See note on v. 15. *I am about to die.* Years later, Joseph spoke these words to his brothers (50:24).

48:7 ᶠS Ge 25:20
ᵍS Ge 42:38
ʰ Ge 35:19; Ru 1:2;
1Sa 16:4
48:8 ⁱS ver 2 ʲver 10
48:9 ᵏS Ge 33:5
ˡS Ge 24:60
48:10 ᵐS Ge 27:1
ⁿS Ge 27:27
ᵒS Ge 29:13
48:11 ᵖS ver 2
qS Ge 44:28
ʳGe 50:23; Job 42:16;
Ps 103:17; 128:6
48:12 ˢGe 50:23;
Job 3:12 ᵗS Ge 19:1;
S 33:3; 37:10
48:13 ᵘPs 16:8;
73:23; 110:1; Mt 25:33
48:14 ᵛS ver 2
ʷver 17,18
ˣS Ge 25:23
ʸS Ge 29:32; S 41:51
48:15 ᶻS Ge 24:60
ᵃS Ge 5:22
ᵇGe 49:24; 2Sa 5:2;
Ps 23:1; 80:1;
Isa 40:11; Jer 23:4
48:16 ᶜS Ge 16:7
ᵈS Ge 24:50;
2Sa 4:9; Ps 71:4;
Jer 15:21; Da 3:17
ᵉS Ge 28:3 ᶠ1Ch 5:1;
Eze 47:13; Heb 11:21
ᵍS Ge 28:13
ʰS Ge 12:2; S 13:14
48:17 ⁱver 13
ʲS ver 14
48:18 ᵏS ver 14
48:19 ˡGe 17:20
ᵐS Ge 25:23
ⁿS Ge 12:2
48:20 ᵒS Ge 24:60
ᵖHeb 11:21 qS ver 2
ʳLev 9:22; Nu 6:23;
Nu 2:18; Jer 31:9
ˢNu 2:18; Jer 31:9
ᵗS Ge 41:51; Nu 2:20;
10:23; Ru 4:11
48:21 ᵘS Ge 26:3

48:21 ʸS Ge 15:16;
S 28:13; Dt 30:3;
Ps 126:1; Jer 29:14;
Eze 34:13
48:22 ʷJos 24:32;
Jn 4:5 ˣS Ge 34:26
49:1 ʸNu 24:14;
Dt 31:29; Jer 23:20;
Da 2:28,45
49:2 ᶻJos 24:1
ᵃ ver 16,28; Ps 34:11
49:3 ᵇS Ge 29:32;
S 41:51 ᶜDt 21:17;
Ps 78:51; 105:36
ᵈS Ge 34:19
49:4 ᵉ Isa 57:20;
Jer 49:23
ᶠS Ge 29:29; S 34:5
49:5 ᵍS Ge 29:33
ʰ Ge 29:34
ⁱS Ge 34:25;
S Pr 4:17
49:6 ʲ Ps 1:1; Pr 1:15;
Eph 5:11 ᵏS Ge 34:26
ˡJos 11:6,9; 2Sa 8:4;
1Ch 18:4
49:7 ᵐGe 34:7
ⁿ Ge 34:25 ᵒJos 19:1,
9; 21:1-42
49:8 ᵖS Ge 29:35
�q Dt 28:48
ʳS Ge 9:25; 1Ch 5:2
49:9 ˢNu 24:9;
Ps 7:2; 10:9; Eze 19:5;
Mic 5:8 ᵗEze 19:2
ᵘRev 5:5 ᵛver 27;
Nu 23:24; Job 38:39;
Ps 17:12; 22:13; 104:21
49:10 ʷNu 24:17,
19; Jdg 1:1-2; 20:18;
1Ch 5:2; 28:4;
Ps 60:7; 108:8

you ᵃ back to the land of your ᵃ fathers. ᵛ ²²And to you I give one more ridge of land ᵇ than to your brothers, ʷ the ridge I took from the Amorites with my sword ˣ and my bow."

JACOB BLESSES HIS SONS
49:1–28Ref — Dt 33:1–29

49 Then Jacob called for his sons and said: "Gather around so I can tell you what will happen to you in days to come. ʸ

² "Assemble ᶻ and listen, sons of Jacob;
    listen to your father Israel. ᵃ
³ "Reuben, you are my firstborn, ᵇ
    my might, the first sign of my strength, ᶜ
    excelling in honor, ᵈ excelling in power.
⁴ Turbulent as the waters, ᵉ you will no longer excel,
    for you went up onto your father's bed,
    onto my couch and defiled it. ᶠ

⁵ "Simeon ᵍ and Levi ʰ are brothers—
    their swords ᶜ are weapons of violence. ⁱ
⁶ Let me not enter their council,
    let me not join their assembly, ʲ
    for they have killed men in their anger ᵏ
    and hamstrung ˡ oxen as they pleased.
⁷ Cursed be their anger, so fierce,
    and their fury, ᵐ so cruel! ⁿ
  I will scatter them in Jacob
    and disperse them in Israel. ᵒ

⁸ "Judah, ᵈᵖ your brothers will praise you;
    your hand will be on the neck ᵠ of your enemies;
    your father's sons will bow down to you. ʳ
⁹ You are a lion's ˢ cub, ᵗ Judah; ᵘ
    you return from the prey, ᵛ my son.
  Like a lion he crouches and lies down,
    like a lioness—who dares to rouse him?
¹⁰ The scepter will not depart from Judah, ʷ
    nor the ruler's staff from between his feet, ᵉ

ᵃ 21 The Hebrew is plural.   ᵇ 22 The Hebrew for *ridge of land* is identical with the place name Shechem.   ᶜ 5 The meaning of the Hebrew for this word is uncertain.   ᵈ 8 *Judah* sounds like and may be derived from the Hebrew for *praise*.   ᵉ 10 Or *from his descendants*

48:22 *ridge of land.* The Hebrew for this phrase is identical with the place-name Shechem, where Joseph was later buried in a plot of ground inherited by his descendants (see Jos 24:32 and note; see also 33:19; Jn 4:5 and note). *I took from the Amorites.* Possibly referring to the event of 34:25–29.
49:2–27 Often called the "Blessing of Jacob," this is the longest poem in Genesis. Its various blessings were intended not only for Jacob's 12 sons but also for the tribes that descended from them (see v. 28). For other poetic blessings in Genesis, see 9:26–27; 14:19–20; 27:27–29; 27:39–40; 48:15–16; 48:20.
49:4 *Turbulent.* Reuben's descendants were characterized by indecision (see Jdg 5:15–16). *you will no longer excel, for you went up onto your father's bed.* See 35:22 and note; see also notes on 37:21; 48:5.
49:5 *Simeon and Levi are brothers.* They shared the traits of violence, anger and cruelty (see vv. 6–7; see also note on 34:25).
49:7 *I will scatter them.* Fulfilled when Simeon's descendants were absorbed into the territory of Judah (see Jos 19:1,9 and note on 19:1) and when Levi's descendants were dispersed throughout the land, living in 48 towns and the surrounding pasturelands (see note on 48:6; see also Nu 35:2,7; Jos 14:4; 21:41).
49:8 Cf. 27:29,40; 37:7,9. *Judah, your brothers … will bow down*

to you. See note on 43:3. As those who would become the leading tribes of southern and northern Israel, respectively, Judah and Joseph were given the longest (vv. 8–12 and vv. 22–26) of Jacob's blessings. Judah was the fourth of Leah's sons and also the fourth son born to Jacob (29:35), but Reuben, Simeon and Levi had forfeited their right of leadership. So Jacob assigns leadership to Judah (a son of Leah) but a double portion to Joseph (a son of Rachel). See also 1Ch 5:2.
49:9 *You are a lion's cub.* A symbol of sovereignty, strength and courage. Judah (or Israel) is often pictured as a lion in later times (see Eze 19:2; Mic 5:8 and notes; and especially Nu 24:9). Judah's greatest descendant, Jesus Christ (see note on 43:3), is himself called "the Lion of the tribe of Judah" (Rev 5:5; see note there).
49:10 Though difficult to translate (see TNIV text note), the verse has been traditionally understood as Messianic. It was initially fulfilled in David, and ultimately in Christ. *scepter.* See Nu 24:17 and note. *until he to whom it belongs shall come.* Repeated almost verbatim in Eze 21:27 (see note there) in a section where Zedekiah, the last king of Judah, is told to "remove the crown" (Eze 21:26) from his head because dominion over Jerusalem will ultimately be given to the one "to whom it rightfully belongs."

until he to whom it belongs[a] shall come[x]
  and the obedience of the nations be his. [y]

[11] He will tether his donkey[z] to a vine,
    his colt to the choicest branch;[a]
  he will wash his garments in wine,
    his robes in the blood of grapes. [b]

[12] His eyes will be darker than wine,
    his teeth whiter than milk. [b][c]

[13] "Zebulun[d] will live by the seashore
    and become a haven for ships;
  his border will extend toward Sidon. [e]

[14] "Issachar[f] is a rawboned[c] donkey
    lying down among the sheep pens. [d][g]

[15] When he sees how good is his resting place
    and how pleasant is his land, [h]
  he will bend his shoulder to the burden[i]
    and submit to forced labor.[j]

[16] "Dan[e][k] will provide justice for his people
    as one of the tribes of Israel. [l]

[17] Dan[m] will be a snake by the roadside,
    a viper along the path, [n]
  that bites the horse's heels[o]
    so that its rider tumbles backward.

[18] "I look for your deliverance,[p] LORD. [q]

[19] "Gad[f][r] will be attacked by a band of raiders,
    but he will attack them at their heels. [s]

[20] "Asher's[t] food will be rich;[u]
  he will provide delicacies fit for a king. [v]

[21] "Naphtali[w] is a doe set free
    that bears beautiful fawns.[g][x]

[22] "Joseph[y] is a fruitful vine,[z]
    a fruitful vine near a spring,
  whose branches[a] climb over a wall. [h]

[23] With bitterness archers attacked him;[b]
    they shot at him with hostility. [c]

[24] But his bow remained steady,[d]
    his strong arms[e] stayed[i] limber,

---

[a] 10 Or *to whom tribute belongs*; the meaning of the Hebrew for this phrase is uncertain.   [b] 12 Or *will be dull from wine, / his teeth white from milk*   [c] 14 Or *strong*   [d] 14 Or *the campfires*; or *the saddlebags*   [e] *Dan* here means *he provides justice*.   [f] 19 *Gad* sounds like the Hebrew for *attack* and also for *band of raiders*.   [g] 21 Or *free; / he utters beautiful words*   [h] 22 Or *Joseph is a wild colt, / a wild colt near a spring, / a wild donkey on a terraced hill*   [i] 23,24 Or *archers will attack . . . will shoot . . . will remain . . . will stay*

49:11 Judah's descendants would someday enjoy a settled and prosperous life.

49:13 Though landlocked by the tribes of Asher and Manasseh, the descendants of Zebulun were close enough to the Mediterranean (within ten miles) to "feast on the abundance of the seas" (Dt 33:19).

49:17 *Dan will be a snake.* The treachery of a group of Danites in later times is described in Jdg 18:27. *bites the horse's heels.* Samson, from the tribe of Dan, would single-handedly hold the Philistines at bay (Jdg 14–16).

49:18 Jacob pauses midway through his series of blessings to utter a brief prayer for God's help.

49:19 *Gad will be attacked.* Located east of the Jordan (see Jos 13:24–27), the descendants of Gad were vulnerable to raids by the Moabites to the south, as the Mesha (see 2Ki 3:4) Stele (a Moabite inscription dating from the late ninth century B.C.) illustrates (see chart, p.xxiii).

49:20 *Asher's food will be rich.* Fertile farmlands near the Mediterranean (see Jos 19:24–30) would ensure the prosperity of Asher's descendants.

49:21 *Naphtali is a doe set free.* Perhaps a reference to an independent spirit fostered in the descendants of Naphtali by their somewhat isolated location in the hill country north of the Sea of Galilee (see Jos 19:32–38).

49:22 *fruitful . . . fruitful.* A pun on the name Ephraim (see TNIV text note on 41:52), who Jacob predicted would be greater than Joseph's firstborn son Manasseh (48:19–20). *branches climb over a wall.* Ephraim's descendants tended to expand their territory (see Jos 17:14–18).

49:24 *his bow remained steady.* The warlike Ephraimites (see Jdg 8:1; 12:1) would often prove victorious in battle (see Jos 17:18). *Mighty One of Jacob.* Stresses the activity of God in saving and redeeming his people (see Isa 49:26). *Shepherd.* See note on 48:15. *Rock of Israel.* Israel's sure defense (see Dt 32:4,15,18,30–31)—a figure often used also in Psalms (see note on Ps 18:2) and Isaiah.

49:10 [x] Eze 21:27
[y] Ps 2:9; 72:8-11;
98:3; 110:2; Isa 2:4;
26:18; 42:1,4; 45:22;
48:20; 49:6; 51:5
49:11 [z] Jdg 5:10;
10:4; Zec 9:9 [a] Dt 8:8;
2Ki 18:32 [b] Dt 32:14;
Isa 63:2
49:12 [c] SS 5:12
49:13 [d] S Ge 30:20
[e] S Ge 10:19
49:14 [f] S Ge 30:18
[g] Jdg 5:16; Ps 68:13
49:15 [h] Jos 19:17-23
[i] Eze 29:18 [j] 1Ki 4:6;
5:13; 9:21; Isa 14:2;
31:8
49:16 [k] Ge 30:6
[l] S ver 2
49:17 [m] Jdg 18:27
[n] Jer 8:17; Am 9:3
[o] ver 19
49:18 [p] S Ge 45:7;
Ps 40:1-3
[q] Ps 119:166,174
49:19 [r] S Ge 30:11
[s] ver 17
49:20 [t] S Ge 30:13
[u] Isa 25:6 [v] Job 29:6
49:21 [w] S Ge 30:8
[x] Job 39:1
49:22 [y] Ge 30:24
[z] S Ge 17:6; Ps 128:3;
Eze 19:10 [a] Ps 80:10
49:23 [b] 1Ch 10:3
[c] S Ge 27:41; S 37:24
49:24 [d] Job 29:20
[e] Ps 18:34; Isa 63:12

49:24 f Ps 132:2, 5;
Isa 1:24; 10:34; 49:26;
60:16 g S Ge 48:15
h Dt 32:4, 15, 18, 31;
1Sa 2:2; 2Sa 22:32;
Ps 18:2, 31; 19:14;
78:35; 89:26; 144:1;
Isa 17:10; 26:4; 30:29;
44:8; Hab 1:12
49:25 i S Ge 28:13
j Ex 18:4; Ps 27:9
k Ge 17:1
l S Ge 27:28
m Isa 66:11 n Dt 7:13;
28:4; Ps 107:38;
Pr 10:22
49:26 o Hab 3:6
p 1Ch 5:1; Eze 47:13
q S Ge 37:8
49:27 r Ge 35:18;
Jdg 20:12-13
s Hab 1:8; Zep 3:3
t S ver 9 u Nu 31:11;
Dt 2:35; Jos 7:21; 8:2;
22:8; Jdg 8:24
49:28 v S ver 2
w S Ge 27:4
49:29 x Ge 50:16
y S Ge 25:8
z S Ge 15:15; 50:25;
2Sa 2:32; 19:37
a S Ge 25:9
49:30 b S Ge 23:9
c S Ge 13:18
d S Ge 23:20
e S Ge 23:4
49:31 f Ge 25:9
g Ge 23:19

because of the hand of the Mighty One of Jacob, f
　because of the Shepherd, g the Rock of Israel, h
[25] because of your father's God, i who helps j you,
　because of the Almighty, a k who blesses you
with blessings of the heavens above,
　blessings of the deep that lies below, l
　blessings of the breast m and womb. n
[26] Your father's blessings are greater
　than the blessings of the ancient mountains,
　than b the bounty of the age-old hills. o
Let all these rest on the head of Joseph, p
　on the brow of the prince among c his brothers. q

[27] "Benjamin r is a ravenous wolf; s
　in the morning he devours the prey, t
　in the evening he divides the plunder." u

[28] All these are the twelve tribes of Israel, v and this is what their father said to them when he blessed them, giving each the blessing w appropriate to him.

THE DEATH OF JACOB

[29] Then he gave them these instructions: x "I am about to be gathered to my people. y Bury me with my fathers z in the cave in the field of Ephron the Hittite, a [30] the cave in the field of Machpelah, b near Mamre c in Canaan, which Abraham bought along with the field d as a burial place e from Ephron the Hittite. [31] There Abraham f and his wife Sarah g

---

a 25 Hebrew *Shaddai*　　b 26 Or *of my progenitors, / as great as*　　c 26 Or *of the one separated from*

49:25 *Almighty.* See note on 17:1. *blessings of the heavens . . . of the deep.* The fertility of the soil watered by rains from above and springs and streams from below. *breast and womb.* The fertility of people and animals. For the later prosperity of Ephraim's descendants, see Hos 12:8.
49:26 *Joseph . . . prince among his brothers.* See notes on v. 8; 48:19. Ephraim would gain supremacy, especially over the northern tribes (see Jos 16:9; Isa 7:1–2; Hos 13:1).

49:27 *Benjamin is a ravenous wolf.* See the exploits of Ehud (Jdg 3:12–30) and Saul and Jonathan (1Sa 11–15). See Jdg 19–21 for examples of the savagery that characterized one group of Benjamin's descendants.
49:28 *twelve tribes of Israel.* See note on vv. 2–27.
49:29 *Bury me with my fathers.* See note on 25:8. Jacob does not forget that the land of his ancestors is his God-appointed homeland (see note on 23:19).

THE TRIBES OF ISRAEL

Wives of Abraham
HAGAR . . . . Ishmael
Abraham
　　　　　REBEKAH
SARAH . . . . Isaac

Esau

Wives of Jacob
LEAH . . . .

Jacob (Israel)*

ZILPAH . . . .
Leah's servant

BILHAH . . . .
Rachel's servant

RACHEL . . . .

Fathers of the tribes of Israel

other child

Reuben
Simeon
Levi**
Judah
Issachar
Zebulun

DINAH

Gad
Asher

Dan
Naphtali

Joseph***
Benjamin

Ephraim
Manasseh

* Jacob's name was symbolically changed to Israel when he wrestled with the divine visitor at Peniel. As patriarch of the 12 tribes, he bequeathed his new name to the nation, which often was still poetically called "Jacob."

** Levi was not included among the tribes given land allotments following the conquest of Canaan (cf. Ge 49:7). Instead, Moses set the Levites apart for national priestly duty as belonging to the Lord (Nu 3:1–4, 49). Joshua awarded them 48 towns scattered throughout Israel (Jos 21:1–45).

*** Joseph became the father of two tribes in Israel since Jacob adopted his two sons, Ephraim and Manasseh.

were buried, there Isaac and his wife Rebekah *h* were buried, and there I buried Leah. *i* ³²The field and the cave in it were bought from the Hittites. *a j*."

³³When Jacob had finished giving instructions to his sons, he drew his feet up into the bed, breathed his last and was gathered to his people. *k*

50 Joseph threw himself on his father and wept over him and kissed him. *l* ²Then Joseph directed the physicians in his service to embalm his father Israel. So the physicians embalmed him, *m* ³taking a full forty days, for that was the time required for embalming. And the Egyptians mourned for him seventy days. *n*

⁴When the days of mourning *o* had passed, Joseph said to Pharaoh's court, *p* "If I have found favor in your eyes, *q* speak to Pharaoh for me. Tell him, ⁵'My father made me swear an oath *r* and said, "I am about to die; *s* bury me in the tomb I dug for myself *t* in the land of Canaan." *u* Now let me go up and bury my father; *v* then I will return.' "

⁶Pharaoh said, "Go up and bury your father, as he made you swear to do."

⁷So Joseph went up to bury his father. All Pharaoh's officials *w* accompanied him—the dignitaries of his court *x* and all the dignitaries of Egypt— ⁸besides all the members of Joseph's household and his brothers and those belonging to his father's household. *y* Only their children and their flocks and herds were left in Goshen. *z* ⁹Chariots *a* and horsemen *b* also went up with him. It was a very large company.

¹⁰When they reached the threshing floor *b* of Atad, near the Jordan, they lamented loudly and bitterly; *c* and there Joseph observed a seven-day period *d* of mourning *e* for his father. *f* ¹¹When the Canaanites *g* who lived there saw the mourning at the threshing floor of Atad, they said, "The Egyptians are holding a solemn ceremony of mourning." *h* That is why that place near the Jordan is called Abel Mizraim. *c*

¹²So Jacob's sons did as he had commanded them: *i* ¹³They carried him to the land of Canaan and buried him in the cave in the field of Machpelah, *j* near Mamre, *k* which Abraham had bought along with the field *l* as a burial place from Ephron the Hittite. *m* ¹⁴After burying his father, Joseph returned to Egypt, together with his brothers and all the others who had gone with him to bury his father. *n*

JOSEPH REASSURES HIS BROTHERS

¹⁵When Joseph's brothers saw that their father was dead, they said, "What if Joseph holds a grudge *o* against us and pays us back for all the wrongs we did to him?" *p* ¹⁶So they sent word to Joseph, saying, "Your father left these instructions *q* before he died: ¹⁷'This is what you are to say to Joseph: I ask you to forgive your brothers the sins *r* and the wrongs they committed in treating you so badly.' *s* Now please forgive the sins of the servants of the God of your father.' " When their message came to him, Joseph wept. *u*

¹⁸His brothers then came and threw themselves down before him. *v* "We are your slaves," *w* they said.

¹⁹But Joseph said to them, "Don't be afraid. Am I in the place of God? *x* ²⁰You intended to harm me, *y* but God intended *z* it for good *a* to accomplish what is now being done, the saving of many lives. *b* ²¹So then, don't be afraid. I will provide for you and your children. *c*" And he reassured them and spoke kindly *d* to them.

---

a 32 Or *the descendants of Heth*   *b 9* Or *charioteers*   *c 11* Abel Mizraim means *mourning of the Egyptians.*

49:31 *h* S Ge 24:67
i S Ge 23:20; S 29:16
49:32 *j* S Ge 10:15
49:33 *k* S Ge 25:8; Ac 7:15
50:1 *l* S Ge 29:11; S 46:4
50:2 *m* ver 26; 2Ch 16:14; Mt 26:12; Mk 16:1; Jn 19:39-40
50:3 *n* S Ge 37:34; S Dt 1:3
50:4 *o* S Ge 27:41
p ver 7 *q* S Ge 30:27; S 32:5
50:5 *r* S Ge 24:37
s ver 24 *t* 2Sa 18:18; 2Ch 16:14; Isa 22:16; Mt 27:60 *u* Ge 47:31
v Mt 8:21
50:7 *w* Ge 45:16
x ver 4
50:8 *y* ver 14
z S Ge 45:10
50:9 *a* S Ge 41:43
50:10 *b* Nu 15:20; Ru 3:2; 2Sa 24:18; 1Ki 22:10 *c* 2Sa 1:17; 3:33; 2Ch 35:25; Eze 32:16; Ac 8:2
d 1Sa 31:13; Job 2:13; Eze 3:15 *e* S Ge 27:41; S Lev 10:6
f S Ge 37:34
50:11 *g* S Ge 10:18
h S Ge 37:34
50:12 *i* Ge 49:29
50:13 *j* S Ge 23:9
k S Ge 13:18
l S Ge 23:20
m S Ge 25:9
50:14 *n* ver 8
50:15 *o* S Ge 27:41
p ver 17; S Ge 9:5;; 37:28; Zep 3:11; 1Pe 3:9
50:16 *q* Ge 49:29
50:17 *r* S Mt 6:14
s S ver 15 *t* S Ge 28:13 *u* S Ge 29:11
50:18 *v* S Ge 37:7
w S Ge 43:18
50:19 *x* S Ge 30:2; S Ex 32:34; Ro 12:19; Heb 10:30
50:20 *y* S Ge 37:20
z Isa 10:7; Mic 4:11-12
a Ro 8:28 *b* S Ge 45:5; Est 4:14
50:21 *c* S Ge 45:11
d S Ge 34:3; Eph 4:32

49:33 *was gathered to his people.* See note on 25:8.

50:1 *wept.* See note on 43:30.

50:2 *physicians embalmed him.* Professional embalmers could have been hired for the purpose, but Joseph perhaps wanted to avoid involvement with the pagan religious ceremonies accompanying their services.

50:3 *forty days ... seventy days.* The two periods probably overlapped.

50:5 *My father made me swear an oath.* See 47:29–31. *dug.* Or "bought," as the Hebrew for this verb is translated in Hos 3:2 (see also Dt 2:6). *go up.* To Hebron, which has a higher elevation than Goshen.

50:10 *threshing floor.* Grain was threshed on a flat, circular area, either of rock or of pounded earth. Threshing floors were located on an elevated, open place exposed to the wind, usually at the edge of town or near the main gate (see 1Ki 22:10). See note on Ru 1:22.

50:15 *holds a grudge ... and pays us back.* Similarly, Esau had

once planned to kill Jacob as soon as Isaac died (see 27:41–45 and note).

◼ 50:17 *Joseph wept.* See note on 43:30. Joseph may have been saddened by the thought that his brothers might be falsely implicating their father in their story. Or he may have regretted his failure to reassure them sooner that he had already forgiven them.

50:18 *threw themselves down.* A final fulfillment of Joseph's earlier dreams (see note on 37:7; see also 37:9). *We are your slaves.* They had earlier expressed a similar willingness, but under quite different circumstances (see 44:9,33).

50:19 *Am I in the place of God?* See note on 30:2.

◼ 50:20 *God intended it for good.* Their act, out of personal animosity toward a brother, had been used by God to save life—the life of the Israelites, the Egyptians and all the nations that came to Egypt to buy food in the face of a famine that threatened the known world. At the same time, God showed by these events that his purpose for the nations is life and that this purpose would be effected through the descendants of Abraham.

50:22 *e* S Ge 25:7;
Jos 24:29
50:23 *f* Job 42:16
g S Ge 41:52
h S Ge 48:11
i Nu 26:29; 27:1;
32:39,40; 36:1;
Dt 3:15; Jos 13:31;
17:1; Jdg 13:31;
j S Ge 41:51
k S Ge 48:12
50:24 *l* ver 5
m Nu 1:6; Ps 35:2;
106:4; Isa 38:14
n S Ge 15:14
o S Ge 13:17
p S Ge 17:19
q S Ge 12:7; S 15:16
50:25 *r* S Ge 24:37
s S Ge 49:29

THE DEATH OF JOSEPH

22Joseph stayed in Egypt, along with all his father's family. He lived a hundred and ten years *e* 23and saw the third generation *f* of Ephraim's *g* children. *h* Also the children of Makir *i* son of Manasseh *j* were placed at birth on Joseph's knees. *a* *k*

24Then Joseph said to his brother Israelites, "I am about to die. *l* But God will surely come to your aid *m* and take you up out of this land to the land *n* he promised on oath to Abraham, *o* Isaac *p* and Jacob." *q* 25And Joseph made the Israelites swear an oath *r* and said, "God will surely come to your aid, and then you must carry my bones *s* up from this place." *t*

26So Joseph died *u* at the age of a hundred and ten. *v* And after they embalmed him, *w* he was placed in a coffin in Egypt.

a 23 That is, were counted as his

50:25 *t* S Ge 47:29-30; Heb 11:22 **50:26** *u* Ex 1:6 *v* S Ge 25:7 *w* S ver 2

50:23 *saw the third generation.* Cf. Job's experience (Job 42:16). *Makir.* Manasseh's firstborn son and the ancestor of the powerful Gileadites (Jos 17:1). The name of Makir later became almost interchangeable with that of Manasseh himself (see Jdg 5:14 and note). *placed at birth on Joseph's knees.* Joseph probably adopted Makir's children (see note on 30:3).

50:24 *I am about to die.* See note on 48:21. *God will... take you up out of this land.* Joseph did not forget God's promises (cf. 15:16; 46:4; 48:21) concerning "the exodus" (Heb 11:22).

50:25 See 47:29–31 for a similar request by Jacob. *carry my bones up from this place.* Centuries later Moses did so to fulfill his ancestor's oath (see Ex 13:19). Joseph's bones were eventually "buried at Shechem in the tract of land that Jacob bought ... from the sons of Hamor" (Jos 24:32; see note there; see also Ge 33:19).

50:26 *Joseph died at the age of a hundred and ten.* See v. 22. Ancient Egyptian records indicate that 110 years was considered to be the ideal life span; to the Egyptians this would have signified divine blessing upon Joseph.

TITLE | EXODUS | INTRODUCTION

"Exodus" is a Latin word derived from the Greek *Exodos,* the name given to the book by those who translated the Septuagint (the pre-Christian Greek translation of the OT). The word means "exit," "departure" (see Lk 9:31; Heb 11:22). The name was retained by the Latin Vulgate, by the Jewish author Philo (a contemporary of Christ) and by the Syriac version. In Hebrew the book is named after its first two words, *we'elleh shemoth* ("And these are the names of"). The same phrase occurs in Ge 46:8, where it likewise introduces a list of the names of those Israelites "who went to Egypt" with Jacob (1:1). Thus Exodus was not intended to exist separately, but was thought of as a continuation of a narrative that began in Genesis and was completed in Leviticus, Numbers and Deuteronomy. The first five books of the Bible are together known as the Pentateuch (see Introduction to Genesis: Author and Date of Writing).

AUTHOR AND DATE OF WRITING

Several statements in Exodus indicate that Moses wrote certain sections of the book (see 17:14; 24:4; 34:27). In addition, Jos 8:31 refers to the command of Ex 20:25 as having been "written in the Book of the Law of Moses." The NT also claims Mosaic authorship for various passages in Exodus (see, e.g., Mk 7:10; 12:26 and TNIV text notes; see also Lk 2:22–23). Taken together, these references strongly suggest that Moses was largely responsible for writing the book of Exodus—a traditional view not convincingly challenged by the commonly held notion that the Pentateuch as a whole contains four underlying sources (see Introduction to Genesis: Author and Date of Writing).

CHRONOLOGY

According to 1Ki 6:1 (see note there), the exodus took place 480 years before "the fourth year of Solomon's reign over Israel." Since that year was c. 966 B.C., it has been traditionally held that the exodus occurred c. 1446. The "three hundred years" of Jdg 11:26 fit comfortably within this time span (see Introduction to Judges: Background). In addition, although Egyptian chronology relating to the 18th dynasty remains somewhat uncertain, some recent research tends to support the traditional view that two of this dynasty's pharaohs, Thutmose III and his son Amunhotep II, were the pharaohs of the oppression and the exodus, respectively (see notes on 2:15,23; 3:10).

B On the other hand, the appearance of the name Rameses in 1:11 has led many to the conclusion that the 19th-dynasty pharaoh Seti I and his son Rameses II were the pharaohs of the oppression and the exodus, respectively. Furthermore, archaeological evidence of the destruction of numerous Canaanite cities in the 13th century B.C. has been interpreted as proof that Joshua's troops invaded the promised land in that century. These and similar lines of argument lead to a date for the exodus of c. 1290 (or, according to some, c. 1280; see Introduction to Joshua: Historical Setting).

The identity of the cities' attackers, however, cannot be positively ascertained. The raids may have been initiated by later Israelite armies, or by Philistines or other outsiders. In addition, the archaeological evidence itself has become

---

KEY **A** APPLICATION FOR LIVING **B** BACKGROUND NOTES **C** CHARACTER INFORMATION

increasingly ambiguous, and recent evaluations have tended to redate some of it to the 18th dynasty. Also, the name Rameses in 1:11 could very well be the result of an editorial updating by someone who lived centuries after Moses—a procedure that probably accounts for the appearance of the same word in Ge 47:11 (see note there).

In short, there are no compelling reasons to modify in any substantial way the traditional 1446 B.C. date for the exodus of the Israelites from Egyptian bondage.

THE ROUTE OF THE EXODUS

B At least three routes of escape from Pithom and Rameses (1:11) have been proposed: (1) a northern route through the land of the Philistines (but see 13:17); (2) a middle route leading eastward across Sinai to Beersheba; and (3) a southern route along the west coast of Sinai to the southeastern extremities of the peninsula. The southern route seems most likely, since several of the sites in Israel's desert itinerary have been tentatively identified along it. See map No. 3 at the end of this study Bible. The exact place where Israel crossed the "Red Sea" is uncertain, however (see notes on 13:18; 14:2).

THEMES AND THEOLOGY

Exodus lays a foundational theology in which God reveals his name, his attributes, his redemption, his law and how he is to be worshiped. It also reports the appointment and work of Moses as the mediator of the Sinaitic covenant, describes the beginnings of the priesthood in Israel, defines the role of the prophet and relates how the ancient covenant relationship between God and his people (see note on Ge 17:2) came under a new administration (the covenant given at Mount Sinai).

Profound insights into the nature of God are found in chs. 3; 6; 33–34. The focus of these texts is on the fact and importance of his presence with his people (as signified by his name Yahweh—see notes on 3:14–15—and by his glory among them). But emphasis is also placed on his attributes of justice, truthfulness, mercy, faithfulness and holiness. Thus to know God's "name" is to know him and to know his character (see 3:13–15; 6:3).

God is also the Lord of history. Neither the affliction of Israel nor the plagues in Egypt were outside his control. The pharaoh, the Egyptians and all Israel saw the power of God. There was no one like him, "majestic in holiness, awesome in glory, working wonders" (15:11; see note there).

It is reassuring to know that God remembers and is concerned about his people (see 2:24). What he had promised centuries earlier to Abraham, Isaac and Jacob he now begins to bring to fruition as Israel is freed from Egyptian bondage and sets out for the land of promise. The covenant at Sinai is but another step in God's fulfillment of his promise to the patriarchs (3:15–17; 6:2–8; 19:3–8).

The Biblical message of salvation is likewise powerfully set forth in this book. The verb "redeem" is used, e.g., in 6:6; 15:13 (see notes on 6:6–8). But the heart of redemption theology is best seen in the Passover narrative of ch. 12, the sealing of the covenant in ch. 24, and the account of God's gracious renewal of that covenant after the Israelites' blatant unfaithfulness to it in their worship of the golden calf (see 34:1–14 and notes). The apostle Paul viewed the death of the Passover lamb as fulfilled in Christ (1Co 5:7). Indeed, John the Baptist called Jesus the "Lamb of God, who takes away the sin of the world" (Jn 1:29).

The foundation of Biblical ethics and morality is laid out first in the gracious character of God as revealed in the exodus itself and then in the Ten Commandments (20:1–17) and the ordinances of the Book of the Covenant (20:22—23:33), which taught Israel how to apply in a practical way the principles of the commandments.

The book concludes with an elaborate discussion of the theology of worship. Though costly in time, effort and monetary value, the tabernacle, in meaning and function, points to the "chief end of man," namely, "to glorify God and to enjoy him forever" (Westminster Shorter Catechism). By means of the tabernacle, the omnipotent, unchanging and transcendent God of the universe came to "dwell" or "tabernacle" with his people, thereby revealing his gracious nearness as well. God is not only mighty in Israel's behalf; he is also present in the nation's midst.

However, these theological elements do not merely sit side by side in the Exodus narrative. They receive their fullest and richest significance from the fact that they are embedded in the account of God's raising up his servant Moses (1) to liberate his people from Egyptian bondage, (2) to inaugurate his earthly kingdom among them by bringing them into a special national covenant with him, and (3) to erect within Israel God's royal tent. And this account of redemption from bondage leading to consecration in covenant and the pitching of God's royal tent in the earth, all through the ministry of a chosen mediator, discloses God's purpose in history—the purpose he would fulfill through Israel, and ultimately through Jesus Christ, the supreme Mediator.

OUTLINE

THE ISRAELITES OPPRESSED

1 These are the names of the sons of Israel[a] who went to Egypt with Jacob, each with his family: [2]Reuben, Simeon, Levi and Judah; [3]Issachar, Zebulun and Benjamin; [4]Dan and Naphtali; Gad and Asher.[b] [5]The descendants of Jacob numbered seventy[a] in all;[c] Joseph was already in Egypt.

[6]Now Joseph and all his brothers and all that generation died,[d] [7]but the Israelites were exceedingly fruitful; they multiplied greatly, increased in numbers[e] and became so numerous that the land was filled with them.

[8]Then a new king, to whom Joseph meant nothing, came to power in Egypt.[f] [9]"Look," he said to his people, "the Israelites have become far too numerous[g] for us.[h] [10]Come, we must deal shrewdly[i] with them or they will become even more numerous and, if war breaks out, will join our enemies, fight against us and leave the country."[j]

[11]So they put slave masters[k] over them to oppress them with forced labor,[l] and they built Pithom and Rameses[m] as store cities[n] for Pharaoh. [12]But the more they were oppressed, the more they multiplied and spread; so the Egyptians came to dread the Israelites [13]and worked them ruthlessly.[o] [14]They made their lives bitter with harsh labor[p] in brick[q] and mortar and with all kinds of work in the fields; in all their harsh labor the Egyptians used them ruthlessly.[r]

[15]The king of Egypt said to the Hebrew midwives,[s] whose names were Shiphrah and Puah, [16]"When you help the Hebrew women in childbirth and observe them on the delivery stool, if it is a boy, kill him; but if it is a girl, let her live."[t] [17]The midwives, however, feared[u] God and did not do what the king of Egypt had told them to do;[v] they let the boys live. [18]Then the king of Egypt summoned the midwives and asked them, "Why have you done this? Why have you let the boys live?"

[19]The midwives answered Pharaoh, "Hebrew women are not like Egyptian women; they are vigorous and give birth before the midwives arrive."[w]

[20]So God was kind to the midwives[x] and the people increased and became even more numerous. [21]And because the midwives feared[y] God, he gave them families[z] of their own.

[22]Then Pharaoh gave this order to all his people: "Every Hebrew boy that is born you must throw into the Nile,[a] but let every girl live."[b]

a 5 Masoretic Text (see also Gen. 46:27); Dead Sea Scrolls and Septuagint (see also Acts 7:14 and note at Gen. 46:27) *seventy-five*

1:21 [z]1Sa 2:35; 2Sa 7:11,27-29; 1Ki 11:38; 14:10 **1:22** [a]S Ge 41:1 [b]ver 16; Ac 7:19

1:1 [a]S Ge 46:8
1:4 [b]Ge 35:22-26; Nu 1:20-43
1:5 [c]S Ge 46:26
1:6 [d]Ge 50:26; Ac 7:15
1:7 [e]ver 9; S Ge 12:2; Dt 7:13; Eze 16:7
1:8 [f]Jer 43:11; 46:2
1:9 [g]S ver 7
[h]S Ge 26:16
1:10 [i]Ge 15:13; Ex 3:7; 18:11; Ps 64:2; 71:10; 83:3; Isa 53:3
[j]Ps 105:24-25; Ac 7:17-19
1:11 [k]Ex 3:7; 5:10, 13,14 [l]S Ge 15:13; Ex 2:11; 5:4; 6:6-7; Jos 9:27; 1Ki 9:21; 1Ch 22:2; Isa 60:10
[m]S Ge 47:11
[n]1Ki 9:19; 2Ch 8:4
1:13 [o]ver 14; Ge 15:13-14; Ex 5:21; 16:3; Lev 25:43,46; 53; Dt 4:20; 26:6; 1Ki 8:51; Ps 129:1; Isa 30:6; 48:10; Jer 11:4
1:14 [p]Dt 26:6; Ezr 9:9; Isa 14:3
[q]S Ge 11:3 [r]Ex 2:23; 3:9; Nu 20:15; 1Sa 10:18; 2Ki 13:4; Ps 66:11; 81:6; Ac 7:19
1:15 [s]S Ge 35:17
1:16 [t]ver 22
1:17 [u]ver 21; Pr 16:6 [v]1Sa 22:17; Da 3:16-18; Ac 4:18-20; 5:29
1:19 [w]Lev 19:11; Jos 2:4-6; 1Sa 19:14; 1Ki 1:19
1:20 [x]Pr 11:18; 22:8; Ecc 8:12; Isa 3:10; Heb 6:10
1:21 [y]S ver 17

1:1—2:25 This first section of Exodus forms a prologue to the book. It describes how God blesses the Israelites to the point where they become a threat to the Egyptians. Oppression follows, but God raises up a deliverer in the person of Moses. Thus the stage is set for the conflict with the pharaoh and for Israel's redemption from Egypt.

1:1–5 These verses clearly indicate that Exodus was written as a continuation of Genesis. The Israelites lived in Egypt 430 years (see 12:40).

1:1 *These are the names of.* The same expression appears in Ge 46:8 at the head of a list of Jacob's descendants. *Israel . . . Jacob.* Jacob had earlier been given the additional name Israel (see Ge 32:28; 35:10 and notes).

1:2–4 The sons of Leah (Reuben through Zebulun) and Rachel (Benjamin; Joseph is not mentioned because the list includes only those "who went to Egypt" with Jacob, v. 1) are listed in the order of their seniority after the sons of Rachel's and Leah's female servants: Bilhah had Dan and Naphtali, Zilpah had Gad and Asher (see Ge 35:23–26).

1:5 *seventy.* See note on Ge 46:27.

1:6–7 From the death of Joseph to the rise of a new king (v. 8) was more than 200 years.

1:7 The language of this verse echoes that of God's benediction on humankind at the time of their creation (see Ge 1:28 and note). This benediction is renewed in the new beginning after the flood (see Ge 9:1 and note on 9:1–7) and subsequently becomes a centerpiece in the blessings promised and covenanted to Abraham (Ge 17:2,6; 22:17), Isaac (Ge 26:4) and Jacob (Ge 28:14; 35:11; 48:4). God's good intentions for humans when he created them were beginning to be realized in a special way in Israel's history—not in the history of Egypt or of any other

world power in which dreams of another, though perhaps lesser, Babel were still cherished. See also notes on 39:32; Nu 1:46. *land.* Goshen (see note on Ge 45:10).

1:8 See Ac 7:18. *new king.* Probably Ahmose, the founder of the 18th dynasty, who expelled the Hyksos (foreign—predominantly Semitic—rulers of Egypt). *to whom Joseph meant nothing.* He did not know about the great blessing Joseph had been to Egypt many years before.

1:11 *slave masters.* The same official Egyptian designation appears on a wall painting in the Theban tomb of Rekhmire during the reign of the 18th-dynasty pharaoh Thutmose III (see Introduction: Chronology). *oppress them with forced labor.* See Ge 15:13. *Rameses.* See note on Ge 47:11. *Pharaoh.* The word, which is Egyptian in origin and means "great house," is a royal title rather than a personal name.

1:14 *made their lives bitter.* A fact commemorated in the Passover meal, which was eaten "with bitter herbs" (12:8). *all kinds of work in the fields.* Including pumping the waters of the Nile into the fields to irrigate them (see Dt 11:10).

1:15 *Hebrew.* See note on Ge 14:13. *Shiphrah and Puah.* Semitic, not Egyptian, names. Since the Israelites were so numerous, there were probably other midwives under Shiphrah and Puah.

1:16 *delivery stool.* The Hebrew term means lit. "two stones"; a woman sat on them while giving birth. *if it is a boy, kill him.* Boy babies are potential warriors and fathers.

1:17 See Ac 5:29 for a parallel in the early church. *feared God.* See note on Ge 20:11.

1:22 *all his people.* Failing to accomplish his purposes through the midwives, the pharaoh mobilized all the Egyptians to deal with the Israelite threat.

2:1 cS Ge 29:34
d ver 2; Ex 6:20;
Nu 26:59
2:2 eS Ge 39:6
f Heb 11:23
2:3 g Isa 18:2
h Ge 6:14 iS Ge 41:2;
S Job 8:11; Ac 7:21
2:4 j Ex 15:20
2:5 kEx 7:15; 8:20
2:10 lISa 1:20
m 2Sa 22:17
2:11 nAc 7:23;
Heb 11:24-26
oS Ex 1:11
2:13 pAc 7:26
2:14 qS Ge 13:8;
Ac 7:27ᵃ
2:15 rEx 4:19
sS Ge 31:21
tHeb 11:27
2:16 uEx 3:1; 18:1
vS Ge 24:11
wS Ge 30:38

THE BIRTH OF MOSES

2 Now a man of the house of Levi c married a Levite woman, d 2and she became pregnant and gave birth to a son. When she saw that he was a fine e child, she hid him for three months. f 3But when she could hide him no longer, she got a papyrus g basketᵃ for him and coated it with tar and pitch. h Then she placed the child in it and put it among the reeds i along the bank of the Nile. 4His sisterj stood at a distance to see what would happen to him.

5Then Pharaoh's daughter went down to the Nile to bathe, and her attendants were walking along the riverbank. k She saw the basket among the reeds and sent her female slave to get it. 6She opened it and saw the baby. He was crying, and she felt sorry for him. "This is one of the Hebrew babies," she said.

7Then his sister asked Pharaoh's daughter, "Shall I go and get one of the Hebrew women to nurse the baby for you?"

8"Yes, go," she answered. And the girl went and got the baby's mother. 9Pharaoh's daughter said to her, "Take this baby and nurse him for me, and I will pay you." So the woman took the baby and nursed him. 10When the child grew older, she took him to Pharaoh's daughter and he became her son. She namedl him Moses,b saying, "I drewm him out of the water."

MOSES FLEES TO MIDIAN

11One day, after Moses had grown up, he went out to where his own peoplen were and watched them at their hard labor. o He saw an Egyptian beating a Hebrew, one of his own people. 12Glancing this way and that and seeing no one, he killed the Egyptian and hid him in the sand. 13The next day he went out and saw two Hebrews fighting. He asked the one in the wrong, "Why are you hitting your fellow Hebrew?"p

14The man said, "Who made you ruler and judge over us?q Are you thinking of killing me as you killed the Egyptian?" Then Moses was afraid and thought, "What I did must have become known."

15When Pharaoh heard of this, he tried to killr Moses, but Moses fleds from Pharaoh and went to live in Midian,t where he sat down by a well. 16Now a priest of Midianu had seven daughters, and they came to draw waterv and fill the troughsw to water their fa-

---

ᵃ 3 The Hebrew can also mean *ark*, as in Gen. 6:14.   ᵇ 10 *Moses* sounds like the Hebrew for *draw out*.

2:1–10 The nativity of Moses. He was born a child of the oppression, was saved by means of an "ark" from the watery death decreed by the pharaoh, and was allowed to grow to maturity in the pharaoh's court. Thus Moses' early life paralleled in fundamental ways the life of Israel in Egypt, even as it contained also foreshadowings of things to come (see note on v. 2). **2:1** *a man ... a Levite woman.* Perhaps Amram and Jochebed (but see note on 6:20).

2:2 *a fine child.* Moses was "no ordinary child" (Ac 7:20; Heb 11:23), "fair in the sight of God" (see TNIV text note on Ac 7:20). The account of Moses' remarkable deliverance in infancy foreshadows Israel's deliverance from Egypt that God would later effect through him.

2:3 *papyrus basket.* Each of the two Hebrew words lying behind this phrase is of Egyptian origin. The word for "basket" is used only here and of Noah's ark (see note on Ge 6:14). Moses' basket was a miniature version of the large, seaworthy "papyrus boats" mentioned in Isa 18:2. *reeds.* A word of Egyptian derivation, reflected in the proper name "Red Sea" (see TNIV text note on 10:19). **2:4** *His sister.* Miriam (see 15:20).

2:5 *Pharaoh's daughter.* Perhaps the famous 18th-dynasty princess who later became Queen Hatshepsut. Throughout this early part of Exodus, all the pharaoh's efforts to suppress Israel were thwarted by women: the midwives (1:17), the Israelite mothers (1:19), Moses' mother and sister (vv. 3–4,7–9), the pharaoh's daughter (here). The pharaoh's impotence to destroy the people of God is thus ironically exposed. **2:6** *baby ... crying.* The only place in the Bible that tells of an infant crying.

2:10 *he became her son.* Thus "Moses was educated in all the wisdom of the Egyptians" (Ac 7:22; see note there).

The narrator here was not interested in describing what this involved. Instead, he cited in the following verses (11–12,13, 16–17) three incidents that illustrated Moses' character as a champion of justice. *Moses.* The name, of Egyptian origin, means "is born" and forms the second element in such pharaonic names as Ahmose (see note on 1:8), Thutmose and Rameses (see note on 1:11). *drew him out.* A Hebrew wordplay on the name Moses (see TNIV text note), emphasizing his providential rescue from the Nile. Thus Moses' name may also have served as a reminder of the great act of deliverance God worked through him at the "Red Sea" (see 13:17—14:31).

2:11–15 See Ac 7:23–29; Heb 11:24–27.
2:11 *Moses had grown up.* He was now 40 years old (see Ac 7:23).
2:14 *Who made you ruler and judge ... ?* Unwittingly, the speaker made a prediction that would be fulfilled 40 years later (see Ac 7:27,30,35). The Hebrew word for "judge" could also refer to a deliverer, as in the book of Judges (see Ac 7:35); it was often a synonym for "ruler" in the OT (see Ge 18:25 and note), as well as in ancient Canaanite usage. *Moses was afraid.* See note on Heb 11:27.

2:15 *Pharaoh.* Probably Thutmose III (see Introduction: Chronology). *Midian.* Named after one of Abraham's younger sons (see Ge 25:2; see also note on Ge 37:25). Midian flanked the eastern arm of the Red Sea (Gulf of Aqaba) on both sides (see map, p. 110). Dry and desolate, it formed a stark contrast to Moses' former home in the royal court. He lived in Midian 40 years (see Ac 7:29–30).

2:16 *priest of Midian.* Reuel (see v. 18), which means "friend of God." His other name, Jethro (see 3:1), may be a title meaning "his excellency."

ther's flock. [17]Some shepherds came along and drove them away, but Moses got up and came to their rescue[x] and watered their flock. [y]

[18]When the girls returned to Reuel[z] their father, he asked them, "Why have you returned so early today?"

[19]They answered, "An Egyptian rescued us from the shepherds. He even drew water for us and watered the flock."

[20]"And where is he?" he asked his daughters. "Why did you leave him? Invite him to have something to eat." [a]

[21]Moses agreed to stay with the man, who gave his daughter Zipporah[b] to Moses in marriage. [22]Zipporah gave birth to a son, and Moses named him Gershom,[a c] saying, "I have become a foreigner[d] in a foreign land."

[23]During that long period,[e] the king of Egypt died. [f]The Israelites groaned in their slavery[g] and cried out, and their cry[h] for help because of their slavery went up to God. [24]God heard their groaning and he remembered[i] his covenant[j] with Abraham, with Isaac and with Jacob. [25]So God looked on the Israelites and was concerned[k] about them.

MOSES AND THE BURNING BUSH

3 Now Moses was tending the flock of Jethro[l] his father-in-law, the priest of Midian,[m] and he led the flock to the far side of the wilderness and came to Horeb,[n] the mountain[o] of God. [2]There the angel of the LORD[p] appeared to him in flames of fire[q] from within a bush. [r] Moses saw that though the bush was on fire it did not burn up. [3]So Moses thought, "I will go over and see this strange sight—why the bush does not burn up."

[4]When the LORD saw that he had gone over to look, God called[s] to him from within the bush, [t] "Moses! Moses!"

And Moses said, "Here I am." [u]

[5]"Do not come any closer," [v] God said. "Take off your sandals, for the place where you are standing is holy ground." [w] [6]Then he said, "I am the God of your father,[b] the God of Abraham, the God of Isaac and the God of Jacob." [x] At this, Moses hid[y] his face, because he was afraid to look at God. [z]

[7]The LORD said, "I have indeed seen[a] the misery[b] of my people in Egypt. I have heard them crying out because of their slave drivers, and I am concerned[c] about their suffering. [d] [8]So I have come down[e] to rescue them from the hand of the Egyptians and to bring

---

[a] 22 *Gershom* sounds like the Hebrew for *a foreigner there.* (see Acts 7:32) *fathers*   [b] 6 Masoretic Text; Samaritan Pentateuch

3:7 [b] ver 16; S Ge 16:11; 1Sa 1:11; Ne 9:9; Ps 106:44 [c] S Ex 2:25; Ac 7:34* [d] S Ex 1:10   **3:8** [e] S Ge 11:5; Ac 7:34*

2:17 [x] Isa 30:8; Ps 31:2 [y] S Ge 29:10
2:18 [z] Ex 3:1; 4:18; 18:1,5,12; Nu 10:29
2:20 [a] Ge 18:2-5
2:21 [b] Ex 4:25; 18:2; Nu 12:1
2:22 [c] Jdg 18:30 [d] S Ge 23:4; Heb 11:13
2:23 [e] Ac 7:30 [f] Ex 4:19 [g] S Ex 1:14 [h] ver 24; Ex 3:7,9; 6:5; Nu 20:15-16; Dt 26:7; Jdg 2:18; 1Sa 12:8; Ps 5:2; 18:6; 39:12; 81:7; 102:1; Jas 5:4
2:24 [i] S Ge 8:1 [j] S Ge 9:15; 15:15; 17:4; 22:16-18; 26:3; 28:13-15; Ex 32:13; 2Ki 13:23; Ps 105:10, 42; Jer 14:21
2:25 [k] Ex 3:7; 4:31; Lk 1:25
3:1 [l] S Ex 2:18; Jdg 1:16 [m] S Ex 2:16 [n] ver 12; Ex 19:11; 19:1-11,5; 33:6; Dt 1:2,6; 4:10; 5:2; 29:1; 1Ki 19:8; Mal 4:4 [o] Ex 4:27; 18:5; 24:13; Dt 4:11,15
3:2 [p] S Ge 16:7; S Ex 12:23; S Ac 5:19 [q] Ex 19:18; 1Ki 19:12 [r] ver 4; Ex 2:2-6; Dt 33:16; Mk 12:26; Lk 20:37; Ac 7:30
3:4 [s] Ex 19:3; Lev 1:1 [t] Ex 4:5 [u] Ge 31:11; 1Sa 3:4; Isa 6:8
3:5 [v] Jer 30:21 [w] S Ge 28:17; Ac 7:33*
3:6 [x] S Ge 24:12; S Ex 4:5; Mt 22:32*; Mk 12:26*; Lk 20:37*; Ac 3:13; 7:32* [y] 1Ki 19:13 [z] Ex 24:11; 33:20; Jdg 13:22; Job 13:11; 23:16; 30:15; Isa 6:5
3:7 [a] Isa 9:16

A **2:23–25** These verses turn the reader's attention back to Israel's miserable plight in Egypt. They show that God truly cares for his people and has not forgotten his covenant promises made to their ancestors. This sets the stage for God's active intervention to bring about Israel's deliverance. Four expressions refer to Israel's suffering: "groaned," "cried out," "cry for help" (v. 23), "groaning" (v. 24); and four verbs describe God's response: "heard," "remembered" (v. 24), "looked on," "was concerned about" (v. 25).

2:23 *During that long period.* Thutmose III (see note on v. 15) enjoyed a long reign.
2:24 *covenant with Abraham.* See Ge 15:17–18; 17:7 and notes. *with Isaac.* See Ge 17:19; 26:24. *with Jacob.* See Ge 35:11–12.
3:1—18:27 The second main section of the book. It describes the deliverance of Israel from Egypt and includes the call of Moses, the plagues, the Passover, the exodus from Egypt, the crossing of the Red Sea and the journey to Sinai.
3:1 Like David (2Sa 7:8), Moses was called from tending the flock to be the shepherd of God's people. *Jethro.* See note on 2:16. *Horeb.* Means "desert," "desolation"; either (1) another name for Mount Sinai or (2) another high mountain in the same vicinity in the southeast region of the Sinai peninsula. Tradition identifies Mount Horeb with Ras es-Safsaf ("willow peak"), 6,500 feet high, and Mount Sinai with Jebel Musa ("mountain of Moses"), 7,400 feet high, but both identifications are uncertain.
3:2 *angel of the LORD.* Used interchangeably with "the LORD" and "God" in v. 4 (see note on Ge 16:7). *appeared to him in flames of* fire. God's revelation of himself and his will was often accompanied by fire (see 13:21; 19:18; 1Ki 18:24,38).
3:4 Every true prophet was called by God (see, e.g., 1Sa 3:4; Isa 6:8; Jer 1:4–5; Eze 2:1–8; Hos 1:2; Am 7:15; Jnh 1:1–2; see also note on 7:1–2). *Moses, Moses!...Here I am.* See notes on Ge 22:1,11.

A **3:5** *Take off your sandals.* A sign of respect and humility in the ancient Near East (see Jos 5:15). This practice is still followed by Muslims before entering a mosque. *holy.* The ground was not holy by nature but was made so by the divine presence (see, e.g., Ge 2:3). Holiness involves being consecrated to the Lord's service and thus being separated from the commonplace.
3:6 See 2:24 and note. *afraid to look at God.* See notes on Ge 16:13; 32:30. Later, as the Lord's servant, Moses would meet with God on Mount Sinai (19:3) and even ask to see God's glory (33:18).

3:8 *I have come down to rescue.* God may also come down to judge (see Ge 11:5–9; 18:21). *land flowing with milk and honey.* The traditional and proverbial description of the hill country of Canaan—in its original pastoral state (see note on Isa 7:15). *honey.* The Hebrew for "honey" refers to both bees' honey and the sweet, syrupy juice of dates. *Canaanites...Jebusites.* See notes on Ge 10:6,15–16; 13:7. The list of the Canaanite nations ranges from two names (see Ge 13:7) to five (see Nu 13:29) to six (as here) to ten (see Ge 15:19–21) to twelve (see Ge 10:15–18). The classic description includes seven names (see, e.g., Dt 7:1), seven being the number of completeness (see note on Ge 4:17–18).

3:8 *f* S Ge 12:7;
S 15:14 *g* ver 17;
Ex 13:5; 33:3;
Lev 20:24; Nu 13:27;
Dt 1:25; 6:3; 8:7-9;
11:9; 26:9; 27:3;
Jos 5:6; Jer 11:5;
32:22; Eze 20:6
h Jos 11:3; Jdg 3:3;
2Sa 24:7 *i* S Ge 15:18-
21; Ezr 9:1
3:9 *j* S Ex 1:14;
S Nu 10:9
3:10 *k* Ex 4:12;
Jos 24:5; Nu 13:2;
Ps 105:26; Ac 7:34*
l Ex 6:13,26; 12:41,51;
20:2; Dt 4:20;
1Sa 12:6; 1Ki 8:16;
Mic 6:4
3:11 *m* Ex 4:10; 6:12,
30; Jdg 6:15; 1Sa 9:21;
15:17; 18:18; 2Sa 7:18;
2Ch 2:6; Isa 6:5;
Jer 1:6
3:12 *n* S Ge 26:3;
S Ex 14:22; Ro 8:31
o Nu 26:10; Jos 2:12;
Jdg 6:17; Ps 86:17;
Isa 7:14; 8:18; 20:3;
Jer 44:29 *p* S ver 1;
Ac 7:7
3:13 *q* S Ge 32:29
3:14 *r* Ex 6:2-3;
Jn 8:58; Heb 13:8;
Rev 1:8; 4:8
3:15 *s* Ge 31:42;
Da 2:23 *t* S Ge 24:12
u Ex 6:3,7; 15:3;
23:21; 34:5-7;
Lev 24:11; Dt 28:58;
Ps 30:4; 83:18; 96:2;
97:12; 135:13; 145:21;
Isa 42:8; Jer 16:21;
33:2; Hos 12:5
v Ps 45:17; 72:17;
102:12
3:16 *w* Ex 4:29; 17:5;
Lev 4:15; Nu 11:16;
16:25; Dt 5:23; 19:12;
Jdg 8:14; Ru 4:2;
Pr 31:23; Eze 8:11
x S Ge 24:12
y Ex 4:31; 2Ki 19:16;
2Ch 6:20; Ps 33:18;
66:7
3:17 *z* S Ge 15:16;
46:4; Ex 6:6 *a* S ver 8
3:18 *b* Ex 4:1,8,31;
6:12,30 *c* S Ge 14:13
d Nu 23:4,16

them up out of that land into a good and spacious land,*f* a land flowing with milk and honey*g*—the home of the Canaanites, Hittites, Amorites, Perizzites, Hivites*h* and Jebusites.*i* 9And now the cry of the Israelites has reached me, and I have seen the way the Egyptians are oppressing*j* them. 10So now, go. I am sending*k* you to Pharaoh to bring my people the Israelites out of Egypt.*l*

11But Moses said to God, "Who am I*m* that I should go to Pharaoh and bring the Israelites out of Egypt?"

12And God said, "I will be with you.*n* And this will be the sign*o* to you that it is I who have sent you: When you have brought the people out of Egypt, you*a* will worship God on this mountain.*p*"

13Moses said to God, "Suppose I go to the Israelites and say to them, 'The God of your fathers has sent me to you,' and they ask me, 'What is his name?'*q* Then what shall I tell them?"

14God said to Moses, "I AM WHO I AM.*b* This is what you are to say to the Israelites: 'I AM*r* has sent me to you.' "

15God also said to Moses, "Say to the Israelites, 'The LORD,*c* the God of your fathers*s*— the God of Abraham, the God of Isaac and the God of Jacob*t*—has sent me to you.'

"This is my name*u* forever,
 the name you shall call me
 from generation to generation.*v*

16"Go, assemble the elders*w* of Israel and say to them, 'The LORD, the God of your fathers—the God of Abraham, Isaac and Jacob*x*—appeared to me and said: I have watched over you and have seen*y* what has been done to you in Egypt. 17And I have promised to bring you up out of your misery in Egypt*z* into the land of the Canaanites, Hittites, Amorites, Perizzites, Hivites and Jebusites—a land flowing with milk and honey.'*a*

18"The elders of Israel will listen*b* to you. Then you and the elders are to go to the king of Egypt and say to him, 'The LORD, the God of the Hebrews,*c* has met*d* with us. Let us take a three-day journey*e* into the wilderness to offer sacrifices*f* to the LORD our God.' 19But I know that the king of Egypt will not let you go unless a mighty hand*g* compels him. 20So I will stretch out my hand*h* and strike the Egyptians with all the wonders*i* that I will perform among them. After that, he will let you go.*j*

21"And I will make the Egyptians favorably disposed*k* toward this people, so that when you leave you will not go empty-handed.*l* 22Every woman is to ask her neighbor and any

---

a 12 The Hebrew is plural.   *b* 14 Or *I WILL BE WHAT I WILL BE*   *c* 15 The Hebrew for LORD sounds like and may be related to the Hebrew for *I AM* in verse 14.

3:18 *e* S Ge 30:36 *f* Ex 4:23; 5:1,3; 6:11; 7:16; 8:20,27; 9:13; 10:9,26   **3:19** *g* Ex 4:21; 6:6; 7:3; 10:1; 11:9; Dt 4:34; 2Ch 6:32   **3:20** *h* Ex 6:1,
6; 7:4-5; 9:15; 13:3,9,14,16; 15:6,12; Dt 4:34,37; 5:15; 7:8; 26:8; 2Ki 17:36; 2Ch 6:32; Ps 118:15-16; 136:12; Isa 41:10; 63:12; Jer 21:5; 51:25;
Da 9:15 *i* Ex 4:21; 7:3; 11:9,10; 15:11; 34:10; Nu 14:11; Dt 3:24; 4:34; 6:22; Ne 9:10; Ps 71:19; 72:18; 77:14; 78:43; 86:10; 105:27; 106:22; 135:9;
136:4; Jer 32:20; Mic 7:15; Ac 7:36 *j* Ex 11:1; 12:31-33   **3:21** *k* S Ge 39:21 *l* Ex 11:2; 2Ch 30:9; Ne 1:11; Ps 105:37; 106:46; Jer 42:12

3:10 *Pharaoh.* Probably Amunhotep II (see Introduction: Chronology).
3:11 Moses' first expression of reluctance (see v. 13; 4:1,10,13).
3:12 *I will be with you.* See note on Ge 26:3. The Hebrew word translated "I will be" is the same as the one translated "I AM" in v. 14. *sign.* A visible proof or guarantee that what God had promised he would surely fulfill (see notes on 4:8; Ge 15:8).
3:13 Moses' second expression of reluctance. *What is his name?* God had not yet identified himself to Moses by name (see v. 6; cf. Ge 17:1).

A **3:14** *I AM WHO I AM.* The name by which God wished to be known and worshiped in Israel—the name that expressed his character as the dependable and faithful God who desires the full trust of his people (see v. 12, where "I will be" is completed by "with you"; see also 34:5–7). *I AM.* The shortened form of the name is perhaps found also in Ps 50:21; Hos 1:9 (see TNIV text notes there). Jesus applied the phrase to himself; in so doing he claimed to be God and risked being stoned for blasphemy (see Jn 8:58–59).
3:15 *The LORD.* The Hebrew for this name is *Yahweh* (often incorrectly spelled "Jehovah"; see note on Dt 28:58). It means "He is" or "He will be" and is the third-person form of the verb translated "I will be" in v. 12 and "I AM" in v. 14. When God speaks of

himself he says, "I AM," and when we speak of him we say, "He is."
3:16 *elders.* The Hebrew for this word means lit. "bearded ones," perhaps reflecting the age, wisdom, experience and influence necessary for a man expected to function as an elder. As heads of local families and tribes, "elders" had a recognized position also among the Babylonians, Hittites, Egyptians (see Ge 50:7), Moabites and Midianites (see Nu 22:7). Their duties included judicial arbitration and sentencing (see Dt 22:13–19), as well as military leadership (see Jos 8:10) and counsel (see 1Sa 4:3).

B **3:18** *Hebrews.* See note on Ge 14:13. *three-day journey.* See note on Ge 22:4. *wilderness.* God had met with Moses there (see vv. 1–2) and would meet with him there again (see v. 12). *to offer sacrifices.* Entries in extant logs of Egyptian supervisors show that such a request was not exceptional.
3:20 *wonders.* A prediction of the plagues that God would send against Egypt (see 7:14—12:30).
3:21–22 See 11:2–3; 12:35–36.
3:21 *when you leave you will not go empty-handed.* God had promised Abraham that after the Israelites had served for 400 years they would "come out with great possessions" (Ge 15:14; see Ps 105:37). Israel was to live by the same principle of providing gifts to a released slave (see Dt 15:12–15).

woman living in her house for articles of silver *m* and gold *n* and for clothing, which you will put on your sons and daughters. And so you will plunder *o* the Egyptians." *p*

SIGNS FOR MOSES

4 Moses answered, "What if they do not believe me or listen *q* to me and say, 'The LORD did not appear to you'?"

²Then the LORD said to him, "What is that in your hand?"

"A staff," *r* he replied.

³The LORD said, "Throw it on the ground."

Moses threw it on the ground and it became a snake, *s* and he ran from it. ⁴Then the LORD said to him, "Reach out your hand and take it by the tail." So Moses reached out and took hold of the snake and it turned back into a staff in his hand. ⁵"This," said the LORD, "is so that they may believe *t* that the LORD, the God of their fathers—the God of Abraham, the God of Isaac and the God of Jacob—has appeared to you." *d*

⁶Then the LORD said, "Put your hand inside your cloak." So Moses put his hand into his cloak, and when he took it out, the skin was leprous *a*—it had become as white as snow. *u*

⁷"Now put it back into your cloak," he said. So Moses put his hand back into his cloak, and when he took it out, it was restored, *v* like the rest of his flesh.

⁸Then the LORD said, "If they do not believe *w* you or pay attention to the first sign, *x* they may believe the second. ⁹But if they do not believe these two signs or listen to you, take some water from the Nile and pour it on the dry ground. The water you take from the river will become blood *y* on the ground."

¹⁰Moses said to the LORD, "Pardon your servant, Lord. I have never been eloquent, neither in the past nor since you have spoken to your servant. I am slow of speech and tongue." *z*

¹¹The LORD said to him, "Who gave human beings their mouths? Who makes them deaf or mute? *a* Who gives them sight or makes them blind? *b* Is it not I, the LORD? ¹²Now go; *c* I will help you speak and will teach you what to say." *d*

¹³But Moses said, "Pardon your servant, Lord. Please send someone else." *e*

¹⁴Then the LORD's anger burned *f* against Moses and he said, "What about your brother, Aaron the Levite? I know he can speak well. He is already on his way to meet *g* you, and his heart will be glad when he sees you. ¹⁵You shall speak to him and put words in his mouth; *h* I will help both of you speak and will teach you what to do. ¹⁶He will speak to the people for you, and it will be as if he were your mouth *i* and as if you were God to him. *j* ¹⁷But take this staff *k* in your hand *l* so you can perform the signs *m* with it."

MOSES RETURNS TO EGYPT

¹⁸Then Moses went back to Jethro his father-in-law and said to him, "Let me return to my own people in Egypt to see if any of them are still alive."

Jethro said, "Go, and I wish you well."

¹⁹Now the LORD had said to Moses in Midian, "Go back to Egypt, for all those who wanted to kill *n* you are dead. *o*" ²⁰So Moses took his wife and sons, *p* put them on a donkey and started back to Egypt. And he took the staff *q* of God in his hand.

²¹The LORD said to Moses, "When you return to Egypt, see that you perform before

---

a 6 The Hebrew word for *leprous* was used for various diseases affecting the skin.

3:22 *m* Job 27:16-17
n Ex 11:2; 12:35;
Ezr 1:4,6; 7:16;
Ps 105:37
o S Ge 15:14;
Eze 39:10 *p* Eze 29:10
4:1 *q* S Ex 3:18
4:2 *r* ver 17,20;
Ge 38:18; Ex 7:19;
8:5,16; 14:16,21; 17:5-
6,9; Nu 17:2; 20:8;
Jos 8:18; Jdg 6:21;
1Sa 14:27; 2Ki 4:29
4:3 *s* Ex 7:8-12,15
4:5 *t* ver 31; S Ex 3:6;
14:31; 19:9
4:6 *u* Lev 13:2,11;
Nu 12:10; Dt 24:9;
2Ki 5:1,27; 2Ch 26:21
4:7 *v* 2Ki 5:14;
Mt 8:3; Lk 17:12-14
4:8 *w* S Ex 3:18
x ver 30; Jdg 6:17;
1Ki 13:3; Isa 7:14;
Jer 44:29
4:9 *y* Ex 7:17-21
4:10 *z* S Ex 3:11
4:11 *a* Lk 1:20,64
b Ps 94:9; 146:8;
Mt 11:5; Jn 10:21
4:12 *c* S Ex 3:10
d ver 15-16; Nu 23:5;
Dt 18:15,18; Isa 50:4;
51:16; Jer 1:9;
Mt 10:19-20;
Mk 13:11; S Lk 12:12
4:13 *e* Jnh 1:1-3
4:14 *f* Nu 11:1,10,33;
12:9; 16:15; 22:22;
24:10; 32:13; Dt 7:25;
Jos 7:1; Job 17:8
g ver 27; 1Sa 10:2-5
4:15 *h* ver 30;
Nu 23:5,12,16;
Dt 18:18; Jos 1:8;
Isa 51:16; 59:21;
Jer 1:9; 31:33
4:16 *i* Ex 7:1-2;
Jer 15:19; 36:6
j Nu 33:1; Ps 77:20;
105:26; Mic 6:4
4:17 *k* S ver 2
l ver 20; Ex 17:9
m Ex 7:9-21; 8:5,16;
9:22; 10:12-15,21-23;
14:15-18,26; Nu 14:11;
Dt 4:34; Ps 74:9;
78:43; 105:27
4:19 *n* Ex 2:15
o Ex 2:23; Mt 2:20
4:20 *p* Ex 2:22; 18:3;
Ac 7:29 *q* S ver 2

3:22 *plunder the Egyptians.* As if they had conquered them in battle.

4:1–17 Moses has already voiced two reasons for his reluctance to obey God's call to rescue Israel from Egyptian bondage (see notes on 3:11,13). Here he states three more (vv. 1,10,13; see notes there). The Lord answers all three. Moses is now ready to return from Midian to Egypt (see vv. 18–31).

4:1 Moses' third expression of reluctance (in spite of God's assurance in 3:18).

4:2 *staff.* Probably a shepherd's crook.

4:3 *snake.* See 7:9–10 and note. Throughout much of Egypt's history the pharaoh wore a cobra made of metal on the front of his headdress as a symbol of his sovereignty.

4:8 *sign.* A supernatural event or phenomenon designed to demonstrate authority, provide assurance (see Jos 2:12–13), bear testimony (see Isa 19:19–20), give warning (see Nu 17:10) or encourage faith. See note on 3:12.

4:10 Moses' fourth expression of reluctance. *I am slow of speech and tongue.* Not in the sense of a speech impediment (see Ac 7:22). He complained, instead, of not being eloquent or quick-witted enough to respond to the pharaoh (see 6:12). Cf. the description of Paul in 2Co 10:10.

4:13 Moses' fifth and final expression of reluctance (see note on 3:11).

4:14 *the LORD's anger burned against Moses.* Although the Lord is "slow to anger" (34:6), he does not withhold his anger or punishment from his disobedient children forever (see 34:7). *Levite.* Under Aaron's leadership Israel's priesthood would come from the tribe of Levi.

4:15–16 See note on 7:1–2.

4:19 *all those ... are dead.* Including Thutmose III (see 2:15,23; see also Introduction: Chronology).

4:20 *sons.* Gershom (see 2:22) and Eliezer. The latter, though unmentioned by name until 18:4, had already been born.

4:21 ʳ S Ex 3:19,20
ˢ Ex 7:3,13; 8:15; 9:12,
35; 10:1,20,27; 11:10;
14:4,8; Dt 2:30;
Jos 11:20; 1Sa 6:6;
Ps 105:25; Isa 6:10;
63:17; Jn 12:40;
Ro 9:18 ᵗ Ex 8:32; 9:17
4:22 ᵘ S Ge 10:15;
Dt 32:6; Isa 9:6;
63:16; 64:8; Jer 3:19;
31:9; Hos 11:1;
Mal 2:10; Ro 9:4;
2Co 6:18
4:23 ᵛ Ex 5:1; 7:16
ʷ Ex 3:18 ˣ Ge 49:3;
Ex 11:5; 12:12,29;
Nu 8:17; 33:4;
Ps 78:51; 105:36;
135:8; 136:10
4:24 ʸ Nu 22:22
4:25 ᶻ S Ex 2:21
ᵃ Ge 17:14; Jos 5:2,3
4:27 ᵇ S Ex 3:1
ᶜ S Ge 27:27; S 29:13
4:29 ᵈ S Ex 3:16
4:30 ᵉ S ver 8
4:31 ᶠ S Ex 3:18
ᵍ S Ex 2:25
ʰ S Ge 16:11
ⁱ S Ge 24:26
5:1 ʲ S Ex 4:23
ᵏ S Ex 3:18
5:2 ˡ Jdg 2:10;
Job 21:15; Mal 3:14
ᵐ Ex 3:19
5:3 ⁿ S Ge 30:36
ᵒ Lev 26:25; Nu 14:12;
Dt 28:21; 2Sa 24:13
5:4 ᵖ S Ex 1:11; 6:6-7
5:5 ᵠ S Ge 12:2
5:6 ʳ S Ge 15:13
5:7 ˢ S Ge 11:3
5:8 ᵗ ver 14,18
ᵘ ver 17 ᵛ Ex 10:11
5:10 ʷ ver 13;
Ex 1:11
5:11 ˣ ver 19

Pharaoh all the wonders ʳ I have given you the power to do. But I will harden his heart ˢ so that he will not let the people go. ᵗ ²²Then say to Pharaoh, 'This is what the Lᴏʀᴅ says: Israel is my firstborn son, ᵘ ²³and I told you, "Let my son go, ᵛ so he may worship ʷ me." But you refused to let him go; so I will kill your firstborn son.' " ˣ

²⁴At a lodging place on the way, the Lᴏʀᴅ met Moses ᵃ and was about to kill ʸ him. ²⁵But Zipporah ᶻ took a flint knife, cut off her son's foreskin ᵃ and touched Moses' feet with it. ᵇ "Surely you are a bridegroom of blood to me," she said. ²⁶So the Lᴏʀᴅ let him alone. (At that time she said "bridegroom of blood," referring to circumcision.)

²⁷The Lᴏʀᴅ said to Aaron, "Go into the wilderness to meet Moses." So he met Moses at the mountain ᵇ of God and kissed ᶜ him. ²⁸Then Moses told Aaron everything the Lᴏʀᴅ had sent him to say, and also about all the signs he had commanded him to perform.

²⁹Moses and Aaron brought together all the elders ᵈ of the Israelites, ³⁰and Aaron told them everything the Lᴏʀᴅ had said to Moses. He also performed the signs ᵉ before the people, ³¹and they believed. ᶠ And when they heard that the Lᴏʀᴅ was concerned ᵍ about them and had seen their misery, ʰ they bowed down and worshiped. ⁱ

BRICKS WITHOUT STRAW

5 Afterward Moses and Aaron went to Pharaoh and said, "This is what the Lᴏʀᴅ, the God of Israel, says: 'Let my people go, ʲ so that they may hold a festival ᵏ to me in the wilderness.' "

²Pharaoh said, "Who is the Lᴏʀᴅ, ˡ that I should obey him and let Israel go? I do not know the Lᴏʀᴅ and I will not let Israel go." ᵐ

³Then they said, "The God of the Hebrews has met with us. Now let us take a three-day journey ⁿ into the wilderness to offer sacrifices to the Lᴏʀᴅ our God, or he may strike us with plagues ᵒ or with the sword."

⁴But the king of Egypt said, "Moses and Aaron, why are you taking the people away from their labor? ᵖ Get back to your work!" ⁵Then Pharaoh said, "Look, the people of the land are now numerous, ᵠ and you are stopping them from working."

⁶That same day Pharaoh gave this order to the slave drivers ʳ and overseers in charge of the people: ⁷"You are no longer to supply the people with straw for making bricks; ˢ let them go and gather their own straw. ⁸But require them to make the same number of bricks as before; don't reduce the quota. ᵗ They are lazy; ᵘ that is why they are crying out, 'Let us go and sacrifice to our God.' ᵛ ⁹Make the work harder for them so that they keep working and pay no attention to lies."

¹⁰Then the slave drivers ʷ and the overseers went out and said to the people, "This is what Pharaoh says: 'I will not give you any more straw. ¹¹Go and get your own straw wherever you can find it, but your work will not be reduced ˣ at all.' " ¹²So the people scattered all over Egypt to gather stubble to use for straw. ¹³The slave drivers kept pressing them, saying, "Complete the work required of you for each day, just as when you had straw."

ᵃ 24 Hebrew *him*   ᵇ 25 The meaning of the Hebrew for this clause is uncertain.

4:21 *wonders.* See note on 3:20. *I will harden his heart.* Nine times in Exodus the hardening of the pharaoh's heart is ascribed to God (here; 7:3; 9:12; 10:1,20,27; 11:10; 14:4,8; see Jos 11:20; Ro 9:17–18 and notes); another nine times the pharaoh is said to have hardened his own heart (7:13–14,22; 8:15,19,32; 9:7,34–35). The pharaoh alone was the agent of the hardening in each of the first five plagues. Not until the sixth plague did God confirm the pharaoh's willful action (see 9:12), as he had told Moses he would do (see similarly Ro 1:24–28).

4:22 *firstborn son.* A figure of speech indicating Israel's special relationship with God (see Jer 31:9; Hos 11:1).

4:23 *kill your firstborn son.* Anticipates the tenth plague (see 11:5; 12:12).

4:24 *lodging place.* Perhaps near water, where travelers could spend the night. *the Lᴏʀᴅ ... was about to kill him.* Evidently because Moses had failed to circumcise his son (see Ge 17:9–14).

4:25 *Zipporah ... cut off her son's foreskin.* Sensing that divine displeasure had threatened Moses' life, she quickly performed the circumcision on their young son. *flint knife.* Continued to be used for circumcision long after metal was introduced, probably because flint knives were sharper than the metal instruments available and thus more efficient for the surgical procedure (see

Jos 5:2 and note). *feet.* Probably a euphemism for "genitals," as in Dt 28:57 ("womb," lit. "feet").

4:26 *bridegroom of blood.* Circumcision may have been repulsive to Zipporah—though it was practiced for various reasons among many peoples of the ancient Near East.

4:27 *kissed.* See note on Ge 29:13.

4:30 *Aaron told them everything the Lᴏʀᴅ had said to Moses.* See note on 7:1–2.

5:1 *Pharaoh.* See note on 3:10.

5:3 See 3:18 and note. The reason for sacrificing where the Egyptians could not see them is given in 8:26 (see note on Ge 43:32).

5:6 *slave drivers.* Probably the same as the Egyptian "slave masters" in 1:11 (see note there). *overseers.* Israelite supervisors whose method of appointment and whose functions are indicated in vv. 14–16.

5:7 *straw.* Chopped and mixed with the clay as binder to make the bricks stronger. Canaanite Amarna letter 148.30–34 probably refers to the use of straw in making bricks.

5:9 *lies.* See 4:29–31. The pharaoh labels all hopes of a quick release for Israel as presumptuous and false.

5:10 *This is what Pharaoh says.* In opposition to "This is what the Lᴏʀᴅ says" (4:22; 5:1). The pharaoh is now set on a collision course with the God of Israel.

¹⁴And Pharaoh's slave drivers beat the Israelite overseers they had appointed,ʸ demanding, "Why haven't you met your quota of bricks yesterday or today, as before?"

¹⁵Then the Israelite overseers went and appealed to Pharaoh: "Why have you treated your servants this way? ¹⁶Your servants are given no straw, yet we are told, 'Make bricks!' Your servants are being beaten, but the fault is with your own people."

¹⁷Pharaoh said, "Lazy, that's what you are—lazy!ᶻ That is why you keep saying, 'Let us go and sacrifice to the LORD.' ¹⁸Now get to work.ᵃ You will not be given any straw, yet you must produce your full quota of bricks."

¹⁹The Israelite overseers realized they were in trouble when they were told, "You are not to reduce the number of bricks required of you for each day." ²⁰When they left Pharaoh, they found Moses and Aaron waiting to meet them, ²¹and they said, "May the LORD look on you and judgeᵇ you! You have made us obnoxiousᶜ to Pharaoh and his officials and have put a swordᵈ in their hand to kill us."ᵉ

GOD PROMISES DELIVERANCE

²²Moses returned to the LORD and said, "Why, Lord, why have you brought trouble on this people?ᶠ Is this why you sent me? ²³Ever since I went to Pharaoh to speak in your name, he has brought trouble on this people, and you have not rescuedᵍ your people at all."

6 Then the LORD said to Moses, "Now you will see what I will do to Pharaoh: Because of my mighty handʰ he will let them go;ⁱ because of my mighty hand he will drive them out of his country."ʲ

²God also said to Moses, "I am the LORD.ᵏ ³I appeared to Abraham, to Isaac and to Jacob as God Almighty,ᵃˡ but by my nameᵐ the LORDᵇⁿ I did not make myself known to them.ᶜ ⁴I also established my covenantᵒ with them to give them the landᵖ of Canaan, where they resided as foreigners.�q ⁵Moreover, I have heard the groaningʳ of the Israelites, whom the Egyptians are enslaving, and I have remembered my covenant.ˢ

⁶"Therefore, say to the Israelites: 'I am the LORD, and I will bring you out from under the yoke of the Egyptians.ᵗ I will free you from being slaves to them, and I will redeemᵘ you with an outstretched armᵛ and with mighty acts of judgment.ʷ ⁷I will take you as my own people, and I will be your God.ˣ Then you will knowʸ that I am the LORD your God, who brought you out from under the yoke of the Egyptians. ⁸And I will bring you to the landᶻ I sw>ᵃ with uplifted handᵇ to give to Abraham, to Isaac and to Jacob.ᶜ I will give it to you as a possession. I am the LORD.' "ᵈ

⁹Moses reported this to the Israelites, but they did not listen to him because of their discouragement and harsh labor.ᵉ

¹⁰Then the LORD said to Moses, ¹¹"Go, tellᶠ Pharaoh king of Egypt to let the Israelites go out of his country."ᵍ

ᵃ 3 Hebrew *El-Shaddai*   ᵇ 3 See note at Exodus 3:15.   ᶜ 3 Or *Almighty, and by my name the LORD did not let myself be known to them?*
6:8 Eze 20:6 ᵇ S Ge 14:22; Rev 10:5-6 ᶜ Ps 136:21-22 ᵈ Lev 18:21   **6:9** ᵉ S Ge 34:30; Ex 2:23   **6:11** ᶠ ver 29 ᵍ S Ex 3:18

5:14 ʸ ver 16; Isa 10:24
5:17 ᶻ ver 8
5:18 ᵃ S Ge 15:13
5:21 ᵇ S Ge 16:5 ᶜ S Ge 34:30 ᵈ Ex 16:3; Nu 14:3; 20:3 ᵉ S Ex 1:13; S 14:11
5:22 ᶠ Nu 11:11; Dt 1:12; Jos 7:7
5:23 ᵍ Jer 4:10; 20:7; Eze 14:9
6:1 ʰ S Ex 3:20; S Dt 5:15 ⁱ S Ex 3:20 ʲ Ex 11:1; 12:31,33,39
6:2 ᵏ ver 6,7,8,29; Ex 3:14,15; 7:5,17; 8:22; 10:2; 12:12; 14:4, 18; 16:12; Lev 11:44; 18:21; 20:7; Isa 25:3; 41:20; 43:11; 49:23; 60:16; Eze 13:9; 25:17; 36:38; 37:6,13; Joel 2:27
6:3 ˡ S Ge 17:1 ᵐ S Ex 3:15; 2Sa 7:26; Ps 48:10; 61:5; 68:4; 83:18; 99:3; Isa 52:6 ⁿ Ex 3:14; Jn 8:58
6:4 ᵒ S Ge 6:18; S 15:18 ᵖ S Ge 12:7; Ac 7:5; Ro 4:13; Gal 3:16; Heb 11:8-10 q S Ge 17:8
6:5 ʳ S Ex 2:23; Ac 7:34 ˢ S Ge 9:15
6:6 ᵗ ver 6,7,8,29; Ex 3:8; 12:17,51; 16:1,6; 18:1; 19:1; 20:2; 29:46; Lev 22:33; 26:13; Dt 6:12; Ps 81:10; 136:11; Jer 2:6; Hos 13:4; Am 2:10; Mic 6:4 ᵘ Ex 15:13; Dt 7:8; 9:26; 1Ch 17:21; Job 19:25; Ps 19:14; 34:22; 74:2; 77:15; 107:2; Isa 29:22; 35:9; 43:1; 44:23; 48:20; Jer 15:21; 31:11; 50:34 ᵛ S Ex 3:19,20; S Jer 32:21; Ac 13:17 ʷ Ex 3:20; Ps 9:16; 105:27
6:7 ˣ S Ge 17:7; S Ex 34:9; Eze 11:19-20; Ro 9:4 ʸ S ver 2; 1Ki 20:13,28; Isa 43:10; 48:7; Eze 39:6; Joel 3:17
6:8 ᶻ S Ge 12:7; Ex 3:8 ᵃ Nu 11:5;

B **5:15** *Israelite overseers … appealed to Pharaoh.* During certain periods of Egyptian history slaves were permitted to appeal directly to the pharaoh, bypassing the ordinary chain of command. Egyptian records show that sometimes they were heard, but more often they were not.
5:21 *May the LORD look on you and judge you!* See Ge 16:5; 31:49 and notes. *obnoxious.* See note on 1Sa 13:4.
6:1 *hand.* Often used figuratively in the Bible for power.
6:2 *I am the LORD.* Appears four times in this passage: (1) to introduce the message; (2) to confirm God's promise of redemption (v. 6) based on the evidence of vv. 2–5; (3) to underscore God's intention to adopt Israel (v. 7); (4) to confirm his promise of the land and to conclude the message (v. 8).
A **6:3** *God Almighty.* See note on Ge 17:1. *by my name the LORD I did not make myself known to them.* See notes on 3:14–15. This does not necessarily mean that the patriarchs were totally ignorant of the name Yahweh ("the LORD"), but it indicates that they did not understand its full implications as the name of the One who would redeem his people (see notes on v. 6; Ge 2:4). That fact could be comprehended only by the Israelites who were to experience the exodus, and by their descendants. *make*

myself known. This experiential sense of the verb "to know" is intended also in its repeated use throughout the account of the plagues (see v. 7; 7:17; 8:10,22; 9:14,29; 10:2; 11:7) and in connection with the exodus itself (see 14:4,18; 16:6,8,12; 18:11).
6:5 *remembered.* See note on Ge 8:1.
A **6:6** *I will bring you out … will free you … will redeem you.* The verbs stress the true significance of the name Yahweh—"the LORD"—who is the Redeemer of his people (see note on v. 3). *outstretched arm.* Used figuratively of God's display of his power in the redemption of his people (see Dt 4:34; 5:15; see also Isa 51:9–11 and note on 51:9). *mighty acts of judgment.* See 7:4. The Lord's acts include redemption (for Israel) and judgment (against Egypt).
A **6:7–8** *brought you out from … will bring you to.* Redemption means not only release from slavery and suffering but also deliverance to freedom and joy.
6:7 *I will take you as my own people, and I will be your God.* Words that anticipate the covenant at Mount Sinai (see 19:5–6; see also Jer 31:33; Zec 8:8 and notes).
6:8 See Ge 22:15–17. *swore with uplifted hand.* See note on Ge 14:22.

6:12 *h* S Ex 3:18
i Ex 4:10
6:13 *j* S Ex 3:10
6:14 *k* Ex 13:3;
Nu 1:1; 26:4
l S Ge 29:32
6:15 *m* S Ge 29:33
6:16 *n* S Ge 29:34
o S Ge 46:11
p Nu 3:17; Jos 21:7;
1Ch 6:1,16
6:17 *q* Nu 3:18;
1Ch 6:17
6:18 *r* Nu 3:27;
1Ch 23:12 *a* Nu 3:19;
1Ch 6:2,18
6:19 *t* Nu 3:20,33;
1Ch 6:19; 23:21
6:20 *u* 1Ch 23:13
v Ex 2:1-2; Nu 26:59
6:21 *w* 1Ch 6:38
6:22 *x* Lev 10:4;
Nu 3:30; 1Ch 15:8;
2Ch 29:13
6:23 *y* Ru 4:19,20;
1Ch 2:10 *z* Nu 1:7; 2:3;
Mt 1:4 *a* Ex 24:1; 28:1;
Lev 10:1 *b* Lev 10:6;
Nu 3:2,32; 16:37,39;
Dt 10:6; Jos 14:1
c Ex 28:1; Lev 10:12,
16; Nu 3:2; 4:28;
26:60; 1Ch 6:3; 24:1
6:24 *d* ver 21;
Nu 16:1; 1Ch 6:22,37
6:25 *e* Nu 25:7,11;
31:6; Jos 24:33;
Ps 106:30
6:26 *f* S Ex 3:10
g Ex 7:4; 12:17,41,51
6:27 *h* Ex 5:1
i Nu 3:1; Ps 77:20
6:29 *j* S ver 2
6:30 *k* S Ex 3:11
7:1 *l* S Ex 4:16
m Ex 4:15; Ac 14:12
7:3 *n* S Ex 4:21;
Ro 9:18 *o* S Ex 3:20;
S 10:1; Ac 7:36

[12] But Moses said to the Lord, "If the Israelites will not listen [h] to me, why would Pharaoh listen to me, since I speak with faltering lips[a]?"[i]

FAMILY RECORD OF MOSES AND AARON

[13] Now the Lord spoke to Moses and Aaron about the Israelites and Pharaoh king of Egypt, and he commanded them to bring the Israelites out of Egypt.[j]

[14] These were the heads of their families[b]:[k]

The sons of Reuben[l] the firstborn son of Israel were Hanok and Pallu, Hezron and Karmi. These were the clans of Reuben. [15] The sons of Simeon[m] were Jemuel, Jamin, Ohad, Jakin, Zohar and Shaul the son of a Canaanite woman. These were the clans of Simeon. [16] These were the names of the sons of Levi[n] according to their records: Gershon,[o] Kohath and Merari.[p] Levi lived 137 years.

[17] The sons of Gershon, by clans, were Libni and Shimei.[q] [18] The sons of Kohath[r] were Amram, Izhar, Hebron and Uzziel.[s] Kohath lived 133 years. [19] The sons of Merari were Mahli and Mushi.[t]

These were the clans of Levi according to their records. [20] Amram[u] married his father's sister Jochebed, who bore him Aaron and Moses.[v] Amram lived 137 years. [21] The sons of Izhar[w] were Korah, Nepheg and Zikri. [22] The sons of Uzziel were Mishael, Elzaphan[x] and Sithri. [23] Aaron married Elisheba, daughter of Amminadab[y] and sister of Nahshon,[z] and she bore him Nadab and Abihu,[a] Eleazar[b] and Ithamar.[c] [24] The sons of Korah[d] were Assir, Elkanah and Abiasaph. These were the Korahite clans. [25] Eleazar son of Aaron married one of the daughters of Putiel, and she bore him Phinehas.[e]

These were the heads of the Levite families, clan by clan.

[26] It was this Aaron and Moses to whom the Lord said, "Bring the Israelites out of Egypt[f] by their divisions."[g] [27] They were the ones who spoke to Pharaoh[h] king of Egypt about bringing the Israelites out of Egypt—this same Moses and Aaron.[i]

AARON TO SPEAK FOR MOSES

[28] Now when the Lord spoke to Moses in Egypt, [29] he said to him, "I am the Lord.[j] Tell Pharaoh king of Egypt everything I tell you."

[30] But Moses said to the Lord, "Since I speak with faltering lips,[k] why would Pharaoh listen to me?"

7 Then the Lord said to Moses, "See, I have made you like God[l] to Pharaoh, and your brother Aaron will be your prophet.[m] [2] You are to say everything I command you, and your brother Aaron is to tell Pharaoh to let the Israelites go out of his country. [3] But I will harden Pharaoh's heart,[n] and though I multiply my signs and wonders[o]

---

[a] 12 Hebrew *I am uncircumcised of lips*; also in verse 30   [b] 14 The Hebrew for *families* here and in verse 25 refers to units larger than clans.

6:12 *I speak with faltering lips.* See note on 4:10.
6:13 *Moses and Aaron.* The genealogy contained in vv. 14–25 gives details concerning the background of Moses and Aaron. Only the first three of Jacob's 12 sons (Reuben, Simeon and Levi) are listed since Moses and Aaron were from the third tribe.
6:16 *Merari.* The name is of Egyptian origin, as are those of Putiel and Phinehas (see v. 25) and of Moses himself (see note on 2:10). *Levi lived 137 years.* See vv. 18,20. In the OT, attention is usually called to a person's life span only when it exceeds 100 years.

C **6:20** *Amram . . . Aaron and Moses.* There is some reason to believe that Amram and Jochebed were not the immediate parents but the ancestors of Aaron and Moses. Kohath, Amram's father (see v. 18), was born before Jacob's (Israel's) descent into Egypt (see Ge 46:11), where the Israelites then stayed 430 years (see 12:40–41). Since Moses was 80 years old at the time of the exodus (see 7:7), he must have been born at least 350 years after Kohath, who consequently could not have been Mo-

ses' grandfather (see v. 18). Therefore Amram must not have been Moses' father, and the Hebrew verb for "bore" must have the same meaning it sometimes has in Ge 10 (see TNIV text note on Ge 10:8, where it is translated "was the father of"). *Jochebed.* The name appears to mean "The Lord is glory." If so, it shows that the name Yahweh (here abbreviated as Jo-) was known before Moses was born (see note on v. 3). *Aaron and Moses.* Aaron, as the firstborn (see 7:7), is listed first in the official genealogy.
6:26 *divisions.* The Hebrew word may imply that Israel is to serve as the Lord's army (also in 7:4; 12:17,41,51).
6:30 *faltering lips.* See v. 12 and note on 4:10.
7:1–2 As God transmits his word through his prophets to his people, so Moses will transmit God's message through Aaron to the pharaoh. The prophet's task was to speak God's word on God's behalf. He was God's "mouth" (4:15–16).
7:3 *harden.* See note on 4:21. *signs.* See notes on 3:12; 4:8.

in Egypt, ⁴he will not listen ᵖ to you. Then I will lay my hand on Egypt and with mighty acts of judgment �q I will bring out my divisions, ʳ my people the Israelites. ⁵And the Egyptians will know that I am the Lord ˢ when I stretch out my hand ᵗ against Egypt and bring the Israelites out of it."

⁶Moses and Aaron did just as the Lord commanded ᵘ them. ⁷Moses was eighty years old ᵛ and Aaron eighty-three when they spoke to Pharaoh.

AARON'S STAFF BECOMES A SNAKE

⁸The Lord said to Moses and Aaron, ⁹"When Pharaoh says to you, 'Perform a miracle, ʷ then say to Aaron, 'Take your staff and throw it down before Pharaoh,' and it will become a snake.'"ˣ

¹⁰So Moses and Aaron went to Pharaoh and did just as the Lord commanded. Aaron threw his staff down in front of Pharaoh and his officials, and it became a snake. ¹¹Pharaoh then summoned wise men and sorcerers, ʸ and the Egyptian magicians ᶻ also did the same things by their secret arts: ᵃ ¹²Each one threw down his staff and it became a snake. But Aaron's staff swallowed up their staffs. ¹³Yet Pharaoh's heart ᵇ became hard and he would not listen ᶜ to them, just as the Lord had said.

THE PLAGUE OF BLOOD

¹⁴Then the Lord said to Moses, "Pharaoh's heart is unyielding; ᵈ he refuses to let the people go. ¹⁵Go to Pharaoh in the morning as he goes out to the river. ᵉ Wait on the bank of the Nile ᶠ to meet him, and take in your hand the staff that was changed into a snake. ¹⁶Then say to him, 'The Lord, the God of the Hebrews, has sent me to say to you: Let my people go, so that they may worship ᵍ me in the wilderness. But until now you have not listened. ʰ ¹⁷This is what the Lord says: By this you will know that I am the Lord: ⁱ With the staff that is in my hand I will strike the water of the Nile, and it will be changed into blood.ʲ ¹⁸The fish in the Nile will die, and the river will stink; ᵏ the Egyptians will not be able to drink its water.' " ˡ

¹⁹The Lord said to Moses, "Tell Aaron, 'Take your staff ᵐ and stretch out your hand ⁿ over the waters of Egypt—over the streams and canals, over the ponds and all the reservoirs—and they will turn to blood.' Blood will be everywhere in Egypt, even in the wooden buckets and stone jars."

²⁰Moses and Aaron did just as the Lord had commanded. ᵒ He raised his staff in the presence of Pharaoh and his officials and struck the water of the Nile, ᵖ and all the water was changed into blood. �q ²¹The fish in the Nile died, and the river smelled so bad that the Egyptians could not drink its water. Blood was everywhere in Egypt.

²²But the Egyptian magicians ʳ did the same things by their secret arts, ˢ and Pharaoh's heart ᵗ became hard; he would not listen to Moses and Aaron, just as the Lord had said. ²³Instead, he turned and went into his palace, and did not take even this to heart. ²⁴And all the Egyptians dug along the Nile to get drinking water ᵘ, because they could not drink the water of the river.

7:4 ᵖ ver 13,16,22; Ex 8:15,19; 9:12; 11:9
q S Ex 3:20; Ac 7:36
ʳ S Ex 6:26
7:5 ˢ S Ex 6:2
ᵗ Ex 3:20; Ps 138:7; Eze 6:14; 25:13
7:6 ᵘ ver 2,10,20; Ge 6:22
7:7 ᵛ Dt 31:2; 34:7; Ac 7:23,30
7:9 ʷ Dt 6:22; 2Ki 19:29; Ps 78:43; 86:17; 105:27; 135:9; Isa 7:11; 37:30; 38:7-8; 55:13; S Jn 2:11
ˣ Ex 4:2-5
7:11 ʸ Ex 22:18; Dt 18:10; 1Sa 6:2; 2Ki 21:6; Isa 2:6; 47:12; Jer 27:9; Mal 3:5 ᶻ S Ge 41:8; 2Ti 3:8 ᵃ ver 22; Ex 8:7,18; S Mt 24:24
7:13 ᵇ S Ex 4:21
ᶜ S ver 4
7:14 ᵈ ver 22; Ex 8:15,32; 9:7; 10:1, 20,27
7:15 ᵉ Ex 8:20
ᶠ S Ge 41:1
7:16 ᵍ S Ex 3:18
ʰ S ver 4
7:17 ⁱ S Ex 6:2; 14:25 ʲ ver 19-21; Ex 4:9; Rev 11:6; 16:4
7:18 ᵏ Isa 19:6
ˡ ver 21,24; Ps 78:44
7:19 ᵐ S Ex 4:2
ⁿ Ex 14:21; 2Ki 5:11
7:20 ᵒ S ver 6
ᵖ Ex 17:5 q Ps 78:44; 105:29; 114:3; Mic 3:8
7:22 ʳ S Ge 41:8
ˢ S ver 11; S Mt 24:24
ᵗ ver 13, S 14; Ex 8:19; Ps 105:28
7:24 ᵘ S ver 18

7:4 *mighty acts of judgment.* See note on 6:6.
7:7 *Moses was eighty years old.* See notes on 2:11,15.
7:9–10 *snake.* The Hebrew for this word is different from that used in 4:3 (see Ps 74:13, "monster"). A related word (also translated "monster") is used in Eze 29:3 as a designation for Egypt and her king.
7:11 *wise men and…magicians.* See note on Ge 41:8. According to tradition, two of the magicians who opposed Moses were named Jannes and Jambres (see 2Ti 3:8; the first is also mentioned in a pre-Christian Dead Sea Scroll). *the Egyptian magicians also did the same things by their secret arts.* Either through sleight of hand or by means of demonic power.
7:12 *Aaron's staff swallowed up their staffs.* Demonstrating God's mastery over the pharaoh and the gods of Egypt.
7:13 *heart became hard.* A hardened heart refers to a stubborn refusal to take God and his word seriously (see also note on 4:21).
7:14—10:29 The first nine plagues can be divided into three groups of three plagues each: 7:14—8:19; 8:20—9:12; 9:13—10:29. The first plague in each group (the first, the fourth and the seventh) is introduced by a warning delivered to the pharaoh in the morning as he went out to the Nile (see v. 15; 8:20; 9:13).
7:17 *my.* Moses'. *the water of the Nile…will be changed into*

blood. See Ps 78:44; 105:29. Some interpreters believe that the first nine plagues may have been a series of unprecedented intensifications of events that were part of the Egyptian experience, events that in their more usual form did not have anything like the catastrophic effects of the disasters God brought on Egypt in order to deliver the Israelites from Egyptian imperial bondage. If that was the case, the first plague may have resulted from an unparalleled quantity of red sediment being washed down from Ethiopia during the annual flooding of the Nile in late summer and early fall, causing the water of Egypt's lifeline to become as red as blood (see v. 24; cf. the incident in 2Ki 3:22–23).
7:19 *your staff.* Aaron was acting on Moses' behalf (see v. 17). *in the wooden buckets and stone jars.* Lit. "in/on the wooden things and in/on the stone things." Some think that, since the Egyptians believed that their gods inhabited idols and images made of wood, clay and stone (see Dt 29:16–17), the plague may have been intended as a rebuke to their religion (see 12:12).
7:20 *Nile.* Egypt's dependence on the life-sustaining waters of the Nile led to its deification as the god Hapi, for whom hymns of adoration were composed. See note on v. 19.
7:24 *dug along the Nile to get drinking water.* Filtered through sandy soil near the river bank, the polluted water would become safe for drinking.

8:1 ᵛEx 3:12,18;
4:23; 5:1; 9:1
8:2 ʷPs 78:45;
105:30; Rev 16:13
8:3 ˣEx 10:6
ʸEx 12:34
8:5 ᶻS Ex 4:2; 7:9-
20; 9:23; 10:13,21-22;
14:27 ªS Ex 4:17
8:6 ᵇPs 78:45;
105:30
8:7 ᶜS Ex 7:11;
S Mt 24:24
8:8 ᵈver 28;
Ex 9:28; 10:17;
Nu 21:7; 1Sa 12:19;
1Ki 13:6; Jer 42:2;
Ac 8:24 ᵉver 25;
Ex 10:8,24; 12:31
8:9 ᶠEx 9:5
8:10 ᵍEx 9:14; 15:11;
Dt 3:24; 4:35; 33:26;
2Sa 7:22; 1Ki 8:23;
1Ch 17:20; 2Ch 6:14;
Ps 71:19; 86:8; 89:6;
113:5; Isa 40:18; 42:8;
46:9; Jer 10:6; 49:19;
Mic 7:18
8:13 ʰJas 5:16-18
8:15 ⁱEcc 8:11
ʲS Ex 7:14
8:16 ᵏS Ex 4:2
8:17 ˡPs 105:31
8:18 ᵐEx 9:11;
Da 5:8 ⁿS Ex 7:11
8:19 ᵒEx 7:5; 10:7;
12:33; 31:18; 1Sa 6:9;
Ne 9:6; Ps 8:3; 33:6;
Lk 11:20 ᵖS Ex 7:22
�q S Ex 7:4
8:20 ʳEx 7:15; 9:13
ˢS Ex 3:18
8:22 ᵗS Ge 45:10

THE PLAGUE OF FROGS

8 25Seven days passed after the Lord struck the Nile. *1Then the Lord said to Moses, "Go to Pharaoh and say to him, 'This is what the Lord says: Let my people go, so that they may worship ᵛ me. 2If you refuse to let them go, I will send a plague of frogs ʷ on your whole country. 3The Nile will teem with frogs. They will come up into your palace and your bedroom and onto your bed, into the houses of your officials and on your people, ˣ and into your ovens and kneading troughs. ʸ 4The frogs will come up on you and your people and all your officials.' "

*5Then the Lord said to Moses, "Tell Aaron, 'Stretch out your hand with your staff ᶻ over the streams and canals and ponds, and make frogs ª come up on the land of Egypt.' "

6So Aaron stretched out his hand over the waters of Egypt, and the frogs ᵇ came up and covered the land. 7But the magicians did the same things by their secret arts; ᶜ they also made frogs come up on the land of Egypt.

8Pharaoh summoned Moses and Aaron and said, "Pray ᵈ to the Lord to take the frogs away from me and my people, and I will let your people go to offer sacrifices ᵉ to the Lord."

9Moses said to Pharaoh, "I leave to you the honor of setting the time ᶠ for me to pray for you and your officials and your people that you and your houses may be rid of the frogs, except for those that remain in the Nile."

10"Tomorrow," Pharaoh said.

Moses replied, "It will be as you say, so that you may know there is no one like the Lord our God. ᵍ 11The frogs will leave you and your houses, your officials and your people; they will remain only in the Nile."

12After Moses and Aaron left Pharaoh, Moses cried out to the Lord about the frogs he had brought on Pharaoh. 13And the Lord did what Moses asked. ʰ The frogs died in the houses, in the courtyards and in the fields. 14They were piled into heaps, and the land reeked of them. 15But when Pharaoh saw that there was relief, ⁱ he hardened his heart ʲ and would not listen to Moses and Aaron, just as the Lord had said.

THE PLAGUE OF GNATS

16Then the Lord said to Moses, "Tell Aaron, 'Stretch out your staff ᵏ and strike the dust of the ground,' and throughout the land of Egypt the dust will become gnats." 17They did this, and when Aaron stretched out his hand with the staff and struck the dust of the ground, gnats ˡ came on people and animals. All the dust throughout the land of Egypt became gnats. 18But when the magicians ᵐ tried to produce gnats by their secret arts, ⁿ they could not.

Since the gnats were on people and animals everywhere, 19the magicians said to Pharaoh, "This is the finger ᵒ of God." But Pharaoh's heart ᵖ was hard and he would not listen, q just as the Lord had said.

THE PLAGUE OF FLIES

20Then the Lord said to Moses, "Get up early in the morning ʳ and confront Pharaoh as he goes to the river and say to him, 'This is what the Lord says: Let my people go, so that they may worship ˢ me. 21If you do not let my people go, I will send swarms of flies on you and your officials, on your people and into your houses. The houses of the Egyptians will be full of flies; even the ground will be covered with them.

22" 'But on that day I will deal differently with the land of Goshen, ᵗ where my people

---

* 8:1-4 is numbered 7:26-29 in Hebrew texts.   * 8:5-32 is numbered 8:1-28 in Hebrew texts.

7:25 *Seven days passed.* The plagues did not follow each other in rapid succession.

8:2 *I will send a plague of frogs.* The frog (or toad) was deified in the goddess Heqt, who assisted women in childbirth.

8:3 *come up.* The frogs abandoned the Nile and swarmed over the land, perhaps because an unusually high concentration of bacteria-laden algae had by now proved fatal to most of the fish, thus polluting the river.

8:13 *the Lord did what Moses asked.* For similar occurrences see v. 31; 1Sa 12:18; 1Ki 18:42–45; Am 7:1–6. *The frogs died.* Probably because they had been infected by bacteria in the Nile algae (see note on v. 3).

8:15 *hardened his heart.* See note on 7:13.

8:16 *dust will become gnats.* The word "dust" is perhaps a reference to the enormous number (see, e.g., Ge 13:16) of the gnats, bred in the flooded fields of Egypt in late autumn.

8:19 *finger of God.* A concise and colorful figure of speech referring to God's miraculous power (see 31:18; Ps 8:3). Jesus drove out demons "by the finger of God" (Lk 11:20). Cf. the similar use of the phrase "hand of the Lord" in 9:3 and "arm of the Lord" in Isa 51:9 (see note there).

8:20 *as he goes to the river.* As he goes to the Nile. Perhaps the pharaoh went there (1) to worship at a shrine or (2) to bathe, as the princess had done in 2:5 (see also 7:15). The specific purpose remains uncertain.

8:21 *I will send swarms of flies.* They probably would have multiplied rapidly as the receding Nile left breeding places in its wake. Full-grown, such flies infest houses and stables and bite people and animals.

8:22 *I will deal differently.* See 33:16. God makes a "distinction" (v. 23) between Moses' people and the pharaoh's people in this plague as well as in the fifth (see 9:4,6), the seventh (see 9:26), live;[u] no swarms of flies will be there, so that you will know[v] that I, the Lord, am in this land. [23]I will make a distinction[a] between my people and your people. [w] This sign will occur tomorrow.'"

[24]And the Lord did this. Dense swarms of flies poured into Pharaoh's palace and into the houses of his officials; throughout Egypt the land was ruined by the flies.[x]

[25]Then Pharaoh summoned[y] Moses and Aaron and said, "Go, sacrifice to your God here in the land."

[26]But Moses said, "That would not be right. The sacrifices we offer the Lord our God would be detestable to the Egyptians.[z] And if we offer sacrifices that are detestable in their eyes, will they not stone us? [27]We must take a three-day journey[a] into the wilderness to offer sacrifices[b] to the Lord our God, as he commands us."

[28]Pharaoh said, "I will let you go to offer sacrifices to the Lord your God in the wilderness, but you must not go very far. Now pray[c] for me."

[29]Moses answered, "As soon as I leave you, I will pray to the Lord, and tomorrow the flies will leave Pharaoh and his officials and his people. Only let Pharaoh be sure that he does not act deceitfully[d] again by not letting the people go to offer sacrifices to the Lord."

[30]Then Moses left Pharaoh and prayed to the Lord,[e] [31]and the Lord did what Moses asked. The flies left Pharaoh and his officials and his people; not a fly remained. [32]But this time also Pharaoh hardened his heart[f] and would not let the people go.

THE PLAGUE ON LIVESTOCK

9 Then the Lord said to Moses, "Go to Pharaoh and say to him, 'This is what the Lord, the God of the Hebrews, says: "Let my people go, so that they may worship[g] me." [2]If you refuse to let them go and continue to hold them back, [3]the hand[h] of the Lord will bring a terrible plague[i] on your livestock in the field—on your horses, donkeys and camels and on your cattle, sheep and goats. [4]But the Lord will make a distinction between the livestock of Israel and that of Egypt,[j] so that no animal belonging to the Israelites will die.'"

[5]The Lord set a time and said, "Tomorrow the Lord will do this in the land." [6]And the next day the Lord did it: All the livestock[k] of the Egyptians died,[l] but not one animal belonging to the Israelites died. [7]Pharaoh investigated and found that not even one of the animals of the Israelites had died. Yet his heart[m] was unyielding and he would not let the people go.[n]

THE PLAGUE OF BOILS

[8]Then the Lord said to Moses and Aaron, "Take handfuls of soot from a furnace and have Moses toss it into the air in the presence of Pharaoh. [9]It will become fine dust over the whole land of Egypt, and festering boils[o] will break out on people and animals throughout the land."

[10]So they took soot from a furnace and stood before Pharaoh. Moses tossed it into the air, and festering boils broke out on people and animals. [11]The magicians[p] could not stand before Moses because of the boils that were on them and on all the Egyptians. [12]But the Lord hardened Pharaoh's heart[q] and he would not listen[r] to Moses and Aaron, just as the Lord had said to Moses.

---

a 23 Septuagint and Vulgate; Hebrew *will put a deliverance*

Cross references (right column)

8:22 [u] Ex 9:4,6,26; 10:23; 11:7; 12:13; 19:5; Dt 4:20; 7:6; 14:2; 26:18; 1Ki 8:36; Job 36:11; Ps 33:12; 135:4; Mal 3:17
[v] Ex 7:5; 9:29
8:23 [w] Ex 9:4,6; 10:23; 11:7; 12:13,23, 27
8:24 [x] Ps 78:45; 105:31
8:25 [y] ver 8; Ex 9:27; 10:16; 12:31
8:26 [z] S Ge 43:32
8:27 [a] S Ge 30:36
[b] S Ex 3:18
8:28 [c] S ver 8; S Jer 37:3; Ac 8:24
8:29 [d] ver 15; Ex 9:30; 10:11; Isa 26:10
8:30 [e] ver 12; Ex 9:33; 10:18
8:32 [f] S Ex 7:14
9:1 [g] S Ex 8:1
9:3 [h] Ex 7:4; 1Sa 5:6; Job 13:21; Ps 32:4; 39:10; Ac 13:11
[i] Lev 26:25; Ps 78:50; Am 4:10
9:4 [j] ver 26; S Ex 8:23
9:6 [k] ver 19-21; Ex 11:5; 12:29
[l] Ps 78:48-50
9:7 [m] S Ex 7:22
[n] Ex 7:14; 8:32
9:9 [o] Lev 13:18,19; Dt 28:27,35; 2Ki 20:7; Job 2:7; Isa 38:21; Rev 16:2
9:11 [p] S Ex 8:18
9:12 [q] S Ex 4:21
[r] S Ex 7:4

Study notes (bottom)

the ninth (see 10:23) and the tenth (see 11:7)—and probably also the sixth and eighth (see 9:11; 10:6)—demonstrating that the Lord can preserve his own people while judging Egypt. *Goshen.* See Ge 45:10 and note.
8:23 *sign.* See 4:8 and note.
8:26 *detestable to the Egyptians.* See Ge 46:34; see also Ge 43:32 and note.
8:31 *the Lord did what Moses asked.* See note on v. 13.
9:3 *hand of the Lord.* See note on 8:19. *terrible plague on your livestock.* The flies of the fourth plague (see note on 8:21) possibly carried the bacteria (see note on 8:13) that would now infect the animals, which had been brought into the fields again as the floodwaters subsided. The Egyptians worshiped many animals and animal-headed deities, including the bull-gods Apis and Mnevis, the cow-god Hathor and the ram-god Khnum. Thus Egyptian religion is again rebuked and ridiculed (see note on 7:19). *camels.* See note on Ge 12:16.
9:4 *distinction.* See note on 8:22.

9:5 *Tomorrow.* To give those Egyptians who feared God time to bring their livestock in from the fields and out of danger (see also v. 20)—mercy in the midst of judgment.
9:6 *All the livestock of the Egyptians died.* That is, all that were left out in the fields. Protected livestock remained alive (see vv. 19–21).
9:8 *Take…soot…toss it into the air.* Perhaps symbolizing either the widespread extent of the plague of boils or their black coloration. *furnace.* Possibly a kiln for firing bricks, the symbol of Israel's bondage (see 1:14; 5:7–19). The same word is used in Ge 19:28 as a simile for the destruction of Sodom and Gomorrah.
9:9 *boils.* Possibly skin anthrax (a variety of the plague that struck the livestock in vv. 1–7), a black, burning abscess that develops into a pustule. *people and animals.* The plague on the livestock now extended to other animals, as well as to the people of Egypt.
9:11 *magicians could not stand.* The "boils of Egypt" (Dt 28:27) seriously affected the knees and legs (see Dt 28:35).
9:12 *the Lord hardened Pharaoh's heart.* See note on 4:21.

9:13 *ᶠ* S Ex 3:18
9:14 *ᵗ* S Ex 8:10
ᵘ Ex 15:11; 1Sa 2:2;
2Sa 7:22; 1Ki 8:23;
1Ch 17:20; Ps 35:10;
71:19; 86:8; 89:6;
Isa 46:9; Jer 10:6;
Mic 7:18
9:15 *ᵛ* Ex 3:20
9:16 *ʷ* Pr 16:4
ˣ Ex 14:4,17,31;
Ps 20:6; 25:11; 68:28;
71:18; 106:8; 109:21;
Ro 9:17*
9:18 *ʸ* ver 23;
Jos 10:11; Ps 78:47-
48; 105:32; 148:8;
Isa 30:30; Eze 38:22;
Hag 2:17 *ᶻ* ver 24;
Ex 10:6
9:20 *ᵃ* Pr 13:13
9:21 *ᵇ* S Ge 19:14;
Eze 33:4-5
9:23 *ᶜ* Ex 20:18;
1Sa 7:10; 12:17;
Ps 18:13; 29:3; 68:33;
77:17; 104:7
ᵈ S ver 18; Rev 8:7;
16:21
9:24 *ᵉ* S ver 18
9:25 *ᶠ* Ps 105:32-33;
Eze 13:13
9:26 *ᵍ* S ver 4;
Isa 32:18-20
ʰ Ex 10:23; 11:7; 12:13;
Am 4:7
9:27 *ⁱ* ver 34;
Ex 10:16; Nu 14:40;
Dt 1:41; Jos 7:11;
Jdg 10:10; 1Sa 15:24;
24:17; 26:21 *ʲ* Ps 11:7;
116:5; 119:137; 129:4;
145:17; Jer 12:1;
La 1:18
9:28 *ᵏ* Ex 8:8;
Ac 8:24 *ˡ* S Ex 8:8
9:29 *ᵐ* ver 33;
1Ki 8:22,38; Job 11:13;
Ps 77:2; 88:9; 143:6;
Isa 1:15 *ⁿ* Ex 19:5;
Job 41:11; Ps 24:1;
50:12; 1Co 10:26
9:30 *ᵒ* S Ex 8:29
9:31 *ᵖ* Dt 8:8;
Ru 1:22; 2:23;
2Sa 14:30; 17:28;
Isa 28:25; Eze 4:9;
Joel 1:11
9:32 *�q* Isa 28:25
9:35 *ʳ* S Ex 4:21
10:1 *ˢ* S Ex 4:21
ᵗ S Ex 3:19; S 7:3;
Jos 24:17; Ne 9:10;
Ps 74:9; 105:26-36
10:2 *ᵘ* Ex 12:26-27;
13:8,14; Dt 4:9; 6:20;
32:7; Jos 4:6; Ps 44:1;
71:18; 78:4,5; Joel 1:3

THE PLAGUE OF HAIL

13Then the LORD said to Moses, "Get up early in the morning, confront Pharaoh and say to him, 'This is what the LORD, the God of the Hebrews, says: Let my people go, so that they may worship *ˢ* me, 14or this time I will send the full force of my plagues against you and against your officials and your people, so you may know *ᵗ* that there is no one like *ᵘ* me in all the earth. 15For by now I could have stretched out my hand and struck you and your people *ᵛ* with a plague that would have wiped you off the earth. 16But I have raised you up*ᵃ* for this very purpose, *ʷ* that I might show you my power*ˣ* and that my name might be proclaimed in all the earth. 17You still set yourself against my people and will not let them go. 18Therefore, at this time tomorrow I will send the worst hailstorm *ʸ* that has ever fallen on Egypt, from the day it was founded till now. *ᶻ* 19Give an order now to bring your livestock and everything you have in the field to a place of shelter, because the hail will fall on every person and animal that has not been brought in and is still out in the field, and they will die.' "

20Those officials of Pharaoh who feared*ᵃ* the word of the LORD hurried to bring their slaves and their livestock inside. 21But those who ignored *ᵇ* the word of the LORD left their slaves and livestock in the field.

22Then the LORD said to Moses, "Stretch out your hand toward the sky so that hail will fall all over Egypt—on people and animals and on everything growing in the fields of Egypt." 23When Moses stretched out his staff toward the sky, the LORD sent thunder*ᶜ* and hail, *ᵈ* and lightning flashed down to the ground. So the LORD rained hail on the land of Egypt; 24hail fell and lightning flashed back and forth. It was the worst storm in all the land of Egypt since it had become a nation. *ᵉ* 25Throughout Egypt hail struck everything in the fields—both people and animals; it beat down everything growing in the fields and stripped every tree. *ᶠ* 26The only place it did not hail was the land of Goshen, *ᵍ* where the Israelites were. *ʰ*

27Then Pharaoh summoned Moses and Aaron. "This time I have sinned," *ⁱ* he said to them. "The LORD is in the right, *ʲ* and I and my people are in the wrong. 28Pray *ᵏ* to the LORD, for we have had enough thunder and hail. I will let you go; *ˡ* you don't have to stay any longer."

29Moses replied, "When I have gone out of the city, I will spread out my hands *ᵐ* in prayer to the LORD. The thunder will stop and there will be no more hail, so you may know that the earth *ⁿ* is the LORD's. 30But I know that you and your officials still do not fear*ᵒ* the LORD God."

31(The flax and barley*ᵖ* were destroyed, since the barley had headed and the flax was in bloom. 32The wheat and spelt, *q* however, were not destroyed, because they ripen later.)

33Then Moses left Pharaoh and went out of the city. He spread out his hands toward the LORD; the thunder and hail stopped, and the rain no longer poured down on the land. 34When Pharaoh saw that the rain and hail and thunder had stopped, he sinned again: He and his officials hardened their hearts. 35So Pharaoh's heart *ʳ* was hard and he would not let the Israelites go, just as the LORD had said through Moses.

THE PLAGUE OF LOCUSTS

10 Then the LORD said to Moses, "Go to Pharaoh, for I have hardened his heart *ˢ* and the hearts of his officials so that I may perform these signs *ᵗ* of mine among them ²that you may tell your children *ᵘ* and grandchildren how I dealt harsh-

ᵃ 16 Or have spared you

A **9:16** Paul quotes this verse as an outstanding illustration of the sovereignty of God (see Ro 9:17).
9:18 *I will send ... hailstorm.* The flooding of the Nile (the possible occasion of the first six plagues) came to an end late in the fall. The hailstorm is thus in the proper chronological position, taking place in January or February when the flax and barley were in flower but the wheat and spelt had not yet germinated (see vv. 31–32).
9:19–21 See note on v. 6.
A **9:19** An example of God's compassion. Even in judgment he allows for the protection of both human beings and animals (see also note on Jnh 4:11).
9:27 *This time I have sinned.* For the first time the pharaoh acknowledges his sinfulness and perceives its devastating results.

B **9:29** *spread out my hands.* See 1Ki 8:22,38,54; 2Ch 6:12–13,29; Ezr 9:5; Ps 44:20; 88:9; 143:6; Isa 1:15; 1Ti 2:8. Statues of men praying with hands upraised have been found by archaeologists at several ancient sites in the Middle East.
9:30 *LORD God.* See note on Ge 2:4.
9:31–32 See note on v. 18.
B **9:32** *spelt.* Grains of spelt, a member of the grass family allied to wheat, have been found in ancient Egyptian tombs. Although inferior to wheat, it grows well in poorer and drier soil.
A **10:2** *tell your children.* The memory of God's redemptive acts is to be kept alive by reciting them to our descendants (see 12:26–27; 13:8,14–15; Dt 4:9; Ps 77:11–20; 78:4–6, 43–53; 105:26–38; 106:7–12; 114:1–3; 135:8–9; 136:10–15).

ly^v with the Egyptians and how I performed my signs among them, and that you may know that I am the LORD."^w

³So Moses and Aaron went to Pharaoh and said to him, "This is what the LORD, the God of the Hebrews, says: 'How long will you refuse to humble^x yourself before me? Let my people go, so that they may worship me. ⁴If you refuse^y to let them go, I will bring locusts^z into your country tomorrow. ⁵They will cover the face of the ground so that it cannot be seen. They will devour what little you have left^a after the hail, including every tree that is growing in your fields. ᵇ ⁶They will fill your houses^c and those of all your officials and all the Egyptians—something neither your parents nor your ancestors have ever seen from the day they settled in this land till now.' "^d Then Moses turned and left Pharaoh.

⁷Pharaoh's officials said to him, "How long will this man be a snare^e to us? Let the people go, so that they may worship the LORD their God. Do you not yet realize that Egypt is ruined?"^f

⁸Then Moses and Aaron were brought back to Pharaoh. "Go, worship^g the LORD your God," he said. "But tell me who will be going."

⁹Moses answered, "We will go with our young and our old, with our sons and our daughters, and with our flocks and herds, because we are to celebrate a festival^h to the LORD."

¹⁰Pharaoh said, "The LORD be with you—if I let you go, along with your women and children! Clearly you are bent on evil.^a ¹¹No! Have only the men go and worship the LORD, since that's what you have been asking for." Then Moses and Aaron were driven out of Pharaoh's presence.

¹²And the LORD said to Moses, "Stretch out your hand^i over Egypt so that locusts swarm over the land and devour everything growing in the fields, everything left by the hail."

¹³So Moses stretched out his staff^j over Egypt, and the LORD made an east wind blow across the land all that day and all that night. By morning the wind had brought the locusts;^k ¹⁴they invaded all Egypt and settled down in every area of the country in great numbers. Never before had there been such a plague of locusts,^l nor will there ever be again. ¹⁵They covered all the ground until it was black. They devoured^m all that was left after the hail—everything growing in the fields and the fruit on the trees. Nothing green remained on tree or plant in all the land of Egypt.

¹⁶Pharaoh quickly summoned^n Moses and Aaron and said, "I have sinned^o against the LORD your God and against you. ¹⁷Now forgive^p my sin once more and pray^q to the LORD your God to take this deadly plague away from me."

¹⁸Moses then left Pharaoh and prayed to the LORD.^r ¹⁹And the LORD changed the wind to a very strong west wind, which caught up the locusts and carried them into the Red Sea.^b Not a locust was left anywhere in Egypt. ²⁰But the LORD hardened Pharaoh's heart,^s and he would not let the Israelites go.

THE PLAGUE OF DARKNESS

²¹Then the LORD said to Moses, "Stretch out your hand toward the sky so that darkness^t spreads over Egypt—darkness that can be felt." ²²So Moses stretched out his hand toward the sky, and total darkness^u covered all Egypt for three days. ²³No one could see anyone else or move about for three days. Yet all the Israelites had light in the places where they lived.^v

²⁴Then Pharaoh summoned Moses and said, "Go,^w worship the LORD. Even your women and children^x may go with you; only leave your flocks and herds behind."^y

---

^a 10 Or Be careful, trouble is in store for you!   ^b 19 Or the Sea of Reeds

---

10:4 I will bring locusts. In March or April the prevailing east winds (see v. 13) would sometimes bring in hordes of migratory locusts. Fifty million of them could occupy a square kilometer and devour as much as 100,000 tons of vegetation in a single night. Such locust plagues were greatly feared in ancient times and became a powerful symbol of divine judgment (see Joel 1:4–7; 2:1–11; Am 7:1–3).

10:7 How long . . . ? The pharaoh's officials ironically echo the phrase used by Moses in v. 3. Egypt is ruined. Human rebellion and disobedience always bring death and destruction in their wake.

10:10 The LORD be with you. This may be irony (see TNIV text note on "Clearly you are bent on evil").

10:11 Have only the men go. From the pharaoh's standpoint,

(1) the women and children should remain behind as hostages, and (2) it was typically only the men who participated fully in worship.

10:13 east wind. See note on v. 4.

10:19 the LORD changed the wind. He used the forces of his own creation to carry out his historical purpose and sovereign will (see v. 4; 14:21; Ps 104:4 and notes; cf. Mt 8:23–27). Red Sea. See TNIV text note.

10:21 darkness spreads over Egypt. Like the third and sixth plagues, this ninth plague was unannounced to the pharaoh. It was possibly caused by the arrival of an unusually severe khamsin, the blinding sandstorm that blows in from the desert each year in the early spring. The darkness was an insult to the sun-god Ra (or Re), one of the chief deities of Egypt.

10:2 ^vIsa 6:6 ^wS Ge 6:2
10:3 ^xIKi 21:29; 2Ki 22:19; 2Ch 7:14; 12:7; 33:23; 34:27; Job 42:6; Isa 58:3; 1Pe 5:6
10:4 ^YEx 8:2; 9:2 ^zDt 28:38; Ps 105:34; Pr 30:27; Joel 1:4; Rev 9:3
10:5 ^aEx 9:32; Joel 1:4 ^bver 15
10:6 ^cJoel 2:9 ^dS Ex 9:18
10:7 ^eEx 23:33; 34:12; Dt 7:16; 12:30; 20:18; Jos 23:13; Jdg 2:3; 8:27; 16:5; 1Sa 18:21; Ps 106:36; Ecc 7:26 ^fS Ge 20:3; S Ex 8:19
10:8 ^gS Ex 8:8
10:9 ^hS Ex 3:18
10:12 ^iEx 7:19
10:13 ^jver 21-22; Ex 4:17; 8:5,17; 9:23; 14:15-16,26-27; 17:5; Nu 20:8 ^kver 4; 1Ki 8:37; Ps 78:46; 105:34; Am 4:9; Na 3:16
10:14 ^lDt 28:38; Ps 78:46; Isa 33:4; Joel 1:4; 2:1-11,25; Am 4:9
10:15 ^mDt 28:38; Ps 105:34-35; Joel 1:4; Am 7:2; Mal 3:11
10:16 ^nS Ex 8:25 ^oS Ex 9:27
10:17 ^pISa 15:25 ^qS Ex 8:8
10:18 ^rS Ex 8:30
10:20 ^sS Ex 4:21
10:21 ^tDt 28:29
10:22 ^uPs 105:28; Isa 13:10; 45:7; 50:3; Rev 16:10
10:23 ^vS Ex 8:22; Am 4:7
10:24 ^wS Ex 8:8 ^xver 8-10 ^yS Ge 45:10

10:25 z S Ge 8:20;
S Ex 18:12
10:27 a S Ex 4:21
10:29 b Ex 11:8;
Heb 11:27
11:1 c S Ex 3:20
d S Ex 6:1
11:2 e S Ex 3:21,22
11:3 f S Ge 39:21
g Dt 34:11; 2Sa 7:9;
8:13; 22:44; 23:1;
Est 9:4; Ps 89:27
11:4 h Ex 12:29;
Job 34:20 i Ex 12:23;
Ps 81:5
11:5 j S Ex 4:23
k Isa 47:2
11:6 l Ex 12:30;
Pr 21:13; Am 5:17
11:7 m S Ex 8:22
11:8 n Ex 12:31-33
o Heb 11:27
11:9 p S Ex 7:4
q S Ex 3:20
11:10 r S Ex 4:21;
Ro 2:5
12:2 s ver 18;
Ex 13:4; 23:15; 34:18;
40:2; Dt 16:1
12:3 t Mk 14:12;
1Co 5:7 u ver 21
12:5 v Ex 29:1;
Lev 1:3; 3:1; 4:3;
22:18-21; 23:12;
Nu 6:14; 15:8; 28:3;
Dt 15:21; 17:1;
Heb 9:14; 1Pe 1:19
12:6 w ver 19;
Lev 23:5; Nu 9:1-3, 5,
11; Jos 5:10; 2Ch 30:2
x Ex 16:12; Dt 16:4, 6

25But Moses said, "You must allow us to have sacrifices and burnt offerings z to present to the Lord our God. 26Our livestock too must go with us; not a hoof is to be left behind. We have to use some of them in worshiping the Lord our God, and until we get there we will not know what we are to use to worship the Lord."

27But the Lord hardened Pharaoh's heart, a and he was not willing to let them go. 28Pharaoh said to Moses, "Get out of my sight! Make sure you do not appear before me again! The day you see my face you will die."

29"Just as you say," Moses replied. "I will never appear b before you again."

THE PLAGUE ON THE FIRSTBORN

11 Now the Lord had said to Moses, "I will bring one more plague on Pharaoh and on Egypt. After that, he will let you go c from here, and when he does, he will drive you out completely. d 2Tell the people that men and women alike are to ask their neighbors for articles of silver and gold." e 3(The Lord made the Egyptians favorably disposed f toward the people, and Moses himself was highly regarded g in Egypt by Pharaoh's officials and by the people.)

4So Moses said, "This is what the Lord says: 'About midnight h I will go throughout Egypt. i 5Every firstborn j son in Egypt will die, from the firstborn son of Pharaoh, who sits on the throne, to the firstborn son of the female slave, who is at her hand mill, k and all the firstborn of the cattle as well. 6There will be loud wailing l throughout Egypt—worse than there has ever been or ever will be again. 7But among the Israelites not a dog will bark at any person or animal.' Then you will know that the Lord makes a distinction m between Egypt and Israel. 8All these officials of yours will come to me, bowing down before me and saying, 'Go, n you and all the people who follow you!' After that I will leave." o Then Moses, hot with anger, left Pharaoh.

9The Lord had said to Moses, "Pharaoh will refuse to listen p to you—so that my wonders q may be multiplied in Egypt." 10Moses and Aaron performed all these wonders before Pharaoh, but the Lord hardened Pharaoh's heart, r and he would not let the Israelites go out of his country.

THE PASSOVER AND THE FESTIVAL OF UNLEAVENED BREAD

12:14-20pp — Lev 23:4-8; Nu 28:16-25; Dt 16:1-8

12 The Lord said to Moses and Aaron in Egypt, 2"This month is to be for you the first month, s the first month of your year. 3Tell the whole community of Israel that on the tenth day of this month each man is to take a lamb a t for his family, one for each household. u 4If any household is too small for a whole lamb, they must share one with their nearest neighbor, having taken into account the number of people there are. You are to determine the amount of lamb needed in accordance with what each person will eat. 5The animals you choose must be year-old males without defect, v and you may take them from the sheep or the goats. 6Take care of them until the fourteenth day of the month, w when all the members of the community of Israel must slaughter them at twilight. x 7Then

---

a 3 The Hebrew word can mean *lamb* or *kid*; also in verse 4.

10:28 The pharaoh declares that he will never again grant Moses an audience. *The day you see my face.* During a plague of darkness, these words are somewhat ironic.

11:1 *and when he does.* The Hebrew for this phrase can also be read "as one sends away [a bride]"—i.e., laden with gifts (see Ge 24:53).

11:2-3 See 3:21-22; 12:35-36.

11:4 *Moses said.* Continuing the speech of 10:29.

11:5 *Every firstborn son in Egypt will die.* See Ps 78:51; 105:36; 135:8; 136:10. This is the ultimate disaster, since all the plans and dreams of a father were bound up in his firstborn son, who received a double share of the family estate when the father died (see Dt 21:17 and note). Moreover, judgment on the firstborn represented judgment on the entire community. *female slave, who is at her hand mill.* The lowliest of occupations (see Isa 47:2).

11:7 *distinction.* See note on 8:22.

11:8 *Moses, hot with anger.* Moses' announcement of the death of the pharaoh's firstborn son is the Lord's response to the death threat to his servant Moses (10:28).

12:2 *This month is ... the first month.* The inauguration of the religious calendar in Israel (see chart, p. 105). In the ancient Near East, new year festivals normally coincided with the new season of life in nature. The designation of this month as Israel's religious New Year reminded Israel that its life as the people of God was grounded in God's redemptive act in the exodus. The Canaanite name for this month was Aviv (see 13:4; 23:15; 34:18; Dt 16:1), which means "young head of grain." Later the Babylonian name Nisan was used (see Ne 2:1; Est 3:7). Israel's agricultural calendar began in the fall (see note on 23:16), and during the monarchy it dominated the nation's civil calendar. Both calendars (civil and religious) existed side by side until after the exile. Judaism today uses only the calendar that begins in the fall.

12:3 *community of Israel.* The Israelites gathered in assembly.

12:5 *animals ... without defect.* See Lev 22:18-25. Similarly, Jesus was like "a lamb without blemish or defect" (1Pe 1:19).

12:6 *at twilight.* Lit. "between the two evenings," an idiom meaning either (1) between the decline of the sun and sunset, or (2) between sunset and nightfall—which has given rise to disputes about when the Sabbath and other holy days begin.

HEBREW CALENDAR AND SELECTED EVENTS

NUMBER OF MONTH		HEBREW NAME	MODERN EQUIVALENT	BIBLICAL REFERENCES	AGRICULTURE	FESTIVALS**
1 Sacred sequence begins	7	Aviv; Nisan	March–April	Ex 12:2; 13:4; 23:15; 34:18; Dt 16:1; Ne 2:1; Est 3:7	Spring (later) rains; barley and flax harvest begins	Passover; Unleavened Bread; Firstfruits
2	8	Ziv (Iyyar)*	April–May	1Ki 6:1,37	Barley harvest; dry season begins	
3	9	Sivan	May–June	Est 8:9	Wheat harvest	Pentecost (Weeks)
4	10	(Tammuz)*	June–July		Tending vines	
5	11	(Ab)*	July–August		Ripening of grapes, figs and olives	
6	12	Elul	August– September	Ne 6:15	Processing grapes, figs and olives	
7	1 Civil sequence	Ethanim (Tishri)*	September– October	1Ki 8:2	Autumn (early) rains begin; plowing	Trumpets; Day of Atonement; Tabernacles (Booths)
8	2	Bul (Marcheshvan)*	October– November	1Ki 6:38	Sowing of wheat and barley	
9	3	Kislev	November– December	Ne 1:1; Zec 7:1	Winter rains begin (snow in some areas)	Hanukkah ("Dedication")
10	4	Tebeth	December– January	Est 2:16		
11	5	Shebat	January– February	Zec 1:7		
12	6	Adar	February– March	Ezr 6:15; Est 3:7,13; 8:12; 9:1,15,17,19,21	Almond trees bloom; citrus fruit harvest	Purim
		(Adar Sheni)* — Second Adar	—	This intercalary month was added about every three years so the lunar calendar would correspond to the solar year.		

*Names of months in parentheses are not in the Bible.   **For more information on the festivals see chart, pp. 180–181.

12:7 ʸ ver 13,23;
Eze 9:6
12:8 ᶻ ver 10;
Ex 16:19; 23:18;
34:25; Lev 7:15;
Nu 9:12 ᵃ Dt 16:7;
2Ch 35:13 ᵇ Nu 9:11
ᶜ ver 19-20; Ex 13:3;
Dt 16:3-4; 1Co 5:8
12:9 ᵈ Ex 29:13,17,
22; Lev 3:3
12:10 ᵉ S ver 8;
Ex 13:7; 29:34;
Lev 22:30; Dt 16:4
12:11 ᶠ ver 33;
Dt 16:3; Isa 48:20;
52:12 ᵍ ver 13,21,27,
43; Lev 23:5; Nu 9:2,
4; 28:16; Dt 16:1;
Jos 5:10; 2Ki 23:21,
23; 2Ch 30:1;
Ezr 6:19; Isa 31:5;
Eze 45:21
12:12 ʰ Am 5:17
ⁱ Isa 10:33; 31:8; 37:36
ʲ ver 29; S Ex 4:23;
13:15 ᵏ Ex 15:11; 18:11;
Nu 33:4; 2Ch 2:5;
Ps 95:3; 97:9; 135:5;
Isa 19:1; Jer 43:12;
44:8 ˡ S Ex 6:2
12:13 ᵐ S ver 11,23;
Heb 11:28 ⁿ S Ex 8:23
12:14 ᵒ Ex 13:9;
23:14; 32:5 ᵖ ver 17,
24; Ex 13:5,10; 27:21;
Lev 3:17; 10:9; 16:29;
17:7; 23:14; 24:3;
Nu 18:23
12:15 ᑫ Ex 13:6-7;
23:15; 34:18;
Lev 23:6; Nu 28:17;
Dt 16:3; 1Co 5:7
ʳ S Ge 17:14
12:16 ˢ Nu 29:35
12:17 ᵗ Ex 23:15;
34:18; Dt 16:16;
2Ch 8:13; 30:21;
Ezr 6:22; Mt 26:17;
Lk 22:1; Ac 12:3
ᵘ ver 41; S Ex 6:6,26;
13:3; Lev 19:36
ᵛ Lev 3:17

they are to take some of the blood ʸ and put it on the sides and tops of the doorframes of the houses where they eat the lambs. ⁸That same night ᶻ they are to eat the meat roasted ᵃ over the fire, along with bitter herbs, ᵇ and bread made without yeast. ᶜ ⁹Do not eat the meat raw or boiled in water, but roast it over a fire—with the head, legs and internal organs. ᵈ ¹⁰Do not leave any of it till morning; ᵉ if some is left till morning, you must burn it. ¹¹This is how you are to eat it: with your cloak tucked into your belt, your sandals on your feet and your staff in your hand. Eat it in haste; ᶠ it is the Lᴏʀᴅ's Passover. ᵍ

¹²"On that same night I will pass through ʰ Egypt and strike down ⁱ every firstborn ʲ of both people and animals, and I will bring judgment on all the gods ᵏ of Egypt. I am the Lᴏʀᴅ. ˡ ¹³The blood will be a sign for you on the houses where you are, and when I see the blood, I will pass over ᵐ you. No destructive plague will touch you when I strike Egypt. ⁿ

¹⁴"This is a day you are to commemorate; ᵒ for the generations to come you shall celebrate it as a festival to the Lᴏʀᴅ—a lasting ordinance. ᵖ ¹⁵For seven days you are to eat bread made without yeast. ᑫ On the first day remove the yeast from your houses, for whoever eats anything with yeast in it from the first day through the seventh must be cut off ʳ from Israel. ¹⁶On the first day hold a sacred assembly, and another one on the seventh day. Do no work ˢ at all on these days, except to prepare food for everyone to eat; that is all you may do.

¹⁷"Celebrate the Festival of Unleavened Bread, ᵗ because it was on this very day that I brought your divisions out of Egypt. ᵘ Celebrate this day as a lasting ordinance for the generations to come. ᵛ ¹⁸In the first month ʷ you are to eat bread made without yeast, from the evening of the fourteenth day until the evening of the twenty-first day. ¹⁹For seven days no yeast is to be found in your houses. And anyone, whether foreigner ˣ or native-born, who eats anything with yeast in it must be cut off ʸ from the community of Israel. ²⁰Eat nothing made with yeast. Wherever you live, ᶻ you must eat unleavened bread." ᵃ

²¹Then Moses summoned all the elders of Israel and said to them, "Go at once and select the animals for your families and slaughter the Passover ᵇ lamb. ²²Take a bunch of hyssop, ᶜ dip it into the blood in the basin and put some of the blood ᵈ on the top and on both sides of the doorframe. None of you shall go out of the door of your house until morning. ²³When the Lᴏʀᴅ goes through the land to strike ᵉ down the Egyptians, he will see the blood ᶠ on the top and sides of the doorframe and will pass over ᵍ that doorway, and he will not permit the destroyer ʰ to enter your houses and strike you down.

²⁴"Obey these instructions as a lasting ordinance ⁱ for you and your descendants.

12:18 ʷ S ver 2 **12:19** ˣ Nu 9:14; 15:14; 35:15; Dt 1:16; Jos 8:33 ʸ S Ge 17:14 **12:20** ᶻ Lev 3:17; Nu 35:29; Eze 6:6 ᵃ Ex 13:6
12:21 ᵇ S ver 11; Mk 14:12-16 **12:22** ᶜ Lev 14:4,6; Nu 19:18; Ps 51:7 ᵈ Heb 11:28 **12:23** ᵉ Isa 19:22 ᶠ S ver 7; Rev 7:3 ᵍ S ver 13
ʰ S Ge 16:7; Isa 37:36; Jer 6:26; 48:8; 1Co 10:10; Heb 11:28 **12:24** ⁱ S ver 14

12:7 *blood.* Symbolizes a sacrifice offered as a substitute, one life laid down for another (see Ge 9:4–6; Lev 17:11 and notes). Thus Israel escapes the judgment about to fall on Egypt only through the mediation of a sacrifice (see Heb 9:22; 1Jn 1:7).

12:8 *bitter herbs.* Endive, chicory and other bitter-tasting plants are indigenous to Egypt. Eating them would recall the bitter years of servitude there (see 1:14 and note). *bread made without yeast.* Reflecting the haste with which the people left Egypt (see vv. 11,39; Dt 16:3; see also note on Ge 19:3).

12:9 *roast it . . . head, legs and internal organs.* The method wandering shepherds used to cook meat.

12:11 *Passover.* Explained in vv. 13,23,27 to mean that the Lord would "pass over" and not destroy the occupants of houses that were under the sign of the blood.

12:12 *judgment on all the gods of Egypt.* Some had already been judged (see notes on 7:19; 8:2; 9:3; 10:21), and now all would be: (1) They would be shown to be powerless to deliver from the impending slaughter, and (2) many animals sacred to the gods would be killed.

12:13 *sign.* Just as the plagues were miraculous signs of judgment on the pharaoh and his people (see 4:8 and note; 8:23), so the Lord's "passing over" the Israelites who placed themselves under the sign of blood was a pledge of God's mercy.

12:14 *celebrate it as . . . a lasting ordinance.* Frequent references to Passover observance occur in the rest of Scripture (see Nu 9:1–5; Jos 5:10; 2Ki 23:21–23; 2Ch 30:1–27; 35:1–19; Ezr 6:19–22; Lk 2:41–43; Jn 2:13,23; 6:4; 11:55—12:1). The ordinance is still kept by practicing Jews today.

12:15 *remove the yeast from your houses.* Yeast later was often used as a symbol of sin, such as "hypocrisy" (Lk 12:1; cf. Mk 8:15 and note) or "malice and wickedness" (1Co 5:8; see note there). Before celebrating Passover, observant Jews today conduct a systematic (often symbolic) search of their house to remove every crumb of leavened bread that might be there (see v. 19). *cut off from Israel.* Removed from the covenant people by execution (see, e.g., 31:14; Lev 20:2–3) or banishment. See also Ge 17:14 and note.

12:17 *Festival of Unleavened Bread.* Began with the Passover meal and continued for seven days (see vv. 18–19; see also Mk 14:12 and note). *divisions.* See note on 6:26.

12:21 *Passover lamb.* Christ (the Messiah) is "our Passover lamb" (1Co 5:7), sacrificed "once for all" (Heb 7:27) for us.

12:22 *hyssop.* Here probably refers to an aromatic plant (*Origanum maru*) of the mint family with a straight stalk (see Jn 19:29) and white flowers. The hairy surface of its leaves and branches held liquids well and made it suitable as a sprinkling device for use in purification rituals (see Lev 14:4,6,49,51–52; Nu 19:6,18; Heb 9:19; see also Ps 51:7). *dip it into the blood.* Today at Passover meals a sprig of parsley or other plant is dipped in salt water to symbolize the lowly diet and tears of the Israelites during their time of slavery.

12:23 *pass over.* See note on v. 11. *the destroyer.* In Ps 78:49 the agent of God's wrath against the Egyptians is described as "a band of destroying angels." God often used angels to bring destructive plagues (see 2Sa 24:15–16; 2Ki 19:35; see also 1Co 10:10, a reference to Nu 16:41–49).

²⁵When you enter the land^j that the LORD will give you as he promised, observe this ceremony. ²⁶And when your children^k ask you, 'What does this ceremony mean to you?' ²⁷then tell them, 'It is the Passover^l sacrifice to the LORD, who passed over the houses of the Israelites in Egypt and spared our homes when he struck down the Egyptians.' "^m Then the people bowed down and worshiped.^n ²⁸The Israelites did just what the LORD commanded^o Moses and Aaron.

²⁹At midnight^p the LORD^q struck down all the firstborn^r in Egypt, from the firstborn of Pharaoh, who sat on the throne, to the firstborn of the prisoner, who was in the dungeon, and the firstborn of all the livestock^s as well. ³⁰Pharaoh and all his officials and all the Egyptians got up during the night, and there was loud wailing^t in Egypt, for there was not a house without someone dead.

THE EXODUS

³¹During the night Pharaoh summoned Moses and Aaron and said, "Up! Leave my people, you and the Israelites! Go, worship^u the LORD as you have requested. ³²Take your flocks and herds,^v as you have said, and go. And also bless^w me."

³³The Egyptians urged the people to hurry^x and leave^y the country. "For otherwise," they said, "we will all die!"^z ³⁴So the people took their dough before the yeast was added, and carried it on their shoulders in kneading troughs^a wrapped in clothing. ³⁵The Israelites did as Moses instructed and asked the Egyptians for articles of silver and gold^b and for clothing.^c ³⁶The LORD had made the Egyptians favorably disposed^d toward the people, and they gave them what they asked for; so they plundered^e the Egyptians.

³⁷The Israelites journeyed from Rameses^f to Sukkoth.^g There were about six hundred thousand men^h on foot, besides women and children. ³⁸Many other people^i went up with them, and also large droves of livestock, both flocks and herds. ³⁹With the dough the Israelites had brought from Egypt, they baked loaves of unleavened bread. The dough was without yeast because they had been driven out^j of Egypt and did not have time to prepare food for themselves.

⁴⁰Now the length of time the Israelite people lived in Egypt^a was 430 years.^k ⁴¹At the end of the 430 years, to the very day, all the LORD's divisions^l left Egypt.^m ⁴²Because the LORD kept vigil that night to bring them out of Egypt, on this night all the Israelites are to keep vigil to honor the LORD for the generations to come.^n

PASSOVER RESTRICTIONS

⁴³The LORD said to Moses and Aaron, "These are the regulations for the Passover:^o

"No foreigner^p is to eat of it. ⁴⁴Any slave you have bought may eat of it after you have circumcised^q him, ⁴⁵but a temporary resident or a hired worker^r may not eat of it.

⁴⁶"It must be eaten inside one house; take none of the meat outside the house. Do not break any of the bones.^s ⁴⁷The whole community of Israel must celebrate it.

⁴⁸"A foreigner residing among you who wants to celebrate the LORD's Passover must have all the males in his household circumcised; then he may take part like one born in the land.^t No uncircumcised^u male may eat of it. ⁴⁹The same law applies both to the native-born and to the foreigner^v residing among you."

⁵⁰All the Israelites did just what the LORD had commanded^w Moses and Aaron. ⁵¹And on that very day the LORD brought the Israelites out of Egypt^x by their divisions.^y

---

^a 40 Masoretic Text; Samaritan Pentateuch and Septuagint *Egypt and Canaan*

12:25 ^j S Ge 15:14; Ex 3:17
12:26 ^k Ex 10:2
12:27 ^l S ver 11
^m S Ex 8:23
^n S Ge 24:26
12:28 ^o ver 50
12:29 ^p S Ex 11:4
^q S Ge 19:13
^r S Ex 4:23 *S Ex 9:6
12:30 ^t S Ex 11:6
12:31 ^u S Ex 8:8
12:32 ^v Ex 10:9,26
^w Ge 27:34
12:33 ^x S ver 11
^y S Ex 6:1; 1Sa 6:6
^z S Ge 20:3; S Ex 8:19
12:34 ^a S Ex 8:3
12:35 ^b S Ex 3:22
^c S Ge 24:53
12:36 ^d S Ge 39:21
^e S Ex 3:22
12:37 ^f S Ge 47:11
^g Ex 13:20; Nu 33:3-5
^h Ge 12:2; Ex 38:26; Nu 1:46; 2:32; 11:13, 21; 26:51
12:38 ^i Nu 11:4; Jos 8:35
12:39 ^j Ex 3:20; 11:1
12:40 ^k Ge 15:13; Ac 7:6; Gal 3:17
12:41 ^l S Ex 6:26
^m S Ex 3:10
12:42 ^n Ex 13:10; Lev 3:17; Nu 9:3; Dt 16:1,6
12:43 ^o S ver 11
^p ver 48; Nu 9:14; 15:14; 2Ch 6:32-33; Isa 1:4; 56:3,6; 60:10
12:44 ^q S Ge 17:12-13
12:45 ^r Lev 22:10
12:46 ^s Nu 9:12; Ps 22:14; 34:20; 51:8; Pr 17:22; Jn 19:36*
12:48 ^t ver 49; Lev 19:18,34; 24:22; Nu 9:14; 10:32
^u Eze 44:7
12:49 ^v Lev 24:22; Nu 15:15-16,29; Dt 1:16
12:50 ^w ver 28
12:51 ^x S Ex 3:10; S 6:6 ^y S Ex 6:26

12:26 *your children ask you, 'What does this ceremony mean to you?'* See 13:14. The Passover was to be observed as a memorial festival commemorating Israel's redemption and appropriating it anew. As observed today, it includes the asking of similar questions by the youngest child present.

12:27 *Passover sacrifice.* See note on v. 21. *passed over.* See note on v. 11.

12:29 *prisoner, who was in the dungeon.* The lowliest of situations (see note on 11:5).

12:31 *Pharaoh summoned Moses.* Though he had sworn never again to grant Moses an audience (see 10:28 and note), the pharaoh now humbles himself by summoning Moses and Aaron into his presence.

12:35-36 See 3:21-22; 11:2-3.

12:36 *plundered the Egyptians.* See note on 3:22.

12:37 *journeyed from Rameses.* See 1:11; see also note on Ge

47:11. The Israelite departure took place "the day after the Passover" (Nu 33:3). *Rameses . . . Sukkoth.* See map, p. 110. *about six hundred thousand men.* A round number for 603,550 (38:26; see Introduction to Numbers: Special Problem; see also Nu 1:46 and note).

12:38 *Many other people.* Possibly including such Egyptians as those mentioned in 9:20.

12:41 *430 years, to the very day.* See notes on Ge 15:13; Ac 7:6.

12:44 See Ge 17:12-13 and note on 17:10.

12:46 *Do not break any of the bones.* See Nu 9:12; Ps 34:20; quoted in Jn 19:36 in reference to Jesus.

12:48 *No uncircumcised male may eat of it.* Only those consecrated to the Lord in covenant commitment could partake of Passover; only for them could it have its full meaning (see Ge 17:9-14). Concerning participants in the Lord's Supper, see 1Co 11:28.

13:2 *z* ver 12,13,15;
Ex 22:29; 34:20;
Lev 27:26; Nu 3:13;
8:17; 18:15; Dt 15:19;
Ne 10:36; Lk 2:23*
13:3 *a* ver 14;
Ex 7:4; Lev 26:13;
Nu 1:1; 9:1; 22:5;
26:4; Dt 4:45; 5:6;
Ps 81:10; 114:1
b S Ex 3:20 *c* S Ex 12:8
13:4 *d* S Ex 12:2
13:5 *e* ver 11
f S Ex 3:8 *g* S Ex 3:8
h Ex 12:25-26
13:6 *i* S Ex 12:15-20
13:8 *j* S Ex 10:2;
Ps 78:5-6
13:9 *k* Isa 44:5
l ver 16; Dt 6:8; 11:18;
Pr 3:3; Mt 23:5
m S Ex 3:20
13:10 *n* S Ex 12:14
o Ps 75:2; 102:13
13:11 *p* S ver 5
q S Ge 22:16; Dt 1:8
r S Ge 12:7; S 17:19;
Ps 105:42-45
13:12 *s* S Ge 4:4;
Lev 27:26; Nu 3:13;
18:15,17; Lk 2:23*
13:13 *t* ver 15;
Lev 27:11 *u* Ex 34:20;
Isa 66:3 *v* Nu 3:46-47
w Nu 18:15
13:14 *x* S Ex 10:2
y Ex 20:2; Dt 7:8;
28:68
13:15 *z* S ver 2
13:16 *a* S ver 9
13:17 *b* Ex 14:11;
Nu 14:1-4; Dt 17:16;
Hos 11:5
13:18 *c* Ex 15:22;
Ps 136:16; Eze 20:10
d Jos 1:14; 4:13
13:19 *e* Jos 24:32;
Ac 7:16; Heb 11:22
f S Ge 47:29-30
13:20 *g* S Ex 12:37
h Nu 33:6
13:21 *i* Ex 32:1;
33:14; Dt 2:7; 31:8;
Jdg 4:14; 5:4; Ps 68:7;
77:20; Jer 2:2;
Hab 3:13 / Ex 14:19,
24; 24:16; 33:9-10;
34:5; 40:38; Nu 9:16;
12:5; 14:14; Dt 1:33;
Ne 9:12,19; Ps 78:14;
99:7; 105:39; Isa 4:5;
1Co 10:1
13:22 *k* Ne 9:19

CONSECRATION OF THE FIRSTBORN

13 The LORD said to Moses, [2]"Consecrate to me every firstborn male.[z] The first offspring of every womb among the Israelites belongs to me, whether human or animal."

[3]Then Moses said to the people, "Commemorate this day, the day you came out of Egypt,[a] out of the land of slavery, because the LORD brought you out of it with a mighty hand.[b] Eat nothing containing yeast.[c] [4]Today, in the month of Aviv,[d] you are leaving. [5]When the LORD brings you into the land of the Canaanites,[e] Hittites, Amorites, Hivites and Jebusites[f]—the land he swore to your ancestors to give you, a land flowing with milk and honey[g]—you are to observe this ceremony[h] in this month: [6]For seven days eat bread made without yeast and on the seventh day hold a festival[i] to the LORD. [7]Eat unleavened bread during those seven days; nothing with yeast in it is to be seen among you, nor shall any yeast be seen anywhere within your borders. [8]On that day tell your children,[j] 'I do this because of what the LORD did for me when I came out of Egypt.' [9]This observance will be for you like a sign on your hand[k] and a reminder on your forehead[l] that this law of the LORD is to be on your lips. For the LORD brought you out of Egypt with his mighty hand.[m] [10]You must keep this ordinance[n] at the appointed time[o] year after year.

[11]"After the LORD brings you into the land of the Canaanites[p] and gives it to you, as he promised on oath[q] to you and your ancestors,[r] [12]you are to give over to the LORD the first offspring of every womb. All the firstborn males of your livestock belong to the LORD.[s] [13]Redeem with a lamb every firstborn donkey,[t] but if you do not redeem it, break its neck.[u] Redeem[v] every firstborn among your sons.

[14]"In days to come, when your children[x] ask you, 'What does this mean?' say to them, 'With a mighty hand the LORD brought us out of Egypt, out of the land of slavery.[y] [15]When Pharaoh stubbornly refused to let us go, the LORD killed the firstborn of both people and animals in Egypt. This is why I sacrifice to the LORD the first male offspring of every womb and redeem each of my firstborn sons.'[z] [16]And it will be like a sign on your hand and a symbol on your forehead[a] that the LORD brought us out of Egypt with his mighty hand."

CROSSING THE SEA

[17]When Pharaoh let the people go, God did not lead them on the road through the Philistine country, though that was shorter. For God said, "If they face war, they might change their minds and return to Egypt."[b] [18]So God led[c] the people around by the desert road toward the Red Sea.[a] The Israelites went up out of Egypt ready for battle.[d]

[19]Moses took the bones of Joseph[e] with him because Joseph had made the Israelites swear an oath. He had said, "God will surely come to your aid, and then you must carry my bones up with you from this place."[b][f]

[20]After leaving Sukkoth[g] they camped at Etham on the edge of the desert.[h] [21]By day the LORD went ahead[i] of them in a pillar of cloud[j] to guide them on their way and by night in a pillar of fire to give them light, so that they could travel by day or night. [22]Neither the pillar of cloud by day nor the pillar of fire by night left[k] its place in front of the people.

---

a 18 Or *the Sea of Reeds*   *b* 19 See Gen. 50:25.

13:2 *Consecrate to me every firstborn male.* God had adopted Israel as his firstborn (see 4:22) and had delivered every firstborn among the Israelites, whether human or animal, from the tenth plague (see 12:12–13). All the firstborn in Israel were therefore his. Jesus, Mary's firstborn son (see Lk 2:7), was presented to the Lord in accordance with this law (see Lk 2:22–23).

13:5 See note on 3:8.

13:9 *like a sign on your hand and a reminder on your forehead.* A figure of speech (see v. 16; Dt 6:8; 11:18; see also Pr 3:3; 6:21; 7:3; SS 8:6). A literal reading of this verse has led to the practice of writing the texts of vv. 1–10, vv. 11–16, Dt 6:4–9 and Dt 11:13–21 on separate strips of parchment and placing them in two small leather boxes, which the observant Jew straps on his forehead and left arm before his morning prayers. The boxes are called "phylacteries" (Mt 23:5). This practice seems to have originated after the exile to Babylon.

13:13 *Redeem.* See 6:6 and note. The verb means "obtain release by means of payment." *every firstborn donkey.* The economic importance of pack animals allowed for their redemption

through sacrificing a lamb. *every firstborn among your sons.* Humans were to be consecrated to the Lord by their life, not by their death (see Ge 22:12; Nu 3:39–51; cf. Ro 12:1 and note).

13:14 See note on 12:26.

13:16 See note on v. 9.

13:17 *road through the Philistine country.* Although the most direct route from Goshen to Canaan, it was heavily guarded by a string of Egyptian fortresses.

13:18 *desert road.* Leading south along the west coast of the Sinai peninsula. *Red Sea.* See TNIV text note. Various locations of the crossing have been proposed along the line of the modern Suez Canal and including the northern end of the Gulf of Suez (see map No. 3 at the end of this study Bible; but see also note on 14:2). *ready for battle.* Probably armed only with spears, bows and slings.

13:19 See notes on Ge 50:24–25.

13:21 *pillar of cloud . . . pillar of fire.* The visible symbol of God's presence among his people (see 14:24; see also note on 3:2). The Lord often spoke to them from the pillar (see Nu 12:5–6; Dt 31:15–16; Ps 99:6–7).

14 Then the LORD said to Moses, [2]"Tell the Israelites to turn back and encamp near Pi Hahiroth, between Migdol[l] and the sea. They are to encamp by the sea, directly opposite Baal Zephon.[m] [3]Pharaoh will think, 'The Israelites are wandering around the land in confusion, hemmed in by the desert.' [4]And I will harden Pharaoh's heart,[n] and he will pursue them.[o] But I will gain glory[p] for myself through Pharaoh and all his army, and the Egyptians will know that I am the LORD."[q] So the Israelites did this.

[5]When the king of Egypt was told that the people had fled,[r] Pharaoh and his officials changed their minds[s] about them and said, "What have we done? We have let the Israelites go and have lost their services!" [6]So he had his chariot made ready and took his army with him. [7]He took six hundred of the best chariots,[t] along with all the other chariots of Egypt, with officers over all of them. [8]The LORD hardened the heart[u] of Pharaoh king of Egypt, so that he pursued the Israelites, who were marching out boldly.[v] [9]The Egyptians—all Pharaoh's horses[w] and chariots, horsemen[a] and troops[x]—pursued the Israelites and overtook[y] them as they camped by the sea near Pi Hahiroth, opposite Baal Zephon.[z]

[10]As Pharaoh approached, the Israelites looked up, and there were the Egyptians, marching after them. They were terrified and cried[a] out to the LORD. [11]They said to Moses, "Was it because there were no graves in Egypt that you brought us to the desert to die?[b] What have you done to us by bringing us out of Egypt? [12]Didn't we say to you in Egypt, 'Leave us alone; let us serve the Egyptians'? It would have been better for us to serve the Egyptians than to die in the desert!"[c]

[13]Moses answered the people, "Do not be afraid.[d] Stand firm and you will see[e] the deliverance the LORD will bring you today. The Egyptians you see today you will never see[f] again. [14]The LORD will fight[g] for you; you need only to be still."[h]

[15]Then the LORD said to Moses, "Why are you crying out to me?[i] Tell the Israelites to move on. [16]Raise your staff[j] and stretch out your hand over the sea to divide the water[k] so that the Israelites can go through the sea on dry ground. [17]I will harden the hearts[l] of the Egyptians so that they will go in after them.[m] And I will gain glory through Pharaoh and all his army, through his chariots and his horsemen. [18]The Egyptians will know that I am the LORD[n] when I gain glory through Pharaoh, his chariots and his horsemen."

[19]Then the angel of God,[o] who had been traveling in front of Israel's army, withdrew and went behind them. The pillar of cloud[p] also moved from in front and stood behind[q] them, [20]coming between the armies of Egypt and Israel. Throughout the night the cloud brought darkness[r] to the one side and light to the other side; so neither went near the other all night long.

[21]Then Moses stretched out his hand[s] over the sea,[t] and all that night the LORD drove the sea back with a strong east wind[u] and turned it into dry land.[v] The waters were divided,[w] [22]and the Israelites went through the sea[x] on dry ground,[y] with a wall[z] of water on their right and on their left.

---

[a] 9 Or *charioteers*; also in verses 17, 18, 23, 26 and 28

14:21 Isa 63:12 **14:22** [x] ver 16; Nu 33:8; Jos 24:6; Isa 43:16; 63:11; 1Co 10:1 [y] ver 21,29; S Ex 3:12; 15:19; Dt 31:6-8; Jos 3:16,17; 4:22; Ne 9:11; Ps 66:6; 77:19; 106:9; Isa 11:15; 41:10; 43:5; 44:27; 50:2; 51:10; 63:13; Jer 46:28; Na 1:4; Heb 11:29 [z] Ex 15:8; Jos 3:13; Ps 78:13

14:2 [l] Nu 33:7; Jer 44:1; Eze 29:10 [m] ver 9
14:4 [n] S Ex 4:21 [o] ver 8,17,23; Ps 71:11 [p] S Ex 9:16; Ro 9:17, 22-23 [q] S Ex 6:2; Eze 32:15
14:5 [r] S Ge 31:21 [s] Ps 105:25
14:7 [t] Ex 15:4
14:8 [u] S Ex 11:10 [v] Nu 33:3; Ac 13:17
14:9 [w] Ge 47:17 [x] ver 6-7,25; Jos 24:6; Isa 43:17 [y] Ex 15:9 [z] ver 2
14:10 [a] Ex 15:25; Jos 24:7; Ne 9:9; Ps 5:2; 34:17; 50:15; 107:6,28
14:11 [b] S Ex 5:21; 16:3; 17:3; Nu 11:1; 14:22; 20:4; 21:5; Dt 9:7
14:12 [c] S Ex 5:21; 15:24; 17:2; Ps 106:7-8
14:13 [d] S Ge 15:1 [e] 1Sa 12:16; 2Ch 20:17 [f] ver 30
14:14 [g] ver 25; Ex 15:3; Dt 1:30; 3:22; 20:4; Jos 10:14; 23:3, 10; 2Sa 5:24; 2Ch 20:29; Ne 4:20; Ps 24:8; 35:1; Isa 42:13; Jer 41:12 [h] 1Sa 12:16; Ps 37:7; 46:10; 116:7; Isa 28:12; 30:15; Zec 2:13
14:15 [i] Jos 7:10
14:16 [j] S Ex 4:2 [k] ver 27; Isa 10:26
14:17 [l] Ex 4:21 [m] S ver 4
14:18 [n] S Ex 6:2; Eze 32:15
14:19 [o] S Ge 16:7; [p] S Ex 13:21; 1Co 10:1 [q] Isa 26:7; 42:16; 49:10; 52:12; 58:8
14:20 [r] Jos 24:7
14:21 [s] S Ex 7:19 [t] S Ex 4:2; Job 26:12; Isa 14:27; 23:11; 51:15; Jer 31:35; Ac 7:36 [u] S Ge 41:6; Ex 15:8; 2Sa 22:16; 1Ki 19:11; Job 38:1; 40:6; Jer 23:19; Na 1:3 [v] S ver 22; S Ge 8:1 [w] 2Ki 2:8; Ps 74:13; 78:13; 114:5; 136:13;

14:2 *turn back.* Northward, in the general direction from which they had come. *Pi Hahiroth.* Located "east of Baal Zephon" (Nu 33:7). *Migdol.* Location unknown. The name means "watchtower." *sea.* The sea that the TNIV, in accordance with established tradition, calls the Red Sea—in Hebrew *Yam Suph,* i.e., Sea of Reeds (see 13:18 and TNIV text note). Reference can hardly be to the northern end of the Gulf of Suez since reeds do not grow in salt water. Moreover, an Egyptian papyrus seems to locate Baal Zephon in the vicinity of Tahpanhes (see note on Jer 2:16), a site near Lake Menzaleh about 20 miles east of Rameses. The crossing of the "Red Sea" thus probably occurred at the southern end of Lake Menzaleh (see map, p. 110; but see note on 13:18). *Baal Zephon.* Means "Baal of the north" or "Baal of North (Mountain)"—also the name of a Canaanite god.
14:4 *harden.* See v. 8 and note on 4:21. *know that I am the LORD.* See note on 6:3.
14:7 *chariots.* Introduced into Egypt from Canaan, they brought about a revolutionary change in the art of warfare. Where the terrain was open and relatively flat, as much of Egypt was, they were especially effective. *officers.* The Hebrew for the

singular of this word means "third man," perhaps referring to his place in a chariot crew.
14:8 *hardened.* See v. 4 and note.

🔺 **14:14** *The LORD will fight for you.* A necessary reminder that although Israel was "ready for battle" (13:18) and "marching out boldly" (v. 8), the victory would be won by God alone.

14:19 *angel of God.* See note on Ge 16:7; here associated with the cloud (see 13:21).

🔺 **14:20** *coming between the armies of Egypt and Israel.* The pillar of cloud (signifying the Lord's presence) protected Israel (see Ps 105:39).

14:21 *strong east wind.* See 10:13. In 15:8 the poet praises the Lord and calls the wind the "blast of your nostrils," affirming (as here) that the miracle occurred in accordance with God's timing and under his direction (see 15:10).
14:22 *through the sea on dry ground.* In later times, psalmists and prophets reminded Israel of what God had done for them (see Ps 66:6; 106:9; 136:13–14; Isa 51:10; 63:11–13). *wall of water.* See v. 29. The waters were "piled up" (15:8) on both sides.

THE EXODUS

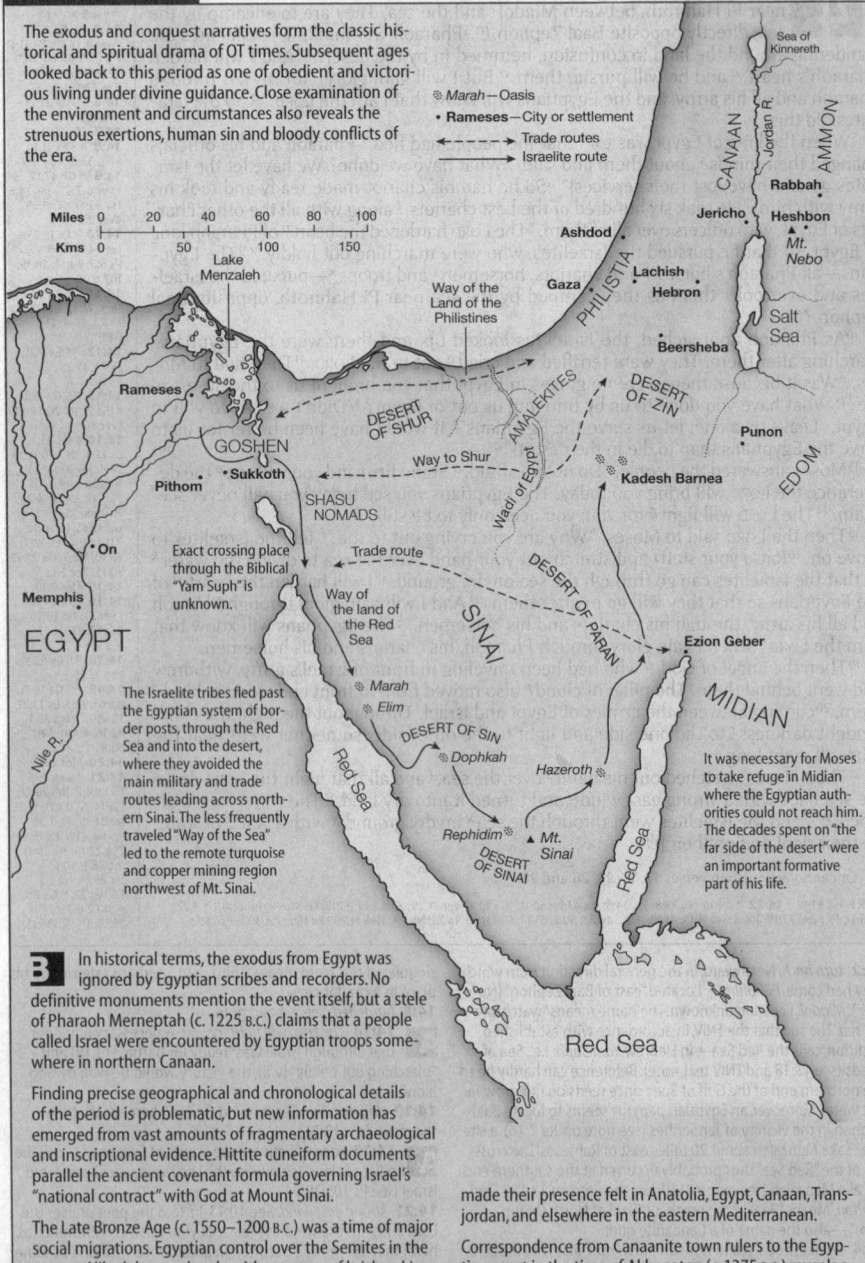

The exodus and conquest narratives form the classic historical and spiritual drama of OT times. Subsequent ages looked back to this period as one of obedient and victorious living under divine guidance. Close examination of the environment and circumstances also reveals the strenuous exertions, human sin and bloody conflicts of the era.

Legend:
⊛ *Marah*—Oasis
• *Rameses*—City or settlement
◄----► Trade routes
→ Israelite route

Miles 0 20 40 60 80 100
Kms 0 50 100 150

Map labels: Sea of Kinnereth, CANAAN, Jordan R., AMMON, Rabbah, Heshbon, Mt. Nebo, Jericho, Ashdod, PHILISTIA, Lachish, Hebron, Gaza, Way of the Land of the Philistines, Beersheba, Salt Sea, DESERT OF ZIN, Punon, EDOM, AMALEKITES, DESERT OF SHUR, Way to Shur, Kadesh Barnea, Lake Menzaleh, Rameses, GOSHEN, Pithom, Sukkoth, SHASU NOMADS, Wadi of Egypt, DESERT OF PARAN, On, Memphis, EGYPT, Nile R., Trade route, Way of the land of the Red Sea, SINAI, Ezion Geber, MIDIAN, Marah, Elim, DESERT OF SIN, Dophkah, Hazeroth, Red Sea, Rephidim, Mt. Sinai, DESERT OF SINAI, Red Sea

Exact crossing place through the Biblical "Yam Suph" is unknown.

The Israelite tribes fled past the Egyptian system of border posts, through the Red Sea and into the desert, where they avoided the main military and trade routes leading across northern Sinai. The less frequently traveled "Way of the Sea" led to the remote turquoise and copper mining region northwest of Mt. Sinai.

It was necessary for Moses to take refuge in Midian where the Egyptian authorities could not reach him. The decades spent on "the far side of the desert" were an important formative part of his life.

B In historical terms, the exodus from Egypt was ignored by Egyptian scribes and recorders. No definitive monuments mention the event itself, but a stele of Pharaoh Merneptah (c. 1225 B.C.) claims that a people called Israel were encountered by Egyptian troops somewhere in northern Canaan.

Finding precise geographical and chronological details of the period is problematic, but new information has emerged from vast amounts of fragmentary archaeological and inscriptional evidence. Hittite cuneiform documents parallel the ancient covenant formula governing Israel's "national contract" with God at Mount Sinai.

The Late Bronze Age (c. 1550–1200 B.C.) was a time of major social migrations. Egyptian control over the Semites in the eastern Nile delta was harsh, with a system of brickmaking quotas imposed on the labor force, often the landless, low-class "Apiru." Numerous Canaanite towns were violently destroyed. New populations, including the "Sea Peoples,"

made their presence felt in Anatolia, Egypt, Canaan, Transjordan, and elsewhere in the eastern Mediterranean.

Correspondence from Canaanite town rulers to the Egyptian court in the time of Akhenaten (c. 1375 B.C.) reveals a weak structure of alliances, with an intermittent Egyptian military presence and an ominous fear of people called "Habiru" ("Apiru").

²³The Egyptians pursued them, and all Pharaoh's horses and chariots and horsemen ª followed them into the sea. ²⁴During the last watch of the night the LORD looked down from the pillar of fire and cloud ᵇ at the Egyptian army and threw it into confusion. ᶜ ²⁵He jammed ª the wheels of their chariots so that they had difficulty driving. And the Egyptians said, "Let's get away from the Israelites! The LORD is fighting ᵈ for them against Egypt." ᵉ

²⁶Then the LORD said to Moses, "Stretch out your hand over the sea so that the waters may flow back over the Egyptians and their chariots and horsemen." ²⁷Moses stretched out his hand over the sea, and at daybreak the sea went back to its place. ᶠ The Egyptians were fleeing toward ᵇ it, and the LORD swept them into the sea. ᵍ ²⁸The water flowed back and covered the chariots and horsemen—the entire army of Pharaoh that had followed the Israelites into the sea. ʰ Not one of them survived. ⁱ

²⁹But the Israelites went through the sea on dry ground, ʲ with a wall ᵏ of water on their right and on their left. ³⁰That day the LORD saved ˡ Israel from the hands of the Egyptians, and Israel saw the Egyptians lying dead on the shore. ³¹And when the Israelites saw the great power ᵐ the LORD displayed against the Egyptians, the people feared ⁿ the LORD and put their trust ᵒ in him and in Moses his servant.

THE SONG OF MOSES AND MIRIAM

15 Then Moses and the Israelites sang this song ᵖ to the LORD:

"I will sing ᑫ to the LORD,
 for he is highly exalted.
Both horse and driver ʳ
 he has hurled into the sea. ˢ

² "The LORD is my strength ᵗ and my defense ᶜ;
 he has become my salvation. ᵘ
He is my God, ᵛ and I will praise him,
 my father's God, and I will exalt ʷ him.
³ The LORD is a warrior; ˣ
 the LORD is his name. ʸ
⁴ Pharaoh's chariots and his army ᶻ
 he has hurled into the sea.
The best of Pharaoh's officers
 are drowned in the Red Sea. ᵈ
⁵ The deep waters ª have covered them;
 they sank to the depths like a stone. ᵇ
⁶ Your right hand, ᶜ LORD,
 was majestic in power.
Your right hand, ᵈ LORD,
 shattered ᵉ the enemy.

ª 25 See Samaritan Pentateuch, Septuagint and Syriac; Masoretic Text *removed*   ᵇ 27 Or *from*   ᶜ 2 Or *song*   ᵈ 4 Or *the Sea of Reeds*; also in verse 22

15:6 ᵉ Nu 24:8; 1Sa 2:10; Ps 2:9

14:23 ª ver 7
14:24 ᵇ S Ex 13:21; 1Co 10:1 ᶜ Ex 23:27; Jos 10:10; 1Sa 5:9; 7:10; 14:15; 2Sa 5:24; 2Ki 7:6; 19:7
14:25 ᵈ S ver 14 ᵉ S ver 9; Dt 32:31; 1Sa 2:2; 4:8
14:27 ᶠ Jos 4:18 ᵍ ver 28; Ex 15:1,21; Dt 1:40; 2:1; 11:4; Ps 78:53; 106:11; 136:15; Heb 11:29
14:28 ʰ ver 23; Ex 15:19; Jos 24:7 ⁱ S ver 27; Ex 15:5; Jdg 4:16; Ne 9:11
14:29 ʲ ver 21,S 22; Jos 24:11; 2Ki 2:8; Ps 74:15 ᵏ Ps 78:13
14:30 ˡ ver 29; 1Sa 14:23; 1Ch 11:14; Ps 44:7; 106:8,10,21; Isa 43:3; 50:2; 51:9-10; 60:16; 63:8,11
14:31 ᵐ S Ex 9:16; Ps 147:5 ⁿ Ex 20:18; Dt 31:13; Jos 4:24; 1Sa 12:18; Ps 76:7; 112:1 ᵒ S Ex 4:5; Ps 22:4; 40:3; 106:12; Jn 2:11; 11:45
15:1 ᵖ Nu 21:17; Jdg 5:1; 2Sa 22:1; 1Ch 16:9; Job 36:24; Ps 59:16; 105:2; Rev 15:3 ᑫ Jdg 5:3; Ps 13:6; 21:13; 27:6; 61:8; 104:33; 106:12; Isa 12:5,6; 42:10; 44:23 ʳ Dt 11:4; Ps 76:6; Jer 51:21 ˢ Ex 14:27
15:2 ᵗ Ps 18:1; 59:17 ᵘ S Ge 45:7; Ex 14:13; Ps 18:2,46; 25:5; 27:1; 62:2; 118:14; Isa 12:2; 33:2; Jnh 2:9; Hab 3:18 ᵛ S Ge 28:21 ʷ Dt 10:21; 2Sa 22:47; Ps 22:3; 30:1; 34:3; 35:27; 99:5; 103:19; 107:32; 108:5; 109:1; 118:28; 145:11; 148:14; Isa 24:15; 25:1; Jer 17:14; Da 4:37
15:3 ˣ S Ex 14:14; Rev 19:11 ʸ S Ex 3:15
15:4 ᶻ Ex 14:6-7; Jer 51:21
15:5 ª S Ex 14:28 ᵇ ver 10; Ne 9:11
15:6 ᶜ Ps 16:11; 17:7; 21:8; 63:8; 74:11; 77:10; 89:13; 98:1; 118:15; 138:7 ᵈ S Ex 3:20; S Job 40:14

14:24 *last watch of the night.* Often the time for surprise attack (see Jos 10:9; 1Sa 11:11). *the LORD looked down.* See note on 13:21.
14:25 *The LORD is fighting for them.* See note on v. 14.
14:27 *the LORD swept them into the sea.* As he had done with the locusts of the eighth plague (see 10:19).
14:31 *feared the LORD.* See note on Ge 20:11. *put their trust in him and in Moses.* Faith in God's mighty power and confidence in Moses' leadership (cf. 1Sa 12:18 and note). *his servant.* Here refers to one who has the status of a high official in the Lord's kingly administration (see notes on Nu 12:6–8; Dt 34:5). See also the same title applied to Joshua (Jos 24:29), Samuel (1Sa 3:10), David (2Sa 3:18) and Elijah (2Ki 9:36).
15:1–18 A hymn celebrating God's spectacular victory over the pharaoh and his army. The focus of the song is God himself (see v. 11 and note); the divine name Yahweh ("the LORD") appears ten times. The first two stanzas (vv. 2–6, 7–11) retell the story of the "deliverance" (14:13) at the Red Sea, and the final

stanza (vv. 12–17) anticipates the future approach to and conquest of Canaan (the promised land).
15:1 *Moses and the Israelites sang.* As though one person, the whole community praises God. *I will sing ... into the sea.* Together with v. 18, this opening couplet frames the song and concentrates its dominant theme. *I will sing.* A common way to begin a hymn of praise (see Jdg 5:3; Ps 89:1; 101:1; 108:1).
15:2–6 The Lord's victory over the pharaoh was decisive.
15:2 The first half of the verse is echoed in Ps 118:14 (see Isa 12:2).
15:3 *The LORD is a warrior.* See note on 14:14. God is often pictured as a king leading his people into battle (see, e.g., Dt 1:30; Jdg 4:14; 2Sa 5:24; 2Ch 20:17–18).
15:4 *officers.* See note on 14:7.
15:5 *sank ... like a stone.* Babylon is similarly described in Jer 51:63–64.
15:6 *right hand.* See Isa 41:10 and note.

15:7 f Dt 33:26;
Ps 150:2 g Ps 2:5;
78:49-50; Jer 12:13;
25:38 h Ex 24:17;
Dt 4:24; 9:3; Ps 18:8;
59:13; Heb 12:29
15:8 i S Ex 14:21;
Ps 18:15 j Jos 3:13;
Ps 78:13; Isa 43:16
k S Ex 14:22 l Ps 46:2
15:9 m Ex 14:5-9;
Dt 28:45; Ps 7:5;
La 1:3 n Jdg 5:30;
Isa 9:3; 53:12;
Lk 11:22
15:10 o Job 4:9;
15:30; Isa 11:4; 30:33;
40:7 p ver 5; Ne 9:11;
Ps 29:3; 32:6; 77:19
15:11 q S Ex 8:10;
Ps 77:13; S Isa 46:5
r Lev 19:2; 1Sa 2:2;
1Ch 16:29; Ps 99:3;
110:3; Isa 6:3; Rev 4:8
s S Ex 14:4; Ps 4:2;
8:1; 26:8; Isa 35:2;
40:5 t S Ex 3:20
15:12 u S Ex 7:5
v Nu 16:32; 26:10;
Dt 11:6; Ps 106:17
15:13 w Ne 9:12;
Ps 77:20 x S Ex 6:6;
Job 33:28; Ps 71:23;
106:10; Isa 1:27;
41:14; 43:14; 44:22-
24; 51:10; 63:9;
Tit 2:14 y ver 17;
Ps 68:16; 76:2; 78:54
15:14 z ver 16;
Ex 23:27; Dt 2:25;
Jos 2:9; 5:1; 9:24;
1Sa 4:7; Est 8:17;
Ps 48:6; 96:9; 99:1;
114:7; Eze 38:20
a Isa 13:8 b Ps 83:7
15:15 c S Ge 15:3;
d Dt 2:4 e Nu 22:3;
Ps 114:7 f Jos 2:9,24
15:16 g S ver 14;
S Ge 35:5 h 1Sa 25:37
i Ps 74:2; 2Pe 2:1
j Dt 2:4
15:17 k Ex 23:20;
32:34; 33:12
l 2Sa 7:10; Ps 44:2;
80:8,15; Isa 5:2;
60:21; Jer 2:21; 11:17;
24:6; Am 9:15
m Dt 33:19; Ps 2:6;
3:4; 15:1; 78:54,68;
133:3; Da 9:16;
Joel 2:1; Ob 1:16;
Zep 3:11 n S ver 13;
Ps 132:13-14
o Ps 78:69; 114:2

7 "In the greatness of your majesty f
  you threw down those who opposed you.
You unleashed your burning anger; g
  it consumed h them like stubble.
8 By the blast of your nostrils i
  the waters piled up. j
The surging waters stood up like a wall; k
  the deep waters congealed in the heart of the sea. l
9 The enemy boasted,
  'I will pursue, m I will overtake them.
I will divide the spoils; n
  I will gorge myself on them.
I will draw my sword
  and my hand will destroy them.'
10 But you blew with your breath, o
  and the sea covered them.
They sank like lead
  in the mighty waters. p
11 Who among the gods
  is like you, q LORD?
Who is like you—
  majestic in holiness, r
awesome in glory, s
  working wonders? t

12 "You stretch out u your right hand,
  and the earth swallows your enemies. v
13 In your unfailing love you will lead w
  the people you have redeemed. x
In your strength you will guide them
  to your holy dwelling. y
14 The nations will hear and tremble; z
  anguish a will grip the people of Philistia. b
15 The chiefs c of Edom d will be terrified,
  the leaders of Moab will be seized with trembling, e
the people a of Canaan will melt f away;
16   terror g and dread will fall on them.
By the power of your arm
  they will be as still as a stone h—
until your people pass by, LORD,
  until the people you bought b i pass by. j
17 You will bring k them in and plant l them
  on the mountain m of your inheritance—
the place, LORD, you made for your dwelling, n
  the sanctuary, o Lord, your hands established.

a 15 Or rulers   b 16 Or created

15:7–8 The Lord's overwhelming victory marks him as incomparable among the gods.
15:8 See note on 14:22. *blast of your nostrils.* See note on 14:21; see also Ps 18:15.
15:10 *you blew with your breath.* See note on 14:21.

A 15:11 *Who is like you . . . ?* See Ps 35:10; 71:19; 89:6; 113:5; Mic 7:18 and note. The Lord, who tolerates no rivals (see 20:3 and note), has defeated all the gods of Egypt and their worshipers.
15:12–17 The Lord's victorious right hand (= power) will surely establish his people in the promised land.
15:12 *earth.* Perhaps refers to Sheol or the grave (see Ps 63:9; 71:20), the "realm of death below" (Dt 32:22), since it was the sea that swallowed the Egyptians.
15:13 *unfailing love.* See note on Ps 6:4. *people you have redeemed.* See note on 6:6. *your holy dwelling.* Perhaps a reference to the house of worship at Shiloh (see Jer 7:12), and ultimately

the temple on Mount Zion (see Ps 76:2), the "place" God would "choose" (Dt 12:14,18,26; 14:25; 16:7,15–16; 17:8,10; 18:6; 31:11) to put "his Name" (Dt 12:5,11,21; 14:23–24; 16:2,6,11; 26:2). But the phrase may refer to the promised land, which is called "your dwelling" and "the sanctuary . . . your hands established" in v. 17. *holy.* See note on 3:5.
15:14–15 *Philistia . . . Edom . . . Moab . . . Canaan.* Israel's potential enemies. The order is roughly that along the route Israel would follow from Mount Sinai to the promised land.
15:15 *chiefs.* The term used earlier of the Edomite rulers (see Ge 36:15–19,21,29–30,40,43).
15:16 *dread will fall on them.* See note on 1Ch 14:17. *bought.* See TNIV text note; see also Dt 32:6 and TNIV text note. In Ps 74:2 the meaning "bought" or "purchased" is found in context with "redeemed" (see note on 13:13).
15:17 *inheritance.* The promised land (see 1Sa 26:19; Ps 79:1).

[18] "The LORD reigns
    for ever and ever." [P]

[19] When Pharaoh's horses, chariots and horsemen [a] went into the sea, [q] the LORD brought the waters of the sea back over them, but the Israelites walked through the sea on dry ground. [r] [20] Then Miriam [s] the prophet, [t] Aaron's sister, took a timbrel in her hand, and all the women followed her, with timbrels [u] and dancing. [v] [21] Miriam sang [w] to them:

"Sing to the LORD,
    for he is highly exalted.
Both horse and driver [x]
    he has hurled into the sea." [y]

THE WATERS OF MARAH AND ELIM

[22] Then Moses led Israel from the Red Sea and they went into the Desert [z] of Shur. [a] For three days they traveled in the desert without finding water. [b] [23] When they came to Marah, they could not drink its water because it was bitter. (That is why the place is called Marah. [b][c]) [24] So the people grumbled [d] against Moses, saying, "What are we to drink?" [e] [25] Then Moses cried out [f] to the LORD, and the LORD showed him a piece of wood. He threw [g] it into the water, and the water became sweet.

There the LORD issued a ruling and instruction for them and put them to the test. [h] [26] He said, "If you listen carefully to the LORD your God and do what is right in his eyes, if you pay attention to his commands and keep [i] all his decrees, [j] I will not bring on you any of the diseases [k] I brought on the Egyptians, for I am the LORD, who heals [l] you."

[27] Then they came to Elim, where there were twelve springs and seventy palm trees, and they camped [m] there near the water.

MANNA AND QUAIL

16

The whole Israelite community set out from Elim and came to the Desert of Sin, [n] which is between Elim and Sinai, on the fifteenth day of the second month after they had come out of Egypt. [o] [2] In the desert the whole community grumbled [p] against Moses and Aaron. [3] The Israelites said to them, "If only we had died by the LORD's hand in Egypt! [q] There we sat around pots of meat and ate all the food [r] we wanted, but you have brought us out into this desert to starve this entire assembly to death." [s]

[4] Then the LORD said to Moses, "I will rain down bread from heaven [t] for you. The people are to go out each day and gather enough for that day. In this way I will test [u] them

---

[a] 19 Or *charioteers*   [b] 23 *Marah* means *bitter.*

16:3 106:14; Jer 44:17 [s] S Ge 47:15; Dt 8:3   **16:4** [t] ver 14-15; Dt 8:3; Ne 9:15; Ps 78:24; 105:40; S Jn 6:31 [u] S Ge 22:1

15:18 [P] S Ge 21:33; Ps 9:7; 29:10; 55:19; 66:7; 80:1; 102:12; 145:13; La 5:19
15:19 [q] S Ex 14:28 [r] S Ex 14:22
15:20 [s] ver 21; Ex 2:4; Nu 12:1; 20:1; 26:59; 1Ch 4:17; 6:3 [t] Jdg 4:4; 2Ki 22:14; 2Ch 34:22; Ne 6:14; Isa 8:3; Eze 13:17 [u] S Ge 31:27; 1Sa 18:6; Ps 81:2; Isa 30:32 [v] S Ge 4:21; Jdg 11:34; 21:21; 1Sa 18:6; 2Sa 6:5,14, 16; Ps 30:11; 149:3; 150:4; S S 6:13; Jer 31:4,13
15:21 [w] 1Sa 18:7 [x] Am 2:15; Hag 2:22 [y] S Ex 14:27
15:22 [z] Ps 78:52 [a] S Ge 16:7 [b] Ex 17:1, 3; Nu 20:2,5; 33:14; Ps 107:5
15:23 [c] Nu 33:8; Ru 1:20
15:24 [d] S Ge 14:12; 16:2; 7:3; Nu 14:2; Jos 9:18; Ps 78:18,42; 106:13,25; Eze 16:43 [e] Mt 6:31
15:25 [f] S Ex 14:10 [g] 2Ki 2:21; 4:41; 6:6 [h] S Ge 22:1; Jdg 3:4; Job 23:10; Ps 81:7; Isa 48:10
15:26 [i] Ex 23:22; Dt 11:13; 15:5; 28:1; Jer 11:6 [j] Lev 19:5-6; 20:2-17; Dt 7:12 [k] Dt 7:15; 28:27,58-60; 32:39; 1Sa 5:6; Ps 30:2; 41:3-4; 103:3 [l] Ex 23:25-26; 2Ki 20:5; Ps 25:11; 103:3; 107:20; Jer 30:17; Hos 11:3
15:27 [m] Nu 33:9
16:1 [n] Ex 17:1; Nu 33:11,12 [o] S Ex 6:6; 12:1-2
16:2 [p] S Ex 15:24; 1Co 10:10
16:3 [q] Ex 17:3; Nu 14:2; 20:3 [r] Nu 11:4,34; Dt 12:20; Ps 78:18;

15:18 See note on v. 1.

15:20 *prophet.* See Nu 12:1–2 for a statement by Miriam concerning her prophetic gift (see note on 7:1–2). Other female prophets in the Bible were Deborah (Jdg 4:4), Isaiah's wife (Isa 8:3, but see note there), Huldah (2Ki 22:14), Noadiah (Ne 6:14), Anna (Lk 2:36) and Philip's daughters (Ac 21:9). *women followed her, with timbrels and dancing.* Such celebration was common after victory in battle (see 1Sa 18:6; 2Sa 1:20).

15:21 Miriam repeats the first four lines of the victory hymn (see v. 1), changing only the form of the first verb.

15:22—18:27 The story of Israel's journey from the Red Sea to Mount Sinai (see Introduction: Outline).

15:22 *Desert of Shur.* Located east of Egypt (see Ge 25:18; 1Sa 15:7) in the northwestern part of the Sinai peninsula. In Nu 33:8 it is called the "Desert of Etham." Shur and Etham both mean "fortress wall" (Shur in Hebrew, Etham in Egyptian).

15:23 *Marah.* Probably modern Ain Hawarah, inland from the western arm of the Red Sea, about 50 miles south of its northern end.

15:24 *grumbled.* During their wilderness wanderings, the Israelites grumbled against Moses and Aaron whenever they faced a crisis (see 16:2; 17:3; Nu 14:2; 16:11,41). In reality, however, they were grumbling "against the LORD" (16:8). Paul warns us not to follow their example (see 1Co 10:10).

15:25 *He threw it into the water, and the water became sweet.* For a similar occurrence see 2Ki 2:19–22. *a ruling and instruction.* Technical presumably referring to what follows in v. 26. *put them to the test.* See note on Ge 22:1. God tested Israel also in connection with his provision of manna (see 16:4; Dt 8:2–3) and the giving of the Ten Commandments (see 20:20).

15:27 *Elim.* Seven miles south of Ain Hawarah (see note on v. 23) in the well-watered valley of Gharandel. *palm trees.* Elim means "large trees."

16:1 *from Elim ... to the Desert of Sin.* See Nu 33:10–11. The Desert of Sin was in southwestern Sinai ("Sin" is probably derived from "Sinai"). *fifteenth day of the second month.* Exactly one month had passed since Israel's exodus from Egypt (see 12:2,6,29,31).

16:2 *grumbled.* See note on 15:24.

16:3 *meat.* Nu 11:5 lists additional items of food from Egypt that the Israelites craved.

16:4 *bread from heaven.* Jesus called himself "the true bread from heaven" (Jn 6:32), "the bread of God" (Jn 6:33), "the bread of life" (Jn 6:35,48), "the living bread that came down from heaven" (Jn 6:51)—all in the spiritual sense (Jn 6:63). For a similar application, see Dt 8:3 and Jesus' quotation of it in Mt 4:4. *go out each day and gather enough for that day.* Probably the background for Jesus' model petition in Mt 6:11; Lk 11:3. *test.* See notes on 15:25; Ge 22:1.

16:5 ᵛver 22;
Lev 25:21
16:6 ʷS Ex 6:6
16:7 ˣver 10;
Ex 24:16; 29:43;
33:18,22; 40:34;
Lev 9:6; Nu 16:19,42;
Dt 5:24; 1Ki 8:11;
Ps 63:2; Isa 6:3; 35:2;
40:5; 44:23; 60:1;
66:18; Eze 1:28; 10:4;
43:5; Hab 2:14;
Hag 2:7; Jn 11:40
ʸver 12; Nu 11:1,18;
14:2,27,28; 17:5
ᶻNu 16:11
16:8 ᵃver 7
ᵇNu 23:21; Dt 33:5;
Jdg 8:23; 1Sa 8:7;
12:12; S Mt 10:40;
Ro 13:2; 1Th 4:8
16:10 ᶜS ver 7;
Jn 11:4 ᵈEx 13:21;
40:34-35; 1Ki 8:10;
2Ch 7:1; Eze 10:4
16:12 ᵉS ver 7
ᶠS Ex 6:2; S 20:2
16:13 ᵍNu 11:31;
Ps 78:27-28; 105:40;
106:15 ʰNu 11:9
16:14 ⁱver 31;
Nu 11:7-9; Dt 8:3,16;
Ps 105:40
16:15 ʲDt 8:16
ᵏS ver 4; Ne 9:20;
S Jn 6:31
16:16 ˡver 32,36
16:18 ᵐ2Co 8:15ˣ
16:19 ⁿver 23;
Ex 12:10
16:20 ᵒver 24
ᵖEx 32:19
16:22 ᵠS ver 5
ʳEx 34:31
16:23 ˢS Ge 2:3;
S Ex 20:8; Dt 5:13-14
16:26 ᵗver 23
16:28 ᵘJos 9:14;
Ps 78:10; 106:13;
107:11; 119:51;
Jer 32:23
16:31 ᵛS ver 14

and see whether they will follow my instructions. ⁵On the sixth day they are to prepare what they bring in, and that is to be twice ᵛ as much as they gather on the other days."

⁶So Moses and Aaron said to all the Israelites, "In the evening you will know that it was the LORD who brought you out of Egypt, ʷ ⁷and in the morning you will see the glory ˣ of the LORD, because he has heard your grumbling ʸ against him. Who are we, that you should grumble against us?" ᶻ ⁸Moses also said, "You will know that it was the LORD when he gives you meat to eat in the evening and all the bread you want in the morning, because he has heard your grumbling ᵃ against him. Who are we? You are not grumbling against us, but against the LORD." ᵇ

⁹Then Moses told Aaron, "Say to the entire Israelite community, 'Come before the LORD, for he has heard your grumbling.' "

¹⁰While Aaron was speaking to the whole Israelite community, they looked toward the desert, and there was the glory ᶜ of the LORD appearing in the cloud. ᵈ

¹¹The LORD said to Moses, ¹²"I have heard the grumbling ᵉ of the Israelites. Tell them, 'At twilight you will eat meat, and in the morning you will be filled with bread. Then you will know that I am the LORD your God.' " ᶠ

¹³That evening quail ᵍ came and covered the camp, and in the morning there was a layer of dew ʰ around the camp. ¹⁴When the dew was gone, thin flakes like frost ⁱ on the ground appeared on the desert floor. ¹⁵When the Israelites saw it, they said to each other, "What is it?" For they did not know ʲ what it was.

Moses said to them, "It is the bread ᵏ the LORD has given you to eat. ¹⁶This is what the LORD has commanded: 'Each one is to gather as much as they need. Take an omer ᵃ ˡ for each person you have in your tent.' "

¹⁷The Israelites did as they were told; some gathered much, some little. ¹⁸And when they measured it by the omer, the one who gathered much did not have too much, and the one who gathered little did not have too little. ᵐ Each one had gathered just as much as they needed.

¹⁹Then Moses said to them, "No one is to keep any of it until morning." ⁿ

²⁰However, some of them paid no attention to Moses; they kept part of it until morning, but it was full of maggots and began to smell. ᵒ So Moses was angry ᵖ with them.

²¹Each morning everyone gathered as much as they needed, and when the sun grew hot, it melted away. ²²On the sixth day, they gathered twice ᵠ as much—two omers ᵇ for each person—and the leaders of the community ʳ came and reported this to Moses. ²³He said to them, "This is what the LORD commanded: 'Tomorrow is to be a day of sabbath rest, a holy sabbath ˢ to the LORD. So bake what you want to bake and boil what you want to boil. Save whatever is left and keep it until morning.' "

²⁴So they saved it until morning, as Moses commanded, and it did not stink or get maggots in it. ²⁵"Eat it today," Moses said, "because today is a sabbath to the LORD. You will not find any of it on the ground today. ²⁶Six days you are to gather it, but on the seventh day, the Sabbath, ᵗ there will not be any."

²⁷Nevertheless, some of the people went out on the seventh day to gather it, but they found none. ²⁸Then the LORD said to Moses, "How long will you ᶜ refuse to keep my commands ᵘ and my instructions? ²⁹Bear in mind that the LORD has given you the Sabbath; that is why on the sixth day he gives you bread for two days. Everyone is to stay where they are on the seventh day; no one is to go out." ³⁰So the people rested on the seventh day.

³¹The people of Israel called the bread manna. ᵈ ᵛ It was white like coriander seed and tasted like wafers made with honey. ³²Moses said, "This is what the LORD has command-

---

ᵃ 16 That is, possibly about 3 pounds or about 1.4 kilograms; also in verses 18, 32, 33 and 36   ᵇ 22 That is, possibly about 6 pounds or about 2.8 kilograms   ᶜ 28 The Hebrew is plural.   ᵈ 31 *Manna* means *What is it?* (see verse 15).

16:5 *sixth day ... twice as much as they gather on the other days.* To provide for "the seventh day, the Sabbath" (v. 26), "a day of sabbath rest" (v. 23). See v. 29.

16:6 *know.* See note on 6:3.

16:8 *meat ... in the evening and ... bread ... in the morning.* See vv. 13–14.

16:10 *glory of the LORD appearing in the cloud.* See 24:15–17; see also notes on 13:21; 40:34; Ps 26:8.

16:12 *twilight.* See note on 12:6.

16:13 *quail came.* For a similar incident, see Nu 11:31–33.

16:14 *thin flakes like frost.* See note on v. 31.

16:15 *What is it?* See v. 31 and TNIV text note.

16:18 See 2Co 8:15, where Paul quotes the heart of the verse to describe Christians who share with each other what they possess.

16:23 *sabbath.* The first occurrence of the word itself, though the principle of the seventh day as a day of rest and holiness is set forth in the account of creation (see note on Ge 2:3).

16:29 See note on v. 5.

16:31 *manna.* Several naturalistic explanations for the manna have been given. For example, some equate it with the sticky and often granular honeydew that is excreted in Sinai in early June by various scale insects and that solidifies rapidly through evaporation. But no naturally occurring substance fits all the data of the ed: 'Take an omer of manna and keep it for the generations to come, so they can see the bread I gave you to eat in the wilderness when I brought you out of Egypt.' "

[33] So Moses said to Aaron, "Take a jar and put an omer of manna [w] in it. Then place it before the Lord to be kept for the generations to come."

[34] As the Lord commanded Moses, Aaron put the manna with the tablets of the covenant law, [x] so that it might be preserved. [35] The Israelites ate manna [y] forty years, [z] until they came to a land that was settled; they ate manna until they reached the border of Canaan. [a]

[36] (An omer [b] is one-tenth of an ephah.) [c]

WATER FROM THE ROCK

17 The whole Israelite community set out from the Desert of Sin, [d] traveling from place to place as the Lord commanded. They camped at Rephidim, [e] but there was no water [f] for the people to drink. [2] So they quarreled with Moses and said, "Give us water [g] to drink." [h]

Moses replied, "Why do you quarrel with me? Why do you put the Lord to the test?" [i]

[3] But the people were thirsty [j] for water there, and they grumbled [k] against Moses. They said, "Why did you bring us up out of Egypt to make us and our children and livestock die [l] of thirst?"

[4] Then Moses cried out to the Lord, "What am I to do with these people? They are almost ready to stone [m] me."

[5] The Lord answered Moses, "Go out in front of the people. Take with you some of the elders of Israel and take in your hand the staff [n] with which you struck the Nile, [o] and go. [6] I will stand there before you by the rock at Horeb. [p] Strike [q] the rock, and water [r] will come out of it for the people to drink." So Moses did this in the sight of the elders of Israel. [7] And he called the place Massah [a] [s] and Meribah [b] [t] because the Israelites quarreled and because they tested the Lord saying, "Is the Lord among us or not?"

THE AMALEKITES DEFEATED

[8] The Amalekites [u] came and attacked the Israelites at Rephidim. [v] [9] Moses said to Joshua, [w] "Choose some of our men and go out to fight the Amalekites. Tomorrow I will stand on top of the hill with the staff [x] of God in my hands."

[10] So Joshua fought the Amalekites as Moses had ordered, and Moses, Aaron and Hur [y] went to the top of the hill. [11] As long as Moses held up his hands, the Israelites were win-

---

[a] 7 *Massah* means *testing.*   [b] 7 *Meribah* means *quarreling.*

16:33 [w] Heb 9:4; Rev 2:17
16:34 [x] Ex 25:16,21, 22; 27:21; 31:18; 40:20; Lev 16:13; Nu 1:50; 7:89; 10:11; 17:4,10; Dt 10:2; 1Ki 8:9; 2Ch 5:10
16:35 [y] Jn 6:31,49 [z] Nu 14:33; 33:38; Dt 1:3; 2:7; 8:2-4; Jos 5:6; Jdg 3:11; Ne 9:21; Ps 95:10; Am 5:25 [a] Jos 5:12
16:36 [b] S ver 16 [c] Lev 5:11; 6:20; Nu 5:15; 15:4; 28:5
17:1 [d] S Ex 16:1 [e] ver 8; Ex 19:2; Nu 33:15 [f] Nu 20:5; 21:5; 33:14
17:2 [g] Nu 20:2; 33:14; Ps 107:5 [h] S Ex 14:12 [i] Dt 6:16; Ps 78:18,41; 106:14; Mt 4:7; 1Co 10:9
17:3 [j] S Ex 15:22 [k] S Ex 15:24 [l] S Ex 14:11
17:4 [m] Nu 14:10; 1Sa 30:6; S Jn 8:59
17:5 [n] S Ex 4:2; S 10:12-13 [o] Ex 7:20
17:6 [p] S Ex 4:2 [q] Nu 20:8 [r] Nu 20:11; Dt 8:15; Jdg 15:19; 2Ki 3:20; Ne 9:15; Ps 74:15; 78:15-16; 105:41; 107:35; 114:8; Isa 30:25; 35:6; 43:19; 48:21; 1Co 10:4
17:7 [s] Dt 6:16; 9:22; 33:8; Ps 95:8 [t] Nu 20:13,24; 27:14; Ps 81:7; 106:32
17:8 [u] S Ge 36:12 [v] S ver 1
17:9 [w] Ex 24:13; 32:17; 33:11; Nu 11:28; 27:22; Dt 1:38; Jos 1:1; Ac 7:45 [x] S Ex 4:17
17:10 [y] ver 10-12; Ex 24:14; 31:2

---

text, and several factors suggest that manna was in fact the Lord's unique provision for his people in the desert: 1. The meaning of the Hebrew word for "manna" suggests that it was something unknown by the people at the time (see TNIV text note). 2. The appearance and taste of the manna suggest that it is not something experienced by other peoples in other times. 3. The daily abundance of the manna and its regular periodic surge and slump (double amounts on the sixth day but none on the seventh day, vv. 22,27) hardly fit a natural phenomenon. 4. Its availability in ample supply for the entire desert experience, no matter where the people were (v. 35), argues against a natural substance. 5. The keeping of a sample of the manna in the ark for future generations (vv. 33–34) suggests that it was a unique food.

16:33 *jar.* Said in Heb 9:4 to be made of gold.
16:34 *covenant law.* Anticipates the later description of the tablets containing the Ten Commandments as the "two tablets of the covenant law" (31:18; 32:15; 34:29), which gave their name to the "ark of the covenant law" (25:22; 26:33) in which they were placed (see 25:16,21), along with the jar of manna (see Heb 9:4; see also Rev 2:17 and note).
16:35 *ate manna forty years … until they reached … Canaan.* The manna stopped at the time the Israelites celebrated their first Passover in Canaan (see Jos 5:10–12).
17:1 *traveling from place to place.* For a list of specific sites see Nu 33:12–14. *Rephidim.* Probably either the Wadi Refayid or the Wadi Feiran, both near Jebel Musa (see note on 3:1) in southern Sinai.
17:2 *put the Lord to the test.* Israel fails the Lord's testing of her (see 16:4) by putting the Lord to the test.
17:3 *grumbled.* See note on 15:24.
17:4 *these people.* The same note of distance and alienation

("these people" instead of "my people") in such situations (see also the interplay in 32:7,9–11; 33:13) is found often in the prophets (see, e.g., Isa 6:9–10 and note; Hag 1:2).
17:6 *I will stand there … by the rock.* Paul may have had this incident in mind when he spoke of Christ as "the spiritual rock that accompanied" Israel (see 1Co 10:4 and note; see also Heb 11:24–26). *Horeb.* See note on 3:1. *Strike the rock, and water will come out.* The event was later celebrated by Israel's hymn writers and prophets (see Ps 78:15–16,20; 105:41; 114:8; Isa 48:21).
17:7 *Massah and Meribah.* Heb 3:7–8,15 (quoting Ps 95:7–8) gives the meaning "testing" for Massah and "rebellion" for Meribah. Another Meribah, where a similar incident occurred near Kadesh Barnea (see note on Ge 14:7), is referred to in Nu 20:13,24; 27:14; Dt 32:51; 33:8; Ps 81:7; 106:32; Eze 47:19; 48:28.
17:8 *Amalekites.* See note on Ge 14:7.
17:9 *Joshua.* The name given by Moses to Hoshea, son of Nun (see Nu 13:16). "Hoshea" means "salvation," while "Joshua" means "The Lord saves." The Greek form of the name Joshua is the same as that of the name Jesus, for the meaning of which see TNIV text note on Mt 1:21. Joshua was from the tribe of Ephraim (Nu 13:8), one of the most powerful of the 12 tribes (see notes on Ge 48:6,19). *fight the Amalekites.* Joshua's military prowess uniquely suited him to be the conqueror of Canaan 40 years later, while his faith in God and loyalty to Moses suited him to be Moses' "aide" (24:13; 33:11) and successor (see Dt 1:38; 3:28; 31:14; 34:9; Jos 1:5).
17:10 *Hur.* Perhaps the same Hur who was the son of Caleb and the grandfather of Bezalel (see 31:2–5), one of the builders of the tabernacle (see 31:2–5).
17:11 *held up his hands.* A symbol of appeal to God for help and enablement (see note on 9:29; see also 9:22; 10:12; 14:16).

17:11 ᶻ Jas 5:16
17:12 ª Jos 8:26
17:13 ᵇ ver 8
17:14 ᶜ Ex 24:4;
34:27; Nu 33:2;
Dt 31:9; Job 19:23;
Isa 30:8; Jer 36:2;
45:1; 51:60
ᵈ Ex 32:33; Dt 29:20;
Job 18:17; Ps 9:5;
34:16; 109:15;
Eze 18:4 ᵉ ver 13;
S Ge 36:12; Nu 24:7;
Jdg 3:13; 1Sa 30:17-
18; Ps 83:7
17:15 ᶠ S Ge 8:20
ᵍ S Ge 22:14
17:16 ʰ Nu 24:7;
1Sa 15:8,32;
1Ch 4:43; Est 3:1; 8:3;
9:24 ⁱ Est 9:5
18:1 ʲ S Ex 2:18
ᵏ S Ex 2:16 ˡ S Ex 6:6
18:2 ᵐ S Ex 2:21
18:3 ⁿ S Ex 4:20;
Ac 7:29 ᵒ Ex 2:22
18:4 ᵖ 1Ch 23:15
�q S Ge 49:25;
S Dt 33:29
18:5 ʳ S Ex 3:1
18:7 ˢ S Ge 17:3;
S 43:28 ᵗ S Ge 29:13
18:8 ᵘ Nu 20:14;
Ne 9:32 ᵛ Ex 15:6,16;
Ps 81:7
18:9 ʷ Jos 21:45;
1Ki 8:66; Ne 9:25;
Ps 145:7; Isa 63:7
18:10 ˣ S Ge 9:26;
S 24:27
18:11 ʸ S Ex 12:12;
S 1Ch 16:25
ᶻ S Ex 1:10; S Lk 1:51
18:12 ª S Ex 3:1
ᵇ Ex 10:25; 20:24;
Lev 1:2-9 ᶜ Ge 31:54;
Ex 24:5 ᵈ S Ge 26:30
ᵉ Dt 12:7
18:15 ᶠ S ver 19;
S Ge 25:22
18:16 ᵍ Ex 24:14
ʰ ver 15; Lev 24:12;
Nu 15:34; Dt 1:17;
2Ch 19:7; Pr 24:23;
Mal 2:9

ning, ᶻ but whenever he lowered his hands, the Amalekites were winning. ¹²When Moses' hands grew tired, they took a stone and put it under him and he sat on it. Aaron and Hur held his hands up—one on one side, one on the other—so that his hands remained steady till sunset. ª ¹³So Joshua overcame the Amalekite ᵇ army with the sword.

¹⁴Then the Lᴏʀᴅ said to Moses, "Write ᶜ this on a scroll as something to be remembered and make sure that Joshua hears it, because I will completely blot out ᵈ the name of Amalek ᵉ from under heaven."

¹⁵Moses built an altar ᶠ and called ᵍ it The Lᴏʀᴅ is my Banner. ¹⁶He said, "Because hands were lifted up against ª the throne of the Lᴏʀᴅ, ᵇ the Lᴏʀᴅ will be at war against the Amalekites ʰ from generation to generation." ⁱ

JETHRO VISITS MOSES

18 Now Jethro, ʲ the priest of Midian ᵏ and father-in-law of Moses, heard of everything God had done for Moses and for his people Israel, and how the Lᴏʀᴅ had brought Israel out of Egypt. ˡ

²After Moses had sent away his wife Zipporah, ᵐ his father-in-law Jethro received her ³and her two sons. ⁿ One son was named Gershom, ᶜ for Moses said, "I have become a foreigner in a foreign land"; ᵒ ⁴and the other was named Eliezer, ᵈ ᵖ for he said, "My father's God was my helper; �q he saved me from the sword of Pharaoh."

⁵Jethro, Moses' father-in-law, together with Moses' sons and wife, came to him in the wilderness, where he was camped near the mountain ʳ of God. ⁶Jethro had sent word to him, "I, your father-in-law Jethro, am coming to you with your wife and her two sons."

⁷So Moses went out to meet his father-in-law and bowed down ˢ and kissed ᵗ him. They greeted each other and then went into the tent. ⁸Moses told his father-in-law about everything the Lᴏʀᴅ had done to Pharaoh and the Egyptians for Israel's sake and about all the hardships ᵘ they had met along the way and how the Lᴏʀᴅ had saved ᵛ them.

⁹Jethro was delighted to hear about all the good things ʷ the Lᴏʀᴅ had done for Israel in rescuing them from the hand of the Egyptians. ¹⁰He said, "Praise be to the Lᴏʀᴅ, ˣ who rescued you from the hand of the Egyptians and of Pharaoh, and who rescued the people from the hand of the Egyptians. ¹¹Now I know that the Lᴏʀᴅ is greater than all other gods, ʸ for he did this to those who had treated Israel arrogantly." ᶻ ¹²Then Jethro, Moses' father-in-law, ª brought a burnt offering ᵇ and other sacrifices ᶜ to God, and Aaron came with all the elders of Israel to eat bread ᵈ with Moses' father-in-law in the presence ᵉ of God.

¹³The next day Moses took his seat to serve as judge for the people, and they stood around him from morning till evening. ¹⁴When his father-in-law saw all that Moses was doing for the people, he said, "What is this you are doing for the people? Why do you alone sit as judge, while all these people stand around you from morning till evening?"

¹⁵Moses answered him, "Because the people come to me to seek God's will. ᶠ ¹⁶Whenever they have a dispute, ᵍ it is brought to me, and I decide between the parties and inform them of God's decrees and instructions." ʰ

¹⁷Moses' father-in-law replied, "What you are doing is not good. ¹⁸You and these people who come to you will only wear yourselves out. The work is too heavy for you; you

---

ª 16 Or to   ᵇ 16 The meaning of the Hebrew for this clause is uncertain.   ᶜ 3 *Gershom* sounds like the Hebrew for *a foreigner there.*   ᵈ 4 *Eliezer* means *my God is helper.*

B **17:14** *Write.* See 24:4; 34:27–28; Nu 33:2; Dt 28:58; 29:20,21,27; 30:10; 31:9,19,22,24; see also Introduction: Author and Date of Writing. *scroll.* A long strip of leather or papyrus on which scribes wrote in columns (see Jer 36:23) with pen (see Isa 8:1) and ink (see Jer 36:18), sometimes on both sides (see Eze 2:10; Rev 5:1). After being rolled up, a scroll was often sealed (see Isa 29:11; Da 12:4; Rev 5:1–2,5,9) to protect its contents. Scrolls were of various sizes (see Isa 8:1; Rev 10:2,9–10). Certain Egyptian examples reached lengths of over 100 feet; Biblical scrolls, however, rarely exceeded 30 feet in length, as in the case of a book like Isaiah (see Lk 4:17). Reading the contents of a scroll involved the awkward procedure of unrolling it with one hand while rolling it up with the other (see Isa 34:4; Eze 2:10; Lk 4:17,20; Rev 6:14). Shortly after the time of Christ the scroll gave way to the book form still used today.

A **17:15** *my Banner.* Recalling Moses' petition with upraised hands (see vv. 11–12,16) and testifying to the power of God displayed in defense of his people.

18:1 *Jethro, the priest of Midian.* See note on 2:16.

18:2 *sent away his wife.* Apparently Moses sent Zipporah to her father with the news that the Lord had blessed his mission (see v. 1) and that he was in the vicinity of Mount Sinai with Israel.

18:5 *mountain of God.* See 3:1 and note.

18:11 *Now I know that the Lᴏʀᴅ is greater than all other gods.* See the similar confession of Naaman in 2Ki 5:15.

18:12 *brought.* The verb means "provided" an animal for sacrifice (see, e.g., 25:2; Lev 12:8), not "officiated at" a sacrifice. *eat bread with.* A token of friendship (contrast the battle with the Amalekites; 17:8–16). Such a meal often climaxed the establishment of a treaty (see Ge 31:54; Ex 24:11).

18:15 *seek God's will.* Inquire of God, usually by going to a place of worship (see Ge 25:22 and note; Nu 27:21) or to a prophet (see 1Sa 9:9; 1Ki 22:8).

18:16 *God's decrees and instructions.* The process of compiling and systematizing the body of divine law that would govern the newly formed nation of Israel may have already begun (see 15:25–26 and note on Ge 26:5).

cannot handle it alone.[i] [19]Listen now to me and I will give you some advice, and may God be with you.[j] You must be the people's representative before God and bring their disputes[k] to him. [20]Teach them his decrees and instructions,[l] and show them the way they are to live[m] and how they are to behave.[n] [21]But select capable men[o] from all the people—men who fear[p] God, trustworthy men who hate dishonest gain[q]—and appoint them as officials[r] over thousands, hundreds, fifties and tens. [22]Have them serve as judges for the people at all times, but have them bring every difficult case[s] to you; the simple cases they can decide themselves. That will make your load lighter, because they will share[t] it with you. [23]If you do this and God so commands, you will be able to stand the strain, and all these people will go home satisfied."

[24]Moses listened to his father-in-law and did everything he said. [25]He chose capable men from all Israel and made them leaders[u] of the people, officials over thousands, hundreds, fifties and tens.[v] [26]They served as judges[w] for the people at all times. The difficult cases[x] they brought to Moses, but the simple ones they decided themselves.[y]

[27]Then Moses sent his father-in-law on his way, and Jethro returned to his own country.[z]

AT MOUNT SINAI

19 On the first day of the third month after the Israelites left Egypt[a]—on that very day—they came to the Desert of Sinai. [b] [2]After they set out from Rephidim,[c] they entered the Desert of Sinai, and Israel camped there in the desert in front of the mountain. [d]

[3]Then Moses went up to God,[e] and the Lord called[f] to him from the mountain and said, "This is what you are to say to the house of Jacob and what you are to tell the people of Israel: [4]'You yourselves have seen what I did to Egypt,[g] and how I carried you on eagles' wings[h] and brought you to myself. [i] [5]Now if you obey me fully[j] and keep my covenant,[k] then out of all nations you will be my treasured possession. [l] Although the whole earth[m] is mine, [6]you[n] will be for me a kingdom of priests[n] and a holy nation.'[o] These are the words you are to speak to the Israelites."

[7]So Moses went back and summoned the elders[p] of the people and set before them all the words the Lord had commanded him to speak.[q] [8]The people all responded together, "We will do everything the Lord has said."[r] So Moses brought their answer back to the Lord.

[9]The Lord said to Moses, "I am going to come to you in a dense cloud,[s] so that the people will hear me speaking[t] with you and will always put their trust[u] in you." Then Moses told the Lord what the people had said.

[10]And the Lord said to Moses, "Go to the people and consecrate[v] them today and tomorrow. Have them wash their clothes[w] [11]and be ready by the third day,[x] because on that

---

[a] 5,6 Or *possession, for the whole earth is mine.* [6]You

19:9 [s] ver 16; Ex 20:21; 24:15-16; 33:9; 34:5; Dt 4:11; 2Sa 22:10,12; 2Ch 6:1; Ps 18:11; 97:2; 99:7; Mt 17:5 [t] Dt 4:12,36; Jn 12:29-30 [u] S Ex 4:5 **19:10** [v] ver 14,22; Lev 11:44; Nu 11:18; 1Sa 16:5; Joel 2:16; Heb 10:22 [w] S Ge 35:2; Rev 22:14 **19:11** [x] ver 16

18:18 [i] Nu 11:11,14, 17; Dt 1:9,12
18:19 [j] Ex 3:12 [k] ver 15; Nu 27:5
18:20 [l] Dt 4:1,5; 5:1; Ps 119:12,26,68 [m] Ps 143:8 [n] S Ge 39:11
18:21 [o] S Ge 47:6; Ac 6:3 [p] S Ge 22:12 [q] Ex 23:8; Dt 16:19; 1Sa 12:3; Ps 15:5; Pr 17:23; 28:8; Ecc 7:7; Eze 18:8; 22:12 [r] Nu 1:16; 7:2; 10:4; Dt 16:18; Ezr 7:25
18:22 [s] Lev 24:11; Dt 1:17-18 [t] Nu 11:17; Dt 1:9
18:25 [u] Nu 1:16; 7:2; 11:16; Dt 16:18 [v] Dt 1:13-15
18:26 [w] Dt 16:18; 2Ch 19:5; Ezr 7:25 [x] Dt 1:17 [y] ver 22
18:27 [z] Nu 10:29-30
19:1 [a] S Ex 6:6 [b] Nu 1:1; 3:14; 33:15
19:2 [c] S Ex 17:1 [d] S ver 17; S Ex 3:1; Dt 5:2-4
19:3 [e] Ex 20:21 [f] S Ex 3:4; S 25:22; Ac 7:38
19:4 [g] Dt 29:2; Jos 24:7 [h] Dt 32:11; Ps 103:5; Isa 40:31; Jer 4:13; 48:40; Rev 12:14 [i] Dt 33:12; Isa 31:5; Eze 16:6
19:5 [j] Ex 15:26; Dt 6:3; Ps 78:10; Jer 7:23 [k] S Ge 17:9; S Ex 3:1 [l] S Ex 8:22; S 34:9; S Dt 8:1; S Tit 2:14 [m] S Ex 9:29; 1Co 10:26
19:6 [n] Isa 61:6; 66:21; S 1Pe 2:5 [o] Ge 18:19; Lev 11:44-45; Dt 4:37; 7:6; 26:19; 28:9; 29:13; 33:3; Isa 4:3; 62:12; Jer 2:3; Am 3:2
19:7 [p] Ex 18:12; Lev 4:15; 9:1; Nu 16:25 [q] Ex 4:30; 1Sa 8:10
19:8 [r] Ex 24:3,7; Dt 5:27; 26:17

18:21 *men who fear God.* See note on Ge 20:11.

19:1 The arrival at Sinai marked a significant milestone in Israel's life. Having been delivered by God from Egyptian bondage and having experienced his care and provision, they were about to enter into a national covenantal relationship with him.

19:2 *Desert of Sinai.* Located in the southeast region of the peninsula (see note on 3:1). The narrator locates there the events recorded in the rest of Exodus, all of Leviticus, and Nu 1:1—10:10.

19:3—24:18 The Sinaitic covenant. It was cast in the form of ancient Near Eastern suzerainty-vassal treaties of the second millennium B.C. It contained the divine pledge to be the Israelites' Suzerain-Protector if they would be faithful to him as their Suzerain Lord and obedient to the stipulations of the covenant as the vassal-people of his kingdom. The covenant had several later renewals, including ch. 34, the whole book of Deuteronomy, and Jos 24. See chart, p. 20; see also note on Jer 31:32.

19:3 *Jacob...Israel.* See note on 1:1.

19:4 *I carried you on eagles' wings.* The description best fits the female golden eagle.

19:5 *if...then.* The covenant between God and Israel at Mount Sinai is the outgrowth and extension of the Lord's covenant with Abraham and his descendants 600 years earlier.

Participation in the divine blessings is conditioned on obedience added to faith (see note on Ge 17:9). *my covenant.* See note on Ge 9:9. *out of all nations...my treasured possession.* The equivalent phrases used of Christians in 1Pe 2:9 are "chosen people" and "God's special possession" (see Dt 7:6; 14:2; 26:18; Ps 135:4; Mal 3:17; cf. Tit 2:14). *the whole earth is mine.* God is the Creator and Possessor of the earth and everything in it (see Ge 14:19,22; Ps 24:1–2).

19:6 *kingdom of priests.* The Israelites were to constitute the Lord's kingdom (the people who acknowledged him as their King) and, like priests, were to be wholly consecrated to his service (see Isa 61:6; cf. 1Pe 2:5; Rev 1:6; 5:10; 20:6). In their priestly role, the Israelites were to be channels of God's grace to the nations (see notes on Ge 12:2–3; Isa 42:1–4; 49:6). *holy nation.* See 1Pe 2:9. God's people, both individually and collectively, are to be "set apart" (see note on 3:5) to do his will (see Dt 7:6; 14:2,21; 26:19; Isa 62:12).

19:8 *We will do everything the Lord has said.* The people promised to obey the terms of the covenant (see 24:3,7; Dt 5:27).

19:9 *dense cloud.* See 13:21 and note. *the people will hear me speaking.* See Dt 4:33. *put their trust in you.* See 14:31 and note.

19:10–11 Outward preparation to meet God symbolizes the inward consecration God requires of his people.

19:11 ʸ S Ge 11:5
ᶻ ver 3, 20; S Ex 3:1;
24:16; 31:18; 34:2, 4,
29, 32; Lev 7:38;
26:46; 27:34; Nu 3:1;
Dt 10:5; Ne 9:13;
Gal 4:24-25
19:12 ᵃ ver 23
19:13 ᵇ Heb 12:20*
ᶜ Jos 6:4; 1Ch 15:28;
Ps 81:3; 98:6 ᵈ ver 21;
Ex 34:3
19:14 ᵉ S Ge 35:2
19:15 ᶠ 1Sa 21:4;
1Co 7:5
19:16 ᵍ 1Sa 2:10;
Isa 29:6 ʰ S ver 9
ⁱ Heb 12:18-19;
Rev 4:1 ʲ S Ge 3:10;
1Sa 13:7; 14:15; 28:5;
Ps 99:1; Heb 12:21
19:17 ᵏ S ver 2;
Dt 4:11
19:18 ˡ Ex 20:18;
Ps 104:32; Isa 6:4;
Rev 15:8 ᵐ S Ex 3:2;
24:17; Lev 9:24;
Dt 4:11, 24, 33, 36; 5:4;
9:3; 1Ki 18:24, 38;
1Ch 21:26; 2Ch 7:1;
Ps 18:8; Heb 12:18
ⁿ S Ge 19:28; Rev 9:2
ᵒ Jdg 5:5; 2Sa 22:8;
Ps 18:7; 68:8;
Isa 2:19; 5:25; 41:15;
64:1; Jer 4:24; 10:10;
Mic 1:4; Na 1:5;
Hab 3:6, 10; Hag 2:6
19:19 ᵖ S ver 9;
Dt 4:33; Ne 9:13
�q Ps 81:7
19:20 ʳ S ver 11
19:21 ˢ Ex 24:10-11;
Nu 4:20; 1Sa 6:19
ᵗ S ver 13
19:22 ᵘ Lev 10:3
ᵛ 1Sa 16:5; 2Ch 29:5;
Joel 2:16 ʷ ver 24;
2Sa 6:7
19:23 ˣ ver 11 ʸ ver 12
19:24 ᶻ Ex 24:1, 9
ᵃ ver 22
20:1 ᵇ Dt 10:4
ᶜ Ne 9:13; Ps 119:9;
147:19; Mal 4:4
20:2 ᵈ S Ge 17:7;
Ex 16:12; Lev 19:2;
20:7; Isa 43:3;
Eze 20:19 ᵉ S Ge 15:7
ᶠ S Ex 6:6

day the LORD will come down ʸ on Mount Sinai ᶻ in the sight of all the people. ¹²Put limits ᵃ for the people around the mountain and tell them, 'Be careful that you do not approach the mountain or touch the foot of it. Whoever touches the mountain is to be put to death. ¹³They are to be stoned ᵇ or shot with arrows; not a hand is to be laid on them. Whether people or animals, they shall not be permitted to live.' Only when the ram's horn ᶜ sounds a long blast may they approach the mountain." ᵈ

¹⁴After Moses had gone down the mountain to the people, he consecrated them, and they washed their clothes. ᵉ ¹⁵Then he said to the people, "Prepare yourselves for the third day. Abstain ᶠ from sexual relations."

¹⁶On the morning of the third day there was thunder ᵍ and lightning, with a thick cloud ʰ over the mountain, and a very loud trumpet blast. ⁱ Everyone in the camp trembled. ʲ ¹⁷Then Moses led the people out of the camp to meet with God, and they stood at the foot of the mountain. ᵏ ¹⁸Mount Sinai was covered with smoke, ˡ because the LORD descended on it in fire. ᵐ The smoke billowed up from it like smoke from a furnace, ⁿ and the whole mountain ᵃ trembled ᵒ violently. ¹⁹As the sound of the trumpet grew louder and louder, Moses spoke and the voice ᵖ of God answered ᑫ him. ᵇ

²⁰The LORD descended to the top of Mount Sinai ʳ and called Moses to the top of the mountain. So Moses went up ²¹and the LORD said to him, "Go down and warn the people so they do not force their way through to see ˢ the LORD and many of them perish. ᵗ ²²Even the priests, who approach ᵘ the LORD, must consecrate ᵛ themselves, or the LORD will break out against them." ʷ

²³Moses said to the LORD, "The people cannot come up Mount Sinai, ˣ because you yourself warned us, 'Put limits ʸ around the mountain and set it apart as holy.' "

²⁴The LORD replied, "Go down and bring Aaron ᶻ up with you. But the priests and the people must not force their way through to come up to the LORD, or he will break out against them." ᵃ

²⁵So Moses went down to the people and told them.

THE TEN COMMANDMENTS
20:1–17pp — Dt 5:6–21

20 And God spoke ᵇ all these words: ᶜ

² "I am the LORD your God, ᵈ who brought you out ᵉ of Egypt, ᶠ out of the land of slavery. ᵍ

³ "You shall have no other gods before ᶜ me. ʰ

⁴ "You shall not make for yourself an image ⁱ in the form of anything in heaven above

ᵃ 18 Most Hebrew manuscripts; a few Hebrew manuscripts and Septuagint *and all the people*
ᵇ 19 Or *and God answered him with thunder*   ᶜ 3 Or *besides*

20:2 ᵍ Ex 13:3; Eze 20:6   **20:3** ʰ ver 23; Ex 34:14; Dt 6:14; 13:10; 2Ki 17:35; Ps 44:20; 81:9; Jer 1:16; 7:6, 9; 11:13; 19:4; 25:6; 35:15
20:4 ⁱ ver 5, 23; Ex 32:8; 34:17; Lev 19:4; 26:1; Dt 4:15-19, 23; 27:15; 2Sa 7:22; 1Ki 14:9; 2Ki 17:12; Isa 40:19; 42:8; 44:9

19:12–13 The whole mountain becomes holy because of God's presence (see 3:5 and note). Israel must keep itself from the mountain even as it is to keep itself from the tabernacle (see Nu 3:10).
19:15 *Abstain from sexual relations.* Not because sex is sinful but because it may leave the participants ceremonially unclean (see Lev 15:18; see also 1Sa 21:4–5).
19:16 *thunder…lightning…trumpet blast.* God's appearance is often accompanied by an impressive display of meteorological sights and sounds (see, e.g., 1Sa 7:10; 12:18; Job 38:1; 40:6; Ps 18:13–14). *thick cloud.* See 13:21 and note.
19:18 *fire…smoke from a furnace.* See Ge 15:17 and note.
19:22 *priests.* See also v. 24. Before the Aaronic priesthood was established (see 28:1), priestly functions were performed either by the elders (see note on 3:16; see also 3:18; 12:21; 18:12) or by designated younger men (see 24:5). But perhaps the verse anticipates the regulations for the Aaronic priests who will be appointed. *who approach the LORD.* To officiate at sacrifices (see 40:32; Lev 21:23).
19:23 *set it apart as holy.* See note on 3:5.
20:1–17 See Dt 5:6–21; see also Mt 5:21,27; 19:17–19; Mk 10:19; Lk 18:20; Ro 13:9; Eph 6:2–3; Jas 2:10–11.
20:1 *words.* A technical term for "(covenant) stipulations" in the ancient Near East (e.g., among the Hittites; see also 24:3,8; 34:28). The basic code in Israel's divine law is found in vv. 2–17,

elsewhere called the "Ten Commandments" (34:28; Dt 4:13; 10:4), the Hebrew words for which mean lit. "Ten Words." "Decalogue," a term of Greek origin often used as a synonym for the Ten Commandments, also means lit. "Ten Words."
20:2 *I am the LORD your God, who brought you out.* The Decalogue reflects the structure of the contemporary royal treaties (see note on Ge 15:7). On the basis of (1) a preamble, in which the great king identified himself ("I am the LORD your God"), and (2) a historical prologue, in which he sketched his previous gracious acts toward the subject king or people ("who brought you out …"), the Lord then set forth (3) the treaty (covenant) stipulations (see Dt 5:1–3, 7–21) to be obeyed (in this case, ten in number, vv. 3–17). Use of this ancient royal treaty pattern shows that the Lord is here formally acknowledged as Israel's King and that Israel is his subject people. As his subjects, his covenant people are to render complete submission, allegiance and obedience to him out of gratitude for his mercies, reverence for his sovereignty, and trust in his continuing care. See chart, p. 20.
20:3 *before.* The Hebrew for this word is translated "in hostility toward" in Ge 16:12; 25:18. Something of that sense may be intended here. In any event, no deity, real or imagined, is to rival the one true God in Israel's heart and life.
20:4 *image in the form of anything.* Because God has no visible form, any idol intended to resemble him would be

or on the earth beneath or in the waters below. ⁵You shall not bow down to them or worship*ʲ* them; for I, the LORD your God, am a jealous God,*ᵏ* punishing the children for the sin of the parents*ˡ* to the third and fourth generation*ᵐ* of those who hate me, ⁶but showing love to a thousand*ⁿ* generations of those who love me and keep my commandments.

⁷"You shall not misuse the name of the LORD your God, for the LORD will not hold anyone guiltless who misuses his name.*ᵒ*

⁸"Remember the Sabbath*ᵖ* day by keeping it holy. ⁹Six days you shall labor and do all your work,*�q* ¹⁰but the seventh day is a sabbath*ʳ* to the LORD your God. On it you shall not do any work, neither you, nor your son or daughter, nor your male or female servant, nor your animals, nor any foreigner residing in your towns. ¹¹For in six days the LORD made the heavens and the earth,*ˢ* the sea, and all that is in them, but he rested*ᵗ* on the seventh day.*ᵘ* Therefore the LORD blessed the Sabbath day and made it holy.

¹²"Honor your father and your mother,*ᵛ* so that you may live long*ʷ* in the land*ˣ* the LORD your God is giving you.

¹³"You shall not murder.*ʸ*

¹⁴"You shall not commit adultery.*ᶻ*

¹⁵"You shall not steal.*ᵃ*

¹⁶"You shall not give false testimony*ᵇ* against your neighbor.*ᶜ*

¹⁷"You shall not covet*ᵈ* your neighbor's house. You shall not covet your neighbor's wife, or his male or female servant, his ox or donkey, or anything that belongs to your neighbor."

¹⁸When the people saw the thunder and lightning and heard the trumpet*ᵉ* and saw the mountain in smoke,*ᶠ* they trembled with fear.*ᵍ* They stayed at a distance ¹⁹and said to

20:5 *ʲ* Ex 23:13,24; Jos 23:7; Jdg 6:10; 2Ki 17:35; Isa 44:15, 17,19; 46:6 *ᵏ* Ex 34:14; Dt 4:24; Jos 24:19; Na 1:2 *ˡ* S Ge 9:25; S Lev 26:39
ᵐ Ex 34:7; Nu 14:18; Jer 32:18
20:6 *ⁿ* Ex 34:7; Nu 14:18; Dt 7:9; Jer 32:18; Lk 1:50; Ro 11:28
20:7 *ᵒ* Ex 22:28; Lev 18:21; 19:12; 22:2; 24:11,16; Dt 6:13; 10:20; Job 2:5,9; Ps 63:11; Isa 8:21; Eze 20:39; 39:7; S Mt 5:33
20:8 *ᵖ* S Ex 16:23; 31:13-16; 35:3; Lev 19:3,30; 26:2; Isa 56:2; Jer 17:21-27; Eze 22:8
20:9 *q* Ex 23:12; 31:13-17; 34:21; 35:2-3; Lev 23:3; Lk 13:14
20:10 *ʳ* S Ge 2:3; Ex 31:14; Lev 23:38; Nu 28:9; Isa 56:2; Eze 20:12,20
20:11 *ˢ* Ge 1:3-2:1 *ᵗ* S Ge 2:2 *ᵘ* Ex 31:17; Heb 4:4
20:12 *ᵛ* S Ge 31:35; S Dt 5:16; Mt 15:4*; 19:19*; Mk 7:10*; 10:19*; Lk 18:20*; Eph 6:2 *ʷ* Dt 6:2; Eph 6:3 *ˣ* Dt 11:9; 25:15; Jer 35:7
20:13 *ʸ* S Ge 4:23; Mt 5:21*; 19:18*; Mk 10:19*; Lk 18:20*;

20:13 Ro 13:9*; Jas 2:11*   **20:14** *ᶻ* Lev 18:20; 20:10; Nu 5:12,13,29; Pr 6:29,32; Mt 5:27*; 19:18*; Mk 10:19*; Lk 18:20*; Ro 13:9*; Jas 2:11*   **20:15** *ᵃ* Lev 19:11,13; Eze 18:7; Mt 19:18*; Mk 10:19*; Lk 18:20*; Ro 13:9*   **20:16** *ᵇ* Lev 19:11; Jer 9:3,5 *ᶜ* Ex 23:1,7; Lev 19:18; Ps 50:20; 101:5; 119:29; Mt 19:18*; Mk 10:19; Lk 3:14*; 18:20*   **20:17** *ᵈ* Lk 12:15; Ro 7:7*; 13:9*; Eph 5:3; Heb 13:5   **20:18** *ᵉ* Ex 19:16-19; Dt 4:36; Isa 58:1; Jer 6:17; Eze 33:3; Heb 12:18-19; Rev 1:10 *ᶠ* S Ex 19:18 *ᵍ* S Ge 3:10; S Ex 14:31; S 19:16

---

a sinful misrepresentation of him (see Dt 4:12,15–18). Since other gods are not to be worshiped (see v. 5), making idols of them would be equally sinful (see Dt 4:19,23–28). Cf. Jn 4:23–24 and note on 4:24.

A **20:5** *jealous God.* God will not put up with rivalry or unfaithfulness. Usually his "jealousy" concerns Israel and assumes the covenant relationship (analogous to marriage) and the Lord's exclusive right to possess Israel and to claim her love and allegiance. Actually, jealousy is part of the vocabulary of love. The "jealousy" of God (1) demands exclusive devotion to himself (see 34:14; 32:16,21; Jos 24:19; Ps 78:58; 1Co 10:22; Jas 4:5 and TNIV text note), (2) delivers to judgment all who oppose him (see Dt 29:20; 1Ki 14:22; Ps 79:5; Isa 42:13; 59:17; Eze 5:13; 16:38; 23:25; 36:5–6; Na 1:2; Zep 1:18; 3:8) and (3) vindicates his people (see 2Ki 19:31; Isa 9:7; 26:11; Eze 39:25; Joel 2:18; Zec 1:14; 8:2). In some of these passages the meaning is closer to "zeal" (the same Hebrew word may be translated either way, depending on context). *to the third and fourth generation of those who hate me.* Those Israelites who blatantly violate God's covenant and thus show that they reject the Lord as their King will bring down judgment on themselves and their households (see, e.g., Nu 16:31–34; Jos 7:24 and note)—households were usually extended to "three or four" generations. See note on Ps 109:12. *hate.* In covenant contexts the terms "hate" and "love" (v. 6) were conventionally used to indicate rejection of or loyalty to the covenant Lord.

B **20:6** *a thousand generations of those.* See Dt 7:9; 1Ch 16:15; Ps 105:8. *love me and keep my commandments.* See Dt 5:10; 7:9,12 and note; Ne 1:5; Da 9:4; Jn 14:15; 1Jn 5:3. In the treaty language of the ancient Near East the "love" owed to the great king was a conventional term for total allegiance and implicit trust expressing itself in obedient service.

A **20:7** *misuse the name of the LORD.* By profaning God's name—e.g., by swearing falsely by it (see Lev 19:12; see also Jer 7:9 and TNIV text note), as on the witness stand in court. Jesus elaborates on oath-taking in Mt 5:33–37.

20:8 See Ge 2:3. *Sabbath.* See note on 16:23. *holy.* See note on 3:5.

20:9 *Six days.* The question of a shorter work week in a modern industrialized culture is not in view.

A **20:10** *On it you shall not do any work.* Two reasons (one here and one in Deuteronomy) are given: (1) Having completed his work of creation God "rested on the seventh day" (v. 11), and the Israelites are to observe the same pattern in their service of God in the creation; (2) the Israelites must cease all labor so that their servants can also participate in the Sabbath-rest—just as God had delivered his people from the burden of slavery in Egypt (see Dt 5:14–15). The Sabbath thus became a "sign" of the covenant between God and Israel at Mount Sinai (see 31:12–17; see also note on Ge 9:12).

A **20:12** *Honor.* (1) Prize highly (see Pr 4:8), (2) care for (see Ps 91:15), (3) show respect for (see Lev 19:3; 20:9), and (4) obey (see Dt 21:18–21; cf. Eph 6:1). *so that you may live long.* "The first commandment with a promise" (Eph 6:2). See also note on Dt 6:2. Honoring those in authority is essential for social stability.

A **20:13** See Mt 5:21–26. *murder.* The Hebrew for this verb usually refers to a premeditated and deliberate act. See note on Nu 35:33.

A **20:14** See Mt 5:27–30. *adultery.* A sin "against God" (Ge 39:9) as well as against the marriage partner. "Marriage should be honored by all" (Heb 13:4).

20:15 *steal.* Stealing deprives others of what God has entrusted to them (see 22:1–15 and notes).

20:16 *false testimony.* Violates others' reputation and deprives them of their rights (see Ps 24:4; Pr 6:19; Jer 5:2 and notes).

A **20:17** *covet.* Desire something with evil motivation (see Mt 15:19). To break God's commandments inwardly is equivalent to breaking them outwardly (see Mt 5:21–30; cf. Col 3:5).

20:18–21 Concludes the account of the giving of the Decalogue. The order of the narrative appears to be different from the order of events, since v. 18 is most likely a continuation of

20:19 h Job 37:4, 5;
40:9; Ps 29:3-4
i Dt 5:5, 23-27; 18:16;
Gal 3:19
20:20 j S Ge 15:1
k S Ge 22:1 l Dt 4:10;
6:2, 24; 10:12;
Ps 111:10; 128:1;
Pr 1:7; Ecc 12:13;
Isa 8:13 m Job 1:8; 2:3;
28:28; Pr 3:7; 8:13;
14:16; 16:6
20:21 n S Ex 19:9;
Dt 5:22; Ps 18:9;
68:4; 97:2; Isa 19:1
20:22 o Dt 5:24, 26;
Ne 9:13
20:23 p S ver 3
q Ex 22:20; 32:4, 8, 31;
34:17; Dt 29:17-18;
Ne 9:18
20:24 r Ex 27:1;
40:29; Nu 16:38;
Dt 27:5; Jos 8:30;
2Ki 16:14; 2Ch 4:1;
Ezr 3:2; Eze 43:13
s S Ge 8:20;
S Ex 18:12 t Dt 12:5;
16:6, 11; 26:2; 1Ki 9:3;
2Ki 21:4, 7; 2Ch 6:6;
12:13; Ezr 6:12
u S Ge 12:2; 22:17
20:25 v Jos 8:31;
1Ki 6:7
20:26 w Eze 43:17
21:1 x Ex 24:3;
34:32; Dt 4:14; 6:1
21:2 y Ex 22:3
z ver 7; Jer 34:8, 14
21:5 a Dt 15:16
21:6 b Ex 22:8-9;
Dt 17:9; 19:17; 25:1

Moses, "Speak to us yourself and we will listen. But do not have God speak [h] to us or we will die." [i]

[20] Moses said to the people, "Do not be afraid. [j] God has come to test [k] you, so that the fear [l] of God will be with you to keep you from sinning." [m]

[21] The people remained at a distance, while Moses approached the thick darkness [n] where God was.

IDOLS AND ALTARS

[22] Then the LORD said to Moses, "Tell the Israelites this: 'You have seen for yourselves that I have spoken to you from heaven: [o] [23] Do not make any gods to be alongside me; [p] do not make for yourselves gods of silver or gods of gold. [q]

[24] " 'Make an altar [r] of earth for me and sacrifice on it your burnt offerings [s] and fellowship offerings, your sheep and goats and your cattle. Wherever I cause my name [t] to be honored, I will come to you and bless [u] you. [25] If you make an altar of stones for me, do not build it with dressed stones, for you will defile it if you use a tool [v] on it. [26] And do not go up to my altar on steps, lest your nakedness [w] be exposed on it.'

21

"These are the laws [x] you are to set before them:

HEBREW SERVANTS

21:2–6pp — Dt 15:12–18
21:2–11Ref — Lev 25:39–55

[2] "If you buy a Hebrew servant, [y] he is to serve you for six years. But in the seventh year, he shall go free, [z] without paying anything. [3] If he comes alone, he is to go free alone; but if he has a wife when he comes, she is to go with him. [4] If his master gives him a wife and she bears him sons or daughters, the woman and her children shall belong to her master, and only the man shall go free.

[5] "But if the servant declares, 'I love my master and my wife and children and do not want to go free,' [a] [6] then his master must take him before the judges. [a] [b] He shall take him

---

a 6 Or *before God*

19:25. On this reading, the proclamation of the Decalogue took place after Moses approached God (v. 21). Biblical writers often did not follow chronological sequence in their narratives for various literary reasons. The purpose of chronological displacement here may have been either to (1) keep the Decalogue distinct from the "Book of the Covenant" (24:7) that follows (20:22—23:19) or (2) to conclude the account with the formal institution of Moses' office as covenant mediator—or both.

A C **20:19** See Heb 12:19–20. Israel requests a mediator to stand between her people and God, a role fulfilled by Moses and subsequently by priests, prophets and kings—and ultimately by Jesus Christ (see 1Ti 2:5).

A **20:20** *Do not be afraid.* Do not think that God's display of his majesty is intended simply to fill you with abject fear. He has come to enter into covenant with you as your heavenly King. *test.* See note on Ge 22:1. *fear of God.* See note on Ge 20:11.

20:22—23:19 The stipulations of the "Book of the Covenant" (24:7), consisting largely of expansions on and expositions of the Ten Commandments. See chart, p. 275.

20:22–26 Initial stipulations governing Israel's basic relationship with God (cf. v. 3).

20:22 *heaven.* God's dwelling place. Even on "top of Mount Sinai" (19:20) God spoke from heaven.

A **20:23** See vv. 3–4. The contrast between the one true God "in heaven," who "does whatever pleases him" (Ps 115:3), and idols of silver or gold, who can do nothing at all (see Ps 115:3–8; see also Ps 135:5–6, 15–17), is striking indeed.

B **20:24** *altar of earth.* Such an altar, with dimensions the same as those of the altar in the tabernacle (see 27:1), has been found in the excavated ruins of a small Iron Age (10th, or possibly 11th, century B.C.) Israelite temple at Arad in southern

Israel. *burnt offerings.* See note on Lev 1:3. *fellowship offerings.* See note on Lev 3:1. *Wherever I cause my name to be honored.* Not the later central sanctuary at Jerusalem, but numerous temporary places of worship (see, e.g., Jos 8:30–31; Jdg 6:24; 21:4; 1Sa 7:17; 14:35; 2Sa 24:25; 1Ki 18:30).

B **20:25** *do not build it with dressed stones.* Many ancient altars of undressed stones (from various periods) have been found in Israel. *defile it if you use a tool on it.* For reasons not now clear, but perhaps related to pagan practices.

B **20:26** *steps.* The oldest stepped altar known in Israel is at Megiddo and dates between 3000 and 2500 B.C. *nakedness be exposed.* Men who ascended to such altars would expose their nakedness in the presence of God. Although Aaron and his descendants served at stepped altars (see Lev 9:22; Eze 43:17), they were instructed to wear linen undergarments (see 28:42–43; Lev 6:10; 16:3–4; Eze 44:17–18).

21:1 This verse functions as the heading for the section 21:2—23:19.

B **21:2–11** See Jer 34:8–22. The list begins with laws regulating servitude. No other ancient Near Eastern law collection begins this way. Hammurapi's law code, e.g., deals with the question of slavery last (see chart, p. xxiii). The fact that the Lord gives priority to regulating servitude in the Book of the Covenant may reflect his recent deliverance of Israel from a painful period of enslavement in Egypt.

21:2 *Hebrew.* See note on Ge 14:13. *in the seventh year, he shall go free.* The Lord's servants are not to be anyone's perpetual slaves (see 20:10 and note).

21:6 *the judges.* See 22:8–9, 28 and TNIV text notes. *pierce his ear with an awl.* See Dt 15:17. Submission to this rite symbolized willing service (see Ps 40:6–8 and note on 40:6).

to the door or the doorpost and pierce ^c his ear with an awl. Then he will be his servant for life. ^d

⁷"If a man sells his daughter as a servant, she is not to go free as male servants do. ⁸If she does not please the master who has selected her for himself, ^a he must let her be redeemed. He has no right to sell her to foreigners, because he has broken faith with her. ⁹If he selects her for his son, he must grant her the rights of a daughter. ¹⁰If he marries another woman, he must not deprive the first one of her food, clothing and marital rights. ^e ¹¹If he does not provide her with these three things, she is to go free, without any payment of money.

PERSONAL INJURIES

¹²"Anyone who strikes someone a fatal blow is to be put to death. ^f ¹³However, if it is not done intentionally, but God lets it happen, they are to flee to a place ^g I will designate. ¹⁴But if anyone schemes and kills someone deliberately, ^h that person is to be taken from my altar and put to death. ⁱ

¹⁵"Anyone who attacks ^b their father or mother is to be put to death.

¹⁶"Anyone who kidnaps someone is to be put to death, ^j whether the victim has been sold ^k or is still in the kidnapper's possession.

¹⁷"Anyone who curses their father or mother is to be put to death. ^l

¹⁸"If two people quarrel and one hits the other with a stone or with a fist ^c and the victim does not die but is confined to bed, ¹⁹the one who struck the blow will not be held liable if the other can get up and walk around outside with a staff; however, the guilty party must pay the injured person for any loss of time and see that the victim is completely healed.

²⁰"Anyone who beats their male or female slave with a rod must be punished if the slave dies as a direct result, ²¹but they are not to be punished if the slave recovers after a day or two, since the slave is their property. ^m

²²"If people are fighting and a pregnant woman is hit and gives birth prematurely ^d but there is no serious injury, the offender must be fined whatever the woman's husband demands ⁿ and the court allows. ²³But if there is serious injury, you are to take life for life, ^o ²⁴eye for eye, tooth for tooth, ^p hand for hand, foot for foot, ²⁵burn for burn, wound for wound, bruise for bruise.

²⁶"An owner who hits a male or female slave in the eye and destroys it must let the slave go free to compensate for the eye. ²⁷And an owner who knocks out the tooth of a male or female slave must let the slave go free to compensate for the tooth.

²⁸"If a bull gores a man or a woman to death, the bull is to be stoned to death, ^q and its meat must not be eaten. But the owner of the bull will not be held responsible. ²⁹If, however, the bull has had the habit of goring and the owner has been warned but has not kept it penned up ^r and it kills a man or woman, the bull is to be stoned and its owner also is to be put to death. ³⁰However, if payment is demanded, the owner's life may be redeemed by the payment of whatever is demanded. ^s ³¹This law also applies if the bull gores a son

^a 8 Or *master so that he does not choose her*   ^b 15 Or *Kills*   ^c 18 Or *with a tool*   ^d 22 Or *and has a miscarriage*

21:6 ^c Ps 40:6
^d Job 39:9; 41:4
21:10 ^e 1Co 7:3-5
21:12 ^f ver 15,17;
S Ge 4:14,23;
Ex 31:15; Lev 20:9,10;
24:16; 27:29; Nu 1:51;
35:16,30-31; Dt 13:5;
19:11; 22:22; 27:16;
Job 31:11; Pr 20:20;
S Mt 26:52
21:13 ^g Nu 35:10-34; Dt 4:42; 19:2-13;
Jos 20:9
21:14 ^h Ge 4:8;
Nu 35:20; 2Sa 3:27;
20:10; Heb 10:26
ⁱ Dt 19:11-12;
1Ki 2:28-34
21:16 ^j Ex 22:4;
Dt 24:7 ^k Ge 37:28
21:17 ^l S ver 12;
S Dt 5:16; Mt 15:4*;
Mk 7:10*
21:21 ^m Lev 25:44-46
21:22 ⁿ ver 30
21:23 ^o Lev 24:19;
Dt 19:21
21:24 ^p S ver 23;
Mt 5:38*
21:28 ^q ver 32;
Ge 9:5
21:29 ^r ver 36
21:30 ^s ver 22

21:12–15 See 20:13 and note; see also Nu 35:16–34; Dt 19:1–13; 21:1–9; 24:7; 27:24–25; Jos 20:1–9.

21:12 See Ge 9:6 and note.

21:13 *not done intentionally.* Related terms and expressions are "accidentally" (Nu 35:11), "without enmity" (Nu 35:22), "was not an enemy" (Nu 35:23), "no harm was intended" (Nu 35:23) and "without malice aforethought" (Dt 19:4). Premeditated murder is thus distinguished from accidental manslaughter. *God lets it happen.* The event is beyond human control—in modern legal terminology, an "act of God." *place.* A city of refuge (see Nu 35:6–32; Dt 19:1–13; Jos 20:1–9; 21:13,21,27, 32,38).

21:14 *from my altar.* Or "even from my altar." The horns of the altar were a final refuge for those subject to judicial action (see 1Ki 1:50–51; 2:28; Am 3:14 and notes).

21:15 See 20:12 and note.

21:16 See 20:15 and note.

21:17 *curses ... father or mother.* Calls down curses on them to effect their destruction.

21:19 *walk around outside with a staff.* Recover in a satisfactory way. *any loss of time.* Lit. "sitting," i.e., enforced idleness.

21:20–21 Benefit of doubt was granted to the slaveholder where no homicidal intentions could be proved.

21:23–25 See Dt 19:21. The so-called law of retaliation, as its contexts show, was meant to limit the punishment to fit the crime. By invoking the law of love, Jesus corrected the popular misunderstanding of the law of retaliation (see Mt 5:38–42). See note on Lev 24:20.

21:23 *serious injury.* Either to mother or to child.

21:26–27 Humane applications of the law of retaliation.

21:28–32 The law of the goring bull.

21:28 *the bull is to be stoned to death.* By killing someone, the bull becomes accountable for that person's life (see Ge 9:5 and note).

21:30 *if payment is demanded.* If the victim's family is willing to accept a ransom payment instead of demanding the death penalty. *life may be redeemed by the payment.* The payment (lit. "ransom," as in Nu 35:31) is not to compensate the victim's family but to save the negligent man's life.

21:32 ᵗGe 37:28;
Zec 11:12-13;
Mt 26:15; 27:3, 9
21:33 ᵘLk 14:5
21:36 ᵛver 29
22:1 ʷLev 6:1-7;
2Sa 12:6; Pr 6:31;
S Lk 19:8
22:2 ˣJob 24:16;
Jer 2:34; Hos 7:1;
Mt 6:19-20; 24:43
ʸNu 35:27
22:3 ᶻver 1
ᵃS Ex 21:2;
S Mt 18:25
22:4 ᵇ1Sa 12:5
ᶜS Ge 43:12
22:5 ᵈver 1
22:6 ᵉJdg 15:5
ᶠver 1
22:7 ᵍver 10;
Lev 6:2 ʰS Ge 43:12
22:8 ⁱS Ex 21:6
22:9 ʲver 8; Dt 25:1
22:10 ᵏS ver 7
22:11 ˡLev 6:3;
1Ki 8:31; 2Ch 6:22;
Heb 6:16
22:12 ᵐver 1
22:13 ⁿGe 31:39
22:14 ᵒver 1
22:15 ᵖLev 19:13;
Job 7:1
22:16 ᑫDt 22:28
ʳS Ge 34:12

or daughter. ³²If the bull gores a male or female slave, the owner must pay thirty shekels ᵃ ᵗ of silver to the master of the slave, and the bull is to be stoned to death.

³³"If anyone uncovers a pit ᵘ or digs one and fails to cover it and an ox or a donkey falls into it, ³⁴the one who opened the pit must pay the owner for the loss and take the dead animal in exchange.

³⁵"If anyone's bull injures the bull of another and it dies, the two parties are to sell the live one and divide both the money and the dead animal equally. ³⁶However, if it was known that the bull had the habit of goring, yet the owner did not keep it penned up, ᵛ the owner must pay, animal for animal, and take the dead animal in exchange.

PROTECTION OF PROPERTY

22 *"Whoever steals an ox or a sheep and slaughters it or sells it must pay back ʷ five head of cattle for the ox and four sheep for the sheep.

*²"If a thief is caught breaking in ˣ and is struck a fatal blow, the defender is not guilty of bloodshed; ʸ ³but if it happens ᵇ after sunrise, the defender is guilty of bloodshed.

"Anyone who steals must certainly make restitution, ᶻ but if they have nothing, they must be sold ᵃ to pay for their theft. ⁴If the stolen animal is found alive in their possession ᵇ—whether ox or donkey or sheep—they must pay back double. ᶜ

⁵"If anyone grazes their livestock in a field or vineyard and lets them stray and they graze in another person's field, restitution ᵈ must be made from the best of the livestock owner's field or vineyard.

⁶"If a fire breaks out and spreads into thornbushes so that it burns shocks ᵉ of grain or standing grain or the whole field, the one who started the fire must make restitution. ᶠ

⁷"If anyone gives a neighbor silver or goods for safekeeping ᵍ and they are stolen from the neighbor's house, the thief, if caught, must pay back double. ʰ ⁸But if the thief is not found, the owner of the house must appear before the judges, ⁱ and they must ᶜ determine whether the owner of the house has laid hands on the other person's property. ⁹In all cases of illegal possession of an ox, a donkey, a sheep, a garment, or any other lost property about which somebody says, 'This is mine,' both parties are to bring their cases before the judges. ᵈ ʲ The one whom the judges declare ᵉ guilty must pay back double to the other.

¹⁰"If anyone gives a donkey, an ox, a sheep or any other animal to a neighbor for safekeeping ᵏ and it dies or is injured or is taken away while no one is looking, ¹¹the issue between them will be settled by the taking of an oath ˡ before the Lᴏʀᴅ that the neighbor did not lay hands on the other person's property. The owner is to accept this, and no restitution is required. ¹²But if the animal was stolen from the neighbor, restitution ᵐ must be made to the owner. ¹³If it was torn to pieces by a wild animal, the neighbor shall bring in the remains as evidence and shall not be required to pay for the torn animal. ⁿ

¹⁴"If anyone borrows an animal from a neighbor and it is injured or dies while the owner is not present, restitution ᵒ must be made. ¹⁵But if the owner is with the animal, the borrower will not have to pay. If the animal was hired, the money paid for the hire covers the loss. ᵖ

SOCIAL RESPONSIBILITY

¹⁶"If a man seduces a virgin ᑫ who is not pledged to be married and sleeps with her, he must pay the bride-price, ʳ and she shall be his wife. ¹⁷If her father absolutely refuses to give her to him, he must still pay the bride-price for virgins.

ᵃ 32 That is, about 12 ounces or about 345 grams   ᵇ 3 Or *if the defender kills the thief*   ᶜ 8 Or *before God, and he will*   ᵈ 9 Or *before God*   ᵉ 9 Or *whom God declares*

* 22:1 is numbered 21:37 in Hebrew texts.   * 22:2-31 is numbered 22:1-30 in Hebrew texts.

21:32 *thirty shekels of silver.* Apparently the standard price for a slave. It was also the amount Judas was willing to accept as his price for betraying Jesus (see Mt 26:14–15; see also Zec 11:12–13 and notes). *shekels.* See note on Ge 20:16.

21:33–36 Laws concerning injuries to animals.

22:1–15 Laws concerning property rights (see 20:15 and note).

22:2 An act of self-defense in darkness does not produce bloodguilt.

22:3 Killing an intruder in broad daylight is not justifiable.

▲ 22:5 *from the best.* Restitution should always err on the side of quality and generosity.

22:6 *thornbushes.* Often used as hedges (see Mic 7:4) bordering cultivated areas.

22:11 See 20:7 and note. *an oath before the Lᴏʀᴅ.* The judges were God's representatives in court cases (see 21:6; 22:8–9,28 and TNIV text notes).

22:12–13 Similar laws apparently existed as early as the patriarchal period (see Ge 31:39).

22:16–31 General laws related to social obligations (see chart, p. 275).

22:16 *bride-price.* A gift, usually substantial, given by the prospective groom to the bride's family as payment for her (see Ge 24:53). The custom is still followed today in parts of the Middle East.

18"Do not allow a sorceress s to live.

19"Anyone who has sexual relations with an animal t is to be put to death.

20"Whoever sacrifices to any god u other than the LORD must be destroyed. a v

21"Do not mistreat or oppress a foreigner, w for you were foreigners x in Egypt.

22"Do not take advantage of a widow or an orphan. y 23If you do and they cry out z to me, I will certainly hear their cry. a 24My anger will be aroused, and I will kill you with the sword; your wives will become widows and your children fatherless. b

25"If you lend money to one of my people among you who is needy, do not treat it like a business deal; charge no interest. c 26If you take your neighbor's cloak as a pledge, d return it by sunset, 27because that cloak is the only covering your neighbor has. What else can your neighbor sleep in? e When he cries out to me, I will hear, for I am compassionate. f

28"Do not blaspheme God b g or curse h the ruler of your people. i

29"Do not hold back offerings j from your granaries or your vats. c

"You must give me the firstborn of your sons. k 30Do the same with your cattle and your sheep. l Let them stay with their mothers for seven days, but give them to me on the eighth day. m

31"You are to be my holy people. n So do not eat the meat of an animal torn by wild beasts; o throw it to the dogs.

LAWS OF JUSTICE AND MERCY

23 "Do not spread false reports. p Do not help a guilty person by being a malicious witness. q

2"Do not follow the crowd in doing wrong. When you give testimony in a lawsuit, do not pervert justice r by siding with the crowd, s 3and do not show favoritism t to the poor in a lawsuit.

4"If you come across your enemy's u ox or donkey wandering off, be sure to return it. v 5If you see the donkey w of someone who hates you fallen down under its load, do not leave it there; be sure you help your enemy with it.

6"Do not deny justice x to your poor people in their lawsuits. 7Have nothing to do with a false charge y and do not put an innocent z or honest person to death, a for I will not acquit the guilty. b

8"Do not accept a bribe, c for a bribe blinds those who see and twists the words of the righteous.

a 20 The Hebrew term refers to the irrevocable giving over of things or persons to the LORD, often by totally destroying them. b 28 Or Do not revile the judges c 29 The meaning of the Hebrew for this phrase is uncertain.

22:29 Pr 3:9; Mal 3:10 k S Ex 13:2; Nu 8:16-17; Lk 2:23 22:30 l Ex 34:19; Dt 15:19 m Ge 17:12; Lev 12:3; 22:27 22:31 n Ex 19:6; Lev 19:2; 22:31; Ezr 9:2 o Lev 7:24; 17:15; 22:8; Dt 14:21; Eze 4:14; 44:31 23:1 p S Ge 39:17; Mt 19:18; Lk 3:14 q S Ex 20:16; Dt 5:20; 19:16-21; Ps 27:12; 35:11; Pr 19:5; Ac 6:11 23:2 r ver 3, 6, 9; Lev 19:15, 33; Dt 1:17; 16:19; 24:17; 27:19; 1Sa 8:3 s Job 31:34 23:3 t Dt 1:17 23:4 u Ro 12:20 v Lev 6:3; 19:11; Dt 22:1-3 23:5 w Dt 22:4 23:6 x S ver 2; Dt 23:16; Pr 22:22 23:7 y S Ex 20:16; S Eph 4:25 z Mt 27:4 a S Ge 18:23 b Ex 34:7; Dt 19:18; 25:1 23:8 c S Ex 18:21; Lev 19:15; Dt 10:17; 27:25; Job 15:34; 36:18; Ps 26:10; Pr 6:35; 15:27; 17:8; Isa 1:23; 5:23; Mic 3:11; 7:3

Right margin cross-references

22:18 s S Ex 7:11; Lev 19:26,31; 20:27; Dt 18:11; 1Sa 28:3; 2Ch 33:6; Isa 57:3
22:19 t Lev 18:23; 20:15; Dt 27:21
22:20 u S Ex 20:23; 34:15; Lev 17:7; Nu 25:2; Dt 32:17; Ps 106:37 v Lev 27:29; Dt 13:5; 17:2-5; 18:20; 1Ki 18:40; 19:1; 2Ki 10:25; 23:20; 2Ch 15:13
22:21 w Ex 23:9; Lev 19:33; 24:22; Nu 15:14; Dt 1:16; 24:17; Eze 22:29 x Dt 10:19; 27:19; Zec 7:10; Mal 3:5
22:22 y ver 26; Dt 10:18; 24:6,10,12, 17; Job 22:6,9; 24:3, 21; Ps 68:5; 146:9; Pr 23:10; Isa 1:17; Jer 7:5,6; 21:12; 22:3; Eze 18:5-9,12; Zec 7:9-10; Mal 3:5; Jas 1:27
22:23 z Lk 18:7 a Dt 10:18; 15:9; 24:15; Job 34:28; 35:9; Ps 10:14,17; 12:5; 18:6; 34:15; Jas 5:4
22:24 b Ps 69:24; 109:9; La 5:3
22:25 c Lev 25:35-37; Dt 15:7-11; 23:20; Ne 5:7,10; Ps 15:5; Eze 18:8
22:26 d S ver 22; Pr 20:16; Eze 33:15; Am 2:8
22:27 e Dt 24:13,17; Job 22:6; 24:7; 29:11; 31:19-20; Eze 18:12, 16 f Ex 34:6; Dt 4:31; 2Ch 30:9; Ne 9:17; Ps 99:8; 103:8; 116:5; 145:8; Joel 2:13; Jnh 4:2
22:28 g S Ex 20:7 h 2Sa 16:5,9; 19:21; 1Ki 21:10; 2Ki 2:23; Ps 102:8 i Ecc 10:20; Ac 23:5
22:29 j Ex 23:15,16, 19; 34:20,26; Lev 19:24; 23:10; Nu 18:13; 28:26; Dt 18:4; 26:2,10; 1Sa 6:3; Ne 10:35;

22:18 Dt 18:9–12 strongly condemns sorcery and all such occult practices (see also 1Sa 28:9; Isa 47:12–14).

22:19 Ancient myths and epics describe acts of bestiality performed by pagan gods and demigods in Babylon and Canaan.

22:20 See 20:3–5. The total destruction (see TNIV text note) of the idolatrous Canaanites was later commanded by the Lord (see Dt 7:2; 13:15; 20:17; Jos 6:17; 10:40; 11:12,20).

22:21–27 That the poor, the widow, the orphan, the foreigner—in fact, all defenseless people—are objects of God's special concern and providential care is clear from the writings of Moses (see 21:26–27; 23:6–12; Lev 19:9–10; Dt 14:29; 16:11,14; 24:19–21; 26:12–13), the psalmists (see Ps 10:14, 17–18; 68:5; 82:3; 146:9) and the prophets (see Isa 1:23; 10:2; Jer 7:6; 22:3; Zec 7:10; Mal 3:5), as well as from the teachings of Jesus (see, e.g., Mt 25:34–45) and the apostles (Ro 15:26; Gal 2:10; Jas 1:27; 2:2–7).

22:25–27 Laws dealing with interest on loans (see Lev 25:35–37; Dt 15:7–11; 23:19–20; see also Ne 5:10 and note; Job 24:9; Ps 15:5; Pr 28:8 and note; Eze 18:13; 22:12). Interest for profit was not to be charged at the expense of the poor. Generosity in such matters was extended even further by Jesus (see Lk 6:34–35).

22:26–27 If all that a person had to offer in pledge for a loan was a cloak, that person was among the poorest of the poor (see Am 2:8 and note).

22:28 Do not … curse the ruler of your people. A ruler was God's representative. A penitent Paul quoted this law after he had unwittingly insulted the high priest (see Ac 23:4–5).
22:29 vats. See note on Hag 2:16. give me the firstborn. See notes on 4:22; 13:2,13; see also 13:15.
22:30 Do the same with your cattle and your sheep. See notes on 13:2,13; see also 13:12,15. give them to me on the eighth day. The same principle applied in a different way to firstborn sons as well (see note on Ge 17:12).
22:31 Since God's people were "a kingdom of priests" (see 19:6 and note), they were to obey a law later specified for members of the Aaronic priesthood (see Lev 22:8) as well.
23:1–9 Most of the regulations in this section pertain to 20:16.
23:1 See Lev 19:16; Dt 22:13–19; 1Ki 21:10–13.
23:4–5 Those hostile to you are to be shown the same consideration as others (see Dt 22:1–4; Pr 25:21). Jesus teaches that this means "love your enemies" (Mt 5:44).
23:8 See Dt 16:19.

23:9 *d* S ver 2;
S Ex 22:21;
Lev 19:33-34;
Eze 22:7
23:11 *e* Lev 25:1-7;
Ne 10:31
23:12 *f* S Ex 20:9;
Lk 13:14 *g* Ge 2:2-3
23:13 *h* Dt 4:9,23;
1Ti 4:16 *i* ver 32;
Dt 12:3; Jos 23:7;
Ps 16:4; Zec 13:2
j Dt 18:20; Jos 23:7;
Ps 16:4; Hos 2:17
23:14 *k* ver 17;
S Ex 12:14; 34:23,24;
Dt 16:16; 1Ki 9:25;
2Ch 8:13; Eze 46:9
23:15 *l* S Ex 12:17;
Mt 26:17; Lk 22:1;
Ac 12:3 *m* S Ex 12:2
n S Ex 22:29
23:16 *o* Lev 23:15-
21; Nu 28:26; Dt 16:9;
2Ch 8:13
p S Ex 22:29; S 34:22
q Ex 34:22; Lev 23:34,
42; Dt 16:16; 31:10;
Ezr 3:4; Ne 8:14;
Zec 14:16 *r* Lev 23:39;
Dt 16:13; Jer 40:10
23:17 *s* S ver 14
23:18 *t* Ex 34:25;
Lev 2:11 *u* S Ex 12:8
23:19 *v* S Ex 22:29;
S 34:22; S Nu 18:12
w Ex 34:26; Dt 14:21
23:20 *x* S Ge 16:7
y Ex 15:17
23:21 *z* Dt 18:19;
Jer 13:15 *a* Dt 29:20;
2Ki 24:4; La 1:17
b Nu 17:10; Dt 9:7;
31:27; Jos 24:19;
Ps 25:7; 78:8,40,56;
106:33; 107:11;
1Jn 5:16 *c* S Ex 3:14
23:22 *d* S Ex 15:26
e S Ge 12:3; Isa 41:11;
Jer 30:20
23:23 *f* Nu 13:29;
21:21; Jos 3:10; 24:8,
11; Ezr 9:1; Ps 135:11
23:24 *g* S Ex 20:5
h Lev 18:3; 20:23;
Dt 9:4; 12:30-31;
Jer 10:2 *i* Ex 34:13;
Nu 33:52; Dt 7:5;
12:3; Jdg 2:2;
2Ki 18:4; 23:14
j Lev 26:1; Dt 16:22;
1Ki 14:23; 2Ki 3:2;

9"Do not oppress a foreigner; *d* you yourselves know how it feels to be foreigners, because you were foreigners in Egypt.

SABBATH LAWS

10"For six years you are to sow your fields and harvest the crops, 11but during the seventh year let the land lie unplowed and unused. *e* Then the poor among your people may get food from it, and the wild animals may eat what they leave. Do the same with your vineyard and your olive grove.

12"Six days do your work, *f* but on the seventh day do not work, so that your ox and your donkey may rest, and so that the slave born in your household and the foreigner living among you may be refreshed. *g*

13"Be careful *h* to do everything I have said to you. Do not invoke the names of other gods; *i* do not let them be heard on your lips. *j*

THE THREE ANNUAL FESTIVALS

14"Three times *k* a year you are to celebrate a festival to me.

15"Celebrate the Festival of Unleavened Bread; *l* for seven days eat bread made without yeast, as I commanded you. Do this at the appointed time in the month of Aviv, *m* for in that month you came out of Egypt.

"No one is to appear before me empty-handed. *n*

16"Celebrate the Festival of Harvest *o* with the firstfruits *p* of the crops you sow in your field.

"Celebrate the Festival of Ingathering *q* at the end of the year, when you gather in your crops from the field. *r*

17"Three times *s* a year all the men are to appear before the Sovereign Lord.

18"Do not offer the blood of a sacrifice to me along with anything containing yeast. *t*

"The fat of my festival offerings must not be kept until morning. *u*

19"Bring the best of the firstfruits *v* of your soil to the house of the Lord your God.

"Do not cook a young goat in its mother's milk. *w*

GOD'S ANGEL TO PREPARE THE WAY

20"See, I am sending an angel *x* ahead of you to guard you along the way and to bring you to the place I have prepared. *y* 21Pay attention to him and listen *z* to what he says. Do not rebel against him; he will not forgive *a* your rebellion, *b* since my Name *c* is in him. 22If you listen carefully to what he says and do *d* all that I say, I will be an enemy *e* to your enemies and will oppose those who oppose you. 23My angel will go ahead of you and bring you into the land of the Amorites, Hittites, Perizzites, Canaanites, Hivites and Jebusites, *f* and I will wipe them out. 24Do not bow down before their gods or worship *g* them or follow their practices. *h* You must demolish *i* them and break their sacred stones *j* to pieces. 25Worship the Lord your God, *k* and his blessing *l* will be on your food and water. I will take

23:24 10:26; 17:10; 2Ch 14:3; Isa 27:9   **23:25** *k* Mt 4:10 *l* Lev 26:3-13; Dt 7:12-15; 28:1-14

23:10–13 Extensions of the principles taught in 20:8–11; Dt 5:12–15.

23:14–19 See 34:18–26; Lev 23:4–44; Nu 28:16—29:40; Dt 16:1–17; see also chart, pp. 180–181.

23:15 *Festival of Unleavened Bread.* Celebrated from the 15th through the 21st days of the first month (usually about mid-March to mid-April; see note on 12:2) at the beginning of the barley harvest; it commemorated the exodus.

23:16 *Festival of Harvest.* Also called the "Festival of Weeks" (34:22) because it was held seven weeks after the Festival of Unleavened Bread. It was celebrated on the sixth day of the third month (usually about mid-May to mid-June) during the wheat harvest. In later Judaism it came to commemorate the giving of the law on Mount Sinai, though there is no evidence of this significance in the OT. In NT times it was called "(the day of) Pentecost" (Ac 2:1; 20:16; 1Co 16:8), which means "50" (see Lev 23:16). *Festival of Ingathering.* Also called the "Festival of Tabernacles" (Lev 23:34; see note on Zec 14:16) or "Booths" because the Israelites lived in temporary shelters when God brought them out of Egypt (see Lev 23:42–43). It was celebrated from the 15th through the 22nd days of the seventh month (usually about mid-September to mid-October) when the produce of the

orchards and vines had been harvested; it commemorated the wilderness wanderings after the exodus. *end of the year.* End of the agricultural year, which began in the fall (see note on 12:2).

23:17 *all the men.* Normally accompanied by their families (see, e.g., 1Sa 1).

23:18 *not . . . with anything containing yeast.* See note on 12:15. *not be kept until morning.* See 12:9–10.

23:19 *firstfruits.* Representative of the whole harvest. The offering of firstfruits was an acknowledgment that the harvest was from the Lord and belonged wholly to him. *Do not cook a young goat in its mother's milk.* The reason for the prohibition is uncertain. In order to fulfill this command, Jewish rabbis at a later period formulated their rule against serving meat and milk at the same meal.

23:20 *angel.* See 14:19; see also note on Ge 16:7. *place I have prepared.* Canaan (cf. the similar statement of Jesus in Jn 14:2–3).

23:21 *Name.* Representing God's presence (see note on Dt 12:5).

23:22 *If.* See note on 19:5.

23:23 See 3:8 and note.

23:25–26 For more expanded lists of God's covenant blessings see Lev 26:3–13; Dt 7:13–15; 28:1–14; 31:1–10.

away sickness *m* from among you, ²⁶and none will miscarry or be barren *n* in your land. I will give you a full life span. *o*

²⁷"I will send my terror *p* ahead of you and throw into confusion *q* every nation you encounter. I will make all your enemies turn their backs and run. *r* ²⁸I will send the hornet *s* ahead of you to drive the Hivites, Canaanites and Hittites *t* out of your way. ²⁹But I will not drive them out in a single year, because the land would become desolate and the wild animals *u* too numerous for you. ³⁰Little by little I will drive them out before you, until you have increased enough to take possession *v* of the land.

³¹"I will establish your borders from the Red Sea *a* to the Mediterranean Sea, *b* and from the desert to the Euphrates River. *w* I will give into your hands the people who live in the land, and you will drive them out *x* before you. ³²Do not make a covenant *y* with them or with their gods. ³³Do not let them live in your land or they will cause you to sin against me, because the worship of their gods will certainly be a snare *z* to you."

THE COVENANT CONFIRMED

24 Then he said to Moses, "Come up to the LORD, you and Aaron, *a* Nadab and Abihu, *b* and seventy of the elders *c* of Israel. You are to worship at a distance, ²but Moses alone is to approach *d* the LORD; the others must not come near. And the people may not come up with him."

³When Moses went and told the people all the LORD's words and laws, *e* they responded with one voice, "Everything the LORD has said we will do." *f* ⁴Moses then wrote *g* down everything the LORD had said.

He got up early the next morning and built an altar *h* at the foot of the mountain and set up twelve stone pillars *i* representing the twelve tribes of Israel. ⁵Then he sent young Israelite men, and they offered burnt offerings *j* and sacrificed young bulls as fellowship offerings *k* to the LORD. ⁶Moses *l* took half of the blood *m* and put it in bowls, and the other half he splashed *n* against the altar. ⁷Then he took the Book of the Covenant *o* and read it to the people. They responded, "We will do everything the LORD has said; we will obey." *p*

⁸Moses then took the blood, sprinkled it on the people *q* and said, "This is the blood of the covenant *r* that the LORD has made with you in accordance with all these words."

⁹Moses and Aaron, Nadab and Abihu, and the seventy elders *s* of Israel went up ¹⁰and saw *t* the God of Israel. Under his feet was something like a pavement made of lapis la-

---

a 31 Or *the Sea of Reeds*   *b* 31 Hebrew *to the Sea of the Philistines*

24:8 Dt 5:2-3; Jos 24:25; 2Ki 11:17; Jer 11:4,8; 31:32; 34:13; Zec 9:11; S Mt 26:28; S Lk 22:20; Heb 9:20*   **24:9** *s* S ver 1

24:10 *t* S Ge 16:13; Nu 12:6; Isa 6:1; Eze 1:1; 8:3; 40:2; S Jn 1:18

23:25 *m* S Ex 15:26
23:26 *n* Lev 26:3-4; Dt 7:14; 28:4;
Mal 3:11 *o* S Ge 15:15; Dt 4:1,40; 32:47; Ps 90:10
23:27 *p* S Ge 35:5; S Ex 15:14
q S Ex 14:24; Dt 7:23 *r* 2Sa 22:41; Ps 18:40; 21:12
23:28 *s* Dt 7:20; Jos 24:12 *t* Ex 33:2; 34:11,24; Nu 13:29; Dt 4:38; 11:23; 18:12; Jos 3:10; 24:11; Ps 78:55
23:29 *u* Dt 7:22
23:30 *v* Jos 23:5
23:31 *w* S Ge 2:14; Dt 34:2; Ezr 4:20 *x* Dt 7:24; 9:3; Jos 21:44; 24:12,18; Ps 80:8
23:32 *y* S Ge 26:28; Ex 34:12; Dt 7:2; Jos 9:7; Jdg 2:2; 1Sa 11:1; 1Ki 15:19; 20:34; Eze 17:13
23:33 *z* S Ex 10:7
24:1 *a* S Ex 19:24
b S Ex 6:23 *c* ver 9; Nu 11:16
24:2 *d* Nu 12:6-8
24:3 *e* S Ex 21:1; Gal 3:19 *f* S Ex 19:8; Jos 24:24
24:4 *g* S Ex 17:14
h S Ge 8:20
i S Ge 28:18; S Dt 27:2
24:5 *j* Lev 1:3
k S Ge 31:54
24:6 *l* Ex 14:15; 32:31; Ps 99:6
m Heb 9:18 *n* Lev 1:11; 3:2,8,13; 5:9; Mt 26:28
24:7 *o* 2Ki 23:2,21; Heb 9:19 *p* Ex 19:8; Jer 40:3; 42:6,21; 43:2
24:8 *q* Heb 9:19; 1Pe 1:2 *r* Lev 26:3;

23:27 *my terror.* See note on 1Ch 14:17.
23:28 *hornet.* The meaning of the Hebrew for this word is uncertain. The Septuagint (the pre-Christian Greek translation of the OT) renders it "wasp," but the translators may have been guessing. In any event, the Lord promises to send some agent to disable or frighten the peoples of Canaan so that they will not be able to resist Israel's invasion. But probably the word involves concrete imagery and the focus of the statement is on the effects—therefore we are not to look for some historical agent to which the word metaphorically refers (cf. Isa 7:18).
23:30 *Little by little.* See Jdg 1.
23:31 See Ge 15:18; 1Ki 4:21. *Red Sea.* The (south)eastern border (here the modern Gulf of Aqaba; see note on 1Ki 9:26). *Mediterranean Sea.* The western border (see TNIV text note). *the desert.* The southern border (northeastern Sinai; see note on Ge 15:18). *Euphrates River.* The northern border.
23:33 *snare.* A symbol of destruction (see 10:7; Job 18:9; Ps 18:5; Pr 13:14; 21:6; Isa 24:17–18).
24:1 *Come up.* The action, temporarily interrupted for the Book of the Covenant (20:22—23:33), is resumed from 20:21. Moses and his associates would ascend the mountain after the events of vv. 3–8. *Nadab and Abihu.* Aaron's two oldest sons. Nadab would have succeeded Aaron as high priest, but he and his brother died because they offered unauthorized fire before the Lord (see Lev 10:2; Nu 3:4 and notes). *seventy . . . elders.* Cf. Nu 11:16; perhaps representing Jacob's 70 descendants (see 1:5; Ge 46:27 and note). *elders.* See note on 3:16. *at a distance.* See 20:21.

24:2 *Moses alone.* The mediator between God and the people of Israel. Jesus, who is greater than Moses (see Heb 3:1–6), is the "mediator of a new covenant" (Heb 12:24).
24:3 *words.* Probably refers to the Ten Commandments (see 20:1 and note). *laws.* Probably refers to the stipulations of the Book of the Covenant (20:22—23:19). *we will do.* See v. 7; see also 19:8 and note.
24:4 *Moses . . . wrote.* See note on 17:14; see also Introduction: Author and Date of Writing. *twelve stone pillars representing.* See Jos 4:5,20; 1Ki 18:31.
24:5 *young Israelite men . . . offered.* See note on 19:22.
24:6 *half the blood . . . the other half.* The division of the blood points to the twofold aspect of the "blood of the covenant" (v. 8): The blood on the altar symbolizes God's forgiveness and his acceptance of the offering; the blood on the people points to an oath that binds them in obedience (see vv. 3,7).
24:7 *Book of the Covenant.* Strictly speaking, 20:22—23:19 (see note there)—but here implying also the stipulations of 20:2–17; 23:20–33. *We will do . . . we will obey.* See v. 3; see also 19:8 and note.

24:8 *then.* Only after the people agreed to obey the Lord could they participate in his covenant with them. *blood of the covenant.* See Mk 14:24 and note.
24:9 *went up.* See v. 1 and note.
24:10 *saw . . . God.* But not in the fullness of his glory (see 33:20; see also notes on 3:6; Ge 16:13; Nu 12:8; Eze 1:28). *sky.* Symbolized by the blue color of the "lapis lazuli" (see Eze 1:26).

24:10 ᵘJob 28:16;
Isa 54:11; Eze 1:26;
10:1 ᵛRev 4:3
24:11 ʷS ver 10;
S Ex 3:6; S 19:21
ˣEze 44:3; Mt 26:29
24:12 ʸEx 31:18;
32:15-16; 34:1,28,29;
Dt 4:13; 5:22; 8:3;
9:9,10,11; 10:4;
2Co 3:3
24:13 ᶻS Ex 17:9
ᵃS Ex 3:1
24:14 ᵇS Ex 17:10
ᶜEx 18:16
24:15 ᵈS Ex 19:9;
Mt 17:5
24:16 ᵉS Ex 16:7;
Lev 9:23; Nu 14:10;
1Sa 4:21,22; Eze 8:4;
11:22 ᶠS Ex 19:11
ᵍPs 99:7
24:17 ʰS Ex 15:7;
S 19:18; Heb 12:18,29
24:18 ⁱ1Ki 19:8
ʲS Ge 7:4; Mt 4:2
25:2 ᵏEx 35:21,22,
26,27,29; 36:2;
2Ki 12:4; 1Ch 29:5,7,
9; 2Ch 24:10; 29:31;
Ezr 2:68; Ne 7:70-72;
2Co 8:11,12; 9:7
25:4 ˡEx 28:4-8
25:5 ᵐNu 4:6,10
ⁿDt 10:3
25:6 ᵒEx 27:20;
30:22-32; 35:28;
39:37; Nu 4:16
ᵖEx 30:1,7,35; 31:11;
35:28; Lev 16:12;
Nu 4:16; 7:14;
2Ch 13:11
25:7 �q Ex 28:4,6-14;
29:5; Jdg 8:27;
Hos 3:4 ʳLev 8:8
25:8 ˢEx 36:1-5;
Lev 4:6; 10:4,7; 21:12,
23; Nu 3:28; Heb 9:1-
2 ᵗEx 29:45;
Lev 26:11-12; Nu 5:3;

²⁴:¹⁰zuli,ᵘ as bright blue as the sky. ᵛ¹¹But God did not raise his hand against these leaders of the Israelites; they sawʷ God, and they ate and drank.ˣ

¹²The LORD said to Moses, "Come up to me on the mountain and stay here, and I will give you the tablets of stoneʸ with the law and commandments I have written for their instruction."

¹³Then Moses set out with Joshuaᶻ his aide, and Moses went up on the mountainᵃ of God. ¹⁴He said to the elders, "Wait here for us until we come back to you. Aaron and Hurᵇ are with you, and anyone involved in a disputeᶜ can go to them."

¹⁵When Moses went up on the mountain, the cloudᵈ covered it, ¹⁶and the gloryᵉ of the LORD settled on Mount Sinai. ᶠFor six days the cloud covered the mountain, and on the seventh day the LORD called to Moses from within the cloud.ᵍ ¹⁷To the Israelites the glory of the LORD looked like a consuming fireʰ on top of the mountain. ¹⁸Then Moses entered the cloud as he went on up the mountain. And he stayed on the mountain fortyⁱ days and forty nights.ʲ

OFFERINGS FOR THE TABERNACLE
25:1–7pp — Ex 35:4–9

25
The LORD said to Moses, ²"Tell the Israelites to bring me an offering. You are to receive the offering for me from everyone whose heart promptsᵏ them to give. ³These are the offerings you are to receive from them: gold, silver and bronze; ⁴blue, purple and scarlet yarnˡ and fine linen; goat hair; ⁵ram skins dyed red and another durable leather ᵃ;ᵐ acacia wood;ⁿ ⁶olive oilᵒ for the light; spices for the anointing oil and for the fragrant incense;ᵖ ⁷and onyx stones and other gems to be mounted on the ephodq and breastpiece.ʳ

⁸"Then have them make a sanctuaryˢ for me, and I will dwellᵗ among them. ⁹Make this tabernacle and all its furnishings exactly like the patternᵘ I will show you.

THE ARK
25:10–20pp — Ex 37:1–9

¹⁰"Have them make an arkᵇ ᵛof acacia wood—two and a half cubits long, a cubit and

---

ᵃ 5 Possibly the hides of dugongs   ᵇ 10 That is, a chest

25:8 Dt 12:11; 1Ki 6:13; Zec 2:10; 2Co 6:16   25:9 ᵘver 40; Ex 26:30; 27:8; 31:11; 39:32,42,43; Nu 8:4; 1Ch 28:11,19; Ac 7:44; Heb 8:5
25:10 ᵛDt 10:1-5; 1Ki 6:19; Heb 9:4

24:11 *raise his hand against.* See 9:15. *leaders.* Lit. "corners," "corner supports"; used in the sense of "leaders" only here. Cf. Gal 2:9. *ate and drank.* A covenant meal (cf. Ge 26:30; 31:54) celebrating the sealing of the covenant described in vv. 3–8. It foreshadows the Lord's Supper, which celebrates the new covenant sealed by Christ's death (see 1Co 11:25–26).
24:12 *Come up.* See note on v. 1. *tablets of stone.* See note on 31:18. *their.* The people's. *instruction.* As instruction from the covenant Lord, the laws were divine directives.
24:13 *Joshua his aide.* See note on 17:9.
24:14 *Hur.* See note on 17:10.
24:17 *glory of the LORD.* See v 10; 16:10 and notes.
24:18 *stayed on the mountain.* Moses did not come down until he had received instructions concerning the tabernacle and its furnishings (see 32:15). *forty days and forty nights.* Jesus, the new Moses (see note on v. 2), fasted for the same length of time (see Mt 4:2).
25:2 *offering.* Here refers to a voluntary contribution.
25:4 *blue, purple and scarlet.* Royal colors. *blue, purple.* Dyes derived from various shellfish (primarily the *murex*) that swarm in the waters of the northeast Mediterranean. See note on Ge 10:6. *scarlet.* Derived from the eggs and carcasses of the worm *Coccus ilicis,* which attaches itself to the leaves of the holly plant. *fine linen.* A very high quality cloth (often used by Egyptian royalty) made from thread spun from the fibers of flax straw. The Hebrew for this term derives ultimately from Egyptian. Excellent examples of unusually white, tightly woven linen have been found in ancient Egyptian tombs. Some are so finely woven that they cannot be distinguished from silk without the use of a magnifying glass. *goat hair.* From long-haired goats. Coarse and black (cf. SS 1:5; 6:5), it was often used to weave cloth for tents.

25:5 *ram skins dyed red.* After all the wool had been removed from the skins. The final product was similar to present-day morocco leather. *durable leather.* See TNIV text note. *acacia.* The wood is darker and harder than oak and is avoided by wood-eating insects. It is common in the Sinai peninsula.
25:6 *spices.* Those used in the anointing oil are identified in 30:23–24 as myrrh (balsam sap), cinnamon (bark of the cinnamon tree, a species of laurel), calamus (pith from the root of a reed plant) and cassia (made from dried flowers of the cinnamon tree). Those used in the fragrant incense are identified in 30:34 as gum resin (a powder taken from the middle of hardened drops of myrrh—rare and very valuable), onycha (made from mollusk shells) and galbanum (a rubbery resin taken from the roots of a flowering plant that thrives in Syria and Persia).
25:7 *other gems.* See 28:17–20. *ephod.* See 28:6 and note. *breastpiece.* See 28:15–30.
25:8 *sanctuary.* Lit. "holy place," "place set apart." See note on 3:5.
25:9 *tabernacle.* Lit. "dwelling place." The word is rarely used of human dwellings; it almost always signifies the place where God dwells among his people (see v. 8; 29:45–46; Lev 26:11; Eze 37:27; cf. Jn 1:14; Rev 21:3). *pattern.* See note on v. 40.
25:10 *ark.* See TNIV text note. Such was its form and function. The Hebrew for this word is translated by the traditional term "ark" throughout Exodus (see note on Dt 10:1–3); it is a different word from that used to refer to Noah's ark and to the reed basket in which the infant Moses was placed (see note on 2:3). Of all the tabernacle furnishings, the ark is mentioned first, probably because it symbolized the throne of the Lord (see 1Sa 4:4; 2Sa 6:2), the great King, who chose to dwell among his people (see note on v. 9).

a half wide, and a cubit and a half high.[a] [11]Overlay[w] it with pure gold, both inside and out, and make a gold molding around it. [12]Cast four gold rings for it and fasten them to its four feet, with two rings[x] on one side and two rings on the other. [13]Then make poles of acacia wood and overlay them with gold.[y] [14]Insert the poles[z] into the rings on the sides of the ark to carry it. [15]The poles are to remain in the rings of this ark; they are not to be removed.[a] [16]Then put in the ark the tablets of the covenant law,[b] which I will give you.

[17]"Make an atonement cover[c] of pure gold—two and a half cubits long and a cubit and a half wide. [18]And make two cherubim[d] out of hammered gold at the ends of the cover. [19]Make one cherub on one end and the second cherub on the other; make the cherubim of one piece with the cover, at the two ends. [20]The cherubim[e] are to have their wings spread upward, overshadowing[f] the cover with them. The cherubim are to face each other, looking toward the cover. [21]Place the cover on top of the ark[g] and put in the ark the tablets of the covenant law[h] that I will give you. [22]There, above the cover between the two cherubim[i] that are over the ark of the covenant law, I will meet[j] with you and give you all my commands for the Israelites.[k]

THE TABLE
25:23–29pp — Ex 37:10–16

[23]"Make a table[l] of acacia wood—two cubits long, a cubit wide and a cubit and a half high.[b] [24]Overlay it with pure gold and make a gold molding around it. [25]Also make around it a rim a handbreadth[c] wide and put a gold molding on the rim. [26]Make four gold rings for the table and fasten them to the four corners, where the four legs are. [27]The rings are to be close to the rim to hold the poles used in carrying the table. [28]Make the poles of acacia wood, overlay them with gold[m] and carry the table with them. [29]And make its plates and dishes of pure gold, as well as its pitchers and bowls for the pouring out of offerings.[n] [30]Put the bread of the Presence[o] on this table to be before me at all times.

THE LAMPSTAND
25:31–39pp — Ex 37:17–24

[31]"Make a lampstand[p] of pure gold. Hammer out its base and shaft, and make its flowerlike cups, buds and blossoms of one piece with them. [32]Six branches are to extend from the sides of the lampstand—three on one side and three on the other. [33]Three cups shaped like almond flowers with buds and blossoms are to be on one branch, three on the next branch, and the same for all six branches extending from the lampstand. [34]And on the lampstand there are to be four cups shaped like almond flowers with buds and blossoms. [35]One bud shall be under the first pair of branches extending from the lampstand, a sec-

---

a 10 That is, about 3 3/4 feet long and 2 1/4 feet wide and high or about 1.1 meters long and 67 centimeters wide and high; also in verse 17   b 23 That is, about 3 feet long, 1 1/2 feet wide and 2 1/4 feet high or about 90 centimeters long, 45 centimeters wide and 67 centimeters high   c 25 That is, about 3 inches or about 7.5 centimeters

25:11 *w* ver 24; Ex 30:3
25:12 *x* ver 26; Ex 30:4
25:13 *y* ver 28; Ex 27:6; 30:5; 37:28
25:14 *z* Ex 27:7; 40:20; 1Ch 15:15
25:15 *a* 1Ki 8:8
25:16 *b* S Ex 16:34; Heb 9:4
25:17 *c* ver 21; Lev 16:13; Ro 3:25
25:18 *d* Ex 26:1,31; 36:35; 1Ki 6:23,27; 8:6; 2Ch 3:10-13; Heb 9:5
25:20 *e* S Ge 3:24 *f* Ex 37:9; 1Ki 8:7; 1Ch 28:18; Heb 9:5
25:21 *g* ver 10-15; Ex 26:34; 40:20; Dt 10:5 *h* S Ex 16:34; Heb 9:4
25:22 *i* Nu 7:89; 1Sa 4:4; 2Sa 6:2; 22:11; 2Ki 19:15; 1Ch 13:6; 28:18; Ps 18:10; 80:1; 99:1; Isa 37:16 *j* S Ex 19:3; 29:42; 30:6,36; Lev 1:1; 16:2; Nu 17:4 *k* Jer 3:16
25:23 *l* ver 30; Ex 26:35; 40:4,22; Lev 24:6; Nu 3:31; 1Ki 7:48; 1Ch 28:16; 2Ch 4:8,19; Eze 41:22; 44:16; Heb 9:2
25:28 *m* S ver 13
25:29 *n* Nu 4:7
25:30 *o* Ex 35:13; 39:36; 40:4,23; Lev 24:5-9; Nu 4:7; 1Sa 21:4-6; 1Ki 7:48; 1Ch 23:29
25:31 *p* Ex 26:35; 31:8; 35:14; 39:37; 40:4,24; Lev 24:4; Nu 3:31; 1Ki 7:49; 2Ch 4:7; Zec 4:2; Heb 9:2; Rev 1:12

25:11 *pure gold.* Uncontaminated by silver or other impurities.

25:12 *rings.* Lit. "houses," "housings," into which poles were inserted to carry the ark (see v. 14).

25:16 *covenant law.* The two tablets on which were inscribed the Ten Commandments as the basic stipulations of the Sinai covenant (see 20:1–17; 31:18). The Hebrew word for "covenant law" is related to a Babylonian word meaning "covenant stipulations." See also notes on v. 22; 16:34.

A **25:17** *atonement.* Reconciliation, the divine act of grace whereby God draws to himself and makes "at one" with him those who were once alienated from him. In the OT, the shed blood of sacrificial offerings effected atonement (see Lev 17:11 and note); in the NT, the blood of Jesus, shed once for all time (see Heb 9:12), does the same (see Ro 3:25; 1Jn 2:2 and notes). *atonement cover.* See Lev 16:2 and note. That God's symbolic throne was capped with an atonement cover signified his great mercy toward his people—only such a God can be revered (see Ps 130:3–4).

B **25:18** *cherubim.* Probably similar to the carvings of winged sphinxes that adorned the armrests of royal thrones (see note on v. 10) in many parts of the ancient Near East (see also note on Ge 3:24). In the OT the cherubim were symbolic attendants that marked the place of the Lord's "enthronement" in his earthly kingdom (see 1Sa 4:4; 2Sa 6:2; 2Ki

19:15; Ps 99:1). From the cover of the ark (God's symbolic throne) the Lord gave directions to Moses (see v. 22; Nu 7:89). Later the ark's presence in the temple at Jerusalem would designate it as God's earthly royal city (see Ps 9:11 and note).

25:22 *ark of the covenant law.* Called this because it contained the two "tablets of the covenant law" (v. 16; see note there). The phrase "ark of the covenant law" is a synonym of the more familiar phrase "ark of the covenant" (see, e.g., Nu 10:33). *I will meet with you.* See note on 27:21.

25:26 *rings.* See note on v. 12.

A **25:30** *bread of the Presence.* Traditionally "showbread." In this phrase, "Presence" refers to the presence of God himself (as in 33:14–15; Isa 63:9). The bread (12 loaves, one for each tribe) represented a perpetual bread offering to the Lord by which the Israelites declared that they consecrated to God the fruits of their labors and by which the nation at the same time acknowledged that all such fruit had been provided only by God's blessing. See Lev 24:5–9.

25:31 *flowerlike cups, buds and blossoms.* The design is patterned after an almond tree (see v. 33), the first of the trees in the Near East to blossom in spring. The cups of the lampstand resemble either the outer covering of the almond flower or the almond nut.

25:36 q ver 18;
Nu 8:4
25:37 r Ex 27:21;
30:8; Lev 24:3-4;
Nu 8:2; 1Sa 3:3;
2Ch 13:11
25:38 s S ver 37;
Nu 4:9
25:40 t S ver 9;
Ac 7:44; Heb 8:5*
26:1 u Ex 29:42;
40:2; Lev 8:10;
Nu 1:50; Jos 22:19,29;
2Sa 7:2; 1Ki 1:39;
Ac 7:44; Heb 8:2,5;
13:10; S Rev 21:3
v S Ex 25:18
26:2 w ver 8
26:6 x ver 11
26:8 y ver 2
26:11 z ver 6
26:14 a Nu 3:25
b Nu 4:25
26:19 c ver 21,25,
32; Ex 38:27

ond bud under the second pair, and a third bud under the third pair—six branches in all. ³⁶The buds and branches shall all be of one piece with the lampstand, hammered out of pure gold. q

³⁷"Then make its seven lamps r and set them up on it so that they light the space in front of it. ³⁸Its wick trimmers and trays s are to be of pure gold. ³⁹A talent a of pure gold is to be used for the lampstand and all these accessories. ⁴⁰See that you make them according to the pattern t shown you on the mountain.

THE TABERNACLE
26:1–37pp — Ex 36:8–38

26 "Make the tabernacle u with ten curtains of finely twisted linen and blue, purple and scarlet yarn, with cherubim v worked into them by skilled hands. ²All the curtains are to be the same size w—twenty-eight cubits long and four cubits wide. b ³Join five of the curtains together, and do the same with the other five. ⁴Make loops of blue material along the edge of the end curtain in one set, and do the same with the end curtain in the other set. ⁵Make fifty loops on one curtain and fifty loops on the end curtain of the other set, with the loops opposite each other. ⁶Then make fifty gold clasps and use them to fasten the curtains together so that the tabernacle is a unit. x

⁷"Make curtains of goat hair for the tent over the tabernacle—eleven altogether. ⁸All eleven curtains are to be the same size y—thirty cubits long and four cubits wide. c ⁹Join five of the curtains together into one set and the other six into another set. Fold the sixth curtain double at the front of the tent. ¹⁰Make fifty loops along the edge of the end curtain in one set and also along the edge of the end curtain in the other set. ¹¹Then make fifty bronze clasps and put them in the loops to fasten the tent together as a unit. z ¹²As for the additional length of the tent curtains, the half curtain that is left over is to hang down at the rear of the tabernacle. ¹³The tent curtains will be a cubit d longer on both sides; what is left will hang over the sides of the tabernacle so as to cover it. ¹⁴Make for the tent a covering a of ram skins dyed red, and over that a covering of the other durable leather. e b

¹⁵"Make upright frames of acacia wood for the tabernacle. ¹⁶Each frame is to be ten cubits long and a cubit and a half wide, f ¹⁷with two projections set parallel to each other. Make all the frames of the tabernacle in this way. ¹⁸Make twenty frames for the south side of the tabernacle ¹⁹and make forty silver bases c to go under them—two bases for each frame, one under each projection. ²⁰For the other side, the north side of the tabernacle,

---

a 39 That is, about 75 pounds or about 34 kilograms   b 2 That is, about 42 feet long and 6 feet wide or about 13 meters long and 1.8 meters wide   c 8 That is, about 45 feet long and 6 feet wide or about 13.5 meters long and 1.8 meters wide   d 13 That is, about 18 inches or about 45 centimeters   e 14 Possibly the hides of dugongs   f 16 That is, about 15 feet long and 2 1/4 feet wide or about 4.5 meters long and 67 centimeters wide

---

B A **25:37** *seven.* Signifying completeness. *lamps.* The ancient lamp was a small clay saucer with part of its rim pinched together to form a spout from which protruded the top of a wick fed by oil contained in the saucer. (Examples of seven-spouted lamps come from the time of Moses; see note on Zec 4:2.) The ruins of Beth Shan and Megiddo have yielded examples of a metal pedestal topped by a ledge designed to carry a lamp. The classic representation of the shape of the tabernacle lampstand comes from the time of Herod the Great and may be seen on the Arch of Titus in Rome. The lamps were to burn all night in the tabernacle, tended by the priests. Oil for the lamps was to be supplied by the people; the light from the lamps represented the glory of the Lord reflected in the consecrated lives of the Israelites—Israel's glory answering to God's glory in the tabernacle (29:43). See 27:20–21.

A **25:40** Quoted in Heb 8:5 in order to contrast the "shadow" (the trappings of the old covenant) with the reality (the Christ of the new covenant). See also Heb 10:1.

A **26:1** *tabernacle.* See note on 25:9; see also diagram, p. 129. Its basic structure was to be 15 feet wide by 45 feet long by 15 feet high. Over an inner lining of embroidered linen (vv. 1–6), it was to have a covering woven of goat hair (vv. 7–13) and two additional coverings of leather, one made from ram skins dyed red and one from "another durable leather" (25:5; see TNIV text note there; cf. 26:14). Internally, the ceiling was

probably flat, but whether the leather coverings had a ridge line with sloping sides (like a tent) is not known. The tabernacle represented God's royal tent. Its form and adornment (like those of the later temples that replaced it) marked it as a symbolic representation of the created cosmos over which God is sovereign as Creator and Lord. As such, it stood for the center of the cosmos from which the Creator reigns, the place where the heavenly and earthly realms converge. There God "lived" among his people (Immanuel, "God with us"), and his people could come near to him. At this sanctuary Israel lived symbolically at the gate of Paradise—very near though still outside, awaiting the fulfillment of God's redemptive program (see vv. 31–35; Ge 3:24 and notes; see also Rev 21:1—22:6 and notes). *finely twisted linen and blue, purple and scarlet yarn.* See note on 25:4. *cherubim.* Signifying a royal chamber (see 25:18 and note).

26:7 *goat hair.* See note on 25:4.

26:14 *ram skins dyed red . . . other durable leather.* See note on 25:5.

26:17 *projections.* Lit. "hands"; probably the two pegs at the bottom of each frame that were inserted into its two bases (see v. 19).

26:19 *forty silver bases.* These plus the 40 in v. 21, the 16 in v. 25 and the 4 in v. 32 make a grand total of 100, the number of talents of silver obtained from the Israelite community to be used to cast the bases (see 38:27).

make twenty frames ²¹and forty silver bases *ᵈ*—two under each frame. ²²Make six frames for the far end, that is, the west end of the tabernacle, ²³and make two frames for the corners at the far end. ²⁴At these two corners they must be double from the bottom all the way to the top and fitted into a single ring; both shall be like that. ²⁵So there will be eight frames and sixteen silver bases—two under each frame.

²⁶"Also make crossbars of acacia wood: five for the frames on one side of the tabernacle, ²⁷five for those on the other side, and five for the frames on the west, at the far end of the tabernacle. ²⁸The center crossbar is to extend from end to end at the middle of the frames. ²⁹Overlay the frames with gold and make gold rings to hold the crossbars. Also overlay the crossbars with gold.

³⁰"Set up the tabernacle *ᵉ* according to the plan *ᶠ* shown you on the mountain.

³¹"Make a curtain *ᵍ* of blue, purple and scarlet yarn and finely twisted linen, with cher-

26:21 *ᵈ*S ver 19
26:30 *ᵉ*Ex 40:2;
Nu 9:15 *ᶠ*S Ex 25:9
26:31 *ᵍ*Nu 4:5;
2Ch 3:14; Mt 27:51;
Lk 23:45; Heb 9:3

26:23 *corners.* Or "angles," perhaps referring to mitered joints at the corners.

26:26 *crossbars.* To strengthen the frames on the north, south and west sides.

26:29 *rings.* Lit. "houses," "housings" (see note on 25:12).

26:30 *plan.* See note on 25:40.

26:31–35 A curtain was to divide the tabernacle into two rooms, the Holy Place and the Most Holy Place, with the former twice as large as the latter. The Most Holy Place probably formed a perfect cube, 15 feet by 15 feet by 15 feet. Enclosed with linen curtains embroidered with cherubim and containing only the ark of the covenant, it represented God's throne room (see note on v. 1). The Holy Place represented his royal guest

chamber where his people symbolically came before him in the bread of the Presence (see note on 25:30), the light from the lampstand (see note on 25:37) and the incense from the altar of incense (see note on 30:1).

A 26:31 *curtain.* To separate the Holy Place from the Most Holy Place (see v. 33). It was called the "shielding curtain" (39:34; 40:21; Nu 4:5) because it shielded the ark (see 27:21; see also notes on 16:34; 25:22). At the moment when Christ died, the curtain of Herod's temple was torn, thereby giving the believer direct access to the presence of God (see Mk 15:38; Heb 6:19–20; 10:19–22). *cherubim.* See v. 1 and note. The curtain at the entrance to the Holy Place did not have cherubim (see v. 36).

THE TABERNACLE

Most Holy Place with the ark of the covenant
10 cubits square (*15 ft. square*)

Curtain

Holy Place, with the golden table
for the bread of the Presence,
golden lampstand, and
altar of incense
length: 20 cubits (*30 ft.*)
width: 10 cubits (*15 ft.*)

50 cubits

100 cubits (*150 ft. long*)

10—20 cubits

High Clearance

W N / S E

CUBITS
FEET

Bronze Basin

Bronze Altar

Entrance 20 cubits (*30 ft. wide*)

The new religious observances taught by Moses in the wilderness centered on rituals connected with the tabernacle and amplified Israel's sense of separateness, purity and oneness under the Lordship of Yahweh.

B A few desert shrines have been found in Sinai, notably at Serabit el-Khadem and at Timnah in the Negev, and show marked Egyptian influence.

Specific cultural antecedents to portable shrines carried on poles and covered with thin sheets of gold can be found in ancient Egypt as early as the Old Kingdom (2800–2250 B.C.),

but were especially prominent in the 18th and 19th dynasties (1570–1180). The best examples come from the fabulous tomb of Tutankhamun, c. 1350.

Comparisons of construction details in the text of Ex 25–40 with the frames, shrines, poles, sheathing, draped fabric covers, gilt rosettes, and winged protective figures from the shrine of Tutankhamun, is instructive. The period, the Late Bronze Age, is equivalent in all dating systems to the era of Moses and the exodus.

26:31 *h* S Ex 25:18
26:32 *i* S ver 19
26:33 *j* Ex 27:21;
35:12; 40:3,21;
Lev 16:2; Nu 3:31;
4:5; 2Ch 3:14
k Lev 16:2,16;
1Ki 6:16; 7:50; 8:6;
2Ch 3:8; 5:7;
Eze 41:4; Heb 9:2-3
26:34 *l* Ex 25:21;
30:6; 37:6; Lev 16:2;
Heb 9:5
26:35 *m* S Ex 25:23;
Heb 9:2 *n* S Ex 25:31
26:36 *o* Ex 35:15;
40:5,28 *p* Ps 45:14;
Eze 16:10; 26:16; 27:7
27:1 *q* S Ex 20:24;
S 40:6; S 1Ki 8:64
27:2 *r* Ex 29:12;
30:2; 37:25; Lev 4:7;
1Ki 1:50; 2:28;
Ps 118:27; Jer 17:1;
Eze 43:15; Am 3:14;
Zec 9:15

ubim *h* worked into it by skilled hands. ³²Hang it with gold hooks on four posts of acacia wood overlaid with gold and standing on four silver bases. *i* ³³Hang the curtain from the clasps and place the ark of the covenant law behind the curtain. *j* The curtain will separate the Holy Place from the Most Holy Place. *k* ³⁴Put the atonement cover *l* on the ark of the covenant law in the Most Holy Place. ³⁵Place the table *m* outside the curtain on the north side of the tabernacle and put the lampstand *n* opposite it on the south side.

³⁶"For the entrance to the tent make a curtain *o* of blue, purple and scarlet yarn and finely twisted linen—the work of an embroiderer. *p* ³⁷Make gold hooks for this curtain and five posts of acacia wood overlaid with gold. And cast five bronze bases for them.

THE ALTAR OF BURNT OFFERING
27:1–8pp — Ex 38:1–7

27 "Build an altar *q* of acacia wood, three cubits *a* high; it is to be square, five cubits long and five cubits wide. *b* ²Make a horn *r* at each of the four corners, so that the horns and the altar are of one piece, and overlay the altar with bronze. ³Make all its utensils of bronze—its pots to remove the ashes, and its shovels, sprinkling

a 1 That is, about 4 1/2 feet or about 1.4 meters   *b 1* That is, about 7 1/2 feet or about 2.3 meters long and wide

---

26:37 *bronze.* Inside the tabernacle, gold was the metal of choice; outside—beginning with the bases of the outer curtain (see v. 36)—the metal of choice was bronze. The furnishings close to the place of God's dwelling were made of, or overlaid with, gold; those farther away (see 27:2–6; 30:18) were made of, or overlaid with, bronze. The bases that supported the frames of the tabernacle and the four posts holding the dividing curtain were of silver (see vv. 19,21,25,32).

27:1 *altar.* The altar of burnt offering (see Lev 4:7,10,18). *acacia wood.* See note on 25:5.
27:2 *horns.* Projections of the four corner posts. They were symbols of help and refuge (see 1Ki 1:50; 2:28). They also symbolized the atoning power of the altar: Some of the blood was put on the horns of the altar before the rest was poured out at the base (see 29:12; Lev 4:7,18,25,30,34; 8:15; 9:9; 16:18).
27:3 *sprinkling bowls.* To catch the blood of the animals slain

---

TABERNACLE FURNISHINGS

The symbolism of God's redemptive covenant was preserved in the tabernacle, making each element an object lesson for the worshiper. Likely reconstructions of the furnishings are based on the detailed descriptions and precise measurements recorded in Exodus 25–40. (The bronze basin is not shown here.)

ARK OF THE COVENANT

B The ark of the covenant compares with the roughly contemporary shrine and funerary furniture of King Tutankhamen (c. 1350 B.C.), which, along with the Nimrud and Samaria ivories from a later period, have been used to guide the graphic interpretation of the text. Both sources show the conventional way of depicting extreme reverence, with facing winged guardians shielding a sacred place.

LAMPSTAND
The traditional form of the lampstand is not attested archaeologically until much later.

TABLE

B The table holding the bread of the Presence was made of wood covered with thin sheets of gold. All of the objects were portable and were fitted with rings and carrying poles, practices typical of Egyptian ritual processions as early as the Old Kingdom.

INCENSE ALTAR

BRONZE ALTAR

B The altar of burnt offering was made of wood overlaid with bronze. The size, five cubits square and three cubits high, matches altars found at Arad and Beersheba from the period of the monarchy.

bowls,ˢ meat forks and firepans.ᵗ ⁴Make a grating for it, a bronze network, and make a bronze ring at each of the four corners of the network. ⁵Put it under the ledge of the altar so that it is halfway up the altar. ⁶Make poles of acacia wood for the altar and overlay them with bronze.ᵘ ⁷The poles are to be inserted into the rings so they will be on two sides of the altar when it is carried.ᵛ ⁸Make the altar hollow, out of boards. It is to be made just as you were shownʷ on the mountain.

THE COURTYARD

27:9–19pp — Ex 38:9–20

⁹"Make a courtyardˣ for the tabernacle. The south side shall be a hundred cubitsª long and is to have curtains of finely twisted linen, ¹⁰with twenty posts and twenty bronze bases and with silver hooks and bands on the posts. ¹¹The north side shall also be a hundred cubits long and is to have curtains, with twenty posts and twenty bronze bases and with silver hooks and bands on the posts.

¹²"The west end of the courtyard shall be fifty cubitsᵇ wide and have curtains, with ten posts and ten bases. ¹³On the east end, toward the sunrise, the courtyard shall also be fifty cubits wide. ¹⁴Curtains fifteen cubitsᶜ long are to be on one side of the entrance, with three posts and three bases, ¹⁵and curtains fifteen cubits long are to be on the other side, with three posts and three bases.

¹⁶"For the entrance to the courtyard, provide a curtainʸ twenty cubitsᵈ long, of blue, purple and scarlet yarn and finely twisted linen—the work of an embroidererᶻ—with four posts and four bases. ¹⁷All the posts around the courtyard are to have silver bands and hooks, and bronze bases. ¹⁸The courtyard shall be a hundred cubits long and fifty cubits wide,ᵉ with curtains of finely twisted linen five cubitsᶠ high, and with bronze bases. ¹⁹All the other articles used in the service of the tabernacle, whatever their function, including all the tent pegs for it and those for the courtyard, are to be of bronze.

OIL FOR THE LAMPSTAND

27:20–21pp — Lev 24:1–3

²⁰"Command the Israelites to bring you clear oilª of pressed olives for the light so that the lamps may be kept burning. ²¹In the tent of meeting,ᵇ outside the curtain that shields the ark of the covenant law,ᶜ Aaron and his sons are to keep the lampsᵈ burning before the LORD from evening till morning. This is to be a lasting ordinanceᵉ among the Israelites for the generations to come.

THE PRIESTLY GARMENTS

28

"Have Aaronᶠ your brother brought to you from among the Israelites, along with his sons Nadab and Abihu,ᵍ Eleazar and Ithamar,ʰ so they may serve me as priests.ⁱ ²Make sacred garmentsʲ for your brother Aaron to give him

---

ᵃ *9* That is, about 150 feet or about 45 meters; also in verse 11   ᵇ *12* That is, about 75 feet or about 22.5 meters; also in verse 13   ᶜ *14* That is, about 22 feet or about 6.8 meters; also in verse 15   ᵈ *16* That is, about 30 feet or about 9 meters   ᵉ *18* That is, about 150 feet long and 75 feet wide or about 45 meters long and 22.5 meters wide   ᶠ *18* That is, about 7 1/2 feet or about 2.3 meters

27:3 ˢ Nu 7:13; 1Ki 7:40, 45; 2Ki 12:13 ᵗ Nu 4:14; 1Ch 28:17; Jer 52:18
27:6 ᵘ S Ex 25:13
27:7 ᵛ Ex 25:14, 28
27:8 ʷ S Ex 25:9
27:9 ˣ Ex 35:17; 40:8, 33; Lev 6:16, 26; Eze 40:14; 42:1
27:16 ʸ Ex 40:33 ᶻ Ex 36:37
27:20 ᵃ S Ex 25:6
27:21 ᵇ Ex 28:43; 29:42; 30:36; 33:7; Lev 1:1; 6:26; 8:3, 31; Nu 1:1; 31:54; Jos 18:1; 1Ki 1:39 ᶜ S Ex 16:34 ᵈ S Ex 25:37 ᵉ Ex 29:9; 30:21; Lev 3:17; 16:34; 17:7; Nu 18:23; 19:21; 1Sa 30:25
28:1 ᶠ Lev 8:30; Ps 99:6; Heb 5:4 ᵍ S Ex 6:23; 24:9 ʰ S Ex 6:23 ⁱ Lev 8:2; 21:1; Nu 18:1-7; Dt 18:5; 1Sa 2:28; Heb 5:1
28:2 ʲ Ex 29:5, 29; 31:10; 35:19; 39:1; Lev 8:7-9, 30; 16:32; Nu 20:26-28

---

beside the altar and to sprinkle it at the base. *meat forks.* Three-pronged forks for arranging the sacrifice or removing the priests' portion from the container in which it was being boiled (see 1Sa 2:13–14). *firepans.* Probably for carrying fire from the altar of burnt offering to the altar of incense inside the Holy Place (see Lev 10:1; 16:12–13).

27:4 *grating.* Placed midway between the top and bottom of the boxlike structure. Since the intense heat of the fire built inside the upper half of the altar would have eventually destroyed it, perhaps the hollow altar (see v. 8) was designed to be filled with earth when it was in use. *ring.* See note on 25:12.

27:12–13 *west end … east end.* The courtyard is described as having two equal parts. The Most Holy Place probably occupied the central position in the western half, the altar of burnt offering the central position in the eastern half.

27:13–14 *toward the sunrise … the entrance.* The entrance to the tabernacle courtyard faced east, as did that of Solomon's temple (see note on 25:9) and of Herod's temple.

27:18 *five cubits.* See TNIV text note; high enough to block the view of people standing outside the courtyard, thus protecting the sanctity and privacy of the worship taking place inside.

27:20 *clear oil of pressed olives.* Unripe olives were crushed in a mortar. The pulpy mass was then placed in a cloth basket through the bottom of which the oil dripped, producing a clear fuel that burned with little or no smoke.

27:21 *tent of meeting.* The tabernacle; it was not a place where God's people met for collective worship but one where God himself met—by appointment, not by accident—with his people (see 29:42–43). *curtain that shields the ark of the covenant law.* See note on 26:31. *lamps burning … from evening till morning.* The lamps were lit in the evening (see 30:8) and apparently extinguished in the morning (1Sa 3:3).

28:1 *Nadab and Abihu.* See note on 24:1. *serve me as priests.* In order "to offer gifts and sacrifices for sins" and "to deal gently with those who are ignorant and are going astray" (Heb 5:1–2). Another important function of the priests was to read the law of Moses to the people and remind them of their covenant obligations (see Dt 31:9–13; Ne 8:2–3; Jer 18:18; Mal 2:5–8).

28:2 *to give him dignity and honor.* The garments were to exalt the office and functions of lesser priests (see v. 40), as well as of the high priest.

28:2 k ver 40
28:3 l Ex 31:6; 35:10,
25,35; 36:1 m Ex 31:3;
Dt 34:9; Isa 11:2;
1Co 12:8; S Eph 1:17
28:4 n ver 15-30
o S Ex 25:7 p ver 31-
35 q ver 39; Lev 10:5
r ver 37
28:5 s Ex 25:4
28:6 t S Ex 25:7
28:8 u Ex 29:5
28:9 v SS 8:6;
Isa 49:16; Hag 2:23
28:12 w Dt 33:12;
Job 31:36 x ver 29;
Ex 30:16; Nu 10:10;
31:54; Jos 4:7;
Zec 6:14
28:15 y S Ex 25:7
28:17 z Eze 28:13;
Rev 21:19-20
a Eze 1:16; 10:9;
Da 10:6
28:21 b Jos 4:8
c Rev 21:12
28:29 d ver 43
28:30 e Lev 8:8;
Nu 27:21; Dt 33:8;
1Sa 28:6; Ezr 2:63;
Ne 7:65

dignity and honor. k 3Tell all the skilled workers l to whom I have given wisdom m in such matters that they are to make garments for Aaron, for his consecration, so he may serve me as priest. 4These are the garments they are to make: a breastpiece, n an ephod, o a robe, p a woven tunic, q a turban r and a sash. They are to make these sacred garments for your brother Aaron and his sons, so they may serve me as priests. 5Have them use gold, and blue, purple and scarlet yarn, and fine linen. s

THE EPHOD

28:6–14pp — Ex 39:2–7

6"Make the ephod t of gold, and of blue, purple and scarlet yarn, and of finely twisted linen—the work of skilled hands. 7It is to have two shoulder pieces attached to two of its corners, so it can be fastened. 8Its skillfully woven waistband u is to be like it—of one piece with the ephod and made with gold, and with blue, purple and scarlet yarn, and with finely twisted linen.

9"Take two onyx stones and engrave v on them the names of the sons of Israel 10in the order of their birth—six names on one stone and the remaining six on the other. 11Engrave the names of the sons of Israel on the two stones the way a gem cutter engraves a seal. Then mount the stones in gold filigree settings 12and fasten them on the shoulder pieces of the ephod as memorial stones for the sons of Israel. Aaron is to bear the names on his shoulders w as a memorial x before the LORD. 13Make gold filigree settings 14and two braided chains of pure gold, like a rope, and attach the chains to the settings.

THE BREASTPIECE

28:15–28pp — Ex 39:8–21

15"Fashion a breastpiece y for making decisions—the work of skilled hands. Make it like the ephod: of gold, and of blue, purple and scarlet yarn, and of finely twisted linen. 16It is to be square—a span a long and a span wide—and folded double. 17Then mount four rows of precious stones z on it. The first row shall be carnelian, chrysolite a and beryl; 18the second row shall be turquoise, lapis lazuli and emerald; 19the third row shall be jacinth, agate and amethyst; 20the fourth row shall be topaz, onyx and jasper. b Mount them in gold filigree settings. 21There are to be twelve stones, one for each of the names of the sons of Israel, b each engraved like a seal with the name of one of the twelve tribes. c

22"For the breastpiece make braided chains of pure gold, like a rope. 23Make two gold rings for it and fasten them to two corners of the breastpiece. 24Fasten the two gold chains to the rings at the corners of the breastpiece, 25and the other ends of the chains to the two settings, attaching them to the shoulder pieces of the ephod at the front. 26Make two gold rings and attach them to the other two corners of the breastpiece on the inside edge next to the ephod. 27Make two more gold rings and attach them to the bottom of the shoulder pieces on the front of the ephod, close to the seam just above the waistband of the ephod. 28The rings of the breastpiece are to be tied to the rings of the ephod with blue cord, connecting it to the waistband, so that the breastpiece will not swing out from the ephod.

29"Whenever Aaron enters the Holy Place, d he will bear the names of the sons of Israel over his heart on the breastpiece of decision as a continuing memorial before the LORD. 30Also put the Urim and the Thummim e in the breastpiece, so they may be over Aaron's heart whenever he enters the presence of the LORD. Thus Aaron will always bear the means of making decisions for the Israelites over his heart before the LORD.

---

a 16 That is, about 9 inches or about 22.5 centimeters   b 20 The precise identification of some of these precious stones is uncertain.

28:6 *ephod.* A sleeveless vestment worn by the high priest. Sometimes the word refers to an otherwise unidentified object of worship (see, e.g., Jdg 8:27; 18:17; Hos 3:4).

28:8 *waistband.* Apparently to hold the front and the back of the ephod to the priest's body.

28:12 *Aaron is to bear the names on his shoulders.* To symbolize the fact that the high priest represents all Israel when he ministers in the tabernacle.

28:15 *for making decisions.* By means of the Urim and Thummim (see note on v. 30).

28:29 *Aaron . . . will bear the names . . . over his heart.* Thus the

nation was doubly represented before the Lord (see v. 12 and note).

28:30 *the Urim and the Thummim.* The Hebrew for this phrase probably means "the curses [traditionally 'lights'] and the perfections." The Hebrew word *Urim* begins with the first letter of the Hebrew alphabet (*aleph*), and *Thummim* begins with the last letter (*taw*). They were sacred lots and were often used in times of crisis to determine the will of God (see Nu 27:21). It has been suggested that if Urim ("curses") dominated when the lots were cast the answer was "no," but if Thummim ("perfections") dominated it was "yes." In any event, their "every decision" was "from the LORD" (Pr 16:33; see note there).

OTHER PRIESTLY GARMENTS

28:31–43pp — Ex 39:22–31

31"Make the robe of the ephod entirely of blue cloth, 32with an opening for the head in its center. There shall be a woven edge like a collar[a] around this opening, so that it will not tear. 33Make pomegranates [f] of blue, purple and scarlet yarn around the hem of the robe, with gold bells between them. 34The gold bells and the pomegranates are to alternate around the hem of the robe. 35Aaron must wear it when he ministers. The sound of the bells will be heard when he enters the Holy Place before the LORD and when he comes out, so that he will not die.

36"Make a plate [g] of pure gold and engrave on it as on a seal: HOLY TO THE LORD. [h] 37Fasten a blue cord to it to attach it to the turban; it is to be on the front of the turban. 38It will be on Aaron's forehead, and he will bear the guilt [i] involved in the sacred gifts the Israelites consecrate, whatever their gifts may be. It will be on Aaron's forehead continually so that they will be acceptable [j] to the LORD.

39"Weave the tunic [k] of fine linen and make the turban [l] of fine linen. The sash is to be the work of an embroiderer. 40Make tunics, sashes and caps for Aaron's sons [m] to give them dignity and honor. [n] 41After you put these clothes [o] on your brother Aaron and his sons, anoint [p] and ordain them. Consecrate them so they may serve me as priests. [q]

42"Make linen undergarments [r] as a covering for the body, reaching from the waist to the thigh. 43Aaron and his sons must wear them whenever they enter the tent of meeting [s] or approach the altar to minister in the Holy Place, [t] so that they will not incur guilt and die. [u]

"This is to be a lasting ordinance [v] for Aaron and his descendants.

CONSECRATION OF THE PRIESTS

29:1–37pp — Lev 8:1–36

29 "This is what you are to do to consecrate [w] them, so they may serve me as priests: Take a young bull and two rams without defect. [x] 2And from the finest wheat flour make round loaves without yeast, thick loaves without yeast and with olive oil mixed in, and thin loaves without yeast and brushed with olive oil. [y] 3Put them in a basket and present them along with the bull and the two rams. [z] 4Then bring Aaron and his sons to the entrance to the tent of meeting and wash them with water. [a] 5Take the garments [b] and dress Aaron with the tunic, the robe of the ephod, the ephod itself and the breastpiece. Fasten the ephod on him by its skillfully woven waistband. [c] 6Put the turban [d] on his head and attach the sacred emblem [e] to the turban. 7Take the anointing oil [f] and anoint him by pouring it on his head. 8Bring his sons and dress them in tunics [g] 9and fasten caps on them. Then tie sashes on Aaron and his sons. [b] [h] The priesthood is theirs by a lasting ordinance. [i] Then you shall ordain Aaron and his sons.

10"Bring the bull to the front of the tent of meeting, and Aaron and his sons shall lay their hands on its head. [j] 11Slaughter it in the LORD's presence [k] at the entrance to the tent of meeting. 12Take some of the bull's blood and put it on the horns [l] of the altar with your finger, and pour out the rest of it at the base of the altar. [m] 13Then take all the fat [n] on the internal organs, [o] the long lobe of the liver, and both kidneys with the fat on them, and

---

[a] 32 The meaning of the Hebrew for this word is uncertain.   [b] 9 Hebrew; Septuagint *on them*

29:13 6:12; 7:3,5,31; 9:10; Nu 18:17; 1Sa 2:15; 1Ki 8:64; 2Ch 7:7; 29:35; 35:14; Isa 43:24; Eze 44:15 [o]S Ex 12:9

28:31 *robe.* Worn under the ephod.
28:35 According to Jewish tradition, one end of a length of rope was tied to the high priest's ankle and the other remained outside the tabernacle. If the bells on his robe stopped tinkling while he was in the Holy Place, the assumption that he had died could be tested by pulling gently on the rope.
28:36 HOLY TO THE LORD. See 3:5 and note; 39:30; Zec 14:20 and note.
28:38 *bear the guilt.* Symbolically.
28:39 *tunic.* Worn under the robe.
28:40 *to give them dignity and honor.* See note on v. 2.
28:42–43 See note on 20:26.
28:43 *tent of meeting.* See note on 27:21.
29:1 *consecrate them.* See note on 19:10–11. *without defect.* See note on 12:5.

29:4 *tent of meeting.* See note on 27:21. *wash them with water.* Symbolizing the removal of ceremonial uncleanness (cf. Heb 10:22) and thus signifying the purity that must characterize them.
29:7 *anoint him.* Symbolizing spiritual endowment for serving God (see 28:41; Isa 61:1 and note).
29:10 *Bring the bull.* As a sin offering (see v. 14) to atone for the past sins of Aaron and his sons (see Lev 4:3 and note). *lay their hands on its head.* As a symbol of (1) the animal's becoming their substitute and (2) transferring their sins to the sin-bearer (see Lev 16:20–22 and note).
29:12 *horns of the altar.* See note on 27:2.
29:13 *fat.* The most select parts of the bull (see Lev 3:3–5,16) were burned on the altar as a sacrifice to the Lord.

28:33 [f]Nu 13:23;
1Sa 14:2; 1Ki 7:18;
SS 4:3; Jer 52:22;
Joel 1:12; Hag 2:19
28:36 [g]ver 37;
Ex 29:6; Lev 8:9
[h]Zec 14:20
28:38 [i]Lev 5:1;
10:17; 16:22; 22:9,16;
Nu 18:1; Isa 53:5,6,
11; Eze 4:4-6;
Heb 9:28; 1Pe 2:24
[j]S Ge 32:20;
Lev 22:20,27; 23:11;
Isa 56:7
28:39 [k]ver 4
[l]Ex 29:6; Lev 16:4;
Eze 24:17,23; 44:18
28:40 [m]ver 4;
Ex 29:8-9; 39:41;
40:14; Lev 8:13 [n]ver 2
28:41 [o]Ex 40:13
[p]Ex 29:7; Lev 6:20;
10:7; 21:12; Nu 35:25
[q]Ex 29:7-9; 30:30;
40:15; Lev 4:3; 6:22;
8:1:36; Nu 3:3;
Heb 7:28
28:42 [r]Lev 6:10;
16:4,23; Eze 44:18
28:43 [s]S Ex 25:22
[t]ver 29 [u]Ex 30:20,21;
Lev 16:13; 22:9;
Nu 1:51; 4:15,20;
18:22 [v]S Ex 27:21
29:1 [w]ver 21,44;
Lev 20:7; Jos 3:5;
1Ch 15:12 [x]Eze 43:23
29:2 [y]ver 23;
Lev 2:1,4; 6:19-23;
Nu 6:15
29:3 [z]ver 15,19
29:4 [a]Ex 40:12;
Lev 14:8; 16:4;
Heb 10:22
29:5 [b]S Ex 28:2
[c]Ex 28:8
29:6 [d]Ex 28:39;
Isa 3:23; Zec 3:5
[e]S Ex 28:36
29:7 [f]ver 21;
S Ex 28:41; 30:25,30,
31; 37:29; 40:9;
Lev 21:10; 1Sa 10:1;
1Ki 1:39; Ps 89:20;
133:2; 141:5
29:8 [g]S Ex 28:4;
Lev 16:4
29:9 [h]Ex 28:40
[i]S Ex 27:21; 40:15;
Nu 3:10; 18:7; 25:13;
Dt 18:5; Jdg 17:5;
1Sa 2:30; 1Ki 12:31
29:10 [j]ver 19;
Lev 1:4; 4:15; 16:21;
Nu 8:12
29:11 [k]Lev 1:5,11;
4:24; 6:16,25; 14:13
29:12 [l]S Ex 27:2
[m]Lev 4:7; 9:9
29:13 [n]ver 22;
Lev 1:8; 3:3,5,9; 4:10;

29:14 *p* Na 3:6;
Mal 2:3 *q* Lev 4:12,21;
16:27; Nu 19:3-5;
Heb 13:11
29:15 *r* S ver 3
s ver 10; Lev 3:2;
2Ch 29:23
29:17 *t* Lev 1:9,13
29:18 *u* S Ge 8:21;
2Co 2:15
29:19 *v* S ver 3
w S ver 10
29:20 *x* Lev 14:14,25
y ver 16; Lev 1:5,11; 3:2
29:21 *z* Heb 9:22
a S ver 7 *b* S ver 1
29:22 *c* S ver 13
29:24 *d* Lev 7:30;
9:21; 10:15; 14:12;
23:11,20; Nu 6:20;
8:11,13,15
29:25 *e* ver 18
29:26 *f* Lev 7:31-34
29:27 *g* Ex 22:29;
Lev 7:31,34; Nu 18:11,
12; Dt 18:3
29:28 *h* ver 22-27;
Lev 7:30,34; 10:15
29:29 *i* S Ex 28:2;
S Lev 16:4 *j* Nu 20:28
29:30 *k* Lev 6:22;
Nu 3:3; 20:28
29:31 *l* Lev 7:37;
2Ch 13:9 *m* Lev 10:14;
Nu 19:9; Eze 42:13
29:32 *n* Mt 12:4
29:33 *o* Lev 22:10,13
29:34 *p* S Ex 12:10
29:36 *q* Heb 10:11
r ver 33,37; Ex 30:10;
Lev 1:4; 4:20; 16:16;
Nu 6:11; 8:12,19; 16:46;
25:13; 2Ch 29:24
s Ex 40:10; Nu 7:10
29:37 *t* Ex 30:28-
29; 40:10; Eze 43:25;
Mt 23:19
29:38 *u* ver 23:2;
Nu 28:3-8; 1Ch 16:40;
2Ch 8:13; Eze 46:13-
15; Da 12:11
29:39 *v* Nu 28:4,8;
1Ki 18:36; 2Ch 13:11;
Ezr 3:3; Ps 141:2;
Da 9:21
29:40 *w* Ex 30:24;
Nu 15:4; 28:5
x S Ge 35:14;
Lev 23:37; 2Ki 16:13
29:41 *y* 1Ki 18:29,36;
2Ki 3:20; 16:15;
Ezr 9:4,5; Ps 141:2;
Da 9:21 *z* Lev 2:1; 5:13;
10:12; Nu 4:16; 6:17;
1Ki 8:64; Isa 43:2
29:42 *a* Ex 30:8,10,
21,31; 31:13
b Eze 46:15
c S Ex 26:1; S 27:21
d ver 43; Ex 25:22;
33:9,11; Nu 7:89
29:43 *e* Ex 33:18;
40:34; Lev 9:6;
1Ki 8:11; 2Ch 5:14;
7:2; Ps 26:8; 85:9;
Eze 1:28; 43:5;
Hag 1:8; 2:7

burn them on the altar. [14]But burn the bull's flesh and its hide and its intestines[p] outside the camp. [q] It is a sin offering. [a]

[15]"Take one of the rams, [r] and Aaron and his sons shall lay their hands on its head. [s] [16]Slaughter it and take the blood and splash it against the sides of the altar. [17]Cut the ram into pieces and wash [t] the internal organs and the legs, putting them with the head and the other pieces. [18]Then burn the entire ram on the altar. It is a burnt offering to the LORD, a pleasing aroma, [u] a food offering presented to the LORD.

[19]"Take the other ram, [v] and Aaron and his sons shall lay their hands on its head. [w] [20]Slaughter it, take some of its blood and put it on the lobes of the right ears of Aaron and his sons, on the thumbs of their right hands, and on the big toes of their right feet. [x] Then splash blood against the sides of the altar. [y] [21]And take some blood [z] from the altar and some of the anointing oil [a] and sprinkle it on Aaron and his garments and on his sons and their garments. Then he and his sons and their garments will be consecrated. [b]

[22]"Take from this ram the fat, [c] the fat tail, the fat on the internal organs, the long lobe of the liver, both kidneys with the fat on them, and the right thigh. (This is the ram for the ordination.) [23]From the basket of bread made without yeast, which is before the LORD, take one round loaf, one thick loaf with olive oil mixed in, and one thin loaf. [24]Put all these in the hands of Aaron and his sons and have them wave them before the LORD as a wave offering. [d] [25]Then take them from their hands and burn them on the altar along with the burnt offering for a pleasing aroma to the LORD, a food offering presented to the LORD. [e] [26]After you take the breast of the ram for Aaron's ordination, wave it before the LORD as a wave offering, and it will be your share. [f]

[27]"Consecrate those parts of the ordination ram that belong to Aaron and his sons: [g] the breast that was waved and the thigh that was presented. [28]This is always to be the perpetual share from the Israelites for Aaron and his sons. It is the contribution the Israelites are to make to the LORD from their fellowship offerings. [h]

[29]"Aaron's sacred garments [i] will belong to his descendants so that they can be anointed and ordained in them. [j] [30]The son [k] who succeeds him as priest and comes to the tent of meeting to minister in the Holy Place is to wear them seven days.

[31]"Take the ram [l] for the ordination and cook the meat in a sacred place. [m] [32]At the entrance to the tent of meeting, Aaron and his sons are to eat the meat of the ram and the bread [n] that is in the basket. [33]They are to eat these offerings by which atonement was made for their ordination and consecration. But no one else may eat [o] them, because they are sacred. [34]And if any of the meat of the ordination ram or any bread is left over till morning, [p] burn it up. It must not be eaten, because it is sacred.

[35]"Do for Aaron and his sons everything I have commanded you, taking seven days to ordain them. [36]Sacrifice a bull each day [q] as a sin offering to make atonement [r]. Purify the altar by making atonement for it, and anoint it to consecrate [s] it. [37]For seven days make atonement for the altar and consecrate it. Then the altar will be most holy, and whatever touches it will be holy. [t]

[38]"This is what you are to offer on the altar regularly each day: [u] two lambs a year old. [39]Offer one in the morning and the other at twilight. [v] [40]With the first lamb offer a tenth of an ephah [b] of the finest flour mixed with a quarter of a hin [c] of oil [w] from pressed olives, and a quarter of a hin of wine as a drink offering. [x] [41]Sacrifice the other lamb at twilight [y] with the same grain offering [z] and its drink offering as in the morning—a pleasing aroma, a food offering presented to the LORD.

[42]"For the generations to come [a] this burnt offering is to be made regularly [b] at the entrance to the tent of meeting [c] before the LORD. There I will meet you and speak to you; [d] [43]there also I will meet with the Israelites, and the place will be consecrated by my glory. [e]

[44]"So I will consecrate the tent of meeting and the altar and will consecrate Aaron and

---

a 14 Or *purification offering*; also in verse 36   *b 40* That is, probably about 3 1/2 pounds or about 1.6 kilograms   *c 40* That is, probably about 1 quart or about 0.9 liter

---

29:14 *flesh ... hide ... intestines.* Thought of as bearing sin, and thus burned outside the camp (see Heb 13:11–13 and notes).

29:18 *burn the entire ram.* Symbolizing total dedication.

29:20 *right ears.* Symbolizing sensitivity to God and his word. *right hands ... right feet.* Symbolizing a life of service to others on God's behalf.

29:24 *wave offering.* See note on Lev 7:30–32.

29:28 *perpetual share ... for Aaron and his sons.* Parts of certain sacrificial animals were set aside as food for the priests and their families (see Lev 10:14).

29:31 *a sacred place.* Probably the tabernacle courtyard.

29:36 *making atonement for it.* Because the altar was corrupted by the sins of the people (see Lev 16:16; Heb 9:21–22).

29:37 *holy ... holy.* Set apart as consecrated to the Lord (see note on 3:5).

29:38–39 *Institution of the daily morning and evening offerings—sometimes observed even during days of apostasy (see 2Ki 16:15).

29:42–43 *I will meet.* See note on 27:21.

29:43 *my glory.* Symbolic of God's presence over the ark of the covenant (see note on 25:10; see also 40:34–35; 1Ki 8:10–13).

his sons to serve me as priests.[f] [45]Then I will dwell[g] among the Israelites and be their God.[h] [46]They will know that I am the LORD their God, who brought them out of Egypt[i] so that I might dwell among them. I am the LORD their God.[j]

THE ALTAR OF INCENSE
30:1–5pp — Ex 37:25–28

30 "Make an altar[k] of acacia wood for burning incense.[l] [2]It is to be square, a cubit long and a cubit wide, and two cubits high[a]—its horns[m] of one piece with it. [3]Overlay the top and all the sides and the horns with pure gold, and make a gold molding around it.[n] [4]Make two gold rings[o] for the altar below the molding—two on each of the opposite sides—to hold the poles used to carry it. [5]Make the poles of acacia wood and overlay them with gold.[p] [6]Put the altar in front of the curtain that shields the ark of the covenant law—before the atonement cover[q] that is over the tablets of the covenant law—where I will meet with you.

[7]"Aaron must burn fragrant incense[r] on the altar every morning when he tends the lamps. [8]He must burn incense again when he lights the lamps at twilight so incense will burn regularly before the LORD for the generations to come.[s] [9]Do not offer on this altar any other incense[t] or any burnt offering or grain offering, and do not pour a drink offering on it. [10]Once a year[u] Aaron shall make atonement[v] on its horns. This annual atonement must be made with the blood of the atoning sin offering[b] [w] for the generations to come.[x] It is most holy to the LORD."

ATONEMENT MONEY

[11]Then the LORD said to Moses, [12]"When you take a census[y] of the Israelites to count them, each one must pay the LORD a ransom[z] for his life at the time he is counted. Then no plague[a] will come on them when you number them. [13]Each one who crosses over to those already counted is to give a half shekel,[c] according to the sanctuary shekel,[b] which weighs twenty gerahs. This half shekel is an offering to the LORD. [14]All who cross over, those twenty years old or more,[c] are to give an offering to the LORD. [15]The rich are not to give more than a half shekel and the poor are not to give less[d] when you make the offering to the LORD to atone for your lives. [16]Receive the atonement[e] money from the Israelites and use it for the service of the tent of meeting.[f] It will be a memorial[g] for the Israelites before the LORD, making atonement for your lives."

BASIN FOR WASHING

[17]Then the LORD said to Moses, [18]"Make a bronze basin,[h] with its bronze stand, for washing. Place it between the tent of meeting and the altar, and put water in it. [19]Aaron and his sons are to wash their hands and feet[i] with water[j] from it. [20]Whenever they enter the tent of meeting, they shall wash with water so that they will not die.[k] Also, when they approach the altar to minister by presenting a food offering to the LORD, [21]they shall wash their hands and feet so that they will not die. This is to be a lasting ordinance[l] for Aaron and his descendants for the generations to come."[m]

---

[a] 2 That is, about 1 1/2 feet long and wide and 3 feet high or about 45 centimeters long and wide and 90 centimeters high   [b] 10 Or *purification offering*   [c] 13 That is, about 1/5 ounce or about 5.7 grams; also in verse 15

29:44 [f] S ver 1
29:45 [g] S Ex 25:8;
Nu 35:34; Jn 14:17;
S Ro 8:10 [h] S Ge 17:7;
2Co 6:16
29:46 [i] S Ex 6:6;
19:4-6; Dt 5:6;
Ps 114:1; Hag 2:5
[j] S Ge 17:7
30:1 [k] Ex 40:5,26;
Nu 4:11; 1Ki 6:20;
Eze 41:22 [l] S Ex 25:6;
37:29; Lk 1:11;
Heb 9:4; Rev 8:3
30:2 [m] S Ex 27:2;
Rev 9:13
30:3 [n] S Ex 25:11
30:4 [o] S Ex 25:12
30:5 [p] S Ex 25:13
30:6 [q] S Ex 25:22;
S 26:34
30:7 [r] S Ex 25:6;
40:27; Nu 3:10;
Dt 33:10; 1Sa 2:28;
1Ch 6:49; 2Ch 2:4;
26:18; 29:7
30:8 [s] S Ex 25:37;
S 29:42
30:9 [t] Lev 10:1;
Nu 16:7,40
30:10 [u] Lev 16:2
[v] Lev 9:7; 16:18-19,
30; 23:27,28; 25:9
[w] Ex 29:14; Lev 4:3;
6:25; 7:7; 8:2,14;
Nu 6:11 [x] S Ex 29:42
30:12 [y] S Ex 38:25;
Nu 1:2,49; 4:2,29;
14:29; 26:2; 31:26;
2Sa 24:1; 2Ki 12:4
[z] Ex 38:26; Nu 31:50;
S Mt 20:28
[a] Nu 14:12; Dt 28:58-
61; 2Sa 24:13;
1Ki 8:37
30:13 [b] ver 24;
Ex 38:24,26;
Lev 5:15; 27:3,25;
Nu 3:47; 7:13; 18:16;
Eze 4:10; 45:12;
Mt 17:24
30:14 [c] S Ex 38:26;
Nu 1:3,18; 14:29;
26:2; 32:11; 2Ch 25:5
30:15 [d] Pr 22:2;
Eph 6:9
30:16 [e] ver 12
[f] Ex 38:25-28;
2Ch 24:5 [g] Nu 31:54
30:18 [h] Ex 31:9;
35:16; 38:8; 39:39;
40:7,30; 1Ki 7:38;
2Ch 4:6
30:19 [i] Ex 40:31-32;
Jn 13:10 / Ex 29:4;
40:12; Lev 8:6;
Ps 26:6; Heb 10:22
30:20 [k] S Ex 28:43
30:21 [l] S Ex 27:21
[m] Ex 29:42

29:45–46 *dwell among.* See note on 25:9.
29:45 *I will … be their God.* Commonly denotes the essence of the divine promise pledged in his covenant with his people (see note on 6:7).
29:46 *I am the LORD … who brought them out.* See note on 20:2.

30:1 *incense.* Its fragrant smoke symbolized the prayers of God's people (see Ps 141:2; Lk 1:10; Rev 5:8; 8:3–4).
30:3 *gold.* See note on 26:37.
30:4 *rings.* See note on 25:12.
30:6 *curtain that shields the ark of the covenant law.* See notes on 25:16,22; 26:31.
30:10 *annual atonement.* See Lev 16:34 and note. *holy to the LORD.* See 29:37 and note.

30:12 *take a census.* Perhaps such censuses were taken on various occasions (and at stated intervals) to enter the

Israelites into an official roll for public duties in the Lord's service (see Nu 1:2; 26:2). *pay … a ransom for his life.* An extension of the principle stated in 13:13,15 (see note on 13:13). Jesus gave "his life as a ransom for many" (see Mt 20:28; Mk 10:45 and notes; cf. 1Ti 2:5–6).
30:13 *shekel.* A unit of weight, not a coin (see note on Ge 20:16). *according to the sanctuary shekel.* In keeping with the standard weights used at the tabernacle. They may have differed slightly from those used in the marketplace.
30:14 *twenty years old or more.* Of military age (see Nu 1:3).
30:16 *tent of meeting.* See note on 27:21. *atonement.* See note on 25:17.
30:18 *basin.* Made from bronze mirrors contributed by Israelite women (see 38:8). *washing.* See note on 29:4.

30:23 *n* S Ge 43:11
o S Ge 37:25
p Pr 7:17; SS 4:14
q SS 4:14; Isa 43:24;
Jer 6:20
30:24 *r* S ver 13
s Ps 45:8; Eze 27:19
30:25 *t* ver 35;
Ex 37:29; 1Ch 9:30
u S Ex 29:7;
S 1Sa 9:16
30:26 *v* Ex 40:9;
Lev 8:10; Nu 7:1
30:29 *w* Ex 8:10-11
x Ex 29:37; Lev 6:18,
27; Mt 23:17
30:30 *y* Ex 29:7;
Lev 8:2,12,30; 10:7;
16:32; 21:10,12;
1Ch 15:12; Ps 133:2
z S Ex 29:42
30:31 *a* S Ex 29:7
b S Ex 29:42
30:32 *c* ver 25,37
30:33 *d* ver 38;
S Ge 17:14
30:34 *e* SS 3:6
30:35 *f* S Ex 25:6
g S ver 25
30:36 *h* S Ex 25:22
i ver 32; Ex 29:37;
Lev 2:3
30:37 *j* S ver 32
30:38 *k* S ver 33
31:2 *l* Ex 36:1,2;
37:1; 38:22; 1Ch 2:20;
2Ch 1:5 *m* S Ex 17:10
31:3 *n* S Ex 28:3
o 1Ki 7:14; 1Co 12:4
31:6 *p* Ex 36:1,2;
38:23 *q* 1Ki 7:14;
2Ch 2:14 *r* S Ex 28:3
31:7 *s* Ex 36:8-38
t Ex 37:1-5 *u* Ex 37:6;
40:20
31:8 *v* Ex 37:10-16
w Ex 37:24;
Lev 24:4 *x* Ex 37:25-
28
31:9 *y* Ex 38:3;
Nu 4:14 *z* S Ex 30:18
31:10 *a* S Ex 28:2
31:11 *b* Ex 30:22-
32; 37:29 *c* S Ex 25:6
d S Ex 25:9
31:13 *e* S Ex 20:8
f ver 17; Isa 56:4;
Eze 20:12,20
g S Ex 29:42
h Lev 11:44; 20:8;
21:8; Eze 37:28
31:14 *i* Ex 35:2;
Nu 15:32-36
31:15 *j* S Ex 20:8-11;
35:2; Lev 16:29; 23:3;
Nu 29:7 *k* S Ge 2:3

ANOINTING OIL

22Then the LORD said to Moses, 23"Take the following fine spices: *n* 500 shekels *a* of liquid myrrh, *o* half as much (that is, 250 shekels) of fragrant cinnamon, *p* 250 shekels *b* of fragrant calamus, *q* 24500 shekels *r* of cassia *s*—all according to the sanctuary shekel—and a hin *c* of olive oil. 25Make these into a sacred anointing oil, a fragrant blend, the work of a perfumer. *t* It will be the sacred anointing oil. *u* 26Then use it to anoint *v* the tent of meeting, the ark of the covenant law, 27the table and all its articles, the lampstand and its accessories, the altar of incense, 28the altar of burnt offering and all its utensils, and the basin with its stand. 29You shall consecrate them *w* so they will be most holy, and whatever touches them will be holy. *x*

30"Anoint Aaron and his sons and consecrate *y* them so they may serve me as priests. *z* 31Say to the Israelites, 'This is to be my sacred anointing oil *a* for the generations to come. *b* 32Do not pour it on anyone else's body and do not make any other oil using the same formula. It is sacred, and you are to consider it sacred. *c* 33Whoever makes perfume like it and puts it on anyone other than a priest must be cut off *d* from their people.' "

INCENSE

34Then the LORD said to Moses, "Take fragrant spices *e*—gum resin, onycha and galbanum—and pure frankincense, all in equal amounts, 35and make a fragrant blend of incense, *f* the work of a perfumer. *g* It is to be salted and pure and sacred. 36Grind some of it to powder and place it in front of the ark of the covenant law in the tent of meeting, where I will meet *h* with you. It shall be most holy *i* to you. 37Do not make any incense with this formula for yourselves; consider it holy *j* to the LORD. 38Whoever makes incense like it to enjoy its fragrance must be cut off *k* from their people."

BEZALEL AND OHOLIAB

31:2–6pp — Ex 35:30–35

31 Then the LORD said to Moses, 2"See, I have chosen Bezalel *l* son of Uri, the son of Hur, *m* of the tribe of Judah, 3and I have filled him with the Spirit of God, with wisdom, with understanding, with knowledge *n* and with all kinds of skills *o*— 4to make artistic designs for work in gold, silver and bronze, 5to cut and set stones, to work in wood, and to engage in all kinds of crafts. 6Moreover, I have appointed Oholiab *p* son of Ahisamak, of the tribe of Dan, *q* to help him. Also I have given ability to all the skilled workers *r* to make everything I have commanded you: 7the tent of meeting, *s* the ark of the covenant law *t* with the atonement cover *u* on it, and all the other furnishings of the tent— 8the table *v* and its articles, the pure gold lampstand *w* and all its accessories, the altar of incense, *x* 9the altar of burnt offering *y* and all its utensils, the basin *z* with its stand— 10and also the woven garments *a*, both the sacred garments for Aaron the priest and the garments for his sons when they serve as priests, 11and the anointing oil *b* and fragrant incense *c* for the Holy Place. They are to make them just as I commanded *d* you."

THE SABBATH

12Then the LORD said to Moses, 13"Say to the Israelites, 'You must observe my Sabbaths. *e* This will be a sign *f* between me and you for the generations to come, *g* so you may know that I am the LORD, who makes you holy. *h*

14" 'Observe the Sabbath, because it is holy to you. Anyone who desecrates it is to be put to death; *i* those who do any work on that day must be cut off from their people. 15For six days work *j* is to be done, but the seventh day is a day of sabbath rest, *k* holy to the LORD.

---

a 23 That is, about 12 1/2 pounds or about 5.8 kilograms; also in verse 24   *b 23* That is, about 6 1/4 pounds or about 2.9 kilograms   *c 24* That is, probably about 1 gallon or about 3.6 liters

---

30:23–24 *myrrh…cinnamon…calamus…cassia.* See note on 25:6.
30:29 *holy…holy.* See 29:37 and note.
30:33 *cut off from their people.* See note on 12:15.
30:34 *gum resin, onycha and galbanum.* See note on 25:6. *frankincense.* A resin from the bark of *Boswellia carteri,* which grows in southern Arabia.
31:2 *Bezalel.* Means "in the shadow/protection of God." *Hur.* See note on 17:10.
31:3 *filled him with the Spirit of God.* Ability to work skillfully in all kinds of crafts was a spiritual gift, equipping a person for special service to God. *wisdom.* See Pr 1:2 and note.
31:6 *Oholiab.* Means "The (divine) father is my tent/ tabernacle." The names of Bezalel (see note on v. 2) and Oholiab were appropriate for the chief craftsmen working on the tabernacle.
31:7 *tent of meeting.* See note on 27:21.
31:13 *observe my Sabbaths.* Instructions for building the tabernacle and making the priestly garments are concluded by impressing on the Israelites the importance and necessity of keeping the Sabbath even while carrying out this special task. *makes you holy.* See 19:6; 29:37 and notes.
31:14 *cut off from their people.* See note on 12:15.

Whoever does any work on the Sabbath day is to be put to death. ¹⁶The Israelites are to observe the Sabbath, *ᶦ* celebrating it for the generations to come as a lasting covenant. ¹⁷It will be a sign *ᵐ* between me and the Israelites forever, for in six days the LORD made the heavens and the earth, and on the seventh day he abstained from work and rested. *ⁿ* " *ᵒ*

¹⁸When the LORD finished speaking to Moses on Mount Sinai, *ᵖ* he gave him the two tablets of the covenant law, the tablets of stone *�q* inscribed by the finger of God. *ʳ*

THE GOLDEN CALF

32 When the people saw that Moses was so long in coming down from the mountain, *ˢ* they gathered around Aaron and said, "Come, make us gods *ᵃ* who will go before *ᵗ* us. As for this fellow Moses who brought us up out of Egypt, we don't know what has happened to him." *ᵘ*

²Aaron answered them, "Take off the gold earrings *ᵛ* that your wives, your sons and your daughters are wearing, and bring them to me." ³So all the people took off their earrings and brought them to Aaron. ⁴He took what they handed him and made it into an idol *ʷ* cast in the shape of a calf, *ˣ* fashioning it with a tool. Then they said, "These are your gods, *ᵇ ʸ* Israel, who brought you up out of Egypt." *ᶻ*

⁵When Aaron saw this, he built an altar in front of the calf and announced, "Tomorrow there will be a festival *ᵃ* to the LORD." ⁶So the next day the people rose early and sacrificed burnt offerings and presented fellowship offerings. *ᵇ* Afterward they sat down to eat and drink *ᶜ* and got up to indulge in revelry. *ᵈ*

⁷Then the LORD said to Moses, "Go down, because your people, whom you brought up out of Egypt, *ᵉ* have become corrupt. *ᶠ* ⁸They have been quick to turn away *ᵍ* from what I commanded them and have made themselves an idol *ʰ* cast in the shape of a calf. *ᶦ* They have bowed down to it and sacrificed *ʲ* to it and have said, 'These are your gods, Israel, who brought you up out of Egypt.' *ᵏ*

⁹"I have seen these people," the LORD said to Moses, "and they are a stiff-necked *ᶦ* people. ¹⁰Now leave me alone *ᵐ* so that my anger may burn against them and that I may destroy *ⁿ* them. Then I will make you into a great nation." *ᵒ*

¹¹But Moses sought the favor *ᵖ* of the LORD his God. "LORD," he said, "why should your anger burn against your people, whom you brought out of Egypt with great power and a

---

ᵃ 1 Or *a god; also in verses 23 and 31*   *ᵇ 4* Or *This is your god; also in verse 8*

32:9 36:13; Ne 9:16; Ps 78:8; Pr 29:1; Isa 46:12; 48:4; Jer 7:26; Eze 2:4; Hos 4:16; Ac 7:51   **32:10** ᵐ1Sa 2:25; Jer 7:16; 11:14; 14:11   *ⁿ Ex 22:24; 33:3,5; Nu 16:21,45; Dt 9:14,19; Ps 106:23; Jer 14:12; Eze 20:13 ᵒNu 14:12; Dt 9:14   **32:11** *ᵖDt 9:18; 2Sa 21:1; 2Ch 15:2; Ps 9:10; 34:4; 106:23; Isa 9:13; Jer 15:1*

31:16 ᶦS Ex 20:8
31:17 ᵐS ver 13
ⁿS Ge 2:2-3
ᵒS Ge 2:2; S Ex 20:9;
Isa 56:2; 58:13; 66:23;
Jer 17:21-22;
Eze 20:12,20
31:18 ᵖS Ex 19:11
�q S Ex 24:12; 2Co 3:3;
Heb 9:4 ʳEx 32:15-
16; 34:1,28; Dt 4:13;
9:10
32:1 ˢS Ge 7:4;
Dt 9:9-12 ᵗS Ex 13:21
ᵘver 23; Ac 7:40*
32:2 ᵛJdg 8:24-27
32:4 ʷS Ex 20:23;
Jdg 17:3-4; Isa 30:22
ˣver 8,24,35;
Dt 9:16; Ne 9:18;
Ps 106:19; Ac 7:41
ʸEx 20:23; Isa 42:17
ᶻ1Ki 12:28; 14:9;
2Ki 10:29; 17:16;
2Ch 13:8; Hos 8:6;
10:5
32:5 ᵃLev 23:2,37;
2Ki 10:20; Joel 2:15
32:6 ᵇEx 20:24;
34:15; Lev 3:1; 4:10;
6:12; 9:4; 22:21;
Nu 6:14; 25:2;
Dt 27:7; Jdg 20:26;
Eze 43:27; Ac 7:41
ᶜJdg 19:4; Ru 3:3;
1Sa 1:9; 2Sa 11:11;
1Ki 13:23; 18:42;
Ne 8:12; Job 1:4;
Ecc 5:18; 8:15;
Jer 16:8 ᵈver 17-19;
1Co 10:7*
32:7 ᵉver 4,11;
Ex 33:1 ᶠS Ge 6:11-12;
Eze 20:8
32:8 ᵍJer 7:26;
16:12; Mal 2:8; 3:7
ʰS Ex 20:4 ᶦS ver 4
ʲEx 22:20 ᵏ1Ki 12:28;
Eze 23:8
32:9 ᶦEx 33:3,5;
34:9; Dt 9:6,13; 10:16;
31:27; Jdg 2:19;
2Ki 17:14; 2Ch 30:8;

31:16–17 *covenant … sign.* In their rhythm of work and rest in the service of God, the Israelites were to emulate God's pattern in creation as an ever-renewed sign of their covenant with God (see note on Ge 9:12).

B **31:18** *two tablets.* In keeping with ancient Near Eastern practice, these were probably duplicates of the covenant document, not two sections of the Ten Commandments. One copy belonged to each party of the covenant. Since Israel's copy was to be laid up in the presence of God (according to custom), both covenant tablets (God's and Israel's) were placed in the ark (see 25:21). *covenant law.* See notes on 16:34; 25:16. *inscribed by the finger of God.* Because it was God's covenant (see 19:5–6 and notes), and the stipulations of the covenant (20:1–17) were his.
32:1 *so long.* Forty days and forty nights (see 24:18 and note). *they.* Probably the tribe and clan leaders. *gods.* See TNIV text note. *Moses who brought us up out of Egypt.* A rebellious contrast to the gracious statement of Israel's covenant Lord (see 20:2 and note; 29:46).
32:2 *gold earrings.* Probably part of the plunder brought from Egypt (see 3:21–22 and note on 3:21; 11:2–3; 12:35–36).

B **32:4** *cast in the shape of a calf.* Either gold plating over a carved wooden calf (it was later burned, v. 20) or crudely cast in solid gold and then further shaped with a tool, later to be melted down in the fire. The calf was probably similar to representations of the Egyptian bull-god Apis (see note on Jer 46:15). Its manufacture was a flagrant violation of the second commandment (20:4–5; see notes there). *they.* The leaders among the people (see note on v. 1). *These are your gods … up out of Egypt.* A parody of 20:2 (see note on v. 1). Centuries later,

King Jeroboam would quote these words when he set up two golden calves in the northern kingdom of Israel (see 1Ki 12:28–29 and notes).
32:5 *altar in front of the calf … festival to the LORD.* Apparently Aaron recognized the idolatrous consequences of his deed and acted quickly to keep the people from turning completely away from the Lord.

A **32:6** *they sat down … indulge in revelry.* A pagan symbol evoked pagan religious practices. Paul quotes this sentence as a vivid example of Israel's tendency toward idolatry (see 1Co 10:7 and note). The Hebrew verb translated "indulge in revelry" often has sexual connotations (see, e.g., "caressing," Ge 26:8). Immoral orgies frequently accompanied pagan worship in ancient times.
32:7,9 *your people … these people.* By not calling Israel "my people" (as, e.g., in 3:10), God indicates that he is disowning them for breaking his covenant with them (see note on 17:4).
32:7 *corrupt.* And, therefore, ripe for destruction (see v. 10; Ge 6:11–13).
32:9 *stiff-necked.* Like unresponsive oxen or horses (see Jer 27:11–12; see also note on Ne 3:5).
32:10 *I will make you into a great nation.* After Israel—Abraham's descendants—has been destroyed, God will transfer to Moses the pledge originally given to Abraham (see Ge 12:2).

A C **32:11** *your people.* Using God's own words (see v. 7 and note on vv.7,9), Moses appeals to God's special relationship to Israel, then to God's need to vindicate his name in the eyes of the Egyptians (see v. 12), and finally to the great patriarchal promises (see v. 13).

32:11 *q* ver 13;
Dt 9:26; 1Sa 7:9;
Ne 1:10; Ps 136:12
32:12 *r* Nu 14:13-16;
Dt 9:28 *s* ver 14;
Ex 33:13
32:13 *t* S Ex 2:24;
33:13 *u* S Ge 22:16;
Heb 6:13 *v* Ge 15:5;
22:17 *w* S Ge 12:7
32:14 *x* Dt 9:19;
1Sa 15:11; 2Sa 24:16;
1Ki 21:29; 1Ch 21:15;
Ps 106:45; Jer 18:8;
26:3,19; Am 7:3,6;
Jnh 3:10
32:15 *y* Ex 31:18;
Heb 9:4 *z* S Ex 19:18;
34:4,29; Dt 9:15
a 2Co 3:3
32:16 *b* S Ex 24:12
32:17 *c* S Ex 17:9
32:19 *d* Dt 9:16
e ver 6; 1Co 10:7
f Ezr 9:3; Ps 119:53,
158 *g* Ex 34:1; Dt 9:17
32:20 *h* Dt 7:25;
12:3; Jos 7:1; 2Ki 23:6;
1Ch 14:12 *i* 2Ch 34:7;
Mic 1:7 *j* Dt 9:21
32:22 *k* S Ge 18:30
l Dt 9:24; 28:20;
2Ki 21:15; Ezr 9:13;
Ne 9:28; Jer 4:4;
44:3; Eze 6:9
32:23 *m* S ver 1;
Ac 7:40
32:24 *n* S ver 4
32:25 *o* S Ge 38:23
32:27 *p* Nu 25:3,5;
Dt 33:9; Eze 9:5

mighty hand?[q] [12]Why should the Egyptians say, 'It was with evil intent that he brought them out, to kill them in the mountains and to wipe them off the face of the earth'?[r] Turn from your fierce anger; relent and do not bring disaster[s] on your people. [13]Remember[t] your servants Abraham, Isaac and Israel, to whom you swore by your own self:[u] 'I will make your descendants as numerous as the stars[v] in the sky and I will give your descendants all this land[w] I promised them, and it will be their inheritance forever.' " [14]Then the LORD relented[x] and did not bring on his people the disaster he had threatened.

[15]Moses turned and went down the mountain with the two tablets of the covenant law[y] in his hands.[z] They were inscribed[a] on both sides, front and back. [16]The tablets were the work of God; the writing was the writing of God, engraved on the tablets.[b]

[17]When Joshua[c] heard the noise of the people shouting, he said to Moses, "There is the sound of war in the camp."

[18]Moses replied:

> "It is not the sound of victory,
> it is not the sound of defeat;
> it is the sound of singing that I hear."

[19]When Moses approached the camp and saw the calf[d] and the dancing,[e] his anger burned[f] and he threw the tablets out of his hands, breaking them to pieces[g] at the foot of the mountain. [20]And he took the calf they had made and burned[h] it in the fire; then he ground it to powder,[i] scattered it on the water[j] and made the Israelites drink it.

[21]He said to Aaron, "What did these people do to you, that you led them into such great sin?"

[22]"Do not be angry,[k] my lord," Aaron answered. "You know how prone these people are to evil.[l] [23]They said to me, 'Make us gods who will go before us. As for this fellow Moses who brought us up out of Egypt, we don't know what has happened to him.'[m] [24]So I told them, 'Whoever has any gold jewelry, take it off.' Then they gave me the gold, and I threw it into the fire, and out came this calf!"[n]

[25]Moses saw that the people were running wild and that Aaron had let them get out of control and so become a laughingstock[o] to their enemies. [26]So he stood at the entrance to the camp and said, "Whoever is for the LORD, come to me." And all the Levites rallied to him.

[27]Then he said to them, "This is what the LORD, the God of Israel, says: 'Each man strap a sword to his side. Go back and forth through the camp from one end to the other, each killing his brother and friend and neighbor.' "[p] [28]The Levites did as Moses commanded, and that day about three thousand of the people died. [29]Then Moses said, "You have been set apart to the LORD today, for you were against your own sons and brothers, and he has blessed you this day."

32:13 *Israel.* Jacob (see 33:1; see also Ge 32:28).

32:14 *the LORD relented.* See note on Jer 18:7–10; see also 2Sa 24:16; Ps 106:45; Am 7:1–6; cf. Jas 5:16.

32:15 *went down the mountain.* See note on 24:18. *two tablets.* See note on 31:18. *covenant law.* See notes on 16:34; 25:16. *inscribed on both sides.* This rather uncommon feature highlights the great importance of these stone tablets as official covenant documents. It is not known whether the reverse side of the tablets contained a repetition of what was inscribed on the front side or the latter half of the Ten Commandments. Elsewhere note is taken of scrolls written on both sides (Eze 2:10; Zec 5:3; Rev 5:1); in each case what is written pertains to God's sovereign involvement in human history, especially his coming judgment.

32:16 *work of God ... writing of God.* See 31:18.

32:17 *Joshua.* Perhaps he had accompanied Moses part of the way up the mountain (see 24:13).

32:19 *breaking them to pieces.* Thus testifying against Israel that the people had broken the covenant.

32:20 *burned it ... ground it to powder.* King Jeroboam's altar (see note on v. 4) at Bethel received the same treatment (see 2Ki 23:15).

32:21 *great sin.* See Ge 20:9 and note.

32:22–24 In his desperation, Aaron blamed the people (cf. Ge 3:12–13 and notes), but the Lord held him ac-countable. Only through Moses' intercession was Aaron spared (see Dt 9:20).

32:24 *out came this calf.* Aaron could hardly have thought that Moses would believe such an incredible story.

32:25 *were running wild ... get out of control.* The same Hebrew root underlies both phrases and is found also in Pr 29:18 ("cast off restraint"). Anarchy reigns among people who refuse to obey and worship the Lord.

32:26 *Whoever is for the LORD, come to me.* See Jos 24:15; 1Ki 18:21; Mt 6:24. *all.* A generalization since Dt 33:9 implies that some of the Levites were also slain. *Levites.* The descendants of Levi (Ge 29:34) may have originally been regarded as priests (Dt 18:6–8). But at some stage they became subordinate to the priests who were descendants of Aaron, the brother of Moses (38:21; Nu 3:9–10; 1Ch 16:4–6,37–42).

32:27 *killing his brother and friend and neighbor.* See Mt 10:37; Lk 14:26.

32:28 *The Levites did as Moses commanded.* Their zeal for the Lord is later matched by Aaron's grandson Phinehas, resulting in a perpetual covenant of the priesthood (see Nu 25:7–13).

32:29 *You have been set apart to the LORD today.* Because of their zeal for the Lord the Levites were set apart to be caretakers of the tabernacle and aides to the priests (see Nu 1:47–53; 3:5–9,12,41,45; 4:2–3).

³⁰The next day Moses said to the people, "You have committed a great sin.^q But now I will go up to the LORD; perhaps I can make atonement^r for your sin."

³¹So Moses went back to the LORD and said, "Oh, what a great sin these people have committed!^s They have made themselves gods of gold.^t ³²But now, please forgive their sin^u—but if not, then blot me^v out of the book^w you have written."

³³The LORD replied to Moses, "Whoever has sinned against me I will blot out^x of my book. ³⁴Now go, lead^y the people to the place^z I spoke of, and my angel^a will go before you. However, when the time comes for me to punish,^b I will punish them for their sin."

³⁵And the LORD struck the people with a plague because of what they did with the calf^c Aaron had made.

33 Then the LORD said to Moses, "Leave this place, you and the people you brought up out of Egypt, and go up to the land I promised on oath^d to Abraham, Isaac and Jacob, saying, 'I will give it to your descendants.'^e ²I will send an angel^f before you and drive out the Canaanites, Amorites, Hittites, Perizzites, Hivites and Jebusites.^g ³Go up to the land flowing with milk and honey.^h But I will not go with you, because you are a stiff-neckedⁱ people and I might destroy^j you on the way."

⁴When the people heard these distressing words, they began to mourn^k and no one put on any ornaments. ⁵For the LORD had said to Moses, "Tell the Israelites, 'You are a stiff-necked people.^l If I were to go with you even for a moment, I might destroy^m you. Now take off your ornaments and I will decide what to do with you.' " ⁶So the Israelites stripped off their ornaments at Mount Horeb.ⁿ

THE TENT OF MEETING

⁷Now Moses used to take a tent and pitch it outside the camp some distance away, calling it the "tent of meeting."^o Anyone inquiring^p of the LORD would go to the tent of meeting outside the camp. ⁸And whenever Moses went out to the tent, all the people rose and stood at the entrances to their tents,^q watching Moses until he entered the tent. ⁹As Moses went into the tent, the pillar of cloud^r would come down and stay at the entrance, while the LORD spoke^s with Moses. ¹⁰Whenever the people saw the pillar of cloud standing at the entrance to the tent, they all stood and worshiped at the entrances to their tents.^t ¹¹The LORD would speak to Moses face to face,^u as one speaks to a friend. Then Moses would return to the camp, but his young aide Joshua^v son of Nun did not leave the tent.

MOSES AND THE GLORY OF THE LORD

¹²Moses said to the LORD, "You have been telling me, 'Lead these people,'^w but you have not let me know whom you will send with me. You have said, 'I know you by name^x and you have found favor^y with me.' ¹³If you are pleased with me, teach me your ways^z so I may know you and continue to find favor with you. Remember that this nation is your people."^a ¹⁴The LORD replied, "My Presence^b will go with you, and I will give you rest."^c

33:14 Hag 1:13; 2:4 ^cDt 12:9,10; 25:19; Jos 1:13; 11:23; 21:44; 22:4; 23:1; 1Ki 8:56; Isa 63:14; Jer 31:2; Mt 11:28; Heb 4:1-11

32:30 ^q1Sa 12:20; Ps 25:11; 85:2 ^rLev 1:4; 4:20,26; 5:6,10,13; 6:7
32:31 ^sEx 34:9; Dt 9:18 ^tS Ex 20:23
32:32 ^uNu 14:19 ^vRo 9:3 ^wPs 69:28; Eze 13:9; Da 7:10; 12:1; Mal 3:16; S Lk 10:20
32:33 ^xS Ex 17:14; S Job 21:20; Rev 3:5
32:34 ^yS Ex 15:17 ^zEx 3:17 ^aS Ex 14:19 ^bS Ge 50:19; Dt 32:35; Ps 89:32; 94:23; 99:8; 109:20; Isa 27:1; Jer 5:9; 11:22; 23:2; 44:13,29; Hos 12:2; Ro 2:5-6
32:35 ^cS ver 4
33:1 ^dS Ex 13:11; S Nu 14:23; Heb 6:13 ^eS Ge 12:7
33:2 ^fS Ex 14:19 ^gS Ex 23:28
33:3 ^hS Ex 3:8 ⁱEx 32:9; Ac 7:51 ^jS Ex 32:10
33:4 ^kNu 14:39; Ezr 9:3; Est 4:1; Ps 119:53
33:5 ^lS Ex 32:9 ^mS Ex 32:10
33:6 ⁿS Ex 3:1
33:7 ^oS Ex 27:21 ^pS Ge 25:22; S 1Ki 22:5
33:8 ^qver 10; Nu 16:27
33:9 ^rEx 13:21; S 19:9; Dt 31:15; 1Co 10:1 ^sS Ex 29:42; 31:18; Ps 99:7
33:10 ^tS ver 8
33:11 ^uNu 12:8; Dt 5:4; 34:10 ^vS Ex 17:9
33:12 ^wEx 3:10; S 15:17 ^xver 17; Isa 43:1; 45:3; 49:1; Jn 10:14-15; 2Ti 2:19 ^yS Ge 6:8
33:13 ^zPs 25:4; 27:11; 51:13; 86:11; 103:7; 143:8 ^aEx 3:7; Dt 9:26,29; Ps 77:15
33:14 ^bS Ex 13:21; Dt 4:37; Isa 63:9;

A **C** **32:30** *make atonement for your sin.* By making urgent intercession before God, as the mediator God had appointed between himself and Israel. No sacrifice that Israel or Moses might bring could atone for this sin. But Moses so identified himself with Israel that he made his own death the condition for God's destruction of the nation (see v. 32). Jesus Christ, the great Mediator, offered himself on the cross to make atonement for his people.

32:32 *blot me out.* Paul made a similar statement (see Ro 9:3 and note). *book you have written.* See notes on Ps 9:5; 51:1; 69:28.

A **32:33** *Whoever has sinned . . . I will blot out.* Moses' gracious offer is refused, because the person who sins is responsible for his own sin (see Dt 24:16; Eze 18:4 and note).

32:34 *Now go, lead the people.* Thus Moses receives assurance that the Lord will continue his covenant with wayward Israel and fulfill his promise concerning the land. *the place I spoke of.* Canaan (see 33:1). *my angel.* See 23:23; 33:2.

33:2 *Canaanites . . . Jebusites.* See note on 3:8.

33:3 *land flowing with milk and honey.* See note on 3:8. *I will not go with you.* The Lord's presence, earlier assured to his people (see 23:21 and note), is now temporarily withdrawn because of sin. *stiff-necked.* See note on 32:9.

33:6 *stripped off their ornaments.* As a sign of mourning (see Eze 26:16-17).

33:7 *tent of meeting outside the camp.* Not the tabernacle (contrast 27:21), which occupied a central location within the Israelite camp, but a temporary structure where the people could consult the Lord until the more durable tabernacle was completed.

33:9 *pillar of cloud would come down.* Symbolizing God's communication with Moses "as one speaks to a friend" (v. 11). Later, a similar descent crowned the completion of the tabernacle (see 40:33-34; see also note on 13:21).

C **33:11** *The LORD would speak to Moses face to face.* God communicated with him directly—but without visually showing his "face." As the OT mediator, Moses was unique among the prophets (see Nu 12:6-8; Dt 34:10,12 and notes). *Joshua . . . did not leave the tent.* Probably his task was to guard the tent against intrusion by others.

C **33:12** *you have not let me know whom you will send with me.* Moses objects that a mere angel is no substitute for God's own presence. *I know you by name.* I have chosen you for my special purpose (see Jer 1:5 and note).

33:13 *teach me your ways.* A prayer that is answered in 34:6-7.

33:14 *My Presence.* Lit "My face." The Lord will not "hide" his face from his people but will cause it to "shine" on them (see Nu 6:25; Ps 13:1 and notes). See also note on v. 12.

33:15 *d* ver 3;
Ex 34:9; 2Ki 13:23;
17:18; 23:27; 24:20;
Ps 51:11; 80:3,7,19;
Jer 7:15; 52:3
33:16 *e* Ex 34:5;
40:34,35; Nu 9:15;
14:14 *f* Ex 34:10;
Lev 20:24,26;
Nu 23:9; Dt 4:7,32,
34; 32:9; 33:28
33:17 *g* Ex 34:28;
Dt 9:18,25; 10:10;
Jas 5:16 *h* S Ge 6:8
33:18 *i* S Ex 16:7;
Jn 1:14; 12:41;
1Ti 6:16; Rev 15:8
33:19 *j* Isa 19:11
k Ex 6:3; 34:5-7
l Ro 9:15*
33:20 *m* S Ge 16:13;
S Ex 3:6; S Dt 5:26;
S Jn 1:18
33:22 *n* Ge 49:24;
1Ki 19:9; Ps 27:5;
31:20; 62:7; 91:1;
Isa 2:21; Jer 4:29
o Ps 91:4; Isa 49:2;
51:16
34:1 *p* S Ex 24:12
q Dt 10:2,4
r S Ex 32:19
34:2 *s* S Ex 19:11
34:3 *t* S Ex 19:13
34:4 *u* Dt 10:3
v S Ex 32:15
34:5 *w* S Ex 13:21;
S 19:9 *x* Ex 6:3; 33:19
34:6 *y* S Ex 22:27;
S Nu 14:20;
S Ps 86:15 *z* Nu 14:18;
Ps 78:38; Jer 15:15;
Ro 2:4 *a* S Ge 19:16
b Ps 61:7; 108:4; 115:1;
138:2; 143:1; La 3:23;
Jas 5:11
34:7 *c* S Ex 20:6;
Dt 5:10 *d* 1Ki 8:30;
Ps 86:5; 103:3; 130:4,
8; Isa 43:25; Da 9:9;
1Jn 1:9 *e* Ex 23:7;
Jos 24:19; Job 7:20-
21; 9:28; 10:14;
Mic 6:1-16; Na 1:3
f S Ex 20:5
34:9 *g* Ex 33:13;
Nu 11:15 *h* S Ex 33:15
i Ex 32:9 *j* Nu 14:19;
1Ki 8:30; 2Ch 6:21;
Ps 19:12; 25:11;
Jer 33:8; Hos 14:2
k S Ex 6:7; 19:5;
Dt 4:20; 7:6; 9:26,29;
14:2; 26:18; 32:9;

[15] Then Moses said to him, "If your Presence *d* does not go with us, do not send us up from here. [16] How will anyone know that you are pleased with me and with your people unless you go with us? *e* What else will distinguish me and my people from all the other people on the face of the earth?" *f*

[17] And the LORD said to Moses, "I will do the very thing you have asked, *g* because I am pleased with you and I know you by name." *h*

[18] Then Moses said, "Now show me your glory." *i*

[19] And the LORD said, "I will cause all my goodness to pass *j* in front of you, and I will proclaim my name, *k* the LORD, in your presence. I will have mercy on whom I will have mercy, and I will have compassion on whom I will have compassion. *l* [20] But," he said, "you cannot see my face, for no one may see *m* me and live."

[21] Then the LORD said, "There is a place near me where you may stand on a rock. [22] When my glory passes by, I will put you in a cleft in the rock *n* and cover you with my hand *o* until I have passed by. [23] Then I will remove my hand and you will see my back; but my face must not be seen."

THE NEW STONE TABLETS

34 The LORD said to Moses, "Chisel out two stone tablets like the first ones, *p* and I will write on them the words that were on the first tablets, *q* which you broke. *r* [2] Be ready in the morning, and then come up on Mount Sinai. *s* Present yourself to me there on top of the mountain. [3] No one is to come with you or be seen anywhere on the mountain; *t* not even the flocks and herds may graze in front of the mountain."

[4] So Moses chiseled *u* out two stone tablets like the first ones and went up Mount Sinai early in the morning, as the LORD had commanded him; and he carried the two stone tablets in his hands. *v* [5] Then the LORD came down in the cloud *w* and stood there with him and proclaimed his name, the LORD. *x* [6] And he passed in front of Moses, proclaiming, "The LORD, the LORD, the compassionate *y* and gracious God, slow to anger, *z* abounding in love *a* and faithfulness, *b* [7] maintaining love to thousands, *c* and forgiving wickedness, rebellion and sin. *d* Yet he does not leave the guilty unpunished; *e* he punishes the children and their children for the sin of the parents to the third and fourth generation." *f*

[8] Moses bowed to the ground at once and worshiped. [9] "Lord," he said, "if I have found favor *g* in your eyes, then let the Lord go with us. *h* Although this is a stiff-necked *i* people, forgive our wickedness and our sin, *j* and take us as your inheritance." *k*

[10] Then the LORD said: "I am making a covenant *l* with you. Before all your people I will do wonders *m* never before done in any nation in all the world. *n* The people you live among will see how awesome is the work that I, the LORD, will do for you. [11] Obey what I command *o* you today. I will drive out before you the Amorites, Canaanites, Hittites, Perizzites, Hivites and Jebusites. *p* [12] Be careful not to make a treaty *q* with those who live in the land where you are going, or they will be a snare *r* among you. [13] Break down their altars,

34:9 1Sa 10:1; 2Sa 14:16; 1Ki 8:51,53; Ps 28:9; 33:12; 74:2; 79:1; 94:14; 106:5,40; Isa 19:25; 63:17; Jer 10:16; 51:19; Mic 7:18; Zec 2:12
34:10 *l* S Ge 6:18; S 9:15; S 15:18; Dt 5:2-3 *m* S Ex 3:20 *n* S Ex 33:16   **34:11** *o* Dt 6:25; Jos 11:15 *p* S Ex 23:28   **34:12** *q* Jdg 2:2
r S Ex 10:7

A **33:17** *because I am pleased with you.* How much more does God hear the prayers of his Son Jesus Christ (see Mt 17:5; Heb 3:1–6)!

C **33:18** *show me your glory.* All that God has done for Israel through Moses has made him very bold. At his first meeting with God he was "afraid to look at God" in the small display of God's glory in the burning bush (see 3:6 and note), and he inquired concerning God's name (3:13). Now he asks to be shown God's glory unveiled and is told he has asked too much, that he must be content with the fuller proclamation of God's name (see vv. 19,22; 34:5–7).

33:19 *goodness.* God's nature and character. *name.* A further symbol of God's nature, character and person (see Ps 20:1; Jn 1:12; 17:6 and note). Here his name implies his mercy (grace) and his compassion (as it does also in 34:6). *I will have mercy on whom ... compassion.* Paul quotes these words in Ro 9:15 to defend his view of God's sovereignty.

33:20 *no one may see me and live.* See note on Ge 16:13; see also Jn 1:18; 6:46; 1Ti 1:17; 1Jn 4:12.

33:21–23 God speaks of himself in human language. See 34:5–7 for the fulfillment of his promise.

34:1 *two stone tablets ... I will write on them.* See note on 31:18. *words.* See note on 20:1.

34:5 *name.* See note on 33:19.

A **34:6–7** See 33:19 and note. The Lord's proclamation of the meaning and implications of his name in these verses became a classic exposition that was frequently recalled elsewhere in the OT (see Nu 14:18; Ne 9:17; Ps 86:15; 103:8; 145:8; Joel 2:13; Jnh 4:2). See also notes on 3:14–15; 6:2–3.

34:7 *thousands.* Or "a thousand generations" (see 20:6). *wickedness, rebellion and sin.* See Isa 59:12 and note.

34:10 *making a covenant.* Renewing the covenant he had earlier made (chs. 19–24). Verses 10–26, many of which are quoted almost verbatim from previous sections of Exodus (compare especially vv. 18–26 with 23:14–19), are sometimes referred to as the Ritual Decalogue since they can be convincingly divided into ten sections (see, e.g., the TNIV paragraphing of vv. 15–26). *wonders.* The same word used for the plagues sent on Egypt (3:20). Here it probably refers to the miracles God performed during the wilderness wanderings and the conquest of Canaan (see Ps 9:1 and note).

34:12 *not to make a treaty with those who live in the land.* Israel smash their sacred stones and cut down their Asherah poles. [a] [s] [14]Do not worship any other god, [t] for the LORD, whose name [u] is Jealous, is a jealous God. [v]

[15]"Be careful not to make a treaty [w] with those who live in the land; for when they prostitute [x] themselves to their gods and sacrifice to them, they will invite you and you will eat their sacrifices. [y] [16]And when you choose some of their daughters as wives [z] for your sons and those daughters prostitute themselves to their gods, [a] they will lead your sons to do the same.

[17]"Do not make any idols. [b]

[18]"Celebrate the Festival of Unleavened Bread. [c] For seven days eat bread made without yeast, [d] as I commanded you. Do this at the appointed time in the month of Aviv, [e] for in that month you came out of Egypt.

[19]"The first offspring [f] of every womb belongs to me, including all the firstborn males of your livestock, whether from herd or flock. [20]Redeem the firstborn donkey with a lamb, but if you do not redeem it, break its neck. [g] Redeem all your firstborn sons. [h]

"No one is to appear before me empty-handed. [i]

[21]"Six days you shall labor, but on the seventh day you shall rest; [j] even during the plowing season and harvest [k] you must rest.

[22]"Celebrate the Festival of Weeks with the firstfruits [l] of the wheat harvest, and the Festival of Ingathering [m] at the turn of the year. [b] [23]Three times [n] a year all your men are to appear before the Sovereign LORD, the God of Israel. [24]I will drive out nations [o] before you and enlarge your territory, [p] and no one will covet your land when you go up three times each year to appear before the LORD your God.

[25]"Do not offer the blood of a sacrifice to me along with anything containing yeast, [q] and do not let any of the sacrifice from the Passover Festival remain until morning. [r]

[26]"Bring the best of the firstfruits [s] of your soil to the house of the LORD your God.

"Do not cook a young goat in its mother's milk." [t]

[27]Then the LORD said to Moses, "Write [u] down these words, for in accordance with these words I have made a covenant [v] with you and with Israel." [28]Moses was there with the LORD forty days and forty nights [w] without eating bread or drinking water. [x] And he wrote on the tablets [y] the words of the covenant—the Ten Commandments. [z]

THE RADIANT FACE OF MOSES

[29]When Moses came down from Mount Sinai [a] with the two tablets of the covenant law in his hands, [b] he was not aware that his face was radiant [c] because he had spoken with the LORD. [30]When Aaron and all the Israelites saw Moses, his face was radiant, and they were afraid to come near him. [31]But Moses called to them; so Aaron and all the leaders of the community [d] came back to him, and he spoke to them. [32]Afterward all the Israelites came near him, and he gave them all the commands [e] the LORD had given him on Mount Sinai.

[a] 13 That is, wooden symbols of the goddess Asherah   [b] 22 That is, in the autumn

34:32 [a] S Ex 21:1; 35:1,4

34:13 [s] S Ex 23:24; Nu 33:52; Dt 7:5; 12:3; Jdg 6:26; 1Ki 15:13; 2Ch 15:16; 17:6; 34:3-4; Mic 5:14
34:14 [t] S Ex 20:3 [u] Isa 9:6 [v] S Ex 20:5
34:15 [w] ver 12; Dt 23:6; Ezr 9:12 [x] Ex 22:20; 32:8; Dt 31:16; Jdg 2:17; 2Ki 17:8; 1Ch 5:25; 2Ch 11:15; Am 2:4 [y] S Ex 32:6; 1Co 8:4
34:16 [z] Dt 7:3; 17:17; Jos 23:12; Jdg 3:6; 14:3; 1Ki 11:1, 2; 16:31; Ezr 9:2; 10:3; Ne 10:30; 13:25,26 [a] Dt 7:4; 12:31; 20:18; 1Ki 11:4; 2Ki 21:3-15; Ps 106:34-41; Mal 2:11
34:17 [b] S Ex 20:4
34:18 [c] S Ex 12:17; Mt 26:17; Lk 22:1; Ac 12:3 [d] S Ex 12:15 [e] S Ex 12:2
34:19 [f] Ex 13:2
34:20 [g] S Ex 13:13 [h] S Ex 13:2 [i] S Ex 22:29; Dt 16:16; Eze 46:9
34:21 [j] Ge 2:2-3 [k] Ne 13:15; Isa 56:2; 58:13
34:22 [l] ver 26; Ex 23:19; Lev 2:12,14; 7:13; 23:10,17; Nu 28:26 [m] S Ex 23:16
34:23 [n] S Ex 23:14
34:24 [o] S Ex 23:28 [p] Dt 12:20; 19:8; Job 12:23
34:25 [q] S Ex 23:18 [r] S Ex 12:8
34:26 [s] S Ex 22:29; S Nu 18:12 [t] S Ex 23:19
34:27 [u] S Ex 17:14 [v] S Ge 6:18; S 15:18
34:28 [w] S Ge 7:4; Mt 4:2; Lk 4:2 [x] Dt 9:9,18; Ezr 10:6 [y] ver 1; Ex 31:18 [z] Dt 4:13; 10:4
34:29 [a] S Ex 19:11 [b] S Ex 32:15 [c] ver 35; Ps 34:5; Isa 60:5; Mt 17:2; 2Co 3:7,13
34:31 [d] Ex 16:22

is not to make a treaty of peace with any of the people of Canaan to let them live in the land. *treaty.* The Hebrew for this word is the same as that for "covenant" in v. 10 (see also v. 15).
34:13 *Asherah poles.* Asherah was the name of the wife of El, the chief Canaanite god. Wooden poles, perhaps carved in her image, were often set up in her honor and placed near other pagan objects of worship (see, e.g., Jdg 6:25).
34:14 *whose name is Jealous.* See note on 20:5.

A **34:15** *prostitute themselves.* A metaphor widely used in the OT to refer to Israel's unfaithfulness to her covenant Lord, who, according to a related metaphor, had become Israel's "husband" (with all that implied in the ancient social world) when he established his special covenant with her (see Isa 54:5-6; Jer 3:14; 31:32; Hos 2:2,7,16; cf. Jer 2:1; 3:1,20; Eze 16:8, 32,45; 23:4,37). Such unfaithfulness took various forms, but most commonly outright idolatry (worshiping other gods and looking to them for fertility of wombs, fields and flocks, for healing wounds and diseases, for deliverance or security from enemies—thus treating the false gods as their "lovers"). *eat their sacrifices.* Partaking of food sacrificed to a pagan deity invites compromise (cf. 1Co 8; 10:18-21).
34:17 *Do not make any idols.* As Aaron had done when he

made the golden calf (see 32:4).
34:18-26 See notes on 23:14-19.
34:21 *even during the plowing season and harvest you must rest.* Just as they were also to rest while building the tabernacle (see notes on 31:13,16-17).
34:24 *no one will covet your land.* The Lord promises to protect the Israelite pilgrim's ownership of his land while he is away attending the three annual festivals that require his presence (see Dt 16:16 and note).
34:27 *Write down these words.* As he had earlier written down similar words (see 24:4).
34:28 *he wrote.* Here the Lord, rather than Moses, is probably the subject (see v. 1). *the words of the covenant—the Ten Commandments.* The two phrases are synonymous (see note on 20:1).

A C **34:29** *covenant law.* See notes on 16:34; 25:16. *was radiant.* He who had asked to see God's glory (see 33:18 and note) now, quite unawares, reflects the divine glory. The Hebrew for "was radiant" is related to the Hebrew noun for "horn." The meaning of the phrase was therefore misunderstood by the Vulgate (the Latin translation), and thus European medieval art often showed horns sprouting from Moses' head.

34:33 *f* 2Co 3:13
34:35 *g* S ver 29
35:1 *h* S Ex 34:32
35:2 *i* S Ge 2:3;
Ex 34:21; Dt 5:13-14
j S Ex 31:14
35:3 *k* Ex 16:23
35:8 *l* S Ex 25:6
35:10 *m* Ex 31:6;
39:43
35:11 *n* Ex 26:1-37;
36:8-38
35:12 *o* Ex 25:10-
22; 37:1-9
p S Ex 26:33
35:13 *q* Ex 25:23-
30; 37:10-16
35:14 *r* S Ex 25:31
35:15 *s* S Ex 25:6
37:25-28 *t* Ex 30:25
u Ex 30:34-38
v S Ex 26:36
35:16 *w* Ex 27:1-8;
38:1-7 *x* S Ex 30:18
35:17 *y* S Ex 27:9;
38:9-20
35:18 *z* Ex 27:19;
38:20
35:19 *a* S Ex 28:2
35:23 *b* S Ex 39:1
35:25 *c* S Ex 28:3
35:27 *d* S Ex 25:2;
1Ch 29:6 *e* 1Ch 29:8
35:28 *f* S Ex 25:6
35:29 *g* S Ex 25:2
h ver 4-9; Ex 25:1-7;
36:3; 2Ki 12:4

[33] When Moses finished speaking to them, he put a veil *f* over his face. [34] But whenever he entered the Lord's presence to speak with him, he removed the veil until he came out. And when he came out and told the Israelites what he had been commanded, [35] they saw that his face was radiant. *g* Then Moses would put the veil back over his face until he went in to speak with the Lord.

SABBATH REGULATIONS

35 Moses assembled the whole Israelite community and said to them, "These are the things the Lord has commanded *h* you to do: [2] For six days, work is to be done, but the seventh day shall be your holy day, a day of sabbath *i* rest to the Lord. Whoever does any work on it is to be put to death. *j* [3] Do not light a fire in any of your dwellings on the Sabbath day. *k*"

MATERIALS FOR THE TABERNACLE

35:4–9pp — Ex 25:1–7
35:10–19pp — Ex 39:32–41

[4] Moses said to the whole Israelite community, "This is what the Lord has commanded: [5] From what you have, take an offering for the Lord. Everyone who is willing is to bring to the Lord an offering of gold, silver and bronze; [6] blue, purple and scarlet yarn and fine linen; goat hair; [7] ram skins dyed red and another durable leather[a]; acacia wood; [8] olive oil *l* for the light; spices for the anointing oil and for the fragrant incense; [9] and onyx stones and other gems to be mounted on the ephod and breastpiece.

[10] "All who are skilled among you are to come and make everything the Lord has commanded: *m* [11] the tabernacle *n* with its tent and its covering, clasps, frames, crossbars, posts and bases; [12] the ark *o* with its poles and the atonement cover and the curtain *p* that shields it; [13] the table *q* with its poles and all its articles and the bread of the Presence; [14] the lampstand *r* that is for light with its accessories, lamps and oil for the light; [15] the altar *s* of incense with its poles, the anointing oil *t* and the fragrant incense; *u* the curtain for the doorway at the entrance to the tabernacle; *v* [16] the altar *w* of burnt offering with its bronze grating, its poles and all its utensils; the bronze basin *x* with its stand; [17] the curtains of the courtyard with its posts and bases, and the curtain for the entrance to the courtyard; *y* [18] the tent pegs *z* for the tabernacle and for the courtyard, and their ropes; [19] the woven garments worn for ministering in the sanctuary—both the sacred garments *a* for Aaron the priest and the garments for his sons when they serve as priests."

[20] Then the whole Israelite community withdrew from Moses' presence, [21] and everyone who was willing and whose heart moved them came and brought an offering to the Lord for the work on the tent of meeting, for all its service, and for the sacred garments. [22] All who were willing, men and women alike, came and brought gold jewelry of all kinds: brooches, earrings, rings and ornaments. They all presented their gold as a wave offering to the Lord. *b* [23] Everyone who had blue, purple or scarlet yarn *b* or fine linen, or goat hair, ram skins dyed red or the other durable leather brought them. [24] Those presenting an offering of silver or bronze brought it as an offering to the Lord, and everyone who had acacia wood for any part of the work brought it. [25] Every skilled woman *c* spun with her hands and brought what she had spun—blue, purple or scarlet yarn or fine linen. [26] And all the women who were willing and had the skill spun the goat hair. [27] The leaders *d* brought onyx stones and other gems *e* to be mounted on the ephod and breastpiece. [28] They also brought spices and olive oil for the light and for the anointing oil and for the fragrant incense. *f* [29] All the Israelite men and women who were willing *g* brought to the Lord freewill offerings *h* for all the work the Lord through Moses had commanded them to do.

a 7 Possibly the hides of dugongs; also in verse 23

C **34:33** *he put a veil over his face.* So that the Israelites would not see the fading away of the radiance but would continue to honor Moses as the one who represented God. For a NT reflection on Moses' action, see 2Co 3:7–18 and notes.

35:1–3 Just as the Israelites had been reminded of the importance of Sabbath observance immediately after the instructions for building the tabernacle and making the priestly garments (see note on 31:13), so now—just before the fulfilling of those instructions—the people are given the same reminder.

35:4—39:43 For the most part repeated from chs. 25–28;

30:1–5; 31:1–11 (see notes on those passages), sometimes verbatim, but with the verbs primarily in the past rather than the future tense and with the topics arranged in a different order. Such repetition was a common feature of ancient Near Eastern literature and was intended to fix the details of a narrative in the reader's mind (see note on Ge 24:34–49).

35:5 *Everyone who is willing.* The voluntary motivation behind the offering of materials and services for the tabernacle is stressed (see vv. 21–22,26,29; 36:2–3).

35:21 *tent of meeting.* See note on 27:21.

BEZALEL AND OHOLIAB

35:30–35pp — Ex 31:2–6

³⁰Then Moses said to the Israelites, "See, the Lᴏʀᴅ has chosen Bezalel son of Uri, the son of Hur, of the tribe of Judah, ³¹and he has filled him with the Spirit of God, with wisdom, with understanding, with knowledge and with all kinds of skills ⁱ— ³²to make artistic designs for work in gold, silver and bronze, ³³to cut and set stones, to work in wood and to engage in all kinds of artistic crafts. ³⁴And he has given both him and Oholiab ʲ son of Ahisamak, of the tribe of Dan, the ability to teach ᵏ others. ³⁵He has filled them with skill to do all kinds of work ˡ as engravers, designers, embroiderers in blue, purple and scarlet

36

yarn and fine linen, and weavers—all of them skilled workers and designers. ¹So Bezalel, Oholiab and every skilled person ᵐ to whom the Lᴏʀᴅ has given skill and ability to know how to carry out all the work of constructing the sanctuary ⁿ are to do the work just as the Lᴏʀᴅ has commanded."

²Then Moses summoned Bezalel ᵒ and Oholiab ᵖ and every skilled person to whom the Lᴏʀᴅ had given ability and who was willing �q to come and do the work. ³They received from Moses all the offerings ʳ the Israelites had brought to carry out the work of constructing the sanctuary. And the people continued to bring freewill offerings morning after morning. ⁴So all the skilled workers who were doing all the work on the sanctuary left what they were doing ⁵and said to Moses, "The people are bringing more than enough ˢ for doing the work the Lᴏʀᴅ commanded to be done."

⁶Then Moses gave an order and they sent this word throughout the camp: "No man or woman is to make anything else as an offering for the sanctuary." And so the people were restrained from bringing more, ⁷because what they already had was more ᵗ than enough to do all the work.

THE TABERNACLE

36:8–38pp — Ex 26:1–37

⁸All those who were skilled among the workers made the tabernacle with ten curtains of finely twisted linen and blue, purple and scarlet yarn, with cherubim worked into them by expert hands. ⁹All the curtains were the same size—twenty-eight cubits long and four cubits wide. ª ¹⁰They joined five of the curtains together and did the same with the other five. ¹¹Then they made loops of blue material along the edge of the end curtain in one set, and the same was done with the end curtain in the other set. ¹²They also made fifty loops on one curtain and fifty loops on the end curtain of the other set, with the loops opposite each other. ¹³Then they made fifty gold clasps and used them to fasten the two sets of curtains together so that the tabernacle was a unit. ᵘ

¹⁴They made curtains of goat hair for the tent over the tabernacle—eleven altogether. ¹⁵All eleven curtains were the same size—thirty cubits long and four cubits wide. ᵇ ¹⁶They joined five of the curtains into one set and the other six into another set. ¹⁷Then they made fifty loops along the edge of the end curtain in one set and also along the edge of the end curtain in the other set. ¹⁸They made fifty bronze clasps to fasten the tent together as a unit. ᵛ ¹⁹Then they made for the tent a covering of ram skins dyed red, and over that a covering of the other durable leather. ᶜ

²⁰They made upright frames of acacia wood for the tabernacle. ²¹Each frame was ten cubits long and a cubit and a half wide, ᵈ ²²with two projections set parallel to each other. They made all the frames of the tabernacle in this way. ²³They made twenty frames for the south side of the tabernacle ²⁴and made forty silver bases to go under them—two bases for each frame, one under each projection. ²⁵For the other side, the north side of the tabernacle, they made twenty frames ²⁶and forty silver bases—two under each frame. ²⁷They made six frames for the far end, that is, the west end of the tabernacle, ²⁸and two frames were made for the corners of the tabernacle at the far end. ²⁹At these two corners the frames were double from the bottom all the way to the top and fitted into a single ring; both were made alike. ³⁰So there were eight frames and sixteen silver bases—two under each frame.

³¹They also made crossbars of acacia wood: five for the frames on one side of the tabernacle, ³²five for those on the other side, and five for the frames on the west, at the far end of the tabernacle. ³³They made the center crossbar so that it extended from end to

35:31 ⁱ ver 35; 2Ch 2:7,14
35:34 ʲ S Ex 31:6
ᵏ 2Ch 2:14
35:35 ˡ ver 31
36:1 ᵐ S Ex 28:3
ⁿ Ex 25:8
36:2 ᵒ S Ex 31:2
ᵖ S Ex 31:6
q S Ex 25:2
36:3 ʳ S Ex 35:29
36:5 ˢ 2Ch 24:14; 31:10; 2Co 8:2-3
36:7 ᵗ 1Ki 7:47
36:13 ᵘ ver 18
36:18 ᵛ ver 13

ª 9 That is, about 42 feet long and 6 feet wide or about 13 meters long and 1.8 meters wide   ᵇ 15 That is, about 45 feet long and 6 feet wide or about 13.5 meters long and 1.8 meters wide   ᶜ 19 Possibly the hides of dugongs   ᵈ 21 That is, about 15 feet long and 2 1/4 feet wide or about 4.5 meters long and 67 centimeters wide end at the middle of the frames. ³⁴They overlaid the frames with gold and made gold rings to hold the crossbars. They also overlaid the crossbars with gold.

³⁵They made the curtain ʷ of blue, purple and scarlet yarn and finely twisted linen, with cherubim worked into it by expert hands. ³⁶They made four posts of acacia wood for it and overlaid them with gold. They made gold hooks for them and cast their four silver bases. ³⁷For the entrance to the tent they made a curtain of blue, purple and scarlet yarn and finely twisted linen—the work of an embroiderer; ˣ ³⁸and they made five posts with hooks for them. They overlaid the tops of the posts and their bands with gold and made their five bases of bronze.

THE ARK

37:1–9pp — Ex 25:10–20

37 Bezalel ʸ made the ark ᶻ of acacia wood—two and a half cubits long, a cubit and a half wide, and a cubit and a half high. ª ²He overlaid it with pure gold, ª both inside and out, and made a gold molding around it. ³He cast four gold rings for it and fastened them to its four feet, with two rings on one side and two rings on the other. ⁴Then he made poles of acacia wood and overlaid them with gold. ⁵And he inserted the poles into the rings on the sides of the ark to carry it.

⁶He made the atonement cover ᵇ of pure gold—two and a half cubits long and a cubit and a half wide. ⁷Then he made two cherubim ᶜ out of hammered gold at the ends of the cover. ⁸He made one cherub on one end and the second cherub on the other; at the two ends he made them of one piece with the cover. ⁹The cherubim had their wings spread upward, overshadowing ᵈ the cover with them. The cherubim faced each other, looking toward the cover. ᵉ

THE TABLE

37:10–16pp — Ex 25:23–29

¹⁰They ᵇ made the table ᶠ of acacia wood—two cubits long, a cubit wide and a cubit and a half high. ᶜ ¹¹Then they overlaid it with pure gold ᵍ and made a gold molding around it. ¹²They also made around it a rim a handbreadth ᵈ wide and put a gold molding on the rim. ¹³They cast four gold rings for the table and fastened them to the four corners, where the four legs were. ¹⁴The rings ʰ were put close to the rim to hold the poles used in carrying the table. ¹⁵The poles for carrying the table were made of acacia wood and were overlaid with gold. ¹⁶And they made from pure gold the articles for the table—its plates and dishes and bowls and its pitchers for the pouring out of drink offerings.

THE LAMPSTAND

37:17–24pp — Ex 25:31–39

¹⁷They made the lampstand ⁱ of pure gold. They hammered out its base and shaft, and made its flowerlike cups, buds and blossoms of one piece with them. ¹⁸Six branches extended from the sides of the lampstand—three on one side and three on the other. ¹⁹Three cups shaped like almond flowers with buds and blossoms were on one branch, three on the next branch and the same for all six branches extending from the lampstand. ²⁰And on the lampstand were four cups shaped like almond flowers with buds and blossoms. ²¹One bud was under the first pair of branches extending from the lampstand, a second bud under the second pair, and a third bud under the third pair—six branches in all. ²²The buds and the branches were all of one piece with the lampstand, hammered out of pure gold. ʲ

²³They made its seven lamps, ᵏ as well as its wick trimmers and trays, of pure gold. ²⁴They made the lampstand and all its accessories from one talent ᵉ of pure gold.

THE ALTAR OF INCENSE

37:25–28pp — Ex 30:1–5

²⁵They made the altar of incense ˡ out of acacia wood. It was square, a cubit long and

---

ª *1* That is, about 3 1/4 feet long and 2 1/4 feet wide and high or about 1.1 meters long and 67 centimeters wide and high; also in verse 6   ᵇ *10* Or *He*; also in verses 11-29   ᶜ *10* That is, about 3 feet long, 1 1/2 feet wide and 2 1/4 feet high or about 90 centimeters long, 45 centimeters wide and 67 centimeters high   ᵈ *12* That is, about 3 inches or about 7.5 centimeters   ᵉ *24* That is, about 75 pounds or about 34 kilograms

---

37:1–29 See note on 35:4–39:43.

C **37:1** *Bezalel made the ark.* The chief craftsman (see 31:2–3 and notes) was given the honor of making the ob-ject that was most sacred (see 25:10 and note) among the furnishings for the tabernacle.

a cubit wide and two cubits high[a]—its horns[m] of one piece with it. [26]They overlaid the top and all the sides and the horns with pure gold, and made a gold molding around it. [27]They made two gold rings[n] below the molding—two on each of the opposite sides—to hold the poles used to carry it. [28]They made the poles of acacia wood and overlaid them with gold.[o]

[29]They also made the sacred anointing oil[p] and the pure, fragrant incense[q]—the work of a perfumer.

THE ALTAR OF BURNT OFFERING

38:1–7pp — Ex 27:1–8

38 They[b] built the altar of burnt offering of acacia wood, three cubits[c] high; it was square, five cubits long and five cubits wide.[d] [2]They made a horn at each of the four corners, so that the horns and the altar were of one piece, and they overlaid the altar with bronze.[r] [3]They made all its utensils[s] of bronze—its pots, shovels, sprinkling bowls, meat forks and firepans. [4]They made a grating for the altar, a bronze network, to be under its ledge, halfway up the altar. [5]They cast bronze rings to hold the poles for the four corners of the bronze grating. [6]They made the poles of acacia wood and overlaid them with bronze. [7]They inserted the poles into the rings so they would be on the sides of the altar for carrying it. They made it hollow, out of boards.

THE BASIN FOR WASHING

[8]They made the bronze basin[t] and its bronze stand from the mirrors of the women[u] who served at the entrance to the tent of meeting.

THE COURTYARD

38:9–20pp — Ex 27:9–19

[9]Next they made the courtyard. The south side was a hundred cubits[e] long and had curtains of finely twisted linen, [10]with twenty posts and twenty bronze bases, and with silver hooks and bands on the posts. [11]The north side was also a hundred cubits long and had twenty posts and twenty bronze bases, with silver hooks and bands on the posts.

[12]The west end was fifty cubits[f] wide and had curtains, with ten posts and ten bases, with silver hooks and bands on the posts. [13]The east end, toward the sunrise, was also fifty cubits wide. [14]Curtains fifteen cubits[g] long were on one side of the entrance, with three posts and three bases, [15]and curtains fifteen cubits long were on the other side of the entrance to the courtyard, with three posts and three bases. [16]All the curtains around the courtyard were of finely twisted linen. [17]The bases for the posts were bronze. The hooks and bands on the posts were silver, and their tops were overlaid with silver; so all the posts of the courtyard had silver bands.

[18]The curtain for the entrance to the courtyard was of blue, purple and scarlet yarn and finely twisted linen—the work of an embroiderer. It was twenty cubits[h] long and, like the curtains of the courtyard, five cubits[i] high, [19]with four posts and four bronze bases. Their hooks and bands were silver, and their tops were overlaid with silver. [20]All the tent pegs[v] of the tabernacle and of the surrounding courtyard were bronze.

THE MATERIALS USED

[21]These are the amounts of the materials used for the tabernacle, the tabernacle of the covenant law,[w] which were recorded at Moses' command by the Levites under the direction of Ithamar[x] son of Aaron, the priest. [22](Bezalel[y] son of Uri, the son of Hur, of the tribe of Judah, made everything the LORD commanded Moses; [23]with him was Oholiab[z] son of Ahisamak, of the tribe of Dan—an engraver and designer, and an embroiderer in blue, purple and scarlet yarn and fine linen.) [24]The total amount of the gold from the wave offering used for all the work on the sanctuary[a] was 29 talents and 730 shekels,[j] according to the sanctuary shekel.[b]

[25]The silver obtained from those of the community who were counted in the census[c]

37:25 *m* S Ex 27:2; Rev 9:13
37:27 *n* ver 14
37:28 *o* S Ex 25:13
37:29 *p* S Ex 31:11
q Ex 30:1,25; 39:38
38:2 *r* 2Ch 1:5
38:3 *s* S Ex 31:9
38:8 *t* S Ex 30:18; S 40:7 *u* Dt 23:17; 1Sa 2:22; 1Ki 14:24
38:20 *v* S Ex 35:18
38:21 *w* Nu 1:50,53; 8:24; 9:15; 10:11; 17:7; 1Ch 23:32; 2Ch 24:6; Ac 7:44; Rev 15:5
x Nu 4:28,33
38:22 *y* S Ex 31:2
38:23 *z* S Ex 31:6
38:24 *a* S Ex 30:16
b S Ex 30:13
38:25 *c* S Ex 30:12

---

a 25 That is, about 1 1/2 feet long and wide and 3 feet high or about 45 centimeters long and wide and 90 centimeters high   *b 1* Or *He*; also in verses 2-9   *c 1* That is, about 4 1/2 feet or about 1.4 meters   *d 1* That is, about 7 1/2 feet or about 2.3 meters long and wide   *e 9* That is, about 150 feet or about 45 meters   *f 12* That is, about 75 feet or about 22.5 meters   *g 14* That is, about 22 feet or about 6.8 meters   *h 18* That is, about 30 feet or about 9 meters   *i 18* That is, about 7 1/2 feet or about 2.3 meters   *j 24* The weight of the gold was a little over a ton or about 1 metric ton.

38:1–31 See note on 35:4—39:43.
38:8 *bronze…mirrors.* Mirrored glass was unknown in ancient times, but highly polished bronze gave adequate reflection (cf. 1Co 13:12 and note). *tent of meeting.* See note on 27:21.

38:26 *d* S Ex 30:12
e S Ex 30:13
f S Ex 30:14
g S Ex 12:37
38:27 *h* S Ex 26:19
39:1 *i* Ex 35:23
j Ex 35:19 *k* ver 41;
Ex 28:2
39:7 *l* Lev 24:7;
Jos 4:7
39:8 *m* Lev 8:8
39:14 *n* Rev 21:12

was 100 talents[a] and 1,775 shekels,[b] according to the sanctuary shekel— [26]one beka per person,[d] that is, half a shekel,[c] according to the sanctuary shekel,[e] from everyone who had crossed over to those counted, twenty years old or more,[f] a total of 603,550 men.[g] [27]The 100 talents of silver were used to cast the bases[h] for the sanctuary and for the curtain—100 bases from the 100 talents, one talent for each base. [28]They used the 1,775 shekels to make the hooks for the posts, to overlay the tops of the posts, and to make their bands.

[29]The bronze from the wave offering was 70 talents and 2,400 shekels.[d] [30]They used it to make the bases for the entrance to the tent of meeting, the bronze altar with its bronze grating and all its utensils, [31]the bases for the surrounding courtyard and those for its entrance and all the tent pegs for the tabernacle and those for the surrounding courtyard.

THE PRIESTLY GARMENTS

39

From the blue, purple and scarlet yarn[i] they made woven garments for ministering in the sanctuary.[j] They also made sacred garments[k] for Aaron, as the LORD commanded Moses.

THE EPHOD

39:2–7pp — Ex 28:6–14

[2]They[e] made the ephod of gold, and of blue, purple and scarlet yarn, and of finely twisted linen. [3]They hammered out thin sheets of gold and cut strands to be worked into the blue, purple and scarlet yarn and fine linen—the work of skilled hands. [4]They made shoulder pieces for the ephod, which were attached to two of its corners, so it could be fastened. [5]Its skillfully woven waistband was like it—of one piece with the ephod and made with gold, and with blue, purple and scarlet yarn, and with finely twisted linen, as the LORD commanded Moses.

[6]They mounted the onyx stones in gold filigree settings and engraved them like a seal with the names of the sons of Israel. [7]Then they fastened them on the shoulder pieces of the ephod as memorial[l] stones for the sons of Israel, as the LORD commanded Moses.

THE BREASTPIECE

39:8–21pp — Ex 28:15–28

[8]They fashioned the breastpiece[m]—the work of a skilled craftsman. They made it like the ephod: of gold, and of blue, purple and scarlet yarn, and of finely twisted linen. [9]It was square—a span[f] long and a span wide—and folded double. [10]Then they mounted four rows of precious stones on it. The first row was carnelian, chrysolite and beryl; [11]the second row was turquoise, lapis lazuli and emerald; [12]the third row was jacinth, agate and amethyst; [13]the fourth row was topaz, onyx and jasper.[g] They were mounted in gold filigree settings. [14]There were twelve stones, one for each of the names of the sons of Israel, each engraved like a seal with the name of one of the twelve tribes.[n]

[15]For the breastpiece they made braided chains of pure gold, like a rope. [16]They made two gold filigree settings and two gold rings, and fastened the rings to two of the corners of the breastpiece. [17]They fastened the two gold chains to the rings at the corners of the breastpiece, [18]and the other ends of the chains to the two settings, attaching them to the shoulder pieces of the ephod at the front. [19]They made two gold rings and attached them to the other two corners of the breastpiece on the inside edge next to the ephod. [20]Then they made two more gold rings and attached them to the bottom of the shoulder pieces on the front of the ephod, close to the seam just above the waistband of the ephod. [21]They tied the rings of the breastpiece to the rings of the ephod with blue cord, connecting it to the waistband so that the breastpiece would not swing out from the ephod—as the LORD commanded Moses.

---

[a] *25* That is, about 3 3/4 tons or about 3.4 metric tons; also in verse 27   [b] *25* That is, about 45 pounds or about 20 kilograms; also in verse 28   [c] *26* That is, about 1/5 ounce or about 5.7 grams   [d] *29* The weight of the bronze was about 2 1/2 tons or about 2.4 metric tons.   [e] *2* Or *He*; also in verses 7, 8 and 22   [f] *9* That is, about 9 inches or about 22.5 centimeters   [g] *13* The precise identification of some of these precious stones is uncertain.

38:25 *100 talents and 1,775 shekels.* Since there are 3,000 shekels in a talent, 100 talents equals 300,000 shekels, which, when added to the 1,775 shekels, gives a grand total of 301,775—half a shekel for each of the 603,550 men of military age (v. 26).

38:26 *603,550 men.* See Introduction to Numbers: Special Problem; see also Nu 1:46 and note.
38:27 *one talent for each base.* See note on 26:19.
39:1–43 See note on 35:4—39:43.

OTHER PRIESTLY GARMENTS

39:22–31pp — Ex 28:31–43

²²They made the robe of the ephod entirely of blue cloth—the work of a weaver—²³with an opening in the center of the robe like the opening of a collar,ᵃ and a band around this opening, so that it would not tear. ²⁴They made pomegranates of blue, purple and scarlet yarn and finely twisted linen around the hem of the robe. ²⁵And they made bells of pure gold and attached them around the hem between the pomegranates. ²⁶The bells and pomegranates alternated around the hem of the robe to be worn for ministering, as the LORD commanded Moses.

²⁷For Aaron and his sons, they made tunics of fine linenᵒ—the work of a weaver—²⁸and the turbanᵖ of fine linen, the linen caps and the undergarments of finely twisted linen. ²⁹The sash was of finely twisted linen and blue, purple and scarlet yarn—the work of an embroiderer—as the LORD commanded Moses.

³⁰They made the plate, the sacred emblem, out of pure gold and engraved on it, like an inscription on a seal: HOLY TO THE LORD. q ³¹Then they fastened a blue cord to it to attach it to the turban,ʳ as the LORD commanded Moses.

MOSES INSPECTS THE TABERNACLE

39:32–41pp — Ex 35:10–19

³²So all the work on the tabernacle, the tent of meeting, was completed. The Israelites did everything just as the LORD commanded Moses. s ³³Then they brought the tabernacleᵗ to Moses: the tent and all its furnishings, its clasps, frames, crossbars, posts and bases; ³⁴the covering of ram skins dyed red and the covering of another durable leatherᵇ and the shielding curtain; ³⁵the ark of the covenant lawᵘ with its poles and the atonement cover; ³⁶the tableᵛ with its articles and the bread of the Presence; ʷ ³⁷the pure gold lampstandˣ with its row of lamps and all its accessories,ʸ and the oilᶻ for the light; ³⁸the gold altar,ᵃ the anointing oil,ᵇ the fragrant incense,ᶜ and the curtainᵈ for the entrance to the tent; ³⁹the bronze altarᵉ with its bronze grating, its poles and all its utensils; the basinᶠ with its stand; ⁴⁰the curtains of the courtyard with its posts and bases, and the curtain for the entrance to the courtyard;ᵍ the ropes and tent pegs for the courtyard; all the furnishings for the tabernacle, the tent of meeting; ⁴¹and the woven garmentsʰ worn for ministering in the sanctuary, both the sacred garments for Aaron the priest and the garments for his sons when serving as priests.

⁴²The Israelites had done all the work just as the LORD had commanded Moses. i ⁴³Moses inspected the work and saw that they had done it just as the LORD had commanded.ʲ So Moses blessedᵏ them.

SETTING UP THE TABERNACLE

40 Then the LORD said to Moses: ²"Set upˡ the tabernacle, the tent of meeting,ᵐ on the first day of the first month. n ³Place the arkᵒ of the covenant law in it and shield the ark with the curtain. ⁴Bring in the tableᵖ and set out what belongs on it. q Then bring in the lampstandʳ and set up its lamps. ⁵Place the gold altarˢ of incense in front of the ark of the covenant law and put the curtain at the entrance to the tabernacle.

⁶"Place the altarᵗ of burnt offering in front of the entrance to the tabernacle, the tent of meeting; ⁷place the basinᵘ between the tent of meeting and the altar and put water in it. ⁸Set up the courtyardᵛ around it and put the curtain at the entrance to the courtyard.

⁹"Take the anointing oil and anointʷ the tabernacle and everything in it; consecrate it and all its furnishings,ˣ and it will be holy. ¹⁰Then anoint the altar of burnt offering and all its utensils; consecrateʸ the altar, and it will be most holy. ¹¹Anoint the basin and its stand and consecrate them.

¹²"Bring Aaron and his sons to the entrance to the tent of meetingᶻ and wash them

---

ᵃ 23 The meaning of the Hebrew for this word is uncertain.   ᵇ 34 Possibly the hides of dugongs

39:27 ᵒ Lev 6:10; 8:2
39:28 ᵖ ver 31; S Ex 28:4; Lev 8:9; Isa 61:10
39:30 �q Isa 23:18; Zec 14:20
39:31 ʳ S ver 28
39:32 ˢ S Ex 25:9
39:33 ᵗ Ex 25:8-40; 36:8-38
39:35 ᵘ S Ex 37:1
39:36 ᵛ Ex 25:23-30; 37:10-16
ʷ S Ex 25:30
39:37 ˣ S Ex 25:31
ʸ Ex 25:31-39
ᶻ S Ex 25:6
39:38 ᵃ Ex 30:1-10
ᵇ Ex 30:22-32; 37:29
ᶜ Ex 30:34-38;
S 37:29 ᵈ S Ex 36:35
39:39 ᵉ Ex 27:1-8;
38:1-7 ᶠ S Ex 30:18
39:40 ᵍ Ex 27:9-19;
38:9-20
39:41 ʰ S ver 1
39:42 ⁱ S Ex 25:9
39:43 ʲ S Ex 25:9
S 35:10 ᵏ Ge 31:55;
Lev 9:22,23;
Nu 6:23-27; Dt 21:5;
26:15; 2Sa 6:18;
1Ki 8:14,55; 1Ch 16:2;
2Ch 30:27
40:2 ˡ S Ex 26:30
ᵐ ver 34,35; Lev 1:1;
3:2; 6:26; 9:23; 16:16;
Nu 1:1; 7:89; 11:16;
17:4; 20:6; Jos 18:1;
19:51; Jer 7:12
ⁿ ver 17; S Ex 12:2;
Nu 9:1
40:3 ᵒ S Ex 26:33
40:4 ᵖ S Ex 25:23
�q S Ex 25:30
ʳ S Ex 25:31
40:5 ˢ S Ex 30:1
40:6 ᵗ S Ex 27:1;
2Ki 16:14; 2Ch 4:1
40:7 ᵘ Ex 30:18
40:8 ᵛ S Ex 27:9
40:9 ʷ S Ex 30:26
ˣ Nu 7:1
40:10 ʸ S Ex 29:36
40:12 ᶻ Nu 8:9

39:30 *sacred emblem.* An official designation (not found in 28:36–37) for the plate of the turban. *HOLY TO THE LORD.* See 28:36 and note.

39:32 *all the work on the tabernacle ... was completed.* Reminiscent of the concluding words of the creation narrative (see Ge 2:1–3). Thus the end of Exodus links with the beginning (see 1:7 and note), marking the complex of events narrated in the book as the beginning of the restoration of the creation order and of the realization of God's redemptive purposes in history

(see also note on 26:1).

A **39:43** *Moses blessed them.* For the faithfulness with which the Israelites had donated their gifts, time and talents in building the tabernacle and all its furnishings—faithfulness in service brings divine benediction.

40:2 *first day of the first month.* The tabernacle was set up almost a year after the institution of the Passover (see v. 17; 12:2,6 and note on 12:2).

40:9–10 *holy ... most holy.* See 3:5; 29:37 and notes.

40:12 *ªS Ex 29:4;
S 30:19
40:13 *ᵇS Ex 28:41
ᶜLev 8:12
40:14 *ᵈS Ex 28:40;
Lev 10:5
40:15 *ᵉS Ex 29:9
40:16 *ᶠS Ge 6:22
40:17 *ᵍNu 7:1
ʰS ver 2
40:18 *i2Ch 1:3
ʲEx 36:20-34
40:19 *ᵏEx 36:19
ˡS Ge 6:22
40:20 *ᵐS Ex 16:34;
Heb 9:4 *ⁿS Ex 25:21
ᵒEx 25:17-22;
S 26:34; S 31:7
40:21 *ᵖS Ex 26:33
ᵠS Ge 6:22
40:22 *ʳS Ex 25:23
40:23 *ˢS Ex 25:30;
Lev 24:5-8
ᵗS Ge 6:22
40:24 *ᵘS Ex 25:31
40:25 *ᵛS Ex 37:23
ʷS Ge 6:22
40:26 *ˣS Ex 30:1
40:27 *ʸS Ge 6:22
40:28 *ᶻS Ex 26:36
40:29 *ᵃS Ex 20:24
ᵇEx 29:38-42
ᶜS Ge 6:22
40:30 *ᵈS ver 7;
S Ex 30:18
40:31 *ᵉEx 30:19-21
40:32 *ᶠEx 30:20
ᵍS Ge 6:22
40:33 *ʰS Ex 27:9;
38:9-20 ʲEx 27:16
40:34 *ʲEx 19:16;
Lev 16:2; Nu 9:15-23;
1Ki 8:12; 2Ch 5:13;
Isa 6:4; Eze 10:4
ᵏS Ex 16:7; Jn 1:14;
12:41; Rev 15:8
40:35 *ˡS Ex 16:10
ᵐ1Ki 8:11; 2Ch 5:13-
14; 7:2
40:36 *ⁿNu 9:17-23;
10:13
40:38 *ᵒS Ex 13:21;
1Co 10:1

with water. ᵃ ¹³Then dress Aaron in the sacred garments, ᵇ anoint him and consecrate ᶜ him so he may serve me as priest. ¹⁴Bring his sons and dress them in tunics. ᵈ ¹⁵Anoint them just as you anointed their father, so they may serve me as priests. Their anointing will be to a priesthood that will continue throughout their generations. ᵉ" ¹⁶Moses did everything just as the LORD commanded ᶠ him.

¹⁷So the tabernacle ᵍ was set up on the first day of the first month ʰ in the second year. ¹⁸When Moses ⁱ set up the tabernacle, he put the bases in place, erected the frames, ʲ inserted the crossbars and set up the posts. ¹⁹Then he spread the tent over the tabernacle and put the covering ᵏ over the tent, as the LORD commanded ˡ him.

²⁰He took the tablets of the covenant law ᵐ and placed them in the ark, ⁿ attached the poles to the ark and put the atonement cover ᵒ over it. ²¹Then he brought the ark into the tabernacle and hung the shielding curtain ᵖ and shielded the ark of the covenant law, as the LORD commanded ᵠ him.

²²Moses placed the table ʳ in the tent of meeting on the north side of the tabernacle outside the curtain ²³and set out the bread ˢ on it before the LORD, as the LORD commanded ᵗ him.

²⁴He placed the lampstand ᵘ in the tent of meeting opposite the table on the south side of the tabernacle ²⁵and set up the lamps ᵛ before the LORD, as the LORD commanded ʷ him.

²⁶Moses placed the gold altar ˣ in the tent of meeting in front of the curtain ²⁷and burned fragrant incense on it, as the LORD commanded ʸ him.

²⁸Then he put up the curtain ᶻ at the entrance to the tabernacle. ²⁹He set the altar ᵃ of burnt offering near the entrance to the tabernacle, the tent of meeting, and offered on it burnt offerings and grain offerings, ᵇ as the LORD commanded ᶜ him.

³⁰He placed the basin ᵈ between the tent of meeting and the altar and put water in it for washing, ³¹and Moses and Aaron and his sons used it to wash ᵉ their hands and feet. ³²They washed whenever they entered the tent of meeting or approached the altar, ᶠ as the LORD commanded ᵍ Moses.

³³Then Moses set up the courtyard ʰ around the tabernacle and altar and put up the curtain ⁱ at the entrance to the courtyard. And so Moses finished the work.

THE GLORY OF THE LORD

³⁴Then the cloud ʲ covered the tent of meeting, and the glory ᵏ of the LORD filled the tabernacle. ³⁵Moses could not enter the tent of meeting because the cloud had settled on it, and the glory ˡ of the LORD filled the tabernacle. ᵐ

³⁶In all the travels of the Israelites, whenever the cloud lifted from above the tabernacle, they would set out; ⁿ ³⁷but if the cloud did not lift, they did not set out—until the day it lifted. ³⁸So the cloud ᵒ of the LORD was over the tabernacle by day, and fire was in the cloud by night, in the sight of all the house of Israel during all their travels.

A C **40:16** *Moses did . . . just as the LORD commanded.* Moses' obedience to God's command is a key theme of the final chapter of Exodus (see vv. 19,21,23,25,27,29,32). The people provided all the resources and made all the components, but only the Lord's servant Moses was authorized to erect the tabernacle and prepare it for the Lord's entry. **40:33** *Moses finished the work.* See note on 39:32.

A C **40:34** With the glory of the Lord entering the tabernacle (cf. 1Ki 8:10–11 and note on 8:10), the great series of events that began with the birth of Moses and his rescue from the Nile, foreshadowing the deliverance of Israel from Egypt, comes to a grand climax. From now on, the Israelites march through the wilderness, and through history, with the Lord tenting among them and leading them to the land of fulfilled promises. **40:38** See note on 13:21.

AUTHOR AND DATE

LEVITICUS

See note on 1:1 and Introduction to Genesis: Author and Date of Writing.

TITLE

Leviticus receives its name from the Septuagint (the pre-Christian Greek translation of the OT) and means "relating to the Levites." Its Hebrew title, *wayyiqra'*, is the first word in the Hebrew text of the book and means "And he [i.e., the LORD] called." Although Leviticus does not deal only with the special duties of the Levites, it is so named because it concerns mainly the service of worship at the tabernacle, which was conducted by the priests who were the sons of Aaron, assisted by many from the rest of the tribe of Levi. Exodus gave the directions for building the tabernacle, and now Leviticus gives the laws and regulations for worship there, including instructions on ceremonial cleanness, moral laws, holy days, the sabbath year and the Year of Jubilee. These laws were given, at least for the most part, during the year that Israel camped at Mount Sinai, when God directed Moses in organizing Israel's worship, government and military forces. The book of Numbers continues the history with preparations for moving on from Sinai to Canaan.

THEOLOGICAL THEMES

Leviticus is a manual of regulations enabling the holy King to set up his earthly throne among the people of his kingdom. It explains how they are to be his holy people and to worship him in a holy manner. Holiness in this sense means to be separated from sin and set apart exclusively to the Lord for his purpose and for his glory. So the key thought of the book is holiness (see notes on 11:44; Ex 3:5)—the holiness of God and his people (they must revere him in "holiness"). In Leviticus spiritual holiness is symbolized by physical perfection. Therefore the book demands perfect animals for its many sacrifices (chs. 1–7) and requires priests without deformity (chs. 8–10). A woman's hemorrhaging after giving birth (ch. 12); sores, burns or baldness (chs. 13–14); a man's bodily discharge (15:1–18); specific activities during a woman's monthly period (15:19–33)—all may be signs of blemish (a lack of perfection) and may symbolize human spiritual defects, which break spiritual wholeness. The person with visible skin disease must be banished from the camp, the place of God's special presence, just as Adam and Eve were banished from the Garden of Eden. Such people can return to the camp (and therefore to God's presence) when they are pronounced whole again by the examining priests. Before they can reenter the camp, however, they must offer the prescribed, perfect sacrifices (symbolizing the perfect, whole sacrifice of Christ).

After the covenant at Sinai, Israel was the earthly representation of God's kingdom (the theocracy), and the Lord, as its King, established his royal administration over all of Israel's life. The Israelites' religious, communal and personal life was so regulated as to establish them as God's holy people and to instruct them in holiness. Special attention was given to Israel's religious ritual. The sacrifices were to be offered at an approved sanctuary, which would symbolize both God's holiness and his compassion. They were to be controlled by the priests, who by care and instruction would preserve them in purity and carefully teach their meaning to the people.

Each particular sacrifice was to have meaning for the people of Israel but would also have spiritual and symbolic import.

For more information on the meaning of sacrifice in general, see the solemn ritual of the Day of Atonement (ch. 16; see note on 16:1—34). For the meaning of the blood of the offering, see 17:11; Ge 9:4 and notes. For the emphasis on substitution, see 16:21.

Some suppose that the OT sacrifices were remains of old agricultural offerings—a human desire to offer part of one's possessions as a love gift to the deity. But the OT sacrifices were specifically prescribed by God and received their meaning from the Lord's covenant relationship with Israel—whatever their superficial resemblances to pagan sacrifices may have been. They indeed include the idea of a gift, but this is accompanied by such other values as dedication, communion, propitiation (appeasing God's judicial wrath against sin) and restitution. The various offerings have differing functions, the primary ones being atonement (see note on Ex 25:17) and worship (see chart, p. 155).

OUTLINE

The subjects treated in Leviticus, as in any book of laws and regulations, cover several categories:

THE BURNT OFFERING

1 The LORD called to Moses[a] and spoke to him from the tent of meeting.[b] He said, [2]"Speak to the Israelites and say to them: 'When you bring an offering to the LORD,[c] bring as your offering an animal from either the herd or the flock.[d]

[3]" 'If the offering is a burnt offering[e] from the herd,[f] you are to offer a male without defect.[g] You must present it at the entrance to the tent[h] of meeting so that you may be acceptable[i] to the LORD. [4]You are to lay your hand on the head[j] of the burnt offering,[k] and it will be accepted[l] on your behalf to make atonement[m] for you. [5]You are to slaughter[n] the young bull[o] before the LORD, and then Aaron's sons[p] the priests shall bring the blood and splash it against the sides of the altar[q] at the entrance to the tent of meeting. [6]You are to skin[r] the burnt offering and cut it into pieces.[s] [7]The sons of Aaron the priest are to put fire on the altar and arrange wood[t] on the fire. [8]Then Aaron's sons the priests shall arrange the pieces, including the head and the fat,[u] on the wood[v] that is burning on the altar. [9]You are to wash the internal organs and the legs with water,[w] and the priest is to burn all of it[x] on the altar.[y] It is a burnt offering,[z] a food offering,[a] an aroma pleasing to the LORD.[b]

[10]" 'If the offering is a burnt offering from the flock, from either the sheep[c] or the goats,[d] you are to offer a male without defect. [11]You are to slaughter it at the north side of the altar[e] before the LORD, and Aaron's sons the priests shall splash its blood against the sides of the altar.[f] [12]You are to cut it into pieces, and the priest shall arrange them, including the head and the fat,[g] on the wood that is burning on the altar. [13]You are to wash the internal organs and the legs with water,[h] and the priest is to bring all of them and burn them[i] on the altar.[j] It is a burnt offering,[k] a food offering, an aroma pleasing to the LORD.

[14]" 'If the offering to the LORD is a burnt offering of birds, you are to offer a dove or a young pigeon.[l] [15]The priest shall bring it to the altar, wring off the head[m] and burn it on the altar; its blood shall be drained out on the side of the altar.[n] [16]He is to remove the crop and the feathers[a] and throw them down east of the altar where the ashes[o] are. [17]He

---

[a] 16 Or *crop with its contents*; the meaning of the Hebrew for this word is uncertain.

1:10 [d]S ver 3; Ex 12:5; Lev 3:12; 4:23,28; 5:6; Nu 15:11 **1:11** [e]S Ex 29:11 [f]S Ex 29:20 **1:12** [g]S ver 8 **1:13** [h]S Ex 29:17 [i]Lev 6:22 [j]S ver 9 [k]Dt 12:27 **1:14** [l]S Ge 15:9; Lk 2:24 **1:15** [m]Lev 5:8 [n]Lev 5:9 **1:16** [o]Lev 4:12; 6:10; Nu 4:13

Side references

1:1 [a]S Ex 3:4; S 25:22 [b]S Ex 27:21; S 40:2
1:2 [c]Lev 7:16,38; 22:21; 23:38; 27:9 [d]Lev 22:18-19; Nu 15:3
1:3 [e]S Ge 8:20 [f]ver 10; Lev 22:27; Ezr 8:35; Mal 1:8 [g]S ver 5; S Ex 12:5; S Lev 22:19,20; Heb 9:14; 1Pe 1:19 [h]Lev 6:25; 17:9; [i]Isa 58:5
1:4 [j]S Ex 29:10,15 [k]ver 3; Lev 4:29; 6:25; Eze 45:15 [l]S Ge 32:20 [m]S Ex 29:36; S 32:30
1:5 [n]Ex 29:11; Lev 3:2,8 [o]S ver 3; Ex 29:1; Nu 15:8; Dt 18:3; Ps 50:9; 69:31 [p]Lev 8:2; 10:6; 21:1 [q]S Ex 29:20; Heb 12:24; 1Pe 1:2
1:6 [r]Lev 7:8
1:7 [t]ver 17; S Ge 22:9; Lev 3:5; 6:12
1:8 [u]ver 12; S Ex 29:13; Lev 8:20
1:9 [w]S Ex 29:17 [x]Lev 6:22 [y]ver 13; Ex 29:18; Lev 9:14 [z]ver 3 [a]Lev 23:8,25, 36; Nu 28:6,19 [b]ver 13; Ge 8:21; Lev 2:2; 3:5,16; 17:6; Nu 18:17; 28:11-13; Eph 5:2
1:10 [c]S Ge 22:7

1:1—7:38 Regulations for the five main offerings: burnt, grain, fellowship, sin and guilt offerings.

1:1 Emphasizes that the contents of Leviticus were given to Moses by God at Mount Sinai. Cf. also the concluding verse (27:34). In more than 50 places it is said that the Lord spoke to Moses. Modern criticism has attributed practically the whole book to priestly legislation written during or after the exile. But this is without objective evidence, is against the repeated claim of the book to be Mosaic, is against the traditional Jewish view, and runs counter to other OT and NT witness (Ro 10:5). Many items in Leviticus are now seen to be best explained in terms of a second-millennium B.C. date, which is also the most likely time for Moses to have written the Pentateuch (see Introduction to Genesis: Author and Date of Writing). There is no convincing reason not to take at face value the many references to Moses and his work. *tent of meeting.* The tabernacle, where God met with Israel (see note on Ex 27:21).

1:2 *bring an offering.* The Hebrew word for "offering" used here (*qorban*) comes from the verb translated "bring." An "offering" is something that people "bring" to God as a gift (most offerings were voluntary, such as the burnt offering). This word for "offering" is also used in Mk 7:11 (Corban), where Mark translates it "devoted to God" (see note there).

1:3 *burnt offering.* See further priestly regulations in 6:8–13 (see also chart, p. 155). A burnt offering was offered every morning and evening for all Israel (Ex 29:39–42). Double burnt offerings were brought on the Sabbath (Nu 28:9–10) and extra ones on festival days (Nu 28–29). In addition, anyone could offer special burnt offerings to express devotion to the Lord. *male.* The burnt offering had to be a male animal because of its greater value, and also perhaps because it was thought to better represent vigor and fertility. It was usually a young sheep or goat (for the average individual), but bulls (for the wealthy) and doves or pigeons (for the poor) were also specified. *without defect.* The ani-

mal had to be unblemished (cf. Mal 1:8; 1Pe 1:19 and note). As in all offerings, the offerers were to lay their hands on the head of the animal to express identification between themselves and the animal (16:21), whose death would then be accepted in "atonement" (v. 4). The blood was splashed on the sides of the great altar (located outside the tabernacle—later the temple—in the eastern half of the courtyard), where the fire of sacrifice was never to go out (6:13). The whole sacrifice was to be burned up (v. 9), including the head, legs, fat and internal organs. It is therefore sometimes called a holocaust offering (*holo* means "whole," and *caust* means "burnt"). When a bull was offered, however, the officiating priest could keep its hide (7:8). The burnt offering may have been the usual sacrifice offered by the patriarchs. It was the most comprehensive in its meaning. Its Hebrew name means "going up," perhaps symbolizing worship and prayer as its aroma ascended to the Lord (v. 17). The completeness of its burning also speaks of dedication on the part of the worshiper. *entrance to the tent of meeting.* Where the altar of burnt offering was (see Ex 40:29). *acceptable to the Lord.* See Ro 12:1; Php 4:18 and note.

1:4 *lay your hand on.* See note on v. 3; Ex 29:10. *atonement.* See notes on 16:20–22; 17:11; Ex 25:17.

1:5 Only after the offerer killed the animal (symbolizing substitution of a perfect animal sacrifice for a sinful human life) did the priestly work begin. *blood.* See notes on 17:11; Heb 9:18. *splash it against the sides of the altar.* See Ex 24:6; Heb 9:19–21.

1:6 *skin.* The whole animal was burned except the hide, which was given to the priest (7:8).

1:9,13,17 *aroma pleasing to the Lord.* The OT sacrifices foreshadowed Christ, who was a "fragrant offering" (Eph 5:2; cf. Php 4:18).

1:11 *north side.* See diagram, p. 129.

1:14 *birds.* Three categories of sacrifices are mentioned: (1) herds (vv. 3–9), (2) flocks (vv. 10–13) and (3) birds (vv. 14–17). Sacrifices of birds were allowed for the poor (see 5:7; 12:8; Lk 2:24).

1:17 *p* S Ge 15:10
q S ver 7
2:1 *r* S Ex 29:41;
Lev 6:14-18 *s* Ex 29:2,
40; Lev 5:11 *t* Nu 15:4;
28:5 *u* S Ex 29:2;
Lev 7:12 *v* ver 2,15,16;
Lev 24:7; Ne 13:9;
Isa 43:23
2:2 *w* Lev 5:11
x Lev 6:15; Isa 1:13;
65:3; 66:3 *y* ver 9,16;
Lev 5:12; 6:15; 24:7;
Nu 5:26; 18:8;
Ps 16:5; 73:26;
Isa 53:12 *z* ver 16
a S Lev 1:9
2:3 *b* ver 10;
Lev 6:16; 10:12,13
c S Ex 30:36
2:4 *d* Lev 7:9; 26:26
e Lev 7:12; 8:26
f S Ex 29:2
2:5 *g* Lev 6:21; 7:9;
Eze 4:3
2:7 *h* Lev 7:9
2:9 *i* S ver 2
j S Ge 8:21
2:10 *k* ver 3
l Ezr 2:63
2:11 *m* S Ex 23:18;
Lev 6:16
2:12 *n* S Ex 34:22
2:13 *o* Mk 9:49
p Nu 18:19; 2Ch 13:5;
Eze 43:24
2:14 *q* S Ex 34:22;
Nu 15:20; Dt 16:13;
26:2; Ru 3:2
2:15 *r* S ver 1
2:16 *s* S ver 2
t S ver 1 *u* Nu 4:16;
Jer 14:12
3:1 *v* S ver 6;
S Ex 32:6; Lev 7:11-
34; S 17:5 *w* S Ex 12:5
3:2 *x* S Ex 29:15;
Nu 8:10 *y* S Lev 1:5

shall tear it open by the wings, not dividing it completely, *p* and then the priest shall burn it on the wood *q* that is burning on the altar. It is a burnt offering, a food offering, an aroma pleasing to the LORD.

THE GRAIN OFFERING

2 " 'When anyone brings a grain offering *r* to the LORD, your offering is to be of the finest flour. *s* You are to pour olive oil *t* on it, *u* put incense on it *v* ²and take it to Aaron's sons the priests. The priest shall take a handful of the flour *w* and oil, together with all the incense, *x* and burn this as a memorial*a* portion *y* on the altar, a food offering, *z* an aroma pleasing to the LORD. *a* ³The rest of the grain offering belongs to Aaron and his sons; *b* it is a most holy *c* part of the food offering presented to the LORD.

⁴" 'If you bring a grain offering baked in an oven, *d* it is to consist of the finest flour: either thick loaves made without yeast and with olive oil mixed in or thin loaves *e* made without yeast and brushed with olive oil. *f* ⁵If your grain offering is prepared on a griddle, *g* it is to be made of the finest flour mixed with oil, and without yeast. ⁶Crumble it and pour oil on it; it is a grain offering. ⁷If your grain offering is cooked in a pan, *h* it is to be made of the finest flour and some olive oil. ⁸Bring the grain offering made of these things to the LORD; present it to the priest, who shall take it to the altar. ⁹He shall take out the memorial portion *i* from the grain offering and burn it on the altar as a food offering, an aroma pleasing to the LORD. *j* ¹⁰The rest of the grain offering belongs to Aaron and his sons; *k* it is a most holy part of the food offerings presented to the LORD. *l*

¹¹" 'Every grain offering you bring to the LORD must be made without yeast, *m* for you are not to burn any yeast or honey in a food offering presented to the LORD. ¹²You may bring them to the LORD as an offering of the firstfruits, *n* but they are not to be offered on the altar as a pleasing aroma. ¹³Season all your grain offerings with salt. *o* Do not leave the salt of the covenant*p* of your God out of your grain offerings; add salt to all your offerings.

¹⁴" 'If you bring a grain offering of firstfruits *q* to the LORD, offer crushed heads of new grain roasted in the fire. ¹⁵Put oil and incense *r* on it; it is a grain offering. ¹⁶The priest shall burn the memorial portion *s* of the crushed grain and the oil, together with all the incense, *t* as a food offering presented to the LORD. *u*

THE FELLOWSHIP OFFERING

3 " 'If your offering is a fellowship offering, *v* and you offer an animal from the herd, whether male or female, you are to present before the LORD an animal without defect. *w* ²You are to lay your hand on the head *x* of your offering and slaughter it *y*

a 2 Or *representative*; also in verses 9 and 16

1:17 *not dividing it completely.* See note on Ge 15:10.
2:1 *grain offering.* See further priestly regulations in 6:14–23; 7:9–10. It was made of grain or fine flour. If baked or cooked, it consisted of cakes or wafers made in a pan or oven or on a griddle. It was the only bloodless offering, but it was to accompany the burnt offering (see Nu 28:3–6), sin offering (see Nu 6:14–15) and fellowship offering (see 9:4; Nu 6:17). The amounts of grain offering ingredients specified to accompany a bull, ram or lamb sacrificed as a burnt offering are given in Nu 28:12–13. A representative handful of flour was to be burned on the altar with the accompanying offerings, and the balance was to be baked without yeast and eaten by the priests in their holy meals (6:14–17). The flour that was burned on the altar was mixed with olive oil for shortening, salted for taste and accompanied by incense, but it was to have no yeast or honey—neither of which was allowed on the altar (vv. 11–13). The cooked product was similar to pie crust. The worshiper was not to eat any of the grain offering, and the priests were not to eat any of their own grain offerings, which were to be totally burned (6:22–23). The Hebrew word for grain offering can mean "present" or "gift" and is often used in that way (see Ge 43:11). The sacred gifts expressed devotion to God (see v. 2). *finest flour.* Grain that was milled and sifted. *oil.* Olive oil is often mentioned in connection with grain and new wine as fresh products of the harvest (see Dt 7:13). Used extensively in cooking, it was a suitable part of the worshiper's gift. *incense.* Frankincense was the chief ingredient (see Ex 30:34–35).

2:2,9,16 *memorial portion.* Either (1) to remind the worshiper that all good things come from the Lord (cf. Jas 1:17), or (2) to cause the Lord to "remember" and bless the offerer in covenant faithfulness (cf. Ge 9:13–16). It may have been a combination of both. See also 5:12; 6:15; 24:7.
2:3 *most holy part.* For this reason, the priests were to eat it in the sanctuary area proper and not feed their families with it (6:16–18). See also v. 10. *holy.* See Ex 29:37 and note.
2:4 *without yeast.* See notes on Ex 12:8,15.
2:5 *griddle.* A clay pan that rested on a stone heated by a fire. Later, iron pans were sometimes used.
2:11 *honey.* It was forbidden on the altar, perhaps because of its use in brewing beer (as an aid to fermentation), though some suggest that it was because of its use in Canaanite cultic practice.
2:12 *firstfruits.* See 23:10–11; Ex 23:16,19; Nu 15:18–20; Dt 18:4–5; 26:1–11.
2:13 *salt of the covenant.* See note on Nu 18:19.
3:1 *fellowship offering.* See further priestly regulations in 7:11–21,28–34. Two basic ideas are included in this offering: peace and fellowship. The traditional translation is "peace offering," a name that comes from the Hebrew word for the offering, which in turn is related to the Hebrew word *shalom,* meaning "peace" or "wholeness." Thus the offering perhaps symbolized peace between God and his people, as well as the inward peace that resulted. The fellowship offering was the only

at the entrance to the tent of meeting. ᶻ Then Aaron's sons the priests shall splash ᵃ the blood against the sides ᵇ of the altar. ᶜ ³From the fellowship offering you are to bring a food offering to the Lord: the internal organs ᵈ and all the fat ᵉ that is connected to them, ⁴both kidneys ᶠ with the fat on them near the loins, and the long lobe of the liver, which you will remove with the kidneys. ⁵Then Aaron's sons ᵍ are to burn it on the altar ʰ on top of the burnt offering ⁱ that is lying on the burning wood; ʲ it is a food offering, an aroma pleasing to the Lord. ᵏ

6 " 'If you offer an animal from the flock as a fellowship offering ˡ to the Lord, you are to offer a male or female without defect. ⁷If you offer a lamb, ᵐ you are to present it before the Lord, ⁿ ⁸lay your hand on its head and slaughter it ᵒ in front of the tent of meeting. Then Aaron's sons shall splash its blood against the sides of the altar. ⁹From the fellowship offering you are to bring a food offering ᵖ to the Lord: its fat, the entire fat tail cut off close to the backbone, the internal organs and all the fat that is connected to them, ¹⁰both kidneys with the fat on them near the loins, and the long lobe of the liver, which you will remove with the kidneys. ¹¹The priest shall burn them on the altar �q as a food offering ʳ presented to the Lord. ˢ

12 " 'If your offering is a goat, ᵗ you are to present it before the Lord, ¹³lay your hand on its head and slaughter it in front of the tent of meeting. Then Aaron's sons shall splash ᵘ its blood against the sides of the altar. ᵛ ¹⁴From what you offer you are to present this food offering to the Lord: the internal organs and all the fat that is connected to them, ¹⁵both kidneys with the fat on them near the loins, and the long lobe of the liver, which you will remove with the kidneys. ʷ ¹⁶The priest shall burn them on the altar ˣ as a food offering, ʸ a pleasing aroma. ᶻ All the fat ᵃ is the Lord's. ᵇ

17 " 'This is a lasting ordinance ᶜ for the generations to come, ᵈ wherever you live: ᵉ You must not eat any fat or any blood. ᶠ ' "

THE SIN OFFERING

4 The Lord said to Moses, ²"Say to the Israelites: 'When anyone sins unintentionally ᵍ and does what is forbidden in any of the Lord's commands ʰ—

3 " 'If the anointed priest ⁱ sins, ʲ bringing guilt on the people, he must bring to the Lord a young bull ᵏ without defect ˡ as a sin offering ᵃ ᵐ for the sin he has committed. ⁿ ⁴He is to present the bull at the entrance to the tent of meeting before the Lord. ᵒ He is to lay his hand on its head and slaughter it there before the Lord. ⁵Then the anointed priest shall take some of the bull's blood ᵖ and carry it into the tent of meeting. ⁶He is to dip his

ᵃ 3 Or *purification offering*; here and throughout this chapter

4:5 ᵖ ver 16; Lev 16:14

3:2 ᶻ S Ex 40:2
ᵃ S Ex 24:6
ᵇ S Ex 29:20
ᶜ Lev 17:6; Nu 18:17
3:3 ᵈ S Ex 12:9
ᵉ S Ex 29:13
3:4 ᶠ ver 10;
Ex 29:13; Lev 4:9
3:5 ᵍ Lev 7:29-34
ʰ ver 11,16; ⁱ Ex 29:13,
38-42; Nu 28:3-10
ʲ S Lev 1:7 ᵏ S Lev 1:9
3:6 ˡ S ver 1;
Lev 22:21; Nu 15:3,8
3:7 ᵐ Lev 17:3;
Nu 15:5; 28:5,7,8
ⁿ Lev 17:8-9; 1Ki 8:62
3:8 ᵒ S Lev 1:5
3:9 ᵖ Isa 34:6;
Jer 46:10; Eze 39:19;
Zep 1:7
3:11 q S ver 5
ʳ ver 16; Lev 21:6,17;
Nu 28:2 ˢ Lev 9:18
3:12 ᵗ S Lev 1:10;
S 43
3:13 ᵘ S Ex 24:6
ᵛ Lev 1:5
3:15 ʷ Lev 7:4
3:16 ˣ S ver 5;
Lev 7:31 ʸ S ver 11
ᶻ S Lev 1:9 ᵃ S Ge 4:4
ᵇ 1Sa 2:16
3:17 ᶜ S Ex 12:14;
S 27:21 ᵈ S Ge 9:12
ᵉ S Lev 23:14 ᶠ Ge 9:4;
Lev 7:25-26; 17:10-
16; Dt 12:16; Ac 15:20
4:2 ᵍ ver 13,27;
Lev 5:15-18; 22:14;
Nu 15:24-29; 35:11-
15; Jos 20:3,9;
Heb 9:7 ʰ ver 22;
Nu 15:22
4:3 ⁱ S Ex 28:41
ʲ S Ge 18:23 ᵏ ver 14;
Lev 3:12; 8:14; 10:16;
16:3,5; Nu 15:27;
Ps 66:15; Eze 43:19,
23 ˡ S Ex 12:5
ᵐ S ver 24;
S Ex 30:10; Lev 5:6-
13; 9:2-22; Heb 9:13-
14 ⁿ ver 32
4:4 ᵒ ver 15,24;
Lev 1:3; Nu 8:12

---

sacrifice of which the offerer might eat a part. Fellowship was involved because the offerer, on the basis of the sacrifice, had fellowship with God and with the priest, who also ate part of the offering (7:14–15,31–34). This sacrifice—along with others—was offered by the thousands during the three annual festivals in Israel (see Ex 23:14–17; Nu 29:39) because multitudes of people came to the temple to worship and share in a communal meal. During the monarchy, the animals offered by the people were usually supplemented by large numbers given by the king. At the dedication of the temple, Solomon offered 20,000 cattle and 120,000 sheep and goats as fellowship offerings over a period of 14 days (1Ki 8:63–65).

3:2 *lay your hand on.* See notes on 1:3; Ex 29:10.

3:5 *on top of the burnt offering.* The burnt offerings for the nation as a whole were offered every morning and evening, and the fellowship offerings were offered on top of them.

3:9 *fat tail.* A breed of sheep still much used in the Middle East has a tail heavy with fat.

3:11,16 *on the altar as a food offering.* Israelite sacrifices were not "food for the gods" (as in other ancient cultures; see Eze 16:20; cf. Ps 50:9–13) but were sometimes called "food" metaphorically (21:6,8,17,21; 22:25) in the sense that they were gifts to God, which he received with delight.

3:16 *All the fat is the Lord's.* Because it signified the best (see 7:23; Ge 4:34 and notes).

3:17 *not eat any fat or any blood.* See note on 17:11.

4:2 *unintentionally.* See 5:15; contrast Nu 15:30–31. Four class-

es of people involved in committing unintentional sins are listed: (1) "the anointed priest" (vv. 3–12), (2) the "whole Israelite community" (vv. 13–21), (3) a "leader" (vv. 22–26) and (4) a "member of the community" (vv. 27–35). Heb 9:7 speaks of sins "committed in ignorance" in referring to the Day of Atonement.

Ⓐ **4:3** *anointed priest.* The high priest (see 6:20,22). *sins.* All high priests sinned except the high priest Jesus Christ (Heb 5:1–3; 7:26–28). *on the people.* The relationship of the priests to the people was so intimate in Israel (as a nation consecrated to God) that the people became guilty when the priest sinned. *must.* Although the burnt, grain and fellowship offerings (chs. 1–3) were voluntary, the sin offering was compulsory (see vv. 14,23,28). *without defect.* A defective sacrifice could not be a substitute for a defective people (see Mal 1:8 and note). The final perfect sacrifice for the sins of God's people was the crucified Christ, who was without any moral defect (Heb 9:13–14; 1Pe 1:19). *sin offering.* See further priestly regulations in 6:24–30; Nu 15:22–29. As soon as an "anointed priest" (or a person from one of the other classes of people) became aware of unintentional sin, he was to bring his sin offering to the Lord. On the other hand, if the priest (or others) should remain unaware of unintentional sin, this lack was atoned for on the Day of Atonement.

4:4 Three principles of atonement are found in this verse: (1) substitution ("present the bull"), (2) identification ("lay his hand on its head") and (3) the death of the substitute ("slaughter it").

Ⓐ **4:5** *blood.* See note on 17:11. There were two types of sin offerings. The first (vv. 3–21) and more important in-

4:6 *q* Ex 24:8
r ver 17; Lev 16:14,19
s S Ex 25:8
4:7 *t* S Ex 27:2
u ver 34; S Ex 29:12;
Lev 8:15 *v* ver 18,30;
Lev 5:9; 9:9; 16:18
4:8 *w* ver 19
4:9 *x* S Lev 3:4
4:10 *y* Lev 9:4
z S Ex 32:6
a S Ex 29:13
4:11 *b* Ex 29:14;
Lev 8:17; 9:11;
Nu 19:5
4:12 *c* S Ex 29:14;
Lev 8:17; 9:11;
Heb 13:11 *d* Lev 6:11;
10:14; Nu 19:9
e S Lev 1:16 *f* Lev 6:30
g Lev 16:3
4:13 *h* S ver 2
4:14 *i* S ver 3
j Nu 15:24
4:15 *k* S Ex 3:16;
S 19:7 *l* 2Ch 29:23
m S Ex 29:10;
Lev 8:14,22; Nu 8:10
n S ver 4
4:16 *o* S ver 5
4:17 *p* Nu 19:4,18
q S ver 6
4:18 *r* Lev 8:15; 17:6;
2Ch 29:22 *s* ver 7;
Lev 6:30; 10:18
t Lev 5:9
4:19 *u* ver 8 *v* ver 26
4:20 *w* S Ex 29:36;
S 32:30; S Ro 3:25;
Heb 10:10-12
x ver 26,31,35;
Nu 15:25
4:21 *y* S ver 12
z Lev 16:5,15;
2Ch 29:21
4:22 *a* Nu 31:13
b ver 2
4:23 *c* S ver 3;
S Lev 1:10
4:24 *d* S ver 4
e S ver 3; Lev 6:25

finger into the blood and sprinkle *q* some of it seven times before the Lord, *r* in front of the curtain of the sanctuary. *s* 7The priest shall then put some of the blood on the horns *t* of the altar of fragrant incense that is before the Lord in the tent of meeting. The rest of the bull's blood he shall pour out at the base of the altar *u* of burnt offering *v* at the entrance to the tent of meeting. 8He shall remove all the fat *w* from the bull of the sin offering—all the fat that is connected to the internal organs, 9both kidneys with the fat on them near the loins, and the long lobe of the liver, which he will remove with the kidneys *x* — 10just as the fat is removed from the ox *a y* sacrificed as a fellowship offering. *z* Then the priest shall burn them on the altar of burnt offering. *a* 11But the hide of the bull and all its flesh, as well as the head and legs, the internal organs and the intestines *b* — 12that is, all the rest of the bull—he must take outside the camp *c* to a place ceremonially clean, *d* where the ashes *e* are thrown, and burn it *f* there in a wood fire on the ash heap. *g*

13" 'If the whole Israelite community sins unintentionally *h* and does what is forbidden in any of the Lord's commands, even though the community is unaware of the matter, when they realize their guilt 14and the sin they committed becomes known, the assembly must bring a young bull *i* as a sin offering *j* and present it before the tent of meeting. 15The elders *k* of the community are to lay their hands *l* on the bull's head *m* before the Lord, and the bull shall be slaughtered before the Lord. *n* 16Then the anointed priest is to take some of the bull's blood *o* into the tent of meeting. 17He shall dip his finger into the blood and sprinkle *p* it before the Lord *q* seven times in front of the curtain. 18He is to put some of the blood *r* on the horns of the altar that is before the Lord *s* in the tent of meeting. The rest of the blood he shall pour out at the base of the altar *t* of burnt offering at the entrance to the tent of meeting. 19He shall remove all the fat *u* from it and burn it on the altar, *v* 20and do with this bull just as he did with the bull for the sin offering. In this way the priest will make atonement *w* for them, and they will be forgiven. *x* 21Then he shall take the bull outside the camp *y* and burn it as he burned the first bull. This is the sin offering for the community. *z*

22" 'When a leader *a* sins unintentionally *b* and does what is forbidden in any of the commands of the Lord his God, when he realizes his guilt 23and the sin he has committed becomes known, he must bring as his offering a male goat *c* without defect. 24He is to lay his hand on the goat's head and slaughter it at the place where the burnt offering is slaughtered before the Lord. *d* It is a sin offering. *e* 25Then the priest shall take some of

---

a 10 The Hebrew word can refer to either male or female.

---

volved sprinkling the blood in the tabernacle in front of the inner curtain or, in the case of the solemn Day of Atonement (ch. 16), on and in front of the atonement cover (traditionally "mercy seat)" itself. This type of sin offering was not eaten. The fat, kidneys and covering of the liver were burned on the great altar, but all the rest was burned outside the camp (v. 12). Heb 13:11–13 clearly draws the parallel to our sin offering, Jesus, who suffered outside the city gate. This type of sin offering was offered by and for a priest or by the elders for the whole community. In general, the animal to be sacrificed was a young bull, but on the Day of Atonement the sin offering was to be a goat (16:9).

The second type of sin offering (4:22—5:13) was for a leader of the nation or a private individual. Some of the blood was applied to the horns of the great altar; the rest was poured out at its base. The fat, etc., was burned on the altar, but the rest of the offering was given to the priest and his male relatives as food to be eaten in a holy place (6:29–30; see 10:16–20). The sin offering brought by a private person was to be a female goat or lamb. If such persons were poor, they could bring a dove or young pigeon (5:7–8; 12:6,8; cf. Lk 2:24), or even about two quarts of flour (5:11). The offering included confession (5:5) and the symbolic transfer of guilt by laying hands on the sacrifice (v. 29; 16:21). Then the priest who offered the sacrifice made atonement for the sin, and the Lord promised forgiveness (5:13). By bringing such a sin offering, a faithful Israelite under conviction of sin sought restoration of fellowship with God.

4:6 *finger.* The right forefinger (see 14:16). *seven.* The number was symbolic of perfection and completeness (see note on Ge

5:5). *curtain.* The great curtain that separated the Holy Place from the Most Holy Place (Ex 26:33).

4:7,30 *horns.* The four horns of the altar (see Ex 30:1–3) were symbols of the atoning power of the sin offering (Ex 30:10).

4:8–10 See 3:3–5.

🔲 **4:12** *outside the camp.* See note on 13:45–46. So also Jesus was crucified outside Jerusalem (Heb 13:11–13; cf. Lev 9:11; 16:26–28; Nu 19:3; Eze 43:21). *ceremonially clean.* The distinction between clean and unclean was a matter of ritual or religious purity, not a concern for physical cleanliness (see chs. 11–15 for examples; see also Mk 7:1–4). *burn.* Since the sins of the offerer were symbolically transferred to the sacrificial bull, the bull had to be entirely destroyed and not thrown on the ash pile of 1:16.

4:15 *elders.* See note on Ex 3:16.

4:18 *altar.* Of incense (see v. 7).

4:20 *sin offering.* The offering of the priest who had sinned (see v. 3 and note). *will be forgiven.* In 4:20—6:7 this is a key phrase, occurring nine times and referring to forgiveness by God.

4:23 *male goat.* Less valuable animals were sacrificed for those with lesser standing in the community or of lesser economic means. Thus a bull was required for the high priest (v. 3) and the whole community (v. 14), but a male goat for a civic leader (here) and a female goat (v. 28) or lamb (v. 32) for an ordinary Israelite. If an offerer was too poor, then doves and pigeons were sufficient (5:7) or even a handful of finest flour (see 5:11–12 and note on 5:11).

4:25 *priest.* The priest who officiated for the civil authority or the lay person (see vv. 30,34).

OLD TESTAMENT SACRIFICES

SACRIFICE	OT REFERENCES	ELEMENTS	PURPOSE
Burnt Offering	Lev 1; 6:8–13; 8:18–21; 16:24	Bull, ram or male bird (dove or young pigeon for the poor); wholly consumed; no defect	Voluntary act of worship; atonement for unintentional sin in general; expression of devotion, commitment and complete surrender to God
Grain Offering	Lev 2; 6:14–23	Grain, finest flour, olive oil, incense, baked bread (cakes or wafers), salt; no yeast or honey; accompanied burnt offering and fellowship offering (along with drink offering)	Voluntary act of worship; recognition of God's goodness and provisions; devotion to God
Fellowship Offering	Lev 3; 7:11–34	Any animal without defect from herd or flock; variety of breads	Voluntary act of worship; thanksgiving and fellowship (it included a communal meal)
Sin Offering	Lev 4:1—5:13; 6:24–30; 8:14–17; 16:3–22	1. Young bull: for high priest and congregation 2. Male goat: for leader 3. Female goat or lamb: for common person 4. Dove or pigeon: for the poor 5. Tenth of an ephah of finest flour: for the very poor	Mandatory atonement for specific unintentional sin; confession of sin; forgiveness of sin; cleansing from defilement
Guilt Offering	Lev 5:14—6:7; 7:1–6	Ram	Mandatory atonement for unintentional sin requiring restitution; cleansing from defilement; make restitution; pay 20% fine

When more than one kind of offering was presented (as in Nu 7:16,17), the procedure was usually as follows: (1) sin offering or guilt offering, (2) burnt offering, (3) fellowship offering and grain offering (along with a drink offering). This sequence furnishes part of the spiritual significance of the sacrificial system. First, sin had to be dealt with (sin offering or guilt offering). Second, the worshipers committed themselves completely to God (burnt offering and grain offering). Third, fellowship or communion between the Lord, the priest and the worshiper (fellowship offering) was established. To state it another way, there were sacrifices of expiation (sin offerings and guilt offerings), consecration (burnt offerings and grain offerings) and communion (fellowship offerings—these included vow offerings, thank offerings and freewill offerings).

4:25 ^f Lev 16:18;
Eze 43:20,22
^g Lev 9:9
4:26 ^h S Ex 32:30
ⁱ Lev 5:10; 12:8
4:27 ^j S ver 2
4:28 ^k Lev 5:6;
Eze 40:39; 44:27
^l S ver 3; S Lev 1:10
4:29 ^m ver 4,24
ⁿ S Lev 1:4
^o S Ge 8:20
4:30 ^p S ver 7
4:31 ^q ver 35
^r S Ge 8:21 ^s Lev 1:4
^t S ver 20
4:32 ^u Ex 29:38;
Lev 9:3; 14:10
^v Lev 1:3
4:33 ^w Lev 1:5
^x Lev 1:4 ^y ver 29
4:34 ^z S ver 7
4:35 ^a ver 31
5:1 ^b Pr 29:24;
Mt 26:63 ^c ver 17;
S Ex 28:38; Lev 7:18;
17:16; 19:8; 20:17;
24:15; Nu 5:31; 9:13;
15:31; 19:20; 30:15
5:2 ^d Lev 11:11,24-
40; Dt 14:8; Isa 52:11
^e ver 3; Lev 7:21; 11:8,
24; 13:45; Nu 19:22;
Job 15:16; Ps 51:5;
Isa 6:5; 64:6;
Eze 36:17; Hag 2:13
5:3 ^f Nu 19:11-16
^g Lev 7:20; 11:25;
14:19; 21:1; Nu 5:2;
9:6; 19:7; Eze 44:25
5:4 ^h Nu 30:6,8
ⁱ Isa 41:23
5:5 ^j Lev 16:21;
26:40; Nu 5:7;
Jos 7:19; 1Ki 8:47;
Pr 28:13
5:6 ^k S Lev 1:10;
S 4:3 ^l S Lev 4:28
^m S Ex 32:30
5:7 ⁿ ver 11;
Lev 12:8; 14:21; 27:8
^o Lev 12:8; 14:22,30
^p S Ge 15:9; Nu 6:10
5:8 ^q Lev 1:15
^r Lev 1:17
5:9 ^s S Ex 24:6
^t Lev 1:15 ^u S Lev 4:7
5:10 ^v Lev 1:14-17;
1Ch 15:13
^w S Ex 32:30
^x S Lev 4:26
5:11 ^y S ver 7
^z S Ge 15:9
^a S Ex 16:36
^b S Lev 2:1
5:12 ^c S Lev 2:2
^d Lev 2:9
5:13 ^e S Ex 32:30

the blood of the sin offering with his finger and put it on the horns of the altar ^f of burnt offering and pour out the rest of the blood at the base of the altar. ^g ²⁶ He shall burn all the fat on the altar as he burned the fat of the fellowship offering. In this way the priest will make atonement ^h for the leader's sin, and he will be forgiven. ⁱ

²⁷ " 'If any member of the community sins unintentionally ^j and does what is forbidden in any of the Lord's commands, when they realize their guilt ²⁸ and the sin they have committed becomes known, they must bring as their offering ^k for the sin they committed a female goat ^l without defect. ²⁹ They are to lay their hand on the head ^m of the sin offering ⁿ and slaughter it at the place of the burnt offering. ^o ³⁰ Then the priest is to take some of the blood with his finger and put it on the horns of the altar of burnt offering ^p and pour out the rest of the blood at the base of the altar. ³¹ They shall remove all the fat, just as the fat is removed from the fellowship offering, and the priest shall burn it on the altar ^q as an aroma pleasing to the Lord. ^r In this way the priest will make atonement ^s for them, and they will be forgiven. ^t

³² " 'If they bring a lamb ^u as their sin offering, they are to bring a female without defect. ^v ³³ They are to lay their hand on its head and slaughter it ^w for a sin offering ^x at the place where the burnt offering is slaughtered. ^y ³⁴ Then the priest shall take some of the blood of the sin offering with his finger and put it on the horns of the altar of burnt offering and pour out the rest of the blood at the base of the altar. ^z ³⁵ They shall remove all the fat, just as the fat is removed from the lamb of the fellowship offering, and the priest shall burn it on the altar ^a on top of the food offerings presented to the Lord. In this way the priest will make atonement for them for the sin they have committed, and they will be forgiven.

5 " 'If anyone sins because they do not speak up when they hear a public charge to testify ^b regarding something they have seen or learned about, they will be held responsible. ^c ² Or if anyone unwittingly touches anything ceremonially unclean— whether the carcass of an unclean animal, wild or domestic, or of any unclean creature that moves along the ground ^d —and they are unaware that they have become unclean, ^e but then they come to realize their guilt; ³ or if they touch human uncleanness ^f —anything that would make them unclean ^g —even though they are unaware of it, but then they learn of it and realize their guilt; ⁴ or if anyone thoughtlessly takes an oath ^h to do anything, whether good or evil ⁱ —in any matter one might carelessly swear about—even though they are unaware of it, but then they learn of it and realize their guilt— ⁵ when anyone realizes their guilt in any of these matters, they must confess ^j in what way they have sinned ⁶ and, as a penalty for the sin they have committed, they must bring to the Lord a female lamb or goat ^k from the flock as a sin offering ^{a;} ^l and the priest shall make atonement ^m for them for their sin.

⁷ " 'Anyone who cannot afford ⁿ a lamb ^o is to bring two doves or two young pigeons ^p to the Lord as a penalty for their sin—one for a sin offering and the other for a burnt offering. ⁸ They are to bring them to the priest, who shall first offer the one for the sin offering. He is to wring its head from its neck, ^q not dividing it completely, ^r ⁹ and is to splash ^s some of the blood of the sin offering against the side of the altar; ^t the rest of the blood must be drained out at the base of the altar. ^u It is a sin offering. ¹⁰ The priest shall then offer the other as a burnt offering in the prescribed way ^v and make atonement ^w for them for the sin they have committed, and they will be forgiven. ^x

¹¹ " 'If, however, they cannot afford ^y two doves or two young pigeons, ^z they are to bring as an offering for their sin a tenth of an ephah ^b ^a of the finest flour ^b for a sin offering. They must not put oil or incense on it, because it is a sin offering. ¹² They are to bring it to the priest, who shall take a handful of it as a memorial ^c portion ^c and burn it on the altar ^d on top of the food offerings presented to the Lord. It is a sin offering. ¹³ In this way the priest will make atonement ^e for them for any of these sins they have committed, and

---

^a 6 Or *purification offering*; here and throughout this chapter   ^b 11 That is, probably about 3 1/2 pounds or about 1.6 kilograms   ^c 12 Or *representative*

4:28 *female goat.* See note on v. 23.
4:29 *lay their hand on.* See notes on 1:3; Ex 29:10.
4:32 *lamb...female.* See note on v. 23.
4:35 *fat...of the fellowship offering.* See 3:3–5.
5:1–4 Four examples of the unintentional sins (see 4:2–3,13,22,27) the law offers covers.
5:2 *ceremonially unclean.* See note on 4:12.
5:3 *human uncleanness.* See chs. 11–15.

5:5 *confess.* The offerers had to acknowledge their sin to God in order to receive forgiveness (cf. Pr 28:13 and note).
5:7 *two doves...pigeons.* See note on 4:23.
5:11 *finest flour.* See note on 4:23. Although no blood was used with a flour offering, it was offered "on top of the food offerings presented to the Lord" (v. 12). Heb 9:22 may refer to such a situation.
5:12 *memorial portion.* See note on 2:2,9,16.

they will be forgiven. The rest of the offering will belong to the priest, *f* as in the case of the grain offering. *g* ' "

THE GUILT OFFERING

[14] The LORD said to Moses: [15] "When anyone is unfaithful to the LORD by sinning unintentionally *h* in regard to any of the LORD's holy things, they are to bring to the LORD as a penalty *i* a ram *j* from the flock, one without defect and of the proper value in silver, according to the sanctuary shekel. *a k* It is a guilt offering. *l* [16] They must make restitution *m* for what they have failed to do in regard to the holy things, pay an additional penalty of a fifth of its value *n* and give it all to the priest. The priest will make atonement for them with the ram as a guilt offering, and they will be forgiven.

[17] "If anyone sins and does what is forbidden in any of the LORD's commands, even though they do not know it, *o* they are guilty and will be held responsible. *p* [18] They are to bring to the priest as a guilt offering *q* a ram from the flock, one without defect and of the proper value. In this way the priest will make atonement for them for the wrong they have committed unintentionally, and they will be forgiven. *r* [19] It is a guilt offering; they have been guilty of *b* wrongdoing against the LORD." *s*

6 *** The LORD said to Moses: [2] "If anyone sins and is unfaithful to the LORD *t* by deceiving a neighbor *u* about something entrusted to them or left in their care *v* or about something stolen, or if they cheat *w* a neighbor, [3] or if they find lost property and lie about it, *x* or if they swear falsely *y* about any such sin that people may commit— [4] when they thus sin and realize their guilt, they must return *z* what they have stolen or taken by extortion, or what was entrusted to them, or the lost property they found, [5] or whatever it was they swore falsely about. They must make restitution *a* in full, add a fifth of the value to it and give it all to the owner on the day they present their guilt offering. *b* [6] And as a penalty they must bring to the priest, that is, to the LORD, their guilt offering, *c* a ram from the flock, one without defect and of the proper value. *d* [7] In this way the priest will make atonement *e* for them before the LORD, and they will be forgiven for any of the things they did that made them guilty."

THE BURNT OFFERING

*** [8] The LORD said to Moses: [9] "Give Aaron and his sons this command: 'These are the regulations for the burnt offering *f*. The burnt offering is to remain on the altar hearth throughout the night, till morning, and the fire must be kept burning on the altar. *g* [10] The priest shall then put on his linen clothes, *h* with linen undergarments next to his body, *i* and shall remove the ashes *j* of the burnt offering that the fire has consumed on the altar and place them beside the altar. [11] Then he is to take off these clothes and put on others, and carry the ashes outside the camp to a place that is ceremonially clean. *k* [12] The fire on the altar must be kept burning; it must not go out. Every morning the priest is to add firewood *l* and arrange the burnt offering on the fire and burn the fat *m* of the fellowship offerings *n* on it. [13] The fire must be kept burning on the altar continuously; it must not go out.

THE GRAIN OFFERING

[14] " 'These are the regulations for the grain offering: *o* Aaron's sons are to bring it before the LORD, in front of the altar. [15] The priest is to take a handful of the finest flour and some olive oil, together with all the incense *p* on the grain offering, *q* and burn the memorial *c*

---

a 15 That is, about 2/5 ounce or about 11.5 grams   *b* 19 Or *have made full expiation for their*
c 15 Or *representative*

** 6:1-7 is numbered 5:20-26 in Hebrew texts.   ** 6:8-30 is numbered 6:1-23 in Hebrew texts.*

5:15 *LORD's holy things.* See note on Ex 3:5. *according to the sanctuary shekel.* See note on Ex 30:13. *guilt offering.* See further priestly regulations in 7:1–6 (see also Isa 53:10). Traditionally called the "trespass offering," it was very similar to the sin offering (cf. 7:7), and the Hebrew words for the two were apparently sometimes interchanged. The major difference between the guilt and sin offerings was that the guilt offering was brought in cases where restitution for the sin was possible and therefore required (v. 16). Thus, in cases of theft and cheating (6:2–5), the stolen property had to be returned along with 20 percent indemnity. By contrast, the sin offering was prescribed in cases of sin where no restitution was possible. The animal sacrificed as a guilt offering was always a ram.

6:3 *lost property.* See Dt 22:1–3.
6:6 *to the priest, that is, to the LORD.* Sacrifices were brought to the Lord, but priests were his authorized representatives.
6:8—7:36 Further regulations concerning the sacrifices, dealing mainly with the portions to be eaten by the priests or, in the case of the fellowship offering, by the one offering the sacrifice.
6:9 *burnt offering.* See ch. 1; Nu 15:1–16 and notes.
6:13 The perpetual fire on the altar represented uninterrupted offering to and appeal to God on behalf of Israel.
6:14 *grain offering.* See ch. 2 and notes.
6:15 *memorial portion.* See note on 2:2,9,16.

5:13 *f* Lev 2:3
g S Ex 29:41
5:15 *h* S Lev 4:2
i Lev 22:14
j S Ex 29:3; Lev 6:6;
Nu 5:8; 6:14; 15:6;
28:11 *k* S Ex 30:13
l ver 16,18; Lev 6:5,6;
7:1,7; 14:12-17; 19:21,
22; Nu 6:12; 18:9;
1Sa 6:3; Ezr 10:19;
Isa 53:10
5:16 *m* Lev 6:4
n ver 15; Lev 27:13;
Nu 5:7
5:17 *o* ver 15
p S ver 1
5:18 *q* Lev 6:6; 14:12
r S ver 15
5:19 *s* 2Ki 12:16
6:2 *t* Nu 5:6;
Ps 73:27; Ac 5:4;
Col 3:9 *u* Lev 19:11;
Jer 9:4,5 *v* S Ex 22:7
w S Ge 31:7
6:3 *x* S Ex 23:4
y S Ex 22:11
6:4 *z* Lev 5:16;
Eze 33:15; S Lk 19:8
6:5 *a* Nu 5:7
b S Lev 5:15
6:6 *c* S Lev 5:15
d Nu 5:8
6:7 *e* S Ex 32:30
6:9 *f* Lev 7:37
g ver 12
6:10 *h* S Ex 39:27
i Ex 28:39-42,43;
39:28 *j* S Lev 1:16
6:11 *k* S Lev 4:12
6:12 *l* S Lev 1:7
m S Ex 29:13
n S Ex 32:6
6:14 *o* S Lev 2:1;
Nu 6:15; 15:4; 28:13
6:15 *p* S Lev 2:1
q Lev 2:9

6:15 ʳS Lev 2:2
6:16 ˢS Lev 2:3
ᵗEze 44:29
ᵘS Lev 2:11 ᵛver 26;
S Ex 29:11; Lev 10:13;
16:24; 24:9; Nu 18:10
ʷS Ex 27:9
ˣEx 29:31; Lev 8:31
6:17 ʸNu 5:9
ᶻEx 29:28; Lev 7:7;
10:16-18 ᵃver 29;
Ex 40:10; Lev 10:12;
21:22; 24:9; Nu 18:9,
10
6:18 ᵇver 29;
Lev 2:3; 7:6; Nu 18:9;
10 ᶜS Ge 9:12
ᵈNu 5:9 ᵉS Ex 30:29
6:20 ᶠS Ex 28:41
ᵍS Ex 16:36
ʰNu 5:9; 28:5
ⁱEx 29:2; Lev 23:13;
Nu 4:16
6:21 ʲLev 2:5
6:22 ᵏS Ex 28:41;
S 29:30 ˡS Lev 1:9
6:25 ᵐS Ex 30:10;
S Lev 4:24 ⁿS Lev 1:3
ᵒS Ex 29:11
6:26 ᵖS ver 16
�q S Ex 27:9
ʳS Ex 27:21; S 40:2
6:27 ˢS Ex 29:37;
Lev 10:10; Eze 44:19;
46:20; Hag 2:12
6:28 ᵗLev 11:33;
15:12; Nu 19:15
6:29 ᵘS ver 18
ᵛS ver 17; Eze 42:13
6:30 ʷEze 45:15
ˣS Lev 4:18
ʸLev 4:12
7:1 ᶻS Lev 5:15;
Eze 40:39
7:3 ᵃS Ex 29:13
7:4 ᵇLev 3:15
7:5 ᶜS Ex 29:13
7:6 ᵈS Lev 6:18
ᵉEze 42:13
7:7 ᶠS Ex 30:10
ᵍS Lev 5:15 ʰver 6;
Lev 2:3; 6:17,26;
14:13; 2Ki 12:16;
1Co 9:13; 10:18
ⁱNu 5:8
7:8 ʲLev 1:6
7:9 ᵏS Lev 2:4
ˡLev 2:7 ᵐS Lev 2:5
7:12 ⁿver 13,15;
Lev 22:29; Ps 50:14;
54:6; 107:22; 116:17;
Jer 33:11 ᵒJer 44:19
ᵖNu 6:19 qS Lev 2:4
ʳS Lev 2:1
7:13 ˢS ver 12;
S Ex 34:22
ᵗLev 23:17; Am 4:5

portion ʳ on the altar as an aroma pleasing to the LORD. ¹⁶Aaron and his sons ˢ shall eat the rest ᵗ of it, but it is to be eaten without yeast ᵘ in the sanctuary area; ᵛ they are to eat it in the courtyard ʷ of the tent of meeting. ˣ ¹⁷It must not be baked with yeast; I have given it as their share ʸ of the food offerings presented to me. ᶻ Like the sin offering ᵃ and the guilt offering, it is most holy. ᵃ ¹⁸Any male descendant of Aaron may eat it. ᵇ For all generations to come ᶜ it is his perpetual share ᵈ of the food offerings presented to the LORD. Whatever touches them will become holy. ᵇ ᵉ’ ”

¹⁹The LORD also said to Moses, ²⁰“This is the offering Aaron and his sons are to bring to the LORD on the day he ᶜ is anointed: ᶠ a tenth of an ephah ᵈ ᵍ of the finest flour ʰ as a regular grain offering, ⁱ half of it in the morning and half in the evening. ²¹It must be prepared with oil on a griddle; ʲ bring it well-mixed and present the grain offering broken ᵉ in pieces as an aroma pleasing to the LORD. ²²The son who is to succeed him as anointed priest ᵏ shall prepare it. It is the LORD’s perpetual share and is to be burned completely. ˡ ²³Every grain offering of a priest shall be burned completely; it must not be eaten.”

THE SIN OFFERING

²⁴The LORD said to Moses, ²⁵“Say to Aaron and his sons: ‘These are the regulations for the sin offering: ᵐ The sin offering is to be slaughtered before the LORD ⁿ in the place ᵒ the burnt offering is slaughtered; it is most holy. ²⁶The priest who offers it shall eat it; it is to be eaten in the sanctuary area, ᵖ in the courtyard q of the tent of meeting. ʳ ²⁷Whatever touches any of the flesh will become holy, ˢ and if any of the blood is spattered on a garment, you must wash it in the sanctuary area. ²⁸The clay pot ᵗ the meat is cooked in must be broken; but if it is cooked in a bronze pot, the pot is to be scoured and rinsed with water. ²⁹Any male in a priest’s family may eat it; ᵘ it is most holy. ᵛ ³⁰But any sin offering whose blood is brought into the tent of meeting to make atonement ʷ in the Holy Place ˣ must not be eaten; it must be burned up. ʸ

THE GUILT OFFERING

7 “ ‘These are the regulations for the guilt offering, ᶻ which is most holy: ²The guilt offering is to be slaughtered in the place where the burnt offering is slaughtered, and its blood is to be splashed against the sides of the altar. ³All its fat ᵃ shall be offered: the fat tail and the fat that covers the internal organs, ⁴both kidneys with the fat on them near the loins, and the long lobe of the liver, which is to be removed with the kidneys. ᵇ ⁵The priest shall burn them on the altar ᶜ as a food offering presented to the LORD. It is a guilt offering. ⁶Any male in a priest’s family may eat it, ᵈ but it must be eaten in the sanctuary area; it is most holy. ᵉ

⁷ ‘The same law applies to both the sin offering ᶠ ᶠ and the guilt offering: ᵍ They belong to the priest ʰ who makes atonement with them. ⁱ ⁸The priest who offers a burnt offering for anyone may keep its hide ʲ for himself. ⁹Every grain offering baked in an oven ᵏ or cooked in a pan ˡ or on a griddle ᵐ belongs to the priest who offers it, ¹⁰and every grain offering, whether mixed with oil or dry, belongs equally to all the sons of Aaron.

THE FELLOWSHIP OFFERING

¹¹“ ‘These are the regulations for the fellowship offering anyone may present to the LORD:

¹²“ ‘If they offer it as an expression of thankfulness, then along with this thank offering ⁿ they are to offer thick loaves ᵒ made without yeast ᵖ and with olive oil mixed in, thin loaves q made without yeast and brushed with olive oil, ʳ and thick loaves of the finest flour well-kneaded and with olive oil mixed in. ¹³Along with their fellowship offering of thanksgiving ˢ they are to present an offering with thick loaves of bread made with yeast. ᵗ

ᵃ 17 Or *purification offering*; also in verses 25 and 30   ᵇ 18 Or *Whoever touches them must be holy*; similarly in verse 27   ᶜ 20 Or *each*   ᵈ 20 That is, probably about 3 1/2 pounds or about 1.6 kilograms   ᵉ 21 The meaning of the Hebrew for this word is uncertain.   ᶠ 7 Or *purification offering*; also in verse 37

6:18 *will become holy.* See Ex 29:37 and note.
6:25 *sin offering.* See 4:1—5:13 and notes.
6:28 *clay.* Ordinary kitchen utensils and domestic ware were made of clay, usually fired in a kiln and often painted or burnished.
7:1 *holy.* See note on Ex 3:5.
7:2 *guilt offering.* See 5:14—6:7 and notes. *place.* On the north side of the altar of burnt offering in front of the tabernacle (1:11; see note there).
7:3 *fat tail.* See note on 3:9.
7:7–10 See Nu 18:8–20; 1Co 9:13 and notes.

7:11–36 This section supplements ch. 3, adding regulations about (1) three types of fellowship offerings (thank, vv. 12–15; vow, v. 16; freewill, v. 16), (2) prohibition on eating fat and blood (vv. 22–27) and (3) the priests’ share (vv. 28–36).

7:12–15 Thank offerings were given in gratitude for deliverance from sickness (Ps 116:17), trouble (Ps 107:22) or death (Ps 56:12) or for a blessing received.
7:13 *with yeast.* This regulation was not against the prohibition of 2:11 or Ex 23:18 since the offering here was not burned on the altar.

[14]They are to bring one of each kind as an offering, a contribution to the LORD; it belongs to the priest who splashes the blood of the fellowship offering against the altar. [15]The meat of their fellowship offering of thanksgiving must be eaten on the day it is offered; they must leave none of it till morning. [u]

[16]" 'If, however, their offering is the result of a vow [v] or is a freewill offering, [w] the sacrifice shall be eaten on the day they offer it, but anything left over may be eaten on the next day. [x] [17]Any meat of the sacrifice left over till the third day must be burned up. [y] [18]If any meat of the fellowship offering [z] is eaten on the third day, the one who offered it will not be accepted. [a] It will not be reckoned [b] to their credit, for it has become impure; the person who eats any of it will be held responsible. [c]

[19]" 'Meat that touches anything ceremonially unclean must not be eaten; it must be burned up. As for other meat, anyone ceremonially clean may eat it. [20]But if anyone who is unclean [d] eats any meat of the fellowship offering belonging to the LORD, they must be cut off from their people. [e] [21]Anyone who touches something unclean [f]—whether human uncleanness or an unclean animal or any unclean creature that moves along the ground [a]—and then eats any of the meat of the fellowship offering belonging to the LORD must be cut off from their people.' "

EATING FAT AND BLOOD FORBIDDEN

[22]The LORD said to Moses, [23]"Say to the Israelites: 'Do not eat any of the fat of cattle, sheep or goats. [g] [24]The fat of an animal found dead or torn by wild animals [h] may be used for any other purpose, but you must not eat it. [25]Anyone who eats the fat of an animal from which a food offering may be [b] presented to the LORD must be cut off from their people. [26]And wherever you live, you must not eat the blood [i] of any bird or animal. [27]Anyone who eats blood [j] must be cut off from their people.' "

THE PRIESTS' SHARE

[28]The LORD said to Moses, [29]"Say to the Israelites: 'Anyone who brings a fellowship offering to the LORD is to bring part of it as their sacrifice to the LORD. [30]With their own hands they are to present the food offering to the LORD; they are to bring the fat, together with the breast, and wave the breast before the LORD as a wave offering. [k] [31]The priest shall burn the fat on the altar, [l] but the breast belongs to Aaron and his sons. [m] [32]You are to give the right thigh of your fellowship offerings to the priest as a contribution. [n] [33]The son of Aaron who offers the blood and the fat of the fellowship offering shall have the right thigh as his share. [34]From the fellowship offerings of the Israelites, I have taken the breast that is waved and the thigh [o] that is presented and have given them to Aaron the priest and his sons [p] as their perpetual share from the Israelites.' "

[35]This is the portion of the food offerings presented to the LORD that were allotted to Aaron and his sons on the day they were presented to serve the LORD as priests. [36]On the day they were anointed, [q] the LORD commanded that the Israelites give this to them as their perpetual share for the generations to come.

[37]These, then, are the regulations for the burnt offering, [r] the grain offering, [s] the sin offering, the guilt offering, the ordination offering [t] and the fellowship offering, [38]which the

---

[a] 21 A few Hebrew manuscripts, Samaritan Pentateuch, Syriac and Targum (see Lev. 5:2); most Hebrew manuscripts *unclean, detestable thing*   [b] 25 Or *offering is*

7:15–18 See 19:5–8. All meat had to be eaten promptly (in the case of the thank offering on the same day and in the case of the vow and freewill offerings within two days). One reason may have been that in Canaan meat spoiled quickly and thus became ceremonially impure (v. 18) because it was not then perfect (1:3; see 21:16–23). The prohibition applied also to the Passover (Ex 12:10).

7:16 *vow.* See 22:18–23. A vow was a solemn promise to offer a gift to God in response to a divine deliverance or blessing. Such vows often accompanied prayers for deliverance or blessing (see note on Ps 7:17; see also Introduction to Psalms: Psalm Types). *freewill offering.* See 22:18–23.

7:19 *ceremonially unclean.* See note on 4:12.

7:20 *cut off from their people.* Removed from the covenant people through direct divine judgment (Ge 17:14), or (as here and in vv. 21,25,27; 17:4,9–10,14; 18:29; 19:8; 20:3,5–6,17–18; 23:29) through execution (see, e.g., 20:2–3; Ex 31:14) or possibly sometimes through banishment.

7:22–27 See note on 17:11.

7:23 *fat.* The prohibition of fat for food was as strict as that of blood, but the reason was different. The fat of the fellowship offerings was the Lord's and was to be burned on the altar (see 3:16 and note). There was no explicit prohibition of eating the fat of hunted animals like the gazelle or deer, but probably that was included (see 3:17; Dt 12:15–22).

7:26 *not eat the blood.* See note on 17:11; see also 3:17; 19:26; Ge 9:4–6; Dt 12:16,23–25; 15:23; 1Sa 14:32–34; Eze 33:25.

7:28–36 See 10:12–15; Nu 18:8–20; Dt 18:1–5.

7:30–32 *breast . . . right thigh.* The breast and right thigh given to the priest were first presented to the Lord with gestures described as waving the breast and presenting the thigh (v. 34). See 8:25–29; 9:21; 10:14–15; Ex 29:26–27; Nu 6:20; 18:11,18.

7:37–38 A summary of chs. 1–7.

7:37 *ordination offering.* See 8:14–36; Ex 29:1–35.

7:15 [u] S Ex 12:10
7:16 [v] S Ge 28:20; S Lev 1:2; Dt 23:21-23 [w] Ex 35:29; Lev 22:18,21; 23:38; Nu 15:3; 29:39; Dt 12:6; Ps 54:6; Eze 46:12 [x] Lev 19:5-8
7:17 [y] Ex 12:10; Lev 19:6
7:18 [z] 2Ch 33:16 [a] Lev 19:7 [b] Nu 18:27 [c] S Lev 5:1
7:20 [d] S Lev 5:3 [e] S Ge 17:14; Lev 22:3-7
7:21 [f] S Lev 5:2
7:23 [g] Lev 17:13-14; Dt 14:4
7:24 [h] S Ex 22:31
7:26 [i] S Ge 9:4
7:27 [j] S Ge 9:4
7:30 [k] S Ex 29:24
7:31 [l] S Ex 29:13 [m] S Ex 29:27
7:32 [n] Ex 29:27; Lev 10:14,15; Nu 5:9; 6:20; 18:18
7:34 [o] Ex 29:22; Lev 10:15; Nu 6:20; 1Sa 9:24 [p] S Ex 29:27
7:36 [q] Lev 8:12,30
7:37 [r] Lev 6:9
[s] Lev 6:14 [t] S Ex 29:31

7:38 *u* Lev 26:46;
Nu 36:13; Dt 4:5; 29:1
v S Ex 19:11
w S Lev 1:2
8:2 *x* S Ex 28:1;
S Lev 1:5 *y* Ex 28:2,4,
43; S 39:27
z Ex 30:23-25,30
a S Ex 30:10 *b* ver 18,
22 *c* Ex 29:2-3
8:3 *d* Nu 8:9
8:5 *e* Ex 29:1
8:6 *f* S Ex 29:4;
S 30:19; S Ac 22:16
8:7 *g* Ex 28:4
8:8 *h* S Ex 25:7
i S Ex 28:30
8:9 *j* S Ex 39:28
k S Ex 28:36
l S Ex 28:2; Lev 21:10
8:10 *m* ver 2
n S Ex 30:26
o S Ex 26:1
8:11 *p* S Ex 30:29
8:12 *q* S Lev 7:36
r S Ex 30:30
8:13 *s* S Ex 28:40
t S Ex 28:4,39; 39:27
u Lev 21:10
8:14 *v* S Lev 4:3
w S Ex 30:10
x S Lev 4:15
8:15 *y* S Lev 4:18
z S Lev 4:7 *a* Heb 9:22
b Eze 43:20
8:17 *c* S Lev 4:11
d S Lev 4:12
8:18 *e* S ver 2
8:20 *f* S Lev 1:8
8:22 *g* S ver 2
h S Lev 4:15
8:23 *i* Lev 14:14,25
8:24 *j* Heb 9:18-22
8:25 *k* Lev 3:3-5
8:26 *l* S Lev 2:4

Lord gave Moses *u* on Mount Sinai *v* in the Desert of Sinai on the day he commanded the Israelites to bring their offerings to the Lord. *w*

THE ORDINATION OF AARON AND HIS SONS
8:1–36pp — Ex 29:1–37

8 The Lord said to Moses, [2]"Bring Aaron and his sons, *x* their garments, *y* the anointing oil, *z* the bull for the sin offering, *a* *a* the two rams *b* and the basket containing bread made without yeast, *c* [3]and gather the entire assembly *d* at the entrance to the tent of meeting." [4]Moses did as the Lord commanded him, and the assembly gathered at the entrance to the tent of meeting.

[5]Moses said to the assembly, "This is what the Lord has commanded to be done. *e*" [6]Then Moses brought Aaron and his sons forward and washed them with water. *f* [7]He put the tunic on Aaron, tied the sash around him, clothed him with the robe and put the ephod on him. He also fastened the ephod with a decorative waistband, which he tied around him. *g* [8]He placed the breastpiece *h* on him and put the Urim and Thummim *i* in the breastpiece. [9]Then he placed the turban *j* on Aaron's head and set the gold plate, the sacred emblem, *k* on the front of it, as the Lord commanded Moses. *l*

[10]Then Moses took the anointing oil *m* and anointed *n* the tabernacle *o* and everything in it, and so consecrated them. [11]He sprinkled some of the oil on the altar seven times, anointing the altar and all its utensils and the basin with its stand, to consecrate them. *p* [12]He poured some of the anointing oil on Aaron's head and anointed *q* him to consecrate him. *r* [13]Then he brought Aaron's sons *s* forward, put tunics *t* on them, tied sashes around them and fastened caps on them, as the Lord commanded Moses. *u*

[14]He then presented the bull *v* for the sin offering, *w* and Aaron and his sons laid their hands on its head. *x* [15]Moses slaughtered the bull and took some of the blood, *y* and with his finger he put it on all the horns of the altar *z* to purify the altar. *a* He poured out the rest of the blood at the base of the altar. So he consecrated it to make atonement for it. *b* [16]Moses also took all the fat around the internal organs, the long lobe of the liver, and both kidneys and their fat, and burned it on the altar. [17]But the bull with its hide and its flesh and its intestines *c* he burned up outside the camp, *d* as the Lord commanded Moses.

[18]He then presented the ram *e* for the burnt offering, and Aaron and his sons laid their hands on its head. [19]Then Moses slaughtered the ram and splashed the blood against the sides of the altar. [20]He cut the ram into pieces and burned the head, the pieces and the fat. *f* [21]He washed the internal organs and the legs with water and burned the whole ram on the altar. It was a burnt offering, a pleasing aroma, a food offering presented to the Lord, as the Lord commanded Moses.

[22]He then presented the other ram, the ram for the ordination, *g* and Aaron and his sons laid their hands on its head. *h* [23]Moses slaughtered the ram and took some of its blood and put it on the lobe of Aaron's right ear, on the thumb of his right hand and on the big toe of his right foot. *i* [24]Moses also brought Aaron's sons forward and put some of the blood on the lobes of their right ears, on the thumbs of their right hands and on the big toes of their right feet. Then he splashed blood against the sides of the altar. *j* [25]After that, he took the fat *k*, the fat tail, all the fat around the internal organs, the long lobe of the liver, both kidneys and their fat and the right thigh. [26]And from the basket of bread made without yeast, which was before the Lord, he took one thick loaf, one thick loaf with olive oil mixed in, and one thin loaf, *l* and he put these on the fat portions and on the right thigh. [27]He put

---

a 2 Or purification offering; also in verse 14

8:1—10:20 The ordination, installation and ministry of Aaron and his sons, and the deaths of Nadab and Abihu and attendant regulations.
8:2 *their garments.* See Ex 39:1–31; 40:12–16. The garments that the high priest was to wear when he ministered are detailed in Ex 28:4–43 (see notes there). *anointing oil.* See note on Ex 25:6. The oil was used to anoint the tabernacle, sacred objects and consecrated priests (vv. 10–12,30). It was later used to anoint leaders and kings (1Sa 10:1; 16:13). See also note on Ex 29:7.
8:6 *washed them with water.* In the bronze basin (see v. 11) in the courtyard of the tabernacle (see Ex 30:17–21).
8:7 *ephod.* See note on Ex 28:6.
8:8 *Urim and Thummim.* See notes on Ex 28:30; 1Sa 2:28.
8:9 *sacred emblem.* See note on Ex 39:30.
8:11 *seven times.* See note on 4:6.

8:12 *oil on Aaron's head.* See Ps 133.
8:14 *sin offering.* See 4:3–11 and notes. The consecration service included a sin offering for atonement, a burnt offering for worship (v. 18) and a "ram for the ordination" (v. 22), whose blood was applied to the high priest on his right ear, thumb and toe (v. 23). After this was done, Aaron offered sacrifices for the people (9:15–21). Then he blessed the people in his capacity as priest, and the Lord accepted his ministry with the sign of miraculous fire (9:23–24). *laid their hands on.* See notes on 1:3; Ex 29:10.
8:15 *make atonement for it.* See 16:16; see also note on Ex 29:36.
8:17 *outside the camp.* See notes on 4:5,12; 13:45–46; Eze 43:21; Heb 13:12–13.
8:23 Putting some of the blood on Aaron's extremities signified his complete consecration to the Lord's service (cf. note on v. 14).

all these in the hands of Aaron and his sons, and they waved them before the LORD *m* as a wave offering. [28]Then Moses took them from their hands and burned them on the altar on top of the burnt offering as an ordination offering, a pleasing aroma, a food offering presented to the LORD. [29]Moses also took the breast, which was his share of the ordination ram, *n* and waved it before the LORD as a wave offering, as the LORD commanded Moses.

[30]Then Moses *o* took some of the anointing oil and some of the blood from the altar and sprinkled them on Aaron and his garments *p* and on his sons and their garments. So he consecrated *q* Aaron and his garments and his sons and their garments.

[31]Moses then said to Aaron and his sons, "Cook the meat at the entrance to the tent of meeting *r* and eat it there with the bread from the basket of ordination offerings, as I was commanded: 'Aaron and his sons are to eat it.' [32]Then burn up the rest of the meat and the bread. [33]Do not leave the entrance to the tent of meeting for seven days, until the days of your ordination are completed, for your ordination will last seven days. *s* [34]What has been done today was commanded by the LORD *t* to make atonement for you. [35]You must stay at the entrance to the tent of meeting day and night for seven days and do what the LORD requires, *u* so you will not die; for that is what I have been commanded." [36]So Aaron and his sons did everything the LORD commanded through Moses.

THE PRIESTS BEGIN THEIR MINISTRY

9 On the eighth day *v* Moses summoned Aaron and his sons and the elders *w* of Israel. [2]He said to Aaron, "Take a bull calf for your sin offering*a* and a ram for your burnt offering, both without defect, and present them before the LORD. [3]Then say to the Israelites: 'Take a male goat*x* for a sin offering, *y* a calf*z* and a lamb*a*—both a year old and without defect—for a burnt offering, [4]and an ox*b b* and a ram for a fellowship offering*c* to sacrifice before the LORD, together with a grain offering mixed with olive oil. For today the LORD will appear to you. *d* '"

[5]They took the things Moses commanded to the front of the tent of meeting, and the entire assembly came near and stood before the LORD. [6]Then Moses said, "This is what the LORD has commanded you to do, so that the glory of the LORD *e* may appear to you."

[7]Moses said to Aaron, "Come to the altar and sacrifice your sin offering and your burnt offering and make atonement for yourself and the people; *f* sacrifice the offering that is for the people and make atonement for them, as the LORD has commanded. *g*"

[8]So Aaron came to the altar and slaughtered the calf as a sin offering *h* for himself. [9]His sons brought the blood to him, *i* and he dipped his finger into the blood and put it on the horns of the altar; the rest of the blood he poured out at the base of the altar. *j k* [10]On the altar he burned the fat, the kidneys and the long lobe of the liver from the sin offering, as the LORD commanded Moses; [11]the flesh and the hide *l* he burned up outside the camp. *m*

[12]Then he slaughtered the burnt offering. *n* His sons handed him the blood, *o* and he splashed it against the sides of the altar. [13]They handed him the burnt offering piece by piece, including the head, and he burned them on the altar. *p* [14]He washed the internal organs and the legs and burned them on top of the burnt offering on the altar. *q*

[15]Aaron then brought the offering that was for the people. *r* He took the goat for the people's sin offering and slaughtered it and offered it for a sin offering as he did with the first one.

[16]He brought the burnt offering and offered it in the prescribed way. *s* [17]He also brought the grain offering, took a handful of it and burned it on the altar in addition to the morning's burnt offering. *t*

[18]He slaughtered the ox and the ram as the fellowship offering for the people. *u* His sons handed him the blood, and he splashed it against the sides of the altar. [19]But the fat portions of the ox and the ram—the fat tail, the layer of fat, the kidneys and the long lobe of the liver— [20]these they laid on the breasts, and then Aaron burned the fat on the altar. [21]Aaron waved the breasts and the right thigh before the LORD as a wave offering, *v* as Moses commanded.

---

a 2 Or *purification offering*; here and throughout this chapter male or female; also in verses 18 and 19. *b* 4 The Hebrew word can refer to either

8:27 *m* Nu 5:25
8:29 *n* Lev 7:31-34
8:30 *o* S Ex 28:1
p S Ex 28:2
q S Lev 7:36
8:31 *r* S Lev 6:16
8:33 *s* Lev 14:8;
15:13,28; Nu 19:11;
Eze 43:25
8:34 *t* Heb 7:16
8:35 *u* Lev 18:30;
22:9; Nu 3:7; 9:19;
Dt 11:1; 1Ki 2:3;
Eze 48:11; Zec 3:7
9:1 *v* Eze 43:27
w S Lev 4:15
9:3 *x* S Lev 4:3
y ver 15; Lev 10:16
z ver 8 *a* S Lev 4:32
9:4 *b* Lev 4:10
c S Ex 32:6 *d* Ex 29:43
9:6 *e* S Ex 16:7
9:7 *f* Lev 16:6
g S Ex 30:10; Heb 5:1,
3; 7:27
9:8 *h* Lev 4:1-12;
10:19
9:9 *i* ver 12,18
j S Ex 29:12
k Eze 43:20
9:11 *l* S Lev 4:11
m S Lev 4:12
9:12 *n* Lev 10:19
o S ver 9
9:13 *p* S Lev 1:8
9:14 *q* S Lev 1:9
9:15 *r* Lev 4:27-31
9:16 *s* Lev 1:1-13
9:17 *t* Lev 3:5
9:18 *u* Lev 3:1-11
9:21 *v* S Ex 29:24,26

8:27 *wave offering.* See note on 7:30–32.
8:28 *on top of the burnt offering.* See note on 3:5.
8:31 *Aaron and his sons are to eat it.* See Ex 29:32.
9:1 *eighth day.* After the seven days of ordination (8:33).
9:2 *sin offering.* See notes on 4:3,5. *burnt offering.* See note on 1:3.
9:4 *fellowship offering.* See note on 3:1. *grain offering.* See note on 2:1. *LORD will appear.* See vv. 6,23; see also note on Ge 12:7.

9:6,23 *glory of the LORD.* See notes on Ex 16:7; 40:34; Ps 26:8; Eze 1:1–28.
9:8 *sin offering for himself.* Contrast Jesus in Heb 7:26–28 (see notes there).
9:11 *outside the camp.* See note on 8:17.
9:17 *morning's burnt offering.* See Ex 29:38–42.
9:21 *wave offering.* See note on 7:30–32.

9:22 ʷ S Ge 48:20;
S Ex 39:43; Lk 24:50
9:23 ˣ S Ex 40:2
ʸ S Ex 24:16
9:24 ᶻ S Ex 19:18;
Jdg 6:21; 13:20
ᵃ 1Ki 18:39
10:1 ᵇ Ex 6:23; 24:1;
28:1; Nu 3:2-4; 26:61;
1Ch 6:3 ᶜ Nu 16:46;
1Ki 7:50; 2Ki 25:15;
2Ch 4:22; Jer 52:19;
Eze 8:11 ᵈ Lev 16:12;
Nu 16:7,18; Isa 6:6
ᵉ S Ex 30:9 ᶠ ver 2;
Lev 16:1 ᵍ Ex 30:9
10:2 ʰ Ps 106:18
ⁱ Nu 11:1; 16:35;
Ps 2:12; 50:3; Isa 29:6
ʲ S Ge 19:24; S 38:7;
Nu 16:35; 1Ch 24:2;
Job 1:16
10:3 ᵏ Ex 19:22
ˡ Ex 30:29; Lev 21:6;
22:32; Nu 16:5; 20:13;
Isa 5:16; Eze 28:22;
38:16 ᵐ Ex 14:4;
Isa 44:23; 49:3; 55:5;
60:21
10:4 ⁿ S Ex 6:22
ᵒ Ex 6:18 ᵖ Ac 5:6,9,
10 ᵍ S Ex 25:8
10:5 ʳ S Lev 8:13
10:6 ˢ S Ex 6:23
ᵗ Lev 13:45; 21:10;
Nu 5:18 ᵘ Jer 41:5;
S Mk 14:63 ᵛ Nu 1:53;
16:22; Jos 7:1; 22:18
ʷ Ge 50:3,10;
Nu 20:29; 1Sa 25:1
10:7 ˣ S Ex 25:8
ʸ S Ex 28:41
10:9 ᶻ Ge 9:21;
Ex 29:40; Lev 23:13;
Nu 15:5; Dt 28:39;
Isa 5:22; 22:13; 28:1;
29:9; 56:12; Jer 35:6;
Hos 4:11; Hab 2:15-16
ᵃ Nu 6:3; 28:7;
Dt 14:26; 29:6;
Jdg 13:4; Pr 20:1;
23:29-35; 31:4-7;
Isa 28:7; Eze 44:21;
Mic 2:11; Lk 1:15;
S Eph 5:18; 1Ti 3:3;
Tit 1:7 ᵇ S Ex 12:14
10:10 ᶜ S Ge 7:2;
S Lev 6:27; 14:57;
20:25; Eze 22:26
10:11 ᵈ 2Ch 15:3;
17:7; Ezr 7:25; Ne 8:7;
Mal 2:7 ᵉ Dt 17:10,11;
24:8; 25:1; 33:10;
Pr 4:27; Hag 2:11;
Mal 2:7
10:12 ᶠ S Ex 29:41
ᵍ Lev 6:14-16
10:13 ʰ S Lev 6:16
ⁱ Eze 42:13

[22]Then Aaron lifted his hands toward the people and blessed them. ʷ And having sacrificed the sin offering, the burnt offering and the fellowship offering, he stepped down. [23]Moses and Aaron then went into the tent of meeting. ˣ When they came out, they blessed the people; and the glory of the Lord ʸ appeared to all the people. [24]Fire ᶻ came out from the presence of the Lord and consumed the burnt offering and the fat portions on the altar. And when all the people saw it, they shouted for joy and fell facedown. ᵃ

THE DEATH OF NADAB AND ABIHU

10 Aaron's sons Nadab and Abihu ᵇ took their censers, ᶜ put fire in them ᵈ and added incense; ᵉ and they offered unauthorized fire before the Lord, ᶠ contrary to his command. ᵍ [2]So fire came out ʰ from the presence of the Lord and consumed them, ⁱ and they died before the Lord. ʲ [3]Moses then said to Aaron, "This is what the Lord spoke of when he said:

" 'Among those who approach me ᵏ
   I will be proved holy; ˡ
in the sight of all the people
   I will be honored.' ᵐ "

Aaron remained silent.

[4]Moses summoned Mishael and Elzaphan, ⁿ sons of Aaron's uncle Uzziel, ᵒ and said to them, "Come here; carry your cousins outside the camp, ᵖ away from the front of the sanctuary. ᵍ" [5]So they came and carried them, still in their tunics, ʳ outside the camp, as Moses ordered.

[6]Then Moses said to Aaron and his sons Eleazar and Ithamar, ˢ "Do not let your hair become unkempt ᵗ and do not tear your clothes, ᵘ or you will die and the Lord will be angry with the whole community. ᵛ But your relatives, all the house of Israel, may mourn ʷ for those the Lord has destroyed by fire. [7]Do not leave the entrance to the tent of meeting ˣ or you will die, because the Lord's anointing oil ʸ is on you." So they did as Moses said.

[8]Then the Lord said to Aaron, [9]"You and your sons are not to drink wine ᶻ or other fermented drink ᵃ whenever you go into the tent of meeting, or you will die. This is a lasting ordinance ᵇ for the generations to come, [10]so that you can distinguish between the holy and the common, between the unclean and the clean, ᶜ [11]and so you can teach ᵈ the Israelites all the decrees the Lord has given them through Moses. ᵉ"

[12]Moses said to Aaron and his remaining sons, Eleazar and Ithamar, "Take the grain offering ᶠ left over from the food offerings prepared without yeast and presented to the Lord and eat it beside the altar, ᵍ for it is most holy. [13]Eat it in the sanctuary area, ʰ because it is your share and your sons' share of the food offerings presented to the Lord; for so I have been commanded. ⁱ [14]But you and your sons and your daughters may eat the breast ʲ that was waved and the thigh that was presented. Eat them in a ceremonially clean place; ᵏ they have been given to you and your children as your share of the Israelites' fellowship offerings. [15]The thigh ˡ that was presented and the breast that was waved must be brought with the fat portions of the food offerings, to be waved before the Lord as a wave offering. ᵐ This will be the perpetual share for you and your children, as the Lord has commanded."

ᵃ 6 Or *Do not uncover your heads*

10:14 ʲ Nu 5:9 ᵏ S Ex 29:31; S Lev 4:12   **10:15** ˡ S Lev 7:34 ᵐ S Ex 29:28

9:22 *blessed.* The Aaronic benediction, a threefold blessing, is given in Nu 6:23–26. Cf. the threefold apostolic benediction in 2Co 13:14.
9:23 *glory of the Lord.* See v. 6; cf. the display of the Lord's glory at the erection of the tabernacle (Ex 40:34–35); cf. also God's acceptance of sacrifices at the dedication of Solomon's temple (2Ch 7:1).
9:24 *Fire came out from the presence of the Lord.* See 10:2; 1Ki 18:38.
10:1 *censers.* Ceremonial vessels containing hot coals and used for burning incense (see 16:12–13; 2Ch 26:19; Rev 8:3–4).

A C **10:2** *died before the Lord.* Aaron's older sons are mentioned also in Ex 6:23; 24:1,9; 28:1; Nu 3:2–4; 26:60–61; 1Ch 6:3; 24:1–2. They are regularly remembered as having died before the Lord and as having had no sons. Their death was tragic and at first seems harsh, but no more so than that of Ananias and Sapphira (Ac 5:1–11). In both cases a new

era was being inaugurated (cf. also the judgment on Achan, Jos 7, and on Uzzah, 2Sa 6:1–7). The new community had to be made aware that it existed for God, not vice versa.
10:3 The quotation reflects the spirit and substance of passages like Ex 14:4; 19:22; 29:1,44; 30:29. *be proved holy.* Act so as to publicly display my holiness (see 11:44 and note; see also Nu 20:13; Isa 5:16; Eze 20:41; 28:22,25; 36:23; 38:16; 39:27). *holy.* See Introduction: Theological Themes.
10:4 *outside the camp.* See note on 8:17.
10:6 *tear your clothes.* See 21:10; see also note on Ge 44:13.
10:7 *Do not leave.* To join the mourners (see 21:11–12).

A **10:10** *between the holy and the common.* The distinction between what was holy (sacred; see note on Ex 3:5) and what was common (not associated with the sacred) was carefully maintained (see Eze 22:26; 42:20; 44:23; 48:14–15).
10:12–15 See 7:28–36; Nu 18:8–20; Dt 18:1–5.

[16]When Moses inquired about the goat of the sin offering[a][n] and found that it had been burned up, he was angry with Eleazar and Ithamar, Aaron's remaining sons, and asked, [17]"Why didn't you eat the sin offering[o] in the sanctuary area? It is most holy; it was given to you to take away the guilt[p] of the community by making atonement for them before the LORD. [18]Since its blood was not taken into the Holy Place,[q] you should have eaten the goat in the sanctuary area, as I commanded.[r]"

[19]Aaron replied to Moses, "Today they sacrificed their sin offering and their burnt offering[s] before the LORD, but such things as this have happened to me. Would the LORD have been pleased if I had eaten the sin offering today?" [20]When Moses heard this, he was satisfied.

CLEAN AND UNCLEAN FOOD

11:1–23pp — Dt 14:3–20

The LORD said to Moses and Aaron, [2]"Say to the Israelites: 'Of all the animals that live on land, these are the ones you may eat:[t] [3]You may eat any animal that has a divided hoof and that chews the cud.

[4]" 'There are some that only chew the cud or only have a divided hoof, but you must not eat them.[u] The camel, though it chews the cud, does not have a divided hoof; it is ceremonially unclean for you. [5]The hyrax, though it chews the cud, does not have a divided hoof; it is unclean for you. [6]The rabbit, though it chews the cud, does not have a divided hoof; it is unclean for you. [7]And the pig,[v] though it has a divided hoof, does not chew the cud; it is unclean for you. [8]You must not eat their meat or touch their carcasses; they are unclean for you.[w]

[9]" 'Of all the creatures living in the water of the seas and the streams you may eat any that have fins and scales. [10]But all creatures in the seas or streams that do not have fins and scales—whether among all the swarming things or among all the other living creatures in the water—you are to regard as unclean.[x] [11]And since you are to regard them as unclean, you must not eat their meat; you must regard their carcasses as unclean.[y] [12]Anything living in the water that does not have fins and scales is to be regarded as unclean by you.[z]

[13]" 'These are the birds you are to regard as unclean and not eat because they are unclean: the eagle,[b] the vulture, the black vulture, [14]the red kite, any kind[a] of black kite, [15]any kind of raven,[b] [16]the horned owl, the screech owl, the gull, any kind of hawk, [17]the little owl, the cormorant, the great owl, [18]the white owl,[c] the desert owl, the osprey, [19]the stork,[d] any kind[e] of heron, the hoopoe and the bat.[f]

[20]" 'All flying insects that walk on all fours are to be regarded as unclean by you.[g] [21]There are, however, some flying insects that walk on all fours that you may eat: those that have jointed legs for hopping on the ground. [22]Of these you may eat any kind of locust,[h] katydid, cricket or grasshopper. [23]But all other flying insects that have four legs you are to regard as unclean.

[24]" 'You will make yourselves unclean by these;[i] whoever touches their carcasses will be unclean till evening.[j] [25]Whoever picks up one of their carcasses must wash their clothes,[k] and they will be unclean till evening.[l]

[26]" 'Every animal that does not have a divided hoof or that does not chew the cud is un-

---

[a] 16 Or *purification offering*; also in verses 17 and 19   [b] 13 The precise identification of some of the birds, insects and animals in this chapter is uncertain.

10:18 *Since its blood was not taken into the Holy Place, you should have eaten.* There were two types of sin offerings: (1) those in which the blood was sprinkled within the tabernacle, and (2) those in which it was splashed only on the great altar. Portions of the second type normally should have been eaten (see note on 4:5). But Moses was satisfied when he learned that Aaron had acted sincerely and not in negligence or rebellion (vv. 19–20).

10:19 *such things as this have happened to me.* Probably referring to the death of his two oldest sons (v. 2), for which he mourned by fasting. Or possibly something had occurred that made him ceremonially unclean.

11:1—15:33 The distinction between clean and unclean (see note on 11:2).

11:2 *the ones you may eat.* Ch. 11 is closely paralleled in Dt 14:3–21 but is more extensive. The animals acceptable for human consumption were those that chewed the cud and had a

divided hoof (v. 3). Of marine life, only creatures with fins and scales were permissible (v. 9). Birds and insects are also covered in the instructions (vv. 13–23). Some distinction between clean and unclean food was as old as the time of Noah (Ge 7:2). The main reason for the laws concerning clean and unclean food is the same as for other laws concerning the clean and unclean—to preserve the sanctity of Israel as God's holy people (see v. 44 and note). Some hold that certain animal life was considered unclean for health considerations, but it is difficult to substantiate this idea. Uncleanness typified sin and defilement. For the uncleanness of disease and bodily discharges see chs. 13–15.

11:6 *rabbit.* Does not technically chew the cud with regurgitation. The apparent chewing movements of the rabbit caused it to be classified popularly with cud chewers.

11:20 *all fours.* Although insects have six legs, perhaps people in ancient times did not count as ordinary legs the two large hind legs used for jumping.

10:16 [n] S Lev 9:3
10:17 [o] Lev 6:24-30; Eze 42:13
[p] S Ex 28:38
10:18 [q] S Lev 4:18; 6:26 [r] S Lev 6:17
10:19 [s] Lev 9:12
11:2 [t] Ac 10:12-14
11:4 [u] Ac 10:14
11:7 [v] Isa 65:4; 66:3,17
11:8 [w] S Lev 5:2; Heb 9:10
11:10 [x] ver 12
11:11 [y] S Lev 5:2
11:12 [z] ver 10
11:14 [a] S Ge 1:11
11:15 [b] S Ge 8:7
11:18 [c] Isa 13:21; Zep 2:14
11:19 [d] Zec 5:9 [e] S Ge 1:11 [f] Isa 2:20
11:20 [g] Ac 10:14
11:22 [h] Mt 3:4; Mk 1:6
11:24 [i] S Lev 5:2 [j] ver 27-40; Lev 13:3; 14:46; 15:5; 22:6; Nu 19:7,19
11:25 [k] ver 28; S Ex 19:10; Lev 13:6; 14:8,47; 15:5; 16:26; Nu 8:7; 19:7 [l] Lev 13:34; Nu 19:8; 31:24

11:28 *m* Heb 9:10
11:29 *n* ver 41
o Isa 66:17
11:32 *p* Lev 15:12;
Nu 19:18; 31:20
11:33 *q* S Lev 6:28
11:39 *r* Lev 17:15;
22:8; Dt 14:21;
Eze 4:14; 44:31
s ver 40; Lev 22:4;
Nu 19:11
11:40 *t* S ver 39
u ver 25; Lev 14:8;
17:15; 22:8;
Eze 44:31; Heb 9:10
11:43 *v* ver 44;
Lev 20:25; 22:5
11:44 *w* S Ex 6:2,7;
20:2; Isa 43:3; 51:15;
Eze 20:5 *x* S Ex 19:10;
Lev 20:7; Nu 15:40;
Jos 3:5; 7:13;
1Ch 15:12; 2Ch 29:5;
35:6 *y* S Ex 22:31;
S Dt 14:2 *z* S Ex 31:13;
Lev 19:2; 20:7;
Jos 24:19; 1Sa 2:2;
Job 6:10; Ps 99:3;
Eph 1:4; 1Th 4:7;
1Pe 1:15,16*
a S ver 43
11:45 *b* Lev 25:38,
55 *c* S Ge 17:7
d S Ex 19:6; 1Pe 1:16*
11:47 *e* Lev 10:10
12:2 *f* Lev 15:19;
18:19; Isa 64:6;
Eze 18:6; 22:10; 36:17
12:3 *g* S Ex 22:30
h S Ge 17:10;
S Lk 1:59

clean for you; whoever touches the carcass of any of them will be unclean. [27]Of all the animals that walk on all fours, those that walk on their paws are unclean for you; whoever touches their carcasses will be unclean till evening. [28]Anyone who picks up their carcasses must wash their clothes, and they will be unclean till evening. [m] These animals are unclean for you.

[29]" 'Of the animals that move about on the ground, these are unclean for you: [n] the weasel, the rat, [o] any kind of great lizard, [30]the gecko, the monitor lizard, the wall lizard, the skink and the chameleon. [31]Of all those that move along the ground, these are unclean for you. Whoever touches them when they are dead will be unclean till evening. [32]When one of them dies and falls on something, that article, whatever its use, will be unclean, whether it is made of wood, cloth, hide or sackcloth. [p] Put it in water; it will be unclean till evening, and then it will be clean. [33]If one of them falls into a clay pot, everything in it will be unclean, and you must break the pot. [q] [34]Any food you are allowed to eat that has come into contact with water from any such pot is unclean, and any liquid that is drunk from such a pot is unclean. [35]Anything that one of their carcasses falls on becomes unclean; an oven or cooking pot must be broken up. They are unclean, and you are to regard them as unclean. [36]A spring, however, or a cistern for collecting water remains clean, but anyone who touches one of these carcasses is unclean. [37]If a carcass falls on any seeds that are to be planted, they remain clean. [38]But if water has been put on the seed and a carcass falls on it, it is unclean for you.

[39]" 'If an animal that you are allowed to eat dies, [r] anyone who touches its carcass [s] will be unclean till evening. [40]Anyone who eats some of its carcass [t] must wash their clothes, and they will be unclean till evening. [u] Anyone who picks up the carcass must wash their clothes, and they will be unclean till evening.

[41]" 'Every creature that moves about on the ground is to be regarded as unclean; it is not to be eaten. [42]You are not to eat any creature that moves about on the ground, whether it moves on its belly or walks on all fours or on many feet; it is unclean. [43]Do not defile yourselves by any of these creatures. [v] Do not make yourselves unclean by means of them or be made unclean by them. [44]I am the Lord your God; [w] consecrate yourselves [x] and be holy, [y] because I am holy. [z] Do not make yourselves unclean by any creature that moves about on the ground. [a] [45]I am the Lord, who brought you up out of Egypt [b] to be your God; [c] therefore be holy, because I am holy. [d]

[46]" 'These are the regulations concerning animals, birds, every living thing that moves in the water and every creature that moves about on the ground. [47]You must distinguish between the unclean and the clean, between living creatures that may be eaten and those that may not be eaten. [e] ' "

PURIFICATION AFTER CHILDBIRTH

12 The Lord said to Moses, [2]"Say to the Israelites: 'A woman who becomes pregnant and gives birth to a son will be ceremonially unclean for seven days, just as she is unclean during her monthly period. [f] [3]On the eighth day [g] the boy is to be circumcised. [h] [4]Then the woman must wait thirty-three days to be purified from her bleeding. She must not touch anything sacred or go to the sanctuary until the days of her purification are over. [5]If she gives birth to a daughter, for two weeks the woman will be unclean, as during her period. Then she must wait sixty-six days to be purified from her bleeding.

11:36 *cistern for collecting water.* The use of waterproof plaster for lining cisterns dug in the ground was an important factor in helping the Israelites to settle the dry areas of Canaan after the conquest (cf. 2Ch 26:10).

11:41 *ground.* Verses 29–30 identify the animals that move about (or swarm) on the ground.

11:44 *be holy.* Quoted in 1Pe 1:16 (see note there; see also Introduction to Leviticus: Theological Themes). Holiness is the key theme of Leviticus, ringing like a refrain in various forms throughout the book (e.g., v. 45; 19:2; 20:7,26; 21:8,15; 22:9,16,32). The word "holy" appears more often in Leviticus than in any other book of the Bible. Israel was to be totally consecrated to God. Her holiness was to be expressed in every aspect of her life, to the extent that all of life had a certain ceremonial quality. Because of who God is and what he has done (v. 45), his people must dedicate themselves fully to him (cf. Mt 5:48). See Ro 12:1. *I am holy.* When God's holiness is spo-

ken of in the Bible, reference is to (1) his incomparably awesome majesty (the mysterious, overwhelming presence of his infinite power, before which the whole creation trembles), and (2) his absolute moral virtue (a presence so infinitely pure that it unmasks and judges every moral flaw or fault). Sometimes one of these aspects is foregrounded, sometimes the other, but often both are evoked together (as in Isa 6:3–5).

11:45 *brought ... out of Egypt.* A refrain found 8 more times in Leviticus (19:36; 22:33; 23:43; 25:38,42,55; 26:13,45) and nearly 60 times in 18 other books of the OT.

11:46–47 A summary of ch. 11.

12:2 *unclean.* The uncleanness came from the bleeding (vv. 4–5,7), not from the birth. It is not clear why the period of uncleanness after the birth of a baby boy (40 days) was half the period for a girl (80 days). *monthly period.* See 15:19–24.

12:3 See notes on Ge 17:10,12.

6" 'When the days of her purification for a son or daughter are over, [i] she is to bring to the priest at the entrance to the tent of meeting a year-old lamb[j] for a burnt offering and a young pigeon or a dove for a sin offering. [a][k] [7]He shall offer them before the LORD to make atonement for her, and then she will be ceremonially clean from her flow of blood.

" 'These are the regulations for the woman who gives birth to a boy or a girl. [8]If she cannot afford a lamb, she is to bring two doves or two young pigeons, [l] one for a burnt offering and the other for a sin offering. [m] In this way the priest will make atonement for her, and she will be clean. [n]' "

REGULATIONS ABOUT DEFILING SKIN DISEASES

13 The LORD said to Moses and Aaron, [2]"When anyone has a swelling[o] or a rash or a shiny spot[p] on their skin that may be a defiling skin disease, [b][q] they must be brought to Aaron the priest[r] or to one of his sons[c] who is a priest. [3]The priest is to examine the sore on the skin, and if the hair in the sore has turned white and the sore appears to be more than skin deep, it is a defiling skin disease. When the priest examines them, he shall pronounce them ceremonially unclean. [s] [4]If the shiny spot[t] on the skin is white but does not appear to be more than skin deep and the hair in it has not turned white, the priest is to isolate the affected person for seven days. [u] [5]On the seventh day[v] the priest is to examine them, [w] and if he sees that the sore is unchanged and has not spread in the skin, he is to isolate them for another seven days. [6]On the seventh day the priest is to examine them again, and if the sore has faded and has not spread in the skin, the priest shall pronounce them clean; [x] it is only a rash. They must wash their clothes, [y] and they will be clean. [z] [7]But if the rash does spread in their skin after they have shown themselves to the priest to be pronounced clean, they must appear before the priest again. [a] [8]The priest is to examine them, and if the rash has spread in the skin, he shall pronounce them unclean; it is a defiling skin disease.

[9]"When anyone has a defiling skin disease, they must be brought to the priest. [10]The priest is to examine them, and if there is a white swelling in the skin that has turned the hair white and if there is raw flesh in the swelling, [11]it is a chronic skin disease[b] and the priest shall pronounce them unclean. He is not to isolate them, because they are already unclean.

[12]"If the disease breaks out all over their skin and, so far as the priest can see, it covers all the skin of the affected person from head to foot, [13]the priest is to examine them, and if the disease has covered their whole body, he shall pronounce them clean. Since it has all turned white, they are clean. [14]But whenever raw flesh appears on them, they will be unclean. [15]When the priest sees the raw flesh, he shall pronounce them unclean. The raw flesh is unclean; they have a defiling disease. [c] [16]If the raw flesh changes and turns white, they must go to the priest. [17]The priest is to examine them, and if the sores have turned white, the priest shall pronounce the affected person clean; [d] then they will be clean.

[18]"When someone has a boil[e] on their skin and it heals, [19]and in the place where the boil was, a white swelling or reddish-white[f] spot[g] appears, they must present themselves to the priest. [20]The priest is to examine it, and if it appears to be more than skin deep and the hair in it has turned white, the priest shall pronounce them unclean. It is a defiling skin disease[h] that has broken out where the boil was. [21]But if, when the priest examines it, there is no white hair in it and it is not more than skin deep and has faded, then the priest is to isolate them for seven days. [22]If it is spreading in the skin, the priest shall pronounce them unclean; it is a defiling disease. [23]But if the spot is unchanged and has not spread, it is only a scar from the boil, and the priest shall pronounce them clean. [i]

[24]"When someone has a burn on their skin and a reddish-white or white spot appears

---

[a] 6 Or *purification offering*; also in verse 8   [b] 2 The Hebrew word for *defiling skin disease*, traditionally translated "leprosy," was used for various diseases affecting the skin; here and throughout verses 3-46.
[c] 2 Or *descendants*

12:6 *burnt offering.* See note on 1:3. *sin offering.* See notes on 4:3,5.
12:7 The last sentence in this verse is a summary of ch. 12.
12:8 An appendix prescribing alternative sacrifices for people who were poor. See 1:14–17 and note on 1:14; see also 5:7–10; 14:21–22; and especially Lk 2:24 (Mary's offering for Jesus).
13:1–46 This section deals with preliminary symptoms of skin diseases (vv. 1–8) and then with the symptoms of (1) raw flesh (vv. 9–17), (2) boils (vv. 18–23), (3) burns (vv. 24–28), (4) sores on the head or chin (vv. 29–37), (5) white spots (vv. 38–39) and (6) skin diseases on the head that cause baldness (vv. 40–44).

13:2 *defiling skin disease.* Occurs often in chs. 13–14; see also 22:4; Nu 5:2. Such diseases show visible defects that could function aptly as a symbol for defilement—as could mold (cf. vv. 47–59). *disease.* See TNIV text note; see also 22:4–8; Nu 5:2–4; Dt 24:8–9. The symptoms described, and the fact that they may rapidly change (vv. 6,26–27,32–37), show that the disease was not true leprosy (Hansen's disease). They apply also to a number of other diseases, as well as to rather harmless skin eruptions. The Hebrew word translated "defiling skin disease" can also mean "mold" (v. 47; 14:34; and especially 14:57).

12:6 [i] Lk 2:22
[j] Ex 29:38; Lev 23:12; Nu 6:12,14; 7:15
[k] Lev 5:7
12:8 [l] S Ge 15:9; Lev 14:22 [m] Lev 5:7; Lk 2:22-24*
[n] S Lev 4:26
13:2 [o] ver 10,19,28, 43 [p] ver 4,38,39; Lev 14:56 [q] ver 3,9, 15; S Lev 4:6; Lev 14:3, 32; Nu 5:2; Dt 24:8
[r] Dt 24:8
13:3 [s] ver 8,11,20, 30; Lev 21:1; Nu 9:6
13:4 [t] S ver 2
[u] ver 5,21,26,33,46; Lev 14:38; Nu 12:14, 15; Dt 24:8
13:5 [v] Lev 14:9
[w] ver 27,32,34,51
13:6 [x] ver 13,17,23, 28,34; Mt 8:3; Lk 5:12-14
[y] S Lev 11:25
[z] Lev 11:25; 14:8,9,20, 48; 15:8; Nu 8:7
13:7 [a] Lk 5:14
13:11 [b] S Ex 4:6; S Lev 14:8; S Nu 12:10; Mt 8:2
13:15 [c] S ver 2
13:17 [d] S ver 6
13:18 [e] S Ex 9:9
13:19 [f] ver 24,42; Lev 14:37 [g] S ver 2
13:20 [h] ver 2
13:23 [i] S ver 6

13:25 /ver 11
13:26 ʰS ver 4
13:27 /S ver 5
13:28 ᵐS ver 2
13:29 ⁿ ver 43, 44
13:31 ᵒ ver 4
13:32 ᵖS ver 5
13:34 ᵠS ver 5
ʳS Lev 11:25
13:36 ˢver 30
13:40 ᵗ Lev 21:5;
2Ki 2:23; Isa 3:24;
15:2; 22:12; Eze 27:31;
29:18; Am 8:10;
Mic 1:16
13:45 ᵘS Lev 10:6
ᵛEze 24:17, 22;
Mic 3:7 ʷS Lev 5:2;
La 4:15; Lk 17:12
13:46 ˣNu 5:1-4;
12:14; 2Ki 7:3; 15:5
13:49 ʸMk 1:44
13:50 ᶻEze 44:23
13:51 ᵃS ver 5
ᵇLev 14:44
13:52 ᶜver 55, 57

in the raw flesh of the burn, [25]the priest is to examine the spot, and if the hair in it has turned white, and it appears to be more than skin deep, it is a defiling disease that has broken out in the burn. The priest shall pronounce them unclean; it is a defiling skin disease.[j] [26]But if the priest examines it and there is no white hair in the spot and if it is not more than skin deep and has faded, then the priest is to isolate them for seven days.[k] [27]On the seventh day the priest is to examine them,[l] and if it is spreading in the skin, the priest shall pronounce them unclean; it is a defiling skin disease. [28]If, however, the spot is unchanged and has not spread in the skin but has faded, it is a swelling from the burn, and the priest shall pronounce them clean; it is only a scar from the burn.[m]

[29]"If a man or woman has a sore on their head[n] or chin, [30]the priest is to examine the sore, and if it appears to be more than skin deep and the hair in it is yellow and thin, the priest shall pronounce them unclean; it is a defiling skin disease on the head or chin. [31]But if, when the priest examines the sore, it does not seem to be more than skin deep and there is no black hair in it, then the priest is to isolate the affected person for seven days.[o] [32]On the seventh day the priest is to examine the sore,[p] and if it has not spread and there is no yellow hair in it and it does not appear to be more than skin deep, [33]then the man or woman must shave themselves, except for the affected area, and the priest is to keep them isolated another seven days. [34]On the seventh day the priest is to examine the sore,[q] and if it has not spread in the skin and appears to be no more than skin deep, the priest shall pronounce the man or woman clean. They must wash their clothes, and they will be clean.[r] [35]But if the sore does spread in the skin after they are pronounced clean, [36]the priest is to examine them, and if he finds that the sore has spread in the skin, he does not need to look for yellow hair; they are unclean.[s] [37]If, however, the sore is unchanged so far as the priest can see, and if black hair has grown in it, the affected person is healed. They are clean, and the priest shall pronounce them clean.

[38]"When a man or woman has white spots on the skin, [39]the priest is to examine them, and if the spots are dull white, it is a harmless rash that has broken out on the skin; they are clean.

[40]"A man who has lost his hair and is bald[t] is clean. [41]If he has lost his hair from the front of his scalp and has a bald forehead, he is clean. [42]But if he has a reddish-white sore on his bald head or forehead, it is a defiling disease breaking out on his head or forehead. [43]The priest is to examine him, and if the swollen sore on his head or forehead is reddish-white like a defiling skin disease, [44]the man is diseased and is unclean. The priest shall pronounce him unclean because of the sore on his head.

[45]"Anyone with such a defiling disease must wear torn clothes,[u] let their hair be unkempt,[a] cover the lower part of their face[v] and cry out, 'Unclean! Unclean!'[w] [46]As long as they have the disease they remain unclean. They must live alone; they must live outside the camp.[x]

REGULATIONS ABOUT DEFILING MOLDS

[47]"As for any fabric that is spoiled with a defiling mold—any woolen or linen clothing, [48]any woven or knitted material of linen or wool, any leather or anything made of leather— [49]if the affected area in the fabric, the leather, the woven or knitted material, or any leather article, is greenish or reddish, it is a defiling mold and must be shown to the priest.[y] [50]The priest is to examine the affected area[z] and isolate the article for seven days. [51]On the seventh day he is to examine it,[a] and if the mold has spread in the fabric, the woven or knitted material, or the leather, whatever its use, it is a persistent defiling mold; the article is unclean.[b] [52]He must burn the fabric, the woven or knitted material of wool or linen, or any leather article that has been spoiled; because the defiling mold is persistent, the article must be burned.[c]

[53]"But if, when the priest examines it, the mold has not spread in the fabric, the woven or knitted material, or the leather article, [54]he shall order that the spoiled article be washed. Then he is to isolate it for another seven days. [55]After the article has been washed,

---

ᵃ 45 Or clothes, uncover their head

13:45-46 The ceremonially unclean were excluded from the camp (the area around the tabernacle and courtyard), where the Israelites lived in tents. Later, no unclean persons were allowed in the temple area, where they could mingle with others. Not only was God present in the tabernacle in a special way, but also in the camp (Nu 5:3; Dt 23:14). Therefore unclean people were not to be in the camp (see Nu 5:1-4; 12:14-15, Miriam; 31:19-24; see also Lev 10:4-5; Nu 15:35-36; 2Ki 7:3-4; 2Ch

26:21, Uzziah). As a result of their separation from God, they were to exhibit their grief by tearing their clothes, by having unkempt hair and by partially covering their faces (v. 45).
13:47 *defiling mold.* During Israel's rainy season (October through March), this is a problem along the coast and by the Sea of Galilee, where it is very humid.
13:54 *washed.* See vv. 34, 55-56, 58. The treatment of disorders commonly included washing.

the priest is to examine it again, and if the mold has not changed its appearance, even though it has not spread, it is unclean. Burn it, no matter which side of the fabric has been spoiled. ⁵⁶If, when the priest examines it, the mold has faded after the article has been washed, he is to tear the spoiled part out of the fabric, the leather, or the woven or knitted material. ⁵⁷But if it reappears in the fabric, in the woven or knitted material, or in the leather article, it is a spreading mold; whatever has the mold must be burned. ⁵⁸Any fabric, woven or knitted material, or any leather article that has been washed and is rid of the mold, must be washed again. Then it will be clean."

⁵⁹These are the regulations concerning defiling molds in woolen or linen clothing, woven or knitted material, or any leather article, for pronouncing them clean or unclean.

CLEANSING FROM DEFILING SKIN DISEASES

14 The Lord said to Moses, ²"These are the regulations for any diseased person at the time of their ceremonial cleansing, when they are brought to the priest: ᵈ ³The priest is to go outside the camp and examine them. ᵉ If they have been healed of their defiling skin disease, ª ᶠ ⁴the priest shall order that two live clean birds and some cedar wood, scarlet yarn and hyssop ᵍ be brought for the person to be cleansed. ʰ ⁵Then the priest shall order that one of the birds be killed over fresh water in a clay pot. ᶦ ⁶He is then to take the live bird and dip it, together with the cedar wood, the scarlet yarn and the hyssop, into the blood of the bird that was killed over the fresh water. ᶦ ⁷Seven times ᵏ he shall sprinkle ˡ the one to be cleansed of the defiling disease, and then pronounce them clean. After that, he is to release the live bird in the open fields. ᵐ

⁸"The person to be cleansed must wash their clothes, ⁿ shave off all their hair and bathe with water; ᵒ then they will be ceremonially clean. ᵖ After this they may come into the camp, �q but they must stay outside their tent for seven days. ⁹On the seventh day ʳ they must shave off all their hair; ˢ they must shave their head, their beard, their eyebrows and the rest of their hair. They must wash their clothes and bathe themselves with water, and they will be clean. ᵗ

¹⁰"On the eighth day ᵘ they must bring two male lambs and one ewe lamb ᵛ a year old, each without defect, along with three-tenths of an ephah ᵇ ʷ of the finest flour mixed with olive oil for a grain offering, ˣ and one log ᶜ of oil. ʸ ¹¹The priest who pronounces them clean shall present ᶻ both the one to be cleansed and their offerings before the Lord at the entrance to the tent of meeting. ª

¹²"Then the priest is to take one of the male lambs and offer it as a guilt offering, ᵇ along with the log of oil; he shall wave them before the Lord as a wave offering. ᶜ ¹³He is to slaughter the lamb in the sanctuary area ᵈ where the sin offering ᵈ and the burnt offering are slaughtered. Like the sin offering, the guilt offering belongs to the priest; ᵉ it is most holy. ¹⁴The priest is to take some of the blood of the guilt offering and put it on the lobe of the right ear of the one to be cleansed, on the thumb of their right hand and on the big toe of their right foot. ᶠ ¹⁵The priest shall then take some of the log of oil, pour it in the palm of his own left hand, ᵍ ¹⁶dip his right forefinger into the oil in his palm, and with his finger sprinkle some of it before the Lord seven times. ʰ ¹⁷The priest is to put some of the oil remaining in his palm on the lobe of the right ear of the one to be cleansed, on the thumb of their right hand and on the big toe of their right foot, on top of the blood of the guilt offering. ᶦ ¹⁸The rest of the oil in his palm the priest shall put on the head of the one to be cleansed ᶦ and make atonement for them before the Lord.

ª 3 The Hebrew word for *defiling skin disease*, traditionally translated "leprosy," was used for various diseases affecting the skin; also in verses 7 and 32.　ᵇ 10 That is, probably about 11 pounds or about 5 kilograms　ᶜ 10 That is, about 1/2 pint or about 0.3 liter; also in verses 12, 15, 21 and 24　ᵈ 13 Or *purification offering*; also in verses 19, 22 and 31

14:2 ᵈLev 13:57; Dt 24:8; Mt 8:2-4; Mk 1:40-44; Lk 5:12-14; 17:14
14:3 ᵉLev 13:46; ᶠS Lev 13:2
14:4 ᵍS Ex 12:22; ʰver 6, 49, 51, 52; Nu 19:6; Ps 51:7
14:5 ᶦver 50
14:6 ᶦS ver 4
14:7 ᵏver 51
14 ᶦ2Ki 5:10, 14; Isa 52:15; Eze 36:25
ᵐver 53
14:8 ⁿS Lev 11:25
ᵒver 9; S Ex 29:4; Lev 15:5; 17:15; 22:6; ᵖver 20
ᑫS Lev 13:11; Nu 5:2, 3; 12:14, 15; 19:20; 31:24; 2Ch 26:21
14:9 ʳS Lev 13:5
ˢNu 6:9; Dt 21:12
ᵗS Lev 13:6
14:10 ᵘNu 6:10; Mt 8:4; Mk 1:44; Lk 5:14 ᵛS Lev 4:32
ʷNu 15:9; 28:20
ˣLev 2:1 ʸver 12, 15, 21, 24
14:11 ᶻNu 6:16
ªNu 6:10
14:12 ᵇS Lev 5:18
ᶜS Ex 29:24
14:13 ᵈS Ex 29:11
ᵉLev 6:24-30; S 7:7
14:14 ᶠS Ex 29:20
14:15 ᵍver 26
14:16 ʰver 27
14:17 ᶦver 26
14:18 ᶦver 31; Lev 15:15

13:59 A summary of ch. 13.

14:1–32 The ritual after the skin disease had been cured had three parts: (1) ritual for the first week (outside the camp, vv. 1–7), (2) ritual for the second week (inside the camp, vv. 8–20) and (3) special permission for the poor (vv. 21–32).

14:4 *hyssop.* A plant used in ceremonial cleansing (see note on Ex 12:22).

14:5 *killed.* Diseases and disorders were a symbol of sin and rendered a person or object ceremonially unclean. The prescribed cleansing included sacrifice as well as washing (see note on 13:54).

14:6 *cedar . . . yarn . . . hyssop.* Also used for cleansing in vv. 51–52; Nu 19:6 (see note there).

14:7,16,51 *Seven times.* See note on 4:6.

14:7 *clean.* Perhaps the yarn and cedar stick were used as well as the hyssop plant to sprinkle the blood for cleansing (see Ps 51:7 and note). Further sacrifices are specified in vv. 10–31. *release the live bird.* Cf. 16:22; see note on 16:5.

14:8 The Levites were similarly cleansed (see Nu 8:7 and note).

14:10 *grain offering.* See note on 2:1.

14:12 *guilt offering.* See 5:14—6:7 and note on 5:15. *wave offering.* See note on 7:30–32.

14:13 *most holy.* See note on Ex 3:5.

14:14 See note on 8:14.

14:18–21,29,31 *atonement.* See notes on 16:20–22; 17:11; Ex 25:17; cf. note and TNIV text note on Ro 3:25.

14:19 *k* ver 31;
S Lev 5:3; 15:15
14:20 *l* Lev 15:30
m ver 8
14:21 *n* S Lev 5:7
o ver 22,32
14:22 *p* S Lev 5:7
q Lev 15:30
14:23 *r* Lev 15:14,29
s S ver 10,11
14:24 *t* Nu 6:14
u S ver 10 *v* ver 12
14:25 *w* S Ex 29:20
14:26 *x* ver 15
14:29 *y* ver 18
14:30 *z* S Lev 5:7
14:31 *a* ver 22;
Lev 5:7; 15:15,30
b S ver 18,19
14:32 *c* S Lev 13:2
d S ver 21
14:34 *e* Ge 12:5;
Ex 6:4; Nu 13:2
f Ge 17:8; 48:4;
Nu 27:12; 32:22;
Dt 3:27; 7:1; 32:49
14:37 *g* S Lev 13:19
14:38 *h* S Lev 13:4
14:39 *i* Lev 13:5
14:40 *j* ver 45
14:44 *k* Lev 13:51
14:46 *l* S Lev 11:24
14:47 *m* S Lev 11:25
14:48 *n* S Lev 13:6
14:49 *o* ver 4;
1Ki 4:33
14:50 *p* ver 5
14:51 *q* ver 6;
Ps 51:7 *r* S ver 4,7

¹⁹"Then the priest is to sacrifice the sin offering and make atonement for the one to be cleansed from their uncleanness. *k* After that, the priest shall slaughter the burnt offering ²⁰and offer it on the altar, together with the grain offering, and make atonement for them, *l* and they will be clean. *m*

²¹"If, however, they are poor *n* and cannot afford these, *o* they must take one male lamb as a guilt offering to be waved to make atonement for them, together with a tenth of an ephah*a* of the finest flour mixed with olive oil for a grain offering, a log of oil, ²²and two doves or two young pigeons, *p* such as they can afford, one for a sin offering and the other for a burnt offering. *q*

²³"On the eighth day they must bring them for their cleansing to the priest at the entrance to the tent of meeting, *r* before the LORD. *s* ²⁴The priest is to take the lamb for the guilt offering, *t* together with the log of oil, *u* and wave them before the LORD as a wave offering. *v* ²⁵He shall slaughter the lamb for the guilt offering and take some of its blood and put it on the lobe of the right ear of the one to be cleansed, on the thumb of their right hand and on the big toe of their right foot. *w* ²⁶The priest is to pour some of the oil into the palm of his own left hand, *x* ²⁷and with his right forefinger sprinkle some of the oil from his palm seven times before the LORD. ²⁸Some of the oil in his palm he is to put on the same places he put the blood of the guilt offering—on the lobe of the right ear of the one to be cleansed, on the thumb of their right hand and on the big toe of their right foot. ²⁹The rest of the oil in his palm the priest shall put on the head of the one to be cleansed, to make atonement for them before the LORD. *y* ³⁰Then he shall sacrifice the doves or the young pigeons, such as the person can afford, *z* ³¹one as a sin offering and the other as a burnt offering, *a* together with the grain offering. In this way the priest will make atonement before the LORD on behalf of the one to be cleansed. *b*"

³²These are the regulations for anyone who has a defiling skin disease *c* and who cannot afford the regular offerings *d* for their cleansing.

CLEANSING FROM DEFILING MOLDS

³³The LORD said to Moses and Aaron, ³⁴"When you enter the land of Canaan, *e* which I am giving you as your possession, *f* and I put a spreading mold in a house in that land, ³⁵the owner of the house must go and tell the priest, 'I have seen something that looks like a defiling mold in my house.' ³⁶The priest is to order the house to be emptied before he goes in to examine the mold, so that nothing in the house will be pronounced unclean. After this the priest is to go in and inspect the house. ³⁷He is to examine the mold on the walls, and if it has greenish or reddish*g* depressions that appear to be deeper than the surface of the wall, ³⁸the priest shall go out the doorway of the house and close it up for seven days. *h* ³⁹On the seventh day*i* the priest shall return to inspect the house. If the mold has spread on the walls, ⁴⁰he is to order that the contaminated stones be torn out and thrown into an unclean place outside the town.*j* ⁴¹He must have all the inside walls of the house scraped and the material that is scraped off dumped into an unclean place outside the town. ⁴²Then they are to take other stones to replace these and take new clay and plaster the house.

⁴³"If the defiling mold reappears in the house after the stones have been torn out and the house scraped and plastered, ⁴⁴the priest is to go and examine it and, if the mold has spread in the house, it is a persistent defiling mold; the house is unclean. *k* ⁴⁵It must be torn down—its stones, timbers and all the plaster—and taken out of the town to an unclean place.

⁴⁶"Anyone who goes into the house while it is closed up will be unclean till evening. *l* ⁴⁷Anyone who sleeps or eats in the house must wash their clothes. *m*

⁴⁸"But if the priest comes to examine it and the mold has not spread after the house has been plastered, he shall pronounce the house clean, *n* because the defiling mold is gone. ⁴⁹To purify the house he is to take two birds and some cedar wood, scarlet yarn and hyssop. *o* ⁵⁰He shall kill one of the birds over fresh water in a clay pot.*p* ⁵¹Then he is to take the cedar wood, the hyssop, *q* the scarlet yarn and the live bird, dip them into the blood of the dead bird and the fresh water, and sprinkle the house seven times. *r* ⁵²He shall purify the house with the bird's blood, the fresh water, the live bird, the cedar wood, the hys-

---

a 21 That is, probably about 3 1/2 pounds or about 1.6 kilograms

---

14:19 *sin offering.* See 4:1—5:13 and notes on 4:3,5. *burnt offering.* See note on 1:3.
14:20 *grain offering.* See note on 2:1.
14:33–53 There are many similarities between this section

and the previous one, particularly in the manner of restoration.
14:45 *torn down.* A house desecrated by mold or fungus would be a defiled place to live in, so drastic measures had to be taken.

sop and the scarlet yarn. [53]Then he is to release the live bird in the open fields[s] outside the town. In this way he will make atonement for the house, and it will be clean. [t]"

[54]These are the regulations for any defiling skin disease, [u] for a sore, [55]for defiling molds[v] in fabric or in a house, [56]and for a swelling, a rash or a shiny spot, [w] [57]to determine when something is clean or unclean.

These are the regulations for defiling skin diseases and defiling molds. [x]

DISCHARGES CAUSING UNCLEANNESS

15 The Lord said to Moses and Aaron, [2]"Speak to the Israelites and say to them: 'When any man has an unusual bodily discharge, [y] such a discharge is unclean. [3]Whether it continues flowing from his body or is blocked, it will make him unclean. This is how his discharge will bring about uncleanness:

[4]" 'Any bed the man with a discharge lies on will be unclean, and anything he sits on will be unclean. [5]Anyone who touches his bed must wash their clothes[z] and bathe with water, [a] and they will be unclean till evening. [b] [6]Whoever sits on anything that the man with a discharge sat on must wash their clothes and bathe with water, and they will be unclean till evening.

[7]" 'Whoever touches the man[c] who has a discharge[d] must wash their clothes and bathe with water, and they will be unclean till evening.

[8]" 'If the man with the discharge spits[e] on anyone who is clean, they must wash their clothes and bathe with water, and they will be unclean till evening.

[9]" 'Everything the man sits on when riding will be unclean, [10]and whoever touches any of the things that were under him will be unclean till evening; whoever picks up those things[f] must wash their clothes and bathe with water, and they will be unclean till evening.

[11]" 'Anyone the man with a discharge touches without rinsing his hands with water must wash their clothes and bathe with water, and they will be unclean till evening.

[12]" 'A clay pot[g] that the man touches must be broken, and any wooden article[h] is to be rinsed with water.

[13]" 'When a man is cleansed from his discharge, he is to count off seven days[i] for his ceremonial cleansing; he must wash his clothes and bathe himself with fresh water, and he will be clean.[j] [14]On the eighth day he must take two doves or two young pigeons[k] and come before the Lord to the entrance to the tent of meeting and give them to the priest. [15]The priest is to sacrifice them, the one for a sin offering[a][l] and the other for a burnt offering. [m] In this way he will make atonement before the Lord for the man because of his discharge. [n]

[16]" 'When a man has an emission of semen, [o] he must bathe his whole body with water, and he will be unclean till evening. [p] [17]Any clothing or leather that has semen on it must be washed with water, and it will be unclean till evening. [18]When a man has sexual relations with a woman and there is an emission of semen, [q] both of them must bathe with water, and they will be unclean till evening.

[19]" 'When a woman has her regular flow of blood, the impurity of her monthly period[r] will last seven days, and anyone who touches her will be unclean till evening.

[20]" 'Anything she lies on during her period will be unclean, and anything she sits on will be unclean. [21]Anyone who touches her bed will be unclean; they must wash their clothes and bathe with water, and they will be unclean till evening. [s] [22]Anyone who touches anything she sits on will be unclean; they must wash their clothes and bathe with water, and they will be unclean till evening. [23]Whether it is the bed or anything she was sitting on, anyone who touches it will be unclean till evening.

[24]" 'If a man has sexual relations with her and her monthly flow[t] touches him, he will be unclean for seven days; any bed he lies on will be unclean.

[a] 15 Or *purification offering*; also in verse 30

14:53 [s] S ver 7
[t] ver 20
14:54 [u] Lev 13:2
14:55 [v] Lev 13:47-52
14:56 [w] Lev 13:2
14:57 [x] S Lev 10:10
15:2 [y] ver 16, 32; Lev 22:4; Nu 5:2; 2Sa 3:29; Mt 9:20
15:5 [z] S Lev 11:25
[a] Lev 14:8
[b] S Lev 11:24
15:7 [c] ver 19; Lev 22:5 [d] ver 16; Lev 22:4
15:8 [e] Nu 12:14
15:10 [f] Nu 19:10
15:12 [g] S Lev 6:28
[h] S Lev 11:32
15:13 [i] S Lev 8:33
[j] ver 5
15:14 [k] Lev 14:22
15:15 [l] Lev 5:7
[m] Lev 14:31
[n] S Lev 14:18,19
15:16 [o] S ver 2; Dt 23:10 [p] ver 5; Dt 23:11
15:18 [q] 1Sa 21:4
15:19 [r] S ver 24
15:21 [s] ver 27
15:24 [t] ver 19; Lev 12:2; 18:19; 20:18; Eze 18:6

14:54–57 A summary of chs. 13; 14.

15:1–33 The chapter deals with (1) male uncleanness caused by bodily discharge (vv. 2–15) or emission of semen (vv. 16–18); (2) female uncleanness caused by her monthly period (vv. 19–24) or lengthy hemorrhaging (vv. 25–30); (3) summary (vv. 31–33).

15:2 *bodily discharge.* Probably either diarrhea or urethral discharge (various kinds of infections). The contamination of anything under the man (v. 10), whether he sat (vv. 4,6,9) or lay (v. 4) on it, indicates that the bodily discharge had to do with the buttocks or genitals.

15:4 *bed.* Something like a mat (cf. 2Sa 11:13).

15:13 *cleansed.* God brought about the healing; the priest could only ascertain that a person was already healed.

15:16 *semen.* Normal sexual activity and a woman's menstruation required no sacrifices but only washing and a minimal period of uncleanness.

15:19 *seven days.* See 12:2. This regulation is the background of 2Sa 11:4 (Bathsheba; see note there).

15:20 See note on Ge 31:35.

15:24 *flow.* During her period a woman was protected from sexual activity. No offering was required for uncleanness contracted by a man in this way, but the uncleanness lasted seven days.

15:25 *u* Mt 9:20;
Mk 5:25; Lk 8:43
15:29 *v* Lev 14:22
15:30 *w* Lev 5:10;
14:20,31; 18:19;
2Sa 11:4; Mk 5:25;
Lk 8:43
15:31 *x* Lev 20:3;
Nu 5:3; 19:13,20;
2Sa 15:25; 2Ki 21:7;
Ps 33:14; 74:7; 76:2;
Eze 5:11; 23:38
15:32 *y* S ver 2
15:33 *z* ver 19,24,25
16:1 *a* S Lev 10:1
16:2 *b* Ex 30:10;
Heb 9:7 *c* S Ex 26:33;
Heb 9:25; 10:19
d S Ex 26:33;
Heb 6:19 *e* S Ex 26:34
f S Ex 25:22
g S Ex 40:34;
S 2Sa 22:10
16:3 *h* ver 6;
Lev 4:1-12; Heb 9:24,
25 *i* S Lev 4:3 *j* ver 5
16:4 *k* S Lev 8:13
l S Ex 28:39 *m* ver 32;
S Ex 28:42; 29:29,30;
Lev 21:10; Nu 20:26,
28 *n* S Ex 29:4;
Heb 10:22 *o* Eze 9:2;
44:17-18
16:5 *p* S Lev 4:13-21
q ver 20; S Lev 4:3;
2Ch 29:23; Ps 50:9

25 " 'When a woman has a discharge of blood for many days at a time other than her monthly period *u* or has a discharge that continues beyond her period, she will be unclean as long as she has the discharge, just as in the days of her period. 26 Any bed she lies on while her discharge continues will be unclean, as is her bed during her monthly period, and anything she sits on will be unclean, as during her period. 27 Anyone who touches them will be unclean; they must wash their clothes and bathe with water, and they will be unclean till evening.

28 " 'When she is cleansed from her discharge, she must count off seven days, and after that she will be ceremonially clean. 29 On the eighth day she must take two doves or two young pigeons *v* and bring them to the priest at the entrance to the tent of meeting. 30 The priest is to sacrifice one for a sin offering and the other for a burnt offering. In this way he will make atonement for her before the LORD for the uncleanness of her discharge. *w*

31 " 'You must keep the Israelites separate from things that make them unclean, so they will not die in their uncleanness for defiling my dwelling place, *a* *x* which is among them.' "

32 These are the regulations for a man with a discharge, for anyone made unclean by an emission of semen, *y* 33 for a woman in her monthly period, for a man or a woman with a discharge, and for a man who has sexual relations with a woman who is ceremonially unclean. *z*

THE DAY OF ATONEMENT

16:2–34pp — Lev 23:26–32; Nu 29:7–11

16 The LORD spoke to Moses after the death of the two sons of Aaron who died when they approached the LORD. *a* 2 The LORD said to Moses: "Tell your brother Aaron that he is not to come whenever he chooses *b* into the Most Holy Place *c* behind the curtain *d* in front of the atonement cover *e* on the ark, or else he will die. For I will appear *f* in the cloud *g* over the atonement cover.

3 "This is how Aaron is to enter the Most Holy Place: *h* He must first bring a young bull *i* for a sin offering *b* and a ram for a burnt offering. *j* 4 He is to put on the sacred linen tunic, *k* with linen undergarments next to his body; he is to tie the linen sash around him and put on the linen turban. *l* These are sacred garments; *m* so he must bathe himself with water *n* before he puts them on. *o* 5 From the Israelite community *p* he is to take two male goats *q* for a sin offering and a ram for a burnt offering.

a 31 Or *my tabernacle*   *b* 3 Or *purification offering*; here and throughout this chapter

---

15:25 *discharge of blood for many days.* As, e.g., the woman in Mt 9:20 (see note on Mk 5:25). *beyond her period.* An unnatural discharge, possibly caused by disease, was treated like a sickness and required an offering upon recovery (vv. 28–30; see vv. 14–15).

15:31 Addressed to the priests, thus emphasizing the importance of the regulations. Since God dwelt in the tabernacle, any unholiness, symbolized by the discharges of ch. 15, could result in death if the people came into his presence. Sin separates all people from a holy God and results in their death, unless atonement is made (see the next chapter).

15:32–33 A summary of ch. 15.

16:1–34 See 23:26–32; 25:9; Ex 30:10; Nu 29:7–11; Heb 9:7. The order of ritual for the Day of Atonement was as follows: 1. The high priest went to the basin in the courtyard, removed his regular garments, washed himself and went into the Holy Place to put on the special garments for the Day of Atonement (v. 4). 2. He went out to sacrifice a bull as the Day of Atonement offering for himself and the other priests (v. 11). 3. He went into the Most Holy Place with some of the bull's blood, with incense and with coals from the altar of burnt offering (vv. 12–13). The incense was placed on the burning coals, and the smoke of the incense hid the ark from view. 4. He sprinkled some of the bull's blood on and in front of the atonement cover of the ark (v. 14). 5. He went outside the tabernacle and cast lots for two goats to see which was to be sacrificed and which was to be the scapegoat (vv. 7–8). 6. At the altar of burnt offering the high priest killed the goat for the sin offering for the people, and for a second time he went into the Most Holy Place, this time to sprinkle the goat's blood in front of and on the atonement cover (vv. 5,9,15–16a). 7. He returned to the Holy Place (called "tent of meeting" in v. 16) and sprinkled the

goat's blood there (v. 16b). 8. He went outside to the altar of burnt offering and sprinkled it (v. 18) with the blood of the bull (for himself, v. 11) and of the goat (for the people, v. 15). 9. While in the courtyard, he laid both hands on the second goat, thus symbolizing the transfer of Israel's sin, and sent it out into the wilderness (vv. 20–22). 10. The man who took the goat away, after he had accomplished his task, washed himself and his clothes outside the camp (v. 26) before rejoining the people. 11. The high priest entered the Holy Place to remove his special garments (v. 23). 12. He went out to the basin to wash and put on his regular priestly clothes (v. 24). 13. As a final sacrifice he went out to the great altar and offered a ram (v. 3) as a burnt offering for himself, and another ram (v. 5) for the people (v. 24). 14. The conclusion of the entire day was the removal of the sacrifices for the sin offerings to a place outside the camp, where they were burned, and there the man who performed this ritual bathed and washed his clothes (vv. 27–28) before rejoining the people.

16:1 *sons of Aaron who died.* See 10:1–3.

16:2 *atonement cover.* See Ex 25:17 and note. Blood sprinkled on the lid of the ark made atonement for Israel on the Day of Atonement (vv. 15–17). In the Septuagint (the pre-Christian Greek translation of the OT) the word for "atonement cover" is the same one used of Christ and translated "sacrifice of atonement" in Ro 3:25 (see TNIV text note there).

16:3 *bull.* For Aaron's cleansing (vv. 6,11). Before Aaron could minister in the Most Holy Place for the nation, he himself had to be cleansed (Heb 5:1–3); not so Christ, who is our high priest and Aaron's antitype (Heb 7:26–28).

16:5 *two male goats for a sin offering.* One was the usual sin offering (see notes on 4:3,5) and the other a scape-

⁶"Aaron is to offer the bull for his own sin offering to make atonement for himself and his household.ʳ ⁷Then he is to take the two goats and present them before the LORD at the entrance to the tent of meeting. ⁸He is to cast lotsˢ for the two goats—one lot for the LORD and the other for the scapegoat.ᵃ ᵗ ⁹Aaron shall bring the goat whose lot falls to the LORD and sacrifice it for a sin offering. ¹⁰But the goat chosen by lot as the scapegoat shall be presented alive before the LORD to be used for making atonementᵘ by sending it into the wilderness as a scapegoat.

¹¹"Aaron shall bring the bull for his own sin offering to make atonement for himself and his household,ᵛ and he is to slaughter the bull for his own sin offering. ¹²He is to take a censer full of burning coalsʷ from the altar before the LORD and two handfuls of finely ground fragrant incenseˣ and take them behind the curtain. ¹³He is to put the incense on the fire before the LORD, and the smoke of the incense will conceal the atonement coverʸ above the tablets of the covenant law, so that he will not die.ᶻ ¹⁴He is to take some of the bull's bloodᵃ and with his finger sprinkle it on the front of the atonement cover; then he shall sprinkle some of it with his finger seven times before the atonement cover.ᵇ

¹⁵"He shall then slaughter the goat for the sin offering for the peopleᶜ and take its blood behind the curtainᵈ and do with it as he did with the bull's blood: He shall sprinkleᵉ it on the atonement cover and in front of it. ¹⁶In this way he will make atonementᶠ for the Most Holy Placeᵍ because of the uncleanness and rebellion of the Israelites, whatever their sins have been. He is to do the same for the tent of meeting,ʰ which is among them in the midst of their uncleanness. ¹⁷No one is to be in the tent of meeting from the time Aaron goes in to make atonement in the Most Holy Place until he comes out, having made atonement for himself, his household and the whole community of Israel.

¹⁸"Then he shall come out to the altarⁱ that is before the LORD and make atonement for it. He shall take some of the bull's blood and some of the goat's blood and put it on all the horns of the altar.ʲ ¹⁹He shall sprinkle some of the blood on it with his finger seven times to cleanse it and to consecrate it from the uncleanness of the Israelites.ᵏ

²⁰"When Aaron has finished making atonement for the Most Holy Place, the tent of meeting and the altar, he shall bring forward the live goat. ²¹He is to lay both hands on the head of the live goatᵐ and confessⁿ over it all the wickedness and rebellion of the Israelites—all their sins—and put them on the goat's head. He shall send the goat away into the wilderness in the care of someone appointed for the task. ²²The goat will carry on itself all their sinsᵒ to a remote place; and the man shall release it in the wilderness.

²³"Then Aaron is to go into the tent of meeting and take off the linen garmentsᵖ he put on before he entered the Most Holy Place, and he is to leave them there.�q ²⁴He shall bathe himself with water in the sanctuary areaʳ and put on his regular garments.ˢ Then he shall come out and sacrifice the burnt offering for himself and the burnt offering for the people,ᵗ to make atonement for himself and for the people.ᵘ ²⁵He shall also burn the fat of the sin offering on the altar.

²⁶"The one who releases the goat as a scapegoatᵛ must wash his clothesʷ and bathe himself with water;ˣ afterward he may come into the camp. ²⁷The bull and the goat for the sin offerings, whose blood was brought into the Most Holy Place to make atonement, must be taken outside the camp;ʸ their hides, flesh and intestines are to be burned up. ²⁸The man who burns them must wash his clothes and bathe himself with water; afterward he may come into the camp.ᶻ

²⁹"This is to be a lasting ordinanceᵃ for you: On the tenth day of the seventh monthᵇ

ᵃ 8 The meaning of the Hebrew for this word is uncertain; also in verses 10 and 26.

---

goat. No single offering could fully typify the atonement of Christ. The one goat was killed, its blood sprinkled in the Most Holy Place and its body burned outside the camp (vv. 15,27), symbolizing the payment of the price of Christ's atonement. The other goat, sent away alive and bearing the sins of the nation (v. 21), symbolized the removal of sin and its guilt. *ram*. For the sins of the people; the one in v. 3 was for the sins of the high priest. Both were sacrificed at the end of the ceremony (v. 24).

16:6–10 An outline of vv. 11–22.

16:8 *scapegoat*. See TNIV text note.

16:11 *make atonement for himself*. See note on v. 3.

16:13 *smoke of the incense*. Covered the ark so that the high priest would not see the glorious presence of God (v. 2) and

thus die. *the tablets of the covenant law*. See note on Ex 25:22.

16:14 See Ro 3:25 and note. *seven times*. See note on 4:6.

16:16 *tent of meeting*. Here and in vv. 17,20,33 the term refers to the Holy Place.

16:20–22 A summary description of substitutionary atonement. The sin of the worshipers was confessed and symbolically transferred to the sacrificial animal, on which hands were laid (see notes on 1:3; Ex 29:10; see also Lev 1:4; 3:8; 4:4; cf. Isa 53:6; Jn 1:29; 1Pe 2:24).

16:24 *sanctuary area*. Cf. 6:26. *burnt offering … burnt offering*. The two rams mentioned in vv. 3,5.

16:25 *fat of the sin offering*. See 4:8–10.

16:27 *outside the camp*. See note on 4:12.

16:6 ʳ Lev 9:7; Heb 7:27; 9:7,12
16:8 ˢ Nu 26:55,56; 33:54; 34:13; Jos 14:2; 18:6; Jdg 20:9; Ne 10:34; Est 3:7; 9:24; Ps 22:18; Pr 16:33 ᵗ ver 10,26
16:10 ᵘ Isa 53:4-10; S Ro 3:25
16:11 ᵛ S ver 6,24, 33
16:12 ʷ S Lev 10:1; Rev 8:5 ˣ S Ex 25:6; 30:34-38
16:13 ʸ S Ex 25:17 ᶻ S Ex 28:43
16:14 ᵃ S Lev 4:5; Heb 9:7,13,25 ᵇ S Lev 4:6
16:15 ᶜ S Lev 4:13-21; Heb 7:27; 9:7,12; 13:11 ᵈ Heb 9:3 ᵉ S Lev 4:17; Nu 19:19; Isa 52:15; Eze 36:25
16:16 ᶠ S Ex 29:36; S Ro 3:25 ᵍ S Ex 26:33; Heb 9:25 ʰ Ex 29:4; S 40:2
16:18 ⁱ S Lev 4:7 ʲ S Lev 4:25
16:19 ᵏ Eze 43:20
16:20 ˡ S ver 5
16:21 ᵐ S Ex 29:10 ⁿ S Lev 5:5
16:22 ᵒ S Ex 28:38; Isa 53:12
16:23 ᵖ S Ex 28:42 q Eze 42:14
16:24 ʳ S Lev 6:16 ˢ ver 3-5 ᵗ Lev 1:3 ᵘ S ver 11
16:26 ᵛ S ver 8 ʷ S Lev 11:25 ˣ Lev 14:8
16:27 ʸ S Ex 29:14
16:28 ᶻ Nu 19:8,10
16:29 ᵃ S Lev 23:14 ᵇ Lev 25:9

16:29 ʿver 31;
Lev 23:27,32;
Nu 29:7; Isa 58:3
ᵈS Ex 31:15;
S Lev 23:28 ᵉEx 12:19
16:30 ʿS Ex 30:10
ᵍPs 51:2; Jer 33:8;
Eze 36:33; Zec 13:1;
Eph 5:26
16:31 ʰEzr 8:21;
Isa 58:3,5; Da 10:12
ⁱAc 27:9
16:32 ʲS Ex 30:30
ᵏS ver 4; S Ex 28:2
16:33 ˡS ver 11,16-
18; Eze 45:18
16:34 ᵐS Ex 27:21
ⁿHeb 9:7,25
17:2 ᵒLev 10:6,12
17:3 ᵖS Lev 3:7
ᵠS Lev 7:23
17:4 ʳver 9; 1Ki 8:4;
2Ch 1:3 ˢDt 12:5-21
ᵗS Ge 17:14
17:5 ᵘS Lev 3:1;
Eze 43:27
17:6 ᵛS Lev 4:18
ʷS Lev 3:2
ˣS Lev 1:9
17:7 ʸS Ex 22:20
ᶻS Ex 34:15; Jer 3:6,
9; Eze 23:3;
1Co 10:20 ᵃS Ex 12:14
ᵇS Ge 9:12
17:9 ᶜS Lev 1:3
ᵈS ver 4 ᵉS Lev 3:7
17:10 ᶠS Ge 9:4
17:11 ᵍver 14
ʰHeb 9:22
17:13 ⁱLev 7:26;
Eze 24:7; 33:25;
Ac 15:20
17:14 ʲS Ge 9:4
17:15 ᵏS Lev 7:24

you must deny yourselves[a][c] and not do any work[d]—whether native-born[e] or a foreigner residing among you— ³⁰because on this day atonement will be made[f] for you, to cleanse you. Then, before the LORD, you will be clean from all your sins.[g] ³¹It is a day of sabbath rest, and you must deny yourselves;[h] it is a lasting ordinance.[i] ³²The priest who is anointed and ordained[j] to succeed his father as high priest is to make atonement. He is to put on the sacred linen garments[k] ³³and make atonement for the Most Holy Place, for the tent of meeting and the altar, and for the priests and all the members of the community.[l]

³⁴"This is to be a lasting ordinance[m] for you: Atonement is to be made once a year[n] for all the sins of the Israelites."

And it was done, as the LORD commanded Moses.

EATING BLOOD FORBIDDEN

17 The LORD said to Moses, ²"Speak to Aaron and his sons[o] and to all the Israelites and say to them: 'This is what the LORD has commanded: ³Any Israelite who sacrifices an ox,[b] a lamb[p] or a goat[q] in the camp or outside of it ⁴instead of bringing it to the entrance to the tent of meeting[r] to present it as an offering to the LORD in front of the tabernacle of the LORD[s]—such persons shall be considered guilty of bloodshed; they have shed blood and must be cut off from their people.[t] ⁵This is so the Israelites will bring to the LORD the sacrifices they are now making in the open fields. They must bring them to the priest, that is, to the LORD, at the entrance to the tent of meeting and sacrifice them as fellowship offerings.[u] ⁶The priest is to splash the blood against the altar[v] of the LORD[w] at the entrance to the tent of meeting and burn the fat as an aroma pleasing to the LORD.[x] ⁷They must no longer offer any of their sacrifices to the goat idols[c][y] to whom they prostitute themselves.[z] This is to be a lasting ordinance[a] for them and for the generations to come.'[b]

⁸"Say to them: 'Any Israelite or any foreigner residing among them who offers a burnt offering or sacrifice ⁹and does not bring it to the entrance to the tent[c] of meeting[d] to sacrifice it to the LORD[e] must be cut off from their people.

¹⁰"'I will set my face against any Israelite or any foreigner residing among them who eats blood,[f] and I will cut them off from their people. ¹¹For the life of a creature is in the blood,[g] and I have given it to you to make atonement for yourselves on the altar; it is the blood that makes atonement for one's life.[d][h] ¹²Therefore I say to the Israelites, "None of you may eat blood, nor may any foreigner residing among you eat blood."

¹³"'Any Israelite or any foreigner residing among you who hunts any animal or bird that may be eaten must drain out the blood and cover it with earth,[i] ¹⁴because the life of every creature is its blood. That is why I have said to the Israelites, "You must not eat the blood of any creature, because the life of every creature is its blood; anyone who eats it must be cut off."[j]

¹⁵"'Anyone, whether native-born or foreigner, who eats anything[k] found dead or torn

---

a 29 Or *must fast*; also in verse 31   b 3 The Hebrew word can refer to either male or female.
c 7 Or *the demons*   d 11 Or *atonement by the life in the blood*

16:29,31 *deny yourselves.* See TNIV text note; more lit. "humble (or afflict) yourselves." The expression came to be used of fasting (Ps 35:13). The Day of Atonement was the only regular fast day stipulated in the OT (see 23:27,29,32 and TNIV text note), though tradition later added other fast days to the Jewish calendar (see Zec 7:5; 8:19 and note).

16:29 *seventh month.* Tishri, the seventh month, begins with the Festival of Trumpets (see note on 23:24). The Day of Atonement follows on the 10th day, and on the 15th day the Festival of Tabernacles begins (see 23:23–36). See chart, pp. 180–181.

16:30 *clean from all your sins.* On the Day of Atonement the repentant Israelite was assured of sins forgiven.

16:34 *once a year.* Heb 9:11—10:14 repeatedly contrasts this with Christ's "once for all" sacrifice.

17:1—26:46 Sometimes called the "Holiness Code," these chapters deal with regulations for holy living and holy practices in various areas (see Introduction: Theological Themes and Outline; see also note on 11:44).

17:4 *tabernacle of the LORD.* The people, with few exceptions (e.g., Dt 12:15,20–21), were directed to sacrifice only at the central sanctuary (Dt 12:5–6). Sennacherib's representa-

tive referred to Hezekiah's requiring worship only in Jerusalem (2Ki 18:22). One reason for such a regulation was to keep the Israelites from becoming corrupted by the Canaanites' pagan worship. *cut off from their people.* See note on 7:20.

17:5 *to the priest, that is, to the LORD.* See note on 6:6.

17:7 *prostitute themselves.* See Ex 34:15 and note.

17:11 *the life of a creature is in the blood.* See note on Ge 9:4. The blood shed in the sacrifices was sacred. It epitomized the life of the sacrificial victim. Since life was sacred, blood (a symbol of life) had to be treated with respect (Ge 9:5–6). Eating blood was therefore strictly forbidden (see 7:26–27; Dt 12:16,23–25; 15:23; 1Sa 14:32–34). *blood ... makes atonement.* Practically every sacrifice included the splashing or sprinkling of blood on the altar or within the tabernacle (v. 6; 1:5; 3:2; 4:6,25; 7:2), thus teaching that atonement involves the substitution of life for life. The blood of the OT sacrifice pointed forward to the blood of the Lamb of God, who obtained for his people "eternal redemption" (Heb 9:12). "Without the shedding of blood there is no forgiveness" (Heb 9:22).

17:15 *found dead or torn.* Such animals would not have had the blood drained from them and therefore would be forbidden.

by wild animals / must wash their clothes and bathe with water, *m* and they will be ceremonially unclean till evening; *n* then they will be clean. ¹⁶But if they do not wash their clothes and bathe themselves, they will be held responsible. *o* ' "

UNLAWFUL SEXUAL RELATIONS

18 The LORD said to Moses, ²"Speak to the Israelites and say to them: 'I am the LORD your God. *p* ³You must not do as they do in Egypt, where you used to live, and you must not do as they do in the land of Canaan, where I am bringing you. Do not follow their practices. *q* ⁴You must obey my laws *r* and be careful to follow my decrees. *s* I am the LORD your God. *t* ⁵Keep my decrees and laws, *u* for whoever obeys them will live by them. *v* I am the LORD.

⁶ 'No one is to approach any close relative to have sexual relations. I am the LORD.

⁷ 'Do not dishonor your father *w* by having sexual relations with your mother. *x* She is your mother; do not have relations with her.

⁸ 'Do not have sexual relations with your father's wife; *y* that would dishonor your father. *z*

⁹ 'Do not have sexual relations with your sister, *a* either your father's daughter or your mother's daughter, whether she was born in the same home or elsewhere. *b*

¹⁰ 'Do not have sexual relations with your son's daughter or your daughter's daughter; that would dishonor you.

¹¹ 'Do not have sexual relations with the daughter of your father's wife, born to your father; she is your sister.

¹² 'Do not have sexual relations with your father's sister; *c* she is your father's close relative.

¹³ 'Do not have sexual relations with your mother's sister, *d* because she is your mother's close relative.

¹⁴ 'Do not dishonor your father's brother by approaching his wife to have sexual relations; she is your aunt. *e*

¹⁵ 'Do not have sexual relations with your daughter-in-law. *f* She is your son's wife; do not have relations with her. *g*

¹⁶ 'Do not have sexual relations with your brother's wife; *h* that would dishonor your brother.

¹⁷ 'Do not have sexual relations with both a woman and her daughter. *i* Do not have sexual relations with either her son's daughter or her daughter's daughter; they are her close relatives. That is wickedness.

¹⁸ 'Do not take your wife's sister *j* as a rival wife and have sexual relations with her while your wife is living.

¹⁹ 'Do not approach a woman to have sexual relations during the uncleanness *k* of her monthly period. *l*

²⁰ 'Do not have sexual relations with your neighbor's wife *m* and defile yourself with her.

17:15 / S Ex 22:31
m S Lev 14:8
n S Lev 11:40
17:16 *o* S Lev 5:1
18:2 *p* S Ge 17:7
18:3 *q* ver 24-30;
S Ex 23:24; Dt 18:9;
2Ki 16:3; 17:8;
1Ch 5:25
18:4 *r* S Ge 26:5
s Dt 4:1; 1Ki 11:11;
Jer 44:10,23;
Eze 11:12 *t* ver 2
18:5 *u* S Ge 26:5
v Dt 4:1; Ne 9:29;
Isa 55:3; Eze 18:9;
20:11; Am 5:4-6;
Mt 19:17; S Ro 10:5*;
Gal 3:12*
18:7 *w* ver 8;
Lev 20:11; Dt 27:20
x Eze 22:10
18:8 *y* 1Co 5:1
z Ge 35:22; Lev 20:11;
Dt 22:30; 27:20
18:9 *a* ver 11;
Lev 20:17; Dt 27:22
b Lev 20:17; Dt 27:22;
2Sa 13:13; Eze 22:11
18:12 *c* ver 13;
Lev 20:19
18:13 *d* S ver 12,14;
Lev 20:20
18:14 *e* S ver 13
18:15 *f* S Ge 11:31;
S 38:16 *g* Eze 22:11
18:16 *h* Lev 20:21;
Mt 14:4; Mk 6:18
18:17 *i* Lev 20:14;
Dt 27:23
18:18 *j* S Ge 30:1
18:19 *k* S Lev 15:25-
30 *l* S Lev 15:24
18:20 *m* S Ex 20:14;
Mt 5:27,28; 1Co 6:9;
Heb 13:4

18:1—20:27 Here God's people are given instructions concerning interpersonal relations and a morality reflecting God's holiness. Israel was thereby prepared for a life different from the Canaanites, whose lifestyle was deplorably immoral. Ch. 18 marks the boundaries for marriage and sexual relations (but see also v. 21 and note); ch. 19 provides specific moral guidance on a variety of matters, many of which are implicitly covered by the Ten Commandments; and ch. 20 specifies the penalties for violating God's standard of morality. See chart, p. 275.

18:2 In chs. 18–26 the phrase "I am the LORD" occurs 47 times. The Lord's name (i.e., his revealed character as Yahweh, "the LORD") is the authority that stands behind his instructions. See note on Ex 3:15.

18:3 Six times in this chapter Israel is warned not to follow the example of pagans (here, two times; see also vv. 24,26–27,30).

18:5 *live.* With God's full blessing. The law was the way of life for the redeemed (see Dt 6:2; 8:2–3; 30:20 and notes; 32:47; Eze 20:11,13,21), not a way of salvation for the lost (see Ro 10:5; Gal 3:12).

18:6 A summary of the laws against incest (vv. 7–18). Penalties for incestuous relations are given in ch. 20. (Cf. 1Co 5.)

18:7 This prohibition applied also after the father's death.

18:8 *your father's wife.* Other than your mother—assuming there is more than one wife.

18:11 *sister.* There would be many half-sisters in a polygamous society. Tamar claimed that an exception to this prohibition could be made (2Sa 13:12–13; but see note there).

18:14 *your aunt.* See 20:20. If the father's brother was alive, the act would be adulterous. If he was dead, one could rationalize such a marriage because the aunt was not a blood relative—but it was still forbidden.

18:15 Cf. the account of Judah and Tamar (Ge 38:18).

18:16 *your brother's wife.* The law also applied to a time after divorce or the brother's death. To marry one's brother's widow was not immoral but might damage the brother's inheritance. The levirate law of Dt 25:5–6 offered an exception that preserved the dead brother's inheritance and continued his line.

18:17 *daughter.* Stepdaughter (granddaughter-in-law is also covered in the verse). The law applied even after the mother's death.

18:18 Cf. the account of Jacob with Leah and Rachel (Ge 29:23–30).

18:19 See Eze 18:6; 22:10.

18:20 See note on Ex 20:14.

18:21 *n* Dt 12:31;
18:10; 2Ki 16:3; 17:17;
21:6; 23:10; 2Ch 28:1-
4; 33:6; Ps 106:37,38;
Isa 57:5; Jer 7:30,31;
19:5; 32:35;
Eze 16:20; Mic 6:7
o Lev 20:2-5; Dt 9:4;
1Ki 11:5,7,33;
Isa 57:9; Jer 32:35;
49:1; Zep 1:5
p Lev 19:12; 21:6;
Isa 48:11; Eze 22:26;
36:20; Am 2:7;
Mal 1:12 *q* S Ex 6:2
18:22 *r* Lev 20:13;
Dt 23:18; Ro 1:27;
1Co 6:9 *s* S Ge 19:5
18:23 *t* Ex 20:12
Lev 20:15; Dt 27:21
18:24 *u* ver 3, 27, 30;
Lev 20:23 *v* Dt 9:4;
18:12
18:25 *w* Nu 35:34;
Dt 21:23 *x* Lev 20:23;
Dt 9:5; 12:31; 18:12
y ver 28; Lev 20:22;
Job 20:15; Jer 51:34
18:26 *z* S Ge 26:5
18:28 *a* Lev 20:22;
Ezr 9:11; La 1:17
b S ver 25
18:30 *c* S Lev 8:35
d ver 2
19:2 *e* Nu 14:5;
Ps 68:26 *f* S Ex 20:2
g S Ex 15:11;
1Pe 1:16 *; *
S Lev 11:44; S 20:26
19:3 *h* Ex 20:12
i S Ex 20:8 / Lev 11:44
19:4 *k* S Ex 20:4;
Jdg 17:3; Ps 96:5;
115:4-7; 135:15
l Lev 11:44
19:6 *m* Lev 7:16-17
19:7 *n* Lev 7:18
19:8 *o* S Lev 5:1
p Lev 22:2,15,16;
Nu 18:32 *q* S Ge 17:14
19:9 *r* Ru 2:2,3,7,16,
17 *s* Lev 23:10,22;
Dt 24:19-22;
Job 24:10
19:10 *t* Lev 24:20
u ver 9 *v* Dt 24:19,21
19:11 *w* Ex 20:15;
S 23:4; Lk 3:14
x S Ex 20:16;
S Eph 4:25 *y* S Lev 6:2
19:12 *z* Jer 5:2; 7:9;
Mal 3:5 *a* Ex 3:13;
20:7; Dt 18:19;
Pr 18:10; Isa 42:8;
Jer 44:16,26;
S Mt 5:33 *b* Jer 34:16
19:13 *c* Lev 25:14,17
d S Ex 20:15
e S Ex 22:15,25-27
f Job 7:2; 24:12; 31:39;
Isa 16:14; Mal 3:5
g Dt 24:15; Jer 22:13;
Mt 20:8; 1Ti 5:18;
Jas 5:4
19:14 *h* S Ex 4:11;

21 " 'Do not give any of your children *n* to be sacrificed to Molek, *o* for you must not profane the name of your God. *p* I am the Lord. *q*

22 " 'Do not have sexual relations with a man as one does with a woman; *r* that is detestable. *s*

23 " 'Do not have sexual relations with an animal and defile yourself with it. A woman must not present herself to an animal to have sexual relations with it; that is a perversion. *t*

24 " 'Do not defile yourselves in any of these ways, because this is how the nations that I am going to drive out before you *u* became defiled. *v* 25 Even the land was defiled; *w* so I punished it for its sin, *x* and the land vomited out its inhabitants. *y* 26 But you must keep my decrees and my laws. *z* The native-born and the foreigners residing among you must not do any of these detestable things, 27 for all these things were done by the people who lived in the land before you, and the land became defiled. 28 And if you defile the land, *a* it will vomit you out *b* as it vomited out the nations that were before you.

29 " 'Everyone who does any of these detestable things—such persons must be cut off from their people. 30 Keep my requirements *c* and do not follow any of the detestable customs that were practiced before you came and do not defile yourselves with them. I am the Lord your God. *d* ' "

VARIOUS LAWS

19 The Lord said to Moses, 2 "Speak to the entire assembly of Israel *e* and say to them: 'Be holy because I, the Lord your God, *f* am holy. *g*

3 " 'Each of you must respect your mother and father, *h* and you must observe my Sabbaths. *i* I am the Lord your God. *j*

4 " 'Do not turn to idols or make metal gods for yourselves. *k* I am the Lord your God. *l*

5 " 'When you sacrifice a fellowship offering to the Lord, sacrifice it in such a way that it will be accepted on your behalf. 6 It shall be eaten on the day you sacrifice it or on the next day; anything left over until the third day must be burned up. *m* 7 If any of it is eaten on the third day, it is impure and will not be accepted. *n* 8 Whoever eats it will be held responsible *o* because they have desecrated what is holy *p* to the Lord; they must be cut off from their people. *q*

9 " 'When you reap the harvest of your land, do not reap to the very edges *r* of your field or gather the gleanings of your harvest. *s* 10 Do not go over your vineyard a second time *t* or pick up the grapes that have fallen. *u* Leave them for the poor and the foreigner. *v* I am the Lord your God.

11 " 'Do not steal. *w*

" 'Do not lie. *x*

" 'Do not deceive one another. *y*

12 " 'Do not swear falsely *z* by my name *a* and so profane *b* the name of your God. I am the Lord.

13 " 'Do not defraud your neighbors *c* or rob *d* them. *e*

" 'Do not hold back the wages of a hired worker *f* overnight. *g*

14 " 'Do not curse the deaf or put a stumbling block in front of the blind, *h* but fear your God. *i* I am the Lord.

15 " 'Do not pervert justice; *j* do not show partiality *k* to the poor or favoritism to the great, *l* but judge your neighbor fairly. *m*

16 " 'Do not go about spreading slander *n* among your people.

" 'Do not do anything that endangers your neighbor's life. *o* I am the Lord.

19:14 Lev 21:18; Dt 27:18 *i* ver 32; Lev 25:17,36 **19:15** *j* S Ex 23:2; Ex 23:2,6 *k* Dt 24:17; Job 13:8,10; 32:21; Pr 28:21 *l* Job 34:19 *m* S Ex 23:8;
Pr 24:23; Mal 2:9; Jas 2:1-4 **19:16** *n* Ps 15:3; 31:13; 41:6; 101:5; Jer 6:28; 9:4; Eze 22:9 *o* Ex 23:7; Dt 10:17; 27:25; Ps 15:5; Eze 22:12

18:21 *Molek.* The god of the Ammonites (see 20:2-5; 1Ki 11:5 and note). The detestable practice of sacrificing children to Molek was common in Phoenicia and other surrounding countries. Cf. 2Ki 3:26-27. King Manasseh evidently sacrificed his sons to Molek (2Ch 33:6; see 2Ki 23:10). Jer 32:35 protests the practice. *profane the name of your God.* Whatever blatantly violates God's revealed will desecrates his name (see note on Ps 5:11) because it fails to honor his holiness (see note on Lev 11:44).

18:22 *have sexual relations with a man.* See 20:13, where the penalty for homosexual acts is stated.

18:29 *detestable.* See note on 7:21. *cut off from their people.* See note on 7:20.

19:1 See note on 18:1—20:27.

19:2 *Be holy.* See note on 11:44.

19:3-4 See 18:30; see also Ex 20:4-6,8-12 and notes; and chart, p. 275.

19:5 *fellowship offering.* See note on 3:1.

19:6 *third day.* See note on 7:15-18.

19:8 *what is holy to the Lord.* See note on Ex 3:5. *cut off from their people.* See note on 7:20.

19:9-10 See 23:22; see also Dt 24:19-21. Ru 2 gives an example of the application of the law of gleaning.

19:11-12 See Ex 20:7,15-16 and notes.

19:13 *wages of a hired worker.* See Dt 24:14-15; Mt 20:8.

¹⁷" 'Do not hate a fellow Israelite in your heart. ᵖ Rebuke your neighbor frankly �q so you will not share in their guilt.

¹⁸" 'Do not seek revenge ʳ or bear a grudge ˢ against anyone among your people, ᵗ but love your neighbor ᵘ as yourself. ᵛ I am the LORD.

¹⁹" 'Keep my decrees. ʷ

" 'Do not mate different kinds of animals.

" 'Do not plant your field with two kinds of seed. ˣ

" 'Do not wear clothing woven of two kinds of material. ʸ

²⁰" 'If a man sleeps with a female slave who is promised to another man ᶻ but who has not been ransomed or given her freedom, there must be due punishment. ᵃ Yet they are not to be put to death, because she had not been freed. ²¹The man, however, must bring a ram to the entrance to the tent of meeting for a guilt offering to the LORD. ᵃ ²²With the ram of the guilt offering the priest is to make atonement for him before the LORD for the sin he has committed, and his sin will be forgiven. ᵇ

²³" 'When you enter the land and plant any kind of fruit tree, regard its fruit as forbidden. ᵇ For three years you are to consider it forbidden ᵇ; it must not be eaten. ²⁴In the fourth year all its fruit will be holy, ᶜ an offering of praise to the LORD. ²⁵But in the fifth year you may eat its fruit. In this way your harvest will be increased. I am the LORD your God.

²⁶" 'Do not eat any meat with the blood still in it. ᵈ

" 'Do not practice divination ᵉ or seek omens. ᶠ

²⁷" 'Do not cut the hair at the sides of your head or clip off the edges of your beard. ᵍ

²⁸" 'Do not cut ʰ your bodies for the dead or put tattoo marks on yourselves. I am the LORD.

²⁹" 'Do not degrade your daughter by making her a prostitute, ⁱ or the land will turn to prostitution and be filled with wickedness. ʲ

³⁰" 'Observe my Sabbaths ᵏ and have reverence for my sanctuary. I am the LORD. ˡ

³¹" 'Do not turn to mediums ᵐ or seek out spiritists, ⁿ for you will be defiled by them. I am the LORD your God.

³²" 'Stand up in the presence of the aged, show respect ᵒ for the elderly ᵖ and revere your God. �q I am the LORD. ʳ

³³" 'When foreigners reside among you in your land, do not mistreat them. ³⁴The foreigners residing among you must be treated as your native-born. ˢ Love them as yourself, ᵗ for you were foreigners ᵘ in Egypt. ᵛ I am the LORD your God.

³⁵" 'Do not use dishonest standards when measuring length, weight or quantity. ʷ ³⁶Use honest scales ˣ and honest weights, an honest ephah ᶜʸ and an honest hin. ᵈᶻ I am the LORD your God, who brought you out of Egypt. ᵃ

³⁷" 'Keep all my decrees ᵇ and all my laws ᶜ and follow them. I am the LORD.' "

PUNISHMENTS FOR SIN

20 The LORD said to Moses, ²"Say to the Israelites: 'Any Israelite or any foreigner residing in Israel who sacrifices any of his children to Molek is to be put to death. ᵈ The members of the community are to stone him. ᵉ ³I myself will set

---

ᵃ 20 Or *be an inquiry*   ᵇ 23 Hebrew *uncircumcised*   ᶜ 36 An ephah was a dry measure having the capacity of about 3/5 of a bushel or about 22 liters.   ᵈ 36 A hin was a liquid measure having the capacity of about 1 gallon or about 3.6 liters.

19:17 *Do not hate a fellow Israelite.* See 1Jn 2:9,11; 3:15; 4:20.

🅰 **19:18** *love your neighbor as yourself.* Quoted by Christ (Mt 22:39; Mk 12:31; Lk 10:27), Paul (Ro 13:9; Gal 5:14) and James (2:8). The stricter Pharisees (school of Shammai) added to this command what they thought it implied: "Hate your enemy" (Mt 5:43; see note there). Jesus' reaction, "Love your enemies," was in line with true OT teaching (see vv. 17,34) and was more in agreement with the middle-of-the-road Pharisees. Rabbi Nahmanides (13th century) caught their sentiments: "One should place no limitations upon the love for the neighbor, but instead a person should love to do an abundance of good for his fellow being as he does for himself." "Neighbor" does not merely mean one who lives nearby, but anyone with whom one comes in contact.

19:19 *Do not mate…plant…wear.* Such mixing symbolically violated the distinction God established in the creation order.

19:21–22 *guilt offering.* See 5:14—6:7 and note on 5:15.

19:26 *meat with the blood.* See note on 17:11. *seek omens.* See v. 31; Ex 22:18; Dt 18:14; 1Sa 28:9; Isa 47:12–14.

19:27 *Do not cut the hair at the sides of your head.* A prohibition still followed by orthodox Jews.

19:28 There was to be no disfiguring of the body, after the manner of the pagans (see note on 21:5).

19:34 *you were foreigners in Egypt.* See Dt 5:15.

🅰 **19:35** *dishonest standards.* In a culture with no bureau of weights and measures, cheating in business transactions by falsification of standards was common (see Dt 25:13–16; Pr 11:1 and note; 16:11 and note; 20:10,23). The prophets also condemned such sin (Am 8:5; Mic 6:10–11).

🅰 **20:1–27** In ch. 20 many of the same sins listed in ch. 18 are mentioned again, but this time usually with the death penalty specified. Israel's God is a jealous God who tolerates no rivals (see note on Ex 20:5). He requires exclusive allegiance (see Ex 20:3 and note). See note on 18:1—20:27.

20:2–5 *Molek.* See note on 18:21.

19:17 ᵖ S 1Jn 2:9
q S Mt 18:15
19:18 ʳ S Ge 4:23;
Ro 12:19; Heb 10:30
ˢ Ps 103:9 ᵗ S Ex 12:48
ᵘ S Ex 20:16 ᵛ ver 34;
S Mt 5:43*; 19:16*;
22:39*; Mk 12:31*;
Lk 10:27*; Jn 13:34;
Ro 13:9*; Gal 5:14*;
Jas 2:8*
19:19 ʷ S Ge 26:5
ˣ Dt 22:9 ʸ Dt 22:11
19:20 ᶻ Dt 22:23-27
19:21 ᵃ S Lev 5:15
19:22 ᵇ S Lev 5:15
19:24 ᶜ S Ex 22:29
19:26 ᵈ S Ge 9:4
ᵉ S Ge 30:27;
S Isa 44:25
ᶠ S Ex 22:18; 2Ki 17:17
19:27 ᵍ Lev 21:5;
Dt 14:1; 2Sa 10:4-5;
Jer 41:5; 48:37;
Eze 5:1-5
19:28 ʰ Lev 21:5;
Dt 14:1; 1Ki 18:28;
Jer 16:6; 41:5; 47:5
19:29 ⁱ Lev 21:9;
Dt 23:18 ʲ Ge 34:7;
Lev 21:9
19:30 ᵏ S Ex 20:8
ˡ Lev 26:2
19:31 ᵐ S Ex 22:18;
1Sa 28:7-20;
1Ch 10:13 ⁿ Lev 20:6;
2Ki 21:6; 23:24;
Isa 8:19; 19:3; 29:4;
47:12; 65:4
19:32 ᵒ 1Ki 12:8
ᵖ Job 32:4; Pr 23:22;
La 5:12; 1Ti 5:1
q S ver 14; Job 29:8
ʳ Lev 11:44; 25:17
19:34 ˢ S Ex 12:48
ᵗ S ver 18 ᵘ S Ex 22:21
ᵛ Ex 23:9; Dt 10:19;
23:7; Ps 146:9
19:35 ʷ Dt 25:13-16
19:36 ˣ Job 31:6;
Pr 11:1; Hos 12:7;
Mic 6:11 ʸ Jdg 6:19;
Ru 2:17; 1Sa 1:24;
17:17; Eze 45:10
ᶻ Dt 25:13-15;
Pr 20:10; Eze 45:11
ᵃ S Ex 12:17
19:37 ᵇ 2Ki 17:37;
2Ch 7:17; Ps 119:5;
Eze 18:9 ᶜ S Ge 26:5
20:2 ᵈ ver 10;
Ge 26:11; Ex 19:12
ᵉ ver 27; Lev 24:14;
Nu 15:35,36;
Dt 21:21; Jos 7:25

20:3 *f* ver 5,6;
Lev 23:30 *o* Ps 74:7;
79:1; Jer 7:30;
Eze 5:11 *h* S Lev 15:31
i S Lev 18:21
20:4 *j* Dt 17:2-5
20:6 *k* S ver 3;
S Lev 19:31
20:7 *l* S Lev 11:44
m S Ex 29:1; 31:13;
Lev 11:45; Eph 1:4;
1Pe 1:16 *n* S Ex 6:2;
S 20:2
20:8 *o* S Ge 26:5
p S Ex 31:13;
Eze 20:12
20:9 *q* Ex 20:12;
Jer 35:16; Mal 1:6;
2:10 *r* S Ex 20:12;
Dt 27:16; Eze 22:7
s Ex 21:17; Dt 21:20-
21; Mt 15:4*;
Mk 7:10* *t* ver 11;
Dt 22:30; Jos 2:19;
2Sa 1:16; 3:29;
1Ki 2:37; Eze 18:13;
33:4,5
20:10 *u* Ex 20:14;
Dt 5:18; 22:22; Jn 8:5
v S Ge 38:24;
S Ex 21:12
20:11 *w* S Lev 18:7
x S ver 9; S Lev 18:8
20:12 *y* S Ge 11:31;
S 38:16
20:13 *z* Lev 18:22
20:14 *a* S Lev 18:17
b Lev 21:9; Nu 16:39;
Jdg 14:15; 15:6
c S Lev 18:8; Dt 27:23
20:15 *d* S Ex 22:19
e ver 10
20:17 *f* S Lev 18:9
g S Ge 17:14
h S Lev 5:1
20:18 *i* S Lev 15:24
j Eze 18:6
20:19 *k* S Lev 18:12
20:20 *l* S Lev 18:13
m ver 21; Ge 15:2
20:21 *n* S Lev 18:16;
Mt 14:4; Mk 6:18
o S ver 20
20:22 *p* S Ge 26:5
q S Lev 18:25-28
20:23 *r* S Lev 18:3
s S Lev 18:24
t S Lev 18:25
20:24 *u* S Ex 3:8;
Nu 14:8; 16:14
v S Ex 33:16
20:25 *w* Lev 10:10;
Dt 14:3-21; Ac 10:14
20:26 *x* Dt 14:2
y ver 8; Lev 19:2;
Jos 24:19; 2Ki 19:22;
Ps 99:3 *z* S Ex 33:16

my face against him and will cut him off from his people;*f* for by sacrificing his children to Molek, he has defiled*g* my sanctuary*h* and profaned my holy name.*i* 4If the members of the community close their eyes when that man sacrifices one of his children to Molek and if they fail to put him to death,*j* 5I myself will set my face against him and his family and will cut them off from their people together with all who follow him in prostituting themselves to Molek.

6" 'I will set my face against anyone who turns to mediums and spiritists to prostitute themselves by following them, and I will cut them off from their people.*k*

7" 'Consecrate yourselves*l* and be holy,*m* because I am the Lord your God.*n* 8Keep my decrees*o* and follow them. I am the Lord, who makes you holy.*p*

9" 'Anyone who curses their father*q* or mother*r* is to be put to death.*s* Because they have cursed their father or mother, their blood will be on their own head.*t*

10" 'If a man commits adultery with another man's wife*u*—with the wife of his neighbor—both the adulterer and the adulteress are to be put to death.*v*

11" 'If a man has sexual relations with his father's wife, he has dishonored his father.*w* Both the man and the woman are to be put to death; their blood will be on their own heads.*x*

12" 'If a man has sexual relations with his daughter-in-law,*y* both of them are to be put to death. What they have done is a perversion; their blood will be on their own heads.

13" 'If a man has sexual relations with a man as one does with a woman, both of them have done what is detestable.*z* They are to be put to death; their blood will be on their own heads.

14" 'If a man marries both a woman and her mother,*a* it is wicked. Both he and they must be burned in the fire,*b* so that no wickedness will be among you.*c*

15" 'If a man has sexual relations with an animal,*d* he is to be put to death,*e* and you must kill the animal.

16" 'If a woman approaches an animal to have sexual relations with it, kill both the woman and the animal. They are to be put to death; their blood will be on their own heads.

17" 'If a man marries his sister,*f* the daughter of either his father or his mother, and they have sexual relations, it is a disgrace. They are to be publicly removed*g* from their people. He has dishonored his sister and will be held responsible.*h*

18" 'If a man has sexual relations with a woman during her monthly period,*i* he has exposed the source of her flow, and she has also uncovered it. Both of them are to be cut off from their people.*j*

19" 'Do not have sexual relations with the sister of either your mother or your father,*k* for that would dishonor a close relative; both of you would be held responsible.

20" 'If a man has sexual relations with his aunt,*l* he has dishonored his uncle. They will be held responsible; they will die childless.*m*

21" 'If a man marries his brother's wife,*n* it is an act of impurity; he has dishonored his brother. They will be childless.*o*

22" 'Keep all my decrees and laws*p* and follow them, so that the land*q* where I am bringing you to live may not vomit you out. 23You must not live according to the customs of the nations*r* I am going to drive out before you.*s* Because they did all these things, I abhorred them.*t* 24But I said to you, "You will possess their land; I will give it to you as an inheritance, a land flowing with milk and honey."*u* I am the Lord your God, who has set you apart from the nations.*v*

25" 'You must therefore make a distinction between clean and unclean animals and between unclean and clean birds.*w* Do not defile yourselves by any animal or bird or anything that moves along the ground—those which I have set apart as unclean for you. 26You are to be holy to me*x* because I, the Lord, am holy,*y* and I have set you apart from the nations*z* to be my own.

20:3 *cut him off from his people.* See note on 7:20.
20:5 *prostituting themselves.* See Ex 34:15 and note.

20:6 *mediums and spiritists.* Practitioners of the occult; consulting a medium was no less a sin than being one (v. 27). See Dt 18:10–11; Isa 3:2–3. Only God was to be consulted—through either the priest or a prophet (see Isa 8:19–20 and notes).
20:7 *be holy.* See note on 11:44.
20:8 *who makes ... holy.* This phrase and the expression "I am the Lord (your God)" are characteristic of chs. 18–26.
20:9 Cf. the penalty of a profligate son in Dt 21:20–21.
20:10 See 18:20.

20:12 See 18:15.
20:13 *detestable.* See note on 7:21.
20:15–16 See 18:23.
20:18 See 18:19.
20:20 See 18:14.
20:21 See 18:16 and note.
20:24 *flowing with milk and honey.* A common phrase in Exodus, Numbers and Deuteronomy (see notes on Ex 3:8; Dt 6:3; see also Jos 5:6; Jer 11:5; 32:22; Eze 20:6,15).
20:25 See ch. 11 and notes.
20:26 See 11:44 and note.

27" 'A man or woman who is a medium *a* or spiritist among you must be put to death. *b* You are to stone them; *c* their blood will be on their own heads.' "

RULES FOR PRIESTS

21 The LORD said to Moses, "Speak to the priests, the sons of Aaron, *d* and say to them: 'A priest must not make himself ceremonially unclean *e* for any of his people who die, *f* 2except for a close relative, such as his mother or father, *g* his son or daughter, his brother, 3or an unmarried sister who is dependent on him since she has no husband—for her he may make himself unclean. *h* 4He must not make himself unclean for people related to him by marriage, *a* and so defile himself.

5" 'Priests must not shave *i* their heads or shave off the edges of their beards *j* or cut their bodies. *k* 6They must be holy to their God *l* and must not profane the name of their God. *m* Because they present the food offerings to the LORD, *n* the food of their God, *o* they are to be holy. *p*

7" 'They must not marry women defiled by prostitution or divorced from their husbands, *q* because priests are holy to their God. *r* 8Regard them as holy, *s* because they offer up the food of your God. *t* Consider them holy, because I the LORD am holy—I who make you holy. *u*

9" 'If a priest's daughter defiles herself by becoming a prostitute, she disgraces her father; she must be burned in the fire. *v*

10" 'The high priest, the one among his brothers who has had the anointing oil poured on his head *w* and who has been ordained to wear the priestly garments, *x* must not let his hair become unkempt *b* or tear his clothes. *y* 11He must not enter a place where there is a dead body. *z* He must not make himself unclean, *a* even for his father or mother, *b* 12nor leave the sanctuary *c* of his God or desecrate it, because he has been dedicated by the anointing oil *d* of his God. I am the LORD.

13" 'The woman he marries must be a virgin. *e* 14He must not marry a widow, a divorced woman, or a woman defiled by prostitution, but only a virgin from his own people, 15so that he will not defile his offspring among his people. I am the LORD, who makes him holy.' "

16The LORD said to Moses, 17"Say to Aaron: 'For the generations to come none of your descendants who has a defect *f* may come near to offer the food of his God. *g* 18No man who has any defect *h* may come near: no man who is blind *i* or lame, *j* disfigured or deformed; 19no man with a crippled foot or hand, 20or who is a hunchback or a dwarf, or who has any eye defect, or who has festering or running sores or damaged testicles. *k* 21No descendant of Aaron the priest who has any defect *l* is to come near to present the food offerings to the LORD. *m* He has a defect; he must not come near to offer the food of his God. *n* 22He may eat the most holy food of his God, *o* as well as the holy food; 23yet because of his defect, *p* he must not go near the curtain or approach the altar, and so desecrate my sanctuary. *q* I am the LORD, who makes them holy.' "

24So Moses told this to Aaron and his sons and to all the Israelites.

22 The LORD said to Moses, 2"Tell Aaron and his sons to treat with respect the sacred offerings *s* the Israelites consecrate to me, so they will not profane my holy name. *t* I am the LORD. *u*

3"Say to them: 'For the generations to come, if any of your descendants is ceremonially unclean and yet comes near the sacred offerings that the Israelites consecrate to the LORD, *v* that person must be cut off from my presence. *w* I am the LORD.

---

a 4 Or *unclean as a leader among his people*   *b* 10 Or *not uncover his head*

20:27 *a* S Ex 22:18
b S Lev 19:31
c S ver 2; S Lev 24:14
21:1 *d* S Ex 28:1;
S Lev 1:5 *e* S Lev 5:3;
S 13:3 *f* ver 11; Nu 5:2;
6:6; 19:11; 31:19
21:2 *g* ver 11
21:3 *h* Nu 6:6
21:5 *i* S Lev 13:40;
Jer 7:29; 16:6
j Eze 5:1; 44:20
k S Lev 19:28
l S Lev 19:28; Ezr 8:28
m Lev 18:21
n S Lev 3:11 *o* ver 17,
22; Lev 22:25
p S Ex 19:22;
S Lev 10:3
21:7 *q* ver 13,14
r Eze 44:22
21:8 *s* ver 6
t Lev 3:11 *u* S Ex 31:13
21:9 *v* S Ge 38:24;
S Lev 19:29
21:10 *w* S Ex 29:7
x S Lev 8:7-9,13;
S 16:4 *y* S Lev 10:6
21:11 *z* Nu 5:2; 6:6;
9:6; 19:11,13,14; 31:19
a Lev 19:28 *b* ver 2
21:12 *c* S Ex 25:8
d S Ex 28:41
21:13 *e* Eze 44:22
21:17 *f* ver 18,21,23
g S ver 6
21:18 *h* Lev 22:19-
25 *i* S Lev 19:14
j 2Sa 4:4; 9:3; 19:26
21:20 *k* Lev 22:24;
Dt 23:1; Isa 56:3
21:21 *l* S ver 17
m S Lev 3:11
n Lev 22:19
21:22 *o* 1Co 9:13
21:23 *p* S ver 17
q S Ex 25:8 *r* Lev 20:8
22:2 *s* S Lev 19:8
t S Ex 20:7; S Mt 5:33
u Eze 44:8
22:3 *v* Ezr 8:28
w Nu 7:20,21;
Nu 19:13

20:27 See note on v. 6.

21:1—22:33 Directions for the priests' conduct, especially about separation from ceremonial uncleanness.

21:1 *for any ... who die.* Touching a corpse (Nu 19:11) or entering the home of a person who had died (Nu 19:14) made one unclean. A priest was to contract such uncleanness only at the death of a close relative (vv. 2–3), and the regulations for the high priest denied him such relief (vv. 11–12).

21:5 *cut their bodies.* See 19:27–28. Such lacerations and disfigurement were common among pagans as signs of mourning and to secure the attention of their deity (see 1Ki 18:28). Israelite faith had a much less grotesque view of death (see, e.g., vv. 1–4; Ge 5:24; 2Sa 12:23; Heb 11:19).

21:6 *They must be holy to their God.* As those especially set

apart for service at God's sanctuary and who represent him in a special way, the priests must be especially careful to retain ceremonial and moral purity (see 11:44; Ex 3:5 and notes). *food of their God.* See note on 3:11,16.

21:8 *I ... am holy.* See note on 11:44.

21:9 See Ge 38:24 and note.

21:11–12 See note on v. 1.

21:17 *defect.* Like the sacrifices that had to be without defect, the priests were to typify Christ's perfection (Heb 9:13–14).

21:23 *curtain.* Between the Holy Place and the Most Holy Place (see Ex 26:33).

22:3 *cut off from my presence.* Excluded from the worshiping community.

22:4 ˣLev 15:2-15
ʸLev 11:24-28,39
22:5 ᶻLev 11:24-28, 43 ᵃS Lev 15:7
22:6 ᵇHag 2:13
ᶜS Lev 11:24
ᵈS Lev 14:8
22:7 ᵉS Lev 11:39
22:8 ᶠS Lev 11:39
ᵍS Ex 22:31
ʰS Lev 11:40
ⁱLev 11:44
22:9 ʲS Lev 8:35
ᵏS Ex 28:38 ˡver 16;
S Ex 28:43 ᵐLev 20:8
22:10 ⁿver 13;
Ex 12:45; 29:33
22:11 ᵒGe 17:13;
Ex 12:44
22:14 ᵖS Lev 4:2
�q Lev 5:15
22:15 ʳS Lev 19:8
ˢNu 18:32
22:16 ᵗNu 18:11
ᵘS Ex 28:38 ᵛS ver 9
ʷLev 20:8
22:18 ˣNu 15:16;
19:10; Jos 8:33
ʸS Lev 1:2 ᶻver 21;
S Ge 28:20; Nu 15:8;
Ps 22:25; 76:11; 116:18
ᵃS Lev 7:16
22:19 ᵇS Lev 1:3;
21:18-21; Nu 28:11;
Dt 15:21 ᶜS Lev 1:2
22:20 ᵈS Lev 1:3;
Dt 15:21; 17:1;
Eze 43:23; 45:18;
46:6; Mal 1:8;
Heb 9:14; 1Pe 1:19
ᵉS Ex 28:38
22:21 ᶠS Lev 1:2
ᵍS Ex 32:6; S Lev 3:6
ʰS Lev 7:16
ⁱS Ex 12:5; Mal 1:14
ʲAm 4:5
22:24 ᵏS Lev 21:20
22:25 ˡS Lev 21:6
ᵐS Lev 1:3; S 3:1;
Nu 19:2
22:27 ⁿS Lev 1:3
ᵒS Ex 22:30
ᵖS Ex 22:30
�q S Ex 28:38
22:28 ʳDt 22:6,7
22:29 ˢS Lev 7:12
22:30 ᵗLev 7:15
ᵘLev 11:44

4" 'If a descendant of Aaron has a defiling skin disease ᵃ or a bodily discharge, ˣ he may not eat the sacred offerings until he is cleansed. He will also be unclean if he touches something defiled by a corpse ʸ or by anyone who has an emission of semen, ⁵or if he touches any crawling thing ᶻ that makes him unclean, or any person ᵃ who makes him unclean, whatever the uncleanness may be. ⁶The one who touches any such thing will be unclean ᵇ till evening. ᶜ He must not eat any of the sacred offerings unless he has bathed himself with water. ᵈ ⁷When the sun goes down, he will be clean, and after that he may eat the sacred offerings, for they are his food. ᵉ ⁸He must not eat anything found dead ᶠ or torn by wild animals, ᵍ and so become unclean ʰ through it. I am the LORD. ⁱ

9" 'The priests are to perform my service ʲ in such a way that they do not become guilty ᵏ and die ˡ for treating it with contempt. I am the LORD, who makes them holy. ᵐ

10" 'No one outside a priest's family may eat the sacred offering, nor may the guest of a priest or his hired worker eat it. ⁿ ¹¹But if a priest buys a slave with money, or if slaves are born in his household, they may eat his food. ᵒ ¹²If a priest's daughter marries anyone other than a priest, she may not eat any of the sacred contributions. ¹³But if a priest's daughter becomes a widow or is divorced, yet has no children, and she returns to live in her father's household as in her youth, she may eat of her father's food. No unauthorized person, however, may eat any of it.

14" 'Anyone who eats a sacred offering by mistake ᵖ must make restitution to the priest for the offering and add a fifth of the value q to it. ¹⁵The priests must not desecrate the sacred offerings ʳ the Israelites present to the LORD ˢ ¹⁶by allowing them to eat ᵗ the sacred offerings and so bring upon them guilt ᵘ requiring payment. ᵛ I am the LORD, who makes them holy. ʷ ' "

UNACCEPTABLE SACRIFICES

¹⁷The LORD said to Moses, ¹⁸"Speak to Aaron and his sons and to all the Israelites and say to them: 'If any of you—whether an Israelite or a foreigner residing in Israel ˣ—presents a gift ʸ for a burnt offering to the LORD, either to fulfill a vow ᶻ or as a freewill offering, ᵃ ¹⁹you must present a male without defect ᵇ from the cattle, sheep or goats in order that it may be accepted on your behalf. ᶜ ²⁰Do not bring anything with a defect, ᵈ because it will not be accepted on your behalf. ᵉ ²¹When anyone brings from the herd or flock ᶠ a fellowship offering ᵍ to the LORD to fulfill a special vow or as a freewill offering, ʰ it must be without defect or blemish ⁱ to be acceptable. ʲ ²²Do not offer to the LORD the blind, the injured or the maimed, or anything with warts or festering or running sores. Do not place any of these on the altar as a food offering presented to the LORD. ²³You may, however, present as a freewill offering an ox ᵇ or a sheep that is deformed or stunted, but it will not be accepted in fulfillment of a vow. ²⁴You must not offer to the LORD an animal whose testicles are bruised, crushed, torn or cut. ᵏ You must not do this in your own land, ²⁵and you must not accept such animals from the hand of a foreigner and offer them as the food of your God. ˡ They will not be accepted on your behalf, because they are deformed and have defects. ᵐ ' "

²⁶The LORD said to Moses, ²⁷"When a calf, a lamb or a goat ⁿ is born, it is to remain with its mother for seven days. ᵒ From the eighth day ᵖ on, it will be acceptable q as a food offering presented to the LORD. ²⁸Do not slaughter a cow or a sheep and its young on the same day. ʳ

²⁹"When you sacrifice a thank offering ˢ to the LORD, sacrifice it in such a way that it will be accepted on your behalf. ³⁰It must be eaten that same day; leave none of it till morning. ᵗ I am the LORD. ᵘ

ᵃ 4 The Hebrew word for *defiling skin disease*, traditionally translated "leprosy," was used for various diseases affecting the skin.　ᵇ 23 The Hebrew word can refer to either male or female.

22:4 See 13:1–46 and note on 13:45–46; 15:1–18 and notes; 21:11.
22:5 See 11:29–31.
22:8 See 17:15 and note.
A 22:9 *die for treating it with contempt.* The laws of cleanness were the same for priests and people, but the penalties were far more severe for the priests, who had greater responsibility. Cf. Nadab and Abihu (10:1–3) and the faithless priests of Malachi's day (Mal 1:6—2:9). *holy.* See note on 11:44.
22:14 *make restitution…add a fifth.* Cf. 5:16 and note on 5:15.
22:16 *holy.* See note on 11:44.
22:18 *burnt offering.* See note on 1:3.

22:20–22 See Mal 1:8.
22:21 *fellowship offering.* See note on 3:1.
22:24 *bruised, crushed, torn or cut.* Castrated animals were not acceptable offerings.
22:28 Perhaps the prohibition was humanitarian (see v. 27), or possibly it was practical: The mother was to be saved to build up the flock (see Dt 22:6–7). Or it may have been a law to avoid an otherwise unknown pagan custom (see note on Ex 23:19).
22:30 *that same day.* The rule applied also to the Passover (Ex 34:25); however, the fellowship offering could be saved and eaten on the following day (7:16).

³¹"Keep ᵛ my commands and follow them. ʷ I am the Lᴏʀᴅ. ³²Do not profane my holy name, ˣ for I must be acknowledged as holy by the Israelites. ʸ I am the Lᴏʀᴅ, who made you holy ᶻ ³³and who brought you out of Egypt ᵃ to be your God. ᵇ I am the Lᴏʀᴅ."

23

The Lᴏʀᴅ said to Moses, ²"Speak to the Israelites and say to them: 'These are my appointed festivals, ᶜ the appointed festivals of the Lᴏʀᴅ, which you are to proclaim as sacred assemblies. ᵈ

THE SABBATH

³" 'There are six days when you may work, ᵉ but the seventh day is a day of sabbath rest, ᶠ a day of sacred assembly. You are not to do any work; ᵍ wherever you live, it is a sabbath to the Lᴏʀᴅ.

THE PASSOVER AND THE FESTIVAL OF UNLEAVENED BREAD

23:4–8pp — Ex 12:14–20; Nu 28:16–25; Dt 16:1–8

⁴" 'These are the Lᴏʀᴅ's appointed festivals, the sacred assemblies you are to proclaim at their appointed times: ʰ ⁵The Lᴏʀᴅ's Passover ⁱ begins at twilight on the fourteenth day of the first month. ʲ ⁶On the fifteenth day of that month the Lᴏʀᴅ's Festival of Unleavened Bread ᵏ begins; for seven days ˡ you must eat bread made without yeast. ⁷On the first day hold a sacred assembly ᵐ and do no regular work. ⁸For seven days present a food offering to the Lᴏʀᴅ. ⁿ And on the seventh day hold a sacred assembly and do no regular work.' "

OFFERING THE FIRSTFRUITS

⁹The Lᴏʀᴅ said to Moses, ¹⁰"Speak to the Israelites and say to them: 'When you enter the land I am going to give you ᵒ and you reap its harvest, ᵖ bring to the priest a sheaf ᑫ of the first grain you harvest. ʳ ¹¹He is to wave the sheaf before the Lᴏʀᴅ ˢ so it will be accepted ᵗ on your behalf; the priest is to wave it on the day after the Sabbath. ¹²On the day you wave the sheaf, you must sacrifice as a burnt offering to the Lᴏʀᴅ a lamb a year old ᵘ without defect, ᵛ ¹³together with its grain offering ʷ of two-tenths of an ephah ᵃ ˣ of the finest flour mixed with olive oil—a food offering presented to the Lᴏʀᴅ, a pleasing aroma—and its drink offering ʸ of a quarter of a hin ᵇ of wine. ᶻ ¹⁴You must not eat any bread, or roasted or new grain, ᵃ until the very day you bring this offering to your God. ᵇ This is to be a lasting ordinance for the generations to come, ᶜ wherever you live. ᵈ

THE FESTIVAL OF WEEKS

23:15–22pp — Nu 28:26–31; Dt 16:9–12

¹⁵" 'From the day after the Sabbath, the day you brought the sheaf of the wave offering, count off seven full weeks. ¹⁶Count off fifty days up to the day after the seventh Sabbath, ᵉ and then present an offering of new grain to the Lᴏʀᴅ. ¹⁷From wherever you live, bring two loaves made of two-tenths of an ephah ᶠ of the finest flour, baked with yeast, as a wave offering of firstfruits ᵍ to the Lᴏʀᴅ. ¹⁸Present with this bread seven male lambs, each a year old and without defect, one young bull and two rams. They will be a burnt offering to the Lᴏʀᴅ, together with their grain offerings and drink offerings ʰ—a food offering, an aroma pleasing to the Lᴏʀᴅ. ¹⁹Then sacrifice one male goat for a sin offering ᶜ and two lambs, each a year old, for a fellowship offering. ²⁰The priest is to wave the two lambs before the Lᴏʀᴅ as a wave offering, ⁱ together with the bread of the firstfruits. They are a sacred offering to the Lᴏʀᴅ for the priest. ²¹On that same day you are to proclaim a sacred

---

ᵃ *13* That is, probably about 7 pounds or about 3.2 kilograms; also in verse 17   ᵇ *13* That is, about 1 quart or about 0.9 liter   ᶜ *19* Or *purification offering*

22:31 ᵛ Dt 4:2,40;
Ps 105:45
ʷ S Ex 22:31
22:32 ˣ Lev 18:21
ʸ S Lev 10:3
ᶻ Lev 20:8
22:33 ᵃ S Ex 6:6
ᵇ S Ge 17:7
23:2 ᶜ ver 4,37,44;
Nu 29:39; Eze 44:24;
Col 2:16 ᵈ ver 21,27
23:3 ᵉ Ex 20:9
ᶠ S Ex 20:10; Heb 4:9,
10 ᵍ ver 7,21,35;
Nu 28:26
23:4 ʰ Na 1:15
23:5 ⁱ S Ex 12:11
ʲ S Ex 12:6
23:6 ᵏ Ex 12:17
ˡ S Ex 12:19
23:7 ᵐ ver 3,8
23:8 ⁿ S Lev 1:9
23:10 ᵒ Nu 15:2,18
ᵖ S Lev 19:9
ᑫ S Lev 19:9
ʳ S Ex 22:29; S 34:22;
Ro 11:16
23:11 ˢ S Ex 29:24
ᵗ S Ex 28:38
23:12 ᵘ S Lev 12:6
ᵛ S Ex 12:5
23:13 ʷ Lev 2:14-
16; S 6:20 ˣ ver 17;
Lev 24:5; Nu 15:6;
28:9 ʸ S Ge 35:14
ᶻ S Lev 10:9
23:14 ᵃ Jos 5:11;
Ru 2:14; 1Sa 17:17;
25:18; 2Sa 17:28
ᵇ Ex 34:26 ᶜ Lev 3:17;
Nu 10:8; 15:21
ᵈ Jer 2:3
23:16 ᵉ Ac 2:1; 20:16
23:17 ᶠ S ver 13
ᵍ S Ex 34:22
23:18 ʰ ver 13;
Ex 29:41; 30:9; 37:16;
Jer 19:13; 44:18
23:20 ⁱ S Ex 29:24

22:32 *holy…holy…holy.* See 11:44; 18:21 and notes.

23:2 *appointed festivals.* See Ex 23:14–17 and notes; 34:18–25; Nu 28–29; Dt 16:1–17. The parallel in Numbers (the fullest and closest to Leviticus) specifies in great detail the offerings to be made at each festival. See chart, pp. 180–181.

23:3 *sabbath.* See notes on Ex 16:23; 20:9–10. The Sabbath is associated with the annual festivals (vv. 4–17 and notes). Two additional lambs were to be sacrificed as a burnt offering every weekly Sabbath (Nu 28:9–10).

23:5 *Passover.* See notes on Ex 12:11,14,21. *first month.* See note on Ex 12:2. The Israelites had three systems of referring to months. In one, the months were simply numbered (as here and in v. 24). In another, the Canaanite names were used (Aviv, Bul,

etc.), of which only four are known. In the third system, the Babylonian names (Nisan, Adar, Tishri, Kislev, etc.) were used—in the exilic and postexilic books only—and are still used today. See chart, p. 105.

23:6 *Festival of Unleavened Bread.* See note on Ex 23:15. During the Festival the first sheaf of the barley harvest was brought (see vv. 10–11).

23:9–14 Festival of Firstfruits (see notes on Ex 23:19; Nu 15:20; Ne 10:35).

23:15 *seven full weeks.* See note on Ex 23:16.

23:16 *fifty days.* The NT name for the Festival of Weeks was Pentecost (see Ac 2:1 and note; 20:16; 1Co 16:8), meaning "fifty."

23:21 *j* S ver 2;
Ex 32:5 *k* S ver 3
23:22 *l* S Lev 19:9
m S Lev 19:10;
Dt 24:19-21; Ru 2:15
n Ru 2:2
23:24 *o* ver 27,36;
Ezr 3:1 *p* Lev 25:9;
Nu 10:9,10; 29:1;
31:6; 2Ki 11:14;
2Ch 13:12; Ps 98:6
23:25 *q* ver 21
r S Lev 1:9
23:27 *s* S Lev 16:29

assembly *j* and do no regular work. *k* This is to be a lasting ordinance for the generations to come, wherever you live.

²² " 'When you reap the harvest *l* of your land, do not reap to the very edges of your field or gather the gleanings of your harvest. *m* Leave them for the poor and for the foreigner residing among you. *n* I am the LORD your God.' "

THE FESTIVAL OF TRUMPETS
23:23–25pp — Nu 29:1–6

²³ The LORD said to Moses, ²⁴ "Say to the Israelites: 'On the first day of the seventh month you are to have a day of sabbath rest, a sacred assembly *o* commemorated with trumpet blasts. *p* ²⁵ Do no regular work, *q* but present a food offering to the LORD.' *r* ' "

THE DAY OF ATONEMENT
23:26–32pp — Lev 16:2–34; Nu 29:7–11

²⁶ The LORD said to Moses, ²⁷ "The tenth day of this seventh month *s* is the Day of Atone-

---

23:22 See note on 19:9–10.
23:24 *first day of the seventh month.* Today known as the Jewish New Year (*Rosh Hashanah,* "the beginning of the year"), but not so called in the Bible (the Hebrew expression is used only in Eze 40:1 in a date formula; see note there). *trumpet blasts.* Trumpets were blown on the first of every month (see Ps 81:3 and note). With no calendars available, the trumpets sounding

across the land were an important signal of the beginning of the new season, the end of the agricultural year. See note on 16:29; see also chart, p. 105.

A **23:27** *Day of Atonement.* For details see notes on 16:1–34. Aaron was to enter the Most Holy Place only once a year (16:29–34) on this day. Modern Jews call it *Yom Kippur.* The day was typological, foreshadowing the atoning work

---

OLD TESTAMENT FESTIVALS AND OTHER SACRED DAYS

NAME	OLD TESTAMENT REFERENCES	OT TIME	MODERN EQUIVALENT
Sabbath	Ex 20:8–11; 31:12–17; Lev 23:3; Dt 5:12–15	7th day	Same
Sabbath Year	Ex 23:10–11; Lev 25:1–7	7th year	Same
Year of Jubilee	Lev 25:8–55; 27:17–24; Nu 36:4	50th year	Same
Passover	Ex 12:1–14; Lev 23:5; Nu 9:1–14; 28:16; Dt 16:1–3a,4b–7	1st month (Aviv) 14	Mar.–Apr.
Unleavened Bread	Ex 12:15–20; 13:3–10; 23:15; 34:18; Lev 23:6–8; Nu 28:17–25; Dt 16:3b,4a,8	1st month (Aviv) 15–21	Mar.–Apr.
Firstfruits	Lev 23:9–14	1st month (Aviv) 16	Mar.–Apr.
Weeks (Pentecost) (Harvest)	Ex 23:16a; 34:22a; Lev 23:15–21; Nu 28:26–31; Dt 16:9–12	3rd month (Sivan) 6	May–June
Trumpets (Later: Rosh Hashanah–New Year's Day)	Lev 23:23–25; Nu 29:1–6	7th month (Tishri) 1	Sept.–Oct.
Day of Atonement (Yom Kippur)	Lev 16; 23:26–32; Nu 29:7–11	7th month (Tishri) 10	Sept.–Oct.
Tabernacles (Booths) (Ingathering)	Ex 23:16b; 34:22b; Lev 23:33–36a,39–43; Nu 29:12–34; Dt 16:13–15; Zec 14:16–19	7th month (Tishri) 15–21	Sept.–Oct.
Sacred Assembly	Lev 23:36b; Nu 29:35–38	7th month (Tishri) 22	Sept.–Oct.
Purim	Est 9:18–32	12th month (Adar) 14,15	Feb.–Mar.

On Kislev 25 (mid-December) Hanukkah, the feast of dedication or festival of lights, commemorated the purification of the temple and altar in the Maccabean period (165/4 B.C.). This festival is mentioned in Jn 10:22 (see note there).

ment.ᵗ Hold a sacred assemblyᵘ and deny yourselves,ᵃ and present a food offering to the Lᴏʀᴅ. ²⁸Do not do any workᵛ on that day, because it is the Day of Atonement, when atonement is made for you before the Lᴏʀᴅ your God. ²⁹Those who do not deny themselves on that day must be cut off from their people. ʷ ³⁰I will destroy from among their peopleˣ anyone who does any work on that day. ³¹You shall do no work at all. This is to be a lasting ordinanceʸ for the generations to come, wherever you live. ³²It is a day of sabbath restᶻ for you, and you must deny yourselves. From the evening of the ninth day of the month until the following evening you are to observe your sabbath." ᵃ

THE FESTIVAL OF TABERNACLES

23:33–43pp — Nu 29:12–39; Dt 16:13–17

³³The Lᴏʀᴅ said to Moses, ³⁴"Say to the Israelites: 'On the fifteenth day of the seventh ᵇ month the Lᴏʀᴅ's Festival of Tabernaclesᶜ begins, and it lasts for seven days. ³⁵The first day is a sacred assembly; ᵈ do no regular work. ᵉ ³⁶For seven days present food offerings to the Lᴏʀᴅ, and on the eighth day hold a sacred assembly ᶠ and present a food offering to the Lᴏʀᴅ. ᵍ It is the closing special assembly; do no regular work.

³⁷(" 'These are the Lᴏʀᴅ's appointed festivals, which you are to proclaim as sacred assemblies for bringing food offerings to the Lᴏʀᴅ—the burnt offerings and grain offerings, sacrifices and drink offerings ʰ required for each day. ³⁸These offerings ⁱ are in addition to

---

ᵃ 27 Or *and fast*; also in verses 29 and 32

---

of Christ, our high priest (see Heb 9:7; 13:11–12 and notes). *deny yourselves.* See note on 16:29,31.
23:29 *cut off from their people.* See note on 7:20.

23:34 *Festival of Tabernacles.* See notes on Ex 23:16; Zec 14:16; Jn 7:37–39. Tabernacles was the last of the three annual pilgrimage festivals (see Ex 23:14–17; Dt 16:16 and notes).

23:27 ᵗ S Ex 30:10
ᵘ S ver 2, S 24
23:28 ᵛ ver 31
23:29 ʷ Ge 17:14;
Lev 7:20; Nu 5:2
23:30 ˣ S Lev 20:3
23:31 ʸ Lev 3:17
23:32 ᶻ S Lev 16:31
ᵃ Ne 13:19
23:34 ᵇ 1Ki 8:2;
Hag 2:1 ᶜ S Ex 23:16;
Jn 7:2
23:35 ᵈ ver 2 ᵉ ver 3
23:36 ᶠ S ver 24;
1Ki 8:2; 2Ch 7:9;
Ne 8:18; Jn 7:37
ᵍ S Lev 1:9
23:37 ʰ ver 13
23:38 ⁱ S Lev 1:2

DESCRIPTION	PURPOSE	NEW TESTAMENT REFERENCES
Day of rest; no work	Rest for people and animals	Mt 12:1–14; 28:1; Lk 4:16; Jn 5:9–10; Ac 13:42; Col 2:16; Heb 4:1–11
Year of rest; fallow fields	Rest for land	
Canceled debts; liberation of slaves and indentured servants; land returned to original family owners	Help for poor; stabilize society	
Slaying and eating a lamb, together with bitter herbs and bread made without yeast, in every household	Remember Israel's deliverance from Egypt	Mt 26:17; Mk 14:12–26; Jn 2:13; 11:55; 1Co 5:7; Heb 11:28
Eating bread made without yeast; holding several assemblies; making designated offerings	Remember how the Lord brought the Israelites out of Egypt in haste	Mk 14:1; Ac 12:3; 1Co 5:6–8
Presenting a sheaf of the first of the barley harvest as a wave offering; making a burnt offering and a grain offering	Recognize the Lord's bounty in the land	Ro 8:23; 1Co 15:20–23
A festival of joy; mandatory and voluntary offerings, including the firstfruits of the wheat harvest	Show joy and thankfulness for the Lord's blessing of harvest	Ac 2:1–4; 20:16; 1Co 16:8
An assembly on a day of rest commemorated with trumpet blasts and sacrifices	Present Israel before the Lord for his favor	
A day of rest, fasting and sacrifices of atonement for priests and people and atonement for the tabernacle and altar	Atone for the sins of priests and people and purify the Holy Place	Ro 3:24–26; Heb 9:7; 10:3,19–22
A week of celebration for the harvest; living in booths (temporary shelters) and offering sacrifices	Memorialize the journey from Egypt to Canaan; give thanks for the productivity of Canaan	Jn 7:2,37
A day of convocation, rest and offering sacrifices	Commemorate the closing of the cycle of festivals	
A day of joy and feasting and giving presents	Remind the Israelites of their national deliverance in the time of Esther	

In addition, new moons were often special feast days (Nu 10:10; 1Ch 23:31; Ezr 3:5; Ne 10:33; Ps 81:3; Isa 1:13–14; 66:23; Hos 5:7; Am 8:5; Col 2:16).

23:38 *j* S Ex 20:10;
2Ch 2:4; Eze 45:17
k S Lev 7:16
23:39 *l* Isa 62:9
m S Ex 23:16
23:40 *n* Ps 118:27
o Ne 8:14-17;
Ps 137:2; Isa 44:4
p Dt 12:7; 14:26;
28:47; Ne 8:10;
Ps 9:2; 66:6; 105:43;
Joel 2:26
23:42 *q* S Ex 23:16
23:43 *r* Ps 78:5
24:3 *s* S Ex 12:14
24:4 *t* S Ex 25:31
24:5 *u* S Ex 25:30;
Heb 9:2 *v* S Lev 23:13
24:6 *w* Ex 25:23-30;
Nu 4:7
24:7 *x* S Lev 2:1
y S Lev 2:2
24:8 *z* Ex 25:30;
Nu 4:7; 1Ch 9:32;
2Ch 2:4 *a* Mt 12:5
24:9 *b* Mt 12:4;
Mk 2:26; Lk 6:4
c S Lev 6:16
d S Lev 6:17
24:11 *e* S Ex 3:15
f S Ex 20:7;
S 2Ki 6:33; S Job 1:11
g S Ex 18:22 *h* Ex 31:2;
Nu 1:4; 7:2; 10:15;
13:2; 17:2; Jos 7:18;
1Ki 7:14
24:12 *i* S Ex 18:16
24:14 *j* ver 23;
S Lev 20:2; Dt 13:9;
17:5,7; Ac 7:58
24:15 *k* S Ex 22:28
l S Lev 5:1
24:16 *m* S Ex 22:28
n S Ex 21:12;
1Ki 21:10,13;
Mt 26:66; Mk 14:64;
Jn 10:33; 19:7;
Ac 7:58
24:17 *o* ver 21;
Ge 9:6; S Ex 21:12;
Dt 27:24
24:18 *p* ver 21

those for the LORD's Sabbaths *j* and *a* in addition to your gifts and whatever you have vowed and all the freewill offerings *k* you give to the LORD.)

39 " 'So beginning with the fifteenth day of the seventh month, after you have gathered the crops of the land, celebrate the festival *l* to the LORD for seven days; *m* the first day is a day of sabbath rest, and the eighth day also is a day of sabbath rest. 40On the first day you are to take branches *n* from luxuriant trees—from palms, willows and other leafy trees *o*—and rejoice *p* before the LORD your God for seven days. 41Celebrate this as a festival to the LORD for seven days each year. This is to be a lasting ordinance for the generations to come; celebrate it in the seventh month. 42Live in temporary shelters *q* for seven days: All native-born Israelites are to live in such shelters 43so your descendants will know *r* that I had the Israelites live in temporary shelters when I brought them out of Egypt. I am the LORD your God.' "

44So Moses announced to the Israelites the appointed festivals of the LORD.

OIL AND BREAD SET BEFORE THE LORD
24:1–3pp — Ex 27:20–21

24 The LORD said to Moses, 2"Command the Israelites to bring you clear oil of pressed olives for the light so that the lamps may be kept burning continually. 3Outside the curtain that shields the ark of the covenant law in the tent of meeting, Aaron is to tend the lamps before the LORD from evening till morning, continually. This is to be a lasting ordinance *s* for the generations to come. 4The lamps on the pure gold lampstand *t* before the LORD must be tended continually.

5"Take the finest flour and bake twelve loaves of bread, *u* using two-tenths of an ephah *b v* for each loaf. 6Arrange them in two stacks, six in each stack, on the table of pure gold *w* before the LORD. 7By each stack put some pure incense *x* as a memorial *c* portion *y* to represent the bread and to be a food offering presented to the LORD. 8This bread is to be set out before the LORD regularly, *z* Sabbath after Sabbath, *a* on behalf of the Israelites, as a lasting covenant. 9It belongs to Aaron and his sons, *b* who are to eat it in the sanctuary area, *c* because it is a most holy *d* part of their perpetual share of the food offerings presented to the LORD."

A BLASPHEMER STONED

10Now the son of an Israelite mother and an Egyptian father went out among the Israelites, and a fight broke out in the camp between him and an Israelite. 11The son of the Israelite woman blasphemed the Name *e* with a curse; *f* so they brought him to Moses. *g* (His mother's name was Shelomith, the daughter of Dibri the Danite.) *h* 12They put him in custody until the will of the LORD should be made clear to them. *i*

13Then the LORD said to Moses: 14"Take the blasphemer outside the camp. All those who heard him are to lay their hands on his head, and the entire assembly is to stone him. *j* 15Say to the Israelites: 'Anyone who curses their God *k* will be held responsible; *l* 16anyone who blasphemes *m* the name of the LORD is to be put to death. *n* The entire assembly must stone them. Whether foreigner or native-born, when they blaspheme the Name they are to be put to death.

17" 'Anyone who takes the life of a human being is to be put to death. *o* 18Anyone who takes the life of someone's animal must make restitution *p*—life for life. 19Anyone who injures a neighbor is to be injured in the same manner: 20fracture for fracture, eye for eye,

---

a 38 Or *These festivals are in addition to the LORD's Sabbaths, and these offerings are*   *b* 5 That is, probably about 7 pounds or about 3.2 kilograms   *c* 7 Or *representative*

23:42 *temporary shelters.* The Hebrew for this phrase is *Sukkot* and is also translated "Tabernacles" (as in v. 34), giving the festival its name. Even today, orthodox Jews construct small shelters (see Ne 8:13–17) to remind them of the shelters they lived in when God brought them out of Egypt at the time of the exodus (v. 43).
24:2–4 See Ex 27:20–21.
24:3 *the ark of the covenant law.* See note on Ex 25:22. *tend the lamps.* So that they would burn all night. *continually.* Every night without interruption, but not throughout the day. See 1Sa 3:3 and note.
24:5 *two-tenths of an ephah.* See TNIV text note. Either the loaves were quite large or a smaller unit of measurement is intended. The Hebrew word *ephah* is not expressed, but since the ephah was the standard measure of capacity (see table, p. 2151), it is the measure most likely implied here.

24:7 *pure incense.* Not used as a condiment for the bread but burned either in piles on the table or in small receptacles alongside the stacks of bread. *memorial portion.* See note on 2:2,9,16.
24:8 *This bread.* Often called the "bread of the Presence" (see Ex 25:30 and note). It represented a gift from the 12 tribes and signified the fact that God sustained his people. It was eaten by the priests (24:9).
24:9 See 1Sa 21:4–6.
24:10 *Egyptian father.* A foreigner. The laws, at least in the judicial sphere, applied equally to both the foreigner and the native-born Israelite (v. 22; see Ex 12:49).
24:11 *blasphemed.* See Ex 20:7 and note.
24:16 *the Name.* See note on Dt 12:5.
24:17,21 See Ge 9:6 and note.

tooth for tooth. *q* The one who has inflicted the injury must suffer the same injury. ²¹Whoever kills an animal must make restitution, *r* but whoever kills a human being is to be put to death. *s* ²²You are to have the same law for the foreigner *t* and the native-born. *u* I am the LORD your God.' "

²³Then Moses spoke to the Israelites, and they took the blasphemer outside the camp and stoned him. *v* The Israelites did as the LORD commanded Moses.

THE SABBATH YEAR

25 The LORD said to Moses on Mount Sinai, *w* ²"Speak to the Israelites and say to them: 'When you enter the land I am going to give you, the land itself must observe a sabbath to the LORD. ³For six years sow your fields, and for six years prune your vineyards and gather their crops. *x* ⁴But in the seventh year the land is to have a year of sabbath rest, *y* a sabbath to the LORD. Do not sow your fields or prune your vineyards. *z* ⁵Do not reap what grows of itself *a* or harvest the grapes *b* of your untended vines. *c* The land is to have a year of rest. ⁶Whatever the land yields during the sabbath year *d* will be food for you—for yourself, your male and female servants, and the hired worker and temporary resident who live among you, ⁷as well as for your livestock and the wild animals *e* in your land. Whatever the land produces may be eaten.

THE YEAR OF JUBILEE

25:8–38Ref — Dt 15:1–11
25:39–55Ref — Ex 21:2–11; Dt 15:12–18

⁸" 'Count off seven sabbath years—seven times seven years—so that the seven sabbath years amount to a period of forty-nine years. ⁹Then have the trumpet *f* sounded everywhere on the tenth day of the seventh month; *g* on the Day of Atonement *h* sound the trumpet throughout your land. ¹⁰Consecrate the fiftieth year and proclaim liberty *i* throughout the land to all its inhabitants. It shall be a jubilee *j* for you; each of you is to return to your family property *k* and to your own clan. ¹¹The fiftieth year shall be a jubilee *l* for you; do not sow and do not reap what grows of itself or harvest the untended vines. *m* ¹²For it is a jubilee and is to be holy for you; eat only what is taken directly from the fields.

¹³" 'In this Year of Jubilee *n* everyone is to return to their own property.

¹⁴" 'If you sell land to any of your own people or buy land from them, do not take advantage of each other. *o* ¹⁵You are to buy from your own people on the basis of the number of years *p* since the Jubilee. And they are to sell to you on the basis of the number of years left for harvesting crops. ¹⁶When the years are many, you are to increase the price, and when the years are few, you are to decrease the price, *q* because what is really being sold to you is the number of crops. ¹⁷Do not take advantage of each other, *r* but fear your God. *s* I am the LORD your God. *t*

¹⁸" 'Follow my decrees and be careful to obey my laws, *u* and you will live safely in the land. *v* ¹⁹Then the land will yield its fruit, *w* and you will eat your fill and live there in safety. *x* ²⁰You may ask, "What will we eat in the seventh year *y* if we do not plant or harvest our crops?" ²¹I will send you such a blessing *z* in the sixth year that the land will yield

---

24:20 *q* S Ex 21:24; Mt 5:38*
24:21 *r* S ver 18   *s* S ver 17
24:22 *t* S Ex 12:49; S 22:21; Eze 47:22   *u* Nu 9:14
24:23 *v* S ver 14
25:1 *w* Ex 19:11
25:3 *x* Ex 23:10
25:4 *y* ver 5,6,20; Lev 26:35; 2Ch 36:21   *z* Isa 36:16; 37:30
25:5 *a* 2Ki 19:29   *b* Ge 40:10; Nu 6:3; 13:20; Dt 23:24; Ne 13:15; Isa 5:2   *c* ver 4,11
25:6 *d* S ver 4
25:7 *e* Ex 23:11
25:9 *f* Lev 23:24; Nu 10:8; Jos 6:4; Jdg 3:27; 7:16; 1Sa 13:3; Isa 27:13; Zec 9:14   *g* S Lev 16:29   *h* S Ex 30:10
25:10 *i* Isa 61:1; S Lk 4:19   *j* ver 11,28, 50; Lev 27:17,21; Nu 36:4; Eze 46:17   *k* ver 27
25:11 *l* S ver 10   *m* S ver 5
25:13 *n* ver 10
25:14 *o* S Lev 19:13; 1Sa 12:3,4; 1Co 6:8
25:15 *p* ver 27; Lev 27:18,23
25:16 *q* ver 27,51,52
25:17 *r* S Lev 19:13; Job 31:16; Pr 22:22; Jer 7:5,6; 21:12; 22:3, 15; Zec 7:9-10; 1Th 4:6   *s* S Lev 19:14   *t* S Lev 19:32
25:18 *u* S Ge 26:5   *v* ver 19; Lev 26:4,5; Dt 12:10; 33:28; Job 5:22; Ps 4:8; Jer 23:6; 30:10; 32:37; 33:16; Eze 28:26; 34:25; 38:14
25:19 *w* Lev 26:4; Dt 11:14; 28:12; Isa 55:10   *x* S ver 18
25:20 *y* S ver 4
25:21 *z* Dt 28:8,12; Ps 133:3; 134:3; 147:13; Eze 44:30; Hag 2:19; Mal 3:10

B **A** **24:20** *eye for eye, tooth for tooth.* See note on Ex 21:23–25. This represents a statement of principle: The penalty is to fit the crime, not exceed it. An actual eye or tooth was not to be required, nor is there evidence that such a penalty was ever exacted. A similar law of "retaliation" is found in the Code of Hammurapi (see chart, p. xxiii), which also seems not to have been literally applied. Christ, like the middle-of-the-road Pharisees (school of Hillel), objected to an extremist use of this judicial principle to excuse private vengeance, such as by the strict Pharisees (school of Shammai); see Mt 5:38–42.
24:22 See note on v. 10.
25:4 *land is to have a...sabbath.* See Ex 23:10–11. The Israelites did not practice crop rotation, but the fallow year (when the crops were not planted) served somewhat the same purpose. And just as the land was to have a sabbath year, so the servitude of a Hebrew slave was limited to six years, apparently whether or not the year he was freed was a sabbath year (see Ex 21:2 and note). Dt 15:1–11 specifies that debts were also to be canceled in the sabbath year. The care for the poor in the laws of Israel (see Ex 23:11) is noteworthy. See 23:7,35; Dt 31:10; Ne 10:31.

25:9 *Day of Atonement.* See notes on 16:1–34; see also 23:27.
25:10 *fiftieth year.* Possibly a fallow year in addition to the seventh sabbath year, or perhaps the same as the 49th year (counting the first and last years). Jewish sources from the period between the Testaments favor the latter interpretation. *proclaim liberty...inhabitants.* See vv. 39–43,47–55. The Liberty Bell in Philadelphia is so named because this statement was written on it. Cf. Isa 61:1–2; Lk 4:16–21. *jubilee.* The Hebrew for this word is the same as, and may be related to, one of the Hebrew words for "[ram's] horn," "trumpet" (see, e.g., Ex 19:13), though in v. 9 a different Hebrew word for "trumpet" is used. Trumpets were blown at the close of the Day of Atonement to inaugurate the Year of Jubilee. Cf. 23:24.

A **25:13** *return to their own property.* See v. 10. The Lord prohibited the accumulation of property to the detriment of the poor. "The land is mine," said the Lord (v. 23). God's people are only tenants (see 1Ch 29:15; Heb 11:13).
25:15 *number of years left for harvesting.* In a way, the sale of land in Israel was a lease until the Year of Jubilee (see 27:18,23).

25:21 *a* S Ex 16:5
25:22 *b* Lev 26:10
25:23 *c* Nu 36:7;
1Ki 21:3; Eze 46:18
d Ex 19:5 *e* S Ge 23:4;
S Heb 11:13
25:24 *f* ver 29, 48;
Ru 4:7
25:25 *g* ver 48;
Ru 2:20; Jer 32:7
h Lev 27:13, 19, 31;
Ru 4:4
25:26 *i* ver 49
25:27 *j* S ver 15
k ver 10
25:28 *l* Lev 27:24
m S ver 10
25:32 *n* Nu 35:1-8;
Jos 21:2
25:34 *o* Nu 35:2-5;
Eze 48:14
25:35 *p* Dt 24:14, 15
q Dt 15:8; Ps 37:21,
26; Pr 21:26; Lk 6:35
25:36 *r* S Ex 22:25;
Jer 15:10 *s* S Lev 19:32
25:37 *t* S Lev 22:25
25:38 *u* S Ge 10:19
v S Ge 17:7
25:39 *w* 1Ki 5:13;
9:22; Jer 34:14
25:40 *x* ver 53
25:41 *y* ver 28
z Jer 34:8
25:42 *a* ver 38
25:43 *b* S Ex 1:13;
Eze 34:4; Col 4:1
c S Ge 42:18
25:47 *d* Ne 5:5;
Job 24:9
25:48 *e* S ver 24
f S ver 25
25:49 *g* ver 26
25:50 *h* S ver 10
i Job 7:1; 14:6;
Isa 16:14; 21:16
25:52 *j* S ver 16
25:53 *k* ver 43
25:55 *l* S Lev 11:45
m Lev 11:44

enough for three years. *a* 22While you plant during the eighth year, you will eat from the old crop and will continue to eat from it until the harvest of the ninth year comes in. *b*

23" 'The land *c* must not be sold permanently, because the land is mine *d* and you reside in my land as foreigners *e* and strangers. 24Throughout the land that you hold as a possession, you must provide for the redemption *f* of the land.

25" 'If anyone among you becomes poor and sells some of their property, their nearest relative *g* is to come and redeem *h* what they have sold. 26If, however, there is no one to redeem it for them but later on they prosper *i* and acquire sufficient means to redeem it themselves, 27they are to determine the value for the years *j* since they sold it and refund the balance to the one to whom they sold it; they can then go back to their own property. *k* 28But if they do not acquire the means to repay, what was sold will remain in the possession of the buyer until the Year of Jubilee. It will be returned *l* in the Jubilee, and they can then go back to their property. *m*

29" 'Anyone who sells a house in a walled city retains the right of redemption a full year after its sale. During that time the seller may redeem it. 30If it is not redeemed before a full year has passed, the house in the walled city shall belong permanently to the buyer and the buyer's descendants. It is not to be returned in the Jubilee. 31But houses in villages without walls around them are to be considered as belonging to the open country. They can be redeemed, and they are to be returned in the Jubilee.

32" 'The Levites always have the right to redeem their houses in the Levitical towns, *n* which they possess. 33So the property of the Levites is redeemable—that is, a house sold in any town they hold—and is to be returned in the Jubilee, because the houses in the towns of the Levites are their property among the Israelites. 34But the pastureland belonging to their towns must not be sold; it is their permanent possession. *o*

35" 'If any of your own people become poor *p* and are unable to support themselves among you, help them *q* as you would a foreigner and stranger, so they can continue to live among you. 36Do not take interest *r* or any profit from them, but fear your God, *s* so that your poor neighbors may continue to live among you. 37You must not lend them money at interest *t* or sell them food at a profit. 38I am the Lord your God, who brought you out of Egypt to give you the land of Canaan *u* and to be your God. *v*

39" 'If any of your own people become poor and sell themselves to you, do not make them work as slaves. *w* 40They are to be treated as hired workers *x* or temporary residents among you; they are to work for you until the Year of Jubilee. 41Then they and their children are to be released, and they will go back to their own clans and to the property *y* of their ancestors. *z* 42Because the Israelites are my servants, whom I brought out of Egypt, *a* they must not be sold as slaves. 43Do not rule over them ruthlessly, *b* but fear your God. *c*

44" 'Your male and female slaves are to come from the nations around you; from them you may buy slaves. 45You may also buy some of the temporary residents living among you and members of their clans born in your country, and they will become your property. 46You can bequeath them to your children as inherited property and can make them slaves for life, but you must not rule over your fellow Israelites ruthlessly.

47" 'If a foreigner residing among you becomes rich and any of your own people become poor and sell themselves *d* to the foreigner or to a member of the foreigner's clan, 48they retain the right of redemption *e* after they have sold themselves. One of their relatives *f* may redeem them: 49An uncle or a cousin or any blood relative in their clan may redeem them. Or if any of them prosper, *g* they may redeem themselves. 50They and their buyer are to count the time from the year they sold themselves up to the Year of Jubilee. *h* The price for their release is to be based on the rate paid to a hired worker *i* for that number of years. 51If many years remain, they must pay for their redemption a larger share of the price paid for them. 52If only a few years remain until the Year of Jubilee, they are to compute that and pay for their redemption accordingly. *j* 53They are to be treated as hired workers from year to year; you must see to it that those to whom they owe service do not rule over them ruthlessly. *k*

54" 'Even if they are not redeemed in any of these ways, they and their children are to be released in the Year of Jubilee, 55for the Israelites belong to me as servants. They are my servants, whom I brought out of Egypt. *l* I am the Lord your God. *m*

25:24 *redemption of the land.* That is, the right to repurchase the land by (or for) the original family.

25:25 *nearest relative is to come and redeem.* See Jer 32:6–15. This is apparently what the nearest relative was to do for Naomi and Ruth (Ru 4:1–4), but he was also obligated to marry the widow and support the family (see Dt 25:5–10). Only Boaz was

willing to do both (Ru 4:9–10). See note on Ru 2:20.
25:33 *towns of the Levites.* See Nu 35:1–8; Jos 21:1–42.
25:35–38 See notes on Ex 22:25–27; Ne 5:10; Pr 28:8.
25:43 *fear your God.* See note on Ge 20:11.
25:55 *servants.* Covenant terminology, similar to "vassals" (see chart, p. 20).

REWARD FOR OBEDIENCE

26 " 'Do not make idols ⁿ or set up an image ᵒ or a sacred stone ᵖ for yourselves, and do not place a carved stone �q in your land to bow down before it. I am the LORD your God.

²" 'Observe my Sabbaths ʳ and have reverence for my sanctuary. ˢ I am the LORD.

³" 'If you follow my decrees and are careful to obey ᵗ my commands, ⁴I will send you rain ᵘ in its season, ᵛ and the ground will yield its crops and the trees their fruit. ʷ ⁵Your threshing will continue until grape harvest and the grape harvest will continue until planting, and you will eat all the food you want ˣ and live in safety in your land. ʸ

⁶" 'I will grant peace in the land, ᶻ and you will lie down ᵃ and no one will make you afraid. ᵇ I will remove wild beasts ᶜ from the land, and the sword will not pass through your country. ⁷You will pursue your enemies, ᵈ and they will fall by the sword before you. ⁸Five ᵉ of you will chase a hundred, and a hundred of you will chase ten thousand, and your enemies will fall by the sword before you. ᶠ

⁹" 'I will look on you with favor and make you fruitful and increase your numbers, ᵍ and I will keep my covenant ʰ with you. ¹⁰You will still be eating last year's harvest when you will have to move it out to make room for the new. ⁱ ¹¹I will put my dwelling place ᵃʲ among you, and I will not abhor you. ᵏ ¹²I will walk ˡ among you and be your God, ᵐ and you will be my people. ⁿ ¹³I am the LORD your God, ᵒ who brought you out of Egypt ᵖ so that you would no longer be slaves to the Egyptians; I broke the bars of your yoke �q and enabled you to walk with heads held high.

PUNISHMENT FOR DISOBEDIENCE

¹⁴" 'But if you will not listen to me and carry out all these commands, ʳ ¹⁵and if you reject my decrees and abhor my laws ˢ and fail to carry out all my commands and so violate my covenant, ᵗ ¹⁶then I will do this to you: I will bring on you sudden terror, wasting diseases and fever ᵘ that will destroy your sight and sap your strength. ᵛ You will plant seed in vain, because your enemies will eat it. ʷ ¹⁷I will set my face ˣ against you so that you will be defeated ʸ by your enemies; ᶻ those who hate you will rule over you, ᵃ and you will flee even when no one is pursuing you. ᵇ

¹⁸" 'If after all this you will not listen to me, ᶜ I will punish ᵈ you for your sins seven times over. ᵉ ¹⁹I will break down your stubborn pride ᶠ and make the sky above you like iron and the ground beneath you like bronze. ᵍ ²⁰Your strength will be spent in vain, ʰ because your soil will not yield its crops, nor will the trees of your land yield their fruit. ⁱ

²¹" 'If you remain hostile ʲ toward me and refuse to listen to me, I will multiply your afflictions seven times over, ᵏ as your sins deserve. ²²I will send wild animals ˡ against you, and they will rob you of your children, destroy your cattle and make you so few ᵐ in number that your roads will be deserted. ⁿ

²³" 'If in spite of these things you do not accept my correction ᵒ but continue to be hostile toward me, ²⁴I myself will be hostile ᵖ toward you and will afflict you for your sins seven times over. ²⁵And I will bring the sword q on you to avenge ʳ the breaking of the covenant. When you withdraw into your cities, I will send a plague ˢ among you, and you will be given into enemy hands. ²⁶When I cut off your supply of bread, ᵗ ten women will be able to bake your bread in one oven, and they will dole out the bread by weight. You will eat, but you will not be satisfied.

ᵃ 11 Or *my tabernacle*

26:18 ᵈPs 99:8; Jer 21:14; Am 3:14 ᵉver 21   **26:19** ᶠPs 10:4; 73:6; Isa 16:6; 25:11; 28:1-3; Jer 13:9; 48:29; Eze 24:21; Am 6:8; Zep 3:11. ᵍDt 28:23; Job 38:38   **26:20** ʰDt 28:38; Ps 127:1; Isa 17:11; 49:4; Jer 12:13; Mic 6:15; Hag 1:6 ⁱDt 11:17; 28:24   **26:21** ʲver 41 ᵏver 18; S Ge 4:15   **26:22** ˡS Ge 37:20 ᵐDt 28:62; Jer 42:2 ⁿJer 5:6; 14:16; 15:3; 16:4; Eze 14:15   **26:23** ᵒJer 2:30; 5:3; 7:28; 17:23; 32:33; Zep 3:2   **26:24** ᵖ2Sa 22:27   **26:25** qJer 5:17; 15:3; 47:6; Eze 11:8; 14:17; 21:4; 33:2 ʳJer 50:28; 51:6,11 ˢEx 5:3; S 9:3; Nu 16:46; 1Ki 8:37; Hab 3:5   **26:26** ᵗ1Ki 8:37; 18:2; 2Ki 4:38; 6:25; 8:1; 25:3; Ps 105:16; Isa 3:1; 9:20; Jer 37:21; 52:6; Eze 4:16,17; 5:16; 14:13; Hos 4:10; Mic 6:14

26:1 ⁿS Ex 20:4
ᵒPs 97:7; Isa 48:5;
Jer 44:19; Hab 2:18
ᵖS Ex 23:24
qNu 33:52
26:2 ʳS Ex 20:8
ˢLev 19:30
26:3 ᵗS Ge 26:5;
S Lev 24:8; Dt 6:17;
7:12; 11:13,22; 28:1,9
26:4 ᵘDt 11:14;
28:12; Ps 68:9;
Jer 5:24; Hos 6:3;
Joel 2:23; Zec 10:1
ᵛJob 5:10; Ps 65:9;
104:13; 147:8; Jer 5:24
ʷS Ex 23:26;
S Lev 25:19;
S Job 14:9; Ps 67:6
26:5 ˣDt 6:11; 11:15;
Eze 36:29-30;
Joel 2:19,26
ʸS Lev 25:18
26:6 ᶻPs 29:11;
37:11; 85:8; 147:14;
Isa 26:3; 54:13; 60:18;
Hag 2:9 ᵃPs 3:5; 4:8;
Pr 3:24 ᵇJob 11:18,19;
Isa 17:2; Jer 30:10;
Mic 4:4; Zep 3:13
ᶜS ver 22; S Ge 37:20
26:7 ᵈPs 18:37; 44:5
26:8 ᵉIsa 30:17
26:9 ᶠDt 28:7; 32:30;
Jos 23:10; Jdg 15:15;
1Ch 12:14
26:9 ᵍS Ge 1:22;
S 17:6; Ne 9:23
ʰS Ge 17:7
26:10 ⁱLev 25:22
26:11 ʲEx 25:8;
Ps 74:7; 76:2;
Eze 37:27 ᵏver 15,43,
44; Dt 31:6; 1Sa 12:22;
1Ki 6:13; 2Ki 17:15
26:12 ˡS Ge 3:8
ᵐS Ge 17:7 ⁿEx 6:7;
Jer 7:23; 11:4; 24:7;
30:22; 31:1; Zec 13:9;
2Co 6:16*
26:13 ᵒLev 11:44
ᵖS Ex 6:6; S 13:3
qIsa 10:27; Jer 2:20;
27:2; 28:10; 30:8;
Eze 30:18; 34:27;
Hos 11:4
26:14 ʳDt 28:15-68;
Mal 2:2
26:15 ˢS ver 11
ᵗS Ge 17:7
26:16 ᵘDt 28:22,
35; Ps 78:33 ᵛver 39;
1Sa 2:33; Ps 107:17;
Eze 4:17; 24:23; 33:10
ʷJdg 6:3-6; Job 31:8
26:17 ˣLev 17:10;
Eze 15:7 ʸDt 28:48;
Jos 7:12; Jdg 2:15;
1Ki 8:33; 2Ch 6:24
ᶻJos 7:4; Jer 19:7;
21:7 ᵃPs 106:41
ᵇver 36,37; Dt 28:7,
25; Ps 53:5; Pr 28:1;
Isa 30:17
26:18 ᶜver 14

26:1 Forbids worshiping God in any material form (see Ex 20:4 and note)."God is spirit" (Jn 4:24; see Dt 4:15–19).

26:3 *obey my commands.* Obedience is the key to blessing (see Gal 6:7–10; Jas 1:22–25). Compare the blessings promised in vv. 3–13 with those in Dt 28:1–14.

26:4 *I will send you rain.* One of the blessings for faithful obedience to the Sinaitic covenant (see Dt 28:12; see also Dt 11:14; Isa 30:23; Jer 14:22; Zec 10:1 and notes). On the other hand, one of the curses for covenant disobedience was God's withholding of rain (v. 19; Dt 28:23–24; see also Dt 11:17; 1Ki 8:35; Isa 5:6; Jer 3:3; 14:4; Zec 14:17–18 and notes).

26:9 *fruitful and increase.* See note on Ge 1:22; contrast Lev 26:22.

26:12 *your God … my people.* Covenantal terms later made famous by Hosea (1:9–10; 2:23). See Jer 31:33; Zec 8:8 and note; Heb 8:10.

26:14 *if you will not listen.* The list of curses for covenant disobedience (see vv. 14–39) is usually much longer than that of blessings for obedience (as in vv. 3–13; see Dt 28:15—29:28; cf. Dt 28:1–14).

26:16 *You will plant seed … your enemies will eat it.* See note on Hag 1:6.

26:17 See v. 36 and the allusion to this statement in Pr 28:1.

26:18,21,24,28 *seven times over.* Thoroughly (cf. note on 4:6).

26:19 *sky … like iron … ground … like bronze.* See note on Dt 28:23.

26:27 *u* ver 14
26:28 *v* Dt 32:19;
Jdg 2:14; Ps 78:59;
106:40 *w* Dt 7:10;
Job 34:11; Isa 59:18;
65:6-7; 66:6;
Jer 17:10; 25:29;
Joel 3:4 *x* ver 18
26:29 *y* 2Ki 6:29;
Jer 19:9; La 4:10;
Eze 5:10 *z* Dt 28:53
26:30 *a* Dt 12:2;
1Sa 9:12; 10:5;
1Ki 3:2,4; 12:31; 13:2,
32; 2Ki 17:29; 23:20;
2Ch 34:3; Ps 78:58;
Eze 6:3; 16:16;
Am 7:9 *b* 2Ch 34:4;
Isa 17:8; 27:9; Eze 6:6
c Isa 21:9; Jer 50:2;
Eze 6:13 *d* Ps 106:40;
Am 6:8
26:31 *e* Ne 1:3;
Isa 1:7; 3:8,26; 6:11;
24:12; 61:4; Jer 4:7;
9:11; 25:11; 34:22;
44:2,6,22; Eze 36:33;
Mic 2:4; 3:12;
Zep 2:5; 3:6
f 2Ki 22:19 *g* Ps 74:3-
7; Isa 63:18; 64:11;
La 2:7; Eze 24:21;
Am 7:9 *h* Am 5:21,22;
8:10
26:32 *i* Isa 5:6;
Jer 9:11; 12:11; 25:11;
26:9; 33:10; 34:22;
44:22 *j* 1Ki 9:8;
2Ch 29:8; Isa 52:14;
Jer 18:16; 19:8; 48:39;
Eze 5:14; 26:16;
27:35; 28:19
26:33 *k* Jer 40:15;
50:17; Eze 34:6;
Joel 3:2 *l* Dt 4:27;
28:64; Ne 1:8;
Ps 44:11; 106:27;
Jer 4:11; 9:16; 13:24;
31:10; Eze 5:10; 12:15;
17:21; 20:23; 22:15;
Zec 7:14 *m* Jer 42:16;
Am 9:4 *n* Isa 49:19;
Jer 7:34 *o* ver 31;
1Sa 15:22; Job 36:11;
Jer 40:3
26:34 *p* Isa 1:7;
Jer 7:34; 25:11; 44:6;
Eze 33:29 *q* ver 43;
2Ch 36:21
26:35 *r* S Lev 25:4
26:36 *s* Job 13:25
t 2Ki 25:5; Ps 58:7;
La 1:3,6; 4:19;
Eze 21:7 *u* S ver 17
26:37 *v* Jer 6:21;
13:16; 46:16;
Eze 3:20; Na 3:3
w Jos 7:12
26:38 *x* Job 4:9;
36:12; Ps 1:6; Isa 1:28;
Jer 16:4; 44:27
y Dt 4:26
26:39 *z* Ex 20:5;
Isa 14:21 *a* S ver 16;
Isa 24:16
26:40 *b* S Lev 5:5
c Ps 32:5; 38:18
d Ne 9:2; Ps 106:6;

27 " 'If in spite of this you still do not listen to me *u* but continue to be hostile toward me, ²⁸then in my anger *v* I will be hostile *w* toward you, and I myself will punish you for your sins seven times over. *x* ²⁹You will eat *y* the flesh of your sons and the flesh of your daughters. *z* ³⁰I will destroy your high places, *a* cut down your incense altars *b* and pile your dead bodies *a* on the lifeless forms of your idols, *c* and I will abhor *d* you. ³¹I will turn your cities into ruins *e* and lay waste *f* your sanctuaries, *g* and I will take no delight in the pleasing aroma of your offerings. *h* ³²I myself will lay waste the land, *i* so that your enemies who live there will be appalled. *j* ³³I will scatter *k* you among the nations *l* and will draw out my sword *m* and pursue you. Your land will be laid waste, *n* and your cities will lie in ruins. *o* ³⁴Then the land will enjoy its sabbath years all the time that it lies desolate *p* and you are in the country of your enemies; *q* then the land will rest and enjoy its sabbaths. ³⁵All the time that it lies desolate, the land will have the rest *r* it did not have during the sabbaths you lived in it.

³⁶ 'As for those of you who are left, I will make their hearts so fearful in the lands of their enemies that the sound of a windblown leaf *s* will put them to flight. *t* They will run as though fleeing from the sword, and they will fall, even though no one is pursuing them. *u* ³⁷They will stumble over one another *v* as though fleeing from the sword, even though no one is pursuing you. So you will not be able to stand before your enemies. *w* ³⁸You will perish *x* among the nations; the land of your enemies will devour you. *y* ³⁹Those of you who are left will waste away in the lands of their enemies because of their sins; also because of their ancestors' *z* sins they will waste away. *a*

⁴⁰ " 'But if they will confess *b* their sins *c* and the sins of their ancestors *d*—their unfaithfulness and their hostility toward me, ⁴¹which made me hostile *e* toward them so that I sent them into the land of their enemies—then when their uncircumcised hearts *f* are humbled *g* and they pay *h* for their sin, ⁴²I will remember my covenant with Jacob *i* and my covenant with Isaac *j* and my covenant with Abraham, *k* and I will remember the land. ⁴³For the land will be deserted *l* by them and will enjoy its sabbaths while it lies desolate without them. They will pay for their sins because they rejected *m* my laws and abhorred my decrees. *n* ⁴⁴Yet in spite of this, when they are in the land of their enemies, *o* I will not reject them or abhor *p* them so as to destroy them completely, *q* breaking my covenant *r* with them. I am the Lᴏʀᴅ their God. ⁴⁵But for their sake I will remember *s* the covenant with their ancestors whom I brought out of Egypt *t* in the sight of the nations to be their God. I am the Lᴏʀᴅ.' "

⁴⁶These are the decrees, the laws and the regulations that the Lᴏʀᴅ established on Mount Sinai *u* between himself and the Israelites through Moses. *v*

REDEEMING WHAT IS THE LORD'S

27 The Lᴏʀᴅ said to Moses, ²"Speak to the Israelites and say to them: 'If anyone makes a special vow *w* to dedicate a person to the Lᴏʀᴅ by giving the equivalent value, ³set the value of a male between the ages of twenty and sixty at fifty shekels *b* of silver, according to the sanctuary shekel *c*; *x* ⁴for a female, set her value at thirty shekels *d*; ⁵for a person between the ages of five and twenty, set the value of a male at twenty shekels *e* *y* and of a female at ten shekels *f*; ⁶for a person between one month and five years, set the value of a male at five shekels *g* *z* of silver and that of a female at three

a 30 Or *your funeral offerings*   *b 3* That is, about 1 1/4 pounds or about 575 grams; also in verse 16
c 3 That is, about 2/5 ounce or about 11.5 grams; also in verse 25   *d 4* That is, about 12 ounces or about 345 grams   *e 5* That is, about 8 ounces or about 230 grams   *f 5* That is, about 4 ounces or about 115 grams; also in verse 7   *g 6* That is, about 2 ounces or about 55 grams

26:40 Jer 3:12-15; 14:20; Hos 5:15; Lk 15:18; 1Jn 1:9   **26:41** *e* S ver 21 *f* Dt 10:16; 30:6; Jer 4:4; 9:25,26; Eze 44:7,9; Ac 7:51 *g* 2Ch 7:14; 12:6; Eze 20:43 *h* Isa 6:7; 33:24; 40:2; 53:5,6,11   **26:42** *i* Ge 28:15; 35:11-12 *j* S Ge 26:5 *k* S Ex 2:24   **26:43** *l* Ps 69:25; Isa 6:11; 32:14; 62:4; Jer 2:15; 44:2; La 1:1; Eze 36:4 *m* Nu 11:20; 14:31; 1Sa 8:7; Ps 106:24 *n* S ver 11; Eze 20:13   **26:44** *o* S ver 33; 2Ki 17:20; 25:11; 2Ch 6:36; 36:20 *p* S ver 11; Ro 11:2 *q* Ex 4:31; Jer 4:27; 5:10; 30:11 *r* Jdg 2:1; Jer 31:37; 33:26; 51:5   **26:45** *s* Dt 4:31 *t* Ex 6:8; Lev 25:38   **26:46** *u* S Ex 19:11 *v* S Lev 7:38; 27:34   **27:2** *w* S Ge 28:20   **27:3** *x* S Ex 30:13   **27:5** *y* S Ge 37:28   **27:6** *z* Nu 3:47; 18:16

26:30 *high places.* See note on 1Sa 9:12. *idols.* The Hebrew term means something like "piles of dung."

26:34 Fulfilled during the Babylonian exile (see note on 2Ch 36:20–21).

26:40 *confess their sins.* See notes on Pr 28:13; 1Jn 1:9.

26:41 *uncircumcised hearts.* See note on Ge 17:10.

26:44 *not reject them.* See Jer 31:37; 33:25–26; Ro 11:1–29 and notes.

26:46 A summary statement concerning chs. 1–26.

27:1–34 This final chapter concerns things promised to the Lord in kind—servants, animals, houses or lands. But provisions

were made to give money instead of the item, in which case the adding of a fifth of its value was usually required. Such vows were expressions of special thanksgiving (cf. Hannah, 1Sa 1:28) and were given over and above the expected sacrifices.

27:2 *to dedicate a person.* Possibly to give a slave to the service of the temple, but more likely to offer oneself or a member of one's family. Since only Levites were acceptable for most work of this kind, other people gave the monetary equivalent—but see 1Sa 1:11 and note.

27:3,25 *according to the sanctuary shekel.* See note on Ex 30:13.

shekels^a of silver; ⁷for a person sixty years old or more, set the value of a male at fifteen shekels^b and of a female at ten shekels. ⁸If anyone making the vow is too poor to pay ^a the specified amount, the person being dedicated is to be presented to the priest, who will set the value ^b according to what the one making the vow can afford.

⁹"'If what anyone vowed is an animal that is acceptable as an offering to the LORD, ^c such an animal given to the LORD becomes holy. ^d ¹⁰They must not exchange it or substitute a good one for a bad one, or a bad one for a good one; ^e if they should substitute one animal for another, both it and the substitute become holy. ¹¹If what they vowed is a ceremonially unclean animal ^f—one that is not acceptable as an offering to the LORD—the animal must be presented to the priest, ¹²who will judge its quality as good or bad. Whatever value the priest then sets, that is what it will be. ¹³If the owner wishes to redeem ^g the animal, a fifth must be added to its value. ^h

¹⁴"'If anyone dedicates their house as something holy to the LORD, the priest will judge its quality as good or bad. Whatever value the priest then sets, so it will remain. ¹⁵If the one who dedicates their house wishes to redeem it, ⁱ they must add a fifth to its value, and the house will again become theirs.

¹⁶"'If anyone dedicates to the LORD part of their family land, its value is to be set according to the amount of seed required for it—fifty shekels of silver to a homer ^c of barley seed. ¹⁷If they dedicate a field during the Year of Jubilee, the value that has been set remains. ¹⁸But if they dedicate a field after the Jubilee, ^j the priest will determine the value according to the number of years that remain ^k until the next Year of Jubilee, and its set value will be reduced. ¹⁹If the one who dedicates the field wishes to redeem it, ^l they must add a fifth to its value, and the field will again become theirs. ²⁰If, however, they do not redeem the field, or if they have sold it to someone else, it can never be redeemed. ²¹When the field is released in the Jubilee, ^m it will become holy, ⁿ like a field devoted to the LORD; ^o it will become priestly property.

²²"'If anyone dedicates to the LORD a field they have bought, which is not part of their family land, ²³the priest will determine its value up to the Year of Jubilee, ^p and that person must pay its value on that day as something holy to the LORD. ²⁴In the Year of Jubilee the field will revert to the person from whom it was bought, ^q the one whose land it was. ²⁵Every value is to be set according to the sanctuary shekel, ^r twenty gerahs ^s to the shekel.

²⁶"'No one, however, may dedicate the firstborn of an animal, since the firstborn already belongs to the LORD; ^t whether an ox ^d or a sheep, it is the LORD's. ²⁷If it is one of the unclean animals, ^u it may be bought back at its set value, adding a fifth of the value to it. If it is not redeemed, it is to be sold at its set value.

²⁸"'But nothing that a person owns and devotes ^e ^v to the LORD—whether a human being or an animal or family land—may be sold or redeemed; everything so devoted is most holy ^w to the LORD.

²⁹"'No persons devoted to destruction ^f may be ransomed; they are to be put to death. ^x

³⁰"'A tithe ^y of everything from the land, whether grain from the soil or fruit from the trees, belongs to the LORD; it is holy ^z to the LORD. ³¹Whoever would redeem ^a any of their tithe must add a fifth of the value ^b to it. ³²Every tithe of the herd and flock—every tenth animal that passes under the shepherd's rod ^c—will be holy to the LORD. ³³No one may pick out the good from the bad or make any substitution. ^d If anyone does make a substitution, both the animal and its substitute become holy and cannot be redeemed. ^e '"

³⁴These are the commands the LORD gave Moses on Mount Sinai ^f for the Israelites. ^g

---

^a 6   That is, about 1 1/4 ounces or about 35 grams   ^b 7   That is, about 6 ounces or about 170 grams   ^c 16   That is, probably about 300 pounds or about 135 kilograms   ^d 26   The Hebrew word can refer to either male or female.   ^e 28   The Hebrew term refers to the irrevocable giving over of things or persons to the LORD.   ^f 29   The Hebrew term refers to the irrevocable giving over of things or persons to the LORD, often by totally destroying them.

27:8 ^a S Lev 5:11
^b ver 12,14
27:9 ^c S Ge 28:20;
S Lev 1:2 ^d ver 21,26,
28; Ex 40:9; Nu 6:20;
18:17; Dt 15:19
27:10 ^e ver 33
27:11 ^f ver 27;
S Ex 13:13; Nu 18:15
27:13 ^g S Lev 25:25
^h S Lev 5:16
27:15 ⁱ ver 13,20
27:18 ^j Lev 25:10
^k Lev 25:15
27:19 ^l S Lev 25:25
27:21 ^m S Lev 25:10
ⁿ ver 9 ^o ver 28;
Nu 18:14; Eze 44:29
27:23 ^p S Lev 25:15
27:24 ^q S Lev 25:25
27:25 ^r S Ex 30:13
^s Nu 3:47; Eze 45:12
27:26 ^t S Ex 13:12
27:27 ^u S ver 11
27:28 ^v Nu 18:14;
Jos 6:17-19 ^w S ver 9
27:29 ^x Dt 7:26
27:30 ^y Nu 18:26;
Dt 12:6,17; 14:22,28;
2Ch 31:6; Ne 10:37;
12:44; 13:5; Mal 3:8
^z Dt 7:6; Ezr 9:2;
Isa 6:13
27:31 ^a S Lev 25:25
^b Lev 5:16
27:32 ^c Ps 89:32;
Jer 33:13; Eze 20:37
27:33 ^d ver 10
^e Nu 18:21
27:34 ^f S Ex 19:11
^g S Lev 7:38; Ac 7:38

27:9 *becomes holy.* See note on Ex 3:5. An animal given for a sacrifice could not be exchanged for another (v. 10). The people of Malachi's day chose the poorest animals, after having vowed to offer good ones (see Mal 1:13–14 and notes). If an unclean animal was given, it could be redeemed with the 20 percent penalty (vv. 11–13).

27:18 See note on 25:15.

27:28 *devotes to the LORD.* See TNIV text note. Devoting something was far more serious than dedicating it to sacred use. The devoted thing became totally the Lord's. Achan's sin was the greater because he stole what had been devoted to the Lord (Jos 7:11). Persons devoted to destruction were usually the captives in the wars of Canaan (cf. 1Sa 15:3,18).

27:29 Saul sinned in this regard when he did not totally destroy the Amalekites (1Sa 15).

27:30 *tithe.* A tenth (see Nu 18:21–29; Dt 12:6–18; 14:22–29; 26:12). From these passages it appears that Israel actually had three tithes: (1) the general tithe (here), paid to the Levites (Nu 18:21), who in turn had to give a tenth of that to the priests (Nu 18:26); (2) the tithe associated with the sacred meal involving offerer and Levite (Dt 14:22–27); and (3) the tithe paid every three years to the poor (Dt 14:28–29).

27:34 *the LORD gave Moses.* See 1:1 and note; 7:37–38; 25:1; 26:46.

NUMBERS

The English name of the book comes from the Septuagint (the pre-Christian Greek translation of the OT) and is based on the census lists found in chs. 1; 26. The Hebrew title of the book (*bemidbar,* "in the Desert," 1:1) is more descriptive of its content. Numbers presents an account of the 38-year period of Israel's wandering in the desert (or wilderness) following the establishment of the Sinaitic covenant (compare 1:1 with Dt 1:1).

AUTHOR AND DATE

The book has traditionally been ascribed to Moses. This conclusion is based on (1) statements concerning Moses' writing activity (e.g., 33:1–2; Ex 17:14; 24:4; 34:27) and (2) the assumption that the first five books of the Bible, the Pentateuch, are a unit and come from one author. See Introduction to Genesis: Author and Date of Writing.

It is not necessary, however, to claim that Numbers came from Moses' hand complete and in final form. Portions of the book were probably added by scribes or editors from later periods of Israel's history. For example, the protestation of the humility of Moses (12:3) would hardly be convincing if it came from his own mouth. But it seems reasonable to assume that Moses wrote the essential content of the book.

CONTENTS

C Numbers relates the story of Israel's journey from Mount Sinai to the plains of Moab on the border of Canaan. Much of its legislation for people and priests is similar to that in Exodus, Leviticus and Deuteronomy. The book tells of the murmuring and rebellion of God's people and of their subsequent judgment. Those whom God had redeemed from slavery in Egypt and with whom he had made a covenant at Mount Sinai responded not with faith, gratitude and obedience but with unbelief, ingratitude and repeated acts of rebellion, which came to extreme expression in their refusal to undertake the conquest of Canaan (ch. 14). The community of the redeemed forfeited its part in the promised land. The Israelites were condemned to live out their lives in the wilderness; only their children would enjoy the fulfillment of the promise that had originally been theirs (cf. Heb 3:7—4:11).

THEOLOGICAL TEACHING

In telling the story of Israel's wilderness wanderings, Numbers offers much that is theologically significant. During the first year after Israel's deliverance from Egypt, the nation entered into covenant with the Lord at Sinai to be the people of his kingdom, among whom he pitched his royal tent (the tabernacle)—this is the story of Exodus. As the account of Numbers begins, the Lord organizes the Israelites into a military camp. Leaving Sinai, they march forth as his conquering army, with the Lord at the head, to establish his kingdom in the promised land in the midst of the nations. The book graphically portrays Israel's identity as the Lord's redeemed covenant people and their vocation as the servant people of God, charged with estab-

---

lishing his kingdom on earth. God's purpose in history is implicitly disclosed: to invade the arena of fallen humanity and effect the redemption of his creation—the mission in which his people are also to be totally engaged.

C Numbers also presents the chastening wrath of God against his disobedient people. Because of their rebellion (and especially the nation's refusal to undertake the conquest of Canaan), Israel was in breach of covenant. The fourth book of the Pentateuch presents a sobering reality: The God who had entered into covenant with Abraham (Ge 15; 17), who had delivered his people from bondage in the exodus (Ex 14–15), who had brought Israel into covenant with himself as his "treasured possession" (Ex 19; see especially Ex 19:5) and who had revealed his holiness and the gracious means of approaching him (Lev 1–7), was also a God of wrath. His wrath extended to his errant children, as well as to the enemy nations of Egypt and Canaan.

C Even Moses, the great prophet and servant of the Lord, was not exempt from God's wrath when he disobeyed God. Ch. 20, which records his error, begins with the notice of Miriam's death (20:1) and concludes with the record of Aaron's death (20:22–29). Here is the passing of the old guard. Those whom God has used to establish the nation are dying before the nation has come into its own.

The questions arise: Is God finished with the nation as a whole (cf. Ro 11:1)? Are his promises a thing of the past? In one of the most remarkable sections of the Bible—the account of Balaam, the pagan diviner (chs. 22–24)—the reply is given. The Lord, working in a providential and direct way, proclaims his continued faithfulness to his purpose for his people despite their unfaithfulness to him.

C Balaam is Moab's answer to Moses, the man of God. He is an internationally known prophet who shares the pagan belief that the God of Israel is like any other deity who might be manipulated by acts of magic or sorcery (see note on 22:5). But from the early part of the narrative, when Balaam first encounters the one true God in visions, and in the narrative of the journey on the donkey (ch. 22), he begins to learn that dealing with the true God is fundamentally different from anything he has ever known. When he attempts to curse Israel at the instigation of Balak, king of Moab, Balaam finds his mouth unable to express the curse he desires to pronounce. Instead, from his lips come blessings on Israel and curses on their enemies (chs. 23–24).

In his seven prophetic messages, Balaam proclaims God's great blessing for his people (see 23:20). Though the immediate enjoyment of this blessing will always depend on the faithfulness of his people, the ultimate realization of God's blessing is sure—because of the character of God (see 23:19). Thus Numbers reaffirms the ongoing purposes of God. Despite his judgment on his rebellious people, God is still determined to bring Israel into the land of promise. His blessing to Israel rests in his sovereign will.

The teaching of the book has lasting significance for Israel and for the church (cf. Ro 15:4; 1Co 10:6,11). God does display his wrath even against his errant people, but his grace is renewed as surely as is the dawn, and his redemptive purpose will not be thwarted.

SPECIAL PROBLEM

The large numbers of men conscripted into Israel's army (see, e.g., the figures in 1:46; 26:51) have puzzled many interpreters. The numbers of men mustered for warfare seem to demand a total population in excess of 2,000,000. Such numbers appear to be exceedingly large for the times, for the locale, for the wilderness wanderings, and in comparison with the inhabitants of Canaan. See note on 3:43.

Various possibilities have been suggested to solve this problem. Some have thought that the numbers may have been corrupted in transmission. The present text, however, does not betray textual difficulties with the numbers.

Others have felt that the Hebrew word for "thousand" might have a different meaning here from its usual numerical connotation. In some passages, for example, the word is a technical term for a company of men that may or may not equal 1,000 (e.g., Jos 22:14, "family division"; 1Sa 23:23, "clans"). Further, some have postulated that this Hebrew word means "chief" (as in Ge 36:15). In this way the figure 53,400 (26:47) would mean "53 chiefs plus 400 men." Such a procedure would yield a greatly reduced total, but it would be at variance with the fact that the Hebrew text adds the "thousands" in the same way it adds the "hundreds" for a large total. Also, this would make the proportion of chiefs to fighting men top-heavy (59 chiefs for 300 men in Simeon).

Another option is to read the Hebrew word for "thousand" with a dual meaning of "chief" and "1,000," with the chiefs numbering one less than the stated figure. For example, the 46,500 of Reuben (1:20) is read as 45 chiefs and 1,500 fighting men, the 59,300 of Simeon (1:23) is read as 58 chiefs and 1,300 fighting men, etc. But in this case, as in the former, the totals of 1:46 and 2:32 must then be regarded as errors of understanding (perhaps by later scribes).

Still another approach is to regard the numbers as symbolic figures rather than as strictly mathematical. The numerical value of the Hebrew letters in the expression *bene yisra'el* ("the whole Israelite community," 1:2) equals 603 (the number of the thousands of the fighting men, 1:46); the remaining 550 (plus 1 for Moses) might come from the numerical equivalent of the Hebrew letters in the expression "all the men . . . who are . . . able to serve in the army" (1:3). This symbolic use of numbers (called "gematria") is not unknown in the Bible (see Rev 13:18), but it is not likely in Numbers, where there are no literary clues pointing in that direction. (For one more option [hyperbole], see note on 1Ch 12:23—37.)

While the problem of the large numbers has not been satisfactorily solved, the Bible does point to a remarkable increase of Jacob's descendants during the four centuries of their sojourn in Egypt (see Ex 1:7—12). With all their difficulties, these numbers also point to the great role of providence and miracles in God's dealings with his people during their life in the wilderness (see note on 1:46).

STRUCTURE AND OUTLINE

The book has three major divisions, based on Israel's geographical locations. Each of the three divisions has two parts, as the following breakdown demonstrates: (1) Israel at Sinai, preparing to depart for the land of promise (1:1—10:10), followed by the journey from Sinai to Kadesh (10:11—12:16); (2) Israel at Kadesh, delayed as a result of rebellion (13:1—20:13), followed by the journey from Kadesh to the plains of Moab (20:14—22:1); (3) Israel on the plains of Moab, anticipating the conquest of the land of promise (22:2—32:42), followed by appendixes dealing with various matters (chs. 33—36).

I. Israel at Sinai, Preparing to Depart for the Promised Land (1:1—10:10)
  A. The Commands for the Census of the People (chs. 1—4)
    1. The numbers of men from each tribe mustered for war (ch. 1)
    2. The placement of the tribes around the tabernacle and their order for march (ch. 2)
    3. The placement of the Levites around the tabernacle, and the numbers of the Levites and the firstborn of Israel (ch. 3)
    4. The numbers of the Levites in their tabernacle service for the Lord (ch. 4)
  B. The Commands for Purity of the People (5:1—10:10)
    1. The test for purity in the law of jealousy (ch. 5)
    2. The Nazirite vow and the Aaronic benediction (ch. 6)

1:1 *a* S Ex 27:21;
S 40:2 *b* S Ex 19:1
c ver 18 *d* S Ex 6:14
1:2 *e* Ex 30:11-16
f ver 18 *g* Nu 3:40
1:3 *h* Ex 4:14;
Nu 17:3 *i* S Ex 30:14
j ver 20; Nu 26:2;
Jos 5:4; 1Ch 5:18
1:4 *k* S Lev 24:11;
S Jos 7:1 *l* ver 16;
Nu 7:2; 30:1; 31:26
m Ex 18:21; Nu 34:18;
Dt 1:15; Jos 22:14
1:5 *n* Nu 17:2
o S Ge 29:32; Rev 7:5
p Nu 2:10; 7:30; 10:18
1:6 *q* ver 22;
Nu 25:14 *r* Nu 2:12;
7:36,41; 10:19
1:7 *s* ver 26;
S Ge 29:35; Ps 78:68
t Ex 6:23; Nu 7:12;
Ru 4:20; 1Ch 2:10;
Mt 1:4; Lk 3:32
1:8 *u* S Ge 30:18;
Nu 10:15 *v* Nu 2:5;
7:18
1:9 *w* ver 30;
Nu 10:16 *x* Nu 2:7;
7:24
1:10 *y* ver 32
z Nu 2:18; 7:48,53;
10:22 *a* ver 34;
Nu 10:23 *b* Nu 2:20;
7:54
1:11 *c* Nu 10:24
d Nu 2:22; 7:60;
Ps 68:27
1:12 *e* ver 38
f Nu 2:25; 7:66; 10:25
1:13 *g* ver 40;
Nu 10:26 *h* Nu 2:27;
7:72
1:14 *i* ver 24;
Nu 10:20 *j* Nu 2:14;
7:42
1:15 *k* ver 42;
Nu 10:27 *l* Nu 2:29;
7:78
1:16 *m* S Ex 18:25
n Nu 32:28 *o* S ver 4
1:18 *p* ver 1
q Ezr 2:59; Heb 7:3
r ver 2 *s* S Ex 30:14
1:19 *t* Ex 30:12;
Nu 26:63; 31:49
1:20 *u* S Ge 29:32;

THE CENSUS

1 The LORD spoke to Moses in the tent of meeting *a* in the Desert of Sinai *b* on the first day of the second month *c* of the second year after the Israelites came out of Egypt. *d* He said: ²"Take a census *e* of the whole Israelite community by their clans and families, *f* listing every man by name, *g* one by one. ³You and Aaron *h* are to count according to their divisions all the men in Israel who are twenty years old or more *i* and able to serve in the army. *j* ⁴One man from each tribe, *k* each of them the head of his family, *l* is to help you. *m* ⁵These are the names *n* of the men who are to assist you:

from Reuben, *o* Elizur son of Shedeur; *p*
⁶from Simeon, *q* Shelumiel son of Zurishaddai; *r*
⁷from Judah, *s* Nahshon son of Amminadab; *t*
⁸from Issachar, *u* Nethanel son of Zuar; *v*
⁹from Zebulun, *w* Eliab son of Helon; *x*
¹⁰from the sons of Joseph:
from Ephraim, *y* Elishama son of Ammihud; *z*
from Manasseh, *a* Gamaliel son of Pedahzur; *b*
¹¹from Benjamin, *c* Abidan son of Gideoni; *d*
¹²from Dan, *e* Ahiezer son of Ammishaddai; *f*
¹³from Asher, *g* Pagiel son of Okran; *h*
¹⁴from Gad, *i* Eliasaph son of Deuel; *j*
¹⁵from Naphtali, *k* Ahira son of Enan. *l* "

¹⁶These were the men appointed from the community, the leaders *m* of their ancestral tribes. *n* They were the heads of the clans of Israel. *o*

¹⁷Moses and Aaron took these men whose names had been specified, ¹⁸and they called the whole community together on the first day of the second month. *p* The people registered their ancestry *q* by their clans and families, *r* and the men twenty years old or more *s* were listed by name, one by one, ¹⁹as the LORD commanded Moses. And so he counted *t* them in the Desert of Sinai:

²⁰From the descendants of Reuben *u* the firstborn son *v* of Israel:
All the men twenty years old or more who were able to serve in the army were listed by name, one by one, according to the records of their clans and families. ²¹The number from the tribe of Reuben *w* was 46,500.

²²From the descendants of Simeon: *x*
All the men twenty years old or more who were able to serve in the army were

1:20 S 46:9; Rev 7:5 *v* S Ge 10:15   **1:21** *w* Nu 26:7   **1:22** *x* S Ge 29:33; Rev 7:7

C **1:1** *The LORD spoke to Moses.* One of the most pervasive emphases in Numbers is the fact that the Lord spoke to Moses and through Moses to Israel. From the opening words to the closing words (36:13), this is stated over 150 times and in more than 20 ways. The Lord's use of Moses as his prophet is described in 12:6–8 (see notes there). One of the Hebrew names for the book is *wayedabber* ("And he [the LORD] spoke"), from the first word in the Hebrew text. *tent of meeting.* The tabernacle. *Desert of Sinai.* The more common Hebrew name for Numbers is *bemidbar* ("in the Desert"), the fifth word in the Hebrew text. The events of Numbers cover a period of 38 years and nine or ten months, i.e., the period of Israel's desert (or wilderness) wanderings. *first day … second month … second year.* Thirteen months after the exodus, Numbers begins. Israel had spent the previous year in the region of Mount Sinai receiving the law and erecting the tabernacle. Now the people were to be mustered as a military force for an orderly march. Dating events from the exodus (for another example, see 1Ki 6:1; see also note there) is similar to the Christian practice of dating years in reference to the incarnation of Christ (B.C. and A.D.). The exodus was God's great act of deliverance of his people from bondage.
1:2 *Take.* The Hebrew for this word is plural, indicating that Moses and Aaron were to complete this task together (see v. 3, "You and Aaron"), but the primary responsibility lay with Moses. *cen-*

sus. Its main purpose was to form a military roster, not a social, political or taxing document.
1:3 *able to serve in the army.* Refers to the principal military purpose of the census. The phrase occurs 14 times in ch. 1 and again in 26:2 (see note on 26:1–51).
1:4 *One man from each tribe.* By having a representative from each tribe assist Moses and Aaron, the count would be regarded as legitimate by all.
1:5–16 The names of these men occur again in chs. 2; 7; 10. Most contain within them a reference to the name of God. Levi is not represented in the list (see vv. 47–53 and notes).
1:19 *And so he counted them in the Desert of Sinai.* A summary statement; vv. 20–43 provide the details.
1:20–43 For each tribe there are two verses in repetitive formulaic structure, giving: (1) the name of the tribe, (2) the specifics of those numbered, (3) the name of the tribe again and (4) the total count for that tribe. The numbers for each tribe are probably rounded off to the hundred (but Gad to the fifty, v. 25). The same numbers are given for each tribe in ch. 2, where there are four triads of tribes. A peculiarity in the numbers that leads some to believe that they are symbolic is that the hundreds are grouped between 200 and 700. Also, various speculations have arisen regarding the meaning of the Hebrew word for "thousand" (see Introduction: Special Problem). In this chapter, the word has been used to mean 1,000 in order for the totals to be achieved.

counted and listed by name, one by one, according to the records of their clans and families. ²³The number from the tribe of Simeon was 59,300. ʸ

²⁴From the descendants of Gad: ᶻ
All the men twenty years old or more who were able to serve in the army were listed by name, according to the records of their clans and families. ²⁵The number from the tribe of Gad ᵃ was 45,650.

²⁶From the descendants of Judah: ᵇ
All the men twenty years old or more who were able to serve in the army were listed by name, according to the records of their clans and families. ²⁷The number from the tribe of Judah ᶜ was 74,600.

²⁸From the descendants of Issachar: ᵈ
All the men twenty years old or more who were able to serve in the army were listed by name, according to the records of their clans and families. ²⁹The number from the tribe of Issachar ᵉ was 54,400. ᶠ

³⁰From the descendants of Zebulun: ᵍ
All the men twenty years old or more who were able to serve in the army were listed by name, according to the records of their clans and families. ³¹The number from the tribe of Zebulun was 57,400. ʰ

³²From the sons of Joseph: ⁱ
From the descendants of Ephraim: ʲ
All the men twenty years old or more who were able to serve in the army were listed by name, according to the records of their clans and families. ³³The number from the tribe of Ephraim ᵏ was 40,500.

³⁴From the descendants of Manasseh: ˡ
All the men twenty years old or more who were able to serve in the army were listed by name, according to the records of their clans and families. ³⁵The number from the tribe of Manasseh was 32,200.

³⁶From the descendants of Benjamin: ᵐ
All the men twenty years old or more who were able to serve in the army were listed by name, according to the records of their clans and families. ³⁷The number from the tribe of Benjamin ⁿ was 35,400.

³⁸From the descendants of Dan: ᵒ
All the men twenty years old or more who were able to serve in the army were listed by name, according to the records of their clans and families. ³⁹The number from the tribe of Dan was 62,700. ᵖ

⁴⁰From the descendants of Asher: �q
All the men twenty years old or more who were able to serve in the army were listed by name, according to the records of their clans and families. ⁴¹The number from the tribe of Asher ʳ was 41,500.

⁴²From the descendants of Naphtali: ˢ
All the men twenty years old or more who were able to serve in the army were listed by name, according to the records of their clans and families. ⁴³The number from the tribe of Naphtali ᵗ was 53,400. ᵘ

⁴⁴These were the men counted by Moses and Aaron ᵛ and the twelve leaders of Israel, each one representing his family. ⁴⁵All the Israelites twenty years old or more ʷ who were able to serve in Israel's army were counted according to their families. ˣ ⁴⁶The total number was 603,550. ʸ

1:23 ʸ Nu 26:14
1:24 ᶻ S Ge 30:11;
S Jos 13:24-28;
Rev 7:5
1:25 ᵃ Ge 46:16;
Nu 26:18; 1Ch 5:11
1:26 ᵇ S ver 7;
Mt 1:2; Rev 7:5
1:27 ᶜ Nu 26:22
1:28 ᵈ S Ge 30:18;
Rev 7:7
1:29 ᵉ S Ge 30:18
ᶠ Nu 26:25
1:30 ᵍ S Ge 30:20;
Rev 7:8
1:31 ʰ Nu 26:27
1:32 ⁱ Ge 49:26
ʲ S Ge 41:52
1:33 ᵏ Nu 26:37;
1Ch 7:20
1:34 ˡ S Ge 41:51;
Rev 7:6
1:36 ᵐ S Ge 35:18;
2Ch 17:17; Jer 32:44;
Ob 1:19; Rev 7:8
1:37 ⁿ Nu 26:41
1:38 ᵒ Ge 30:6;
Dt 33:22
1:39 ᵖ Nu 26:43
1:40 q S Ge 30:13;
Nu 26:44; Rev 7:6
1:41 ʳ Nu 26:47
1:42 ˢ S Ge 30:8;
Rev 7:6
1:43 ᵗ Nu 26:50
ᵘ S Ex 1:1-4
1:44 ᵛ Nu 26:64
1:45 ʷ ver 3;
Nu 14:29 ˣ Nu 2:32
1:46 ʸ S Ex 12:37;
2Sa 24:9

1:32–35 Because the descendants of Levi were excluded from the census (see note on v. 47), the descendants of Joseph are listed according to the families of his two sons, Ephraim (vv. 32–33) and Manasseh (vv. 34–35). In this way the traditional tribal number of 12 is maintained, and Joseph is given the "double portion" of the ranking heir (cf. Ge 49:22–26; Dt 33:13–17; 2Ki 2:9 and notes).
1:46 *603,550.* Except for Joshua and Caleb, all these died in the wilderness. The mathematics of these numbers is accurate and complex. It is complex in that the totals are reached in two ways: (1) a linear listing of 12 units (vv. 20–43), with the total given (v. 46); (2) four sets of triads, each with a subtotal, and

then the grand total (2:3–32). These figures are also consistent with those in Ex 12:37; 38:26. This large number of men conscripted for the army suggests a population for the entire community in excess of 2,000,000 (see Introduction: Special Problem). Ex 1:7 describes the remarkable growth of the Hebrew people in Egypt during the 400-year sojourn. They had become so numerous that they were regarded as a grave threat to the security of Egypt (Ex 1:9–10,20). Israel's amazing growth from the 70 who entered Egypt (Ex 1:5) was an evidence of God's great blessing and his faithfulness to his covenant with Abraham (Ge 12:2; 15:5; 17:4–6; 22:17).

1:47 ᶻS Nu 3:17-20
ᵃNu 4:3,49
1:50 ᵇEx 25:9;
S 26:1 ᶜS 16:34;
Ac 7:44; Rev 15:5
ᵈNu 3:31
1:51 ᵉS Ex 26:1
ᶠNu 4:5 ᵍNu 3:38;
4:15 ʰS Ex 21:12
1:52 ⁱNu 10:14;
Ps 20:5; SS 2:4; 6:4
1:53 ʲNu 2:10; 3:23,
29,38 ᵏLev 10:6;
Nu 16:46; 18:5;
Dt 9:22 ˡS Ex 38:21;
Nu 18:2-4
2:2 ᵐPs 74:4;
Isa 31:9; Jer 4:21
2:3 ⁿS Ex 6:23
2:5 ᵒNu 10:15
ᵖS Nu 1:8
2:7 �ۑNu 1:9; 10:16
2:9 ʳNu 10:14;
Jdg 1:1
2:10 ˢS Nu 1:53
ᵗNu 1:5
2:12 ᵘNu 10:19
ᵛS Nu 1:6
2:14 ʷNu 10:20
ˣNu 1:14; 10:20

⁴⁷The ancestral tribe of the Levites,ᶻ however, was not counted ᵃ along with the others. ⁴⁸The Lᴏʀᴅ had said to Moses: ⁴⁹"You must not count the tribe of Levi or include them in the census of the other Israelites. ⁵⁰Instead, appoint the Levites to be in charge of the tabernacle ᵇ of the covenant law ᶜ—over all its furnishings ᵈ and everything belonging to it. They are to carry the tabernacle and all its furnishings; they are to take care of it and encamp around it. ⁵¹Whenever the tabernacle ᵉ is to move, ᶠ the Levites are to take it down, and whenever the tabernacle is to be set up, the Levites shall do it. ᵍ Anyone else who approaches it is to be put to death. ʰ ⁵²The Israelites are to set up their tents by divisions, each of them in their own camp under their standard. ⁱ ⁵³The Levites, however, are to set up their tents around the tabernacle ʲ of the covenant law so that my wrath will not fall ᵏ on the Israelite community. The Levites are to be responsible for the care of the tabernacle of the covenant law. ˡ "

⁵⁴The Israelites did all this just as the Lᴏʀᴅ commanded Moses.

THE ARRANGEMENT OF THE TRIBAL CAMPS

2 The Lᴏʀᴅ said to Moses and Aaron: ²"The Israelites are to camp around the tent of meeting some distance from it, each of them under their standard ᵐ and holding the banners of their family."

³On the east, toward the sunrise, the divisions of the camp of Judah are to encamp under their standard. ⁿ ⁴His division numbers 74,600.

⁵The tribe of Issachar ᵒ will camp next to them. The leader of the people of Issachar is Nethanel son of Zuar. ᵖ ⁶His division numbers 54,400.

⁷The tribe of Zebulun will be next. The leader of the people of Zebulun is Eliab son of Helon. ᵠ ⁸His division numbers 57,400.

⁹All the men assigned to the camp of Judah, according to their divisions, number 186,400. They will set out first. ʳ

¹⁰On the south ˢ will be the divisions of the camp of Reuben under their standard. The leader of the people of Reuben is Elizur son of Shedeur. ᵗ ¹¹His division numbers 46,500.

¹²The tribe of Simeon ᵘ will camp next to them. The leader of the people of Simeon is Shelumiel son of Zurishaddai. ᵛ ¹³His division numbers 59,300.

¹⁴The tribe of Gad ʷ will be next. The leader of the people of Gad is Eliasaph son of Deuel. ᵃˣ ¹⁵His division numbers 45,650.

ᵃ 14 Many manuscripts of the Masoretic Text, Samaritan Pentateuch and Vulgate (see also Num. 1:14); most manuscripts of the Masoretic Text *Reuel*

1:47 Because of their special tasks, the Levites were excluded from this military count. They too had to perform service to the Lord, but they were to be engaged in the ceremonies and maintenance of the tabernacle (see note on vv. 32–35).

1:50,53 *the covenant law.* The Ten Commandments written on stone tablets (see Ex 31:18; 32:15; 34:29), which were placed in the ark (Ex 25:16,21; 40:20), leading to the phrase the "ark of the covenant law" (Ex 25:22; 26:33,34). See notes on Ex 16:34; 25:16,22.

1:51 *Anyone else.* The Hebrew for this phrase is often translated "stranger" or "foreigner" (e.g., Isa 1:7; Hos 7:9). Thus a non-Levite Israelite was considered a "stranger" to the religious duties of the tabernacle (see Ex 29:33; 30:33; Lev 22:12). *death.* See 3:10,38; 18:7; cf. 16:31–33; 1Sa 6:19.

1:53 *their tents around the tabernacle.* See 3:21–38 and diagram, p. 195. *wrath.* The Levites formed a protective hedge against trespassing by the non-Levites to keep them from experiencing divine wrath.

A **1:54** *as the Lᴏʀᴅ commanded Moses.* In view of Israel's great disobedience in the later chapters of Numbers, these words of initial compliance have a special poignancy.

2:1–34 This chapter is symmetrically structured:
　Summary command (vv. 1–2)
　　Details of execution (vv. 3–33)
　　　Eastern camp (vv. 3–9)
　　　Southern camp (vv. 10–16)
　　　Tent and Levites (v. 17)
　　　Western camp (vv. 18–24)
　　　Northern camp (vv. 25–31)

　Summary totals (vv. 32–33)
　Summary conclusion (v. 34)
In ch. 1 the nation is mustered, and the genealogical relationships are clarified. In ch. 2 the nation is put in structural order, and the line of march and place of encampment are established. The numbers of ch. 1 are given in a new pattern, and the same leaders are named here again.

2:2 *some distance from it.* See 1:52–53. *each of them.* Each was to know his exact position within the camp. *standard … banners.* Each tribe had its banner, and each triad of tribes had its standard. Jewish tradition suggests that the tribal banners corresponded in color to the 12 stones in the breastpiece of the high priest (Ex 28:15–21). Tradition also holds that the standard of the triad led by Judah had the figure of a lion, that of Reuben the figure of a man, that of Ephraim the figure of an ox and that of Dan the figure of an eagle (see the four living creatures described by Eze 1:10; cf. Rev 4:7). But these traditions are not otherwise substantiated. See diagram, p. 195.

C **2:3–7** *Judah … Issachar … Zebulun.* The fourth, fifth and sixth sons of Jacob and Leah. It is somewhat surprising to have these three tribes first in the order of march, since Reuben is regularly noted as Jacob's firstborn son (1:20). However, because of the failure of the older brothers (Reuben, Simeon and Levi; see Ge 49:3–7), Judah is granted pride of place among his brothers (Ge 49:8). Judah produced the royal line from which the Messiah came (Ge 49:10; Ru 4:18–21; Mt 1:1–16).

2:10–12 *Reuben … Simeon.* The first and second sons of Jacob and Leah.

[16]All the men assigned to the camp of Reuben,[y] according to their divisions, number 151,450. They will set out second.

[17]Then the tent of meeting and the camp of the Levites[z] will set out in the middle of the camps. They will set out in the same order as they encamp, each in their own place under their standard.

[18]On the west[a] will be the divisions of the camp of Ephraim[b] under their standard. The leader of the people of Ephraim is Elishama son of Ammihud.[c] [19]His division numbers 40,500.

[20]The tribe of Manasseh[d] will be next to them. The leader of the people of Manasseh is Gamaliel son of Pedahzur.[e] [21]His division numbers 32,200.

[22]The tribe of Benjamin[f] will be next. The leader of the people of Benjamin is Abidan son of Gideoni.[g] [23]His division numbers 35,400.

[24]All the men assigned to the camp of Ephraim,[h] according to their divisions, number 108,100. They will set out third.[i]

[25]On the north[j] will be the divisions of the camp of Dan under their standard.[k] The leader of the people of Dan is Ahiezer son of Ammishaddai.[l] [26]His division numbers 62,700.

[27]The tribe of Asher will camp next to them. The leader of the people of Asher is Pagiel son of Okran.[m] [28]His division numbers 41,500.

[29]The tribe of Naphtali[n] will be next. The leader of the people of Naphtali is Ahira son of Enan.[o] [30]His division numbers 53,400.

[31]All the men assigned to the camp of Dan number 157,600. They will set out last,[p] under their standards.

[32]These are the Israelites, counted according to their families.[q] All the men in the

2:16 [y] Nu 10:18
2:17 [z] Nu 1:50; 10:21
2:18 [a] S Nu 1:53
[b] S Ge 48:20;
Jer 31:18-20 [c] Nu 1:10
2:20 [d] S Ge 48:20
[e] S Nu 1:10
2:22 [f] Nu 10:24
[g] S Nu 1:11
2:24 [h] Nu 10:22
[i] Ps 80:2
2:25 [j] S Nu 1:53
[k] Nu 10:25 [l] S Nu 1:12
2:27 [m] Nu 1:13;
10:26
2:29 [n] Nu 10:27
[o] Nu 1:15; 10:27
2:31 [p] Nu 10:25;
Jos 6:9
2:32 [q] Nu 1:45

2:14 *Gad.* The first son of Jacob and Zilpah (Leah's servant). Levi, Leah's third son, is not included with the divisions of the congregation. *Deuel.* See TNIV text note. The Hebrew letters for *d* and *r* were easily confused by scribes (copyists) because of their similarity in form (see note on Ge 10:4).
2:17 *tent of meeting.* Representing God's presence in the heart of the camp (see 1:1 and note). *Levites.* In the line of march, the Judah and Reuben triads would lead the community, then would come the tabernacle with the attendant protective hedge of Levites (see note on 1:53), and last would come the Ephraim and Dan triads.

2:18–22 The Rachel tribes (Joseph and Benjamin) were on the west. Joseph's two sons, Manasseh and Ephraim, received a special blessing from their grandfather Jacob, but the younger son, Ephraim, was given precedence over Manasseh (see Ge 48:5–20 and notes). Here, true to Jacob's words, Ephraim is ahead of Manasseh. Last comes Benjamin, the last son born to Jacob.
2:25 *Dan.* The first son of Bilhah, Rachel's servant.
2:27 *Asher.* The second son of Zilpah, Leah's servant.
2:29 *Naphtali.* The second son of Bilhah.

ENCAMPMENT OF THE TRIBES OF ISRAEL

2:32 ʳ S Ex 12:37
2:33 ˢ Nu 1:47;
26:57-62
3:1 ᵗ S Ex 6:27
ᵘ S Ex 19:11
3:2 ᵛ Nu 1:20
ʷ S Ex 6:23
3:3 ˣ S Ex 28:41;
S 29:30
3:4 ʸ S Lev 10:2
ᶻ S Lev 10:1
ᵃ Lev 10:6,12;
Nu 4:28 ᵇ 1Ch 24:1
3:6 ᶜ Dt 10:8; 31:9;
1Ch 15:2 ᵈ Nu 8:6-22;
18:1-7; 2Ch 29:11
3:7 ᵉ Nu 1:53; 8:19
ᶠ S Lev 8:35
3:9 ᵍ ver 12,45;
Nu 8:19; 18:6
3:10 ʰ S Ex 30:7
ⁱ S Ex 29:9 ʲ Nu 1:51
3:12 ᵏ Ne 13:29;
Mal 2:4 ˡ ver 41;
Nu 8:16,18 ᵐ S ver 9;
Ex 13:2; Nu 8:14; 16:9
3:13 ⁿ S Ex 13:12
ᵒ Lev 11:44
3:14 ᵖ S Ex 19:1
3:15 �q ver 39;
S Nu 1:19 ʳ ver 22;
Nu 18:16; 26:62
3:17 ˢ S Ge 29:34;
S 46:11; Nu 1:47;
1Ch 15:4, 20 ᵗ Ge 46:11;
2Ch 29:12 ᵘ Jos 21:6
ᵘ Jos 21:4 ᵛ S Ex 6:16

camps, by their divisions, number 603,550. ʳ 33 The Levites, however, were not counted ˢ along with the other Israelites, as the LORD commanded Moses.

34 So the Israelites did everything the LORD commanded Moses; that is the way they encamped under their standards, and that is the way they set out, each of them with their clan and family.

THE LEVITES

3 This is the account of the family of Aaron and Moses ᵗ at the time the LORD spoke to Moses on Mount Sinai. ᵘ

2 The names of the sons of Aaron were Nadab the firstborn ᵛ and Abihu, Eleazar and Ithamar. ʷ 3 Those were the names of Aaron's sons, the anointed priests, ˣ who were ordained to serve as priests. 4 Nadab and Abihu, however, died before the LORD ʸ when they made an offering with unauthorized fire before him in the Desert of Sinai. ᶻ They had no sons, so Eleazar and Ithamar ᵃ served as priests during the lifetime of their father Aaron. ᵇ

5 The LORD said to Moses, 6 "Bring the tribe of Levi ᶜ and present them to Aaron the priest to assist him. ᵈ 7 They are to perform duties for him and for the whole community ᵉ at the tent of meeting by doing the work ᶠ of the tabernacle. 8 They are to take care of all the furnishings of the tent of meeting, fulfilling the obligations of the Israelites by doing the work of the tabernacle. 9 Give the Levites to Aaron and his sons; ᵍ they are the Israelites who are to be given wholly to him. ᵃ 10 Appoint Aaron ʰ and his sons to serve as priests; ⁱ anyone else who approaches the sanctuary is to be put to death." ʲ

11 The LORD also said to Moses, 12 "I have taken the Levites ᵏ from among the Israelites in place of the first male offspring ˡ of every Israelite woman. The Levites are mine, ᵐ 13 for all the firstborn are mine. ⁿ When I struck down all the firstborn in Egypt, I set apart for myself every firstborn in Israel, whether human or animal. They are to be mine. I am the LORD." ᵒ

14 The LORD said to Moses in the Desert of Sinai, ᵖ 15 "Count q the Levites by their families and clans. Count every male a month old or more." ʳ 16 So Moses counted them, as he was commanded by the word of the LORD.

17 These were the names of the sons of Levi: ˢ
Gershon, ᵗ Kohath ᵘ and Merari. ᵛ

ᵃ 9 Most manuscripts of the Masoretic Text; some manuscripts of the Masoretic Text, Samaritan Pentateuch and Septuagint (see also Num. 8:16) *to me*

2:32 *603,550.* See 1:46 and note.
2:33 *Levites.* See notes on 1:47,53.

2:34 *did everything the LORD commanded Moses.* As in 1:54 (see note there), these words of absolute compliance contrast with Israel's later folly. *under their standards ... each of them with their clan and family.* A major accomplishment for a people so numerous, so recently enslaved and more recently a mob in disarray. It may have been the orderliness of this encampment that led Balaam to say: "How beautiful are your tents, Jacob, / your dwelling places, Israel!" (24:5).

3:1 *Aaron and Moses.* At first glance, the names seem out of order, but the emphasis is correct: It is the family of Aaron that is about to be described (see v. 2).

3:3 *anointed priests.* Ex 28:41 records God's command to Moses to anoint his brother Aaron and his sons as priests of the Lord (see Ex 30:30; Lev 8:30). By this solemn act they were consecrated in a special way to the Lord. Kings (see 1Sa 16:13 and note) were also anointed with oil for special service to God. Physical objects could be anointed as well (see Ge 28:18 and note; Ex 29:36). The Hebrew term for "anointed" (*mashiah*) later became the specific term for the Messiah (Christ); see TNIV text note on Mt 1:1. *ordained.* The Hebrew for this word means lit. "fill the hand of" (see Ex 32:29 and note). By this act there was an investing of authority, a consecration and a setting apart.

3:4 *Nadab and Abihu.* See Lev 10:1–3 and notes. *unauthorized fire.* Or "strange fire." This seems to be a deliberately obscure expression, as though the narrator finds the very concept distasteful. They were using fire that the Lord had not commanded (see Lev 10:1). Proximity to God's holiness requires righteousness and obedience from his priests. For all time, the deaths of Aaron's newly consecrated sons serve to

warn God's ministers of the awesome seriousness of their tasks (cf. 1Sa 2:12–17,22–25, 27–36; 3:11–14; 4:1–11). For similar divine judgments at the beginning of new stages in salvation history see Jos 7:1–26; 2Sa 6:7; Ac 5:1 and notes.

3:5–10 These commands are not followed by a report of obedience, as were the commands in chs. 1–2, but further details are given in ch. 8. Clear distinctions are made here between the priestly house (the sons of Aaron) and the Levites. The latter were to be aides to the priests, and they served not only Aaron but the whole nation in the process (see vv. 7–8).

3:9 *to him.* See TNIV text note. It appears that the issue here is service to Aaron (and through him to the Lord); in 8:16 the service is to the Lord.

3:10 *anyone else.* Lit. "stranger"—anyone lacking authorization. Service at the tabernacle may be performed only at the express appointment of the Lord. The words of v. 10 follow the paragraph telling of the deaths of Aaron's sons. They were authorized persons but used unauthorized means. If the sons of Aaron were put to death at the commencement of their duties, how dare an unauthorized person even think to trespass! See v. 38; 18:1–7 and notes.

3:12–13 See note on Ex 13:2. *mine.* Repeated for emphasis.

3:12 *in place of.* An example of the practice of substitution (see Ge 22:13; Mt 20:28 and notes).

3:15 *a month old or more.* The counting of the Levites corresponds to that of the other tribes in chs. 1–2, except that all males from the age of one month, rather than from 20 years, were to be counted. The Levites were not being mustered for war, but for special service in the sacred precincts of the Lord.

3:16 *as he was commanded.* The obedience of Moses to the Lord's command is explicit and total.

¹⁸ These were the names of the Gershonite clans:
Libni and Shimei.^w
¹⁹ The Kohathite clans:
Amram, Izhar, Hebron and Uzziel.^x
²⁰ The Merarite clans:^y
Mahli and Mushi.^z
These were the Levite clans, according to their families.

²¹ To Gershon^a belonged the clans of the Libnites and Shimeites;^b these were the Gershonite clans. ²² The number of all the males a month old or more who were counted was 7,500. ²³ The Gershonite clans were to camp on the west, behind the tabernacle.^c ²⁴ The leader of the families of the Gershonites was Eliasaph son of Lael. ²⁵ At the tent of meeting the Gershonites were responsible for the care of the tabernacle^d and tent, its coverings,^e the curtain at the entrance^f to the tent of meeting,^g ²⁶ the curtains of the courtyard^h, the curtain at the entrance to the courtyard surrounding the tabernacle and altar,ⁱ and the ropes^j—and everything^k related to their use.

²⁷ To Kohath^l belonged the clans of the Amramites, Izharites, Hebronites and Uzzielites;^m these were the Kohathiteⁿ clans. ²⁸ The number of all the males a month old or more^o was 8,600.^a The Kohathites were responsible^p for the care of the sanctuary.^q ²⁹ The Kohathite clans were to camp on the south side^r of the tabernacle. ³⁰ The leader of the families of the Kohathite clans was Elizaphan^s son of Uzziel. ³¹ They were responsible for the care of the ark,^t the table,^u the lampstand,^v the altars,^w the articles^x of the sanctuary used in ministering, the curtain,^y and everything related to their use.^z ³² The chief leader of the Levites was Eleazar^a son of Aaron, the priest. He was appointed over those who were responsible^b for the care of the sanctuary.^c

³³ To Merari belonged the clans of the Mahlites and the Mushites;^d these were the Merarite clans.^e ³⁴ The number of all the males a month old or more^f who were counted was 6,200. ³⁵ The leader of the families of the Merarite clans was Zuriel son of Abihail; they were to camp on the north side of the tabernacle.^g ³⁶ The Merarites were appointed^h to take care of the frames of the tabernacle,ⁱ its crossbars,^j posts,^k bases, all its equipment, and everything related to their use,^l ³⁷ as well as the posts of the surrounding courtyard^m with their bases, tent pegsⁿ and ropes.

³⁸ Moses and Aaron and his sons were to camp to the east^o of the tabernacle, toward the sunrise, in front of the tent of meeting.^p They were responsible for the care of the sanctuary^q on behalf of the Israelites. Anyone else who approached the sanctuary was to be put to death.^r

³⁹ The total number of Levites counted^s at the LORD's command by Moses and Aaron according to their clans, including every male a month old or more, was 22,000.^t

^a *28* Hebrew; some Septuagint manuscripts *8,300*

3:18 ^w Ex 6:17
3:19 ^x S Ex 6:18
3:20 ^y S Ge 46:11
^z S Ex 6:19
3:21 ^a S Ge 46:11
^b Ex 6:17
3:23 ^c S Nu 2:18
3:25 ^d Ex 25:9;
Nu 7:1 ^e Ex 26:14
^f Ex 26:36; Nu 4:25
^g Ex 40:2
3:26 ^h Ex 27:9
ⁱ ver 31 / Ex 35:18
^k Nu 4:26
3:27 ^l S Ge 46:11;
S Ex 6:18 ^m Ex 6:18;
1Ch 26:23 ⁿ Nu 4:15, 37
3:28 ^o ver 15
^p Nu 4:4,15
^q S Ex 25:8; 30:13;
2Ch 30:19; Ps 15:1;
20:2; Eze 44:27
3:29 ^r S Nu 1:53
3:30 ^s S Ex 6:22
3:31 ^t S Ex 25:10-22; Dt 10:1-8;
2Ch 5:2; Jer 3:16
^u S Ex 25:23
^v S Ex 25:31;
1Ch 28:15; Jer 52:19
^w ver 26 ^x Nu 1:50
^y S Ex 26:33; Nu 4:5
^z Nu 4:15; 18:3
3:32 ^a S Ex 6:23
^b ver 28 ^c Nu 4:19;
18:3
3:33 ^d S Ex 6:19
^e S Ge 46:11
3:34 ^f ver 15
3:35 ^g S Nu 2:25
3:36 ^h Nu 4:32
ⁱ Ex 26:15-25; 35:20-29 / Ex 26:26-29
^k Ex 36:36 ^l Nu 18:3
3:37 ^m Ex 27:10-17
ⁿ Ex 27:19
3:38 ^o Nu 2:3
^p S Nu 1:53; 1Ch 9:27;
23:32 ^q ver 7; Nu 18:5
^r ver 10; Nu 1:51
3:39 ^s S ver 15
^t Nu 26:62

3:21–38 The words of 1:53, "their tents around the tabernacle of the covenant law," are detailed by the four paragraphs in this section: (1) Gershon to the west (vv. 21–26); (2) Kohath to the south (vv. 27–32); (3) Merari to the north (vv. 33–37); (4) Moses and Aaron and sons to the east (v. 38). The other tribes began with the most favored: (1) Judah on the east (2:3); (2) Reuben on the south (2:10); (3) Ephraim on the west (2:18); (4) Dan on the north (2:25). The Levitical clans lead up to the most favored. The leaders of the Levitical houses correspond to the leaders of the other tribes (see note on 1:5–16). As the names of the other tribal leaders include a form of God's name, so do these names.
3:24 *Eliasaph.* Means "(My) God has added." *Lael.* Means "belonging to God."
3:25–26 There were three curtains or covering screens for the tabernacle: (1) at the gate of the courtyard (v. 26; 4:26); (2) at the entrance to the tent (vv. 25,31; 4:25); (3) between the Most Holy Place and the Holy Place (4:5).
3:27 *Amramites.* Aaron was an Amramite (see Ex 6:20 and note); thus he and Moses were from the family of Kohath. To the

Kohathites was given the care of the most holy things (see 4:4–18).
3:28 *8,600.* The total number of Levites given in v. 39 is 22,000—300 less than the totals of 7,500 Gershonites (v. 22), 8,600 Kohathites (here) and 6,200 Merarites (v. 34). Many believe that a copyist may have made a mistake here and that the correct number is 8,300 (see TNIV text note).
3:30 *Elizaphan.* Means "(My) God has protected." *Uzziel.* Means "My strength is God."
3:35 *Zuriel.* Means "My Rock is God." *Abihail.* Means "My (divine) Father is powerful."

A **3:38** *toward the sunrise.* The most honored location, but Moses and Aaron were placed there for a representative ministry (on behalf of the Israelites). *Anyone else . . . was to be put to death.* Service in the tabernacle was an act of mercy, a means for the people to come before God. Yet it was marked by strict discipline—it had to be done in God's way. The sovereignty of God was evident in his limitations on the means to approach him (see v. 10; 1:51; 18:1–7 and notes).

3:40 *u* ver 15
v Nu 1:2
3:41 *w* ver 12
x Lev 11:44
3:43 *y* ver 15
z ver 39
3:45 *a* S ver 9
b Lev 11:44
3:46 *c* Ex 13:13;
Nu 18:15
3:47 *d* S Lev 27:6
e S Ex 30:13
f S Lev 27:25
3:48 *g* ver 51
h ver 50
3:49 *i* ver 48
3:50 *i* ver 41,45
k S ver 46-48
4:2 *l* S Ex 30:12
4:3 *m* S Nu 1:47
n ver 23; Nu 8:25;
1Ch 23:3,24,27;
Ezr 3:8
4:4 *o* S Nu 3:28
p Nu 7:9 *q* ver 19
4:5 *r* Nu 1:51
s S Ex 26:31,33
t 1Ch 23:26
4:6 *u* S Ex 25:5
v S Ex 25:13-15;
1Ki 8:7; 2Ch 5:8
4:7 *w* S Lev 24:6
x Ex 39:36; Jer 52:19
y S Ex 25:30
4:8 *z* Ex 26:26-28
4:9 *a* S Ex 25:38
4:10 *b* ver 12
4:11 *c* S Ex 30:1
d Ex 30:4
4:12 *e* Nu 3:31
f ver 10
4:13 *g* S Lev 1:16
h Ex 27:1-8; Nu 3:31
4:14 *i* S Ex 31:9
j S Ex 27:3
k 1Ch 28:17; 2Ch 4:16
l 2Ch 4:11 *m* Ex 27:3;
Nu 7:84; 2Ch 4:8;
Jer 52:18 *n* Ex 27:6
4:15 *o* ver 5
p S Nu 3:27

⁴⁰The Lord said to Moses, "Count all the firstborn Israelite males who are a month old or more *u* and make a list of their names. *v* ⁴¹Take the Levites for me in place of all the firstborn of the Israelites, *w* and the livestock of the Levites in place of all the firstborn of the livestock of the Israelites. I am the Lord." *x*

⁴²So Moses counted all the firstborn of the Israelites, as the Lord commanded him. ⁴³The total number of firstborn males a month old or more, *y* listed by name, was 22,273. *z*

⁴⁴The Lord also said to Moses, ⁴⁵"Take the Levites in place of all the firstborn of Israel, and the livestock of the Levites in place of their livestock. The Levites are to be mine. *a* I am the Lord. *b* ⁴⁶To redeem *c* the 273 firstborn Israelites who exceed the number of the Levites, ⁴⁷collect five shekels *a d* for each one, according to the sanctuary shekel, *e* which weighs twenty gerahs. *f* ⁴⁸Give the money for the redemption *g* of the additional Israelites to Aaron and his sons." *h*

⁴⁹So Moses collected the redemption money *i* from those who exceeded the number redeemed by the Levites. ⁵⁰From the firstborn of the Israelites *j* he collected silver weighing 1,365 shekels, *b k* according to the sanctuary shekel. ⁵¹Moses gave the redemption money to Aaron and his sons, as he was commanded by the word of the Lord.

THE KOHATHITES

4 The Lord said to Moses and Aaron: ²"Take a census *l* of the Kohathite branch of the Levites by their clans and families. ³Count *m* all the men from thirty to fifty years of age *n* who come to serve in the work at the tent of meeting.

⁴"This is the work *o* of the Kohathites *p* at the tent of meeting: the care of the most holy things. *q* ⁵When the camp is to move, *r* Aaron and his sons are to go in and take down the shielding curtain *s* and put it over the ark of the covenant law. *t* ⁶Then they are to cover the curtain with a durable leather, *c u* spread a cloth of solid blue over that and put the poles *v* in place.

⁷"Over the table of the Presence *w* they are to spread a blue cloth and put on it the plates, dishes and bowls, and the jars for drink offerings; *x* the bread that is continually there *y* is to remain on it. ⁸They are to spread a scarlet cloth over them, cover that with the durable leather and put the poles *z* in place.

⁹"They are to take a blue cloth and cover the lampstand that is for light, together with its lamps, its wick trimmers and trays, *a* and all its jars for the olive oil used to supply it. ¹⁰Then they are to wrap it and all its accessories in a covering of the durable leather and put it on a carrying frame. *b*

¹¹"Over the gold altar *c* they are to spread a blue cloth and cover that with the durable leather and put the poles *d* in place.

¹²"They are to take all the articles *e* used for ministering in the sanctuary, wrap them in a blue cloth, cover that with the durable leather and put them on a carrying frame. *f*

¹³"They are to remove the ashes *g* from the bronze altar *h* and spread a purple cloth over it. ¹⁴Then they are to place on it all the utensils *i* used for ministering at the altar, including the firepans, *j* meat forks, *k* shovels *l* and sprinkling bowls. *m* Over it they are to spread a covering of the durable leather and put the poles *n* in place.

¹⁵"After Aaron and his sons have finished covering the holy furnishings and all the holy articles, and when the camp is ready to move, *o* only then are the Kohathites *p* to come and

---

a 47 That is, about 2 ounces or about 55 grams   *b 50* That is, about 35 pounds or about 16 kilograms
c 6 Possibly the hides of dugongs; also in verses 8, 10, 11, 12, 14 and 25

3:41 *I am the Lord.* What is being commanded conforms to God's character as Yahweh ("the Lord"; see note on Ex 3:14).

3:43 *22,273.* Seems too small for a population in excess of 2,000,000 and is used as an argument for attempting to find a means of reducing the total number of the people (calculations based on this number suggest a total population of about 250,000). Some suggest that the 22,273 firstborn of Israel were those born since the exodus, all the firstborn at the time of the exodus having already been set apart for the Lord at the first Passover (see Ex 12:22–23). This, however, creates a new problem since nowhere is that allegedly distinct group assigned any special service of the Lord. See Introduction: Special Problem.

3:47,50 *according to the sanctuary shekel.* See note on Ex 30:13.

4:3 *thirty to fifty years.* Ch. 3 listed all males over the age of one

month (3:15). Ch. 4 lists those Levites who were of age to serve in the tabernacle. Of the 22,000 Levite males (3:39), 8,580 were of age for service (v. 48). From 8:24 we learn that the beginning age for service was 25; perhaps the first five years were something of an apprenticeship.

4:4 *most holy things.* See note on Ex 3:5. Despite the fact that the primary care of these holy things was given to the Kohathites, they were forbidden to touch them (v. 15) or even to look at them (v. 20), on pain of death. All the work of the Kohathites was to be strictly supervised by Aaron and his sons, and only the priests were able to touch and look at the unveiled holy things.

4:5 *covenant law.* See note on Ex 25:22.

4:6 *durable leather.* See TNIV text note.

4:7 *table of the Presence.* See note on Ex 25:30.

do the carrying. *q* But they must not touch the holy things *r* or they will die. *s t* The Kohathites are to carry those things that are in the tent of meeting.

¹⁶"Eleazar *u* son of Aaron, the priest, is to have charge of the oil for the light, *v* the fragrant incense, *w* the regular grain offering *x* and the anointing oil. He is to be in charge of the entire tabernacle and everything in it, including its holy furnishings and articles."

¹⁷The LORD said to Moses and Aaron, ¹⁸"See that the Kohathite tribal clans are not destroyed from among the Levites. ¹⁹So that they may live and not die when they come near the most holy things, *y* do this for them: Aaron and his sons *z* are to go into the sanctuary and assign to each man his work and what he is to carry. *a* ²⁰But the Kohathites must not go in to look *b* at the holy things, even for a moment, or they will die."

THE GERSHONITES

²¹The LORD said to Moses, ²²"Take a census also of the Gershonites by their families and clans. ²³Count all the men from thirty to fifty years of age *c* who come to serve in the work at the tent of meeting.

²⁴"This is the service of the Gershonite clans in their carrying and their other work: ²⁵They are to carry the curtains of the tabernacle, *d* that is, the tent of meeting, *e* its covering *f* and its outer covering of durable leather, the curtains for the entrance to the tent of meeting, ²⁶the curtains of the courtyard surrounding the tabernacle and altar, *g* the curtain for the entrance to the courtyard, *h* the ropes and all the equipment *i* used in the service of the tent. The Gershonites are to do all that needs to be done with these things. ²⁷All their service, whether carrying or doing other work, is to be done under the direction of Aaron and his sons. *j* You shall assign to them as their responsibility *k* all they are to carry. ²⁸This is the service of the Gershonite clans *l* at the tent of meeting. Their duties are to be under the direction of Ithamar *m* son of Aaron, the priest.

THE MERARITES

²⁹"Count *n* the Merarites by their clans and families. *o* ³⁰Count all the men from thirty to fifty years of age who come to serve in the work at the tent of meeting. ³¹As part of all their service at the tent, they are to carry the frames of the tabernacle, its crossbars, posts and bases, *p* ³²as well as the posts of the surrounding courtyard with their bases, tent pegs, ropes, *q* all their equipment and everything related to their use. Assign to each man the specific things he is to carry. ³³This is the service of the Merarite clans as they work at the tent of meeting under the direction of Ithamar *r* son of Aaron, the priest."

THE NUMBERING OF THE LEVITE CLANS

³⁴Moses, Aaron and the leaders of the community counted the Kohathites *s* by their clans and families. ³⁵All the men from thirty to fifty years of age *t* who came to serve in the work at the tent of meeting, ³⁶counted by clans, were 2,750. ³⁷This was the total of all those in the Kohathite clans *u* who served at the tent of meeting. Moses and Aaron counted them according to the LORD's command through Moses.

³⁸The Gershonites *v* were counted by their clans and families. ³⁹All the men from thirty to fifty years of age who came to serve in the work at the tent of meeting, ⁴⁰counted by their clans and families, were 2,630. ⁴¹This was the total of those in the Gershonite clans who served at the tent of meeting. Moses and Aaron counted them according to the LORD's command.

⁴²The Merarites were counted by their clans and families. ⁴³All the men from thirty to fifty years of age *w* who came to serve in the work at the tent of meeting, ⁴⁴counted by their clans, were 3,200. ⁴⁵This was the total of those in the Merarite clans. *x* Moses and Aaron counted them according to the LORD's command through Moses.

⁴⁶So Moses, Aaron and the leaders of Israel counted *y* all the Levites by their clans and families. ⁴⁷All the men from thirty to fifty years of age *z* who came to do the work of serving and carrying the tent of meeting ⁴⁸numbered 8,580. *a* ⁴⁹At the LORD's command through Moses, each was assigned his work and told what to carry.

Thus they were counted, *b* as the LORD commanded Moses.

4:15 *q* Nu 7:9 *r* ver 4
s S Ex 28:43 *t* Nu 1:51;
2Sa 6:6,7
4:16 *u* Lev 10:6;
Nu 3:32 *v* S Ex 25:6
w S Ex 25:6
x S Ex 29:41;
Lev 6:14-23
4:19 *y* S ver 15
z ver 27 *a* S Nu 3:32
4:20 *b* S Ex 19:21
4:23 *c* S ver 3
4:25 *d* Ex 27:10-18
e Nu 3:25 *f* Ex 26:14
4:26 *g* Ex 27:9
h Ex 27:16 *i* Nu 3:26
4:27 *j* ver 19
k Nu 3:25,26
4:28 *l* Nu 7:7
m S Ex 6:23
4:29 *n* S Ex 30:12
o S Ge 46:11
4:31 *p* Nu 3:36
4:32 *q* Nu 3:37
4:33 *r* S Ex 38:21
4:34 *s* ver 2
4:35 *t* ver 3
4:37 *u* S Nu 3:27
4:38 *v* S Ge 46:11
4:43 *w* ver 3
4:45 *x* ver 29
4:46 *y* Nu 1:19
4:47 *z* ver 3
4:48 *a* Nu 3:39
4:49 *b* S Nu 1:47

4:16 *Eleazar . . . , the priest, is to have charge.* The high priest could draw near to the most holy things on behalf of the people. If he had not been able to do so, there could have been no worship by the community.

5:2 c S Lev 13:2
d S Lev 15:2; Mt 9:20
e Lev 13:3; Nu 9:6-10
f S Lev 21:11
5:3 g S Ex 29:45;
Lev 26:12; 2Co 6:16
5:6 h S Lev 6:2
i Lev 5:14–6:7
5:7 j S Lev 5:5;
S Lk 19:8 k S Lev 5:16
5:8 l S Lev 5:15
m Lev 6:6,7
5:9 n Lev 6:17
5:10 o Lev 7:29-34
5:12 p ver 19-21;
S Ex 20:14
5:13 q S Ex 20:14
5:14 r ver 30;
Pr 6:34; 27:4; SS 8:6
5:15 s S Ex 16:36
t S Lev 6:20

THE PURITY OF THE CAMP

5 The LORD said to Moses, [2]"Command the Israelites to send away from the camp anyone who has a defiling skin disease[a][c] or a discharge[d] of any kind, or who is ceremonially unclean[e] because of a dead body.[f] [3]Send away male and female alike; send them outside the camp so they will not defile their camp, where I dwell among them.[g]" [4]The Israelites did so; they sent them outside the camp. They did just as the LORD had instructed Moses.

RESTITUTION FOR WRONGS

[5]The LORD said to Moses, [6]"Say to the Israelites: 'Any man or woman who wrongs another in any way[b] and so is unfaithful[h] to the LORD is guilty[i] [7]and must confess[j] the sin they have committed. They must make full restitution[k] for the wrong they have done, add a fifth of the value to it and give it all to the person they have wronged. [8]But if that person has no close relative to whom restitution can be made for the wrong, the restitution belongs to the LORD and must be given to the priest, along with the ram[l] with which atonement is made for the wrongdoer.[m] [9]All the sacred contributions the Israelites bring to a priest will belong to him.[n] [10]All sacred gifts belong to the donors, but what they give to the priest will belong to the priest.[o]'"

THE TEST FOR AN UNFAITHFUL WIFE

[11]Then the LORD said to Moses, [12]"Speak to the Israelites and say to them: 'If a man's wife goes astray[p] and is unfaithful to him [13]so that another man has sexual relations with her,[q] and this is hidden from her husband and her impurity is undetected (since there is no witness against her and she has not been caught in the act), [14]and if feelings of jealousy[r] come over her husband and he suspects his wife and she is impure—or if he is jealous and suspects her even though she is not impure— [15]then he is to take his wife to the priest. He must also take an offering of a tenth of an ephah[c][s] of barley flour[t] on her be-

a 2 The Hebrew word for *defiling skin disease*, traditionally translated "leprosy," was used for various diseases affecting the skin.   b 6 Or *woman who commits any wrong common to humankind*   c 15 That is, probably about 3 1/2 pounds or about 1.6 kilograms

A **5:2** *defiling skin disease.* See TNIV text note; see also note on Lev 13:2; cf. Lk 5:12–16; 17:11–19. *discharge of any kind.* See note on Lev 15:2. Such discharges were primarily from the sexual organs and were chronic in nature (cf. Lk 8:43–48). The people who suffered from them became living object lessons to the whole camp on the necessity for all people to be "clean" in their approach to God. *unclean.* Ceremonially unfit to be with the community, and a possible contaminant to the tabernacle and the pure worship of the Lord. Aspects of uncleanness were not left in the abstract or theoretical; the focus was on tangible issues, such as clearly evident skin diseases and discharges. *dead body.* The ultimate tangible sign of uncleanness. Processes of decay and disease in dead flesh were evident to all. Physical contact with a corpse was a sure mark of uncleanness; normal contacts with the living would have to be curtailed until proper cleansing had been made. See note on 6:6 for application to the Nazirite vow. Jesus reached out to the dead as well as to the living; his raising of Jairus's daughter began with holding her limp hand (Lk 8:54).

A **5:3** *male and female alike.* The concept of clean versus unclean cuts across sexual lines. The essential issue was the presence of the Lord in the camp; there can be no uncleanness where he dwells. In the new Jerusalem (Rev 21:2–3) the dwelling of God with his people will be uncompromised by any form of uncleanness (Rev 21:27).

A **5:5–10** The connection of these verses (on personal wrongs) with the first paragraph (on ritual uncleanness) may be that of moving from the outward, visible defects to the inward, more secret faults that mar the purity of the community. Those with evident marks of uncleanness are to be expelled for the duration of their malady. But more insidious are those who have overtly sinned against others in the community, and who think that they may continue to function as though they had done nothing wrong.

5:8 *atonement.* See notes on Ex 25:17; Lev 17:11; Ro 3:25.

5:11–31 Again, the connection with the preceding two paragraphs seems to be a movement from the more open, obvious sins to the more personal, hidden ones. Issues of purity begin with physical marks (vv. 1–4), are expanded to interpersonal relationships (vv. 5–10), and then intrude into the most intimate of relationships—the purity of a man and woman in their marriage bed (cf. Ex 20:14 and note). A test for marital fidelity is far more difficult to prove than a test for a skin disorder; hence, the larger part of the chapter is given to this most sensitive of issues.

5:14 *feelings of jealousy.* These may have been provoked on the basis of good cause, and the issue must be faced. The concern is not just for the bruised feelings of the husband but is ultimately based on the reality of God's dwelling among his people (v. 3). Yet the chapter is designed to prevent unfounded charges of unfaithfulness. This text was not to be used by a capricious, petty or malevolent husband to badger an innocent woman. *impure.* The subject of the chapter is consistent; the purity of the camp where God dwells (v. 3) is the burden of the passage.

5:15–28 The actions presented here seem severe and harsh. But the consequences would have been worse for a woman charged with adultery by an angry husband if there was no provision for her guilt or innocence to be demonstrated. That she was taken to the priest (v. 15) is finally an act of mercy. The gravity of the ritual for a suspected unfaithful wife shows that the law regards marital infidelity most seriously. This was not just a concern of a jealous husband. The entire community was affected by this breach of faith; hence, the judgment was in the context of the community.

5:15,18 *reminder-offering.* A grain offering apparently designed to stimulate reflection on sin and guilt.

half. He must not pour oil on it or put incense on it, because it is a grain offering for jealousy, [u] a reminder-offering [v] to draw attention to wrongdoing.

16 " 'The priest shall bring her and have her stand before the Lord. 17 Then he shall take some holy water in a clay jar and put some dust from the tabernacle floor into the water. 18 After the priest has had the woman stand before the Lord, he shall loosen her hair [w] and place in her hands the reminder-offering, the grain offering for jealousy, [x] while he himself holds the bitter water that brings a curse. [y] 19 Then the priest shall put the woman under oath and say to her, "If no other man has had sexual relations with you and you have not gone astray [z] and become impure while married to your husband, may this bitter water that brings a curse [a] not harm you. 20 But if you have gone astray [b] while married to your husband and you have made yourself impure by having sexual relations with a man other than your husband"— 21 here the priest is to put the woman under this curse [c]— "may the Lord cause you to become a curse [a] among your people when he makes your womb miscarry and your abdomen swell. 22 May this water [d] that brings a curse [e] enter your body so that your abdomen swells or your womb miscarries."

" 'Then the woman is to say, "Amen. So be it. [f] "

23 " 'The priest is to write these curses on a scroll [g] and then wash them off into the bitter water. 24 He shall make the woman drink the bitter water that brings a curse, and this water that brings a curse and causes bitter suffering will enter her. 25 The priest is to take from her hands the grain offering for jealousy, wave it before the Lord [h] and bring it to the altar. 26 The priest is then to take a handful of the grain offering as a memorial [b] offering [i] and burn it on the altar; after that, he is to have the woman drink the water. 27 If she has made herself impure and been unfaithful to her husband, this will be the result: When she is made to drink the water that brings a curse and causes bitter suffering, it will enter her, her abdomen will swell and her womb will miscarry, and she will become a curse. [j] 28 If, however, the woman has not made herself impure, but is clean, she will be cleared of guilt and will be able to have children.

29 " 'This, then, is the law of jealousy when a woman goes astray [k] and makes herself impure while married to her husband, 30 or when feelings of jealousy [l] come over a man because he suspects his wife. The priest is to have her stand before the Lord and is to apply this entire law to her. 31 The husband will be innocent of any wrongdoing, but the woman will bear the consequences [m] of her sin.' "

THE NAZIRITE

6 The Lord said to Moses, 2 "Speak to the Israelites and say to them: 'If a man or woman wants to make a special vow [n], a vow of dedication [o] to the Lord as a Nazirite, [p] 3 they must abstain from wine [q] and other fermented drink and must not drink vinegar [r] made from wine or other fermented drink. They must not drink grape juice or eat grapes [s] or raisins. 4 As long as they remain under their Nazirite vow, they must not eat anything that comes from the grapevine, not even the seeds or skins.

5 " 'During the entire period of the Nazirite's vow, no razor [t] may be used on their head. [u]

---

a 21 That is, may he cause your name to be used in cursing (see Jer. 29:22); or, may others see that you are cursed; similarly in verse 27.   b 26 Or *representative*

5:15 [u] ver 18,25
[v] Eze 21:23; 29:16
5:18 [w] S Lev 10:6;
1Co 11:6 [x] ver 15
[y] ver 19
5:19 [z] ver 12,29
[a] ver 18
5:20 [b] ver 12
5:21 [c] Jos 6:26;
1Sa 14:24; Ne 10:29
5:22 [d] Ps 109:18
[e] ver 18 [f] Dt 27:15
5:23 [g] Jer 45:1
5:25 [h] Lev 8:27
5:26 [i] S Lev 2:2
5:27 [j] Isa 43:28;
65:15; Jer 26:6; 29:18;
42:18; 44:12,22;
Zec 8:13
5:29 [k] S ver 19
5:30 [l] S ver 14
5:31 [m] S Lev 5:1
6:2 [n] ver 5;
S Ge 28:20; Ac 21:23
[o] ver 6 [p] Jdg 13:5;
16:17
6:3 [q] S Lev 10:9;
S Lk 1:15 [r] Ru 2:14;
Ps 69:21; Pr 10:26
[s] S Lev 25:5
6:5 [t] Ps 52:2; 57:4;
59:7; Isa 7:20; Eze 5:1
[u] 1Sa 1:11

5:17 *holy water.* Pure water perhaps taken from the bronze basin (Ex 38:8) and placed in a consecrated vessel and dedicated to God's service. This rendered it ritually clean for use in this ceremony.

5:18 *loosen her hair.* A sign of openness; for the guilty, an expectation of judgment and mourning. *bitter water that brings a curse.* Or "curse-bringing water of bitterness." It is not just that the water was bitter tasting but that the water had the potential of bringing with it a bitter curse. The Lord's role in the proceedings (vv. 16,21,25) is emphasized repeatedly to show that this potion was neither simply a tool of magic nor merely a psychological device to determine stress. The verdict with respect to the woman was precipitated by her physiological and psychological responses to the bitter water, but the judgment was from the Lord.

5:21 *your womb miscarry and your abdomen swell.* Speaks of the loss of the capacity for childbearing (and, if pregnant, the miscarriage of the child). This is demonstrated by the determination of the fate of a woman wrongly charged (v. 28). For a woman in the ancient Near East to be denied the ability to bear children was a personal loss of inestimable proportions. Since it was in the bearing of children that a woman's worth was realized in the ancient world, this was a grievous punishment indeed.

A 6:2 *man or woman.* See ch. 30 for the differences between the vows of men and women. *vow … Nazirite.* Involved separation or consecration for a specific period of special devotion to God—on occasion even for life (see notes on Jdg 13:5; 1Sa 1:11). Attention is usually given to the prohibitions for the Nazirite; more important to the Lord is the positive separation (see v. 8). This was not just a vow of personal self-discipline; it was an act of total devotion to the Lord.

6:4 *anything that comes from the grapevine.* Not only was the fermented beverage forbidden, but even the seed and skin of the grape. During the period of a Nazirite's vow, three areas of his (or her) life were governed: (1) diet, (2) appearance and (3) associations. Every Israelite was regulated in these areas, but for the Nazirite each regulation was heightened.

6:5 *no razor.* See Jdg 13:5 and note. The unusually long hair of a Nazirite would become a physical mark of his (or her) vow of special devotion to the Lord. Cf. Lev 21:5. *They must be holy.* See note on Ex 3:5.

6:6 ʸS Lev 21:1-3;
Nu 19:11-22
6:7 ʷNu 9:6
6:9 ˣ ver 18
ʸS Lev 14:9
6:10 ᶻS Lev 14:10
ᵃS Lev 5:7 ᵇLev 14:11
6:11 ᶜS Lev 30:10
ᵈS Ge 8:20
ᵉS Ex 29:36
6:12 ᶠS Lev 12:6
ᵍS Lev 5:15
6:13 ʰAc 21:26
ⁱLev 14:11
6:14 ʲS Ex 12:5
ᵏ ver 11; Lev 4:3; 14:10
ˡS Lev 5:15 ᵐLev 3:1
6:15 ⁿLev 2:1;
S 6:14 ᵒS Ge 35:14
ᵖS Ex 29:2
6:16 �q Lev 1:3
ʳ ver 10 ˢ ver 11
6:17 ᵗLev 3:1
ᵘS Ex 29:41
ᵛLev 23:13
6:18 ʷ ver 9;
Ac 21:24
6:19 ˣLev 7:12
6:20 ʸLev 7:30
ᶻS Lev 27:9
ᵃS Lev 7:34 ᵇEcc 9:7
6:21 ᶜ ver 13 ᵈ ver 2
6:23 ᵉDt 21:5;
1Ch 23:13
6:24 ᶠS Ge 28:3;
Dt 28:3-6; Ps 28:9;
128:5 ᵍ1Sa 2:9;
Ps 17:8
6:25 ʰ Job 29:24;
Ps 4:6; 31:16; 80:3;
119:135 ⁱGe 43:29;
Ps 25:16; 86:16;
119:29

They must be holy until the period of their dedication to the LORD is over; they must let their hair grow long.

6 " 'Throughout the period of their dedication to the LORD, the Nazirite must not go near a dead body. ᵛ ⁷Even if their own father or mother or brother or sister dies, they must not make themselves ceremonially unclean ʷ on account of them, because the symbol of their dedication to God is on their head. ⁸Throughout the period of their dedication, they are consecrated to the LORD.

9 " 'If someone dies suddenly in the Nazirite's presence, thus defiling the hair that symbolizes their dedication, ˣ they must shave their head on the seventh day—the day of their cleansing. ʸ ¹⁰Then on the eighth day ᶻ they must bring two doves or two young pigeons ᵃ to the priest at the entrance to the tent of meeting. ᵇ ¹¹The priest is to offer one as a sin offering ᵃ ᶜ and the other as a burnt offering ᵈ to make atonement ᵉ for the Nazirite because they sinned by being in the presence of the dead body. That same day they are to consecrate their head again. ¹²They must rededicate themselves to the LORD for the same period of dedication and must bring a year-old male lamb ᶠ as a guilt offering. ᵍ The previous days do not count, because they became defiled during their period of dedication.

13 " 'Now this is the law for the Nazirite when the period of their dedication is over. ʰ The Nazirite is to be brought to the entrance to the tent of meeting. ⁱ ¹⁴There they are to present their offerings to the LORD: a year-old male lamb without defect ʲ for a burnt offering, a year-old ewe lamb without defect for a sin offering, ᵏ a ram ˡ without defect for a fellowship offering, ᵐ ¹⁵together with their grain offerings ⁿ and drink offerings, ᵒ and a basket of bread made with the finest flour and without yeast—thick loaves with olive oil mixed in, and thin loaves brushed with olive oil. ᵖ

16 " 'The priest is to present the Nazirite q before the LORD ʳ and make the sin offering and the burnt offering. ˢ ¹⁷He is to present the basket of unleavened bread and is to sacrifice the ram as a fellowship offering ᵗ to the LORD, together with its grain offering ᵘ and drink offering. ᵛ

18 " 'Then at the entrance to the tent of meeting, the Nazirite must shave off the hair that symbolizes their dedication. ʷ They are to take the hair and put it in the fire that is under the sacrifice of the fellowship offering.

19 " 'After the Nazirite has shaved off the hair that symbolizes their dedication, the priest is to place in their hands a boiled shoulder of the ram, and one thick loaf and one thin loaf from the basket, both made without yeast. ˣ ²⁰The priest shall then wave these before the LORD as a wave offering; ʸ they are holy ᶻ and belong to the priest, together with the breast that was waved and the thigh that was presented. ᵃ After that, the Nazirite may drink wine. ᵇ

21 " 'This is the law of the Nazirite ᶜ who vows offerings to the LORD in accordance with their dedication, in addition to whatever else they can afford. They must fulfill the vows ᵈ they have made, according to the law of the Nazirite.' "

THE PRIESTLY BLESSING

22The LORD said to Moses, 23"Tell Aaron and his sons, 'This is how you are to bless ᵉ the Israelites. Say to them:

24 " ' "The LORD bless you ᶠ
         and keep you; ᵍ
25 the LORD make his face shine on you ʰ
         and be gracious to you; ⁱ

ᵃ 11 Or *purification offering*; also in verses 14 and 16

6:6 *dead body.* See note on 5:2. For the Nazirite, the prohibition on contact with dead bodies extended even to the deceased within his (or her) own family (v. 7; contrast Lev 21:1-3).
6:9–12 The provisions of the Nazirite vow concerned areas where he (or she) was able to make conscious decisions. This section deals with the unexpected and the unplanned events of daily living.
6:13–20 The offerings of the Nazirite at the completion of the period of the vow were extensive, expensive and expressive of the spirit of total commitment to the Lord during this time of special devotion. In addition to these several offerings, the Nazirite burned his (or her) hair (the sign of the vow).

6:21 A summary of vv. 1–20.
6:24–26 The Aaronic benediction. The threefold repetition of the divine name Yahweh ("the LORD") is for emphasis and gives force to the expression in v. 27: "So they will put my name on the Israelites." Each verse conveys two elements of benediction, and the verses are progressively longer (in the Hebrew text, the first verse has three words, the second has five and the third has seven). This benediction is echoed in Ps 67:1 (see note there). In 1979 a condensed version of these verses was found in a burial cave in Jerusalem. The words were inscribed in Hebrew on two silver amulets dating to c. 600 B.C.
6:25 *make his face shine on you.* In acceptance and favor.

26the LORD turn his face[j] toward you
  and give you peace.[k]' "

27"So they will put my name[l] on the Israelites, and I will bless them."

OFFERINGS AT THE DEDICATION OF THE TABERNACLE

When Moses finished setting up the tabernacle,[m] he anointed[n] and consecrated it and all its furnishings.[o] He also anointed and consecrated the altar and all its utensils.[p] 2Then the leaders of Israel,[q] the heads of families who were the tribal leaders in charge of those who were counted,[r] made offerings. 3They brought as their gifts before the LORD six covered carts[s] and twelve oxen—an ox from each leader and a cart from every two. These they presented before the tabernacle.

4The LORD said to Moses, 5"Accept these from them, that they may be used in the work at the tent of meeting. Give them to the Levites as each man's work requires."

6So Moses took the carts and oxen and gave them to the Levites. 7He gave two carts and four oxen to the Gershonites,[t] as their work required, 8and he gave four carts and eight oxen to the Merarites,[u] as their work required. They were all under the direction of Ithamar son of Aaron, the priest. 9But Moses did not give any to the Kohathites,[v] because they were to carry on their shoulders[w] the holy things, for which they were responsible.

10When the altar was anointed,[x] the leaders brought their offerings for its dedication[y] and presented them before the altar. 11For the LORD had said to Moses, "Each day one leader is to bring his offering for the dedication of the altar."

12The one who brought his offering on the first day was Nahshon[z] son of Amminadab of the tribe of Judah.

13His offering was one silver plate weighing a hundred and thirty shekels[a] and one silver sprinkling bowl[a] weighing seventy shekels,[b] both according to the sanctuary shekel,[c] each filled with the finest flour mixed with olive oil as a grain offering;[d] 14one gold dish[e] weighing ten shekels,[c] [f] filled with incense;[g] 15one young bull,[h] one ram and one male lamb a year old for a burnt offering;[i] 16one male goat for a sin offering;[d] [j] 17and two oxen, five rams, five male goats and five male lambs a year old to be sacrificed as a fellowship offering.[k] This was the offering of Nahshon son of Amminadab.[l]

18On the second day Nethanel son of Zuar,[m] the leader of Issachar, brought his offering. 19The offering he brought was one silver plate weighing a hundred and thirty shekels and one silver sprinkling bowl weighing seventy shekels, both according to the sanctuary shekel, each filled with the finest flour mixed with olive oil as a grain offering; 20one gold dish[n] weighing ten shekels, filled with incense; 21one young bull, one ram and one male lamb a year old for a burnt offering; 22one male goat for a sin offering; 23and two oxen, five rams, five male goats and five male lambs a year old to be sacrificed as a fellowship offering. This was the offering of Nethanel son of Zuar.

24On the third day, Eliab son of Helon,[o] the leader of the people of Zebulun, brought his offering.
25His offering was one silver plate weighing a hundred and thirty shekels and one silver sprinkling bowl weighing seventy shekels, both according to the sanctuary

---

a 13 That is, about 3 1/4 pounds or about 1.5 kilograms; also elsewhere in this chapter   b 13 That is, about 1 3/4 pounds or about 800 grams; also elsewhere in this chapter   c 14 That is, about 4 ounces or about 115 grams; also elsewhere in this chapter   d 16 Or purification offering; also elsewhere in this chapter

6:26 [j] Ps 4:6; 44:3
[k] Ps 4:8; 29:11; 37:11, 37; 127:2; Isa 14:7; Jer 33:6; Jn 14:27
6:27 [l] Dt 28:10; 2Sa 7:23; 2Ch 7:14; Ne 9:10; Jer 25:29; Eze 36:23
7:1 [m] Ex 40:17
[n] S Ex 30:26
[o] S Ex 40:9 [p] ver 84, 88; Ex 40:10; 2Ch 7:9
7:2 [q] Nu 1:5-16
[r] Nu 1:19
7:3 [s] Ge 45:19; 1Sa 6:7-14; 1Ch 13:7
7:7 [t] Nu 4:24-26, 28
7:8 [u] Nu 4:31-33
7:9 [v] Nu 4:4
[w] Nu 4:15
7:10 [x] ver 1; S Ex 29:36 [y] 2Ch 7:9
7:12 [z] S Nu 1:7
7:13 [a] S Ex 27:3
[b] ver 85 [c] S Ex 30:13; Lev 27:3-7 [d] Lev 2:1; Nu 6:15; 15:4
7:14 [e] ver 20; 1Ki 7:50; 2Ki 25:14; 2Ch 4:22; 24:14
[f] ver 86 [g] S Ex 25:6
7:15 [h] Ex 24:5; 29:3; Nu 28:11 [i] Lev 1:3
7:16 [j] Lev 4:3
7:17 [k] Lev 3:1
[l] Nu 1:7
7:18 [m] S Nu 1:8
7:20 [n] S ver 14
7:24 [o] S Nu 1:9

6:26 *peace.* The Hebrew for this word is *shalom,* here seen in its most expressive fullness—not the absence of war, but a positive state of rightness and well-being. Such peace comes only from the Lord (cf. Jn 14:27 and note).

7:1–89 See Ex 40, which describes the setting up of the tabernacle and ends with the report of the cloud covering and the presence of the Lord filling the tabernacle. With much repetition of language, this chapter (the longest in the Pentateuch) records the magnificent (and identical) gifts to the Lord for tabernacle service from the leaders of the 12 tribes. The fact that the record of these gifts follows the text of the Aaronic benediction (6:24–26) seems fitting: In response to God's prom-

ise to bless his people, they bring gifts to him in 12 sequential days of celebrative pageantry.

7:12–78 The leaders of the 12 tribes have already been named in 1:5–15; 2:3–32. The order of the presentation of their offerings to the Lord is the same as the order of march: first, the triad of tribes camped east of the tabernacle (Judah, Issachar and Zebulun: 2:3–9; 7:12,18,24); second, the triad camped to the south (Reuben, Simeon and Gad: 2:10–16; 7:30,36,42); third, the triad to the west (Ephraim, Manasseh and Benjamin: 2:18–24; 7:48,54,60); finally, those to the north (Dan, Asher and Naphtali: 2:25–31; 7:66,72,78). See diagram, p. 195.

7:17,23 *fellowship offering.* See note on Lev 3:1.

7:19 *according to the sanctuary shekel.* See note on Ex 30:13.

7:30 P S Nu 1:5
7:36 q S Nu 1:6
7:42 r S Nu 1:14
7:48 s S Nu 1:10
7:53 t S Nu 1:10
7:54 u S Nu 1:10
7:60 v S Nu 1:11

shekel, each filled with the finest flour mixed with olive oil as a grain offering; ²⁶one gold dish weighing ten shekels, filled with incense; ²⁷one young bull, one ram and one male lamb a year old for a burnt offering; ²⁸one male goat for a sin offering; ²⁹and two oxen, five rams, five male goats and five male lambs a year old to be sacrificed as a fellowship offering. This was the offering of Eliab son of Helon.

³⁰On the fourth day Elizur son of Shedeur,^p the leader of the people of Reuben, brought his offering.

³¹His offering was one silver plate weighing a hundred and thirty shekels and one silver sprinkling bowl weighing seventy shekels, both according to the sanctuary shekel, each filled with the finest flour mixed with olive oil as a grain offering; ³²one gold dish weighing ten shekels, filled with incense; ³³one young bull, one ram and one male lamb a year old for a burnt offering; ³⁴one male goat for a sin offering; ³⁵and two oxen, five rams, five male goats and five male lambs a year old to be sacrificed as a fellowship offering. This was the offering of Elizur son of Shedeur.

³⁶On the fifth day Shelumiel son of Zurishaddai,^q the leader of the people of Simeon, brought his offering.

³⁷His offering was one silver plate weighing a hundred and thirty shekels and one silver sprinkling bowl weighing seventy shekels, both according to the sanctuary shekel, each filled with the finest flour mixed with olive oil as a grain offering; ³⁸one gold dish weighing ten shekels, filled with incense; ³⁹one young bull, one ram and one male lamb a year old for a burnt offering; ⁴⁰one male goat for a sin offering; ⁴¹and two oxen, five rams, five male goats and five male lambs a year old to be sacrificed as a fellowship offering. This was the offering of Shelumiel son of Zurishaddai.

⁴²On the sixth day Eliasaph son of Deuel,^r the leader of the people of Gad, brought his offering.

⁴³His offering was one silver plate weighing a hundred and thirty shekels and one silver sprinkling bowl weighing seventy shekels, both according to the sanctuary shekel, each filled with the finest flour mixed with olive oil as a grain offering; ⁴⁴one gold dish weighing ten shekels, filled with incense; ⁴⁵one young bull, one ram and one male lamb a year old for a burnt offering; ⁴⁶one male goat for a sin offering; ⁴⁷and two oxen, five rams, five male goats and five male lambs a year old to be sacrificed as a fellowship offering. This was the offering of Eliasaph son of Deuel.

⁴⁸On the seventh day Elishama son of Ammihud,^s the leader of the people of Ephraim, brought his offering.

⁴⁹His offering was one silver plate weighing a hundred and thirty shekels and one silver sprinkling bowl weighing seventy shekels, both according to the sanctuary shekel, each filled with the finest flour mixed with olive oil as a grain offering; ⁵⁰one gold dish weighing ten shekels, filled with incense; ⁵¹one young bull, one ram and one male lamb a year old for a burnt offering; ⁵²one male goat for a sin offering; ⁵³and two oxen, five rams, five male goats and five male lambs a year old to be sacrificed as a fellowship offering. This was the offering of Elishama son of Ammihud.^t

⁵⁴On the eighth day Gamaliel son of Pedahzur,^u the leader of the people of Manasseh, brought his offering.

⁵⁵His offering was one silver plate weighing a hundred and thirty shekels and one silver sprinkling bowl weighing seventy shekels, both according to the sanctuary shekel, each filled with the finest flour mixed with olive oil as a grain offering; ⁵⁶one gold dish weighing ten shekels, filled with incense; ⁵⁷one young bull, one ram and one male lamb a year old for a burnt offering; ⁵⁸one male goat for a sin offering; ⁵⁹and two oxen, five rams, five male goats and five male lambs a year old to be sacrificed as a fellowship offering. This was the offering of Gamaliel son of Pedahzur.

⁶⁰On the ninth day Abidan son of Gideoni,^v the leader of the people of Benjamin, brought his offering.

⁶¹His offering was one silver plate weighing a hundred and thirty shekels and one silver sprinkling bowl weighing seventy shekels, both according to the sanctuary shekel, each filled with the finest flour mixed with olive oil as a grain offering; ⁶²one gold dish weighing ten shekels, filled with incense; ⁶³one young bull, one ram and one male lamb a year old for a burnt offering; ⁶⁴one male goat for a sin offering; ⁶⁵and two oxen, five rams, five male goats and five male lambs a year old to be sacrificed as a fellowship offering. This was the offering of Abidan son of Gideoni.

66On the tenth day Ahiezer son of Ammishaddai,[w] the leader of the people of Dan, brought his offering.
67His offering was one silver plate weighing a hundred and thirty shekels and one silver sprinkling bowl weighing seventy shekels, both according to the sanctuary shekel, each filled with the finest flour mixed with olive oil as a grain offering; 68one gold dish weighing ten shekels, filled with incense; 69one young bull, one ram and one male lamb a year old for a burnt offering; 70one male goat for a sin offering; 71and two oxen, five rams, five male goats and five male lambs a year old to be sacrificed as a fellowship offering. This was the offering of Ahiezer son of Ammishaddai.

72On the eleventh day Pagiel son of Okran,[x] the leader of the people of Asher, brought his offering.
73His offering was one silver plate weighing a hundred and thirty shekels and one silver sprinkling bowl weighing seventy shekels, both according to the sanctuary shekel, each filled with the finest flour mixed with olive oil as a grain offering; 74one gold dish weighing ten shekels, filled with incense; 75one young bull, one ram and one male lamb a year old for a burnt offering; 76one male goat for a sin offering; 77and two oxen, five rams, five male goats and five male lambs a year old to be sacrificed as a fellowship offering. This was the offering of Pagiel son of Okran.

78On the twelfth day Ahira son of Enan,[y] the leader of the people of Naphtali, brought his offering.
79His offering was one silver plate weighing a hundred and thirty shekels and one silver sprinkling bowl weighing seventy shekels, both according to the sanctuary shekel, each filled with the finest flour mixed with olive oil as a grain offering; 80one gold dish weighing ten shekels, filled with incense; 81one young bull, one ram and one male lamb a year old for a burnt offering; 82one male goat for a sin offering; 83and two oxen, five rams, five male goats and five male lambs a year old to be sacrificed as a fellowship offering. This was the offering of Ahira son of Enan.

84These were the offerings of the Israelite leaders for the dedication of the altar when it was anointed:[z] twelve silver plates, twelve silver sprinkling bowls[a] and twelve gold dishes.[b] 85Each silver plate weighed a hundred and thirty shekels, and each sprinkling bowl seventy shekels. Altogether, the silver dishes weighed two thousand four hundred shekels,[a] according to the sanctuary shekel.[c] 86The twelve gold dishes filled with incense weighed ten shekels each, according to the sanctuary shekel.[d] Altogether, the gold dishes weighed a hundred and twenty shekels.[b] 87The total number of animals for the burnt offering[e] came to twelve young bulls, twelve rams and twelve male lambs a year old, together with their grain offering.[f] Twelve male goats were used for the sin offering.[g] 88The total number of animals for the sacrifice of the fellowship offering[h] came to twenty-four oxen, sixty rams, sixty male goats and sixty male lambs[i] a year old. These were the offerings for the dedication of the altar after it was anointed.[j]

89When Moses entered the tent of meeting[k] to speak with the Lord,[l] he heard the voice speaking to him from between the two cherubim above the atonement cover[m] on the ark of the covenant law.[n] In this way the Lord spoke to him.

SETTING UP THE LAMPS

8 The Lord said to Moses, 2"Speak to Aaron and say to him, 'When you set up the lamps, see that all seven light up the area in front of the lampstand.[o]'"
3Aaron did so; he set up the lamps so that they faced forward on the lampstand, just as the Lord commanded Moses. 4This is how the lampstand was made: It was made of hammered gold[p]—from its base to its blossoms. The lampstand was made exactly like the pattern[q] the Lord had shown Moses.

THE SETTING APART OF THE LEVITES

5The Lord said to Moses: 6"Take the Levites from among all the Israelites and make

7:66 w S Nu 1:12
7:72 x S Nu 1:13
7:78 y S Nu 1:15
7:84 z ver 1,10
a S Nu 4:14 b ver 14
7:85 c ver 13
7:86 d ver 13
7:87 e ver 15 f ver 13
g ver 16
7:88 h ver 17
i Ge 32:14 j S ver 1,10
7:89 k S Ex 40:2
l S Ex 29:42
m S Ex 16:34; Ps 80:1;
99:1 n Nu 3:31
8:2 o Ex 25:37
8:4 p S Ex 25:18,36
q S Ex 25:9

---

a 85 That is, about 61 pounds or about 28 kilograms   b 86 That is, about 3 pounds or about 1.4 kilograms

---

7:84–88 The totals of the 12 sets of gifts.
7:89 The climax: Communion is established between the Lord and his prophet. The people have an advocate with God. *covenant law.* See note on Ex 25:22.
8:2 *area in front of the lampstand.* The Holy Place in the tabernacle (see Ex 25:37; 26:31–35; 27:21 and notes).

8:5–26 Describes the cleansing of the Levites and may be compared with the account of the ordination of Aaron and his sons to the priesthood (Lev 8). The Levites are helpers to the priests, and the language describing their consecration is somewhat different from that of the priests. The priests were made holy, the Levites clean; the priests were anointed and washed,

8:6 ʳLev 22:2;
Isa 1:16; 52:11
8:7 ˢNu 19:9,17;
31:23 ᵗS Lev 14:9;
Nu 6:9; Dt 21:12
ᵘS Ge 35:2; Lev 14:8
ᵛS Ge 35:2
8:8 ʷLev 2:1;
Nu 15:8-10 ˣLev 4:3
8:9 ʸEx 40:12
ᶻLev 8:3
8:10 ᵃS Lev 3:2;
Ac 6:6
8:11 ᵇS Ex 29:24
8:12 ᶜS Ex 29:10
ᵈLev 4:3; Nu 6:11
ᵉLev 1:3 ᶠS Ex 29:36
8:13 ᵍS Ex 29:24
8:14 ʰS Nu 3:12
8:15 ⁱS Ex 29:24
ʲEx 40:2
8:16 ᵏNu 1:20
ˡS Nu 3:12
8:17 ᵐS Ex 4:23
ⁿS Ex 22:29
ᵒS Ex 13:2
8:18 ᵖS Nu 3:12
8:19 ᵍS Nu 3:9
ʳS Nu 3:7 ˢNu 16:46
8:21 ᵗver 7;
S Ge 35:2 ᵘNu 16:47
ᵛver 12
8:22 ʷver 11
8:24 ˣ1Ch 23:3
ʸS Ex 38:21
8:25 ᶻS Nu 4:3
8:26 ᵃver 11
9:1 ᵇS Ex 40:2
ᶜNu 1:1
9:2 ᵈS Ex 12:11
ᵉver 7
9:3 ᶠS Ex 12:6,42
ᵍEx 12:2-11,43-49;
Lev 23:5-8; Dt 16:1-8

them ceremonially clean. ʳ ⁷To purify them, do this: Sprinkle the water of cleansing ˢ on them; then have them shave their whole bodies ᵗ and wash their clothes. ᵘ And so they will purify themselves. ᵛ ⁸Have them take a young bull with its grain offering of the finest flour mixed with olive oil; ʷ then you are to take a second young bull for a sin offering. ᵃ ˣ ⁹Bring the Levites to the front of the tent of meeting ʸ and assemble the whole Israelite community. ᶻ ¹⁰You are to bring the Levites before the Lᴏʀᴅ, and the Israelites are to lay their hands on them. ᵃ ¹¹Aaron is to present the Levites before the Lᴏʀᴅ as a wave offering ᵇ from the Israelites, so that they may be ready to do the work of the Lᴏʀᴅ.

¹²"Then the Levites are to lay their hands on the heads of the bulls, ᶜ using one for a sin offering ᵈ to the Lᴏʀᴅ and the other for a burnt offering, ᵉ to make atonement ᶠ for the Levites. ¹³Have the Levites stand in front of Aaron and his sons and then present them as a wave offering ᵍ to the Lᴏʀᴅ. ¹⁴In this way you are to set the Levites apart from the other Israelites, and the Levites will be mine. ʰ

¹⁵"After you have purified the Levites and presented them as a wave offering, ⁱ they are to come to do their work at the tent of meeting. ʲ ¹⁶They are the Israelites who are to be given wholly to me. I have taken them as my own in place of the firstborn, ᵏ the first male offspring ˡ from every Israelite woman. ¹⁷Every firstborn male in Israel, whether human or animal, ᵐ is mine. When I struck down all the firstborn in Egypt, I set them apart for myself. ⁿ ᵒ ¹⁸And I have taken the Levites in place of all the firstborn sons in Israel. ᵖ ¹⁹From among all the Israelites, I have given the Levites as gifts to Aaron and his sons ᵍ to do the work at the tent of meeting on behalf of the Israelites ʳ and to make atonement for them ˢ so that no plague will strike the Israelites when they go near the sanctuary."

²⁰Moses, Aaron and the whole Israelite community did with the Levites just as the Lᴏʀᴅ commanded Moses. ²¹The Levites purified themselves and washed their clothes. ᵗ Then Aaron presented them as a wave offering before the Lᴏʀᴅ and made atonement ᵘ for them to purify them. ᵛ ²²After that, the Levites came to do their work ʷ at the tent of meeting under the supervision of Aaron and his sons. They did with the Levites just as the Lᴏʀᴅ commanded Moses.

²³The Lᴏʀᴅ said to Moses, ²⁴"This applies to the Levites: Men twenty-five years old or more ˣ shall come to take part in the work at the tent of meeting, ʸ ²⁵but at the age of fifty, ᶻ they must retire from their regular service and work no longer. ²⁶They may assist their brothers in performing their duties at the tent of meeting, but they themselves must not do the work. ᵃ This, then, is how you are to assign the responsibilities of the Levites."

THE PASSOVER

9 The Lᴏʀᴅ spoke to Moses in the Desert of Sinai in the first month ᵇ of the second year after they came out of Egypt. ᶜ He said, ²"Have the Israelites celebrate the Passover ᵈ at the appointed time. ᵉ ³Celebrate it at the appointed time, at twilight on the fourteenth day of this month, ᶠ in accordance with all its rules and regulations. ᵍ"

ᵃ 8 Or *purification offering*; also in verse 12

---

the Levites sprinkled; the priests were given new garments, while the Levites washed theirs; blood was applied to the priests but was waved over the Levites.

8:7 *shave their whole bodies.* Symbolic of the completeness of their cleansing, as in the case of the ritual cleansing of one cured of skin disease (see Lev 14:8 and note).

8:10 *Israelites are to lay their hands on them.* The Levites were substitutes for the nation; by laying hands on them, the other people of the nation were acknowledging this substitutionary act (see vv. 16–18).

8:16 *to me.* See note on 3:9.

8:19 *I have given the Levites as gifts to Aaron and his sons.* The Levites were given to the Lord for his exclusive use (see v. 14). Now the Lord gives his Levites to the priests as their aides for the work of ministry in the tabernacle worship. *so that no plague will strike the Israelites.* The Levites were a protective hedge for the community against trespassing in the sacred precincts of the tabernacle (see note on 1:53).

C A **8:20** *as the Lᴏʀᴅ commanded Moses.* See vv. 4,22; 1:54; 2:34; 3:16,51; 4:49; 5:4; 9:5,23. The implicit obedience of Moses and the Israelites to God's commands in the areas of ritual and regimen stands in sharp contrast to the people's complaints against the Lord's loving character and to

their breaches of faith that begin in ch. 11.

8:24 *twenty-five years old.* See note on 4:3. The age at which the Levites entered service was reduced to 20 by David (see 1Ch 23:3,24,27 and note on 23:3), as the circumstances of their work had greatly changed by the time of the monarchy (see 1Ch 23:26). It is difficult to imagine a change in circumstances between 4:3 and this verse, however. Therefore the Rabbinical suggestion that these two verses indicate a five-year period of apprenticeship seems reasonable.

8:26 *They may assist.* After a Levite had reached the mandatory retirement age of 50 (see v. 25), he was still free to assist his younger co-workers (perhaps at festivals), but he was no longer to do the difficult work he had done in his prime.

9:1–14 This unit is in four parts: (1) the command to keep the Passover (vv. 1–5); (2) the question concerning those ceremonially unclean (vv. 6–8); (3) the response of the Lord—giving permission for legitimate delay, but judgment for willful neglect (vv. 9–13); (4) the rights of the foreigner at Passover (v. 14). The first Passover was held in Egypt (see Ex 12). The second is here at Sinai a year later. Because of Israel's rebellion and God's judgment on her (ch. 14), Israel would not celebrate the Passover again until she entered the promised land (see Jos 5:10 and note).

⁴So Moses told the Israelites to celebrate the Passover,^h ⁵and they did so in the Desert of Sinaiⁱ at twilight on the fourteenth day of the first month.^j The Israelites did everything just as the LORD commanded Moses.^k

⁶But some of them could not celebrate the Passover on that day because they were ceremonially unclean^l on account of a dead body.^m So they came to Moses and Aaronⁿ that same day ⁷and said to Moses, "We have become unclean because of a dead body, but why should we be kept from presenting the LORD's offering with the other Israelites at the appointed time?^o"

⁸Moses answered them, "Wait until I find out what the LORD commands concerning you."^p

⁹Then the LORD said to Moses, ¹⁰"Tell the Israelites: 'When any of you or your descendants are unclean because of a dead body^q or are away on a journey, they are still to celebrate^r the LORD's Passover, ¹¹but they are to do it on the fourteenth day of the second month^s at twilight. They are to eat the lamb, together with unleavened bread and bitter herbs.^t ¹²They must not leave any of it till morning^u or break any of its bones.^v When they celebrate the Passover, they must follow all the regulations.^w ¹³But if anyone who is ceremonially clean and not on a journey fails to celebrate the Passover, they must be cut off from their people^x for not presenting the LORD's offering at the appointed time. They will bear the consequences of their sin.

¹⁴" 'A foreigner^y residing among you is also to celebrate the LORD's Passover in accordance with its rules and regulations. You must have the same regulations for both the foreigner and the native-born.' "

THE CLOUD ABOVE THE TABERNACLE

¹⁵On the day the tabernacle, the tent of the covenant law,^z was set up,^a the cloud^b covered it. From evening till morning the cloud covered the tabernacle looked like fire.^c ¹⁶That is how it continued to be; the cloud covered it, and at night it looked like fire.^d ¹⁷Whenever the cloud lifted from above the tent, the Israelites set out;^e wherever the cloud settled, the Israelites encamped.^f ¹⁸At the LORD's command the Israelites set out, and at his command they encamped. As long as the cloud stayed over the tabernacle, they remained^g in camp. ¹⁹When the cloud remained over the tabernacle a long time, the Israelites obeyed the LORD's order^h and did not set out.ⁱ ²⁰Sometimes the cloud was over the tabernacle only a few days; at the LORD's command they would encamp, and then at his command they would set out. ²¹Sometimes the cloud stayed only from evening till morning, and when it lifted in the morning, they set out. Whether by day or by night, whenever the cloud lifted, they set out. ²²Whether the cloud stayed over the tabernacle for two days or a month or a year, the Israelites would remain in camp and not set out; but when it lifted, they would set out. ²³At the LORD's command they encamped, and at the LORD's command they set out. They obeyed the LORD's order, in accordance with his command through Moses.

9:4 ^hver 2;
S Ex 12:11
9:5 ⁱver 1 / S Ex 12:6
^kver 3
9:6 ^lS Lev 5:3;
S 13:3 ^mS Lev 21:11
ⁿEx 18:15; Nu 27:2
9:7 ^over 2
9:8 ^pEx 18:15;
Lev 24:12; Nu 15:34;
27:5,21; Ps 85:8
9:10 ^qver 6
^r2Ch 30:2
9:11 ^sS Ex 12:6
^tEx 12:8
9:12 ^uS Ex 12:8
^vS Ex 12:46;
Jn 19:36* ^wver 3
9:13 ^xS Ge 17:14
9:14 ^yS Ex 12:19,43
9:15 ^zS Ex 38:21
^aS Ex 26:30
^bS Ex 33:16 ^cEx 13:21
9:16 ^dS Ex 40:38
9:17 ^ever 21
^f1Co 10:1
9:18 ^gEx 40:37
9:19 ^hS Lev 8:35
ⁱEx 40:37

9:1 *first month of the second year.* The events of this chapter preceded the beginning of the census in ch. 1 (see 1:1 and note).

9:3 *twilight.* Traditional Jewish practice regards this period as the end of one day and the beginning of the next.

9:7 *why should we be kept from presenting the LORD's offering …?* Those with ceremonial uncleanness had a keen desire to worship the Lord "in the Spirit and in truth" (Jn 4:24; see note there).

9:10 *they are still to celebrate.* God's gracious provision for these people was an alternative day one month later (v. 11) so that they would not be excluded totally from the Passover celebration. The Lord thus demonstrates the reality of the distance that uncleanness brings between a believer and his or her participation in the worship of the community, but he also provides a merciful alternative.

9:12 *not … break any of its bones.* When Jesus ("our Passover lamb," 1Co 5:7; cf. Jn 1:29) was crucified, it was reported that none of his bones was broken, in fulfillment of Scripture (Jn 19:36). See also Ex 12:46; Ps 34:20.

9:13 *fails to celebrate … cut off.* The NT also issues grave warnings concerning the abuse or misuse of the cele-

bration of the Lord's Supper (1Co 11:28–30). See note on Ex 12:15.

9:14 *foreigner.* Must first be circumcised before participating in the Passover celebration (see Ex 12:48 and note).

9:15 *covenant law.* See note on Ex 25:22. *cloud covered it.* See notes on Ex 13:21; 40:34. The cloud was the visible symbol of the Lord's presence hovering above the tabernacle. That this was no ordinary cloud is attested not only by its spontaneous appearance at the completion of the setting up of the tabernacle, but also by the fact that at night it had the appearance of fire. The Lord also directed the movements of his people by means of the cloud (vv. 17–18).

9:18 *At the LORD's command.* The lifting and settling of the cloud are identified with the Lord's command.

9:23 *obeyed the LORD's order.* The repetitious nature of vv. 15–23 enhances the expectation of continued complete obedience to the Lord's direction of Israel's movements through the wilderness. The role of Moses is mentioned for balance: Moses was the Lord's agent, who interpreted the movement of the cloud as signaling the movement of the people. The tragedy of their subsequent disobedience (ch. 11) is heightened by this paragraph on their obedience.

10:2 *i* ver 8, 9;
Nu 31:6; Ne 12:35;
Ps 47:5; 98:6; 150:3
k Ne 4:18; Jer 4:5,19;
6:1; Hos 5:8; 8:1;
Joel 2:1,15; Am 3:6
l Nu 33:3
10:4 *m* S Ex 18:21
10:5 *n* ver 14
10:6 *o* ver 18
10:7 *p* Jer 4:5; 6:1;
Eze 33:3; Joel 2:1
q 1Co 14:8
10:8 *r* S Ge 9:12;
Nu 15:14; 35:29
10:9 *s* Ex 3:9;
Jdg 2:18; 6:9;
1Sa 10:18; 2Ki 13:4;
Ps 106:42
t S Lev 23:24
u S Ge 8:1
v 2Ch 13:12; Ps 106:4
10:10 *w* Nu 28:11;
1Sa 20:5,24;
2Ki 4:23; 2Ch 8:13;
Ps 81:3; Isa 1:13;
Eze 45:17; 46:6;
Am 8:5 *x* S Lev 23:24
y Lev 1:3 *z* Lev 3:1;
Nu 6:14 *a* Lev 11:44
10:11 *b* Ex 40:17
c Nu 9:17 *d* S Ex 38:21
10:12 *e* S Ge 14:6;
Dt 1:1; 33:2
10:13 *f* Dt 1:6
10:14 *g* S Nu 1:52;
S 2:3-9 *h* Nu 1:7
10:15 *i* S Lev 24:11
j S Nu 1:8
10:16 *k* S Nu 2:7
l S Nu 1:9
10:17 *m* ver 21;
Nu 4:21-32
10:18 *n* Nu 2:16
o Nu 2:10-16
p S Nu 1:5
10:19 *q* Nu 1:6
10:20 *r* S Nu 1:14
10:21 *s* S Nu 2:17
t Nu 4:20 *u* S ver 17
10:22 *v* Nu 2:24
w S Nu 1:10
10:23 *x* S Nu 1:10
10:24 *y* Nu 1:11
10:25 *z* S Nu 2:31
a S Nu 1:12
10:26 *b* S Nu 1:13
10:27 *c* S Nu 1:15
10:29 *d* Jdg 4:11
e S Ex 2:18 *f* S Ex 3:1
g S Ge 12:7; S 15:14

THE SILVER TRUMPETS

10 The Lord said to Moses: [2]"Make two trumpets *j* of hammered silver, and use them for calling the community *k* together and for having the camps set out. *l* [3]When both are sounded, the whole community is to assemble before you at the entrance to the tent of meeting. [4]If only one is sounded, the leaders *m*—the heads of the clans of Israel—are to assemble before you. [5]When a trumpet blast is sounded, the tribes camping on the east are to set out. *n* [6]At the sounding of a second blast, the camps on the south are to set out. *o* The blast will be the signal for setting out. [7]To gather the assembly, blow the trumpets, *p* but not with the signal for setting out. *q*

[8]"The sons of Aaron, the priests, are to blow the trumpets. This is to be a lasting ordinance for you and the generations to come. *r* [9]When you go into battle in your own land against an enemy who is oppressing you, *s* sound a blast on the trumpets. *t* Then you will be remembered *u* by the Lord your God and rescued from your enemies. *v* [10]Also at your times of rejoicing—your appointed festivals and New Moon feasts *w*—you are to sound the trumpets *x* over your burnt offerings *y* and fellowship offerings, *z* and they will be a memorial for you before your God. I am the Lord your God. *a*"

THE ISRAELITES LEAVE SINAI

[11]On the twentieth day of the second month of the second year, *b* the cloud lifted *c* from above the tabernacle of the covenant law. *d* [12]Then the Israelites set out from the Desert of Sinai and traveled from place to place until the cloud came to rest in the Desert of Paran. *e* [13]They set out, this first time, at the Lord's command through Moses. *f*

[14]The divisions of the camp of Judah went first, under their standard. *g* Nahshon son of Amminadab *h* was in command. [15]Nethanel son of Zuar was over the division of the tribe *i* of Issachar, *j* [16]and Eliab son of Helon *k* was over the division of the tribe of Zebulun. *l* [17]Then the tabernacle was taken down, and the Gershonites and Merarites, who carried it, set out. *m*

[18]The divisions of the camp of Reuben *n* went next, under their standard. *o* Elizur son of Shedeur *p* was in command. [19]Shelumiel son of Zurishaddai was over the division of the tribe of Simeon, *q* [20]and Eliasaph son of Deuel was over the division of the tribe of Gad. *r* [21]Then the Kohathites *s* set out, carrying the holy things. *t* The tabernacle was to be set up before they arrived. *u*

[22]The divisions of the camp of Ephraim *v* went next, under their standard. Elishama son of Ammihud *w* was in command. [23]Gamaliel son of Pedahzur was over the division of the tribe of Manasseh, *x* [24]and Abidan son of Gideoni was over the division of the tribe of Benjamin. *y*

[25]Finally, as the rear guard *z* for all the units, the divisions of the camp of Dan set out under their standard. Ahiezer son of Ammishaddai *a* was in command. [26]Pagiel son of Okran was over the division of the tribe of Asher, *b* [27]and Ahira son of Enan was over the division of the tribe of Naphtali. *c* [28]This was the order of march for the Israelite divisions as they set out.

[29]Now Moses said to Hobab *d* son of Reuel *e* the Midianite, Moses' father-in-law, *f* "We are setting out for the place about which the Lord said, 'I will give it to you.' *g* Come with us and we will treat you well, for the Lord has promised good things to Israel."

10:2 *trumpets.* Long, straight, slender metal tubes with flared ends. They were blown for order and discipline.
10:3 *sounded.* Not only for assembling but also for marching (vv. 5–6), battle (v. 9) and festivals (v. 10). Since different signals were used (v. 7), a guild of priestly musicians was developed (v. 8). See Jos 6:4 (see also note there) for the use of seven trumpets of rams' horns (Hebrew *shophar*) in the battle of Jericho.
10:10 *at your ... appointed festivals ... sound the trumpets.* To prepare the people for communion with God. Later, David expanded the instruments to include the full orchestra in the worship of the Lord (see, e.g., 1Ch 25), but he maintained the playing of the silver trumpets regularly before the ark of the covenant (1Ch 16:6).
10:11—22:1 The sordid account of the Israelites' long trek from Sinai to Kadesh (13:26) to the plains of Moab (see Introduction: Structure and Outline).
10:11–28 The structure of this section is: (1) v. 11, time frame; (2) vv. 12–13, introductory summary of setting out; (3) vv. 14–17, setting out of the tribes led by Judah (see 2:3–9); (4) vv. 18–21, setting out of the tribes led by Reuben (see 2:10–16);

(5) vv. 22–24, setting out of the tribes led by Ephraim (see 2:18–24); (6) vv. 25–27, setting out of the tribes led by Dan (see 2:25–31); (7) v. 28, concluding summary of the line of march.
10:11 *twentieth day of the second month.* After 11 months in the region of Mount Sinai, the people set out for the promised land, led by the cloud. Israel leaves on a journey that in a few months should have led to the conquest of Canaan. *covenant law.* See note on Ex 25:22.
10:14–27 The names of the leaders of the 12 tribes are given for the fourth time in the book (see 1:5–15; 2:3–31; 7:12–83). The order of the line of march is essentially the same as that in ch. 2. The new details are that the Gershonites and Merarites, who carry the tabernacle, follow the triad of the Judah tribes (v. 17), and the Kohathites, who carry the holy things, follow the triad of the Reuben tribes (v. 21) (see diagram, p. 195).
10:14 *standard.* As in 2:3,10,18,25, each of the four triads of tribes had a standard or banner for rallying and organization.
10:29 *Hobab son of Reuel.* Thus Hobab was Moses' brother-in-law. *Reuel.* Jethro (see Ex 2:18; 3:1).

³⁰He answered, "No, I will not go; ^h I am going back to my own land and my own people. ⁱ"
³¹But Moses said, "Please do not leave us. You know where we should camp in the wilderness, and you can be our eyes. ^j ³²If you come with us, we will share with you ^k whatever good things the LORD gives us. ^l"

³³So they set out ^m from the mountain of the LORD and traveled for three days. The ark of the covenant of the LORD ⁿ went before them during those three days to find them a place to rest. ^o ³⁴The cloud of the LORD was over them by day when they set out from the camp. ^p

³⁵Whenever the ark set out, Moses said,

"Rise up, ^q LORD!
May your enemies be scattered; ^r
may your foes flee before you. ^s" ^t

³⁶Whenever it came to rest, he said,

"Return, ^u LORD,
to the countless thousands of Israel. ^v"

FIRE FROM THE LORD

11

Now the people complained ^w about their hardships in the hearing of the LORD, ^x and when he heard them his anger was aroused. ^y Then fire from the LORD burned among them ^z and consumed ^a some of the outskirts of the camp. ²When the people cried out to Moses, he prayed ^b to the LORD ^c and the fire died down. ³So that place was called Taberah, ^a ^d because fire from the LORD had burned among them. ^e

QUAIL FROM THE LORD

⁴The rabble with them began to crave other food, ^f and again the Israelites started wailing ^g and said, "If only we had meat to eat! ⁵We remember the fish we ate in Egypt at no cost—also the cucumbers, melons, leeks, onions and garlic. ^h ⁶But now we have lost our appetite; we never see anything but this manna! ⁱ"

⁷The manna was like coriander seed ^j and looked like resin. ^k ⁸The people went around gathering it, ^l and then ground it in a hand mill or crushed it in a mortar. They cooked it in a pot or made it into loaves. And it tasted like something made with olive oil. ⁹When the dew ^m settled on the camp at night, the manna also came down.

¹⁰Moses heard the people of every family wailing ⁿ at the entrance to their tents. The LORD became exceedingly angry, and Moses was troubled. ¹¹He asked the LORD, "Why have you

---

^a 3 *Taberah* means *burning.*

10:30 ^h Mt 21:29
ⁱ S Ex 18:27
10:31 ^j Job 29:15
10:32 ^k S Ex 12:48;
Dt 10:18 / Ps 22:27-
31; 67:5-7
10:33 ^m ver 12;
Dt 1:33 ⁿ Dt 10:8;
31:9; Jos 3:3;
Jdg 20:27; 2Sa 15:24
^o Jer 31:2
10:34 ^p Nu 9:15-23
10:35 ^q 2Ch 6:41;
Ps 17:13; 44:26; 94:2;
132:8 ^r Jdg 5:31;
1Sa 2:1; Ps 68:1; 92:9
^s Dt 5:9; 7:10; 32:41;
Ps 68:2; Isa 17:12-14
^t Isa 59:18
10:36 ^u Isa 52:8;
63:17 ^v Ge 15:5; 26:4;
Dt 1:10; 10:22;
Ne 9:23
11:1 ^w S Ex 14:11;
S 16:7; La 3:39
^x Nu 12:2; Dt 1:34
^y S Ex 4:14
^z S Lev 10:2
^a Nu 21:28; Ps 78:63;
Isa 26:11
11:2 ^b Dt 9:19;
1Sa 2:25; 12:23;
Ps 106:23 ^c S Ge 20:7;
Nu 21:7; Dt 9:20;
Jnh 2:1
11:3 ^d Dt 9:22
^e Nu 16:35; Job 1:16;
Isa 10:17
11:4 ^f S Ex 16:3
^g ver 18
11:5 ^h S Ex 16:3;
Nu 21:5
11:6 ⁱ Ex 16:14
11:7 ^j S Ex 16:31
^k Ge 2:12
11:8 ^l Ex 16:16
11:9 ^m Ex 16:13
11:10 ⁿ ver 4

10:31 *be our eyes.* Jdg 1:16 indicates that Hobab acceded to Moses's request.

10:33 *three days.* Because of the huge numbers of people in the tribes of Israel, and because this was their first organized march, it is not likely that this first journey covered much territory (cf. note on Ge 22:4).

10:35–36 Reinforces the portrayal of Israel as the Lord's army on the march, with the Lord in the vanguard.

10:35 Later used in the opening words of a psalm celebrating God's triumphal march from Sinai to Jerusalem (see Ps 68:1 and note on 68:1–3).

11:1 *people complained.* The first ten chapters of Numbers repeatedly emphasize the complete obedience of Moses and the people to the dictates of the Lord. But only three days into their march, the people reverted to disloyal complaints. They had expressed the same complaints a year earlier, only three days after their deliverance at the waters of the "Red Sea" (Ex 15:22–27), and had subsequently complained about manna (Ex 16) and a lack of water (Ex 17:1–7). *fire from the LORD.* By God's mercy, this purging fire was limited to the outskirts of the camp. The phrase sometimes refers to fire ignited by lightning (as probably in 1Ki 18:38; see note on 18:24).

11:3 *Taberah.* See TNIV text note.

11:4 *rabble.* An apt term for the non-Israelite mixed group of people who followed the Israelites out of Egypt, pointing to a recurring source of complaints and trouble in the camp.

Those who did not know the Lord and his mercies incited those who did know him to rebel against him. *If only we had meat to eat!* As in Ex 16, the people began to complain about their diet, forgetting what God had done for them (see Ps 106:14). Certainly meat was not their common fare when they were slaves in Egypt. Now that they were in a new type of distress, the people romanticized the past and minimized its discomforts.

11:5 *fish … cucumbers … garlic.* Suggestive of the varieties of foods available in Egypt, in contrast to the diet of manna in the desert.

11:7 *manna.* See note on Ex 16:31.

11:10 *The LORD became exceedingly angry.* The rejection of his gracious gift of heavenly food (called "bread from heaven" in Ex 16:4) angered the Lord. God had said that the reception of the manna by the people would be a significant test of their obedience (Ex 16:4). In view of the good things he was to give them (10:32), the people were expected to receive each day's supply of manna as a gracious gift of a merciful God and a promise of abundance to come. In spurning the manna, the people had spurned the Lord. They had failed the test of faith. *Moses was troubled.* The people's reaction to God's provision of manna was troubling to Moses as well. Instead of asking the Lord to understand the substance of their complaint, Moses asked him why he was given such an ungrateful people to lead.

11:11–15 A prayer of distress and complaint, filled with urgency, irony and passion.

11:11 °S Ge 34:30
P S Ex 5:22; S 18:18
11:12 q Isa 40:11;
49:23; 66:11,12
r Nu 14:16 s S Ge 12:7;
Ex 13:5
11:13 t S Ex 12:37;
Jn 6:5-9
11:14 u S Ex 18:18
11:15 v Ex 32:32;
1Ki 19:4; Job 6:9;
7:15-16; 9:21; 10:1;
Isa 38:12; Jnh 4:3
11:16 w S Ex 3:16
x S Ex 18:25
y S Ex 40:2
11:17 z Ex 19:20
a ver 25,29; 1Sa 10:6;
2Ki 2:9,15; 3:12;
Isa 32:15; 40:5; 63:11;
Joel 2:28; Hag 2:5
b S Ex 18:18; Jer 19:1
11:18 c S Ex 19:10
d S Ex 16:7 e ver 5;
Ac 7:39 f Ps 78:20
11:20 g Ps 78:29;
106:14,15
h S Lev 26:43;
Jos 24:27; Jdg 8:23;
1Sa 10:19; Job 31:28;
Isa 59:13; Hos 13:11
i ver 33; Job 20:13,23
11:21 j S Ex 12:37
11:22 k Mt 15:33
11:23 l Isa 50:2;
59:1 m Nu 23:19;
1Sa 15:29; Eze 12:25;
24:14
11:25 n S Ex 19:9;
Nu 12:5 o ver 17
p ver 29; 1Sa 10:6;
19:23 q S Ac 2:17
r ver 26; Nu 24:2;
Jdg 3:10; 1Sa 10:10;
19:20; 2Ch 15:1
11:26 s S ver 25;
1Ch 12:18; Rev 1:10
11:28 t Ex 17:9;
Nu 13:8; 26:65;
Jos 14:10 u Ex 33:11;
Jos 1:1 v Mk 9:38-40
11:29 w 1Sa 10:5;
19:20; 2Ch 24:19;
Jer 7:25; 44:4;
1Co 14:5 x S ver 17
y Nu 27:18
11:31 z S Ex 16:13;
Ps 78:26-28

brought this trouble° on your servant? What have I done to displease you that you put the burden of all these people on me? P [12] Did I conceive all these people? Did I give them birth? Why do you tell me to carry them in my arms, as a nurse carries an infant, q to the land you promised on oath r to their ancestors? s [13] Where can I get meat for all these people? t They keep wailing to me, 'Give us meat to eat!' [14] I cannot carry all these people by myself; the burden is too heavy for me. u [15] If this is how you are going to treat me, please go ahead and kill me v—if I have found favor in your eyes—and do not let me face my own ruin."

[16] The LORD said to Moses: "Bring me seventy of Israel's elders w who are known to you as leaders and officials among the people. x Have them come to the tent of meeting, y that they may stand there with you. [17] I will come down and speak with you z there, and I will take some of the power of the Spirit that is on you and put it on them. a They will share the burden of the people with you so that you will not have to carry it alone. b

[18] "Tell the people: 'Consecrate yourselves c in preparation for tomorrow, when you will eat meat. The LORD heard you when you wailed, d "If only we had meat to eat! We were better off in Egypt!" e Now the LORD will give you meat, f and you will eat it. [19] You will not eat it for just one day, or two days, or five, ten or twenty days, [20] but for a whole month—until it comes out of your nostrils and you loathe it g—because you have rejected the LORD, h who is among you, and have wailed before him, saying, "Why did we ever leave Egypt?" ' " i

[21] But Moses said, "Here I am among six hundred thousand men j on foot, and you say, 'I will give them meat to eat for a whole month!' [22] Would they have enough if flocks and herds were slaughtered for them? Would they have enough if all the fish in the sea were caught for them?" k

[23] The LORD answered Moses, "Is the LORD's arm too short? l Now you will see whether or not what I say will come true for you. m"

[24] So Moses went out and told the people what the LORD had said. He brought together seventy of their elders and had them stand around the tent. [25] Then the LORD came down in the cloud n and spoke with him, o and he took some of the power of the Spirit P that was on him and put it on the seventy elders. q When the Spirit rested on them, they prophesied r—but did not do so again.

[26] However, two men, whose names were Eldad and Medad, had remained in the camp. They were listed among the elders, but did not go out to the tent. Yet the Spirit also rested on them, s and they prophesied in the camp. [27] A young man ran and told Moses, "Eldad and Medad are prophesying in the camp."

[28] Joshua son of Nun, t who had been Moses' aide u since youth, spoke up and said, "Moses, my lord, stop them!" v

[29] But Moses replied, "Are you jealous for my sake? I wish that all the LORD's people were prophets w and that the LORD would put his Spirit x on them!" y [30] Then Moses and the elders of Israel returned to the camp.

[31] Now a wind went out from the LORD and drove quail z in from the sea. It scattered them up to two cubits a deep all around the camp, as far as a day's walk in any direction.

a 31 That is, about 3 feet or about 90 centimeters

11:12 *Did I conceive all these people?* The implication is that the Lord conceived the people of Israel, that he was their nurse and that their promises were his. Moses asks that he be relieved of his mediatorial office, for "the burden is too heavy for me" (v. 14; cf. Elijah, 1Ki 19). Even death, Moses asserts (v. 15), would be preferable to facing the continuing complaints of the people.

11:16–34 The Lord's response to the great distress of his prophet was twofold—mercy and curse: 1. There was mercy to Moses in that his responsibility was now to be shared by 70 leaders (vv. 16–17). 2. There was a curse on the people that was analogous to their complaint: They asked for meat and would now become sick with meat (vv. 18–34; cf. Ps 78:27–31).

11:18 *you will eat meat.* Their distress at the lack of variety in the daily manna had led the people to challenge the Lord's goodness. They had wailed for meat. Now they were going to get their fill of meat, so much that it would make them physically ill (v. 20).

11:20 *you have rejected the LORD.* The principal issue was not meat at all, but a failure to demonstrate proper gratitude to the Lord, who was in their midst and who was their constant source of good.

11:21 *six hundred thousand men on foot.* The numbers are consistent: A marching force of this size suggests a total population of over 2,000,000 (see note on 1:46). Moses' distress at providing meat for this immense number of people (v. 22) is nearly comical—the task is impossible for him.

11:23 *Is the LORD's arm too short?* The human impossibility is an occasion for demonstrating the Lord's power. Cf. Isa 59:1.

11:25 *the Spirit.* God's empowering presence (cf. Jdg 3:10 and note). *they prophesied.* Probably means that they gave ecstatic expression to an intense religious experience (see 1Sa 10:5; 18:10; 19:20,24; 1Ki 18:29 and notes). *but did not do so again.* It seems that the temporary gift of prophecy to the elders was primarily to establish their credentials as Spirit-empowered leaders.

11:29 *Are you jealous for my sake?* Here the true spirit of Moses is demonstrated. Rather than being threatened by the public demonstration of the gifts of the Spirit by Eldad and Medad, Moses desired that all God's people might have the full gifts of the Spirit (cf. Joel 2:28 and note; Php 1:15–18). This verse is a fitting introduction to the inexcusable challenge to Moses' leadership in ch. 12.

11:31–32 Cf. the great provision of Jesus in the feeding of the 5,000 (Jn 6:5–13) and the 4,000 (Mt 15:29–39). In

[32]All that day and night and all the next day the people went out and gathered quail. No one gathered less than ten homers. [a] Then they spread them out all around the camp. [33]But while the meat was still between their teeth [a] and before it could be consumed, the anger [b] of the LORD burned against the people, and he struck them with a severe plague. [c] [34]Therefore the place was named Kibroth Hattaavah, [b] [d] because there they buried the people who had craved other food.

[35]From Kibroth Hattaavah the people traveled to Hazeroth [e] and stayed there.

MIRIAM AND AARON OPPOSE MOSES

12 Miriam [f] and Aaron began to talk against Moses because of his Cushite wife, [g] for he had married a Cushite. [2]"Has the LORD spoken only through Moses?" they asked. "Hasn't he also spoken through us?" [h] And the LORD heard this. [i]

[3](Now Moses was a very humble man, [j] more humble than anyone else on the face of the earth.)

[4]At once the LORD said to Moses, Aaron and Miriam, "Come out to the tent of meeting, all three of you." So the three of them went out. [5]Then the LORD came down in a pillar of cloud; [k] he stood at the entrance to the tent and summoned Aaron and Miriam. When the two of them stepped forward, [6]he said, "Listen to my words:

"When there are prophets of the LORD among you,
    I reveal [l] myself to them in visions, [m]
    I speak to them in dreams. [n]
[7]But this is not true of my servant Moses; [o]
    he is faithful in all my house. [p]
[8]With him I speak face to face,
    clearly and not in riddles; [q]
    he sees the form of the LORD. [r]
Why then were you not afraid
    to speak against my servant Moses?" [s]

[9]The anger of the LORD burned against them, [t] and he left them. [u]

[10]When the cloud lifted from above the tent, [v] Miriam's skin was leprous [c]—it became as white as snow. [w] Aaron turned toward her and saw that she had a defiling skin disease, [x] [11]and he said to Moses, "Please, my lord, I ask you not to hold against us the sin we have so foolishly committed. [y] [12]Do not let her be like a stillborn infant coming from its mother's womb with its flesh half eaten away."

[13]So Moses cried out to the LORD, "Please, God, heal her! [z]"

---

[a] 32 That is, possibly about 1 3/4 tons or about 1.6 metric tons   [b] 34 *Kibroth Hattaavah* means *graves of craving.*   [c] 10 The Hebrew for *leprous* was used for various diseases affecting the skin.

11:33 [a] Ps 78:30
[b] Nu 14:18; Dt 9:7;
Jdg 2:12; 2Ki 22:17;
Ps 106:29; Jer 44:3;
Eze 8:17 [c] S ver 18-
20; Ps 106:15;
Isa 10:16
11:34 [d] Nu 33:16;
Dt 9:22
11:35 [e] Nu 33:17
12:1 [f] S Ex 15:20
[g] S Ex 2:21
12:2 [h] Nu 16:3
[i] S Nu 11:1
12:3 [j] Mt 11:29
12:5 [k] S Ex 13:21;
S Nu 11:25
12:6 [l] 1Sa 3:7,21
[m] S Ge 15:1
[n] S Ge 20:3;
S Mt 27:19; Heb 1:1
12:7 [o] Dt 34:5;
Jos 1:1-2; Ps 105:26
[p] Heb 3:2,5
12:8 [q] Jdg 14:12;
1Ki 10:1; Ps 49:4;
Pr 1:6; Da 5:12
[r] Ex 20:4; Job 19:26;
Ps 17:15; 140:13;
Isa 6:1 [s] Ex 24:2
12:9 [t] S Ex 4:14
[u] S Ge 17:22
12:10 [v] Ex 40:2
[w] S Ex 4:6; Dt 24:9
[x] S Lev 13:11; 2Ki 5:1,
27; 2Ch 16:12; 21:12-
15; 26:19
12:11 [y] 2Sa 19:19;
24:10
12:13 [z] Ex 15:26;
Ps 6:2; 147:3; Isa 1:6;
30:26; 53:5; Jer 17:14;
Hos 6:1

---

those cases the feeding was a demonstration of God's grace; in this instance it was accompanied by God's wrath.

11:34 *Kibroth Hattaavah.* See TNIV text note. These graves marked the death camp of those who had turned against the food of the Lord's mercy.

12:1 *his Cushite wife.* Ham had a son named Cush. His descendants, as named in Ge 10:7, were all located in Arabia (see note on Ge 10:7). Nimrod, a descendant of perhaps another Cush, is identified as a great empire builder in lower Mesopotamia (Ge 10:8–12; see note on 10:8). Elsewhere "Cush" also frequently refers to a region lying just south of Egypt (ancient Nubia, modern Sudan; see note on Ge 10:6). Because of this diversity, we cannot know with any certainty the ethnic identity of Moses' wife here referred to. Perhaps Hab 3:7 provides a better clue. There "the tents of Cushan" appear to be identified with "the dwellings of Midian." It is possible that one from "the tents of Cushan" could be referred to as "a Cushite." In that case, the wife of Moses in question is Zipporah, a daughter of the Midianite priest Jethro (Ex 3:1; see note there). The attack on Moses because of his Cushite wife was a pretext; its focus was the prophetic gift of Moses and his special relationship with the Lord (v. 2).

12:2 *Hasn't he also spoken through us?* Of course he had. Mic 6:4 speaks of Moses, Aaron and Miriam as God's gracious provision for Israel. The prophetic gifting of the 70 elders (11:24–30) seems to have been the immediate provocation for the attack of Miriam and Aaron on their brother.

12:3 Perhaps a later addition to the text, alerting the reader to the great unfairness of the charge of arrogance against Moses.

A **12:5** *came down.* Often used of divine manifestations. In 11:25 the Lord came down in grace; here and in Ge 11:5 he came down in judgment. In a sense every theophany (appearance of God) is a picture and promise of the grand theophany, the incarnation of Jesus, both in grace and in judgment.

C **12:6–8** The poetic cast of these words adds a sense of solemnity to them. The point of the poem is clear: All true prophetic vision is from the Lord, but in the case of Moses his position and faithfulness enhance his special relationship with the Lord.

12:7 *my servant.* See notes on Ex 14:31; Ps 18 title; Isa 41:8–9; 42:1. *my house.* The household of God's people Israel (see notes on Heb 3:5–6).

C **12:8** *clearly and not in riddles.* God's revelation does not come with equal clarity to his servants. There may be oracles of the Lord that a prophet might not fully understand at the time; to him they may be riddles and mysteries (cf. 1Pe 1:10–11). But to Moses God spoke with special clarity, as though "face to face" (see also Dt 34:10 and note).

12:10 *leprous.* See TNIV text note. Miriam, the principal offender against her brother Moses, has become an outcast, as she now suffers from a skin disease that would exclude her from the community of Israel (see 5:1–4).

12:14 *a* Dt 25:9;
Job 17:6; 30:9-10;
Isa 50:6 *b* S Lev 13:46
12:15 *c* S Lev 14:8
d S Lev 13:4
12:16 *e* Nu 11:35
f Ge 21:21; Nu 10:12;
15:32
13:2 *g* ver 16;
Dt 1:22 *h* S Lev 14:34
i Jos 1:3 *j* S Lev 24:11
13:3 *k* Nu 1:16
13:6 *l* ver 30;
Nu 14:6,24; 34:19;
Dt 1:36; Jdg 1:12-15
13:8 *m* S Nu 11:28
13:16 *n* S ver 2
o ver 8 *p* Dt 32:44
13:17 *q* ver 2;
Jos 14:7 *r* S Ge 12:9
s Dt 1:7; Jos 9:1;
Jdg 1:9
13:20 *t* Dt 1:25
u S Lev 25:5
13:21 *v* Nu 20:1;
27:14; 33:36;
Dt 32:51; Jos 15:1
w Jos 19:28; Jdg 1:31;
18:28; 2Sa 10:6;
1Ch 6:75 *x* Nu 34:8;
Jos 13:5; Jdg 3:3;
1Ki 8:65; 2Ki 14:25;
1Ch 13:5; 2Ch 7:8;
Jer 52:9; Eze 47:16,
20; Am 6:14
13:22 *y* S Ge 13:18;
S 23:19 *z* Jos 15:14;
Jdg 1:10 *a* ver 28;
Dt 2:10; 9:2; Jos 11:21;
15:13; Jdg 1:20
b Ps 78:12,43;
Isa 19:11,13; 30:4;
Eze 30:14
13:23 *c* S Ge 14:13

[14]The LORD replied to Moses, "If her father had spit in her face,[a] would she not have been in disgrace for seven days? Confine her outside the camp[b] for seven days; after that she can be brought back." [15]So Miriam was confined outside the camp[c] for seven days,[d] and the people did not move on till she was brought back.

[16]After that, the people left Hazeroth[e] and encamped in the Desert of Paran.[f]

EXPLORING CANAAN

13 The LORD said to Moses, [2]"Send some men to explore[g] the land of Canaan,[h] which I am giving to the Israelites.[i] From each ancestral tribe[j] send one of its leaders."

[3]So at the LORD's command Moses sent them out from the Desert of Paran. All of them were leaders of the Israelites.[k] [4]These are their names:

from the tribe of Reuben, Shammua son of Zakkur;
[5]from the tribe of Simeon, Shaphat son of Hori;
[6]from the tribe of Judah, Caleb son of Jephunneh;[l]
[7]from the tribe of Issachar, Igal son of Joseph;
[8]from the tribe of Ephraim, Hoshea son of Nun;[m]
[9]from the tribe of Benjamin, Palti son of Raphu;
[10]from the tribe of Zebulun, Gaddiel son of Sodi;
[11]from the tribe of Manasseh (a tribe of Joseph), Gaddi son of Susi;
[12]from the tribe of Dan, Ammiel son of Gemalli;
[13]from the tribe of Asher, Sethur son of Michael;
[14]from the tribe of Naphtali, Nahbi son of Vophsi;
[15]from the tribe of Gad, Geuel son of Maki.

[16]These are the names of the men Moses sent to explore[n] the land. (Moses gave Hoshea son of Nun[o] the name Joshua.)[p]

[17]When Moses sent them to explore Canaan,[q] he said, "Go up through the Negev[r] and on into the hill country.[s] [18]See what the land is like and whether the people who live there are strong or weak, few or many. [19]What kind of land do they live in? Is it good or bad? What kind of towns do they live in? Are they unwalled or fortified? [20]How is the soil? Is it fertile or poor? Are there trees in it or not? Do your best to bring back some of the fruit of the land.[t]" (It was the season for the first ripe grapes.)[u]

[21]So they went up and explored the land from the Desert of Zin[v] as far as Rehob,[w] toward Lebo Hamath.[x] [22]They went up through the Negev and came to Hebron,[y] where Ahiman, Sheshai and Talmai,[z] the descendants of Anak,[a] lived. (Hebron had been built seven years before Zoan in Egypt.)[b] [23]When they reached the Valley of Eshkol,[a][c] they cut off a branch bearing a single cluster of grapes. Two of them carried it on a pole between

a 23 Eshkol means cluster; also in verse 24.

12:14 *disgrace for seven days.* An act of public rebuke (see Dt 25:9) demands a period of public shame. A period of seven days was a standard time for uncleanness occasioned by being in contact with a dead body (see 19:11,14,16).

12:16 *Desert of Paran.* The southernmost region of the promised land. The people's opportunity to conquer the land was soon to come.

13:2 *Send some men to explore the land of Canaan.* The use of spies was a common practice in the ancient Near East (see note on Jos 2:1–24). From Dt 1:22–23 it appears that this directive of the Lord was in response to the people's request.

13:4–15 The names listed here are different from those in chs. 1–2; 7; 10. Presumably the tribal leaders in the four earlier lists were older men. The task for the spies called for men who were younger and more robust, but no less respected by their peers.

13:6 Although Caleb was not a native Israelite since he was a Kenizzite (32:12) and Kenaz was an Edomite (Ge 36:6,9,11), he became associated with the tribe of Judah. See note on 14:24.

C **13:16** *Moses gave Hoshea son of Nun the name Joshua.* A parenthetical statement anticipating the later prominence of Joshua. The reader is alerted to the significance of this name in the list of the spies; here is a man of destiny. Hoshea means "salvation"; Joshua means "The LORD saves" (see TNIV text note on Mt 1:21).

13:17–20 Moses' instruction to the 12 spies was comprehensive; a thorough report of the land and its produce and the peoples and their towns was required in their reconnaissance mission.

13:21 *explored the land.* The journey of the spies began in the southernmost extremity of the land (the Desert of Zin) and took them to the northernmost point (Rehob, near Lebo Hamath; see 34:8). This journey of about 250 miles each way took them 40 days (v. 25), perhaps a round number.

13:22 *Hebron.* The first city the spies came to in Canaan. The parenthetical comment about the city's being built seven years before Zoan in Egypt (see note on Ps 78:12,43) may have been prompted by their amazement at the size and fortifications of the city that was so closely associated with the lives of their ancestors four centuries before this time (see Ge 13:14–18; 14:13; 23:2; 25:9; 35:27–29; 50:13). In the stories of the ancestors of their people, Hebron had not been a great city but a dwelling and trading place for shepherds and herdsmen. *descendants of Anak.* The Anakites were men of great stature; their physical size brought fear to the people (see vv. 32–33). In a later day of faith, Caleb was to drive them from their city (Jos 15:14; Jdg 1:10).

13:23 *Valley of Eshkol.* See TNIV text note. This valley is near Hebron. The size of the grape cluster should have indicated the goodness of the land God was giving them.

them, along with some pomegranates ^{d} and figs. ^{e} ^{24}That place was called the Valley of Eshkol because of the cluster of grapes the Israelites cut off there. ^{25}At the end of forty days ^{f} they returned from exploring the land. ^{g}

REPORT ON THE EXPLORATION

^{26}They came back to Moses and Aaron and the whole Israelite community at Kadesh ^{h} in the Desert of Paran. ^{i} There they reported to them ^{j} and to the whole assembly and showed them the fruit of the land. ^{k} ^{27}They gave Moses this account: "We went into the land to which you sent us, and it does flow with milk and honey! ^{l} Here is its fruit. ^{m} ^{28}But the people who live there are powerful, and the cities are fortified and very large. ^{n} We even saw descendants of Anak ^{o} there. ^{p} ^{29}The Amalekites ^{q} live in the Negev; the Hittites, ^{r} Jebusites ^{s} and Amorites ^{t} live in the hill country; ^{u} and the Canaanites ^{v} live near the sea and along the Jordan. ^{w}"

^{30}Then Caleb ^{x} silenced the people before Moses and said, "We should go up and take possession of the land, for we can certainly do it."

^{31}But the men who had gone up with him said, "We can't attack those people; they are stronger than we are." ^{y} ^{32}And they spread among the Israelites a bad report ^{z} about the land they had explored. They said, "The land we explored devours ^{a} those living in it. All the people we saw there are of great size. ^{b} ^{33}We saw the Nephilim ^{c} there (the descendants of Anak ^{d} come from the Nephilim). We seemed like grasshoppers ^{e} in our own eyes, and we looked the same to them."

THE PEOPLE REBEL

14 That night all the members of the community raised their voices and wept aloud. ^{f} ^{2}All the Israelites grumbled ^{g} against Moses and Aaron, and the whole assembly said to them, "If only we had died in Egypt! ^{h} Or in this wilderness! ^{i} ^{3}Why is the LORD bringing us to this land only to let us fall by the sword? ^{j} Our wives and children ^{k} will be taken as plunder. ^{l} Wouldn't it be better for us to go back to Egypt? ^{m}" ^{4}And they said to each other, "We should choose a leader and go back to Egypt. ^{n}"

^{5}Then Moses and Aaron fell facedown ^{o} in front of the whole Israelite assembly ^{p} gathered there. ^{6}Joshua son of Nun ^{q} and Caleb son of Jephunneh, who were among those who had explored the land, tore their clothes ^{r} ^{7}and said to the entire Israelite assembly, "The land we passed through and explored is exceedingly good. ^{s} ^{8}If the LORD is pleased with us, ^{t} he will lead us into that land, a land flowing with milk and honey, ^{u} and will give it to us. ^{v} ^{9}Only do not rebel ^{w} against the LORD. And do not be afraid ^{x} of the people of the land, ^{y} because we will devour them. Their protection is gone, but the LORD is with ^{z} us. ^{a} Do not be afraid of them." ^{b}

^{10}But the whole assembly talked about stoning ^{c} them. Then the glory of the LORD ^{d} appeared at the tent of meeting to all the Israelites. ^{11}The LORD said to Moses, "How long will these people treat me with contempt? ^{e} How long will they refuse to believe in me, ^{f} in spite of all the signs ^{g} I have performed among them? ^{12}I will strike them down with a

14:9 ^{w} Dt 1:26; 9:7,23,24 ^{x} Ge 26:24; 2Ch 32:7; Ps 118:6; Jer 41:18; 42:11 ^{y} Dt 1:21; 7:18; 20:1 ^{z} Hag 2:4 ^{a} S Ge 21:22; Dt 1:30; 2Ch 13:12; Jer 15:20; 46:28; Hag 1:13 ^{b} ver 24   **14:10** ^{c} S Ex 17:4 ^{d} S Ex 24:16   **14:11** ^{e} Ex 23:21; Nu 15:31; 16:30; 1Sa 2:17; Eze 31:14; Mal 1:13 ^{f} Dt 1:32; Ps 78:22; 106:24; Jn 3:18 ^{g} S Ex 3:20; S 4:17; S 10:1

13:23 ^{d} S Ex 28:33
^{e} Ge 3:7; Nu 20:5;
Dt 8:8; 2Ki 18:31;
Ne 13:15
13:25 ^{f} S Ge 7:4
^{g} Nu 14:34
13:26 ^{h} S Ge 14:7
^{i} S Ge 14:6 / Nu 32:8
^{k} Dt 1:25
13:27 ^{l} S Ex 3:3
^{m} Dt 1:25; Jer 2:7
13:28 ^{n} Dt 1:28;
9:1,2 ^{o} S ver 22
^{p} Jos 14:12
13:29 ^{q} S Ge 14:7
^{r} S Ge 10:15; Dt 7:1;
20:17; 1Ki 9:20;
10:29; 2Ki 7:6
^{s} S Ge 3:8 ^{t} S Ge 10:16
^{u} ver 17 ^{v} Ge 10:18
^{w} S Ge 13:10; Nu 22:1;
32:5; Dt 1:1; Jos 1:2;
Jdg 3:28; Ps 42:6
13:30 ^{x} S ver 6
13:31 ^{y} Dt 9:1;
Jos 14:8
13:32 ^{z} Nu 14:36,37
^{a} Eze 36:13,14
^{b} Dt 1:28; Am 2:9
13:33 ^{c} Ge 6:4
^{d} ver 28; Dt 1:28;
Jos 11:22; 14:12
^{e} Ecc 12:5; Isa 40:22
14:1 ^{f} S Ge 27:38;
Ex 33:4; Nu 25:6;
Dt 1:45; Jdg 20:23,26;
2Sa 3:32; Job 31:29
14:2 ^{g} Ex 16:2;
Heb 3:16 ^{h} S Ex 16:3
^{i} S Nu 11:1; 16:13;
20:4; 21:5
14:3 ^{j} S Ex 5:21
^{k} ver 31 ^{l} S Ge 34:29;
Dt 1:39; Ps 109:11;
Isa 33:4; Eze 7:21;
25:7; 26:5 ^{m} Ac 7:39
14:4 ^{n} Ne 9:17
14:5 ^{o} S Lev 9:24;
Nu 16:4,22,45; 20:6;
Jos 5:14; 2Sa 14:4;
1Ch 21:16; Eze 1:28
^{p} S Lev 19:2
14:6 ^{q} Nu 11:28
^{r} S Ge 37:29,34;
Jdg 11:35; 2Sa 13:31;
2Ki 19:1; Ezr 9:3;
Est 4:1; S Mk 14:63
14:7 ^{s} Nu 13:27;
Dt 1:25
14:8 ^{t} Dt 7:8; 10:15;
Ps 18:19; 22:8; 37:23;
41:11; 56:9; 147:11;
Pr 11:20; Isa 62:4;
Mal 2:17 ^{u} Nu 13:27
^{v} Dt 1:21

13:26–29 The first part of the spies' report was truthful, but the goodness of the land was offset in their fearful eyes by the powerful peoples who lived there.

13:26 *Kadesh.* See note on Ge 14:7.

13:27 *flow with milk and honey.* See notes on Ex 3:8; Dt 6:3.

[A] [C] **13:30** *Caleb silenced the people.* Only Caleb and Joshua gave a report prompted by faith in God.

[A] **13:32** *bad report about the land.* The promised land was a good land, a gracious gift from God. By speaking bad things about it, the faithless spies were speaking evil of the Lord (cf. 10:29).

[A] **13:33** Their words became exaggerations and distortions. The Anakites were now said to be Nephilim (see note on Ge 6:4). The reference to the Nephilim seems deliberately intended to evoke fear. The exaggeration of the faithless led to their final folly: "We seemed like grasshoppers."

[A] **14:1** *all the members . . . wept.* The frightening words of the faithless spies led to mourning by the entire community and to their great rebellion against the Lord. They forgot all the miracles the Lord had done for them, they despised his mer-

cies and spurned his might. In their ingratitude they preferred death (v. 2).

14:2,29 *grumbled.* See Introduction: Contents; see also note on Ex 15:24.

14:3 *children.* The most reprehensible charge against God's grace was that concerning their children. Only their children would survive (see vv. 31–33).

14:8 *flowing with milk and honey.* See notes on Ex 3:8; Dt 6:3.

[A] **14:9** *the LORD is with us.* There are no walls, no fortifications, no factors of size or bearing, and certainly no gods that can withstand the onslaught of God's people when the Lord is with them.

14:10 *glory of the LORD appeared.* This manifestation of God must have been staggering in its sudden and intense display of his majesty and wrath (see vv. 21–22; see also note on Ex 16:7).

[A] **14:11** *treat me with contempt.* By refusing to believe in the Lord's power, especially in view of all the wonders they had experienced, the people of Israel were holding him in contempt.

14:12 ʰ S Ex 5:3;
S 30:12 ʲ S Ex 32:10
ʲ Dt 9:14; 29:20;
32:26; Ps 109:13
14:13 ᵏ Ex 32:11-14;
Ps 106:23
14:14 ˡ Ex 15:14
ᵐ Nu 5:3; 16:3;
Jos 2:9 ⁿ Dt 5:4; 34:10
ᵒ S Ex 33:16
ᵖ S Ex 13:21
14:16 ᑫ Nu 11:12
ʳ Ex 32:12; Jos 7:7
14:18 ˢ S Ex 20:6;
34:6; Ps 145:8;
Jnh 4:2; Jas 5:11
ᵗ Ex 20:5
14:19 ᵘ S Ex 34:9;
1Ki 8:34; Ps 85:2;
103:3 ᵛ Ps 106:45
ʷ Ps 78:38
14:20 ˣ Ex 34:6;
Ps 99:8; 106:23;
Mic 7:18-20
14:21 ʸ ver 28;
Dt 32:40; Jdg 8:19;
Ru 3:13; 1Sa 14:39;
19:6; Isa 49:18;
Jer 4:2; Eze 5:11;
Zep 2:9 ᶻ Lev 9:6
ᵃ Ps 72:19; Isa 6:3;
40:5; Hab 2:14
14:22 ᵇ ver 11
ᶜ S Ex 14:11; 17:7;
32:1; Ps 81:7; 1Co 10:5
14:23 ᵈ ver 16;
S Ex 33:1; Nu 32:11;
Dt 1:34; Ps 95:11;
106:26 ᵉ ver 11
ᶠ Heb 3:18
14:24 ᵍ Nu 13:6
ʰ ver 6-9; Dt 1:36;
Jos 14:8,14
ⁱ Nu 26:65; 32:12;
Ps 25:13; 37:9,11
14:25 ʲ S Ge 14:7
ᵏ S Ge 10:18 ˡ Dt 1:40
ᵐ Ex 23:31; Nu 21:4;
1Ki 9:26
14:27 ⁿ Ex 16:12;
Dt 1:34,35
14:28 ᵒ S ver 21
ᵖ Nu 33:56
14:29 ᑫ ver 23,30,
32; Nu 26:65; 32:13;
1Co 10:5; Heb 3:17;
Jude 1:5 ʳ S Nu 1:45
ˢ S Ex 30:12
14:30 ᵗ S ver 29
ᵘ Ex 6:8; Dt 32:40;
Ne 9:15; Ps 106:26;
Eze 20:5; 36:7
ᵛ Nu 13:6 ʷ Nu 11:28
14:31 ˣ S Lev 26:43
14:32 ʸ S ver 29,35

plague ʰ and destroy them, but I will make you into a nation ⁱ greater and stronger than they." ʲ

¹³Moses said to the LORD, "Then the Egyptians will hear about it! By your power you brought these people up from among them. ᵏ ¹⁴And they will tell the inhabitants of this land about it. They have already heard ˡ that you, LORD, are with these people ᵐ and that you, LORD, have been seen face to face, ⁿ that your cloud stays over them, ᵒ and that you go before them in a pillar of cloud by day and a pillar of fire by night. ᵖ ¹⁵If you put these people to death all at one time, the nations who have heard this report about you will say, ¹⁶'The LORD was not able to bring these people into the land he promised them on oath, ᑫ so he slaughtered them in the wilderness.' ʳ

¹⁷"Now may the Lord's strength be displayed, just as you have declared: ¹⁸'The LORD is slow to anger, abounding in love and forgiving sin and rebellion. ˢ Yet he does not leave the guilty unpunished; he punishes the children for the sin of the parents to the third and fourth generation.' ᵗ ¹⁹In accordance with your great love, forgive ᵘ the sin of these people, ᵛ just as you have pardoned them from the time they left Egypt until now." ʷ

²⁰The LORD replied, "I have forgiven them, ˣ as you asked. ²¹Nevertheless, as surely as I live ʸ and as surely as the glory of the LORD ᶻ fills the whole earth, ᵃ ²²not one of those who saw my glory and the signs ᵇ I performed in Egypt and in the wilderness but who disobeyed me and tested me ten times ᶜ— ²³not one of them will ever see the land I promised on oath ᵈ to their ancestors. No one who has treated me with contempt ᵉ will ever see it. ᶠ ²⁴But because my servant Caleb ᵍ has a different spirit and follows me wholeheartedly, ʰ I will bring him into the land he went to, and his descendants will inherit it. ⁱ ²⁵Since the Amalekites ʲ and Canaanites ᵏ are living in the valleys, turn ˡ back tomorrow and set out toward the desert along the route to the Red Sea. ᵃ ᵐ"

²⁶The LORD said to Moses and Aaron: ²⁷"How long will this wicked community grumble against me? I have heard the complaints of these grumbling Israelites. ⁿ ²⁸So tell them, 'As surely as I live, ᵒ declares the LORD, I will do to you ᵖ the very thing I heard you say: ²⁹In this wilderness your bodies will fall ᑫ—every one of you twenty years old or more ʳ who was counted in the census ˢ and who has grumbled against me. ³⁰Not one of you will enter the land ᵗ I swore with uplifted hand ᵘ to make your home, except Caleb son of Jephunneh ᵛ and Joshua son of Nun. ʷ ³¹As for your children that you said would be taken as plunder, I will bring them in to enjoy the land you have rejected. ˣ ³²But as for you, your bodies will fall ʸ in this wilderness. ³³Your children will be shepherds here for forty years, ᶻ suffering for your unfaithfulness, until the last of your bodies lies in the wilderness. ³⁴For forty years ᵃ—one year for each of the forty days you explored the land ᵇ—you will suffer for your sins and know what it is like to have me against you.' ³⁵I, the LORD, have spoken, and I will surely do these things ᶜ to this whole wicked community, which has banded together against me. They will meet their end in this wilderness; here they will die. ᵈ"

³⁶So the men Moses had sent ᵉ to explore the land, who returned and made the whole community grumble ᶠ against him by spreading a bad report ᵍ about it— ³⁷these men who

---

ᵃ 25 Or *the Sea of Reeds*

14:33 ᶻ ver 34; S Ex 16:35; Ac 13:18; Heb 3:9   **14:34** ᵃ S ver 33 ᵇ Nu 13:25   **14:35** ᶜ Nu 23:19 ᵈ S ver 32   **14:36** ᵉ Nu 13:4-16 ᶠ ver 2
ᵍ S Nu 13:32

14:12 *I will make you into a nation.* For the second time since the exodus, God speaks of starting over with Moses in creating a people faithful to himself (see Ex 32:10).

🅰 **14:13** *Egyptians will hear about it!* Moses desires to protect the Lord's reputation. The enemies of God's people will charge the Lord with inability to complete his deliverance and will be contemptuous of his power.

🅰 **14:17–19** Moses now moves from the Lord's reputation to his character, presenting a composite quotation of his own words of loyal love and faithful discipline of his people (see Ex 20:6; 34:6–7 and notes).

14:22 *ten times.* Perhaps to be enumerated as follows: (1) Ex 14:10–12; (2) Ex 15:22–24; (3) Ex 16:1–3; (4) Ex 16:19–20; (5) Ex 16:27–30; (6) Ex 17:1–4; (7) Ex 32:1–35; (8) Nu 11:1–3; (9) 11:4–34; (10) 14:3. But "ten times" may also be a way of saying "many times."

🅲 **14:24** *Caleb … follows me wholeheartedly.* Caleb may be singled out—even though Joshua—because although he was not a native Israelite (see note on 13:6), he was faithful to the Lord. His ultimate vindication came 45 years later (see note

on 13:22; see also Jos 14:10).

🅰 **14:28** *I will do to you the very thing I heard you say.* The people of Israel brought upon themselves their punishment. They had said that they would rather die in the wilderness (v. 2) than be led into Canaan to die by the sword. All those 20 years old or more, who were counted in the census, were to die in the wilderness (v. 29). The only exceptions would be Joshua and Caleb (v. 30). Only the people's children would survive (v. 31)—the very children they had said God would allow to die in the wilderness (v. 3).

14:32 See Heb 3:17.

🅰 **14:34** The 40 days of the travels of the spies became the numerical pattern for their suffering: one year for one day—for 40 years they would recount their misjudgment, and for 40 years the people 20 years old or more would be dying, so that only the young generation might enter the land. Significantly, Israel's refusal to carry out the Lord's commission to conquer his land is the climactic act of rebellion for which God condemns Israel to die in the wilderness.

14:37 *these men who were responsible for spreading the bad* were responsible for spreading the bad report ^{h} about the land were struck down and died of a plague ^{i} before the LORD. ^{38}Of the men who went to explore the land, ^{j} only Joshua son of Nun and Caleb son of Jephunneh survived. ^{k}

^{39}When Moses reported this ^{l} to all the Israelites, they mourned ^{m} bitterly. ^{40}Early the next morning they set out for the highest point in the hill country, ^{n} saying, "Now we are ready to go up to the land the LORD promised. Surely we have sinned! ^{o}"

^{41}But Moses said, "Why are you disobeying the LORD's command? This will not succeed! ^{p} ^{42}Do not go up, because the LORD is not with you. You will be defeated by your enemies, ^{q} ^{43}for the Amalekites ^{r} and Canaanites ^{s} will face you there. Because you have turned away from the LORD, he will not be with you ^{t} and you will fall by the sword."

^{44}Nevertheless, in their presumption they went up ^{u} toward the highest point in the hill country, though neither Moses nor the ark of the LORD's covenant moved from the camp. ^{v} ^{45}Then the Amalekites and Canaanites ^{w} who lived in that hill country ^{x} came down and attacked them and beat them down all the way to Hormah. ^{y}

SUPPLEMENTARY OFFERINGS

15 The LORD said to Moses, ^{2}"Speak to the Israelites and say to them: 'After you enter the land I am giving you ^{z} as a home ^{3}and you present to the LORD food offerings from the herd or the flock, ^{a} as an aroma pleasing to the LORD ^{b}— whether burnt offerings ^{c} or sacrifices, for special vows or freewill offerings ^{d} or festival offerings ^{e}— ^{4}then the person who brings an offering shall present to the LORD a grain offering ^{f} of a tenth of an ephah ^{a} of the finest flour ^{g} mixed with a quarter of a hin ^{b} of olive oil. ^{5}With each lamb ^{h} for the burnt offering or the sacrifice, prepare a quarter of a hin of wine ^{i} as a drink offering. ^{j}

^{6} "'With a ram ^{k} prepare a grain offering ^{l} of two-tenths of an ephah ^{c} ^{m} of the finest flour mixed with a third of a hin ^{d} of olive oil, ^{n} ^{7}and a third of a hin of wine ^{o} as a drink offering. ^{p} Offer it as an aroma pleasing to the LORD. ^{q}

^{8} "'When you prepare a young bull ^{r} as a burnt offering or sacrifice, for a special vow ^{s} or a fellowship offering ^{t} to the LORD, ^{9}bring with the bull a grain offering ^{u} of three-tenths of an ephah ^{e} ^{v} of the finest flour mixed with half a hin ^{f} of olive oil, ^{10}and also bring half a hin of wine ^{w} as a drink offering. ^{x} This will be a food offering, an aroma pleasing to the LORD. ^{y} ^{11}Each bull or ram, each lamb or young goat, is to be prepared in this manner. ^{12}Do this for each one, for as many as you prepare. ^{z}

^{13} "'Everyone who is native-born ^{a} must do these things in this way when they present a food offering as an aroma pleasing to the LORD. ^{b} ^{14}For the generations to come, ^{c} whenever a foreigner ^{d} or anyone else living among you presents a food ^{e} offering ^{f} as an aroma pleasing to the LORD, they must do exactly as you do. ^{15}The community is to have the same rules for you and for the foreigner residing among you; this is a lasting ordinance for the generations to come. ^{g} You and the foreigner shall be the same before the LORD: ^{16}The same laws and regulations will apply both to you and to the foreigner residing among you. ^{h}'"

^{17}The LORD said to Moses, ^{18}"Speak to the Israelites and say to them: 'When you enter the land to which I am taking you ^{i} ^{19}and you eat the food of the land, ^{j} present a portion

---

^{a} 4 That is, probably about 3 1/2 pounds or about 1.6 kilograms ^{b} 4 That is, about 1 quart or about 0.9 liter; also in verse 5 ^{c} 6 That is, probably about 7 pounds or about 3.2 kilograms ^{d} 6 That is, about 2 2/3 pints or about 1.2 liters; also in verse 7 ^{e} 9 That is, probably about 11 pounds or about 5 kilograms ^{f} 9 That is, about 1/2 gallon or about 1.8 liters; also in verse 10

14:37 ^{h} S Nu 13:32; 1Co 10:10; Heb 3:17
^{i} Nu 16:49; 5:9; 26:1; 31:16; Dt 4:3
14:38 ^{j} ver 30; Nu 13:4-16 ^{k} ver 24; Jos 14:6
14:39 ^{l} ver 28-35
^{m} S Ex 33:4
14:40 ^{n} ver 45; Nu 13:17 ^{o} S Ex 9:27
14:41 ^{p} 2Ch 24:20
14:42 ^{q} Dt 1:42
14:43 ^{r} Jdg 3:13
^{s} ver 45; Nu 13:29
^{t} S Ge 39:23; Dt 31:8; Jos 6:27; Jdg 1:19; 6:16; 1Sa 3:19; 18:14; 2Ch 1:1
14:44 ^{u} Dt 1:43
^{v} Nu 31:6
14:45 ^{w} S ver 43
^{x} S ver 40 ^{y} Nu 21:3; Dt 1:44; Jos 12:14; 15:30; 19:4; Jdg 1:17; 1Sa 30:30; 1Ch 4:30
15:2 ^{z} S Lev 23:10
15:3 ^{a} S Lev 1:2
^{b} ver 24; S Lev 1:9
^{c} Lev 1:3; Nu 28:13
^{d} S Lev 7:16; S Ezr 1:4
^{e} Lev 23:1-44
15:4 ^{f} S Lev 6:14
^{g} S Ex 16:36
15:5 ^{h} S Lev 3:7
^{i} S Lev 10:9
^{j} S Ge 35:14
15:6 ^{k} S Lev 5:15
^{l} Nu 28:12; 29:14
^{m} S Lev 23:13
^{n} Eze 46:14
15:7 ^{o} ver 5
15:9 ^{p} Lev 23:13; Nu 28:14; 29:18 ^{q} S Lev 1:9
15:8 ^{r} S Ex 12:5; S Lev 1:5
^{s} S Lev 22:18
^{t} S Lev 3:6
15:9 ^{u} Lev 2:1
^{v} S Lev 14:10
15:10 ^{w} Nu 28:14
^{x} Lev 23:13 ^{y} Lev 1:9
15:12 ^{z} Ezr 7:17
15:13 ^{a} S Lev 16:29
^{b} Lev 1:9
15:14 ^{c} Lev 3:17; Nu 10:8 ^{d} S Ex 12:19, 43; S 22:21 ^{e} ver 25
^{f} S Lev 22:18
15:15 ^{g} ver 14,21
15:16 ^{h} Lev 12:49; S Lev 22:18; Nu 9:14
15:18 ^{i} S Lev 23:10
15:19 ^{j} Jos 5:11,12

---

report ... were struck down. The judgment on the ten evil spies was immediate; the generation that they influenced would live out their lives in the wilderness.

14:40 *Now we are ready to go up.* Now, too late, the people determine to go up to the land. Such a course of action was doomed to failure. Not only was the Lord not with them; he was against them (v. 41). Their subsequent defeat (v. 45) was another judgment the rebellious people brought down on their own heads (see note on Eze 16:43).

15:1–41 This chapter is divided into three units, each introduced by the phrase, "The LORD said to Moses" (vv. 1,17,37). The people were under terrible judgment because they had disobeyed the specific commands of the Lord and had despised his character.

15:2 *After you enter the land.* The juxtaposition of this clause with the sad ending of ch. 14 is dramatic. The sins

of the people were manifold; they would be judged. The grace and mercy of the Lord are magnified as he points to the ultimate realization of his ancient promise to Abraham (Ge 12:7), as well as to his continuing promise to the nation that they would indeed enter the land.

15:3–12 Grain and wine offerings were to accompany the food offerings; the grain was to be mixed with oil. The offerings increased in amounts with the increase of size of the sacrificial animal (vv. 6–12).

15:14 *foreigner.* As in the case of the celebration of the Passover (see note on 9:14), the foreigner had the same regulations as the native-born Israelite. The commonwealth of Israel would always be open to proselytes. Indeed, God's promise to Abraham embraces all peoples of the earth (see note on Ge 12:2–3).

15:19 *k* Nu 18:8
15:20 *l* S Lev 23:14
m S Lev 2:14;
S Nu 18:27
n S Ge 50:10
15:21 *o* S Lev 23:14
p Eze 44:30; Ro 11:16
15:22 *q* S Lev 4:2
15:23 *r* ver 21
15:24 *s* ver 25,26
t S Lev 5:15 *u* Lev 4:14
v S ver 3 *w* Lev 2:1
x Lev 23:13; Nu 6:15
y Lev 4:3
15:25 *z* Lev 4:20;
S Ro 3:25 *a* ver 22,
S 24 *b* ver 14
c Lev 4:3
15:26 *d* S ver 24
15:27 *e* Lev 4:27
f Lev 4:3; Nu 6:14
15:28 *g* Nu 8:12;
28:22 *h* Lev 4:20
15:29 *i* S Ex 12:49
15:30 *j* Nu 14:40-
44; Dt 1:43; 17:13;
Ps 19:13 *k* ver 14
l 2Ki 19:6,20;
Isa 37:6,23;
Eze 20:27
m S Ge 17:14;
S Job 31:22
15:31 *n* S Nu 14:11
o 1Sa 15:23,26;
2Sa 11:27; 12:9;
Ps 119:126; Pr 13:13
p S Lev 5:1; Eze 18:20
15:32 *q* S Nu 12:16
r Ex 31:14,15; 35:2,3
15:34 *s* Nu 9:8
15:35 *t* Ex 31:14,15
u S Lev 20:2; Lk 4:29;
Ac 7:58
15:36 *v* S Lev 20:2
w S Ex 31:14
x Jer 17:21
15:38 *y* Lev 3:17;
Nu 10:8 *z* Dt 22:12;
Mt 23:5
15:39 *a* Dt 4:23;
6:12; Ps 73:27
b S Lev 17:7; Jdg 2:17;
Ps 106:39; Jer 3:2;
Hos 4:12 *c* Ps 78:37;
Jer 7:24; Eze 20:16
15:40 *d* S Ge 26:5;
Dt 11:13; Ps 103:18;
119:56 *e* S Lev 11:44;
Ro 12:1; Col 1:22;
1Pe 1:15
15:41 *f* S Ge 17:7
g S Ex 20:2

as an offering to the LORD. *k* 20Present a loaf from the first of your ground meal *l* and present it as an offering from the threshing floor. *m n* 21Throughout the generations to come *o* you are to give this offering to the LORD from the first of your ground meal. *p*

OFFERINGS FOR UNINTENTIONAL SINS

22" 'Now if you as a community unintentionally fail to keep any of these commands the LORD gave Moses *q*— 23any of the LORD's commands to you through him, from the day the LORD gave them and continuing through the generations to come *r*— 24and if this is done unintentionally *s* without the community being aware of it, *t* then the whole community is to offer a young bull for a burnt offering *u* as an aroma pleasing to the LORD, *v* along with its prescribed grain offering *w* and drink offering, *x* and a male goat for a sin offering. *a y* 25The priest is to make atonement for the whole Israelite community, and they will be forgiven, *z* for it was not intentional *a* and they have presented to the LORD for their wrong a food offering *b* and a sin offering. *c* 26The whole Israelite community and the foreigners residing among them will be forgiven, because all the people were involved in the unintentional wrong. *d*

27" 'But if just one person sins unintentionally, *e* that person must bring a year-old female goat for a sin offering. *f* 28The priest is to make atonement *g* before the LORD for the one who erred by sinning unintentionally, and when atonement has been made for them, they will be forgiven. *h* 29One and the same law applies to everyone who sins unintentionally, whether a native-born Israelite or a foreigner residing among you. *i*

30" 'But anyone who sins defiantly, *j* whether native-born or foreigner, *k* blasphemes the LORD *l* and must be cut off from their people. *m* 31Because they have despised *n* the LORD's word and broken his commands, *o* they must surely be cut off; their guilt remains on them. *p*' "

THE SABBATH-BREAKER PUT TO DEATH

32While the Israelites were in the wilderness, *q* a man was found gathering wood on the Sabbath day. *r* 33Those who found him gathering wood brought him to Moses and Aaron and the whole assembly, 34and they kept him in custody, because it was not clear what should be done to him. *s* 35Then the LORD said to Moses, "The man must die. *t* The whole assembly must stone him outside the camp. *u*" 36So the assembly took him outside the camp and stoned him *v* to death, *w* as the LORD commanded Moses. *x*

TASSELS ON GARMENTS

37The LORD said to Moses, 38"Speak to the Israelites and say to them: 'Throughout the generations to come *y* you are to make tassels on the corners of your garments, *z* with a blue cord on each tassel. 39You will have these tassels to look at and so you will remember *a* all the commands of the LORD, that you may obey them and not prostitute yourselves *b* by chasing after the lusts of your own hearts *c* and eyes. 40Then you will remember to obey all my commands *d* and will be consecrated to your God. *e* 41I am the LORD your God, who brought you out of Egypt to be your God. *f* I am the LORD your God. *g*' "

---

a 24 Or *purification offering*; also in verses 25 and 27

A **15:20** *Present a loaf from the first.* This law also looks forward to the time when the Israelites would be in the land. The first of the threshed grain was to be made into a loaf and presented to the Lord. This concept of the firstfruits is a symbol that all blessing is from the Lord and all produce belongs to him.

15:22 *unintentionally fail.* Sins may be unintentional, but they still need to be dealt with (see note on Lev 4:2). Such unintentional sins may be committed by the people as a whole (vv. 22–26) or by an individual (vv. 27–29).

A **15:30** *defiantly.* Lit. "with a high hand." Unlike unintentional sins, for which there are provisions of God's mercy, one who sets his hand defiantly to despise the word of God and to blaspheme his name must be punished. This was the experience of the nation in ch. 14, and it is described in the case of an individual here in vv. 32–36. *cut off from their people.* See note on Ex 12:15.

15:32 *gathering wood on the Sabbath day.* The penalty for

breaking the Sabbath was death (v. 36; Ex 31:15; 35:2). As in the case of the willful blasphemer (Lev 24:10–16), the Sabbath-breaker was guilty of high-handed rebellion (see note on v. 30) and was judged with death. By the time of Christ, Sabbath-keeping had become distorted to the point that its regulations were regarded as more important than the needs of people. Jesus confronted the Pharisees on this issue on several occasions (see, e.g., Mt 12:1–14). From their point of view, these regulations (vv. 32–36) gave them reasons to seek his death (Mt 12:14).

15:38 *tassels on the corners of your garments.* As one would walk along, the tassels would swirl about at the edge of one's garment (cf. v. 39), serving as excellent memory prods to obey God's commands (cf. Dt 6:4–9 and notes).

15:39 *prostitute yourselves.* See Ex 34:15 and note.

A **15:41** *I am the LORD your God, who brought you out.* The demands that God made upon his people were grounded in his act of redemption (see Ex 20:2 and note).

KORAH, DATHAN AND ABIRAM

16 Korah [h] son of Izhar, the son of Kohath, the son of Levi, and certain Reubenites—Dathan and Abiram [i], sons of Eliab, [j] and On son of Peleth—became insolent [a] [2] and rose up against Moses. [k] With them were 250 Israelite men, well-known community leaders who had been appointed members of the council. [l] [3] They came as a group to oppose Moses and Aaron [m] and said to them, "You have gone too far! The whole community is holy, [n] every one of them, and the Lord is with them. [o] Why then do you set yourselves above the Lord's assembly?" [p]

[4] When Moses heard this, he fell facedown. [q] [5] Then he said to Korah and all his followers: "In the morning the Lord will show who belongs to him and who is holy, [r] and he will have that person come near him. [s] The one he chooses [t] he will cause to come near him. [6] You, Korah, and all your followers [u] are to do this: Take censers [v] [7] and tomorrow put burning coals [w] and incense [x] in them before the Lord. The man the Lord chooses [y] will be the one who is holy. [z] You Levites have gone too far!"

[8] Moses also said to Korah, "Now listen, you Levites! [9] Isn't it enough [a] for you that the God of Israel has separated you from the rest of the Israelite community and brought you near himself to do the work at the Lord's tabernacle and to stand before the community and minister to them? [b] [10] He has brought you and all your fellow Levites near himself, but now you are trying to get the priesthood too. [c] [11] It is against the Lord that you and all your followers have banded together. Who is Aaron that you should grumble [d] against him? [e]"

[12] Then Moses summoned Dathan and Abiram, [f] the sons of Eliab. But they said, "We will not come! [g] [13] Isn't it enough that you have brought us up out of a land flowing with milk and honey [h] to kill us in the wilderness? [i] And now you also want to lord it over us! [j] [14] Moreover, you haven't brought us into a land flowing with milk and honey [k] or given us an inheritance of fields and vineyards. [l] Do you want to treat these men like slaves [b] [m] No, we will not come! [n]"

[15] Then Moses became very angry [o] and said to the Lord, "Do not accept their offering. I have not taken so much as a donkey [p] from them, nor have I wronged any of them."

[16] Moses said to Korah, "You and all your followers are to appear before the Lord tomorrow—you and they and Aaron. [q] [17] Each one is to take his censer and put incense in it—250 censers in all—and present it before the Lord. You and Aaron are to present your censers also. [r] " [18] So each one took his censer, [s] put burning coals and incense in it, and stood with Moses and Aaron at the entrance to the tent of meeting. [19] When Korah had gathered all his followers in opposition to them [t] at the entrance to the tent of meeting, the glory of the Lord [u] appeared to the entire assembly. [20] The Lord said to Moses and Aaron, [21] "Separate yourselves [v] from this assembly so I can put an end to them at once." [w]

[22] But Moses and Aaron fell facedown [x] and cried out, "O God, God of every human spirit, [y] will you be angry with the entire assembly [z] when only one man sins?" [a]

[23] Then the Lord said to Moses, [24] "Say to the assembly, 'Move away from the tents of Korah, Dathan and Abiram.' "

[25] Moses got up and went to Dathan and Abiram, and the elders of Israel [b] followed him.

---

[a] 1 Or Peleth—took men   [b] 14 Or to deceive these men; Hebrew Will you gouge out the eyes of these men

16:1 [h] S Ex 6:24; Jude 1:11 [i] ver 24; Ps 106:17 [j] Nu 26:8; Dt 11:6
16:2 [k] Nu 27:3 [l] Nu 1:16; 26:9
16:3 [m] ver 7; Ps 106:16 [n] Ex 19:6 [o] S Nu 14:14 [p] Nu 12:2
16:4 [q] Nu 14:5
16:5 [r] S Lev 10:3; 2Ti 2:19 [*] [*] Jer 30:21 [t] Nu 17:5; Ps 65:4; 105:26; Jer 50:44
16:6 [u] ver 7,16 [v] S Lev 10:1; Rev 8:3
16:7 [w] S Lev 10:1 [x] S Nu 30:9 [y] S ver 6 [z] ver 5
16:9 [a] S Ge 30:15 [b] Nu 3:6; Dt 10:8; 17:12; 21:5; 1Sa 2:11; Ps 134:1; Eze 44:11
16:10 [c] Nu 3:10; 18:7; Jdg 17:5,12
16:11 [d] ver 41; 1Co 10:10 [e] S Ex 16:7
16:12 [f] S ver 1,27 [g] ver 14
16:13 [h] Nu 13:27 [i] Nu 14:2 [j] S Ge 13:8; Ac 7:27,35
16:14 [k] S Lev 20:24 [l] Ex 22:5; 23:11; Nu 20:5; 1Ki 4:25; Ne 13:15; Ps 105:33; Jer 5:17; Hos 2:12; Joel 2:22; Hag 2:19; Zec 3:10 [m] Jdg 16:21; 1Sa 11:2; Jer 39:7 [n] ver 12
16:15 [o] S Ex 4:14 [p] 1Sa 12:3
16:16 [q] S ver 6
16:17 [r] Eze 8:11
16:18 [s] Lev 10:1
16:19 [t] ver 12; Nu 20:2 [u] S Ex 16:7; Nu 14:10; 20:6
16:21 [v] ver 24 [w] S Ge 19:14; S Ex 32:10
16:22 [x] S Nu 14:5 [y] Nu 27:16; Job 12:10; 27:8; 33:4; 34:14; Jer 32:27; Eze 18:4; Heb 12:9 [z] S Lev 10:6 [a] S Ge 18:23; S Job 21:20
16:25 [b] S Ex 19:7

16:1–7 Earlier, Miriam and Aaron had led a rebellion against the leadership of Moses (ch. 12). Now Korah and his allies attack the leadership of Moses and Aaron. Korah was descended from Levi through Kohath. As a Kohathite, he had high duties in the service of the Lord at the tabernacle (see 4:1–20), but he desired more. His passion was to assume the role of priest, and he used deception to advance his claim. Korah was joined by the Reubenites, Dathan, Abiram and On, and about 250 other leaders of Israel who had their own complaints. Their charge was that Moses had "gone too far" (v. 3) in taking the role of spiritual leadership of the people; "the whole community is holy" (v. 3). To this abusive charge Moses retorts, "You Levites have gone too far!" (v. 7), and sets up a trial by fire.
16:3 *The whole community is holy.* See notes on Ex 3:5; 19:6.
16:6 *censers.* See note on Lev 10:1.
16:12 *Dathan and Abiram.* Their charge against Moses was that he had not led them into the land of promise. They claimed that Moses had in fact led the people "out of a land flowing with milk and honey" (v. 13). By this strange alchemy, in their minds the land of Egypt has been transformed from prison to paradise.

16:13–14 *flowing with milk and honey.* See notes on Ex 3:8; Dt 6:3.
16:15 *nor have I wronged any of them.* Moses' humanity is seen in his plea of innocence.
16:18–21 The trial was to be by fire: Which men would the Lord accept as his priests in the holy tabernacle? The 250 men allied with Korah came with arrogance to withstand Moses and Aaron at the entrance to the tent of meeting. The revelation of the Lord's glory was sure and sudden (v. 19), with words of impending doom for the rebellious people (v. 21). The punishment was fittingly ironic. Those 250 men who dared to present themselves as priests before the Lord with fire in their censers were themselves put to death by fire (perhaps lightning) from the Lord (see v. 35).
16:19,42 *glory of the Lord.* See note on Ex 16:7.
16:24 *Move away.* God's judgment was going to be severe, but he did not want to lash out against bystanders. It appears that Korah himself had left the 250 false priests and was standing with Dathan and Abiram to continue their opposition to Moses.

16:26 ᶜIsa 52:11
ᵈS Ge 19:15 ᵉJer 51:6
16:27 ᶠS ver 12
ᵍver 32; Jos 7:24;
Isa 13:16; 14:21
ʰS Ex 33:8
16:28 ʲ1Ki 18:36
ʲEx 3:12; Jn 5:36; 6:38
16:29 ᵏNu 24:13;
Job 31:2; Ecc 3:19
16:30 ˡPs 141:7;
Isa 5:14 ᵐver 33;
S Ge 37:35; 1Sa 2:6;
Job 5:26; 21:13;
Ps 9:17; 16:10; 55:15;
Isa 14:11; 38:18
ⁿS Nu 14:11;
S Eze 26:20
16:31 ᵒIsa 64:1-2;
Eze 47:1-12; Mic 1:3-
4; Zec 14:4
16:32 ᵖS Ex 15:12
16:33 ᵠS ver 30;
S Ecc 9:10
16:35 ʳS Nu 11:1-3;
26:10; Rev 11:5
ˢS Lev 10:2
16:37 ᵗS Ex 6:23
ᵘver 6
16:38 ᵛLev 10:1;
Pr 20:2 ʷS Ex 20:24;
38:1-7 ˣNu 26:10;
Dt 28:46; Jer 44:29;
Eze 14:8; 2Pe 2:6
16:39 ʸ2Ch 26:18
ᶻS Lev 20:14
16:40 ᵃS Ex 30:1;
2Ki 12:3; Isa 1:13;
66:3; Jer 41:5; 44:3
ᵇS Ex 30:9;
2Ch 26:18 ᶜS Nu 3:10
16:42 ᵈS ver 19
ᵉEx 16:7; Nu 14:10
16:45 ᶠS Ex 32:10
16:46 ᵍS Lev 10:1
ʰLev 10:6
ʲS Ex 29:36
ʲS Ex 30:12
ᵏS Lev 26:25;
Nu 8:19; Ps 106:29
16:47 ˡNu 25:6-8
16:48 ᵐNu 25:8;
Ps 106:30
16:49 ⁿver 32
17:2 ᵒS Ge 32:10;
S Ex 4:2 ᵖNu 1:4
17:3 ᵠS Nu 1:3

²⁶He warned the assembly, "Move back from the tents of these wicked men!ᶜ Do not touch anything belonging to them, or you will be swept awayᵈ because of all their sins.ᵉ" ²⁷So they moved away from the tents of Korah, Dathan and Abiram.ᶠ Dathan and Abiram had come out and were standing with their wives, childrenᵍ and little ones at the entrances to their tents.ʰ

²⁸Then Moses said, "This is how you will knowⁱ that the Lᴏʀᴅ has sent meʲ to do all these things and that it was not my idea: ²⁹If these men die a natural death and suffer the common fate of all human beings, then the Lᴏʀᴅ has not sent me.ᵏ ³⁰But if the Lᴏʀᴅ brings about something totally new, and the earth opens its mouthˡ and swallows them, with everything that belongs to them, and they go down alive into the realm of the dead,ᵐ then you will know that these men have treated the Lᴏʀᴅ with contempt.ⁿ"

³¹As soon as he finished saying all this, the ground under them split apartᵒ ³²and the earth opened its mouth and swallowed themᵖ and their households, and all those associated with Korah, together with their possessions. ³³They went down alive into the realm of the dead,ᵠ with everything they owned; the earth closed over them, and they perished and were gone from the community. ³⁴At their cries, all the Israelites around them fled, shouting, "The earth is going to swallow us too!"

³⁵And fire came out from the Lᴏʀᴅʳ and consumedˢ the 250 men who were offering the incense.

*³⁶The Lᴏʀᴅ said to Moses, ³⁷"Tell Eleazarᵗ son of Aaron, the priest, to remove the censersᵘ from the charred remains and scatter the coals some distance away, for the censers are holy— ³⁸the censers of the men who sinned at the cost of their lives.ᵛ Hammer the censers into sheets to overlay the altar,ʷ for they were presented before the Lᴏʀᴅ and have become holy. Let them be a signˣ to the Israelites."

³⁹So Eleazar the priestʸ collected the bronze censers brought by those who had been burned to death,ᶻ and he had them hammered out to overlay the altar, ⁴⁰as the Lᴏʀᴅ directed him through Moses. This was to remind the Israelites that no one except a descendant of Aaron should come to burn incenseᵃ before the Lᴏʀᴅ,ᵇ or he would become like Korah and his followers.ᶜ

⁴¹The next day the whole Israelite community grumbled against Moses and Aaron. "You have killed the Lᴏʀᴅ's people," they said.

⁴²But when the assembly gathered in oppositionᵈ to Moses and Aaron and turned toward the tent of meeting, suddenly the cloud covered it and the glory of the Lᴏʀᴅᵉ appeared. ⁴³Then Moses and Aaron went to the front of the tent of meeting, ⁴⁴and the Lᴏʀᴅ said to Moses, ⁴⁵"Get away from this assembly so I can put an endᶠ to them at once." And they fell facedown.

⁴⁶Then Moses said to Aaron, "Take your censerᵍ and put incense in it, along with burning coals from the altar, and hurry to the assemblyʰ to make atonementⁱ for them. Wrath has come out from the Lᴏʀᴅ;ʲ the plagueᵏ has started." ⁴⁷So Aaron did as Moses said, and ran into the midst of the assembly. The plague had already started among the people,ˡ but Aaron offered the incense and made atonement for them. ⁴⁸He stood between the living and the dead, and the plague stopped.ᵐ ⁴⁹But 14,700 people died from the plague, in addition to those who had died because of Korah.ⁿ ⁵⁰Then Aaron returned to Moses at the entrance to the tent of meeting, for the plague had stopped.

THE BUDDING OF AARON'S STAFF

17 *The Lᴏʀᴅ said to Moses, ²"Speak to the Israelites and get twelve staffsᵒ from them, one from the leader of each of their ancestral tribes.ᵖ Write the name of each man on his staff. ³On the staff of Levi write Aaron's name,ᵠ for there

---

*16:36-50 is numbered 17:1-15 in Hebrew texts.   *17:1-13 is numbered 17:16-28 in Hebrew texts.

16:30 *something totally new.* Moses wished to assure the people that the imminent judgment was the direct work of the Lord and not a chance event that might be interpreted differently. The opening of the earth to swallow the rebels was a sure sign of the wrath of God and the vindication of Moses and Aaron. *realm of the dead.* See v. 33; see also note on Ge 37:35.

16:32 *swallowed them and their households.* The sons of Korah did not die (26:11); apparently they did not join their father in his rash plan. The households of the other rebels died with them.

16:37 *remove the censers.* The true priests took the censers of the 250 deceased impostors from their charred remains and

hammered them into bronze sheets for the altar as a memorial of the folly of a self-proclaimed priest (v. 40).

16:41 *the whole Israelite community grumbled.* Again the community attacked Moses, unfairly charging him with the deaths of the Lord's people. Except for the intervention of Moses and Aaron (see vv. 4,22), the entire nation might have been destroyed because of their continued rebellion (see v. 45).

16:49 *14,700 people died.* The number makes sense only if the community is as large as the census lists of ch. 2 suggest.

17:1-13 This story follows the account of the divine judgment of Korah (16:1-35), the narrative of the symbolic use given to the censers of the rebels and its aftermath (16:36-50). Ch. 17 is must be one staff for the head of each ancestral tribe. ⁴Place them in the tent of meeting^r in front of the ark of the covenant law,^s where I meet with you.^t ⁵The staff belonging to the man I choose^u will sprout,^v and I will rid myself of this constant grumbling^w against you by the Israelites."

⁶So Moses spoke to the Israelites, and their leaders gave him twelve staffs, one for the leader of each of their ancestral tribes, and Aaron's staff was among them. ⁷Moses placed the staffs before the Lord in the tent of the covenant law.^x

⁸The next day Moses entered the tent^y and saw that Aaron's staff,^z which represented the house of Levi, had not only sprouted but had budded, blossomed and produced almonds.^a ⁹Then Moses brought out all the staffs^b from the Lord's presence to all the Israelites. They looked at them, and each of the leaders took his own staff.

¹⁰The Lord said to Moses, "Put back Aaron's staff^c in front of the ark of the covenant law, to be kept as a sign to the rebellious.^d This will put an end to their grumbling against me, so that they will not die." ¹¹Moses did just as the Lord commanded him.

¹²The Israelites said to Moses, "We will die! We are lost, we are all lost!^e ¹³Anyone who even comes near the tabernacle of the Lord will die.^f Are we all going to die?"

DUTIES OF PRIESTS AND LEVITES

18 The Lord said to Aaron, "You, your sons and your ancestral family are to bear the responsibility for offenses connected with the sanctuary,^g and you and your sons alone are to bear the responsibility for offenses connected with the priesthood. ²Bring your fellow Levites from your ancestral tribe to join you and assist you when you and your sons minister^h before the tent of the covenant law. ³They are to be responsible to youⁱ and are to perform all the duties of the tent,^j but they must not go near the furnishings of the sanctuary or the altar. Otherwise both they and you will die.^k ⁴They are to join you and be responsible for the care of the tent of meeting—all the work at the tent—and no one else may come near where you are.^l

⁵"You are to be responsible for the care of the sanctuary and the altar,^m so that my wrath will not fall on the Israelites again. ⁶I myself have selected your fellow Levites from among the Israelites as a gift to you,ⁿ dedicated to the Lord to do the work at the tent of meeting.^o ⁷But only you and your sons may serve as priests in connection with everything at the altar and inside the curtain.^p I am giving you the service of the priesthood as a gift.^q Anyone else who comes near the sanctuary is to be put to death.^r"

OFFERINGS FOR PRIESTS AND LEVITES

⁸Then the Lord said to Aaron, "I myself have put you in charge of the offerings presented to me; all the holy offerings the Israelites give me I give to you and your sons as your portion,^s your perpetual share.^t ⁹You are to have the part of the most holy offerings^u that

17:4 ^r S Ex 40:2
^s ver 7; Ex 16:34
^t Ex 25:22
17:5 ^u S Nu 16:5
^v ver 8 ^w S Ex 16:7
17:7 ^x S Ex 38:21
17:8 ^y ver 7; Nu 1:50
^z ver 2,10 ^a Eze 17:24;
Heb 9:4
17:9 ^b ver 2
17:10 ^c S ver 8
^d S Ex 23:21; Dt 9:24;
Ps 66:7; 68:18;
Pr 24:21
17:12 ^e Jdg 13:22;
Isa 6:5; 15:1
17:13 ^f Nu 1:51
18:1 ^g S Ex 28:38
18:2 ^h Nu 3:10
18:3 ⁱ S Nu 3:32
^j Nu 1:51 ^k ver 7
18:4 ^l S Nu 3:38
18:5 ^m ver 3;
Lev 6:12
18:6 ⁿ S Nu 3:9
^o Nu 3:8
18:7 ^p Heb 9:3,6
^q ver 20; Ex 29:9;
40:13; Heb 5:4
^r ver 3; Nu 3:10
18:8 ^s S Lev 2:2
^t Lev 6:16; 7:6,31-34,
36; Dt 18:1; 2Ch 31:4
18:9 ^u S Lev 6:17

---

thus the third in a series of accounts vindicating the Aaronic priesthood against all opposition. The selection of 12 staffs, one from each tribe, was a symbolic act whereby the divine choice of Aaron would be indicated again.

17:3 *On the staff of Levi write Aaron's name.* The test needed to be unequivocal because of the wide support given to Korah's rebellion. The 250 who had joined with Korah were from many, perhaps all, of the tribes.

17:4 *in front of the ark of the covenant law.* In front of the ark, with the Ten Commandments, thus probably in the Holy Place, near the altar of incense (see vv. 7–8,10; see also note on Ex 25:22).

17:8 *had not only sprouted but had budded, blossomed and produced almonds.* God exceeded the demands of the test so that there might be no uncertainty as to who had acted or what he intended by his action.

17:10 *in front of the ark of the covenant law.* Aaron's rod joined the stone tablets of the law of Moses (see note on Ex 25:16) and the jar of manna (Ex 16:33–34) within or near the ark of the covenant (see Heb 9:4). These holy symbols were ever before the Lord as memorials of his special deeds on behalf of his people. Moreover, if anyone of a later age should dare to question the unique and holy place of the Aaronic priests in the Lord's service, this symbolic memorial of God's choice of Aaron would stand in opposition to their audacity. It is difficult to overestimate the importance of the role of Aaron and his sons in the worship of Israel (see note on 18:1–7).

17:12 *We will die!* At last the people realized the sin of their arrogance in challenging Aaron's role. The appropriate ways of approaching the Lord are detailed in chs. 18–19.

18:1–7 Aaron and his family, chosen by the Lord to be the true priests of holy worship, faced a burdensome task. The lament of the people in 17:12–13 was real; grievous sins against the holy meeting place of the Lord and his people would be judged by death. The Lord's mercy in providing a legitimate priesthood was actually an aspect of his grace (cf. Ps 99:6–8), because it was the people's only hope for deliverance from judgment.

18:2 *Bring your fellow Levites.* The Aaronic priests were to be assisted by the others in the tribe of Levi, but the assistants were not to go beyond their serving role. If they did so, not only would they die, but so would the priests who were responsible (v. 3). *covenant law.* See note on Ex 25:22.

18:7 *the service of the priesthood as a gift.* Of all men, the priests were privileged to approach the Holy Place and minister before the Lord. The priesthood was a gift of God's grace to both priests and people.

18:8 *your portion, your perpetual share.* The priests were to be supported in their work of ministry (see Lev 6:14—7:36). Since the Levites as a whole and the priests in particular had no part in the land that God was going to give them, it was necessary that the means for their provision be spelled out fully. They were not to have a part in the land; their share was the Lord himself (v. 20).

18:9 ᵛLev 2:1
ʷLev 6:25
ˣS Lev 5:15
18:10 ʸS Lev 6:16
ᶻLev 6:17,18
18:11 ªEx 29:26;
Lev 7:30; Nu 6:20
ᵇLev 7:31-34
ᶜLev 13:3; 22:1-16
18:12 ᵈDt 7:13;
11:14; 12:17; 28:51;
2Ki 18:32; 2Ch 31:5;
Ne 10:37; Jer 31:12;
Eze 23:41; Hos 2:8;
Joel 1:10; Hag 1:11
ᵉS Ge 4:3 ᶠEx 23:19;
34:26; Ne 10:35
18:13 ᵍS Ex 29:27
ʰver 11
18:14 ⁱS Lev 27:21;
Jos 6:17-19
18:15 ʲEx 13:2
ᵏS Nu 3:46
ˡS Ge 10:15
ᵐS Ex 13:13
18:16 ⁿS Nu 3:15
ᵒS Lev 27:6
ᵖS Ex 30:13
�q Nu 3:47
18:17 ʳS Lev 27:9
ˢS Lev 3:2
ᵗS Ex 29:13
ᵘS Lev 1:9
18:18 ᵛLev 7:30
ʷver 11
18:19 ˣ2Ki 12:4
ʸS Lev 2:13
18:20 ᶻNu 26:62;
Dt 12:12 ªver 24;
Dt 10:9; 14:27; 18:1-2;
Jos 13:33; Eze 44:28
18:21 ᵇver 24;
S Ge 28:22; Nu 31:28;
Dt 14:22; Ne 10:37;
13:5; Mal 3:8
ᶜLev 27:30-33;
Heb 7:5 ᵈNu 1:53
18:22 ᵉS Ex 28:43
18:23 ᶠS Ex 12:14;
S 27:21 ᵍNu 10:8
ʰver 20; Nu 26:62;
Dt 10:9 / Eze 44:10
18:24 ⁱLev 27:30;
Dt 26:12
18:26 ᵏver 21
ʲver 28; Ne 10:38
18:27 ᵐLev 7:18
ⁿGe 50:10; Dt 15:14;
Jdg 6:37; Ru 3:3,6,14;
1Sa 23:1 ᵒver 12,30
18:28 ᵖMal 3:8
18:30 ᵠS ver 27
18:31 ʳver 23
18:32 ˢLev 22:15
ᵗver 29 ᵘS Lev 19:8
19:2 ᵛS Ge 15:9;
Heb 9:13
ʷS Lev 22:19-25
ˣDt 21:3; 1Sa 6:7

is kept from the fire. From all the gifts they bring me as most holy offerings, whether grain ᵛ or sin ª ʷ or guilt offerings, ˣ that part belongs to you and your sons. ¹⁰Eat it as something most holy; every male shall eat it. ʸ You must regard it as holy. ᶻ

¹¹"This also is yours: whatever is set aside from the gifts of all the wave offerings ª of the Israelites. I give this to you and your sons and daughters as your perpetual share. ᵇ Everyone in your household who is ceremonially clean ᶜ may eat it.

¹²"I give you all the finest olive oil and all the finest new wine and grain ᵈ they give the Lᴏʀᴅ ᵉ as the firstfruits of their harvest. ᶠ ¹³All the land's firstfruits that they bring to the Lᴏʀᴅ will be yours. ᵍ Everyone in your household who is ceremonially clean may eat it. ʰ

¹⁴"Everything in Israel that is devoted ᵇ to the Lᴏʀᴅ ⁱ is yours. ¹⁵The first offspring of every womb, both human and animal, that is offered to the Lᴏʀᴅ is yours. ʲ But you must redeem ᵏ every firstborn ˡ son and every firstborn male of unclean animals. ᵐ ¹⁶When they are a month old, ⁿ you must redeem them at the redemption price set at five shekels ᶜ ᵒ of silver, according to the sanctuary shekel, ᵖ which weighs twenty gerahs. ᵠ

¹⁷"But you must not redeem the firstborn of a cow, a sheep or a goat; they are holy. ʳ Splash their blood ˢ against the altar and burn their fat ᵗ as a food offering, an aroma pleasing to the Lᴏʀᴅ. ᵘ ¹⁸Their meat is to be yours, just as the breast of the wave offering ᵛ and the right thigh are yours. ʷ ¹⁹Whatever is set aside from the holy ˣ offerings the Israelites present to the Lᴏʀᴅ I give to you and your sons and daughters as your perpetual share. It is an everlasting covenant of salt ʸ before the Lᴏʀᴅ for both you and your offspring."

²⁰The Lᴏʀᴅ said to Aaron, "You will have no inheritance in their land, nor will you have any share among them; ᶻ I am your share and your inheritance ª among the Israelites.

²¹"I give to the Levites all the tithes ᵇ in Israel as their inheritance ᶜ in return for the work they do while serving at the tent of meeting. ᵈ ²²From now on the Israelites must not go near the tent of meeting, or they will bear the consequences of their sin and will die. ᵉ ²³It is the Levites who are to do the work at the tent of meeting and bear the responsibility for any offenses they commit against it. This is a lasting ordinance ᶠ for the generations to come. ᵍ They will receive no inheritance ʰ among the Israelites. ⁱ ²⁴Instead, I give to the Levites as their inheritance the tithes that the Israelites present as an offering to the Lᴏʀᴅ. ʲ That is why I said concerning them: 'They will have no inheritance among the Israelites.' "

²⁵The Lᴏʀᴅ said to Moses, ²⁶"Speak to the Levites and say to them: 'When you receive from the Israelites the tithe I give you ᵏ as your inheritance, you must present a tenth of that tithe as the Lᴏʀᴅ's offering. ˡ ²⁷Your offering will be reckoned ᵐ to you as grain from the threshing floor ⁿ or juice from the winepress. ᵒ ²⁸In this way you also will present an offering to the Lᴏʀᴅ from all the tithes ᵖ you receive from the Israelites. From these tithes you must give the Lᴏʀᴅ's portion to Aaron the priest. ²⁹You must present as the Lᴏʀᴅ's portion the best and holiest part of everything given to you.'

³⁰"Say to the Levites: 'When you present the best part, it will be reckoned to you as the product of the threshing floor or the winepress. ᵠ ³¹You and your households may eat the rest of it anywhere, for it is your wages for your work at the tent of meeting. ʳ ³²By presenting the best part ˢ of it you will not be guilty in this matter; ᵗ then you will not defile the holy offerings ᵘ of the Israelites, and you will not die.' "

THE WATER OF CLEANSING

19 The Lᴏʀᴅ said to Moses and Aaron: ²"This is a requirement of the law that the Lᴏʀᴅ has commanded: Tell the Israelites to bring you a red heifer ᵛ without defect or blemish ʷ and that has never been under a yoke. ˣ ³Give it to Elea-

---

ª 9 Or *purification*   ᵇ 14 The Hebrew term refers to the irrevocable giving over of things or persons to the Lᴏʀᴅ.   ᶜ 16 That is, about 2 ounces or about 55 grams

---

18:11 *your sons and daughters.* Provision was made not only for the priests, but for their families as well. Only family members who were ceremonially unclean were forbidden to eat the gifts and offerings of the people (see v. 13). Provisions for cleansing were stated in Lev 22:4-8.

18:12 *finest olive oil … finest new wine and grain.* Since the best items of produce were to be given to the Lord, these became the special foods of the priests and their families. The NT writers similarly argue that those who minister the word of God in the present period should also be paid suitably for their work (see, e.g., 1Co 9:3-10 and notes).

18:16 *according to the sanctuary shekel.* See note on Ex 30:13.

18:19 *everlasting covenant of salt.* A permanent provision for the priests. The phrase "covenant of salt" (see 2Ch 13:5) remains ob-

scure. In Lev 2:13 the salt that must accompany grain offerings is called the "salt of the covenant." According to Eze 43:24, salt is also to be sprinkled on burnt offerings, and Ex 30:35 specifies salt as one of the ingredients in the special incense compounded for the sanctuary. A "covenant of salt" is perhaps an allusion to the salt used in the sacrificial meal that commonly accompanied the making of a covenant (see Ge 31:54; Ex 24:5-11; Ps 50:5).

18:26-32 Although the Levites were the recipients of the tithe given to the Lord, they were not themselves exempt from tithing. They in turn were to give a tenth of their income to Aaron (v. 28) and were to be sure that the best part was given as the Lord's portion (v. 29). By obedient compliance the Levites would escape judicial death (v. 32).

19:2 *red heifer.* The qualifying words, "without defect or blemzar[y] the priest; it is to be taken outside the camp[z] and slaughtered in his presence. [4]Then Eleazar the priest is to take some of its blood on his finger and sprinkle[a] it seven times toward the front of the tent of meeting. [5]While he watches, the heifer is to be burned— its hide, flesh, blood and intestines.[b] [6]The priest is to take some cedar wood, hyssop[c] and scarlet wool[d] and throw them onto the burning heifer. [7]After that, the priest must wash his clothes and bathe himself with water.[e] He may then come into the camp, but he will be ceremonially unclean till evening. [8]The man who burns it must also wash his clothes and bathe with water, and he too will be unclean till evening.

[9]"A man who is clean shall gather up the ashes of the heifer[f] and put them in a ceremonially clean place[g] outside the camp. They are to be kept by the Israelite community for use in the water of cleansing;[h] it is for purification from sin.[i] [10]The man who gathers up[j] the ashes of the heifer must also wash his clothes, and he too will be unclean till evening.[k] This will be a lasting ordinance[l] both for the Israelites and for the foreigners residing among them.[m]

[11]"Whoever touches a human corpse[n] will be unclean for seven days.[o] [12]They must purify themselves with the water on the third day and on the seventh day;[p] then they will be clean. But if they do not purify themselves on the third and seventh days, they will not be clean.[q] [13]If they fail to purify themselves after touching a human corpse,[r] they defile the LORD's tabernacle.[s] They must be cut off from Israel.[t] Because the water of cleansing has not been sprinkled on them, they are unclean;[u] their uncleanness remains on them.

[14]"This is the law that applies when a person dies in a tent: Anyone who enters the tent and anyone who is in it will be unclean for seven days, [15]and every open container[v] without a lid fastened on it will be unclean.

[16]"Anyone out in the open who touches someone who has been killed with a sword or someone who has died a natural death,[w] or anyone who touches a human bone[x] or a grave,[y] will be unclean for seven days.[z]

[17]"For the unclean person, put some ashes[a] from the burned purification offering into a jar and pour fresh water[b] over them. [18]Then a man who is ceremonially clean is to take some hyssop,[c] dip it in the water and sprinkle[d] the tent and all the furnishings and the people who were there. He must also sprinkle anyone who has touched a human bone or a grave[e] or anyone who has been killed or anyone who has died a natural death. [19]The man who is clean is to sprinkle[f] those who are unclean on the third and seventh days, and on the seventh day he is to purify them.[g] Those who are being cleansed must wash their clothes[h] and bathe with water, and that evening they will be clean. [20]But if those who are unclean do not purify themselves, they must be cut off from the community, because they have defiled[i] the sanctuary of the LORD.[j] The water of cleansing has not been sprinkled on them, and they are unclean.[k] [21]This is a lasting ordinance[l] for them.

"The man who sprinkles the water of cleansing must also wash his clothes, and anyone who touches the water of cleansing will be unclean till evening. [22]Anything that an unclean[m] person touches becomes unclean, and anyone who touches it becomes unclean till evening."

19:3 [y] Nu 3:4
[z] S Ex 29:14
19:4 [a] S Lev 4:17
19:5 [b] S Ex 29:14
19:6 [c] ver 18; Ps 51:7
[d] S Lev 14:4
19:7 [e] S Lev 11:25; S 14:8
19:9 [f] Heb 9:13
[g] S Ex 29:31;
S Lev 4:12 [h] ver 13;
Nu 8:7 [i] S Ge 35:2
19:10 [j] Lev 15:10
[k] Lev 14:46 [l] Lev 3:17
[m] S Lev 22:18
19:11 [n] S Lev 21:1
[o] S Lev 8:33; Nu 31:19
19:12 [p] ver 19;
Nu 31:19 [q] ver 20;
2Ch 26:21
19:13 [r] S Lev 21:11
[s] S Lev 15:31;
2Ch 36:14; Ps 79:1
[t] Lev 7:20; 22:3
[u] ver 22; Hag 2:13
19:15 [v] S Lev 6:28
19:16 [w] Nu 31:19
[x] 1Ki 13:2; 2Ki 23:14;
Eze 6:5 [y] 2Ki 23:6;
Mt 23:27 [z] S Lev 5:3
19:17 [a] ver 9
[b] S Nu 8:7
19:18 [c] ver 6;
S Ex 12:22
[d] S Lev 4:17 [e] ver 16
19:19 [f] S Lev 16:14-15 [g] Nu 31:19;
Eze 36:25; Heb 10:22
[h] S Ge 35:2
19:20 [i] Ps 74:7
[j] S Lev 15:31
[k] S ver 12; S Lev 14:8
19:21 [l] S Ex 27:21
19:22 [m] S Lev 5:2; 15:4-12

---

ish," are familiar in contexts of sacrificial worship in the OT. But this is not a sacrificial animal. It is a cow, not an ox; it is to be slaughtered, not sacrificed; and it is to be killed outside the camp, not at the holy altar. The ashes of the red heifer (v. 9) are the primary focus of this act, for they will be used in the ritual of the water of cleansing. The burning of the animal with its "blood and intestines" (v. 5) is unprecedented in the OT. The normal pattern for the sacrifice of the burnt offering is given in Lev 1:3–9. In every respect the killing of the red heifer is distinct: A female animal was taken outside the camp to be killed; the priest had to be present, but he did not identify himself with it; and a bit of the heifer's blood was sprinkled from the priest's finger toward the tabernacle seven times. The rest of the animal was to be burned in its entirety, without the draining of its blood or the cleansing of its intestines.
19:6 *cedar wood, hyssop and scarlet wool.* Associated with the cleansing properties of the ashes of the red heifer.
19:12 *purify themselves with the water.* The ashes from the red

heifer were kept outside the camp and would be mixed as needed with water to provide a means of cleansing after contact with dead bodies.
19:13 *defile the LORD's tabernacle.* Willful neglect of the provision for cleansing brought not only judgment on the person but pollution of the tabernacle itself. *cut off from Israel.* See note on Ex 12:15.
19:14 *anyone who is in it.* There would be many occasions in which a person would become unclean, not because of deliberate contact with a dead body, but just by being in the proximity of one who died.

A **19:18** *hyssop, dip it in the water and sprinkle.* Here the method of the cleansing ritual is explained. A ceremonially clean person had to sprinkle the ceremonially unclean person or thing. The cleansing power of the blood of Christ is specifically contrasted ("much more"; Heb 9:13–14) with the cleansing effectiveness of the water of the ashes of the red heifer.

20:1 ⁿ Nu 13:21
º ver 14; Nu 13:26;
33:36; Dt 1:46;
Jdg 11:17; Ps 29:8
ᵖ S Ex 15:20
20:2 ᑫ S Ex 15:22
ʳ Ex 17:1 ᔆ S Nu 16:19
20:3 ᵗ ver 13;
S Ge 13:7; Ex 17:2;
21:18 ᵘ S Ex 5:21
ᵛ S Nu 14:2; 16:31-35
20:4 ʷ S Nu 14:2
ˣ S Ex 14:11; Nu 14:3;
16:13
20:5 ʸ Nu 13:23;
16:14 ᶻ S Ex 17:1
20:6 ᵃ S Ex 40:2
ᵇ Nu 14:5 ᶜ S Nu 16:19
20:8 ᵈ S Ex 4:2;
S 10:12-13 ᵉ Ex 17:6;
Isa 41:18; 43:20;
Jer 31:9
20:9 ᶠ Nu 17:2
ᵍ Nu 17:10
20:10 ʰ ver 8
ⁱ Ps 106:32,33
20:11 ʲ S Ex 17:6;
S Isa 33:21
20:12 ᵏ Nu 27:14;
Dt 32:51; Isa 5:16;
8:13 ˡ ver 24; Dt 1:37;
3:27
20:13 ᵐ S Ex 17:7
ⁿ S ver 3 º S Lev 10:3
20:14 ᵖ S ver 1
ᑫ S ver 16;
S Ge 25:30; S 36:16
ʳ Ge 24:3; Dt 4:39;
Jos 2:11; 9:9
ᔆ S Ex 18:8
20:15 ᵗ S Ge 46:6
ᵘ S Ge 15:13
ᵛ S Ex 1:14
20:16 ʷ S Ge 16:11;
S 21:17; S Ex 2:23
ˣ Ex 14:19 ʸ Ex 12:42;
Dt 26:8 ᶻ ver 14,23;
Nu 33:37

WATER FROM THE ROCK

20 In the first month the whole Israelite community arrived at the Desert of Zin, ⁿ and they stayed at Kadesh. º There Miriamᵖ died and was buried.

²Now there was no waterᑫ for the community, ʳ and the people gathered in oppositionᔆ to Moses and Aaron. ³They quarreledᵗ with Moses and said, "If only we had died when our brothers fell deadᵘ before the Lord! ᵛ ⁴Why did you bring the Lord's community into this wilderness, ʷ that we and our livestock should die here?ˣ ⁵Why did you bring us up out of Egypt to this terrible place? It has no grain or figs, grapevines or pomegranates. ʸ And there is no water to drink!ᶻ"

⁶Moses and Aaron went from the assembly to the entrance to the tent of meetingᵃ and fell facedown,ᵇ and the glory of the Lordᶜ appeared to them. ⁷The Lord said to Moses, ⁸"Take the staff, ᵈ and you and your brother Aaron gather the assembly together. Speak to that rock before their eyes and it will pour out its water. ᵉ You will bring water out of the rock for the community so they and their livestock can drink."

⁹So Moses took the staffᶠ from the Lord's presence, ᵍ just as he commanded him. ¹⁰He and Aaron gathered the assembly togetherʰ in front of the rock and Moses said to them, "Listen, you rebels, must we bring you water out of this rock?"ⁱ ¹¹Then Moses raised his arm and struck the rock twice with his staff. Waterʲ gushed out, and the community and their livestock drank."

¹²But the Lord said to Moses and Aaron, "Because you did not trust in me enough to honor me as holyᵏ in the sight of the Israelites, you will not bring this community into the land I give them." ˡ

¹³These were the waters of Meribah, ᵃ ᵐ where the Israelites quarreledⁿ with the Lord and where he was proved holy among them. º

EDOM DENIES ISRAEL PASSAGE

¹⁴Moses sent messengers from Kadeshᵖ to the king of Edom, ᑫ saying:

"This is what your brother Israel says: You knowʳ about all the hardshipsᔆ that have come on us. ¹⁵Our ancestors went down into Egypt, ᵗ and we lived there many years. ᵘ The Egyptians mistreatedᵛ us and our ancestors, ¹⁶but when we cried out to the Lord, he heard our cryʷ and sent an angelˣ and brought us out of Egypt. ʸ

"Now we are here at Kadesh, a town on the edge of your territory. ᶻ ¹⁷Please let us

---

ᵃ 13 *Meribah* means *quarreling.*

20:1–29 This chapter begins with the death of Miriam (v. 1), concludes with the death of Aaron (v. 28), includes the record of the conflict with Edom (vv. 14–21) and centers on the tragic sin of Moses (vv. 11–12). Such was the sad beginning of Israel's last year in the wilderness.

20:1 *first month.* The year is not given, but a comparison of vv. 22–29 with 33:38 leads to the conclusion that this chapter begins in the 40th year after the exodus (see notes on 1:1; 9:1). Most of the people 20 years old or more at the time of the rebellion at Kadesh (chs. 13–14) would already have died. *at Kadesh.* See note on Ge 14:7. The larger part of the wilderness wandering (see 32:13) is left without record. The people may have traveled about, seeking the water sources and the sparse vegetation, supported primarily by manna. But their circuits would bring them back to the central camp at Kadesh, the scene of their great rebellion (chs. 13–14). They have now come full circle; the land of promise lies before them again.

20:2 *no water.* Forty years earlier the Lord had instructed Moses to take the staff he had used to strike the Nile (Ex 7:17) and to strike the rock at Horeb to initiate a flow of water (Ex 17:1–7). Now, 40 years later, at the place of Israel's worst acts of rebellion, the scene was recurring. The children of the rebellious nation now desire to die with their parents; the parents' complaints about the bread from heaven are repeated by the children.

20:6 *glory of the Lord.* See note on Ex 16:7.

20:8 *Speak to that rock.* Moses was told to take his staff, through which God had performed wonders in Egypt and in the wilderness all these years, but this time he was merely to speak to the rock and it would pour out its water for the people. Cf. Ps 114:8 and note.

20:10 *Listen, you rebels.* At once the accumulated anger, exasperation and frustration of 40 years came to expression (see Ps 106:33 and note).

A C **20:11** *struck the rock twice with his staff.* In his rage Moses disobeyed the Lord's instruction to speak to the rock (v. 8). Moses' rash action brought a stern rebuke from the Lord (v. 12). The nature of Moses' offense is not clearly stated in this text, but these factors appear to have been involved: 1. Moses' action was a lack of trust in God (v. 12), as though he believed that a word alone would not suffice. 2. God's holiness was offended by Moses' rash action (v. 12), for he had not shown proper deference to God's presence.

C **20:12** *to honor me as holy.* See note on Lev 11:44. *you will not bring this community into the land.* The end result of Moses' action is sure: Neither Aaron nor Moses would enter the land of promise. Of their contemporaries only Joshua and Caleb would survive to enter the land. The inclusion of Aaron demonstrates his partnership with his brother in the breach against God's holiness.

20:13 *Meribah.* See TNIV text note. The same name was used 40 years earlier at the first occasion of bringing water from the rock (Ex 17:7, where it is also called Massah, "testing"; see note there). Ps 95:8 (see note there) laments the rebellion at Meribah and Massah. *was proved holy.* See Lev 10:3 and note.

20:14–21 Moses' attempt to pass through the territory of Edom by peaceful negotiation and payment for services rendered is met with arrogant rebuff.

20:14 *your brother Israel.* The people of Edom were descended from Esau, the brother of Jacob (see Ge 36:1; Ob 10 and notes).

pass through your country. We will not go through any field or vineyard, or drink water from any well. We will travel along the King's Highway and not turn to the right or to the left until we have passed through your territory. *a*"

[18] But Edom *b* answered:

"You may not pass through here; if you try, we will march out and attack you with the sword. *c*"

[19] The Israelites replied:

"We will go along the main road, and if we or our livestock *d* drink any of your water, we will pay for it. *e* We only want to pass through on foot—nothing else."

[20] Again they answered:

"You may not pass through. *f*"

Then Edom *g* came out against them with a large and powerful army. [21] Since Edom refused to let them go through their territory, *h* Israel turned away from them. *i*

THE DEATH OF AARON

[22] The whole Israelite community set out from Kadesh *j* and came to Mount Hor. *k* [23] At Mount Hor, near the border of Edom, *l* the LORD said to Moses and Aaron, [24] "Aaron will be gathered to his people. *m* He will not enter the land I give the Israelites, because both of you rebelled against my command *n* at the waters of Meribah. *o* [25] Get Aaron and his son Eleazar and take them up Mount Hor. *p* [26] Remove Aaron's garments *q* and put them on his son Eleazar, for Aaron will be gathered to his people; *r* he will die there."

[27] Moses did as the LORD commanded: They went up Mount Hor *s* in the sight of the whole community. [28] Moses removed Aaron's garments and put them on his son Eleazar. *t* And Aaron died there *u* on top of the mountain. Then Moses and Eleazar came down from the mountain, [29] and when the whole community learned that Aaron had died, *v* the entire house of Israel mourned for him *w* thirty days.

ARAD DESTROYED

21 When the Canaanite king of Arad, *x* who lived in the Negev, *y* heard that Israel was coming along the road to Atharim, he attacked the Israelites and captured some of them. [2] Then Israel made this vow *z* to the LORD: "If you will deliver these people into our hands, we will totally destroy *a a* their cities." [3] The LORD listened to Israel's plea and gave the Canaanites *b* over to them. They completely destroyed them *c* and their towns; so the place was named Hormah. *b d*

THE BRONZE SNAKE

[4] They traveled from Mount Hor *e* along the route to the Red Sea, *c f* to go around Edom. *g* But the people grew impatient on the way; *h* [5] they spoke against God *i* and against Moses,

---

a 2 The Hebrew term refers to the irrevocable giving over of things or persons to the LORD, often by totally destroying them; also in verse 3.   *b 3* *Hormah* means *destruction.*   *c 4* Or *the Sea of Reeds*

20:17 *King's Highway.* The major north-south trade route in Transjordan, extending from Arabia to Damascus.

20:20 *large and powerful army.* The show of force by Edom caused Israel to turn away so as not to risk conflict with this brother nation. Israel was forbidden by the Lord to take even a foothold in Edom (see Dt 2:4–6).

20:22 *Mount Hor.* Somewhere near the border of Edom (v. 23).

20:24 *gathered to his people.* A euphemism for death (see, e.g., Ge 25:8,17; 35:29). *both of you.* Aaron had joined Moses in rebellion against God (v. 12); his impending death was a precursor of Moses' death as well (see Dt 34).

20:25 *Aaron and his son Eleazar.* There was no doubt about Aaron's successor, just as there was none about Moses' successor (see Dt 34).

20:26–28 While Aaron was still alive, his garments were to be placed on his son; only then did he die.

20:29 *mourned for him.* Aaron's death (and that of Moses) marked the passing of a generation. The old generation was now nearly gone; in 40 years there had been almost a complete turnover of the people 20 years old or older.

21:1–3 The first battle of the new community against the Canaanites was provoked by the king of Arad, perhaps as he was raiding them. The result was a complete victory for the Israelites—a new day for them, since they had been defeated by the Amalekites and Canaanites a generation before (14:41–45).

21:1 *Negev.* See note on Ge 12:9.

21:2 *totally destroy.* See TNIV text note.

21:3 *Hormah.* See TNIV text note; the association with Israel's earlier defeat is made certain by the use of this place-name (cf. 14:45).

21:4 With Moses' determination not to engage Edom in battle (see note on 20:20), the people became impatient with him and with the direction the Lord was taking them. Flushed with victory, they were confident in themselves. They forgot that their victory over Arad had been granted by the Lord in response to their solemn pledge (v. 2); now they were ready to rebel again.

20:17 *a* ver 20;
Nu 21:22; Dt 2:27;
Jdg 11:17
20:18 *b* ver 14
c Nu 21:23
20:19 *d* Ex 12:38
e Dt 2:6,28
20:20 *f* S ver 17,18
g ver 14
20:21 *h* Nu 21:23
i Nu 21:4; Dt 2:8;
Jdg 11:18
20:22 *j* Dt 1:46
k Nu 33:37; 34:7;
Dt 32:50
20:23 *l* S ver 16
20:24 *m* S Ge 25:8
n S ver 10 *o* S Ex 17:7
20:25 *p* Nu 33:38
20:26 *q* Ex 28:1-4;
40:13; S Lev 16:4
r ver 24; Nu 27:13;
31:2
20:27 *s* Nu 33:38
20:28 *t* S Ex 29:29
u ver 26; Nu 33:38;
Dt 10:6; 32:50
20:29 *v* Dt 32:50
S Ge 27:41;
S Lev 10:6; S Dt 34:8
21:1 *x* Nu 33:40;
Jos 12:14 *y* S Ge 12:9;
Nu 13:17; Dt 1:7;
Jdg 1:9,16
21:2 *z* Lev 7:16
a ver 3; Ex 22:20;
Jos 2:34; Jos 2:10;
8:26; Jer 25:9; 50:21
21:3 *b* S Ge 10:18
c S ver 2 *d* S Nu 14:45
21:4 *e* Nu 20:22
f Nu 14:25; Dt 2:1;
11:4 *g* S Nu 20:21
h Dt 2:8; Jdg 11:18
21:5 *i* Ps 78:19

21:5 / Nu 11:20
k S Ex 14:11; Nu 14:2,
3 / Nu 20:5
m S Nu 11:5
21:6 n ver 7;
Dt 8:15; 32:33;
Job 20:14; Ps 58:4;
140:3; Jer 8:17
o 1Co 10:9
21:7 p Ps 78:34;
Hos 5:15 q Nu 14:40
r Ex 8:8; 1Sa 7:8;
Jer 27:18; 37:3;
Ac 8:24 s S Nu 11:2
21:8 t Jn 3:14
21:9 u 2Ki 18:4
v Jn 3:14-15
21:10 w Nu 33:43
21:11 x S Ge 36:35;
Nu 33:44; Dt 34:8;
Jer 40:11
21:12 y Dt 2:13,14
21:13 z Nu 22:36;
Dt 2:24; Jos 12:1;
Jdg 11:13,18;
2Ki 10:33; Isa 16:2;
Jer 48:20 a S Ge 10:16
21:14 b 1Sa 17:47;
18:17; 25:28
21:15 c ver 28;
Dt 2:9,18; 1Sa 15:1
21:16 d Nu 25:1;
33:49; Jdg 9:21;
Isa 15:8
21:17 e S Ex 15:1
21:20 f Nu 23:14;
Dt 3:17,27; 34:1;
Jos 12:3; 13:20
21:21 g S Ge 32:3
h Nu 32:33; Dt 1:4;
Jos 2:10; 12:2,4; 13:10;
Jdg 11:19-21; 1Ki 4:19;
Ne 9:22; Ps 135:11;
136:19; Jer 48:45
i S Ex 23:23
21:22 j S Nu 20:17
21:23 k Nu 20:21
l Dt 2:32; Jos 13:18;
21:36; Jdg 11:20;
Isa 15:4; Jer 48:21,34

and said, "Why have you brought us up out of Egypt[j] to die in the wilderness?[k] There is no bread! There is no water![l] And we detest this miserable food!"[m]

[6]Then the LORD sent venomous snakes[n] among them; they bit the people and many Israelites died.[o] [7]The people came to Moses[p] and said, "We sinned[q] when we spoke against the LORD and against you. Pray that the LORD[r] will take the snakes away from us." So Moses prayed[s] for the people.

[8]The LORD said to Moses, "Make a snake and put it up on a pole;[t] anyone who is bitten can look at it and live." [9]So Moses made a bronze snake[u] and put it up on a pole. Then when anyone was bitten by a snake and looked at the bronze snake, they lived.[v]

THE JOURNEY TO MOAB

[10]The Israelites moved on and camped at Oboth.[w] [11]Then they set out from Oboth and camped in Iye Abarim, in the wilderness that faces Moab[x] toward the sunrise. [12]From there they moved on and camped in the Zered Valley.[y] [13]They set out from there and camped alongside the Arnon[z], which is in the wilderness extending into Amorite territory. The Arnon is the border of Moab, between Moab and the Amorites.[a] [14]That is why the Book of the Wars[b] of the LORD says:

> ". . . Zahab[a] in Suphah and the ravines,
>   the Arnon [15]and[b] the slopes of the ravines
> that lead to the settlement of Ar[c]
>   and lie along the border of Moab."

[16]From there they continued on to Beer,[d] the well where the LORD said to Moses, "Gather the people together and I will give them water."

[17]Then Israel sang this song:[e]

> "Spring up, O well!
>   Sing about it,
> [18]about the well that the princes dug,
>   that the nobles of the people sank—
> the nobles with scepters and staffs."

Then they went from the wilderness to Mattanah, [19]from Mattanah to Nahaliel, from Nahaliel to Bamoth, [20]and from Bamoth to the valley in Moab where the top of Pisgah[f] overlooks the wasteland.

DEFEAT OF SIHON AND OG

[21]Israel sent messengers[g] to say to Sihon[h] king of the Amorites:[i]

[22]"Let us pass through your country. We will not turn aside into any field or vineyard, or drink water from any well. We will travel along the King's Highway until we have passed through your territory.[j]"

[23]But Sihon would not let Israel pass through his territory.[k] He mustered his entire army and marched out into the wilderness against Israel. When he reached Jahaz,[l] he

---

a 14 Septuagint; Hebrew *Waheb*   b 14,15 Or *"I have been given from Suphah and the ravines / of the Arnon* [15]*to*

21:5 *we detest this miserable food!* The people's impatience (v. 4) led them to blaspheme God, to reject his servant Moses and to despise the "bread from heaven" (Ex 16:4; see note there). This is the most bitter of their several complaints about the manna (see note on 11:7). Just as Moses' attack on the rock was more than it appeared to be (see note on 20:11), so the people's contempt for the heavenly bread was more serious than one might think. Rejecting the heavenly manna was tantamount to spurning God's grace (cf. Jn 6:32–35,48–51,58).

21:8–9 In response to the people's confession of sin (v. 7), God directed Moses to make an image of a snake and put it on a pole, so that anyone who had been bitten could look at it and live. See the typological use of this incident in Jn 3:14–15.

21:10–13 The people skirt Edom and make their way to the Arnon, the wadi that serves as the border between Moab and the region of the Amorites and that flows west into the midpoint of the Dead Sea.

21:12 *Zered.* See note on Dt 2:13.

21:14 *Book of the Wars of the LORD.* Mentioned only here in the OT. This is not in existence today; it was presumably an ancient collection of songs of war in praise of God (see note on 10:3 for music in war). Cf. the "Book of Jashar" (Jos 10:13 [see note there]; 2Sa 1:18).

21:16 *I will give them water.* The quest for water had been a constant problem during the desert experience (see ch. 20; Ex 17).

21:17–18 The song about the well may also come from the "Book of the Wars of the LORD" (v. 14).

21:21–26 As they had done with Edom (20:14–19), Israel requested freedom to pass through the land of the Amorites. When Sihon their king tried to meet Israel with a show of force, he suffered an overwhelming defeat. The land of the Amorites referred to here was in Transjordan, extending from the Arnon River (at the midpoint of the Dead Sea) to the Jabbok River (v. 24), which flows into the Jordan some 24 miles north of the Dead Sea.

fought with Israel.[m] [24]Israel, however, put him to the sword[n] and took over his land[o] from the Arnon to the Jabbok,[p] but only as far as the Ammonites,[q] because their border was fortified. [25]Israel captured all the cities of the Amorites[r] and occupied them,[s] including Heshbon[t] and all its surrounding settlements. [26]Heshbon was the city of Sihon[u] king of the Amorites,[v] who had fought against the former king of Moab[w] and had taken from him all his land as far as the Arnon.[x]

[27]That is why the poets say:

> "Come to Heshbon and let it be rebuilt;
>   let Sihon's city be restored.

[28] "Fire went out from Heshbon,
>   a blaze from the city of Sihon.[y]
> It consumed[z] Ar[a] of Moab,
>   the citizens of Arnon's heights.[b]
[29] Woe to you, Moab![c]
>   You are destroyed, people of Chemosh![d]
> He has given up his sons as fugitives[e]
>   and his daughters as captives[f]
> to Sihon king of the Amorites.

[30] "But we have overthrown them;
>   Heshbon's dominion has been destroyed all the way to Dibon.[g]
> We have demolished them as far as Nophah,
>   which extends to Medeba."[h]

[31]So Israel settled in the land of the Amorites.[i]

[32]After Moses had sent spies[j] to Jazer,[k] the Israelites captured its surrounding settlements and drove out the Amorites who were there. [33]Then they turned and went up along the road toward Bashan,[l],[m] and Og king of Bashan and his whole army marched out to meet them in battle at Edrei.[n]

[34]The LORD said to Moses, "Do not be afraid of him, for I have delivered him into your hands, along with his whole army and his land. Do to him what you did to Sihon king of the Amorites, who reigned in Heshbon.[o]"

[35]So they struck him down, together with his sons and his whole army, leaving them no survivors.[p] And they took possession of his land.[q]

BALAK SUMMONS BALAAM

22 Then the Israelites traveled to the plains of Moab[r] and camped along the Jordan[s] across from Jericho.[t] [2]Now Balak son of Zippor[u] saw all that Israel had done to the Amorites, [3]and Moab was terrified because there were so many people. Indeed, Moab was filled with dread[v] because of the Israelites.

[4]The Moabites[w] said to the elders of Midian,[x] "This horde is going to lick up everything[y] around us, as an ox licks up the grass of the field.[z]"

So Balak son of Zippor, who was king of Moab at that time, [5]sent messengers to summon Balaam son of Beor,[a] who was at Pethor, near the Euphrates River,[b] in his native land. Balak said:

> "A people has come out of Egypt;[c] they cover the face of the land and have set-

21:23 [m] Nu 20:18
21:24 [n] Dt 2:33; 3:3; 29:7; Ps 135:10-11; Am 2:9 [o] ver 35; Dt 3:4 [p] S Ge 32:22; Nu 32:33; Jdg 11:13, 22 [q] S Ge 19:38; Dt 2:37; Jos 13:10
21:25 [r] Nu 13:29; Jdg 10:11; Am 2:10 [s] Jdg 11:26 [t] ver 30; Nu 32:3; Dt 1:4; 29:7; Jos 9:10; 12:2; Isa 15:4; 16:8; Jer 48:2,34
21:26 [u] ver 21; Dt 2:9; Ps 135:11 [v] Nu 13:29 [w] ver 11 [x] ver 13
21:28 [y] Jer 48:45 [z] S Nu 11:1 [a] S ver 15 [b] Nu 22:41; Dt 12:2; Jos 13:17; Isa 15:2; Jer 19:5
21:29 [c] Nu 24:17; 2Sa 8:2; 1Ch 18:2; Ps 60:8; Isa 25:10; Jer 48:46 [d] Jdg 10:6; 11:24; Ru 1:15; 1Ki 11:7, 33; 2Ki 23:13; Jer 48:7, 46 [e] Isa 15:5 [f] Isa 16:2
21:30 [g] Nu 32:3; Jos 13:9, 17; Ne 11:25; Isa 15:2; Jer 48:18, 22 [h] Jos 13:16; 1Ch 19:7
21:31 [i] Nu 13:29
21:32 [j] Jos 2:1; 6:22; 7:2; Jdg 18:2; 2Sa 10:3; 1Ch 19:3 [k] Nu 32:1,3, 35; Jos 13:25; 2Sa 24:5; 1Ch 6:81; Isa 16:8; Jer 48:32
21:33 [l] Nu 32:33; Dt 3:3; 31:4; Jos 2:10; 12:4; 13:30; 1Ki 4:19; Ne 9:22; Ps 135:11; 136:20 [m] Dt 3:4; 32:14; Jos 9:10; 1Ki 4:13 [n] Dt 1:4; 3:1, 10; Jos 12:4; 13:12,31; 19:37
21:34 [o] Dt 3:2
21:35 [p] Jos 9:10 [q] S ver 24
22:1 [r] S Nu 21:11 [s] S Nu 13:29; S Jos 2:7 [t] Nu 31:12; 33:48; Dt 32:49; Jos 2:1
22:2 [u] Nu 23:1-3; Jos 24:9; Jdg 11:25; Mic 6:5; Rev 2:14
22:3 [v] S Ex 15:15
22:4 [w] S Ge 19:37 [x] S Ge 25:2 [y] Nu 32:17,18,29 [z] Job 5:25; Ps 72:16
22:5 [a] ver 7; Nu 24:25; 31:8,16; Dt 23:4; Jos 13:22; Ne 13:2; Mic 6:5; S 2Pe 2:15 [b] S Ge 2:14 [c] S Ex 13:3

21:27–30 This third ancient poem in ch. 21 was an Amorite taunt song about their earlier victory over Moab (v. 29). Perhaps the song about Heshbon was also preserved in the "Book of the Wars of the LORD" (v. 14).
21:33 *Bashan*. The region northeast of the Sea of Galilee.
21:35 *struck him down*. By defeating Og, Israel now controlled Transjordan from Moab to the heights of Bashan in the vicinity of Mount Hermon. The victory over Sihon and Og became a subject of song (Ps 135:11; 136:19–20), and is now a regular part of the commemoration of the works of the Lord in the Passover celebration.
22:1 *plains of Moab*. The Israelites now marched back to their staging area east of the Jordan and just north of the Dead Sea. From this point they would launch their attack on Canaan, beginning with the ancient city of Jericho. Moab did not trust Israel's intentions, however. Moab's fear leads to a remarkable interval in the story of Israel: the account of Balak and Balaam (chs. 22–24).

22:3 *Moab was filled with dread*. Balak, king of Moab, did not know that Israel had no plans against them.
22:4 *said to the elders of Midian*. Balak made an alliance with the Midianites to oppose Israel (see v. 7). *as an ox licks up the grass of the field*. A proverbial simile particularly fitting for a pastoral people.

22:5 *summon Balaam*. Since Balak believed that there was no military way to withstand the Israelites, he sought to oppose them through pagan divination (vv. 6–7), sending for a diviner with an international reputation. (One of Balaam's non-Biblical prophecies is preserved in an Aramaic [or, according to some, a dialect of Hebrew] inscription from Deir 'Alla—east of the Jordan River, just north of the Jabbok River—dating to the eighth or seventh century B.C.) *Pethor*. Located in Northwest Mesopotamia and mentioned in Assyrian inscriptions.

22:6 d ver 12,17;
Nu 23:7,11,13; 24:9,
10 e ver 11
22:7 f S Ge 30:27
22:8 g ver 19
22:9 h S Ge 20:3
i ver 20; Nu 23:5;
24:4,16
22:12 j S Ge 12:2
22:17 k ver 37;
Nu 24:11 l S ver 6
22:18 m ver 38;
Nu 23:12,26; 24:13;
1Ki 22:14; 2Ch 18:13;
Jer 42:4
22:19 n ver 8
22:20 o S Ge 20:3
p ver 35,38; Nu 23:5,
12,16,26; 24:13;
2Ch 18:13
22:22 q S Ex 4:14
r S Ge 16:7; Jdg 13:3,
6,13
22:23 s Jos 5:13
t ver 25,27
22:27 u Nu 11:1;
Jas 1:19
22:28 v 2Pe 2:16
w ver 32
22:29 x ver 33;
Dt 25:4; Pr 12:10;
27:23-27; Mt 15:19

tled next to me. [6]Now come and put a curse d on these people, because they are too powerful for me. Perhaps then I will be able to defeat them and drive them out of the land. e For I know that whoever you bless is blessed, and whoever you curse is cursed."

[7]The elders of Moab and Midian left, taking with them the fee for divination. f When they came to Balaam, they told him what Balak had said.

[8]"Spend the night here," Balaam said to them, "and I will report back to you with the answer the LORD gives me. g" So the Moabite officials stayed with him.

[9]God came to Balaam h and asked, i "Who are these men with you?"

[10]Balaam said to God, "Balak son of Zippor, king of Moab, sent me this message: [11]'A people that has come out of Egypt covers the face of the land. Now come and put a curse on them for me. Perhaps then I will be able to fight them and drive them away.' "

[12]But God said to Balaam, "Do not go with them. You must not put a curse on those people, because they are blessed. j"

[13]The next morning Balaam got up and said to Balak's officials, "Go back to your own country, for the LORD has refused to let me go with you."

[14]So the Moabite officials returned to Balak and said, "Balaam refused to come with us."

[15]Then Balak sent other officials, more numerous and more distinguished than the first. [16]They came to Balaam and said:

"This is what Balak son of Zippor says: Do not let anything keep you from coming to me, [17]because I will reward you handsomely k and do whatever you say. Come and put a curse l on these people for me."

[18]But Balaam answered them, "Even if Balak gave me all the silver and gold in his palace, I could not do anything great or small to go beyond the command of the LORD my God. m [19]Now spend the night here so that I can find out what else the LORD will tell me. n"

[20]That night God came to Balaam o and said, "Since these men have come to summon you, go with them, but do only what I tell you." p

BALAAM'S DONKEY

[21]Balaam got up in the morning, saddled his donkey and went with the Moabite officials. [22]But God was very angry q when he went, and the angel of the LORD r stood in the road to oppose him. Balaam was riding on his donkey, and his two servants were with him. [23]When the donkey saw the angel of the LORD standing in the road with a drawn sword s in his hand, it turned off the road into a field. Balaam beat it t to get it back on the road.

[24]Then the angel of the LORD stood in a narrow path through the vineyards, with walls on both sides. [25]When the donkey saw the angel of the LORD, it pressed close to the wall, crushing Balaam's foot against it. So he beat the donkey again.

[26]Then the angel of the LORD moved on ahead and stood in a narrow place where there was no room to turn, either to the right or to the left. [27]When the donkey saw the angel of the LORD, it lay down under Balaam, and he was angry u and beat it with his staff. [28]Then the LORD opened the donkey's mouth, v and it said to Balaam, "What have I done to you to make you beat me these three times? w"

[29]Balaam answered the donkey, "You have made a fool of me! If only I had a sword in my hand, I would kill you right now. x"

[30]The donkey said to Balaam, "Am I not your own donkey, which you have always ridden, to this day? Have I been in the habit of doing this to you?"

22:6 *put a curse on these people.* See note on Ge 12:3.

A **22:8** *the answer the LORD gives me.* The language here and in v. 18 ("the LORD my God") has led some to believe that Balaam was a believer in Yahweh ("the LORD"), God of Israel. Based on the subsequent narrative, however, it seems best to take Balaam's words as claiming to be the spokesman for any god. Balaam is universally condemned in Scripture for moral, ethical and religious faults (see 31:7–8,15–16; Dt 23:3–6; Jos 13:22; 24:9–10; Ne 13:1–3; Mic 6:5; 2Pe 2:15–16; Jude 11; Rev 2:14).

22:9 That God spoke to Balaam is not to be denied, but Balaam did not yet realize that the God of Israel was unlike the supposed deities that he usually schemed against.

22:12 *they are blessed.* Israel was under the Lord's blessing promised to Abraham (see note on Ge 12:2–3).

22:20 *go with them.* There appears to be a contradiction between the permission God grants Balaam here and the prohibition he had given earlier (v. 12), and then the anger the Lord displayed against Balaam on his journey (v. 22). The difficulty is best understood as lying in the contrary character of Balaam. God had forbidden him to go to curse Israel. He then allowed Balaam to go, but only if he would follow the Lord's direction. But Balaam's real intentions were known to the Lord, and so with severe displeasure he confronted the pagan prophet.

22:23 *the donkey saw the angel of the LORD.* As a pagan prophet, Balaam was a specialist in animal divination, but his dumb beast saw what Balaam was blind to observe.

22:29 *If only I had a sword.* A ridiculous picture of the hapless Balaam. A sword was nearby (see vv. 23,31–33), but its victim was not going to be the donkey.

"No," he said.

³¹Then the LORD opened Balaam's eyes,ʸ and he saw the angel of the LORD standing in the road with his sword drawn. So he bowed low and fell facedown.

³²The angel of the LORD asked him, "Why have you beaten your donkey these three times? I have come here to oppose you because your path is a reckless one before me.ᵃ ³³The donkey saw me and turned away from me these three times. If it had not turned away, I would certainly have killed you by now,ᶻ but I would have spared it."

³⁴Balaam said to the angel of the LORD, "I have sinned.ᵃ I did not realize you were standing in the road to oppose me. Now if you are displeased, I will go back."

³⁵The angel of the LORD said to Balaam, "Go with the men, but speak only what I tell you." So Balaam went with Balak's officials.

³⁶When Balakᵇ heard that Balaam was coming, he went out to meet him at the Moabite town on the Arnonᶜ border, at the edge of his territory. ³⁷Balak said to Balaam, "Did I not send you an urgent summons? Why didn't you come to me? Am I really not able to reward you?"

³⁸"Well, I have come to you now," Balaam replied. "But I can't say whatever I please. I must speak only what God puts in my mouth."ᵈ

³⁹Then Balaam went with Balak to Kiriath Huzoth. ⁴⁰Balak sacrificed cattle and sheep,ᵉ and gave some to Balaam and the officials who were with him. ⁴¹The next morning Balak took Balaam up to Bamoth Baal,ᶠ and from there he could see the outskirts of the Israelite camp.ᵍ

BALAAM'S FIRST MESSAGE

23 Balaam said, "Build me seven altars here, and prepare seven bulls and seven ramsʰ for me." ²Balak did as Balaam said, and the two of them offered a bull and a ram on each altar.ⁱ

³Then Balaam said to Balak, "Stay here beside your offering while I go aside. Perhaps the LORD will come to meet with me.ʲ Whatever he reveals to me I will tell you." Then he went off to a barren height.

⁴God met with him,ᵏ and Balaam said, "I have prepared seven altars, and on each altar I have offered a bull and a ram."

⁵The LORD put a word in Balaam's mouthˡᵐ and said, "Go back to Balak and give him this word."ⁿ

⁶So he went back to him and found him standing beside his offering, with all the Moabite officials.ᵒ ⁷Then Balaamᵖ spoke his message:ᑫ

"Balak brought me from Aram,ʳ
    the king of Moab from the eastern mountains.ˢ
'Come,' he said, 'curse Jacob for me;
    come, denounce Israel.'ᵗ
⁸How can I curse
    those whom God has not cursed?ᵘ
How can I denounce
    those whom the LORD has not denounced?ᵛ

ᵃ 32 The meaning of the Hebrew for this clause is uncertain.

22:31 ʸGe 21:19
22:33 ᶻS ver 29
22:34 ᵃGe 39:9; Nu 14:40; 1Sa 15:24, 30; 2Sa 12:13; 24:10; Job 33:27; Ps 51:4
22:36 ᵇver 2
ᶜS Nu 21:13
22:38 ᵈNu 23:5,16, 26
22:40 ᵉNu 23:1,14, 29; Eze 45:23
22:41 ᶠS Nu 21:28
ᵍNu 23:13
23:1 ʰS Nu 22:40
23:2 ⁱver 14,30
23:3 ʲver 15
23:4 ᵏver 16
23:5 ˡS Ex 4:12; Isa 59:21 ᵐS Ex 4:15
ⁿS Nu 22:20
23:6 ᵒver 17
23:7 ᵖNu 22:5; Jos 24:9 ᑫver 18; Nu 24:3,21; 2Sa 23:1
ʳ2Ki 5:1 ˢS Ge 24:10
ᵗS Nu 22:6; Ne 13:2
23:8 ᵘNu 22:12
ᵛver 20; Isa 43:13

22:31 *Then the LORD opened Balaam's eyes.* The language follows the same structure as the opening words of v. 28. In some ways, the opening of the eyes of the pagan prophet to see the reality of the angel was the greater miracle.

22:35 *speak only what I tell you.* The one great gain was that Balaam was now more aware of the seriousness of the task before him; he would not be able to change the word the Lord would give him (see 23:12,20,26).

22:37 *Did I not send you an urgent summons?* The comic element of the story is seen not only in the hapless Balaam but also in the frustrated Balak (see 23:11,25; 24:10).

22:40 The pieces given to Balaam would have included the livers, for, as a pagan diviner, Balaam was a specialist in liver divination. Balaam subsequently gave up his acts of sorcery as the power of the Lord's word came upon him (24:1).

23:1 *seven altars ... seven bulls and seven rams.* These sacrifices were prepared as a part of Balaam's pagan actions. The number seven (signifying completeness) was held in high regard among

Semitic peoples in general. The many animals would provide abundant liver and other organ materials for the diviner from Northwest Mesopotamia.

23:2 *Balak did as Balaam said.* Balaam is in charge; Balak is now his subordinate.

23:7—24:24 There are seven poetic oracles here. The first four are longer, have introductory narrative bridges and are written in exquisite poetry (23:7–10; 23:18–24; 24:3–9; 24:15–19). The last three are brief, are much more difficult to understand, and follow one another in a staccato pattern (24:20, 21–22,23–24).

23:7 *message.* Hebrew *mashal,* usually translated "proverb," but here "message" is appropriate. By this word the distinctive nature of Balaam's prophecies is established; none of the prophecies of Israel's true prophets is described by this term.

23:8 *How can I curse those whom God has not cursed?* That which Balaam had been hired to do he was unable to do. God kept him from pronouncing a curse on his people, who were unlike the nations of the world (v. 9).

23:9 ʷ Nu 22:41
ˣ S Ex 33:16;
S Dt 32:8
23:10 ʸ S Ge 13:16
ᶻ Ps 16:3; 116:15;
Isa 57:1 ᵃ Ps 37:37
23:11 ᵇ S Nu 22:6
ᶜ Nu 24:10; Jos 24:10;
Ne 13:2
23:12 ᵈ S Nu 22:18,
20
23:13 ᵉ ver 27
ᶠ Nu 22:41
ᵍ S Nu 22:6
23:14 ʰ S Nu 21:20;
27:12 ⁱ S ver 2
23:16 ʲ S Ex 4:15;
S Nu 22:38
23:17 ᵏ ver 6
23:18 ˡ S ver 7
ᵐ Nu 22:2
23:19 ⁿ Job 9:32;
Isa 55:9; Hos 11:9
ᵒ S Nu 11:23
ᵖ 1Sa 15:29; Job 12:13;
36:5; Ps 33:11; 89:34;
102:27; 110:4;
Jer 4:28; 7:16;
Mal 3:6; Tit 1:2;
Heb 6:18; 7:21;
Jas 1:17 �q 2Sa 7:25;
Ps 119:38
23:20 ʳ ver 5,16;
Nu 24:1 ˢ Ge 22:17;
Nu 22:12 ᵗ S ver 8;
S Job 9:12
23:21 ᵘ Ps 32:2,5;
85:2; Ro 4:7-8
ᵛ Isa 33:24; 40:2;
Jer 50:20 ʷ S Ge 26:3;
Ex 29:45,46; Dt 4:7;
Ps 34:17-18; 145:18;
Zec 2:10 ˣ Dt 32:15;
33:5; Ps 89:15-18;
Isa 44:2
23:22 ʸ Nu 24:8;
Jos 2:10; 9:9
ᶻ Dt 33:17; Job 39:9;
Ps 22:21; 29:6; 92:10;
Isa 34:7
23:23 ᵃ ver 3;
S Ge 30:27; Nu 24:1
23:24 ᵇ Nu 24:9;
Eze 19:2; Na 2:11
ᶜ S Ge 49:9
ᵈ Isa 49:26

> [9] From the rocky peaks I see them,
> from the heights I view them. ʷ
> I see a people who live apart
> and do not consider themselves one of the nations. ˣ
> [10] Who can count the dust of Jacob ʸ
> or number the fourth part of Israel?
> Let me die the death of the righteous, ᶻ
> and may my final end be like theirs! ᵃ”

[11] Balak said to Balaam, "What have you done to me? I brought you to curse my enemies, ᵇ but you have done nothing but bless them!" ᶜ

[12] He answered, "Must I not speak what the LORD puts in my mouth?" ᵈ

BALAAM'S SECOND MESSAGE

[13] Then Balak said to him, "Come with me to another place ᵉ where you can see them; you will not see them all but only the outskirts of their camp. ᶠ And from there, curse them for me. ᵍ" [14] So he took him to the field of Zophim on the top of Pisgah, ʰ and there he built seven altars and offered a bull and a ram on each altar. ⁱ

[15] Balaam said to Balak, "Stay here beside your offering while I meet with him over there."

[16] The LORD met with Balaam and put a word in his mouth ʲ and said, "Go back to Balak and give him this word."

[17] So he went to him and found him standing beside his offering, with the Moabite officials. ᵏ Balak asked him, "What did the LORD say?"

[18] Then he spoke his message: ˡ

> "Arise, Balak, and listen;
> hear me, son of Zippor. ᵐ
> [19] God is not a human, ⁿ that he should lie, ᵒ
> not a human being, that he should change his mind. ᵖ
> Does he speak and then not act?
> Does he promise �q and not fulfill?
> [20] I have received a command to bless; ʳ
> he has blessed, ˢ and I cannot change it. ᵗ
>
> [21] "No misfortune is seen in Jacob, ᵘ
> no misery observed ᵃ in Israel. ᵛ
> The LORD their God is with them; ʷ
> the shout of the King ˣ is among them.
> [22] God brought them out of Egypt; ʸ
> they have the strength of a wild ox. ᶻ
> [23] There is no divination against ᵇ Jacob,
> no evil omens ᵃ against ᵇ Israel.
> It will now be said of Jacob
> and of Israel, 'See what God has done!'
> [24] The people rise like a lioness; ᵇ
> they rouse themselves like a lion ᶜ
> that does not rest till it devours its prey
> and drinks the blood ᵈ of its victims."

ᵃ 21 Or He has not looked on Jacob's offenses / or on the wrongs found   ᵇ 23 Or in

---

23:10 *Let me die the death of the righteous.* A wish not granted (see 31:8,16). *may my final end be like theirs!* He who had come to curse desired to share in Israel's blessing.

23:13 *not see them all but only the outskirts.* Balak attempted to reduce Israel's power by selecting a point where their immense numbers would be obscured. Unfortunately for Balak, the oracle that followed (vv. 18–24) exceeded the first in its blessing on Israel.

23:19 *God is not a human, that he should lie.* These sublime words describe the immutability of the Lord and the integrity of his word. Balaam is a foil to God—constantly shifting, prevaricating, equivocating, changing—a prime example of the distinction between God and human beings.

23:21 *the shout of the King is among them.* That the first explicit declaration of the Lord's kingship in the Pentateuch was made by Balaam is a suitable improbability. Because God is King (Sovereign), he was able to use Balaam for his own ends—to bless his people in a new and wonderful manner.

23:22 *wild ox.* "Aurochs," a traditional image of power in the ancient Near East (see also 24:8); or possibly "oryx," a large, straight-horned antelope.

23:23 *no divination against Jacob.* Balaam speaks from his frightful experience. He had no means in his bag of tricks to withstand God's blessing of Israel.

23:24 *like a lioness.* Israel was about to arise and devour its foes, like a lioness on the hunt (see 24:9; Ge 49:9 and note).

²⁵Then Balak said to Balaam, "Neither curse them at all nor bless them at all!"
²⁶Balaam answered, "Did I not tell you I must do whatever the LORD says?" *e*

BALAAM'S THIRD MESSAGE

²⁷Then Balak said to Balaam, "Come, let me take you to another place. *f* Perhaps it will please God to let you curse them for me *g* from there." ²⁸And Balak took Balaam to the top of Peor, *h* overlooking the wasteland.

²⁹Balaam said, "Build me seven altars here, and prepare seven bulls and seven rams for me." ³⁰Balak did as Balaam had said, and offered a bull and a ram on each altar. *i*

24 Now when Balaam saw that it pleased the LORD to bless Israel, *j* he did not resort to divination *k* as at other times, but turned his face toward the wilderness. *l* ²When Balaam looked out and saw Israel encamped tribe by tribe, the Spirit of God came on him *m* ³and he spoke his message:

"The prophecy of Balaam son of Beor,
   the prophecy of one whose eye sees clearly, *n*
⁴ the prophecy of one who hears the words of God, *o*
   who sees a vision from the Almighty, *a p*
   who falls prostrate, and whose eyes are opened:

⁵ "How beautiful are your tents, *q* Jacob,
   your dwelling places, Israel!

⁶ "Like valleys they spread out,
   like gardens beside a river, *r*
   like aloes *s* planted by the LORD,
   like cedars beside the waters. *t*
⁷ Water will flow from their buckets;
   their seed will have abundant water.

   "Their king will be greater than Agag; *u*
   their kingdom will be exalted. *v*

⁸ "God brought them out of Egypt;
   they have the strength of a wild ox.
They devour hostile nations
   and break their bones in pieces; *w*
   with their arrows they pierce them. *x*
⁹ Like a lion they crouch and lie down,
   like a lioness *y*—who dares to rouse them?

   "May those who bless you be blessed *z*
   and those who curse you be cursed!" *a*

¹⁰Then Balak's anger burned *b* against Balaam. He struck his hands together *c* and said to him, "I summoned you to curse my enemies, *d* but you have blessed them *e* these three times. *f* ¹¹Now leave at once and go home! *g* I said I would reward you handsomely, *h* but the LORD has kept you from being rewarded."

¹²Balaam answered Balak, "Did I not tell the messengers you sent me, *i* ¹³'Even if Balak gave me all the silver and gold in his palace, I could not do anything of my own ac-

---

a 4 Hebrew *Shaddai*; also in verse 16

24:1 *divination as at other times.* Balaam's magic and divination are identified here (see notes on 22:40; 23:1).
24:2 *the Spirit of God came on him.* This unexpected language indicates that God has overpowered the pagan prophet for his own purposes. Cf. note on Jdg 3:10.
24:3–4 The extensive introduction of this oracle describes Balaam's experience in the Lord's presence. Now Balaam's eyes were opened (see note on 22:31).
24:6–7 Balaam speaks here in general, but luxuriant, terms of the blessings that will come to the Israelites as they settle in their new land. The lushness of their blessing from the Lord is reminiscent of Eden.
24:7 *Agag.* Possibly a throne name for the king of the Amalekites (cf. 1Sa 15:32–33). The allusion here may be to the Amalekites who attacked Israel when they came out of Egypt

(see Ex 17:8–13) and again when they first approached Canaan (see 14:45).
24:8 *God brought them out of Egypt.* These central words about Israel's salvation are recited by one who was a hostile outsider (see notes on 23:21; 25:1–18).
24:9 *May those who bless you be blessed . . . cursed!* The theology of blessing and cursing in the promises made to Abraham (Ge 12:2–3; see note there) is now a part of this oracle of blessing. Perhaps here Balaam was reasserting his desire to be a part of Israel's blessing (see 23:10–11 and note on 23:10).
24:11 *the LORD has kept you from being rewarded.* In his disgust with Balaam's failure to curse Israel, Balak now dismisses him without pay—the ultimate insult to his greed (see 2Pe 2:15 and note).

23:26 *e* S Nu 22:18, 20
23:27 *f* ver 13
   g Nu 24:10
23:28 *h* Nu 25:3,18; 31:16; Dt 3:29; 4:3; Jos 22:17; Ps 106:28; Hos 9:10
23:30 *i* S ver 2
24:1 *j* S Nu 23:20
   k S Nu 23:23
24:2 *m* S Nu 11:25, 26
24:3 *n* ver 15
24:4 *o* S Nu 22:9
   p S Ge 15:1
   a Jer 4:20; 30:18; Mal 2:12
24:6 *r* S Ge 2:10
   s Ps 45:8; SS 4:14
   t Job 29:19; Ps 1:3; 104:16; Eze 31:5
24:7 *u* S Ex 17:8-16
   v Dt 28:1; 2Sa 5:12; 1Ch 14:2; Ps 89:27; 145:11-13
24:8 *w* S Ex 15:6; Jer 50: 17 *x* 2Sa 18:14; Ps 45:5
24:9 *y* S Nu 23:24
   z S Ge 12:2
   a S Ge 12:3
24:10 *b* S Ex 4:14
   c Job 27:23; 34:37; La 2:15; Eze 21:14; 22:13; 25:6
   d S Nu 22:6
   S Nu 23:11;
   S Dt 23:5 *e* ver 3-9;
   Nu 23:7-10,18-24
24:11 *g* ver 14,25
   h S Nu 22:17
24:12 *i* Nu 22:18

24:13 /S Nu 22:18
k S Nu 22:20
24:14 /S Ge 49:1;
Nu 31:8,16; Mic 6:5
24:16 m S Nu 22:9
n Ge 14:18; Isa 14:14
24:17 o Rev 1:7
p Mt 2:2 q S Ge 49:10
r S Ge 19:37;
S Nu 21:29;
S Dt 23:6;
Isa 15:1–16:14
s Jer 48:45
24:18 t 2Sa 8:12;
1Ch 18:11; Ps 60:8;
Isa 11:14; Am 9:12
u S Ge 14:6; Dt 1:44;
Jos 12:7; 15:10;
Jdg 5:4 v Ob 1:2
w S Ge 9:25
24:19 x S Ge 49:10;
Mic 5:2
24:20 y S Ge 14:7;
S Ex 17:14 z Dt 25:19;
1Sa 15:20; 30:17-20;
2Sa 8:12; 1Ch 18:11
24:21 a S Ge 15:19
b Ps 37:27; Pr 1:33;
Isa 32:18; Eze 34:27
24:22 c S Ge 10:22
24:24 d S Ge 10:4
e ver 22 f S Ge 10:21
g ver 20
24:25 h S Nu 22:5

cord, good or bad, to go beyond the command of the Lord[j]—and I must say only what the Lord says'? [k] [14]Now I am going back to my people, but come, let me warn you of what this people will do to your people in days to come." [l]

BALAAM'S FOURTH MESSAGE

[15]Then he spoke his message:

"The prophecy of Balaam son of Beor,
   the prophecy of one whose eye sees clearly,
[16]the prophecy of one who hears the words [m] of God,
   who has knowledge from the Most High, [n]
who sees a vision from the Almighty,
   who falls prostrate, and whose eyes are opened:

[17]"I see him, but not now;
   I behold him, but not near. [o]
A star will come out of Jacob; [p]
   a scepter will rise out of Israel. [q]
He will crush the foreheads of Moab, [r]
   the skulls[a][s] of[b] all the people of Sheth. [c]
[18]Edom [t] will be conquered;
   Seir, [u] his enemy, will be conquered, [v]
   but Israel [w] will grow strong.
[19]A ruler will come out of Jacob [x]
   and destroy the survivors of the city."

BALAAM'S FIFTH MESSAGE

[20]Then Balaam saw Amalek [y] and spoke his message:

"Amalek was first among the nations,
   but they will come to ruin at last." [z]

BALAAM'S SIXTH MESSAGE

[21]Then he saw the Kenites [a] and spoke his message:

"Your dwelling place is secure, [b]
   your nest is set in a rock;
[22]yet you Kenites will be destroyed
   when Ashur [c] takes you captive."

BALAAM'S SEVENTH MESSAGE

[23]Then he spoke his message:

"Ah, who can live when God does this? [d]
[24]   Ships will come from the shores of Cyprus; [d]
   they will subdue Ashur [e] and Eber, [f]
   but they too will come to ruin. [g]"

[25]Then Balaam [h] got up and returned home, and Balak went his own way.

---

a 17 Samaritan Pentateuch (see also Jer. 48:45); the meaning of the word in the Masoretic Text is uncertain.   b 17 Or possibly Moab, / batter   c 17 Or all the noisy boasters   d 23 Masoretic Text; with a different word division of the Hebrew The people from the islands will gather from the north.

24:14 *in days to come.* The distant (Messianic) future is usually indicated by this expression (see, e.g., Jer 48:47 and note).
24:15–16 As in the third oracle (see vv. 3–4), the introduction to the fourth oracle is lengthy, helping to prepare the reader for the startling words of the prophecy.

A C **24:17** *star . . . scepter.* Perhaps fulfilled initially in David, but ultimately in the coming Messianic ruler. Israel's future Deliverer will be like a star (cf. 2Pe 1:19; Rev 22:16); he will wield a royal scepter and bring victory over the enemies of his people (see v. 19). *Sheth.* Possibly the early inhabitants of Moab, known as the Shutu people in ancient Egyptian documents (but see TNIV text note; see also Jer 48:45–46 and note).
24:20 *Amalek was first.* The first to attack Israel and oppose the

Lord's purpose with his people (see Ex 17:8–13).
24:21 *Kenites.* The name suggests a tribe of metal workers. In other passages the Kenites are allied with Israel (see, e.g., Jdg 1:16; 4:11; 1Sa 15:6 and note). Since Moses' father-in-law was a Kenite but also associated with Midian (see Ex 2:16), it may be that Balaam's reference is to Midianites (see 22:4,7). *nest.* Hebrew *qen,* a wordplay on the word for Kenites (Hebrew *qeni*).
24:22 *Ashur.* Assyria.
24:24 *they will subdue Ashur and Eber, but . . . ruin.* One nation will rise and supplant another, only to face its own doom. By contrast, there is the implied ongoing blessing on Israel and the sure promise of a future deliverer who will have the final victory (vv. 17–19).

MOAB SEDUCES ISRAEL

25 While Israel was staying in Shittim, [i] the men began to indulge in sexual immorality[j] with Moabite[k] women, [l] 2who invited them to the sacrifices[m] to their gods. [n] The people ate the sacrificial meal and bowed down before these gods. 3So Israel yoked themselves to[o] the Baal of Peor. [p] And the LORD's anger burned against them.

4The LORD said to Moses, "Take all the leaders[q] of these people, kill them and expose[r] them in broad daylight before the LORD, [s] so that the LORD's fierce anger[t] may turn away from Israel."

5So Moses said to Israel's judges, "Each of you must put to death[u] those of your people who have yoked themselves to the Baal of Peor."[v]

6Then an Israelite man brought into the camp a Midianite[w] woman right before the eyes of Moses and the whole assembly of Israel while they were weeping[x] at the entrance to the tent of meeting. 7When Phinehas[y] son of Eleazar, the son of Aaron, the priest, saw this, he left the assembly, took a spear[z] in his hand 8and followed the Israelite into the tent. He drove the spear into both of them, right through the Israelite man and into the woman's stomach. Then the plague against the Israelites was stopped; [a] 9but those who died in the plague[b] numbered 24,000. [c]

10The LORD said to Moses, 11"Phinehas son of Eleazar, the son of Aaron, the priest, has turned my anger away from the Israelites. [d] Since he was as zealous for my honor[e] among them as I am, I did not put an end to them in my zeal. 12Therefore tell him I am making my covenant of peace[f] with him. 13He and his descendants will have a covenant of a lasting priesthood, [g] because he was zealous[h] for the honor[i] of his God and made atonement[j] for the Israelites."[k]

14The name of the Israelite who was killed with the Midianite woman[l] was Zimri son of Salu, the leader of a Simeonite family. [m] 15And the name of the Midianite woman who was put to death was Kozbi[n] daughter of Zur, a tribal chief of a Midianite family. [o]

16The LORD said to Moses, [p] 17"Treat the Midianites[q] as enemies[r] and kill them. [s] 18They treated you as enemies when they deceived you in the Peor incident[t] involving their sister Kozbi, the daughter of a Midianite leader, the woman who was killed when the plague came as a result of that incident."

THE SECOND CENSUS

26 After the plague[u] the LORD said to Moses and Eleazar son of Aaron, the priest, 2"Take a census[v] of the whole Israelite community by families—all those twenty years old or more who are able to serve in the army[w] of Israel." 3So on

25:17 21:8; 74:23 [s] Dt 21:1; 1Sa 17:9,35; 2Ki 9:27; 10:25 **25:18** [t] S Nu 23:28 **26:1** [u] S Nu 14:37; 25:8 **26:2** [v] Ex 30:11-16 [w] S Nu 1:3

25:1 [i] S Nu 21:16; Jos 2:1; Isa 66:11; Joel 3:18; Mic 6:5
[j] Jer 5:7; 7:9; 9:2; 1Co 10:8; Rev 2:14
[k] S Ge 19:37
[l] Nu 31:16
25:2 [m] S Ex 32:6
[n] Ex 20:5; Dt 32:38; 1Co 10:20
25:3 [o] Dt 4:19; Jdg 2:19; 1Ki 9:9; Jer 1:16; 44:3
[p] S Nu 23:28
25:4 [q] Nu 7:2; 13:3
[r] 2Sa 21:6 [d] Dt 4:3
[t] Ex 32:12; Dt 13:17; Jos 7:26; 2Ki 23:26; 2Ch 28:11; 29:10; 30:8; Ezr 10:14; Jer 44:3
25:5 [u] S Ex 32:27
[v] Hos 9:10
25:6 [w] S Ge 25:2
[x] S Nu 14:1; Jdg 2:4; Ru 1:9; 1Sa 11:4; 2Sa 15:30; Ezr 10:1; Ps 126:6; Jer 41:6
25:7 [y] S Ex 6:25; Jos 22:13; Jdg 20:28
[z] Jdg 5:8; 1Sa 13:19, 22; 1Ki 18:28; Ps 35:3; 46:9; Joel 3:10; Mic 4:3
25:8 [a] Ps 106:30
25:9 [b] S Nu 14:37; 1Co 10:8 [c] Nu 31:16
25:11 [d] Ps 106:30
[e] Ex 20:5; Dt 32:16, 21; Ps 78:58
25:12 [f] Isa 11:9; 54:10; Eze 34:25; 37:26; Mal 2:4,5
25:13 [g] S Ex 29:9
[h] 1Ki 19:10; 2Ki 10:16
[i] ver 11 [j] S Ex 29:36; S Ro 3:25 [k] Ps 106:31; Jer 33:18
25:14 [l] ver 6
[m] S Nu 1:6
25:15 [n] ver 18
[o] Nu 31:8; Jos 13:21; Hab 3:7
25:16 [p] Nu 31:7
25:17 [q] Nu 31:1-3
[r] Ex 23:22; Jdg 2:16-18; Ne 9:27; Ps 8:2;

25:1–18 It is not until 31:8,16 that we learn that the principal instigator of Israel's apostasy here was Balaam (see notes on 22:5,8). Failing to destroy Israel by means of a curse, Balaam seduced Israel by the Canaanite fertility rites of Baal.

25:1 *Shittim.* Another name for the region of Israel's staging for the conquest of Canaan; it was across the Jordan River opposite the ancient city of Jericho (see Jos 2:1). *indulge in sexual immorality.* Israel's engagement in the fertility rites of Baal involved not only the evil of sexual immorality. It was also a breach of covenant with the Lord (see Ex 20:3–4 and notes), a worship of the gods of the land (vv. 2–3) and a foretaste of the people's ruin in the unfolding of their history.

25:4 *kill them and expose them in broad daylight.* The special display of the corpses would warn survivors of the consequences of sin.

25:6 *brought into the camp a Midianite woman.* The contempt for the holy things and the word of the Lord shown by Zimri (v. 14) and his lover Kozbi (v. 15) is unimaginable.

25:9 *24,000.* The number of those who died because of the flagrant actions of the people in their worship of Baal exceeded even that of those who had died in the rebellion of Korah and his allies (14,700; see 16:49 and note). Again, the large number of those who died fits well with the immense number of the people stated in the first census (see 1:46 and note) and the second (see 26:51 and note).

25:11 *he was as zealous for my honor among them as I am.* Cf. Ex

20:4–6. The zeal of Phinehas for the Lord's honor became the occasion for the Lord's covenanting with him and his descendants as God's true priests (see note on Ge 9:9; see also v. 12 and chart, p. 20). This son of Eleazar contrasts with the casual wickedness of his uncles, Nadab and Abihu (see Lev 10:1–3 and notes).

25:12 *covenant of peace.* Cf. note on Isa 54:10.

25:17 *Treat the Midianites as enemies.* Because of their active participation in the seduction of the Israelites, Midianites had been in league with Balak from the beginning of the confrontation (see 22:4,7) and became the objects of a holy war (31:1–24).

26:1–51 The first census of those who were mustered for the war of conquest had been taken more than 38 years earlier. That first generation of men 20 years old or more had nearly all died. It was now time for the new generation to be numbered and mustered for the campaign that awaited them. The aged Moses was joined in the task this time by his nephew Eleazar; Aaron was dead (see 20:28). In this second census the prominent clans of each tribe are listed. The numbers of many of the tribes increase, but those of Reuben show a decline. It is possible that the reduction of the families of Reuben was brought about by the judgment on their members during the rebellion of Korah and his Reubenite allies (see note on v. 9). In the intervening years the family of Reuben had nearly caught up with its former numbers (see note on v. 14). Note the comparison of the numbers of each tribe from the first census to the second:

26:3 x ver 63;
Nu 33:48; Jos 13:32
y Nu 22:1
26:4 z S Ex 6:14;
S 13:3
26:5 a Nu 1:20
b S Ge 46:9 c 1Ch 5:3
26:6 d 1Ch 5:3
e Ge 46:9
26:9 f Nu 16:1
g Nu 1:16 h S Nu 16:2
26:10 i S Ex 15:12
j S Nu 16:35
k S Ex 3:12;
S Nu 16:38
26:11 l Ex 6:24
m Nu 16:33; Dt 5:9;
24:16; 2Ki 14:6;
2Ch 25:4; Eze 18:20
26:12 n S Ge 46:10
o 1Ch 4:24
26:13 p S Ge 46:10
26:14 q S Ge 46:10
r Nu 1:23
26:15 s Ge 46:16
26:18 t S Ge 30:11;
S Nu 1:25;
S Jos 13:24-28
26:19 u Nu 16:1
v S Ge 38:4 w Ge 38:7
26:20 x S Ge 38:5
y S Ge 38:29 z Jos 7:17
26:21 a S Ge 38:29
b Ru 4:19; 1Ch 2:9
26:22 c Nu 1:27
26:23 d S Ge 46:13

the plains of Moab[x] by the Jordan across from Jericho,[y] Moses and Eleazar the priest spoke with them and said, [4]"Take a census of the men twenty years old or more, as the LORD commanded Moses."

These were the Israelites who came out of Egypt:[z]

[5]The descendants of Reuben,[a] the firstborn son of Israel, were:

through Hanok,[b] the Hanokite clan;

through Pallu,[c] the Palluite clan;

[6]through Hezron,[d] the Hezronite clan;

through Karmi,[e] the Karmite clan.

[7]These were the clans of Reuben; those numbered were 43,730.

[8]The son of Pallu was Eliab, [9]and the sons of Eliab[f] were Nemuel, Dathan and Abiram. The same Dathan and Abiram were the community[g] officials who rebelled against Moses and Aaron and were among Korah's followers when they rebelled against the LORD.[h] [10]The earth opened its mouth and swallowed them[i] along with Korah, whose followers died when the fire devoured the 250 men.[j] And they served as a warning sign.[k] [11]The line of Korah,[l] however, did not die out.[m]

[12]The descendants of Simeon by their clans were:

through Nemuel,[n] the Nemuelite clan;

through Jamin,[o] the Jaminite clan;

through Jakin, the Jakinite clan;

[13]through Zerah,[p] the Zerahite clan;

through Shaul, the Shaulite clan.

[14]These were the clans of Simeon;[q] those numbered were 22,200.[r]

[15]The descendants of Gad by their clans were:

through Zephon,[s] the Zephonite clan;

through Haggi, the Haggite clan;

through Shuni, the Shunite clan;

[16]through Ozni, the Oznite clan;

through Eri, the Erite clan;

[17]through Arodi,[a] the Arodite clan;

through Areli, the Arelite clan.

[18]These were the clans of Gad;[t] those numbered were 40,500.

[19]Er[u] and Onan[v] were sons of Judah, but they died[w] in Canaan.

[20]The descendants of Judah by their clans were:

through Shelah,[x] the Shelanite clan;

through Perez,[y] the Perezite clan;

through Zerah, the Zerahite clan.[z]

[21]The descendants of Perez[a] were:

through Hezron,[b] the Hezronite clan;

through Hamul, the Hamulite clan.

[22]These were the clans of Judah;[c] those numbered were 76,500.

[23]The descendants of Issachar by their clans were:

through Tola,[d] the Tolaite clan;

through Puah, the Puite[b] clan;

---

a 17 Samaritan Pentateuch and Syriac (see also Gen. 46:16); Masoretic Text *Arod*   b 23 Samaritan Pentateuch, Septuagint, Vulgate and Syriac (see also 1 Chron. 7:1); Masoretic Text *through Puvah, the Punite*

Tribe	First Census	Second Census
Reuben	46,500	43,730
Simeon	59,300	22,200
Gad	45,650	40,500
Judah	74,600	76,500
Issachar	54,400	64,300
Zebulun	57,400	60,500
Ephraim	40,500	32,500
Manasseh	32,200	52,700
Benjamin	35,400	45,600
Dan	62,700	64,400
Asher	41,500	53,400
Naphtali	53,400	45,400
Total	603,550	601,730

26:9 *Dathan and Abiram.* The listing of Reuben's families becomes an occasion to remind the reader of the part that certain of their number played in Korah's rebellion (see 16:1–7 and note; cf. Jude 11 and note).

26:14 *22,200.* The greatest loss was in the tribe of Simeon (down from 59,300). Zimri was from the house of Simeon (25:14). Perhaps most of the 24,000 who died in the plague of that time were from Simeon. The judgment was so recent that the tribe had not had time to recover, as had the tribe of Reuben (see note on vv. 1–51).

26:19 *Er and Onan.* The names of the evil sons of Judah had not been forgotten, but they had no heritage (see Ge 38:1–10).

26:20 *Perez.* The line of David and Jesus would be traced through him (see Ru 4:18–22 and note; Mt 1:1–3).

²⁴through Jashub,ᵉ the Jashubite clan;
   through Shimron, the Shimronite clan.
²⁵These were the clans of Issachar;ᶠ those numbered were 64,300.

²⁶The descendants of Zebulunᵍ by their clans were:
   through Sered, the Seredite clan;
   through Elon, the Elonite clan;
   through Jahleel, the Jahleelite clan.
²⁷These were the clans of Zebulun;ʰ those numbered were 60,500.

²⁸The descendants of Josephⁱ by their clans through Manasseh and Ephraimʲ were:

²⁹The descendants of Manasseh:ᵏ
   through Makir,ˡ the Makirite clan (Makir was the father of Gileadᵐ);
   through Gilead, the Gileadite clan.
³⁰These were the descendants of Gilead:ⁿ
      through Iezer,ᵒ the Iezerite clan;
      through Helek, the Helekite clan;
   ³¹through Asriel, the Asrielite clan;
      through Shechem, the Shechemite clan;
   ³²through Shemida, the Shemidaite clan;
      through Hepher, the Hepherite clan.
³³(Zelophehadᵖ son of Hepher had no sons;�q he had only daughters, whose names were Mahlah, Noah, Hoglah, Milkah and Tirzah.)ʳ
³⁴These were the clans of Manasseh; those numbered were 52,700.ˢ

³⁵These were the descendants of Ephraimᵗ by their clans:
   through Shuthelah, the Shuthelahite clan;
   through Beker, the Bekerite clan;
   through Tahan, the Tahanite clan.
³⁶These were the descendants of Shuthelah:
      through Eran, the Eranite clan.
³⁷These were the clans of Ephraim;ᵘ those numbered were 32,500.

These were the descendants of Joseph by their clans.

³⁸The descendants of Benjaminᵛ by their clans were:
   through Bela, the Belaite clan;
   through Ashbel, the Ashbelite clan;
   through Ahiram, the Ahiramite clan;
   ³⁹through Shupham,ᵃ the Shuphamite clan;
   through Hupham, the Huphamite clan.
⁴⁰The descendants of Bela through Ardʷ and Naaman were:
      through Ard,ᵇ the Ardite clan;
      through Naaman, the Naamite clan.
⁴¹These were the clans of Benjamin;ˣ those numbered were 45,600.

⁴²These were the descendants of Danʸ by their clans:ᶻ
   through Shuham,ᵃ the Shuhamite clan.
These were the clans of Dan: ⁴³All of them were Shuhamite clans; and those numbered were 64,400.

⁴⁴The descendants of Asherᵇ by their clans were:
   through Imnah, the Imnite clan;
   through Ishvi, the Ishvite clan;
   through Beriah, the Beriite clan;
   ⁴⁵and through the descendants of Beriah:
      through Heber, the Heberite clan;
      through Malkiel, the Malkielite clan.

ᵃ 39 A few manuscripts of the Masoretic Text, Samaritan Pentateuch, Vulgate and Syriac (see also Septuagint); most manuscripts of the Masoretic Text *Shephupham*   ᵇ 40 Samaritan Pentateuch and Vulgate (see also Septuagint); Masoretic Text does not have *through Ard*.

26:29,35 *Manasseh . . . Ephraim.* The order of the tribes is the same as in ch. 1, except for the inversion of Ephraim and Manasseh, perhaps due to the much larger relative growth of Manasseh's tribe (see note on vv. 1–51; see also note on v. 34).

26:33 *Zelophehad . . . daughters.* See 27:1–11; 36.
26:34 *52,700.* The greatest gain was in the tribe of Manasseh (up from 32,200). The reason for this increase is not known.

26:24 ᵉ Ge 46:13
26:25 ᶠ S Ge 30:18
26:26 ᵍ Nu 1:30
26:27 ʰ S Ge 30:20
26:28 ⁱ Nu 1:32; 36:1
   ʲ Ge 41:52
26:29 ᵏ Nu 1:34
   ˡ S Ge 50:23
   ᵐ Jdg 11:1
26:30 ⁿ Nu 27:1;
   36:1; 1Ch 7:14,17
   ᵒ Jos 17:2; Jdg 6:11;
   8:2
26:33 ᵖ Nu 27:1;
   36:2; Jos 17:3;
   1Ch 7:15 q Nu 27:3
   ʳ Nu 36:11
26:34 ˢ Nu 1:35
26:35 ᵗ Nu 1:32
26:37 ᵘ S Nu 1:33
26:38 ᵛ Ge 46:21;
   Nu 1:36; 1Ch 8:40
26:40 ʷ S Ge 46:21
26:41 ˣ Nu 1:37
26:42 ʸ Nu 1:38
   ᶻ Jdg 18:19 ᵃ Ge 46:23
26:44 ᵇ S Nu 1:40

26:47 ^c Nu 1:41
26:48 ^d S Ge 30:8
26:50 ^e Nu 1:43
^f Nu 1:42
26:51 ^g S Ex 12:37
26:53 ^h ver 55;
Jos 11:23; 14:1;
Eze 45:8
26:54 ⁱ Nu 33:54
^j Nu 35:8
26:55 ^k S Lev 16:8
26:57 ^l S Ge 46:11
26:58 ^m Ex 6:20
26:59 ⁿ S Ex 2:1
^o S Ex 6:20 ^p S Ex 2:4
^q S Ex 15:20
26:60 ^r Ex 6:23
26:61 ^s S Lev 10:1-2
^t Nu 3:4
26:62 ^u Nu 3:39
^v Nu 1:47
^w S Nu 18:23
^x S Nu 2:33
26:63 ^y S Nu 1:19
^z ver 3 ^a Nu 22:1
26:64 ^b S Nu 14:29
^c Nu 1:44
26:65 ^d Nu 14:28;
1Co 10:5 ^e Nu 13:6
^f S Nu 11:28
27:1 ^g S Nu 26:33
^h Jos 17:2,3
ⁱ S Nu 26:30
^j S Ge 50:23; 1Ch 2:21
27:2 ^k S Nu 9:6
^l Nu 1:16; 31:13; 32:2;
36:1 ^m Ex 40:2,17
27:3 ⁿ Nu 26:65

⁴⁶ (Asher had a daughter named Serah.)

⁴⁷ These were the clans of Asher; ^c those numbered were 53,400.

⁴⁸ The descendants of Naphtali ^d by their clans were:

through Jahzeel, the Jahzeelite clan;

through Guni, the Gunite clan;

⁴⁹ through Jezer, the Jezerite clan;

through Shillem, the Shillemite clan.

⁵⁰ These were the clans of Naphtali; ^e those numbered were 45,400. ^f

⁵¹ The total number of the men of Israel was 601,730. ^g

⁵² The LORD said to Moses, ⁵³ "The land is to be allotted to them as an inheritance based on the number of names. ^h ⁵⁴ To a larger group give a larger inheritance, and to a smaller group a smaller one; each is to receive its inheritance according to the number ⁱ of those listed. ^j ⁵⁵ Be sure that the land is distributed by lot. ^k What each group inherits will be according to the names for its ancestral tribe. ⁵⁶ Each inheritance is to be distributed by lot among the larger and smaller groups."

⁵⁷ These were the Levites ^l who were counted by their clans:

through Gershon, the Gershonite clan;

through Kohath, the Kohathite clan;

through Merari, the Merarite clan.

⁵⁸ These also were Levite clans:

the Libnite clan,

the Hebronite clan,

the Mahlite clan,

the Mushite clan,

the Korahite clan.

(Kohath was the forefather of Amram; ^m ⁵⁹ the name of Amram's wife was Jochebed, ⁿ a descendant of Levi, who was born to the Levites ^a in Egypt. To Amram she bore Aaron, Moses ^o and their sister ^p Miriam. ^q ⁶⁰ Aaron was the father of Nadab and Abihu, Eleazar and Ithamar. ^r ⁶¹ But Nadab and Abihu ^s died when they made an offering before the LORD with unauthorized fire.) ^t

⁶² All the male Levites a month old or more numbered 23,000. ^u They were not counted ^v along with the other Israelites because they received no inheritance ^w among them. ^x

⁶³ These are the men counted ^y by Moses and Eleazar the priest when they counted the Israelites on the plains of Moab ^z by the Jordan across from Jericho. ^a ⁶⁴ Not one of them was among those counted ^b by Moses and Aaron ^c the priest when they counted the Israelites in the Desert of Sinai. ⁶⁵ For the LORD had told those Israelites they would surely die in the wilderness, ^d and not one of them was left except Caleb ^e son of Jephunneh and Joshua son of Nun. ^f

ZELOPHEHAD'S DAUGHTERS

27:1–11pp — Nu 36:1–12

27 The daughters of Zelophehad ^g son of Hepher, ^h the son of Gilead, ⁱ the son of Makir, ^j the son of Manasseh, belonged to the clans of Manasseh son of Joseph. The names of the daughters were Mahlah, Noah, Hoglah, Milkah and Tirzah. They came forward ² and stood before Moses, ^k Eleazar the priest, the leaders ^l and the whole assembly at the entrance to the tent of meeting ^m and said, ³ "Our father died in the wilderness. ⁿ He was not among Korah's followers, who banded together against the

^a 59 Or *Jochebed, a daughter of Levi, who was born to Levi*

26:46 *daughter named Serah.* The listing of this solitary daughter is striking.

26:51 *601,730.* Despite all that the people had been through during the years of wilderness experience, their total number was nearly the same as that of those who were first numbered. This remarkable fact is to be regarded as the blessing of the Lord, in fulfillment of his many promises to give numerical strength to the people descended from Abraham through Jacob (see note on Ge 12:2–3). This grand total and its parts are in accord with the general pattern of the numbers in the book (see note on 1:46).

26:53–56 Larger tribes would receive larger shares, but decisions of place would be made by lot (see v. 56; 33:54).

26:57 *Levites.* As in the first census (ch. 3), the Levites were counted separately.

27:1–11 The daughters of a man who had no son (see 26:33) were concerned about their rights of inheritance and the preservation of their father's name in the land (v. 4). Their action in approaching Moses, Eleazar and the leaders of the nation was unprecedented, an act of courage and conviction.

LORD, [o] but he died for his own sin and left no sons. [p] 4Why should our father's name disappear from his clan because he had no son? Give us property among our father's relatives."

5So Moses brought their case [q] before the LORD, [r] 6and the LORD said to him, 7"What Zelophehad's daughters are saying is right. You must certainly give them property as an inheritance [s] among their father's relatives and give their father's inheritance to them. [t]

8"Say to the Israelites, 'If a man dies and leaves no son, give his inheritance to his daughter. 9If he has no daughter, give his inheritance to his brothers. 10If he has no brothers, give his inheritance to his father's brothers. 11If his father had no brothers, give his inheritance to the nearest relative in his clan, that he may possess it. This is to have the force of law [u] for the Israelites, as the LORD commanded Moses.' "

JOSHUA TO SUCCEED MOSES

12Then the LORD said to Moses, "Go up this mountain [v] in the Abarim Range [w] and see the land [x] I have given the Israelites. [y] 13After you have seen it, you too will be gathered to your people, [z] as your brother Aaron [a] was, 14for when the community rebelled at the waters in the Desert of Zin, [b] both of you disobeyed my command to honor me as holy [c] before their eyes." (These were the waters of Meribah [d] Kadesh, in the Desert of Zin.)

15Moses said to the LORD, 16"May the LORD, the God of every human spirit, [e] appoint someone over this community 17to go out and come in before them, one who will lead them out and bring them in, so the LORD's people will not be like sheep without a shepherd." [f]

18So the LORD said to Moses, "Take Joshua son of Nun, a man in whom is the spirit of leadership, [a] [g] and lay your hand on him. [h] 19Have him stand before Eleazar the priest and the entire assembly and commission him [i] in their presence. [j] 20Give him some of your authority so the whole Israelite community will obey him. [k] 21He is to stand before Eleazar the priest, who will obtain decisions for him by inquiring [l] of the Urim [m] before the LORD. At his command he and the entire community of the Israelites will go out, and at his command they will come in."

22Moses did as the LORD commanded him. He took Joshua and had him stand before Eleazar the priest and the whole assembly. 23Then he laid his hands on him and commissioned him, [n] as the LORD instructed through Moses.

DAILY OFFERINGS

28 The LORD said to Moses, 2"Give this command to the Israelites and say to them: 'Make sure that you present to me at the appointed time [o] my food [p] offerings, as an aroma pleasing to me.' [q] 3Say to them: 'This is the food offering you are to present to the LORD: two lambs a year old without defect, [r] as a regular burnt offering each day. [s] 4Offer one lamb in the morning and the other at twilight, [t] 5together with a grain offering [u] of a tenth of an ephah [b] of the finest flour [v] mixed with a quarter of a hin [c] of oil [w] from pressed olives. 6This is the regular burnt offering [x] instituted at Mount Sinai [y] as a pleasing aroma, a food offering presented to the LORD. [z] 7The accompanying

[a] 18 Or *the Spirit*   [b] 5 That is, probably about 3 1/2 pounds or about 1.6 kilograms; also in verses 13, 21 and 29   [c] 5 That is, about 1 quart or about 0.9 liter; also in verses 7 and 14

27:3 *he died for his own sin.* A particular case from among those who died in the wilderness (see 26:64–65). These pious women had a sound understanding of the nature of the wilderness experience and a just claim for their family.

27:5 *Moses brought their case before the LORD.* This verse indicates how case law might have operated in Israel. The general laws would be proclaimed. Then legitimate exceptions or special considerations would come to the elders, and perhaps to Moses himself. He would then await a decision from the Lord. In this case, the Lord gave a favorable decision for these women. Ch. 36 provides an appendix to this account.

27:12–23 The juxtaposition of the story of Zelophehad's daughters' request for an inheritance in the land (vv. 1–11) and the Lord's words to Moses about his own exclusion from the land (vv. 12–14) is striking. Provisions are made for exceptions and irregularities in the inheritance laws, but there is no provision for Moses. His sin at the waters of Meribah at Kadesh (20:1–13) was always before him.

27:14 *honor me as holy.* See 20:12 and note.

27:16 *appoint someone.* Moses' reaction to this reassertion of his restriction is a prayer for a successor.

27:18 *Take Joshua.* As Moses and Aaron needed to determine the true successor of Aaron before his death (20:22–29), so the true successor of Moses also needed to be established. Joshua and Caleb were the two heroes in the darkest hour of Israel's apostasy (chs. 13–14). It was fitting that the Lord selected one of them (cf. Ex 17:9–14; 24:13; 32:17; 33:11).

27:20 *Give him some of your authority.* The transition from Moses' leadership to that of any successor would have been difficult. The change would be made smoother by a gradual shift of power while Moses was still alive.

27:21 *Urim.* See notes on Ex 28:30; 1Sa 2:28.

28:1—29:40 These chapters attest to the all-pervasiveness of sacrifice in the life of the people and to the enormity of the work of the priests. Perhaps the reason for these passages at this time is to give continuity to the impending transition from the leadership of Moses to that of Joshua (27:12–23).

28:1–8 See Ex 29:38–41; Lev 1–7 and notes.

27:3 [o] Nu 16:2
[p] Nu 26:33
27:5 [q] S Ge 25:22;
S Ex 18:19 [r] S Nu 9:8
27:7 [s] Job 42:15
[t] ver 8; Jos 17:4
27:11 [u] Nu 35:29
27:12 [v] Nu 23:14
[w] Nu 33:47; Jer 22:20
[x] Dt 3:23-27; 32:48-
52 [y] S Lev 14:34
27:13 [z] Nu 20:12;
31:2; Dt 4:22; 31:14;
32:50; 1Ki 2:1
[a] Nu 20:28
27:14 [b] S Nu 20:1,
2-5 [c] S Nu 20:12
[d] S Ex 17:7
27:16 [e] S Nu 16:22;
S Job 21:20
27:17 [f] 1Ki 22:17;
2Ch 18:16; Eze 34:5;
Zec 10:2; S Mt 9:36
27:18 [g] S Ge 41:38;
Nu 11:25-29 [h] ver 23;
Dt 34:9; Ac 6:6
27:19 [i] ver 23;
Dt 3:28; 31:14,23
[j] Dt 31:7
27:20 [k] Jos 1:16,17
27:21 [l] S Ge 25:22;
Jos 9:14; Ps 106:13;
Isa 8:19; Hag 1:13;
Mal 2:7; 3:1
[m] S Ex 28:30
27:23 [n] S ver 19
28:2 [o] Lev 23:1-44
[p] S Lev 3:11 [q] Lev 1:9
28:3 [r] S Lev 12:5
[s] Ex 29:38; Am 4:4
28:4 [t] S Ex 29:39
28:5 [u] Nu 29:6
[v] Lev 6:20 [w] S Lev 2:1
28:6 [x] Lev 1:3
[y] Ex 19:3 [z] S Lev 1:9

28:7 *a* Nu 6:15
b S Lev 10:9; S 23:13
c S Lev 3:7; Nu 3:28
28:8 *d* S Ex 29:39
e S Lev 3:7 *f* ver 2;
Lev 1:9
28:9 *g* S Ex 20:10;
Mt 12:5 *h* ver 3
i S Lev 23:13 *j* ver 5
28:10 *k* S Lev 23:38
l ver 3
28:11 *m* S Nu 10:10
n S Nu 7:15
o S Lev 5:15 *p* Lev 1:3
28:12 *q* S Nu 15:6;
S 29:3 *r* Nu 15:9
s ver 20
28:13 *t* S Lev 6:14
u ver 21 *v* S Nu 15:3
w Lev 1:9
28:14 *x* S Nu 15:7
y ver 11; 2Ch 2:4;
Ezr 3:5
28:15 *z* ver 3,23,24
a ver 30 *b* Lev 4:3;
Nu 29:16,19
28:16 *c* S Ex 12:11;
2Ch 30:13; 35:1
28:17 *d* S Ex 12:19
e S Ex 12:15
28:18 *f* S Ex 12:16
28:19 *g* S Lev 1:9
h ver 11
28:20 *i* S Lev 14:10
j ver 12
28:21 *k* ver 13
28:22 *l* Lev 4:3;
Ro 8:3 *m* S Nu 15:28
28:24 *n* Lev 1:9
28:26 *o* S Ex 34:22
p S Ex 23:16 *q* ver 18
28:27 *r* ver 19
28:28 *s* ver 12
28:29 *t* ver 13
28:30 *u* ver 15
28:31 *v* ver 3,19

drink offering *a* is to be a quarter of a hin of fermented drink *b* with each lamb. Pour out the drink offering to the Lord at the sanctuary. *c* [8]Offer the second lamb at twilight, *d* along with the same kind of grain offering and drink offering that you offer in the morning. *e* This is a food offering, an aroma pleasing to the Lord. *f*

SABBATH OFFERINGS

[9]" 'On the Sabbath *g* day, make an offering of two lambs a year old without defect, *h* together with its drink offering and a grain offering of two-tenths of an ephah *a i* of the finest flour mixed with olive oil. *j* [10]This is the burnt offering for every Sabbath, *k* in addition to the regular burnt offering *l* and its drink offering.

MONTHLY OFFERINGS

[11]" 'On the first of every month, *m* present to the Lord a burnt offering of two young bulls, *n* one ram *o* and seven male lambs a year old, all without defect. *p* [12]With each bull there is to be a grain offering *q* of three-tenths of an ephah *b r* of the finest flour mixed with oil; with the ram, a grain offering of two-tenths *s* of an ephah of the finest flour mixed with oil; [13]and with each lamb, a grain offering *t* of a tenth *u* of an ephah of the finest flour mixed with oil. This is for a burnt offering, *v* a pleasing aroma, a food offering presented to the Lord. *w* [14]With each bull there is to be a drink offering *x* of half a hin *c* of wine; with the ram, a third of a hin *d*; and with each lamb, a quarter of a hin. This is the monthly burnt offering to be made at each new moon *y* during the year. [15]Besides the regular burnt offering *z* with its drink offering, one male goat *a* is to be presented to the Lord as a sin offering. *e b*

THE PASSOVER

28:16–25pp — Ex 12:14–20; Lev 23:4–8; Dt 16:1–8

[16]" 'On the fourteenth day of the first month the Lord's Passover *c* is to be held. [17]On the fifteenth day of this month there is to be a festival; for seven days *d* eat bread made without yeast. *e* [18]On the first day hold a sacred assembly and do no regular work. *f* [19]Present to the Lord a food offering *g* consisting of a burnt offering of two young bulls, one ram and seven male lambs a year old, all without defect. *h* [20]With each bull offer a grain offering of three-tenths of an ephah *i* of the finest flour mixed with oil; with the ram, two-tenths; *j* [21]and with each of the seven lambs, one-tenth. *k* [22]Include one male goat as a sin offering *l* to make atonement for you. *m* [23]Offer these in addition to the regular morning burnt offering. [24]In this way present the food offering every day for seven days as an aroma pleasing to the Lord; *n* it is to be offered in addition to the regular burnt offering and its drink offering. [25]On the seventh day hold a sacred assembly and do no regular work.

THE FESTIVAL OF WEEKS

28:26–31pp — Lev 23:15–22; Dt 16:9–12

[26]" 'On the day of firstfruits, *o* when you present to the Lord an offering of new grain during the Festival of Weeks, *p* hold a sacred assembly and do no regular work. *q* [27]Present a burnt offering of two young bulls, one ram and seven male lambs a year old as an aroma pleasing to the Lord. *r* [28]With each bull there is to be a grain offering of three-tenths of an ephah of the finest flour mixed with oil; with the ram, two-tenths; *s* [29]and with each of the seven lambs, one-tenth. *t* [30]Include one male goat *u* to make atonement for you. [31]Offer these together with their drink offerings, in addition to the regular burnt offering *v* and its grain offering. Be sure the animals are without defect.

---

a 9 That is, probably about 7 pounds or about 3.2 kilograms; also in verses 12, 20 and 28   *b 12* That is, probably about 11 pounds or about 5 kilograms; also in verses 20 and 28   *c 14* That is, about 1/2 gallon or about 1.8 liters   *d 14* That is, about 2 2/3 pints or about 1.2 liters   *e 15* Or *purification offering;* also in verse 22

28:9–10 The Sabbath offerings were in addition to the daily offerings.

28:11–15 The sacrifices at the beginning of the month were of great significance. These were times for celebration and blowing of trumpets in worship (see 10:10 and note).

28:16–25 The priests are instructed as to the proper preparation for the Passover in the first month of the year. Passover is also associated with the Festival of Unleavened Bread (see Ex 12:15 and note on 12:17; Lev 23:4–8). The number 7 (and 14, its multiple) reappears frequently in the paragraph.

28:26–31 The Festival of Weeks came 50 days after the Festival of Unleavened Bread (see Lev 23:9–22); from this number the term "Pentecost" (meaning "fifty") was used in the NT (see Ac 2:1 and note).

THE FESTIVAL OF TRUMPETS
29:1–6pp — Lev 23:23–25

29 " 'On the first day of the seventh month hold a sacred assembly and do no regular work. [w] It is a day for you to sound the trumpets. [2]As an aroma pleasing to the Lord, [x] offer a burnt offering [y] of one young bull, one ram and seven male lambs a year old, [z] all without defect. [a] [3]With the bull offer a grain offering [b] of three-tenths of an ephah [a] of the finest flour mixed with olive oil; with the ram, two-tenths [b]; [4]and with each of the seven lambs, one-tenth. [c] [c] [5]Include one male goat [d] as a sin offering [d] to make atonement for you. [6]These are in addition to the monthly [e] and daily burnt offerings [f] with their grain offerings [g] and drink offerings [h] as specified. They are food offerings presented to the Lord, a pleasing aroma. [i]

THE DAY OF ATONEMENT
29:7–11pp — Lev 16:2–34; 23:26–32

[7]" 'On the tenth day of this seventh month hold a sacred assembly. You must deny yourselves [e] [j] and do no work. [k] [8]Present as an aroma pleasing to the Lord a burnt offering of one young bull, one ram and seven male lambs a year old, all without defect. [l] [9]With the bull offer a grain offering [m] of three-tenths of an ephah of the finest flour mixed with olive oil; with the ram, two-tenths; [n] [10]and with each of the seven lambs, one-tenth. [o] [11]Include one male goat [p] as a sin offering, in addition to the sin offering for atonement and the regular burnt offering [q] with its grain offering, and their drink offerings. [r]

THE FESTIVAL OF TABERNACLES
29:12–39pp — Lev 23:33–43; Dt 16:13–17

[12]" 'On the fifteenth day of the seventh [s] month, [t] hold a sacred assembly and do no regular work. Celebrate a festival to the Lord for seven days. [13]Present as an aroma pleasing to the Lord [u] a food offering consisting of a burnt offering of thirteen young bulls, two rams and fourteen male lambs a year old, all without defect. [v] [14]With each of the thirteen bulls offer a grain offering [w] of three-tenths of an ephah of the finest flour mixed with olive oil; with each of the two rams, two-tenths; [15]and with each of the fourteen lambs, one-tenth. [x] [16]Include one male goat as a sin offering, [y] in addition to the regular burnt offering with its grain offering and drink offering. [z]

[17]" 'On the second day [a] offer twelve young bulls, two rams and fourteen male lambs a year old, all without defect. [b] [18]With the bulls, rams and lambs, offer their grain offerings [c] and drink offerings [d] according to the number specified. [e] [19]Include one male goat as a sin offering, [f] in addition to the regular burnt offering [g] with its grain offering, and their drink offerings. [h]

[20]" 'On the third day offer eleven bulls, two rams and fourteen male lambs a year old, all without defect. [i] [21]With the bulls, rams and lambs, offer their grain offerings and drink offerings according to the number specified. [j] [22]Include one male goat as a sin offering, in addition to the regular burnt offering with its grain offering and drink offering.

[23]" 'On the fourth day offer ten bulls, two rams and fourteen male lambs a year old, all without defect. [24]With the bulls, rams and lambs, offer their grain offerings and drink offerings according to the number specified. [25]Include one male goat as a sin offering, in addition to the regular burnt offering with its grain offering and drink offering.

[26]" 'On the fifth day offer nine bulls, two rams and fourteen male lambs a year old, all without defect. [27]With the bulls, rams and lambs, offer their grain offerings and drink offerings according to the number specified. [28]Include one male goat as a sin offering, in addition to the regular burnt offering with its grain offering and drink offering.

[29]" 'On the sixth day offer eight bulls, two rams and fourteen male lambs a year old, all without defect. [30]With the bulls, rams and lambs, offer their grain offerings and drink of-

29:1 w Nu 28:18
29:2 x Nu 28:2
y Lev 1:9; Nu 28:11
z ver 36 a Lev 1:3;
Nu 28:3
29:3 b ver 14;
Nu 28:12
29:4 c Nu 28:13
29:5 d Nu 28:15
29:6 e Nu 28:11
f Nu 28:3 g Nu 28:5
h Nu 28:7 i Lev 1:9;
Nu 28:2
29:7 j Ac 27:9
k Ex 31:15
29:8 l ver 2
29:9 m S ver 3,18
n Nu 28:12
29:10 o Nu 28:13
29:11 p ver 5;
Nu 28:15 q S Lev 16:3
r S ver 6
29:12 s 1Ki 8:2;
12:32 t S Lev 23:24
29:13 u ver 2;
Nu 28:2 v Nu 28:3
29:14 w S ver 3;
S Nu 15:6
29:15 x ver 4;
Nu 28:13
29:16 y ver 5;
S Nu 28:15 z ver 6
29:17 a Lev 23:36
b ver 2; Nu 28:3
29:18 c S ver 9
d Nu 28:7 e Nu 15:4-
12
29:19 f S Nu 28:15
g Nu 28:3 h ver 6
29:20 i S ver 17
29:21 j S ver 18

---

a 3 That is, probably about 11 pounds or about 5 kilograms; also in verses 9 and 14   b 3 That is, probably about 7 pounds or about 3.2 kilograms; also in verses 9 and 14   c 4 That is, probably about 3 1/2 pounds or about 1.6 kilograms; also in verses 10 and 15   d 5 Or *purification offering*; also elsewhere in this chapter   e 7 Or *must fast*

29:1–6 The Festival of Trumpets came at the beginning of the seventh month, a busy month for the worship of the Lord in holy festivals (see Lev 23:23–25; see also chart, pp. 180–181). Later in Jewish tradition this festival came to commemorate the New Year (Rosh Hashanah). The trumpet used was the ram's horn (*shophar*).
29:7–11 The Festival of Trumpets leads into the Day of Atonement, a time of confession, contrition and celebration (see Lev

16:1–34 and note; 23:26–32).
29:12–34 In the seventh month the Festival of Trumpets took place on the first day, the Day of Atonement occurred on the tenth day, and the Festival of Tabernacles began on the 15th day and lasted for seven days (see Lev 23:33–44). Each day of the Festival of Tabernacles had its own order for sacrifice (see note on Zec 14:16).

29:35 ᵏS Lev 23:36
29:36 ˡLev 1:9
ᵐver 2
29:39 ⁿNu 6:2
ᵒS Lev 7:16
ᵖS Lev 23:2 ᑫLev 1:3;
1Ch 23:31; 2Ch 31:3
ʳLev 3:1
30:1 ˢS Nu 1:4
30:2 ᵗDt 23:21-23;
Jdg 11:35; Job 22:27;
Ps 22:25; 50:14;
61:5,8; 76:11; 116:14;
Pr 20:25; Ecc 5:4,5;
Isa 19:21; Jnh 1:16; 2:9
30:4 ᵘver 7
30:5 ᵛver 8,12,15
30:6 ʷS Lev 5:4
30:8 ˣS Ge 3:16
ʸver 5
30:12 ᶻEph 5:22;
Col 3:18
30:15 ᵃS ver 5

ferings according to the number specified. [31] Include one male goat as a sin offering, in addition to the regular burnt offering with its grain offering and drink offering.

[32] "'On the seventh day offer seven bulls, two rams and fourteen male lambs a year old, all without defect. [33] With the bulls, rams and lambs, offer their grain offerings and drink offerings according to the number specified. [34] Include one male goat as a sin offering, in addition to the regular burnt offering with its grain offering and drink offering.

[35] "'On the eighth day hold a closing special assembly ᵏ and do no regular work. [36] Present as an aroma pleasing to the Lᴏʀᴅ ˡ a food offering consisting of a burnt offering of one bull, one ram and seven male lambs a year old, ᵐ all without defect. [37] With the bull, the ram and the lambs, offer their grain offerings and drink offerings according to the number specified. [38] Include one male goat as a sin offering, in addition to the regular burnt offering with its grain offering and drink offering.

[39] "'In addition to what you vow ⁿ and your freewill offerings, ᵒ offer these to the Lᴏʀᴅ at your appointed festivals: ᵖ your burnt offerings, ᑫ grain offerings, drink offerings and fellowship offerings.' ʳ"

*[40] Moses told the Israelites all that the Lᴏʀᴅ commanded him.

VOWS

30 *Moses said to the heads of the tribes of Israel: ˢ "This is what the Lᴏʀᴅ commands: [2] When a man makes a vow to the Lᴏʀᴅ or takes an oath to obligate himself by a pledge, he must not break his word but must do everything he said. ᵗ

[3] "When a young woman still living in her father's household makes a vow to the Lᴏʀᴅ or obligates herself by a pledge [4] and her father hears about her vow or pledge but says nothing to her, then all her vows and every pledge by which she obligated herself will stand. ᵘ [5] But if her father forbids her ᵛ when he hears about it, none of her vows or the pledges by which she obligated herself will stand; the Lᴏʀᴅ will release her because her father has forbidden her.

[6] "If she marries after she makes a vow ʷ or after her lips utter a rash promise by which she obligates herself [7] and her husband hears about it but says nothing to her, then her vows or the pledges by which she obligated herself will stand. [8] But if her husband ˣ forbids her when he hears about it, he nullifies the vow that obligates her or the rash promise by which she obligates herself, and the Lᴏʀᴅ will release her. ʸ

[9] "Any vow or obligation taken by a widow or divorced woman will be binding on her.

[10] "If a woman living with her husband makes a vow or obligates herself by a pledge under oath [11] and her husband hears about it but says nothing to her and does not forbid her, then all her vows or the pledges by which she obligated herself will stand. [12] But if her husband nullifies them when he hears about them, then none of the vows or pledges that came from her lips will stand. ᶻ Her husband has nullified them, and the Lᴏʀᴅ will release her. [13] Her husband may confirm or nullify any vow she makes or any sworn pledge to deny herself. ᵃ [14] But if her husband says nothing to her about it from day to day, then he confirms all her vows or the pledges binding on her. He confirms them by saying nothing to her when he hears about them. [15] If, however, he nullifies them ᵃ some time after he hears about them, then he must bear the consequences of her wrongdoing."

[16] These are the regulations the Lᴏʀᴅ gave Moses concerning relationships between a man and his wife, and between a father and his young daughter still living at home.

ᵃ 13 Or *to fast*

* 29:40 is numbered 30:1 in Hebrew texts.   * 30:1-16 is numbered 30:2-17 in Hebrew texts.

29:40 *Moses told the Israelites.* The recapitulation of these festivals was a necessary part of the transfer of power from Moses to Joshua.

30:1–16 The principal OT passage on vows (see Dt 23:21–23). A vow is not to be made rashly (cf. Ecc 5:1–7), and a vow to the Lord must be kept.

30:3–8 In Near Eastern society, women were subject to the authority of their fathers (vv. 3–5) or husbands (vv. 6–8), who could disallow the carrying out of a vow.

30:9 *widow or divorced woman.* Such women remained responsible for the vows they made.

30:10–15 Further examples of the complications that come in the making of vows within the husband-wife relationship. Such complications may have come up much as in the case of Zelophehad's daughters (27:1–11). One case after another presented itself, resulting in this final codification. Presumably, in the centuries leading up to the NT, the legal decisions on vows became even more complex. The words of Jesus that one is to avoid complications connected with oaths (Mt 5:33–37) are liberating.

VENGEANCE ON THE MIDIANITES

31 The Lord said to Moses, [2]"Take vengeance on the Midianites [b] for the Israelites. After that, you will be gathered to your people. [c]" [3]So Moses said to the people, "Arm some of your men to go to war against the Midianites so that they may carry out the Lord's vengeance [d] on them. [4]Send into battle a thousand men from each of the tribes of Israel." [5]So twelve thousand men armed for battle, [e] a thousand from each tribe, were supplied from the clans of Israel. [6]Moses sent them into battle, [f] a thousand from each tribe, along with Phinehas [g] son of Eleazar, the priest, who took with him articles from the sanctuary [h] and the trumpets [i] for signaling.

[7]They fought against Midian, as the Lord commanded Moses, [j] and killed every man. [k] [8]Among their victims were Evi, Rekem, Zur, Hur and Reba [l]—the five kings of Midian. [m] They also killed Balaam son of Beor [n] with the sword. [o] [9]The Israelites captured the Midianite women [p] and children and took all the Midianite herds, flocks and goods as plunder. [q] [10]They burned [r] all the towns where the Midianites had settled, as well as all their camps. [s] [11]They took all the plunder and spoils, including the people and animals, [t] [12]and brought the captives, spoils [u] and plunder to Moses and Eleazar the priest and the Israelite assembly [v] at their camp on the plains of Moab, by the Jordan across from Jericho. [w]

[13]Moses, Eleazar the priest and all the leaders of the community went to meet them outside the camp. [14]Moses was angry with the officers of the army [x]—the commanders of thousands and commanders of hundreds—who returned from the battle.

[15]"Have you allowed all the women to live?" he asked them. [16]"They were the ones who followed Balaam's advice [y] and enticed the Israelites to be unfaithful to the Lord in the Peor incident, [z] so that a plague [a] struck the Lord's people. [17]Now kill all the boys. And kill every woman who has slept with a man, [b] [18]but save for yourselves every girl who has never slept with a man.

[19]"Anyone who has killed someone or touched someone who was killed [c] must stay outside the camp seven days. [d] On the third and seventh days you must purify yourselves [e] and your captives. [20]Purify every garment [f] as well as everything made of leather, goat hair or wood. [g]"

[21]Then Eleazar the priest said to the soldiers who had gone into battle, [h] "This is what is required by the law that the Lord gave Moses: [22]Gold, silver, bronze, iron, [i] tin, lead [23]and anything else that can withstand fire must be put through the fire, [j] and then it will be clean. But it must also be purified with the water of cleansing. [k] And whatever cannot withstand fire must be put through that water. [24]On the seventh day wash your clothes and you will be clean. [l] Then you may come into the camp. [m]"

DIVIDING THE SPOILS

[25]The Lord said to Moses, [26]"You and Eleazar the priest and the family heads [n] of the community are to count all the women [o] and animals that were captured. [p] [27]Divide [q] the spoils equally between the soldiers who took part in the battle and the rest of the community. [28]From the soldiers who fought in the battle, set apart as tribute for the Lord [r] one out of every five hundred, whether women, cattle, donkeys or sheep. [29]Take this tribute from their half share and give it to Eleazar the priest as the Lord's part. [30]From the Israelites' half, select one out of every fifty, whether women, cattle, donkeys, sheep or other

---

31:2 [b] S Ge 25:2
[c] S Nu 20:26
31:3 [d] Jdg 11:36;
1Sa 24:12; 2Sa 4:8;
22:48; Ps 94:1; 149:7;
Isa 34:8; Jer 11:20;
46:10; Eze 25:17
31:5 [e] ver 6,21
31:6 [f] S ver 5
[g] S Ex 6:25
[h] Nu 14:44
[i] S Nu 10:2
31:7 [j] Nu 25:16
[k] Dt 20:13; Jdg 21:11;
1Ki 11:15,16
31:8 [l] Jos 13:21
[m] S Nu 25:15
[n] S Nu 22:5; S 24:14
[o] Jos 13:22
31:9 [p] ver 15
31:10 [r] Jos 6:24;
8:28; 11:11; Jdg 18:27
[s] Ge 25:16; 1Ch 6:54;
Ps 69:25; Eze 25:4
31:11 [t] ver 26;
Dt 20:14; 2Ch 28:8
31:12 [u] ver 32,53;
Ge 49:27; Ex 15:9
[v] S Nu 27:2 [w] Nu 22:1
31:14 [x] ver 48;
Ex 18:21; Dt 1:15;
2Sa 18:1
31:16 [y] S Nu 22:5;
S 24:14; S 2Pe 2:15
[z] S Nu 23:28; 25:1-9
[a] S Nu 14:37
31:17 [b] Dt 7:2;
20:16-18; Jdg 21:11
31:19 [c] Nu 19:16
[d] S Lev 21:1
[e] Nu 19:12
31:20 [f] Nu 19:19
[g] S Lev 11:32
31:21 [h] S ver 5
31:22 [i] Jos 6:19;
22:8
31:23 [j] S 1Co 3:13
[k] S Nu 8:7
31:24 [l] S Lev 11:25
[m] S Lev 14:8
31:26 [n] S Nu 1:4
[o] S Nu 1:19 [p] S ver 11,
12
31:27 [q] Jos 22:8;
1Sa 25:13; 30:24
31:28 [r] ver 37-41;
S Nu 18:21

31:1–24 The Lord declares war (see essay, p. 294) against the Midianites as one of Moses' last actions before the end of his life. Moses was not motivated by petty jealousy; rather, the war was "the Lord's vengeance" (v. 3) for the Midianites' part in seducing the Israelites to engage in sexual immorality and to worship the Baal of Peor. (See 25:16–18, where the specific mention of Kozbi, a Midianite woman, heightens the anger expressed in ch. 31.)
31:2 *be gathered to your people.* In death (see note on Ge 25:8).
31:4 *a thousand men from each of the tribes of Israel.* The burden of the Lord's war had to be shared equally among the tribes.
31:6 *Phinehas.* His zeal for the Lord's honor led him to execute Zimri and Kozbi (25:8). Now he leads in the sacred aspects of the battle to demonstrate that this is the Lord's war. *trumpets.* See note on 10:3.
31:8 *They also killed Balaam.* Ch. 25 lacks the name of the principal instigator of the seduction of the Israelite men to the de-

praved worship of Baal. But here he is found among the dead. What Balaam had been unable to accomplish through acts of magic or sorcery (chs. 22–24) he was almost able to achieve by his advice to the Midianites (v. 16).
31:9–18 While the troops killed the men of Midian, they spared the women and children as plunder. Moses commanded that only the virgin women (who were thus innocent of the indecencies at Peor) could be spared; the guilty women and the boys (who might endanger the inheritance rights of Israelite men) were to be put to death (vv. 15–17).
31:16 *the Peor incident.* See notes on v. 8; 25:1–18.
31:19–24 Since this was the Lord's war, both people (vv. 19–20) and things (vv. 21–24) had to be cleansed (cf. 19:11–13).
31:26–35 Another aspect of the Lord's war was the fair distribution of the spoils of war, both among those who fought in the battle and among those who stayed with the community, with appropriate shares to be given to the Lord, whose battle it was (v. 28).

31:30 ⁿ Nu 3:7; 18:3
31:32 ˢ See ver 12
31:37 ᵘ ver 38-41
31:41 ᵛ Nu 5:9; 18:8
ʷ ver 21,28
31:48 ˣ See ver 14
31:49 ʸ S Nu 1:19
ᶻ Jer 23:4
31:50 ᵃ S Ex 30:16
31:53 ᵇ S Ge 34:29;
Dt 20:14
31:54 ᶜ S Ex 27:21;
40:2 ᵈ S Ex 28:12
32:1 ᵉ ver 24,36;
Jdg 5:16 ᶠ S Nu 21:32
ᵍ S Ge 31:21
ʰ Ex 12:38
32:2 ⁱ Lev 4:22;
Nu 27:2
32:3 ʲ ver 34;
Jos 16:2,7; 18:13
ᵏ ver 34; S Nu 21:30
ˡ ver 1 ᵐ ver 36;
Jos 13:27 ⁿ Nu 21:25
ᵒ ver 37; Isa 15:4;
16:9; Jer 48:34
ᵖ Jos 13:19; Isa 16:8,9;
Jer 48:32 ᵍ Nu 33:47;
Dt 32:49; 34:1;
1Ch 5:8 ʳ ver 38;
Jos 13:17; Eze 25:9
32:4 ˢ Nu 21:34
ᵗ Ex 12:38
32:5 ᵘ S Nu 13:29
32:7 ᵛ Nu 13:27-
14:4
32:8 ʷ Nu 13:3,26;
Dt 1:19-25
32:9 ˣ Nu 13:23;
Dt 1:24
32:10 ʸ Nu 11:1
ᶻ S Nu 14:20-23
32:11 ᵃ S Ex 30:14
ᵇ Nu 1:1 ᶜ S Nu 14:23
ᵈ Nu 14:28-30
32:12 ᵉ Nu 14:24,30
32:13 ᶠ S Ex 4:14
ᵍ Nu 14:28-35; 26:64,
65
32:14 ʰ S ver 10;
Dt 1:34; Ps 78:59
32:15 ⁱ Dt 30:17-18;
2Ch 7:20
32:16 ʲ ver 24,36;
1Sa 24:3; Ps 50:9;
78:70

animals. Give them to the Levites, who are responsible for the care of the LORD's tabernacle. ˢ" ³¹So Moses and Eleazar the priest did as the LORD commanded Moses.

³²The plunder remaining from the spoils ᵗ that the soldiers took was 675,000 sheep, ³³72,000 cattle, ³⁴61,000 donkeys ³⁵and 32,000 women who had never slept with a man. ³⁶The half share of those who fought in the battle was:

337,500 sheep, ³⁷of which the tribute for the LORD ᵘ was 675;
³⁸36,000 cattle, of which the tribute for the LORD was 72;
³⁹30,500 donkeys, of which the tribute for the LORD was 61;
⁴⁰16,000 women, of whom the tribute for the LORD was 32.

⁴¹Moses gave the tribute to Eleazar the priest as the LORD's part, ᵛ as the LORD commanded Moses. ʷ

⁴²The half belonging to the Israelites, which Moses set apart from that of the fighting men— ⁴³the community's half—was 337,500 sheep, ⁴⁴36,000 cattle, ⁴⁵30,500 donkeys ⁴⁶and 16,000 women. ⁴⁷From the Israelites' half, Moses selected one out of every fifty women and animals, as the LORD commanded him, and gave them to the Levites, who were responsible for the care of the LORD's tabernacle.

⁴⁸Then the officers ˣ who were over the units of the army—the commanders of thousands and commanders of hundreds—went to Moses ⁴⁹and said to him, "Your servants have counted ʸ the soldiers under our command, and not one is missing. ᶻ ⁵⁰So we have brought as an offering to the LORD the gold articles each of us acquired—armlets, bracelets, signet rings, earrings and necklaces—to make atonement for ourselves ᵃ before the LORD."

⁵¹Moses and Eleazar the priest accepted from them the gold—all the crafted articles. ⁵²All the gold from the commanders of thousands and commanders of hundreds that Moses and Eleazar presented as a gift to the LORD weighed 16,750 shekels. ᵃ ⁵³Each soldier had taken plunder ᵇ for himself. ⁵⁴Moses and Eleazar the priest accepted the gold from the commanders of thousands and commanders of hundreds and brought it into the tent of meeting ᶜ as a memorial ᵈ for the Israelites before the LORD.

THE TRANSJORDAN TRIBES

32 The Reubenites and Gadites, who had very large herds and flocks, ᵉ saw that the lands of Jazer ᶠ and Gilead ᵍ were suitable for livestock. ʰ ²So they came to Moses and Eleazar the priest and to the leaders of the community, ⁱ and said, ³"Ataroth, ʲ Dibon, ᵏ Jazer, ˡ Nimrah, ᵐ Heshbon, ⁿ Elealeh, ᵒ Sebam, ᵖ Nebo ᵍ and Beon ʳ— ⁴the land the LORD subdued ˢ before the people of Israel—are suitable for livestock, ᵗ and your servants have livestock. ⁵If we have found favor in your eyes," they said, "let this land be given to your servants as our possession. Do not make us cross the Jordan. ᵘ"

⁶Moses said to the Gadites and Reubenites, "Should your own people go to war while you sit here? ⁷Why do you discourage the Israelites from crossing over into the land the LORD has given them? ᵛ ⁸This is what your fathers did when I sent them from Kadesh Barnea to look over the land. ʷ ⁹After they went up to the Valley of Eshkol ˣ and viewed the land, they discouraged the Israelites from entering the land the LORD had given them. ¹⁰The LORD's anger was aroused ʸ that day and he swore this oath: ᶻ ¹¹'Because they have not followed me wholeheartedly, not one of those who were twenty years old or more ᵃ when they came up out of Egypt ᵇ will see the land I promised on oath ᶜ to Abraham, Isaac and Jacob ᵈ— ¹²not one except Caleb son of Jephunneh the Kenizzite and Joshua son of Nun, for they followed the LORD wholeheartedly.' ᵉ ¹³The LORD's anger burned against Israel ᶠ and he made them wander in the wilderness forty years, until the whole generation of those who had done evil in his sight was gone. ᵍ

¹⁴"And here you are, a brood of sinners, standing in the place of your fathers and making the LORD even more angry with Israel. ʰ ¹⁵If you turn away from following him, he will again leave all this people in the wilderness, and you will be the cause of their destruction. ⁱ"

¹⁶Then they came up to him and said, "We would like to build pens ʲ here for our live-

---

ᵃ 52 That is, about 420 pounds or about 190 kilograms

32:1 *Reubenites and Gadites.* The abundance of fertile grazing land in Transjordan prompted the leaders of these two tribes to request that they be allowed to settle there and not cross the Jordan. This area too was a gift of God won by conquest.
32:8 *This is what your fathers did.* Moses' fear was that the failure of these two tribes to stay with the whole community in

conquering Canaan would be the beginning of a general revolt against entering the land. It would be the failure of Kadesh (chs. 13–14) all over again. Moreover, the conquest of Canaan was a commission to all Israel.
32:12 *followed the LORD wholeheartedly.* See note on 14:24.

stock*k* and cities for our women and children. 17But we will arm ourselves for battle*a* and go ahead of the Israelites *l* until we have brought them to their place. *m* Meanwhile our women and children will live in fortified cities, for protection from the inhabitants of the land. 18We will not return to our homes until all the Israelites have received their inheritance. *n* 19We will not receive any inheritance with them on the other side of the Jordan, because our inheritance *o* has come to us on the east side of the Jordan."*p*

20Then Moses said to them, "If you will do this—if you will arm yourselves before the LORD for battle*q* 21and if all of you who are armed cross over the Jordan before the LORD until he has driven his enemies out before him*r*— 22then when the land is subdued before the LORD, you may return*s* and be free from your obligation to the LORD and to Israel. And this land will be your possession*t* before the LORD. *u*

23"But if you fail to do this, you will be sinning against the LORD; and you may be sure that your sin will find you out. *v* 24Build cities for your women and children, and pens for your flocks, *w* but do what you have promised.*x*"

25The Gadites and Reubenites said to Moses, "We your servants will do as our lord commands. *y* 26Our children and wives, our flocks and herds will remain here in the cities of Gilead. *z* 27But your servants, every man who is armed for battle, will cross over to fight*a* before the LORD, just as our lord says."

28Then Moses gave orders about them *b* to Eleazar the priest and Joshua son of Nun *c* and to the family heads of the Israelite tribes. *d* 29He said to them, "If the Gadites and Reubenites, all those armed for battle, cross over the Jordan with you before the LORD, then when the land is subdued before you, *e* you must give them the land of Gilead as their possession. *f* 30But if they do not cross over*g* with you armed, they must accept their possession with you in Canaan. *h*"

31The Gadites and Reubenites answered, "Your servants will do what the LORD has said. *i* 32We will cross over before the LORD into Canaan armed, *j* but the property we inherit will be on this side of the Jordan. *k*"

33Then Moses gave to the Gadites, *l* the Reubenites and the half-tribe of Manasseh *m* son of Joseph the kingdom of Sihon king of the Amorites *n* and the kingdom of Og king of Bashan *o*—the whole land with its cities and the territory around them. *p*

34The Gadites built up Dibon, Ataroth, Aroer, *q* 35Atroth Shophan, Jazer, *r* Jogbehah, *s* 36Beth Nimrah *t* and Beth Haran as fortified cities, and built pens for their flocks. *u* 37And the Reubenites rebuilt Heshbon, *v* Elealeh *w* and Kiriathaim, *x* 38as well as Nebo *y* and Baal Meon (these names were changed) and Sibmah. *z* They gave names to the cities they rebuilt.

39The descendants of Makir *a* son of Manasseh went to Gilead, *b* captured it and drove out the Amorites *c* who were there. 40So Moses gave Gilead to the Makirites, *d* the descendants of Manasseh, and they settled there. 41Jair, *e* a descendant of Manasseh, captured their settlements and called them Havvoth Jair. *b f* 42And Nobah captured Kenath*g* and its surrounding settlements and called it Nobah *h* after himself. *i*

STAGES IN ISRAEL'S JOURNEY

33 Here are the stages in the journey*j* of the Israelites when they came out of Egypt *k* by divisions under the leadership of Moses and Aaron. *l* 2At the LORD's command Moses recorded *m* the stages in their journey *n*. This is their journey by stages:

a 17 Septuagint; Hebrew *will be quick to arm ourselves*   *b* 41 Or *them the settlements of Jair*

32:16 *k* Ex 12:38; Dt 3:19
32:17 *l* Dt 3:18; Jos 4:12,13
m S Nu 22:4; Dt 3:20
32:18 *n* Jos 22:1-4
32:19 *o* ver 22,29
p Nu 21:33; Jos 12:1; 22:7
32:20 *q* ver 17
32:21 *r* ver 17
32:22 *s* Jos 22:4
t S Lev 14:34
u Dt 3:18-20
32:23 *v* S Ge 4:7; S Isa 3:9
32:24 *w* S ver 1,16
x Nu 30:2
32:25 *y* ver 29;
Jos 1:16,18; 22:2
32:26 *z* ver 16,24;
Jos 1:14; 12:2; 22:9;
2Sa 2:9; 1Ch 5:9
32:27 *a* ver 17,21
32:28 *b* ver 29;
Dt 3:18-20; Jos 1:13
c Nu 11:28 *d* Nu 1:16
32:29 *e* S Nu 22:4
f S ver 19
32:30 *g* ver 23
h ver 29,32
32:31 *i* ver 29
32:32 *j* ver 17
k S ver 30; Jos 12:6
32:33 *l* Jos 13:24-28; 1Sa 13:7 *m* Jos 1:12
n Nu 21:21; Dt 2:26
o S ver 19; S Jos 12:5
p S Nu 21:24; 34:14;
Dt 2:36; Jos 12:6
32:34 *q* Dt 2:36; 3:12;
4:48; Jos 12:2; 13:9;
Jdg 11:26; 1Sa 30:28;
1Ch 5:8; Jer 48:19
32:35 *r* ver 3
s Jdg 8:11
32:36 *t* S ver 3
u S ver 1
32:37 *v* Nu 21:25
w S ver 3 *x* Jos 13:19;
1Ch 6:76; Jer 48:1,23;
Eze 25:9
32:38 *y* S ver 3;
Isa 15:2; Jer 48:1,22
z S ver 3
32:39 *a* S Ge 50:23
b Nu 26:29; Dt 2:36
c S Ge 10:16
32:40 *d* S Ge 50:23;
Dt 3:15
32:41 *e* 1Ki 4:13
f Dt 3:14; Jos 13:30;
Jdg 10:4; 1Ch 2:23
32:42 *g* 1Ch 2:23
h Jdg 8:11 *i* 1Sa 15:12;
2Sa 18:18; Ps 49:11;
Isa 22:16; 56:5
33:1 *j* Ex 17:1; 40:36
k Nu 1:1 *l* Ex 4:16;
6:26
33:2 *m* S Ex 17:14
n S ver 1

32:17 *we will arm ourselves for battle.* The leaders of Reuben and Gad sought to assure Moses that they did not wish to shirk their duty to serve in the Lord's army in conquering the land. They would join their brothers in battle but wished to leave their families and livestock behind in the territory of their choosing.

32:23 *your sin will find you out.* The bargain was struck, but not without strong warnings if they failed to live up to their word.

32:33 *and the half-tribe of Manasseh.* It appears that after the requirements for Transjordan settlement were established with the tribes of Reuben and Gad, half the tribe of Manasseh joined with them.

33:1-49 The numerous places (significantly 40 in number between Rameses and the plains of Moab) in Israel's wilderness experience are listed. Unfortunately, most of the sites were

wilderness encampments, not cities with lasting archaeological records; so they are difficult to locate. Many of the places (e.g., in vv. 19-29) are not recorded elsewhere in Exodus and Numbers, while some of the places mentioned elsewhere (e.g., Taberah, 11:3; see 21:19) are missing here. The data warrant these conclusions: 1. Moses recorded the list at the Lord's command (v. 2). 2. The list should be taken seriously, as an accurate recapitulation of the stages of the journey, despite difficulty in locating many of the sites. 3. The numerical factor of 40 sites between Rameses and the plains of Moab suggests some styling of the list, which helps to account for the sites not included. 4. As in the case of genealogies in the Pentateuch, some factors of ancient significance may not be clear to us today. 5. Ultimately the record is a recital of the Lord's blessing on his people for the extended period of their wilderness experience. Although certainly not without geo-

33:3 *o* Nu 10:2
p S Ge 47:11 *q* Jos 5:10
r S Ex 14:8
33:4 *s* S Ex 4:23
t 2Ch 24:24; Jer 15:3;
Eze 14:21 *u* S Ex 12:12
33:5 *v* Ex 12:37
33:6 *w* Ex 13:20
33:7 *x* Ex 14:9
y S Ex 14:2
33:8 *z* Ex 14:2
a S Ex 14:22
b S Ex 15:23
33:9 *c* Ex 15:27
33:10 *d* Ex 16:1
33:11 *e* S Ex 16:1
33:14 *f* S Ex 15:22;
S 17:2
33:15 *g* S Ex 17:1
h S Ex 19:1
33:16 *i* S Nu 11:34
33:17 *j* Nu 11:35
33:20 *k* Jos 10:29;
12:15; 15:42; 21:13;
2Ki 8:22; 19:8; 23:31;
1Ch 6:57; 2Ch 21:10;
Isa 37:8; Jer 52:1
33:30 *l* Dt 10:6
33:31 *m* Dt 10:6
33:33 *n* Dt 10:7
33:35 *o* Dt 2:8;
1Ki 9:26; 22:48
33:36 *p* S Nu 13:21
33:37 *q* S Nu 20:22
r S Ge 36:16;
S Nu 20:16
33:38 *s* S Nu 27:13
t S Ex 16:35
u Nu 20:25-28
33:40 *v* S Ge 10:18
w S Nu 21:1
x S Ge 12:9
33:43 *y* Nu 21:10
33:44 *z* S Nu 21:11
33:47 *a* Nu 27:12
b Nu 32:3
33:48 *c* Nu 27:12
d S Nu 26:3

³The Israelites set out *o* from Rameses *p* on the fifteenth day of the first month, the day after the Passover. *q* They marched out defiantly *r* in full view of all the Egyptians, ⁴who were burying all their firstborn, *s* whom the LORD had struck down among them; for the LORD had brought judgment *t* on their gods. *u*

⁵The Israelites left Rameses and camped at Sukkoth. *v*

⁶They left Sukkoth and camped at Etham, on the edge of the desert. *w*

⁷They left Etham, turned back to Pi Hahiroth, to the east of Baal Zephon, *x* and camped near Migdol. *y*

⁸They left Pi Hahiroth ᵃᶻ and passed through the sea ᵃ into the desert, and when they had traveled for three days in the Desert of Etham, they camped at Marah. *b*

⁹They left Marah and went to Elim, where there were twelve springs and seventy palm trees, and they camped *c* there.

¹⁰They left Elim *d* and camped by the Red Sea. *b*

¹¹They left the Red Sea and camped in the Desert of Sin. *e*

¹²They left the Desert of Sin and camped at Dophkah.

¹³They left Dophkah and camped at Alush.

¹⁴They left Alush and camped at Rephidim, where there was no water for the people to drink. *f*

¹⁵They left Rephidim *g* and camped in the Desert of Sinai. *h*

¹⁶They left the Desert of Sinai and camped at Kibroth Hattaavah. *i*

¹⁷They left Kibroth Hattaavah and camped at Hazeroth. *j*

¹⁸They left Hazeroth and camped at Rithmah.

¹⁹They left Rithmah and camped at Rimmon Perez.

²⁰They left Rimmon Perez and camped at Libnah. *k*

²¹They left Libnah and camped at Rissah.

²²They left Rissah and camped at Kehelathah.

²³They left Kehelathah and camped at Mount Shepher.

²⁴They left Mount Shepher and camped at Haradah.

²⁵They left Haradah and camped at Makheloth.

²⁶They left Makheloth and camped at Tahath.

²⁷They left Tahath and camped at Terah.

²⁸They left Terah and camped at Mithkah.

²⁹They left Mithkah and camped at Hashmonah.

³⁰They left Hashmonah and camped at Moseroth. *l*

³¹They left Moseroth and camped at Bene Jaakan. *m*

³²They left Bene Jaakan and camped at Hor Haggidgad.

³³They left Hor Haggidgad and camped at Jotbathah. *n*

³⁴They left Jotbathah and camped at Abronah.

³⁵They left Abronah and camped at Ezion Geber. *o*

³⁶They left Ezion Geber and camped at Kadesh, in the Desert of Zin. *p*

³⁷They left Kadesh and camped at Mount Hor, *q* on the border of Edom. *r* ³⁸At the LORD's command Aaron the priest went up Mount Hor, where he died *s* on the first day of the fifth month of the fortieth year *t* after the Israelites came out of Egypt. *u* ³⁹Aaron was a hundred and twenty-three years old when he died on Mount Hor.

⁴⁰The Canaanite king *v* of Arad, *w* who lived in the Negev *x* of Canaan, heard that the Israelites were coming.

⁴¹They left Mount Hor and camped at Zalmonah.

⁴²They left Zalmonah and camped at Punon.

⁴³They left Punon and camped at Oboth. *y*

⁴⁴They left Oboth and camped at Iye Abarim, on the border of Moab. *z*

⁴⁵They left Iye Abarim and camped at Dibon Gad.

⁴⁶They left Dibon Gad and camped at Almon Diblathaim.

⁴⁷They left Almon Diblathaim and camped in the mountains of Abarim, *a* near Nebo. *b*

⁴⁸They left the mountains of Abarim *c* and camped on the plains of Moab *d* by the

---

ᵃ 8 Many manuscripts of the Masoretic Text, Samaritan Pentateuch and Vulgate; most manuscripts of the Masoretic Text *left from before Hahiroth*   ᵇ 10 Or *the Sea of Reeds; also in verse 11*

---

graphical importance, the listing of the stages of Israel's experience in the wilderness is fundamentally a religious document, a litany of the LORD's deliverance of his people.
33:40 *Negev.* See note on Ge 12:9.

33:50—36:13 A summary statement dealing with matters of land and other property in the promised land. The first and last verses—with their several verbal links—frame the section.

Jordan *e* across from Jericho. *f* 49There on the plains of Moab they camped along the Jordan from Beth Jeshimoth *g* to Abel Shittim. *h*

50On the plains of Moab by the Jordan across from Jericho *i* the LORD said to Moses, 51"Speak to the Israelites and say to them: 'When you cross the Jordan into Canaan, *j* 52drive out all the inhabitants of the land before you. Destroy all their carved images and their cast idols, and demolish all their high places. *k* 53Take possession of the land and settle in it, for I have given you the land to possess. *l* 54Distribute the land by lot, *m* according to your clans. *n* To a larger group give a larger inheritance, and to a smaller group a smaller one. *o* Whatever falls to them by lot will be theirs. Distribute it according to your ancestral tribes. *p*

55" 'But if you do not drive out the inhabitants of the land, those you allow to remain will become barbs in your eyes and thorns *q* in your sides. They will give you trouble in the land where you will live. 56And then I will do to you what I plan to do to them. *r* ' "

BOUNDARIES OF CANAAN

34 The LORD said to Moses, 2"Command the Israelites and say to them: 'When you enter Canaan, *s* the land that will be allotted to you as an inheritance *t* is to have these boundaries: *u*

3" 'Your southern side will include some of the Desert of Zin *v* along the border of Edom. Your southern boundary will start in the east from the southern end of the Dead Sea, *w* 4cross south of Scorpion Pass, *x* continue on to Zin and go south of Kadesh Barnea. *y* Then it will go to Hazar Addar and over to Azmon, *z* 5where it will turn, join the Wadi of Egypt *a* and end at the Mediterranean Sea. *p*

6" 'Your western boundary will be the coast of the Mediterranean Sea. *b* This will be your boundary on the west. *c*

7" 'For your northern boundary, *d* run a line from the Mediterranean Sea to Mount Hor *e* 8and from Mount Hor to Lebo Hamath. *f* Then the boundary will go to Zedad, 9continue to Ziphron and end at Hazar Enan. This will be your boundary on the north.

10" 'For your eastern boundary, *g* run a line from Hazar Enan to Shepham. 11The boundary will go down from Shepham to Riblah *h* on the east side of Ain *i* and continue along the slopes east of the Sea of Galilee. *a j* 12Then the boundary will go down along the Jordan and end at the Dead Sea.

" 'This will be your land, with its boundaries on every side.' "

13Moses commanded the Israelites: "Assign this land by lot *k* as an inheritance. *l* The LORD has ordered that it be given to the nine and a half tribes, 14because the families of the tribe of Reuben, the tribe of Gad and the half-tribe of Manasseh have received their inheritance. *m* 15These two and a half tribes have received their inheritance east of the Jordan across from Jericho, toward the sunrise."

16The LORD said to Moses, 17"These are the names of the men who are to assign the land for you as an inheritance: Eleazar the priest and Joshua *n* son of Nun. 18And appoint one leader from each tribe to help *o* assign the land. *p* 19These are their names: *q*

Caleb *r* son of Jephunneh,
　from the tribe of Judah; *s*
20Shemuel son of Ammihud,
　from the tribe of Simeon; *t*
21Elidad son of Kislon,
　from the tribe of Benjamin; *u*
22Bukki son of Jogli,
　the leader from the tribe of Dan;
23Hanniel son of Ephod,
　the leader from the tribe of Manasseh *v* son of Joseph;

---

a 11 Hebrew *Kinnereth*

33:52 *drive out all the inhabitants of the land … Destroy all their …idols.* What Israel had accomplished in the war against the Midianites (ch. 31) was now to be extended to all the inhabitants of Canaan. Particularly important was the command to destroy all symbols of the pagan religious system of the Canaanites.
33:54 See note on 26:53–56.
34:3–12 The listing of the four boundaries displays the dimensions of God's great gift to his people.

34:13–15 The new realities that the settlement of Reuben, Gad and the half-tribe of Manasseh in Transjordan brought about (see ch. 32).
34:16–29 The listing of the new tribal leaders recalls the listing of the leaders of the first generation (1:5–16). This time the promise will be realized; these new leaders will assist Eleazar and Joshua in actually allotting the land.
34:19 *Caleb … Judah.* See note on 13:6.

33:48 *e* S Ge 13:10
f Nu 22:1; Jos 12:9
33:49 *g* Jos 12:3;
13:20; Eze 25:9
h S Nu 21:16
33:50 *i* ver 48
33:51 *j* Nu 34:2;
Jos 3:17
33:52 *k* 34:13;
S Lev 26:1;
Ps 106:34-36
33:53 *l* Dt 11:31;
17:14; Jos 1:11; 21:43
33:54 *m* S Lev 16:8;
Nu 36:2 *n* Nu 26:54
o Nu 35:8 *p* Jos 18:10
33:55 *q* Jos 23:13;
Jdg 2:3; Ps 106:36;
Isa 55:13; Eze 2:6;
28:24; Mic 7:4;
2Co 12:7
33:56 *r* Nu 14:28
34:2 *s* S Nu 33:51
t Ge 17:8; Dt 1:7-8;
Jos 23:4; Ps 78:54-55;
105:11 *u* Eze 47:15
34:3 *v* Nu 13:21;
Jos 15:1-3 *w* S Ge 14:3
34:4 *x* Jos 15:3;
Jdg 1:36 *y* Nu 32:8
z Jos 15:4
34:5 *a* Ge 15:18
34:6 *b* Jos 1:4; 9:1;
15:12,47; 23:4;
Eze 47:10,15; 48:28
c Eze 47:19-20
34:7 *d* Eze 47:15-17
e S Nu 20:22
34:8 *f* Nu 13:21;
Jos 13:5
34:10 *g* Jos 15:5
34:11 *h* 2Ki 23:33;
25:6,21; Jer 39:5;
52:9,27 *i* Jos 15:32;
21:16; 1Ch 4:32
j Dt 3:17; Jos 11:2;
13:27
34:13 *k* S Lev 16:8;
Jos 18:10; Mic 2:5
l Jos 13:6; 14:1-5;
Isa 49:8; 65:9;
Eze 45:1
34:14 *m* Nu 32:19;
Dt 33:21; Jos 14:3
34:17 *n* Nu 11:28;
Dt 1:38
34:18 *o* S Nu 1:4
p Jos 14:1
34:19 *q* ver 29
r S Nu 26:65
s Ge 29:35; Dt 33:7;
Ps 60:7
34:20 *t* S Ge 29:33
34:21 *u* Ge 49:27;
Jdg 5:14; Ps 68:27
34:23 *v* Nu 1:34

34:24 ʷ Nu 1:32
34:25 ˣ S Ge 30:20
34:27 ʸ Nu 1:40
34:29 ᶻ ver 19
35:1 ᵃ Nu 22:1
35:2 ᵇ Lev 25:32-
34; Jos 14:3,4
ᶜ Jos 21:1-42
35:3 ᵈ Dt 18:6;
Jos 14:4; 21:2
35:5 ᵉ Jos 3:4
ᶠ Lev 25:34;
2Ch 11:14; 13:9; 23:2;
31:19
35:6 ᵍ ver 11;
Jos 21:13
35:8 ʰ Nu 26:54;
33:54
35:10 ⁱ Nu 33:51;
Dt 9:1; Jos 1:2,11
35:11 ʲ ver 22-25
ᵏ S Ex 21:13
35:12 ˡ ver 19;
Dt 19:6; Jos 20:3;
2Sa 14:11 ᵐ ver 26,27,
28 ⁿ ver 24,25
35:13 ᵒ ver 6,14
35:16 ᵖ S Ex 21:12
35:19 �q S ver 12
ʳ ver 21
35:20 ˢ S Ex 21:14
35:21 ᵗ Ex 21:14
ᵘ ver 19

²⁴ Kemuel son of Shiphtan,
the leader from the tribe of Ephraim ʷ son of Joseph;
²⁵ Elizaphan son of Parnak,
the leader from the tribe of Zebulun; ˣ
²⁶ Paltiel son of Azzan,
the leader from the tribe of Issachar;
²⁷ Ahihud son of Shelomi,
the leader from the tribe of Asher; ʸ
²⁸ Pedahel son of Ammihud,
the leader from the tribe of Naphtali."

²⁹ These are the men the Lᴏʀᴅ commanded to assign the inheritance to the Israelites in the land of Canaan. ᶻ

TOWNS FOR THE LEVITES

35 On the plains of Moab by the Jordan across from Jericho, ᵃ the Lᴏʀᴅ said to Moses, ²"Command the Israelites to give the Levites towns to live in ᵇ from the inheritance the Israelites will possess. And give them pasturelands ᶜ around the towns. ³Then they will have towns to live in and pasturelands for the cattle they own and all their other animals. ᵈ

⁴"The pasturelands around the towns that you give the Levites will extend a thousand cubits ᵃ from the town wall. ⁵Outside the town, measure two thousand cubits ᵇ ᵉ on the east side, two thousand on the south side, two thousand on the west and two thousand on the north, with the town in the center. They will have this area as pastureland for the towns. ᶠ

CITIES OF REFUGE

35:6–34Ref — Dt 4:41–43; 19:1–14; Jos 20:1–9

⁶"Six of the towns you give the Levites will be cities of refuge, to which a person who has killed someone may flee. ᵍ In addition, give them forty-two other towns. ⁷In all you must give the Levites forty-eight towns, together with their pasturelands. ⁸The towns you give the Levites from the land the Israelites possess are to be given in proportion to the inheritance of each tribe: Take many towns from a tribe that has many, but few from one that has few." ʰ

⁹Then the Lᴏʀᴅ said to Moses: ¹⁰"Speak to the Israelites and say to them: 'When you cross the Jordan into Canaan, ⁱ ¹¹select some towns to be your cities of refuge, to which a person who has killed someone ʲ accidentally ᵏ may flee. ¹²They will be places of refuge from the avenger, ˡ so that anyone accused of murder ᵐ may not die before standing trial before the assembly. ⁿ ¹³These six towns you give will be your cities of refuge. ᵒ ¹⁴Give three on this side of the Jordan and three in Canaan as cities of refuge. ¹⁵These six towns will be a place of refuge for Israelites and for foreigners residing among them, so that anyone who has killed another accidentally can flee there.

¹⁶ 'If anyone strikes someone a fatal blow with an iron object, that person is a murderer; the murderer is to be put to death. ᵖ ¹⁷Or if anyone is holding a stone and strikes someone a fatal blow with it, that person is a murderer; the murderer is to be put to death. ¹⁸Or if anyone is holding a wooden object and strikes someone a fatal blow with it, that person is a murderer; the murderer is to be put to death. ¹⁹The avenger of blood q shall put the murderer to death; when the avenger comes upon the murderer, the avenger shall put the murderer to death. ʳ ²⁰If anyone with malice aforethought shoves another or throws something at them intentionally ˢ so that they die ²¹or if out of enmity one person hits another with their fist so that the other dies, that person is to be put to death; ᵗ that person is a murderer. The avenger of blood ᵘ shall put the murderer to death when they meet.

²² 'But if without enmity someone suddenly pushes another or throws something at

---

ᵃ 4 That is, about 1,500 feet or about 450 meters   ᵇ 5 That is, about 3,000 feet or about 900 meters

---

35:1–5 Since the Levites would not receive an allotment with the other tribes in the land (1:47–53), they would need towns in which to live and to raise their families and care for their livestock. The Levites were to be spread throughout the land (see Ge 49:5,7 and notes), not in an isolated encampment. Jos 21 presents the fulfillment of this command.
35:6–15 Six Levitical cities were to be stationed strategically in the land—three in Transjordan and three in Canaan proper—as

cities of refuge, where a person guilty of unintentional manslaughter might escape blood revenge. Jos 20 describes the sites that were chosen. See map on p. 245 and accompanying text.
35:16–21 Various descriptions of willful murder.
35:21 avenger of blood. See note on Jos 20:3.
35:22 without enmity. The cities of refuge were to be established for the person who had committed an act of involuntary manslaughter.

them unintentionally [v] [23]or, without seeing them, drops on them a stone heavy enough to kill them, and they die, then since that other person was not an enemy and no harm was intended, [24]the assembly [w] must judge between the accused and the avenger of blood according to these regulations. [25]The assembly must protect the one accused of murder from the avenger of blood and send the accused back to the city of refuge to which they fled. The accused must stay there until the death of the high priest, [x] who was anointed [y] with the holy oil. [z]

[26]" 'But if the accused ever goes outside the limits of the city of refuge in which refuge was taken [27]and the avenger of blood finds that person outside the city, the avenger of blood may kill the accused without being guilty of murder. [28]The accused must stay in the city of refuge until the death of the high priest; only after the death of the high priest may an accused person return home.

[29]" 'This is to have the force of law [a] for you throughout the generations to come, [b] wherever you live. [c]

[30]" 'Anyone who kills a person is to be put to death as a murderer only on the testimony of witnesses. But no one is to be put to death on the testimony of only one witness. [d]

[31]" 'Do not accept a ransom [e] for the life of a murderer, who deserves to die. A murderer is to be put to death.

[32]" 'Do not accept a ransom for anyone who has fled to a city of refuge and so allow them to go back and live on their own land before the death of the high priest.

[33]" 'Do not pollute the land where you are. Bloodshed pollutes the land, [f] and atonement cannot be made for the land on which blood has been shed, except by the blood of the one who shed it. [34]Do not defile the land [g] where you live and where I dwell, [h] for I, the LORD, dwell among the Israelites.' "

35:22 [v] S Ex 21:13
35:24 [w] S ver 12
35:25 [x] ver 32
[y] S Ex 28:41
[z] S Ex 29:7
35:29 [a] Nu 27:11
[b] Nu 10:8 [c] S Ex 12:20
35:30 [d] Dt 17:6;
19:15; S Mt 18:16;
Jn 7:51
35:31 [e] Ex 21:30;
Job 6:22; Ps 49:8;
Pr 13:8
35:33 [f] S Ge 4:10
35:34 [g] Lev 18:24,
25 [h] S Ex 29:45

35:24 *according to these regulations.* Any gracious provision is subject to abuse. For this reason the case of the involuntary slayer had to be determined by the judges. Further, the accused had to stay in the city of refuge until the death of the high priest, which probably atoned for the act of manslaughter. Any accused person who left the city of refuge would become fair game again for the avenger of blood.
35:25–28 See note on Jos 20:6.

35:25 *send the accused back.* The trial of the accused apparently took place outside the city of refuge.
35:30 *witnesses.* To avoid the possibility of an innocent party being accused and sentenced to death on insufficient evidence.
35:32 Not even an involuntary slayer could leave the city of refuge on the payment of a ransom.

35:33 *Bloodshed pollutes the land.* The crime of murder is not only an offense against the sanctity of life but also a pollutant to the Lord's sacred land (cf. Ge 4:10–11 and notes).

CITIES OF REFUGE

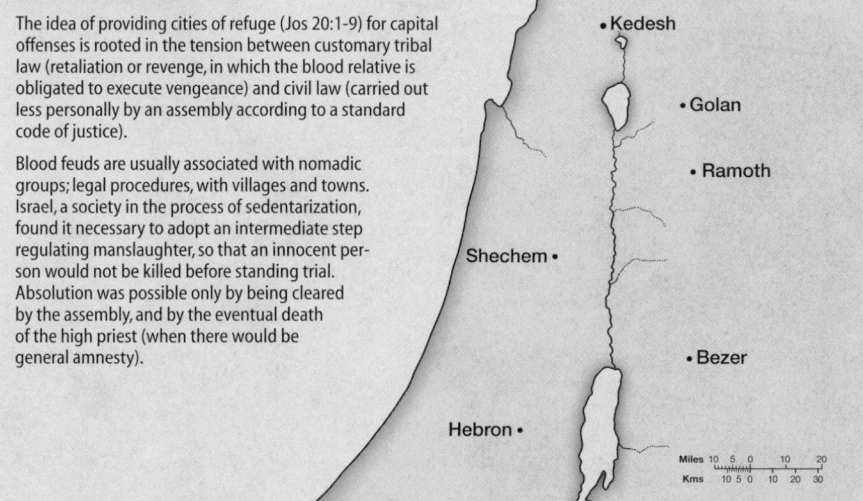

The idea of providing cities of refuge (Jos 20:1-9) for capital offenses is rooted in the tension between customary tribal law (retaliation or revenge, in which the blood relative is obligated to execute vengeance) and civil law (carried out less personally by an assembly according to a standard code of justice).

Blood feuds are usually associated with nomadic groups; legal procedures, with villages and towns. Israel, a society in the process of sedentarization, found it necessary to adopt an intermediate step regulating manslaughter, so that an innocent person would not be killed before standing trial. Absolution was possible only by being cleared by the assembly, and by the eventual death of the high priest (when there would be general amnesty).

• Kedesh

• Golan

• Ramoth

Shechem •

• Bezer

Hebron •

Miles 10 5   0   10   20
Kms   10 5 0   10   20   30

INHERITANCE OF ZELOPHEHAD'S DAUGHTERS

36:1–12pp — Nu 27:1–11

36 The family heads of the clan of Gilead *i* son of Makir, *j* the son of Manasseh, who were from the clans of the descendants of Joseph, *k* came and spoke before Moses and the leaders, *l* the heads of the Israelite families. ²They said, "When the LORD commanded my lord to give the land as an inheritance to the Israelites by lot, *m* he ordered you to give the inheritance of our brother Zelophehad *n* to his daughters. ³Now suppose they marry men from other Israelite tribes; then their inheritance will be taken from our ancestral inheritance and added to that of the tribe they marry into. And so part of the inheritance allotted to us will be taken away. ⁴When the Year of Jubilee *o* for the Israelites comes, their inheritance will be added to that of the tribe into which they marry, and their property will be taken from the tribal inheritance of our ancestors."

⁵Then at the LORD's command Moses gave this order to the Israelites: "What the tribe of the descendants of Joseph is saying is right. ⁶This is what the LORD commands for Zelophehad's daughters: They may marry anyone they please as long as they marry within their father's tribal clan. ⁷No inheritance *p* in Israel is to pass from one tribe to another, for each of the Israelites shall keep the tribal inheritance of their ancestors. ⁸Every daughter who inherits land in any Israelite tribe must marry someone in her father's tribal clan, *q* so that all Israelites will possess the inheritance of their ancestors. ⁹No inheritance may pass from one tribe to another, for each Israelite tribe is to keep the land it inherits."

¹⁰So Zelophehad's daughters did as the LORD commanded Moses. ¹¹Zelophehad's daughters—Mahlah, Tirzah, Hoglah, Milkah and Noah *r*—married their cousins on their father's side. ¹²They married within the clans of the descendants of Manasseh son of Joseph, and their inheritance remained in their father's tribe and clan. *s*

¹³These are the commands and regulations the LORD gave through Moses *t* to the Israelites on the plains of Moab by the Jordan across from Jericho. *u*

36:1–13 Presents an interesting further development of the account of Zelophehad's daughters (see 27:1–11). Since the Lord had instructed Moses that the women might inherit their father's land, new questions arose: What will happen to the family lands if these daughters marry among other tribes? Will not the original intention of the first provision be frustrated? Such questions led to the decision that marriage is to be kept within one's own tribe, so that the family allotments will not "pass from one tribe to another" (v. 9).

36:4 *Year of Jubilee.* See Lev 25:10 and note.

36:10 *Zelophehad's daughters did as the LORD commanded.* The book of Numbers, which so often presents the rebellion of God's people against his grace and in defiance of his will, ends on a happy note. These noble women, who were concerned for their father's name and their own place in the land, obeyed the Lord.

36:11 See note on 33:50—36:13; cf. Lev. 27:34.

DEUTERONOMY | INTRODUCTION

TITLE

The Hebrew name of the book is *'elleh haddebarim* ("These are the words") or, more simply, *debarim* ("words"; see 1:1). The word "Deuteronomy" (meaning "repetition of the law") arose from a mistranslation in the Septuagint (the pre-Christian Greek translation of the OT) and the Latin Vulgate of a phrase in Dt 17:18, which in Hebrew means "copy of this law." The error is not serious, however, since Deuteronomy is, in a certain sense, a "repetition of the law" (see Structure and Outline).

AUTHOR AND DATE OF WRITING

The book itself ascribes most of its content to Moses (see 1:1,5; 31:24 and notes). For that reason, the OT elsewhere ascribes the bulk of Deuteronomy and other Penta-teuchal legislation to Moses (see, e.g., Jos 1:7–8; 23:6; 1Ki 2:3; 8:53; Mal 4:4 and notes; see also 2Ki 14:6 and TNIV text note). Similarly Jesus attributed Dt 24:1 to Moses (Mt 19:7–8; Mk 10:3–5), Peter attributed Dt 18:15,18–19 to Moses (Ac 3:22–23), as did Stephen (see Ac 7:37–38 and notes), and Paul attributed Dt 32:21 to Moses (Ro 10:19). See also Mt 22:24 and note; Mk 12:18–19; Lk 20:27–28. At the same time, it seems clear that the narrative framework within which the Mosaic material is placed (e.g., the preamble [1:1–5] and the conclusion [ch. 34]; see also 5:1; 27:1,9,11; 29:1–2; 31:1,7,9–10,14–25,30; 32:44–46, 48–52; 33:1–2) comes from another—and unknown—hand. See Introduction to Genesis: Author and Date of Writing.

HISTORICAL SETTING

Deuteronomy locates Moses and the Israelites in the territory of Moab in the area where the Jordan River flows into the Dead Sea (1:5). As his final act at this impor-tant time of transferring leadership to Joshua, Moses delivered his farewell address-es to prepare the people for their entrance into Canaan. In them, Moses emphasized the laws that were especially needed at such a time, and he presented them in a way appropriate to the situation. In contrast to the matter-of-fact narratives of Leviticus and Numbers, here the words of Moses come to us from his heart as this servant of the Lord presses God's claims on his people Israel.

SPECIAL FUNCTION IN THE BIBLE

The trajectory of the story that unfolds in Genesis–Numbers seems to call for an account of the conquest of Canaan as found in Joshua to bring closure to the move-ment from promise to fulfillment (see Introduction to Joshua: Title and Theme). But Deuteronomy intervenes as a massive interruption. Here there is very little forward movement. At the end of Numbers, Israel is "on the plains of Moab by the Jordan across from Jericho" (Nu 36:13) and at the end of Deuteronomy, the people are still there (Dt 34:8), waiting to cross the Jordan (see Jos 1:2). All that has happened is the transition from the ministry of Moses as God's spokesman and official representa-tive to that of Joshua in his place (Dt 34:9; see Jos 1:1–2). But Moses' final acts as the Lord's appointed servant for dealing with Israel are so momentous that Deuteron-omy's account of them marks the conclusion to the Pentateuch, while the book of

KEY   **A** APPLICATION FOR LIVING   **B** BACKGROUND NOTES   **C** CHARACTER INFORMATION

Joshua, which narrates the initial fulfillment of the promises made to the patriarchs and the conclusion to the mission on which Moses had been sent (see Nu 17:15–23; Jos 21:43–45), serves as the introduction to the Former Prophets.

So Deuteronomy creates a long pause in the advancement of the story of redemption:

(1) of deliverance from bondage to a world power (Egypt) to a place in the earth where Israel can be a free people under the rule of God;

(2) of deliverance from rootlessness in the post-Babel world (Abraham, Isaac and Jacob) to security and "rest" (see Dt 3:20 and note; 12:10; 25:19) in the promised land;

(3) of deliverance from a life of banishment from God's garden (Ge 3) to a life in the Lord's own land where he has pitched his tent (Jos 22:19).

But in that long pause on the threshold of the promised land Moses, in this renewal of the Sinaitic covenant, reminded Israel at length of what the Lord required of them as his people if they were to cross the Jordan, take possession of the promised land and there enjoy the promised "rest" in fellowship with him. It was a word that Israel needed to hear over and over again. Upon reading the Pentateuch, Israel was brought ever anew to the threshold of the promised land and its promised "rest" to hear again this final word from God through his servant Moses (see also Ps 95:7b–22). For this reason, all the history of Israel in Canaan as narrated in the Former Prophets is brought under the judgment of this word.

THEOLOGICAL TEACHING AND PURPOSE

The book of Deuteronomy was cast in the form of ancient Near Eastern suzerainty-vassal treaties of the second millennium B.C. It contained the Great King's pledge to be Israel's Suzerain and Protector if they would be faithful to him as their covenant Lord and obedient to the covenant stipulations as the vassal people of his kingdom. There would be blessings for such obedience, but curses for disobedience (chs. 27–30). Deuteronomy's purpose was to prepare the new generation of the Lord's chosen people to be his kingdom representatives in the land he had unconditionally promised them in the Abrahamic covenant (see Structure and Outline below; see also notes on 3:27; 17:14,18).

The love relationship of the Lord to his people, and that of the people to the Lord as their sovereign God, pervade the whole book. Deuteronomy's spiritual emphasis and its call to total commitment to the Lord in worship and obedience inspired references to its message throughout the rest of Scripture. In particular, the division of the Hebrew Bible called the Former Prophets (Joshua, Judges, Samuel, Kings) is thoroughly imbued with the style, themes and motifs of Deuteronomy. Among the Latter Prophets, Jeremiah also reflects strong influence from this book.

STRUCTURE AND OUTLINE

Deuteronomy's literary structure supports its historical setting. By its interpretive, repetitious, reminiscent and somewhat irregular style it shows that it is a series of more or less extemporaneous addresses, sometimes describing events in nonchronological order (see, e.g., 10:3). But it also bears in its structure clear reflections of the suzerain-vassal treaties (see chart, p. 20) of the preceding and then-current Near Eastern states, a structure that lends itself to the Biblical emphasis on the covenant between the Lord and his people. In this sense Deuteronomy is a covenant-renewal document, as the following outline shows:

I. Preamble (1:1–5)

II. Historical Prologue (1:6—4:43)

1:1 *a*S Nu 13:29;
Dt 4:46 *b*ver 7;
Dt 2:8; 3:17; Jos 3:16;
8:14; 11:2; Eze 47:8
*c*S Nu 10:12
1:2 *d*S Ex 3:1
*e*S Ge 14:7; Dt 2:14;
9:23; Jos 15:3
*f*S Nu 24:18 *g*ver 19
1:3 *h*Nu 14:33;
32:13; Dt 8:2;
Heb 3:7-9 *i*Ge 50:3;
Dt 34:8; Jos 4:19
*j*Dt 4:1-2
1:4 *k*Nu 21:21-26
*l*S Ge 10:16; S 14:7
*m*S Nu 21:25
*n*Nu 21:33-35;
Dt 3:10 *o*Jos 9:10;
12:4; 1Ch 11:44
1:5 *p*S Nu 21:11
1:6 *q*Nu 10:13
*r*S Ex 3:1 *s*Dt 2:3
1:7 *t*ver 19; Dt 2:24;
7:1; Jos 10:5 *u*S ver 1
*v*S Nu 21:1; Jos 11:16;
12:8; 2Sa 24:7
*w*S Ge 10:18
*x*Dt 11:24 *y*S Ge 2:14
1:8 *z*S Jos 23:13
*a*S Nu 34:2
*b*S Ex 13:11;
S Nu 14:23;
Heb 6:13-14
1:9 *c*S Nu 11:14;
Ps 38:4 *d*S Ex 18:18
1:10 *e*ver 11;
Eze 16:7 *f*S Dt 7:13
*g*S Ge 15:5; Isa 51:2;
60:22; Eze 33:24
*h*S Ge 22:17;
S Nu 10:36
1:11 *i*S ver 10
*j*ver 8; Ex 32:13;
2Sa 24:3; 1Ch 21:3
1:12 *k*S Ex 5:22;
S 18:18
1:13 *l*S Ge 47:6
1:15 *m*Ex 18:25
*n*Ex 5:14; Nu 11:16;
Jos 1:10; 3:2
*o*S Ge 47:6
*p*Nu 31:14; 1Sa 8:12;
22:7; 1Ki 14:27
*q*S Nu 1:4
1:16 *r*1Ki 3:9;
Ps 72:1; Pr 2:9
*s*S Ge 31:37; Jer 7:24

THE COMMAND TO LEAVE HOREB

1 These are the words Moses spoke to all Israel in the wilderness east of the Jordan *a*—that is, in the Arabah *b*—opposite Suph, between Paran *c* and Tophel, Laban, Hazeroth and Dizahab. ²(It takes eleven days to go from Horeb *d* to Kadesh Barnea *e* by the Mount Seir *f* road.) *g*

³In the fortieth year, *h* on the first day of the eleventh month, *i* Moses proclaimed *j* to the Israelites all that the LORD had commanded him concerning them. ⁴This was after he had defeated Sihon *k* king of the Amorites, *l* who reigned in Heshbon, *m* and at Edrei had defeated Og *n* king of Bashan, who reigned in Ashtaroth. *o*

⁵East of the Jordan in the territory of Moab, *p* Moses began to expound this law, saying:

⁶The LORD our God said to us *q* at Horeb, *r* "You have stayed long enough *s* at this mountain. ⁷Break camp and advance into the hill country of the Amorites; *t* go to all the neighboring peoples in the Arabah, *u* in the mountains, in the western foothills, in the Negev *v* and along the coast, to the land of the Canaanites *w* and to Lebanon, *x* as far as the great river, the Euphrates. *y* ⁸See, I have given you this land *z*. *a* Go in and take possession of the land the LORD swore *b* he would give to your fathers—to Abraham, Isaac and Jacob—and to their descendants after them."

THE APPOINTMENT OF LEADERS

⁹At that time I said to you, "You are too heavy a burden *c* for me to carry alone. *d* ¹⁰The LORD your God has increased *e* your numbers *f* so that today you are as many *g* as the stars in the sky. *h* ¹¹May the LORD, the God of your ancestors, increase *i* you a thousand times and bless you as he has promised! *j* ¹²But how can I bear your problems and your burdens and your disputes all by myself? *k* ¹³Choose some wise, understanding and respected men *l* from each of your tribes, and I will set them over you."

¹⁴You answered me, "What you propose to do is good."

¹⁵So I took *m* the leading men of your tribes, *n* wise and respected men, *o* and appointed them to have authority over you—as commanders *p* of thousands, of hundreds, of fifties and of tens and as tribal officials. *q* ¹⁶And I charged your judges at that time: Hear the disputes between your people and judge *r* fairly, *s* whether the case is between two Israelites or between an Israelite and a foreigner residing among you. *t* ¹⁷Do not show partiality *u* in judging; hear both small and great alike. Do not be afraid of anyone, *v* for judgment belongs to God. Bring me any case too hard for you, and I will hear it. *w* ¹⁸And at that time I told you everything you were to do. *x*

SPIES SENT OUT

¹⁹Then, as the LORD our God commanded us, we set out from Horeb and went toward

1:16 *t*S Ex 12:19, 49; S 22:21 **1:17** *u*S Ex 18:16; S Lev 19:15; Ac 10:34; Jas 2:1 *v*Pr 29:25 *w*Ex 18:26 **1:18** *x*S Ge 39:11

1:1–5 The preamble gives the historical setting for the entire book and introduces Moses, the Great King's covenant mediator.

1:1 *Moses spoke.* Almost all of Deuteronomy is presented as speeches by Moses during the final months of his life, just before the Israelites crossed the Jordan to enter Canaan. *Arabah.* Includes the valley of the Jordan (from the Sea of Galilee to the southern end of the Dead Sea) and the valley extending down to the Gulf of Aqaba. *Suph ... Paran ... Tophel, Laban, Hazeroth and Dizahab.* Places along the route from Sinai to the territory of Moab (see, e.g., Nu 12:16 and note).

1:2 *Horeb.* The usual name for Mount Sinai in Deuteronomy (the only exception is in 33:2). *Kadesh Barnea.* See notes on Ge 14:7; Nu 20:11. *Seir.* See notes on Ge 36:8; Eze 35:2.

1:3 *fortieth year.* After leaving Egypt. The Lord had condemned the Israelites to 40 years of wandering in Sinai as punishment for not entering Canaan as he had commanded them to do at Kadesh (Nu 14:33–34). The 40 years included the time spent at Sinai and on the journey to Kadesh, as well as the next 38 years (see 2:14). See 8:2–5; 29:5–6; Nu 14:29–35; 32:13; Ac 7:36; Heb 3:7–19. *eleventh month.* January–February.

1:4 *Sihon ... Og.* See notes on Nu 21:21–26, 35. *Heshbon.* See note on Isa 15:4.

1:5 *this law.* The Ten Commandments and other laws given at Mount Sinai and recorded in Ex 20–24, Leviticus and Numbers.

In Deuteronomy the laws are summarized, interpreted and adjusted to the new, specific situation Israel would face in Canaan. Thus Deuteronomy is, in essence, a covenant renewal (and updating) document (see Introduction: Theological Teaching and Purpose; Structure and Outline).

1:6 *The LORD our God.* Together with "the LORD your God," this title occurs almost 300 times in Deuteronomy, in addition to the many times that "LORD" is used alone or in other combinations (see notes on 28:58; Ge 2:4; Ex 3:14–15; 6:3,6; Lev 18:2).

1:7 See Jos 1:4. The land is described by its various geographical areas (see map No. 2 at the end of this study Bible). *Arabah.* See note on v. 1. *mountains.* The midsection running north and south. *western foothills.* Sloping toward the Mediterranean. *Negev.* See note on Ge 12:9. *coast.* The Mediterranean coastal strip. The "land of the Canaanites" and "Lebanon, as far as ... the Euphrates" make up the northern sector. The "hill country of the Amorites" is, in general, the central and southern mountains. This description of the land agrees with that in the promise (see v. 8) to Abraham in Ge 15:18–21, a promise later limited to Isaac's descendants (Ge 26:2–4) and still later to the descendants of Jacob (Ge 35:11–12).

1:9–18 Cf. 16:18–20; Ex 18:13–26.

1:10 *as the stars in the sky.* See 10:22; 28:62; Ge 13:16 and note; 15:5 and note; 22:17; 26:4; Ex 32:13.

1:19–46 See Nu 13–14 and notes.

the hill country of the Amorites ᵛ through all that vast and dreadful wilderness ᶻ that you have seen, and so we reached Kadesh Barnea. ª ²⁰Then I said to you, "You have reached the hill country of the Amorites, which the LORD our God is giving us. ²¹See, the LORD your God has given you the land. Go up and take possession ᵇ of it as the LORD, the God of your ancestors, told you. Do not be afraid; ᶜ do not be discouraged." ᵈ

²²Then all of you came to me and said, "Let us send men ahead to spy ᵉ out the land ᶠ for us and bring back a report about the route we are to take and the towns we will come to."

²³The idea seemed good to me; so I selected ᵍ twelve of you, one man from each tribe. ²⁴They left and went up into the hill country, and came to the Valley of Eshkol ʰ and explored it. ²⁵Taking with them some of the fruit of the land, they brought it down to us and reported, ⁱ "It is a good land ʲ that the LORD our God is giving us." ᵏ

REBELLION AGAINST THE LORD

²⁶But you were unwilling to go up; ˡ you rebelled ᵐ against the command of the LORD your God. ²⁷You grumbled ⁿ in your tents and said, "The LORD hates us; so he brought us out of Egypt to deliver us into the hands of the Amorites to destroy us. ²⁸Where can we go? Our brothers have made our hearts melt in fear. They say, 'The people are stronger and taller ᵒ than we are; the cities are large, with walls up to the sky. We even saw the Anakites ᵖ there.'"

²⁹Then I said to you, "Do not be terrified; do not be afraid �q of them. ʳ ³⁰The LORD your God, who is going before you, will fight ˢ for you, as he did for you in Egypt, before your very eyes, ³¹and in the wilderness. There you saw how the LORD your God carried ᵗ you, as a father carries his son, all the way you went until you reached this place." ᵘ

³²In spite of this, ᵛ you did not trust ʷ in the LORD your God, ³³who went ahead of you on your journey, in fire by night and in a cloud by day, ˣ to search ʸ out places for you to camp and to show you the way you should go.

³⁴When the LORD heard ᶻ what you said, he was angry ª and solemnly swore: ᵇ ³⁵"No one from this evil generation shall see the good land ᶜ I swore to give your ancestors, ³⁶except Caleb ᵈ son of Jephunneh. He will see it, and I will give him and his descendants the land he set his feet on, because he followed the LORD wholeheartedly. ᵉ"

³⁷Because of you the LORD became angry ᶠ with me also and said, "You shall not enter ᵍ it, either. ³⁸But your assistant, Joshua ʰ son of Nun, will enter it. Encourage ⁱ him, because he will lead ʲ Israel to inherit ᵏ it. ³⁹And the little ones that you said would be taken captive, ˡ your children who do not yet know ᵐ good from bad—they will enter the land. I will give it to them and they will take possession of it. ⁴⁰But as for you, turn around and set out toward the desert along the route to the Red Sea. ª ⁿ"

⁴¹Then you replied, "We have sinned against the LORD. We will go up and fight, as the LORD our God commanded us." So every one of you put on his weapons, thinking it easy to go up into the hill country.

⁴²But the LORD said to me, "Tell them, 'Do not go up and fight, because I will not be with you. You will be defeated by your enemies.'" ᵒ

⁴³So I told you, but you would not listen. You rebelled against the LORD's command and

ª 40 Or the Sea of Reeds

1:19 ᵛ S ver 7
ᶻ Dt 2:7; 8:15; 32:10; Ps 136:16; Jer 2:2,6; Hos 13:5 ª ver 2; Nu 13:26
1:21 ᵇ Dt 9:23
ᶜ S Nu 14:9; Jos 1:6,9, 18; 2Sa 10:12; Ps 27:14 ᵈ Dt 7:18; Jos 8:1; 10:8
1:22 ᵉ Nu 13:1-3
ᶠ S Ge 42:9
1:23 ᵍ Nu 13:1-3
1:24 ʰ Nu 13:21-25; S 32:9
1:25 ⁱ S Nu 13:27
ʲ S Nu 14:7 ᵏ Jos 1:2
1:26 ˡ Nu 14:1-4
ᵐ S Nu 14:9
1:27 ⁿ Dt 9:28; Ps 106:25
1:28 ᵒ S Nu 13:32
ᵖ S Nu 13:33; Dt 9:1-3
1:29 q Dt 3:22; 20:3; Ne 4:14 ʳ Dt 7:18; 20:1; 31:6
1:30 ˢ S Ex 14:14
1:31 ᵗ Ex 19:4; Dt 32:10-12; Ps 28:9; Isa 46:3-4; 63:9; Hos 11:3; Ac 13:18
ᵘ Jer 31:32
1:32 ᵛ S Nu 14:11
ʷ Dt 9:23; Ps 78:22; 106:24; Zep 3:2; Heb 3:19; Jude 1:5
1:33 ˣ Ex 13:21; Nu 9:15-23; Ne 9:12; Ps 78:14 ʸ S Nu 10:33
1:34 ᶻ S Nu 11:1
ª S Nu 32:14
ᵇ S Nu 14:23,28-30; Eze 20:15; Heb 3:11
1:35 ᶜ S Nu 14:29
1:36 ᵈ S Nu 13:6
ᵉ S Nu 14:24
1:37 ᶠ Ps 106:32
ᵍ S Nu 20:12
1:38 ʰ S Nu 11:28
ⁱ Dt 31:7 ʲ Dt 3:28
ᵏ Jos 1:23; Ps 78:55; 136:21
1:39 ˡ S Nu 14:3
ᵐ Isa 7:15-16
1:40 ⁿ S Ex 14:27; Jdg 11:16
1:42 ᵒ S Nu 14:41-43

1:21 *as the LORD … told you.* The promise of the land (see note on v. 7) was reaffirmed to Moses (v. 8) at the burning bush (Ex 3:8,17). Now the Israelites are told to enter the land and conquer it. *Do not be afraid … discouraged.* See 31:8; Jos 1:9; 8:1; 10:25.
1:23 *twelve.* They are named in Nu 13:4–15.
1:24 *Eshkol.* See note on Nu 13:23.
1:27 *grumbled.* See note on Ex 15:24. *The LORD hates us.* The people's statement is ironic indeed in the light of Deuteronomy's major theme of love (see Introduction: Theological Teaching and Purpose).
1:28 *Anakites.* Earlier inhabitants of Canaan, described as giants (see 2:10,21; 9:2; Nu 13:32–33).
1:29 *Do not be terrified … afraid.* See notes on Isa 41:10,13; 43:1–2.
1:30 *as he did for you in Egypt.* See Ex 14:1—15:19.
1:31 *God carried you.* Cf. Isa 40:11; Jer 31:10; Eze 34:11–16.
1:33 *in fire by night and in a cloud by day.* The presence of the Lord was in the cloud over the tabernacle to guide

the Israelites through their desert journeys (see Ex 13:21 and note; 40:34–38).
1:36 *Caleb.* See Nu 13:30—14:38; Jos 14:6–15. *followed the LORD wholeheartedly.* See note on Nu 14:24.
1:37 *Because of you.* See 3:26; 4:21. God was angry with Moses who, failing to honor the Lord as holy, struck the rock at Meribah to get water (see Nu 20:9–13 and note on 20:11; 27:12–14). And since it was the Israelites who had incited him to sin, God was angry with them too. This event (v. 37) occurred almost 40 years after that of the preceding verses (vv. 34–36), but Moses, interested in telling about the Israelites' sin and his own, brings the two events together.
1:39 *do not yet know good from bad.* See notes on Ge 2:9; Isa 7:15.
1:41 *We will go up.* See v. 26; Nu 14:40 and note.
1:43 *You rebelled against the LORD's command.* The same charge as in v. 26. First the people rebelled against the Lord's command to go into the land, then against his command not to enter after they had rebelled. After their first rebellion the Lord would not go with them. His presence was essential, and Israel needed to learn that lesson.

1:44 p Ps 118:12
q S Nu 24:18
r S Nu 14:45
1:45 s S Nu 14:1
t Job 27:9; 35:13;
Ps 18:41; 66:18;
Pr 1:28; Isa 1:15;
Jer 14:12; La 3:8;
Mic 3:4; S Jn 9:31
u Ps 28:1; 39:12;
Pr 28:9
1:46 v S Nu 20:1
2:1 w S Ex 14:27;
S Nu 21:4
x S Nu 24:18
2:3 y Dt 1:6
2:4 z Nu 20:14-21
a Ge 36:8 b ver 1
c Ex 15:16
2:5 d Jos 24:4
2:7 e Dt 8:2-4
f S Ex 13:21; S Dt 1:19
g ver 14; S Nu 14:33;
32:13; Jos 5:6
h Ne 9:21; Am 2:10
2:8 i S Nu 20:21
j S Dt 1:1 k Nu 33:35;
1Ki 9:26 l S Nu 21:4
2:9 m S Nu 21:15
n Ge 19:38; Ps 83:8
2:10 o Ge 14:5
p S Nu 13:22,33
2:11 q S Ge 14:5
2:12 r S Ge 14:6
s Nu 21:35,35
2:13 t S Nu 21:12
2:14 u S ver 7
v S Dt 1:2
w Nu 14:29-35
x Dt 1:34-35; Jos 5:6
2:15 y Ps 106:26;
Jude 1:5
2:18 z S Nu 21:15
2:19 a S Ge 19:38
b 2Ch 20:10 c S ver 9
2:20 d S Ge 14:5
2:21 e ver 10

in your arrogance you marched up into the hill country. ⁴⁴The Amorites who lived in those hills came out against you; they chased you like a swarm of bees p and beat you down from Seir q all the way to Hormah. r ⁴⁵You came back and wept before the LORD, s but he paid no attention t to your weeping and turned a deaf ear u to you. ⁴⁶And so you stayed in Kadesh v many days—all the time you spent there.

WANDERINGS IN THE WILDERNESS

2 Then we turned back and set out toward the wilderness along the route to the Red Sea, a w as the LORD had directed me. For a long time we made our way around the hill country of Seir. x

²Then the LORD said to me, ³"You have made your way around this hill country long enough; y now turn north. ⁴Give the people these orders: z 'You are about to pass through the territory of your relatives the descendants of Esau, a who live in Seir. b They will be afraid c of you, but be very careful. ⁵Do not provoke them to war, for I will not give you any of their land, not even enough to put your foot on. I have given Esau the hill country of Seir as his own. d ⁶You are to pay them in silver for the food you eat and the water you drink.' "

⁷The LORD your God has blessed you in all the work of your hands. He has watched e over your journey through this vast wilderness. f These forty years g the LORD your God has been with you, and you have not lacked anything. h

⁸So we went on past our relatives the descendants of Esau, who live in Seir. We turned from i the Arabah j road, which comes up from Elath and Ezion Geber, k and traveled along the desert road of Moab. l

⁹Then the LORD said to me, "Do not harass the Moabites or provoke them to war, for I will not give you any part of their land. I have given Ar m to the descendants of Lot n as a possession."

¹⁰(The Emites o used to live there—a people strong and numerous, and as tall as the Anakites. p ¹¹Like the Anakites, they too were considered Rephaites, q but the Moabites called them Emites. ¹²Horites r used to live in Seir, but the descendants of Esau drove them out. They destroyed the Horites from before them and settled in their place, just as Israel did s in the land the LORD gave them as their possession.)

¹³And the LORD said, "Now get up and cross the Zered Valley. t" So we crossed the valley.

¹⁴Thirty-eight years u passed from the time we left Kadesh Barnea v until we crossed the Zered Valley. By then, that entire generation w of fighting men had perished from the camp, as the LORD had sworn to them. x ¹⁵The LORD's hand was against them until he had completely eliminated y them from the camp.

¹⁶Now when the last of these fighting men among the people had died, ¹⁷the LORD said to me, ¹⁸"Today you are to pass by the region of Moab at Ar. z ¹⁹When you come to the Ammonites, a do not harass them or provoke them to war, b for I will not give you possession of any land belonging to the Ammonites. I have given it as a possession to the descendants of Lot. c"

²⁰(That too was considered a land of the Rephaites, d who used to live there; but the Ammonites called them Zamzummites. ²¹They were a people strong and numerous, and as tall as the Anakites. e The LORD destroyed them from before the Ammonites, who drove them out and settled in their place. ²²The LORD had done the same for the descendants

---

a 1 Or *the Sea of Reeds*

1:44 *bees.* See note on Ex 23:28.

1:45 *before the LORD.* At the tabernacle.

2:1—3:11 See Nu 20:14—21:35 and notes.

2:1 *Red Sea.* Here probably the Gulf of Aqaba (see note on 1Ki 9:26). *hill country of Seir.* The mountainous area south of the Dead Sea (Edom).

2:5 *I will not give you any of their land.* See vv. 9,19. The Lord told Moses to bypass Edom, Moab and Ammon because of their blood relationship to Israel. The Israelites were to take over only those lands east of the Jordan that were in the hands of the Amorites (see v. 24; 3:2). *I have given.* See vv. 9,19. The Lord had given the descendants of Esau (Edomites) and Lot (Moabites and Ammonites) their lands, just as he was giving the Israelites the territories of Transjordan and Canaan.

2:6,28 *silver.* See note on 14:25.

2:8 *Elath and Ezion Geber.* Towns at the head of the Gulf of Aqa-

ba. The "Arabah road" ran from the head of the gulf northward and to the east of Moab.

2:10 *Anakites.* See note on 1:28.

2:11 *Rephaites.* People of large stature (see 3:11).

2:12 *Horites.* See note on Ge 14:6. *the land the LORD gave them.* Either (1) the Transjordan regions (see 2:24—3:20), (2) Canaan itself or (3) Transjordan and Canaan. If either (2) or (3) is intended, editorial updating is involved (see note on Ge 14:14).

2:13 *Zered.* The main stream (intermittent) that flows into the southern end of the Dead Sea from the east. It marked the border between Edom and Moab (see map No. 4 at the end of this study Bible).

2:14 *Thirty-eight years.* See note on 1:3.

2:20 *Zamzummites.* Perhaps to be identified with the Zuzites of Ge 14:5.

of Esau, who lived in Seir, [f] when he destroyed the Horites from before them. They drove them out and have lived in their place to this day. [23] And as for the Avvites [g] who lived in villages as far as Gaza, [h] the Caphtorites [i] coming out from Caphtor [a][j] destroyed them and settled in their place.)

DEFEAT OF SIHON KING OF HESHBON

[24] "Set out now and cross the Arnon Gorge. [k] See, I have given into your hand Sihon the Amorite, [l] king of Heshbon, and his country. Begin to take possession of it and engage [m] him in battle. [25] This very day I will begin to put the terror [n] and fear [o] of you on all the nations under heaven. They will hear reports of you and will tremble [p] and be in anguish because of you."

[26] From the Desert of Kedemoth [q] I sent messengers to Sihon [r] king of Heshbon offering peace [s] and saying, [27] "Let us pass through your country. We will stay on the main road; we will not turn aside to the right or to the left. [t] [28] Sell us food to eat [u] and water to drink for their price in silver. Only let us pass through on foot [v]— [29] as the descendants of Esau, who live in Seir, and the Moabites, who live in Ar, did for us—until we cross the Jordan into the land the LORD our God is giving us." [30] But Sihon king of Heshbon refused to let us pass through. For the LORD [w] your God had made his spirit stubborn [x] and his heart obstinate [y] in order to give him into your hands, [z] as he has now done.

[31] The LORD said to me, "See, I have begun to deliver Sihon and his country over to you. Now begin to conquer and possess his land." [a]

[32] When Sihon and all his army came out to meet us in battle [b] at Jahaz, [33] the LORD our God delivered [c] him over to us and we struck him down, [d] together with his sons and his whole army. [34] At that time we took all his towns and completely destroyed [b][e] them— men, women and children. We left no survivors. [35] But the livestock [f] and the plunder [g] from the towns we had captured we carried off for ourselves. [36] From Aroer [h] on the rim of the Arnon Gorge, and from the town in the gorge, even as far as Gilead, [i] not one town was too strong for us. The LORD our God gave [j] us all of them. [37] But in accordance with the command of the LORD our God, [k] you did not encroach on any of the land of the Ammonites, [l] neither the land along the course of the Jabbok [m] nor that around the towns in the hills.

DEFEAT OF OG KING OF BASHAN

3 Next we turned and went up along the road toward Bashan, and Og king of Bashan [n] with his whole army marched out to meet us in battle at Edrei. [o] [2] The LORD said to me, "Do not be afraid [p] of him, for I have delivered him into your hands, along with his whole army and his land. Do to him what you did to Sihon king of the Amorites, who reigned in Heshbon."

[3] So the LORD our God also gave into our hands Og king of Bashan and all his army. We struck them down, [q] leaving no survivors. [r] [4] At that time we took all his cities. [s] There was not one of the sixty cities that we did not take from them—the whole region of Argob, Og's kingdom [t] in Bashan. [u] [5] All these cities were fortified with high walls and with gates and bars, and there were also a great many unwalled villages. [6] We completely destroyed [b] them, as we had done with Sihon king of Heshbon, destroying [b][v] every city—men, women and children. [7] But all the livestock [w] and the plunder from their cities we carried off for ourselves.

---

[a] 23 That is, Crete   [b] 34,6 The Hebrew term refers to the irrevocable giving over of things or persons to the LORD, often by totally destroying them.

2:22 [f] S Ge 14:6
2:23 [g] Jos 13:3; 18:23; 2Ki 17:31
[h] S Ge 10:19
[i] S Ge 10:14; Jer 47:4; Am 9:7
2:24 [k] Nu 21:13-14; Jdg 11:13,18; [l] S Dt 1:7
[m] Dt 3:6
2:25 [n] S Ge 35:5; Dt 11:25 [o] Jos 2:9,11; 1Ch 14:17; 2Ch 14:14; 17:10; 20:29; Isa 2:19; 13:13; 19:16
[p] Ex 15:14-16
2:26 [q] Jos 13:18; 1Ch 6:79 [r] Dt 1:4; Jdg 11:21-22
[s] Dt 20:10; Jdg 21:13; 2Sa 20:19
2:27 [t] Nu 21:21-22
2:28 [u] Dt 23:4
[v] S Nu 20:19
2:30 [w] Jdg 14:4; 1Ki 12:15 [x] S Ex 4:21; Ro 9:18 [y] S Ex 14:17
[z] La 3:65
2:31 [a] S Ge 12:7
2:32 [b] S Nu 21:23
2:33 [c] Ex 23:31; Dt 7:2; 31:5
[d] S Nu 21:24
2:34 [e] S Nu 21:2; Dt 3:6; 7:2; Ps 106:34
2:35 [f] Dt 3:7
[g] S Ge 34:29; S 49:27
2:36 [h] S Nu 32:34
[i] S Nu 32:39 / Ps 44:3
2:37 [k] ver 18-19
[l] S Nu 21:24
[m] S Ge 32:22
3:1 [n] S Nu 32:19
[o] S Nu 21:33
3:2 [p] Jos 10:8; 2Ki 19:6; Isa 7:4
3:3 [q] S Nu 21:24
[r] Nu 21:35
3:4 [s] S Nu 21:24
[t] ver 13 [u] S Nu 21:33
3:6 [v] Dt 2:24
3:7 [w] Dt 2:35

2:23 *Avvites.* Pre-Philistine people otherwise unknown (Jos 13:3). *Caphtorites.* See note on Ge 10:14.
2:24 *Arnon.* See note on Nu 21:10–13. *Sihon . . . Heshbon.* See 1:4 and note.
2:26 *Kedemoth.* Means "eastern regions."
2:30 *God had made his spirit stubborn and his heart obstinate.* In the OT, actions are often attributed to God without the mention of mediate or contributing situations or persons. Sihon by his own conscious will refused Israel passage, but it was God who would give Sihon's land to Israel (see note on Ex 4:21).
2:32 *Jahaz.* See Nu 21:23; see also note on Isa 15:4.
2:34 *completely destroyed.* See TNIV text note. The Hebrew for this expression usually refers to the destruction of everyone and everything that could be destroyed. Objects like gold, silver and bronze, not subject to destruction, were put in a secure place as

God's possession. Destruction of people and things made them useless to the conquerors but put them in the hands of God. So the word is sometimes translated "destroyed" and sometimes "devoted" (see, e.g., Nu 18:14; Jos 6:17). God sometimes permitted exclusion from this practice, as when he assigned captured livestock and other plunder to his people as recompense for service in his army (see v. 35; 3:7; Jos 8:2).
2:36 *Aroer.* See note on Isa 17:2. *Gilead.* See note on Ge 31:21.
2:37 *Jabbok.* See note on Ge 32:22.
3:3 *gave into our hands Og.* As in 2:26–37. See 1:4 and note.
3:4 *sixty cities.* These were "large walled cities" (1Ki 4:13), implying a heavily populated territory (see v. 5). *region of Argob.* An otherwise unidentified area in Bashan (see vv. 13–14; 1Ki 4:13), which was northeast of the Sea of Galilee.
3:6–7 See note on 2:34.

3:8 ˣNu 32:33;
Jos 13:8-12 ʸDt 4:48;
Jos 11:3,17; 12:1; 13:5;
Jdg 3:3; 1Ch 5:23;
Ps 42:6; 89:12; 133:3;
SS 4:8
3:9 ᶻPs 29:6
ᵃ1Ch 5:23; SS 4:8;
Eze 27:5
3:10 ᵇJos 12:5;
1Ch 5:11
3:11 ᶜGe 14:5
ᵈJos 13:25; 15:60;
2Sa 11:1; 12:26; 17:27;
1Ch 20:1; Jer 49:2;
Eze 21:20; 25:5;
Am 1:14
3:12 ᵉDt 2:36
3:13 ᶠDt 29:8
ᵍS Ge 14:5
3:14 ʰS Nu 32:41
ⁱJos 12:5; 13:11,13;
2Sa 10:6; 23:34;
2Ki 25:23; 1Ch 4:19;
Jer 40:8 ʲJos 19:47;
Ps 49:11
3:15 ᵏS Ge 50:23;
Nu 32:39-40
3:16 ˡS Nu 21:24
3:17 ᵐ2Sa 2:29;
4:7; Eze 47:8
ⁿS Nu 34:11 ᵒS Dt 1:1
ᵖS Ge 14:3
3:18 ᵠJos 1:13
ʳS Nu 32:17
3:19 ˢJos 1:14
ᵗS Nu 32:16
3:22 ᵘS Dt 1:29
ᵛDt 7:18; 20:1; 31:6;
2Ch 32:8; Ps 23:4;
Isa 41:10 ʷS Ex 14:14
3:23 ˣDt 1:37; 31:2;
32:52; 34:4
3:24 ʸDt 5:24; 11:2;
32:3 ᶻS Ex 8:10
ᵃPs 71:16; 106:2;
145:12; 150:2
ᵇ2Sa 7:22
3:25 ᶜDt 4:22
ᵈDt 1:7; Jos 1:4; 9:1;
11:17; 12:7; 13:5;
Jdg 3:3; 9:15; 1Ki 4:33
3:26 ᵉver 27;
Dt 1:37; 31:2

⁸So at that time we took from these two kings of the Amorites ˣ the territory east of the Jordan, from the Arnon Gorge as far as Mount Hermon. ʸ ⁹(Hermon is called Sirion ᶻ by the Sidonians; the Amorites call it Senir.) ᵃ ¹⁰We took all the towns on the plateau, and all Gilead, and all Bashan as far as Salekah ᵇ and Edrei, towns of Og's kingdom in Bashan. ¹¹(Og king of Bashan was the last of the Rephaites. ᶜ His bed was decorated with iron and was more than nine cubits long and four cubits wide. ᵃ It is still in Rabbah ᵈ of the Ammonites.)

DIVISION OF THE LAND

¹²Of the land that we took over at that time, I gave the Reubenites and the Gadites the territory north of Aroer ᵉ by the Arnon Gorge, including half the hill country of Gilead, together with its towns. ¹³The rest of Gilead and also all of Bashan, the kingdom of Og, I gave to the half-tribe of Manasseh. ᶠ (The whole region of Argob in Bashan used to be known as a land of the Rephaites. ᵍ ¹⁴Jair, ʰ a descendant of Manasseh, took the whole region of Argob as far as the border of the Geshurites and the Maakathites; ⁱ it was named ʲ after him, so that to this day Bashan is called Havvoth Jair. ᵇ) ¹⁵And I gave Gilead to Makir. ᵏ ¹⁶But to the Reubenites and the Gadites I gave the territory extending from Gilead down to the Arnon Gorge (the middle of the gorge being the border) and out to the Jabbok River, ˡ which is the border of the Ammonites. ¹⁷Its western border was the Jordan in the Arabah, ᵐ from Kinnereth ⁿ to the Sea of the Arabah ᵒ (that is, the Dead Sea ᵖ), below the slopes of Pisgah.

¹⁸I commanded you at that time: "The LORD your God has given ᵠ you this land to take possession of it. But all your able-bodied men, armed for battle, must cross over ahead of the other Israelites. ʳ ¹⁹However, your wives, ˢ your children and your livestock ᵗ (I know you have much livestock) may stay in the towns I have given you, ²⁰until the LORD gives rest to all your people as he has to you, and they too have taken over the land that the LORD your God is giving them across the Jordan. After that, each of you may go back to the possession I have given you."

MOSES FORBIDDEN TO CROSS THE JORDAN

²¹At that time I commanded Joshua: "You have seen with your own eyes all that the LORD your God has done to these two kings. The LORD will do the same to all the kingdoms over there where you are going. ²²Do not be afraid ᵘ of them; ᵛ the LORD your God himself will fight ʷ for you."

²³At that time I pleaded ˣ with the LORD: ²⁴"Sovereign LORD, you have begun to show to your servant your greatness ʸ and your strong hand. For what god ᶻ is there in heaven or on earth who can do the deeds and mighty works ᵃ you do? ᵇ ²⁵Let me go over and see the good land ᶜ beyond the Jordan—that fine hill country and Lebanon. ᵈ"

²⁶But because of you the LORD was angry ᵉ with me and would not listen to me. "That

---

ᵃ 11 That is, about 13 feet long and 6 feet wide or about 4 meters long and 1.8 meters wide
ᵇ 14 Or called the settlements of Jair

3:8 *Mount Hermon.* Rising to a height of over 9,200 feet and snowcapped throughout the year, it is one of the most prominent and beautiful mountains in Lebanon.

B **3:9** *Sirion.* This name for Mount Hermon is found also in a Canaanite document contemporary with Moses. *Senir.* This name for Mount Hermon is also found in Assyrian sources.

3:10 *Salekah.* A city marking the eastern boundary of Bashan (see Jos 13:11).

B **3:11** *bed … with iron.* Possibly a sarcophagus made of black basalt. Such sarcophagi (stone coffins) have been found in Bashan, and the Hebrew for "bed" and "iron" may reflect this. If an actual bed, it was probably made of wood but with certain iron fixtures, as were the "chariots fitted with iron" (see note on Jos 17:16). *Rabbah of the Ammonites.* Called Philadelphia in NT times, Rabbah was the capital of ancient Ammon (Am 1:13–14). Today its name is Amman, the capital of the kingdom of Jordan.

3:12–20 See Nu 32; 34:13–15 and notes.

3:14 *Jair … Havvoth Jair.* See TNIV text note; see also note on Jdg 10:3. *the Geshurites and the Maakathites.* Two comparatively small kingdoms, Geshur was east of the Sea of Galilee and Maakah was east of the Waters of Merom (see note on Jos 11:5) and north of Geshur.

3:15 *Makir.* See note on Ge 50:23.

3:17 *Kinnereth.* See note on Mk 1:16. The Hebrew word *kinnor* means "harp"; the Sea of Galilee is a harp-shaped lake. Or reference may be to the town on the northwestern shore of the Sea of Galilee that gave its name to the lake (see Jos 11:2). *Pisgah.* On the edge of the high plateau overlooking the Dead Sea from the east (see Nu 21:20).

3:18 *you.* The tribes of Reuben and Gad and the half-tribe of Manasseh.

3:20 *rest.* A peaceful situation—free from external threat and oppression, and untroubled within by conflict, famine or plague (see 12:9–10; 25:19; see also notes on Jos 1:13; 1Ki 5:4; Heb 4:1–11).

A **3:22** *God himself.* The conquest narratives emphasize the truth that without the Lord's help Israel's victory would be impossible. The Lord's power, not Israel's unaided strength, achieved victory. Moses bolstered Israel's resolve and faith by giving this assurance (see 1:30; 2:21–22,31; 20:4).

3:23–25 Moses' final plea to be allowed to enter the land (see 1:37 and note; 31:2).

3:26 *because of you.* See note on 1:37.

is enough," the LORD said. "Do not speak to me anymore about this matter. ²⁷Go up to the top of Pisgah ᶠ and look west and north and south and east. ᵍ Look at the land with your own eyes, since you are not going to cross ʰ this Jordan. ⁱ ²⁸But commission ʲ Joshua, and encourage ᵏ and strengthen him, for he will lead this people across ˡ and will cause them to inherit the land that you will see." ²⁹So we stayed in the valley near Beth Peor. ᵐ

OBEDIENCE COMMANDED

4 Now, Israel, hear the decrees ⁿ and laws I am about to teach ᵒ you. Follow them so that you may live ᵖ and may go in and take possession of the land the LORD, the God of your ancestors, is giving you. ²Do not add �q to what I command you and do not subtract ʳ from it, but keep ˢ the commands ᵗ of the LORD your God that I give you.

³You saw with your own eyes what the LORD did at Baal Peor. ᵘ The LORD your God destroyed from among you everyone who followed the Baal of Peor, ⁴but all of you who held fast to the LORD your God are still alive today.

⁵See, I have taught ᵛ you decrees and laws ʷ as the LORD my God commanded ˣ me, so that you may follow them in the land you are entering ʸ to take possession of it. ⁶Observe ᶻ them carefully, for this will show your wisdom ᵃ and understanding to the nations, who will hear about all these decrees and say, "Surely this great nation is a wise and understanding people." ᵇ ⁷What other nation is so great ᶜ as to have their gods near ᵈ them the way the LORD our God is near us whenever we pray to him? ⁸And what other nation is so great as to have such righteous decrees and laws ᵉ as this body of laws I am setting before you today?

⁹Only be careful, ᶠ and watch yourselves closely so that you do not forget the things your eyes have seen or let them slip from your heart as long as you live. Teach ᵍ them to your children ʰ and to their children after them. ¹⁰Remember the day you stood before the LORD your God at Horeb, ⁱ when he said to me, "Assemble the people before me to hear my words so that they may learn ʲ to revere ᵏ me as long as they live in the land ˡ and may teach ᵐ them to their children." ¹¹You came near and stood at the foot of the mountain ⁿ while it blazed with fire ᵒ to the very heavens, with black clouds and deep darkness. ᵖ ¹²Then the LORD spoke q to you out of the fire. You heard the sound of words but saw no form; ʳ there was only a voice. ˢ ¹³He declared to you his covenant, ᵗ the Ten Commandments, ᵘ which he commanded you to follow and then wrote them on two stone tablets. ¹⁴And the LORD directed me at that time to teach you the decrees and laws ᵛ you are to follow in the land that you are crossing the Jordan to possess.

IDOLATRY FORBIDDEN

¹⁵You saw no form ʷ of any kind the day the LORD spoke to you at Horeb ˣ out of the fire. Therefore watch yourselves very carefully, ʸ ¹⁶so that you do not become corrupt ᶻ and make for yourselves an idol, ᵃ an image of any shape, whether formed like a man or a woman, ¹⁷or like any animal on earth or any bird that flies in the air, ᵇ ¹⁸or like any creature that moves along the ground or any fish in the waters below. ¹⁹And when you look up to the sky and see the sun, ᶜ the moon and the stars ᵈ—all the heavenly array ᵉ—do

4:15 ʷ Isa 40:18; 41:22-24 ˣ S Ge 3:1 ʸ Jos 23:11; Mal 2:15   **4:16** ᶻ S Ge 6:11-12; Dt 9:12; 31:29; 32:5; Jdg 2:19 ᵃ Ex 20:4-5; Ro 1:23
4:17 ᵇ Ro 1:23   **4:19** ᶜ Dt 17:3; 2Ki 23:11; Job 31:26; Jer 8:2; 43:13; Eze 8:16 ᵈ S Ge 1:16 ᵉ S Ge 2:1; S 37:9; Ro 1:25

3:27 ʳ S Nu 21:20
ᵍ S Ge 13:14
ʰ S ver 26;
S Nu 20:12; Dt 32:52
ⁱ S Nu 27:12
3:28 ʲ Nu 27:18-23
ᵏ Dt 31:7 ˡ Dt 1:38;
31:3,23
3:29 ᵐ S Nu 23:28;
Dt 4:46; 34:6;
Jos 13:20
4:1 ⁿ S Lev 18:4
ᵒ Dt 1:3 ᵖ S Lev 18:5;
Dt 30:15-20;
S Ro 10:5
4:2 q Dt 12:32;
Jos 1:7; Pr 30:6;
Rev 22:18-19
ʳ Jer 26:2
ˢ S Lev 22:31
ᵗ Dt 10:12-13;
Ecc 12:13
4:3 ᵘ Nu 25:1-9;
Ps 106:28
4:5 ᵛ Ps 71:17;
119:102; Jer 32:33
ʷ S Ex 18:20
ˣ S Lev 27:34
ʸ Ezr 9:11
4:6 ᶻ Dt 29:9;
1Ki 2:3 ᵃ Dt 30:19-20;
32:46-47; Ps 19:7;
119:98; Pr 1:7;
2Ti 3:15 ᵇ Job 1:1;
28:28; Ps 111:10;
Pr 2:5; 3:7; 9:10;
Ecc 12:13; Eze 5:5
4:7 ᶜ ver 32-34;
2Sa 7:23
ᵈ S Nu 23:21;
S Ps 46:1; Ac 17:27
4:8 ᵉ Ps 89:14; 97:2;
119:7,62,144,160,172;
Ro 3:2
4:9 ᶠ S Ex 23:13
ᵍ S Ge 14:14; 18:19;
Dt 6:20-25; Eph 6:4
ʰ S Ex 10:2
4:10 ⁱ S Ex 3:1
ʲ Dt 14:23; 17:19;
31:12-13; Ps 2:11;
111:10; 147:11; Isa 8:13;
Jer 32:40 ᵏ S Ex 20:20
ˡ Dt 12:1 ᵐ ver 9
4:11 ⁿ S Ex 3:1;
S 19:17 ᵒ S Ex 19:18
ᵖ S Ex 19:9; Ps 18:11;
97:2
4:12 q Ex 20:22;
Dt 5:4,22; S Mt 3:17;
Heb 12:19 ʳ Jn 5:37
ˢ S Ex 19:9
4:13 ᵗ Dt 9:9; Ro 9:4
ᵘ S Ex 24:12
4:14 ᵛ S Ex 21:1

C **3:27** *Go up to the top of Pisgah.* Moses did so after he had expounded the law to the Israelites to prepare them for life in the promised land (see 32:48–52; 34:1–6). *Pisgah.* See note on v. 17. *look west and north and south and east.* Like Abraham (see Ge 13:14), Moses would inherit the promised land only through his descendants (see 34:1–4).

3:28 *commission Joshua.* See 31:7–8.

3:29 *Beth Peor.* Means "house/sanctuary of Peor." Very likely, reference is to the place where the Baal of Peor was worshiped (see Nu 23:28; 25:3,5).

A **4:1** *Israel, hear.* God's call to his people to hear and obey is a frequent theme in Deuteronomy (see, e.g., 5:1; 6:3–4; 9:1; 20:3) and elsewhere in the OT. See also note on 6:4–9.

A **4:2** *Do not add ... do not subtract.* The revelation the Lord gives is sufficient. All of it must be obeyed, and anything that adulterates or contradicts it cannot be tolerated (see 12:32; Pr 30:6; Gal 3:15; Rev 22:18–19).

4:4 *held fast.* See note on 10:20.

A **4:7** *near us whenever we pray.* The Israelites always had access to the Lord in prayer. His presence was symbolized

by the tabernacle in the center of the camp, and by the pillar of cloud over the tabernacle (see Ex 40:34–38; Nu 23:21).

4:9 *Teach them to your children.* See v. 10; 6:7; 11:19; Ps 78:4–8; cf. Ex 12:26–27.

4:10–14 See Ex 19–24 and notes.

A **4:10** *Remember.* The divine call to Israel to remember the Lord's past redemptive acts—especially how he delivered them from slavery in Egypt—is a common theme in Deuteronomy (5:15; 7:18; 8:2,18; 9:7,27; 11:2; 15:15; 16:3,12; 24:9,18,22; 25:17) and is summarized in 32:7: "Remember the days of old."

4:12 *no form.* See v. 15; see also note on Ex 20:4. "God is spirit" (Jn 4:24; cf. Isa 31:3). *only a voice.* See v. 36; 5:23–26; Nu 7:89; 1Ki 19:13.

4:13 *his covenant, the Ten Commandments.* See notes on Ex 20:1; 34:28. *two stone tablets.* See note on Ex 31:18.

4:15–18 See note on Ex 20:4.

4:19 Cf. 17:3. *do not be enticed.* As kings of Judah would be later (2Ki 17:16; 21:3,5; 23:4–5).

4:19 ʳDt 13:5
ᵍS Nu 25:3
4:20 ʰS Ex 1:13
ⁱS Ex 3:10 ʲS Ge 17:7;
S Ex 8:22; S 34:9;
Tit 2:14
4:21 ᵏNu 20:12;
Dt 1:37
4:22 ʲNu 27:13-14
ᵐDt 3:25
4:23 ⁿver 9
ᵒS Ex 20:4
4:24 ᵖS Ex 15:7;
S 19:18; Heb 12:29
ᵠS Ex 23
4:25 ʳver 16 ˢver 23
ᵗ1Ki 11:6; 15:26;
16:25,30; 2Ki 17:2,17;
21:2
4:26 ᵘGe 31:50;
Pr 14:5 ᵛDt 30:18-19;
31:28; 32:1; Ps 50:4;
Isa 1:2; 34:1; Jer 6:19;
Mic 6:2 ʷDt 6:15; 7:4
4:27 ˣS Lev 26:33;
Dt 28:36,64; 29:28;
1Ki 8:46; 2Ki 17:6;
Ps 44:11; 106:27;
Jer 3:8; Mic 1:16
ʸIsa 17:6; 21:17;
Ob 1:5
4:28 ᶻDt 13:2;
28:36,64; 1Sa 26:19;
Jer 5:19; 16:13;
Ac 19:26 ᵃDt 29:17
ᵇPs 115:4-8; 135:15-
18; Isa 8:19; 26:14;
44:17-20; Rev 9:20
4:29 ᶜ1Sa 13:12;
2Ki 13:4; 2Ch 7:14;
15:4; 33:12; Ps 78:34;
119:58; Isa 45:19,22;
55:6; Jer 26:19;
Da 9:13; Hos 3:5;
Am 5:4 ᵈ1Sa 7:3;
1Ki 8:48; Jer 29:13
ᵉDt 6:5; 30:1-3,10
4:30 ᶠLev 26:41;
Dt 31:17,21; Ps 4:1;
18:6; 46:1; 59:16;
107:6 ᵍDt 31:29;
Jer 23:20; Hos 3:5;
Heb 1:2 ʰDt 30:2;
1Ki 8:48; Ne 1:9;
Jer 3:1,12,22; 4:1;
18:11; Joel 2:12
4:31 ⁱEx 34:6;
Ne 9:31; Ps 111:4
ʲDt 31:6,8; Jos 1:5;
1Ki 8:57; 1Ch 28:9,
20; Ps 9:10; 27:9;
71:9; Isa 42:16;
Heb 13:5
ᵏS Lev 26:44
ˡLev 26:45
4:32 ᵐDt 32:7
ⁿS Ge 1:27; Isa 45:12
ᵒDt 28:64; 30:1;
Jer 9:16; Mt 24:31

not be enticed ᶠ into bowing down to them and worshiping ᵍ things the LORD your God has apportioned to all the nations under heaven. ²⁰But as for you, the LORD took you and brought you out of the iron-smelting furnace, ʰ out of Egypt, ⁱ to be the people of his inheritance, ʲ as you now are.

²¹The LORD was angry with me ᵏ because of you, and he solemnly swore that I would not cross the Jordan and enter the good land the LORD your God is giving you as your inheritance. ²²I will die in this land; ˡ I will not cross the Jordan; but you are about to cross over and take possession of that good land. ᵐ ²³Be careful not to forget the covenant ⁿ of the LORD your God that he made with you; do not make for yourselves an idol ᵒ in the form of anything the LORD your God has forbidden. ²⁴For the LORD your God is a consuming fire, ᵖ a jealous God. ᵠ

²⁵After you have had children and grandchildren and have lived in the land a long time—if you then become corrupt ʳ and make any kind of idol, ˢ doing evil ᵗ in the eyes of the LORD your God and arousing his anger, ²⁶I call the heavens and the earth as witnesses ᵘ against you ᵛ this day that you will quickly perish ʷ from the land that you are crossing the Jordan to possess. You will not live there long but will certainly be destroyed. ²⁷The LORD will scatter ˣ you among the peoples, and only a few of you will survive ʸ among the nations to which the LORD will drive you. ²⁸There you will worship gods ᶻ of wood and stone made by human hands, ᵃ which cannot see or hear or eat or smell. ᵇ ²⁹But if from there you seek ᶜ the LORD your God, you will find him if you seek him with all your heart ᵈ and with all your soul. ᵉ ³⁰When you are in distress ᶠ and all these things have happened to you, then in later days ᵍ you will return ʰ to the LORD your God and obey him. ³¹For the LORD your God is a merciful ⁱ God; he will not abandon ʲ or destroy ᵏ you or forget ˡ the covenant with your ancestors, which he confirmed to them by oath.

THE LORD IS GOD

³²Ask ᵐ now about the former days, long before your time, from the day God created human beings on the earth; ⁿ ask from one end of the heavens to the other. ᵒ Has anything so great ᵖ as this ever happened, or has anything like it ever been heard of? ³³Has any other people heard the voice of God ᵃ speaking out of fire, as you have, and lived? ᵠ ³⁴Has any god ever tried to take for himself one nation out of another nation, ʳ by testings, ˢ by signs ᵗ and wonders, ᵘ by war, by a mighty hand and an outstretched arm, ᵛ or by great and awesome deeds, ʷ like all the things the LORD your God did for you in Egypt before your very eyes?

³⁵You were shown these things so that you might know that the LORD is God; besides him there is no other. ˣ ³⁶From heaven he made you hear his voice ʸ to discipline ᶻ you. On earth he showed you his great fire, and you heard his words from out of the fire. ³⁷Because he loved ᵃ your ancestors and chose their descendants after them, he brought you out of Egypt by his Presence and his great strength, ᵇ ³⁸to drive out before you nations

---

ᵃ 33 Or *of a god*

4:32 ᵖver 7; 2Sa 7:23   **4:33** ᵠEx 20:22; Dt 5:24-26   **4:34** ʳEx 14:30 ˢIsa 7:12 ᵗS Ex 4:17 ᵘDt 7:19; 26:8; 29:3; 1Ch 16:12; Ps 9:1; 40:5; Jer 32:20 ᵛS Ex 3:20; Dt 5:15; 6:21; 15:15 ʷEx 15:11; Dt 34:12; Ps 45:4; 65:5   **4:35** ˣver 39; Ex 8:10; Dt 7:9; 32:4,12; 1Sa 2:2; 1Ki 8:60; 2Ki 19:19; Isa 43:10; Mk 12:32   **4:36** ʸS Ex 19:19; Heb 12:25 ᶻDt 8:5   **4:37** ᵃDt 7:8; 10:15; 23:5; 33:3; Ps 44:3; Jer 31:3; Hos 11:1; Mal 1:2; 2:11 ᵇS Ex 3:20; S 13:14

4:20 *iron-smelting furnace.* The period in Egypt was a time of affliction for the Israelites (see 1Ki 8:51; Jer 11:4; see also Isa 48:10 and note).

4:21 *because of you.* See note on 1:37.

4:24 *consuming fire.* See 9:3; see also Ex 24:17; Isa 33:14 and notes; Heb 12:29. *jealous God.* See 5:9; 6:15; see also note on Ex 20:5.

4:25 *After you ... have lived in the land.* The pattern of the Israelites' rebellion, resulting in expulsion from the land, and then their repentance, leading to restoration to the land, is prominent in Deuteronomy (see, e.g., the blessing and curse formulas in chs. 27–28).

4:26 *the heavens and the earth as witnesses.* See notes on 30:19; Ps 50:1; Isa 1:2.

4:27 *will scatter you.* See note on 28:64.

4:29 *with all your heart and ... soul.* Indicates total involvement and commitment. The phrase is applied not

only to how the Lord's people should seek him, but also to how they should fear (revere) him, live in obedience to him, love and serve him (6:5; 10:12; 11:13; 13:3; 30:6), and, after forsaking him, renew their allegiance and commitment to him (26:16; 30:2,10).

4:31 *covenant ... confirmed ... by oath.* See notes on Ge 21:23; 22:16; Ex 19:5; Heb 6:13,18. In ancient times, parties to a covenant were expected to confirm their intentions by means of a self-maledictory oath (see note on Ge 15:17).

4:35 *so that you might know.* See v. 10. *besides him there is no other.* See v. 39; 5:7; 6:4 and note; 32:39. Moses insists that there is only one God (see also note on Ge 1:1).

4:37 *he loved.* The first reference in Deuteronomy to God's love for his people (see Introduction: Theological Teaching and Purpose). See 5:10; 7:9,13; 10:15; 23:5. The corollary truth is that his people should love him (see note on 6:5). *Presence.* See notes on Ex 25:30; 33:14.

greater and stronger than you and to bring you into their land to give it to you for your inheritance, *c* as it is today.

[39]Acknowledge *d* and take to heart this day that the LORD is God in heaven above and on the earth below. There is no other. *e* [40]Keep *f* his decrees and commands, *g* which I am giving you today, so that it may go well *h* with you and your children after you and that you may live long *i* in the land the LORD your God gives you for all time.

CITIES OF REFUGE

4:41–43Ref — Nu 35:6–34; Dt 19:1–14; Jos 20:1–9

[41]Then Moses set aside three cities east of the Jordan, [42]to which anyone who had killed a person could flee if they had unintentionally *j* killed a neighbor without malice aforethought. They could flee into one of these cities and save their life. [43]The cities were these: Bezer in the wilderness plateau, for the Reubenites; Ramoth *k* in Gilead, for the Gadites; and Golan in Bashan, for the Manassites.

INTRODUCTION TO THE LAW

[44]This is the law Moses set before the Israelites. [45]These are the stipulations, decrees and laws Moses gave them when they came out of Egypt [46]and were in the valley near Beth Peor east of the Jordan, in the land of Sihon *l* king of the Amorites, who reigned in Heshbon and was defeated by Moses and the Israelites as they came out of Egypt. [47]They took possession of his land and the land of Og king of Bashan, the two Amorite kings east of the Jordan. [48]This land extended from Aroer *m* on the rim of the Arnon Gorge to Mount Sirion *a n* (that is, Hermon *o*), [49]and included all the Arabah east of the Jordan, as far as the Dead Sea, *b* below the slopes of Pisgah.

THE TEN COMMANDMENTS

5:6–21pp — Ex 20:1–17

5 Moses summoned all Israel and said:
Hear, Israel, the decrees and laws *p* I declare in your hearing today. Learn them and be sure to follow them. [2]The LORD our God made a covenant *q* with us at Horeb. *r* [3]It was not with our ancestors *c* that the LORD made this covenant, but with us, *s* with all of us who are alive here today. *t* [4]The LORD spoke *u* to you face to face *v* out of the fire *w* on the mountain. [5](At that time I stood between *x* the LORD and you to declare to you the word of the LORD, because you were afraid *y* of the fire and did not go up the mountain.) And he said:

[6]"I am the LORD your God, who brought you out of Egypt, *z* out of the land of slavery. *a*

[7]"You shall have no other gods before *d* me.

[8]"You shall not make for yourself an image in the form of anything in heaven above or on the earth beneath or in the waters below. *b* [9]You shall not bow down to them or worship them; for I, the LORD your God, am a jealous God, punishing the children for the sin of the parents *c* to the third and fourth generation of those who hate me, *d* [10]but showing love to a thousand *e* generations of those who love me and keep my commandments. *f*

[11]"You shall not misuse the name *g* of the LORD your God, for the LORD will not hold anyone guiltless who misuses his name. *h*

---

a 48 Syriac (see also Deut. 3:9); Hebrew *Siyon*   *b 49* Hebrew *the Sea of the Arabah*   *c 3* Or *not only with our parents*   *d 7* Or *besides*

4:39 See v. 35 and note.

4:40 *it may go well with you.* That is, you will receive the covenant benefits. This assurance occurs ten times in Deuteronomy (here; 5:16,29; 6:3,18; 8:16; 12:25,28; 19:13; 22:7). Cf. also 28:1–14; 30:1–10.

4:41–43 See 19:1–13; Nu 35:9–28; Jos 20 and notes.

4:43 *Bezer … Ramoth … Golan.* See map, p. 245.

5:1 *Hear, Israel.* See note on 4:1.

5:2 *covenant with us at Horeb.* See note on Ex 19:5. God's covenant with Israel, given at Mount Horeb (Sinai) and now being confirmed, bound the Israelites to the Lord as their absolute Sovereign, and to his laws and regulations as their way of life. Adherence to the covenant would bring God's people the blessings of the Lord, while breaking the covenant would bring against them the punishments described as "curses" (see, e.g., 28:15–20).

Jer 31:31–34 predicted the establishing of a new covenant, which made the Sinaitic covenant obsolete (see Heb 7:18–22; see also Heb 8:6–13; 10:15–18 and notes). See chart, p. 20.

5:3 *not with our ancestors … but with us.* See TNIV text note. The covenant was made with those who were present at Sinai, but since they were representatives of the nation it was made with all succeeding generations as well.

5:5 See vv. 23–27; Ex 20:18–21.

5:6–21 The Ten Commandments are the central stipulations of God's covenant with Israel made at Sinai. It is almost impossible to exaggerate their effect on subsequent history. They constitute the basis of the moral principles found throughout the Western world and summarize what the one true God expects of his people in terms of faith, worship and conduct (see notes on Ex 20:2–17).

4:38 *c* Nu 34:14-15; Dt 7:1; 9:5
4:39 *d* Ex 8:10
e S ver 35; Ex 15:11
4:40 *f* S Lev 22:31
g ver 1; S Ge 26:5; Dt 5:29; 11:1; Ps 105:45; Isa 48:18
h Dt 5:16; 12:25; Isa 3:10 *i* S Ex 23:26; Eph 6:2-3
4:42 *j* S Ex 21:13
4:43 *k* Jos 21:38; 1Ki 22:3; 2Ki 8:28; 9:14
4:46 *l* Nu 21:26
4:48 *m* Dt 2:36
n Dt 3:9 *o* S Dt 3:8
5:1 *p* S Ex 18:20
5:2 *q* Ex 19:5; Jer 11:2; Heb 9:15; 10:15-17 *r* S Ge 17:9; S Ex 3:1
5:3 *s* Dt 11:2-7
t Nu 26:63-65; Heb 8:9
5:4 *u* S Dt 4:12
v S Nu 14:14
w S Ex 19:18
5:5 *x* Gal 3:19
y S Ge 3:10; Heb 12:18-21
5:6 *z* S Ex 13:3; S 29:46 *a* Lev 26:1; Dt 6:4; Ps 81:10
5:8 *b* Lev 26:1; Dt 4:15-18; Ps 78:58; 97:7
5:9 *c* S Nu 26:11
d Ex 34:7; S Nu 10:35; 14:18
5:10 *e* S Ex 34:7
f Nu 14:18; Dt 7:9; Ne 1:5; Jer 32:18; Da 9:4
5:11 *g* Ps 139:20
h Lev 19:12; Dt 10:20; Mt 5:33-37

5:12 *i* Ex 16:23-30;
31:13-17; Mk 2:27-28
5:14 *j* S Ge 2:2;
Mt 12:2; Mk 2:27;
Heb 4:4 *k* Job 31:13;
Jer 34:9-11 *l* Jer 17:21,
24
5:15 *m* S Ge 15:13
n Ex 6:1; Ps 108:6;
Jer 32:21 *o* S Dt 4:34
5:16 *p* Mal 1:6
q Ex 21:17; Lev 19:3;
Eze 22:7; Mt 15:4*;
19:19*; Mk 7:10*;
10:19*; Lk 18:20*;
Eph 6:2-3*
r S Dt 4:40; 11:9;
Pr 3:1-2
5:17 *s* Ge 9:6;
Lev 24:17; Ecc 3:3;
Jer 40:15; 41:3;
Mt 5:21-22*; 19:19*;
Mk 10:19*; Lk 18:20*;
Ro 13:9*; Jas 2:11*
5:18 *t* Lev 20:10;
Mt 5:27-30; 19:18*;
Mk 10:19*; Lk 18:20*;
Ro 13:9*; Jas 2:11*
5:19 *u* Lev 19:11;
Mt 19:19*;
Mk 10:19*; Lk 18:20*;
Ro 13:9*
5:20 *v* S Ex 23:1;
Mt 19:18*;
Mk 10:19*; Lk 18:20*
5:21 *w* Ro 7:7*;
13:9*
5:22 *x* S Ex 20:21
y S Ex 24:12
5:23 *z* S Ex 3:16
5:24 *a* Dt 4:34; 8:5;
11:2; Isa 53:4
b S Dt 3:24 *c* Ex 19:19
5:25 *d* Ex 20:18-19;
Dt 18:16; Heb 12:19
5:26 *e* S Ex 33:20;
Dt 4:33; Jdg 6:22-23;
13:22; Isa 6:5
5:27 *f* S Ex 19:8
g S Ex 24:7
5:28 *h* Dt 18:17
5:29 *i* Ps 81:8,13
j Jos 22:5; Ps 78:7
k ver 33; S Dt 4:1,40;
12:25; 22:7
5:31 *l* Ex 24:12
5:32 *m* S Dt 4:29;
10:12 *n* Dt 17:11,20;
28:14; Jos 1:7;
1Ki 15:5; 2Ki 22:2;
Pr 4:27
5:33 *o* Isa 3:10;
Jer 7:23; 38:20;
S Lk 1:6 *p* S ver 29
6:2 *q* S Ex 20:20;
S 1Sa 12:24 *r* Dt 4:9
s S Ge 26:5
t S Ex 20:12
6:3 *u* S Ex 19:5

[12] "Observe the Sabbath day by keeping it holy, [i] as the Lord your God has command- ed you. [13]Six days you shall labor and do all your work, [14]but the seventh day [j] is a sabbath to the Lord your God. On it you shall not do any work, neither you, nor your son or daughter, nor your male or female servant, [k] nor your ox, your donkey or any of your animals, nor any foreigner residing in your towns, so that your male and female servants may rest, as you do. [l] [15]Remember that you were slaves [m] in Egypt and that the Lord your God brought you out of there with a mighty hand [n] and an outstretched arm. [o] Therefore the Lord your God has commanded you to observe the Sabbath day.

[16] "Honor your father [p] and your mother, [q] as the Lord your God has commanded you, so that you may live long [r] and that it may go well with you in the land the Lord your God is giving you.

[17] "You shall not murder. [s]

[18] "You shall not commit adultery. [t]

[19] "You shall not steal. [u]

[20] "You shall not give false testimony against your neighbor. [v]

[21] "You shall not covet your neighbor's wife. You shall not set your desire on your neigh- bor's house or land, his male or female servant, his ox or donkey, or anything that belongs to your neighbor." [w]

[22]These are the commandments the Lord proclaimed in a loud voice to your whole as- sembly there on the mountain from out of the fire, the cloud and the deep darkness; [x] and he added nothing more. Then he wrote them on two stone tablets [y] and gave them to me. [23]When you heard the voice out of the darkness, while the mountain was ablaze with fire, all the leaders of your tribes and your elders [z] came to me. [24]And you said, "The Lord our God has shown us [a] his glory and his majesty, [b] and we have heard his voice from the fire. Today we have seen that people can live even if God speaks with them. [c] [25]But now, why should we die? This great fire will consume us, and we will die if we hear the voice of the Lord our God any longer. [d] [26]For what mortal has ever heard the voice of the living God speaking out of fire, as we have, and survived? [e] [27]Go near and listen to all that the Lord our God says. [f] Then tell us whatever the Lord our God tells you. We will listen and obey." [g]

[28]The Lord heard you when you spoke to me, and the Lord said to me, "I have heard what this people said to you. Everything they said was good. [h] [29]Oh, that their hearts would be inclined to fear me [i] and keep all my commands [j] always, so that it might go well with them and their children forever! [k]

[30]"Go, tell them to return to their tents. [31]But you stay here [l] with me so that I may give you all the commands, decrees and laws you are to teach them to follow in the land I am giving them to possess."

[32]So be careful to do what the Lord your God has commanded you; [m] do not turn aside to the right or to the left. [n] [33]Walk in obedience to all that the Lord your God has com- manded you, [o] so that you may live and prosper and prolong your days [p] in the land that you will possess.

LOVE THE LORD YOUR GOD

6 These are the commands, decrees and laws the Lord your God directed me to teach you to observe in the land that you are crossing the Jordan to possess, [2]so that you, your children and their children after them may fear [q] the Lord your God as long as you live [r] by keeping all his decrees and commands [s] that I give you, and so that you may enjoy long life. [t] [3]Hear, Israel, and be careful to obey [u] so that it may go well with

---

5:12 *as the Lord your God has commanded you.* Missing from the parallel verse in Exodus (20:8), this clause reminds the peo- ple of the divine origin of the Ten Commandments 40 years ear- lier at Mount Sinai (see vv. 15–16).
5:14 *so that your male and female servants may rest.* See v. 15; see also note on Ex 20:10.
5:15 *Remember.* See note on 4:10.
5:16–21 The NT quotes often from this section of the Ten Commandments (see cross references on these verses).
5:16 *that it may go well with you.* Missing from the parallel in Ex 20:12, this clause explains that the life the Lord desires for his people is not to be measured merely in terms of longevity (see note on 4:40).

5:20 See 19:18–19; Lev 19:11–13; 1Ki 21:10,13.
5:22 *commandments.* Lit. "words" (see note on Ex 20:1). *two stone tablets.* See note on Ex 31:18.
5:25 *we will die.* See notes on Ge 16:13; 32:30.
5:27 *We will listen and obey.* See note on Ex 19:8.
6:2 *fear the Lord.* See note on Ge 20:11. *enjoy long life.* See 4:40; 5:16 and note. By obeying the Lord and keeping his decrees, in- dividual Israelites would enjoy long life in the land, and the peo- ple as a whole would enjoy a long national existence there.
6:3 *Hear, Israel.* See v. 4 and note on 4:1. *land flowing with milk and honey.* See note on Ex 3:8. The phrase is used 14 times from Exodus through Deuteronomy and 5 times elsewhere in the OT.

you and that you may increase greatly ^v in a land flowing with milk and honey, ^w just as the Lord, the God of your ancestors, promised ^x you.

⁴Hear, O Israel: The Lord our God, the Lord is one. ^{a y 5}Love ^z the Lord your God with all your heart ^a and with all your soul and with all your strength. ^{b 6}These commandments that I give you today are to be on your hearts. ^{c 7}Impress them on your children. Talk about them when you sit at home and when you walk along the road, when you lie down and when you get up. ^{d 8}Tie them as symbols on your hands and bind them on your foreheads. ^{e 9}Write them on the doorframes of your houses and on your gates. ^f

¹⁰When the Lord your God brings you into the land he swore to your fathers, to Abraham, Isaac and Jacob, to give you—a land with large, flourishing cities you did not build, ^{g 11}houses filled with all kinds of good things you did not provide, wells you did not dig, ^h and vineyards and olive groves you did not plant—then when you eat and are satisfied, ^{i 12}be careful that you do not forget ^j the Lord, who brought you out of Egypt, out of the land of slavery.

¹³Fear the Lord ^k your God, serve him only ^l and take your oaths ^m in his name. ^{n 14}Do not follow other gods, the gods of the peoples around you; ¹⁵for the Lord your God ^o, who is among you, is a jealous God and his anger will burn against you, and he will destroy you from the face of the land. ¹⁶Do not put the Lord your God to the test ^p as you did at Massah. ¹⁷Be sure to keep ^q the commands of the Lord your God and the stipulations and decrees he has given you. ^{r 18}Do what is right and good in the Lord's sight, ^s so that it may go well ^t with you and you may go in and take over the good land the Lord promised on oath to your ancestors, ¹⁹thrusting out all your enemies ^u before you, as the Lord said.

²⁰In the future, when your children ask you, ^v "What is the meaning of the stipulations, decrees and laws the Lord our God has commanded you?" ²¹tell them: "We were slaves of Pharaoh in Egypt, but the Lord brought us out of Egypt with a mighty hand. ^{w 22}Before our eyes the Lord sent signs and wonders—great and terrible—on Egypt and Pharaoh and his whole household. ²³But he brought us out from there to bring us in and give us the land he promised on oath to our ancestors. ²⁴The Lord commanded us to obey all these decrees and to fear the Lord our God, ^x so that we might always prosper and be kept alive, as is the case today. ^{y 25}And if we are careful to obey all this law ^z before the Lord our God, as he has commanded us, that will be our righteousness. ^a"

^a 4 Or *The Lord our God is one Lord*; or *The Lord is our God, the Lord is one*; or *The Lord is our God, the Lord alone*

6:24 ^y Ps 27:12; 41:2; S Ro 10:5   **6:25** ^z Ps 103:18; 119:34, 55 ^a Dt 24:13; S Ro 9:31; Ro 10:3, 5

6:3 ^v Ge 15:5; Dt 5:33 ^w S Ex 3:8; Dt 32:13-14 ^x Ex 13:5
6:4 ^y Dt 4:35, 39; Ne 9:6; Ps 86:10; Isa 44:6; Zec 14:9; Mk 12:29*; Jn 10:30; 1Co 8:4; Eph 4:6; Jas 2:19
6:5 ^z Dt 11:1, 22; Mt 22:37*; Mk 12:30*; Lk 10:27* ^a 1Sa 12:24 ^b Dt 4:29; 10:12; Jos 22:5
6:6 ^c ver 8; Dt 11:18; 30:14; 32:46; Ps 26:2; 37:31; 40:8; 119:11; Pr 3:3; Isa 51:7; Jer 17:1; 31:33; Eze 40:4
6:7 ^d Dt 4:9; 11:19; Pr 22:6; Eph 6:4
6:8 ^e S ver 6; S Ex 13:9; Mt 23:5
6:9 ^f Dt 11:20
6:10 ^g S Ge 11:4; Dt 12:29; 19:1; Jos 24:13; Ps 105:44
6:11 ^h Jer 2:13 ⁱ S Lev 26:5; Dt 8:10; 14:29; 31:20
6:12 ^j Dt 4:9, 23; 2Ki 17:38; Ps 44:17; 78:7; 103:2
6:13 ^k Ps 33:8; 34:9 ^l Dt 13:4; 1Sa 7:3; Jer 44:10; Mt 4:10*; Lk 4:4*; 4:8* ^m 1Sa 20:3 ⁿ S Ex 20:7; S Mt 5:33
6:15 ^o Dt 4:24; 5:9
6:16 ^p S Ex 17:2; Mt 4:7*; Lk 4:12*
6:17 ^q S Lev 26:3 ^r Dt 11:22; Ps 119:4, 56, 100, 134, 168
6:18 ^s 2Ki 18:6; Isa 36:7; 38:3 ^t Dt 4:40
6:19 ^u Ex 23:27; Jos 21:44; Ps 78:53; 107:2; 136:24
6:20 ^v S Ex 10:2
6:21 ^w S Dt 4:34
6:24 ^x Dt 10:12; 30:6; Ps 86:11; Jer 32:39

6:4–9 See Mk 12:29–30; see also Mt 22:37–38; Lk 10:27. This passage in Deuteronomy is known as the *Shema* (Hebrew for "Hear"). It has become the Jewish confession of faith, recited daily by the pious and every Sabbath day in the synagogue.

6:4 *the Lord is one.* The truth revealed to Israel that God is one and that this one God created all things, sustains all things and governs all things stood in radical opposition to all the religions of the ancient Near Eastern world. All of Israel's neighbors had to come to terms in their daily lives with scores of gods, each with its own sphere of influence, its own limitations, its own petty self-interests and its own morally erratic ways. But Israel could live serenely in the knowledge that all things and all times were under the rule of one divine King, whose ways are righteous and whose purpose with her and through her (as Yahweh, her God) is salvation for humankind—from sin and judgment and every evil that has burdened human life. Such serenity in the midst of the ragings of history and all its seeming chaos remains the precious gift of faith for all who know and trust the God of Israel.

6:5 *Love the Lord.* Primarily in view here is the love shown by a subject to a king. To love King Yahweh is to be his loyal and obedient servant (Israel was the Lord's kingdom people). Love for God and neighbor (see Lev 19:18) is built on the love that the Lord has for his people (see 4:37 and note; 7:8–9, 13; 23:5; 1Jn 4:19–21) and on his identification with

them. Such love is to be total, involving one's whole being (see notes on 4:29; Jos 22:5).

6:6 *commandments…on your hearts.* A feature that would especially characterize the "new covenant" (see Jer 31:31–33; 1Co 3:3).

6:8–9 Many Jews take these verses literally and tie phylacteries (see note on Mt 23:5) to their foreheads and left arms. They also attach mezuzot (small wooden or metal containers in which passages of Scripture are placed) to the doorframes of their houses. But a figurative interpretation is supported by 11:18–20; Ex 13:9,16. See note on Ex 13:9.

6:10–12 Because the emphasis in Scripture is always on what God does and not on what his people achieve, they are never to forget what he has done for them. See note on 4:10.

6:13 Quoted in part by Jesus in response to Satan's temptation (Mt 4:10; Lk 4:8). Jesus quoted from Deuteronomy in response to the devil's other two temptations as well (see notes on v. 16; 8:3). *Fear the Lord.* See note on Ge 20:11.

6:15 *jealous God.* See 4:24; 5:9; see also note on Ex 20:5.

6:16 Quoted in part by Jesus in Mt 4:7; Lk 4:12 (see also note on v. 13 here). *as you did at Massah.* See 9:22; 33:8; see also note on Ex 17:7.

6:20 See Ex 12:26 and note.

6:23 *brought us out…to bring us in.* See note on Ex 6:7–8.

6:25 *righteousness.* Probably here refers to a true, personal relationship with the covenant Lord that manifests itself in the daily lives of God's people (see 24:13).

7:1 *b* S Lev 14:34;
S Dt 4:38 *c* Dt 20:16-
18; 31:3 *d* Ge 15:20
e S Ge 10:16 *f* S Dt 1:7
g Ge 13:7 *h* S Ge 10:17
i Jos 3:10
7:2 *j* S Dt 2:33
k S Dt 2:34 *l* Nu 31:17;
Dt 33:27; Jos 11:11
m S Ex 23:32 *n* ver 16;
Dt 13:8; 19:13; 25:12
7:3 *o* Ex 34:15-16;
Jos 22:16; Da 9:7
7:4 *p* Jdg 3:6
q S Dt 4:26
7:5 *r* S Ex 34:13;
Dt 16:21 *s* S Ex 23:24
7:6 *t* S Ex 19:6;
S Lev 27:30
u Dt 26:19; Ps 30:4;
37:28; 50:5; 52:9
v Dt 14:2; 1Ki 3:8;
Isa 41:9; Eze 20:5
w S Ge 17:7;
S Ex 8:22; S 34:9;
Isa 43:1; Ro 9:4;
Tit 2:14
7:7 *x* S Ge 22:17
y Ge 34:30 *z* Dt 4:37;
10:22
7:8 *a* S Dt 4:37;
1Ki 10:9; 2Ch 2:11;
Ps 44:3 *b* Ex 32:13;
S Nu 14:8; Ro 11:28
c S Ex 3:20 *d* S Ex 6:6
e S Ex 13:14
7:9 *f* S Dt 4:35
g Ps 18:25; 33:4;
108:4; 145:13; 146:6;
Isa 49:7; Jer 42:5;
Hos 11:12; S 1Co 1:9
h ver 12; 1Ki 8:23;
2Ch 6:14; Ne 1:5; 9:32
i S Ex 20:6 *j* S Dt 5:10
7:10 *k* S Lev 26:28;
S Nu 10:35; Na 1:2
7:12 *l* Lev 26:3-13;
Dt 28:1-14; Ps 105:8-
9; Mic 7:20
7:13 *m* Ps 11:5;
146:8; Pr 15:9;
Isa 51:1; Jn 14:21
n S Ge 17:6; Ex 1:7;
Dt 1:10; 13:17; 30:5;
Ps 107:38
o S Ge 49:25
p S Ge 27:28
q S Nu 18:12 *r* Dt 28:4
7:14 *s* Ex 23:26
7:15 *t* S Ex 15:26
u S Ex 9:9

DRIVING OUT THE NATIONS

7 When the Lord your God brings you into the land you are entering to possess *b* and drives out before you many nations *c*—the Hittites, *d* Girgashites, *e* Amorites, *f* Canaanites, Perizzites, *g* Hivites *h* and Jebusites, *i* seven nations larger and stronger than you— ²and when the Lord your God has delivered *j* them over to you and you have defeated them, then you must destroy *k* them totally. *a l* Make no treaty *m* with them, and show them no mercy. *n* ³Do not intermarry with them. *o* Do not give your daughters to their sons or take their daughters for your sons, ⁴for they will turn your children away from following me to serve other gods, *p* and the Lord's anger will burn against you and will quickly destroy *q* you. ⁵This is what you are to do to them: Break down their altars, smash their sacred stones, cut down their Asherah poles *b r* and burn their idols in the fire. *s* ⁶For you are a people holy *t* to the Lord your God. *u* The Lord your God has chosen *v* you out of all the peoples on the face of the earth to be his people, his treasured possession. *w*

⁷The Lord did not set his affection on you and choose you because you were more numerous *x* than other peoples, for you were the fewest *y* of all peoples. *z* ⁸But it was because the Lord loved *a* you and kept the oath he swore *b* to your ancestors that he brought you out with a mighty hand *c* and redeemed *d* you from the land of slavery, *e* from the power of Pharaoh king of Egypt. ⁹Know therefore that the Lord your God is God; *f* he is the faithful God, *g* keeping his covenant of love *h* to a thousand generations *i* of those who love him and keep his commandments. *j* ¹⁰But

> those who hate him he will repay to their face by destruction;
> he will not be slow to repay to their face those who hate him. *k*

¹¹Therefore, take care to follow the commands, decrees and laws I give you today.

¹²If you pay attention to these laws and are careful to follow them, then the Lord your God will keep his covenant of love with you, as he swore to your ancestors. *l* ¹³He will love you and bless you *m* and increase your numbers. *n* He will bless the fruit of your womb, *o* the crops of your land—your grain, new wine *p* and olive oil *q*—the calves of your herds and the lambs of your flocks in the land he swore to your ancestors to give you. *r* ¹⁴You will be blessed more than any other people; none of your men or women will be childless, nor will any of your livestock be without young. *s* ¹⁵The Lord will keep you free from every disease. *t* He will not inflict on you the horrible diseases you knew in Egypt, *u* but he will inflict them on all who hate you. *v* ¹⁶You must destroy all the peoples the Lord your God gives over to you. *w* Do not look on them with pity *x* and do not serve their gods, *y* for that will be a snare *z* to you.

¹⁷You may say to yourselves, "These nations are stronger than we are. How can we drive

---

a 2 The Hebrew term refers to the irrevocable giving over of things or persons to the Lord, often by totally destroying them; also in verse 26. *b 5* That is, wooden symbols of the goddess Asherah; here and elsewhere in Deuteronomy

7:15 *v* S Ex 23:25; Dt 30:8-10 **7:16** *w* ver 24; Jos 6:2; 10:26 *x* S ver 2 *y* Jdg 3:6; Ezr 9:1; Ps 106:36 *z* ver 25; S Ex 10:7

7:1–6 When this passage is carefully examined together with 1Ki 11:1–13; Ezr 9:1–2,10–12,14, it seems clear that what was prohibited was intermarriage with idolatrous and immoral foreigners (see note on v. 4). On the other hand, outsiders who placed themselves under the Lord's rule and thus became affiliated with the covenant community were treated for the most part just like ordinary Israelites (see Ex 12:48–49; Lev 17:8–9; 19:33–34; Nu 9:14; 15:13–16,26–31; Dt 16:11–14; cf. Mal 2:11 and note; see also Rahab [Jos 2; 6:17,22–25] and Ruth [the book of Ruth]; see further Mt 1:5).

7:1 *Hittites … Jebusites.* See 20:17; see also notes on Ge 10:6,15–18; 13:7; Jos 9:7. *seven nations.* See note on Ex 3:8.

7:2–5 *Make no treaty … Do not intermarry … Break down their altars.* Israel was to have no association—political, social or religious—with the idol worshipers of Canaan (see v. 16; cf. Mal 2:11 and note).

7:2 *destroy them totally.* See note on 2:34.

7:4 *turn your children away … to serve other gods.* See note on vv.1–6. The Lord's command against intermarriage with foreigners was not racially motivated but was intended to prevent spiritual contamination and apostasy (see, e.g., 1Ki 11:1–11; Ne 13:25–27).

7:5 *altars … sacred stones … Asherah poles.* Objects of Canaan-

ite idolatrous worship (see 12:3; 16:21–22). See also TNIV text note; Ex 34:13 and note.

7:6 *holy.* Separated from all corrupting people or things and consecrated totally to the Lord (see note on Ex 3:5). *treasured possession.* See note on Ex 19:5.

7:8 *because the Lord loved you.* See 4:37 and note.

7:9,12 *his covenant of love.* See 1Ki 8:23; 1Ch 6:14; Ne 1:5; 9:32; Da 9:4; cf. Ps 89:28; 106:45; Isa 54:10; 55:3; i.e., the covenant in which God pledges on oath to show the Israelites his unfailing love (kindness, mercy; see note on Ps 6:4) in all his ways with them through the vicissitudes of their history so that all his particular promises to them (see vv. 13–15; 19:24; 28:1–14; 30:1–10; see also Ge 22:17–18; Lev 26:3–13) might be fulfilled. A closely related phrase is "covenant of peace" (Nu 25:12; Isa 54:10; Eze 34:25; 37:26).

7:9 *Know … that the Lord … is God.* See 11:28; Ps 100:3 and notes. *thousand generations … keep his commandments.* See note on Ex 20:6.

7:12–15 The blessings are stated more fully in 28:1–14; 30:1–10.

7:13 *grain, new wine and olive oil.* A common OT summary of the produce of field, vineyard and olive grove (see, e.g., 11:14; 14:23; 18:4; 28:51).

7:15 *not inflict … diseases.* See note on 28:60.

7:16 See essay, p. 294.

them out? *ᵃ* ¹⁸But do not be afraid *ᵇ* of them; remember well what the LORD your God did to Pharaoh and to all Egypt. *ᶜ* ¹⁹You saw with your own eyes the great trials, the signs and wonders, the mighty hand *ᵈ* and outstretched arm, with which the LORD your God brought you out. The LORD your God will do the same to all the peoples you now fear. *ᵉ* ²⁰Moreover, the LORD your God will send the hornet *ᶠ* among them until even the survivors who hide from you have perished. ²¹Do not be terrified by them, for the LORD your God, who is among you, *ᵍ* is a great and awesome God. *ʰ* ²²The LORD your God will drive out those nations before you, little by little. *ⁱ* You will not be allowed to eliminate them all at once, or the wild animals will multiply around you. ²³But the LORD your God will deliver them over to you, throwing them into great confusion until they are destroyed. *ʲ* ²⁴He will give their kings *ᵏ* into your hand, *ˡ* and you will wipe out their names from under heaven. No one will be able to stand up against you; *ᵐ* you will destroy them. *ⁿ* ²⁵The images of their gods you are to burn *ᵒ* in the fire. Do not covet *ᵖ* the silver and gold on them, and do not take it for yourselves, or you will be ensnared *q* by it, for it is detestable *ʳ* to the LORD your God. ²⁶Do not bring a detestable thing into your house or you, like it, will be set apart for destruction. *ˢ* Regard it as vile and utterly detest it, for it is set apart for destruction.

DO NOT FORGET THE LORD

8 Be careful to follow every command I am giving you today, so that you may live *ᵗ* and increase and may enter and possess the land the LORD promised on oath to your ancestors. *ᵘ* ²Remember how the LORD your God led *ᵛ* you all the way in the wilderness these forty years, to humble and test *ʷ* you in order to know what was in your heart, whether or not you would keep his commands. ³He humbled *ˣ* you, causing you to hunger and then feeding you with manna, *ʸ* which neither you nor your ancestors had known, to teach *ᶻ* you that people do not live on bread *ᵃ* alone but on every word that comes from the mouth *ᵇ* of the LORD. *ᶜ* ⁴Your clothes did not wear out and your feet did not swell during these forty years. *ᵈ* ⁵Know then in your heart that as a man disciplines his son, so the LORD your God disciplines you. *ᵉ*

⁶Observe the commands of the LORD your God, walking in obedience to him *ᶠ* and revering him. *ᵍ* ⁷For the LORD your God is bringing you into a good land *ʰ*—a land with streams and pools of water, with springs flowing in the valleys and hills; *ⁱ* ⁸a land with wheat and barley, *ʲ* vines *ᵏ* and fig trees, *ˡ* pomegranates, olive oil and honey; *ᵐ* ⁹a land where bread *ⁿ* will not be scarce and you will lack nothing; *ᵒ* a land where the rocks are iron and you can dig copper out of the hills. *ᵖ*

¹⁰When you have eaten and are satisfied, *q* praise the LORD your God for the good land he has given you. ¹¹Be careful that you do not forget *ʳ* the LORD your God, failing to observe his commands, his laws and his decrees that I am giving you this day. ¹²Otherwise, when you eat and are satisfied, when you build fine houses and settle down, *ˢ* ¹³and when your herds and flocks grow large and your silver and gold increase and all you have is multiplied, ¹⁴then your heart will become proud and you will forget *ᵗ* the LORD your God, who brought you out of Egypt, out of the land of slavery. ¹⁵He led you through the vast and dreadful wilderness, *ᵘ* that thirsty and waterless land, with its venomous snakes *ᵛ* and scorpions. He brought you water out of hard rock. *ʷ* ¹⁶He gave you manna *ˣ* to eat in the wilderness, something your ancestors had never known, *ʸ* to humble and test *ᶻ* you so that in the end it might go well with you. ¹⁷You may say to yourself, *ᵃ* "My power and the strength

8:15 Isa 14:29; 30:6 *ʷ* Ex 17:6; Dt 32:13; Job 28:9; Ps 78:15; 114:8 **8:16** *ˣ* S Ex 16:14 *ʸ* Ex 16:15 *ᶻ* S Ge 22:1 **8:17** *ᵃ* Dt 9:4,7,24; 31:27

7:17 *ᵃ* Nu 33:53
7:18 *ᵇ* S Nu 14:9; S Dt 1:21,29
ᶜ Ps 105:5; 119:52
7:19 *ᵈ* Ps 136:12
ᵉ Dt 4:34
7:20 *ᶠ* S Ex 23:28
7:21 *ᵍ* S Ge 17:7; Jos 3:10 *ʰ* Dt 10:17; Ne 1:5; 9:32; Ps 47:2; 66:3; 68:35; Isa 9:6; Da 9:4
7:22 *ⁱ* Ex 23:28-30
7:23 *ʲ* Ex 23:27; Jos 10:10
7:24 *ᵏ* Jos 10:24; Ps 110:5 *ˡ* S ver 16 *ᵐ* S Ex 23:31; Dt 11:25; Jos 1:5; 10:8; 23:9 *ⁿ* Jos 21:44
7:25 *ᵒ* S Ex 4:14; S 32:20 *ᵖ* Ex 20:17; Jos 7:21 *q* S ver 16 *ʳ* Dt 17:1
7:26 *ˢ* Lev 27:28-29
8:1 *ᵗ* Dt 4:1
ᵘ S Ex 19:5; Job 36:11; Ps 16:11; Eze 20:19
8:2 *ᵛ* Dt 29:5; Ps 136:16; Am 2:10
ʷ S Ge 22:1
8:3 *ˣ* 2Ch 36:12; Ps 44:9; Pr 18:12; Isa 2:11; Jer 44:10 *ʸ* S Ex 16:4 *ᶻ* 1Ki 8:36; Ps 25:5; 94:12; 119:171 *ᵃ* ver 9; S Ge 3:19; Job 23:12; Ps 104:15; Pr 28:21; Isa 51:14; Jer 42:14 *ᵇ* Job 22:22; Ps 119:13; 138:4 *ᶜ* S Ex 16:2-3; Mt 4:4; Lk 4:4
8:4 *ᵈ* Dt 29:5; Ne 9:21
8:5 *ᵉ* Dt 4:36; 2Sa 7:14; Job 5:17; 33:19; Pr 3:11-12; Heb 12:5-11; Rev 3:19
8:6 *ᶠ* S Ex 33:13; 1Ki 3:14; Ps 81:13; 95:10 *ᵍ* Dt 5:33
8:7 *ʰ* Ps 106:24; Jer 3:19; Eze 20:6 *ⁱ* Dt 11:9-12; Jer 2:7
8:8 *ʲ* S Ex 9:31 *ᵏ* S Ge 49:11 *ˡ* S Nu 13:23; S 1Ki 4:25 *ᵐ* Dt 32:13; Ps 81:16
8:9 *ⁿ* S ver 3 *ᵒ* Jdg 18:10 *ᵖ* Job 28:2
8:10 *q* Dt 6:10-12
8:11 *ʳ* Dt 4:9
8:12 *ˢ* Pr 30:9; Hos 13:6
8:14 *ᵗ* ver 11; Ps 78:7; 106:21
8:15 *ᵘ* S Dt 1:19; S 32:10 *ᵛ* Nu 21:6;

7:18 *remember.* See note on 4:10.
7:20 *hornet.* See note on Ex 23:28.
7:22 *God will drive out.* See note on 3:22. *wild animals will multiply.* The rapid expulsion of the Canaanites would leave much of the land deserted and therefore open to wild animals.
7:25–26 Cf. the story of Achan (Jos 6:17–19; 7:1,20–25).
7:26 *set apart for destruction.* See note on 2:34.
8:2 *Remember.* See note on 4:10. *test.* See v. 16; see also note on Ge 22:1.

A **8:3** *manna.* See v. 16; see also note on Nu 11:7. *people do not live on bread alone.* See note on 6:13; quoted by Jesus in response to the devil's temptation (see Mt 4:4; Lk 4:4). Bread sustains but does not guarantee life, which is God's gift to those who trust in and live by his word: his commands and promises (see vv. 1,18). God's "discipline" (v. 5) of his people by bringing them through the wilderness taught them this fundamental truth. There they were humbled (v. 16; cf. v. 14) by being

cast on the Lord in total dependence.
8:7–9 A concise description of the rich and fertile land of promise that the Israelites were about to enter and possess (see 11:8–12). See map No. 2 at the end of this study Bible.

B **8:9** *iron … copper.* The mountains of southern Lebanon and the regions east of the Sea of Galilee and south of the Dead Sea contain iron. Both copper and iron were plentiful in the part of the Arabah south of the Dead Sea. Some of the copper mines date to the time of Solomon and earlier. Zarethan, located in the Jordan Valley north of the Dead Sea, was a center for bronze works in Solomon's time (1Ki 7:45–46). Some bronze objects from this site precede the Solomonic period, and today there are copper works at Timnah in the Negev.
8:11 *not forget.* See note on 4:10; cf. 8:14,19.
8:15 *water out of hard rock.* See Ex 17:6 and note.
8:16 *test.* See v. 2; see also note on Ge 22:1.
8:17–18 See Zec 4:6 and note.

8:17 *b* Jdg 7:2;
Ps 44:3; Isa 10:13
8:18 *c* Ge 26:13;
Dt 26:10; 28:4;
1Sa 2:7; Ps 25:13;
112:3; Pr 8:18; 10:22;
Ecc 9:11; Hos 2:8
8:19 *d* Dt 6:14;
Ps 16:4; Jer 7:6; 13:10;
25:6 *e* Dt 4:26; 30:18
8:20 *f* 2Ki 21:2;
Ps 10:16 *g* Eze 5:5-17
9:1 *h* S Nu 35:10
i Dt 4:38 *j* S Nu 13:28
k S Ge 11:4
9:2 *l* Nu 13:22;
Jos 11:22
9:3 *m* Dt 31:3;
Jos 3:11 *n* S Ex 15:7;
S 19:18; Heb 12:29
o S Ex 23:31
9:4 *p* S Dt 8:17
q 2Ki 16:3; 17:8; 21:2;
Ezr 9:11 *r* S Ex 23:24;
S Lev 18:21, 24-30;
Dt 18:9-14
9:5 *s* S Eph 2:9
t Dt 18:9 *u* S Lev 18:25
v Dt 4:38; 11:23
w S Ge 12:7
x Eze 36:32
9:6 *y* S Ex 32:9;
Ac 7:51
9:7 *z* S Nu 11:33
a S Ex 23:21
b S Ex 14:11
9:8 *c* Nu 16:46;
1Sa 28:18; Job 20:28;
Ps 2:12; 7:11; 69:24;
110:5; Isa 9:19;
Eze 20:13 *d* Ex 32:7-
10; Ezr 9:14;
Ps 106:19
9:9 *e* S Dt 4:13
f S Ge 7:4
g S Ex 24:12
9:10 *h* S Ex 31:18
i Dt 10:4; Heb 8:10
9:11 *j* S Ge 7:4
k S Ex 24:12
9:12 *l* S Dt 4:16
m Jdg 2:17
9:13 *n* ver 6;
Dt 10:16
9:14 *o* Ex 32:10
p S Nu 14:12 *q* Jer 7:16
9:15 *r* S Ex 32:15
9:16 *s* S Ex 32:4
9:18 *t* S Ex 34:28
u ver 9 *v* S Ex 32:31

of my hands *b* have produced this wealth for me." [18]But remember the LORD your God, for it is he who gives you the ability to produce wealth, *c* and so confirms his covenant, which he swore to your ancestors, as it is today.

[19]If you ever forget the LORD your God and follow other gods *d* and worship and bow down to them, I testify against you today that you will surely be destroyed. *e* [20]Like the nations *f* the LORD destroyed before you, so you will be destroyed for not obeying the LORD your God. *g*

NOT BECAUSE OF ISRAEL'S RIGHTEOUSNESS

9 Hear, Israel: You are now about to cross the Jordan *h* to go in and dispossess nations greater and stronger than you, *i* with large cities *j* that have walls up to the sky. *k* [2]The people are strong and tall—Anakites! You know about them and have heard it said: "Who can stand up against the Anakites?" *l* [3]But be assured today that the LORD your God is the one who goes across ahead of you *m* like a devouring fire. *n* He will destroy them; he will subdue them before you. And you will drive them out and annihilate them quickly, *o* as the LORD has promised you.

[4]After the LORD your God has driven them out before you, do not say to yourself, *p* "The LORD has brought me here to take possession of this land because of my righteousness." No, it is on account of the wickedness *q* of these nations *r* that the LORD is going to drive them out before you. [5]It is not because of your righteousness or your integrity *s* that you are going in to take possession of their land; but on account of the wickedness *t* of these nations, *u* the LORD your God will drive them out *v* before you, to accomplish what he swore *w* to your fathers, to Abraham, Isaac and Jacob. *x* [6]Understand, then, that it is not because of your righteousness that the LORD your God is giving you this good land to possess, for you are a stiff-necked people. *y*

THE GOLDEN CALF

[7]Remember this and never forget how you aroused the anger *z* of the LORD your God in the wilderness. From the day you left Egypt until you arrived here, you have been rebellious *a* against the LORD. *b* [8]At Horeb you aroused the LORD's wrath *c* so that he was angry enough to destroy you. *d* [9]When I went up on the mountain to receive the tablets of stone, the tablets of the covenant *e* that the LORD had made with you, I stayed on the mountain forty days *f* and forty nights; I ate no bread and drank no water. *g* [10]The LORD gave me two stone tablets inscribed by the finger of God. *h* On them were all the commandments the LORD proclaimed to you on the mountain out of the fire, on the day of the assembly. *i*

[11]At the end of the forty days and forty nights, *j* the LORD gave me the two stone tablets, *k* the tablets of the covenant. [12]Then the LORD told me, "Go down from here at once, because your people whom you brought out of Egypt have become corrupt. *l* They have turned away quickly *m* from what I commanded them and have made an idol for themselves."

[13]And the LORD said to me, "I have seen this people *n*, and they are a stiff-necked people indeed! [14]Let me alone, *o* so that I may destroy them and blot out *p* their name from under heaven. *q* And I will make you into a nation stronger and more numerous than they."

[15]So I turned and went down from the mountain while it was ablaze with fire. And the two tablets of the covenant were in my hands. *r* [16]When I looked, I saw that you had sinned against the LORD your God; you had made for yourselves an idol cast in the shape of a calf. *s* You had turned aside quickly from the way that the LORD had commanded you. [17]So I took the two tablets and threw them out of my hands, breaking them to pieces before your eyes. [18]Then once again I fell *t* prostrate before the LORD for forty days and forty nights; I ate no bread and drank no water, *u* because of all the sin you had committed, *v* doing what was evil in the LORD's sight and so arousing his anger. [19]I feared the anger and wrath of the

---

8:18 *remember.* See note on 4:10.
9:1 *Hear, Israel.* See note on 4:1.
9:2 *Anakites.* See note on 1:28.
9:3 *devouring fire.* See 4:24 and note. *he will subdue them before you ... you will drive them out.* The Lord not only went ahead of the Israelites but also exerted his power alongside them and through them to assure victory. The Lord's involvement, together with that of the Israelite armies, continues throughout Deuteronomy and the conquest narratives.
9:4 *because of my righteousness.* See note on 7:8. *wickedness of these nations.* See on Ge 15:16.
9:6,13 *stiff-necked.* See 10:16; 31:27; see also note on Ex 32:9.

9:7,27 *Remember.* See note on 4:10.
9:9 *tablets of the covenant.* See notes on Ex 20:1; 34:28.
9:10 *two stone tablets ... finger of God.* See Ex 31:18 and note; see also note on Ex 8:19.
9:11–21 See Ex 31:18—32:20 and notes.
9:12–13 *your people ... this people.* See note on Ex 17:4.

B **9:14** *blot out their name.* The Phoenician cognate of the Hebrew for this phrase appears in a ninth-century B.C. inscription on a gateway: "If ... a man ... blots out the name of Azitawadda from this gate ... may (the gods) wipe out ... that man!"

LORD, for he was angry enough with you to destroy you. *w* But again the LORD listened to me. *x* 20And the LORD was angry enough with Aaron to destroy him, but at that time I prayed for Aaron too. 21Also I took that sinful thing of yours, the calf you had made, and burned it in the fire. Then I crushed it and ground it to powder as fine as dust *y* and threw the dust into a stream that flowed down the mountain. *z*

22You also made the LORD angry *a* at Taberah, *b* at Massah *c* and at Kibroth Hattaavah. *d*

23And when the LORD sent you out from Kadesh Barnea, *e* he said, "Go up and take possession *f* of the land I have given you." But you rebelled *g* against the command of the LORD your God. You did not trust *h* him or obey him. 24You have been rebellious against the LORD ever since I have known you. *i*

25I lay prostrate before the LORD those forty days and forty nights *j* because the LORD had said he would destroy you. *k* 26I prayed to the LORD and said, "Sovereign LORD, do not destroy your people, *l* your own inheritance *m* that you redeemed *n* by your great power and brought out of Egypt with a mighty hand. *o* 27Remember your servants Abraham, Isaac and Jacob. Overlook the stubbornness *p* of this people, their wickedness and their sin. 28Otherwise, the country *q* from which you brought us will say, 'Because the LORD was not able to take them into the land he had promised them, and because he hated them, *r* he brought them out to put them to death in the wilderness.' *s* 29But they are your people, *t* your inheritance *u* that you brought out by your great power and your outstretched arm. *v*"

TABLETS LIKE THE FIRST ONES

10 At that time the LORD said to me, "Chisel out two stone tablets *w* like the first ones and come up to me on the mountain. Also make a wooden ark. *a* 2I will write on the tablets the words that were on the first tablets, which you broke. Then you are to put them in the ark." *x*

3So I made the ark out of acacia wood *y* and chiseled *z* out two stone tablets like the first ones, and I went up on the mountain with the two tablets in my hands. 4The LORD wrote on these tablets what he had written before, the Ten Commandments *a* he had proclaimed *b* to you on the mountain, out of the fire, on the day of the assembly. *c* And the LORD gave them to me. 5Then I came back down the mountain *d* and put the tablets in the ark *e* I had made, *f* as the LORD commanded me, and they are there now. *g*

6(The Israelites traveled from the wells of Bene Jaakan to Moserah. *h* There Aaron died *i* and was buried, and Eleazar *j* his son succeeded him as priest. *k* 7From there they traveled to Gudgodah and on to Jotbathah, a land with streams of water. *l* 8At that time the LORD set apart the tribe of Levi *m* to carry the ark of the covenant *n* of the LORD, to stand before the LORD to minister *o* and to pronounce blessings *p* in his name, as they still do today. *q* 9That is why the Levites have no share or inheritance among their fellow Israelites; the LORD is their inheritance, *r* as the LORD your God told them.)

10Now I had stayed on the mountain forty days and nights, as I did the first time, and the LORD listened to me at this time also. It was not his will to destroy you. *s* 11"Go," the LORD said to me, "and lead the people on their way, so that they may enter and possess the land I swore to their ancestors to give them."

FEAR THE LORD

12And now, Israel, what does the LORD your God ask of you *t* but to fear *u* the LORD your God, to walk *v* in obedience to him, to love him, *w* to serve the LORD *x* your God with all your heart *y* and with all your soul, *z* 13and to observe the LORD's commands *a* and decrees that I am giving you today for your own good? *b*

---

a 1 That is, a chest

9:19 *w* S Ex 32:14;
Heb 12:21^k *x* ver 26;
Ex 34:10; S Nu 11:2;
1Sa 7:9; Jer 15:1
9:21 *y* Ps 18:42;
Isa 29:5; 40:15
z Ex 32:20; Isa 2:18;
Mic 1:7
9:22 *a* S Nu 1:53
b Nu 11:3 *c* S Ex 17:7
d Nu 11:34
9:23 *e* S Dt 1:2
f Dt 1:21 *g* S Nu 14:9
h S Dt 1:32; Ps 106:24
9:24 *i* S Dt 8:17
9:25 *j* S Ge 7:4
k ver 18; S Ex 33:17
9:26 *l* S Ex 33:13
m S Ex 34:9
n S Ex 6:6; Dt 15:15;
2Sa 7:23; Ps 78:35
o S ver 19; S Ex 32:11
9:27 *p* ver 6;
S Ex 32:9
9:28 *q* Dt 32:27
r S Dt 1:27
s S Ex 32:12; Jos 7:9
9:29 *t* S Ex 33:13
u S Ex 34:9; Dt 32:9
v Dt 4:34; Ne 1:10;
Jer 27:5; 32:17
10:1 *w* Ex 34:1-2
10:2 *x* Ex 25:16,21;
2Ch 5:10; 6:11
10:3 *y* Ex 37:1-9
z Ex 34:4
10:4 *a* S Ex 24:12;
S 34:28 *b* Ex 20:1
c S Dt 9:10
10:5 *d* S Ex 19:11
e S Ex 25:10;
S 1Sa 3:3 *f* S Ex 25:21
g 1Ki 8:9
10:6 *h* Nu 33:30
i S Nu 27:13
j S Ex 6:23
k S Nu 20:25-28
10:7 *l* Nu 33:32-34;
Ps 42:1; SS 5:12;
Isa 32:2
10:8 *m* S Nu 3:6
n S Nu 10:33
o S Nu 16:9
p S Ge 48:20
q 1Ch 23:26
10:9 *r* S Nu 18:20
10:10 *s* S Ex 33:17
10:12 *t* Mic 6:8
u S Ex 20:20 *v* 1Ki 2:3;
3:3; 9:4 *w* Dt 5:33;
6:13; Mt 22:37; 1Ti 1:5
x Dt 11:13; 28:47;
Ps 100:2 *y* S Dt 6:5;
Ps 119:2 *z* S Dt 5:32
10:13 *a* S Dt 4:2
b Dt 5:33; 6:24

C A **9:19** *But again the LORD listened to me.* Moses' intercessory prayer on this occasion (vv. 26–29) ranks among the great prayers for Israel's national survival (see Ex 32:11–13 and notes; see also Ezr 9:6–15; Ne 9:5–38; Da 9:4–19).

9:22 *Taberah.* See Nu 11:3 and TNIV text note. *Massah.* See 6:16; 33:8; see also note on Ex 17:7. *Kibroth Hattaavah.* See Nu 11:34 and TNIV text note.

9:23 *Kadesh Barnea.* See notes on Ge 14:7; Nu 20:1.

9:27 *Overlook.* See note on Ac 17:30.

10:1–3 *ark.* The Hebrew word means "chest" or "box" (see TNIV text note on v.1; see also note on Ex 25:10).

10:1 *two stone tablets.* See note on Ex 31:18.

10:2 *put them in the ark.* See notes on Ex 16:34; 25:16.

10:3 The order of events here is different from that in Exodus 34–37 (see Introduction to Deuteronomy: Structure and Outline).

10:6–9 A historical parenthesis, apparently stemming from Moses' prayer for Aaron and the Israelites (9:26–29) and the reference to the ark (vv. 1–5).

10:8 *carry the ark.* See note on Nu 1:50. *to minister... to pronounce blessings.* See note on 21:5.

10:9 See 12:12 and note.

10:12 *what does the LORD... ask of you...?* See Mic 6:8 and note. *fear the LORD.* See note on Ge 20:11. *love him.* See notes on 4:29,37; 6:5.

10:13 *for your own good.* See 6:24; see also note on 6:2.

10:14 *c* Ps 148:4;
Isa 19:1; Hab 3:8
d Ne 9:6; Job 35:5;
Ps 8:3; 89:11; 104:3
e Dt 33:26 *f* Ps 115:16
g 1Ki 8:27 *h* Ex 19:5;
Ps 24:1; Ac 17:24
10:15 *i* S Dt 4:37
j Ps 105:6; 135:4
k S Nu 14:8; Ro 11:28;
1Pe 2:9
10:16 *l* S Ge 17:11
m S Lev 26:41;
Dt 30:6; Jer 32:39
n S Ex 32:9; S Dt 9:13
10:17 *o* Jos 22:22;
Ps 135:5; 136:2;
Da 2:47; 11:36
p Ps 136:3; S 1Ti 6:15
q S Dt 7:21 *f* Dt 1:17;
Mal 2:9 *s* Ex 23:8;
S Lev 19:16
10:18 *t* Ex 22:21,22-
24; 23:9; Lev 19:33;
Dt 27:19; Job 29:13;
Ps 94:6; Isa 10:2;
Jer 49:11 *u* S Nu 10:32
10:19 *v* Dt 7:12
w S Ex 22:21;
S Dt 24:19
x S Lev 19:34;
Eze 47:22-23
10:20 *y* Mt 4:10
z Dt 11:22; 13:4;
30:20; Jos 23:8;
Ru 1:14; 2Ki 18:6;
Ps 119:31; Isa 38:3
a S Ex 20:7
10:21 *b* S Ex 15:2
c 1Sa 12:24; Ps 126:2
d 2Sa 7:23
10:22 *e* S Ge 34:30;
S 46:26; Ac 7:14
f S Ge 12:2;
S Nu 10:36
11:1 *g* S Dt 6:5
h S Lev 8:35
11:2 *i* Dt 31:13;
Ps 78:6 *j* S Dt 5:24
k S Dt 3:24 *l* Ps 136:12
11:3 *m* Ex 7:8-21
11:4 *n* S Ex 15:1
o S Ex 14:27;
S Nu 21:4
11:6 *p* Nu 16:1-35;
Ps 106:16-18
q Isa 24:19
11:7 *f* Dt 5:3
11:8 *s* Ezr 9:10
t Dt 31:6-7,23; Jos 1:7
11:9 *u* S Dt 5:16
v Dt 9:5 *w* S Ex 3:8
11:10 *x* Isa 11:15;
37:25
11:11 *y* Eze 36:4
z Dt 8:7; Ne 9:25
11:12 *a* 1Ki 8:29; 9:3
11:13 *b* S Dt 6:17
c S Dt 10:12 *d* Dt 4:29;
Jer 17:24
11:14 *e* S Lev 26:4;

[14] To the LORD your God belong the heavens, *cde* even the highest heavens, *fg* the earth and everything in it. *h* [15] Yet the LORD set his affection on your ancestors and loved *i* them, and he chose you, *j* their descendants, above all the nations—as it is today. *k* [16] Circumcise *l* your hearts, *m* therefore, and do not be stiff-necked *n* any longer. [17] For the LORD your God is God of gods *o* and Lord of lords, *p* the great God, mighty and awesome, *q* who shows no partiality *r* and accepts no bribes. *s* [18] He defends the cause of the fatherless and the widow, *t* and loves the foreigners residing among you, giving them food and clothing. *u* [19] And you are to love *v* those who are foreigners, *w* for you yourselves were foreigners in Egypt. *x* [20] Fear the LORD your God and serve him. *y* Hold fast *z* to him and take your oaths in his name. *a* [21] He is the one you praise; *b* he is your God, who performed for you those great *c* and awesome wonders *d* you saw with your own eyes. [22] Your ancestors who went down into Egypt were seventy in all, *e* and now the LORD your God has made you as numerous as the stars in the sky. *f*

LOVE AND OBEY THE LORD

11 Love *g* the LORD your God and keep his requirements, his decrees, his laws and his commands always. *h* [2] Remember today that your children *i* were not the ones who saw and experienced the discipline of the LORD your God: *j* his majesty, *k* his mighty hand, his outstretched arm; *l* [3] the signs he performed and the things he did in the heart of Egypt, both to Pharaoh king of Egypt and to his whole country; *m* [4] what he did to the Egyptian army, to its horses and chariots, *n* how he overwhelmed them with the waters of the Red Sea *a o* as they were pursuing you, and how the LORD brought lasting ruin on them. [5] It was not your children who saw what he did for you in the wilderness until you arrived at this place, [6] and what he did *p* to Dathan and Abiram, sons of Eliab the Reubenite, when the earth opened *q* its mouth right in the middle of all Israel and swallowed them up with their households, their tents and every living thing that belonged to them. [7] But it was your own eyes that saw all these great things the LORD has done. *r*

[8] Observe therefore all the commands *s* I am giving you today, so that you may have the strength to go in and take over the land that you are crossing the Jordan to possess, *t* [9] and so that you may live long *u* in the land the LORD swore *v* to your ancestors to give to them and their descendants, a land flowing with milk and honey. *w* [10] The land you are entering to take over is not like the land of Egypt, *x* from which you have come, where you planted your seed and irrigated it by foot as in a vegetable garden. [11] But the land you are crossing the Jordan to take possession of is a land of mountains and valleys *y* that drinks rain from heaven. *z* [12] It is a land the LORD your God cares for; the eyes *a* of the LORD your God are continually on it from the beginning of the year to its end.

[13] So if you faithfully obey *b* the commands I am giving you today—to love *c* the LORD your God and to serve him with all your heart and with all your soul *d*— [14] then I will send rain *e* on your land in its season, both autumn and spring rains, *f* so that you may gather in your grain, new wine and olive oil. [15] I will provide grass *g* in the fields for your cattle, and you will eat and be satisfied. *h*

[16] Be careful, or you will be enticed to turn away and worship other gods and bow down to them. *i* [17] Then the LORD's anger *j* will burn against you, and he will shut *k* the heavens so that it will not rain and the ground will yield no produce, *l* and you will soon perish *m*

---

a 4 Or *the Sea of Reeds*

11:14 Ac 14:17 *f* Ps 147:8; Jer 3:3; 5:24; Joel 2:23; Jas 5:7 **11:15** *g* Ps 104:14 *h* S Lev 26:5 **11:16** *i* Dt 4:19; 8:19; 29:18; Job 31:9,27
11:17 *j* Dt 6:15; 9:19 *k* 1Ki 17:1; 2Ch 6:26; 7:13 *l* S Lev 26:20 *m* Dt 4:26; 28:12,24

10:15 *set his affection...loved.* See 7:7–8 and note on 7:8. *ancestors.* The patriarchs (cf. v. 22).

10:16 *Circumcise your hearts.* See note on Ge 17:10. *stiff-necked.* See 9:6,13; 31:27; see also note on Ex 32:9.

10:20 *Hold fast.* As a man is "united" to his wife (Ge 2:24), and as Ruth "clung" to Naomi (Ru 1:14). See 4:4; 11:22; 13:4; 30:20.

10:21 *He is the one you praise.* See Ps 22:3 and note.

10:22 *seventy.* See notes on Ge 10:2; 46:26–27; see also Ex 1:5. *as the stars in the sky.* See note on 1:10.

11:1 *Love.* See note on 6:5. *keep.* Love and obedience are frequently linked in Scripture (e.g., 6:5–6; Jn 14:15; 1Jn 5:3; see note on Ex 20:2).

11:2–7 Moses continually emphasizes the involvement of his listeners in the Lord's works of providence and deliverance. In 5:3 it was not the patriarchs (but see TNIV text note there: "not only...parents") but they themselves with whom the covenant

was made at Sinai. Here it is not their children but they themselves who saw God's great deeds.

11:2 *Remember.* See note on 4:10.

11:8–12 See note on 8:7–9.

11:9 *live long.* See note on 6:2.

11:10 *irrigated it by foot.* Irrigation channels dug by foot and/or fed by devices powered by foot brought the water of the Nile to the gardens in Egypt, in contrast to the rains that watered Canaan (v. 11).

11:13 See note on 4:29.

11:14 *autumn and spring rains.* The rainy season in Israel begins in October and ends in April.

11:17 *shut the heavens.* The all-important seasonal rains (see v. 14) were controlled by the Lord—not by Baal, as the inhabitants of Canaan thought (cf. Jer 14:22; Hos 2:8 and notes).

from the good land the LORD is giving you. [18]Fix these words of mine in your hearts and minds; tie them as symbols on your hands and bind them on your foreheads. [n] [19]Teach them to your children, [o] talking about them when you sit at home and when you walk along the road, when you lie down and when you get up. [p] [20]Write them on the doorframes of your houses and on your gates, [q] [21]so that your days and the days of your children may be many [r] in the land the LORD swore to give your ancestors, as many as the days that the heavens are above the earth. [s]

[22]If you carefully observe [t] all these commands I am giving you to follow—to love [u] the LORD your God, to walk in obedience to him and to hold fast [v] to him— [23]then the LORD will drive out [w] all these nations [x] before you, and you will dispossess nations larger and stronger than you. [y] [24]Every place where you set your foot will be yours: [z] Your territory will extend from the desert to Lebanon, and from the Euphrates River [a] to the Mediterranean Sea. [25]No one will be able to stand against you. The LORD your God, as he promised you, will put the terror [b] and fear of you on the whole land, wherever you go. [c]

[26]See, I am setting before you today a blessing [d] and a curse [e]— [27]the blessing [f] if you obey the commands of the LORD your God that I am giving you today; [28]the curse if you disobey [g] the commands of the LORD your God and turn from the way that I command you today by following other gods, [h] which you have not known. [29]When the LORD your God has brought you into the land you are entering to possess, you are to proclaim on Mount Gerizim [i] the blessings, and on Mount Ebal [j] the curses. [k] [30]As you know, these mountains are across the Jordan, westward, toward the setting sun, near the great trees of Moreh, [l] in the territory of those Canaanites living in the Arabah in the vicinity of Gilgal. [m] [31]You are about to cross the Jordan to enter and take possession [n] of the land the LORD your God is giving [o] you. When you have taken it over and are living there, [32]be sure that you obey all the decrees and laws I am setting before you today.

THE ONE PLACE OF WORSHIP

12 These are the decrees [p] and laws you must be careful to follow in the land that the LORD, the God of your ancestors, has given you to possess—as long as you live in the land. [q] [2]Destroy completely all the places on the high mountains, [r] on the hills and under every spreading tree, [s] where the nations you are dispossessing worship their gods. [3]Break down their altars, smash [t] their sacred stones and burn [u] their Asherah [v] poles in the fire; cut down the idols of their gods and wipe out their names [w] from those places.

[4]You must not worship the LORD your God in their way. [x] [5]But you are to seek the place the LORD your God will choose from among all your tribes to put his Name [y] there for his dwelling. [z] To that place you must go; [6]there bring your burnt offerings and sacrifices, your tithes [a] and special gifts, what you have vowed [b] to give and your freewill offerings, and the firstborn of your herds and flocks. [c] [7]There, in the presence [d] of the LORD your God, you and your families shall eat and shall rejoice [e] in everything you have put your hand to, because the LORD your God has blessed you.

[8]You are not to do as we do here today, everyone doing as they see fit, [f] [9]since you have

11:18 [n] S Ex 13:9; Dt 6:6-8
11:19 [o] S Ex 12:26; Dt 6:7; Ps 145:4; Isa 38:19; Jer 32:39
[p] Dt 4:9-10
11:20 [q] Dt 6:9
11:21 [r] Job 5:26; Pr 3:2; 4:10; 9:11
[s] Ps 72:5
11:22 [t] S Dt 6:17
[u] S Dt 6:5 [v] S Dt 10:20
11:23 [w] S Dt 9:5
[x] S Ex 23:28 [y] Dt 9:1
11:24 [z] Ge 15:18; Dt 1:36; 12:20; 19:8; Jos 1:3; 14:9
[a] S Ge 2:14
11:25 [b] S Dt 2:25
[c] Ex 23:27; Dt 7:24
11:26 [d] Ps 24:5
[e] Lev 26:14-17; Dt 27:13-26; 30:1,15, 19; La 2:17; Da 9:11; Hag 1:11; Mal 2:2; 3:9; 4:6
11:27 [f] Dt 28:1-14; Ps 24:5
11:28 [g] 2Ch 24:20; Jer 42:13; 44:16
[h] S Dt 4:28; 13:6,13; 29:26; 1Sa 26:19
11:29 [i] Jdg 9:7
[j] Dt 27:4; Jos 8:30
[k] Dt 27:12-13; Jos 8:33; Jn 4:20
11:30 [l] S Ge 12:6
[m] Jos 4:19; 5:9; 9:6; 10:6; 14:6; 15:7; Jdg 2:1; 2Ki 2:1; Mic 6:5
11:31 [n] S Nu 33:53
[o] Dt 12:10; Jos 11:23
12:1 [p] Ps 119:5
[q] Dt 4:9-10; 6:15; 1Ki 8:40; Eze 20:19
12:2 [r] S Nu 21:28
[s] 1Ki 14:23; 2Ki 17:10; Isa 57:5; Jer 2:20; 3:6, 13
12:3 [t] 2Ki 11:18
[u] S Dt 7:5
[v] Ex 34:13; 1Ki 14:15, 23 [w] S Ex 23:13
12:4 [x] ver 30; 2Ki 17:15; Jer 10:2
12:5 [y] S Ex 20:24; S 2Sa 7:13 [z] ver 11,13; Dt 14:23; 15:20; 16:2, 11; 18:6; 26:2; 1Sa 2:29; 1Ki 5:5; 8:16; 9:3; 2Ch 2:4; 6:6; 7:12,16; Ezr 6:12; 7:15; Ps 26:8; 78:68; Zec 2:12
12:6 [a] S Lev 27:30

12:6 [b] S Ge 28:20 [c] Jos 22:27; Isa 66:20 **12:7** [d] S Ex 18:12 [e] S Lev 23:40; Ecc 3:12-13; 5:18-20; S Isa 62:9 **12:8** [f] Jdg 17:6; 21:25

11:18–20 See note on 6:8–9.
11:21 *as many as the days ... earth.* That is, as long as the present creation endures.
11:22 *hold fast.* See note on 10:20.
11:24 *Every place where you set your foot.* See 1:7 and note; Jos 1:3.
11:26–30 The blessings and curses proclaimed on Mount Gerizim and Mount Ebal are detailed in chs. 27–28.
11:28 *known.* Experienced or acknowledged (see 13:2,6,13; 28:64; 29:26; 32:17; see also note on Ex 6:3).
11:30 *great trees of Moreh.* See note on Ge 12:6. *Arabah.* See note on 1:1. The Canaanites who lived there controlled the territory around Gerizim and Ebal. *Gilgal.* See Jos 4:19 and note.
12:2 *under every spreading tree.* See note on 2Ki 16:4.
12:3 *altars ... sacred stones ... Asherah poles.* See note on 7:5.
[A] **12:4** *in their way.* The rituals and accessories of idolatrous worship were not to be used to worship the Lord, the one true God (cf. vv. 29–31). Everything that does not honor him must be eliminated from his people's worship (see Mic 5:10–14 and note).

12:5 *the place the LORD ... will choose ... to put his Name.* The tabernacle, the Lord's dwelling place during the desert journey, will be located in the city in Canaan where the Lord would choose to dwell. Moses stresses the importance of centralizing the place of worship as he prepares the people for settlement in the promised land, where the Canaanites had established many places of worship. See vv. 11,14,18,21,26; 14:23–24; 16:2,6,11; 26:2. *his Name.* Since in the ancient Semitic world "name" often stood for the essence of the thing named, God's "Name" is equivalent to "his presence" (see notes on Ex 3:13–15; 23:21; 2Sa 7:13; 1Ki 5:5).
12:6 See v. 11 and chart, p. 155.
[A] **12:7** *rejoice in everything you have put your hand to.* The Lord wants his people to enjoy the fruit of their labor, because it is the result of his blessing (see v. 18; cf. Ecc 2:24–25 and note; 5:18–20).
12:8 *as we do here today.* The Israelites were not able to follow all the procedures of the sacrificial system during the wilderness wandering and conquest periods. Moses was giving directives for their worship and way of life when settled in the land (vv. 10–14). *as they see fit.* See note on Jdg 17:6.

12:9 *g* S Ex 33:14;
Dt 3:20; Ps 95:11;
Mic 2:10 *h* Dt 4:21
12:10 *i* S Dt 11:31
j S Ex 33:14
12:11 *k* S ver 5
l S Lev 1:3; Jos 22:23
12:12 *m* ver 7
n Dt 26:11-13
o S Nu 18:20
12:13 *p* S ver 5
12:14 *q* ver 11
12:15 *r* ver 22;
Dt 14:5; 15:22
12:16 *s* S Ge 9:4;
Ac 15:20 *t* ver 23-24;
S Ge 35:14; 1Ch 11:18;
Jer 7:18 *u* S Lev 17:13;
S Dt 15:23; Jn 19:34
12:17 *v* S Lev 27:30
w S Nu 18:12 *x* ver 26;
Nu 18:19 *y* Dt 14:23;
15:20
12:18 *z* Dt 14:23;
15:20 *a* ver 5 *b* ver 7,
12; Dt 14:26; Ne 8:10;
Ecc 3:12-13; 5:18-20
12:19 *c* ver 12;
Dt 14:27; Ne 13:10
d Mal 3:8
12:20 *e* S Ex 34:24
f S Ge 15:8; S Dt 11:24
g S Ex 16:3
12:21 *h* Dt 14:24
i Lev 17:4
12:22 *j* S ver 15
12:23 *k* Ge 9:4;
S Lev 7:26 *l* Eze 33:25
12:24 *m* ver 16
12:25 *n* S Dt 4:40
o ver 28; Ex 15:26;
Dt 13:18; 1Ki 11:38;
2Ki 12:2
12:26 *p* S ver 17;
Nu 5:9-10
12:27 *q* S Lev 1:13
r Lev 3:1-17
12:28 *s* Dt 4:40;
Ecc 8:12
12:29 *t* Jos 23:4
u S Dt 6:10
12:30 *v* S Ex 10:7
w S ver 4
12:31 *x* S Lev 18:25
y S Lev 18:21
z S 2Ki 3:27
12:32 *a* S Dt 4:2;
Rev 22:18-19
13:1 *b* Mt 24:24;
Mk 13:22; 2Th 2:9
c S Ge 20:3; Jer 23:25;
27:9; 29:8
13:2 *d* Dt 18:22;
1Sa 2:34; 10:9;
2Ki 19:29; 20:9;
Isa 7:11 *e* S Dt 11:28

not yet reached the resting place *g* and the inheritance *h* the LORD your God is giving you. ¹⁰But you will cross the Jordan and settle in the land the LORD your God is giving *i* you as an inheritance, and he will give you rest *j* from all your enemies around you so that you will live in safety. ¹¹Then to the place the LORD your God will choose as a dwelling for his Name *k*—there you are to bring everything I command you: your burnt offerings and sacrifices, your tithes and special gifts, and all the choice possessions you have vowed to the LORD. *l* ¹²And there rejoice *m* before the LORD your God—you, your sons and daughters, your male and female servants, and the Levites *n* from your towns who have no allotment or inheritance *o* of their own. ¹³Be careful not to sacrifice your burnt offerings anywhere you please. *p* ¹⁴Offer them only at the place the LORD will choose *q* in one of your tribes, and there observe everything I command you.

¹⁵Nevertheless, you may slaughter your animals in any of your towns and eat as much of the meat as you want, as if it were gazelle or deer, *r* according to the blessing the LORD your God gives you. Both the ceremonially unclean and the clean may eat it. ¹⁶But you must not eat the blood; *s* pour *t* it out on the ground like water. *u* ¹⁷You must not eat in your own towns the tithe *v* of your grain and new wine and olive oil, *w* or the firstborn of your herds and flocks, or whatever you have vowed to give, *x* or your freewill offerings or special gifts. *y* ¹⁸Instead, you are to eat *z* them in the presence of the LORD your God at the place the LORD your God will choose *a*—you, your sons and daughters, your male and female servants, and the Levites from your towns—and you are to rejoice *b* before the LORD your God in everything you put your hand to. ¹⁹Be careful not to neglect the Levites *c* as long as you live in your land. *d*

²⁰When the LORD your God has enlarged your territory *e* as he promised *f* you, and you crave meat *g* and say, "I would like some meat," then you may eat as much of it as you want. ²¹If the place where the LORD your God chooses to put his Name *h* is too far away from you, you may slaughter animals from the herds and flocks the LORD has given you, as I have commanded you, and in your own towns you may eat as much of them as you want. *i* ²²Eat them as you would gazelle or deer. *j* Both the ceremonially unclean and the clean may eat. ²³But be sure you do not eat the blood, *k* because the blood is the life, and you must not eat the life with the meat. *l* ²⁴You must not eat the blood; pour it out on the ground like water. *m* ²⁵Do not eat it, so that it may go well *n* with you and your children after you, because you will be doing what is right *o* in the eyes of the LORD.

²⁶But take your consecrated things and whatever you have vowed to give, *p* and go to the place the LORD will choose. ²⁷Present your burnt offerings *q* on the altar of the LORD your God, both the meat and the blood. The blood of your sacrifices must be poured beside the altar of the LORD your God, but you may eat *r* the meat. ²⁸Be careful to obey all these regulations I am giving you, so that it may always go well *s* with you and your children after you, because you will be doing what is good and right in the eyes of the LORD your God.

²⁹The LORD your God will cut off *t* before you the nations you are about to invade and dispossess. But when you have driven them out and settled in their land, *u* ³⁰and after they have been destroyed before you, be careful not to be ensnared *v* by inquiring about their gods, saying, "How do these nations serve their gods? We will do the same." *w* ³¹You must not worship the LORD your God in their way, because in worshiping their gods, they do all kinds of detestable things the LORD hates. *x* They even burn their sons *y* and daughters in the fire as sacrifices to their gods. *z*

*³²See that you do all I command you; do not add *a* to it or take away from it.

WORSHIPING OTHER GODS

13 *If a prophet, *b* or one who foretells by dreams, *c* appears among you and announces to you a sign or wonder, ²and if the sign *d* or wonder spoken of takes place, and the prophet says, "Let us follow other gods" *e* (gods you have not

---

* 12:32 is numbered 13:1 in Hebrew texts.   * 13:1-18 is numbered 13:2-19 in Hebrew texts.

12:9 *resting place.* See note on 3:20.
12:11 *dwelling for his Name.* See note on v. 5.

A **12:12** *rejoice before the LORD.* Joy, based on the Lord's blessings, was to be a major feature of Hebrew life and worship in the promised land (vv. 7,18). *Levites . . . have no . . . inheritance.* See 10:9; Nu 18:1–8,20,24 and note on 18:1.
12:13 *not . . . anywhere you please.* Sacrifices and offerings to the Lord were to be brought only to the central sanctuary, not to the various Canaanite worship sites (see v. 5 and note).

12:15,22 *ceremonially unclean.* See note on Lev 4:12.
12:16,24 *you must not eat the blood.* See notes on Ge 9:4; Lev 17:11.
12:31 *burn . . . sons and daughters . . . as sacrifices.* See 18:10; see also note on Lev 18:21.
12:32 *do not add . . . or take away.* See note on 4:2.

A **13:1–5** Eventual fulfillment is one test of true prophecy (18:21–22), but the more stringent rule given here guards against intelligent foresight masquerading as prophecy and known) "and let us worship them," ³you must not listen to the words of that prophet ᶠ or dreamer. ᵍ The Lᴏʀᴅ your God is testing ʰ you to find out whether you love ⁱ him with all your heart and with all your soul. ⁴It is the Lᴏʀᴅ your God you must follow, ʲ and him you must revere. ᵏ Keep his commands and obey him; serve him and hold fast ˡ to him. ⁵That prophet or dreamer must be put to death ᵐ for inciting rebellion against the Lᴏʀᴅ your God, who brought you out of Egypt and redeemed you from the land of slavery. That prophet or dreamer tried to turn ⁿ you from the way the Lᴏʀᴅ your God commanded you to follow. You must purge the evil ᵒ from among you.

⁶If your very own brother, or your son or daughter, or the wife you love, or your closest friend secretly entices ᵖ you, saying, "Let us go and worship other gods" �q (gods that neither you nor your ancestors have known, ⁷gods of the peoples around you, whether near or far, from one end of the land to the other), ⁸do not yield ʳ to them or listen to them. Show them no pity. ˢ Do not spare them or shield them. ⁹You must certainly put them to death. ᵗ Your hand ᵘ must be the first in putting them to death, and then the hands of all the people. ¹⁰Stone them to death, because they tried to turn you away ᵛ from the Lᴏʀᴅ your God, who brought you out of Egypt, out of the land of slavery. ¹¹Then all Israel will hear and be afraid, ʷ and no one among you will do such an evil thing again.

¹²If you hear it said about one of the towns the Lᴏʀᴅ your God is giving you to live in ¹³that wicked persons ˣ have arisen among you and have led the people of their town astray, saying, "Let us go and worship other gods" (gods you have not known), ¹⁴then you must inquire, probe and investigate it thoroughly. ʸ And if it is true and it has been proved that this detestable thing has been done among you, ᶻ ¹⁵you must certainly put to the sword all who live in that town. Destroy it completely, ᵃ ᵃ both its people and its livestock. ᵇ ¹⁶Gather all the plunder of the town into the middle of the public square and completely burn the town ᶜ and all its plunder as a whole burnt offering to the Lᴏʀᴅ your God. ᵈ It is to remain a ruin ᵉ forever, never to be rebuilt. ¹⁷None of those condemned things ᵃ shall be found in your hands, so that the Lᴏʀᴅ will turn from his fierce anger; ᶠ he will show you mercy, ᵍ have compassion ʰ on you, and increase your numbers, ⁱ as he promised ʲ on oath to your ancestors, ¹⁸because you obey the Lᴏʀᴅ your God, keeping all his commands that I am giving you today and doing what is right ᵏ in his eyes.

CLEAN AND UNCLEAN FOOD

14:3–20pp — Lev 11:1–23

14 You are the children ˡ of the Lᴏʀᴅ your God. Do not cut yourselves or shave the front of your heads for the dead, ²for you are a people holy ᵐ to the Lᴏʀᴅ your God. ⁿ Out of all the peoples on the face of the earth, the Lᴏʀᴅ has chosen you to be his treasured possession. ᵒ

³Do not eat any detestable thing. ᵖ ⁴These are the animals you may eat: q the ox, the sheep, the goat, ʳ ⁵the deer, ˢ the gazelle, the roe deer, the wild goat, ᵗ the ibex, the antelope and the mountain sheep. ᵇ ⁶You may eat any animal that has a divided hoof and that chews the cud. ⁷However, of those that chew the cud or that have a divided hoof you may not eat the camel, the rabbit or the hyrax. Although they chew the cud, they do not have a divided hoof; they are ceremonially unclean for you. ⁸The pig is also unclean; although

---

ᵃ *15,17* The Hebrew term refers to the irrevocable giving over of things or persons to the Lᴏʀᴅ, often by totally destroying them.   ᵇ *5* The precise identification of some of the birds and animals in this chapter is uncertain.

13:3 ᶠ 2Pe 2:1
ᵍ 1Sa 28:6,15
ʰ S Ge 22:1; 1Ki 13:18;
22:22-23; Jer 29:31;
43:2; Eze 13:9;
1Co 11:19 ⁱ Dt 6:5
13:4 ʲ 2Ki 23:3;
2Ch 34:31; 2Jn 1:6
ᵏ S Dt 6:13; S Ps 5:7
ˡ S Dt 10:20
13:5 ᵐ S Ex 21:12;
S 22:20 ⁿ ver 10;
Dt 4:19 ᵒ Dt 17:7,12;
19:19; 24:7; Jdg 20:13;
S 1Co 5:13
13:6 ᵖ Dt 17:2-7;
29:18 q S Dt 11:28
13:8 ʳ Pr 1:10
ˢ S Dt 7:2
13:9 ᵗ ver 5
ᵘ S Lev 24:14
13:10 ᵛ S Ex 20:3
13:11 ʷ Dt 17:13;
19:20; 21:21; 1Ti 5:20
13:13 ˣ ver 2,6;
Jdg 19:22; 20:13;
1Sa 2:12; 10:27; 11:12;
25:17; 1Ki 21:10
13:14 ʸ Jdg 20:12
ᶻ Dt 17:4
13:15 ᵃ Isa 24:6;
34:5; 43:28; 47:6;
La 2:6; Da 9:11;
Zec 8:13; Mal 4:6
ᵇ Ex 22:20
13:16 ᶜ 2Ki 25:9;
Jer 39:8; 52:13;
Eze 16:41 ᵈ Dt 7:25,
26; Jos 6:24
ᵉ Jos 8:28; Isa 7:16;
17:1; 24:10; 25:2;
27:10; 32:14,19;
37:26; Jer 49:2;
Mic 1:6
13:17 ᶠ Ex 32:12;
Nu 25:4 ᵍ S Ge 43:14
ʰ Dt 30:3 ⁱ S Dt 7:13
ʲ S Ge 12:2; S 13:14;
S 26:24
13:18 ᵏ S Dt 12:25
14:1 ˡ 19:28;
S Jn 1:12; S Ro 8:14;
9:8
14:2 ᵐ S Ge 28:14;
Ex 23:31; Isa 6:13;
Mal 2:15
ⁿ S Lev 20:26; Ro 12:1
ᵒ S Ex 8:22; S Dt 7:6
14:3 ᵖ Eze 4:14
14:4 q Ac 10:14
ʳ S Lev 7:23
14:5 ˢ S Dt 12:15
ᵗ Job 39:1; Ps 104:18

---

against coincidental fulfillment of the predictions of false prophets (cf. Isa 8:20).
13:3 *testing.* See note on Ge 22:1. *all your heart.* See note on 4:29.
13:4 *hold fast.* See note on 10:20.
13:5 *prophet . . . must be put to death.* See 18:20; Jer 28:15–17. *You must purge the evil from among you.* Repeated in 17:7; 19:19; 21:21; 22:21,24; 24:7, and quoted in 1Co 5:13. The purpose was to eliminate the evildoers as well as the evil itself.

⊂   **13:13** *wicked.* See 1Sa 1:16; 2:12; 25:17. The same Hebrew word is also used, e.g., in 1Sa 30:22 ("troublemakers"); 1Sa 10:27; 1Ki 21:10,13 ("scoundrels"); Job 34:18 ("worthless"); Pr 6:12 ("Troublemakers"). Later, this word (*Belial* in Hebrew) was used as a name for Satan (2Co 6:15), who is the personification of wickedness and lawlessness.

13:15 *Destroy it completely.* See TNIV text note and note on 2:34.
14:1 *cut yourselves.* A pagan religious custom (see 1Ki 18:28). *shave the front of your heads.* Shaving the forehead was a practice of mourners in Canaan.
14:2,21 *holy to the Lᴏʀᴅ.* See note on Lev 11:44. The regulations regarding clean and unclean foods were intended to separate Israel from things the Lord had identified as detestable and ceremonially unclean.
14:2 *a people holy to the Lᴏʀᴅ.* See Ex 3:5 and note; 19:6. *treasured possession.* See note on Ex 19:5.
14:3–21 The subject of clean and unclean food is discussed in greater detail in Lev 11 (see notes there).
14:7 *ceremonially unclean.* See note on Lev 4:12.

14:8 ^{u}S Lev 5:2
14:13 ^{v}S Ge 1:11
^{w}Isa 34:15
14:14 ^{x}S Ge 8:7
14:17 ^{y}Ps 102:6;
Isa 13:21; 14:23; 34:11;
Zep 2:14
14:20 ^{z}S Lev 20:25
14:21 ^{a}S Lev 11:39
^{b}ver 2 ^{c}S Ex 23:19
14:22 ^{d}S Ge 14:20;
S Lev 27:30;
S Nu 18:21
14:23 ^{e}S Dt 12:17,
18 ^{f}Ps 4:7 ^{g}S Dt 12:5;
1Ki 3:2 ^{h}S Dt 4:10
^{i}Ps 22:23; 33:8;
Mal 2:5
14:25 ^{j}Mt 21:12;
Jn 2:14
14:26 ^{k}S Lev 10:9;
Ecc 10:16-17
^{l}S Lev 23:40;
S Dt 12:18
14:27 ^{m}S Dt 12:19
^{n}S Nu 18:20; 26:62;
Dt 18:1-2
14:28 ^{o}S Lev 27:30
^{p}Dt 26:12
14:29 ^{q}Ge 47:22
^{r}Nu 26:62 ^{s}Dt 16:11;
24:19-21; Ps 94:6;
Isa 1:17; 58:6
^{t}S Dt 6:11 ^{u}Dt 15:10;
Ps 41:1; Pr 22:9;
Mal 3:10
15:1 ^{v}Dt 31:10;
Ne 10:31
15:3 ^{w}S Ge 31:15;
Dt 23:20; 28:12;
Ru 2:10
15:4 ^{x}Dt 28:8
15:5 ^{y}S Ex 15:26;
Dt 7:12; 28:1

it has a divided hoof, it does not chew the cud. You are not to eat their meat or touch their carcasses. ^{u}

^{9}Of all the creatures living in the water, you may eat any that has fins and scales. ^{10}But anything that does not have fins and scales you may not eat; for you it is unclean.

^{11}You may eat any clean bird. ^{12}But these you may not eat: the eagle, the vulture, the black vulture, ^{13}the red kite, the black kite, any kind ^{v} of falcon, ^{w} ^{14}any kind of raven, ^{x} ^{15}the horned owl, the screech owl, the gull, any kind of hawk, ^{16}the little owl, the great owl, the white owl, ^{17}the desert owl, ^{y} the osprey, the cormorant, ^{18}the stork, any kind of heron, the hoopoe and the bat.

^{19}All flying insects that swarm are unclean to you; do not eat them. ^{20}But any winged creature that is clean you may eat. ^{z}

^{21}Do not eat anything you find already dead. ^{a} You may give it to the foreigners residing in any of your towns, and they may eat it, or you may sell it to any other foreigner. But you are a people holy to the LORD your God. ^{b}

Do not cook a young goat in its mother's milk. ^{c}

TITHES

^{22}Be sure to set aside a tenth ^{d} of all that your fields produce each year. ^{23}Eat ^{e} the tithe of your grain, new wine ^{f} and olive oil, and the firstborn of your herds and flocks in the presence of the LORD your God at the place he will choose as a dwelling for his Name, ^{g} so that you may learn ^{h} to revere ^{i} the LORD your God always. ^{24}But if that place is too distant and you have been blessed by the LORD your God and cannot carry your tithe (because the place where the LORD will choose to put his Name is so far away), ^{25}then exchange ^{j} your tithe for silver, and take the silver with you and go to the place the LORD your God will choose. ^{26}Use the silver to buy whatever you like: cattle, sheep, wine or other fermented drink, ^{k} or anything you wish. Then you and your household shall eat there in the presence of the LORD your God and rejoice. ^{l} ^{27}And do not neglect the Levites ^{m} living in your towns, for they have no allotment or inheritance of their own. ^{n}

^{28}At the end of every three years, bring all the tithes ^{o} of that year's produce and store it in your towns, ^{p} ^{29}so that the Levites (who have no allotment ^{q} or inheritance ^{r} of their own) and the foreigners, ^{s} the fatherless and the widows who live in your towns may come and eat and be satisfied, ^{t} and so that the LORD your God may bless ^{u} you in all the work of your hands.

THE YEAR FOR CANCELING DEBTS

15:1–11Ref — Lev 25:8–38

15 At the end of every seven years you must cancel debts. ^{v} ^{2}This is how it is to be done: Every creditor shall cancel any loan they have made to another Israelite. They shall not require payment from anyone among their own people, because the LORD's time for canceling debts has been proclaimed. ^{3}You may require payment from a foreigner, ^{w} but you must cancel any debt one of your people owes you. ^{4}However, there need be no poor people among you, for in the land the LORD your God is giving you to possess as your inheritance, he will richly bless ^{x} you, ^{5}if only you fully obey the LORD your God and are careful to follow ^{y} all these commands I am giving you today. ^{6}For the LORD your God will bless you as he has promised, and you will lend to many na-

---

14:21 *Do not eat … already dead.* Because of the prohibition against eating blood, since the dead animal's blood would not be properly drained (see 12:16,24; see also notes on Ge 9:4; Lev 17:11). *Do not cook a young goat in its mother's milk.* See note on Ex 23:19.

14:22–29 See Nu 18:21–29. Taken together, the two passages suggest the following: 1. Annually, a tenth of all Israelite produce was to be taken to the city of the central sanctuary for distribution to the Levites. 2. At that time, at an initial festival, all Israelites ate part of the tithe. 3. The rest, which would be by far the major part of it, belonged to the Levites. 4. Every third year the tithe was gathered in the towns and stored for distribution to the Levites and the less fortunate: aliens, fatherless and widows (see 26:12). 5. The Levites were to present to the Lord a tenth of their tithe. See note on Lev 27:30.

14:22 *set aside a tenth.* See notes on Ge 14:20; 28:22.

14:23 *dwelling for his Name.* See note on 12:5.

14:25 *silver.* Pieces of silver of various weights were a common

medium of exchange, but not in the form of coins (see note on Ge 20:16).

15:1 *every seven years.* See Ex 23:10–11; Lev 25:1–7 and note on 25:4.

15:3 *require payment from a foreigner.* Since he was not subject to the command to allow his fields to lie fallow during the seventh year, a foreigner would probably be financially able to pay his debts if asked to do so.

15:4 *there need be no poor people among you.* Because of the Lord's reward for obedience (vv. 4–6) and because of the sabbath-year arrangement (vv. 7–11), this "year for canceling debts" (v. 9) gave Israelites who had experienced economic reverses a way to gain release from indebtedness and so, in a measure, a way to equalize wealth. Cf. the provisions of the Year of Jubilee (Lev 25:8–38).

15:6 *you will lend.* If Israel failed to follow the Lord's commands, the reverse would be true (see 28:43–44).

tions but will borrow from none. You will rule over many nations but none will rule over you. [z]

[7]If anyone is poor [a] among your people in any of the towns of the land the LORD your God is giving you, do not be hardhearted or tightfisted [b] toward them. [8]Rather, be open-handed [c] and freely lend them whatever they need. [9]Be careful not to harbor this wicked thought: "The seventh year, the year for canceling debts, [d] is near," so that you do not show ill will [e] toward the needy among your people and give them nothing. They may then appeal to the LORD against you, and you will be found guilty of sin. [f] [10]Give generously to them and do so without a grudging heart; [g] then because of this the LORD your God will bless [h] you in all your work and in everything you put your hand to. [11]There will always be poor people [i] in the land. Therefore I command you to be openhanded toward those of your people who are poor and needy in your land. [j]

FREEING SERVANTS
15:12–18pp — Ex 21:2–6
15:12–18Ref — Lev 25:38–55

[12]If any of your people, men or women, sell themselves to you and serve you six years, in the seventh year you must let them go free. [k] [13]And when you release them, do not send them away empty-handed. [14]Supply them liberally from your flock, your threshing floor [l] and your winepress. Give to them as the LORD your God has blessed you. [15]Remember that you were slaves [m] in Egypt and the LORD your God redeemed you. [n] That is why I give you this command today.

[16]But if your servant says to you, "I do not want to leave you," because he loves you and your family and is well off with you, [17]then take an awl and push it through his ear lobe into the door, and he will become your servant for life. Do the same for your female servant.

[18]Do not consider it a hardship to set your servants free, because their service to you these six years has been worth twice as much as that of a hired hand. And the LORD your God will bless you in everything you do.

THE FIRSTBORN ANIMALS

[19]Set apart for the LORD [o] your God every firstborn male [p] of your herds and flocks. [q] Do not put the firstborn of your cows to work, and do not shear the firstborn of your sheep. [r] [20]Each year you and your family are to eat them in the presence of the LORD your God at the place he will choose. [s] [21]If an animal has a defect, [t] is lame or blind, or has any serious flaw, you must not sacrifice it to the LORD your God. [u] [22]You are to eat it in your own towns. Both the ceremonially unclean and the clean may eat it, as if it were gazelle or deer. [v] [23]But you must not eat the blood; pour it out on the ground like water. [w]

THE PASSOVER
16:1–8pp — Ex 12:14–20; Lev 23:4–8; Nu 28:16–25

16
Observe the month of Aviv [x] and celebrate the Passover [y] of the LORD your God, because in the month of Aviv he brought you out of Egypt by night. [2]Sacrifice as the Passover to the LORD your God an animal from your flock or herd at the place the LORD will choose as a dwelling for his Name. [z] [3]Do not eat it with bread made with yeast, but for seven days eat unleavened bread, the bread of affliction, [a] because you left Egypt in haste [b]—so that all the days of your life you may remember the time of your departure from Egypt. [c] [4]Let no yeast be found in your possession in all your land for sev-

15:6 [z] Dt 28:12-13, 44
15:7 [a] ver 11; Mt 26:11 [b] 1Jn 3:17
15:8 [c] Mt 5:42; Lk 6:34; S Ac 24:17
15:9 [d] ver 1 [e] Mt 20:15 [f] S Ex 22:23; S Job 5:15; Jas 5:4
15:10 [g] 2Co 9:5 [h] S Dt 14:29
15:11 [i] S ver 7 [j] Mt 26:11; Mk 14:7; Jn 12:8
15:12 [k] Jer 34:14
15:14 [l] S Nu 18:27
15:15 [m] Ex 13:3; [n] Ex 20:2; S Dt 4:34; S 9:26; 16:12; 24:18; Jer 16:14; 23:7
15:19 [o] S Lev 27:9 [p] S Ex 13:2 [q] S Ge 4:4 [r] S Ex 22:30
15:20 [s] S Lev 7:15-18; Dt 12:5-7,17,18
15:21 [t] S Ex 12:5 [u] S Lev 22:19-25; Dt 17:1; Mal 1:8,13
15:22 [v] S Dt 12:15
15:23 [w] S Ge 9:4; Dt 12:16; Eze 33:25
16:1 [x] S Ex 12:2 [y] S Ex 12:11; 2Ki 23:21; Mt 26:17-29
16:2 [z] Dt 12:5,26
16:3 [a] Ex 12:8,39; 34:18; 1Co 5:8 [b] S Ex 12:11 [c] Dt 4:9

15:11 *There will always be poor people.* See also Jesus' statement in Mt 26:11. Even in the best of societies under the most enlightened laws, the uncertainties of life and the variations among citizens result in some people becoming poor. In such cases the Lord commands that generosity and kindness be extended to them.
15:15 *Remember.* See note on 4:10.
15:16 *because he loves you.* In Ex 21:5 an additional reason is given: The servant may want to stay with his family.
15:17 *take an awl and push it through his ear lobe.* See note on Ex 21:6.

15:18 *worth twice as much.* A Hebrew servant worked twice as many years as the Code of Hammurapi, e.g., required for release from debt (see chart, p. xxiii). Other ancient le-

gal texts, however, support "equivalent to" as a possible translation of the phrase.
15:19 *Set apart…every firstborn male.* Because the Lord saved his people from the plague of death on the firstborn in Egypt (see Ex 12:12,29; 13:2,15 and note on 13:2).
15:21 *If an animal has a defect…you must not sacrifice it.* See note on Lev 1:3.
15:22 *ceremonially unclean.* See note on Lev 4:12.
15:23 See 12:16,24; see also notes on Ge 9:4; Lev 17:11.
16:1–17 See chart, pp. 180–181; see also Ex 23:14–19; 34:18–26; Lev 23:4–44; Nu 28:16—29:40 and notes.
16:1–8 See Ex 12:1–28; 13:1–16 and notes.
16:1 *Aviv.* See chart, p. 105.
16:3,12 *remember.* See note on 4:10.

16:4 *d* S Ex 12:6
e S Ex 12:8; Mk 14:12
16:6 *f* S Ex 12:42
16:7 *g* S Ex 12:8
16:8 *h* 13:6;
S Lev 23:8 *i* Mt 26:17;
Lk 2:41; 22:7; Jn 2:13
16:9 *j* Ac 2:1
k S Ex 23:16
16:11 *l* Dt 12:7
m S Ex 20:24;
S 2Sa 7:13 *n* Dt 12:12
o S Dt 14:29 *p* Ne 8:10
16:12 *q* S Dt 15:15
16:13 *r* S Lev 2:14
s S Ge 27:37;
S Ex 23:16
16:14 *t* ver 11
16:15 *u* Job 38:7;
Ps 4:7; 28:7; 30:11
16:16 *v* Dt 31:11;
Ps 84:7 *w* S Ex 12:17
x S Ex 23:14,16;
Ezr 3:4 *y* S Ex 34:20
16:18 *z* S Ex 18:21,
26 *a* S Ge 31:37
16:19 *b* S Ex 23:2
c S Lev 19:15
d S Ex 18:21; S 1Sa 8:3
16:21 *e* S Dt 7:5
f Ex 34:13; 1Ki 14:15;
2Ki 17:16; 21:3;
2Ch 33:3
16:22 *g* S Ex 23:24
17:1 *h* S Ex 12:5;
S Lev 22:20 *i* Dt 7:25
j S Dt 15:21
17:2 *k* Dt 13:6-11
17:3 *l* Jer 7:31
m Ex 22:20
n S Ge 1:16 *o* S Ge 2:1;
S 37:9
17:4 *p* Dt 22:20
q Dt 13:12-14
17:5 *r* S Lev 24:14

en days. Do not let any of the meat you sacrifice on the evening *d* of the first day remain until morning. *e*

⁵You must not sacrifice the Passover in any town the Lord your God gives you ⁶except in the place he will choose as a dwelling for his Name. There you must sacrifice the Passover in the evening, when the sun goes down, on the anniversary *a f* of your departure from Egypt. ⁷Roast *g* it and eat it at the place the Lord your God will choose. Then in the morning return to your tents. ⁸For six days eat unleavened bread and on the seventh day hold an assembly *h* to the Lord your God and do no work. *i*

THE FESTIVAL OF WEEKS
16:9–12pp — Lev 23:15–22; Nu 28:26–31

⁹Count off seven weeks *j* from the time you begin to put the sickle to the standing grain. *k* ¹⁰Then celebrate the Festival of Weeks to the Lord your God by giving a freewill offering in proportion to the blessings the Lord your God has given you. ¹¹And rejoice *l* before the Lord your God at the place he will choose as a dwelling for his Name *m*—you, your sons and daughters, your male and female servants, the Levites *n* in your towns, and the foreigners, *o* the fatherless and the widows living among you. *p* ¹²Remember that you were slaves in Egypt, *q* and follow carefully these decrees.

THE FESTIVAL OF TABERNACLES
16:13–17pp — Lev 23:33–43; Nu 29:12–39

¹³Celebrate the Festival of Tabernacles for seven days after you have gathered the produce of your threshing floor *r* and your winepress. *s* ¹⁴Be joyful *t* at your festival—you, your sons and daughters, your male and female servants, and the Levites, the foreigners, the fatherless and the widows who live in your towns. ¹⁵For seven days celebrate the festival to the Lord your God at the place the Lord will choose. For the Lord your God will bless you in all your harvest and in all the work of your hands, and your joy *u* will be complete.

¹⁶Three times a year all your men must appear *v* before the Lord your God at the place he will choose: at the Festival of Unleavened Bread, *w* the Festival of Weeks and the Festival of Tabernacles. *x* No one should appear before the Lord empty-handed: *y* ¹⁷Each of you must bring a gift in proportion to the way the Lord your God has blessed you.

JUDGES

¹⁸Appoint judges *z* and officials for each of your tribes in every town the Lord your God is giving you, and they shall judge the people fairly. *a* ¹⁹Do not pervert justice *b* or show partiality. *c* Do not accept a bribe, *d* for a bribe blinds the eyes of the wise and twists the words of the righteous. ²⁰Follow justice and justice alone, so that you may live and possess the land the Lord your God is giving you.

WORSHIPING OTHER GODS

²¹Do not set up any wooden Asherah pole *e* beside the altar you build to the Lord your God, *f* ²²and do not erect a sacred stone, *g* for these the Lord your God hates.

17 Do not sacrifice to the Lord your God an ox or a sheep that has any defect *h* or flaw in it, for that would be detestable *i* to him. *j*

²If a man or woman living among you in one of the towns the Lord gives you is found doing evil in the eyes of the Lord your God in violation of his covenant, *k* ³and contrary to my command *l* has worshiped other gods, *m* bowing down to them or to the sun *n* or the moon or the stars in the sky, *o* ⁴and this has been brought to your attention, then you must investigate it thoroughly. If it is true *p* and it has been proved that this detestable thing has been done in Israel, *q* ⁵take the man or woman who has done this evil deed to your city gate and stone that person to death. *r* ⁶On the testimony of two or three wit-

a 6 Or *down, at the time of day*

16:7 *to your tents.* To wherever they were staying while in the festival, whether in permanent or temporary quarters.
16:8 *assembly.* That is, the closing assembly (see Lev 23:36).
16:9 *seven weeks.* Symbolizing the full season of grain harvest.
16:10 *giving ... in proportion to.* See v. 17; cf. 1Co 16:2; 2Co 8:12 and notes.
16:15 *your joy will be complete.* As a result of God's blessing (cf. Jn 3:29; 15:11; 16:24; Php 2:2; 1Jn 1:4; 2Jn 12).
16:16 *Three times a year.* The three annual pilgrimage festivals (see Ex 23:14,17; 34:23; see also chart, p. 105).

16:18–20 Cf. 1:9–18; Ex 18:13–26.
16:19 Israel must emulate the Lord in these matters (see 10:17; see also Ex 23:8 and note).
16:21–22 *Asherah pole ... sacred stone.* See note on 7:5.
17:1 *defect or flaw.* See note on Lev 1:3.
17:3 *bowing down to ... the sun or the moon or the stars.* See 4:19 and note.
17:6 *two or three witnesses.* A further specification of the law set forth in Nu 35:30 (see note there). See 19:15; cf. Mt 18:16; 2Co 13:1; 1Ti 5:19; Heb 10:28.

nesses a person is to be put to death, but no one is to be put to death on the testimony of only one witness. ^{s} ^{7}The hands of the witnesses must be the first in putting that person to death, ^{t} and then the hands of all the people. ^{u} You must purge the evil ^{v} from among you.

LAW COURTS

^{8}If cases come before your courts that are too difficult for you to judge ^{w}—whether bloodshed, lawsuits or assaults ^{x}—take them to the place the LORD your God will choose. ^{y} ^{9}Go to the Levitical ^{z} priests and to the judge ^{a} who is in office at that time. Inquire of them and they will give you the verdict. ^{b} ^{10}You must act according to the decisions they give you at the place the LORD will choose. Be careful to do everything they instruct you to do. ^{11}Act according to whatever they teach you and the decisions they give you. Do not turn aside from what they tell you, to the right or to the left. ^{c} ^{12}Anyone who shows contempt ^{d} for the judge or for the priest who stands ministering ^{e} there to the LORD your God is to be put to death. ^{f} You must purge the evil from Israel. ^{g} ^{13}All the people will hear and be afraid, and will not be contemptuous again. ^{h}

THE KING

^{14}When you enter the land the LORD your God is giving you and have taken possession ^{i} of it and settled in it, ^{j} and you say, "Let us set a king over us like all the nations around us," ^{k} ^{15}be sure to appoint ^{l} over you the king the LORD your God chooses. He must be from among your own people. ^{m} Do not place a foreigner over you, one who is not an Israelite. ^{16}The king, moreover, must not acquire great numbers of horses ^{n} for himself ^{o} or make the people return to Egypt ^{p} to get more of them, ^{q} for the LORD has told you, "You are not to go back that way again." ^{r} ^{17}He must not take many wives, ^{s} or his heart will be led astray. ^{t} He must not accumulate ^{u} large amounts of silver and gold. ^{v}

^{18}When he takes the throne ^{w} of his kingdom, he is to write ^{x} for himself on a scroll a copy ^{y} of this law, taken from that of the Levitical priests. ^{19}It is to be with him, and he is to read it all the days of his life ^{z} so that he may learn to revere the LORD his God and follow carefully all the words of this law and these decrees ^{a} ^{20}and not consider himself better than his fellow Israelites and turn from the law ^{b} to the right or to the left. ^{c} Then he and his descendants will reign a long time over his kingdom in Israel. ^{d}

OFFERINGS FOR PRIESTS AND LEVITES

18 The Levitical ^{e} priests—indeed, the whole tribe of Levi—are to have no allotment or inheritance with Israel. They shall live on the food offerings ^{f} presented to the LORD, for that is their inheritance. ^{g} ^{2}They shall have no inheritance among their fellow Israelites; the LORD is their inheritance, ^{h} as he promised them. ^{i}

^{3}This is the share due the priests ^{j} from the people who sacrifice a bull ^{k} or a sheep: the shoulder, the jowls and the internal organs. ^{l} ^{4}You are to give them the firstfruits of your grain, new wine and olive oil, and the first wool from the shearing of your sheep, ^{m} ^{5}for the LORD your God has chosen them ^{n} and their descendants out of all your tribes to stand and minister ^{o} in the LORD's name always. ^{p}

^{6}If a Levite moves from one of your towns anywhere in Israel where he is living, and comes in all earnestness to the place the LORD will choose, ^{q} ^{7}he may minister in the name ^{r} of the LORD his God like all other Levites who serve there in the presence of the LORD. ^{8}He is to share equally in their benefits, even though he has received money from the sale of family possessions. ^{s}

18:7 Ps 118:26   18:8 ^{s} Nu 18:24; 2Ch 31:4; Ne 12:44,47; 13:12

17:6 ^{s} Nu 35:30;
Dt 19:15; S Mt 18:16
17:7 ^{t} Jn 8:7
^{u} S Lev 24:14; Ac 7:58
^{v} S Dt 13:5; 1Co 5:13*
17:8 ^{w} Ex 21:6
x 2Ch 19:10 ^{y} Dt 12:5;
Ps 122:3-5
17:9 ^{z} Dt 24:8; 27:9
^{a} S Ex 21:6
^{b} S Ge 25:22;
Dt 19:17; Eze 44:24;
Hag 2:11
17:11 ^{c} S Lev 10:11;
S Dt 5:32
17:12 ^{d} Nu 15:30
^{e} S Nu 16:9 ^{f} ver 13;
S Ge 17:14; Dt 13:11;
18:20; 19:20;
1Ki 18:40; Jer 14:14;
Hos 4:4; Zec 13:3
^{g} S Dt 13:5
17:13 ^{h} S ver 12
17:14 ^{i} S Nu 33:53
^{j} Jos 21:43 ^{k} 1Sa 8:5,
19-20; 10:19
17:15 ^{l} 1Sa 16:3;
2Sa 5:3 ^{m} Jer 30:21
17:16 ^{n} Isa 2:7;
30:16 ^{o} 1Sa 8:11;
1Ki 4:26; 9:19; 10:26;
2Ch 1:14; Ps 20:7
^{p} 1Ki 10:29; Isa 31:1;
Jer 42:14 ^{q} 1Ki 10:28;
Isa 31:1; Eze 17:15
^{r} S Ex 13:17
17:17 ^{s} S Ex 34:16;
2Sa 5:13; 12:11;
1Ki 11:3; 2Ch 11:21
^{t} 1Ki 11:2; Pr 31:3
^{u} 1Ki 10:27 ^{v} 2Ch 1:11;
Isa 2:7
17:18 ^{w} 1Ki 1:46;
1Ch 29:23 ^{x} Dt 31:22,
24; Jos 24:26;
1Sa 10:25 ^{y} 2Ch 23:11
17:19 ^{z} Dt 4:9-10;
Jos 1:8 ^{a} Dt 11:13;
1Ki 3:3; 11:38;
2Ki 22:2
17:20 ^{b} Jos 23:6;
Job 23:12; Ps 119:102
^{c} S Dt 5:32; S 1Ki 9:4
^{d} 1Sa 8:5; 10:25;
1Ki 2:3; 1Ch 28:8
18:1 ^{e} Jer 33:18,21
^{f} S Nu 18:8
^{g} S Nu 18:20;
1Co 9:13
18:2 ^{h} Nu 18:20
^{i} Jos 13:14
18:3 ^{j} S Ex 29:27
^{k} S Lev 1:5 ^{l} Lev 7:28-
34; Nu 18:12
18:4 ^{m} Ex 22:29;
Nu 18:12
18:5 ^{n} S Ex 28:1
^{o} Dt 10:8 ^{p} S Ex 29:9
18:6 ^{q} S Nu 35:2-3;
S Dt 12:5
18:7 ^{r} ver 19;
1Ki 18:32; 22:16;

17:7 *You must purge the evil from among you.* See v. 12; see also note on 13:5.

A C **17:14** *a king … like all the nations around us.* Moses, Joshua and a succession of judges were chosen directly by the Lord to govern Israel on his behalf. As Gideon later said, "The LORD will rule over you" (Jdg 8:23; see note there). Moses here, however, anticipates a time when the people would ask for a king (see 1Sa 8:4–9) contrary to the Lord's ideal for them (see notes on 7:2–5; 1Sa 8:1—12:25; see also Lev 20:23). So Moses gives guidance concerning the eventual selection of a king (vv. 14–20).

A **17:16–17** The very things that later kings were guilty of, beginning especially with Solomon (1Ki 4:26; 10:14–22; 11:1–4)—except that they did not make Israel return to Egypt (but see Jer 42:13—43:7).

B **17:18** *write for himself … a copy of this law.* As a sign of submission to the Lord as his King, and as a guide for his rule in obedience to his heavenly Suzerain. This was required procedure for vassal kings under the suzerainty treaties among the Hittites and others before and during this period (see note on 31:9). See chart, p. 20. *copy of this law.* See Introduction: Title.

A **17:20** *not consider himself better.* The king was not above God's law, any more than were the humblest of his subjects.

18:1 *no allotment or inheritance.* No private ownership of land. Towns and surrounding pasturelands were set aside for the use of the Levites (Jos 21:41–42), as were the tithes and parts of sacrifices (see 14:22–29; Lev 27:30 and notes; Nu 18:21–29).

18:4 *firstfruits.* See Ex 23:19 and note; 34:26; Lev 23:10–11; Nu 15:18–20; 18:12–13.

18:5 See note on 21:5.

18:9 *f* Dt 9:5; 12:29-31 *u* S Lev 18:3; 2Ki 21:2; 2Ch 28:3; 33:2; 34:33; Ezr 6:21; 9:11; Jer 44:4
18:10 *v* S Lev 18:21 *w* 1Sa 15:23 *x* S Ex 7:11 *y* S Lev 19:31
18:11 *z* Isa 47:9 *a* S Ex 22:18; S 1Sa 28:13
18:12 *b* S Lev 18:24
18:13 *c* S Ge 6:9; Ps 119:1 *d* Mt 5:48
18:14 *e* 2Ki 21:6
18:15 *f* S Mt 21:11; Lk 2:25-35; Jn 1:21; Ac 3:22*; 7:37*
18:16 *g* S Ex 20:19; Dt 5:23-27
18:18 *h* S Ge 20:7 *i* Isa 2:3; 26:8; 51:4; Mic 4:2 *j* S Ex 4:12 *k* Jn 4:25-26; S 14:24; Ac 3:22*
18:19 *l* Jos 22:23; Ac 3:23*; Heb 12:25 *m* S Ex 23:21 *n* S ver 7; S Lev 19:12; 2Ki 2:24
18:20 *o* S Ex 23:13 *p* Dt 13:1-5; S 17:12
18:22 *q* S Dt 13:2; 1Sa 3:20 *r* 1Ki 22:28; Jer 28:9 *s* ver 20
19:1 *t* Dt 6:10-11
19:6 *u* S Nu 35:12
19:8 *v* S Ex 34:24 *w* S Ge 15:8; S Dt 11:24
19:9 *x* Dt 6:5
19:10 *y* Pr 6:17; Jer 7:6; 26:15 *z* Dt 21:1-9
19:11 *a* S Ex 21:12; 1Jn 3:15

OCCULT PRACTICES

⁹When you enter the land the LORD your God is giving you, do not learn to imitate the detestable ways of the nations there. ¹⁰Let no one be found among you who sacrifices their son or daughter in the fire, who practices divination or sorcery, interprets omens, engages in witchcraft, ¹¹or casts spells, or who is a medium or spiritist or who consults the dead. ¹²Anyone who does these things is detestable to the LORD, and because of these detestable practices the LORD your God will drive out those nations before you. ¹³You must be blameless before the LORD your God.

THE PROPHET

¹⁴The nations you will dispossess listen to those who practice sorcery or divination. But as for you, the LORD your God has not permitted you to do so. ¹⁵The LORD your God will raise up for you a prophet like me from among you, from your own people. You must listen to him. ¹⁶For this is what you asked of the LORD your God at Horeb on the day of the assembly when you said, "Let us not hear the voice of the LORD our God nor see this great fire anymore, or we will die."

¹⁷The LORD said to me: "What they say is good. ¹⁸I will raise up for them a prophet like you from among their people, and I will put my words in his mouth. He will tell them everything I command him. ¹⁹I myself will call to account anyone who does not listen to my words that the prophet speaks in my name. ²⁰But a prophet who presumes to speak in my name anything I have not commanded, or a prophet who speaks in the name of other gods, is to be put to death."

²¹You may say to yourselves, "How can we know when a message has not been spoken by the LORD?" ²²If what a prophet proclaims in the name of the LORD does not take place or come true, that is a message the LORD has not spoken. That prophet has spoken presumptuously. No one should be alarmed.

CITIES OF REFUGE

19:1–14Ref — Nu 35:6–34; Dt 4:41–43; Jos 20:1–9

19 When the LORD your God has destroyed the nations whose land he is giving you, and when you have driven them out and settled in their towns and houses, ²then set aside for yourselves three cities in the land the LORD your God is giving you to possess. ³Build roads to them and divide into three parts the land the LORD your God is giving you as an inheritance, so that anyone who kills someone else may flee there.

⁴This is the rule concerning anyone who kills a person and flees there for safety—anyone who kills a neighbor unintentionally, without malice aforethought. ⁵For instance, a man may go into the forest with his neighbor to cut wood, and as he swings his ax to fell a tree, the head may fly off and hit his neighbor and kill him. That man may flee to one of these cities and save his life. ⁶Otherwise, the avenger of blood might pursue him in a rage, overtake him if the distance is too great, and kill him even though he is not deserving of death, since he did it to his neighbor without malice aforethought. ⁷This is why I command you to set aside for yourselves three cities.

⁸If the LORD your God enlarges your territory, as he promised on oath to your ancestors, and gives you the whole land he promised them, ⁹because you carefully follow all these laws I command you today—to love the LORD your God and to walk always in obedience to him—then you are to set aside three more cities. ¹⁰Do this so that innocent blood will not be shed in your land, which the LORD your God is giving you as your inheritance, and so that you will not be guilty of bloodshed.

¹¹But if out of hate someone lies in wait, assaults and kills a neighbor, and then flees

---

18:9 *detestable ways of the nations.* What follows is the most complete list of magical or spiritistic arts in the OT. All were practiced in Canaan, and all are condemned and prohibited. The people are not to resort to such sources for their information, guidance or revelation. Rather, they are to listen to the Lord's true prophets (see vv. 14–22; Isa 8:19–20).

18:10 *sacrifices their son or daughter.* See 12:31; see also note on Lev 18:21.

18:15 *prophet like me.* See 34:10. Verse 16, as well as the general context (see especially vv. 20–22), indicates that a series of prophets is meant. At Mount Horeb the people requested that Moses take the message from God and deliver it to them (see Ex 20:19 and note). But now that Moses is

to leave them, he says that another spokesman will take his place, and then another will be necessary for the next generation. This is therefore a collective reference to the prophets who will follow. As such, it is also the basis for later Messianic expectation and receives a unique fulfillment in Jesus (see Jn 1:21,25,45; 5:46; 6:14; 7:40; Ac 3:22–26; 7:37).

18:16 See Ex 20:18–21; Heb 12:18–21 and notes.

18:18 *my words in his mouth.* See Ex 4:15–16; see also notes on Ex 7:1–2; Jer 1:9.

18:20 *prophet who presumes to speak.* See note on 13:1–5. *is to be put to death.* See 13:5; Jer 28:15–17.

18:21–22 See note on 13:1–5.

19:1–13 See 4:41–43; Nu 35:9–28; Jos 20 and notes.

to one of these cities, [12]the killer shall be sent for by the town elders, be brought back from the city, and be handed over to the avenger of blood to die. [13]Show no pity. [b] You must purge from Israel the guilt of shedding innocent blood, [c] so that it may go well with you.

[14]Do not move your neighbor's boundary stone set up by your predecessors in the inheritance you receive in the land the LORD your God is giving you to possess. [d]

WITNESSES

[15]One witness is not enough to convict anyone accused of any crime or offense they may have committed. A matter must be established by the testimony of two or three witnesses. [e]

[16]If a malicious witness [f] takes the stand to accuse someone of a crime, [17]the two involved in the dispute must stand in the presence of the LORD before the priests and the judges [g] who are in office at the time. [18]The judges must make a thorough investigation, [h] and if the witness proves to be a liar, giving false testimony, [19]then do to the false witness as that witness intended to do to the other party. [i] You must purge the evil from among you. [20]The rest of the people will hear of this and be afraid, [j] and never again will such an evil thing be done among you. [21]Show no pity: [k] life for life, eye for eye, tooth for tooth, hand for hand, foot for foot. [l]

GOING TO WAR

20 When you go to war against your enemies and see horses and chariots and an army greater than yours, [m] do not be afraid [n] of them, [o] because the LORD your God, who brought you up out of Egypt, will be with [p] you. [2]When you are about to go into battle, the priest shall come forward and address the army. [3]He shall say: "Hear, Israel: Today you are going into battle against your enemies. Do not be fainthearted [q] or afraid; do not be terrified or give way to panic before them. [4]For the LORD your God is the one who goes with you [r] to fight [s] for you against your enemies to give you victory. [t]"

[5]The officers shall say to the army: "Has anyone built a new house and not yet begun to live in [u] it? Let him go home, or he may die in battle and someone else may begin to live in it. [6]Has anyone planted [v] a vineyard and not begun to enjoy it? [w] Let him go home, or he may die in battle and someone else enjoy it. [7]Has anyone become pledged to a woman and not married her? Let him go home, or he may die in battle and someone else may marry her. [x]" [8]Then the officers shall add, "Is anyone afraid or fainthearted? Let him go home so that the others will not become disheartened too." [y] [9]When the officers have finished speaking to the army, they shall appoint commanders over it.

[10]When you march up to attack a city, make its people an offer of peace. [z] [11]If they accept and open their gates, all the people in it shall be subject [a] to forced labor [b] and shall work for you. [12]If they refuse to make peace and they engage you in battle, lay siege to that city. [13]When the LORD your God delivers it into your hand, put to the sword all the men in it. [c] [14]As for the women, the children, the livestock [d] and everything else in the city, [e] you may take these as plunder [f] for yourselves. And you may use the plunder the LORD your God gives you from your enemies. [15]This is how you are to treat all the cities that are at a distance [g] from you and do not belong to the nations nearby.

[16]However, in the cities of the nations the LORD your God is giving you as an inheritance, do not leave alive anything that breathes. [h] [17]Completely destroy [a] them—the Hittites, Amorites, Canaanites, Perizzites, Hivites and Jebusites—as the LORD your God has

---

[a] *17* The Hebrew term refers to the irrevocable giving over of things or persons to the LORD, often by totally destroying them.

19:13 [b] Dt 7:2
[c] Dt 21:9; 1Ki 2:31
19:14 [d] Dt 27:17;
Job 24:2; Ps 16:6;
Pr 15:25; 22:28;
23:10; Isa 1:23;
Hos 5:10
19:15 [e] S Dt 17:6;
S Mt 18:16*; 26:60;
2Co 13:1*
19:16 [f] Ex 23:1;
Pr 6:19
19:17 [g] S Ex 21:6
19:18 [h] S Ex 23:7
19:19 [i] Pr 19:5,9;
1Co 5:13*
19:20 [j] S Dt 13:11
19:21 [k] ver 13
[l] S Ex 21:24; Mt 5:38*
20:1 [m] Ps 20:7;
Isa 31:1 [n] S Nu 14:9
[o] S Dt 3:22;
S 1Sa 17:45
[p] Isa 41:10
20:3 [q] 1Sa 17:32;
Job 23:16; Ps 22:14;
Isa 7:4; 35:4;
Jer 51:46
20:4 [r] 2Ch 20:14-22
[s] S Ex 14:14;
1Ch 5:22; Ne 4:20
[t] Jdg 12:3; 15:18;
Ps 44:7; 144:10
20:5 [u] Ne 12:27
20:6 [v] Jer 31:5;
Eze 28:26; Mic 1:6
[w] 1Co 9:7
20:7 [x] Dt 24:5;
Pr 5:18
20:8 [y] Jdg 7:3
20:10 [z] S Dt 2:26;
Lk 14:31-32
20:11 [a] ver 15;
2Ki 6:22 [b] 1Ki 9:21;
1Ch 22:2; Isa 31:8
20:13 [c] Nu 31:7
20:14 [d] Jos 8:2; 22:8
[e] S Nu 31:11
[f] S Nu 31:53
20:15 [g] S ver 11;
Jos 9:9
20:16 [h] Ex 23:31-33;
Nu 21:2-3; S Dt 7:2;
Jos 6:21; 10:1; 11:14

B **19:14** *boundary stone.* Such stones were set up to indicate the perimeters of fields and landed estates. Moving them illegally to increase one's own holdings was considered a serious crime (see 27:17; Pr 15:25 and note). Amenemope's (Egyptian) Wisdom (see chart, p. xxiii) has a similar prohibition in ch. 6 of that work.

19:15 See note on 17:6.

19:18 *giving false testimony.* See 5:20; Lev 19:11–12; 1Ki 21:10,13.

19:19 *You must purge the evil from among you.* See note on 13:5.

19:21 *life for life.* See notes on Ex 21:23–25; Lev 24:20; see also Mt 5:38–42.

20:2 *priest shall … address.* Priests sometimes accompanied

the army when it went into battle (see, e.g., Jos 6:4–21; 2Ch 20:14–22).

20:3 *Hear, Israel.* See note on 4:1.

20:4 See note on 3:22.

A **20:5–8** Cf. the curses in 28:30. *Let him go home.* Israel was not to trust in the size of its army but in the Lord (see notes on 2Sa 24:1; Ps 30:6–7). The number of exemptions from military duty was sometimes extensive (see, e.g., Jdg 7:2–8).

20:10–15 Rules regarding warfare against nations outside the promised land.

20:11 *subject to forced labor.* A fulfillment of Noah's curse on Canaan (see Ge 9:25 and note).

20:17 *Hittites … Jebusites.* See 7:1; see also notes on Ge 10:6, 15–18; 13:7; Jos 9:7.

20:18 *i* S Ex 34:16
j S Ex 10:7
20:20 *k* Jer 6:6
21:1 *l* S Nu 25:17
21:3 *m* S Nu 19:2
21:5 *n* S Ge 48:20;
S Ex 39:43 *o* Dt 17:8-
11
21:6 *p* Mt 27:24
21:8 *q* Nu 35:33-34
21:9 *r* Dt 19:13
21:10 *s* Jos 21:44
t 1Ki 8:46; 1Ch 9:1;
Ezr 5:12; Jer 40:1;
Eze 1:1; 17:12;
Da 2:25; Mic 4:10
21:11 *u* Ge 6:2
v S Ge 34:8
21:12 *w* S Lev 14:9;
S Nu 8:7; 1Co 11:5
21:13 *x* Ps 45:10
21:14 *y* S Ge 34:2
21:15 *z* S Ge 4:19
a Ge 29:33
21:16 *b* 1Ch 26:10
21:17 *c* 2Ki 2:9;
Isa 40:2; 61:7;
Zec 9:12 *d* S Ge 49:3
e Ge 25:31; Lk 15:12
21:18 *f* Ps 78:8;
Jer 5:23; Zep 3:1
g Pr 30:17

commanded you. [18]Otherwise, they will teach you to follow all the detestable things they do in worshiping their gods, *i* and you will sin *j* against the LORD your God.

[19]When you lay siege to a city for a long time, fighting against it to capture it, do not destroy its trees by putting an ax to them, because you can eat their fruit. Do not cut them down. Are the trees people, that you should besiege them? *a* [20]However, you may cut down trees that you know are not fruit trees *k* and use them to build siege works until the city at war with you falls.

ATONEMENT FOR AN UNSOLVED MURDER

21 If someone is found slain, lying in a field in the land the LORD your God is giving you to possess, and it is not known who the killer was, *l* [2]your elders and judges shall go out and measure the distance from the body to the neighboring towns. [3]Then the elders of the town nearest the body shall take a heifer that has never been worked and has never worn a yoke *m* [4]and lead it down to a valley that has not been plowed or planted and where there is a flowing stream. In the valley they are to break the heifer's neck. [5]The priests, the sons of Levi, shall step forward, for the LORD your God has chosen them to minister and to pronounce blessings *n* in the name of the LORD and to decide all cases of dispute and assault. *o* [6]Then all the elders of the town nearest the body shall wash their hands *p* over the heifer whose neck was broken in the valley, [7]and they shall declare: "Our hands did not shed this blood, nor did our eyes see it done. [8]Accept this atonement for your people Israel, whom you have redeemed, LORD, and do not hold your people guilty of the blood of an innocent person." And the bloodshed will be atoned for. *q* [9]So you will purge *r* from yourselves the guilt of shedding innocent blood, since you have done what is right in the eyes of the LORD.

MARRYING A CAPTIVE WOMAN

[10]When you go to war against your enemies and the LORD your God delivers them into your hands *s* and you take captives, *t* [11]if you notice among the captives a beautiful *u* woman and are attracted to her, *v* you may take her as your wife. [12]Bring her into your home and have her shave her head, *w* trim her nails [13]and put aside the clothes she was wearing when captured. After she has lived in your house and mourned her father and mother for a full month, *x* then you may go to her and be her husband and she shall be your wife. [14]If you are not pleased with her, let her go wherever she wishes. You must not sell her or treat her as a slave, since you have dishonored her. *y*

THE RIGHT OF THE FIRSTBORN

[15]If someone has two wives, *z* and he loves one but not the other, and both bear him sons but the firstborn is the son of the wife he does not love, *a* [16]when he wills his property to his sons, he must not give the rights of the firstborn to the son of the wife he loves in preference to his actual firstborn, the son of the wife he does not love. *b* [17]He must acknowledge the son of his unloved wife as the firstborn by giving him a double *c* share of all he has. That son is the first sign of his father's strength. *d* The right of the firstborn belongs to him. *e*

A REBELLIOUS SON

[18]If someone has a stubborn and rebellious *f* son *g* who does not obey his father and

---

a 19   Or *down to use in the siege, for the fruit trees are for the benefit of people.*

20:19 *do not destroy its trees.* The failure of later armies to follow this wise rule stripped bare much of the land (though the absence of woodlands there today is of relatively recent origin).
21:5 *to minister.* To officiate at the place of worship before the Lord on behalf of the people (see 10:8; 18:5). *to pronounce blessings.* See Nu 6:22–27.
21:6 *wash their hands.* Symbolic of a declaration of innocence (v. 7; see Mt 27:24).
21:10 *take captives.* The enemies here were those outside Canaan (see 20:14–15), so they were not subject to total destruction (see 20:17 and TNIV text note there).
21:12 *shave her head.* Indicative of leaving her former life and beginning a new life, or perhaps symbolic of mourning (v. 13; see, e.g., Jer 47:5; Mic 1:16) or of humiliation (see note on Isa 7:20). For cleansing rites see Lev 14:8; Nu 8:7 and note; cf. 2Sa 19:24.
21:14 *dishonored.* Twelve other times the Hebrew for this word

is used of men forcing women to have sexual intercourse with them (22:24,29; Ge 34:2; Jdg 19:24; 20:5; 2Sa 13:12,14,22,32; La 5:11; Eze 22:10–11).
21:15 *two wives.* See notes on Ge 4:19; 25:6.
21:16 *in preference to.* The order of birth rather than parental favoritism governed succession, though the rule was sometimes set aside with divine approval (cf., e.g., Jacob or Solomon).

21:17 *double share.* In Israel the oldest son enjoyed a double share of the inheritance. Parallels to this practice come from Nuzi, Larsa in the Old Babylonian period, and Assyria in the Middle Assyrian period (see chart, p. xxiv). Receiving a double portion of an estate was also tantamount to succession. Thus Elisha succeeded Elijah (see 2Ki 2:9 and note). *first sign of his father's strength.* The first result of a man's procreative ability.
21:18 *stubborn and rebellious … does not obey.* In wicked defiance of the fifth commandment (see 5:16; Ex 20:12 and note).

mother [h] and will not listen to them when they discipline him, [19]his father and mother shall take hold of him and bring him to the elders at the gate of his town. [20]They shall say to the elders, "This son of ours is stubborn and rebellious. He will not obey us. He is a profligate and a drunkard." [21]Then all the men of his town are to stone him to death. [i] You must purge the evil [j] from among you. All Israel will hear of it and be afraid. [k]

VARIOUS LAWS

[22]If anyone guilty of a capital offense [l] is put to death and their body is exposed on a pole, [23]you must not leave the body hanging on the pole overnight. [m] Be sure to bury [n] it that same day, because anyone who is hung on a pole is under God's curse. [o] You must not desecrate [p] the land the LORD your God is giving you as an inheritance.

22 If you see someone else's ox or sheep straying, do not ignore it but be sure to take it back to its owner. [q] [2]If the owner does not live near you or if you do not know who owns it, take it home with you and keep it until the owner comes looking for it. Then give it back. [3]Do the same if you find someone's donkey or cloak or anything else they have lost. Do not ignore it.

21:21 *stone him to death.* See 5:16; 27:16; Ex 21:15,17. *You must purge the evil from among you.* See note on 13:5.
21:22 *put to death and … exposed on a pole.* The offender was first executed, then the body was impaled on a pole (see Ge 40:19; Est 2:23 and note).
21:23 *not leave the body hanging on the pole overnight.* Prolonged exposure gives undue attention to the crime and the criminal and would desecrate the land. *under God's*

curse. God had condemned murder, and hanging on a pole symbolized divine judgment and rejection. Christ accepted the full punishment of our sins, thus becoming "a curse for us" (Gal 3:13; see note there).
22:1 *do not ignore it.* See vv. 3–4. The Biblical legislation was intended not only to punish criminal behavior but also to express concern for people and their possessions. See chart below.

21:18 [h] S Ge 31:35; Pr 1:8; Isa 30:1; Eph 6:1-3
21:21 [i] S Lev 20:9 / Dt 19:19; 1Co 5:13*
[k] S Dt 13:11
21:22 [l] Dt 22:26; Mt 26:66; Mk 14:64; Ac 23:29
21:23 [m] Jos 8:29; 10:27; Jn 19:31
[n] Eze 39:12 [o] Ezr 6:11; Est 2:23; 7:9; 8:7; 9:13,25; Isa 50:11; Gal 3:13*
[p] S Lev 18:25
22:1 [q] Ex 23:4-5; Pr 27:10; Zec 7:9

MAJOR SOCIAL CONCERNS IN THE COVENANT

1. Personhood
Everyone's person is to be secure (Ex 20:13; Dt 5:17; Ex 21:16–21,26–32; Lev 19:14; Dt 24:7; 27:18).

2. False Accusation
Everyone is to be secure against slander and false accusation (Ex 20:16; Dt 5:20; Ex 23:1–3,6–8; Lev 19:16; Dt 19:15–21).

3. Woman
No woman is to be taken advantage of within her subordinate status in society (Ex 21:7–11,20,26–32; 22:16–17; Dt 21:10–14; 22:13–30; 24:1–5).

4. Punishment
Punishment for wrongdoing shall not be excessive so that the culprit is dehumanized (Dt 25:1–5).

5. Dignity
Every Israelite's dignity and right to be God's servant are to be honored and safeguarded (Ex 21:2,5–6; Lev 25; Dt 15:12–18).

6. Inheritance
Every Israelite's inheritance in the promised land is to be secure (Lev 25; Nu 27:5–7; 36:1–9; Dt 25:5–10).

7. Property
Everyone's property is to be secure (Ex 20:15; Dt 5:19; Ex 21:33–36; 22:1–15; 23:4–5; Lev 19:35–36; Dt 22:1–4; 25:13–15).

8. Fruit of Labor
Everyone is to receive the fruit of their labors (Lev 19:13; Dt 24:14; 25:4).

9. Fruit of the Ground
Everyone is to share the fruit of the ground (Ex 23:10–11; Lev 19:9–10; 23:22; 25:3–55; Dt 14:28–29; 24:19–21).

10. Rest on Sabbath
Everyone, down to the humblest servant and the resident alien, is to share in the weekly rest of God's Sabbath (Ex 20:8–11; Dt 5:12–15; Ex 23:12).

11. Marriage
The marriage relationship is to be kept inviolate (Ex 20:14; Dt 5:18; see also Lev 18:6–23; 20:10–21; Dt 22:13–30).

12. Exploitation
No one, however disabled, impoverished or powerless, is to be oppressed or exploited (Ex 22:21–27; Lev 19:14,33–34; 25:35–36; Dt 23:19; 24:6,12–15,17; 27:18).

13. Fair Trial
Everyone is to have free access to the courts and is to be afforded a fair trial (Ex 23:6–8; Lev 19:15; Dt 1:17; 10:17–18; 16:18–20; 17:8–13; 19:15–21).

14. Social Order
Every person's God-given place in the social order is to be honored (Ex 20:12; Dt 5:16; Ex 21:15,17; 22:28; Lev 19:3,32; 20:9; Dt 17:8–13; 21:15–21; 27:16).

15. Law
No one shall be above the law, not even the king (Dt 17:18–20).

16. Animals
Concern for the welfare of other creatures is to be extended to the animal world (Ex 23:5,11; Lev 25:7; Dt 22:4,6–7; 25:4).

22:4 ʳ Ex 23:5
ˢ 1Co 9:9
22:6 ᶠ Lev 22:28
22:7 ᵘ S Lev 22:28
ᵛ S Dt 5:29
22:8 ʷ Jos 2:8;
1Sa 9:25; 2Sa 11:2
22:9 ˣ Lev 19:19
22:10 ʸ 2Co 6:14
22:11 ᶻ Lev 19:19
22:12 ᵃ Nu 15:37-
41; Mt 23:5
22:13 ᵇ Dt 24:1
22:15 ᶜ S Ge 23:10
22:18 ᵈ Ex 18:21;
Dt 1:9-18
22:20 ᵉ Dt 17:4
22:21 ᶠ S Ge 34:7;
S 38:24; S Lev 19:29;
Dt 23:17-18;
1Co 5:13*
22:22 ᵍ 2Sa 11:4
ʰ S Ge 38:24;
S Ex 21:12; Mt 5:27-
28; Jn 8:5; 1Co 6:9;
Heb 13:4
22:24 ⁱ 1Co 5:13*
22:27 ʲ S Ge 39:14
22:28 ᵏ Ex 22:16
22:30 ˡ S Ge 29:29;
S Lev 18:8; S 20:9;
1Co 5:1

⁴If you see someone's donkey ʳ or ox fallen on the road, do not ignore it. Help the owner get it to its feet. ˢ

⁵A woman must not wear men's clothing, nor a man wear women's clothing, for the LORD your God detests anyone who does this.

⁶If you come across a bird's nest beside the road, either in a tree or on the ground, and the mother is sitting on the young or on the eggs, do not take the mother with the young. ᵗ ⁷You may take the young, but be sure to let the mother go, ᵘ so that it may go well with you and you may have a long life. ᵛ

⁸When you build a new house, make a parapet around your roof so that you may not bring the guilt of bloodshed on your house if someone falls from the roof. ʷ

⁹Do not plant two kinds of seed in your vineyard; ˣ if you do, not only the crops you plant but also the fruit of the vineyard will be defiled. ᵃ

¹⁰Do not plow with an ox and a donkey yoked together. ʸ

¹¹Do not wear clothes of wool and linen woven together. ᶻ

¹²Make tassels on the four corners of the cloak you wear. ᵃ

MARRIAGE VIOLATIONS

¹³If a man takes a wife and, after sleeping with her ᵇ, dislikes her ¹⁴and slanders her and gives her a bad name, saying, "I married this woman, but when I approached her, I did not find proof of her virginity," ¹⁵then the young woman's father and mother shall bring to the town elders at the gate ᶜ proof that she was a virgin. ¹⁶Her father will say to the elders, "I gave my daughter in marriage to this man, but he dislikes her. ¹⁷Now he has slandered her and said, 'I did not find your daughter to be a virgin.' But here is the proof of my daughter's virginity." Then her parents shall display the cloth before the elders of the town, ¹⁸and the elders ᵈ shall take the man and punish him. ¹⁹They shall fine him a hundred shekels ᵇ of silver and give them to the young woman's father, because this man has given an Israelite virgin a bad name. She shall continue to be his wife; he must not divorce her as long as he lives.

²⁰If, however, the charge is true ᵉ and no proof of the young woman's virginity can be found, ²¹she shall be brought to the door of her father's house and there the men of her town shall stone her to death. She has done an outrageous thing ᶠ in Israel by being promiscuous while still in her father's house. You must purge the evil from among you.

²²If a man is found sleeping with another man's wife, both the man who slept ᵍ with her and the woman must die. ʰ You must purge the evil from Israel.

²³If a man happens to meet in a town a virgin pledged to be married and he sleeps with her, ²⁴you shall take both of them to the gate of that town and stone them to death—the young woman because she was in a town and did not scream for help, and the man because he violated another man's wife. You must purge the evil from among you. ⁱ

²⁵But if out in the country a man happens to meet a young woman pledged to be married and rapes her, only the man who has done this shall die. ²⁶Do nothing to the woman; she has committed no sin deserving death. This case is like that of someone who attacks and murders a neighbor, ²⁷for the man found the young woman out in the country, and though the betrothed woman screamed, ʲ there was no one to rescue her.

²⁸If a man happens to meet a virgin who is not pledged to be married and rapes her and they are discovered, ᵏ ²⁹he shall pay her father fifty shekels ᶜ of silver. He must marry the young woman, for he has violated her. He can never divorce her as long as he lives. ˡ

*³⁰A man is not to marry his father's wife; he must not dishonor his father's bed. ˡ

ᵃ 9 Or *be forfeited to the sanctuary*   ᵇ 19 That is, about 2 1/2 pounds or about 1.2 kilograms
ᶜ 29 That is, about 1 1/4 pounds or about 575 grams

* 22:30 is numbered 23:1 in Hebrew texts.

A **22:5** Probably intended to prohibit such perversions as transvestism and homosexual practices, especially under religious auspices. The God-created differences between men and women are not to be disregarded (see Lev 18:22; 20:13).
22:9–11 See note on Lev 19:19.
22:12 *tassels.* See note on Nu 15:38; cf. Mt 23:5.
22:14 *proof of her virginity.* A blood-stained cloth or garment (see vv. 15,17,20).
22:15 *elders at the gate.* See 21:19; 25:7; see also notes on Ge 19:1; Ru 4:1; La 5:14.
A **22:19** *hundred shekels of silver.* A heavy fine—several times what Hosea paid to buy Gomer back (Hos 3:2) or what Jeremiah paid for the field at Anathoth (Jer 32:9). It may

have been about twice the average bride-price (see note on v. 29). The high fine, in addition to the no-divorce rule, was intended to restrain not only a husband's charges against his wife but also easy divorce. *shekels.* See note on Ge 20:16.
22:21,24 *You must purge the evil from among you.* See v. 22; see also note on 13:5.
22:22 See Lev 20:10.
22:29 *fifty shekels of silver.* Probably equaled the average bride-price, which must have varied with the economic status of the participants (see note on Ex 22:16).
22:30 *his father's wife.* Refers to a wife other than his mother (see 27:20). *dishonor his father's bed.* Lit. "uncover the corner of his father's garment" (cf. notes on Ru 3:9; Eze 16:8).

EXCLUSION FROM THE ASSEMBLY

23 *No one who has been emasculated *m* by crushing or cutting may enter the assembly of the LORD. ²No one born of a forbidden marriage ᵃ nor any offspring from such a marriage may enter the assembly of the LORD, not even in the tenth generation.

³No Ammonite ⁿ or Moabite or any of their descendants may enter the assembly of the LORD, not even in the tenth generation. ᵒ ⁴For they did not come to meet you with bread and water ᵖ on your way when you came out of Egypt, and they hired Balaam �q son of Beor from Pethor in Aram Naharaim ᵇ ʳ to pronounce a curse on you. ˢ ⁵However, the LORD your God would not listen to Balaam but turned the curse ᵗ into a blessing for you, because the LORD your God loves ᵘ you. ⁶Do not seek a treaty ᵛ of friendship with them as long as you live. ʷ

⁷Do not despise an Edomite, ˣ for the Edomites are related to you. ʸ Do not despise an Egyptian, because you resided as foreigners in their country. ᶻ ⁸The third generation of children born to them may enter the assembly of the LORD.

UNCLEANNESS IN THE CAMP

⁹When you are encamped against your enemies, keep away from everything impure. ᵃ ¹⁰If one of your men is unclean because of a nocturnal emission, he is to go outside the camp and stay there. ᵇ ¹¹But as evening approaches he is to wash himself, and at sunset ᶜ he may return to the camp. ᵈ

¹²Designate a place outside the camp where you can go to relieve yourself. ¹³As part of your equipment have something to dig with, and when you relieve yourself, dig a hole and cover up your excrement. ¹⁴For the LORD your God moves ᵉ about in your camp to protect you and to deliver your enemies to you. Your camp must be holy, ᶠ so that he will not see among you anything indecent and turn away from you.

MISCELLANEOUS LAWS

¹⁵If a slave has taken refuge ᵍ with you, do not hand them over to their master. ʰ ¹⁶Let them live among you wherever they like and in whatever town they choose. Do not oppress ⁱ them.

¹⁷No Israelite man ʲ or woman is to become a shrine prostitute. ᵏ ¹⁸You must not bring the earnings of a female prostitute or of a male prostitute ᶜ into the house of the LORD your God to pay any vow, because the LORD your God detests them both. ˡ

¹⁹Do not charge an Israelite interest, whether on money or food or anything else that may earn interest. ᵐ ²⁰You may charge a foreigner ⁿ interest, but not another Israelite, so that the LORD your God may bless ᵒ you in everything you put your hand to in the land you are entering to possess.

²¹If you make a vow to the LORD your God, do not be slow to pay it, ᵖ for the LORD your God will certainly demand it of you and you will be guilty of sin. �q ²²But if you refrain from making a vow, you will not be guilty. ʳ ²³Whatever your lips utter you must be sure to do, because you made your vow freely to the LORD your God with your own mouth.

²⁴If you enter your neighbor's vineyard, you may eat all the grapes you want, but do not put any in your basket. ²⁵If you enter your neighbor's grainfield, you may pick kernels with your hands, but you must not put a sickle to the standing grain. ˢ

ᵃ 2 Or *one of illegitimate birth*   ᵇ 4 That is, Northwest Mesopotamia   ᶜ 18 Hebrew *of a dog*
* 23:1-25 is numbered 23:2-26 in Hebrew texts.

23:1 For blessings on eunuchs in later times, see Isa 56:4–5; Ac 8:26–39.
23:2–3 *not even in the tenth generation.* Perhaps forever, since ten is symbolic of completeness or finality. In v. 6 the equivalent expression is "as long as you live" (lit. "all your days forever").
23:4 *Balaam son of Beor.* See Nu 22:4—24:25 and notes.
23:6 See the prophets' denunciation of Moab and Ammon (Isa 15–16; Jer 48:1—49:6; Eze 25:1–11; Am 1:13—2:3; Zep 2:8–11).
23:7 *Edomite . . . related to you.* Edom (Esau) is often condemned for his hostility against his "brother" Jacob (Israel; see Am 1:11; Ob 10; see also notes on Ge 25:22,26).
23:9–14 Sanitary rules for Israel's military camps. For similar rules for the people in general, see Lev 15 and notes.

23:14 *Your camp must be holy.* Even as the Lord is holy (see Lev 11:44 and note).
23:15 *If a slave has taken refuge.* A foreign slave seeking freedom in Israel.
23:17–18 See notes on Ge 38:21; Ex 34:15; Jdg2:17; 1Ki 14:24; Mic 1:7.
23:18 *male prostitute.* Lit. "dog" (see TNIV text note), a word often associated with moral or spiritual impurity (cf. Mt 7:6; 15:26; Php 3:2; Rev 22:15 and note).
23:19 *interest.* See note on Ex 22:25–27.
23:20 *charge a foreigner.* A foreign merchant would come into Israel for financial advantage and so would be subject to paying interest.
23:21–23 See notes on Nu 30; Ecc 5:1–7.

23:1 *m* S Lev 21:20
23:3 *n* S Ge 19:38
o ver 4; Ne 13:2
23:4 *p* Dt 2:28
q S Nu 23:7;
S 2Pe 2:15
r S Ge 24:10 *s* S ver 3
23:5 *t* Nu 24:10;
Jos 24:10; Pr 26:2
u S Dt 4:37
23:6 *v* S Nu 24:17;
Isa 15:1; 25:10;
Jer 25:21; 27:3; 48:1;
Eze 25:8; Zep 2:9
w Ezr 9:12; Mt 5:43
23:7 *x* S Ge 25:30
y S Ge 25:26
z S Lev 19:34
23:9 *a* Lev 15:1-33
23:10 *b* Lev 15:16
23:11 *c* S Lev 15:16
d 1Sa 21:5
23:14 *e* S Ge 3:8
f Ex 3:5
23:15 *g* 2Sa 22:3;
Ps 2:12; 71:1
h 1Sa 30:15
23:16 *i* Ex 22:21;
S 23:6
23:17 *j* 1Ki 14:24;
15:12; 22:46;
2Ki 23:7; Job 36:14
k S Ge 38:21
23:18 *l* S Ge 19:5;
S Lev 20:13;
Rev 22:15
23:19 *m* S Lev
25:35-37; Ne 5:2-7
23:20 *n* S Ge 31:15;
S Dt 15:3 *o* Dt 15:10
23:21 *p* S Nu 6:21;
Jdg 11:35; Ps 15:4
q Nu 30:1-2;
Job 22:27; Ps 61:8;
65:1; 76:11; Isa 19:21;
S Mt 5:33; Ac 5:3
23:22 *r* Ac 5:4
23:25 *s* Mt 12:1;
Mk 2:23; Lk 6:1

24:1 *t* Dt 22:13
u ver 3; 2Ki 17:6;
Isa 50:1; Jer 3:8;
Mal 2:16; Mt 1:19;
5:31*; 19:7-9;
Mk 10:4-5
24:4 *v* Jer 3:1
24:5 *w* S Dt 20:7
24:6 *x* S Ex 22:22
24:7 *y* S Ex 21:16
z 1Co 5:13*
24:8 *a* S Dt 17:9
b Lev 13:1-46; S 14:2
24:9 *c* S Nu 12:10
24:10 *d* S Ex 22:25-27
24:12 *e* S Ex 22:26
24:13 *f* Ex 22:26
g S Ex 22:27
h Dt 6:25; Ps 106:31;
Da 4:27
24:14 *i* Lev 19:13;
25:35-43; Dt 15:12-
18; Job 24:4; Pr 14:31;
19:17; Am 4:1; 1Ti 5:18
24:15 *j* S Lev 25:35
k S Lev 19:13; Mt 20:8
l S Ex 22:23;
S Job 12:19; Jas 5:4
24:16 *m* S Nu 26:11;
Jer 31:29-30
24:17 *n* Ex 22:22;
Job 6:27; 24:9; 29:12;
Ps 10:18; 82:3;
Pr 23:10; Eze 22:7
o S Ex 22:21; S 23:2;
S Dt 10:18
24:18 *p* S Dt 15:15
24:19 *q* S Lev 19:9
r Dt 10:19; 27:19;
Eze 47:22; Zec 7:10;
Mal 3:5 *s* ver 20;
Dt 14:29 *t* S Dt 14:29;
Pr 19:17; 28:27;
Ecc 11:1
24:20 *u* Lev 19:10
24:22 *v* ver 18
25:1 *w* S Ex 21:6
x Dt 17:8-13; 19:17;
Ac 23:3 *y* 1Ki 8:32
z S Ex 23:7; Dt 1:16-17
25:2 *a* Pr 10:13;
19:29; Lk 12:47-48
25:3 *b* Mt 22:26;
Jn 19:1; 2Co 11:24
c Jer 20:2
25:4 *d* S Nu 22:29;
1Co 9:9*; 1Ti 5:18*

24 If a man marries a woman who becomes displeasing to him *t* because he finds something indecent about her, and he writes her a certificate of divorce, *u* gives it to her and sends her from his house, ²and if after she leaves his house she becomes the wife of another man, ³and her second husband dislikes her and writes her a certificate of divorce, gives it to her and sends her from his house, or if he dies, ⁴then her first husband, who divorced her, is not allowed to marry her again after she has been defiled. That would be detestable in the eyes of the LORD. Do not bring sin upon the land the LORD *v* your God is giving you as an inheritance.

⁵If a man has recently married, he must not be sent to war or have any other duty laid on him. For one year he is to be free to stay at home and bring happiness to the wife he has married. *w*

⁶Do not take a pair of millstones—not even the upper one—as security for a debt, because that would be taking a person's livelihood as security. *x*

⁷If someone is caught kidnapping another Israelite and treating or selling that Israelite as a slave, the kidnapper must die. *y* You must purge the evil from among you. *z* ⁸In cases of defiling skin diseases, *a* be very careful to do exactly as the Levitical *a* priests instruct you. You must follow carefully what I have commanded them. *b* ⁹Remember what the LORD your God did to Miriam along the way after you came out of Egypt. *c*

¹⁰When you make a loan of any kind to a neighbor, do not go into the neighbor's house to get what is offered to you as a pledge. *d* ¹¹Stay outside and let the neighbor to whom you are making the loan bring the pledge out to you. ¹²If the neighbor is poor, do not go to sleep with that pledge *e* in your possession. ¹³Return the cloak by sunset *f* so that your neighbor may sleep in it. *g* Then you will be thanked, and it will be regarded as a righteous act in the sight of the LORD your God. *h*

¹⁴Do not take advantage of a hired worker who is poor and needy, whether that worker is an Israelite or is a foreigner residing in one of your towns. *i* ¹⁵Pay them their wages each day before sunset, because they are poor *j* and are counting on it. *k* Otherwise they may cry to the LORD against you, and you will be guilty of sin. *l*

¹⁶Parents are not to be put to death for their children, nor children put to death for their parents; each of you will die for your own sin. *m*

¹⁷Do not deprive the foreigner or the fatherless *n* of justice, *o* or take the cloak of the widow as a pledge. ¹⁸Remember that you were slaves in Egypt *p* and the LORD your God redeemed you from there. That is why I command you to do this.

¹⁹When you are harvesting in your field and you overlook a sheaf, do not go back to get it. *q* Leave it for the foreigner, *r* the fatherless and the widow, *s* so that the LORD your God may bless *t* you in all the work of your hands. ²⁰When you beat the olives from your trees, do not go over the branches a second time. *u* Leave what remains for the foreigner, the fatherless and the widow. ²¹When you harvest the grapes in your vineyard, do not go over the vines again. Leave what remains for the foreigner, the fatherless and the widow. ²²Remember that you were slaves in Egypt. That is why I command you to do this. *v*

25 When people have a dispute, they are to take it to court and the judges *w* will decide the case, *x* acquitting *y* the innocent and condemning the guilty. *z* ²If the one who is guilty deserves to be beaten, *a* the judge shall make them lie down and have them flogged in his presence with the number of lashes the crime deserves, ³but the judge must not impose more than forty lashes. *b* If the guilty party is flogged more than that, your Israelite neighbor will be degraded in your eyes. *c*

⁴Do not muzzle an ox while it is treading out the grain. *d*

---

a 8 The Hebrew word for *defiling skin diseases,* traditionally translated "leprosy," was used for various diseases affecting the skin.

24:1–4 In the books of Moses divorce was permitted and regulated (see Lev 21:7,14; 22:13; Nu 30:9). Jesus commented on the law of 24:1 in the Sermon on the Mount (Mt 5:31–32). On another occasion, he cited the higher law of creation (Mt 19:3–9).

24:5 *happiness.* Marital bliss was held in high regard.

24:6 *millstones.* Used for grinding grain for flour and daily food (see note on Jdg 9:53).

24:7 *as a slave.* Cf. 23:15. *You must purge the evil from among you.* See note on 13:5.

24:8 *defiling skin diseases.* See TNIV text note; see also note on Lev 13:2.

24:9,18,22 *Remember.* See note on 4:10.

24:10–13 See notes on 6:25; Ex 22:26–27.

24:16 *each of you will die for your own sin.* See Eze 18:4 and note.

24:17–18 See 10:18–19. When the Israelites were in trouble, the Lord helped them. Therefore they were not to take advantage of others in difficulty.

24:19–21 See note on Lev 19:9–10.

25:3 *not . . . more than forty lashes.* Beating could subject the culprit to abuse, so the law kept the punishment from becoming inhumane. Cf. Paul's experience (see 2Co 11:24–25 and note).

25:4 Applied to ministers of Christ in 1Co 9:9–10; 1Ti 5:17–18. *treading out the grain.* See notes on Ge 50:10; Ru 1:22.

⁵If brothers are living together and one of them dies without a son, his widow must not marry outside the family. Her husband's brother shall take her and marry her and fulfill the duty of a brother-in-law to her. *ᵉ* ⁶The first son she bears shall carry on the name of the dead brother so that his name will not be blotted out from Israel. *f*

⁷However, if a man does not want to marry his brother's wife, *g* she shall go to the elders at the town gate *h* and say, "My husband's brother refuses to carry on his brother's name in Israel. He will not fulfill the duty of a brother-in-law to me." *i* ⁸Then the elders of his town shall summon him and talk to him. If he persists in saying, "I do not want to marry her," ⁹his brother's widow shall go up to him in the presence of the elders, take off one of his sandals, *j* spit in his face *k* and say, "This is what is done to the man who will not build up his brother's family line." ¹⁰That man's line shall be known in Israel as The Family of the Unsandaled.

¹¹If two men are fighting and the wife of one of them comes to rescue her husband from his assailant, and she reaches out and seizes him by his private parts, ¹²you shall cut off her hand. Show her no pity. *l*

¹³Do not have two differing weights in your bag—one heavy, one light. *m* ¹⁴Do not have two differing measures in your house—one large, one small. ¹⁵You must have accurate and honest weights and measures, so that you may live long *n* in the land the Lᴏʀᴅ your God is giving you. ¹⁶For the Lᴏʀᴅ your God detests anyone who does these things, anyone who deals dishonestly. *o*

¹⁷Remember what the Amalekites *p* did to you along the way when you came out of Egypt. ¹⁸When you were weary and worn out, they met you on your journey and attacked all who were lagging behind; they had no fear of God. *q* ¹⁹When the Lᴏʀᴅ your God gives you rest *r* from all the enemies *s* around you in the land he is giving you to possess as an inheritance, you shall blot out the name of Amalek *t* from under heaven. Do not forget!

FIRSTFRUITS AND TITHES

26

When you have entered the land the Lᴏʀᴅ your God is giving you as an inheritance and have taken possession of it and settled in it, ²take some of the firstfruits *u* of all that you produce from the soil of the land the Lᴏʀᴅ your God is giving you and put them in a basket. Then go to the place the Lᴏʀᴅ your God will choose as a dwelling for his Name *v* ³and say to the priest in office at the time, "I declare today to the Lᴏʀᴅ your God that I have come to the land the Lᴏʀᴅ swore to our ancestors to give us." ⁴The priest shall take the basket from your hands and set it down in front of the altar of the Lᴏʀᴅ your God. ⁵Then you shall declare before the Lᴏʀᴅ your God: "My father was a wandering *w* Aramean, *x* and he went down into Egypt with a few people *y* and lived there and became a great nation, *z* powerful and numerous. ⁶But the Egyptians mistreated us and made us suffer, *a* subjecting us to harsh labor. *b* ⁷Then we cried out to the Lᴏʀᴅ, the God of our ancestors, and the Lᴏʀᴅ heard our voice *c* and saw *d* our misery, *e* toil and oppression. *f* ⁸So the Lᴏʀᴅ brought us out of Egypt *g* with a mighty hand and an outstretched arm, *h* with great terror and with signs and wonders. *i* ⁹He brought us to this place and gave us this land, a land flowing with milk and honey; *j* ¹⁰and now I bring the firstfruits of the soil that you, Lᴏʀᴅ, have given me. *k*" Place the basket before the Lᴏʀᴅ your God and bow down before him. ¹¹Then you and the Levites *l* and the foreigners residing among you shall rejoice *m* in all the good things the Lᴏʀᴅ your God has given to you and your household.

¹²When you have finished setting aside a tenth *n* of all your produce in the third year, the year of the tithe, *o* you shall give it to the Levite, the foreigner, the fatherless and the

---

25:5 *ᵉ* Ru 4:10,13; Mt 22:24; Mk 12:19; Lk 20:28
25:6 *f* Ge 38:9; Ru 4:5,10
25:7 *g* Ru 1:15 *h* S Ge 23:10 *i* Ru 4:1-2,5-6
25:9 *j* Jos 24:22; Ru 4:7-8,11 *k* Nu 12:14; Job 17:6; 30:10; Isa 50:6
25:12 *l* S Dt 7:2
25:13 *m* Pr 11:1; 20:23; Mic 6:11
25:15 *n* S Ex 20:12
25:16 *o* Pr 11:1
25:17 *p* S Ge 36:12
25:18 *q* Ps 36:1; Ro 3:18
25:19 *r* S Ex 33:14; Heb 3:18-19 *s* Est 9:16 *t* S Ge 36:12
26:2 *u* S Ex 22:29 *v* S Dt 12:5
26:5 *w* S Ge 20:13 *x* S Ge 25:20 *y* S Ge 34:30; 43:14 *z* S Ge 12:2
26:6 *a* S Nu 20:15 *b* S Ex 1:13
26:7 *c* S Ge 21:17 *d* Ex 3:9; 2Ki 13:4; 14:26 *e* S Ge 16:11 *f* Ps 42:9; 44:24; 72:14
26:8 *g* S Nu 20:16 *h* S Ex 3:20 *i* S Dt 4:34; 34:11-12
26:9 *j* S Ex 3:8
26:10 *k* S Dt 8:18
26:11 *l* Dt 12:12 *m* S Dt 16:11
26:12 *n* S Ge 14:20 *o* S Nu 18:24; Dt 14:28-29; Heb 7:5,9

25:5–6 The continuity of each family and the decentralized control of land through family ownership were basic to the Mosaic economy (see note on Ge 38:8).

25:7 *if a man does not want to marry his brother's wife.* See vv. 8–10; note the experiences, with some variations, described in Ge 38:8–10; Ru 4:1–12.

elders at the town gate. See 21:19; 22:15; see also notes on Ge 19:1; Ru 4:1.

25:11–12 Cf. Ex 21:22–25 and notes.

25:13–16 See note on Lev 19:35.

25:14 *measures.* Of quantity.

25:17 *Remember.* See note on 4:10. *Amalekites.* See Ex 17:8–16; Nu 14:45; 1Sa 15:2–3; 30:1–20.

25:18 *fear of God.* See note on Ge 20:11.

25:19 *rest.* See note on 3:20.

26:1 *inheritance.* See note on Ex 15:17.

26:2 *firstfruits.* The offering described here occurred only once and must not be confused with the annual offerings of firstfruits (see 18:4 and note). *the place the Lᴏʀᴅ . . . will choose as a dwelling for his Name.* See note on 12:5.

26:5 *wandering Aramean.* A reference to Jacob, who had wandered from southern Canaan to Harran in Aram (see note on Ge 10:22 and maps, pp. 23, 508) and back (Ge 27–35) and who later migrated to Egypt (see Ge 46:3–7). He also married two Aramean women (see Ge 28:5; 29:16,28). The Arameans were a Semitic people who spoke a form of the Aramaic language (see also Ge 22:23–24 and note; 25:20; 31:20,24; 1Ch 18:5 and note). *with a few people . . . became a great nation.* See Ex 1:5,7 and note on 1:7.

26:11 *rejoice.* See note on 12:12.

26:12 See note on 14:22–29.

26:13 ᴾ Ps 119:141,
153,176
26:14 ᵠ Lev 7:20;
Hos 9:4
26:15 ʳ Ps 68:5;
80:14; 102:19;
Isa 63:15; Zec 2:13
ˢ S Ex 39:43
26:16 ᵗ Dt 4:29
26:17 ᵘ Ex 19:8;
Ps 48:14
26:18 ᵛ Ex 6:7;
Dt 7:6
26:19 ʷ Isa 62:7;
Zep 3:20 ˣ Dt 4:7-8;
28:1,13,44; 1Ch 14:2;
Ps 148:14; Isa 40:11
ʸ S Dt 7:6
27:1 ᶻ Ps 78:7
27:2 ᵃ Jos 4:1
ᵇ Ex 24:4; Jos 24:26;
1Sa 7:12 ᶜ Jos 8:31
27:3 ᵈ S Ex 3:8
27:4 ᵉ S Dt 11:29
27:5 ᶠ S Ex 20:24
ᵍ Ex 20:25
27:7 ʰ S Ex 32:6
ⁱ S Dt 16:11 ʲ Jos 8:31
27:8 ᵏ Isa 8:1; 30:8;
Hab 2:2 ˡ Jos 8:32
27:9 ᵐ S Dt 17:9
ⁿ Dt 26:18
27:12 ᵒ S Dt 11:29
ᵖ S Ge 30:18
ᵠ Jos 8:35
27:13 ʳ S Dt 11:29
27:15 ˢ S Ex 20:4
ᵗ 1Ki 11:5,7; 2Ki 23:13;
Isa 44:19; 66:3
ᵘ Nu 5:22;
S 1Co 14:16

widow, so that they may eat in your towns and be satisfied. ¹³Then say to the Lᴏʀᴅ your God: "I have removed from my house the sacred portion and have given it to the Levite, the foreigner, the fatherless and the widow, according to all you commanded. I have not turned aside from your commands nor have I forgotten any of them. ᵖ ¹⁴I have not eaten any of the sacred portion while I was in mourning, nor have I removed any of it while I was unclean, ᵠ nor have I offered any of it to the dead. I have obeyed the Lᴏʀᴅ my God; I have done everything you commanded me. ¹⁵Look down from heaven, ʳ your holy dwelling place, and bless ˢ your people Israel and the land you have given us as you promised on oath to our ancestors, a land flowing with milk and honey."

FOLLOW THE LORD'S COMMANDS

¹⁶The Lᴏʀᴅ your God commands you this day to follow these decrees and laws; carefully observe them with all your heart and with all your soul. ᵗ ¹⁷You have declared this day that the Lᴏʀᴅ is your God and that you will walk in obedience to him, that you will keep his decrees, commands and laws—that you will listen to him. ᵘ ¹⁸And the Lᴏʀᴅ has declared this day that you are his people, his treasured possession ᵛ as he promised, and that you are to keep all his commands. ¹⁹He has declared that he will set you in praise, ʷ fame and honor high above all the nations ˣ he has made and that you will be a people holy ʸ to the Lᴏʀᴅ your God, as he promised.

THE ALTAR ON MOUNT EBAL

27 Moses and the elders of Israel commanded the people: "Keep all these commands ᶻ that I give you today. ²When you have crossed the Jordan ᵃ into the land the Lᴏʀᴅ your God is giving you, set up some large stones ᵇ and coat them with plaster. ᶜ ³Write on them all the words of this law when you have crossed over to enter the land the Lᴏʀᴅ your God is giving you, a land flowing with milk and honey, ᵈ just as the Lᴏʀᴅ, the God of your ancestors, promised you. ⁴And when you have crossed the Jordan, set up these stones on Mount Ebal, ᵉ as I command you today, and coat them with plaster. ⁵Build there an altar ᶠ to the Lᴏʀᴅ your God, an altar of stones. Do not use any iron tool ᵍ on them. ⁶Build the altar of the Lᴏʀᴅ your God with fieldstones and offer burnt offerings on it to the Lᴏʀᴅ your God. ⁷Sacrifice fellowship offerings ʰ there, eating them and rejoicing ⁱ in the presence of the Lᴏʀᴅ your God. ʲ ⁸And you shall write very clearly all the words of this law on these stones ᵏ you have set up." ˡ

CURSES FROM MOUNT EBAL

⁹Then Moses and the Levitical ᵐ priests said to all Israel, "Be silent, Israel, and listen! You have now become the people of the Lᴏʀᴅ your God. ⁿ ¹⁰Obey the Lᴏʀᴅ your God and follow his commands and decrees that I give you today."

¹¹On the same day Moses commanded the people:

¹²When you have crossed the Jordan, these tribes shall stand on Mount Gerizim ᵒ to bless the people: Simeon, Levi, Judah, Issachar, ᵖ Joseph and Benjamin. ᵠ ¹³And these tribes shall stand on Mount Ebal ʳ to pronounce curses: Reuben, Gad, Asher, Zebulun, Dan and Naphtali.

¹⁴The Levites shall recite to all the people of Israel in a loud voice:

¹⁵"Cursed is anyone who makes an idol ˢ—a thing detestable ᵗ to the Lᴏʀᴅ, the work of skilled hands—and sets it up in secret."

Then all the people shall say, "Amen!" ᵘ

26:16 *with all your heart...soul.* See note on 4:29.
26:17 The terminology is that of a covenant or treaty, involving a renewal of Israel's vow that the Lord was God and that they would obey him (see 5:27; see also note on Ex 19:8).
26:18 *treasured possession.* See note on Ex 19:5.
26:19 *a people holy to the Lᴏʀᴅ.* See 14:2 and note.
27:2–8 Setting up stones inscribed with messages to be remembered was a common practice in the ancient Near East.
27:2,4 *coat them with plaster.* So that the writing inscribed on them would stand out clearly (see v. 8).
27:3,8 *all the words of this law.* The stipulations (see note on Ex 20:1) of the covenant that Moses' reaffirmation contained.
27:4 *Mount Ebal.* See note on Jos 8:30.
27:5 *Build...an altar of stones.* Different from the altars of the tabernacle, both in form and in use (see note on Ex 20:25).
27:9 *You have now become the people of the Lᴏʀᴅ.* The language

of covenant renewal.
27:12 *these tribes shall stand on Mount Gerizim.* All six were descendants of Jacob by Leah and Rachel (see Ge 35:23–24). See 11:30 and note. *Mount Gerizim.* See note on Jn 4:20. *to bless.* No blessings appear in vv. 15–26, which consist entirely of 12 curses (see 28:15–68). Blessings, however, are listed and described in 28:1–14.
27:13 *these tribes shall stand on Mount Ebal.* Reuben and Zebulun were descendants of Jacob by Leah; the rest were his descendants by the female servants Zilpah and Bilhah (see Ge 35:23,25–26).
27:15 *makes an idol.* In violation of the first and second commandments of the Decalogue (see notes on Ex 20:1,4). See 4:28; 5:6–10; 31:29; Isa 40:19–20; 41:7; 44:9–20; 45:16; Jer 10:3–9; Hos 8:4–6; 13:2. *Amen!* Not simply approval but a solemn, formal assertion that the people accept and agree to the covenant with its curses and blessings (see vv. 16–26).

¹⁶"Cursed is anyone who dishonors their father or mother." ^v

Then all the people shall say, "Amen!"

¹⁷"Cursed is anyone who moves their neighbor's boundary stone." ^w

Then all the people shall say, "Amen!"

¹⁸"Cursed is anyone who leads the blind astray on the road." ^x

Then all the people shall say, "Amen!"

¹⁹"Cursed is anyone who withholds justice from the foreigner, ^y the fatherless or the widow." ^z

Then all the people shall say, "Amen!"

²⁰"Cursed is anyone who sleeps with his father's wife, for he dishonors his father's bed." ^a

Then all the people shall say, "Amen!"

²¹"Cursed is anyone who has sexual relations with any animal." ^b

Then all the people shall say, "Amen!"

²²"Cursed is anyone who sleeps with his sister, the daughter of his father or the daughter of his mother." ^c

Then all the people shall say, "Amen!"

²³"Cursed is anyone who sleeps with his mother-in-law." ^d

Then all the people shall say, "Amen!"

²⁴"Cursed is anyone who kills ^e their neighbor secretly." ^f

Then all the people shall say, "Amen!"

²⁵"Cursed is anyone who accepts a bribe to kill an innocent person." ^g

Then all the people shall say, "Amen!"

²⁶"Cursed is anyone who does not uphold the words of this law by carrying them out." ^h

Then all the people shall say, "Amen!" ⁱ

BLESSINGS FOR OBEDIENCE

28

If you fully obey the Lord your God and carefully follow ^j all his commands ^k I give you today, the Lord your God will set you high above all the nations on earth. ²All these blessings will come on you ^m and accompany you if you obey the Lord your God:

³You will be blessed ⁿ in the city and blessed in the country. ^o

⁴The fruit of your womb will be blessed, and the crops of your land and the young of your livestock—the calves of your herds and the lambs of your flocks. ^p

⁵Your basket and your kneading trough will be blessed.

⁶You will be blessed when you come in and blessed when you go out. ^q

⁷The Lord will grant that the enemies ^r who rise up against you will be defeated before you. They will come at you from one direction but flee from you in seven. ^s

⁸The Lord will send a blessing on your barns and on everything you put your hand to. The Lord your God will bless ^t you in the land he is giving you.

⁹The Lord will establish you as his holy people, ^u as he promised you on oath, if you keep the commands ^v of the Lord your God and walk in obedience to him. ¹⁰Then all the peoples on earth will see that you are called by the name ^w of the Lord, and they will fear you. ¹¹The Lord will grant you abundant prosperity—in the fruit of your womb, the young of your livestock ^x and the crops of your ground—in the land he swore to your ancestors to give you. ^y

¹²The Lord will open the heavens, the storehouse ^z of his bounty, ^a to send rain ^b on your land in season and to bless ^c all the work of your hands. You will lend to many nations but will borrow from none. ^{d 13}The Lord will make you the head, not the tail. If you pay attention to the commands of the Lord your God that I give you this day and careful-

27:16 ^vS Ge 31:35; S Ex 21:12; S Dt 5:16
27:17 ^wS Dt 19:14
27:18 ^xS Lev 19:14
27:19 ^yS Ex 22:21; S Dt 24:19
^zS Ex 23:2; S Dt 10:18
27:20 ^aS Ge 34:5; S Lev 18:7
27:21 ^bS Ex 22:19
27:22 ^cS Lev 18:9
27:23 ^dS Lev 20:14
27:24 ^eS Ge 4:23
^fEx 21:12
27:25 ^gEx 23:7-8; S Lev 19:16
27:26 ^hS Lev 26:14; Dt 28:15; Ps 119:21; Jer 11:3; Gal 3:10*
ⁱJer 11:5
28:1 ^jS Dt 15:5
^kS Lev 26:3
^lS Dt 26:19
28:2 ^mJer 32:24; Zec 1:6
28:3 ⁿPs 144:15
^oS Ge 39:5
28:4 ^pS Ge 49:25; S Dt 8:18
28:6 ^qPs 121:8
28:7 ^r2Ch 6:34
^sS Lev 26:8,17
28:8 ^tDt 15:4
28:9 ^uS Ex 19:6
^vS Lev 26:3
28:10 ^wS Nu 6:27; 1Ki 8:43; Jer 25:29; Da 9:18
28:11 ^xS Ge 30:27
^yver 4; Dt 30:9
28:12 ^zJob 38:22; Ps 135:7; Jer 10:13; 51:16 ^aPs 65:11; 68:10; Jer 31:12
^bS Lev 26:4; 1Ki 8:35-36; 18:1; Ps 104:13; Isa 5:6; 30:23; 32:20
^cIsa 61:9; 65:23; Jer 32:38-41; Mal 3:12
^dver 44; S Lev 25:19; S Dt 15:3,6; Eze 34:26

27:16 See 5:16; Ex 20:12 and note.
27:17 See note on 19:14.
27:19 See 24:17–18 and note.
27:20 See 22:30; Lev 18:8 and notes.
27:21 See Ex 22:19 and note; Lev 18:23; 20:15–16.
27:22 See Lev 18:9,11 and note.
27:24–25 See 5:17; Ex 20:13 and note; 21:12; Lev 24:17,21.
27:26 Quoted in Gal 3:10 to prove that humankind is under a curse because no one follows the law of God fully (cf. Jas 2:10; 1Jn 1:8,10).

28:1–14 These blessings are the opposites of the curses in vv. 15–44 (compare especially vv. 3–6 with vv. 16–19).
28:5,17 *basket...kneading trough.* Used for storage and for the preparation of foods, particularly bread.
28:7 For the reverse, see v. 25.
28:9 *establish you as his holy people.* See 7:6 and note.
28:12 *the heavens, the storehouse.* For the heavens as the storehouse of rain, snow, hail and wind, see Job 38:22; Ps 135:7; Jer 10:13; 51:16. *You will lend.* For the opposite, see v. 44; see also note on 15:6.
28:13 *the head, not the tail.* For the reverse, see v. 44.

28:13 *e* Jer 11:6;
f S Dt 26:19
28:14 *g* S Dt 5:32;
Jos 1:7
28:15 *h* 1Ki 9:6;
2Ch 7:19 *i* S Dt 27:26
j Dt 29:27; Jos 23:15;
2Ch 12:5; Da 9:11;
Mal 2:2
28:16 *k* ver 3
28:17 *l* ver 5
28:18 *m* ver 4
28:19 *n* ver 6
28:20 *o* ver 8,15;
Lev 26:16; Jer 42:18;
Mal 2:2; 3:9; 4:6
p Ps 39:11; 76:6;
80:16; Isa 17:13;
51:20; 54:9; 66:15;
Eze 5:15 *q* Dt 4:26
r S Ex 32:22
28:21 *s* Lev 26:25;
Nu 14:12; Jer 24:10;
Am 4:10
28:22 *t* ver 48;
Dt 32:24 *u* Lev 26:16;
2Ki 8:1; Job 12:15;
Ps 105:16; Jer 14:1;
Hag 1:11; Mal 3:9
v Hag 2:17
w S Lev 26:25
x Dt 4:26; Am 4:9
28:23 *y* S Lev 26:19
28:24 *z* Lev 26:19;
Dt 11:17; 1Ki 8:35;
17:1; Isa 5:6; Jer 14:1;
Hag 1:10
28:25 *a* 1Sa 4:10;
Ps 78:62
b S Lev 26:17 *c* ver 37
d 2Ch 29:8; 30:7;
Jer 15:4; 24:9; 26:6;
29:18; 44:12;
Eze 23:46
28:26 *e* S Ge 40:19
f Ps 79:2; Isa 18:6;
Jer 7:33; 12:9; 15:2;
16:4; 19:7; 34:20
28:27 *d* Dt 7:15
28:29 *h* Ge 19:11;
Ex 10:21; Job 5:14;
12:25; 24:13; 38:15;
Isa 59:10 *i* Jdg 3:9;
2Ki 13:5; Est 4:14;
Isa 19:20; 43:11;
Hos 13:4; Ob 1:21
28:30 *j* Job 31:10
k Isa 65:22; Am 5:11
l Jer 12:13
28:32 *m* ver 41
28:33 *n* ver 6:6;
22:17 *o* Jer 5:15-17;
Eze 25:4
28:34 *p* ver 67
28:35 *q* Dt 7:15;
Rev 16:2 *r* Job 2:7; 7:5;
13:28; 30:17,30; Isa 1:6
28:36 *s* 1Sa 12:25
t S Dt 4:27; 2Ki 24:14;
25:7,11; 2Ch 33:11;
36:21; Jer 5:12;
Jer 15:14; 16:13;
27:20; 39:1-9; 52:28;
La 1:3 *u* S Dt 4:28
28:37 *v* ver 25;
Jer 42:18; Eze 5:15
w Ps 22:7; 39:8; 44:13;
64:8; Jer 18:16; 48:27;
Mic 6:16 *x* 2Ch 7:20;
Ezr 9:7; Jer 44:8
y 1Ki 9:7; Ps 44:14;
Jer 19:8; 24:9; 25:9,
18; 29:18; La 2:15
28:38 *z* Lev 26:20;
Ps 129:7; Isa 5:10;
Jer 12:13; Hos 8:7;

ly follow *e* them, you will always be at the top, never at the bottom. *f* **14**Do not turn aside from any of the commands I give you today, to the right or to the left, *g* following other gods and serving them.

CURSES FOR DISOBEDIENCE

15However, if you do not obey *h* the Lord your God and do not carefully follow all his commands and decrees I am giving you today, *i* all these curses will come on you and overtake you: *j*

16You will be cursed in the city and cursed in the country. *k*

17Your basket and your kneading trough will be cursed. *l*

18The fruit of your womb will be cursed, and the crops of your land, and the calves of your herds and the lambs of your flocks. *m*

19You will be cursed when you come in and cursed when you go out. *n*

20The Lord will send on you curses, *o* confusion and rebuke *p* in everything you put your hand to, until you are destroyed and come to sudden ruin *q* because of the evil *r* you have done in forsaking him. *a* **21**The Lord will plague you with diseases until he has destroyed you from the land you are entering to possess. *s* **22**The Lord will strike you with wasting disease, *t* with fever and inflammation, with scorching heat and drought, *u* with blight *v* and mildew, which will plague *w* you until you perish. *x* **23**The sky over your head will be bronze, the ground beneath you iron. *y* **24**The Lord will turn the rain *z* of your country into dust and powder; it will come down from the skies until you are destroyed.

25The Lord will cause you to be defeated *a* before your enemies. You will come at them from one direction but flee from them in seven, *b* and you will become a thing of horror *c* to all the kingdoms on earth. *d* **26**Your carcasses will be food for all the birds *e* and the wild animals, and there will be no one to frighten them away. *f* **27**The Lord will afflict you with the boils of Egypt *g* and with tumors, festering sores and the itch, from which you cannot be cured. **28**The Lord will afflict you with madness, blindness and confusion of mind. **29**At midday you will grope *h* about like a blind person in the dark. You will be unsuccessful in everything you do; day after day you will be oppressed and robbed, with no one to rescue *i* you.

30You will be pledged to be married to a woman, but another will take her and ravish her. *j* You will build a house, but you will not live in it. *k* You will plant a vineyard, but you will not even begin to enjoy its fruit. *l* **31**Your ox will be slaughtered before your eyes, but you will eat none of it. Your donkey will be forcibly taken from you and will not be returned. Your sheep will be given to your enemies, and no one will rescue them. **32**Your sons and daughters will be given to another nation, *m* and you will wear out your eyes watching for them day after day, powerless to lift a hand. **33**A people that you do not know will eat what your land and labor produce, and you will have nothing but cruel oppression *n* all your days. *o* **34**The sights you see will drive you mad. *p* **35**The Lord will afflict your knees and legs with painful boils *q* that cannot be cured, spreading from the soles of your feet to the top of your head. *r*

36The Lord will drive you and the king *s* you set over you to a nation unknown to you or your ancestors. *t* There you will worship other gods, gods of wood and stone. *u* **37**You will become a thing of horror, *v* a byword *w* and an object of ridicule *x* among all the peoples where the Lord will drive you. *y*

38You will sow much seed in the field but you will harvest little, *z* because locusts *a* will devour *b* it. **39**You will plant vineyards and cultivate them but you will not drink the wine *c* or gather the grapes, because worms will eat *d* them. *e* **40**You will have olive trees throughout your country but you will not use the oil, because the olives will drop off. *f* **41**You will have sons and daughters but you will not keep them, because they will go into captivity. *g* **42**Swarms of locusts *h* will take over all your trees and the crops of your land.

43The foreigners who reside among you will rise above you higher and higher, but you will sink lower and lower. *i* **44**They will lend to you, but you will not lend to them. *j* They will be the head, but you will be the tail. *k*

a 20 Hebrew *me*

28:38 Mic 6:15; Hag 1:6,9; 2:16 *a* S Ex 10:4 *b* S Ex 10:15 28:39 *c* S Lev 10:9 *d* Joel 1:4; 2:25; Mal 3:11 *e* Isa 5:10; 17:10-11; Zep 1:13
28:40 *f* Jer 11:16; Mic 6:15 28:41 *g* ver 32 28:42 *h* ver 38; Jdg 6:5; 7:12; Jer 46:23 28:43 *i* ver 13 28:44 *j* S ver 12 *k* S Dt 26:19

28:16–19 The opposites of vv. 3–6 (see note on vv. 1–14).

28:23 *sky…bronze…ground…iron.* No rain would pierce the sky or penetrate the ground (see v. 22).

28:25 For the reverse, see v. 7.

28:27 *boils of Egypt.* See note on Ex 9:9.

28:30–33 See Mic 6:14–15; Hag 1:6 and note.

28:30 See 20:5–8 and note; contrast Isa 65:21–22.

28:35 See note on Ex 9:11.

28:44 See notes on vv. 12–13.

⁴⁵All these curses will come on you. They will pursue you and overtake you *ᶦ* until you are destroyed, *ᵐ* because you did not obey the LORD your God and observe the commands and decrees he gave you. *ⁿ* ⁴⁷Because you did not serve *ᵒ* the LORD your God joyfully and gladly *ᵖ* in the time of prosperity, ⁴⁸therefore in hunger and thirst, *q* in nakedness and dire poverty, you will serve the enemies the LORD sends against you. He will put an iron yoke *ʳ* on your neck *ˢ* until he has destroyed you.

⁴⁹The LORD will bring a nation against you *ᵗ* from far away, from the ends of the earth, *ᵘ* like an eagle *ᵛ* swooping down, a nation whose language you will not understand, *ʷ* ⁵⁰a fierce-looking nation without respect for the old *ˣ* or pity for the young. ⁵¹They will devour the young of your livestock and the crops of your land until you are destroyed. They will leave you no grain, new wine *ʸ* or olive oil, *ᶻ* nor any calves of your herds or lambs of your flocks until you are ruined. *ᵃ* ⁵²They will lay siege *ᵇ* to all the cities throughout your land until the high fortified walls in which you trust fall down. They will besiege all the cities throughout the land the LORD your God is giving you. *ᶜ*

⁵³Because of the suffering that your enemy will inflict on you during the siege, you will eat the fruit of the womb, the flesh of the sons and daughters the LORD your God has given you. *ᵈ* ⁵⁴Even the most gentle and sensitive man among you will have no compassion on his own brother or the wife he loves or his surviving children, ⁵⁵and he will not give to one of them any of the flesh of his children that he is eating. It will be all he has left because of the suffering your enemy will inflict on you during the siege of all your cities. *ᵉ* ⁵⁶The most gentle and sensitive *ᶠ* woman among you—so sensitive and gentle that she would not venture to touch the ground with the sole of her foot—will begrudge the husband she loves and her own son or daughter *ᵍ* ⁵⁷the afterbirth from her womb and the children she bears. For in her dire need she intends to eat them *ʰ* secretly because of the suffering your enemy will inflict on you during the siege of your cities.

⁵⁸If you do not carefully follow all the words of this law, *ᶦ* which are written in this book, and do not revere *ʲ* this glorious and awesome name *ᵏ*—the LORD your God— ⁵⁹the LORD will send fearful plagues on you and your descendants, harsh and prolonged disasters, and severe and lingering illnesses. ⁶⁰He will bring on you all the diseases of Egypt *ᶦ* that you dreaded, and they will cling to you. ⁶¹The LORD will also bring on you every kind of sickness and disaster not recorded in this Book of the Law, *ᵐ* until you are destroyed. *ⁿ* ⁶²You who were as numerous as the stars in the sky *ᵒ* will be left but few *ᵖ* in number, because you did not obey the LORD your God. ⁶³Just as it pleased *q* the LORD to make you prosper and increase in number, so it will please *ʳ* him to ruin and destroy you. *ˢ* You will be uprooted *ᵗ* from the land you are entering to possess.

⁶⁴Then the LORD will scatter *ᵘ* you among all nations, *ᵛ* from one end of the earth to the other. *ʷ* There you will worship other gods—gods of wood and stone, which neither you nor your ancestors have known. *ˣ* ⁶⁵Among those nations you will find no repose, no resting place *ʸ* for the sole of your foot. There the LORD will give you an anxious mind, eyes *ᶻ* weary with longing, and a despairing heart. *ᵃ* ⁶⁶You will live in constant suspense, filled with dread both night and day, never sure of your life. ⁶⁷In the morning you will say, "If only it were evening!" and in the evening, "If only it were morning!"—because of the terror that will fill your hearts and the sights that your eyes will see. *ᵇ* ⁶⁸The LORD will send you

28:65 *ᵃ* Lev 26:16,36; Hos 9:17   **28:67** *ᵇ* ver 34

28:45 *ᶦ* S Ex 15:9
ᵐ ver 15; Dt 4:25-26
28:46 *ⁿ* S Nu 16:38;
Ps 71:7; Isa 8:18;
20:3; Eze 5:15;
Zec 3:8
28:47 *ᵒ* S Dt 10:12
ᵖ S Lev 23:40;
Ne 9:35
28:48 *q* Jer 14:3;
La 4:4 *ʳ* Jer 28:13-14;
La 1:14 *ˢ* Ge 49:8
28:49 *ᵗ* S Lev 26:44
ᵘ Isa 5:26-30,26;
7:18-20; 39:3;
Jer 4:16; 5:15; 6:22;
25:32; 31:8; Hab 1:6
ᵛ 2Sa 1:23; Jer 4:13;
48:40; 49:22; La 4:19;
Eze 17:3 *ʷ* S Ge 11:7;
1Co 14:21*
28:50 *ˣ* Isa 47:6
28:51 *ʸ* Ps 4:7;
Isa 36:17; Hag 1:11
ᶻ S Nu 18:12 *ᵃ* ver 33;
Jdg 6:4
28:52 *ᵇ* 2Ki 6:24
ᶜ Jer 10:18; Eze 6:10;
Zep 1:14-16,17
28:53 *ᵈ* ver 57;
Lev 26:29; 2Ki 6:28-
29; La 2:20
28:55 *ᵉ* 2Ki 6:29
28:56 *ᶠ* Isa 47:1
ᵍ La 4:10
28:57 *ʰ* S ver 53
28:58 *ᶦ* Dt 31:24
ʲ Ps 96:4; Jer 5:22;
Mal 1:14; 2:5; 3:5,16;
4:2 *ᵏ* S Ex 3:15;
S Jos 7:9
28:60 *ᶦ* Ex 15:26
28:61 *ᵐ* Dt 29:21;
30:10; 31:26; Jos 1:8;
8:34; 23:6; 24:26;
2Ki 14:6; 22:8;
2Ch 17:9; 25:4;
Ne 8:1,18; Mal 4:4
ⁿ Dt 4:25-26
28:62 *ᵒ* S Ge 22:17;
Dt 4:27; 10:22
ᵖ S Lev 26:22
28:63 *q* Dt 30:9;
Isa 62:5; 65:19;
Jer 32:41; Zep 3:17
ʳ Pr 1:26 *ˢ* S Ge 6:7
ᵗ Ps 52:5; Jer 12:14;
31:28; 45:4
28:64 *ᵘ* S Dt 4:27;
Ezr 9:7; Isa 6:12;
Jer 32:23; 43:11; 52:27
ᵛ Ne 1:8; Ps 44:11;
Jer 13:24; 18:17; 22:22
ʷ S Dt 4:32;
S Jer 8:19 *ˣ* Dt 11:28;
32:17
28:65 *ʸ* La 1:3
ᶻ Job 11:20

28:49 *ends of the earth.* An indefinite figurative expression meaning "far away"—anywhere from the visible horizon to the outer perimeter of the then-known world. *eagle swooping down.* Later used to symbolize the speed and power of the Assyrians (see Hos 8:1) and Babylonians (see Jer 48:40; 49:22). *whose language you will not understand.* The Lord's threat was fulfilled through the actions of Assyria and Babylonia, whose languages, though related to Hebrew, were not understood by the average Israelite (see Isa 28:11; 33:19 and note; cf. 1Co 14:21).

▲ **28:53** *suffering that your enemy will inflict on you during the siege.* See vv. 55,57. The repetition of the clause emphasizes the distress that the Israelites would suffer if they refused to obey the Lord. *you will eat . . . sons and daughters.* For the actualizing of this curse, see 2Ki 6:24–29; La 2:20; 4:10; cf. Zec 11:9 and note.

▲ **28:58** *words of this law.* See note on 31:24. *this glorious and awesome name—the LORD.* See note and TNIV text

note on Ex 3:15. One of the oddities of history is the loss of the proper pronunciation of the Hebrew word *YHWH*, the personal and covenant name of God in the OT (see note on Ge 2:4). "Jehovah" is a spelling that developed from combining the consonants of the name with the vowels of a word for "Lord" (*Adonai*). "Yahweh" is probably the original pronunciation. The name eventually ceased to be pronounced because later Jews thought it too holy to be uttered and feared violating Ex 20:7; Lev 24:16. It is translated "LORD" in this version (see the end of the Introduction to this study Bible: The Divine Name Yahweh).
28:60 *diseases of Egypt.* Those brought on the Egyptians during the plagues (see 7:15; Ex 15:26).
28:61 *Book of the Law.* See note on 31:24.
28:62 *as the stars in the sky.* See 1:10; see also notes on 1:10; Ge 13:16; 15:5.
28:64 *will scatter you.* Experienced by Israel in the Assyrian (722–721 B.C.) and Babylonian (586 B.C.) exiles (see 2Ki 17:6; 25:21).

28:68 ^c S Ex 13:14
29:1 ^d S Lev 7:38
^e S Ex 3:1
29:2 ^f Ex 19:4
29:3 ^g S Dt 4:34
29:4 ^h Isa 6:10; 32:3;
48:8; Jer 5:21;
Eze 12:2; S Mt 13:15;
Eph 4:18
29:5 ⁱ S Dt 8:2
^j S Dt 8:4
29:6 ^k S Lev 10:9
^l Dt 8:3
29:7 ^m S Nu 21:26
ⁿ S Nu 21:25
^o Nu 21:21-24, 33-35;
Dt 2:26–3:11
29:8 ^p Ps 78:55;
135:12; 136:22
^q Nu 32:33; Dt 3:12-
13
29:9 ^r S Dt 4:6;
S Jos 1:7 ^s Ex 19:5;
Ps 25:10; 103:18
^t Jos 1:8; 2Ch 31:21
29:11 ^u Jos 9:21, 23,
27; 1Ch 20:3
29:13 ^v S Ge 6:18;
S Ex 19:6 ^w S Ge 17:7
29:14 ^x Ex 19:5;
Isa 59:21; Jer 31:31;
32:40; 50:5;
Eze 16:62; 37:26;
Heb 8:7-8
29:15 ^y S Ge 6:18;
Ac 2:39
29:17 ^z Ex 20:23;
Dt 4:28
29:18 ^a S Dt 13:6
^b S Dt 11:16;
Heb 12:15
29:19 ^c Ps 72:17;
Isa 65:16 ^d Ps 36:2
29:20 ^e S Ex 23:21
^f Ex 34:14; Eze 23:25;
Zep 1:18 ^g Ps 74:1;
79:5; 80:4; Eze 36:5
^h 2Ki 13:23; 14:27;
Rev 3:5
29:21 ⁱ Dt 32:23;
Eze 7:26 ^j S Dt 28:61
29:22 ^k Jer 19:8;
49:17; 50:13
29:23 ^l Isa 1:7; 6:11;
9:18; 64:10; Jer 12:11;
44:2,6; Mic 5:11
^m S Ge 13:10;
Eze 47:11
ⁿ S Ge 19:24, 25;
Zep 2:9; S Mt 10:15;
Ro 9:29

back in ships to Egypt on a journey I said you should never make again. ^c There you will offer yourselves for sale to your enemies as male and female slaves, but no one will buy you.

RENEWAL OF THE COVENANT

29 [*]These are the terms of the covenant the LORD commanded Moses to make with the Israelites in Moab, ^d in addition to the covenant he had made with them at Horeb. ^e

^{*2}Moses summoned all the Israelites and said to them:

Your eyes have seen all that the LORD did in Egypt to Pharaoh, to all his officials and to all his land. ^f ³With your own eyes you saw those great trials, those signs and great wonders. ^g ⁴But to this day the LORD has not given you a mind that understands or eyes that see or ears that hear. ^h ⁵During the forty years that I led ⁱ you through the wilderness, your clothes did not wear out, nor did the sandals on your feet. ^j ⁶You ate no bread and drank no wine or other fermented drink. ^k I did this so that you might know that I am the LORD your God. ^l

⁷When you reached this place, Sihon ^m king of Heshbon ⁿ and Og king of Bashan came out to fight against us, but we defeated them. ^o ⁸We took their land and gave it as an inheritance ^p to the Reubenites, the Gadites and the half-tribe of Manasseh. ^q

⁹Carefully follow ^r the terms of this covenant, ^s so that you may prosper in everything you do. ^t ¹⁰All of you are standing today in the presence of the LORD your God—your leaders and chief men, your elders and officials, and all the other men of Israel, ¹¹together with your children and your wives, and the foreigners living in your camps who chop your wood and carry your water. ^u ¹²You are standing here in order to enter into a covenant with the LORD your God, a covenant the LORD is making with you this day and sealing with an oath, ¹³to confirm you this day as his people, ^v that he may be your God ^w as he promised you and as he swore to your fathers, Abraham, Isaac and Jacob. ¹⁴I am making this covenant, ^x with its oath, not only with you ¹⁵who are standing here with us today in the presence of the LORD our God but also with those who are not here today. ^y

¹⁶You yourselves know how we lived in Egypt and how we passed through the countries on the way here. ¹⁷You saw among them their detestable images and idols of wood and stone, of silver and gold. ^z ¹⁸Make sure there is no man or woman, clan or tribe among you today whose heart turns ^a away from the LORD our God to go and worship the gods of those nations; make sure there is no root among you that produces such bitter poison. ^b

¹⁹When such persons hear the words of this oath and invoke a blessing ^c on themselves, thinking, "I will be safe, even though I persist in going my own way," ^d they will bring disaster on the watered land as well as the dry. ²⁰The LORD will never be willing to forgive ^e them; his wrath and zeal ^f will burn ^g against them. All the curses written in this book will fall on them, and the LORD will blot ^h out their names from under heaven. ²¹The LORD will single them out from all the tribes of Israel for disaster, ⁱ according to all the curses of the covenant written in this Book of the Law. ^j

²²Your children who follow you in later generations and foreigners who come from distant lands will see the calamities that have fallen on the land and the diseases with which the LORD has afflicted it. ^k ²³The whole land will be a burning waste ^l of salt ^m and sulfur— nothing planted, nothing sprouting, no vegetation growing on it. It will be like the destruction of Sodom and Gomorrah, ⁿ Admah and Zeboyim, which the LORD overthrew in

28:68 *a journey I said you should never make again.* See 17:16; Ex 13:17; Nu 14:3–4.

29:1 See notes on 5:2–3.

29:2 *Your eyes have seen.* Only those who were less than 20 years old (Nu 14:29) when Israel followed the majority spy report at Kadesh Barnea and refused to enter Canaan would have actually experienced life in Egypt before the exodus. But Moses is speaking to the people as a nation and referring to the national experience (see note on 5:3).

29:4 Quoted in Ro 11:8 and applied to hardened Israel.

29:7 *Sihon . . . Og.* See 1:4 and note.

29:8 *gave it as an inheritance.* See 3:12–17.

29:9–15 A clear summary of the nature of covenant reaffirmation.

29:13 *his people . . . your God.* See note on Zec 8:8.

29:17 *idols.* See note on Lev 26:30.

29:18 *root . . . that produces such bitter poison.* The poison of idolatry, involving the rejection of the Lord (see Ex 20:3–4 and notes).

29:19 *oath.* God's covenant with his people (vv. 12–14). *watered land . . . dry.* A disaster of major proportions is indicated (vv. 20–21).

29:20 *The LORD will never be willing to forgive them.* Not to be taken as contradictory to 2Pe 3:9 ("not wanting anyone to perish"). Peter, too, says that those who deny the "sovereign Lord" bring "swift destruction on themselves" (2Pe 2:1). See note on 2Pe 3:9. *this book.* See note on 31:24. *blot out their names.* See 9:14 and note.

29:21 *Book of the Law.* See note on 31:24.

29:23 *destruction of Sodom.* See Ge 19:24–25; see also notes on Ge 10:19; 13:10.

fierce anger. *o* 24All the nations will ask: "Why has the LORD done this to this land? *p* Why this fierce, burning anger?"

25And the answer will be: "It is because this people abandoned the covenant of the LORD, the God of their ancestors, the covenant he made with them when he brought them out of Egypt. *q* 26They went off and worshiped other gods and bowed down to them, gods they did not know, gods he had not given them. 27Therefore the LORD's anger burned against this land, so that he brought on it all the curses written in this book. *r* 28In furious anger and in great wrath *s* the LORD uprooted *t* them from their land and thrust them into another land, as it is now."

29The secret things belong to the LORD our God, *u* but the things revealed belong to us and to our children forever, that we may follow all the words of this law. *v*

PROSPERITY AFTER TURNING TO THE LORD

When all these blessings and curses *w* I have set before you come on you and you take them to heart wherever the LORD your God disperses you among the nations, *x* 2and when you and your children return *y* to the LORD your God and obey him with all your heart *z* and with all your soul according to everything I command you today, 3then the LORD your God will restore your fortunes *a* *a* and have compassion *b* on you and gather *c* you again from all the nations where he scattered *d* you. *e* 4Even if you have been banished to the most distant land under the heavens, *f* from there the LORD your God will gather *g* you and bring you back. *h* 5He will bring *i* you to the land that belonged to your ancestors, and you will take possession of it. He will make you more prosperous and numerous *j* than your ancestors. 6The LORD your God will circumcise your hearts and the hearts of your descendants, *k* so that you may love *l* him with all your heart and with all your soul, and live. 7The LORD your God will put all these curses *m* on your enemies who hate and persecute you. *n* 8You will again obey the LORD and follow all his commands I am giving you today. 9Then the LORD your God will make you most prosperous in all the work of your hands and in the fruit of your womb, the young of your livestock and the crops of your land. *o* The LORD will again delight *p* in you and make you prosperous, just as he delighted in your ancestors, 10if you obey the LORD your God and keep his commands and decrees that are written in this Book of the Law *q* and turn to the LORD your God with all your heart and with all your soul. *r*

THE OFFER OF LIFE OR DEATH

11Now what I am commanding you today is not too difficult for you or beyond your reach. *s* 12It is not up in heaven, so that you have to ask, "Who will ascend into heaven *t* to get it and proclaim it to us so we may obey it?" *u* 13Nor is it beyond the sea, *v* so that you have to ask, "Who will cross the sea to get it and proclaim it to us so we may obey it?" *w* 14No, the word is very near you; it is in your mouth and in your heart so you may obey it. *x*

15See, I set before you today life *y* and prosperity, *z* death *a* and destruction. *b* 16For I command you today to love *c* the LORD your God, to walk in obedience to him, and to keep his commands, decrees and laws; then you will live *d* and increase, and the LORD your God will bless you in the land you are entering to possess.

17But if your heart turns away and you are not obedient, and if you are drawn away to bow down to other gods and worship them, 18I declare to you this day that you will certainly be destroyed. *e* You will not live long in the land you are crossing the Jordan to enter and possess.

19This day I call the heavens and the earth as witnesses against you *f* that I have set before you life and death, blessings and curses. *g* Now choose life, so that you and your chil-

---

a 3 Or *will bring you back from captivity*

29:23 *o* S Ge 14:8
29:24 *p* 1Ki 9:8;
2Ch 36:19; Jer 16:10;
22:8-9; 52:13
29:25 *q* 2Ki 17:23;
2Ch 36:21
29:27 *r* S Dt 28:15
29:28 *s* Ps 7:11
t 1Ki 14:15; 2Ch 7:20;
Ps 9:6; 52:5; Pr 2:22;
Jer 12:14; 31:28;
42:10; Eze 19:12
29:29 *u* Ac 1:7
v Jn 5:39; Ac 17:11;
2Ti 3:16
30:1 *w* S Dt 11:26
x Lev 26:40-45;
S Dt 4:32; 29:28
30:2 *y* S Dt 4:30
z Dt 4:29; Ps 119:2
30:3 *a* Ps 14:7; 53:6;
85:1; 126:4; Jer 30:18;
33:11; Eze 16:53;
Joel 3:1; Zep 2:7
b Dt 13:17
c S Ge 48:21
d S Ge 11:4; Dt 4:27
e Isa 11:11; Jer 12:15;
16:15; 24:6; 29:14;
48:47; 49:6
30:4 *f* Ps 19:6
g Isa 17:6; 24:13;
27:12; 40:11; 49:5;
56:8; Eze 20:34,41;
34:13 *h* Ne 1:8-9;
Isa 11:12; 41:5; 42:10;
43:6; 48:20; 62:11;
Jer 31:8,10; 50:2
30:5 *i* Jer 29:14
j S Dt 7:13
30:6 *k* S Dt 6:24;
S 10:16 *l* Dt 6:5
30:7 *m* S Ge 12:3
n Dt 7:15
30:9 *o* Jer 1:10; 24:6;
31:28; 32:41; 42:10;
45:4 *p* S Dt 28:63
30:10 *q* S Dt 28:61
r S Dt 4:29
30:11 *s* Ps 19:8;
Isa 45:19,23; 63:1
30:12 *t* Pr 30:4
u Ro 10:6*
30:13 *v* Job 28:14
w Ro 10:7*
30:14 *x* S Dt 6:6;
Ro 10:8*
30:15 *y* Pr 10:16;
11:19; 12:28; Jer 21:8
z Dt 28:11; Job 36:11;
Ps 25:13; 106:5;
Pr 3:1-2 *a* S Ge 2:17
b S Dt 11:26
30:16 *c* Dt 6:5
d ver 19; Dt 4:1;
32:47; Ne 9:29
30:18 *e* S Dt 8:19
30:19 *f* Dt 4:26
g S Dt 11:26

29:27 *this book.* See note on 31:24.
29:28 *as it is now.* This would be said when Israel was in exile (see vv. 22–25).
29:29 *secret things.* The hidden events of Israel's future relative to the blessings and curses; but the phrase can also have wider application. *things revealed.* Primarily the "words of this law."
30:2,6,10 *with all your heart and ... soul.* See note on 4:29.
30:3 *restore your fortunes.* See TNIV text note.
30:6 *circumcise your hearts.* See 10:16; see also note on Ge 17:10.
30:7 *curses on your enemies.* Cf. Ge 12:3.
30:9 *your ancestors.* The patriarchs (see v. 20).

30:10 *Book of the Law.* See note on 31:24.

■ **30:12,14** *It is not up in heaven ... the word is very near you.* Moses declares that understanding, believing and obeying the covenant were not beyond them. Paul applies this passage to the availability of the "message concerning faith" (Ro 10:6–10).

30:16 *love ... keep.* See notes on 6:5; 11:1.

■ **30:19** *I call the heavens and the earth as witnesses.* The typical ancient covenant outside the OT contained a list of gods who served as "witnesses" to its provisions. The covenant in Deuteronomy was "witnessed" by the heavens and the earth (see 31:28; 32:1; see also notes on Ps 50:1; Isa 1:2).

30:20 ^{h} Dt 6:5
^{i} Dt 4:1; S 8:3; 32:47;
Ps 27:1; Pr 3:22;
S Jn 5:26; Ac 17:28
^{j} Ge 12:7 ^{k} Ps 37:3
31:2 ^{l} S Ex 7:7
^{m} Nu 27:17; 1Ki 3:7
^{n} S Dt 3:23,26
31:3 ^{o} Nu 27:18
^{p} S Dt 9:3 ^{q} S Dt 7:1
^{r} S Dt 3:28
31:4 ^{s} S Nu 21:33
31:5 ^{t} S Dt 2:33
31:6 ^{u} ver 7,23;
Jos 1:6,9,18; 10:25;
1Ch 22:13; 28:20;
2Ch 32:7 ^{v} Jer 1:8,17;
Eze 2:6 ^{w} S Ge 28:15;
S Dt 1:29; Zec 4:6;
S Mt 28:20 ^{x} Ps 56:9;
118:6 ^{y} S Dt 4:31;
1Sa 12:22; 1Ki 6:13;
Ps 94:14; Isa 41:17;
Heb 13:5*
31:7 ^{z} ver 23;
Nu 27:23 ^{a} Jos 1:6
31:8 ^{b} S Ex 13:21
^{c} S Ge 28:15; S Dt 4:31
31:9 ^{d} S Ex 17:14
^{e} ver 25; 1Ch 15:2
31:10 ^{f} S Dt 15:1
^{g} S Ex 23:16; Dt 16:13
31:11 ^{h} S Dt 16:16
^{i} Dt 12:5 ^{j} Jos 8:34-35;
2Ki 23:2; Ne 8:2
31:12 ^{k} Dt 4:10
^{l} Hag 1:12; Mal 1:6;
3:5,16
31:13 ^{m} S Dt 11:2
31:14 ^{n} S Ge 25:8;
S Nu 27:13
^{o} Nu 27:23; Dt 34:9;
Jos 1:1-9 ^{p} S Nu 27:19
^{q} Ex 33:9-11
31:15 ^{r} S Ex 33:9
31:16 ^{s} S Ge 15:15
^{t} S Ex 34:15; Dt 4:25-
28; Jdg 2:12
^{u} Jdg 10:6,13; 1Ki 9:9;
18:18; 19:10; Jer 2:13;
5:19; 19:4
31:17 ^{v} Dt 32:16;
Jdg 2:14,20; 10:7;
2Ki 13:3; 22:13;
Ps 106:29,40;
Jer 7:18; 21:5; 36:7
^{w} Jdg 6:13; 2Ch 15:2;
24:20; Ezr 8:22;
Ps 44:9; Isa 2:6
^{x} Dt 32:20; Isa 1:15;
45:15; 53:3; 54:8
^{y} Job 13:24; Ps 13:1;
27:9; 30:7; 104:29;
Isa 50:6; Jer 33:5;
Eze 39:29; Mic 3:4
^{z} Jer 4:20; Eze 7:26

dren may live ^{20} and that you may love ^{h} the LORD your God, listen to his voice, and hold fast to him. For the LORD is your life, ^{i} and he will give ^{j} you many years in the land ^{k} he swore to give to your fathers, Abraham, Isaac and Jacob.

JOSHUA TO SUCCEED MOSES

31 Then Moses went out and spoke these words to all Israel: ^{2}"I am now a hundred and twenty years old ^{l} and I am no longer able to lead you. ^{m} The LORD has said to me, 'You shall not cross the Jordan.' ^{n} ^{3} The LORD your God himself will cross ^{o} over ahead of you. ^{p} He will destroy these nations ^{q} before you, and you will take possession of their land. Joshua also will cross ^{r} over ahead of you, as the LORD said. ^{4} And the LORD will do to them what he did to Sihon and Og, ^{s} the kings of the Amorites, whom he destroyed along with their land. ^{5} The LORD will deliver ^{t} them to you, and you must do to them all that I have commanded you. ^{6} Be strong and courageous. ^{u} Do not be afraid or terrified ^{v} because of them, for the LORD your God goes with you; ^{w} he will never leave you ^{x} nor forsake ^{y} you."

^{7} Then Moses summoned Joshua and said ^{z} to him in the presence of all Israel, "Be strong and courageous, for you must go with this people into the land that the LORD swore to their ancestors to give them, ^{a} and you must divide it among them as their inheritance. ^{8} The LORD himself goes before you and will be with you; ^{b} he will never leave you nor forsake you. ^{c} Do not be afraid; do not be discouraged."

PUBLIC READING OF THE LAW

^{9} So Moses wrote ^{d} down this law and gave it to the priests, the sons of Levi, who carried ^{e} the ark of the covenant of the LORD, and to all the elders of Israel. ^{10} Then Moses commanded them: "At the end of every seven years, in the year for canceling debts, ^{f} during the Festival of Tabernacles, ^{g} ^{11} when all Israel comes to appear ^{h} before the LORD your God at the place he will choose, ^{i} you shall read this law ^{j} before them in their hearing. ^{12} Assemble the people—men, women and children, and the foreigners residing in your towns—so they can listen and learn ^{k} to fear ^{l} the LORD your God and follow carefully all the words of this law. ^{13} Their children, ^{m} who do not know this law, must hear it and learn to fear the LORD your God as long as you live in the land you are crossing the Jordan to possess."

ISRAEL'S REBELLION PREDICTED

^{14} The LORD said to Moses, "Now the day of your death ^{n} is near. Call Joshua ^{o} and present yourselves at the tent of meeting, where I will commission him. ^{p}" So Moses and Joshua came and presented themselves at the tent of meeting. ^{q}

^{15} Then the LORD appeared at the tent in a pillar of cloud, and the cloud stood over the entrance to the tent. ^{r} ^{16} And the LORD said to Moses: "You are going to rest with your ancestors, ^{s} and these people will soon prostitute ^{t} themselves to the foreign gods of the land they are entering. They will forsake ^{u} me and break the covenant I made with them. ^{17} And in that day I will become angry ^{v} with them and forsake ^{w} them; I will hide ^{x} my face ^{y} from them, and they will be destroyed. Many disasters ^{z} and calamities will come on them, and in that day they will ask, 'Have not these disasters come on us because our God is not

---

A **30:20** *hold fast.* See note on 10:20. *the LORD is your life.* When they chose the Lord, they chose life (v. 19). In 32:46–47 "all the words of this law" are said to be their life. The law, the Lord and life are bound together. "Life" in this context refers to all that makes life rich, full and productive—as God created it to be (cf. Lev 18:5; Jn 10:10 and notes).

31:2 *no longer able to lead.* Not a reference to physical disability (see 34:7). Because of his sin, the Lord did not allow Moses to lead the people into Canaan (see 1:37; 3:23–27; 4:21–22; 32:48–52; Nu 20:2–13 and notes).

31:4 *what he did to Sihon and Og.* See 2:26—3:11; see also note on 1:4.

A **31:6** *Be strong and courageous.* The Lord's exhortation, often through his servants, to the people of Israel (Jos 10:25), to Joshua (vv. 7,23; Jos 1:6–7,9,18), to Solomon (1Ch 22:13; 28:20) and to Hezekiah's military officers (2Ch 32:7). By trusting in the Lord and obeying him, his followers would be victorious in spite of great obstacles. *he will never leave you nor forsake you.* See v. 8; Jos 1:5; 1Ki 8:57; see also note on Ge 28:15. The clause is quoted in

the first person in Heb 13:5 and applied to God's faithfulness in providing for the material needs of his people.

B **31:9** *wrote down this law and gave it to the priests.* Ancient treaties specified that a copy of the treaty was to be placed before the gods at the religious centers of the nations involved. For Israel, that meant to place it in the ark of the covenant (see notes on 33:9; Ex 16:34; 31:18).

31:10 *every seven years.* See 15:4 and note; Ex 23:10–11; Lev 25:1–7; see also chart, pp. 180–181.

A **31:11** *place he will choose.* See note on 12:5. *read this law before them.* Reading the law to the Israelites (and teaching it to them) was one of the main duties of the priests (see 33:10; Mal 2:4–9).

31:12 *fear the LORD.* See notes on Ge 20:11; Ps 34:8–14. *words of this law.* See note on v. 24.

31:14 *I will commission him.* See v. 23; cf. Nu 27:18–23 and notes on 27:18,20.

31:16 *prostitute themselves.* See Ex 34:15 and note.

31:17–18 *hide my face.* See 32:20; see also note on Ps 13:1.

with us?'[a] [18]And I will certainly hide my face in that day because of all their wickedness in turning to other gods.

[19]"Now write[b] down this song and teach it to the Israelites and have them sing it, so that it may be a witness[c] for me against them. [20]When I have brought them into the land flowing with milk and honey, the land I promised on oath to their ancestors,[d] and when they eat their fill and thrive, they will turn to other gods[e] and worship them,[f] rejecting me and breaking my covenant.[g] [21]And when many disasters and calamities come on them,[h] this song will testify against them, because it will not be forgotten by their descendants. I know what they are disposed to do,[i] even before I bring them into the land I promised them on oath." [22]So Moses wrote[j] down this song that day and taught it to the Israelites.

[23]The LORD gave this command[k] to Joshua son of Nun: "Be strong and courageous,[l] for you will bring the Israelites into the land I promised them on oath, and I myself will be with you."

[24]After Moses finished writing[m] in a book the words of this law[n] from beginning to end, [25]he gave this command to the Levites who carried[o] the ark of the covenant of the LORD: [26]"Take this Book of the Law and place it beside the ark of the covenant of the LORD your God. There it will remain as a witness against you.[p] [27]For I know how rebellious[q] and stiff-necked[r] you are. If you have been rebellious against the LORD while I am still alive and with you, how much more will you rebel after I die! [28]Assemble before me all the elders of your tribes and all your officials, so that I can speak these words in their hearing and call the heavens and the earth to testify against them.[s] [29]For I know that after my death you are sure to become utterly corrupt[t] and to turn from the way I have commanded you. In days to come, disaster[u] will fall on you because you will do evil in the sight of the LORD and arouse his anger by what your hands have made."

THE SONG OF MOSES

[30]And Moses recited the words of this song from beginning to end in the hearing of the whole assembly of Israel:

32 Listen,[v] you heavens,[w] and I will speak;
    hear, you earth, the words of my mouth.[x]
[2]Let my teaching fall like rain[y]
    and my words descend like dew,[z][a]
    like showers[b] on new grass,
    like abundant rain on tender plants.

[3]I will proclaim[c] the name of the LORD.[d]
    Oh, praise the greatness[e] of our God!
[4]He is the Rock,[f] his works are perfect,[g]
    and all his ways are just.
A faithful God[h] who does no wrong,
    upright[i] and just is he.[j]

[5]They are corrupt and not his children;
    to their shame they are a warped and crooked generation.[k]
[6]Is this the way you repay[l] the LORD,
    you foolish[m] and unwise people?[n]
Is he not your Father,[o] your Creator,[a]
    who made you and formed you?[p]

---

[a] 6 Or *Father, who bought you*

31:17 [a]Nu 14:42; Hos 9:12
31:19 [b]ver 22
[c]S Ge 31:50
31:20 [d]Dt 6:10-12
[e]Ps 4:2; 16:4; 40:4; Jer 13:25; Da 3:28; Am 2:4 [f]Dt 8:19; 11:16-17 [g]ver 16
31:21 [h]S Dt 4:30
[i]1Ch 28:9; Hos 5:3; Jn 2:24-25
31:22 [j]ver 19
31:23 [k]S ver 7
[l]Jos 1:6
31:24 [m]Dt 17:18; 2Ki 22:8 [n]Dt 28:58
31:25 [o]S ver 9
31:26 [p]ver 19
31:27 [q]S Ex 23:21
[r]S Dt 9:27
31:28 [s]Dt 4:26; 30:19; 32:1; Job 20:27; Isa 26:21
31:29 [t]S Dt 4:16; Rev 9:20 [u]1Ki 9:9; 22:23; 2Ki 22:16
32:1 [v]Ps 49:1; Mic 1:2 [w]Jer 2:12
[x]S Dt 4:26
32:2 [y]2Sa 23:4
[z]Ps 107:20; Isa 9:8; 55:11 [a]Mic 5:7
[b]Ps 65:10; 68:9; 72:6; 147:8
32:3 [c]Ps 118:17; 145:6 [d]Ex 33:19; 34:5-6 [e]S Dt 3:24
32:4 [f]S Ge 49:24
[g]2Sa 22:31; Ps 18:30; 19:7 [h]S Dt 4:35
[i]Ps 92:15 / S Ge 18:25
32:5 [k]ver 20; Mt 17:17; Lk 9:41; Ac 2:40
32:6 [l]Ps 116:12
[m]Ps 94:8; Jer 5:21
[n]ver 28 [o]S Ex 4:22; 2Sa 7:24 [p]ver 15

31:19 *write down this song and teach it.* See v. 22; 31:30—32:44.
31:23 *Be strong and courageous.* See note on v. 6.
31:24 *words of this law from beginning to end.* The book of Deuteronomy up to this place (see note on v. 9).
31:26 *place it beside the ark.* See note on v. 9.
31:27 *stiff-necked.* See 9:6,13; 10:16; see also note on Ex 32:9.
31:28 *the heavens and the earth to testify.* See note on 30:19.
31:29 *what your hands have made.* A reference to idols (see 4:28; 27:15 and note).

A **31:30—32:44** The song of Moses (see notes on Ex 15:1–18; Rev 15:3) set within the narrative frame of 31:30 and 32:44. The song may be outlined as follows: (1) summoning

of covenant witnesses and description of the covenant God (32:1–4), (2) charges against the people (32:5–6), (3) review of God's covenant benefits (32:7–14), (4) the people's disobedience to the covenant stipulations (32:15–18), (5) covenant curses for such disobedience (32:19–27), (6) the impotence of false gods (32:28–38) and (7) the Lord's vindication and vengeance (32:39–43).
32:1 *Listen, you heavens.* For similar introductions see Isa 1:2 and note; 34:1; Mic 1:2; 6:1–2.
32:4 *He is the Rock.* A major theme of the song of Moses (see vv. 15,18,30–31; see also notes on Ge 49:24; Ps 18:2).
32:5 *warped and crooked generation.* See Php 2:15 and note.
32:6 *Father.* See Isa 63:16; 64:8.

32:7 ^qPs 44:1; 74:2;
77:5; Isa 51:9; 63:9
^rDt 4:32; Job 8:8;
20:4; Ps 78:4;
Isa 46:9 ^sS Ex 10:2;
Job 15:18
32:8 ^tPs 7:8
^uS Ge 11:8; Ac 8:1
^vPs 74:17 ^wNu 23:9;
Dt 33:12,28; Jer 23:6
32:9 ^xPs 16:5;
73:26; 119:57; 142:5;
Jer 10:16 ^yS Dt 9:29;
S 1Sa 26:19
32:10 ^zS Dt 1:19
^aDt 8:15; Job 12:24;
Ps 107:40 ^bPs 32:10;
Jer 31:22 ^cPs 17:8;
Pr 7:2; Hos 13:5;
Zec 2:8
32:11 ^dS Ex 19:4
^ePs 17:8; 18:10-19;
61:4
32:12 ^fPs 106:9;
Isa 63:13; Jer 31:32
^gDt 4:35 ^hver 39;
Jdg 2:12; Ps 18:31;
81:9; Isa 43:12; 45:5
32:13 ⁱDt 33:29;
2Sa 22:34; Ps 18:33;
Isa 33:16; 58:14;
Eze 36:2; Hab 3:19
^jS Dt 8:8 ^kDt 33:24;
Job 29:6
32:14 ^lS Nu 21:33
^mPs 65:9; 81:16;
147:14 ⁿS Ge 49:11
32:15 ^oDt 33:5,26;
Isa 44:2 ^pDt 31:20;
Jer 5:28 ^qDt 31:16;
Isa 1:4,28; 58:2;
65:11; Jer 15:6;
Eze 14:5 ^rS Ge 49:24
32:16 ^sS Nu 25:11;
S 1Co 10:22
^tS Dt 31:17;
S 1Ki 14:9
32:17 ^uS Ex 32:8
^vS Ex 22:20;
1Co 10:20
^wS Dt 28:64 ^xJdg 5:8
32:18 ^yJdg 3:7;
1Sa 12:9; Ps 44:17,20;
106:21; Jer 2:32;
Eze 23:35; Hos 8:14;
13:6
32:19 ^zLev 26:30;
Ps 78:59 ^aAm 6:8
32:20 ^bDt 31:17,29;
Ps 4:6; 44:24
^cS ver 5 ^dDt 9:23

⁷Remember the days of old; ^q
  consider the generations long past. ^r
Ask your father and he will tell you,
  your elders, and they will explain to you. ^s
⁸When the Most High ^t gave the nations their inheritance,
  when he divided all the human race, ^u
he set up boundaries ^v for the peoples
  according to the number of the sons of Israel. ^a ^w
⁹For the LORD's portion ^x is his people,
  Jacob his allotted inheritance. ^y

¹⁰In a desert ^z land he found him,
  in a barren and howling waste. ^a
He shielded ^b him and cared for him;
  he guarded him as the apple of his eye, ^c
¹¹like an eagle that stirs up its nest
  and hovers over its young, ^d
that spreads its wings to catch them
  and carries them aloft. ^e
¹²The LORD alone led ^f him; ^g
  no foreign god was with him. ^h

¹³He made him ride on the heights ⁱ of the land
  and fed him with the fruit of the fields.
He nourished him with honey from the rock, ^j
  and with oil ^k from the flinty crag,
¹⁴with curds and milk from herd and flock
  and with fattened lambs and goats,
with choice rams of Bashan ^l
  and the finest kernels of wheat. ^m
You drank the foaming blood of the grape. ⁿ

¹⁵Jeshurun ^b ^o grew fat ^p and kicked;
  filled with food, he became heavy and sleek.
He abandoned ^q the God who made him
  and rejected the Rock ^r his Savior.
¹⁶They made him jealous ^s with their foreign gods
  and angered ^t him with their detestable idols.
¹⁷They sacrificed ^u to demons, ^v which are not God—
  gods they had not known, ^w
gods that recently appeared, ^x
  gods your ancestors did not fear.
¹⁸You deserted the Rock, who bore you;
  you forgot ^y the God who gave you birth.

¹⁹The LORD saw this and rejected them ^z
  because he was angered by his sons and daughters. ^a
²⁰"I will hide my face ^b from them," he said,
  "and see what their end will be;
for they are a perverse generation, ^c
  children who are unfaithful. ^d

---

^a 8 Masoretic Text; Dead Sea Scrolls (see also Septuagint) *sons of God*   ^b 15 *Jeshurun* means *the upright one,* that is, Israel.

32:7 *Remember the days of old.* See note on 4:10.

A 32:8 *Most High.* The only occurrence in Deuteronomy of this name for God (see note on Ge 14:19). It emphasizes the Lord's sovereignty over all creation. *gave the nations their inheritance.* See Ge 10. *according to the number of the sons of Israel.* Perhaps referring to the number (70; see 10:22) of the sons of Jacob (Israel) who went down to Egypt (see Ge 46:27; Ex 1:5; see also note on Ge 10:2). But see TNIV text note.

32:10 *apple of his eye.* Referring to the pupil, a delicate part of the eye that is essential for vision and that therefore must be protected at all costs.

32:11 *hovers over.* See note on Ge 1:2.

32:13 *honey from the rock.* See Ps 81:16. In Canaan, bees sometimes built their hives in crevices in the rocks (cf. Isa 7:18–19). *oil from the flinty crag.* Olive trees often grew on rocky hillsides, as on the Mount of Olives east of Jerusalem.

32:14 *choice rams of Bashan.* See note on Eze 39:18. *foaming blood of the grape.* Red wine (see Ge 49:11).

32:15 *Jeshurun.* See TNIV text note; see also Isa 44:2 and note. *Rock.* See v. 18 and note on v. 4.

32:17 *demons.* See Ps 106:7 and note.

32:20 *hide my face.* See note on 31:17–18.

21 They made me jealous [e] by what is no god
and angered me with their worthless idols. [f]
I will make them envious by those who are not a people;
I will make them angry by a nation that has no understanding. [g]
22 For a fire will be kindled by my wrath, [h]
one that burns down to the realm of the dead below. [i]
It will devour [j] the earth and its harvests [k]
and set afire the foundations of the mountains. [l]

23 "I will heap calamities [m] on them
and spend my arrows [n] against them.
24 I will send wasting famine [o] against them,
consuming pestilence [p] and deadly plague; [q]
I will send against them the fangs of wild beasts, [r]
the venom of vipers [s] that glide in the dust. [t]
25 In the street the sword will make them childless;
in their homes terror [u] will reign. [v]
The young men and young women will perish,
the infants and those with gray hair. [w]
26 I said I would scatter [x] them
and erase their name from human memory, [y]
27 but I dreaded the taunt of the enemy,
lest the adversary misunderstand [z]
and say, 'Our hand has triumphed;
the LORD has not done all this.' " [a]

28 They are a nation without sense,
there is no discernment [b] in them.
29 If only they were wise and would understand this [c]
and discern what their end will be! [d]
30 How could one man chase a thousand,
or two put ten thousand to flight, [e]
unless their Rock had sold them, [f]
unless the LORD had given them up? [g]
31 For their rock is not like our Rock, [h]
as even our enemies concede. [i]
32 Their vine comes from the vine of Sodom [j]
and from the fields of Gomorrah.
Their grapes are filled with poison, [k]
and their clusters with bitterness. [l]
33 Their wine is the venom of serpents,
the deadly poison of cobras. [m]

34 "Have I not kept this in reserve
and sealed it in my vaults? [n]
35 It is mine to avenge; [o] I will repay. [p]
In due time their foot will slip; [q]
their day of disaster is near
and their doom rushes upon them. [r]"

36 The LORD will vindicate his people [s]
and relent [t] concerning his servants [u]
when he sees their strength is gone
and no one is left, slave [v] or free. [a]

---

[a] 36 Or *and they are without a ruler or leader*

Cross references (right column):

32:21 [e] S Nu 25:11;
S 1Co 10:22 [f] ver 17;
1Ki 16:13,26;
2Ki 17:15; Ps 31:6;
Jer 2:5; 8:19; 10:8;
16:19; Jnh 2:8
[g] Ro 10:19*
32:22 [h] Ps 7:11
[i] Nu 16:31-35;
Ps 18:7-8; Jer 15:14;
La 4:11 [j] Am 7:4
[k] Lev 26:20 [l] Ps 83:14
32:23 [m] S Dt 29:21
[n] ver 42; 2Sa 22:15;
Job 6:4; Ps 7:13;
18:14; 45:5; 77:17;
120:4; Isa 5:28; 49:2;
Eze 5:16; Hab 3:9,11
32:24 [o] Ge 26:1;
S 41:55; 42:5;
2Sa 24:13; 1Ch 21:12
[p] S Dt 28:22 [q] Ps 91:6
[r] S Ge 37:20 [s] ver 33;
Job 20:16; Ps 58:4;
Jer 8:17; Am 5:18-19;
Mic 7:17 [t] Job 20:16
32:25 [u] Isa 24:17
[v] Jer 14:18; La 1:20;
Eze 7:15; 2Co 7:5
[w] 2Ch 36:17;
Isa 13:18; Jer 4:31;
La 2:21
32:26 [x] Dt 4:27
[y] S Nu 14:12;
Job 18:17; Ps 34:16;
37:28; 109:15;
Isa 14:20
32:27 [z] Dt 9:26-28
[a] Ps 140:8; Isa 10:13;
Jer 40:2-3
32:28 [b] Isa 1:3; 5:13;
27:11; Jer 8:7
32:29 [c] Dt 5:29;
Ps 81:13 [d] Isa 47:7;
La 1:9
32:30 [e] S Lev 26:8
[f] Jdg 2:14; 3:8; 4:2;
10:7; 1Sa 12:9
[g] Nu 21:34; 1Sa 23:7;
Isa 50:1; 54:6
32:31 [h] S Ge 49:24
[i] S Ex 14:25
32:32 [j] Jer 23:14
[k] Job 6:4; 20:16
[l] Dt 29:18
32:33 [m] S ver 24
32:34 [n] Job 14:17;
Jer 2:22; Hos 13:12
32:35 [o] S ver 41;
S Ge 4:24; S Jer 51:6
[p] S Ge 30:2;
S Ex 32:34; S Ps 54:5;
S Ro 12:19*;
Heb 10:30* [q] Ps 17:5;
35:6; 37:31; 38:16;
66:9; 73:2,18; 94:18;
121:3; Pr 4:19;
Jer 23:12 [r] Eze 7:8-9
32:36 [s] Heb 10:30*
[t] Am 7:3 [u] Lev 26:43-
45; Dt 30:1-3;
Jdg 2:18; Ps 90:13;
102:13; 103:13;
106:45; 135:14;
Joel 2:14 [v] 1Ki 14:10;
21:21; 2Ki 9:8

32:21 Quoted in part in Ro 10:19 to illustrate Israel's failure to understand the good news about Christ. See also v. 16. *those who are not a people*. See note on Ro 10:19.
32:22 *realm of the dead below*. See notes on Ge 37:35; Job 17:16; Ps 6:5; Pr 15:11; Am 9:2–4; see also Job 3:13–19; 11:8; 26:6; Ps 139:8; Pr 23:14; 27:20; Isa 7:11; 14:9–11,15–20; 38:10.
32:26 *I said I would scatter them*. See 28:64 and note; see also 4:27. *erase their name from human memory*. See 9:14 and note; cf. 25:19.

32:30 *their Rock*. Israel's God (see note on v.4).
32:31 *their rock*. The god of Israel's enemy.

32:34 *sealed it in my vaults*. The Lord's plans for the future are fixed and certain. Sin will be punished in due time.

32:35–36 Quoted in part in Heb 10:30 as a warning against rejecting the Son of God.

32:35 *It is mine to avenge; I will repay.* Quoted in Ro 12:19 to affirm that avenging is God's prerogative, not ours.

32:37 w Jdg 10:14;
Jer 2:28; 11:12
32:38 x Nu 25:1-2;
Jer 11:12; 44:8,25
32:39 y Isa 41:4;
43:10; 44:7; 46:4;
48:12 z S ver 12
a 1Sa 2:6 b 1Sa 2:6;
2Ki 5:7; Ps 68:20;
Jn 11:25-26
c Ex 15:26; Job 5:18;
15:11; Ps 147:3;
Isa 6:10; 19:22; 30:26;
53:5; 57:18; Jer 33:6;
Hos 6:1; Mal 4:2;
1Pe 2:24 d Job 9:12;
10:7; Ps 7:2; 50:22;
Isa 43:13; Da 4:35;
Hos 5:14
32:40 e S Ge 14:22
f S Ge 21:33; Rev 1:18
32:41 g Jdg 7:20;
Ps 7:12; 45:3;
Isa 27:1; 34:6; 66:16;
Jer 12:12; Eze 21:9-10
h ver 35; Ps 149:7;
Jer 46:10; Na 1:2
i Ps 137:8; Jer 25:14;
50:29; 51:24,56
32:42 j S ver 23
k 2Sa 2:26; Jer 12:12;
44:1; 46:10,14
32:43 l Ps 137:6;
Isa 25:9; 65:18; 66:10;
Ro 15:10* m 2Ki 9:7;
S Rev 6:10 n Isa 1:24;
Jer 9:9 o Ps 65:3; 79:9
32:44 p Nu 13:8,16
32:46 q S Dt 6:6;
Jn 1:17; 7:19 r Dt 6:7
32:47 s S Dt 30:20
t S Ex 23:26;
Dt 33:25; Isa 65:22
32:48 u Nu 27:12
32:49 v Nu 27:12
w S Nu 32:3
x S Nu 22:1
y S Lev 14:34
32:50 z S Ge 25:8;
S Nu 27:13
a Nu 20:29
b S Nu 20:22
32:51 c Eze 47:19
d S Nu 13:21; 20:11-13
e Nu 27:14
32:52 f Dt 34:1-3
g S Dt 3:27
33:1 h S Ge 27:4
i Jos 14:6; 1Sa 2:27;
9:6; 1Ki 12:22; 13:1;
2Ki 1:9-13; 5:8;
Jer 35:4
33:2 j Ex 19:18;
Ps 68:8 k Jos 11:17;
Jdg 5:4

37 He will say: "Now where are their gods,
  the rock they took refuge in, w
38 the gods who ate the fat of their sacrifices
  and drank the wine of their drink offerings? x
Let them rise up to help you!
  Let them give you shelter!

39 "See now that I myself am He! y
  There is no god besides me. z
I put to death a and I bring to life, b
  I have wounded and I will heal, c
  and no one can deliver out of my hand. d
40 I lift my hand e to heaven and declare:
  As surely as I live forever, f
41 when I sharpen my flashing sword g
  and my hand grasps it in judgment,
I will take vengeance h on my adversaries
  and repay those who hate me. i
42 I will make my arrows drunk with blood, j
  while my sword devours flesh: k
the blood of the slain and the captives,
  the heads of the enemy leaders."

43 Rejoice, l you nations, with his people, a,b
  for he will avenge the blood of his servants; m
he will take vengeance on his enemies n
  and make atonement for his land and people. o

44Moses came with Joshua c p son of Nun and spoke all the words of this song in the hearing of the people. 45When Moses finished reciting all these words to all Israel, 46he said to them, "Take to heart all the words I have solemnly declared to you this day, q so that you may command r your children to obey carefully all the words of this law. 47They are not just idle words for you—they are your life. s By them you will live long t in the land you are crossing the Jordan to possess."

MOSES TO DIE ON MOUNT NEBO

48On that same day the Lord told Moses, u 49"Go up into the Abarim v Range to Mount Nebo w in Moab, across from Jericho, x and view Canaan, y the land I am giving to the Israelites as their own possession. 50There on the mountain that you have climbed you will die z and be gathered to your people, just as your brother Aaron died a on Mount Hor b and was gathered to his people. 51This is because both of you broke faith with me in the presence of the Israelites at the waters of Meribah Kadesh c in the Desert of Zin d and because you did not uphold my holiness among the Israelites. e 52Therefore, you will see the land only from a distance; f you will not enter g the land I am giving to the people of Israel."

MOSES BLESSES THE TRIBES

33:1–29Ref — Ge 49:1–28

33 This is the blessing h that Moses the man of God i pronounced on the Israelites before his death. 2He said:

  "The Lord came from Sinai j
    and dawned over them from Seir; k

a 43 Or *Make his people rejoice, you nations*   b 43 Masoretic Text; Dead Sea Scrolls (see also Septuagint) *people, /and let all the angels worship him /*   c 44 Hebrew *Hoshea*, a variant of *Joshua*

32:39 *I myself am He.* See Ex 3:12–15 and notes; cf. Jn 4:26 and note. *no god besides me.* See note on 4:35. *I put to death and I bring to life.* See note on 1Sa 2:6–8.
32:40 *lift my hand.* See Ge 14:22 and note.

■ **32:43** *Rejoice, you nations, with his people.* One of the Dead Sea Scrolls adds a clause in Deuteronomy (see TNIV text note), and the clause is quoted in Ro 15:10; Heb 1:6 (see note there).
32:47 *they are your life.* See note on 30:20.
32:50 *gathered to your people.* See note on Ge 25:8. *Aaron died*

on Mount Hor. See 10:6; Nu 20:22–29 and notes.
32:51 *you broke faith with me.* See 1:37; 3:23–27; 4:21–22; 31:2; Nu 20:12. *Meribah Kadesh in the Desert of Zin.* See 33:8; see also notes on Ex 17:7; Nu 20:13.
33:1 *blessing.* See Ge 12:1–3; 22:15–18; 27:27–29; 28:10–15. Moses' blessings on the tribes (vv. 6–25) should be compared particularly with Jacob's blessings on his sons in Ge 49:3–27. *man of God.* The first occurrence of this title. It appears next in Jos 14:6 (also of Moses; see Ps 90 title). Later it designates other messengers of God (see note on 1Sa 2:27).

he shone forth *l* from Mount Paran. *m*
He came with *a* myriads of holy ones *n*
from the south, from his mountain slopes. *b*
³ Surely it is you who love *o* the people;
all the holy ones are in your hand. *p*
At your feet they all bow down, *q*
and from you receive instruction,
⁴ the law that Moses gave us, *r*
the possession of the assembly of Jacob. *s*
⁵ He was king *t* over Jeshurun *c u*
when the leaders of the people assembled,
along with the tribes of Israel.

⁶ "Let Reuben live and not die,
nor *d* his people be few." *v*

⁷ And this he said about Judah: *w*

"Hear, LORD, the cry of Judah;
bring him to his people.
With his own hands he defends his cause.
Oh, be his help against his foes!"

⁸ About Levi *x* he said:

"Your Thummim and Urim *y* belong
to your faithful servant. *z*
You tested *a* him at Massah;
you contended with him at the waters of Meribah. *b*
⁹ He said of his father and mother, *c*
'I have no regard for them.'
He did not recognize his brothers
or acknowledge his own children,
but he watched over your word
and guarded your covenant. *d*
¹⁰ He teaches *e* your precepts to Jacob
and your law to Israel. *f*
He offers incense before you *g*
and whole burnt offerings on your altar. *h*
¹¹ Bless all his skills, LORD,
and be pleased with the work of his hands. *i*
Strike down those who rise against him,
his foes till they rise no more."

¹² About Benjamin *j* he said:

"Let the beloved of the LORD rest secure in him, *k*
for he shields him all day long, *l*
and the one the LORD loves *m* rests between his shoulders. *n*"

¹³ About Joseph *o* he said:

"May the LORD bless his land
with the precious dew from heaven above
and with the deep waters that lie below; *p*

---

a 2 Or *from*   *b 2* The meaning of the Hebrew for this phrase is uncertain.   *c 5 Jeshurun* means *the upright one,* that is, Israel; also in verse 26.   *d 6* Or *but let*

33:2 *l* Ps 50:2; 80:1; 94:1 *m* S Nu 10:12
n Ps 89:7; Da 4:13; 7:10; 8:13; Zec 14:5; Ac 7:53; Gal 3:19; Heb 2:2; Rev 5:11
33:3 *o* S Dt 4:37
p Dt 7:6 *q* Lk 10:39; Rev 4:10
33:4 *r* Dt 4:2; Jn 1:17; 7:19
s Ps 119:111
33:5 *t* S Ex 16:8; 1Sa 10:19; Ps 10:16; 149:2 *u* S Nu 23:21; S Dt 32:15
33:6 *v* S Ge 34:5
33:7 *w* S Ge 49:10
33:8 *x* S Ge 29:34
y Ex 28:30 *z* Ps 106:16
a S Nu 14:22
b S Ex 17:7
33:9 *c* Ex 32:26-29
d Pr 61:5; Mal 2:5
33:10 *e* Ezr 7:10; Ne 8:18; Ps 119:151; Jer 23:22; Mal 2:6
f S Lev 10:11; Dt 17:8-11; 31:9-13
g S Ex 30:7; Lev 16:12-13
h Ps 51:19
33:11 *i* 2Sa 24:23; Ps 20:3; 51:19
33:12 *j* S Ge 35:18
k Dt 4:37-38; 12:10; S 32:8 *l* S Ex 19:4
m Ps 60:5; 127:2; Isa 5:1 *n* S Ex 28:12
33:13 *o* S Ge 30:24
p Ge 27:28; Ps 148:7

33:2 *Sinai... Seir... Paran.* Mountains associated with the giving of the law (see Ge 21:21 and note; Jdg 5:4–5; Hab 3:3 and note). *holy ones.* Angels.
33:3 *holy ones.* Israelites (see 7:6 and note; 14:2; 26:19; 28:9).
33:5 *king.* The Lord, not an earthly monarch, was to be king over Israel (see Jdg 8:23 and note). *Jeshurun.* See TNIV text note; see also Isa 44:2 and note.
33:6 *Reuben.* For the boundaries of the tribal territories see map No. 4 at the end of this study Bible.
33:8 *Thummim and Urim.* See note on Ex 28:30. *Massah.* See

6:16; 9:22; see also note on Ex 17:7. *Meribah.* See note on 32:51.
33:9 *he watched over your word.* The Levites had charge of the tabernacle with its ark, in which the Book of the Law was placed (see note on 31:9).
33:10 *teaches your precepts to Jacob.* See note on 31:11.
33:12 *between his shoulders.* See Isa 49:22; cf. Dt 33:27.
33:13 *About Joseph.* Moses included the blessing on the two tribes of Ephraim and Manasseh (v. 17), Joseph's sons, with that of Joseph himself. *dew from heaven... deep waters.* See note on Ge 49:25.

33:15 q Hab 3:6
33:16 r S Ex 3:2
s S Ge 37:8
33:17 t 1Sa 2:10;
2Sa 22:3; Eze 34:21
u Nu 23:22
v 1Ki 22:11; Ps 44:5
w S Ge 41:52
x S Ge 41:51
33:18 y S Ge 30:20
z S Ge 30:18
33:19 a S Ex 15:17;
Ps 48:1; Isa 2:3; 65:11;
66:20; Jer 31:6
b Ps 4:5; 51:19
c Isa 18:7; 23:18;
45:14; 60:5, 11; 61:6;
Hag 2:7; Zec 14:14
33:20 d Ge 30:11
e Dt 3:12-17
33:21 f Nu 32:1-5,
31-32 g S Nu 34:14
h Jos 22:1-3
33:22 i Ge 49:16;
S Nu 1:38
33:23 j S Ge 30:8
33:24 k S Ge 30:13
l S Ge 49:20;
S Dt 32:13
33:25 m Ne 3:3; 7:3;
Ps 147:13
n S Dt 32:47
33:26 o S Dt 32:15
p Ps 18:10; 68:33
q S Dt 10:14;
S Ps 104:3
r 2Sa 22:10; Ps 18:9;
68:4; Da 7:13
s S Ex 15:7
33:27 t Ex 15:18;
Isa 40:28; 57:15
u Ps 9:9; 84:1; 90:1;
91:9

14 with the best the sun brings forth
 and the finest the moon can yield;
15 with the choicest gifts of the ancient mountains q
 and the fruitfulness of the everlasting hills;
16 with the best gifts of the earth and its fullness
 and the favor of him who dwelt in the burning bush. r
 Let all these rest on the head of Joseph,
 on the brow of the prince among a his brothers. s
17 In majesty he is like a firstborn bull;
 his horns t are the horns of a wild ox. u
 With them he will gore v the nations,
 even those at the ends of the earth.
 Such are the ten thousands of Ephraim; w
 such are the thousands of Manasseh. x"

18 About Zebulun y he said:

 "Rejoice, Zebulun, in your going out,
 and you, Issachar, z in your tents.
19 They will summon peoples to the mountain a
 and there offer the sacrifices of the righteous; b
 they will feast on the abundance of the seas, c
 on the treasures hidden in the sand."

20 About Gad d he said:

 "Blessed is he who enlarges Gad's domain! e
 Gad lives there like a lion,
 tearing at arm or head.
21 He chose the best land for himself; f
 the leader's portion was kept for him. g
 When the heads of the people assembled,
 he carried out the LORD's righteous will, h
 and his judgments concerning Israel."

22 About Dan i he said:

 "Dan is a lion's cub,
 springing out of Bashan."

23 About Naphtali j he said:

 "Naphtali is abounding with the favor of the LORD
 and is full of his blessing;
 he will inherit southward to the lake."

24 About Asher k he said:

 "Most blessed of sons is Asher;
 let him be favored by his brothers,
 and let him bathe his feet in oil. l
25 The bolts of your gates will be iron and bronze, m
 and your strength will equal your days. n

26 "There is no one like the God of Jeshurun, o
 who rides p on the heavens to help you q
 and on the clouds r in his majesty. s
27 The eternal t God is your refuge, u

---

a 16 Or *of the one separated from*

33:15–16 See Ge 49:26 and note.
33:16 *best gifts of the earth.* Under the Lord's blessing, Joseph's land in the central part of Canaan was to be unusually fertile and productive. *who dwelt in the burning bush.* See Ex 3:1–6.
33:19 *abundance of the seas . . . treasures hidden in the sand.* References to maritime wealth (see note on Ge 49:13).
33:21 *He chose the best land.* For his livestock (see 3:12–20 and notes).

33:22 *springing out of Bashan.* The lion's cub, not Dan, is the subject. Another possible translation is "keeping away from the viper." Although someday he would be like a viper himself (see Ge 49:17 and note), the early history of Dan pictured him as being somewhat more timid (see Jdg 18).
33:23 *lake.* The Sea of Galilee.
33:26 *Jeshurun.* See note on 32:15. *rides . . . on the clouds.* See note on Ps 68:4.

and underneath are the everlasting ^{v} arms.
He will drive out your enemies before you, ^{w}
saying, 'Destroy them!' ^{x}
28 So Israel will live in safety; ^{y}
Jacob will dwell ^{a} secure
in a land of grain and new wine,
where the heavens drop dew. ^{z}
29 Blessed are you, Israel! ^{a}
Who is like you, ^{b}
a people saved by the LORD? ^{c}
He is your shield and helper ^{d}
and your glorious sword.
Your enemies will cower before you,
and you will tread on their heights. ^{e}"

THE DEATH OF MOSES

34 Then Moses climbed Mount Nebo ^{f} from the plains of Moab to the top of Pisgah, ^{g} across from Jericho. ^{h} There the LORD showed ^{i} him the whole land—from Gilead to Dan, ^{j} 2 all of Naphtali, the territory of Ephraim and Manasseh, all the land of Judah as far as the Mediterranean Sea, ^{k} 3 the Negev ^{l} and the whole region from the Valley of Jericho, the City of Palms, ^{m} as far as Zoar. ^{n} 4 Then the LORD said to him, "This is the land I promised on oath ^{o} to Abraham, Isaac and Jacob ^{p} when I said, 'I will give it ^{q} to your descendants.' I have let you see it with your eyes, but you will not cross ^{r} over into it."

5 And Moses the servant of the LORD ^{s} died ^{t} there in Moab, as the LORD had said. 6 He buried him ^{b} in Moab, in the valley opposite Beth Peor, ^{u} but to this day no one knows where his grave is. ^{v} 7 Moses was a hundred and twenty years old ^{w} when he died, yet his eyes were not weak ^{x} nor his strength gone. ^{y} 8 The Israelites grieved for Moses in the plains of Moab ^{z} thirty days, ^{a} until the time of weeping and mourning ^{b} was over.

9 Now Joshua son of Nun was filled with the spirit ^{c} of wisdom ^{c} because Moses had laid his hands on him. ^{d} So the Israelites listened to him and did what the LORD had commanded Moses.

10 Since then, no prophet ^{e} has risen in Israel like Moses, ^{f} whom the LORD knew face to face, ^{g} 11 who did all those signs and wonders ^{h} the LORD sent him to do in Egypt—to Pharaoh and to all his officials ^{i} and to his whole land. 12 For no one has ^{j} ever shown the mighty power or performed the awesome deeds ^{k} that Moses did in the sight of all Israel.

---

^{a} 28 Septuagint; Hebrew *Jacob's spring is* ^{b} 6 Or *He was buried* ^{c} 9 Or *Spirit*

33:27 *underneath are the everlasting arms.* See v. 12 and note.
33:29 *shield.* See note on Ge 15:1. *tread on their heights.* See Mic 1:3 and note; cf. Dt 32:13.
34:1 *Moses climbed Mount Nebo.* In obedience to the Lord's command in 32:48–52.
34:3 *Negev.* See note on Ge 12:9. *as far as Zoar.* See Isa 15:5 and note.
34:4 *land I promised.* See 1:8; Ge 12:1; 15:18 and note; Ex 33:1.

A C **34:5** *servant of the LORD.* A special title used to refer to those whom the Lord, as the Great King, has taken into his service; they serve as members of God's royal administration. For example, it was used especially of Abraham (Ge 26:24), Moses (Ex 14:31), Joshua (Jos 24:29), David (2Sa 3:18; 7:5), the prophets (2Ki 9:7), Israel collectively (Isa 41:8–9),

and even a foreign king the Lord used to carry out his purposes (Jer 25:9). See notes on Ex 14:31; Isa 41:8–9; 42:1–4.
34:6 *Beth Peor.* See note on 3:29.
34:7 *a hundred and twenty years old.* See 31:2; perhaps a round number, indicating three generations of about 40 years each (see Ac 7:23 and note).
34:8 *grieved…thirty days.* See Ge 50:3 and note.

C **34:10** *no prophet has risen in Israel like Moses.* See note on 18:15. *face to face.* See Nu 12:8 and note.

A **34:12** *no one has ever.* Until Jesus came, no one was superior to Moses. See Heb 3:1–6, where Moses the "servant in all God's house" (v. 5) is contrasted with Christ the "Son over God's house" (v. 6).

33:27 ^{v} S Ge 21:33
^{w} Ex 34:11; Jos 24:18
^{x} S Dt 7:2
33:28 ^{y} S Ex 33:16;
S Lev 25:18;
S Dt 32:8; Ps 16:9;
Pr 1:33; Isa 14:30
^{z} ver 13; Ge 27:28
33:29 ^{a} Ps 1:1; 32:1-2; 144:15 ^{b} 2Sa 22:45;
Ps 18:44; 66:3; 81:15
^{c} Dt 4:7 ^{d} Ge 15:1;
Ex 18:4; Ps 10:14;
18:1; 27:1,9; 30:10;
54:4; 70:5; 115:9-11;
118:7; Isa 45:24;
Hos 13:9; Hab 3:19
^{e} S Nu 33:52;
S Dt 32:13
34:1 ^{f} S Nu 32:3
^{g} S Nu 21:20
^{h} Dt 32:49 / Dt 32:52
^{i} S Ge 14:14
34:2 ^{k} S Ge 23:31
34:3 ^{l} S Ge 12:9
^{m} Jdg 1:16; 3:13;
2Ch 28:15
^{n} S Ge 13:10
34:4 ^{o} Ge 28:13
^{p} Jos 21:43 ^{q} Ge 12:7
^{r} S Dt 3:23
34:5 ^{s} S Nu 12:7
^{t} S Ge 25:8
34:6 ^{u} S Dt 3:29
^{v} Jude 1:9
34:7 ^{w} S Ex 7:7
^{x} S Ge 27:1
^{y} S Ge 15:15
34:8 ^{z} S Nu 21:11
^{a} S Ge 37:34; S Dt 1:3
^{b} 2Sa 11:27
34:9 ^{c} S Ge 41:38;
S Ex 28:3; Isa 11:2
^{d} S Dt 31:14; Ac 6:6
34:10 ^{e} S Ge 20:7
^{f} Dt 18:15,18
^{g} S Ex 33:11
34:11 ^{h} Dt 4:34
^{i} S Ex 11:3
34:12 ^{j} Heb 3:1-6
^{k} S Dt 4:34

Many readers of Joshua (and other OT books) are deeply troubled by the role that warfare plays in Joshua's account of God's dealings with his people. Not a few relieve their ethical scruples by ascribing the author's perspective to a pre-Christian (and sub-Christian) stage of moral development that the Christian, in the light of Christ's teaching, must repudiate and transcend. Hence the main thread of the narrative line of Joshua is an offense to them.

It must be remembered, however, that the book of Joshua does not address itself to the abstract ethical question of war as a means for gaining human ends. It can only be understood in the context of the history of redemption unfolding in the Pentateuch, with its interplay of divine grace and judgment. Of that story it is the direct continuation.

Joshua is not an epic account of Israel's heroic generation or the story of Israel's conquest of Canaan with the aid of her national deity. It is rather the story of how God, to whom the whole world belongs, at one stage in the history of redemption reconquered a portion of the earth from the powers of this world that had claimed it for themselves, defending their claims by force of arms and reliance on their false gods. It tells how God commissioned his people to serve as his army under the leadership of his servant Joshua, to take Canaan in his name out of the hands of the idolatrous and dissolute Canaanites (whose measure of sin was now full; see Ge 15:16 and note). It further tells how he aided them in the enterprise and gave them conditional tenancy in his land in fulfillment of the ancient pledge he had made to Israel's ancestors, Abraham, Isaac and Jacob.

Joshua is the story of the kingdom of God breaking into the world of nations at a time when national and political entities were viewed as the creation of the gods and living proofs of their power. Thus the Lord's triumph over the Canaanites testified to the world that the God of Israel is the one true and living God, whose claim on the world is absolute. It was also a warning to the nations that the irresistible advance of the kingdom of God would ultimately disinherit all those who opposed it, giving place in the earth only to those who acknowledge and serve the Lord. At once an act of redemption and judgment, it gave notice of the outcome of history and anticipated the final destiny of humankind and the creation.

The battles for Canaan were therefore the Lord's war, undertaken at a particular time in the program of redemption. God gave his people under Joshua no commission or license to conquer the world with the sword but a particular, limited mission. The conquered land itself would not become Israel's national possession by right of conquest, but it belonged to the Lord. So the land had to be cleansed of all remnants of paganism. Its people and their wealth were not for Israel to seize as the booty of war from which to enrich themselves (as Achan tried to do, ch. 7) but were placed under God's ban (were to be devoted to God to dispense with as he pleased). On that land Israel was to establish a commonwealth faithful to the righteous rule of God and thus be a witness (and a blessing) to the nations. If Israel became unfaithful and conformed to Canaanite culture and practice, it would in turn lose its place in the Lord's land—as Israel almost did in the days of the judges, and as it eventually did in the exile.

War is a terrible curse that the human race brings on itself as it seeks to possess the earth by its own unrighteous ways. But it pales before the curse that awaits all those who do not heed God's testimony to himself or his warnings—those who oppose the rule of God and reject his offer of grace. The God of the second Joshua (Jesus) is the God of the first Joshua also. Although now for a time he reaches out to the whole world with the gospel (and commissions his people urgently to carry his offer of peace to all nations), the sword of his judgment waits in the wings—and his second Joshua will wield it (Rev 19:11–16; see notes there).

JOSHUA

Joshua is a story of conquest and fulfillment for the people of God. After many years of slavery in Egypt and 40 years in the wilderness, the Israelites were finally allowed to enter the land promised to their ancestors. Abraham, always a migrant, never possessed the country to which he was sent, but he left to his children the legacy of God's covenant that made them the eventual heirs of all of Canaan (see Ge 15:13, 16,18; 17:8). Joshua was destined to turn that promise into reality.

Where Deuteronomy ends, the book of Joshua begins: The tribes of Israel are still camped on the east side of the Jordan River. The narrative opens with God's command to move forward and pass through the river on dry land. Then it relates the series of victories in central, southern and northern Canaan that gave the Israelites control of all the hill country and the Negev. It continues with a description of the tribal allotments and ends with Joshua's final addresses to the people. The theme of the book, therefore, is the establishment of God's people Israel in the Lord's land, the land he had promised to give them as their place of "rest" in the earth (1:13,15; 21:44; 22:4; 23:1; see also Dt 3:20 and note; 12:9–10; 25:19; 1Ki 5:4 and note; 8:56). So the Great King's promise to the partriarchs and Moses to give the land of Canaan to the chosen people of his kingdom is now historically fulfilled (1:1–6; 21:43–45).

In the story the book tells, three primary actors play a part: "the LORD" (as Israel's God), his servant Joshua and his people Israel (the last a collective "character" in the story). We meet all three immediately in ch. 1, where all three are clearly presented in the distinctive roles they will play in the story that follows. Ch. 1 also introduces the reader to the main concern of the book as a whole.

The role of the central human actor in the events narrated here is reinforced by the name he bears. Earlier in his life Joshua was called simply Hoshea (Nu 13:8,16), meaning "salvation." But later Moses changed his name to Joshua, meaning "The LORD saves" (or "The LORD gives victory"). When this same name (the Greek form of which is Jesus; see TNIV text note on Mt 1:21) was given to Mary's firstborn son, it identified him as the servant of God who would complete what God did for Israel in a preliminary way through the first Joshua; namely, overcome all powers of evil in the world and bring God's people into their eternal "rest" (see Heb 4:1–11 and notes).

In the Hebrew Bible the book of Joshua initiates a division called the Former Prophets, including also Judges, Samuel and Kings. These are all historical in content but are written from a prophetic standpoint. They do more than merely record the nation's history from Moses to the fall of Judah in 586 B.C. They prophetically interpret God's covenant ways with Israel in history—how he fulfills and remains true to his promises (especially through his servants such as Joshua, the judges, Samuel and David) and how he deals with the waywardness of the Israelites. In Joshua it was the Lord who won the victories and "gave Israel all the land he had sworn to give their ancestors" (21:43).

AUTHOR AND DATE

In the judgment of many scholars Joshua was not written until the end of the period of the kings, some 800 years after the actual events. But there are significant reasons to question this conclusion and to place the time of composition much earlier. The

---

KEY   **A** APPLICATION FOR LIVING   **B** BACKGROUND NOTES   **C** CHARACTER INFORMATION

earliest Jewish traditions (Talmud) claim that Joshua wrote his own book except for the final section about his funeral, which is attributed to Eleazar, son of Aaron (the last verse must have been added by a later editor).

On at least two occasions the text reports writing at Joshua's command or by Joshua himself. We are told that when the tribes received their territories, Joshua instructed his men to "make a survey of the land and write a description of it" (18:8). Then in the last scene of the book, when Joshua led Israel in a renewal of the covenant with the Lord, it is said that "he reaffirmed for them decrees and laws" (24:25) and "recorded these things" (24:26). On another occasion the narrator speaks as if he had been a participant in the event; he uses the pronoun "us" (5:6).

Moreover, the author seems to be familiar with ancient names of cities, such as "the Jebusite city" (15:8; 18:16,28) for Jerusalem, Kiriath Arba (14:15; 15:54; 20:7; 21:11) for Hebron, and Greater Sidon (11:8; 19:28) for what later became simply Sidon. And Tyre is never mentioned, probably because in Joshua's day it had not yet developed into a port of major importance.

But if some features suggest an author of Joshua's own lifetime, others point to a writer of a somewhat later period. The account of the long day when the sun stood still at Aijalon is substantiated by a quotation from another source, the Book of Jashar (10:13). This would hardly be natural for an eyewitness of the miracle who was writing shortly after it happened. Also, there are 12 instances where the phrase "until this day" occurs.

It seems safe to conclude that the book draws on early sources. It may date from the beginning of the monarchy. Some think that Samuel may have had a hand in shaping or compiling the materials of the book, but in fact we are unsure who the final author or editor was.

THE LIFE OF JOSHUA

Joshua's remarkable life was filled with excitement, variety, success and honor. He was known for his deep trust in God and as "a man in whom is the spirit" of leadership (Nu 27:18). As a youth he lived through the bitter realities of slavery in Egypt, but he also witnessed the supernatural plagues and the miracle of Israel's escape from the army of the Egyptians when the waters of the Red Sea opened before them. In the Sinai peninsula it was Joshua who led the troops of Israel to victory over the Amalekites (Ex 17:8–13). He alone was allowed to accompany Moses up the holy mountain where the tablets of the law were received (Ex 24:13–14). And it was he who stood watch at the temporary "tent of meeting" Moses set up before the tabernacle was erected (Ex 33:11).

Joshua was elected to represent his own tribe of Ephraim when the 12 spies were sent into Canaan to look over the land. Only Joshua and Caleb, representing the tribe of Judah, were ready to follow God's will and take immediate possession of the land (see Nu 14:26–34). The rest of the Israelites of that generation were condemned to die in the wilderness. Even Moses died short of the goal and was told to turn everything over to Joshua. God promised to guide and strengthen Joshua, just as he had Moses (Dt 31:23; cf. Jos 1:5 and note).

Joshua was God's chosen servant (see 24:29 and note on Dt 34:5) to bring Moses' work to completion and establish Israel in the promised land. To that special divine appointment he was faithful—as the leader of God's army, as the administrator of God's division of the land and as God's spokesman for promoting Israel's covenant faithfulness. In all this he was a striking OT type (foreshadowing) of Christ (see notes on Heb 4:1,6–8).

HISTORICAL SETTING

At the time of the Israelite migration into Canaan the superpowers of the ancient Near East were relatively weak. The Hittites had faded from the scene. Neither Babylon nor Egypt could maintain a standing military presence in Canaan, and the Assyrians would not send in their armies until centuries later.

As the tribes circled east of the Dead Sea, the Edomites refused them passage, so Israel bypassed them to the east. However, when Sihon and Og, two regional Amorite kings of Transjordan, tried to stop the Israelites, they were easily defeated and their lands occupied. Moab was forced to let Israel pass through her territory and camp in her plains. Also the Midianites were dealt a severe blow.

B Biblical archaeologists call this period the Late Bronze Age (1550–1200 B.C.). Today thousands of artifacts give testimony to the richness of the Canaanite material culture, which was in many ways superior to that of the Israelites. When the ruins of the ancient kingdom of Ugarit were discovered at modern Ras Shamra on the northern coast of Syria (see chart, p. xxiv), a wealth of new information came to light concerning the domestic, commercial and religious life of the Canaanites. From a language close to Hebrew came stories of ancient kings and gods that revealed their immoral behavior and cruelty. In addition, pagan temples, altars, tombs and ritual vessels have been uncovered, throwing more light on the culture and customs of the peoples surrounding Israel.

Excavations at the ancient sites of Megiddo, Beth Shan and Gezer show how powerfully fortified these cities were and why they were not captured and occupied by Israel in Joshua's day. Many other fortified towns were taken, however, so that Israel became firmly established in the land as the dominant power. Apart from Jericho and Ai, Joshua is reported to have burned only Hazor (11:13), so attempts to date these events by destruction levels in the mounds of Canaan's ancient cities are questionable undertakings. It must also be remembered that other groups were involved in campaigns in the region about this time, among whom were Egyptian rulers and the Sea Peoples (including the Philistines). There had also been much intercity warfare among the Canaanites, and afterward the period of the judges was marked by general turbulence.

Much of the data from archaeology appears to support a date for Joshua's invasion c. 1250 B.C. This fits well with an exodus that would then have taken place 40 years earlier under the famous Rameses II, who ruled from the Nile delta at a city with the same name (Ex 1:11). It also places Joseph in Egypt in a favorable situation. Four hundred years before Rameses II the pharaohs were the Semitic Hyksos, who also ruled from the delta near the land of Goshen.

On the other hand, a good case can be made for the traditional viewpoint that the invasion occurred c. 1406 B.C. The oppression would have taken place under Amunhotep II after the death of his father Thutmose III, who is known to have used slave labor in his building projects. The earlier date also fits better with the two numbers found in Jdg 11:26 and 1Ki 6:1, since it allows for an additional 150 years between Moses and the monarchy. See also Introductions to Genesis: Author and Date of Writing; Exodus: Chronology; Judges: Background; and note on 1Ki 6:1.

OUTLINE

THE LORD COMMANDS JOSHUA

1 After the death of Moses the servant of the LORD, *a* the LORD said to Joshua *b* son of Nun, Moses' aide: ²"Moses my servant is dead. Now then, you and all these people, get ready to cross the Jordan River *c d* into the land *e* I am about to give to them *f*—to the Israelites. ³I will give you every place where you set your foot, *g* as I promised Moses. *h* ⁴Your territory will extend from the desert to Lebanon, *i* and from the great river, the Euphrates *j*—all the Hittite *k* country—to the Mediterranean Sea in the west. *l* ⁵No one will be able to stand against you *m* all the days of your life. As I was with *n* Moses, so I will be with you; I will never leave you nor forsake *o* you. ⁶Be strong *p* and courageous, *q* because you will lead these people to inherit the land I swore to their ancestors *r* to give them.

⁷"Be strong and very courageous. Be careful to obey *s* all the law *t* my servant Moses *u* gave you; do not turn from it to the right or to the left, *v* that you may be successful wherever you go. *w* ⁸Keep this Book of the Law *x* always on your lips; *y* meditate *z* on it day and night, so that you may be careful to do everything written in it. Then you will be prosperous and successful. *a* ⁹Have I not commanded you? Be strong and courageous. Do not be afraid; *b* do not be discouraged, *c* for the LORD your God will be with you wherever you go." *d*

¹⁰So Joshua ordered the officers of the people: *e* ¹¹"Go through the camp *f* and tell the people, 'Get your provisions *g* ready. Three days *h* from now you will cross the Jordan *i* here to go in and take possession *j* of the land the LORD your God is giving you for your own.' "

¹²But to the Reubenites, the Gadites and the half-tribe of Manasseh, *k* Joshua said, ¹³"Remember the command that Moses the servant of the LORD gave you after he said, 'The LORD your God will give you rest *l* by giving you this land.' ¹⁴Your wives, *m* your children and your livestock may stay in the land *n* that Moses gave you east of the Jordan, but all your fighting men, ready for battle, *o* must cross over ahead of the other Israelites. *p* You are to help them ¹⁵until the LORD gives them rest, as he has done for you, and until they too have taken possession of the land the LORD your God is giving them. After that, you may go back and occupy your own land, which Moses the servant of the LORD gave you east of the Jordan toward the sunrise." *q*

1:9 *c* S Dt 1:21; Job 4:5 *d* S ver 7; Dt 31:7-8; Jer 1:8 **1:10** *e* S Dt 1:15 **1:11** *f* Jos 3:2 *g* Isa 17:22; Isa 10:28 *h* S Ge 40:13 *i* S Nu 35:10 *j* S Nu 33:53 **1:12** *k* Nu 32:33 **1:13** *l* S Ex 33:14; Ps 55:6; Isa 11:10; 28:12; 30:15; 32:18; 40:31; Jer 6:16; 45:3; La 5:5 **1:14** *m* Dt 3:19 *n* S Nu 32:26 *o* S Ex 13:18 *p* Jos 4:12 **1:15** *q* Nu 32:20-22; Jos 22:1-4

1:1 *a* Ex 14:31; Dt 34:5; Rev 15:3
b S Ex 17:9
1:2 *c* S Nu 13:29
d S Nu 35:10
e S Ge 15:14 *f* Ge 12:7; Dt 1:25
1:3 *g* S Dt 11:24
h Ge 50:24; Nu 13:2; Dt 1:8
1:4 *i* S Dt 3:25
j S Ge 2:14
k S Ge 10:15; 23:10; Ex 3:8 *l* Nu 34:2-12; Ezr 4:20
1:5 *m* S Dt 7:24
n ver 17; S Ge 26:3; S 39:2; Jdg 6:12;
1Sa 10:7; Jer 1:8; 30:11
o S Ge 28:15; S Dt 4:31
1:6 *p* 2Sa 2:7; 1Ki 2:2; Isa 41:6; Joel 3:9-10
q S Dt 1:21; S 31:6; S Jdg 5:21 *r* Jer 3:18; 7:7
1:7 *s* Dt 29:9;
1Ki 2:3; 3:3 *t* Ezr 7:26; Ps 78:10; 119:136;
Isa 42:24; Jer 26:4-6; 32:23; 44:10 *u* ver 2, 15; S Nu 12:7; Job 1:8; 42:7 *v* S Dt 5:32;
Jos 23:6 *w* ver 9; S Dt 4:2; 5:33; S 11:8; Jos 11:15
1:8 *x* S Dt 28:61; S Ps 147:19
y S Ex 4:15; Isa 59:21
z S Ge 24:63
a Dt 29:9; 1Sa 18:14; Ps 1:1-3; Isa 52:13; 53:10; Jer 23:5
1:9 *b* S Dt 31:6; Jos 10:8; 2Ki 19:6; Isa 35:4; 37:6

1:1-18 The Lord initiates the action by charging Joshua, his chosen replacement for Moses (see Dt 31:1-8), to lead Israel across the Jordan and take possession of the promised land. He urges courage and promises success—but only if Israel obeys the law of God that Moses has given them. The chapter consists of speeches significant in their content and order: The Lord commands Joshua as his appointed leader over his people (vv. 1-9); Joshua, as the Lord's representative, addresses Israel (vv. 10-15); Israel responds to Joshua as the Lord's representative and successor to Moses (vv. 16-18). Thus the events of the book are set in motion and the roles of the main actors indicated.
1:1 *After the death of Moses.* Immediately the time and occasion of the action are set forth, showing that the story will continue where Deuteronomy ended, with the death of Moses. Cf. "After the death of Joshua" (Jdg 1:1). *servant of the LORD.* See notes on Ex 14:31; Dt 34:5; Ps 18 title; Isa 41:8-9; 42:1. *Moses' aide.* The title by which Joshua served for many years as second in command (see Nu 11:28; see also Ex 24:13; 33:11; Dt 1:38).
1:2 *Jordan River.* The flow of the Jordan near Jericho was not large during most of the year (less than 100 feet wide), but at flood stage in the spring it filled its wider bed, which at places was a mile wide and far more treacherous to cross. *I am about to give to them.* A central theme of the Pentateuch (see Ge 12:1; 50:24; Ex 3:8; 23:31; Dt 1:8). The book of Joshua relates the fulfillment of this promise of God.
1:3-5 See Dt 11:24-25.
1:4 The dimensions of the land promised to Israel vary (compare this text and Ge 15:18 with Dt 34:1-4), but these are the farthest limits—conquered and held only by David and Solomon. Canaan was still called "Hatti-land" centuries after the Hittites had withdrawn to the north. But Joshua was to take all he set out to conquer; wherever he set his foot was his (v. 3). His victories gave the 12 tribes control over most of the central hill country and much of the Negev.

1:5 *I will be with you.* To direct, sustain and assure success.
1:6 *land I swore to their ancestors.* The long-awaited inheritance pledged to the descendants of Abraham (Ge 15:7,8-21) and of Jacob (Ge 28:13).
1:7 *Be careful to obey.* Success was not guaranteed unconditionally (see Dt 8:1; 11:8-9, 22-25).
1:8 *Book of the Law.* See Dt 28:58,61; 29:17,20-21; 30:10; 31:24. *lips; meditate.* See Ps 1:2. In the ancient world, reading written texts and even meditating on them were rarely done in complete silence (see Ex 13:9; Dt 30:14; Ps 19:14; 119:13; Ac 8:30). *day and night.* See Ps 1:2.
1:9 *Have I not commanded you?* A rhetorical question that emphasizes the authority of the speaker.
1:10 *Joshua ordered.* At this point Joshua assumes full command. *officers.* May refer to those whom Moses had appointed over the divisions within the tribes (Ex 18:21; Dt 1:15).
1:11 *provisions.* Foodstuffs needed for the next several days' march.
1:12-15 The threat from the two kings of Transjordan was overcome by military victory and the occupation of the lands north of Moab and east of the Jordan River. The two and a half tribes who asked to remain had been charged by Moses to send their fighting men across with the rest to conquer Canaan (Nu 21:21-35; 32:1-27). The conquest of the promised land must be an undertaking by all Israel.
1:13,15 *rest.* An important OT concept (see notes on Dt 3:20; 2Sa 7:1,11), implying secure borders, peace with neighboring countries and absence of threat to life and well-being within the land (see 1Ki 5:4; 8:56 and notes).
1:14 *your fighting men.* Those over 20 (see Nu 1:3,18-45) who were fit for the rigors of war.

1:16 ʳ S Nu 27:20;
S 32:25
1:17 ˢ S Nu 27:20
1:18 ᵗ S Nu 32:25
ᵘ S Dt 1:21; S 31:6
2:1 ᵛ S ver 4;
S Ge 42:9
ʷ S Nu 25:1; Jos 3:1;
Joel 3:18 ˣ S Nu 21:32;
Jdg 18:2 ʸ S Nu 33:48
ᶻ Jos 6:17,25;
S Heb 11:31
2:3 ᵃ Jos 6:23
2:4 ᵇ ver 1; Jos 6:22
ᶜ Jos 6:17
2:5 ᵈ Jdg 5:8; 9:35;
16:2 ᵉ S Heb 11:31
2:6 ᶠ Jdg 15:14;
Pr 31:13; Isa 19:9
ᵍ S Ex 1:17,19;
Jos 6:25; Jnh 1:5
2:7 ʰ Nu 22:1;
Jdg 3:28; 7:24; 12:5,6;
Isa 16:2 ᶦ ver 16,22
2:8 ʲ S Dt 22:8;
Jdg 16:27; 2Sa 16:22;
Ne 8:16; Isa 15:3;
22:1; Jer 32:29
2:9 ᵏ S Ge 35:5;
S Ex 15:14
2:10 ˡ S Ge 8:1;
Ex 14:21; Jos 3:17;
Ps 74:15 ᵐ S Nu 23:22
ⁿ S Nu 21:21
ᵒ S Ge 10:16; S 14:7
ᵖ Jos 9:10 �q S Nu 21:2
2:11 ʳ S Ge 42:28
ˢ S Dt 2:25;
Ps 107:26; Jnh 1:5
ᵗ Ex 15:14; Jos 5:1; 7:5;
2Sa 4:1; Ps 22:14;
Isa 13:7; 19:1;
Jer 51:30; Na 2:10
ᵘ 2Ki 5:15; 19:15;
Da 6:26 ᵛ S Ge 14:19;
S Nu 20:14
2:12 ʷ S Ge 24:8;
S 47:31 ˣ S Ge 24:12;
Ru 3:10 ʸ S Ge 24:14;
S Ex 3:12; Jos 4:6;
1Sa 2:34; 2Ki 19:29

¹⁶Then they answered Joshua, "Whatever you have commanded us we will do, and wherever you send us we will go. ʳ ¹⁷Just as we fully obeyed Moses, so we will obey you. ˢ Only may the Lᴏʀᴅ your God be with you as he was with Moses. ¹⁸Whoever rebels against your word and does not obey ᵗ it, whatever you may command them, is to be put to death. Only be strong and courageous! ᵘ"

RAHAB AND THE SPIES

2 Then Joshua son of Nun secretly sent two spies ᵛ from Shittim. ʷ "Go, look over ˣ the land," he said, "especially Jericho. ʸ" So they went and entered the house of a prostitute named Rahab ᶻ and stayed there.

²The king of Jericho was told, "Look! Some of the Israelites have come here tonight to spy out the land." ³So the king of Jericho sent this message to Rahab: ᵃ "Bring out the men who came to you and entered your house, because they have come to spy out the whole land."

⁴But the woman had taken the two men ᵇ and hidden them. ᶜ She said, "Yes, the men came to me, but I did not know where they had come from. ⁵At dusk, when it was time to close the city gate, ᵈ they left. I don't know which way they went. Go after them quickly. You may catch up with them." ᵉ ⁶(But she had taken them up to the roof and hidden them under the stalks of flax ᶠ she had laid out on the roof.) ᵍ ⁷So the men set out in pursuit of the spies on the road that leads to the fords of the Jordan, ʰ and as soon as the pursuers ᶦ had gone out, the gate was shut.

⁸Before the spies lay down for the night, she went up on the roof ʲ ⁹and said to them, "I know that the Lᴏʀᴅ has given you this land and that a great fear ᵏ of you has fallen on us, so that all who live in this country are melting in fear because of you. ¹⁰We have heard how the Lᴏʀᴅ dried up ˡ the water of the Red Sea ᵃ for you when you came out of Egypt, ᵐ and what you did to Sihon and Og, ⁿ the two kings of the Amorites ᵒ east of the Jordan, ᵖ whom you completely destroyed. ᵇ q ¹¹When we heard of it, our hearts melted in fear ʳ and everyone's courage failed ˢ because of you, ᵗ for the Lᴏʀᴅ your God ᵘ is God in heaven above and on the earth ᵛ below.

¹²"Now then, please swear to me ʷ by the Lᴏʀᴅ that you will show kindness ˣ to my family, because I have shown kindness to you. Give me a sure sign ʸ ¹³that you will spare

---

ᵃ 10 Or *the Sea of Reeds*   ᵇ 10 The Hebrew term refers to the irrevocable giving over of things or persons to the Lᴏʀᴅ, often by totally destroying them.

A **1:18** *Whoever rebels.* Having just taken the oath of allegiance to Joshua, they now agree to the death penalty for any rebellious act (e.g., the sin of Achan, 7:15). *be strong and courageous.* The people's words of encouragement to Joshua echo and reinforce those from the Lord (vv. 6–7,9).

A C **2:1–24** The mission of the two spies and the account of Rahab. The practice of reconnaissance and espionage is as old as war itself (cf. Jdg 7:10–11; 1Sa 26:6–12). Rahab became a convert to the God of Israel and a famous woman among the Hebrews. She is honored in the NT for her faith (Heb 11:31) and good works (Jas 2:25).

In this first encounter of the Israelites (represented by the two spies) and the Canaanites (represented by Rahab and the men sent by the king of Jericho), the outcome of the mission on which God had sent his army under Joshua (ch.1) is foreshadowed, and God's assurances of success (1:5) are confirmed.
2:1 *sent . . . from Shittim.* The invasion point was in the plains of Moab facing toward the Jordan and Jericho (Nu 33:48–49). The Hebrew word *Shittim* means "acacia trees," which grow in the semi-arid conditions of the wilderness. *especially Jericho.* The primary focus of the spies. It was a fortified city, was well supplied with water by strong springs and was located just five miles west of the Jordan (see note on 6:1). *prostitute.* Josephus and other early sources refer to Rahab as an "innkeeper," but see Heb 11:31; Jas 2:25.

B **2:2** *king of Jericho.* The major cities of Canaan were in reality small kingdoms, each ruled by a local king (attested also in the Amarna letters of the 14th century B.C.; see chart, p. xxiii).
2:6 *hidden . . . under the stalks of flax.* Rooftops in the Near East

are still used for drying grain or stalks. Rahab's cunning saved the lives of the two Israelites but put her own life in jeopardy.
2:7 *fords of the Jordan.* Shallow crossings of the Jordan, where the depth of normal flow averages only three feet.
2:9–11 Rahab's confession has a significant concentric structure:
  a "I know";
    b "a great fear . . . has fallen on us . . . all who live in this country";
      c "We have heard";
    b´ "our hearts melted in fear and everyone's courage failed";
  a´ "the Lᴏʀᴅ your God is God."
Rahab's personal confession forms the outer frame (a–a´); the inner frame (b–b´) offers the military intelligence that the spies report back to Joshua; the center (c., v. 10) sums up the news about the Lord that occasioned both the Canaanite fear and Rahab's abandonment of Canaan and its gods to side with the Lord and Israel. That the hearts of the Canaanites were "melting in fear" (v. 9) was vital information to the spies. Rahab's word is the decisive turning point in the narrator's account of this event. The whole outcome of the spies' venture into Jericho hinges on her actions.
2:10 *completely destroyed.* See TNIV text note.
2:12 *show kindness to my family.* The Hebrew for "kindness" is frequently translated "love" or "unfailing love" and often summarizes God's covenant favor toward his people or the love that people are to show to others (see note on Ps 6:4). Rahab had acted toward the spies as a friend of Israel, and now she asks that Israel treat her similarly. *sure sign.* They gave her their oath to spare her whole family (v. 14).

the lives of my father and mother, my brothers and sisters, and all who belong to them[z]— and that you will save us from death."

[14]"Our lives for your lives!"[a] the men assured her. "If you don't tell what we are doing, we will treat you kindly and faithfully[b] when the LORD gives us the land."

[15]So she let them down by a rope[c] through the window,[d] for the house she lived in was part of the city wall. [16]She said to them, "Go to the hills[e] so the pursuers[f] will not find you. Hide yourselves there three days[g] until they return, and then go on your way."[h]

[17]Now the men had said to her, "This oath[i] you made us swear will not be binding on us [18]unless, when we enter the land, you have tied this scarlet cord[j] in the window[k] through which you let us down, and unless you have brought your father and mother, your brothers and all your family[l] into your house. [19]If any of them go outside your house into the street, their blood will be on their own heads;[m] we will not be responsible. As for those who are in the house with you, their blood will be on our head[n] if a hand is laid on them. [20]But if you tell what we are doing, we will be released from the oath you made us swear.[o]"

[21]"Agreed," she replied. "Let it be as you say." So she sent them away, and they departed. And she tied the scarlet cord[p] in the window.[q]

[22]When they left, they went into the hills and stayed there three days,[r] until the pursuers[s] had searched all along the road and returned without finding them. [23]Then the two men started back. They went down out of the hills, forded the river and came to Joshua son of Nun and told him everything that had happened to them. [24]They said to Joshua, "The LORD has surely given the whole land into our hands;[t] all the people are melting in fear[u] because of us."

CROSSING THE JORDAN

3 Early in the morning Joshua and all the Israelites set out from Shittim[v] and went to the Jordan,[w] where they camped before crossing over. [2]After three days[x] the officers[y] went throughout the camp,[z] [3]giving orders to the people: "When you see the ark of the covenant[a] of the LORD your God, and the Levitical[b] priests[c] carrying it, you are to move out from your positions and follow it. [4]Then you will know which way to go, since you have never been this way before. But keep a distance of about two thousand cubits[a][d] between you and the ark; do not go near it."

[5]Joshua told the people, "Consecrate yourselves,[e] for tomorrow the LORD will do amazing things[f] among you."

[a] 4 That is, about 3,000 feet or about 900 meters

2:13 [z] ver 18; Jos 6:23
2:14 [a] 1Ki 20:39, 42; 2Ki 10:24
2:15 [c] Jer 38:6, 11
[b] S Ge 47:29
[d] ver 18, 21; Ge 26:8; Jdg 5:28; 1Sa 19:12
2:16 [e] S Ge 14:10
[f] S ver 7 [g] ver 22
[h] S Heb 11:31
2:17 [i] S Ge 24:8
2:18 [j] ver 21
[k] S ver 15 [l] S ver 13
2:19 [m] S Lev 20:9
[n] Mt 27:25
2:20 [o] S Ge 24:8; S 47:31
2:21 [p] ver 18
[q] S ver 16
2:22 [r] ver 16
[s] S ver 7
2:24 [t] Jos 10:8; 11:6; Jdg 3:28; 7:9, 14; 20:28; 1Sa 14:10
[u] S Ex 15:15
3:1 [v] S Jos 2:1
[w] S Ge 13:10; Job 40:23
3:2 [x] S Ge 40:13; Jos 2:16 [y] S Dt 1:15
[z] Jos 1:11
3:3 [a] S Nu 10:33
[b] 1Sa 6:15 [c] ver 8, 17; Nu 4:15; Dt 31:9; 1Ki 8:3
3:4 [d] Nu 35:5
3:5 [e] S Ex 29:1; S Lev 11:44 [f] Jdg 6:13; 1Ch 16:9, 24; Ps 26:7; 75:1

2:14 *kindly and faithfully.* The terms of the pledge made by the spies echo Rahab's request (v. 12). *when the LORD gives us the land.* Rahab's words had added to their assurance of the inevitable victory of the Israelites over Jericho.

2:15 *the house . . . was part of the city wall.* There is archaeological evidence that the people of Jericho would occasionally integrate living quarters into the city wall. Although this evidence predates the time of Joshua, it may still serve to illumine this verse. The Late Bronze fortifications at Jericho may have included a casemate wall (a hollow wall with partitions), and Rahab may have occupied one or more rooms inside it.

2:16 *Go to the hills.* The opposite direction from the fords of the Jordan where the spies' pursuers had gone (see v. 7).

2:18 *scarlet cord in the window.* The function of the red marker was similar to that of the blood of the Passover lamb when the Lord struck down the firstborn of Egypt (see Ex 12:13, 22–23). The early church viewed the blood-colored cord as a type (symbol) of Christ's atonement.

2:19 *their blood will be on our head.* A vow that accepted responsibility for the death of another, with its related guilt and the retribution meted out by either relatives or the state.

2:22 *into the hills.* Directly west of ancient Jericho were the high, honeycombed hills of the central mountain ridge in Canaan. They are honeycombed with caves, making the concealment and escape of the two spies relatively easy.

2:24 The spies' mission (see v. 1) concludes with a reassuring word to Joshua (cf. Nu 13:26–33).

3:1—4:24 Details of the river crossing and the memorial of 12 stones set up in the camp at Gilgal. The great significance of this

account can hardly be overemphasized, since it marks the crossing of the boundary into the promised land and parallels the miracle of the Red Sea crossing in the exodus (Ex 14–15). The Israelites' faith in the God of their ancestors was renewed and strengthened when it was about to be most severely challenged, while at the same time the Canaanites' fear was greatly increased (5:1). In this account the author uses an overlay technique in which, having narrated the crossing to its conclusion (ch. 3), he returns to various points in the event to enlarge on several details: the stones for a memorial (4:1–9); the successful crossing by all Israel (4:10–14); the renewed flow of the river after the crossing was completed (4:15–18). The final paragraph of ch. 4 (vv. 19–24) picks up the story again from 3:17 and completes the account by noting Israel's encampment at Gilgal and the erecting of the stone memorial.

3:3 *ark of the covenant.* The most sacred of the tabernacle furnishings (see Ex 25:10–22). Since it signified the Lord's throne, the Lord himself went into the Jordan ahead of his people as he led them into the land of rest (see Nu 10:33–36; Dt 31:7).

3:4 *distance of about two thousand cubits.* See TNIV text note. There was evidently a line of march, with the priests and ark leading the way. Respect for the sacred symbol of the Lord's holy presence accounts for this gap between the people and the priests bearing the ark.

3:5 *Consecrate yourselves.* Before their meeting with God at Sinai this had involved washing all their garments, as well as their bodies, and also abstinence from sexual intercourse (see Ex 19:10, 14–15).

3:7 *a* Jos 4:14;
1Ch 29:25 *b* Jos 1:5
3:8 *i* S ver 3
3:10 *j* Dt 5:26;
1Sa 17:26,36;
2Ki 19:4,16; Ps 18:46;
42:2; 84:2; Isa 37:4,
17; Jer 10:10; 23:36;
Da 6:26; Hos 1:10;
S Mt 16:16 *k* S Dt 7:21
l S Ge 26:34
m Jos 17:15; 24:11;
Jdg 1:4; 3:5 *n* S Ex 3:8;
S 23:23; S Dt 7:1;
Jos 9:1; 11:3; 12:8;
Jdg 19:11; 1Ch 11:4
3:11 *o* ver 13;
Ex 19:5; Dt 10:14;
Job 9:10; 28:24; 41:11;
Ps 50:12; 97:5;
Zec 6:5 *p* S Dt 9:3
3:12 *q* Jos 4:2,4
3:13 *r* S ver 11
s ver 16 *t* Jos 4:7
u S Ex 14:22;
S Isa 11:15
3:14 *v* Ps 132:8
w Ac 7:44-45
3:15 *x* 2Ki 2:6
y Jos 4:18; 1Ch 12:15;
Isa 8:7 *z* S Ge 8:22
3:16 *a* Ps 66:6;
74:15; 114:3
b Job 38:37; Ps 33:7
c 1Ki 4:12; 7:46
d ver 13 *e* S Dt 1:1
f S Ge 14:3 *g* S Ge 8:1;
S Ex 14:22 *h* 2Ki 2:4
3:17 *i* S ver 3
j Jos 4:3,5,8,9,10
k S Ex 14:22;
S Jos 2:10
4:1 *l* Dt 27:2
4:2 *m* S Jos 3:12
4:3 *n* ver 20
o S Jos 3:17 *p* ver 19
4:4 *q* S Jos 3:12
4:5 *r* S Jos 3:17
4:6 *s* S Jos 2:12
t S Ex 10:2 *u* ver 21;
Ex 12:26; S 13:14
4:7 *v* Jos 3:13

⁶Joshua said to the priests, "Take up the ark of the covenant and pass on ahead of the people." So they took it up and went ahead of them.

⁷And the Lord said to Joshua, "Today I will begin to exalt you *g* in the eyes of all Israel, so they may know that I am with you as I was with Moses. *h* ⁸Tell the priests *i* who carry the ark of the covenant: 'When you reach the edge of the Jordan's waters, go and stand in the river.' "

⁹Joshua said to the Israelites, "Come here and listen to the words of the Lord your God. ¹⁰This is how you will know that the living God *j* is among you *k* and that he will certainly drive out before you the Canaanites, Hittites, *l* Hivites, Perizzites, *m* Girgashites, Amorites and Jebusites. *n* ¹¹See, the ark of the covenant of the Lord of all the earth *o* will go into the Jordan ahead of you. *p* ¹²Now then, choose twelve men *q* from the tribes of Israel, one from each tribe. ¹³And as soon as the priests who carry the ark of the Lord—the Lord of all the earth *r*—set foot in the Jordan, its waters flowing downstream *s* will be cut off *t* and stand up in a heap. *u* "

¹⁴So when the people broke camp to cross the Jordan, the priests carrying the ark of the covenant *v* went ahead *w* of them. ¹⁵Now the Jordan *x* is at flood stage *y* all during harvest. *z* Yet as soon as the priests who carried the ark reached the Jordan and their feet touched the water's edge, ¹⁶the water from upstream stopped flowing. *a* It piled up in a heap *b* a great distance away, at a town called Adam in the vicinity of Zarethan, *c* while the water flowing down *d* to the Sea of the Arabah *e* (that is, the Dead Sea *f*) was completely cut off. *g* So the people crossed over opposite Jericho. *h* ¹⁷The priests *i* who carried the ark of the covenant of the Lord stopped in the middle of the Jordan and stood on dry ground, *j* while all Israel passed by until the whole nation had completed the crossing on dry ground. *k*

4 When the whole nation had finished crossing the Jordan, *l* the Lord said to Joshua, ²"Choose twelve men *m* from among the people, one from each tribe, ³and tell them to take up twelve stones *n* from the middle of the Jordan, *o* from right where the priests are standing, and carry them over with you and put them down at the place where you stay tonight. *p* "

⁴So Joshua called together the twelve men *q* he had appointed from the Israelites, one from each tribe, ⁵and said to them, "Go over before the ark of the Lord your God into the middle of the Jordan. *r* Each of you is to take up a stone on his shoulder, according to the number of the tribes of the Israelites, ⁶to serve as a sign *s* among you. In the future, when your children *t* ask you, 'What do these stones mean?' *u* ⁷tell them that the flow of the Jordan was cut off *v* before the ark of the covenant of the Lord. When it crossed the Jordan,

---

3:7 *I will begin to exalt you.* A prime objective for the divine intervention at the Jordan was to validate the leadership of Joshua. With a miraculous event so much like that of the Red Sea crossing, Joshua's position as the Lord's servant would be shown to be comparable to that of Moses.

3:10 *This is how you will know.* The manner by which God is about to bring the Israelites across the Jordan River, the watery boundary of the promised land, will bring assurance that the one true God is with them and that he will surely dislodge the present inhabitants of Canaan. Two fundamental issues are at stake: 1. Who is the true and mighty God—the God of Israel or the god on whom the Canaanites depend (Baal, who was believed to reign as king among the gods because he had triumphed over the sea-god)? By opening the way through the flooded Jordan the Lord would show both Israel and the Canaanites that he is Lord over the waters (as he was at the Red Sea, at the flood and at creation) and that he is able to establish his own order in the world. See 1Ki 20:23; 2Ki 18:32–35. 2. Who has the rightful claim to the land—the Lord or the Canaanites? (For the juridical aspect of such wars, see Jdg 11:27.) By passing safely through the Jordan at the head of his army, the Lord showed the rightness of his claim on the land. In the ancient Near East a common way for obtaining the judicial verdict of the gods was by compelling the accused to submit to trial by water ordeal. Usually this involved casting them into a river (if the accused drowned, the gods had found them guilty; if not, the gods had declared them innocent). For another form of trial by water ordeal, see Nu 5:16–28. Significantly, the Lord would enter the Jordan first and then remain there until his whole

army had crossed safely over. Thus his claim to the land was vindicated before the eyes of all who heard about it. And it was his claim, not Israel's; they came through the Jordan only with him and as his army, "baptized" into his service. *Canaanites . . . Jebusites.* See notes on Ge 9:25; 10:6,15–16; 13:7; 15:16; 23:3; Ex 3:8; Jdg 3:3; 6:10.

3:12 *choose twelve men.* Joshua seems to anticipate the Lord's instructions concerning a stone monument of the event (see 4:2–3).

3:13 *cut off.* Blocked, stopped in its flow. *stand up in a heap.* The Hebrew for "heap" is found here, in v. 16 and also in the poetic accounts of the Red Sea crossing (Ex 15:8; Ps 78:13). It is possible that God used a physical means (such as a landslide) to dam up the Jordan at the place called Adam (v. 16), near the entrance of the Jabbok River. (As recently as 1927 a blockage of the water in this area was recorded that lasted over 20 hours.) But, even if so, the miraculous element is not diminished (see Ex 14:21).

3:15 *at flood stage.* Because of the spring rains and the melting of snow on Mount Hermon. *harvest.* Grain harvest took place in April and May. *as soon as.* The stoppage nearly 20 miles upstream (v. 16) would have happened several hours earlier to make the events coincide.

3:17 *The priests who carried the ark . . . stood on dry ground.* Signifying that the Lord himself remained in the place of danger—under the threat of the waters of judgment—until all Israel had crossed the Jordan.

4:6 *What do these stones mean?* A stone monument was commonly used as a memorial to remind future generations of what had happened at a particular place (24:26; 1Sa 7:12).

the waters of the Jordan were cut off. These stones are to be a memorial [w] to the people of Israel forever."

[8]So the Israelites did as Joshua commanded them. They took twelve stones [x] from the middle of the Jordan, [y] according to the number of the tribes of the Israelites, as the LORD had told Joshua; [z] and they carried them over with them to their camp, where they put them down. [9]Joshua set up the twelve stones [a] that had been [a] in the middle of the Jordan at the spot where the priests who carried the ark of the covenant had stood. And they are there to this day. [b]

[10]Now the priests who carried the ark remained standing in the middle of the Jordan until everything the LORD had commanded Joshua was done by the people, just as Moses had directed Joshua. The people hurried over, [11]and as soon as all of them had crossed, the ark of the LORD and the priests came to the other side while the people watched. [12]The men of Reuben, [c] Gad [d] and the half-tribe of Manasseh [e] crossed over, ready for battle, in front of the Israelites, [f] as Moses had directed them. [g] [13]About forty thousand armed for battle [h] crossed over [i] before the LORD to the plains of Jericho for war.

[14]That day the LORD exalted [j] Joshua in the sight of all Israel; and they stood in awe of him all the days of his life, just as they had stood in awe of Moses.

[15]Then the LORD said to Joshua, [16]"Command the priests carrying the ark of the covenant law [k] to come up out of the Jordan."

[17]So Joshua commanded the priests, "Come up out of the Jordan."

[18]And the priests came up out of the river carrying the ark of the covenant of the LORD. No sooner had they set their feet on the dry ground than the waters of the Jordan returned to their place [l] and ran at flood stage [m] as before.

[19]On the tenth day of the first month the people went up from the Jordan and camped at Gilgal [n] on the eastern border of Jericho. [20]And Joshua set up at Gilgal the twelve stones [o] they had taken out of the Jordan. [21]He said to the Israelites, "In the future when your descendants ask their parents, 'What do these stones mean?' [p] [22]tell them, 'Israel crossed the Jordan on dry ground.' [q] [23]For the LORD your God dried up the Jordan before you until you had crossed over. The LORD your God did to the Jordan what he had done to the Red Sea [b] when he dried it up before us until we had crossed over. [r] [24]He did this so that all the peoples of the earth might know [s] that the hand of the LORD is powerful [t] and so that you might always fear the LORD your God. [u]"

5 Now when all the Amorite kings west of the Jordan and all the Canaanite kings along the coast [v] heard how the LORD had dried up the Jordan before the Israelites until they [c] had crossed over, their hearts melted in fear [w] and they no longer had the courage to face the Israelites.

[a] 9 Or Joshua also set up twelve stones   [b] 23 Or the Sea of Reeds   [c] 1 Another textual tradition we

4:7 [w] S Ex 28:12
4:8 [x] Ex 28:21
[y] S Jos 3:17 [z] ver 20
4:9 [a] S Ge 28:18; Jos 24:26; 1Sa 7:12
[b] S Ge 35:20
4:12 [c] S Ge 29:32
[d] S Ge 30:11
[e] S Ge 41:51
[f] S Nu 32:27
[g] Nu 32:29
4:13 [h] S Ex 13:18
4:14 [i] S Jos 3:7
4:16 [k] Ex 25:22
4:18 [l] Ex 14:27
[m] S Jos 3:15
4:19 [n] S Dt 11:30
4:20 [o] ver 3,8
4:21 [p] S ver 6
4:22 [q] S Ex 14:22
4:23 [r] Ex 14:19-22
4:24 [s] 1Ki 8:60; 18:36; 2Ki 5:15; Ps 67:2; 83:18; 106:8; Isa 37:20; 52:10
[t] Ex 15:16; 1Ch 29:12; Ps 44:3; 89:13; 98:1; 118:15-16 [u] S Ex 14:31
5:1 [v] S Nu 13:29
[w] S Ge 42:28

4:9 *Joshua set up the twelve stones.* Each tribe brought a stone for the monument from the riverbed to the new campsite at Gilgal, and Joshua constructed the monument there (see v. 20). An alternative translation suggests that Joshua set up a second pile in the middle of the river (see TNIV text note). The monument at Gilgal was the first of many others that came to dot the countryside as memorials to how Israel came to be established in the promised land: the ruins of Jericho (6:26), the pile of rocks raised over Achan's body (7:26), the pile of rocks raised over the body of the king of Ai (8:29), the altar of covenant renewal on Mount Ebal (8:30–31), the pile of rocks that closed the cave where five Canaanite kings were buried (10:27), the altar built in the Jordan Valley as a witness to the tribes west of the Jordan that those east of the Jordan had equal share in the Lord (22:26–28) and the stone of covenant witness that Joshua set up at Shechem (24:26–27).

4:13 *About forty thousand.* Seems too few for the number of men listed in Nu 26 for Reuben, Gad and half of Manasseh; the contingents were very likely representative since it would have been imprudent to leave the people undefended who settled in Transjordan (cf. 22:8, "the other members of your tribes"; Nu 32:17).

4:14 See 3:7 and note.

4:19 *tenth day of the first month.* The day the Passover lamb was to be selected (Ex 12:3). *Gilgal.* Usually identified with the ruins at Khirbet el-Mafjer, two miles northeast of Jericho (see map, p. 317).

4:22 *Israel crossed the Jordan.* Earlier Joshua had instructed Israel to answer that the waters of the Jordan were "cut off" so that "the ark of the covenant of the LORD" could cross the Jordan (vv. 6–7). That was the primary fact to be remembered: God crossed the Jordan to take possession of Canaan as the place in his creation where he would establish his kingdom—and he brought Israel as his people (army) with him.

4:23 *God dried up the Jordan.* Still another descriptive phrase for the miracle, along with "the waters . . . cut off," "piled up in a heap" and "stopped flowing" (3:16).

4:24 *so that all . . . might know.* The Lord's revelation of his power to the Israelites was a public event that all the Canaanites heard about (see 5:1), just as they had heard of the crossing of the Red Sea and the defeat of Sihon and Og (2:10). *fear the LORD.* Worship and serve him according to his commandments.

5:1–12 Circumcision and the celebration of the Passover, the two basic covenant rites, were resumed at Gilgal. Both were significant preparations for the conquest of the promised land. Only as a people who had consecrated themselves to God (circumcision; see note on Ge 17:10) and who remembered that God had set them free from Egyptian bondage to be his people (Passover; Ex 12:11,17) could Israel expect to be given possession of Canaan.

5:1 *Amorite . . . Canaanite.* Usually interchangeable, these general names included the many smaller nations in the land. Amorite meant "westerner," and Canaanite referred to the people living along the Mediterranean coast. This verse perhaps concludes the account of the crossing since it notes the effect of that event on the peoples of Canaan (see note on 3:10).

5:2 ˣ S Ex 4:25
ʸ S Ge 17:10,12,14
5:4 ᶻ S Nu 1:3
ᵃ Dt 2:14
5:6 ᵇ Nu 32:13;
Jos 14:10; Ps 107:4
ᶜ S Ex 16:35
ᵈ Nu 14:23,29-35;
Dt 2:14 ᵉ S Ex 3:8
5:8 ᶠ Ge 34:25
5:9 ᵍ S Dt 11:30
5:10 ʰ S Ex 12:6
ⁱ S Ex 12:11
5:11 ʲ S Nu 15:19
ᵏ Ex 12:15
ˡ S Lev 23:14
5:12 ᵐ Ex 16:35
5:13 ⁿ S Ge 18:2
ᵒ Nu 22:23
5:14 ᵖ S Ge 17:3
ᵠ S Ge 19:1
5:15 ʳ S Ge 28:17;
Ex 3:5; Ac 7:33

CIRCUMCISION AND PASSOVER AT GILGAL

²At that time the LORD said to Joshua, "Make flint knives ˣ and circumcise ʸ the Israelites again." ³So Joshua made flint knives and circumcised the Israelites at Gibeath Haaraloth. ᵃ

⁴Now this is why he did so: All those who came out of Egypt—all the men of military age ᶻ—died in the wilderness on the way after leaving Egypt. ᵃ ⁵All the people that came out had been circumcised, but all the people born in the wilderness during the journey from Egypt had not. ⁶The Israelites had moved about in the wilderness ᵇ forty years ᶜ until all the men who were of military age when they left Egypt had died, since they had not obeyed the LORD. For the LORD had sworn to them that they would not see the land he had solemnly promised their ancestors to give us, ᵈ a land flowing with milk and honey. ᵉ ⁷So he raised up their sons in their place, and these were the ones Joshua circumcised. They were still uncircumcised because they had not been circumcised on the way. ⁸And after the whole nation had been circumcised, they remained where they were in camp until they were healed. ᶠ

⁹Then the LORD said to Joshua, "Today I have rolled away the reproach of Egypt from you." So the place has been called Gilgal ᵇ ᵍ to this day.

¹⁰On the evening of the fourteenth day of the month, ʰ while camped at Gilgal on the plains of Jericho, the Israelites celebrated the Passover. ⁱ ¹¹The day after the Passover, that very day, they ate some of the produce of the land: ʲ unleavened bread ᵏ and roasted grain. ˡ ¹²The manna stopped the day after ᶜ they ate this food from the land; there was no longer any manna for the Israelites, but that year they ate of the produce of Canaan. ᵐ

THE FALL OF JERICHO

¹³Now when Joshua was near Jericho, he looked up and saw a man ⁿ standing in front of him with a drawn sword ᵒ in his hand. Joshua went up to him and asked, "Are you for us or for our enemies?"

¹⁴"Neither," he replied, "but as commander of the army of the LORD I have now come." Then Joshua fell facedown ᵖ to the ground ᵠ in reverence, and asked him, "What message does my Lord ᵈ have for his servant?"

¹⁵The commander of the LORD's army replied, "Take off your sandals, for the place where you are standing is holy." ʳ And Joshua did so.

ᵃ 3 *Gibeath Haaraloth* means *the hill of foreskins.*   ᵇ 9 *Gilgal* sounds like the Hebrew for *roll.*
ᶜ 12 Or *the day*   ᵈ 14 Or *lord*

5:2 *flint knives.* Metal knives were available, but flint made a more efficient surgical tool, as modern demonstrations have shown. *circumcise.* Circumcision marked every male as a son of Abraham (Ge 17:10–11), bound to the service of the Lord, and it was a prerequisite for the Passover (Ex 12:48). *again.* Explained in vv. 4–8.

5:3 *Gibeath Haaraloth.* See TNIV text note.

5:6 *forty years.* The time between their departure from Egypt and the crossing of the Jordan. Only 38 years had passed since they turned back at Kadesh Barnea (Nu 14:20–22; Dt 2:14). *milk and honey.* See notes on Ex 3:8; Dt 6:3.

5:9 *reproach of Egypt.* Although the reference may be to Egypt's enslavement of Israel, it is much more likely that the author had in mind the reproach the Egyptians would have cast upon them and their God if they had perished in the wilderness (see Ex 32:12; Nu 14:13; Dt 9:28). Now that the wilderness journey is over and Israel is safely in the promised land as God's special people consecrated to him by circumcision, the reproach of Egypt is rolled away.

5:10 *Passover.* The ceremonies took place in the month of Aviv, the first month of the year (Ex 12:2). At twilight on the 14th day of the month the Passover lamb was to be slaughtered, then roasted and eaten that same night (Ex 12:5–8). The Israelites had not celebrated Passover since Sinai, one year after their release from Egypt (Nu 9:1–5). Before the next season they rebelled at the border of Canaan, and the generation of the exodus had been condemned to die in the wilderness (Nu 14:21–23,29–35). For that generation the celebration of Passover (deliverance from the judgment that God brought on Egypt; see Ex 12:12–13,23) could have had little meaning.

5:11 *unleavened bread.* Bread baked without yeast. It was to be eaten during the seven festival days that followed (Ex 12:15; Lev 23:6).

5:12 *manna stopped.* This transition from eating manna to eating the "produce of the land" (v. 11) ended 40 years of dependence on God's special provision. Manna was God's gift for the wilderness journey; from now on he provided Israel with food from the promised land.

5:13–15 The narration of the conquest of Jericho (5:13—6:27) is introduced by the sudden appearance of a heavenly figure who calls himself the "commander of the army of the LORD" (v. 14).

5:13 *Joshua was near Jericho.* The leader of God's army went to scout the nearest Canaanite stronghold, but another warrior was already on the scene. *a man standing.* The experience is taken by many to be an encounter with God in human form (theophany), or with Christ (Christophany). But angels also were sent on missions of this kind (Jdg 6:11; 13:3), and some were identified as captains over the heavenly armies (Da 10:5,20; 12:1).

5:14 *Neither.* Joshua and Israel must know their place—it is not that God is on their side; rather, they must fight God's battles. *commander of the army of the LORD.* God has sent the commander of his heavenly armies to take charge of the battle on earth. Joshua must take orders from him (6:2–5), and he can also know that the armies of heaven are committed to this war—as later events confirm. *my Lord.* A term of respect for a superior.

5:15 Joshua is commissioned to undertake the Lord's battles for Canaan, just as Moses had been commissioned to confront the pharaoh (Ex 3:5). *place…is holy.* See Ex 3:5 and note.

6 Now the gates of Jericho ^{s} were securely barred because of the Israelites. No one went out and no one came in.

^{2}Then the LORD said to Joshua, "See, I have delivered ^{t} Jericho into your hands, along with its king and its fighting men. ^{3}March around the city once with all the armed men. Do this for six days. ^{4}Have seven priests carry trumpets of rams' horns ^{u} in front of the ark. On the seventh day, march around the city seven times, with the priests blowing the trumpets. ^{v} ^{5}When you hear them sound a long blast ^{w} on the trumpets, have the whole army give a loud shout; ^{x} then the wall of the city will collapse and the army will go up, everyone straight in."

^{6}So Joshua son of Nun called the priests and said to them, "Take up the ark of the covenant of the LORD and have seven priests carry trumpets in front of it." ^{y} ^{7}And he ordered the army, "Advance ^{z}! March around the city, with an armed guard going ahead of the ark ^{a} of the LORD."

^{8}When Joshua had spoken to the people, the seven priests carrying the seven trumpets before the LORD went forward, blowing their trumpets, and the ark of the LORD's covenant followed them. ^{9}The armed guard marched ahead of the priests who blew the trumpets, and the rear guard ^{b} followed the ark. All this time the trumpets were sounding. ^{10}But Joshua had commanded the army, "Do not give a war cry, do not raise your voices, do not say a word until the day I tell you to shout. Then shout! ^{c}" ^{11}So he had the ark of the LORD carried around the city, circling it once. Then the army returned to camp and spent the night there.

^{12}Joshua got up early the next morning and the priests took up the ark of the LORD. ^{13}The seven priests carrying the seven trumpets went forward, marching before the ark of the LORD and blowing the trumpets. The armed men went ahead of them and the rear guard followed the ark of the LORD, while the trumpets kept sounding. ^{14}So on the second day they marched around the city once and returned to the camp. They did this for six days.

^{15}On the seventh day, they got up at daybreak and marched around the city seven times in the same manner, except that on that day they circled the city seven times. ^{d} ^{16}The seventh time around, when the priests sounded the trumpet blast, Joshua commanded the army, "Shout! For the LORD has given you the city! ^{e} ^{17}The city and all that is in it are to be devoted ^{a} ^{f} to the LORD. Only Rahab the prostitute ^{g} and all who are with her in her house

---

^{a} 17 The Hebrew term refers to the irrevocable giving over of things or persons to the LORD, often by totally destroying them; also in verses 18 and 21.

6:1 ^{s} Jos 24:11
6:2 ^{t} ver 16; Dt 7:24; Jos 8:1
6:4 ^{u} S Ex 19:13
^{v} S Lev 25:9
6:5 ^{w} Ex 19:13
^{x} ver 20; 1Sa 4:5;
2Sa 6:15; Ezr 3:11;
10:12; Ps 42:4; 95:1;
Isa 8:9; 42:13
6:6 ^{y} ver 4
6:7 ^{z} Ex 14:15
^{a} Nu 10:35; 1Sa 4:3;
7:1
6:9 ^{b} ver 13;
S Nu 2:31; Isa 52:12
6:10 ^{c} ver 20;
1Sa 4:5; Ezr 3:11
6:15 ^{d} 1Ki 18:44;
2Ki 4:35; 5:14
6:16 ^{e} S ver 2
6:17 ^{f} ver 21;
Lev 27:28; Dt 20:17;
Isa 13:5; 24:1; 34:2,5;
Mal 4:6 ^{g} S Jos 2:1

6:1 *Jericho.* Modern Tell es-Sultan. Archaeological excavations have revealed that Jericho may have been the first site of village settlement in Canaan. (People who moved about and lived by hunting and gathering had been present in the area for thousands of years.) The earliest settled occupation dates from c. 7000 B.C. By Joshua's day, more than two dozen cities had already been built and destroyed on the site, one above the other, over a period of some 5,000 years. Many of them had powerful double walls. The present-day tell (mound) is roughly 400 by 200 yards in size, and about 65 feet high. Jericho may have been a center for the worship of the moon god (Jericho probably means "moon city"). If so, God was destroying not only Canaanite cities, but also Canaanite religion. See map No. 3 at the end of this study Bible.

6:2 *the LORD.* The Lord's command no doubt comes to Joshua through the "commander of the army of the LORD" (5:14), who orders the first conquest of a Canaanite city.

6:3 *March around the city.* A ritual act, signifying a siege of the city, that was to be repeated for six days.

6:4 *trumpets of rams' horns.* Instruments not of music but of signaling, in both religious and military contexts (which appear to come together here). The trumpets were to be sounded (v. 8), as on the seventh day, announcing the presence of the Lord (see 2Sa 6:15; 1Ch 15:28; Zec 9:14). *ark.* Signified that the Lord was laying siege to the city. *seventh day.* No note is taken of the Sabbath during this seven-day siege, but perhaps that was the day the Lord gave the city to Israel as the first pledge of the land of rest. To arrive at the goal of a long march on the seventh day is a motif found also in other ancient Near Eastern literature. In any event, the remarkable constellation of sevens (seven priests with trumpets, seven days, seven encirclements on the seventh

day) underscores the sacred significance of the event and is, perhaps, a deliberate evoking of the seven days of creation to signal the beginning of God's new order in the world.

6:5 *long blast...loud shout.* Signaling the onset of the attack—psychological warfare, intended to create panic and confusion (see Jdg 7). In the Dead Sea Scroll of "The War of the Sons of Light against the Sons of Darkness," the Levites are instructed to blow in unison a great battle fanfare to melt the heart of the enemy. (For Dead Sea Scrolls see essay, pp. 1595–1597.) *everyone straight in.* Not a breach here and there but a general collapse of the walls, giving access to the city from all sides.

6:7 *armed guard.* The Hebrew for this term differs from that in v. 3 but may be synonymous with it. It is to be expected that the ark led the procession. If so, the present reference may be to a kind of royal guard (but see v. 9 and note).

6:8–14 Throughout these verses the ark of the Lord is made the center of focus (as it was in the account of the crossing of the Jordan), highlighting the fact that the Lord himself besieged the city.

6:9 *rear guard.* If the rear guard was made up of the final contingents of the army (see Nu 10:25), the armed guard of vv. 7,9 constituted the main body of troops.

6:12–14 Literary repetition reflects repetition in action, a common feature in ancient Near Eastern literature.

6:17 *devoted.* See TNIV text note. The ban placed all of Jericho's inhabitants under the curse of death and all of the city's treasures that could not be destroyed under consignment to the Lord's house (v. 19). According to the law of Moses this ban could be applied to animals for sacrifice, to property given to God, or to any person found worthy of death (Lev 27:28–29). It was Moses himself who ruled that all the inhabitants of Canaan be "devoted" by execution for their idolatry and all its accompa-

6:17 *h* ver 25;
Jos 2:4
6:18 *i* Jos 7:1;
1Ch 2:7 *j* Jos 7:12
k Jos 7:25,26
6:19 *l* ver 24;
Nu 31:22
6:20 *m* Lev 25:9;
Jdg 6:34; 7:22;
1Ki 1:41; Isa 18:3;
27:13; Jer 4:21; 42:14;
Am 2:2 *n* S ver 5; S 10
o Heb 11:30
6:21 *p* S ver 17
q S Dt 20:16
6:22 *r* S Ge 42:9;
S Jos 2:4 *s* S Nu 21:32
t Jos 2:14; Heb 11:31
6:23 *u* S Jos 2:13
6:24 *v* S Nu 31:10
w S ver 19 *x* S Dt 13:16
6:25 *y* Jdg 1:25
z S Jos 2:1 *a* S ver 17;
S Jos 2:6
6:26 *b* 1Sa 14:24
c S Nu 5:21
d 1Ki 16:34
6:27 *e* S Ge 39:2;
S Nu 14:43 *f* Jos 9:1;
1Ch 14:17
7:1 *a* S Jos 6:18
b ver 26; 1Ch 2:7
i Jos 22:20 *j* ver 18;
Nu 1:4 *k* S Ex 4:14;
S 32:20 *l* S Lev 10:6
7:2 *m* S Ge 12:8;
S Jos 8:1,28
n Jos 18:12; 1Sa 13:5;
14:23; Hos 4:15; 5:8;
10:5 *o* Ge 12:8;
Jos 12:16; 16:1;
Jdg 1:22; 1Sa 30:27;
2Ki 23:15; Jer 48:13;
Am 3:14; 4:4; 5:5-6;
7:10,13 *p* S Nu 21:32
7:4 *q* S Lev 26:17;
S Dt 28:25
7:5 *r* Jos 22:20

shall be spared, because she hid[h] the spies we sent. [18]But keep away from the devoted things,[i] so that you will not bring about your own destruction by taking any of them. Otherwise you will make the camp of Israel liable to destruction[j] and bring trouble[k] on it. [19]All the silver and gold and the articles of bronze and iron[l] are sacred to the LORD and must go into his treasury.

[20]When the trumpets sounded,[m] the army shouted, and at the sound of the trumpet, when the men gave a loud shout,[n] the wall collapsed; so everyone charged straight in, and they took the city.[o] [21]They devoted[p] the city to the LORD and destroyed[q] with the sword every living thing in it—men and women, young and old, cattle, sheep and donkeys.

[22]Joshua said to the two men[r] who had spied out[s] the land, "Go into the prostitute's house and bring her out and all who belong to her, in accordance with your oath to her.[t]" [23]So the young men who had done the spying went in and brought out Rahab, her father and mother, her brothers and sisters and all who belonged to her.[u] They brought out her entire family and put them in a place outside the camp of Israel.

[24]Then they burned the whole city[v] and everything in it, but they put the silver and gold and the articles of bronze and iron[w] into the treasury of the LORD's house.[x] [25]But Joshua spared[y] Rahab the prostitute,[z] with her family and all who belonged to her, because she hid the men Joshua had sent as spies to Jericho[a]—and she lives among the Israelites to this day.

[26]At that time Joshua pronounced this solemn oath:[b] "Cursed[c] before the LORD is anyone who undertakes to rebuild this city, Jericho:

"At the cost of his firstborn son
   he will lay its foundations;
at the cost of his youngest
   he will set up its gates."[d]

[27]So the LORD was with Joshua,[e] and his fame spread[f] throughout the land.

ACHAN'S SIN

7 But the Israelites were unfaithful in regard to the devoted things[a];[g] Achan[h] son of Karmi, the son of Zimri,[b] the son of Zerah,[i] of the tribe of Judah,[j] took some of them. So the LORD's anger burned[k] against Israel.[l]

[2]Now Joshua sent men from Jericho to Ai,[c][m] which is near Beth Aven[n] to the east of Bethel,[o] and told them, "Go up and spy out[p] the region." So the men went up and spied out Ai.

[3]When they returned to Joshua, they said, "Not all the army will have to go up against Ai. Send two or three thousand men to take it and do not weary the whole army, for only a few people live there." [4]So about three thousand went up; but they were routed by the men of Ai,[q] [5]who killed about thirty-six[r] of them. They chased the Israelites from the city

---

[a] *1* The Hebrew term refers to the irrevocable giving over of things or persons to the LORD, often by totally destroying them; also in verses 11, 12, 13 and 15.   [b] *1* See Septuagint and 1 Chron. 2:6; Hebrew *Zabdi*; also in verses 17 and 18.   [c] *2* *Ai* means *the ruin*.

---

nying moral corruption (Dt 20:16–18). See note on Dt 2:34. *Rahab . . . and . . . her house shall be spared.* Honoring the pledge made by the two spies (2:14).

6:18 *your own destruction.* See TNIV text note on v. 17. If the Israelites took for themselves anything that was under God's ban, they themselves would fall under the ban.

A C **6:25** *she lives among the Israelites.* The faith of Rahab is noted twice in the NT (Heb 11:31; Jas 2:25).

6:26 *Cursed . . . is anyone.* Jericho itself was to be devoted to the Lord as a perpetual sign of God's judgment on the wicked Canaanites (a second memorial in the land; see note on 4:9) and as a firstfruits offering of the land. This was a way of signifying that the conquered land belonged to the Lord. The curse was fulfilled in the rebellious days of King Ahab (see 1Ki 16:34 and note).

A C **7:1–26** The tragic story of Achan, which stands in sharp contrast to the story of Rahab. In the earlier event a Canaanite prostitute, because of her courageous allegiance to Israel and her acknowledgment of the Lord, was spared and received into Israel. She abandoned Canaan and its gods on account of the Lord and Israel and so received Canaan

back. In the present event an Israelite (of the tribe of Judah, no less), because of his disloyalty to the Lord and Israel is executed as the Canaanites were. He stole the riches of Canaan from the Lord and so lost his inheritance in the promised land. This is also a story of how one man's sin adversely affected the entire nation. Throughout this account (as often in the OT) Israel is considered a corporate unity in covenant with and in the service of the Lord. Thus even in the acts of one (Achan) or a few (the 3,000 defeated at Ai) all Israel is involved (see vv. 1,11; 22:20).

7:2 *from Jericho to Ai.* An uphill march of some 15 miles through a ravine to the top of the central Canaanite ridge. Strategically, an advance from Gilgal to Ai would bring Israel beyond the Jordan Valley and provide a foothold in the central highlands. Ai in Hebrew means "the ruin." It is usually identified with et-Tell (meaning "the ruin" in Arabic), just two miles east of Bethel, but some dispute this precise identification. *Beth Aven.* Means "house of wickedness," a derogatory designation of either Bethel itself or a pagan shrine nearby (see 1Sa 13:5; Hos 4:15; Am 5:5). *spy out the region.* See note on 2:1–24.

gate as far as the stone quarries and struck them down on the slopes. At this the hearts of the people melted in fear^s and became like water.

⁶Then Joshua tore his clothes^t and fell facedown^u to the ground before the ark of the LORD, remaining there till evening.^v The elders of Israel^w did the same, and sprinkled dust^x on their heads. ⁷And Joshua said, "Ah, Sovereign LORD, why^y did you ever bring this people across the Jordan to deliver us into the hands of the Amorites to destroy us?^z If only we had been content to stay on the other side of the Jordan! ⁸Pardon your servant, Lord. What can I say, now that Israel has been routed by its enemies? ⁹The Canaanites and the other people of the country will hear about this and they will surround us and wipe out our name from the earth. ^a What then will you do for your own great name?^b"

¹⁰The LORD said to Joshua, "Stand up! What are you doing down on your face? ¹¹Israel has sinned; ^c they have violated my covenant, ^d which I commanded them to keep. They have taken some of the devoted things; they have stolen, they have lied, ^e they have put them with their own possessions. ^f ¹²That is why the Israelites cannot stand against their enemies; ^g they turn their backs ^h and run ⁱ because they have been made liable to destruction. ^j I will not be with you anymore ^k unless you destroy whatever among you is devoted to destruction.

¹³"Go, consecrate the people. Tell them, 'Consecrate yourselves ^l in preparation for tomorrow; for this is what the LORD, the God of Israel, says: There are devoted things among you, Israel. You cannot stand against your enemies until you remove them.

¹⁴"'In the morning, present ^m yourselves tribe by tribe. The tribe the LORD chooses ⁿ shall come forward clan by clan; the clan the LORD chooses shall come forward family by family; and the family the LORD chooses shall come forward man by man. ¹⁵Whoever is caught with the devoted things ^o shall be destroyed by fire, ^p along with all that belongs to him. ^q He has violated the covenant ^r of the LORD and has done an outrageous thing in Israel!' " ^s

¹⁶Early the next morning Joshua had Israel come forward by tribes, and Judah was chosen. ¹⁷The clans of Judah came forward, and the Zerahites were chosen. ^t He had the clan of the Zerahites come forward by families, and Zimri was chosen. ¹⁸Joshua had his family come forward man by man, and Achan son of Karmi, the son of Zimri, the son of Zerah, of the tribe of Judah, ^u was chosen. ^v

¹⁹Then Joshua said to Achan, "My son, give glory ^w to the LORD, the God of Israel, and honor him. Tell ^x me what you have done; do not hide it from me."

²⁰Achan replied, "It is true! I have sinned against the LORD, the God of Israel. This is what I have done: ²¹When I saw in the plunder ^y a beautiful robe from Babylonia, ^a two hundred shekels ^b of silver and a bar of gold weighing fifty shekels, ^c I coveted ^z them and took them. They are hidden in the ground inside my tent, with the silver underneath."

²²So Joshua sent messengers, and they ran to the tent, and there it was, hidden in his tent, with the silver underneath. ²³They took the things from the tent, brought them to Joshua and all the Israelites and spread them out before the LORD.

²⁴Then Joshua, together with all Israel, took Achan son of Zerah, the silver, the robe, the

---

^a 21 Hebrew Shinar   ^b 21 That is, about 5 pounds or about 2.3 kilograms   ^c 21 That is, about 1 1/4 pounds or about 575 grams

---

7:6 *Joshua tore his clothes.* A sign of great distress (see Ge 37:34 and note; 44:13; Jdg 11:35). Joshua's dismay (and that of the people), as indicated by his prayer, arose from his recognition that the Lord had not been with Israel's troops in the battle. And without the Lord the whole venture for which Israel had crossed the Jordan would be impossible. Moreover, the Canaanites would now judge that Israel and its God were not invincible. They would pour out of their fortified cities, combine forces and descend on Israel in the Jordan Valley, from which Israel could not escape across the flooding Jordan. *sprinkled dust on their heads.* See Job 2:12; La 2:10 and notes.

7:9 *your own great name.* Joshua pleads, as Moses had (Nu 14:13–16; Dt 9:28–29), that God's honor in the eyes of all the world was at stake in the fortunes of his people.

7:11 *Israel has sinned.* One soldier's theft of the devoted goods brought collective guilt on the entire nation (see 22:20). *violated my covenant.* This is the main indictment; what follows is further specification.

7:12 *devoted to destruction.* See note on 6:18.

7:13 *Consecrate yourselves.* A series of purifications to be un-

dertaken by every Israelite in preparation for meeting with God, as before a solemn religious festival or a special assembly called by the Lord (see note on 3:5). Here God summons his people before him for his judgment.

7:14 *tribe the LORD chooses.* When the lots are cast, one of the tribes is taken by the Lord so that the search is narrowed until the Lord exposes the guilty persons. The lots may have been the Urim and Thummim from the ephod of the high priest (see notes on Ex 28:30; 1Sa 2:28; see also TNIV text note on 1Sa 14:41).

7:15 *outrageous thing in Israel.* An act that within Israel, as the covenant people of the Lord, is an outrage of utter folly (see Dt 22:21; Jdg 19:23–24 and notes; 20:6,10; 2Sa 13:12).

7:19 *My son.* Joshua took a fatherly attitude toward Achan.

7:21 *robe from Babylonia.* A valuable import. *two hundred shekels . . . fifty shekels.* See TNIV text notes.

7:23 *before the LORD.* Who is here the Judge.

7:24 *Joshua . . . all Israel.* Joshua and all Israel were God's agents for executing his judgment on both the Canaanites and this violator of the covenant. *all that he had.* As the head of (and example for) his family, Achan involved his whole household in his

7:5 ^s S Ge 42:28;
Ps 22:14; Isa 13:7;
Eze 21:7; Na 2:10
7:6 ^t S Ge 37:29
^u S Ge 17:3;
1Ch 21:16; Eze 9:8
^v Jdg 20:23 ^w Jos 8:10;
9:11; 20:4; 23:2
^x 1Sa 4:12; 2Sa 13:19;
15:32; Ne 9:1;
Job 2:12; La 2:10;
Eze 27:30; Rev 18:19
7:7 ^y 1Sa 4:3
^z S Ex 5:22;
S Nu 14:16
7:9 ^a Ex 32:12;
S Dt 9:28 ^b Dt 28:58;
1Sa 12:22; Ps 48:10;
106:8; Jer 14:21
7:11 ^c S Ex 9:27;
Dt 27:25; Jos 24:16-
27; 2Ki 17:7; Hos 10:9
^d ver 15; Jos 6:17-19;
23:16; Jdg 2:20;
1Sa 15:24; Ps 78:10
^e Ac 5:1-2 ^f ver 21
7:12 ^g Lev 26:37
^h Ps 18:40; 21:12
ⁱ S Lev 26:17 ^j Jos 6:18
^k Ps 44:9; 60:10
7:13 ^l S Lev 11:44
7:14 ^m 1Sa 10:19
ⁿ Pr 16:33
7:15 ^o Jos 6:18
^p Dt 7:25; 2Ki 25:9;
1Ch 14:12; Isa 37:19;
Jer 43:12; Eze 30:16
^q 1Sa 14:39 ^r S ver 11
^s Ge 34:7
7:17 ^t Nu 26:20
7:18 ^u S ver 1;
S Lev 24:11 ^v Jnh 1:7
7:19 ^w Ex 14:17;
1Sa 6:5; Ps 96:8;
Isa 42:12; Jer 13:16;
Jn 9:24* ^x S Lev 5:5;
1Sa 14:43
7:21 ^y S Ge 34:29;
S 49:27 ^z S Dt 7:25;
Eph 5:5; 1Ti 6:10

7:24 *a* S Nu 16:27
b ver 26; Jos 15:7;
Isa 65:10; Hos 2:15
7:25 *c* S Jos 6:18
d S Lev 20:2; Dt 17:5;
1Ki 12:18; 2Ch 10:18;
24:21; Ne 9:26
e S Ge 38:24
7:26 *f* 2Sa 18:17
g S Ge 35:20
h S Nu 25:4 *i* S ver 24
8:1 *j* Ge 26:24;
Dt 31:6 *k* S Nu 14:9;
S Dt 1:21 *l* Jos 10:7
m Jos 7:2; 9:3; 10:1;
12:9 *n* S Jos 6:2
8:2 *o* S Ge 49:27
p ver 27; Dt 20:14
q ver 4,12; Jdg 9:43;
20:29
8:7 *r* Jdg 7:7;
1Sa 23:4
8:8 *s* Jdg 20:29-38
t ver 19
8:9 *u* 2Ch 13:13
8:10 *v* Ge 22:3
w S Jos 7:6
8:14 *x* S Dt 1:1
y Jdg 20:34
8:15 *z* Jdg 20:36
a Jos 15:61; 16:1; 18:12
8:16 *b* Jdg 20:31
8:18 *c* Job 41:26;
Ps 35:3 *d* S Ex 4:2;
17:9-12 *e* ver 26
8:19 *f* Jdg 20:33
g S ver 8
8:20 *h* Jdg 20:40

gold bar, his sons *a* and daughters, his cattle, donkeys and sheep, his tent and all that he had, to the Valley of Achor. *b* 25Joshua said, "Why have you brought this trouble *c* on us? The LORD will bring trouble on you today."

Then all Israel stoned him, *d* and after they had stoned the rest, they burned them. *e* 26Over Achan they heaped *f* up a large pile of rocks, which remains to this day. *g* Then the LORD turned from his fierce anger. *h* Therefore that place has been called the Valley of Achor *a i* ever since.

AI DESTROYED

8 Then the LORD said to Joshua, "Do not be afraid; *j* do not be discouraged. *k* Take the whole army *l* with you, and go up and attack Ai. *m* For I have delivered *n* into your hands the king of Ai, his people, his city and his land. 2You shall do to Ai and its king as you did to Jericho and its king, except that you may carry off their plunder *o* and livestock for yourselves. *p* Set an ambush *q* behind the city."

3So Joshua and the whole army moved out to attack Ai. He chose thirty thousand of his best fighting men and sent them out at night 4with these orders: "Listen carefully. You are to set an ambush behind the city. Don't go very far from it. All of you be on the alert. 5I and all those with me will advance on the city, and when the men come out against us, as they did before, we will flee from them. 6They will pursue us until we have lured them away from the city, for they will say, 'They are running away from us as they did before.' So when we flee from them, 7you are to rise up from ambush and take the city. The LORD your God will give it into your hand. *r* 8When you have taken the city, set it on fire. *s* Do what the LORD has commanded. *t* See to it; you have my orders."

9Then Joshua sent them off, and they went to the place of ambush *u* and lay in wait between Bethel and Ai, to the west of Ai—but Joshua spent that night with the people.

10Early the next morning *v* Joshua mustered his army, and he and the leaders of Israel *w* marched before them to Ai. 11The entire force that was with him marched up and approached the city and arrived in front of it. They set up camp north of Ai, with the valley between them and the city. 12Joshua had taken about five thousand men and set them in ambush between Bethel and Ai, to the west of the city. 13So the soldiers took up their positions—with the main camp to the north of the city and the ambush to the west of it. That night Joshua went into the valley.

14When the king of Ai saw this, he and all the men of the city hurried out early in the morning to meet Israel in battle at a certain place overlooking the Arabah. *x* But he did not know *y* that an ambush had been set against him behind the city. 15Joshua and all Israel let themselves be driven back *z* before them, and they fled toward the wilderness. *a* 16All the men of Ai were called to pursue them, and they pursued Joshua and were lured away *b* from the city. 17Not a man remained in Ai or Bethel who did not go after Israel. They left the city open and went in pursuit of Israel.

18Then the LORD said to Joshua, "Hold out toward Ai the javelin *c* that is in your hand, *d* for into your hand I will deliver the city." So Joshua held out toward the city the javelin that was in his hand. *e* 19As soon as he did this, the men in the ambush rose quickly *f* from their position and rushed forward. They entered the city and captured it and quickly set it on fire. *g*

20The men of Ai looked back and saw the smoke of the city rising against the sky, *h* but they had no chance to escape in any direction; the Israelites who had been fleeing toward the wilderness had turned back against their pursuers. 21For when Joshua and all Israel saw

a 26 Achor means *trouble.*

---

guilt and punishment. This is in accordance with the principle of corporate solidarity—the whole community is represented in one member (especially the head of that community).

7:25 *stoned him.* Because he had been found guilty of violating the covenant of the holy Lord (see Ex 19:13; Lev 24:23; Nu 15:36). Afterward the bodies were burned to purge the land of the evil.

7:26 *large pile of rocks.* A third monument in the land to the events of the conquest (see note on 4:9). *Achor.* See TNIV text note. Achor was also another form of Achan's name (see 1Ch 2:7, "Achar," and TNIV text note there).

8:1–29 Renewal of the conquest and the taking of Ai.

8:1 *Do not be afraid.* Now that Israel is purged, the Lord reassures Joshua once more (see 1:3–5; 3:11–13; 6:2–5).

8:2 *you may carry off their plunder.* The Lord now assigns the

wealth of Canaan to his troops who fight his battles. *Set an ambush.* Still in command, the Lord directs the attack.

8:12 *five thousand.* Verse 3 speaks of a contingent of 30,000 assigned to the ambush. Perhaps Joshua assigned two different units to the task to assure success. Or from the original 30,000 a unit of 5,000 may have been designated to attack Ai itself while the remaining 25,000 served as a covering force to block the threat from Bethel (see v. 17).

8:13 *the main camp to the north.* In full visibility Joshua's main force moved north of the city, then pretended to flee to the east, drawing out the entire army of defenders.

8:14 *Arabah.* See note on Dt 1:1.

8:17 *Ai or Bethel.* Their joint action indicates that the two cities were closely allied, though each is said to have had a king (12:9,16).

that the ambush had taken the city and that smoke was going up from it, they turned around[i] and attacked the men of Ai. [22]Those in the ambush also came out of the city against them, so that they were caught in the middle, with Israelites on both sides. Israel cut them down, leaving them neither survivors nor fugitives.[j] [23]But they took the king of Ai alive[k] and brought him to Joshua.

[24]When Israel had finished killing all the men of Ai in the fields and in the wilderness where they had chased them, and when every one of them had been put to the sword, all the Israelites returned to Ai and killed those who were in it. [25]Twelve thousand men and women fell that day—all the people of Ai.[l] [26]For Joshua did not draw back the hand that held out his javelin[m] until he had destroyed[a][n] all who lived in Ai.[o] [27]But Israel did carry off for themselves the livestock and plunder of this city, as the LORD had instructed Joshua.[p]

[28]So Joshua burned[q] Ai[b][r] and made it a permanent heap of ruins,[s] a desolate place to this day.[t] [29]He impaled the body of the king of Ai on a pole and left it there until evening. At sunset,[u] Joshua ordered them to take the body from the pole and throw it down at the entrance of the city gate. And they raised a large pile of rocks[v] over it, which remains to this day.

THE COVENANT RENEWED AT MOUNT EBAL

[30]Then Joshua built on Mount Ebal[w] an altar[x] to the LORD, the God of Israel, [31]as Moses the servant of the LORD had commanded the Israelites. He built it according to what is written in the Book of the Law of Moses—an altar of uncut stones, on which no iron tool[y] had been used. On it they offered to the LORD burnt offerings and sacrificed fellowship offerings.[z] [32]There, in the presence of the Israelites, Joshua copied on stones the law of Moses, which he had written.[a] [33]All the Israelites, with their elders, officials and judges, were standing on both sides of the ark of the covenant of the LORD, facing the Levitical[b] priests who carried it. Both the foreigners living among them and the native-born[c] were there. Half of the people stood in front of Mount Gerizim and half of them in front of Mount Ebal,[d] as Moses the servant of the LORD had formerly commanded when he gave instructions to bless the people of Israel.

[34]Afterward, Joshua read all the words of the law—the blessings and the curses—just as it is written in the Book of the Law.[e] [35]There was not a word of all that Moses had commanded that Joshua did not read to the whole assembly of Israel, including the women and children, and the foreigners who lived among them.[f]

---

[a] 26 The Hebrew term refers to the irrevocable giving over of things or persons to the LORD, often by totally destroying them.   [b] 28 Ai means the ruin.

8:21 [i] Jdg 20:41
8:22 [j] Dt 7:2; Jos 10:1
8:23 [k] 1Sa 15:8
8:25 [l] Dt 20:16-18
8:26 [m] ver 18
[n] S Nu 21:2 o Ex 17:12
8:27 [p] S ver 2
8:28 [q] S Nu 31:10
[r] Jos 7:2; Jer 49:3
[s] Dt 13:16; Jos 10:1
[t] S Ge 35:20
8:29 [u] S Dt 21:23; Jn 19:31 [v] 2Sa 18:17
8:30 [w] ver 33; S Dt 11:29
[x] S Ex 20:24
8:31 [y] S Ex 20:25
[z] Dt 27:6-7
8:32 [a] Dt 27:8
8:33 [b] Dt 31:12
[c] S Lev 16:29
[d] Dt 11:29; Jn 4:20
8:34 [e] S Dt 28:61; 31:11
8:35 [f] S Ex 12:38; Dt 31:12

8:26 *he had destroyed.* For the second time Joshua ordered the holy ban on the inhabitants of a Canaanite city (see TNIV text note).

8:28 *burned Ai.* As he had Jericho (6:24) and would later do to Hazor (11:11).

8:29 *impaled the body of the king of Ai on a pole.* The Israelites did not execute by hanging (see note on Dt 21:22). *until evening.* According to Mosaic instructions (see Dt 21:22–23). *large pile of rocks.* A fourth monument in the land memorializing the conquest (see note on 4:9).

8:30–35 The renewal of the covenant with the Lord as Moses had ordered (Dt 11:26–30; 27:1–8) concludes the account of the initial battles (see Introduction: Outline). The conquest of Canaan has already been put into rich theological perspective. This final event (see also Joshua's final official act, ch. 24) underscores the Israelites' servant relationship to the Lord. In conquest and occupation they must faithfully acknowledge their unique identity as the people of the kingdom of God, subject to his commission and rule (see note on 5:14).

How Israel could assemble peacefully between Mount Ebal and Mount Gerizim without further conquest is a worrisome question—and has led to some radical reconstructions of Israel's history. It must be noted, however, that Biblical narrators at times followed a thematic rather than a strictly chronological order of events. That may be the case here, since it is clear that the story of the Gibeonite deception and submission (ch. 9) is included in the thematic development of how Israel came into

possession of the rest of Canaan (see the author's introduction in 9:1–2). The Shechemites (Shechem was a major city lying between the two mountains mentioned) were Hivites (or were under Hivite domination; see Ge 34:2) and thus were related to the people of the Gibeonite cities (9:7; 11:19). Also, there was no important town between Gibeon and Shechem (Bethel and Ai had been subdued). Perhaps the treaty of submission established between Israel and the Gibeonites (ch. 9) applied also to the Hivites of Shechem, and the covenant renewal ceremony that concludes ch. 8 (and the previous narrative section) actually took place chronologically after the events narrated in ch. 9. If this suggestion is correct, the Gibeonites or their representatives would have been among the "foreigners" who participated with Israel in the covenant event (vv. 33,35).

8:30 *Mount Ebal.* At the foot of this peak was the fortress city of Shechem, where Abraham had built an altar (Ge 12:6–7).

8:31 *burnt offerings.* See Lev 1:1–17. *fellowship offerings.* See Lev 3:1–17; 7:11–18; see also chart, p. 155.

8:32 *copied on stones.* Moses had ordered the people first to plaster the stones, then to inscribe on them the words of the law (Dt 27:2–4). These stones are a fifth monument in the land (see note on 4:9).

8:33 *foreigners … and the native-born.* Israel now included the "other people" (Ex 12:38) who had come out of Egypt, plus those who had joined them during the wilderness wanderings (see note on vv. 30–35).

8:34 *the blessings and the curses.* See Dt 27–28 and notes.

9:1 *g* S Nu 13:17
h S Nu 34:6
i S Dt 3:25 *j* Ge 13:7;
S Jos 3:10 *k* ver 7;
Jos 11:19 *l* S Jos 3:10
9:3 *m* ver 17;
Jos 10:10; 11:19; 18:25;
21:17; 2Sa 2:12; 5:25;
20:8; 1Ki 3:4; 9:2;
1Ch 8:29; 14:16;
16:39; 21:29; 2Ch 1:3;
Ne 3:7; Isa 28:21;
Jer 28:1; 41:12
n Ge 12:8; S Jos 8:1
9:6 *o* S Dt 11:30
p ver 22 *q* S Ge 26:28
9:7 *r* S ver 1
s S Ex 23:32;
S 1Ki 5:12
9:8 *t* 2Ki 10:5
9:9 *u* S Dt 20:15
v ver 24 *w* S Nu 23:22
9:10 *x* S Nu 21:25
y S Nu 21:33
z S Nu 21:24,35;
Jos 2:10
9:14 *a* S Ex 16:28;
S Nu 27:21
9:15 *b* S ver 3,7;
Jos 10:1,4; 11:19;
2Sa 21:2; 24:1
c ver 21; Jdg 1:21;
Ps 106:34
9:16 *d* ver 22
9:17 *e* Jos 18:25;
2Sa 4:2; 23:37
f Jos 15:9,60; 18:14,
15; Jdg 18:12;
1Sa 6:21; 7:2;
Ps 132:6; Jer 26:20
9:18 *g* ver 15;
Jdg 21:1,7,18;
1Sa 20:17; Ps 15:4
h S Ex 15:24
9:20 *i* S Ge 24:8
9:21 *j* S ver 15
k S Dt 29:11
9:22 *l* ver 6 *m* ver 16

THE GIBEONITE DECEPTION

9 Now when all the kings west of the Jordan heard about these things—those in the hill country,[g] in the western foothills, and along the entire coast of the Mediterranean Sea[h] as far as Lebanon[i] (the kings of the Hittites, Amorites, Canaanites, Perizzites,[j] Hivites[k] and Jebusites)[l]— [2]they came together to make war against Joshua and Israel.

[3]However, when the people of Gibeon[m] heard what Joshua had done to Jericho and Ai,[n] [4]they resorted to a ruse: They went as a delegation whose donkeys were loaded[a] with worn-out sacks and old wineskins, cracked and mended. [5]They put worn and patched sandals on their feet and wore old clothes. All the bread of their food supply was dry and moldy. [6]Then they went to Joshua in the camp at Gilgal[o] and said to him and the Israelites, "We have come from a distant country;[p] make a treaty[q] with us."

[7]The Israelites said to the Hivites,[r] "But perhaps you live near us, so how can we make a treaty[s] with you?"

[8]"We are your servants,[t]" they said to Joshua.

But Joshua asked, "Who are you and where do you come from?"

[9]They answered: "Your servants have come from a very distant country[u] because of the fame of the LORD your God. For we have heard reports[v] of him: all that he did in Egypt,[w] [10]and all that he did to the two kings of the Amorites east of the Jordan—Sihon king of Heshbon,[x] and Og king of Bashan,[y] who reigned in Ashtaroth.[z] [11]And our elders and all those living in our country said to us, 'Take provisions for your journey; go and meet them and say to them, "We are your servants; make a treaty with us." ' [12]This bread of ours was warm when we packed it at home on the day we left to come to you. But now see how dry and moldy it is. [13]And these wineskins that we filled were new, but see how cracked they are. And our clothes and sandals are worn out by the very long journey."

[14]The Israelites sampled their provisions but did not inquire[a] of the LORD. [15]Then Joshua made a treaty of peace[b] with them to let them live,[c] and the leaders of the assembly ratified it by oath.

[16]Three days after they made the treaty with the Gibeonites, the Israelites heard that they were neighbors, living near[d] them. [17]So the Israelites set out and on the third day came to their cities: Gibeon, Kephirah, Beeroth[e] and Kiriath Jearim.[f] [18]But the Israelites did not attack them, because the leaders of the assembly had sworn an oath[g] to them by the LORD, the God of Israel.

The whole assembly grumbled[h] against the leaders, [19]but all the leaders answered, "We have given them our oath by the LORD, the God of Israel, and we cannot touch them now. [20]This is what we will do to them: We will let them live, so that God's wrath will not fall on us for breaking the oath[i] we swore to them." [21]They continued, "Let them live,[j] but let them be woodcutters and water carriers[k] for the entire community." So the leaders' promise to them was kept.

[22]Then Joshua summoned the Gibeonites and said, "Why did you deceive us by saying, 'We live a long way[l] from you,' while actually you live near[m] us? [23]You are now un-

---

a 4 Most Hebrew manuscripts; some Hebrew manuscripts, Vulgate and Syriac (see also Septuagint) *They prepared provisions and loaded their donkeys*

9:1–27 The account of how the Gibeonites deceived the leaders of the tribes and obtained a treaty of submission to Israel. It is the first of three sections telling how Israel came into possession of the bulk of the land. Verses 1–2 introduce the three units.
9:1 *kings west of the Jordan.* Small, independent city-kingdoms were scattered over Canaan, inhabited by a variety of peoples who had come earlier from outside the land (compare vv. 1–2 with Ge 15:19; see also note on Ex 3:8).
9:3 *Gibeon.* A site just north of Jerusalem called el-Jib, showing the remains of a Late Bronze Age city with an excellent water supply. The Gibeonites were in league with a number of neighboring towns (v. 17) but seem to have been dominant in the confederation.
9:4 *they resorted to a ruse.* Motivated by their fear of Israel's God, the Gibeonites used pretense to trick Joshua into a treaty that would allow them to live.
9:6 *make a treaty with us.* In this request they were offering to submit themselves by treaty to be subjects of the Israelites (see v. 11, where they call themselves "your servants"—unmistakable language in the international diplomacy of that day). They

chose submission rather than certain death (v. 24).
9:7 *Hivites.* Possibly Horites, an ethnic group living in Canaan related to the Hurrians of northern Mesopotamia (see 11:19; Ge 10:17; 34:2; 36:2; Ex 23:23; Jdg 3:3; see also note on Jos 8:30–35).
9:9 *heard reports of him.* The same reports that had been heard in Jericho (see 2:10).
9:14 *did not inquire of the LORD.* Did not consult their King, whose mission they were on.
9:15 *treaty of peace.* A covenant to let them live was sworn by the heads of the tribes—i.e., an oath was taken in the holy name of God. All such oaths were binding in Israel (see Ex 20:7; Lev 19:12; 1Sa 14:24).
9:18 *The whole assembly grumbled.* Perhaps the people feared the consequences of not following through on the earlier divine order to destroy all the Canaanites, but more likely they grumbled because they could not take over the Gibeonite cities and possessions.
9:21 *woodcutters and water carriers.* A conventional phrase for household servants (see Dt 19:11).

der a curse: [n] You will never cease to serve as woodcutters and water carriers for the house of my God."

[24]They answered Joshua, "Your servants were clearly told [o] how the LORD your God had commanded his servant Moses to give you the whole land and to wipe out all its inhabitants from before you. So we feared for our lives because of you, and that is why we did this. [25]We are now in your hands. [p] Do to us whatever seems good and right [q] to you."

[26]So Joshua saved them from the Israelites, and they did not kill them. [27]That day he made the Gibeonites [r] woodcutters and water carriers [s] for the community and for the altar of the LORD at the place the LORD would choose. [t] And that is what they are to this day.

THE SUN STANDS STILL

10 Now Adoni-Zedek [u] king of Jerusalem [v] heard that Joshua had taken Ai [w] and totally destroyed[a][x] it, doing to Ai and its king as he had done to Jericho and its king, and that the people of Gibeon [y] had made a treaty of peace [z] with Israel and had become their allies. [2]He and his people were very much alarmed at this, because Gibeon was an important city, like one of the royal cities; it was larger than Ai, and all its men were good fighters. [3]So Adoni-Zedek king of Jerusalem appealed to Hoham king of Hebron, [a] Piram king of Jarmuth, [b] Japhia king of Lachish [c] and Debir [d] king of Eglon. [e] [4]"Come up and help me attack Gibeon," he said, "because it has made peace [f] with Joshua and the Israelites."

[5]Then the five kings [g] of the Amorites [h]—the kings of Jerusalem, Hebron, Jarmuth, Lachish and Eglon—joined forces. They moved up with all their troops and took up positions against Gibeon and attacked it.

[6]The Gibeonites then sent word to Joshua in the camp at Gilgal: [i] "Do not abandon your servants. Come up to us quickly and save us! Help us, because all the Amorite kings from the hill country have joined forces against us."

[7]So Joshua marched up from Gilgal with his entire army, [j] including all the best fighting men. [8]The LORD said to Joshua, "Do not be afraid [k] of them; I have given them into your hand. [l] Not one of them will be able to withstand you." [m]

[9]After an all-night march from Gilgal, Joshua took them by surprise. [10]The LORD threw them into confusion [n] before Israel, [o] so Joshua and the Israelites defeated them completely at Gibeon. [p] Israel pursued them along the road going up to Beth Horon [q] and cut them down all the way to Azekah [r] and Makkedah. [s] [11]As they fled before Israel on the road down from Beth Horon to Azekah, the LORD hurled large hailstones [t] down on them, [u] and more of them died from the hail than were killed by the swords of the Israelites.

[12]On the day the LORD gave the Amorites [v] over to Israel, Joshua said to the LORD in the presence of Israel:

---

[a] [1] The Hebrew term refers to the irrevocable giving over of things or persons to the LORD, often by totally destroying them; also in verses 28, 35, 37, 39 and 40.

9:23 [n] S Ge 9:25
9:24 [o] ver 9
9:25 [p] Ge 16:6
[q] Jer 26:14
9:27 [r] S Ex 1:11
[s] S Dt 29:11 [t] Dt 12:5
10:1 [u] ver 3
[v] Jos 12:10; 15:8,63; 18:28; Jdg 1:7
[w] S Jos 8:1
[x] S Dt 20:16; S Jos 8:22 [y] Jos 9:3
[z] S Jos 9:15
10:3 [a] S Ge 13:18
[b] ver 5; Jos 12:11; 15:35; 21:29; Ne 11:29
[c] ver 5,31; Jos 12:11; 15:39; 2Ki 14:19; 2Ch 11:9; 25:27; 32:9; Ne 11:30; Isa 36:2; 37:8; Jer 34:7;
Mic 1:13 [d] ver 38; Jos 11:21; 12:13; 13:26; 15:7,49; 21:15;
Jdg 1:11; 1Ch 6:58
[e] ver 23,34,36; Jos 12:12; 15:39
10:4 [f] S Jos 9:15
10:5 [g] ver 16
[h] Nu 13:29; S Dt 1:7
10:6 [i] S Dt 11:30
10:7 [j] Jos 8:1
10:8 [k] S Dt 3:2; S Jos 1:9 [l] S Jos 2:24
[m] S Dt 7:24
10:10 [n] S Ex 14:24
[o] S Dt 7:23 [p] S Jos 9:3
[q] Jos 16:3,5; 18:13,14; 21:22; 1Sa 13:18;
1Ki 9:17; 1Ch 6:68; 7:24; 2Ch 8:5; 25:13
[r] Jos 15:35; 1Sa 17:1; 2Ch 11:9; Ne 11:30;
Jer 34:7 [s] ver 16,17, 21; Jos 12:16; 15:41
10:11 [t] S Ex 9:18; Ps 18:12; Isa 28:2,17; 32:19; Eze 13:11,13
[u] Jdg 5:20
10:12 [v] Am 2:9

9:23 *under a curse.* Noah's prediction that Canaan would someday "be the slave of Shem" (Ge 9:25–26) has part of its fulfillment in this event. *for the house of my God.* Probably specifies how the Gibeonites were to serve "the entire community" (v. 21). Worship at the tabernacle (and later at the temple) required much wood and water (for sacrifices and washing) and consequently a great deal of menial labor. From now on, that labor was to be supplied by the Gibeonites, perhaps on a rotating basis. In this way they entered the Lord's service. When Solomon became king, the tabernacle and the altar of burnt offering were at Gibeon (2Ch 1:3,5).
9:27 *place the LORD would choose.* Joshua moved the tabernacle (and its altar) to Shiloh, and there it would reside at least until the days of Samuel (1Sa 4:3). Later, the Lord chose Jerusalem (1Ki 9:3).
10:1–43 The army under Joshua comes to the defense of Gibeon and defeats the coalition of southern kings at Aijalon, then subdues all the southern cities of Judah and the Negev.
10:1 *Adoni-Zedek.* Means "lord of righteousness" or "My (divine) lord is righteous." An earlier king of Jerusalem had a similar name (Melchizedek; see Ge 14:18 and note). *Jerusalem.* City of the Jebusites.
10:2 *important city.* Gibeon was not only larger in size than Bethel or Ai but also closer to Jerusalem. With Bethel and Ai conquered and the Gibeonite league in submission, the Israel-

ites were well established in the central highlands, virtually cutting the land in two. Naturally the king of Jerusalem felt threatened, and he wanted to reunite all the Canaanites against Israel. Perhaps he also held (or claimed) some political dominion over the Gibeonite cities and viewed their submission to Israel as rebellion. *good fighters.* Men known to be effective in battle. Yet they were wise enough to have made peace with the Israelites.
10:5 *five kings of the Amorites.* Rulers over five of the major cities in the southern hill country. The Amorites of the hills are here distinguished from the Canaanites along the coast.
10:6 *Come ... and save us!* An urgent appeal for deliverance to a man whose name means "The LORD saves." A treaty such as Joshua had made with the Gibeonites usually obliged the ruling nation to come to the aid of the subject peoples if they were attacked.
10:9 *all-night march.* Gilgal was about 20 miles east of Gibeon, a steep uphill climb for Joshua's men. *by surprise.* Joshua attacked early in the morning, perhaps while the moon was still up (v. 12).
10:10 *confusion.* The Hebrew for this word implies terror or panic.
10:11 *down from Beth Horon.* A long descent to the plain of Aijalon below, following the main east-west crossroad just north of Jerusalem. *large hailstones.* For the Lord's use of the elements of nature as his armaments, see Jdg 5:20; 1Sa 7:10; Job 38:22–23; Ps 18:12–14.

10:12 ʷ Jos 19:42;
21:24; Jdg 1:35; 12:12;
1Sa 14:31; 1Ch 6:69;
8:13; 2Ch 11:10; 28:18
10:13 ˣ Hab 3:11
ʸ 2Sa 1:18 ᶻ Isa 38:8
10:14 ᵃ ver 42;
S Ex 14:14; Ps 106:43;
136:24; Isa 63:10;
Jer 21:5
10:15 ᵇ ver 43
10:16 ᶜ Ps 68:12
10:20 ᵈ Dt 20:16
ᵉ 2Ch 11:10; Jer 4:5;
5:17; 8:14; 35:11
10:24 ᶠ S Dt 7:24
ᵍ Mal 4:3
ʰ 2Sa 22:40; Ps 110:1;
Isa 51:23
10:25 ⁱ S Dt 31:6
10:27 ʲ S Dt 21:23
ᵏ S Ge 35:20
10:28 ˡ Dt 20:16
ᵐ ver 30,32,35,39;
Jos 6:21
10:29 ⁿ S Nu 33:20
10:31 ᵒ S ver 3
10:33 ᵖ Jos 12:12;
16:3,10; 21:21;
Jdg 1:29; 2Sa 5:25;
1Ki 9:15; 1Ch 6:67

"Sun, stand still over Gibeon,
  and you, moon, over the Valley of Aijalon. ʷ"
¹³So the sun stood still, ˣ
  and the moon stopped,
  till the nation avenged itself on ᵃ its enemies,

as it is written in the Book of Jashar. ʸ

The sun stopped ᶻ in the middle of the sky and delayed going down about a full day. ¹⁴There has never been a day like it before or since, a day when the LORD listened to a human being. Surely the LORD was fighting ᵃ for Israel!

¹⁵Then Joshua returned with all Israel to the camp at Gilgal. ᵇ

FIVE AMORITE KINGS KILLED

¹⁶Now the five kings had fled ᶜ and hidden in the cave at Makkedah. ¹⁷When Joshua was told that the five kings had been found hiding in the cave at Makkedah, ¹⁸he said, "Roll large rocks up to the mouth of the cave, and post some guards there. ¹⁹But don't stop; pursue your enemies! Attack them from the rear and don't let them reach their cities, for the LORD your God has given them into your hand."

²⁰So Joshua and the Israelites defeated them completely, ᵈ but a few survivors managed to reach their fortified cities. ᵉ ²¹The whole army then returned safely to Joshua in the camp at Makkedah, and no one uttered a word against the Israelites.

²²Joshua said, "Open the mouth of the cave and bring those five kings out to me." ²³So they brought the five kings out of the cave—the kings of Jerusalem, Hebron, Jarmuth, Lachish and Eglon. ²⁴When they had brought these kings ᶠ to Joshua, he summoned all the men of Israel and said to the army commanders who had come with him, "Come here and put your feet ᵍ on the necks of these kings." So they came forward and placed their feet ʰ on their necks.

²⁵Joshua said to them, "Do not be afraid; do not be discouraged. Be strong and courageous. ⁱ This is what the LORD will do to all the enemies you are going to fight." ²⁶Then Joshua put the kings to death and exposed their bodies on five poles, and they were left hanging on the poles until evening.

²⁷At sunset ʲ Joshua gave the order and they took them down from the poles and threw them into the cave where they had been hiding. At the mouth of the cave they placed large rocks, which are there to this day. ᵏ

SOUTHERN CITIES CONQUERED

²⁸That day Joshua took Makkedah. He put the city and its king to the sword and totally destroyed everyone in it. He left no survivors. ˡ And he did to the king of Makkedah as he had done to the king of Jericho. ᵐ

²⁹Then Joshua and all Israel with him moved on from Makkedah to Libnah ⁿ and attacked it. ³⁰The LORD also gave that city and its king into Israel's hand. The city and everyone in it Joshua put to the sword. He left no survivors there. And he did to its king as he had done to the king of Jericho.

³¹Then Joshua and all Israel with him moved on from Libnah to Lachish; ᵒ he took up positions against it and attacked it. ³²The LORD gave Lachish into Israel's hands, and Joshua took it on the second day. The city and everyone in it he put to the sword, just as he had done to Libnah. ³³Meanwhile, Horam king of Gezer ᵖ had come up to help Lachish, but Joshua defeated him and his army—until no survivors were left.

ᵃ 13 Or *nation triumphed over*

10:13 *Book of Jashar.* An early account of Israel's wars (perhaps all in poetic form; see 2Sa 1:18; see also note on Jdg 5:1–31), but now lost. *delayed going down.* Some believe that God extended the hours of daylight for the Israelites to defeat their enemies. Others suggest that the sun remained cool (perhaps the result of an overcast sky) for an entire day, allowing the fighting to continue through the afternoon. The fact is that we do not know what happened, except that it involved divine intervention.
10:16 *Makkedah.* A town near Azekah (v. 10) in the western foothills where Joshua's troops made their camp.
10:19 *pursue your enemies.* Most of the fighting men defending the southern cities were caught and killed before they could reach the safety of their fortresses.
10:21 *no one uttered a word.* The thought here appears to be that

no one dared even to raise his voice against the Israelites anymore.
10:24 *put your feet on the necks.* Public humiliation of defeated enemy chieftains was the usual climax of warfare in the ancient Near East.
10:26 *exposed their bodies on five poles.* See note on Dt 21:22.
10:27 *they placed large rocks.* A sixth monument in the land to the events of the conquest (see note on 4:9).
10:28 *totally destroyed everyone.* The holy ban was placed on the people of Makkedah, meaning that they were "devoted to death" for their wicked deeds (see TNIV text note on v. 1). The same fate came to the other major cities of the south (vv. 29–42).
10:33 *Horam king of Gezer.* An important detail: the defeat of the king of the most powerful city in the area. Gezer was eventually taken over by the Egyptians and given to King Solomon as a wedding gift (see 1Ki 9:16).

³⁴Then Joshua and all Israel with him moved on from Lachish to Eglon; ⁹ they took up positions against it and attacked it. ³⁵They captured it that same day and put it to the sword and totally destroyed everyone in it, just as they had done to Lachish.

³⁶Then Joshua and all Israel with him went up from Eglon to Hebron ʳ and attacked it. ³⁷They took the city and put it to the sword, together with its king, its villages and everyone ˢ in it. They left no survivors. Just as at Eglon, they totally destroyed it and everyone in it.

³⁸Then Joshua and all Israel with him turned around and attacked Debir. ᵗ ³⁹They took the city, its king and its villages, and put them to the sword. Everyone in it they totally destroyed. They left no survivors. They did to Debir and its king as they had done to Libnah and its king and to Hebron. ᵘ

⁴⁰So Joshua subdued the whole region, including the hill country, the Negev, ᵛ the western foothills and the mountain slopes, ʷ together with all their kings. ˣ He left no survivors. He totally destroyed all who breathed, just as the LORD, the God of Israel, had commanded. ʸ ⁴¹Joshua subdued them from Kadesh Barnea ᶻ to Gaza ᵃ and from the whole region of Goshen ᵇ to Gibeon. ⁴²All these kings and their lands Joshua conquered in one campaign, because the LORD, the God of Israel, fought ᶜ for Israel.

⁴³Then Joshua returned with all Israel to the camp at Gilgal. ᵈ

NORTHERN KINGS DEFEATED

11 When Jabin ᵉ king of Hazor ᶠ heard of this, he sent word to Jobab king of Madon, to the kings of Shimron ᵍ and Akshaph, ʰ ²and to the northern kings who were in the mountains, in the Arabah ⁱ south of Kinnereth, ʲ in the western foothills and in Naphoth Dor ᵏ on the west; ³to the Canaanites in the east and west; to the Amorites, Hittites, Perizzites ˡ and Jebusites in the hill country; ᵐ and to the Hivites ⁿ below Hermon ᵒ in the region of Mizpah. ᵖ ⁴They came out with all their troops and a large number of horses and chariots—a huge army, as numerous as the sand on the seashore. ⁹ ⁵All these kings joined forces ʳ and made camp together at the Waters of Merom ˢ to fight against Israel.

⁶The LORD said to Joshua, "Do not be afraid of them, because by this time tomorrow I will hand ᵗ all of them, slain, over to Israel. You are to hamstring ᵘ their horses and burn their chariots." ᵛ

⁷So Joshua and his whole army came against them suddenly at the Waters of Merom and attacked them, ⁸and the LORD gave them into the hand of Israel. They defeated them and pursued them all the way to Greater Sidon, ʷ to Misrephoth Maim, ˣ and to the Valley of Mizpah on the east, until no survivors were left. ⁹Joshua did to them as the LORD had directed: He hamstrung their horses and burned their chariots.

¹⁰At that time Joshua turned back and captured Hazor and put its king to the sword. ʸ (Hazor had been the head of all these kingdoms.) ¹¹Everyone in it they put to the sword. They totally destroyed ᵃ them, ᶻ not sparing anyone that breathed, ᵃ and he burned ᵇ Hazor itself.

ᵃ 11 The Hebrew term refers to the irrevocable giving over of things or persons to the LORD, often by totally destroying them; also in verses 12, 20 and 21.

10:38 *Debir*. Also known as Kiriath Sepher (15:15). This city was at one time identified with Tell Beit Mirsim. More recently, however, it has been equated with Khirbet Rabud, about five miles southwest of Hebron.

10:41 *Kadesh Barnea to Gaza*. The south-to-north limits in the western part of the region. *Goshen*. A seldom-used name for the eastern Negev, not to be confused with the Goshen in the delta of Egypt; it is also the name of a town (15:51). Goshen and Gibeon mark the south-to-north limits in the eastern part of the region.

11:1–23 Only the northern cities remained to be conquered. The major battle for the hills of Galilee is fought and won against Hazor and the coalition of other northern city-states. A summary follows of all Joshua's victories in the southern and central regions as well.

11:1 *Jabin king of Hazor*. Jabin is perhaps a dynastic name, used again in the days of Deborah (Jdg 4:2).

11:2 *Kinnereth*. Means "harp"; the Sea of Galilee (but see note on Dt 3:17).

11:4 *as numerous as the sand*. A widely used figure of speech for indicating large numbers (see note on Ge 22:17).

11:5 *All these kings*. Jabin's muster extended as far as the Arabah (v. 2) in the Jordan Valley and Dor on the Mediterranean, south of Mount Carmel. *Merom*. Probably modern Meirun, about eight miles northwest of the Sea of Galilee.

11:6 *hamstring their horses*. Done by cutting the tendon above the hock or ankle, crippling the horse so that it cannot walk again. *burn their chariots*. These advanced implements of war were not used by the armies of Israel until the time of Solomon (see 1Ki 9:22; 10:26–29).

11:10 *Joshua … captured Hazor*. Perhaps his greatest victory. Hazor's armed forces, however, had been defeated earlier at Merom. The archaeological site reveals extensive damage and the burning of the Canaanite city c. 1400 B.C., c. 1300 and again c. 1230. Since the destruction level at c. 1300 probably indicates the burning of the city by Pharaoh Seti I, this leaves the destruction levels at c. 1400 and c. 1230 for Joshua's conquest. Those who hold to the late date of the conquest opt for the 1230 level; those who hold to the early date opt for 1400 (see Introduction: Historical Setting). Once again the ban of total destruction was applied (v. 11).

10:34 ⁹ S ver 3
10:36 ʳ S Ge 13:18; Jos 14:13; 15:13; 20:7; 21:11; Jdg 16:3
10:37 ˢ S ver 28
10:38 ᵗ S ver 3
10:39 ᵘ S ver 28
10:40 ᵛ S Ge 12:9; Jos 12:8; 15:19,21; 18:25; 19:8; 1Sa 30:27
ʷ S Dt 1:7 ˣ Dt 7:24
ʸ Dt 20:16-17
10:41 ᶻ S Ge 14:7
ᵃ S Ge 10:19
ᵇ Jos 11:16; 15:51
10:42 ᶜ S ver 14
10:43 ᵈ ver 15;
Jos 5:9; 1Sa 7:16; 10:8; 11:14; 13:12
11:1 ᵉ Jdg 4:2,7,23; Ps 83:9 ᶠ ver 10;
Jos 12:19; 15:23,25; 19:36; Jdg 4:2,17;
1Sa 12:9; 1Ki 9:15;
2Ki 15:29; Ne 11:33;
Jer 49:28,33
ᵍ Jos 19:15 ʰ Jos 12:20; 19:25
11:2 ⁱ ver 16;
S Dt 1:1; Jos 12:1;
18:18 ʲ S Nu 34:11;
Dt 3:17; Jos 19:35;
1Ki 15:20 ᵏ Jos 12:23; 17:11; Jdg 1:27;
1Ki 4:11; 1Ch 7:29
11:3 ˡ S Jos 3:10
ᵐ Nu 13:17 ⁿ S Ex 3:8;
Dt 7:1; Jdg 3:3,5;
1Ki 9:20 ᵒ S Dt 3:8
ᵖ ver 8; S Ge 31:49;
Jos 15:38; 18:26;
Jdg 11:11; 20:1; 21:1;
1Sa 7:5,6; 1Ki 15:22;
2Ki 25:23
11:4 ⁹ S Ge 12:2;
Jdg 7:12; 1Sa 13:5
11:5 ʳ Jdg 5:19
ˢ ver 7
11:6 ᵗ S Jos 2:24
ᵘ S Ge 49:6 ᵛ ver 9
11:8 ʷ S Ge 10:15;
S Jdg 18:7 ˣ Jos 13:6
11:10 ʸ Isa 3:25;
Jer 41:2; 44:18
11:11 ᶻ S Dt 7:2
ᵃ Dt 20:16-17
ᵇ S Nu 31:10

11:12 ^cNu 33:50-
52; Dt 7:2
11:14 ^dS Dt 20:16
11:15 ^eEx 34:11;
Dt 7:2; S Jos 1:7
11:16 ^fNu 13:17
^gS Dt 1:7
^hS Jos 10:41
11:17 ⁱS Ge 14:6;
S Nu 24:18; S Dt 33:2
^jJos 13:5 ^kS Dt 3:25;
Jos 12:7 ^lDt 3:9;
Jos 12:8 ^mDt 7:24
11:19 ⁿS Jos 9:1
^oS Jos 9:3
^pS Jos 9:15
11:20 ^qS Ex 4:21;
S 14:17; Ro 9:18
^rDt 7:16; Jdg 14:4
11:21 ^sS Nu 13:22,
33 ^tS Jos 10:3
^uJos 15:50
11:22 ^vS Ge 10:19
^wJos 12:17; 19:13;
1Sa 5:8; 17:4;
1Ki 2:39; 2Ki 14:25;
1Ch 8:13; Am 6:2
^xJos 15:47; 1Sa 5:1;
Isa 20:1
11:23 ^yJos 21:43-
45; Ne 9:24
^zS Dt 1:38; 12:9-10;
S 25:19; S Jos 13:7
^aS Nu 26:53
^bPs 105:44
^cS Ex 33:14
^dJos 14:15
12:1 ^ePs 136:21
^fS Nu 32:19
^gS Nu 21:13
^hS Dt 3:8 ⁱS Jos 11:2
12:2 ^jver 5;
S Nu 21:21,25;
Jos 13:10; Jdg 11:19
^kS Nu 32:34;
S Jos 13:16
^lS Ge 32:22
^mS Ge 19:38
ⁿS Ge 31:21;
S Nu 32:26; Dt 2:36;
S 3:15; Jos 13:11,25;
17:1; 20:8; 21:38;
Jdg 5:17; 7:3; 10:8
12:3 ^oJos 11:2
^pS Ge 14:3
^qS Nu 33:49;
Jos 13:20 ^rS Nu 21:20
12:4 ^sS Nu 21:21,
33; Jos 13:30
^tS Ge 14:5 ^uS Dt 1:4
12:5 ^vS Dt 3:10
^wNu 32:33; Jos 17:1;
20:8; 21:27; 22:7
^xJos 13:2,13; 1Sa 27:8
^yS Dt 3:14 ^zver 2
12:6 ^aS Dt 3:8
^bNu 32:29,33;
Jos 13:8

¹²Joshua took all these royal cities and their kings and put them to the sword. He totally destroyed them, as Moses the servant of the LORD had commanded. ^c ¹³Yet Israel did not burn any of the cities built on their mounds—except Hazor, which Joshua burned. ¹⁴The Israelites carried off for themselves all the plunder and livestock of these cities, but all the people they put to the sword until they completely destroyed them, not sparing anyone that breathed. ^d ¹⁵As the LORD commanded his servant Moses, so Moses commanded Joshua, and Joshua did it; he left nothing undone of all that the LORD commanded Moses. ^e

¹⁶So Joshua took this entire land: the hill country, ^f all the Negev, ^g the whole region of Goshen, the western foothills, ^h the Arabah and the mountains of Israel with their foothills, ¹⁷from Mount Halak, which rises toward Seir, ⁱ to Baal Gad ^j in the Valley of Lebanon ^k below Mount Hermon. ^l He captured all their kings and put them to death. ^m ¹⁸Joshua waged war against all these kings for a long time. ¹⁹Except for the Hivites ⁿ living in Gibeon, ^o not one city made a treaty of peace ^p with the Israelites, who took them all in battle. ²⁰For it was the LORD himself who hardened their hearts ^q to wage war against Israel, so that he might destroy them totally, exterminating them without mercy, as the LORD had commanded Moses. ^r

²¹At that time Joshua went and destroyed the Anakites ^s from the hill country: from Hebron, Debir ^t and Anab, ^u from all the hill country of Judah, and from all the hill country of Israel. Joshua totally destroyed them and their towns. ²²No Anakites were left in Israelite territory; only in Gaza, ^v Gath ^w and Ashdod ^x did any survive.

²³So Joshua took the entire land, ^y just as the LORD had directed Moses, and he gave it as an inheritance ^z to Israel according to their tribal divisions. ^{a b} Then the land had rest ^c from war. ^d

LIST OF DEFEATED KINGS

12 These are the kings of the land whom the Israelites had defeated and whose territory they took ^e over east of the Jordan, ^f from the Arnon ^g Gorge to Mount Hermon, ^h including all the eastern side of the Arabah: ⁱ

²Sihon king of the Amorites, who reigned in Heshbon. ^j
He ruled from Aroer ^k on the rim of the Arnon Gorge—from the middle of the gorge—to the Jabbok River, ^l which is the border of the Ammonites. ^m This included half of Gilead. ⁿ ³He also ruled over the eastern Arabah from the Sea of Galilee ^{a o} to the Sea of the Arabah (that is, the Dead Sea ^p), to Beth Jeshimoth, ^q and then southward below the slopes of Pisgah. ^r

⁴And the territory of Og king of Bashan, ^s one of the last of the Rephaites, ^t who reigned in Ashtaroth ^u and Edrei.
⁵He ruled over Mount Hermon, Salekah, ^v all of Bashan ^w to the border of the people of Geshur ^x and Maakah, ^y and half of Gilead ^z to the border of Sihon king of Heshbon.

⁶Moses, the servant of the LORD, and the Israelites conquered them. ^a And Moses the servant of the LORD gave their land to the Reubenites, the Gadites and the half-tribe of Manasseh to be their possession. ^b

---

^a 3 Hebrew *Kinnereth*

11:13 *mounds.* The Hebrew word is *tel* (Arabic *tell*), a hill formed by the accumulated debris of many ancient settlements one on top of another (see notes on 7:2; Jer 30:18).

11:15 *he left nothing undone.* Joshua's success should be measured in the light of the specific orders given by God, which he carried out fully, rather than by the total area that eventually would have to be occupied by Israel.

11:16 *this entire land.* A lesson in the geography of Canaan follows. See map No. 2 at the end of this study Bible.

11:17 *Mount Halak.* A wilderness peak to the east of Kadesh Barnea marking Israel's southern extremity. *Baal Gad.* The first valley west of Mount Hermon.

11:18 *for a long time.* An estimation of the duration of Joshua's conquests can be made from the life span of Caleb: Seven years had elapsed from the beginning of the conquest (age 78; compare 14:7 with Dt 2:14) until he took Hebron (age 85; see 14:10).

11:20 *the LORD ... hardened their hearts.* See notes on Ex 4:21; 7:13.

11:21 *Anakites.* Had been reported by the 12 spies to be a people "of great size" (Nu 13:32), whom the Israelites had feared so much that they had refused to undertake the conquest. They were related to the Nephilim (see note on Ge 6:4) and were named after their forefather, Anak. Joshua shared with Caleb his victory over the Anakites (14:12–15).

12:1–24 A conclusion to the first section of Joshua, and a summary of the victories of the Israelites and the cities whose kings had been defeated (see map No. 3 at the end of this study Bible).

12:1 *territory ... east of the Jordan.* The unity of the nation is reaffirmed by the inclusion of these lands in Transjordan. *Arnon Gorge.* Marked the border with Moab to the south. *Mount Hermon.* The upper limits of Israel's land to the north.

12:4 *Og king of Bashan.* Sihon and Og (v. 2) were defeated by Israel under Moses' leadership, a long-remembered sign of God's mighty power (see Ne 9:22; Ps 135:11).

[7]These are the kings of the land that Joshua and the Israelites conquered on the west side of the Jordan, from Baal Gad in the Valley of Lebanon[c] to Mount Halak, which rises toward Seir (their lands Joshua gave as an inheritance to the tribes of Israel according to their tribal divisions— [8]the hill country, the western foothills, the Arabah, the mountain slopes, the wilderness and the Negev[d]—the lands of the Hittites, Amorites, Canaanites, Perizzites, Hivites and Jebusites):[e]

[9]the king of Jericho[f]	one
the king of Ai[g] (near Bethel[h])	one
[10]the king of Jerusalem[i]	one
the king of Hebron	one
[11]the king of Jarmuth	one
the king of Lachish[j]	one
[12]the king of Eglon[k]	one
the king of Gezer[l]	one
[13]the king of Debir[m]	one
the king of Geder	one
[14]the king of Hormah[n]	one
the king of Arad[o]	one
[15]the king of Libnah[p]	one
the king of Adullam[q]	one
[16]the king of Makkedah[r]	one
the king of Bethel[s]	one
[17]the king of Tappuah[t]	one
the king of Hepher[u]	one
[18]the king of Aphek[v]	one
the king of Lasharon	one
[19]the king of Madon	one
the king of Hazor[w]	one
[20]the king of Shimron Meron	one
the king of Akshaph[x]	one
[21]the king of Taanach[y]	one
the king of Megiddo[z]	one
[22]the king of Kedesh[a]	one
the king of Jokneam[b] in Carmel[c]	one
[23]the king of Dor (in Naphoth Dor[d])	one
the king of Goyim in Gilgal	one
[24]the king of Tirzah[e]	one
thirty-one kings in all.[f]	

LAND STILL TO BE TAKEN

13 When Joshua had grown old,[g] the LORD said to him, "You are now very old, and there are still very large areas of land to be taken over.

[2]"This is the land that remains: all the regions of the Philistines[h] and Geshurites,[i] [3]from the Shihor River[j] on the east of Egypt to the territory of Ekron[k] on the north, all of it counted as Canaanite though held by the five Philistine rulers[l] in Gaza, Ashdod,[m] Ashkelon,[n] Gath and Ekron; the territory of the Avvites[o] [4]on the south; all the land of the Canaanites, from Arah of the Sidonians as far as Aphek[p] and the border

---

12:7 *c* S Jos 11:17
12:8 *d* S Dt 1:7
e S Jos 3:10; S 11:17; Ezr 9:1
12:9 *f* S Nu 33:48
g S Ge 12:8; S Jos 8:1
h S Jos 7:2; 8:9; 18:13; Jdg 1:23; 4:5; 20:18; 21:2; Ne 11:31
12:10 *i* S Jos 10:1
12:11 *j* S Jos 10:3
12:12 *k* S Jos 10:3
l S Jos 10:33
12:13 *m* S Jos 10:3
12:14 *n* S Nu 14:45
o S Nu 21:1
12:15 *p* S Nu 33:20
q S Ge 38:1; Jos 15:35; Mic 1:15
12:16 *r* S Jos 10:10
s S Jos 7:2
12:17 *t* Jos 15:34; 16:8; 17:8
u S Jos 11:22; 1Ki 4:10
12:18 *v* Jos 13:4; 19:30; Jdg 1:31; 1Sa 4:1; 29:1
12:19 *w* S Jos 11:1
12:20 *x* S Jos 11:1
12:21 *y* Jos 17:11; 21:25 *z* Jdg 1:27; 5:19; 1Ki 4:12
12:22 *a* Jos 15:23; 19:37; 20:7; 21:32; Jdg 4:6,9 *b* Jos 19:11; 21:34 *c* Jos 15:55; 19:26; 1Sa 15:12; 2Sa 23:35
12:23 *d* S Jos 11:2
12:24 *e* 1Ki 14:17; 15:33; 16:8,23; SS 6:4 *f* Ps 135:11; 136:18
13:1 *g* Ge 24:1; Jos 14:10; 23:1,2; 1Ki 1:1
13:2 *h* S Ge 10:14; S Jdg 3:31 *i* S Jos 12:5
13:3 *j* 1Ch 13:5; Isa 23:3; Jer 2:18 *k* Jos 15:11,45; 19:43; Jdg 1:18; 1Sa 5:10; 7:14 *l* Jdg 3:3; 16:5,18; 1Sa 6:4,17; Isa 14:29; Jer 25:20; Eze 25:15 *m* S Jos 11:22; Am 3:9 *n* Jdg 1:18; 14:19; 2Sa 1:20 *o* S Dt 2:23
13:4 *p* S Jos 12:18

12:7 *the land ... on the west side.* Canaan proper (9:1; 11:16–17; 24:11; Ge 15:18–19).

12:12 *king of Gezer.* Had been defeated in the siege of Lachish (10:33), but the city itself was not captured by Joshua, nor were the cities of Aphek, Taanach, Megiddo or Dor (vv. 18–23; see Jdg 1:27–31).

13:1–32 The heavenly King, who has conquered the land, begins the administration of his realm by assigning specific territories to the several tribes. Much of chs. 13–21 reads like administrative documents. The account begins by noting the land still to be subdued (but to be allotted) and by recalling the assignments already made by Moses to the two and a half

tribes east of the Jordan (see map No. 4 at the end of this study Bible).

13:1 *Joshua had grown old.* Between 90 and 100 years of age; Caleb was 85 (14:10).

13:3 *Shihor River.* Elsewhere Shihor apparently refers to a branch of the Nile (see 1Ch 13:5; Isa 23:3 and notes; see also TNIV text note on Jer 2:18). Here, however, it appears to be another name for the Wadi el-Arish below Gaza at the eastern entrance to the Sinai ("on the east of Egypt"). *Ekron.* See note on 1Sa 5:10. *rulers.* The Hebrew for this word may be related to the Greek term *tyrannos* (from which comes English "tyrant"). In the OT it is used only of Philistine rulers and so may indicate the Aegean background of the Philistines. See map, p. 338.

13:4 *q* S Ge 14:7;
S 15:16; Am 2:10
13:5 *r* 1Ki 5:18;
Ps 83:7; Eze 27:9
s S Jos 11:17 *t* S Dt 3:8
u S Nu 13:21; 34:8;
Jdg 3:3
13:6 *v* Jos 11:8
w Ps 80:8 *x* Nu 33:54;
S 34:13
13:7 *y* S Jos 11:23;
Ps 78:55
13:8 *z* S Jos 12:6
a Jos 18:7
13:9 *b* ver 16;
S Nu 32:34; Dt 2:36;
Jdg 11:26; 2Sa 24:5
c ver 17,21; Jer 48:8,
21 *d* S 32:3; Isa 15:2;
Jer 48:18,22
13:10 *e* S Jos 12:2
f S Nu 21:24
13:11 *g* S Jos 12:2
h Jos 12:5
13:12 *i* S Dt 1:4
i Jos 12:4 *k* S Nu 21:33

of the Amorites; *q* 5the area of Byblos; *r* and all Lebanon *s* to the east, from Baal Gad below Mount Hermon *t* to Lebo Hamath. *u*

6"As for all the inhabitants of the mountain regions from Lebanon to Misrephoth Maim, *v* that is, all the Sidonians, I myself will drive them out *w* before the Israelites. Be sure to allocate this land to Israel for an inheritance, as I have instructed you, *x* 7and divide it as an inheritance *y* among the nine tribes and half of the tribe of Manasseh."

DIVISION OF THE LAND EAST OF THE JORDAN

8The other half of Manasseh, *a* the Reubenites and the Gadites had received the inheritance that Moses had given them east of the Jordan, as he, the servant of the LORD, had assigned *z* it to them. *a*

9It extended from Aroer *b* on the rim of the Arnon Gorge, and from the town in the middle of the gorge, and included the whole plateau *c* of Medeba as far as Dibon, *d* 10and all the towns of Sihon king of the Amorites, who ruled in Heshbon, *e* out to the border of the Ammonites. *f* 11It also included Gilead, *g* the territory of the people of Geshur and Maakah, all of Mount Hermon and all Bashan as far as Salekah *h*— 12that is, the whole kingdom of Og in Bashan, *i* who had reigned in Ashtaroth *j* and Edrei. *k*

a 8 Hebrew *With it* (that is, with the other half of Manasseh)

13:5 *Byblos.* Just north of modern Beirut. The Phoenicians and the Philistines held most of the territory still to be occupied by Israel.

13:9 *Aroer.* This town on the Arnon River marked the southern boundary of Israel east of the Jordan. From here the land extended north through Gilead and Bashan to the slopes of Mount Hermon, the territory once dominated by the two kings of the Amorites, Sihon and Og.

CONQUEST OF CANAAN: ENTRY AND CENTRAL CAMPAIGN

ENTRY INTO CANAAN

When the Israelite tribes approached Canaan after four decades of desert existence, they had to overcome the two Amorite kingdoms on the Medeba plateau and in Bashan. Under Moses' leadership, they also subdued the Midianites in order to consolidate their control over the Transjordanian region.

The conquest of Canaan followed a course that in retrospect appears as though it had been planned by a brilliant strategist. Taking Jericho gave Israel control of its strategic plains, fords and roads as a base of operations. When Israel next gained control of the Bethel, Gibeon and Upper Beth Horon region, it dominated the center of the north-south Palestinian ridge. Subsequently, Israel was able to break the power of the allied urban centers in separate campaigns south and north.

THE CENTRAL CAMPAIGN

The destruction of both Jericho and Ai led to a major victory against the Canaanites in the Valley of Aijalon—the "battle of the long day"—which then allowed Joshua to proceed against the cities of the western foothills.

(He was the last of the Rephaites.[l]) Moses had defeated them and taken over their land.[m] [13]But the Israelites did not drive out the people of Geshur[n] and Maakah,[o] so they continue to live among the Israelites to this day.[p]

[14]But to the tribe of Levi he gave no inheritance, since the food offerings presented to the LORD, the God of Israel, are their inheritance, as he promised them.[q]

[15]This is what Moses had given to the tribe of Reuben, according to its clans:

[16]The territory from Aroer[r] on the rim of the Arnon Gorge, and from the town in the middle of the gorge, and the whole plateau past Medeba[s] [17]to Heshbon and all its towns on the plateau,[t] including Dibon,[u] Bamoth Baal,[v] Beth Baal Meon,[w] [18]Jahaz,[x] Kedemoth,[y] Mephaath,[z] [19]Kiriathaim,[a] Sibmah,[b] Zereth Shahar on the hill in the valley, [20]Beth Peor,[c] the slopes of Pisgah, and Beth Jeshimoth— [21]all the towns on the plateau[d] and the entire realm of Sihon king of the Amorites, who ruled at Heshbon. Moses had defeated him and the Midianite chiefs,[e] Evi, Rekem, Zur, Hur and Reba[f]—princes allied with Sihon—who lived in that country. [22]In addition to those slain in battle, the Israelites had put to the sword Balaam son of Beor,[g] who practiced divination.[h] [23]The boundary of the Reubenites was the bank of the Jordan.

13:12 [l] S Ge 14:5
[m] S Dt 3:8
13:13 [n] S Jos 12:5
[o] S Dt 3:14 [p] Dt 3:12
13:14 [q] ver 33;
Dt 18:1-2; Jos 14:3
13:16 [r] S ver 9;
Jos 12:2; 1Sa 30:28
[s] S Nu 21:30; Isa 15:2
13:17 [t] S ver 9
[u] S Nu 32:3
[v] Nu 22:41 [w] 1Ch 5:8;
Jer 48:23; Eze 25:9
13:18 [x] S Nu 21:23
[y] S Dt 2:26
[z] Jos 21:37; Jer 48:21
13:19 [a] S Nu 32:37
[b] S Nu 32:3
13:20 [c] S Dt 3:29
13:21 [d] S ver 9
[e] S Ge 25:2;
S Nu 25:15 [f] Nu 31:8
13:22 [g] S Nu 22:5
[h] S Ge 30:27;
S Nu 23:23

13:14 *the food offerings...are their inheritance.* See Dt 18:1–8 and note on 18:1.
13:15 *what Moses had given to...Reuben.* The land east of the Dead Sea between the Arnon River (boundary of Moab) and Heshbon (the old royal city of Sihon).

13:22 *Balaam son of Beor.* The one who supposedly had influence with the gods (Nu 22–24) was slain when the Lord punished the Midianites for trying to seduce Israel into idolatry and sexual immorality (see Nu 25; 31:8 and notes on Nu 22:5,8).

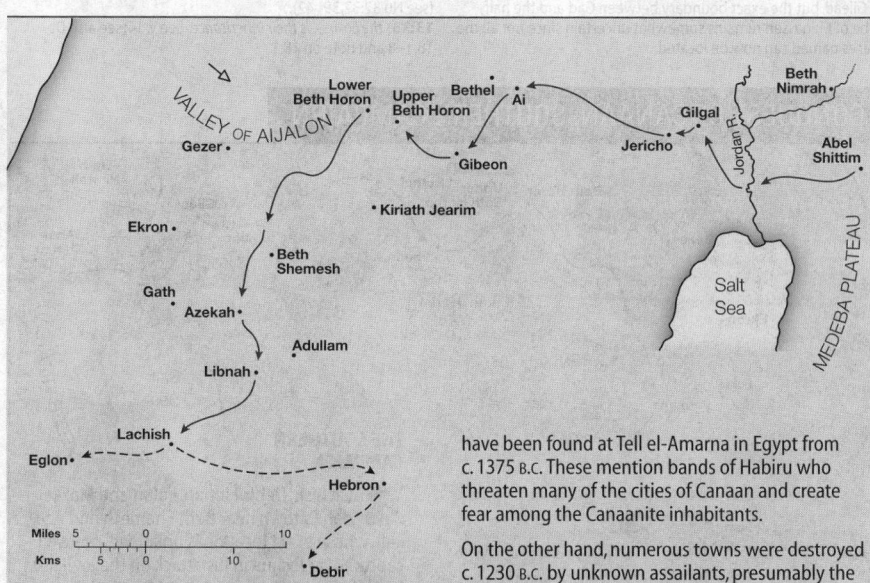

Archaeological evidence for the conquest is mixed, in part because the chronological problems are unsolved. On the one hand, clay tablets containing cuneiform letters to the Egyptian court have been found at Tell el-Amarna in Egypt from c. 1375 B.C. These mention bands of Habiru who threaten many of the cities of Canaan and create fear among the Canaanite inhabitants.

On the other hand, numerous towns were destroyed c. 1230 B.C. by unknown assailants, presumably the "Sea Peoples," but possibly including the Israelites as well. The Biblical chronology based on 1Ki 6:1 seems to demand an even earlier dating, near the end of the 15th century (see Introduction to Joshua: Historical Setting).

13:23 ᶦ1Ch 5:7
13:25 ʲS Nu 21:32;
Jos 21:39 ᵏS Jos 12:2
ˡS Dt 3:11
13:26 ᵐS Nu 21:25;
Jer 49:3 ⁿS Ge 32:2
ᵒS Jos 10:3
13:27 ᵖS Nu 32:3
ᑫS Ge 33:17
ʳJdg 12:1; Ps 48:2
ˢS Nu 34:11
13:28 ᵗGe 46:16;
S Nu 32:33;
Eze 48:27
13:30 ᵘS Ge 32:2
ᵛS Nu 21:33
ʷS Jos 12:4
ˣS Nu 32:41
13:31 ʸNu 21:33
ᶻS Ge 50:23 ᵃJos 17:5
13:32 ᵇS Nu 26:3
ᶜS Nu 22:1
13:33 ᵈNu 26:62
ᵉS Nu 18:20
ᶠS ver 14; Jos 18:7;
Eze 44:28

These towns and their villages were the inheritance of the Reubenites, according to their clans.ᶦ

24This is what Moses had given to the tribe of Gad, according to its clans:

25The territory of Jazer,ʲ all the towns of Gileadᵏ and half the Ammonite country as far as Aroer, near Rabbah;ˡ 26and from Heshbonᵐ to Ramath Mizpah and Betonim, and from Mahanaimⁿ to the territory of Debir; ᵒ 27and in the valley, Beth Haram, Beth Nimrah,ᵖ Sukkothᑫ and Zaphonʳ with the rest of the realm of Sihon king of Heshbon (the east side of the Jordan, the territory up to the end of the Sea of Galileeᵃ ˢ). 28These towns and their villages were the inheritance of the Gadites,ᵗ according to their clans.

29This is what Moses had given to the half-tribe of Manasseh, that is, to half the family of the descendants of Manasseh, according to its clans:

30The territory extending from Mahanaimᵘ and including all of Bashan,ᵛ the entire realm of Og king of Bashanʷ—all the settlements of Jairˣ in Bashan, sixty towns, 31half of Gilead, and Ashtaroth and Edrei (the royal cities of Og in Bashan).ʸ This was for the descendants of Makirᶻ son of Manasseh—for half of the sons of Makir, according to their clans.ᵃ

32This is the inheritance Moses had given when he was in the plains of Moabᵇ across the Jordan east of Jericho. ᶜ 33But to the tribe of Levi, Moses had given no inheritance;ᵈ the LORD, the God of Israel, is their inheritance,ᵉ as he promised them.ᶠ

ᵃ 27 Hebrew *Kinnereth*

13:24 *what Moses had given to ... Gad.* The central area, beginning near Heshbon on the south and reaching, along the Jordan, to the southern end of the Sea of Galilee. It included most of Gilead, but the exact boundary between Gad and the half-tribe of Manasseh remains somewhat uncertain since not all the places named can now be located.

13:29 *what Moses had given to the half-tribe of Manasseh.* The lands east and north of the Sea of Galilee, but also including the upper part of Gilead. Makir led in the occupation of these lands (see Nu 32:32,39–42).
13:33 *the LORD ... is their inheritance.* See v. 14; see also Dt 18:1–8 and note on 18:1.

CONQUEST OF CANAAN: SOUTHERN CAMPAIGN

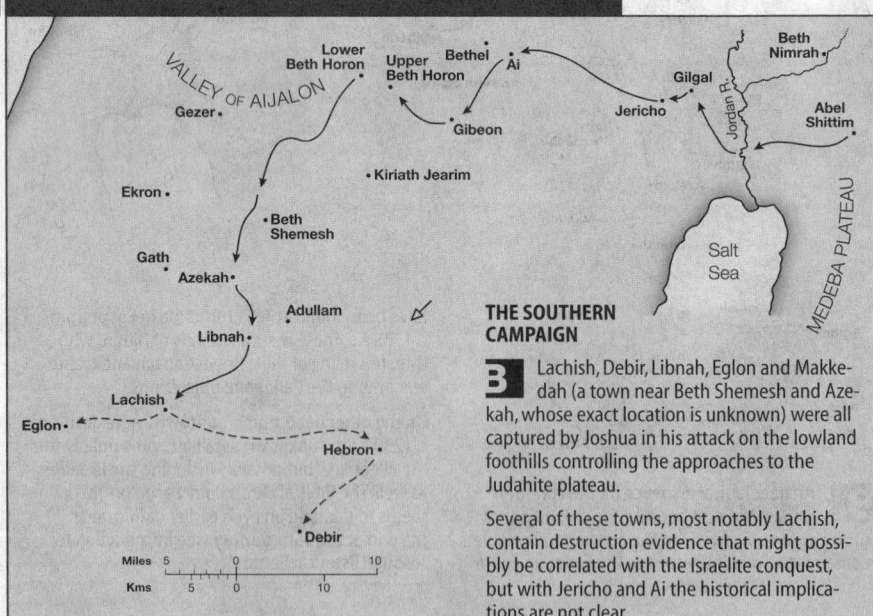

THE SOUTHERN CAMPAIGN

B Lachish, Debir, Libnah, Eglon and Makkedah (a town near Beth Shemesh and Azekah, whose exact location is unknown) were all captured by Joshua in his attack on the lowland foothills controlling the approaches to the Judahite plateau.

Several of these towns, most notably Lachish, contain destruction evidence that might possibly be correlated with the Israelite conquest, but with Jericho and Ai the historical implications are not clear.

DIVISION OF THE LAND WEST OF THE JORDAN

14 Now these are the areas the Israelites received as an inheritance[g] in the land of Canaan, which Eleazar[h] the priest, Joshua son of Nun and the heads of the tribal clans of Israel[i] allotted[j] to them.[k] [2]Their inheritances were assigned by lot[l] to the nine-and-a-half tribes,[m] as the LORD had commanded through Moses. [3]Moses had granted the two-and-a-half tribes their inheritance east of the Jordan[n] but had not granted the Levites an inheritance among the rest,[o] [4]for the sons of Joseph had become two tribes—Manasseh and Ephraim.[p] The Levites received no share of the land but only towns to live in, with pasturelands for their flocks and herds.[q] [5]So the Israelites divided the land, just as the LORD had commanded Moses.[r]

ALLOTMENT FOR CALEB

[6]Now the people of Judah approached Joshua at Gilgal,[s] and Caleb son of Jephunneh[t] the Kenizzite said to him, "You know what the LORD said to Moses the man of God[u] at Kadesh Barnea[v] about you and me.[w] [7]I was forty years old when Moses the servant of the LORD sent me from Kadesh Barnea[x] to explore the land.[y] And I brought him back a report according to my convictions,[z] [8]but the others who went up with me made the hearts of the people melt in fear.[a] I, however, followed the LORD my God wholeheartedly.[b] [9]So on that day Moses swore to me, 'The land on which your feet have walked will be your in-

14:1 [g] S Jos 11:23; Ps 16:6; 136:21
[h] S Ex 6:23 [i] Jos 21:1
[j] S Nu 26:53
[k] Nu 34:17-18; Jos 19:51
14:2 [l] S Lev 16:8
[m] Nu 34:13
14:3 [n] S Nu 32:33; S 34:14 [o] S Nu 35:2; S Jos 13:14
14:4 [p] S Ge 41:52; S Jdg 1:29
[q] S Nu 35:2-3; Jos 21:2
14:5 [r] S Nu 34:13
14:6 [s] S Dt 11:30
[t] Nu 13:6; 14:30
[u] S Dt 33:1 [v] Nu 13:26
[w] S Nu 14:38
14:7 [x] Jos 15:3
[y] S Nu 13:17
[z] Nu 13:30; S 14:6-9
14:8 [a] S Nu 13:31
[b] S Nu 14:24; S 32:12

14:1–5 An introduction to the allotment of territories in Canaan.
14:1 *Eleazar the priest.* Son of Aaron, Eleazar as high priest was the highest official over the casting of the lots. The Urim and Thummim (see notes on Ex 28:30; 1Sa 2:28) may have been used.
14:4 *Manasseh and Ephraim.* Sons of Joseph. Since Jacob had adopted them as his own sons (Ge 48:5), they constituted two separate tribes. This made possible the 12-part nation, with the Levites serving as a nonpolitical tribe.

14:6–15 Assignment of Hebron to Caleb—in accordance with Moses' pledge to him for his faithful service as one of Israel's spies sent to explore the promised land (see Nu 14:24,30; 32:12 and note on 14:24). Assignment of cities in Canaan to Caleb (Judah) and Joshua (Ephraim) frame the account of territorial divisions west of the Jordan (see 19:49–50 and note on 19:49).
14:6 *what the LORD said.* Caleb now recalls the promise from the Lord 38 years earlier at Kadesh Barnea when he brought back a good report of the land (Nu 13:30; 14:6–9; Dt 1:34–36).
14:8 *followed … wholeheartedly.* See Nu 14:24 and note; 32:12.

CONQUEST OF CANAAN: NORTHERN CAMPAIGN

Mt. Hermon ▲

Kedesh

Waters of Merom

Hazor

Akshaph

Madon

Shimron

Sea of Kinnereth

Miles 5 0 10 20
Kms 5 0 10 20 30

THE NORTHERN CAMPAIGN

B Late Bronze Age Hazor was burned by Joshua (Jos 11:13). Excavations have revealed three clearly datable destruction layers, one of which may provide the strongest evidence yet for a historically verifiable date for the conquest.

The excavator thought Joshua burned the latest level (c. 1230 B.C.), but others argue that it must actually have been the earliest of the three levels, c. 1400 B.C. (see note on 11:10).

14:9 c Dt 11:24
d S Nu 14:24
14:10 e S Nu 11:28;
14:30 f S Jos 5:6
g S Jos 13:1
14:11 h S Dt 34:7
i S Ge 15:15
14:12 j S Nu 14:24
k S Nu 13:33
l Nu 13:28
14:13 m Jos 22:6,7
n 1Sa 25:3; 30:14
o S Ge 23:19;
S Jos 10:36 j Jdg 1:20;
1Ch 6:56
14:14 q S Nu 14:24
14:15 r S Ge 23:2
a Jos 15:13 t Jos 11:23;
Jdg 3:11; 1Ki 4:24;
5:4; 1Ch 22:9
15:1 u Nu 34:3
v S Nu 13:21
w Jos 18:5
15:2 x S Ge 14:3
15:3 y S Nu 34:4
z S Dt 1:2
15:4 a Nu 34:4
b S Ge 15:18
15:5 c Nu 34:10
d S Ge 14:3
e Jos 18:15-19
15:6 f Jos 18:19,21
g ver 61; Jos 18:18
h Jos 18:17
15:7 i S Jos 10:3
j S Jos 7:24
k S Dt 11:30 l Jos 18:17
m Jos 18:16; 2Sa 17:17;
1Ki 1:9
15:8 n 2Ch 28:3;
Jer 19:6 o ver 63;
Jos 18:16,28; Jdg 1:21;
19:10; 2Sa 5:6;
1Ch 11:4; Ezr 9:1
p S Jos 10:1
q 2Ki 23:10; Jer 7:31;
19:2 r 2Sa 5:18,22;
1Ch 14:9; Isa 17:5
15:9 s Jos 18:15
t ver 10,11,29;
2Sa 6:2; 1Ch 13:6
u S Jos 9:17
15:10 v S ver 9
w S Nu 24:18
x Jos 19:22,38; 21:16;
Jdg 1:33; 1Sa 6:9;
1Ki 4:9; 2Ki 14:11
y S Ge 38:12
15:11 z S Jos 13:3
a S ver 9 b Jos 19:33
15:12 c S Nu 34:6
15:13 d 1Sa 25:3;
30:14 e S Ge 23:2
f S Jos 10:36; 21:12;
1Ch 6:56 g S Nu 13:22
15:14 h S Nu 13:33
i S Nu 13:22 j Jdg 1:10,
20

heritance c and that of your children d forever, because you have followed the LORD my God wholeheartedly.'ᵃ

¹⁰"Now then, just as the LORD promised, e he has kept me alive for forty-five years since the time he said this to Moses, while Israel moved f about in the wilderness. So here I am today, eighty-five years old! g ¹¹I am still as strong h today as the day Moses sent me out; I'm just as vigorous i to go out to battle now as I was then. ¹²Now give me this hill country that the LORD promised me that day. j You yourself heard then that the Anakites k were there and their cities were large and fortified, l but, the LORD helping me, I will drive them out just as he said."

¹³Then Joshua blessed m Caleb son of Jephunneh n and gave him Hebron o as his inheritance. p ¹⁴So Hebron has belonged to Caleb son of Jephunneh the Kenizzite ever since, because he followed the LORD, the God of Israel, wholeheartedly. q ¹⁵(Hebron used to be called Kiriath Arba r after Arba, s who was the greatest man among the Anakites.)

Then the land had rest t from war.

ALLOTMENT FOR JUDAH

15:15–19pp — Jdg 1:11–15

15 The allotment for the tribe of Judah, according to its clans, extended down to the territory of Edom, u to the Desert of Zin v in the extreme south. w ²Their southern boundary started from the bay at the southern end of the Dead Sea, x ³crossed south of Scorpion Pass, y continued on to Zin and went over to the south of Kadesh Barnea. z Then it ran past Hezron up to Addar and curved around to Karka. ⁴It then passed along to Azmon a and joined the Wadi of Egypt, b ending at the Mediterranean Sea. This is their b southern boundary.

⁵The eastern boundary c is the Dead Sea d as far as the mouth of the Jordan.

The northern boundary e started from the bay of the sea at the mouth of the Jordan, ⁶went up to Beth Hoglah f and continued north of Beth Arabah g to the Stone of Bohan h son of Reuben. ⁷The boundary then went up to Debir i from the Valley of Achor j and turned north to Gilgal, k which faces the Pass of Adummim south of the gorge. It continued along to the waters of En Shemesh l and came out at En Rogel. m ⁸Then it ran up the Valley of Ben Hinnom n along the southern slope of the Jebusite o city (that is, Jerusalem p). From there it climbed to the top of the hill west of the Hinnom Valley q at the northern end of the Valley of Rephaim. r ⁹From the hilltop the boundary headed toward the spring of the waters of Nephtoah, s came out at the towns of Mount Ephron and went down toward Baalah t (that is, Kiriath Jearim). u ¹⁰Then it curved westward from Baalah v to Mount Seir, w ran along the northern slope of Mount Jearim (that is, Kesalon), continued down to Beth Shemesh x and crossed to Timnah. y ¹¹It went to the northern slope of Ekron, z turned toward Shikkeron, passed along to Mount Baalah a and reached Jabneel. b The boundary ended at the sea.

¹²The western boundary is the coastline of the Mediterranean Sea. c

These are the boundaries around the people of Judah by their clans.

¹³In accordance with the LORD's command to him, Joshua gave to Caleb d son of Jephunneh a portion in Judah—Kiriath Arba e, that is, Hebron. f (Arba was the ancestor of Anak.) g ¹⁴From Hebron Caleb drove out the three Anakites h —Sheshai, Ahiman and Talmai, i the sons of Anak. j ¹⁵From there he marched against the people living in Debir (for-

---

ᵃ 9 Deut. 1:36   ᵇ 4 Septuagint; Hebrew *your*

14:12 *this hill country.* Hebron is situated high in the Judahite hill country, about 25 miles south of Jerusalem. *Anakites.* See note on 11:21.

14:15 *Kiriath Arba.* Means "the town of Arba" and was named for Arba, the father of the Anakites (15:13; 21:11). It can also mean "the town of four," possibly referring to Anak and his three descendants (see 15:14; Nu 13:22 and note; Jdg 1:20). *Then the land had rest from war.* Since the Judahites and Caleb approached Joshua concerning their territory while he was still headquartered at Gilgal, it may be that they did so shortly before the wars fought under Joshua were ended (see 11:23).

15:1–63 Judah is the first of the west bank tribes to have its territory delineated. First the outer limits are listed, then the area apportioned to Caleb and Othniel; finally the Canaanite cities allotted to the clans of Judah are named region by region.

15:1 *tribe of Judah.* Judah's priority is anchored in the oracle of Jacob (Ge 49:8–12) and upheld in the history of the nation (Jdg 1:1–2; 20:18; 2Ki 17:18; Ps 78:68).

15:4 *southern boundary.* The points listed formed a curved line beginning at the lower tip of the Dead Sea and moving under Kadesh Barnea to join the Mediterranean coast at the mouth of the Wadi el-Arish (see note on 13:3).

15:5 *northern boundary.* Judah's border with Benjamin ran in a westerly line from the mouth of the Jordan through the Hinnom Valley, just south of Jerusalem, over to Timnah, then northwest to the coastal city of Jabneel (later called Jamnia), about ten miles south of Joppa.

15:7 *Gilgal.* See note on Jdg 3:19.

15:15 *he marched against . . . Debir.* See note on 10:38.

merly called Kiriath Sepher). [16]And Caleb said, "I will give my daughter Aksah[k] in marriage to the man who attacks and captures Kiriath Sepher." [17]Othniel[l] son of Kenaz, Caleb's brother, took it; so Caleb gave his daughter Aksah to him in marriage.

[18]One day when she came to Othniel, she urged him[a] to ask her father for a field. When she got off her donkey, Caleb asked her, "What can I do for you?"

[19]She replied, "Do me a special favor. Since you have given me land in the Negev,[m] give me also springs of water." So Caleb gave her the upper and lower springs.[n]

[20]This is the inheritance of the tribe of Judah, according to its clans:

[21]The southernmost towns of the tribe of Judah in the Negev[o] toward the boundary of Edom were:

Kabzeel,[p] Eder,[q] Jagur, [22]Kinah, Dimonah, Adadah, [23]Kedesh,[r] Hazor,[s] Ithnan, [24]Ziph,[t] Telem, Bealoth, [25]Hazor Hadattah, Kerioth Hezron (that is, Hazor),[u] [26]Amam, Shema, Moladah,[v] [27]Hazar Gaddah, Heshmon, Beth Pelet, [28]Hazar Shual,[w] Beersheba,[x] Biziothiah, [29]Baalah,[y] Iyim, Ezem,[z] [30]Eltolad,[a] Kesil, Hormah,[b] [31]Ziklag,[c] Madmannah,[d] Sansannah, [32]Lebaoth, Shilhim, Ain[e] and Rimmon[f]—a total of twenty-nine towns and their villages.

[33]In the western foothills:

Eshtaol,[g] Zorah,[h] Ashnah,[i] [34]Zanoah,[j] En Gannim,[k] Tappuah,[l] Enam, [35]Jarmuth,[m] Adullam,[n] Sokoh,[o] Azekah,[p] [36]Shaaraim,[q] Adithaim and Gederah[r] (or Gederothaim)[b]—fourteen towns and their villages.

[37]Zenan, Hadashah, Migdal Gad, [38]Dilean, Mizpah,[s] Joktheel,[t] [39]Lachish,[u] Bozkath,[v] Eglon,[w] [40]Kabbon, Lahmas, Kitlish, [41]Gederoth,[x] Beth Dagon,[y] Naamah and Makkedah[z]—sixteen towns and their villages.

[42]Libnah,[a] Ether, Ashan,[b] [43]Iphtah, Ashnah,[c] Nezib, [44]Keilah,[d] Akzib[e] and Mareshah[f]—nine towns and their villages.

[45]Ekron,[g] with its surrounding settlements and villages; [46]west of Ekron, all that were in the vicinity of Ashdod,[h] together with their villages; [47]Ashdod,[i] its surrounding settlements and villages; and Gaza, its settlements and villages, as far as the Wadi of Egypt[j] and the coastline of the Mediterranean Sea.[k]

[48]In the hill country:

Shamir,[l] Jattir,[m] Sokoh,[n] [49]Dannah, Kiriath Sannah (that is, Debir[o]), [50]Anab,[p] Eshtemoh,[q] Anim, [51]Goshen,[r] Holon[s] and Giloh[t]—eleven towns and their villages.

[52]Arab, Dumah,[u] Eshan, [53]Janim, Beth Tappuah, Aphekah, [54]Humtah, Kiriath Arba[v] (that is, Hebron) and Zior—nine towns and their villages.

[55]Maon,[w] Carmel,[x] Ziph,[y] Juttah,[z] [56]Jezreel,[a] Jokdeam, Zanoah,[b] [57]Kain, Gibeah[c] and Timnah[d]—ten towns and their villages.

[58]Halhul, Beth Zur,[e] Gedor,[f] [59]Maarath, Beth Anoth and Eltekon—six towns and their villages.[c]

[60]Kiriath Baal[g] (that is, Kiriath Jearim[h]) and Rabbah[i]—two towns and their villages.

[61]In the wilderness:[j]

Beth Arabah,[k] Middin, Sekakah, [62]Nibshan, the City of Salt and En Gedi[l]—six towns and their villages.

[63]Judah could not[m] dislodge the Jebusites[n], who were living in Jerusalem;[o] to this day the Jebusites live there with the people of Judah.[p]

---

a 18 Hebrew and some Septuagint manuscripts; other Septuagint manuscripts (see also note at Judges 1:14) *Othniel, he urged her*   *b 36* Or *Gederah and Gederothaim*   *c 59* The Septuagint adds another district of eleven towns, including Tekoa and Ephrathah (Bethlehem).

15:56 *a* Jos 17:16; 19:18; Jdg 6:33; 1Sa 25:43; 1Ki 18:45; 1Ch 3:1; Hos 1:5 *b* S ver 34   **15:57** *c* Jos 18:28; 24:33; Jdg 19:12; 20:4; 2Sa 23:29; 1Ch 11:31 *d* S Ge 38:12   **15:58** *e* 1Ch 2:45; 2Ch 11:7; Ne 3:16 *f* 1Ch 4:39; 12:7   **15:60** *g* ver 9 *h* S Jos 9:17 *i* S Dt 3:11   **15:61** *j* S Jos 8:15 *k* S ver 6   **15:62** *l* 1Sa 23:29; 24:1; Eze 47:10   **15:63** *m* Jos 16:10; 17:12; Jdg 1:21; 1Ki 9:21 *n* S ver 8 *o* S Jos 10:1 *p* Eze 48:7

15:16 *k* 1Ch 2:49
15:17 *l* Jdg 3:9, 11;
1Ch 4:13; 27:15
15:19 *m* S Jos 10:40
n Ge 36:24
15:21 *o* S Jos 10:40
p 2Sa 23:20;
1Ch 11:22 *q* Ge 35:21
15:23 *r* S Jos 12:22
s S Jos 11:1
15:24 *t* ver 55;
1Sa 23:14; 2Ch 11:8
15:25 *u* S Jos 11:1
15:26 *v* Jos 19:2;
1Ch 4:28; Ne 11:26
15:28 *w* Jos 19:3;
1Ch 4:28 *x* S Ge 21:14
15:29 *y* S ver 9
z Jos 19:3; 1Ch 4:29
15:30 *a* Jos 19:4
b S Nu 14:45
15:31 *c* Jos 19:5;
1Sa 27:6; 1Ch 4:30;
12:1; Ne 11:28
d 1Ch 2:49
15:32 *e* S Nu 34:11
f Jos 19:7; Jdg 20:45;
21:13; Zec 14:10
15:33 *g* Jos 19:41;
Jdg 13:25; 16:31; 18:2
h Jdg 13:2; 18:11;
2Ch 11:10; Ne 11:29
i ver 43
15:34 *j* ver 56;
1Ch 4:18; Ne 3:13;
11:30 *k* Jos 19:21;
21:29 *l* S Jos 12:17
15:35 *m* S Jos 10:3
n S Ge 38:1 *o* ver 48;
1Ki 4:10 *p* S Jos 10:10
15:36 *q* 1Sa 17:52;
1Ch 4:31 *r* 1Ch 12:4
15:38 *s* S Jos 11:3
t 2Ki 14:7
15:39 *u* S Jos 10:3
v 2Ki 22:1 *w* S Jos 10:3
15:41 *x* 2Ch 28:18
y Jos 19:27
z S Jos 10:10
15:42 *a* S Nu 33:20
b Jos 19:7; 1Sa 30:30;
1Ch 4:32; 6:59
15:43 *c* ver 33
15:44 *d* 1Sa 23:1-2,
1; 1Ch 4:19; Ne 3:17,
18 *e* Jos 19:29;
Jdg 1:31; Mic 1:14
f Mic 1:15
15:45 *g* S Jos 13:3
15:46 *h* Jos 11:22
15:47 *i* S Jos 11:22
j S Ge 15:18
k S Nu 34:6
15:48 *l* Jdg 10:1
m Jos 21:14;
1Sa 30:27; 1Ch 6:57
n S ver 35
15:49 *o* S Jos 10:3
15:50 *p* Jos 11:21
15:51 *r* S Jos 10:41
s Jos 21:15; Jer 48:21
t 2Sa 15:12
15:52 *u* S Ge 25:14
15:54 *v* S Ge 35:27
15:55 *w* Jdg 10:12;
1Sa 23:24, 25; 25:1, 2;
1Ch 2:45 *x* S Jos 12:22
y S ver 24 *z* Jos 21:16

15:17 *Othniel.* See Jdg 3:7–11 for his service as judge in Israel.

15:21 *southernmost towns.* Most of the first 29 villages were assigned to the tribe of Simeon (cf. 19:1–9).

15:33 *western foothills.* This area between the highlands of central Judah and the Philistine coast was for the most part not occupied by Israel until the victories of King David. Some of the places on this list were reassigned to the tribe of Dan (cf. 19:41–43).

15:48 *hill country.* The high region south of Jerusalem. The Septuagint (the pre-Christian Greek translation of the OT) adds 11 names, including Tekoa and Bethlehem, to this list.

B **15:61–62** The "wilderness" is the chalky, dry region east and south of Jerusalem that borders the Dead Sea. Of the places named, only En Gedi can be positively located. However, either Sekakah or the City of Salt may have been the ancient name of the site of Qumran, where the scribes who produced the Dead Sea Scrolls lived.

15:63 *Jebusites.* A victory over the city of the Jebusites by the men of Judah is recorded in Jdg 1:8, but evidently this did not result in its permanent occupation. Both Benjamin and Judah failed to take the Jebusite fortress of Jerusalem (Jdg 1:21).

16:1 *S Jos 8:15
*S Jos 12:9
16:2 *S Ge 28:19
*2Sa 15:32 *S ver 5;
S Nu 32:3
16:3 *S Jos 10:10
*S Jos 10:33
16:4 *Jos 18:5
16:5 *ver 2;
Jos 18:13 *S Jos 10:10
16:6 *Jos 17:7
*ver 7; 2Ki 15:29
16:7 *S ver 6
*S Nu 32:3
16:8 *S Jos 12:17
*Jos 17:9; 19:28
16:9 *Eze 48:5
16:10 *S Jos 15:63;
17:13; Jdg 1:28-29;
1Ki 9:16
17:1 *S Nu 1:34;
1Ch 7:14 *S Ge 41:51
*S Ge 50:23
*S Jos 12:2
*S Jos 12:5
17:2 *Jos 22:7
*S Nu 26:30;
Jdg 6:11,34; 8:2;
1Ch 7:18 *1Ch 7:14
*S Nu 27:1 *1Ch 7:19
17:3 *S Nu 27:1
*S Nu 26:33
17:4 *Nu 27:5-7
17:5 *Jos 13:30-31
17:7 *ver 10;
Jos 19:24,31; 21:6,30;
Jdg 1:31; 5:17; 6:35;
7:23 *Jos 16:6
*S Ge 12:6; Jos 21:21;
24:25; Jdg 9:1
17:8 *S Jos 12:17
17:9 *S Jos 16:8
17:10 *S ver 7
*S Ge 30:18
*Eze 48:5
17:11 *ver 10
*ver 16; Jdg 1:27;
1Sa 31:10; 2Sa 21:12;
1Ki 4:12; 1Ch 7:29
*2Ki 9:27 *S Jos 11:2
*1Sa 28:7; Ps 83:10
*S Jos 12:21 *1Ki 9:15
*Eze 48:4

ALLOTMENT FOR EPHRAIM AND MANASSEH

16 The allotment for Joseph began at the Jordan, east of the springs of Jericho, and went up from there through the desert *q* into the hill country of Bethel. *r* 2It went on from Bethel (that is, Luz *s*),*a* crossed over to the territory of the Arkites *t* in Ataroth, *u* 3descended westward to the territory of the Japhletites as far as the region of Lower Beth Horon *v* and on to Gezer, *w* ending at the Mediterranean Sea.

4So Manasseh and Ephraim, the descendants of Joseph, received their inheritance. *x*

5This was the territory of Ephraim, according to its clans:

The boundary of their inheritance went from Ataroth Addar *y* in the east to Upper Beth Horon *z* 6and continued to the Mediterranean Sea. From Mikmethath *a* on the north it curved eastward to Taanath Shiloh, passing by it to Janoah *b* on the east. 7Then it went down from Janoah *c* to Ataroth *d* and Naarah, touched Jericho and came out at the Jordan. 8From Tappuah *e* the border went west to the Kanah Ravine *f* and ended at the Mediterranean Sea. This was the inheritance of the tribe of the Ephraimites, according to its clans. 9It also included all the towns and their villages that were set aside for the Ephraimites within the inheritance of the Manassites. *g*

10They did not dislodge the Canaanites living in Gezer; to this day the Canaanites live among the people of Ephraim but are required to do forced labor. *h*

17 This was the allotment for the tribe of Manasseh *i* as Joseph's firstborn, *j* that is, for Makir, *k* Manasseh's firstborn. Makir was the ancestor of the Gileadites, who had received Gilead *l* and Bashan *m* because the Makirites were great soldiers. 2So this allotment was for the rest of the people of Manasseh *n*—the clans of Abiezer, *o* Helek, Asriel, *p* Shechem, Hepher *q* and Shemida. *r* These are the other male descendants of Manasseh son of Joseph by their clans.

3Now Zelophehad son of Hepher, *s* the son of Gilead, the son of Makir, the son of Manasseh, had no sons but only daughters, *t* whose names were Mahlah, Noah, Hoglah, Milkah and Tirzah. 4They went to Eleazar the priest, Joshua son of Nun, and the leaders and said, "The LORD commanded Moses to give us an inheritance among our relatives." So Joshua gave them an inheritance along with the brothers of their father, according to the LORD's command. *u* 5Manasseh's share consisted of ten tracts of land besides Gilead and Bashan east of the Jordan, *v* 6because the daughters of the tribe of Manasseh received an inheritance among the sons. The land of Gilead belonged to the rest of the descendants of Manasseh.

7The territory of Manasseh extended from Asher *w* to Mikmethath *x* east of Shechem. *y* The boundary ran southward from there to include the people living at En Tappuah. 8(Manasseh had the land of Tappuah, but Tappuah *z* itself, on the boundary of Manasseh, belonged to the Ephraimites.) 9Then the boundary continued south to the Kanah Ravine. *a* There were towns belonging to Ephraim lying among the towns of Manasseh, but the boundary of Manasseh was the northern side of the ravine and ended at the Mediterranean Sea. 10On the south the land belonged to Ephraim, on the north to Manasseh. The territory of Manasseh reached the Mediterranean Sea and bordered Asher *b* on the north and Issachar *c* on the east. *d*

11Within Issachar *e* and Asher, Manasseh also had Beth Shan, *f* Ibleam *g* and the people of Dor, *h* Endor, *i* Taanach *j* and Megiddo, *k* together with their surrounding settlements (the third in the list is Naphoth *b*). *l*

---

a 2 Septuagint; Hebrew Bethel to Luz   *b 11 That is, Naphoth Dor*

16:1—17:18 Two chapters are devoted to the lands given to the "house of Joseph" (Ephraim and the half-tribe of Manasseh that settled west of the Jordan). Following Judah, the Joseph tribes were given priority in the allotting of territory.

16:1 *allotment for Joseph.* The southern border of the Joseph tribes moved west from Jericho past Bethel and down to Gezer and the Mediterranean coast.

16:5 *boundary.* Ephraim's northern border began at the edge of the Jordan Valley and ran west near Shiloh, but south of Shechem, then followed the Wadi Kanah down to the Mediterranean Sea.

16:10 *Gezer.* See note on 10:33. *required to do forced labor.* On projects undertaken by public officials, usually the king (2Sa 12:13; 1Ki 9:15,20–21).

17:1 *Manasseh as Joseph's firstborn.* A reminder that Manasseh was the firstborn, though Jacob had given priority to Ephraim when he adopted Joseph's two sons (Ge 48:14,19).

17:3 *Zelophehad…had…only daughters.* See notes on Nu 27:1–11; 36:1–3.

17:5 *ten tracts of land.* Manasseh's territory was second only to Judah's in size. The ten portions went to the five brothers (minus Hepher) and to the five granddaughters of Hepher.

17:11 *Beth Shan…Megiddo.* These powerfully fortified cities (and others) were not conquered until later. When King Saul died in battle, the victorious Philistines fastened his body to the wall of Beth Shan (see 1Sa 31:10), which suggests that that city was in league with the Philistines.

¹²Yet the Manassites were not able ^m to occupy these towns, for the Canaanites were determined to live in that region. ¹³However, when the Israelites grew stronger, they subjected the Canaanites to forced labor but did not drive them out completely. ⁿ

¹⁴The people of Joseph said to Joshua, "Why have you given us only one allotment and one portion for an inheritance? We are a numerous people, and the LORD has blessed us abundantly." ^o

¹⁵"If you are so numerous," Joshua answered, "and if the hill country of Ephraim is too small for you, go up into the forest ^p and clear land for yourselves there in the land of the Perizzites ^q and Rephaites. ^r"

¹⁶The people of Joseph replied, "The hill country is not enough for us, and all the Canaanites who live in the plain have chariots fitted with iron, ^s both those in Beth Shan ^t and its settlements and those in the Valley of Jezreel." ^u

¹⁷But Joshua said to the house of Joseph—to Ephraim and Manasseh—"You are numerous and very powerful. You will have not only one allotment ^v ¹⁸but the forested hill country ^w as well. Clear it, and its farthest limits will be yours; though the Canaanites have chariots fitted with iron ^x and though they are strong, you can drive them out."

DIVISION OF THE REST OF THE LAND

18 The whole assembly of the Israelites gathered at Shiloh ^y and set up the tent of meeting ^z there. The country was brought under their control, ²but there were still seven Israelite tribes who had not yet received their inheritance.

³So Joshua said to the Israelites: "How long will you wait before you begin to take possession of the land that the LORD, the God of your ancestors, has given you? ⁴Appoint three men from each tribe. I will send them out to make a survey of the land and to write a description of it, ^a according to the inheritance of each. ^b Then they will return to me. ⁵You are to divide the land into seven parts. Judah is to remain in its territory on the south ^c and the house of Joseph in its territory on the north. ^d ⁶After you have written descriptions of the seven parts of the land, bring them here to me and I will cast lots ^e for you in the presence of the LORD our God. ⁷The Levites, however, do not get a portion among you, because the priestly service of the LORD is their inheritance. ^f And Gad, Reuben and the half-tribe of Manasseh have already received their inheritance on the east side of the Jordan. Moses the servant of the LORD gave it to them. ^g"

⁸As the men started on their way to map out the land, Joshua instructed them, "Go and make a survey of the land and write a description of it. ^h Then return to me, and I will cast lots for you here at Shiloh ⁱ in the presence of the LORD." ⁹So they left and went through the land. They wrote its description on a scroll, town by town, in seven parts, and returned to Joshua in the camp at Shiloh. ¹⁰Joshua then cast lots ^j for them in Shiloh in the presence ^k of the LORD, and there he distributed the land to the Israelites according to their tribal divisions. ^l

17:12 ^m S Jos 15:63
17:13 ⁿ Jdg 1:27-28
17:14 ^o Nu 26:28-37
17:15 ^p 2Sa 18:6
^q S Jos 3:10
^r S Ge 14:5; Jos 15:8; 18:16; 2Sa 5:18; 23:13; Isa 17:5
17:16 ^s ver 18; Jdg 1:19; 4:3,13
^t S ver 11
^u S Jos 15:56; S 1Sa 29:1
17:17 ^v Eze 48:5
17:18 ^w 1Sa 1:1
^x S ver 16
18:1 ^y ver 8; Jos 19:51; 21:2; Jdg 18:31; 21:12,19; 1Sa 1:3; 3:21; 4:3; 1Ki 14:2; Ps 78:60; Jer 7:12; 26:6; 41:5
^z S ver 10; S Ex 27:21; S 40:2; Ac 7:45
18:4 ^a ver 8
^b Mic 2:5
18:5 ^c Jos 15:1
^d Jos 16:1-4
18:6 ^e S Lev 16:8
18:7 ^f S Jos 13:33
^g Jos 13:8
18:8 ^h ver 4 ⁱ S ver 1
18:10 ^j S Nu 34:13
^k S ver 1; Jer 7:12
^l Nu 33:54; Jos 19:51

17:13 *when the Israelites grew stronger.* Possibly referring to the days of David and Solomon (see note on 16:10).

17:14 *people of Joseph ... numerous.* The reference is to both Ephraim and Manasseh (see v. 17). The allotment to the Joseph tribes is here handled as one (see 16:1,4)—though the two subdivisions are then described separately (16:5—17:11).

17:15 *hill country of Ephraim.* The territory of the Joseph tribes—under the name of the legal firstborn (see note on v. 1). *clear land for yourselves.* This region of Canaan was still heavily forested. It seems that the Israelites viewed their assigned territories primarily in terms of the number of cities that had their land cleared for farming and pasturage, not in terms of the size of the region in which these cities were located. The region assigned to the Joseph tribes was at the time not as heavily populated as others. *Perizzites and Rephaites.* Here listed as neighboring peoples, though elsewhere the Perizzites are said to have lived on the west bank in Canaan (3:10; 12:8) and the Rephaites in the Transjordan kingdom of Og (12:4; 13:12). See notes on Ge 13:7; Dt 2:11.

17:16 *in the plain.* Only in the plains were chariots effective. *chariots fitted with iron.* Wooden chariots with certain parts made of iron (see note on 2Sa 8:7), perhaps the axles. This use of

iron was a new development. Israel did not employ chariots until much later (see note on 11:6).

18:1—19:51 Seven tribes remained to be assigned land: Benjamin, Simeon, Zebulun, Issachar, Asher, Naphtali and Dan. Their lots were cast at Shiloh.

18:1 *Shiloh.* About ten miles northeast of Bethel, a little east of the main road from Bethel to Shechem. *tent of meeting.* The tabernacle (see note on Ex 27:21) with its sacred ark of the covenant. It would remain at Shiloh until the time of Samuel (1Sa 4:3).

18:3 *take possession.* Conquest had to be followed by settlement, which required a survey, then a fair distribution, and then a full occupation of the land. A distinction must therefore be made between the national wars of conquest (Joshua) and the tribal wars of occupation (Jdg 1–2).

18:5 *north.* Relative to the territory of Judah.

18:6 *I will cast lots for you.* See note on 14:1.

18:7 *priestly service of the LORD is their inheritance.* See 13:14; see also Dt 18:1–8 and note on 18:1.

18:9 *scroll.* Presumed form of the document; the Hebrew for this word is not specific.

18:12 *m* S Jos 8:15
n S Jos 7:2
18:13 *o* S Ge 28:19
p S Jos 12:9
q S Nu 32:3;
S Jos 16:5
18:14 *r* Jos 10:10
s S Jos 9:17
18:15 *t* Jos 15:9
18:16 *u* S Jos 17:15
v Jos 15:8 *w* S Jos 15:7
18:17 *x* Jos 22:10
y Jos 15:7 *z* Jos 15:6
18:18 *a* S Jos 15:6
b S Jos 11:2
18:19 *c* S Jos 15:6
d S Ge 14:3
18:20 *e* 1Sa 9:3
18:21 *f* S Jos 15:6
18:22 *g* Jos 15:6
h 2Ch 13:4 *i* Jos 16:1
18:23 *j* S Dt 2:23
k Jdg 6:11,24; 8:27,32;
9:5; 1Sa 13:17
18:24 *l* Jos 21:17;
1Sa 13:3,16; 14:5;
1Ki 15:22; 2Ki 23:8;
Isa 10:29
18:25 *m* Jos 9:3
n S Jos 10:40; Jdg 4:5;
19:13; Isa 10:29;
Jer 31:15; 40:1
o S Jos 9:17; Ezr 2:25;
Ne 7:29
18:26 *p* S Jos 11:3
q Jos 9:17; Ezr 2:25;
Ne 7:29
18:28 *r* 2Sa 21:14
s S Jos 15:8 *t* S Jos 10:1
u S Jos 15:57
v S Jos 9:17
w Eze 48:23
19:1 *x* S Ge 49:7
19:2 *y* S Ge 21:14;
1Ki 19:3 *z* S Jos 15:26
19:3 *a* S Jos 15:28
b S Jos 15:29
19:4 *c* Jos 15:30
d S Nu 14:45
19:5 *e* S Jos 15:31
19:7 *f* S Jos 15:32
g S Jos 15:42
19:8 *h* S Jos 10:40
19:9 *i* S Ge 49:7
j Eze 48:24
19:10 *k* ver 16,27,
34; Jos 21:7,34
l ver 12
19:11 *m* S Jos 12:22

ALLOTMENT FOR BENJAMIN

[11] The first lot came up for the tribe of Benjamin according to its clans. Their allotted territory lay between the tribes of Judah and Joseph:

[12] On the north side their boundary began at the Jordan, passed the northern slope of Jericho and headed west into the hill country, coming out at the wilderness *m* of Beth Aven. *n* [13] From there it crossed to the south slope of Luz *o* (that is, Bethel *p*) and went down to Ataroth Addar *q* on the hill south of Lower Beth Horon.

[14] From the hill facing Beth Horon *r* on the south the boundary turned south along the western side and came out at Kiriath Baal (that is, Kiriath Jearim), *s* a town of the people of Judah. This was the western side.

[15] The southern side began at the outskirts of Kiriath Jearim on the west, and the boundary came out at the spring of the waters of Nephtoah. *t* [16] The boundary went down to the foot of the hill facing the Valley of Ben Hinnom, north of the Valley of Rephaim. *u* It continued down the Hinnom Valley *v* along the southern slope of the Jebusite city and so to En Rogel. *w* [17] It then curved north, went to En Shemesh, continued to Geliloth, *x* which faces the Pass of Adummim, *y* and ran down to the Stone of Bohan *z* son of Reuben. [18] It continued to the northern slope of Beth Arabah *a a* and on down into the Arabah. *b* [19] It then went to the northern slope of Beth Hoglah *c* and came out at the northern bay of the Dead Sea, *d* at the mouth of the Jordan in the south. This was the southern boundary.

[20] The Jordan formed the boundary on the eastern side.

These were the boundaries that marked out the inheritance of the clans of Benjamin on all sides. *e*

[21] The tribe of Benjamin, according to its clans, had the following towns:

Jericho, Beth Hoglah, *f* Emek Keziz, [22] Beth Arabah, *g* Zemaraim, *h* Bethel, *i* [23] Avvim, *j* Parah, Ophrah, *k* [24] Kephar Ammoni, Ophni and Geba *l*—twelve towns and their villages.

[25] Gibeon, *m* Ramah, *n* Beeroth, *o* [26] Mizpah, *p* Kephirah, *q* Mozah, [27] Rekem, Irpeel, Taralah, [28] Zelah, *r* Haeleph, the Jebusite city *s* (that is, Jerusalem *t*), Gibeah *u* and Kiriath—fourteen towns and their villages. *v*

This was the inheritance of Benjamin for its clans. *w*

ALLOTMENT FOR SIMEON

19:2–10pp — 1Ch 4:28–33

19 The second lot came out for the tribe of Simeon according to its clans. Their inheritance lay within the territory of Judah. *x* [2] It included:

Beersheba *y* (or Sheba), *b* Moladah, *z* [3] Hazar Shual, *a* Balah, Ezem, *b* [4] Eltolad, *c* Bethul, Hormah, *d* [5] Ziklag, *e* Beth Markaboth, Hazar Susah, [6] Beth Lebaoth and Sharuhen—thirteen towns and their villages—

[7] Ain, Rimmon, *f* Ether and Ashan *g*—four towns and their villages— [8] and all the villages around these towns as far as Baalath Beer (Ramah in the Negev). *h*

This was the inheritance of the tribe of the Simeonites, according to its clans. [9] The inheritance of the Simeonites was taken from the share of Judah, *i* because Judah's portion was more than they needed. So the Simeonites received their inheritance within the territory of Judah. *j*

ALLOTMENT FOR ZEBULUN

[10] The third lot came up for Zebulun *k* according to its clans:

The boundary of their inheritance went as far as Sarid. *l* [11] Going west it ran to Maralah, touched Dabbesheth, and extended to the ravine near Jokneam. *m* [12] It turned

---

a 18 Septuagint; Hebrew *slope facing the Arabah*   *b 2* Or *Beersheba, Sheba;* 1 Chron. 4:28 does not have *Sheba.*

18:11 *lot . . . for . . . Benjamin.* Benjamin's northern border was the same as Ephraim's southern border, and Benjamin's southern border was the same as Judah's northern boundary (see note on 15:5). The areas allotted to Benjamin and Dan (19:40–48) constituted a buffer zone between Judah and Ephraim, the two dominant tribes in Israel. The accounts of allotments to Benjamin and Dan frame the account of allotments made at Shiloh. These two tribes and the location of their allotments would play a significant role in the cycles of narratives related in the book of Judges (see Introduction to Judges: Literary Features and notes on Jdg 3:12–36; 13:1—16:31).

18:23 *Avvim.* The people of Ai.

19:1 *second lot . . . for . . . Simeon.* Cities in the Negev within the borders of Judah (15:21; 1Ch 4:24–42; see also Jdg 1:3).

19:10 *third lot . . . for Zebulun.* To this tribe went a portion of lower Galilee midway between the Sea of Galilee and the Mediterranean.

east from Sarid [n] toward the sunrise to the territory of Kisloth Tabor and went on to Daberath [o] and up to Japhia. [13] Then it continued eastward to Gath Hepher [p] and Eth Kazin; it came out at Rimmon [q] and turned toward Neah. [14] There the boundary went around on the north to Hannathon and ended at the Valley of Iphtah El. [r] [15] Included were Kattath, Nahalal, [s] Shimron, [t] Idalah and Bethlehem. [u] There were twelve towns and their villages.

[16] These towns and their villages were the inheritance of Zebulun, [v] according to its clans. [w]

ALLOTMENT FOR ISSACHAR

[17] The fourth lot came out for Issachar [x] according to its clans. [18] Their territory included:

Jezreel, [y] Kesulloth, Shunem, [z] [19] Hapharaim, Shion, Anaharath, [20] Rabbith, Kishion, [a] Ebez, [21] Remeth, En Gannim, [b] En Haddah and Beth Pazzez. [22] The boundary touched Tabor, [c] Shahazumah and Beth Shemesh, [d] and ended at the Jordan. There were sixteen towns and their villages.

[23] These towns and their villages were the inheritance of the tribe of Issachar, [e] according to its clans. [f]

ALLOTMENT FOR ASHER

[24] The fifth lot came out for the tribe of Asher [g] according to its clans. [25] Their territory included:

Helkath, Hali, Beten, Akshaph, [h] [26] Allammelek, Amad and Mishal. [i] On the west the boundary touched Carmel [j] and Shihor Libnath. [27] It then turned east toward Beth Dagon, [k] touched Zebulun [l] and the Valley of Iphtah El, [m] and went north to Beth Emek and Neiel, passing Kabul [n] on the left. [28] It went to Abdon, [a][o] Rehob, [p] Hammon [q] and Kanah, [r] as far as Greater Sidon. [s] [29] The boundary then turned back toward Ramah [t] and went to the fortified city of Tyre, [u] turned toward Hosah and came out at the Mediterranean Sea [v] in the region of Akzib, [w] [30] Ummah, Aphek [x] and Rehob. [y] There were twenty-two towns and their villages.

[31] These towns and their villages were the inheritance of the tribe of Asher, [z] according to its clans.

ALLOTMENT FOR NAPHTALI

[32] The sixth lot came out for Naphtali according to its clans:

[33] Their boundary went from Heleph and the large tree in Zaanannim, [a] passing Adami Nekeb and Jabneel [b] to Lakkum and ending at the Jordan. [34] The boundary ran west through Aznoth Tabor and came out at Hukkok. [c] It touched Zebulun [d] on the south, Asher on the west and the Jordan [b] on the east. [35] The fortified towns were Ziddim, Zer, Hammath, [e] Rakkath, Kinnereth, [f] [36] Adamah, Ramah, [g] Hazor, [h] [37] Kedesh, [i] Edrei, [j] En Hazor, [38] Iron, Migdal El, Horem, Beth Anath [k] and Beth Shemesh. [l] There were nineteen towns and their villages.

[39] These towns and their villages were the inheritance of the tribe of Naphtali, according to its clans. [m]

ALLOTMENT FOR DAN

[40] The seventh lot came out for the tribe of Dan according to its clans. [41] The territory of their inheritance included:

Zorah, Eshtaol, [n] Ir Shemesh, [42] Shaalabbin, Aijalon, [o] Ithlah, [43] Elon, Timnah, [p] Ekron, [q] [44] Eltekeh, Gibbethon, [r] Baalath, [s] [45] Jehud, Bene Berak, Gath Rimmon, [t] [46] Me Jarkon and Rakkon, with the area facing Joppa. [u]

[47] (When the territory of the Danites was lost to them, [v] they went up and attacked Le-

---

19:12 [n] ver 10
[o] Jos 21:28; 1Ch 6:72
19:13 [p] S Jos 11:22
[q] Jos 15:32
19:14 [r] ver 27
19:15 [s] Jos 21:35
[t] Jos 11:1 [u] S Ge 35:19
19:16 [v] S ver 10
[w] Eze 48:26
19:17 [x] S Ge 30:18
19:18 [y] S Jos 15:56
[z] 1Sa 28:4; 1Ki 1:3;
2Ki 4:8
19:20 [a] Jos 21:28
19:21 [b] S Jos 15:34
19:22 [c] Jdg 4:6,12;
8:18; Ps 89:12;
Jer 46:18 [d] S Jos 15:10
19:23 [e] Jos 17:10
[f] Ge 49:15; Eze 48:25
19:24 [g] S Jos 17:7
19:25 [h] S Jos 11:1
19:26 [i] Jos 21:30
[j] S Jos 12:22;
1Ki 18:19; 2Ki 2:25
19:27 [k] Jos 15:41
[l] S ver 10 [m] ver 14
[n] 1Ki 9:13
19:28 [o] Jos 21:30;
1Ch 6:74 [p] ver 30;
Nu 13:21; Jos 21:31;
Jdg 1:31 [q] 1Ch 6:76
[r] S Jos 16:8
[s] S Ge 10:19
19:29 [t] Jos 18:25
[u] 2Sa 5:11; 24:7;
Ezr 3:7; Ps 45:12;
Isa 23:1; Jer 25:22;
Eze 26:2 [v] Jdg 5:17
[w] S Jos 15:44
19:30 [x] S Jos 12:18
[y] S ver 28
19:31 [z] S Ge 30:13;
S Jos 17:7; Eze 48:2
19:33 [a] Jdg 4:11
[b] Jos 15:11
19:34 [c] 1Ch 6:75
[d] S ver 10
19:35 [e] 1Ch 2:55
[f] S Jos 11:2
19:36 [g] Jos 18:25
[h] S Jos 11:1
19:37 [i] S Jos 12:22
[j] S Nu 21:33
19:38 [k] Jdg 1:33
[l] S Jos 15:10
19:39 [m] Eze 48:3
19:41 [n] S Jos 15:33
19:42 [o] S Jos 10:12
19:43 [p] S Ge 38:12
[q] S Jos 13:3
19:44 [r] Jos 21:23;
1Ki 15:27; 16:15
[s] 1Ki 9:18; 2Ch 8:6
19:45 [t] Jos 21:24;
1Ch 6:69
19:46 [u] 2Ch 2:16;
Ezr 3:7; Jnh 1:3;
Ac 9:36
19:47 [v] Jdg 18:1

---

[a] 28 Some Hebrew manuscripts (see also Joshua 21:30); most Hebrew manuscripts Ebron
[b] 34 Septuagint; Hebrew west, and Judah, the Jordan,

19:17 fourth lot ... for Issachar. Southwest of the Sea of Galilee reaching down to the vicinity of Beth Shan and west to the Jezreel Valley. Mount Tabor marked its northern border.
19:24 fifth lot ... for ... Asher. Asher was given the coastal area as far north as Sidon in Phoenicia and as far south as Mount Carmel.
19:32 sixth lot ... for Naphtali. An area mostly to the north of the Sea of Galilee, including the mountains bordering on Asher and Zebulun to the west. Its southernmost point was at the southern end of the Sea of Galilee.

19:40 seventh lot ... for ... Dan. An elbow of land squeezed between Ephraim and Judah and west of Benjamin (see note on 18:11). The port of Joppa marked the northwestern corner of Dan.
19:47 territory of the Danites was lost to them. The Amorites of this area "confined the Danites to the hill country" (Jdg 1:34), so most of the tribe migrated to the upper Jordan Valley, where they seized the town of Leshem (or Laish, Jdg 18:2–10,27–29) and renamed it Dan.

19:47 ʷJdg 18:7,14
ˣS Dt 3:14
ʸJdg 18:27,29
19:48 ᶻS Ge 30:6
19:50 ᵃJos 24:30;
Jdg 2:9
19:51 ᵇJos 23:4
ᶜS Jos 14:1; S 18:10;
Ac 13:19
20:3 ᵈS Lev 4:2
ᵉS Nu 35:12
20:4 ᶠS Ge 23:10;
Jer 38:7 ᵍS Jos 7:6
20:6 ʰS Nu 35:12
20:7 ⁱS Jos 12:22
ʲS Ge 12:6
ᵏS Ge 35:27
ˡS Jos 10:36 ᵐLk 1:39
20:8 ⁿJos 21:36;
1Ch 6:78 ᵒ1Ch 6:80
ᵖS Jos 12:2
�q S Jos 12:5; 1Ch 6:71
20:9 ʳS Lev 4:2
ˢS Ex 21:13

shem ʷ, took it, put it to the sword and occupied it. They settled in Leshem and named ˣ it Dan after their ancestor.) ʸ 48These towns and their villages were the inheritance of the tribe of Dan, ᶻ according to its clans.

ALLOTMENT FOR JOSHUA

49When they had finished dividing the land into its allotted portions, the Israelites gave Joshua son of Nun an inheritance among them, 50as the LORD had commanded. They gave him the town he asked for—Timnath Serah ᵃ ᵃ in the hill country of Ephraim. And he built up the town and settled there.

51These are the territories that Eleazar the priest, Joshua son of Nun and the heads of the tribal clans of Israel assigned by lot at Shiloh in the presence of the LORD at the entrance to the tent of meeting. And so they finished dividing ᵇ the land. ᶜ

CITIES OF REFUGE

20:1–9Ref — Nu 35:9–34; Dt 4:41–43; 19:1–14

20 Then the LORD said to Joshua: 2"Tell the Israelites to designate the cities of refuge, as I instructed you through Moses, 3so that anyone who kills a person accidentally and unintentionally ᵈ may flee there and find protection from the avenger of blood. ᵉ 4When they flee to one of these cities, they are to stand in the entrance of the city gate ᶠ and state their case before the elders ᵍ of that city. Then the elders are to admit them into their city and give them a place to live with them. 5If the avenger of blood pursues them, the elders must not surrender the accused, because they killed their neighbor unintentionally and without malice aforethought. 6They are to stay in that city until they have stood trial before the assembly ʰ and until the death of the high priest who is serving at that time. Then they may go back to their own home in the town from which they fled."

7So they set apart Kedesh ⁱ in Galilee in the hill country of Naphtali, Shechem ʲ in the hill country of Ephraim, and Kiriath Arba ᵏ (that is, Hebron ˡ) in the hill country of Judah. ᵐ 8East of the Jordan (on the other side from Jericho) they designated Bezer ⁿ in the wilderness on the plateau in the tribe of Reuben, Ramoth in Gilead ᵒᵖ in the tribe of Gad, and Golan in Bashan q in the tribe of Manasseh. 9Any of the Israelites or any foreigner residing among them who killed someone accidentally ʳ could flee to these designated cities and not be killed by the avenger of blood prior to standing trial before the assembly. ˢ

ᵃ 50 Also known as *Timnath Heres* (see Judges 2:9)

19:49 *gave Joshua … an inheritance.* In the account of the distribution of the promised land (the territory west of the Jordan), the assignment to Caleb is treated first (14:6–15), the assignment to Joshua last. Thus the allotting of inheritance to these two dauntless servants of the Lord from the wilderness generation (see Nu 13:30; 14:6,24,30) frames the whole account—and both received the territory they asked for. Appropriately, Joshua's allotment came last; he was not a king or a warlord but the servant of God commissioned to bring the Lord's people into the promised land.
19:50 *Timnath Serah.* Located in the southwestern corner of Ephraim, facing out to the sea. Here Joshua was also buried (24:30).
20:1–9 Having distributed the land to the tribes, the Lord's next administrative regulation (see note on 13:1–32) provided an elementary system of government, specifically a system of regional courts to deal with capital offenses having to do with manslaughter. Thus this most inflammatory of cases was removed from local jurisdiction, and a safeguard was created against the easy miscarriage of justice (with its potential for endless blood feuds) when retribution for manslaughter was left in the hands of family members. The cities chosen were among those also assigned to the Levites, where ideally the law of Moses would es-

pecially be known and honored. See map, p. 245.
20:2 *as I instructed you through Moses.* See Nu 35:6–34.
20:3 *avenger of blood.* The Hebrew word is also translated "family guardians" (Ru 2:20; see note and TNIV text note there) and "Redeemer" (see Isa 41:14 and note). The avenger was a near relative with the obligation of exacting retribution (see Lev 24:17; Nu 35:16–28).
20:4 *city gate.* Traditional place for trials, where the elders sat to hold court (see Ru 4:1 and note; see also Job 29:7).
20:6 *assembly.* Perhaps the assembly in the town where the crime was committed (see Nu 35:24–25). *death of the high priest.* See Nu 35:25–28 and note on 35:24.
20:7 *they set apart Kedesh.* A wordplay in the Hebrew: "they consecrated (the town of) consecration." The other two cities west of the Jordan already had sacred associations: For Shechem see 8:30–35 and note; Ge 12:6–7; for Hebron see Ge 23:2; 49:29–32. The geographical distribution of the cities was important: one in the north, one in the midlands and one in the south. (See v. 8, where the order of the three cities of refuge that served in Transjordan is reversed: Bezer in the south, Ramoth in the midlands and Golan in the north.) See map, p. 245.
20:9 *or any foreigner.* Evidence of the equal protection granted to the foreigners living in Israel (cf. Lev 19:33–34; Dt 10:18–19).

TOWNS FOR THE LEVITES

21:4–39pp — 1Ch 6:54–80

21 Now the family heads of the Levites approached Eleazar the priest, Joshua son of Nun, and the heads of the other tribal families of Israel [t] [2]at Shiloh [u] in Canaan and said to them, "The LORD commanded through Moses that you give us towns [v] to live in, with pasturelands for our livestock." [w] [3]So, as the LORD had commanded, the Israelites gave the Levites the following towns and pasturelands out of their own inheritance:

[4]The first lot came out for the Kohathites, [x] according to their clans. The Levites who were descendants of Aaron the priest were allotted thirteen towns from the tribes of Judah, Simeon and Benjamin. [y] [5]The rest of Kohath's descendants were allotted ten towns from the clans of the tribes of Ephraim, Dan and half of Manasseh. [z]

[6]The descendants of Gershon [a] were allotted thirteen towns from the clans of the tribes of Issachar, [b] Asher, [c] Naphtali and the half-tribe of Manasseh in Bashan.

[7]The descendants of Merari, [d] according to their clans, received twelve [e] towns from the tribes of Reuben, Gad and Zebulun. [f]

[8]So the Israelites allotted to the Levites these towns and their pasturelands, as the LORD had commanded through Moses.

[9]From the tribes of Judah and Simeon they allotted the following towns by name [10](these towns were assigned to the descendants of Aaron who were from the Kohathite clans of the Levites, because the first lot fell to them):

[11]They gave them Kiriath Arba [g] (that is, Hebron [h]), with its surrounding pastureland, in the hill country of Judah. (Arba was the ancestor of Anak.) [12]But the fields and villages around the city they had given to Caleb son of Jephunneh as his possession. [i]

[13]So to the descendants of Aaron the priest they gave Hebron (a city of refuge [j] for one accused of murder), Libnah, [k] [14]Jattir, [l] Eshtemoa, [m] [15]Holon, [n] Debir, [o] [16]Ain, [p] Juttah [q] and Beth Shemesh, [r] together with their pasturelands—nine towns from these two tribes.

[17]And from the tribe of Benjamin they gave them Gibeon, [s] Geba, [t] [18]Anathoth [u] and Almon, together with their pasturelands—four towns.

[19]The total number of towns [v] for the priests, the descendants of Aaron, came to thirteen, together with their pasturelands. [w]

[20]The rest of the Kohathite clans of the Levites were allotted towns from the tribe of Ephraim:

[21]In the hill country of Ephraim they were given Shechem [x] (a city of refuge for one accused of murder) and Gezer, [y] [22]Kibzaim and Beth Horon, [z] together with their pasturelands—four towns. [a]

[23]Also from the tribe of Dan they received Eltekeh, Gibbethon, [b] [24]Aijalon [c] and Gath Rimmon, [d] together with their pasturelands—four towns.

[25]From half the tribe of Manasseh they received Taanach [e] and Gath Rimmon, together with their pasturelands—two towns.

[26]All these ten towns and their pasturelands were given to the rest of the Kohathite clans. [f]

[27]The Levite clans of the Gershonites were given:

from the half-tribe of Manasseh,

Golan in Bashan [g] (a city of refuge for one accused of murder [h]) and Be Eshterah, together with their pasturelands—two towns;

[28]from the tribe of Issachar, [i]

Kishion, [j] Daberath, [k] [29]Jarmuth [l] and En Gannim, [m] together with their pasturelands—four towns;

[30]from the tribe of Asher, [n]

Mishal, [o] Abdon, [p] [31]Helkath and Rehob, [q] together with their pasturelands—four towns;

[32]from the tribe of Naphtali,

21:1–45 Finally the Levites are allotted their towns and adjoining pasturelands—with the priestly families being given precedence (see v. 10).
21:4 *Kohathites.* The three sons of Levi were Kohath, Gershon and Merari (Ex 6:16; Nu 3:17). *Judah, Simeon and Benjamin.* Tribal areas close to Jerusalem, which would later be the site of the temple.

The remaining Kohathites received cities in adjoining tribes.
21:11 *Hebron.* Caleb's city (14:13–15). The priests and Levites were to be given space in their assigned cities along with the other inhabitants.
21:27 *Gershonites.* Received cities in the northern tribes of Asher, Naphtali and Issachar.

21:1 [t] Jos 14:1
21:2 [u] S Jos 18:1
[v] S Lev 25:32
[w] S Nu 35:2-3;
S Jos 14:4
21:4 [x] Nu 3:17
[y] ver 19
21:5 [z] ver 26
21:6 [a] Nu 3:17
[b] S Ge 30:18
[c] S Jos 17:7
21:7 [d] S Ex 6:16
[e] ver 40 [f] S Jos 19:10
21:11 [g] S Ge 23:2
[h] S Jos 10:36
21:12 [i] S Jos 15:13
21:13 [j] Nu 35:6
[k] S Nu 33:20
21:14 [l] S Jos 15:48
[m] S Jos 15:50
21:15 [n] S Jos 15:51
[o] S Jos 10:3
21:16 [p] S Nu 34:11
[q] Jos 15:55
[r] S Jos 15:10
21:17 [s] S Jos 9:3
[t] S Jos 18:24;
S Ne 11:31
21:18 [u] 2Sa 23:27;
1Ki 2:26; Ezr 2:23;
Ne 7:27; 11:32;
Isa 10:30; Jer 1:1;
11:21; 32:7
21:19 [v] 2Ch 31:15
[w] ver 4
21:21 [x] S Jos 17:7
[y] S Jos 10:33
21:22 [z] S Jos 10:10
[a] 1Sa 1:1
21:23 [b] S Jos 19:44
21:24 [c] S Jos 10:12
[d] S Jos 19:45
21:25 [e] S Jos 12:21
21:26 [f] ver 5
21:27 [g] S Jos 12:5
[h] Nu 35:6
21:28 [i] S Ge 30:18
[j] Jos 19:20
[k] S Jos 19:12
21:29 [l] S Jos 10:3
[m] S Jos 15:34
21:30 [n] S Jos 17:7
[o] Jos 19:26
[p] S Jos 19:28
21:31 [q] S Jos 19:28

21:32 ʳS Jos 12:22
ˢNu 35:6
21:33 ᵗver 6
21:34 ᵘS Jos 19:10
ᵛS Jos 12:22
21:35 ʷJos 19:15
21:36 ˣS Jos 20:8
ʸS Nu 21:23; Dt 2:32;
Jdg 11:20
21:37 ᶻS Jos 13:18
21:38 ᵃS Dt 4:43
ᵇS Jos 12:2
ᶜS Ge 32:2
21:39 ᵈS Jos 13:25
21:40 ᵉver 7
21:41 ᶠNu 35:7
21:43 ᵍDt 11:31 ⁱS Dt 17:14
21:44 ʲS Ex 33:14
ᵏS Dt 6:19
ˡS Ex 23:31
ᵐDt 21:10
21:45 ⁿJos 23:14;
Ne 9:8
22:2 ᵒS Nu 32:25
22:4 ᵖS Ex 33:14
�q Nu 32:22; Dt 3:20
ʳNu 32:18; S Jos 1:13-
15
22:5 ˢIsa 43:22;
Mal 3:14 ᵗJos 23:11
ᵘS Dt 5:29 ᵛS Dt 6:5
22:6 ʷS Ge 24:60;
S Ex 39:43
22:7 ˣS Nu 32:19;
S Jos 12:5 ʸJos 17:2
ᶻS Jos 14:13; Lk 24:50
22:8 ᵃS Dt 20:14
ᵇS Nu 31:22
ᶜS Nu 31:27
ᵈS Ge 49:27;
1Sa 30:16; 2Sa 1:1;
Isa 9:3
22:9 ᵉJos 18:1
ᶠS Nu 32:26
22:10 ᵍJos 18:17

Kedesh ʳ in Galilee (a city of refuge for one accused of murder ˢ), Hammoth Dor and Kartan, together with their pasturelands—three towns.

³³The total number of towns of the Gershonite ᵗ clans came to thirteen, together with their pasturelands.

³⁴The Merarite clans (the rest of the Levites) were given:

from the tribe of Zebulun, ᵘ
Jokneam, ᵛ Kartah, ³⁵Dimnah and Nahalal, ʷ together with their pasturelands—four towns;

³⁶from the tribe of Reuben,
Bezer, ˣ Jahaz, ʸ ³⁷Kedemoth and Mephaath, ᶻ together with their pasturelands—four towns;

³⁸from the tribe of Gad,
Ramoth ᵃ in Gilead ᵇ (a city of refuge for one accused of murder), Mahanaim, ᶜ ³⁹Heshbon and Jazer, ᵈ together with their pasturelands—four towns in all.

⁴⁰The total number of towns allotted to the Merarite clans, who were the rest of the Levites, came to twelve. ᵉ

⁴¹The towns of the Levites in the territory held by the Israelites were forty-eight in all, together with their pasturelands. ᶠ ⁴²Each of these towns had pasturelands surrounding it; this was true for all these towns.

⁴³So the LORD gave Israel all the land he had sworn to give their ancestors, ᵍ and they took possession ʰ of it and settled there. ⁱ ⁴⁴The LORD gave them rest ʲ on every side, just as he had sworn to their ancestors. Not one of their enemies ᵏ withstood them; the LORD gave all their enemies ˡ into their hands. ᵐ ⁴⁵Not one of all the LORD's good promises ⁿ to the house of Israel failed; every one was fulfilled.

EASTERN TRIBES RETURN HOME

22 Then Joshua summoned the Reubenites, the Gadites and the half-tribe of Manasseh ²and said to them, "You have done all that Moses the servant of the LORD commanded, ᵒ and you have obeyed me in everything I commanded. ³For a long time now—to this very day—you have not deserted the other Israelites but have carried out the mission the LORD your God gave you. ⁴Now that the LORD your God has given them rest ᵖ as he promised, return to your homes �q in the land that Moses the servant of the LORD gave you on the other side of the Jordan. ʳ ⁵But be very careful to keep the commandment ˢ and the law that Moses the servant of the LORD gave you: to love the LORD ᵗ your God, to walk in obedience to him, to keep his commands, ᵘ to hold fast to him and to serve him with all your heart and with all your soul. ᵛ"

⁶Then Joshua blessed ʷ them and sent them away, and they went to their homes. ⁷(To the half-tribe of Manasseh Moses had given land in Bashan, ˣ and to the other half of the tribe Joshua gave land on the west side ʸ of the Jordan along with the other Israelites.) When Joshua sent them home, he blessed them, ᶻ ⁸saying, "Return to your homes with your great wealth—with large herds of livestock, ᵃ with silver, gold, bronze and iron, ᵇ and a great quantity of clothing—and divide ᶜ the plunder ᵈ from your enemies with the other members of your tribes."

⁹So the Reubenites, the Gadites and the half-tribe of Manasseh left the Israelites at Shiloh ᵉ in Canaan to return to Gilead, ᶠ their own land, which they had acquired in accordance with the command of the LORD through Moses.

¹⁰When they came to Geliloth ᵍ near the Jordan in the land of Canaan, the Reubenites,

---

21:34 *Merarite clans.* Their 12 cities were scattered throughout Reuben, Gad and Zebulun.

21:43–45 A concluding summary statement of how the Lord had fulfilled his sworn promise to give Israel this land (see Ge 15:18–21). The occupation of the land was not yet complete (see 23:4–5; Jdg 1–2), but the national campaign was over and Israel was finally established in the promised land. No power was left in Canaan that could threaten to dislodge her.

21:44 *rest on every side.* See note on 1:13.

21:45 *good promises.* Refers to the good things God had covenanted to give his people (23:14–15; 1Ki 8:56; Jer 33:14).

22:1–34 The two and a half tribes from east of the Jordan, faithful in battle, are now commended by Joshua and sent to their homes. But their altar of "witness" (see vv. 26–27,34) was misunderstood, and disciplinary action against them was narrowly averted.

22:2 *all that Moses … commanded.* Moses had ordered them to join the other tribes in the conquest of Canaan (Nu 32:16–27; Dt 3:18).

22:5 *love the LORD … serve him with all your heart.* Both Moses and Joshua saw that obedience to the laws of God would require love and service from the heart. In the ancient Near East, "love" was also a political term, indicating truehearted loyalty to one's king (see notes on Dt 6:5; 11:1).

22:8 *divide … with the other members of your tribes.* Moses also had seen the need for a fair sharing of the spoils of war (Nu 31:25–27).

22:10 *Geliloth.* Understood in the Septuagint (the pre-Christian Greek translation of the OT) to be Gilgal, next to Jericho; more likely it was a site east of Shiloh along the Jordan River (18:17).

the Gadites and the half-tribe of Manasseh built an imposing altar[h] there by the Jordan. [11]And when the Israelites heard that they had built the altar on the border of Canaan at Geliloth near the Jordan on the Israelite side, [12]the whole assembly of Israel gathered at Shiloh[i] to go to war against them.

[13]So the Israelites sent Phinehas[j] son of Eleazar,[k] the priest, to the land of Gilead—to Reuben, Gad and the half-tribe of Manasseh. [14]With him they sent ten of the chief men, one from each of the tribes of Israel, each the head of a family division among the Israelite clans.[l]

[15]When they went to Gilead—to Reuben, Gad and the half-tribe of Manasseh—they said to them: [16]"The whole assembly of the LORD says: 'How could you break faith[m] with the God of Israel like this? How could you turn away from the LORD and build yourselves an altar in rebellion[n] against him now? [17]Was not the sin of Peor[o] enough for us? Up to this very day we have not cleansed ourselves from that sin, even though a plague fell on the community of the LORD! [18]And are you now turning away from the LORD?

" 'If you rebel against the LORD today, tomorrow he will be angry with the whole community[p] of Israel. [19]If the land you possess is defiled, come over to the LORD's land, where the LORD's tabernacle[q] stands, and share the land with us. But do not rebel against the LORD or against us by building an altar[r] for yourselves, other than the altar of the LORD our God. [20]When Achan son of Zerah was unfaithful in regard to the devoted things,[a s] did not wrath[t] come on the whole community[u] of Israel? He was not the only one who died for his sin.' "[v]

[21]Then Reuben, Gad and the half-tribe of Manasseh replied to the heads of the clans of Israel: [22]"The Mighty One, God, the LORD! The Mighty One, God,[w] the LORD![x] He knows![y] And let Israel know! If this has been in rebellion or disobedience to the LORD, do not spare us this day. [23]If we have built our own altar to turn away from the LORD and to offer burnt offerings and grain offerings,[z] or to sacrifice fellowship offerings on it, may the LORD himself call us to account.[a]

[24]"No! We did it for fear that some day your descendants might say to ours, 'What do you have to do with the LORD, the God of Israel? [25]The LORD has made the Jordan a boundary between us and you—you Reubenites and Gadites! You have no share in the LORD.' So your descendants might cause ours to stop fearing the LORD.

[26]"That is why we said, 'Let us get ready and build an altar—but not for burnt offerings or sacrifices.' [27]On the contrary, it is to be a witness[b] between us and you and the generations that follow, that we will worship the LORD at his sanctuary with our burnt offerings, sacrifices and fellowship offerings.[c] Then in the future your descendants will not be able to say to ours, 'You have no share in the LORD.'

[28]"And we said, 'If they ever say this to us, or to our descendants, we will answer: Look at the replica of the LORD's altar, which our people built, not for burnt offerings and sacrifices, but as a witness[d] between us and you.'

[29]"Far be it from us to rebel[e] against the LORD and turn away from him today by building an altar for burnt offerings, grain offerings and sacrifices, other than the altar of the LORD our God that stands before his tabernacle.[f]"

[30]When Phinehas the priest and the leaders of the community—the heads of the clans of the Israelites—heard what Reuben, Gad and Manasseh had to say, they were pleased. [31]And Phinehas son of Eleazar, the priest, said to Reuben, Gad and Manasseh, "Today we

---

[a] 20 The Hebrew term refers to the irrevocable giving over of things or persons to the LORD, often by totally destroying them.

22:10 [h] ver 19,26-27; Isa 19:19; 56:7
22:12 [i] Jos 18:1
22:13 [j] S Nu 25:7
[k] Nu 3:32; Jos 24:33
22:14 [l] ver 32; S Nu 1:4
22:16 [m] S Dt 7:3; 1Sa 13:13; 15:11
[n] Dt 12:13-14
22:17 [o] S Nu 23:28; 25:1-9
22:18 [p] S Lev 10:6
22:19 [q] S Ex 26:1
[r] S ver 10
22:20 [s] Jos 7:1
[t] Ps 7:11 [u] Lev 10:6
[v] Jos 7:5
22:22 [w] S Dt 10:17
[x] Ps 50:1 [y] 1Sa 2:3; 16:7; 1Ki 8:39; 1Ch 28:9; Ps 11:4; 40:9; 44:21; 139:4; Jer 17:10
22:23 [z] Jer 41:5
[a] S Dt 12:11; S 18:19; 1Sa 20:16
22:27 [b] S Ge 21:30; Jos 24:27; Isa 19:20
[c] S Dt 12:6
22:28 [d] S Ge 21:30
22:29 [e] Jos 24:16
[f] S Ex 26:1

22:11 *when the Israelites heard.* Anxiety about apostasy led to hasty conclusions. They thought the altar had been set up as a rival to the true altar at Shiloh.

22:12 *gathered at Shiloh.* In the presence of God at the tabernacle. *to go to war against them.* To take disciplinary action (cf. Dt 13:12–18; Jdg 20).

22:13–14 A prestigious delegation is sent to try to turn the Transjordan tribes from their (supposed) act of rebellion against the Lord.

22:16 *How could you . . . ?* The accusations were very grave: You have committed apostasy and rebellion.

22:17 *Peor.* Where some of the Israelites became involved in the Moabite worship of Baal of Peor (Nu 25:1–5).

22:19 *is defiled.* By pagan worship, corrupting its inhabitants. *the LORD's land.* The promised land proper had never included

Transjordan territory. Canaan was the land the Lord especially claimed as his own and promised to the descendants of Abraham, Isaac and Jacob.

22:20 *Achan . . . the whole community of Israel.* See note on 7:1–26.

22:22 *The Mighty One, God, the LORD!* See note on Ps 50:1. The repetition of the sacred names gives an oath-like quality to this strong denial of any wrongdoing.

22:27 *witness.* The altar, presumably of uncut stone (see 8:31; Ex 20:25), was to serve as a testimony to the commitment of the Transjordan tribes to remain loyal to the Lord, and to their continued right to worship the Lord at the tabernacle—even though they lived outside the land of promise. It constitutes a seventh memorial monument in the land noted by the author of Joshua (see note on 4:9).

22:31 *g* 2Ch 15:2
22:32 *h* S ver 14
22:33 *i* 1Ch 29:20;
Da 2:19; Lk 2:28
22:34 *j* S Ge 21:30
23:1 *k* S Dt 12:9;
Jos 21:44 *l* S Jos 13:1
23:2 *m* S Jos 7:6
n Jos 24:1 *o* S Jos 13:1
23:3 *p* S Ex 14:14;
S Dt 20:4
23:4 *q* Jos 19:51
r S Nu 34:2; Ps 78:55
s S Nu 34:6
23:5 *t* ver 13;
Jdg 2:21 *u* Ps 44:5;
Jer 46:15 *v* Ex 23:30
23:6 *w* S Dt 28:61
x S Dt 17:20 *y* Jos 1:7
23:7 *z* Ex 23:13;
Jer 5:7; 12:16
a S Ex 20:5
23:8 *b* S Dt 10:20
23:9 *c* Dt 11:23
d Dt 7:24
23:10 *e* Lev 26:8;
Jdg 3:31 *f* S Ex 14:14
23:11 *g* S Dt 4:15
h Jos 22:5
23:12 *i* S Ge 34:9
j S Ex 34:16;
Ps 106:34-35
23:13 *k* S ver 5
l S Ex 10:7
m S Nu 33:55
n Dt 1:8; 1Ki 9:7;
2Ki 25:21
23:14 *o* 1Ki 2:2
p Ps 119:140; 145:13
q S Jos 21:45
23:15 *r* 1Ki 8:56;
Jer 33:14 *s* 1Ki 14:10;
2Ki 22:16; Isa 24:6;
34:5; 43:28; Jer 6:19;
11:8; 35:17; 39:16;
Mal 4:6 *t* Jos 24:20
u Lev 26:17; Dt 28:15;
Jer 40:2
23:16 *v* Dt 4:25-26
24:1 *w* Ge 49:2
x S Ge 12:6 *y* 1Sa 12:7;
1Ki 8:14 *z* Jos 7:6
a Jos 23:2

know that the LORD is with us, *g* because you have not been unfaithful to the LORD in this matter. Now you have rescued the Israelites from the LORD's hand."

³²Then Phinehas son of Eleazar, the priest, and the leaders returned to Canaan from their meeting with the Reubenites and Gadites in Gilead and reported to the Israelites. *h* ³³They were glad to hear the report and praised God. *i* And they talked no more about going to war against them to devastate the country where the Reubenites and the Gadites lived.

³⁴And the Reubenites and the Gadites gave the altar this name: A Witness *j* Between Us—that the LORD is God.

JOSHUA'S FAREWELL TO THE LEADERS

23 After a long time had passed and the LORD had given Israel rest *k* from all their enemies around them, Joshua, by then a very old man, *l* ²summoned all Israel—their elders, *m* leaders, judges and officials *n*—and said to them: "I am very old. *o* ³You yourselves have seen everything the LORD your God has done to all these nations for your sake; it was the LORD your God who fought for you. *p* ⁴Remember how I have allotted *q* as an inheritance *r* for your tribes all the land of the nations that remain—the nations I conquered—between the Jordan and the Mediterranean Sea *s* in the west. ⁵The LORD your God himself will push them out *t* for your sake. He will drive them out *u* before you, and you will take possession of their land, as the LORD your God promised you. *v*

⁶"Be very strong; be careful to obey all that is written in the Book of the Law *w* of Moses, without turning aside *x* to the right or to the left. *y* ⁷Do not associate with these nations that remain among you; do not invoke the names of their gods or swear *z* by them. You must not serve them or bow down *a* to them. ⁸But you are to hold fast to the LORD *b* your God, as you have until now.

⁹"The LORD has driven out before you great and powerful nations; *c* to this day no one has been able to withstand you. *d* ¹⁰One of you routs a thousand, *e* because the LORD your God fights for you, *f* just as he promised. ¹¹So be very careful *g* to love the LORD *h* your God.

¹²"But if you turn away and ally yourselves with the survivors of these nations that remain among you and if you intermarry with them *i* and associate with them, *j* ¹³then you may be sure that the LORD your God will no longer drive out *k* these nations before you. Instead, they will become snares *l* and traps for you, whips on your backs and thorns in your eyes, *m* until you perish from this good land, *n* which the LORD your God has given you.

¹⁴"Now I am about to go the way of all the earth. *o* You know with all your heart and soul that not one of all the good promises the LORD your God gave you has failed. Every promise *p* has been fulfilled; not one has failed. *q* ¹⁵But just as all the good things *r* the LORD your God has promised you have come to you, so he will bring on you all the evil things *s* he has threatened, until the LORD your God has destroyed you *t* from this good land he has given you. *u* ¹⁶If you violate the covenant of the LORD your God, which he commanded you, and go and serve other gods and bow down to them, the LORD's anger will burn against you, and you will quickly perish from the good land he has given you. *v*"

THE COVENANT RENEWED AT SHECHEM

24 Then Joshua assembled *w* all the tribes of Israel at Shechem. *x* He summoned *y* the elders, *z* leaders, judges and officials of Israel, *a* and they presented themselves before God.

22:31 *you have rescued the Israelites.* Their words prevented a terrible punishment that the other tribes were about to inflict as an act of divine judgment (consider the implications of v. 20).

A C **23:1–16** Joshua, the Lord's servant, delivers a farewell address recalling the victories the Lord has given, but also reminding the people of areas yet to be possessed and of the need to be loyal to God's covenant laws. Their mission remains—to be the people of God's kingdom in the world.

23:1 *rest.* See note on 1:13. *very old man.* Joshua was approaching the age of 110 (24:29).

23:6 *be careful to obey.* Echoing the Lord's instructions at the beginning (1:7–8; see 22:5). *Book of the Law.* See note on 1:8.

23:10 *One of you routs a thousand.* See, e.g., Jdg 15:15–16.

23:11 *love the LORD your God.* A concluding summation (see note on 22:5).

A **23:12** *But if you turn away.* Remaining in the promised land was conditioned on faithfulness to the Lord and separation from the idolaters still around them. Failure to meet these conditions would bring Israel's banishment from the land (cf. vv. 13,15–16; 2Ki 17:7–8; 2Ch 7:14–20). *ally yourselves ... intermarry.* The Lord prohibited alliances, either national or domestic, with the peoples of Canaan because such alliances would tend to compromise Israel's loyalty to the Lord (see Ex 34:15–16; Dt 7:2–4).

23:13 *snares and traps.* Joshua's warning echoes Ex 23:33; 34:12; Dt 7:16.

23:14 *go the way of all the earth.* To the grave.

A C **24:1–33** Once more Joshua assembled the tribes at Shechem to call Israel to a renewal of the covenant (see 8:30–35). It was his final official act as the Lord's servant, mediator of the Lord's rule over his people. In this he followed the example of Moses, whose final official act was also a call to covenant renewal—of which Deuteronomy is the preserved document.

[2]Joshua said to all the people, "This is what the LORD, the God of Israel, says: 'Long ago your ancestors, including Terah the father of Abraham and Nahor, [b] lived beyond the Euphrates River and worshiped other gods. [c] [3]But I took your father Abraham from the land beyond the Euphrates and led him throughout Canaan [d] and gave him many descendants. [e] I gave him Isaac, [f] [4]and to Isaac I gave Jacob and Esau. [g] I assigned the hill country of Seir [h] to Esau, but Jacob and his family went down to Egypt. [i]

[5]" 'Then I sent Moses and Aaron, [j] and I afflicted the Egyptians by what I did there, and I brought you out. [k] [6]When I brought your people out of Egypt, you came to the sea, [l] and the Egyptians pursued them with chariots and horsemen [a] [m] as far as the Red Sea. [b] [n] [7]But they cried [o] to the LORD for help, and he put darkness [p] between you and the Egyptians; he brought the sea over them and covered them. [q] You saw with your own eyes what I did to the Egyptians. [r] Then you lived in the wilderness for a long time. [s]

[8]" 'I brought you to the land of the Amorites [t] who lived east of the Jordan. They fought against you, but I gave them into your hands. I destroyed them from before you, and you took possession of their land. [u] [9]When Balak son of Zippor, [v] the king of Moab, prepared to fight against Israel, he sent for Balaam son of Beor [w] to put a curse on you. [x] [10]But I would not listen to Balaam, so he blessed you [y] again and again, and I delivered you out of his hand.

[11]" 'Then you crossed the Jordan [z] and came to Jericho. [a] The citizens of Jericho fought against you, as did also the Amorites, Perizzites, [b] Canaanites, Hittites, Girgashites, Hivites and Jebusites, [c] but I gave them into your hands. [d] [12]I sent the hornet [e] ahead of you, which drove them out [f] before you—also the two Amorite kings. You did not do it with your own sword and bow. [g] [13]So I gave you a land [h] on which you did not toil and cities you did not build; and you live in them and eat from vineyards and olive groves that you did not plant.' [i]

[14]"Now fear the LORD [j] and serve him with all faithfulness. [k] Throw away the gods [l] your ancestors worshiped beyond the Euphrates River and in Egypt, [m] and serve the LORD. [15]But if serving the LORD seems undesirable to you, then choose for yourselves this day whom you will serve, whether the gods your ancestors served beyond the Euphrates, or the gods of the Amorites, [n] in whose land you are living. But as for me and my household, [o] we will serve the LORD." [p]

[16]Then the people answered, "Far be it from us to forsake [q] the LORD to serve other gods! [17]It was the LORD our God himself who brought us and our parents up out of Egypt, from that land of slavery, [r] and performed those great signs [s] before our eyes. He protected us on our entire journey and among all the nations through which we traveled. [18]And the LORD drove out [t] before us all the nations, [u] including the Amorites, who lived in the land. [v] We too will serve the LORD, because he is our God. [w]"

[19]Joshua said to the people, "You are not able to serve the LORD. He is a holy God; [x] he is a jealous God. [y] He will not forgive [z] your rebellion [a] and your sins. [20]If you forsake the LORD [b] and serve foreign gods, he will turn [c] and bring disaster [d] on you and make an end of you, [e] after he has been good to you."

[21]But the people said to Joshua, "No! We will serve the LORD."

[22]Then Joshua said, "You are witnesses [f] against yourselves that you have chosen [g] to serve the LORD."

"Yes, we are witnesses, [h]" they replied.

---

[a] 6 Or *charioteers*   [b] 6 Or *the Sea of Reeds*

24:2 *Ge 11:26*
c Ge 11:32
24:3 *d* S Ge 12:1
e S Ge 1:28; S 12:2
f S Ge 21:3
24:4 *g* S Ge 25:26
h S Ge 14:6;
S Nu 24:18
i Ge 46:5-6
24:5 *j* S Ex 3:10
k Ex 12:51
24:6 *l* S Ex 14:22
m S Ex 14:9 *n* Ex 14:23
24:7 *o* S Ex 14:10
p Ex 14:20
q S Ex 14:28
r S Ex 19:4 *s* Dt 1:46
24:8 *t* S Ex 23:23
u S Nu 21:31
24:9 *v* Nu 22:2
w S Nu 23:31
x S Nu 22:6
24:10 *y* S Nu 23:11;
S Dt 23:5
24:11 *z* S Ex 14:29
a Jos 6:1 *b* S Jos 3:10
c S Ge 15:18-21
d Ex 23:23; Dt 7:1
24:12 *e* S Ex 23:28;
Ps 44:3,6-7
f S Ex 23:31
g Ps 135:11
24:13 *h* Ex 6:8
i Dt 6:10-11
24:14 *j* 1Sa 12:14;
Job 23:15; Ps 19:9;
119:120 *k* Dt 10:12;
18:13; 1Sa 12:24;
2Co 1:12 *l* ver 23;
S Ge 31:19; Ex 12:12;
18:11; 20:3; Nu 25:2;
Dt 11:28; Jdg 10:16;
Ru 1:15; Isa 55:7
m Eze 23:3
24:15 *n* Jdg 6:10;
Ru 1:15 *o* S Ge 35:2
p Ru 1:16; 2:12;
1Ki 18:21; Da 3:18
24:16 *q* Jos 22:29
24:17 *r* Jdg 6:8
s S Ex 10:1
24:18 *t* S Ex 23:31
u S Dt 33:27 *v* Ac 7:45
w S Ge 28:21
24:19 *x* S Lev 11:44;
S 20:26 *y* S Ex 20:5
z S Ex 34:7
a S Ex 23:21
24:20 *b* 1Ch 28:9,
20; 2Ch 24:18
c Ac 7:42 *d* 1Sa 12:25;
Hos 13:11 *e* Jos 23:15
24:22 *f* ver 27;
Ru 4:10; Isa 8:2;
43:10; 44:8; Jer 42:5;
Mal 2:14 *g* Ps 119:30,
173 *h* S Dt 25:9

B **24:2** *This is what the LORD . . . says.* Only a divinely appointed mediator would dare to speak for God with direct discourse, as in vv. 2–13. *Long ago.* In accordance with the common ancient Near Eastern practice of making treaties (covenants), a brief recital of the past history of the relationship precedes the making of covenant commitments. Joshua here focuses on the separation of Abraham from his polytheistic family, the deliverance of Israel from Egypt and the Lord's establishment of his people in Canaan.

24:10 *I would not listen to Balaam.* Not only did the Lord reject Balaam's prayers, he also turned his curse into a blessing (see Nu 23–24; Ne 13:2; Mic 6:5).

24:12 *hornet.* See note on Ex 23:28.

B **A** **24:14** *fear the LORD.* Trust, serve and worship him (see note on Ge 20:11). *gods your ancestors worshiped beyond the Euphrates and in Egypt.* See v. 2. Joshua appealed to the Israelites to put away the gods their ancestors

had worshiped in Mesopotamia and Egypt. In Ur and Harran, Terah's family would have been exposed to the worship of the moon god, Nanna(r) or Sin. The golden calf of Ex 32:4 may be an example of their worship of the gods of Egypt. It was probably patterned after Apis, the sacred bull of Egypt; see note on Ex 32:4. (Jeroboam's golden calves at Bethel and Dan, on the other hand, probably represented mounts or pedestals for a riding or standing deity; see 1Ki 12:28–29 and note.)

A **24:15** *as for me.* Joshua publicly makes his commitment, hoping to elicit the same from Israel.

A **24:17–18** A confessional statement based on the miraculous events of the exodus.

A **24:19** *You are not able.* Strong words to emphasize the danger of overconfidence. *He is a holy God.* See Lev 11:44 and note. *he is a jealous God.* See Ex 20:5; Zec 1:14 and notes.

24:22 *witnesses.* See v. 27; a normal part of treaty/covenant-making (see Dt 30:19).

24:23 ʲS ver 14
ʲ1Ki 8:58; Ps 119:36;
141:4; Jer 31:33
24:24 ᵏEx 19:8;
Jer 42:6
24:25 ʲS Ex 24:8
ᵐS Jos 17:7
ⁿEx 15:25
24:26 ºS Dt 17:18
ᵖS Dt 28:61; S 31:24
ᵠS Ge 28:18;
S Dt 27:2 ʳS Ge 12:6;
S Jdg 4:11
24:27 ˢS Ge 28:18;
Hab 2:11 ᵗS ver 22;
S Ge 21:30;
S Jos 22:27
ᵘS Jos 7:11
ᵛS Nu 11:20;
S Pr 30:9
24:28 ʷJdg 21:23,
24
24:29 ˣJdg 1:1
ʸS Ge 50:22
24:30 ᶻS Jos 19:50
ᵃ2Sa 23:30
24:31 ᵇJos 7:6
24:32 ᶜHeb 11:22
ᵈS Ge 47:29-30
ᵉGe 33:19; Jn 4:5;
Ac 7:16
24:33 ᶠS Jos 22:13
ᵍS Jos 15:57
ʰS Ex 6:25 ʲ1Sa 9:4;
1Ki 4:8

²³"Now then," said Joshua, "throw away the foreign gods ⁱ that are among you and yield your hearts ʲ to the LORD, the God of Israel."

²⁴And the people said to Joshua, "We will serve the LORD our God and obey him." ᵏ

²⁵On that day Joshua made a covenant ˡ for the people, and there at Shechem ᵐ he re-affirmed for them decrees and laws. ⁿ ²⁶And Joshua recorded º these things in the Book of the Law of God. ᵖ Then he took a large stone ᵠ and set it up there under the oak ʳ near the holy place of the LORD.

²⁷"See!" he said to all the people. "This stone ˢ will be a witness ᵗ against us. It has heard all the words the LORD has said to us. It will be a witness against you if you are untrue ᵘ to your God." ᵛ

²⁸Then Joshua dismissed the people, each to their own inheritance. ʷ

BURIED IN THE PROMISED LAND
24:29–31pp — Jdg 2:6–9

²⁹After these things, Joshua son of Nun, the servant of the LORD, died ˣ at the age of a hundred and ten. ʸ ³⁰And they buried him in the land of his inheritance, at Timnath Se-rah ᵃᶻ in the hill country of Ephraim, north of Mount Gaash. ᵃ

³¹Israel served the LORD throughout the lifetime of Joshua and of the elders ᵇ who out-lived him and who had experienced everything the LORD had done for Israel.

³²And Joseph's bones, ᶜ which the Israelites had brought up from Egypt, ᵈ were buried at Shechem in the tract of land ᵉ that Jacob bought for a hundred pieces of silver ᵇ from the sons of Hamor, the father of Shechem. This became the inheritance of Joseph's de-scendants.

³³And Eleazar son of Aaron ᶠ died and was buried at Gibeah, ᵍ which had been allotted to his son Phinehas ʰ in the hill country ⁱ of Ephraim.

ᵃ 30 Also known as *Timnath Heres* (see Judges 2:9)   ᵇ 32 Hebrew *hundred kesitahs*; a kesitah was a unit of money of unknown weight and value.

24:23 *foreign gods.* The other gods were represented by idols of wood and metal, which could be thrown away and destroyed.

24:25 *covenant for the people.* Consisting of the pledges they had agreed to and the decrees and laws from God.

24:26 *Book of the Law of God.* Probably a list of decrees and laws Joshua had drawn up for the people (v. 25). *large stone.* Set up as a witness to the covenant renewal that closed Joshua's ministry, this is the eighth memorial in the land reminding the Israelites of what the Lord had done for them through his ser-vant (see note on 4:9). Thus the promised land itself bore full testimony to God's people—how they had come into posses-sion of the land and how they would remain in the land only by fulfilling the covenant conditions. The land shouted its own story. *oak.* See note on Ge 12:6.

🔺 **24:29–33** *Three burials.* Since it was a deep desire of the ancients to be buried in their homeland, these notices not only mark the conclusion of the story and the close of an era but also underscore the fact that Israel had indeed been estab-

lished in the promised homeland—the Lord had kept his cov-enant promises.

24:29 *a hundred and ten.* For the significance of this number see note on Ge 50:26.

24:30 *buried him…at Timnath Serah.* See 19:50 and note.

🔺 **24:31** The story told in Joshua is a testimony to Israel's faithfulness in that generation. The author anticipates the quite different story that would follow in Judges.

24:32 *Joseph's bones.* Returning his bones to Shechem was sig-nificant not only because of the ancient plot of land Jacob bought from Hamor (Ge 33:19), but also because Shechem was to be the center of the tribes of Ephraim and Manasseh, the two sons of Joseph. Also, the return fulfilled an oath sworn to Joseph on his deathbed (Ge 50:25; Ex 13:19).

24:33 *Eleazar.* The high priest who served Joshua, as Aaron had served Moses. *Gibeah.* Not the Benjamite city, but a place in Ephraim near Shiloh.

TITLE | JUDGES | INTRODUCTION

The title refers to the leaders Israel had from the time of the elders who outlived Joshua until the time of the monarchy. Their principal purpose is best expressed in 2:16: "Then the LORD raised up judges, who saved them out of the hands of . . . raiders." Since it was God who permitted the oppressions and raised up deliverers, he himself was Israel's ultimate Judge and Deliverer (11:27; see 8:23, where Gideon, a judge, insists that the Lord is Israel's true ruler).

AUTHOR AND DATE

Although tradition ascribes the book to Samuel, the author is actually unknown. It is possible that Samuel assembled some of the accounts from the period of the judges and that such prophets as Nathan and Gad, both of whom were associated with David's court, had a hand in shaping and editing the material (see 1Ch 29:29).

The date of composition is also unknown, but it was undoubtedly during the monarchy. The frequent expression "In those days Israel had no king" (17:6; 18:1; 19:1; 21:25) suggests a date after the establishment of the monarchy. The observation that the Jebusites still controlled Jerusalem (1:21) has been taken to indicate a time before David's capture of the city c. 1000 B.C. (see 2Sa 5:6–10). But the new conditions in Israel alluded to in chs. 17–21 suggest a time after the Davidic dynasty had been effectively established (tenth century B.C.).

THEMES AND THEOLOGY

The book of Judges depicts the life of Israel in the promised land from the death of Joshua to the rise of the monarchy. On the one hand, it is an account of frequent apostasy, provoking divine chastening. On the other hand, it tells of urgent appeals to God in times of crisis, moving the Lord to raise up leaders (judges) through whom he throws off foreign oppressors and restores the land to peace.

With Israel's conquest of the promised land through the leadership of Joshua, many of the covenant promises God had made to their ancestors were fulfilled (see Jos 21:43–45). The Lord's land, where Israel was to enter into rest, lay under their feet; it remained only for them to occupy it, to displace the Canaanites and to cleanse it of paganism. The time had come for Israel to be the kingdom of God in the form of an established commonwealth on earth.

But in Canaan Israel quickly forgot the acts of God that had given them birth and had established them in the land. Consequently they lost sight of their unique identity as God's people, chosen and called to be his army and the loyal citizens of his emerging kingdom. They settled down and attached themselves to Canaan's peoples together with Canaanite morals, gods, and religious beliefs and practices as readily as to Canaan's agriculture and social life.

Throughout Judges the fundamental issue is the lordship of God in Israel, especially Israel's acknowledgment of and loyalty to his rule. His kingship over Israel had been uniquely established by the covenant at Sinai (Ex 19–24), which was later renewed by Moses on the plains of Moab (Dt 29) and by Joshua at Shechem (Jos 24). The author accuses the Israelites of having rejected the kingship of the Lord again and again. They stopped fighting the Lord's battles, turned to the gods of Canaan to secure the blessings of family, flocks and fields, and abandoned God's laws for daily living. In the very center of the cycle of the judges (see Outline), Gideon had to remind Israel that the Lord was its King (see note on 8:23). The recurring lament, and indictment, of chs. 17–21 (see Outline) is: "In those days Israel had no king; everyone did as they saw fit" (17:6; see note there). The primary reference here is doubtless to the earthly mediators of the Lord's rule (i.e., human kings), but the implicit charge is that Israel did not truly acknowledge or obey her heavenly King either.

Only by the Lord's sovereign use of foreign oppression to chasten his people—thereby implementing the covenant curses (see Lev 26:14–45; Dt 28:15–68)—and by his raising up deliverers when his people cried out to him did he maintain his kingship in Israel and preserve his embryonic kingdom from extinction. The Israelites' flawed condition was graphically exposed; they continued to need new saving acts by God in order to enter into the promised rest (see note on Jos 1:13).

Out of the recurring cycles of disobedience, foreign oppression, cries of distress, and deliverance (see 2:11–19; Ne 9:26–31) emerges another important theme—the covenant faithfulness of the Lord. The amazing patience and long-suffering of God are no better demonstrated than during this unsettled period.

Remarkably, this age of Israel's failure, following directly on the redemptive events that came through Moses and Joshua, is in a special way the OT age of the Spirit. God's Spirit enabled people to accomplish feats of victory in the Lord's war against the powers that threatened his kingdom (see 3:10; 6:34; 11:29; 13:25; 14:6,19; 15:14; see also 1Sa 10:6,10; 11:6; 16:13). This same Spirit, poured out on the church following the redemptive work of the second Joshua (Jesus), empowered the people of the Lord to begin the task of preaching the gospel to all nations and of advancing the kingdom of God (see notes on Ac 1:2,8; 2:4,33).

BACKGROUND

Fixing precise dates for the judges is difficult and complex. The dating system followed here is based primarily on 1Ki 6:1, which speaks of an interval of 480 years between the exodus and the fourth year of Solomon's reign. This would place the exodus c. 1446 B.C. and the period of the judges between c. 1380 and the rise of Saul, c. 1050. Jephthah's statement that Israel had occupied Heshbon for 300 years (11:26) generally agrees with these dates. And the reference to "Israel" in the Merneptah Stele demonstrates that Israel was established in Canaan before 1210 B.C. (see chart, p. xxiv).

Some maintain, however, that the number 480 in 1Ki 6:1 is somewhat artificial, arrived at by multiplying 12 (perhaps in reference to the 12 judges) by 40 (a conventional number of years for a generation). They point out the frequent use of the round numbers 10, 20, 40 and 80 in the book of Judges itself. A later date for the exodus would of course require a much shorter period of time for the judges (see Introduction to Exodus: Chronology; see also note on 1Ki 6:1).

LITERARY FEATURES

Even a quick reading of Judges discloses its basic threefold division: (1) a prologue (1:1—3:6), (2) a main body (3:7—16:31) and (3) an epilogue (chs. 17–21). Closer study brings to light a more complex structure, with interwoven themes that bind the whole into an intricately designed portrayal of the character of an age.

The prologue (1:1—3:6) has two parts, and each serves a different purpose. They are not chronologically related, nor does either offer a strict chronological scheme of the time as a whole. The first part (1:1—2:5) sets the stage historically for the narratives that follow. It describes the Israelites' occupation of the promised land—from their initial success to their large-scale failure and divine rebuke.

The second part (2:6—3:6) indicates a basic perspective on the period from the time of Joshua to the rise of the monarchy, a time characterized by recurring cycles of apostasy, oppression, cries of distress and gracious divine deliverance. The author summarizes and explains the Lord's dealings with his rebellious people and introduces some of the basic vocabulary and formulas he will use in the later narratives: "did evil in the eyes of the LORD," 2:11 (see 3:7,12; 4:1; 6:1; 10:6); "gave them into the hands of," 2:14 (see 6:1; 13:1); and "sold them," 2:14 (see 3:8; 4:2; 10:7).

The main body of the book (3:7—16:31), which gives the actual accounts of the recurring cycles (apostasy, oppression, distress, deliverance), has its own unique design. Each cycle has a similar beginning ("The Israelites did evil in the eyes of the LORD"; see note on 3:7) and a recognizable conclusion ("the land had peace . . . years" or "led Israel . . . years"; see note on 3:11). The first of these cycles (Othniel; see 3:7–11 and note) provides the "report form" used for each successive story of oppression and deliverance.

The remaining five cycles form the following narrative units, each of which focuses on one of the major judges:

1. Ehud (3:12–30), a lone hero from the tribe of Benjamin who delivers Israel from oppression from the east.

2. Deborah (chs. 4–5), a woman from one of the Joseph tribes (Ephraim, west of the Jordan), who judges at a time when Israel is being overrun by a coalition of Canaanites under Sisera.

3. Gideon and his son Abimelek (chs. 6–9), whose story forms the central account. In many ways Gideon is the ideal judge, evoking memory of Moses, while his son is the very antithesis of a responsible and faithful judge.

4. Jephthah (10:6—12:7), a social outcast from the other Joseph tribe (Manasseh, east of the Jordan), who judges at a time when Israel is being threatened by a coalition of powers under the king of Ammon.

5. Samson (chs. 13–16), a lone hero from the tribe of Dan who delivers Israel from oppression from the west.

The arrangement of these narrative units is significant. The central accounts of Gideon (the Lord's ideal judge) and Abimelek (the anti-judge) are bracketed by the parallel narratives of the woman Deborah and the social outcast Jephthah—which in turn are framed by the stories of the lone heroes Ehud and Samson. In this way even the structure focuses attention on the crucial issue of the period of the judges: Israel's attraction to the Baals of Canaan (shown by Abimelek; see note on 9:1–57) versus the Lord's kingship over his people (encouraged by Gideon; see note on 8:23).

The epilogue (chs. 17–21) characterizes the era in yet another way, depicting religious and moral corruption on the part of individuals, cities and tribes. Like the introduction, it has two divisions that are neither chronologically related nor expressly dated to the careers of specific judges. The events must have taken place, however, rather early in the period of the judges (see notes on 18:30; 20:1,28).

By dating the events of the epilogue only in relationship to the monarchy (see the recurring refrain in 17:6; 18:1; 19:1; 21:25), the author contrasts the age of the judges with the better time that the monarchy inaugurated, undoubtedly having in view the rule of David and his dynasty (see note on 17:1—21:25). The book mentions two instances of the Lord's assigning leadership to the tribe of Judah: (1) in driving out the Canaanites (1:1–2), and (2) in disciplining a tribe in Israel (20:18). The author views the ruler from the tribe of Judah as the savior of the nation.

The first division of the epilogue (chs. 17–18) relates the story of Micah's development of a paganized place of worship and tells of the tribe of Dan abandoning their allotted territory while adopting Micah's corrupted religion. The second division (chs. 19–21) tells the story of a Levite's sad experience at Gibeah in Benjamin and records the disciplinary removal of the tribe of Benjamin because it had defended the degenerate town of Gibeah.

The two divisions have several interesting parallels:

1. Both involve a Levite's passing between Bethlehem (in Judah) and Ephraim across the Benjamin-Dan corridor.

2. Both mention 600 warriors—those who led the tribe of Dan and those who survived from the tribe of Benjamin.

3. Both conclude with the emptying of a tribal area in that corridor (Dan and Benjamin).

Not only are these Benjamin-Dan parallels significant within the epilogue, but they also form a notable link to the main body of the book. The tribe of Benjamin, which in the epilogue undertook to defend gross immorality, setting ties of blood above loyalty to the Lord, was the tribe from which the Lord raised up the deliverer Ehud (3:15). The tribe of Dan, which in the epilogue retreated from its assigned inheritance and adopted pagan religious practices, was the tribe from which the Lord raised up the deliverer Samson (13:2,5). Thus the tribes that in the epilogue depict the religious and moral corruption of Israel are the very tribes from which the deliverers were chosen whose stories frame the central account of the book (Gideon-Abimelek).

The whole design of the book from prologue to epilogue, the unique manner in which each section deals with the age as a whole, and the way the three major divisions are interrelated clearly portray an age gone awry—an age when "Israel had no king" and "everyone did as they saw fit" (see note on 17:6). Of no small significance is the fact that the story is in episodes and cycles. It is given as the story of all Israel, though usually only certain areas are directly involved. The book portrays the centuries after Joshua as a time of the Israelites' unfaithfulness to the Lord and of their surrender to the allurements of Canaan. Only by the mercies of God were the Israelites not overwhelmed and absorbed by the pagan nations around them. Meanwhile, the history of redemption virtually stood still—awaiting the forward movement that came with the Lord's servant David and the establishment of his dynasty.

OUTLINE

I. Prologue: Incomplete Conquest and Apostasy (1:1—3:6)
  A. First Episode: Israel's Failure to Purge the Land (1:1—2:5)
  B. Second Episode: God's Dealings with Israel's Rebellion (2:6—3:6)
II. Oppression and Deliverance (3:7—16:31)

Major Judges	*Minor Judges*
A. Othniel Defeats Aram Naharaim (3:7–11)	
B. Ehud Defeats Moab (3:12–30)	1. Shamgar (3:31)
C. Deborah Defeats Canaan (chs. 4–5)	
D. Gideon Defeats Midian (chs. 6–8)	
(Abimelek, the anti-judge, ch. 9)	
	2. Tola (10:1–2)
	3. Jair (10:3–5)
E. Jephthah Defeats Ammon (10:6—12:7)	
	4. Ibzan (12:8–10)
	5. Elon (12:11–12)
	6. Abdon (12:13–15)
F. Samson Checks Philistia (chs. 13–16)	

III. Epilogue: Religious and Moral Disorder (chs. 17–21)
  A. First Episode (chs. 17–18; see 17:6; 18:1)
    1. Micah's corruption of religion (ch. 17)
    2. The Danites' departure from their tribal territory (ch. 18)
  B. Second Episode (chs. 19–21; see 19:1; 21:25)
    1. Gibeah's corruption of morals (ch. 19)
    2. The Benjamites' near removal from their tribal territory (chs. 20–21)

ISRAEL FIGHTS THE REMAINING CANAANITES

1:11–15pp — Jos 15:15–19

After the death *a* of Joshua, the Israelites asked the LORD, "Who of us is to go up first *b* to fight against the Canaanites? *c*"

²The LORD answered, "Judah *d* shall go up; I have given the land into their hands. *e*"

³The men of Judah then said to the Simeonites their fellow Israelites, "Come up with us into the territory allotted to us, to fight against the Canaanites. We in turn will go with you into yours." So the Simeonites *f* went with them.

⁴When Judah attacked, the LORD gave the Canaanites and Perizzites *g* into their hands, and they struck down ten thousand men at Bezek. *h* ⁵It was there that they found Adoni-Bezek *i* and fought against him, putting to rout the Canaanites and Perizzites. ⁶Adoni-Bezek fled, but they chased him and caught him, and cut off his thumbs and big toes.

⁷Then Adoni-Bezek said, "Seventy kings with their thumbs and big toes cut off have picked up scraps under my table. Now God has paid me back *j* for what I did to them." They brought him to Jerusalem, *k* and he died there.

⁸The men of Judah attacked Jerusalem *l* also and took it. They put the city to the sword and set it on fire.

⁹After that, Judah went down to fight against the Canaanites living in the hill country, *m* the Negev *n* and the western foothills. ¹⁰They advanced against the Canaanites living in Hebron *o* (formerly called Kiriath Arba *p*) and defeated Sheshai, Ahiman and Talmai. *q*

¹¹From there they advanced against the people living in Debir *r* (formerly called Kiriath Sepher). ¹²And Caleb said, "I will give my daughter Aksah in marriage to the man who attacks and captures Kiriath Sepher." ¹³Othniel son of Kenaz, Caleb's younger brother, took it; so Caleb gave his daughter Aksah to him in marriage.

¹⁴One day when she came to Othniel, she urged him *a* to ask her father for a field. When she got off her donkey, Caleb asked her, "What can I do for you?"

¹⁵She replied, "Do me a special favor. Since you have given me land in the Negev, give me also springs of water." So Caleb gave her the upper and lower springs. *s*

¹⁶The descendants of Moses' father-in-law, *t* the Kenite, *u* went up from the City of Palms *b v* with the people of Judah to live among the inhabitants of the Desert of Judah in the Negev near Arad. *w*

---

a 14 Hebrew; Septuagint and Vulgate *Othniel, he urged her*   *b* 16 That is, Jericho

---

*Marginal references (right column):*

1:1 *a* Jos 24:29
b S Nu 2:3-9;
Jdg 20:18; 1Ki 20:14
c ver 27; S Ge 10:18;
Jdg 3:1-6
1:2 *d* S Ge 49:10
e ver 4; Jdg 3:28; 4:7,
14; 7:9
1:3 *f* ver 17
1:4 *g* S Ge 13:7;
S Jos 3:10 *h* 1Sa 11:8
1:5 *i* ver 6,7
1:7 *j* Lev 24:19;
Jer 25:12 *k* S Jos 10:1
1:8 *l* ver 21;
Jos 15:63; 2Sa 5:6
1:9 *m* S Nu 13:17
n S Ge 12:9;
S Nu 21:1; Isa 30:6
1:10 *o* S Ge 13:18
p S Ge 35:27 *q* ver 20;
S Nu 13:22; Jos 15:14
1:11 *r* Jos 10:38
1:15 *s* S Nu 13:6
1:16 *t* Nu 10:29
u S Ge 15:19
v Dt 34:3; Jdg 3:13;
2Ch 28:15 *w* Nu 21:1;
Jos 12:14

1:1—3:6 An introduction in two parts: (1) an account of the Israelites' failure to lay claim completely to the promised land as the Lord had directed (1:1–36) and of his rebuke for their disloyalty (2:1–5); (2) an overview of the main body of the book (3:7—16:31), portraying Israel's rebellious ways in the centuries after Joshua's death and showing how the Lord dealt with her in that period (2:6—3:6). See Introduction: Literary Features.

1:1–36 Judah is assigned leadership in occupying the land (v. 2; see 20:18). Her vigorous efforts (together with those of Simeon) highlight by contrast the sad story of failure that follows. Only Ephraim's success at Bethel (vv. 22–26) breaks the monotony of that story.

1:1 *After the death of Joshua.* The book of Judges, like that of Joshua, tells of an era following the death of a leading figure in the history of redemption (see Jos 1:1). Joshua probably died c. 1390 B.C. (but see Introduction: Background). The battles under his leadership broke the power of the Canaanites to drive the Israelites out of the land. The task that now confronted Israel was the actual occupation of Canaanite territory (see notes on Jos 13:1). *asked the LORD.* Probably by the priestly use of Urim and Thummim (see notes on Ex 28:30; 1Sa 2:28). *go up.* The main Israelite encampment was at Gilgal, near Jericho in the Jordan Valley (about 800 feet below sea level), while the Canaanite cities were mainly located in the central hill country (about 2,500–3,500 feet above sea level).

1:2 *Judah shall go up.* See 20:18. Judah was also the first to be assigned territory west of the Jordan (Jos 15). The leadership role of the tribe of Judah had been anticipated in the blessing of Jacob (Ge 49:8–12; see also note on Jos 15:1).

1:3 *Simeonites.* Joshua assigned to Simeon cities within the territory of Judah (Jos 19:1,9; see Ge 49:5–7).

1:4 *Canaanites.* See note on Ge 10:6. *Perizzites.* See note on Ge 13:7. *Bezek.* Saul marshaled his army there before going to Jabesh Gilead (see 1Sa 11:8 and note).

1:5 *Adoni-Bezek.* Means "lord of Bezek."

1:6 *cut off his thumbs and big toes.* Physically mutilating prisoners of war was a common practice in the ancient Near East (see note on 16:21). It rendered them unfit for military service.

1:7 *Seventy kings.* Canaan was made up of many small city-states, each of which was ruled by a king. "Seventy" may be a round number, or it may be symbolic of a large number. *under my table.* Humiliating treatment, like that given to a dog (see Mt 15:27; Lk 16:21). *God has paid me back.* See note on Ex 21:23–25.

1:8 *attacked Jerusalem.* Although the city was defeated, it was not occupied by the Israelites at this time (see v. 21). Israel did not permanently control the city until David captured it c. 1000 B.C. (2Sa 5:6–10).

1:10 *Kiriath Arba.* See note on Jos 14:15.

1:11–15 Virtually a word-for-word repetition of Jos 15:15–19. In Joshua the passage functions as part of the description of the territory allotted to the tribe of Judah. Here it serves as part of the account of Judah's success in taking possession of its tribal territory.

1:11 *Debir.* See note on Jos 10:38.

1:12 *Caleb.* He and Joshua had brought back an optimistic report about the prospects of conquering Canaan (Nu 14:6–9). *daughter . . . in marriage.* Victory in battle was one way to pay the bride-price for a girl (see 1Sa 18:25).

1:13 *Othniel.* First major judge (see 3:7–11).

1:16 *Moses' father-in-law.* See note on Ex 2:16.

1:17 ˣ ver 3
ʸ S Nu 14:45
1:18 ᶻ Jos 11:22
ᵃ S Jos 13:3
1:19 ᵇ S Nu 14:43
ᶜ Nu 13:17
ᵈ S Jos 17:16
1:20 ᵉ Jos 10:36
ᶠ S ver 10; S Jos 14:13
1:21 ᵍ S Jos 9:15;
S 15:63 ʰ S ver 8
1:22 ⁱ Jdg 10:9
ʲ S Jos 7:2

¹⁷Then the men of Judah went with the Simeonites ˣ their fellow Israelites and attacked the Canaanites living in Zephath, and they totally destroyed ᵃ the city. Therefore it was called Hormah. ᵇ ʸ ¹⁸Judah also took ᶜ Gaza, ᶻ Ashkelon ᵃ and Ekron—each city with its territory.

¹⁹The LORD was with ᵇ the men of Judah. They took possession of the hill country, ᶜ but they were unable to drive the people from the plains, because they had chariots fitted with iron. ᵈ ²⁰As Moses had promised, Hebron ᵉ was given to Caleb, who drove from it the three sons of Anak. ᶠ ²¹The Benjamites, however, did not drive out ᵍ the Jebusites, who were living in Jerusalem; ʰ to this day the Jebusites live there with the Benjamites.

²²Now the house of Joseph ⁱ attacked Bethel, ʲ and the LORD was with them. ²³When

ᵃ 17 The Hebrew term refers to the irrevocable giving over of things or persons to the LORD, often by totally destroying them.　ᵇ 17 Hormah means *destruction*.　ᶜ 18 Hebrew; Septuagint *Judah did not take*

1:17 men of Judah … Simeonites. The Judahites were fulfilling their commitment (v. 3).
1:18 Gaza, Ashkelon and Ekron. Three of the five main cities inhabited by the Philistines (see map, below).
1:19 unable to drive the people from. Israel failed to comply with God's commands (Dt 7:1–5; 20:16–18) to drive the Canaanites out of the land. Five factors were involved in that failure: (1) The Canaanites possessed superior weapons (here); (2) Israel disobeyed God by making treaties with the Canaanites (2:1–3); (3) Israel took up the worship of other gods and so violated the covenant the Lord had made with their ancestors (2:20–21); (4) God was testing Israel's faithfulness to obey his commands (2:22–23; 3:4); (5) God was giving the Israelites, as his army, the

opportunity to develop their skills in warfare (3:1–2). chariots fitted with iron. Wooden vehicles with certain iron fittings, perhaps axles (see note on Jos 17:16).
1:20 As Moses had promised. See Nu 14:24; Dt 1:36; Jos 14:9–14. Anak. See notes on Nu 13:22; Jos 14:15.
1:21 Benjamites … did not drive out. See note on v. 8. Jerusalem lay on the border between Benjamin and Judah but was allotted to Benjamin (Jos 18:28). Jebusites. See note on Ge 10:16.

B **1:22** house of Joseph. Ephraim and West Manasseh. Bethel. See note on Ge 12:8. There is archaeological evidence of a destruction in the 13th century B.C. that may reflect the battle mentioned in this verse.

FIVE CITIES OF THE PHILISTINES

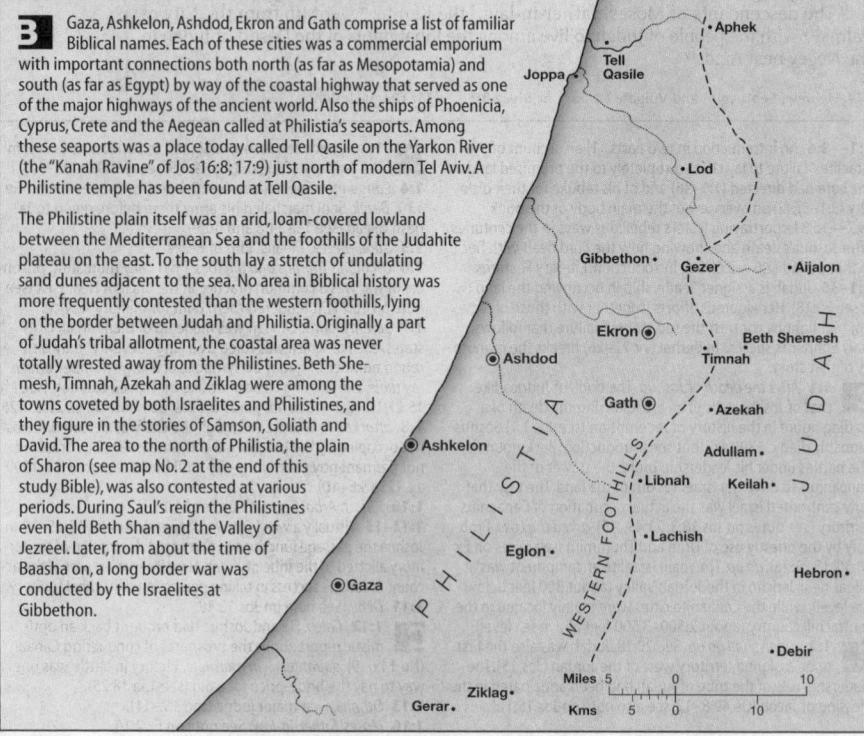

B Gaza, Ashkelon, Ashdod, Ekron and Gath comprise a list of familiar Biblical names. Each of these cities was a commercial emporium with important connections both north (as far as Mesopotamia) and south (as far as Egypt) by way of the coastal highway that served as one of the major highways of the ancient world. Also the ships of Phoenicia, Cyprus, Crete and the Aegean called at Philistia's seaports. Among these seaports was a place today called Tell Qasile on the Yarkon River (the "Kanah Ravine" of Jos 16:8; 17:9) just north of modern Tel Aviv. A Philistine temple has been found at Tell Qasile.

The Philistine plain itself was an arid, loam-covered lowland between the Mediterranean Sea and the foothills of the Judahite plateau on the east. To the south lay a stretch of undulating sand dunes adjacent to the sea. No area in Biblical history was more frequently contested than the western foothills, lying on the border between Judah and Philistia. Originally a part of Judah's tribal allotment, the coastal area was never totally wrested away from the Philistines. Beth Shemesh, Timnah, Azekah and Ziklag were among the towns coveted by both Israelites and Philistines, and they figure in the stories of Samson, Goliath and David. The area to the north of Philistia, the plain of Sharon (see map No. 2 at the end of this study Bible), was also contested at various periods. During Saul's reign the Philistines even held Beth Shan and the Valley of Jezreel. Later, from about the time of Baasha on, a long border war was conducted by the Israelites at Gibbethon.

Aphek
Joppa
Tell Qasile
Lod
Gibbethon
Gezer
Aijalon
Ekron
Beth Shemesh
Ashdod
Timnah
JUDAH
Gath
Azekah
Ashkelon
Adullam
PHILISTIA
Libnah
Keilah
WESTERN FOOTHILLS
Eglon
Lachish
Gaza
Hebron
Debir
Miles 5　0　10
Ziklag
Gerar
Kms 5　0　10

they sent men to spy out Bethel (formerly called Luz),ᵏ ²⁴the spies saw a man coming out of the city and they said to him, "Show us how to get into the city and we will see that you are treated well.ʲ" ²⁵So he showed them, and they put the city to the sword but sparedᵐ the man and his whole family. ²⁶He then went to the land of the Hittites,ⁿ where he built a city and called it Luz,ᵒ which is its name to this day.

²⁷But Manasseh did notᵖ drive out the people of Beth Shan or Taanach or Dor�q or Ibleamʳ or Megiddoˢ and their surrounding settlements, for the Canaanitesᵗ were determined to live in that land. ²⁸When Israel became strong, they pressed the Canaanites into forced labor but never drove them out completely.ᵘ ²⁹Nor did Ephraimᵛ drive out the Canaanites living in Gezer,ʷ but the Canaanites continued to live there among them.ˣ ³⁰Neither did Zebulun drive out the Canaanites living in Kitron or Nahalol, so these Canaanites lived among them, but Zebulun did subject them to forced labor. ³¹Nor did Asherʸ drive out those living in Akko or Sidonᶻ or Ahlab or Akzibᵃ or Helbah or Aphekᵇ or Rehob.ᶜ ³²The Asherites lived among the Canaanite inhabitants of the land because they did not drive them out. ³³Neither did Naphtali drive out those living in Beth Shemeshᵈ or Beth Anathᵉ; but the Naphtalites too lived among the Canaanite inhabitants of the land, and those living in Beth Shemesh and Beth Anath became forced laborers for them. ³⁴The Amoritesᶠ confined the Danitesᵍ to the hill country, not allowing them to come down into the plain.ʰ ³⁵And the Amorites were determined also to hold out in Mount Heres,ⁱ Aijalonʲ and Shaalbim,ᵏ but when the power of the house of Joseph increased, they too were pressed into forced labor. ³⁶The boundary of the Amorites was from Scorpion Passˡ to Selaᵐ and beyond.ⁿ

THE ANGEL OF THE LORD AT BOKIM

2 The angel of the LORDᵒ went up from Gilgalᵖ to Bokimq and said, "I brought you up out of Egyptʳ and led you into the land I swore to give to your ancestors.ˢ I said, 'I will never break my covenant with you,ᵗ ²and you shall not make a covenant with the people of this land,ᵘ but you shall break down their altars.ᵛ Yet you have disobeyedʷ me. Why have you done this? ³And I have also said, 'I will not drive them out before you;ˣ they will become trapsʸ for you, and their gods will become snaresᶻ to you.' "

⁴When the angel of the LORD had spoken these things to all the Israelites, the people wept aloud,ᵃ ⁵and they called that place Bokim.ᵃ ᵇ There they offered sacrifices to the LORD.

DISOBEDIENCE AND DEFEAT

2:6–9pp — Jos 24:29–31

⁶After Joshua had dismissed the Israelites, they went to take possession of the land, each to their own inheritance. ⁷The people served the LORD throughout the lifetime of

---

ᵃ 5 *Bokim* means *weepers.*

1:23 ᵏ S Ge 28:19
1:24 ˡ S Ge 47:29
1:25 ᵐ Jos 6:25
1:26 ⁿ S Dt 7:1;
Eze 16:3 ᵒ S Ge 28:19
1:27 ᵖ 1Ki 9:21
q S Jos 11:2
ʳ S Jos 17:11
ˢ S Jos 12:21 ᵗ S ver 1
1:28 ᵘ Jos 17:12-13
1:29 ᵛ Jos 14:4;
Jdg 5:14 ʷ S Jos 10:33
ˣ Jos 16:10
1:31 ʸ S Jos 17:7
ᶻ S Ge 49:13
ᵃ S Jos 15:44
ᵇ S Jos 12:18
ᶜ S Nu 13:21
1:33 ᵈ S Jos 15:10
ᵉ Jos 19:38
1:34 ᶠ Nu 13:29;
Jdg 10:11; 1Sa 7:14
ᵍ S Ge 30:6 ʰ Jdg 18:1
1:35 ⁱ Jdg 8:13
ʲ Jos 19:42 ᵏ 1Ki 4:9
1:36 ˡ Jos 15:3
ᵐ 2Ki 14:7; Isa 16:1;
42:11 ⁿ Ps 106:34
2:1 ᵒ S Ge 16:7
ᵖ S Dt 11:30 q ver 5
ʳ Ex 20:2; Jdg 6:8
ˢ Ge 17:8
ᵗ S Lev 26:42-44;
Dt 7:9
2:2 ᵘ S Ex 23:32;
S 34:12; Dt 7:2
ᵛ S Ex 23:24; 34:13;
Dt 7:5; 2Ch 14:3
ʷ Jer 7:28
2:3 ˣ Jos 23:13
ʸ S Nu 33:55
ᶻ S Ex 10:7
2:4 ᵃ S Ge 27:38;
S Nu 25:6; 2Ki 17:13
2:5 ᵇ ver 1

1:23 *spy out.* See note on Nu 13:2.
1:25 *spared the man.* Cf. the treatment of Rahab (Jos 6:25).
1:26 *land of the Hittites.* A name for Aram (Syria) at the time of the conquest (see note on Ge 10:15).
1:27–29 See Jos 17:16–18.
1:28 *forced labor.* See note on Jos 16:10.
1:33 *Beth Shemesh.* Location unknown. The name means "house of the sun (god)." There was also a Beth Shemesh in Judah (see note on v. 35). *Beth Anath.* Means "house of (the goddess) Anath" (see notes on 3:31; Jer 1:1).
1:34 *Amorites.* See note on Ge 10:16. *confined the Danites.* Joshua had defeated the Amorites earlier (Jos 10:5–11), but they were still strong enough to withstand the Danites. For this reason a large number of Danites migrated northward a short time later (see ch. 18).
1:35 *Mount Heres.* Means "mountain of the sun (god)"; probably the Beth Shemesh in Judah, which is also called Ir Shemesh, "city of the sun (god)" (Jos 19:41).
1:36 *boundary of the Amorites.* Their southern boundary (see Jos 15:2–3).
2:1–5 Because Israel had not zealously laid claim to the land as the Lord had directed (see 1:27–36), he withdrew his helping hand. On this note the first half of the introduction ends. Although the actual time of the Lord's rebuke is not indicated, it

was probably early in the period of the judges and may even have been connected with the event in Jos 9 (or possibly Jos 18:1–3).

2:1 *angel of the LORD.* See note on Ge 16:7. The role of the angel of the Lord in this passage parallels that of the unnamed prophet in 6:8–10 and the word of the Lord in 10:11–14, calling his people to account. *Gilgal.* The place where Israel first became established in the land under Joshua (see Jos 4:19—5:12). *out of Egypt.* The theme of Exodus, frequently referred to as the supreme evidence of God's redemptive love for his people in the OT (see Ex 20:2). *swore to give.* See Ge 15:18; see also note on Heb 6:13.
2:2 *not make a covenant.* To have done so would have broken their covenant with the Lord (see Ex 23:32).

2:6—3:6 The second half of the introduction continues the narrative of Jos 24:28–31. It is a preliminary survey of the accounts narrated in Jdg 3:7—16:31, showing that Israel's first centuries in the promised land are a recurring cycle of apostasy, oppression, cries of distress and gracious deliverance (see Introduction: Literary Features). The author reminds the Israelites that they will enjoy God's promised rest in the promised land only when they are loyal to him and to his covenant.
2:6 *take possession of the land.* See note on 1:1.

2:7 c ver 17
2:8 d Jos 1:1
2:9 e S Jos 19:50
2:10 f S Ex 5:2;
Gal 4:8
2:11 g 1Ki 15:26
h Jdg 3:12; 4:1; 6:1;
10:6 i Jdg 3:7; 8:33;
1Ki 16:31; 22:53;
2Ki 10:18; 17:16
2:12 j S Dt 32:12;
Ps 106:36
k S Dt 31:16; Jdg 10:6
l S Nu 11:33
m Dt 4:25; Ps 78:58;
106:40
2:13 n 1Sa 7:3;
1Ki 11:5,33; 2Ki 23:13
o Jdg 3:7; 5:8; 6:25;
8:33; 10:6; 1Sa 31:10;
Ne 9:26; Ps 78:56;
Jer 11:10
2:14 p S Dt 31:17
q Ne 9:27; Ps 106:41
r Ps 44:10; 89:41;
Eze 34:8
s S Dt 32:30;
S Jdg 3:8 t S Dt 28:25
2:15 u Ru 1:13;
Job 19:21; Ps 32:4
v Ge 35:3; 2Sa 22:7;
2Ch 15:4; Job 5:5;
20:22; Ps 4:1; 18:6
2:16 w Ru 1:1;
1Sa 4:18; 7:6,15;
2Sa 7:11; 1Ch 17:10;
Ac 13:20 x 1Sa 11:3;
Ps 106:43
2:17 y S Ex 34:15;
S Nu 15:39 z S Ps 4:2
a Ne 9:28; Ps 106:36
b Dt 9:12 c ver 7
2:18 d 1Sa 7:3;
2Ki 13:5; Isa 19:20;
43:3,11; 45:15,21;
49:26; 60:16; 63:8
e S Dt 32:36
f S Ex 2:23
g S Nu 10:9
2:19 h S Ge 6:11;
S Dt 4:16 i Dt 32:17;
Ne 9:2; Ps 78:57;
Jer 44:3,9 j Jdg 4:1;
8:33 k S Ex 32:9
2:20 l S Dt 31:17;

Joshua and of the elders who outlived him and who had seen all the great things the Lord had done for Israel. c

[8]Joshua son of Nun, d the servant of the Lord, died at the age of a hundred and ten. [9]And they buried him in the land of his inheritance, at Timnath Heres a e in the hill country of Ephraim, north of Mount Gaash.

[10]After that whole generation had been gathered to their ancestors, another generation grew up who knew neither the Lord nor what he had done for Israel. f [11]Then the Israelites did evil g in the eyes of the Lord h and served the Baals. i [12]They forsook the Lord, the God of their ancestors, who had brought them out of Egypt. They followed and worshiped various gods j of the peoples around them. k They aroused l the Lord's anger m [13]because they forsook n him and served Baal and the Ashtoreths. o [14]In his anger p against Israel the Lord gave them into the hands q of raiders who plundered r them. He sold them s into the hands of their enemies all around, whom they were no longer able to resist. t [15]Whenever Israel went out to fight, the hand of the Lord was against them u to defeat them, just as he had sworn to them. They were in great distress. v

[16]Then the Lord raised up judges, b w who saved x them out of the hands of these raiders. [17]Yet they would not listen to their judges but prostituted y themselves to other gods z and worshiped them. a Unlike their ancestors, they quickly turned b from following the way of their ancestors, the way of obedience to the Lord's commands. c [18]Whenever the Lord raised up a judge for them, he was with the judge and saved d them out of the hands of their enemies as long as the judge lived; for the Lord relented e because of their groaning f under those who oppressed and afflicted g them. [19]But when the judge died, the people returned to ways even more corrupt h than those of their ancestors, i following other gods and serving and worshiping them. j They refused to give up their evil practices and stubborn k ways.

[20]Therefore the Lord was very angry l with Israel and said, "Because this nation has violated the covenant m I ordained for their ancestors and has not listened to me, [21]I will no longer drive out n before them any of the nations Joshua left when he died. [22]I will use them to test o Israel and see whether they will keep the way of the Lord and walk in it as their ancestors did." [23]The Lord had allowed those nations to remain; he did not drive them out at once by giving them into the hands of Joshua. p

3 These are the nations the Lord left to test q all those Israelites who had not experienced any of the wars in Canaan [2](he did this only to teach warfare to the descendants of the Israelites who had not had previous battle experience): [3]the

a 9 Also known as *Timnath Serah* (see Joshua 19:50 and 24:30)   b 16 Or *leaders*; similarly in verses 17-19

2:20 Jos 23:16 m S Jos 7:11; S 2Ki 17:15   **2:21** n Jos 23:5   **2:22** o S Ge 22:1; S Ex 15:25   **2:23** p Jdg 1:1   **3:1** q S Ex 15:25

2:8 *servant of the Lord.* Joshua is identified as the Lord's official representative (see notes on Ex 14:31; Ps 18 title; Isa 41:8–9; 42:1). *a hundred and ten.* For the significance of this number see note on Ge 50:26.

2:10–15 The Lord withdraws his help because of Israel's apostasy. He "sells" the people he had "bought" (Ex 15:16) and redeemed (Ex 15:13; cf. Ps 74:2).

2:10 *gathered to their ancestors.* See Ge 15:15; see also note on Ge 25:8. *who knew neither the Lord ... Israel.* They had no direct experience of the Lord's acts (see Ex 1:8).

2:11 *did evil in the eyes of the Lord.* The same expression is used in 3:7,12; 4:1; 6:1; 10:6. *Baals.* The many local forms of this Canaanite deity (see note on v. 13).

2:12 *aroused the Lord's anger.* See Dt 4:25; see also note on Zec 1:2.

2:13 *Baal.* Means "lord." Baal, the god worshiped by the Canaanites and Phoenicians, was variously known to them as the son of Dagon and the son of El. In Aram (Syria) he was called Hadad and in Babylonia Adad. Believed to give fertility to the womb and life-giving rain to the soil, he is pictured as standing on a bull, a popular symbol of fertility and strength (see 1Ki 12:28). The storm cloud was his chariot, thunder his voice, and lightning his spear and arrows. The worship of Baal involved sacred prostitution and sometimes even child sacrifice (see Jer 19:5). The stories of Elijah and Elisha (1Ki 17–2Ki 13), as well as many other OT passages, directly or indirectly protest Baalism (e.g., Ps 29:3–9; 68:1–4,32–34; 93:1–5; 97:1–5; Jer 10:12–16;

14:22; Hos 2:8,16–17; Am 5:8). *Ashtoreths.* Female deities such as Ashtoreth (wife of Baal) and Asherah (wife of El, the chief god of the Canaanite pantheon). Ashtoreth was associated with the evening star and was the beautiful goddess of war and fertility. She was worshiped as Ishtar in Babylonia and as Athtart in Aram. To the Greeks she was Astarte or Aphrodite, and to the Romans, Venus. Worship of the Ashtoreths involved extremely lascivious practices (1Ki 14:24; 2Ki 23:7).

2:14 *gave them into the hands of.* The same Hebrew expression is used in 6:1; 13:1. *sold them.* The same expression is used in 3:8; 4:2; 10:7.

2:16–19 The Lord was merciful to his people in times of distress, sending deliverers to save them from oppression. But Israel continually forgot these saving acts, just as they had forgotten those God had performed through Moses and Joshua.

2:16 *judges.* See Introduction: Title. There were six major judges (Othniel, Ehud, Deborah, Gideon, Jephthah and Samson) and six minor ones (Shamgar, Tola, Jair, Ibzan, Elon and Abdon).

2:17 *prostituted themselves.* See Ex 34:15 and note.

2:18 *groaning ... oppressed.* The language of the Egyptian bondage (see Ex 2:24; 3:9; 6:5).

2:20–23 The Lord decided to leave the remaining nations to test Israel's loyalty.

3:1–6 The list of nations the Lord left roughly describes an arc along the western and northern boundaries of the area actually occupied by Israel at the death of Joshua (vv. 1–4). Within Israelite-occupied territory there were large groups of native peoples five [r] rulers of the Philistines, [s] all the Canaanites, the Sidonians, and the Hivites [t] living in the Lebanon mountains from Mount Baal Hermon [u] to Lebo Hamath. [v] 4They were left to test [w] the Israelites to see whether they would obey the Lord's commands, which he had given their ancestors through Moses.

5The Israelites lived [x] among the Canaanites, Hittites, Amorites, Perizzites, [y] Hivites and Jebusites. [z] 6They took their daughters [a] in marriage and gave their own daughters to their sons, and served their gods. [b][c]

OTHNIEL

7The Israelites did evil in the eyes of the Lord; they forgot the Lord [d] their God and served the Baals and the Asherahs. [e] 8The anger of the Lord burned against Israel so that he sold [f] them into the hands of Cushan-Rishathaim [g] king of Aram Naharaim, [a][h] to whom the Israelites were subject for eight years. 9But when they cried out [i] to the Lord, he raised up for them a deliverer, [j] Othniel [k] son of Kenaz, Caleb's younger brother, who saved them. 10The Spirit of the Lord came on him, [l] so that he became Israel's judge [b] and went to war. The Lord gave Cushan-Rishathaim [m] king of Aram [n] into the hands of Othniel, who overpowered him. 11So the land had peace [o] for forty years, [p] until Othniel son of Kenaz [q] died.

EHUD

12Again the Israelites did evil in the eyes of the Lord, [r] and because they did this evil the Lord gave Eglon king of Moab [s] power over Israel. 13Getting the Ammonites [t] and Amalekites [u] to join him, Eglon came and attacked Israel, and they took possession of the City of Palms. [c][v] 14The Israelites were subject to Eglon king of Moab [w] for eighteen years.

15Again the Israelites cried out to the Lord, and he gave them a deliverer [x]—Ehud [y], a left-handed [z] man, the son of Gera the Benjamite. The Israelites sent him with tribute [a] to Eglon king of Moab. 16Now Ehud [b] had made a double-edged sword about a cubit [d] long, which he strapped to his right thigh under his clothing. 17He presented the tribute [c] to Eg-

---

[a] 8 That is, Northwest Mesopotamia   [b] 10 Or leader   [c] 13 That is, Jericho   [d] 16 That is, about 18 inches or about 45 centimeters

3:15 x S ver 9 y ver 16; Jdg 4:1 z Jdg 20:16; 1Ch 12:2 a ver 17,18; 2Sa 8:2,6; 1Ki 4:21; 2Ki 17:3; Est 10:1; Ps 68:29; 72:10; 89:22; Ecc 2:8; Isa 60:5; Hos 10:6   **3:16** b S ver 15   **3:17** c S ver 15

Right margin cross-references

3:3 r S Jos 13:3
s S Ge 10:14
t S Ge 10:17; 1S S Ex 3:8
u S Dt 3:8
v S Nu 13:21
3:4 w S Ex 15:25
3:5 x Ps 106:35
y S Jos 3:10
z S Jos 11:3; Ezr 9:1
3:6 a Ezr 10:18;
Ne 13:23; Mal 2:11
b S Ex 34:16; Dt 7:3-4
c S Dt 7:16
3:7 d Dt 4:9;
S 32:18; Jdg 8:34;
Ps 78:11,42; 106:7;
Jer 23:27 e S Ex 34:13;
1Ki 16:33; 2Ch 34:7;
Isa 17:8
3:8 f Jdg 2:14;
Ps 44:12; Isa 50:1;
52:3 g ver 10
h S Ge 24:10
3:9 i ver 15; Jdg 6:6,
7; 10:10; 1Sa 12:10;
Ps 106:44; 107:13
j S Dt 28:29; Ne 9:27
k S Jos 15:17
3:10 l S Nu 11:25,29;
Jdg 6:34; 11:29; 13:25;
14:6,19; 15:14;
1Sa 11:6; 16:13;
1Ki 18:46; 1Ch 12:18;
2Ch 24:20; Isa 11:2
m ver 8 n S Ge 10:22
3:11 o ver 30;
S Jos 14:15; Jdg 5:31;
8:28 p S Ex 16:35
q S Jos 15:17
3:12 r S Jdg 2:11,14
s 1Sa 12:9
3:13 t S Ge 19:38;
Jdg 10:11 u S Ge 14:7
v S Jdg 1:16
3:14 w Jer 48:1

(v. 5; see 1:27–36) with whom the Israelites intermingled, often adopting their religions (v. 6).

3:2 only to teach warfare. As his covenant servant, Israel was the Lord's army for fighting against the powers of the world that were settled in his land. Because of the incomplete conquest, succeeding generations in Israel needed to become capable warriors. "Only" probably here means "especially."

3:3 five rulers. See note on Jos 13:3. These rulers had control of a five-city confederacy (see map, p. 338). At one point Judah defeated three of the cities (1:18) but was unable to hold them. Sidonians. Here used collectively of the Phoenicians. Hivites. Here identified with a region in northern Canaan reaching all the way to Hamath (see Jos 11:3 and note). Mount Baal Hermon. The same as Mount Hermon (see 1Ch 5:23).

3:6 took their daughters … and served their gods. See note on Jos 23:12. The degenerating effect of such intermarriage is well illustrated in Solomon's experience (1Ki 11:1–8).

3:7–11 In the account of Othniel's judgeship the author provides the basic literary form he uses in his accounts of the major judges (i.e., beginning statement; cycle of apostasy, oppression, distress, deliverance; recognizable conclusion), filling it out in each case with the materials he considered necessary to his purpose (see Introduction: Literary Features).

3:7 did evil in the eyes of the Lord. A recurring expression (see v. 12; 4:1; 6:1; 10:6; 13:1) used to introduce the cycles of the judges (see Introduction: Literary Features). Baals. See note on 2:13. Asherahs. See notes on 2:13; Ex 34:13.

3:8 Cushan-Rishathaim. Probably means "doubly wicked Cushan," perhaps a caricature of his actual name (see note on 10:6 regarding Baal-Zebub). Aram Naharaim. See note on Ge 24:10.

3:9 they cried out to the Lord. The Israelites' cries of distress occurred in each recurring cycle of the judges (see Introduction: Literary Features). Othniel. See 1:13.

3:10 Spirit of the Lord came on him. The Spirit empowered Othniel to deliver his people, as he did Gideon (6:34), Jephthah (11:29), Samson (14:6,19)—and also David (1Sa 16:13). Cf. Nu 11:25–29.

3:11 the land had peace … years. A recognizable conclusion to the cycle of a judge (noted only here and in v. 30; 5:31; 8:28). After the judgeship of Gideon this formula is replaced by "led Israel … years" (12:7; 15:20; 16:31). See Introduction: Literary Features. forty years. A conventional number of years for a generation (see Introduction: Background).

3:12–30 Ehud's triumph over Eglon, king of Moab. The left-handed Benjamite was an authentic hero. All alone, and purely by his wits, he cut down the king of Moab, who had established himself in Canaan near Jericho. This account balances that of Samson in the five narrative units central to the book of Judges (see Introduction: Literary Features).

3:12 Moab. See note on Ge 19:36–38.

3:13 Ammonites. See note on Ge 19:33. Amalekites. These descendants of Esau (Ge 36:12,16) lived in the Negev (Nu 13:29). See note on Ge 14:7.

3:14 Israelites. Here mainly Benjamin and Ephraim.

3:15 left-handed man. Left-handedness was noteworthy among Benjamites (see 20:15–16)—which is ironic since Benjamin means "son of (my) right hand." Being left-handed, Ehud could conceal his dagger on the side where it was not expected (see v. 21). tribute. An annual payment, perhaps of agricultural products (cf. 2Ki 3:4).

3:16 made a double-edged sword. That is, a straight-bladed sword useful for a stabbing thrust, in distinction from the more common cycle sword intended for slashing blows. During the period of the judges, Israelite weapons were often fashioned or improvised for the occasion: Shamgar's oxgoad (v. 31), Jael's tent peg (4:21–22), Gideon's jars and torches (7:20), the woman's millstone (9:53) and Samson's donkey jawbone (15:15). See 1Sa 13:19.

3:17 *d*Job 15:27;
Ps 73:4
3:20 *e*Am 3:15
*f*Ne 8:5
3:21 *g*2Sa 2:16;
3:27; 20:10
3:24 *h*1Sa 24:3
3:25 *i*2Ki 2:17; 8:11
3:27 *j*S Lev 25:9;
Jdg 6:34; 7:18;
2Sa 2:28; Isa 18:3;
Jer 42:14
3:28 *k*S Ge 19:37
*l*S Jos 2:24; S Jdg 1:2
*m*S Nu 13:29;
S Jos 2:7
3:30 *n*S Ge 36:35
*o*S ver 11
3:31 *p*Jdg 5:6
*q*S Jos 23:10
*r*Jos 13:2; Jdg 10:11;
13:1; 1Sa 5:1; 31:1;
2Sa 8:1; Jer 25:20;
47:1
4:1 *s*S Jdg 2:19
*t*S Jdg 2:11
*u*S Jdg 3:15
4:2 *v*S Dt 32:30
*w*S Jos 11:1 *x*1Sa 12:9;
Ps 83:9
4:3 *y*S Jos 17:16
*z*Jdg 10:12; Ps 106:42
4:4 *a*Jdg 5:1,7,12,15
*b*S Ex 15:20

lon king of Moab, who was a very fat man. *d* 18After Ehud had presented the tribute, he dismissed those who had carried it. 19But on reaching the stone images near Gilgal he himself went back to Eglon and said, "Your Majesty, I have a secret message for you."

The king said to his attendants, "Leave us!" And they all left.

20Ehud then approached him while he was sitting alone in the upper room of his palace *a e* and said, "I have a message from God for you." As the king rose *f* from his seat, 21Ehud reached with his left hand, drew the sword*g* from his right thigh and plunged it into the king's belly. 22Even the handle sank in after the blade, and his bowels discharged. Ehud did not pull the sword out, and the fat closed in over it. 23Then Ehud went out to the porch*b*; he shut the doors of the upper room behind him and locked them.

24After he had gone, the servants came and found the doors of the upper room locked. They said, "He must be relieving himself*h* in the inner room of the palace." 25They waited to the point of embarrassment, *i* but when he did not open the doors of the room, they took a key and unlocked them. There they saw their lord fallen to the floor, dead.

26While they waited, Ehud got away. He passed by the stone images and escaped to Seirah. 27When he arrived there, he blew a trumpet*j* in the hill country of Ephraim, and the Israelites went down with him from the hills, with him leading them.

28"Follow me," he ordered, "for the LORD has given Moab, *k* your enemy, into your hands. *l*" So they followed him down and took possession of the fords of the Jordan *m* that led to Moab; they allowed no one to cross over. 29At that time they struck down about ten thousand Moabites, all vigorous and strong; not one escaped. 30That day Moab*n* was made subject to Israel, and the land had peace *o* for eighty years.

SHAMGAR

31After Ehud came Shamgar son of Anath, *p* who struck down six hundred *q* Philistines *r* with an oxgoad. He too saved Israel.

DEBORAH

4 Again the Israelites did evil *s* in the eyes of the LORD, *t* now that Ehud *u* was dead. 2So the LORD sold them *v* into the hands of Jabin king of Canaan, who reigned in Hazor. *w* Sisera, *x* the commander of his army, was based in Harosheth Haggoyim. 3Because he had nine hundred chariots fitted with iron*y* and had cruelly oppressed*z* the Israelites for twenty years, they cried to the LORD for help.

4Now Deborah, *a* a prophet, *b* the wife of Lappidoth, was leading*c* Israel at that time.

a 20 The meaning of the Hebrew for this word is uncertain; also in verse 24.   *b 23* The meaning of the Hebrew for this word is uncertain.   *c 4* Traditionally *judging*

3:19 *stone images.* Lit. "carved (stone) things," a frequent Hebrew way of referring to stone idols. But here the reference may be to carved stone statues of Eglon, marking the boundary of the territory he now claims as part of his expanded realm—a common practice in the ancient Near East. *Gilgal.* Perhaps the one mentioned in Jos 15:7, located on the border between Benjamin and Judah, not the well-known city east of Jericho.
3:20 *upper room.* Rooms built on the flat roofs of houses (2Ki 4:10–11) and palaces (Jer 22:13–14) had latticed windows (2Ki 1:2) that provided comfort in the heat of summer.
3:28 *took possession of the fords.* This move enabled the Israelites to cut off the Moabites fleeing Jericho and also prevented the Moabites from sending reinforcements.
3:30 *eighty years.* Round numbers are frequently used in Judges (see Introduction: Background).
3:31 *Shamgar.* The first of six minor judges and a contemporary of Deborah (see 5:6–7). His name is foreign, so he was probably not an Israelite. *son of Anath.* Indicates either that Shamgar came from the town of Beth Anath (see 1:33 and note) or that his family worshiped the goddess Anath. Since Anath, Baal's sister, was a goddess of war who fought for Baal, the expression "son of Anath" may have been a military title, meaning "a warrior." *oxgoad.* A long, wooden rod, sometimes having a metal tip, used for driving draft animals (see 1Sa 13:21).
4:1—5:31 Deborah's triumph over Sisera (commander of a Canaanite army)—first narrated in prose (ch. 4), then celebrated in song (ch. 5). At the time of the Canaanite threat from the north, the Israelites remained incapable of united action until a woman (Deborah) summoned them to the Lord's battle. Because the warriors of Israel lacked the courage to rise up and face the enemy, the glory of victory went to a woman (Jael)—and she may not have been an Israelite.
4:1–2 Except for the Canaanites, Israel's enemies came from outside the territory they occupied. Nations like Aram Naharaim, Moab, Midian and Ammon were mainly interested in plunder, but the Canaanite uprising of chs. 4–5 was an attempt to restore Canaanite power in the north. The Philistines engaged in continual struggle with Israel for permanent control of the land in the southern and central regions.
4:2 *Jabin.* See Ps 83:9–10. The name was possibly royal rather than personal. Joshua is credited with having earlier slain a king by the same name (Jos 11:1,10). *Hazor.* The original royal city of the Jabin dynasty; it may still have been in ruins (see note on Jos 11:10). Sisera sought to recover the territory once ruled by the kings of Hazor. *Sisera.* His name suggests he was not a Canaanite.
4:3 *nine hundred.* The number probably represents a coalition rather than the chariot force of one city. In the 15th century B.C., Pharaoh Thutmose III boasted of having captured 924 chariots at the battle of Megiddo. *Israelites.* Mainly Zebulun and Naphtali, but West Manasseh, Issachar and Asher were also affected.
4:4 *Deborah.* Means "bee"; cf. Dt 1:44. She is the only judge said to have been a prophet. Other women spoken of as prophets are Miriam (Ex 15:20), Huldah (2Ki 22:14), Noadiah (Ne 6:14) and Anna (Lk 2:36), but see also Ac 21:9.

4:5 c 1Sa 14:2; 22:6
d S Jos 18:25
e S Jos 12:9
4:6 f Jdg 5:1,12,15;
1Sa 12:11; Heb 11:32
g S Jos 12:22
h S Ge 30:8 / Jdg 5:18;
6:35 / S Jos 19:22
4:7 k S Jos 11:1
l ver 13; Jdg 5:21;
1Ki 18:40; Ps 83:9
m S Jdg 1:2
4:9 n S Jos 12:22
4:10 o 2Ch 36:23;
Ezr 1:2; Isa 41:2; 42:6;
45:3; 46:11; 48:15
4:11 p S Ge 15:19
q Nu 10:29
r Jos 24:26; Jdg 9:6
s Jos 19:33
4:12 t S Jos 19:22
4:13 u S ver 7;
Jdg 5:19 v S Jos 17:16
4:14 w S Jdg 1:2
x Dt 9:3; Jdg 4:6;
2Sa 5:24; Ps 68:7
4:15 y S Jos 10:10
4:16 z S Ex 14:28;
Ps 83:9
4:17 a ver 18,21,22;
Jdg 5:6,24
b S Ge 15:19
c S Jos 11:1
4:18 d S ver 17
4:19 e S Ge 18:8
4:21 f S ver 17
g Ge 2:21; 15:12;
1Sa 26:12; Isa 29:10;
Jnh 1:5 h Jdg 5:26

⁵She held court c under the Palm of Deborah between Ramah d and Bethel e in the hill country of Ephraim, and the Israelites went up to her to have their disputes decided. ⁶She sent for Barak son of Abinoam f from Kedesh g in Naphtali and said to him, "The LORD, the God of Israel, commands you: 'Go, take with you ten thousand men of Naphtali h and Zebulun i and lead them up to Mount Tabor. j ⁷I will lead Sisera, the commander of Jabin's k army, with his chariots and his troops to the Kishon River l and give him into your hands. m ' "

⁸Barak said to her, "If you go with me, I will go; but if you don't go with me, I won't go."

⁹"Certainly I will go with you," said Deborah. "But because of the course you are taking, the honor will not be yours, for the LORD will deliver Sisera into the hands of a woman." So Deborah went with Barak to Kedesh. n ¹⁰There Barak summoned o Zebulun and Naphtali, and ten thousand men went up under his command. Deborah also went up with him.

¹¹Now Heber the Kenite had left the other Kenites, p the descendants of Hobab, q Moses' brother-in-law, a and pitched his tent by the great tree r in Zaanannim s near Kedesh.

¹²When they told Sisera that Barak son of Abinoam had gone up to Mount Tabor, t ¹³Sisera summoned from Harosheth Haggoyim to the Kishon River u all his men and his nine hundred chariots fitted with iron. v

¹⁴Then Deborah said to Barak, "Go! This is the day the LORD has given Sisera into your hands. w Has not the LORD gone ahead x of you?" So Barak went down Mount Tabor, with ten thousand men following him. ¹⁵At Barak's advance, the LORD routed y Sisera and all his chariots and army by the sword, and Sisera got down from his chariot and fled on foot.

¹⁶Barak pursued the chariots and army as far as Harosheth Haggoyim, and all Sisera's troops fell by the sword; not a man was left. z ¹⁷Sisera, meanwhile, fled on foot to the tent of Jael, a the wife of Heber the Kenite, b because there was an alliance between Jabin king of Hazor c and the family of Heber the Kenite.

¹⁸Jael d went out to meet Sisera and said to him, "Come, my lord, come right in. Don't be afraid." So he entered her tent, and she covered him with a blanket.

¹⁹"I'm thirsty," he said. "Please give me some water." She opened a skin of milk, e gave him a drink, and covered him up.

²⁰"Stand in the doorway of the tent," he told her. "If anyone comes by and asks you, 'Is there a man in here?' say 'No.' "

²¹But Jael, f Heber's wife, picked up a tent peg and a hammer and went quietly to him while he lay fast asleep, g exhausted. She drove the peg through his temple into the ground, and he died. h

---

a 11 Or father-in-law

4:5 *Palm of Deborah.* The Hebrew word for "honey" refers to both bees' honey and the sweet, syrupy juice of dates. Deborah, the Bee, dispensed the sweetness of justice as she held court, not in a city gate where male judges sat, but under the shade of a "honey" tree. See also note on 1Sa 14:2.

4:6 *Barak.* Means "thunderbolt"—which suggests that he is summoned to be the Lord's "flashing sword" (Dt 32:41). He is named among the heroes of faith in Heb 11:32. *Kedesh in Naphtali.* A town affected by the Canaanite oppression. *Naphtali and Zebulun.* Issachar, a near neighbor of these tribes, is not mentioned here but is included in the poetic description of the battle in 5:15. In all, six tribes are mentioned as having participated in the battle. *Mount Tabor.* A mountain about 1,300 feet high, northeast of the battle site.

4:7 With the Israelites encamped on the slopes of Mount Tabor, safe from chariot attack, the Lord's strategy was to draw Sisera into a trap. For the battle site, Sisera cleverly chose the Valley of Jezreel along the Kishon River, where his chariot forces would have ample maneuvering space to range the battlefield and attack in numbers from any quarter. But that was his undoing, for he did not know the power of the Lord, who would fight from heaven for Israel with storm and flood (see 5:20–21), as he had done in the days of Joshua (Jos 10:11–14). Even in modern times storms have rendered the plain along the Kishon virtually impassable. In April of 1799 the flooded Kishon River aided Napoleon's victory over a Turkish army.

4:9 *a woman.* Barak's timidity (and that of Israel's other warriors, whom he exemplified) was due to lack of trust in the Lord and was thus rebuked (see note on 9:54).

4:11 *Heber the Kenite.* Since one meaning of Heber's name is

"ally," and since "Kenite" identifies him as belonging to a clan of metalworkers, the author hints at the truth that this member of a people allied with Israel since the days of Moses has moved from south to north to ally himself (see v. 17) with the Canaanite king who is assembling a large force of "chariots fitted with iron" (v. 3; see note on Jos 17:16). It is no doubt he who informs Sisera of Barak's military preparations. *other Kenites.* Settled in the south not far from Kadesh Barnea in the Negev (see 1:16). *Hobab.* See Nu 10:29.

4:14 *gone ahead of you.* As a king at the head of his army (see 1Sa 8:20). See also Ex 15:3 ("the LORD is a warrior"); Jos 10:10–11; 2Sa 5:24; 2Ch 20:15–17, 22–24. *Barak went down Mount Tabor.* The Lord's "thunderbolt" (see note on v. 6) descends the mountain to attack the Canaanite army.

4:15 *routed.* See note on v. 7. The Hebrew for this word is also used of the panic that overcame the Egyptians at the Red Sea (Ex 14:24) and the Philistines at Mizpah (1Sa 7:10).

4:18 *he entered her tent.* Since ancient Near Eastern custom prohibited any man other than a woman's husband or father from entering her tent, Jael seemed to offer Sisera an ideal hiding place.

4:19 *skin.* Containers for liquids were normally made from the skins of goats or lambs. *milk.* See note on 5:25. Jael, whose name means "mountain goat," gave him milk to drink—and it was most likely goat's milk (see Ex 23:19; Pr 27:27).

4:21 *drove the peg through his temple.* The laws of hospitality normally meant that one tried to protect a guest from any harm (see 19:23; Ge 19:8). Jael remained true to her family's previous alliance with Israel (she may not have been an Israelite) and so undid her husband's deliberate breach of faith. Armed only with domestic implements, this dauntless woman destroyed the great warrior whom Barak had earlier feared.

4:22 ᶦS ver 17
ʲJdg 5:27
4:23 ᵏNe 9:24;
Ps 18:47; 44:2; 47:3;
144:2 ᶦS Jos 11:1
4:24 ᵐPs 83:9;
106:43
5:1 ⁿS Jdg 4:4
ᵒS Jdg 4:6
ᵖS Ex 15:1; Ps 32:7
5:2 ᵠ2Ch 17:16;
Ps 110:3 ʳver 9
5:3 ˢS Ex 15:1
ᵗPs 27:6
5:4 ᵘS Ex 13:21
ᵛS Nu 24:18;
S Dt 33:2 ʷ2Sa 22:8;
Ps 18:7; 77:18; 82:5;
Isa 2:19, 21; 13:13;
24:18; 64:3; Jer 10:10;
50:46; Joel 3:16; Na 1:5;
Hab 3:6 ˣPs 68:8;
77:17
5:5 ʸS Ex 19:18;
Ps 29:6; 46:3; 77:18;
114:4; Isa 64:3
5:6 ᶻJdg 3:31
ᵃS Jdg 4:17
ᵇLev 26:22; Isa 33:8
ᶜPs 125:5; Isa 59:8
5:7 ᵈS Jdg 4:4
5:8 ᵉDt 32:17;
S Jdg 2:13 ᶠver 11;
S Jos 2:5 ᵍS Nu 25:7
5:9 ʰS ver 2
5:10 ᶦS Ge 49:11;
Jdg 10:4; 12:14

²²Just then Barak came by in pursuit of Sisera, and Jael ᶦ went out to meet him. "Come," she said, "I will show you the man you're looking for." So he went in with her, and there lay Sisera with the tent peg through his temple—dead. ʲ

²³On that day God subdued ᵏ Jabin ᶦ king of Canaan before the Israelites. ²⁴And the hand of the Israelites pressed harder and harder against Jabin king of Canaan until they destroyed him. ᵐ

THE SONG OF DEBORAH

5 On that day Deborah ⁿ and Barak son of Abinoam ᵒ sang this song: ᵖ

² "When the princes in Israel take the lead,
    when the people willingly offer ᵠ themselves—
      praise the LORD! ʳ

³ "Hear this, you kings! Listen, you rulers!
    I, even I, will sing to ᵃ the LORD; ˢ
    I will praise the LORD, the God of Israel, in song. ᵗ

⁴ "When you, LORD, went out ᵘ from Seir, ᵛ
    when you marched from the land of Edom,
    the earth shook, ʷ the heavens poured,
      the clouds poured down water. ˣ
⁵ The mountains quaked ʸ before the LORD, the One of Sinai,
    before the LORD, the God of Israel.

⁶ "In the days of Shamgar son of Anath, ᶻ
    in the days of Jael, ᵃ the highways ᵇ were abandoned;
    travelers took to winding paths. ᶜ
⁷ Villagers in Israel would not fight;
    they held back until I, Deborah, ᵈ arose,
    until I arose, a mother in Israel.
⁸ God chose new leaders ᵉ
    when war came to the city gates, ᶠ
    but not a shield or spear ᵍ was seen
      among forty thousand in Israel.
⁹ My heart is with Israel's princes,
    with the willing volunteers ʰ among the people.
    Praise the LORD!

¹⁰ "You who ride on white donkeys, ᶦ
    sitting on your saddle blankets,
    and you who walk along the road,
    consider ¹¹the voice of the singers ᵇ at the watering places.

ᵃ 3 Or of   ᵇ 11 The meaning of the Hebrew for this word is uncertain.

4:22 *there lay Sisera...dead.* With Sisera dead the kingdom of Jabin was no longer a threat. The land "flowing with milk and honey" had been saved by the courage and faithfulness of "Bee" (see note on v. 4) and "Mountain Goat" (see note on v. 19).

5:1–31 To commemorate a national victory with songs was a common practice (see Ex 15:1–18; Nu 21:27–30; Dt 32:1–43; 1Sa 18:7). The Book of the Wars of the LORD (see note on Nu 21:14) and the Book of Jashar (see note on Jos 10:13) were probably collections of such songs.

    The song was probably written by Deborah or a contemporary (see vv. 1,3,7). It highlights some of the central themes of the narrative (cf. Ex 15:1–18; 1Sa 2:1–10; 2Sa 22; 23:1–7; Lk 1:46–55,68–79). In particular, it celebrates before the nations (v. 3) the righteous acts of the Lord and of his warriors (v. 11). The song may be divided into the following sections: (1) the purpose of the song (praise) and the occasion for the deeds it celebrates (vv. 2–9); (2) the exhortation to the Israelites to act in accordance with their heroic past (vv. 10–11a); (3) the people's appeal to Deborah (vv. 11b–12); (4) the gathering of warriors (vv. 13–18); (5) the battle (vv. 19–23); (6) the crafty triumph of

Jael over Sisera (vv. 24–27); (7) the anxious waiting of Sisera's mother (vv. 28–30); and (8) the conclusion (v. 31).

5:4–5 Poetic recalling of the Lord's terrifying appearance in a storm cloud many years before, when he had brought Israel through the wilderness into Canaan (see Dt 33:2; Ps 68:7–8; Mic 1:3–4; see also Ps 18:7–15).

5:4 *Seir.* Mt. Seir (in Edom). For a similar association of Seir (and Mount Paran) with Sinai, see Dt 33:2. *the heavens poured.* See Ps 68:7–10.

5:5 *the One of Sinai.* See Ps 68:8. An earthquake and thunderstorm occurred when God appeared at Mount Sinai (Ex 19:16–18).

5:6 *Shamgar.* See note on 3:31. *highways were abandoned.* Because of enemy garrisons and marauding bands (see note on 4:1–2) the roads were unsafe.

5:8 *not a shield or spear was seen.* Either because Israel had made peace with the native Canaanites (see 3:5–6) or because she had been disarmed (see 1Sa 13:19–22).

5:10 *who ride on white donkeys.* An allusion to the nobles and the wealthy (see 10:4; 12:14).

5:11 *voice of the singers.* The leaders are encouraged by the

They recite the victories[j] of the LORD,
the victories of his villagers in Israel.

"Then the people of the LORD
went down to the city gates.[k]
12 'Wake up,[l] wake up, Deborah![m]
Wake up, wake up, break out in song!
Arise, Barak![n]
Take captive your captives,[o] son of Abinoam.'

13 "The remnant of the nobles came down;
the people of the LORD came down to me against the mighty.
14 Some came from Ephraim,[p] whose roots were in Amalek;[q]
Benjamin[r] was with the people who followed you.
From Makir[s] captains came down,
from Zebulun those who bear a commander's[a] staff.
15 The princes of Issachar[t] were with Deborah;[u]
yes, Issachar was with Barak,[v]
sent under his command into the valley.
In the districts of Reuben
there was much searching of heart.
16 Why did you stay among the sheep pens[b][w]
to hear the whistling for the flocks?[x]
In the districts of Reuben
there was much searching of heart.
17 Gilead[y] stayed beyond the Jordan.
And Dan, why did he linger by the ships?
Asher[z] remained on the coast[a]
and stayed in his coves.
18 The people of Zebulun[b] risked their very lives;
so did Naphtali[c] on the terraced fields.[d]

19 "Kings came[e], they fought,
the kings of Canaan fought.
At Taanach, by the waters of Megiddo,[f]
they took no plunder of silver.[g]
20 From the heavens[h] the stars fought,
from their courses they fought against Sisera.
21 The river Kishon[i] swept them away,
the age-old river, the river Kishon.
March on, my soul; be strong![j]
22 Then thundered the horses' hooves—

---

[a] 14 The meaning of the Hebrew for this word is uncertain. [b] 16 Or *the campfires*; or *the saddlebags*

5:11 [j] 1Sa 12:7;
Da 9:16; Mic 6:5
[k] S ver 8
5:12 [l] Ps 44:23;
57:8; Isa 51:9,17
[m] S Jdg 4:4
[n] S Jdg 4:6 [o] Ps 68:18;
Eph 4:8
5:14 [p] S Ge 41:52;
S Jdg 1:29 [q] Jdg 3:13
[r] S Nu 34:21
[s] S Ge 50:23
5:15 [t] S Ge 30:18
[u] S Jdg 4:4 [v] S Jdg 4:6
5:16 [w] S Ge 49:14
[x] S Nu 32:1
5:17 [y] S Jos 12:2
[z] S Jos 17:7 [a] Jos 19:29
5:18 [b] S Ge 30:20
[c] S Ge 30:8; Ps 68:27
[d] S Jdg 4:6,10
5:19 [e] Jos 11:5;
S Jdg 4:13; Rev 16:16
[f] S Jos 12:21 [g] ver 30
5:20 [h] S Jos 10:11
5:21 [i] S Jdg 4:7
[j] Jos 1:6

---

songs of the minstrels at the watering places—songs that rehearse the past heroic achievements of the Lord and his warriors.

5:12 *Wake up.* A plea to take action (see Ps 44:23; Isa 51:9). *Take captive your captives.* The same action is applied to God in Ps 68:18 and to Christ in Eph 4:8 (see notes on those verses).

5:13–18 The warriors of the Lord who gathered for the battle. The tribes who came were Ephraim, Benjamin, Manasseh ("Makir" is possibly both East and West Manasseh; see Dt 3:15; Jos 13:29–31; 17:1), Zebulun (vv. 14,18), Issachar (v. 15) and Naphtali (v. 18). Especially involved were Zebulun and Naphtali (v. 18; see 4:10), the tribes most immediately affected by Sisera's tyranny. Reuben (vv. 15–16) and Gad (here referred to as Gilead, v. 17), from east of the Jordan, and Dan and Asher, from along the coast (v. 17), are rebuked for not responding. Judah and Simeon are not even mentioned, perhaps because they were already engaged with the Philistines. Levi is not mentioned because it did not have military responsibilities in the theocracy (kingdom of God).

5:14 *roots . . . in Amalek.* Some Amalekites apparently once lived in the hill country of Ephraim (see 12:15). *Makir.* The firstborn son of Manasseh (Jos 17:1). Although the descendants of

Makir settled on both sides of the Jordan (see Dt 3:15; Jos 13:29–31; 17:1; 1Ch 7:14–19), reference here is to those west of the Jordan (see v. 17; Jos 17:5).

5:19 *Megiddo.* Megiddo and Taanach dominated the main pass that runs northeast through the hill country from the plain of Sharon to the Valley of Jezreel. Because of its strategic location, the "plain of Megiddo" (2Ch 35:22) has been a frequent battleground from the earliest times. There Pharaoh Thutmose III defeated a Canaanite coalition in 1468 B.C., and there in A.D. 1917 the British under General Allenby ended the rule of the Turks in Palestine by vanquishing them in the Valley of Jezreel opposite Megiddo. In Biblical history the forces of Israel under Deborah and Barak crushed the Canaanites "by the waters of Megiddo," and there Judah's good king Josiah died in battle against Pharaoh Necho II in 609 B.C. (2Ki 23:29). See also the reference in Rev 16:16 (see note there) to "the place that in Hebrew is called Armageddon" (i.e., "Mount Megiddo") as the site of the "battle on the great day of God Almighty" (Rev 16:14).

5:20 *stars fought.* A poetic way of saying that the powers of heaven fought in Israel's behalf (see notes on 4:7; Jos 10:11; Ps 18:7–15).

5:21 *swept them away.* See note on 4:7.

5:22 *k* Jer 8:16
5:24 *l* Lk 1:42
m S Jdg 4:17
n S Ge 15:19
5:25 *o* S Ge 18:8
5:26 *p* Jdg 4:21
5:27 *q* Jdg 4:22
5:28 *r* S Jos 2:15
s Pr 7:6
5:30 *t* Ex 15:9;
1Sa 30:24; Ps 68:12
u Ps 45:14; Eze 16:10
v ver 19; 2Sa 1:24
5:31 *w* S Nu 10:35
x 2Sa 23:4; Job 37:21;
Ps 19:4; 89:36;
Isa 18:4 *y* 2Sa 18:32
z S Jdg 3:11
6:1 *a* S Jdg 2:11
b S Ge 25:2
6:2 *c* 1Sa 13:6;
Isa 5:30; 8:21; 26:16;
37:3 *d* Isa 2:19;
Jer 48:28; 49:8, 30
e Job 24:8; Jer 41:9;
Heb 11:38
6:3 *f* Nu 13:29

galloping, galloping go his mighty steeds. *k*
23 'Curse Meroz,' said the angel of the LORD.
'Curse its people bitterly,
because they did not come to help the LORD,
to help the LORD against the mighty.'

24 "Most blessed of women *l* be Jael, *m*
the wife of Heber the Kenite, *n*
most blessed of tent-dwelling women.
25 He asked for water, and she gave him milk; *o*
in a bowl fit for nobles she brought him curdled milk.
26 Her hand reached for the tent peg,
her right hand for the laborer's hammer.
She struck Sisera, she crushed his head,
she shattered and pierced his temple. *p*
27 At her feet he sank,
he fell; there he lay.
At her feet he sank, he fell;
where he sank, there he fell—dead. *q*

28 "Through the window *r* peered Sisera's mother;
behind the lattice she cried out, *s*
'Why is his chariot so long in coming?
Why is the clatter of his chariots delayed?'
29 The wisest of her ladies answer her;
indeed, she keeps saying to herself,
30 'Are they not finding and dividing the spoils: *t*
a woman or two for each man,
colorful garments as plunder for Sisera,
colorful garments embroidered,
highly embroidered garments *u* for my neck—
all this as plunder?' *v*

31 "So may all your enemies perish, *w* LORD!
But may all who love you be like the sun *x*
when it rises in its strength." *y*

Then the land had peace *z* forty years.

GIDEON

6 The Israelites did evil in the eyes of the LORD, *a* and for seven years he gave them into the hands of the Midianites. *b* 2Because the power of Midian was so oppressive, *c* the Israelites prepared shelters for themselves in mountain clefts, caves *d* and strongholds. *e* 3Whenever the Israelites planted their crops, the Midianites, Amalekites *f*

5:23 *Meroz.* Because of its refusal to help the army of the Lord, this Israelite town in Naphtali was cursed. Other cities were also punished severely for refusing to participate in the wars of the Lord (see 8:15–17; 21:5–10).

5:25 *curdled milk.* Artificially soured milk made by shaking milk in a skin-bottle and then allowing it to ferment (due to bacteria that remained in the skin from previous use).

5:28 This graphic picture of the anxious waiting of Sisera's mother heightens the triumph of Jael over the powerful Canaanite general and presents a contrast between this mother in Canaan and the triumphant Deborah, "a mother in Israel" (v. 7).

5:31 The song ends with a prayer that the present victory would be the pattern for all future battles against the Lord's enemies (see Nu 10:35; Ps 68:1–2). *your enemies ... all who love you.* The two basic attitudes of people toward the Lord. As Lord of the covenant and royal Head of his people Israel, he demanded their love (see Ex 20:6), just as kings in the ancient Near East demanded the love of their subjects. *forty years.* A conventional number of years for a generation (see Introduction: Background).

6:1—9:57 The Gideon and Abimelek narratives are a literary unit and constitute the central account of the judges. They are bracketed by the stories of Deborah (from Ephraim, a son of Joseph; west of the Jordan) and Jephthah (from Manasseh, the other son of Joseph; east of the Jordan)—which in turn are bracketed by the stories of the heroes Ehud (from Benjamin) and Samson (from Dan). In this central narrative, the crucial issues of the period of the judges are emphasized: the worship of Baal and the Lord's kingship over his covenant people Israel (see note on 8:23).

6:1 *Midianites.* See notes on Ge 37:25; Ex 2:15. Since they were apparently not numerous enough to wage war against the Israelites alone, they often formed coalitions with surrounding peoples—as with the Moabites (Nu 22:4–6; 25:6–18), the Amalekites and other tribes from the east (v. 3). Their defeat was an event long remembered in Hebrew history (see Ps 83:9; Isa 9:4; 10:26; Hab 3:7).

6:3 *Amalekites.* See note on Ge 14:7. Normally they were a people of the Negev, but they are in coalition here with the Midianites and other eastern peoples, who were nomads from the desert east of Moab and Ammon.

and other eastern peoples *g* invaded the country. [4]They camped on the land and ruined the crops *h* all the way to Gaza *i* and did not spare a living thing for Israel, neither sheep nor cattle nor donkeys. [5]They came up with their livestock and their tents like swarms of locusts. *j* It was impossible to count them or their camels; *k* they invaded the land to ravage it. [6]Midian so impoverished the Israelites that they cried out *l* to the Lord for help.

[7]When the Israelites cried out *m* to the Lord because of Midian, [8]he sent them a prophet, *n* who said, "This is what the Lord, the God of Israel, says: I brought you up out of Egypt, *o* out of the land of slavery. *p* [9]I rescued you from the hand of the Egyptians. And I delivered you from the hand of all your oppressors; *q* I drove them out before you and gave you their land. *r* [10]I said to you, 'I am the Lord your God; do not worship *s* the gods of the Amorites, *t* in whose land you live.' But you have not listened to me."

[11]The angel of the Lord *u* came and sat down under the oak in Ophrah *v* that belonged to Joash *w* the Abiezrite, *x* where his son Gideon *y* was threshing *z* wheat in a winepress *a* to keep it from the Midianites. [12]When the angel of the Lord appeared to Gideon, he said, "The Lord is with you, *b* mighty warrior. *c*"

[13]"Pardon me, my lord," Gideon replied, "but if the Lord is with us, why has all this happened to us? Where are all his wonders *d* that our ancestors told *e* us about when they said, 'Did not the Lord bring us up out of Egypt?' But now the Lord has abandoned *f* us and given us into the hand of Midian."

[14]The Lord turned to him and said, "Go in the strength you have *g* and save *h* Israel out of Midian's hand. Am I not sending you?"

[15]"Pardon me, my lord," Gideon replied, "but how can I save Israel? My clan *i* is the weakest in Manasseh, and I am the least in my family. *j*"

[16]The Lord answered, "I will be with you *k*, and you will strike down all the Midianites together."

[17]Gideon replied, "If now I have found favor in your eyes, give me a sign *l* that it is really you talking to me. [18]Please do not go away until I come back and bring my offering and set it before you."

And the Lord said, "I will wait until you return."

[19]Gideon went in, prepared a young goat, *m* and from an ephah *a n* of flour he made bread without yeast. Putting the meat in a basket and its broth in a pot, he brought them out and offered them to him under the oak. *o*

[20]The angel of God said to him, "Take the meat and the unleavened bread, place them on this rock, *p* and pour out the broth." And Gideon did so. [21]With the tip of the staff *q* that was in his hand, the angel of the Lord touched the meat and the unleavened bread. *r* Fire flared from the rock, consuming the meat and the bread. And the angel of the Lord disappeared. [22]When Gideon realized *s* that it was the angel of the Lord, he exclaimed, "Ah, Sovereign Lord! I have seen the angel of the Lord face to face!" *t*

[23]But the Lord said to him, "Peace! Do not be afraid. *u* You are not going to die." *v*

[24]So Gideon built an altar to the Lord there and called *w* it The Lord Is Peace. To this day it stands in Ophrah *x* of the Abiezrites.

[25]That same night the Lord said to him, "Take the second bull from your father's herd, the one seven years old. *b* Tear down your father's altar to Baal and cut down the Asherah

---

a 19 That is, probably about 36 pounds or about 16 kilograms
from your father's herd

b 25 Or *Take a full-grown, mature bull*

6:3 *g* S Ge 25:6;
Isa 11:14; Jer 49:28
6:4 *h* Lev 26:16;
Dt 28:30, 51; Isa 10:6;
39:6; 42:22
i S Ge 10:19
6:5 *j* S Dt 28:42
k Jdg 8:10; Isa 21:7;
60:6; Jer 49:32
6:6 *l* S Jdg 3:9
6:7 *m* S Jdg 3:9
6:8 *n* Dt 18:15;
1Ki 20:13, 22;
2Ki 17:13, 23;
Ne 9:29; Job 36:10;
Jer 25:5; Eze 18:30-31
o S Jdg 2:1 *p* Jos 24:17
6:9 *q* S Nu 10:9;
Ps 136:24 *r* Ps 44:2
6:10 *s* S Ex 20:5
t S Jos 24:15
6:11 *u* S Ge 16:7
v S Jos 18:23 *w* ver 29;
Jdg 7:14; 8:13, 29
x S Nu 26:30
y Jdg 7:1; 8:1;
Heb 11:32 *z* Ru 2:17;
3:2; 1Sa 23:1;
1Ch 21:20 *a* Ne 13:15;
Isa 16:10; 63:3;
La 1:15; Joel 3:13
6:12 *b* S Jos 1:5;
Ru 2:4; 1Sa 10:7;
Ps 129:8 *c* Jdg 11:1
6:13 *d* S Jos 3:5
e 2Sa 7:22; Ps 44:1;
78:3 *f* S Dt 31:17
6:14 *g* Heb 11:34
h ver 36; Jdg 10:1;
2Ki 14:27
6:15 *i* Isa 60:22
j 1Sa 9:21
6:16 *k* Ex 3:12;
S Nu 14:43; Jos 1:5
6:17 *l* ver 36-37;
S Ge 24:14; S Ex 3:12;
S 4:8
6:19 *m* Jdg 13:15
n S Lev 19:36
o Ge 18:7-8
6:20 *p* Jdg 13:19
6:21 *q* S Ex 4:2
r S Lev 9:24
6:22 *s* Jdg 13:16, 21
t Ge 32:30; Jdg 13:22
6:23 *u* Da 10:19
v S Ge 16:13;
S Dt 5:26
6:24 *w* S Ge 22:14
x S Jos 18:23

6:5 *swarms of locusts.* A vivid picture of the marauders who swarmed across the land, leaving it stripped bare (see 7:12; Ex 10:13–15; Joel 1:4). *camels.* The earliest OT reference to the use of mounted camels in warfare (cf. note on Ge 12:16).

6:7 *cried out to the Lord.* The Israelites' cries of distress occurred in each recurring cycle of the judges (see Introduction: Literary Features).

6:8 *prophet.* See notes on 2:1; 10:11. The unnamed prophet rebuked Israel for forgetting that the Lord had saved them from Egyptian bondage and had given them the land (vv. 9–10).

6:10 *Amorites.* Probably here includes all the inhabitants of Canaan (see note on Ge 10:16).

6:11 *angel of the Lord.* See note on Ge 16:7. *Ophrah.* To be distinguished from the Benjamite Ophrah (Jos 18:23). *Abiezrite.* The Abiezrites (v. 24) were from the tribe of Manasseh (Jos 17:2). *threshing wheat in a winepress.* Rather than in the usual, exposed area (see note on Ru 1:22). Gideon felt more secure threshing in this better protected but very confined space.

6:12 *mighty warrior.* Apparently Gideon belonged to the upper class, perhaps a kind of aristocracy (see v. 27), in spite of his disclaimer in v. 15.

6:14 *Lord turned.* See v. 23; see also note on Ge 16:7. *Go…Am I not sending you?* Gideon was commissioned to deliver Israel as Moses had been (see Ex 3:7–10).

6:15 *how can I…?* Cf. Moses' and Jeremiah's reactions to God's call to serve (Ex 3:11; 4:10; see Jer 1:6–7 and notes). The Lord usually calls the lowly rather than the mighty to act for him (see Nu 12:3 and notes on Ge 25:23; 1Sa 9:21; cf. 1Co 1:26–31 and note).

6:17 *give me a sign.* See vv. 36–40; cf. the signs the Lord gave Moses as assurance that he would be with him in his undertaking (see Ex 3:12; 4:1–17).

6:21 *consuming the meat.* Indicating that Gideon's offering was accepted (see Lev 9:24).

6:23 *not going to die.* See 13:22 and notes on Ge 16:13; 32:30.

6:25 *Tear down…altar.* Gideon's first task as the Lord's warrior

6:25 *y* ver 26, 28, 30;
Ex 34:13; S Jdg 2:13
6:26 *z* S Ge 8:20
6:28 *a* ver 30;
1Ki 16:32; 2Ki 21:3
6:29 *b* S ver 11
6:30 *c* S ver 28
6:31 *d* 1Sa 24:15;
Ps 43:1; Jer 30:13
6:32 *e* Jdg 7:1; 8:29,
35; 9:1; 1Sa 12:11
6:33 *f* Nu 13:29
g S Ge 25:6
h S Jos 15:56;
Eze 25:4; Hos 1:5
6:34 *i* S Jdg 3:10
j S Jos 6:20;
S Jdg 3:27 *k* S Jos 17:2
6:35 *l* S Jos 17:7
m S Jdg 4:6 *n* Jdg 7:23
6:36 *o* S ver 14
6:37 *p* Job 31:20
q S Nu 18:27; 2Sa 6:6;
24:16 *r* S Ge 24:14
6:39 *s* Ge 18:32
6:40 *t* Ex 3:4-7;
Isa 38:7
7:1 *u* S Jdg 6:32
v S Jdg 6:11
w 2Sa 23:25
x S Ge 25:2
y S Ge 12:6
7:2 *z* S Dt 8:17;
2Co 4:7
7:3 *a* Dt 20:8;
S Jos 12:2
7:4 *b* 1Sa 14:6

pole[a][y] beside it. [26]Then build a proper kind of[b] altar to the Lord your God on the top of this height. Using the wood of the Asherah pole that you cut down, offer the second[c] bull as a burnt offering.[z]"

[27]So Gideon took ten of his servants and did as the Lord told him. But because he was afraid of his family and the townspeople, he did it at night rather than in the daytime.

[28]In the morning when the people of the town got up, there was Baal's altar,[a] demolished, with the Asherah pole beside it cut down and the second bull sacrificed on the newly built altar!

[29]They asked each other, "Who did this?"

When they carefully investigated, they were told, "Gideon son of Joash[b] did it."

[30]The people of the town demanded of Joash, "Bring out your son. He must die, because he has broken down Baal's altar[c] and cut down the Asherah pole beside it."

[31]But Joash replied to the hostile crowd around him, "Are you going to plead Baal's cause?[d] Are you trying to save him? Whoever fights for him shall be put to death by morning! If Baal really is a god, he can defend himself when someone breaks down his altar." [32]So that day they gave Gideon the name Jerub-Baal,[d][e] saying, "Let Baal contend with him," because he broke down Baal's altar.

[33]Now all the Midianites, Amalekites[f] and other eastern peoples[g] joined forces and crossed over the Jordan and camped in the Valley of Jezreel.[h] [34]Then the Spirit of the Lord came on[i] Gideon, and he blew a trumpet,[j] summoning the Abiezrites[k] to follow him. [35]He sent messengers throughout Manasseh, calling them to arms, and also into Asher,[l] Zebulun and Naphtali,[m] so that they too went up to meet them.[n]

[36]Gideon said to God, "If you will save[o] Israel by my hand as you have promised— [37]look, I will place a wool fleece[p] on the threshing floor.[q] If there is dew only on the fleece and all the ground is dry, then I will know[r] that you will save Israel by my hand, as you said." [38]And that is what happened. Gideon rose early the next day; he squeezed the fleece and wrung out the dew—a bowlful of water.

[39]Then Gideon said to God, "Do not be angry with me. Let me make just one more request.[s] Allow me one more test with the fleece, but this time make the fleece dry and let the ground be covered with dew." [40]That night God did so. Only the fleece was dry; all the ground was covered with dew.[t]

GIDEON DEFEATS THE MIDIANITES

7 Early in the morning, Jerub-Baal[u] (that is, Gideon[v]) and all his men camped at the spring of Harod.[w] The camp of Midian[x] was north of them in the valley near the hill of Moreh.[y] [2]The Lord said to Gideon, "You have too many men. I cannot deliver Midian into their hands, or Israel would boast against me, 'My own strength[z] has saved me.' [3]Now announce to the army, 'Anyone who trembles with fear may turn back and leave Mount Gilead.[a]'" So twenty-two thousand men left, while ten thousand remained.

[4]But the Lord said to Gideon, "There are still too many[b] men. Take them down to the water, and I will sift them for you there. If I say, 'This one shall go with you,' he shall go; but if I say, 'This one shall not go with you,' he shall not go."

---

[a] 25 That is, a wooden symbol of the goddess Asherah; also in verses 26, 28 and 30   [b] 26 Or *build with layers of stone an*   [c] 26 Or *full-grown*; also in verse 28   [d] 32 *Jerub-Baal* probably means *let Baal contend.*

---

was to tear down his father's altar to Baal (cf. 2:2; Ex 34:13; Dt 7:5). *Baal.* See note on 2:13. *Asherah pole.* See TNIV text note; see also notes on 2:13; Ex 34:13.

6:26 *proper kind of altar.* See Ex 20:25.

6:30 *He must die.* The Israelites were so apostate that they were willing to kill one of their own people for the cause of Baal (contrast Dt 13:6–10, where God told Moses that idolaters must be stoned).

6:32 *Jerub-Baal.* See TNIV text note. This name later occurs as Jerub-Besheth (2Sa 11:21) by substituting a degrading term (Hebrew *bosheth,* "shameful thing") for the name of Baal (see note on Jer 2:26), as in the change of the names Esh-Baal and Merib-Baal (1Ch 8:33–34) to Ish-Bosheth and Mephibosheth (see notes on 2Sa 2:8; 4:4). *Let Baal contend with him.* Let Baal defend himself against Gideon.

6:33 *Valley of Jezreel.* See note on 5:19.

6:34 *Spirit … came on.* Lit. "Spirit … clothed himself with." This vivid figure, used only three times (here; 1Ch 12:18; 2Ch 24:20), emphasizes that the Spirit of the Lord empowered the human

agent and acted through him (see note on 3:10).

6:35 *Manasseh.* West Manasseh. *Asher.* This tribe had earlier failed to answer the call to arms (5:17).

6:39 *not be angry … just one more request.* Cf. Abraham's words in Ge 18:32.

7:1–8 As supreme commander of Israel, the Lord reduced the army so that Israel would know that the victory was by his power, not theirs.

7:1 *Harod.* Means "trembling" and may refer to either the timidity of the Israelites (v. 3) or the great panic of the Midianites when Gideon attacked (v. 21). The Hebrew verb form is translated "routing" in 8:12. *valley.* That is, the Valley of Jezreel. *hill of Moreh.* Located across the valley from Harod, approximately four miles from the Israelite army.

7:3 *may turn back.* Those who were afraid to fight the Lord's battle were not to go out with his army so that they would not demoralize the others (Dt 20:8). *Mount Gilead.* Perhaps used here as another name for Mount Gilboa.

7:6 ᶜGe 14:14
7:7 ᵈS Jos 8:7
ᵉ1Sa 14:6
7:9 ᶠver 13-15;
S Jos 2:24; S Jdg 1:2
7:12 ᵍNu 13:29
ʰS Dt 28:42;
Jer 46:23 ⁱJer 49:29
ʲS Jos 11:4

⁵So Gideon took the men down to the water. There the Lᴏʀᴅ told him, "Separate those who lap the water with their tongues like a dog from those who kneel down to drink." ⁶Three hundred of them ᶜ lapped with their hands to their mouths. All the rest got down on their knees to drink.

⁷The Lᴏʀᴅ said to Gideon, "With the three hundred men that lapped I will save you and give the Midianites into your hands. ᵈ Let all the others go, each to his own place." ᵉ ⁸So Gideon sent the rest of the Israelites to their tents but kept the three hundred, who took over the provisions and trumpets of the others.

Now the camp of Midian lay below him in the valley. ⁹During that night the Lᴏʀᴅ said to Gideon, "Get up, go down against the camp, because I am going to give it into your hands. ᶠ ¹⁰If you are afraid to attack, go down to the camp with your servant Purah ¹¹and listen to what they are saying. Afterward, you will be encouraged to attack the camp." So he and Purah his servant went down to the outposts of the camp. ¹²The Midianites, the Amalekites ᵍ and all the other eastern peoples had settled in the valley, thick as locusts. ʰ Their camels ⁱ could no more be counted than the sand on the seashore. ʲ

¹³Gideon arrived just as a man was telling a friend his dream. "I had a dream," he was saying. "A round loaf of barley bread came tumbling into the Midianite camp. It struck the tent with such force that the tent overturned and collapsed."

7:6 *lapped.* The 300 remained on their feet, prepared for any emergency.

7:8–14 The Lord provided Gideon with encouraging military intelligence for the battle.

7:13–14 Although revelations by dreams are frequently mentioned in the OT, here both dreamer and interpreter are non-Israelite. Contrast Joseph, who interpreted dreams in Egypt (Ge 40:1–22; 41:1–32), and Daniel, who interpreted dreams in Babylon (Da 2:1–45; 4:4–27).

7:13 *round loaf of barley bread.* Since barley was considered an inferior grain and only half the value of wheat (see 2Ki 7:1), it is a fitting symbol for Israel, which was inferior in numbers.

GIDEON'S BATTLES

The story of Gideon begins with a graphic portrayal of one of the most striking facts of life in the Fertile Crescent: the periodic migration of nomadic people from the Aramean desert into the settled areas of Canaan. Each spring the tents of the bedouin herdsmen appeared overnight almost as if by magic, scattered on the hills and fields of the farming districts. Conflict between these two ways of life (herdsmen and farmers) was inevitable.

In the Biblical period, the vast numbers and warlike practice of the herdsmen reduced the village people to near vassalage. God's answer was twofold: (1) religious reform, starting with Gideon's own family; and (2) military action, based on a coalition of northern Israelite tribes. The location of Gideon's hometown, "Ophrah of the Abiezrites," is not known with certainty, but probably was ancient Aper (modern Afula) in the Valley of Jezreel.

The battle at the spring of Harod is justly celebrated for its strategic brilliance. Denied the use of the only local water source, the Midianites camped in the valley and fell victim to the small band of Israelites, who attacked them from the heights of the hill of Moreh.

The main battle took place north of the hill near the village of Endor at the foot of Mount Tabor. Fleeing by way of the Jordan Valley, the Midianites were trapped when the Ephraimites seized the fords of the Jordan from below Beth Shan to Beth Barah near Adam.

7:14 *k* S Jdg 6:11
7:15 *l* 1Sa 15:31
m S ver 9
7:16 *n* Ge 14:15
o Jdg 9:43; 1Sa 11:11;
2Sa 18:2 *p* S Lev 25:9
q ver 19; Ge 24:14
r S Ge 15:17
7:18 *s* S Jdg 3:27
7:19 *t* S ver 16
7:20 *u* S Ge 15:17
v S Dt 32:41
7:21 *w* 2Ki 7:7
7:22 *x* S Jos 6:20
y 1Sa 14:20;
2Ch 20:23; Isa 9:21;
19:2; Eze 38:21;
Hag 2:22; Zec 14:13
z Hab 3:14
a 1Sa 18:19; 1Ki 4:12;
19:16
7:23 *b* S Jos 17:7
c Jdg 6:35 *d* Ps 83:9
7:24 *e* S Jos 2:7
7:25 *f* Jdg 8:3;
Ps 83:11 *g* Isa 10:26
h Isa 9:4; Jdg 8:4;
Ps 106:43
8:1 *i* S Jdg 6:11
k S Ge 25:2 *j* Jdg 12:1
m 2Sa 19:41
8:2 *n* S Nu 26:30
8:3 *o* S Jdg 7:25
8:4 *p* Jdg 7:25
8:5 *q* S Ge 33:17
r Job 16:7; Ps 6:6;
Jer 45:3 *s* ver 7,12;
Ps 83:11
8:6 *t* ver 14
u 1Sa 25:11 *v* ver 15

[14]His friend responded, "This can be nothing other than the sword of Gideon son of Joash, *k* the Israelite. God has given the Midianites and the whole camp into his hands."

[15]When Gideon heard the dream and its interpretation, he bowed down and worshiped. *l* He returned to the camp of Israel and called out, "Get up! The LORD has given the Midianite camp into your hands." *m* [16]Dividing the three hundred men *n* into three companies, *o* he placed trumpets *p* and empty jars *q* in the hands of all of them, with torches *r* inside.

[17]"Watch me," he told them. "Follow my lead. When I get to the edge of the camp, do exactly as I do. [18]When I and all who are with me blow our trumpets, *s* then from all around the camp blow yours and shout, 'For the LORD and for Gideon.' "

[19]Gideon and the hundred men with him reached the edge of the camp at the beginning of the middle watch, just after they had changed the guard. They blew their trumpets and broke the jars *t* that were in their hands. [20]The three companies blew the trumpets and smashed the jars. Grasping the torches *u* in their left hands and holding in their right hands the trumpets they were to blow, they shouted, "A sword *v* for the LORD and for Gideon!" [21]While each man held his position around the camp, all the Midianites ran, crying out as they fled. *w*

[22]When the three hundred trumpets sounded, *x* the LORD caused the men throughout the camp to turn on each other *y* with their swords. *z* The army fled to Beth Shittah toward Zererah as far as the border of Abel Meholah *a* near Tabbath. [23]Israelites from Naphtali, Asher *b* and all Manasseh were called out, *c* and they pursued the Midianites. *d* [24]Gideon sent messengers throughout the hill country of Ephraim, saying, "Come down against the Midianites and seize the waters of the Jordan *e* ahead of them as far as Beth Barah."

So all the men of Ephraim were called out and they seized the waters of the Jordan as far as Beth Barah. [25]They also captured two of the Midianite leaders, Oreb and Zeeb *f*. They killed Oreb at the rock of Oreb, *g* and Zeeb at the winepress of Zeeb. They pursued the Midianites *h* and brought the heads of Oreb and Zeeb to Gideon, who was by the Jordan. *i*

ZEBAH AND ZALMUNNA

8 Now the Ephraimites asked Gideon, *j* "Why have you treated us like this? Why didn't you call us when you went to fight Midian? *k* *l* And they challenged him vigorously. *m*

[2]But he answered them, "What have I accomplished compared to you? Aren't the gleanings of Ephraim's grapes better than the full grape harvest of Abiezer? *n* [3]God gave Oreb and Zeeb, *o* the Midianite leaders, into your hands. What was I able to do compared to you?" At this, their resentment against him subsided.

[4]Gideon and his three hundred men, exhausted yet keeping up the pursuit, came to the Jordan *p* and crossed it. [5]He said to the men of Sukkoth, *q* "Give my troops some bread; they are worn out, *r* and I am still pursuing Zebah and Zalmunna, *s* the kings of Midian."

[6]But the officials of Sukkoth *t* said, "Do you already have the hands of Zebah and Zalmunna in your possession? Why should we give bread *u* to your troops?" *v*

7:16 *three companies.* A strategy adopted by Israel on several occasions (9:43; 1Sa 11:11; 2Sa 18:2). *trumpets.* Rams' horns (see Ex 19:13).

7:19 *middle watch.* The Israelites divided the night into three watches (see note on Mt 14:25). The "beginning of the middle watch" would be after the enemy had gone to sleep.

7:22 *three hundred trumpets.* Normally only a comparatively small number of men in an army carried trumpets. *turn on each other.* A similar panic occurred among the Ammonites, Moabites and Edomites (2Ch 20:23) and, on a somewhat smaller scale, among the Philistines at Gibeah (1Sa 14:20). See Eze 38:21; Zec 14:13; see also note on Jdg 4:15. *toward Zererah.* Toward the southeast.

7:23 *were called out.* Encouraged by the turn of events, many of those who had departed now joined the battle.

7:24 *hill country of Ephraim.* Gideon needed the aid of the Ephraimites to cut off the retreat of the Midianites into the Jordan Valley. *waters of the Jordan.* Probably the river crossings in the vicinity of Beth Shan. By controlling the river the Israelites could prevent the escape of the fleeing Midianites (see note on 3:28). *Beth Barah.* Exact location unknown, but it must have been some distance down the river. Gideon's pursuit of the enemy across the

river took him to Sukkoth, a town near the Jabbok River (8:5).

7:25 *Oreb.* Means "raven" (see Isa 10:26). *Zeeb.* Means "wolf." *heads.* Frequently parts of the bodies of dead victims, such as heads, hands (8:6) and foreskins (1Sa 18:25), were cut off and brought back as a kind of body count.

8:1 *Ephraimites.* Contrast Gideon, who placates the wrath of this tribe (vv. 2–3), with Jephthah, who brings humiliation and defeat to it (12:1–6).

8:2 *gleanings.* Leftover grain after the main gathering of the harvest (see note on Ru 1:22). Here Gideon implies that Ephraim has accomplished more than he and all the other forces involved in the initial attack. *Abiezer.* Gideon's clan (see note on 6:11). The name means "My (divine) Father is helper" or "My (divine) Father is strong."

A **8:3** *their resentment ... subsided.* "A gentle answer turns away wrath" (Pr 15:1).

8:5 *kings of Midian.* Zebah and Zalmunna may have belonged to different Midianite tribes (see Nu 31:8).

8:6 *hands.* See note on 7:25. *Why should we give bread ... ?* The officials of Sukkoth doubted Gideon's ability to defeat the Midianite coalition and feared reprisal if they gave his army food.

⁷Then Gideon replied, "Just for that, when the LORD has given Zebah and Zalmunna ʷ into my hand, I will tear your flesh with desert thorns and briers."

⁸From there he went up to Peniel ᵃˣ and made the same request of them, but they answered as the men of Sukkoth had. ⁹So he said to the men of Peniel, "When I return in triumph, I will tear down this tower." ʸ

¹⁰Now Zebah and Zalmunna were in Karkor with a force of about fifteen thousand men, all that were left of the armies of the eastern peoples; a hundred and twenty thousand swordsmen had fallen. ᶻ ¹¹Gideon went up by the route of the nomads east of Nobah ᵃ and Jogbehah ᵇ and attacked the unsuspecting army. ¹²Zebah and Zalmunna, the two kings of Midian, fled, but he pursued them and captured them, routing their entire army.

¹³Gideon son of Joash ᶜ then returned from the battle by the Pass of Heres. ᵈ ¹⁴He caught a young man of Sukkoth and questioned him, and the young man wrote down for him the names of the seventy-seven officials of Sukkoth, ᵉ the elders ᶠ of the town. ¹⁵Then Gideon came and said to the men of Sukkoth, "Here are Zebah and Zalmunna, about whom you taunted me by saying, 'Do you already have the hands of Zebah and Zalmunna in your possession? Why should we give bread to your exhausted troops? ᵍ' " ¹⁶He took the elders of the town and taught the men of Sukkoth a lesson ʰ by punishing them with desert thorns and briers. ¹⁷He also pulled down the tower of Peniel ⁱ and killed the men of the town.ʲ

¹⁸Then he asked Zebah and Zalmunna, "What kind of men did you kill at Tabor? ᵏ"

"Men like you," they answered, "each one with the bearing of a prince."

¹⁹Gideon replied, "Those were my brothers, the sons of my own mother. As surely as the LORD lives, ˡ if you had spared their lives, I would not kill you." ²⁰Turning to Jether, his oldest son, he said, "Kill them!" But Jether did not draw his sword, because he was only a boy and was afraid.

²¹Zebah and Zalmunna said, "Come, do it yourself. 'As is the man, so is his strength.' " So Gideon stepped forward and killed them, and took the ornaments ᵐ off their camels' necks.

GIDEON'S EPHOD

²²The Israelites said to Gideon, "Rule over us—you, your son and your grandson—because you have saved us from the hand of Midian."

²³But Gideon told them, "I will not rule over you, nor will my son rule over you. The LORD will rule ⁿ over you." ²⁴And he said, "I do have one request, that each of you give me an earring ᵒ from your share of the plunder. ᵖ" (It was the custom of the Ishmaelites �q to wear gold earrings.)

²⁵They answered, "We'll be glad to give them." So they spread out a garment, and each of them threw a ring from his plunder onto it. ²⁶The weight of the gold rings he asked for came to seventeen hundred shekels, ᵇ not counting the ornaments, the pendants and the purple garments worn by the kings of Midian or the chains ʳ that were on their camels' necks. ²⁷Gideon made the gold into an ephod, ˢ which he placed in Ophrah, ᵗ his town. All Israel prostituted themselves by worshiping it there, and it became a snare ᵘ to Gideon and his family. ᵛ

GIDEON'S DEATH

²⁸Thus Midian was subdued before the Israelites and did not raise its head ʷ again. During Gideon's lifetime, the land had peace ˣ forty years.

²⁹Jerub-Baal ʸ son of Joash ᶻ went back home to live. ³⁰He had seventy sons ᵃ of his own,

---

ᵃ 8 Hebrew *Penuel*, a variant of *Peniel*; also in verses 9 and 17   ᵇ 26 That is, about 43 pounds or about
20 kilograms

8:7 ʷ S ver 5
8:8 ˣ ver 9,17;
Ge 32:30; 1Ki 12:25
8:9 ʸ ver 17
8:10 ᶻ S Jdg 6:5;
Isa 9:4
8:11 ᵃ Nu 32:42
ᵇ Nu 32:35
8:13 ᶜ S Jdg 6:11
ᵈ Jdg 1:35
8:14 ᵉ ver 6
ᶠ S Ex 3:16
8:15 ᵍ ver 6
8:16 ʰ 1Sa 14:12
8:17 ⁱ S ver 8 / ver 9
8:18 ᵏ S Jos 19:22
8:19 ˡ S Nu 14:21
8:21 ᵐ ver 26;
Isa 3:18
8:23 ⁿ S Ex 16:8;
S Nu 11:20; 1Sa 12:12
8:24 ᵒ S Ge 35:4
ᵖ S Ge 49:27
�q S Ge 16:11
8:26 ʳ S ver 21
8:27 ˢ S Ex 25:7;
Jdg 17:5; 18:14
ᵗ S Jos 18:23
ᵘ S Ex 10:7
ᵛ S Ex 32:2
8:28 ʷ Ps 83:2
ˣ S Jdg 3:11
8:29 ʸ S Jdg 6:32
ᶻ S Jdg 6:11
8:30 ᵃ Jdg 9:2,5,18,
24; 12:14; 2Ki 10:1

8:8 *Peniel.* The place where Jacob had wrestled with God (Ge 32:30–31).

8:19 *sons of my own mother.* In an age when men often had several wives it was necessary to distinguish between full brothers and half brothers.

8:21 *do it yourself.* Dying at the hands of a boy may have been considered a disgrace (see 1Sa 17:42). *ornaments.* Crescent necklaces, as in Isa 3:18.

▲ **8:23** *I will not rule … The LORD will rule.* Gideon, like Samuel (1Sa 8:4–20), rejected the establishment of a monarchy because he regarded it as a replacement of the Lord's rule. God's rule over Israel (theocracy) is a central issue in Judges.

8:24 *earring.* Or possibly "nose ring" (see Ge 24:47; Eze 16:12).

Ishmaelites. Related to the Midianites (Ge 25:1–2) and sometimes identified with them (vv. 22,24; Ge 37:25–28; 39:1). See note on Ge 37:25.

8:27 *ephod.* Sometimes a holy garment associated with the priesthood (Ex 28:6–30; 39:2–26; Lev 8:7) and at other times a pagan object associated with idols (17:5; 18:14,17). *prostituted themselves.* See Ex 34:15 and note.

8:28 *forty years.* A conventional number of years for a generation (see Introduction: Background).

8:29 *Jerub-Baal.* See note on 6:32.

8:30 *seventy sons.* A sign of power and prosperity (see 12:14; 2Ki 10:1).

8:31 ^b S Ge 22:24
^c Jdg 9:1; 10:1;
2Sa 11:21
8:32 ^d S Ge 15:15
8:33 ^e S Jdg 2:11,13,
19 ^f Jdg 9:4
^g Jdg 9:27,46
8:34 ^h S Jdg 3:7;
S Ne 9:17
8:35 ⁱ S Jdg 6:32
^j Jdg 9:16
9:1 ^k S Jdg 8:31
^l S Jdg 6:32
9:2 ^m S Ge 29:14
9:4 ⁿ S Jdg 8:33
^o Jdg 11:3; 1Sa 25:25;
2Ch 13:7; Job 30:8
9:5 ^p S Jdg 8:30
^q ver 7, 21,57
^r 2Ki 11:2; 2Ch 22:9
9:6 ^s ver 20;
2Ki 12:20 ^t S Ge 12:6;
S Jdg 4:11
9:7 ^u S ver 5
^v S Dt 11:29; Jn 4:20

for he had many wives. ³¹His concubine, ^b who lived in Shechem, also bore him a son, whom he named Abimelek. ^{c 32}Gideon son of Joash died at a good old age ^d and was buried in the tomb of his father Joash in Ophrah of the Abiezrites.

³³No sooner had Gideon died than the Israelites again prostituted themselves to the Baals. ^e They set up Baal-Berith ^f as their god ^{g 34}and did not remember ^h the LORD their God, who had rescued them from the hands of all their enemies on every side. ³⁵They also failed to show any loyalty to the family of Jerub-Baal ⁱ (that is, Gideon) in spite of all the good things he had done for them. ^j

ABIMELEK

9 Abimelek ^k son of Jerub-Baal ^l went to his mother's brothers in Shechem and said to them and to all his mother's clan, ²"Ask all the citizens of Shechem, 'Which is better for you: to have all seventy of Jerub-Baal's sons rule over you, or just one man?' Remember, I am your flesh and blood. ^m"

³When the brothers repeated all this to the citizens of Shechem, they were inclined to follow Abimelek, for they said, "He is related to us." ⁴They gave him seventy shekels^a of silver from the temple of Baal-Berith, ⁿ and Abimelek used it to hire reckless scoundrels, ^o who became his followers. ⁵He went to his father's home in Ophrah and on one stone murdered his seventy brothers, ^p the sons of Jerub-Baal. But Jotham, ^q the youngest son of Jerub-Baal, escaped by hiding. ^{r 6}Then all the citizens of Shechem and Beth Millo ^s gathered beside the great tree ^t at the pillar in Shechem to crown Abimelek king.

⁷When Jotham ^u was told about this, he climbed up on the top of Mount Gerizim ^v and shouted to them, "Listen to me, citizens of Shechem, so that God may listen to you. ⁸One day the trees went out to anoint a king for themselves. They said to the olive tree, 'Be our king.'

⁹"But the olive tree answered, 'Should I give up my oil, by which both gods and human beings are honored, to hold sway over the trees?'

¹⁰"Next, the trees said to the fig tree, 'Come and be our king.'

¹¹"But the fig tree replied, 'Should I give up my fruit, so good and sweet, to hold sway over the trees?'

^a 4 That is, about 1 3/4 pounds or about 800 grams

A **8:31** *concubine.* She was originally a slave in his household (9:18; see note on Ge 16:2). *Abimelek.* Appears elsewhere as a royal title (Ge 20:2; 26:1; Ps 34 title) and means "My (divine) Father is King." Gideon, in naming his son, acknowledges that the Lord (here called "Father") is King.

8:32 *at a good old age.* A phrase used elsewhere only of Abraham (Ge 15:15; 25:8) and David (1Ch 29:28).

8:33 *prostituted themselves.* See Ex 34:15 and note. *Baals.* See notes on 2:11,13. *Baal-Berith.* Means "lord of the covenant"; the same deity is called El-Berith ("god of the covenant") in 9:46. There was a temple dedicated to him (see 9:4) in Shechem. The word "covenant" in his name probably refers to a solemn treaty that bound together a league of Canaanite cities whose people worshiped him as their god. Ironically, Shechem (v. 31), near Mount Ebal, was the site at which Joshua had twice renewed the Lord's covenant with the Israelites after they had entered Canaan (Jos 8:30–35; 24:25–27). See also note on 2:11.

A **9:1–57** The stories of Gideon and Abimelek form the literary center of Judges (see Introduction: Literary Features). Abimelek, who tried to set himself up like a Canaanite city king with the help of Baal (v. 4), stands in sharp contrast to his father, Gideon (Jerub-Baal), who had attacked Baal worship and insisted that the Lord ruled over Israel. Abimelek attempted this Canaanite revival in the very place where Joshua had earlier reaffirmed Israel's allegiance to the Lord (Jos 24:14–27). In every respect Abimelek was the antithesis of the Lord's appointed judges.

B **9:1** *Shechem.* See note on Ge 33:18. Ruins dating from the Canaanite era give evidence of a sacred area, probably to be associated with the temple of Baal-Berith or El-Berith (vv. 4,46). Archaeological evidence, which is compatible with the destruction of Shechem by Abimelek, indicates that its sacred area was never rebuilt after this time.

9:2 *citizens.* The singular form of the Hebrew for this word is *ba'al.* It means "lord" or "owner" and probably refers here to the aristocracy or landowners of the city. *flesh and blood.* Being half-Canaanite, Abimelek intimated that it was in their best interest to make him king rather than be under the rule of Gideon's other 70 sons. The following he gathered was based on this relationship and became a threat to the people of Israel.

B **9:4** *from the temple.* Ancient temples served as depositories for personal and civic funds. The payments of vows and penalties, as well as gifts, were also part of the temple treasury. The temple of Baal-Berith is probably to be identified with a large building found at Shechem by archaeologists. *reckless scoundrels.* Use of mercenaries to accomplish political or military goals was common in ancient times. Others who used them are Jephthah (11:3), David (1Sa 22:1–2), Absalom (2Sa 15:1), Adonijah (1Ki 1:5), Rezon (1Ki 11:23–24) and Jeroboam (2Ch 13:6–7).

9:5 *one on stone.* Abimelek's 70 brothers were slaughtered like sacrificial animals (see 13:19–20; 1Sa 14:33–34). In effect, he inaugurated his kingship by using his Israelite half brothers as his coronation sacrifices (see 2Sa 15:10,12; 1Ki 1:5,9; 3:4).

9:6 *Beth Millo.* "Millo" is derived from a Hebrew verb meaning "to fill" and perhaps refers to the earthen fill on which walls and other large structures were built. Beth Millo may be identical to the "stronghold" of v. 46. *great tree.* See Jos 24:25–26; see also note on Ge 12:6.

9:7 *top.* Probably a ledge that overlooked the city.

9:8 *trees went out.* Fables of this type, in which inanimate objects speak and act, were popular among Eastern peoples of that time (see 2Ki 14:9).

9:9–13 The olive tree, the fig tree and the vine were all plants that produced fruit of great importance to the people of the Near East.

¹²"Then the trees said to the vine, 'Come and be our king.'

¹³"But the vine answered, 'Should I give up my wine,^w which cheers both gods and human beings, to hold sway over the trees?'

¹⁴"Finally all the trees said to the thornbush, 'Come and be our king.'

¹⁵"The thornbush said to the trees, 'If you really want to anoint me king over you, come and take refuge in my shade;^x but if not, then let fire come out^y of the thornbush and consume the cedars of Lebanon!'^z

¹⁶"Have you acted honorably and in good faith by making Abimelek king? Have you been fair to Jerub-Baal and his family? Have you treated him as he deserves? ¹⁷Remember that my father fought for you and risked^a his life to rescue you from the hand of Midian. ¹⁸But today you have revolted against my father's family. You have murdered his seventy sons^b on a single stone and have made Abimelek, the son of his female slave, king over the citizens of Shechem because he is related to you. ¹⁹So have you acted honorably and in good faith toward Jerub-Baal and his family today?^c If you have, may Abimelek be your joy, and may you be his, too! ²⁰But if you have not, let fire come out^d from Abimelek and consume you, the citizens of Shechem^e and Beth Millo,^f and let fire come out from you, the citizens of Shechem and Beth Millo, and consume Abimelek!"

²¹Then Jotham^g fled, escaping to Beer,^h and he lived there because he was afraid of his brother Abimelek.

²²After Abimelek had governed Israel three years, ²³God stirred up animosityⁱ between Abimelek and the citizens of Shechem so that they acted treacherously against Abimelek. ²⁴God did this in order that the crime against Jerub-Baal's seventy sons,^j the shedding^k of their blood, might be avenged^l on their brother Abimelek and on the citizens of Shechem, who had helped him^m murder his brothers. ²⁵In opposition to him these citizens of Shechem set an ambush on the hilltops to rob everyone who passed by, and this was reported to Abimelek.

²⁶Now Gaal son of Ebedⁿ moved with his brothers into Shechem, and its citizens put their confidence in him. ²⁷After they had gone out into the fields and gathered the grapes and trodden^o them, they held a festival in the temple of their god.^p While they were eating and drinking, they cursed Abimelek. ²⁸Then Gaal son of Ebed^q said, "Who^r is Abimelek, and who is Shechem, that we should be subject to him? Isn't he Jerub-Baal's son, and isn't Zebul his deputy? Serve the people of Hamor,^s Shechem's father! Why should we serve Abimelek? ²⁹If only this people were under my command!^t Then I would get rid of him. I would say to Abimelek, 'Call out your whole army!'"^a^u

³⁰When Zebul the governor of the city heard what Gaal son of Ebed said, he was very angry. ³¹Under cover he sent messengers to Abimelek, saying, "Gaal son of Ebed and his relatives have come to Shechem and are stirring up the city against you. ³²Now then, during the night you and your men should come and lie in wait^v in the fields. ³³In the morning at sunrise, advance against the city. When Gaal and his men come out against you, do whatever your hand finds to do.^w"

³⁴So Abimelek and all his troops set out by night and took up concealed positions near Shechem in four companies. ³⁵Now Gaal son of Ebed had gone out and was standing at

---

^a 29 Septuagint; Hebrew *him.*" Then he said to Abimelek, "Call out your whole army!"

9:13 ^w S Ge 14:18; Ecc 2:3; SS 4:10
9:15 ^x Isa 30:2 ^y ver 20 ^z S Dt 3:25; 1Ki 5:6; Ps 29:5; 92:12; Isa 2:13
9:17 ^a Jdg 12:3; 1Sa 19:5; 28:21; Job 13:14; Ps 119:109
9:18 ^b S Jdg 8:30
9:19 ^c ver 16
9:20 ^d ver 15 ^e ver 45 ^f S ver 6
9:21 ^g S ver 5 ^h Nu 21:16
9:23 ⁱ 1Sa 16:14,23; 18:10; 19:9; 1Ki 22:22
9:24 ^j S Jdg 8:30 ^k S Ge 9:6; Nu 35:33; 1Ki 2:32 ^l ver 56-57 ^m Dt 27:25
9:26 ⁿ ver 28,31,41
9:27 ^o Isa 16:10; Am 5:11; 9:13 ^p S Jdg 8:33
9:28 ^q S ver 26 ^r 1Sa 25:10 ^s S Ge 33:19
9:29 ^t 2Sa 15:4 ^u ver 38
9:32 ^v Jos 8:2
9:33 ^w 1Sa 10:7

9:13 *gods.* It was commonly believed that the gods participated in such human experiences as drinking wine (cf. Ex 29:40).

9:14 *thornbush.* Probably the well-known buckthorn, a scraggly bush common in the hills of Israel and a constant menace to farming. It produced nothing of value and was an apt figure for Abimelek.

9:15 *shade.* Ironically, in offering shade to the trees, the thornbush symbolized the traditional role of kings as protectors of their subjects (see Isa 30:2–3; 32:1–2; La 4:20; Da 4:12). *cedars of Lebanon.* The most valuable of Near Eastern trees, here symbolic of the leading men of Shechem (see v. 20).

9:20 *fire come out … and consume.* A grim prediction that Abimelek and the people of Shechem would destroy each other. Fire spreads rapidly through bramble bushes and brings about swift destruction (see Ex 22:6; Isa 9:18).

9:21 *Beer.* A very common name, meaning "a well."

9:22 *Israel.* Those Israelites who recognized Abimelek's authority, mainly in the vicinity of Shechem.

9:23 *animosity.* The Hebrew for "animosity" is frequently rendered "evil spirit" or "harmful spirit" (cf., e.g, 1Sa 16:14 and TNIV text note); here perhaps a "spirit" of distrust and bitterness. The Hebrew for "spirit" is often used to describe an attitude or disposition. *acted treacherously.* The one who founded his kingdom by treachery is himself undone by treachery.

9:26 *put their confidence in him.* Just as the fickle population had followed Abimelek, so they are now swayed by the deceptive proposals of Gaal.

9:27 *held a festival.* The vintage harvest was one of the most joyous times of the year (see Isa 16:9–10; Jer 25:30), but festivals and celebrations held at pagan temples often degenerated into debauched drinking affairs.

9:28 *Hamor.* The Hivite ruler who had founded the city of Shechem (Ge 33:19; 34:2; Jos 24:32).

9:32 *lie in wait.* Ambush succeeded against Gibeah in Benjamin (20:37) and against Ai (Jos 8:2).

9:34 *four companies.* Smaller segments meant less chance of detection. Also, attack from several directions was a good tactical strategy.

9:35 ˣ S Jos 2:5
ʸ Ps 32:7; Isa 28:15,
17; Jer 49:10
9:38 ᶻ ver 28-29
9:43 ᵃ S Jdg 7:16
ᵇ Jos 8:2
9:45 ᶜ ver 20
ᵈ Jer 48:9
9:46 ᵉ S Jdg 8:33
9:48 ᶠ Ps 68:14
9:50 ᵍ 2Sa 11:21
9:53 ʰ 2Sa 11:21
9:54 ⁱ 1Sa 31:4;
2Sa 1:9
9:57 ʲ ver 24;
Ps 94:23 ᵏ S ver 5
10:1 ˡ S Jdg 8:31
ᵐ Ge 30:18
ⁿ S Ge 46:13
ᵒ S Jdg 6:14
ᵖ Jos 15:48

the entrance of the city gate ˣ just as Abimelek and his troops came out from their hiding place. ʸ

³⁶When Gaal saw them, he said to Zebul, "Look, people are coming down from the tops of the mountains!"

Zebul replied, "You mistake the shadows of the mountains for men."

³⁷But Gaal spoke up again: "Look, people are coming down from the central hill, ᵃ and a company is coming from the direction of the diviners' tree."

³⁸Then Zebul said to him, "Where is your big talk now, you who said, 'Who is Abimelek that we should be subject to him?' Aren't these the men you ridiculed? ᶻ Go out and fight them!"

³⁹So Gaal led out ᵇ the citizens of Shechem and fought Abimelek. ⁴⁰Abimelek chased him all the way to the entrance of the gate, and many fell slain as they fled. ⁴¹Abimelek stayed in Arumah, and Zebul drove Gaal and his relatives out of Shechem.

⁴²The next day the people of Shechem went out to the fields, and this was reported to Abimelek. ⁴³So he took his troops, divided them into three companies ᵃ and set an ambush ᵇ in the fields. When he saw the people coming out of the city, he rose to attack them. ⁴⁴Abimelek and the companies with him rushed forward to a position at the entrance of the city gate. Then two companies attacked those in the fields and struck them down. ⁴⁵All that day Abimelek pressed his attack against the city until he had captured it and killed its people. Then he destroyed the city ᶜ and scattered salt ᵈ over it.

⁴⁶On hearing this, the citizens in the tower of Shechem went into the stronghold of the temple ᵉ of El-Berith. ⁴⁷When Abimelek heard that they had assembled there, ⁴⁸he and all his men went up Mount Zalmon. ᶠ He took an ax and cut off some branches, which he lifted to his shoulders. He ordered the men with him, "Quick! Do what you have seen me do!" ⁴⁹So all the men cut branches and followed Abimelek. They piled them against the stronghold and set it on fire with the people still inside. So all the people in the tower of Shechem, about a thousand men and women, also died.

⁵⁰Next Abimelek went to Thebez ᵍ and besieged it and captured it. ⁵¹Inside the city, however, was a strong tower, to which all the men and women—all the people of the city—had fled. They had locked themselves in and climbed up on the tower roof. ⁵²Abimelek went to the tower and attacked it. But as he approached the entrance to the tower to set it on fire, ⁵³a woman dropped an upper millstone on his head and cracked his skull. ʰ ⁵⁴Hurriedly he called to his armor-bearer, "Draw your sword and kill me, ⁱ so that they can't say, 'A woman killed him.' " So his servant ran him through, and he died. ⁵⁵When the Israelites saw that Abimelek was dead, they went home.

⁵⁶Thus God repaid the wickedness that Abimelek had done to his father by murdering his seventy brothers. ⁵⁷God also made the people of Shechem pay for all their wickedness. ʲ The curse of Jotham ᵏ son of Jerub-Baal came on them.

TOLA

10

After the time of Abimelek, ˡ a man of Issachar ᵐ named Tola son of Puah, ⁿ the son of Dodo, rose to save ᵒ Israel. He lived in Shamir, ᵖ in the hill country of Ephraim. ²He led ᶜ Israel twenty-three years; then he died, and was buried in Shamir.

ᵃ 37 The Hebrew for this phrase means *the navel of the earth.* ᵇ 39 Or *Gaal went out in the sight of*
ᶜ 2 Traditionally *judged*; also in verse 3

9:37 *central hill.* See TNIV text note; see also note on Eze 38:12, where the same Hebrew is translated "center of the land." *diviners' tree.* Probably a sacred tree in some way related to the temple of Baal-Berith (see note on Ge 12:6).

9:43 *three companies.* See note on 7:16.

9:45 *scattered salt over it.* To condemn it to perpetual barrenness and desolation (see Dt 29:23; Ps 107:33–34; Jer 17:6; Zep 2:9).

9:46 *stronghold.* Probably the Beth Millo of v. 6. *El-Berith.* Baal-Berith (v. 4).

9:49 *set it on fire.* In fulfillment of Jotham's curse (v. 20).

9:53 *woman.* While the men used bows, arrows and spears, women helped to defend the tower by dropping heavy stones on those who came near it. *upper millstone.* See note on 3:16. The upper, revolving stone of a mill was circular, with a hole in the center. Grinding grain was women's work (see Ex 11:5), usu-

ally considered too lowly for men to perform (see 16:21). Abimelek was killed by a woman using a domestic implement (see also 4:21).

9:54 *armor-bearer.* In Israel's earlier years in Canaan, military leaders were usually served by a personal attendant (see 1Sa 14:6; 31:4), but no armor-bearers are mentioned after the time of David. *A woman killed him.* It was considered a disgrace for a soldier to die at the hands of a woman. Abimelek's shameful death was long remembered (2Sa 11:21).

A **9:56** *God repaid.* God was in control of the events. As Israel's true King, he brought Abimelek's wickedness to a quick and shameful end.

9:57 *curse of Jotham.* See v. 20.

10:1 *a man of Issachar named Tola son of Puah.* Tola and Puah bear names of two of the sons of Issachar (Ge 46:13; Nu 26:23; 1Ch 7:1).

JAIR

³He was followed by Jair *q* of Gilead, who led Israel twenty-two years. ⁴He had thirty sons, who rode thirty donkeys. *r* They controlled thirty towns in Gilead, which to this day are called Havvoth Jair. *a s* ⁵When Jair *t* died, he was buried in Kamon.

JEPHTHAH

⁶Again the Israelites did evil in the eyes of the LORD. *u* They served the Baals and the Ashtoreths, *v* and the gods of Aram, *w* the gods of Sidon, *x* the gods of Moab, the gods of the Ammonites *yz* and the gods of the Philistines. *a* And because the Israelites forsook the LORD *b* and no longer served him, ⁷he became angry *c* with them. He sold them *d* into the hands of the Philistines and the Ammonites, ⁸who that year shattered and crushed them. For eighteen years they oppressed all the Israelites on the east side of the Jordan in Gilead, *e* the land of the Amorites. ⁹The Ammonites also crossed the Jordan to fight against Judah, *f* Benjamin and the house of Ephraim; *g* and Israel was in great distress. ¹⁰Then the Israelites cried *h* out to the LORD, "We have sinned *i* against you, forsaking our God and serving the Baals." *j*

¹¹The LORD replied, "When the Egyptians, *k* the Amorites, *l* the Ammonites, *m* the Philistines, *n* ¹²the Sidonians, the Amalekites *o* and the Maonites *b p* oppressed you *q* and you cried to me for help, did I not save you from their hands? ¹³But you have forsaken *r* me and served other gods, *s* so I will no longer save you. ¹⁴Go and cry out to the gods you have chosen. Let them save *t* you when you are in trouble! *u*"

¹⁵But the Israelites said to the LORD, "We have sinned. Do with us whatever you think best, *v* but please rescue us now." ¹⁶Then they got rid of the foreign gods among them and served the LORD. *w* And he could bear Israel's misery *x* no longer. *y*

¹⁷When the Ammonites were called to arms and camped in Gilead, the Israelites assembled and camped at Mizpah. *z* ¹⁸The leaders of the people of Gilead said to each other, "Whoever will take the lead in attacking the Ammonites will be head *a* over all who live in Gilead."

11 Jephthah *b* the Gileadite was a mighty warrior. *c* His father was Gilead; *d* his mother was a prostitute. *e* ²Gilead's wife also bore him sons, and when they were grown up, they drove Jephthah away. "You are not going to get any inheritance in our family," they said, "because you are the son of another woman." ³So Jephthah fled from his brothers and settled in the land of Tob, *f* where a gang of scoundrels *g* gathered around him and followed him.

⁴Some time later, when the Ammonites *h* were fighting against Israel, ⁵the elders of

---

a 4 Or *called the settlements of Jair*   *b 12* Hebrew; some Septuagint manuscripts *Midianites*

### Cross references (right margin)

10:3 *q* S Nu 32:41
10:4 *r* S Ge 49:11; S 1Ki 1:33
s S Nu 32:41
10:5 *t* S Nu 32:41
10:6 *u* S Jdg 2:11
v S Jdg 2:13
w Eze 27:16
x S Ge 10:15
y S Ge 19:38
z S Nu 21:29
a S Ge 26:1; S Jdg 2:12
b S Dt 32:15
10:7 *c* S Dt 31:17
d S Dt 32:30
10:8 *e* S Jos 12:2
10:9 *f* ver 17; Jdg 11:4 *g* Jdg 1:22
10:10 *h* S Jdg 3:9
i S Ex 9:27; Ps 32:5; Jer 3:25; 8:14; 14:20
j Jer 2:27
10:11 *k* Ex 14:30
l S Ge 14:7
m S Jdg 3:13
n S Jdg 3:31
10:12 *o* S Ge 14:7
p S Jos 15:55
q S Jdg 4:3
10:13 *r* S Dt 32:15
s Jer 11:10; 13:10
10:14 *t* Isa 44:17; 57:13 *u* Dt 32:37;
Jer 2:28; 11:12; Hab 2:18
10:15 *v* 1Sa 3:18; Job 1:21; Isa 39:8
10:16 *w* Jos 24:23; Jer 18:8 *x* Isa 63:9
y S Dt 32:36
10:17 *z* S Ge 31:49; Jdg 11:29
10:18 *a* Jdg 11:8, 9
11:1 *b* Jdg 12:1; 1Sa 12:11; Heb 11:32
c Jdg 6:12 *d* Nu 26:29
e S Ge 38:15
11:3 *f* ver 5; 2Sa 10:6,8 *g* S Jdg 9:4
11:4 *h* S Jdg 10:9

10:3 *Jair.* Since Jair came from Gilead (the territory assigned to Manasseh) and since a descendant of Manasseh bore the same name (Nu 32:41; Dt 3:14; 1Ki 4:13), it appears that Jair was a Manassite.

10:4 *thirty sons … thirty donkeys … thirty towns.* Evidence of wealth and position. *Havvoth Jair.* See TNIV text note.

10:6—12:7 Israel now turned to Jephthah, a social outcast whom they had driven from the land and caused to become an outlaw without an inheritance in Israel. The author notes this to Israel's shame. The account of Jephthah's judgeship balances that of Deborah in the story of the judges (see note on 4:1—5:31; see also Introduction: Literary Features).

10:6 *gods of Aram.* The chief gods were Hadad (Baal), Mot, Anath and Rimmon. *gods of Sidon.* The Sidonians worshiped essentially the same gods as the Canaanites (see notes on 2:11,13). *gods of Moab.* The chief deity of Moab was Chemosh. *gods of the Ammonites.* Molek was the chief Ammonite deity (see 1Ki 11:7) and was sometimes worshiped by the offering of human sacrifice (Lev 18:21; 20:2–5; 2Ki 23:10). This god is also called Milkom in Hebrew. Both Molek and Milkom are forms of a Semitic word for "king." *gods of the Philistines.* While the Philistines worshiped most of the Canaanite gods, their most popular deities appear to have been Dagon and Baal-Zebub. The name Dagon is the same as a Hebrew word for "grain," suggesting that he was a vegetation deity. He was worshiped in Babylonia as early as the second millennium B.C. Baal-Zebub was worshiped in Ekron (2Ki 1:2–3,6,16). The name means "lord of the flies," a deliberate

change by followers of the Lord (Yahweh) to ridicule and protest the worship of Baal-Zebul ("Baal the Prince"), a name known from ancient Canaanite texts. See Mt 10:25 and note; 12:24.

10:7 *Philistines.* The account of Philistine oppression is resumed in 13:1.

10:11 *The LORD replied.* See note on 2:1. The Lord rebuked the Israelites for forgetting that he had delivered them from their oppressors in Canaan (see notes on 2:16–19; 6:8).

10:12 *Maonites.* See TNIV text note; or perhaps the same as the Meunites, who along with the Philistines and Arabs opposed Israel (2Ch 26:7).

10:17 *Mizpah.* Means "watchtower." Several places bore this name. Jephthah's headquarters was a town or fortress in Gilead (11:11) called "Mizpah of Gilead" (11:29). It may have been the same as Ramath Mizpah (Jos 13:26), located about 30 miles east of Beth Shan.

10:18 The Gileadites wanted to resist the Ammonite incursion but lacked the courageous military leadership to press their cause. *people.* Fighting men.

11:1 *his mother was a prostitute.* Therefore Jephthah was a social outcast.

11:3 *the land of Tob.* The Hebrew name sounds exactly like "the good land," a common way of referring to the promised land in Deuteronomy. The narrator appears to call attention to the irony of this outcast from Israel finding a refuge in "a land of good (things)." The men of Tob were later allied with the Ammonites against David (2Sa 10:6–8). *scoundrels.* See note on 9:4.

11:7 ʲS Ge 26:16
11:8 ʲS Jdg 10:18
11:10 ᵏS Ge 31:50;
S Isa 1:2
11:11 ʲ1Sa 8:4;
2Sa 3:17 ᵐEx 19:9;
1Sa 8:21 ⁿS Jos 11:3
11:13 ᵒS Nu 21:13
ᵖS Nu 21:24
11:15 ᵖDt 2:9
ʳDt 2:19
11:16 ˢNu 14:25;
S Dt 1:40 ᵗS Ge 14:7
11:17 ᵘver 19;
S Ge 32:3; Nu 20:14
ᵛS Nu 20:17
ʷJer 48:1 ˣS Jos 24:9
11:18 ʸS Nu 20:21
ᶻDt 2:8 ᵃS Nu 21:13
11:19 ᵇS ver 17
ᶜS Jos 12:2
ᵈNu 21:21-22
11:20 ᵉNu 21:23
11:22 ᶠNu 21:21-26;
S Dt 2:26
11:24 ᵍS Nu 21:29;
S Jos 3:10 ʰDt 2:36
11:25 ᶦNu 22:2
ʲS Jos 24:9
11:26 ᵏNu 21:25
ʲS Nu 32:34;
S Jos 13:9

Gilead went to get Jephthah from the land of Tob. ⁶"Come," they said, "be our commander, so we can fight the Ammonites."

⁷Jephthah said to them, "Didn't you hate me and drive me from my father's house? ⁱ Why do you come to me now, when you're in trouble?"

⁸The elders of Gilead said to him, "Nevertheless, we are turning to you now; come with us to fight the Ammonites, and you will be head ʲ over all of us who live in Gilead."

⁹Jephthah answered, "Suppose you take me back to fight the Ammonites and the Lᴏʀᴅ gives them to me—will I really be your head?"

¹⁰The elders of Gilead replied, "The Lᴏʀᴅ is our witness; ᵏ we will certainly do as you say." ¹¹So Jephthah went with the elders ˡ of Gilead, and the people made him head and commander over them. And he repeated ᵐ all his words before the Lᴏʀᴅ in Mizpah. ⁿ

¹²Then Jephthah sent messengers to the Ammonite king with the question: "What do you have against me that you have attacked my country?"

¹³The king of the Ammonites answered Jephthah's messengers, "When Israel came up out of Egypt, they took away my land from the Arnon ᵒ to the Jabbok, ᵖ all the way to the Jordan. Now give it back peaceably."

¹⁴Jephthah sent back messengers to the Ammonite king, ¹⁵saying:

"This is what Jephthah says: Israel did not take the land of Moab �q or the land of the Ammonites. ʳ ¹⁶But when they came up out of Egypt, Israel went through the wilderness to the Red Sea ᵃ ˢ and on to Kadesh. ᵗ ¹⁷Then Israel sent messengers ᵘ to the king of Edom, saying, 'Give us permission to go through your country,' ᵛ but the king of Edom would not listen. They sent also to the king of Moab, ʷ and he refused. ˣ So Israel stayed at Kadesh.

¹⁸"Next they traveled through the wilderness, skirted the lands of Edom ʸ and Moab, passed along the eastern side ᶻ of the country of Moab, and camped on the other side of the Arnon. ᵃ They did not enter the territory of Moab, for the Arnon was its border.

¹⁹"Then Israel sent messengers ᵇ to Sihon king of the Amorites, who ruled in Heshbon, ᶜ and said to him, 'Let us pass through your country to our own place.' ᵈ ²⁰Sihon, however, did not trust Israel ᵇ to pass through his territory. He mustered all his army and encamped at Jahaz and fought with Israel. ᵉ

²¹"Then the Lᴏʀᴅ, the God of Israel, gave Sihon and his whole army into Israel's hands, and they defeated them. Israel took over all the land of the Amorites who lived in that country, ²²capturing all of it from the Arnon to the Jabbok and from the desert to the Jordan. ᶠ

²³"Now since the Lᴏʀᴅ, the God of Israel, has driven the Amorites out before his people Israel, what right have you to take it over? ²⁴Will you not take what your god Chemosh ᵍ gives you? Likewise, whatever the Lᴏʀᴅ our God has given us, ʰ we will possess. ²⁵Are you any better than Balak son of Zippor, ⁱ king of Moab? Did he ever quarrel with Israel or fight with them? ʲ ²⁶For three hundred years Israel occupied ᵏ Heshbon, Aroer, ˡ the surrounding settlements and all the towns along the Arnon. Why didn't you retake them during that time? ²⁷I have not wronged you, but you are

---

ᵃ 16 Or *the Sea of Reeds*   ᵇ 20 Or *however, would not make an agreement for Israel*

11:8 *you will be head over all of us.* In addition to their initial offer of military command during the war with Ammon (v. 6), the Gileadites now also offer to make Jephthah regional head after the fighting is over.

11:11 The proposal of the elders was ratified by the people, a process followed later in the election of Saul (1Sa 11:15), Rehoboam (1Ki 12:1) and Jeroboam (1Ki 12:20). Jephthah's final act here suggests that the agreement reached between himself and the elders had the formal status of a covenant (compare David's "pact" with the representatives of the northern tribes, 2Sa 5:3). In any event, Jephthah lays his conditions "before the Lᴏʀᴅ" as a way of calling on the Lord to enforce the pledge made to him by the elders of Gilead.

11:13 *my land.* When the Israelites had first approached Canaan, this area was ruled by the Amorite king Sihon, who had taken it from the Moabites (Nu 21:29). The Ammonites had since become dominant over Moab and now claimed all previous Moabite territory.

B **11:14–27** Jephthah responded in accordance with international policies of the time; his letter is a classic example of contemporary international correspondence. It also reflects—and appeals to—the common recognition that the god(s) of a people established and protected their political boundaries and decided all boundary disputes. Jephthah's defense of Israel's claim to the land is threefold: (1) Israel took it from Sihon, king of the Amorites, not from the Ammonites (vv. 15–22); (2) the Lord gave the land to Israel (vv. 23–25); and (3) Israel had long possessed it (vv. 26–27).

11:16 *Kadesh.* Kadesh Barnea; see note on Nu 20:1.

11:21 *Lᴏʀᴅ, the God of Israel.* War was viewed not only in military terms but also as a contest between deities (see v. 24; Ex 12:12; Nu 33:4).

11:24 *Chemosh.* The chief deity of the Moabites. At this time either the king of Ammon also ruled Moab or there was a military confederacy of the two peoples.

11:25 *Balak.* See Nu 22–24.

11:26 *three hundred years.* For the relevance of this phrase in establishing the time span for Judges, see Introduction: Background.

doing me wrong by waging war against me. Let the Lord, the Judge, [a] [m] decide [n] the dispute this day between the Israelites and the Ammonites. [o] "

28 The king of Ammon, however, paid no attention to the message Jephthah sent him.

29 Then the Spirit [p] of the Lord came on Jephthah. He crossed Gilead and Manasseh, passed through Mizpah [q] of Gilead, and from there he advanced against the Ammonites. [r] 30 And Jephthah made a vow [s] to the Lord: "If you give the Ammonites into my hands, 31 whatever comes out of the door of my house to meet me when I return in triumph [t] from the Ammonites will be the Lord's, and I will sacrifice it as a burnt offering. [u] "

32 Then Jephthah went over to fight the Ammonites, and the Lord gave them into his hands. 33 He devastated twenty towns from Aroer to the vicinity of Minnith, [v] as far as Abel Keramim. Thus Israel subdued Ammon.

34 When Jephthah returned to his home in Mizpah, who should come out to meet him but his daughter, dancing [w] to the sound of timbrels! [x] She was an only child. [y] Except for her he had neither son nor daughter. 35 When he saw her, he tore his clothes [z] and cried, "Oh! My daughter! You have brought me down and I am devastated. I have made a vow to the Lord that I cannot break. [a] "

36 "My father," she replied, "you have given your word to the Lord. Do to me just as you promised, [b] now that the Lord has avenged you [c] of your enemies, [d] the Ammonites. 37 But grant me this one request," she said. "Give me two months to roam the hills and weep with my friends, because I will never marry."

38 "You may go," he said. And he let her go for two months. She and her friends went into the hills and wept because she would never marry. 39 After the two months, she returned to her father, and he did to her as he had vowed. And she was a virgin.

From this comes the Israelite tradition 40 that each year the young women of Israel go out for four days to commemorate the daughter of Jephthah the Gileadite.

JEPHTHAH AND EPHRAIM

12 The Ephraimite forces were called out, and they crossed over to Zaphon [e] and said to Jephthah, [f] "Why did you go to fight the Ammonites without calling us to go with you? [g] We're going to burn down your house over your head."

2 Jephthah answered, "I and my people were engaged in a great struggle with the Ammonites, and although I called, you didn't save me out of their hands. 3 When I saw that you wouldn't help, I took my life in my hands [h] and crossed over to fight the Ammonites, and the Lord gave me the victory [i] over them. Now why have you come up today to fight me?"

4 Jephthah then called together the men of Gilead [j] and fought against Ephraim. The Gileadites struck them down because the Ephraimites had said, "You Gileadites are renegades from Ephraim and Manasseh. [k] " 5 The Gileadites captured the fords of the Jordan [l] leading to Ephraim, and whenever a survivor of Ephraim said, "Let me cross over," the Gileadites asked him, "Are you an Ephraimite?" If he replied, "No," 6 they said, "All right, say 'Shibboleth.' " If he said, "Sibboleth," because he could not pronounce the word correct-

[a] 27 Or *Ruler*

11:27 [m] S Ge 18:25
[n] S Ge 16:5
[o] 2Ch 20:12
11:29 [p] S Jdg 3:10
[q] S Ge 31:49
[r] S Jdg 10:17
11:30 [s] S Ge 28:20;
Nu 30:10; 1Sa 1:11;
Pr 31:2
11:31 [t] Ge 28:21
[u] S Ge 8:20; Lev 1:3;
Jdg 13:16
11:33 [v] Eze 27:17
11:34 [w] S Ex 15:20
[x] S Ge 31:27;
S Ex 15:20 [y] Zec 12:10
11:35 [z] S Nu 14:6
Ecc 5:2,4,5
11:36 [b] Lk 1:38
[c] S Nu 31:3
[d] 2Sa 18:19
12:1 [e] S Jos 13:27
[f] S Jdg 11:1 [g] Jdg 8:1
12:3 [h] S Jdg 9:17
[i] S Dt 20:4
12:4 [j] 1Ki 17:1
[k] S Ge 46:20;
Isa 9:21; 19:2
12:5 [l] S Jos 2:7

11:27 *Judge.* See 1Sa 24:15. As the divine Judge, the Lord is the final court of appeal. It is significant that in the book of Judges the singular noun "judge" is found only here, where it is used of the Lord, Israel's true Judge.

11:29 *Spirit of the Lord.* See note on 3:10. In the OT the unique empowering of the Spirit was given to individuals primarily to enable them to carry out the special responsibilities God had given them.

11:30 *made a vow.* A common practice among the Israelites (see Ge 28:20; 1Sa 1:11; 2Sa 15:8). Here Jephthah was seeking to assure the outcome of the battle by bargaining for God's help. The precise nature of this vow has been the subject of wide speculation, but v. 31 indicates the promise of a burnt offering and leads to the conclusion that Jephthah probably offered his daughter as a human sacrifice (v. 39). A vow was not to be broken (see Nu 30:2; Dt 23:21–23; see also Ecc 5:4–5).

11:34 *dancing.* It was customary for women to greet armies returning victoriously from battle in this way (see Ex 15:20; 1Sa 18:6).

11:35 *tore his clothes.* A common practice for expressing extreme grief (see Ge 37:34 and note). *a vow to the Lord*

that I cannot break. In his determination to secure the position of leadership over his old adversaries, Jephthah had laid their pledge to him "before the Lord" for him to enforce (see v. 11 and note). Now, accordingly, he cannot go back on his own vow (pledge) to the Lord. Thus all his efforts to assure himself a position of power in Israel by manipulating God backfired. God will not be used!

11:37 *I will never marry.* To be kept from marrying and rearing children was a bitter prospect for an Israelite woman.

11:39 *Israelite tradition.* Probably a local custom, since no other mention of it is found in the OT.

12:1 *burn down your house.* The Philistines issued a similar threat to Samson's wife (14:15). See also 20:48.

12:2 *answered.* Again Jephthah tried diplomacy first (see 11:12,14; see also note on 8:1). *I called.* New information on the sequence of events.

12:6 *Shibboleth.* Ironically, the word meant "floods" (see, e.g., Ps 69:2,15). Apparently the Israelites east of the Jordan pronounced its initial letter with a strong "sh" sound, while those in Canaan gave it a softer "s" sound. (Peter was similarly betrayed by his accent; see Mt 26:73.)

12:8 *m* S Ge 35:19
12:12 *n* S Jos 10:12
12:13 *o* ver 15;
2Sa 23:30; 1Ch 11:31;
27:14
12:14 *p* S Jdg 8:30
q S Jdg 5:10
12:15 *r* Jdg 5:14
13:1 *s* S Jdg 3:31
t Jdg 14:4
13:2 *u* S Jos 15:33
v ver 8; Jdg 16:31
w S Ge 30:6
x S Ge 11:30
13:3 *y* S Ge 16:7
z ver 10 *a* Isa 7:14;
Lk 1:13
13:4 *b* S Lev 10:9
c ver 14; Nu 6:2-4;
S Lk 1:15
13:5 *d* S Ge 3:15
e 1Sa 1:11 *f* S Nu 6:2,
13; Am 2:11,12
g Isa 7:13
13:6 *h* ver 8;
1Sa 2:27; 9:6;
1Ki 13:1; 17:18
i S Nu 22:22 *j* Ps 66:5
13:7 *k* Jer 35:6
l Lev 10:9 *m* 1Sa 1:11,
28
13:8 *n* S ver 2

ly, they seized him and killed him at the fords of the Jordan. Forty-two thousand Ephraimites were killed at that time.

[7]Jephthah led[a] Israel six years. Then Jephthah the Gileadite died and was buried in a town in Gilead.

IBZAN, ELON AND ABDON

[8]After him, Ibzan of Bethlehem[m] led Israel. [9]He had thirty sons and thirty daughters. He gave his daughters away in marriage to those outside his clan, and for his sons he brought in thirty young women as wives from outside his clan. Ibzan led Israel seven years. [10]Then Ibzan died and was buried in Bethlehem.

[11]After him, Elon the Zebulunite led Israel ten years. [12]Then Elon died and was buried in Aijalon[n] in the land of Zebulun.

[13]After him, Abdon son of Hillel, from Pirathon,[o] led Israel. [14]He had forty sons and thirty grandsons,[p] who rode on seventy donkeys.[q] He led Israel eight years. [15]Then Abdon son of Hillel died and was buried at Pirathon in Ephraim, in the hill country of the Amalekites.[r]

THE BIRTH OF SAMSON

13 Again the Israelites did evil in the eyes of the LORD, so the LORD delivered them into the hands of the Philistines[s] for forty years.[t] [2]A certain man of Zorah,[u] named Manoah,[v] from the clan of the Danites,[w] had a wife who was childless,[x] unable to give birth. [3]The angel of the LORD[y] appeared to her[z] and said, "You are barren and childless, but you are going to become pregnant and give birth to a son.[a] [4]Now see to it that you drink no wine or other fermented drink[b] and that you do not eat anything unclean.[c] [5]You will become pregnant and have a son[d] whose head is never to be touched by a razor[e] because the boy is to be a Nazirite,[f] dedicated to God from the womb. He will begin[g] to deliver Israel from the hands of the Philistines."

[6]Then the woman went to her husband and told him, "A man of God[h] came to me. He looked like an angel of God,[i] very awesome.[j] I didn't ask him where he came from, and he didn't tell me his name. [7]But he said to me, 'You will become pregnant and have a son. Now then, drink no wine[k] or other fermented drink[l] and do not eat anything unclean, because the boy will be a Nazirite of God from the womb until the day of his death.[m]' "

[8]Then Manoah[n] prayed to the LORD: "Pardon your servant, Lord. I beg you to let the

---

a 7 Traditionally *judged*; also in verses 8-14

12:7 *led Israel ... years.* A new formula for closing out the account of a judge (see note on 3:11; see also Introduction: Literary Features).

12:8 *Bethlehem.* Probably the Bethlehem in western Zebulun (see Ge 35:19; 48:7; Jos 19:15).

12:9 *thirty sons and thirty daughters.* See note on 10:4.

12:11 *Elon.* Also the name of a clan in the tribe of Zebulun (Ge 46:14; Nu 26:26).

12:14 *forty sons and thirty grandsons.* A total of 70 (see notes on 8:30; 10:4).

12:15 *hill country of the Amalekites.* See note on 5:14. The background of this reference is unknown; the Amalekites are otherwise associated with the Negev (Nu 13:29).

A C **13:1—16:31** Samson (from the tribe of Dan), like Ehud (from the tribe of Benjamin), was a loner, whose heroic exploits involved single-handed triumphs over powerful enemies. His story therefore balances that of Ehud (see note on 3:12–30). Significantly, this last of the judges typifies the nation of Israel. Born by special divine provision to a barren woman, consecrated to the Lord from birth and endowed by God's Spirit with unique powers to overcome Israel's enemies, he was however drawn to Philistine women, which ultimately led to his destruction—just as God's consecrated (by circumcision) and especially empowered (for the conquest of Canaan) people Israel were continually drawn to the gods and ways of the Canaanites to their destruction (see note on Ex 34:15). The story of Samson is the story of Israel in cameo. The author provides a mirror image of Israel in the days of the judges—and of God's unfailing mercies to his wayward people whom he would not abandon.

13:1–25 The account of Samson's birth helps the author to point out the parallels between Samson and Israel that he wanted his readers to see.

13:1 *did evil in the eyes of the LORD.* See note on 3:7.

13:2 *Zorah.* A town first assigned to Judah (Jos 15:33) but later given to Dan (Jos 19:41). It became the point of departure for the Danite migration northward (18:2,8,11). *Danites.* See 1:34 and note. *childless, unable to give birth.* The same condition, before divine intervention, as that of Sarah, the mother of Isaac (Ge 11:30; 16:1), and Rebekah, the mother of Jacob (Ge 25:21). Cf. also Hannah, the mother of Samuel (1Sa 1:2), and Elizabeth, the mother of John the Baptist (Lk 1:7).

13:3 *angel of the LORD.* See note on Ge 16:7. *you are going to ... give birth to a son.* See the announcement of Isaac's birth (Ge 18:10). Cf. the announcements of the births of Ishmael (Ge 16:11), Immanuel (Isa 7:14), John the Baptist (Lk 1:13) and Jesus (Lk 1:31).

13:5 *Nazirite.* From a Hebrew word meaning "separated" or "dedicated." For the stipulations of this vow see Nu 6:1–21 and notes. Samson's Nazirite-like consecration was not voluntary—like Israel, he was consecrated to special service by God himself—and his consecration applied to his whole lifetime (v. 7). The same was true of Samuel (1Sa 1:11) and John the Baptist (Lk 1:15). *begin to deliver ... from ... the Philistines.* The deliverance was continued in the time of Samuel (1Sa 7:10–14) and completed under David (2Sa 5:17–25; 8:1).

13:6 *man of God.* An expression often used of prophets (see Dt 33:1; 1Sa 2:27; 9:6–10; 1Ki 12:22), though it is clear from vv. 3,21 that this messenger was the angel of the Lord.

man of God *o* you sent to us come again to teach us how to bring up the boy who is to be born."

[9] God heard Manoah, and the angel of God came again to the woman while she was out in the field; but her husband Manoah was not with her. [10] The woman hurried to tell her husband, "He's here! The man who appeared to me *p* the other day!"

[11] Manoah got up and followed his wife. When he came to the man, he said, "Are you the man who talked to my wife?"

"I am," he said.

[12] So Manoah asked him, "When your words are fulfilled, what is to be the rule that governs the boy's life and work?"

[13] The angel of the LORD answered, "Your wife must do all that I have told her. [14] She must not eat anything that comes from the grapevine, nor drink any wine or other fermented drink *q* nor eat anything unclean. *r* She must do everything I have commanded her."

[15] Manoah said to the angel of the LORD, "We would like you to stay until we prepare a young goat *s* for you."

[16] The angel of the LORD replied, "Even though you detain me, I will not eat any of your food. But if you prepare a burnt offering, *t* offer it to the LORD." (Manoah did not realize *u* that it was the angel of the LORD.)

[17] Then Manoah inquired of the angel of the LORD, "What is your name, *v* so that we may honor you when your word comes true?"

[18] He replied, "Why do you ask my name? *w* It is beyond understanding. *a* " [19] Then Manoah took a young goat, together with the grain offering, and sacrificed it on a rock *x* to the LORD. And the LORD did an amazing thing while Manoah and his wife watched: [20] As the flame *y* blazed up from the altar toward heaven, the angel of the LORD ascended in the flame. Seeing this, Manoah and his wife fell with their faces to the ground. *z* [21] When the angel of the LORD did not show himself again to Manoah and his wife, Manoah realized *a* that it was the angel of the LORD.

[22] "We are doomed *b* to die!" he said to his wife. "We have seen *c* God!"

[23] But his wife answered, "If the LORD had meant to kill us, he would not have accepted a burnt offering and grain offering from our hands, nor shown us all these things or now told us this." *d*

[24] The woman gave birth to a boy and named him Samson. *e* He grew *f* and the LORD blessed him, *g* [25] and the Spirit of the LORD began to stir *h* him while he was in Mahaneh Dan, *i* between Zorah and Eshtaol.

SAMSON'S MARRIAGE

14

Samson *j* went down to Timnah *k* and saw there a young Philistine woman. [2] When he returned, he said to his father and mother, "I have seen a Philistine woman in Timnah; now get her for me as my wife." *l*

a 18 Or is wonderful

13:8 *o* S ver 6
13:10 *p* ver 3
13:14 *q* Lev 10:9
r S ver 4
13:15 *s* Jdg 6:19
13:16 *t* S Jdg 11:31
u S Jdg 6:22
13:17 *v* S Ge 32:29
13:18 *w* S Ge 32:29
13:19 *x* Jdg 6:20
13:20 *y* S Lev 9:24
z S Ge 17:3
13:21 *a* S Jdg 6:22
13:22 *b* S Nu 17:12; S Dt 5:26
c S Ge 16:13; S Ex 3:6; S 24:10; S Jdg 6:22
13:23 *d* Ps 25:14
13:24 *e* Jdg 14:1; 15:1; 16:1; Heb 11:32
f 1Sa 2:21,26; 3:19
g Lk 1:80
13:25 *h* S Jdg 3:10
i Jdg 18:12
14:1 *j* S Jdg 13:24
k S Ge 38:12
14:2 *l* S Ge 21:21

13:8 *teach us.* Not the usual parental concern, but a special concern based on the boy's special calling.

[A] 13:12 A declaration of faith. To Manoah it was not a matter of whether these events would occur, but of when (v. 17).

13:15 *stay until we prepare a young goat.* Such food was considered a special delicacy. Hospitality of this kind was common in the ancient Near East (see 6:18–19; Ge 18:1–8).

13:17 *What is your name . . . ?* A messenger's identity was considered very important. *when your word comes true.* Fulfilled prophecy was a sign of the authenticity of a prophet (Dt 18:21–22; 1Sa 9:6).

[A] 13:18 *beyond understanding.* See TNIV text note. In Isa 9:6 the Hebrew for this phrase (translated "Wonderful") applies to One who would come as "Mighty God."

13:22 *doomed to die.* See 6:23 and notes on Ge 16:13; 32:30.

[C] 13:24 *Samson.* The name is derived from a Hebrew word meaning "sun" or "brightness," and is used here as an expression of joy over the birth of the child. *He grew and the LORD blessed him.* Cf. 1Sa 2:26 (Samuel) and Lk 2:52 (Jesus).

13:25 *began to stir him.* See notes on 3:10; 11:29. *Mahaneh Dan.* Means "Dan's camp" (see TNIV text note on 18:12).

[C] 14:1—16:31 The account of Samson's extraordinary exploits and flawed character has a literary structure of special

note. His first encounter with a Philistine woman (14:1–20) and its aftermath (15:1–8) are closely balanced by the account of his last encounter with a Philistine woman (16:4–22) and its aftermath (16:23–31). And what happens in his first encounter foreshadows what happens in his final encounter. Between these two major cycles are three episodes: (1) Judah's attempt to appease the Philistines by binding Samson over to them (15:9–17); (2) God's rescue of Samson from life-threatening dehydration (15:18–19); and (3) Samson's escape from Gaza, the gates of which he deposits on a hill overlooking Hebron, Judah's main city (16:1–3). The author reminds his readers in the brief centerpiece (15:18–19) that mighty Samson shared in the universal vulnerabilities of human life.

[B] 14:1 *Timnah.* Identified as Tell Batash in the Sorek Valley, west of Beth Shemesh (see map, p. 338). Archaeologists have uncovered the Philistine layer of the town. *young Philistine woman.* The disappointment of Samson's parents (v. 3; cf. Esau, Ge 26:35; 27:46; 28:1) is understandable in light of the prohibition against marriage with the pagan peoples of Canaan (Ex 34:11,16; Dt 7:1,3; see also Jdg 3:5–6).

14:2 *get her for me.* See Ge 34:4. As the head of the family, the father exercised authority in all matters, often including the choice of wives for his sons (see 12:9; Ge 24:3–9; Ne 10:30).

14:3 *m* S Ge 24:4
n S Ge 34:14;
S 1Sa 14:6
o S Ex 34:16
14:4 *p* S Dt 2:30
q S Jos 11:20
r Jdg 13:1; 15:11
14:6 *s* S Jdg 3:10
t 1Sa 17:35
14:10 *u* S Ge 29:22
14:12 *v* S Nu 12:8;
Eze 17:2; 20:49; 24:3;
Hos 12:10 *w* Ge 29:27
x S Ge 45:22;
S 2Ki 5:5
14:14 *y* ver 18
14:15 *z* Jdg 16:5;
Ecc 7:26
a S Lev 20:14;
Jdg 15:6
14:16 *b* Jdg 16:15

³His father and mother replied, "Isn't there an acceptable woman among your relatives or among all our people? *m* Must you go to the uncircumcised *n* Philistines to get a wife? *o* "

But Samson said to his father, "Get her for me. She's the right one for me." ⁴(His parents did not know that this was from the LORD, *p* who was seeking an occasion to confront the Philistines; *q* for at that time they were ruling over Israel.) *r*

⁵Samson went down to Timnah together with his father and mother. As they approached the vineyards of Timnah, suddenly a young lion came roaring toward him. ⁶The Spirit of the LORD came on him in power *s* so that he tore the lion apart *t* with his bare hands as he might have torn a young goat. But he told neither his father nor his mother what he had done. ⁷Then he went down and talked with the woman, and he liked her.

⁸Some time later, when he went back to marry her, he turned aside to look at the lion's carcass, and in it he saw a swarm of bees and some honey. ⁹He scooped out the honey with his hands and ate as he went along. When he rejoined his parents, he gave them some, and they too ate it. But he did not tell them that he had taken the honey from the lion's carcass.

¹⁰Now his father went down to see the woman. And there Samson held a feast, *u* as was customary for young men. ¹¹When the people saw him, they chose thirty men to be his companions.

¹²"Let me tell you a riddle, *v* " Samson said to them. "If you can give me the answer within the seven days of the feast, *w* I will give you thirty linen garments and thirty sets of clothes. *x* ¹³If you can't tell me the answer, you must give me thirty linen garments and thirty sets of clothes."

"Tell us your riddle," they said. "Let's hear it."

¹⁴He replied,

> "Out of the eater, something to eat;
> out of the strong, something sweet." *y*

For three days they could not give the answer.

¹⁵On the fourth *a* day, they said to Samson's wife, "Coax *z* your husband into explaining the riddle for us, or we will burn you and your father's household to death. *a* Did you invite us here to steal our property?"

¹⁶Then Samson's wife threw herself on him, sobbing, "You hate me! You don't really love me. *b* You've given my people a riddle, but you haven't told me the answer."

"I haven't even explained it to my father or mother," he replied, "so why should I ex-

---

a 15 Some Septuagint manuscripts and Syriac; Hebrew *seventh*

14:3 *uncircumcised.* A term of scorn, referring to those not bound by covenant to the Lord, used especially of the Philistines (see note on 1Sa 14:6). *right one for me.* The Hebrew for this expression ("is right in my eyes") is similar to that translated "did as they saw fit" (lit. "did what was right in their own eyes") in 17:6; 21:25. The author anticipates this theme, which recurs in chs. 17–21.

14:4 *this was from the LORD.* See Jos 11:20; 1Ki 12:15. The Lord uses even sinful human weaknesses to accomplish his purposes and bring praise to his name (see Ge 45:8; 50:20; 2Ch 25:20; Ac 2:23; 4:28; Ro 8:28–29).

14:5 *vineyards of Timnah.* The Sorek Valley (in which Timnah was located) and its surrounding areas were noted for their luxuriant vineyards. For anyone under Nazirite vows, vineyards could be a powerful source of temptation (see Nu 6:1–4). *a young lion came roaring toward him.* The author's language anticipates his later "the Philistines came toward him shouting" (15:14). This helps the reader to catch the author's intention to use the lion out of the Philistine vineyards as a symbol of the Philistines themselves, the very enemies of Israel against whom Samson was called to be God's champion (cf. 1Sa 17 for the roles of Goliath and David in a later confrontation between the Philistines and Israel). *young lion.* Lions were once common in southern Canaan (see 1Sa 17:34; 2Sa 23:20; 1Ki 13:24; 20:36).

14:6 *Spirit . . . came on him.* See also notes on 3:10; 11:29. *tore the lion apart.* With such unique power God's Spirit endowed Samson to overcome the Philistines. Later, David (1Sa 17:34–37) and Benaiah (2Sa 23:20)

performed similar feats.

14:8–9 *carcass . . . honey. He scooped out the honey with his hands.* Samson thus violated his Nazirite vows (Nu 6:6–7) in order to delight himself with something sweet.

14:10 *feast.* Such a special feast was common in the ancient Near East (see Ge 29:22) and here lasted seven days (v. 12; see Ge 29:27). Since it would have included drinking wine, Samson may have violated his Nazirite vow (see 13:4,7).

14:11 *companions.* These are the "guests of the bridegroom" (cf. Mt 9:15). They were probably charged with protecting the wedding party against marauders.

14:12 *riddle.* The use of riddles at feasts and special occasions was popular in the ancient world. *sets of clothes.* Mentioned, together with silver, as gifts of great value in Ge 45:22; 2Ki 5:22 (see also Zec 14:14).

14:14 *the eater . . . the strong.* Samson refers to the lion he had killed, from the carcass of which he had taken honey to eat. He confidently uses his riddle as his opening shot in a battle of wits with the Philistines. The author, however, uses Samson's riddle to chillingly foreshadow Samson's sorry end. He has just shown us Samson "the eater" (of honey) and Samson "the strong" (killer of a powerful lion). In the end, he shows us blinded Samson grinding grain in prison for his captors (16:21: out of the eater the Philistines get something to eat) and entertaining his captors with feats of strength (16:25: out of the strong the Philistines get something sweet).

14:16 *don't really love me.* Delilah used the same tactics (16:15).

plain it to you?" [17]She cried the whole seven days [c] of the feast. So on the seventh day he finally told her, because she continued to press him. She in turn explained the riddle to her people.

[18]Before sunset on the seventh day the men of the town said to him,

> "What is sweeter than honey?
> What is stronger than a lion?" [d]

Samson said to them,

> "If you had not plowed with my heifer,
> you would not have solved my riddle."

[19]Then the Spirit of the LORD came on him in power. [e] He went down to Ashkelon, [f] struck down thirty of their men, stripped them of everything and gave their clothes to those who had explained the riddle. Burning with anger, [g] he returned to his father's home. [20]And Samson's wife was given to one of his companions [h] who had attended him at the feast.

SAMSON'S VENGEANCE ON THE PHILISTINES

15 Later on, at the time of wheat harvest, [i] Samson [j] took a young goat [k] and went to visit his wife. He said, "I'm going to my wife's room." [l] But her father would not let him go in.

[2]"I was so sure you hated her," he said, "that I gave her to your companion. [m] Isn't her younger sister more attractive? Take her instead."

[3]Samson said to them, "This time I have a right to get even with the Philistines; I will really harm them." [4]So he went out and caught three hundred foxes [n] and tied them tail to tail in pairs. He then fastened a torch [o] to every pair of tails, [5]lit the torches [p] and let the foxes loose in the standing grain of the Philistines. He burned up the shocks [q] and standing grain, together with the vineyards and olive groves.

[6]When the Philistines asked, "Who did this?" they were told, "Samson, the Timnite's son-in-law, because his wife was given to his companion. [r]"

So the Philistines went up and burned her [s] and her father to death. [t] [7]Samson said to them, "Since you've acted like this, I swear that I won't stop until I get my revenge on you." [8]He attacked them viciously and slaughtered many of them. Then he went down and stayed in a cave in the rock [u] of Etam. [v]

[9]The Philistines went up and camped in Judah, spreading out near Lehi. [w] [10]The people of Judah asked, "Why have you come to fight us?"

"We have come to take Samson prisoner," they answered, "to do to him as he did to us."

[11]Then three thousand men from Judah went down to the cave in the rock of Etam and said to Samson, "Don't you realize that the Philistines are rulers over us? [x] What have you done to us?"

14:17 [c] Est 1:5
14:18 [d] ver 14
14:19 [e] S Jdg 3:10
[f] S Jos 13:3 [g] 1Sa 11:6
14:20 [h] Jdg 15:2,6; Jn 3:29
15:1 [i] S Ge 30:14
[j] S Jdg 13:24
[k] S Ge 38:17
[l] Ge 29:21
15:2 [m] S Jdg 14:20
15:4 [n] SS 2:15
[o] S Ge 15:17
15:5 [p] S Ge 15:17
[q] Ex 22:6; 2Sa 14:30-31
15:6 [r] S Jdg 14:20
[s] S Ge 38:24
15:8 [u] Isa 2:21
[v] ver 11
15:9 [w] ver 14,17,19
15:11 [x] S Jdg 14:4; Ps 106:40-42

C **14:18** *sweeter than honey ... stronger than a lion.* The Philistines answer riddle with riddle. And the answer to their riddle exposes Samson's great weakness. The answer to their riddle is "love," or at least "sexual passion," the very thing that kept drawing Samson to the Philistines—and would ultimately lead to his downfall. Moreover, his downfall is already foreshadowed here where a Philistine girl, the object of Samson's passion, defeats him with her beauty and feminine wiles. *my heifer.* Samson's wife (see v. 15). Since heifers were not used for plowing, Samson is accusing their of unfairness.

14:19 *Spirit ... came on him.* God's purposes for Samson included humbling the Philistines. *Ashkelon.* One of the five principal cities of the Philistines (see map, p. 338).

14:20 *one of his companions.* See 15:2; probably the young man who had attended Samson (cf. Jn 3:29), in all likelihood one of his 30 companions (v. 11).

15:1 *time of wheat harvest.* Near the end of May or the beginning of June (see note on Ru 1:22). *young goat.* Such a gift was customary, as with Judah and Tamar (Ge 38:17).

15:2 *younger sister.* Samson's father-in-law felt he had to make a counterproposal because he had received the bride-price from Samson. Similar marital transactions were made by Laban and Jacob (Ge 29:16–28) and Saul and David (1Sa 18:19–21).

15:5 *burned up.* The wheat harvest (v. 1) comes at the end of a

long dry season, thus making the fields extremely vulnerable to fire. Samson's burning of the grainfields foreshadows his destruction of the temple of Dagon (whose name means "grain") in his last attack on the Philistines (16:23–30; see also note on 10:6).

15:7 *revenge.* A common feature of life in the ancient Near East. Six cities of refuge were designated by the Lord to prevent endless killings (see 20:1–9 and note). Samson's act of revenge against the Philistines for murdering the one who had pleased his eyes (see note on 14:3; see also Eze 24:16) foreshadows his act of revenge against them for gouging out his eyes (16:28).

15:9–17 See note on 14:1—16:31.

15:9 *Lehi.* Means "jawbone." This locality probably did not receive the name until after the events described here; the author uses the name in anticipation of those events—a common device in Hebrew narrative. The exact site of Lehi is not known.

15:11 *three thousand men from Judah.* The only time a force from Judah is explicitly mentioned in connection with any of the judges (but see note on 1:2). The men of Judah were well aware of Samson's capabilities, and even with a large force they did not attempt to tie him up without his consent (vv. 12–13). *Philistines are rulers over us.* Much of Judah was under Philistine rule, and the tribe was apparently content to accept it. They mustered a force, not to support Samson, but to capture him for the Philistines. Contrast the role assigned Judah in 1:2 and 20:18.

15:12 ʸS Ge 47:31
15:13 ᶻJdg 16:11,12
15:14 ᵃS ver 9
ᵇS Jdg 3:10
ᶜS Jos 2:6
15:15 ᵈS Lev 26:8
15:16 ᵉJer 22:19
15:17 ᶠS ver 9
15:18 ᵍJdg 16:28
ʰS Dt 20:4
15:19 ⁱGe 45:27;
1Sa 30:12; Isa 40:29
ʲS Ex 17:6
15:20 ᵏJdg 16:31
16:1 ˡS Jdg 13:24
ᵐS Ge 10:19
ⁿS Ge 38:15
16:2 ᵒS Jos 2:5
ᵖ1Sa 19:11
16:3 �qS Jos 10:36
16:4 ʳGe 24:67;
S 34:3 ˢver 6
16:5 ᵗS Jdg 13:3
ᵘS Ex 10:7;
S Jdg 14:15 ᵛver 6,15
ʷver 18
16:6 ˣver 4

He answered, "I merely did to them what they did to me."

¹²They said to him, "We've come to tie you up and hand you over to the Philistines." Samson said, "Swear to me ʸ that you won't kill me yourselves."

¹³"Agreed," they answered. "We will only tie you up and hand you over to them. We will not kill you." So they bound him with two new ropes ᶻ and led him up from the rock. ¹⁴As he approached Lehi, ᵃ the Philistines came toward him shouting. The Spirit of the Lord came on him in power. ᵇ The ropes on his arms became like charred flax, ᶜ and the bindings dropped from his hands. ¹⁵Finding a fresh jawbone of a donkey, he grabbed it and struck down a thousand men. ᵈ

¹⁶Then Samson said,

"With a donkey's jawbone
    I have made donkeys of them.ᵃ ᵉ
With a donkey's jawbone
    I have killed a thousand men."

¹⁷When he finished speaking, he threw away the jawbone; and the place was called Ramath Lehi.ᵇ ᶠ

¹⁸Because he was very thirsty, he cried out to the Lord, ᵍ "You have given your servant this great victory. ʰ Must I now die of thirst and fall into the hands of the uncircumcised?" ¹⁹Then God opened up the hollow place in Lehi, and water came out of it. When Samson drank, his strength returned and he revived. ⁱ So the spring ʲ was called En Hakkore, ᶜ and it is still there in Lehi.

²⁰Samson led ᵈ Israel for twenty years ᵏ in the days of the Philistines.

SAMSON AND DELILAH

16 One day Samson ˡ went to Gaza, ᵐ where he saw a prostitute. ⁿ He went in to spend the night with her. ²The people of Gaza were told, "Samson is here!" So they surrounded the place and lay in wait for him all night at the city gate. ᵒ They made no move during the night, saying, "At dawn ᵖ we'll kill him."

³But Samson lay there only until the middle of the night. Then he got up and took hold of the doors of the city gate, together with the two posts, and tore them loose, bar and all. He lifted them to his shoulders and carried them to the top of the hill that faces Hebron. q

⁴Some time later, he fell in love ʳ with a woman in the Valley of Sorek whose name was Delilah. ˢ ⁵The rulers of the Philistines ᵗ went to her and said, "See if you can lure ᵘ him into showing you the secret of his great strength ᵛ and how we can overpower him so we may tie him up and subdue him. Each one of us will give you eleven hundred shekels ᵉ of silver." ʷ

⁶So Delilah ˣ said to Samson, "Tell me the secret of your great strength and how you can be tied up and subdued."

⁷Samson answered her, "If anyone ties me with seven fresh thongs ᶠ that have not been dried, I'll become as weak as any other man."

ᵃ 16 Or *made a heap or two*; the Hebrew for *donkey* sounds like the Hebrew for *heap*. ᵇ 17 *Ramath Lehi* means *jawbone hill*. ᶜ 19 *En Hakkore* means *caller's spring*. ᵈ 20 Traditionally *judged* ᵉ 5 That is, about 28 pounds or about 13 kilograms ᶠ 7 Or *bowstrings*; also in verses 8 and 9

15:14 *shouting.* A battle cry (see 1Sa 17:52). They came shouting against Samson as the lion had come roaring against him (14:5). *Spirit of the Lord.* See notes on 3:10; 11:29; 14:19.

15:15 *struck down a thousand men.* Cf. the exploits of Shamgar, who struck down 600 Philistines with an oxgoad (3:31).

15:18–19 See note on 14:1—16:31.

15:18 *Must I now die of thirst . . . ?* Mighty Samson was, after all, only a mortal man.

15:19 *water came out of it.* God provided for Samson as he had for Israel in the desert. See Ex 17:1–7 (Massah and Meribah); Nu 20:2–13 (Meribah).

15:20 *led Israel . . . years.* See note on 12:7. *twenty years.* Round numbers are frequently used in Judges (see Introduction: Background).

16:1–3 See note on 14:1—16:31.

16:1 *Gaza.* An important Philistine seaport on the Mediterranean coast of southwest Canaan. *prostitute.* While Samson certainly possessed physical strength, he lacked moral strength, which ultimately led to his ruin.

16:2 *dawn.* By that time they expected Samson to be exhausted and sleeping soundly.

16:3 *bar.* Probably made of bronze (1Ki 4:13) or iron (Ps 107:16; Isa 45:2). *faces Hebron.* That is, in the direction of Hebron, which was 38 miles away in the hill country. Since Hebron was the chief city of Judah, this must be seen as Samson's response to what the men of Judah had done to him (see 15:11–13).

16:4–31 See note on 14:1—16:31.

16:5 *rulers of the Philistines.* See note on 3:3. *subdue him.* The Philistines were not interested in killing him quickly; they sought revenge by a prolonged period of torture. *eleven hundred shekels.* An extraordinarily generous payment in light of 17:10 (see note there). (The total amount paid by the five Philistines would have been equivalent to the price of 275 slaves, at the rate offered for Joseph centuries earlier; see Ge 37:28.) Micah stole a similar amount of silver from his mother (17:2). *shekels.* See note on Ge 20:16.

16:7 *seven fresh thongs.* The number seven had special significance to the ancients, symbolizing completeness or fullness. Note that Samson's hair was divided into seven braids (v. 13).

⁸Then the rulers of the Philistines brought her seven fresh thongs that had not been dried, and she tied him with them. ⁹With men hidden in the room, ʸ she called to him, "Samson, the Philistines are upon you!" ᶻ But he snapped the thongs as easily as a piece of string snaps when it comes close to a flame. So the secret of his strength was not discovered.

¹⁰Then Delilah said to Samson, "You have made a fool of me; ᵃ you lied to me. Come now, tell me how you can be tied."

¹¹He said, "If anyone ties me securely with new ropes ᵇ that have never been used, I'll become as weak as any other man."

¹²So Delilah took new ropes and tied him with them. Then, with men hidden in the room, she called to him, "Samson, the Philistines are upon you!" ᶜ But he snapped the ropes off his arms as if they were threads.

¹³Delilah then said to Samson, "Until now, you have been making a fool of me and lying to me. Tell me how you can be tied."

He replied, "If you weave the seven braids of my head into the fabric ⌐on the loom⌐ and tighten it with the pin, I'll become as weak as any other man." So while he was sleeping, Delilah took the seven braids of his head, wove them into the fabric ¹⁴andᵃ tightened it with the pin.

Again she called to him, "Samson, the Philistines are upon you!" ᵈ He awoke from his sleep and pulled up the pin and the loom, with the fabric.

¹⁵Then she said to him, "How can you say, 'I love you,' ᵉ when you won't confide in me? This is the third time ᶠ you have made a fool of me and haven't told me the secret of your great strength. ᵍ" ¹⁶With such nagging she prodded him day after day until he was tired to death.

¹⁷So he told her everything. ʰ "No razor has ever been used on my head," he said, "because I have been a Nazirite ᶦ dedicated to God from my mother's womb. If my head were shaved, my strength would leave me, and I would become as weak as any other man."

¹⁸When Delilah saw that he had told her everything, she sent word to the rulers of the Philistines,ʲ "Come back once more; he has told me everything." So the rulers of the Philistines returned with the silver in their hands. ᵏ ¹⁹Having put him to sleep on her lap, she called for someone to shave off the seven braids of his hair, and so began to subdue him. ᵇ And his strength left him. ˡ

²⁰Then she called, "Samson, the Philistines are upon you!" ᵐ

He awoke from his sleep and thought, "I'll go out as before and shake myself free." But he did not know that the Lᴏʀᴅ had left him. ⁿ

²¹Then the Philistines ᵒ seized him, gouged out his eyes ᵖ and took him down to Gaza. �q Binding him with bronze shackles, they set him to grinding grain ʳ in the prison. ²²But the hair on his head began to grow again after it had been shaved.

THE DEATH OF SAMSON

²³Now the rulers of the Philistines assembled to offer a great sacrifice to Dagon ˢ their god and to celebrate, saying, "Our god has delivered Samson, our enemy, into our hands."
²⁴When the people saw him, they praised their god, ᵗ saying,

> "Our god has delivered our enemy
> into our hands, ᵘ

ᵃ 13,14 Some Septuagint manuscripts; Hebrew *"⌐I can⌐ if you weave the seven braids of my head into the fabric ⌐on the loom⌐."* ¹⁴*So she*   ᵇ 19 Hebrew; some Septuagint manuscripts *and he began to weaken*

16:9 ʸ ver 12 ᶻ ver 14
16:10 ᵃ ver 13
16:11 ᵇ S Jdg 15:13
16:12 ᶜ ver 14
16:14 ᵈ ver 9,20
16:15 ᵉ Jdg 14:16
ᶠ Nu 24:10 ᵍ S ver 5
16:17 ʰ ver 18;
Mic 7:5 ᶦ S Nu 6:2
1Sa 5:8 ᵏ ver 5
16:19 ˡ Pr 7:26-27
16:20 ᵐ S ver 14
ⁿ Nu 14:42; Jos 7:12;
1Sa 16:14; 18:12; 28:15
16:21 ᵒ Jer 47:1
ᵖ S Nu 16:14
q S Ge 10:19
ʳ Job 31:10; Isa 47:2
16:23 ˢ 1Sa 5:2;
1Ch 10:10
16:24 ᵗ Da 5:4
ᵘ 1Sa 31:9; 1Ch 10:9

16:11 *new ropes.* The Philistines apparently did not know that this method had already been tried and had failed (15:13–14).
16:13 Out of disdain, Samson arrogantly played with his Philistine adversaries. *tighten it with the pin.* Probably from a weaver's shuttle. The details of the account suggest that the loom in question was the vertical type with a crossbeam from which warp threads were suspended. Samson's long hair was woven into the warp and beaten up into the web with the pin, thus forming a tight fabric.

A **16:19–20** *his strength left him ... the Lᴏʀᴅ had left him.* The source of Samson's strength was ultimately God himself.

A **C** **16:20** *he did not know.* One of the most tragic statements in the OT. Samson was unaware that he had betrayed his calling. He had permitted a Philistine woman to rob him of the sign of his special consecration to the Lord.

The Lord's champion lay asleep and helpless in the arms of his paramour.

16:21 *gouged out his eyes.* Brutal treatment of prisoners of war to humiliate and incapacitate them was common (see 1Sa 11:2; 2Ki 25:7; see also note on Jdg 1:6). *to Gaza.* In shame and weakness, Samson was led to Gaza, the place where he had displayed great strength (vv. 1–3). *set him to grinding.* See notes on 9:53; 14:14.

A **16:22** *hair ... began to grow again.* The author hints at the great truth that shines through the Samson story and would soon receive its final confirmation for Samson, namely, that God had not and would not abandon his flawed servant—or his flawed people Israel.

16:23 *Dagon.* See notes on 10:6; 15:5. *Our god has delivered.* It was common to attribute a victory to the national deities.

16:25 ᵛ Jdg 9:27;
19:6,9,22; Ru 3:7;
Est 1:10
16:27 ʷ S Jos 2:8
16:28 ˣ Jdg 15:18
ʸ Jer 15:15
16:31 ᶻ S Jdg 13:2
ᵃ Ru 1:1; 1Sa 4:18; 7:6
ᵇ Jdg 15:20
17:1 ᶜ Jdg 18:2,13
17:2 ᵈ Ru 2:20; 3:10;
1Sa 15:13; 23:21;
2Sa 2:5
17:3 ᵉ S Ex 20:4
17:4 ᶠ S Ex 32:4;
S Isa 17:8

> the one who laid waste our land
> and multiplied our slain."

²⁵While they were in high spirits, ᵛ they shouted, "Bring out Samson to entertain us." So they called Samson out of the prison, and he performed for them.

When they stood him among the pillars, ²⁶Samson said to the servant who held his hand, "Put me where I can feel the pillars that support the temple, so that I may lean against them." ²⁷Now the temple was crowded with men and women; all the rulers of the Philistines were there, and on the roof ʷ were about three thousand men and women watching Samson perform. ²⁸Then Samson prayed to the LORD, ˣ "Sovereign LORD, remember me. Please, God, strengthen me just once more, and let me with one blow get revenge ʸ on the Philistines for my two eyes." ²⁹Then Samson reached toward the two central pillars on which the temple stood. Bracing himself against them, his right hand on the one and his left hand on the other, ³⁰Samson said, "Let me die with the Philistines!" Then he pushed with all his might, and down came the temple on the rulers and all the people in it. Thus he killed many more when he died than while he lived.

³¹Then his brothers and his father's whole family went down to get him. They brought him back and buried him between Zorah and Eshtaol in the tomb of Manoah ᶻ his father. He had led ᵃ ᵃ Israel twenty years. ᵇ

MICAH'S IDOLS

17 Now a man named Micah ᶜ from the hill country of Ephraim ²said to his mother, "The eleven hundred shekels ᵇ of silver that were taken from you and about which I heard you utter a curse—I have that silver with me; I took it."

Then his mother said, "The LORD bless you, ᵈ my son!"

³When he returned the eleven hundred shekels of silver to his mother, she said, "I solemnly consecrate my silver to the LORD for my son to make an image overlaid with silver. ᵉ I will give it back to you."

⁴So after he returned the silver to his mother, she took two hundred shekels ᶜ of silver and gave them to a silversmith, who used them to make the idol. ᶠ And it was put in Micah's house.

ᵃ 31 Traditionally *judged*   ᵇ 2 That is, about 28 pounds or about 13 kilograms   ᶜ 4 That is, about 5 pounds or about 2.3 kilograms

---

16:25 *to entertain us.* See note on 14:14.

16:27 *on the roof.* The temple complex probably surrounded an open court and had a flat roof where a large number of people had gathered to get a glimpse of the fallen champion.

16:28 *revenge ... for my two eyes.* See note on 15:7.

🅱 🄲 **16:30** *pushed.* Samson pushed the wooden pillars from their stone bases. Archaeologists have discovered a Philistine temple at Tell Qasile with a pair of closely spaced pillar bases (see archaeology note in map, p. 338). *killed many more.* Samson previously had slain well over 1,000 people (see 15:15; see also 14:19; 15:8). His final exploit was a mighty demonstration that the Philistine celebration of their god's victory over the Lord's champion was premature. *when he died.* If the Nazirite vow was violated and the uncut hair marking special dedication to God had become "defiled," that hair had to be cut off and the period of special consecration started all over again. The Nazirites "must rededicate themselves to the LORD for the same period of dedication ...The previous days do not count, because they became defiled during their period of dedication." And they must bring to the Lord "a year-old male lamb as a guilt offering" (Nu 6:9–12). When Samson's hair of dedication was cut off by Delilah, God showed that it had been defiled by Samson's many defiling acts and was not acceptable to him. But when his hair "began to grow again," a new time of Samson's consecration began (see v. 22 and note). Samson had no lamb to offer God as a guilt offering or lifetime ("from the womb until the day of his death," 13:7) to consecrate to the Lord. But he could offer up his life as God's champion warrior against the Philistines. And that is what he did.

16:31 *went down to get him.* The freedom of his family to secure his body and give it a burial indicates that the Philistines had no intention of further dishonoring him (contrast Saul's

death, 1Sa 31:9–10). *led Israel ... years.* See note on 12:7. *twenty years.* Round numbers are frequently used in Judges (see Introduction: Background).

🄲 **17:1—21:25** Two cycles of events forming an epilogue to the story of the judges (see Introduction: Literary Features). The events narrated evidently took place fairly early in the period of the judges (see notes on 18:30; 20:1,28). They illustrate the religious and moral degeneracy that characterized the age— when "Israel had no king" and "everyone did as they saw fit" (17:6; 21:25). Writing at a time when the monarchy under the Davidic dynasty had brought cohesion and order to the land and had reestablished a center for the worship of the Lord, the author portrays this earlier era of the judges as a dismal period of national decay, from which it was to be rescued by the house of David.

🄲 **17:1—18:31** The first cycle of events illustrates corruption in Israelite worship by telling of Micah's establishment of a local place of worship in Ephraim, aided by a Levite claiming descent from Moses. This paganized worship of the Lord is taken over by the tribe of Dan when that tribe abandons its appointed inheritance and migrates to Israel's northern frontier.

17:2 *eleven hundred shekels.* See note on 16:5. *I heard you utter a curse.* Fear of the curse seems to have motivated his returning the stolen money. *The LORD bless you.* A blessing to counteract the curse.

17:3 *mother ... son.* With their paganized view of the God of Israel, both were idolaters in disobedience to the law (Ex 20:4,23; Dt 4:16). *image.* Probably made of wood overlaid with silver.

17:4 *silversmith.* A maker of idols, as in Ac 19:24 (cf. Isa 40:19 and Jer 10:9, where the Hebrew for this word is translated "goldsmith").

⁵Now this man Micah had a shrine,ᵍ and he made an ephodʰ and some household godsⁱ and installedʲ one of his sons as his priest.ᵏ ⁶In those days Israel had no king;ˡ everyone did as they saw fit.ᵐ

⁷A young Leviteⁿ from Bethlehem in Judah,ᵒ who had been living within the clan of Judah, ⁸left that town in search of some other place to stay. On his wayᵃ he came to Micah's house in the hill country of Ephraim.

⁹Micah asked him, "Where are you from?"

"I'm a Levite from Bethlehem in Judah,ᵖ" he said, "and I'm looking for a place to stay."

¹⁰Then Micah said to him, "Live with me and be my fatherᑫ and priest,ʳ and I'll give you ten shekelsᵇ of silver a year, your clothes and your food." ¹¹So the Levite agreed to live with him, and the young man became like one of his sons to him. ¹²Then Micah installedˢ the Levite, and the young man became his priestᵗ and lived in his house. ¹³And Micah said, "Now I know that the Lᴏʀᴅ will be good to me, since this Levite has become my priest."ᵘ

THE DANITES SETTLE IN LAISH

18 In those days Israel had no king.ᵛ
And in those days the tribe of the Danites was seeking a place of their own where they might settle, because they had not yet come into an inheritance among the tribes of Israel.ʷ ²So the Danitesˣ sent five of their leading menʸ from Zorah and Eshtaol to spy outᶻ the land and explore it. These men represented all the Danites. They told them, "Go, explore the land."ᵃ

So they entered the hill country of Ephraim and came to the house of Micah,ᵇ where they spent the night. ³When they were near Micah's house, they recognized the voice of the young Levite;ᶜ so they turned in there and asked him, "Who brought you here? What are you doing in this place? Why are you here?"

⁴He told them what Micah had done for him, and said, "He has hired me and I am his priest.ᵈ"

⁵Then they said to him, "Please inquire of Godᵉ to learn whether our journey will be successful."

⁶The priest answered them, "Go in peace.ᶠ Your journey has the Lᴏʀᴅ's approval."

⁷So the five menᵍ left and came to Laish,ʰ where they saw that the people were living in safety, like the Sidonians, unsuspecting and secure.ⁱ And since their land lacked nothing, they were prosperous.ᶜ Also, they lived a long way from the Sidoniansʲ and had no relationship with anyone else.ᵈ

---

a 8 Or *To carry on his profession*   *b 10* That is, about 4 ounces or about 115 grams   *c 7* The meaning of the Hebrew for this clause is uncertain.   *d 7* Hebrew; some Septuagint manuscripts *with the Arameans*

17:5 ᵍ Isa 44:13; Eze 8:10 ʰ S Jdg 8:27
ⁱ S Ge 31:19
ʲ S Nu 16:10
ᵏ S Ex 29:9
17:6 ˡ Jdg 18:1; 19:1; 21:25 ᵐ S Dt 12:8
17:7 ⁿ Jdg 18:3
ᵒ S Ge 35:19; Mt 2:1
17:9 ᵖ Ru 1:1
17:10 ᑫ S Ge 45:8
ʳ Jdg 18:19
17:12 ˢ S Nu 16:10
ᵗ Jdg 18:4
17:13 ᵘ Nu 18:7
18:1 ᵛ S Jdg 17:6
ʷ Jos 19:47; Jdg 1:34
18:2 ˣ S Ge 30:6
ʸ ver 17 ᶻ S Nu 21:32
ᵃ S Jos 2:1 ᵇ S Jdg 17:1
18:3 ᶜ Jdg 17:7
18:4 ᵈ Jdg 17:12
18:5 ᵉ S Ge 25:22; Jdg 20:18, 23, 27; 1Sa 14:18; 2Sa 5:19; 2Ki 1:2; 8:8
18:6 ᶠ 1Ki 22:6
18:7 ᵍ ver 17
ʰ S Jos 19:47
ⁱ S Ge 34:25 ʲ ver 28; Jos 11:8

17:5 *ephod.* See 8:27 and note on Ex 28:6. *household gods.* Used in this case for divining (cf. Eze 21:21; Zec 10:2). Some of them were in human form (1Sa 19:13).

17:6 *had no king.* See 18:1; 19:1; 21:25; suggests that Judges was written after the establishment of the monarchy (see Introduction: Author and Date). *did as they saw fit.* The expression implies that Israel had departed from the covenant standards of conduct found in the law (see Dt 12:8).

17:7 *Levite.* His name was Jonathan (see 18:30 and note). *Bethlehem in Judah.* Not among the 48 designated Levitical cities (Jos 21).

17:8 *left that town.* The failure of the Israelites to obey the law probably resulted in a lack of support for the Levites, which explains the man's wandering in search of his fortune.

17:10 *father.* A term of respect used also for Elijah (2Ki 2:12) and Elisha (2Ki 6:21; 13:14). See Ge 45:8; Mt 23:9. *ten shekels.* See TNIV text note. In the light of this remuneration for a year's service, the stated amounts in 16:5 and 17:2 take on special significance. The offer of wages, clothing and food was more than this Levite could resist (v. 11). Clearly material concerns were at the root of his decision, because later he accepts an even more attractive offer (18:19–20).

17:12 *installed the Levite.* An attempt to make his shrine legitimate and give it prestige. Micah probably removed his son (see v. 5).

18:1 *seeking a place.* The Danite allotment was at the west end of the strip of land between Judah and Ephraim (Jos 19:41–46), but, due to the opposition of the Amorites (Jdg 1:34) and the

Philistines, the Danites were unable to occupy that territory (see note on 13:2).

18:2 *spy out.* See 1:23 and note on Nu 13:2.

18:3 *recognized the voice.* Perhaps they recognized him by his dialect or accent.

18:5 *inquire of God.* The request is for an oracle, probably by using the ephod and household gods (see note on 17:5). God had already revealed his will by the allotments given to the various tribes (Jos 14–20). They were searching for an oracle that would guarantee the success of their journey.

18:6 *Go in peace.* The Levite gave them the message they wanted to hear. He was even careful to use the name of the Lord to give the message credibility and authority.

18:7 *Laish.* The journey northward was about 100 miles from Zorah and Eshtaol (v. 2). This town is called Leshem in Jos 19:47. After its capture by the Danites, Laish was renamed Dan (v. 29), and it was Israel's northernmost settlement (see 20:1; 1Sa 3:20; 2Sa 3:10). Excavations there have disclosed that the earliest Israelite occupation of Dan was in the 12th century B.C. and that the first Israelite inhabitants apparently lived in tents or temporary huts. Occupation of the site continued into the Assyrian period, but the town was destroyed and rebuilt many times. A large high place attached to the city was often extensively rebuilt and refurbished and was in use into the Hellenistic period. *Sidonians.* A peaceful Phoenician people who engaged in commerce throughout the Mediterranean world. *had no relationship.* They did not feel threatened by other powers and therefore sought no treaties for mutual defense.

18:9 *k* Nu 13:30;
1Ki 22:3
18:10 *l* Dt 8:9
m 1Ch 4:40
18:11 *n* ver 16,17
o Jdg 13:2
18:12 *p* S Jos 9:17
q Jdg 13:25
18:13 *r* S Jdg 17:1
18:14 *s* S Jos 19:47
t S Jdg 8:27
u S Ge 31:19
18:16 *v* S ver 11
18:17 *w* S Ge 31:19;
Mic 5:13 *x* ver 11
18:18 *y* ver 24;
Isa 46:2; Jer 43:11;
48:7; 49:3; Hos 10:5
z S Ge 31:19
18:19 *a* Job 13:5;
21:5; 29:9; 40:4;
Isa 52:15; Mic 7:16
b Jdg 17:10 *c* Nu 26:42
18:24 *d* S ver 17-18
18:26 *e* 2Sa 3:39;
Ps 18:17; 35:10
18:27 *f* S Ge 34:25
g S Nu 31:10
h Ge 49:17;
S Jos 19:47
18:28 *i* S ver 7;
S Ge 10:19
j S Nu 13:21
18:29 *k* S Ge 14:14
l S Jos 19:47;
1Ki 15:20
18:30 *m* Ex 2:22
18:31 *n* ver 17
o Jdg 19:18; 20:18
p S Jos 18:1; Jer 7:14

[8]When they returned to Zorah and Eshtaol, the Danites asked them, "How did you find things?"

[9]They answered, "Come on, let's attack them! We have seen the land, and it is very good. Aren't you going to do something? Don't hesitate to go there and take it over. [k] [10]When you get there, you will find an unsuspecting people and a spacious land that God has put into your hands, a land that lacks nothing [l] whatever. [m]"

[11]Then six hundred men [n] of the Danites, [o] armed for battle, set out from Zorah and Eshtaol. [12]On their way they set up camp near Kiriath Jearim [p] in Judah. This is why the place west of Kiriath Jearim is called Mahaneh Dan [a] [q] to this day. [13]From there they went on to the hill country of Ephraim and came to Micah's house. [r]

[14]Then the five men who had spied out the land of Laish [s] said to their fellow Danites, "Do you know that one of these houses has an ephod, [t] some household gods and an image overlaid with silver? [u] Now you know what to do." [15]So they turned in there and went to the house of the young Levite at Micah's place and greeted him. [16]The six hundred Danites, [v] armed for battle, stood at the entrance of the gate. [17]The five men who had spied out the land went inside and took the idol, the ephod and the household gods [w] while the priest and the six hundred armed men [x] stood at the entrance of the gate.

[18]When the five went into Micah's house and took [y] the idol, the ephod and the household gods, [z] the priest said to them, "What are you doing?"

[19]They answered him, "Be quiet! [a] Don't say a word. Come with us, and be our father and priest. [b] Isn't it better that you serve a tribe and clan [c] in Israel as priest rather than just one man's household?" [20]The priest was very pleased. He took the ephod, the household gods and the idol and went along with the people. [21]Putting their little children, their livestock and their possessions in front of them, they turned away and left.

[22]When they had gone some distance from Micah's house, the men who lived near Micah were called together and overtook the Danites. [23]As they shouted after them, the Danites turned and said to Micah, "What's the matter with you that you called out your men to fight?"

[24]He replied, "You took [d] the gods I made, and my priest, and went away. What else do I have? How can you ask, 'What's the matter with you?' "

[25]The Danites answered, "Don't argue with us, or some of the men may get angry and attack you, and you and your family will lose your lives." [26]So the Danites went their way, and Micah, seeing that they were too strong for him, [e] turned around and went back home.

[27]Then they took what Micah had made, and his priest, and went on to Laish, against a peaceful and unsuspecting people. [f] They attacked them with the sword and burned [g] down their city. [h] [28]There was no one to rescue them because they lived a long way from Sidon [i] and had no relationship with anyone else. The city was in a valley near Beth Rehob. [j]

The Danites rebuilt the city and settled there. [29]They named it Dan [k] after their ancestor Dan, who was born to Israel—though the city used to be called Laish. [l] [30]There the Danites set up for themselves the idol, and Jonathan son of Gershom, [m] the son of Moses, [b] and his sons were priests for the tribe of Dan until the time of the captivity of the land. [31]They continued to use the idol Micah had made, [n] all the time the house of God [o] was in Shiloh. [p]

---

[a] 12 *Mahaneh Dan* means *Dan's camp.*   [b] 30 Many Hebrew manuscripts, some Septuagint manuscripts and Vulgate; many other Hebrew manuscripts and some other Septuagint manuscripts *Manasseh*

18:11 *six hundred men.* As leaders of the tribe of Dan, they represented the entire tribe's migration to its new location in the north. Cf. the 600 men who constituted the remnant of the tribe of Benjamin (20:47).

18:19 *father.* See note on 17:10. *a tribe and clan.* Only one clan from the tribe of Dan is ever mentioned—Shuham (Nu 26:42; called Hushim in Ge 46:23). The Danites appealed to the Levite's vanity and materialism.

18:21 *in front of them.* For protection in case of attack by Micah and his neighbors (cf. Ge 33:2–3, Jacob and Esau).

18:24 *You took the gods.* Micah was concerned about the loss of gods that could not even protect themselves. *What else do I have?* The agonizing cry of one whose faith is centered in helpless gods.

18:28 *Beth Rehob.* Probably the same as Rehob in Nu 13:21 (see also 2Sa 10:6,8).

18:29 *named it Dan.* For the city's location see map No. 4 at the end of this study Bible.

18:30 *Jonathan.* The Levite is here identified as Jonathan, son of Gershom, the son of Moses (Ex 2:22; 18:3; 1Ch 23:14–15). In an effort to prevent desecration of the name of Moses, later scribes modified the name slightly, making it read "Manasseh" (see TNIV text note). If Jonathan was the grandson of Moses, the events in this chapter must have occurred early in the period of the judges (see notes on 20:1,28). *captivity of the land.* The date of this captivity has not been determined (see note on v. 7 regarding Laish).

18:31 *all the time the house of God was in Shiloh.* See Jos 18:1. For Shiloh's destruction see Ps 78:60; Jer 7:12,14; 26:6. Archaeological work at Shiloh indicates that the site was destroyed c. 1050 B.C. and was left uninhabited for many centuries.

A LEVITE AND HIS CONCUBINE

19

In those days Israel had no king.

Now a Levite who lived in a remote area in the hill country of Ephraim q took a concubine from Bethlehem in Judah. r 2But she was unfaithful to him. She left him and went back to her parents' home in Bethlehem, Judah. After she had been there four months, 3her husband went to her to persuade her to return. He had with him his servant and two donkeys. She took him into her parents' home, and when her father saw him, he gladly welcomed him. 4His father-in-law, the woman's father, prevailed on him to stay; so he remained with him three days, eating and drinking, s and sleeping there.

5On the fourth day they got up early and he prepared to leave, but the woman's father said to his son-in-law, "Refresh yourself t with something to eat; then you can go." 6So the two of them sat down to eat and drink together. Afterward the woman's father said, "Please stay tonight and enjoy yourself. u" 7And when the man got up to go, his father-in-law persuaded him, so he stayed there that night. 8On the morning of the fifth day, when he rose to go, the woman's father said, "Refresh yourself. Wait till afternoon!" So the two of them ate together.

9Then when the man, with his concubine and his servant, got up to leave, his father-in-law, the woman's father, said, "Now look, it's almost evening. Spend the night here; the day is nearly over. Stay and enjoy yourself. Early tomorrow morning you can get up and be on your way home." 10But, unwilling to stay another night, the man left and went toward Jebus v (that is, Jerusalem), with his two saddled donkeys and his concubine.

11When they were near Jebus and the day was almost gone, the servant said to his master, "Come, let's stop at this city of the Jebusites w and spend the night."

12His master replied, "No. We won't go into any city whose people are not Israelites. We will go on to Gibeah." 13He added, "Come, let's try to reach Gibeah or Ramah x and spend the night in one of those places." 14So they went on, and the sun set as they neared Gibeah in Benjamin. y 15There they stopped to spend the night. z They went and sat in the city square, a but no one took them in for the night.

16That evening b an old man from the hill country of Ephraim, c who was living in Gibeah (the inhabitants of the place were Benjamites), came in from his work in the fields. 17When he looked and saw the traveler in the city square, the old man asked, "Where are you going? Where did you come from?" d

18He answered, "We are on our way from Bethlehem in Judah to a remote area in the hill country of Ephraim where I live. I have been to Bethlehem in Judah and now I am going to the house of the Lord. a e No one has taken me in for the night. 19We have both straw and fodder f for our donkeys g and bread and wine h for ourselves your servants—me, the woman and the young man with us. We don't need anything."

20"You are welcome at my house," the old man said. "Let me supply whatever you need. Only don't spend the night in the square." 21So he took him into his house and fed his donkeys. After they had washed their feet, they had something to eat and drink. i

22While they were enjoying themselves, j some of the wicked men k of the city sur-

---

a 18 Hebrew, Vulgate, Syriac and Targum; Septuagint *going home*

19:1 q ver 16,18
r Ru 1:1
19:4 s ver 6,8;
S Ex 32:6
19:5 t ver 8; Ge 18:5
19:6 u S Jdg 16:25
19:10 v S Ge 10:16;
S Jos 15:8
19:11 w S Ge 10:16;
S Jos 3:10
19:13 x S Jos 18:25
19:14 y Jos 15:57;
1Sa 10:26; 11:4; 13:2;
15:34; Isa 10:29
19:15 z S Ge 24:23
a S Ge 19:2
19:16 b Ps 104:23
c S ver 1
19:17 d S Ge 29:4
19:18 e S Jdg 18:31
19:19 f Ge 24:25
g S Ge 42:27
h S Ge 14:18
19:21 i Ge 24:32-
33; Lk 7:44
19:22 j S Jdg 16:25
k S Dt 13:13

C **19:1—21:25** The second cycle of events in the epilogue (see note on 17:1—18:31). It illustrates Israel's moral corruption by telling of the degenerate act of the men of Gibeah—an act remembered centuries later (Hos 9:9; 10:9). Although that town showed itself to be as wicked as any Canaanite town, it was defended by the rest of the tribe of Benjamin against the Lord's discipline through the Israelites, until nearly the whole tribe was destroyed.

19:1–30 An account of an Israelite town (Gibeah) that revived the ways of Sodom (see Ge 19).

19:1 *Levite.* Unlike the Levite of chs. 17–18, this man is not named. *concubine.* See note on Ge 25:6.

19:3 *gladly welcomed him.* The separation of the concubine from the Levite was probably a matter of family disgrace, so his father-in-law was glad for the prospect of the two being reunited.

19:10 *Jebus.* See 1:21; see also note on Ge 10:16.

19:12 *city whose people are not Israelites.* With the city under the control of the Jebusites, the Levite was afraid that he would receive no hospitality and might be in mortal danger.

19:14 *Gibeah in Benjamin.* Distinguished from the Gibeah in

Judah (Jos 15:20,57) and the Gibeah in the hill country of Ephraim (Jos 24:33). As the political capital of Saul's kingdom, it is called Gibeah of Saul in 1Sa 11:4; see also 1Sa 13:15.

19:15 *took them in.* See notes on 13:15; Ge 18:2.

19:18 *house of the Lord.* Apparently the Levite was planning to go to Shiloh (see 18:31; Jos 18:1) to present a thank offering to the Lord or a sin offering for himself and his concubine.

19:21 *washed their feet.* An evidence of hospitality in the ancient Near East, where travelers commonly wore sandals as they walked the dusty roads (see Ge 18:4; 24:32; 43:24; Lk 7:44; Jn 13:5–14).

C **19:22** *wicked men.* The Hebrew for this expression refers to the morally depraved (see note on Dt 13:13). Elsewhere the expression is associated with idolatry (Dt 13:13), drunkenness (1Sa 1:16) and rebellion (1Sa 2:12). Here the reference is to homosexual acts. *Bring out the man.* The sexual perversion of these wicked men is yet another example of the decadence of an age when "everyone did as they saw fit" (17:6; 21:25). A similar request was made by the men of Sodom (Ge 19:5). Homosexual practices were common among the Canaanites.

19:22 *¹* Ge 19:4-5;
Jdg 20:5; Ro 1:26-27
19:23 *ᵐ* Ge 19:6
ⁿ S Ge 34:7;
S Lev 19:29;
S Jos 7:15; S Jdg 20:6;
Ro 1:27
19:24 *ᵒ* Ge 19:8
19:25 *ᵖ* Jdg 20:5
q 1Sa 31:4
19:29 *ʳ* S Ge 22:6
ˢ Jdg 20:6; 1Sa 11:7
19:30 *ᵗ* Hos 9:9
ᵘ Jdg 20:7; Pr 13:10
20:1 *ᵛ* Jdg 21:5
ʷ S Ge 21:14;
1Sa 3:20; 2Sa 3:10;
17:11; 24:15; 1Ki 4:25;
2Ch 30:5 *ˣ* ver 11;
1Sa 11:7 *ʸ* 1Sa 7:5
ᶻ S Jos 11:3
20:2 *ᵃ* 1Sa 11:8
20:4 *ᵇ* S Jos 15:57
ᶜ S Ge 24:23
20:5 *ᵈ* S Jdg 19:22
ᵉ Jdg 19:25-26
20:6 *ᶠ* S Jdg 19:29
ᵍ S Jdg 19:23;
2Sa 13:12
20:7 *ʰ* S Jdg 19:30
20:9 *ⁱ* S Lev 16:8
20:11 *ʲ* S ver 1

rounded the house. Pounding on the door, they shouted to the old man who owned the house, "Bring out the man who came to your house so we can have sex with him.*¹*"

²³The owner of the house went outside*ᵐ* and said to them, "No, my friends, don't be so vile. Since this man is my guest, don't do this outrageous thing.*ⁿ* ²⁴Look, here is my virgin daughter,*ᵒ* and his concubine. I will bring them out to you now, and you can use them and do to them whatever you wish. But as for this man, don't do such an outrageous thing."

²⁵But the men would not listen to him. So the man took his concubine and sent her outside to them, and they raped her*ᵖ* and abused her*q* throughout the night, and at dawn they let her go. ²⁶At daybreak the woman went back to the house where her master was staying, fell down at the door and lay there until daylight.

²⁷When her master got up in the morning and opened the door of the house and stepped out to continue on his way, there lay his concubine, fallen in the doorway of the house, with her hands on the threshold. ²⁸He said to her, "Get up; let's go." But there was no answer. Then he put her on his donkey and set out for home.

²⁹When he reached home, he took a knife*ʳ* and cut up his concubine, limb by limb, into twelve parts and sent them into all the areas of Israel.*ˢ* ³⁰Everyone who saw it said, "Such a thing has never been seen or done, not since the day the Israelites came up out of Egypt.*ᵗ* Think about it! Consider it! Tell us what to do!*ᵘ*"

THE ISRAELITES PUNISH THE BENJAMITES

20 Then all the Israelites*ᵛ* from Dan to Beersheba*ʷ* and from the land of Gilead came out with one accord*ˣ* and assembled*ʸ* before the LORD in Mizpah.*ᶻ* ²The leaders of all the people of the tribes of Israel took their places in the assembly of the people of God, four hundred thousand soldiers*ᵃ* armed with swords. ³(The Benjamites heard that the Israelites had gone up to Mizpah.) Then the Israelites said, "Tell us how this awful thing happened."

⁴So the Levite, the husband of the murdered woman, said, "I and my concubine came to Gibeah*ᵇ* in Benjamin to spend the night.*ᶜ* ⁵During the night the men of Gibeah came after me and surrounded the house, intending to kill me.*ᵈ* They raped my concubine, and she died.*ᵉ* ⁶I took my concubine, cut her into pieces and sent one piece to each region of Israel's inheritance,*ᶠ* because they committed this lewd and outrageous act*ᵍ* in Israel. ⁷Now, all you Israelites, speak up and give your verdict.*ʰ*"

⁸All the people rose with one accord, saying, "None of us will go home. No, not one of us will return to his house. ⁹But now this is what we'll do to Gibeah: We'll go up against it as the lot directs.*ⁱ* ¹⁰We'll take ten men out of every hundred from all the tribes of Israel, and a hundred from a thousand, and a thousand from ten thousand, to get provisions for the army. Then, when the army arrives at Gibeah*ᵃ* in Benjamin, it can give them what they deserve for this outrageous act done in Israel." ¹¹So all the Israelites got together and united against the city with one accord.*ʲ*

---

a 10 One Hebrew manuscript; most Hebrew manuscripts *Geba,* a variant of *Gibeah*

A   **19:23** *don't be so vile.* An expression of outrage at the willful perversion of what is right and natural (see Ge 19:7; 2Sa 13:12; see also Ro 1:27).

A   **19:24** *my virgin daughter, and his concubine.* The tragedy of this story lies not only in the decadence of Gibeah but also in the callous selfishness of men who would betray defenseless women to be brutally violated for a whole night. Cf. Ge 19:8, where Lot offered his two daughters to the men of Sodom.

19:25 *took.* Here the Hebrew for this verb suggests taking by force.

19:29 *cut up his concubine.* Dismembering the concubine's body and sending parts to each of the 12 tribes was intended to awaken Israel from its moral lethargy and to marshal the tribes to face up to their responsibility. It is ironic that the one who issued such a call was himself so selfish and insensitive. See also Saul's similar action in 1Sa 11:7.

20:1–48 All Israel (except Jabesh Gilead; see 21:8–9) assembled before the Lord to deal with the moral outrage committed by the men of Gibeah. Having first inquired of God for divine direction, they marched against Gibeah and the Benjamites as the

disciplinary arm of the Lord (see Jos 22:11–34), following him as their King.

20:1 *Dan to Beersheba.* A conventional way of speaking of all Israel from north (Dan) to south (Beersheba); see 1Sa 3:20; 2Sa 3:10; 24:2; 1Ch 21:2; 2Ch 30:5. The use of this expression, however, does not mean that the events of this chapter occurred after Dan's move to the north (18:27–29); rather, it indicates the author's perspective at the time of writing (Judges was probably written after the Davidic dynasty was fully established; see Introduction: Author and Date). Here the expression refers to the disciplinary action of all Israel (except Jabesh Gilead; see 21:8–9) against Gibeah and the rest of the Benjamites. Such a united response must have occurred early in the time of the judges, before the period of foreign domination of various parts of the land. *with one accord.* Cf. vv. 8,11; 1Sa 11:7. *assembled . . . in Mizpah.* A place where the tribes gathered to meet before the Lord also during the days of Saul (1Sa 7:5–17; 10:17).

20:9 *lot.* Casting lots was a common method of determining the will of God (see notes on Ex 28:30; Jnh 1:7; Ac 1:26).

20:10 *ten men.* Support for the large army had to be well organized and efficient. One man was responsible for providing food for nine men fighting at the front.

¹²The tribes of Israel sent messengers throughout the tribe of Benjamin, saying, "What about this awful crime that was committed among you? *ᵏ* ¹³Now turn those wicked men *ˡ* of Gibeah over to us so that we may put them to death and purge the evil from Israel. *ᵐ*"

But the Benjamites would not listen to their fellow Israelites. ¹⁴From their towns they came together at Gibeah to fight against the Israelites. ¹⁵At once the Benjamites mobilized twenty-six thousand swordsmen from their towns, in addition to seven hundred able young men from those living in Gibeah. ¹⁶Among all these soldiers there were seven hundred who were left-handed, *ⁿ* each of whom could sling a stone at a hair and not miss.

¹⁷Israel, apart from Benjamin, mustered four hundred thousand swordsmen, all of them fighting men.

¹⁸The Israelites went up to Bethel *ᵃ ᵒ* and inquired of God. *ᵖ* They said, "Who of us is to go up first *�q* to fight *ʳ* against the Benjamites?"

The Lᴏʀᴅ replied, "Judah *ˢ* shall go first."

¹⁹The next morning the Israelites got up and pitched camp near Gibeah. ²⁰The Israelites went out to fight the Benjamites and took up battle positions against them at Gibeah. ²¹The Benjamites came out of Gibeah and cut down twenty-two thousand Israelites *ᵗ* on the battlefield that day. ²²But the Israelites encouraged one another and again took up their positions where they had stationed themselves the first day. ²³The Israelites went up and wept before the Lᴏʀᴅ *ᵘ* until evening, *ᵛ* and they inquired of the Lᴏʀᴅ. *ʷ* They said, "Shall we go up again to fight *ˣ* against the Benjamites, our fellow Israelites?"

The Lᴏʀᴅ answered, "Go up against them."

²⁴Then the Israelites drew near to Benjamin the second day. ²⁵This time, when the Benjamites came out from Gibeah to oppose them, they cut down another eighteen thousand Israelites, *ʸ* all of them armed with swords.

²⁶Then all the Israelites, the whole army, went up to Bethel, and there they sat weeping before the Lᴏʀᴅ. *ᶻ* They fasted *ᵃ* that day until evening and presented burnt offerings *ᵇ* and fellowship offerings *ᶜ* to the Lᴏʀᴅ. *ᵈ* ²⁷And the Israelites inquired of the Lᴏʀᴅ. *ᵉ* (In those days the ark of the covenant of God *ᶠ* was there, ²⁸with Phinehas son of Eleazar, *ᵍ* the son of Aaron, ministering before it.) *ʰ* They asked, "Shall we go up again to fight against the Benjamites, our fellow Israelites, or not?"

The Lᴏʀᴅ responded, "Go, for tomorrow I will give them into your hands. *ⁱ*"

²⁹Then Israel set an ambush *ʲ* around Gibeah. ³⁰They went up against the Benjamites on the third day and took up positions against Gibeah as they had done before. ³¹The Benjamites came out to meet them and were drawn away *ᵏ* from the city. They began to inflict casualties on the Israelites as before, so that about thirty of them fell in the open field and on the roads—the one leading to Bethel *ˡ* and the other to Gibeah.

³²While the Benjamites were saying, "We are defeating them as before," *ᵐ* the Israelites were saying, "Let's retreat and draw them away from the city to the roads."

³³All the men of Israel moved from their places and took up positions at Baal Tamar, and the Israelite ambush charged out of its place *ⁿ* on the west *ᵇ* of Gibeah. *ᶜ* ³⁴Then ten thousand of Israel's able young men made a frontal attack on Gibeah. The fighting was so heavy that the Benjamites did not realize *ᵒ* how near disaster was. *ᵖ* ³⁵The Lᴏʀᴅ defeated Benjamin *q* before Israel, and on that day the Israelites struck down 25,100 Benjamites, all armed with swords. ³⁶Then the Benjamites saw that they were beaten.

Now the men of Israel had given way *ʳ* before Benjamin, because they relied on the ambush *ˢ* they had set near Gibeah. ³⁷Those who had been in ambush made a sudden

20:12 *ᵏ* Dt 13:14
20:13 *ˡ* S Dt 13:13
ᵐ S Dt 13:5;
S 1Co 5:13
20:16 *ⁿ* S Jdg 3:15
20:18 *ᵒ* S Jos 12:9;
S Jdg 18:31
ᵖ S Jdg 18:5 *q* S Jdg 1:1
ʳ ver 23,28
ˢ S Ge 49:10
20:21 *ᵗ* ver 25
20:23 *ᵘ* S Nu 14:1
ᵛ Jos 7:6 *ʷ* S Jdg 18:5
ˣ S ver 18
20:25 *ʸ* ver 21
20:26 *ᶻ* S Nu 14:1
ᵃ 2Sa 12:21 *ᵇ* Lev 1:3
ᶜ S Ex 32:6 *ᵈ* Jdg 21:4
20:27 *ᵉ* S Jdg 18:5
ᶠ S Nu 10:33
20:28 *ᵍ* Nu 25:7
ʰ Dt 18:5 *ⁱ* S Jos 2:24
20:29 *ʲ* S Jos 8:2,4
20:31 *ᵏ* Jos 8:16
ˡ Jos 16:1
20:32 *ᵐ* ver 39
20:33 *ⁿ* Jos 8:19
20:34 *ᵒ* Jos 8:14
ᵖ ver 41
20:35 *q* 1Sa 9:21
20:36 *ʳ* Jos 8:15
ˢ Jos 8:2

ᵃ 18 Or *to the house of God*; also in verse 26   *ᵇ 33* Some Septuagint manuscripts and Vulgate; the meaning of the Hebrew for this word is uncertain.   *ᶜ 33* Hebrew *Geba*, a variant of *Gibeah*

20:13 *turn those wicked men . . . over to us.* The demand of Israel was not unreasonable. The intent was to punish only those directly involved in the crime. *wicked men.* See note on Dt 13:13. *put them to death.* The sin of the men of Gibeah called for the death penalty, and Israel had to punish the sin if she was to avoid guilt herself (see Dt 13:5; 17:7; 19:19–20).

20:16 *left-handed.* The Benjamite Ehud was also left-handed (3:15). *sling a stone.* Cf. Zec 9:15. The sling was a very effective weapon, as David later demonstrated in his encounter with Goliath (1Sa 17:49). A slingstone, weighing one pound or more, could be hurled at 90–100 miles an hour. *miss.* In other contexts the Hebrew for this word is translated "to sin."

20:18 *Bethel.* At this time the ark of the covenant and the high priest Phinehas were at Bethel (see vv. 26–28). *inquired of God.* Probably by priestly use of the Urim and Thummim (see notes

on Ex 28:30; 1Sa 2:28). *Who of us is to go up first . . . ?* See 1:1–36. *Judah.* See note on 1:2.

20:21 *twenty-two thousand Israelites.* A rousing victory for the Benjamites, who numbered 26,700 (v. 15) and therefore had struck down nearly one man apiece.

20:27 *ark.* The only mention of the ark in Judges.

20:28 *Phinehas.* Phinehas was the priest in the tabernacle in the days of Joshua (Jos 22:13), and the fact that he was still serving is further evidence that these events took place early in the days of the judges (see notes on v. 1; 18:30).

20:29 *set an ambush.* See 9:32; Jos 8:2.

20:33 *Baal Tamar.* Location unknown.

20:35 *25,100.* Apparently 1,000 Benjamites had been killed in the first two battles (see note on v. 21).

20:36b–45 Details of the account in vv. 29–36a.

20:37 ᵗ Jos 8:19
20:38 ᵘ Jos 8:20
ᵛ Jos 8:4-8
20:39 ʷ ver 32;
Ps 78:9
20:40 ˣ Jos 8:20
20:41 ʸ Jos 8:21
ᶻ ver 34
20:44 ᵃ 1Sa 10:26;
Ps 76:5
20:45 ᵇ S Jos 15:32
20:46 ᶜ 1Sa 9:21
20:48 ᵈ Jdg 21:23
21:1 ᵉ S Jos 9:18
ᶠ S Jos 11:3 ᵍ ver 18,22
21:3 ʰ ver 6,17
21:4 ⁱ Jdg 20:26
21:5 ʲ Jdg 20:1
21:7 ᵏ S Jos 9:18
21:8 ˡ 1Sa 11:1; 31:11;
2Sa 2:4; 21:12;
1Ch 10:11
21:11 ᵐ S Nu 31:7
ⁿ Nu 31:17-18
21:12 ᵒ S Jos 18:1

dash into Gibeah, spread out and put the whole city to the sword. ᵗ ³⁸The Israelites had arranged with the ambush that they should send up a great cloud of smoke ᵘ from the city, ᵛ ³⁹and then the Israelites would turn in the battle.

The Benjamites had begun to inflict casualties on the Israelites (about thirty), and they said, "We are defeating them as in the first battle." ʷ ⁴⁰But when the column of smoke began to rise from the city, the Benjamites turned and saw the smoke of the whole city going up into the sky. ˣ ⁴¹Then the Israelites turned on them, ʸ and the Benjamites were terrified, because they realized that disaster had come ᶻ on them. ⁴²So they fled before the Israelites in the direction of the wilderness, but they could not escape the battle. And the Israelites who came out of the towns cut them down there. ⁴³They surrounded the Benjamites, chased them and easily ᵃ overran them in the vicinity of Gibeah on the east. ⁴⁴Eighteen thousand Benjamites fell, all of them valiant fighters. ᵃ ⁴⁵As they turned and fled toward the wilderness to the rock of Rimmon, ᵇ the Israelites cut down five thousand men along the roads. They kept pressing after the Benjamites as far as Gidom and struck down two thousand more.

⁴⁶On that day twenty-five thousand Benjamite ᶜ swordsmen fell, all of them valiant fighters. ⁴⁷But six hundred men turned and fled into the wilderness to the rock of Rimmon, where they stayed four months. ⁴⁸The men of Israel went back to Benjamin and put all the towns to the sword, including the animals and everything else they found. All the towns they came across they set on fire. ᵈ

WIVES FOR THE BENJAMITES

21 The men of Israel had taken an oath ᵉ at Mizpah: ᶠ "Not one of us will give ᵍ his daughter in marriage to a Benjamite."

²The people went to Bethel, ᵇ where they sat before God until evening, raising their voices and weeping bitterly. ³"LORD, God of Israel," they cried, "why has this happened to Israel? Why should one tribe be missing ʰ from Israel today?"

⁴Early the next day the people built an altar and presented burnt offerings and fellowship offerings. ⁱ

⁵Then the Israelites asked, "Who from all the tribes of Israel ʲ has failed to assemble before the LORD?" For they had taken a solemn oath that anyone who failed to assemble before the LORD at Mizpah was to be put to death.

⁶Now the Israelites grieved for Benjamin, one of their tribes. "Today one tribe is cut off from Israel," they said. ⁷"How can we provide wives for those who are left, since we have taken an oath ᵏ by the LORD not to give them any of our daughters in marriage?" ⁸Then they asked, "Which one of the tribes of Israel failed to assemble before the LORD at Mizpah?" They discovered that no one from Jabesh Gilead ˡ had come to the camp for the assembly. ⁹For when they counted the people, they found that none of the people of Jabesh Gilead were there.

¹⁰So the assembly sent twelve thousand fighting men with instructions to go to Jabesh Gilead and put to the sword those living there, including the women and children. ¹¹"This is what you are to do," they said. "Kill every male ᵐ and every woman who is not a virgin. ⁿ" ¹²They found among the people living in Jabesh Gilead four hundred young women who had never slept with a man, and they took them to the camp at Shiloh ᵒ in Canaan.

ᵃ 43 The meaning of the Hebrew for this word is uncertain. ᵇ 2 Or *to the house of God*

20:46 *twenty-five thousand.* A round number for 25,100 (v. 35).
20:47 *six hundred men.* If these had not escaped, the tribe of Benjamin would have been annihilated. The same number of Danites went to Laish (18:11).
21:1–25 Second thoughts about the slaughter of their Benjamite brothers caused the Israelites to grieve over the loss. Only 600 Benjamites were left alive, and the men of Israel decided to provide wives for them in order to keep the tribe from disappearing. After slaughtering most of the people of Jabesh Gilead, the Israelites took 400 young women from the survivors and gave them to 400 Benjamites. Shortly afterward, each of the remaining Benjamites seized a wife from the women of Shiloh, and Benjamin began to be restored.
21:1 *taken an oath.* This vow, probably taken in the name of the Lord, was not an ordinary vow but invoked a curse on oneself if the vow was broken (v. 18; see also Ac 23:12–15).
21:2 *Bethel.* See 20:18,26–27. *weeping bitterly.* Earlier the Israelites wept because they were defeated by the Benjamites

(20:23,26). Now they weep because the disciplinary action against the Benjamites has nearly annihilated one of the tribes (see v. 3).
21:5 *failed to assemble.* The tribes had a mutual responsibility in times of military action (see note on 5:13–18). Those who failed to participate were often singled out and sometimes punished (5:15–17,23). *solemn oath.* Complicating the situation for Israel was the fact that they had taken a second oath, calling for the deaths of those who had not participated in the battle.
21:10 *twelve thousand.* A thousand from each tribe (see Nu 31:6), with 1,000 supplied to represent the tribe of Benjamin.
21:11 *Kill every male.* The punishment of Jabesh Gilead seems brutal, but the covenant bond between the tribes was extremely important. Even though delinquency on some occasions was not punished (5:15–17), the nature of the crime in this case, coupled with Benjamin's refusal to turn over the criminals, caused Israel to take this oath (v. 5).
21:12 *in Canaan.* Emphasizes the fact that the women were brought across the Jordan from the east.

¹³Then the whole assembly sent an offer of peace^p to the Benjamites at the rock of Rimmon. ^q ¹⁴So the Benjamites returned at that time and were given the women of Jabesh Gilead who had been spared. But there were not enough for all of them.

¹⁵The people grieved for Benjamin, ^r because the LORD had made a gap in the tribes of Israel. ¹⁶And the elders of the assembly said, "With the women of Benjamin destroyed, how shall we provide wives for the men who are left? ¹⁷The Benjamite survivors must have heirs," they said, "so that a tribe of Israel will not be wiped out. ^s ¹⁸We can't give them our daughters as wives, since we Israelites have taken this oath: ^t 'Cursed be anyone who gives ^u a wife to a Benjamite.' ¹⁹But look, there is the annual festival of the LORD in Shiloh, ^v to the north of Bethel ^w, and east of the road that goes from Bethel to Shechem, ^x and to the south of Lebonah."

²⁰So they instructed the Benjamites, saying, "Go and hide in the vineyards ²¹and watch. When the young women of Shiloh come out to join in the dancing, ^y then rush from the vineyards and each of you seize a wife from the young women of Shiloh and go to the land of Benjamin. ²²When their fathers or brothers complain to us, we will say to them, 'Do us a kindness by helping them, because we did not get wives for them during the war, and you are innocent, since you did not give ^z your daughters to them.' "

²³So that is what the Benjamites did. While the young women were dancing, ^a each man caught one and carried her off to be his wife. Then they returned to their inheritance ^b and rebuilt the towns and settled in them. ^c

²⁴At that time the Israelites left that place and went home to their tribes and clans, each to his own inheritance.

²⁵In those days Israel had no king; everyone did as they saw fit. ^d

21:13 ^p S Dt 2:26
^q S Jos 15:32
21:15 ^r ver 6
21:17 ^s S ver 3
21:18 ^t S Jos 9:18
^u S ver 1
21:19 ^v S Jos 18:1
^w Jos 16:1 ^x S Jos 17:7
21:21 ^y S Ex 15:20
21:22 ^z S ver 1;
ver 1,18
21:23 ^a ver 21
^b S Jos 24:28
^c Jdg 20:48
21:25 ^d S Dt 12:8

21:19 *festival of the LORD.* In light of the mention of vineyards (v. 20), it is likely that this reference is to the Festival of Tabernacles (see note on 1Sa 1:3), though it may have been a local festival. *north of Bethel … south of Lebonah.* This detailed description of Shiloh's location may indicate that this material was written at a time when Shiloh was in ruins, perhaps after its destruction during the battle of Aphek (1Sa 4:1–11).

21:21 *seize a wife.* With the Benjamites securing wives in this manner, the other tribes were not actually "giving" their daughters to them (see note on v. 22).

21:22 *When their fathers or brothers complain.* It was customary for the brothers of a young woman who had been abducted to demand satisfaction (see Ge 34:7–31; 2Sa 13:20–38). It was therefore important that the elders anticipate this response and be prepared to get cooperation from the young women's families.

21:24 *went home.* These soldiers had probably been away from home at least five months (see 20:47).

21:25 *Israel had no king.* See Introduction: Author and Date; see also note on 17:6. *did as they saw fit.* See note on 17:6; see also Introduction: Themes and Theology; Literary Features.

TITLE   RUTH   INTRODUCTION

C The book is named after one of its main characters, a young woman of Moab, the great-grandmother of David and an ancestor of Jesus (4:21–22; Mt 1:1,5). The only other Biblical book bearing the name of a woman is Esther.

BACKGROUND

The story is set in the time of the judges, a time characterized in the book of Judges as a period of religious and moral degeneracy, national disunity and frequent foreign oppression. The book of Ruth reflects a time of peace between Israel and Moab (contrast Jdg 3:12–30). Like 1Sa 1–2, it gives a series of intimate glimpses into the private lives of the members of an Israelite family. It also presents a delightful account of the remnant of true faith and piety in the period of the judges, relieving an otherwise wholly dark picture of that era.

AUTHOR AND DATE OF WRITING

The author is unknown. Jewish tradition points to Samuel, but it is unlikely that he is the author because the mention of David (4:17,22) implies a later date. Further, the literary style of Hebrew used in Ruth suggests that it was written during the period of the monarchy.

THEME AND THEOLOGY

C The importance of faithful love in human relationships among God's kingdom people is powerfully underscored. The author focuses on Ruth's unswerving and selfless devotion to desolate Naomi (1:16–17; 2:11–12; 3:10; 4:15) and on Boaz's kindness to these two widows (chs. 2–4). He presents striking examples of lives that embody in their daily affairs the self-giving love that fulfills God's law (Lev 19:18; cf. Ro 13:10). Such love also reflects God's love, in a marvelous joining of human and divine actions (compare 2:12 with 3:9). In God's benevolence such lives are blessed and are made a blessing.

It may seem surprising that one who reflects God's love so clearly is a Moabite (see map, p. 375). Yet her complete loyalty to the Israelite family into which she has been received by marriage and her total devotion to her desolate mother-in-law mark her as a true daughter of Israel and a worthy ancestor of David. She strikingly exemplifies the truth that participation in the coming kingdom of God is decided, not by blood and birth, but by the conformity of one's life to the will of God through "faith and obedience" (Ro 1:5). Her place in the ancestry of David signifies that all nations will be represented in the kingdom of David's greater Son.

As an episode in the ancestry of David, the book of Ruth sheds light on his role in the history of redemption. Redemption is a key concept throughout the account; the Hebrew word in its various forms occurs 23 times. The book is primarily a story of Naomi's transformation from despair to happiness through the selfless, God-blessed acts of Ruth and Boaz. She moves from emptiness to fullness (1:21; 3:17; see notes on 1:1,3,5–6,12,21–22; 3:17; 4:15), from destitution (1:1–5) to security

KEY   **A** APPLICATION FOR LIVING   **B** BACKGROUND NOTES   **C** CHARACTER INFORMATION

and hope (4:13–17). Similarly, Israel was transformed from national desperation at the death of Eli (1Sa 4:18) to peace and prosperity in the early days of Solomon (1Ki 4:20–34; 5:4) through the selfless devotion of David, a true descendant of Ruth and Boaz. The author thus reminded Israel that the reign of the house of David, as the means of God's benevolent rule in Israel, held the prospect of God's promised peace and rest. But this rest would continue only so long as those who participated in the kingdom—prince and people alike—reflected in their daily lives the selfless love exemplified by Ruth and Boaz. In Jesus, the great "son of David" (Mt 1:1), and his redemptive work, the promised blessings of the kingdom of God find their fulfillment.

LITERARY FEATURES

The book of Ruth is a Hebrew short story, told with consummate skill. Among historical narratives in Scripture it is unexcelled in its compactness, vividness, warmth, beauty and dramatic effectiveness—an exquisitely wrought jewel of Hebrew narrative art.

Marvelously symmetrical throughout (see Outline), the action moves from a briefly sketched account of distress (1:1–5; 71 words in Hebrew) through four episodes to a concluding account of relief and hope that is drawn with equal brevity (4:13–17; 71 words in Hebrew). The crucial turning point occurs exactly midway (see note on 2:20). The opening line of each of the four episodes signals its main development (1:6, the return; 2:1, the meeting with Boaz; 3:1, finding a home for Ruth; 4:1, the decisive event at the gate), while the closing line of each episode facilitates transition to what follows (see notes on 1:22; 2:23; 3:18; 4:12). Contrast is also used to good effect: pleasant (the meaning of "Naomi") and bitter (1:20), full and empty (1:21), and the living and the dead (2:20). Most striking is the contrast between two of the main characters, Ruth and Boaz: The one is a young, foreign, destitute widow, while the other is a middle-aged, well-to-do Israelite securely established in his home community. For each there is a corresponding character whose actions highlight, by contrast, his or her selfless acts: Ruth—Orpah, Boaz—the unnamed family guardian.

When movements in space, time and circumstance all correspond in some way, a harmony results that both satisfies the reader's artistic sense and helps open doors to understanding. The author of Ruth keeps his readers from being distracted from the central story—Naomi's passage from emptiness to fullness through the selfless acts of Ruth and Boaz (see Theme and Theology). That passage, or restoration, first takes place in connection with her return from Moab to the promised land and to Bethlehem ("house of food"; see note on 1:1). It then progresses with the harvest season, when the fullness of the land is gathered in. All aspects of the story keep the reader's attention focused on the central issue. Consideration of these and other literary devices (mentioned throughout the notes) will aid understanding of the book of Ruth.

OUTLINE

NAOMI LOSES HER HUSBAND AND SONS

1 In the days when the judges ruled,[a] [a] there was a famine in the land.[b] So a man from Bethlehem in Judah,[c] together with his wife and two sons, went to live for a while[d] in the country of Moab.[e] [2]The man's name was Elimelek,[f] his wife's name was Naomi, and the names of his two sons were Mahlon and Kilion.[g] They were Ephrathites[h] from Bethlehem,[i] Judah. And they went to Moab and lived there.

[3]Now Elimelek, Naomi's husband, died, and she was left with her two sons. [4]They married Moabite women,[j] one named Orpah and the other Ruth.[k] After they had lived there about ten years, [5]both Mahlon and Kilion[l] also died,[m] and Naomi was left without her two sons and her husband.

NAOMI AND RUTH RETURN TO BETHLEHEM

[6]When Naomi heard in Moab[n] that the LORD had come to the aid of his people[o] by providing food[p] for them, she and her daughters-in-law[q] prepared to return home from there. [7]With her two daughters-in-law she left the place where she had been living and set out on the road that would take them back to the land of Judah.

[8]Then Naomi said to her two daughters-in-law, "Go back, each of you, to your moth-

---

[a] 1 Traditionally *judged*

1:1 [a] Jdg 2:16-18
[b] S Ge 12:10;
2Ki 6:25; Ps 105:16;
Hag 1:11 [c] S Ge 35:19
[d] Ge 47:4
[e] S Ge 36:35
1:2 [f] ver 3; Ru 2:1;
4:3 [g] ver 5; Ru 4:9
[h] S Ge 35:16
[i] S Ge 35:19; 1Sa 16:18
1:4 [j] 1Ki 11:1;
2Ch 24:26; Ezr 9:2;
Ne 13:23 [k] ver 14;
Ru 4:13; Mt 1:5
1:5 [l] S ver 2 [m] ver 8;
Ru 2:11
1:6 [n] S Ge 36:35
Jer 29:10; Zep 2:7
[o] Ps 132:15; Mt 6:11
[q] S Ge 11:31; S 38:16

1:1 *when the judges ruled.* Probably from c. 1380 to c. 1050 B.C. (see Introduction to Judges: Background). By mentioning the judges, the author calls to mind that period of Israel's apostasy, moral degradation and oppression. *famine.* Not mentioned in Judges. *Bethlehem in Judah.* David's hometown (1Sa 16:18). Bethlehem (the name suggests "house of food") is empty.
1:2 *Elimelek.* Means "(My) God is King" (see note on Jdg 8:23). *Naomi.* See TNIV text note on v. 20. *Ephrathites.* Ephrathah was a name for the area around Bethlehem (see 4:11; Ge 35:19; 1Sa 17:12; Mic 5:2).
1:3 *Elimelek, Naomi's husband, died.* Naomi's emptying begins (see v. 21).

C 1:4 *They married.* The prospect of continuing the family line remained. *Moabite women.* See Ge 19:36–37. Marriage with Moabite women was not forbidden, though no Moabite—or his descendents to the tenth generation—was allowed to "enter the assembly of the LORD" (Dt 23:3). *Ruth.* The

name sounds like the Hebrew for "friendship." Ruth is one of five women in Matthew's genealogy of Jesus. The others are Tamar, Rahab, Bathsheba and Mary (Mt 1:3,5–6,16).
1:5 *Mahlon.* Ruth's husband (4:10), whose name probably means "weakling." *Naomi was left.* Naomi's emptiness is complete: She has neither husband nor sons. She has only two young daughters-in-law, both of them foreigners and childless.
1:6–22 Act I in the drama: Naomi's sense of desolation is exposed.

A 1:6 *the LORD had come to the aid of his people.* At several points in the account, God's sovereign control of events is acknowledged (here; vv. 13,21; 2:20; 4:12–15). *food.* Bethlehem ("house of food") again has food. *prepared to return home.* Empty Naomi returns to the newly filled land of promise.
1:8 *Go back.* Desolate Naomi repeatedly urges her daughters-in-law to return to their original homes in Moab (here; vv. 11–12,15); she has nothing to offer them.

THE BOOK OF RUTH

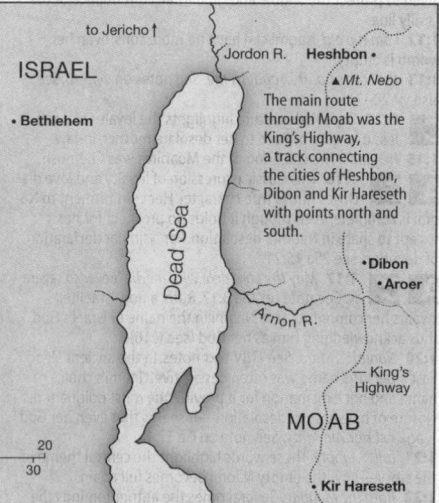

B Set in the dark and bloody days of the judges, the story of Ruth is silent about the underlying hostility and suspicion the two peoples—Judahites and Moabites—felt for each other. The original onslaught of the invading Israelite tribes against towns that were once Moabite had never been forgotten or forgiven, while the Hebrew prophets denounced Moab's pride and arrogance for trying to bewitch, seduce and oppress Israel from the time of Balaam on. The Mesha Stele (c. 830 B.C.) boasts of the massacre of entire Israelite towns.

Moab encompassed the expansive, grain-filled plateau between the Dead Sea and the eastern desert on both sides of the enormous rift of the Arnon River gorge. Much of eastern Moab was steppeland—semiarid wastes not profitable for cultivation, but excellent for grazing flocks of sheep and goats. The tribute Moab paid to Israel in the days of Ahab was 100,000 lambs and the wool of 100,000 rams (see 2Ki 3:4 and note).

to Jericho ↑

ISRAEL

Jordon R. Heshbon •

▲ Mt. Nebo

• Bethlehem

The main route through Moab was the King's Highway, a track connecting the cities of Heshbon, Dibon and Kir Hareseth with points north and south.

Dead Sea

• Dibon
• Aroer

Arnon R.

— King's Highway

MOAB

• Kir Hareseth

Miles 10 5 0 10 20
Kms 10 5 0 10 20 30

1:8 'Ge 38:11
*S Ge 19:19; 2Ti 1:16
'S ver 5
1:9 "Ru 3:1
"S Ge 27:27; S 29:11
"S Ge 27:38;
S Nu 25:6
1:11 "Ge 38:11;
Dt 25:5
1:13 "Ge 38:11
"ver 20; Ex 1:14;
15:23; 1Sa 30:6
*S Jdg 2:15; S Job 4:5
1:14 "ver 9
"Ru 2:11; 3:1; Mic 7:6
"S Ge 31:28
"S Dt 10:20
1:15 "Dt 25:7
"S Jos 24:14
1:16 "2Ki 2:2
'Ge 24:58 / Ps 45:10
"S Jos 24:15
1:17 'I1Sa 3:17;
14:44; 20:13; 25:22;
2Sa 3:9,35; 2Sa 19:13;
1Ki 2:23; 19:2; 20:10;
2Ki 6:31 "2Sa 15:21
1:18 "Ac 21:14
1:19 "S Jdg 17:7
"Mt 21:10
1:20 "S Ge 15:1;
S 17:1; Ps 91:1
"S ver 13
1:21 "Job 1:21
"Job 30:11; Ps 88:7;
Isa 53:4
1:22 "Ru 2:2,6,21;
4:5,10 "S Ge 11:31
"S Ex 9:31;
S Lev 19:9 *2Sa 21:9

er's home.' May the LORD show you kindness,* as you have shown kindness to your dead' and to me. ⁹May the LORD grant that each of you will find rest" in the home of another husband."

Then she kissed them good-by and they wept aloud™ ¹⁰and said to her, "We will go back with you to your people."

¹¹But Naomi said, "Return home, my daughters. Why would you come with me? Am I going to have any more sons, who could become your husbands?* ¹²Return home, my daughters; I am too old to have another husband. Even if I thought there was still hope for me—even if I had a husband tonight and then gave birth to sons— ¹³would you wait until they grew up?⁷ Would you remain unmarried for them? No, my daughters. It is more bitter² for me than for you, because the LORD's hand has turned against me!ᵃ"

¹⁴At this they wept ᵇ aloud again. Then Orpah kissed her mother-in-law ᶜ good-by, ᵈ but Ruth clung to her. ᵉ

¹⁵"Look," said Naomi, "your sister-in-law ᶠ is going back to her people and her gods. ᵍ Go back with her."

¹⁶But Ruth replied, "Don't urge me to leave you ʰ or to turn back from you. Where you go I will go, ' and where you stay I will stay. Your people will be my people ʲ and your God my God. ᵏ ¹⁷Where you die I will die, and there I will be buried. May the LORD deal with me, be it ever so severely,' if even death separates you and me." ᵐ ¹⁸When Naomi realized that Ruth was determined to go with her, she stopped urging her. ⁿ

¹⁹So the two women went on until they came to Bethlehem. ᵒ When they arrived in Bethlehem, the whole town was stirred ᵖ because of them, and the women exclaimed, "Can this be Naomi?"

²⁰"Don't call me Naomi,ᵃ" she told them. "Call me Mara,ᵇ because the Almightyᶜ �q has made my life very bitter. ʳ ²¹I went away full, but the LORD has brought me back empty. ˢ Why call me Naomi? The LORD has afflictedᵈ me; ᵗ the Almighty has brought misfortune upon me."

²²So Naomi returned from Moab accompanied by Ruth the Moabite, " her daughter-in-law, ᵛ arriving in Bethlehem as the barley harvest ʷ was beginning. ˣ

ᵃ 20 *Naomi* means *pleasant*; also in verse 21.   ᵇ 20 *Mara* means *bitter*.   ᶜ 20 Hebrew *Shaddai*; also in verse 21   ᵈ 21 Or *has testified against*

1:11 *sons, who could become your husbands.* Naomi alludes to the Israelite law (Dt 25:5–6) regarding levirate marriage (see notes on Ge 38:8; Dt 25:5–10; see also Mk 12:18–23), which was given to protect the widow and guarantee continuance of the family line.

1:12 *I am too old.* Naomi can have no more sons; even her womb is empty.

1:13 *the LORD's hand . . . against me.* See notes on vv. 5–6; see also vv. 20–21.

1:14 Orpah's departure highlights the loyalty and selfless devotion of Ruth to her desolate mother-in-law.

1:15 *her gods.* The chief god of the Moabites was Chemosh.

1:16 This classic expression of loyalty and love discloses Ruth's true character. Her commitment to Naomi is complete, even though it holds no prospect for her except to share in Naomi's desolation. For a similar declaration of devotion, see 2Sa 15:21.

1:17 *May the LORD deal with me, be it ever so severely.* See note on 1Sa 3:17. Ruth, a non-Israelite, swears her commitment to Naomi in the name of Israel's God, thus acknowledging him as her God (see v. 16).

1:20 *Naomi . . . Mara.* See TNIV text notes. In the ancient Near East a person's name was often descriptive. Naomi's choice of name and her explanation for it provide the most poignant disclosure of her sense of desolation—it seems that even her God is against her. *Almighty.* See note on Ge 17:1.

1:21 *full . . . empty.* These words highlight the central theme of the story—how the empty Naomi becomes full again.

1:22 *Ruth the Moabite.* Several times the author reminds the

reader that Ruth is a foreigner from a despised people (2:2,6,21; 4:5,10; see 2:10). *harvest.* Harvesting grain in ancient Canaan took place in April and May (barley first, wheat a few weeks later; see 2:23). It involved the following steps: (1) cutting the ripened standing grain with hand sickles (Dt 16:9; 23:25; Jer 50:16; Joel 3:13)—usually done by men; (2) binding the grain into sheaves—usually done by women; (3) gleaning, i.e., gathering stalks of grain left behind (2:7); (4) transporting the sheaves to the threshing floor—often by donkey, sometimes by cart (Am 2:13); (5) threshing, i.e., loosening the grain from the straw—usually done by the treading of cattle (Dt 25:4; Hos 10:11), but sometimes by toothed threshing sledges (Isa 41:15; Am 1:3) or the wheels of carts (Isa 28:28); (6) winnowing—done by tossing the grain into the air with winnowing forks (Jer 15:7) so that the wind, which usually came up for a few hours in the afternoon, blew away the straw and chaff (Ps 1:4), leaving the grain at the winnower's feet; (7) sifting the grain (Am 9:9) to remove any residual foreign matter; (8) bagging for transportation and storage (Ge 42–44). Threshing floors, where both threshing and winnowing occurred, were hard, smooth, open places, prepared on either rock or clay and carefully chosen for favorable exposure to the prevailing winds. They were usually on the east side—i.e., downwind—of the village. *was beginning.* Naomi and Ruth arrive in Bethlehem just as the renewed fullness of the land is beginning to be harvested—an early hint that Naomi will be full again. Reference to the barley harvest also prepares the reader for the next major scene in the harvest fields (see Introduction: Literary Features).

RUTH MEETS BOAZ IN THE GRAIN FIELD

2 Now Naomi had a relative[y] on her husband's side, a man of standing[z] from the clan of Elimelek,[a] whose name was Boaz.[b] ²And Ruth the Moabite[c] said to Naomi, "Let me go to the fields and pick up the leftover grain[d] behind anyone in whose eyes I find favor.[e]"

Naomi said to her, "Go ahead, my daughter." ³So she went out, entered a field and began to glean behind the harvesters.[f] As it turned out, she found herself working in a field belonging to Boaz, who was from the clan of Elimelek.[g]

⁴Just then Boaz arrived from Bethlehem and greeted the harvesters, "The Lord be with you![h]"

"The Lord bless you![i]" they answered.

⁵Boaz asked the overseer of his harvesters, "Who does that young woman belong to?"

⁶The overseer replied, "She is the Moabite[j] who came back from Moab with Naomi. ⁷She said, 'Please let me glean and gather among the sheaves[k] behind the harvesters.' She came into the field and has remained here from morning till now, except for a short rest[l] in the shelter."

⁸So Boaz said to Ruth, "My daughter, listen to me. Don't go and glean in another field and don't go away from here. Stay here with the women who work for me. ⁹Watch the field where the harvesters are working, and follow along after the women. I have told the men not to lay a hand on you. And whenever you are thirsty, go and get a drink from the water jars the men have filled."

¹⁰At this, she bowed down with her face to the ground.[m] She asked him, "Why have I found such favor in your eyes that you notice me[n]—a foreigner?[o]"

¹¹Boaz replied, "I've been told all about what you have done for your mother-in-law[p] since the death of your husband[q]—how you left your father and mother and your homeland and came to live with a people you did not know[r] before.[s] ¹²May the Lord repay you for what you have done. May you be richly rewarded by the Lord,[t] the God of Israel,[u] under whose wings[v] you have come to take refuge.[w]"

¹³"May I continue to find favor in your eyes,[x] my lord," she said. "You have reassured me and have spoken kindly to your servant—though I do not have the standing of one of your servants."

¹⁴At mealtime Boaz said to her, "Come over here. Have some bread[y] and dip it in the wine vinegar."

When she sat down with the harvesters,[z] he offered her some roasted grain.[a] She ate all she wanted and had some left over.[b] ¹⁵As she got up to glean, Boaz gave orders to his men, "Let her gather among the sheaves[c] and don't reprimand her. ¹⁶Even pull out some stalks for her from the bundles and leave them for her to pick up, and don't rebuke[d] her."

¹⁷So Ruth gleaned in the field until evening. Then she threshed[e] the barley she had gathered, and it amounted to about an ephah.[a][f] ¹⁸She carried it back to town, and her mother-in-law saw how much she had gathered. Ruth also brought out and gave her what she had left over[g] after she had eaten enough.

¹⁹Her mother-in-law asked her, "Where did you glean today? Where did you work? Blessed be the man who took notice of you![h]"

ᵃ 17 That is, probably about 30 pounds or about 13 kilograms

2:1 ʸRu 3:2; Pr 7:4
ᶻ1Sa 9:1; 1Ki 11:28
ᵃS Ru 1:2 ᵇRu 4:21;
1Ch 2:12; Mt 1:5;
Lk 3:32
2:2 ᶜS Ru 1:22
ᵈLev 19:9; S 23:22
ᵉS Ge 6:8; S 18:3
2:3 ᶠver 14;
2Ki 4:18; Jer 9:22;
Am 9:13 ᵍver 1
2:4 ʰS Jdg 6:12;
Lk 1:28; 2Th 3:16
ⁱS Ge 28:3; S Nu 6:24
2:6 ʲS Ru 1:22
2:7 ᵏS Ge 37:7;
S Lev 19:9 ˡIsa 4:5
2:10 ᵐS Ge 19:1;
S 1Sa 20:41 ⁿver 19;
Ps 41:1 ᵒS Ge 31:15;
S Dt 15:3
2:11 ᵖS Ru 1:14
�q S Ru 1:5 ʳIsa 55:5
ˢRu 1:16-17
2:12 ᵗ1Sa 24:19;
26:23,25; Ps 18:20;
Pr 25:22; Jer 31:16
ᵘS Jos 24:15
ᵛPs 17:8; 36:7; 57:1;
61:4; 63:7; 91:4
ʷPs 71:1
2:13 ˣS Ge 18:3
2:14 ʸS Ge 3:19
ᶻS ver 3 ᵃS Lev 23:14
ᵇver 18
2:15 ᶜS Ge 37:7;
S Lev 19:9
2:16 ᵈS Ge 37:10
2:17 ᵉS Jdg 6:11
ᶠS Lev 19:36
2:18 ᵍver 14
2:19 ʰS ver 10

2:1–23 Act II in the drama: What is done by Ruth and Boaz awakens hope in Naomi's heart.

2:1 *relative.* A sign of hope (see note on v. 20). *Boaz.* Probably means "In him is strength." Boaz is included in both genealogies of Jesus (Mt 1:5; Lk 3:32).

2:2 *Let me go.* Although Ruth is a foreigner and, as a young woman alone, obviously quite vulnerable in the harvest fields, she undertakes to provide for her mother-in-law. In 3:1 Naomi undertakes to provide for Ruth. *pick up the leftover grain.* The law of Moses instructed landowners to leave what the harvesters missed so that the poor, the foreigner, the widow and the fatherless could glean for their needs (Lev 19:9; 23:22; Dt 24:19).

2:3 *As it turned out.* Divine providence is at work (vv. 19–20).

2:4 The exchange of greetings between Boaz and his laborers characterizes Boaz as a godly man with a kind spirit.

2:9 *follow along after the women.* It was customary for the men to cut the grain and for the female servants to go behind them to bind the grain into sheaves. Then Ruth could glean what they had left behind (see note on 1:22). *not to lay a hand on you.* This little word from Boaz indicates the risk Ruth had taken and discloses the measure of Boaz's care for her.

2:11 *what you have done for your mother-in-law.* Ruth's commitment to care for her desolate mother-in-law remains the center of attention throughout the book.

2:12 *under whose wings.* A figure of a bird protecting her young under her wings (see Mt 23:37; see also note on 3:9).

2:13 *your servant.* A polite reference to herself.

2:15 *gave orders to his men.* Boaz goes beyond the requirement of the law in making sure that Ruth's labors are abundantly productive (see 3:15 and note).

2:17 *threshed.* See note on 1:22. In Ruth's case, as in that of Gideon (Jdg 6:11), the amount was small and could be threshed by hand simply by beating it with a club or stick. *ephah.* See TNIV text note; an unusually large amount for one day's gleaning.

2:20 ʰS Jdg 17:2;
S 1Sa 23:21
ʲS Ge 11:31
ᵏS Ge 19:19
ˡS Lev 25:25
ᵐRu 3:9,12; 4:1,14
2:21 ⁿS Ru 1:22
2:23 ᵒS Ex 9:31
ᵖS Ge 30:14;
S 1Sa 6:13
3:1 ᵠRu 1:14 ʳRu 1:9
3:2 ˢS Ru 2:1
ᵗS Lev 2:14;
S Nu 18:27; S Jdg 6:11
3:3 ᵘ2Sa 12:20;
2Ki 5:10; Ps 26:6;
51:2; Isa 1:16; Jer 4:14;
Eze 16:9 ᵛ2Sa 14:2;
Isa 61:3 ᵂS Ge 41:14
ˣS Ex 32:6; S Ecc 2:3;
S Jer 15:17
3:5 ʸEph 6:1;
Col 3:20
3:6 ᶻS Nu 18:27
3:7 ᵃJdg 19:6,9,22;
1Sa 25:36; 2Sa 13:28;
1Ki 21:7; Est 1:10
ᵇ2Ch 31:6; SS 7:2;
Jer 50:26; Hag 2:16
3:9 ᶜEze 16:8
ᵈS Ru 2:20
3:10 ᵉS Jdg 17:2
ᶠS Jos 2:12
3:11 ᵍPr 12:4; 14:1;
31:10
3:12 ʰS Ru 2:20
ⁱRu 4:1

Then Ruth told her mother-in-law about the one at whose place she had been working. "The name of the man I worked with today is Boaz," she said.

²⁰"The Lᴏʀᴅ bless him!ⁱ" Naomi said to her daughter-in-law.ʲ "He has not stopped showing his kindnessᵏ to the living and the dead." She added, "That man is our close relative;ˡ he is one of our family guardians.ᵃᵐ"

²¹Then Ruth the Moabiteⁿ said, "He even said to me, 'Stay with my workers until they finish harvesting all my grain.'"

²²Naomi said to Ruth her daughter-in-law, "It will be good for you, my daughter, to go with the women who work for him, because in someone else's field you might be harmed."

²³So Ruth stayed close to the women of Boaz to glean until the barleyᵒ and wheat harvestsᵖ were finished. And she lived with her mother-in-law.

RUTH AND BOAZ AT THE THRESHING FLOOR

3 One day Naomi her mother-in-lawᵠ said to her, "My daughter, I must find a homeᵇʳ for you, where you will be well provided for. ²Now Boaz, with whose women you have worked, is a relativeˢ of ours. Tonight he will be winnowing barley on the threshing floor.ᵗ ³Washᵘ and perfume yourself,ᵛ and put on your best clothes.ᵂ Then go down to the threshing floor, but don't let him know you are there until he has finished eating and drinking.ˣ ⁴When he lies down, note the place where he is lying. Then go and uncover his feet and lie down. He will tell you what to do."

⁵"I will do whatever you say,"ʸ Ruth answered. ⁶So she went down to the threshing floorᶻ and did everything her mother-in-law told her to do.

⁷When Boaz had finished eating and drinking and was in good spirits,ᵃ he went over to lie down at the far end of the grain pile.ᵇ Ruth approached quietly, uncovered his feet and lay down. ⁸In the middle of the night something startled the man; he turned—and there was a woman lying at his feet!

⁹"Who are you?" he asked.

"I am your servant Ruth," she said. "Spread the corner of your garmentᶜ over me, since you are a family guardian.ᵈ"

¹⁰"The Lᴏʀᴅ bless you,ᵉ my daughter," he replied. "This kindness is greater than that which you showed earlier:ᶠ You have not run after the younger men, whether rich or poor. ¹¹And now, my daughter, don't be afraid. I will do for you all you ask. All the people of my town know that you are a woman of noble character.ᵍ ¹²Although it is true that I am a family guardian,ʰ there is another who is more closely related than I ⁱ. ¹³Stay here for the

---

ᵃ 20 The Hebrew word for *family guardian* is a legal term for one who has the obligation to redeem a relative in serious difficulty (see Lev. 25:25-55).   ᵇ 1 Hebrew *find rest* (see Ruth 1:9)

2:20 *He has not stopped showing his kindness.* In 3:10 Boaz credits Ruth with demonstrating this same virtue. *family guardians.* See TNIV text note. Redemption is a key concept in Ruth (see Introduction: Theme and Theology). The family guardian was responsible for protecting the interests of needy members of the extended family—e.g., to provide an heir for a brother who had died (Dt 25:5–10), to redeem land that a poor relative had sold outside the family (Lev 25:25–28), to redeem a relative who had been sold into slavery (Lev 25:47–49) and to avenge the killing of a relative (Nu 35:19–21; "avenger" and "family guardian" are translations of the same Hebrew word). When Naomi hears about the day's events, she takes courage. This moment of her awakened hope is the crucial turning point of the story (see Introduction: Literary Features).

2:23 *until the barley and wheat harvests were finished.* This phrase rounds out the harvest episode and prepares for the next major scene on the threshing floor (see Introduction: Literary Features).

3:1–18 Act III in the drama: Hopeful Naomi takes the initiative.

3:2 *Tonight he will be winnowing.* See note on 1:22. In the threshing season it was customary for the landowner and his men to spend the night near the threshing floor to protect his grain from theft.

3:3 Ruth is instructed to prepare herself like a bride (see Eze 16:9–12 and notes). *go down to the threshing floor.* At winnowing time the threshing floor was a place for male camaraderie and revelry (v. 14). *eating and drinking.* Harvest was a time of festivity (Isa 9:3; 16:9–10; Jer 48:33).

3:4 *uncover his feet and lie down.* Although Naomi's instructions may appear forward, the moral integrity of Naomi, Ruth and Boaz is never in doubt (see v. 11). Naomi's advice to Ruth is clearly for the purpose of appealing to Boaz's family guardian obligation. Ruth's actions were a request for marriage. Tamar, the mother of Perez (4:12), had also laid claim to the provision of the levirate (or family guardian) law (Ge 38:13–30).

3:9 *Spread the corner of your garment over me.* A request for marriage (see Eze 16:8); a similar custom is still practiced in some parts of the Middle East today. With a striking play on words Ruth confronts Boaz with his moral obligations. In the harvest field he had wished her well at the hands of the Lord "under whose wings you have come to take refuge" (2:12). Now on the threshing floor Ruth asks him to spread the "wings" (i.e., the corners) of his garment over her. Boaz is vividly reminded that he must serve as the Lord's protective wings over Ruth.

3:10 *kindness ... you showed earlier.* See 2:11–12; see also note on 2:20.

3:11 *woman of noble character.* See Pr 12:4; 31:10, the only other places where the Hebrew for this phrase occurs in the OT. The Hebrew for "noble character" is the same as that used to describe Boaz in 2:1; thus the author maintains a balance between his descriptions of Ruth and Boaz.

3:12 *another ... more closely related.* How Boaz was related to Ruth's former husband (Mahlon) is unknown, but the closest male relative had the primary responsibility to marry a widow. Naomi instructed Ruth to approach Boaz because he had already shown himself willing to be Ruth's protector. Boaz, how-night, and in the morning if he wants to do his duty as your family guardian,[j] good; let him redeem you. But if he is not willing, as surely as the LORD lives[k] I will do it.[l] Lie here until morning."

[14]So she lay at his feet until morning, but got up before anyone could be recognized; and he said, "No one must know that a woman came to the threshing floor.[m][n]

[15]He also said, "Bring me the shawl[o] you are wearing and hold it out." When she did so, he poured into it six measures of barley and put it on her. Then he[a] went back to town.

[16]When Ruth came to her mother-in-law, Naomi asked, "How did it go, my daughter?" Then she told her everything Boaz had done for her [17]and added, "He gave me these six measures of barley, saying, 'Don't go back to your mother-in-law empty-handed.' "

[18]Then Naomi said, "Wait, my daughter, until you find out what happens. For the man will not rest until the matter is settled today."[p]

BOAZ MARRIES RUTH

4 Meanwhile Boaz went up to the town gate[q] and sat down there just as the family guardian[r] he had mentioned[s] came along. Boaz said, "Come over here, my friend, and sit down." So he went over and sat down.

[2]Boaz took ten of the elders[t] of the town and said, "Sit here," and they did so. [u] [3]Then he said to the family guardian, "Naomi, who has come back from Moab, is selling the piece of land that belonged to our relative Elimelek.[v] [4]I thought I should bring the matter to your attention and suggest that you buy it in the presence of these seated here and in the presence of the elders of my people. If you will redeem it, do so. But if you[b] will not, tell me, so I will know. For no one has the right to do it except you,[w] and I am next in line."

"I will redeem it," he said.

[5]Then Boaz said, "On the day you buy the land from Naomi, you also acquire Ruth the Moabite,[x] the[c] dead man's widow, in order to maintain the name of the dead with his property."[y]

[6]At this, the family guardian said, "Then I cannot redeem[z] it because I might endanger my own estate. You redeem it yourself. I cannot do it."[a]

[7](Now in earlier times in Israel, for the redemption[b] and transfer of property to become final, one party took off his sandal[c] and gave it to the other. This was the method of legalizing transactions[d] in Israel.)[e]

[8]So the family guardian said to Boaz, "Buy it yourself." And he removed his sandal.[f]

[9]Then Boaz announced to the elders and all the people, "Today you are witnesses[g] that I have bought from Naomi all the property of Elimelek, Kilion and Mahlon. [10]I have also

---

[a] 15 Most Hebrew manuscripts; many Hebrew manuscripts, Vulgate and Syriac *she*   [b] 4 Many Hebrew manuscripts, Septuagint, Vulgate and Syriac; most Hebrew manuscripts *he*   [c] 5 Vulgate and Syriac; Hebrew (see also Septuagint) *Naomi and from Ruth the Moabite, you acquire the*

3:13 *j* Dt 25:5;
Ru 4:5; Mt 22:24
k S Nu 14:21; Hos 4:15
l Ru 4:6
3:14 *m* S Nu 18:27
n Ro 14:16; 2Co 8:21
3:15 *o* Isa 3:22
3:18 *p* Ps 37:3-5
4:1 *q* S Ge 18:1;
S 23:10 *r* S Ru 2:20
s Ru 3:12
4:2 *t* S Ex 3:16
u S Dt 25:7
4:3 *v* S Lev 25:25;
S Ru 1:2
4:4 *w* S Lev 25:25;
Jer 32:7-8
4:5 *x* S Ru 1:22
y S Ge 38:8; S Ru 3:13
4:6 *z* Lev 25:25;
a Lev 25:25
4:7 *b* S Lev 25:24
c ver 8 *d* Isa 8:1-2,16,
20 *e* Dt 25:7-9
4:8 *f* Dt 25:9
4:9 *g* Isa 8:2;
Jer 32:10,44

---

ever, would not bypass the directives of the law, which clearly gave priority to the nearest relative.

3:13 *as surely as the LORD lives.* Boaz commits himself by oath (cf. 1:17 and note) to redeem the family property and to arrange Ruth's honorable marriage.

3:15 Boaz goes beyond the requirement of the law in supplying Ruth with grain from the threshing floor (see 2:15).

3:17 *empty-handed.* Again the empty/full motif (see note on 1:21).

3:18 *Wait.* The Hebrew underlying this word is translated "sat" in 4:1. Thus the author prepares the reader for the next major scene, in which Boaz sits at the town gate to see the matter through.

4:1–12 Act IV in the drama: Boaz arranges to fulfill his pledge to Ruth.

4:1 *town gate.* The "town hall" of ancient Israel, the normal place for business and legal transactions, where witnesses were readily available (vv. 9–12; see note on Ge 19:1). *my friend.* The other kinsman remains unnamed.

4:2 *ten of the elders.* A full court for legal proceedings.

4:3 *selling the piece of land.* See note on 2:20. Two interpretations are possible: 1. Naomi owns the land but is so destitute that she is forced to sell. It was the duty of the family guardian to buy any land in danger of being sold outside the family. 2. Naomi does not own the land—it had been sold by Elimelek

before the family left for Moab—but by law she retains the right of redemption to buy the land back. Lacking funds to do so herself, she is dependent on a family guardian to do it for her. It is the right of redemption that Naomi is "selling."

4:5 *you also acquire ... the dead man's widow.* Now Boaz reveals the other half of the obligation—the acquisition of Ruth. Levirate law (Dt 25:5–6; see note on Lev 25:25) provided that Ruth's firstborn son would keep Mahlon's name alive and retain ownership of the family inheritance.

C **4:6** *I cannot redeem it.* Possibly he fears that, if he has a son by her and if that son is his only surviving heir, his own property will transfer to the family of Elimelek (see note on Ge 38:9). In that case his risk was no greater than that assumed by Boaz. This kinsman's refusal to assume the family guardian's role highlights the kindness and generosity of Boaz toward the two widows—just as Orpah's return to her family highlights Ruth's selfless devotion and loyalty to Naomi.

B **4:7** *one party took off his sandal.* The process of renouncing one's property rights and passing them to another was publicly attested by taking off a sandal and transferring it to the new owner (cf. Am 2:6; 8:6). The Nuzi documents (see chart, p. xxiv) refer to a similar custom.

4:9 *witnesses.* The role of public witnesses was to attest to all legal transactions and other binding agreements.

4:10 *h* S Ru 1:22
i S Dt 25:5 / S Dt 25:6
k S Jos 24:22
4:11 *l* S Ge 23:10
m S Dt 25:9
n S Ge 4:19; S 29:16
o S Ge 35:16 *p* Ru 1:19
4:12 *q* S Ge 38:29
r Ge 38:6,24
4:13 *s* S Ge 8:1;
S 29:31 *t* S Ge 29:32;
S 30:6; Lk 1:57
4:14 *u* Lk 1:58
v S Ge 24:27
w S Ru 2:20
4:15 *x* S Ge 11:31
y 1Sa 1:8; 2:5; Job 1:2
4:17 *z* ver 22;
1Sa 16:1,18; 17:12,17,
58; 1Ch 2:12,13;
Ps 72:20 *a* 1Sa 16:13;
1Ch 2:15
4:18 *b* S Ge 38:29
c Nu 26:21
4:19 *d* S Ex 6:23
4:20 *e* S Nu 7:12
4:21 *f* S Ru 2:1

acquired Ruth the Moabite, [h] Mahlon's widow, as my wife, [i] in order to maintain the name of the dead with his property, so that his name will not disappear from among his family or from his hometown. [j] Today you are witnesses! [k]"

[11] Then the elders and all the people at the gate [l] said, "We are witnesses. [m] May the LORD make the woman who is coming into your home like Rachel and Leah, [n] who together built up the house of Israel. May you have standing in Ephrathah [o] and be famous in Bethlehem. [p] [12] Through the offspring the LORD gives you by this young woman, may your family be like that of Perez, [q] whom Tamar [r] bore to Judah."

NAOMI GAINS A SON

[13] So Boaz took Ruth and she became his wife. When he made love to her, the LORD enabled her to conceive, [s] and she gave birth to a son. [t] [14] The women [u] said to Naomi: "Praise be to the LORD, [v] who this day has not left you without a family guardian. [w] May he become famous throughout Israel! [15] He will renew your life and sustain you in your old age. For your daughter-in-law, [x] who loves you and who is better to you than seven sons, [y] has given him birth."

[16] Then Naomi took the child in her arms and cared for him. [17] The women living there said, "Naomi has a son!" And they named him Obed. He was the father of Jesse, [z] the father of David. [a]

THE GENEALOGY OF DAVID

4:18–22pp — 1Ch 2:5–15; Mt 1:3–6; Lk 3:31–33

[18] This, then, is the family line of Perez [b]:

Perez was the father of Hezron, [c]
[19] Hezron the father of Ram,
    Ram the father of Amminadab, [d]
[20] Amminadab the father of Nahshon, [e]
    Nahshon the father of Salmon, [a]
[21] Salmon the father of Boaz, [f]
    Boaz the father of Obed,
[22] Obed the father of Jesse,
    and Jesse the father of David.

a 20 A few Hebrew manuscripts, some Septuagint manuscripts and Vulgate (see also verse 21 and Septuagint of 1 Chron. 2:11); most Hebrew manuscripts Salma

---

4:10 *name of the dead.* See Dt 25:5–7 and notes.
4:11 *Rachel and Leah … built up the house of Israel.* Cf. Dt 25:9. The Israelite readers of Ruth would have associated the house of Jacob (Israel), built up by Rachel and Leah, with the house of Israel, rebuilt by David, the descendant of Ruth and Boaz, after it had been threatened with extinction (1Sa 4). They also knew that the Lord had covenanted to "build" the house of David as an enduring dynasty, through which Israel's blessed destiny would be assured (see 2Sa 7:27–29). *Ephrathah.* See note on 1:2.
4:12 *Perez, whom Tamar bore to Judah.* Perez was Boaz's ancestor (vv. 18–21; Mt 1:3; Lk 3:33). His birth to Judah was from a union based on the levirate practice (Ge 38:27–30; see note on 1:11). Perez was therefore an appropriate model within Boaz's ancestry for the blessing the elders gave to Boaz. Moreover, the descendants of Perez had raised the tribe of Judah to a prominent place in Israel. So the blessing of the elders—that, through the offspring Ruth would bear to Boaz, his family would be like that of Perez—was fully realized in David and his dynasty. Thus also v. 12 prepares the reader for the events briefly narrated in the conclusion.
4:13–17 The conclusion of the story balances the introduction (1:1–5): (1) In the Hebrew both have the same number of words; (2) both compress much into a short space; (3) both focus on Naomi; (4) the introduction emphasizes Naomi's emptiness, and the conclusion portrays her fullness.
4:13 *the LORD enabled her to conceive.* See note on 1:6.
4:14 *family guardian.* The child Obed, as vv. 15–17 make clear.

May he become famous. This same wish is expressed concerning Boaz in v. 11.
4:15 *better to you than seven sons.* See 1Sa 1:8. Since seven was considered a number of completeness, to have seven sons was the epitome of all family blessings in Israel (see 1Sa 2:5; Job 1:2; 42:13). Ruth's selfless devotion to Naomi receives its climactic acknowledgment.
4:16 *took the child in her arms.* Possibly symbolizing adoption (see v. 17 and note on Ge 30:3).
4:17 *Naomi has a son.* Through Ruth, aged Naomi, who can no longer bear children, obtains an heir in place of Mahlon. *Obed.* The name means "servant," in its full form possibly "servant of the LORD."
4:18–22 See 1Ch 2:5–15; Mt 1:3–6; Lk 3:31–33. Like the genealogies of Ge 5:3–32; 11:10–26, this genealogy has ten names (see note on Ge 5:5). It brings to mind the reign of David, during which, in contrast to the turbulent period of the judges recalled in 1:1, Israel finally entered into rest in the promised land (see 1Ki 5:4 and note). It signifies that, just as Naomi was brought from emptiness to fullness through the selfless love of Ruth and Boaz, so the Lord brought Israel from unrest to rest through their descendant David, who selflessly gave himself to fight Israel's battles on the Lord's behalf. The ultimate end of this genealogy is Jesus Christ, the great "son of David" (Mt 1:1; see note there), who fulfills prophecy and will bring the Lord's people into final rest (see Introduction to Joshua: Title and Theological Theme; see also Heb 3:7—4:11 and notes).

TITLE 1 SAMUEL INTRODUCTION

C 1 and 2 Samuel are named after the person God used to establish monarchy in
Israel. Samuel not only anointed both Saul and David, Israel's first two kings,
but he also gave definition to the new order of God's rule over Israel. Samuel's role
as God's representative in this period of Israel's history is close to that of Moses (see
Ps 99:6; Jer 15:1 and notes) since he, more than any other person, provided for covenant continuity in the transition from the rule of the judges to that of the monarchy.

    1 and 2 Samuel were originally one book. It was divided into two parts by
the translators of the Septuagint (the pre-Christian Greek translation of the OT)—a
division subsequently followed by Jerome (in the Latin Vulgate, c. A.D. 400) and by
modern versions. The title of the book has varied from time to time, having been
designated "The First and Second Books of Kingdoms" (Septuagint), "First and Second Kings" (Vulgate) and "First and Second Samuel" (Hebrew tradition and most
modern versions).

LITERARY FEATURES, AUTHORSHIP AND DATE

Many questions have arisen pertaining to the literary character, authorship and date
of 1,2 Samuel. Certain features of the book suggest that it was compiled with the use
of a number of originally independent sources, which the author may have incorporated into his own composition as much as possible in their original, unedited form.

    Who the author was cannot be known since the book itself gives no indica-
tion of his identity. Whoever he was, he doubtless had access to records of the life
and times of Samuel, Saul and David. Explicit reference in the book itself is made to
only one such source (the Book of Jashar, 2Sa 1:18), but the writer of Chronicles
refers to four others that pertain to this period (the book of the annals of King David,
1Ch 27:24; the records of Samuel the seer; the records of Nathan the prophet; and
the records of Gad the seer, 1Ch 29:29). For the dates of the period, see Chronology
on p. 383.

CONTENTS AND THEME: KINGSHIP AND COVENANT

1 Samuel relates God's establishment of a political system in Israel headed by a
human king. Before the author describes this momentous change in the structure of
the theocracy (God's kingly rule over his people), he effectively depicts the complexi-
ty of its context. The following events provide both historical and theological background for the beginning of the monarchy:

C 1. *The birth, youth and call of Samuel (chs. 1–3).* In a book dealing for the most
part with the reigns of Israel's first two kings, Saul and David, it is significant
that the author chose not to include a birth narrative of either of these men, but to
describe the birth of their forerunner and anointer, the prophet Samuel. This in itself
accentuates the importance the author attached to Samuel's role in the events that
follow. He seems to be saying in a subtle way that flesh and blood are to be subordinated to word and Spirit in the process of the establishment of kingship. For this reason chs. 1–3 should be viewed as integrally related to what follows, not as a more
likely component of the book of Judges or as a loosely attached prefix to the rest of
1,2 Samuel. Kingship is given its birth and then nurtured by the prophetic word and

work of the prophet Samuel. Moreover, the events of Samuel's nativity thematically anticipate the story of God's working that is narrated in the rest of the book.

2. *The "ark narratives" (chs. 4–6)*. This section describes how the ark of God was captured by the Philistines and then, after God had wreaked havoc on several Philistine cities, returned to Israel. These narratives reveal the folly of Israel's notion that possession of the ark automatically guaranteed victory over her enemies. They also display the awesome power of the Lord (Yahweh, the God of Israel) and his superiority over the Philistine god Dagon. The Philistines were forced to confess openly their helplessness against God's power by their return of the ark to Israel. The entire ark episode performs a vital function in placing Israel's subsequent sinful desire for a human king in proper perspective.

3. *Samuel as a judge and deliverer (ch. 7)*. When Samuel called Israel to repentance and renewed dedication to the Lord, the Lord intervened mightily in Israel's behalf and gave victory over the Philistines. This narrative reaffirms the authority of Samuel as a divinely ordained leader; at the same time it provides evidence of divine protection and blessing for God's people when they place their confidence in the Lord and live in obedience to their covenant obligations.

All the material in chs. 1–7 serves as a necessary preface for the narratives of chs. 8–12, which describe the rise and establishment of kingship in Israel. The author has masterfully arranged the stories in chs. 8–12 in order to accentuate the serious theological conflict surrounding the historical events. In the study of these chapters, scholars have often noted the presence of a tension or ambivalence in the attitude toward the monarchy: On the one hand, Samuel is commanded by the Lord to give the people a king (8:7,9,22; 9:16–17; 10:24; 12:13); on the other hand, their request for a king is considered a sinful rejection of the Lord (8:7; 10:19; 12:12,17, 19–20). These seemingly conflicting attitudes toward the monarchy must be understood in the context of Israel's covenant relationship with the Lord.

Moses had anticipated Israel's desire for a human king (see Dt 17:14–20 and notes), but Israelite kingship was to be compatible with the continued rule of the Lord over his people as their Great King. Instead, when the elders asked Samuel to give them a king (8:5,19–20), they rejected the Lord's kingship over them. Their desire was for a king such as the nations around them had—to lead them in battle and give them a sense of national security and unity. The request for a king constituted a denial of their covenant relationship to the Lord, who was their King. Moreover, the Lord not only had promised to be their protector but had also repeatedly demonstrated his power in their behalf, most recently in the ark narratives (chs. 4–6), as well as in the great victory won over the Philistines under the leadership of Samuel (ch. 7).

Nevertheless the Lord instructed Samuel to give the people a king. By divine appointment Saul was brought into contact with Samuel, and Samuel was directed to anoint him privately as king (9:1—10:16). Subsequently, Samuel gathered the people at Mizpah, where, after again admonishing them concerning their sin in desiring a king (10:18–19), he presided over the selection of a king by lot. The lot fell on Saul and publicly designated him as the one whom God had chosen (10:24). Saul did not immediately assume his royal office but returned home to work his fields (11:5,7). When the inhabitants of Jabesh Gilead were threatened by Nahash the Ammonite, Saul rose to the challenge, gathered an army and led Israel to victory in battle. His success placed a final seal of divine approval on Saul's selection to be king (cf. 10:24; 11:12–13) and occasioned the inauguration of his reign at Gilgal (11:14—12:25).

The question that still needed resolution, then, was not so much whether Israel should have a king (it was clearly the Lord's will to give them one), but rather how they could maintain their covenant with God (i.e., preserve the theocracy) now that they had a human king. The problem was resolved when Samuel called the people to repentance and renewal of their allegiance to the Lord on the very occasion of the inauguration of Saul (see note on 10:25). By establishing kingship in the context of covenant renewal, Samuel placed the monarchy in Israel on a radically different footing from that in surrounding nations. The king in Israel was not to be autonomous in his authority and power; rather, he was to be subject to the law of the Lord and the word of the prophet (10:25; 12:23). This was to be true not only for Saul but also for all the kings who would occupy the throne in Israel in the future. The king was to be an instrument of the Lord's rule over his people, and the people as well as the king were to continue to recognize the Lord as their ultimate Sovereign (see 12:14–15 and notes).

Saul soon demonstrated that he was unwilling to submit to the requirements of his theocratic office (chs. 13–15). When he disobeyed the instructions of the prophet Samuel in preparation for battle against the Philistines (see 13:13 and notes), and when he refused to totally destroy the Amalekites as he had been commanded to do by the word of the Lord through Samuel (ch. 15), he ceased to be an instrument of the Lord's rule over his people. These abrogations of the requirements of his theocratic office led to his rejection as king (see 15:22–23 and notes).

The remainder of 1 Samuel (chs. 16–31) depicts the Lord's choice of David to be Saul's successor and then describes the long road by which David is prepared for accession to the throne. Although Saul's rule became increasingly antitheocratic in nature, David refused to usurp the throne by forceful means but left his accession to office in the Lord's hands. Eventually Saul was wounded in a battle with the Philistines and, fearing capture, took his own life. Three of Saul's sons, including David's loyal friend Jonathan, were killed in the same battle (ch. 31).

CHRONOLOGY

Even though the narratives of 1,2 Samuel contain some statements of chronological import (see, e.g., 1Sa 6:1; 7:2; 8:1,5; 13:1; 25:1; 2Sa 2:10–11; 5:4–5; 14:28; 15:7), the data are insufficient to establish a precise chronology for the major events of this period of Israel's history. Except for the dates of David's birth and the duration of his reign, which are quite firm (see 2Sa 5:4–5), most other dates can only be approximated. The textual problem with the chronological data on the age of Saul when he became king and the length of his reign (see TNIV text notes on 1Sa 13:1) contributes to uncertainty concerning the precise time of his birth and the beginning of his reign. No information is given concerning the time of Samuel's birth (1Sa 1:20) or death (25:1). His lifetime probably overlapped that of Samson and that of Obed, son of Ruth and Boaz and grandfather of David. It is indicated that he was well along in years when the elders of Israel asked him to give them a king (see 8:1,5 and note on 8:1).

One other factor contributing to chronological uncertainty is that the author has not always arranged his material in strict chronological sequence. It seems clear, e.g., that 2Sa 7 is to be placed chronologically after David's conquests described in 2Sa 8:1–14 (see notes on 2Sa 7:1; 8:1). The story of the famine sent by God on Israel during the reign of David because of Saul's violation of a treaty with the Gibeonites is found in 2Sa 21:1–14, though chronologically it occurred prior to the time of Absalom's rebellion recorded in 2Sa 15–18 (see further the notes on 2Sa 21:1–14). The following dates, however, provide an approximate chronological framework for the times of Samuel, Saul and David.

1105 B.C.	Birth of Samuel (1Sa 1:20)
1080	Birth of Saul
1050	Saul anointed to be king (1Sa 10:1)
1040	Birth of David
1025	David anointed to be Saul's successor (1Sa 16:1–13)
1010	Death of Saul and beginning of David's reign over Judah in Hebron (1Sa 31:4–6; 2Sa 2:1,4,11)

1003	Beginning of David's reign over all Israel and capture of Jerusalem (2Sa 5)
997–992	David's wars (2Sa 8:1–14)
991	Birth of Solomon (2Sa 12:24)
980	David's census (2Sa 24:1–9)
970	End of David's reign (2Sa 5:4–5; 1Ki 2:10–11)

OUTLINE

THE BIRTH OF SAMUEL

1 There was a certain man from Ramathaim,*a* a Zuphite*a b* from the hill country*c* of Ephraim,*d* whose name was Elkanah*e* son of Jeroham, the son of Elihu, the son of Tohu, the son of Zuph, an Ephraimite. ²He had two wives;*f* one was called Hannah and the other Peninnah. Peninnah had children, but Hannah had none.

³Year after year*g* this man went up from his town to worship*h* and sacrifice to the LORD Almighty at Shiloh,*i* where Hophni and Phinehas, the two sons of Eli,*j* were priests of the LORD. ⁴Whenever the day came for Elkanah to sacrifice,*k* he would give portions of the meat to his wife Peninnah and to all her sons and daughters.*l* ⁵But to Hannah he gave a double portion*m* because he loved her, and the LORD had closed her womb.*n* ⁶Because the LORD had closed Hannah's womb, her rival kept provoking her in order to irritate her.*o* ⁷This went on year after year. Whenever Hannah went up to the house of the LORD, her rival provoked her till she wept and would not eat.*p* ⁸Her husband Elkanah would say to her, "Hannah, why are you weeping? Why don't you eat? Why are you downhearted? Don't I mean more to you than ten sons?*q*"

⁹Once when they had finished eating and drinking in Shiloh, Hannah stood up. Now Eli the priest was sitting on his chair by the doorpost of the LORD's house.*r* ¹⁰In her deep anguish*s* Hannah prayed to the LORD, weeping bitterly. ¹¹And she made a vow,*t* saying, "LORD Almighty*u*, if you will only look on your servant's misery and remember*v* me, and not forget your servant but give her a son, then I will give him to the LORD for all the days of his life,*w* and no razor*x* will ever be used on his head."

¹²As she kept on praying to the LORD, Eli observed her mouth. ¹³Hannah was praying in her heart, and her lips were moving but her voice was not heard. Eli thought she was drunk ¹⁴and said to her, "How long are you going to stay drunk? Put away your wine."

¹⁵"Not so, my lord," Hannah replied, "I am a woman who is deeply troubled.*y* I have not been drinking wine or beer; I was pouring*z* out my soul to the LORD. ¹⁶Do not take your servant for a wicked woman; I have been praying here out of my great anguish and grief."*a*

---

a 1 See Septuagint and 1 Chron. 6:26-27,33-35; or *from Ramathaim Zuphim.*

1:1 *a* S Jos 18:25
b 1Sa 9:5 *c* Jos 17:17-18 *d* Jos 21:20-22
1Ch 6:27,34
1:2 *f* S Ge 4:19
1:3 *g* ver 21;
Ex 23:14; 1Sa 2:19;
20:6,29; Lk 2:41
h Dt 12:5-7 *i* S Jos 18:1
j 1Sa 2:31; 14:3
1:4 *k* Lev 7:15-18;
Dt 12:17-18
l S Ge 29:34
1:5 *m* S Ge 37:3
n S Ge 11:30; S 29:31
1:6 *o* S Ge 16:4
1:7 *p* 2Sa 12:17;
Ps 102:4
1:8 *q* S Ru 4:15
1:9 *r* 1Sa 3:3
1:10 *s* Job 3:20; 7:11;
10:1; 21:25; 23:2;
27:2; Isa 38:15;
Jer 20:18
1:11 *t* S Jdg 11:30
u S Ge 17:1; Ps 24:10;
46:7; Isa 1:9
v S Ge 8:1 *w* S Jdg 13:7
x Nu 6:1-21; Jdg 13:5;
Lk 1:15
1:15 *y* 2Ki 4:27
z Ps 42:4; 62:8;
La 2:19
1:16 *a* Ps 55:2

1:1 *Ramathaim.* The name occurs only here in the OT and appears to be another name for Ramah (see v. 19; 2:11; 7:17; 19:18; 25:1). It is perhaps to be identified with Arimathea (see Mt 27:57 and note; Jn 19:38). *Zuphite.* See TNIV text note. It is not clear whether this word refers to the man or the place. If it refers to the man, it indicates his descent from Zuph (see later in this verse; see also 1Ch 6:34-35). If it refers to the place, it designates the general area in which Ramathaim was located (see 9:5). *Ephraimite.* Although Elkanah is here called an Ephraimite, he was probably a Levite whose family belonged to the Kohathite clans that had been allotted towns in Ephraim (see Jos 21:20-21; 1Ch 6:22-27). **1:2** *two wives.* See notes on Ge 4:19; 16:2; 25:6.

1:3 *Year after year this man went up.* Three times a year every Israelite male was required to appear before the Lord at the central sanctuary (Ex 23:14-19; 34:23; Dt 16:16-17). The festival referred to here was probably the Festival of Tabernacles, which not only commemorated God's care for his people during the wilderness journey to Canaan (see Lev 23:43) but more especially celebrated, with joy and feasting, God's blessing on the year's crops (see Dt 16:13-15). On such festive occasions Hannah's deep sorrow because of her own barrenness was the more poignant. *the LORD Almighty.* Traditionally "the LORD of hosts," a royal title. This is the first time in the Bible that God is so designated. It now becomes prominent at the onset of monarchy in Israel. The Hebrew for "host(s)" can refer to (1) human armies (Ex 7:4, "divisions"; Ps 44:9); (2) the celestial bodies such as the sun, moon and stars (Ge 2:1, "vast array"; Dt 4:19; Isa 40:26); or (3) the heavenly creatures such as angels (Jos 5:14; 1Ki 22:19; Ps 148:2). The title, "the LORD of hosts," is perhaps best understood as a general reference to the sovereignty of God over all comers in the universe (hence the TNIV rendering, "the LORD Almighty"). In the account of the establishment of kingship in Israel it became particularly appropriate as a reference to God as the God of armies—both of the heavenly armies (cf. Dt 33:2; Jos 5:14; Ps 68:17; Hab 3:8) and the armies of Israel (1Sa 17:45). *Shiloh.* The town in Ephraim between Bethel and Shechem, where the central sanctuary and the ark of the covenant were located (see 4:3; Jos 18:1 and note; Jdg 21:19).

1:4 *sacrifice.* Here refers to a fellowship offering, a sacrifice that was combined with a festive meal signifying fellowship and communion with the Lord and grateful acknowledgment of his mercies (see 7:11-18).
1:5 *the LORD had closed her womb.* The Lord gives and withholds children (see Ge 18:10; 29:31; 30:2,22 and note on 30:2).
1:6 *her rival.* See Ge 16:4 and note.
1:8 *more to you than ten sons.* See 2:5; see also note on Ru 4:15.
1:9 *house.* Here and in 3:3 the central sanctuary, the tabernacle, is referred to as "the LORD's house" or "the house of the LORD" (also in v. 7; 3:15) and "the tent of meeting" (2:22), and the Lord calls it "my dwelling" (2:32). The references to the tabernacle as a "house," as well as references to sleeping quarters and doors (3:2,15), give the impression that at this time the tabernacle was part of a larger, more permanent building complex to which the term "house" could legitimately be applied (cf. Jer 7:12,14 and note on 7:12; 26:6).
1:11 *vow.* See Ge 28:20-22; Nu 21:2; Ps 50:14 and note; 76:11; 116:14,18; 132:2-5; Pr 20:25 and note; 31:2. Regulations for the making of vows by women are found in Nu 30. *remember.* To remember is more than simply to recall that Hannah existed. It is to go into action in her behalf (see vv. 19-20; see also note on Ge 8:1). *your servant.* That is, me (see note on Ge 18:2). *no razor.* Hannah voluntarily vows for her son what God had required of Samson (see Jdg 13:5 and note). Long hair was a symbol of dedication to the service of the Lord and was one of the characteristics of the Nazirite vow, which was normally taken for a limited time rather than for life (see Nu 6:1-21 and notes).

1:13 *drunk.* Eli's mistake suggests that in those days it was not uncommon for drunken people to enter the sanctuary. Further evidence of the religious and moral deterioration of the time is found in the stories of Jdg 17-21.
1:15 *beer.* Written texts from Mesopotamia as early as 2500 B.C. portray the brewing of beer as a major industry.
1:16 *wicked.* See note on Dt 13:13.

1:17 b Nu 6:26;
1Sa 20:42; 2Ki 5:19;
S Ac 15:33
c S Ge 25:21;
Ps 20:3-5
1:18 d S Ge 18:3;
Ru 2:13 e Ro 15:13
1:19 f S Jos 18:25
g S Ge 8:1; S 29:31
1:20 h S Ge 17:19;
S 29:32; S 30:6
i Ex 2:10; Mt 1:21
j 1Sa 7:5; 12:23;
1Ch 6:27; Jer 15:1;
Heb 11:32
1:21 k S ver 3
l S Ge 28:20; Nu 30:2;
Dt 12:11
1:22 m Ex 13:2;
Lk 2:22
1:23 n S Ge 25:21
o Ge 21:8
1:24 p Nu 15:8-10
1:27 q 1Sa 2:20;
Ps 66:19-20
1:28 r S Jdg 13:7
2:1 s Lk 1:46-55
t Ps 13:5; 33:21;
Zec 10:7 u Ps 18:2;
89:17,24; 148:14
v Ps 6:8 w S Nu 10:35;
Ps 6:10

[17] Eli answered, "Go in peace, [b] and may the God of Israel grant you what you have asked of him. [c]"

[18] She said, "May your servant find favor in your eyes. [d]" Then she went her way and ate something, and her face was no longer downcast. [e]

[19] Early the next morning they arose and worshiped before the LORD and then went back to their home at Ramah. [f] Elkanah made love to his wife Hannah, and the LORD remembered [g] her. [20] So in the course of time Hannah became pregnant and gave birth to a son. [h] She named [i] him Samuel, [a][j] saying, "Because I asked the LORD for him."

HANNAH DEDICATES SAMUEL

[21] When Elkanah went up with all his family to offer the annual [k] sacrifice to the LORD and to fulfill his vow, [l] [22] Hannah did not go. She said to her husband, "After the boy is weaned, I will take him and present [m] him before the LORD, and he will live there always." [b]

[23] "Do what seems best to you," her husband Elkanah told her. "Stay here until you have weaned him; only may the LORD make good [n] his [c] word." So the woman stayed at home and nursed her son until she had weaned [o] him.

[24] After he was weaned, she took the boy with her, young as he was, along with a three-year-old bull, [d][p] an ephah [e] of flour and a skin of wine, and brought him to the house of the LORD at Shiloh. [25] When the bull had been sacrificed, they brought the boy to Eli, [26] and she said to him, "Pardon me, my lord. As surely as you live, I am the woman who stood here beside you praying to the LORD. [27] I prayed [q] for this child, and the LORD has granted me what I asked of him. [28] So now I give him to the LORD. For his whole life [r] he will be given over to the LORD." And he worshiped the LORD there.

HANNAH'S PRAYER

2 Then Hannah prayed and said: [s]

"My heart rejoices [t] in the LORD;
    in the LORD my horn [f][u] is lifted high.
My mouth boasts [v] over my enemies, [w]
    for I delight in your deliverance.

---

a *20* *Samuel* sounds like the Hebrew for *heard by God.*   b *22* Masoretic Text; Dead Sea Scrolls *always.*
I have dedicated him as a Nazirite—all the days of his life.   c *23* Masoretic Text; Dead Sea Scrolls,
Septuagint and Syriac *your*   d *24* Dead Sea Scrolls, Septuagint and Syriac; Masoretic Text *with three
bulls*   e *24* That is, probably about 36 pounds or about 16 kilograms   f *1* *Horn* here symbolizes
strength; also in verse 10.

1:20 *Samuel.* See TNIV text note.

A **1:21** *annual sacrifice.* See notes on vv. 3–4. *his vow.* Making vows to God was a common feature of OT piety, usually involving thank offerings and praise (see Ps 50:14; 56:12; 116:17–18). Elkanah no doubt annually made vows to the Lord as he prayed for God's blessing on his crops and flocks, and fulfilled those vows at the Festival of Tabernacles (see note on v. 3).

1:22 *weaned.* It was customary in the East to nurse children for three years or longer (in the Apocrypha see 2 Maccabees 7:27) since there was no way to keep milk sweet.

1:23 *his word.* No previous word from God is mentioned, unless this refers to the pronouncement of Eli in v. 17. The Dead Sea Scrolls, Septuagint (the pre-Christian Greek translation of the OT) and Syriac version (see TNIV text note) resolve this problem by reading "your word." But "his word" may refer to an earlier, unrecorded word from the Lord.

1:26 *As surely as you live.* A customary way of emphasizing the truthfulness of one's words.

1:27 *I prayed for this child.* In the nativity account of Samuel, which also serves as the nativity account of the monarchy in Israel, Hannah serves as a cameo of Israel. As Hannah in her distress "asked" for a child, so Israel in her distress "asked" for a king, and Hannah's hymnic prayer that follows Samuel's birth (2:1–10) became Israel's hymn of praise as they reflected on the inauguration of the Davidic dynasty.

1:28 *given over.* The unusual Hebrew term used here sounds precisely like the Hebrew for the name Saul. It appears that the author already here hints that Saul, the one "asked for" by Israel,

should also have been Saul, the one "given over" to the service of the Lord—that every king in Israel should be a "Saul" in this latter sense.

2:1–10 Hannah's prayer is constructed of two balanced parts (vv. 1–5,6–10). While there is considerable overlapping of themes between the first and second halves, the focus of Hannah's praise shifts from a celebration of the ways of God that "lifted high" her "horn" to a celebration of the ways of God that will "exalt" the "horn" of his anointed.

A **2:1** *prayed.* Hannah's prayer (vv. 1–10) is a song of praise and thanksgiving to God (see Ps 72:20, where the psalms of David are designated "prayers"). This song has sometimes been termed the "Magnificat of the OT" because it is so similar to the Magnificat of the NT (Mary's song, Lk 1:46–55). It also has certain resemblances to the "Benedictus" (Zechariah's song, Lk 1:67–79). Hannah's song of praise finds many echoes in David's song near the end of the book (2Sa 22). These two songs frame the main narrative, and their themes highlight the ways of God that the narrative relates—they contain the theology of the book in the form of praise. Hannah speaks prophetically at a time when Israel is about to enter an important new period of her history with the establishment of kingship through her son, Samuel. *rejoices in the LORD.* The supreme source of Hannah's joy is not in the child, but in the God who has answered her prayer. *my horn is lifted high.* See TNIV text note; cf. Dt 33:17; Ps 75:4 and note; 92:10; 112:9; Lk 1:69 and note. To have one's horn "lifted high" by God is to be delivered from disgrace to a position of honor and strength.

2 "There is no one holy[x] like[y] the LORD;
  there is no one besides you;
  there is no Rock[z] like our God.

3 "Do not keep talking so proudly
  or let your mouth speak such arrogance,[a]
  for the LORD is a God who knows,[b]
  and by him deeds[c] are weighed.[d]

4 "The bows of the warriors are broken,[e]
  but those who stumbled are armed with strength.[f]
5 Those who were full hire themselves out for food,
  but those who were hungry[g] are hungry no more.
  She who was barren[h] has borne seven children,
  but she who has had many sons pines away.

6 "The LORD brings death and makes alive;[i]
  he brings down to the grave and raises up.[j]
7 The LORD sends poverty and wealth;[k]
  he humbles and he exalts.[l]
8 He raises[m] the poor[n] from the dust[o]
  and lifts the needy[p] from the ash heap;
he seats them with princes
  and has them inherit a throne of honor.[q]

  "For the foundations[r] of the earth are the LORD's;
  on them he has set the world.
9 He will guard the feet[s] of his faithful servants,[t]
  but the wicked will be silenced in the place of darkness.[u]

  "It is not by strength[v] that one prevails;
10 those who oppose the LORD will be broken.[w]
The Most High will thunder[x] from heaven;
  the LORD will judge[y] the ends of the earth.

  "He will give strength[z] to his king
  and exalt the horn[a] of his anointed."

2:10 [y] Ps 96:13; 98:9; Mt 25:31-32 [z] Ps 18:1; 21:1; 59:16 [a] S Dt 33:17; Ps 89:24; S Lk 1:69

2:2 [x] S Ex 15:11;
S Lev 11:44
[y] S Ex 8:10; Isa 40:25;
46:5 [z] S Ge 49:24;
S Ex 33:22; Dt 32:37;
2Sa 22:2,32; 23:3;
Ps 31:3; 71:3
2:3 [a] Ps 17:10; 31:18;
73:8; 75:4; 94:4
[b] S Jos 22:22
[c] 1Sa 16:7; 1Ki 8:39;
1Ch 28:9; 2Ch 6:30;
Pr 15:11; Jer 11:20;
17:10 [d] Pr 16:2; 24:11-
12
2:4 [e] 2Sa 1:27;
Ps 37:15; 46:9; 76:3
[f] Job 17:9; Isa 40:31;
41:1; 52:1; 57:10
2:5 [g] Lk 1:53
[h] Ps 113:9; Isa 54:1;
Jer 15:9
2:6 [i] Dt 32:39
[j] Isa 26:19; Eze 37:3,
12
2:7 [k] S Dt 8:18
[l] Job 5:11; 40:12;
Ps 75:7; Isa 2:12;
13:11; 22:19; Da 4:37
2:8 [m] Ps 113:7-8
[n] Jas 2:5 [o] 1Ki 16:2
[p] Ps 72:12; 107:41;
145:14; 146:8;
S Mt 23:12 [q] 2Sa 7:8;
Job 36:7; Isa 22:23;
Eze 21:26 [r] Job 15:7;
38:4; Ps 104:5;
Pr 8:29; Isa 40:12;
Jer 10:12
2:9 [s] Ps 91:12; 121:3;
Pr 3:26 [t] Pr 2:8
[u] Job 10:22; Isa 5:30;
8:22; 59:9; 60:2;
Jer 13:16; Am 5:18,20;
Zep 1:14-15; Mt 8:12
[v] 1Sa 17:47; Ps 33:16-
17; Zec 4:6
2:10 [w] S Ex 15:6
[x] S Ex 19:16; 1Sa 7:10;
12:17; 2Sa 22:14;
Job 37:4,5; 38:1;
Ps 18:13; 29:3;
Isa 66:6

2:2 *no one holy like the LORD.* See Lev 11:44 and note. *no one besides you.* See 2Sa 7:22; 22:32; Dt 4:35 and note; Isa 45:6. *Rock.* A metaphor to depict the strength and stability of the God of Israel as the unfailing source of security for his people (see 2Sa 22:2 and note; Ps 19:14; Isa 17:10 and note).

2:3 *so proudly ... such arrogance.* After the manner of Peninnah (and others in the narratives of 1,2 Samuel—Eli's sons, the Philistines, Saul, Nabal, Goliath, Absalom, Shimei and Sheba). *the LORD is a God who knows.* See 16:7; 1Ki 8:39; Ps 139:1-6 and note; Jn 2:24-25.

2:4-5 In a series of examples derived from everyday life Hannah shows that God often works contrary to natural expectations and brings about surprising reversals—seen frequently in the stories that follow.

2:5 *seven children.* See 1:8 and note on Ru 4:15.

2:6-8 Hannah declares that life and death, prosperity and adversity, are determined by the sovereign power of God—a theme richly illustrated in the following narrative (see also 2Sa 22:2; 1Ki 17:20-24; 2Ki 4:32-35; Jn 5:21; 11:41-44).

2:6 *grave.* See note on Ge 37:35.

2:8 *foundations of the earth.* A common figure in the OT for the solid base on which the earth (the dry land on which people live, not planet Earth; Ge 1:10) is founded. The phrase does not teach a particular theory of the structure of the universe (see Job 9:6; 38:6; Ps 24:2 and note; 75:3; 104:5; Zec 12:1).

2:9 *guard the feet.* Travel in ancient Israel was for the most part by foot over trails that were often rocky and dangerous (see Ps 91:11-12; 121:3). *his faithful servants.* People who faithfully serve the Lord. The Hebrew root underlying this word is used of both

God and his people in 2Sa 22:26 to characterize the nature of their mutual relationship. The word is also translated "faithful" (Ps 12:1; 32:6) and "faithful ones" (Pr 2:8). See Ps 4:3 and note.

2:10 *judge.* Impose his righteous rule upon (see Ps 96:13; 98:9). *ends of the earth.* All nations and peoples (see Dt 33:17; Isa 45:22). *his king.* Hannah's prayer is here prophetic, anticipating the establishment of kingship in Israel and the initial realization of the Messianic ideal in David (Lk 1:69). Ultimately her expectation finds fulfillment in Christ and his complete triumph over the enemies of God. *exalt the horn.* The expected king's horn will be "lifted high/exalted" as surely as Hannah's had been (see v. 1). This word about the horns frames the song and highlights its central theme. *anointed.* The first reference in the Bible to the Lord's anointed—i.e., his anointed king. (Priests were also anointed for God's service; see Ex 28:41; Lev 4:3.) The word is often synonymous with "king" (as here) and provides part of the vocabulary basis for the Messianic idea in the Bible. "Anointed" and "Messiah" are the translation and transliteration, respectively, of the same Hebrew word. The Greek translation of this Hebrew term is *Christos*, from which comes the English word "Christ" (see TNIV text note on Mt 1:1). A king (coming from the tribe of Judah) is first prophesied by Jacob (Ge 49:10); kingship is further anticipated in the oracles of Balaam in Nu 24:7,17. Also Dt 17:14-20 looks forward to the time when the Lord will place a king of his choice over his people after they enter the promised land. 1,2 Samuel shows how this expectation of the theocratic king is realized in the person of David. Hannah's prophetic anticipation of a king at the time of the dedication of her son Samuel, who was to be God's agent for establishing kingship in Israel, is entirely appropriate.

2:11 *b* S Jos 18:25
c ver 18; S Nu 16:9;
1Sa 3:1
2:12 *d* Jer 2:8; 9:6
2:13 *e* Dt 18:3
f Lev 7:35-36
2:16 *g* Lev 3:3,14-
16; 7:29-34
2:17 *h* ver 22,29;
S Nu 14:11; Jer 7:21;
Eze 22:26; Mal 2:7-9
2:18 *i* S ver 11
j ver 28; 1Sa 22:18;
23:9; 2Sa 6:14;
1Ch 15:27
2:19 *k* S 1Sa 1:3
2:20 *l* S 1Sa 1:27
2:21 *m* Ge 21:1
n S Jdg 13:24; Lk 1:80;
2:40
2:22 *o* S ver 17
p S Ex 38:8
2:25 *q* Ex 4:21;
Jos 11:20 *r* S Ex 32:10;
S Nu 11:2; 1Sa 3:14;
1Ki 13:6; Job 9:33;
Ps 106:30; Isa 1:18;
22:14; Jer 15:1;
Heb 10:26
2:26 *s* S Jdg 13:24;
Lk 2:52 *t* Pr 3:4

[11]Then Elkanah went home to Ramah,[b] but the boy ministered[c] before the LORD under Eli the priest.

ELI'S WICKED SONS

[12]Eli's sons were scoundrels; they had no regard[d] for the LORD. [13]Now it was the practice[e] of the priests that, whenever any of the people offered a sacrifice, the priest's servant would come with a three-pronged fork in his hand while the meat[f] was being boiled [14]and would plunge the fork into the pan or kettle or caldron or pot. Whatever the fork brought up the priest would take for himself. This is how they treated all the Israelites who came to Shiloh. [15]But even before the fat was burned, the priest's servant would come and say to the person who was sacrificing, "Give the priest some meat to roast; he won't accept boiled meat from you, but only raw."

[16]If the person said to him, "Let the fat[g] be burned first, and then take whatever you want," the servant would answer, "No, hand it over now; if you don't, I'll take it by force."

[17]This sin of the young men was very great in the LORD's sight, for they[a] were treating the LORD's offering with contempt.[h]

[18]But Samuel was ministering[i] before the LORD—a boy wearing a linen ephod.[j] [19]Each year his mother made him a little robe and took it to him when she went up with her husband to offer the annual[k] sacrifice. [20]Eli would bless Elkanah and his wife, saying, "May the LORD give you children by this woman to take the place of the one she prayed[l] for and gave to[b] the LORD." Then they would go home. [21]And the LORD was gracious to Hannah;[m] she gave birth to three sons and two daughters. Meanwhile, the boy Samuel grew[n] up in the presence of the LORD.

[22]Now Eli, who was very old, heard about everything[o] his sons were doing to all Israel and how they slept with the women[p] who served at the entrance to the tent of meeting. [23]So he said to them, "Why do you do such things? I hear from all the people about these wicked deeds of yours. [24]No, my sons; the report I hear spreading among the LORD's people is not good. [25]If anyone sins against another human being, God[c] may mediate for the offender; but if anyone sins against the LORD, who will[q] intercede[r] for them?" His sons, however, did not listen to their father's rebuke, for it was the LORD's will to put them to death.

[26]And the boy Samuel continued to grow[s] in stature and in favor with the LORD and with people.[t]

---

[a] 17 Dead Sea Scrolls and Septuagint; Masoretic Text *people*   [b] 20 Dead Sea Scrolls; Masoretic Text *and asked from*   [c] 25 Or *the judges*

2:11 *ministered.* Performed such services as a boy might render while assisting the high priest. *before the LORD.* At the "house of the LORD" (1:24).

2:12 *scoundrels.* See 1:16 and note. *had no regard for.* Lit. "did not know." In OT usage, to "know" the Lord is not just intellectual or theoretical recognition. It is to enter into fellowship with him and acknowledge his claims on one's life. The term often has a covenantal connotation (see Jer 31:34; Hos 2:20 and note).

2:13–16 Apparently vv. 13–14 describe the practice that had come to be accepted for determining the priests' portion of the fellowship offerings (Lev 7:31–36; 10:14–15; Dt 18:1–5)—a tradition presumably based on the assumption that a random thrust of the fork would providentially determine a fair portion. Verses 15–16 then describe how Eli's sons arrogantly violated that custom and the law.

2:15 *before the fat was burned.* On the altar as the Lord's portion, which he was to receive first (see Lev 3:16 and note; 4:10,26,31,35; 7:30–31; 17:6). *roast.* Boiling is the only form of cooking specified in the law for the priests' portion (Nu 6:19–20). Roasting this portion is nowhere expressly forbidden in the law, but it is specified only for the Passover lamb (Ex 12:8–9; Dt 16:7). The present passage seems to imply that for the priests to roast their portion of the sacrifices was unlawful.

2:16 *by force.* Presenting the priests' portion was to be a voluntary act on the part of the worshipers (see Lev 7:28–36; Dt 18:3).

2:18 *But Samuel.* Between 2:12 and 4:1 the author presents a series of sharp contrasts between Samuel and Eli's sons. *linen ephod.* A priestly garment worn by those who served before the

Lord at his sanctuary (see 22:18; 2Sa 6:14). Samuel's garment was similar to the ephod worn by the high priest (see note on v. 28; cf. Ex 39:1–7).

2:19 *little robe.* A sleeveless garment reaching to the knees, worn over the undergarment and under the ephod. *annual sacrifice.* See note on 1:3.

2:22 *slept with the women who served.* See Ex 38:8. There is no further reference to such women in the OT. Their service is not to be confused with that of the Levites, which is prescribed in the Pentateuch (Nu 1:50; 3:6–8; 8:15; 16:9; 18:2–3). The immoral acts of Eli's sons are reminiscent of the religious prostitution (fertility rites) at the Canaanite sanctuaries—acts that were an abomination to the Lord and a desecration of his house (Dt 23:17–18).

2:23 *he said to them.* Eli rebuked his sons but did not remove them from office. God would do that.

2:25 *God.* See TNIV text note. Eli's argument is that when someone commits an offense against another person, there is recourse to a third party to decide the issue (whether this be understood as God or as God's representatives, the judges; see TNIV text notes on Ex 22:8–9 and note on Ps 82:1); but when the offense is against the Lord there is no recourse, for God is both the one wronged and the judge. *the LORD's will to put them to death.* This comment by the author of the narrative is not intended to excuse Eli's sons but to indicate that Eli's warning was much too late. Eli's sons had persisted in their evil ways for so long that God's judgment on them was determined (v. 34; see Jos 11:20).

2:26 *grow in stature and in favor with the LORD and with people.* Cf. Luke's description of Jesus (Lk 2:52).

PROPHECY AGAINST THE HOUSE OF ELI

²⁷Now a man of God ᵘ came to Eli and said to him, "This is what the LORD says: 'Did I not clearly reveal myself to the family of your ancestor when they were in Egypt under Pharaoh? ²⁸I chose ᵛ your ancestor out of all the tribes of Israel to be my priest, to go up to my altar, to burn incense, ʷ and to wear an ephod ˣ in my presence. I also gave your ancestor's family all the food offerings ʸ presented by the Israelites. ²⁹Why do you ᵃ scorn my sacrifice and offering ᶻ that I prescribed for my dwelling? ᵃ Why do you honor your sons more than me by fattening yourselves on the choice parts of every offering made by my people Israel?'

³⁰"Therefore the LORD, the God of Israel, declares: 'I promised that the members of your family would minister before me forever. ᵇ But now the LORD declares: 'Far be it from me! Those who honor me I will honor, ᶜ but those who despise ᵈ me will be disdained. ᵉ ³¹The time is coming when I will cut short your strength and the strength of the members of your family, so that no one in it will reach old age, ᶠ ³²and you will see distress ᵍ in my dwelling. Although good will be done to Israel, no one in your family line will ever reach old age. ʰ ³³Every one of you that I do not cut off from serving at my altar I will spare only to destroy your sight and sap your strength, and all your descendants ⁱ will die in the prime of life.

³⁴" 'And what happens to your two sons, Hophni and Phinehas, will be a sign ʲ to you—they will both die ᵏ on the same day. ˡ ³⁵I will raise up for myself a faithful priest, ᵐ who will do according to what is in my heart and mind. I will firmly establish his family line, and he will minister before my anointed ⁿ one always. ³⁶Then everyone left in your family line will come and bow down before him for a piece of silver and a loaf of bread and plead, ᵒ "Appoint me to some priestly office so I can have food to eat." ' "

THE LORD CALLS SAMUEL

3 The boy Samuel ministered ᑫ before the LORD under Eli. In those days the word of the LORD was rare; ʳ there were not many visions. ˢ ²One night Eli, whose eyes ᵗ were becoming so weak that he could barely see, ᵘ was lying down in his usual place. ³The lamp ᵛ of God had not yet gone out, and Samuel

ᵃ 29 The Hebrew is plural.

2:27 ᵘ S Dt 33:1; S Jdg 13:6
2:28 ᵛ S Ex 28:1 ʷ S Ex 30:7 ˣ 1Sa 22:18; 23:6,9; 30:7 ʸ Lev 7:35-36
2:29 ᶻ ver 12-17 ᵃ S Dt 12:5
2:30 ᵇ S Ex 29:9 ᶜ Ps 50:23; 91:15; Pr 8:17 ᵈ Isa 53:3; Na 3:6; Mal 2:9 ᵉ Jer 18:10
2:31 ᶠ 1Sa 4:11-18; 22:16
2:32 ᵍ 1Sa 4:3; 22:17-20; Jer 7:12,14 ʰ 1Ki 2:26-27
2:33 ⁱ Jer 29:32; Mal 2:12
2:34 ʲ S Dt 13:2 ᵏ 1Sa 4:11 ˡ 1Ki 13:3
2:35 ᵐ 2Sa 8:17; 20:25; 1Ki 1:8,32; 2:35; 4:4; 1Ch 16:39; 29:22; Eze 44:15-16 ⁿ 1Sa 9:16; 10:1; 16:13; 2Sa 2:4; 12:7; 23:1; 1Ki 1:34; Ps 89:20
2:36 ᵒ Eze 44:10-14 ᵖ 1Sa 3:12; 1Ki 2:27
3:1 ᑫ S 1Sa 2:11 ʳ Ps 74:9; La 2:9; Eze 7:26 ˢ Am 8:11
3:2 ᵗ 1Sa 4:15 ᵘ S Ge 27:1
3:3 ᵛ Ex 25:31-38; Lev 24:1-4

2:27 *man of God.* Often a designation for a prophet (see 9:6,9–10; Dt 33:1; Jos 14:6; 1Ki 13:1; 17:24; 2Ki 4:9). *family of your ancestor.* The descendants of Aaron.
2:28 *to be my priest.* Three tasks of the priests are mentioned: 1. *to go up to my altar.* To perform the sacrificial rites at the altar of burnt offering in the courtyard of the tabernacle. 2. *to burn incense.* At the altar of incense in the Holy Place (Ex 30:1–10). 3. *to wear an ephod.* See note on v. 18. It would appear that the reference here is to the special ephod of the high priest (see Ex 28:6–14). The breastpiece containing the Urim and Thummim was attached to the ephod. The Urim and Thummim were a divinely ordained means of obtaining guidance from God, placed in the custody of the high priest (see Ex 28:30 and note; see also 1Sa 23:9–12; 30:7–8).
2:30 *I promised.* See Ex 29:9; Lev 8–9; Nu 16–17; 25:13. *Far be it from me!* This is not to say that the promise of the priesthood to Aaron's house has been annulled, but that Eli and his house are to be excluded from participation in this privilege because of their sin. *Those who honor me I will honor.* See v. 29. Spiritual privileges bring responsibilities and obligations; they are not to be treated as irrevocable rights (see 2Sa 22:26–27).
2:31 *strength . . . strength.* Lit. "arm . . . arm," symbolic of strength. Eli's "arm" and that of his priestly family will be cut off (contrast David, 2Sa 22:35). *no one in it will reach old age.* A prediction of the decimation of Eli's priestly family in the death of his sons (4:11), in the massacre of his descendants by Saul at Nob (22:18–19) and in the removal of Abiathar from his priestly office (1Ki 2:26–27).
2:32 *distress in my dwelling.* Including the capture of the ark by the Philistines (4:1–11), the destruction of Shiloh (Jer 7:14) and the relocation of the tabernacle to Nob (21:1–6; see note on 21:1).
2:33 A reference apparently to Abiathar, who was expelled from office by Solomon (see 1Ki 2:26–27) after an unsuccessful attempt to make Adonijah king as the successor to David.

2:34 *a sign to you.* The death of Hophni and Phinehas (4:11) will confirm the longer-term predictions. Such confirmation of a prophetic word was not uncommon (see 10:7–9; 1Ki 13:3 and note; Jer 28:15–17; Lk 1:18–20,64).
2:35 *I will raise up for myself a faithful priest.* Initially fulfilled in the person of Zadok, who served as a priest during the time of David (see 2Sa 8:17; 15:24,35; 20:25) and who eventually replaced Abiathar as high priest in the time of Solomon (see 1Ki 2:35; 1Ch 29:22). *firmly establish his family line.* Lit. "build for him a faithful house"; the faithful priest will be given a "faithful" (i.e., enduring) priestly family. See the similar word spoken concerning David (25:28, "lasting dynasty"; see also 2Sa 7:16; 1Ki 11:38). The line of Zadok was continued by his son Azariah (see 1Ki 4:2) and was still on the scene at the time of the exile and return (see 1Ch 6:8–15; Ezr 3:2). It continued in intertestamental times until Antiochus IV Epiphanes (175–164 B.C.) sold the priesthood to Menelaus (in the Apocrypha see 2 Maccabees 4:23–50), who was not of the priestly line. *my anointed one.* David and his successors (see note on v. 10).
3:1 *boy Samuel.* See 2:11,18. Samuel is now no longer a little child (see 2:21,26). The Jewish historian Josephus places his age at 12 years; he may have been older. *the word of the LORD was rare.* See Pr 29:18 and note; Am 8:11. During the entire period of the judges, apart from the prophet of 2:27–36, we are told of only two prophets (Jdg 4:4; 6:8) and of five revelations (Jdg 2:1–3; 6:11–26; 7:2–11; 10:11–14; 13:3–21). Possibly 2Ch 15:3 also refers to this period. *visions.* Cf. Ge 15:1.
3:3 *The lamp of God had not yet gone out.* The reference is to the golden lampstand, which stood opposite the table of the bread of the Presence (Ex 25:31–40) in the Holy Place. It was still night, but the early morning hours were approaching when the flame would grow dim or go out (see Ex 27:20–21; 30:7–8; Lev 24:3–4; 2Ch 13:11; Pr 31:18). For the lamp to be permitted to go out before morning was a violation of the Pentateuchal regulations. *house.* See note on 1:9.

3:3 ʷ1Sa 1:9
ˣDt 10:1-5; 1Ki 6:19;
8:1
3:4 ʸS Ge 22:1;
S Ex 3:4
3:7 ᶻ1Sa 2:12
ᵃJer 1:2 ᵇS Nu 12:6;
Am 3:7
3:10 ᶜEx 3:4
3:11 ᵈ2Ki 21:12;
Job 15:21; Jer 19:3
3:12 ᵃS 1Sa 2:27-36
3:13 ᶠ1Ki 1:6
3:14 ᵍS 1Sa 2:25
3:17 ʰ1Ki 22:14;
Jer 23:28; 38:14; 42:4
ⁱS Ru 1:17
3:18 ʲS Jdg 10:15
3:19 ᵏS Ge 21:22;
S Nu 14:43
ˡS Jdg 13:24
ᵐ1Sa 9:6
3:20 ⁿS Jdg 20:1
ᵒS Dt 18:22;
Eze 33:33
3:21 ᵖS Nu 12:6
4:1 ᵠ1Sa 5:1; 7:12
ʳJos 12:18; 1Sa 29:1;
1Ki 20:26

was lying down in the house ʷ of the LORD, where the ark ˣ of God was. ⁴Then the LORD called Samuel.

Samuel answered, "Here I am. ʸ" ⁵And he ran to Eli and said, "Here I am; you called me."

But Eli said, "I did not call; go back and lie down." So he went and lay down.

⁶Again the LORD called, "Samuel!" And Samuel got up and went to Eli and said, "Here I am; you called me."

"My son," Eli said, "I did not call; go back and lie down."

⁷Now Samuel did not yet know ᶻ the LORD: The word ᵃ of the LORD had not yet been revealed ᵇ to him.

⁸A third time the LORD called, "Samuel!" And Samuel got up and went to Eli and said, "Here I am; you called me."

Then Eli realized that the LORD was calling the boy. ⁹So Eli told Samuel, "Go and lie down, and if he calls you, say, 'Speak, LORD, for your servant is listening.' " So Samuel went and lay down in his place.

¹⁰The LORD came and stood there, calling as at the other times, "Samuel! Samuel! ᶜ"

Then Samuel said, "Speak, for your servant is listening."

¹¹And the LORD said to Samuel: "See, I am about to do something in Israel that will make the ears of everyone who hears about it tingle. ᵈ ¹²At that time I will carry out against Eli everything ᵉ I spoke against his family—from beginning to end. ¹³For I told him that I would judge his family forever because of the sin he knew about; his sons blasphemed God, ᵃ and he failed to restrain ᶠ them. ¹⁴Therefore I swore to the house of Eli, 'The guilt of Eli's house will never be atoned ᵍ for by sacrifice or offering.' "

¹⁵Samuel lay down until morning and then opened the doors of the house of the LORD. He was afraid to tell Eli the vision, ¹⁶but Eli called him and said, "Samuel, my son."

Samuel answered, "Here I am."

¹⁷"What was it he said to you?" Eli asked. "Do not hide ʰ it from me. May God deal with you, be it ever so severely, ⁱ if you hide from me anything he told you." ¹⁸So Samuel told him everything, hiding nothing from him. Then Eli said, "He is the LORD; let him do what is good in his eyes." ʲ

¹⁹The LORD was with ᵏ Samuel as he grew ˡ up, and he let none ᵐ of Samuel's words fall to the ground. ²⁰And all Israel from Dan to Beersheba ⁿ recognized that Samuel was attested as a prophet of the LORD. ᵒ ²¹The LORD continued to appear at Shiloh, and there he revealed ᵖ himself to Samuel through his word.

4

And Samuel's word came to all Israel.

THE PHILISTINES CAPTURE THE ARK

Now the Israelites went out to fight against the Philistines. The Israelites camped at Ebenezer, ᵠ and the Philistines at Aphek. ʳ ²The Philistines deployed their forces to meet Is-

---

ᵃ 13 An ancient Hebrew scribal tradition (see also Septuagint); Masoretic Text *sons made themselves contemptible*

3:4 *Here I am.* See note on Ge 22:1.

3:5 *I did not call.* Eli's failure to recognize at once that the Lord had called Samuel may be indicative of his own unfamiliarity with the Lord.

3:7 *did not yet know the LORD.* In the sense of having a direct experience of him (see Ex 1:8), such as receiving a revelation from him (see the last half of the verse).

3:10 *Samuel! Samuel!* See note on Ge 22:11.

3:11–14 The Lord's first revelation to Samuel summarizes the message Eli had already received from the "man of God" (2:27–36), thus confirming the fact that the youth had indeed received a revelation from God.

3:11 *make the ears . . . tingle.* See note on Jer 19:3.

3:13 *blasphemed God.* See TNIV text note and Lev 24:14–16.

3:15 *doors of the house of the LORD.* See note on 1:9. *vision.* See notes on vv. 1, 11–14.

3:17 *May God deal with you, be it ever so severely.* A curse formula (see 14:44; 20:13; 25:22; 2Sa 3:9,35; 19:13; Ru 1:17; 1Ki 2:23; 2Ki 6:31), usually directed against the speaker but here used by Eli against Samuel if he conceals anything the Lord said (see also note on 14:24).

3:18 *let him do what is good in his eyes.* Eli bows before God, accepting the judgment as righteous (see Ex 34:5–7).

3:19 *The LORD was with Samuel.* Said also of David (see 16:18 and note). *he let none of Samuel's words fall to the ground.* Because none of Samuel's words proved unreliable, he was recognized as a prophet who spoke the word of the Lord (see vv. 20–21; 9:6).

3:20 *Dan to Beersheba.* A conventional expression often used in Samuel, Kings and Chronicles to denote the entire land (Dan was located in the far north and Beersheba in the far south).

3:21 *continued to appear at Shiloh.* But not after the events narrated in chs. 4–6 (see Jer 7:12–14; 26:6).

4:1 *Samuel's word came to all Israel.* Contrast 3:1. *Ebenezer.* Means "stone of help." The precise location is unknown, but it was probably a short distance (see v. 6) to the east of Aphek—not to be confused with the location of the stone named Ebenezer that was later erected by Samuel between Mizpah and Shen (see 7:12) to commemorate a victory over the Philistines. *Aphek.* A town about 12 miles northeast of the coastal city of Joppa. Philistine presence this far north suggests an attempt to spread their control over the Israelite tribes of central Canaan (see v. 9; Jdg 15:11).

rael, and as the battle spread, Israel was defeated by the Philistines, who killed about four thousand of them on the battlefield. ³When the soldiers returned to camp, the elders of Israel asked, "Why ˢ did the LORD bring defeat on us today before the Philistines? Let us bring the ark ᵗ of the LORD's covenant from Shiloh, ᵘ so that he may go with us ᵛ and save us from the hand of our enemies."

⁴So the people sent men to Shiloh, and they brought back the ark of the covenant of the LORD Almighty, who is enthroned between the cherubim. ʷ And Eli's two sons, Hophni and Phinehas, were there with the ark of the covenant of God.

⁵When the ark of the LORD's covenant came into the camp, all Israel raised such a great shout ˣ that the ground shook. ⁶Hearing the uproar, the Philistines asked, "What's all this shouting in the Hebrew ʸ camp?"

When they learned that the ark of the LORD had come into the camp, ⁷the Philistines were afraid. ᶻ "A god has ᵃ come into the camp," they said. "We're in trouble! Nothing like this has happened before. ⁸Woe to us! Who will deliver us from the hand of these mighty gods? They are the gods who struck ᵃ the Egyptians with all kinds of plagues ᵇ in the wilderness. ⁹Be strong, Philistines! Be men, or you will be subject to the Hebrews, as they ᶜ have been to you. Be men, and fight!"

¹⁰So the Philistines fought, and the Israelites were defeated ᵈ and every man fled to his tent. The slaughter was very great; Israel lost thirty thousand foot soldiers. ¹¹The ark of God was captured, and Eli's two sons, Hophni and Phinehas, died. ᵉ

DEATH OF ELI

¹²That same day a Benjamite ᶠ ran from the battle line and went to Shiloh with his clothes torn and dust ᵍ on his head. ¹³When he arrived, there was Eli ʰ sitting on his chair by the side of the road, watching, because his heart feared for the ark of God. When the man entered the town and told what had happened, the whole town sent up a cry.

¹⁴Eli heard the outcry and asked, "What is the meaning of this uproar?"

The man hurried over to Eli, ¹⁵who was ninety-eight years old and whose eyes ⁱ had failed so that he could not see. ¹⁶He told Eli, "I have just come from the battle line; I fled from it this very day."

Eli asked, "What happened, my son?"

¹⁷The one who brought the news replied, "Israel fled before the Philistines, and the army has suffered heavy losses. Also your two sons, Hophni and Phinehas, are dead, ʲ and the ark of God has been captured." ᵏ

¹⁸When he mentioned the ark of God, Eli fell backward off his chair by the side of the gate. His neck was broken and he died, for he was an old man, and he was heavy. He had led ᵇ/ Israel forty years. ᵐ

ᵃ 7 Or "Gods have (see Septuagint)   ᵇ 18 Traditionally judged

---

4:3 ˢ Jos 7:7
ᵗ S Jos 6:7 ᵘ S Jos 18:1;
S 1Sa 2:32 ᵛ 2Ch 13:8
4:4 ʷ S Ge 3:24;
S Ex 25:22
4:5 ˣ S Jos 6:5,10
4:6 ʸ S Ge 14:13
4:7 ᶻ S Ex 15:14
4:8 ᵃ Ex 12:30;
1Sa 5:12 ᵇ Rev 11:6
4:9 ᶜ S Jdg 13:1
4:10 ᵈ S Dt 28:25
4:11 ᵉ Ps 78:64;
Jer 7:12
4:12 ᶠ Eze 24:26;
33:21 ᵍ S Jos 7:6;
S 2Sa 1:2
4:13 ʰ ver 18
4:15 ⁱ S 1Sa 3:2
4:17 ʲ 1Sa 22:18;
Ps 78:64 ᵏ Ps 78:61
4:18 / S Jdg 2:16;
S 16:31 ᵐ 1Sa 2:31

4:3 *Why did the LORD bring defeat . . . ?* The elders understood that their defeat was more an indication of God's displeasure than it was of Philistine military might. Israel's pagan neighbors also believed that the outcome of battle was decided by the gods. *so that he may go with us and save us.* In an attempt to secure the Lord's presence with them in the struggle against the Philistines, the elders sent for the ark of the covenant. They were correct in thinking there was a connection between God's presence with his people and the ark (cf. v. 4), and no doubt they remembered the presence of the ark at notable victories in Israel's past history (see Nu 10:33–36; Jos 3:3,11,14–17; 6:6,12–20). But they incorrectly believed that the Lord's presence with the ark was guaranteed, rather than being subject to his free decision. They reflect the pagan notion that the deity is identified with the symbol of his presence and that God's favor could automatically be gained by manipulating the symbol.

4:4 *enthroned between the cherubim.* On each end of the atonement cover of the ark of the covenant were cherubim of gold with their wings spread upward over the ark (see Ex 25:17–22). In the space between these cherubim God's presence with his people was localized in a special way, so that the atonement cover of the ark came to be viewed as the throne of Israel's divine King (see 2Sa 6:2; Ps 80:1; 99:1; see also note on Ex 25:18). *Hophni and Phinehas.* These wicked priests (see 2:12) did not restrain the army from its improper use of the ark but actually accompanied the ark to the battlefield.

4:6 *Hebrew.* See note on Ge 14:13.

4:7 *A god has come into the camp.* The Philistines also identified the God of Israel with the symbol of his presence (see note on v. 3).

4:8 *mighty gods.* The Philistines could think only in polytheistic terms. *Egyptians . . . plagues.* See note on 6:6.

4:11 *The ark of God was captured.* This phrase or a variation of it occurs five times in the chapter (here, vv. 17,19,21–22) and is the focal point of the narrative. In this disastrous event, God's word in 3:11 finds a swift fulfillment. *Hophni and Phinehas, died.* The fulfillment of 2:34; 3:12.

4:12 *his clothes torn and dust on his head.* A sign of grief and sorrow, here marking the messenger as a bearer of bad news (see 2Sa 1:2; 13:19; 15:32).

4:13 *his heart feared for the ark of God.* Eli had sufficient spiritual sensitivity to be aware of the danger inherent in the sinful and presumptuous act of taking the ark of God into the battle. And he seems to have been even more concerned for the ark than for his sons (see v. 18).

4:18 *he died.* The death of Eli marked the end of an era that had begun with the deaths of Joshua and the elders who served with him (see Jos 24:29,31). Incapable of restraining Israel or his sons from their wicked ways, and weakened and blinded by age, the old priest is an apt symbol of the flawed age now coming to its tragic close. He is also a striking contrast to the reign of David, which is the main focus of this narrative. *heavy.* A bit of information that not only helps explain why Eli's

4:21 ⁿ S Ge 35:18
ᵒ S Ex 24:16;
Ps 106:20; Jer 2:11;
Eze 1:28; 9:3; 10:18
4:22 ᵖ S Ex 24:16;
Ps 78:61 ᵍ Jer 7:12
5:1 ʳ S 1Sa 4:1
ˢ S Jos 11:22; S 13:3
5:2 ᵗ S Jdg 16:23;
Isa 2:18; 19:1; 46:1
5:3 ᵘ Isa 40:20; 41:7;
46:7; Jer 10:4
5:4 ᵛ Eze 6:6;
Mic 1:7
5:5 ʷ Zep 1:9
5:6 ˣ S Ex 9:3;
Ac 13:11 ʸ 2Sa 6:7;
Ps 78:66 ᶻ S Ex 15:26;
1Sa 6:5
5:8 ᵃ S Jdg 16:18
ᵇ S Jos 11:22

¹⁹His daughter-in-law, the wife of Phinehas, was pregnant and near the time of delivery. When she heard the news that the ark of God had been captured and that her father-in-law and her husband were dead, she went into labor and gave birth, but was overcome by her labor pains. ²⁰As she was dying, the women attending her said, "Don't despair; you have given birth to a son." But she did not respond or pay any attention.

²¹She named the boy Ichabod,ᵃ ⁿ saying, "The Gloryᵒ has departed from Israel"—because of the capture of the ark of God and the deaths of her father-in-law and her husband. ²²She said, "The Gloryᵖ has departed from Israel, for the ark of God has been captured."ᵍ

THE ARK IN ASHDOD AND EKRON

5 After the Philistines had captured the ark of God, they took it from Ebenezerʳ to Ashdod.ˢ ²Then they carried the ark into Dagon's temple and set it beside Dagon.ᵗ ³When the people of Ashdod rose early the next day, there was Dagon, fallenᵘ on his face on the ground before the ark of the Lᴏʀᴅ! They took Dagon and put him back in his place. ⁴But the following morning when they rose, there was Dagon, fallen on his face on the ground before the ark of the Lᴏʀᴅ! His head and hands had been brokenᵛ off and were lying on the threshold; only his body remained. ⁵That is why to this day neither the priests of Dagon nor any others who enter Dagon's temple at Ashdod step on the threshold.ʷ

⁶The Lᴏʀᴅ's handˣ was heavy on the people of Ashdod and its vicinity; he brought devastationʸ on them and afflicted them with tumors.ᵇ ᶻ ⁷When the people of Ashdod saw what was happening, they said, "The ark of the god of Israel must not stay here with us, because his hand is heavy on us and on Dagon our god." ⁸So they called together all the rulersᵃ of the Philistines and asked them, "What shall we do with the ark of the god of Israel?"

They answered, "Have the ark of the god of Israel moved to Gath. ᵇ" So they moved the ark of the God of Israel.

ᵃ 21 *Ichabod* means *no glory*.   ᵇ 6 Hebrew; Septuagint and Vulgate *tumors. And rats appeared in their land, and there was death and destruction throughout the city*

---

fall was fatal but also links his death with the judgment announced earlier:"Why do you honor your sons more than me by fattening yourselves ...?" (2:29). *He had led Israel forty years.* See TNIV text note. Eli is here included among the judges (see 2Sa 7:11; Jdg 2:16–19; Ru 1:1), who served as leaders of Israel in the period between the deaths of Joshua and of the elders who outlived him and the establishment of kingship. Eli's leadership of 40 years may have overlapped that of some of the judges, such as Jephthah and Samson.

A **4:21** *The Glory has departed.* The glory of Israel was Israel's God, not the ark (see 15:29; Heb 9:5 and notes), and loss of the ark did not mean that God had abandoned his people—God was not inseparably bound to the ark (see Jer 3:16–17). Yet the removal of the ark from Israel did signal estrangement in the relationship between God and his people, and it demonstrated the gravity of their error in thinking that in spite of their wickedness they had the power to coerce God into doing their will simply because they possessed the ark.

5:1 *Ashdod.* One of the five major cities of the Philistines (Jos 13:3), it was located near the Mediterranean coast about 35 miles west of Jerusalem. See note on Isa 20:1; see also map, p. 338.

B **5:2** *Dagon.* In Canaanite mythology the son (or brother) of El and the father of Baal. He was the principal god of the Philistines and was worshiped in temples at Gaza (Jdg 16:21,23,26), Ashdod (here) and Beth Shan (31:10–12; 1Ch 10:10). Veneration of this deity was widespread in the ancient world, extending from Mesopotamia to the Aramean and Canaanite area and attested in non-Biblical sources dating from the late third millennium B.C. until Maccabean times (second century B.C.; in the Apocrypha see 1 Maccabees 10:83–84). The precise nature of the worship of Dagon is obscure. Some have considered Dagon to be a fish god, but more recent evidence suggests either a storm or grain god. His name is related to a Hebrew word for "grain" (see note on Jdg 10:6).

5:3 *Dagon, fallen on his face.* The ark was placed next to the idol of Dagon by the Philistines in order to demonstrate Dagon's

superiority over the God of Israel, but the symbolism was reversed when Dagon was toppled to a position of homage before the ark of the Lord.

5:4 *head and hands had been broken off.* Proving that the Lord had defeated Dagon. In the ancient Near East, the heads and/or right hands of slain enemy soldiers were often brought back to the victors' camp as trophies of war (1Ch 10:10) and to establish a body count (cf. 18:27 and note).

5:5 *this day.* The time of the writing of 1,2 Samuel (see Introduction: Literary Features, Authorship and Date). *step on the threshold.* Apparently the threshold was considered to possess supernatural power because of its contact with parts of the fallen image of Dagon. Zep 1:9 appears to be a reference to a more general and rather widespread pagan idea that the threshold was the dwelling place of spirits.

5:6 *The Lᴏʀᴅ's hand.* A pervasive motif in the ark narratives; it or its equivalent occurs eight times (here and in vv. 7,9,11; 6:3,5,9; 7:13; cf. also 4:8). *was heavy.* Dagon's broken hands lay on the threshold (v. 4), but the Lord showed the reality and strength of his own hand by bringing a plague (see note on 6:4) on the people of Ashdod and the surrounding area (see vv. 9,11). God would not be manipulated by his own people (see note on 4:3), nor would he permit the Philistines to think that their victory over the Israelites and the capture of the ark demonstrated the superiority of their god over the God of Israel. *tumors.* One of the many covenant curses that would be inflicted on the Israelites if they disobeyed God (Dt 28:58–60). Here the affliction fell on the Philistines. See also TNIV text note on v. 9.

5:8 *rulers.* Of the five major cities of the Philistines (see 6:16; Jos 13:3; Jdg 3:3; see also map, p. 338). *Have the ark of the god of Israel moved to Gath.* Evidently the leaders of the Philistines did not share the opinion of the Ashdodites that there was a direct connection between what had happened in Ashdod and the presence of the ark; they seem to have suspected that the sequence of events was merely coincidental (see 6:9). The removal of the ark to Gath (12 miles southeast of Ashdod) put the matter to a test.

⁹But after they had moved it, the LORD's hand was against that city, throwing it into a great panic. ᶜ He afflicted the people of the city, both young and old, with an outbreak of tumors. ᵃ ¹⁰So they sent the ark of God to Ekron. ᵈ

As the ark of God was entering Ekron, the people of Ekron cried out, "They have brought the ark of the god of Israel around to us to kill us and our people." ¹¹So they called together all the rulers ᵉ of the Philistines and said, "Send the ark of the god of Israel away; let it go back to its own place, or it ᵇ will kill us and our people." For death had filled the city with panic; God's hand was very heavy on it. ¹²Those who did not die ᶠ were afflicted with tumors, and the outcry of the city went up to heaven.

THE ARK RETURNED TO ISRAEL

6 When the ark of the LORD had been in Philistine territory seven months, ²the Philistines called for the priests and the diviners ᵍ and said, "What shall we do with the ark of the LORD? Tell us how we should send it back to its place."

³They answered, "If you return the ark of the god of Israel, do not send it back to him without a gift; ʰ by all means send a guilt offering ⁱ to him. Then you will be healed, and you will know why his hand ʲ has not been lifted from you."

⁴The Philistines asked, "What guilt offering should we send to him?"

They replied, "Five gold tumors and five gold rats, according to the number ᵏ of the Philistine rulers, because the same plague ˡ has struck both you and your rulers. ⁵Make models of the tumors ᵐ and of the rats that are destroying the country, and give glory ⁿ to Israel's god. Perhaps he will lift his hand from you and your gods and your land. ⁶Why do you harden ᵒ your hearts as the Egyptians and Pharaoh did? When Israel's god dealt harshly with them, ᵖ did they �q not send the Israelites out so they could go on their way?

⁷"Now then, get a new cart ʳ ready, with two cows that have calved and have never been yoked. ˢ Hitch the cows to the cart, but take their calves away and pen them up. ⁸Take the ark of the LORD and put it on the cart, and in a chest beside it put the gold objects you are sending back to him as a guilt offering. Send it on its way, ⁹but keep watching it. If it goes up to its own territory, toward Beth Shemesh, ᵗ then the LORD has brought this great disaster on us. But if it does not, then we will know that it was not his hand that struck us but that it happened to us by chance."

¹⁰So they did this. They took two such cows and hitched them to the cart and penned up their calves. ¹¹They placed the ark of the LORD on the cart and along with it the chest containing the gold rats and the models of the tumors. ¹²Then the cows went straight up toward Beth Shemesh, keeping on the road and lowing all the way; they did not turn to the right or to the left. The rulers of the Philistines followed them as far as the border of Beth Shemesh.

¹³Now the people of Beth Shemesh were harvesting their wheat ᵘ in the valley, and when they looked up and saw the ark, they rejoiced at the sight. ¹⁴The cart came to the field of Joshua of Beth Shemesh, and there it stopped beside a large rock. The people chopped up the wood of the cart and sacrificed the cows as a burnt offering ᵛ to the LORD. ¹⁵The Levites ʷ took down the ark of the LORD, together with the chest containing the gold

---

ᵃ 9 Or *with tumors in the groin* (see Septuagint)   ᵇ 11 Or *he*

5:9 ᶜ S Ex 14:24
5:10 ᵈ S Jos 13:3
5:11 ᵉ ver 8
5:12 ᶠ S 1Sa 4:8
6:2 ᵍ S Ex 7:11; S Isa 44:25
6:3 ʰ S Ex 22:29; S 34:20 ⁱ S Lev 5:15 ʲ ver 9
6:4 ᵏ S Jos 13:3 ˡ 2Sa 24:25
6:5 ᵐ S 1Sa 5:6-11 ⁿ S Jos 7:19; Rev 14:7
6:6 ᵒ S Ex 4:21 ᵖ Ex 10:2 q S Ex 12:33
6:7 ʳ 2Sa 6:3; 1Ch 13:7 ˢ S Nu 19:2
6:9 ᵗ S Jos 15:10; 2l:16
6:13 ᵘ S Ge 30:14; Ru 2:23; 1Sa 12:17
6:14 ᵛ 1Sa 11:7; 2Sa 24:22; 1Ki 19:21
6:15 ʷ Jos 3:3

5:10 *Ekron.* The northernmost of the five major Philistine cities (see Jos 13:3), located 11 miles northeast of Ashdod and close to Israelite territory (see map, p. 338).

5:11 *Send the ark of the god of Israel away.* After three successive towns had been struck by disease upon the arrival of the ark, there was little doubt in the people's minds that the power of the God of Israel was the cause of their distress.

6:2 *priests and … diviners.* The experts on religious matters (priests) and the discerners of hidden knowledge by interpretation of omens (diviners) were consulted (see Dt 18:10; Isa 2:6; Eze 21:21).

6:3 *guilt offering.* The priests and diviners suggest returning the ark with a gift, signifying recognition of guilt in taking the ark from Israel and compensation for this violation of the Lord's honor (see v. 5). For the guilt offering in Israel see Lev 5:14—6:7.

6:4 *Five gold tumors.* Corresponding to the symptoms of the plague (see 5:6). *five gold rats.* The disease was accompanied by an infestation of rats (v. 5). The pre-Christian Greek translation of the OT (the Septuagint) includes this information earlier in the narrative (see TNIV text note on 5:6). It is likely that the rats

were carriers of the disease.

6:5 *Make models … and give glory to Israel's god.* The gold models were an acknowledgment that the disease and the rats were a judgment from the hand of the God of Israel (see note on v. 3).

6:6 *harden your hearts.* See notes on Ex 4:21; Dt 2:3; Jos 11:20. *the Egyptians and Pharaoh.* The plagues that God inflicted on the Egyptians at the time of the exodus made a lasting impression on the surrounding nations (see 4:8; Jos 2:10).

6:7 *have never been yoked.* Have not been trained to pull a cart. *take their calves away.* Normally cows do not willingly leave their suckling calves.

6:9 *Beth Shemesh.* A town near the Philistine border, belonging to Judah (see Jos 15:10). *by chance.* See note on 5:8.

6:12 *the cows went … keeping on the road.* Further indication that the Lord was directing them (see v. 7 and note).

6:13 *harvesting their wheat.* The time of wheat harvest is from mid-April until mid-June.

6:14–15 The arrival of the ark at Beth Shemesh is just as much a revelation of the hand of God as the journey itself, because it was one of the priestly towns (see Jos 21:13–16).

objects, and placed them on the large rock.ˣ On that day the people of Beth Shemeshʸ offered burnt offerings and made sacrifices to the LORD. ¹⁶The five rulers of the Philistines saw all this and then returned that same day to Ekron.

¹⁷These are the gold tumors the Philistines sent as a guilt offering to the LORD—one eachᶻ for Ashdod, Gaza, Ashkelon, Gath and Ekron. ¹⁸And the number of the gold rats was according to the number of Philistine towns belonging to the five rulers—the fortified towns with their country villages. The large rock on which the Levites set the ark of the LORD is a witness to this day in the field of Joshua of Beth Shemesh.

¹⁹But God struck downª some of the inhabitants of Beth Shemesh, putting seventyª of them to death because they lookedᵇ into the ark of the LORD. The people mourned because of the heavy blow the LORD had dealt them. ²⁰And the people of Beth Shemesh asked, "Who can standᶜ in the presence of the LORD, this holyᵈ God? To whom will the ark go up from here?"

²¹Then they sent messengers to the people of Kiriath Jearim,ᵉ saying, "The Philistines have returned the ark of the LORD. Come down and take it up to your town." ¹So the men of Kiriath Jearim came and took up the arkᶠ of the LORD. They brought it to Abinadab'sᵍ house on the hill and consecrated Eleazar his son to guard the ark of the LORD. ²The ark remained at Kiriath Jearimʰ a long time—twenty years in all.

SAMUEL SUBDUES THE PHILISTINES AT MIZPAH

Then all the people of Israel turned back to the LORD.ⁱ ³So Samuel said to the whole house of Israel, "If you are returningʲ to the LORD with all your hearts, then ridᵏ yourselves of the foreign gods and the Ashtorethsˡ and commitᵐ yourselves to the LORD and serve him only,ⁿ and he will deliver° you out of the hand of the Philistines." ⁴So the Israelites put away their Baals and Ashtoreths, and served the LORD only.

⁵Then Samuelᵖ said, "Assemble all Israel at Mizpah,q and I will intercedeʳ with the LORD for you." ⁶When they had assembled at Mizpah,ˢ they drew water and poured it out before the LORD. On that day they fasted and there they confessed, "We have sinned against the LORD." Now Samuel was serving as leaderᵇ ᵘ of Israel at Mizpah.

⁷When the Philistines heard that Israel had assembled at Mizpah, the rulers of the Philistines came up to attack them. When the Israelites heard of it, they were afraidᵛ be-

---

ª 19 A few Hebrew manuscripts; most Hebrew manuscripts and Septuagint *50,070*   ᵇ 6 Traditionally *judge*; also in verse 15

6:17 *guilt offering.* See note on v. 3.
6:18 *witness.* A kind of monument to the event. *this day.* The time of the writing of 1,2 Samuel (see Introduction: Literary Features, Authorship and Date).
6:19 *seventy.* The additional 50,000 in most Hebrew manuscripts (see TNIV text note) is apparently a copyist's mistake because it is added in an ungrammatical way (no conjunction). Furthermore, this small town could not have contained that many inhabitants. *looked into the ark.* The men of Beth Shemesh (Levites and priests among them) were judged by God for their irreverent curiosity. Because God had so closely linked the manifestation of his own presence among his people with the ark, it was to be treated with great honor (see 2Sa 6:7; Nu 4:15,17–20). This attitude of respect, however, is quite different from the superstitious attitude that led the elders to take the ark into battle against the Philistines, thus treating it as an object with magical power (see note on 4:3).
6:20 *this holy God.* See 2:2 and note. *To whom will the ark go up from here?* The inhabitants of Beth Shemesh respond to God's judgment in much the same way as the inhabitants of Ashdod, Gath and Ekron (see 5:8–10).
6:21 *Kiriath Jearim.* Located nine miles west of Jerusalem.
7:1 *Abinadab's house.* The ark remained in relative obscurity at Abinadab's house until David brought it to Jerusalem (2Sa 6:2–3). Somehow the tent of meeting (and the altar of burnt offering) escaped the destruction of Shiloh (Jer 7:12,14; 26:6). It apparently was first moved to Nob (21:1–9). In David's and Solomon's days it was located at Gibeon, five miles northwest of Jerusalem (1Ki 3:4; 1Ch 16:39; 21:29; 2Ch 1:3,13). The Gibeonites had been condemned to be menial laborers at the Lord's sanctuary (Jos 9:23,27). After Solomon completed the construction

of the temple, he brought the ark and the tent of meeting to it (see 1Ki 8:3–6 and note on 8:4).
7:2 *twenty years in all.* Probably the 20-year interval between the return of the ark to Israel and the assembly called by Samuel at Mizpah (see v. 5).
7:3 *Ashtoreths.* A general term for foreign goddesses, as elsewhere in the ancient Near East. More specifically, however, Ashtoreth herself was a goddess of love, fertility and war, worshiped in various forms by many peoples, including the Canaanites (see note on Jdg 2:13). The worship of Ashtoreth is frequently combined with the worship of Baal (see v. 4; 12:10; Jdg 2:13; 10:6), in accordance with the common practice in fertility religions to associate male and female deities.
7:5 *Mizpah.* See note on 2Ki 25:23; a town in the territory of Benjamin (Jos 18:26), located about seven and a half miles north of Jerusalem (see map, p. 586). It was here that the Israelites had previously gathered to undertake disciplinary action against Benjamin (Jdg 20:1; 21:1) after the abuse and murder of the concubine of a traveling Levite in Gibeah of Benjamin. Several other places bore the same name (see 22:3; Ge 31:49; Jos 11:3,8; 15:38). *I will intercede.* See 7:8–9 and note on 7:8; 8:6; 12:17–19,23; 15:11. Samuel, like Moses, was later remembered as a great intercessor (see Ps 99:6; Jer 15:1). Both were appointed by God to mediate his rule over his people, representing God to Israel and speaking on Israel's behalf to God.
7:6 *they drew water and poured it out before the LORD.* There is no other reference to this type of ceremony in the OT. It appears to symbolize the pouring out of one's heart in repentance and humility before the Lord. For related expressions see 1:15; Ps 62:8; La 2:19 and note. *Samuel was . . . leader.* See TNIV text note and v. 15; see also note on 4:18.

cause of the Philistines. [8]They said to Samuel, "Do not stop crying[w] out to the LORD our God for us, that he may rescue us from the hand of the Philistines." [9]Then Samuel[x] took a suckling lamb and sacrificed it as a whole burnt offering to the LORD. He cried out to the LORD on Israel's behalf, and the LORD answered him.[y]

[10]While Samuel was sacrificing the burnt offering, the Philistines drew near to engage Israel in battle. But that day the LORD thundered[z] with loud thunder against the Philistines and threw them into such a panic[a] that they were routed before the Israelites. [11]The men of Israel rushed out of Mizpah and pursued the Philistines, slaughtering them along the way to a point below Beth Kar.

[12]Then Samuel took a stone[b] and set it up between Mizpah and Shen. He named it Ebenezer,[a c] saying, "Thus far the LORD has helped us."

[13]So the Philistines were subdued[d] and they stopped invading Israel's territory. Throughout Samuel's lifetime, the hand of the LORD was against the Philistines. [14]The towns from Ekron[e] to Gath that the Philistines had captured from Israel were restored, and Israel delivered the neighboring territory from the hands of the Philistines. And there was peace between Israel and the Amorites.[f]

[15]Samuel[g] continued as Israel's leader[h] all[i] the days of his life. [16]From year to year he went on a circuit from Bethel[j] to Gilgal[k] to Mizpah, judging[l] Israel in all those places. [17]But he always went back to Ramah,[m] where his home was, and there he also held court[n] for Israel. And he built an altar[o] there to the LORD.

ISRAEL ASKS FOR A KING

8 When Samuel grew old, he appointed[p] his sons as Israel's leaders.[b 2]The name of his firstborn was Joel and the name of his second was Abijah,[q] and they served at Beersheba.[r 3]But his sons[s] did not follow his ways. They turned aside[t] after dishonest gain and accepted bribes[u] and perverted[v] justice.

[4]So all the elders[w] of Israel gathered together and came to Samuel at Ramah.[x 5]They said to him, "You are old, and your sons do not follow your ways; now appoint a king[y] to lead[c z] us, such as all the other nations[a] have."

[6]But when they said, "Give us a king[b] to lead us," this displeased[c] Samuel; so he prayed to the LORD. [7]And the LORD told him: "Listen[d] to all that the people are saying to you; it is not you they have rejected,[e] but they have rejected me as their king.[f 8]As they have

---

[a] 12 Ebenezer means stone of help.   [b] 1 Traditionally judges   [c] 5 Traditionally judge; also in verses 6 and 20

7:8 [w] ver 5; S Ex 32:30; S Nu 21:7; 1Sa 12:19,23; 1Ki 18:24; Isa 37:4; Jer 15:1; 27:18
7:9 [x] Ps 99:6
[y] S Ex 32:11; S Dt 9:19
7:10 [z] S Ex 9:23; S 1Sa 2:10
[a] S Ge 35:5; S Ex 14:24
7:12 [b] S Ge 28:22; S Dt 27:2; Jos 4:9
[c] S 1Sa 4:1
7:13 [d] Jdg 13:1,5
7:14 [e] S Jos 13:3
[f] S Jdg 1:34
7:15 [g] ver 6; 1Sa 12:11 [h] S Jdg 2:16
[i] Jdg 2:18
7:16 [j] S Ge 12:8
[k] S Jos 10:43;
S 1Sa 10:8; Am 5:5
[l] ver 6; Ac 13:20
7:17 [m] S Jos 18:25; 1Sa 8:4; 15:34; 19:18; 25:1; 28:3 [n] ver 6
[o] 1Sa 9:12; 14:35; 20:6; 2Sa 24:25
8:1 [p] Dt 16:18-19
8:2 [q] 1Ch 6:28
[r] Ge 22:19; 1Ki 19:3; Am 5:4-5
8:3 [s] 1Sa 2:12
[t] Ne 9:29; Job 34:27; Ps 14:3; 58:3; Isa 53:6
[u] Ex 23:8; 1Sa 12:3; Job 8:22; Pr 17:23
[v] S Ex 23:2
8:4 [w] S Jdg 11:11; 1Sa 11:3 [x] S 1Sa 7:17
8:5 [y] ver 19; S Dt 17:14-20; 1Sa 10:19; 12:12,13; Hos 13:11 [z] Isa 3:20; 12:2 [a] ver 20
8:6 [b] Hos 13:10
[c] 1Sa 12:17; 15:11; 16:1
8:7 [d] ver 22; 1Sa 12:1 [e] S Nu 11:20
[f] S Ex 16:8

7:8 *Do not stop crying out to the LORD our God for us.* As persons who were called out from among the people to mediate God's word to them, prophets were given unique access to God's council chamber (see 1Ki 22:19 and note). This privilege of having such access to God as to be mediators of God's rule over his people brought with it the special responsibility to be intercessors for God's people—as Moses was (Ex 32:11–14; 34:8–9; Nu 14:13–19), and as were Isaiah (2Ki 19:4), Jeremiah (see Jer 7:16; 15:1 and notes) and Amos (Am 7:2–3,5–6).

7:10 *the LORD thundered with loud thunder.* The Lord had promised to be the protector of his people when they were obedient to their covenant obligations (see Ex 23:22; Dt 20:1–4; see also 2Sa 5:19–25; Jos 10:11–14; Jdg 5:20–21; 2Ki 7:6; 19:35; 2Ch 20:17,22).

7:12 *Ebenezer.* See TNIV text note and note on 4:1.

7:13 *stopped invading Israel's territory.* Some interpreters see a contradiction between this statement and subsequent references to the Philistines in 9:16; 10:5; 13:3,5; 17:1; 23:27. This statement, however, only indicates that the Philistines did not immediately counterattack. See 2Ki 6:23–24 for a similar situation.

7:14 *Amorites.* See note on Ge 10:16.

7:15 A summary statement marking the end of the author's account of Samuel's ministry as Israel's leader (see v. 6).

7:16 *from Bethel to Gilgal to Mizpah.* A relatively small area (see map No. 4 at the end of this study Bible). *judging Israel.* See note on 4:18.

7:17 *Ramah.* See note on 1:1.

8:1—12:25 See Introduction: Contents and Theme.

8:1 *When Samuel grew old.* Probably about 20 years after the victory at Mizpah (see 7:11), when Samuel was approximately

65 years old (see Introduction: Chronology).

8:2 *Joel.* Means "The LORD is God." *Abijah.* Means "The LORD is my Father." Despite their names, Samuel's two sons "did not follow his ways" (v. 3). *Beersheba.* Located 45 miles southwest of Jerusalem (see also note on Ge 21:31).

8:3 *accepted bribes.* Contrast 12:3. Perversion of justice through bribery was explicitly forbidden in Pentateuchal law (see Ex 23:8; Dt 16:19).

8:5 *appoint a king to lead us.* The elders cite Samuel's age and the misconduct of his sons as justifications for their request for a king. It soon becomes apparent, however, that the more basic reason for their request was a desire to be like the surrounding nations—to have a human king as a symbol of national power and unity, one who would lead them in battle and guarantee their security (see v. 20; 10:19; 12:12; see also Introduction: Contents and Theme).

8:7 *Listen to all that the people are saying to you.* Anticipations of kingship in Israel are present already in the Pentateuch (Ge 49:10; Nu 24:7,17; Dt 17:14–20); Samuel is therefore instructed to listen to the people's request (see vv. 9,22). *it is not you they have rejected, but they have rejected me as their king.* Cf. Jdg 8:23. The sin of Israel in requesting a king (see 10:19; 12:12,17,19–20) did not rest in any evil inherent in kingship itself, but in the kind of kingship the people envisioned and their reasons for requesting it (see Introduction: Contents and Theme). Their desire was for a form of kingship that denied their covenant relationship with the Lord, who himself was pledged to be their savior and deliverer. In requesting a king "like all the other nations" (v. 20) they broke the covenant, rejected the Lord who was their King (12:12; Nu 23:21; Dt 33:5) and forgot his constant provision for their protection in the past (10:18; 12:8–11).

8:8 *g* 1Sa 12:10;
2Ki 21:22; Jer 2:17
8:9 *h* ver 11–18;
S Dt 17:14–20;
1Sa 10:25
8:10 *i* S Ex 19:7
8:11 *j* 1Sa 14:52
k S Ge 41:46
l S Dt 17:16; 2Sa 15:1;
1Ki 1:5; 2Ch 1:14;
9:25; SS 3:7
8:12 *m* Dt 1:15
8:14 *n* Eze 46:18
o 1Ki 21:7,15; Mic 2:2
p 2Ki 22:12
8:15 *q* S Ge 41:34;
1Sa 17:25
8:18 *r* 1Sa 28:6;
Job 27:9; 35:12,13;
Ps 18:41; 66:18;
Pr 1:28; Isa 1:15; 58:4;
59:2; Jer 14:12;
Eze 8:18; Mic 3:4
s 1Sa 10:25; 1Ki 12:4
8:19 *t* Pr 1:24;
Isa 50:2; 66:4;
Jer 7:13; 8:12; 13:10;
44:16 *u* Ac 13:21
v S ver 5
8:20 *w* S ver 5
8:21 *x* S Jdg 11:11
8:22 *y* S ver 7
9:1 *z* Jos 18:11–20
a S Ru 2:1 *b* 1Sa 14:51;
1Ch 8:33; 9:39;
Est 2:5; Ac 13:21
9:2 *c* S Ge 39:6
d 1Sa 10:24
e 1Sa 10:23
9:3 *f* ver 20;
1Sa 10:14,16
9:4 *g* S Jos 24:33
h 2Ki 4:42 *i* 1Sa 10:2
9:5 *j* 1Sa 1:1
k 1Sa 10:2
9:6 *l* S Dt 33:1;
S Jdg 13:6 *m* 1Sa 3:19
9:7 *n* S Ge 32:20;
1Ki 13:7; 14:3;
2Ki 4:42; 5:5,15;
Jer 40:5

done from the day I brought them up out of Egypt until this day, forsaking *g* me and serving other gods, so they are doing to you. ⁹Now listen to them; but warn them solemnly and let them know *h* what the king who will reign over them will claim as his rights."

¹⁰Samuel told *i* all the words of the Lᴏʀᴅ to the people who were asking him for a king. ¹¹He said, "This is what the king who will reign over you will claim as his rights: He will take *j* your sons and make them serve *k* with his chariots and horses, and they will run in front of his chariots. *l* ¹²Some he will assign to be commanders *m* of thousands and commanders of fifties, and others to plow his ground and reap his harvest, and still others to make weapons of war and equipment for his chariots. ¹³He will take your daughters to be perfumers and cooks and bakers. ¹⁴He will take the best of your *n* fields and vineyards *o* and olive groves and give them to his attendants. *p* ¹⁵He will take a tenth *q* of your grain and of your vintage and give it to his officials and attendants. ¹⁶Your male and female servants and the best of your cattle *a* and donkeys he will take for his own use. ¹⁷He will take a tenth of your flocks, and you yourselves will become his slaves. ¹⁸When that day comes, you will cry out for relief from the king you have chosen, but the Lᴏʀᴅ will not answer *r* you in that day. *s*"

¹⁹But the people refused *t* to listen to Samuel. "No!" they said. "We want *u* a king *v* over us. ²⁰Then we will be like all the other nations, *w* with a king to lead us and to go out before us and fight our battles."

²¹When Samuel heard all that the people said, he repeated *x* it before the Lᴏʀᴅ. ²²The Lᴏʀᴅ answered, "Listen *y* to them and give them a king."

Then Samuel said to the Israelites, "Everyone go back to your own town."

SAMUEL ANOINTS SAUL

9 There was a Benjamite, *z* a man of standing, *a* whose name was Kish *b* son of Abiel, the son of Zeror, the son of Bekorath, the son of Aphiah of Benjamin. ²Kish had a son named Saul, as handsome *c* a young man as could be found *d* anywhere in Israel, and he was a head taller *e* than anyone else.

³Now the donkeys *f* belonging to Saul's father Kish were lost, and Kish said to his son Saul, "Take one of the servants with you and go and look for the donkeys." ⁴So he passed through the hill *g* country of Ephraim and through the area around Shalisha, *h* but they did not find them. They went on into the district of Shaalim, but the donkeys *i* were not there. Then he passed through the territory of Benjamin, but they did not find them.

⁵When they reached the district of Zuph, *j* Saul said to the servant who was with him, "Come, let's go back, or my father will stop thinking about the donkeys and start worrying *k* about us."

⁶But the servant replied, "Look, in this town there is a man of God; *l* he is highly respected, and everything *m* he says comes true. Let's go there now. Perhaps he will tell us what way to take."

⁷Saul said to his servant, "If we go, what can we give the man? The food in our sacks is gone. We have no gift *n* to take to the man of God. What do we have?"

---

a 16 Septuagint; Hebrew *young men*

8:9,11 *what the king ... will claim as his rights.* Using a description of the policies of contemporary Canaanite kings (vv. 11–17), Samuel warns the people of the burdens associated with the type of kingship they long for.

8:11 *chariots.* See note on Jos 11:6; see also Dt 17:16 and note on 17:16–17.

8:15 *tenth.* This king's portion would be over and above the tenth Israel was to devote to the Lᴏʀᴅ (Lev 27:30–32; Nu 18:26; Dt 14:22,28; 26:12). In fact, the demands of the king would parallel all that Israel was to consecrate to the Lord as her Great King (persons, lands, crops, livestock)—even the whole population (v. 17).

8:18 *cry out for relief from the king.* See 1Ki 12:4; Jer 22:13–17.

8:20 *like all the other nations.* See notes on vv. 5,7.

9:1—11:15 God's establishment of Saul as King over Israel took place in three distinct stages: He was (1) anointed by Samuel (9:1—10:16), (2) chosen by lot (10:17–27) and (3) confirmed by public acclamation (11:1–15).

9:1 *man of standing.* Saul (v. 2) and David are each depicted as descending from an ancestor who was a noteworthy member of his community (see Ru 2:1; 4:21–22).

9:2 *a head taller than anyone else.* Physically of kingly stature (see 10:23).

9:3 *donkeys ... were lost.* Saul is introduced as a donkey wrangler sent in search of donkeys that had strayed from home—perhaps symbolizing Saul and the rebellious people who had asked for a king (cf. Isa 1:3). David would be introduced as a shepherd caring for his father's flock (16:11–13) and later pictured as the shepherd over the Lᴏʀᴅ's flock (2Sa 5:2; 7:7–8; Ps 78:70–72).

9:5 *Zuph.* Perhaps the region in which Ramah was located (see notes on v. 6; 1:1).

9:6 *But the servant replied.* Saul's ignorance of Samuel is an early hint of his character. *this town.* Probably Ramah (see 7:17), the hometown of Samuel, to which he had just returned from a journey (see v. 12). *man of God.* See note on 2:27; here a reference to Samuel. *everything he says comes true.* See 3:19 and note.

9:7 *what can we give the man?* Other examples of gifts offered to prophets are found in 1Ki 14:3; 2Ki 4:42; 5:15–16; 8:8–9. Whether Samuel accepted the gift and whether he was dependent on such gifts for a livelihood are not clear. Elisha refused the gift of Naaman (2Ki 5:16). False prophets usually

⁸The servant answered him again. "Look," he said, "I have a quarter of a shekel^a of silver. I will give it to the man of God so that he will tell us what way to take." ⁹(Formerly in Israel, if people went to inquire^o of God, they would say, "Come, let us go to the seer," because the prophet of today used to be called a seer.)^p

¹⁰"Good," Saul said to his servant. "Come, let's go." So they set out for the town where the man of God was.

¹¹As they were going up the hill to the town, they met some young women coming out to draw^q water, and they asked them, "Is the seer here?"

¹²"He is," they answered. "He's ahead of you. Hurry now; he has just come to our town today, for the people have a sacrifice^r at the high place.^s ¹³As soon as you enter the town, you will find him before he goes up to the high place to eat. The people will not begin eating until he comes, because he must bless^t the sacrifice; afterward, those who are invited will eat. Go up now; you should find him about this time."

¹⁴They went up to the town, and as they were entering it, there was Samuel, coming toward them on his way up to the high place.

¹⁵Now the day before Saul came, the LORD had revealed this to Samuel: ¹⁶"About this time tomorrow I will send you a man from the land of Benjamin. Anoint^u him ruler^v over my people Israel; he will deliver^w them from the hand of the Philistines.^x I have looked on my people, for their cry^y has reached me."

¹⁷When Samuel caught sight of Saul, the LORD said to him, "This^z is the man I spoke to you about; he will govern my people."

¹⁸Saul approached Samuel in the gateway and asked, "Would you please tell me where the seer's house is?"

¹⁹"I am the seer," Samuel replied. "Go up ahead of me to the high place, for today you are to eat with me, and in the morning I will send you on your way and will tell you all that is in your heart. ²⁰As for the donkeys^a you lost three days ago, do not worry about them; they have been found. And to whom is all the desire^b of Israel turned, if not to you and your whole family line?"

²¹Saul answered, "But am I not a Benjamite, from the smallest tribe^c of Israel, and is not my clan the least^d of all the clans of the tribe of Benjamin?^e Why do you say such a thing to me?"

²²Then Samuel brought Saul and his servant into the hall and seated them at the head of those who were invited—about thirty in number. ²³Samuel said to the cook, "Bring the piece of meat I gave you, the one I told you to lay aside."

²⁴So the cook took up the thigh^f with what was on it and set it in front of Saul. Samuel said, "Here is what has been kept for you. Eat, because it was set aside for you for this

---

^a 8 That is, about 1/10 ounce or about 3 grams

9:9 ^o S Ge 25:22
^p 2Sa 15:27; 24:11;
2Ki 17:13; 1Ch 9:22;
21:9; 26:28; 29:29;
2Ch 19:2; Isa 29:10;
30:10; Am 7:12
9:11 ^q S Ge 24:11,13
9:12 ^r Nu 28:11-15;
S 1Sa 7:17
^s S Lev 26:30
9:13 ^t S Mt 14:19;
1Co 10:16; 1Ti 4:3-5
9:16 ^u Ex 30:25;
S 1Sa 2:35; 12:3; 15:1;
26:9; 2Ki 11:12; Ps 2:2
^v 2Sa 7:8; 1Ki 8:16;
1Ch 5:2 ^w Ex 3:7-9
^x 1Sa 23:4; 2Sa 3:18
^y S Ge 16:11; Ps 102:1
9:17 ^z 1Sa 16:12
9:20 ^a S ver 3
^b 1Sa 12:13; Ezr 6:8;
Isa 60:4-9; Da 2:44;
Hag 2:7; Mal 3:1
9:21 ^c Ps 68:27
^d S Ex 3:11; Mt 2:6;
1Co 15:9 ^e Jdg 6:15;
20:35,46; 1Sa 18:18
9:24 ^f S Lev 7:32-34

---

adjusted their message to the desires of those who supported them (1Ki 22:6,8,18; Jer 28; Mic 3:5,11).

9:8 *a quarter of a shekel of silver.* See TNIV text note. Before the use of coins, gold or silver was weighed out for each monetary transaction (see 13:21; Job 28:15).

9:9 *the prophet of today used to be called a seer.* There was no essential difference between a seer and a prophet. The person popularly designated as a prophet at the time of the writing of 1,2 Samuel was termed a seer in the time of Saul. This need not mean that the term "prophet" was unknown in the time of Saul or that the term "seer" was unknown in later times (see Isa 30:10). The reference is to popular usage.

9:11 *young women coming out to draw water.* In the cool of the evening (see Ge 24:11).

B **9:12** *high place.* After entrance into the promised land, the Israelites often followed the custom of the Canaanites in building local altars on hills. (At this time the central sanctuary was not functioning because the ark of God was separated from the tabernacle; Shiloh had been destroyed, and the priestly family, after the death of Eli's sons, was apparently still inactive.) In later times, worship at these high places provided a means for the entrance of pagan practices into Israel's religious observances and, for this reason, it was condemned (see note on 1Ki 3:2).

9:13 *he must bless the sacrifice.* Samuel presided over the sacrificial meal (see 1:4; 2:13–16), at which he gave a prayer, probably similar to those referred to in the NT (see Mt 26:26–27; Jn 6:11,23; 1Ti 4:3–5).

9:16 *Anoint him.* Priests were also anointed (see Ex 29:7; 40:12–15; Lev 4:3; 8:12), but from this point in the OT it is usually the king who is referred to as "the LORD's anointed" (see note on 2:10; see also 24:6; 26:9,11,16; 2Sa 1:14,16; 19:21; cf. Ps 2:2; but see also Zec 4:14). Anointing signifies separation to the Lord for a particular task and divine equipping for the task (see 10:1,6; 16:13; Isa 61:1). *ruler.* The Hebrew for this word (see 10:1; 13:14; 25:30) indicates one designated by the Lord to be the ruler of his people (see also 2Sa 5:2; 7:8; 1Ch 11:2; 17:7). It served as a useful term to ease the transition between the leadership of the judges and that of the kings. *Philistines.* See note on 7:13.

9:20 *all the desire of Israel.* A reference to Israel's desire for a king.

A **9:21** *smallest tribe ... least of all the clans.* Saul's origins were among the humblest in Israel (Benjamin was the youngest of Jacob's sons, and the tribe had been greatly reduced in the time of the judges; see Jdg 20:46–48). His elevation to king shows that God "exalts" whomever he will (2:7), which is one of the central themes running throughout Samuel. God's use of the powerless to promote his kingdom on earth is a common feature in the Biblical testimony and underscores the truth that his kingdom is not of this world.

9:24 *thigh.* Normally reserved for the Lord's consecrated priest (see Ex 29:22,27; Lev 7:32–33,35; Nu 6:20; 18:18). The presentation of this choice piece of the sacrificial animal to Saul was a distinct honor and anticipated his being designated the Lord's anointed.

9:25 *g*S Dt 22:8;
S Jos 2:8; S Mt 24:17;
Lk 5:19
10:1 *h*1Sa 16:1;
2Ki 9:1,3,6
*i*S Ex 29:7;
S 1Sa 9:16; S 1Ki 1:39
*j*S Ex 34:9;
2Sa 20:19; Ps 78:62,
71
10:2 *k*Ge 35:20
*l*1Sa 9:4 *m*1Sa 9:5
10:3 *n*S Ge 35:7-8
10:4 *o*ver 27;
1Sa 16:20; Pr 18:16
10:5 *p*ver 26;
1Sa 11:4; 15:34
*q*1Sa 13:3
*r*S Nu 11:29;
1Ki 20:35; 2Ki 2:3,15;
4:1; 6:1; 9:1; Am 7:14
*s*S Lev 26:30
*t*S Ge 31:27; Jer 31:4
*u*1Ki 1:40; Isa 30:29
*v*1Sa 16:16; 18:10;
19:9; 2Ki 3:15;
Ps 92:3 *w*ver 10;
1Sa 19:20; 1Ch 25:1;
1Co 14:1
10:6 *x*S Nu 11:25
*y*ver 9
10:7 *z*2Sa 7:3;
1Ki 8:17; 1Ch 22:7;
28:2; 2Ch 6:7;
Ecc 9:10 *a*Jdg 9:33
*b*S Jos 1:5; Lk 1:28;
Heb 13:5
10:8 *c*Jos 4:20;
S 10:43; 1Sa 7:16;
11:14-15 *d*1Sa 13:8
10:9 *e*ver 6
*f*S Dt 13:2 *g*ver 7
10:10 *h*S Nu 11:25;
1Sa 11:6 *i*S ver 5-6
10:11 *j*Mt 13:54;
Jn 7:15 *k*ver 12;
1Sa 19:24; 2Ki 9:11;
Jer 29:26; Hos 9:7

occasion from the time I said, 'I have invited guests.' " And Saul dined with Samuel that day.

²⁵After they came down from the high place to the town, Samuel talked with Saul on the roof*g* of his house. ²⁶They rose about daybreak, and Samuel called to Saul on the roof, "Get ready, and I will send you on your way." When Saul got ready, he and Samuel went outside together. ²⁷As they were going down to the edge of the town, Samuel said to Saul, "Tell the servant to go on ahead of us"—and the servant did so—"but you stay here for a while, so that I may give you a message from God."

10

Then Samuel took a bottle*h* of olive oil and poured it on Saul's head and kissed him, saying, "Has not the Lᴏʀᴅ anointed*i* you ruler over his inheritance?*a j* ²When you leave me today, you will meet two men near Rachel's tomb,*k* at Zelzah on the border of Benjamin. They will say to you, 'The donkeys*l* you set out to look for have been found. And now your father has stopped thinking about them and is worried*m* about you. He is asking, "What shall I do about my son?" '

³"Then you will go on from there until you reach the great tree of Tabor. Three men going up to God at Bethel*n* will meet you there. One will be carrying three young goats, another three loaves of bread, and another a skin of wine. ⁴They will greet you and offer you two loaves of bread,*o* which you will accept from them.

⁵"After that you will go to Gibeah*p* of God, where there is a Philistine outpost.*q* As you approach the town, you will meet a procession of prophets*r* coming down from the high place*s* with lyres, timbrels,*t* pipes*u* and harps*v* being played before them, and they will be prophesying.*w* ⁶The Spirit*x* of the Lᴏʀᴅ will come on you in power, and you will prophesy with them; and you will be changed*y* into a different person. ⁷Once these signs are fulfilled, do whatever*z* your hand*a* finds to do, for God is with*b* you.

⁸"Go down ahead of me to Gilgal.*c* I will surely come down to you to sacrifice burnt offerings and fellowship offerings, but you must wait seven*d* days until I come to you and tell you what you are to do."

SAUL MADE KING

⁹As Saul turned to leave Samuel, God changed*e* Saul's heart, and all these signs*f* were fulfilled*g* that day. ¹⁰When he and his servant arrived at Gibeah, a procession of prophets met him; the Spirit*h* of God came on him in power, and he joined in their prophesying.*i* ¹¹When all those who had formerly known him saw him prophesying with the prophets, they asked each other, "What is this*j* that has happened to the son of Kish? Is Saul also among the prophets?"*k*

¹²A man who lived there answered, "And who is their father?" So it became a saying:

a 1 Hebrew; Septuagint and Vulgate *over his people Israel? You will reign over the Lᴏʀᴅ's people and save them from the power of their enemies round about. And this will be a sign to you that the Lᴏʀᴅ has anointed you ruler over his inheritance:*

9:25 *on the roof.* Where they could catch the cool evening breeze (see v. 11; 2Sa 11:2 and notes) and where Saul would sleep that night (see v. 26).

10:1 *olive oil.* Perhaps spiced (see Ex 30:22–33). *Has not the Lᴏʀᴅ anointed you …?* See note on 9:16. *ruler.* See 9:16 and note. *his inheritance.* "My people Israel" (9:16). The Lord's inheritance includes both the people (see Ex 34:9) and the land (see Ex 15:17). After departing from Samuel, Saul is to receive three signs (see vv. 2–7) to authenticate Samuel's words and to assure him that the Lord has indeed chosen him to be king.

10:2 *Rachel's tomb.* Rachel, Jacob's favorite wife, had died on the road to Bethlehem while giving birth to Benjamin. Her tomb had become a notable landmark (see Ge 35:20 and note).

10:3 *great tree.* A large tree was often a conspicuous point of reference for pilgrims and other travelers (see Ge 12:6 and note). *Bethel.* Located ten miles north of Jerusalem (see note on Ge 12:8).

10:5 *Gibeah of God.* Gibeah was Saul's hometown (see v. 26; 11:4), located in the tribal area of Benjamin (Jos 18:28; Jdg 19:12–14). It was usually called "Gibeah" or "Gibeah in Benjamin" (as in 13:2,15), but three times "Gibeah of Saul" (11:4; 15:34; 2Sa 21:6). The present designation (used only here) may have been Samuel's way of reminding Saul that the land of Canaan belonged to God and not to the Philistines (see Dt 32:43; Isa 14:2; Hos 9:3). *prophets.* The bands of prophets with which

Samuel was associated (as also the "company of the prophets" with whom Elijah and Elisha were associated; see note on 1Ki 20:35) appear to have been small communities of men who banded together in spiritually decadent times for mutual cultivation of their religious zeal. *lyres … harps.* The actions of individual prophets or groups of prophets were sometimes accompanied by musical instruments (see 2Ki 3:15; 1Ch 25:1). *prophesying.* Here (and in vv. 6,10–11,13) appears to designate an ecstatic praising of God inspired by the Spirit of the Lord (see Nu 11:24–30 for similar use of the term).

10:6 *changed into a different person.* God's Spirit would enable Saul to be Israel's king.

10:7 *do whatever your hand finds to do.* Saul is to take whatever action is appropriate when the situation presents itself to manifest publicly his royal leadership (see 11:4–11).

10:8 *Go down ahead of me to Gilgal.* At some unspecified future time, perhaps previously discussed (see 9:25), Saul is to go to Gilgal and wait seven days for Samuel's arrival (see 13:7–14). *Gilgal.* See note on Jos 4:19.

10:11 *Is Saul also among the prophets?* See 19:24 and note; an expression of surprise at Saul's behavior by those who had known him previously—another subtle indication of his character (see notes on 9:3,6).

10:12 *who is their father?* Some understand the question as an expression of contempt for prophets generally, others as imply-

"Is Saul also among the prophets?" [l] [13] After Saul stopped prophesying, [m] he went to the high place.

[14] Now Saul's uncle [n] asked him and his servant, "Where have you been?"

"Looking for the donkeys, [o] " he said. "But when we saw they were not to be found, we went to Samuel."

[15] Saul's uncle said, "Tell me what Samuel said to you."

[16] Saul replied, "He assured us that the donkeys [p] had been found." But he did not tell his uncle what Samuel had said about the kingship.

[17] Samuel summoned the people of Israel to the LORD at Mizpah [q] [18] and said to them, "This is what the LORD, the God of Israel, says: 'I brought Israel up out of Egypt, and I delivered you from the power of Egypt and all the kingdoms that oppressed [r] you.' [19] But you have now rejected [s] your God, who saves [t] you out of all your disasters and calamities. And you have said, 'No, appoint a king [u] over us.' [v] So now present [w] yourselves before the LORD by your tribes and clans."

[20] When Samuel had all Israel come forward by tribes, the tribe of Benjamin was taken by lot. [21] Then he brought forward the tribe of Benjamin, clan by clan, and Matri's clan was taken. [x] Finally Saul son of Kish was taken. But when they looked for him, he was not to be found. [22] So they inquired [y] further of the LORD, "Has the man come here yet?"

And the LORD said, "Yes, he has hidden himself among the supplies."

[23] They ran and brought him out, and as he stood among the people he was a head taller [z] than any of the others. [24] Samuel said to all the people, "Do you see the man the LORD has chosen? [a] There is no one like [b] him among all the people."

Then the people shouted, "Long live [c] the king!"

[25] Samuel explained [d] to the people the rights and duties [e] of kingship. [f] He wrote them down on a scroll and deposited it before the LORD. Then Samuel dismissed the people to go to their own homes.

[26] Saul also went to his home in Gibeah, [g] accompanied by valiant men [h] whose hearts God had touched. [27] But some scoundrels [i] said, "How can this fellow save us?" They despised him and brought him no gifts. [j] But Saul kept silent.

SAUL RESCUES THE CITY OF JABESH

11

Nahash [a] [k] the Ammonite went up and besieged Jabesh Gilead. [l] And all the men of Jabesh said to him, "Make a treaty [m] with us, and we will be subject to you."

[a] 1 Masoretic Text; Dead Sea Scrolls *gifts. Now Nahash king of the Ammonites oppressed the Gadites and Reubenites severely. He gouged out all their right eyes and struck terror and dread in Israel. Not a man remained among the Israelites beyond the Jordan whose right eye was not gouged out by Nahash king of the Ammonites, except that seven thousand men fled from the Ammonites and entered Jabesh Gilead. About a month later,* [l] *Nahash*

10:12 [l] S ver 11
10:13 [m] 1Sa 19:23
10:14 [n] 1Sa 14:50
[o] S 1Sa 9:3
10:16 [p] S 1Sa 9:3
10:17 [q] S 1Sa 7:5
10:18 [r] S Ex 1:14;
S Nu 10:9
10:19 [s] S Nu 11:20;
S Dt 33:5 [t] Ps 7:10;
18:48; 68:20; 145:19
[u] S 1Sa 8:5-7
[v] S Dt 17:14 [w] Jos 7:14
10:21 [x] Est 3:7;
Pr 16:33
10:22 [y] S Ge 25:22;
S Jdg 18:5
10:23 [z] 1Sa 9:2
10:24 [a] Dt 17:15;
2Sa 21:6 [b] 1Sa 9:2
[c] 1Ki 1:25,34,39;
2Ki 11:12
10:25 [d] S 1Sa 8:9
[e] S Dt 17:14-20;
S 1Sa 8:11-18;
2Ki 11:12 [f] 1Sa 11:14
10:26 [g] S ver 5;
S Jdg 19:14
[h] S Jdg 20:44
10:27 [i] S Dt 13:13;
S 1Sa 20:7 [j] S ver 4;
1Ki 10:25; 2Ch 17:5;
32:23; Ps 68:29
11:1 [k] S Ge 19:38;
1Sa 12:12; 2Sa 10:2;
17:27; 1Ch 19:1
[l] Jdg 21:8; 1Sa 31:11;
2Sa 2:4,5; 21:12
[m] S Ex 23:32;
S Jer 37:1

ing the recognition that prophetic inspiration comes from God and therefore could be imparted to whomever God chose. However, since leading prophets were sometimes called "father" (2Ki 2:12; 6:21; 13:14), the speaker may have intended a disdainful reference to Samuel or an ironical gibe at Saul.

10:17 *Samuel summoned the people.* After the private designation and anointing of Saul to be king (9:15–17,20–21,27; 10:1), an assembly is called by Samuel to make the Lord's choice known to the people (v. 21) and to define the king's task (v. 25). *Mizpah.* See note on 7:5.

10:18 *I delivered you.* Speaking through Samuel, the Lord emphasizes to the people that he has been their deliverer throughout their history. He brought them out of Egypt and delivered them from all their enemies during the time of the judges. Although the judges themselves are sometimes referred to as Israel's deliverers (see Jdg 3:9,15,31; 6:14; 10:1; 13:5), this was true only in a secondary sense, for they were instruments of the Lord's deliverance (see Jdg 2:18). It was the Lord who sent them (see 12:11; Jdg 6:14).

10:19 *rejected your God.* See note on 8:7.

10:20 *tribe of Benjamin was taken by lot.* See 14:41–42; Jos 7:16–18. The Urim and Thummim were used for this purpose (see notes on 2:28; Ex 28:30).

10:23 *a head taller.* See 9:2 and note.

10:24 *Long live the king!* See note on Ps 62:4.

10:25 *rights and duties of kingship.* Samuel here takes the first

step toward resolving the tension that existed between Israel's misdirected desire for a king (and their misconceived notion of what the king's role and function should be) and the Lord's intent to give them one (see Introduction: Contents and Theme). This description of the duties and prerogatives of the Israelite king was given for the benefit of both the people and the king-designate. It was intended to clearly distinguish Israelite kingship from that of the surrounding nations and to ensure that the king's role in Israel was compatible with the continued rule of the Lord over Israel as her Great King (see Dt 17:14–20). *scroll.* See note on Ex 17:14. *deposited it before the LORD.* Cf. note on Ex 31:9. The legal document defining the role of the king in governing God's covenant people was preserved at the sanctuary (the tabernacle, later the temple).

10:27 *scoundrels.* See 2:12; see also note on Dt 13:13. *How can this fellow save us?* Reflects the people's continued apostate idea that national security was to be sought in the person of the human king (see note on v. 18; see also 8:20).

11:1 *Ammonite.* The Ammonites were descended from Lot (see Ge 19:36–38 and note; Dt 2:19) and lived east of the Jordan River and south of the Jabbok (see Dt 2:37; Jos 12:2). Previous attempts by the Ammonites to occupy Israelite territory are referred to in Jdg 3:13; 11:4–33. The Philistine threat to Israel in the west presented the Ammonites with an opportunity to move against Israel from the east with supposed impunity. *Jabesh Gilead.* A town east of the Jordan (see map No. 4 at the end of this study Bible).

11:2 *n* Ge 34:15
o S Nu 16:14
p 1Sa 17:26
11:3 *q* S 1Sa 8:4
r S Jdg 2:16 *s* ver 10
11:4 *t* S 1Sa 10:5, 26
u S Ge 27:38;
S Nu 25:6
11:6 *v* S Jdg 3:10
11:7 *w* S 1Sa 6:14
x S Jdg 19:29
y Jdg 21:5 *z* S Jdg 20:1
11:8 *a* Jdg 20:2
b Jdg 1:4
11:10 *c* ver 3
11:11 *d* S Jdg 7:16
e S Ge 19:38
11:12 *f* S Dt 13:13;
Lk 19:27
11:13 *g* 2Sa 19:22
h 1Sa 19:5; 1Ch 11:14
11:14 *i* S Jos 10:43;
S 1Sa 10:8 *j* 1Sa 10:25
11:15 *k* S Jos 5:9;
2Sa 19:15 *l* 1Sa 12:1
12:1 *m* S 1Sa 8:7
n 1Sa 11:15
12:2 *o* S 1Sa 8:5
p 1Sa 8:3

[2] But Nahash the Ammonite replied, "I will make a treaty with you only on the condition [n] that I gouge [o] out the right eye of every one of you and so bring disgrace [p] on all Israel."

[3] The elders [q] of Jabesh said to him, "Give us seven days so we can send messengers throughout Israel; if no one comes to rescue [r] us, we will surrender [s] to you."

[4] When the messengers came to Gibeah [t] of Saul and reported these terms to the people, they all wept [u] aloud. [5] Just then Saul was returning from the fields, behind his oxen, and he asked, "What is wrong with everyone? Why are they weeping?" Then they repeated to him what the men of Jabesh had said.

[6] When Saul heard their words, the Spirit [v] of God came on him in power, and he burned with anger. [7] He took a pair of oxen, [w] cut them into pieces, and sent the pieces by messengers throughout Israel, [x] proclaiming, "This is what will be done to the oxen of anyone [y] who does not follow Saul and Samuel." Then the terror of the LORD fell on the people, and they turned out with one accord. [z] [8] When Saul mustered [a] them at Bezek, [b] the men of Israel numbered three hundred thousand and those of Judah thirty thousand.

[9] They told the messengers who had come, "Say to the men of Jabesh Gilead, 'By the time the sun is hot tomorrow, you will be rescued.' " When the messengers went and reported this to the men of Jabesh, they were elated. [10] They said to the Ammonites, "Tomorrow we will surrender [c] to you, and you can do to us whatever you like."

[11] The next day Saul separated his men into three divisions; [d] during the last watch of the night they broke into the camp of the Ammonites [e] and slaughtered them until the heat of the day. Those who survived were scattered, so that no two of them were left together.

SAUL CONFIRMED AS KING

[12] The people then said to Samuel, "Who [f] was it that asked, 'Shall Saul reign over us?' Turn these men over to us so that we may put them to death." [13] But Saul said, "No one will be put to death today, [g] for this day the LORD has rescued [h] Israel."

[14] Then Samuel said to the people, "Come, let us go to Gilgal [i] and there renew the kingship. [j] " [15] So all the people went to Gilgal [k] and made Saul king [l] in the presence of the LORD. There they sacrificed fellowship offerings before the LORD, and Saul and all the Israelites held a great celebration.

SAMUEL'S FAREWELL SPEECH

12 Samuel said to all Israel, "I have listened [m] to everything you said to me and have set a king [n] over you. [2] Now you have a king as your leader. [o] As for me, I am old and gray, and my sons [p] are here with you. I have been your leader from

---

11:2 *gouge out the right eye.* Besides causing humiliation (see note on Jdg 16:21), the loss of the right eye would destroy the military capability of the archers.

11:4 *Gibeah of Saul.* See 10:26 and note on 10:5. Close family ties undoubtedly prompted the inhabitants of Jabesh to seek help from the tribe of Benjamin (see Jdg 21:12–14).

11:5 *Saul was returning from the fields.* After Saul's public selection as the king-designate at Mizpah (10:17–25), he returned home (10:26) to resume his normal private activities and to wait for the Lord's leading for the next step in his elevation to the throne (see notes on v. 15; 16:2).

11:6 *the Spirit of God came on him in power.* See 10:6,10. For similar endowment of Israel's deliverers with extraordinary vigor by God's Spirit see 11:29 and note; Jdg 14:6,19; 15:14.

11:7 *sent the pieces by messengers throughout Israel.* For a similar case see Jdg 19:29 and note.

11:8 *Bezek.* Located north of Shechem, west of the Jordan River but within striking distance of Jabesh Gilead.

11:11 *last watch of the night.* The third watch (2:00–6:00 A.M.; see note on Mt 14:25).

11:13 *the LORD has rescued Israel.* Saul recognizes Israel's true deliverer (see note on 10:18). The victory, in combination with Saul's confession, places yet another seal of divine approval on Saul as the man the Lord has chosen to be king.

11:14 *let us go to Gilgal and there renew the kingship.* Samuel perceives that it is now the appropriate time for the people to renew their allegiance to the Lord. The kingship he speaks of is the Lord's, not Saul's. Samuel calls for an assembly to restore the cov-

enant relationship between the Lord and his people. He wants to inaugurate Saul's rule in a manner demonstrating that the continued rule of the Lord as Israel's Great King is in no way diminished or violated in the new era of the monarchy (see Introduction: Contents and Theme). Verses 14–15 are a brief synopsis of the Gilgal assembly and are prefaced to the more detailed account of the same assembly in ch. 12. *Gilgal.* Located east of Jericho near the Jordan River. It was a particularly appropriate place for Israel to renew her allegiance to the Lord (see Jos 4:19—5:10; 10:7–15).

11:15 *made Saul king in the presence of the LORD.* Saul had previously been anointed in private by Samuel at Ramah (10:1) and publicly selected as the king-designate at Mizpah (10:17–27). In the subsequent Ammonite crisis (vv. 1–13) his leadership did not rest on public recognition of his royal authority but on the military victory. Now at Gilgal Saul is inaugurated as God's chosen king and formally assumes the privileges and responsibilities of this office. *fellowship offerings.* This type of offering was an important element in the original ceremony of covenant ratification at Sinai (Ex 24:5,11). It represented the communion or peace between the Lord and his people when the people lived in conformity with their covenant obligations (see Lev 7:11–21; 22:21–23). *held a great celebration.* Here the rejoicing is the expression of people who have renewed their commitment to the Lord, confessed their sin (see 12:19) and been given a king.

12:2 *your leader.* Lit. "one who goes before you." The Hebrew imagery is probably that of a king or leader as shepherd of his people (see 2Sa 5:2; Eze 34:23; cf. note on Ps 23:1; Mic 2:12–13 and ultimately Jesus in Jn 10:3–4,11,14–15,27).

my youth until this day. ³Here I stand. Testify against me in the presence of the LORD and his anointed. ⁹ Whose ox have I taken? Whose donkey ʳ have I taken? Whom have I cheated? Whom have I oppressed? From whose hand have I accepted a bribe ˢ to make me shut my eyes? If I have done ᵗ any of these things, I will make it right." ᵘ

⁴"You have not cheated or oppressed us," they replied. "You have not taken anything from anyone's hand."

⁵Samuel said to them, "The LORD is witness ᵛ against you, and also his anointed is witness this day, that you have not found anything ʷ in my hand. ˣ"

"We agree," they said.

⁶Then Samuel said to the people, "It is the LORD who appointed Moses and Aaron and brought ʸ your ancestors up out of Egypt. ⁷Now then, stand ᶻ here, because I am going to confront ᵃ you with evidence before the LORD as to all the righteous acts ᵇ performed by the LORD for you and your ancestors.

⁸"After Jacob ᶜ entered Egypt, they cried ᵈ to the LORD for help, and the LORD sent ᵉ Moses and Aaron, who brought your ancestors out of Egypt and settled them in this place.

⁹"But they forgot ᶠ the LORD their God; so he sold them ᵍ into the hand of Sisera, ʰ the commander of the army of Hazor, ⁱ and into the hands of the Philistines ʲ and the king of Moab, ᵏ who fought against them. ¹⁰They cried ˡ out to the LORD and said, 'We have sinned; we have forsaken ᵐ the LORD and served the Baals and the Ashtoreths. ⁿ But now deliver us from the hands of our enemies, and we will serve you.' ¹¹Then the LORD sent Jerub-Baal, ᵃ ᵒ Barak, ᵇ ᵖ Jephthah �q and Samuel, ᶜ ʳ and he delivered you from the hands of your enemies all around you, so that you lived in safety.

¹²"But when you saw that Nahash ˢ king ᵗ of the Ammonites was moving against you, you said to me, 'No, we want a king to rule ᵘ over us'—even though the LORD your God was your king. ¹³Now here is the king ᵛ you have chosen, the one you asked ʷ for; see, the LORD has set a king over you. ¹⁴If you fear ˣ the LORD and serve and obey him and do not rebel ʸ against his commands, and if both you and the king who reigns over you follow the LORD your God—good! ¹⁵But if you do not obey the LORD, and if you rebel against ᶻ his commands, his hand will be against you, as it was against your ancestors.

¹⁶"Now then, stand still ᵃ and see ᵇ this great thing the LORD is about to do before your

---

ᵃ *11* Also called *Gideon*   ᵇ *11* Some Septuagint manuscripts and Syriac; Hebrew *Bedan*   ᶜ *11* Hebrew; some Septuagint manuscripts and Syriac *Samson*

12:3 *Testify against me.* Court language. When Samuel presents the newly inaugurated king to the people, he seeks to establish publicly his own past faithfulness to the covenant as leader of the nation. His purpose is to exonerate himself and provide an example for Saul in his new responsibilities. *Whose ox have I taken? Whose donkey have I taken?* See Ex 20:17; 22:1,4,9. Unlike his sons, Samuel has not used his position for personal gain (see 8:3 and note; cf. Nu 16:15). *Whom have I cheated? Whom have I oppressed?* See Lev 19:13; Dt 24:14. *From whose hand have I accepted a bribe …?* Contrast 8:3. See Ex 23:8; Dt 16:19.

12:6 *Samuel said to the people.* Samuel now turns to the matter of the people's request for a king, which he views as a covenant-breaking act and a serious apostasy. *It is the LORD.* Samuel emphasizes that in the past the Lord had provided the necessary leadership for the nation.

12:7 *confront you with evidence.* The terminology is that of a legal proceeding, as in vv. 2–5, but now the relationship of the parties is reversed. This time Samuel is the accuser, the people are the defendants, and the Lord is the Judge. *righteous acts performed by the LORD.* These acts (see vv. 8–11) not only demonstrate the constancy of the Lord's covenant faithfulness toward his people in the past but also serve to expose their present apostasy.

12:9–11 A summary of the dreary cycle of apostasy, divine chastening, urgent appeals to God, and divine restoration that characterized the period of the judges (see, e.g., Jdg 2:10–15 and note; see also Introduction to Judges: Theme and Theology).

12:9 *forgot the LORD.* This would become Israel's persistent failure (see Hos 2:13 and note).

12:10 *the Baals and the Ashtoreths.* See notes on 7:3; Jdg 2:13.

12:11 *he delivered you.* The Lord repeatedly rescued Israel from her enemies right up to Samuel's own lifetime (see 7:3,8,10,12),

demonstrating again the people's apostasy in desiring a king.

12:12 *when you saw that Nahash … was moving against you.* In the face of the combined threat from the Philistines in the west (9:16) and the Ammonites in the east (11:1–13), the Israelites sought to find security in the person of a human king. *No, we want a king … the LORD your God was your king.* The Israelite desire for and trust in a human leader constituted a rejection of the kingship of the Lord and betrayed a loss of confidence in his care, in spite of his faithfulness during the time of the exodus, conquest and judges (see 8:7 and note).

12:13 *the LORD has set a king over you.* In spite of the sinfulness of the people's request, the Lord had chosen to incorporate kingship into the structure of the theocracy (his kingdom). Kingship was given by the Lord to his people and was to function as an instrument of his rule over them (see Introduction: Contents and Theme).

12:14 *If you …* Samuel relates the covenant conditions (see Ex 19:5–6; Dt 8:19; 11:13–15, 22–23; 28:1,15; 30:17–18; Jos 24:20) to the new era Israel is entering with the establishment of the monarchy. *if both you and the king … follow the LORD your God—good!* Israel and her king are to demonstrate that although human kingship has been established, they will continue to recognize the Lord as their true King. In this new era where potential for divided loyalty between the Lord and the human king arises, Israel's loyalty to the Lord must remain inviolate.

12:15 *But if you do not obey.* Samuel confronts Israel with the same alternatives Moses had expressed centuries earlier (see Dt 28:1,15; 30:15–20). The introduction of kingship into Israel's social and political structures has not changed the fundamental nature of her relationship to the Lord.

12:16 *see this great thing.* See v. 24. Samuel calls the people to

---

12:3 ⁹ S Ge 9:16; 24:6; 26:9,11; 2Sa 1:14; 19:21; Ps 105:15 ʳ Nu 16:15 ˢ S Ex 18:21; S 1Sa 8:3 ᵗ Ex 20:17; Ac 20:33 ᵘ S Lev 25:14
12:5 ᵛ S Ge 31:50 ʷ Ac 23:9; 24:20 ˣ Ex 22:4
12:6 ʸ S Ex 3:10; Mic 6:4
12:7 ᶻ S Jos 24:1 ᵃ Isa 1:18; 3:14; Jer 2:9; 25:31; Eze 17:20; 20:35; Mic 6:1-5 ᵇ S Jdg 5:11
12:8 ᶜ S Ge 46:6 ᵈ S Ex 2:23 ᵉ S Ex 3:10; 4:16
12:9 ᶠ S Dt 32:18; S Jdg 3:7 ᵍ S Dt 32:30 ʰ Jdg 4:2 ⁱ S Jos 11:1 ʲ Jdg 10:7 ᵏ Jdg 3:12
12:10 ˡ S Jdg 3:9 ᵐ S 1Sa 8:8 ⁿ S 1Sa 7:3
12:11 ᵒ Jdg 6:32 ᵖ S Jdg 4:6 q S Jdg 11:1 ʳ S 1Sa 7:15
12:12 ˢ S 1Sa 11:1 ᵗ S 1Sa 8:5 ᵘ 1Sa 25:30; 2Sa 5:2; 1Ch 5:2
12:13 ᵛ S 1Sa 8:5 ʷ S 1Sa 9:20
12:14 ˣ S Jos 24:14 ʸ Jer 4:17; La 1:18
12:15 ᶻ Lev 26:16; Jos 24:20; Isa 1:20; Jer 4:17; 26:4
12:16 ᵃ S Ex 14:14 ᵇ S Ex 14:13

12:17 c S Ge 30:14;
S 1Sa 6:13 d 1Ki 18:42;
Jas 5:18 e S Ex 9:23;
S 1Sa 2:10 f Ge 7:12;
Ex 9:18; Job 37:13;
Pr 26:1 g S 1Sa 8:6-7
12:18 h Ps 99:6
i S Ge 3:10; S Ex 14:31
12:19 j S Ex 8:8;
S 1Sa 7:8; S Jer 37:3;
Jas 5:18; 1Jn 5:16
k S Dt 9:19
12:20 l S Ex 32:30
12:21 m Isa 40:20;
41:24,29; 44:9;
Jer 2:5,11; 14:22;
16:19; Jnh 2:8;
Hab 2:18; Ac 14:15
n Dt 11:16
12:22 o Ps 25:11;
106:8; Isa 48:9,11;
Jer 14:7; Da 9:19
p S Jos 7:9; 2Sa 7:23;
Jn 17:12 q S Lev 26:11;
S Dt 31:6 r Dt 7:7;
1Pe 2:9
12:23 s S Nu 11:2;
S 1Sa 1:20; S 7:8;
Ro 1:9-10 t Ki 8:36;
Ps 25:4; 34:11; 86:11;
94:12; Pr 4:11
12:24 u Dt 6:2;
Ecc 12:13 v Dt 6:5;
S Jos 24:14
w Job 34:27; Isa 5:12;
22:11; 26:10
x S Dt 10:21
12:25 y 1Sa 31:1-5
z Dt 28:36
a S Jos 24:20;
S 1Ki 14:10
13:2 b ver 15 c ver 5,
11,23; Ne 11:31;
Isa 10:28 d S Jdg 19:14
13:3 e S 1Sa 10:5
f S Jos 18:24
g S Lev 25:9;
S Jdg 3:27
13:4 h S Ge 34:30
13:5 i 1Sa 17:1
j S Jos 11:4; Rev 20:8
k S ver 2 l S Jos 7:2
13:6 m 1Sa 14:11,22
n S Jdg 6:2; Eze 33:27
13:7 o S Nu 32:33
p S Ge 35:5;
S Ex 19:16
13:8 q 1Sa 10:8

eyes! [17]Is it not wheat harvest c now? I will call d on the LORD to send thunder e and rain. f And you will realize what an evil g thing you did in the eyes of the LORD when you asked for a king."

[18]Then Samuel called on the LORD, h and that same day the LORD sent thunder and rain. So all the people stood in awe i of the LORD and of Samuel.

[19]The people all said to Samuel, "Pray j to the LORD your God for your servants so that we will not die, k for we have added to all our other sins the evil of asking for a king."

[20]"Do not be afraid," Samuel replied. "You have done all this evil; l yet do not turn away from the LORD, but serve the LORD with all your heart. [21]Do not turn away after useless m idols. n They can do you no good, nor can they rescue you, because they are useless. [22]For the sake o of his great name p the LORD will not reject q his people, because the LORD was pleased to make r you his own. [23]As for me, far be it from me that I should sin against the LORD by failing to pray s for you. And I will teach t you the way that is good and right. [24]But be sure to fear u the LORD and serve him faithfully with all your heart; v consider w what great x things he has done for you. [25]Yet if you persist y in doing evil, both you and your king z will perish." a

SAMUEL REBUKES SAUL

13 Saul was thirty a years old when he became king, and he reigned over Israel forty- b two years. [2]Saul chose three thousand men from Israel; two thousand b were with him at Mikmash c and in the hill country of Bethel, and a thousand were with Jonathan at Gibeah d in Benjamin. The rest he sent back to their homes.

[3]Jonathan attacked the Philistine outpost e at Geba, f and the Philistines heard about it. Then Saul had the trumpet g blown throughout the land and said, "Let the Hebrews hear!" [4]So all Israel heard the news: "Saul has attacked the Philistine outpost, and now Israel has become obnoxious h to the Philistines." And the people were summoned to join Saul at Gilgal.

[5]The Philistines assembled i to fight Israel, with three thousand c chariots, six thousand charioteers, and soldiers as numerous as the sand j on the seashore. They went up and camped at Mikmash, k east of Beth Aven. l [6]When the Israelites saw that their situation was critical and that their army was hard pressed, they hid m in caves and thickets, among the rocks, and in pits and cisterns. n [7]Some Hebrews even crossed the Jordan to the land of Gad o and Gilead.

Saul remained at Gilgal, and all the troops with him were quaking p with fear. [8]He waited seven q days, the time set by Samuel; but Samuel did not come to Gilgal, and Saul's

---

a 1 A few late manuscripts of the Septuagint; Hebrew does not have *thirty*.　　b 1 Probable reading of the original Hebrew text (see Acts 13:21); Masoretic Text does not have *forty-*.　　c 5 Some Septuagint manuscripts and Syriac; Hebrew *thirty thousand*

---

observe as the Lord himself demonstrates his existence and power and authenticates the truthfulness and seriousness of Samuel's words.

12:17 *wheat harvest.* See note on 6:13.

12:18 *stood in awe of the LORD and of Samuel.* See Ex 14:31 and note.

12:19 *Pray to the LORD your God.* Samuel's indictment (vv. 6–15), combined with the awesome sign of thunder and rain in the dry season (vv. 16–18), prompted the people to confess their sin and request Samuel's intercession for them.

12:20 *yet do not turn away from the LORD.* Samuel again brings into focus the central issue in the controversy surrounding the establishment of kingship in Israel.

12:21 *useless idols.* No rivals to the Lord can deliver or guarantee security (see Ex 20:3 and note).

12:23 *by failing to pray for you.* See 7:8 and note. *I will teach you the way that is good and right.* Samuel is not retiring from his prophetic role when he presents the people with their king. He will continue to intercede for the people (see v. 19; 7:8–9) and will instruct them in their covenant obligations (see Dt 6:18; 12:28). Saul and all future kings are to be subject to instruction and correction by the Lord's prophets.

12:24 *fear the LORD.* See notes on Ge 20:11; Ps 15:4; 111:10; Pr 1:7. Samuel summarizes Israel's obligation of loyalty to the Lord as an expression of gratitude for the great things he has done for them.

12:25 *you and your king will perish.* If the nation persists in covenant-breaking conduct, it will bring upon itself its own destruction.

13:1 *thirty years old…forty-two years.* See TNIV text notes. The wording of the verse follows the regularly used formula that introduces the reigns of later kings (see, e.g., 2Sa 2:10; 5:4; 1Ki 14:21; 2Ki 8:26).

13:2 *Mikmash.* Located southeast of Bethel and northeast of Gibeah near a pass (see v. 23; see also map, p. 565). *Jonathan.* Saul's oldest son (see 14:49; 31:2), mentioned here for the first time.

13:3,7 *Hebrews.* See note on Ge 14:13.

13:3 *Geba.* Located across a ravine and south of Mikmash.

13:4 *obnoxious.* A metaphor depicting an object of strong hostility, as in 2Sa 10:6; 16:21; Ge 34:30; Ex 5:21. *Gilgal.* See note on 11:14. By prearrangement Saul had been instructed to wait for Samuel there (see notes on v. 8; 10:8).

13:5 *three thousand chariots.* The Israelites did not acquire chariots until the time of Solomon (see 1Ki 4:26). *six thousand charioteers.* See note on 1Ki 22:34.

13:8 *time set by Samuel.* See note on 10:8. Saul is fully aware that Samuel's previous instructions had reference to this gathering at Gilgal. *Saul's men began to scatter.* The seven-day delay heightened the fear of the Israelite soldiers.

men began to scatter. [9]So he said, "Bring me the burnt offering and the fellowship offerings." And Saul offered [r] up the burnt offering. [10]Just as he finished making the offering, Samuel [s] arrived, and Saul went out to greet [t] him.

[11]"What have you done?" asked Samuel.

Saul replied, "When I saw that the men were scattering, and that you did not come at the set time, and that the Philistines were assembling at Mikmash, [u] [12]I thought, 'Now the Philistines will come down against me at Gilgal, [v] and I have not sought the LORD's favor. [w]' So I felt compelled to offer the burnt offering."

[13]"You have done a foolish thing, [x]" Samuel said. "You have not kept [y] the command the LORD your God gave you; if you had, he would have established your kingdom over Israel for all time. [z] [14]But now your kingdom [a] will not endure; the LORD has sought out a man after his own heart [b] and appointed [c] him ruler [d] of his people, because you have not kept [e] the LORD's command."

[15]Then Samuel left Gilgal [a] and went up to Gibeah [f] in Benjamin, and Saul counted the men who were with him. They numbered about six hundred. [g]

ISRAEL WITHOUT WEAPONS

[16]Saul and his son Jonathan and the men with them were staying in Gibeah [b] [h] in Benjamin, while the Philistines camped at Mikmash. [17]Raiding [i] parties went out from the Philistine camp in three detachments. One turned toward Ophrah [j] in the vicinity of Shual, [18]another toward Beth Horon, [k] and the third toward the borderland overlooking the Valley of Zeboyim [l] facing the wilderness.

[19]Not a blacksmith [m] could be found in the whole land of Israel, because the Philistines had said, "Otherwise the Hebrews will make swords or spears! [n]" [20]So all Israel went down to the Philistines to have their plowpoints, mattocks, axes and sickles [c] sharpened. [21]The price was two-thirds of a shekel [d] for sharpening plowpoints and mattocks, and a third of a shekel [e] for sharpening forks and axes and for repointing goads.

[22]So on the day of the battle not a soldier with Saul and Jonathan [o] had a sword or spear [p] in his hand; only Saul and his son Jonathan had them.

JONATHAN ATTACKS THE PHILISTINES

14 [23]Now a detachment of Philistines had gone out to the pass [q] at Mikmash. [r] [1]One day Jonathan son of Saul said to his young armor-bearer, "Come, let's go over to the Philistine outpost on the other side." But he did not tell his father. [2]Saul was staying [s] on the outskirts of Gibeah [t] under a pomegranate tree [u] in Migron. [v] With him were about six hundred men, [3]among whom was Ahijah, who was wearing an

---

[a] 15 Hebrew; Septuagint *Gilgal and went his way; the rest of the people went after Saul to meet the army, and they went out of Gilgal*   [b] 16 Two Hebrew manuscripts; most Hebrew manuscripts *Geba*, a variant of *Gibeah*   [c] 20 Septuagint; Hebrew *plowpoints*   [d] 21 That is, about 1/4 ounce or about 8 grams   [e] 21 That is, about 1/8 ounce or about 4 grams

---

13:9 [r] Dt 12:5-14; 2Sa 24:25; 1Ki 3:4
13:10 [s] 1Sa 15:13; [t] 1Sa 25:14
13:11 [u] S ver 2
13:12 [v] S Jos 10:43; [w] S Dt 4:29; Ps 119:58; Jer 26:19
13:13 [x] 2Ch 16:9; [y] ver 14; S Jos 22:16; 1Sa 15:23,24; 2Sa 7:15; 1Ch 10:13; [z] Ps 72:5
13:14 [a] 1Sa 15:28; 18:8; 24:20; 1Ch 10:14; [b] Ac 7:46; 13:22; [c] 2Sa 6:21; [d] 1Sa 25:30; 2Sa 5:2; Ps 18:43; Isa 16:5; 55:4; Jer 30:9; Eze 34:23-24; 37:24; Da 9:25; Hos 3:5; Mic 5:2 [e] 1Sa 15:26; 16:1; 2Sa 12:9; 1Ki 13:21; Hos 13:11
13:15 [f] 1Sa 14:2; [g] ver 2
13:16 [h] S Jos 18:24
13:17 [i] 1Sa 14:15; [j] S Jos 18:23
13:18 [k] S Jos 10:10; [l] Ne 11:34
13:19 [m] S Ge 4:22; [n] S Nu 25:7
13:22 [o] 1Ch 9:39; [p] S Nu 25:7; 1Sa 14:6; 17:47; Zec 4:6
13:23 [q] 1Sa 14:4; [r] S ver 2
14:2 [s] S Jdg 4:5; [t] 1Sa 13:15; [u] S Ex 28:33; [v] Isa 10:28

13:9 *Saul offered up the burnt offering.* Samuel had promised to make these offerings himself (see 10:8) before Israel went to battle (see 7:9), and he had directed Saul to await his arrival and instructions.

C **13:13** *You have done a foolish thing.* The foolish and sinful aspect (see 26:21; 2Sa 24:10; 2Ch 16:9; Isa 32:6) of Saul's act was that he thought he could strengthen Israel's chances against the Philistines while disregarding the instruction of the Lord's prophet Samuel. *You have not kept the command the LORD your God gave you.* Saul was to recognize the word of the prophet Samuel as the word of the Lord (see 3:20; 15:1; Ex 20:18–19; see also note on Ex 7:1–2). In disobeying Samuel's instructions, Saul violated a fundamental requirement of his theocratic office. His kingship was not to function independently of the law and the prophets (see notes on 12:14,23; 15:11).

C **13:14** *your kingdom will not endure.* Saul will not be followed by his sons; there will be no dynasty bearing his name (contrast the Lord's word to David, 2Sa 7:11–16). There is a striking parallel in the word of the Lord to Eli (see 2:30,35 and notes). *the LORD has sought out a man after his own heart and appointed him.* Paul quotes from this passage (Ac 13:22). *ruler.* See note on 9:16.

13:15 *six hundred.* The seven-day delay had greatly depleted Saul's forces (see vv. 2,4,6–8,11).

13:17 *Raiding parties.* The purpose of these Philistine contingents was not to engage the Israelites in battle, but to plunder the land and demoralize its inhabitants.

13:18 *Valley of Zeboyim.* Located to the east toward the Jordan Valley.

13:19 *Not a blacksmith.* A Philistine monopoly on the technology of iron production placed the Israelites at a great disadvantage in the fashioning and maintenance of agricultural implements and military weapons.

13:20 *plowpoints.* See note on Isa 2:4.

B **13:21** *price.* Probably exorbitant. *two thirds of a shekel.* The Hebrew word (*pim*) for this phrase, which occurs only here in the OT, has now been found on weights that have turned up in various excavations.

13:22 *not . . . a sword or spear.* The Israelites fought with bow and arrow and slingshot.

14:1 *on the other side.* The Philistines were encamped to the north of the pass and the Israelites to the south.

14:2 *Gibeah.* Saul had retreated farther south from Geba (13:3) to Gibeah. *under a pomegranate tree.* It appears to have been customary for leaders in early Israel to hold court under well-known trees (see 22:6; Jdg 4:5).

14:3 *Ahijah.* Either the brother and predecessor of Ahimelek son of Ahitub (referred to in 21:1; 22:9,11) or an alternative

14:3 ʷS Ge 35:18
ˣ1Sa 22:11,20
ʸS 1Sa 1:3 ᶻPs 78:60
14:4 ᵃ1Sa 13:23
14:5 ᵇS Jos 18:24
14:6 ᶜJdg 14:3;
1Sa 17:26,36; 31:4;
Jer 9:26; Eze 28:10
ᵈS 1Sa 13:22;
S 1Ki 19:12;
S Mt 19:26; Heb 11:34
ᵉJdg 7:4 ᶠPs 33:16
14:10 ᵍS Ge 24:14
ʰS Jos 2:24
14:11 ⁱS Ge 14:13
ʲS 1Sa 13:6
14:12 ᵏJdg 8:16
ˡ1Sa 17:46; 2Sa 5:24
14:15 ᵐS Ge 35:5;
S Ex 14:24; S 19:16;
2Ki 7:5-7 ⁿ1Sa 13:17
14:16 ᵒ2Sa 18:24;
2Ki 9:17; Isa 52:8;
Eze 33:2
14:18 ᵖ1Sa 30:7
�q S Jdg 18:5
14:19 ʳNu 27:21
14:20 ˢS Jdg 7:22;
Eze 38:21; Zec 14:13
14:21 ᵗ1Sa 29:4
14:22 ᵘS 1Sa 13:6
14:23 ᵛS Ex 14:30
ʷS Jos 7:2

ephod. He was a son of Ichabod's ʷ brother Ahitub ˣ son of Phinehas, the son of Eli, ʸ the LORD's priest in Shiloh. ᶻ No one was aware that Jonathan had left.

⁴On each side of the pass ᵃ that Jonathan intended to cross to reach the Philistine outpost was a cliff; one was called Bozez and the other Seneh. ⁵One cliff stood to the north toward Mikmash, the other to the south toward Geba. ᵇ

⁶Jonathan said to his young armor-bearer, "Come, let's go over to the outpost of those uncircumcised ᶜ fellows. Perhaps the LORD will act in our behalf. Nothing ᵈ can hinder the LORD from saving, whether by many ᵉ or by few. ᶠ"

⁷"Do all that you have in mind," his armor-bearer said. "Go ahead; I am with you heart and soul."

⁸Jonathan said, "Come on, then; we will cross over toward them and let them see us. ⁹If they say to us, 'Wait there until we come to you,' we will stay where we are and not go up to them. ¹⁰But if they say, 'Come up to us,' we will climb up, because that will be our sign ᵍ that the LORD has given them into our hands. ʰ"

¹¹So both of them showed themselves to the Philistine outpost. "Look!" said the Philistines. "The Hebrews ⁱ are crawling out of the holes they were hiding ʲ in." ¹²The men of the outpost shouted to Jonathan and his armor-bearer, "Come up to us and we'll teach you a lesson. ᵏ"

So Jonathan said to his armor-bearer, "Climb up after me; the LORD has given them into the hand ˡ of Israel."

¹³Jonathan climbed up, using his hands and feet, with his armor-bearer right behind him. The Philistines fell before Jonathan, and his armor-bearer followed and killed behind him. ¹⁴In that first attack Jonathan and his armor-bearer killed some twenty men in an area of about half an acre.

ISRAEL ROUTS THE PHILISTINES

¹⁵Then panic ᵐ struck the whole army—those in the camp and field, and those in the outposts and raiding ⁿ parties—and the ground shook. It was a panic sent by God. ᵃ

¹⁶Saul's lookouts ᵒ at Gibeah in Benjamin saw the army melting away in all directions. ¹⁷Then Saul said to the men who were with him, "Muster the forces and see who has left us." When they did, it was Jonathan and his armor-bearer who were not there.

¹⁸Saul said to Ahijah, "Bring ᵖ the ark ᑫ of God." (At that time it was with the Israelites.) ᵇ ¹⁹While Saul was talking to the priest, the tumult in the Philistine camp increased more and more. So Saul said to the priest, ʳ "Withdraw your hand."

²⁰Then Saul and all his men assembled and went to the battle. They found the Philistines in total confusion, striking ˢ each other with their swords. ²¹Those Hebrews who had previously been with the Philistines and had gone up with them to their camp went ᵗ over to the Israelites who were with Saul and Jonathan. ²²When all the Israelites who had hidden ᵘ in the hill country of Ephraim heard that the Philistines were on the run, they joined the battle in hot pursuit. ²³So on that day the LORD saved ᵛ Israel, and the battle moved on beyond Beth Aven. ʷ

ᵃ 15 Or *a terrible panic*   ᵇ 18 Hebrew; Septuagint *"Bring the ephod." (At that time he wore the ephod before the Israelites.)*

---

name for Ahimelek. *wearing an ephod.* See note on 2:28. *Ichabod's brother.* See 4:21.

14:6 *uncircumcised fellows.* A term of contempt (see 17:26,36; 31:4; 2Sa 1:20; Jdg 14:3; 15:18), which draws attention to Israel's covenant relationship to the Lord (see Ge 17:10 and note) and, by implication, to the illegitimacy of the Philistine presence in the land. *by many or by few.* See note on 17:47. Jonathan's bold plan is undertaken as an act of faith (cf. Heb 11:32–34) founded on God's promise (9:16).

14:10 *our sign.* See Jdg 6:36–40; Isa 7:11.

14:11 *Hebrews.* See v. 21; 4:6; 13:3,7 and note on Ge 14:13.

14:15 *ground shook.* See 7:10; 2Sa 22:12–16; Jos 10:11–14; Ps 77:18 for other instances of divine intervention in nature to bring deliverance to Israel.

14:18 *Bring the ark of God.* Saul decides to seek God's will before entering into battle with the Philistines (see Nu 27:21; Dt 20:2–4). Here the Septuagint (the pre-Christian Greek translation of the OT) may preserve the original text (see TNIV text

note) for the following reasons: 1. In 7:1 the ark was located at Kiriath Jearim, where it remained until David brought it to Jerusalem (2Sa 6), but the ephod was present in Saul's camp at Gibeah (see v. 3). 2. Nowhere else in the OT is the ark used to determine God's will, but the ephod (with the Urim and Thummim) was given for this purpose (see 23:9; 30:7 and notes on 2:18,28). 3. The command to the priest to withdraw his hand (v. 19) is more appropriate with the ephod than with the ark.

14:19 *Withdraw your hand.* Stop the priestly action I asked you to perform. Due to the urgency of the moment, Saul decides that to wait for the word of the Lord might jeopardize his military advantage. As in 13:8–12, his decision rests on his own insight rather than on dependence on the Lord and a commitment to obey him.

14:23 *So on that day the LORD saved Israel.* The writer attributes the victory to the Lord, not to either Saul or Jonathan (see vv. 6,10,12,15; 11:13).

JONATHAN EATS HONEY

²⁴Now the Israelites were in distress that day, because Saul had bound the people under an oath,ˣ saying, "Cursed be anyone who eats food before evening comes, before I have avenged myself on my enemies!" So none of the troops tasted food.

²⁵The entire army entered the woods, and there was honey on the ground. ²⁶When they went into the woods, they saw the honey oozing out; yet no one put his hand to his mouth, because they feared the oath. ²⁷But Jonathan had not heard that his father had bound the people with the oath, so he reached out the end of the staff that was in his hand and dipped it into the honeycomb.ʸ He raised his hand to his mouth, and his eyes brightened.ᵃ ²⁸Then one of the soldiers told him, "Your father bound the army under a strict oath, saying, 'Cursed be anyone who eats food today!' That is why the men are faint."

²⁹Jonathan said, "My father has made troubleᶻ for the country. See how my eyes brightenedᵇ when I tasted a little of this honey. ³⁰How much better it would have been if the men had eaten today some of the plunder they took from their enemies. Would not the slaughter of the Philistines have been even greater?"

³¹That day, after the Israelites had struck down the Philistines from Mikmashᵃ to Aijalon,ᵇ they were exhausted. ³²They pounced on the plunderᶜ and, taking sheep, cattle and calves, they butchered them on the ground and ate them, together with the blood.ᵈ ³³Then someone said to Saul, "Look, the men are sinning against the Lᴏʀᴅ by eating meat that has bloodᵉ in it."

"You have broken faith," he said. "Roll a large stone over here at once." ³⁴Then he said, "Go out among the men and tell them, 'Each of you bring me your cattle and sheep, and slaughter them here and eat them. Do not sin against the Lᴏʀᴅ by eating meat with blood still ᶠ in it.' "

So everyone brought his ox that night and slaughtered it there. ³⁵Then Saul built an altarᵍ to the Lᴏʀᴅ; it was the first time he had done this.

³⁶Saul said, "Let us go down and pursue the Philistines by night and plunder them till dawn, and let us not leave one of them alive."

"Do whatever seems best to you," they replied.

But the priest said, "Let us inquireʰ of God here."

³⁷So Saul asked God, "Shall I go down and pursue the Philistines? Will you give them into Israel's hand?" But God did not answerⁱ him that day.

³⁸Saul therefore said, "Come here, all you who are leaders of the army, and let us find out what sin has been committedʲ today. ³⁹As surely as the Lᴏʀᴅ who rescues Israel lives,ᵏ even if it lies with my son Jonathan,ˡ he must die."ᵐ But not one of them said a word.

⁴⁰Saul then said to all the Israelites, "You stand over there; I and Jonathan my son will stand over here."

"Do what seems best to you," they replied.

ᵃ 27 Or *his strength was renewed*   ᵇ 29 Or *my strength was renewed*

14:24 ˣ Jos 6:26
14:27 ʸ ver 43;
Ps 19:10; Pr 16:24;
24:13
14:29 ᶻ Jos 7:25;
1Ki 18:18
14:31 ᵃ ver 5
ᵇ S Jos 10:12
14:32 ᶜ 1Sa 15:19;
Est 9:10 ᵈ S Ge 9:4
14:33 ᵉ S Ge 9:4
14:34 ᶠ Lev 19:26
14:35 ᵍ S 1Sa 7:17
14:36 ʰ S Ge 25:22;
S Jdg 18:5
14:37 ⁱ 1Sa 28:6,15;
2Sa 22:42; Ps 18:41
14:38 ʲ Jos 7:11
14:39 ᵏ S Nu 14:21;
2Sa 12:5; Job 19:25;
Ps 18:46; 42:2 ˡ ver 44
ᵐ Jos 7:15

C 14:24–46 Following the account of the great victory the Lord had given, the author relates Saul's actions that strikingly illustrated his lack of fitness to be king. His foolish curse before the battle (see v. 24 and note) brought "distress" to the army and, as Jonathan tellingly observed, "made trouble for the country" (v. 29) rather than contributing to the victory (cf. Jos 7:25; 1Ki 18:17–18). And later, when hindered from taking advantage of the battle's outcome by the Lord's refusal to answer (v. 37), Saul was ready to execute Jonathan as the cause, though Jonathan had contributed most to the victory, as everyone else recognized (v. 45). Saul's growing egocentrism was turning into an all-consuming passion that threatened the very welfare of the nation. Rather than serving the cause of the Lord and his people, he was in fact becoming a king "such as all the other nations have" (8:5).

C 14:24 *in distress.* Saul's rash action in requiring his troops to fast placed them at an unnecessary disadvantage in the battle (see vv. 29–30). *Cursed.* Thus Saul as king "bound the army under a strict oath" (v. 28), a most serious matter because an oath directly invoked God's involvement, whether it concerned giving testimony (Ex 20:7; Lev 19:12), making commitments (Ge 21:23–24; 24:3–4) or prohibiting action (here). It appealed to God as the supreme enforcement power and the all-knowing Judge of human actions. *I have*

avenged myself on my enemies. Saul perceives the conflict with the Philistines more as a personal vendetta (see note on 15:12) than as a battle for the honor of the Lord and the security of the Lord's people (note the contrast between his attitude and that of Jonathan in vv. 6,10,12).

14:31 *Aijalon.* Located to the west near the Philistines' own territory (see Jos 10:12 and map, p. 338).

14:33 *eating meat that has blood in it.* The Israelites were not permitted to eat blood (see Ge 9:4; Lev 17:10–11; 19:26; Dt 12:16,24; Eze 33:25; Ac 15:20 and notes). *broken faith.* See Mal 2:10–11. The same Hebrew term is translated "faithless" (Ps 78:57), "unfaithful" (Jer 3:7–8,10–11) and "treacherous" (Isa 48:8).

C 14:35 *first time he had done this.* Another indication of Saul's personal lack of interest in religious matters (see notes on 9:3,6; 10:11).

14:36 *priest.* Ahijah (see v. 3).

14:37 *Saul asked God.* The means of ascertaining God's will appears to have been the ephod with its Urim and Thummim (see v. 3 and note on v. 18). *God did not answer.* Because an oath had been broken in the battle, God refused to answer Saul's inquiry concerning further military action.

14:39,45 *As surely as the Lᴏʀᴅ ... lives.* An oath formula (see note on v. 24; 19:6; see also Ge 42:15; Hos 4:15 and notes).

14:42 ⁿ Jnh 1:7
14:43 ᵒ S Jos 7:19
ᵖ S ver 27
14:44 ᑫ S Ru 1:17
ʳ ver 39
14:45 ˢ 1Ki 1:52;
S Mt 10:30 ᵗ 2Sa 14:11
14:47 ᵘ S Ge 19:37
ᵛ S Ge 19:38;
2Sa 12:31 ʷ 1Sa 21:7
ˣ 2Sa 8:3; 10:6; 23:36
14:48 ʸ S Ge 36:12;
Nu 13:29; Jdg 3:13;
1Sa 15:2,7; 27:8;
28:18; 30:13; 2Sa 1:1;
1Ch 4:43
14:49 ᶻ 1Sa 31:2;
1Ch 8:33 ᵃ S Ge 29:26
14:50 ᵇ 2Sa 2:8; 3:6;
1Ki 2:5 ᶜ 1Sa 10:14
14:51 ᵈ S 1Sa 9:1
14:52 ᵉ 1Sa 8:11
15:1 ᶠ S 1Sa 9:16
15:2 ᵍ S Ge 14:7;
S 1Sa 14:48; S 2Sa 1:8
15:3 ʰ ver 9,19;
S Ge 14:23; Jos 6:17;
1Sa 22:19; 27:9;
28:18; Est 3:13; 9:5
15:6 ⁱ S Ge 15:19;
Nu 24:22; Jdg 1:16;
1Sa 30:29

⁴¹Then Saul prayed to the Lᴏʀᴅ, the God of Israel, "Why have you not answered your servant today? If the fault is in me or my son Jonathan, respond with Urim, but if the men of Israel are at fault,ᵃ respond with Thummim." Jonathan and Saul were taken by lot, and the men were cleared. ⁴²Saul said, "Cast the lot ⁿ between me and Jonathan my son." And Jonathan was taken.

⁴³Then Saul said to Jonathan, "Tell me what you have done." ᵒ

So Jonathan told him, "I tasted a little honeyᵖ with the end of my staff. And now I must die!"

⁴⁴Saul said, "May God deal with me, be it ever so severely,ᑫ if you do not die, Jonathan.ʳ"

⁴⁵But the men said to Saul, "Should Jonathan die—he who has brought about this great deliverance in Israel? Never! As surely as the Lᴏʀᴅ lives, not a hairˢ of his head will fall to the ground, for he did this today with God's help." So the men rescuedᵗ Jonathan, and he was not put to death.

⁴⁶Then Saul stopped pursuing the Philistines, and they withdrew to their own land.

⁴⁷After Saul had assumed rule over Israel, he fought against their enemies on every side: Moab,ᵘ the Ammonites,ᵛ Edom,ʷ the kingsᵇ of Zobah,ˣ and the Philistines. Wherever he turned, he inflicted punishment on them.ᶜ ⁴⁸He fought valiantly and defeated the Amalekites,ʸ delivering Israel from the hands of those who had plundered them.

SAUL'S FAMILY

⁴⁹Saul's sons were Jonathan, Ishvi and Malki-Shua.ᶻ The name of his older daughter was Merab, and that of the younger was Michal.ᵃ ⁵⁰His wife's name was Ahinoam daughter of Ahimaaz. The name of the commander of Saul's army was Abnerᵇ son of Ner, and Ner was Saul's uncle.ᶜ ⁵¹Saul's father Kishᵈ and Abner's father Ner were sons of Abiel.

⁵²All the days of Saul there was bitter war with the Philistines, and whenever Saul saw a mighty or brave man, he tookᵉ him into his service.

THE LORD REJECTS SAUL AS KING

15 Samuel said to Saul, "I am the one the Lᴏʀᴅ sent to anointᶠ you king over his people Israel; so listen now to the message from the Lᴏʀᴅ. ²This is what the Lᴏʀᴅ Almighty says: 'I will punish the Amalekitesᵍ for what they did to Israel when they waylaid them as they came up from Egypt. ³Now go, attack the Amalekites and totallyʰ destroyᵈ all that belongs to them. Do not spare them; put to death men and women, children and infants, cattle and sheep, camels and donkeys.' "

⁴So Saul summoned the men and mustered them at Telaim—two hundred thousand foot soldiers and ten thousand from Judah. ⁵Saul went to the city of Amalek and set an ambush in the ravine. ⁶Then he said to the Kenites,ⁱ "Go away, leave the Amalekites so that

---

ᵃ 41 Septuagint; Hebrew does not have "Why . . . at fault."   ᵇ 47 Masoretic Text; Dead Sea Scrolls and Septuagint *king*   ᶜ 47 Hebrew; Septuagint *he was victorious*   ᵈ 3 The Hebrew term refers to the irrevocable giving over of things or persons to the Lᴏʀᴅ, often by totally destroying them; also in verses 8, 9, 15, 18, 20 and 21.

14:41 *taken by lot.* See 10:20–21; Jos 7:14–18; Pr 16:33.

14:44 A curse formula (see note on v. 24; see also 3:17 and note).

14:45 *he did this today with God's help.* The men of Saul's army recognize the inappropriateness of taking the life of the one through whom God has delivered his people.

14:47–48 A summary of Saul's military victories to the east (Moab and the Ammonites), south (Edom), north (Zobah) and west (Philistines).

14:47 *Ammonites.* See Dt 2:19–21,37.

14:48 *Amalekites.* See note on 15:2.

14:49 *Saul's sons.* See 31:2; 1Ch 9:39 and notes. *Merab . . . Michal.* See 18:17,20; 19:11–17; 25:44; 2Sa 6:16–23.

14:50 *Ahinoam.* The only reference to a wife of Saul. His concubine Rizpah is mentioned in 2Sa 3:7; 21:8–11.

14:52 *All the days of Saul.* Closes the main account of Saul's reign. *he took him into his service.* Saul developed a special cadre of professional soldiers bound to himself, much as David was to do later (Philistines). See 22:2; 23:13; 25:13; 27:2–3; 29:2; 30:1,9–10; 2Sa 2:3; 5:6; 8:18; 15:18; 23:8–39).

15:1–35 The event that occasioned Saul's rejection as king. Although no time designation is given, it evidently occurred after the conflicts of 14:47, in a time of relative peace

and security. It is likely that David was anointed (16:1–13) shortly after the rejection of Saul (vv. 23,26,28), thus c. 1025 B.C.

15:2 *Amalekites.* A nomadic people descended from Esau (see Ge 36:12,16), usually living in the Negev and Sinai regions (see 27:8; 30:1; 2Sa 17:1–15; Ge 14:7 and note; Ex 17:8; Nu 13:29). *what they did to Israel.* See 14:48; Ex 17:8–15; Nu 14:43, 45; Dt 25:17–19; cf. Jdg 3:13; 6:3–5,33; 7:12; 10:12.

15:3 *totally destroy.* See TNIV text note; Dt 13:12–18; see also notes on Lev 27:28–29; Jos 6:17–18. Saul is given an opportunity as king to demonstrate his allegiance to the Lord by obedience in this assigned task.

15:4 *Telaim.* Probably the same as Telem in Jos 15:24, located in the southern part of Judah. *foot soldiers.* From the northern tribes (see 11:8).

15:5 *city of Amalek.* A settlement of Amalekites, most likely located between Telaim and Kadesh Barnea, possibly the residence of their king.

15:6 *Kenites.* A nomadic people of the Sinai, closely related to the Midianites. Moses had married a Kenite woman (see Ex 2:16,21–22; Nu 10:29; Jdg 1:16; 4:11), and some of the Kenites had accompanied the Israelites when they settled in the land of Canaan (see 27:10; Jdg 1:16; 4:17–23; 5:24; 1Ch 2:55).

I do not destroy you along with them; for you showed kindness to all the Israelites when they came up out of Egypt." So the Kenites moved away from the Amalekites.

[7]Then Saul attacked the Amalekites[j] all the way from Havilah to Shur,[k] near the eastern border of Egypt. [8]He took Agag[l] king of the Amalekites alive,[m] and all his people he totally destroyed with the sword. [9]But Saul and the army spared[n] Agag and the best of the sheep and cattle, the fat calves[a] and lambs—everything that was good. These they were unwilling to destroy completely, but everything that was despised and weak they totally destroyed.

[10]Then the word of the LORD came to Samuel: [11]"I regret[o] that I have made Saul king, because he has turned[p] away from me and has not carried out my instructions."[q] Samuel was angry,[r] and he cried out to the LORD all that night.

[12]Early in the morning Samuel got up and went to meet Saul, but he was told, "Saul has gone to Carmel.[s] There he has set up a monument[t] in his own honor and has turned and gone on down to Gilgal."

[13]When Samuel reached him, Saul said, "The LORD bless you! I have carried out the LORD's instructions."

[14]But Samuel said, "What then is this bleating of sheep in my ears? What is this lowing of cattle that I hear?"

[15]Saul answered, "The soldiers brought them from the Amalekites; they spared the best of the sheep and cattle to sacrifice to the LORD your God, but we totally destroyed the rest."

[16]"Enough!" Samuel said to Saul. "Let me tell you what the LORD said to me last night."

"Tell me," Saul replied.

[17]Samuel said, "Although you were once small[u] in your own eyes, did you not become the head of the tribes of Israel? The LORD anointed you king over Israel. [18]And he sent you on a mission, saying, 'Go and completely destroy those wicked people, the Amalekites; make war on them until you have wiped them out.' [19]Why did you not obey the LORD? Why did you pounce on the plunder[v] and do evil in the eyes of the LORD?"

[20]"But I did obey[w] the LORD," Saul said. "I went on the mission the LORD assigned me. I completely destroyed the Amalekites and brought back Agag their king. [21]The soldiers took sheep and cattle from the plunder, the best of what was devoted to God, in order to sacrifice them to the LORD your God at Gilgal."

[22]But Samuel replied:

> "Does the LORD delight in burnt offerings and sacrifices
>   as much as in obeying the LORD?
> To obey is better than sacrifice,[x]
>   and to heed is better than the fat of rams.
> [23]For rebellion is like the sin of divination,[y]

---

a 9 Or *the grown bulls*; the meaning of the Hebrew for this phrase is uncertain.

15:7 *j* S 1Sa 14:48
k S Ge 16:7
15:8 *l* Ex 17:8-16;
S Nu 24:7
m S Jos 8:23
15:9 *n* S ver 3
15:11 *o* S Ge 6:6;
S Ex 32:14
p S Jos 22:16
q Job 21:14; 34:27;
Ps 28:5; Isa 5:12;
53:6; Jer 48:10;
Eze 18:24 *r* S ver 35;
S 1Sa 8:6
15:12 *s* Jos 15:55
t S Nu 32:42
15:17 *u* S Ex 3:11
15:19 *v* S Ge 14:23;
S 1Sa 8:6
15:20 *w* 1Sa 28:18
15:22 *x* Ps 40:6-8;
51:16; Pr 21:3;
Isa 1:11-15; Jer 7:22;
Hos 6:6; Am 5:25;
Mic 6:6-8; S Mk 12:33
15:23 *y* Dt 18:10

15:7 *Havilah to Shur.* Ishmael's descendants occupied this area (see Ge 25:18). The location of Havilah is uncertain. Shur was on the eastern frontier of Egypt (see 27:8; Ge 16:7; 20:1).

15:8 *Agag king of the Amalekites.* His descendants would later oppress Israel (see note on Est 3:1). *all his people.* All the Amalekites they encountered. Some Amalekites survived (see 27:8; 30:1,18; 2Sa 1:8,13; 8:12; 1Ch 4:43).

15:9 When the Israelites refused to obey the Lord's command (v. 3), their holy war against the Amalekites degenerated into personal aggrandizement, much like that of Achan at the time of the conquest of Canaan (see Jos 7:1). Giving to the Lord by destruction only what was despised and weak was a contemptible act (see Mal 1:7–12 and notes), not to be excused (see v. 19) by the protestation that the best had been preserved for sacrifice to the Lord (vv. 15,21).

15:11 *regret.* See note on v. 29. *he has turned away from me.* A violation of the fundamental requirement of his office as king (see notes on 12:14–15).

15:12 *Carmel.* Located about seven miles south of Hebron (see 25:2; Jos 15:55). *monument in his own honor.* Saul's self-glorification here contrasts sharply with his self-abasement after the victory over the Ammonites (see note on 11:13; cf. v. 17; 2Sa 18:18). *Gilgal.* Saul returns to the place where he was inaugurated and instructed in the responsibilities of his office (see 11:14–15). This was also the place where he had

been told that he would not have a continuing dynasty because of his disobedience (see 13:13–14).

15:13 *I have carried out the LORD's instructions.* Here and in v. 20 Saul is clearly less than honest in his statements to Samuel.

15:15 *The soldiers ... spared the best ... to sacrifice.* Saul attempts to shift responsibility from himself to the army and to excuse their action by claiming pious intentions. *the LORD your God.* Saul's use of the pronoun "your" instead of "my" here and in vv. 21,30 indicates an awareness of his own alienation from the Lord (see 12:19 for a similar case), even though he speaks of obedience and the intent to honor God by sacrifice.

15:17 *you were once small in your own eyes.* See 9:21; 10:22.

15:22 Samuel does not suggest that sacrifice is unimportant but that it is acceptable only when brought with an attitude of obedience and devotion to the Lord (see Ps 51:16–17 and notes; Isa 1:11–17; Hos 6:6; Am 5:21–24; Mic 6:6–8). *fat of rams.* The fat of sacrificed animals belonged to the Lord (see 2:15 and note; Ex 23:18; Lev 3:14–16; 7:30).

15:23 *rebellion.* Samuel charges Saul with violating the central requirement of the covenant condition given to him when he became king (see 12:14–15). *sin of divination.* A serious offense against the Lord (see Lev 19:26; Dt 18:9–12), which Saul himself condemned (28:3,9). *you have rejected the word of the LORD.* A king who sets his own will above

15:23 ʳ S 1Sa 13:13
15:24 ᵃ S Ex 9:27;
S Nu 22:34; Ps 51:4
ᵇ S 1Sa 13:13
ᶜ Pr 29:25; Isa 51:12-
13; Jer 42:11
15:25 ᵈ Ex 10:17
15:26 ᵉ S Nu 15:31;
S 1Sa 13:14;
S 1Ki 14:10
15:27 ᶠ 1Sa 28:14
ᵍ 1Ki 11:11,31; 14:8;
2Ki 17:21
15:28 ʰ 1Sa 28:17
ⁱ S 1Sa 13:14
ʲ 2Sa 6:21; 7:15
15:29 ᵏ Tit 1:2
ˡ S Nu 23:19;
Heb 7:21
15:30 ᵐ S Nu 22:34
ⁿ Isa 29:13; Jn 12:43
15:33 ᵒ Est 9:7-10;
Jer 18:21
15:34 ᵖ S 1Sa 7:17
�q S Jdg 19:14;
S 1Sa 10:5
15:35 ʳ 1Sa 19:24
ˢ ver 11; 1Sa 16:1
ᵗ S Ge 6:6
16:1 ᵘ S 1Sa 8:6;
S 15:35 ᵛ S 1Sa 13:14
ʷ S 1Sa 10:1
ˣ S Ru 4:17 ʸ 2Sa 5:2;
7:8; 1Ki 8:16;
1Ch 12:23; Ps 78:70;
Ac 13:22
16:3 ᶻ Ex 4:15
ᵃ S Dt 17:15

and arrogance like the evil of idolatry.
Because you have rejected ᶻ the word of the Lᴏʀᴅ,
he has rejected you as king."

²⁴Then Saul said to Samuel, "I have sinned. ᵃ I violated ᵇ the Lᴏʀᴅ's command and your instructions. I was afraid ᶜ of the men and so I gave in to them. ²⁵Now I beg you, forgive ᵈ my sin and come back with me, so that I may worship the Lᴏʀᴅ."

²⁶But Samuel said to him, "I will not go back with you. You have rejected ᵉ the word of the Lᴏʀᴅ, and the Lᴏʀᴅ has rejected you as king over Israel!"

²⁷As Samuel turned to leave, Saul caught hold of the hem of his robe, ᶠ and it tore. ᵍ ²⁸Samuel said to him, "The Lᴏʀᴅ has torn ʰ the kingdom ⁱ of Israel from you today and has given it to one of your neighbors—to one better than you. ʲ ²⁹He who is the Glory of Israel does not lie ᵏ or change ˡ his mind; for he is not a human being, that he should change his mind."

³⁰Saul replied, "I have sinned. ᵐ But please honor ⁿ me before the elders of my people and before Israel; come back with me, so that I may worship the Lᴏʀᴅ your God." ³¹So Samuel went back with Saul, and Saul worshiped the Lᴏʀᴅ.

³²Then Samuel said, "Bring me Agag king of the Amalekites."
Agag came to him in chains. ᵃ And he thought, "Surely the bitterness of death is past."
³³But Samuel said,

"As your sword has made women childless,
so will your mother be childless among women." ᵒ

And Samuel put Agag to death before the Lᴏʀᴅ at Gilgal.

³⁴Then Samuel left for Ramah, ᵖ but Saul went up to his home in Gibeah q of Saul. ³⁵Until the day Samuel ʳ died, he did not go to see Saul again, though Samuel mourned ˢ for him. And the Lᴏʀᴅ regretted ᵗ that he had made Saul king over Israel.

SAMUEL ANOINTS DAVID

16 The Lᴏʀᴅ said to Samuel, "How long will you mourn ᵘ for Saul, since I have rejected ᵛ him as king over Israel? Fill your horn with oil ʷ and be on your way; I am sending you to Jesse ˣ of Bethlehem. I have chosen ʸ one of his sons to be king."

²But Samuel said, "How can I go? If Saul hears about it, he will kill me."
The Lᴏʀᴅ said, "Take a heifer with you and say, 'I have come to sacrifice to the Lᴏʀᴅ.' ³Invite Jesse to the sacrifice, and I will show ᶻ you what to do. You are to anoint ᵃ for me the one I indicate."

ᵃ 32 The meaning of the Hebrew for this phrase is uncertain.

---

the command of the Lord ceases to be an instrument of the Lord's rule over his people, violating the very nature of his theocratic office. *he has rejected you as king.* The judgment here goes beyond the one given earlier (see note on 13:14). Now Saul himself is to be set aside as king. Although this did not happen immediately, as chs. 16–31 show, the process began that led to his death. It included in its relentless course the removal of God's Spirit and favor from him (16:14), the defection of his son Jonathan and daughter Michal to David (18:1–4,20; 19:11–17) and the insubordination of his own officials (22:17).

A **15:24** Saul's confession retains an element of self-justification and a shift of blame (contrast David's confession; see 2Sa 12:13; Ps 51:4 and notes). Previously (vv. 15,21) he had attempted to justify his soldiers' actions.
15:25 *come back with me.* Saul's greatest concern was not to worship God but to avoid an open break with the prophet Samuel, a break that would undermine his authority as king (see v. 30).
15:28 *one of your neighbors.* David (see 28:17 and note on 13:14).
15:29 *Glory of Israel.* In Ps 106:20; Jer 2:11; Hos 4:7 God is called "glorious God" (see 4:21; Heb 9:5 and notes). Cf. 2Sa 1:19; Ps 89:17; Isa 13:19. *does not lie or change his mind.* See Nu 23:19; Mal 3:6 and notes; see also Ps 110:4; Jer 4:28. There is no conflict between this statement and vv. 11,35, where the Lord is said to "regret" that he had made Saul king.
15:31 *So Samuel went back with Saul.* Samuel's purpose in

agreeing to Saul's request is not to honor Saul, but to carry out the divine sentence on Agag and in so doing to reemphasize Saul's neglect of duty.
15:34 *Ramah.* Samuel's home (see 7:17; see also note on 1:1). *Gibeah of Saul.* See note on 10:5.
15:35 *Samuel mourned.* Samuel regarded Saul as though dead (see the use of "mourned" in 6:19). Even though his love for him remained (see v. 11; 16:1), he sought no further contact with him because God had rejected him as king. Saul did come to Samuel on one other occasion (see 19:24).
16:1 *The Lᴏʀᴅ said to Samuel.* Probably c. 1025 B.C. (see note on 15:1–35). *Jesse.* For Jesse's genealogy see Ru 4:18–22; Mt 1:3–6. *Bethlehem.* A town five miles south of Jerusalem, formerly known as Ephrath (see Ge 35:16 and note). It was later to become renowned as the "town of David" and the birthplace of the Messiah (Mic 5:2; Mt 2:1; Lk 2:4–7). *I have chosen one of his sons to be king.* See notes on 13:14; 15:28.
16:2 *Saul ... will kill me.* The road from Ramah (where Samuel was, 15:34) to Bethlehem passed through Gibeah of Saul. Saul already knew that the Lord had chosen someone to replace him as king (see 15:28). Samuel fears that jealousy will incite Saul to violence. Later incidents (18:10–11; 19:10; 20:33) demonstrate that Samuel's fears were well-founded. *say, 'I have come to sacrifice to the Lᴏʀᴅ.'* This response is true but incomplete, and it was intended to deceive Saul.
16:3 *anoint.* See vv. 1,13 and note on 9:16.

⁴Samuel did what the LORD said. When he arrived at Bethlehem,ᵇ the elders of the town trembledᶜ when they met him. They asked, "Do you come in peace?ᵈ"

⁵Samuel replied, "Yes, in peace; I have come to sacrifice to the LORD. Consecrateᵉ yourselves and come to the sacrifice with me." Then he consecrated Jesse and his sons and invited them to the sacrifice.

⁶When they arrived, Samuel saw Eliabᶠ and thought, "Surely the LORD's anointed stands here before the LORD."

⁷But the LORD said to Samuel, "Do not consider his appearance or his height, for I have rejected him. The LORD does not look at the things human beings look at. People look at the outward appearance,ᵍ but the LORD looks at the heart."ʰ

⁸Then Jesse called Abinadabⁱ and had him pass in front of Samuel. But Samuel said, "The LORD has not chosen this one either." ⁹Jesse then had Shammahʲ pass by, but Samuel said, "Nor has the LORD chosen this one." ¹⁰Jesse had seven of his sons pass before Samuel, but Samuel said to him, "The LORD has not chosen these." ¹¹So he asked Jesse, "Are these allᵏ the sons you have?"

"There is still the youngest," Jesse answered. "He is tending the sheep."ˡ

Samuel said, "Send for him; we will not sit down until he arrives."

¹²So heᵐ sent and had him brought in. He was glowing with health and had a fine appearance and handsomeⁿ features.

Then the LORD said, "Rise and anoint him; this is the one."

¹³So Samuel took the horn of oil and anointedᵒ him in the presence of his brothers, and from that day on the Spirit of the LORDᵖ came on David in power.�q Samuel then went to Ramah.

DAVID IN SAUL'S SERVICE

¹⁴Now the Spirit of the LORD had departedʳ from Saul, and an evilᵃ spiritˢ from the LORD tormented him.ᵗ

¹⁵Saul's attendants said to him, "See, an evil spirit from God is tormenting you. ¹⁶Let our lord command his servants here to search for someone who can play the lyre.ᵘ He will play when the evil spirit from God comes on you, and you will feel better."

¹⁷So Saul said to his attendants, "Find someone who plays well and bring him to me."

¹⁸One of the servants answered, "I have seen a son of Jesseᵛ of Bethlehem who knows how to play the lyre. He is a brave man and a warrior.ʷ He speaks well and is a fine-looking man. And the LORD is withˣ him."

¹⁹Then Saul sent messengers to Jesse and said, "Send me your son David, who is with

---

ᵃ **14** Or *harmful*; also in verses 15, 16 and 23

16:4 ᵇ S Ge 48:7;
Lk 2:4 ᶜ 1Sa 21:1
ᵈ 1Ki 2:13; 2Ki 9:17
16:5 ᵉ S Ex 19:10,22
16:6 ᶠ 1Sa 17:13;
1Ch 2:13
16:7 ᵍ Ps 147:10
ʰ S 1Sa 2:3; 2Sa 7:20;
S Ps 44:21; S 139:23;
S Rev 2:23
16:8 ⁱ 1Sa 17:13
16:9 ʲ 1Sa 17:13;
2Sa 13:3; 21:21
16:11 ᵏ 1Sa 17:12
ˡ S Ge 37:2; 2Sa 7:8
16:12 ᵐ 1Sa 9:17
ⁿ S Ge 39:6
16:13 ᵒ S 1Sa 2:35;
S 2Sa 22:51
ᵖ 1Sa 18:12
q 1Sa 11:6
16:14 ʳ S Jdg 16:20
ˢ ver 23; S Jdg 9:23;
1Sa 18:10 ᵗ 2Sa 7:15
16:16 ᵘ ver 23;
S 1Sa 10:5,6;
2Ch 29:26-27;
Ps 49:4
16:18 ᵛ S Ru 4:17
ʷ 2Sa 17:8
ˣ S Ge 39:2;
1Sa 17:32-37; 20:13;
1Ch 22:11; Mt 1:23

16:5 *Consecrate yourselves.* Involves preparing oneself spiritually as well as making oneself ceremonially clean by washing and putting on clean clothes (see Ex 19:10,14; Lev 15; Nu 19:11–22).

16:6 *Eliab.* Jesse's oldest son (17:13).

16:7 *his appearance or his height.* Samuel is not to focus on these outward features, which had characterized Saul (see 9:2; 10:23–24). *heart.* The Lord is concerned with a person's inner disposition and character (see 1Ki 8:39; 1Ch 28:9; Lk 16:15; Jn 2:25; Ac 1:24).

16:8 *Abinadab.* Jesse's second son (17:13).

16:9 *Shammah.* Jesse's third son (17:13).

16:11 *He is tending the sheep.* The Lord's chosen one is a shepherd (see note on 9:3; see also 2Sa 7:7–8; Ps 78:71–72).

16:13–14 Taken together, these verses describe not only the transfer of God's Spirit from Saul to David but also the beginning of God's effective displacement of Saul by David as Israel's king. This transition, occurring as it does at the center of 1 Samuel, serves as the literary, historical and theological crux of this book. Cf. Ps 51:11 and note.

16:13 *in the presence of his brothers.* The small circle of witnesses to David's anointing assured its confidentiality but also provided ample testimony for the future that David had been anointed by Samuel and that he was not merely a usurper of Saul's office. *the Spirit of the LORD came on David in power.* See 10:5–6,10; 11:6; 14:6,19; Jdg 3:10 and note; 11:29 and note; 15:14. This is the first mention of David by name in 1 Samuel.

16:14—17:58 In the next two episodes, David is introduced to Saul's court and to Israel as a gifted musician

and warrior. With these two gifts he would become famous in Israel and would lead the nation to spiritual and political vigor (see 2Sa 22; 23:1–7). Also through these two gifts Saul would become dependent on David.

16:14 *the Spirit of the LORD had departed from Saul.* Cf. Jdg 16:20. The removal of the Spirit from Saul and the giving of the Spirit to David (v. 13) determined the contrasting courses of their lives. *evil spirit from the LORD.* This statement and similar ones in Scripture indicate that evil spirits are subject to God's control and operate only within divinely determined boundaries (see 1Ki 22:19–23; Job 1:12; 2:6 and notes; see also 2Sa 24:1 and note). Saul's disobedience continued to be punished by the assaults of an evil spirit (vv. 15–16,23; 18:10; 19:9). *tormented him.* Saul's increasing tendencies to despondency, jealousy and violence were no doubt occasioned by his knowledge of his rejection as king (see 13:13–14; 15:22–26; 18:9; 20:30–33; 22:16–18) and his awareness of David's growing popularity, but an evil spirit was also involved in these psychological aberrations (see 18:10–12; 19:9–10).

16:16 *you will feel better.* The soothing effect of certain types of music on a troubled spirit is a generally recognized phenomenon (see 2Ki 3:15). Beyond this natural effect of music, however, it would appear that in this instance the Spirit of the Lord was active in David's music to suppress the evil spirit temporarily (see v. 23).

16:18 *the LORD is with him.* Said also of Samuel (see 3:1 and note). The fact that God was with David (see also 17:37; 18:12,14,28; 2Sa 5:10) outweighs everything David was.

16:19 *Send me your son David.* Saul unknowingly invites to the court the person God chose to be his replacement. In this way

16:19 ʸ1Sa 17:15
16:20 ᶻS Ge 32:13;
S 1Sa 10:4
16:21 ᵃS Ge 41:46
16:23 ᵇS ver 14;
S Jdg 9:23
17:1 ᶜ1Sa 13:5
ᵈJos 15:35; 2Ch 28:18
ᵉS Jos 10:10,11
17:2 ᶠ1Sa 21:9
17:4 ᵍ1Sa 21:9;
2Sa 21:19
17:6 ʰver 45;
1Sa 18:10
17:7 ⁱ2Sa 21:19;
1Ch 11:23; 20:5
ʲver 41
17:8 ᵏ2Sa 2:12-17
17:10 ˡver 26,45;
2Sa 21:21 ᵐver 23
17:12 ⁿS Ge 35:16;
S 48:7; Ps 132:6
ᵒS Ru 4:17
ᵖS Ge 35:19
�q1Sa 16:11
17:13 ʳS 1Sa 16:6
ˢ1Sa 16:8 ᵗS 1Sa 16:9
17:15 ᵘS Ge 37:2
ᵛ1Sa 16:19
17:17 ʷS Lev 19:36
ˣS Lev 23:14;
1Sa 25:18
17:18 ʸGe 37:14
17:22 ᶻS Jos 1:11
17:23 ᵃver 8-10

the sheep.ʸ ²⁰So Jesse took a donkey loaded with bread,ᶻ a skin of wine and a young goat and sent them with his son David to Saul.

²¹David came to Saul and entered his service.ᵃ Saul liked him very much, and David became one of his armor-bearers. ²²Then Saul sent word to Jesse, saying, "Allow David to remain in my service, for I am pleased with him."

²³Whenever the spirit from God came on Saul, David would take up his lyre and play. Then relief would come to Saul; he would feel better, and the evil spiritᵇ would leave him.

DAVID AND GOLIATH

17 Now the Philistines gathered their forces for war and assembledᶜ at Sokoh in Judah. They pitched camp at Ephes Dammim, between Sokohᵈ and Azekah.ᵉ ²Saul and the Israelites assembled and camped in the Valley of Elahᶠ and drew up their battle line to meet the Philistines. ³The Philistines occupied one hill and the Israelites another, with the valley between them.

⁴A champion named Goliath,ᵍ who was from Gath, came out of the Philistine camp. His height was six cubits and a span.ᵃ ⁵He had a bronze helmet on his head and wore a coat of scale armor of bronze weighing five thousand shekelsᵇ; ⁶on his legs he wore bronze greaves, and a bronze javelinʰ was slung on his back. ⁷His spear shaft was like a weaver's rod,ⁱ and its iron point weighed six hundred shekels.ᶜ His shield bearerʲ went ahead of him.

⁸Goliath stood and shouted to the ranks of Israel, "Why do you come out and line up for battle? Am I not a Philistine, and are you not the servants of Saul? Chooseᵏ a man and have him come down to me. ⁹If he is able to fight and kill me, we will become your subjects; but if I overcome him and kill him, you will become our subjects and serve us." ¹⁰Then the Philistine said, "This day I defyˡ the armies of Israel! Give me a man and let us fight each other."ᵐ ¹¹On hearing the Philistine's words, Saul and all the Israelites were dismayed and terrified.

¹²Now David was the son of an Ephrathiteⁿ named Jesse,ᵒ who was from Bethlehemᵖ in Judah. Jesse had eightq sons, and in Saul's time he was very old. ¹³Jesse's three oldest sons had followed Saul to the war: The firstborn was Eliab;ʳ the second, Abinadab;ˢ and the third, Shammah.ᵗ ¹⁴David was the youngest. The three oldest followed Saul, ¹⁵but David went back and forth from Saul to tendᵘ his father's sheepᵛ at Bethlehem.

¹⁶For forty days the Philistine came forward every morning and evening and took his stand.

¹⁷Now Jesse said to his son David, "Take this ephahᵈʷ of roasted grainˣ and these ten loaves of bread for your brothers and hurry to their camp. ¹⁸Take along these ten cheeses to the commander of their unit. See how your brothersʸ are and bring back some assuranceᵉ from them. ¹⁹They are with Saul and all the men of Israel in the Valley of Elah, fighting against the Philistines."

²⁰Early in the morning David left the flock in the care of a shepherd, loaded up and set out, as Jesse had directed. He reached the camp as the army was going out to its battle positions, shouting the war cry. ²¹Israel and the Philistines were drawing up their lines facing each other. ²²David left his things with the keeper of supplies,ᶻ ran to the battle lines and asked his brothers how they were. ²³As he was talking with them, Goliath, the Philistine champion from Gath, stepped out from his lines and shouted his usualᵃ defi-

---

ᵃ 4 That is, about 9 1/2 feet or about 2.9 meters　　ᵇ 5 That is, about 125 pounds or about 57 kilograms　　ᶜ 7 That is, about 15 pounds or about 6.9 kilograms　　ᵈ 17 That is, probably about 36 pounds or about 16 kilograms　　ᵉ 18 Or *some token*; or *some pledge of spoils*

David is brought into contact with Saul, and his introduction to Israel begins.

C **16:21** *David became one of his armor-bearers.* May refer to a later time after David's victory over Goliath (see 18:2).
17:1 *Sokoh.* Located about 15 miles west of Bethlehem (see 2Ch 28:18) near the Philistine border. *Azekah.* Located a little over a mile northwest of Sokoh.
17:2 *Valley of Elah.* Located between Azekah and Sokoh.
17:4 *champion.* The ancient Greeks, to whom the Philistines were apparently related, sometimes decided issues of war through chosen champions who met in combat between the armies. Through this economy of warriors the judgment of the gods on the matter at stake was determined (trial by battle ordeal). Israel too may have known this practice (see 2Sa 2:14-16). *Gath.* See 5:8 and note.

C **17:11** *Saul and all the Israelites were … terrified.* Israel's giant warrior (see 9:2; 10:23) quails before the Philistine champion. The fear of Saul and the Israelite army (see vv. 24,32) betrays a loss of faith in the covenant promises of the Lord (see Ex 23:22; Dt 3:22; 20:1-4). Their fear also demonstrates that the Israelite search for security in a human king (apart from trust in the Lord; see notes on 8:5,7) had failed. On the basis of God's covenant promises, Israel was never to fear her enemies but to trust in the Lord (see 2Sa 10:12; Ex 14:13-14; Nu 14:9; Jos 10:8; 2Ch 20:17).
17:12 *Ephrathite.* See note on Ru 1:2.
17:15 *David went back and forth from Saul.* David's position at the court (see 16:21-23) was not permanent, but was performed on an intermittent basis. For the relationship between chs. 16 and 17, see note on v. 55.

ance, and David heard it. ²⁴Whenever the Israelites saw the man, they all fled from him in great fear.

²⁵Now the Israelites had been saying, "Do you see how this man keeps coming out? He comes out to defy Israel. The king will give great wealth to the man who kills him. He will also give him his daughter *b* in marriage and will exempt his family line from taxes *c* in Israel."

²⁶David asked those standing near him, "What will be done for the man who kills this Philistine and removes this disgrace *d* from Israel? Who is this uncircumcised *e* Philistine that he should defy *f* the armies of the living *g* God?"

²⁷They repeated to him what they had been saying and told him, "This is what will be done for the man who kills him."

²⁸When Eliab, David's oldest brother, heard him speaking with the men, he burned with anger *h* at him and asked, "Why have you come down here? And with whom did you leave those few sheep in the wilderness? I know how conceited you are and how wicked your heart is; you came down only to watch the battle."

17:25 *b* 1Sa 18:17
c S 1Sa 8:15
17:26 *d* 1Sa 11:2
e S 1Sa 14:6 *f* S ver 10
g Dt 5:26; S Jos 3:10;
2Ki 18:35
17:28 *h* S Ge 27:41;
Pr 18:19

17:24 *great fear.* See on v. 11.
17:25 *The king will give great wealth.* See 8:14; 22:7. *give him his daughter in marriage.* See 18:17–27; cf. Jos 15:16.
17:26,36 *uncircumcised.* See note on 14:6.
17:26 *Who is this …?* David sees the issues clearly—which sets him apart from Saul and all the other Israelites on that battlefield. Because of the Philistine threat and the cowering of Saul and his army in the face of it, the coming of the kingdom of God into the world through God's ways with Israel

was at stake. David seems to have been aware of this. It marked him as one who was more worthy than Saul—or any other man there—to wear the crown in Israel.
17:28 *he burned with anger.* Eliab's anger may arise from jealousy toward his brother and a sense of guilt for the defeatist attitude of the Israelites. His evaluation of David stands in sharp contrast to that of Saul's attendant (see 16:18). Eliab does not comprehend David's indomitable spirit (see 16:13).

DAVID'S FAMILY TREE

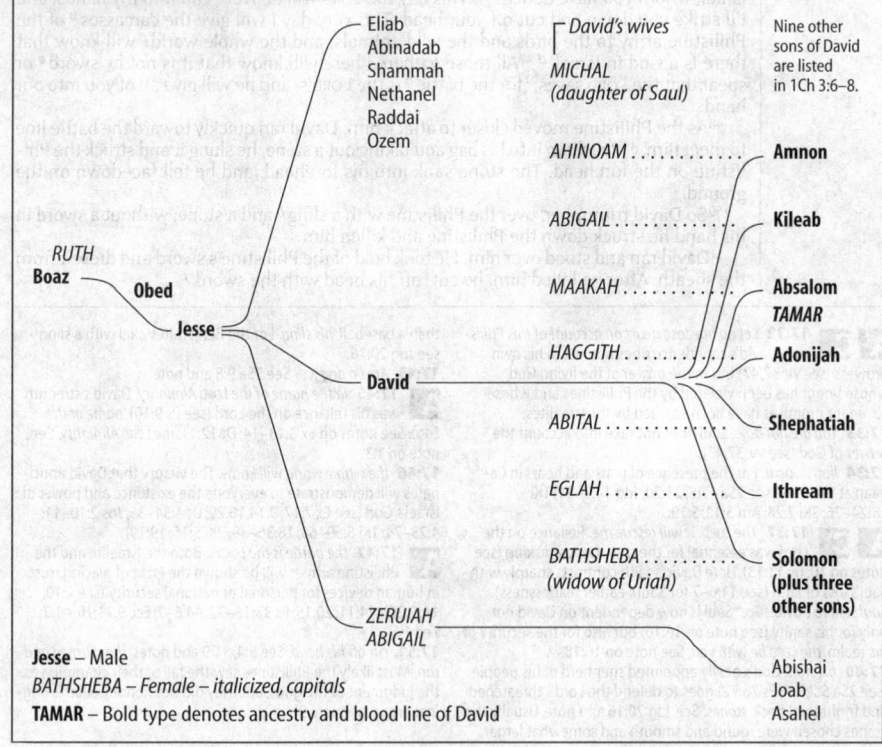

Eliab
Abinadab
Shammah
Nethanel
Raddai
Ozem

David's wives
MICHAL
(daughter of Saul)

AHINOAM .... — **Amnon**

ABIGAIL .... — **Kileab**

MAAKAH .... — **Absalom**
TAMAR

HAGGITH .... — **Adonijah**

ABITAL .... — **Shephatiah**

EGLAH .... — **Ithream**

BATHSHEBA .... — **Solomon**
(widow of Uriah) **(plus three other sons)**

Nine other sons of David are listed in 1Ch 3:6–8.

RUTH
Boaz — **Obed** — **Jesse** — **David**

ZERUIAH
ABIGAIL

Abishai
Joab
Asahel

Jesse – Male
BATHSHEBA – Female – italicized, capitals
TAMAR – Bold type denotes ancestry and blood line of David

17:32 *t* S Dt 20:3;
Ps 18:45; Isa 7:4;
Jer 4:9; 38:4;
Da 11:30
17:33 *j* Nu 13:31
17:34 *k* Job 10:16;
Isa 31:4; Jer 49:19;
Hos 13:8; Am 3:12
17:35 *l* Jdg 14:6
17:36 *m* 1Ch 11:22
17:37 *n* 2Co 1:10
o 2Ti 4:17
p S 1Sa 16:18; S 18:12
17:38 *q* S Ge 41:42
17:41 *r* ver 7
17:42 *s* 1Sa 16:12
t Ps 123:3-4; Pr 16:18
17:43 *u* 1Sa 24:14;
2Sa 3:8; 9:8; 2Ki 8:13
17:44 *v* S Ge 40:19;
Rev 19:17 *w* 2Sa 21:10;
Jer 34:20
17:45 *x* S ver 6
y Dt 20:1; 2Ch 13:12;
14:11; 32:8; Ps 20:7-8;
124:8; Heb 11:32-34
z S ver 10
17:46 *a* S 1Sa 14:12
b S Dt 28:26
c S Jos 4:24; S Isa 11:9
d 1Ki 18:36; 2Ki 5:8;
19:19; Isa 37:20
17:47 *e* Hos 1:7
f 1Sa 14:6; 2Ch 14:11;
Jer 39:18 *g* S Ex 14:14;
S Nu 21:14; S 1Sa 2:9;
2Ch 20:15; Ps 44:6-7
17:50 *h* 1Sa 25:29
17:51 *i* Heb 11:34
j 1Sa 21:9; 22:10

29"Now what have I done?" said David. "Can't I even speak?" 30He then turned away to someone else and brought up the same matter, and the men answered him as before. 31What David said was overheard and reported to Saul, and Saul sent for him.

32David said to Saul, "Let no one lose heart *i* on account of this Philistine; your servant will go and fight him."

33Saul replied, *j* "You are not able to go out against this Philistine and fight him; you are little more than a boy, and he has been a warrior from his youth."

34But David said to Saul, "Your servant has been keeping his father's sheep. When a lion *k* or a bear came and carried off a sheep from the flock, 35I went after it, struck it and rescued the sheep from its mouth. When it turned on me, I seized *l* it by its hair, struck it and killed it. 36Your servant has killed both the lion *m* and the bear; this uncircumcised Philistine will be like one of them, because he has defied the armies of the living God. 37The LORD who rescued *n* me from the paw of the lion *o* and the paw of the bear will rescue me from the hand of this Philistine."

Saul said to David, "Go, and the LORD be with *p* you."

38Then Saul dressed David in his own *q* tunic. He put a coat of armor on him and a bronze helmet on his head. 39David fastened on his sword over the tunic and tried walking around, because he was not used to them.

"I cannot go in these," he said to Saul, "because I am not used to them." So he took them off. 40Then he took his staff in his hand, chose five smooth stones from the stream, put them in the pouch of his shepherd's bag and, with his sling in his hand, approached the Philistine.

41Meanwhile, the Philistine, with his shield bearer *r* in front of him, kept coming closer to David. 42He looked David over and saw that he was little more than a boy, glowing with health and handsome, *s* and he despised *t* him. 43He said to David, "Am I a dog, *u* that you come at me with sticks?" And the Philistine cursed David by his gods. 44"Come here," he said, "and I'll give your flesh to the birds *v* and the wild animals! *w*"

45David said to the Philistine, "You come against me with sword and spear and javelin, *x* but I come against me in the name *y* of the LORD Almighty, the God of the armies of Israel, whom you have defied. *z* 46This day the LORD will deliver *a* you into my hands, and I'll strike you down and cut off your head. This very day I will give the carcasses *b* of the Philistine army to the birds and the wild animals, and the whole world *c* will know that there is a God in Israel. *d* 47All those gathered here will know that it is not by sword *e* or spear that the LORD saves; *f* for the battle *g* is the LORD's, and he will give all of you into our hands."

48As the Philistine moved closer to attack him, David ran quickly toward the battle line to meet him. 49Reaching into his bag and taking out a stone, he slung it and struck the Philistine on the forehead. The stone sank into his forehead, and he fell facedown on the ground.

50So David triumphed over the Philistine with a sling *h* and a stone; without a sword in his hand he struck down the Philistine and killed him.

51David ran and stood over him. He took hold of the Philistine's sword and drew it from the sheath. After he killed him, he cut *i* off his head with the sword. *j*

17:32 *Let no one lose heart on account of this Philistine.* David's confidence does not rest in his own prowess (see vv. 37,47) but in the power of the living God, whose honor has been violated by the Philistines and whose covenant promises have been scorned by the Israelites.

17:33 *You are not able.* Saul does not take into account the power of God (see vv. 37,47).

17:34 *lion . . . bear.* For the presence of lions and bears in Canaan at that time see 2Sa 17:8; 23:20; Jdg 14:5–11; 1Ki 13:24–26; 2Ki 2:24; Am 3:12; 5:19.

17:37 *The LORD . . . will rescue me.* Reliance on the Lord was essential for the true theocratic king (see notes on 10:18; 11:13). Here David's faith contrasts sharply with Saul's loss of faith (see 11:6–7 for Saul's earlier fearlessness). *Saul said to David, "Go."* Saul was now dependent on David not only for his sanity (see note on 16:16) but also for the security of his realm. *the LORD be with you.* See note on 16:18.

17:40 *his staff.* God's newly appointed shepherd of his people (see 2Sa 5:2; 7:7; Ps 78:72) goes to defend the Lord's threatened and frightened flock. *stones.* See Jdg 20:16 and note. Usually the stones chosen were round and smooth and somewhat larger

than a baseball. *his sling.* For the Benjamites' skill with a sling see Jdg 20:16.

17:43 *Am I a dog . . . ?* See 2Sa 9:8 and note.

17:45 *in the name of the LORD Almighty.* David's strength was his reliance on the Lord (see Ps 9:10). *name of the LORD.* See notes on Ex 3:13–14; Dt 12:11. *the LORD Almighty.* See note on 1:3.

17:46 *the whole world will know.* The victory that David anticipates will demonstrate to everyone the existence and power of Israel's God (see Ex 7:17; 9:14,16,29; Dt 4:34–35; Jos 2:10–11; 4:23–24; 1Ki 8:59–60; 18:36–39; 2Ki 5:15; 19:19).

17:47 *the battle is the LORD's.* Both the Israelite and the Philistine armies will be shown the error of placing trust in human devices for personal or national security (see 2:10; 14:6; 2Ch 14:11; 20:15; Ps 33:16–22; 44:6–7; Ecc 9:11; Hos 1:7; Zec 4:6).

17:51 *cut off his head.* See 5:4; 31:9 and notes. *they turned and ran.* Most likely the Philistines saw the fall of their champion as the judgment of the gods, but they did not honor Goliath's original proposal (see v. 9).

When the Philistines saw that their hero was dead, they turned and ran. ⁵²Then the men of Israel and Judah surged forward with a shout and pursued the Philistines to the entrance of Gath[a] and to the gates of Ekron.[k] Their dead were strewn along the Shaaraim[l] road to Gath and Ekron. ⁵³When the Israelites returned from chasing the Philistines, they plundered their camp.

⁵⁴David took the Philistine's head and brought it to Jerusalem; he put the Philistine's weapons in his own tent.

⁵⁵As Saul watched David[m] going out to meet the Philistine, he said to Abner, commander of the army, "Abner,[n] whose son is that young man?"

Abner replied, "As surely as you live, Your Majesty, I don't know."

⁵⁶The king said, "Find out whose son this young man is."

⁵⁷As soon as David returned from killing the Philistine, Abner took him and brought him before Saul, with David still holding the Philistine's head.

⁵⁸"Whose son are you, young man?" Saul asked him.

David said, "I am the son of your servant Jesse[o] of Bethlehem."

SAUL'S GROWING FEAR OF DAVID

18 After David had finished talking with Saul, Jonathan[p] became one in spirit with David, and he loved[q] him as himself.[r] ²From that day Saul kept David with him and did not let him return home to his family. ³And Jonathan made a covenant[s] with David because he loved him as himself. ⁴Jonathan took off the robe[t] he was wearing and gave it to David, along with his tunic, and even his sword, his bow and his belt.[u]

⁵Whatever mission Saul sent him on, David was so successful[v] that Saul gave him a high rank in the army.[w] This pleased all the troops, and Saul's officers as well.

⁶When the men were returning home after David had killed the Philistine, the women came out from all the towns of Israel to meet King Saul with singing and dancing,[x] with joyful songs and with timbrels[y] and lyres. ⁷As they danced, they sang:[z]

> "Saul has slain his thousands,
> and David his tens[a] of thousands."

⁸Saul was very angry; this refrain displeased him greatly. "They have credited David with tens of thousands," he thought, "but me with only thousands. What more can he get but the kingdom?[b]" ⁹And from that time on Saul kept a close[c] eye on David.

¹⁰The next day an evil[b] spirit[d] from God came forcefully on David. He was prophesying in his house, while David was playing the lyre,[e] as he usually[f] did. Saul had a spear[g] in

---

a 52 Some Septuagint manuscripts; Hebrew *of a valley*   b 10 Or *harmful*

17:52 ᵏ Jos 15:11
ˡ S Jos 15:36
17:55 ᵐ 1Sa 16:21
ⁿ 1Sa 26:5
17:58 ᵒ S Ru 4:17
18:1 ᵖ 1Sa 19:1;
20:16; 31:2; 2Sa 4:4
q 2Sa 1:26
ʳ S Ge 44:30
18:3 ˢ 1Sa 20:8,16,
17,42; 22:8; 23:18;
24:21; 2Sa 21:7
18:4 ᵗ S Ge 41:42
ᵘ 2Sa 18:11
18:5 ᵛ ver 30
ʷ 2Sa 5:2
18:6 ˣ S Ex 15:20;
2Sa 1:20 ʸ Ps 68:25
18:7 ᶻ Ex 15:21
ᵃ 1Sa 21:11; 29:5;
2Sa 18:3
18:8 ᵇ S 1Sa 13:14;
1Sa 15:8
18:9 ᶜ 1Sa 19:1
18:10 ᵈ S Jdg 9:23;
S 1Sa 16:14
ᵉ S 1Sa 10:5
ᶠ 1Sa 16:21; 19:7
ᵍ S 1Sa 17:6

17:54 *brought it to Jerusalem.* Jerusalem had not at this time been conquered by the Israelites. David may have kept Goliath's head as a trophy of victory and brought the skull with him to Jerusalem when he took that city and made it his capital (see 2Sa 5:6–9). Or, having grown up almost under the shadow of the Jebusite city, he may have displayed Goliath's head to its defiant inhabitants as a warning of what the God of Israel was able to do and eventually would do. *put the Philistine's weapons in his own tent.* As his personal spoils of the battle. Since Goliath's sword is later in the custody of the priest at Nob (see 21:9), David must have dedicated it to the Lord, the true victor in the fight (cf. 31:10).
17:55 *whose son is that young man?* The seeming contradiction between vv. 55–58 and 16:16–23 may be resolved by noting that prior to this time David was not a permanent resident at Saul's court (see v. 15; 18:2; see also note on 16:21), so that Saul's knowledge of David and his family may have been minimal. Further, Saul may have been so incredulous at David's courage that he was wondering whether his family background and social standing might explain his extraordinary conduct.
18:1 It appears that David spoke with Saul at length, and he may have explained his actions as an expression of his faith in the Lord, thus attracting the love and loyalty of Jonathan (see v. 3; 14:6; 19:5). Their friendship endured even when it became clear that David was to replace him as the successor to his father's throne.
18:2 *Saul kept David with him.* See note on 17:15.
18:3 *Jonathan made a covenant with David.* The initiative comes from Jonathan. The terms of the agreement are not here

specified (see further 19:1; 20:8,12–16,41–42; 23:18) but would appear to involve a pledge of mutual loyalty and friendship. At the very least, Jonathan accepts David as his equal.
18:4 *took off the robe ... and gave it to David.* Jonathan ratifies the covenant in an act that symbolizes giving himself to David. His act may even signify his recognition that David was to assume his place as successor to Saul (see 20:14–15,31; 23:17)—a possibility that seems the more likely in that he also gave David "even his sword, his bow and his belt" (cf. 13:22).
18:5 *Whatever mission Saul sent him on.* During the rest of the campaign.
18:6 *women came out ... with timbrels.* See Ex 15:20 and note.
18:7 *David his tens of thousands.* See 21:11; 29:5. In accordance with the normal conventions of Hebrew poetry, this was the women's way of saying "Saul and David have slain thousands" (10,000 was normally used as the parallel of 1,000—see Dt 32:30; Ps 91:7 and note; Da 7:10; Mic 6:7; also in Canaanite poetry found at Ugarit). It is a measure of Saul's insecurity and jealousy that he read their intentions incorrectly and took offense (see v. 8). His resentment may have been initially triggered by the mention of David's name alongside his own. See note on 21:11 for how the Philistines interpreted the song.
18:10 *evil spirit from God.* See note on 16:14. *prophesying.* The Hebrew for this word is sometimes used to indicate uncontrolled ecstatic behavior (see note on 1Ki 18:29) and is best understood in that sense in this context (see also note on 10:5). *as he usually did.* See 16:23.

18:11 ʰver 25;
1Sa 20:7,33
ⁱ1Sa 19:10 / Ps 132:1
18:12 ᵏver 29
ⁱ1Sa 16:13 ᵐJos 1:5;
1Sa 17:37; 20:13;
1Ch 22:11
ⁿS Jdg 16:20
18:13 ᵒNu 27:17
ᵖ2Sa 5:2
18:14 ᵠS Ge 39:3
ʳS Ge 39:2;
S Nu 14:43; 2Sa 7:9
18:16 ˢ2Sa 5:2
18:17 ᵗ1Sa 17:25
ᵘS Ge 29:26
ᵛS Nu 21:14 ʷver 25;
1Sa 20:33
18:18 ˣS Ge 3:11;
S 1Sa 9:21 ʸver 23
18:19 ᶻ2Sa 21:8
ᵃS Jdg 7:22
18:20 ᵇver 28;
S Ge 29:26 ᶜver 29
18:21 ᵈS Ex 10:7;
S Dt 7:16
18:23 ᵉver 18
18:25 ᶠS Ge 34:12
ᵍPs 8:2; 44:16;
Jer 20:10 ʰS ver 11,
S 17; ver 17
18:27 ⁱ2Sa 3:14;
6:16
18:28 ʲS ver 20
18:29 ᵏver 12
18:30 ⁱver 5
19:1 ᵐS 1Sa 18:1
ⁿ1Sa 18:9
19:2 ᵒ1Sa 20:5,19
19:3 ᵖ1Sa 20:12
19:4 ᵠ1Sa 20:32;
22:14; Pr 31:8,9;
Jer 18:20

his hand ¹¹and he hurled it, saying to himself, ʰ "I'll pin David to the wall." But David eluded ⁱ him twice.ʲ

¹²Saul was afraid ᵏ of David, because the Lᴏʀᴅ ⁱ was with ᵐ David but had departed from ⁿ Saul. ¹³So he sent David away from him and gave him command over a thousand men, and David led ᵒ the troops in their campaigns. ᵖ ¹⁴In everything he did he had great success, ᵠ because the Lᴏʀᴅ was with ʳ him. ¹⁵When Saul saw how successful he was, he was afraid of him. ¹⁶But all Israel and Judah loved David, because he led them in their campaigns. ˢ

¹⁷Saul said to David, "Here is my older daughter ᵗ Merab. I will give her to you in marriage; ᵘ only serve me bravely and fight the battles ᵛ of the Lᴏʀᴅ." For Saul said to himself, ʷ "I will not raise a hand against him. Let the Philistines do that!"

¹⁸But David said to Saul, "Who am I, ˣ and what is my family or my clan in Israel, that I should become the king's son-in-law?ʸ ¹⁹Soᵃ when the time came for Merab, ᶻ Saul's daughter, to be given to David, she was given in marriage to Adriel of Meholah. ᵃ

²⁰Now Saul's daughter Michal ᵇ was in love with David, and when they told Saul about it, he was pleased. ᶜ ²¹"I will give her to him," he thought, "so that she may be a snare ᵈ to him and so that the hand of the Philistines may be against him." So Saul said to David, "Now you have a second opportunity to become my son-in-law."

²²Then Saul ordered his attendants: "Speak to David privately and say, 'Look, the king likes you, and his attendants all love you; now become his son-in-law.' "

²³They repeated these words to David. But David said, "Do you think it is a small matter to become the king's son-in-law?ᵉ I'm only a poor man and little known."

²⁴When Saul's servants told him what David had said, ²⁵Saul replied, "Say to David, 'The king wants no other price ᶠ for the bride than a hundred Philistine foreskins, to take revengeᵍ on his enemies.' " Saul's plan ʰ was to have David fall by the hands of the Philistines.

²⁶When the attendants told David these things, he was pleased to become the king's son-in-law. So before the allotted time elapsed, ²⁷David took his men with him and went out and killed two hundred Philistines and brought back their foreskins. They counted out the full number to the king so that David might become the king's son-in-law. Then Saul gave him his daughter Michal ⁱ in marriage.

²⁸When Saul realized that the Lᴏʀᴅ was with David and that his daughter Michalʲ loved David, ²⁹Saul became still more afraid ᵏ of him, and he remained his enemy the rest of his days.

³⁰The Philistine commanders continued to go out to battle, and as often as they did, David met with more success ⁱ than the rest of Saul's officers, and his name became well known.

SAUL TRIES TO KILL DAVID

19 Saul told his son Jonathan ᵐ and all the attendants to kill ⁿ David. But Jonathan had taken a great liking to David ²and warned him, "My father Saul is looking for a chance to kill you. Be on your guard tomorrow morning; go into hidingᵒ and stay there. ³I will go out and stand with my father in the field where you are. I'll speakᵖ to him about you and will tell you what I find out."

⁴Jonathan spokeᵠ well of David to Saul his father and said to him, "Let not the king do

---

ᵃ 19 Or However,

18:12 *the Lᴏʀᴅ was with David.* See 16:18 and note. *but had departed from Saul.* See 16:14 and note.
18:13 *he sent David away.* His apparent motive was the hope that David would be killed in battle (see vv. 17,21,25; 19:1), but the result was greater acclaim for David (see vv. 14,16,30).
18:14 *the Lᴏʀᴅ was with him.* See note on 16:18.
18:17 *Here is my older daughter.* David was entitled to have Saul's daughter as his wife because of his victory over Goliath (see 17:25). This promise had not been kept and is now made conditional on further military service, in which Saul hoped David would be killed. *battles of the Lᴏʀᴅ.* See 25:28.
18:20 *Michal was in love with David.* See v. 28 and note.
18:21 *second opportunity to become my son-in-law.* For the first, see 17:25.
18:25 *no other price.* Normally a bride-price was paid by the bridegroom to the father of the bride (see Ge 34:12; Ex 22:16) as compensation for the loss of his daughter and insurance for her support if widowed. Saul requires David instead to pass a test

appropriate for a great warrior, hoping that he will "fall" (see vv. 17,21).

18:28 *the Lᴏʀᴅ was with David.* See note on 16:18. *Michal loved David.* God's favor on David is revealed not only in his military accomplishments but also in Michal's love for him—now added to that of Jonathan. Everything Saul seeks to use against David turns to David's advantage.

18:29 *Saul became still more afraid of him.* Saul's perception that God's hand was on David did not lead him to repentance and acceptance of his own lot (see 15:26) but to greater fear and jealousy toward David.
19:1 *Saul told his son . . . to kill David.* Saul now abandons his indirect attempts on David's life (see 18:13,17,21,25) and adopts a more direct approach, leading to David's departure from the court and from service to Saul (see vv. 12,18; 20:42).
19:4 *Jonathan spoke well of David.* Jonathan does not let his own personal ambition distort his perception of David's true theocratic spirit (see v. 5 and notes on 14:6; 17:11; 18:1).

wrong[r] to his servant David; he has not wronged you, and what he has done has benefited you greatly. [5]He took his life[s] in his hands when he killed the Philistine. The LORD won a great victory[t] for all Israel, and you saw it and were glad. Why then would you do wrong to an innocent[u] man like David by killing him for no reason?"

[6]Saul listened to Jonathan and took this oath: "As surely as the LORD lives, David will not be put to death."

[7]So Jonathan called David and told him the whole conversation. He brought him to Saul, and David was with Saul as before.[v]

[8]Once more war broke out, and David went out and fought the Philistines. He struck them with such force that they fled before him.

[9]But an evil[a] spirit[w] from the LORD came on Saul as he was sitting in his house with his spear in his hand. While David was playing the lyre,[x] [10]Saul tried to pin him to the wall with his spear, but David eluded[y] him as Saul drove the spear into the wall. That night David made good his escape.

[11]Saul sent men to David's house to watch[z] it and to kill him in the morning.[a] But Michal, David's wife, warned him, "If you don't run for your life tonight, tomorrow you'll be killed." [12]So Michal let David down through a window,[b] and he fled and escaped. [13]Then Michal took an idol[c] and laid it on the bed, covering it with a garment and putting some goats' hair at the head.

[14]When Saul sent the men to capture David, Michal said,[d] "He is ill."

[15]Then Saul sent the men back to see David and told them, "Bring him up to me in his bed so that I may kill him." [16]But when the men entered, there was the idol in the bed, and at the head was some goats' hair.

[17]Saul said to Michal, "Why did you deceive me like this and send my enemy away so that he escaped?"

Michal told him, "He said to me, 'Let me get away. Why should I kill you?' "

[18]When David had fled and made his escape, he went to Samuel at Ramah[e] and told him all that Saul had done to him. Then he and Samuel went to Naioth and stayed there. [19]Word came to Saul: "David is in Naioth at Ramah"; [20]so he sent men to capture him. But when they saw a group of prophets[f] prophesying, with Samuel standing there as their leader, the Spirit of God came on[g] Saul's men, and they also prophesied.[h] [21]Saul was told about it, and he sent more men, and they prophesied too. Saul sent men a third time, and they also prophesied. [22]Finally, he himself left for Ramah and went to the great cistern at Seku. And he asked, "Where are Samuel and David?"

"Over in Naioth at Ramah," they said.

[23]So Saul went to Naioth at Ramah. But the Spirit of God came even on him, and he walked along prophesying[i] until he came to Naioth. [24]He stripped[j] off his garments, and he too prophesied in Samuel's[k] presence. He lay naked all that day and all that night. This is why people say, "Is Saul also among the prophets?"[l]

DAVID AND JONATHAN

20 Then David fled from Naioth at Ramah and went to Jonathan and asked, "What have I done? What is my crime? How have I wronged[m] your father, that he is trying to take my life?"[n]

[2]"Never!" Jonathan replied. "You are not going to die! Look, my father doesn't do anything, great or small, without letting me know. Why would he hide this from me? It isn't so!"

[3]But David took an oath[o] and said, "Your father knows very well that I have found favor in your eyes, and he has said to himself, 'Jonathan must not know this or he will be

---

[a] 9 Or *harmful*

19:4 [r] 1Sa 25:21; Pr 17:13
19:5 [s] Jdg 9:17; S 12:3 [t] 1Sa 11:13 [u] S Ge 31:36; Dt 19:10-13
19:7 [v] S 1Sa 18:2,13
19:9 [w] S Jdg 9:23 [x] S 1Sa 10:5
19:10 [y] 1Sa 18:11
19:11 [z] Ps 59 Title [a] Jdg 16:2
19:12 [b] S Jos 2:15; Ac 9:25; 2Co 11:33
19:13 [c] S Ge 31:19
19:14 [d] S Ex 1:19; Jos 2:4
19:18 [e] S 1Sa 7:17
19:20 [f] S Nu 11:29 [g] S Nu 11:25 [h] S 1Sa 10:5
19:23 [i] 1Sa 10:13
19:24 [j] 2Sa 6:20; Isa 20:2 [k] 1Sa 15:35 [l] S 1Sa 10:11
20:1 [m] 1Sa 24:9 [n] 1Sa 22:23; 23:15; 24:11; 25:29; Ps 40:14; 54:3; 63:9; 70:2
20:3 [o] Dt 6:13

19:5 *The LORD won a great victory.* See notes on 10:18; 12:11; 14:23.

19:6 *Saul listened to Jonathan and took this oath.* See 14:24,44 for previous oaths that Saul did not keep (see note on 14:39).

19:9 *evil spirit from the LORD.* See note on 16:14; cf. 18:10–11.

19:10 *with his spear.* See 18:10–11; 20:33.

19:12 *through a window.* For similar escapes, see Jos 2:15; Ac 9:25.

19:18 *Ramah.* Samuel's home (see 7:17 and note on 1:1). *Naioth.* Means "habitations" or "dwellings." The term appears to designate a complex of houses in a certain section of Ramah where a company of prophets resided (see vv. 19–20,22–23).

19:20 *group of prophets.* See 10:5 and note. *prophesying.* See

notes on 10:5; 18:10.

19:24 *He lay naked all that day and all that night.* Saul was so overwhelmed by the power of the Spirit of God that he was prevented from carrying out his intention to take David's life. His frustrated attempts to kill David—his own inability to harm David and the thwarting of his plans by Jonathan's loyalty, by Michal's deception and by David's own cleverness—all reach their climax here. *Is Saul also among the prophets?* This second occasion reinforced the first (see 10:11 and note). Its repetition underscores how alien Saul's spirit was from that of these zealous servants of the Lord.

20:1 *Naioth at Ramah.* See note on 19:18.

20:5 ᵖ S Nu 10:10
ᑫ S 1Sa 19:2
20:6 ʳ ver 28
ˢ 1Sa 17:58; ᵗ S 1Sa 1:3
20:7 ᵘ 1Sa 10:27;
25:17; ᵛ S 1Sa 18:11
20:8 ʷ S 1Sa 18:3
ˣ 2Sa 14:32
20:12 ʸ 1Sa 19:3
20:13 ᶻ S Ru 1:17
ᵃ S 1Sa 16:18; S 18:12
20:14 ᵇ S Ge 40:14
20:15 ᶜ 1Sa 24:21;
2Sa 9:7

grieved.' Yet as surely as the Lᴏʀᴅ lives and as you live, there is only a step between me and death."

⁴Jonathan said to David, "Whatever you want me to do, I'll do for you."

⁵So David said, "Look, tomorrow is the New Moon feast,ᵖ and I am supposed to dine with the king; but let me go and hideᑫ in the field until the evening of the day after tomorrow. ⁶If your father misses me at all, tell him, 'David earnestly asked my permissionʳ to hurry to Bethlehem,ˢ his hometown, because an annualᵗ sacrifice is being made there for his whole clan.' ⁷If he says, 'Very well,' then your servant is safe. But if he loses his temper,ᵘ you can be sure that he is determinedᵛ to harm me. ⁸As for you, show kindness to your servant, for you have brought him into a covenantʷ with you before the Lᴏʀᴅ. If I am guilty, then killˣ me yourself! Why hand me over to your father?"

⁹"Never!" Jonathan said. "If I had the least inkling that my father was determined to harm you, wouldn't I tell you?"

¹⁰David asked, "Who will tell me if your father answers you harshly?"

¹¹"Come," Jonathan said, "let's go out into the field." So they went there together.

¹²Then Jonathan said to David, "I swear by the Lᴏʀᴅ, the God of Israel, that I will surely soundʸ out my father by this time the day after tomorrow! If he is favorably disposed toward you, will I not send you word and let you know? ¹³But if my father intends to harm you, may the Lᴏʀᴅ deal with Jonathan, be it ever so severely,ᶻ if I do not let you know and send you away in peace. May the Lᴏʀᴅ be withᵃ you as he has been with my father. ¹⁴But show me unfailing kindnessᵇ like the Lᴏʀᴅ's kindness as long as I live, so that I may not be killed, ¹⁵and do not ever cut off your kindness from my familyᶜ—not even when the Lᴏʀᴅ has cut off every one of David's enemies from the face of the earth."

20:3 *as surely as the Lᴏʀᴅ lives.* See note on 14:39,45.

20:5 *New Moon feast.* Each month of the year was consecrated to the Lord by bringing special sacrifices (Nu 28:11–15) and blowing trumpets (Nu 10:10; Ps 81:3). This observance also involved cessation from normal work, especially at the beginning of the seventh month (Lev 23:24–25; Nu 29:1–6; 2Ki 4:23; Isa 1:13; Am 8:5).

20:6 *annual sacrifice.* David's statement indicates that it was customary for families to observe the New Moon feast together once in the year. There is no other reference in the OT to this practice.

20:8 *covenant.* See note on 18:3.

20:11 *let's go out into the field.* Jonathan acted to save David. Cain had said the same to Abel, but in order to kill him (Ge 4:8; but see TNIV text note there).

20:13 *may the Lᴏʀᴅ deal with Jonathan, be it ever so severely.* A common curse formula (see note on 3:17). *May the Lᴏʀᴅ be with you as he has been with my father.* A clear indication that Jonathan expects David to become king.

20:14 *that I may not be killed.* It was quite common in the ancient world for the first ruler of a new dynasty to secure his position by murdering all potential claimants to the throne from the preceding dynasty (see 1Ki 15:29; 16:11; 2Ki 10:7; 11:1).

20:15 *your kindness from my family.* This request was based on the covenant previously concluded between Jonathan and David (see note on 18:3) and was subsequently honored in David's dealings with Jonathan's son Mephibosheth (see 2Sa 9:3,7; 21:7).

DAVID THE FUGITIVE

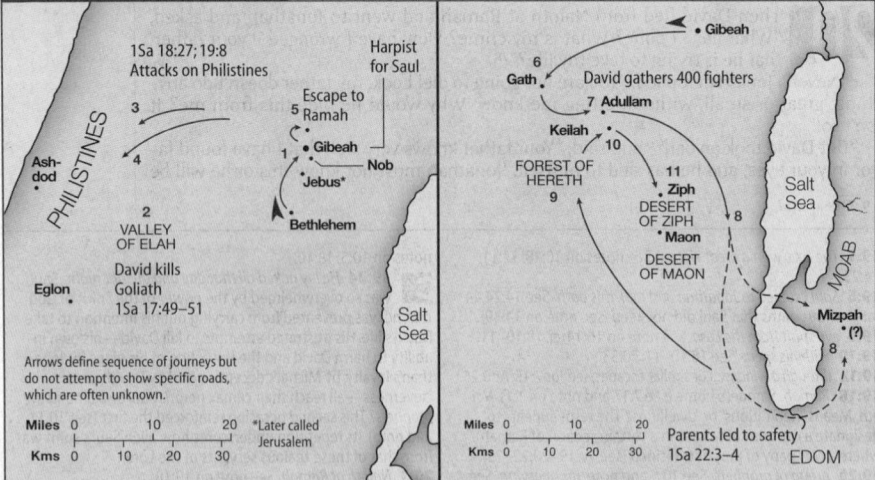

¹⁶So Jonathan ^d made a covenant ^e with the house of David, saying, "May the LORD call David's enemies to account. ^f" ¹⁷And Jonathan had David reaffirm his oath ^g out of love for him, because he loved him as he loved himself.

¹⁸Then Jonathan said to David, "Tomorrow is the New Moon feast. You will be missed, because your seat will be empty. ^h ¹⁹The day after tomorrow, toward evening, go to the place where you hid ⁱ when this trouble began, and wait by the stone Ezel. ²⁰I will shoot three arrows ^j to the side of it, as though I were shooting at a target. ²¹Then I will send a boy and say, 'Go, find the arrows.' If I say to him, 'Look, the arrows are on this side of you; bring them here,' then come, because, as surely as the LORD lives, you are safe; there is no danger. ²²But if I say to the boy, 'Look, the arrows are beyond ^k you,' then you must go, because the LORD has sent you away. ²³And about the matter you and I discussed—remember, the LORD is witness ^l between you and me forever."

²⁴So David hid in the field, and when the New Moon feast ^m came, the king sat down to eat. ²⁵He sat in his customary place by the wall, opposite Jonathan, ^a and Abner sat next to Saul, but David's place was empty. ⁿ ²⁶Saul said nothing that day, for he thought, "Something must have happened to David to make him ceremonially unclean—surely he is unclean. ^o" ²⁷But the next day, the second day of the month, David's place was empty again. Then Saul said to his son Jonathan, "Why hasn't the son of Jesse come to the meal, either yesterday or today?"

²⁸Jonathan answered, "David earnestly asked me for permission ^p to go to Bethlehem. ²⁹He said, 'Let me go, because our family is observing a sacrifice ^q in the town and my brother has ordered me to be there. If I have found favor in your eyes, let me get away to see my brothers.' That is why he has not come to the king's table."

³⁰Saul's anger flared up at Jonathan and he said to him, "You son of a perverse and rebellious woman! Don't I know that you have sided with the son of Jesse to your own shame and to the shame of the mother who bore you? ³¹As long as the son of Jesse lives on this earth, neither you nor your kingdom ^r will be established. Now send someone to bring him to me, for he must die!"

³²"Why ^s should he be put to death? What ^t has he done?" Jonathan asked his father. ³³But Saul hurled his spear at him to kill him. Then Jonathan knew that his father intended ^u to kill David.

³⁴Jonathan got up from the table in fierce anger; on that second day of the feast he did not eat, because he was grieved at his father's shameful treatment of David.

³⁵In the morning Jonathan went out to the field for his meeting with David. He had a small boy with him, ³⁶and he said to the boy, "Run and find the arrows I shoot." As the boy ran, he shot an arrow beyond him. ³⁷When the boy came to the place where Jonathan's arrow had fallen, Jonathan called out after him, "Isn't the arrow beyond ^v you?" ³⁸Then he shouted, "Hurry! Go quickly! Don't stop!" The boy picked up the arrow and returned to his master. ³⁹(The boy knew nothing about all this; only Jonathan and David knew.) ⁴⁰Then Jonathan gave his weapons to the boy and said, "Go, carry them back to town."

⁴¹After the boy had gone, David got up from the south side of the stone and bowed down before Jonathan three times, with his face to the ground. ^w Then they kissed each other and wept together—but David wept the most.

⁴²Jonathan said to David, "Go in peace, ^x for we have sworn friendship ^y with each other in the name of the LORD, ^z saying, 'The LORD is witness ^a between you and me, and be-

20:16 ^d 1Sa 18:1
^e S 1Sa 18:3
^f S Jos 22:23
20:17 ^g S Jos 9:18; S 1Sa 18:3
20:18 ^h ver 25
20:19 ⁱ S 1Sa 19:2
20:20 ^j 2Ki 13:15
20:22 ^k ver 37
20:23 ^l S Ge 31:50
20:24 ^m S Nu 10:10
20:25 ⁿ ver 18
20:26 ^o Lev 7:20-21
20:28 ^p ver 6
20:29 ^q S Ge 8:20
20:31 ^r 1Sa 23:17; 24:20
20:32 ^s S 1Sa 19:4; Mt 27:23 ^t S Ge 31:36
20:33 ^u S 1Sa 18:11, 17
20:37 ^v ver 22
20:41 ^w S Ge 33:3; Ru 2:10; 1Sa 24:8; 25:23; 2Sa 1:2
20:42 ^x S 1Sa 1:17; S Ac 15:33
^y S Ge 40:14; 2Sa 1:26; Pr 18:24
^z Isa 48:1
^a S Ge 31:50; S 1Sa 18:3

---

^a 25 Septuagint; Hebrew *wall. Jonathan arose*

20:16 *May the LORD call David's enemies to account.* Jonathan aligns himself completely with David, calling for destruction of his enemies, even if that should include his father, Saul.
20:17 *reaffirm his oath.* See vv. 14–15,42; 18:3. *he loved him as he loved himself.* See 18:3; 2Sa 1:26.
20:18 *New Moon feast.* See note on v. 5.
20:19 *the place where you hid.* Perhaps the place referred to in 19:2.
20:21 *as surely as the LORD lives.* See note on 14:39,45.
20:23 *the matter you and I discussed.* See vv. 14–17. *the LORD is witness.* Invoking God to act as witness and judge between them ensures that their agreement will be kept.
20:25 *Abner.* Saul's cousin and the commander of his army (see 14:50).

20:26 *ceremonially unclean.* See note on 16:5; cf. Lev 7:19–21; 15:16; Dt 23:10.
20:27,30–31 *son of Jesse.* A contemptuous way of referring to David (see 22:7–9,13; 25:10; cf. 2Sa 16:10; Isa 7:4).
20:30 *son of a perverse and rebellious woman.* The Hebrew idiom intends to characterize Jonathan, not his mother.
20:31 *neither you nor your kingdom will be established.* Saul is now convinced that David will succeed him if David is not killed (see notes on 18:13,17,29; 19:1), and he is incapable of understanding Jonathan's lack of concern for his own succession to the throne.
20:33 *hurled his spear.* See 18:11; 19:10.
20:41 *bowed … three times.* A sign of submission and respect (see Ge 33:3 and note; 42:6).
20:42 *sworn friendship.* See vv. 14–15,23; 18:3. *the town.* Gibeah (see 10:26).

20:42 *b* 2Sa 9:1
21:1 *c* 1Sa 22:9,19;
Ne 11:32; Isa 10:32
d 1Sa 16:4
21:4 *e* Lev 24:8-9
f Mt 12:4 *S* Ex 19:15;
S Lev 15:18
21:5 *h* Dt 23:9-11;
Jos 3:5; 2Sa 11:11
i 1Th 4:4
21:6 *j* S Ex 25:30;
1Sa 22:10; Mt 12:3-4;
Mk 2:25-28; Lk 6:1-5
21:7 *k* 1Sa 22:9,22
l 1Sa 14:47; Ps 52
Title
21:9 *m* S 1Sa 17:51
n S 1Sa 17:4 *o* 1Sa 17:2
21:10 *p* 1Sa 25:13;
27:2
21:11 *q* S 1Sa 18:7
21:13 *r* Ps 34 Title

tween your descendants and my descendants forever. *b* " " *Then David left, and Jonathan went back to the town.

DAVID AT NOB

21 *David went to Nob, *c* to Ahimelek the priest. Ahimelek trembled *d* when he met him, and asked, "Why are you alone? Why is no one with you?" ²David answered Ahimelek the priest, "The king sent me on a mission and said to me, 'No one is to know anything about the mission I am sending you on.' As for my men, I have told them to meet me at a certain place. ³Now then, what do you have on hand? Give me five loaves of bread, or whatever you can find."

⁴But the priest answered David, "I don't have any ordinary bread *e* on hand; however, there is some consecrated *f* bread here—provided the men have kept *g* themselves from women."

⁵David replied, "Indeed women have been kept from us, as usual *h* whenever *a* I set out. The men's bodies are holy *i* even on missions that are not holy. How much more so today!" ⁶So the priest gave him the consecrated bread, *j* since there was no bread there except the bread of the Presence that had been removed from before the LORD and replaced by hot bread on the day it was taken away.

⁷Now one of Saul's servants was there that day, detained before the LORD; he was Doeg *k* the Edomite, *l* Saul's chief shepherd.

⁸David asked Ahimelek, "Don't you have a spear or a sword here? I haven't brought my sword or any other weapon, because the king's mission was urgent."

⁹The priest replied, "The sword *m* of Goliath *n* the Philistine, whom you killed in the Valley of Elah, *o* is here; it is wrapped in a cloth behind the ephod. If you want it, take it; there is no sword here but that one."

David said, "There is none like it; give it to me."

DAVID AT GATH

¹⁰That day David fled from Saul and went *p* to Achish king of Gath. ¹¹But the servants of Achish said to him, "Isn't this David, the king of the land? Isn't he the one they sing about in their dances:

" 'Saul has slain his thousands,
　　and David his tens of thousands'?" *q*

¹²David took these words to heart and was very much afraid of Achish king of Gath. ¹³So he pretended to be insane *r* in their presence; and while he was in their hands he acted like a madman, making marks on the doors of the gate and letting saliva run down his beard.

¹⁴Achish said to his servants, "Look at the man! He is insane! Why bring him to me? ¹⁵Am I so short of madmen that you have to bring this fellow here to carry on like this in front of me? Must this man come into my house?"

---

a 5 Or *from us in the past few days since*

* This sentence (20:42b) is numbered 21:1 in Hebrew texts.　　* 21:1-15 is numbered 21:2-16 in Hebrew texts.

21:1 *Nob.* A town northeast of Jerusalem and southeast of Gibeah (see map, p. 416) where the tabernacle was relocated after the destruction of Shiloh (4:3; Jer 7:12). Although it appears that no attempt was made to bring the ark to this sanctuary (see note on 7:1), Ahimelek the high priest, 85 other priests (22:16–18), the ephod (v. 9) and the consecrated bread (v. 6) are mentioned in connection with it. *Ahimelek the priest.* See note on 14:3. It appears from 22:10,15 that David's purpose in coming to Nob was to seek the Lord's guidance by means of the Urim and Thummim (see notes on 2:28; Ex 28:30).

21:2 It is not clear why David resorts to deception in his response to Ahimelek. Perhaps it was an attempt to protect Ahimelek from the charge of involvement in David's escape from Saul. If so, his strategy was not successful (see 22:13–19).

A **21:4** *consecrated bread.* The "bread of the Presence" (v. 6; see Ex 25:30 and note), which was placed in the Holy Place in the tabernacle and later in the temple as a thank offering to the Lord, symbolizing his provision of daily bread. *provided the men have kept themselves from women.* Although the bread was to be eaten only by the priests (see Lev 24:9), Ahimelek agreed to

give it to David and his men on the condition that they were ceremonially clean (see Ex 19:15; Lev 15:18). Jesus uses this incident to illustrate the principle that the ceremonial law was not to be viewed in a legalistic manner (see Mt 12:3–4). He also teaches that it is always lawful to do good and to save life (see Lk 6:9). Such compassionate acts are within the true spirit of the law.

21:5 *are holy.* That is, have been consecrated to God (see note on Ex 3:5).

21:9 *sword of Goliath.* See note on 17:54. *ephod.* See note on 2:28.

B **21:10** *Achish.* See note on Ps 34 title. The name may have been a traditional title used by Philistine rulers (see note on 1Ki 2:39). It appears as the title of a king of Ekron several centuries later (as attested in the annals of the Assyrian kings Esarhaddon and Ashurbanipal, as well as in an inscription found at Ekron in 1996). *Gath.* See 5:8 and note.

21:11 See 29:5 and note on 18:7. *king of the land.* The designation of David as "king" by the Philistines may be understood as a popular exaggeration expressing an awareness of the enormous success and popularity of David among the Israelite people.

DAVID AT ADULLAM AND MIZPAH

22 David left Gath and escaped to the cave *s* of Adullam. *t* When his brothers and his father's household heard about it, they went down to him there. ²All those who were in distress or in debt or discontented gathered *u* around him, and he became their commander. About four hundred men were with him.

³From there David went to Mizpah in Moab and said to the king of Moab, "Would you let my father and mother come and stay with you until I learn what God will do for me?" ⁴So he left them with the king of Moab, *v* and they stayed with him as long as David was in the stronghold.

⁵But the prophet Gad *w* said to David, "Do not stay in the stronghold. Go into the land of Judah." So David left and went to the forest of Hereth. *x*

SAUL KILLS THE PRIESTS OF NOB

⁶Now Saul heard that David and his men had been discovered. And Saul was seated, *y* spear in hand, under the tamarisk *z* tree on the hill at Gibeah, with all his officials standing at his side. ⁷He said to them, "Listen, men of Benjamin! Will the son of Jesse give all of you fields and vineyards? Will he make all of you commanders *a* of thousands and commanders of hundreds? ⁸Is that why you have all conspired *b* against me? No one tells me when my son makes a covenant *c* with the son of Jesse. *d* None of you is concerned *e* about me or tells me that my son has incited my servant to lie in wait for me, as he does today."

⁹But Doeg *f* the Edomite, who was standing with Saul's officials, said, "I saw the son of Jesse come to Ahimelek son of Ahitub *g* at Nob. *h* ¹⁰Ahimelek inquired *i* of the Lᴏʀᴅ for him; he also gave him provisions *j* and the sword *k* of Goliath the Philistine."

¹¹Then the king sent for the priest Ahimelek son of Ahitub and all the men of his family, who were the priests at Nob, and they all came to the king. ¹²Saul said, "Listen now, son of Ahitub."

"Yes, my lord," he answered.

¹³Saul said to him, "Why have you conspired *l* against me, you and the son of Jesse, giving him bread and a sword and inquiring of God for him, so that he has rebelled against me and lies in wait for me, as he does today?"

¹⁴Ahimelek answered the king, "Who *m* of all your servants is as loyal as David, the king's son-in-law, captain of your bodyguard and highly respected in your household? ¹⁵Was that day the first time I inquired of God for him? Of course not! Let not the king accuse your servant or any of his father's family, for your servant knows nothing at all about this whole affair."

¹⁶But the king said, "You will surely die, Ahimelek, you and your whole family. *n*"

¹⁷Then the king ordered the guards at his side: "Turn and kill the priests of the Lᴏʀᴅ, because they too have sided with David. They knew he was fleeing, yet they did not tell me."

But the king's officials were unwilling *o* to raise a hand to strike the priests of the Lᴏʀᴅ.

¹⁸The king then ordered Doeg, "You turn and strike down the priests." *p* So Doeg the Edomite turned and struck them down. That day he killed eighty-five men who wore the linen ephod. *q* ¹⁹He also put to the sword *r* Nob, *s* the town of the priests, with its men and women, its children and infants, and its cattle, donkeys and sheep.

22:1 *s* Ps 57 Title;
142 Title *t* S Ge 38:1
22:2 *u* 1Sa 23:13;
25:13; 2Sa 15:20
22:4 *v* S Ge 19:37
22:5 *w* 2Sa 24:11;
1Ch 21:9; 29:29;
2Ch 29:25
x 2Sa 23:14
22:6 *y* S Jdg 4:5
z S Ge 21:33
22:7 *a* S Dt 1:15
22:8 *b* ver 13
c S 1Sa 18:3 *d* 2Sa 20:1
e 1Sa 23:21
22:9 *f* S 1Sa 21:7
g 1Sa 14:3 *h* S 1Sa 21:1
22:10 *i* S Ge 25:22;
S 1Sa 23:2 *j* S 1Sa 21:6
k S 1Sa 17:51
22:13 *l* ver 8
22:14 *m* S 1Sa 19:4
22:16 *n* S 1Sa 2:31
22:17 *o* S Ex 1:17
22:18 *p* S 1Sa 4:17
q S 1Sa 2:18,31
22:19 *r* S 1Sa 15:3
s S 1Sa 21:1

22:1 *cave of Adullam.* See 2Sa 23:13; Ge 38:1 and note; Jos 12:15; 15:35.

22:2 *four hundred men were with him.* David, officially an outlaw, was joined by others in similar circumstances, so that he began to develop a military power base that would sustain him throughout his later years as king (see note on 14:52).

22:3 *let my father and mother come and stay with you.* The king of Moab was a natural ally for David because Saul had warred against Moab (see 14:47) and David's own great-grandmother was a Moabite (see Ru 4:5,13,22).

22:4 *stronghold.* Perhaps a specific fortress, but more likely a reference to a geographical area in which it was easy to hide (see 23:14; 2Sa 5:17; 23:14).

22:5 *prophet Gad.* The king-designate is now served also by a prophet. Later a priest would come to him (v. 20) and complete the basic elements of a royal entourage—and they were all refugees from Saul's administration. This is the first appearance of the prophet who later assisted David in musical arrangements for the temple services (see 2Ch 29:25), wrote a history of David's reign (see 1Ch 29:29) and confronted David

with the Lord's rebuke for his sin of numbering the Israelites (see 2Sa 24:11–25). *forest of Hereth.* Located in the tribal area of Judah.

22:6 *tamarisk tree.* See note on Ge 21:33. *Gibeah.* See note on 10:5.

22:7–9,13 *son of Jesse.* See note on 20:27,30–31.

22:7 *men of Benjamin.* Saul, a Benjamite (9:1–2; 10:21), seeks to strengthen his position with his own officials by emphasizing tribal loyalty. David was from the tribe of Judah (see note on 16:1; 2Sa 2:4). *give all of you fields and vineyards?* Saul does exactly what Samuel had warned him that he would do—become like the kings of other nations (see 8:14). His actions are contrary to the covenantal ideal for kingship (see notes on 8:7; 10:25). *commanders of thousands . . . hundreds.* See 8:12.

22:10 *Ahimelek inquired of the Lᴏʀᴅ for him.* See note on 21:1.

22:17 *They knew he was fleeing.* How much the priests really knew is not clear. David himself had not told them (see 21:2–3,8).

22:18 *linen ephod.* See note on 2:18.

22:19 *put to the sword Nob.* Thus the prophecy of judgment against the house of Eli is fulfilled (see 2:31 and note).

22:20 *s* 1Sa 14:3
u 1Sa 23:6,9; 30:7;
2Sa 15:24; 20:25;
1Ki 1:7; 2:22,26,27;
4:4; 1Ch 15:11; 27:34
v S 1Sa 2:32
22:22 *w* S 1Sa 21:7
22:23 *x* S 1Sa 20:1
23:1 *y* S Jos 15:44
z S Nu 18:27;
S Jdg 6:11
23:2 *a* ver 4,12;
1Sa 22:10; 30:8;
2Sa 2:1; 5:19,23;
Ps 50:15
23:4 *b* S ver 2
c S 1Sa 9:16
d S Jos 8:7
23:6 *e* S 1Sa 22:20
f S 1Sa 2:28
23:7 *g* S Dt 32:30
h Ps 31:21
23:9 *i* S 1Sa 22:20
j S 1Sa 2:18
23:12 *k* ver 20
23:13 *l* S 1Sa 22:2
23:14 *m* Ps 55:7
n S Jos 15:24,55
o Ps 54:3-4 *p* Ps 32:7
23:15 *q* S 1Sa 20:1
23:16 *r* 1Sa 30:6;
Ps 18:2; 27:14
23:17 *s* S 1Sa 20:31
23:18 *t* S 1Sa 18:3;
2Sa 9:1
23:19 *u* 1Sa 26:1
v Ps 54 Title
w 1Sa 26:3
23:20 *x* ver 12
23:21 *y* Ru 2:20;
2Sa 2:5 *z* 1Sa 22:8

²⁰But one son of Ahimelek son of Ahitub, *t* named Abiathar, *u* escaped and fled to join David. *v* ²¹He told David that Saul had killed the priests of the LORD. ²²Then David said to Abiathar, "That day, when Doeg *w* the Edomite was there, I knew he would be sure to tell Saul. I am responsible for the death of your whole family. ²³Stay with me; don't be afraid. The man who wants to take your life *x* is trying to kill me too. You will be safe with me."

DAVID SAVES KEILAH

23 When David was told, "Look, the Philistines are fighting against Keilah *y* and are looting the threshing floors," *z* ²he inquired *a* of the LORD, saying, "Shall I go and attack these Philistines?"

The LORD answered him, "Go, attack the Philistines and save Keilah."

³But David's men said to him, "Here in Judah we are afraid. How much more, then, if we go to Keilah against the Philistine forces!"

⁴Once again David inquired *b* of the LORD, and the LORD answered him, "Go down to Keilah, for I am going to give the Philistines *c* into your hand. *d* " ⁵So David and his men went to Keilah, fought the Philistines and carried off their livestock. He inflicted heavy losses on the Philistines and saved the people of Keilah. ⁶(Now Abiathar *e* son of Ahimelek had brought the ephod *f* down with him when he fled to David at Keilah.)

SAUL PURSUES DAVID

⁷Saul was told that David had gone to Keilah, and he said, "God has delivered him into my hands, *g* for David has imprisoned himself by entering a town with gates and bars." *h* ⁸And Saul called up all his forces for battle, to go down to Keilah to besiege David and his men.

⁹When David learned that Saul was plotting against him, he said to Abiathar *i* the priest, "Bring the ephod. *j* " ¹⁰David said, "LORD, God of Israel, your servant has heard definitely that Saul plans to come to Keilah and destroy the town on account of me. ¹¹Will the citizens of Keilah surrender me to him? Will Saul come down, as your servant has heard? LORD, God of Israel, tell your servant."

And the LORD said, "He will."

¹²Again David asked, "Will the citizens of Keilah surrender *k* me and my men to Saul?"

And the LORD said, "They will."

¹³So David and his men, *l* about six hundred in number, left Keilah and kept moving from place to place. When Saul was told that David had escaped from Keilah, he did not go there.

¹⁴David stayed in the wilderness *m* strongholds and in the hills of the Desert of Ziph. *n* Day after day Saul searched *o* for him, but God did not *p* give David into his hands.

¹⁵While David was at Horesh in the Desert of Ziph, he learned that Saul had come out to take his life. *q* ¹⁶And Saul's son Jonathan went to David at Horesh and helped him find strength *r* in God. ¹⁷"Don't be afraid," he said. "My father Saul will not lay a hand on you. You will be king *s* over Israel, and I will be second to you. Even my father Saul knows this." ¹⁸The two of them made a covenant *t* before the LORD. Then Jonathan went home, but David remained at Horesh.

¹⁹The Ziphites *u* went up to Saul at Gibeah and said, "Is not David hiding among us *v* in the strongholds at Horesh, on the hill of Hakilah, *w* south of Jeshimon? ²⁰Now, Your Majesty, come down whenever it pleases you to do so, and we will be responsible for giving *x* him into your hands."

²¹Saul replied, "The LORD bless *y* you for your concern *z* for me. ²²Go and get more in-

---

C **22:20** *Abiathar, escaped and fled to join David.* See note on v. 5. Abiathar brought the high priestly ephod with him (see 23:6) and subsequently "inquired of the LORD" for David (see 23:2 and note; see also 23:4,9; 30:7–8; 2Sa 2:1; 5:19,23). He served as high priest until removed from office by Solomon for participating in the rebellion of Adonijah (see 1Ki 2:26–27).
23:1 *Keilah.* Located about three miles southeast of Adullam (see map, p. 416).
23:2,4 *inquired of the LORD.* By means of the Urim and Thummim through the high priest Abiathar (see vv. 6,9 and note on 2:28).
23:5 *saved the people of Keilah.* God uses David rather than Saul to be Israel's protective "shepherd"—so again David protects Saul's "flock."
23:9 *Bring the ephod.* See note on v. 2.

23:13 *about six hundred.* The number of David's men has grown significantly (cf. 22:2).
23:14 *wilderness strongholds.* Inaccessible places (see note on 22:4). *Desert of Ziph.* Located south of Hebron. *God did not give David into his hands.* The reality of God's protection over David portrayed here contrasts sharply with the wishful thinking of Saul in v. 7.
C **23:17** *You will be king over Israel.* See notes on 18:4; 20:13,16,31. *I will be second to you.* Jonathan's love and respect for David enable him to accept a role subordinate to David without any sign of resentment or jealousy (see notes on 18:3; 19:4). This is the last recorded meeting between Jonathan and David. *Saul knows this.* See 18:8 and note on 20:31.
23:18 *covenant.* See notes on 18:3; 20:14–15.

formation. Find out where David usually goes and who has seen him there. They tell me he is very crafty. ²³Find out about all the hiding places he uses and come back to me with definite information. Then I will go with you; if he is in the area, I will track ᵃ him down among all the clans of Judah."

²⁴So they set out and went to Ziph ahead of Saul. Now David and his men were in the Desert of Maon, ᵇ in the Arabah south of Jeshimon. ᶜ ²⁵Saul and his men began the search, and when David was told about it, he went down to the rock and stayed in the Desert of Maon. When Saul heard this, he went into the Desert of Maon in pursuit of David.

²⁶Saul ᵈ was going along one side of the mountain, and David and his men were on the other side, hurrying to get away from Saul. As Saul and his forces were closing in on David and his men to capture them, ²⁷a messenger came to Saul, saying, "Come quickly! The Philistines are raiding the land." ²⁸Then Saul broke off his pursuit of David and went to meet the Philistines. That is why they call this place Sela Hammahlekoth. ᵃ *²⁹And David went up from there and lived in the strongholds ᵉ of En Gedi. ᶠ

DAVID SPARES SAUL'S LIFE

24 *After Saul returned from pursuing the Philistines, he was told, "David is in the Desert of En Gedi. ᵍ" ²So Saul took three thousand able young men from all Israel and set out to look ʰ for David and his men near the Crags of the Wild Goats.

³He came to the sheep pens along the way; a cave ⁱ was there, and Saul went in to relieve ʲ himself. David and his men were far back in the cave. ⁴The men said, "This is the day the LORD spoke ᵏ of when he said ᵇ to you, 'I will give your enemy into your hands for you to deal with as you wish.'" ˡ Then David crept up unnoticed and cut ᵐ off a corner of Saul's robe.

⁵Afterward, David was conscience-stricken ⁿ for having cut off a corner of his robe. ⁶He said to his men, "The LORD forbid that I should do such a thing to my master, the LORD's anointed, ᵒ or lay my hand on him; for he is the anointed of the LORD." ⁷With these words David sharply rebuked his men and did not allow them to attack Saul. And Saul left the cave and went his way.

⁸Then David went out of the cave and called out to Saul, "My lord the king!" When Saul looked behind him, David bowed down and prostrated himself with his face to the ground. ᵖ ⁹He said to Saul, "Why do you listen ۹ when men say, 'David is bent on harming ʳ you'? ¹⁰This day you have seen with your own eyes how the LORD delivered you into my hands in the cave. Some urged me to kill you, but I spared ˢ you; I said, 'I will not lay my hand on my lord, because he is the LORD's anointed.' ¹¹See, my father, look at this piece

ᵃ 28 Sela Hammahlekoth means rock of parting.　　ᵇ 4 Or "Today the LORD is saying

* 23:29 is numbered 24:1 in Hebrew texts.　　* 24:1-22 is numbered 24:2-23 in Hebrew texts.

23:23 ᵃS Ge 31:36
23:24 ᵇS Jos 15:55
ᶜ1Sa 26:1
23:26 ᵈPs 17:9
23:29 ᵉ1Sa 24:22
ᶠS Jos 15:62;
2Ch 20:2; SS 1:14
24:1 ᵍS Jos 15:62
24:2 ʰ1Sa 26:2
24:3 ⁱPs 57 Title;
142 Title ʲJdg 3:24
24:4 ᵏ1Sa 25:28-30
ˡ2Sa 4:8 ᵐver 10,11
24:5 ⁿ1Sa 26:9;
2Sa 24:10
24:6 ᵒS 1Sa 26:11;
S 1Sa 12:3
24:8 ᵖS 1Sa 20:41
24:9 ۹1Sa 26:19
ʳ1Sa 20:1
24:10 ˢS ver 4

23:29 En Gedi. See note on SS 1:14.
C 24:1—26:25 In each of the three episodes in these chapters, David is put to a severe test in the desert as the Lord's anointed (16:1–13; cf. Dt 8, the testing of Israel in the wilderness; Mt 4:1–11, the testing of Jesus in the wilderness). In all three events, circumstances place David in a position of power with opportunity to use that power for purely personal ends (avenging wrongs done to him) rather than in the service of the Lord and Israel. To have failed this test would have disqualified David—as it had disqualified Saul—from serving as the Lord's appointed king over Israel.

Within these three chapters the final two confrontations between Saul and David take place. In both, the tables are turned and Saul is at the mercy of David. These two episodes (chs. 24; 26) bracket another (ch. 25) in which David has dealings with Nabal, a wealthy Judahite whose flocks David and his men had protected—as they have protected Saul's "flock" from Philistine aggression. In this center episode, Nabal serves as a literary picture of Saul, who is thus exposed as a fool whom the Lord will soon strike down (see 25:38; cf. 26:10; 28:19; 31:4).
24:1–22 Saul at the mercy of David while seeking privacy in a cave.
C 24:4 This is the day the LORD spoke of when he said. There is no previous record of the divine revelation here alluded to by David's men. Perhaps this was their own interpretation of

the anointing of David to replace Saul (see 16:13–14), or of assurances given to David that he would survive Saul's vendetta against him and ultimately become king (see 20:14–15; 23:17). If the alternative given in the TNIV text note is taken, the reference would not be to a verbal communication from the Lord but to the providential nature of the incident itself, which David's men understood as a revelation from God that David should not ignore. I will give your enemy into your hands. So it seemed to David's men (see also 26:8). Cf. what David says to Saul in v. 10 and contrast what the author has stated in 23:14. cut off a corner of Saul's robe. Perhaps David was symbolically depriving Saul of his royal authority and transferring it to himself (see v. 11; cf. also 15:27–28; 18:4).
24:6 for he is the anointed of the LORD. See v. 10; 26:9,11,16,23; 2Sa 1:14,16. Because Saul's royal office carried divine sanction by virtue of his anointing (see note on 9:16), David is determined not to wrest the kingship from Saul but to leave its disposition to the Lord who gave it (see vv. 12,15; 26:10).
24:11 my father. See also Saul's address to David as "my son" (v. 16). David uses this form of address either because (1) Saul was David's father-in-law (see 18:27) or because (2) the special relationship between father and son was at times used as a metaphor for an intimate relationship between king and subject (see notes on 2Sa 7:14; Ps 2:7; see also chart, p. 20).

24:11 ᵗS ver 4
ᵘ Ps 7:3 ᵛ1Sa 25:28
ʷPs 35:7
ˣ S Ge 31:36;
1Sa 26:20 ʸ S 1Sa 20:1
24:12 ᶻ S Ge 16:5;
S 1Sa 25:38;
S Job 9:15 ᵃ S Nu 31:3
24:13 ᵇ Mt 7:20
24:14 ᶜ S 1Sa 17:43
ᵈ 1Sa 26:20
24:15 ᵉ ver 12
ᶠ S Ge 16:5 ᵍPs 35:1,
23; Isa 49:25
ʰ Ps 26:1; 35:24; 43:1;
50:4; 54:1; 135:14
ⁱ Ps 119:134,154
24:16 ʲ 1Sa 26:17
24:17 ᵏ Ge 38:26
ˡ Mt 5:44 ᵐ S Ex 9:27
24:18 ⁿ 1Sa 26:23
24:19 ᵒ S Ru 2:12;
S 2Ch 15:7
24:20 ᵖ S 1Sa 20:31
�q S 1Sa 13:14
24:21 ʳ Ge 21:23;
S 47:31; S 1Sa 18:3;
2Sa 21:1-9
ˢ S 1Sa 20:14-15
24:22 ᵗ 1Sa 23:29
25:1 ᵘ1Sa 28:3
ᵛ S Lev 10:6; Dt 34:8
ʷ S 1Sa 7:17
25:2 ˣ S Jos 15:55
ʸ 2Sa 19:32
ᶻ S Ge 31:19
25:3 ᵃPr 31:10
ᵇ S Jos 14:13; S 15:13
25:6 ᶜPs 122:7;
Mt 10:12 ᵈ1Ch 12:18

of your robe in my hand! I cut ᵗ off the corner of your robe but did not kill you. See that there is nothing in my hand to indicate that I am guilty ᵘ of wrongdoing ᵛ or rebellion. I have not wronged ʷ you, but you are hunting ˣ me down to take my life. ʸ ¹²May the LORD judge ᶻ between you and me. And may the LORD avenge ᵃ the wrongs you have done to me, but my hand will not touch you. ¹³As the old saying goes, 'From evildoers come evil deeds, ᵇ' so my hand will not touch you.

¹⁴"Against whom has the king of Israel come out? Whom are you pursuing? A dead dog? ᶜ A flea? ᵈ ¹⁵May the LORD be our judge ᵉ and decide ᶠ between us. May he consider my cause and uphold ᵍ it; may he vindicate ʰ me by delivering ⁱ me from your hand."

¹⁶When David finished saying this, Saul asked, "Is that your voice, ʲ David my son?" And he wept aloud. ¹⁷"You are more righteous than I," ᵏ he said. "You have treated me well, ˡ but I have treated you badly. ᵐ ¹⁸You have just now told me about the good you did to me; the LORD delivered ⁿ me into your hands, but you did not kill me. ¹⁹When a man finds his enemy, does he let him get away unharmed? May the LORD reward ᵒ you well for the way you treated me today. ²⁰I know that you will surely be king ᵖ and that the kingdom �q of Israel will be established in your hands. ²¹Now swear ʳ to me by the LORD that you will not kill off my descendants or wipe out my name from my father's family. ˢ"

²²So David gave his oath to Saul. Then Saul returned home, but David and his men went up to the stronghold. ᵗ

DAVID, NABAL AND ABIGAIL

25 Now Samuel died, ᵘ and all Israel assembled and mourned ᵛ for him; and they buried him at his home in Ramah. ʷ Then David moved down into the Desert of Paran. ᵃ

²A certain man in Maon, ˣ who had property there at Carmel, was very wealthy. ʸ He had a thousand goats and three thousand sheep, which he was shearing ᶻ in Carmel. ³His name was Nabal and his wife's name was Abigail. ᵃ She was an intelligent and beautiful woman, but her husband was surly and mean in his dealings—he was a Calebite. ᵇ

⁴While David was in the wilderness, he heard that Nabal was shearing sheep. ⁵So he sent ten young men and said to them, "Go up to Nabal at Carmel and greet him in my name. ⁶Say to him: 'Long life to you! Good health ᶜ to you and your household! And good health to all that is yours! ᵈ

ᵃ 1 Hebrew and some Septuagint manuscripts; other Septuagint manuscripts *Maon*

24:14 *dead dog.* See note on 2Sa 9:8. *flea.* See note on 26:20.
24:16 *he wept aloud.* Saul experiences temporary remorse (see 26:21) for his actions against David but quickly reverts to his former determination to kill him (see 26:2).
24:21 *not kill off my descendants.* See notes on 20:14–15.
24:22 *stronghold.* An inaccessible place (see note on 22:4). From previous experience David did not place any confidence in Saul's words of repentance.

■ **25:1–44** David's dealings with Nabal (see note on 24:1—26:25). Nabal, the "fool" (see v. 25 and note), lived near Carmel, where Saul had erected a monument in his own honor (see 15:12 and note). The account of Nabal effectively serves the author's purpose in a number of ways: 1. Nabal's general character, his disdainful attitude toward David though David had guarded his flocks, and his sudden death at the Lord's hand all parallel Saul (whose "flock" David had also protected). Thus the author indirectly characterizes Saul as a fool (see 13:13; 26:21) and foreshadows his end. 2. David's vengeful attitude toward Nabal displays his natural tendency and highlights his restraint toward Saul, the Lord's anointed (this event is sandwiched between the two instances in which David spared Saul in spite of the urging of his men). 3. Abigail's prudent action prevents David from using his power as leader for personal vengeance (the very thing Saul was doing). In this way the Lord (who avenged his servant) keeps David's sword clean, teaching him a lesson he does not forget. 4. Abigail's confident acknowledgment of David's future accession to the throne foreshadows that event and even anticipates the Lord's commitment to establish David's house as a "lasting dynasty" (v. 28; cf. 2Sa 7:11–16). 5. Abigail's marriage to David provides him a wise and worthy wife, while Saul gives away David's wife Michal to another, illustrating how the Lord

counters every move Saul makes against David.

■ **25:1** The author begins the David-Nabal episode by noting David's loss of his chief protector in Israel (see 19:18–24) and ends it with a notation that David also loses his wife Michal, one of his protectors in the royal family itself (see 19:11–17). Meanwhile he obtains a wife whose wisdom rivals that of Ahithophel (see 2Sa 16:23). She is one of two wives who link him with the aristocracy of Judah. This account of how David obtained Nabal's wife serves as a foil to the later account of how David obtained the wife of Uriah the Hittite (2Sa 11). There it is David who acts the fool. *all Israel … mourned for him.* Samuel was recognized as a leader of national prominence who played a key role in the restructuring of the theocracy with the establishment of the monarchy (see chs. 8–12). The loss of his leadership was mourned much like that of other prominent figures in Israel's past history, including Jacob (Ge 50:10), Aaron (Nu 20:29) and Moses (Dt 34:8). *Ramah.* See 7:17 and note on 1:1.
25:2 In ancient times wealth often consisted primarily of livestock (see Ge 12:16; 13:2).

■ **25:3** *intelligent and beautiful … surly and mean.* The stark contrast between the foolish Nabal and the wise Abigail is played out through the rest of the chapter. *Calebite.* A descendant of Caleb (see Nu 14:24), who settled at Hebron (see Jos 14:13) after the conquest of Canaan. Since Caleb's name can mean "dog," Nabal is subtly depicted as a dog, as well as a fool. He would soon be a dead dog (see note on 2Sa 9:8), when the Lord would avenge his acts of contempt toward David. The hint is strong that, when the Lord avenges Saul's sins against David (see 24:12,15), the king will no longer pursue a dead dog (see 24:14) but will himself become one—a case of biting irony.
25:4 *shearing sheep.* A festive occasion (see v. 8; 2Sa 13:23–24).

7" 'Now I hear that it is sheep-shearing time. When your shepherds were with us, we did not mistreat[e] them, and the whole time they were at Carmel nothing of theirs was missing. [8]Ask your own servants and they will tell you. Therefore be favorable toward my men, since we come at a festive time. Please give your servants and your son David whatever[f] you can find for them.' "

[9]When David's men arrived, they gave Nabal this message in David's name. Then they waited.

[10]Nabal answered David's servants, "Who[g] is this David? Who is this son of Jesse? Many servants are breaking away from their masters these days. [11]Why should I take my bread[h] and water, and the meat I have slaughtered for my shearers, and give it to men coming from who knows where?"

[12]David's men turned around and went back. When they arrived, they reported every word. [13]David said to his men[i], "Each of you strap on your sword!" So they did, and David strapped his on as well. About four hundred men went[j] up with David, while two hundred stayed with the supplies.[k]

[14]One of the servants told Abigail, Nabal's wife, "David sent messengers from the wilderness to give our master his greetings,[l] but he hurled insults at them. [15]Yet these men were very good to us. They did not mistreat[m] us, and the whole time we were out in the fields near them nothing was missing.[n] [16]Night and day they were a wall[o] around us the whole time we were herding our sheep near them. [17]Now think it over and see what you can do, because disaster is hanging over our master and his whole household. He is such a wicked[p] man that no one can talk to him."

[18]Abigail acted quickly. She took two hundred loaves of bread, two skins of wine, five dressed sheep, five seahs[a] of roasted grain,[q] a hundred cakes of raisins[r] and two hundred cakes of pressed figs, and loaded them on donkeys. [s] [19]Then she told her servants, "Go on ahead;[t] I'll follow you." But she did not tell[u] her husband Nabal.

[20]As she came riding her donkey into a mountain ravine, there were David and his men descending toward her, and she met them. [21]David had just said, "It's been useless—all my watching over this fellow's property in the wilderness so that nothing of his was missing. [v] He has paid[w] me back evil[x] for good. [22]May God deal with David,[b] be it ever so severely,[y] if by morning I leave alive one male[z] of all who belong to him!"

[23]When Abigail saw David, she quickly got off her donkey and bowed down before David with her face to the ground. [a] [24]She fell at his feet and said: "Pardon your servant, my lord,[b] and let me speak to you; hear what your servant has to say. [25]Please pay no attention, my lord, to that wicked man Nabal. He is just like his name—his name means Fool[c], [d] and folly goes with him. And as for me, your servant, I did not see the men my lord sent. [26]And now, my lord, as surely as the LORD your God lives and as you live, since the LORD has kept you from bloodshed[e] and from avenging[f] yourself with your own hands, may your enemies and all who are intent on harming my lord be like Nabal.[g] [27]And let this gift,[h] which your servant has brought to my lord, be given to the men who follow you.

[28]"Please forgive[i] your servant's presumption. The LORD your God will certainly make a lasting[j] dynasty for my lord, because you fight the LORD's battles,[k] and no wrongdoing[l] will be found in you as long as you live. [29]Even though someone is pursuing you to take your life,[m] the life of my lord will be bound securely in the bundle of the living by the

---

25:7 [e] ver 15
25:8 [f] Ne 8:10
25:10 [g] Jdg 9:28
25:11 [h] Jdg 8:6
25:13 [i] S 1Sa 22:2
[j] S 1Sa 21:10
[k] S Nu 31:27
25:14 [l] 1Sa 13:10
25:15 [m] ver 7
[n] ver 21
25:16 [o] Ex 14:22;
Job 1:10; Ps 139:5
25:17 [p] S Dt 13:13;
S 1Sa 20:7
25:18 [q] S Lev 23:14;
S 1Sa 17:17
[r] 1Ch 12:40
[s] S Ge 42:26;
2Sa 16:1; 1Sa 30:6
25:19 [t] Ge 32:20
[u] ver 36
25:21 [v] ver 15
[x] S 1Sa 19:4
25:22 [y] S Ru 1:17
[z] 1Ki 14:10; 21:21;
2Ki 9:8
25:23 [a] S Ge 19:1;
1Sa 20:41
25:24 [b] 2Sa 14:9
25:25 [c] Pr 17:12
[d] Pr 12:16; 14:16; 20:3;
Isa 32:5
25:26 [e] ver 33
[f] Heb 10:30 [g] ver 34;
2Sa 18:32
25:27 [h] S Ge 33:11
25:28 [i] ver 24;
2Sa 14:9 [j] 2Sa 7:11,26
[k] 1Sa 18:17 [l] 1Sa 24:11
25:29 [m] S 1Sa 20:1

---

[a] 18 That is, probably about 60 pounds or about 27 kilograms Hebrew with David's enemies

[b] 22 Some Septuagint manuscripts;

25:8 give…whatever you can find for them. David and his men ask for some consideration for their protection of Nabal's shepherds and flocks against pillage (see vv. 15–16,21).

25:10 son of Jesse. See note on 20:27,30–31.

25:17 wicked man. See note on Dt 13:13. no one can talk to him. In this way, too, Nabal is like Saul (cf., e.g., 20:27–33).

25:18 She took…bread…wine…sheep…grain…raisins… figs. A feast for a king. Cf. what Nabal had mentioned in v. 11.

25:19 did not tell her husband. Cf. Michal's treatment of Saul (19:11–17).

25:22 May God deal with David, be it ever so severely. See note on 3:17. David invokes a curse on himself if he should fail to kill every male in Nabal's household and so obliterate Nabal's family.

25:24 Pardon your servant. Abigail begins her appeal to David on an apologetic note (she is not taking on herself the blame for Nabal's action) as she does again when she begins the second half of her appeal (v. 28). Contrast Nabal's high-handed treatment of David.

25:25 wicked man. See v. 17 and note on Dt 13:13. He is just like his name. In ancient times a person's name was believed to reflect his nature and character.

25:26 as surely as the LORD…lives. See note on 14:39,45.

25:28 The LORD…will certainly make a lasting dynasty. While the idea that David was destined to become king in place of Saul may have spread among the general populace, Abigail's assessment of David contrasts sharply with that of her husband (see v. 10). you fight the LORD's battles. Abigail is familiar with David's victories over the Philistines, in which he sought to glorify the Lord rather than advance his own honor (see 17:26,45–47; 18:17). no wrongdoing will be found in you. See v. 39. Abigail shows concern for the preservation of David's integrity in view of the office he was later to assume (see vv. 30–31).

25:29 bound securely in the bundle of the living. Using the figure of placing a valuable possession in a carefully wrapped

25:29 *n* Jer 10:18;
22:26 *o* 1Sa 17:50;
2Sa 4:8
25:30 *p* S 1Sa 12:12;
S 13:14
25:31 *q* S Ge 40:14
r 2Sa 3:10
25:32 *s* S Ge 24:27
25:33 *t* ver 26
25:34 *u* S ver 26
25:35 *v* S Ge 19:21
25:36 *w* S Ru 3:7
x Pr 20:1; Ecc 10:17;
Isa 5:11,22; 22:13;
28:7; 56:12; Hos 4:11
y ver 19
25:37 *z* Ex 15:16
25:38 *a* Dt 32:35;
1Sa 24:12; 26:10;
2Sa 6:7; 12:15
25:42 *b* 2Sa 2:2; 3:3;
1Ch 3:1
25:43 *c* 2Sa 3:2;
1Ch 3:1 *d* 1Sa 27:3;
30:5; 2Sa 2:2
25:44 *e* 2Sa 3:15
f Isa 10:30
26:1 *g* 1Sa 23:19
h Ps 54 Title
i 1Sa 23:24
26:2 *j* 1Sa 24:2
26:3 *k* 1Sa 23:19
26:5 *l* 1Sa 17:55

LORD your God, but the lives of your enemies he will hurl *n* away as from the pocket of a sling. *o* 30When the LORD has fulfilled for my lord every good thing he promised concerning him and has appointed him ruler *p* over Israel, 31my lord will not have on his conscience the staggering burden of needless bloodshed or of having avenged himself. And when the LORD your God has brought my lord success, remember *q* your servant." *r*

32David said to Abigail, "Praise *s* be to the LORD, the God of Israel, who has sent you today to meet me. 33May you be blessed for your good judgment and for keeping me from bloodshed *t* this day and from avenging myself with my own hands. 34Otherwise, as surely as the LORD, the God of Israel, lives, who has kept me from harming you, if you had not come quickly to meet me, not one male belonging to Nabal *u* would have been left alive by daybreak."

35Then David accepted from her hand what she had brought him and said, "Go home in peace. I have heard your words and granted *v* your request."

36When Abigail went to Nabal, he was in the house holding a banquet like that of a king. He was in high *w* spirits and very drunk. *x* So she told *y* him nothing at all until daybreak. 37Then in the morning, when Nabal was sober, his wife told him all these things, and his heart failed him and he became like a stone. *z* 38About ten days later, the LORD struck *a* Nabal and he died.

39When David heard that Nabal was dead, he said, "Praise be to the LORD, who has upheld my cause against Nabal for treating me with contempt. He has kept his servant from doing wrong and has brought Nabal's wrongdoing down on his own head."

Then David sent word to Abigail, asking her to become his wife. 40His servants went to Carmel and said to Abigail, "David has sent us to you to take you to become his wife." 41She bowed down with her face to the ground and said, "I am your servant and am ready to serve you and wash the feet of my lord's servants." 42Abigail *b* quickly got on a donkey and, attended by her five female servants, went with David's messengers and became his wife. 43David had also married Ahinoam *c* of Jezreel, and they both were his wives. *d* 44But Saul had given his daughter Michal, David's wife, to Paltiel *a* *e* son of Laish, who was from Gallim. *f*

DAVID AGAIN SPARES SAUL'S LIFE

26 The Ziphites *g* went to Saul at Gibeah and said, "Is not David hiding *h* on the hill of Hakilah, which faces Jeshimon? *i*"

2So Saul went down to the Desert of Ziph, with his three thousand able young Israelites, to search *j* there for David. 3Saul made his camp beside the road on the hill of Hakilah *k* facing Jeshimon, but David stayed in the wilderness. When he saw that Saul had followed him there, 4he sent out scouts and learned that Saul had definitely arrived.

5Then David set out and went to the place where Saul had camped. He saw where Saul and Abner *l* son of Ner, the commander of the army, had lain down. Saul was lying inside the camp, with the army encamped around him.

a 44 Hebrew *Palti*, a variant of *Paltiel*

---

package for safekeeping, Abigail assures David that the Lord will preserve his life in the midst of danger. *hurl away as from the pocket of a sling.* A word that soon comes true for Nabal after he becomes "like a stone" (v. 37).

25:30 *ruler.* See note on 9:16.

25:31 *needless bloodshed.* See note on v. 28.

25:32–34 Cf. David's words in vv. 21–22. His words there and here bracket the account of his meeting with Abigail and highlight the crucial role of wise Abigail's actions.

25:32 *who has sent you.* David recognizes the providential leading of the Lord in his encounter with Abigail (see v. 39).

25:33 *your good judgment.* See v. 3 and note.

25:36 *holding a banquet.* See Pr 30:21–22. *like that of a king.* Another clue that the author is using Nabal as a subtle portrayal of Saul.

25:37 *when Nabal was sober.* Lit. "when the wine had gone out of Nabal"—containing a clever wordplay on Nabal's name, which sounds very much like the Hebrew word for wineskin (as in v. 18). *became like a stone.* Perhaps he suffered a stroke—he who was without moral sensitivity (was a *nabal*; see v. 25 and note) became as senseless as a stone.

25:42 *became his wife.* She who acknowledged the Lord's anointed came to share in his kingdom while her fool of a husband ended up a dead dog, a dead fool, an empty wineskin, a stone flung from a sling. He typifies Saul and all who reject the Lord's anointed.

25:43 *Ahinoam.* The mother of David's first son, Amnon (see 2Sa 3:2). *Jezreel.* Located near Carmel (see v. 2; Jos 15:55–56) and not to be confused with the northern town of the same name, where Israel camped against the Philistines (see 29:1,11) and where Ahab resided in later times (see 1Ki 18:45–46; 21:1).

25:44 *Michal, David's wife.* See 18:27.

26:1–25 Saul is at the mercy of David while sleeping in the midst of his army encampment (see notes on 24:1—26:25; 24:1–22).

26:1 *Ziphites.* See 23:19; see also note on 23:14. *Gibeah.* The site of Saul's royal residence (see 10:26).

26:2 *Desert of Ziph.* See 23:19; see also note on 23:14. *three thousand.* Apparently Saul's standing army (see 24:2).

26:5 *Abner.* Saul's cousin (see 14:50). *lain down.* David arrived at Saul's camp during the night when the men were sleeping.

⁶David then asked Ahimelek the Hittite *m* and Abishai *n* son of Zeruiah, *o* Joab's brother, "Who will go down into the camp with me to Saul?"

"I'll go with you," said Abishai.

⁷So David and Abishai went to the army by night, and there was Saul, lying asleep inside the camp with his spear stuck in the ground near his head. Abner and the soldiers were lying around him.

⁸Abishai said to David, "Today God has delivered your enemy into your hands. Now let me pin him to the ground with one thrust of the spear; I won't strike him twice."

⁹But David said to Abishai, "Don't destroy him! Who can lay a hand on the LORD's anointed *p* and be guiltless? *q* ¹⁰As surely as the LORD lives," he said, "the LORD himself will strike *r* him, or his time *s* will come and he will die, *t* or he will go into battle and perish. ¹¹But the LORD forbid that I should lay a hand on the LORD's anointed. Now get the spear and water jug that are near his head, and let's go."

¹²So David took the spear and water jug near Saul's head, and they left. No one saw or knew about it, nor did anyone wake up. They were all sleeping, because the LORD had put them into a deep sleep. *u*

¹³Then David crossed over to the other side and stood on top of the hill some distance away; there was a wide space between them. ¹⁴He called out to the army and to Abner son of Ner, "Aren't you going to answer me, Abner?"

Abner replied, "Who are you who calls to the king?"

¹⁵David said, "You're a man, aren't you? And who is like you in Israel? Why didn't you guard your lord the king? Someone came to destroy your lord the king. ¹⁶What you have done is not good. As surely as the LORD lives, you and your men must die, because you did not guard your master, the LORD's anointed. Look around you. Where are the king's spear and water jug that were near his head?"

¹⁷Saul recognized David's voice and said, "Is that your voice, *v* David my son?"

David replied, "Yes it is, my lord the king." ¹⁸And he added, "Why is my lord pursuing his servant? What have I done, and what wrong *w* am I guilty of? ¹⁹Now let my lord the king listen *x* to his servant's words. If the LORD has incited you against me, then may he accept an offering. *y* If, however, people have done it, may they be cursed before the LORD! They have driven me today from my share in the LORD's inheritance *z* and have said, 'Go, serve other gods.' *a* ²⁰Now do not let my blood *b* fall to the ground far from the presence of the LORD. The king of Israel has come out to look for a flea *c*—as one hunts a partridge in the mountains. *d*"

²¹Then Saul said, "I have sinned. *e* Come back, David my son. Because you considered my life precious *f* today, I will not try to harm you again. Surely I have acted like a fool and have been terribly wrong."

²²"Here is the king's spear," David answered. "Let one of your servants come over and get it. ²³The LORD rewards *g* every man for his righteousness *h* and faithfulness. The LORD delivered *i* you into my hands today, but I would not lay a hand on the LORD's anointed. ²⁴As surely as I valued your life today, so may the LORD value my life and deliver *j* me from all trouble."

26:6 *m* S Ge 10:15
n 2Sa 2:18; 10:10;
16:9; 18:2; 19:21;
23:18; 1Ch 11:20; 19:11
o 1Ch 2:16
26:9 *p* ver 16;
S Ge 26:11;
S 1Sa 9:16; 2Sa 1:14;
19:21; La 4:20
q S 1Sa 24:5
26:10 *r* S Ge 16:5;
S 1Sa 25:38;
S Ro 12:19 *s* Dt 31:14;
Ps 37:13 *t* 1Sa 31:6;
2Sa 1:1
26:12 *u* S Jdg 4:21
26:17 *v* 1Sa 24:16
26:18 *w* Job 13:23;
Jer 37:18
26:19 *x* 1Sa 24:9
y 2Sa 16:11 *z* Dt 20:16;
32:9; 2Sa 14:16;
20:19; 21:3
a S Dt 4:28; S 11:28
26:20 *b* S 1Sa 24:11
c 1Sa 24:14 *d* Jer 4:29;
16:16; Am 9:3
26:21 *e* S Ex 9:27
f Ps 72:14
26:23 *g* S Ge 16:5;
S Ru 2:12; Ps 62:12
h 2Sa 22:21,25;
Ps 7:8; 18:20,24
i 1Sa 24:18
26:24 *j* Ps 54:7

26:6 *Ahimelek the Hittite.* Not referred to elsewhere. Hittites had long resided in Canaan (see note on Ge 10:15; see also Ge 15:20; 23:3–20; Dt 7:1; 20:17). Another Hittite in David's service was Uriah (see 2Sa 11:6–7; 23:39). *Abishai son of Zeruiah, Joab's brother.* See note on 1Sa 26:6. Zeruiah was David's sister (1Ch 2:16), so Abishai and Joab (and their brother Asahel, 2Sa 2:18) were David's nephews, as well as trusted military leaders. Joab would serve as the commander of his army for a long time.
26:8 *delivered your enemy into your hands.* See 24:4 and note. *pin him to the ground with … the spear.* Just as Saul had tried to pin David to the wall with his spear (see 18:11; 19:10).
26:9,11 See note on 24:6.
26:10,16 *As surely as the LORD lives.* See note on 14:39,45.
26:12 *David took the spear and water jug.* In this way he sought to prove again to Saul that he did not seek his life. But he also showed Saul that God had given him the power to take away the spear with which Saul had often tried to kill him and the water jug on which Saul's very life depended in the hot and dry Desert of Ziph.
26:19 *may he accept an offering.* David knows no reason why God should be angry with him; but if for some reason God is be-

hind Saul's determined effort to kill him, David appeals for God to accept an offering of appeasement (cf. 16:5)—in any event, to let the matter be settled between David and God without Saul's involvement. *may they be cursed before the LORD!* David commits any such men to the judgment of God. *the LORD's inheritance.* See note on 10:1. David appeals to Saul's conscience by describing his present exclusion from the fellowship of God's people and from living at peace in the Lord's land. *Go, serve other gods.* In their view, to be expelled from the Lord's land was to be separated from the Lord's sanctuary (an OT form of excommunication) and left to serve the gods of whatever land in which one might settle (see Jos 22:24–27 and note on 1Ki 5:17).
26:20 *look for a flea.* See 24:14. David suggests that Saul is making a fool of himself in his fanatical pursuit of an innocent and undesigning man.
26:21 *I have sinned.* See 24:17. *I have acted like a fool.* Saul confesses that his behavior has been not only unwise but also ungodly (see notes on 13:13; 25:2–44).
26:23 *I would not lay a hand on the LORD's anointed.* See v. 9 and note on 24:6.

²⁵Then Saul said to David, "May you be blessed, *k* David my son; you will do great things and surely triumph."

So David went on his way, and Saul returned home.

DAVID AMONG THE PHILISTINES

27 But David thought to himself, "One of these days I will be destroyed by the hand of Saul. The best thing I can do is to escape to the land of the Philistines. Then Saul will give up searching for me anywhere in Israel, and I will slip out of his hand."

²So David and the six hundred men *l* with him left and went *m* over to Achish *n* son of Maok king of Gath. ³David and his men settled in Gath with Achish. Each man had his family with him, and David had his two wives: *o* Ahinoam of Jezreel and Abigail of Carmel, the widow of Nabal. ⁴When Saul was told that David had fled to Gath, he no longer searched for him.

⁵Then David said to Achish, "If I have found favor in your eyes, let a place be assigned to me in one of the country towns, that I may live there. Why should your servant live in the royal city with you?"

⁶So on that day Achish gave him Ziklag, *p* and it has belonged to the kings of Judah ever since. ⁷David lived *q* in Philistine territory a year and four months.

⁸Now David and his men went up and raided the Geshurites, *r* the Girzites and the Amalekites. *s* (From ancient times these peoples had lived in the land extending to Shur *t* and Egypt.) ⁹Whenever David attacked an area, he did not leave a man or woman alive, *u* but took sheep and cattle, donkeys and camels, and clothes. Then he returned to Achish.

¹⁰When Achish asked, "Where did you go raiding today?" David would say, "Against the Negev of Judah" or "Against the Negev of Jerahmeel *v*" or "Against the Negev of the Kenites. *w*" ¹¹He did not leave a man or woman alive to be brought to Gath, for he thought, "They might inform on us and say, 'This is what David did.' " And such was his practice as long as he lived in Philistine territory. ¹²Achish trusted David and said to himself, "He has become so obnoxious *x* to his people, the Israelites, that he will be my servant for life. *y*"

28 In those days the Philistines gathered *z* their forces to fight against Israel. Achish said to David, "You must understand that you and your men will accompany me in the army."

²David said, "Then you will see for yourself what your servant can do." Achish replied, "Very well, I will make you my bodyguard *a* for life."

26:25 *you will … triumph.* Saul makes a veiled reference to his own conviction that David will replace him as king (see 24:20).
27:1 *I will be destroyed by the hand of Saul.* Under the pressure of Saul's superior forces David feels compelled to seek security outside Israel's borders. *land of the Philistines.* For the second time David seeks refuge in Philistia (see 21:10–15).
27:2 *Achish … king of Gath.* See 21:10 and note. In contrast to David's previous excursion into Philistia, Achish is now ready to receive him because he has become known as a formidable adversary of Saul. Moreover, to offer sanctuary under the circumstances would obligate David and his men to serve at his call in any military venture (see 28:1).
27:3 *Ahinoam.* See note on 25:43. *Abigail.* See 25:39–42.
27:4 *he no longer searched for him.* Saul did not have sufficient military strength to make incursions into Philistine territory, and with David out of the country he no longer faced an internal threat to his throne.
27:5 *in one of the country towns.* David desired more independence and freedom of movement than was possible while residing under the very eyes of the king of Gath. *Why should your servant live in the royal city with you?* David implies that he is not worthy of this honor.
27:6 *Ziklag.* Location unknown, but it is included in a list of towns in southern Judah (see Jos 15:31). It was given to the tribe of Simeon (see Jos 19:1–5) and was presumably occupied by them (cf. Jdg 1:17–18), only to be lost to the Philistines at a later, undisclosed time. *it has belonged to the kings of Judah ever since.* As royal property.
27:7 *David lived in Philistine territory a year and four months.* It

was not until after the death of Saul that David moved his residence from Ziklag (see 2Sa 1:1; 2:1–3) to Hebron.
27:8 *Geshurites.* A people residing in the area south of Philistia who were not defeated by the Israelites at the time of the conquest (see Jos 13:1–3) and who are to be distinguished from the Geshurites residing in the north near the upper Jordan in Aram (see 2Sa 3:3; 13:37–38; Dt 3:14; Jos 12:5). *Girzites.* Not mentioned elsewhere in the OT. *Amalekites.* See note on 15:2. *Shur.* See note on 15:7.
27:9 *he did not leave a man or woman alive.* David's reason for this is given in v. 11; his action conformed to that of Joshua in the conquest of Canaan (see, e.g., Jos 6:21 and note on 6:17).
27:10 *Negev of Judah.* Negev in Hebrew means "dry" and designates a large area from Beersheba to the highlands of the Sinai peninsula. *Jerahmeel.* The Jerahmeelites were descendants of Judah through Hezron (see 1Ch 2:9,25). *Kenites.* See note on 15:6.
27:12 *Achish trusted David.* David led Achish to believe that he was raiding outposts of Israelite territory when in actuality he was attacking the Geshurites, Girzites and Amalekites (see v. 8 and map, p. 427).
28:1 *accompany me in the army.* In the ancient Near East, to accept sanctuary in a country involved obligations of military service (see note on 27:2).
28:2 *you will see for yourself what your servant can do.* Perhaps an ambiguous answer. *I will make you my bodyguard.* Very likely this was conditional on David's proof of his loyalty and effectiveness in the projected campaign. Later, David would have a personal guard made up largely of Philistines (see 2Sa 15:18 and note).

SAUL AND THE MEDIUM AT ENDOR

³Now Samuel was dead, [b] and all Israel had mourned for him and buried him in his own town of Ramah. [c] Saul had expelled [d] the mediums and spiritists [e] from the land.

⁴The Philistines assembled and came and set up camp at Shunem, [f] while Saul gathered all Israel and set up camp at Gilboa. [g] ⁵When Saul saw the Philistine army, he was afraid; terror [h] filled his heart. ⁶He inquired [i] of the LORD, but the LORD did not answer him by dreams [j] or Urim [k] or prophets. [l] ⁷Saul then said to his attendants, "Find me a woman who is a medium, [m] so I may go and inquire of her."

"There is one in Endor, [n]" they said.

⁸So Saul disguised [o] himself, putting on other clothes, and at night he and two men went to the woman. "Consult [p] a spirit for me," he said, "and bring up for me the one I name."

⁹But the woman said to him, "Surely you know what Saul has done. He has cut off [q] the mediums and spiritists from the land. Why have you set a trap [r] for my life to bring about my death?"

¹⁰Saul swore to her by the LORD, "As surely as the LORD lives, you will not be punished for this."

¹¹Then the woman asked, "Whom shall I bring up for you?"

"Bring up Samuel," he said.

28:3 ᵇ1Sa 25:1
ᶜS 7:17 ᵈver 9
ᵉS Ex 22:18
28:4 ᶠS Jos 19:18
ᵍ1Sa 31:1,3; 2Sa 1:6,
21; 21:12
28:5 ʰS Ex 19:16
28:6 ᶦS 1Sa 8:18;
14:37 ʲS Dt 13:3
ᵏS Ex 28:30;
S Lev 8:8 ˡEze 20:3;
Am 8:11; Mic 3:7
28:7 ᵐ1Ch 10:13;
Ac 16:16 ⁿJos 17:11;
Ps 83:10
28:8 ᵒ1Ki 22:30;
2Ch 18:29; 35:22
ᵖ2Ki 1:3; Isa 8:19
28:9 ᵈver 3
ʳJob 18:10; Ps 31:4;
69:22; Isa 8:14

28:3 *Now Samuel was dead.* See 25:1. Saul could not turn to him, even in desperation. *expelled … from the land.* Possibly a euphemism for "put to death," in agreement with Pentateuchal law (see vv. 9,21). *mediums and spiritists.* See Lev 19:31; 20:6,27; Dt 18:11.

28:4 *Shunem.* The Philistines assembled their forces far to the north, along the plain of Jezreel in the territory of Issachar (see Jos 19:18). *Gilboa.* A range of mountains east of the plain of Jezreel.

28:5 *terror filled his heart.* Because he was estranged from the Lord and was not performing his role as the true theocratic king (see note on 17:11).

28:6 *He inquired of the LORD.* Presumably through the agency of a priest. Saul seems to sense disaster in the approaching battle and seeks divine revelation concerning its outcome. *dreams.* Direct personal revelation (see Nu 12:6 and note on 12:6–8). *Urim.*

Revelation through the priest (see note on 2:28). Since the authentic ephod and its Urim were with Abiathar, who was aligned with David (see 23:2,6,9), either Saul had fabricated another ephod for his use or the author used a conventional statement, including the three visual forms of revelation, to underscore his point. *prophets.* David had a prophet (Gad, 22:5), but after Samuel's alienation from Saul (15:35) no prophet served Saul.

28:7 *Find me a woman who is a medium.* In his desperation Saul turns to a pagan practice that he himself had previously outlawed (v. 3) in accordance with the Mosaic law (see Lev 19:31). *Endor.* Located about six miles northwest of Shunem (see v. 4; Jos 17:11).

28:9 *Why have you set a trap for my life …?* The woman is very cautious about practicing her trade with strangers, lest she be betrayed to Saul (see note on v. 3).

28:10 *As surely as the LORD lives.* See note on 14:39,45.

EXPLOITS OF DAVID

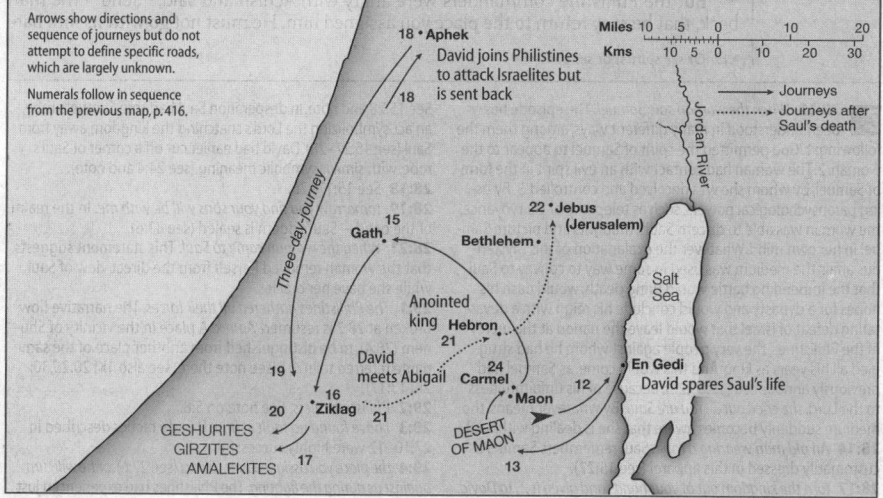

Arrows show directions and sequence of journeys but do not attempt to define specific roads, which are largely unknown.

Numerals follow in sequence from the previous map, p. 416.

18 • Aphek
David joins Philistines to attack Israelites but is sent back

Miles 10 5 0   10   20
Kms 10 5 0   10   20   30

→ Journeys
⇢ Journeys after Saul's death

Jordan River

Three-day journey

15
Gath •

22 • Jebus (Jerusalem)
Bethlehem •

Salt Sea

Anointed king
Hebron
21

24
Carmel

En Gedi
David spares Saul's life

19
David meets Abigail

12
• Maon

16
20   Ziklag   21

DESERT OF MAON

13

GESHURITES
GIRZITES
AMALEKITES   17

28:12 *S Ge 27:36;
1Ki 14:6
28:13 *t* ver 15;
S Lev 19:31; 2Ch 33:6
28:14 *u* 1Sa 15:27
28:15 *v* S Jdg 16:20
w S 1Sa 14:37
x Dt 13:3
28:17 *y* 1Sa 15:28
28:18 *z* 1Sa 15:20
a S Dt 9:8; S 1Sa 15:3
b S Ge 14:7;
S 1Sa 14:48
28:19 *c* 1Sa 31:2;
1Ch 8:33
28:21 *d* S Jdg 9:17;
S 12:3
28:23 *e* 1Ki 21:4
28:24 *f* S Ge 18:7
29:1 *g* 1Sa 28:1
h S 1Sa 4:1; *i* Jos 17:16;
1Ki 18:45; 21:1,23;
2Ki 9:30; Jer 50:5;
Hos 1:4,5,11; 2:22
29:2 *j* 1Sa 28:2
29:3 *k* 1Ch 12:19
l 1Sa 27:7
29:4 *m* 1Ch 12:19

¹²When the woman saw Samuel, she cried out at the top of her voice and said to Saul, "Why have you deceived me?*s* You are Saul!"

¹³The king said to her, "Don't be afraid. What do you see?"

The woman said, "I see a ghostly figure*a* coming up out of the earth."*t*

¹⁴"What does he look like?" he asked.

"An old man wearing a robe*u* is coming up," she said.

Then Saul knew it was Samuel, and he bowed down and prostrated himself with his face to the ground.

¹⁵Samuel said to Saul, "Why have you disturbed me by bringing me up?"

"I am in great distress," Saul said. "The Philistines are fighting against me, and God has departed*v* from me. He no longer answers*w* me, either by prophets or by dreams.*x* So I have called on you to tell me what to do."

¹⁶Samuel said, "Why do you consult me, now that the LORD has departed from you and become your enemy? ¹⁷The LORD has done what he predicted through me. The LORD has torn*y* the kingdom out of your hands and given it to one of your neighbors—to David. ¹⁸Because you did not obey*z* the LORD or carry out his fierce wrath*a* against the Amalekites,*b* the LORD has done this to you today. ¹⁹The LORD will deliver both Israel and you into the hands of the Philistines, and tomorrow you and your sons*c* will be with me. The LORD will also give the army of Israel into the hands of the Philistines."

²⁰Immediately Saul fell full length on the ground, filled with fear because of Samuel's words. His strength was gone, for he had eaten nothing all that day and all that night.

²¹When the woman came to Saul and saw that he was greatly shaken, she said, "Look, your servant has obeyed you. I took my life*d* in my hands and did what you told me to do. ²²Now please listen to your servant and let me give you some food so you may eat and have the strength to go on your way."

²³He refused*e* and said, "I will not eat."

But his men joined the woman in urging him, and he listened to them. He got up from the ground and sat on the couch.

²⁴The woman had a fattened calf*f* at the house, which she butchered at once. She took some flour, kneaded it and baked bread without yeast. ²⁵Then she set it before Saul and his men, and they ate. That same night they got up and left.

ACHISH SENDS DAVID BACK TO ZIKLAG

29 The Philistines gathered*g* all their forces at Aphek,*h* and Israel camped by the spring in Jezreel.*i* ²As the Philistine rulers marched with their units of hundreds and thousands, David and his men were marching at the rear*j* with Achish. ³The commanders of the Philistines asked, "What about these Hebrews?"

Achish replied, "Is this not David,*k* who was an officer of Saul king of Israel? He has already been with me for over a year,*l* and from the day he left Saul until now, I have found no fault in him."

⁴But the Philistine commanders were angry with Achish and said, "Send*m* the man back, that he may return to the place you assigned him. He must not go with us into bat-

a 13 Or see spirits; or see gods

28:12 *When the woman saw Samuel.* The episode has been understood in many different ways, among them the following: 1. God permitted the spirit of Samuel to appear to the woman. 2. The woman had contact with an evil spirit in the form of Samuel, by whom she was deceived and controlled. 3. By using parapsychological powers, such as telepathy or clairvoyance, the woman was able to discern Saul's thoughts and picture Samuel in her own mind. Whatever the explanation of this mysterious affair, the medium was used in some way to convey to Saul that the impending battle would bring death, would dash his hopes for a dynasty and would conclude his reign with a devastating defeat of Israel that would leave the nation at the mercy of the Philistines, the very people against whom he had struggled all his years as king. And this would come, as Samuel had previously announced (15:26,28), because of his unfaithfulness to the Lord. *she cried out … You are Saul!* By whatever means, the medium suddenly becomes aware that she is dealing with Saul.
28:14 *An old man wearing a robe.* Saul remembers Samuel as customarily dressed in this apparel (see 15:27).
28:17 *torn the kingdom out of your hands and given it … to David.*

See 15:28 and note. In desperation Saul had torn Samuel's robe, an act symbolizing the Lord's snatching the kingdom away from Saul (see 15:27–28). David had earlier cut off a corner of Saul's robe, with similar symbolic meaning (see 24:4 and note).
28:18 See 15:17–26.
28:19 *tomorrow you and your sons will be with me.* In the realm of the dead—Saul's doom is sealed (see 31:6).
28:21 *When the woman came to Saul.* This statement suggests that the woman removed herself from the direct view of Saul while she gave him oracles.
29:1 *The Philistines gathered all their forces.* The narrative flow broken at 28:2 is resumed. *Aphek.* A place in the vicinity of Shunem (28:4), to be distinguished from another place of the same name referred to in 4:1 (see note there; see also 1Ki 20:26,30; 2Ki 13:17).
29:2 *Philistine rulers.* See note on 5:8.
29:3 *I have found no fault in him.* David's tactics described in 27:10–12 were highly successful.
29:4 *the place you assigned him.* Ziklag (see 27:6). *or he will turn against us during the fighting.* The Philistines had experienced just

tle, or he will turn [n] against us during the fighting. How better could he regain his master's favor than by taking the heads of our own men? [5]Isn't this the David they sang about in their dances:

> " 'Saul has slain his thousands,
> and David his tens of thousands'?" [o]

[6]So Achish called David and said to him, "As surely as the LORD lives, you have been reliable, and I would be pleased to have you serve with me in the army. From the day [p] you came to me until today, I have found no fault in you, but the rulers [q] don't approve of you. [7]Now turn back and go in peace; do nothing to displease the Philistine rulers."

[8]"But what have I done?" asked David. "What have you found against your servant from the day I came to you until now? Why can't I go and fight against the enemies of my lord the king?"

[9]Achish answered, "I know that you have been as pleasing in my eyes as an angel [r] of God; nevertheless, the Philistine commanders [s] have said, 'He must not go up with us into battle.' [10]Now get up early, along with your master's servants who have come with you, and leave [t] in the morning as soon as it is light."

[11]So David and his men got up early in the morning to go back to the land of the Philistines, and the Philistines went up to Jezreel.

DAVID DESTROYS THE AMALEKITES

30 David and his men reached Ziklag [u] on the third day. Now the Amalekites [v] had raided the Negev and Ziklag. They had attacked Ziklag and burned [w] it, [2]and had taken captive the women who were in it, both young and old. They killed none of them, but carried them off as they went on their way.

[3]When David and his men reached Ziklag, they found it destroyed by fire and their wives and sons and daughters taken captive. [x] [4]So David and his men wept [y] aloud until they had no strength left to weep. [5]David's two wives [z] had been captured—Ahinoam of Jezreel and Abigail, the widow of Nabal of Carmel. [6]David was greatly distressed because the men were talking of stoning [a] him; each one was bitter [b] in spirit because of his sons and daughters. But David found strength [c] in the LORD his God.

[7]Then David said to Abiathar [d] the priest, the son of Ahimelek, "Bring me the ephod. [e]" Abiathar brought it to him, [8]and David inquired [f] of the LORD, "Shall I pursue this raiding party? Will I overtake them?"

"Pursue them," he answered. "You will certainly overtake them and succeed [g] in the rescue. [h]"

[9]David and the six hundred men [i] with him came to the Besor Valley, where some stayed behind. [10]Two hundred of them were too exhausted [j] to cross the valley, but David and the other four hundred continued the pursuit.

[11]They found an Egyptian in a field and brought him to David. They gave him water to drink and food to eat— [12]part of a cake of pressed figs and two cakes of raisins. He ate and was revived, [k] for he had not eaten any food or drunk any water for three days and three nights.

[13]David asked him, "Who do you belong to? Where do you come from?"

He said, "I am an Egyptian, the slave of an Amalekite. [l] My master abandoned me when I became ill three days ago. [14]We raided the Negev of the Kerethites, [m] some territory belonging to Judah and the Negev of Caleb. [n] And we burned [o] Ziklag."

29:4 [n] 1Sa 14:21
29:5 [o] S 1Sa 18:7
29:6 [p] 1Sa 27:8-12
[q] ver 3
29:9 [r] 2Sa 14:17,20; 19:27 [s] ver 4
29:10 [t] 1Ch 12:19
30:1 [u] S 1Sa 27:6
[v] S 1Sa 27:8 [w] ver 14
30:3 [x] S Ge 31:26
30:4 [y] S Ge 27:38
30:5 [z] S 1Sa 25:43
30:6 [a] S Ex 17:4; Jn 8:59 [b] S Ru 1:13
[c] S 1Sa 23:16; Ro 4:20
30:7 [d] S 1Sa 22:20
[e] S 1Sa 2:28
30:8 [f] S 1Sa 23:2
30:9 [g] S 1Sa 25:43
[h] S Ex 2:17
30:9 [i] S 1Sa 27:2
30:10 [j] ver 21
30:12 [k] S Jdg 15:19
30:13 [l] S 1Sa 14:48
30:14 [m] 2Sa 8:18; 15:18; 20:7,23; 1Ki 1:38,44; 1Ch 18:17; Eze 25:16; Zep 2:5 [n] S Jos 14:13; S 15:13 [o] ver 1

---

such a reversal on a previous occasion (see 14:21). *taking the heads.* As trophies of victory (see 17:51; see also 5:4; 31:9 and notes).

29:5 See 21:11 and note on 18:7.

29:6 *As surely as the LORD lives.* See note on 14:39,45. Achish swears by the God of Israel apparently as a means of proving his sincerity to David.

29:8 *But what have I done?* David pretends disappointment in order to keep intact his strategy of deception. In reality this turn of events rescued David from a serious dilemma. *Why can't I go and fight against the enemies of my lord the king?* David again uses an ambiguous statement (see 28:2). To whom was he referring as "my lord the king"—Achish or Saul or the Lord?

29:9 *as an angel of God.* A common simile (see 2Sa 14:17 and note).

29:11 *Jezreel.* The place of Israel's camp (see v. 1).

30:1—31:13 While Saul goes to his death at the hands of the

Philistines, David is drawn into and pursues the Lord's continuing war with the Amalekites (see 15:2–3 and notes).

30:1 *Ziklag.* See note on 27:6. *Amalekites.* See 27:8 and note on 15:2. The absence of David and his warriors gave the Amalekites opportunity for revenge. *Negev.* See note on 27:10.

30:5 *Ahinoam.* See note on 25:43. *Abigail.* See 25:42.

30:6 *David found strength in the LORD.* As he had throughout his life (see 17:37 and note).

30:7 *Abiathar the priest.* See note on 22:20. *ephod.* See note on 2:28.

30:14 *Negev.* See note on 27:10. *Kerethites.* Along with the Pelethites, they later contributed contingents of professional warriors to David's private army (see 2Sa 8:18 and note; 15:18; 20:7; 1Ki 1:38). The name may indicate that they originally came from the island of Crete (see Jer 47:4 and note). *Negev of Caleb.* The area south of Hebron (see Jos 14:13).

30:15 *P* Dt 23:15
30:16 *q* Lk 12:19
r S ver 17; S Jos 22:8
30:17 *s* ver 16;
1Sa 11:11; 2Sa 1:1
t 2Sa 1:8
30:18 *u* S Ge 14:16
30:21 *v* ver 10
30:24 *w* S Nu 31:27;
S Jdg 5:30
30:26 *x* S Ge 33:11
30:27 *y* S Jos 7:2
z S Jos 10:40
a S Jos 15:48
30:28 *b* S Nu 32:34;
S Jos 13:16
c 1Ch 27:27
d S Jos 15:50
30:29 *e* 1Sa 27:10
f S 1Sa 15:6
30:30 *g* S Nu 14:45;
S 21:3 *h* S Jos 15:42
30:31 *i* Nu 13:22;
S Jos 10:36; 2Sa 2:1,4
31:1 *j* S 1Sa 28:4
31:2 *k* S 1Sa 28:19
l S 1Sa 18:1
m S 1Sa 14:49
31:3 *n* S 1Sa 28:4
31:4 *o* S Jdg 9:54
P Ge 34:14;
S 1Sa 14:6
31:6 *q* S 1Sa 26:10
31:8 *r* 2Sa 1:20

¹⁵David asked him, "Can you lead me down to this raiding party?"

He answered, "Swear to me before God that you will not kill me or hand me over to my master, *P* and I will take you down to them."

¹⁶He led David down, and there they were, scattered over the countryside, eating, drinking and reveling *q* because of the great amount of plunder *r* they had taken from the land of the Philistines and from Judah. ¹⁷David fought *s* them from dusk until the evening of the next day, and none of them got away, except four hundred young men who rode off on camels and fled. *t* ¹⁸David recovered *u* everything the Amalekites had taken, including his two wives. ¹⁹Nothing was missing: young or old, boy or girl, plunder or anything else they had taken. David brought everything back. ²⁰He took all the flocks and herds, and his men drove them ahead of the other livestock, saying, "This is David's plunder."

²¹Then David came to the two hundred men who had been too exhausted *v* to follow him and who were left behind at the Besor Valley. They came out to meet David and the men with him. As David and his men approached, he asked them how they were. ²²But all the evil men and troublemakers among David's followers said, "Because they did not go out with us, we will not share with them the plunder we recovered. However, each man may take his wife and children and go."

²³David replied, "No, my brothers, you must not do that with what the LORD has given us. He has protected us and delivered into our hands the raiding party that came against us. ²⁴Who will listen to what you say? The share of the man who stayed with the supplies is to be the same as that of him who went down to the battle. All will share alike. *w* ²⁵David made this a statute and ordinance for Israel from that day to this.

²⁶When David reached Ziklag, he sent some of the plunder to the elders of Judah, who were his friends, saying, "Here is a gift *x* for you from the plunder of the LORD's enemies."

²⁷David sent it to those who were in Bethel, *y* Ramoth *z* Negev and Jattir; *a* ²⁸to those in Aroer, *b* Siphmoth, *c* Eshtemoa *d* ²⁹and Rakal; to those in the towns of the Jerahmeelites *e* and the Kenites; *f* ³⁰to those in Hormah, *g* Bor Ashan, *h* Athak ³¹and Hebron; *i* and to those in all the other places where he and his men had roamed.

SAUL TAKES HIS LIFE

31:1–13pp — 2Sa 1:4–12; 1Ch 10:1–12

31 Now the Philistines fought against Israel; the Israelites fled before them, and many fell dead on Mount Gilboa. *j* ²The Philistines were in hot pursuit of Saul and his sons, *k* and they killed his sons Jonathan, *l* Abinadab and Malki-Shua. *m* ³The fighting grew fierce around Saul, and when the archers overtook him, they wounded *n* him critically.

⁴Saul said to his armor-bearer, "Draw your sword and run me through, *o* or these uncircumcised *P* fellows will come and run me through and abuse me."

But his armor-bearer was terrified and would not do it; so Saul took his own sword and fell on it. ⁵When the armor-bearer saw that Saul was dead, he too fell on his sword and died with him. ⁶So Saul and his three sons and his armor-bearer and all his men died *q* together that same day.

⁷When the Israelites along the valley and those across the Jordan saw that the Israelite army had fled and that Saul and his sons had died, they abandoned their towns and fled. And the Philistines came and occupied them.

⁸The next day, when the Philistines *r* came to strip the dead, they found Saul and his

---

30:17 *camels.* The mount of choice for the Amalekites and other eastern peoples (see Jdg 6:3,5 and note on 6:5).

30:22 *troublemakers.* See note on Dt 13:13.

30:23 *what the LORD has given us.* See 25:28 and note. David gently but firmly rejects the idea that their victory is to be attributed to their own prowess. Because the Lord gave the victory, no segment of David's men could claim any greater right to the spoils than any other.

30:24 *All will share alike.* Cf. Ex 16:18 and note.

30:26 *elders of Judah, who were his friends.* David sent the plunder as an expression of gratitude to those who had assisted him during his flight from Saul (see v. 31), thus preparing the way for his later elevation to kingship in Judah (see 2Sa 2:1–4).

30:29 *Jerahmeelites.* See note on 27:10. *Kenites.* See note on 15:6.

30:31 *Hebron.* The most important city in the central part of Judah. The other locations mentioned are to the southwest and

southeast of Hebron.

31:1,8 *Mount Gilboa.* A range of hills (see 2Sa 1:21) at the southeast end of the Plain of Jezreel and at the head of the valley that leads down to Beth Shan. It is referred to elsewhere in the OT only as the place where Saul died (see 2Sa 1:6,21; 21:12).

31:2 *Jonathan, Abinadab and Malki-Shua.* See note on 14:49. The surviving son, Ish-Bosheth or Esh-Baal (1Ch 8:33; 9:39), was afterward promoted by Abner, who somehow survived the battle, to succeed his father as king (2Sa 2:8–9).

31:4 *uncircumcised fellows.* See 14:6 and note. *abuse me.* A practice that was not uncommon; previously the Philistines had mutilated and humiliated Samson after his capture (see Jdg 16:21–25). *took his own sword and fell on it.* The culmination of a long process of self-destruction.

31:6 *all his men.* Those who had served around him in his administration (but see note on v. 2).

three sons fallen on Mount Gilboa. ⁹They cut off his head and stripped off his armor, and they sent messengers throughout the land of the Philistines to proclaim the news *s* in the temple of their idols and among their people. *t* ¹⁰They put his armor in the temple of the Ashtoreths *u* and fastened his body to the wall of Beth Shan. *v*

¹¹When the people of Jabesh Gilead *w* heard what the Philistines had done to Saul, ¹²all their valiant men *x* marched through the night to Beth Shan. They took down the bodies of Saul and his sons from the wall of Beth Shan and went to Jabesh, where they burned *y* them. ¹³Then they took their bones *z* and buried them under a tamarisk *a* tree at Jabesh, and they fasted *b* seven days. *c*

31:9 *s* 2Sa 1:20; 4:4
t S Jdg 16:24
31:10 *u* S Jdg 2:12-13; S 1Sa 7:3
v Jos 17:11
31:11 *w* S Jdg 21:8; S 1Sa 11:1
31:12 *x* Ps 76:5
y S Ge 38:24; Am 6:10
31:13 *z* 2Sa 21:12-14
a S Ge 21:33
b 2Sa 3:35; 12:19-23
c S Ge 50:10

31:9 *They cut off his head.* David had done the same to Goliath (see 17:51). *sent messengers throughout the land.* Probably bearing Saul's head and armor as proof and trophies of their victory (see 5:4 and note).

31:10 *They put his armor in the temple.* Symbolic of ascribing the victory to the Philistine gods. *Ashtoreths.* See note on 7:3. *Beth Shan.* See note on Jos 17:11.

31:11 *Jabesh Gilead.* See note on 11:1.

31:12 *They took down the bodies of Saul and his sons.* The men of Jabesh Gilead had not forgotten how Saul had come to their

defense when they were threatened by the Ammonites (see 11:1–11). *burned them.* Cremation was not customary in ancient Israel and here appears to have been done to prevent any further abuse of the bodies of Saul and his sons by the Philistines.

31:13 *took their bones and buried them.* David later had their remains removed from Jabesh and placed in the family burial grounds of Zela in Benjamin (see 2Sa 21:11–14). *fasted seven days.* As an indication of their mourning for Saul (cf. 2Sa 1:12; 3:35; 12:16,21–23).

1 and 2 Samuel were originally one book (see Introduction to 1 Samuel: Title).

LITERARY FEATURES, AUTHORSHIP AND DATE

See Introduction to 1 Samuel: Literary Features, Authorship and Date.

CONTENTS AND THEME: KINGSHIP AND COVENANT

C 2 Samuel depicts David as a true (though imperfect) representative of the ideal theocratic king. David was initially acclaimed king at Hebron by the tribe of Judah (chs. 1–4), and subsequently was accepted by the remaining tribes after the murder of Ish-Bosheth, one of Saul's surviving sons (5:1–5). David's leadership was decisive and effective. He captured Jerusalem from the Jebusites and made it his royal city and residence (5:6–13). Shortly afterward he brought the ark of the Lord from the house of Abinadab to Jerusalem, publicly acknowledging the Lord's kingship and rule over himself and the nation (ch. 6; Ps 132:3–5).

Under David's rule the Lord caused the nation to prosper, to defeat its enemies and, in fulfillment of his promise (see Ge 15:18), to extend its borders from Egypt to the Euphrates (ch. 8). David wanted to build a temple for the Lord—as his royal house, as a place for his throne (the ark) and as a place for Israel to worship him. But the prophet Nathan told David that he was not to build the Lord a house (temple); rather, the Lord would build David a house (dynasty). Ch. 7 announces the Lord's promise that this Davidic dynasty would endure forever. This climactic chapter also describes the establishment of the Davidic covenant (see notes on 7:1–29,11,16; Ps 89:30–37). Later the prophets make clear that a descendant of David who sits on David's throne will perfectly fulfill the role of the theocratic king. He will complete the redemption of God's people (see Isa 9:6–7; 11:1–16; Jer 23:5–6; 30:8–9; 33:14–16; Eze 34:23–24; 37:24–25), thus enabling them to achieve the promised victory with him (Ro 16:20).

After the description of David's rule in its glory and success, chs. 10–20 depict the darker side of his reign and describe David's weaknesses and failures. Even though David remained a king after God's own heart because he was willing to acknowledge his sin and repent (12:13), he nevertheless fell far short of the theocratic ideal and suffered the disciplinary results of his disobedience (12:10–12). His sin with Bathsheba (chs. 11–12) and his leniency with regard both to the wickedness of his sons (13:12–39; 21; 14:1,33; 19:4–6) and to the insubordination of Joab (3:28–39; 20:10,23) led to intrigue, violence and bloodshed within his own family and the nation. It eventually drove him from Jerusalem at the time of Absalom's rebellion. Nonetheless the Lord was gracious to David, and his reign became a standard by which the reigns of later kings were measured (see 2Ki 18:3; 22:2).

The book ends with David's own words of praise to God, who had delivered him from all his enemies (22:31–51), and with words of expectation for the fulfillment of God's promise that a king will come from the house of David and rule "over people in righteousness" (23:3–5). These songs echo many of the themes of Hannah's song (1Sa 2:1–10), and together they frame (and interpret) the basic narrative.

CHRONOLOGY

See Introduction to 1 Samuel: Chronology.

OUTLINE

Below is an outline for 2 Samuel. For an outline of both 1 and 2 Samuel see Introduction to 1 Samuel: Outline.

1:1 a S 1Sa 26:10;
1Ch 10:13
b S Jos 22:8;
S 1Sa 30:17
c S Ge 14:7; Nu 13:29
1:2 d 2Sa 4:10
e S 1Sa 4:12; Job 2:12;
Eze 27:30
f S 1Sa 20:41
g S Ge 37:7
1:6 h ver 21;
S 1Sa 28:4
1:8 i ver 13;
S 1Sa 15:2; S 27:8;
30:13,17
1:9 j S Jdg 9:54
1:10 k 2Ki 11:12
1:11 l S Ge 37:29;
S Nu 14:6
1:13 m S ver 8;
S 1Sa 14:48
1:14 n S 1Sa 12:3;
S 26:9
1:15 o 2Sa 4:12
p 2Sa 4:10
1:16 q S Lev 20:9;
Mt 27:24-25; Ac 18:6
1:17 r S Ge 50:10;
S Eze 32:2 # ver 26
1:18 t Jos 10:13
1:19 u 2Sa 23:8;
Ps 29:1; 45:3
v 2Sa 3:38

DAVID HEARS OF SAUL'S DEATH
1:4–12pp — 1Sa 31:1–13; 1Ch 10:1–12

1 After the death a of Saul, David returned from striking down b the Amalekites c and stayed in Ziklag two days. 2On the third day a man d arrived from Saul's camp with his clothes torn and dust on his head. e When he came to David, he fell f to the ground to pay him honor. g

3"Where have you come from?" David asked him.

He answered, "I have escaped from the Israelite camp."

4"What happened?" David asked. "Tell me."

"The men fled from the battle," he replied. "Many of them fell and died. And Saul and his son Jonathan are dead."

5Then David said to the young man who brought him the report, "How do you know that Saul and his son Jonathan are dead?"

6"I happened to be on Mount Gilboa, h" the young man said, "and there was Saul, leaning on his spear, with the chariots and their drivers in hot pursuit. 7When he turned around and saw me, he called out to me, and I said, 'What can I do?'

8"He asked me, 'Who are you?'

" 'An Amalekite,i' I answered.

9"Then he said to me, 'Stand here by me and kill me!j I'm in the throes of death, but I'm still alive.'

10"So I stood beside him and killed him, because I knew that after he had fallen he could not survive. And I took the crown k that was on his head and the band on his arm and have brought them here to my lord."

11Then David and all the men with him took hold of their clothes and tore l them. 12They mourned and wept and fasted till evening for Saul and his son Jonathan, and for the army of the LORD and the house of Israel, because they had fallen by the sword.

13David said to the young man who brought him the report, "Where are you from?"

"I am the son of a foreigner, an Amalekite, m" he answered.

14David asked him, "Why weren't you afraid to lift your hand to destroy the LORD's anointed? n"

15Then David called one of his men and said, "Go, strike him down!" o So he struck him down, and he died. p 16For David had said to him, "Your blood be on your own head. q Your own mouth testified against you when you said, 'I killed the LORD's anointed.' "

DAVID'S LAMENT FOR SAUL AND JONATHAN

17David took up this lament r concerning Saul and his son Jonathan, s 18and he ordered that the people of Judah be taught this lament of the bow (it is written in the Book of Jashar): t

19"A gazellea lies slain on your heights, Israel.
How the mighty u have fallen!v

---

a 19 *Gazelle* here symbolizes a human dignitary.

1:1 *After the death of.* See Jos 1:1; Jdg 1:1; 2Ki 1:1. The narrative thread of 1 Samuel is continued. 1 and 2 Samuel were originally one book (see Introduction to 1 Samuel: Title). *David returned from striking down the Amalekites.* See 1Sa 30:26. *Ziklag.* See note on 1Sa 27:6.
1:2 *his clothes torn … dust on his head.* See note on 1Sa 4:12; see also Jos 7:6; Ac 14:14 and notes.
1:8 *Amalekite.* It is not necessary to conclude from v. 3 that this Amalekite was a member of Saul's army. His statement that he "happened to be on Mount Gilboa" (v. 6) is probably not as innocent as it appears. He may have been there as a scavenger to rob the fallen soldiers of their valuables and weapons. It is ironic that Saul's death is reported by an Amalekite (see 1Sa 15).
1:10 *I stood beside him and killed him.* The Amalekite's story conflicts with 1Sa 31:3–6, where Saul is depicted as taking his own life. It appears that the Amalekite fabricated this version of Saul's death, expecting David to reward him (see 4:10). His miscalculation of David's response cost him his life (see v. 15). *I took the crown.* Apparently he got to Saul before the Philistines did (see 1Sa 31:8–9).
1:11 *took hold of their clothes and tore them.* See note on v. 9.
1:12 *mourned and wept.* David and his men expressed their

grief in typical Near Eastern fashion (see Ge 23:2; 1Ki 13:30; Jer 22:18). *fasted.* See note on 1Sa 31:13.
1:13 *Amalekite.* The man was probably unaware of David's recent hostile encounters with the Amalekites (see v. 1; 1Sa 30; see also note on 1Sa 15:2).
1:14 The Amalekite understood nothing of the deep significance that David attached to the sanctity of the royal office in Israel (see 1Sa 24:6 and note). *the LORD's anointed.* See note on 1Sa 9:16.
1:15 *strike him down!* David displays no personal satisfaction over Saul's death and condemns to death the one he believes to be his murderer (see note on v. 10; see also 4:10).
1:16 *Your blood be on your own head.* The Amalekite's own testimony brought about his execution (see Jos 2:19; 1Ki 2:37).
1:17 *lament.* It was a common practice in the ancient Near East to compose laments for fallen leaders, heroes and royal cities (see 2Ch 35:25 and note; Lamentations, particularly its Introduction: Themes and Theology).
1:18 *lament of the bow.* Perhaps David taught his men to sing this lament while they practiced with the bow (Israel's most common weapon; see, e.g., 22:35) as a motivation to master the weapon thoroughly so they would not experience a similar defeat (see note on Eze 21:9). *Book of Jashar.* See note on Jos 10:13.

20 "Tell it not in Gath,[w]
    proclaim it not in the streets of Ashkelon,[x]
lest the daughters of the Philistines[y] be glad,
    lest the daughters of the uncircumcised rejoice.[z]

21 "Mountains of Gilboa,[a]
    may you have neither dew[b] nor rain,[c]
    may no showers fall on your terraced fields.[a][d]
For there the shield of the mighty was despised,
    the shield of Saul—no longer rubbed with oil.[e]

22 "From the blood[f] of the slain,
    from the flesh of the mighty,
the bow[g] of Jonathan did not turn back,
    the sword of Saul did not return unsatisfied.

23 Saul and Jonathan—
    in life they were loved and admired,
    and in death they were not parted.
They were swifter than eagles,[h]
    they were stronger than lions.[i]

24 "Daughters of Israel,
    weep for Saul,
who clothed you in scarlet and finery,
    who adorned your garments with ornaments of gold.[j]

25 "How the mighty have fallen in battle!
    Jonathan lies slain on your heights.
26 I grieve[k] for you, Jonathan[l] my brother;[m]
    you were very dear to me.
Your love for me was wonderful,[n]
    more wonderful than that of women.

27 "How the mighty have fallen!
    The weapons of war have perished!"[o]

DAVID ANOINTED KING OVER JUDAH

2 In the course of time, David inquired[p] of the LORD. "Shall I go up to one of the towns of Judah?" he asked.
The LORD said, "Go up."

---

a 21 Or / nor fields that yield grain for offerings

1:19 *A gazelle.* See TNIV text note; probably a reference to Jonathan (see v. 25, a kind of refrain; for the imagery cf. 2:18; 1Ch 12:8). Or the Hebrew may be rendered "Your glory," referring to both Saul and Jonathan (vv. 22–23). *heights.* Of Gilboa (see v. 25; 1Sa 31:1,8 and note). *How the mighty have fallen!* The theme of David's lament (see vv. 25,27). David's words contain no suggestion of bitterness toward Saul but rather recall the good qualities and accomplishments of Saul and Jonathan. However, David's lament over "fallen" Saul is Saul's epitaph and stands in significant contrast to Hannah's song in 1Sa 2:1–10 and David's song in 2Sa 22.
1:20 *Tell it not in Gath … Ashkelon.* As the major Philistine cities located the closest and farthest from Israel's borders, Gath and Ashkelon represent the entire Philistine nation. David does not want the enemies of God's covenant people to take pleasure in Israel's defeat (as he knew they would; see 1Sa 31:9–10) and thus bring reproach on the name of the Lord (see Ex 32:12; Nu 14:13–19; Dt 9:28; see also Jos 7:9; Mic 1:10 and notes). *uncircumcised.* See note on 1Sa 14:6.
1:21 *Mountains of Gilboa.* As an expression of profound grief, David rhetorically pronounces a curse on the place where Israel was defeated and Saul and Jonathan were killed (for other such rhetorical curses, see Job 3:3–26; Jer 20:14–18). *no longer rubbed with oil.* Leather shields were rubbed with oil to preserve them (see Isa 21:5).

1:23 *in death they were not parted.* Even though Jonathan opposed his father's treatment of David, he gave his life beside his father in Israel's defense.
1:26 *more wonderful than that of women.* David is not suggesting that marital love is inferior to that of friendship, nor do his remarks have any sexual implications. He is simply calling attention to Jonathan's nearly inexplicable self-denying commitment to David, whom he had long recognized as the Lord's choice to succeed Jonathan's own father, Saul (see notes on 1Sa 20:13–16).
1:27 *weapons of war.* Probably a metaphor for Saul and Jonathan.
2:1 *In the course of time.* This phrase introduces significant episodes in David's life: his anointing as king over Judah (here), his most notable military victories (8:1), his adultery with Bathsheba and murder of Uriah (10:1), the death of his firstborn son, Amnon (13:1), and the conspiracy of his son Absalom (15:1). *David inquired of the LORD.* By means of the ephod through the priest Abiathar (see notes on Ex 28:30; 1Sa 2:28; 23:2). *one of the towns of Judah.* Even though Saul was dead and David had many friends and contacts among the people of his own tribe (see 1Sa 30:26–31), David did not presume to return from Philistine territory to assume the kingship promised to him without first seeking the Lord's guidance. *Hebron.* An old and important city (see Ge 13:18; 23:2; Jos 15:13–14; see also note on 1Sa 30:31) centrally located in the tribe of Judah.

1:20 [w]Mic 1:10
[x]S Jos 13:3 [y]1Sa 31:8
[z]S 1Sa 18:6
1:21 [a]S ver 6
[b]S Ge 27:28;
S Isa 18:4 [c]Dt 11:17;
1Ki 8:35; 17:1; 18:1;
2Ch 6:26; Job 36:27;
38:28; Ps 65:10;
147:8; Isa 5:6;
Jer 5:24; 14:4; Am 1:2
[d]Jer 12:4; Eze 31:15
[e]Isa 21:5
1:22 [f]Isa 34:3,7;
49:26 [g]Dt 32:42
1:23 [h]S Dt 28:49
[i]Jdg 14:18
1:24 [j]S Jdg 5:30
1:26 [k]Jer 22:18;
34:5 [l]ver 17
[m]S 1Sa 20:42
[n]S 1Sa 18:1
1:27 [o]S 1Sa 2:4
2:1 [p]S 1Sa 23:2,11-
12

David asked, "Where shall I go?"

"To Hebron," ⁹ the Lᴏʀᴅ answered.

²So David went up there with his two wives, ʳ Ahinoam of Jezreel and Abigail, ˢ the widow of Nabal of Carmel. ³David also took the men who were with him, ᵗ each with his family, and they settled in Hebron ᵘ and its towns. ⁴Then the men of Judah came to Hebron, ᵛ and there they anointed ʷ David king over the house of Judah.

When David was told that it was the men from Jabesh Gilead ˣ who had buried Saul, ⁵he sent messengers to them to say to them, "The Lᴏʀᴅ bless ʸ you for showing this kindness to Saul your master by burying him. ⁶May the Lᴏʀᴅ now show you kindness and faithfulness, ᶻ and I too will show you the same favor because you have done this. ⁷Now then, be strong ᵃ and brave, for Saul your master is dead, and the house of Judah has anointed me king over them."

WAR BETWEEN THE HOUSES OF DAVID AND SAUL

3:2–5pp — 1Ch 3:1–4

⁸Meanwhile, Abner ᵇ son of Ner, the commander of Saul's army, had taken Ish-Bosheth ᶜ son of Saul and brought him over to Mahanaim. ᵈ ⁹He made him king over Gilead, ᵉ Ashuri ᶠ and Jezreel, and also over Ephraim, Benjamin and all Israel. ᵍ

¹⁰Ish-Bosheth son of Saul was forty years old when he became king over Israel, and he reigned two years. The house of Judah, however, remained loyal to David. ¹¹The length of time David was king in Hebron over the house of Judah was seven years and six months. ʰ ¹²Abner son of Ner, together with the men of Ish-Bosheth son of Saul, left Mahanaim and went to Gibeon. ⁱ ¹³Joab ʲ son of Zeruiah and David's men went out and met them at the pool of Gibeon. One group sat down on one side of the pool and one group on the other side.

¹⁴Then Abner said to Joab, "Let's have some of the soldiers get up and fight hand to hand in front of us."

"All right, let them do it," Joab said.

¹⁵So they stood up and were counted off—twelve men for Benjamin and Ish-Bosheth son of Saul, and twelve for David. ¹⁶Then each man grabbed his opponent by the head

---

2:2 *Ahinoam of Jezreel.* See note on 1Sa 25:43. *Abigail.* See 1Sa 25.

2:3 *men who were with him.* See note on v. 13.

■ **2:4** *anointed David king.* See notes on 1Sa 2:10; 9:16. David had previously been anointed privately by Samuel in the presence of his own family (see note on 1Sa 16:13). Here the anointing ceremony is repeated as a public recognition by his own tribe of his divine calling to be king. *over the house of Judah.* Very likely the tribe of Simeon was also involved (see Jos 19:1; Jdg 1:3), but the Judahites in every way dominated the area. *men from Jabesh Gilead.* See notes on 1Sa 11:1; 31:12. *buried Saul.* See note on 1Sa 31:13.

2:7 *your master is dead, and the house of Judah has anointed me king over them.* David's concluding statement to the men of Jabesh Gilead is a veiled invitation to them to recognize him as their king, just as the tribe of Judah had done. This appeal for their support, however, was ignored.

■ **2:8** *Abner son of Ner.* See 1Sa 14:50–51. *Saul's army.* His small standing army of professionals loyal to him and his family (see 1Sa 13:2,15; 14:2,52). *Ish-Bosheth.* The name was originally Ish-(or Esh-)Baal (1Ch 8:33) but was changed by the author of Samuel to Ish-Bosheth, meaning "man of the shameful thing" (see notes on 4:4; Jdg 6:32; Jer 2:26; 3:24–25; 11:13). Evidently Baal (meaning "lord" or "master") was at this time still used to refer to the Lord. Later this was discontinued because of confusion with the Canaanite god Baal, and the author of Samuel reflects the later sensitivity. *son of Saul.* See note on 1Sa 31:2. *brought him.* Abner takes the initiative in the power vacuum created by Saul's death, using the unassertive Ish-Bosheth as a pawn for his own ambitions (see 3:11 and more on 4:1). There is no evidence that Ish-Bosheth had strong support among the Israelites generally. *Mahanaim.* A Gileadite town east of the Jordan River and thus beyond the sphere of Philistine domination—a kind of refugee capital.

2:9 *He made him king.* As a relative of Saul (see 1Sa 14:50–51), Abner had both a family and a career interest in ensuring dy-

nastic succession for Saul's house. *Gilead . . . all Israel.* This delineation of Ish-Bosheth's realm suggests that his actual rule, while involving territory both east and west of the Jordan, was quite limited and that "all Israel" was more claim than reality. David ruled over Judah and Simeon, and the Philistines controlled large sections of the northern tribal regions.

2:11 *seven years and six months.* Cf. Ish-Bosheth's two-year reign in Mahanaim (v. 10). Because it appears that David was made king over all Israel shortly after Ish-Bosheth's death (5:1–5) and moved his capital to Jerusalem not long afterward (5:6–12), reconciling the lengths of David's and Ish-Bosheth's reigns is difficult. The difficulty is best resolved by assuming that it took Ish-Bosheth a number of years to be recognized as his father's successor, and that the two years of his reign roughly correspond to the last two or three years of David's reign in Hebron.

2:12 Abner initiates an action to prevent David's sphere of influence from spreading northward out of Judah. Gibeon was located in the tribal area of Benjamin (see Jos 18:21,25), to which Saul and his family belonged, and which the Philistines had not occupied.

■ ■ **2:13** *Joab son of Zeruiah.* See note on 1Sa 26:6. Joab became a figure of major importance during David's reign as a competent but ruthless military leader (see 10:7–14; 11:1; 12:26; 1Ki 11:15–16). At times David was unable to control him (3:39; 18:5,14; 1Ki 2:5–6), and he was eventually executed for his wanton assassinations and his part in the conspiracy to place Adonijah rather than Solomon on David's throne (1Ki 2:28–34). *David's men.* Some, at least, of David's small force of professionals who had gathered around him (see 1Sa 22:2; 23:13; 27:2; 30:3,9). *pool of Gibeon.* See Jer 41:12. In 1956 archaeologists uncovered a large, cylindrical pool at el-Jib (ancient Gibeon), probably the one near which the battle recorded in vv. 15–16 took place.

2:15 *Benjamin.* At this time Ish-Bosheth seems to have been supported mainly by his own tribesmen.

and thrust his dagger[k] into his opponent's side, and they fell down together. So that place in Gibeon was called Helkath Hazzurim.[a]

[17]The battle that day was very fierce, and Abner and the Israelites were defeated[l] by David's men.[m]

[18]The three sons of Zeruiah[n] were there: Joab,[o] Abishai[p] and Asahel.[q] Now Asahel was as fleet-footed as a wild gazelle.[r] [19]He chased Abner, turning neither to the right nor to the left as he pursued him. [20]Abner looked behind him and asked, "Is that you, Asahel?"

"It is," he answered.

[21]Then Abner said to him, "Turn aside to the right or to the left; take on one of the soldiers and strip him of his weapons." But Asahel would not stop chasing him.

[22]Again Abner warned Asahel, "Stop chasing me! Why should I strike you down? How could I look your brother Joab in the face?"[s]

[23]But Asahel refused to give up the pursuit; so Abner thrust the butt of his spear into Asahel's stomach,[t] and the spear came out through his back. He fell there and died on the spot. And every man stopped when he came to the place where Asahel had fallen and died.[u]

[24]But Joab and Abishai pursued Abner, and as the sun was setting, they came to the hill of Ammah, near Giah on the way to the wasteland of Gibeon. [25]Then the men of Benjamin rallied behind Abner. They formed themselves into a group and took their stand on top of a hill.

[26]Abner called out to Joab, "Must the sword devour[v] forever? Don't you realize that this will end in bitterness? How long before you order your men to stop pursuing their fellow Israelites?"

[27]Joab answered, "As surely as God lives, if you had not spoken, the men would have continued pursuing them until morning."

[28]So Joab[w] blew the trumpet,[x] and everyone came to a halt; they no longer pursued Israel, nor did they fight anymore.

[29]All that night Abner and his men marched through the Arabah.[y] They crossed the Jordan, continued through the morning hours[b] and came to Mahanaim.[z]

[30]Then Joab stopped pursuing Abner and assembled the whole army. Besides Asahel, nineteen of David's men were found missing. [31]But David's men had killed three hundred and sixty Benjamites who were with Abner. [32]They took Asahel and buried him in his father's tomb[a] at Bethlehem. Then Joab and his men marched all night and arrived at Hebron by daybreak.

3 The war between the house of Saul and the house of David lasted a long time.[b] David grew stronger and stronger,[c] while the house of Saul grew weaker and weaker.[d]

[2]Sons were born to David in Hebron:

His firstborn was Amnon[e] the son of Ahinoam[f] of Jezreel;

[3]his second, Kileab the son of Abigail[g] the widow of Nabal of Carmel;

the third, Absalom[h] the son of Maakah daughter of Talmai king of Geshur;[i]

[4]the fourth, Adonijah[j] the son of Haggith;

---

[a] 16 *Helkath Hazzurim* means *field of daggers* or *field of hostilities.* [b] 29 Or See Septuagint; the meaning of the Hebrew for this phrase is uncertain.

2:17 *The battle that day was very fierce.* Because the representative combat (see note on 1Sa 17:4) by 12 men from each side was indecisive, a full-scale battle ensued in which David's forces were victorious. The attempt to use representative combat to avoid the decimation of civil war failed (see 3:1).

2:21 *Turn aside.* Abner tried unsuccessfully to avoid the necessity of killing Asahel.

2:22 *How could I look your brother Joab in the face?* Abner did not want the hostility between himself and Joab to be intensified by the practice of blood revenge (see note on 3:27).

2:23 Stabbing an enemy in the stomach was the method of execution noted also in 3:27; 4:6 (cf. Jdg 3:21).

2:26 *Must the sword devour forever?* Abner proposes an armistice as a means of avoiding the awful consequences of civil war.

2:27 *As surely as God lives.* An oath formula (see note on 1Sa 14:39,45).

2:28 *nor did they fight anymore.* For the present the open conflict ceased, but the hostility remained (see 3:1).

2:29 *Arabah.* See note on Dt 1:1.

3:2–5 The list of six sons born to David in Hebron is given as an evidence of the strengthening of David's house in contrast to that of Saul (v. 1). That these six sons were each born of a different mother indirectly informs us that David married four additional wives (see 2:2) during his time in Hebron.

3:2 *Amnon.* Later raped his sister Tamar and was killed by his brother Absalom (see ch. 13). *Ahinoam of Jezreel.* See note on 1Sa 25:43.

3:3 *Kileab.* Called Daniel in 1Ch 3:1. *Abigail.* See 1Sa 25. *Absalom.* Later avenged the rape of Tamar by killing Amnon, and conspired against his father David in an attempt to make himself king (see chs. 13–18). *Maakah daughter of Talmai.* David's marriage to Maakah undoubtedly had political implications. With Talmai as an ally on Ish-Bosheth's northern border, David flanked the northern kingdom both south and north. *Geshur.* A small Aramean city kingdom (see 15:8) located northeast of the Sea of Galilee (see Jos 12:5; 13:11–13).

3:4 *Adonijah.* Was put to death for attempting to take over the throne before Solomon could be crowned (see 1Ki 1–2).

2:16 ᵏS Jdg 3:21
2:17 ˡ2Sa 3:1
ᵐS 1Sa 17:8
2:18 ⁿ2Sa 3:39; 16:10; 19:22
ᵒ2Sa 3:30; 10:7; 11:1; 14:1; 18:14; 20:8; 24:3; 1Ki 1:7; 2:5,34
ᵖS 1Sa 26:6
�q2Sa 23:24; 1Ch 2:16; 11:26; 27:7 ʳ1Ch 12:8; Pr 6:5; SS 2:9
2:22 ˢ2Sa 3:27
2:23 ᵗ2Sa 3:27; 4:6
ᵘ2Sa 20:12
2:26 ᵛS Dt 32:42; Jer 46:10,14; Na 2:13; 3:15
2:28 ʷ2Sa 18:16; 20:23 ˣS Jdg 3:27
2:29 ʸS Dt 3:17
ᶻS Ge 32:2
2:32 ᵃS Ge 49:29
3:1 ᵇ1Ki 14:30
ᶜ2Sa 5:10 ᵈ2Sa 2:17; 22:44; Est 9:4
3:2 ᵉ2Sa 13:1
ᶠS 1Sa 25:43
3:3 ᵍS 1Sa 25:42
ʰ2Sa 13:1,28
ⁱ2Sa 13:37; 14:32; 15:8
3:4 ʲ1Ki 1:5,11; 2:13, 22

3:6 *S 1Sa 14:50
3:7 *S Ge 22:24;
2Sa 16:21-22;
S 1Ki 1:3 *m 2Sa 21:8-
11
3:8 *S 1Sa 17:43;
2Sa 9:8; 16:9;
2Ki 8:13
3:9 *S 1Sa 15:28
3:10 *S Jdg 20:1;
1Sa 25:28-31;
2Sa 24:2
3:13 *S Ge 43:5
3:14 *S 1Sa 18:27
3:15 *Dt 24:1-4
*1Sa 25:44
3:16 *2Sa 16:5;
17:18
3:17 *S Jdg 11:11
3:18 *S 1Sa 9:16
*2Sa 8:6
3:19 *1Ch 12:2,16,
29
3:20 *1Ch 12:39
3:21 *2Sa 5:3
*1Ki 11:37

the fifth, Shephatiah the son of Abital;
⁵and the sixth, Ithream the son of David's wife Eglah.
These were born to David in Hebron.

ABNER GOES OVER TO DAVID

⁶During the war between the house of Saul and the house of David, Abner *k* had been strengthening his own position in the house of Saul. ⁷Now Saul had had a concubine *l* named Rizpah *m* daughter of Aiah. And Ish-Bosheth said to Abner, "Why did you sleep with my father's concubine?"

⁸Abner was very angry because of what Ish-Bosheth said. So he answered, "Am I a dog's head *n*—on Judah's side? This very day I am loyal to the house of your father Saul and to his family and friends. I haven't handed you over to David. Yet now you accuse me of an offense involving this woman! ⁹May God deal with Abner, be it ever so severely, if I do not do for David what the LORD promised *o* him on oath ¹⁰and transfer the kingdom from the house of Saul and establish David's throne over Israel and Judah from Dan to Beersheba." *p* ¹¹Ish-Bosheth did not dare to say another word to Abner, because he was afraid of him.

¹²Then Abner sent messengers on his behalf to say to David, "Whose land is it? Make an agreement with me, and I will help you bring all Israel over to you."

¹³"Good," said David. "I will make an agreement with you. But I demand one thing of you: Do not come into my presence unless you bring Michal daughter of Saul when you come to see me." *q* ¹⁴Then David sent messengers to Ish-Bosheth son of Saul, demanding, "Give me my wife Michal, *r* whom I betrothed to myself for the price of a hundred Philistine foreskins."

¹⁵So Ish-Bosheth gave orders and had her taken away from her husband *s* Paltiel *t* son of Laish. ¹⁶Her husband, however, went with her, weeping behind her all the way to Bahurim. *u* Then Abner said to him, "Go back home!" So he went back.

¹⁷Abner conferred with the elders *v* of Israel and said, "For some time you have wanted to make David your king. ¹⁸Now do it! For the LORD promised David, 'By my servant David I will rescue my people Israel from the hand of the Philistines *w* and from the hand of all their enemies.' *x* '"

¹⁹Abner also spoke to the Benjamites in person. Then he went to Hebron to tell David everything that Israel and the whole house of Benjamin *y* wanted to do. ²⁰When Abner, who had twenty men with him, came to David at Hebron, David prepared a feast *z* for him and his men. ²¹Then Abner said to David, "Let me go at once and assemble all Israel for my lord the king, so that they may make a covenant *a* with you, and that you may rule over all that your heart desires." *b* So David sent Abner away, and he went in peace.

JOAB MURDERS ABNER

²²Just then David's men and Joab returned from a raid and brought with them a great deal of plunder. But Abner was no longer with David in Hebron, because David had sent

---

3:7 *Rizpah.* See 21:8–11. *Why did you sleep with my father's concubine?* Ish-Bosheth suspects that Abner's act was part of a conspiracy to seize the kingship (cf. v. 6). Great significance was attached to taking the concubine of a former king (see notes on 12:8; 16:21; 1Ki 2:22).

3:8 *dog's head.* Cf. note on 9:8.

3:9 *May God deal with Abner, be it ever so severely.* A curse formula (see note on 1Sa 3:17). *what the LORD promised him on oath.* The knowledge of David's divine designation as successor to Saul had spread widely (see notes on 2:4; 1Sa 16:13; 25:28).

3:10 *transfer the kingdom.* Abner was the real power behind the throne. *Dan to Beersheba.* See note on 1Sa 3:20.

3:12 *Whose land is it?* Possibly a rhetorical question that presumed that the land belonged either to Abner or to David. The former seems more likely from the following sentence. *Make an agreement with me.* Abner wants assurance that he will face no reprisals for his past loyalty to the house of Saul.

3:13 *Michal daughter of Saul.* Although Saul had given Michal to David (1Sa 18:27), he later gave her to another man after David fled from his court (1Sa 25:44). David probably sensed that in the minds of the northern elders, his reunion with Michal would strengthen his claim to the throne as a legitimate son-in-law of Saul.

3:14 *David sent messengers to Ish-Bosheth.* David wanted Michal

returned as an open and official act of Ish-Bosheth himself, rather than as part of a subterfuge planned by Abner. David knew that Ish-Bosheth would not dare to defy Abner's wishes (see v. 11). *a hundred Philistine foreskins.* See 1Sa 18:25. Saul had required 100 Philistine foreskins; David presented him with 200 (1Sa 18:27).

3:16 *Bahurim.* Near the Mount of Olives.

3:17 *elders of Israel.* The collective leadership of the various tribes comprised an informal national ruling body (see notes on Ex 3:16; Joel 1:2; see also 1Sa 8:4; 2Sa 5:3; 1Ki 8:1,3; 20:7; 2Ki 10:1; 23:1). *you have wanted to make David your king.* Apparently Ish-Bosheth's support came mainly from the tribe of Benjamin (see 2:15 and note) and from Gilead east of the Jordan River (see 2:8; 1Sa 11:9–11; 31:11–13).

3:18 *the LORD promised David.* By this time Samuel's anointing of David must have become common knowledge (see 5:2). Abner probably interpreted the anointing as a promise from the Lord, since Samuel was the Lord's much-revered prophet.

3:19 *Abner also spoke to the Benjamites in person.* Because Saul and his family were from the tribe of Benjamin, Abner was careful to consult the Benjamites concerning the transfer of kingship to the tribe of Judah. Apparently they consented, but Abner was not above representing matters in a way that was favorable to his purpose.

3:21 *make a covenant with you.* See 5:3 and note.

him away, and he had gone in peace. [23]When Joab and all the soldiers with him arrived, he was told that Abner son of Ner had come to the king and that the king had sent him away and that he had gone in peace.

[24]So Joab went to the king and said, "What have you done? Look, Abner came to you. Why did you let him go? Now he is gone! [25]You know Abner son of Ner; he came to deceive you and observe your movements and find out everything you are doing."

[26]Joab then left David and sent messengers after Abner, and they brought him back from the cistern at Sirah. But David did not know it. [27]Now when Abner[c] returned to Hebron, Joab took him aside into an inner chamber, as if to speak with him privately. And there, to avenge the blood of his brother Asahel, Joab stabbed him[d] in the stomach, and he died.[e]

[28]Later, when David heard about this, he said, "I and my kingdom are forever innocent[f] before the Lord concerning the blood of Abner son of Ner. [29]May his blood[g] fall on the head of Joab and on his whole family![h] May Joab's family never be without someone who has a running sore[i] or leprosy[a] or who leans on a crutch or who falls by the sword or who lacks food."

[30](Joab and his brother Abishai murdered Abner because he had killed their brother Asahel in the battle at Gibeon.)

[31]Then David said to Joab and all of Joab's men, "Tear your clothes and put on sackcloth[j] and walk in mourning[k] in front of Abner." King David himself walked behind the bier. [32]They buried Abner in Hebron, and the king wept[l] aloud at Abner's tomb. All of Joab's men wept also.

[33]The king sang this lament[m] for Abner:

"Should Abner have died as the lawless die?
[34] Your hands were not bound,
      your feet were not fettered.[n]
  You fell as one falls before the wicked."

And all of Joab's men wept over him again.

[35]Then they all came and urged David to eat something while it was still day; but David took an oath, saying, "May God deal with me, be it ever so severely,[o] if I taste bread[p] or anything else before the sun sets!"

[36]All of Joab's men took note and were pleased; indeed, everything the king did pleased them. [37]So on that day all of Joab's men and all Israel knew that the king had no part[q] in the murder of Abner son of Ner.

[38]Then the king said to his men, "Don't you realize that a great commander has fallen[r] in Israel this day? [39]And today, though I am the anointed king, I am weak, and these sons of Zeruiah[s] are too strong[t] for me. [u] May the Lord repay[v] the evildoer according to his evil deeds!"

ISH-BOSHETH MURDERED

4 When Ish-Bosheth son of Saul heard that Abner[w] had died in Hebron, he lost courage, and all Israel became alarmed. [2]Now Saul's son had two leaders of raiding bands. One was named Baanah and the other Rekab; they were sons of Rim-

---

[a] 29 The Hebrew for *leprosy* was used for various diseases affecting the skin.

3:27 [e]2Sa 2:8; 4:1; 1Ki 2:5,32
[d]S Ex 21:14; S Jdg 3:21; S 2Sa 2:23
[e]2Sa 2:22
3:28 [f]ver 37; Dt 21:9
3:29 [g]S Lev 20:9
[h]1Ki 2:31-33
[i]S Lev 15:2
3:31 [j]Ps 30:11; 35:13; 69:11; Isa 20:2
[k]S Ge 37:34
3:32 [l]S Nu 14:1; Pr 24:17
3:33 [m]S Ge 50:10
3:34 [n]Job 36:8; Ps 2:3; 149:8; Isa 45:14; Na 3:10
3:35 [o]S Ru 1:17
[p]S 1Sa 31:13; 2Sa 12:17; Jer 16:7
3:37 [q]S ver 28
3:38 [r]2Sa 1:19
3:39 [s]S 2Sa 2:18
[t]2Sa 16:9; 18:11
[u]S Jdg 18:26
[v]1Ki 2:32; Ps 41:10; 101:8
4:1 [w]S 2Sa 3:27

3:25 *he came to deceive you.* Joab despised Abner for killing his brother (2:18,23; 3:27) and sought to discredit him in David's eyes as a mere opportunist. Perhaps he also sensed that his own position of leadership would be threatened if Abner joined forces with David, since Abner was obviously a power among the northern tribes.

3:27 *inner chamber ... privately.* City gateways usually had small side chambers. *Joab stabbed him in the stomach, and he died.* Joab's murder of Abner is not to be excused either as an act of war or as justifiable blood revenge (cf. Nu 35:12; Dt 19:11-13). Asahel had been killed by Abner in the course of battle (see v. 30; see also 2:21,23 and notes).

3:29 *May his blood fall on the head of Joab and on his whole family!* After disclaiming any personal or official involvement in the plot to assassinate Abner (v. 28), David cursed Joab and thereby called on God to judge his wicked act. In this crucial hour when David's relationship to the northern tribes hung in the balance, he appears not to have felt sufficiently secure in his own position to bring Joab publicly to justice (see v. 39). The crime went

unpunished until early in the reign of Solomon (1Ki 2:5-6, 29-34).

3:31 *Joab.* He too was compelled to join the mourners. It may be that Joab's involvement was not widely known and that David hoped to keep the matter secret for the time being.

3:32 *Hebron.* David's royal city at the time. *the king wept aloud at Abner's tomb.* Because Abner's murder had the potential of destroying the union of the nation under David's rule, David did everything possible to demonstrate his innocence to the people. In this he was successful (see vv. 36-37).

3:33-34 For another lament sung by David over fallen leaders, see 1:19-27.

3:35 *urged David to eat ... but.* See 1:12; see also 1Sa 31:13 and note. *May God deal with me, be it ever so severely.* A curse formula (see note on 1Sa 3:17).

3:39 *May the Lord repay the evildoer.* See note on v. 29.

4:1 *he lost courage.* Ish-Bosheth was very much aware of his dependence on Abner (see note on 2:8). *all Israel became alarmed.* Civil strife threatened, and the northern tribes were now without a strong leader.

4:2 ˣ S Jos 9:17
4:3 ʸ Ne 11:33
4:4 ᶻ S 1Sa 18:1
ᵃ S 1Sa 31:9
ᵇ S Lev 21:18
ᶜ 2Sa 9:8,12; 16:1-4;
19:24; 21:7-8;
1Ch 8:34; 9:40
4:5 ᵈ S 2Sa 2:8
ᵉ Ru 2:7
4:6 ᶠ S 2Sa 2:23
4:7 ᵍ S Dt 3:17
4:8 ʰ 2Sa 20:21;
2Ki 10:7 ¹ 1Sa 24:4;
25:29 ʲ S Nu 31:3
4:9 ᵏ S Ge 48:16;
1Ki 1:29
4:10 ˡ 2Sa 1:2-16
4:11 ᵐ S Ge 4:10;
9:5; Ps 9:12; 72:14
4:12 ⁿ 2Sa 1:15
5:1 ᵒ 2Sa 19:43
ᵖ S Ge 29:14; 35:26
5:2 �q 1Sa 18:5,13,16
ʳ S 1Sa 11:6
ˢ S Ge 48:15;
S 1Sa 16:1; 2Sa 7:7;
Mt 2:6; Jn 21:16
ᵗ S 1Sa 12:12; S 13:14;
S 2Sa 6:21
5:3 ᵘ 2Sa 3:21
ᵛ S Dt 17:15; 2Sa 2:4

mon the Beerothite from the tribe of Benjamin—Beeroth ˣ is considered part of Benjamin, ³because the people of Beeroth fled to Gittaim ʸ and have resided there as foreigners to this day.

⁴(Jonathan ᶻ son of Saul had a son who was lame in both feet. He was five years old when the news ᵃ about Saul and Jonathan came from Jezreel. His nurse picked him up and fled, but as she hurried to leave, he fell and became disabled. ᵇ His name was Mephibosheth.) ᶜ

⁵Now Rekab and Baanah, the sons of Rimmon the Beerothite, set out for the house of Ish-Bosheth, ᵈ and they arrived there in the heat of the day while he was taking his noonday rest. ᵉ ⁶They went into the inner part of the house as if to get some wheat, and they stabbed ᶠ him in the stomach. Then Rekab and his brother Baanah slipped away.

⁷They had gone into the house while he was lying on the bed in his bedroom. After they stabbed and killed him, they cut off his head. Taking it with them, they traveled all night by way of the Arabah. ᵍ ⁸They brought the head ʰ of Ish-Bosheth to David at Hebron and said to the king, "Here is the head of Ish-Bosheth son of Saul, ¹ your enemy, who tried to take your life. This day the LORD has avengedʲ my lord the king against Saul and his offspring."

⁹David answered Rekab and his brother Baanah, the sons of Rimmon the Beerothite, "As surely as the LORD lives, who has delivered ᵏ me out of every trouble, ¹⁰when someone told me, 'Saul is dead,' and thought he was bringing good news, I seized him and put him to death in Ziklag. ˡ That was the reward I gave him for his news! ¹¹How much more— when wicked men have killed an innocent man in his own house and on his own bed— should I not now demand his blood ᵐ from your hand and rid the earth of you!"

¹²So David gave an order to his men, and they killed them. ⁿ They cut off their hands and feet and hung the bodies by the pool in Hebron. But they took the head of Ish-Bosheth and buried it in Abner's tomb at Hebron.

DAVID BECOMES KING OVER ISRAEL
5:1-3pp — 1Ch 11:1-3

5 All the tribes of Israel ᵒ came to David at Hebron and said, "We are your own flesh and blood. ᵖ ²In the past, while Saul was king over us, you were the one who led Israel on their military campaigns. �q And the LORD said ʳ to you, 'You will shepherd ˢ my people Israel, and you will become their ruler.' " ᵗ

³When all the elders of Israel had come to King David at Hebron, the king made a covenant ᵘ with them at Hebron before the LORD, and they anointed ᵛ David king over Israel.

4:2 *Beeroth.* One of the Gibeonite cities (Jos 9:17) assigned to Benjamin (Jos 18:21,25).

4:4 *Jonathan son of Saul had a son who was lame in both feet.* The writer emphasizes that with the death of Ish-Bosheth (see v. 6) there was no other viable claimant to the throne from the house of Saul. *news about Saul and Jonathan.* See 1:4; 1Sa 31:2–6. *Mephibosheth.* See 9:1–13; 16:1–4; 19:24–30; 21:7. The name was originally Merib-Baal (apparently meaning "opponent of Baal"; see 1Ch 8:34), perhaps to be spelled "Meri-Baal" (meaning "loved by Baal"), but was changed by the author of Samuel to Mephibosheth (meaning "from the mouth of the shameful thing"). See note on 2:8.

4:6 *stabbed him in the stomach.* See 2:23 and note.

4:7 *cut off his head.* See 1Sa 5:4 and note. *Arabah.* See note on Dt 1:1.

4:8 *This day the LORD has avenged my lord the king against Saul.* Rekab and Baanah depict their assassination of Ish-Bosheth in pious terms, expecting David to commend them for their act— a serious miscalculation.

4:9 *As surely as the LORD lives.* An oath formula (see note on 1Sa 14:39,45).

4:11 *demand his blood from your hand.* A call for the death penalty (see Ge 9:5–6). David here does what he was unable to do with Joab (see note on 3:29).

4:12 *their hands and feet.* The hands that had assassinated Ish-Bosheth and the feet that had run with the news (cf. note on 1Sa 5:4).

5:1—24:25 Beginning with ch. 5 there are sections of 2 Samuel (see also 3:2–5) that have parallel passages in 1 Chronicles (they are listed at the sectional headings). In some instances these par-

allel accounts are nearly identical; in others there are variations. **5:1** *All the tribes of Israel.* Representatives of each tribe, including elders and armed soldiers (see 1Ch 12:23–40). *your own flesh and blood.* The representatives of the various tribes cite three reasons for recognizing David as their king. The first of these is the acknowledgment that David is an Israelite. Even though national unity had been destroyed in the civil strife following Saul's death (2:8—3:1), this blood relationship had not been forgotten.

5:2 *the one who led Israel on their military campaigns.* The second reason (see note on v. 1) for recognizing David as king (see 1Sa 18:5,13–14,16,30). *the LORD said to you.* The third and most important reason (see 1Sa 13:13–14; 16:1,13; 23:17; 25:26–31). *shepherd...ruler.* "Shepherd" was often used as a metaphor for political rule in the OT (see Ps 23:1; Jer 2:8; Eze 34:2 and notes) and elsewhere in the ancient Near East (see, e.g., the prologue to Hammurapi's Code—see chart, p. xxiii). See also note on 1Sa 12:2 ("your leader").

5:3 *the king made a covenant with them...before the LORD.* David and Israel entered into a covenant in which both the king and the people obligated themselves before the Lord to carry out their mutual responsibilities (see 2Ki 11:17 and note). Thus, while David was king over Judah as the one elevated to that position by his tribe and later became king over Jerusalem by conquest (vv. 6–10), his rule over the northern tribes was by virtue of a treaty (covenant) of submission. That treaty was not renewed with David's grandson Rehoboam because he refused to negotiate its terms at the time of his accession to the throne (1Ki 12:1–16). *they anointed David king over Israel.* The third time David was anointed (see note on 2:4).

⁴David was thirty years old^w when he became king, and he reigned^x forty^y years. ⁵In Hebron he reigned over Judah seven years and six months,^z and in Jerusalem he reigned over all Israel and Judah thirty-three years.

DAVID CONQUERS JERUSALEM
5:6–10pp — 1Ch 11:4–9
5:11–16pp — 1Ch 3:5–9; 14:1–7

⁶The king and his men marched to Jerusalem^a to attack the Jebusites,^b who lived there. The Jebusites said to David, "You will not get in here; even the blind and the lame can ward you off." They thought, "David cannot get in here." ⁷Nevertheless, David captured the fortress of Zion^c—which is the City of David. ^{de}

⁸On that day David had said, "Anyone who conquers the Jebusites will have to use the water shaft^f to reach those 'lame and blind'^g who are David's enemies.^a" That is why they say, "The 'blind and lame' will not enter the palace."

^a 8 Or *are hated by David*

5:5 *In Hebron he reigned … seven years and six months.* See 2:11. *Israel and Judah.* The specific relationship of David to these two segments of his realm appears to have remained distinct (see note on v. 3).

5:6 *Jerusalem.* One of the most significant accomplishments of David's reign was the establishment of Jerusalem as his royal city and the nation's capital (see Introduction: Contents and Theme). The site was first occupied in the third millennium B.C. and was a royal city in the time of Abraham (see note on Ge 14:18). It was located on the border between Judah and Benjamin but was controlled by neither tribe. At the time of the conquest both Judah and Benjamin had attacked the city (see notes on Jdg 1:8,21), but it was quickly lost again to the Jebusites (Jos 15:63) and was sometimes referred to by the name Jebus (see Jdg 19:10; 1Ch 11:4). The city David conquered covered somewhat less than 11 acres and could have housed not many more than 3,500 inhabitants. By locating his royal city in a newly conquered town on the border between the two segments of his realm, David united the kingdom under his rule without seeming to subordinate one part to the other. *Jebusites.* A Canaanite people (Ge 10:15–16) inhabiting Jerusalem (Jos 15:8; 18:16). *the blind and the lame can ward you off.* Jerusalem was a natural fortress because of its location on a rise surrounded on three sides by deep valleys; so the Jebusites were confident that their walls could easily be defended.

5:7 *fortress.* Probably the fortified city itself. *Zion.* The first occurrence of the name in the OT. Originally the name appears to have been given to the southernmost hill of the city on which the Jebusite fortress was located. As the city expanded (from the days of Solomon onward), the name continued to be applied to the entire city (see Isa 1:8 and note; 2:3). *City of David.* As Jerusalem's conqueror, David becomes its owner and gives it his name. Jerusalem's southeast hill (Ophel; see note on Ne 3:26) continued to bear the name long after David's time (see Isa 22:19; cf. also Isa 29:1).

5:8 *On that day David had said.* 1Ch 11:6 may be combined with this verse for a more complete account. Joab's part in the conquest of the city demonstrated again his military

THE CITY OF THE JEBUSITES/DAVID'S JERUSALEM

Substantial historical evidence, both Biblical and extra-Biblical, places the temple of Solomon on the holy spot where King David built an altar to the Lord. David had purchased the land from Araunah the Jebusite, who was using the exposed bedrock as a threshing floor (2Sa 24:18–25). Tradition claims a much older sanctity for the site, associating it with the altar of Abraham on Mount Moriah (Ge 22:1–19). The writer of Genesis equates Moriah with "the mountain of the Lord" (Ge 22:14).

c. 1000 B.C.

Less than 11 acres in size, Jebus, a Canaanite city, could well defend itself against attack, with walls atop steep canyons and shafts reaching an underground water source. David captured the stronghold c. 1000 B.C. and made it his capital.

Jerusalem is shown from above and at an angle, and therefore wall shapes appear different from those on flat maps. Wall locations have been determined from limited archaeological evidence; houses are artist's concept.

© Hugh Claycombe 1982

5:9 *h* 1Ki 9:15,24
5:10 *i* 2Sa 3:1
j Ps 24:10 *k* 2Sa 7:9
5:11 *l* 1Ki 5:1,18;
2Ch 2:3
5:12 *m* S Nu 24:7
5:13 *n* S Dt 17:17
5:14 *o* 1Ch 3:5
p Lk 3:31
5:17 *q* 2Sa 23:14;
1Ch 11:16
5:18 *r* S Jos 15:8;
S 17:15
5:19 *s* S Jdg 18:5;
S 1Sa 23:2
5:20 *t* S Ge 38:29
5:21 *u* Dt 7:5;
Isa 46:2
5:24 *v* S Ex 14:24

⁹David then took up residence in the fortress and called it the City of David. He built up the area around it, from the terraces ᵃ *h* inward. ¹⁰And he became more and more powerful, *i* because the LORD God Almighty *j* was with him. *k*

¹¹Now Hiram *l* king of Tyre sent messengers to David, along with cedar logs and carpenters and stonemasons, and they built a palace for David. ¹²And David knew that the LORD had established him as king over Israel and had exalted his kingdom *m* for the sake of his people Israel.

¹³After he left Hebron, David took more concubines and wives *n* in Jerusalem, and more sons and daughters were born to him. ¹⁴These are the names of the children born to him there: *o* Shammua, Shobab, Nathan, *p* Solomon, ¹⁵Ibhar, Elishua, Nepheg, Japhia, ¹⁶Elishama, Eliada and Eliphelet.

DAVID DEFEATS THE PHILISTINES
5:17–25pp — 1Ch 14:8–17

¹⁷When the Philistines heard that David had been anointed king over Israel, they went up in full force to search for him, but David heard about it and went down to the stronghold. *q* ¹⁸Now the Philistines had come and spread out in the Valley of Rephaim; *r* ¹⁹so David inquired *s* of the LORD, "Shall I go and attack the Philistines? Will you deliver them into my hands?"

The LORD answered him, "Go, for I will surely deliver the Philistines into your hands."

²⁰So David went to Baal Perazim, and there he defeated them. He said, "As waters break out, the LORD has broken out against my enemies before me." So that place was called Baal Perazim. *b* *t* ²¹The Philistines abandoned their idols there, and David and his men carried them off. *u*

²²Once more the Philistines came up and spread out in the Valley of Rephaim; ²³so David inquired of the LORD, and he answered, "Do not go straight up, but circle around behind them and attack them in front of the poplar trees. ²⁴As soon as you hear the sound *v* of marching in the tops of the poplar trees, move quickly, because that will mean the LORD

ᵃ 9 Or *the Millo*   ᵇ 20 *Baal Perazim* means *the lord who breaks out.*

---

prowess and reconfirmed him in the position of commander of David's armies. *water shaft.* Although the Hebrew for this term is obscure, it appears that David knew of a secret tunnel—perhaps running from the Gihon spring outside the city into the fortress—that gave access to water when the city was under siege (see 2Ch 32:30). *lame and blind.* An ironic reference to the Jebusites (cf. v. 6 and note). *The 'blind and lame' will not enter the palace.* The proverb may mean that the Jebusites did not have access to the royal palace, though they were allowed to remain in the city and its environs.
5:9 *terraces.* Stone terraces on the steep slopes of the hill, creating additional space for buildings (but see TNIV text note; see also note on Jdg 9:6).
5:10 *the LORD ... was with him.* See note on 1Sa 16:18.

C **5:11** *Hiram king of Tyre.* This Phoenician king was the first to accord the newly established King David international recognition. It was vital to him that he have good relations with the king of Israel since Israel dominated the inland trade routes to Tyre, and Tyre was dependent on Israelite agriculture for much of its food (also true in the first century A.D.; see Ac 12:20). A close relationship existed between these two realms until the Babylonian invasions. *Tyre.* An important Phoenician seaport on the Mediterranean coast north of Israel (see Eze 26–27). *cedar.* A strong, durable wood used by the powerful and wealthy throughout the ancient Near East for building and decorating temples and palaces (see 1Ki 5:6 and note; 6:9; SS 5:15 and note; 8:9; Jer 22:14–15; Hag 1:4 and note).
C **5:12** *David knew that the LORD had established him as king.* In the ideology of the ancient Near East the king's possession of a palace was the chief symbolic indication of his status. *for the sake of his people Israel.* David acknowledged that his elevation to kingship over all Israel was the Lord's doing and that it was an integral part of his continuing redemptive program for Israel—just as the ministries of Moses, Joshua, the judges and Samuel had been.

5:13 *David took more concubines and wives.* See notes on 3:2–5; Ge 25:6.
5:14 *Shammua, Shobab, Nathan, Solomon.* 1Ch 3:5 designates Bathsheba as their mother.
5:17 *When the Philistines heard that David had been anointed king.* Chronologically it is likely that the Philistine attack followed immediately after the events of v. 3 and before the capture of Jerusalem (vv. 6–10). (The author arranged his narrative by topics; see note on 7:1.) The Philistines had not been disturbed by David's reign over Judah, but now they acted to protect their interests in the north, much of which they dominated after the defeat of Saul (1Sa 31). *stronghold.* Probably a reference to the wilderness area in southern Judah where David had hidden from Saul (see notes on 1Sa 22:4; 23:14). This action of David suggests that he had not yet taken Jerusalem.
5:18,22 *Valley of Rephaim.* Bordering ancient Jerusalem on the west and southwest (see Jos 15:8; 18:16; see also note on Isa 17:5).
5:19 *David inquired of the LORD.* See notes on 2:1; 1Sa 2:28; 22:20; 23:2.
C **5:20** *the LORD has broken out ... Baal Perazim.* See TNIV text note. As a true theocratic king, David attributes the victory to the Lord and does not claim the glory for himself (see notes on 1Sa 10:18,27; 11:13; 12:11; 14:23; 17:11,45–47).
5:21 *abandoned their idols there.* As the Israelites had taken the ark into battle (see note on 1Sa 4:3), so the Philistines carried images of their deities into battle in the hope that this would ensure victory. *carried them off.* In compliance with the instruction of Dt 7:5, they also burned them (1Ch 14:12).
5:23 *he answered.* As had been true in the case of the conquest under Joshua, the Lord ordered the battle and he himself marched against the enemy with his heavenly host (see Jos 6:2–5; 8:1–2; 10:8,14; 11:6). David's wars were a continuation and completion of the wars fought by Joshua.
5:24 *sound of marching.* The heavenly host of the Lord going into battle.

has gone out in front ^w of you to strike the Philistine army." ²⁵So David did as the LORD commanded him, and he struck down the Philistines ^x all the way from Gibeon ^{a y} to Gezer. ^z

THE ARK BROUGHT TO JERUSALEM
6:1–11pp — 1Ch 13:1–14
6:12–19pp — 1Ch 15:25–16:3

6 David again brought together all the able young men of Israel—thirty thousand. ²He and all his men went to Baalah ^{b a} in Judah to bring up from there the ark ^b of God, which is called by the Name, ^{c c} the name of the LORD Almighty, who is enthroned ^d between the cherubim ^e on the ark. ³They set the ark of God on a new cart ^f and brought it from the house of Abinadab, which was on the hill. ^g Uzzah and Ahio, sons of Abinadab, were guiding the new cart ⁴with the ark of God on it, ^d and Ahio was walking in front of it. ⁵David and the whole house of Israel were celebrating ^h with all their might before the LORD, with castanets, ^e harps, lyres, timbrels, sistrums and cymbals. ⁱ

⁶When they came to the threshing floor of Nakon, Uzzah reached out and took hold of ^j the ark of God, because the oxen stumbled. ⁷The LORD's anger burned against Uzzah because of his irreverent act; ^k therefore God struck him down, ^l and he died there beside the ark of God.

⁸Then David was angry because the LORD's wrath ^m had broken out against Uzzah, and to this day that place is called Perez Uzzah. ^{f n}

⁹David was afraid of the LORD that day and said, "How ^o can the ark of the LORD ever come to me?" ¹⁰He was not willing to take the ark of the LORD to be with him in the City of David. Instead, he took it to the house of Obed-Edom ^p the Gittite. ¹¹The ark of the LORD remained in the house of Obed-Edom the Gittite for three months, and the LORD blessed him and his entire household. ^q

¹²Now King David ^r was told, "The LORD has blessed the household of Obed-Edom and everything he has, because of the ark of God." So David went to bring up the ark of God from the house of Obed-Edom to the City of David with rejoicing. ¹³When those who were carrying the ark of the LORD had taken six steps, he sacrificed ^s a bull and a fattened calf. ¹⁴Wearing a linen ephod, ^t David was dancing ^u before the LORD with all his might, ¹⁵while

^a 25 Septuagint (see also 1 Chron. 14:16); Hebrew *Geba*   ^b 2 That is, Kiriath Jearim (see 1 Chron. 13:6)
^c 2 Hebrew; Septuagint and Vulgate do not have *the Name.*   ^d 3,4 Dead Sea Scrolls and some
Septuagint manuscripts; Masoretic Text *cart ⁴and they brought it with the ark of God from the house of
Abinadab, which was on the hill*   ^e 5 Masoretic Text; Dead Sea Scrolls and Septuagint (see also 1 Chron.
13:8) *songs*   ^f 8 *Perez Uzzah* means *outbreak against Uzzah.*

5:24 ^w Jdg 4:14
5:25 ^x 2Sa 8:12;
21:15 ^y Isa 28:21
^z S Jos 10:33
6:2 ^a S Jos 15:9
^b 1Sa 4:4; 7:1
^c Lev 24:16; Dt 28:10;
Isa 63:14 ^d Ps 99:1;
132:14 ^e S Ge 3:24;
S Ex 25:22
6:3 ^f ver 7; Nu 7:4-
9; S 1Sa 6:7 ^g 2Sa 7:1
6:5 ^h S Ex 15:20
ⁱ Ezr 3:10; Ne 12:27;
Ps 150:5
6:6 ^j S Nu 4:15,19-
20
6:7 ^k 1Ch 15:13-15
^l S Ex 19:22;
S 1Sa 5:6; 6:19;
S 25:38
6:8 ^m Ps 7:11
ⁿ S Ge 38:29
6:9 ^o S 1Sa 6:20
6:10 ^p 1Ch 15:18;
26:4-5
6:11 ^q S Ge 30:27;
39:5
6:12 ^r 1Ki 8:1
6:13 ^s 1Ki 8:5,62;
Ezr 6:17
6:14 ^t Ex 19:6;
S 1Sa 2:18
^u S Ex 15:20

5:25 *Gibeon.* See notes on 2:12–13; Jos 9:3. *Gezer.* Fifteen miles west of Gibeon, overlooking the Philistine plain (see note on Jos 10:33).

6:2 *Baalah in Judah.* See TNIV text note; see also Jos 15:60; 18:14; 1Sa 7:1. *ark of God.* See Ex 25:10–22; see also notes on 1Sa 4:3–4,21. The ark had remained at Kiriath Jearim during the reign of Saul. *called by the Name.* Used elsewhere to designate ownership (see 12:28; Dt 28:10; Isa 4:1; 63:19). *LORD Almighty.* See note on 1Sa 1:3. *enthroned between the cherubim.* See note on 1Sa 4:4; see also 1Ch 28:2 ("footstool of our God"). David recognized the great significance of the ark as the earthly throne of Israel's God. As a true theocratic king, he wished to acknowledge the Lord's kingship and rule over both himself and the people by restoring the ark to a place of prominence in the nation.

6:3 *new cart.* David follows the example of the Philistines (see 1Sa 6:7) rather than the instructions of Ex 25:12–15; Nu 4:5–6, 15, which require that the ark be carried on the shoulders of the Levites (see 1Ch 15:13–15). *from the house of Abinadab.* See 1Sa 7:1. *Uzzah and Ahio, sons of Abinadab.* 1Sa 7:1 speaks of Eleazar as the son of Abinadab. The Hebrew word for "son" can have the broader meaning of "descendant."

6:5 *sistrums.* Percussion instruments played by shaking with the hand; mentioned only here in the Bible.

6:7 *his irreverent act.* Although Uzzah's intent may have been good, he violated the clear instructions the Lord had given for handling the ark (see notes on v. 3; 1Sa 6:19). At this important new beginning in Israel's life with the Lord, the Lord gives

a shocking and vivid reminder to David and Israel that those who claim to serve him must acknowledge his rule with absolute seriousness (see Lev 10:1–3; Jos 7:24–25; 24:19–20; Ac 5:1–11).

6:8 *David was angry.* David's initial reaction was resentment that his attempt to honor the Lord had resulted in a display of God's wrath. *to this day.* Until the time of the writing of 2 Samuel. *Perez Uzzah.* See TNIV text note. The place-name memorialized a divine warning that was not soon forgotten (see Jos 7:26 and TNIV text note). Evenhanded in his judgment against sinners, the Lord plays no favorites as he "breaks out" against friend and foe alike (see 5:20 and note).

6:9 *David was afraid of the LORD.* David's anger was accompanied by fear—not the wholesome fear of proper honor and respect for the Lord (see 1Sa 12:24; Jos 24:14; see also notes on Ge 20:11; Pr 1:7) but an anxiety arising from an acute sense of his own guilt (Ge 3:10; Dt 5:5).

6:10 *Gittite.* He appears to have been a Levite (see note on 1Ch 13:13; cf. 1Ch 15:18,24; 16:5; 26:4–8,15; 2Ch 25:24), though many think the term "Gittite" fixes his place of birth at the Philistine city of Gath (see 15:18 and note). However, Gittite may be a reference to the Levitical city Gath Rimmon in Dan or Manasseh (Jos 21:20–25).

6:12 *David went to bring up the ark.* God's blessing on the household of Obed-Edom showed David that God's anger had been appeased.

6:13 *those . . . carrying the ark.* David had become aware of his previous error (1Ch 15:13–15).

6:14 *linen ephod.* See note on 1Sa 2:18.

he and the entire house of Israel were bringing up the ark of the Lᴏʀᴅ with shouts ᵛ and the sound of trumpets. ʷ

¹⁶As the ark of the Lᴏʀᴅ was entering the City of David, ˣ Michal ʸ daughter of Saul watched from a window. And when she saw King David leaping and dancing before the Lᴏʀᴅ, she despised him in her heart.

¹⁷They brought the ark of the Lᴏʀᴅ and set it in its place inside the tent that David had pitched for it, ᶻ and David sacrificed burnt offerings ᵃ and fellowship offerings before the Lᴏʀᴅ. ¹⁸After he had finished sacrificing ᵇ the burnt offerings and fellowship offerings, he blessed ᶜ the people in the name of the Lᴏʀᴅ Almighty. ¹⁹Then he gave a loaf of bread, a cake of dates and a cake of raisins ᵈ to each person in the whole crowd of Israelites, both men and women. ᵉ And all the people went to their homes.

²⁰When David returned home to bless his household, Michal daughter of Saul came out to meet him and said, "How the king of Israel has distinguished himself today, going around half-naked ᶠ in full view of the slave girls of his servants as any vulgar fellow would!"

²¹David said to Michal, "It was before the Lᴏʀᴅ, who chose me rather than your father or anyone from his house when he appointed ᵍ me ruler ʰ over the Lᴏʀᴅ's people Israel— I will celebrate before the Lᴏʀᴅ. ²²I will become even more undignified than this, and I will be humiliated in my own eyes. But by these slave girls you spoke of, I will be held in honor."

²³And Michal daughter of Saul had no children to the day of her death.

GOD'S PROMISE TO DAVID

7:1–17pp — 1Ch 17:1–15

7 After the king was settled in his palace ⁱ and the Lᴏʀᴅ had given him rest from all his enemies ʲ around him, ᵏ ²he said to Nathan ˡ the prophet, "Here I am, living in a house ᵐ of cedar, while the ark of God remains in a tent." ⁿ

³Nathan replied to the king, "Whatever you have in mind, ᵒ go ahead and do it, for the Lᴏʀᴅ is with you."

⁴But that night the word of the Lᴏʀᴅ came to Nathan, saying:

⁵"Go and tell my servant David, 'This is what the Lᴏʀᴅ says: Are you ᵖ the one to build me a house to dwell in? q ⁶I have not dwelt in a house from the day I brought the Israelites up out of Egypt to this day. ʳ I have been moving from place to place with a tent ˢ as my dwelling. ᵗ ⁷Wherever I have moved with all the Israelites, ᵘ did I ever say to any of their rulers whom I commanded to shepherd ᵛ my people Israel, "Why have you not built me a house ʷ of cedar?"'

⁸"Now then, tell my servant David, 'This is what the Lᴏʀᴅ Almighty says: I took you from the pasture, from tending the flock, ʸ and appointed you ruler ᶻ over my people Israel. ᵃ ⁹I have been with you wherever you have gone, ᵇ and I have cut off

---

6:16 *she despised him.* Michal had no appreciation for the significance of the event and deeply resented David's public display as unworthy of the dignity of a king (see vv. 20–23).

6:17 *burnt offerings.* See note on Lev 1:3. *fellowship offerings.* See notes on Lev 3:1; 1Sa 11:15.

6:18 *he blessed the people.* As Solomon would later do at the dedication of the temple (1Ki 8:55–61). *Lᴏʀᴅ Almighty.* See note on 1Sa 1:3.

6:21 *ruler.* See note on 1Sa 9:16.

6:23 *Michal…had no children.* Probably a punishment for her pride and at the same time another manifestation of God's judgment on the house of Saul.

7:1–29 God's great promise to David (see Introduction: Contents and Theme). Although it is not expressly called a covenant here, it is elsewhere (23:5; Ps 89:3,28,34,39; cf. Ps 132:11), and David responds with language suggesting his recognition that a covenant had been made (see also notes on vv. 11,16,20,28).

7:1 *After the king was settled in his palace.* See 5:11; see also note on 5:12. *the Lᴏʀᴅ had given him rest from all his enemies.* Chronologically the victories noted in 8:1–14 probably preceded the events of this chapter. The arrangement of material is topical (see notes on 5:17; 8:1)—ch. 6 records the bringing of the ark to Jerusalem; ch. 7 tells of David's desire to build a temple in Jerusalem in which to house the ark.

7:2 *Nathan.* The first reference to this prophet. *cedar.* See note on 5:11. *tent.* See v. 6; 6:17. Now that he himself had a royal palace (symbolic of his established kingship), a tent did not seem to David to be an appropriate place for the throne of Israel's divine King (see note on 6:2; see also Ps 132:2–5; Ac 7:46). He wanted to build Israel's heavenly King a royal house in the capital city of his kingdom.

7:3 *Nathan replied.* In consulting a prophet, David sought God's will, but Nathan boldly voiced approval of David's plans in the Lord's name before he had received a revelation from the Lord. *the Lᴏʀᴅ is with you.* See v. 9; see also note on 1Sa 16:18.

7:5–16 The Davidic covenant (see note on v. 11).

7:5 *Are you the one…?* David's desire was commendable (1Ki 8:18–19), but his gift and mission were to fight the Lord's battles until Israel was securely at rest in the promised land (see v. 10; 1Ki 5:3; 1Ch 22:8–9 and note).

7:7 *did I ever say…, "Why have you not built me a house …?"* David misunderstood the Lord's priorities. He reflected the pagan notion that the gods were interested in human beings only as builders and maintainers of their temples and as practitioners of their religion. Instead, the Lord had raised up rulers in Israel only to shepherd his people (that is also why he had brought David "from the pasture," v. 8).

7:9 *I have cut off all your enemies.* See note on v. 1.

all your enemies from before you. *c* Now I will make your name great, like the names of the greatest men on earth. *d* 10And I will provide a place for my people Israel and will plant *e* them so that they can have a home of their own and no longer be disturbed. *f* Wicked *g* people will not oppress them anymore, *h* as they did at the beginning 11and have done ever since the time I appointed leaders *a* *i* over my people Israel. I will also give you rest from all your enemies. *j*

" 'The LORD declares *k* to you that the LORD himself will establish *l* a house *m* for you: 12When your days are over and you rest *n* with your ancestors, I will raise up your offspring to succeed you, who will come from your own body, *o* and I will establish his kingdom. *p* 13He is the one who will build a house *q* for my Name, *r* and I will establish the throne of his kingdom forever. *s* 14I will be his father, and he will be my son. *t* When he does wrong, I will punish him *u* with a rod *v* wielded by human beings, with floggings inflicted by human hands. 15But my love will never be taken away from him, *w* as I took it away from Saul, *x* whom I removed from before you. 16Your house and your kingdom will endure forever before me *b*; your throne *y* will be established *z* forever. *a* ' "

17Nathan reported to David all the words of this entire revelation.

DAVID'S PRAYER
7:18–29pp — 1Ch 17:16–27

18Then King David went in and sat before the LORD, and he said:

"Who am I, *b* Sovereign LORD, and what is my family, that you have brought me this far? 19And as if this were not enough in your sight, Sovereign LORD, you have also spoken about the future of the house of your servant—and this decree, *c* Sovereign LORD, is for a human being! *c*

20"What more can David say *d* to you? For you know *e* your servant, *f* Sovereign LORD. 21For the sake of your word and according to your will, you have done this great thing and made it known to your servant.

---

a 11 Traditionally *judges*   *b* 16 Some Hebrew manuscripts and Septuagint; most Hebrew manuscripts *you*   *c* 19 Or *for the human race*

7:16 *z* Ps 93:2; 103:19 *a* S ver 13   **7:18** *b* S Ex 3:11   **7:19** *c* Isa 55:8-9   **7:20** *d* Isa 38:15 *e* Jn 21:17 *f* 1Sa 16:7

7:9 *c* Ps 18:37-42
d S Ex 11:3
7:10 *e* S Ex 15:17;
Isa 5:1-7 *f* 2Ki 21:8;
2Ch 33:8 *g* Ps 89:22-
23 *h* Ps 147:14;
Isa 54:14; 60:18
7:11 *i* S Jdg 2:16;
1Sa 12:9-11 *j* ver 1
k 1Ki 2:24 *l* 1Sa 25:28;
Ps 89:35-37; S Mt 1:1;
Lk 1:32-33; Ac 13:22-
23; 2Ti 2:8
m S Ex 1:21; Isa 7:2
7:12 *n* S Ge 15:15;
1Ki 2:1; Ac 13:36
o 1Ki 8:20; Ps 132:11-
12; Jer 30:21; 33:15
p 2Ch 23:3
7:13 *q* S Dt 12:5;
1Ki 5:12 *r* Dt 16:11;
1Ki 5:5; 8:19,29;
2Ki 21:4,7 *s* ver 16;
S Ge 9:16; 2Sa 22:51;
1Ki 2:4,45; 1Ch 22:10;
28:6; 2Ch 6:16; 7:18;
13:5; 21:7; Ps 89:3-4,
29,35-37; Pr 25:5;
Isa 9:7; 16:5;
Jer 17:25; 33:17,21;
Da 7:27
7:14 *t* Ps 2:7; 89:26;
Jer 3:19; S Mt 3:17;
Jn 1:49; 2Co 6:18*;
Heb 1:5*; Rev 21:7
u S Dt 8:5; 1Ki 11:34;
1Ch 22:10; Heb 12:7
v Ps 89:30-33;
Pr 13:24
7:15 *w* ver 25;
1Ki 2:4; 6:12; 8:25; 9:5;
11:13,32; 2Ki 19:34;
2Ch 6:16; 7:18; 21:7;
Ps 89:24,33; Jer 33:17
x 1Sa 13:13; S 15:28;
16:14
7:16 *y* Ps 89:36-37;
S Lk 1:33

7:10 *I will provide a place for my people Israel.* It is for this purpose that the Lord has made David king, and through David he will do it. *at the beginning.* In Egypt.

A C **7:11** *leaders.* During the period of the judges (see TNIV text note). *I will also give you rest from all your enemies.* See vv. 1,9. David's victories over threatening powers will be complete, so that the rest already enjoyed will be assured for the future. *the LORD himself will establish a house for you.* Compare this statement with the rhetorical question of v. 5. In a beautiful play on words God says that David is not to build him a house (temple); rather, God will build David a house (royal dynasty) that will last forever (v. 16). God has been building Israel ever since the days of Abraham, and now he commits himself to build David's royal house so that the promise to Israel may be fulfilled—rest in the promised land. It is God's building that effects his kingdom. This covenant with David is unconditional, like those with Noah, Abram and Phinehas (see note on Ge 9:9; see also chart, p. 20), grounded only in God's firm and gracious purpose. It finds its ultimate fulfillment in the kingship of Christ, who was born of the tribe of Judah and the house of David (see 23:5; Ps 89:3-4,30-37 and note; 132:11-18; Isa 9:1-7; 55:3; Mt 1:1; Lk 1:32-33,69; Ac 2:29-30; 13:22-23; Ro 1:2-3; 2Ti 2:8; Rev 3:7; 5:5; 22:16).

7:12 *raise up your offspring to succeed you.* The royal line of David, in contrast to that of Saul, would continue after David's death by dynastic succession.

7:13 *He is the one who will build a house for my Name.* God's priorities are that his own royal house, where his throne (the ark) can finally come to rest (1Ch 6:31; 28:2), will wait until Israel is at rest and David's dynasty (in the person of his son Solomon) is secure. "Name" is equivalent to "me" in v. 5 (see note on 1Sa 25:25).

A C **7:14** *his father ... my son.* This familial language expresses the special relationship God promises to

maintain with the descendant(s) of David whom he will establish on David's throne. It marks him as the one whom God has chosen and enthroned to rule in his name as the official representative of God's rule over his people (see notes on Ps 2:7; 45:6; 89:27; see also 89:26). In Jesus Christ this promise comes to ultimate fulfillment (see Mk 1:11; Heb 1:5 and notes).

A **7:15** *my love.* God's special and unfailing favor (see note on Ps 6:4).

A **7:16** *your throne will be established forever.* See note on v. 11; see also Introduction: Contents and Theme. The promise of an everlasting kingdom for the house of David became the focal point for many later prophecies and powerfully influenced the development of the Messianic hope in Israel.

C **7:18–29** David's prayer expresses wonder that God would make such commitments to him and his descendants. But he also acknowledges that what God had pledged to him is for Israel's sake, that its purpose is the fulfillment of God's covenantal promises to his people, and that its ultimate effect will be the honor and praise of God throughout the world.

7:18 *went in.* Presumably into the tent (6:17) in which the ark was kept. *sat before the LORD.* The ark was the symbol of God's presence with his people (see Ex 25:22; see also notes on 1Sa 4:3–4,21).

7:19 *this decree ... is for a human being!* Probably referring to David and his "house" (cf. 1Ch 17:17). The meaning of this clause, however, is uncertain (see TNIV text note).

7:20 *know.* Or "especially acknowledge" (see Hos 2:20; 6:6) or "choose" (see Ge 18:19; Am 3:2). David recognizes God's promise as a covenant (23:5).

7:21 *your word.* Probably God's covenant word of promise to his people.

7:22 *g* Ps 48:1;
77:13; 86:10; Jer 10:6
h Dt 3:24 *i* Ex 9:14
j S Ex 8:10; S 20:4
k Ex 10:2; S Jdg 6:13;
Ps 44:1
7:23 *l* Dt 4:32-38;
S 33:29; S 1Sa 12:22
m S Nu 6:27
n Dt 10:21 *o* Dt 7:7-8;
S 9:26
7:24 *p* Dt 26:18
q Ex 6:6-7; Ps 48:14
7:25 *r* S ver 15;
S Nu 23:19; 2Ch 1:9
7:26 *s* S Ex 6:3;
Ne 9:5; Ps 72:19;
96:8; Mt 6:9
t S 1Sa 25:28
7:28 *u* Ex 34:6;
Jn 17:17
7:29 *v* Nu 6:23-27
8:1 *w* Ps 60:8; 87:4;
108:9 *x* Heb 11:32-33
8:2 *y* S Ge 19:37;
S Nu 21:29
z S Jdg 3:15;
S Isa 45:14
8:3 *a* 2Sa 10:16,19;
1Ki 11:23
b S 1Sa 14:47
c S Ge 2:14
8:4 *d* S Ge 49:6;
Jos 11:9
8:5 *e* S Ge 14:15;
2Sa 10:6; 1Ki 11:24;
2Ki 8:7; 14:28
8:6 *f* 1Ki 20:34
g 2Sa 10:19 *h* 2Sa 3:18

²²"How great *g* you are, *h* Sovereign LORD! There is no one like *i* you, and there is no God *j* but you, as we have heard with our own ears. *k* ²³And who is like your people Israel *l*—the one nation on earth that God went out to redeem as a people for himself, and to make a name *m* for himself, and to perform great and awesome wonders *n* by driving out nations and their gods from before your people, whom you redeemed *o* from Egypt? *a* ²⁴You have established your people Israel as your very own *p* forever, and you, LORD, have become their God. *q*

²⁵"And now, LORD God, keep forever the promise *r* you have made concerning your servant and his house. Do as you promised, ²⁶so that your name *s* will be great forever. Then people will say, 'The LORD Almighty is God over Israel!' And the house of your servant David will be established *t* in your sight.

²⁷"LORD Almighty, God of Israel, you have revealed this to your servant, saying, 'I will build a house for you.' So your servant has found courage to pray this prayer to you. ²⁸Sovereign LORD, you are God! Your covenant is trustworthy, *u* and you have promised these good things to your servant. ²⁹Now be pleased to bless the house of your servant, that it may continue forever in your sight; for you, Sovereign LORD, have spoken, and with your blessing *v* the house of your servant will be blessed forever."

DAVID'S VICTORIES
8:1–14pp — 1Ch 18:1–13

8 In the course of time, David defeated the Philistines *w* and subdued *x* them, and he took Metheg Ammah from the control of the Philistines. ²David also defeated the Moabites. *y* He made them lie down on the ground and measured them off with a length of cord. Every two lengths of them were put to death, and the third length was allowed to live. So the Moabites became subject to David and brought him tribute. *z*

³Moreover, David defeated Hadadezer *a* son of Rehob, king of Zobah, *b* when he went to restore his monument at *b* the Euphrates *c* River. ⁴David captured a thousand of his chariots, seven thousand charioteers *c* and twenty thousand foot soldiers. He hamstrung *d* all but a hundred of the chariot horses.

⁵When the Arameans of Damascus *e* came to help Hadadezer king of Zobah, David struck down twenty-two thousand of them. ⁶He put garrisons *f* in the Aramean kingdom of Damascus, and the Arameans became subject *g* to him and brought tribute. The LORD gave David victory wherever he went. *h*

---

a 23 See Septuagint and 1 Chron. 17:21; Hebrew *wonders for your land and before your people, whom you redeemed from Egypt, from the nations and their gods.*   *b* 3 Or *his control along*   *c* 4 Septuagint (see also Dead Sea Scrolls and 1 Chron. 18:4); Masoretic Text *captured seventeen hundred of his charioteers*

7:22 *no God but you.* See 22:32; 1Sa 2:2; cf. Ex 20:3; Dt 6:4 and notes.

C **7:23** *the one nation on earth that God went out to redeem as a people for himself.* Israel's uniqueness did not consist in her national achievements but in God's choice of her to be his own people (see Dt 7:6–8; 33:26–29). *to make a name for himself.* The basis for God's electing love, revealed in his dealings with Israel, did not lie in any meritorious characteristic of the Israelite people but in his own sovereign purposes (see 1Sa 12:22; Dt 7:6–8; 9:4–6; Ne 9:10; Isa 63:12; Jer 32:20–21; Eze 36:22–38).

7:24 David recalls the essence of God's covenant relationship with his people (see Jer 7:23 and note). *you, LORD, have become their God.* What God has pledged to David, he has pledged as the God of Israel.

7:27 *your servant has found courage to pray this prayer to you.* David's prayer lays claim to God's promise.

7:28 *good things.* A common summary expression for covenant benefits from God (see, e.g., 1Sa 2:32, "good"; Nu 10:29,32; Dt 26:11; Jos 21:45, "good promises"; 23:14, "good promises"; Isa 63:7; Jer 29:32; 32:40–41, "good"; 33:9).

8:1 *In the course of time.* See note on 2:1. Chronologically the events of this chapter, or many of them, are probably to be placed between chs. 5 and 6 (see 7:1 and note). *Metheg Ammah.* Perhaps a way of referring to Gath and its environs (see 1Ch 18:1).

C **8:2** *Moabites.* Descendants of Lot (see Ge 19:36–38 and note), occupying territory east of the Dead Sea. Saul

fought against the Moabites (1Sa 14:47), and David sought refuge in Moab for his parents during his exile from Israel (1Sa 22:3–4). David's great-grandmother Ruth was from Moab (see Ru 1:4; 4:13, 21–22).

8:3 *Hadadezer.* Means "Hadad is (my) help." Hadad was an Aramean deity equivalent to the Canaanite Baal. *Zobah.* Saul had previously fought against the kings of Zobah (1Sa 14:47), whose territory was apparently located in the Beqaa Valley between the Lebanon and Anti-Lebanon mountains, thus on Israel's northern border. *restore.* Saul's earlier victories over the kings of Zobah had extended Israelite control, if only briefly, as far as the fringes of the Euphrates Valley. *Euphrates River.* The land promised to Abraham had included borders from Egypt to the Euphrates (see Ge 15:18–21; Dt 1:7 and note; 11:24; Jos 1:4 and note). Here is at least another provisional fulfillment of this promise (see 1Ki 4:21,24 and notes; see also Ge 17:8; Jos 21:43–45). See map No. 5 at the end of this study Bible.

8:4 See TNIV text note. *hamstrung all but a hundred of the chariot horses.* See Jos 11:6 and note. David's action is often attributed to his supposed ignorance of the value of the chariot as a military weapon. It is more likely, however, that he was acting in obedience to the ancient divine command not to "acquire great numbers of horses for himself" (Dt 17:16; cf. 1Sa 8:11 and note).

8:5 *Arameans.* See notes on Dt 26:5; 1Ch 18:5. *came to help Hadadezer.* They feared Israelite expansion to the north.

8:6,14 *The LORD … wherever he went.* The sentence summarizes David's victories at two critical points in this section (vv. 1–14)

⁷David took the gold shieldsⁱ that belonged to the officers of Hadadezer and brought them to Jerusalem. ⁸From Tebah^a and Berothai,^j towns that belonged to Hadadezer, King David took a great quantity of bronze.

⁹When Tou^b king of Hamath^k heard that David had defeated the entire army of Hadadezer,^l ¹⁰he sent his son Joram^c to King David to greet him and congratulate him on his victory in battle over Hadadezer, who had been at war with Tou. Joram brought with him articles of silver, of gold and of bronze.

¹¹King David dedicated^m these articles to the Lord, as he had done with the silver and gold from all the nations he had subdued: ¹²Edom^{d n} and Moab,^o the Ammonites^p and the Philistines,^q and Amalek.^r He also dedicated the plunder taken from Hadadezer son of Rehob, king of Zobah.

¹³And David became famous^s after he returned from striking down eighteen thousand Edomites^e in the Valley of Salt.^t

¹⁴He put garrisons throughout Edom, and all the Edomites^u became subject to David.^v The Lord gave David victory^w wherever he went.^x

DAVID'S OFFICIALS
8:15–18pp — 1Ch 18:14–17

¹⁵David reigned over all Israel, doing what was just and right^y for all his people. ¹⁶Joab^z son of Zeruiah was over the army; Jehoshaphat^a son of Ahilud was recorder;^b ¹⁷Zadok^c son of Ahitub and Ahimelek son of Abiathar^d were priests; Seraiah was secretary;^e ¹⁸Benaiah^f son of Jehoiada was over the Kerethites^g and Pelethites; and David's sons were priests.^f

DAVID AND MEPHIBOSHETH

9 David asked, "Is there anyone still left of the house of Saul to whom I can show kindness for Jonathan's sake?"^h ²Now there was a servant of Saul's household named Ziba.ⁱ They summoned him to appear before David, and the king said to him, "Are you Ziba?"

"At your service," he replied.

---

^a 8 See some Septuagint manuscripts (see also 1 Chron. 18:8); Hebrew *Betah.*   ^b 9 Hebrew *Toi,* a variant of *Tou;* also in verse 10   ^c 10 A variant of *Hadoram*   ^d 12 Some Hebrew manuscripts, Septuagint and Syriac (see also 1 Chron. 18:11); most Hebrew manuscripts *Aram*   ^e 13 A few Hebrew manuscripts, Septuagint and Syriac (see also 1 Chron. 18:12); most Hebrew manuscripts *Aram* (that is, Arameans)   ^f 18 Or *were chief officials* (see Septuagint and Targum; see also 1 Chron. 18:17)

8:7 ⁱ1Ki 10:16; 14:26; 2Ki 11:10
8:8 ^jEze 47:16
8:9 ^k1Ki 8:65; 2Ki 14:28; 2Ch 8:4 ^lLk 14:31-32
8:11 ^mver 12; 1Ki 7:51; 15:15; 1Ch 26:26; 2Ch 5:1
8:12 ⁿS Nu 24:18 ^over 2 ^p2Sa 10:14 ^qS 2Sa 5:25 ^rS Nu 24:20; S 1Sa 27:8
8:13 ^s2Sa 7:9 ^t2Ki 14:7; 1Ch 18:12; Ps 60 Title
8:14 ^uNu 24:17-18; Ps 108:9; Isa 34:5; 63:1; Jer 49:7; Eze 25:12 ^vS Ge 27:29,37-40 ^wPs 144:10 ^x2Sa 22:44; Ps 18:43
8:15 ^yS Ge 18:19; 1Ki 11:38; 14:8; 15:11; 22:43; 2Ki 12:2; Job 29:14; Ps 5:12; 119:121; Heb 11:33
8:16 ^zS 2Sa 2:13 ^a2Sa 20:24; 1Ki 4:3 ^bIsa 36:3,22
8:17 ^cS 1Sa 2:35; 2Sa 15:24,29; 20:25; 1Ki 1:8; 4:4; 1Ch 6:8, 53; 16:39; 24:3; 27:17; 2Ch 31:10; Eze 40:46; 43:19; 44:15; 48:11 ^dMk 2:26 ^e1Ki 4:3; 2Ki 12:10; 19:2; 22:3; Isa 36:3; Jer 36:12
8:18 ^f2Sa 20:23; 23:20; 1Ki 1:8,38; 2:25,35,46; 4:4 ^g1Sa 30:14
9:1 ^hS 1Sa 20:14-17, 42; S 23:18
9:2 ⁱ2Sa 16:1-4; 19:17,26,29

---

and reminds the reader that God, not David, is the true Savior of his people.

8:7 *gold shields.* Shields adorned with gold—the phrase is similar to "iron chariots" (see Jos 17:16 and note).

8:8 *bronze.* Later used by Solomon in the construction of the temple (see 1Ch 18:8 and note).

8:9 *Hamath.* A kingdom centered on the Orontes River, north of Zobah (see v. 3 and note).

8:13 *eighteen thousand.* As king, David receives the credit for striking down 18,000 Edomites. Abishai, however, was one of David's army commanders in this battle (see 1Ch 18:12 and note). The 12,000 Edomites struck down under Joab's leadership according to the title of Ps 60 were probably part of the 18,000. *Valley of Salt.* See 2Ki 14:7 and note; see also Ps 60 title.

A C **8:15** *just and right.* As a true theocratic king, David's reign was characterized by adherence to God's standards of right rule (see notes on 1Sa 8:3; 12:3; Ps 119:121), as no doubt laid down in Samuel's "rights and duties of kingship" (see 1Sa 10:25; 1Ki 2:3–4 and notes).

8:16 *Joab son of Zeruiah was over the army.* See notes on 2:13; 5:8. *recorder.* The precise duties of this official are not indicated, though the position was an important one in the court and was maintained throughout the period of the monarchy (see 2Ki 18:18,37; 2Ch 34:8). He may have been a kind of chancellor or chief administrator of royal affairs, responsible among other things for the royal chronicles and annals.

C **8:17** *Zadok son of Ahitub.* First mentioned here, Zadok was a descendant of Eleazar, son of Aaron (see 1Ch 6:4–8,50–52; 24:1–3). His father, Ahitub, is not to be identified with Ichabod's brother of the same name (1Sa 14:3). Zadok remained loyal to David throughout his reign (15:24–29; 17:15–16;

19:11). Zadok and the prophet Nathan eventually anointed Solomon as David's successor (1Ki 1:43–45). *Ahimelek son of Abiathar.* A copyist's error may have occurred here (see also 1Ch 24:6) in which these two names have been transposed. Abiathar is referred to as son of Ahimelek in 1Sa 22:20. While it is true that the Abiathar of 1Sa 22:20 could have had a son named Ahimelek (after his grandfather), such a person does not appear elsewhere in the narratives of Samuel and Kings as a colleague of Zadok, but Abiathar consistently does (15:29,35; 17:15; 19:11; 20:25; 1Ki 1:7–8; 2:35; 4:4). *Seraiah.* Perhaps the same person elsewhere called Sheva (20:25), Shisha (1Ki 4:3) and Shavsha (1Ch 18:16). *secretary.* His duties presumably included domestic and foreign correspondence, perhaps keeping records of important political events, and various administrative functions (2Ki 12:10–12).

8:18 *Kerethites.* See note on 1Sa 30:14. *Pelethites.* Probably an alternate form of "Philistines." *priests.* See TNIV text note; see also 20:26. Several early translations render the term by some word other than "priests." Chronicles calls these men "chief officials at the king's side" (1Ch 18:17; see note there).

9:1—20:26 These chapters, together with 1Ki 1:1—2:46, are one of the finest examples of historical narrative ever produced in the ancient world.

9:1–13 The events of this chapter occurred a number of years after David's capture of Jerusalem. Mephibosheth was five years old at the time of his father's death (4:4); now he has a son of his own (v. 12).

9:1 *I can show kindness for Jonathan's sake.* David has not forgotten his promise to Jonathan (cf. 1Sa 20:14–17,42).

9:2 *Ziba.* The chief steward of Saul's estate, which had been inherited by Mephibosheth, son of Jonathan, Saul's firstborn (see 16:1–4; 19:17).

9:3 *i* 1Ch 8:34;
1Sa 20:14
k S Lev 21:18
9:4 *l* 2Sa 17:27-29
9:6 *m* S Ge 37:7
9:7 *n* S 1Sa 20:14-15
o ver 13; 2Sa 19:28;
21:7; 1Ki 2:7;
2Ki 25:29; Jer 52:33
9:8 *p* S 2Sa 4:4
q 2Sa 3:8
9:10 *r* 2Sa 16:3
9:11 *s* Job 36:7;
Ps 113:8
9:12 *t* S 2Sa 4:4
10:2 *u* S 1Sa 11:1
10:3 *v* S Nu 21:32
10:4 *w* S Lev 19:27;
Isa 7:20; 15:2; 50:6;
52:14; Jer 48:37;
Eze 5:1 *x* Isa 20:4

³The king asked, "Is there no one still left of the house of Saul to whom I can show God's kindness?"

Ziba answered the king, "There is still a son of Jonathan; *j* he is lame *k* in both feet."

⁴"Where is he?" the king asked.

Ziba answered, "He is at the house of Makir *l* son of Ammiel in Lo Debar."

⁵So King David had him brought from Lo Debar, from the house of Makir son of Ammiel.

⁶When Mephibosheth son of Jonathan, the son of Saul, came to David, he bowed down to pay him honor. *m*

David said, "Mephibosheth!"

"At your service," he replied.

⁷"Don't be afraid," David said to him, "for I will surely show you kindness for the sake of your father Jonathan. *n* I will restore to you all the land that belonged to your grandfather Saul, and you will always eat at my table. *o*"

⁸Mephibosheth *p* bowed down and said, "What is your servant, that you should notice a dead dog *q* like me?"

⁹Then the king summoned Ziba, Saul's steward, and said to him, "I have given your master's grandson everything that belonged to Saul and his family. ¹⁰You and your sons and your servants are to farm the land for him and bring in the crops, so that your master's grandson *r* may be provided for. And Mephibosheth, grandson of your master, will always eat at my table." (Now Ziba had fifteen sons and twenty servants.)

¹¹Then Ziba said to the king, "Your servant will do whatever my lord the king commands his servant to do." So Mephibosheth ate at David's *a* table like one of the king's sons. *s*

¹²Mephibosheth had a young son named Mika, and all the members of Ziba's household were servants of Mephibosheth. *t* ¹³And Mephibosheth lived in Jerusalem, because he always ate at the king's table; he was lame in both feet.

DAVID DEFEATS THE AMMONITES
10:1–19pp — 1Ch 19:1–19

10 In the course of time, the king of the Ammonites died, and his son Hanun succeeded him as king. ²David thought, "I will show kindness to Hanun son of Nahash, *u* just as his father showed kindness to me." So David sent a delegation to express his sympathy to Hanun concerning his father.

When David's men came to the land of the Ammonites, ³the Ammonite commanders said to Hanun their lord, "Do you think David is honoring your father by sending envoys to you to express sympathy? Hasn't David sent them to you only to explore the city and spy it out *v* and overthrow it?" ⁴So Hanun seized David's envoys, shaved off half of each man's beard, *w* cut off their garments at the buttocks, *x* and sent them away.

a 11 Septuagint; Hebrew *my*

9:3,13 *lame in both feet.* And thus disqualified from contesting David's position as king (see 4:4 and note).

9:3 *There is still a son of Jonathan.* Saul had other descendants (see 21:8), but Ziba mentions only the one in whom David would be chiefly interested.

9:4 *Makir.* Apparently a wealthy benefactor of Mephibosheth who later also came to David's aid (17:27). *Lo Debar.* A town deep in Gileadite territory in Transjordan.

9:6 *Mephibosheth.* See 4:4 and note.

9:7 *restore to you.* Either the property Saul had acquired as king had been taken over by David, or Ziba as steward had virtually taken possession of it and was profiting from its income (see 16:1–4; 19:26–30). *you will always eat at my table.* A matter of honor—but probably also so that David could keep a watchful eye on him (cf. 1Sa 20:24–27; 2Ki 25:29). In any event, Mephibosheth's general financial needs were to be cared for by the produce of Saul's estate (v. 10).

9:8 *dead dog like me.* An expression of deep self-abasement. The author has used the "(dead) dog" motif with great effect. First Goliath, scornfully disdaining the young warrior David, asks, "Am I a dog...?" (1Sa 17:43)—and unwittingly foreshadows his own end. Then David, in a self-deprecating manner, describes himself as a "dead dog" (1Sa 24:14) to sug-

gest to Saul that the king of Israel should not consider him worth so much attention. In the Nabal episode, that "dog" (a "Calebite") and his sudden death characterize Saul and foreshadow his unhappy end (see note on 1Sa 25:3). Here a grandson of Saul and in 16:9 a relative of Saul who curses David are similarly described. For the author, "dead dog" fittingly characterizes those who foolishly scorn or oppose the Lord's anointed, while David's own self-deprecation (see 7:18; 1Sa 18:18) is conducive to his exaltation.

9:12 *had a young son named Mika.* Who also had descendants (1Ch 8:35–39).

10:1 *In the course of time.* See note on 2:1. *king.* Nahash (see v. 2; 1Sa 11). *Ammonites.* See note on 1Sa 11:1.

10:2 *show kindness.* The Hebrew for this expression suggests that a formal treaty existed between the Israelites and the Ammonites (cf. 1Sa 20:8).

10:3,14 *city.* Rabbah, the capital (11:1; 12:26). See note on Dt 3:11.

10:4 *shaved off half of each man's beard.* In the world of that time this was considered an insult of the most serious kind (cf. Isa 7:20). *cut off their garments at the buttocks.* A customary way of degrading prisoners of war (cf. Isa 20:4).

⁵When David was told about this, he sent messengers to meet the men, for they were greatly humiliated. The king said, "Stay at Jericho till your beards have grown, and then come back."

⁶When the Ammonites realized that they had become obnoxious ʸ to David, they hired twenty thousand Aramean ᶻ foot soldiers from Beth Rehob ᵃ and Zobah, ᵇ as well as the king of Maakah ᶜ with a thousand men, and also twelve thousand men from Tob. ᵈ

⁷On hearing this, David sent Joab ᵉ out with the entire army of fighting men. ⁸The Ammonites came out and drew up in battle formation at the entrance of their city gate, while the Arameans of Zobah and Rehob and the men of Tob and Maakah were by themselves in the open country.

⁹Joab saw that there were battle lines in front of him and behind him; so he selected some of the best troops in Israel and deployed them against the Arameans. ¹⁰He put the rest of the men under the command of Abishai ᶠ his brother and deployed them against the Ammonites. ¹¹Joab said, "If the Arameans are too strong for me, then you are to come to my rescue; but if the Ammonites are too strong for you, then I will come to rescue you. ¹²Be strong, ᵍ and let us fight bravely for our people and the cities of our God. The LORD will do what is good in his sight." ʰ

¹³Then Joab and the troops with him advanced to fight the Arameans, and they fled before him. ¹⁴When the Ammonites ⁱ realized that the Arameans were fleeing, they fled before Abishai and went inside the city. So Joab returned from fighting the Ammonites and came to Jerusalem.

¹⁵After the Arameans saw that they had been routed by Israel, they regrouped. ¹⁶Hadadezer had Arameans brought from beyond the Euphrates River; they went to Helam, with Shobak the commander of Hadadezer's army leading them.

¹⁷When David was told of this, he gathered all Israel, crossed the Jordan and went to Helam. The Arameans formed their battle lines to meet David and fought against him. ¹⁸But they fled before Israel, and David killed seven hundred of their charioteers and forty thousand of their foot soldiers. ᵃ He also struck down Shobak the commander of their army, and he died there. ¹⁹When all the kings who were vassals of Hadadezer saw that they had been routed by Israel, they made peace with the Israelites and became subject ʲ to them.

So the Arameans ᵏ were afraid to help the Ammonites anymore.

DAVID AND BATHSHEBA

11 In the spring, ˡ at the time when kings go off to war, David sent Joab ᵐ out with the king's men and the whole Israelite army. ⁿ They destroyed the Ammonites and besieged Rabbah. ᵒ But David remained in Jerusalem.

²One evening David got up from his bed and walked around on the roof ᵖ of the palace. From the roof he saw �q a woman bathing. The woman was very beautiful, ³and David sent someone to find out about her. The man said, "She is Bathsheba, ʳ the daughter of Eliam ˢ and the wife of Uriah ᵗ the Hittite." ⁴Then David sent messengers to get her. ᵘ

ᵃ *18* Some Septuagint manuscripts (see also 1 Chron. 19:18); Hebrew *horsemen*

10:5 *Jericho.* See notes on Jos 6:1; 1Ki 16:34. Jericho remained unrestored during the centuries between Joshua's conquest and the time of Ahab.

10:6 *obnoxious.* See note on 1Sa 13:4. *Beth Rehob.* See Nu 13:21; Jdg 18:28 and notes. *Zobah.* See note on 8:3. *Maakah.* See Dt 3:14 and note; Jos 12:5; 13:13. *Tob.* See Jdg 11:3–6 and note on 11:3.

10:10 *Abishai.* See note on 1Sa 26:6.

10:16 *Hadadezer.* See note on 8:3.

10:18 *seven hundred.* Perhaps a copyist's mistake; in 1Ch 19:18 the figure is 7,000.

10:19 *they made peace with the Israelites.* There is no indication that Hadadezer himself made peace with Israel as his vassals did in the aftermath of this defeat. These events represent David's last major campaign against combined foreign powers.

11:1–27 This detailed account of David's sin has as its foil the story of how David came to receive Nabal's wife Abigail as his wife (1Sa 25). There the Lord removes the husband because of his disdain for the Lord's anointed, and Abigail comes to David as the one who has prevented him from using his incipient royal power for personal ends. Here David abuses his royal power to obtain the wife of another whom he callously

removes by royal manipulation of events. David commits the great sin of those entrusted by God with power—using it for personal ends. Contrast what David's greatest Son said about his own ministry (Mk 10:45).

11:1 *the spring.* Of the year following the events reported in ch. 10. *the time when kings go off to war.* When the rains have ended. At that time the roads became passable and the spring harvest provided food for armies on the march as well as fodder for their animals. *Rabbah.* See note on 10:3,14. Though now alone (see 10:19), the Ammonites had not yet been subjugated.

11:2 *walked around on the roof.* Where he could enjoy the cool evening air (see note on 1Sa 9:25).

11:3 *Eliam.* Perhaps the same Eliam who was a member of David's personal bodyguard (23:34) and a son of his counselor Ahithophel (see 15:12 and note). *Uriah.* Also listed among those comprising David's royal guard (23:39). His name suggests that even though he was a Hittite, he had adopted the Israelite faith (Uriah means "The LORD is my light"). *Hittite.* See note on 1Sa 26:6.

11:4 *David sent messengers to get her.* Through this and subsequent actions David broke the sixth, seventh and tenth commandments (Ex 20:13–14,17). *She came to him, and he slept with her.* Bathsheba appears to have been an unprotest-

---

10:6 ʸ S Ge 34:30
ᶻ S 2Sa 8:5
ᵃ S Nu 13:21
ᵇ S 1Sa 14:47
ᶜ S Dt 3:14
ᵈ Jdg 11:3-5
10:7 ᵉ S 2Sa 2:18
10:10 ᶠ S 1Sa 26:6
10:12 ᵍ S Dt 1:21;
31:6; S Eph 6:10
ʰ S Jdg 10:15; Ne 4:14
10:14 ⁱ 2Sa 8:12
10:19 ʲ 2Sa 8:6
ᵏ 1Ki 11:25; 22:31;
2Ki 5:1
11:1 ˡ 1Ki 20:22,26
ᵐ S 2Sa 2:18
ⁿ 1Ch 20:1 ᵒ S Dt 3:11
11:2 ᵖ S Dt 22:8;
S Jos 2:8 q Mt 5:28
11:3 ʳ 1Ch 3:5
ˢ 2Sa 23:34
ᵗ 2Sa 23:39
11:4 ᵘ S Lev 20:10;
Ps 51 Title; Jas 1:14-15

11:4 ᵛDt 22:22
ᵂS Lev 15:25-30
11:6 ˣ1Ch 11:41
11:8 ʸS Ge 18:4
11:11 ᶻ2Sa 7:2
ᵃS 1Sa 21:5
11:14 ᵇ1Ki 21:8
11:15 ᶜver 14-17;
2Sa 12:9 ᵈ2Sa 12:12
11:21 ᵉS Jdg 8:31
ᶠJdg 9:50-54

She came to him, and he slept ᵛwith her. (Now she was purifying herself from her month-ly uncleanness.) ᵂ Then she went back home. ⁵The woman conceived and sent word to David, saying, "I am pregnant."

⁶So David sent this word to Joab: "Send me Uriah ˣ the Hittite." And Joab sent him to David. ⁷When Uriah came to him, David asked him how Joab was, how the soldiers were and how the war was going. ⁸Then David said to Uriah, "Go down to your house and wash your feet." ʸ So Uriah left the palace, and a gift from the king was sent after him. ⁹But Uriah slept at the entrance to the palace with all his master's servants and did not go down to his house.

¹⁰David was told, "Uriah did not go home." So he asked Uriah, "Haven't you just come from a military campaign? Why didn't you go home?"

¹¹Uriah said to David, "The ark ᶻ and Israel and Judah are staying in tents, ᵃ and my com-mander Joab and my lord's men are camped in the open country. How could I go to my house to eat and drink and make love ᵃ to my wife? As surely as you live, I will not do such a thing!"

¹²Then David said to him, "Stay here one more day, and tomorrow I will send you back." So Uriah remained in Jerusalem that day and the next. ¹³At David's invitation, he ate and drank with him, and David made him drunk. But in the evening Uriah went out to sleep on his mat among his master's servants; he did not go home.

¹⁴In the morning David wrote a letter ᵇ to Joab and sent it with Uriah. ¹⁵In it he wrote, "Put Uriah out in front where the fighting is fiercest. Then withdraw from him so he will be struck down ᶜ and die. ᵈ"

¹⁶So while Joab had the city under siege, he put Uriah at a place where he knew the strongest defenders were. ¹⁷When the men of the city came out and fought against Joab, some of the men in David's army fell; moreover, Uriah the Hittite died.

¹⁸Joab sent David a full account of the battle. ¹⁹He instructed the messenger: "When you have finished giving the king this account of the battle, ²⁰the king's anger may flare up, and he may ask you, 'Why did you get so close to the city to fight? Didn't you know they would shoot arrows from the wall? ²¹Who killed Abimelek ᵉ son of Jerub-Besheth ᵇ? Didn't a woman drop an upper millstone on him from the wall, ᶠ so that he died in The-bez? Why did you get so close to the wall?' If he asks you this, then say to him, 'Moreover, your servant Uriah the Hittite is dead.' "

²²The messenger set out, and when he arrived he told David everything Joab had sent him to say. ²³The messenger said to David, "The men overpowered us and came out against us in the open, but we drove them back to the entrance of the city gate. ²⁴Then the archers shot arrows at your servants from the wall, and some of the king's men died. Moreover, your servant Uriah the Hittite is dead."

ᵃ 11 Or staying at Sukkoth   ᵇ 21 Also known as Jerub-Baal (that is, Gideon)

---

ing partner in this adulterous relationship with David. (Now she was purifying herself from her monthly uncleanness.) The pur-pose of this statement is to indicate Bathsheba's condition at the time of her sexual relations with David. She was just becom-ing ceremonially clean (Lev 15:28–30) after the seven-day peri-od of monthly impurity due to menstruation (Lev 15:19). It is thus clear that she was not already pregnant by her own hus-band when David took her.
11:5 I am pregnant. Bathsheba leaves the next step up to Da-vid. The law prescribed the death penalty for both David and Bathsheba (Lev 20:10), as they well knew.
11:6 Send me Uriah. Under the pretense of seeking information about the course of the war, David brings Uriah back to Jerusalem.
11:8 Go down to your house and wash your feet. In essence, Da-vid tells Uriah to go home and relax. What he does not say specifically is what is most important, and well understood by Uriah (v. 11). a gift from the king was sent after him. The Hebrew word for "gift" has the meaning of "food" in Ge 43:34 ("portions" from the king's table). David wanted Uriah and Bathsheba to en-joy their evening together.
11:11 ark. Uriah's statement suggests that the ark was in the field camp with the army rather than in the tent that David had set up for it in Jerusalem (6:17). If so, it was probably there for purposes of worship and to seek guidance for the war. But then the circumstances are even more damning for Da-

vid—the Lord is in the field with his army while David stays at home in leisure. How could I go to my house to eat . . . ? See note on v. 8 ("gift"). Uriah's devotion to duty exposes by sharp con-trast David's dalliance at home while his men are in the field. As surely as you live. See note on 1Sa 14:39,45.
11:13 David made him drunk. In the hope that in this condition he would relent and go to Bathsheba.
11:14 Uriah is unaware that he is carrying his own death war-rant to Joab.
11:15 so he will be struck down and die. Unsuccessful in making it appear that Uriah was the father of Bathsheba's child, David plotted Uriah's death so he could marry Bathsheba himself as quickly as possible.
11:16 city. Rabbah (see note on 10:3,14).
11:17 Uriah the Hittite died. This phrase or its equivalent ech-oes like a death knell throughout the rest of the chapter (vv. 21,24; cf. also vv. 15,26).
11:21 Jerub-Besheth. Another possible spelling is "Jerub-Bo-sheth." In Judges he is called Jerub-Baal (see note on Jdg 6:32; see also TNIV text note here). For similar name changes else-where in 2 Samuel, see notes on 2:8; 4:4. millstone. See Jdg 9:53 and note. Uriah . . . is dead. Joab knows that this news is of great importance to David, and he uses it to squelch any criticism Da-vid might otherwise have had of the battle tactics.
11:24 some of the king's men died. Other brave soldiers were

²⁵David told the messenger, "Say this to Joab: 'Don't let this upset you; the sword devours one as well as another. Press the attack against the city and destroy it.' Say this to encourage Joab."

²⁶When Uriah's wife heard that her husband was dead, she mourned for him. ²⁷After the time of mourning *g* was over, David had her brought to his house, and she became his wife and bore him a son. But the thing David had done displeased *h* the LORD.

NATHAN REBUKES DAVID

11:1; 12:29–31pp — 1Ch 20:1–3

12 The LORD sent Nathan *i* to David. *j* When he came to him, *k* he said, "There were two men in a certain town, one rich and the other poor. ²The rich man had a very large number of sheep and cattle, ³but the poor man had nothing except one little ewe lamb he had bought. He raised it, and it grew up with him and his children. It shared his food, drank from his cup and even slept in his arms. It was like a daughter to him.

⁴"Now a traveler came to the rich man, but the rich man refrained from taking one of his own sheep or cattle to prepare a meal for the traveler who had come to him. Instead, he took the ewe lamb that belonged to the poor man and prepared it for the one who had come to him."

⁵David *l* burned with anger *m* against the man *n* and said to Nathan, "As surely as the LORD lives, *o* the man who did this must die! ⁶He must pay for that lamb four times over, *p* because he did such a thing and had no pity."

⁷Then Nathan said to David, "You are the man! *q* This is what the LORD, the God of Israel, says: 'I anointed *r* you *s* king over Israel, and I delivered you from the hand of Saul. ⁸I gave you your master's house to you, *t* and your master's wives into your arms. I gave you the house of Israel and Judah. And if all this had been too little, I would have given you even more. ⁹Why did you despise *u* the word of the LORD by doing what is evil in his eyes? You struck down *v* Uriah *w* the Hittite with the sword and took his wife to be your own. You killed *x* him with the sword of the Ammonites. ¹⁰Now, therefore, the sword *y* will never depart from your house, because you despised me and took the wife of Uriah the Hittite to be your own.'

¹¹"This is what the LORD says: 'Out of your own household *z* I am going to bring calamity on you. *a* Before your very eyes I will take your wives and give them to one who is close to you, and he will sleep with your wives in broad daylight. *b* ¹²You did it in secret, *c* but I will do this thing in broad daylight *d* before all Israel.' "

¹³Then David said to Nathan, "I have sinned *e* against the LORD."
Nathan replied, "The LORD has taken away *f* your sin. *g* You are not going to die. *h* ¹⁴But

---

11:27 *g* Dt 34:8
h 2Sa 12:9; Ps 51:4-5
12:1 *i* S 2Sa 7:2
j Ps 51 Title *k* 2Sa 14:4
12:5 *l* 1Ki 20:40
m S Ge 34:7 *n* Ro 2:1
o S 1Sa 14:39
12:6 *p* Ex 22:1
12:7 *q* 2Sa 14:13;
Da 4:22 *r* S 1Sa 2:35
s 1Ki 20:42
12:8 *t* S 2Sa 9:7
12:9 *u* S Nu 15:31;
S 1Sa 13:14
v S 2Sa 11:15
w 1Ki 15:5 *x* Ps 26:9;
51:14
12:10 *y* 2Sa 13:28;
18:14-15; 1Ki 2:25
12:11 *z* 2Sa 16:11
a Dt 28:30; 2Sa 16:21-
22 *b* S Dt 17:17
12:12 *c* 2Sa 11:4-15
d 2Sa 16:22
12:13 *e* S Ge 13:13;
S 20:6; S Nu 22:34
f Ps 32:1-5; 51:1,9;
103:12; Isa 43:25;
44:22; Zec 3:4,9
g Pr 28:13; Jer 2:35;
Mic 7:18-19
h Lev 20:10; 24:17

---

sacrificed along with Uriah, a fact that exposes David's callousness, as well as the enormity of his sinful cover-up.

11:25 *David told the messenger.* David hid his satisfaction over the news with a hypocritical statement that war is war and the death of Uriah should not be a discouragement.

▲ ◯ **11:27** *time of mourning was over.* Presumably a period of seven days (see 1Sa 31:13 and note; Ge 50:10). *she became his wife.* See note on 5:14. *the thing David had done displeased the LORD.* Not only had David brazenly violated God's laws (see note on v. 4) but, even worse, he had shamelessly abused his royal power, which the Lord had entrusted to him to shepherd the Lord's people (see 5:2; 7:7 and note).

12:1 *The LORD sent.* Prophets were messengers from the Lord. Here the Great King sends his emissary to rebuke and announce judgment on the king he had enthroned over his people. *Nathan.* See note on 7:2.

12:5 *As surely as the LORD lives.* See note on 1Sa 14:39,45.

12:6 *four times over.* In agreement with the requirements of Ex 22:1.

◯ **12:7** *You are the man!* Nathan identifies David as the rich man in the parable of vv. 1–4. David's sentence of fourfold retribution against that man (v. 6) came true in his own experience: As a result of his engineering Uriah's death, David lost four of his sons (see vv. 10,18 and note on v. 10). Indeed, his sin against Uriah became a permanent stain on his otherwise godly life (see 1Ki 15:5).

12:8 *your master's wives.* Earlier narratives refer to only one

wife of Saul (Ahinoam, 1Sa 14:50) and one concubine (Rizpah, 2Sa 3:7; 21:8–11). This statement suggests that there were others. But since it was customary for new kings to assume the harem of their predecessors (see note on 3:7), it may be that Nathan merely uses conventional language to emphasize that the Lord had placed David on Saul's throne. *I gave you the house of Israel and Judah.* See 2:1,4; 5:2–3.

◯ **12:9** *despise the word of the LORD.* See notes on 11:4,27. *You killed him.* David is held directly responsible for Uriah's death even though he fell in battle (see 11:15 and note).

◯ **12:10** *the sword will never depart from your house.* Three of David's sons died violently: Amnon (13:28–29), Absalom (18:14–15) and Adonijah (1Ki 2:25).

◯ **12:11** *Out of your own household I am going to bring calamity on you.* David was driven from Jerusalem by Absalom's conspiracy to seize the kingship from his own father (15:1–17). *he will sleep with your wives in broad daylight.* Fulfilled at the time of Absalom's rebellion (see note on 16:22).

▲ ◯ **12:13** *I have sinned against the LORD.* David recognizes his guilt and confesses his sin in response to Nathan's rebuke (see Ps 51:4 and note). There is a clear contrast between David's confession and Saul's (see note on 1Sa 15:24). *The LORD has taken away your sin.* David experienced the joy of knowing his sin has been forgiven (see Ps 32:1,5; cf. Ps 51:8,12). *You are not going to die.* The Lord, in his grace, released David from the customary death penalty for adultery and murder (Lev 20:10; 24:17, 21).

12:14 *i* Isa 52:5;
Ro 2:24
12:15 *j* S 1Sa 25:38
12:16 *k* Ps 5:7; 95:6
12:17 *l* S Ge 37:35;
S 1Sa 1:7
m S 2Sa 3:35; Da 6:18
12:20 *n* Mt 6:17
o S Ge 41:14
12:21 *p* Jdg 20:26
12:22 *q* Jnh 3:9
r Isa 38:1-5
12:23 *s* Ge 37:35
t S 1Sa 31:13;
2Sa 13:39; Job 7:10;
10:21
12:24 *u* 1Ki 1:11
v 1Ki 1:10; 1Ch 22:9;
28:5; Mt 1:6
12:25 *w* Ne 13:26
12:26 *x* S Dt 3:11
12:30 *y* Est 8:15;
Ps 21:3; 132:18
12:31 *z* S 1Sa 14:47

because by doing this you have shown utter contempt for[a] the LORD,[i] the son born to you will die."

[15]After Nathan had gone home, the LORD struck[j] the child that Uriah's wife had borne to David, and he became ill. [16]David pleaded with God for the child. He fasted and spent the nights lying[k] in sackcloth[b] on the ground. [17]The elders of his household stood beside him to get him up from the ground, but he refused,[l] and he would not eat any food with them. [m]

[18]On the seventh day the child died. David's attendants were afraid to tell him that the child was dead, for they thought, "While the child was still living, he wouldn't listen to us when we spoke to him. How can we now tell him the child is dead? He may do something desperate."

[19]David noticed that his attendants were whispering among themselves, and he realized the child was dead. "Is the child dead?" he asked.

"Yes," they replied, "he is dead."

[20]Then David got up from the ground. After he had washed,[n] put on lotions and changed his clothes,[o] he went into the house of the LORD and worshiped. Then he went to his own house, and at his request they served him food, and he ate.

[21]His attendants asked him, "Why are you acting this way? While the child was alive, you fasted and wept,[p] but now that the child is dead, you get up and eat!"

[22]He answered, "While the child was still alive, I fasted and wept. I thought, 'Who knows?[q] The LORD may be gracious to me and let the child live.'[r] [23]But now that he is dead, why should I go on fasting? Can I bring him back again? I will go to him,[s] but he will not return to me."[t]

[24]Then David comforted his wife Bathsheba,[u] and he went to her and made love to her. She gave birth to a son, and they named him Solomon.[v] The LORD loved him; [25]and because the LORD loved him, he sent word through Nathan the prophet to name him Jedidiah.[c][w]

[26]Meanwhile Joab fought against Rabbah[x] of the Ammonites and captured the royal citadel. [27]Joab then sent messengers to David, saying, "I have fought against Rabbah and taken its water supply. [28]Now muster the rest of the troops and besiege the city and capture it. Otherwise I will take the city, and it will be named after me."

[29]So David mustered the entire army and went to Rabbah, and attacked and captured it. [30]David took the crown[y] from their king's[d] head, and it was placed on his own head. It weighed a talent[e] of gold, and it was set with precious stones. David took a great quantity of plunder from the city [31]and brought out the people who were there, consigning them to labor with saws and with iron picks and axes, and he made them work at brickmaking.[f] David did this to all the Ammonite[z] towns. Then he and his entire army returned to Jerusalem.

---

[a] 14 An ancient Hebrew scribal tradition; Masoretic Text *for the enemies of*   [b] 16 Dead Sea Scrolls and Septuagint; Masoretic Text does not have *in sackcloth.*   [c] 25 *Jedidiah* means *loved by the LORD.*
[d] 30 Or *from Milkom's* (that is, Molek's)   [e] 30 That is, about 75 pounds or about 34 kilograms
[f] 31 The meaning of the Hebrew for this clause is uncertain.

12:14 *you have shown utter contempt for the LORD.* See TNIV text note.

12:16 *pleaded . . . fasted.* See note on Ezr 8:23.

12:18 *seventh day.* If reference is to the child's age, his life was so short that he remained uncircumcised and unnamed (see Lk 1:59; 2:21; cf. Ge 21:3–4)—and therefore was not counted among the Israelites.

12:20 *put on lotions.* A practice associated with the cessation of mourning (see 14:2). *changed his clothes.* Took off his mourning garments and put on his normal clothing. *went into the house of the LORD and worshiped.* In this way David openly demonstrated his humble acceptance of the disciplinary results of his sin. Again (see note on v. 13) there is a contrast between David's attitude and Saul's (see note on 1Sa 15:25).

12:23 *I will go to him.* David too will die and join his child in the grave (see note on Ge 37:35). *he will not return to me.* See Job 7:9 and note.

12:24 *Solomon.* See 1Ch 22:9 and TNIV text note.

12:25 *Jedidiah.* See TNIV text note. The giving of this name suggests that the Lord's special favor rested on Solomon from his birth. And since the name also contained an echo of David's name, it provided assurance to David that the Lord also loved him and would continue his dynasty.

12:26 *Joab fought against Rabbah.* The writer now returns to the outcome of the attack against the Ammonites (11:1,25), which provided the background for the story of David and Bathsheba. Even while the Lord was displeased with David (11:27), he gave the Israelites victory over a people who had abused them.

12:30 *the crown . . . was placed on his own head.* A crown of such weight (see TNIV text note) would have been worn only briefly and on very special occasions. Perhaps it was worn only once in a symbolic act of transferring to David sovereignty over Ammon.

12:31 *consigning them to labor.* Victorious kings often used prisoners of war as menial laborers in royal building projects (see 1Ki 9:20–21; cf. also Ex 1:11).

Once he had become king over all Israel (2Sa 5:1–5), David:

1. Conquered the Jebusite fortress of Zion/Jerusalem and made it his royal city (5:6–10);

2. Received the recognition of and assurance of friendship from Hiram of Tyre, king of the Phoenicians (5:11–12);

3. Decisively defeated the Philistines so that their hold on Israelite territory was broken and their threat to Israel eliminated (5:17–25; 8:1);

4. Defeated the Moabites and imposed his authority over them (8:2);

5. Crushed the Aramean kingdoms of Hadadezer (king of Zobah), Damascus and Maakah and put them under tribute (8:3–8; 10:6–19). Talmai, the Aramean king of Geshur, apparently had made peace with David while he was still reigning in Hebron and sealed the alliance by giving his daughter in marriage to David (3:3; cf. 1Ch 2:23);

6. Subdued Edom and incorporated it into his empire (8:13–14);

7. Defeated the Ammonites and brought them into subjection (12:26–31);

8. Subjugated the remaining Canaanite cities that had previously maintained their independence from Israel, such as Beth Shan, Megiddo, Taanach and Dor.

Since David had earlier crushed the Amalekites (1Sa 30:17–18), his wars thus completed the conquest begun by Joshua and secured all the borders of Israel. His empire (united Israel plus the subjugated kingdoms) reached from Ezion Geber on the eastern arm of the Red Sea to the Euphrates River.

13:1 *a* 2Sa 3:2
b 2Sa 14:27; 1Ch 3:9
c S 2Sa 3:3
13:3 *d* S 1Sa 16:9
13:9 *e* Ge 45:1
13:11 *f* S Ge 39:12
g S Ge 38:16
13:12 *h* Lev 20:17
i S Ge 34:7
13:13 *j* S Lev 18:9;
S Dt 22:21,23-24
13:14 *k* S Ge 34:2;
Eze 22:11
13:18 *l* S Ge 37:23
13:19 *m* S Jos 7:6;
Est 4:1; Da 9:3
13:21 *n* S Ge 34:7
13:22 *o* Ge 31:24
p Lev 19:17-18;
1Jn 2:9-11

AMNON AND TAMAR

13 In the course of time, Amnon *a* son of David fell in love with Tamar, *b* the beautiful sister of Absalom *c* son of David. ²Amnon became so obsessed with his sister Tamar that he made himself ill. She was a virgin, and it seemed impossible for him to do anything to her.

³Now Amnon had an adviser named Jonadab son of Shimeah, *d* David's brother. Jonadab was a very shrewd man. ⁴He asked Amnon, "Why do you, the king's son, look so haggard morning after morning? Won't you tell me?"

Amnon said to him, "I'm in love with Tamar, my brother Absalom's sister."

⁵"Go to bed and pretend to be ill," Jonadab said. "When your father comes to see you, say to him, 'I would like my sister Tamar to come and give me something to eat. Let her prepare the food in my sight so I may watch her and then eat it from her hand.' "

⁶So Amnon lay down and pretended to be ill. When the king came to see him, Amnon said to him, "I would like my sister Tamar to come and make some special bread in my sight, so I may eat from her hand."

⁷David sent word to Tamar at the palace: "Go to the house of your brother Amnon and prepare some food for him." ⁸So Tamar went to the house of her brother Amnon, who was lying down. She took some dough, kneaded it, made the bread in his sight and baked it. ⁹Then she took the pan and served him the bread, but he refused to eat.

"Send everyone out of here," *e* Amnon said. So everyone left him. ¹⁰Then Amnon said to Tamar, "Bring the food here into my bedroom so I may eat from your hand." And Tamar took the bread she had prepared and brought it to her brother Amnon in his bedroom. ¹¹But when she took it to him to eat, he grabbed *f* her and said, "Come to bed with me, my sister." *g*

¹²"No, my brother!" she said to him. "Don't force me! Such a thing should not be done in Israel! *h* Don't do this wicked thing. *i* ¹³What about me? *j* Where could I get rid of my disgrace? And what about you? You would be like one of the wicked fools in Israel. Please speak to the king; he will not keep me from being married to you." ¹⁴But he refused to listen to her, and since he was stronger than she, he raped her. *k*

¹⁵Then Amnon hated her with intense hatred. In fact, he hated her more than he had loved her. Amnon said to her, "Get up and get out!"

¹⁶"No!" she said to him. "Sending me away would be a greater wrong than what you have already done to me."

But he refused to listen to her. ¹⁷He called his personal servant and said, "Get this woman out of my sight and bolt the door after her." ¹⁸So his servant put her out and bolted the door after her. She was wearing a richly ornamented *a* robe, *l* for this was the kind of garment the virgin daughters of the king wore. ¹⁹Tamar put ashes *m* on her head and tore the ornamented *b* robe she was wearing. She put her hands on her head and went away, weeping aloud as she went.

²⁰Her brother Absalom said to her, "Has that Amnon, your brother, been with you? Be quiet for now, my sister; he is your brother. Don't take this thing to heart." And Tamar lived in her brother Absalom's house, a desolate woman.

²¹When King David heard all this, he was furious. *n* ²²And Absalom never spoke to Amnon again; *o* he hated *p* Amnon because he had disgraced his sister Tamar.

---

a 18 The meaning of the Hebrew for this phrase is uncertain.   *b 19* The meaning of the Hebrew for this word is uncertain.

13:1–39 The trouble within David's family begins (see note on 12:10).

13:1 *In the course of time.* See note on 2:1. *Amnon.* David's firstborn son (3:2). *Tamar.* David's daughter by Maakah of Geshur (cf. 3:3), and Absalom's full sister.

13:3 *Shimeah.* Called Shammah in 1Sa 16:9.

13:6 *When the king came to see him.* Amnon used his father, David, to obtain his illicit purpose, just as David had used Joab (see 11:14–17).

13:12 *wicked thing.* Hebrew *nebalah,* from the same root word as the name Nabal (see 1Sa 25:25).

13:13 *what about you?* This act would jeopardize Amnon's position as crown prince and heir to the throne. *one of the wicked fools.* That is, a *nabal* (see note on v. 12; see also TNIV text note on Pr 1:7). David's wicked folly in his dealings with Bathsheba yields the bitter fruit of imitation by his oldest son, who by his act becomes another Nabal.

13:15 *Amnon hated her.* The reversal in Amnon's feelings toward Tamar demonstrates that his former "love" (v. 1) was nothing but sensual desire.

13:16 *Sending me away would be a greater wrong.* No longer a virgin, she could not be offered by her father to any other potential husband (see v. 21 and note).

13:18 *richly ornamented robe.* See Ge 37:3 and note.

13:19 *put ashes on her head and tore the … robe she was wearing.* Signs of grief (see 1Sa 4:12 and note), expressing her anguish and announcing that her virginity had been violated.

13:20 *Be quiet for now, my sister … Don't take this thing to heart.* Absalom urges his sister not to make the matter a public scandal. Meanwhile, he formulates his own secret plans for revenge (see vv. 22,28,32).

13:21 *he was furious.* Although David was incensed by Amnon's rape of Tamar, there is no record that he took any punitive action against him. Perhaps the memory of his

ABSALOM KILLS AMNON

13:23 q1Sa 25:7
13:28 rS 2Sa 3:3
sS Ru 3:7
tS 2Sa 12:10
13:31 uS Nu 14:6
13:37 vS 2Sa 3:3
13:39 w2Sa 14:13
xS 2Sa 12:19-23
14:1 yS 2Sa 2:18
14:2 zNe 3:5;
Jer 6:1; Am 1:1
a2Sa 20:16

23Two years later, when Absalom's sheepshearers q were at Baal Hazor near the border of Ephraim, he invited all the king's sons to come there. 24Absalom went to the king and said, "Your servant has had shearers come. Will the king and his attendants please join me?" 25"No, my son," the king replied. "All of us should not go; we would only be a burden to you." Although Absalom urged him, he still refused to go but gave him his blessing.

26Then Absalom said, "If not, please let my brother Amnon come with us."

The king asked him, "Why should he go with you?" 27But Absalom urged him, so he sent with him Amnon and the rest of the king's sons.

28Absalom r ordered his men, "Listen! When Amnon is in high s spirits from drinking wine and I say to you, 'Strike Amnon down,' then kill him. Don't be afraid. Haven't I given you this order? Be strong and brave. t " 29So Absalom's men did to Amnon what Absalom had ordered. Then all the king's sons got up, mounted their mules and fled.

30While they were on their way, the report came to David: "Absalom has struck down all the king's sons; not one of them is left." 31The king stood up, tore u his clothes and lay down on the ground; and all his attendants stood by with their clothes torn.

32But Jonadab son of Shimeah, David's brother, said, "My lord should not think that they killed all the princes; only Amnon is dead. This has been Absalom's express intention ever since the day Amnon raped his sister Tamar. 33My lord the king should not be concerned about the report that all the king's sons are dead. Only Amnon is dead."

34Meanwhile, Absalom had fled.

Now the man standing watch looked up and saw many people on the road west of him, coming down the side of the hill. The watchman went and told the king, "I see men in the direction of Horonaim, on the side of the hill." a

35Jonadab said to the king, "See, the king's sons have come; it has happened just as your servant said."

36As he finished speaking, the king's sons came in, wailing loudly. The king, too, and all his attendants wept very bitterly.

37Absalom fled and went to Talmai v son of Ammihud, the king of Geshur. But King David mourned many days for his son.

38After Absalom fled and went to Geshur, he stayed there three years. 39And King David longed to go to Absalom, w for he was consoled x concerning Amnon's death.

ABSALOM RETURNS TO JERUSALEM

14 Joab y son of Zeruiah knew that the king's heart longed for Absalom. 2So Joab sent someone to Tekoa z and had a wise woman a brought from there. He said to her, "Pretend you are in mourning. Dress in mourning clothes, and don't

a 34 Septuagint; Hebrew does not have this sentence.

own sin with Bathsheba adversely affected his judicious handling of the matter. Whatever the reason, David abdicated his responsibility both as king and as father. This disciplinary leniency toward his sons (see notes on 14:33; 1Ki 1:6) eventually led to the death of Amnon and the revolts of Absalom and Adonijah.

13:22 *Absalom never spoke to Amnon again; he hated Amnon.* He quietly bided his time.

13:23 *Two years later.* After two years it was clear to Absalom that King David was not going to do anything to Amnon for raping Tamar. *he invited all the king's sons.* The time of sheepshearing was a festive occasion (see 1Sa 25:4,8).

13:26 *let my brother Amnon come.* Upon David's refusal of the invitation, Absalom diplomatically requested that Amnon, the crown prince and oldest son, be his representative. *Why should he go with you?* David's question suggests some misgivings because of the strained relationship between the two half brothers (see v. 22).

A C **13:28** *kill him.* Absalom arranged for the murder of his half brother in violation of Eastern hospitality. In the wicked acts of Amnon and Absalom, David's oldest sons became guilty of sexual immorality and murder, as their father had before them. With the murder of Amnon, Absalom not only avenged the rape of his sister but also secured for himself the position of successor to the throne (see 3:3; 15:1–6). Kileab, David's second son (3:3), may have died in his youth since there is no reference to him beyond the announcement of his birth.

13:29 *mules.* Apparently the normal mount for royalty in David's kingdom (see 18:9; 1Ki 1:33,38,44; see also note on 1Ki 1:33).

13:31 *tore his clothes and lay down on the ground.* Common ways of expressing grief (see v. 19; Jos 7:6; 1Ki 21:27; Est 4:1,3; Job 1:20; 2:8).

13:34 *Horonaim.* The Levitical cities of Upper and Lower Beth Horon, located in Ephraim (see Jos 21:20,22; 1Ch 7:24) two miles apart and about eleven miles northwest of Jerusalem (see note on Ne 2:10, "Horonite"; see also map, p. 317).

13:37 *Talmai son of Ammihud, the king of Geshur.* Absalom's grandfather (see 3:3 and note).

C **13:39** *longed to go to Absalom.* With Absalom a refugee, David had lost both of his oldest living sons. Moreover, he could not bring Absalom to account for what he had done to Amnon since David himself had blood on his hands.

14:1 *Joab son of Zeruiah.* See notes on 2:13; 1Sa 26:6. *the king's heart longed for Absalom.* Torn between anger and love (and perhaps remorse), David again leaves the initiative to others.

C **14:2** *So Joab sent.* Joab appears to have been motivated by a concern for the political implications of the unresolved dispute between David and the son in line for the throne. He attempts to move David to action by means of a story designed to elicit a response clearly applicable, by analogy, to David's own predicament. A similar technique was used by Nathan the prophet (12:1–7; see also 1Ki 20:38–43). *Tekoa.* A town a few miles south of Bethlehem, from which the prophet Amos also came (Am 1:1).

14:2 *b* S Ru 3:3;
S Isa 1:6
14:3 *c* ver 19
14:7 *d* Nu 35:19
e Mt 21:38 *f* Dt 19:10-
13
14:8 *g* 1Sa 25:35
14:9 *h* 1Sa 25:24
i Mt 27:25 *j* 1Sa 25:28
14:11 *k* S Nu 35:12,
21 *l* S Mt 10:30
m S 1Sa 14:45
14:13 *n* S 2Sa 12:7;
1Ki 20:40
o 2Sa 13:38-39
14:14 *p* Job 14:11;
Ps 58:7; Isa 19:5
q Job 10:8; 17:13;
30:23; Ps 22:15;
Heb 9:27 *r* Nu 35:15,
25-28
14:16 *s* S Ex 34:9;
S 1Sa 26:19
14:17 *t* S 1Sa 29:9
u 1Ki 3:9; Da 2:21

use any cosmetic lotions. *b* Act like a woman who has spent many days grieving for the dead. ³Then go to the king and speak these words to him." And Joab *c* put the words in her mouth.

⁴When the woman from Tekoa went *a* to the king, she fell with her face to the ground to pay him honor, and she said, "Help me, Your Majesty!"

⁵The king asked her, "What is troubling you?"

She said, "I am a widow; my husband is dead. ⁶I your servant had two sons. They got into a fight with each other in the field, and no one was there to separate them. One struck the other and killed him. ⁷Now the whole clan has risen up against your servant; they say, 'Hand over the one who struck his brother down, so that we may put him to death *d* for the life of his brother whom he killed; then we will get rid of the heir *e* as well.' They would put out the only burning coal I have left, *f* leaving my husband neither name nor descendant on the face of the earth."

⁸The king said to the woman, "Go home, *g* and I will issue an order in your behalf."

⁹But the woman from Tekoa said to him, "Let my lord the king pardon *h* me and my family, *i* and let the king and his throne be without guilt. *j* "

¹⁰The king replied, "If anyone says anything to you, bring them to me, and they will not bother you again."

¹¹She said, "Then let the king invoke the LORD his God to prevent the avenger *k* of blood from adding to the destruction, so that my son will not be destroyed."

"As surely as the LORD lives," he said, "not one hair *l* of your son's head will fall to the ground. *m* "

¹²Then the woman said, "Let your servant speak a word to my lord the king."

"Speak," he replied.

¹³The woman said, "Why then have you devised a thing like this against the people of God? When the king says this, does he not convict himself, *n* for the king has not brought back his banished son? *o* ¹⁴Like water *p* spilled on the ground, which cannot be recovered, so we must die. *q* But that is not what God desires; rather, he devises ways so that a banished person *r* does not remain banished from him.

¹⁵"And now I have come to say this to my lord the king because the people have made me afraid. Your servant thought, 'I will speak to the king; perhaps he will grant his servant's request. ¹⁶Perhaps the king will agree to deliver his servant from the hand of the man who is trying to cut off both me and my son from God's inheritance.' *s*

¹⁷"And now your servant says, 'May the word of my lord the king secure my inheritance, for my lord the king is like an angel *t* of God in discerning *u* good and evil. May the LORD your God be with you.' "

¹⁸Then the king said to the woman, "Don't keep from me the answer to what I am going to ask you."

---

a 4 Many Hebrew manuscripts, Septuagint, Vulgate and Syriac; most Hebrew manuscripts *spoke*

14:7 *the whole clan has risen up against your servant.* It was customary in Israel for a murder victim's next of kin to avenge the blood of his relative by putting the murderer to death (see note on 3:27; see also map, p. 245, and accompanying text). In the case presented, however, blood revenge would have wiped out the family line, which Israelite law and custom tried to avoid if at all possible (see notes on Dt 25:5–6; Ru 2:20). *we will get rid of the heir as well.* The woman suggests that the motivation for blood revenge was more a selfish desire to acquire the family inheritance than a desire for justice (see Nu 27:11). *leaving my husband neither name nor descendant.* The implication is that it would be a more serious offense to terminate the woman's family line than to permit a murder to go unpunished by blood revenge. Apparently Joab hoped subtly to suggest to David that if he did not restore Absalom, a struggle for the throne would eventually ensue.
14:8 *I will issue an order in your behalf.* David's judicial action may have rested on the legal ground that the murder was not premeditated (see Dt 19:4–6).
14:11 *let the king invoke the LORD his God.* The woman wants David to confirm his promise by an oath in the Lord's name. *As surely as the LORD lives.* An oath formula (see notes on Ge 42:15; 1Sa 14:39,45) that solemnly binds David to his commitment.
14:13 *against the people of God.* The woman's suggestion is

that David has done the same thing to Israel that her family members have done to her. The people of Israel want their crown prince returned safely to them. *does he not convict himself…?* The argument is that when David exempted the fictitious murderer from blood revenge, he in effect rendered himself guilty for not doing the same in the case of Absalom. The analogy places David in the position of the blood avenger.
14:14 *Like water spilled on the ground.* Blood revenge will not return the victim of murder to life, just as water spilled on the ground cannot be recovered. *that is not what God desires.* In the suggestion that the avenging of blood is contrary to God's ways of dealing with people, the woman apparently distorts Biblical teaching of God's justice (see note on Ge 9:6). But she dwells on the mercy of God, who would rather preserve life than take it (see Eze 18:32; 33:11 and notes). David's own guilt and subsequent experience of God's mercy appear to give added weight to the woman's argument (see notes on 12:13; 13:21).
14:15 *the people have made me afraid.* The woman reverts to her own fabricated story. "The people" are evidently those of her own family who are seeking blood revenge.
14:17 *like an angel of God in discerning good and evil.* Possessing superhuman powers of discernment—as a king ideally should (see v. 20; 19:27).

"Let my lord the king speak," the woman said.

[19]The king asked, "Isn't the hand of Joab [v] with you in all this?"

The woman answered, "As surely as you live, my lord the king, no one can turn to the right or to the left from anything my lord the king says. Yes, it was your servant Joab who instructed me to do this and who put all these words into the mouth of your servant. [20]Your servant Joab did this to change the present situation. My lord has wisdom [w] like that of an angel of God—he knows everything that happens in the land. [x]"

[21]The king said to Joab, "Very well, I will do it. Go, bring back the young man Absalom."

[22]Joab fell with his face to the ground to pay him honor, and he blessed the king. [y] Joab said, "Today your servant knows that he has found favor in your eyes, my lord the king, because the king has granted his servant's request."

[23]Then Joab went to Geshur and brought Absalom back to Jerusalem. [24]But the king said, "He must go to his own house; he must not see my face." So Absalom went to his own house and did not see the face of the king.

[25]In all Israel there was not a man so highly praised for his handsome appearance as Absalom. From the top of his head to the sole of his foot there was no blemish in him. [26]Whenever he cut the hair of his head [z]—he used to cut his hair once a year because it became too heavy for him—he would weigh it, and its weight was two hundred shekels [a] by the royal standard.

[27]Three sons [a] and a daughter were born to Absalom. His daughter's name was Tamar, [b] and she became a beautiful woman.

[28]Absalom lived two years in Jerusalem without seeing the king's face. [29]Then Absalom sent for Joab in order to send him to the king, but Joab refused to come to him. So he sent a second time, but he refused to come. [30]Then he said to his servants, "Look, Joab's field is next to mine, and he has barley [c] there. Go and set it on fire." So Absalom's servants set the field on fire.

[31]Then Joab did go to Absalom's house, and he said to him, "Why have your servants set my field on fire? [d]"

[32]Absalom said to Joab, "Look, I sent word to you and said, 'Come here so I can send you to the king to ask, "Why have I come from Geshur? [e] It would be better for me if I were still there!" ' Now then, I want to see the king's face, and if I am guilty of anything, let him put me to death." [f]

[33]So Joab went to the king and told him this. Then the king summoned Absalom, and he came in and bowed down with his face to the ground before the king. And the king kissed [g] Absalom.

ABSALOM'S CONSPIRACY

15 In the course of time, [h] Absalom provided himself with a chariot [i] and horses and with fifty men to run ahead of him. [2]He would get up early and stand by the side of the road leading to the city gate. [j] Whenever anyone came with a complaint to be placed before the king for a decision, Absalom would call out to him, "What town are you from?" He would answer, "Your servant is from one of the tribes of Israel." [3]Then Absalom would say to him, "Look, your claims are valid and proper, but

---

[a] 26 That is, about 5 pounds or about 2.3 kilograms

14:19 [v] ver 3
14:20 [w] 1Ki 3:12, 28; 10:23-24; Isa 28:6
[x] 2Sa 18:13
14:22 [y] S Ge 47:7
14:26 [z] 2Sa 18:9
14:27 [a] 2Sa 18:18
[b] S 2Sa 13:1
14:30 [c] S Ex 9:31
14:31 [d] S Jdg 15:5
14:32 [e] S 2Sa 3:3
[f] 1Sa 20:8
14:33 [g] Lk 15:20
15:1 [h] S 2Sa 12:11
[i] S 1Sa 8:11
15:2 [j] S Ge 23:10; 2Sa 19:8

14:21 *Joab.* He appears to have been present the whole time.

14:23 *Joab went to Geshur.* See 13:37.

14:24 *he must not see my face.* David still vacillates (see note on v. 1); he does not offer forgiveness and restoration.

14:25 *not a man so highly praised.* Absalom's handsomeness brought him attention and popular favor—which he was soon to cultivate.

14:26 *hair of his head.* For the people of that time, hair was a sign of vigor. Kings and heroic figures were usually portrayed with abundant locks, while baldness was a disgrace (see 2Ki 2:23 and note). In this, too, Absalom seemed destined for the throne. *royal standard.* The royal shekel was perhaps heavier than the sanctuary shekel (see Ex 30:13).

14:27 *Three sons.* Their names are unknown; 18:18 suggests that they died in their youth. *Tamar.* Absalom named his daughter after his sister (13:1). Maakah (see 1Ki 15:2 and note) was probably a daughter of Tamar and thereby Absalom's granddaughter (see note on 2Ch 11:20).

14:32 *if I am guilty of anything, let him put me to death.* Absa-

lom demands either full pardon and restoration or death, but he still gives no sign of repentance.

C **14:33** *the king kissed Absalom.* Signifying his forgiveness and Absalom's reconciliation with the royal family. David sidesteps repentance and justice, and in this way he probably contributes to the fulfillment of the prophecy of Nathan (see 12:10–11 and notes).

15:1 *In the course of time.* See note on 2:1. *chariot and horses.* As far as is known, Absalom was the first Israelite leader to acquire a chariot and horses (cf. Dt 17:16). *fifty men.* They probably functioned as bodyguards and provided a display of royal pomp that appealed to the masses. Absalom and his brother Adonijah (see 1Ki 1:5 and note) are parade examples of precisely what Samuel had warned against (see 1Sa 8:11 and note).

15:2 The main gateway of a city was the primary site where legal cases were settled (see notes on Ge 19:1; Ru 4:1).

15:3 *your claims are valid.* Absalom seeks to ingratiate himself with the people by endorsing their grievances apart from any investigation into their merit.

15:3 k Pr 12:2
15:4 l Jdg 9:29
15:6 m Ro 16:18
15:8 n S 2Sa 3:3
  o S Ge 28:20
15:10 p 1Ki 1:34,39;
2Ki 9:13
15:12 q ver 31,34;
2Sa 16:15,23; 17:14;
23:34; 1Ch 27:33
  r Job 19:14; Ps 41:9;
55:13; Jer 9:4
  s Jos 15:51 t Ps 3:1
15:14 u 1Ki 2:26;
Ps 132:1; Ps 3 Title
  v 2Sa 19:9
15:16 w 2Sa 16:21-
22; 20:3
15:18 x S 1Sa 30:14;
2Sa 20:7,23; 1Ki 1:38,
44; 1Ch 18:17
15:19 y 2Sa 18:2
  z S Ge 31:15
15:20 a S 1Sa 22:2
  b 2Sa 2:6
15:21 c Ru 1:16-17;
Pr 17:17

there is no representative of the king to hear you." [k] [4]And Absalom would add, "If only I were appointed judge in the land! [l] Then everyone who has a complaint or case could come to me and I would see that they receive justice."

[5]Also, whenever anyone approached him to bow down before him, Absalom would reach out his hand, take hold of him and kiss him. [6]Absalom behaved in this way toward all the Israelites who came to the king asking for justice, and so he stole the hearts [m] of the people of Israel.

[7]At the end of four[a] years, Absalom said to the king, "Let me go to Hebron and fulfill a vow I made to the LORD. [8]While your servant was living at Geshur [n] in Aram, I made this vow: [o] 'If the LORD takes me back to Jerusalem, I will worship the LORD in Hebron. [b] ' "

[9]The king said to him, "Go in peace." So he went to Hebron.

[10]Then Absalom sent secret messengers throughout the tribes of Israel to say, "As soon as you hear the sound of the trumpets, [p] then say, 'Absalom is king in Hebron.' " [11]Two hundred men from Jerusalem had accompanied Absalom. They had been invited as guests and went quite innocently, knowing nothing about the matter. [12]While Absalom was offering sacrifices, he also sent for Ahithophel [q] the Gilonite, David's counselor, [r] to come from Giloh, [s] his hometown. And so the conspiracy gained strength, and Absalom's following kept on increasing. [t]

DAVID FLEES

[13]A messenger came and told David, "The hearts of the people of Israel are with Absalom."

[14]Then David said to all his officials who were with him in Jerusalem, "Come! We must flee, [u] or none of us will escape from Absalom. [v] We must leave immediately, or he will move quickly to overtake us and bring ruin on us and put the city to the sword."

[15]The king's officials answered him, "Your servants are ready to do whatever our lord the king chooses."

[16]The king set out, with his entire household following him; but he left ten concubines [w] to take care of the palace. [17]So the king set out, with all the people following him, and they halted at the edge of the city. [18]All his men marched past him, along with all the Kerethites [x] and Pelethites; and all the six hundred Gittites who had accompanied him from Gath marched before the king.

[19]The king said to Ittai [y] the Gittite, "Why should you come along with us? Go back and stay with King Absalom. You are a foreigner, [z] an exile from your homeland. [20]You came only yesterday. And today shall I make you wander [a] about with us, when I do not know where I am going? Go back, and take your people with you. May the LORD show you kindness and faithfulness." [c] [b]

[21]But Ittai replied to the king, "As surely as the LORD lives, and as my lord the king lives, wherever my lord the king may be, whether it means life or death, there will your servant be." [c]

---

[a] 7 Some Septuagint manuscripts, Syriac and Josephus; Hebrew *forty*   [b] 8 Some Septuagint manuscripts; Hebrew does not have *in Hebron*.   [c] 20 Septuagint; Hebrew *May kindness and faithfulness be with you*

15:4 *If only I were appointed judge in the land!* Absalom presents himself as the solution to the people's legal grievances. In the case of Amnon, Absalom had taken matters into his own hands because of his father's laxity. Now he has found, he believes, the weakness in his father's reign, and he capitalizes on it with political astuteness.

15:7 *four years.* After Absalom's return to the court (14:33). By this time he must have been about 30 years old, so his revolt must be dated early in the last decade of David's reign. *Hebron.* Where David was first proclaimed king (see notes on 2:1,4; 5:3,5) and where Absalom was born (3:2–3). Absalom may have had reason to believe that he could count on some local resentment over David's transfer of the capital to Jerusalem. Hebron was also the site of an important sanctuary. *fulfill a vow I made to the LORD.* Absalom piously lies to his father in order to mask his true intentions; cf. David's masking his intentions in the matter of Uriah (11:7–15).

15:8 *Geshur.* See 13:37.

C 15:12 *Ahithophel.* Bathsheba's grandfather (see 11:3; 23:34 and notes) and a wise and respected counselor (16:23). He appears to have secretly aligned himself with Absa-

lom's rebellion in its planning stage, perhaps in retaliation against David for his treatment of Bathsheba and Uriah. This unsuspected betrayal by a trusted friend may have prompted David's statements in Ps 41:9; 55:12–14. *Giloh.* Near Hebron (see Jos 15:51,54).

15:14 *none of us will escape from Absalom.* Uncertain of the extent of Absalom's support (see v. 13), David fears being trapped in Jerusalem, and he wants to spare the city a bloodbath.

15:16 *he left ten concubines to take care of the palace.* See 5:13; see also note on 3:2. David unknowingly arranges for the fulfillment of one of Nathan's prophecies (see notes on 12:11; 16:22; see also 20:3).

15:18 *Kerethites and Pelethites.* See notes on 8:18; Jer 47:4. *six hundred Gittites.* Philistine soldiers who had joined David's personal military force. Their commander was Ittai (v. 19; 18:2).

15:19 *Go back and stay with King Absalom.* David releases the Philistine contingent from further obligations to him.

15:21 *As surely as the LORD lives.* An oath of loyalty taken in the name of Israel's God (see note on 1Sa 14:39,45). *wherever my lord ... may be, ... there will your servant be.* For a similar declaration of commitment, see Ru 1:16–17.

²²David said to Ittai, "Go ahead, march on." So Ittai the Gittite marched on with all his men and the families that were with him.

²³The whole countryside wept aloud ᵈ as all the people passed by. The king also crossed the Kidron Valley, ᵉᶠ and all the people moved on toward the wilderness.

²⁴Zadok ᵍ was there, too, and all the Levites who were with him were carrying the ark ʰ of the covenant of God. They set down the ark of God, and Abiathar ⁱ offered sacrifices until all the people had finished leaving the city.

²⁵Then the king said to Zadok, "Take the ark of God back into the city. If I find favor in the LORD's eyes, he will bring me back and let me see it and his dwelling place ʲ again. ²⁶But if he says, 'I am not pleased with you,' then I am ready; let him do to me whatever seems good to him. ᵏ"

²⁷The king also said to Zadok the priest, "Do you understand? ˡ Go back to the city with my blessing. Take your son Ahimaaz with you, and also Abiathar's son Jonathan. ᵐ You and Abiathar return with your two sons. ²⁸I will wait at the fords ⁿ in the wilderness until word comes from you to inform me." ²⁹So Zadok and Abiathar took the ark of God back to Jerusalem and stayed there.

³⁰But David continued up the Mount of Olives, weeping ᵒ as he went; his head ᵖ was covered and he was barefoot. All the people with him covered their heads too and were weeping as they went up. ³¹Now David had been told, "Ahithophel �q is among the conspirators with Absalom." So David prayed, "LORD, turn Ahithophel's counsel into foolishness."

³²When David arrived at the summit, where people used to worship God, Hushai ʳ the Arkite ˢ was there to meet him, his robe torn and dust ᵗ on his head. ³³David said to him, "If you go with me, you will be a burden ᵘ to me. ³⁴But if you return to the city and say to Absalom, 'Your Majesty, I will be your servant; I was your father's servant in the past, but now I will be your servant,' ᵛ then you can help me by frustrating ʷ Ahithophel's advice. ³⁵Won't the priests Zadok and Abiathar be there with you? Tell them anything you hear in the king's palace. ˣ ³⁶Their two sons, Ahimaaz ʸ son of Zadok and Jonathan ᶻ son of Abiathar, are there with them. Send them to me with anything you hear."

³⁷So Hushai, ª David's confidant, arrived at Jerusalem as Absalom ᵇ was entering the city.

DAVID AND ZIBA

16 When David had gone a short distance beyond the summit, there was Ziba, ᶜ the steward of Mephibosheth, waiting to meet him. He had a string of donkeys saddled and loaded with two hundred loaves of bread, a hundred cakes of raisins, a hundred cakes of figs and a skin of wine. ᵈ

²The king asked Ziba, "Why have you brought these?"

Ziba answered, "The donkeys are for the king's household to ride on, the bread and fruit are for the men to eat, and the wine is to refresh ᵉ those who become exhausted in the wilderness."

³The king then asked, "Where is your master's grandson?" ᶠ

15:23 ᵈ1Sa 11:4; Job 2:12 ⁺1Ki 2:37; 2Ki 23:12; 2Ch 15:16; 29:16; 30:14; Jer 31:40 ᶠJn 18:1
15:24 ᵍS 2Sa 8:17; 19:11 ʰNu 4:15; S 10:33; 1Ki 2:26 ⁱS 1Sa 22:20
15:25 ʲEx 15:13; S Lev 15:31; Ps 43:3; 46:4; 84:1; 132:7
15:26 ᵏS Jdg 10:15; 2Sa 22:20
15:27 ˡS 1Sa 9:9 ᵐver 36; 2Sa 17:17; 1Ki 1:42
15:28 ⁿ2Sa 17:16
15:30 ᵒS Nu 25:6; S Ps 30:5 ᵖEst 6:12
15:31 qS ver 12
15:32 ʳver 37; 2Sa 16:16; 17:5; 1Ki 4:16 ˢJos 16:2 ᵗS Jos 7:6
15:33 ᵘ2Sa 19:35
15:34 ᵛ2Sa 16:19 ʷ2Sa 17:14; Pr 11:14
15:35 ˣ2Sa 17:15-16
15:36 ʸ2Sa 18:19 ᶻS ver 27; 2Sa 17:17; 1Ki 1:42
15:37 ª1Ch 27:33 ᵇ2Sa 16:15
16:1 ᶜ2Sa 9:1-13 ᵈS 1Sa 25:18; 1Ch 12:40
16:2 ᵉ2Sa 17:27-29
16:3 ᶠ2Sa 9:9-10

15:23 *Kidron Valley.* Just east of Jerusalem (see note on Isa 22:7). *wilderness.* The northern part of the Desert of Judah that lies between Jerusalem and the Dead Sea.
15:24 *Zadok.* See note on 8:17. *Abiathar.* See note on 8:17; see also 1Sa 22:20–23 and note on 22:20.
15:25 *Take the ark of God back into the city.* David reveals a true understanding of the connection between the ark and God's presence with his people. He knows that possession of the ark does not guarantee God's blessing (see notes on 1Sa 4:3,21). He also recognizes that the ark belongs in the capital city as a symbol of the Lord's rule over the nation (see note on 6:2), no matter who the king might be.
15:26 *let him do to me whatever seems good to him.* David confesses that he has no exclusive claim to the throne and that Israel's divine King is free to confer the kingship on whomever he chooses.
15:27 *Do you understand?* Perhaps an allusion to the high priest's custody of the Urim and Thummim as a means of divine revelation (see notes on Ex 28:30; 1Sa 2:28). See also note on 1Sa 9:9.

15:28 *fords in the wilderness.* Fords across the Jordan in the vicinity of Gilgal.
15:30 *Mount of Olives.* See notes on Zec 14:4; Mk 11:1. *his head was covered.* A sign of sorrow (see Est 6:12; Jer 14:3–4; cf. 2Sa 19:4 and note). *he was barefoot.* A sign of mourning (see Eze 24:17; Mic 1:8) and shame (see Isa 20:4).
15:31 *Ahithophel.* See note on v. 12.
15:32 *Hushai the Arkite.* The Arkites were a clan (some think non-Israelite) that inhabited an area southwest of Bethel (Jos 16:2). Since Hushai was a trusted member of David's court (see note on v. 37), his appearance was the beginning of an answer to David's prayer (v. 31).
15:37 *Hushai, David's confidant.* 1Ch 27:33 calls him the "king's confidant," which seems to be an official title for the king's most trusted adviser (see 1Ki 4:5, where the Hebrew for "king's confidant" is translated "adviser to the king").
16:1 *Ziba.* See ch. 9. *Mephibosheth.* See note on 4:4.
16:2 *Ziba answered.* Since David assumed control of Saul's estate (9:7–10), Ziba, always the opportunist, seeks to profit from the political crisis.
16:3 *your master's grandson.* Mephibosheth (see 9:2–3,9).

16:3 9 S 2Sa 9:2
16:4 h S 2Sa 4:4
16:5 i S 2Sa 3:16
j 2Sa 19:16-23;
1Ki 2:8-9,36,44
k S Ex 22:28
16:8 l 2Sa 19:28;
21:9 m 2Sa 19:19;
Ps 55:3
16:9 n S 1Sa 26:6
o S 2Sa 3:8
p S 2Sa 3:39; Lk 9:54
16:10 q S 2Sa 2:18;
19:22 r Ro 9:20
16:11 s 2Sa 12:11
t S Ge 45:5; 1Sa 26:19
16:12 u Ps 4:1; 25:18
v Dt 23:5; Ro 8:28
w Ps 109:28
16:14 x 2Sa 17:2
16:15 y S 2Sa 15:37
z S 2Sa 15:12
16:16 a S 2Sa 15:32
16:17 b 2Sa 19:25
16:19 c 2Sa 15:34
16:22 d S 2Sa 3:7;
12:11-12; S 15:16
16:23 e 2Sa 17:14,
23 f S 2Sa 15:12

Ziba g said to him, "He is staying in Jerusalem, because he thinks, 'Today the house of Israel will restore to me my grandfather's kingdom.' "

[4] Then the king said to Ziba, "All that belonged to Mephibosheth h is now yours."

"I humbly bow," Ziba said. "May I find favor in your eyes, my lord the king."

SHIMEI CURSES DAVID

[5] As King David approached Bahurim, i a man from the same clan as Saul's family came out from there. His name was Shimei j son of Gera, and he cursed k as he came out. [6] He pelted David and all the king's officials with stones, though all the troops and the special guard were on David's right and left. [7] As he cursed, Shimei said, "Get out, get out, you murderer, you scoundrel! [8] The LORD has repaid you for all the blood you shed in the household of Saul, in whose place you have reigned. l The LORD has given the kingdom into the hands of your son Absalom. You have come to ruin because you are a murderer!" m

[9] Then Abishai n son of Zeruiah said to the king, "Why should this dead dog o curse my lord the king? Let me go over and cut off his head." p

[10] But the king said, "What does this have to do with you, you sons of Zeruiah? q If he is cursing because the LORD said to him, 'Curse David,' who can ask, 'Why do you do this?' " r

[11] David then said to Abishai and all his officials, "My son, s who is of my own flesh, is trying to take my life. How much more, then, this Benjamite! Leave him alone; let him curse, for the LORD has told him to. t [12] It may be that the LORD will look upon my misery u and restore to me his covenant blessing v instead of his curse today. w "

[13] So David and his men continued along the road while Shimei was going along the hillside opposite him, cursing as he went and throwing stones at him and showering him with dirt. [14] The king and all the people with him arrived at their destination exhausted. x And there he refreshed himself.

THE ADVICE OF AHITHOPHEL AND HUSHAI

[15] Meanwhile, Absalom y and all the men of Israel came to Jerusalem, and Ahithophel z was with him. [16] Then Hushai a the Arkite, David's confidant, went to Absalom and said to him, "Long live the king! Long live the king!"

[17] Absalom said to Hushai, "So this is the love you show your friend? If he's your friend, why didn't you go with him?" b

[18] Hushai said to Absalom, "No, the one chosen by the LORD, by these people, and by all the men of Israel—his I will be, and I will remain with him. [19] Furthermore, whom should I serve? Should I not serve the son? Just as I served your father, so I will serve you." c

[20] Absalom said to Ahithophel, "Give us your advice. What should we do?"

[21] Ahithophel answered, "Sleep with your father's concubines whom he left to take care of the palace. Then all Israel will hear that you have made yourself obnoxious to your father, and the hands of everyone with you will be more resolute." [22] So they pitched a tent for Absalom on the roof, and he slept with his father's concubines in the sight of all Israel. d

[23] Now in those days the advice e Ahithophel gave was like that of one who inquires of God. That was how both David f and Absalom regarded all of Ahithophel's advice.

16:4 *All that belonged to Mephibosheth is now yours.* Because the revolt was so widespread and loyalties so uncertain, David was quick to assume the worst.

16:5 *Bahurim.* Near the Mount of Olives. *same clan as Saul's family.* The clan of Matri (see 1Sa 10:21). *Gera.* See note on 1Ki 2:8.

16:6 *the troops and the special guard.* The Kerethites, Pelethites and 600 Gittites (see 15:18 and note).

16:7 *scoundrel.* See note on Dt 13:13.

16:8 *blood you shed in the household of Saul.* Shimei may be referring to the executions reported in 21:1–14, but the time of that event is uncertain (see note on 21:1).

16:9 *Abishai.* See note on 1Sa 26:6. *this dead dog.* An expression of absolute contempt (see note on 9:8).

16:10 *sons of Zeruiah.* Intended as an insult (cf. note on 1Sa 20:27,30–31). *If … because the LORD said to him, 'Curse David.'* David leaves open the possibility that God has seen fit to termi-

nate his rule—the verdict is not yet in (see 15:26 and note). For David's later actions regarding Shimei, see 19:18–23; 1Ki 2:8–9.

16:15 *Ahithophel.* See note on 15:12.

16:16 *Hushai the Arkite, David's confidant.* See notes on 15:32,37. *Long live the king!* See note on Ps 62:4.

16:18 Hushai's statement is deliberately ambiguous. Nowhere is Absalom referred to as God's "chosen" one, but David is often called the Lord's "chosen" one or its equivalent (see 6:21; 1Sa 16:8–13; 1Ki 8:16; 11:34; 1Ch 28:4; Ps 78:70).

16:21 *Sleep with your father's concubines.* This would signify Absalom's assumption of royal power; it would also be a definitive and irreversible declaration of the break between father and son (see notes on 3:7; 12:8; 1Ki 2:22). *obnoxious.* See note on 1Sa 13:4.

16:22 *he slept with his father's concubines.* A fulfillment of Nathan's prophecy (12:11–12). For additional significance see note on v. 21.

17:2 ᵍ 2Sa 16:14
ʰ 1Ki 22:31; Zec 13:7
17:5 ⁱ S 2Sa 15:32
17:8 ʲ Hos 13:8
ᵏ 1Sa 16:18
17:9 ⁱ Jer 41:9
17:10 ᵐ 1Ch 12:8
ⁿ Jos 2:9,11; Eze 21:15
ᵒ 2Sa 23:8; 1Ch 11:11
17:11 ᵖ S Jdg 20:1
�q S Ge 12:2; S Jos 11:4
17:13 ʳ Mic 1:6
17:14 ˢ S 2Sa 16:23
ᵗ S 2Sa 15:12
ᵘ S 2Sa 15:34; Ne 4:15
ᵛ Ps 9:16 ʷ 2Ch 10:8
17:16 ˣ 2Sa 15:28
ʸ 2Sa 15:35
17:17 ᶻ S 2Sa 15:27,
36 ᵃ Jos 15:7; 18:16;
1Ki 1:9
17:18 ᵇ S 2Sa 3:16
17:19 ᶜ S Jos 2:6
17:20 ᵈ S Ex 1:19
17:23 ᵉ 2Sa S 2Sa 1
6:23 ᶠ 2Ki 20:1

17

Ahithophel said to Absalom, "I would ᵃ choose twelve thousand men and set out tonight in pursuit of David. ²I would attack him while he is weary and weak.ᵍ I would strike him with terror, and then all the people with him will flee. I would strike down only the king ʰ ³and bring all the people back to you. The death of the man you seek will mean the return of all; all the people will be unharmed." ⁴This plan seemed good to Absalom and to all the elders of Israel.

⁵But Absalom said, "Summon also Hushai ⁱ the Arkite, so we can hear what he has to say as well." ⁶When Hushai came to him, Absalom said, "Ahithophel has given this advice. Should we do what he says? If not, give us your opinion."

⁷Hushai replied to Absalom, "The advice Ahithophel has given is not good this time. ⁸You know your father and his men; they are fighters, and as fierce as a wild bear robbed of her cubs.ʲ Besides, your father is an experienced fighter;ᵏ he will not spend the night with the troops. ⁹Even now, he is hidden in a cave or some other place.ⁱ If he should attack your troops first,ᵇ whoever hears about it will say, 'There has been a slaughter among the troops who follow Absalom.' ¹⁰Then even the bravest soldier, whose heart is like the heart of a lion,ᵐ will melt ⁿ with fear, for all Israel knows that your father is a fighter and that those with him are brave.ᵒ

¹¹"So I advise you: Let all Israel, from Dan to Beershebaᵖ—as numerous as the sandq on the seashore—be gathered to you, with you yourself leading them into battle. ¹²Then we will attack him wherever he may be found, and we will fall on him as dew settles on the ground. Neither he nor any of his men will be left alive. ¹³If he withdraws into a city, then all Israel will bring ropes to that city, and we will drag it down to the valley ʳ until not so much as a pebble is left."

¹⁴Absalom and all the men of Israel said, "The advice ˢ of Hushai the Arkite is better than that of Ahithophel." ᵗ For the LORD had determined to frustrate ᵘ the good advice of Ahithophel in order to bring disaster ᵛ on Absalom. ʷ

¹⁵Hushai told Zadok and Abiathar, the priests, "Ahithophel has advised Absalom and the elders of Israel to do such and such, but I have advised them to do so and so. ¹⁶Now send a message at once and tell David, 'Do not spend the night at the fords in the wilderness;ˣ cross over without fail, or the king and all the people with him will be swallowed up.ʸ ' "

¹⁷Jonathan ᶻ and Ahimaaz were staying at En Rogel.ᵃ A female servant was to go and inform them, and they were to go and tell King David, for they could not risk being seen entering the city. ¹⁸But a young man saw them and told Absalom. So the two of them left at once and went to the house of a man in Bahurim.ᵇ He had a well in his courtyard, and they climbed down into it. ¹⁹His wife took a covering and spread it out over the opening of the well and scattered grain over it. No one knew anything about it.ᶜ

²⁰When Absalom's men came to the woman ᵈ at the house, they asked, "Where are Ahimaaz and Jonathan?"

The woman answered them, "They crossed over the brook." ᶜ The men searched but found no one, so they returned to Jerusalem.

²¹After they had gone, the two climbed out of the well and went to inform King David. They said to him, "Set out and cross the river at once; Ahithophel has advised such and such against you." ²²So David and all the people with him set out and crossed the Jordan. By daybreak, no one was left who had not crossed the Jordan.

²³When Ahithophel saw that his advice ᵉ had not been followed, he saddled his donkey and set out for his house in his hometown. He put his house in order ᶠ and then hanged himself. So he died and was buried in his father's tomb.

ᵃ 1 Or Let me   ᵇ 9 Or When some of the men fall at the first attack   ᶜ 20 Or "They passed by the sheep pen toward the water."

17:1–3 Ahithophel's advice to Absalom envisioned a cheap and easy victory that would not leave the nation weakened.
17:4 *all the elders of Israel.* See note on 3:17. Absalom's rebellion appears to have gained extensive backing from prominent tribal leaders.
17:5 *Hushai the Arkite.* See 16:16–19; see also notes on 15:32, 37.
17:7–13 Hushai's advice subtly capitalizes on Absalom's uncertainty, his fear and his egotism.
17:11 *from Dan to Beersheba.* See note on 1Sa 3:20.
17:12–13 *we ... we ... we.* Hushai carefully links himself with the revolt.
17:14 *the LORD had determined to frustrate the good advice of Ahithophel.* An answer to David's prayer (see 15:31; cf. Ps 33:10; Pr 21:30).

17:15 *Zadok and Abiathar.* See 15:24–29, 35–36.
17:16 *fords in the wilderness.* See 15:28 and note. *cross over.* Hushai advises David to cross the Jordan River, knowing that Absalom might change his mind and immediately set out after him.
17:17 *Jonathan and Ahimaaz.* See 15:36. *En Rogel.* A spring in the Kidron Valley just outside the walls of Jerusalem. *A female servant.* A servant going to the spring for water would attract no attention.
17:18 *Bahurim.* See note on 16:5.
17:23 *his hometown.* Giloh (see 15:12 and note). *hanged himself.* Ahithophel was convinced that the rebellion would fail and that he would be found guilty of treason as a co-conspirator.

17:24 ⁹ S Ge 32:2
17:25 ʰ 2Sa 19:13;
20:4, 9-12; 1Ki 2:5, 32;
1Ch 12:18 ¹ 1Ch 2:13-
17
17:27 ʲ S 1Sa 11:1
ᵏ S Dt 3:11 ¹ 2Sa 9:4
ᵐ 2Sa 19:31-39;
1Ki 2:7 ⁿ 2Sa 19:31;
Ezr 2:61
17:29 ᵒ 1Ch 12:40
ᵖ 2Sa 16:2; S Ro 12:13
18:2 ᑫ Jdg 7:16;
1Sa 11:11 ʳ S 1Sa 26:6
ˢ 2Sa 15:19
18:3 ᵗ S 1Sa 18:7
ᵘ 2Sa 21:17
18:6 ᵛ S Jos 17:15
18:9 ʷ 2Sa 14:26
18:11 ˣ S 2Sa 3:39
ʸ 1Sa 18:4

ABSALOM'S DEATH

²⁴David went to Mahanaim,⁹ and Absalom crossed the Jordan with all the men of Israel. ²⁵Absalom had appointed Amasaʰ over the army in place of Joab. Amasa was the son of Jether,ᵃⁱ an Ishmaeliteᵇ who had married Abigal, the daughter of Nahash and sister of Zeruiah the mother of Joab. ²⁶The Israelites and Absalom camped in the land of Gilead.

²⁷When David came to Mahanaim, Shobi son of Nahashʲ from Rabbahᵏ of the Ammonites, and Makirˡ son of Ammiel from Lo Debar, and Barzillaiᵐ the Gileaditeⁿ from Rogelim ²⁸brought bedding and bowls and articles of pottery. They also brought wheat and barley, flour and roasted grain, beans and lentils,ᶜ ²⁹honey and curds, sheep, and cheese from cows' milk for David and his people to eat. ᵒ For they said, "The people have become exhausted and hungry and thirsty in the wilderness.ᵖ"

18 David mustered the men who were with him and appointed over them commanders of thousands and commanders of hundreds. ²David sent out his troops,ᑫ a third under the command of Joab, a third under Joab's brother Abishaiʳ son of Zeruiah, and a third under Ittaiˢ the Gittite. The king told the troops, "I myself will surely march out with you."

³But the men said, "You must not go out; if we are forced to flee, they won't care about us. Even if half of us die, they won't care; but you are worth tenᵗ thousand of us.ᵈ It would be better now for you to give us support from the city."ᵘ

⁴The king answered, "I will do whatever seems best to you."

So the king stood beside the gate while all his men marched out in units of hundreds and of thousands. ⁵The king commanded Joab, Abishai and Ittai, "Be gentle with the young man Absalom for my sake." And all the troops heard the king giving orders concerning Absalom to each of the commanders.

⁶David's army marched out of the city to fight Israel, and the battle took place in the forestᵛ of Ephraim. ⁷There Israel's troops were routed by David's men, and the casualties that day were great—twenty thousand men. ⁸The battle spread out over the whole countryside, and the forest swallowed up more men that day than the sword.

⁹Now Absalom happened to meet David's men. He was riding his mule, and as the mule went under the thick branches of a large oak, Absalom's hairʷ got caught in the tree. He was left hanging in midair, while the mule he was riding kept on going.

¹⁰When one of the men saw what had happened, he told Joab, "I just saw Absalom hanging in an oak tree."

¹¹Joab said to the man who had told him this, "What! You saw him? Why didn't you strikeˣ him to the ground right there? Then I would have had to give you ten shekelsᵉ of silver and a warrior's belt.ʸ"

¹²But the man replied, "Even if a thousand shekelsᶠ were weighed out into my hands, I would not lay a hand on the king's son. In our hearing the king commanded you and Abishai and Ittai, 'Protect the young man Absalom for my sake.ᵍ' ¹³And if I had put my life

---

ᵃ 25 Hebrew *Ithra*, a variant of *Jether*   ᵇ 25 Some Septuagint manuscripts (see also 1 Chron. 2:17); Hebrew and other Septuagint manuscripts *Israelite*   ᶜ 28 Most Septuagint manuscripts and Syriac; Hebrew *lentils, and roasted grain*   ᵈ 3 Two Hebrew manuscripts, some Septuagint manuscripts and Vulgate; most Hebrew manuscripts *care; for now there are ten thousand like us*   ᵉ 11 That is, about 4 ounces or about 115 grams   ᶠ 12 That is, about 25 pounds or about 11 kilograms   ᵍ 12 A few Hebrew manuscripts, Septuagint, Vulgate and Syriac; most Hebrew manuscripts may be translated *Absalom, whoever you may be.*

17:24 *Mahanaim.* Ironically the same place where Ish-Bosheth had sought refuge after Saul's death (see 2:8 and note).

17:25 *Amasa.* Nephew of David and cousin of both Absalom and Joab, son of Zeruiah. *Abigail, the daughter of Nahash and sister of Zeruiah.* Zeruiah was David's sister (1Ch 2:16). Since the father of Abigail and Zeruiah is Nahash rather than Jesse, their unnamed mother may have married Jesse after the death of Nahash.

17:27 *Shobi son of Nahash.* Apparently the brother of Hanun (see 10:2–4), whom David had defeated earlier in his reign (11:1; 12:26–31). *Rabbah of the Ammonites.* See note on 10:3. *Makir.* See note on 9:4. *Barzillai.* A wealthy benefactor of David during his flight to Mahanaim (see 19:32; 1Ki 2:7). After the Babylonian exile, there were claimants to the priesthood among his descendants (Ezr 2:61–63).

18:2 *Ittai the Gittite.* See 15:18–22.

18:3 *You must not go out.* In addition to the reason given, David was growing old and was no longer the warrior he had been. This is essentially the same idea that Ahithophel had expressed to Absalom (see 17:2).

18:5 *Be gentle with . . . Absalom for my sake.* David's love for his (now) oldest son was undying—and almost his undoing (see 19:5–7 and note on 19:5).

18:6 *Israel.* Absalom's army (see 15:13; 16:15; 17:4, 11, 24–26). *forest of Ephraim.* The battle was apparently fought in Gilead, east of the Jordan (see 17:24,26). The name "forest of Ephraim" may have derived from an Ephraimite claim on the area (see Jdg 12:1–4).

18:8 *The battle spread out.* The armies apparently became dispersed, and many of the men got lost in the forest.

18:9 *his mule.* See note on 13:29. *Absalom's hair got caught in the tree.* His handsome head of hair (see 14:25,26) was in the end—ironically—his undoing.

18:11 *I would have had to give you.* Joab must be referring to an announced intent on his part to reward anyone killing Absalom. His actions and interests did not always coincide with David's wishes (see note on 2:13).

in jeopardy^a—and nothing is hidden from the king^z—you would have kept your distance from me."

¹⁴Joab^a said, "I'm not going to wait like this for you." So he took three javelins in his hand and plunged them into Absalom's heart while Absalom was still alive in the oak tree. ¹⁵And ten of Joab's armor-bearers surrounded Absalom, struck him and killed him.^b

¹⁶Then Joab^c sounded the trumpet, and the troops stopped pursuing Israel, for Joab halted them. ¹⁷They took Absalom, threw him into a big pit in the forest and piled up^d a large heap of rocks^e over him. Meanwhile, all the Israelites fled to their homes.

¹⁸During his lifetime Absalom had taken a pillar and erected it in the King's Valley^f as a monument^g to himself, for he thought, "I have no son^h to carry on the memory of my name." He named the pillar after himself, and it is called Absalom's Monument to this day.

DAVID MOURNS

¹⁹Now Ahimaazⁱ son of Zadok said, "Let me run and take the news to the king that the LORD has vindicated him by delivering him from the hand of his enemies.^j"

²⁰"You are not the one to take the news today," Joab told him. "You may take the news another time, but you must not do so today, because the king's son is dead."

²¹Then Joab said to a Cushite, "Go, tell the king what you have seen." The Cushite bowed down before Joab and ran off.

²²Ahimaaz son of Zadok again said to Joab, "Come what may, please let me run behind the Cushite."

But Joab replied, "My son, why do you want to go? You don't have any news that will bring you a reward."

²³He said, "Come what may, I want to run."

So Joab said, "Run!" Then Ahimaaz ran by way of the plain^b and outran the Cushite.

²⁴While David was sitting between the inner and outer gates, the watchman^k went up to the roof of the gateway by the wall. As he looked out, he saw a man running alone. ²⁵The watchman called out to the king and reported it.

The king said, "If he is alone, he must have good news." And the runner came closer and closer.

²⁶Then the watchman saw another runner, and he called down to the gatekeeper, "Look, another man running alone!"

The king said, "He must be bringing good news,^l too."

²⁷The watchman said, "It seems to me that the first one runs like^m Ahimaaz son of Zadok."

"He's a good man," the king said. "He comes with good news."

²⁸Then Ahimaaz called out to the king, "All is well!" He bowed down before the king with his face to the ground and said, "Praise be to the LORD your God! He has delivered up those who lifted their hands against my lord the king."

²⁹The king asked, "Is the young man Absalom safe?"

Ahimaaz answered, "I saw great confusion just as Joab was about to send the king's servant and me, your servant, but I don't know what it was."

³⁰The king said, "Stand aside and wait here." So he stepped aside and stood there.

³¹Then the Cushite arrived and said, "My lord the king, hear the good news! The LORD has vindicated you today by delivering you from the hand of all who rose up against you."

³²The king asked the Cushite, "Is the young man Absalom safe?"

The Cushite replied, "May the enemies of my lord the king and all who rise up to harm you be like that young man."ⁿ

*³³The king was shaken. He went up to the room over the gateway and wept. As he

---

^a 13 Or *Otherwise, if I had acted treacherously toward him*   ^b 23 That is, the plain of the Jordan

* 18:33 is numbered 19:1 in Hebrew texts.

18:13 ^z 2Sa 14:19-20
18:14 ^a S 2Sa 2:18
18:15 ^b S 2Sa 12:10
18:16 ^c S 2Sa 2:28
18:17 ^d Jos 7:26
^e Jos 8:29
18:18 ^f Ge 14:17
^g S Ge 50:5;
S Nu 32:42
^h 2Sa 14:27
18:19 ⁱ S 2Sa 15:36
^j Jdg 11:36
18:24 ^k S 1Sa 14:16;
S Jer 51:12
18:26 ^l 1Ki 1:42;
Isa 52:7; 61:1
18:27 ^m 2Ki 9:20
18:32 ⁿ Jdg 5:31;
S 1Sa 25:26

18:15 *killed him.* The easiest and most certain way of ending the rebellion—but the brutal overkill is indicative of the deep animosity felt by David's men toward Absalom.

18:17 *large heap of rocks.* A mound of rocks that mocked the monument Absalom himself had erected (v. 18). *all the Israelites.* See note on v. 6.

B **18:18** *erected it . . . as a monument to himself.* As Saul had done (see 1Sa 15:12 and note). *King's Valley.* Near Jerusalem (see Ge 14:17; Josephus, *Antiquities*, 7.10.3). *I have no son.* See 14:27 and note. *Absalom's Monument.* Not to be confused with the much later monument of the same name that is

still visible today in the valley east of Jerusalem.

18:19 *Ahimaaz son of Zadok.* See 15:27; 17:17–21.

18:20 *not the one to take the news.* The choice of a messenger depended on the content of the message (see v. 27 and note).

18:21 *Cushite.* A foreigner (see note on Nu 12:1).

18:27 *He comes with good news.* David presumed that Joab would not have sent someone like Ahimaaz to carry bad news (see v. 20 and note).

18:29 *I saw great confusion.* Ahimaaz avoids a direct answer to David's question, though he knew Absalom was dead.

18:33 °Ex 32:32
ᵖS Ge 43:14;
2Sa 19:4
19:7 �qPr 14:28
19:8 ʳS 2Sa 15:2
19:9 ˢ2Sa 8:1-14
ᵗ2Sa 15:14
19:11 ᵘS 2Sa 15:24
19:13 ᵛS 2Sa 17:25
ʷS Ge 29:14
ˣS Ru 1:17
ʸS 2Sa 2:13
19:15 ᶻS 1Sa 11:15
19:16 ᵃ2Sa 16:5-13
19:17 ᵇS 2Sa 9:2
ᶜS Ge 43:16
19:19 ᵈS 2Sa 16:6-8

went, he said: "O my son Absalom! My son, my son Absalom! If only I had died ° instead of you—O Absalom, my son, my son!" ᵖ

19 *Joab was told, "The king is weeping and mourning for Absalom." ²And for the whole army the victory that day was turned into mourning, because on that day the troops heard it said, "The king is grieving for his son." ³The men stole into the city that day as men steal in who are ashamed when they flee from battle. ⁴The king covered his face and cried aloud, "O my son Absalom! O Absalom, my son, my son!"

⁵Then Joab went into the house to the king and said, "Today you have humiliated all your men, who have just saved your life and the lives of your sons and daughters and the lives of your wives and concubines. ⁶You love those who hate you and hate those who love you. You have made it clear today that the commanders and their men mean nothing to you. I see that you would be pleased if Absalom were alive today and all of us were dead. ⁷Now go out and encourage your men. I swear by the LORD that if you don't go out, not a man will be left with you by nightfall. This will be worse for you than all the calamities that have come on you from your youth till now." �q

⁸So the king got up and took his seat in the gateway. When the men were told, "The king is sitting in the gateway, ʳ" they all came before him.

Meanwhile, the Israelites had fled to their homes.

DAVID RETURNS TO JERUSALEM

⁹Throughout the tribes of Israel, all the people were arguing among themselves, saying, "The king delivered us from the hand of our enemies; he is the one who rescued us from the hand of the Philistines. ˢ But now he has fled the country to escape from Absalom; ᵗ ¹⁰and Absalom, whom we anointed to rule over us, has died in battle. So why do you say nothing about bringing the king back?"

¹¹King David sent this message to Zadok ᵘ and Abiathar, the priests: "Ask the elders of Judah, 'Why should you be the last to bring the king back to his palace, since what is being said throughout Israel has reached the king at his quarters? ¹²You are my relatives, my own flesh and blood. So why should you be the last to bring back the king?' ¹³And say to Amasa, ᵛ 'Are you not my own flesh and blood? ʷ May God deal with me, be it ever so severely, ˣ if you are not the commander of my army for life in place of Joab. ʸ' "

¹⁴He won over the hearts of the men of Judah so that they were all of one accord. They sent word to the king, "Return, you and all your men." ¹⁵Then the king returned and went as far as the Jordan.

Now the men of Judah had come to Gilgal ᶻ to go out and meet the king and bring him across the Jordan. ¹⁶Shimei ᵃ son of Gera, the Benjamite from Bahurim, hurried down with the men of Judah to meet King David. ¹⁷With him were a thousand Benjamites, along with Ziba, ᵇ the steward of Saul's household, ᶜ and his fifteen sons and twenty servants. They rushed to the Jordan, where the king was. ¹⁸They crossed at the ford to take the king's household over and to do whatever he wished.

When Shimei son of Gera crossed the Jordan, he fell prostrate before the king ¹⁹and said to him, "May my lord not hold me guilty. Do not remember how your servant did wrong on the day my lord the king left Jerusalem. ᵈ May the king put it out of his mind.

*19:1-43 is numbered 19:2-44 in Hebrew texts.

A C **18:33** *O my son Absalom!* One of the most moving expressions in all literature of a father's grief over his son's death—in spite of all that Absalom had done. *If only I had died instead of you.* The intensity of David's grief springs in no small part from his recognition that he himself bore large responsibility for the course of events that led to Absalom's death. His own actions had set a negative example for his children and at the same time had rendered him incapable of acting judicially as a king ought—all of which led up to Absalom's rebellion. In Absalom's violent death at the hands of Joab, David's sinful abuse of royal power had finally produced its most bitter fruit.
19:4 *covered his face.* Cf. note on 15:30.
19:5 *Joab went . . . to the king.* Apparently confident that the king was unaware of Joab's part in Absalom's death. David never indicates that he learned of it (see 1Ki 2:5). *you have humiliated all your men.* Joab boldly rebukes David for allowing his personal grief to keep him from expressing his appreciation for the loyalty of those who risked their lives to preserve his throne. Joab warns David that his love for Absalom can still undo him.

19:9 *The king delivered us.* With Absalom dead, the northern tribes remember what David had done for them (see 3:17–18; 5:2).
19:11 *Ask the elders of Judah.* Even though the rebellion had begun in Hebron in Judah (see 15:9–12), David appeals to the elders of his own tribe to take the initiative in restoring him to the throne in Jerusalem (see 2:4; 1Sa 30:26 and notes). This appeal produced the desired result, but it also led to the arousal of tribal jealousies (see vv. 41–43).
19:13 *Amasa . . . my own flesh and blood.* See 17:25 and note. Although Amasa deserved death for treason, David appointed him commander of his army in place of Joab, hoping to secure the allegiance of those who had followed Amasa, especially the Judahites (see 20:4 and note). *May God deal with me, be it ever so severely.* A curse formula (see note on 1Sa 3:17).
19:15 *Gilgal.* See note on Jos 4:19.
19:17 *a thousand Benjamites.* No doubt they feared they would be suspected by the king of being implicated in Shimei's deed.
19:19 *your servant did wrong.* See 16:5–13.

²⁰For I your servant know that I have sinned, but today I have come here as the first of the whole house of Joseph to come down and meet my lord the king."

²¹Then Abishai ^e son of Zeruiah said, "Shouldn't Shimei be put to death for this? He cursed ^f the LORD's anointed." ^g

²²David replied, "What does this have to do with you, you sons of Zeruiah? ^h What right do you have to interfere? Should anyone be put to death in Israel today? ⁱ Don't I know that today I am king over Israel?" ²³So the king said to Shimei, "You shall not die." And the king promised him on oath. ^j

²⁴Mephibosheth, ^k Saul's grandson, also went down to meet the king. He had not taken care of his feet or trimmed his mustache or washed his clothes from the day the king left until the day he returned safely. ²⁵When he came from Jerusalem to meet the king, the king asked him, "Why didn't you go with me, ^l Mephibosheth?"

²⁶He said, "My lord the king, since I your servant am lame, ^m I said, 'I will have my donkey saddled and will ride on it, so I can go with the king.' But Ziba ⁿ my servant betrayed me. ²⁷And he has slandered your servant to my lord the king. My lord the king is like an angel ^o of God; so do whatever you wish. ²⁸All my grandfather's descendants deserved nothing but death ^p from my lord the king, but you gave your servant a place among those who eat at your table. ^q So what right do I have to make any more appeals to the king?"

²⁹The king said to him, "Why say more? I order you and Ziba to divide the land."

³⁰Mephibosheth said to the king, "Let him take everything, now that my lord the king has returned home safely."

³¹Barzillai ^r the Gileadite also came down from Rogelim to cross the Jordan with the king and to send him on his way from there. ³²Now Barzillai was very old, eighty years of age. He had provided for the king during his stay in Mahanaim, for he was a very wealthy ^s man. ³³The king said to Barzillai, "Cross over with me and stay with me in Jerusalem, and I will provide for you."

³⁴But Barzillai answered the king, "How many more years will I live, that I should go up to Jerusalem with the king? ³⁵I am now eighty ^t years old. Can I tell the difference between what is enjoyable and what is not? Can your servant taste what he eats and drinks? Can I still hear the voices of male and female singers? ^u Why should your servant be an added ^v burden to my lord the king? ³⁶Your servant will cross over the Jordan with the king for a short distance, but why should the king reward me in this way? ³⁷Let your servant return, that I may die in my own town near the tomb of my father ^w and mother. But here is your servant Kimham. ^x Let him cross over with my lord the king. Do for him whatever you wish."

³⁸The king said, "Kimham shall cross over with me, and I will do for him whatever you wish. And anything you desire from me I will do for you."

³⁹So all the people crossed the Jordan, and then the king crossed over. The king kissed Barzillai and bid him farewell, ^y and Barzillai returned to his home.

⁴⁰When the king crossed over to Gilgal, Kimham crossed with him. All the troops of Judah and half the troops of Israel had taken the king over.

⁴¹Soon all the men of Israel were coming to the king and saying to him, "Why did our brothers, the men of Judah, steal the king away and bring him and his household across the Jordan, together with all his men?" ^z

⁴²All the men of Judah answered the men of Israel, "We did this because the king is

19:21 ^e S 1Sa 26:6
^f S Ex 22:28
^g S 1Sa 12:3; S 26:9
19:22 ^h S 2Sa 2:18;
S 16:10 ⁱ 1Sa 11:13
19:23 ^j 1Ki 2:8,42
19:24 ^k S 2Sa 4:4
19:25 ^l 2Sa 16:17
19:26 ^m S Lev 21:18
ⁿ S 2Sa 9:2
19:27 ^o S 1Sa 29:9
19:28 ^p S 2Sa 16:8
^q S 2Sa 9:7,13
19:31 ^r S 2Sa 17:27-
29; 1Ki 2:7
19:32 ^s 1Sa 25:2
19:35 ^t Ps 90:10
^u 2Ch 35:25; Ezr 2:65;
Ecc 2:8; 12:1
^v 2Sa 15:33
19:37 ^w S Ge 49:29
^x Jer 41:17
19:39 ^y S Ge 47:7
19:41 ^z Jdg 8:1; 12:1

19:20 *I your servant know that I have sinned.* Shimei's guilt was common knowledge; he could only seize the most appropriate time to plead for mercy. *house of Joseph.* A common way of referring to the northern tribes (see Jos 18:5; Jdg 1:22; 1Ki 11:28; Am 5:6; Zec 10:6)—of which Ephraim and Manasseh (sons of Joseph) were the most prominent (see Nu 26:28).

19:21 *Abishai.* See 16:9; see also note on 1Sa 26:6. *the LORD's anointed.* See note on 1Sa 9:16; see also 1Sa 24:6; 26:9,11; Ex 22:28; 1Ki 21:10.

19:22 *sons of Zeruiah.* See note on 16:10. *Should anyone be put to death in Israel today?* It was a day for general amnesty (see 1Sa 11:13).

19:23 *You shall not die.* David kept his pledge; he would not himself avenge the wrong committed against him (see note on 1Sa 25:1–44). But on his deathbed he instructed Solomon to take Shimei's case in hand (see 1Ki 2:8–9,36–46).

19:24 *Mephibosheth.* See 9:6–13.

19:25 *Why didn't you go with me …?* David remembers Ziba's previous allegations (see 16:3).

19:26 *lame.* See 4:4; 9:3.

19:27 *he has slandered your servant.* See 16:3. *like an angel of God.* See 14:17 and note. *do whatever you wish.* Mephibosheth discreetly requests David to reconsider the grant of his property to Ziba (see 16:4).

19:29 *divide the land.* Faced with conflicting testimony that could not be corroborated, David withholds judgment and orders the division of Saul's estate (cf. 1Ki 3:25 and note).

19:31 *Barzillai.* See note on 17:27.

19:35 Cf. Ecc 12:2–5 and note. *difference between what is enjoyable and what is not.* At his age, he would be indifferent to all the pleasures of the court.

19:37 *Kimham.* Likely a son of Barzillai (see 1Ki 2:7).

19:40 *Gilgal.* See v. 15 and note.

19:43 a S 2Sa 5:1
20:1 b S Ge 31:14
c S Ge 29:14;
1Ki 12:16 d 1Sa 22:7-8
20:3 e S 2Sa 15:16
20:4 f S 2Sa 17:25
20:6 g 2Sa 21:17
20:7 h S 1Sa 30:14;
S 2Sa 15:18
20:8 i S Jos 9:3
j S 2Sa 2:18
20:10 k S Jdg 3:21
l 1Ki 2:5
20:12 m S 2Sa 2:23

closely related to us. Why are you angry about it? Have we eaten any of the king's provisions? Have we taken anything for ourselves?"

[43] Then the men of Israel [a] answered the men of Judah, "We have ten shares in the king; so we have a greater claim on David than you have. Why then do you treat us with contempt? Weren't we the first to speak of bringing back our king?"

But the men of Judah responded even more harshly than the men of Israel.

SHEBA REBELS AGAINST DAVID

20 Now a troublemaker named Sheba son of Bikri, a Benjamite, happened to be there. He sounded the trumpet and shouted,

"We have no share [b] in David, [c]
no part in Jesse's son! [d]
Everyone to your tents, Israel!"

[2] So all the men of Israel deserted David to follow Sheba son of Bikri. But the men of Judah stayed by their king all the way from the Jordan to Jerusalem.

[3] When David returned to his palace in Jerusalem, he took the ten concubines [e] he had left to take care of the palace and put them in a house under guard. He provided for them but had no sexual relations with them. They were kept in confinement till the day of their death, living as widows.

[4] Then the king said to Amasa, [f] "Summon the men of Judah to come to me within three days, and be here yourself." [5] But when Amasa went to summon Judah, he took longer than the time the king had set for him.

[6] David said to Abishai, [g] "Now Sheba son of Bikri will do us more harm than Absalom did. Take your master's men and pursue him, or he will find fortified cities and escape from us." [a] [7] So Joab's men and the Kerethites [h] and Pelethites and all the mighty warriors went out under the command of Abishai. They marched out from Jerusalem to pursue Sheba son of Bikri.

[8] While they were at the great rock in Gibeon, [i] Amasa came to meet them. Joab [j] was wearing his military tunic, and strapped over it at his waist was a belt with a dagger in its sheath. As he stepped forward, it dropped out of its sheath.

[9] Joab said to Amasa, "How are you, my brother?" Then Joab took Amasa by the beard with his right hand to kiss him. [10] Amasa was not on his guard against the dagger [k] in Joab's [l] hand, and Joab plunged it into his belly, and his intestines spilled out on the ground. Without being stabbed again, Amasa died. Then Joab and his brother Abishai pursued Sheba son of Bikri.

[11] One of Joab's men stood beside Amasa and said, "Whoever favors Joab, and whoever is for David, let him follow Joab!" [12] Amasa lay wallowing in his blood in the middle of the road, and the man saw that all the troops came to a halt [m] there. When he realized that everyone who came up to Amasa stopped, he dragged him from the road into a field and threw a garment over him. [13] After Amasa had been removed from the road, everyone went on with Joab to pursue Sheba son of Bikri.

[14] Sheba passed through all the tribes of Israel to Abel Beth Maakah and through the en-

---

a 6 Or and do us serious injury

19:43 *ten shares.* The ten tribes, excluding Judah and Simeon (see note on 2:4). *we have a greater claim on David.* The grounds for this assertion may be that the Lord had chosen David to reign in the place of Saul (see 3:17–18; 5:2).

20:1 *troublemaker.* See note on Dt 13:13. *Benjamite.* Tribal jealousy still simmered over the transfer of the royal house from Benjamin (Saul's tribe) to Judah. *there.* In Gilgal (19:40). *We have no share in David.* Sheba appeals to the Israelite suspicion that David favored his own tribe (Judah) over the other tribes (see 1Ki 12:16). *Jesse's son.* See note on 1Sa 20:27,30–31.

20:2 *all the men of Israel.* Those referred to in 19:41–43.

20:3 *ten concubines.* See notes on 15:16; 16:22.

20:4 *Amasa.* See notes on 17:25; 19:13. David bypasses Joab.

20:6 *Abishai.* David bypasses Joab a second time (see v. 7). *your master's men.* "Joab's men" (v. 7).

20:7 *Joab's men.* See 18:2. It becomes clear that Joab also accompanied the soldiers and, though not in command (by the king's order), he was obviously the leader recognized by the soldiers (see vv. 7,11,15). *Kerethites and Pelethites.* See note on 8:18.

mighty warriors. See 23:8–39. Once more in a time of crisis David depended mainly on the small force of professionals (many of them non-Israelite) who made up his private army.

20:8 *Gibeon.* See note on 2:12. *Amasa came.* Apparently with some troops (see v. 11 and note).

20:10 *into his belly.* See 2:23; 3:27. For the second time Joab commits murder to secure his position as commander of David's army (see 1Ki 2:5–6). *Joab and his brother Abishai.* In defiance of David's order, Joab reassumes command on his own initiative (see v. 23).

20:11 *Whoever favors Joab, and whoever is for David.* To dispel any idea that Joab was aligned with Sheba's conspiracy, an appeal is made to Amasa's troops to support Joab if they are truly loyal to David.

20:14 *Abel Beth Maakah.* Located to the north of Dan (see 1Ki 15:20; 2Ch 16:4 and TNIV text note). Sheba's strategy was to gather as many volunteers for his revolt as possible, but he was obviously afraid to assemble his ragtag army anywhere within close reach of David's warriors.

tire region of the Bikrites,ᵃ ⁿ who gathered together and followed him. ¹⁵All the troops with Joab came and besieged Sheba in Abel Beth Maakah.ᵒ They built a siege rampᵖ up to the city, and it stood against the outer fortifications. While they were battering the wall to bring it down, ¹⁶a wise woman ᑫ called from the city, "Listen! Listen! Tell Joab to come here so I can speak to him." ¹⁷He went toward her, and she asked, "Are you Joab?"

"I am," he answered.

She said, "Listen to what your servant has to say."

"I'm listening," he said.

¹⁸She continued, "Long ago they used to say, 'Get your answer at Abel,' and that settled it. ¹⁹We are the peaceful ʳ and faithful in Israel. You are trying to destroy a city that is a mother in Israel. Why do you want to swallow up the LORD's inheritance?"ˢ

²⁰"Far be it from me!" Joab replied, "Far be it from me to swallow up or destroy! ²¹That is not the case. A man named Sheba son of Bikri, from the hill country of Ephraim, has lifted up his hand against the king, against David. Hand over this one man, and I'll withdraw from the city."

The woman said to Joab, "His head ᵗ will be thrown to you from the wall."

²²Then the woman went to all the people with her wise advice, ᵘ and they cut off the head of Sheba son of Bikri and threw it to Joab. So he sounded the trumpet, and his men dispersed from the city, each returning to his home. And Joab went back to the king in Jerusalem.

DAVID'S OFFICIALS

²³Joab ᵛ was over Israel's entire army; Benaiah son of Jehoiada was over the Kerethites and Pelethites; ²⁴Adoniram ᵇ ʷ was in charge of forced labor; Jehoshaphat ˣ son of Ahilud was recorder; ²⁵Sheva was secretary; Zadok ʸ and Abiathar were priests; ²⁶and Ira the Jairite ᶜ was David's priest.

THE GIBEONITES AVENGED

21 During the reign of David, there was a famine ᶻ for three successive years; so David sought ᵃ the face of the LORD. The LORD said, "It is on account of Saul and his blood-stained house; it is because he put the Gibeonites to death."

ᵃ 14 See Septuagint and Vulgate; Hebrew *Berites*.   ᵇ 24 Some Septuagint manuscripts (see also 1 Kings 4:6 and 5:14); Hebrew *Adoram*   ᶜ 26 Hebrew; some Septuagint manuscripts and Syriac (see also 2 Samuel 23:38) *Ithrite*

20:14 ⁿ Nu 21:16
20:15 ᵒ 1Ki 15:20;
2Ki 15:29 ᵖ Isa 37:33;
Jer 6:6; 32:24
20:16 ᑫ 2Sa 14:2
20:19 ʳ S Dt 2:26
ˢ S 1Sa 26:19
20:21 ᵗ S 2Sa 4:8
20:22 ᵘ Ecc 9:13
20:23 ᵛ S 2Sa 2:28;
8:16-18; 24:2
20:24 ʷ 1Ki 4:6;
5:14; 12:18; 2Ch 10:18
ˣ S 2Sa 8:16
20:25 ʸ S 1Sa 2:35;
S 2Sa 8:17
21:1 ᶻ S Ge 12:10;
S Dt 32:24
ᵃ S Ex 32:11

20:18 *Get your answer at Abel.* The city was famous for the wisdom of its inhabitants.

20:19 *a mother in Israel.* A town that produced faithful Israelites—cities were commonly personified as women (see Jer 50:12; Gal 4:26). *the LORD's inheritance.* See note on 1Sa 10:1.

20:21 *hill country of Ephraim.* Either Sheba, a Benjamite (see v. 1), lived in the tribal territory of Ephraim or this was the designation of a geographical, rather than a strictly tribal, region.

20:22 *Joab went back to the king in Jerusalem.* See notes on vv. 7,10.

20:23–26 These royal officials apparently served David during most of his reign (see 8:15–18).

20:23 *Joab was over Israel's entire army.* Though in some disfavor, he held this position until he participated in Adonijah's conspiracy (1Ki 1:7; 2:28–35). *Kerethites and Pelethites.* See note on 8:18.

20:24 *Adoniram was in charge of forced labor.* A position not established in the early years of David's reign (see 8:15–16). Adoniram must have been a late appointee of David since he continued to serve under Solomon (1Ki 4:6; 5:14) and was eventually killed in the early days of the reign of Rehoboam (1Ki 12:18). *forced labor.* Labor usually performed by prisoners of war from defeated nations (see 12:31 and note; 1Ki 9:15, 20–21). *recorder.* See note on 8:16.

20:25 *Sheva.* See note on 8:17 ("Seraiah"). *secretary.* See note on 8:17. *Zadok and Abiathar.* See note on 8:17.

20:26 *Jairite.* A reference either to Jair of the tribe of Manasseh or to an inhabitant of one of the settlements known as Havvoth Jair (Nu 32:41; 1Ki 4:13). *priest.* See note on 8:18.

C **21:1—24:25** This concluding section forms an appendix to 1,2 Samuel and contains additional materials (without concern for chronology) relating to David's reign. Its topical arrangement is striking in that it employs the literary pattern *a-b-c/c-b-a*, frequently found elsewhere in OT literature (cf., e.g., Ps 25 and its introduction; 45; cf. also Isa 6:10 and note). The first and last units (21:1–14; 24:1–25) are narratives of two events in which David had to deal with God's wrath against Israel (the first occasioned by an act of Saul, the second by his own). The second and fifth units (21:15–22; 23:8–39) are accounts of David's warriors (the second much longer than the first). At the center (22:1—23:7) are two songs of David (the first much longer than the second), one of which celebrates David's victories as warrior-king, while the other recalls his role as psalmist (see note on 1Sa 16:14—17:58). It is unknown whether motivation for this *a-b-c/c-b-a* arrangement went beyond aesthetic considerations. But it is possible that the author appended these materials and did so in that way to recall to mind again the triumph song of the women who came to meet King Saul and David after their victories over the Philistines ("Saul has slain his thousands, and David his tens of thousands," 1Sa 18:7). If so, he suggests that what the women said of Saul and David in their victories over foreign enemies came true (bitterly) also as a result of their royal sins, but now those "slain" were Israelites. However that may be, King David's triumph song in ch. 22 and Hannah's song in 1Sa 2:1–10 form a literary frame around the main body of the book (see note on 1Sa 2:1) and poetically highlight its central themes.

21:1–14 This event appears to have occurred after David's kindness was extended to Mephibosheth (ch. 9) and before Absalom's rebellion (16:7–8; 18:28; see note on 16:8).

21:1 *he put the Gibeonites to death.* Saul's action against the Gibeonites is not related elsewhere but appears to have been instituted early in his reign, motivated by an excessive nationalism.

21:2 *b* S Jos 9:15
21:3 *c* S 1Sa 26:19
21:4 *d* Nu 35:33-34
21:6 *e* Nu 25:4
f S 1Sa 10:24
21:7 *g* 2Sa 4:4
h S 1Sa 18:3;
S 2Sa 9:7
21:8 *i* 2Sa 3:7
j 1Sa 18:19
21:9 *k* S 2Sa 16:8
l S Ru 1:22
21:10 *m* S Ge 40:19;
S 1Sa 17:44
21:12 *n* 1Sa 31:11-13
o S Jdg 21:8; S 1Sa 11:1
p S Jos 7:11
q 1Sa 31:10
r S 1Sa 28:4
21:14 *s* Jos 18:28
t Jos 7:26 *u* 2Sa 24:25
v 1Ch 8:34
21:15 *w* S 2Sa 5:25

²The king summoned the Gibeonites *b* and spoke to them. (Now the Gibeonites were not a part of Israel but were survivors of the Amorites; the Israelites had sworn to ⌞spare⌟ them, but Saul in his zeal for Israel and Judah had tried to annihilate them.) ³David asked the Gibeonites, "What shall I do for you? How shall I make atonement so that you will bless the LORD's inheritance?" *c*

⁴The Gibeonites answered him, "We have no right to demand silver or gold from Saul or his family, nor do we have the right to put anyone in Israel to death." *d*

"What do you want me to do for you?" David asked.

⁵They answered the king, "As for the man who destroyed us and plotted against us so that we have been decimated and have no place anywhere in Israel, ⁶let seven of his male descendants be given to us to be killed and their bodies exposed *e* before the LORD at Gibeah of Saul—the LORD's chosen *f* one."

So the king said, "I will give them to you."

⁷The king spared Mephibosheth *g* son of Jonathan, the son of Saul, because of the oath *h* before the LORD between David and Jonathan son of Saul. ⁸But the king took Armoni and Mephibosheth, the two sons of Aiah's daughter Rizpah, *i* whom she had borne to Saul, together with the five sons of Saul's daughter Merab, *a* whom she had borne to Adriel son of Barzillai the Meholathite. *j* ⁹He handed them over to the Gibeonites, who killed them and exposed their bodies on a hill before the LORD. All seven of them fell together; they were put to death *k* during the first days of the harvest, just as the barley harvest was beginning. *l*

¹⁰Rizpah daughter of Aiah took sackcloth and spread it out for herself on a rock. From the beginning of the harvest till the rain poured down from the heavens on the bodies, she did not let the birds touch them by day or the wild animals by night. *m* ¹¹When David was told what Aiah's daughter Rizpah, Saul's concubine, had done, ¹²he went and took the bones of Saul *n* and his son Jonathan from the citizens of Jabesh Gilead. *o* (They had stolen their bodies from the public square at Beth Shan, *p* where the Philistines had hung *q* them after they struck Saul down on Gilboa.) *r* ¹³David brought the bones of Saul and his son Jonathan from there, and the bones of those who had been killed and exposed were gathered up.

¹⁴They buried the bones of Saul and his son Jonathan in the tomb of Saul's father Kish, at Zela *s* in Benjamin, and did everything the king commanded. After that, *t* God answered prayer *u* in behalf of the land. *v*

WARS AGAINST THE PHILISTINES
21:15–22pp — 1Ch 20:4–8

¹⁵Once again there was a battle between the Philistines *w* and Israel. David went down with his men to fight against the Philistines, and he became exhausted. ¹⁶And Ishbi-Benob, one of the descendants of Rapha, whose bronze spearhead weighed three hundred

---

a 8 Two Hebrew manuscripts, some Septuagint manuscripts and Syriac (see also 1 Samuel 18:19); most Hebrew and Septuagint manuscripts *Michal*

Perhaps tribalism was also involved, since the Gibeonites occupied territory partly assigned to Benjamin, and Saul's great-grandfather was known as the "father of Gibeon" (1Ch 8:29; 9:35).
21:2 *Amorites.* A comprehensive name sometimes used to designate all the pre-Israelite inhabitants of Canaan (Ge 15:16; Jos 24:18; Jdg 6:10; Am 2:10). More precisely, the Gibeonites were called Hivites (Jos 9:7; 11:19). *the Israelites had sworn to ⌞spare⌟ them.* A pledge sworn in the name of the Lord (Jos 9:15, 18–21). *tried to annihilate them.* The reason Saul was unsuccessful is not known.
21:3 *bless.* Since the oath sworn to them in the Lord's name had been violated, they could rightly call down his curse on the land. *the LORD's inheritance.* See note on 1Sa 10:1.
21:5 *the man.* Saul. *no place anywhere in Israel.* Those who escaped Saul's attack had been driven from their towns and lands (see 4:2–3).
21:6 *seven.* Because it would represent a full number (seven symbolized completeness)—though many more Gibeonites had been slain. *Gibeah.* The place of Saul's residence (see 1Sa 10:26).
21:7 *oath before the LORD between David and Jonathan.* See 9:1–13; 1Sa 18:3; 20:15 and note.
21:8 *Rizpah.* See 3:7. *Merab.* See 1Sa 18:19. *Barzillai the Meholathite.* Not to be confused with Barzillai the Gileadite (17:27; 19:31).

21:9 *All seven of them fell together.* This nearly extinguished the house of Saul, which God had rejected (see 1Sa 13:13–14; 15:23–26). In 1Ch 8:29–39; 9:35–44 no descendants of Saul are listed other than from the line of Jonathan. *barley harvest was beginning.* About the middle of April (see note on Ru 1:22).
21:10 *sackcloth.* See note on Ge 37:34. *rain poured down.* An indication that the famine was caused by drought and evidence that the judgment on Israel for breaking the oath sworn to the Gibeonites (see v. 1) was now over.
21:12–14 *bones of Saul and his son Jonathan.* See 1Sa 31:11–13. David's final act toward Saul and Jonathan was a deed of deep respect for the king he had honored and the friend he had loved.
21:14 *God answered prayer in behalf of the land.* Concludes the first unit of the *a-b-c/c-b-a* literary structure that characterizes the last four chapters of 2 Samuel, just as its echo in 24:25 concludes the last unit (see note on 21:1—24:25).
21:15–21 These four Philistine episodes (vv. 15–17, 18, 19, 20–21) cannot be chronologically located with any certainty (see note on 21:1—24:25). Each involves a heroic accomplishment by one of David's mighty men, resulting in the death of a descendant of Rapha (see v. 22).
21:16,18,20,22 *Rapha.* The ancestor of at least one group of Rephaites (see 1Ch 20:4,8). In calling the four formidable enemy

shekels[a] and who was armed with a new ⌊sword⌋, said he would kill David. [17]But Abishai[x] son of Zeruiah came to David's rescue; he struck the Philistine down and killed him. Then David's men swore to him, saying, "Never again will you go out with us to battle, so that the lamp[y] of Israel will not be extinguished.[z]"

[18]In the course of time, there was another battle with the Philistines, at Gob. At that time Sibbekai[a] the Hushathite killed Saph, one of the descendants of Rapha.

[19]In another battle with the Philistines at Gob, Elhanan son of Jair[b] the Bethlehemite killed the brother of[c] Goliath the Gittite,[b] who had a spear with a shaft like a weaver's rod.[c]

[20]In still another battle, which took place at Gath, there was a huge man with six fingers on each hand and six toes on each foot—twenty-four in all. He also was descended from Rapha. [21]When he taunted[d] Israel, Jonathan son of Shimeah,[e] David's brother, killed him. [22]These four were descendants of Rapha in Gath, and they fell at the hands of David and his men.

DAVID'S SONG OF PRAISE
22:1–51pp — Ps 18:1–50

22 David sang[f] to the LORD the words of this song when the LORD delivered him from the hand of all his enemies and from the hand of Saul. [2]He said:

> "The LORD is my rock,[g] my fortress[h] and my deliverer;[i]
> 3   my God is my rock, in whom I take refuge,[j]
>   my shield[d][k] and the horn[e][l] of my salvation.
> He is my stronghold,[m] my refuge and my savior—
>   from violent people you save me.
>
> 4 "I called to the LORD, who is worthy[n] of praise,
>   and have been saved from my enemies.
> 5 The waves[o] of death swirled about me;
>   the torrents of destruction overwhelmed me.
> 6 The cords of the grave[p] coiled around me;
>   the snares of death confronted me.
>
> 7 "In my distress[q] I called[r] to the LORD;

---

[a] 16 That is, about 7 1/2 pounds or about 3.5 kilograms   [b] 19 See 1 Chron. 20:5; Hebrew *Jaare-Oregim.*   [c] 19 See 1 Chron. 20:5; Hebrew does not have *the brother of.*   [d] 3 Or *sovereign*   [e] 3 *Horn* here symbolizes strength.

21:17 *x*2Sa 20:6
*y*1Ki 11:36; 15:4;
2Ki 8:19; 2Ch 21:7;
Ps 132:17 *z*2Sa 18:3
21:18 *a*1Ch 11:29;
27:11
21:19 *b*S 1Sa 17:4
*c*S 1Sa 17:7
21:21 *d*S 1Sa 17:10
*e*S 1Sa 16:9
22:1 *f*S Ex 15:1
22:2 *g*S 1Sa 2:2
*h*Ps 31:3; 91:2
*i*Ps 144:2
22:3 *j*S Dt 23:15;
S 32:37; Ps 14:6; 31:2;
59:16; 71:7; 91:2;
94:22; Pr 10:29;
Isa 25:4; Jer 16:19;
Joel 3:16 *k*S Ge 15:1
*l*S Dt 33:17; S Lk 1:69
*m*Ps 9:9; 52:7
22:4 *n*Ps 48:1; 96:4;
145:3
22:5 *o*Ps 69:14-15;
Jnh 2:3
22:6 *p*Ps 116:3;
Ac 2:24
22:7 *q*Ge 35:3;
S Jdg 2:15; 2Ch 15:4;
Ps 4:1; 77:2; 120:1;
Isa 26:16 *r*Ps 34:6,15;
116:4

---

warriors referred to in this series "descendants of Rapha" (v. 22), the writer most likely identifies them as giants (see v. 20; Dt 2:10–11,20–21). In that case, they may have been related to the Anakites (see Nu 13:28,32–33; Jos 11:21–22). The list of the ten peoples of Canaan in Ge 15:19–21 mentions Rephaites but not Anakites, though the Anakites (but not Rephaites) figure significantly in the accounts of the conquest (Dt 9:2; Jos 14:12,15; Jdg 1:20).
21:17 *Abishai.* See note on 1Sa 26:6. *so that the lamp of Israel will not be extinguished.* A striking metaphor depicting Israel's dependence on David for its security and continuing existence as a nation—its national hope (see 22:29; 23:3–4; 1Ki 11:36 and note; cf. 2Sa 22:29; 23:3–4).
21:18–19 *Gob.* Mentioned nowhere else in the OT, it may have been in the near vicinity of Gezer, where 1Ch 20:4 locates this same battle. On the other hand, many Hebrew manuscripts read "Nob," a well-known town northeast of Jerusalem (see 1Sa 21:1 and note). In that case, the text nicely echoes the proper name Ishbi-Benob (v. 16), which apparently means "inhabitant of Nob."
21:19 *Elhanan . . . killed the brother of Goliath.* See TNIV text note. Since it is clear from 1Sa 17 that David killed Goliath, an early copyist probably misread the Hebrew for "Lahmi the brother of" (see 1Ch 20:5) as "the Bethlehemite" (in Hebrew the word for "killed" stands first in the clause). *Jair.* See TNIV text note. The Hebrew for "Oregim" occurs also at the end of the verse, where it is translated "weaver's." An early copyist probably inserted it in the name by mistake, since 1Ch 20:5 reads "Jair" (apparently correctly) instead of "Jaare-Oregim."
21:21 *taunted Israel.* As Goliath had done (see 1Sa 17:10,25). *Shimeah.* Also called Shammah (1Sa 16:9; 17:13).

22:1–51 For the relationship of this song to Hannah's song in the overall literary structure of 1 and 2 Samuel, see notes on 1Sa 2:1–10, especially on 2:1. David's song is preserved also as Ps 18 (see notes on that psalm). Besides an introduction (vv. 2–4) and conclusion (vv. 47–51), the song consists of three major sections: The first describes David's deliverance from mortal danger at the hands of his enemies (vv. 5–20); the second sets forth the moral grounds for God's saving help (vv. 21–30); the third recounts the help the Lord gave him (vv. 31–46). The song was probably composed shortly after David's victories over foreign enemies (8:1–14) and before his sins against Bathsheba and Uriah (11:2–4,14–17; compare vv. 21–25 with 1Ki 15:5).
22:1 *from . . . all his enemies.* See 8:1–14. *from . . . Saul.* See 1Sa 18–27.
22:2 *rock.* A figure particularly appropriate to David's experience (see vv. 3,32,47; 23:3; cf. Dt 32:4,15,18,31; Ps 28:1; 31:2; 61:2; 78:35; 89:26; 94:22; 95:1). He had often taken refuge among the rocks of the desert (1Sa 23:25; 24:2), but he realized that true security was found only in the Lord. *fortress.* The Hebrew for this word occurs in 5:17; 23:14; 1Sa 22:4–5; 24:22, referring to one or more strongholds where David sought refuge.
22:3 *my shield.* See v. 31; Ge 15:1 and note. *horn.* See TNIV text note; Dt 33:17; Jer 48:25.
22:5 *waves of death.* In vv. 5–6 David depicts his experiences in poetic figures of mortal danger.
22:6 *grave.* See note on 30:3; Jnh 2:2 ("realm of the dead").
22:7 *his temple.* Heaven, where the Lord is enthroned as King (see Ps 11:4; Isa 6:1 and notes; see also Jnh 2:7).

22:8 ˢJdg 5:4;
Ps 97:4 ᵗS Ex 19:18;
S Jdg 5:4; Ps 68:8;
77:18; Jer 10:10
ᵘJob 9:6; 26:11;
Ps 75:3
22:9 ᵛPs 50:3; 97:3;
Heb 12:29; S Rev 11:5
ʷIsa 6:6; Eze 1:13;
10:2
22:10 ˣS Ex 19:9;
Lev 16:2; S Dt 33:26;
1Ki 8:12; Job 26:9;
Ps 104:3; Isa 19:1;
Jer 4:13; Na 1:3
22:11 ʸS Ge 3:24;
S Ex 25:22 ᶻPs 104:3
22:12 ᵃS Ex 19:9
22:13 ᵇJob 37:3;
Ps 77:18
22:14 ᶜS 1Sa 2:10
22:15 ᵈS Dt 32:23
22:16 ᵉPs 6:1; 50:8,
21; 106:9; Na 1:4
ᶠS Ex 14:21;
Isa 30:33; 40:24
22:17 ᵍPs 144:7
ʰEx 2:10
22:18 ⁱLk 1:71
22:19 ʲPs 23:4
22:20 ᵏJob 36:16;
Ps 31:8 ˡPs 118:5
ᵐPs 22:8; Isa 42:1;
Mt 12:18
ⁿS 2Sa 15:26
22:21 ᵒS 1Sa 26:23
ᵖPs 26:6 ᑫJob 17:9;
22:30; 42:7-8;
Ps 24:4
22:22 ʳGe 18:19;
Ps 128:1; Pr 8:32
22:23 ˢDt 6:4-9;
Ps 119:30-32
ᵗPs 119:102
22:24 ᵘS Ge 6:9;
Eph 1:4
22:25 ᵛS 1Sa 26:23

I called out to my God.
From his temple he heard my voice;
my cry came to his ears.
⁸The earth ˢ trembled and quaked, ᵗ
the foundations ᵘ of the heavens ᵃ shook;
they trembled because he was angry.
⁹Smoke rose from his nostrils;
consuming fire ᵛ came from his mouth,
burning coals ʷ blazed out of it.
¹⁰He parted the heavens and came down;
dark clouds ˣ were under his feet.
¹¹He mounted the cherubim ʸ and flew;
he soared ᵇ on the wings of the wind. ᶻ
¹²He made darkness ᵃ his canopy around him—
the dark ᶜ rain clouds of the sky.
¹³Out of the brightness of his presence
bolts of lightning ᵇ blazed forth.
¹⁴The LORD thundered ᶜ from heaven;
the voice of the Most High resounded.
¹⁵He shot his arrows ᵈ and scattered the enemy,
with great bolts of lightning he routed them.
¹⁶The valleys of the sea were exposed
and the foundations of the earth laid bare
at the rebuke ᵉ of the LORD,
at the blast ᶠ of breath from his nostrils.

¹⁷"He reached down from on high ᵍ and took hold of me;
he drew ʰ me out of deep waters.
¹⁸He rescued ⁱ me from my powerful enemy,
from my foes, who were too strong for me.
¹⁹They confronted me in the day of my disaster,
but the LORD was my support. ʲ
²⁰He brought me out into a spacious ᵏ place;
he rescued ˡ me because he delighted ᵐ in me. ⁿ

²¹"The LORD has dealt with me according to my righteousness; ᵒ
according to the cleanness ᵖ of my hands ᑫ he has rewarded me.
²²For I have kept ʳ the ways of the LORD;
I am not guilty of turning from my God.
²³All his laws are before me; ˢ
I have not turned ᵗ away from his decrees.
²⁴I have been blameless ᵘ before him
and have kept myself from sin.
²⁵The LORD has rewarded me according to my righteousness, ᵛ
according to my cleanness ᵈ in his sight.

²⁶"To the faithful you show yourself faithful,
to the blameless you show yourself blameless,

ᵃ 8 Hebrew; Vulgate and Syriac (see also Psalm 18:7) *mountains*   ᵇ 11 Many Hebrew manuscripts (see also Psalm 18:10); most Hebrew manuscripts *appeared*   ᶜ 12 Septuagint (see also Psalm 18:11); Hebrew *massed*   ᵈ 25 Hebrew; Septuagint and Vulgate (see also Psalm 18:24) *to the cleanness of my hands*

22:8–16 See note on Ps 18:7-15.
22:9 *Smoke rose from his nostrils.* See note on Ps 18:8.
22:10 *parted the heavens and came down.* See Isa 64:1 and note.
22:11 *mounted the cherubim and flew.* See notes on 1Sa 4:4; Ge 3:24; Ps 18:10; Eze 1:5.
22:14 *The LORD thundered.* The reference to thunder as the voice of God is common in the OT (see Ps 29; Job 37:2–5). Thunder is particularly suited to expressing God's power and majesty.
22:17 *He reached down from on high.* In vv. 17–20 David describes his deliverance, initially in figurative terms (v. 17; cf. v. 5) and subsequently in more literal language (vv. 18–20).
22:20 *spacious place.* See note on Ps 18:19. *delighted in.* The

Hebrew underlying this expression is used in 15:26 ("pleased with"); Ps 22:8 (cf. Mt 3:17, "with ... well pleased") and expresses the idea of the sovereign good pleasure and favor of God toward his anointed one (v. 51).

22:21,25 *according to my righteousness.* See 1Ki 15:5. In vv. 21–25 David refers to the Lord's deliverances as a reward for his own righteousness. While these statements may give the impression of self-righteous boasting and a meritorious basis for divine favor, they should be understood in their context as: (1) David's desire to please the Lord in his service as the Lord's anointed (see note on v. 51); (2) his recognition that the Lord rewards those who faithfully seek to serve him.
22:26–30 See notes on Ps 18:25–29.

²⁷to the pure^w you show yourself pure,
  but to the devious you show yourself shrewd.^x
²⁸You save the humble,^y
  but your eyes are on the haughty^z to bring them low. ^a
²⁹You, Lord, are my lamp;^b
  the Lord turns my darkness into light.
³⁰With your help I can advance against a troop^a;
  with my God I can scale a wall.

³¹"As for God, his way is perfect;^c
  the Lord's word is flawless.^d
  He shields^e all who take refuge in him.
³²For who is God besides the Lord?
  And who is the Rock^f except our God?^g
³³It is God who arms me with strength^b
  and keeps my way secure.
³⁴He makes my feet like the feet of a deer^h
  and causes me to stand on the heights. ⁱ
³⁵He trains my hands^j for battle;
  my arms can bend a bow^k of bronze.
³⁶You make your saving help my shield;^l
  your help has made^c me great.
³⁷You provide a broad path^m for my feet,
  so that my ankles do not give way.

³⁸"I pursued my enemies and crushed them;
  I did not turn back till they were destroyed.
³⁹I crushedⁿ them completely, and they could not rise;
  they fell beneath my feet.
⁴⁰You armed me with strength for battle;
  you humbled my adversaries before me. ^o
⁴¹You made my enemies turn their backs^p in flight,
  and I destroyed my foes.
⁴²They cried for help,^q but there was no one to save them— ^r
  to the Lord, but he did not answer. ^s
⁴³I beat them as fine as the dust^t of the earth;
  I pounded and trampled^u them like mud^v in the streets.

⁴⁴"You have delivered^w me from the attacks of the peoples;
  you have preserved^x me as the head of nations.
  People^y I did not know now serve me,
⁴⁵ foreigners cower^z before me;
  as soon as they hear of me, they obey me. ^a
⁴⁶They all lose heart;
  they come trembling^{d b} from their strongholds.

⁴⁷"The Lord lives! Praise be to my Rock!
  Exalted^c be my God, the Rock, my Savior!^d
⁴⁸He is the God who avenges^e me, ^f
  who puts the nations under me,
⁴⁹ who sets me free from my enemies. ^g
You exalted me^h above my foes;
  from violent people you rescued me.
⁵⁰Therefore I will praise you, Lord, among the nations;
  I will sing the praisesⁱ of your name.^j

---

^a 30 Or *can run through a barricade*   ^b 33 Dead Sea Scrolls, some Septuagint manuscripts, Vulgate and Syriac (see also Psalm 18:32); Masoretic Text *who is my strong refuge*   ^c 36 Dead Sea Scrolls; Masoretic Text *shield; / you stoop down to make*   ^d 46 Some Septuagint manuscripts and Vulgate (see also Psalm 18:45); Masoretic Text *they arm themselves*

22:29 *You . . . are my lamp.* The Lord causes David's life and undertakings to flourish (see Job 18:5–6; 21:17; see also note on Ps 27:1).
22:31 *his way is perfect.* The remainder of the song (vv. 31–51) accentuates David's praise to God for his deliverances.
22:32,47 *Rock.* See note on v. 2.

22:34 See Hab 3:19 and note.
22:47 *The Lord lives!* See note on Ps 18:46.
22:50 *I will praise you, Lord, among the nations.* For Paul's reference to this vow, see Ro 15:9.

22:27 ^wMt 5:8
^xLev 26:23-24
22:28 ^yS Ex 3:8;
1Sa 2:8-9; Ps 72:12-13 ; ^zPs 131:1; Pr 30:13;
Da 4:31; Zep 3:11
^aIsa 2:12,17; 5:15;
S Lk 1:51
22:29 ^bPs 27:1;
Isa 2:5; Mic 7:8;
Rev 21:23; 22:5
22:31 ^cS Dt 32:4;
Mt 5:48 ^dPs 12:6;
119:140; Pr 30:5-6
^eS Ge 15:1
22:32 ^fS 1Sa 2:2
^gS 2Sa 7:22
22:34 ^hIsa 35:6;
Hab 3:19 ⁱS Dt 32:13
22:35 ^jPs 144:1
^kPs 7:12; 11:2;
Zec 9:13
22:36 ^lEph 6:16
22:37 ^mPr 4:11
22:39 ⁿPs 44:5;
110:6; Mal 4:3
22:40 ^oS Jos 10:24;
S 1Ki 5:3
22:41 ^pS Ex 23:27
22:42 ^qIsa 1:15
^rPs 50:22
^sS 1Sa 14:37
22:43 ^t1Ki 20:10;
2Ki 13:7; Isa 41:2;
Am 1:3 ^uPs 7:5;
Isa 41:25; Mic 7:10;
Zec 10:5 ^vIsa 5:25;
10:6; 22:5; Mic 7:10
22:44 ^wS Ex 11:3;
S 2Sa 3:1 ^xDt 28:13
^yS 2Sa 8:1-14;
Isa 55:3-5
22:45 ^zPs 66:3;
81:15 ^aS Dt 33:29
22:46 ^bMic 7:17
22:47 ^cS Ex 15:2
^dDt 32:15; Ps 18:31;
89:26; 95:1
22:48 ^eS Nu 31:3
^fPs 144:2
22:49 ^gPs 140:1,4
^hPs 27:6
22:50 ⁱPs 9:11; 47:6;
68:4 / Ro 15:9*

22:51 *k* Ps 21:1;
144:9-10; *l* 1Sa 16:13;
Ps 89:20; Ac 13:23
m S 2Sa 7:13
n Ps 89:24,29
23:1 *o* S Ex 11:3;
Ps 78:70-71; 89:27
p 1Sa 2:10,35;
Ps 18:50; 20:6; 84:9;
Isa 45:1; Hab 3:13
23:2 *q* Mt 22:43;
Mk 12:36; 2Pe 1:21
23:3 *r* Dt 32:4;
S 1Sa 2:2; Ps 18:31
s Ps 72:2 *t* S Ge 42:18
u Isa 11:1-5
23:4 *v* Jn 1:5
w Ps 119:147; 130:6;
Pr 4:18 *x* S Jdg 5:31;
Mt 13:43 *y* S Dt 32:2
23:5 *z* S Ge 9:16;
Ps 89:29
23:6 *a* Isa 5:6; 9:18;
10:17; 27:4; 33:12;
Mic 7:4; Na 1:10;
Mt 13:40-41
23:8 *b* S 2Sa 17:10
c 1Ch 27:2
23:9 *d* 1Ch 27:4
e 1Ch 8:4

[51] "He gives his king great victories; [k]
    he shows unfailing kindness to his anointed, [l]
    to David [m] and his descendants forever." [n]

DAVID'S LAST WORDS

23

These are the last words of David:

"The inspired utterance of David son of Jesse,
    the utterance of the man exalted [o] by the Most High,
the man anointed [p] by the God of Jacob,
    the hero of Israel's songs:

[2] "The Spirit [q] of the LORD spoke through me;
    his word was on my tongue.
[3] The God of Israel spoke,
    the Rock [r] of Israel said to me:
'When one rules over people in righteousness, [s]
    when he rules in the fear [t] of God, [u]
[4] he is like the light [v] of morning [w] at sunrise [x]
    on a cloudless morning,
like the brightness after rain [y]
    that brings grass from the earth.'

[5] "If my house were not right with God,
    surely he would not have made with me an everlasting covenant, [z]
    arranged and secured in every part;
surely he would not bring to fruition my salvation
    and grant me my every desire.
[6] But evil men are all to be cast aside like thorns, [a]
    which are not gathered with the hand.
[7] Whoever touches thorns
    uses a tool of iron or the shaft of a spear;
    they are burned up where they lie."

DAVID'S MIGHTY WARRIORS
23:8–39pp — 1Ch 11:10–41

[8] These are the names of David's mighty warriors: [b]

Josheb-Basshebeth, [a c] a Tahkemonite, [b] was chief of the Three; he raised his spear against eight hundred men, whom he killed [c] in one encounter.

[9] Next to him was Eleazar son of Dodai [d] the Ahohite. [e] As one of the three mighty warriors, he was with David when they taunted the Philistines gathered ⌊at Pas Dammim⌋ [d] for battle. Then the Israelites retreated, [10] but Eleazar stood his ground and struck down

---

[a] 8 Hebrew; some Septuagint manuscripts suggest *Ish-Bosheth*, that is, *Esh-Baal* (see also 1 Chron. 11:11 *Jashobeam*).   [b] 8 Probably a variant of *Hakmonite* (see 1 Chron. 11:11)   [c] 8 Some Septuagint manuscripts (see also 1 Chron. 11:11); Hebrew and other Septuagint manuscripts *Three; it was Adino the Eznite who killed eight hundred men*   [d] 9 See 1 Chron. 11:13; Hebrew *gathered there*.

22:51 *his king … his anointed.* See notes on 1Sa 2:10; 10:25; 12:14–15. David refers to himself in the third person in a way that acknowledges the covenantal character of his kingship. It is in the context of David's official capacity as the Lord's anointed that the entire song is to be read and understood (see note on vv. 21,25). *his descendants forever.* David speaks of God's promise through Nathan (see 7:12–16).

C **23:1** *last words of David.* Probably to be understood as David's last poetic testimony (in the manner of his psalms), perhaps composed at the time of his final instructions and warnings to his son Solomon (see 1Ki 2:1–10).

23:2 See notes on 2Ti 3:16; 2Pe 1:20.

A C **23:3** *Rock.* See note on 22:2; see also 1Sa 2:2 and note; Dt 32:4,15,18,30–31. *When one rules over people in righteousness.* In brief and vivid strokes David portrays the ideal theocratic king—to be fully realized only in the rule of great David's greater Son, Jesus Christ. This prophetic utterance complements that of 7:12–16 and anticipates those of Isa 9:7;

11:1–5; Jer 23:5–6; 33:15–16; Zec 9:9.

23:4 *like the light of morning.* See notes on Ps 27:1; 36:9.

23:5 *If my house were not right with God.* David recalls God's covenant with him and his dynasty (see 7:12–16). *everlasting covenant.* David expressly calls God's promise to him a covenant that will not be abrogated (see notes on 7:20,28; Isa 55:3; see also Ps 89:3–4,28–29,34–37; 132:11–12). *bring to fruition.* Through David's promised descendants.

23:6 *evil men … cast aside.* Godless people who have no interest in the righteous king will be destroyed (see Ps 2:8–9; 110:5–6).

23:8–39 See note on 21:1—24:25. This list of 37 (see v. 39) of David's most valiant warriors and the description of some of their exploits are paralleled in 1Ch 11:11–41. There the list is expanded by 16 names (1Ch 11:41–47).

23:8 *Three.* Two groups of three warriors (vv. 8–12 and 13–23) and one group of thirty warriors (vv. 24–39) are mentioned (see v. 39 for the total number of warriors).

the Philistines till his hand grew tired and froze to the sword. The LORD brought about a great victory that day. The troops returned to Eleazar, but only to strip the dead.

[11]Next to him was Shammah son of Agee the Hararite. When the Philistines banded together at a place where there was a field full of lentils, Israel's troops fled from them. [12]But Shammah took his stand in the middle of the field. He defended it and struck the Philistines down, and the LORD brought about a great victory.

[13]During harvest time, three of the thirty chief warriors came down to David at the cave of Adullam, [f] while a band of Philistines was encamped in the Valley of Rephaim. [g] [14]At that time David was in the stronghold, [h] and the Philistine garrison was at Bethlehem. [i] [15]David longed for water and said, "Oh, that someone would get me a drink of water from the well near the gate of Bethlehem!" [16]So the three mighty warriors broke through the Philistine lines, drew water from the well near the gate of Bethlehem and carried it back to David. But he refused to drink it; instead, he poured [j] it out before the LORD. [17]"Far be it from me, LORD, to do this!" he said. "Is it not the blood [k] of men who went at the risk of their lives?" And David would not drink it.

Such were the exploits of the three mighty warriors.

[18]Abishai [l] the brother of Joab son of Zeruiah was chief of the Three. [a] He raised his spear against three hundred men, whom he killed, and so he became as famous as the Three. [19]Was he not held in greater honor than the Three? He became their commander, even though he was not included among them.

[20]Benaiah [m] son of Jehoiada, a valiant fighter from Kabzeel, [n] performed great exploits. He struck down Moab's two mightiest warriors. He also went down into a pit on a snowy day and killed a lion. [21]And he struck down a huge Egyptian. Although the Egyptian had a spear in his hand, Benaiah went against him with a club. He snatched the spear from the Egyptian's hand and killed him with his own spear. [22]Such were the exploits of Benaiah son of Jehoiada; he too was as famous as the three mighty warriors. [23]He was held in greater honor than any of the Thirty, but he was not included among the Three. And David put him in charge of his bodyguard.

[24]Among the Thirty were:
Asahel [o] the brother of Joab,
Elhanan son of Dodo from Bethlehem,
[25]Shammah the Harodite, [p]
Elika the Harodite,
[26]Helez [q] the Paltite,
Ira [r] son of Ikkesh from Tekoa,
[27]Abiezer [s] from Anathoth, [t]
Sibbekai [b] the Hushathite,
[28]Zalmon the Ahohite,
Maharai [u] the Netophathite, [v]
[29]Heled [c] [w] son of Baanah the Netophathite,
Ithai son of Ribai from Gibeah [x] in Benjamin,
[30]Benaiah the Pirathonite, [y]
Hiddai [d] from the ravines of Gaash, [z]
[31]Abi-Albon the Arbathite,
Azmaveth the Barhumite, [a]
[32]Eliahba the Shaalbonite,
the sons of Jashen,

23:13 [f] S Ge 38:1;
S Jos 12:15
[g] S Jos 17:15
23:14 [h] 1Sa 22:4-5;
S 2Sa 5:17 [i] Ru 1:19
23:16 [j] S Ge 35:14
23:17 [k] Lev 17:10-12
23:18 [l] S 1Sa 26:6
23:20 [m] S 2Sa 8:18;
1Ch 27:5 [n] Jos 15:21
23:24 [o] S 2Sa 2:18
23:25 [p] Jdg 7:1
23:26 [q] 1Ch 27:10
[r] 1Ch 27:9
23:27 [s] 1Ch 27:12
[t] S Jos 21:18
23:28 [u] 1Ch 27:13
[v] 2Ki 25:23; Ezr 2:22;
Ne 7:26; Jer 40:8
23:29 [w] 1Ch 27:15
[x] S Jos 15:57
23:30 [y] S Jdg 12:13
[z] Jos 24:30
23:31 [a] 2Sa 3:16

---

[a] 18 Most Hebrew manuscripts (see also 1 Chron. 11:20); two Hebrew manuscripts and Syriac *Thirty*
[b] 27 Some Septuagint manuscripts (see also 21:18; 1 Chron. 11:29); Hebrew *Mebunnai* [c] 29 Some Hebrew manuscripts and Vulgate (see also 1 Chron. 11:30); most Hebrew manuscripts *Heleb*
[d] 30 Hebrew; some Septuagint manuscripts (see also 1 Chron. 11:32) *Hurai*

23:13 *harvest time.* See 11:1 and note. The circumstances of this event suggest that it happened shortly after David had fled from Saul, when men first began to gather to his cause (see 1Sa 22:1–4), or shortly after his conquest of Jerusalem (see 2Sa 5:17–18). *three.* Probably not the same as the three mighty men of v. 9. *thirty chief warriors.* See vv. 23–24,39. *cave of Adullam.* See 1Sa 22:1. *Rephaim.* See 5:18.
23:14 *stronghold.* See note on 1Sa 22:4.
23:15–17 See note on 1Ch 11:15–19.
23:15 *Bethlehem.* David's hometown (1Sa 17:58).
23:18 *Abishai.* See 10:10,14; 18:2; see also note on 1Sa 26:6. *Three.* Presumably those referred to in vv. 13–17.

23:20 *Benaiah son of Jehoiada.* Commander of the Kerethites and Pelethites (see 8:18 and note; 20:23; see also v. 23 below) and of the division of troops for the third month of the year (1Ch 27:5). He supported Solomon's succession to the throne (1Ki 1–2) and eventually replaced Joab as commander of the army (1Ki 2:35).
23:24 *Thirty.* At least 30 names are listed in vv. 24–39. Since the three of vv. 13–17 are also included in the Thirty (see v. 13), the total number of warriors mentioned is at least 33. 1Ch 11:41–47 lists 16 additional names for this group and apparently includes the names of replacements for vacancies when a warrior either dropped out or died. *Asahel.* See 2:18–23.

23:34 *b* S Dt 3:14
c S 2Sa 11:3
d S 2Sa 15:12
23:35 *e* S Jos 12:22
23:36 *f* S 1Sa 14:47
23:37 *g* S Jos 9:17
23:38 *h* 1Ch 2:53
23:39 *i* 2Sa 11:3
24:1 *j* S Jos 9:15
k Job 1:6; Zec 3:1
l S Ex 30:12;
1Ch 27:23
24:2 *m* S 2Sa 20:23
n S 2Sa 3:10
o 2Ch 2:17; 17:14;
25:5
24:3 *p* S 2Sa 2:18
q S Dt 1:11
24:5 *r* S Jos 13:9
s S Nu 21:32
24:6 *t* S Ge 10:19;
Jdg 1:31
24:7 *u* S Jos 19:29
v S Ex 3:8 *w* Ge 21:31
x S Dt 1:7
24:9 *y* S Nu 1:44-46

Jonathan [33]son of[a] Shammah the Hararite,
Ahiam son of Sharar[b] the Hararite,
[34] Eliphelet son of Ahasbai the Maakathite,[b]
Eliam[c] son of Ahithophel[d] the Gilonite,
[35] Hezro the Carmelite,[e]
Paarai the Arbite,
[36] Igal son of Nathan from Zobah,[f]
the son of Hagri,[c]
[37] Zelek the Ammonite,
Naharai the Beerothite,[g] the armor-bearer of Joab son of Zeruiah,
[38] Ira the Ithrite,[h]
Gareb the Ithrite
[39] and Uriah[i] the Hittite.
There were thirty-seven in all.

DAVID ENROLLS THE FIGHTING MEN
24:1–17pp — 1Ch 21:1–17

24 Again[j] the anger of the LORD burned against Israel,[k] and he incited David against them, saying, "Go and take a census of[l] Israel and Judah."

[2] So the king said to Joab[m] and the army commanders[d] with him, "Go throughout the tribes of Israel from Dan to Beersheba[n] and enroll[o] the fighting men, so that I may know how many there are."

[3] But Joab[p] replied to the king, "May the LORD your God multiply the troops a hundred times over,[q] and may the eyes of my lord the king see it. But why does my lord the king want to do such a thing?"

[4] The king's word, however, overruled Joab and the army commanders; so they left the presence of the king to enroll the fighting men of Israel.

[5] After crossing the Jordan, they camped near Aroer,[r] south of the town in the gorge, and then went through Gad and on to Jazer. [s] [6] They went to Gilead and the region of Tahtim Hodshi, and on to Dan Jaan and around toward Sidon. [t] [7] Then they went toward the fortress of Tyre[u] and all the towns of the Hivites[v] and Canaanites. Finally, they went on to Beersheba[w] in the Negev[x] of Judah.

[8] After they had gone through the entire land, they came back to Jerusalem at the end of nine months and twenty days.

[9] Joab reported the number of the fighting men to the king: In Israel there were eight hundred thousand able-bodied men who could handle a sword, and in Judah five hundred thousand.[y]

---

a 33 Some Septuagint manuscripts (see also 1 Chron. 11:34); Hebrew does not have *son of.*
b 33 Hebrew; some Septuagint manuscripts (see also 1 Chron. 11:35) *Sakar*   *c 36* Some Septuagint manuscripts (see also 1 Chron. 11:38); Hebrew *Haggadi*   *d 2* Septuagint (see also verse 4 and 1 Chron. 21:2); Hebrew *Joab the army commander*

23:34 *Eliam.* Father of Bathsheba (see 11:3 and note) and son of David's counselor Ahithophel, who joined in Absalom's conspiracy (see 15:12 and note; 16:20–23; 17:1–23).

23:39 *Uriah.* Husband of Bathsheba (see 11:3–27; see also notes on 11:17; 12:7).

A C **24:1** *Again.* The previous occasion may have been the famine of 21:1. *the anger of the LORD burned against Israel.* The specific reason for the Lord's displeasure is not stated. Because the anger is said to be directed against Israel rather than David, some have concluded that it was occasioned by the widespread support among the people for the rebellions of Absalom and Sheba against David (see 15:12; 17:11,24–26; 18:7; 20:1–2), the divinely chosen and anointed theocratic king. This would mean that the events of this chapter are to be placed chronologically shortly after those of chs. 15–20 and so after 980 B.C. (see note on 15:7). *the LORD ... incited David against them.* 1Ch 21:1 says that Satan inspired David to take the census. Although Scripture is clear that God does not cause anyone to sin (Jas 1:13–14), it is also clear that the evil acts of people and Satan are under God's sovereign control (see Ex 4:21; 7:3; 9:12; 10:1,20,27; 11:10; 14:4,8; Jos 11:20; 1Ki 22:22–23; Job 1:12; 2:6; Eze 3:20; 14:9; Ac 4:28). *take a census of Israel and Judah.* David's military census (see vv. 2–3) does not

appear to have been prompted by any immediate external threat. Since he wanted to "know how many there are" (v. 2), it is evident that his action was motivated by pride in the size of the empire he had acquired, by reliance for his security on the size of the reserve of manpower he could muster in an emergency or, still more likely, by both. The mere taking of a census was hardly sinful (see Nu 1:2–3; 26:2–4), but in this instance it represented an unwarranted glorying in and dependence upon human power rather than the Lord (not much different from Israel's initial desire to have a king for its security; see 1Sa 8–12). The act was uncharacteristic of David (see 22:2–4,47–51; 1Sa 17:26,37, 45–47).

24:2,15 *from Dan to Beersheba.* See note on 1Sa 3:20.

24:3 *But why ...?* David's directive does not go unchallenged. The fact that he does not answer suggests that he knew his reasons were highly questionable. In any event, Joab's challenge renders David the more guilty.

24:5–8 The military census was begun in southern Transjordan and moved northward, then west across the Jordan, moving from north to south.

24:9 *eight hundred thousand ... five hundred thousand.* These figures differ from those of 1Ch 21:5 (see notes on 1Ch 21:5–6).

¹⁰David was conscience-stricken ᶻ after he had counted the fighting men, and he said to the Lord, "I have sinned ᵃ greatly in what I have done. Now, Lord, I beg you, take away the guilt of your servant. I have done a very foolish thing. ᵇ"

¹¹Before David got up the next morning, the word of the Lord had come to Gad ᶜ the prophet, David's seer: ᵈ ¹²"Go and tell David, 'This is what the Lord says: I am giving you three options. Choose one of them for me to carry out against you.' "

¹³So Gad went to David and said to him, "Shall there come on you three ᵃ years of famine ᵉ in your land? Or three months of fleeing from your enemies while they pursue you? Or three days of plague ᶠ in your land? Now then, think it over and decide how I should answer the one who sent me."

¹⁴David said to Gad, "I am in deep distress. Let us fall into the hands of the Lord, for his mercy ᵍ is great; but do not let me fall into human hands."

¹⁵So the Lord sent a plague on Israel from that morning until the end of the time designated, and seventy thousand of the people from Dan to Beersheba died. ʰ ¹⁶When the angel stretched out his hand to destroy Jerusalem, the Lord relented ⁱ concerning the disaster and said to the angel who was afflicting the people, "Enough! Withdraw your hand." The angel of the Lord ʲ was then at the threshing floor of Araunah the Jebusite.

¹⁷When David saw the angel who was striking down the people, he said to the Lord, "I have sinned; I, the shepherd, ᵇ have done wrong. These are but sheep. ᵏ What have they done? ⁱ Let your hand fall on me and my family." ᵐ

DAVID BUILDS AN ALTAR
24:18–25pp — 1Ch 21:18–26

¹⁸On that day Gad went to David and said to him, "Go up and build an altar to the Lord on the threshing floor of Araunah ⁿ the Jebusite." ¹⁹So David went up, as the Lord had commanded through Gad. ²⁰When Araunah looked and saw the king and his officials coming toward him, he went out and bowed down before the king with his face to the ground.

²¹Araunah said, "Why has my lord the king come to his servant?"

"To buy your threshing floor," David answered, "so I can build an altar to the Lord, that the plague on the people may be stopped." ᵒ

²²Araunah said to David, "Let my lord the king take whatever he wishes and offer it up. Here are oxen ᵖ for the burnt offering, and here are threshing sledges and ox yokes for the wood. ²³Your Majesty, Araunah ᶜ gives �q all this to the king." Araunah also said to him, "May the Lord your God accept you."

²⁴But the king replied to Araunah, "No, I insist on paying you for it. I will not sacrifice to the Lord my God burnt offerings that cost me nothing." ʳ

So David bought the threshing floor and the oxen and paid fifty shekels ᵈ ˢ of silver for them. ²⁵David built an altar ᵗ to the Lord there and sacrificed burnt offerings and fellowship offerings. Then the Lord answered his prayer ᵘ in behalf of the land, and the plague on Israel was stopped.

ᵃ 13 Septuagint (see also 1 Chron. 21:12); Hebrew *seven*   ᵇ 17 Dead Sea Scrolls and Septuagint; Masoretic Text does not have *the shepherd.*   ᶜ 23 Some Hebrew manuscripts and Septuagint; most Hebrew manuscripts *King Araunah*   ᵈ 24 That is, about 1 1/4 pounds or about 575 grams

24:10 *I have sinned greatly.* See note on v. 1.

24:11 *Gad the prophet, David's seer.* See notes on 1Sa 9:9; 22:5.

24:12 *Go and tell David.* See 12:1 and note. *three options.* The three alternative judgments (v. 13) were all included in the curses that Moses said would come on God's people when they failed to adhere to their covenant obligations (see Dt 28:15–25).

24:14 *not ... into human hands.* David, who knew both God and war, knew that even in his anger God is more merciful than humans let loose in the rampages of war (see Ps 30:5). **24:16** *angel.* Angels appear elsewhere in Scripture as instruments of God's judgment (see Ex 33:2; 2Ki 19:35; Ps 35:5–6; 78:49; Mt 13:41; Ac 12:23). *the Lord relented.* See note on 1Sa 15:29. *threshing floor of Araunah.* Located on Mount Moriah, immediately north of David's city and overlooking it. Later it would become the site of the temple (see 1Ch 21:28—22:1; 2Ch 3:1). *Jebusite.* See note on 5:6.

24:17 *Let your hand fall on me and my family.* Although the people of Israel were not without guilt (see v. 1), Da-

vid assumes full blame for his own act and acknowledges his responsibility as king for the well-being of the Lord's people (see 5:2; 7:7–8).

24:19 *as the Lord had commanded.* The Lord himself appointed the atoning sacrifice in answer to David's prayer.

24:21 *To buy your threshing floor.* David does not simply expropriate the property for his royal purposes (see 1Sa 8:14).

24:22 *threshing sledges.* See Am 1:3 and note on Ru 1:22.

24:24 *burnt offerings.* See Lev 1:1–17. *David bought the threshing floor.* Thus the later site of the temple (see note on v. 16) became the royal property of the house of David. *and the oxen.* David's haste could not wait for oxen to be brought some distance from his own herds. *fifty shekels.* See note on 1Ch 21:25.

24:25 *fellowship offerings.* See note on 1Sa 11:15. Reconciliation and restoration of covenant fellowship were obtained by the king's repentance, intercessory prayer and the offering of sacrifices. *the Lord answered his prayer in behalf of the land.* See note on 21:14.

24:10 ᶻ S 1Sa 24:5
ᵃ Nu 22:34
ᵇ S Nu 12:11
24:11 ᶜ S 1Sa 22:5
ᵈ 1Sa 9:9
24:13 ᵉ Dt 28:38-42, 48; S 32:24; Eze 14:21 ᶠ S Ex 5:3; S 30:12; S Lev 26:25; Dt 28:21-22, 27-28, 35
24:14 ᵍ Ne 9:28; Ps 4:1; 51:1; 86:5; 103:8,13; 119:132; 130:4; Isa 54:7; 55:7; Jer 33:8; 42:12; Da 9:9
24:15 ʰ 1Ch 27:24
24:16 ⁱ S Ge 6:6
ʲ S Ge 16:7; S 19:13; S Ex 12:23; Ac 12:23
24:17 ᵏ Ps 74:1; 100:3; Jer 49:20
ⁱ S Ge 18:23
ᵐ Jnh 1:12
24:18 ⁿ Ge 22:2; 2Ch 3:1
24:21 ᵒ Nu 16:44-50
24:22 ᵖ S 1Sa 6:14
24:23 �q Ge 23:11
24:24 ʳ Mal 1:13-14
ˢ S Ge 23:16
24:25 ᵗ S 1Sa 7:17
ᵘ 2Sa 21:14

TITLE

1 KINGS

INTRODUCTION

1 and 2 Kings (like 1 and 2 Samuel and 1 and 2 Chronicles) are actually one literary work, called in Hebrew tradition simply "Kings." The division of this work into two books was introduced by the translators of the Septuagint (the pre-Christian Greek translation of the OT) and subsequently followed in the Latin Vulgate (c. A.D. 400) and most modern versions. In 1448 the division into two sections also appeared in a Hebrew manuscript and was perpetuated in later printed editions of the Hebrew text. Both the Septuagint and the Latin Vulgate further designated Samuel and Kings in a way that emphasized the relationship of these two works (Septuagint: First, Second, Third and Fourth Book of Kingdoms; Latin Vulgate: First, Second, Third and Fourth Kings). Together Samuel and Kings relate the whole history of the monarchy, from its rise under the ministry of Samuel to its fall at the hands of the Babylonians.

The division between 1 and 2 Kings has been made at a somewhat arbitrary and yet appropriate place, shortly after the deaths of Ahab of the northern kingdom (1Ki 22:37) and Jehoshaphat of the southern kingdom (22:50). Placing the division at this point causes the account of the reign of Ahaziah of Israel to overlap the end of 1 Kings (22:51–53) and the beginning of 2 Kings (ch. 1). The same is true of the narration of the ministry of Elijah, which for the most part appears in 1 Kings (chs. 17–19). However, his final act of judgment and the passing of his cloak to Elisha at the moment of his ascension to heaven in a whirlwind are contained in 2 Kings (1:1—2:17).

AUTHOR, SOURCES AND DATE

There is little conclusive evidence as to the identity of the author of 1,2 Kings. Although Jewish tradition credits Jeremiah, few today accept this as likely. Whoever the author was, it is clear that he was familiar with the book of Deuteronomy—as were many of Israel's prophets. It is also clear that he used a variety of sources in compiling his history of the monarchy. Three such sources are named: "the book of the annals of Solomon" (11:41), "the book of the annals of the kings of Israel" (14:19) and "the book of the annals of the kings of Judah" (14:29). It is likely that other written sources were also employed (such as those mentioned in Chronicles; see below).

Although some scholars have concluded that the three sources specifically cited in 1,2 Kings are to be viewed as official court annals from the royal archives in Jerusalem and Samaria, this is by no means certain. It seems at least questionable whether official court annals would have included details of conspiracies such as those referred to in 16:20; 2Ki 15:15. It is also questionable whether official court annals would have been readily accessible for public scrutiny, as the author clearly implies in his references to them. Such considerations have led some scholars to conclude that these sources were probably records of the reigns of the kings of Israel and Judah compiled by the succession of Israel's prophets spanning the kingdom period. 1,2 Chronicles makes reference to a number of such writings: "the records of Samuel the seer, the records of Nathan the prophet and the records of Gad the seer" (1Ch 29:29), "the prophecy of Ahijah the Shilonite" and "the visions of Iddo the seer" (2Ch 9:29), "the records of Shemaiah the prophet" (2Ch 12:15), "the annals of Jehu son of Hanani" (2Ch 20:34), "the annotations on the book of the kings" (2Ch 24:27), the "events of Uzziah's reign . . . recorded by the prophet Isaiah son of Amoz" (2Ch 26:22; see also 2Ch 32:32)—and there may have been others. It is most likely, for example, that for the ministries of Elijah and Elisha the author depended on a prophetic source (perhaps from the eighth century) that had drawn up an account of those two prophets in which they were already compared with Moses and Joshua.

Some scholars place the date of composition of 1,2 Kings in the time subsequent to Jehoiachin's release from prison (562 B.C.; 2Ki 25:27–30) and prior to the end of the Babylonian exile in 538. This position is challenged by others on the basis of statements in 1,2 Kings that speak of certain things in the preexilic period that are said to have continued in existence "to this day" (see, e.g., 8:8, the poles used to carry the ark; 9:20–21, conscripted labor; 12:19, Israel in rebellion against the house of David; 2Ki 8:22, Edom in rebellion against the kingdom of Judah). From such statements it is argued that the writer must have been a person living in Judah in the preexilic period rather than in Babylon in postexilic times. If this argument is accepted, one must conclude that the original book was composed about the time of the death of Josiah and that the material pertaining to the time subsequent to his reign was added during the exile c. 550. While this "two-edition" viewpoint is possible, it rests largely on the "to this day" statements.

An alternative is to understand these statements as those of the original source used by the author rather than statements of the author himself. A comparison of 2Ch 5:9 with 1Ki 8:8 suggests that this is a legitimate conclusion. Chronicles is clearly a postexilic writing, yet the wording of the statement concerning the poles used to carry the ark ("they are still there today") is the same in Chronicles as it is in Kings. Probably the Chronicler was simply quoting his source, namely, 1Ki 8:8. There is no reason that the author of 1,2 Kings could not have done the same thing in quoting from his earlier sources. This explanation allows for positing a single author living in exile and using the source materials at his disposal.

THEME: KINGSHIP AND COVENANT

1,2 Kings contains no explicit statement of purpose or theme. Reflection on its content, however, reveals that the author has selected and arranged his material in a manner that provides a sequel to the history found in 1,2 Samuel—a history of kingship regulated by covenant. In general, 1,2 Kings describes the history of the kings of Israel and Judah in the light of God's covenants. The guiding thesis of the book is that the welfare of Israel and her kings depended on their submission to and reliance on Israel's covenant God—their obedience to the Sinaitic covenant regulations and their faithful response to God's prophets.

B It is clearly not the author's intention to present a social, political and economic history of Israel's monarchy in accordance with the principles of modern historiography. The author repeatedly refers the reader to other sources for more detailed information about the reigns of the various kings (see, e.g., 11:41; 14:19,29; 15:7,31; 16:5,14,20,27), and he gives a covenantal rather than a social or political or economic assessment of their reigns. From the standpoint of a political historian, Omri would be considered one of the more important rulers in the northern kingdom. He established a powerful dynasty and made Samaria the capital city. According to the Moabite Stone (see chart, p. xxiv), Omri was the ruler who subjugated the Moabites to the northern kingdom. Long after Omri's death, the Assyrian king Shalmaneser III referred to Jehu as the "son of Omri" (either mistakenly or merely in accordance with their literary conventions when speaking of a later king of a realm). Yet in spite of Omri's political importance, his reign is dismissed in six verses (16:23–28) with the statement that he "did evil in the eyes of the LORD and sinned more than all those before him" (16:25). Similarly, the reign of Jeroboam II, who presided over the northern kingdom during the time of its greatest political and economic power, is treated only briefly (2Ki 14:23–29).

Another example of the writer's covenantal rather than merely political or economic interest can be seen in the description of the reign of Josiah of Judah. Nothing is said about the early years of his reign, but a detailed description is given of the reformation and renewal of the covenant that he promoted in his 18th year as king (2Ki 22:3—23:28). Nor is anything said of the motives leading Josiah to oppose Pharaoh Necho of Egypt at Megiddo, or of the major shift in geopolitical power from Assyria to Babylon that was connected with this incident (see notes on 2Ki 23:29–30).

It becomes apparent, then, that the kings who receive the most attention in 1,2 Kings are those during whose reigns there was either notable deviation from or affirmation of the covenant (or significant interaction between a king and God's prophet; see below). Ahab, son of Omri, is an example of the former (16:29—22:39). His reign is given extensive treatment, not so much because of its extraordinary political importance but because of the serious threat to covenant fidelity and continuity that arose in the northern kingdom during his reign. Ultimately the pagan influence of Ahab's wife Jezebel through Ahab's daughter Athaliah (whether she was Jezebel's daughter is unknown) nearly led to the extermination of the house of David in Judah (see 2Ki 11:1–3).

B Manasseh (2Ki 21:1–18) is an example of a similar sort. Here again it is deviation from the covenant that is emphasized in the account of his reign rather than political features, such as involvement in the Assyrian-Egyptian conflict (mentioned in Assyrian records but not in 2 Kings). The extreme apostasy characterizing Manasseh's reign made exile for Judah inevitable (2Ki 21:10–15; 23:26–27; Jer 15:4).

On the positive side, Hezekiah (2Ki 18:1—20:21) and Josiah (2Ki 22:1—23:29) are given extensive treatment because of their involvement in covenant renewal. These are the only two kings given unqualified approval by the writer for their loyalty to the Lord (2Ki 18:3; 22:2). It is noteworthy that all the kings of the northern kingdom are said to have done evil in the eyes of the Lord and walked in the ways of Jeroboam, who caused Israel to sin (see, e.g., 16:26,31; 22:52; 2Ki 3:3; 10:29). It was Jeroboam who established the golden calf worship at Bethel and Dan shortly after the division of the kingdom (see 12:26–33; 13:1–6).

While the writer depicts Israel's obedience or disobedience to the Sinai covenant as decisive for her historical destiny, he also recognizes the far-reaching historical significance of the Davidic covenant, which promised that David's dynasty would endure forever. This is particularly noticeable in references to the "lamp" that the Lord had promised David (see 11:36 and note; 15:4; 2Ki 8:19; see also note on 2Sa 21:17). It also appears in more general references to the promise to David (8:20,25) and its consequences for specific historical developments in Judah's later history (11:12–13,32; 2Ki 19:34; 20:6). In addition, the writer uses the life and reign of David as a standard by which the lives of later kings are measured (see, e.g., 9:4; 11:4,6, 33,38; 14:8; 15:3,5,11; 2Ki 16:2; 18:3; 22:2).

Another prominent feature of the narratives of 1,2 Kings is the emphasis on the relationship between prophecy and fulfillment in the historical developments of the monarchy. On at least 11 occasions a prophecy is recorded that is later said to have been fulfilled (see, e.g., 2Sa 7:13 and 1Ki 8:20; 1Ki 11:29–39 and 1Ki 12:15; 1Ki 13 and 2Ki 23:16–18). The result of this emphasis is that the history of the kingdom is not presented as a chain of chance occurrences or the mere interplay of human actions but as the unfolding of Israel's historical destiny under the guidance of an omniscient and omnipotent God—Israel's covenant Lord, who rules all history in accordance with his sovereign purposes (see 8:56; 2Ki 10:10).

The author also stresses the importance of the prophets themselves in their role as official emissaries from the court of Israel's covenant Lord, the Great King to whom Israel and her king were bound in service through the covenant. The Lord sent a long succession of such prophets to call king and people back to covenant loyalty (2Ki 17:13). For the most part their warnings and exhortations fell on deaf ears. Many of these prophets are mentioned in the narratives of 1,2 Kings (see, e.g., Ahijah, 11:29–40; 14:5–18; Shemaiah, 12:22–24; Micaiah, 22:8–28; Jonah, 2Ki 14:25; Isaiah, 2Ki 19:1–7,20–34; Huldah, 2Ki 22:14–20), but particular attention is given to the ministries of Elijah and Elisha (1Ki 17–19; 2Ki 1–13).

C Reflection on these features of 1,2 Kings suggests that it was written to explain to a people in exile that the reason for their condition of humiliation was their stubborn persistence in breaking the covenant. In bringing the exile upon his people, God, after much patience, imposed the curses of the covenant, which had stood as a warning to them from the beginning (see Lev 26:27–45; Dt 28:64–68). This is made explicit with respect to the captivity of the northern kingdom in 2Ki 17:7–23; 18:9–12, and with respect to the southern kingdom in 2Ki 21:12–15. The reformation under Josiah in the southern kingdom is viewed as too little, too late (see 2Ki 23:26–27; 24:3).

The books of Kings, then, provide a retrospective analysis of Israel's history. They explain the reasons both for the destruction of Samaria and Jerusalem and their respective kingdoms and for the bitter experience of being forced into exile. This does not mean, however, that there is no hope for the future. The writer consistently keeps the promise to David in view as a basis on which Israel in exile may look to the future with hope rather than with despair. In this connection the final four verses of 2 Kings, reporting Jehoiachin's release from prison in Babylon and his elevation to a place of honor in the court there (2Ki 25:27–30), take on added significance. The future remains open for a new work of the Lord in faithfulness to his promise to the house of David.

It is important to note that, although the author was undoubtedly a Judahite exile, and although the northern kingdom had been dispersed for well over a century and a half at the time of his writing, the scope of his concern was all Israel—the whole covenant people. Neither he nor the prophets (see Isa 10:20–21; 11:11–13; Jer 31; Eze 48:1–29; Hos 11:8–11; Am 9:11–15; Zec 9:10–13) viewed the division of the Israelite kingdom as a divine rejection of the ten tribes, nor did they see the earlier exile of the northern kingdom as a final exclusion of the northern tribes from Israel's future. As a matter of fact, many from the north had fled south during the Assyrian invasions, so that a significant remnant of the northern tribes lived on in the kingdom of Judah and shared in its continuing history.

CHRONOLOGY

1,2 Kings presents the reader with abundant chronological data. Not only is the length of the reign of each king given, but during the period of the divided kingdom the beginning of the reign of each king is synchronized with the regnal year of the ruling king in the opposite kingdom. Often additional data, such as the age of the ruler at the time of his accession, are also provided.

B By integrating Biblical data with those derived from Assyrian chronological records, the year 853 B.C. can be fixed as the year of Ahab's death and 841 as the year Jehu began to reign. The years in which Ahab and Jehu had contacts with Shalmaneser III of Assyria can also be given definite dates (by means of astronomical calculations based on an Assyrian reference to a solar eclipse). With these fixed points, it is then possible to work both forward and backward in the lines of the kings of Israel and Judah to give dates for each king. By the same means it can be determined that the division of the kingdom occurred in 930, that Samaria fell to the Assyrians in 722–721 and that Jerusalem fell to the Babylonians in 586.

The synchronistic data correlating the reigns of the kings of Israel and Judah present some knotty problems, which have long been considered nearly insoluble. In more recent times, most of these problems have been resolved in a satisfactory way through recognizing such possibilities as overlapping reigns, coregencies of sons with their fathers, differences in the time of the year in which the reign of a king officially began, and differences in the way a king's first year was reckoned (e.g., see notes on 15:33; 2Ki 8:25; see also charts, pp. 512–513 and p. 482).

CONTENT

1,2 Kings narrates the history of Israel during the period of the monarchy from the closing days of David's rule until the time of the Babylonian exile. After an extensive account of Solomon's reign, the narrative relates the division of the kingdom and then presents an interrelated account of developments within the two kingdoms. In this account, special attention is given to the ministries of Elijah and Elisha in the northern kingdom, with almost a third of the book (nearly equal to the amount of narrative given to Solomon's reign) devoted to God's efforts through his prophets to turn that kingdom away from its apostasies back to covenant faithfulness (see note on 1Ki 12:25—2Ki 17:41).

Kingship in the northern kingdom was plagued with instability and violence. Twenty rulers represented nine different dynasties during the approximately 210 years from the division of the kingdom in 930 B.C. to the fall of Samaria in 722–721. In the southern kingdom there were also 20 rulers, but these were all descendants of David (except Athaliah, whose usurping of the throne interrupted the sequence for a few years) and spanned a period of about 345 years from the division of the kingdom until the fall of Jerusalem in 586.

OUTLINE

1,2 Kings can be broadly outlined by relating its contents to the major historical periods it describes and to the ministries of Elijah and Elisha.

B. Manasseh (21:1–18)
C. Amon (21:19–26)
D. Josiah (22:1—23:30)
  1. Repair of the temple; discovery of the Book of the Law (ch. 22)
  2. Renewal of the covenant; end of Josiah's reign (23:1–30)
E. Jehoahaz Exiled to Egypt (23:31–35)
F. Jehoiakim: First Babylonian Deportation (23:36—24:7)
G. Jehoiachin: Second Babylonian Deportation (24:8–17)
H. Zedekiah: Third Babylonian Deportation (24:18—25:21)
I. Removal of the Remnant to Egypt (25:22–26)
J. Elevation of Jehoiachin in Babylon (25:27–30)

CHRONOLOGY OF FOREIGN KINGS

This is a chronology of selected foreign kings mentioned in this study Bible.

ASSYRIA	Tiglath-Pileser III	745–727*
	Shalmaneser V	727–722
	Sargon II	721–705
	Sennacherib	705–681
	Esarhaddon	681–669
	Ashurbanipal	669–627
BABYLONIA	Nebuchadnezzar II	605–562
	Nabonidus	556–539
	Belshazzar	*Coregency with Nabonidus* 553(?)–539
PERSIA	Cyrus the Great	559–530
	Cambyses	530–522
	Darius I the Great	522–486
	Xerxes (Ahasuerus)	486–465
	Artaxerxes I	465–424
	Darius II	423–404

*All dates are B.C. and are those of the kings' reigns.

ADONIJAH SETS HIMSELF UP AS KING

1 When King David was very old, he could not keep warm even when they put covers over him. ²So his attendants said to him, "Let us look for a young virgin to serve the king and take care of him. She can lie beside him so that our lord the king may keep warm."

³Then they searched throughout Israel for a beautiful girl and found Abishag, *a* a Shunammite, *b* and brought her to the king. ⁴The girl was very beautiful; she took care of the king and waited on him, but the king had no sexual relations with her.

⁵Now Adonijah, *c* whose mother was Haggith, put himself forward and said, "I will be king." So he got chariots *d* and horses*a* ready, with fifty men to run ahead of him. ⁶(His father had never rebuked *e* him by asking, "Why do you behave as you do?" He was also very handsome and was born next after Absalom.)

⁷Adonijah conferred with Joab *f* son of Zeruiah and with Abiathar *g* the priest, and they gave him their support. ⁸But Zadok *h* the priest, Benaiah *i* son of Jehoiada, Nathan *j* the prophet, Shimei *k* and Rei and David's special guard *l* did not join Adonijah.

⁹Adonijah then sacrificed sheep, cattle and fattened calves at the Stone of Zoheleth near En Rogel. *m* He invited all his brothers, the king's sons, *n* and all the royal officials of Judah, ¹⁰but he did not invite *o* Nathan the prophet or Benaiah or the special guard or his brother Solomon. *p*

¹¹Then Nathan asked Bathsheba, *q* Solomon's mother, "Have you not heard that Adonijah, *r* the son of Haggith, has become king, and our lord David knows nothing about it? ¹²Now then, let me advise *s* you how you can save your own life and the life of your son Solomon. ¹³Go in to King David and say to him, 'My lord the king, did you not swear *t* to me your servant: "Surely Solomon your son shall be king after me, and he will sit on my throne"? Why then has Adonijah become king?' ¹⁴While you are still there talking to the king, I will come in and add my word to what you have said."

¹⁵So Bathsheba went to see the aged king in his room, where Abishag *u* the Shunammite was attending him. ¹⁶Bathsheba bowed down, prostrating herself before the king.

"What is it you want?" the king asked.

---

a 5 Or charioteers

1:3 *a* ver 15;
  S 2Sa 3:7; 1Ki 2:17,22
  b S Jos 19:18
1:5 *c* S 2Sa 3:4
  d S 1Sa 8:11
1:6 *e* 1Sa 3:13
1:7 *f* S 2Sa 2:13,18
  g S 1Sa 22:20
1:8 *h* S 1Sa 2:35;
  S 2Sa 8:17
  i S 2Sa 8:18
  j S 2Sa 7:2 *k* 1Ki 4:18
  l 2Sa 23:8
1:9 *m* S 2Sa 17:17
  n 1Ch 29:24
1:10 *o* ver 26
  p S 2Sa 12:24
1:11 *q* 2Sa 12:24
  r S 2Sa 3:4
1:12 *s* Pr 15:22
1:13 *t* ver 17,30
1:15 *u* S ver 3

1:1—12:24 The narrative of the Solomonic era is an exquisite example of literary inversion, in this case consisting of nine sections. The first and last are parallel, as well as the second and eighth, etc.—and the fifth section, which occupies the central position in the structure, is the longest of the nine and describes Solomon's building projects (see Introduction: Outline).
1:1 *very old.* 2Sa 5:4 indicates that David died at about 70 years of age (cf. 1Ki 2:11).
1:2 *may keep warm.* The Jewish historian Josephus (first century A.D.) and the Greek physician Galen (second century A.D.) both refer to the ancient medical practice of using a healthy person's body to provide warmth for one who is ill.
1:3 *Shunammite.* Abishag came from Shunem (2Ki 4:8; Jos 19:18; 1Sa 28:4), located near the plain of Jezreel in the tribal territory of Issachar.
1:4 *had no sexual relations with her.* Significant in connection with Adonijah's request to be given Abishag as his wife after the death of David (see notes on 2:17,22).
1:5 *Adonijah.* The fourth son of David (see 2Sa 3:4), who was at this time approximately 35 years of age. It is likely that he was the oldest surviving son of David (see note on 2Sa 13:28; see also 2Sa 18:14). *put himself forward.* A unilateral attempt to usurp the throne, bypassing King David's right to designate his own successor (Adonijah must at least have known that his father favored Solomon; see v. 10). If successful, it would have thwarted God's and David's choice of Solomon (see vv. 13,17,30; 1Ch 22:9–10; see also note on 2Sa 12:25). *fifty men to run ahead of him.* Adonijah here follows the example of Absalom before him (see note on 2Sa 15:1).
1:6 *never rebuked him.* David appears to have been consistently negligent in disciplining his sons (see notes on 2Sa 13:21; 14:33). *very handsome.* Attractive physical appearance was an important asset to an aspirant to the throne (see 1Sa 9:2; 16:12; 2Sa 14:25).

1:7 *Joab son of Zeruiah.* See notes on 1Sa 26:6; 2Sa 2:13; 19:13; 20:10,23. Joab's alignment with Adonijah may have been motivated by a struggle for power with Benaiah (see v. 8; 2Sa 8:18; 20:23; 23:20–23). Joab held his position more by his standing with the army than by the favor and confidence of David (see 2:5–6). *Abiathar the priest.* See note on 2Sa 8:17.
1:8 *Zadok the priest.* See note on 2Sa 8:17. *Benaiah son of Jehoiada.* See note on 2Sa 23:20. *Nathan the prophet.* See 2Sa 12:1–25. *Shimei.* Not the Shimei of 2:8,46; 2Sa 16:5–8; perhaps the same as Shimei, son of Ela (4:18). *Rei.* Or possibly "his friends." There is no other OT reference to Rei if taken as a proper name. *David's special guard.* See 2Sa 23:8–39.
1:9 *Adonijah then sacrificed.* Here also (see note on v. 5) Adonijah followed the example of Absalom (see 2Sa 15:7–12). *En Rogel.* Means "the spring of Rogel"; located just south of Jerusalem in the Kidron Valley. Apparently the site of a spring had some kind of symbolic significance for the business at hand (see v. 33 and note).
1:11 *Bathsheba, Solomon's mother.* The queen mother held an important and influential position in the royal court (see 2:19; 15:13; 2Ki 10:13; 2Ch 15:16). *has become king.* Although the preceding narrative does not relate the actual proclamation of Adonijah's kingship, it can be assumed (see v. 25; 2:15; cf. 2Sa 15:10).
1:12 *save your own life and the life of your son Solomon.* It was common in the ancient Near East for a usurper to liquidate all potential claimants to the throne in an attempt to secure his own position (see 15:29; 2Ki 10:11; 11:1).
1:13 *did you not swear to me ...?* Although 2 Samuel does not record David's oath concerning the succession of Solomon, it does suggest that Solomon was the son through whom the Lord's promise to David for an eternal dynasty would be carried forward (see note on v. 5).
1:15 *Shunammite.* See note on v. 3.

1:17 ᵛS ver 13
1:19 ʷver 9
1:21 ˣS Ge 15:15;
1Ki 2:10
1:26 ʸver 10
1:29 ᶻS 2Sa 4:9
1:30 ᵃS ver 13;
1Ch 23:1
1:32 ᵇS 1Sa 2:35
1:33 ᶜJdg 10:4;
Zec 9:9 ᵈver 38;
2Ch 32:30; 33:14
1:34 ᵉS 1Sa 2:35;
10:1 ᶠS 2Sa 15:10
1:37 ᵍJos 1:5,17
ʰver 47
1:38 ⁱver 8
ʲS 1Sa 30:14;
S 2Sa 15:18 ᵏS ver 33
1:39 ˡS Ex 29:7;
S 1Sa 10:1; 2Ki 11:12;
Ps 89:20 ᵐS Ex 26:1;
S 27:21 ⁿS 2Sa 15:10;
2Ki 11:14 ᵒver 34;
Nu 23:21; Ps 47:5;
Zec 9:9

¹⁷She said to him, "My lord, you yourself swore ᵛto me your servant by the Lᴏʀᴅ your God: 'Solomon your son shall be king after me, and he will sit on my throne.' ¹⁸But now Adonijah has become king, and you, my lord the king, do not know about it. ¹⁹He has sacrificed ʷ great numbers of cattle, fattened calves, and sheep, and has invited all the king's sons, Abiathar the priest and Joab the commander of the army, but he has not invited Solomon your servant. ²⁰My lord the king, the eyes of all Israel are on you, to learn from you who will sit on the throne of my lord the king after him. ²¹Otherwise, as soon as my lord the king is laid to rest ˣ with his ancestors, I and my son Solomon will be treated as criminals."

²²While she was still speaking with the king, Nathan the prophet arrived. ²³And the king was told, "Nathan the prophet is here." So he went before the king and bowed with his face to the ground.

²⁴Nathan said, "Have you, my lord the king, declared that Adonijah shall be king after you, and that he will sit on your throne? ²⁵Today he has gone down and sacrificed great numbers of cattle, fattened calves, and sheep. He has invited all the king's sons, the commanders of the army and Abiathar the priest. Right now they are eating and drinking with him and saying, 'Long live King Adonijah!' ²⁶But me your servant, and Zadok the priest, and Benaiah son of Jehoiada, and your servant Solomon he did not invite. ʸ ²⁷Is this something my lord the king has done without letting his servants know who should sit on the throne of my lord the king after him?"

DAVID MAKES SOLOMON KING
1:28–53pp — 1Ch 29:21–25

²⁸Then King David said, "Call in Bathsheba." So she came into the king's presence and stood before him.

²⁹The king then took an oath: "As surely as the Lᴏʀᴅ lives, who has delivered me out of every trouble, ᶻ ³⁰I will surely carry out this very day what I swore ᵃ to you by the Lᴏʀᴅ, the God of Israel: Solomon your son shall be king after me, and he will sit on my throne in my place."

³¹Then Bathsheba bowed down with her face to the ground, prostrating herself before the king, and said, "May my lord King David live forever!"

³²King David said, "Call in Zadok ᵇ the priest, Nathan the prophet and Benaiah son of Jehoiada." When they came before the king, ³³he said to them: "Take your lord's servants with you and have Solomon my son mount my own mule ᶜ and take him down to Gihon. ᵈ ³⁴There have Zadok the priest and Nathan the prophet anoint ᵉ him king over Israel. Blow the trumpet ᶠ and shout, 'Long live King Solomon!' ³⁵Then you are to go up with him, and he is to come and sit on my throne and reign in my place. I have appointed him ruler over Israel and Judah."

³⁶Benaiah son of Jehoiada answered the king, "Amen! May the Lᴏʀᴅ, the God of my lord the king, so declare it. ³⁷As the Lᴏʀᴅ was with my lord the king, so may he be with ᵍ Solomon to make his throne even greater ʰ than the throne of my lord King David!"

³⁸So Zadok ⁱ the priest, Nathan the prophet, Benaiah son of Jehoiada, the Kerethites ʲ and the Pelethites went down and had Solomon mount King David's mule, and they escorted him to Gihon. ᵏ ³⁹Zadok the priest took the horn of oil ˡ from the sacred tent ᵐ and anointed Solomon. Then they sounded the trumpet ⁿ and all the people shouted, ᵒ "Long

---

1:17 *you yourself swore to me … by the Lᴏʀᴅ your God.* An oath taken in the Lord's name was inviolable (see Ex 20:7; Lev 19:12; Jos 9:15,18,20; Jdg 11:30,35; Ecc 5:4–7).

1:21 *laid to rest with his ancestors.* A conventional expression for death (see Ge 47:30; Dt 31:16).

1:24 Nathan approached David diplomatically by raising a question that revealed the dilemma. Either David had secretly encouraged Adonijah to claim the throne and thereby had broken his oath to Bathsheba and Solomon (see v. 27), or he had been betrayed by Adonijah.

1:25 *Long live King Adonijah!* An expression of recognition and acclamation of the new king (see 1Sa 10:24; 2Sa 16:16; 2Ki 11:12).

1:31 *May my lord King David live forever!* An expression of Bathsheba's thanks in the stereotyped hyperbolic language of the court (see Ne 2:3; Da 2:4; 3:9; 5:10; 6:21).

1:33 *your lord's servants.* Presumably including the Kerethites and Pelethites (see v. 38). *my own mule.* Although crossbreeding was forbidden in the Mosaic law (Lev 19:19), mules (perhaps imported; see Eze 27:14) were used in the time of David, at least

as mounts for royalty (see 2Sa 13:29; 18:9). To ride on David's own mule was a public proclamation that Solomon's succession to the throne was sanctioned by David (see Ge 41:43 and first TNIV text note; Est 6:7–8). *Gihon.* The site of a spring on the eastern slope of Mount Zion (see notes on v. 9; 2Sa 5:8).

1:34 *anoint him.* See notes on 1Sa 2:10; 9:16. *Blow the trumpet.* See 2Ki 9:13; 2Sa 15:10; 20:1. *Long live King Solomon!* See note on v. 25.

1:35 *Israel and Judah.* The distinction between Israel and Judah was rooted in the separate arrangements by which David became king over these two tribal units (see 2Sa 2:4; 5:3).

1:36 *Amen! May the Lᴏʀᴅ … so declare it.* See Jer 28:6.

1:37 *even greater.* Not a deprecation of David's accomplishments, but an expression of total loyalty to David and Solomon. Benaiah shared David's own desire for his chosen successor (see vv. 47–48).

1:38 *the Kerethites and the Pelethites.* See note on 2Sa 8:18.

1:39 *Zadok … anointed Solomon.* Kings chosen by God to rule over his people who were not in a line of dynastic succession live King Solomon!" [40]And all the people went up after him, playing pipes[p] and rejoicing greatly, so that the ground shook with the sound.

[41]Adonijah and all the guests who were with him heard it as they were finishing their feast. On hearing the sound of the trumpet, Joab asked, "What's the meaning of all the noise in the city?"[q]

[42]Even as he was speaking, Jonathan[r] son of Abiathar the priest arrived. Adonijah said, "Come in. A worthy man like you must be bringing good news."[s]

[43]"Not at all!" Jonathan answered. "Our lord King David has made Solomon king. [44]The king has sent with him Zadok the priest, Nathan the prophet, Benaiah son of Jehoiada, the Kerethites and the Pelethites, and they have put him on the king's mule, [45]and Zadok the priest and Nathan the prophet have anointed him king at Gihon. From there they have gone up cheering, and the city resounds[t] with it. That's the noise you hear. [46]Moreover, Solomon has taken his seat[u] on the royal throne. [47]Also, the royal officials have come to congratulate our lord King David, saying, 'May your God make Solomon's name more famous than yours and his throne greater[v] than yours!' And the king bowed in worship on his bed [48]and said, 'Praise be to the Lord, the God of Israel, who has allowed my eyes to see a successor[w] on my throne today.' "

[49]At this, all Adonijah's guests rose in alarm and dispersed. [50]But Adonijah, in fear of Solomon, went and took hold of the horns[x] of the altar. [51]Then Solomon was told, "Adonijah is afraid of King Solomon and is clinging to the horns of the altar. He says, 'Let King Solomon swear to me today that he will not put his servant to death with the sword.' "

[52]Solomon replied, "If he shows himself to be worthy, not a hair[y] of his head will fall to the ground; but if evil is found in him, he will die." [53]Then King Solomon sent men, and they brought him down from the altar. And Adonijah came and bowed down to King Solomon, and Solomon said, "Go to your home."

DAVID'S CHARGE TO SOLOMON
2:10–12pp — 1Ch 29:26–28

2 When the time drew near for David to die,[z] he gave a charge to Solomon his son. [2]"I am about to go the way of all the earth,"[a] he said. "So be strong,[b] act like a man, [3]and observe[c] what the Lord your God requires: Walk in obedience to him, and keep his decrees and commands, his laws and regulations, as written in the Law of Moses. Do this so that you may prosper[d] in all you do and wherever you go [4]and that the

1:40 *p* S 1Sa 10:5
1:41 *q* 2Ch 23:12-13
1:42 *r* S 2Sa 15:27,
36 *s* S 2Sa 18:26
1:45 *t* ver 40
1:46 *u* S Dt 17:18
1:47 *v* ver 37
1:48 *w* 1Ki 3:6
1:50 *x* S Ex 27:2
1:52 *y* S 1Sa 14:45
2:1 *z* S Ge 27:2;
S Nu 27:13
2:2 *a* Jos 23:14
b S Jos 1:6
2:3 *c* S Dt 4:6;
S 10:12; S 17:14-20;
S Jos 1:7 *d* 1Ch 22:13

---

were anointed by prophets (Saul, 1Sa 9:16; David, 1Sa 16:12; Jehu, 2Ki 9). Kings who assumed office in the line of dynastic succession were anointed by priests (Solomon, here; Joash, 2Ki 11:12). The distinction seems to be that the priest worked within the established order while the prophets introduced new divine initiatives. *horn of oil.* Perhaps containing the anointing oil described in Ex 30:22–33. *sacred tent.* The tent David had erected in Jerusalem to house the ark (see 2Sa 6:17) rather than the tabernacle at Gibeon (see 3:4 and note; 2Ch 1:3).
1:41 *heard it.* Although Gihon may not have been visible from En Rogel, the distance was not great and the sound would carry down the Kidron Valley.
1:42 *Jonathan son of Abiathar.* See 2Sa 17:17–21.
1:47 *more famous.* See note on v. 37.
1:48 *successor.* In Solomon's succession to the throne David sees a fulfillment of the promise in 2Sa 7:12,16.
1:49 *dispersed.* No one wanted to be identified with Adonijah's abortive coup now that it appeared certain to fail.
1:50 *took hold of the horns of the altar.* The horns of the altar were vertical projections at each corner. The idea of seeking asylum at the altar was rooted in the Pentateuch (see Ex 21:13–14). The priest smeared the blood of the sacrifice on the horns of the altar (see Ex 29:12; Lev 4:7,18,25,30,34) during the sacrificial ritual. Adonijah thus seeks to place his own destiny under the protection of God.
1:52 *worthy.* One who recognizes and submits to Solomon's office and authority. *if evil is found in him.* If he shows evidence of continuing opposition to Solomon's succession to the throne.
2:1 *he gave a charge.* Moses (Dt 31:1–8), Joshua (Jos 23:1–16) and Samuel (1Sa 12:1–25), as representatives of the Lord's rule, had all given final instructions and admonitions shortly before their deaths.

2:2 *the way of all the earth.* To the grave (see Jos 23:14). *be strong.* See Dt 31:7,23; Jos 1:6–7,9,18.

A **2:3** *observe what the Lord your God requires.* See Ge 26:5; Lev 18:30; Dt 11:1. *Walk in obedience to him.* A characteristic expression of Deuteronomy for obedience to covenant obligations (Dt 5:33; 8:6; 10:12; 11:22; 19:9; 26:17; 28:9; 30:16). *his decrees and commands, his laws and regulations.* Four generally synonymous terms for covenant obligations (see 6:12; 8:58; 2Ki 17:37; Dt 8:11; 11:1; 26:17; 28:15,45; 30:10,16). *that you may prosper.* See Dt 29:9.

A **C** **2:4** *that the Lord may keep his promise to me.* David here alludes to the covenanted promise of an everlasting dynasty given to him by God through Nathan the prophet (see notes on 2Sa 7:11–16). Although the covenant promise to David was unconditional, individual participation in its blessing on the part of David's royal descendants was conditioned on obedience to the obligations of the Sinaitic covenant (see 2Ch 7:17–22). *with all their heart and soul.* See Dt 4:29; 6:5; 10:12; 30:6. *you will never fail to have a successor on the throne of Israel.* Both Solomon and his descendants fell short of their covenant obligations. This led to the division of the kingdom and eventually to the exile of both the northern and southern kingdoms. It was only in the coming of Christ that the fallen tent of David would be restored (see notes on Am 9:11–15; Ac 15:16) and the promise of David's eternal dynasty ultimately fulfilled. When the nation and its king turned away from the requirements of the Sinai covenant, they experienced the covenant curses rather than blessings; but in all this God remained faithful to his covenant promises to Abraham and to David (see Lev 26:42–45; Isa 9:6–7; 11:1–16; 16:5; 55:3; Jer 23:5–6; 30:9; 33:17,20–22,25–26; Eze 34:23–24; 37:24–28).

2:4 ᵉS 2Sa 7:13,25;
2Ch 23:3 ᶠ2Ki 18:3-6;
20:3; Ps 26:1-3;
132:12
2:5 ᵍS 2Sa 2:18
ʰS 1Sa 14:50;
S 2Sa 3:27
ⁱS 2Sa 20:10
2:6 ʲver 9
2:7 ᵏS Ge 40:14
ˡS 2Sa 17:27; 19:31-
39 ᵐS 2Sa 9:7
2:8 ⁿver 36-46;
2Sa 16:5-13
ᵒS Ge 32:2
ᵖ2Sa 19:18-23
2:9 �q ver 6
2:10 ʳAc 2:29
ˢS 2Sa 5:7
2:11 ᵗS 2Sa 5:4,5
2:12 ᵘ1Ch 17:14;
29:23; 2Ch 9:8
ᵛver 46; 2Ch 1:1;
12:13; 17:1; 21:4
2:13 ʷS 2Sa 3:4
ˣS 1Sa 16:4

LORD may keep his promise ᵉ to me: 'If your descendants watch how they live, and if they walk faithfully ᶠ before me with all their heart and soul, you will never fail to have a successor on the throne of Israel.'

⁵"Now you yourself know what Joab ᵍ son of Zeruiah did to me—what he did to the two commanders of Israel's armies, Abner ʰ son of Ner and Amasa ⁱ son of Jether. He killed them, shedding their blood in peacetime as if in battle, and with that blood he stained the belt around his waist and the sandals on his feet. ⁶Deal with him according to your wisdom, ʲ but do not let his gray head go down to the grave in peace.

⁷"But show kindness ᵏ to the sons of Barzillai ˡ of Gilead and let them be among those who eat at your table. ᵐ They stood by me when I fled from your brother Absalom.

⁸"And remember, you have with you Shimei ⁿ son of Gera, the Benjamite from Bahurim, who called down bitter curses on me the day I went to Mahanaim. ᵒ When he came down to meet me at the Jordan, I swore ᵖ to him by the LORD: 'I will not put you to death by the sword.' ⁹But now, do not consider him innocent. You are a man of wisdom; �q you will know what to do to him. Bring his gray head down to the grave in blood."

¹⁰Then David rested with his ancestors and was buried ʳ in the City of David. ˢ ¹¹He had reigned ᵗ forty years over Israel—seven years in Hebron and thirty-three in Jerusalem. ¹²So Solomon sat on the throne ᵘ of his father David, and his rule was firmly established. ᵛ

SOLOMON'S THRONE ESTABLISHED

¹³Now Adonijah, ʷ the son of Haggith, went to Bathsheba, Solomon's mother. Bathsheba asked him, "Do you come peacefully?" ˣ

He answered, "Yes, peacefully." ¹⁴Then he added, "I have something to say to you."
"You may say it," she replied.

2:5 *Joab son of Zeruiah.* See note on 1:7. *Abner son of Ner.* See notes on 2Sa 3:25–32. *Amasa son of Jether.* See 2Sa 20:10. *shedding their blood in peacetime.* Joab's actions were unlawful assassinations (see Dt 19:1–13; 21:1–9) and only served his own self-interest. In addition, he murdered David's son Absalom (see 2Sa 18:14–15) and participated in Adonijah's conspiracy to usurp the throne (see 1:7,19).

2:7 *sons of Barzillai.* See note on 2Sa 17:27. *eat at your table.* A position of honor that brought with it other benefits (see 18:19; 2Ki 25:29; 2Sa 9:7; 19:28; Ne 5:17).

2:8 See 2Sa 16:5–13. *Shimei son of Gera, the Benjamite.* Gera was probably the ancestor of Shimei's particular line of descent

rather than his immediate father (see Ge 46:21; Jdg 3:15). See TNIV text notes on Ge 10:2; Da 5:22.

2:9 *do not consider him innocent.* The Mosaic law prohibited cursing a ruler (21:10; Ex 22:28).

2:10 *rested with his ancestors.* See note on 1:21. *City of David.* See 2Sa 5:7 and note. Peter implies that David's tomb was still known in his day (Ac 2:29).

2:11 *forty years.* See 2Sa 5:4–5. David ruled c. 1010–970 B.C. (see Introduction to 1Samuel: Chronology).

2:13 *Adonijah, the son of Haggith.* See note on 1:5. *Do you come peacefully?* The question (see 1Sa 16:4; 2Ki 9:22) reveals Bathsheba's apprehension concerning Adonijah's intention (see 1:5).

SOLOMON'S JERUSALEM

c. 950 B.C.

Solomon extended the city northward from the original site and there built his magnificent temple.

His royal residence was nearby; however, its architecture and location are unknown.

Temple

Hinnom Valley

Hinnom Valley

Kidron Valley

Meters
Feet
100 200 300 1000
500

Mt. of Olives

Jerusalem is shown from above and at an angle; therefore wall shapes appear different from those on flat maps. Wall locations have been determined from limited archaeological evidence; houses are artist's concept.

¹⁵"As you know," he said, "the kingdom was mine. All Israel looked to me as their king. But things changed, and the kingdom has gone to my brother; for it has come to him from the LORD. ¹⁶Now I have one request to make of you. Do not refuse me."

"You may make it," she said.

¹⁷So he continued, "Please ask King Solomon—he will not refuse you—to give me Abishag ^y the Shunammite as my wife."

¹⁸"Very well," Bathsheba replied, "I will speak to the king for you."

¹⁹When Bathsheba went to King Solomon to speak to him for Adonijah, the king stood up to meet her, bowed down to her and sat down on his throne. He had a throne brought for the king's mother, ^z and she sat down at his right hand. ^a

²⁰"I have one small request to make of you," she said. "Do not refuse me."

The king replied, "Make it, my mother; I will not refuse you."

²¹So she said, "Let Abishag ^b the Shunammite be given in marriage to your brother Adonijah."

²²King Solomon answered his mother, "Why do you request Abishag ^c the Shunammite for Adonijah? You might as well request the kingdom for him—after all, he is my older brother ^d—yes, for him and for Abiathar ^e the priest and Joab son of Zeruiah!"

²³Then King Solomon swore by the LORD: "May God deal with me, be it ever so severely, ^f if Adonijah does not pay with his life for this request! ²⁴And now, as surely as the LORD lives—he who has established me securely on the throne of my father David and has founded a dynasty for me as he promised ^g—Adonijah shall be put to death today!" ²⁵So King Solomon gave orders to Benaiah ^h son of Jehoiada, and he struck down Adonijah and he died. ⁱ

²⁶To Abiathar ^j the priest the king said, "Go back to your fields in Anathoth. ^k You deserve to die, but I will not put you to death now, because you carried the ark ^l of the Sovereign LORD before my father David and shared all my father's hardships." ^m ²⁷So Solomon removed Abiathar from the priesthood of the LORD, fulfilling ⁿ the word the LORD had spoken at Shiloh about the house of Eli.

²⁸When the news reached Joab, who had conspired with Adonijah though not with Absalom, he fled to the tent of the LORD and took hold of the horns ^o of the altar. ²⁹King Solomon was told that Joab had fled to the tent of the LORD and was beside the altar. ^p Then Solomon ordered Benaiah ^q son of Jehoiada, "Go, strike him down!"

³⁰So Benaiah entered the tent ^r of the LORD and said to Joab, "The king says, 'Come out! ^s'"

But he answered, "No, I will die here."

Benaiah reported to the king, "This is how Joab answered me."

³¹Then the king commanded Benaiah, "Do as he says. Strike him down and bury him, and so clear me and my family line of the guilt of the innocent blood ^t that Joab shed. ³²The LORD will repay ^u him for the blood he shed, ^v because without my father David knowing it he attacked two men and killed them with the sword. Both of them—Abner son of Ner, commander of Israel's army, and Amasa ^w son of Jether, commander of Judah's

2:17 ^y S 1Ki 1:3
2:19 ^z 1Ki 15:13;
2Ki 10:13; 24:15;
2Ch 15:16; Jer 13:18;
22:26; 29:2 ^a Ps 45:9
2:21 ^b 1Ki 1:3
2:22 ^c S Ge 22:24;
S 1Ki 1:3 ^d 1Ch 3:2
^e S 1Sa 22:20
2:23 ^f S Ru 1:17
2:24 ^g 2Sa 7:11
2:25 ^h S 2Sa 8:18
ⁱ S 2Sa 12:10
2:26 ^j S 1Sa 22:20
^k S Jos 21:18
^l S 2Sa 15:24
^m S 2Sa 15:14
2:27 ⁿ S 1Sa 2:27-36
2:28 ^o S Ex 27:2
2:29 ^p Ex 21:14
^q ver 25
2:30 ^r 2Ki 11:15
^s Ex 21:14
2:31 ^t S Dt 19:13
2:32 ^u Jdg 9:57
^v S Ge 4:14;
S Jdg 9:24
^w S 2Sa 17:25

2:15 *the kingdom was mine.* See 1:11. *All Israel looked to me as their king.* A gross exaggeration (see 1:7–8). *it has come to him from the LORD.* Adonijah professes to view Solomon's kingship as God's will and to have no further intentions of seeking the position for himself.

2:17 *give me Abishag the Shunammite as my wife.* Adonijah's request has the appearance of being innocent (but see note on v. 22) since Abishag had remained a virgin throughout the period of her care for David (see 1:1–4; Dt 22:30).

2:19 *right hand.* The position of honor (see Ps 110:1; Mt 20:21).

2:20 *one small request.* Bathsheba does not seem to have attached any great significance to Adonijah's request.

2:22 *You might as well request the kingdom for him.* Solomon immediately understood Adonijah's request as another attempt to gain the throne. Possession of the royal harem was widely regarded as signifying the right of succession to the throne (see notes on 2Sa 3:7; 12:8; 16:21). Although Abishag was a virgin, she would be regarded by the people as belonging to David's harem; so marriage to Abishag would greatly strengthen Adonijah's claim to the throne. *for Abiathar the priest and Joab son of Zeruiah.* See note on 1:7. Solomon assumes that Abiathar and Joab continue to be involved in Adonijah's treacherous schemes.

2:23 *May God deal with me, be it ever so severely.* A curse formula (see note on 1Sa 3:17).

2:24 *has founded a dynasty for me.* Solomon's son and successor, Rehoboam, was born shortly before Solomon became king (cf. 11:42; 14:21). *as he promised.* See 1Ch 22:9–10.

2:25 *Benaiah son of Jehoiada.* See notes on 1:7; 2Sa 23:20.

2:26 *you carried the ark.* See 2Sa 15:24–25,29; 1Ch 15:11–12. *shared all my father's hardships.* See 1Sa 22:20–23; 23:6–9; 30:7; 2Sa 17:15; 19:11.

2:27 *fulfilling the word the LORD had spoken at Shiloh about the house of Eli.* See notes on 1Sa 2:30–35.

2:28 *news.* Of Adonijah's death and Abiathar's banishment. *conspired with Adonijah.* See 1:7. *tent of the LORD.* See note on 1:39. *took hold of the horns of the altar.* See note on 1:50.

2:29 *strike him down!* The right of asylum was extended only to those who accidentally caused someone's death (see Ex 21:14). Solomon was completely justified in denying this right to Joab, not only for his complicity in Adonijah's conspiracy, but also for his murder of Abner and Amasa (see vv. 31–33). In this incident Solomon finds a suitable occasion for carrying out his father's instruction (see vv. 5–6).

2:32 *he attacked two men and killed them.* See 2Sa 3:27; 20:9–10. *Israel's army.* See 2Sa 2:8–9. *Judah's army.* See 2Sa 20:4.

2:32 ˣ 2Ch 21:13
2:34 ʸ ver 25
ᶻ S 2Sa 2:18
2:35 ᵃ S 2Sa 8:18
ᵇ S 1Sa 2:35
2:36 ᶜ S 2Sa 16:5
2:37 ᵈ S 2Sa 15:23;
Jn 18:1 ᵉ S Lev 20:9
2:39 ᶠ 1Sa 27:2
2:42 ᵍ S 2Sa 19:23
2:44 ʰ 2Sa 16:5-13
2:45 ⁱ S 2Sa 7:13
2:46 ʲ S 2Sa 8:18
ᵏ S ver 8 ˡ S ver 12
3:1 ᵐ 1Ki 7:8; 11:1-13
ⁿ 1Ki 9:24; 2Ch 8:11
ᵒ 2Sa 5:7; 1Ki 2:10
ᵖ S 2Sa 7:2; 1Ki 9:10
3:2 �q Lev 17:3-5;
S 26:30; Dt 12:14;
1Ki 15:14; 22:43

army—were better ˣ men and more upright than he. ³³May the guilt of their blood rest on the head of Joab and his descendants forever. But on David and his descendants, his house and his throne, may there be the LORD's peace forever."

³⁴So Benaiah ʸ son of Jehoiada went up and struck down Joab ᶻ and killed him, and he was buried at his home out in the country. ³⁵The king put Benaiah ᵃ son of Jehoiada over the army in Joab's position and replaced Abiathar with Zadok ᵇ the priest.

³⁶Then the king sent for Shimei ᶜ and said to him, "Build yourself a house in Jerusalem and live there, but do not go anywhere else. ³⁷The day you leave and cross the Kidron Valley, ᵈ you can be sure you will die; your blood will be on your own head." ᵉ

³⁸Shimei answered the king, "What you say is good. Your servant will do as my lord the king has said." And Shimei stayed in Jerusalem for a long time.

³⁹But three years later, two of Shimei's slaves ran off to Achish ᶠ son of Maakah, king of Gath, and Shimei was told, "Your slaves are in Gath." ⁴⁰At this, he saddled his donkey and went to Achish at Gath in search of his slaves. So Shimei went away and brought the slaves back from Gath.

⁴¹When Solomon was told that Shimei had gone from Jerusalem to Gath and had returned, ⁴²the king summoned Shimei and said to him, "Did I not make you swear by the LORD and warn ᵍ you, 'On the day you leave to go anywhere else, you can be sure you will die'? At that time you said to me, 'What you say is good. I will obey.' ⁴³Why then did you not keep your oath to the LORD and obey the command I gave you?"

⁴⁴The king also said to Shimei, "You know in your heart all the wrong ʰ you did to my father David. Now the LORD will repay you for your wrongdoing. ⁴⁵But King Solomon will be blessed, and David's throne will remain secure ⁱ before the LORD forever."

⁴⁶Then the king gave the order to Benaiah ʲ son of Jehoiada, and he went out and struck Shimei ᵏ down and he died.

The kingdom was now established ˡ in Solomon's hands.

SOLOMON ASKS FOR WISDOM
3:4–15pp — 2Ch 1:2–13

3 Solomon made an alliance with Pharaoh king of Egypt and married ᵐ his daughter. ⁿ He brought her to the City of David ᵒ until he finished building his palace ᵖ and the temple of the LORD, and the wall around Jerusalem. ²The people, however, were still sacrificing at the high places, �q because a temple had not yet been built for

---

2:34 *at his home out in the country.* The tomb of Joab's father was located near Bethlehem (see 2Sa 2:32).

2:35 *Benaiah son of Jehoiada.* See note on 2Sa 23:20. *Zadok the priest.* See notes on 1Sa 2:35; 2Sa 8:17.

2:36 *do not go anywhere else.* Confinement to Jerusalem would greatly reduce the possibility of Shimei's (see v. 8) conspiring with any remaining followers of Saul against Solomon's rule.

2:37 *Kidron Valley.* See map, p. 486.

2:39 *Achish son of Maakah, king of Gath.* Gath was a major Philistine city (see Jos 13:3; 1Sa 6:16–17). It is likely that Gath was ruled successively by Maok, Achish the elder (1Sa 27:2), Maakah and Achish the younger (here).

2:43 See v. 36 and note.

2:46 *struck Shimei down and he died.* The third execution carried out by Benaiah (see vv. 25,34). It brought to completion the tasks assigned to Solomon by David just before his death (vv. 6,9).

B C **3:1** *made an alliance with Pharaoh.* It appears likely that Solomon established his marriage alliance with Siamun, one of the last kings of the 21st Egyptian dynasty. (Siamun was pharaoh of Egypt 979/978–960/959 B.C.) Such an alliance attests Egyptian recognition of the growing importance and strength of the Israelite state. 1Ki 9:16 indicates that the pharaoh gave his daughter the Canaanite town of Gezer as a dowry at the time of her marriage to Solomon. Gezer was located near the crossing of two important trade routes. One, to the west of Gezer, went from Egypt to the north and was very important for Egypt's commercial interests. The other, to the north of Gezer, went from Jerusalem to the Mediterranean Sea and the port of Joppa and was important to Solomon as a supply line for his building projects. The marriage alliance enabled both Solomon and the pharaoh to accomplish important eco-

nomic and political objectives. No precise date is given for the conclusion of the marriage alliance, though it appears to have occurred in the third or fourth year of Solomon's reign (see 2:39). Solomon began construction of the temple in his fourth year (6:1), and control of the Gezer area was important to him for the beginning of this project. *married his daughter.* See 7:8; 9:16,24. Solomon had already married Rehoboam's mother, Naamah (see 14:21,31), and may have had other wives also (cf. 11:1–3). *City of David.* The Egyptian princess was given a temporary residence in the old fortress (see 2Sa 5:7 and note) until a separate palace of her own could be constructed some 20 years later (7:8; 9:10; 2Ch 8:11).

3:2 *high places.* Upon entering Canaan, the Israelites often followed the Canaanite custom of locating their altars on high hills, probably on the old Baal sites. The question of the legitimacy of Israelite worship at these high places has long been a matter of debate. It is clear that the Israelites were forbidden to take over pagan altars and high places and use them for the worship of the Lord (Nu 33:52; Dt 7:5; 12:3). It is also clear that altars were to be built only at divinely sanctioned sites (see Ex 20:24; Dt 12:5,8,13–14). It is not so clear whether multiplicity of altars was totally forbidden, provided the above conditions were met (see 19:10,14; Lev 26:30–31; Dt 12; 1Sa 9:12). It seems, however, that these conditions were not followed even in the time of Solomon, when pagan high places were being used for the worship of the Lord. This would eventually lead to religious apostasy and syncretism and was strongly condemned (2Ki 17:7–18; 21:2–9; 23:4–25). *because a temple had not yet been built.* Worship at a variety of places was apparently considered normal prior to the building of the temple (see Jdg 6:24; 13:19; 1Sa 7:17; 9:12–13). *Name of the LORD.* See notes on Dt 12:5; Ps 5:11.

the Name ^{r} of the LORD. ^{3}Solomon showed his love ^{s} for the LORD by walking ^{t} according to the instructions ^{u} given him by his father David, except that he offered sacrifices and burned incense on the high places. ^{v}

^{4}The king went to Gibeon ^{w} to offer sacrifices, for that was the most important high place, and Solomon offered a thousand burnt offerings on that altar. ^{5}At Gibeon the LORD appeared ^{x} to Solomon during the night in a dream, ^{y} and God said, "Ask ^{z} for whatever you want me to give you."

^{6}Solomon answered, "You have shown great kindness to your servant, my father David, because he was faithful ^{a} to you and righteous and upright in heart. You have continued this great kindness to him and have given him a son ^{b} to sit on his throne this very day.

^{7}"Now, LORD my God, you have made your servant king in place of my father David. But I am only a little child ^{c} and do not know how to carry out my duties. ^{8}Your servant is here among the people you have chosen, ^{d} a great people, too numerous to count or number. ^{e} ^{9}So give your servant a discerning ^{f} heart to govern your people and to distinguish ^{g} between right and wrong. For who is able ^{h} to govern this great people of yours?"

^{10}The Lord was pleased that Solomon had asked for this. ^{11}So God said to him, "Since you have asked ^{i} for this and not for long life or wealth for yourself, nor have asked for the death of your enemies but for discernment ^{j} in administering justice, ^{12}I will do what you have asked. ^{k} I will give you a wise ^{l} and discerning heart, so that there will never have been anyone like you, nor will there ever be. ^{13}Moreover, I will give you what you have not ^{m} asked for—both wealth and honor ^{n}—so that in your lifetime you will have no equal ^{o} among kings. ^{14}And if you walk ^{p} in obedience to me and keep my decrees and commands as David your father did, I will give you a long life." ^{q} ^{15}Then Solomon awoke ^{r}—and he realized it had been a dream. ^{s}

He returned to Jerusalem, stood before the ark of the Lord's covenant and sacrificed burnt offerings ^{t} and fellowship offerings. ^{u} Then he gave a feast ^{v} for all his court.

A WISE RULING

^{16}Now two prostitutes came to the king and stood before him. ^{17}One of them said, "Pardon me, my lord. This woman and I live in the same house, and I had a baby while she was there with me. ^{18}The third day after my child was born, this woman also had a baby. We were alone; there was no one in the house but the two of us.

^{19}"During the night this woman's son died because she lay on him. ^{20}So she got up in the middle of the night and took my son from my side while I your servant was asleep. She put him by her breast and put her dead son by my breast. ^{21}The next morning, I got up to nurse my son—and he was dead! But when I looked at him closely in the morning light, I saw that it wasn't the son I had borne."

^{22}The other woman said, "No! The living one is my son; the dead one is yours."

3:2 ^{r}S Dt 14:23
3:3 ^{s}Dt 6:5;
Ps 31:23; 145:20
^{t}S Dt 10:12; S Jos 1:7
^{u}S Dt 17:19;
S 1Ki 14:8 ^{v}S ver 2;
Lev 17:3-5; 2Ki 12:3;
15:4, 35; 16:4; 21:3
3:4 ^{w}S Jos 9:3
3:5 ^{x}1Ki 9:2; 11:9
^{y}S Mt 27:19
^{z}S Mt 7:7
3:6 ^{a}S Ge 17:1
^{b}1Ki 1:48
3:7 ^{c}Nu 27:17;
1Ch 22:5; 29:1; Jer 1:6
3:8 ^{d}S Dt 7:6
^{e}S Ge 12:2; 15:5;
3:9 ^{f}S 2Sa 14:17;
Jas 1:5 ^{g}S Dt 1:16
^{h}2Co 2:16
3:11 ^{i}Jas 4:3
^{j}1Ch 22:12
3:12 ^{k}1Jn 5:14-15
^{l}S 2Sa 14:20;
1Ki 4:29, 30, 31; 5:12;
10:23; Ecc 1:16
3:13 ^{m}Mt 6:33;
Eph 3:20 ^{n}Pr 3:1-2,
16; 8:18 ^{o}1Ki 10:23;
2Ch 9:22; Ne 13:26
3:14 ^{p}1Ki 9:4;
Ps 25:13; 101:2; 128:1;
Pr 3:1-2, 16 ^{q}Ps 61:6
3:15 ^{r}S Ge 28:16
^{s}ver 5 ^{t}Lev 6:8-13
^{u}Lev 7:11-21 ^{v}Est 1:3,
9; 2:18; 5:8; 6:14;
9:17; Da 5:1

3:3 *except.* Solomon's one major fault early in his reign was inconsistency in meeting the Mosaic requirements concerning places of legitimate worship.

3:4 *Gibeon.* The Gibeonites tricked Joshua and Israel into a peace treaty at the time of the conquest of Canaan (see Jos 9:3–27). The city was subsequently given to the tribe of Benjamin and set apart for the Levites (Jos 18:25; 21:17). David avenged Saul's violation of the Gibeonite treaty by the execution of seven of Saul's descendants (see 2Sa 21:1–9). *most important high place.* The reason for Gibeon's importance was the presence there of the tabernacle and the ancient bronze altar (see 1Ch 21:29; 2Ch 1:2–6). These must have been salvaged after the destruction of Shiloh by the Philistines (see note on 1Sa 7:1).

3:5 *dream.* Revelation through dreams is found elsewhere in the OT (see Ge 28:12; 31:11; 46:2; Nu 12:6; Jdg 7:13; Da 2:4; 7:1), as well as in the NT (see, e.g., Mt 1:20; 2:12,22).

3:6 *kindness.* The Hebrew for this word often refers to God's covenant favors (see notes on 2Sa 7:15; Ps 6:4). Solomon is praising the Lord for faithfulness to his promises to David (2Sa 7:8–16). *because.* See note on 2Sa 22:21.

3:7 *I am only a little child.* The birth of Solomon is generally placed in approximately the middle of David's 40-year reign, meaning that Solomon was about 20 years old at the beginning of his own reign (see 2:11–12) and lacked experience in assuming the responsibilities of his office (cf. Jer 1:6).

3:8 *great people, too numerous to count.* From the small beginnings of a single family living in Egypt (see Ge 46:26–27; Dt 7:7), the Israelites had increased to an extent approaching that anticipated in the promise given to Abraham (Ge 13:16; 22:17–18) and Jacob (Ge 32:12). See 4:20 and note.

3:9 *a discerning heart.* Lit. "a hearing heart." The phrase indicates the ability to listen patiently to all sides of an issue in order to come to true and wise decisions—a characteristic traditionally associated with a good king in the ancient Near East (cf. Isa 11:2–5).

3:11 *long life … wealth … death of your enemies.* Typical desires of ancient Near Eastern monarchs.

3:12 *never … anyone like you.* See 4:29–34; 10:1–13.

3:13 *I will give you what you have not asked for.* Cf. Jesus' promise in Lk 12:31.

3:14 *if you walk in obedience to me … I will give you a long life.* Echoes Dt 6:2; 17:20; 22:7. Unfortunately Solomon did not remain obedient to the covenant as his father David had (11:6), and he did not live to be much more than 60 years of age (see note on v. 7; cf. 11:42).

3:15 *ark of the Lord's covenant.* See notes on 6:19; 2Sa 6:2. *fellowship offerings.* See note on 1Sa 11:15.

3:16 *two prostitutes came to the king.* It was possible for Israelites (and others within the realm) to bypass lower judicial officials (Dt 16:18) and appeal directly before the king (see 2Ki 8:3; 2Sa 15:2).

3:17 *live in the same house.* Brothels were common in ancient Near Eastern cities.

3:26 ʷPs 102:13;
Isa 49:15; 63:15;
Jer 3:12; 31:20;
Hos 11:8
3:28 ˣS 2Sa 14:20;
Col 2:3
4:2 ʸ1Ki 12:6;
Job 12:12 ᶻ1Ch 6:10;
2Ch 26:17
4:3 ªS 2Sa 8:17
ᵇS 2Sa 8:16
4:4 ᶜS 2Sa 8:18
ᵈS 2Sa 8:17
4:6 ᵉS Ge 41:40
ᶠS 2Sa 20:24
ᵍS Ge 49:15
4:7 ʰver 27
4:8 ʲS Jos 24:33
4:9 ʲJdg 1:35
ᵏS Jos 15:10
4:10 ˡS Jos 15:35
ᵐS Jos 12:17
4:11 ⁿS Jos 11:2
4:12 ᵒS Jos 17:11
ᵖS Jos 3:16
ᵠS Jdg 7:22
ʳ1Ch 6:68
4:13 ˢS Nu 32:41
ᵗNu 32:40 ᵘDt 3:4
4:14 ᵛJos 13:26

But the first one insisted, "No! The dead one is yours; the living one is mine." And so they argued before the king.

²³The king said, "This one says, 'My son is alive and your son is dead,' while that one says, 'No! Your son is dead and mine is alive.'"

²⁴Then the king said, "Bring me a sword." So they brought a sword for the king. ²⁵He then gave an order: "Cut the living child in two and give half to one and half to the other."

²⁶The woman whose son was alive was deeply moved ʷ out of love for her son and said to the king, "Please, my lord, give her the living baby! Don't kill him!"

But the other said, "Neither I nor you shall have him. Cut him in two!"

²⁷Then the king gave his ruling: "Give the living baby to the first woman. Do not kill him; she is his mother."

²⁸When all Israel heard the verdict the king had given, they held the king in awe, because they saw that he had wisdom ˣ from God to administer justice.

SOLOMON'S OFFICIALS AND GOVERNORS

4 So King Solomon ruled over all Israel. ²And these were his chief officials: ʸ

Azariah ᶻ son of Zadok—the priest;

³Elihoreph and Ahijah, sons of Shisha—secretaries; ª
Jehoshaphat ᵇ son of Ahilud—recorder;

⁴Benaiah ᶜ son of Jehoiada—commander in chief;
Zadok ᵈ and Abiathar—priests;

⁵Azariah son of Nathan—in charge of the district governors;
Zabud son of Nathan—a priest and adviser to the king;

⁶Ahishar—palace administrator; ᵉ
Adoniram ᶠ son of Abda—in charge of forced labor. ᵍ

⁷Solomon had twelve district governors ʰ over all Israel, who supplied provisions for the king and the royal household. Each one had to provide supplies for one month in the year. ⁸These are their names:

Ben-Hur—in the hill country ⁱ of Ephraim;
⁹Ben-Deker—in Makaz, Shaalbim, ʲ Beth Shemesh ᵏ and Elon Bethhanan;
¹⁰Ben-Hesed—in Arubboth (Sokoh ˡ and all the land of Hepher ᵐ were his);
¹¹Ben-Abinadab—in Naphoth Dor ⁿ (he was married to Taphath daughter of Solomon);
¹²Baana son of Ahilud—in Taanach and Megiddo, and in all of Beth Shan ᵒ next to Zarethan ᵖ below Jezreel, from Beth Shan to Abel Meholah ᵠ across to Jokmeam; ʳ
¹³Ben-Geber—in Ramoth Gilead (the settlements of Jair ˢ son of Manasseh in Gilead ᵗ were his, as well as the region of Argob in Bashan and its sixty large walled cities ᵘ with bronze gate bars);
¹⁴Ahinadab son of Iddo—in Mahanaim; ᵛ

3:25 *Cut the living child in two.* This royal command, whereby Solomon in his wisdom resolved a judicial enigma and restored a violated relationship, served the author as a narrative foil to expose more effectively the folly Solomon later displayed, which led to God's judicial cutting of the kingdom in two, giving one part to Solomon's son and one part to Jeroboam (see 11:9–13). In the prophetic literature, these two kingdoms are often compared to prostitutes (see v. 16; see also Jer 3:6–12; Eze 16:15–46; 23:3–5; Hos 1:2 and notes).

3:28 *they saw that he had wisdom from God.* This episode strikingly demonstrated that the Lord had answered Solomon's prayer for a discerning heart (vv. 9,12).

4:1 *ruled over all Israel.* Solomon ruled over an undivided kingdom, as his father had before him (see 2Sa 8:15).

4:2 *son.* According to 2Sa 15:27,36 and 1Ch 6:8–9, Azariah was the son of Ahimaaz and the grandson of Zadok (see note on 2:8). Apparently Zadok's son Ahimaaz had died, so that Zadok was succeeded by his grandson Azariah. *Zadok.* See 2:27,35.

4:3 *Shisha.* See note on 2Sa 8:17. *secretaries.* See note on 2Sa 8:17. *Jehoshaphat son of Ahilud.* The same person who served in David's court (see 2Sa 8:16). *recorder.* See note on 2Sa 8:16.

4:4 *Benaiah.* Replaced Joab as commander of the army (see 2:35; 2Sa 8:18). *Zadok and Abiathar.* Abiathar was banished at the beginning of Solomon's reign (2:27,35), and Zadok was suc-

ceeded by his grandson Azariah (v. 2).

4:5 *Nathan.* Either the prophet (1:11) or the son of David (2Sa 5:14). *district governors.* See vv. 7–19. *priest.* See note on 2Sa 8:18. *adviser to the king.* See note on 2Sa 15:37.

4:6 *palace administrator.* The first OT reference to an office mentioned frequently in 1,2 Kings (1Ki 16:9; 18:3; 2Ki 18:18,37; 19:2). It is likely that this official was administrator of the palace and steward of the king's properties. *Adoniram.* Served not only under Solomon, but also under David before him (2Sa 20:24) and Rehoboam after him (1Ki 12:18). *forced labor.* See notes on 9:15; 2Sa 20:24.

4:7 *Solomon had twelve district governors.* The 12 districts were not identical to tribal territories, possibly because the tribes varied greatly in agricultural productivity. But Solomon's administrative decision violated traditional tribal boundaries and probably stirred up ancient tribal loyalties, eventually contributing to the disruption of the united kingdom.

4:8 *Ben-Hur.* The Hebrew *Ben* means "son of."

4:11 *Ben-Abinadab.* Most likely the "son of" David's brother Abinadab (see 1Sa 16:8; 17:13), making him Solomon's first cousin (he was also his son-in-law).

4:12 *Baana son of Ahilud.* Probably a brother of Jehoshaphat the recorder (v. 3).

[15] Ahimaaz [w]—in Naphtali (he had married Basemath daughter of Solomon);
[16] Baana son of Hushai [x]—in Asher and in Aloth;
[17] Jehoshaphat son of Paruah—in Issachar;
[18] Shimei [y] son of Ela—in Benjamin;
[19] Geber son of Uri—in Gilead (the country of Sihon [z] king of the Amorites and the country of Og [a] king of Bashan). He was the only governor over the district.

SOLOMON'S DAILY PROVISIONS

[20] The people of Judah and Israel were as numerous as the sand [b] on the seashore; they ate, they drank and they were happy. [c] [*21]And Solomon ruled [d] over all the kingdoms from the Euphrates River [e] to the land of the Philistines, as far as the border of Egypt. [f] These countries brought tribute [g] and were Solomon's subjects all his life.

[22] Solomon's daily provisions [h] were thirty cors [a] of the finest flour and sixty cors [b] of meal, [23] ten head of stall-fed cattle, twenty of pasture-fed cattle and a hundred sheep and goats, as well as deer, gazelles, roebucks and choice fowl. [i] [24] For he ruled over all the kingdoms west of the Euphrates River, from Tiphsah [j] to Gaza, and had peace [k] on all sides. [25] During Solomon's lifetime Judah and Israel, from Dan to Beersheba, [l] lived in safety, [m] everyone under their own vine and fig tree. [n]

[26] Solomon had four [c] thousand stalls for chariot horses, [o] and twelve thousand horses. [d]

[27] The district governors, [p] each in his month, supplied provisions for King Solomon and all who came to the king's table. They saw to it that nothing was lacking. [28] They also brought to the proper place their quotas of barley and straw for the chariot horses and the other horses.

SOLOMON'S WISDOM

[29] God gave Solomon wisdom [q] and very great insight, and a breadth of understanding as measureless as the sand [r] on the seashore. [30] Solomon's wisdom was greater than the wisdom of all the people of the East, [s] and greater than all the wisdom of Egypt. [t] [31] He was wiser [u] than anyone else, including Ethan the Ezrahite—wiser than Heman, Kalkol and Darda, the sons of Mahol. And his fame spread to all the surrounding nations. [32] He spoke three thousand proverbs [v] and his songs [w] numbered a thousand and five. [33] He spoke about plant life, from the cedar of Lebanon to the hyssop [x] that grows out of walls. He also spoke about animals and birds, reptiles and fish. [34] From all nations people came to listen to Solomon's wisdom, sent by all the kings [y] of the world, who had heard of his wisdom.

---

[a] 22 That is, probably about 5 1/2 tons or about 5 metric tons [b] 22 That is, probably about 11 tons or about 10 metric tons [c] 26 Some Septuagint manuscripts (see also 2 Chron. 9:25); Hebrew *forty* [d] 26 Or *charioteers*

[*] 4:21-34 is numbered 5:1-14 in Hebrew texts.

4:15 [w] 2Sa 15:27
4:16 [x] S 2Sa 15:32
4:18 [y] 1Ki 1:8
4:19 [z] S Jos 12:2
  [a] Dt 3:8-10; S Jos 12:4
4:20 [b] S Ge 12:2;
  S 32:12 [c] 1Ch 22:9
4:21 [d] 2Ch 9:26;
  Ezr 4:20; Ps 72:11;
  La 1:1 [e] S Ge 2:14;
  Ps 72:8 [f] S Ex 23:31
  [g] S Jdg 3:15; Eze 16:13
4:22 [h] 1Ki 10:5
4:23 [i] Ne 5:18
4:24 [j] 2Ki 15:16
  [k] S Jos 14:15
4:25 [l] S Jdg 20:1
  [m] 1Ch 22:9; Jer 23:6;
  [n] Dt 8:8; 2Ki 18:31;
  Jer 5:17; Joel 2:22;
  Mic 4:4; Zec 3:10
4:26 [o] S Dt 17:16
4:27 [p] ver 7
4:29 [q] S 1Ki 3:12
  [r] S Ge 32:12
4:30 [s] Ge 25:6;
  S Jdg 6:3; Da 1:20;
  Mt 2:1 [t] Isa 19:11;
  Ac 7:22
4:31 [u] S 1Ki 3:12
4:32 [v] Pr 1:1; 10:1;
  25:1; Ecc 12:9
  [w] Ps 78:63; SS 1:1;
  Eze 33:32
4:33 [x] S Lev 14:49
4:34 [y] 2Ch 9:23

4:16 *Baana son of Hushai.* Perhaps the son of David's trusted adviser (see notes on 2Sa 15:32,37).
4:18 *Shimei son of Ela.* Perhaps the same Shimei mentioned in 1:8.
4:20 *as numerous as the sand on the seashore.* See 3:8 and note; see also v. 29; Ge 22:17; 2Sa 17:11; Isa 10:22; Jer 33:22; Hos 1:10; cf. Ge 41:49; Jos 11:4; Jdg 7:12; Ps 78:27. *they ate, they drank and they were happy.* Judah and Israel prospered (see 5:4).
4:21 *from the Euphrates River to the land of the Philistines, as far as the border of Egypt.* The borders of Solomon's empire extended to the limits originally promised to Abraham (see note on 2Sa 8:3). However, rebellion was brewing in Edom (11:14–21) and Damascus (11:23–25). *brought tribute.* From the outset of his reign, Solomon enjoyed the submission of the peoples David had conquered (cf. note on Ps 2:1–3).
4:22 *Solomon's daily provisions.* For all his household, his palace servants and his court officials and their families.
4:24 *Tiphsah.* A city on the west bank of the Euphrates River. *Gaza.* The southernmost city of the Philistines on the Mediterranean coast.
4:25 *from Dan to Beersheba.* See note on 1Sa 3:20.
4:26 *four thousand.* See TNIV text note. 1Ki 10:26 and 2Ch 1:14 indicate that Solomon had 1,400 chariots, meaning that he maintained stalls for two horses for each chariot, with places for about 1,200 reserve horses. By way of comparison, an Assyrian account of the battle of Qarqar in 853 B.C. (about a cen-

tury after Solomon) speaks of 1,200 chariots from Damascus, 700 chariots from Hamath and 2,000 chariots from Israel (the northern kingdom). *chariot horses.* See 2Sa 15:1 and note.
4:27 *district governors.* See v. 7 and note.
4:29 *as measureless as the sand on the seashore.* See note on v. 20.
4:30 *people of the East.* The phrase is general and appears to refer to the peoples of Mesopotamia (see Ge 29:1) and Arabia (see Jer 49:28; Eze 25:4,10)—those associated with Israel's northeastern and eastern horizons, just as Egypt was the main region on her southwestern horizon. Many examples of Mesopotamian wisdom literature have been recovered (see essay, p. 750, last paragraph). *wisdom of Egypt.* See Ge 41:8; Ex 7:11; Ac 7:22. Examples of Egyptian wisdom literature are to be found in the proverbs of Ptahhotep (c. 2450 B.C.) and Amenemope (see Introduction to Proverbs: Date; see also chart, p. xxiii).
4:31 *He was wiser than anyone else.* Until Jesus came (see Lk 11:31). *Ethan the Ezrahite.* See Ps 89 title. *Heman, Kalkol and Darda.* See note on 1Ch 2:6. *his fame spread.* See, e.g., 10:1.
4:32 *three thousand proverbs.* Only some of these are preserved in the book of Proverbs.
4:33 *cedar of Lebanon.* See notes on 5:6; Jdg 9:15; Isa 9:10. *hyssop.* See note on Ex 12:22. *animals and birds, reptiles and fish.* Examples of Solomon's knowledge of these creatures are found in Pr 6:6–8; 26:2–3,11; 27:8; 28:1,15.
4:34 *all nations … all the kings of the world.* A general statement referring to the Near Eastern world (cf. Ge 41:57).

5:1 z S 2Sa 5:11
5:3 a 1Ch 22:8; 28:3
b 2Sa 7:5
c 2Sa 22:40; Ps 8:6;
110:1; S Mt 22:44;
1Co 15:25
5:4 d S Jos 14:15;
1Ch 22:9; Lk 2:14
e 1Ki 11:14,23
5:5 f S Dt 12:5;
1Ch 17:12; 1Co 3:16;
Rev 21:22 g Dt 12:5;
2Sa 7:13
5:6 h 1Ch 14:1; 22:4
5:7 i 1Ki 10:9;
Isa 60:6
5:9 j Ezr 3:7 k ver 11;
Eze 27:17; Ac 12:20
5:11 l S ver 9
5:12 m S 1Ki 3:12
n Jos 9:7; 1Ki 15:19;
Am 1:9
5:13 o S Ge 49:15;
S Lev 25:39; 1Ki 9:15
5:14 p S 2Sa 20:24;
1Ki 4:6; 2Ch 10:18
5:16 q 1Ki 9:23

PREPARATIONS FOR BUILDING THE TEMPLE
5:1–16pp — 2Ch 2:1–18

5 *When Hiram z king of Tyre heard that Solomon had been anointed king to succeed his father David, he sent his envoys to Solomon, because he had always been on friendly terms with David. 2Solomon sent back this message to Hiram:

3"You know that because of the wars a waged against my father David from all sides, he could not build b a temple for the Name of the LORD his God until the LORD put his enemies under his feet. c 4But now the LORD my God has given me rest d on every side, and there is no adversary e or disaster. 5I intend, therefore, to build a temple f for the Name of the LORD my God, as the LORD told my father David, when he said, 'Your son whom I will put on the throne in your place will build the temple for my Name.' g

6"So give orders that cedars h of Lebanon be cut for me. My men will work with yours, and I will pay you for your men whatever wages you set. You know that we have no one so skilled in felling timber as the Sidonians."

7When Hiram heard Solomon's message, he was greatly pleased and said, "Praise be to the LORD i today, for he has given David a wise son to rule over this great nation." 8So Hiram sent word to Solomon:

"I have received the message you sent me and will do all you want in providing the cedar and juniper logs. 9My men will haul them down from Lebanon to the Mediterranean Sea j, and I will float them as rafts by sea to the place you specify. There I will separate them and you can take them away. And you are to grant my wish by providing food k for my royal household."

10In this way Hiram kept Solomon supplied with all the cedar and juniper logs he wanted, 11and Solomon gave Hiram twenty thousand cors a of wheat as food l for his household, in addition to twenty thousand baths b, c of pressed olive oil. Solomon continued to do this for Hiram year after year. 12The LORD gave Solomon wisdom, m just as he had promised him. There were peaceful relations between Hiram and Solomon, and the two of them made a treaty. n

13King Solomon conscripted laborers o from all Israel—thirty thousand men. 14He sent them off to Lebanon in shifts of ten thousand a month, so that they spent one month in Lebanon and two months at home. Adoniram p was in charge of the forced labor. 15Solomon had seventy thousand carriers and eighty thousand stonecutters in the hills, 16as well as thirty-three hundred d overseers q who supervised the project and directed the work.

a 11 That is, probably about 3,600 tons or about 3,250 metric tons   b 11 Septuagint (see also 2 Chron. 2:10); Hebrew *twenty cors*   c 11 That is, about 120,000 gallons or about 440,000 liters   d 16 Hebrew; some Septuagint manuscripts (see also 2 Chron. 2:2, 18) *thirty-six hundred*

* 5:1-18 is numbered 5:15-32 in Hebrew texts.

5:1 *Hiram king of Tyre.* Hiram ruled over Tyre c. 978–944 B.C. He may have also served as coregent with his father, Abibaal, as early as 993. Before Solomon was born, Hiram provided timber and workmen for the building of David's palace (see 2Sa 5:11).

5:3 *he could not build a temple.* Although David was denied the privilege of building the temple, he did make plans and supply provisions for its construction (see 1Ch 22:2–5; 28:2; cf. also Ps 30 title).

5:4 *rest.* Described here as "no adversary or disaster." God's promises to his people (see Ex 33:14; Dt 25:19; Jos 1:13,15) and to David (2Sa 7:11) have now been fulfilled (see 8:56 and note), so that the Israelites are free to concentrate their strength and resources on building their Great King's royal house (see note on 2Sa 7:11).

5:5 *Name of the LORD.* See 3:2 and note. *as the LORD told my father David.* See 2Sa 7:12–13; 1Ch 22:8–10.

5:6 *So give orders.* A more detailed account of Solomon's request is found in 2Ch 2:3–10. *cedars of Lebanon.* Widely used in the ancient Near East in the construction of royal houses and temples.

5:7 *Praise be to the LORD.* In polytheistic cultures it was common practice for the people of one nation to recognize the deities of another nation (see 10:9; 11:5) and even to ascribe certain powers to them (see 2Ki 18:25; see also 2Ch 2:12).

5:9 *place you specify.* Joppa (2Ch 2:16; see note on 1Ki 3:1). *providing food for my royal household.* Provision of food for Hiram's

court personnel appears to have covered only the cost of the wood itself. In addition, Solomon would have to provide for the wages of the Phoenician laborers (v. 6). Comparison of v. 11 with 2Ch 2:10 indicates that besides wheat and olive oil for Hiram's court, Solomon also sent barley and wine for labor costs. Hiram may have sold some of these provisions in order to pay the laborers. See also note on 9:11.

5:11 *twenty thousand cors of wheat.* See TNIV text note. By way of comparison, Solomon's court received 10,950 cors of flour and 21,900 cors of meal on an annual basis (see 4:22). Solomon's whole grain payment to Hiram of 20,000 cors of wheat and 20,000 cors of barley (2Ch 2:10) would probably have yielded about 26,666 cors of refined flour and meal, or about 20 percent less than the requirements of Solomon's own court.

5:13 *conscripted laborers.* See notes on 9:15; 2Sa 20:24. Resentment among the people toward this sort of forced labor eventually led to a civil uprising and the division of Solomon's kingdom immediately after his death (12:1–18).

5:15 *seventy thousand carriers and eighty thousand stonecutters.* Conscripted from the non-Israelite population that David had subdued and incorporated into his kingdom (see 2Ch 2:17–18). *hills.* The limestone hills of the surrounding area where the stone was quarried.

5:16 *thirty-three hundred overseers.* 1Ki 9:23 refers to 550 su-

5:17 ʳ1Ki 6:7
ˢ1Ch 22:2
5:18 ᵗS 2Sa 5:11
ᵘS Jos 13:5
6:1 ᵛEzr 3:8
ʷEzr 5:11
6:2 ˣEx 26:1
6:3 ʸEze 40:49
6:4 ᶻEze 41:16
6:5 ᵃJer 35:2;
Eze 41:5-6
6:7 ᵇS Ex 20:25
ᶜS Dt 27:5
6:9 ᵈSS 1:17
6:11 ᵉ1Ki 12:22;
13:20; 16:1,7; 17:2;
21:17; Jer 40:1
6:12 ᶠ1Ki 11:10
ᵍ2Sa 7:12-16; 1Ki 9:5
6:13 ʰS Lev 26:11;
S Dt 31:6; Jn 14:18;
Heb 13:5
6:14 ⁱAc 7:47
ʲ1Ch 28:20; 2Ch 5:1
6:15 ᵏ1Ki 7:7
ˡEze 41:15-16

¹⁷At the king's command they removed from the quarry ʳ large blocks of high-grade stone ˢ to provide a foundation of dressed stone for the temple. ¹⁸The skilled workers of Solomon and Hiram ᵗ and those from Byblos ᵘ cut and prepared the timber and stone for the building of the temple.

SOLOMON BUILDS THE TEMPLE
6:1–29pp — 2Ch 3:1–14

6 In the four hundred and eightieth ᵃ year after the Israelites came out of Egypt, in the fourth year of Solomon's reign over Israel, in the month of Ziv, the second month, ᵛ he began to build the temple of the LORD. ʷ

²The temple ˣ that King Solomon built for the LORD was sixty cubits long, twenty wide and thirty high. ᵇ ³The portico ʸ at the front of the main hall of the temple extended the width of the temple, that is twenty cubits, ᶜ and projected ten cubits ᵈ from the front of the temple. ⁴He made narrow windows ᶻ high up in the temple walls. ⁵Against the walls of the main hall and inner sanctuary he built a structure around the building, in which there were side rooms. ᵃ ⁶The lowest floor was five cubits ᵉ wide, the middle floor six cubits ᶠ and the third floor seven. ᵍ He made offset ledges around the outside of the temple so that nothing would be inserted into the temple walls.

⁷In building the temple, only blocks dressed ᵇ at the quarry were used, and no hammer, chisel or any other iron tool ᶜ was heard at the temple site while it was being built.

⁸The entrance to the lowest ʰ floor was on the south side of the temple; a stairway led up to the middle level and from there to the third. ⁹So he built the temple and completed it, roofing it with beams and cedar ᵈ planks. ¹⁰And he built the side rooms all along the temple. The height of each was five cubits, and they were attached to the temple by beams of cedar.

¹¹The word of the LORD came ᵉ to Solomon: ¹²"As for this temple you are building, if you follow my decrees, observe my laws and keep all my commands ᶠ and obey them, I will fulfill through you the promise ᵍ I gave to David your father. ¹³And I will live among the Israelites and will not abandon ʰ my people Israel."

¹⁴So Solomon ⁱ built the temple and completed ʲ it. ¹⁵He lined its interior walls with cedar boards, paneling them from the floor of the temple to the ceiling, ᵏ and covered the floor of the temple with planks of juniper. ˡ ¹⁶He partitioned off twenty cubits at the rear

---

ᵃ 1 Hebrew; Septuagint *four hundred and fortieth*   ᵇ 2 That is, about 90 feet long, 30 feet wide and 45 feet high or about 27 meters long, 9 meters wide and 13.5 meters high   ᶜ 3 That is, about 30 feet or about 9 meters; also in verses 16 and 20   ᵈ 3 That is, about 15 feet or about 4.5 meters; also in verse 23   ᵉ 6 That is, about 7 1/2 feet or about 2.3 meters; also in verses 10 and 24   ᶠ 6 That is, about 9 feet or about 2.7 meters   ᵍ 6 That is, about 10 1/2 feet or about 3.2 meters   ʰ 8 Septuagint; Hebrew *middle*

---

pervisors. If these are two different categories of supervisory personnel, the total is 3,850 men. 2Ch 2:2 refers to 3,600 supervisors, and 2Ch 8:10 speaks of 250 supervisors, which again yields a total of 3,850 men in a supervisory capacity.
5:17 *large blocks of high-grade stone.* For the size of these stones, see 7:10. Transportation of such stones to Jerusalem would require enormous manpower.
5:18 *Byblos.* See Eze 27:9 and note.
6:1–38 See diagram, p. 494.
6:1 *four hundred and eightieth year ... fourth year.* Synchronizations between certain events in the reigns of later Israelite kings and Assyrian chronological records fix the fourth year of Solomon's reign at c. 966 B.C. (see Introduction: Chronology). If Israel's exodus is placed 480 years prior to 966, it would have occurred c. 1446 (the chronology followed in this study Bible) during the rule of the 18th-dynasty Egyptian pharaoh Amunhotep II. On the basis of Ex 1:11 and certain other historical considerations, however, some have concluded that the exodus could not have occurred prior to the rule of the 19th-dynasty pharaoh, Rameses II—thus not until c. 1290 (see note on Ge 47:11). This would mean that the 480 years of this verse would be understood as either a schematic (perhaps representative of 12 generations multiplied by the conventional, but not always actual, 40-year length of a generation) or aggregate figure (the combined total of a number of subsidiary time periods, which in reality were partly concurrent, examples of which are to be found in Egyptian and Mesopotamian records). See Introduction to Exodus: Chronology.

6:2 *temple that King Solomon built.* The temple was patterned after the tabernacle (and, in general, other temples of the time) and was divided into three major areas: the Most Holy Place, the Holy Place and the outer courtyard. The Most Holy Place in the temple was cubical, as it probably was in the tabernacle. The dimensions of the temple in most instances seem to be double those of the tabernacle (see Ex 26:15–30; 36:20–34).
6:6 *offset ledges.* To avoid making holes in the temple wall, it was built with a series of ledges on which the beams for the three floors of side chambers rested. This accounts for the different widths of the rooms on each floor.
6:8 *entrance to the lowest floor.* Of the side chambers.
6:11 *The word of the LORD came to Solomon.* As the temple neared completion the Lord spoke to Solomon, perhaps through an unnamed prophet (but see 3:5,11–14; 9:2–9).
6:12 *if you follow my decrees ... I will fulfill through you the promise.* In words similar to those spoken by David (see 2:1–4 and notes), the Lord assures Solomon of a continuing dynasty (see 2Sa 7:12–16), but Solomon must remain faithful to the Sinaitic covenant if he is to experience the fulfillment of the Davidic covenant promise (see "through you"; see also chart, p. 20).
6:13 *I will live among the Israelites.* In the temple being built (see 9:3). To avoid any apprehension among the Israelites concerning his presence with them (cf. Ps 78:60; Jer 26:6,9; see note on 1Sa 7:1), the Lord gives assurance that he will dwell in their midst (see 8:10–13; Lev 26:11).

6:16 *m* S Ex 26:33
6:18 *n* ver 29;
Ps 74:6; Eze 41:18
6:19 *o* 1Ki 8:6
p S Ex 25:10;
S 1Sa 3:3
6:20 *q* Eze 41:3-4
r S Ex 30:1

of the temple with cedar boards from floor to ceiling to form within the temple an inner sanctuary, the Most Holy Place. *m* [17] The main hall in front of this room was forty cubits *a* long. [18] The inside of the temple was cedar, *n* carved with gourds and open flowers. Everything was cedar; no stone was to be seen.

[19] He prepared the inner sanctuary *o* within the temple to set the ark of the covenant *p* of the LORD there. [20] The inner sanctuary *q* was twenty cubits long, twenty wide and twenty high. He overlaid the inside with pure gold, and he also overlaid the altar of cedar. *r* [21] Solomon covered the inside of the temple with pure gold, and he extended gold chains across the front of the inner sanctuary, which was overlaid with gold. [22] So he overlaid the whole interior with gold. He also overlaid with gold the altar that belonged to the inner sanctuary.

a 17 That is, about 60 feet or about 18 meters

6:16 *Most Holy Place.* The same terminology was used for the inner sanctuary housing the ark in the tabernacle (see Ex 26:33–34; Lev 16:2,16–17,20,23).

6:19 *ark of the covenant of the LORD.* The Ten Commandments are called the "words of the covenant" in Ex 34:28. The stone tablets on which the Ten Commandments were inscribed are called the "tablets of the covenant" in Dt 9:9. The ark in which the tablets were kept (see Ex 25:16,21; 40:20; Dt 10:1–5) is thus sometimes called the "ark of the covenant of the LORD" (see Dt 10:8; 31:9,25; Jos 3:11). Elsewhere the ark is variously designated as the "ark of the LORD" (Jos 3:13; 4:11), the "ark of the cov-

enant law" (Ex 30:6; 31:7) and the "ark of God" (1Sa 3:3; 4:11,17,21; 5:1–2).

6:20 *pure gold.* The extensive use of gleaming gold probably symbolized the glory of God and his heavenly temple (cf. Rev 21:10–11,18,21).

6:21 *gold chains.* The curtain covering the entrance to the Most Holy Place was probably hung on these chains (see 2Ch 3:14; Mt 27:51; Heb 6:19).

6:22 *altar that belonged to the inner sanctuary.* The incense altar (see 7:48; Ex 30:1,6; 37:25–28; Heb 9:3–4 and note on 9:4).

SOLOMON'S TEMPLE

960–586 B.C.

Temple source materials are subject to academic interpretation, and subsequent art reconstructions vary.

Side rooms

Most Holy Place with ark of the covenant

Holy Place (30 cubits high) with golden tables for bread of the Presence, gold lampstands and altar of incense

Portico

This reconstruction recognizes influence from the desert tabernacle, accepts general Near Eastern cultural diffusion and rejects overt pagan Canaanite symbols. It uses known archaeological parallels to supplement the text and assumes interior dimensions from 1Ki 6:17–20.

20

40 cubits

CUBITS

FEET

Movable stands of bronze

The ornate cast bronze pillars, "Jakin and Boaz"

Sea

Altar

N

The temple of Solomon, located adjacent to the king's palace, functioned as God's royal palace and Israel's national center of worship. The Lord said to Solomon, "I have consecrated this temple... by putting my Name there forever. My eyes and my heart will always be there" (1Ki 9:3). By its cosmological and royal symbolism, the sanctuary taught the absolute sovereignty of the Lord over the whole creation and his special headship over Israel.

B The floor plan is a type that has a long history in Semitic religion, particularly among the West Semites. An early example of the tripartite division into portico, main hall and inner sanctuary has been found at Syrian Ebla (c. 2300 B.C.) and, much later but more contemporaneous with Solomon, at Tell Tainat in the Orontes basin (c. 900 B.C.). Like Solomon's, the temple at Tell Tainat had three divisions, had two columns

supporting the entrance and was located adjacent to the royal palace.

Many archaeological parallels can be drawn to the methods of construction used in the temple, e.g., the "stone and cedar beam" technique described in 1Ki 6:36. Interestingly, evidence for the largest bronze-casting industry ever found in the Holy Land comes from the same locale and period as that indicated in Scripture: Zarethan in the Jordan Valley c. 1000 B.C.

©1986 Hugh Claycombe

²³For the inner sanctuary he made a pair of cherubim *s* out of olive wood, each ten cubits high. ²⁴One wing of the first cherub was five cubits long, and the other wing five cubits—ten cubits from wing tip to wing tip. ²⁵The second cherub also measured ten cubits, for the two cherubim were identical in size and shape. ²⁶The height of each cherub was ten cubits. ²⁷He placed the cherubim *t* inside the innermost room of the temple, with their wings spread out. The wing of one cherub touched one wall, while the wing of the other touched the other wall, and their wings touched each other in the middle of the room. ²⁸He overlaid the cherubim with gold.

²⁹On the walls *u* all around the temple, in both the inner and outer rooms, he carved cherubim, *v* palm trees and open flowers. ³⁰He also covered the floors of both the inner and outer rooms of the temple with gold.

³¹For the entrance to the inner sanctuary he made doors out of olive wood that were one fifth of the width of the sanctuary. ³²And on the two olive-wood doors *w* he carved cherubim, palm trees and open flowers, and overlaid the cherubim and palm trees with hammered gold. ³³In the same way, for the entrance to the main hall he made doorframes out of olive wood that were one fourth of the width of the hall. ³⁴He also made two doors out of juniper wood, each having two leaves that turned in sockets. ³⁵He carved cherubim, palm trees and open flowers on them and overlaid them with gold hammered evenly over the carvings.

³⁶And he built the inner courtyard *x* of three courses *y* of dressed stone and one course of trimmed cedar beams.

³⁷The foundation of the temple of the Lᴏʀᴅ was laid in the fourth year, in the month of Ziv. ³⁸In the eleventh year in the month of Bul, the eighth month, the temple was finished in all its details *z* according to its specifications. *a* He had spent seven years building it.

SOLOMON BUILDS HIS PALACE

7 It took Solomon thirteen years, however, to complete the construction of his palace. *b* ²He built the Palace *c* of the Forest of Lebanon *d* a hundred cubits long, fifty wide and thirty high, *a* with four rows of cedar columns supporting trimmed cedar beams. ³It was roofed with cedar above the beams that rested on the columns—forty-five beams, fifteen to a row. ⁴Its windows were placed high in sets of three, facing each other. ⁵All the doorways had rectangular frames; they were in the front part in sets of three, facing each other. *b*

⁶He made a colonnade fifty cubits long and thirty wide. *c* In front of it was a portico, and in front of that were pillars and an overhanging roof.

⁷He built the throne hall, the Hall of Justice, where he was to judge, *e* and he covered it with cedar from floor to ceiling. *d f* ⁸And the palace in which he was to live, set farther back, was similar in design. Solomon also made a palace like this hall for Pharaoh's daughter, whom he had married. *g*

---

a 2 That is, about 150 feet long, 75 feet wide and 45 feet high or about 45 meters long, 22.5 meters wide and 13.5 meters high   *b 5* The meaning of the Hebrew for this verse is uncertain.   *c 6* That is, about 75 feet long and 45 feet wide or about 22.5 meters long and 13.5 meters wide   *d 7* Vulgate and Syriac; Hebrew *floor*

6:23 ᵉS Ex 37:1-9
6:27 ᶠS Ge 3:24; S Ex 25:18
6:29 ᵘS ver 18 ᵛver 32,35; Eze 41:18,25
6:32 ʷEze 41:23
6:36 ˣ2Ch 4:9
ʸ1Ki 7:12; Ezr 6:4
6:38 ᶻ1Ch 28:19
ᵃEx 25:9; Heb 8:5
7:1 ᵇS 2Sa 7:2
7:2 ᶜS 2Sa 7:2
ᵈ1Ki 10:17; 2Ch 9:16; Isa 22:8; 37:24; Jer 22:6,23
7:7 ᵉ1Sa 7:15; Ps 122:5; Pr 20:8
ᶠ1Ki 6:15
7:8 ᵍS 1Ki 3:1

6:23 *cherubim.* See note on Ex 25:18. They were to stand as sentries on either side of the ark (8:6–7; 2Ch 3:10–13). Two additional cherubim stood on the ark—one on each end of its atonement cover (Ex 25:17–22). *ten cubits high.* The Most Holy Place, where the cherubim stood, was 20 cubits high (v. 16).
6:29 *he carved cherubim.* Not a violation of the second commandment, which prohibited making anything to serve as a representation of God and worshiping it (see note on Ex 20:4). *palm trees and open flowers.* The depiction of cherubim and beautiful trees and flowers is reminiscent of the Garden of Eden, from which Adam and Eve had been driven as a result of sin (Ge 3:24). In a symbolic sense, readmission to the paradise of God is now to be had only by means of atonement for sin at the sanctuary (see note on Ex 26:1, "tabernacle"). Early Jewish synagogues were adorned with similar motifs.
6:36 *inner courtyard.* Suggests that there was an outer courtyard (see 8:64). 2Ch 4:9 refers to the "courtyard of the priests" (inner) and the "large court" (outer). The inner courtyard is also called the upper courtyard (Jer 36:10) because of its higher position on the temple mount.

6:37 *fourth year.* Of Solomon's reign (see v. 1 and note). *Ziv.* See chart, p. 105.
6:38 *eleventh year.* Of Solomon's reign (959 B.C.). *Bul.* See chart, p. 105.
7:1 *thirteen years.* Solomon spent almost twice as long building his own house as he did the Lord's house (see 6:38; see also Hag 1:2–4).
7:2 *Palace of the Forest of Lebanon.* Four rows of cedar pillars in the palace created the impression of a great forest. *a hundred cubits long, fifty wide and thirty high.* See TNIV text note. Compare these measurements with those of the temple in 6:2.
7:3 *forty-five beams, fifteen to a row.* Suggests that there were three floors in the building above the main hall on the ground level. The building included storage space for weaponry (see 10:16–17).
7:6 *colonnade.* Apparently an entrance hall to the Palace of the Forest of Lebanon. Its length (50 cubits) corresponds to the width of the palace.
7:7 *throne hall.* It is not clear whether the throne hall (the Hall of Justice), Solomon's own living quarters (v. 8) and the palace

7:12 h S 1Ki 6:36
7:13 i ver 45;
2Ch 2:13; 4:16
7:14 j Ex 31:2-5;
S 35:31 k 2Ch 4:11,16
7:15 l 2Ki 11:14;
23:3; 25:17; 2Ch 3:15;
23:13; 34:31;
Jer 27:19; 52:17,21;
Eze 40:49

⁹All these structures, from the outside to the great courtyard and from foundation to eaves, were made of blocks of high-grade stone cut to size and trimmed with a saw on their inner and outer faces. ¹⁰The foundations were laid with large stones of good quality, some measuring ten cubits ᵃ and some eight. ᵇ ¹¹Above were high-grade stones, cut to size, and cedar beams. ¹²The great courtyard was surrounded by a wall of three courses ʰ of dressed stone and one course of trimmed cedar beams, as was the inner courtyard of the temple of the LORD with its portico.

THE TEMPLE'S FURNISHINGS

7:23–26pp — 2Ch 4:2–5
7:38–51pp — 2Ch 4:6,10—5:1

¹³King Solomon sent to Tyre and brought Huram, ᶜ ¹⁴whose mother was a widow from the tribe of Naphtali and whose father was from Tyre and a skilled worker in bronze. Huram was filled with wisdom, ʲ with understanding and with knowledge to do all kinds of bronze work. He came to King Solomon and did all ᵏ the work assigned to him.

¹⁵He cast two bronze pillars, ˡ each eighteen cubits high and twelve cubits in circum-

---

ᵃ 10 That is, about 15 feet or about 4.5 meters; also in verse 23   ᵇ 10 That is, about 12 feet or about 3.6 meters   ᶜ 13 Hebrew *Hiram*, a variant of *Huram*; also in verses 40 and 45

---

for the pharaoh's daughter (v. 8) were separate buildings or locations within the Palace of the Forest of Lebanon.
7:9 *trimmed with a saw.* The pinkish white limestone of the Holy Land is easily cut when originally quarried, but gradually hardens with exposure.
7:12 *great courtyard.* Constructed in the same way as the inner courtyard of the temple (6:36).
7:13 *King Solomon sent.* Prior to the completion of the temple and the construction of Solomon's palace (see 2Ch 2:7,13–14). *Huram.* See TNIV text note. His full name is Huram-Abi (2Ch 2:13).

7:14 *widow from the tribe of Naphtali.* 2Ch 2:14 indicates that Huram-Abi's mother was from Dan. Apparently she was born in the city of Dan in northern Israel close to the tribe of Naphtali, from which came her first husband. After he died, she married a man from Tyre. *all kinds of bronze work.* Huram-Abi had a much wider range of skills as well (see 2Ch 2:7,14).

7:15 *two bronze pillars.* One was placed on each side of the main entrance to the temple (v. 21). Surely decorative, they may also have embodied a symbolism not known to us. Some believe that the pillars were freestanding, like those found

TEMPLE FURNISHINGS

Glimpses of the rich ornamentation of Solomon's temple can be gained through recent discoveries that illumine the text of 1Ki 6-7.

ARK OF THE COVENANT

Cherubs with wings shielding a sacred place are attested in Egyptian and Phoenician art.

MOVABLE BRONZE BASIN

An extremely close parallel to the wheeled portable basins used in the courtyard of the temple has come from archaeological excavations on Cyprus. This representation combines elements from the Biblical text with the archaeological evidence.

LAMPSTAND

Ten lampstands were in the temple, five on each side of the sanctuary (1Ki 7:49), to which were added ten tables (2 Ch 4:8). Ritual sevenfold lamps have been found at several places in Israel, including Hazor and Dothan. The stand itself is modeled on bronze stands from the excavations at Megiddo.

TABLE FOR THE BREAD OF THE PRESENCE

A stone incense altar having four horns on the corners was found at Megiddo. It provides a clear idea of the shape of the gold incense altar in the temple. The table for the bread of the Presence was also made of gold.

INCENSE ALTAR

ference.^a ¹⁶He also made two capitals ^m of cast bronze to set on the tops of the pillars; each capital was five cubits^b high. ¹⁷A network of interwoven chains adorned the capitals on top of the pillars, seven for each capital. ¹⁸He made pomegranates in two rows^c encircling each network to decorate the capitals on top of the pillars.^d He did the same for each capital. ¹⁹The capitals on top of the pillars in the portico were in the shape of lilies, four cubits^e high. ²⁰On the capitals of both pillars, above the bowl-shaped part next to the network, were the two hundred pomegranates ⁿ in rows all around. ²¹He erected the pillars at the portico of the temple. The pillar to the south he named Jakin^f and the one to the north Boaz.^{g o} ²²The capitals on top were in the shape of lilies. And so the work on the pillars^p was completed.

²³He made the Sea ^q of cast metal, circular in shape, measuring ten cubits from rim to rim and five cubits high. It took a line^r of thirty cubits^h to measure around it. ²⁴Below the rim, gourds encircled it—ten to a cubit. The gourds were cast in two rows in one piece with the Sea.

²⁵The Sea stood on twelve bulls,^s three facing north, three facing west, three facing south and three facing east. The Sea rested on top of them, and their hindquarters were toward the center. ²⁶It was a handbreadthⁱ in thickness, and its rim was like the rim of a cup, like a lily blossom. It held two thousand baths.^j

²⁷He also made ten movable stands^t of bronze; each was four cubits long, four wide and three high.^k ²⁸This is how the stands were made: They had side panels attached to uprights. ²⁹On the panels between the uprights were lions, bulls and cherubim—and on the uprights as well. Above and below the lions and bulls were wreaths of hammered work. ³⁰Each stand^u had four bronze wheels with bronze axles, and each had a basin resting on four supports, cast with wreaths on each side. ³¹On the inside of the stand there was an opening that had a circular frame one cubit^l deep. This opening was round, and with its basework it measured a cubit and a half.^m Around its opening there was engraving. The panels of the stands were square, not round. ³²The four wheels were under the panels, and the axles of the wheels were attached to the stand. The diameter of each wheel was a cubit and a half. ³³The wheels were made like chariot wheels; the axles, rims, spokes and hubs were all of cast metal.

³⁴Each stand had four handles, one on each corner, projecting from the stand. ³⁵At the top of the stand there was a circular band half a cubitⁿ deep. The supports and panels were attached to the top of the stand. ³⁶He engraved cherubim, lions and palm trees on the surfaces of the supports and on the panels, in every available space, with wreaths all around. ³⁷This is the way he made the ten stands. They were all cast in the same molds and were identical in size and shape.

³⁸He then made ten bronze basins,^v each holding forty baths^o and measuring four cubits across, one basin to go on each of the ten stands. ³⁹He placed five of the stands on the south side of the temple and five on the north. He placed the Sea on the south side, at the southeast corner of the temple. ⁴⁰He also made the pots^p and shovels and sprinkling bowls.^w

---

^a *15* That is, about 27 feet high and 18 feet in circumference or about 8.2 meters high and 5.4 meters in circumference   ^b *16* That is, about 7 1/2 feet or about 2.3 meters; also in verse 23   ^c *18* Two Hebrew manuscripts and Septuagint; most Hebrew manuscripts *made the pillars, and there were two rows*   ^d *18* Many Hebrew manuscripts and Syriac; most Hebrew manuscripts *pomegranates*   ^e *19* That is, about 6 feet or about 1.8 meters; also in verse 38   ^f *21* *Jakin* probably means *he establishes.*   ^g *21* *Boaz* probably means *in him is strength.*   ^h *23* That is, about 45 feet or about 13.5 meters   ⁱ *26* That is, about 3 inches or about 7.5 centimeters   ^j *26* That is, about 12,000 gallons or about 44,000 liters; the Septuagint does not have this sentence.   ^k *27* That is, about 6 feet long and wide and about 4 1/2 feet high or about 1.8 meters long and wide and 1.4 meters high   ^l *31* That is, about 18 inches or about 45 centimeters   ^m *31* That is, about 2 1/4 feet or about 67 centimeters; also in verse 32   ⁿ *35* That is, about 9 inches or about 22.5 centimeters   ^o *38* That is, about 240 gallons or about 880 liters   ^p *40* Many Hebrew manuscripts, Septuagint, Syriac and Vulgate (see also verse 45 and 2 Chron. 4:11); many other Hebrew manuscripts *basins*

7:16 ^m ver 20, 42;
2Ki 25:17; Jer 52:22
7:20 ⁿ ver 18;
2Ch 3:16; 4:13
7:21 ^o 2Ch 3:17
7:22 ^p 2Ki 25:17
7:23 ^q ver 47;
2Ki 25:13; 1Ch 18:8;
2Ch 4:18; Jer 52:17;
Rev 4:6 ^r Jer 31:39;
Zec 2:1
7:25 ^s Jer 52:20
7:27 ^t 2Ki 16:17
7:30 ^u 2Ki 16:17
7:38 ^v S Ex 30:18
7:40 ^w S Ex 27:3;
Jer 52:18

---

at certain excavations in the Near East. Others think that they supported a roof (forming a portico to the temple) and an architrave.

7:16 *five cubits.* See 2Ki 25:17 and note.

7:21 *pillar to the south.* The temple, like the tabernacle before it, faced east (see Eze 8:16).

7:23 *Sea of cast metal.* This enormous reservoir of water corresponded to the bronze basin made for the tabernacle (see Ex 30:17–21; 38:8). Its water was used by the priests for ritual cleansing (2Ch 4:6). *thirty cubits.* Technically speaking, this should be 31.416 cubits because of the ten-cubit diameter of the circular top. Thirty may be a round number here.

7:24 *ten to a cubit.* With ten gourds to a cubit it took 300 gourds to span the entire reservoir, or 600 gourds counting both rows.

7:26 *two thousand baths.* See 2Ch 4:5 and note.

7:27 *ten movable stands.* These movable bronze stands were designed to hold water basins (see v. 38) of much smaller dimensions than the bronze Sea. The water from the basins was used to wash certain prescribed parts of the animals that were slaughtered for burnt offerings (see Lev 1:9,13; 2Ch 4:6).

7:36 *He engraved cherubim, lions and palm trees.* See note on 6:29.

7:40 *pots.* See TNIV text note; perhaps used for cooking meat to be eaten in connection with the fellowship offerings (see Lev

7:42 ˣS ver 16
7:45 ʸS Ex 27:3;
Jer 52:18 ᶻS ver 13
7:46 ᵃS Ge 13:10
ᵇS Ge 33:17 ᶜJos 3:16
7:47 ᵈ1Ch 22:3;
Jer 52:20 ᵉEx 36:5-7
ᶠS ver 23
7:48 ᵍEx 39:32-43
ʰS Ex 25:23
ⁱS Ex 25:30
7:49 ʲS Ex 25:31-38
7:50 ᵏS Nu 7:14
ˡ2Ki 25:13; Jer 52:19
7:51 ᵐS 2Sa 8:11
ⁿ2Ki 12:13; 24:13;
Jer 27:19
8:1 ᵒNu 7:2
ᵖS 1Sa 3:3; Rev 11:19
�q S 2Sa 5:7
8:2 ʳver 65;
S Lev 23:36; Ne 8:17
ˢS Lev 23:34;
S Nu 29:12
8:3 ᵗS Jos 3:3
8:4 ᵘS Lev 17:4
ᵛ1Ch 15:13
8:5 ʷS 2Sa 6:13;
S 2Ch 30:24
8:6 ˣS Ex 26:33;
S 2Sa 6:17; Rev 11:19
ʸS Ex 26:33
ᶻS Ge 3:24;
S Ex 25:18

So Huram finished all the work he had undertaken for King Solomon in the temple of the LORD:

⁴¹the two pillars;
 the two bowl-shaped capitals on top of the pillars;
 the two sets of network decorating the two bowl-shaped capitals on top of the pillars;
⁴²the four hundred pomegranates for the two sets of network (two rows of pomegranates for each network decorating the bowl-shaped capitals ˣ on top of the pillars);
⁴³the ten stands with their ten basins;
⁴⁴the Sea and the twelve bulls under it;
⁴⁵the pots, shovels and sprinkling bowls. ʸ

All these objects that Huram ᶻ made for King Solomon for the temple of the LORD were of burnished bronze. ⁴⁶The king had them cast in clay molds in the plain ᵃ of the Jordan between Sukkoth ᵇ and Zarethan. ᶜ ⁴⁷Solomon left all these things unweighed, ᵈ because there were so many; ᵉ the weight of the bronze ᶠ was not determined.

⁴⁸Solomon also made all ᵍ the furnishings that were in the LORD's temple:

the golden altar;
the golden table ʰ on which was the bread of the Presence; ⁱ
⁴⁹the lampstands ʲ of pure gold (five on the right and five on the left, in front of the inner sanctuary);
the gold floral work and lamps and tongs;
⁵⁰the pure gold basins, wick trimmers, sprinkling bowls, dishes ᵏ and censers; ˡ
  and the gold sockets for the doors of the innermost room, the Most Holy Place, and
  also for the doors of the main hall of the temple.

⁵¹When all the work King Solomon had done for the temple of the LORD was finished, he brought in the things his father David had dedicated ᵐ—the silver and gold and the furnishings ⁿ—and he placed them in the treasuries of the LORD's temple.

THE ARK BROUGHT TO THE TEMPLE
8:1–21pp — 2Ch 5:2—6:11

8 Then King Solomon summoned into his presence at Jerusalem the elders of Isra-el, all the heads of the tribes and the chiefs ᵒ of the Israelite families, to bring up the ark ᵖ of the LORD's covenant from Zion, the City of David. q ²All the Israelites came together to King Solomon at the time of the festival ʳ in the month of Ethanim, the seventh month. ˢ

³When all the elders of Israel had arrived, the priests ᵗ took up the ark, ⁴and they brought up the ark of the LORD and the tent of meeting ᵘ and all the sacred furnishings in it. The priests and Levites ᵛ carried them up, ⁵and King Solomon and the entire assembly of Is-rael that had gathered about him were before the ark, sacrificing ʷ so many sheep and cattle that they could not be recorded or counted.

⁶The priests then brought the ark of the LORD's covenant ˣ to its place in the inner sanc-tuary of the temple, the Most Holy Place, ʸ and put it beneath the wings of the cherubim. ᶻ

7:11–17; 22:21–23). *shovels.* Used for removing ashes from the altar. *sprinkling bowls.* For use by the priests in various rites in-volving the sprinkling of blood or water (see Ex 27:3).
7:41 *two sets of network.* See v. 17.
7:42 *four hundred pomegranates.* See vv. 18,20.
7:43 *ten stands with their ten basins.* See vv. 27–37.
7:44 *the Sea and the twelve bulls.* See vv. 23–26.
7:45 *pots, shovels and sprinkling bowls.* See v. 40 and note.

7:46 *Sukkoth.* Located on the east side of the Jordan (Ge 33:17; Jos 13:27; Jdg 8:4–5) just north of the Jabbok River. Excavations in this area have confirmed that Sukkoth was a cen-ter of metallurgy during the period of the monarchy. *Zarethan.* Located near Adam (see Jos 3:16) and Abel Meholah (4:12).
7:48 *golden altar.* See 6:22. *golden table.* The bread of the Pres-ence was placed on this table (see Ex 25:23–30; 1Ch 9:32; 2Ch 13:11; 29:18). Ten such golden tables are mentioned in 1Ch 28:16 and 2Ch 4:8,19, five placed on the north and five on the south side of the temple.
7:49 *lampstands of pure gold.* Only one lampstand with seven arms had stood in the tabernacle, opposite the table for the bread of the Presence (Ex 25:31–40; 26:35). The ten lampstands

in the temple, five on the north and five on the south side, cre-ated a lane of light in the Holy Place. *gold floral work.* See Ex 25:33. *lamps.* See Ex 25:37. *tongs.* See 2Ch 4:21; Isa 6:6.
7:50 *censers.* See 2Ki 25:15; 2Ch 4:22; Jer 52:18–19.
7:51 *things his father David had dedicated.* Valuable objects of silver and gold, either taken as booty in war or received as trib-ute from kings seeking David's favor (see 2Sa 8:9–12; 1Ch 18:7–11; 2Ch 5:1). *treasuries of the LORD's temple.* See 15:18; 2Ki 12:18; 1Ch 9:26; 26:20–26; 28:12.
8:1 *bring up the ark of the LORD's covenant.* David had previously brought the ark from the house of Obed-Edom to Jerusalem (see 2Sa 6). *Zion, the City of David.* See note on 2Sa 5:7.
8:2 *festival.* It is probable that Solomon waited 11 months (see 6:38) to dedicate the temple during the Festival of Tabernacles, which was observed in the seventh month of the year (Lev 23:34; Dt 16:13–15). *seventh month.* Presumably in the 12th year of Solomon's reign.
8:4 *tent of meeting.* The tabernacle, which had been preserved at Gibeon (see notes on 3:4; 1Sa 7:1; see also 2Ch 5:4–5).
8:6 *put it beneath the wings of the cherubim.* See 6:23–28.

8:7 *a* S Ex 25:20
8:8 *b* Ex 25:13-15
8:9 *c* S Ex 16:34;
S 25:16; Heb 9:4
8:10 *d* S Ex 16:10;
S Lev 16:2; Rev 15:8
8:11 *e* 2Ch 7:2;
Rev 15:8 *f* S Ex 16:7;
S 29:43
8:12 *g* S Ex 40:34;
S 2Sa 22:10
8:13 *h* Ex 15:17;
Ps 132:13; 135:21;
Mt 23:21
8:14 *i* S Ex 39:43
8:15 *j* 1Ch 16:36;
Lk 1:68
8:16 *k* S Ex 3:10
l S Dt 12:5
m S 1Sa 9:16; S 16:1
n Ps 89:3-4
8:17 *o* S 1Sa 10:7;
Ac 7:46 *p* 2Sa 7:27;
1Ch 22:7; Ps 26:8;
132:5
8:19 *q* S 2Sa 7:5
r S 2Sa 7:13
8:20 *s* S 2Sa 7:12
t 1Ch 28:6
8:22 *u* S Ex 9:29
8:23 *v* S Ex 9:14
w S Dt 7:9,12; Ne 1:5;
9:32; Da 9:4
8:25 *x* S 2Sa 7:15;
1Ch 17:23; 2Ch 1:9
8:26 *y* S 2Sa 7:25
8:27 *z* Ac 7:48; 17:24
a S Dt 10:14
b 2Ch 2:6; Ps 139:7-
16; Isa 66:1; Jer 23:24

[7]The cherubim spread their wings over the place of the ark and overshadowed[a] the ark and its carrying poles. [8]These poles were so long that their ends could be seen from the Holy Place in front of the inner sanctuary, but not from outside the Holy Place; and they are still there today.[b] [9]There was nothing in the ark except the two stone tablets[c] that Moses had placed in it at Horeb, where the LORD made a covenant with the Israelites after they came out of Egypt.

[10]When the priests withdrew from the Holy Place, the cloud[d] filled the temple of the LORD. [11]And the priests could not perform their service[e] because of the cloud, for the glory[f] of the LORD filled his temple.

[12]Then Solomon said, "The LORD has said that he would dwell in a dark cloud;[g] [13]I have indeed built a magnificent temple for you, a place for you to dwell[h] forever."

[14]While the whole assembly of Israel was standing there, the king turned around and blessed[i] them. [15]Then he said:

"Praise be to the LORD,[j] the God of Israel, who with his own hand has fulfilled what he promised with his own mouth to my father David. For he said, [16]'Since the day I brought my people Israel out of Egypt,[k] I have not chosen a city in any tribe of Israel to have a temple built that my Name[l] might be there, but I have chosen[m] David[n] to rule my people Israel.'

[17]"My father David had it in his heart[o] to build a temple[p] for the Name of the LORD, the God of Israel. [18]But the LORD said to my father David, 'You did well to have it in your heart to build a temple for my Name. [19]Nevertheless, you[q] are not the one to build the temple, but your son, who is your own flesh and blood—he is the one who will build the temple for my Name.'[r]

[20]"The LORD has kept the promise he made: I have succeeded[s] David my father and now I sit on the throne of Israel, just as the LORD promised, and I have built[t] the temple for the Name of the LORD, the God of Israel. [21]I have provided a place there for the ark, in which is the covenant of the LORD that he made with our ancestors when he brought them out of Egypt."

SOLOMON'S PRAYER OF DEDICATION
8:22–53pp — 2Ch 6:12–40

[22]Then Solomon stood before the altar of the LORD in front of the whole assembly of Israel, spread out his hands[u] toward heaven [23]and said:

"LORD, the God of Israel, there is no God like[v] you in heaven above or on earth below—you who keep your covenant of love[w] with your servants who continue wholeheartedly in your way. [24]You have kept your promise to your servant David my father; with your mouth you have promised and with your hand you have fulfilled it—as it is today.

[25]"Now LORD, the God of Israel, keep for your servant David my father the promises[x] you made to him when you said, 'You shall never fail to have a successor to sit before me on the throne of Israel, if only your descendants are careful in all they do to walk before me faithfully as you have done.' [26]And now, God of Israel, let your word that you promised[y] your servant David my father come true.

[27]"But will God really dwell[z] on earth? The heavens, even the highest heaven,[a] cannot contain[b] you. How much less this temple I have built! [28]Yet give attention to

---

8:8 *their ends could be seen.* The carrying poles were always to remain in the gold rings of the ark (Ex 25:15). *they are still there today.* These words must be those of the original author of this description of the dedication of the temple rather than those of the final compiler of the books of Kings (see Introduction: Author, Sources and Date; see also 2Ch 5:9).
8:9 *two stone tablets.* See Ex 25:16; 40:20. *the LORD made a covenant.* See Ex 24.
8:10 ▲ *the cloud filled the temple.* Just as a visible manifestation of the presence of the Lord had descended on the tabernacle at Sinai, so now the Lord came to take up his abode in the temple (see Ex 40:33–35; Eze 10:3–5,18–19; 43:4–5).
8:12 *he would dwell in a dark cloud.* See Ex 19:9; 24:15,18; 33:9–10; 34:5; Lev 16:2; Dt 4:11; 5:22; Ps 18:10–11.
8:15 *what he promised.* See 2Sa 7:5–16.
8:16 *have not chosen a city.* See Dt 12:5 and note. *my Name.* See 3:2 and note.

8:21 *covenant of the LORD.* The two tablets containing the Ten Commandments (see Ex 25:16 and note; Heb 9:4).
8:22 *spread out his hands.* In prayer (see Ex 9:29 and note).
8:23 ▲ *no God like you.* No other god has acted in history as has the God of Israel, performing great miracles and directing the course of events so that his long-range covenant promises are fulfilled (see Ex 15:11; Dt 4:39; 7:9; Ps 86:8–10). *who keep your covenant of love.* See Dt 7:9,12 and note. *who continue . . . in your way.* Cf. Ex 20:6 and note.
8:24 *your promise.* See v. 15; 2Sa 7:5–16.
8:25 *if only your descendants . . . walk before me faithfully.* See 9:4–9; 2Ch 7:17–22; see also note on 1Ki 2:4.
8:27 ▲ *How much less this temple I have built!* With the construction of the temple and the appearance of a visible manifestation of the presence of God within its courts, the erroneous notion that God was irreversibly and exclusively bound to the temple in a way that guaranteed his assistance to Israel

8:29 c ver 52;
2Ki 19:16; 2Ch 7:15;
Ne 1:6; Ps 5:1; 31:2;
102:17; 130:2; Isa 37:17
d Ps 28:2; 138:2;
Da 6:10 e S Dt 11:12;
12:11; S 2Sa 7:13
8:30 f ver 40;
Lev 26:40; Ne 1:6;
Jer 29:12; Da 9:4
g ver 39; Ps 34:6
h S Ex 34:7, 9;
Lev 26:40-42;
Ps 85:2
8:31 i S Ex 22:11
8:32 j Dt 25:1;
Eze 18:20
8:33 k S Lev 26:17
l Lev 26:39 m Isa 37:1,
14, 38
8:35 n S Dt 28:24;
S 2Sa 1:21 o Jer 5:25
8:36 p S Dt 8:3;
S 1Sa 12:23 q Ps 5:8;
27:11; 107:7; Pr 11:5;
Isa 45:13; Jer 6:16;
7:23; 31:21 r ver 35;
1Ki 17:1; 18:1, 45;
Jer 5:24; 10:3; 14:22;
Zec 10:1
8:37 s S Lev 26:26
t S Ex 30:12;
S Lev 26:25
u S Dt 28:22
v S Ex 10:13;
Ps 105:34
8:38 w S Ex 9:29
8:39 x S ver 30
y Ps 130:4
z S Jos 22:22;
S Ps 44:21; Jn 2:24;
S Rev 2:23
8:40 a ver 39-40;
Dt 6:13; Ps 103:11;
130:4 b S Dt 12:1
8:41 c S Ge 31:15;
Isa 56:3, 6; 61:5
8:42 d 1Ki 10:1;
Isa 60:3; Ac 8:27
e Dt 3:24

your servant's prayer and his plea for mercy, LORD my God. Hear the cry and the prayer that your servant is praying in your presence this day. 29May your eyes be open c toward d this temple night and day, this place of which you said, 'My Name e shall be there,' so that you will hear the prayer your servant prays toward this place. 30Hear the supplication of your servant and of your people Israel when they pray f toward this place. Hear g from heaven, your dwelling place, and when you hear, forgive. h

31"When anyone wrongs their neighbor and is required to take an oath and they come and swear the oath i before your altar in this temple, 32then hear from heaven and act. Judge between your servants, condemning the guilty by bringing down on their heads what they have done, and vindicating the innocent by treating them in accordance with their innocence. j

33"When your people Israel have been defeated k by an enemy because they have sinned l against you, and when they turn back to you and give praise to your name, praying and making supplication to you in this temple, m 34then hear from heaven and forgive the sin of your people Israel and bring them back to the land you gave to their ancestors.

35"When the heavens are shut up and there is no rain n because your people have sinned o against you, and when they pray toward this place and give praise to your name and turn from their sin because you have afflicted them, 36then hear from heaven and forgive the sin of your servants, your people Israel. Teach p them the right way q to live, and send rain r on the land you gave your people for an inheritance.

37"When famine s or plague t comes to the land, or blight u or mildew, locusts or grasshoppers, v or when an enemy besieges them in any of their cities, whatever disaster or disease may come, 38and when a prayer or plea is made by anyone among your people Israel—being aware of the afflictions of their own hearts, and spreading out their hands w toward this temple— 39then hear x from heaven, your dwelling place. Forgive y and act; deal with everyone according to all they do, since you know z their hearts (for you alone know every human heart), 40so that they will fear a you all the time they live in the land b you gave our ancestors.

41"As for the foreigners c who do not belong to your people Israel but have come from a distant land because of your name— 42for they will hear d of your great name and your mighty hand e and your outstretched arm—when they come and pray toward this temple, 43then hear from heaven, your dwelling place. Do whatever the

---

no matter how the people lived could very easily arise (see Jer 7:4–14; Mic 3:11). Solomon confessed that even though God had chosen to dwell among his people in a special and localized way, he far transcended containment by anything in all creation.

8:29 *My Name.* See note on 3:2.

8:30 *pray toward this place.* When an Israelite was unable to pray in the temple itself, he was to direct his prayers toward the place where God had pledged to be present among his people (see Da 6:10). *heaven, your dwelling place.* See note on v. 27.

8:31 *required to take an oath.* In cases such as default in pledges (Ex 22:10–12) or alleged adultery (Nu 5:11–31), when there was insufficient evidence to establish the legitimacy of the charge, the supposed offender was required to take an oath of innocence at the sanctuary. Such an oath, with its attendant blessings and curses, was considered a divinely given means of determining innocence or guilt since the consequences of the oath became apparent in the life of the individual either by his experiencing the blessing or the curse or by direct divine revelation through the Urim and Thummim (see Ex 28:29–30; Lev 8:8; Nu 27:21).

8:32 *hear from heaven.* It is clear that Solomon viewed the oath as an appeal to God to act and not as an automatic power that worked in a magical way.

8:33 *defeated by an enemy because they have sinned against you.* Defeat by enemies was listed in Dt 28:25 as one of the curses that would come on Israel if she disobeyed the covenant. Solomon's prayer reflects an awareness of the covenant obligations the Lord had placed on his people and a knowledge of the consequences that disobedience would entail.

8:34 *bring them back to the land.* A reference to prisoners taken in battle.

8:35 *no rain.* Drought was another of the covenant curses listed in Dt 28:22–24.

8:36 *right way to live.* In accordance with covenant obligations (see Dt 6:18; 12:25; 13:18; 1Sa 12:23).

8:37 *famine.* See Dt 32:24. *plague.* See Dt 28:21–22; 32:24. *locusts or grasshoppers.* See Dt 28:38,42. *an enemy besieges them in any of their cities.* See Dt 28:52. *disaster.* See Dt 28:61; 31:29; 32:23–25.

8:38 *aware of the afflictions of their own hearts.* Conscious of their guilt before God, with an attitude of repentance and the desire for God's forgiveness and grace (see 2Ch 6:29; Ps 38:17–18; Jer 17:9).

8:39 *deal with everyone according to all they do.* Not to be viewed as a request for retribution for the wrong committed (forgiveness and retribution are mutually exclusive), but as a desire for whatever discipline God in his wisdom may use to correct his people and to instruct them in the way of the covenant (see v. 40; Pr 3:11; Heb 12:5–15).

8:40 *fear you.* Honor and obediently serve you (see notes on Ge 20:11; Pr 1:7; see also Dt 5:29; 6:1–2; 8:6; 31:13; 2Ch 6:31; Ps 130:4).

8:41 *foreigners who do not belong to your people Israel.* Those who come from foreign lands to pray to Israel's God at the temple, as distinguished from resident aliens.

8:42 *they will hear.* See 9:9 (foreign nations generally); 10:1 (queen of Sheba); Jos 2:9–11 (Rahab); 1Sa 4:6–8 (Philistines). *your great name and your mighty hand and your outstretched arm.* God's great power, demonstrated by his interventions in the history of his people (see Dt 4:34; 5:15; 7:19; 11:2; 26:8).

foreigners ask of you, so that all the peoples of the earth may know [f] your name and fear [g] you, as do your own people Israel, and may know that this house I have built bears your Name. [h]

⁴⁴"When your people go to war against their enemies, wherever you send them, and when they pray [i] to the Lᴏʀᴅ toward the city you have chosen and the temple I have built for your Name, ⁴⁵then hear from heaven their prayer and their plea, and uphold their cause. [j]

⁴⁶"When they sin against you—for there is no one who does not sin [k]—and you become angry with them and give them over to their enemies, who take them captive [l] to their own lands, far away or near; ⁴⁷and if they have a change of heart in the land where they are held captive, and repent and plead [m] with you in the land of their captors and say, 'We have sinned, we have done wrong, we have acted wickedly'; [n] ⁴⁸and if they turn back [o] to you with all their heart [p] and soul in the land of their enemies who took them captive, and pray [q] to you toward the land you gave their ancestors, toward the city you have chosen and the temple [r] I have built for your Name; [s] ⁴⁹then from heaven, your dwelling place, hear their prayer and their plea, and uphold their cause. ⁵⁰And forgive your people, who have sinned against you; forgive all the offenses they have committed against you, and cause their captors to show them mercy; [t] ⁵¹for they are your people and your inheritance, [u] whom you brought out of Egypt, out of that iron-smelting furnace. [v]

⁵²"May your eyes be open [w] to your servant's plea and to the plea of your people Israel, and may you listen to them whenever they cry out to you. [x] ⁵³For you singled them out from all the nations of the world to be your own inheritance, [y] just as you declared through your servant Moses when you, Sovereign Lᴏʀᴅ, brought our ancestors out of Egypt."

⁵⁴When Solomon had finished all these prayers and supplications to the Lᴏʀᴅ, he rose from before the altar of the Lᴏʀᴅ, where he had been kneeling with his hands spread out toward heaven. ⁵⁵He stood and blessed [z] the whole assembly of Israel in a loud voice, saying:

⁵⁶"Praise be to the Lᴏʀᴅ, who has given rest [a] to his people Israel just as he promised. Not one word has failed of all the good promises [b] he gave through his servant Moses. ⁵⁷May the Lᴏʀᴅ our God be with us as he was with our ancestors; may he never leave us nor forsake [c] us. ⁵⁸May he turn our hearts [d] to him, to walk in obedience to him and keep the commands, decrees and laws he gave our ancestors. ⁵⁹And may these words of mine, which I have prayed before the Lᴏʀᴅ, be near to the Lᴏʀᴅ our God day and night, that he may uphold the cause of his servant and the cause of his people Israel according to each day's need, ⁶⁰so that all the peoples [e] of the earth may know that the Lᴏʀᴅ is God and that there is no other. [f] ⁶¹And may your hearts [g] be fully committed [h] to the Lᴏʀᴅ our God, to live by his decrees and obey his commands, as at this time."

THE DEDICATION OF THE TEMPLE
8:62–66pp — 2Ch 7:1–10

⁶²Then the king and all Israel with him offered sacrifices [i] before the Lᴏʀᴅ. ⁶³Solomon offered a sacrifice of fellowship offerings to the Lᴏʀᴅ: twenty-two thousand cattle and a

8:43 [f] S Jos 4:24;
S 1Sa 17:46
[g] Ps 102:15
[h] S Dt 28:10
8:44 [i] 1Ch 5:20;
2Ch 14:11
8:45 [j] Ps 9:4; 140:12
8:46 [k] Ps 130:3;
143:2; Pr 20:9;
S Ro 3:9 [l] Lev 26:33-
39; S Dt 4:27;
S 21:10; S 28:64;
2Ki 25:21
8:47 [m] S ver 30;
S Lev 5:5; Ezr 9:15;
Ne 1:6; Jer 14:20
[n] Ezr 9:7; Ps 106:6;
Jer 3:25
8:48 [o] S Dt 4:30
[p] S Dt 4:29 [q] 1Jn 1:8-
10 [r] Ps 5:7; 11:4;
Jnh 2:4 [s] Dt 12:11-14;
Ne 1:9; Jer 23:3; 31:8
8:50 [t] 2Ki 25:28;
2Ch 30:9; Ps 106:46;
Da 1:9
8:51 [u] S Ex 34:9;
S Dt 9:29 [v] S Ex 1:13;
Isa 48:10; Jer 11:4
8:52 [w] S ver 29
[x] Job 30:20; Ps 3:4;
22:2; 77:1; 142:1
8:53 [y] Ex 19:5;
S 34:9
8:55 [z] S Ex 39:43;
Nu 6:23
8:56 [a] S Ex 33:14;
Dt 12:10; Heb 4:8
[b] S Jos 23:15;
S Jer 29:10
8:57 [c] S Dt 4:31;
S 31:6; S Mt 28:20;
Heb 13:5
8:58 [d] S Jos 24:23
8:60 [e] S Jos 4:24
[f] S Dt 4:35
8:61 [g] Dt 6:5
[h] 1Ki 9:4; 11:4; 15:3,
14; 22:43; 2Ki 20:3;
1Ch 28:9; 29:19;
2Ch 16:9; 17:6; 25:2;
Ps 119:80; Isa 38:3
8:62 [i] S 2Sa 6:13;
1Ch 29:21; Eze 45:17

8:44 *go to war ... wherever you send them.* Military initiatives undertaken with divine sanction (see, e.g., Lev 26:7; Dt 20; 21:10; 1Sa 15:3; 23:2,4; 30:8; 2Sa 5:19,24). *toward the city you have chosen.* See note on v. 30.

A **8:46** *no one who does not sin.* A striking acknowledgment that sin is universal (see Ps 14:1 and note; see also Ge 6:5; 8:21; Ro 3:10–23). *their enemies, who take them captive.* On the basis of Lev 26:33–45; Dt 28:64–68; 30:1–5 Solomon knew that stubborn disobedience would lead to exile from the promised land.

8:51 *iron-smelting furnace.* See Dt 4:20 and note.

8:53 *you singled them out ... to be your own inheritance.* Solomon began his prayer with an appeal to the Davidic covenant (vv. 23–30), and he closes with an appeal to the Sinaitic covenant (Ex 19:5; Lev 20:24,26; Dt 7:6; 32:9).

8:54 *he had been kneeling.* Cf. v. 22; see 2Ch 6:13; see also 2Sa 7:18; Lk 22:41; Eph 3:14.

8:56 *Praise be to the Lᴏʀᴅ.* Solomon understood this historic

day to be a testimony to God's covenant faithfulness. *rest to his people.* After the conquest of Canaan under the leadership of Joshua, the Lord gave the Israelites a period of rest from their enemies (Jos 11:23; 21:44; 22:4), even though there remained much land to be possessed (Jos 13:1; Jdg 1). It was only with David's victories that the rest was made durable and complete (see 2Sa 7:1; see also note on 1Ki 5:4). *as he promised.* See Dt 12:9–10. *good promises.* See Jos 21:44–45 and note on 21:45.

A **8:58** *turn our hearts to him.* Solomon asks for a divine work of grace within his people that will enable them to be faithful to the covenant (see Dt 30:6; Ps 51:10; Php 2:13).

8:59 *his servant.* The king, who, as the Lord's anointed, serves as the earthly representative of God's rule over his people (see notes on Ps 2:2,7).

8:60 *so that all ... may know.* See note on Ps 46:10.

8:63 *fellowship offerings.* Involved a communion meal (see note on 1Sa 11:15). *twenty-two thousand cattle and a hundred*

8:63 ʲEzr 6:16
8:64 ᵏS Ex 29:13
ʲS Ex 27:1; 2Ki 16:14;
2Ch 4:1; 8:12; 15:8;
Eze 43:13-17
ᵐS 2Sa 6:17
8:65 ⁿS ver 2
ᵒS Nu 13:21
ᵖS Ge 15:18
8:66 ᵠS Ex 18:9
9:1 ʳS 2Sa 7:2
9:2 ˢS 1Ki 3:5
9:3 ᵗS 1Sa 9:16;
2Ki 19:20; 20:5;
Ps 10:17; 34:17
ᵘS Ex 20:24;
S Dt 12:5 ᵛS Dt 11:12
9:4 ʷS Ge 17:1
ˣDt 17:20; 1Ki 14:8;
15:5 ʸS 1Ki 3:14;
1Ch 28:9; Pr 4:4
9:5 ᶻ1Ch 22:10
ᵃS 2Sa 7:15
9:6 ᵇDt 28:15;
2Sa 7:14; 2Ki 18:12;
Jer 17:27; 26:4; 32:23;
44:23 ᶜ1Ki 11:10
9:7 ᵈLev 18:24-28;
Dt 4:26; S Jos 23:13;
2Ki 17:23; Jer 24:10
ᵉDt 12:5; Jer 7:14
ᶠJob 17:6; Ps 44:14;
Jer 24:9; Joel 2:17
ᵍS Dt 28:37; Eze 5:15
9:8 ʰS Lev 26:32
ⁱS Dt 29:24; Jer 7:4-
15; Mt 23:38
9:9 ʲDt 29:25;
2Ki 22:17; Jer 5:19;
13:22; 16:11,13; 22:9
ᵏS Nu 25:3; Jer 40:3;
44:23; La 4:12
ˡS Dt 31:29

hundred and twenty thousand sheep and goats. So the king and all the Israelites dedicated ʲ the temple of the LORD.

⁶⁴On that same day the king consecrated the middle part of the courtyard in front of the temple of the LORD, and there he offered burnt offerings, grain offerings and the fat ᵏ of the fellowship offerings, because the bronze altar ˡ that stood before the LORD was too small to hold the burnt offerings, the grain offerings and the fat of the fellowship offerings. ᵐ

⁶⁵So Solomon observed the festival ⁿ at that time, and all Israel with him—a vast assembly, people from Lebo Hamath ᵒ to the Wadi of Egypt. ᵖ They celebrated it before the LORD our God for seven days and seven days more, fourteen days in all. ⁶⁶On the following day he sent the people away. They blessed the king and then went home, joyful and glad in heart for all the good ᵠ things the LORD had done for his servant David and his people Israel.

THE LORD APPEARS TO SOLOMON
9:1–9pp — 2Ch 7:11–22

9 When Solomon had finished ʳ building the temple of the LORD and the royal palace, and had achieved all he had desired to do, ²the LORD appeared ˢ to him a second time, as he had appeared to him at Gibeon. ³The LORD said to him:

"I have heard ᵗ the prayer and plea you have made before me; I have consecrated this temple, which you have built, by putting my Name ᵘ there forever. My eyes ᵛ and my heart will always be there.

⁴"As for you, if you walk before me faithfully with integrity of heart ʷ and uprightness, as David ˣ your father did, and do all I command and observe my decrees and laws, ʸ ⁵I will establish ᶻ your royal throne over Israel forever, as I promised David your father when I said, 'You shall never fail ᵃ to have a successor on the throne of Israel.'

⁶"But if you ᵃ or your descendants turn away ᵇ from me and do not observe the commands and decrees I have given you ᵃ and go off to serve other gods ᶜ and worship them, ⁷then I will cut off Israel from the land ᵈ I have given them and will reject this temple I have consecrated for my Name. ᵉ Israel will then become a byword ᶠ and an object of ridicule ᵍ among all peoples. ⁸This temple will become a heap of rubble. All ᵇ who pass by will be appalled ʰ and will scoff and say, 'Why has the LORD done such a thing to this land and to this temple?' ⁱ ⁹People will answer, ʲ 'Because they have forsaken ᵏ the LORD their God, who brought their ancestors out of Egypt, and have embraced other gods, worshiping and serving them—that is why the LORD brought all this disaster ˡ on them.'"

SOLOMON'S OTHER ACTIVITIES
9:10–28pp — 2Ch 8:1–18

¹⁰At the end of twenty years, during which Solomon built these two buildings—the temple of the LORD and the royal palace— ¹¹King Solomon gave twenty towns in Galilee

---

ᵃ 6 The Hebrew is plural.   ᵇ 8 See some Septuagint manuscripts, Old Latin, Syriac, Arabic and Targum; Hebrew *And though this temple is now imposing, all*

---

and twenty thousand sheep and goats. Although these numbers may seem large, there were vast numbers of people who participated in the dedication ceremony, which lasted 14 days (see vv. 1–2; see also v. 65).
8:65 *Lebo Hamath.* See note on Eze 47:15. *Wadi of Egypt.* Probably Wadi el-Arish (see note on Ge 15:18). People came to Jerusalem for the dedication of the temple from nearly the entire area of Solomon's dominion (see note on 4:21). *seven days and seven days more, fourteen days in all.* It appears that the seven-day celebration for the dedication of the temple was followed by the seven-day Festival of Tabernacles (see note on v. 2), which was observed from the 15th to the 21st of the seventh month. According to Chronicles, this was followed by a final assembly on the next day, in accordance with Lev 23:33–36; then on the 23rd of the month the people were sent to their homes (see 2Ch 7:8–10).
9:1 *When Solomon had finished.* At the earliest this would be in the 24th year (4 + 7 + 13 = 24) of Solomon's reign—946 B.C. (see 6:1,37–38; 7:1; 9:10).

9:2 *he had appeared to him at Gibeon.* See 3:4–15.
9:3 *putting my Name there forever.* See notes on 3:2; 8:16. *My eyes and my heart will always be there.* See 8:29.

9:4–5 *if you walk before me faithfully with integrity of heart . . . I will establish your royal throne over Israel forever.* See 8:25 and note on 2:4. The Lord reemphasizes to Solomon the importance of obedience to the covenant in order to experience its blessings rather than its curses. This was particularly necessary as Solomon's kingdom grew in influence and wealth, with all the potential for covenant-breaking that prosperity brought (see Dt 8:12–14,17; 31:20; 32:15).
9:6 *serve other gods and worship them.* See 11:4–8.
9:7 *a byword and an object of ridicule among all peoples.* See the covenant curse in Dt 28:37.
9:9 *that is why the LORD brought all this disaster on them.* See Dt 29:22–28; Jer 22:8–30.
9:10–28 See map No. 5 at the end of this study Bible.
9:11 *Solomon gave twenty towns in Galilee to Hiram king of Tyre.* Comparison of vv. 10–14 with 5:1–12 suggests that during

to Hiram king of Tyre, because Hiram had supplied him with all the cedar and juniper and gold *m* he wanted. ¹²But when Hiram went from Tyre to see the towns that Solomon had given him, he was not pleased with them. ¹³"What kind of towns are these you have given me, my brother?" he asked. And he called them the Land of Kabul,ᵃ *n* a name they have to this day. ¹⁴Now Hiram had sent to the king 120 talentsᵇ of gold. *o*

¹⁵Here is the account of the forced labor King Solomon conscripted*p* to build the LORD's temple, his own palace, the terraces,ᶜ *q* the wall of Jerusalem, and Hazor, *r* Megiddo and Gezer. *s* ¹⁶(Pharaoh king of Egypt had attacked and captured Gezer. He had set it on fire. He killed its Canaanite inhabitants and then gave it as a wedding gift to his daughter, *t* Solomon's wife. ¹⁷And Solomon rebuilt Gezer.) He built up Lower Beth Horon, *u* ¹⁸Baalath, *v* and Tadmorᵈ in the desert, within his land, ¹⁹as well as all his store cities *w* and the towns for his chariotsˣ and for his horsesᵉ—whatever he desired to build in Jerusalem, in Lebanon and throughout all the territory he ruled.

²⁰There were still people left from the Amorites, Hittites, *y* Perizzites, Hivites and Jebusitesᶻ (these peoples were not Israelites). ²¹Solomon conscripted the descendantsᵃ of all these peoples remaining in the land—whom the Israelites could not exterminateᶠᵇ—to serve as slave labor,ᶜ as it is to this day. ²²But Solomon did not make slavesᵈ of any of the Israelites; they were his fighting men, his government officials, his officers, his captains, and the commanders of his chariots and charioteers. ²³They were also the chief officialsᵉ in charge of Solomon's projects—550 officials supervising those who did the work.

²⁴After Pharaoh's daughterᶠ had come up from the City of David to the palace Solomon had built for her, he constructed the terraces.ᵍ

²⁵Threeʰ times a year Solomon sacrificed burnt offerings and fellowship offerings on the altar he had built for the LORD, burning incense before the LORD along with them, and so fulfilled the temple obligations.

²⁶King Solomon also built shipsⁱ at Ezion Geber,ʲ which is near Elathᵏ in Edom, on the shore of the Red Sea. ᵍ ²⁷And Hiram sent his servants—sailors *l* who knew the sea—to serve in the fleet with Solomon's servants. ²⁸They sailed to Ophir *m* and brought back 420 talentsʰ of gold, *n* which they delivered to King Solomon.

ᵃ 13 *Kabul* sounds like the Hebrew for *good-for-nothing.*   ᵇ 14 That is, about 4 1/2 tons or about 4 metric tons   ᶜ 15 Or *the Millo;* also in verse 24   ᵈ 18 The Hebrew may also be read *Tamar.*   ᵉ 19 Or *charioteers*   ᶠ 21 The Hebrew term refers to the irrevocable giving over of things or persons to the LORD, often by totally destroying them.   ᵍ 26 Or *the Sea of Reeds*   ʰ 28 That is, about 16 tons or about 14 metric tons

---

Solomon's 20 years of building activity he became more indebted to Hiram than anticipated in their original agreement (see note on 5:9), which had provided for payment for labor (5:6) and wood (5:10–11). From vv. 11,14 it is evident that in addition to wood and labor Solomon had also acquired great quantities of gold from Hiram. It appears that Solomon gave Hiram the 20 towns in the Phoenician-Galilee border area as a surety for repayment of the gold. 2Ch 8:1–2 indicates that at some later date when Solomon's gold reserves were increased, perhaps after the return of the expedition to Ophir (1Ki 9:26–28; 10:11) or the visit of the queen of Sheba (10:1–13), he settled his debt with Hiram and recovered the 20 towns held as collateral.
9:13 *my brother.* A term used in international diplomacy indicating a relationship of alliance between equals (see 20:32 and note; see also chart, p. 20).
9:15 *forced labor.* Non-Israelite slave labor of a permanent nature (in contrast to the temporary conscription of Israelite workmen described in 5:13–16). *terraces.* Probably for Solomon's expansion of Jerusalem on the ridge north from David's city (see note on 2Sa 5:9). *Hazor.* Solomon's building activity at Hazor, Megiddo and Gezer was intended to strengthen the fortifications of these ancient, strategically located towns (Solomonic gates, probably built by the same masons, have been found at all three sites). Hazor was the most important fortress in the northern Galilee area, controlling the trade route running from the Euphrates River to Egypt. *Megiddo.* Another fortress along the great north-south trade route; it commanded the pass through the Carmel range from the plain of Jezreel to the coastal plain of Sharon. *Gezer.* See note on 3:1.
9:16 *Pharaoh.* See note on 3:1. *killed its Canaanite inhabitants.* Although Joshua had killed the king of Gezer at the time of the conquest (Jos 10:33; 12:12), the tribe of Ephraim had been un-

able to drive out its inhabitants (Jos 16:10; Jdg 1:29).
9:17 *Lower Beth Horon.* Located about nine miles northwest of Jerusalem at a pass giving entrance to the Judahite highlands and Jerusalem from the coastal plain.
9:18 *Baalath.* To be identified with either the Bealoth of Jos 15:24 located to the south of Hebron in the tribe of Judah or the Baalath southwest of Beth Horon in the tribe of Dan (Jos 19:44). *Tadmor.* See TNIV text note; see also 2Ch 8:4; Eze 47:19.
9:19 *towns for his chariots and ... horses.* These towns are not mentioned by name but must have been strategically located throughout the land. Although Solomon was a man of peace, he was fully prepared for war (cf. Dt 17:16–17 and note).
9:20 *Amorites ... Jebusites.* See Dt 7:1; 20:17; see also notes on Ge 10:15–18; 13:7; 15:16; 23:9; Jos 5:1; Jdg 3:3; 6:10; 2Sa 21:2.
9:22 *Solomon did not make slaves of any of the Israelites.* See note on v. 15.
9:23 *550 officials supervising.* See note on 5:16.
9:25 *Three times a year.* On the occasion of the three important annual festivals: the Festival of Unleavened Bread, the Festival of Weeks, and the Festival of Tabernacles (see Ex 23:14–17; 2Ch 8:13).
9:26 *ships.* Used in a large trading business that brought great wealth to Solomon's court (see v. 28; 10:11). *Ezion Geber.* Located at the northern tip of the Gulf of Aqaba (see 22:48; Nu 33:35; Dt 2:8). *Red Sea.* The Hebrew for this term, normally read as *Yam Suph* ("sea of reeds"; see TNIV text note), refers to the body of water through which the Israelites passed at the time of the exodus (see notes on Ex 13:18; 14:2). It can also be read, however, as *Yam Soph* ("sea of land's end"), a more likely reading when referring to the Red Sea, and especially (as here) to its eastern arm (the Gulf of Aqaba).
9:28 *Ophir.* A source for gold (2Ch 8:18; Job 28:16; Ps 45:9; Isa 13:12), almugwood and precious stones (10:11), and

Cross references (right column)

9:11 *m* ver 14
9:13 *n* Jos 19:27
9:14 *o* ver 11
9:15 *p* 1Ki 5:13
ᵍ S 2Sa 5:9
r Jos 11:10-11
s S Jos 10:33
9:16 ᶠ 1Ki 3:1;
Ps 45:12; 68:29; 72:10
9:17 *u* S Jos 10:10
9:18 *v* S Jos 19:44
9:19 *w* S Ex 1:11
ˣ S Dt 17:16; 1Ki 4:26;
2Ch 1:14; 9:25
9:20 *y* S Nu 13:29
ᶻ S Jos 11:3
9:21 ᵃ S Ge 9:25-26
ᵇ S Jos 15:63
ᶜ S Ge 49:15;
S Ex 1:11; S Dt 20:11
9:22 ᵈ S Lev 25:39
9:23 ᵉ 1Ki 5:16
9:24 ᶠ S 1Ki 3:1
ᵍ 2Sa 5:9; 1Ki 11:27
9:25 ʰ S Ex 23:14
9:26 ⁱ 1Ki 10:22;
22:48; 2Ch 20:37;
Isa 2:16 *j* S Nu 33:35
ᵏ 2Ki 14:22; 16:6
9:27 *l* Eze 27:8
9:28 *m* S Ge 10:29
n ver 14; 1Ki 10:10,11,
14,21; 2Ch 1:15;
Ecc 2:8

10:1 °S Ge 10:7,28;
S 25:3; Mt 12:42;
Lk 11:31 ᵖ Eze 16:14
�q S Nu 12:8;
S Jdg 14:12
10:2 ʳ S Ge 24:10
10:5 ˢ 1Ki 4:22
10:7 ᵗ S Ge 45:26
ᵘ 1Ch 29:25
10:8 ᵛ Pr 8:34
10:9 ʷ S 1Ki 5:7;
S Isa 42:10 ˣ S Dt 7:8
ʸ Ps 11:7; 33:5; 72:2;
99:4; 103:6
10:10 ᶻ S 1Ki 9:28;
Isa 60:6
10:11 ᵃ S Ge 10:29
10:14 ᵇ S 1Ki 9:28
10:16 ᶜ S 2Sa 8:7

THE QUEEN OF SHEBA VISITS SOLOMON

10:1–13pp — 2Ch 9:1–12

10 When the queen of Sheba ᵒ heard about the fame ᵖ of Solomon and his relationship to the LORD, she came to test Solomon with hard questions. �q ²Arriving at Jerusalem with a very great caravan ʳ—with camels carrying spices, large quantities of gold, and precious stones—she came to Solomon and talked with him about all that she had on her mind. ³Solomon answered all her questions; nothing was too hard for the king to explain to her. ⁴When the queen of Sheba saw all the wisdom of Solomon and the palace he had built, ⁵the food on his table, ˢ the seating of his officials, the attending servants in their robes, his cupbearers, and the burnt offerings he made at ᵃ the temple of the LORD, she was overwhelmed.

⁶She said to the king, "The report I heard in my own country about your achievements and your wisdom is true. ⁷But I did not believe ᵗ these things until I came and saw with my own eyes. Indeed, not even half was told me; in wisdom and wealth ᵘ you have far exceeded the report I heard. ⁸How happy your people must be! How happy your officials, who continually stand before you and hear ᵛ your wisdom! ⁹Praise ʷ be to the LORD your God, who has delighted in you and placed you on the throne of Israel. Because of the LORD's eternal love ˣ for Israel, he has made you king to maintain justice ʸ and righteousness."

¹⁰And she gave the king 120 talents ᵇ of gold, ᶻ large quantities of spices, and precious stones. Never again were so many spices brought in as those the queen of Sheba gave to King Solomon.

¹¹(Hiram's ships brought gold from Ophir; ᵃ and from there they brought great cargoes of almugwood ᶜ and precious stones. ¹²The king used the almugwood to make supports ᵈ for the temple of the LORD and for the royal palace, and to make harps and lyres for the musicians. So much almugwood has never been imported or seen since that day.)

¹³King Solomon gave the queen of Sheba all she desired and asked for, besides what he had given her out of his royal bounty. Then she left and returned with her retinue to her own country.

SOLOMON'S SPLENDOR

10:14–29pp — 2Ch 1:14–17; 9:13–28

¹⁴The weight of the gold ᵇ that Solomon received yearly was 666 talents, ᵉ ¹⁵not including the revenues from merchants and traders and from all the Arabian kings and the governors of the territories.

¹⁶King Solomon made two hundred large shields ᶜ of hammered gold; six hundred shek-

---

ᵃ 5 Or *the ascent by which he went up to*   ᵇ 10 That is, about 4 1/2 tons or about 4 metric tons
ᶜ 11 Probably a variant of *algumwood*; also in verse 12   ᵈ 12 The meaning of the Hebrew for this word is uncertain.   ᵉ 14 That is, about 25 tons or about 23 metric tons

---

silver, ivory, apes and baboons (10:22). Such a place is attested on a Hebrew ostracon (see note on Jer 34:7) that dates perhaps to the eighth century B.C. It contains this note: "Gold of Ophir for Beth Horon—30 shekels." However, Ophir's location is disputed: Southeastern Arabia, southwestern Arabia, the northeastern African coast (in the area of Somalia), India and Zimbabwe have all been suggested. If Ophir was located in Arabia, it was probably a trading center for goods from farther east, as well as from east Africa. But the three-year voyages of Solomon's merchant vessels (10:22) suggest a more distant location than the Arabian coast.

B **10:1** *Sheba.* Archaeological evidence suggests that Sheba is to be identified with a mercantile kingdom (Saba) that flourished in southwest Arabia (see notes on Ge 10:28; Joel 3:8) c. 900–450 B.C. It profited from the sea trade of India and east Africa by transporting luxury commodities north to Damascus and Gaza on caravan routes through the Arabian Desert. It is possible that Solomon's fleet of ships threatened Sheba's continued dominance of this trading business. *fame of Solomon.* See 4:31. *his relationship to the LORD.* The queen of Sheba recognized a connection between the wisdom of Solomon and the God he served. Jesus used her example to condemn the people of his own day who had not recognized that "one greater than Solomon" was in their midst (Mt 12:42; Lk 11:31).

C **10:9** *Praise be to the LORD your God.* The queen of Sheba's confession is beautifully worded and reflects a profound understanding of Israel's covenant relationship with the Lord.

However, it does not necessarily imply anything more than her recognition of the Lord as Israel's national God, in conformity with the ideas of polytheistic paganism (see note on 5:7; see also 2Ch 2:12; Da 3:28–29). There is no confession that Solomon's God has become her God to the exclusion of all others.

10:10 *120 talents of gold.* See notes on 9:11,28.

10:11 *Hiram's ships.* See 9:26–28. Hiram had supplied the wood, the sailors and the expertise in construction that Israel lacked. *almugwood.* Perhaps juniper; see TNIV text note and 2Ch 9:10–11. It was apparently available from Lebanon as well as Ophir (2Ch 2:8).

10:13 *all she desired and asked for.* The exchange of gifts between Solomon and the queen may have signified the effecting of a trade agreement (see note on v. 1). There is no basis for the idea sometimes suggested that she desired offspring fathered by Solomon and left Jerusalem carrying his child.

10:15 *revenues from … Arabian kings.* Tribute for passage of their caravans through Israelite territory. *governors of the territories.* Perhaps those of 4:7–19.

B **10:16** *large shields.* Rectangular shields that afforded maximum protection (in distinction from the smaller round shields). These gold shields were probably not intended for battle but for ceremonial use, symbolizing Israel's wealth and glory. They were probably made of wood overlaid with gold. Shishak of Egypt carried them off as plunder in the fifth regnal year of Solomon's son Rehoboam (see 14:25–26). Ancient Greek sources also refer to gold shields.

els^a of gold went into each shield. ¹⁷He also made three hundred small shields of hammered gold, with three minas^b of gold in each shield. The king put them in the Palace of the Forest of Lebanon. ^d

¹⁸Then the king made a great throne inlaid with ivory and overlaid with fine gold. ¹⁹The throne had six steps, and its back had a rounded top. On both sides of the seat were armrests, with a lion standing beside each of them. ²⁰Twelve lions stood on the six steps, one at either end of each step. Nothing like it had ever been made for any other kingdom. ²¹All King Solomon's goblets were gold, and all the household articles in the Palace of the Forest of Lebanon were pure gold. ^e Nothing was made of silver, because silver was considered of little value in Solomon's days. ²²The king had a fleet of trading ships^{c f} at sea along with the ships^g of Hiram. Once every three years it returned, carrying gold, silver and ivory, and apes and baboons.

²³King Solomon was greater in riches^h and wisdomⁱ than all the other kings of the earth. ²⁴The whole world sought audience with Solomon to hear the wisdom^j God had put in his heart. ²⁵Year after year, everyone who came brought a gift^k—articles of silver and gold, robes, weapons and spices, and horses and mules.

²⁶Solomon accumulated chariots and horses;^l he had fourteen hundred chariots and twelve thousand horses,^d which he kept in the chariot cities and also with him in Jerusalem. ²⁷The king made silver as common^m in Jerusalem as stones,ⁿ and cedar as plentiful as sycamore-fig^o trees in the foothills. ²⁸Solomon's horses were imported from Egypt and from Kue^e—the royal merchants purchased them from Kue at the current price. ²⁹They imported a chariot from Egypt for six hundred shekels of silver, and a horse for a hundred and fifty.^f They also exported them to all the kings of the Hittites^p and of the Arameans.

SOLOMON'S WIVES

11 King Solomon, however, loved many foreign women^q besides Pharaoh's daughter—Moabites, Ammonites,^r Edomites, Sidonians and Hittites. ²They were from nations about which the LORD had told the Israelites, "You must not intermarry^s with them, because they will surely turn your hearts after their gods." Nevertheless, Solomon held fast to them in love. ³He had seven hundred wives of royal birth and three hundred concubines,^t and his wives led him astray. ^{u 4}As Solomon grew old, his wives turned his heart after other gods,^v and his heart was not fully devoted^w to the LORD his God, as the heart of David his father had been. ⁵He followed Ashtoreth^x the goddess of the Sidonians, and Molek^y the detestable god of the Ammonites. ⁶So Solomon did evil^z in the eyes of the LORD; he did not follow the LORD completely, as David his father had done.

^a 16 That is, about 15 pounds or about 6.9 kilograms; also in verse 29   ^b 17 That is, about 3 3/4 pounds or about 1.7 kilograms; or perhaps reference is to double minas, that is, about 7 1/2 pounds or about 3.5 kilograms.   ^c 22 Hebrew *of ships of Tarshish*   ^d 26 Or *charioteers*   ^e 28 Probably *Cilicia*
^f 29 That is, about 3 3/4 pounds or about 1.7 kilograms

10:17 ^d S 1Ki 7:2
10:21 ^e Isa 60:17
10:22 ^f S 1Ki 9:26
^g 1Ki 9:27; Ps 48:7;
Isa 2:16; 23:1,14;
60:6,9
10:23 ^h 1Ki 3:13;
Mt 6:29 ⁱ S 1Ki 3:12;
Mt 12:42
10:24 ^j S 2Sa 14:20
10:25 ^k S 1Sa 10:27
10:26 ^l S Dt 17:16
10:27 ^m Dt 17:17
ⁿ Job 27:16; Isa 60:17
^o 1Ch 27:28; Am 7:14
10:29 ^p S Nu 13:29
11:1 ^q S ver 3;
S Ex 34:16 ^r 1Ki 14:21,
31
11:2 ^s S Ex 34:16;
1Ki 16:31
11:3 ^t S Ge 22:24;
S Est 2:14 ^u ver 1;
Dt 17:17; Ne 13:26;
Pr 31:3
11:4 ^v S Ex 34:16
^w S 1Ki 8:61;
S 1Ch 29:19
11:5 ^x S Jdg 2:13
^y ver 7; S Lev 18:21;
Isa 57:9; Zep 1:5
11:6 ^z S Dt 4:25

10:17 *Palace of the Forest of Lebanon.* See 7:2 and note.
10:22 *fleet of trading ships.* See TNIV text note; 2Ch 9:21. The same fleet is referred to in v. 11; 9:26–28. "Ships of Tarshish" are not necessarily ships that sail to Tarshish (see note on Jnh 1:3) but can designate large trading vessels.
10:26 *chariots and horses.* See note on 4:26. Accumulation of horses by the king was forbidden in the Mosaic law (Dt 17:16).
10:27 *sycamore-fig trees.* See note on Am 7:14.
10:29 *imported … exported.* Through his agents (v. 28) Solomon was the middleman in a lucrative trading business. *Hittites.* See note on Ge 10:15. *Arameans.* An ancient people who occupied a large area north and east of the Sea of Galilee (cf. notes on Ge 10:22; Dt 26:5; 1Ch 18:15).

C **11:1–13** Solomon's folly—counterpoint to his wisdom (see ch. 3 and note on 1:1—12:24).

C **11:1** *loved many foreign women.* Many of Solomon's marriages were no doubt for the purpose of sealing international relationships with various kingdoms, large and small—a common practice in the ancient Near East. But this violated not only Dt 17:17 with respect to the multiplicity of wives, but also the prohibition against taking wives from the pagan peoples among whom Israel settled (see Ex 34:16; Dt 7:1–3; Jos 23:12–13; Ezr 9:2; 10:2–3; Ne 13:23–27). *Moabites.* See note on Ge 19:36–38. *Ammonites.* See note on Ge 19:36–38; see also 14:21; Dt 23:3. *Edomites.* See notes on Ge 25:26; 36:1; Am 1:11; 9:12; see also Dt

23:7–8. *Sidonians.* See 16:31. *Hittites.* See note on Ge 10:15.

A **11:2** *they will surely turn your hearts after their gods.* As indeed they did (v.4). An example in Israel's earlier history is found in Nu 25:1–15.
11:3 *seven hundred … three hundred.* Cf. SS 6:8, but see note there. *concubines.* See note on Ge 25:6.

A C **11:4** *his wives turned his heart after other gods.* As the Lord had warned (v. 2). *his heart was not fully devoted to the LORD.* See 8:61. The atmosphere of paganism and idolatry introduced into Solomon's court by his foreign wives gradually led Solomon into syncretistic religious practices.
11:5 *Ashtoreth.* See v. 33; 14:15; 2Ki 23:13; see also notes on Jdg 2:13; 1Sa 7:3. *Molek.* See 2Sa 12:30 and TNIV text note there. Molek and Milkom are alternative names for the same pagan deity. Worship of this god not only severely jeopardized the continued recognition of the absolute kingship of the Lord over his people but also involved (on rare occasions) the abomination of child sacrifice (see 2Ki 16:3; 17:17; 21:6; Lev 18:21 and note; 20:2–5; see also notes on Ge 15:16; Jdg 10:6). The names Ashtoreth and Molek have been given the vowel pattern of Hebrew *bosheth* ("shameful thing"). *Bosheth* is often substituted as a degrading name for Baal (see notes on Jdg 6:32; Jer 7:31).

A **11:6** *as David his father had done.* Although David committed grievous sins, he was repentant, and he was never involved in idolatrous worship.

11:7 a 2Ki 23:13
b S Nu 21:29
c S Lev 18:21; 20:2-5;
Ac 7:43
11:9 d S 1Ki 3:5
11:10 e S 1Ki 9:6
f 1Ki 6:12
11:11 g S Lev 18:4
h ver 31; S 1Sa 15:27;
2Ki 17:21; Mt 21:43
11:12 i Ps 89:33
11:13 j 1Ki 12:20
k S 2Sa 7:15 l Dt 12:11
11:14 m S 1Ki 5:4
11:15 n 1Ch 18:12
11:18 o Nu 10:12
11:23 p S 1Ki 5:4
q S 2Sa 8:3
11:24 r S 2Sa 8:5
11:25 s S Ge 10:22;
S 2Sa 10:19

[7]On a hill east [a] of Jerusalem, Solomon built a high place for Chemosh [b] the detestable god of Moab, and for Molek [c] the detestable god of the Ammonites. [8]He did the same for all his foreign wives, who burned incense and offered sacrifices to their gods.

[9]The LORD became angry with Solomon because his heart had turned away from the LORD, the God of Israel, who had appeared [d] to him twice. [10]Although he had forbidden Solomon to follow other gods, [e] Solomon did not keep the LORD's command. [f] [11]So the LORD said to Solomon, "Since this is your attitude and you have not kept my covenant and my decrees, [g] which I commanded you, I will most certainly tear [h] the kingdom away from you and give it to one of your subordinates. [12]Nevertheless, for the sake of David [i] your father, I will not do it during your lifetime. I will tear it out of the hand of your son. [13]Yet I will not tear the whole kingdom from him, but will give him one tribe [j] for the sake [k] of David my servant and for the sake of Jerusalem, which I have chosen." [l]

SOLOMON'S ADVERSARIES

[14]Then the LORD raised up against Solomon an adversary, [m] Hadad the Edomite, from the royal line of Edom. [15]Earlier when David was fighting with Edom, Joab the commander of the army, who had gone up to bury the dead, had struck down all the men in Edom. [n] [16]Joab and all the Israelites stayed there for six months, until they had destroyed all the men in Edom. [17]But Hadad, still only a boy, fled to Egypt with some Edomite officials who had served his father. [18]They set out from Midian and went to Paran. [o] Then taking people from Paran with them, they went to Egypt, to Pharaoh king of Egypt, who gave Hadad a house and land and provided him with food.

[19]Pharaoh was so pleased with Hadad that he gave him a sister of his own wife, Queen Tahpenes, in marriage. [20]The sister of Tahpenes bore him a son named Genubath, whom Tahpenes brought up in the royal palace. There Genubath lived with Pharaoh's own children.

[21]While he was in Egypt, Hadad heard that David rested with his ancestors and that Joab the commander of the army was also dead. Then Hadad said to Pharaoh, "Let me go, that I may return to my own country."

[22]"What have you lacked here that you want to go back to your own country?" Pharaoh asked.

"Nothing," Hadad replied, "but do let me go!"

[23]And God raised up against Solomon another adversary, [p] Rezon son of Eliada, who had fled from his master, Hadadezer [q] king of Zobah. [24]When David destroyed Zobah's army, Rezon gathered a band of men around him and became their leader; they went to Damascus, [r] where they settled and took control. [25]Rezon was Israel's adversary as long as Solomon lived, adding to the trouble caused by Hadad. So Rezon ruled in Aram [s] and was hostile toward Israel.

11:7 *high place.* See note on 3:2. *Chemosh.* See note on 2Ki 3:27.
11:9 *appeared to him twice.* See 3:4–5; 9:1–9.

A C 11:11 *not kept my covenant.* Solomon had broken the most basic demands of the covenant (see Ex 20:2–5) and thereby severely undermined the entire covenant relationship between God and his people.

11:12 *for the sake of David your father.* Because of David's unwavering loyalty to the Lord and God's covenant with him (see 2Sa 7:11–16).

11:13 *one tribe.* Judah (see note on vv. 31–32; see also 12:20). *for the sake of Jerusalem, which I have chosen.* Now that Jerusalem contained the temple built by David's son in accordance with 2Sa 7:13, the destiny of Jerusalem and the Davidic dynasty were closely linked (see 2Ki 19:34; 21:7–8; Ps 132). The temple represented God's royal palace, where his earthly throne (the ark) was situated and where he had pledged to be present as Israel's Great King (9:3).

11:14 *Hadad.* The name of a Semitic storm god (see notes on Jdg 2:13; Zec 12:11) that was also taken by many Aramean (see 15:18; 20:1 and note) and Edomite kings (see Ge 36:35,39) as their royal name.

11:15 *David was fighting with Edom.* See 2Sa 8:13–14; see also map, p. 508.

11:16 *all the Israelites . . . all the men in Edom.* All those, on both sides, who took part in the campaign.

11:17 *only a boy.* Probably in his early teens.

11:18 *Midian.* At this time Midianites inhabited a region on the eastern borders of Moab and Edom. *Paran.* A desert area southeast of Kadesh in the central area of the Sinai peninsula (see Nu 10:12; 12:16; 13:3). *Pharaoh king of Egypt.* See note on 3:1. *gave Hadad a house and land and . . . food.* In a time of Israel's growing strength it was in Egypt's interest to befriend those who would harass Israel and keep her power in check.

11:21 *Let me go.* It appears that Hadad returned to Edom during the early days of Solomon's reign.

11:22 *What have you lacked here . . . ?* Because Egypt had by this time established relatively good relations with Israel (see note on 3:1), the pharaoh was reluctant to see Hadad return to Edom and provoke trouble with Solomon.

11:23 *Zobah.* See note on 2Sa 8:3; see also map No. 5 at the end of this study Bible.

11:24 *Rezon gathered a band of men . . . and became their leader.* As David had done (1Sa 22:1–2), and Jephthah before him (Jdg 11:3). *they went to Damascus, where they settled and took control.* Presumably this took place in the early part of Solomon's reign (see 2Sa 8:6 for the situation in Damascus during the time of David). It is likely that Solomon's expedition (2Ch 8:3) against Hamath Zobah (the kingdom formerly ruled by Hadadezer, 2Sa 8:3–6) was provoked by opposition led by Rezon. Even though Solomon was able to retain control of the territory north of Damascus to the Euphrates (4:21,24), he was not able to drive Rezon from Damascus itself.

JEROBOAM REBELS AGAINST SOLOMON

²⁶Also, Jeroboam son of Nebat rebelled ᵗ against the king. He was one of Solomon's officials, an Ephraimite from Zeredah, and his mother was a widow named Zeruah.

²⁷Here is the account of how he rebelled against the king: Solomon had built the terraces ᵃ ᵘ and had filled in the gap in the wall of the city of David his father. ²⁸Now Jeroboam was a man of standing, ᵛ and when Solomon saw how well ʷ the young man did his work, he put him in charge of the whole labor force of the house of Joseph.

²⁹About that time Jeroboam was going out of Jerusalem, and Ahijah ˣ the prophet of Shiloh met him on the way, wearing a new cloak. The two of them were alone out in the country, ³⁰and Ahijah took hold of the new cloak he was wearing and tore ʸ it into twelve pieces. ³¹Then he said to Jeroboam, "Take ten pieces for yourself, for this is what the LORD, the God of Israel, says: 'See, I am going to tear ᶻ the kingdom out of Solomon's hand and give you ten tribes. ³²But for the sake ᵃ of my servant David and the city of Jerusalem, which I have chosen out of all the tribes of Israel, he will have one tribe. ³³I will do this because they have ᵇ forsaken me and worshiped ᵇ Ashtoreth the goddess of the Sidonians, Chemosh the god of the Moabites, and Molek the god of the Ammonites, and have not walked ᶜ in obedience to me, nor done what is right in my eyes, nor kept my decrees ᵈ and laws as David, Solomon's father, did.

³⁴" 'But I will not take the whole kingdom out of Solomon's hand; I have made him ruler all the days of his life for the sake of David my servant, whom I chose and who obeyed my commands and decrees. ³⁵I will take the kingdom from his son's hands and give you ten tribes. ³⁶I will give one tribe ᵉ to his son so that David my servant may always have a lamp ᶠ before me in Jerusalem, the city where I chose to put my Name. ³⁷However, as for you, I will take you, and you will rule ᵍ over all that your heart desires; ʰ you will be king over Israel. ³⁸If you do whatever I command you and walk in obedience to me and do what is right ⁱ in my eyes by obeying my decrees ʲ and commands, as David my servant did, I will be with you. I will build you a dynasty ᵏ as enduring as the one I built for David and will give Israel to you. ³⁹I will humble David's descendants because of this, but not forever.' "

⁴⁰Solomon tried to kill Jeroboam, but Jeroboam fled ˡ to Egypt, to Shishak ᵐ the king, and stayed there until Solomon's death.

ᵃ 27 Or *the Millo*   ᵇ 33 Hebrew; Septuagint, Vulgate and Syriac *because he has*

11:26 ᵗ 2Ch 13:6
11:27 ᵘ S 1Ki 9:24
11:28 ᵛ S Ru 2:1
ʷ S Ge 39:4; Pr 22:29
11:29 ˣ 1Ki 12:15;
14:2; 2Ch 9:29; 10:15
11:30 ʸ 1Sa 15:27
11:31 ᶻ S ver 11;
S 1Sa 15:27
11:32 ᵃ S 2Sa 7:15
11:33 ᵇ S Jdg 2:13
ᶜ 2Ki 21:22 ᵈ 1Ki 3:3
11:36 ᵉ 1Ki 12:17
ᶠ S 2Sa 21:17
11:37 ᵍ 1Ki 14:7
ʰ 2Sa 3:21
11:38 ⁱ S Dt 12:25;
S 2Sa 8:15 ʲ S Dt 17:19
ᵏ S Ex 1:21
11:40 ˡ 1Ki 12:2;
2Ch 10:2 ᵐ 2Ch 12:2

11:26 *rebelled against the king.* See note on v. 40.
11:27 *terraces.* See 9:15 and note.
11:28 *whole labor force of the house of Joseph.* See 5:13–18. Jeroboam's supervision of the conscripted laborers from the tribes of Ephraim and Manasseh made him aware of the smoldering discontent among the people over Solomon's policies (see 12:4 and note).

🔒 11:31–32 *ten tribes . . . one tribe.* The tradition of considering the ten northern tribes as a unit distinct from the southern tribes (Judah and Simeon—Levi received no territorial inheritance; see Jos 21) goes back to the period of the judges (see Jdg 5:13–18). The reason, no doubt, was the continuing presence of a non-Israelite corridor (Jerusalem, Gibeonite league, Gezer) that separated the two Israelite regions (see map, p. 508; see also map No. 4 at the end of this study Bible). Political division along the same line during the early years of David's reign and the different arrangements that brought the southern and northern segments under David's rule (see 2Sa 2:4; 5:3) reinforced this sense of division. With the conquest of Jerusalem by David (2Sa 5:6–7) and the pharaoh's gift of Gezer to Solomon's wife (9:16–17), all Israel was for the first time territorially united. (Now that Jerusalem and Gezer were under Israelite control, the Gibeonite league, which had submitted already to Joshua—see Jos 9—could be effectively absorbed politically.) In the division here announced, the "one tribe" refers to the area dominated by Judah (but including Simeon; see Jos 19:1–9), and the "ten tribes" refers to the region that came under David's rule at the later date (Ephraim and Manasseh, Joseph's sons, being counted as two tribes; see Ge 48:5; see also note on Jos 14:4). For further refinement of the new boundaries that came about, see note on 12:21.

11:33 *forsaken me.* See vv. 5–7. *have not walked in obedience to me.* See vv. 1–2; 3:14.
11:34 *I have made him ruler all the days of his life.* See vv. 12–13.
11:35 *from his son's hands.* From Rehoboam (see 12:1–24).
11:36 *a lamp before me in Jerusalem.* Symbolizes the continuance of the Davidic dynasty in the city where God had chosen to cause his Name to dwell (see v. 13 and note). In a number of passages, the burning or snuffing out of one's lamp signifies the flourishing or ceasing of one's life (Job 18:6; 21:17; Pr 13:9; 20:20; 24:20). Here (and in 15:4; 2Ki 8:19; 2Ch 21:7; Ps 132:17) the same figure is applied to David's dynasty (see especially Ps 132:17, where "set up a lamp for my anointed" is parallel to "make a horn grow for David"). In David's royal sons his "lamp" continues to burn before the Lord in Jerusalem.
11:37 *Israel.* The northern ten tribes.
11:38 *If you do whatever I command you . . . I will be with you.* Jeroboam was placed under the same covenant obligations as David and Solomon before him (see 2:3–4; 3:14; 6:12–13).

🔒 11:39 *humble David's descendants.* The division of the kingdom considerably reduced the status and power of the house of David. *not forever.* Anticipates a restoration (announced also in the Messianic prophecies of Jer 30:9; Eze 34:23; 37:15–28; Hos 3:5; Am 9:11–12) in which the nation is reunited under the rule of the house of David.
11:40 *Solomon tried to kill Jeroboam.* Jeroboam, perhaps indifferent to the timing announced by Ahijah (vv. 34–35), may have made an abortive attempt to wrest the kingdom from Solomon (see v. 26). *Shishak the king.* See 14:25–26 and note on 14:25. This first Egyptian pharaoh to be mentioned by name in the OT was the Libyan founder of the 22nd dynasty (945–924 B.C.). Solomon's marriage ties were with the previous dynasty (see note on 3:1).

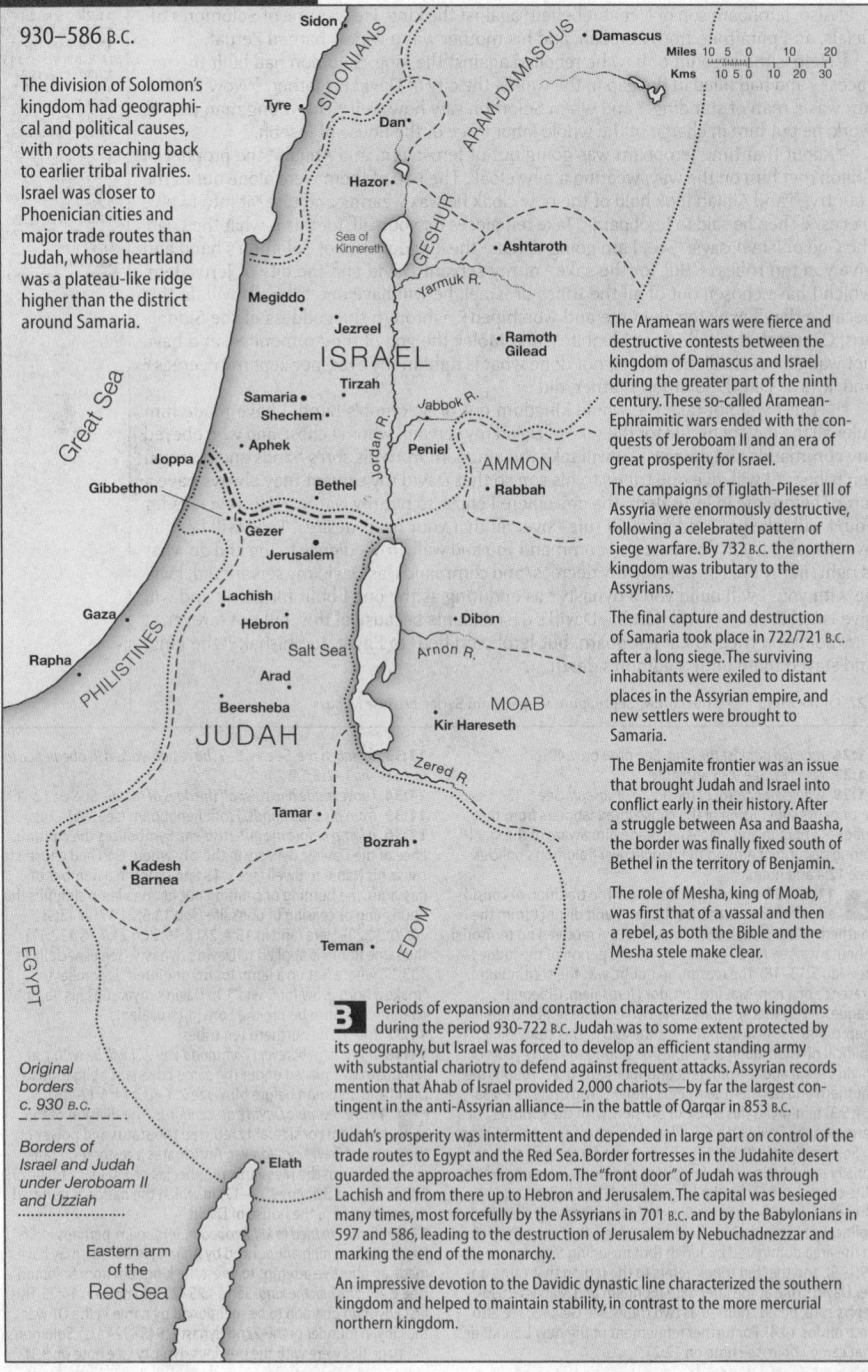

THE DIVIDED KINGDOM

930–586 B.C.

The division of Solomon's kingdom had geographical and political causes, with roots reaching back to earlier tribal rivalries. Israel was closer to Phoenician cities and major trade routes than Judah, whose heartland was a plateau-like ridge higher than the district around Samaria.

The Aramean wars were fierce and destructive contests between the kingdom of Damascus and Israel during the greater part of the ninth century. These so-called Aramean-Ephraimitic wars ended with the conquests of Jeroboam II and an era of great prosperity for Israel.

The campaigns of Tiglath-Pileser III of Assyria were enormously destructive, following a celebrated pattern of siege warfare. By 732 B.C. the northern kingdom was tributary to the Assyrians.

The final capture and destruction of Samaria took place in 722/721 B.C. after a long siege. The surviving inhabitants were exiled to distant places in the Assyrian empire, and new settlers were brought to Samaria.

The Benjamite frontier was an issue that brought Judah and Israel into conflict early in their history. After a struggle between Asa and Baasha, the border was finally fixed south of Bethel in the territory of Benjamin.

The role of Mesha, king of Moab, was first that of a vassal and then a rebel, as both the Bible and the Mesha stele make clear.

3 Periods of expansion and contraction characterized the two kingdoms during the period 930–722 B.C. Judah was to some extent protected by its geography, but Israel was forced to develop an efficient standing army with substantial chariotry to defend against frequent attacks. Assyrian records mention that Ahab of Israel provided 2,000 chariots—by far the largest contingent in the anti-Assyrian alliance—in the battle of Qarqar in 853 B.C.

Judah's prosperity was intermittent and depended in large part on control of the trade routes to Egypt and the Red Sea. Border fortresses in the Judahite desert guarded the approaches from Edom. The "front door" of Judah was through Lachish and from there up to Hebron and Jerusalem. The capital was besieged many times, most forcefully by the Assyrians in 701 B.C. and by the Babylonians in 597 and 586, leading to the destruction of Jerusalem by Nebuchadnezzar and marking the end of the monarchy.

An impressive devotion to the Davidic dynastic line characterized the southern kingdom and helped to maintain stability, in contrast to the more mercurial northern kingdom.

Map labels

Sidon
Damascus
Tyre
Dan
Hazor
SIDONIANS
ARAM-DAMASCUS
GESHUR
Sea of Kinnereth
Ashtaroth
Yarmuk R.
Megiddo
Jezreel
Ramoth Gilead
ISRAEL
Tirzah
Samaria
Shechem
Jabbok R.
Aphek
Peniel
AMMON
Joppa
Gibbethon
Bethel
Rabbah
Jordan R.
Gezer
Jerusalem
Great Sea
Lachish
Gaza
Hebron
Dibon
Salt Sea
Arnon R.
Rapha
PHILISTINES
Arad
Beersheba
MOAB
Kir Hareseth
JUDAH
Zered R.
Tamar
Bozrah
Kadesh Barnea
Teman
EDOM
EGYPT

Miles 10 5 0 10 20
Kms 10 5 0 10 20 30

Original borders
c. 930 B.C.

Borders of Israel and Judah under Jeroboam II and Uzziah

Eastern arm of the Red Sea

Elath

11:43 ⁿ Mt 1:7
12:1 ᵒ ver 25;
S Ge 12:6; Jos 24:32
12:2 ᵖ S 1Ki 11:40
12:4 �q S 1Sa 8:11-18;
1Ki 4:20-28
12:6 ʳ S 1Ki 4:2
12:7 ˢ Pr 15:1
12:8 ᵗ Lev 19:32
12:14 ᵘ Ex 1:14
12:15 ᵛ S Dt 2:30;
2Ch 25:20
ʷ S 1Ki 11:29

SOLOMON'S DEATH

11:41–43pp — 2Ch 9:29–31

⁴¹As for the other events of Solomon's reign—all he did and the wisdom he displayed—are they not written in the book of the annals of Solomon? ⁴²Solomon reigned in Jerusalem over all Israel forty years. ⁴³Then he rested with his ancestors and was buried in the city of David his father. And Rehoboam ⁿ his son succeeded him as king.

ISRAEL REBELS AGAINST REHOBOAM

12:1–24pp — 2Ch 10:1—11:4

12

Rehoboam went to Shechem, ᵒ for all Israel had gone there to make him king. ²When Jeroboam son of Nebat heard this (he was still in Egypt, where he had fled ᵖ from King Solomon), he returned from ᵃ Egypt. ³So they sent for Jeroboam, and he and the whole assembly of Israel went to Rehoboam and said to him: ⁴"Your father put a heavy yoke �q on us, but now lighten the harsh labor and the heavy yoke he put on us, and we will serve you."

⁵Rehoboam answered, "Go away for three days and then come back to me." So the people went away.

⁶Then King Rehoboam consulted the elders ʳ who had served his father Solomon during his lifetime. "How would you advise me to answer these people?" he asked.

⁷They replied, "If today you will be a servant to these people and serve them and give them a favorable answer, ˢ they will always be your servants."

⁸But Rehoboam rejected ᵗ the advice the elders gave him and consulted the young men who had grown up with him and were serving him. ⁹He asked them, "What is your advice? How should we answer these people who say to me, 'Lighten the yoke your father put on us'?"

¹⁰The young men who had grown up with him replied, "These people have said to you, 'Your father put a heavy yoke on us, but make our yoke lighter.' Now tell them, 'My little finger is thicker than my father's waist. ¹¹My father laid on you a heavy yoke; I will make it even heavier. My father scourged you with whips; I will scourge you with scorpions.' "

¹²Three days later Jeroboam and all the people returned to Rehoboam, as the king had said, "Come back to me in three days." ¹³The king answered the people harshly. Rejecting the advice given him by the elders, ¹⁴he followed the advice of the young men and said, "My father made your yoke heavy; I will make it even heavier. My father scourged ᵘ you with whips; I will scourge you with scorpions." ¹⁵So the king did not listen to the people, for this turn of events was from the LORD, ᵛ to fulfill the word the LORD had spoken to Jeroboam son of Nebat through Ahijah ʷ the Shilonite.

ᵃ 2 Or *he remained in*

11:41 *annals of Solomon.* A written source concerning Solomon's life and administration, which was used by the writer of 1,2 Kings (see Introduction: Author, Sources and Date; see also 15:7,23).

11:43 *rested with his ancestors.* See note on 1:21.

12:1 *Shechem.* A city of great significance located in the hill country of northern Ephraim (see Ge 12:6; 33:18–20; Jos 8:30–35 and note on 8:30; see also Jos 20:7; 21:21; 24:1–33). *all Israel.* That is, representatives of the northern tribes (see v. 16). The fact that David became king over the northern tribes on the basis of a covenant (see 2Sa 5:3) suggests that their act of submission was to be renewed with each new king and that it was subject to negotiation.

12:2 *heard this.* Heard about the death of Solomon (11:43). *returned from Egypt.* See 2Ch 10:2.

C 12:4 *put a heavy yoke on us.* Smoldering discontent with Solomon's heavy taxation and conscription of labor and military forces flared up into strong expression (see 4:7, 22–23,27–28; 5:13–14; 9:22; see also notes on 9:15; 11:28). Conditions had progressively worsened since the early days of Solomon's rule (see 4:20).

12:6 *elders who had served his father Solomon.* Officials of Solomon's government such as Adoniram (4:6) and the district governors (4:7–19).

A 12:7 Authority in the kingdom of God is for service, not for personal aggrandizement.

12:8 *young men.* Young in comparison to the officials who had served Solomon. Rehoboam was 41 years old when he became king (14:21). *serving him.* Apparently Rehoboam had quickly established new administrative positions for friends and associates of his own generation.

12:10 *My little finger is thicker than my father's waist.* A proverb claiming that Rehoboam's weakest measures will be far stronger than his father's strongest measures.

12:11 *scorpions.* Metal-spiked leather lashes. Not only will governmental burdens on the people be increased, but the punishment for not complying with the government's directives will also be intensified.

C 12:14 *followed the advice of the young men.* Rehoboam's answer reflects a despotic spirit completely contrary to the covenantal character of Israelite kingship (see Dt 17:14–20; see also note on 1Sa 10:25).

A 12:15 *this turn of events was from the LORD.* By this statement the writer of Kings does not condone either the foolish act of Rehoboam or the revolutionary spirit of the northern tribes, but he reminds the reader that all these things occurred to bring about the divinely announced punishment on the house of David for Solomon's idolatry and breach of the covenant (11:9–13). For the relationship between divine sovereignty over all things and human responsibility for evil acts, see note on 2Sa 24:1. *the word the LORD had spoken to Jeroboam . . . through Ahijah.* See 11:29–39.

12:16 ˣ S Ge 31:14
ʸ 2Sa 20:1 ᶻ Isa 7:17
12:17 ᵃ 1Ki 11:13,36
12:18 ᵇ S 2Sa 20:24
ᶜ S Jos 7:25
12:19 ᵈ 2Ki 17:21
12:20 ᵉ 1Ki 11:13,32;
Eze 37:16
12:21 ᶠ 1Ki 14:30;
15:6,16; 2Ch 11:1
12:22 ᵍ 2Ch 12:5-7
ʰ S Dt 33:1; 2Ki 4:7
12:25 ⁱ S ver 1
ʲ S Jdg 8:8,17

¹⁶When all Israel saw that the king refused to listen to them, they answered the king:

> "What share ˣ do we have in David,
> what part in Jesse's son?
> To your tents, Israel! ʸ
> Look after your own house, David!"

So the Israelites went home. ᶻ ¹⁷But as for the Israelites who were living in the towns of Judah, ᵃ Rehoboam still ruled over them.

¹⁸King Rehoboam sent out Adoniram, ᵃ ᵇ who was in charge of forced labor, but all Israel stoned him to death. ᶜ King Rehoboam, however, managed to get into his chariot and escape to Jerusalem. ¹⁹So Israel has been in rebellion against the house of David ᵈ to this day.

²⁰When all the Israelites heard that Jeroboam had returned, they sent and called him to the assembly and made him king over all Israel. Only the tribe of Judah remained loyal to the house of David. ᵉ

²¹When Rehoboam arrived in Jerusalem, he mustered the whole house of Judah and the tribe of Benjamin—a hundred and eighty thousand able young men—to make war ᶠ against the house of Israel and to regain the kingdom for Rehoboam son of Solomon.

²²But this word of God came to Shemaiah ᵍ the man of God: ʰ ²³"Say to Rehoboam son of Solomon king of Judah, to the whole house of Judah and Benjamin, and to the rest of the people, ²⁴'This is what the LORD says: Do not go up to fight against your brothers, the Israelites. Go home, every one of you, for this is my doing.'" So they obeyed the word of the LORD and went home again, as the LORD had ordered.

GOLDEN CALVES AT BETHEL AND DAN

²⁵Then Jeroboam fortified Shechem ⁱ in the hill country of Ephraim and lived there. From there he went out and built up Peniel. ᵇ ʲ

²⁶Jeroboam thought to himself, "The kingdom will now likely revert to the house of

---

ᵃ 18 Some Septuagint manuscripts and Syriac (see also 1 Kings 4:6 and 5:14); Hebrew *Adoram*
ᵇ 25 Hebrew *Penuel*, a variant of *Peniel*

12:16 *all Israel.* The northern tribes (see note on v. 1). *David.* The Davidic dynasty (see 2Sa 20:1 for an earlier expression of the same sentiment).

12:17 *Israelites who were living in the towns of Judah.* People originally from the northern tribes who had settled in Judah. They were later to be joined by others from the north who desired to serve the Lord and worship at the temple (see 2Ch 11:16–17).

12:18 *Adoniram, who was in charge of forced labor.* He had served in the same capacity under both David (2Sa 20:24) and Solomon (1Ki 4:6; 5:14).

12:19 *house of David.* An early non-Biblical reference to the "house of David" was found in 1993 on a fragment of a stele at Tell Dan. The reading "house of David" is clear, but two other names had to be partially restored. If the restorations are correct, the king of Damascus (probably Hazael) is boasting of victories over "Joram son of Ahab, king of Israel" and "Ahaziah son of Jehoram, king of the house of David." Since Joram ruled over Israel 852–841 B.C. and Ahaziah over Judah in 841, this would date the inscription to 841 or shortly after—less than a century and a half after David's reign (1010–970). *this day.* The time of the writing of the source from which the author of 1 Kings derived this account (see Introduction: Author, Sources and Date).

12:20–24 The kingdom is divided (see map, p. 508; see also chart, pp. 512–513, and note on 12:25—2Ki 17:41).

12:21 *tribe of Benjamin.* Although the bulk of Benjamin was aligned with the northern tribes (see note on 11:31–32), the area around Jerusalem remained under Rehoboam's control (as did the Gibeonite cities and Gezer). The northern boundary of Judah must have reached almost to Bethel (12 miles north of Jerusalem)—which Abijah, Rehoboam's son, even held for a short while (see 2Ch 13:19). *a hundred and eighty thousand able young men.* Probably includes all support personnel, together with those who would actually be committed to battle.

12:22 *Shemaiah.* Wrote a history of Rehoboam's reign (2Ch

12:15). Another of his prophecies is recorded in 2Ch 12:5–8. *man of God.* A common way of referring to a prophet (see, e.g., 13:1; Dt 18:18; 33:1; 1Sa 2:27; 9:9–10).

12:23 *rest of the people.* See note on v. 17.

12:24 *went home again.* Although full-scale civil war was averted, intermittent skirmishes and battles between Israel and Judah continued throughout the reigns of Rehoboam, Abijah and Asa, until political instability in Israel after the death of Baasha finally brought the conflict to a halt. Asa's son Jehoshaphat entered into an alliance with Ahab and sealed the relationship by the marriage of his son Jehoram to Ahab's daughter Athaliah (see 14:30; 15:6,16; 22:2,44; 2Ki 8:18).

12:25—2Ki 17:41 The period of the two kingdoms (see note on 12:20–24). In this large central section of 1,2 Kings major attention is given to the northern kingdom (of 839 verses only 157 are devoted to the Davidic kings of Judah)—to the acts of its kings and the prophetic activities related to them. It was in the north that the emerging kingdom of God was most at risk, the movement toward apostasy more powerful, and the Lord's struggle for the hearts of his people the more intense. In the face of apostatizing kings, with their puppet priests and prophets, the only faithful representatives of God's rule were the prophets he raised up, especially Elijah and Elisha (see Introduction: Content). Through their ministries the Lord was uniquely present among his people, not through the unfaithful kings and their paid religious functionaries. In the southern kingdom he was uniquely present among his people primarily through his own presence and his priests at the temple in Jerusalem.

12:25 *Peniel.* A town in Transjordan (see Ge 32:31; Jdg 8:9,17) of strategic importance for defense against the Arameans of Damascus (see 11:23–25) and the Ammonites.

12:26 *revert to the house of David.* Jeroboam did not have confidence in the divine promise given to him through Ahijah (see 11:38) and thus took action that forfeited the theocratic basis for his kingship.

David. ²⁷If these people go up to offer sacrifices at the temple of the LORD in Jerusalem, ᵏ they will again give their allegiance to their lord, Rehoboam king of Judah. They will kill me and return to King Rehoboam."

²⁸After seeking advice, the king made two golden calves. ˡ He said to the people, "It is too much for you to go up to Jerusalem. Here are your gods, Israel, who brought you up out of Egypt." ᵐ ²⁹One he set up in Bethel, ⁿ and the other in Dan. ᵒ ³⁰And this thing became a sin; ᵖ the people came to worship the one at Bethel and went as far as Dan to worship the other. ᵃ

³¹Jeroboam built shrines �q on high places and appointed priests ʳ from all sorts of people, even though they were not Levites. ³²He instituted a festival on the fifteenth day of the eighth ˢ month, like the festival held in Judah, and offered sacrifices on the altar. This he did in Bethel, ᵗ sacrificing to the calves he had made. And at Bethel he also installed priests at the high places he had made. ³³On the fifteenth day of the eighth month, a month of his own choosing, he offered sacrifices on the altar he had built at Bethel. ᵘ So he instituted the festival for the Israelites and went up to the altar to make offerings.

THE MAN OF GOD FROM JUDAH

13 By the word of the LORD a man of God ᵛ came from Judah to Bethel, ʷ as Jeroboam was standing by the altar to make an offering. ²He cried out against the altar by the word of the LORD: "Altar, altar! This is what the LORD says: 'A son named Josiah ˣ will be born to the house of David. On you he will sacrifice the priests of the high places ʸ who make offerings here, and human bones will be burned on you.' " ³That same day the man of God gave a sign: ᶻ "This is the sign the LORD has declared: The altar will be split apart and the ashes on it will be poured out."

⁴When King Jeroboam heard what the man of God cried out against the altar at Bethel, he stretched out his hand from the altar and said, "Seize him!" But the hand he stretched out toward the man shriveled up, so that he could not pull it back. ⁵Also, the altar was split apart and its ashes poured out according to the sign given by the man of God by the word of the LORD.

⁶Then the king said to the man of God, "Intercede ᵃ with the LORD your God and pray for me that my hand may be restored." So the man of God interceded with the LORD, and the king's hand was restored and became as it was before.

ᵃ 30 Probable reading of the original Hebrew text; Masoretic Text *people went to the one as far as Dan*

12:27 ᵏDt 12:5-6
12:28 ˡS Ex 32:4;
2Ch 11:15
ᵐS Ex 32:8
12:29 ⁿS Ge 12:8;
S Jos 7:2 ᵒJdg 18:27-
31; Am 8:14
12:30 ᵖ1Ki 13:34;
14:16; 15:26,30; 16:2;
2Ki 3:3; 10:29; 13:2;
17:21
12:31 �q S Lev 26:30;
1Ki 13:32; 2Ki 17:29
ʳS Ex 29:9; 1Ki 13:33;
2Ki 17:32; 2Ch 11:14-
15; 13:9
12:32 ˢ S Nu 29:12
ᵗ 2Ki 10:29
12:33 ᵘ 2Ki 23:15;
Am 7:13
13:1 ᵛS Lev 26:30;
S Jdg 13:6 ʷAm 7:13
13:2 ˣ2Ki 23:15-16,
20; 2Ch 34:5
ʸS Lev 26:30
13:3 ᶻS Ge 24:14;
S Ex 4:8; S Jn 2:11
13:6 ᵃS Ge 20:7;
S Nu 11:2; S Jer 37:3;
Ac 8:24

B **12:28** *two golden calves.* Pagan gods of the Arameans and Canaanites were often represented as standing on calves or bulls as symbols of their strength and fertility (see note on Jdg 2:13). *Here are your gods, Israel, who brought you out of Egypt.* Like Aaron (Ex 32:4–5), Jeroboam attempted to combine the pagan calf symbol with the worship of the Lord, though he attempted no physical representation of the Lord—no "god" stood on the backs of his bulls.

B **12:29** *Bethel.* Located about 12 miles north of Jerusalem close to the border of Ephraim but within the territory of Benjamin (Jos 18:11–13,22). Bethel held a prominent place in the history of Israel's worship of the Lord (see Ge 12:8; 28:11–19; 35:6–7; Jdg 20:26–28; 1Sa 7:16). *Dan.* Located in the far north of the land near Mount Hermon. A similarly paganized worship was practiced here during the period of the judges (Jdg 18:30–31). A raised platform ("high place") and shrine found at Dan may be the ones built by Jeroboam I and used by his successors (see vv. 30–31).

A C **12:30** *this thing became a sin.* Jeroboam's royal policy promoted violation of the second commandment (Ex 20:4–6). It inevitably led to Israel's violation of the first commandment also (Ex 20:3) and opened the door for the entrance of fully pagan practices into Israel's religious rites (especially in the time of Ahab; see 16:29–34). Jeroboam foolishly abandoned religious principle for political expediency and in so doing forfeited the promise given him by the prophet Ahijah (see 11:38).

12:31 *Jeroboam built shrines on high places.* See note on 3:2. *not Levites.* Many of the priests and Levites of the northern kingdom migrated to Judah because Jeroboam bypassed them when appointing priests in the north (see 2Ch 11:13–16).

C **12:32** *festival held in Judah.* Apparently the Festival of Tabernacles, observed in Judah on the 15th to the 21st of the seventh month (see 8:2; Lev 23:34). *offered sacrifices on the altar.* Jeroboam overstepped the limits of his prerogatives as king and assumed the role of a priest (see 2Ch 26:16–21).

13:1 *man of God.* See note on 12:22. *from Judah to Bethel.* God sent a prophet from the southern kingdom to Bethel in the northern kingdom. Possibly he did this to emphasize that the divinely appointed political division (11:11,29–39; 12:15,24) was not intended to establish rival religious systems in the two kingdoms. Two centuries later the prophet Amos from Tekoa in Judah also went to Bethel in the northern kingdom to pronounce God's judgment on Jeroboam II (Am 7:10–17).

13:2 *Josiah.* A prophetic announcement of the rule of King Josiah, who came to the throne in Judah nearly 300 years after the division of the kingdom. *will sacrifice the priests of the high places.* Fulfilled in 2Ki 23:15–20.

13:3 *sign.* The immediate fulfillment of a short-term prediction would serve to authenticate the reliability of the longer-term prediction (see Dt 18:21–22 and note).

13:5 *its ashes poured out.* Visibly demonstrating God's power to fulfill the words of the prophet (see note on v. 3) and providing a clear sign to Jeroboam that his offering was unacceptable to the Lord (see Lev 6:10–11).

13:6 *your God.* Should not be taken as implying that Jeroboam no longer considered the Lord as his own God (cf. 2:3; Ge 27:20) but as suggesting his recognition that the prophet had a privileged access to God. *king's hand was restored.* The Lord's gracious response to Jeroboam's request is to be seen as an additional sign (see v. 3) given to confirm the word of the prophet and to move Jeroboam to repentance.

RULERS OF THE DIVIDED KINGDOM OF ISRAEL AND JUDAH

DATA AND DATES IN ORDER OF SEQUENCE

SCRIPTURE	KINGS	SYNCHRONISM OR CORRELATION	LENGTH OF REIGN	HISTORICAL DATA	DATES
1. 1Ki 12:1–24 1Ki 14:21–31	**Rehoboam** (Judah)		17 years		930–913
2. 1Ki 12:25—14:20	**Jeroboam I** (Israel)		22 years		930–909
3. 1Ki 15:1–8	**Abijah** (Judah)	18th of Jeroboam	3 years		913–910
4. 1Ki 15:9–24	**Asa** (Judah)	20th of Jeroboam	41 years		910–869
5. 1Ki 15:25–31	**Nadab** (Israel)	2nd of Asa	2 years		909–908
6. 1Ki 15:32—16:7	**Baasha** (Israel)	3rd of Asa	24 years		908–886
7. 1Ki 16:8–14	**Elah** (Israel)	26th of Asa	2 years		886–885
8. 1Ki 16:15–20	**Zimri** (Israel)	27th of Asa	7 days		885
9. 1Ki 16:21–22	**Tibni** (Israel)			Overlap with Omri	885–880
10. 1Ki 16:23–28	**Omri** (Israel)	27th of Asa 31st of Asa	12 years	Made king by the people Overlap with Tibni Official reign = 11 actual years Sole reign	885 885–880 885–874 880–874
11. 1Ki 16:29—22:40	**Ahab** (Israel)	38th of Asa	22 years	Official reign = 21 actual years	874–853
12. 1Ki 22:41–50	**Jehoshaphat** (Judah)	4th of Ahab	25 years	Coregency with Asa Official reign Sole reign Has Jehoram as regent	872–869 872–848 869–853 853–848
13. 1Ki 22:51— 2Ki 1:18	**Ahaziah** (Israel)	17th of Jehoshaphat	2 years	Official reign = 1 yr. actual reign	853–852
14. 2Ki 1:17 2Ki 3:1—8:15	**Joram** (Israel)	2nd of Jehoram 18th of Jehoshaphat	12 years	Official reign = 11 actual years	852 852–841
15. 2Ki 8:16–24	**Jehoram** (Judah)	5th of Joram 8 years		Coregency with Jehoshaphat Sole reign Official reign = 7 actual years	853–848 848–841 848–841
16. 2Ki 8:25–29 2Ki 9:29	**Ahaziah** (Judah)	12th of Joram 11th of Joram	1 year	Nonaccession-year reckoning Accession-year reckoning	841 841
17. 2Ki 9:30—10:36	**Jehu** (Israel)		28 years		841–814
18. 2Ki 11	**Athaliah** (Judah)		7 years		841–835
19. 2Ki 12	**Joash** (Judah)	7th of Jehu	40 years		835–796
20. 2Ki 13:1–9	**Jehoahaz** (Israel)	23rd of Joash	17 years		814–798
21. 2Ki 13:10–25	**Jehoash** (Israel)	37th of Joash	16 years		798–782

Adapted from: A Chronology of the Hebrew Kings by Edwin R. Thiele. ©1977 by The Zondervan Corporation. Used by permission.

SCRIPTURE	KINGS	SYNCHRONISM OR CORRELATION	LENGTH OF REIGN	HISTORICAL DATA	DATES
22. 2Ki 14:1–22	*Amaziah* (Judah)	2nd of Jehoash	29 years		796–767
				Overlap with Azariah	792–767
23. 2Ki 14:23–29	**Jeroboam II** (Israel)			Coregency with Jehoash	793–782
			41 years	Total reign	793–753
		15th of Amaziah		Sole reign	782–753
24. 2Ki 15:1–7	*Azariah* (Judah)			Overlap with Amaziah	792–767
	(= Uzziah)		52 years	Total reign	792–740
		27th of Jeroboam		Sole reign	767–750
25. 2Ki 15:8–12	**Zechariah** (Israel)	38th of Azariah	6 months		753
26. 2Ki 15:13–15	**Shallum** (Israel)	39th of Azariah	1 month		752
27. 2Ki 15:16–22	**Menahem** (Israel)	39th of Azariah	10 years	Ruled in Samaria	752–742
28. 2Ki 15:23–26	**Pekahiah** (Israel)	50th of Azariah	2 years		742–740
29. 2Ki 15:27–31	**Pekah** (Israel)			In Gilead; overlapping years	752–740
			20 years	Total reign	752–732
		52nd of Azariah		Sole reign	740–732
30. 2Ki 15:32–38	*Jotham* (Judah)	2nd of Pekah		Coregency with Azariah	750–740
2Ki 15:30			16 years	Official reign	750–735
				Reign to his 20th year	750–732
31. 2Ki 16	*Ahaz* (Judah)			Total reign	735–715
		17th of Pekah			735
			16 years	From 20th of Jotham	732–715
32. 2Ki 15:30	**Hoshea** (Israel)			20th of Jotham	732
2Ki 17		12th of Ahaz	9 years		732–722
33. 2Ki 18:1—20:21	*Hezekiah* (Judah)	3rd of Hoshea	29 years		715–686
				Coregency with Ahaz	729–715
34. 2Ki 21:1–18	*Manasseh* (Judah)			Coregency with Hezekiah	697–686
			55 years	Total reign	697–642
35. 2Ki 21:19–26	*Amon* (Judah)		2 years		642–640
36. 2Ki 22:1—23:30	*Josiah* (Judah)		31 years		640–609
37. 2Ki 23:31–33	*Jehoahaz* (Judah)		3 months		609
38. 2Ki 23:34—24:7	*Jehoiakim* (Judah)		11 years		609–598
39. 2Ki 24:8–17	*Jehoiachin* (Judah)		3 months		598–597
40. 2Ki 24:18—25:26	*Zedekiah* (Judah)		11 years		597–586

Italics denote kings of **Judah**.
Non-italic type denotes kings of **Israel**.

13:7 b S 1Sa 9:7
13:8 c Nu 22:18
d ver 16
13:16 e ver 8
13:18 f 1Ki 22:6,12;
2Ch 35:21; Isa 36:10
g S Ge 19:14;
S Dt 13:3
13:21 h ver 26;
S 1Sa 13:14; 1Ki 20:35
13:24 i 1Ki 20:36
13:26 j S ver 21
13:30 k 2Ki 23:17
l Jer 22:18

⁷The king said to the man of God, "Come home with me for a meal, and I will give you a gift." b

⁸But the man of God answered the king, "Even if you were to give me half your possessions, c I would not go with you, nor would I eat bread d or drink water here. ⁹For I was commanded by the word of the LORD: 'You must not eat bread or drink water or return by the way you came.' " ¹⁰So he took another road and did not return by the way he had come to Bethel.

¹¹Now there was a certain old prophet living in Bethel, whose sons came and told him all that the man of God had done there that day. They also told their father what he had said to the king. ¹²Their father asked them, "Which way did he go?" And his sons showed him which road the man of God from Judah had taken. ¹³So he said to his sons, "Saddle the donkey for me." And when they had saddled the donkey for him, he mounted it ¹⁴and rode after the man of God. He found him sitting under an oak tree and asked, "Are you the man of God who came from Judah?"

"I am," he replied.

¹⁵So the prophet said to him, "Come home with me and eat."

¹⁶The man of God said, "I cannot turn back and go with you, nor can I eat bread e or drink water with you in this place. ¹⁷I have been told by the word of the LORD: 'You must not eat bread or drink water there or return by the way you came.' "

¹⁸The old prophet answered, "I too am a prophet, as you are. And an angel said to me by the word of the LORD: f 'Bring him back with you to your house so that he may eat bread and drink water.' " (But he was lying g to him.) ¹⁹So the man of God returned with him and ate and drank in his house.

²⁰While they were sitting at the table, the word of the LORD came to the old prophet who had brought him back. ²¹He cried out to the man of God who had come from Judah, "This is what the LORD says: 'You have defied h the word of the LORD and have not kept the command the LORD your God gave you. ²²You came back and ate bread and drank water in the place where he told you not to eat or drink. Therefore your body will not be buried in the tomb of your ancestors.' "

²³When the man of God had finished eating and drinking, the prophet who had brought him back saddled his donkey for him. ²⁴As he went on his way, a lion i met him on the road and killed him, and his body was left lying on the road, with both the donkey and the lion standing beside it. ²⁵Some people who passed by saw the body lying there, with the lion standing beside the body, and they went and reported it in the city where the old prophet lived.

²⁶When the prophet who had brought him back from his journey heard of it, he said, "It is the man of God who defied j the word of the LORD. The LORD has given him over to the lion, which has mauled him and killed him, as the word of the LORD had warned him."

²⁷The prophet said to his sons, "Saddle the donkey for me," and they did so. ²⁸Then he went out and found the body lying on the road, with the donkey and the lion standing beside it. The lion had neither eaten the body nor mauled the donkey. ²⁹So the prophet picked up the body of the man of God, laid it on the donkey, and brought it back to his own city to mourn for him and bury him. ³⁰Then he laid the body in his own tomb, k and they mourned over him and said, "Alas, my brother!" l

³¹After burying him, he said to his sons, "When I die, bury me in the grave where the

---

13:7 *Come home with me.* Jeroboam attempted to renew his prestige in the eyes of the people by creating the impression that there was no fundamental break between himself and the prophetic order (see 1Sa 15:30 for a similar situation).

A **13:9** *You must not.* The prophet's refusal of Jeroboam's invitation rested on a previously given divine command. It underscored God's extreme displeasure with the apostate worship at Bethel.

13:18 *I too am a prophet, as you are.* A half-truth. It is likely that the old prophet in Bethel had faithfully proclaimed the word of the Lord in former days, but those days had long since passed.

13:19 *the man of God returned with him.* Neither the old prophet's lie nor his own need justified disobedience to the direct and explicit command of the Lord. His public action in this matter undermined respect for the divine authority of all he had said at Bethel.

13:20 *the word of the LORD came to the old prophet.* The fundamental distinction between a true and a false prophecy here becomes apparent. The false prophecy arises from one's own

imagination (Jer 23:16; Eze 13:2,7), while the true prophecy is from God (Ex 4:16; Dt 18:18; Jer 1:9; 2Pe 1:21).

13:22 *your body will not be buried in the tomb of your ancestors.* The man of God from Judah will die far from his own home and family burial plot.

C **13:24** *killed him.* A stern warning to Jeroboam that God takes his word very seriously. *the donkey and the lion standing beside it.* The remarkable fact that the donkey did not run and the lion did not attack the donkey or disturb the man's body (v. 28) clearly stamped the incident as a divine judgment. This additional miracle was reported in Bethel (v. 25) and provided yet another sign authenticating the message that the man of God from Judah had delivered at Jeroboam's altar. But Jeroboam was still not moved to repentance (v. 33).

13:30 *laid the body in his own tomb.* See v. 22. The old prophet did the only thing left for him to do in order to make amends for his deliberate and fatal deception.

13:31 *grave where the man of God is buried.* The old prophet man of God is buried; lay my bones ^{m} beside his bones. ^{32}For the message he declared by the word of the LORD against the altar in Bethel and against all the shrines on the high places ^{n} in the towns of Samaria ^{o} will certainly come true." ^{p}

^{33}Even after this, Jeroboam did not change his evil ways, ^{q} but once more appointed priests for the high places from all sorts ^{r} of people. Anyone who wanted to become a priest he consecrated for the high places. ^{34}This was the sin ^{s} of the house of Jeroboam that led to its downfall and to its destruction ^{t} from the face of the earth.

AHIJAH'S PROPHECY AGAINST JEROBOAM

14 At that time Abijah son of Jeroboam became ill, ^{2}and Jeroboam said to his wife, "Go, disguise yourself, so you won't be recognized as the wife of Jeroboam. Then go to Shiloh. Ahijah ^{u} the prophet is there—the one who told me I would be king over this people. ^{3}Take ten loaves of bread ^{v} with you, some cakes and a jar of honey, and go to him. He will tell you what will happen to the boy." ^{4}So Jeroboam's wife did what he said and went to Ahijah's house in Shiloh.

Now Ahijah could not see; his sight was gone because of his age. ^{5}But the LORD had told Ahijah, "Jeroboam's wife is coming to ask you about her son, for he is ill, and you are to give her such and such an answer. When she arrives, she will pretend to be someone else."

^{6}So when Ahijah heard the sound of her footsteps at the door, he said, "Come in, wife of Jeroboam. Why this pretense? ^{w} I have been sent to you with bad news. ^{7}Go, tell Jeroboam that this is what the LORD, the God of Israel, says: ^{x} 'I raised you up from among the people and appointed you ruler ^{y} over my people Israel. ^{8}I tore ^{z} the kingdom away from the house of David and gave it to you, but you have not been like my servant David, who kept my commands and followed me with all his heart, doing only what was right ^{a} in my eyes. ^{9}You have done more evil ^{b} than all who lived before you. ^{c} You have made for yourself other gods, idols ^{d} made of metal; you have aroused ^{e} my anger and thrust me behind your back. ^{f}

^{10}" 'Because of this, I am going to bring disaster ^{g} on the house of Jeroboam. I will cut off from Jeroboam every last male in Israel—slave or free. $^{a\,h}$ I will burn up the house of Jeroboam as one burns dung, until it is all gone. ^{i} ^{11}Dogs ^{j} will eat those belonging to Jeroboam who die in the city, and the birds ^{k} will feed on those who die in the country. The LORD has spoken!'

^{12}"As for you, go back home. When you set foot in your city, the boy will die. ^{13}All Israel will mourn for him and bury him. He is the only one belonging to Jeroboam who will

---

^{a} 10 Or Israel—every ruler or leader

13:31 ^{m} 2Ki 23:18
13:32 ^{n} S Lev 26:30; S 1Ki 12:31
^{o} 1Ki 16:24,28; 20:1; 2Ki 10:1; 15:13
^{p} 2Ki 23:16
13:33 ^{q} 1Ki 15:26
^{r} S 1Ki 12:31
13:34 ^{s} S 1Ki 12:30
^{t} 1Ki 14:10; 15:29; 2Ki 9:9; Jer 35:17; Am 7:9
14:2 ^{u} S 1Ki 11:29
14:3 ^{v} S 1Sa 9:7
14:6 ^{w} S 1Sa 28:12
14:7 ^{x} 1Ki 15:29
^{y} 1Ki 11:37
14:8 ^{z} S 1Sa 15:27
^{a} S 2Sa 8:15; 1Ki 3:3; 15:5; 2Ki 14:3; 15:3, 34; 16:2; 18:3; 20:3; 22:2
14:9 ^{b} 1Ki 16:30,33; 21:25; 2Ki 21:9,11; 24:3 ^{c} 1Ki 16:2
^{d} S Ex 20:4; S 32:4; 2Ch 11:15 ^{e} Dt 32:16; 1Ki 16:2; Ps 78:58; Jer 7:18; 8:19; 32:32; 44:3; Eze 8:17; 16:26
^{f} Ne 9:26; Ps 50:17; Jer 2:27; 32:33; Eze 23:35
14:10 ^{g} S Jos 23:15; S 1Ki 13:34
^{h} S Dt 32:36; 2Ki 9:8-9 ^{i} 1Sa 12:25; 15:26; 1Ki 15:29; Hos 13:11
14:11 ^{j} 1Ki 16:4; 21:24 ^{k} S Ge 40:19; S Dt 28:26

---

chose in this way to identify himself with the message that the man of God from Judah had given at Bethel.
13:32 *Samaria.* As the capital of the northern kingdom, Samaria is used to designate the entire territory of the northern ten tribes (see note on 16:24). However, Samaria was not established until about 50 years after this (16:23–24). The use of the name here reflects the perspective of the author of Kings (see note on Ge 14:14 for a similar instance of the use of a place-name—Dan—of later origin than the historical incident with which it is connected).
13:33 *appointed priests ... from all sorts of people.* See 12:31 and note.
13:34 *sin.* The sin in 12:30 was the establishment of a paganized worship; here it is persistence in this worship with all its attendant evils.
14:1 *At that time.* Probably indicating a time not far removed from the event narrated in ch. 13. *Abijah.* Means "My (divine) Father is the LORD," suggesting that Jeroboam, at least to some degree, desired to be regarded as a worshiper of the LORD.
14:2 *disguise yourself.* Jeroboam's attempt to mislead the prophet Ahijah into giving a favorable prophecy concerning the sick boy indicates (1) his consciousness of his own guilt, (2) his superstition that prophecy worked in a magical way and (3) his confused but real respect for the power of the LORD's prophet. *Shiloh.* See note on 1Sa 1:3. *who told me I would be king over this people.* See 11:29–39.
14:5 *the LORD had told Ahijah.* See 1Sa 9:15–17; 2Ki 6:32 for other examples of divine revelation concerning an imminent visit.
14:6 *Come in, wife of Jeroboam.* Ahijah's recognition of the

woman and his knowledge of the purpose of her visit served to authenticate his message as truly being the word of the Lord.
14:7–8 *raised you up ... appointed you ruler ... tore the kingdom away.* Jeroboam is first reminded of the gracious acts of the Lord in his behalf (see 11:26,30–38).
14:8 *you have not been like my servant David.* Jeroboam had not responded to God's gracious acts and had ignored the requirements given when Ahijah told him he would become king (see 11:38).
14:9 *all who lived before you.* Jeroboam's wickedness surpassed that of Saul, David and Solomon in that he implemented a paganized system of worship for the entire populace of the northern kingdom. *other gods.* See notes on 12:28,30.
14:10 *slave or free.* Without exception (see 21:21; 2Ki 9:8; 14:26), but see TNIV text note.
14:11 *birds will feed on those who die in the country.* See note on 16:4. The covenant curse of Dt 28:26 is applied to Jeroboam's male descendants, none of whom will receive an honorable burial.
14:12 *boy.* The Hebrew for this word allows for wide latitude in age (the same term is used for the young advisers of Rehoboam; see 12:8 and note). *will die.* Although the death of Abijah was a severe disappointment to Jeroboam and his wife, it was an act of God's mercy to the prince, sparing him the disgrace and suffering that were to come on his father's house (see Isa 57:1–2).
14:13 *All Israel will mourn for him and bury him.* Perhaps an indication that Abijah was the crown prince, and was well known and loved by the people. *buried.* He alone of Jeroboam's descendants would receive an honorable burial.

14:13 *f* 2Ch 12:12;
19:3
14:15 *m* S Dt 29:28;
S 2Ch 7:20 *n* Jer 44:3
o S Dt 12:3
14:16 *p* S 1Ki 12:30;
S 15:26
14:17 *q* S Jos 12:24;
S 1Ki 15:33
14:21 *r* S 1Ki 11:1
14:22 *s* 2Ki 17:19;
2Ch 12:1 *t* Dt 32:21;
Ps 78:58; Jer 44:3;
S 1Co 10:22
14:23 *u* S Ex 23:24;
Dt 16:22; Hos 10:1
v S Dt 12:3
w S Dt 12:2; Eze 6:13
14:24 *x* S Dt 23:17
y 1Ki 11:5-7; 2Ki 21:2;
Ezr 9:11; Pr 21:27;
Isa 1:13; Jer 16:18;
32:35; 44:4
14:25 *z* 2Ch 12:2
14:26 *a* 1Ki 15:15,18
b 2Sa 8:7

be buried, because he is the only one in the house of Jeroboam in whom the LORD, the God of Israel, has found anything good. *f*

¹⁴"The LORD will raise up for himself a king over Israel who will cut off the family of Jeroboam. Even now this is beginning to happen.*a* ¹⁵And the LORD will strike Israel, so that it will be like a reed swaying in the water. He will uproot *m* Israel from this good land that he gave to their ancestors and scatter them beyond the Euphrates River, because they aroused *n* the LORD's anger by making Asherah *o* poles.*b* ¹⁶And he will give Israel up because of the sins *p* Jeroboam has committed and has caused Israel to commit."

¹⁷Then Jeroboam's wife got up and left and went to Tirzah. *q* As soon as she stepped over the threshold of the house, the boy died. ¹⁸They buried him, and all Israel mourned for him, as the LORD had said through his servant the prophet Ahijah.

¹⁹The other events of Jeroboam's reign, his wars and how he ruled, are written in the book of the annals of the kings of Israel. ²⁰He reigned for twenty-two years and then rested with his ancestors. And Nadab his son succeeded him as king.

REHOBOAM KING OF JUDAH
14:21,25–31pp — 2Ch 9:9–16

²¹Rehoboam son of Solomon was king in Judah. He was forty-one years old when he became king, and he reigned seventeen years in Jerusalem, the city the LORD had chosen out of all the tribes of Israel in which to put his Name. His mother's name was Naamah; she was an Ammonite. *r*

²²Judah *s* did evil in the eyes of the LORD. By the sins they committed they stirred up his jealous anger *t* more than those who were before them had done. ²³They also set up for themselves high places, sacred stones *u* and Asherah poles *v* on every high hill and under every spreading tree. *w* ²⁴There were even male shrine prostitutes *x* in the land; the people engaged in all the detestable *y* practices of the nations the LORD had driven out before the Israelites.

²⁵In the fifth year of King Rehoboam, Shishak king of Egypt attacked *z* Jerusalem. ²⁶He carried off the treasures of the temple *a* of the LORD and the treasures of the royal palace. He took everything, including all the gold shields *b* Solomon had made. ²⁷So King Rehoboam made bronze shields to replace them and assigned these to the command-

---

a 14 The meaning of the Hebrew for this sentence is uncertain. *b 15* That is, wooden symbols of the goddess Asherah; here and elsewhere in 1 Kings

---

14:14 *a king … who will cut off the family of Jeroboam.* Ahijah looked beyond the brief reign of Nadab, Jeroboam's son (15:25–26), to the revolt of Baasha (15:27—16:7).

C **14:15** *like a reed swaying in the water.* Descriptive of the instability of the royal house in the northern kingdom, which was to be characterized by assassinations and revolts (see 15:27–28; 16:16; 2Ki 9:24; 15:10,14,25,30). *He will uproot Israel.* See 2Ki 17:22–23 for the fulfillment of this prophecy; see also the list of curses for covenant breaking found in Dt 28:63–64; 29:25–28. *Asherah poles.* See TNIV text note. Ahijah perceived that Jeroboam's use of golden bulls in worship would inevitably lead to the adoption of other elements of Canaanite nature religion. The goddess Asherah was the consort of El, and the Asherah poles were probably wooden representations of the goddess (see notes on Ex 34:13; Jdg 2:13).

14:16 *sins Jeroboam has committed.* See 12:26–33; 13:33–34. *caused Israel to commit.* A phrase repeated often in 1,2 Kings (e.g., 15:26; 16:2,13,19,26).

B **14:17** *Tirzah.* Used by the kings of Israel as the royal city until Omri purchased and built up Samaria to serve that purpose (16:24). It is probably modern Tell el-Far'ah, about seven miles north of Shechem (see note on SS 6:4).

14:19 *his wars.* See v. 30; 15:6; 2Ch 13:2–20. *annals of the kings of Israel.* A record of the reigns of the kings of the northern kingdom used by the author of 1,2 Kings and apparently accessible to those interested in further details of the history of the reigns of Israelite kings. It is not to be confused with the canonical book of 1,2 Chronicles, which was written later than 1,2 Kings and contains the history of the reigns of the kings of Judah only (see Introduction: Author, Sources and Date).

14:20 *twenty-two years.* 930–909 B.C. *rested with his ancestors.*

See note on 1:21. *Nadab.* See 15:25–32.

14:21 *seventeen years.* 930–913 B.C. *city the LORD had chosen … to put his Name.* See 9:3; Ps 132:13.

C **14:22** *Judah did evil in the eyes of the LORD.* The reign of Rehoboam is described in greater detail in 2Ch 11–12. The priests and Levites who immigrated to Judah from the north led the country to follow the way of David and Solomon for the first three years of Rehoboam's reign (see 12:24; 2Ch 11:17). In later years Rehoboam and the people of Judah turned away from the LORD (2Ch 12:1).

14:23 *high places.* See note on 3:2. *sacred stones.* Stone pillars, bearing a religious significance, that were placed next to the altars. The use of such pillars was common among the Canaanites but was explicitly forbidden to the Israelites in the Mosaic law (Ex 23:24; Lev 26:1; Dt 16:21–22). It is likely that the pillars were intended to be representations of the deity (2Ki 3:2). For legitimate uses of stone pillars, see Ge 28:18; 31:45; Ex 24:4. *Asherah poles.* See note on v. 15.

14:24 *male shrine prostitutes.* Ritual prostitution was an important feature of Canaanite fertility religion. The Israelites had been warned by Moses not to engage in this abominable practice (see Dt 23:17–18; see also 1Ki 15:12; 2Ki 23:7; Hos 4:14).

B **14:25** *fifth year of King Rehoboam.* 926 B.C. *Shishak.* See note on 11:40. *attacked Jerusalem.* Shishak's invasion is described in more detail in 2Ch 12:2–4 (see note on 12:2) and is also attested in a victory inscription found on the walls of the temple of Amun in Thebes, where more than 15 towns that Shishak plundered in Judah and Israel are listed. 2Ch 12:5–8 indicates that fear of the impending invasion led to a temporary reformation in Judah.

14:26 *gold shields Solomon had made.* See note on 10:16.

ers of the guard on duty at the entrance to the royal palace. *c* 28Whenever the king went to the LORD's temple, the guards bore the shields, and afterward they returned them to the guardroom.

29As for the other events of Rehoboam's reign, and all he did, are they not written in the book of the annals of the kings of Judah? 30There was continual warfare *d* between Rehoboam and Jeroboam. 31And Rehoboam rested with his ancestors and was buried with them in the City of David. His mother's name was Naamah; she was an Ammonite. *e* And Abijah*a* his son succeeded him as king.

ABIJAH KING OF JUDAH
15:1–2,6–8pp — 2Ch 13:1–2,22—14:1

15 In the eighteenth year of the reign of Jeroboam son of Nebat, Abijah*b* became king of Judah, 2and he reigned in Jerusalem three years. His mother's name was Maakah*f* daughter of Abishalom.*c*

3He committed all the sins his father had done before him; his heart was not fully devoted*g* to the LORD his God, as the heart of David his forefather had been. 4Nevertheless, for David's sake the LORD his God gave him a lamp*h* in Jerusalem by raising up a son to succeed him and by making Jerusalem strong. 5For David had done what was right in the eyes of the LORD and had not failed to keep*i* any of the LORD's commands all the days of his life—except in the case of Uriah*j* the Hittite.

6There was war*k* between Abijah*d* and Jeroboam throughout Abijah's lifetime. 7As for the other events of Abijah's reign, and all he did, are they not written in the book of the annals of the kings of Judah? There was war between Abijah and Jeroboam. 8And Abijah rested with his ancestors and was buried in the City of David. And Asa his son succeeded him as king.

ASA KING OF JUDAH
15:9–22pp — 2Ch 14:2–3; 15:16—16:6
15:23–24pp — 2Ch 16:11—17:1

9In the twentieth year of Jeroboam king of Israel, Asa became king of Judah, 10and he reigned in Jerusalem forty-one years. His grandmother's name was Maakah*l* daughter of Abishalom.

11Asa did what was right in the eyes of the LORD, as his father David *m* had done. 12He expelled the male shrine prostitutes *n* from the land and got rid of all the idols *o* his ancestors had made. 13He even deposed his grandmother Maakah*p* from her position as queen mother, *q* because she had made a repulsive image for the worship of Asherah. Asa cut it

14:27 *c* 2Ki 11:5
14:30 *d* 2Sa 3:1; S 1Ki 12:21
14:31 *e* S 1Ki 11:1
15:2 *f* ver 10,13; 2Ch 11:20
15:3 *g* S 1Ki 8:61
15:4 *h* S 2Sa 21:17
15:5 *i* S Dt 5:32; S 1Ki 9:4 / 2Sa 11:2-27; 12:9
15:6 *k* ver 16,32; S 1Ki 12:21; 2Ch 16:9
15:10 *l* S ver 2
15:11 *m* 1Ki 9:4
15:12 *n* 1Ki 14:24
o 2Ch 15:8
15:13 *p* S ver 2
q S 1Ki 2:19

---

a 31 Some Hebrew manuscripts and Septuagint (see also 2 Chron. 12:16); most Hebrew manuscripts *Abijam* *b* 1 Some Hebrew manuscripts and Septuagint (see also 2 Chron. 12:16); most Hebrew manuscripts *Abijam*; also in verses 7 and 8 *c* 2 A variant of *Absalom*; also in verse 10 *d* 6 Some Hebrew manuscripts and Syriac *Abijam* (that is, Abijah); most Hebrew manuscripts *Rehoboam*

14:27 *bronze shields.* The reduced realm could not match the great wealth Solomon had accumulated in Jerusalem (see 10:21,23,27).

14:29 *annals of the kings of Judah.* A record of the reigns of the kings of Judah similar to the one for the kings of the northern kingdom (see note on v. 19; see also Introduction: Author, Sources and Date).

14:30 *continual warfare.* See notes on v. 19; 12:24.

14:31 *rested with his ancestors.* See note on 1:21.

15:1 *eighteenth year of the reign of Jeroboam.* The first of numerous synchronisms in 1,2 Kings between the reigns of the kings in the north and those in Judah (see, e.g., vv. 9,25,33; 16:8,15,29; see also chart, pp. 512–513, and Introduction: Chronology). *Abijah.* See note on 14:1. Both Rehoboam and Jeroboam had sons by this name.

15:2 *three years.* 913–910 B.C. *Maakah daughter of Abishalom.* See TNIV text note. Abijah's mother is said to be a daughter of Uriel of Gibeah in 2Ch 13:2. It is likely that Maakah was the granddaughter of Absalom and the daughter of a marriage between Tamar (Absalom's daughter; see 2Sa 14:27) and Uriel. Absalom's mother was also named Maakah (2Sa 3:3).

15:3 *sins his father had done.* See 14:22–24. *not fully devoted to the LORD his God, as ... David his forefather had been.* Although David fell into grievous sin, his heart

was never divided between serving the Lord and serving the nature deities of the Canaanites.

15:4 *lamp in Jerusalem.* See note on 11:36.

15:5 *Uriah the Hittite.* See 2Sa 11.

15:6 *Abijah.* See TNIV text note; see also note on 12:24.

15:7 *other events of Abijah's reign.* See 2Ch 13. *annals of the kings of Judah.* See note on 14:29. *war between Abijah and Jeroboam.* Cf. v. 6; 14:30. From 2Ch 13 it is clear that the chronic hostile relations of preceding years flared into serious combat in which Abijah defeated Jeroboam and took several towns from him, including Bethel (2Ch 13:19).

15:8 *rested with his ancestors.* See note on 1:21.

15:9 *twentieth year of Jeroboam.* 910 B.C. (see note on 14:20).

15:10 *forty-one years.* 910–869 B.C. *Maakah daughter of Abishalom.* See note on v. 2.

15:12 *male shrine prostitutes.* See note on 14:24. *got rid of all the idols his ancestors had made.* See 14:23. *idols.* See note on Lev 26:30.

15:13 *deposed his grandmother Maakah.* 2Ch 14:1—15:16 indicates a progression in Asa's reform over a period of years. Although Asa had destroyed pagan idols and altars early in his reign (2Ch 14:2–3), it was not until after a victory over Zerah the Cushite (2Ch 14:8–15) that Asa responded to the message of the prophet Azariah, son of Oded, by calling for a covenant

15:13 ʳS Ex 34:13
15:14 ˢ2Ch 14:5;
17:6 ᵗS 1Ki 8:61
15:15 ᵘS 2Sa 8:11
15:16 ᵛS ver 6;
S 1Ki 12:21
15:17 ʷS Jos 18:25
15:18 ˣS 1Ki 14:26
ʸ2Ki 12:18; 16:8;
18:14-16,15; Joel 3:5
ᶻver 18-20; 1Ki 20:1;
2Ki 6:24; 13:3;
Jer 49:27
15:19 ᵃS Ex 23:32;
S 1Ki 5:12
15:20 ᵇ1Ki 20:34
15:21 ᶜS Jos 18:25
ᵈ1Ki 16:15-17
15:22 ᵉver 17
ᶠver 9-24; Jer 41:9
ᵍS Jos 24:24;
2Ki 23:8 ʰS Jos 11:3
15:24 ⁱMt 1:8
15:26 ʲS Dt 4:25
ᵏS 1Ki 12:30

down ʳ and burned it in the Kidron Valley. ¹⁴Although he did not remove ˢ the high places, Asa's heart was fully committed ᵗ to the Lᴏʀᴅ all his life. ¹⁵He brought into the temple of the Lᴏʀᴅ the silver and gold and the articles that he and his father had dedicated. ᵘ

¹⁶There was war ᵛ between Asa and Baasha king of Israel throughout their reigns. ¹⁷Baasha king of Israel went up against Judah and fortified Ramah ʷ to prevent anyone from leaving or entering the territory of Asa king of Judah.

¹⁸Asa then took all the silver and gold that was left in the treasuries of the Lᴏʀᴅ's temple ˣ and of his own palace. He entrusted it to his officials and sent ʸ them to Ben-Hadad ᶻ son of Tabrimmon, the son of Hezion, the king of Aram, who was ruling in Damascus. ¹⁹"Let there be a treaty ᵃ between me and you," he said, "as there was between my father and your father. See, I am sending you a gift of silver and gold. Now break your treaty with Baasha king of Israel so he will withdraw from me."

²⁰Ben-Hadad agreed with King Asa and sent the commanders of his forces against the towns of Israel. He conquered ᵇ Ijon, Dan, Abel Beth Maakah and all Kinnereth in addition to Naphtali. ²¹When Baasha heard this, he stopped building Ramah ᶜ and withdrew to Tirzah. ᵈ ²²Then King Asa issued an order to all Judah—no one was exempt—and they carried away from Ramah ᵉ the stones and timber Baasha had been using there. With them King Asa ᶠ built up Geba ᵍ in Benjamin, and also Mizpah. ʰ

²³As for all the other events of Asa's reign, all his achievements, all he did and the cities he built, are they not written in the book of the annals of the kings of Judah? In his old age, however, his feet became diseased. ²⁴Then Asa rested with his ancestors and was buried with them in the city of his father David. And Jehoshaphat ⁱ his son succeeded him as king.

NADAB KING OF ISRAEL

²⁵Nadab son of Jeroboam became king of Israel in the second year of Asa king of Judah, and he reigned over Israel two years. ²⁶He did evil ʲ in the eyes of the Lᴏʀᴅ, following the ways of his father ᵏ and committing the same sin his father had caused Israel to commit.

renewal assembly in Jerusalem in the 15th year of his reign (2Ch 15:10). After this assembly Asa deposed his grandmother Maakah because of her idolatry (2Ch 15:16). *made a repulsive image for the worship of Asherah.* See note on 14:15. It appears that Maakah's action was a deliberate attempt to counter Asa's reform. *Kidron Valley.* See note on Isa 22:7 and map, p. 486. For similar use of the Kidron Valley during reform efforts by kings of Judah, see 2Ki 23:4, 6,12 (King Josiah) and 2Ch 29:16; 30:14 (King Hezekiah).

15:14 *did not remove the high places.* The reference here and in 2Ch 15:17 is to those high places, where the Lord was worshiped (for the question of legitimacy of worship of the Lord at high places, see note on 3:2). When 2Ch 14:3 indicates that Asa removed the high places, it is to be taken as a reference to the high places that were centers of pagan Canaanite worship (see 2Ch 17:6; 20:33 for the same distinction). This same statement of qualified approval that is made of Asa is made of five other kings of Judah prior to the time of Hezekiah (Jehoshaphat, 22:43; Joash, 2Ki 12:3; Amaziah, 2Ki 14:4; Azariah, 2Ki 15:4; Jotham, 2Ki 15:35). *fully committed to the Lᴏʀᴅ.* See note on v. 3.

15:15 *silver and gold and the articles.* Most likely consisting of war booty that Abijah had taken from Jeroboam (2Ch 13) and that Asa acquired from Zerah the Cushite (2Ch 14:8–15).

15:16 *war between Asa and Baasha ... throughout their reigns.* A reference to the chronic hostile relations that had existed ever since the division of the kingdom, rather than to full-scale combat (see notes on v. 7; 12:24; see also 2Ch 15:19).

15:17 *fortified Ramah.* Baasha had recaptured the territory previously taken from Jeroboam by Abijah (see note on v. 7; see also 2Ch 13:19) since Ramah was located south of Bethel and only about five miles north of Jerusalem. *prevent anyone from leaving or entering the territory of Asa.* See 2Ch 15:9–10.

15:18 *silver and gold that was left.* That which remained after the plundering of Jerusalem by Shishak of Egypt (see 14:25). *Hezion.* It is not clear whether Hezion is to be identified with Rezon of Damascus (see 11:23–25) or regarded as the founder of a new dynasty.

15:19 *treaty ... between my father and your father.* A reference to a previously unmentioned treaty be-

tween Abijah and Tabrimmon of Aram. When Tabrimmon died, Baasha succeeded in establishing a treaty with his successor Ben-Hadad. Asa saw no hope for success against Baasha without the assistance provided by a renewal of the old treaty with Aram. Although his plan seemed to be successful, it was condemned by Hanani the prophet as a foolish act and a denial of reliance on the Lord (see 2Ch 16:7–10). The true theocratic king was never to fear his enemies but to trust in the God of the covenant for security and protection (see note on 1Sa 17:11). Ahaz was later to follow Asa's bad example and seek Assyria's help when he was attacked by Israel and Aram (see 2Ki 16:5–9; Isa 7).

15:20 *Naphtali.* The cities that Ben-Hadad conquered in Naphtali were of particular importance because the major trade routes from Damascus going west to Tyre and southwest through the plain of Jezreel to the coastal plain and Egypt transversed this area. This same territory was later seized by the Assyrian ruler Tiglath-Pileser III (2Ki 15:29). See note on 14:17.

15:21 *Tirzah.* See note on 14:17.

15:22 *order to all Judah.* Asa's action is reminiscent of the labor force conscripted by Solomon (5:13–14; 11:28). *Geba ... Mizpah.* Asa established two border fortresses to check Baasha's desire to expand his territory southward. Geba was east of Ramah, and Mizpah was southwest of Ramah.

15:23 *other events of Asa's reign.* See 2Ch 14:2—16:14. *annals of the kings of Judah.* See note on 14:29. *feet became diseased.* See 2Ch 16:12.

15:24 *rested with his ancestors.* See note on 1:21. *Jehoshaphat his son succeeded him.* For the reign of Jehoshaphat, see 22:41–50; 2Ch 17:1—21:1.

15:25 *second year of Asa.* See note on v. 1. The second year of Asa of Judah corresponded to the 22nd and last year of Jeroboam of Israel (see v. 9; 14:20). *two years.* 909–908 B.C.

15:26 *same sin his father had caused Israel to commit.* Jeroboam's sin (see note on 14:16). Although Abijah of Judah occupied Bethel during the reign of Jeroboam (see note on v. 7), it is probable that the paganized worship Jeroboam initiated was continued elsewhere until control of Bethel was regained by Baasha.

²⁷Baasha son of Ahijah of the house of Issachar plotted against him, and he struck him down *l* at Gibbethon, *m* a Philistine town, while Nadab and all Israel were besieging it. ²⁸Baasha killed Nadab in the third year of Asa king of Judah and succeeded him as king.

²⁹As soon as he began to reign, he killed Jeroboam's whole family. *n* He did not leave Jeroboam anyone that breathed, but destroyed them all, according to the word of the LORD given through his servant Ahijah the Shilonite. ³⁰This happened because of the sins *o* Jeroboam had committed and had caused *p* Israel to commit, and because he aroused the anger of the LORD, the God of Israel.

³¹As for the other events of Nadab's reign, and all he did, are they not written in the book of the annals *q* of the kings of Israel? ³²There was war *r* between Asa and Baasha king of Israel throughout their reigns.

BAASHA KING OF ISRAEL

³³In the third year of Asa king of Judah, Baasha son of Ahijah became king of all Israel in Tirzah, *s* and he reigned twenty-four years. ³⁴He did evil *t* in the eyes of the LORD, following the ways of Jeroboam and committing the same sin Jeroboam had caused Israel to commit.

16

Then the word of the LORD came to Jehu *u* son of Hanani *v* concerning Baasha: ²"I lifted you up from the dust *w* and appointed you ruler *x* over my people Israel, but you followed the ways of Jeroboam and caused *y* my people Israel to sin and to arouse my anger by their sins. ³So I am about to wipe out Baasha *z* and his house, *a* and I will make your house like that of Jeroboam son of Nebat. ⁴Dogs *b* will eat those belonging to Baasha who die in the city, and birds *c* will feed on those who die in the country."

⁵As for the other events of Baasha's reign, what he did and his achievements, are they not written in the book of the annals *d* of the kings of Israel? ⁶Baasha rested with his ancestors and was buried in Tirzah. *e* And Elah his son succeeded him as king.

⁷Moreover, the word of the LORD came *f* through the prophet Jehu *g* son of Hanani to Baasha and his house, because of all the evil he had done in the eyes of the LORD, arousing his anger by the things he did, becoming like the house of Jeroboam—and also because he destroyed it.

ELAH KING OF ISRAEL

⁸In the twenty-sixth year of Asa king of Judah, Elah son of Baasha became king of Israel, and he reigned in Tirzah two years.

⁹Zimri, one of his officials, who had command of half his chariots, plotted against him. Elah was in Tirzah at the time, getting drunk *h* in the home of Arza, who was in charge *i* of the palace at Tirzah. ¹⁰Zimri came in, struck him down and killed him in the twenty-seventh year of Asa king of Judah. Then he succeeded him as king. *j*

15:27 *l* 1Ki 14:14
m S Jos 19:44
15:29 *n* S 1Ki 13:34
15:30 *o* S 1Ki 12:30
p 1Ki 16:26; 2Ki 3:3;
14:24; 15:28; 21:16
15:31 *q* 1Ki 11:41
15:32 *r* S ver 6
15:33 *s* 1Ki 14:17;
16:6,23; 2Ki 15:14;
SS 6:4
15:34 *t* ver 26
16:1 *u* ver 7;
2Ch 19:2; 20:34
v 2Ch 16:7
16:2 *w* 1Sa 2:8
x S 1Ki 14:7-9
y S 1Ki 12:30
16:3 *z* 2Ki 9:9
a ver 11; 1Ki 21:22
16:4 *b* S 1Ki 14:11
c S Ge 40:19
16:5 *d* 1Ki 15:31
16:6 *e* S 1Ki 15:33
16:7 *f* S 1Ki 6:11
g S ver 1
16:9 *h* 1Ki 20:12,16;
Pr 31:4-5 *i* 1Ki 18:3
16:10 *j* 2Ki 9:31

15:27 *Gibbethon.* A town located between Jerusalem and Joppa (probably a few miles west of Gezer) in the territory originally assigned to Dan (Jos 19:43–45). This Levitical city (Jos 21:23) probably fell into Philistine hands at the time of the Philistine expansion in the period of the judges.

15:28 *third year of Asa.* 908 B.C. (see note on v. 10). It is likely that Baasha was a commander in Nadab's army and was able to secure the support of the military for his revolt.

15:29 *the word . . . given through . . . Ahijah.* See 14:10–11.

15:30 *sins Jeroboam had committed and had caused Israel to commit.* See note on 14:16.

15:31 *annals of the kings of Israel.* See note on 14:19.

15:32 *war . . . throughout their reigns.* See v. 16. The demise of Jeroboam's dynasty did not improve relations between the two kingdoms.

15:33 *third year of Asa.* 908 B.C. (see note on v. 10). *Tirzah.* See note on 14:17. *twenty-four years.* 908–886 B.C. His official years were counted as 24, though his actual years were 23 (see 16:8; see also Introduction: Chronology).

15:34 *same sin Jeroboam had caused Israel to commit.* See note on 14:16. The assessment of Baasha's reign indicates no improvement over the reign of Nadab, whom he replaced (see v. 26).

16:1 *Jehu.* Like his father before him (see 2Ch 16:7–10), Jehu brought God's word of condemnation to a king. Much as the man of God from Judah (see note on 13:1) and lat-

er the prophet Amos, he was sent from the south to a northern king. His ministry continued for about 50 years until the reign of Jehoshaphat of Judah (2Ch 19:2; 20:34).

16:2 *I lifted you up from the dust.* Cf. 14:7. *followed the ways of Jeroboam.* See note on 14:16.

16:3 *wipe out Baasha and his house.* Cf. 14:10 (the house of Jeroboam); 21:21 (the house of Omri and Ahab).

16:4 Identical to the prophecy against Jeroboam's dynasty in 14:11.

16:5 *his achievements.* For the purposes of the writer of Kings (see Introduction: Theme), it was not necessary to list any of Baasha's achievements. He may have been a very successful ruler from a military-political point of view. *annals of the kings of Israel.* See note on 14:19.

16:6 *rested with his ancestors.* See note on 1:21.

16:7 *evil he had done . . . like the house of Jeroboam.* See v. 2; 15:34. *he destroyed it.* Although Baasha fulfilled God's purpose (14:10,14) in destroying the house of Jeroboam, he remained responsible for this violent and unlawful act (cf. Ge 50:20; Isa 10:5–7,12).

16:8 *twenty-sixth year of Asa.* 886 B.C. (see note on 15:10; see also Introduction: Chronology). *two years.* 886–885 B.C.

16:9 *getting drunk.* The fact that Elah was carousing at Tirzah while the army was laying siege to Gibbethon (v. 15) indicates that he had little perception of his responsibilities as king.

16:10 *twenty-seventh year of Asa.* 885 B.C.

16:11 ᵏ S ver 3
16:13 ˡ S Dt 32:21
16:15 ᵐ S Jos 19:44
16:23 ⁿ S Jos 12:24;
S 1Ki 15:33
16:24 ° S 1Ki 13:32;
S Mt 10:5
16:25 ᵖ ver 25-26;
S Dt 4:25; Mic 6:16
16:26 �⁹ S 1Ki 15:30
ʳ S Dt 32:21

¹¹As soon as he began to reign and was seated on the throne, he killed off Baasha's whole family. ᵏ He did not spare a single male, whether relative or friend. ¹²So Zimri destroyed the whole family of Baasha, in accordance with the word of the Lord spoken against Baasha through the prophet Jehu— ¹³because of all the sins Baasha and his son Elah had committed and had caused Israel to commit, so that they aroused the anger of the Lord, the God of Israel, by their worthless idols. ˡ

¹⁴As for the other events of Elah's reign, and all he did, are they not written in the book of the annals of the kings of Israel?

ZIMRI KING OF ISRAEL

¹⁵In the twenty-seventh year of Asa king of Judah, Zimri reigned in Tirzah seven days. The army was encamped near Gibbethon, ᵐ a Philistine town. ¹⁶When the Israelites in the camp heard that Zimri had plotted against the king and murdered him, they proclaimed Omri, the commander of the army, king over Israel that very day there in the camp. ¹⁷Then Omri and all the Israelites with him withdrew from Gibbethon and laid siege to Tirzah. ¹⁸When Zimri saw that the city was taken, he went into the citadel of the royal palace and set the palace on fire around him. So he died, ¹⁹because of the sins he had committed, doing evil in the eyes of the Lord and following the ways of Jeroboam and committing the same sin Jeroboam had caused Israel to commit.

²⁰As for the other events of Zimri's reign, and the rebellion he carried out, are they not written in the book of the annals of the kings of Israel?

OMRI KING OF ISRAEL

²¹Then the people of Israel were split into two factions; half supported Tibni son of Ginath for king, and the other half supported Omri. ²²But Omri's followers proved stronger than those of Tibni son of Ginath. So Tibni died and Omri became king.

²³In the thirty-first year of Asa king of Judah, Omri became king of Israel, and he reigned twelve years, six of them in Tirzah. ⁿ ²⁴He bought the hill of Samaria from Shemer for two talentsᵃ of silver and built a city on the hill, calling it Samaria, ° after Shemer, the name of the former owner of the hill.

²⁵But Omri did evilᵖ in the eyes of the Lord and sinned more than all those before him. ²⁶He followed completely the ways of Jeroboam son of Nebat, committing the same sin Jeroboam had caused ⁹ Israel to commit, so that they aroused the anger of the Lord, the God of Israel, by their worthless idols. ʳ

ᵃ 24 That is, about 150 pounds or about 68 kilograms

16:11 *killed off Baasha's whole family.* See 15:29; 2Ki 10:1-7; 11:1. *friend.* Probably the chief adviser to the king (see note on 2Sa 15:37).

16:12 *word of the Lord . . . through the prophet Jehu.* See vv. 1-4. Zimri did not consciously decide to fulfill Jehu's prophecy, but unwittingly he became the instrument by which Jehu's prediction was fulfilled (see note on v. 7) when he conspired against Elah and destroyed the dynasty of Baasha.

16:13 *sins Baasha and his son Elah had committed.* See 15:34. *worthless idols.* A reference to all the paganism in Israel's religious observances, including the use of the golden calves in worship (see 12:28; 14:9).

16:14 *annals of the kings of Israel.* See note on 14:19.

16:15 *twenty-seventh year of Asa.* 885 B.C. (see notes on 15:1,10). *Gibbethon.* See notes on v. 9; 15:27.

16:16 *plotted against the king and murdered him.* See vv. 9-12. *Omri, the commander of the army.* He held a higher rank than Zimri did under Elah (v. 9).

16:17 *Tirzah.* The royal residence (see vv. 8-10; see also note on 14:17).

16:19 *ways of Jeroboam.* See note on 14:16.

16:20 *annals of the kings of Israel.* See note on 14:19.

16:22 *Tibni died.* It is not clear whether Tibni's death was due to natural causes or the result of the military struggle for control of the land.

16:23 *thirty-first year of Asa.* 880 B.C. (see note on 15:10; see also Introduction: Chronology). *became king.* Became sole king. The struggle for control of the northern kingdom between Omri and Tibni lasted four years (compare this verse with v. 15).

twelve years. 885-874. The 12 years of Omri's reign include the four years of struggle between Omri and Tibni (cf. vv. 15,29). *Tirzah.* See note on 14:17. Omri had been able to capture Tirzah in a matter of days (vv. 15-19).

16:24 *Samaria.* Seven miles northwest of Shechem, Samaria rose about 300 feet above the surrounding fertile valleys (referred to as a "wreath" in Isa 28:1). The original owner may have been persuaded to sell his property (see 21:3) on the condition that the city be named after him (cf. Ru 4:5). The site provided an ideal location for a nearly impregnable capital city for the northern kingdom (see 20:1-21; 2Ki 6:25; 18:9-10). With the establishment of this royal city, the kings of the north came to possess a royal citadel-city like that of the Davidic dynasty (see 2Sa 5:6-12). Archaeologists have discovered that Omri and Ahab also adorned it with magnificent structures to rival those Solomon had erected in Jerusalem. From this time on, the northern kingdom could be designated by the name of the royal city, just as the southern kingdom could be designated by its capital, Jerusalem (see, e.g., 21:1; Isa 10:10; Am 6:1).

16:25 *sinned more than all.* Omri's alliance with Ethbaal of Tyre and Sidon (Omri's son Ahab married Ethbaal's daughter Jezebel to seal the alliance) led to widespread Baal worship in the northern kingdom (vv. 31-33) and eventually to the near extinction of the Davidic line in the southern kingdom (see 2Ki 11; see also note on 2Ki 8:18). This marriage alliance must have been established in the early years of Omri's reign (see note on v. 23), perhaps to strengthen his hand against Tibni (see vv. 21-22).

16:26 *same sin Jeroboam had caused Israel to commit.* See 12:26-33; see also note on 14:16. *worthless idols.* See note on v. 13.

²⁷As for the other events of Omri's reign, what he did and the things he achieved, are they not written in the book of the annals of the kings of Israel? ²⁸Omri rested with his ancestors and was buried in Samaria. ˢ And Ahab his son succeeded him as king.

AHAB BECOMES KING OF ISRAEL

²⁹In the thirty-eighth year of Asa king of Judah, Ahab son of Omri became king of Israel, and he reigned in Samaria over Israel twenty-two years. ³⁰Ahab son of Omri did more ᵗ evil in the eyes of the LORD than any of those before him. ³¹He not only considered it trivial to commit the sins of Jeroboam son of Nebat, but he also married ᵘ Jezebel daughter ᵛ of Ethbaal king of the Sidonians, and began to serve Baal ʷ and worship him. ³²He set up an altar ˣ for Baal in the temple ʸ of Baal that he built in Samaria. ³³Ahab also made an Asherah pole ᶻ and did more ᵃ to arouse the anger of the LORD, the God of Israel, than did all the kings of Israel before him.

³⁴In Ahab's time, Hiel of Bethel rebuilt Jericho. He laid its foundations at the cost of his firstborn son Abiram, and he set up its gates at the cost of his youngest son Segub, in accordance with the word of the LORD spoken by Joshua son of Nun. ᵇ

ELIJAH FED BY RAVENS

17 Now Elijah ᶜ the Tishbite, from Tishbe ᵃ in Gilead, ᵈ said to Ahab, "As the LORD, the God of Israel, lives, whom I serve, there will be neither dew nor rain ᵉ in the next few years except at my word."

²Then the word of the LORD came to Elijah: ³"Leave here, turn eastward and hide ᶠ in

ᵃ 1 Or *Tishbite, of the settlers*

16:28 ˢ S 1Ki 13:32
16:30 ᵗ S 1Ki 14:9
16:31 ᵘ S 1Ki 11:2
ᵛ S Jdg 3:6; 2Ki 9:34
ʷ S Jdg 2:11
16:32 ˣ S Jdg 6:28
ʸ 2Ki 10:21,27; 11:18;
Jer 43:12
16:33 ᶻ S Jdg 3:7;
2Ki 13:6 ᵃ S 1Ki 14:9;
21:25
16:34 ᵇ Jos 6:26
17:1 ᶜ Mal 4:5;
Mt 11:14; 17:3
ᵈ Jdg 12:4 ᵉ S Dt 11:17;
S 28:24; S 2Sa 1:21;
S 1Ki 8:36; Job 12:15;
S Lk 4:25
17:3 ᶠ 1Ki 18:4,10;
Jer 36:19,26

16:27 *things he achieved.* Omri's military and political accomplishments were not of importance for the purposes of the writer of Kings (see Introduction: Theme). Apart from establishing Samaria as the capital of the northern kingdom, about all that is known of him from the Biblical account is that he organized a governmental structure in the northern kingdom that was in place during the rule of his son, Ahab (see 20:14–15). Omri's dynasty, however, endured for over 40 years. A century and a half later (732 B.C.) Tiglath-Pileser III of Assyria referred to Israel as the "house of Omri" in his annals. *annals of the kings of Israel.* See note on 14:19.

16:28 *rested with his ancestors.* See note on 1:21.

16:29 *thirty-eighth year of Asa.* 874 B.C. (see notes on 15:9–10). *twenty-two years.* 874–853 B.C.

16:30 *more evil . . . than any.* Omri sinned more than those before him (see v. 25), and Ahab sinned more than his father had. Evil became progressively worse in the royal house of the northern kingdom. Nearly a third of the narrative material in 1,2 Kings concerns the 34-year period of the reigns of Ahab and his two sons, Ahaziah and Joram. In this period the struggle between the kingdom of God (championed especially by Elijah and Elisha) and the kingdom of Satan was especially intense.

16:31 *married Jezebel daughter of Ethbaal.* The first-century Jewish historian Josephus refers to Ethbaal as a king-priest who ruled over Tyre and Sidon for 32 years. Ahab had already married Jezebel during the reign of his father (see note on v. 25). *Baal.* Perhaps Melqart, the local manifestation of Baal in Tyre, whose worship was brought to Israel by Jezebel. It is probable that Ahab participated in the worship of this deity at the time of his marriage. The names of Ahab's sons (Ahaziah, "The LORD grasps"; Joram, "The LORD is exalted") suggest that Ahab did not intend to replace the worship of the Lord with the worship of Baal but to worship both deities in a syncretistic way.

16:32 *temple of Baal that he built in Samaria.* Ahab imported the Phoenician Baal worship of his wife Jezebel into the northern kingdom by constructing a temple of Baal in Samaria, just as Solomon had erected the temple of the Lord in Jerusalem. This pagan temple and its sacred stone (see note on 14:23) were later destroyed by Jehu (2Ki 10:21–27).

16:33 *Asherah pole.* See note on 14:15. *than did all the kings of Is-*

rael. See note on v. 30. Ahab elevated the worship of Baal to an official status in the northern kingdom at the beginning of his reign.

16:34 *rebuilt Jericho.* Does not mean that Jericho had remained uninhabited since its destruction by Joshua (see Jos 18:21; Jdg 1:16; 3:13; 2Sa 10:5), but that it had remained an unwalled town or village. During the rule of Ahab, Hiel fortified the city by reconstructing its walls and gates (see 9:17 for a similar use of "rebuild"). This violated God's intention that the ruins of Jericho be a perpetual reminder that Israel had received the land of Canaan from God's hand as a gift of grace. Accordingly, Hiel suffered the curse Joshua had pronounced (Jos 6:26).

17:1—2Ki 8:15 The ministries of Elijah and Elisha and other prophets from Ahab/Asa to Joram/Jehoshaphat.

17:1 *Elijah.* Elijah's name (meaning "The LORD is my God") was the essence of his message (18:21,39). He was sent to oppose vigorously, by word and action, both Baal worship and those who engaged in it. *from Tishbe in Gilead.* See TNIV text note. Gilead was in the northern Transjordan area. The precise location of Tishbe is unknown, but see map, p. 527, and map No. 7 at the end of this study Bible. *whom I serve.* Lit. "before whom I stand," a technical expression indicating one who stands in the service of a king. Kings and priests in Israel were anointed to serve as official representatives of the Lord, Israel's Great King, leading Israel in the way of faithfulness to the Lord and channeling his covenantal care and blessings to them. Since the days of Jeroboam the northern kingdom had not had such a priest (12:31), and its kings had all been unfaithful. Now, in the great crisis brought on by Ahab's promotion of Baal worship, the Lord sent Elijah (and after him Elisha) to serve as his representative (instead of king and priest), much as he had sent Moses long ago. The author of Kings highlights many parallels between the ministries of Elijah and Moses. *neither dew nor rain.* The drought was not only a divine judgment on a nation that had turned to idolatry but also a demonstration that even though Baal was considered the god of fertility and lord of the rain clouds, he was powerless to give rain (cf. Lev 26:3–4; Hos 2:5,8).

17:3 *Leave here.* With this command God withdrew his prophet from his land and people to leave them isolated from his word and blessings. The absence of the prophet confirmed and intensified the judgment. *Kerith Ravine, east of the Jordan.* Perhaps a gorge leading into the Jordan Valley (see map, p. 527, and map No. 7 at the end of this study Bible).

17:4 ᵍ S Ge 8:7
17:6 ʰ Ex 16:8
17:9 ⁱ Ob 1:20
/ Lk 4:26
17:10 ᵏ S Ge 24:17;
Jn 4:7
17:12 ˡ 2Ki 4:2
17:14 ᵐ ver 1
17:18 ⁿ Lk 5:8

the Kerith Ravine, east of the Jordan. ⁴You will drink from the brook, and I have directed the ravens ᵍ to supply you with food there."

⁵So he did what the Lᴏʀᴅ had told him. He went to the Kerith Ravine, east of the Jordan, and stayed there. ⁶The ravens brought him bread and meat in the morning ʰ and bread and meat in the evening, and he drank from the brook.

THE WIDOW AT ZAREPHATH

⁷Some time later the brook dried up because there had been no rain in the land. ⁸Then the word of the Lᴏʀᴅ came to him: ⁹"Go at once to Zarephath ⁱ in the region of Sidon and stay there. I have directed a widow ʲ there to supply you with food." ¹⁰So he went to Zarephath. When he came to the town gate, a widow was there gathering sticks. He called to her and asked, "Would you bring me a little water in a jar so I may have a drink?" ᵏ ¹¹As she was going to get it, he called, "And bring me, please, a piece of bread."

¹²"As surely as the Lᴏʀᴅ your God lives," she replied, "I don't have any bread—only a handful of flour in a jar and a little olive oil ˡ in a jug. I am gathering a few sticks to take home and make a meal for myself and my son, that we may eat it—and die."

¹³Elijah said to her, "Don't be afraid. Go home and do as you have said. But first make a small loaf of bread for me from what you have and bring it to me, and then make something for yourself and your son. ¹⁴For this is what the Lᴏʀᴅ, the God of Israel, says: 'The jar of flour will not be used up and the jug of oil will not run dry until the day the Lᴏʀᴅ sends rain ᵐ on the land.' "

¹⁵She went away and did as Elijah had told her. So there was food every day for Elijah and for the woman and her family. ¹⁶For the jar of flour was not used up and the jug of oil did not run dry, in keeping with the word of the Lᴏʀᴅ spoken by Elijah.

¹⁷Some time later the son of the woman who owned the house became ill. He grew worse and worse, and finally stopped breathing. ¹⁸She said to Elijah, "What do you have against me, man of God? Did you come to remind me of my sin ⁿ and kill my son?"

¹⁹"Give me your son," Elijah replied. He took him from her arms, carried him to the

---

17:4 *ravens to supply you with food there.* The Lord's faithful servant Elijah was miraculously sustained beyond the Jordan (like Israel in the desert in the time of Moses) while Israel in the promised land was going hungry—a clear testimony against Israel's reliance on Baal. The fact that Elijah was sustained in a miraculous way while not living among his own people demonstrated that the word of God was not dependent on the people, but the people were dependent on the word of God. *ravens.* Lived mainly on the carcasses of birds and animals they found in the fields and on the leftovers of wild kills. Since they normally fed on these where they found them, a flock of circling ravens would suggest to an observer only the presence of a dead body, thus keeping Elijah's hiding place secure. And the fact that birds of such habit here served as carriers of food heightens the miraculous element.

17:6 *meat.* Since the ravens themselves were not to be eaten (Lev 11:15; Dt 14:14) and the meat they normally ate was also forbidden food (Lev 7:24; Dt 14:21; Eze 4:14), the kind of "meat" referred to and its source remain mysterious. *in the morning . . . in the evening.* To eat meat every day, to say nothing of twice a day, was not common fare for common people. Among them meat was reserved for special occasions. Kings, on the other hand, seem to have had meat daily on their table (see 1Ki 4:23). It appears, then, that Yahweh's servant Elijah is here depicted as eating at King Yahweh's table (see Ex 29:38–41; Nu 28:4–8; cf. 2Ki 4:42 and note; see also 1Ki 18:19, where Elijah speaks of the "prophets . . . who eat at Jezebel's table") while apostate Israel goes hungry.

17:9 *Zarephath in the region of Sidon.* A coastal town located between Tyre and Sidon in the territory ruled by Jezebel's father Ethbaal (16:31). Elijah is commanded to go and reside in the heart of the very land from which the Baal worship now being promoted in Israel had come. *I have directed a widow there to supply you with food.* Elijah, as the bearer of God's word, was now to be sustained by human hands, but they were the hands of a poor widow facing starvation (v. 12). She was, moreover, from outside the circle of God's own people (cf. Lk 4:25–26)—in fact, she was from the pagan nation that at that time (much like Egypt earlier and Babylon

later) represented the forces arrayed against God's kingdom.

17:10 *So he went.* Elijah's reliance on the Lord demonstrated the faith in the Lord that Israel should have been living by.

17:12 *As surely as the Lᴏʀᴅ your God lives.* Her oath in the name of the Lord was either an accommodation to Elijah, whom she recognized as an Israelite (see notes on 5:7; 10:9), or a genuine expression of previous knowledge of and commitment to the God of Israel.

17:13 *first make a small loaf of bread for me . . . then make something for yourself and your son.* As a prophet, Elijah's words are the command of the Lord. The widow is asked to give all she has to sustain the bearer of the word of God. The demand to give her all is in essence the demand of the covenant that Israel had broken.

17:14 *what the Lᴏʀᴅ, the God of Israel, says.* Elijah can tell the widow "Don't be afraid" (v. 13) because the demand of the covenant is not given without the promise of the covenant. The Lord does not ask more than he promises to give.

17:15 *did as Elijah had told her.* By an act of faith the woman received the promised blessing. Israel had forsaken the covenant and followed Baal and Asherah in search of prosperity. Now in the midst of a pagan kingdom a widow realized that trustful obedience to the word of God is the way that leads to life.

17:16 *jar of flour was not used up.* God miraculously provided for this non-Israelite who, in an act of faith in the Lord's word, had laid her life on the line. He gave her "manna" from heaven even while he was withholding food from his unfaithful people in the promised land. The warning of Dt 32:21 was being fulfilled (cf. Ro 10:19; 11:11,14).

17:18 *Did you come to remind me of my sin and kill my son?* The widow concluded that Elijah's presence in her house had called God's attention to her sin, and that the death of her son was a divine punishment for this sin. Although her sense of guilt seems to have been influenced by pagan ideas, both she and Elijah are confronted with the question: Why did the God who promised life bring death instead?

upper room where he was staying, and laid him on his bed. ²⁰Then he cried° out to the LORD, "LORD my God, have you brought tragedy even on this widow I am staying with, by causing her son to die?" ²¹Then he stretchedᵖ himself out on the boy three times and cried out to the LORD, "LORD my God, let this boy's life return to him!"

²²The LORD heard Elijah's cry, and the boy's life returned to him, and he lived. ²³Elijah picked up the child and carried him down from the room into the house. He gave him to his mother�q and said, "Look, your son is alive!"

²⁴Then the woman said to Elijah, "Now I knowʳ that you are a man of Godˢ and that the word of the LORD from your mouth is the truth."ᵗ

ELIJAH AND OBADIAH

18 After a long time, in the third ᵘ year, the word of the LORD came to Elijah: "Go and present ᵛ yourself to Ahab, and I will send rain ʷ on the land." ²So Elijah went to present himself to Ahab.

Now the famine was severe ˣ in Samaria, ³and Ahab had summoned Obadiah, who was in chargeʸ of his palace. (Obadiah was a devout believerᶻ in the LORD. ⁴While Jezebelᵃ was killing off the LORD's prophets, Obadiah had taken a hundred prophets and hidden ᵇ them in two caves, fifty in each, and had suppliedᶜ them with food and water.) ⁵Ahab had said to Obadiah, "Go through the land to all the springs ᵈ and valleys. Maybe we can find some grass to keep the horses and mules alive so we will not have to kill any of our animals."ᵉ ⁶So they divided the land they were to cover, Ahab going in one direction and Obadiah in another.

⁷As Obadiah was walking along, Elijah met him. Obadiah recognizedᶠ him, bowed down to the ground, and said, "Is it really you, my lord Elijah?"

⁸"Yes," he replied. "Go tell your master, 'Elijah is here.'"

⁹"What have I done wrong," asked Obadiah, "that you are handing your servant over to Ahab to be put to death? ¹⁰As surely as the LORD your God lives, there is not a nation or kingdom where my master has not sent someone to lookᵍ for you. And whenever a nation or kingdom claimed you were not there, he made them swear they could not find you. ¹¹But now you tell me to go to my master and say, 'Elijah is here.' ¹²I don't know where the Spiritʰ of the LORD may carry you when I leave you. If I go and tell Ahab and he doesn't find you, he will kill me. Yet I your servant have worshiped the LORD since my youth. ¹³Haven't you heard, my lord, what I did while Jezebel was killing the prophets of the LORD? I hid a hundred of the LORD's prophets in two caves, fifty in each, and supplied them with food and water. ¹⁴And now you tell me to go to my master and say, 'Elijah is here.' He will kill me!"

¹⁵Elijah said, "As the LORD Almighty lives, whom I serve, I will surely present ⁱ myself to Ahab today."

17:20 ° 2Ki 4:33
17:21 ᵖ 2Ki 4:34;
Ac 20:10
17:23 q Heb 11:35
17:24 ʳ Jn 16:30
ˢ ver 18 1Ki 22:16;
Ps 119:43; Jn 17:17
18:1 ᵘ 1Ki 17:1;
Lk 4:25 ᵛ ver 18
ʷ S Dt 28:12
18:2 ˣ S Lev 26:26
18:3 ʸ 1Ki 16:9
ᶻ Ne 7:2
18:4 ᵃ 1Ki 21:23;
2Ki 9:7 ᵇ S 1Ki 17:3;
Isa 16:3; 25:4; 32:2;
Ob 1:14 ᶜ Jer 26:24
18:5 ᵈ Jer 14:3
ᵉ S Ge 47:4
18:7 f 2Ki 1:8;
Zec 13:4
18:10 ᵍ S 1Ki 17:3
18:12 ʰ 2Ki 2:16;
Eze 3:14; Ac 8:39
18:15 ⁱ ver 1

C **17:21** *stretched himself out on the boy three times.* The apparent intent of this physical contact was to transfer the bodily warmth and stimulation of the prophet to the child. Elijah's prayer, however, makes it clear that he expected the life of the child to return as an answer to prayer, not as a result of bodily contact. *let this boy's life return to him.* Moved by a faith like that of Abraham (Ro 4:17; Heb 11:19), Elijah prayed for the child's return to life so that the veracity and trustworthiness of God's word might be demonstrated.

17:22 *the boy's life returned to him.* The first instance of raising the dead recorded in Scripture. This non-Israelite widow was granted the supreme covenant blessing, the gift of life rescued from the power of death. This blessing came in the person of her son, the only hope for a widow in ancient society (see 2Ki 4:14; Ru 1:11–12; 4:15–17; Lk 7:12).

A **17:24** *you are a man of God.* See note on 1Sa 2:27. The widow had addressed Elijah as a man of God previously (v. 18), but now she knew in a much more experiential way that he truly was a prophet of the Lord (see note on 12:22). *the word of the LORD from your mouth is the truth.* God used this experience to convince the Phoenician widow that his word was completely reliable. Her confession was one that the Lord's own people in Israel had failed to make.

18:1 *third year.* Apparently of the drought. Later Jewish tradition indicates that the drought lasted three and a half years (cf.

Lk 4:25; Jas 5:17), but that probably represents a symbolic number for a drought cut short (half of seven years; see Ge 41:27; 2Ki 8:1). *present yourself to Ahab, and I will send rain on the land.* Elijah's return is not occasioned by repentance in Israel but by the command of the Lord, who in his sovereign grace determined to reveal himself anew to his people.

18:3 *Obadiah.* A common OT name, meaning "servant of the LORD." *in charge of his palace.* See note on 4:6.

B **18:5** The famine did not move Ahab to repentance (contrast Ahab's response to the famine with that of David years earlier, 2Sa 21:1). But when his military strength seemed to be jeopardized, he scoured the land for food and water (see 10:26; according to the annals of the Assyrian ruler Shalmaneser III, Ahab could bring 2,000 chariots against him).

18:8 *tell your master, 'Elijah is here.'* This action would publicly identify Obadiah with Elijah in contrast to his previous clandestine support of the prophets sought by Jezebel (see vv. 4, 13).

18:12 *I don't know where the Spirit of the LORD may carry you.* Elijah's disappearance earlier and now his sudden reappearance suggested to Obadiah that God's Spirit was miraculously transporting the prophet about (see 2Ki 2:16).

18:13 *Jezebel was killing the prophets.* Possibly in an attempt to please Baal so he would send rain. *prophets of the LORD.* Probably members of the communities of "prophets" that had sprung up in Israel during this time of apostasy (see note on 20:35).

18:17 *j* Jos 7:25;
1Sa 14:29; 1Ki 21:20;
Jer 38:4
18:18 *k* 1Ki 16:31,33;
21:25 *l* S Dt 31:16
18:19 *m* 2Ki 10:19
n S Jos 19:26
o 2Ki 9:22
18:20 *p* 2Ki 2:25;
4:25
18:21 *q* Jos 24:15;
2Ki 17:41; Ps 119:113;
Mt 6:24 *r* ver 39;
Ps 100:3; 118:27
18:22 *s* 1Ki 19:10
t Jer 2:8; 23:13
18:24 *u* S 1Sa 7:8
v S Ge 4:26
w S ver 38; S Ex 19:18;
S Lev 9:24
18:26 *x* Isa 44:17;
45:20 *y* Ps 115:4-5;
135:16; Isa 41:26,28;
46:7; Jer 10:5;
1Co 8:4; 12:2
18:27 *z* Hab 2:19
18:28 *a* S Lev 19:28
18:29 *b* S Ex 29:41
c 2Ki 19:12; Isa 16:12;
Jer 10:5
18:30 *d* 1Ki 19:10
18:31 *e* S Ge 17:5;
2Ki 17:34
18:32 *f* S Dt 18:7;
Col 3:17

ELIJAH ON MOUNT CARMEL

¹⁶So Obadiah went to meet Ahab and told him, and Ahab went to meet Elijah. ¹⁷When he saw Elijah, he said to him, "Is that you, you troubler *j* of Israel?"

¹⁸"I have not made trouble for Israel," Elijah replied. "But you *k* and your father's family have. You have abandoned *l* the LORD's commands and have followed the Baals. ¹⁹Now summon *m* the people from all over Israel to meet me on Mount Carmel. *n* And bring the four hundred and fifty prophets of Baal and the four hundred prophets of Asherah, who eat at Jezebel's table." *o*

²⁰So Ahab sent word throughout all Israel and assembled the prophets on Mount Carmel. *p* ²¹Elijah went before the people and said, "How long will you waver *q* between two opinions? If the LORD *r* is God, follow him; but if Baal is God, follow him."

But the people said nothing.

²²Then Elijah said to them, "I am the only one of the LORD's prophets left, *s* but Baal has four hundred and fifty prophets. *t* ²³Get two bulls for us. Let Baal's prophets choose one for themselves, and let them cut it into pieces and put it on the wood but not set fire to it. I will prepare the other bull and put it on the wood but not set fire to it. ²⁴Then you call *u* on the name of your god, and I will call on the name of the LORD. *v* The god who answers by fire *w*—he is God."

Then all the people said, "What you say is good."

²⁵Elijah said to the prophets of Baal, "Choose one of the bulls and prepare it first, since there are so many of you. Call on the name of your god, but do not light the fire." ²⁶So they took the bull given them and prepared it.

Then they called *x* on the name of Baal from morning till noon. "Baal, answer us!" they shouted. But there was no response; *y* no one answered. And they danced around the altar they had made.

²⁷At noon Elijah began to taunt them. "Shout louder!" he said. "Surely he is a god! Perhaps he is deep in thought, or busy, or traveling. Maybe he is sleeping and must be awakened." *z* ²⁸So they shouted louder and slashed *a* themselves with swords and spears, as was their custom, until their blood flowed. ²⁹Midday passed, and they continued their frantic prophesying until the time for the evening sacrifice. *b* But there was no response, no one answered, no one paid attention. *c*

³⁰Then Elijah said to all the people, "Come here to me." They came to him, and he repaired the altar *d* of the LORD, which had been torn down. ³¹Elijah took twelve stones, one for each of the tribes descended from Jacob, to whom the word of the LORD had come, saying, "Your name shall be Israel." *e* ³²With the stones he built an altar in the name *f* of the LORD, and he dug a trench around it large enough to hold two seahs *a* of seed. ³³He ar-

---

a 32 That is, probably about 24 pounds or about 11 kilograms

18:17 *you troubler of Israel.* Ahab holds Elijah responsible for the drought and charges him with a crime against the state worthy of death (he calls him a "trouble bringer"; see Jos 7:25).

A C **18:18** *You have abandoned the LORD's commands and have followed the Baals.* The source of Israel's trouble was not Elijah or even the drought, but Ahab's breach of covenantal loyalty.

18:19 *Mount Carmel.* A high ridge next to the Mediterranean Sea, where the effects of the drought would be least apparent (see Am 1:2) and the power of Baal to nurture life would seem to be strongest. *prophets of Baal . . . prophets of Asherah.* See v. 29 and note. *Asherah.* See note on 14:15. *eat at Jezebel's table.* See note on 2:7.

A **18:21** *waver.* The Hebrew for this word is the same as that used for "danced" in v. 26 (see note there). Elijah speaks with biting irony: In her religious ambivalence Israel is but engaging in a wild and futile religious "dance." *If the LORD is God, follow him; but if Baal is God, follow him.* Elijah placed a clear choice before the people. He drew a sharp contrast between the worship of the Lord and that of Baal to eliminate the apostate idea that people could worship both deities.

18:22 *only one . . . left.* At least the only one to stand boldly and publicly against the king and the prophets of Baal (but see v. 4; 19:10,14; 20:13,28,35; 22:6,8; cf. 19:18 and note; Ro 11:4).

18:24 *I will call . . . who answers.* See note on Ps 118:5. *The god who answers by fire—he is God.* Both the Lord and Baal were said to ride the thunderstorm as their divine chariot (see Ps

104:3 and note); thunder was their voice (see Ps 29:3–9 and note) and lightning ("fire") their weapon (see Ps 18:14 and note). Elijah's challenge is direct. Cf. Lev 9:24.

18:26 *danced around the altar.* The ecstatic dance was part of the pagan ritual intended to arouse the deity to perform some desired action (see note on v. 21).

18:27 *deep in thought . . . sleeping.* Elijah ridicules, but as he does he shows knowledge of the Baal myths that depict the gods as having very human characteristics.

18:28 *until their blood flowed.* Self-inflicted wounds (causing blood to flow) were symbolic of self-sacrifice as an extreme method of arousing the deity to action. Such mutilation of the body was strictly forbidden in the Mosaic law (Lev 19:28; Dt 14:1).

18:29 *frantic prophesying.* Indicative of ecstatic raving, in which the ritual reached its climax (see notes on 1Sa 10:5; 10:10). *time for the evening sacrifice.* See Ex 29:38–41; Nu 28:3–8. *no response.* Dramatic demonstration of Baal's impotence (see Ps 115:5–8; 135:15–18; Jer 10:5).

18:30 *altar of the LORD, which had been torn down.* It is possible that the altar had been built by people of the northern ten tribes after the division of the kingdom (see note on 3:2) and that it had been destroyed by the agents of Jezebel (vv. 4,13; 19:10,14).

18:31 *twelve stones, one for each of the tribes.* In this way Elijah called attention to the covenant unity of Israel as the people of God in spite of her political division. What was about to happen concerned the entire nation, not just the northern ten tribes.

ranged ^{g} the wood, cut the bull into pieces and laid it on the wood. Then he said to them, "Fill four large jars with water and pour it on the offering and on the wood."

^{34}"Do it again," he said, and they did it again.

"Do it a third time," he ordered, and they did it the third time. ^{35}The water ran down around the altar and even filled the trench.

^{36}At the time ^{h} of sacrifice, the prophet Elijah stepped forward and prayed: "LORD, the God of Abraham, ^{i} Isaac and Israel, let it be known ^{j} today that you are God in Israel and that I am your servant and have done all these things at your command. ^{k} ^{37}Answer me, LORD, answer me, so these people will know ^{l} that you, LORD, are God, and that you are turning their hearts back again."

^{38}Then the fire ^{m} of the LORD fell and burned up the sacrifice, the wood, the stones and the soil, and also licked up the water in the trench.

^{39}When all the people saw this, they fell prostrate ^{n} and cried, "The LORD—he is God! The LORD—he is God!" ^{o}

^{40}Then Elijah commanded them, "Seize the prophets of Baal. Don't let anyone get away!" They seized them, and Elijah had them brought down to the Kishon Valley ^{p} and slaughtered ^{q} there.

^{41}And Elijah said to Ahab, "Go, eat and drink, for there is the sound of a heavy rain." ^{42}So Ahab went off to eat and drink, but Elijah climbed to the top of Carmel, bent down to the ground and put his face between his knees. ^{r}

^{43}"Go and look toward the sea," he told his servant. And he went up and looked.

"There is nothing there," he said.

Seven times Elijah said, "Go back."

^{44}The seventh time ^{s} the servant reported, "A cloud ^{t} as small as a man's hand is rising from the sea."

So Elijah said, "Go and tell Ahab, 'Hitch up your chariot and go down before the rain stops you.'"

^{45}Meanwhile, the sky grew black with clouds, the wind rose, a heavy rain ^{u} came on and Ahab rode off to Jezreel. ^{v} ^{46}The power ^{w} of the LORD came on Elijah and, tucking his cloak into his belt, ^{x} he ran ahead of Ahab all the way to Jezreel.

ELIJAH FLEES TO HOREB

19 Now Ahab told Jezebel ^{y} everything Elijah had done and how he had killed ^{z} all the prophets with the sword. ^{2}So Jezebel sent a messenger to Elijah to say, "May the gods deal with me, be it ever so severely, ^{a} if by this time tomorrow I do not make your life like that of one of them." ^{b}

^{3}Elijah was afraid ^{a} and ran ^{c} for his life. ^{d} When he came to Beersheba ^{e} in Judah, he left his servant there, ^{4}while he himself went a day's journey into the wilderness. He came to

---

^{a} 3 Or *Elijah saw*

18:33 ^{g} S Ge 22:9
18:36 ^{h} S Ex 29:39, 41 ^{i} S Ge 24:12; S Ex 4:5; Mt 22:32 ^{j} S Jos 4:24; S 1Sa 17:46; S Ps 46:10 ^{k} Nu 16:28
18:37 ^{l} S Jos 4:24
18:38 ^{m} ver 24; S Ex 19:18; S Lev 9:24; 2Ki 1:10; 1Ch 21:26; 2Ch 7:1; Job 1:16
18:39 ^{n} S Lev 9:24 ^{o} S ver 24; S Ps 46:10
18:40 ^{p} S Jdg 4:7 ^{q} S Ex 22:20; S Dt 17:12; S 2Ki 11:18
18:42 ^{r} S 1Sa 12:17; Jas 5:18
18:44 ^{s} S Jos 6:15 ^{t} Lk 12:54
18:45 ^{u} S 1Ki 8:36; Job 37:13 ^{v} S 1Sa 29:1; S Hos 1:4
18:46 ^{w} S Jdg 3:10; S 1Sa 11:6; Lk 1:35; 4:14 ^{x} 2Ki 4:29; 9:1
19:1 ^{y} 1Ki 16:31 ^{z} S Ex 22:20
19:2 ^{a} S Ru 1:17 ^{b} Ps 13:4; Jer 20:10; 26:21; 36:26
19:3 ^{c} S Ge 31:21 ^{d} S Ge 19:17 ^{e} S Jos 19:2

18:33 *water.* By drenching the whole installation Elijah showed to all that he was using no tricks.

18:36 *prayed.* Elijah's simple but earnest prayer stands in sharp contrast to the frantic shouts and "dancing" and self-mutilation of the Baal prophets. *God of Abraham, Isaac and Israel.* An appeal to the Lord to remember his ancient covenant with the patriarchs, and to Israel to remember all that the Lord has done for her since the days of her ancestors.

18:38 *fire of the LORD fell.* See note on v. 24.

18:40 *Kishon Valley.* The Kishon River flows below Mount Carmel (see map, p. 527). *slaughtered there.* Elijah, acting on the authority of the Lord, who sent him, carried out the sentence pronounced in the Mosaic law for prophets of pagan deities (Dt 13:13–18; 17:2–5).

18:41 *sound of a heavy rain.* Now that Baal worship has been struck a devastating blow, there is the promise of rain (see 17:1). Significantly, Ahab takes no action—either to carry out the Mosaic sentence or to halt Elijah. He still wavers between two opinions (see v. 21 and note).

18:42 *Elijah ... bent down to the ground and put his face between his knees.* Now that the people had confessed that the Lord alone is God, Elijah prayed for the covenant curse to be lifted (see note on 17:1) by the coming of rain (see 8:35; 2Ch 7:13–14).

18:43 *Seven times.* The number symbolic of completeness.

18:44 *rising from the sea.* Appearing on the western horizon above the Mediterranean.

18:46 *ran ahead of Ahab all the way to Jezreel.* Divinely energized by extraordinary strength, Elijah ran before Ahab's chariot to Jezreel (a distance of c. 16 miles). This dramatic scene, with the Lord's prophet running before the king and the Lord himself racing behind him riding his mighty thundercloud chariot (see note on v. 24), served as a powerful appeal to Ahab to break once for all with Baal and henceforth to rule as the servant of the Lord.

19:1 *Jezebel.* Ahab's wife and a worshiper of Baal-Melqart, the god of Phoenicia (see notes on 16:25, 31–32; 18:13).

19:2 *May the gods deal with me, be it ever so severely.* A curse formula (see note on 1Sa 3:17). *one of them.* The dead prophets of Baal (v. 1).

19:3 *Elijah was afraid and ran for his life.* In spite of Elijah's great triumph in the trial on Mount Carmel and the dramatic demonstration that his God is the Lord of heaven and earth and the source of Israel's blessings, Jezebel is undaunted. Hers is no empty threat, and Ahab has shown that he is either unwilling or unable to restrain her. So Elijah knows that one of the main sources of Israel's present apostasy is still spewing out its poison and that his own life is in danger. *Beersheba.* The southernmost city in Judah (see notes on Ge 21:31; Am 5:5; see also Jdg 20:1).

19:4 *f* Job 30:4
g S Nu 11:15; Job 6:9;
7:16; 10:1; Ps 69:19;
Jer 20:18; Jnh 4:8
19:5 *h* Ge 28:11
i S Ge 16:7
19:8 *j* Ex 24:18;
Mt 4:2 *k* S Ex 3:1
19:9 *l* S Ex 33:22
m S Ge 3:9
19:10 *n* S Nu 25:13;
Ac 22:3; Gal 4:18
o S Dt 31:16
p 1Ki 18:30 *q* 1Ki 18:4,
22; Jer 5:11; 9:2;
Ro 11:3*
19:11 *r* Ex 34:2;
Mt 17:1-3 *s* Ex 33:19
t S Ex 14:21; S 2Ki 2:1
u Na 1:6
19:12 *v* S Ex 3:2
w ver 11; S 1Sa 14:6;
Job 4:16; Zec 4:6;
2Co 12:9
19:13 *x* Ex 3:6
19:14 *y* 1Ki 18:22;
Ro 11:3*
19:15 *z* 2Ki 8:7-15
19:16 *a* 2Ki 9:1-3,6
b ver 21; 2Ki 2:1; 3:11
c S Jdg 7:22

a broom bush, *f* sat down under it and prayed that he might die. "I have had enough, LORD," he said. "Take my life; *g* I am no better than my ancestors." 5 Then he lay down under the tree and fell asleep. *h*

All at once an angel *i* touched him and said, "Get up and eat." 6 He looked around, and there by his head was some bread baked over hot coals, and a jar of water. He ate and drank and then lay down again.

7 The angel of the LORD came back a second time and touched him and said, "Get up and eat, for the journey is too much for you." 8 So he got up and ate and drank. Strengthened by that food, he traveled forty *j* days and forty nights until he reached Horeb, *k* the mountain of God. 9 There he went into a cave *l* and spent the night.

THE LORD APPEARS TO ELIJAH

And the word of the LORD came to him: "What are you doing here, Elijah?" *m*

10 He replied, "I have been very zealous *n* for the LORD God Almighty. The Israelites have rejected your covenant, *o* torn down your altars, *p* and put your prophets to death with the sword. I am the only one left, *q* and now they are trying to kill me too."

11 The LORD said, "Go out and stand on the mountain *r* in the presence of the LORD, for the LORD is about to pass by." *s*

Then a great and powerful wind *t* tore the mountains apart and shattered *u* the rocks before the LORD, but the LORD was not in the wind. After the wind there was an earthquake, but the LORD was not in the earthquake. 12 After the earthquake came a fire, *v* but the LORD was not in the fire. And after the fire came a gentle whisper. *w* 13 When Elijah heard it, he pulled his cloak over his face *x* and went out and stood at the mouth of the cave.

Then a voice said to him, "What are you doing here, Elijah?"

14 He replied, "I have been very zealous for the LORD God Almighty. The Israelites have rejected your covenant, torn down your altars, and put your prophets to death with the sword. I am the only one left, *y* and now they are trying to kill me too."

15 The LORD said to him, "Go back the way you came, and go to the Desert of Damascus. When you get there, anoint Hazael *z* king over Aram. 16 Also, anoint *a* Jehu son of Nimshi king over Israel, and anoint Elisha *b* son of Shaphat from Abel Meholah *c* to succeed you as

---

A C **19:4** *broom bush.* A desert shrub, sometimes large enough to offer some shade. *prayed that he might die.* Cf. Jnh 4:3,8. Elijah concluded that his work was fruitless and consequently that life was not worth living. He had lost his confidence in the triumph of the kingdom of God and was withdrawing from the arena of conflict.

19:7 *angel of the LORD.* See note on Ge 16:7. God in his mercy provided sustenance and rest for his discouraged servant. *the journey is too much for you.* Evidently Elijah had already determined to go to Mount Horeb, where God had established his covenant with his people. There is no indication that the Lord had instructed him to do this as he had previously directed him to go to Kerith (17:2–3) and to Zarephath (17:8–9) and to meet Ahab (18:1).

19:8 *forty days and forty nights.* Sustained by the Lord as Moses had been for the same length of time on Mount Sinai (Ex 24:18; 34:28) and as Jesus would be in the desert (Mt 4:2,11). *Horeb, the mountain of God.* Probably an alternative name for Mount Sinai (see Ex 3:1; 19:1–3), located in the desert apparently about 250 miles south of Beersheba.

19:9 *What are you doing here, Elijah?* The question implies that Elijah had come to Sinai for his own misguided reasons and not because the Lord had sent him.

19:10 Elijah did not give a direct answer to the Lord's question but implied that the work the Lord had begun centuries earlier with the establishment of the Sinai covenant had now come to nothing. Whereas Moses had interceded for Israel when they sinned with the golden calf (Ex 32:11–13), Elijah condemned the Israelites for breaking the covenant, and bitterly complained over the fruitlessness of his own work. *only one left.* See note on 18:22.

A **19:12** *gentle whisper.* In the symbolism of these occurrences (vv. 11–12) the Lord appears to be telling Elijah that although his servant's indictment of Israel was a call for God to judge his people with windstorm, earthquake and fire, it was not God's will to do so now. Elijah must return to continue God's mission to his people, and Elisha is to carry it on for an-

other generation (v. 16).

19:13 *What are you doing here, Elijah?* After demonstrating his presence in the gentle whisper rather than in the wind, earthquake or fire, the Lord gave Elijah an opportunity to revise the answer he had previously given to the same question (vv. 9–10).

19:14 Elijah's unrevised answer demonstrated that he did not understand the significance of the divine revelation he had just witnessed.

B **19:15** *The LORD said to him.* Giving instructions to Elijah that revealed his sovereign power over people and nations. Even though Israel would experience divine judgment through Hazael, Jehu and Elisha, God would continue to preserve a remnant faithful to himself among the people. *go to the Desert of Damascus.* Apparently Elijah is to go back by way of the road east of the Dead Sea and the Jordan. As it turns out, all three anointings take place east of the Jordan, though it is Elisha who effects the anointing of the two kings. *anoint.* Appears to mean here no more than "designate as divinely appointed." This anointing was actually done by Elijah's successor Elisha (see 2Ki 8:7–15). *Hazael.* Subsequently became a serious threat to Israel during the reigns of Joram, Jehu and Jehoahaz (see 2Ki 8:28–29; 10:32–33; 12:17–18; 13:3,22). There are references to him on ivory fragments from Arslan Tash (north Syria) and Nimrud (Assyria). Tiglath-Pileser III, king of Assyria, called Damascus (Aram) the "House of Hazael."

C **19:16** *anoint Jehu.* Jehu was a military commander under Ahab and Joram, Ahab's son (2Ki 9:5–6). He was anointed king over Israel by a "man from the company of the prophets" at the instruction of Elisha (2Ki 9:1–16), with the mandate to destroy the house of Ahab. *Elisha.* As with Elijah (see note on 17:1), Elisha's name (meaning "God is salvation" or "God saves") was the essence of his ministry. His name evokes memory of Joshua ("The LORD saves"). Elijah is given someone to finish his work, just as Moses was, and Elisha channels the covenant blessings to the faithful in Israel just as Joshua brought Israel into the promised land (see the account of Elisha's ministry prophet. [17]Jehu will put to death any who escape the sword of Hazael, *d* and Elisha will put to death any who escape the sword of Jehu. *e* [18]Yet I reserve *f* seven thousand in Israel—all whose knees have not bowed down to Baal and whose mouths have not kissed *g* him."

THE CALL OF ELISHA

[19]So Elijah went from there and found Elisha son of Shaphat. He was plowing with twelve yoke of oxen, and he himself was driving the twelfth pair. Elijah went up to him and threw his cloak *h* around him. [20]Elisha then left his oxen and ran after Elijah. "Let me kiss my father and mother good-by," *i* he said, "and then I will come with you."

"Go back," Elijah replied. "What have I done to you?"

[21]So Elisha left him and went back. He took his yoke of oxen *j* and slaughtered them. He burned the plowing equipment to cook the meat and gave it to the people, and they ate. Then he set out to follow Elijah and became his servant. *k*

19:17 *d* 2Ki 8:12,29; 10:32; 12:17; 13:3,7, 22; Am 1:4 *e* Jer 48:44
19:18 *f* Ro 11:4*
g Hos 13:2
19:19 *h* S Ge 41:42; 2Ki 2:8,14
19:20 *i* Lk 9:61
19:21 *j* S 1Sa 6:14
k S ver 16

in 2Ki 2:19—8:15; 9:1–3; 13:14–20). In the NT John the Baptist ("Elijah," Mt 11:14; 17:12–13) was followed by Jesus ("Joshua"; see TNIV text note on Mt 1:21) to complete God's saving work. *son of Shaphat.* Shaphat means "He judges," which is also in accordance with Elisha's ministry. *Abel Meholah.* See map, p. 527.
19:17 *Jehu will put to death any who escape the sword of Hazael.* See 2Ki 9:24. *Elisha will put to death any who escape the sword of Jehu.* How this may have been fulfilled we are not told, but see 2Ki 2:24; 8:1 (see also Hos 6:5).

19:18 *seven thousand.* A round number, no doubt symbolic of the fullness or completeness of the divinely pre-

served godly remnant (Ro 11:2–4). In any case Elijah had been mistaken in his conclusion that he alone had remained faithful (see vv. 10,14; 18:22 and note). *not kissed him.* See Hos 13:2.
19:19 *threw his cloak around him.* Thus designating Elisha as his successor (see note on v. 16).
19:21 *slaughtered them … burned the plowing equipment.* Elisha's break with his past vocation was complete, though he obviously came from a wealthy family. *servant.* In Hebrew the same designation as used for Joshua's relationship to Moses ("aide," Ex 24:13; 33:11).

LIVES OF ELIJAH AND ELISHA

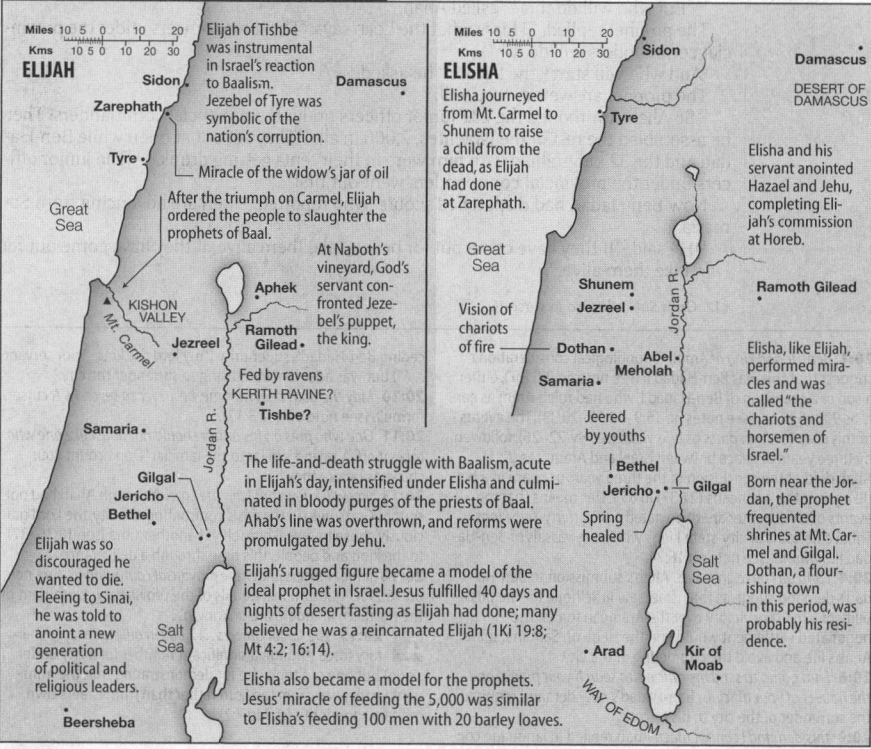

ELIJAH

Miles 10 5 0   10   20
Kms 10 5 0 10 20 30

Sidon
Zarephath
Damascus
Tyre
Miracle of the widow's jar of oil
Great Sea
After the triumph on Carmel, Elijah ordered the people to slaughter the prophets of Baal.
KISHON VALLEY
Mt. Carmel
Aphek
Ramoth Gilead
Jezreel
At Naboth's vineyard, God's servant confronted Jezebel's puppet, the king.
Fed by ravens
KERITH RAVINE?
Tishbe?
Samaria
Jordan R.
Gilgal
Jericho
Bethel
Elijah was so discouraged he wanted to die. Fleeing to Sinai, he was told to anoint a new generation of political and religious leaders.
Salt Sea
Beersheba

Elijah of Tishbe was instrumental in Israel's reaction to Baalism. Jezebel of Tyre was symbolic of the nation's corruption.

The life-and-death struggle with Baalism, acute in Elijah's day, intensified under Elisha and culminated in bloody purges of the priests of Baal. Ahab's line was overthrown, and reforms were promulgated by Jehu.

Elijah's rugged figure became a model of the ideal prophet in Israel. Jesus fulfilled 40 days and nights of desert fasting as Elijah had done; many believed he was a reincarnated Elijah (1Ki 19:8; Mt 4:2; 16:14).

Elisha also became a model for the prophets. Jesus' miracle of feeding the 5,000 was similar to Elisha's feeding 100 men with 20 barley loaves.

ELISHA

Miles 10 5 0   10   20
Kms 10 5 0 10 20 30

Sidon
Damascus
DESERT OF DAMASCUS
Tyre
Elisha journeyed from Mt. Carmel to Shunem to raise a child from the dead, as Elijah had done at Zarephath.
Elisha and his servant anointed Hazael and Jehu, completing Elijah's commission at Horeb.
Great Sea
Shunem
Jezreel
Ramoth Gilead
Vision of chariots of fire
Dothan
Abel Meholah
Jordan R.
Samaria
Jeered by youths
Bethel
Jericho
Gilgal
Spring healed
Salt Sea
Arad
Kir of Moab
WAY OF EDOM

Elisha, like Elijah, performed miracles and was called "the chariots and horsemen of Israel."

Born near the Jordan, the prophet frequented shrines at Mt. Carmel and Gilgal. Dothan, a flourishing town in this period, was probably his residence.

20:1 *l* S 1Ki 15:18
m S 1Ki 13:32
20:7 *n* 1Sa 11:3
o 2Ki 5:7
20:10 *p* S 2Sa 22:43
20:11 *q* Pr 27:1;
Jer 9:23; Am 2:14
20:12 *r* S 1Ki 16:9
20:13 *s* S Jdg 6:8
t S Ex 6:7
20:14 *u* S Jdg 1:1
20:16 *v* S 1Ki 16:9

BEN-HADAD ATTACKS SAMARIA

20 Now Ben-Hadad *l* king of Aram mustered his entire army. Accompanied by thirty-two kings with their horses and chariots, he went up and besieged Samaria *m* and attacked it. ²He sent messengers into the city to Ahab king of Israel, saying, "This is what Ben-Hadad says: ³'Your silver and gold are mine, and the best of your wives and children are mine.' "

⁴The king of Israel answered, "Just as you say, my lord the king. I and all I have are yours."

⁵The messengers came again and said, "This is what Ben-Hadad says: 'I sent to demand your silver and gold, your wives and your children. ⁶But about this time tomorrow I am going to send my officials to search your palace and the houses of your officials. They will seize everything you value and carry it away.' "

⁷The king of Israel summoned all the elders *n* of the land and said to them, "See how this man is looking for trouble! *o* When he sent for my wives and my children, my silver and my gold, I did not refuse him."

⁸The elders and the people all answered, "Don't listen to him or agree to his demands."

⁹So he replied to Ben-Hadad's messengers, "Tell my lord the king, 'Your servant will do all you demanded the first time, but this demand I cannot meet.' " They left and took the answer back to Ben-Hadad.

¹⁰Then Ben-Hadad sent another message to Ahab: "May the gods deal with me, be it ever so severely, if enough dust *p* remains in Samaria to give each of my men a handful."

¹¹The king of Israel answered, "Tell him: 'One who puts on his armor should not boast *q* like one who takes it off.' "

¹²Ben-Hadad heard this message while he and the kings were drinking *r* in their tents,ᵃ and he ordered his men: "Prepare to attack." So they prepared to attack the city.

AHAB DEFEATS BEN-HADAD

¹³Meanwhile a prophet *s* came to Ahab king of Israel and announced, "This is what the LORD says: 'Do you see this vast army? I will give it into your hand today, and then you will know *t* that I am the LORD.' "

¹⁴"But who will do this?" asked Ahab.

The prophet replied, "This is what the LORD says: 'The junior officers under the provincial commanders will do it.' "

"And who will start *u* the battle?" he asked.

The prophet answered, "You will."

¹⁵So Ahab summoned the 232 junior officers under the provincial commanders. Then he assembled the rest of the Israelites, 7,000 in all. ¹⁶They set out at noon while Ben-Hadad and the 32 kings allied with him were in their tents getting drunk. *v* ¹⁷The junior officers under the provincial commanders went out first.

Now Ben-Hadad had dispatched scouts, who reported, "Men are advancing from Samaria."

¹⁸He said, "If they have come out for peace, take them alive; if they have come out for war, take them alive."

ᵃ *12* Or *in Sukkoth*; also in verse 16

20:1 *Ben-Hadad king of Aram.* Chronological considerations suggest that this was Ben-Hadad II (see note on 2Ki 8:7), either a son or a grandson of Ben-Hadad I, who had ruled Aram as early as 900–895 B.C. (see notes on 15:9–10,18–20,33). The events of this chapter span parts of two years (see vv. 22–26), followed by three years of peace between Israel and Aram (see 22:1). Ahab died at the conclusion of the three years of peace in a battle against the Arameans (22:37) in 853. This means that the events of this chapter are to be dated c. 857. *thirty-two kings.* Tribal chieftains or city-state kings who were vassals of Ben-Hadad II. *Samaria.* See note on 16:24.

20:4 *I and all I have are yours.* Ahab's submission to Ben-Hadad's demand suggests that Israel saw little hope for the possibility of a military victory over the Aramean forces. The negotiated settlement would end the siege on Samaria, spare Ahab's life and avoid the plundering of the city.

20:6 *I am going to send my officials to search your palace and the houses of your officials.* Ben-Hadad's new demand required the surrender of the city to his forces.

20:9 *this demand I cannot meet.* Ahab replied in language conceding Ben-Hadad's superiority ("my lord the king, 'Your servant …'") but was adamant in refusing to surrender the city.

20:10 *May the gods deal with me, be it ever so severely.* A curse formula (see note on 1Sa 3:17).

20:11 *One who puts on his armor should not boast like one who takes it off.* A saying similar to the familiar "Don't count your chickens before they hatch."

20:13 *you will know that I am the LORD.* Although Ahab had not sought God's help in the crisis confronting the city, the Lord graciously chose to reveal himself yet another time (see 18:36–37) to the king and people, this time through a deliverance.

20:14 *junior officers under the provincial commanders.* See note on 16:27. Organizational details of the provincial government of the northern kingdom are unknown.

A **20:15** *232 junior officers…7,000 in all.* Not a large military force (though a significant number for a city under siege) but one of fitting size for demonstrating that the imminent victory was from the Lord rather than from Israel's own military superiority (cf. Jdg 7:2).

¹⁹The junior officers under the provincial commanders marched out of the city with the army behind them ²⁰and each one struck down his opponent. At that, the Arameans fled, with the Israelites in pursuit. But Ben-Hadad king of Aram escaped on horseback with some of his horsemen. ²¹The king of Israel advanced and overpowered the horses and chariots and inflicted heavy losses on the Arameans.

²²Afterward, the prophet ^w came to the king of Israel and said, "Strengthen your position and see what must be done, because next spring ^x the king of Aram will attack you again."

²³Meanwhile, the officials of the king of Aram advised him, "Their gods are gods ^y of the hills. That is why they were too strong for us. But if we fight them on the plains, surely we will be stronger than they. ²⁴Do this: Remove all the kings from their commands and replace them with other officers. ²⁵You must also raise an army like the one you lost—horse for horse and chariot for chariot—so we can fight Israel on the plains. Then surely we will be stronger than they." He agreed with them and acted accordingly.

²⁶The next spring ^z Ben-Hadad mustered the Arameans and went up to Aphek ^a to fight against Israel. ²⁷When the Israelites were also mustered and given provisions, they marched out to meet them. The Israelites camped opposite them like two small flocks of goats, while the Arameans covered the countryside. ^b

²⁸The man of God came up and told the king of Israel, "This is what the LORD says: 'Because the Arameans think the LORD is a god of the hills and not a god ^c of the valleys, I will deliver this vast army into your hands, and you will know ^d that I am the LORD.' "

²⁹For seven days they camped opposite each other, and on the seventh day the battle was joined. The Israelites inflicted a hundred thousand casualties on the Aramean foot soldiers in one day. ³⁰The rest of them escaped to the city of Aphek, ^e where the wall collapsed ^f on twenty-seven thousand of them. And Ben-Hadad fled to the city and hid ^g in an inner room.

³¹His officials said to him, "Look, we have heard that the kings of the house of Israel are merciful. ^h Let us go to the king of Israel with sackcloth ⁱ around our waists and ropes around our heads. Perhaps he will spare your life."

³²Wearing sackcloth around their waists and ropes around their heads, they went to the king of Israel and said, "Your servant Ben-Hadad says: 'Please let me live.' "

The king answered, "Is he still alive? He is an old ally."

³³The men took this as a good sign and were quick to pick up his word. "Yes, your old ally Ben-Hadad!" they said.

"Go and get him," the king said. When Ben-Hadad came out, Ahab had him come up into his chariot.

³⁴"I will return the cities ^j my father took from your father," Ben-Hadad ^k offered. "You may set up your own market areas ^l in Damascus, ^m as my father did in Samaria."

20:22 ^w S Jdg 6:8
^x S 2Sa 11:1
20:23 ^y ver 28;
Isa 36:20; Ro 1:21-23
20:26 ^z S 2Sa 11:1
^a ver 30; S 1Sa 4:1;
2Ki 13:17
20:27 ^b Jdg 6:6;
S 1Sa 13:6
20:28 ^c S ver 23
^d S Ex 6:7; Jer 16:19-21
20:30 ^e S ver 26
^f Ps 62:4; Isa 26:21;
30:13 ^g 1Ki 22:25
20:31 ^h Job 41:3
ⁱ S Ge 37:34
20:34 ^j 1Ki 15:20
^k S Ge 10:22 ^l 2Sa 8:6
^m S Ge 14:15;
Jer 49:23-27

20:20 *each one struck down his opponent.* Apparently they were met by a small advance force like their own (see 2Sa 2:15–16). *escaped on horseback with some of his horsemen.* Since fighting on horseback did not come until later, reference must be to chariot horses and charioteers. After their defeat, the Arameans seem to have withdrawn to Damascus.

20:22 *the king of Aram will attack you again.* The anonymous prophet (see v. 13) warned Ahab against undue self-confidence. The prophet's announcement of an impending renewed attack by Ben-Hadad should have driven Ahab to more complete reliance on the God who had revealed himself on Mount Carmel and in the recent military victory.

20:23 *gods of the hills.* An expression of the pagan idea that a deity's power extended only over the limited area of his particular jurisdiction. *That is why they were too strong for us.* The Arameans believed that the outcome of military conflicts depended on the relative strength of the gods of the opposing forces rather than on the inherent strength of the two armies. For this reason, their strategy was to fight the next battle in a way that advantageously maximized the supposed strengths and weaknesses of the deities involved.

20:26 *Aphek.* Presumably the Aphek located a few miles east of the Sea of Galilee (see map, p. 527). The battle apparently took place in the Jordan Valley near the juncture of the Yarmuk and Jordan rivers.

20:28 *man of God.* Apparently the same prophet mentioned in vv. 13,22. *you will know that I am the LORD.* See note on v. 13. God will again demonstrate that he is the sovereign ruler over all nature and history and that the pagan nature deities are powerless before him.

20:29 *a hundred thousand casualties.* For the problem of apparently excessive numbers of people in Biblical narrative, see Introduction to Numbers: Special Problem.

20:30 *wall collapsed.* The God of Israel not only gave Israel's army a victory in battle but also caused an additional disaster to fall on the Aramean army. *twenty-seven thousand.* See note on v. 29.

20:31 *kings of the house of Israel are merciful.* The Arameans recognized that Israel's kings were different from, e.g., the ruthless Assyrian kings. *sackcloth...ropes.* Perhaps here symbolic of humility and submission.

20:32 *Your servant.* In the diplomatic language of the time, Ben-Hadad acknowledged his inferiority and subordination to Ahab by designating himself Ahab's servant (see note on v. 9). *an old ally.* Lit. "my brother." Ahab disregarded Ben-Hadad's concession and responded in terminology used by rulers who considered themselves equals (see 9:13 and note). In doing this, Ahab gave much more than Ben-Hadad had asked or expected.

20:33 *come up into his chariot.* Not the treatment normally accorded a defeated military opponent.

20:34 *cities my father took from your father.* Perhaps Ramoth Gil-

20:34 ⁿ S Ex 23:32
20:35 ° S 1Sa 10:5;
Am 7:14 ᵖ S 1Ki 13:21
20:36 ᑫ 1Ki 13:24
20:39 ʳ S Jos 2:14
20:40 ˢ 2Sa 12:5;
S 14:13
20:42 ᵗ S 2Sa 12:7
ᵘ Jer 48:10
ᵛ S Jos 2:14
20:43 ʷ 1Ki 21:4
21:1 ˣ 2Ki 9:21
ʸ S 1Sa 29:1; 2Ki 10:1
21:3 ᶻ S Lev 25:23
21:4 ᵃ 1Ki 20:43
ᵇ 1Sa 28:23

ₗAhab said,ₗ "On the basis of a treaty ⁿ I will set you free." So he made a treaty with him, and let him go.

A PROPHET CONDEMNS AHAB

³⁵By the word of the Lᴏʀᴅ one of the company of the prophets ° said to his companion, "Strike me with your weapon," but he refused. ᵖ

³⁶So the prophet said, "Because you have not obeyed the Lᴏʀᴅ, as soon as you leave me a lion ᑫ will kill you." And after the man went away, a lion found him and killed him.

³⁷The prophet found another man and said, "Strike me, please." So the man struck him and wounded him. ³⁸Then the prophet went and stood by the road waiting for the king. He disguised himself with his headband down over his eyes. ³⁹As the king passed by, the prophet called out to him, "Your servant went into the thick of the battle, and someone came to me with a captive and said, 'Guard this man. If he is missing, it will be your life for his life, ʳ or you must pay a talentᵃ of silver.' ⁴⁰While your servant was busy here and there, the man disappeared."

"That is your sentence," ˢ the king of Israel said. "You have pronounced it yourself."

⁴¹Then the prophet quickly removed the headband from his eyes, and the king of Israel recognized him as one of the prophets. ⁴²He said to the king, "This is what the Lᴏʀᴅ says: 'You ᵗ have set free a man I had determined should die. ᵇ ᵘ Therefore it is your life for his life, ᵛ your people for his people.' " ⁴³Sullen and angry, ʷ the king of Israel went to his palace in Samaria.

NABOTH'S VINEYARD

21 Some time later there was an incident involving a vineyard belonging to Naboth ˣ the Jezreelite. The vineyard was in Jezreel, ʸ close to the palace of Ahab king of Samaria. ²Ahab said to Naboth, "Let me have your vineyard to use for a vegetable garden, since it is close to my palace. In exchange I will give you a better vineyard or, if you prefer, I will pay you whatever it is worth."

³But Naboth replied, "The Lᴏʀᴅ forbid that I should give you the inheritance ᶻ of my ancestors."

⁴So Ahab went home, sullen and angry ᵃ because Naboth the Jezreelite had said, "I will not give you the inheritance of my ancestors." He lay on his bed sulking and refused ᵇ to eat.

⁵His wife Jezebel came in and asked him, "Why are you so sullen? Why won't you eat?"

ᵃ 39 That is, about 75 pounds or about 34 kilograms   ᵇ 42 The Hebrew term refers to the irrevocable giving over of things or persons to the Lᴏʀᴅ, often by totally destroying them.

---

ead (see 22:3) along with some of the cities Ben-Hadad I had taken from Baasha (15:20) at an even earlier time. *your own market areas.* Outlets for engaging in the lucrative international trade—a distinct economic advantage; usually such privileges were a jealously guarded local monopoly. *made a treaty with him, and let him go.* A parity treaty (a peace treaty between equals) that included among its provisions the political and trade agreements proposed by Ben-Hadad. In all this, the Lord was not consulted.

20:35 *company of the prophets.* See 2Ki 2:3,5,7,15; 4:1,38; 5:22; 6:1; 9:1. "Son" ("company" is lit. "sons") is not to be understood here as "male child" or "descendant" but as the member of a group. These companies of prophets were apparently religious communities that sprang up in the face of general indifference and apostasy for the purpose of mutual edification and the cultivation of the experience of God. It seems likely that they were known as prophets because their religious practices (sometimes ecstatic) were called prophesying (see 18:29; Nu 11:25–27; 1Sa 10:5–6, 10–11; 18:10; 19:20–24)—to be distinguished from "prophet" in the sense of one bringing ("prophesying") a word from the Lord. The relationship of the Lord's great prophets (such as Samuel, Elijah and Elisha) to these communities was understandably a close one, the Lord's prophets probably being viewed as their spiritual mentors.

20:36 *as soon as you leave me a lion will kill you.* A penalty reminiscent of what happened to the man of God from Judah (13:23–24).

20:39 *talent.* See TNIV text note. Because few soldiers could have paid such a large sum, it would appear to Ahab that the man's life was at stake.

20:40 *That is your sentence.* Ahab refused to grant clemency. Little did he know that he was pronouncing his own death sentence (cf. the similar technique used by Nathan the prophet, 2Sa 12:1–12).

20:42 *a man I had determined should die.* See TNIV text note and notes on Lev 27:28; Jos 6:17. It is not clear whether Ahab violated a previous revelation or erred by simply neglecting to inquire of the Lord before releasing Ben-Hadad. In any case, the Lord had given Ben-Hadad into Ahab's hand (see v. 28), and Ahab was responsible to the Lord for his custody. *your life for his life, your people for his people.* Because Ahab sinned in his official capacity as king, the sentence fell not only on Ahab personally but also on the people of the northern kingdom. Ahab died in battle against the Arameans (22:29–39), and Israel was severely humiliated by them during the reigns of Jehu and Jehoahaz (2Ki 10:32; 13:3).

21:1 *close to the palace of Ahab.* Ahab maintained a residence in Jezreel, in addition to his official palace in Samaria (see 18:45; 2Ki 9:30). *Samaria.* The entire northern kingdom is here represented by its capital city (see note on 16:24).

21:2 *Let me have your vineyard.* Because royal power in Israel was limited by covenantal law (see Dt 17:14–20; 1Sa 10:25), Ahab was unable simply to confiscate privately held land, as was customary with Canaanite kings (see note on v. 7; see also 1Sa 8:9–17).

21:3 Naboth's refusal to dispose of his land was based on the conviction that the land was the Lord's, that he had granted a perpetual lease to each Israelite family and that this lease was to be jealously preserved as the family's permanent inheritance in the promised land.

⁶He answered her, "Because I said to Naboth the Jezreelite, 'Sell me your vineyard; or if you prefer, I will give you another vineyard in its place.' But he said, 'I will not give you my vineyard.' "

⁷Jezebel his wife said, "Is this how you act as king over Israel? Get up and eat! Cheer up. I'll get you the vineyard ᶜ of Naboth the Jezreelite."

⁸So she wrote letters ᵈ in Ahab's name, placed his seal ᵉ on them, and sent them to the elders and nobles who lived in Naboth's city with him. ⁹In those letters she wrote:

"Proclaim a day of fasting and seat Naboth in a prominent place among the people. ¹⁰But seat two scoundrels ᶠ opposite him and have them bring charges that he has cursed ᵍ both God and the king. Then take him out and stone him to death."

¹¹So the elders and nobles who lived in Naboth's city did as Jezebel directed in the letters she had written to them. ¹²They proclaimed a fast ʰ and seated Naboth in a prominent place among the people. ¹³Then two scoundrels came and sat opposite him and brought charges against Naboth before the people, saying, "Naboth has cursed both God and the king." So they took him outside the city and stoned him to death. ⁱ ¹⁴Then they sent word to Jezebel: "Naboth has been stoned to death."

¹⁵As soon as Jezebel heard that Naboth had been stoned to death, she said to Ahab, "Get up and take possession of the vineyard ʲ of Naboth the Jezreelite that he refused to sell you. He is no longer alive, but dead." ¹⁶When Ahab heard that Naboth was dead, he got up and went down to take possession of Naboth's vineyard.

¹⁷Then the word of the LORD came to Elijah the Tishbite: ¹⁸"Go down to meet Ahab king of Israel, who rules in Samaria. He is now in Naboth's vineyard, where he has gone to take possession of it. ¹⁹Say to him, 'This is what the LORD says: Have you not murdered a man and seized his property?' ᵏ Then say to him, 'This is what the LORD says: In the place where dogs licked up Naboth's blood, ˡ dogs ᵐ will lick up your blood—yes, yours!' "

²⁰Ahab said to Elijah, "So you have found me, my enemy!" ⁿ

"I have found you," he answered, "because you have sold ᵒ yourself to do evil in the eyes of the LORD. ²¹He says, 'I am going to bring disaster on you. I will wipe out your descendants and cut off from Ahab every last male ᵖ in Israel—slave or free. ᵃ ��q ²²I will make your house ʳ like that of Jeroboam son of Nebat and that of Baasha son of Ahijah, because you have aroused my anger and have caused Israel to sin.' ˢ

²³"And also concerning Jezebel the LORD says: 'Dogs ᵗ will devour Jezebel by the wall of ᵇ Jezreel.'

²⁴"Dogs ᵘ will eat those belonging to Ahab who die in the city, and the birds ᵛ will feed on those who die in the country."

²⁵(There was never ʷ anyone like Ahab, who sold himself to do evil in the eyes of the LORD, urged on by Jezebel his wife. ²⁶He behaved in the vilest manner by going after idols, like the Amorites ˣ the LORD drove out before Israel.)

ᵃ 21 Or Israel—every ruler or leader   ᵇ 23 Most Hebrew manuscripts; a few Hebrew manuscripts, Vulgate and Syriac (see also 2 Kings 9:26) the plot of ground at

---

21:7 ᶜ 1Sa 8:14
21:8 ᵈ 2Sa 11:14
ᵉ S Ge 38:18
21:10 ᶠ S Dt 13:13;
Ac 6:11 ᵍ S Ex 22:28;
Lev 24:15-16
21:12 ʰ Isa 58:4
21:13 ⁱ S Lev 24:16
21:15 ʲ S 1Sa 8:14
21:19 ᵏ Job 24:6;
31:39 ˡ 2Ki 9:26;
Ps 9:12; Isa 14:20
ᵐ 1Ki 22:38; Ps 68:23;
Jer 15:3
21:20 ⁿ S 1Ki 18:17
ᵒ 2Ki 17:17; Ro 7:14
21:21 ᵖ Jdg 9:5;
2Ki 10:7 ᑫ S Dt 32:36
21:22 ʳ 1Ki 16:3
ˢ S 1Ki 12:30
21:23 ᵗ 2Ki 9:10,34-36
21:24 ᵘ 1Ki 14:11
ᵛ S Ge 40:19;
S Dt 28:26
21:25 ʷ S 1Ki 14:9;
S 16:33
21:26 ˣ S Ge 15:16

21:7 *Is this how you act as king over Israel?* A sarcastic remark of incredulity spoken by one accustomed to the despotic practices of the Phoenician and Canaanite kings, who would not hesitate a moment to use their power to satisfy personal interests (contrast the attitude and practice of Samuel in the exercise of his civil power, 1Sa 12:3–4).

21:9 *Proclaim a day of fasting.* Jezebel attempted to create the impression that a disaster threatened the people that could be averted only if they would humble themselves before the Lord and remove any person whose sin had brought God's judgment on them (cf. Jdg 20:26; 1Sa 7:5–6; 2Ch 20:2–4).

21:10 *two.* Mosaic law required two witnesses for capital offenses (Nu 35:30; Dt 17:6; 19:15). *scoundrels.* See note on Dt 13:13 ("wicked"). *have them bring charges.* The entire scenario was designed to give an appearance of legitimate judicial procedure (see Ex 20:16; 23:7; Lev 19:16). *he has cursed both God and the king.* For this the Mosaic law prescribed death by stoning (Lev 24:15–16).

21:13 *outside the city.* In accordance with Mosaic law (Lev 24:14; Nu 15:35–36). Naboth was stoned on his own field (compare v. 19 with 2Ki 9:21,26), and his sons were stoned with him

(see 2Ki 9:26; cf. the case of Achan, Jos 7:24–25), thus also eliminating his heirs.

21:19 *Have you not murdered a man and seized his property?* Ahab's willing compliance with Jezebel's scheme made him guilty of murder and theft. *In the place where dogs licked up Naboth's blood, dogs will lick up your blood.* Ahab's subsequent repentance (v. 29) occasioned the postponement of certain aspects of this prophecy until the time of his son Joram, whose body was thrown on the field of Naboth (2Ki 9:25–26). Ahab himself was killed in battle at Ramoth Gilead (22:29–37) and his body brought to Samaria, where the dogs licked the blood being washed from his chariot (22:38).

21:21 *slave or free.* See note on 14:10.

21:22 *like that of Jeroboam.* See 14:10; 15:28–30. *that of Baasha.* See 16:3–4,11–13.

21:24 See notes on 14:11; 16:4.

21:25 *urged on by Jezebel.* See 16:31; 18:4; 19:1–2; 21:7.

21:26 *idols.* See note on Lev 26:30. *Amorites.* Here a designation for the entire pre-Israelite population of Canaan (see Ge 15:16; Dt 1:7).

21:27 *sackcloth.* See note on Ge 37:34.

21:27 ʸ S Ge 37:34;
S Jer 4:8 ᶻ Isa 38:15
21:29 ᵃ S Ex 10:3
ᵇ S Ex 32:14;
2Ki 22:20 ᶜ Ex 20:5;
2Ki 9:26; 10:6-10
22:3 ᵈ S Dt 4:43
22:4 ᵉ 2Ki 3:7
22:5 ᶠ Ex 33:7;
2Ki 3:11; Job 38:2;
Ps 32:8; 73:24; 107:11
22:6 ᵍ S Jdg 18:6
ʰ S 1Ki 13:18
22:7 ⁱ Dt 18:15;
2Ki 3:11; 5:8
ʲ S Nu 27:21; 2Ki 3:11
22:8 ᵏ Am 5:10
ˡ ver 13; Isa 5:20;
30:10; Jer 23:17
22:10 ᵐ S Jdg 6:37

²⁷When Ahab heard these words, he tore his clothes, put on sackcloth ʸ and fasted. He lay in sackcloth and went around meekly. ᶻ

²⁸Then the word of the Lᴏʀᴅ came to Elijah the Tishbite: ²⁹"Have you noticed how Ahab has humbled himself before me? Because he has humbled ᵃ himself, I will not bring this disaster in his day, ᵇ but I will bring it on his house in the days of his son." ᶜ

MICAIAH PROPHESIES AGAINST AHAB
22:1–28pp — 2Ch 18:1–27

22 For three years there was no war between Aram and Israel. ²But in the third year Jehoshaphat king of Judah went down to see the king of Israel. ³The king of Israel had said to his officials, "Don't you know that Ramoth Gilead ᵈ belongs to us and yet we are doing nothing to retake it from the king of Aram?"

⁴So he asked Jehoshaphat, "Will you go with me to fight ᵉ against Ramoth Gilead?"

Jehoshaphat replied to the king of Israel, "I am as you are, my people as your people, my horses as your horses." ⁵But Jehoshaphat also said to the king of Israel, "First seek the counsel ᶠ of the Lᴏʀᴅ."

⁶So the king of Israel brought together the prophets—about four hundred men—and asked them, "Shall I go to war against Ramoth Gilead, or shall I refrain?"

"Go," ᵍ they answered, "for the Lord will give it into the king's hand." ʰ

⁷But Jehoshaphat asked, "Is there no longer a prophet ⁱ of the Lᴏʀᴅ here whom we can inquire ʲ of?"

⁸The king of Israel answered Jehoshaphat, "There is still one through whom we can inquire of the Lᴏʀᴅ, but I hate ᵏ him because he never prophesies anything good ˡ about me, but always bad. He is Micaiah son of Imlah."

"The king should not say such a thing," Jehoshaphat replied.

⁹So the king of Israel called one of his officials and said, "Bring Micaiah son of Imlah at once."

¹⁰Dressed in their royal robes, the king of Israel and Jehoshaphat king of Judah were sitting on their thrones at the threshing floor ᵐ by the entrance of the gate of Samaria, with

21:29 *Because . . . , I will not bring this disaster.* See Jnh 3:10 and note. *in the days of his son.* The judgment was postponed but not rescinded (see note on v. 19).

22:1 *three years.* See note on 20:1. *no war between Aram and Israel.* The annals of the Assyrian ruler Shalmaneser III (859–824 B.C.) record the participation of both "Ahab the Israelite" and Hadadezer (Ben-Hadad) of Damascus in a coalition of 12 rulers that fought against Assyrian forces at Qarqar on the Orontes River in 853. According to the Assyrian records, Ahab contributed 2,000 chariots and 10,000 foot soldiers to the allied forces. Assyrian claims of victory appear exaggerated since they withdrew and did not venture westward again for four or five years.

22:2 *Jehoshaphat king of Judah went down to see the king of Israel.* Perhaps to congratulate him on the success of the western alliance against the Assyrian threat (see notes on v. 1; 2Ch 18:2).

22:3 *Ramoth Gilead.* Located near the Yarmuk River in Transjordan; an Israelite city since the days of Moses (see 4:13; Dt 4:43; Jos 20:8). *belongs to us.* Israel could lay claim to Ramoth Gilead also by virtue of the treaty concluded with Ben-Hadad a few years earlier (see 20:34), the provisions of which he had apparently failed to honor.

22:4 *he asked Jehoshaphat.* Ironically, the king whom Ahab asked to go with him to battle to secure his victory bore the name Jehoshaphat, which means "The Lᴏʀᴅ judges/rules." Little did he realize—and he would not believe—that the judging Lord would "go with" him into the battle to guide a certain arrow. Significantly, in this episode the king of Israel is named only once, and that by the Lord in the heavenly court scene (v. 20). But the narrator bombards the reader with the fateful name Jehoshaphat 12 times. And then there is Zedekiah ("The Lᴏʀᴅ is righteous"), and there is Micaiah ("Who is like the Lᴏʀᴅ?"). Even though Ahab had just been allied with the Arameans against the Assyrians, now that the Assyrian threat was over he did not hesitate to seize an opportunity to free Ramoth Gilead from Aramean control. *I am*

as you are, my people as your people, my horses as your horses. In this alliance Jehoshaphat completely reversed the policy of his father, Asa, who had entered into an alliance with the Arameans against Baasha of the northern kingdom (see 15:17–23). Of the two allies, only Jehoshaphat realized that the two Israelite kings had actually to do with two other kings: the king of Aram and the King sitting on the heavenly throne (see v. 19). Jehoshaphat was later to be condemned by the prophet Jehu (2Ch 19:2) for violating the Lord's will by joining forces with Ahab.

22:5 *First seek the counsel of the Lᴏʀᴅ.* Jehoshaphat hesitated to proceed with the planned action without the assurance of the Lord's favor (see 1Sa 23:1–4; 2Sa 2:1).

22:6 *prophets.* No doubt associated with the paganized worship at Bethel (see notes on 12:28–29), they exercised their "office" by proclaiming messages designed to please the king (see Am 7:10–13).

22:7 *Is there no longer a prophet of the Lᴏʀᴅ here . . . ?* Jehoshaphat recognized that the 400 prophets were not to be relied on (see Eze 13:2–3) and asked for consultation with a true prophet of the Lord.

22:8 *never prophesies anything good.* Ahab's assessment of a prophet depended on whether his message was favorable to him (see 18:17; 21:20).

22:10 A pause in the action to describe a scene on earth (kings in royal splendor on their thrones surrounded by Ahab's minions and confidently planning a campaign of conquest), a scene that will shortly be outmatched by the description of a scene in heaven (Israel's Great King on his throne surrounded by his heavenly host and planning his campaign against King Ahab [vv. 19–23]). By reporting that Ahab and Jehoshaphat were sitting "at the threshing floor [where sheaves are crushed (Mic 4:12) and grain is winnowed (Jer 15:7)] by the entrance of the gate [where courts sit in judgment (Dt 21:19; Ru 4:1,11)] of Samaria," the author hints with biting irony at the outcome of Ahab's grand design.

all the prophets prophesying before them. [11]Now Zedekiah [n] son of Kenaanah had made iron horns [o] and he declared, "This is what the LORD says: 'With these you will gore the Arameans until they are destroyed.' "

[12]All the other prophets were prophesying the same thing. "Attack Ramoth Gilead and be victorious," they said, "for the LORD will give it into the king's hand."

[13]The messenger who had gone to summon Micaiah said to him, "Look, the other prophets without exception are predicting success for the king. Let your word agree with theirs, and speak favorably." [p]

[14]But Micaiah said, "As surely as the LORD lives, I can tell him only what the LORD tells me." [q]

[15]When he arrived, the king asked him, "Micaiah, shall we go to war against Ramoth Gilead, or not?"

"Attack and be victorious," he answered, "for the LORD will give it into the king's hand."

[16]The king said to him, "How many times must I make you swear to tell me nothing but the truth in the name of the LORD?"

[17]Then Micaiah answered, "I saw all Israel scattered [r] on the hills like sheep without a shepherd, [s] and the LORD said, 'These people have no master. Let each one go home in peace.' "

[18]The king of Israel said to Jehoshaphat, "Didn't I tell you that he never prophesies anything good about me, but only bad?"

[19]Micaiah continued, "Therefore hear the word of the LORD: I saw the LORD sitting on his throne [t] with all the host [u] of heaven standing around him on his right and on his left. [20]And the LORD said, 'Who will entice Ahab into attacking Ramoth Gilead and going to his death there?'

"One suggested this, and another that. [21]Finally, a spirit came forward, stood before the LORD and said, 'I will entice him.'

[22]" 'By what means?' the LORD asked.

" 'I will go out and be a lying [v] spirit in the mouths of all his prophets,' he said.

" 'You will succeed in enticing him,' said the LORD. 'Go and do it.'

[23]"So now the LORD has put a lying [w] spirit in the mouths of all these prophets [x] of yours. The LORD has decreed disaster [y] for you."

[24]Then Zedekiah [z] son of Kenaanah went up and slapped [a] Micaiah in the face. "Which way did the spirit from [a] the LORD go when he went from me to speak [b] to you?" he asked.

[25]Micaiah replied, "You will find out on the day you go to hide [c] in an inner room."

[26]The king of Israel then ordered, "Take Micaiah and send him back to Amon the ruler of the city and to Joash the king's son [27]and say, 'This is what the king says: Put this fellow in prison [d] and give him nothing but bread and water until I return safely.' "

[28]Micaiah declared, "If you ever return safely, the LORD has not spoken [e] through me." Then he added, "Mark my words, all you people!"

[a] 24 Or *Spirit of*

22:11 [n] ver 24
[o] Dt 33:17; Jer 27:2; 28:10; Zec 1:18-21
22:13 [p] S ver 8
22:14 [q] S Nu 22:18; S 1Sa 3:17
22:17 [r] S Ge 11:4; Na 3:18 [s] Nu 27:17; Isa 13:14; S Mt 9:36
22:19 [t] Ps 47:8; Isa 6:1; 63:15; Eze 1:26; Da 7:9
[u] Job 1:6; 15:8; 38:7; Ps 103:20-21; 148:2; Jer 23:18,22; Lk 2:13
22:22 [v] S Jdg 9:23; 2Th 2:11
22:23 [w] S Dt 13:3
[x] Eze 14:9
[y] S Dt 31:29
22:24 [z] ver 11
[a] Ac 23:2 [b] Job 26:4
22:25 [c] 1Ki 20:30
22:27 [d] 2Ch 16:10; Jer 20:2; 26:21; 37:15; Heb 11:36
22:28 [e] S Dt 18:22

22:11 *Zedekiah.* Evidently the spokesman for the 400 prophets. *iron horns.* A symbol of power (see Dt 33:17).
22:13 *Let your word agree with theirs.* A bit of advice reflecting the view that all prophets were merely self-serving.
22:15 *we.* A subtle shift (see v. 6) that seeks a favorable response by including Jehoshaphat as a cosponsor of the enterprise. *Attack ... for the LORD will give it into the king's hand.* Micaiah sarcastically mimics the 400 false prophets (see v. 12).
22:16 *tell me nothing but the truth.* Micaiah apparently betrayed his lack of seriousness, and Ahab immediately recognized this.
22:17 *like sheep without a shepherd ... These people have no master.* Using the imagery of shepherd and sheep (see Nu 27:16–17; Zec 13:7; Mt 9:36; 26:31), Micaiah depicts Ahab's death in the upcoming battle.
22:19 *I saw the LORD sitting on his throne.* A true prophet was one who had, as it were, been made privy to what had transpired in God's heavenly throne room and so could truthfully declare what God intended to do (see Isa 6:1; Jer 23:16–22). Micaiah's description of the heavenly scene puts the earthly scene into which he had been brought (see v. 10 and note) in its true light—a powerful portrayal of where the true power lies and of the folly of human pretensions.

22:23 *the LORD has put a lying spirit in the mouths of all these prophets.* Some view the lying spirit as Satan or one of his agents. Others have suggested a spirit of God who undertakes the task of a lying spirit (but see 1Sa 15:29). Still others understand the lying spirit as a symbolic picture of the power of the lie. The Lord had given the 400 prophets over to the power of the lie because they did not love the truth and had chosen to speak out of their own hearts (see Jer 14:14; 23:16, 26; Eze 13:2–3,17; see also note on 2Sa 24:1; cf. 2Th 2:9–12 and note on 2:11). King Ahab, who was content to live by a lie and hated the prophet who spoke the truth, was fittingly lured by God to his execution through a lie he wanted to believe (see also Nu 11:18–20; Ps 18:25– 26; Eze 14:9 and note).
22:24 *Which way did the spirit from the LORD go when he went from me to speak to you?* By this sarcastic question Zedekiah suggests that one prophet can be a liar just as well as another.
22:25 *hide in an inner room.* Where Zedekiah will seek refuge (cf. 20:30). This will vindicate Micaiah's prophetic authority.
22:26 *king's son.* Probably a royal official (see note on Jer 36:26).
22:27 *This is what the king says.* Ahab speaks his royal word against the Lord's prophet because he trusts the (false) divine word proclaimed by his paid prophet (see v. 11).

22:30 *f* S 1Sa 28:8
22:31 *g* S Ge 10:22;
S 2Sa 10:19
h S 2Sa 17:2
22:34 *i* 2Ki 9:24;
2Ch 35:23
22:36 *j* 2Ki 14:12
22:38 *k* S 1Ki 21:19
22:39 *l* 2Ch 9:17;
Ps 45:8; Am 3:15
22:43 *m* S 1Ki 8:61;
2Ch 17:3 *n* S 1Ki 3:2
22:46 *o* S Dt 23:17
22:47 *p* 1Ki 11:14-18;
2Ki 3:9; 8:20

AHAB KILLED AT RAMOTH GILEAD

22:29–36pp — 2Ch 18:28–34

²⁹So the king of Israel and Jehoshaphat king of Judah went up to Ramoth Gilead. ³⁰The king of Israel said to Jehoshaphat, "I will enter the battle in disguise, *f* but you wear your royal robes." So the king of Israel disguised himself and went into battle.

³¹Now the king of Aram *g* had ordered his thirty-two chariot commanders, "Do not fight with anyone, small or great, except the king *h* of Israel." ³²When the chariot commanders saw Jehoshaphat, they thought, "Surely this is the king of Israel." So they turned to attack him, but when Jehoshaphat cried out, ³³the chariot commanders saw that he was not the king of Israel and stopped pursuing him.

³⁴But someone drew his bow *i* at random and hit the king of Israel between the breastplate and the scale armor. The king told his chariot driver, "Wheel around and get me out of the fighting. I've been wounded." ³⁵All day long the battle raged, and the king was propped up in his chariot facing the Arameans. The blood from his wound ran onto the floor of the chariot, and that evening he died. ³⁶As the sun was setting, a cry spread through the army: "Everyone to your own town; everyone to your land!" *j*

³⁷So the king died and was brought to Samaria, and they buried him there. ³⁸They washed the chariot at a pool in Samaria (where the prostitutes bathed), *a* and the dogs *k* licked up his blood, as the word of the Lord had declared.

³⁹As for the other events of Ahab's reign, including all he did, the palace he built and inlaid with ivory, *l* and the cities he fortified, are they not written in the book of the annals of the kings of Israel? ⁴⁰Ahab rested with his ancestors. And Ahaziah his son succeeded him as king.

JEHOSHAPHAT KING OF JUDAH

22:41–50pp — 2Ch 20:31—21:1

⁴¹Jehoshaphat son of Asa became king of Judah in the fourth year of Ahab king of Israel. ⁴²Jehoshaphat was thirty-five years old when he became king, and he reigned in Jerusalem twenty-five years. His mother's name was Azubah daughter of Shilhi. ⁴³In everything he followed the ways of his father Asa *m* and did not stray from them; he did what was right in the eyes of the Lord. *The high places, *n* however, were not removed, and the people continued to offer sacrifices and burn incense there. *⁴⁴Jehoshaphat was also at peace with the king of Israel.

⁴⁵As for the other events of Jehoshaphat's reign, the things he achieved and his military exploits, are they not written in the book of the annals of the kings of Judah? ⁴⁶He rid the land of the rest of the male shrine prostitutes *o* who remained there even after the reign of his father Asa. ⁴⁷There was then no king *p* in Edom; a provincial governor ruled.

---

a 38 Or *Samaria and cleaned the weapons*
* This sentence (22:43b) is numbered 22:44 in Hebrew texts.　　* 22:44-53 is numbered 22:45-54 in Hebrew texts.

22:30 *The king of Israel said.* Ahab still thought he was in control. *disguise.* By this strategy he thought he could direct attention away from himself and so minimize any chance for fulfillment of Micaiah's prediction. The king who loved the lie thought he could escape the truth by living a lie.
22:31 *except the king of Israel.* If the leader was killed or captured, ancient armies usually fell apart (cf. vv. 35–36).
22:34 *drew his bow at random.* The heavenly King aimed the arrow. *chariot driver.* A war chariot normally carried two men—a fighter and a driver. Sometimes, it appears, there were three men, but the third seems to have been an officer who commanded a chariot unit (see 9:22; 2Ki 9:25; Ex 14:7; 15:4, where these officers are called lit. "the third").
22:35 *that evening he died.* Fulfilling Micaiah's prophecy (vv. 17,28).
22:38 *as the word of the Lord had declared.* A partial fulfillment of Elijah's prophecy concerning Ahab's death (see note on 21:19).
22:39 *the palace he built and inlaid with ivory.* Excavators of Samaria have found ivory inlays in the ruins of some of the buildings dating from this period of Israel's history. Ahab's use of ivory is indicative of the realm's economic prosperity during his reign. *cities he fortified.* Excavators have found evidence

that Ahab strengthened the fortifications of Megiddo and Hazor. *annals of the kings of Israel.* See note on 14:19.
22:40 *rested with his ancestors.* See note on 1:21. *Ahaziah his son succeeded him.* For the reign of Ahaziah, see vv. 51–53; 2Ki 1.
22:41 *Jehoshaphat … became king of Judah in the fourth year of Ahab.* Appears to refer to the beginning of Jehoshaphat's reign as sole king in 869 b.c. (see notes on v. 42; 16:29; see also Introduction: Chronology).
22:42 *twenty-five years.* 872–848 b.c. The full span of Jehoshaphat's reign dates from the 39th year of King Asa, when he became coregent with his father (see note on 15:10; see also 2Ch 16:12).
22:43 *The high places, however, were not removed.* See notes on 3:2; 15:14.
22:44 *king.* Probably to be understood in the collective sense and as including Ahab, Ahaziah and Joram, all of whom ruled in the north during the reign of Jehoshaphat in the south (see note on v. 4).
22:45 *military exploits.* See 2Ki 3; 2Ch 17:11; 20. *annals of the kings of Judah.* See note on 14:29.
22:46 *male shrine prostitutes.* See note on 14:24.
22:47 *no king in Edom.* Suggests that Edom was subject to Judah (see 2Sa 8:14; 2Ki 8:20).

⁴⁸Now Jehoshaphat built a fleet of trading ships ᵃ ᑫ to go to Ophir for gold, but they never set sail—they were wrecked at Ezion Geber. ʳ ⁴⁹At that time Ahaziah son of Ahab said to Jehoshaphat, "Let my men sail with yours," but Jehoshaphat refused.

⁵⁰Then Jehoshaphat rested with his ancestors and was buried with them in the city of David his father. And Jehoram his son succeeded him as king.

AHAZIAH KING OF ISRAEL

⁵¹Ahaziah son of Ahab became king of Israel in Samaria in the seventeenth year of Jehoshaphat king of Judah, and he reigned over Israel two years. ⁵²He did evil ˢ in the eyes of the LORD, because he followed the ways of his father and mother and of Jeroboam son of Nebat, who caused Israel to sin. ⁵³He served and worshiped Baal ᵗ and aroused the anger of the LORD, the God of Israel, just as his father ᵘ had done.

ᵃ 48 Hebrew *of ships of Tarshish*

22:48 ᑫ S 1Ki 9:26
ʳ S Nu 33:35
22:52 ˢ 1Ki 15:26
22:53 ᵗ S Jdg 2:11
ᵘ 1Ki 21:25

22:48 *Ophir.* See note on 9:28. *wrecked at Ezion Geber.* The destruction of the trading ships was a judgment of God on Jehoshaphat for entering into an alliance with Ahaziah of the northern kingdom (see 2Ch 20:35–37).
22:50 *rested with his ancestors.* See note on 1:21. *Jehoram his son*

succeeded him. For the reign of Jehoram, see 2Ki 8:16–24; 2Ch 21.
22:51 *seventeenth year of Jehoshaphat.* 853 B.C. (see notes on vv. 41–42). *two years.* 853–852 (see note on 2Ki 1:17).
22:52 *ways of his father and mother.* See 16:30–33. *and of Jeroboam.* See 12:28–33.

See Introduction to 1 Kings.

OUTLINE

Below is an outline for 2 Kings. For an outline of both 1 and 2 Kings see Introduction to 1 Kings: Outline.

1:1 *a* S Ge 19:37; 2Ki 3:5
1:2 *b* ver 16 *c* S Mk 3:22 *d* 1Sa 6:2; Isa 2:6; 14:29 *e* S Jdg 18:5
1:3 *f* ver 15 *g* 1Ki 17:1 *h* S 1Sa 28:8
1:4 *i* ver 6,16; Ps 41:8
1:6 *j* S ver 4
1:8 *k* S 1Ki 18:7; Mt 3:4; Mk 1:6
1:9 *l* 2Ki 6:14 *m* Ex 18:25; Isa 3:3
1:10 *n* S 1Ki 18:38; S Rev 11:5; S 13:13
1:13 *o* Ps 72:14

THE LORD'S JUDGMENT ON AHAZIAH

1 After Ahab's death, Moab *a* rebelled against Israel. ²Now Ahaziah had fallen through the lattice of his upper room in Samaria and injured himself. So he sent messengers, *b* saying to them, "Go and consult Baal-Zebub, *c* the god of Ekron, *d* to see if I will recover *e* from this injury."

³But the angel *f* of the LORD said to Elijah *g* the Tishbite, "Go up and meet the messengers of the king of Samaria and ask them, 'Is it because there is no God in Israel *h* that you are going off to consult Baal-Zebub, the god of Ekron?' ⁴Therefore this is what the LORD says: 'You will not leave *i* the bed you are lying on. You will certainly die!' " So Elijah went.

⁵When the messengers returned to the king, he asked them, "Why have you come back?"

⁶"A man came to meet us," they replied. "And he said to us, 'Go back to the king who sent you and tell him, "This is what the LORD says: Is it because there is no God in Israel that you are sending messengers to consult Baal-Zebub, the god of Ekron? Therefore you will not leave *j* the bed you are lying on. You will certainly die!" ' "

⁷The king asked them, "What kind of man was it who came to meet you and told you this?"

⁸They replied, "He had a garment of hair *a k* and had a leather belt around his waist." The king said, "That was Elijah the Tishbite."

⁹Then he sent *l* to Elijah a captain *m* with his company of fifty men. The captain went up to Elijah, who was sitting on the top of a hill, and said to him, "Man of God, the king says, 'Come down!' "

¹⁰Elijah answered the captain, "If I am a man of God, may fire come down from heaven and consume you and your fifty men!" Then fire *n* fell from heaven and consumed the captain and his men.

¹¹At this the king sent to Elijah another captain with his fifty men. The captain said to him, "Man of God, this is what the king says, 'Come down at once!' "

¹²"If I am a man of God," Elijah replied, "may fire come down from heaven and consume you and your fifty men!" Then the fire of God fell from heaven and consumed him and his fifty men.

¹³So the king sent a third captain with his fifty men. This third captain went up and fell on his knees before Elijah. "Man of God," he begged, "please have respect for my life *o*

a 8 Or He was a hairy man

1:1 *After Ahab's death.* See 1Ki 22:37; see also Jos 1:1; Jdg 1:1; 2Sa 1:1. *Moab rebelled.* Moab had been brought into subjection by David (see 2Sa 8:2), but when the northern and Transjordan tribes rebelled and made Jeroboam their king, political domination of Moab probably also shifted to the northern kingdom. An inscription of Mesha, king of Moab (see chart, p. xxiv) indicates that during the reign of Omri's "son" (probably a reference to his grandson Joram, not to Ahab) the Moabites were able to free the area of Medeba from Israelite control (see map No. 5 at the end of this study Bible).
1:2 *Baal-Zebub.* See note on Jdg 10:6. *Ekron.* The northernmost of the five major Philistine cities (see Jos 13:3; 1Sa 5:10 and notes). *if I will recover.* Ahaziah appears to have feared that his injury would be fatal. He turned to the pagan deity for a revelatory oracle, not for healing.
1:3 *angel of the LORD.* See 1Ki 19:7; see also note on Ge 16:7. The Lord usually spoke directly to the consciousness of the prophet (1Ki 17:2,8; 18:1; 19:9; 21:17). Perhaps the means of revelation was changed in this instance to heighten the contrast between the messengers of Ahaziah (vv. 2–3,5) and the angel (which means "messenger") of the Lord. *Elijah the Tishbite.* See note on 1Ki 17:1. *king of Samaria.* See note on 1Ki 21:1.
1:4 *You will certainly die!* Ahaziah will receive the oracle he sought, but it will come from the Lord through Elijah, not from Baal-Zebub.
1:5 *Why have you come back?* Ahaziah realized the messengers could not have traveled so quickly to Ekron and back.
1:8 *garment of hair.* Elijah's cloak (1Ki 19:19) was probably of sheepskin or camel's hair, tied with a simple leather thong (cf. Mt 3:4). His dress contrasted sharply with the fine linen clothing (see Jer 13:1) of his wealthy contemporaries and constituted a protest against the materialistic attitudes of the king and the

upper classes (cf. Mt 11:7–8; Lk 7:24–25). *That was Elijah the Tishbite.* Ahaziah was familiar with Elijah's appearance because of the prophet's many encounters with Ahab, his father.
1:9 *he sent to Elijah a captain with his company of fifty men.* The pagan people of that time thought that the magical power of curses could be nullified either by forcing the pronouncer of the curse to retract his statement or by killing him so that his curse would go with him to the netherworld. It appears that Ahaziah shared this view and desired to take Elijah prisoner in order to counteract the pronouncement of his death. *Man of God, the king says, 'Come down!'* Ahaziah attempted to place the prophet under the authority of the king. This constituted a violation of the covenant nature of Israelite kingship, in which the king's actions were always to be placed under the scrutiny and authority of the word of the Lord spoken by his prophets (see notes on 1Sa 10:25; 12:23).
1:10 *fire fell from heaven and consumed the captain and his men.* Another link between the ministries of Elijah and Moses (see Lev 10:2; Nu 16:35). At stake in this incident was the question of who was sovereign in Israel. Would Ahaziah recognize that the king in Israel was only a vice-regent under the authority and kingship of the Lord, or would he exercise despotic power, like pagan kings (see notes on 1Sa 12:14–15)? At Mount Carmel the Lord had revealed himself and authenticated his prophet by fire from heaven (see 1Ki 18:38–39). Now this previous revelation is confirmed to Ahaziah.
1:11 *the king sent to Elijah another captain.* Ahaziah refused to submit to the word of the Lord in spite of the dramatic revelation of God's power.
1:13 *fell on his knees before Elijah.* The third captain, recognizing that Elijah was the bearer of the word of the Lord, feared for his life and bowed before him with a humble request.

and the lives of these fifty men, your servants! [14]See, fire has fallen from heaven and consumed the first two captains and all their men. But now have respect for my life!"

[15]The angel[p] of the LORD said to Elijah, "Go down with him; do not be afraid[q] of him." So Elijah got up and went down with him to the king.

[16]He told the king, "This is what the LORD says: Is it because there is no God in Israel for you to consult that you have sent messengers[r] to consult Baal-Zebub, the god of Ekron? Because you have done this, you will never leave[s] the bed you are lying on. You will certainly die!" [17]So he died,[t] according to the word of the LORD that Elijah had spoken.

Because Ahaziah had no son, Joram[a][u] succeeded him as king in the second year of Jehoram son of Jehoshaphat king of Judah. [18]As for all the other events of Ahaziah's reign, and what he did, are they not written in the book of the annals of the kings of Israel?

ELIJAH TAKEN UP TO HEAVEN

2 When the LORD was about to take[v] Elijah up to heaven in a whirlwind,[w] Elijah and Elisha[x] were on their way from Gilgal.[y] [2]Elijah said to Elisha, "Stay here;[z] the LORD has sent me to Bethel."

But Elisha said, "As surely as the LORD lives and as you live, I will not leave you."[a] So they went down to Bethel.

[3]The company[b] of the prophets at Bethel came out to Elisha and asked, "Do you know that the LORD is going to take your master from you today?"

"Yes, I know," Elisha replied, "so be quiet."

[4]Then Elijah said to him, "Stay here, Elisha; the LORD has sent me to Jericho.[c]"

And he replied, "As surely as the LORD lives and as you live, I will not leave you." So they went to Jericho.

[5]The company[d] of the prophets at Jericho went up to Elisha and asked him, "Do you know that the LORD is going to take your master from you today?"

"Yes, I know," he replied, "so be quiet."

[6]Then Elijah said to him, "Stay here;[e] the LORD has sent me to the Jordan."[f]

And he replied, "As surely as the LORD lives and as you live, I will not leave you."[g] So the two of them walked on.

[7]Fifty men from the company of the prophets went and stood at a distance, facing the place where Elijah and Elisha had stopped at the Jordan. [8]Elijah took his cloak,[h] rolled it up and struck[i] the water with it. The water divided[j] to the right and to the left, and the two of them crossed over on dry[k] ground.

[9]When they had crossed, Elijah said to Elisha, "Tell me, what can I do for you before I am taken from you?"

"Let me inherit a double[l] portion of your spirit," Elisha replied.

[10]"You have asked a difficult thing," Elijah said, "yet if you see me when I am taken from you, it will be yours—otherwise, it will not."

a 17 Hebrew *Jehoram*, a variant of *Joram*

1:15 *The angel of the LORD said to Elijah.* See note on v. 3.
1:17 *died, according to the word of the LORD.* In the end Ahaziah was punished for turning away from the God of Israel to a pagan deity, and the word of the Lord was shown to be both reliable and beyond the power of the king to annul. *Joram.* Ahaziah's younger brother (see 3:1; 1Ki 22:51). *second year of Jehoram son of Jehoshaphat.* Jehoram's reign overlapped that of his father, Jehoshaphat, from 853 to 848 B.C. (see note on 8:16). The reference here is to the second year of that coregency. The 18th year of Jehoshaphat (3:1) is therefore the same as the second year of Jehoram's coregency (852).
1:18 *annals of the kings of Israel.* See note on 1Ki 14:19.
2:1 *Gilgal.* Probably not the well-known town in the Jordan Valley, since they "went down" from it to Bethel (v. 2; see also 4:38); rather, it is more likely the Gilgal located some eight miles north of Bethel.
2:2 *I will not leave you.* Elisha was aware that Elijah's ministry was almost finished and that his departure was near (v. 5). He was determined to accompany him until the moment the Lord took him. His commitment to Elijah and to Elijah's ministry was unfailing (see v. 9; 1Ki 19:21).
2:3 *company of.* Lit. "sons of" (see note on 1Ki 20:35). During the days of Elijah and Elisha, companies of prophets were locat-

ed at Bethel (here), Jericho (v. 5) and Gilgal (4:38). It appears that Elijah journeyed by divine instruction to Gilgal (v. 1), Bethel (v. 2) and Jericho (v. 4) for a last meeting with each of these companies.
2:7 *Fifty men.* Israel's heavenly King could also muster 50 companies of 50 men (see 1:9,11,13; 2:16–17; 1Ki 18:4). The present company of 50 men were to witness the miracle by which Elijah and Elisha crossed the river.
2:8 *Elijah took his cloak ... and struck the water with it.* Elijah used his cloak much as Moses had used his staff at the time of Israel's passage through the "Red Sea" (see Ex 14:16,21,26).
2:9 *Let me inherit a double portion.* Elisha was not expressing a desire for a ministry twice as great as Elijah's, but he was using terms derived from inheritance law to express his desire to carry on Elijah's ministry. Inheritance law assigned a double portion of a father's possessions to the firstborn son (see Dt 21:17 and note).
2:10 *difficult thing.* Although Elijah had previously been told to anoint Elisha as his successor (1Ki 19:16,19–21), Elijah's response clearly showed that the issue rested solely with the Lord's sovereign good pleasure. *if you see me ... it will be yours—otherwise, it will not.* Elijah left the answer to Elisha's request in the Lord's hands.

1:15 [p] ver 3
[q] Isa 51:12; 57:11; Jer 1:17; Eze 2:6
1:16 [r] S ver 2 [s] ver 4
1:17 [t] 2Ki 8:15; Jer 20:6; 28:17
[u] 2Ki 3:1; 8:16
2:1 [v] S Ge 5:24
[w] ver 11; 1Ki 19:11; Isa 5:28; 66:15; Jer 4:13; Na 1:3
[x] S 1Ki 19:16,21
[y] S Dt 11:30; 2Ki 4:38
2:2 [z] ver 6 [a] Ru 1:16
2:3 [b] S 1Sa 10:5
2:4 [c] Jos 3:16
2:5 [d] ver 3
2:6 [e] ver 2 [f] Jos 3:15
[g] Ru 1:16
2:8 [h] S 1Ki 19:19
[i] ver 14 / S Ex 14:21
[k] Ex 14:22,29
2:9 [l] S Dt 21:17
[m] S Nu 11:17

2:11 *n* 2Ki 6:17;
Ps 68:17; 104:3, 4;
Isa 66:15; Hab 3:8;
Zec 6:1 *o* S Ge 5:24
p S ver 1
2:12 *q* 2Ki 6:17;
13:14 *r* S Ge 37:29
2:14 *s* S 1Ki 19:19
t ver 8
2:15 *u* S 1Sa 10:5
v S Nu 11:17
2:16 *w* S 1Ki 18:12
x Ac 8:39
2:17 *y* S Jdg 3:25
2:21 *z* S Ex 15:25;
2Ki 4:41; 6:6
2:22 *a* Ex 15:25
2:23 *b* S Ex 22:28;
2Ch 30:10; 36:16;
Job 19:18; Ps 31:18

[11]As they were walking along and talking together, suddenly a chariot of fire [n] and horses of fire appeared and separated the two of them, and Elijah went up to heaven [o] in a whirlwind. [p] [12]Elisha saw this and cried out, "My father! My father! The chariots [q] and horsemen of Israel!" And Elisha saw him no more. Then he took hold of his garment and tore [r] it in two.

[13]He picked up the cloak that had fallen from Elijah and went back and stood on the bank of the Jordan. [14]Then he took the cloak [s] that had fallen from him and struck [t] the water with it. "Where now is the LORD, the God of Elijah?" he asked. When he struck the water, it divided to the right and to the left, and he crossed over.

[15]The company [u] of the prophets from Jericho, who were watching, said, "The spirit [v] of Elijah is resting on Elisha." And they went to meet him and bowed to the ground before him. [16]"Look," they said, "we your servants have fifty able men. Let them go and look for your master. Perhaps the Spirit [w] of the LORD has picked him up [x] and set him down on some mountain or in some valley."

"No," Elisha replied, "do not send them."

[17]But they persisted until he was too embarrassed [y] to refuse. So he said, "Send them." And they sent fifty men, who searched for three days but did not find him. [18]When they returned to Elisha, who was staying in Jericho, he said to them, "Didn't I tell you not to go?"

HEALING OF THE WATER

[19]The people of the city said to Elisha, "Look, our lord, this town is well situated, as you can see, but the water is bad and the land is unproductive."

[20]"Bring me a new bowl," he said, "and put salt in it." So they brought it to him. [21]Then he went out to the spring and threw [z] the salt into it, saying, "This is what the LORD says: 'I have healed this water. Never again will it cause death or make the land unproductive.' " [22]And the water has remained pure [a] to this day, according to the word Elisha had spoken.

ELISHA IS JEERED

[23]From there Elisha went up to Bethel. As he was walking along the road, some boys came out of the town and jeered [b] at him. "Get out of here, baldy!" they said. "Get out of

---

2:11 *chariot of fire and horses of fire.* The Lord's heavenly host has accompanied and supported Elijah's ministry (as it had that of Moses; see Ex 15:1–10), and now at his departure Elisha is allowed to see it (cf. 6:17). *Elijah went up to heaven in a whirlwind.* Elijah, like Enoch before him (Ge 5:24), was taken up to heaven bodily without experiencing death; like Moses (Dt 34:4–6), he was outside the promised land when he was taken away.

A **C** **2:12** *chariots and horsemen of Israel!* Elisha depicted Elijah as embodying the true strength of the nation. He, rather than the apostate king, is the Lord's representative. The same description was later used of Elisha (see 13:14 and note). *tore it.* See Ge 44:13 and note.

2:13 *He picked up the cloak.* See note on v. 8. Possession of Elijah's cloak symbolized Elisha's succession to Elijah's ministry (see 1Ki 19:19).

C **2:14** *When he struck the water, it divided.* See v. 8. The Lord authenticated Elisha's succession to Elijah's ministry and demonstrated that the same divine power that had accompanied Elijah's ministry was now operative in the ministry of Elisha. In crossing the Jordan as Joshua had before him, Elisha is shown to be Elijah's "Joshua" (Elisha and Joshua are very similar names, Elisha meaning "God saves" and Joshua "The LORD saves").

2:15 *bowed to the ground before him.* Indicated their recognition of Elisha's succession to Elijah's position. Elisha was now the Lord's official representative in this time of royal apostasy.

2:16 *Perhaps the Spirit of the LORD has picked him up and set him down.* Obadiah expressed the same idea years earlier (see 1Ki 18:12). *do not send them.* Elisha knew their search would be fruitless.

2:17 *too embarrassed.* The same Hebrew word is used in Jdg 3:25 ("to the point of embarrassment"). Under pressure to allow the prophets to send men to look for Elijah, Elisha no longer had the heart to say no. *Send them.* When the company of prophets refused to be satisfied with Elisha's answer, he permitted them to go so that the authority and truth of his words would be confirmed to them.

2:19 *city.* Evidently Jericho (see v. 18). *the water is bad and the land is unproductive.* The inhabitants of Jericho were experiencing the effects of the covenant curse (contrast Dt 28:15–18 with Ex 23:25–26; Lev 26:9; Dt 28:1–4). See 1Ki 16:34; Jos 6:26.

2:20 *new bowl.* That which was to be used in the service of the Lord was to be undefiled by profane use (see Lev 1:3,10; Nu 19:2; Dt 21:3; 1Sa 6:7). *put salt in it.* Elisha may have used salt because of its known preservative qualities, but it is more likely that he used it to symbolize the covenant faithfulness of the Lord (see note on Nu 18:19; see also 2Ch 13:5).

2:21 *I have healed this water.* Any idea of a magical effect of the salt in the purification of the water is excluded by the explicit statement that the Lord himself healed (purified) the water. In this symbolic way Elisha was able, as the first act of his ministry, to proclaim to the people that in spite of their disobedience the Lord was merciful and was still reaching out to them in his grace (see 13:23).

2:23 *Get out of here.* Since Bethel was the royal religious center of the northern kings (1Ki 12:29; Am 7:13) and Elijah and Elisha were known to frequent Samaria (perhaps even as their main residence; see note on 5:3), the youths from Bethel no doubt assumed that Elisha was going up to Samaria to continue Elijah's struggle against royal apostasy. *baldy!* Baldness was uncommon among the ancient Jews, and luxuriant hair seems to have been viewed as a sign of strength and vigor (see note on 2Sa 14:26). By calling Elisha "baldy," the youths from Bethel expressed that city's utter disdain for the Lord's representative, who, they felt, had no power.

here, baldy!" ²⁴He turned around, looked at them and called down a curse ᶜ on them in the name ᵈ of the LORD. Then two bears came out of the woods and mauled forty-two of the boys. ²⁵And he went on to Mount Carmel ᵉ and from there returned to Samaria.

MOAB REVOLTS

3 Joram ᵃ ᶠ son of Ahab became king of Israel in Samaria in the eighteenth year of Jehoshaphat king of Judah, and he reigned twelve years. ²He did evil ᵍ in the eyes of the LORD, but not as his father ʰ and mother had done. He got rid of the sacred stone ⁱ of Baal that his father had made. ³Nevertheless he clung to the sins ʲ of Jeroboam son of Nebat, which he had caused Israel to commit; he did not turn away from them.

⁴Now Mesha king of Moab ᵏ raised sheep, and he had to pay the king of Israel a tribute of a hundred thousand lambs ˡ and the wool of a hundred thousand rams. ⁵But after Ahab died, the king of Moab rebelled ᵐ against the king of Israel. ⁶So at that time King Joram set out from Samaria and mobilized all Israel. ⁷He also sent this message to Jehoshaphat king of Judah: "The king of Moab has rebelled against me. Will you go with me to fight ⁿ against Moab?"

"I will go with you," he replied. "I am as you are, my people as your people, my horses as your horses."

⁸"By what route shall we attack?" he asked.

"Through the Desert of Edom," he answered.

⁹So the king of Israel set out with the king of Judah and the king of Edom. ᵒ After a roundabout march of seven days, the army had no more water for themselves or for the animals with them.

¹⁰"What!" exclaimed the king of Israel. "Has the LORD called us three kings together only to deliver us into the hands of Moab?"

¹¹But Jehoshaphat asked, "Is there no prophet of the LORD here, through whom we may inquire ᵖ of the LORD?"

An officer of the king of Israel answered, "Elisha �q son of Shaphat is here. He used to pour water on the hands of Elijah. ᵇ ʳ"

¹²Jehoshaphat said, "The word ˢ of the LORD is with him." So the king of Israel and Jehoshaphat and the king of Edom went down to him.

¹³Elisha said to the king of Israel, "Why do you want to involve me? Go to the prophets of your father and the prophets of your mother."

ᵃ 1 Hebrew *Jehoram*, a variant of *Joram*; also in verse 6   ᵇ 11 That is, he was Elijah's personal servant.

2:24 ᶜ S Ge 4:11
ᵈ S Dt 18:19
2:25 ᵉ S 1Ki 18:20
3:1 ᶠ S 2Ki 1:17
3:2 ᵍ 1Ki 15:26
ʰ 1Ki 16:30-32
ⁱ S Ex 23:24
3:3 ʲ S 1Ki 12:28-32
3:4 ᵏ S Ge 19:37;
2Ki 1:1 ˡ Ezr 7:17;
Isa 16:1
3:5 ᵐ S 2Ki 1:1
3:7 ⁿ 1Ki 22:4
3:9 ᵒ S 1Ki 22:47
3:11 ᵖ S Ge 25:22;
S 1Ki 22:5 q S Ge 20:7
ʳ S 1Ki 19:16
3:12 ˢ S Nu 11:17

Ⓐ Ⓒ 2:24 *called down a curse on them in the name of the LORD.* Elisha pronounced a curse similar to the covenant curse of Lev 26:21–22. The result gave warning of the judgment that would come on the entire nation should it persist in disobedience and apostasy (see 2Ch 36:16). Thus Elisha's first acts were indicative of his ministry that would follow: God's covenant blessings would come to those who looked to him (vv. 19–22), but God's covenant curses would fall on those who turned away from him (cf. 1Ki 19:17 and note).

3:1 *Joram son of Ahab became king … in the eighteenth year of Jehoshaphat.* See note on 1:17. *twelve years.* 852–841 B.C.

3:2 *not as his father and mother had done.* Not as Ahab (see notes on 1Ki 16:30–34) and Jezebel (see 1Ki 18:4; 19:1–2; 21:7–15). *sacred stone of Baal that his father had made.* Apparently a reference to the stone representation of the male deity (see note on 1Ki 16:32–33) that Ahab placed in the temple he had constructed for Jezebel in Samaria (see 1Ki 16:32–33). From 10:27 it appears that this stone was later reinstated, perhaps by Jezebel, then destroyed by Jehu.

3:3 *sins of Jeroboam … he had caused Israel to commit.* See note on 1Ki 14:16.

3:4 *Mesha king of Moab.* See note on 1:1. *a hundred thousand lambs and the wool of a hundred thousand rams.* The heavy annual tribute (see Isa 16:1) that Israel required from the Moabites as a vassal state.

3:5 *king of Moab rebelled.* See note on 1:1.

Ⓒ 3:7 *Will you go with me to fight against Moab?* Joram wished to attack Moab from the rear (v. 8), but to do that his army had to pass through Judah. *I am as you are, my people as your people, my horses as your horses.* See 1Ki 22:4. Jehoshaphat

had already been condemned by prophets of the Lord for his alliance with the northern kings Ahab (see 2Ch 18:1; 19:1–2) and Ahaziah (2Ch 20:35–37), yet he agreed to join with Joram against Moab. Perhaps he was disturbed by the potential danger to Judah posed by the growing strength of Moab (see 2Ch 20), and he may have considered Joram less evil than his predecessors (see v. 2).

3:8 *Through the Desert of Edom.* This route of attack took the armies of Israel and Judah south of the Dead Sea, enabling them to circumvent the fortifications of Moab's northern frontier and to avoid the possibility of a rearguard action against them by the Arameans of Damascus. The Edomites, who were subject to Judah, were in no position to resist the movement of Israel's army through their territory.

3:9 *king of Edom.* Although here designated a king, he was in reality a governor appointed by Jehoshaphat (see 8:20; 1Ki 22:47).

3:11 *Is there no prophet of the LORD here…?* See 1Ki 22:7. Only after the apparent failure of their own strategies did the three rulers seek the word of the Lord (v. 12). *Elisha son of Shaphat is here.* Since Elijah is reported to have sent a letter to Jehoshaphat's son Jehoram after his father's death (2Ch 21:12–15), it seems that Elisha accompanied the armies on this campaign as the representative of the aged Elijah. The event is narrated here after the account of Elisha's initiation as Elijah's successor and the two events that foreshadowed the character of his ministry. Following this introduction to Elisha's ministry, the present episode is topically associated with the series of Elisha's acts that now occupies the narrative.

3:13 *Go to the prophets of your father and … mother.* See 1Ki 22:6.

3:15 ʳS 1Sa 10:5
ᵘ Jer 15:17; Eze 1:3
3:17 ᵛPs 107:35;
Isa 12:3; 32:2; 35:6;
41:18; 65:13
3:18 ʷS Ge 18:14;
2Ki 20:10; Isa 49:6;
Jer 32:17,27;
Mk 10:27
3:20 ˣS Ex 29:41
ʸS Ex 17:6
3:25 ᶻIsa 15:1; 16:7;
Jer 48:31,36
3:27 ᵃS Dt 12:31;
2Ki 16:3; 21:6;
2Ch 28:3; Ps 106:38;
Jer 19:4-5; Mic 6:7
4:1 ᵇS 1Sa 10:5
ᶜS Ex 22:26;
Lev 25:39-43;
Ne 5:3-5; Job 22:6;
24:9
4:2 ᵈS 1Ki 17:12

"No," the king of Israel answered, "because it was the Lord who called us three kings together to deliver us into the hands of Moab."

¹⁴Elisha said, "As surely as the Lord Almighty lives, whom I serve, if I did not have respect for the presence of Jehoshaphat king of Judah, I would not pay any attention to you. ¹⁵But now bring me a harpist." ᵗ

While the harpist was playing, the hand ᵘ of the Lord came on Elisha ¹⁶and he said, "This is what the Lord says: I will fill this valley with pools of water. ¹⁷For this is what the Lord says: You will see neither wind nor rain, yet this valley will be filled with water, ᵛ and you, your cattle and your other animals will drink. ¹⁸This is an easy ʷ thing in the eyes of the Lord; he will also deliver Moab into your hands. ¹⁹You will overthrow every fortified city and every major town. You will cut down every good tree, stop up all the springs, and ruin every good field with stones."

²⁰The next morning, about the time ˣ for offering the sacrifice, there it was—water flowing from the direction of Edom! And the land was filled with water. ʸ

²¹Now all the Moabites had heard that the kings had come to fight against them; so every man, young and old, who could bear arms was called up and stationed on the border. ²²When they got up early in the morning, the sun was shining on the water. To the Moabites across the way, the water looked red—like blood. ²³"That's blood!" they said. "Those kings must have fought and slaughtered each other. Now to the plunder, Moab!"

²⁴But when the Moabites came to the camp of Israel, the Israelites rose up and fought them until they fled. And the Israelites invaded the land and slaughtered the Moabites. ²⁵They destroyed the towns, and each man threw a stone on every good field until it was covered. They stopped up all the springs and cut down every good tree. Only Kir Hareseth ᶻ was left with its stones in place, but men armed with slings surrounded it and attacked it.

²⁶When the king of Moab saw that the battle had gone against him, he took with him seven hundred swordsmen to break through to the king of Edom, but they failed. ²⁷Then he took his firstborn ᵃ son, who was to succeed him as king, and offered him as a sacrifice on the city wall. The fury against Israel was great; they withdrew and returned to their own land.

THE WIDOW'S OIL

4 The wife of a man from the company ᵇ of the prophets cried out to Elisha, "Your servant my husband is dead, and you know that he revered the Lord. But now his creditor ᶜ is coming to take my two boys as his slaves."

²Elisha replied to her, "How can I help you? Tell me, what do you have in your house?"

"Your servant has nothing there at all," she said, "except a little olive oil." ᵈ

³Elisha said, "Go around and ask all your neighbors for empty jars. Don't ask for just a few. ⁴Then go inside and shut the door behind you and your sons. Pour oil into all the jars, and as each is filled, put it to one side."

3:14 *if I did not have respect for . . . Jehoshaphat . . . I would not pay any attention to you.* Joram will share in the blessing of the word of God only because of his association with Jehoshaphat.
3:15 *bring me a harpist.* To create a disposition conducive to receiving the word of the Lord. *hand of the Lord.* See note on Eze 1:3.
3:16 *this valley.* The Israelite armies were encamped in the broad valley (the Arabah) between the highlands of Moab on the east and those of Judah on the west, just south of the Dead Sea.

A **3:17** *will be filled with water.* The word of the Lord contained a promise and a directive. The Lord will graciously provide for his people, but they must respond to his word in faith and obedience (v. 16).
3:19 The two armies will devastate the rebellious country.
3:20 *time for offering.* See Ex 29:38–39; Nu 28:3–4. *water flowing from the direction of Edom.* Flash floods in the distant mountains of Edom caused water to flow north through the broad, usually dry, valley that sloped toward the Dead Sea (see note on v. 16).
3:23 *Those kings must have . . . slaughtered each other.* The Moabites would have good reason to suspect that an internal conflict had arisen between the parties of an alliance whose members had previously been mutually hostile.
3:25 *Kir Hareseth.* The capital city of Moab (see Isa 16:7,11; Jer 48:31,36), usually identified with present-day Kerak, located

about 11 miles east of the Dead Sea and 15 miles south of the Arnon River.
3:26 *break through to the king of Edom.* A desperate attempt by the king of Moab to induce Edom to turn against Israel and Judah.
3:27 *offered him as a sacrifice on the city wall.* King Mesha offered his oldest son, the crown prince, as a burnt offering (see 16:3; Jer 7:31) to the Moabite god Chemosh (see 1Ki 11:7; Nu 21:29; Jer 48:46) in an attempt to induce the deity to come to his aid. *The fury against Israel was great.* It seems that just when total victory appeared to be in Israel's grasp, God's displeasure with the Ahab dynasty showed itself in some way that caused the Israelite kings to give up the campaign.
4:1 *company of the prophets.* See notes on 2:3; 1Ki 20:35. *take my two boys as his slaves.* Servitude as a means of debt payment by labor was permitted in the Mosaic law (Ex 21:1–2; Lev 25:39–41; Dt 15:1–11). It appears that the practice was much abused (see Ne 5:5,8; Am 2:6; 8:6), even though the law limited the term of such bondage and required that those so held be treated as hired workers.

C **4:4** *shut the door behind you and your sons.* The impending miracle was not intended to be a public sensation but to demonstrate privately God's mercy and grace to this widow (cf. Ps 68:5). She did not hesitate to respond to the instructions of the Lord's prophet in faith and obedience.

4:7 *e* S 1Ki 12:22
4:8 *f* S Jos 19:18
4:10 *g* Mt 10:41;
S Ro 12:13
4:12 *h* 2Ki 8:1
4:16 *i* S Ge 18:10
4:18 *j* S Ru 2:3
4:21 *k* ver 32
4:23 *l* S Nu 10:10;
1Ch 23:31; Ps 81:3
4:25 *m* S 1Ki 18:20

[5]She left him and shut the door behind her and her sons. They brought the jars to her and she kept pouring. [6]When all the jars were full, she said to her son, "Bring me another one."

But he replied, "There is not a jar left." Then the oil stopped flowing.

[7]She went and told the man of God, *e* and he said, "Go, sell the oil and pay your debts. You and your sons can live on what is left."

THE SHUNAMMITE'S SON RESTORED TO LIFE

[8]One day Elisha went to Shunem. *f* And a well-to-do woman was there, who urged him to stay for a meal. So whenever he came by, he stopped there to eat. [9]She said to her husband, "I know that this man who often comes our way is a holy man of God. [10]Let's make a small room on the roof and put in it a bed and a table, a chair and a lamp for him. Then he can stay *g* there whenever he comes to us."

[11]One day when Elisha came, he went up to his room and lay down there. [12]He said to his servant Gehazi, "Call the Shunammite." *h* So he called her, and she stood before him. [13]Elisha said to him, "Tell her, 'You have gone to all this trouble for us. Now what can be done for you? Can we speak on your behalf to the king or the commander of the army?' "

She replied, "I have a home among my own people."

[14]"What can be done for her?" Elisha asked.

Gehazi said, "She has no son, and her husband is old."

[15]Then Elisha said, "Call her." So he called her, and she stood in the doorway. [16]"About this time *i* next year," Elisha said, "you will hold a son in your arms."

"No, my lord!" she objected. "Please, man of God, don't mislead your servant!"

[17]But the woman became pregnant, and the next year about that same time she gave birth to a son, just as Elisha had told her.

[18]The child grew, and one day he went out to his father, who was with the reapers. *j* [19]He said to his father, "My head! My head!"

His father told a servant, "Carry him to his mother." [20]After the servant had lifted him up and carried him to his mother, the boy sat on her lap until noon, and then he died. [21]She went up and laid him on the bed *k* of the man of God, then shut the door and went out.

[22]She called her husband and said, "Please send me one of the servants and a donkey so I can go to the man of God quickly and return."

[23]"Why go to him today?" he asked. "It's not the New Moon *l* or the Sabbath."

"That's all right," she said.

[24]She saddled the donkey and said to her servant, "Lead on; don't slow down for me unless I tell you." [25]So she set out and came to the man of God at Mount Carmel. *m*

When he saw her in the distance, the man of God said to his servant Gehazi, "Look! There's the Shunammite! [26]Run to meet her and ask her, 'Are you all right? Is your husband all right? Is your child all right?' "

"Everything is all right," she said.

4:8 *Shunem.* See note on 1Ki 1:3.

C **4:9** *holy man of God.* The woman recognized that Elisha was a person set apart to the Lord's work in a very special sense (see note on Ex 3:5). Nowhere else in the OT is the term "holy" applied to a prophet.

C **4:10** *he can stay there whenever he comes to us.* By her hospitality the woman was able to assist in sustaining the proclamation of God's word through Elisha.

4:12 *Gehazi.* Referred to here for the first time; he appears to have served Elisha in some of the same ways as Elisha had served Elijah, though the two men were of drastically different character (see 5:19–27; 6:15).

4:13 *I have a home among my own people.* The Shunammite woman felt secure and content in the community of her own family and tribe, and she had no need or desire for favors from high government officials.

4:14 *She has no son, and her husband is old.* A great disappointment because it meant that the family's name would cease and its land and possessions would pass on to others. It was also a great threat to this young wife's future in that she faced the likelihood of many years as a widow with no provider or protector—children were a widow's only social security in old age (see 8:1–6; see also note on 1Ki 17:22).

4:16 *About this time next year.* See Ge 17:21; 18:14. *man of God, don't mislead your servant!* The woman's response revealed the depths of her desire for a son and her fear of disappointment more than it showed a lack of confidence in the word of Elisha.

4:17 *just as Elisha had told her.* The trustworthiness of Elisha's word was confirmed, and the birth of the son was shown to be the result of God's gracious intervention in her behalf.

A **4:20** *he died.* The child, given as an evidence of God's grace and the reliability of his word, was suddenly taken from the woman in a severe test of her faith. Her subsequent actions demonstrate the strength of her faith in the face of great calamity.

4:21 *laid him on the bed of the man of God.* In this way the woman concealed the child's death from the rest of the household while she went to seek the prophet at whose word the child had been born.

4:23 *Why go to him today?* The question suggests that it was not uncommon for the woman to go to Elisha but that on this occasion the timing of her visit was unusual.

4:26 *Everything is all right.* The woman was determined to share her distress with no one but the prophet from whom she had received the promise of the birth of her son.

4:27 ⁿ1Sa 1:15
4:29 ᵒS 1Ki 18:46
ᵖS Ex 4:2
4:32 ᵠver 21
4:33 ʳ1Ki 17:20;
Mt 6:6
4:34 ˢ1Ki 17:21;
Ac 20:10
4:35 ᵗS Jos 6:15
ᵘ2Ki 8:5
4:36 ᵛHeb 11:35
4:38 ʷS 2Ki 2:1
ˣS Lev 26:26; 2Ki 8:1
4:41 ʸS Ex 15:25;
S 2Ki 2:21
4:42 ᶻ1Sa 9:4
ᵃMt 14:17; 15:36
ᵇS 1Sa 9:7
4:43 ᶜLk 9:13
ᵈMt 14:20; Jn 6:12

²⁷When she reached the man of God at the mountain, she took hold of his feet. Gehazi came over to push her away, but the man of God said, "Leave her alone! She is in bitter distress, ⁿ but the Lᴏʀᴅ has hidden it from me and has not told me why."

²⁸"Did I ask you for a son, my lord?" she said. "Didn't I tell you, 'Don't raise my hopes'?"

²⁹Elisha said to Gehazi, "Tuck your cloak into your belt, ᵒ take my staff ᵖ in your hand and run. Don't greet anyone you meet, and if anyone greets you, do not answer. Lay my staff on the boy's face."

³⁰But the child's mother said, "As surely as the Lᴏʀᴅ lives and as you live, I will not leave you." So he got up and followed her.

³¹Gehazi went on ahead and laid the staff on the boy's face, but there was no sound or response. So Gehazi went back to meet Elisha and told him, "The boy has not awakened."

³²When Elisha reached the house, there was the boy lying dead on his couch. ᵠ ³³He went in, shut the door on the two of them and prayed ʳ to the Lᴏʀᴅ. ³⁴Then he got on the bed and lay on the boy, mouth to mouth, eyes to eyes, hands to hands. As he stretched ˢ himself out on him, the boy's body grew warm. ³⁵Elisha turned away and walked back and forth in the room and then got on the bed and stretched out on him once more. The boy sneezed seven times ᵗ and opened his eyes. ᵘ

³⁶Elisha summoned Gehazi and said, "Call the Shunammite." And he did. When she came, he said, "Take your son." ᵛ ³⁷She came in, fell at his feet and bowed to the ground. Then she took her son and went out.

DEATH IN THE POT

³⁸Elisha returned to Gilgal ʷ and there was a famine ˣ in that region. While the company of the prophets was meeting with him, he said to his servant, "Put on the large pot and cook some stew for this company."

³⁹One of them went out into the fields to gather herbs and found a wild vine. He gathered some of its gourds and filled the fold of his cloak. When he returned, he cut them up into the pot of stew, though no one knew what they were. ⁴⁰The stew was poured out for the men, but as they began to eat it, they cried out, "Man of God, there is death in the pot!" And they could not eat it.

⁴¹Elisha said, "Get some flour." He put it into the pot and said, "Serve it to the people to eat." And there was nothing harmful in the pot. ʸ

FEEDING OF A HUNDRED

⁴²A man came from Baal Shalishah, ᶻ bringing the man of God twenty loaves ᵃ of barley bread ᵇ baked from the first ripe grain, along with some heads of new grain. "Give it to the people to eat," Elisha said.

⁴³"How can I set this before a hundred men?" his servant asked.

But Elisha answered, "Give it to the people to eat. ᶜ For this is what the Lᴏʀᴅ says: 'They will eat and have some left over.' ᵈ ' " ⁴⁴Then he set it before them, and they ate and had some left over, according to the word of the Lᴏʀᴅ.

4:28 *Didn't I tell you, 'Don't raise my hopes'?* The woman struggled with the question of why the Lord would take from her that which she had been given as a special demonstration of his grace and the trustworthiness of his word.

4:29 *Lay my staff on the boy's face.* It appears that Elisha expected the Lord to restore the boy's life when the staff was placed on him. This does not suggest that Elisha attributed magical power to the staff but that he viewed it as a representation of his own presence and a symbol of divine power (see note on 2:8; cf. Ex 14:16; Ac 19:12).

4:30 *I will not leave you.* The woman was not convinced that Gehazi's mission would be successful and insisted that Elisha himself accompany her to Shunem.

C **4:33** *shut the door on the two of them and prayed.* Just as Elijah had done in a similar situation years before (see 1Ki 17:20–22), Elisha first turned to the Lord in earnest prayer for restoration of life to the dead child. His prayer is clear evidence that his subsequent actions were not intended as a magical means of restoring life.

4:34 *lay on the boy.* See note on 1Ki 17:21. Perhaps Elisha was familiar with the earlier similar action of Elijah.

4:37 *fell at his feet and bowed to the ground.* The woman gratefully acknowledged the special favor granted to her by the Lord

through Elisha, and silently reaffirmed the verbal confession of the widow of Zarephath (see 1Ki 17:24).

4:38 *Gilgal.* See note on 2:1. *famine in that region.* Perhaps the same famine mentioned in 8:1. Famine was a covenant curse (see Lev 26:19–20,26; Dt 28:18,23–24; 1Ki 8:36–37) and evidence of God's anger with his people's disobedience to their covenant obligations. *company of the prophets.* See note on 2:3.

4:39 *wild vine…gourds.* The precise type of plant is not specified.

4:41 *flour.* The flour itself did not make the stew edible (see 2:21 and note). It was simply a means by which the Lord provided for those who were faithful to the covenant, at a time when others suffered under the covenant curse.

C **4:42** *first ripe grain.* Instead of bringing the firstfruits of the new harvest (see Lev 2:14; 23:15–17; Dt 18:3–5) to the apostate priests at Bethel and Dan (see 1Ki 12:28–31), godly people in the northern kingdom may have contributed their offerings for the sustenance of Elisha and those associated with him (see note on v. 23). Thus they looked upon Elisha rather than the apostate king and priests as the true representative of their covenant Lord.

4:43 *the Lᴏʀᴅ says.* The bread was multiplied at the word of the Lord through Elisha apart from any intermediate means (contrast v. 41; 2:20; cf. Mk 6:35–43 and note on 6:43).

NAAMAN HEALED OF LEPROSY

5 Now Naaman was commander of the army of the king of Aram. *e* He was a great man in the sight of his master and highly regarded, because through him the LORD had given victory to Aram. He was a valiant soldier, but he had leprosy. *a f*

²Now bands of raiders *g* from Aram had gone out and had taken captive a young girl from Israel, and she served Naaman's wife. ³She said to her mistress, "If only my master would see the prophet *h* who is in Samaria! He would cure him of his leprosy."

⁴Naaman went to his master and told him what the girl from Israel had said. ⁵"By all means, go," the king of Aram replied. "I will send a letter to the king of Israel." So Naaman left, taking with him ten talents *b* of silver, six thousand shekels *c* of gold and ten sets of clothing. *i* ⁶The letter that he took to the king of Israel read: "With this letter I am sending my servant Naaman to you so that you may cure him of his leprosy."

⁷As soon as the king of Israel read the letter, *j* he tore his robes and said, "Am I God? *k* Can I kill and bring back to life? *l* Why does this fellow send someone to me to be cured of his leprosy? See how he is trying to pick a quarrel *m* with me!"

⁸When Elisha the man of God heard that the king of Israel had torn his robes, he sent him this message: "Why have you torn your robes? Have the man come to me and he will know that there is a prophet *n* in Israel." ⁹So Naaman went with his horses and chariots and stopped at the door of Elisha's house. ¹⁰Elisha sent a messenger to say to him, "Go, wash *o* yourself seven times *p* in the Jordan, and your flesh will be restored and you will be cleansed."

¹¹But Naaman went away angry and said, "I thought that he would surely come out to me and stand and call on the name of the LORD his God, wave his hand *q* over the spot and cure me of my leprosy. ¹²Are not Abana and Pharpar, the rivers of Damascus, better than all the waters *r* of Israel? Couldn't I wash in them and be cleansed?" So he turned and went off in a rage. *s*

¹³Naaman's servants went to him and said, "My father, *t* if the prophet had told you to do some great thing, would you not have done it? How much more, then, when he tells you, 'Wash and be cleansed'!" ¹⁴So he went down and dipped himself in the Jordan sev-

---

a 1 The Hebrew for *leprosy* was used for various diseases affecting the skin; also in verses 3, 6, 7, 11 and 27.   *b 5* That is, about 750 pounds or about 340 kilograms   *c 5* That is, about 150 pounds or about 68 kilograms

---

5:1 *e* S Ge 10:22;
S 2Sa 10:19 *f* S Ex 4:6;
S Nu 12:10; Lk 4:27
5:2 *g* 2Ki 6:23;
13:20; 24:2
5:3 *h* S Ge 20:7
5:5 *i* ver 22;
S Ge 24:53; Jdg 14:12;
S 1Sa 9:7
5:7 *j* 2Ki 19:14
k S Ge 30:2
l S Dt 32:39
m 1Ki 20:7
5:8 *n* S 1Ki 22:7
5:10 *o* Jn 9:7
p S Ge 33:3;
S Lev 14:7
5:11 *q* S Ex 7:19
5:12 *r* Isa 8:6
s Pr 14:17,29; 19:11;
29:11
5:13 *t* 2Ki 6:21; 13:14

5:1 *king of Aram.* Probably Ben-Hadad II (see notes on 8:7; 13:3; 1Ki 20:1). *the LORD had given victory to Aram.* Probably a reference to an otherwise undocumented Aramean victory over the Assyrians in the aftermath of the battle of Qarqar in 853 B.C. (see note on 1Ki 22:1). In the narrator's theological perspective, this victory is attributable to the sovereignty of the God of Israel, who is seen as the ruler and controller of the destinies of all nations, not just that of Israel (see Eze 30:24; Am 2:1–3; 9:7).

5:2 *bands of raiders from Aram.* Although Israel had concluded a peace treaty with the Arameans during the reign of Ahab (see 1Ki 20:34), minor border skirmishes continued between the two states in the aftermath of the battle for control of Ramoth Gilead, in which Ahab had been killed (see note on 1Ki 22:4; see also 1Ki 22:35). *young girl from Israel.* In sharp contrast to the Israelite king in Samaria, this young girl held captive in Damascus was very much aware of God's saving presence with his people through his servant Elisha, and she selflessly shared that knowledge with her Aramean captors.

5:3 *prophet who is in Samaria.* Elisha, who maintained a residence in Samaria (see v. 9; 2:25; 6:19).

5:5 *I will send a letter to the king of Israel.* The border skirmishes had not nullified the official peace between the two nations as established by treaty. The king of Israel was Joram (see 1:17; 3:1; 9:24). *ten talents of silver.* See TNIV text note. An idea of the relative value of this amount of silver can be seen by comparing it with the price Omri paid for the hill of Samaria (see 1Ki 16:24).

5:6 *so that you may cure him of his leprosy.* Ben-Hadad (king of Aram) assumed that the prophet described by the Israelite slave girl was subject to the authority of the king and that his services could be bought with a sufficiently large gift. He thought he could buy with worldly wealth one of the chief blessings of God's saving presence among his people.

5:7 *he is trying to pick a quarrel with me!* Joram concluded that the entire incident was an attempt by Ben-Hadad to create a pretext for a declaration of war. So blind was the king to God's saving presence through Elisha that he could think only of international intrigue.

5:8 *Why have you torn your robes?* Elisha chided Joram for his fear (see note on 1Sa 17:11) and for his failure to consult the Lord's prophet (see 3:13–14 for evidence of the tension that existed between Joram and Elisha).

5:9 *with his horses and chariots.* This proud pagan would command the healing by his lordly presence.

5:10 *wash yourself seven times in the Jordan.* The instruction is designed to demonstrate to Naaman that healing would come by the power of the God of Israel, but only if he obeyed the word of the Lord's prophet. The prophet himself was not a healer. Ritual washings were practiced among Eastern religions as a purification rite, and the number seven was generally known as a symbol of completeness. Naaman was to wash in the muddy waters of the Jordan River, demonstrating that there was no natural connection between the washing and the desired healing. Perhaps it also suggested that one needed to pass through the Jordan, as Israel had done, in order to obtain healing from the God of Israel (see notes on Jos 3:1—4:24; 3:10).

5:11 *wave his hand over the spot and cure me of my leprosy.* Naaman expected to be healed by the magical technique of the prophet rather than by the power of God operative in connection with his own obedient response to God's word.

5:12 *Abana and Pharpar.* The Abana was termed the Golden River by the Greeks. It is usually identified with the Barada River of today, rising in the Anti-Lebanon mountains and flowing through the city of Damascus. The Pharpar River flows east from Mount Hermon just to the south of Damascus (see map, p. 1721).

5:14 uS Ge 33:3;
S Lev 14:7; S Jos 6:15
vS Ex 4:7 wJob 33:25
5:15 xS Jos 2:11
yS Jos 4:24;
S 1Sa 17:46
zS 1Sa 9:7
5:16 aver 20,26;
Ge 14:23; Da 5:17
5:17 bEx 20:24
5:18 c2Ki 7:2
5:19 d1Sa 1:17;
S Ac 15:33
5:20 eEx 20:7
5:22 fS ver 5;
S Ge 45:22
5:26 gS ver 16
hJer 45:5
5:27 iS Nu 12:10

en times, u as the man of God had told him, and his flesh was restored v and became clean like that of a young boy. w

15 Then Naaman and all his attendants went back to the man of God x. He stood before him and said, "Now I know y that there is no God in all the world except in Israel. So please accept a gift z from your servant."

16 The prophet answered, "As surely as the LORD lives, whom I serve, I will not accept a thing." And even though Naaman urged him, he refused. a

17 "If you will not," said Naaman, "please let me, your servant, be given as much earth b as a pair of mules can carry, for your servant will never again make burnt offerings and sacrifices to any other god but the LORD. 18 But may the LORD forgive your servant for this one thing: When my master enters the temple of Rimmon to bow down and he is leaning c on my arm and I have to bow there also—when I bow down in the temple of Rimmon, may the LORD forgive your servant for this."

19 "Go in peace," d Elisha said.

After Naaman had traveled some distance, 20 Gehazi, the servant of Elisha the man of God, said to himself, "My master was too easy on Naaman, this Aramean, by not accepting from him what he brought. As surely as the LORD e lives, I will run after him and get something from him."

21 So Gehazi hurried after Naaman. When Naaman saw him running toward him, he got down from the chariot to meet him. "Is everything all right?" he asked.

22 "Everything is all right," Gehazi answered. "My master sent me to say, 'Two young men from the company of the prophets have just come to me from the hill country of Ephraim. Please give them a talent a of silver and two sets of clothing.' " f

23 "By all means, take two talents," said Naaman. He urged Gehazi to accept them, and then tied up the two talents of silver in two bags, with two sets of clothing. He gave them to two of his servants, and they carried them ahead of Gehazi. 24 When Gehazi came to the hill, he took the things from the servants and put them away in the house. He sent the men away and they left.

25 When he went in and stood before his master, Elisha asked him, "Where have you been, Gehazi?"

"Your servant didn't go anywhere," Gehazi answered.

26 But Elisha said to him, "Was not my spirit with you when the man got down from his chariot to meet you? Is this the time g to take money or to accept clothes—or olive groves and vineyards, or flocks and herds, or male and female slaves? h 27 Naaman's leprosy i will

---

a 22 That is, about 75 pounds or about 34 kilograms

5:14 *his flesh was restored and became clean like that of a young boy.* Physically he was reborn (see also v. 15 and note). As he obeyed God's word, Naaman received the gift of God's grace. Naaman is here a sign to disobedient Israel that God's blessing is found only in the path of trustful obedience. When his own people turn away from covenant faithfulness, God will raise up those who will follow his word from outside the covenant nation (see notes on 1Ki 17:9–24; see also Mt 8:10–12; Lk 4:27).

5:15 *no God in all the world except in Israel.* Naaman's confession put to shame the Israelites who continued to waver in their opinion on whether Baal and the Lord (Yahweh) were both gods or whether Yahweh alone was God (see note on 1Ki 18:21).

5:16 *I will not accept a thing.* Elisha did not seek monetary gain for proclaiming the word of the Lord (see Mt 10:8). Naaman was healed solely by divine grace, not by the power of Elisha.

5:17 *let me . . . be given as much earth as a pair of mules can carry.* In the ancient world it was commonly thought that a deity could be worshiped only on the soil of the nation to which he was bound (see v. 15). For this reason Naaman wanted to take Israelite soil with him in order to have a place in Damascus for the worship of the Lord.

5:18 *my master.* Ben-Hadad, king of Aram. *Rimmon.* Also known as Hadad (and in Canaan and Phoenicia as Baal), this Aramean deity was the god of storm ("Rimmon" means "thunder-er") and war. The two names were sometimes combined (see note on Zec 12:11).

5:19 *Go in peace.* Elisha did not directly address Naaman's problem of conscience (v. 18), but commended him to the leading and grace of God as he returned to his pagan environment and official responsibilities.

5:20 *As surely as the LORD lives.* An oath formula (see note on 1Sa 14:39,45).

5:22 *company of the prophets.* See note on 2:3. *Please give them a talent of silver and two sets of clothing.* Gehazi deceived Naaman in order to satisfy his desire for material gain. The evil of his lie was compounded in that it obscured the gracious character of the Lord's work in Naaman's healing and blurred the distinction between Elisha's function as a true prophet of the Lord and the self-serving actions of false prophets and pagan soothsayers.

5:24 *house.* Of Elisha (see v. 9).

5:26 *Is this the time to take money . . . ?* Gehazi sought to use the grace of God granted to another individual for his own material advantage. This was equivalent to making merchandise of God's grace (see note on 2Co 2:17). "Money" here and elsewhere in 2 Kings refers to gold or silver in various weights, not to coins, which were a later invention. *clothes . . . female slaves.* Evidently what Gehazi secretly hoped to acquire with the two talents of silver (see note on v. 5).

5:27 *leprosy.* See TNIV text note on v. 1. *to you and to your descendants forever.* For the extension of punishment to the children of an offender of God's law, see Ex 20:5 and note; see also note on Jos 7:24. *white as snow.* See Ex 4:6.

cling to you and to your descendants forever." Then Gehazi[j] went from Elisha's presence and his skin was leprous—it had become as white as snow.[k]

AN AXHEAD FLOATS

6 The company[l] of the prophets said to Elisha, "Look, the place where we meet with you is too small for us. ²Let us go to the Jordan, where each of us can get a pole; and let us build a place there for us to meet."

And he said, "Go."

³Then one of them said, "Won't you please come with your servants?"

"I will," Elisha replied. ⁴And he went with them.

They went to the Jordan and began to cut down trees. ⁵As one of them was cutting down a tree, the iron axhead fell into the water. "Oh no, my lord!" he cried out. "It was borrowed!"

⁶The man of God asked, "Where did it fall?" When he showed him the place, Elisha cut a stick and threw[m] it there, and made the iron float. ⁷"Lift it out," he said. Then the man reached out his hand and took it.

ELISHA TRAPS BLINDED ARAMEANS

⁸Now the king of Aram was at war with Israel. After conferring with his officers, he said, "I will set up my camp in such and such a place."

⁹The man of God sent word to the king[n] of Israel: "Beware of passing that place, because the Arameans are going down there." ¹⁰So the king of Israel checked on the place indicated by the man of God. Time and again Elisha warned[o] the king, so that he was on his guard in such places.

¹¹This enraged the king of Aram. He summoned his officers and demanded of them, "Tell me! Which of us is on the side of the king of Israel?"

¹²"None of us, my lord the king[p]," said one of his officers, "but Elisha, the prophet who is in Israel, tells the king of Israel the very words you speak in your bedroom."

¹³"Go, find out where he is," the king ordered, "so I can send men and capture him." The report came back: "He is in Dothan."[q] ¹⁴Then he sent[r] horses and chariots and a strong force there. They went by night and surrounded the city.

¹⁵When the servant of the man of God got up and went out early the next morning, an army with horses and chariots had surrounded the city. "Oh no, my lord! What shall we do?" the servant asked.

¹⁶"Don't be afraid,"[s] the prophet answered. "Those who are with us are more[t] than those who are with them."

¹⁷And Elisha prayed, "Open his eyes, LORD, so that he may see." Then the LORD opened the servant's eyes, and he looked and saw the hills full of horses and chariots[u] of fire all around Elisha.

¹⁸As the enemy came down toward him, Elisha prayed to the LORD, "Strike this army with blindness."[v] So he struck them with blindness, as Elisha had asked.

¹⁹Elisha told them, "This is not the road and this is not the city. Follow me, and I will lead them to the man you are looking for." And he led them to Samaria.

5:27 j Col 3:5
k S Ex 4:6
6:1 l S 1Sa 10:5
6:6 m S Ex 15:25; S 2Ki 2:21
6:9 n ver 12
6:10 o Jer 11:18
6:12 p ver 9
6:13 q Ge 37:17
6:14 r 2Ki 1:9
6:16 s S Ge 15:1
t 2Ch 32:7; Ps 55:18; Ro 8:31; 1Jn 4:4
6:17 u S 2Ki 2:11,12
6:18 v Ge 19:11; Ac 13:11

6:1 *company of the prophets.* See note on 2:3.

6:2 *a place there for us to meet.* Referring to some type of assembly hall. It is implied in 4:1–7 that there were separate dwellings for the members of the prophetic companies to live in (see note on 1Sa 19:18).

6:5 *It was borrowed.* At that time an iron axhead was a costly tool, too expensive for the members of the prophetic company to purchase. Having lost it, the borrower faced the prospect of having to work off the value as a bondservant.

6:6 *Elisha cut a stick and threw it there, and made the iron float.* The Lord demonstrated here his concern for the welfare of his faithful ones.

6:8 *king of Aram.* Probably Ben-Hadad II (see note on 5:1). *war with Israel.* A reference to border clashes rather than full-scale hostility (see v. 23; see also note on 5:2). Some indication of Israelite weakness and Aramean strength is seen in the ability of the Arameans to send forces to Dothan (only about 11 miles north of Samaria) without apparent difficulty (see vv. 13–14).

6:9 *man of God.* Elisha (see v. 10). *king of Israel.* Probably Joram (see 1:17; 3:1; 9:24).

6:11 *Which of us is on the side of the king of Israel?* Repeated evidence that Israel possessed advance knowledge of Aramean

military plans led the king of Aram to suspect that there was a traitor among his top officials.

6:12 *king of Israel.* Joram (see 3:1).

6:13 *capture him.* The king of Aram thought he could eliminate Elisha's influence by denying him contact with Israel's king. *Dothan.* Located on a hill about halfway between Jezreel and Samaria, where the main royal residences were (see 1:2; 3:1; 8:29; 9:15; 10:1; 1Ki 21:1).

6:16 *Those who are with us are more than those who are with them.* Elisha knew that there was greater strength in the unseen reality of the hosts of heaven than in the visible reality of the Aramean forces (see 2Ch 32:7–8; Ps 34:7; 1Jn 4:4).

6:17 *saw the hills full of horses and chariots.* In response to Elisha's prayer, his servant was able to see the protecting might of the heavenly hosts gathered about Elisha (see Ge 32:1–2; Ps 34:7; 91:11–12; Mt 18:10; 26:53; see also note on 2Ki 2:11).

6:18 *Strike this army with blindness.* Elisha had prayed for the eyes of his servant to be opened to the unseen reality of the heavenly hosts; now he prays for the eyes of the Aramean soldiers to be closed to earthly reality (see Ge 19:11).

6:19 *This is not the road and this is not the city.* Elisha's statement led the Aramean soldiers to believe that they were being

6:21 ʷS 2Ki 5:13
6:22 ˣS Dt 20:11;
2Ch 28:8-15
6:23 ʸS 2Ki 5:2
6:24 ᶻS 1Ki 15:18;
2Ki 8:7 ᵃDt 28:52
6:25 ᵇS Lev 26:26;
S Ru 1:1 ᶜIsa 36:12
6:29 ᵈS Lev 26:29;
Dt 28:53-55
6:30 ᵉ2Ki 18:37;
Isa 22:15 ᶠS Ge 37:34
6:32 ᵍEze 8:1; 14:1;
20:1 ʰ1Ki 18:4 ⁱver 31
6:33 ʲLev 24:11;
Job 2:9; 14:14;
Isa 40:31

20After they entered the city, Elisha said, "Lᴏʀᴅ, open the eyes of these men so they can see." Then the Lᴏʀᴅ opened their eyes and they looked, and there they were, inside Samaria.

21When the king of Israel saw them, he asked Elisha, "Shall I kill them, my father? ʷ Shall I kill them?"

22"Do not kill them," he answered. "Would you kill those you have captured ˣ with your own sword or bow? Set food and water before them so that they may eat and drink and then go back to their master." 23So he prepared a great feast for them, and after they had finished eating and drinking, he sent them away, and they returned to their master. So the bands ʸ from Aram stopped raiding Israel's territory.

FAMINE IN BESIEGED SAMARIA

24Some time later, Ben-Hadad ᶻ king of Aram mobilized his entire army and marched up and laid siege ᵃ to Samaria. 25There was a great famine ᵇ in the city; the siege lasted so long that a donkey's head sold for eighty shekels ᵃ of silver, and a quarter of a cab ᵇ of seed pods ᶜ ᶜ for five shekels. ᵈ

26As the king of Israel was passing by on the wall, a woman cried to him, "Help me, my lord the king!"

27The king replied, "If the Lᴏʀᴅ does not help you, where can I get help for you? From the threshing floor? From the winepress?" 28Then he asked her, "What's the matter?"

She answered, "This woman said to me, 'Give up your son so we may eat him today, and tomorrow we'll eat my son.' 29So we cooked my son and ate ᵈ him. The next day I said to her, 'Give up your son so we may eat him,' but she had hidden him."

30When the king heard the woman's words, he tore ᵉ his robes. As he went along the wall, the people looked, and they saw that, under his robes, he had sackcloth ᶠ on his body. 31He said, "May God deal with me, be it ever so severely, if the head of Elisha son of Shaphat remains on his shoulders today!"

32Now Elisha was sitting in his house, and the elders ᵍ were sitting with him. The king sent a messenger ahead, but before he arrived, Elisha said to the elders, "Don't you see how this murderer ʰ is sending someone to cut off my head? ⁱ Look, when the messenger comes, shut the door and hold it shut against him. Is not the sound of his master's footsteps behind him?" 33While he was still talking to them, the messenger came down to him.

The king said, "This disaster is from the Lᴏʀᴅ. Why should I wait ʲ for the Lᴏʀᴅ any longer?"

ᵃ 25 That is, about 2 pounds or about 920 grams   ᵇ 25 That is, probably about 1/4 pound or about 100 grams   ᶜ 25 Or of doves' dung   ᵈ 25 That is, about 2 ounces or about 55 grams

---

directed to the city where Elisha could be found. Technically this statement was not an untruth, since Elisha accompanied them to Samaria, but it was a means of deceiving the Aramean soldiers into a trap inside Samaria, the fortress-like capital city of the northern kingdom (see Ex 1:19–20; Jos 2:6; 1Sa 16:1–2 for other instances of deception recorded in the OT).
6:20 *there they were, inside Samaria.* The power of the Lord operative through Elisha turned the intended captors into captives.
6:21 *king of Israel.* Joram (see note on v. 9).
6:22 *Do not kill them.* In reality the Aramean soldiers had been taken captive by the power of the Lord, not by Joram's military prowess. The Lord's purpose was to demonstrate to them and their king and to the Israelites and their king that Israel's national security ultimately was grounded in the Lord, not in military forces or strategies.
6:23 *bands from Aram stopped raiding Israel's territory.* See notes on v. 8; 5:2. Temporarily the Arameans recognized the futility of opposition to the power of the God of Israel.
6:24 *Ben-Hadad.* The same Ben-Hadad who had besieged Samaria on a previous occasion (see notes on 13:3; 1Ki 20:1). This siege is probably to be dated c. 850 B.C.
6:25 *donkey's head.* According to Pentateuchal law the donkey was unclean and not to be eaten (see Lev 11:2–7; Dt 14:4–8). The severity of the famine caused the inhabitants of Samaria not only to disregard the laws of uncleanness but also to place a

high value on the least edible part of the donkey. *eighty shekels of silver.* See TNIV text note; see also note on 5:5.
6:27 *If the Lᴏʀᴅ does not help you, where can I get help for you?* Joram correctly recognized his own inability to assist the woman if the Lord himself did not act in Israel's behalf, but he wrongly implied that the Lord was to be blamed for a situation brought on by Israel's own disobedience and idolatry.
6:28 *tomorrow we'll eat my son.* The sins of the king and people were so great that the covenant curses of Lev 26:29 and Dt 28:53,57 were being inflicted (cf. La 4:10).
6:30 *tore his robes.* More an expression of anger toward Elisha and the Lord (see v. 31) than one of repentance and sorrow for the sins that had provoked the covenant curse. *sackcloth.* A coarse cloth usually worn as a sign of mourning (see notes on Ge 37:34; Rev 11:3).
6:31 *May God deal with me, be it ever so severely.* A curse formula (see note on 1Sa 3:17). *if the head of Elisha . . . remains on his shoulders today!* Joram considered Elisha in some way responsible for the conditions in the city. Cf. Ahab's attitude toward Elijah (1Ki 18:10,16–17; 21:20).
6:32 *elders.* Leaders of the city (see notes on Ex 3:16; 2Sa 3:17). They sit with Elisha rather than with the king.
6:33 *Why should I wait for the Lᴏʀᴅ any longer?* Joram felt himself deceived by Elisha and abandoned by the Lord, whom he blamed for the disastrous conditions in the city.

7:1 ᵏ ver 16
7:2 ˡ 2Ki 5:18
ᵐ ver 19; Ge 7:11;
Ps 78:23; Mal 3:10
ⁿ ver 17
7:3 ᵒ Lev 13:45-46;
Nu 5:1-4
7:6 ᵖ S Ex 14:24;
Eze 1:24 ᵠ 2Sa 10:6;
Jer 46:21 ʳ S Nu 13:29
7:7 ˢ Jdg 7:21;
Ps 48:4-6; Pr 28:1;
Isa 30:17
7:8 ᵗ Isa 33:23; 35:6
7:12 ᵘ Jos 8:4
7:15 ᵛ Job 27:22
7:16 ʷ Isa 33:4,23
ˣ ver 1
7:17 ʸ S ver 2

Elisha replied, "Hear the word of the Lᴏʀᴅ. This is what the Lᴏʀᴅ says: About this time tomorrow, a seah ᵃ of the finest flour will sell for a shekel ᵇ and two seahs ᶜ of barley for a shekel ᵏ at the gate of Samaria."

²The officer on whose arm the king was leaning ˡ said to the man of God, "Look, even if the Lᴏʀᴅ should open the floodgates ᵐ of the heavens, could this happen?"

"You will see it with your own eyes," answered Elisha, "but you will not eat ⁿ any of it!"

THE SIEGE LIFTED

³Now there were four men with leprosy ᵈ ᵒ at the entrance of the city gate. They said to each other, "Why stay here until we die? ⁴If we say, 'We'll go into the city'—the famine is there, and we will die. And if we stay here, we will die. So let's go over to the camp of the Arameans and surrender. If they spare us, we live; if they kill us, then we die."

⁵At dusk they got up and went to the camp of the Arameans. When they reached the edge of the camp, no one was there, ⁶for the Lord had caused the Arameans to hear the sound ᵖ of chariots and horses and a great army, so that they said to one another, "Look, the king of Israel has hired ᵠ the Hittite ʳ and Egyptian kings to attack us!" ⁷So they got up and fled ˢ in the dusk and abandoned their tents and their horses and donkeys. They left the camp as it was and ran for their lives.

⁸The men who had leprosy ᵗ reached the edge of the camp, entered one of the tents and ate and drank. Then they took silver, gold and clothes, and went off and hid them. They returned and entered another tent and took some things from it and hid them also.

⁹Then they said to each other, "What we're doing is not right. This is a day of good news and we are keeping it to ourselves. If we wait until daylight, punishment will overtake us. Let's go at once and report this to the royal palace."

¹⁰So they went and called out to the city gatekeepers and told them, "We went into the Aramean camp and no one was there—not a sound of anyone—only tethered horses and donkeys, and the tents left just as they were." ¹¹The gatekeepers shouted the news, and it was reported within the palace.

¹²The king got up in the night and said to his officers, "I will tell you what the Arameans have done to us. They know we are starving; so they have left the camp to hide ᵘ in the countryside, thinking, 'They will surely come out, and then we will take them alive and get into the city.' "

¹³One of his officers answered, "Have some men take five of the horses that are left in the city. Their plight will be like that of all the Israelites left here—yes, they will only be like all these Israelites who are doomed. So let us send them to find out what happened."

¹⁴So they selected two chariots with their horses, and the king sent them after the Aramean army. He commanded the drivers, "Go and find out what has happened." ¹⁵They followed them as far as the Jordan, and they found the whole road strewn with the clothing and equipment the Arameans had thrown away in their headlong flight. ᵛ So the messengers returned and reported to the king. ¹⁶Then the people went out and plundered ʷ the camp of the Arameans. So a seah of the finest flour sold for a shekel, and two seahs of barley sold for a shekel, ˣ as the Lᴏʀᴅ had said.

¹⁷Now the king had put the officer on whose arm he leaned in charge of the gate, and the people trampled him in the gateway, and he died, ʸ just as the man of God had foretold when the king came down to his house. ¹⁸It happened as the man of God had said to

---

ᵃ *1* That is, probably about 12 pounds or about 5.6 kilograms; also in verses 16 and 18   ᵇ *1* That is, about 2/5 ounce or about 11.5 grams; also in verses 16 and 18   ᶜ *1* That is, probably about 20 pounds or about 9 kilograms; also in verses 16 and 18   ᵈ *3* The Hebrew for *leprosy* was used for various diseases affecting the skin; also in verse 8.

7:1 *a seah of the finest flour will sell for a shekel.* See TNIV text notes. This was about double the normal cost of flour, but a phenomenal improvement over the highly inflated prices the famine had caused.

7:2 *floodgates of the heavens.* See v. 19; Ge 8:2; Isa 24:18.

7:3 *entrance of the city gate.* Pentateuchal law excluded persons with defiling skin diseases from residence in the community (Lev 13:46; Nu 5:2–3).

7:6 *the Lᴏʀᴅ had caused the Arameans to hear the sound.* See 2Sa 5:24 and note. *Hittite . . . kings.* Kings of small city-states ruled by dynasties of Hittite origin, which had arisen in northern Aram after the fall of the Hittite empire c. 1200 B.C.

A **7:9** Fear of punishment can be a valid motive for changing one's behavior.

7:12 *what the Arameans have done to us.* Joram's unbelief caused him to conclude that the report of the four leprous men was part of an Aramean war strategy rather than an evidence of the fulfillment of Elisha's prophecy (see v. 1).

A C **7:16–20** *as the Lᴏʀᴅ had said . . . as the man of God had foretold . . . as the man of God had said . . . that is exactly what happened to him.* Emphasizing the trustworthiness of the prophetic word spoken by Elisha. In the fulfillment of Elisha's prophecy Israel was reminded that deliverance from her enemies was a gift of God's grace and that rejection of God's word provoked the wrath of divine judgment.

7:19 *S ver 2
8:1 *2Ki 4:8-37
*S Lev 26:26;
S Dt 28:22; S Ru 1:1
*S Ge 12:10
8:5 *2Ki 4:35
8:7 *S 2Sa 8:5
*S 2Ki 6:24
8:8 *1Ki 19:15
*S Ge 32:20;
S 1Sa 9:7 *S Jdg 18:5
8:10 *Isa 38:1
8:11 *S Jdg 3:25
*Lk 19:41
8:12 *S 1Ki 19:17

the king: "About this time tomorrow, a seah of the finest flour will sell for a shekel and two seahs of barley for a shekel at the gate of Samaria."

¹⁹The officer had said to the man of God, "Look, even if the LORD should open the floodgates ² of the heavens, could this happen?" The man of God had replied, "You will see it with your own eyes, but you will not eat any of it!" ²⁰And that is exactly what happened to him, for the people trampled him in the gateway, and he died.

THE SHUNAMMITE'S LAND RESTORED

8 Now Elisha had said to the woman ª whose son he had restored to life, "Go away with your family and stay for a while wherever you can, because the LORD has decreed a famine ᵇ in the land that will last seven years." ᶜ ²The woman proceeded to do as the man of God said. She and her family went away and stayed in the land of the Philistines seven years.

³At the end of the seven years she came back from the land of the Philistines and went to appeal to the king for her house and land. ⁴The king was talking to Gehazi, the servant of the man of God, and had said, "Tell me about all the great things Elisha has done." ⁵Just as Gehazi was telling the king how Elisha had restored ᵈ the dead to life, the woman whose son Elisha had brought back to life came to appeal to the king for her house and land.

Gehazi said, "This is the woman, my lord the king, and this is her son whom Elisha restored to life." ⁶The king asked the woman about it, and she told him.

Then he assigned an official to her case and said to him, "Give back everything that belonged to her, including all the income from her land from the day she left the country until now."

HAZAEL MURDERS BEN-HADAD

⁷Elisha went to Damascus, ᵉ and Ben-Hadad ᶠking of Aram was ill. When the king was told, "The man of God has come all the way up here," ⁸he said to Hazael, ᵍ "Take a gift ʰ with you and go to meet the man of God. Consult ¹ the LORD through him; ask him, 'Will I recover from this illness?' "

⁹Hazael went to meet Elisha, taking with him as a gift forty camel-loads of all the finest wares of Damascus. He went in and stood before him, and said, "Your son Ben-Hadad king of Aram has sent me to ask, 'Will I recover from this illness?' "

¹⁰Elisha answered, "Go and say to him, 'You will certainly recover.'ʲ Nevertheless,ª the LORD has revealed to me that he will in fact die." ¹¹He stared at him with a fixed gaze until Hazael was embarrassed. ᵏ Then the man of God began to weep. ¹

¹²"Why is my lord weeping?" asked Hazael.

"Because I know the harm ᵐ you will do to the Israelites," he answered. "You will set

---

ª 10 The Hebrew may also be read *Go and say, 'You will certainly not recover,' for.*

8:1 *the LORD has decreed a famine.* The famine should have been perceived by the people of the northern kingdom as a covenant curse sent on them because of their sin (see note on 4:38). *seven years.* It is not clear whether this famine began before or after the Aramean siege of Samaria (see 4:38; 6:24—7:20).

8:2 *She and her family went away.* Elisha's instruction enabled this godly woman and her family to escape the privations of the famine.

8:3 *went to … the king.* See note on 1Ki 3:16. *appeal … for her house and land.* Either someone had illegally occupied the woman's property during her absence, or it had fallen to the domain of the king by virtue of its abandonment.

8:4 *Tell me about all the great things Elisha has done.* The king's lack of familiarity with Elisha's ministry is perhaps an indication that this incident occurred in the early days of the reign of Jehu rather than in the time of Joram, who had had numerous contacts with Elisha (see 3:13–14; 5:7–10; 6:10–23; 6:24—7:20). But see note on 5:7.

8:6 *Give back everything that belonged to her.* The widow and her son were living examples of the Lord's provision and blessing for those who were obedient to the word of the Lord through his prophets.

8:7 *Elisha went to Damascus.* The time had come for Elisha to carry out one of the three tasks originally given to Elijah at Mount Horeb (see notes on 1Ki 19:15–16). The annals of

the Assyrian ruler Shalmaneser III record Assyrian victories over Ben-Hadad (Hadadezer) of Damascus in 846 B.C. and Hazael of Damascus in 842. Elisha's visit to Damascus is to be dated c. 843.

8:8 *Consult the LORD through him.* In a reversal of the situation described in 1:1–4, a pagan king seeks an oracle from Israel's God. *Will I recover…?* The question is the same as that of Ahaziah in 1:2.

8:9 *forty camel-loads of all the finest wares of Damascus.* Damascus was the center for trade between Egypt, Asia Minor and Mesopotamia. Ben-Hadad evidently thought a generous gift would favorably influence Elisha's oracle (cf. Naaman's gift in 5:5). *Your son Ben-Hadad.* Use of father-son terminology is a tacit acknowledgment by Ben-Hadad of Elisha's superiority (see 6:21; 1Sa 25:8).

8:10 *You will certainly recover.* An assertion that Ben-Hadad's illness was not terminal. *in fact die.* By the hand of Hazael (vv. 14–15).

8:12 *harm you will do to the Israelites.* The Lord gave Elisha a clear picture of the severity of the judgment he was about to send on Israel by the hand of Hazael (see 9:14–16; 10:32; 12:17–18; 13:3,22). *rip open their pregnant women.* This vicious act was often carried out by victorious armies at that time (see 15:16; Hos 13:16; Am 1:13). Such an atrocity likely was intended to make sure that no male children would be born to provide a remnant of the conquered people, which could rise up again and reclaim the land. Elisha's words do not sanction such acts but simply describe Hazael's future attacks on Israel.

fire to their fortified places, kill their young men with the sword, dash [n] their little children [o] to the ground, and rip open [p] their pregnant women."

[13] Hazael said, "How could your servant, a mere dog, [q] accomplish such a feat?"

"The LORD has shown me that you will become king [r] of Aram," answered Elisha.

[14] Then Hazael left Elisha and returned to his master. When Ben-Hadad asked, "What did Elisha say to you?" Hazael replied, "He told me that you would certainly recover." [15] But the next day he took a thick cloth, soaked it in water and spread it over the king's face, so that he died. [s] Then Hazael succeeded him as king.

JEHORAM KING OF JUDAH

8:16–24pp — 2Ch 21:5–10,20

[16] In the fifth year of Joram [t] son of Ahab king of Israel, when Jehoshaphat was king of Judah, Jehoram [u] son of Jehoshaphat began his reign as king of Judah. [17] He was thirty-two years old when he became king, and he reigned in Jerusalem eight years. [18] He followed the ways of the kings of Israel, as the house of Ahab had done, for he married a daughter [v] of Ahab. He did evil in the eyes of the LORD. [19] Nevertheless, for the sake of his servant David, the LORD was not willing to destroy [w] Judah. He had promised to maintain a lamp [x] for David and his descendants forever.

[20] In the time of Jehoram, Edom rebelled against Judah and set up its own king. [y] [21] So Jehoram [a] went to Zair with all his chariots. The Edomites surrounded him and his chariot commanders, but he rose up and broke through by night; his army, however, fled back home. [22] To this day Edom has been in rebellion [z] against Judah. Libnah [a] revolted at the same time.

[23] As for the other events of Jehoram's reign, and all he did, are they not written in the book of the annals of the kings of Judah? [24] Jehoram rested with his ancestors and was buried with them in the City of David. And Ahaziah his son succeeded him as king.

AHAZIAH KING OF JUDAH

8:25–29pp — 2Ch 22:1–6

[25] In the twelfth [b] year of Joram son of Ahab king of Israel, Ahaziah son of Jehoram king of Judah began to reign. [26] Ahaziah was twenty-two years old when he became king, and he reigned in Jerusalem one year. His mother's name was Athaliah, [c] a granddaughter of Omri [d] king of Israel. [27] He followed the ways of the house of Ahab [e] and did evil [f] in the eyes of the LORD, as the house of Ahab had done, for he was related by marriage to Ahab's family.

---

[a] 21 Hebrew *Joram*, a variant of *Jehoram*; also in verses 23 and 24

8:12 [n] Ps 137:9;
Isa 13:16; Hos 13:16;
Na 3:10; Lk 19:44
[o] S Ge 34:29
[p] 2Ki 15:16; Am 1:13
8:13 [q] S 1Sa 17:43;
S 2Sa 3:8 [r] 1Ki 19:15
8:15 [s] S 2Ki 1:17
8:16 [t] S 2Ki 1:17
[u] 2Ch 21:1-4
8:18 [v] ver 26;
2Ki 11:1
8:19 [w] S Ge 6:13
[x] S 2Sa 21:17;
Rev 21:23
8:20 [y] S 1Ki 22:47
8:22 [z] Ge 27:40
[a] S Nu 33:20;
Jos 21:13; 2Ki 19:8
8:25 [b] 2Ki 9:29
8:26 [c] S ver 18
[d] 2Ch 16:23
8:27 [e] 1Ki 16:30
[f] 1Ki 15:26

B **8:13** *How could your servant, a mere dog, accomplish such a feat?* See 2Sa 9:8 and note. Hazael did not show repulsion at these violent acts but saw no possibility to gain the power necessary to accomplish them. *you will become king of Aram.* Elisha's prophecy suggests that Hazael was not a legitimate successor to Ben-Hadad. In an Assyrian inscription Hazael is designated "the son of a nobody" (i.e., a commoner) who usurped the throne.
8:15 *died.* Elisha's prophecy of Hazael's kingship did not legitimize the assassination. Hazael's murder of Ben-Hadad, as well as his future acts of violence against Israel, were wicked acts arising out of his own sinful heart (see Isa 10:5–19). He was followed by a son he named Ben-Hadad (13:24).
8:16 *fifth year of Joram.* 848 B.C. Jehoram had been coregent with his father since 853 (see note on 1:17), but he now began his reign as sole king.
8:17 *reigned in Jerusalem eight years.* Jehoram's sole reign is to be dated 848–841 B.C.
8:18 *as the house of Ahab had done.* Jehoram introduced Baal worship in Judah, as Ahab had done in the northern kingdom (see 11:18). Baal worship now spread to the southern kingdom at the same time it was being restricted in the northern kingdom by Ahab's son Joram (see 3:1–2). *married a daughter of Ahab.* Jehoram's wife was Athaliah, a daughter of Ahab but probably not of Jezebel (see v. 26; 2Ch 18:1). Athaliah's influence on Jehoram paralleled that of Jezebel on Ahab (see 1Ki 16:31; 18:4; 19:1–2; 2Ch 21:6).
8:19 *lamp for David.* See note on 1Ki 11:36; see also Ps 132:17.

The Lord spared Judah and its royal house the judgment he brought on the house of Ahab because of the covenant he had made with David (see 2Sa 7:16,29; 2Ch 21:7).
8:20 *set up its own king.* Previously Edom had been subject to Judah and had been ruled by a deputy (see note on 3:9; see also 1Ki 22:47).
8:22 *To this day.* Until the time of the writing of the account of Jehoram's reign used by the author of 1,2 Kings (see Introduction to 1 Kings: Author, Sources and Date; see also note on 1Ki 8:8). Later, Amaziah of Judah was able to inflict a serious defeat on Edom (14:7), and his successor Azariah regained control of the trade route to Elath through Edomite territory (14:22; 2Ch 26:2). *Libnah revolted at the same time.* Libnah appears to have been located close to the Philistine border near Lachish (see 19:8). It is likely that the revolt of Libnah was connected with that of the Philistines and Arabs described in 2Ch 21:16–17.
8:23 *other events of Jehoram's reign.* See 2Ch 21:4–20. *annals of the kings of Judah.* See note on 1Ki 14:29.
8:24 *rested with his ancestors.* See notes on 1Ki 1:21; 2Ch 21:20.
8:25 *twelfth year of Joram.* 841 B.C. In 9:29 the first year of Joram's reign was counted as his accession year and his second year as the first year of his reign, whereas here his accession year was counted as the first year of his reign (see Introduction to 1 Kings: Chronology).
8:26 *twenty-two years old when he became king.* See note on 2Ch 22:2. *Athaliah.* See note on v. 18.
8:27 *ways of the house of Ahab.* See 2Ch 22:3–5.

8:28 ᵍS Dt 4:43;
2Ki 9:1,14
8:29 ʰ1Ki 21:29;
2Ki 9:21 ⁱ1Ki 19:15,17
ʲ2Ki 10:13
9:1 ᵏS 1Sa 10:5
ˡS 1Ki 18:46
ᵐS 1Sa 10:1
ⁿS 2Ki 8:28
9:3 ᵒ1Ki 19:16
9:6 ᵖ1Ki 19:16
9:7 ᵍS Ge 4:24;
S Rev 6:10
ʳS Dt 32:43
ˢS 1Ki 18:4
9:8 ᵗ2Ki 10:17
ᵘS 1Sa 25:22
9:9 ᵛS 1Ki 13:34;
S 14:10 ʷ1Ki 16:3
9:10 ˣS 1Ki 21:23
9:11 ʸS 1Sa 10:11;
S Jn 10:20
9:13 ᶻMt 21:8;
Lk 19:36 ᵃS 2Sa 15:10
9:14 ᵇS Dt 4:43;
S 2Ki 8:28
9:15 ᶜS 2Ki 8:29
9:16 ᵈ2Ch 22:7
9:17 ᵉS 1Sa 14:16;
Isa 21:6

²⁸Ahaziah went with Joram son of Ahab to war against Hazael king of Aram at Ramoth Gilead. ᵍ The Arameans wounded Joram; ²⁹so King Joram returned to Jezreel ʰ to recover from the wounds the Arameans had inflicted on him at Ramoth ᵃ in his battle with Hazael ⁱ king of Aram.

Then Ahaziah ʲ son of Jehoram king of Judah went down to Jezreel to see Joram son of Ahab, because he had been wounded.

JEHU ANOINTED KING OF ISRAEL

9 The prophet Elisha summoned a man from the company ᵏ of the prophets and said to him, "Tuck your cloak into your belt, ˡ take this flask of oil ᵐ with you and go to Ramoth Gilead. ⁿ ²When you get there, look for Jehu son of Jehoshaphat, the son of Nimshi. Go to him, get him away from his companions and take him into an inner room. ³Then take the flask and pour the oil ᵒ on his head and declare, 'This is what the Lᴏʀᴅ says: I anoint you king over Israel.' Then open the door and run; don't delay!"

⁴So the young prophet went to Ramoth Gilead. ⁵When he arrived, he found the army officers sitting together. "I have a message for you, commander," he said.

"For which of us?" asked Jehu.

"For you, commander," he replied.

⁶Jehu got up and went into the house. Then the prophet poured the oil ᵖ on Jehu's head and declared, "This is what the Lᴏʀᴅ, the God of Israel, says: 'I anoint you king over the Lᴏʀᴅ's people Israel. ⁷You are to destroy the house of Ahab your master, and I will avenge ᵍ the blood of my servants ʳ the prophets and the blood of all the Lᴏʀᴅ's servants shed by Jezebel. ˢ ⁸The whole house ᵗ of Ahab will perish. I will cut off from Ahab every last male ᵘ in Israel—slave or free. ᵇ ⁹I will make the house of Ahab like the house of Jeroboam ᵛ son of Nebat and like the house of Baasha ʷ son of Ahijah. ¹⁰As for Jezebel, dogs ˣ will devour her on the plot of ground at Jezreel, and no one will bury her.' " Then he opened the door and ran.

¹¹When Jehu went out to his fellow officers, one of them asked him, "Is everything all right? Why did this maniac ʸ come to you?"

"You know the man and the sort of things he says," Jehu replied.

¹²"That's not true!" they said. "Tell us."

Jehu said, "Here is what he told me: 'This is what the Lᴏʀᴅ says: I anoint you king over Israel.' "

¹³They quickly took their cloaks and spread ᶻ them under him on the bare steps. Then they blew the trumpet ᵃ and shouted, "Jehu is king!"

JEHU KILLS JORAM AND AHAZIAH

9:21–29pp — 2Ch 22:7–9

¹⁴So Jehu son of Jehoshaphat, the son of Nimshi, conspired against Joram. (Now Joram and all Israel had been defending Ramoth Gilead ᵇ against Hazael king of Aram, ¹⁵but King Joram ᶜ had returned to Jezreel to recover ᶜ from the wounds the Arameans had inflicted on him in the battle with Hazael king of Aram.) Jehu said, "If you desire to make me king, don't let anyone slip out of the city to go and tell the news in Jezreel." ¹⁶Then he got into his chariot and rode to Jezreel, because Joram was resting there and Ahaziah ᵈ king of Judah had gone down to see him.

¹⁷When the lookout ᵉ standing on the tower in Jezreel saw Jehu's troops approaching, he called out, "I see some troops coming."

ᵃ 29 Hebrew *Ramah*, a variant of *Ramoth*   ᵇ 8 Or *Israel—every ruler or leader*   ᶜ 15 Hebrew *Jehoram*, a variant of *Joram*; also in verses 17 and 21-24

8:28 *Ahaziah went with Joram...to war against Hazael...at Ramoth Gilead.* As Jehoshaphat had joined Ahab in battle against the Arameans at Ramoth Gilead (1Ki 22), so now Ahaziah joined his uncle Joram in a similar venture. On the previous occasion Ahab met his death (1Ki 22:37). On this occasion Joram was wounded and, while recuperating in Jezreel (see note on 1Ki 21:1), both he and his nephew Ahaziah were assassinated by Jehu (see 9:14–28). *Hazael.* See note on 1Ki 19:15.
9:1 *company of the prophets.* See note on 2:3.
9:3 *I anoint you king.* See notes on 1Sa 2:10; 9:16; 1Ki 19:16.
9:7 *destroy the house of Ahab.* Jehu learned that he was the divinely appointed agent to inflict the judgment Elijah had pronounced many years earlier in his own hearing against the house of Ahab (see vv. 25–26; 1Ki 21:21–24). *blood of all the*

Lᴏʀᴅ's *servants shed by Jezebel.* See 1Ki 18:4; 21:13.
9:8 *slave or free.* See note on 1Ki 14:10.
9:9 *like the house of Jeroboam.* See 1Ki 14:7–11; 15:27–30. *like the house of Baasha.* See 1Ki 16:1–4, 8–12. Elijah had spoken the same words to Ahab years before (see 1Ki 21:21–24).
9:11 *this maniac.* The epithet betrays a scornful attitude on the part of the military officers of the northern kingdom toward members of the prophetic companies. Cf 1Sa 21:13–15.
9:15 *Jezreel.* About 45 miles from Ramoth Gilead. Joram apparently had a summer palace there (see 1Ki 21:1 and note). *don't let anyone...go and tell the news in Jezreel.* For the success of Jehu's revolt and to avoid a civil conflict, it was important to take Joram totally by surprise.
9:16 *Ahaziah...had gone down to see him.* See 8:29.

"Get a horseman," Joram ordered. "Send him to meet them and ask, 'Do you come in peace?[f]'"

[18]The horseman rode off to meet Jehu and said, "This is what the king says: 'Do you come in peace?'"

"What do you have to do with peace?" Jehu replied. "Fall in behind me."

The lookout reported, "The messenger has reached them, but he isn't coming back."

[19]So the king sent out a second horseman. When he came to them he said, "This is what the king says: 'Do you come in peace?'"

Jehu replied, "What do you have to do with peace? Fall in behind me."

[20]The lookout reported, "He has reached them, but he isn't coming back either. The driving is like[g] that of Jehu son of Nimshi—he drives like a maniac."

[21]"Hitch up my chariot," Joram ordered. And when it was hitched up, Joram king of Israel and Ahaziah king of Judah rode out, each in his own chariot, to meet Jehu. They met him at the plot of ground that had belonged to Naboth[h] the Jezreelite. [22]When Joram saw Jehu he asked, "Have you come in peace, Jehu?"

"How can there be peace," Jehu replied, "as long as all the idolatry and witchcraft of your mother Jezebel[i] abound?"

[23]Joram turned about and fled, calling out to Ahaziah, "Treachery,[j] Ahaziah!"

[24]Then Jehu drew his bow[k] and shot Joram between the shoulders. The arrow pierced his heart and he slumped down in his chariot. [25]Jehu said to Bidkar, his chariot officer, "Pick him up and throw him on the field that belonged to Naboth the Jezreelite. Remember how you and I were riding together in chariots behind Ahab his father when the LORD spoke this prophecy[l] against him: [26]'Yesterday I saw the blood of Naboth[m] and the blood of his sons, declares the LORD, and I will surely make you pay for it on this plot of ground, declares the LORD.'[a] Now then, pick him up and throw him on that plot, in accordance with the word of the LORD."[n]

[27]When Ahaziah king of Judah saw what had happened, he fled up the road to Beth Haggan.[b] Jehu chased him, shouting, "Kill him too!" They wounded him in his chariot on the way up to Gur near Ibleam,[o] but he escaped to Megiddo[p] and died there. [28]His servants took him by chariot[q] to Jerusalem and buried him with his ancestors in his tomb in the City of David. [29](In the eleventh[r] year of Joram son of Ahab, Ahaziah had become king of Judah.)

JEZEBEL KILLED

[30]Then Jehu went to Jezreel. When Jezebel heard about it, she painted[s] her eyes, arranged her hair and looked out of a window. [31]As Jehu entered the gate, she asked, "Have you come in peace, you Zimri,[t] you murderer of your master?"[c]

[32]He looked up at the window and called out, "Who is on my side? Who?" Two or three eunuchs looked down at him. [33]"Throw her down!" Jehu said. So they threw her down, and some of her blood spattered the wall and the horses as they trampled her underfoot.[u]

[34]Jehu went in and ate and drank. "Take care of that cursed woman," he said, "and bury her, for she was a king's daughter."[v] [35]But when they went out to bury her, they found nothing except her skull, her feet and her hands. [36]They went back and told Jehu, who said, "This is the word of the LORD that he spoke through his servant Elijah the Tishbite: On the plot of ground at Jezreel dogs[w] will devour Jezebel's flesh.[d][x] [37]Jezebel's body will be like dung[y] on the ground in the plot at Jezreel, so that no one will be able to say, 'This is Jezebel.'"

---

[a] 26 See 1 Kings 21:19.   [b] 27 Or *fled by way of the garden house*   [c] 31 Or *"Was there peace for Zimri, who murdered his master?"*   [d] 36 See 1 Kings 21:23.

9:17 [f] S 1Sa 16:4
9:20 [g] 2Sa 18:27
9:21 [h] 1Ki 21:1-7,15-19
9:22 [i] 1Ki 18:19; Rev 2:20
9:23 [j] 2Ki 11:14
9:24 [k] S 1Ki 22:34
9:25 [l] 1Ki 21:19-22, 24-29
9:26 [m] S 1Ki 21:19
[n] S 1Ki 21:29
9:27 [o] S Jdg 1:27
[p] 2Ki 23:29
9:28 [q] 2Ki 14:20; 23:30
9:29 [r] 2Ki 8:25
9:30 [s] Jer 4:30;
9:31 [t] 1Ki 16:9-10
9:33 [u] Ps 7:5
9:34 [v] S 1Ki 16:31
9:36 [w] Ps 68:23; Jer 15:3 [x] S 1Ki 21:23
9:37 [y] Ps 83:10; Isa 5:25; Jer 8:2; 9:22; 16:4; 25:33; Zep 1:17

9:21 *plot of ground that had belonged to Naboth.* See notes on 1Ki 21:2-3,13,19.

9:22 *idolatry and witchcraft.* Both punishable by death (see Dt 13; 18:10-12).

9:25 *chariot officer.* See note on 1Ki 22:34.

9:26 *in accordance with the word of the LORD.* Jehu saw himself providentially placed in the position of fulfilling the prophecy of Elijah given years before (see 1Ki 21:18-24). Even though Ahab's own blood was not shed on Naboth's field (see 1Ki 21:29 and note), Jehu saw in Joram's death the fulfillment of Elijah's prophecy (see note on 1Ki 21:19).

9:27 *escaped to Megiddo and died there.* It may be questioned

whether Jehu was justified in extending the purge of Ahab's house (see Hos 1:4) to the descendants of the house of David through Ahab's daughter Athaliah (see 8:18,26).

9:31 *Zimri, you murderer of your master.* In bitter sarcasm Jezebel called Jehu by the name Zimri. About 45 years earlier Zimri had seized the throne from Elah by assassination and then had destroyed the whole house of Baasha. He ruled, however, for only seven days before Omri seized power (see 1Ki 16:8-20).

9:36 *the word of the LORD that he spoke through his servant Elijah.* In the manner of Jezebel's death the word of the Lord was confirmed—the word she had defied during her life (see 1Ki 21:23).

10:1 ᶻ S 1Ki 13:32
ᵃ S Jdg 8:30
ᵇ S 1Ki 21:1 ᶜ ver 5
10:5 ᵈ Jos 9:8
10:7 ᵉ S 1Ki 21:21
ᶠ S 2Sa 4:8
10:10 ᵍ 2Ki 9:7-10
ʰ S 1Ki 21:29
10:11 ⁱ Hos 1:4
ʲ ver 14; Job 18:19;
Mal 4:1
10:13 ᵏ 2Ki 8:24,29;
2Ch 22:8 ᶦ S 1Ki 2:19
10:14 ᵐ S ver 11
10:15 ⁿ Jer 35:6,14-
19 ᵒ 1Ch 2:55;
Jer 35:2

AHAB'S FAMILY KILLED

10 Now there were in Samaria ᶻ seventy sons ᵃ of the house of Ahab. So Jehu wrote letters and sent them to Samaria: to the officials of Jezreel, ᵃ ᵇ to the elders and to the guardians ᶜ of Ahab's children. He said, ²"You have your master's sons with you and you have chariots and horses, a fortified city and weapons. Now as soon as this letter reaches you, ³choose the best and most worthy of your master's sons and set him on his father's throne. Then fight for your master's house."

⁴But they were terrified and said, "If two kings could not resist him, how can we?"

⁵So the palace administrator, the city governor, the elders and the guardians sent this message to Jehu: "We are your servants ᵈ and we will do anything you say. We will not appoint anyone as king; you do whatever you think best."

⁶Then Jehu wrote them a second letter, saying, "If you are on my side and will obey me, take the heads of your master's sons and come to me in Jezreel by this time tomorrow."

Now the royal princes, seventy of them, were with the leading men of the city, who were rearing them. ⁷When the letter arrived, they took the princes and slaughtered all seventy ᵉ of them. They put their heads ᶠ in baskets and sent them to Jehu in Jezreel. ⁸When the messenger arrived, he told Jehu, "They have brought the heads of the princes."

Then Jehu ordered, "Put them in two piles at the entrance of the city gate until morning."

⁹The next morning Jehu went out. He stood before all the people and said, "You are innocent. It was I who conspired against my master and killed him, but who killed all these? ¹⁰Know, then, that not a word the LORD has spoken against the house of Ahab will fail. The LORD has done what he announced ᵍ through his servant Elijah." ʰ ¹¹So Jehu ⁱ killed everyone in Jezreel who remained of the house of Ahab, as well as all his chief men, his close friends and his priests, leaving him no survivor. ʲ

¹²Jehu then set out and went toward Samaria. At Beth Eked of the Shepherds, ¹³he met some relatives of Ahaziah king of Judah and asked, "Who are you?"

They said, "We are relatives of Ahaziah, ᵏ and we have come down to greet the families of the king and of the queen mother. ᶦ"

¹⁴"Take them alive!" he ordered. So they took them alive and slaughtered them by the well of Beth Eked—forty-two of them. He left no survivor. ᵐ

¹⁵After he left there, he came upon Jehonadab ⁿ son of Rekab, ᵒ who was on his way to meet him. Jehu greeted him and said, "Are you in accord with me, as I am with you?"

"I am," Jehonadab answered.

ᵃ 1 Hebrew; some Septuagint manuscripts and Vulgate *of the city*

10:1 *Samaria.* In order to consolidate his coup and establish control of the northern kingdom, Jehu still faced the formidable problems of taking the nearly impregnable fortress of Samaria (see note on 1Ki 16:24) and then of completing the destruction of Ahab's house. *seventy sons of the house of Ahab.* The 70 could include both sons and grandsons (see 1Ki 4:1–6). *officials.* Officers appointed by the king (see 1Ki 4:6). *elders.* Local leaders by virtue of their position in the tribal and family structure (see notes on Ex 3:16; 2Sa 3:17). *guardians of Ahab's children.* Those entrusted with the care and upbringing of the princes in the royal family.

10:3 *fight for your master's house.* Jehu's strategy was to induce the leaders of Samaria into submission to his rule by bluffing a military confrontation.

10:4 *terrified.* The leaders of Samaria were completely intimidated by Jehu's challenge. *two kings.* Joram and Ahaziah (see 9:24,27).

10:5 *palace administrator.* See note on 1Ki 4:6. *city governor.* Probably an official appointed by the king, who served as commander of the militia of the capital city. *the elders and the guardians.* See notes on these in v. 1.

10:6 *take the heads of your master's sons and come to me.* The wording of Jehu's command contains what appears to be a deliberate ambiguity. The "heads of your master's sons" could be understood as a reference to the leading figures among the 70 descendants of Ahab, such as the crown prince and several other sons of special ability and standing. On the other hand, the expression could be taken as a reference to the literal heads of all 70 princes.

10:7 *slaughtered all seventy.* The leaders of the city understood the communique in the literal sense, as Jehu most certainly had

hoped they would. *put their heads in baskets and sent them to Jehu.* The leaders of Samaria did not carry the heads of the princes to Jezreel themselves as they had been ordered to do by Jehu (see v. 6). It is likely that they feared for their lives.

10:8 *Put them in two piles at the entrance of the city gate.* This gruesome procedure imitated the barbaric practice of the Assyrian rulers Ashurnasirpal and Shalmaneser III, whose reigns were characterized by acts of terror.

10:9 *It was I who … killed him.* Jehu openly confessed his own part in the overthrow of the government of Joram. *who killed all these?* Because of the ambiguous communique Jehu sent to the leaders of Samaria (see note on v. 6), he can now deny any personal responsibility for the slaughter of the 70 sons of Ahab and can lay the blame for it on the leaders of Samaria.

10:10 *what he announced through his servant Elijah.* See 1Ki 21:20–24,29. Jehu implies a divine sanction not only for what had already been done but also for his intent to continue the purge of Ahab's house and associates.

▐ 10:11 *all his chief men, his close friends and his priests.* Jehu went beyond the responsibility given to him (see 9:7; Hos 1:4) and acted solely on grounds of political self-interest. Jehu himself had been in the service of Ahab (see 9:25).

10:13 *relatives of Ahaziah.* See 2Ch 22:17. *families of the king and of the queen mother.* Members of the royal family from Judah who had not yet heard of the deaths of Joram and Jezebel.

▐ 10:15 *Jehonadab son of Rekab.* Jehonadab was the leader of a conservative movement among the Israelites that was characterized by strong opposition to Baalism, as well as to various practices of a settled agricultural society, including

"If so," said Jehu, "give me your hand."[P] So he did, and Jehu helped him up into the chariot. [16]Jehu said, "Come with me and see my zeal[q] for the LORD." Then he had him ride along in his chariot.

[17]When Jehu came to Samaria, he killed all who were left there of Ahab's family;[r] he destroyed them, according to the word of the LORD spoken to Elijah.

SERVANTS OF BAAL KILLED

[18]Then Jehu brought all the people together and said to them, "Ahab served[s] Baal a little; Jehu will serve him much. [19]Now summon[t] all the prophets of Baal, all his servants and all his priests. See that no one is missing, because I am going to hold a great sacrifice for Baal. Anyone who fails to come will no longer live." But Jehu was acting deceptively in order to destroy the servants of Baal.

[20]Jehu said, "Call an assembly[u] in honor of Baal." So they proclaimed it. [21]Then he sent word throughout Israel, and all the servants of Baal came; not one stayed away. They crowded into the temple of Baal until it was full from one end to the other. [22]And Jehu said to the keeper of the wardrobe, "Bring robes for all the servants of Baal." So he brought out robes for them.

[23]Then Jehu and Jehonadab son of Rekab went into the temple of Baal. Jehu said to the servants of Baal, "Look around and see that no one who serves the LORD is here with you—only servants of Baal." [24]So they went in to make sacrifices and burnt offerings. Now Jehu had posted eighty men outside with this warning: "If one of you lets any of the men I am placing in your hands escape, it will be your life for his life."[v]

[25]As soon as Jehu had finished making the burnt offering, he ordered the guards and officers: "Go in and kill[w] them; let no one escape."[x] So they cut them down with the sword. The guards and officers threw the bodies out and then entered the inner shrine of the temple of Baal. [26]They brought the sacred stone[y] out of the temple of Baal and burned it. [27]They demolished the sacred stone of Baal and tore down the temple[z] of Baal, and people have used it for a latrine to this day.

[28]So Jehu[a] destroyed Baal worship in Israel. [29]However, he did not turn away from the sins[b] of Jeroboam son of Nebat, which he had caused Israel to commit—the worship of the golden calves[c] at Bethel[d] and Dan.

[30]The LORD said to Jehu, "Because you have done well in accomplishing what is right in my eyes and have done to the house of Ahab all I had in mind to do, your descendants will sit on the throne of Israel to the fourth generation."[e] [31]Yet Jehu was not careful[f] to keep the law of the LORD, the God of Israel, with all his heart. He did not turn away from the sins[g] of Jeroboam, which he had caused Israel to commit.

[32]In those days the LORD began to reduce[h] the size of Israel. Hazael[i] overpowered the Israelites throughout their territory [33]east of the Jordan in all the land of Gilead (the region of Gad, Reuben and Manasseh), from Aroer[j] by the Arnon[k] Gorge through Gilead to Bashan.

10:15 *P* Ezr 10:19; Eze 17:18
10:16 *q* S Nu 25:13
10:17 *r* 2Ki 9:8
10:18 *s* S Jdg 2:11
10:19 *t* 1Ki 18:19
10:20 *u* S Ex 32:5
10:24 *v* S Jos 2:14
10:25 *w* S Ex 22:20; S 2Ki 11:18
x S 1Ki 18:40
10:26 *y* S Ex 23:24
10:27 *z* S 1Ki 16:32
10:28 *a* 1Ki 19:17
10:29 *b* S 1Ki 12:30
c S Ex 32:4 *d* 1Ki 12:32
10:30 *e* 2Ki 15:12
10:31 *f* Dt 4:9; Pr 4:23 *g* 1Ki 12:30
10:32 *h* 2Ki 13:25; Ps 107:39 *i* S 1Ki 19:17
10:33 *j* S Nu 32:34; Dt 2:36; Jdg 11:26; Isa 17:2 *k* S Nu 21:13

the building of houses, the sowing of crops and the use of wine. His followers still adhered to these principles over 200 years later and were known as Rekabites (see Jer 35:6–10).

10:16 *had him ride along.* Public association with Jehonadab gave Jehu added credentials among the rural populace as a follower of the Lord.

10:18 *Ahab served Baal a little; Jehu will serve him much.* After settling in Samaria, Jehu gave the appearance of having previously appealed to the word of the Lord as a mere political maneuver.

10:19 *will no longer live.* Jehu's reputation made this no idle threat.

10:26 *burned it.* May refer to the Asherah pole (see note on 1Ki 14:15) that usually accompanied a sacred stone (see 1Ki 16:32–33).

10:27 *sacred stone of Baal.* See note on 1Ki 14:23. *to this day.* See note on 8:22.

10:29 *sins of Jeroboam ... he had caused Israel to commit.* See 1Ki 12:26–32; 13:33–34; 14:16.

10:30 *Because you have done ... to the house of Ahab all I had in mind.* Jehu was the Lord's instrument to bring judgment on the house of Ahab, for which he was commended.

But he was later condemned by the prophet Hosea for the killing of all Ahab's associates, as well as Ahaziah of Judah and the 42 Judahite princes—the "massacre at Jezreel" (Hos 1:4). *fourth generation.* The restriction of this blessing to four generations is reflective of the qualified approval given to Jehu's reign. Nevertheless, his dynasty survived longer than any other dynasty of the northern kingdom, lasting nearly 100 years. It included the reigns of Jehoahaz, Jehoash, Jeroboam II and Zechariah (see note on 15:12).

10:31 *was not careful to keep the law of the LORD ... with all his heart.* Jehu seems to have been driven more by a political desire to secure his own position on the throne of the northern kingdom than by a desire to serve the Lord. In this he was guilty of using God's judgment on the house of Ahab to serve his self-interest.

10:32 *the LORD began to reduce the size of Israel.* The climax of the covenant curses enumerated in Lev 26 and Dt 28 was Israel's expulsion from Canaan. During the rule of Jehu the northern kingdom experienced the beginnings of this curse (see 17:7–18 for its full realization).

10:33 All of Transjordan was lost to Hazael and the Arameans of Damascus.

10:34 /1Ki 15:31
11:1 ᵐS 2Ki 8:18
11:2 ⁿ2Ki 12:1
ᵒS Jdg 9:5
11:4 ᵖver 19
11:5 ᵠ1Ch 9:25
ʳ1Ki 14:27
11:10 ˢS 2Sa 8:7
11:12 ᵗEx 25:16;
2Ki 23:3 ᵘS 1Sa 9:16;
S 1Ki 1:39 ᵛPs 47:1;
98:8; 1Sa 55:12
ʷS 1Sa 10:24

³⁴As for the other events of Jehu's reign, all he did, and all his achievements, are they not written in the book of the annals ᶦ of the kings of Israel?

³⁵Jehu rested with his ancestors and was buried in Samaria. And Jehoahaz his son succeeded him as king. ³⁶The time that Jehu reigned over Israel in Samaria was twenty-eight years.

ATHALIAH AND JOASH

11:1–21pp — 2Ch 22:10—23:21

11 When Athaliah ᵐ the mother of Ahaziah saw that her son was dead, she proceeded to destroy the whole royal family. ²But Jehosheba, the daughter of King Jehoram ᵃ and sister of Ahaziah, took Joash ⁿ son of Ahaziah and stole him away from among the royal princes, who were about to be murdered. She put him and his nurse in a bedroom to hide him from Athaliah; so he was not killed. ᵒ ³He remained hidden with his nurse at the temple of the LORD for six years while Athaliah ruled the land.

⁴In the seventh year Jehoiada sent for the commanders of units of a hundred, the Carites ᵖ and the guards and had them brought to him at the temple of the LORD. He made a covenant with them and put them under oath at the temple of the LORD. Then he showed them the king's son. ⁵He commanded them, saying, "This is what you are to do: You who are in the three companies that are going on duty on the Sabbath ᵠ—a third of you guarding the royal palace, ʳ ⁶a third at the Sur Gate, and a third at the gate behind the guard, who take turns guarding the temple— ⁷and you who are in the other two companies that normally go off Sabbath duty are all to guard the temple for the king. ⁸Station yourselves around the king, each of you with weapon in hand. Anyone who approaches your ranks ᵇ is to be put to death. Stay close to the king wherever he goes."

⁹The commanders of units of a hundred did just as Jehoiada the priest ordered. Each one took his men—those who were going on duty on the Sabbath and those who were going off duty—and came to Jehoiada the priest. ¹⁰Then he gave the commanders the spears and shields ˢ that had belonged to King David and that were in the temple of the LORD. ¹¹The guards, each with weapon in hand, stationed themselves around the king—near the altar and the temple, from the south side to the north side of the temple.

¹²Jehoiada brought out the king's son and put the crown on him; he presented him with a copy of the covenant ᵗ and proclaimed him king. They anointed ᵘ him, and the people clapped their hands ᵛ and shouted, "Long live the king!" ʷ

¹³When Athaliah heard the noise made by the guards and the people, she went to the people at the temple of the LORD. ¹⁴She looked and there was the king, standing by the pil-

---

ᵃ 2 Hebrew *Joram*, a variant of *Jehoram*   ᵇ 8 Or *approaches the precincts*

10:34 *other events of Jehu's reign.* The Black Obelisk of the Assyrian ruler Shalmaneser III informs us that Jehu paid tribute to the Assyrians shortly after coming to the throne of the northern kingdom in 841 B.C. In the Assyrian inscription Jehu is incorrectly called the "son of Omri," but this may simply be Shalmaneser's way of identifying Jehu with Samaria (or Israel). There is no reference to this payment of tribute in the Biblical narratives of Jehu's reign. *annals of the kings of Israel.* See note on 1Ki 14:19.
10:35 *rested with his ancestors.* See note on 1Ki 1:21. *Jehoahaz his son succeeded him.* For the reign of Jehoahaz, see 13:1–9.
10:36 *twenty-eight years.* 841–814 B.C.
11:1 *Athaliah.* See note on 8:18. *her son was dead.* See 9:27. *destroy the whole royal family.* To secure the throne in Judah for herself. By this time the royal family in Judah had already been reduced to a mere remnant. Jehoram, the late husband of Athaliah and the father of Ahaziah, had killed all his brothers when he succeeded his father Jehoshaphat on the throne (see 2Ch 21:4). Jehu had slain another 42 members of the royal house of Judah, perhaps including many of the sons of Jehoram's brothers (10:12–14; 2Ch 22:8–9), and the brothers of Ahaziah had been killed by marauding Arabs (2Ch 22:1). It is likely that Athaliah's purge focused primarily on the children of Ahaziah, i.e., her own grandchildren. Ahaziah had died at the young age of 22 (see 8:26). This attempt to completely destroy the house of David was an attack on God's redemptive plan—a plan that centered in the Messiah, which the Davidic covenant promised (see notes on 2Sa 7:11,16; 1Ki 8:25).

11:2 *daughter of King Jehoram and sister of Ahaziah.* It is likely that Jehosheba was the daughter of Jehoram by a wife other than Athaliah, and thus she was a half sister of Ahaziah. She was married to the high priest Jehoiada (see 2Ch 22:11). *him and his nurse.* The child was not more than a year old and had not yet been weaned (see vv. 3,21).
11:4 *seventh year.* Of Athaliah's rule. *commanders of units of a hundred.* 2Ch 23:1 lists the names of five commanders, all native Israelites. *Carites.* Mercenary soldiers from Caria in southwest Asia Minor who served as royal bodyguards. *had them brought to him at the temple.* 2Ch 23:2 includes the Levites and family leaders of Judah in the conspiracy.
11:10 *shields that had belonged to King David and that were in the temple.* David had taken gold shields as plunder in his battle with Hadadezer and then dedicated them to the Lord (see 2Sa 8:7–11). The temple and palace were plundered by Shishak, king of Egypt, during Rehoboam's reign (see 1Ki 14:26). Apparently David's shields had been hidden and were not taken.
11:12 *covenant.* Probably (1) the Ten Commandments, (2) the entire Sinaitic covenant or (3) a document dealing more specifically with the covenant responsibilities of the king (see Dt 17:14–20; see also note on 1Sa 10:25). The third option is most likely. *anointed him.* See notes on 1Sa 2:10; 9:16; 1Ki 1:39. *Long live the king!* See note on Ps 62:4.
11:14 *pillar.* Apparently one of the two bronze pillars of the portico of the temple, named Jakin and Boaz (see 23:3; 1Ki 7:15–22; 2Ch 23:13). *all the people of the land.* It is likely that Je-

lar,[x] as the custom was. The officers and the trumpeters were beside the king, and all the people of the land were rejoicing and blowing trumpets.[y] Then Athaliah tore[z] her robes and called out, "Treason! Treason!"[a]

[15]Jehoiada the priest ordered the commanders of units of a hundred, who were in charge of the troops: "Bring her out between the ranks[a] and put to the sword anyone who follows her." For the priest had said, "She must not be put to death in the temple[b] of the Lord." [16]So they seized her as she reached the place where the horses enter[c] the palace grounds, and there she was put to death.[d]

[17]Jehoiada then made a covenant[e] between the Lord and the king and people that they would be the Lord's people. He also made a covenant between the king and the people.[f] [18]All the people of the land went to the temple[g] of Baal and tore it down. They smashed[h] the altars and idols to pieces and killed Mattan the priest[i] of Baal in front of the altars.

Then Jehoiada the priest posted guards at the temple of the Lord. [19]He took with him the commanders of hundreds, the Carites,[j] the guards and all the people of the land, and together they brought the king down from the temple of the Lord and went into the palace, entering by way of the gate of the guards. The king then took his place on the royal throne. [20]All the people of the land rejoiced,[k] and the city was calm, because Athaliah had been slain with the sword at the palace.

*[21]Joash[b] was seven years old when he began to reign.

JOASH REPAIRS THE TEMPLE
12:1–21pp — 2Ch 24:1–14; 24:23–27

12 *[In the seventh year of Jehu, Joash[c][l] became king, and he reigned in Jerusalem forty years. His mother's name was Zibiah; she was from Beersheba. [2]Joash did what was right[m] in the eyes of the Lord all the years Jehoiada the priest instructed him. [3]The high places,[n] however, were not removed; the people continued to offer sacrifices and burn incense there.

[4]Joash said to the priests, "Collect[o] all the money that is brought as sacred offerings[p] to the temple of the Lord—the money collected in the census,[q] the money received from personal vows and the money brought voluntarily[r] to the temple. [5]Let every priest receive the money from one of the treasurers, then use it to repair[s] whatever damage is found in the temple."

[6]But by the twenty-third year of King Joash the priests still had not repaired the temple. [7]Therefore King Joash summoned Jehoiada the priest and the other priests and asked

---

[a] 15 Or *out from the precincts*   [b] 21 Hebrew *Jehoash*, a variant of *Joash*   [c] 1 Hebrew *Jehoash*, a variant of *Joash*; also in verses 2, 4, 6, 7 and 18

* 11:21 is numbered 12:1 in Hebrew texts.   * 12:1-21 is numbered 12:2-22 in Hebrew texts.

11:14 [x] S 1Ki 7:15
[y] S 1Ki 1:39
[z] S Ge 37:29
[a] 2Ki 9:23
11:15 [b] 1Ki 2:30
11:16 [c] Ne 3:28;
Jer 31:40 [d] S Ge 4:14
11:17 [e] S Ex 24:8;
2Sa 5:3; 2Ch 15:12;
23:3; 29:10; 34:31;
Ezr 10:3 [f] 2Ki 23:3;
Jer 34:8
11:18 [g] S 1Ki 16:32
[h] S Dt 12:3
[i] 1Ki 18:40; 2Ki 10:25;
23:20
11:19 [j] ver 4
11:20 [k] Pr 11:10;
28:12; 29:2
12:1 [l] 2Ki 11:2
12:2 [m] S Dt 12:25;
S 2Sa 8:15
12:3 [n] S 1Ki 3:3;
S 2Ki 18:4
12:4 [o] 2Ki 22:4
[p] Nu 18:19
[q] S Ex 30:12
[r] S Ex 25:2; S 35:29
12:5 [s] 2Ki 22:5

---

hoiada had chosen to stage his coup on a Sabbath during one of the major religious festivals, when many from the realm who were loyal to the Lord would be in Jerusalem.

11:15 *not be put to death in the temple.* So as not to defile God's holy house (see Ex 21:14 and note).

11:17 *covenant between the Lord and the king and people that they would be the Lord's people.* A renewal of the Sinaitic covenant, by which Israel had been constituted as the Lord's people (see Ex 19:5–6; Dt 4:20). The years of apostasy, involving both the royal house and the people of Judah, necessitated a renewal of allegiance to the Lord at the time of an important new beginning for the southern kingdom (see notes on 1Sa 11:14–15; 12:14–15,24–25). *covenant between the king and the people.* Defined responsibilities and mutual obligations of king and people that were compatible with Israel's covenant relationship with the Lord (see notes on 1Sa 10:25; 2Sa 5:3).

11:18 *idols.* Stone pillars (see note on 1Ki 14:23) and Asherah poles (see note on 1Ki 14:15).

11:19 *commanders of hundreds, the Carites, the guards.* See note on v. 4.

11:21 See v. 3. The Lord had preserved a lamp for David in Jerusalem (see 1Ki 11:36).

12:1 *seventh year of Jehu.* 835 B.C. (see note on 10:36). *forty years.* 835–796.

12:2 *all the years Jehoiada the priest instructed him.* After Jehoiada died, Joash turned away from the Lord (see 2Ch 24:17–27).

12:3 *high places . . . were not removed.* These were high places where the Lord was worshiped rather than pagan deities (see note on 1Ki 15:14). They were nevertheless potential sources for the entrance of pagan practices into Israel's worship (see note on 1Ki 3:2).

12:4 *money . . . brought as sacred offerings to the temple.* The money was derived from three different sources: 1. *money collected in the census.* At the age of 20, Israelite youths were required to register for military service and to make an offering of half a shekel (see note on 5:26) for use in the service of the central sanctuary (see Ex 30:11–16; 38:25–26). 2. *money received from personal vows.* Various types of vows and their equivalence in monetary assessments are described in Lev 27:1–25. 3. *money brought voluntarily to the temple.* For voluntary offerings, see Lev 22:18–23; Dt 16:10.

12:5 *treasurers.* Temple functionaries who handled financial matters for the priests relative to the people's sacrifices and offerings. *whatever damage is found in the temple.* Construction of the temple had been completed 124 years before the beginning of the reign of Joash (see notes on v. 1; 1Ki 6:38). In addition to deterioration due to age, it had fallen into disrepair and abuse during the rule of Athaliah (see 2Ch 24:7).

12:6 *twenty-third year of King Joash.* Joash may have instituted his plan for restoration of the temple a few years before the 23rd year of his reign. Now at age 30 he asserts his royal authority and takes charge of the temple repairs.

12:9 ⁱ2Ki 25:18;
Jer 35:4; 52:24
ᵘMk 12:41; Lk 21:1
12:10 ᵛS 2Sa 8:17
12:12 ʷ2Ki 22:5-6
12:13 ˣS 1Ki 7:48-
51
12:15 ʸ2Ki 22:7;
1Co 4:2
12:16 ᶻLev 5:14-19
ᵃLev 4:1-35
ᵇS Lev 7:7
12:17 ᶜ2Ki 8:12
12:18 ᵈS 1Ki 15:18;
S 2Ch 21:16-17
ᵉ1Ki 15:21; 2Ki 15:20;
19:36
12:20 ᶠ2Ki 14:5
ᵍ2Ki 14:19; 15:10,14,
25,30; 21:23; 25:25
ʰJdg 9:6

them, "Why aren't you repairing the damage done to the temple? Take no more money from your treasurers, but hand it over for repairing the temple." ⁸The priests agreed that they would not collect any more money from the people and that they would not repair the temple themselves.

⁹Jehoiada the priest took a chest and bored a hole in its lid. He placed it beside the altar, on the right side as one enters the temple of the LORD. The priests who guarded the entrance ᵗ put into the chest all the money ᵘ that was brought to the temple of the LORD. ¹⁰Whenever they saw that there was a large amount of money in the chest, the royal secretary ᵛ and the high priest came, counted the money that had been brought into the temple of the LORD and put it into bags. ¹¹When the amount had been determined, they gave the money to the men appointed to supervise the work on the temple. With it they paid those who worked on the temple of the LORD—the carpenters and builders, ¹²the masons and stonecutters. ʷ They purchased timber and blocks of dressed stone for the repair of the temple of the LORD, and met all the other expenses of restoring the temple.

¹³The money brought into the temple was not spent for making silver basins, wick trimmers, sprinkling bowls, trumpets or any other articles of gold ˣ or silver for the temple of the LORD; ¹⁴it was paid to the workers, who used it to repair the temple. ¹⁵They did not require an accounting from those to whom they gave the money to pay the workers, because they acted with complete honesty. ʸ ¹⁶The money from the guilt offerings ᶻ and sin offerings ᵃ ᵃ was not brought into the temple of the LORD; it belonged ᵇ to the priests.

¹⁷About this time Hazael ᶜ king of Aram went up and attacked Gath and captured it. Then he turned to attack Jerusalem. ¹⁸But Joash king of Judah took all the sacred objects dedicated by his predecessors—Jehoshaphat, Jehoram and Ahaziah, the kings of Judah—and the gifts he himself had dedicated and all the gold found in the treasuries of the temple of the LORD and of the royal palace, and he sent ᵈ them to Hazael king of Aram, who then withdrew ᵉ from Jerusalem.

¹⁹As for the other events of the reign of Joash, and all he did, are they not written in the book of the annals of the kings of Judah? ²⁰His officials ᶠ conspired against him and assassinated ᵍ him at Beth Millo, ʰ on the road down to Silla. ²¹The officials who murdered him were Jozabad son of Shimeath and Jehozabad son of Shomer. He died and was buried with his ancestors in the City of David. And Amaziah his son succeeded him as king.

ᵃ 16 Or *purification offerings*

12:7 *Take no more money from your treasurers.* The proceeds from the sources of revenue mentioned in v. 4 were no longer to be given to the priests.

12:8 *priests agreed.* Apparently a compromise was reached: The priests would no longer take the money received from the people, but neither would they pay for the temple repairs from the money they had already received.

12:9 *priests who guarded the entrance.* Three high-ranking priests charged with protecting the temple from unlawful (profane) entry (see 25:18; Jer 52:24). *put into the chest all the money.* When the people were assured that all their offerings would be used for the temple restoration, they responded with greater generosity. See 22:3–7 for continuation (or renewal) of this practice in the reign of Josiah.

12:10 *royal secretary.* See note on 2Sa 8:17. Joash arranges for direct royal supervision of the temple's monetary affairs.

12:11 *men appointed.* The whole matter is taken out of the hands of the priests.

12:13 *articles of gold or silver for the temple.* All the money was initially designated for the restoration of the temple. When the restoration was completed, additional funds were used for the acquisition of silver and gold articles for use in the temple service (see 2Ch 24:14).

12:16 *money from the guilt offerings.* See Lev 5:16; 6:5; Nu 5:7–10 for references to priestly income in connection with the bringing of a guilt offering.

12:17 *About this time.* These events must have taken place toward the end of Joash's reign. From 2Ch 24:17–24 it is clear that the Aramean attack was occasioned by Joash's turning away from the Lord after Jehoiada's death. Joash's apostasy reached its climax in the stoning of Jehoiada's son Zechariah (2Ch 24:22). Probably because of Joash's earlier zeal for the

temple, the author of Kings did not choose to relate these matters. *Hazael.* See 8:7–15; 10:32–33; 13:3,22; see also note on 1Ki 19:15. *Gath.* One of the major Philistine cities (see Jos 13:3) that David had conquered (1Ch 18:1) and that continued to be subject to Judah during the reign of Rehoboam (2Ch 11:8). In the latter years of the reign of Joash of Judah (835–796 B.C.) and during the reign of Jehoahaz of Israel (814–798; see 13:3,7), the Arameans had virtually overrun the northern kingdom, enabling them to advance against the Philistines and the kingdom of Judah with little resistance. *he turned to attack Jerusalem.* See 2Ch 24:23–24.

12:18 *sacred objects ... gold ... he sent them to Hazael.* Years earlier, Asa had sought to secure assistance from the Arameans with a similar gift (see 1Ki 15:18).

12:19 *annals of the kings of Judah.* See note on 1Ki 14:29. A fuller account of the reign of Joash is also found in 2Ch 22:10—24:27.

12:20 *conspired against him.* The conspiracy was aroused in response to Joash's murder of Zechariah, son of Jehoiada (see 2Ch 24:25). *Beth Millo.* Beth means "house"; for the meaning of Millo see note on Jdg 9:6. Here the reference may be to a building (perhaps a kind of barracks) built on the "Millo" in the old City of David (see 2Ch 5:9 and note; 1Ki 11:27). Perhaps the king was staying there temporarily with his troops at the time of his assassination; Chronicles says he was killed "in his bed" (2Ch 24:25).

12:21 *officials.* Sons of Ammonite and Moabite mothers (2Ch 24:26), suggesting that they may have been mercenary military officers whose services could have been bought by others. *buried with his ancestors.* But see 2Ch 24:25. *Amaziah his son succeeded him.* For the reign of Amaziah, see 14:1–22.

JEHOAHAZ KING OF ISRAEL

13 In the twenty-third year of Joash son of Ahaziah king of Judah, Jehoahaz son of Jehu became king of Israel in Samaria, and he reigned seventeen years. ²He did evil *i* in the eyes of the LORD by following the sins of Jeroboam son of Nebat, which he had caused Israel to commit, and he did not turn away from them. ³So the LORD's anger *j* burned against Israel, and for a long time he kept them under the power *k* of Hazael king of Aram and Ben-Hadad *l* his son.

⁴Then Jehoahaz sought *m* the LORD's favor, and the LORD listened to him, for he saw *n* how severely the king of Aram was oppressing *o* Israel. ⁵The LORD provided a deliverer *p* for Israel, and they escaped from the power of Aram. So the Israelites lived in their own homes as they had before. ⁶But they did not turn away from the sins *q* of the house of Jeroboam, which he had caused Israel to commit; they continued in them. Also, the Asherah pole *a r* remained standing in Samaria.

⁷Nothing had been left *s* of the army of Jehoahaz except fifty horsemen, ten chariots and ten thousand foot soldiers, for the king of Aram had destroyed the rest and made them like the dust *t* at threshing time.

⁸As for the other events of the reign of Jehoahaz, all he did and his achievements, are they not written in the book of the annals of the kings of Israel? ⁹Jehoahaz rested with his ancestors and was buried in Samaria. And Jehoash *b* his son succeeded him as king.

JEHOASH KING OF ISRAEL

¹⁰In the thirty-seventh year of Joash king of Judah, Jehoash son of Jehoahaz became king of Israel in Samaria, and he reigned sixteen years. ¹¹He did evil in the eyes of the LORD and did not turn away from any of the sins of Jeroboam son of Nebat, which he had caused Israel to commit; he continued in them.

¹²As for the other events of the reign of Jehoash, all he did and his achievements, including his war against Amaziah *u* king of Judah, are they not written in the book of the annals *v* of the kings of Israel? ¹³Jehoash rested with his ancestors, and Jeroboam *w* succeeded him on the throne. Jehoash was buried in Samaria with the kings of Israel.

¹⁴Now Elisha was suffering from the illness from which he died. Jehoash king of Israel went down to see him and wept over him. "My father! My father!" he cried. "The chariots *x* and horsemen of Israel!"

¹⁵Elisha said, "Get a bow and some arrows," *y* and he did so. ¹⁶"Take the bow in your hands," he said to the king of Israel. When he had taken it, Elisha put his hands on the king's hands.

---

a 6 That is, a wooden symbol of the goddess Asherah; here and elsewhere in 2 Kings   *b 9* Hebrew *Joash,* a variant of *Jehoash;* also in verses 12-14 and 25

13:2 *i* 1Ki 12:26-33
13:3 *j* S Dt 31:17
k S 1Ki 19:17 *l* ver 24
13:4 *m* S Dt 4:29
n S Dt 26:7
o S Nu 10:9; 2Sa 7:10
13:5 *p* S Ge 45:7;
S Dt 28:29; S Jdg 2:18
13:6 *q* 1Ki 12:30
r S 1Ki 16:33
13:7 *s* 2Ki 10:32-33
t S 2Sa 22:43
13:12 *u* 2Ki 14:15
v 1Ki 15:31
13:13 *w* 2Ki 14:23;
Hos 1:1
13:14 *x* S 2Ki 2:12
13:15 *y* 1Sa 20:20

13:1 *twenty-third year of Joash.* 814 B.C. (see note on 12:1; see also Introduction to 1 Kings: Chronology). *seventeen years.* 814–798.
13:2 *sins of Jeroboam.* See 1Ki 12:26–32; 13:33–34; 14:16.
13:3 *Hazael.* See notes on 8:12,13,15; 10:33; 1 Ki 19:15. *Ben-Hadad.* See v. 24. His reign began in either 806 or 796 B.C.
13:4 *the LORD listened to him.* Although deliverance did not come during the lifetime of Jehoahaz (see v. 22), the Lord was merciful to his people in spite of their sin, because of his covenant with Abraham, Isaac and Jacob (v. 23).
13:5 *deliverer for Israel.* Probably (1) the Assyrian ruler Adadnirari III (810–783 B.C.), whose attacks on the Arameans of Damascus in 806 and 804 enabled the Israelites to break Aramean control over Israelite territory (see v. 25; 14:25); or (2) Jehoash, son of Jehoahaz (vv. 17,19,25); or (3) Jeroboam II, who was able to extend Israel's boundaries far to the north (see 14:25,27) after the Assyrians had broken the military power of the Arameans.
13:6 *Asherah pole remained standing.* This idol had been set up by Ahab (see 1Ki 16:33) and had either escaped destruction by Jehu when he purged Baal worship from Samaria (see 10:27–28) or been reintroduced during the reign of Jehoahaz.
13:7 *ten chariots.* In effect, a very small police force. Cf. the 2,000 chariots that Ahab was able to deploy against the Assyrians at the battle of Qarqar in 853 B.C. (see note on 1Ki 22:1). *ten thousand foot soldiers.* At the battle of Qarqar Ahab had supplied 10,000 foot soldiers to the coalition of forces opposing the Assyrians. At that time this would have represented only a con-

tingent of Israel's army, while now it represented the entire Israelite infantry. In 857 Ahab had inflicted 100,000 casualties on the Aramean foot soldiers in one day (see 1Ki 20:29).
13:8 *annals of the kings of Israel.* See note on 1Ki 14:19.
13:9 *rested with his ancestors.* See note on 1Ki 1:21.
13:10 *thirty-seventh year of Joash.* 798 B.C. (see note on 12:1). *sixteen years.* 798–782.
13:11 *sins of Jeroboam.* See 1Ki 12:26–32; 13:33–34; 14:16.
13:12 *war against Amaziah.* See 14:8–14; 2Ch 25:17–24. *annals of the kings of Israel.* See note on 1Ki 14:19.
13:13 *rested with his ancestors.* See note on 1Ki 1:21. *Jeroboam succeeded him.* For the reign of Jeroboam II, see 14:23–29.
13:14 *Elisha was suffering.* Ch. 9 contains the last previous reference to Elisha. Since Jehu had been anointed in 841 B.C. (see note on 10:36) and Jehoash began to reign in 798 (see note on v. 10), there is at least a 43-year period in which we are told nothing of Elisha's activities. Based on Elisha's relationship with Elijah, he must have been born prior to 880 and have lived to be more than 80 years of age. *The chariots and horsemen of Israel!* An expression of recognition by Jehoash that Elisha was of greater significance for Israel's military success than Israel's military forces were (see notes on 2:12; 6:13,16–23).
13:16 *put his hands on the king's hands.* By this symbolic act Elisha indicated that Jehoash was to engage the Arameans in battle with the Lord's blessing on him.

13:17 *z* Jos 8:18
a S 1Ki 20:26
13:19 *b* ver 25
13:20 *c* S 2Ki 5:2
13:21 *d* Mt 27:52
13:22 *e* S 1Ki 19:17
13:23 *f* S Ex 2:24
g S Dt 29:20
h S Ex 33:15;
2Ki 17:18; 24:3,20
13:24 *i* ver 3
13:25 *j* ver 18,19
k S 2Ki 10:32
14:4 *l* 2Ki 12:3
14:5 *m* 2Ki 21:24
n 2Ki 12:20
14:6 *o* S Dt 28:61
p S Nu 26:11;
Job 21:20; Jer 31:30;
44:3; Eze 18:4,20
14:7 *q* S 2Sa 8:13
r S Jdg 1:36

¹⁷"Open the east window," he said, and he opened it. "Shoot!"*z* Elisha said, and he shot. "The LORD's arrow of victory, the arrow of victory over Aram!" Elisha declared. "You will completely destroy the Arameans at Aphek."*a*

¹⁸Then he said, "Take the arrows," and the king took them. Elisha told him, "Strike the ground." He struck it three times and stopped. ¹⁹The man of God was angry with him and said, "You should have struck the ground five or six times; then you would have defeated Aram and completely destroyed it. But now you will defeat it only three times."*b*

²⁰Elisha died and was buried.

Now Moabite raiders*c* used to enter the country every spring. ²¹Once while some Israelites were burying a man, suddenly they saw a band of raiders; so they threw the man's body into Elisha's tomb. When the body touched Elisha's bones, the man came to life*d* and stood up on his feet.

²²Hazael king of Aram oppressed*e* Israel throughout the reign of Jehoahaz. ²³But the LORD was gracious to them and had compassion and showed concern for them because of his covenant*f* with Abraham, Isaac and Jacob. To this day he has been unwilling to destroy*g* them or banish them from his presence.*h*

²⁴Hazael king of Aram died, and Ben-Hadad*i* his son succeeded him as king. ²⁵Then Jehoash son of Jehoahaz recaptured from Ben-Hadad son of Hazael the towns he had taken in battle from his father Jehoahaz. Three times*j* Jehoash defeated him, and so he recovered*k* the Israelite towns.

AMAZIAH KING OF JUDAH
14:1–7pp — 2Ch 25:1–4,11–12
14:8–22pp — 2Ch 25:17—26:2

14 In the second year of Jehoash*a* son of Jehoahaz king of Israel, Amaziah son of Joash king of Judah began to reign. ²He was twenty-five years old when he became king, and he reigned in Jerusalem twenty-nine years. His mother's name was Jehoaddan; she was from Jerusalem. ³He did what was right in the eyes of the LORD, but not as his father David had done. In everything he followed the example of his father Joash. ⁴The high places,*l* however, were not removed; the people continued to offer sacrifices and burn incense there.

⁵After the kingdom was firmly in his grasp, he executed*m* the officials*n* who had murdered his father the king. ⁶Yet he did not put the children of the assassins to death, in accordance with what is written in the Book of the Law*o* of Moses where the LORD commanded: "Parents are not to be put to death for their children, nor children put to death for their parents; each of you will die for your own sin."*b p*

⁷He was the one who defeated ten thousand Edomites in the Valley of Salt*q* and captured Sela*r* in battle, calling it Joktheel, the name it has to this day.

a 1 Hebrew *Joash*, a variant of *Jehoash*; also in verses 13, 23 and 27   *b 6* Deut. 24:16

13:17 *east window.* Faced Transjordan, which was controlled by the Arameans (see 10:32–33). *Aphek.* About 60 years earlier Ahab had won a decisive victory at Aphek over the Arameans and Ben-Hadad II (see 1Ki 20:26–30 and note on 20:26).
13:18 *struck it three times and stopped.* The moderately enthusiastic response to Elisha's directive reflected insufficient zeal for accomplishing the announced task.
13:19 *defeat it only three times.* Jehoash's moderate enthusiasm in striking the ground with arrows symbolized the moderate success he would have against the Arameans. It would be left for Jeroboam II, son of Jehoash, to gain complete victory over them (see 14:25,28).
C **13:21** *When the body touched Elisha's bones, the man came to life.* The life-giving power of the God Elisha represented is demonstrated once again in this last OT reference to Elisha (for previous demonstrations of this power, see 4:32–37 and 1Ki 17:17–24; for Elijah's translation to heaven without dying, see 2:11–12).
A **13:23** *To this day.* Until the time of the writing of the source from which the author derived this account (see note on 1Ki 8:8; see also Introduction to 1 Kings: Author, Sources and Date). *unwilling to destroy them or banish them.* In his mercy and grace the Lord was long-suffering toward his people and refrained from full implementation of the covenant curse of ex-

ile from Canaan (see note on 10:32). This postponement of judgment provided Israel with the opportunity to repent and return to covenant faithfulness.
13:24 *Ben-Hadad.* See note on v. 3.
13:25 *towns he had taken . . . from . . . Jehoahaz.* Probably towns west of the Jordan, since the area east of the Jordan had been lost already in the time of Jehu (see 10:32–33). It was not until the time of Jeroboam II that the area east of the Jordan was fully recovered for Israel (see 14:25). *Three times.* In fulfillment of Elisha's prophecy (v. 19).
14:1 *second year of Jehoash.* See note on 13:10).
14:2 *twenty-nine years.* 796–767. Amaziah's 29-year reign included a 24-year coregency with his son Azariah (see notes on v. 21; 15:1–2).
C **14:3** *not as his father David.* Amaziah did not remain completely free from involvement with the worship of pagan deities (see 2Ch 25:14–16). His loyalty to the Lord fell short of that of Asa and Jehoshaphat before him (see 1Ki 15:11,14; 22:43; see also 1Ki 9:4; 11:4).
14:4 *high places, however, were not removed.* See note on 1Ki 15:14.
14:7 *defeated ten thousand Edomites.* Amaziah was able to regain temporarily (see 2Ch 28:17) some of Judah's control over the Edomites, which had been lost during the reign of Jehoram

14:9 ⁸ Jdg 9:8-15
14:10 ¹ 2Ch 26:16;
32:25
14:11 ᵘ S Jos 15:10
14:12 ᵛ 1Ki 22:36
14:13 ʷ 1Ki 3:1;
2Ch 33:14; 36:19;
Jer 39:2 ˣ Ne 8:16;
12:39 ʸ 2Ch 26:9;
Jer 31:38; Zec 14:10
14:15 ᶻ 2Ki 13:12
14:19 ᵃ S 2Ki 12:20
ᵇ S Jos 10:3
14:20 ᶜ S 2Ki 9:28
14:21 ᵈ 2Ki 15:1;
2Ch 26:23; Isa 1:1;
Hos 1:1; Am 1:1
14:22 ᵉ S 1Ki 9:26
14:23 ᶠ S 2Ki 13:13;
1Ch 5:17; Am 1:1; 7:10

⁸Then Amaziah sent messengers to Jehoash son of Jehoahaz, the son of Jehu, king of Israel, with the challenge: "Come, meet me face to face."

⁹But Jehoash king of Israel replied to Amaziah king of Judah: "A thistle ˢ in Lebanon sent a message to a cedar in Lebanon, 'Give your daughter to my son in marriage.' Then a wild beast in Lebanon came along and trampled the thistle underfoot. ¹⁰You have indeed defeated Edom and now you are arrogant. ᵗ Glory in your victory, but stay at home! Why ask for trouble and cause your own downfall and that of Judah also?"

¹¹Amaziah, however, would not listen, so Jehoash king of Israel attacked. He and Amaziah king of Judah faced each other at Beth Shemesh ᵘ in Judah. ¹²Judah was routed by Israel, and every man fled to his home. ᵛ ¹³Jehoash king of Israel captured Amaziah king of Judah, the son of Joash, the son of Ahaziah, at Beth Shemesh. Then Jehoash went to Jerusalem and broke down the wall ʷ of Jerusalem from the Ephraim Gate ˣ to the Corner Gate ʸ—a section about four hundred cubits long. ᵃ ¹⁴He took all the gold and silver and all the articles found in the temple of the LORD and in the treasuries of the royal palace. He also took hostages and returned to Samaria.

¹⁵As for the other events of the reign of Jehoash, what he did and his achievements, including his war ᶻ against Amaziah king of Judah, are they not written in the book of the annals of the kings of Israel? ¹⁶Jehoash rested with his ancestors and was buried in Samaria with the kings of Israel. And Jeroboam his son succeeded him as king.

¹⁷Amaziah son of Joash king of Judah lived for fifteen years after the death of Jehoash son of Jehoahaz king of Israel. ¹⁸As for the other events of Amaziah's reign, are they not written in the book of the annals of the kings of Judah?

¹⁹They conspired ᵃ against him in Jerusalem, and he fled to Lachish, ᵇ but they sent men after him to Lachish and killed him there. ²⁰He was brought back by horse ᶜ and was buried in Jerusalem with his ancestors, in the City of David.

²¹Then all the people of Judah took Azariah, ᵇ ᵈ who was sixteen years old, and made him king in place of his father Amaziah. ²²He was the one who rebuilt Elath ᵉ and restored it to Judah after Amaziah rested with his ancestors.

JEROBOAM II KING OF ISRAEL

²³In the fifteenth year of Amaziah son of Joash king of Judah, Jeroboam ᶠ son of Jehoash king of Israel became king in Samaria, and he reigned forty-one years. ²⁴He did evil

ᵃ 13 That is, about 600 feet or about 180 meters   ᵇ 21 Also called Uzziah

---

(see 8:20–22). *Valley of Salt.* The same battlefield on which David had defeated the Edomites (see 2Sa 8:13; 1Ch 18:12; Ps 60 title), generally identified with the Arabah directly south of the Dead Sea. *Sela.* Means "rock"; often regarded as the Edomite stronghold presently known as Petra (a Greek word meaning "rock"; see Jdg 1:36; Isa 16:1; 42:11; Ob 3). *to this day.* Until the time of the writing of the account of Amaziah's reign used by the author (see note on 1Ki 8:8; see also Introduction to 1 Kings: Author, Sources and Date).
14:8 *meet me face to face.* A challenge amounting to a declaration of war. Perhaps it was provoked by the hostile actions of mercenary troops from the northern kingdom after their dismissal from the Judahite army (see 2Ch 25:10,13) and by the refusal of Jehoash to establish a marriage alliance with Amaziah (see v. 9).
14:9 *Jehoash...replied.* For his reply Jehoash used a fable (see Jdg 9:8–15) in which he represented himself as a strong cedar and Amaziah as an insignificant thistle that could easily be trampled underfoot.
14:11 *would not listen.* See 2Ch 25:20. *Beth Shemesh.* A town about 15 miles west of Jerusalem (see Jos 15:10; 1Sa 6:9 and note).
14:13 *Jehoash...captured Amaziah.* It is likely that Amaziah was taken back to the northern kingdom as a prisoner, where he remained until being released to return to Judah after the death of Jehoash (see vv. 15–16; see also note on v. 21). *Ephraim Gate to the Corner Gate.* The Corner Gate (see Jer 31:38; Zec 14:10) was at the northwest corner of the wall around Jerusalem. The Ephraim Gate was on the north side of Jerusalem (see Ne 12:39), 600 feet east of the Corner Gate. This northwestern section of the wall of Jerusalem was the point at which the city was most vulnerable to attack.

14:14 *gold and silver and all the articles found in the temple...and ...the royal palace.* The value of the plundered articles was probably not great, because Joash had previously stripped the temple and palace to pay tribute to Hazael of Damascus (see 12:17–18). *took hostages.* The hostages were probably intended to secure additional payments of tribute in view of the meager war booty.
14:15 *annals of the kings of Israel.* See note on 1Ki 14:19.
14:16 *rested with his ancestors.* See 13:12–13; see also note on 1Ki 1:21.
14:17 *lived for fifteen years after the death of Jehoash.* Jehoash died in 782 B.C. and Amaziah in 767.
14:18 *annals of the kings of Judah.* See note on 1Ki 14:29.
■ 14:19 *conspired against him.* 2Ch 25:27 connects the conspiracy against Amaziah with his turning away from the Lord, but it did not serve the purpose of the author of Kings to note this. *Lachish.* A fortress city in southern Judah 15 miles west of Hebron, presently known as Tell ed-Duweir (see 18:14; 2Ch 11:9).
14:21 *Then all the people of Judah took Azariah, who was.* Or "Now all the people of Judah had taken Azariah, when he was." See TNIV text note and 15:13. *made him king in place of his father Amaziah.* It is likely that this occurred after Amaziah had been taken prisoner by Jehoash (see v. 13). Thus Azariah's reign substantially overlapped that of his father, Amaziah (see notes on v. 2; 15:2).
■ 14:22 *rebuilt Elath and restored it to Judah.* Azariah extended the subjection of the Edomites begun by his father (see v. 7) and reestablished Israelite control over the important port city on the Gulf of Aqaba (see 1Ki 9:26). A royal seal inscribed "belonging to Jotham" (see 15:32) found near the site of ancient Elath attests Judahite presence there during this period. *rested with his ancestors.* See note on 1Ki 1:21.
14:23 *fifteenth year of Amaziah.* 782 B.C. (see note on v. 2). This

14:24 ᵍ S 1Ki 15:30
14:25 ʰ S Nu 13:21
ⁱ Dt 3:17 / Jnh 1:1;
Mt 12:39
14:26 ᵏ Dt 32:36
ˡ 2Ki 13:4 ᵐ Ps 18:41;
22:11; 72:12; 107:12;
Isa 63:5; La 1:7
14:27 ⁿ S Dt 29:20
ᵒ S Jdg 6:14
14:28 ᵖ S 2Sa 8:5
ᵍ S 2Sa 8:9 ʳ 1Ki 15:31
15:1 ˢ S ver 32;
S 2Ki 14:21
15:3 ᵗ S 1Ki 14:8
15:5 ᵘ S Ge 12:17
ᵛ Lev 13:46 ʷ ver 7,
32; 2Ch 27:1; Mic 1:1
ˣ S Ge 41:40
15:7 ʸ Isa 6:1; 14:28
ᶻ S ver 5

in the eyes of the LORD and did not turn away from any of the sins of Jeroboam son of Nebat, which he had caused Israel to commit. ᵍ ²⁵He was the one who restored the boundaries of Israel from Lebo Hamath ʰ to the Dead Sea, ᵃ ⁱ in accordance with the word of the LORD, the God of Israel, spoken through his servant Jonah ʲ son of Amittai, the prophet from Gath Hepher.

²⁶The LORD had seen how bitterly everyone in Israel, whether slave or free, ᵏ was suffering; ᵇ ˡ there was no one to help them. ᵐ ²⁷And since the LORD had not said he would blot out ⁿ the name of Israel from under heaven, he saved ᵒ them by the hand of Jeroboam son of Jehoash.

²⁸As for the other events of Jeroboam's reign, all he did, and his military achievements, including how he recovered for Israel both Damascus ᵖ and Hamath, ᵍ which had belonged to Judah, are they not written in the book of the annals ʳ of the kings of Israel? ²⁹Jeroboam rested with his ancestors, the kings of Israel. And Zechariah his son succeeded him as king.

AZARIAH KING OF JUDAH

15:1–7pp — 2Ch 26:3–4,21–23

15 In the twenty-seventh year of Jeroboam king of Israel, Azariah ᶜ ˢ son of Amaziah king of Judah began to reign. ²He was sixteen years old when he became king, and he reigned in Jerusalem fifty-two years. His mother's name was Jekoliah; she was from Jerusalem. ³He did what was right ᵗ in the eyes of the LORD, just as his father Amaziah had done. ⁴The high places, however, were not removed; the people continued to offer sacrifices and burn incense there.

⁵The LORD afflicted ᵘ the king with leprosy ᵈ until the day he died, and he lived in a separate house. ᵉ ᵛ Jotham ʷ the king's son had charge of the palace ˣ and governed the people of the land.

⁶As for the other events of Azariah's reign, and all he did, are they not written in the book of the annals of the kings of Judah? ⁷Azariah rested ʸ with his ancestors and was buried near them in the City of David. And Jotham ᶻ his son succeeded him as king.

ᵃ 25 Hebrew *the Sea of the Arabah*   ᵇ 26 Or *Israel was suffering. They were without a ruler or leader, and*   ᶜ 1 Also called *Uzziah*; also in verses 6, 7, 8, 17, 23 and 27   ᵈ 5 The Hebrew for *leprosy* was used for various diseases affecting the skin.   ᵉ 5 Or *in a house where he was relieved of responsibilities*

---

was the beginning of Jeroboam's sole reign. He had previously served as coregent with his father, Jehoash. *forty-one years.* 793–753 (including the coregency with his father).

14:24 *sins of Jeroboam.* See 1Ki 12:26–32; 13:33–34; 14:16; Am 3:13–14; 4:4–5; 5:4–6; 7:10–17.

C 14:25 *from Lebo Hamath.* Jeroboam II was able to free the northern kingdom from the oppression it had suffered at the hands of Hazael and Ben-Hadad (see 10:32; 12:17; 13:3,22,25). He also extended Israelite political control over the Arameans of Damascus, an undertaking that had been begun by his father, Jehoash (see 13:25). Assyrian pressure on the Arameans, including attacks on Damascus by Shalmaneser IV in 773 B.C. and Ashur-Dan III in 772, had weakened the Arameans enough to enable Jeroboam II to gain the upper hand over them. Meanwhile, Assyria also became too weak to suppress Jeroboam's expansion. *Dead Sea.* See TNIV text note. According to Am 6:14 the southern limit of Jeroboam's kingdom in Transjordan was the "valley of the Arabah"— probably to be connected with the Valley of Salt (see note on v. 7). If so, Jeroboam had also subdued Moab and the Ammonites. *word of the LORD ... spoken through ... Jonah.* Not found in the book of Jonah. However, mention of the prophet here helps to date his ministry. *Gath Hepher.* Located in the tribe of Zebulun, northeast of Nazareth (see Jos 19:13).

14:26 *slave or free.* See TNIV text note; see also note on 1Ki 14:10. *suffering.* At the hands of the Arameans (see note on 10:32–33; 13:3–7), the Moabites (13:20) and the Ammonites (Am 1:13).

14:27 *had not said.* The sin of the Israelites had not yet reached its full measure, and the Lord mercifully extended to the nation an additional period of grace in which there was opportunity to repent (see note on 13:23). Persistence in apostasy, however, would bring certain judgment (see Am 4:2–3; 6:14). *saved them*

by the hand of Jeroboam. See note on 13:5.

C 14:28 *all he did.* During Jeroboam's reign the northern kingdom enjoyed greater material prosperity than at any time since the rule of David and Solomon. Unfortunately, it was also a time of religious formalism and apostasy, as well as social injustice (see the books of Amos and Hosea, who prophesied during Jeroboam's reign). *Damascus and Hamath.* See note on v. 25. *annals of the kings of Israel.* See note on 1Ki 14:19.

14:29 *rested with his ancestors.* See note on 1Ki 1:21. *Zechariah his son succeeded him.* For the reign of Zechariah, see 15:8–12.

15:1 *twenty-seventh year of Jeroboam.* 767 B.C., based on dating the beginning of Jeroboam's coregency with Jehoash in 793 (see note on 14:23). *Azariah ... began to reign.* He began his sole reign, after a 24-year coregency with his father, Amaziah (see notes on v. 2; 14:2,21). (His actual years were one less than his official years.)

15:2 *fifty-two years.* 792–740 B.C. (but he was coregent with his father, Amaziah 792–767). See note on v. 1.

15:3 *as his father Amaziah had done.* See note on 14:3.

15:4 *high places, however, were not removed.* See 14:4; see also note on 1Ki 15:14.

15:5 *afflicted the king with leprosy.* See TNIV text note; a punishment for usurping the priestly function of burning incense on the altar in the temple (see 2Ch 26:16–21; cf. Lev 13:46). *had charge of the palace and governed the people of the land.* Jotham ruled for his father for the remainder of Azariah's life (750–740 B.C.; see note on v. 33).

15:6 *all he did.* A more detailed account of Azariah's accomplishments is found in 2Ch 26:1–15. *annals of the kings of Judah.* See note on 1Ki 14:29.

15:7 *rested with his ancestors.* See note on 1Ki 1:21. *Jotham his son succeeded him.* For the reign of Jotham, see vv. 32–38.

ZECHARIAH KING OF ISRAEL

⁸In the thirty-eighth year of Azariah king of Judah, Zechariah son of Jeroboam became king of Israel in Samaria, and he reigned six months. ⁹He did evil ᵃ in the eyes of the LORD, as his predecessors had done. He did not turn away from the sins of Jeroboam son of Nebat, which he had caused Israel to commit.

¹⁰Shallum son of Jabesh conspired against Zechariah. He attacked him in front of the people, ᵃ assassinated ᵇ him and succeeded him as king. ¹¹The other events of Zechariah's reign are written in the book of the annals ᶜ of the kings of Israel. ¹²So the word of the LORD spoken to Jehu was fulfilled: ᵈ "Your descendants will sit on the throne of Israel to the fourth generation." ᵇ

SHALLUM KING OF ISRAEL

¹³Shallum son of Jabesh became king in the thirty-ninth year of Uzziah king of Judah, and he reigned in Samaria ᵉ one month. ¹⁴Then Menahem son of Gadi went from Tirzah ᶠ up to Samaria. He attacked Shallum son of Jabesh in Samaria, assassinated ᵍ him and succeeded him as king.

¹⁵The other events of Shallum's reign, and the conspiracy he led, are written in the book of the annals ʰ of the kings of Israel.

¹⁶At that time Menahem, starting out from Tirzah, attacked Tiphsah ⁱ and everyone in the city and its vicinity, because they refused to open ʲ their gates. He sacked Tiphsah and ripped open all the pregnant women.

MENAHEM KING OF ISRAEL

¹⁷In the thirty-ninth year of Azariah king of Judah, Menahem son of Gadi became king of Israel, and he reigned in Samaria ten years. ¹⁸He did evil ᵏ in the eyes of the LORD. During his entire reign he did not turn away from the sins of Jeroboam son of Nebat, which he had caused Israel to commit.

¹⁹Then Pul ᶜ ˡ king of Assyria invaded the land, and Menahem gave him a thousand talents ᵈ of silver to gain his support and strengthen his own hold on the kingdom. ²⁰Menahem exacted this money from Israel. Every wealthy person had to contribute fifty shekels ᵉ of silver to be given to the king of Assyria. So the king of Assyria withdrew ᵐ and stayed in the land no longer.

²¹As for the other events of Menahem's reign, and all he did, are they not written in the book of the annals of the kings of Israel? ²²Menahem rested with his ancestors. And Pekahiah his son succeeded him as king.

ᵃ 10 Hebrew; some Septuagint manuscripts *in Ibleam*   ᵇ 12 2 Kings 10:30   ᶜ 19 Also called *Tiglath-Pileser*   ᵈ 19 That is, about 38 tons or about 34 metric tons   ᵉ 20 That is, about 1 1/4 pounds or about 575 grams

---

15:9 ᵃ1Ki 15:26
15:10 ᵇS 2Ki 12:20
15:11 ᶜ1Ki 15:31
15:12 ᵈ2Ki 10:30
15:13 ᵉS 1Ki 13:32
15:14 ᶠS 1Ki 15:33
ᵍS 2Ki 12:20
15:15 ʰ1Ki 15:31
15:16 ⁱ1Ki 4:24
ʲS 2Ki 8:12;
S Hos 13:16
15:18 ᵏ1Ki 15:26
15:19 ˡ1Ch 5:6,26
15:20 ᵐS 2Ki 12:18

15:8 *thirty-eighth year of Azariah.* 753 B.C. (see note on v. 2).

15:9 *sins of Jeroboam.* See 1Ki 12:26–32; 13:33–34; 14:16.

15:11 *annals of the kings of Israel.* See note on 1Ki 14:19.

C **15:12** *word of the LORD ... was fulfilled.* See TNIV text note. With the downfall of Jehu's dynasty, the northern kingdom entered a period of political instability (see Hos 1:4). The remaining five kings of the northern kingdom were all assassinated, with the exception of Menahem, who reigned ten years, and Hoshea, who was imprisoned by the Assyrians. From the strength and wealth of the reign of Jeroboam II, the decline and fall of the northern kingdom was swift.

15:13 *thirty-ninth year of Uzziah.* 752 B.C. (see note on v. 2). Uzziah is another name for Azariah (see note on 14:21).

15:14 *Menahem ... went from Tirzah up to Samaria.* It is likely that Menahem was the commander of a military garrison at Tirzah, the former capital of the northern kingdom (see 1Ki 14:17; 15:21, 33). *succeeded him.* For the reign of Menahem, see vv. 17–22.

15:15 *annals of the kings of Israel.* See note on 1Ki 14:19.

15:16 *Tiphsah.* There was a Tiphsah located far to the north of Hamath (see 14:25) on the Euphrates River (see 1Ki 4:24). It is unlikely that this was the city intended. Some interpreters prefer the reading "Tappuah" of the Septuagint (the pre-Christian Greek translation of the OT). Tappuah was a city on the border between Ephraim and Manasseh (Jos 16:8; 17:7–8). Perhaps there was a Tiphsah in Israel not otherwise mentioned. *ripped open all the pregnant women.* See 8:12 and note.

15:17 *thirty-ninth year of Azariah.* 752 B.C. (see note on v. 2). *ten years.* 752–742.

15:18 *sins of Jeroboam.* See 1Ki 12:26–32; 13:33–34; 14:16.

B **15:19** *Pul.* The Babylonian name (see 1Ch 5:26) of the Assyrian ruler Tiglath-Pileser III (745–727 B.C.; see TNIV text note). *invaded the land.* Assyrian annals of Tiglath-Pileser III indicate that he marched west with his army in 743 and took tribute from, among others, Carchemish, Hamath, Tyre, Byblos, Damascus, and Menahem of Samaria (see map 7 and maps No. 7 and 8 at the end of this study Bible). *thousand talents.* See TNIV text note. This was an enormous sum of money. For the relative value of a talent of silver see note on 5:5. *gain his support and strengthen his own hold.* It appears that as a usurper Menahem still felt insecure on the throne. The opposition to his rule may have come from those following the leadership of Pekah, who favored an alliance with the Arameans of Damascus in order to resist the Assyrian threat (see note on v. 27). Hosea denounced the policy of seeking aid from the Assyrians and predicted that it would fail (Hos 5:13–15).

15:20 *fifty shekels.* See TNIV text note. A simple calculation reveals that it would require approximately 60,000 men of means to provide the 1,000 talents of tribute. This gives some indication of the prosperity the northern kingdom had enjoyed during the time of Jeroboam II.

15:21 *annals of the kings of Israel.* See note on 1Ki 14:19.

15:22 *rested with his ancestors.* See note on 1Ki 1:21.

The Assyrian invasions of the eighth century B.C. were the most traumatic political events in the entire history of Israel.

The brutal Assyrian style of warfare relied on massive armies, superbly equipped with the world's first great siege machines, manipulated by an efficient corps of engineers.

Psychological terror, however, was Assyria's most effective weapon. It was ruthlessly applied, with corpses impaled on stakes, severed heads stacked in heaps, and captives skinned alive.

The shock of bloody military sieges on both Israel and Judah was profound. The prophets did not fail to scream out against their horror, while at the same time pleading with the people to see God's hand in history, to recognize spiritual causes in the present punishment.

1. CAMPAIGNS OF TIGLATH-PILESER III (738–732 B.C.)

King Tiglath-Pileser of Assyria (745–727 B.C.) proved to be a vigorous campaigner, first exacting tribute from Menahem and then annexing Hamath, Philistia, Galilee, Gilead and Aram-Damascus (738–732 B.C.) during the reign of Pekah.

The ferocious onslaught against the northern tribes left only central Israel and the capital city of Samaria intact.

By this time Israel was a tiny nation wracked by pro- and anti-Assyrian factions, multiple assassinations, hypocrisy, arrogance and fear.

Campaign of 738 B.C.
Campaign of 734 B.C.
Campaign of 733 B.C.
Capture of Damascus 732 B.C.

Hamath
Orontes R.
738
734
732
Damascus
732
Ijon
Abel Beth Maakah
Kedesh
Janoah
Hazor
Litani R.
Megiddo
Dor
Dothan
733
Samaria
734
Joppa
Jerusalem
PHILISTIA

Miles 0 20 40
Kms 0 20 40 60

Orontes R.
Hamath
Sidon
Tyre
Akko
Litani R.
Damascus
Gezer
Ashdod
Gaza
Rapha
Samaria
Jerusalem
Nile R.
Wadi of Egypt
EGYPT

3. SENNACHERIB'S CAMPAIGN AGAINST JUDAH (701 B.C.)

B In the 14th year of Hezekiah, the Assyrians finally attacked Judah. The Prism of Sennacherib calls Hezekiah "overbearing and proud," indicating that he was part of Philistia's and Egypt's effort to rebel against Assyria.

A battle in the plain of Eltekeh was won by Assyria; the Egyptian and Cushite charioteers fled. Lachish was besieged and taken. Sennacherib's annals note: "As for Hezekiah the Jew, he did not submit to my yoke. I laid siege to 46 of his strong cities, walled forts and the countless small villages in their vicinity, and conquered them by means of well-stamped earth ramps and battering-rams brought near to the walls combined with the attack by foot-soldiers, using mines, breaches and sapper work. I drove out 200,150 people, young and old, male and female, horses, mules, donkeys, camels, big and small cattle beyond counting, and considered them booty. Himself I made a prisoner in Jerusalem, his royal residence, like a bird in a cage."

Nowhere, however, does the boastful Assyrian king record the disaster mentioned in 2Ki 19:35–36; 2Ch 32:21; Isa 37:36–37.

2. CAMPAIGN OF SHALMANESER V (725–722 B.C.)

The last king of Israel, Hoshea, conspired with Egypt and withheld the annual tribute to the Assyrians.

A protracted three-year siege conducted by Shalmaneser and concluded by Sargon II saw the end of the Israelite kingdom in 722–721 B.C.

B At that time, according to Assyrian annals, "I (Sargon) besieged and conquered Samaria, led away as booty 27,290 inhabitants ... I installed over (those remaining) an officer of mine and imposed upon them the tribute of the former king."

15:24 *n* 1Ki 15:26
15:25 *o* 2Ch 28:6;
Isa 7:1 *P* S 2Ki 12:20
15:27 *a* 2Ch 28:6;
Isa 7:1 *r* Isa 7:4
15:29 *s* 2Ki 16:7;
17:6; 1Ch 5:26;
2Ch 28:20; Jer 50:17
t 1Ki 15:20 *u* 2Ki 16:9;
17:24; 2Ch 16:4;
Isa 7:9; 9:1; 10:9,10;
28:1; 36:19; 37:18
v 2Ki 24:14-16;
1Ch 5:22; Isa 14:6,17;
36:17; 45:13
15:30 *w* 2Ki 17:1
x S 2Ki 12:20
15:31 *y* 1Ki 15:31
15:32 *z* ver 1,S 5;
1Ch 5:17; Isa 1:1;
Hos 1:1
15:34 *a* S 1Ki 14:8
15:35 *b* 2Ki 12:3
c S Ge 23:10;
2Ch 23:20
15:37 *d* 2Ki 16:5;
Isa 7:1; 8:6; 9:11

PEKAHIAH KING OF ISRAEL

23 In the fiftieth year of Azariah king of Judah, Pekahiah son of Menahem became king of Israel in Samaria, and he reigned two years. 24 Pekahiah did evil *n* in the eyes of the LORD. He did not turn away from the sins of Jeroboam son of Nebat, which he had caused Israel to commit. 25 One of his chief officers, Pekah *o* son of Remaliah, conspired against him. Taking fifty Gileadites with him, he assassinated *p* Pekahiah, along with Argob and Arieh, in the citadel of the royal palace at Samaria. So Pekah killed Pekahiah and succeeded him as king.

26 The other events of Pekahiah's reign, and all he did, are written in the book of the annals of the kings of Israel.

PEKAH KING OF ISRAEL

27 In the fifty-second year of Azariah king of Judah, Pekah *q* son of Remaliah *r* became king of Israel in Samaria, and he reigned twenty years. 28 He did evil in the eyes of the LORD. He did not turn away from the sins of Jeroboam son of Nebat, which he had caused Israel to commit.

29 In the time of Pekah king of Israel, Tiglath-Pileser *s* king of Assyria came and took Ijon, *t* Abel Beth Maakah, Janoah, Kedesh and Hazor. He took Gilead and Galilee, including all the land of Naphtali, *u* and deported *v* the people to Assyria. 30 Then Hoshea *w* son of Elah conspired against Pekah son of Remaliah. He attacked and assassinated *x* him, and then succeeded him as king in the twentieth year of Jotham son of Uzziah.

31 As for the other events of Pekah's reign, and all he did, are they not written in the book of the annals *y* of the kings of Israel?

JOTHAM KING OF JUDAH
15:33–38pp — 2Ch 27:1–4,7–9

32 In the second year of Pekah son of Remaliah king of Israel, Jotham *z* son of Uzziah king of Judah began to reign. 33 He was twenty-five years old when he became king, and he reigned in Jerusalem sixteen years. His mother's name was Jerusha daughter of Zadok. 34 He did what was right *a* in the eyes of the LORD, just as his father Uzziah had done. 35 The high places, *b* however, were not removed; the people continued to offer sacrifices and burn incense there. Jotham rebuilt the Upper Gate *c* of the temple of the LORD.

36 As for the other events of Jotham's reign, and what he did, are they not written in the book of the annals of the kings of Judah? 37 (In those days the LORD began to send Rezin *d* king of Aram and Pekah son of Remaliah against Judah.) 38 Jotham rested with his ancestors and was buried with them in the City of David, the city of his father. And Ahaz his son succeeded him as king.

15:23 *fiftieth year of Azariah.* 742 B.C. (see note on v. 2). *two years.* 742–740.
15:24 *sins of Jeroboam.* See 1Ki 12:26–32; 13:33–34; 14:16.
15:25 *One of his chief officers.* Pekah was probably the ranking official in the Transjordan provinces, but his allegiance to Menahem and Pekahiah may well have been more apparent than real (see note on v. 27). *conspired against him.* Differences over foreign policy probably played an important role in fomenting Pekah's revolution. Pekahiah undoubtedly followed the policy of his father Menahem in seeking Assyria's friendship (see v. 20). Pekah advocated friendly relations with the Arameans of Damascus in order to counter potential Assyrian aggression (see 16:1–9; Isa 7:1–2,4–6).
15:26 *annals of the kings of Israel.* See note on 1Ki 14:19.
15:27 *fifty-second year of Azariah.* 740 B.C. (see note on v. 2). *twenty years.* 752–732, based on the assumptions (which the data seem to require) that Pekah had established in Transjordan virtually a rival government to that of Menahem when Menahem assassinated Shallum (see notes on vv. 17,19,25) and that the number of regnal years given here includes this period of rival rule.
15:28 *sins of Jeroboam.* See 1Ki 12:26–32; 13:33–34; 14:16.
15:29 *Tiglath-Pileser king of Assyria came.* See note on v. 19; see also map, p. 564. The historical background for this attack is found in 16:5–9; 2Ch 28:16–21; Isa 7:1–17. *Ijon … Naphtali.* Over 150 years earlier Ben-Hadad I of Damascus had taken this same territory from the northern kingdom in response to an appeal by a king of Judah (see notes on 1Ki 15:19–20). *deported the people to Assyria.* See 1Ch 5:26. The forced exile of Israelites from their homeland

was a fulfillment of the covenant curse (see note on 10:32).
15:30 *Hoshea … conspired against Pekah.* Hoshea probably represented the faction in the northern kingdom that favored cooperation with Assyria rather than resistance. In one of his annals Tiglath-Pileser III claims to have placed Hoshea on the throne of the northern kingdom and to have taken ten talents of gold and 1,000 talents of silver as tribute from him. *twentieth year of Jotham.* 732 B.C. (see notes on vv. 32–33). Reference is to his 20th official year, which was his 19th actual year.
15:31 *annals of the kings of Israel.* See note on 1Ki 14:19.
15:32 *second year of Pekah.* 750 B.C. (see note on v. 27).
15:33 *sixteen years.* 750–735 B.C. Jotham was coregent with his father 750–740 (see note on v. 5). Jotham's reign was in some sense terminated in 735, and his son Ahaz took over. However, Jotham continued to live until at least 732 (see notes on vv. 30,37).
15:34 *as his father Uzziah had done.* See note on v. 3; see also 2Ch 27:2.
15:35 *high places, however, were not removed.* See v. 4; see also note on 1Ki 15:14. *Upper Gate of the temple.* See 2Ch 23:20; Jer 20:2; Eze 9:2. Additional information on Jotham's building activities is given in 2Ch 27:3–4.
15:36 *other events of Jotham's reign.* See 2Ch 27:1–6. *annals of the kings of Judah.* See note on 1Ki 14:29.
15:37 This parenthetical statement concerning Jotham's reign supports the idea of an overlap between the reigns of Jotham and Ahaz (see note on v. 33), since 16:5–12; 2Ch 28:5–21; Isa 7:1–17 all place the major effort of Rezin and Pekah in the time of Ahaz.
15:38 *rested with his ancestors.* See note on 1Ki 1:21.

AHAZ KING OF JUDAH
16:1–20pp — 2Ch 28:1–27

16

In the seventeenth year of Pekah son of Remaliah, Ahaz *e* son of Jotham king of Judah began to reign. ²Ahaz was twenty years old when he became king, and he reigned in Jerusalem sixteen years. Unlike David his father, he did not do what was right *f* in the eyes of the LORD his God. ³He followed the ways of the kings of Israel *g* and even sacrificed his son *h* in the fire, engaging in the detestable *i* practices of the nations the LORD had driven out before the Israelites. ⁴He offered sacrifices and burned incense *j* at the high places, on the hilltops and under every spreading tree. *k*

⁵Then Rezin *l* king of Aram and Pekah son of Remaliah king of Israel marched up to fight against Jerusalem and besieged Ahaz, but they could not overpower him. ⁶At that time, Rezin *m* king of Aram recovered Elath *n* for Aram by driving out the people of Judah. Edomites then moved into Elath and have lived there to this day.

⁷Ahaz sent messengers to say to Tiglath-Pileser *o* king of Assyria, "I am your servant and vassal. Come up and save *p* me out of the hand of the king of Aram and of the king of Israel, who are attacking me." ⁸And Ahaz took the silver and gold found in the temple of the LORD and in the treasuries of the royal palace and sent it as a gift *q* to the king of Assyria. ⁹The king of Assyria complied by attacking Damascus *r* and capturing it. He deported its inhabitants to Kir *s* and put Rezin to death.

¹⁰Then King Ahaz went to Damascus to meet Tiglath-Pileser king of Assyria. He saw an altar in Damascus and sent to Uriah *t* the priest a sketch of the altar, with detailed plans for its construction. ¹¹So Uriah the priest built an altar in accordance with all the plans that King Ahaz had sent from Damascus and finished it before King Ahaz returned.

Cross references
16:1 *e* Isa 1:1; 7:1; 14:28; Hos 1:1; Mic 1:1
16:2 *f* S 1Ki 14:8
16:3 *g* 2Ki 17:19
h S Lev 18:21;
S 2Ki 3:27
i S Lev 18:3; S Dt 9:4
16:4 *j* 2Ki 22:17;
23:5 *k* Dt 12:2;
Eze 6:13
16:5 *l* S 2Ki 15:37
16:6 *m* Isa 9:12
n S 1Ki 9:26
16:7 *o* S 2Ki 15:29
p Isa 2:6; 10:20;
Jer 2:18; 3:1;
Eze 16:28; 23:5;
Hos 10:6
16:8 *q* S 1Ki 15:18;
2Ki 12:18
16:9 *r* S Ge 14:15;
S 2Ki 15:29 *s* Isa 22:6;
Am 1:5; 9:7
16:10 *t* ver 11,15,16;
Isa 8:2

16:1 *seventeenth year of Pekah.* 735 B.C. (see note on 15:27). The reign of Ahaz apparently overlapped that of Jotham, with Ahaz serving as a senior partner beginning in 735 (see notes on 15:33,37; see also notes on v. 2; 17:1 and chart, p. 513). *Ahaz son of Jotham king of Judah.* In 1996 a clay seal impression reading "Belonging to Ahaz (son of) Jotham king of Judah" came to light. Written in the ancient Hebrew script used during the divided monarchy, it is the first authentic seal inscription that can be attributed to a king of Judah.

16:2 *twenty years old when he became king.* Perhaps the age at which Ahaz became a senior coregent with his father, Jotham, in 735 B.C. (see note on v. 1). Otherwise, according to the ages and dates provided, Ahaz would have been 11 or 12 instead of 14 or 15 years old when his son Hezekiah was born (cf. 18:1–2). *sixteen years.* The synchronizations of the reigns of Ahaz and Hezekiah of Judah with those of Pekah and Hoshea of the northern kingdom present some apparent chronological difficulties (see notes on v. 1; 17:1; 18:1,9–10). It seems best to take the 16 years specified here as the number of years Ahaz reigned after the death of Jotham, thus 732–715 (see notes on 15:30,33). The beginning of his reign appears to be dated in a variety of ways in the Biblical text: (1) in 744/743, which presupposes a coregency with his grandfather Azariah at the tender age of 11 or 12 (see 17:1); (2) in 735, when he became senior coregent with Jotham (see v. 1); and (3) in 732, when he began his sole reign after the death of Jotham. *Unlike David his father.* Ahaz does not even receive the qualified approval given to Amaziah (14:3), Azariah (15:3) and Jotham (15:34).

16:3 *ways of the kings of Israel.* It is unlikely that Ahaz adhered to the calf worship introduced by Jeroboam I at Bethel and Dan (see 1Ki 12:26–32; 13:33–34; 14:16). The reference here is probably to Baal worship in the spirit of Ahab (see notes on 1Ki 16:31–33; see also 2Ch 28:2). *sacrificed his son.* Israel had been warned by Moses not to engage in this pagan rite (see Lev 18:21; Dt 18:10). In Israel the firstborn son in each household was to be consecrated to the Lord and redeemed by a payment of five shekels to the priests (see Ex 13:1,11–13; Nu 18:16). See also 3:27; 17:17; 21:6; 23:10; 2Ch 28:3; Jer 7:31; 32:35.

16:4 *high places.* See 15:4,35; see also note on 1Ki 15:14. These high places appear to be those assimilated from pagan Baal worship and used by those who worshiped Baal even while also worshiping the Lord. *under every spreading tree.* Large trees

were viewed as symbols of fertility by the pre-Israelite inhabitants of Canaan. Immoral pagan rites were performed at shrines located under such trees. Contrary to the explicit prohibition of the Mosaic covenant, the Israelites adopted this pagan custom (see 17:10; 1Ki 14:23; Dt 12:2; Jer 2:20; 3:6; 17:2; Eze 6:13; 20:28; Hos 4:13–14).

16:5 *Rezin … and Pekah … marched up to fight against Jerusalem.* See notes on 15:25,37. *could not overpower.* See Isa 7:1–17; 2Ch 28:5–21. Rezin and Pekah desired to replace Ahaz on the throne of the southern kingdom with the son of Tabeel in order to gain another ally in their anti-Assyrian political policy (see notes on 15:19,25). The Lord delivered Judah and Ahaz from this threat in spite of their wickedness because of the promises of the Davidic covenant (see 1Ki 11:36; 2Sa 7:13; Isa 7:3–7,14).

16:6 *Rezin king of Aram recovered Elath.* See note on 14:22. *Edomites then moved into Elath.* See 2Ch 28:17. The Philistines also took this opportunity to avenge previous defeats (compare 2Ch 26:5–7 with 2Ch 28:18). *to this day.* See note on 1Ki 8:8.

16:7 *Tiglath-Pileser.* See notes on 15:19,29. *your servant and vassal.* Ahaz preferred to seek security for Judah by means of a treaty with Assyria rather than by obedience to the Lord and trust in his promises (see Ex 23:22; Isa 7:10–16).

16:8 *silver and gold found in the temple.* The temple treasure must have been restored to some degree by Jotham (see 12:18; 14:14). The name "Jehoahaz of Judah" (Ahaz) appears on an inscription of Tiglath-Pileser that contains a list of rulers (including those of the Philistines, Ammonites, Moabites and Edomites) who brought tribute to him in 734 B.C.

16:9 *attacking Damascus and capturing it.* In 732 B.C. Tiglath-Pileser III moved against Damascus and destroyed it (see the prophecies of Isa 7:16; Am 1:3–5). *deported its inhabitants to Kir.* The Arameans were sent back to the place from which they had come (Am 9:7) in fulfillment of the prophecy of Amos (Am 1:5). The location of Kir is unknown, though it is mentioned in connection with Elam in Isa 22:6.

16:10 *Ahaz went to Damascus to meet Tiglath-Pileser.* As a vassal king to express his gratitude and loyalty to the victorious Assyrian ruler. *altar in Damascus.* Perhaps that of the god Rimmon (see 5:18; 2Ch 28:23), but more likely a royal altar of Tiglath-Pileser. Ahaz's reproduction of such an altar would have been a further sign of submission to the Assyrians.

16:12 *u* 2Ch 26:16
16:13 *v* Lev 6:8-13
w Lev 6:14-23
x Ex 29:40
y Lev 7:11-21
16:14 *z* S Ex 20:24;
S 40:6; S 1Ki 8:64
16:15 *a* Ex 29:38-41
b 1Sa 9:9
16:17 *c* 1Ki 7:27
16:18 *d* Eze 16:28
16:20 *e* Isa 14:28
17:1 *f* 2Ki 15:30
17:2 *g* S Dt 4:25
17:3 *h* Hos 10:14
i S Jdg 3:15
17:4 *j* Ps 146:3;
Isa 30:1,7; 36:6;
Jer 2:36; Hos 12:1
k Hos 13:10
17:5 *l* Hos 13:16
17:6 *m* ver 20;
S 2Ki 15:29; Isa 42:24

¹²When the king came back from Damascus and saw the altar, he approached it and presented offerings ᵃ ᵘ on it. ¹³He offered up his burnt offering ᵛ and grain offering, ʷ poured out his drink offering, ˣ and splashed the blood of his fellowship offerings ʸ against the altar. ¹⁴As for the bronze altar ᶻ that stood before the Lᴏʀᴅ, he brought it from the front of the temple—from between the new altar and the temple of the Lᴏʀᴅ—and put it on the north side of the new altar.

¹⁵King Ahaz then gave these orders to Uriah the priest: "On the large new altar, offer the morning ᵃ burnt offering and the evening grain offering, the king's burnt offering and his grain offering, and the burnt offering of all the people of the land, and their grain offering and their drink offering. Splash against this altar the blood of all the burnt offerings and sacrifices. But I will use the bronze altar for seeking guidance." ᵇ ¹⁶And Uriah the priest did just as King Ahaz had ordered.

¹⁷King Ahaz cut off the side panels and removed the basins from the movable stands. He removed the Sea from the bronze bulls that supported it and set it on a stone base. ᶜ ¹⁸He took away the Sabbath canopy ᵇ that had been built at the temple and removed the royal entryway outside the temple of the Lᴏʀᴅ, in deference to the king of Assyria. ᵈ

¹⁹As for the other events of the reign of Ahaz, and what he did, are they not written in the book of the annals of the kings of Judah? ²⁰Ahaz rested ᵉ with his ancestors and was buried with them in the City of David. And Hezekiah his son succeeded him as king.

HOSHEA LAST KING OF ISRAEL

17:3–7pp — 2Ki 18:9–12

In the twelfth year of Ahaz king of Judah, Hoshea ᶠ son of Elah became king of Israel in Samaria, and he reigned nine years. ²He did evil ᵍ in the eyes of the Lᴏʀᴅ, but not like the kings of Israel who preceded him.

³Shalmaneser ʰ king of Assyria came up to attack Hoshea, who had been Shalmaneser's vassal and had paid him tribute. ⁱ ⁴But the king of Assyria discovered that Hoshea was a traitor, for he had sent envoys to So ᶜ king of Egypt, ʲ and he no longer paid tribute to the king of Assyria, as he had done year by year. Therefore Shalmaneser seized him and put him in prison. ᵏ ⁵The king of Assyria invaded the entire land, marched against Samaria and laid siege ˡ to it for three years. ⁶In the ninth year of Hoshea, the king of Assyria ᵐ cap-

---

ᵃ 12 Or *and went up*   ᵇ 18 Or *the dais of his throne* (see Septuagint)   ᶜ 4 *So* is probably an abbreviation for *Osorkon*.

16:13 *burnt offering . . . grain offering . . . drink offering . . . fellowship offerings.* See chart, p. 155. With the exception of the drink offering, these same sacrifices were offered at the dedication of the temple (1Ki 8:64).

16:14 *north side of the new altar.* Ahaz removed the bronze altar from its prominent place in front of the temple and gave it a place alongside the new stone altar.

B **16:15** *large new altar.* Even though fire from heaven had inaugurated and sanctioned the use of the bronze altar for the worship of the Lord (see 2Ch 7:1), Ahaz now replaced it with an altar built on the pattern of the pagan altar from Damascus. Although the bronze altar was quite large (see 2Ch 4:1), the new altar was larger. *morning burnt offering.* See 3:20; Ex 29:38–39; Nu 28:3–4. *evening grain offering.* See note on 1Ki 18:29. *king's burnt offering and his grain offering.* There is no other reference to these special offerings of the king in the OT, with the possible exception of Ezekiel's depiction of the offerings of a future prince (Eze 46:12). *I will use the bronze altar for seeking guidance.* Seeking omens by the examination of the entrails of sacrificed animals is well attested in ancient Near Eastern texts. Here Ahaz states his intention to follow an Assyrian divination technique in an attempt to secure the Lord's guidance.

16:17 *side panels and . . . basins from the movable stands.* See 1Ki 7:27–39. *removed the Sea from the bronze bulls.* See 1Ki 7:23–26. Perhaps the bronze was needed for tribute required by Tiglath-Pileser III.

16:18 *in deference to the king of Assyria.* As a vassal of Tiglath-Pileser, Ahaz was forced to relinquish some of the symbols of his own royal power.

C **16:19** *other events of the reign of Ahaz.* See 2Ch 28, where, among other things, it is said that Ahaz went so far

as to "shut the doors of the temple" (2Ch 28:24). *annals of the kings of Judah.* See note on 1Ki 14:29.

16:20 *rested with his ancestors.* See note on 1Ki 1:21; see also 2Ch 28:27. *Hezekiah his son succeeded him.* For the reign of Hezekiah, see 18:1—20:21.

17:1 *twelfth year of Ahaz.* 732 B.C. (see note on 15:30), on the assumption that Ahaz began a coregency with Azariah in 744/743 (see notes on 16:1–2). *nine years.* 732–722 (see Introduction to 1 Kings: Chronology).

17:3 *Shalmaneser.* Hoshea had become a vassal to Assyria under the rule of Tiglath-Pileser III (see note on 15:30). The latter was succeeded on the Assyrian throne by Shalmaneser V, who ruled 727–722 B.C. (see chart, p. 482).

17:5 *three years.* 725–722 B.C. Samaria was a strongly fortified city and extremely difficult to subdue (see note on 1Ki 16:24).

B **17:6** *ninth year of Hoshea.* 722 B.C. (see note on v. 1). *king of Assyria captured Samaria.* In the winter (December) of 722–721 Shalmaneser V died (possibly by assassination), and the Assyrian throne was seized by Sargon II (721–705). In his annals Sargon lays claim to the capture of Samaria at the beginning of his reign, but it was hardly more than a mopping-up operation. *deported the Israelites.* Because the northern kingdom refused to be obedient to its covenant obligations, the Lord brought on its citizens the judgment pronounced already by Ahijah during the reign of the northern kingdom's first king, Jeroboam I (see note on 1Ki 14:15). In his annals Sargon II claims to have deported 27,290 Israelites. He then settled other captured people in the vacated towns of the northern kingdom (see v. 24). *Gozan on the Habor River.* Gozan was an Assyrian provincial capital located on a tributary (the Habor) of the Euphrates River. *towns of the Medes.* Towns located in the area south of the Caspian Sea and northeast of the Tigris River.

tured Samaria [n] and deported [o] the Israelites to Assyria. He settled them in Halah, in Gozan [p] on the Habor River and in the towns of the Medes.

ISRAEL EXILED BECAUSE OF SIN

[7] All this took place because the Israelites had sinned [q] against the LORD their God, who had brought them up out of Egypt [r] from under the power of Pharaoh king of Egypt. They worshiped other gods [8] and followed the practices of the nations [s] the LORD had driven out before them, as well as the practices that the kings of Israel had introduced. [9] The Israelites secretly did things against the LORD their God that were not right. From watchtower to fortified city [t] they built themselves high places in all their towns. [10] They set up sacred stones [u] and Asherah poles [v] on every high hill and under every spreading tree. [w] [11] At every high place they burned incense, as the nations whom the LORD had driven out before them had done. They did wicked things that aroused the LORD's anger. [12] They worshiped idols, [x] though the LORD had said, "You shall not do this." [a] [13] The LORD warned [y] Israel and Judah through all his prophets and seers: [z] "Turn from your evil ways. [a] Observe my commands and decrees, in accordance with the entire Law that I commanded your ancestors to obey and that I delivered to you through my servants the prophets." [b]

[14] But they would not listen and were as stiff-necked [c] as their ancestors, who did not trust in the LORD their God. [15] They rejected his decrees and the covenant [d] he had made with their ancestors and the statutes he had warned them to keep. They followed worthless idols [e] and themselves became worthless. [f] They imitated the nations [g] around them although the LORD had ordered them, "Do not do as they do."

[16] They forsook all the commands of the LORD their God and made for themselves two idols cast in the shape of calves, [h] and an Asherah [i] pole. They bowed down to all the starry hosts, [j] and they worshiped Baal. [k] [17] They sacrificed [l] their sons and daughters in the fire. They practiced divination and sought omens [m] and sold [n] themselves to do evil in the eyes of the LORD, arousing his anger.

[18] So the LORD was very angry with Israel and removed them from his presence. [o] Only the tribe of Judah was left, [19] and even Judah did not keep the commands of the LORD their God. They followed the practices Israel had introduced. [p] [20] Therefore the LORD rejected all the people of Israel; he afflicted them and gave them into the hands of plunderers, [q] until he thrust them from his presence. [r]

[a] 12 Exodus 20:4,5

17:6 [n] Isa 10:9
[o] S Dt 4:27; S 24:1;
S 2Ki 15:29; Am 7:17
[p] 1Ch 5:26
17:7 [q] S Jos 7:11
[r] Ex 14:15-31
17:8 [s] S Ex 34:15;
S Lev 18:3; S Dt 9:4
17:9 [t] 2Ki 18:8
17:10 [u] S Ex 23:24
[v] Ex 34:13; Isa 17:8;
Mic 5:14 [w] S Dt 12:2
17:12 [x] S Ex 20:4
17:13 [y] S Jdg 6:8;
S 2Ch 7:14;
S Job 34:33;
Eze 3:17-19
[z] S 1Sa 9:9 [a] Jer 4:1;
18:11; 23:22; 25:5;
35:15; 36:3; Zec 1:4
[b] Mt 23:34
17:14 [c] S Ex 32:9;
Ac 7:51
17:15 [d] S Lev 26:11;
Dt 29:25; Jdg 2:20;
1Ki 11:11; 2Ki 18:12;
Ps 78:10; Eze 5:6;
Mal 2:10 [e] S Dt 32:21;
Hos 11:2; Ro 1:21-23
[f] Jer 2:5 [g] S Dt 12:4
17:16 [h] S Ex 32:4
[i] S Dt 16:21 / S Ge 2:1;
Isa 40:26; Jer 19:13
[k] S Jdg 2:11
17:17 [l] S Dt 12:31;
18:10-12; 2Ki 16:3;
Eze 16:21
[m] S Lev 19:26
[n] S 1Ki 21:20; Ro 7:14
17:18 [o] S Ge 4:14;
S Ex 33:15;
S 2Ki 13:23; 2Th 1:9
17:19 [p] 2Ki 16:3;
Jer 3:6-10; Eze 23:13
17:20 [q] S ver 6
[r] Jer 7:15; 15:1

17:7–23 A theological explanation for the downfall of the northern kingdom. Israel had repeatedly spurned the Lord's gracious acts, had refused to heed the prophets' warnings of impending judgment (vv. 13–14,23) and had failed to keep her covenant obligations (v. 15). The result was the implementation of the covenant curse precisely as it had been presented to the Israelites by Moses before they entered Canaan (Dt 28:49–68; 32:1–47).

17:7 *brought them up out of Egypt.* The deliverance from Egypt was the fundamental redemptive event in Israel's history. She owed her very existence as a nation to this gracious and mighty act of the Lord (see Ex 20:2; Dt 5:15; 26:8; Jos 24:5–7,17; Jdg 10:11; 1Sa 12:6; Ne 9:9–13; Mic 6:4). *worshiped other gods.* A violation of the most basic obligation of Israel's covenant with the Lord (see v. 35; Dt 5:7; 6:14; Jos 24:14–16,20; Jer 1:16; 2:5–6; 25:6; 35:15).

17:8 *practices of the nations.* See Dt 18:9; Jdg 2:12–13. *practices that the kings of Israel had introduced.* See, e.g., 10:31 (Jehu); 14:24 (Jeroboam II); 1Ki 12:28–33 (Jeroboam I); 16:25–26 (Omri); 16:30–34 (Ahab).

17:9 *high places in all their towns.* See 14:4; 15:4,35; see also notes on 16:4; 1Ki 3:2; 15:14.

17:10 *sacred stones.* See note on 1Ki 14:23. *Asherah poles.* See note on 1Ki 14:15. *on every high hill and under every spreading tree.* See 16:4; 1Ki 14:23; Jer 2:20; 3:6,13; 17:2.

17:11 *wicked things.* Perhaps a reference to ritual prostitution (see note on 1Ki 14:24; see also Hos 4:13–14).

17:12 *idols.* See note on Lev 26:30. *You shall not do this.* See TNIV text note; see also Ex 23:13; Lev 26:1; Dt 5:6–10.

17:13 *warned Israel and Judah through all his prophets.* Israel not only violated the requirements of the Sinai cov-

enant but also spurned the words of prophets the Lord had graciously sent to call his people back to the covenant (see, e.g., 1Ki 13:1–3; 14:6–16; Jdg 6:8–10; 1Sa 3:19–21, as well as the ministries of Elijah, Elisha, Amos and Hosea). *seers.* See note on 1Sa 9:9.

17:14 *stiff-necked.* A figure derived from the obstinate resistance of an ox to being placed under a yoke (see Dt 10:16; Jer 2:20; 7:26; 17:23; 19:15; Hos 4:16).

17:15 *followed worthless idols.* See Dt 32:21; Jer 2:5; 8:19; 10:8; 14:22; 51:18.

17:16 *two idols cast in the shape of calves.* The golden calves of Bethel and Dan (see 1Ki 12:28–30). *Asherah pole.* See note on 1Ki 14:15. *all the starry hosts.* Israel had been commanded not to worship the stars like her pagan neighbors (see Dt 4:19; 17:3). Although this form of idolatry is not mentioned previously in 1,2 Kings, the prophet Amos apparently alludes to its practice in the northern kingdom during the reign of Jeroboam II (see note on Am 5:26). It was later introduced into the southern kingdom during the reign of Manasseh (see 21:3,5) and abolished during the reformation of Josiah (see 23:4–5,12; see also Eze 8:16).

17:17 *sacrificed their sons and daughters.* See note on 16:3. *practiced divination and sought omens.* Such practices were forbidden in the Mosaic covenant (see note on 16:15; see also Lev 19:26; Dt 18:10).

17:18 *removed them from his presence.* The exile of the northern kingdom (see v. 6; 23:27). *Only the tribe of Judah was left.* The southern kingdom included elements of the tribes of Simeon and Benjamin, but Judah was the only tribe in the south to retain its complete integrity (see notes on 1Ki 11:31–32; see also note on 2Ki 19:4).

17:20 *afflicted them and gave them into the hands of plunderers.* See 10:32–33; 13:3,20; 24:2; 2Ch 21:16; 28:18; Am 1:13.

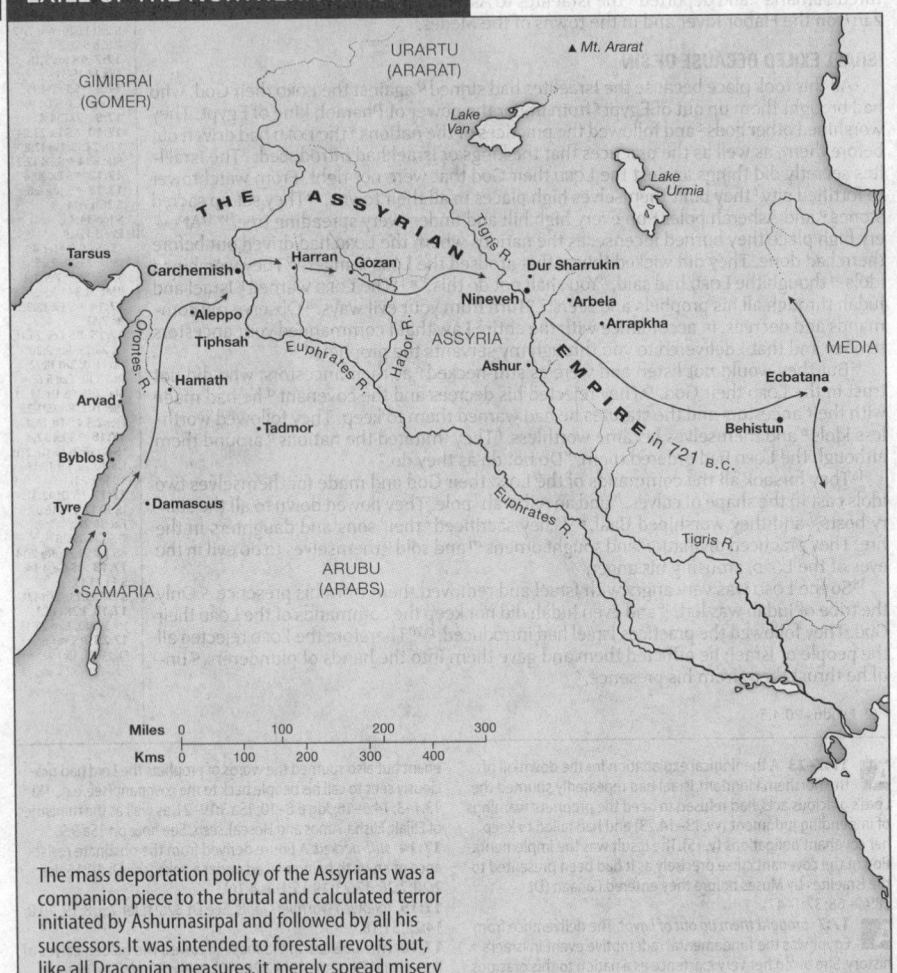

URARTU (ARARAT)

▲ Mt. Ararat

GIMIRRAI (GOMER)

Lake Van

Lake Urmia

THE ASSYRIAN EMPIRE in 721 B.C.

Tarsus

Carchemish • Harran → Gozan

Tigris R.

Dur Sharrukin

Aleppo

Nineveh • Arbela

Tiphsah

Euphrates R.

Habor R.

ASSYRIA

• Arrapkha

Hamath

Ashur

MEDIA

Arvad

Orontes R.

Ecbatana

Tadmor

Behistun

Byblos

Euphrates R.

Tyre

• Damascus

Tigris R.

ARUBU (ARABS)

SAMARIA

Miles 0 — 100 — 200 — 300
Kms 0 — 100 — 200 — 300 — 400

The mass deportation policy of the Assyrians was a companion piece to the brutal and calculated terror initiated by Ashurnasirpal and followed by all his successors. It was intended to forestall revolts but, like all Draconian measures, it merely spread misery and engendered hatred. In the end, it hastened the disintegration of the Assyrian empire.

B There is some evidence that Israel experienced its first deportations under Tiglath-Pileser III (745–727 B.C.), a cruelty repeated by Sargon II (721–705 B.C.) at the time of the fall of Samaria. The latter king's inscriptions boast of carrying away 27,290 inhabitants of the city "as booty." According to 2Ki 17:6, they were sent to Assyria, to Halah, to Gozan on the Habor River, and apparently to the eastern frontiers of the empire (to the towns of the Medes, most probably somewhere in the vicinity of Ecbatana, the modern Hamadan).

B The sequel is provided by the inscriptions of Sargon: "The Arabs who live far away in the

desert, who know neither overseers nor officials, and who had not yet brought their tribute to any king, I deported ... and settled them in Samaria."

Much mythology has developed around the theme of the so-called ten lost tribes of Israel. A close examination of Assyrian records reveals that the deportations approximated only a limited percentage of the population, usually consisting of noble families. Agricultural workers, no doubt the majority, were deliberately left to care for the crops (cf. the Babylonian practice, 2Ki 24:14; 25:12).

17:21 ᔢS 1Sa 15:27;
S 1Ki 11:11 ᵗ1Ki 12:20
ᵘS 1Ki 12:30
17:23 ᵛEze 39:23-
24 ʷS Jdg 6:8
ˣS 1Ki 9:7
17:24 ʸ2Ki 19:37;
Ezr 4:2,10; Isa 37:38
ᶻver 31; S 2Ki 15:29;
18:34; Isa 36:19;
37:13; Am 6:2
17:25 ᵃS Ge 37:20;
Isa 5:29; 15:9;
Jer 50:17
17:29 ᵇJer 2:28;
11:13 ᶜS Lev 26:30;
S 1Ki 12:31 ᵈMic 4:5
17:31 ᵉ2Ki 19:37
ᶠS ver 24
17:32 ᵍS 1Ki 12:31
17:34 ʰS Ge 17:5;
S Isa 18:31
17:35 ⁱS Ex 20:5
ʲS Ex 20:3
17:36 ᵏS Ex 3:20;
Ps 136:12

²¹When he tore ˢ Israel away from the house of David, they made Jeroboam son of Nebat their king.ᵗ Jeroboam enticed Israel away from following the LORD and caused them to commit a great sin.ᵘ ²²The Israelites persisted in all the sins of Jeroboam and did not turn away from them ²³until the LORD removed them from his presence,ᵛ as he had warned ʷ through all his servants the prophets. So the people of Israel were taken from their homeland ˣ into exile in Assyria, and they are still there.

SAMARIA RESETTLED

²⁴The king of Assyria ʸ brought people from Babylon, Kuthah, Avva, Hamath and Sepharvaim ᶻ and settled them in the towns of Samaria to replace the Israelites. They took over Samaria and lived in its towns. ²⁵When they first lived there, they did not worship the LORD; so he sent lions ᵃ among them and they killed some of the people. ²⁶It was reported to the king of Assyria: "The people you deported and resettled in the towns of Samaria do not know what the god of that country requires. He has sent lions among them, which are killing them off, because the people do not know what he requires."

²⁷Then the king of Assyria gave this order: "Have one of the priests you took captive from Samaria go back to live there and teach the people what the god of the land requires." ²⁸So one of the priests who had been exiled from Samaria came to live in Bethel and taught them how to worship the LORD.

²⁹Nevertheless, each national group made its own gods in the several towns ᵇ where they settled, and set them up in the shrines ᶜ the people of Samaria had made at the high places. ᵈ ³⁰The people from Babylon made Sukkoth Benoth, those from Kuthah made Nergal, and those from Hamath made Ashima; ³¹the Avvites made Nibhaz and Tartak, and the Sepharvites burned their children in the fire as sacrifices to Adrammelek ᵉ and Anammelek, the gods of Sepharvaim. ᶠ ³²They worshiped the LORD, but they also appointed all sorts ᵍ of their own people to officiate for them as priests in the shrines at the high places. ³³They worshiped the LORD, but they also served their own gods in accordance with the customs of the nations from which they had been brought.

³⁴To this day they persist in their former practices. They neither worship the LORD nor adhere to the decrees and regulations, the laws and commands that the LORD gave the descendants of Jacob, whom he named Israel. ʰ ³⁵When the LORD made a covenant with the Israelites, he commanded them: "Do not worship ⁱ any other gods or bow down to them, serve them or sacrifice to them.ʲ ³⁶But the LORD, who brought you up out of Egypt with mighty power and outstretched arm, ᵏ is the one you must worship. To him you shall

---

17:21 *tore Israel away from the house of David.* See 1Ki 11:11, 31; 12:24. The division of the kingdom was of the Lord, but it came to the nation as a punishment for its sins. *Jeroboam . . . caused them to commit a great sin.* See 1Ki 12:26–32; 13:33–34; see also note on Ge 20:9.

17:23 *warned through all his servants the prophets.* See 1Ki 14:15–16; Hos 10:1–7; 11:5; Am 5:27.

17:24 *king of Assyria.* Primarily Sargon II (721–705 B.C.), though later Assyrian rulers, including Esarhaddon (681–669) and Ashurbanipal (669–627), settled additional non-Israelites in Samaria (see Ezr 4:2,9–10). *Babylon, Kuthah.* Babylon and Kuthah (located about eight miles northeast of Babylon) were forced to submit to Assyrian rule by Sargon II in 709. *Avva.* Probably the same as Ivvah (see 18:34; 19:13). Its association with Hamath and Arpad suggests a location somewhere in Aram (Syria). *Hamath.* Located on the Orontes River (see 14:25; 18:34; see also note on Ge 47:15). In 720 Sargon II made the kingdom of Hamath into an Assyrian province. *Sepharvaim.* See note on Isa 36:19. *Samaria.* Here a designation for the entire northern kingdom (see note on 1Ki 13:32).

17:25 *did not worship the LORD.* They worshiped their own national deities. *sent lions among them.* Lions had always been present in Canaan (see 1Ki 13:24; 20:36; Jdg 14:5; 1Sa 17:34; Am 3:12). In the aftermath of the disruption and depopulation caused by the conflict with the Assyrians, the lions greatly increased in number (see Ex 23:29). This was viewed by the inhabitants of the land and the writer of Kings as a punishment from the Lord (see Lev 26:21–22).

17:26 *king of Assyria.* Sargon II. *what the god of that country requires.* According to the religious ideas of that time, each regional deity required special ritual observances, which, if ig-

nored or violated, would bring disaster on the land.

17:27 *one of the priests.* Probably a priest of the religion Jeroboam I established in the northern kingdom (see 1Ki 12:31 and note).

17:28 *came to live in Bethel.* Bethel continued to be the center for the apostate form of Yahweh worship that had been promoted in the northern kingdom since the time of Jeroboam I (see notes on 1Ki 12:28–30).

17:29 *people of Samaria.* The mixed population of the former territory of the northern kingdom. These people of mixed ancestry eventually came to be known as Samaritans. In later times the Samaritans rejected the idolatry of their polytheistic origins and followed the teachings of Moses, including monotheism. In NT times Jesus testified to a Samaritan woman (Jn 4:4–26), and many Samaritans were converted under the ministry of Philip (Ac 8:4–25).

17:32 *officiate for them as priests.* See note on 1Ki 12:31.

17:33 *They worshiped the LORD, but they also served their own gods.* A classic statement of a mixed religion.

17:34 *To this day.* Until the time of the writing of 1,2 Kings. *worship the LORD.* Here used in the sense of faithful worship. In vv. 32–33 "worship the LORD" refers to a paganized worship.

17:35 *Do not worship any other gods.* The Mosaic covenant demanded exclusive worship of the Lord (Ex 20:5; Dt 5:9). This was the "first and greatest commandment" (Mt 22:38), and it was to distinguish Israel from all other peoples.

17:36 *the LORD, who brought you up out of Egypt . . . you must worship.* Here, as in v. 7 (see note there), the deliverance from Egypt is cited as the gracious act of the Lord par excellence that entitled him to exclusive claim on Israel's loyalty.

bow down and to him offer sacrifices. ³⁷You must always be careful ˡ to keep the decrees ᵐ and regulations, the laws and commands he wrote for you. Do not worship other gods. ³⁸Do not forget ⁿ the covenant I have made with you, and do not worship other gods. ³⁹Rather, worship the Lᴏʀᴅ your God; it is he who will deliver you from the hand of all your enemies."

⁴⁰They would not listen, however, but persisted in their former practices. ⁴¹Even while these people were worshiping the Lᴏʀᴅ, ᵒ they were serving their idols. To this day their children and grandchildren continue to do as their ancestors did.

HEZEKIAH KING OF JUDAH

18:2–4pp — 2Ch 29:1–2; 31:1
18:5–7pp — 2Ch 31:20–21
18:9–12pp — 2Ki 17:3–7

18 In the third year of Hoshea son of Elah king of Israel, Hezekiah ᵖ son of Ahaz king of Judah began to reign. ²He was twenty-five years old when he became king, and he reigned in Jerusalem twenty-nine years. ᵍ His mother's name was Abijah ᵃ daughter of Zechariah. ³He did what was right ʳ in the eyes of the Lᴏʀᴅ, just as his father David ˢ had done. ⁴He removed ᵗ the high places, ᵘ smashed the sacred stones ᵛ and cut down the Asherah poles. He broke into pieces the bronze snake ʷ Moses had made, for up to that time the Israelites had been burning incense to it. (It was called Nehushtan. ᵇ)

⁵Hezekiah trusted ˣ in the Lᴏʀᴅ, the God of Israel. There was no one like him among all the kings of Judah, either before him or after him. ⁶He held fast ʸ to the Lᴏʀᴅ and did not cease to follow him; he kept the commands the Lᴏʀᴅ had given Moses. ⁷And the Lᴏʀᴅ was with him; he was successful ᶻ in whatever he undertook. He rebelled ᵃ against the king of Assyria and did not serve him. ⁸From watchtower to fortified city, ᵇ he defeated the Philistines, as far as Gaza and its territory.

⁹In King Hezekiah's fourth year, ᶜ which was the seventh year of Hoshea son of Elah king of Israel, Shalmaneser king of Assyria marched against Samaria and laid siege to it. ¹⁰At the end of three years the Assyrians took it. So Samaria was captured in Hezekiah's sixth year, which was the ninth year of Hoshea king of Israel. ¹¹The king ᵈ of Assyria deported Israel to Assyria and settled them in Halah, in Gozan on the Habor River and in

---

ᵃ 2 Hebrew *Abi*, a variant of *Abijah*   ᵇ 4 *Nehushtan* sounds like the Hebrew for both *bronze* and *snake*.

17:39 *will deliver you from … all your enemies.* See Ex 23:22; Dt 20:1–4; 23:14.

17:41 *To this day.* See note on v. 34.

18:1 *third year of Hoshea … Hezekiah … began to reign.* 729 B.C. (see 17:1). Hezekiah was coregent with his father Ahaz from 729 to 715 (see notes on 16:2; Isa 36:1). *Hezekiah son of Ahaz king of Judah.* In 1998 a clay impression of a royal stamp seal came to light that reads "Belonging to Hezekiah (son of) Ahaz king of Judah." It is one of only two such royal Judahite seals known (see note on 14:22).

18:2 *became king.* Became sole king of Judah. *twenty-nine years.* 715–686 B.C. See 2Ch 29–32 and Isa 36–39 for a description of the events of his reign, including a more detailed account of the reformation he led (2Ch 29–31). One of his first acts was to reopen the temple, which had been closed by his father, Ahaz (see note on 16:19; see also 2Ch 29:3).

18:3 *right … as his father David.* Hezekiah is one of the few kings who are compared favorably with David. The others are Asa (1Ki 15:11), Jehoshaphat (1Ki 22:43) and Josiah (2Ki 22:2). A qualification is introduced, however, with both Asa and Jehoshaphat: They did not remove the high places (see 1Ki 15:14; 22:43).

18:4 *removed the high places.* Hezekiah was not the first king to destroy high places (see notes on 1Ki 3:2; 15:14), but he was the first to destroy high places dedicated to the worship of the Lord (see 12:3; 14:4; 15:4,35; 17:9; 1Ki 22:43). This became known even to the Assyrian king, Sennacherib (see v. 22). *sacred stones.* See 3:2; 10:26–27; 17:10; see also note on 1Ki 14:23. *Asherah poles.* See 13:6; 17:10,16; 1Ki 16:23; see also note on 1Ki 14:15. *Israelites had been burning incense to it.* It is unlikely that the bronze snake had been an object of worship all through the centuries of Israel's existence as a nation. Perhaps the idolatrous

significance attached to it occurred during the reign of Hezekiah's father, Ahaz (see ch. 16). Snake worship of various types was common among ancient Near Eastern peoples. See note on Nu 21:8–9.

18:5 *no one like him … either before him or after him.* A difference of emphasis is to be seen in this statement when compared to that of 23:25. Hezekiah's uniqueness is to be found in his trust in the Lord, while Josiah's uniqueness is to be found in his scrupulous observance of the Mosaic law.

18:7 *rebelled against the king of Assyria.* Judah had become a vassal to Assyria under Ahaz (see 16:7)—which required at least formal recognition of Assyrian deities. Hezekiah reversed the policy of his father, Ahaz, and sought independence from Assyrian dominance. It is likely that sometime shortly after 705 B.C., when Sennacherib replaced Sargon II on the Assyrian throne, Hezekiah refused to pay the annual tribute due the Assyrians.

18:8 *defeated the Philistines.* In a reversal of the conditions existing during the time of Ahaz, in which the Philistines captured Judahite cities in the hill country and Negev (see 2Ch 28:18), Hezekiah was able once again to subdue the Philistines. Probably Hezekiah tried to coerce the Philistines into joining his anti-Assyrian policy. In one of his annals Sennacherib tells of forcing Hezekiah to release Padi, king of the Philistine city of Ekron, whom Hezekiah held prisoner in Jerusalem. This occurred in connection with Sennacherib's military campaign in 701 B.C.

18:9 *Hezekiah's fourth year.* 725 B.C., the fourth year of Hezekiah's coregency with Ahaz (see notes on v. 1; 17:1). *Shalmaneser.* See note on 17:3.

18:10 *three years.* See note on 17:5. *ninth year of Hoshea.* See note on 17:6.

18:11 *king of Assyria deported Israel.* See note on 17:6.

towns of the Medes. *e* ¹²This happened because they had not obeyed the LORD their God, but had violated his covenant *f*—all that Moses the servant of the LORD commanded. *g* They neither listened to the commands *h* nor carried them out.

¹³In the fourteenth year *i* of King Hezekiah's reign, Sennacherib king of Assyria attacked all the fortified cities of Judah *j* and captured them. ¹⁴So Hezekiah king of Judah sent this message to the king of Assyria at Lachish: *k* "I have done wrong. *l* Withdraw from me, and I will pay whatever you demand of me." The king of Assyria exacted from Hezekiah king of Judah three hundred talents *a* of silver and thirty talents *b* of gold. ¹⁵So Hezekiah gave *m* him all the silver that was found in the temple of the LORD and in the treasuries of the royal palace.

¹⁶At this time Hezekiah king of Judah stripped off the gold with which he had covered the doors *n* and doorposts of the temple of the LORD, and gave it to the king of Assyria.

SENNACHERIB THREATENS JERUSALEM

18:13, 17–37pp — Isa 36:1–22
18:17–35pp — 2Ch 32:9–19

¹⁷The king of Assyria sent his supreme commander, *o* his chief officer and his field commander with a large army, from Lachish to King Hezekiah at Jerusalem. They came up to Jerusalem and stopped at the aqueduct of the Upper Pool, *p* on the road to the Washerman's Field. ¹⁸They called for the king; and Eliakim *q* son of Hilkiah the palace administrator, Shebna *r* the secretary, and Joah son of Asaph the recorder went out to them.

¹⁹The field commander said to them, "Tell Hezekiah:

" 'This is what the great king, the king of Assyria, says: On what are you basing this confidence *s* of yours? ²⁰You say you have the counsel and the might for war—but you speak only empty words. On whom are you depending, that you rebel against me? ²¹Look, I know you are depending on Egypt, *t* that splintered reed of a staff, *u* which pierces the hands of anyone who leans on it! Such is Pharaoh king of Egypt to all who depend on him. ²²But if you say to me, "We are depending on the LORD our God"—isn't he the one whose high places and altars Hezekiah removed, saying to Judah and Jerusalem, "You must worship before this altar in Jerusalem"?

²³" 'Come now, make a bargain with my master, the king of Assyria: I will give you two thousand horses—if you can put riders on them! ²⁴How can you repulse one officer *v* of the least of my master's officials, even though you are depending on Egypt for chariots and horsemen *c*? ²⁵Furthermore, have I come to attack and destroy this place without word from the LORD? *w* The LORD himself told me to march against this country and destroy it.' "

---

a 14 That is, about 11 tons or about 10 metric tons   *b 14* That is, about 1 ton or about 1 metric ton
c 24 Or *charioteers*

18:11 *e* Eze 16:39; 23:9
18:12 *f* S 2Ki 17:15
g 2Ki 21:8; Da 9:6,10
h S 1Ki 9:6
18:13 *i* S ver 2
i Isa 1:7; Mic 1:9
18:14 *k* 2Ki 19:8
i Isa 24:5; 33:8
18:15 *m* S 1Ki 15:18; Isa 39:2
18:16 *n* 2Ch 29:3
18:17 *o* Isa 20:1
p 2Ki 20:20;
2Ch 32:4,30; Ne 2:14;
Isa 22:9
18:18 *q* 2Ki 19:2;
Isa 22:20; 36:3,11,22;
37:2 *r* ver 26,37;
Isa 22:15
18:19 *s* S ver 5;
S Job 4:6
18:21 *t* Isa 20:5;
31:1; Eze 29:6
u 2Ki 24:7; Isa 20:6;
30:5, 7; Jer 25:19;
37:7; 46:2
18:24 *v* Isa 10:8
18:25 *w* 2Ki 19:6,22;
24:3; 2Ch 35:21

18:12 *violated his covenant.* See 17:7–23.

18:13 *fourteenth year.* Of Hezekiah's sole reign: 701 B.C. (see note on v. 2). *Sennacherib . . . attacked.* See chart, p. 482. Verses 13–16 correspond very closely with Sennacherib's own account of his 701 campaign against Phoenicia, Judah and Egypt. *captured them.* In his annals, Sennacherib claims to have captured 46 of Hezekiah's fortified cities, as well as numerous open villages, and to have taken 200,150 of the people captive. He says he made Hezekiah "a prisoner in Jerusalem his royal residence, like a bird in a cage," but he does not say he took Jerusalem.

18:14 *Lachish.* See notes on 14:19; Isa 36:2. *three hundred talents of silver and thirty talents of gold.* See TNIV text notes. The Assyrian and Biblical reports of the amount of tribute paid by Hezekiah to Sennacherib agree with respect to the 30 talents of gold, but Sennacherib claims to have received 800 talents of silver rather than the 300 specified in the Biblical text.

18:15 *silver . . . in the temple . . . and in the treasuries of the royal palace.* See 12:10,18; 14:14; 16:8; 1Ki 7:51; 14:26; 15:18.

18:17—19:37 See Isa 36–37; cf. 2Ch 32.

18:17 *aqueduct . . . Field.* See note on Isa 7:3. It is ironic that the Assyrian officials demand Judah's surrender on the very spot where Isaiah had warned Ahaz to trust in the Lord rather than in an alliance with Assyria for deliverance from the threat

against him from Aram and the northern kingdom of Israel (see 16:5–10; Isa 7:1–17).

18:18 *palace administrator.* See note on 1Ki 4:6. *secretary.* See note on 2Sa 8:17. *recorder.* See note on 2Sa 8:16.

18:19 *great king.* A frequently used title of the Assyrian rulers—and occasionally of the Lord (Ps 47:2; 48:2; 95:3; Mal 1:14; Mt 5:35). *says.* The following address is a masterpiece of calculated intimidation and psychological warfare designed to destroy the morale of the inhabitants of Jerusalem (see vv. 26–27; cf. note on Jos 6:5).

18:21 *depending on Egypt.* See 19:9; Isa 30:1–5; 31:1–3.

18:22 *isn't he the one whose high places and altars Hezekiah removed . . . ?* The Assyrians cleverly attempted to drive a wedge between Hezekiah and the people. They attempted to exploit any resentment that may have existed among those who opposed Hezekiah's reformation and his destruction of the high places (see note on v. 4).

18:23 *if you can put riders on them!* With this sarcastic taunt, the Assyrians undoubtedly accurately suggest that the Judahites were so weak in military personnel that they could not even take advantage of such a generous offer. In contrast with the Assyrians, the army of Judah at the time consisted largely of foot soldiers. The city under siege would have contained few chariots, and it is not known whether the Israelites ever employed mounted men in combat.

18:26 ˣ Ezr 4:7
18:29 ʸ 2Ki 19:10
18:31 ᶻ S Nu 13:23;
S 1Ki 4:25 ᵃ Jer 14:3;
La 4:4
18:32 ᵇ Dt 30:19
18:33 ᶜ 2Ki 19:12
18:34 ᵈ S 2Ki 17:24;
S Jer 49:23 ᵉ Isa 10:9
18:35 ᶠ Ps 2:1-2
18:37 ᵍ S ver 18;
Isa 33:7; 36:3,22
ʰ S 2Ki 6:30
19:1 ⁱ S Ge 37:34;
S Nu 14:6
19:2 ʲ S Ge 37:34
ᵏ Jer 19:1 ˡ S Ge 37:34
ᵐ Isa 1:1
19:3 ⁿ Hos 13:13

²⁶Then Eliakim son of Hilkiah, and Shebna and Joah said to the field commander, "Please speak to your servants in Aramaic,ˣ since we understand it. Don't speak to us in Hebrew in the hearing of the people on the wall."

²⁷But the commander replied, "Was it only to your master and you that my master sent me to say these things, and not to the people sitting on the wall—who, like you, will have to eat their own excrement and drink their own urine?"

²⁸Then the commander stood and called out in Hebrew, "Hear the word of the great king, the king of Assyria! ²⁹This is what the king says: Do not let Hezekiah deceiveʸ you. He cannot deliver you from my hand. ³⁰Do not let Hezekiah persuade you to trust in the LORD when he says, 'The LORD will surely deliver us; this city will not be given into the hand of the king of Assyria.'

³¹"Do not listen to Hezekiah. This is what the king of Assyria says: Make peace with me and come out to me. Then every one of you will eat from your own vine and fig treeᶻ and drink water from your own cistern, ᵃ ³²until I come and take you to a land like your own— a land of grain and new wine, a land of bread and vineyards, a land of olive trees and honey. Choose lifeᵇ and not death!

"Do not listen to Hezekiah, for he is misleading you when he says, 'The LORD will deliver us.' ³³Has the godᶜ of any nation ever delivered his land from the hand of the king of Assyria? ³⁴Where are the gods of Hamathᵈ and Arpad?ᵉ Where are the gods of Sepharvaim, Hena and Ivvah? Have they rescued Samaria from my hand? ³⁵Who of all the gods of these countries has been able to save his land from me? How then can the LORD deliver Jerusalem from my hand?"ᶠ ³⁶But the people remained silent and said nothing in reply, because the king had commanded, "Do not answer him."

³⁷Then Eliakimᵍ son of Hilkiah the palace administrator, Shebna the secretary, and Joah son of Asaph the recorder went to Hezekiah, with their clothes torn,ʰ and told him what the field commander had said.

JERUSALEM'S DELIVERANCE FORETOLD

19:1-13pp — Isa 37:1-13

19 When King Hezekiah heard this, he toreⁱ his clothes and put on sackcloth and went into the temple of the LORD. ²He sent Eliakimʲ the palace administrator, Shebna the secretary and the leading priests,ᵏ all wearing sackcloth,ˡ to the prophet Isaiahᵐ son of Amoz. ³They told him, "This is what Hezekiah says: This day is a day of distress and rebuke and disgrace, as when children come to the momentⁿ of birth and there is no strength to deliver them. ⁴It may be that the LORD your God will hear all

---

18:26 *Aramaic.* Had become the international language of the Near East, known and used by those engaged in diplomacy and commerce. It is surprising that the Assyrian officials were able to speak the Hebrew dialect of the common people of Judah (see 2Ch 32:18).

18:27 *people sitting on the wall.* The Assyrian strategy was to negotiate in the hearing of the people in order to demoralize them and turn them against Hezekiah. *eat their own excrement and drink their own urine.* A vivid portrayal of the potential hardship of a prolonged siege.

18:29 *the king says.* The Assyrian officials now address their remarks directly to the populace rather than to the officials of Hezekiah, as in vv. 19–27. *Do not let Hezekiah deceive you.* Here and in vv. 30–31 the people are urged three times to turn against Hezekiah.

18:30 *this city will not be given into the hand of the king of Assyria.* Hezekiah could say this on the basis of God's promise to him (see 20:6; see also note on Isa 38:6).

18:31 *eat from your own vine and fig tree and drink water from your own cistern.* Depicting peaceful and prosperous times (see 1Ki 4:25; Mic 4:4; Zec 3:10).

18:32 *until I come and take you to a land like your own.* Ultimately surrender meant deportation, but Sennacherib pictured it as something desirable. *Choose life and not death!* The alternatives depicted for the people are: (1) Trust in the Lord and Hezekiah and die, or (2) trust in the Assyrians and enjoy prosperity and peace. These words directly contradict the alternatives placed before Israel by Moses in Dt 30:15–20.

18:33–35 *Has the god of any nation ever delivered his land from the hand of the king of Assyria? ... How then can the LORD deliver Jerusalem from my hand?* The flaw in the Assyrian reasoning was to equate the one true and living God with the no-gods (Dt 32:21) of the pagan peoples the Assyrians had defeated (see 19:4,6; 2Ch 32:13–19; Isa 10:9–11).

18:34 *Hamath.* See notes on 14:25; 17:24. *Arpad.* A city located near Hamath and taken by the Assyrians in 740 B.C. (see 19:13; Isa 10:9; Jer 49:23). *Ivvah.* See note on 17:24.

18:36 *because the king had commanded, "Do not answer him."* The Assyrian attempt to stir up a popular revolt against the leadership and authority of Hezekiah had failed.

18:37 *clothes torn.* An expression of great emotion (see 6:30; 1Ki 21:27). Perhaps in this instance it was motivated by the Assyrian blasphemy against the true God (see 19:4,6; Mt 26:65; Mk 14:63–64).

19:1 *sackcloth.* See note on 6:30.

19:2 *palace administrator.* See note on 1Ki 4:6. *secretary.* See note on 2Sa 8:17. *leading priests.* Probably the oldest members of various priestly families (see Jer 19:1). The crisis involved not only the city of Jerusalem but also the temple. *prophet Isaiah.* The first reference to Isaiah in the book of Kings, though he had been active in the reigns of Uzziah, Jotham and Ahaz (see Isa 1:1).

19:3 *as when children come to the moment of birth and there is no strength to deliver them.* Depicts the critical nature of the threat facing the city.

the words of the field commander, whom his master, the king of Assyria, has sent to ridicule ^{o} the living God, and that he will rebuke ^{p} him for the words the LORD your God has heard. Therefore pray for the remnant ^{q} that still survives."

^{5}When King Hezekiah's officials came to Isaiah, ^{6}Isaiah said to them, "Tell your master, 'This is what the LORD says: Do not be afraid ^{r} of what you have heard—those words with which the underlings of the king of Assyria have blasphemed ^{s} me. ^{7}Listen! When he hears a certain report, ^{t} I will make him want to return to his own country, and there I will have him cut down with the sword. $^{u\,\prime}$"

^{8}When the field commander heard that the king of Assyria had left Lachish, ^{v} he withdrew and found the king fighting against Libnah. ^{w}

^{9}Now Sennacherib received a report that Tirhakah, the king of Cush, ^{a} was marching out to fight against him. So he again sent messengers to Hezekiah with this word: ^{10}"Say to Hezekiah king of Judah: Do not let the god you depend ^{x} on deceive ^{y} you when he says, 'Jerusalem will not be given into the hands of the king of Assyria.' ^{11}Surely you have heard what the kings of Assyria have done to all the countries, destroying them completely. And will you be delivered? ^{12}Did the gods of the nations that were destroyed by my ancestors deliver ^{z} them—the gods of Gozan, ^{a} Harran, ^{b} Rezeph and the people of Eden who were in Tel Assar? ^{13}Where is the king of Hamath or the king of Arpad? Where are the kings of Lair, Sepharvaim, Hena and Ivvah?" ^{c}

HEZEKIAH'S PRAYER
19:14–19pp — Isa 37:14–20

^{14}Hezekiah received the letter ^{d} from the messengers and read it. Then he went up to the temple of the LORD and spread it out before the LORD. ^{15}And Hezekiah prayed to the LORD: "LORD, the God of Israel, enthroned between the cherubim, ^{e} you alone ^{f} are God over all the kingdoms of the earth. You have made heaven and earth. ^{16}Give ear, ^{g} LORD, and hear; ^{h} open your eyes, ^{i} LORD, and see; listen to the words Sennacherib has sent to ridicule the living God.

^{17}"It is true, LORD, that the Assyrian kings have laid waste these nations and their lands. ^{18}They have thrown their gods into the fire and destroyed them, for they were not gods ^{j} but only wood and stone, fashioned by human hands. ^{k} ^{19}Now, LORD our God, deliver ^{l} us from his hand, so that all the kingdoms ^{m} of the earth may know ^{n} that you alone, LORD, are God."

ISAIAH PROPHESIES SENNACHERIB'S FALL
19:20–37pp — Isa 37:21–38
19:35–37pp — 2Ch 32:20–21

^{20}Then Isaiah son of Amoz sent a message to Hezekiah: "This is what the LORD, the God of Israel, says: I have heard ^{o} your prayer concerning Sennacherib king of Assyria. ^{21}This is the word that the LORD has spoken against ^{p} him:

---

^{a} 9 That is, the upper Nile region

19:4 ^{o} S 1Sa 17:26
^{p} 2Sa 16:12
^{q} S Ge 45:7;
^{q} Jer 37:3
19:6 ^{r} S Dt 3:2;
S Jos 1:9 ^{s} S 2Ki 18:25
19:7 ^{t} S Ex 14:24;
Jer 51:46 ^{u} ver 37;
2Ch 32:21; Isa 10:12
19:8 ^{v} 2Ki 18:14
^{w} S Nu 33:20;
S 2Ki 8:22
19:10 ^{x} S 2Ki 18:5
^{y} 2Ki 18:29
19:12 ^{z} 2Ki 18:33;
2Ch 32:17 ^{a} 2Ki 17:6
^{b} S Ge 11:31
19:13 ^{c} Isa 10:9-11;
Jer 49:23
19:14 ^{d} 2Ki 5:7
19:15 ^{e} S Ge 3:24;
S Ex 25:22 ^{f} S Ge 1:1;
S Jos 2:11
19:16 ^{g} Ps 31:2;
71:2; 88:2; 102:2
^{h} S 1Ki 8:29
^{i} S Ex 3:16
19:18 ^{j} Isa 44:9-11;
Jer 10:3-10 ^{k} Dt 4:28;
Ps 115:4; Ac 17:29
19:19 ^{l} 1Sa 12:10;
Job 6:23; Ps 3:7; 71:4
^{m} S 1Ki 8:43; 1Ch 16:8
^{n} S Jos 4:24;
S 1Sa 17:46
19:20 ^{o} S 1Ki 9:3
19:21 ^{p} Isa 10:5;
33:1

19:4 *living God.* In contrast to the no-gods of 18:33–35. See 1Sa 17:26,36,45 for another example of ridiculing the living and true God. *pray.* Intercessory prayer was an important aspect of the ministry of the prophets (see, e.g., the intercession of Moses and Samuel: Ex 32:31–32; 33:12–17; Nu 14:13–19; 1Sa 7:8–9; 12:19,23; Ps 99:6; Jer 15:1). *remnant.* Those left in Judah after Sennacherib's capture of many towns and numerous people (see note on 18:13; cf. Isa 10:28–32). Archaeological evidence reveals that many Israelites fled the northern kingdom during the Assyrian assaults and settled in Judah, so that the nation of Judah became the remnant of all Israel.

19:7 *report.* Some interpreters link this report with the challenge to Sennacherib from Tirhakah of Egypt (v. 9). Others regard it as disturbing information from Sennacherib's homeland. *make him want to return.* Because of a spirit of insecurity and fear. *cut down with the sword.* See v. 37. Here the eventual murder of Sennacherib is connected with his blasphemy against the living God.

19:8 *Libnah.* See note on 8:22.
19:9 *Tirhakah.* See note on Isa 37:9. *Cush.* See TNIV text note.
19:12 *Gozan.* See note on 17:6. *Harran.* See note on Ge 11:31. It is not known just when Harran was taken by the Assyrians.

Rezeph. Located south of the Euphrates River and northeast of Hamath. *Eden.* A district along the Euphrates River south of Harran (see Eze 27:23; Am 1:5), not to be confused with the Garden of Eden. It was incorporated into the Assyrian empire by Shalmaneser III in 855 B.C.

19:13 *Hamath … Ivvah.* See note on 17:24.
19:14 *letter.* See 2Ch 32:17.
19:15 *enthroned between the cherubim.* See notes on Ex 25:18; 1Sa 4:4. *you alone are God.* See v. 19; Dt 4:35,39; see also 2Ki 18:33–35; Isa 43:11 and notes.
19:18 *fashioned by human hands.* For the foolishness and futility of idolatry see Ps 115:3–8; 135:15–18; Isa 2:20; 40:19–20; 41:7; 44:9–20.
19:19 *that all the kingdoms of the earth may know.* Hezekiah recognizes that the Lord's reputation is at stake in the welfare of his covenant people (see 1Sa 12:22; see also Jos 7:9; 2Sa 7:23; Ps 23:3; Eze 5:13; 6:7 and notes).
19:20 *heard your prayer.* On this occasion Isaiah's message to Hezekiah was unsolicited by the king (contrast v. 2).
19:21–28 The arrogance of the Assyrians and their ridicule of the Israelites and their God are countered with

19:21 q Isa 47:1;
Jer 14:17; 18:13; 31:4;
46:11; La 2:13; Am 5:2
r Ps 53:5 s Pr 1:26;
3:34 t Job 16:4;
Ps 44:14; 64:8;
109:25; Jer 18:16
19:22 u S 2Ki 18:25
v Lev 19:2; 1Sa 2:2;
Job 6:10; Ps 16:10;
22:3; 71:22; 78:41;
89:18; Isa 1:4; 6:3;
57:15; Hos 11:9
19:23 w Isa 10:18;
Jer 21:14; Eze 20:47
x Ps 20:7; Jer 50:37
y Isa 10:34; 14:8;
33:9; Eze 31:3
19:25 z Isa 40:21,28
a Isa 22:11 b Mic 1:6
19:26 c Isa 13:7;
Eze 7:17; Zep 3:16
d Ps 6:10; 71:24;
83:17; Isa 41:23;
Jer 8:9 e Isa 4:2; 11:1;
53:2; Jer 23:5
f Job 8:12; Ps 37:2;
129:6
19:27 g Ps 139:1-4
19:28 h 2Ch 33:11;
Eze 19:9; 29:4; 38:4;
Am 4:2 i Isa 30:28
j ver 33
19:29 k S Ex 7:9;
S Dt 13:2; Lk 2:12
l Lev 25:5

" 'Virgin Daughter q Zion
    despises r you and mocks s you.
Daughter Jerusalem
    tosses her head t as you flee.
22 Who is it you have ridiculed and blasphemed? u
    Against whom have you raised your voice
    and lifted your eyes in pride?
    Against the Holy One v of Israel!
23 By your messengers
    you have ridiculed the Lord.
And you have said, w
    "With my many chariots x
I have ascended the heights of the mountains,
    the utmost heights of Lebanon.
I have cut down y its tallest cedars,
    the choicest of its junipers.
I have reached its remotest parts,
    the finest of its forests.
24 I have dug wells in foreign lands
    and drunk the water there.
With the soles of my feet
    I have dried up all the streams of Egypt."

25 " 'Have you not heard? z
    Long ago I ordained it.
In days of old I planned a it;
    now I have brought it to pass,
that you have turned fortified cities
    into piles of stone. b
26 Their people, drained of power, c
    are dismayed d and put to shame.
They are like plants in the field,
    like tender green shoots, e
like grass sprouting on the roof,
    scorched f before it grows up.

27 " 'But I know g where you are
    and when you come and go
    and how you rage against me.
28 Because you rage against me
    and because your insolence has reached my ears,
I will put my hook h in your nose
    and my bit i in your mouth,
and I will make you return j
    by the way you came.'

29 "This will be the sign k for you, Hezekiah:

"This year you will eat what grows by itself, l
    and the second year what springs from that.

---

a derisive pronouncement of judgment (cf. Ps 2) on the misconceived Assyrian pride (see Isa 10:5–34).
19:21 *Virgin Daughter Zion ... Daughter Jerusalem.* In Hebrew poetry (mainly) a conventional way of referring to a royal city, a nation or a people when these are personified as a woman, found often in the prophetic literature, with special concentration in Lamentations.
19:22 *Holy One of Israel.* A designation of the God of Israel characteristic of Isaiah (see Lev 11:44; Isa 1:4 and notes).
19:23 *Lebanon ... its tallest cedars.* See note on 1Ki 5:6.
19:24 *dried up all the streams of Egypt.* A presumptuous boast for one who had not even conquered Egypt.

A **19:25** *I ordained it ... now I have brought it to pass.* The God of Israel is the ruler of all nations and history. The Assyrians attributed their victories to their own military superiori-

ty. However, Isaiah said that God alone ordained these victories (see Isa 10:5–19; cf. Eze 30:24–26).

B **19:28** *hook in your nose.* At the top of an Assyrian obelisk an Assyrian king (probably Esarhaddon, 681–669 B.C.) is pictured holding ropes attached to rings in the noses of four of his enemies. Here Isaiah portrays the same thing happening to Sennacherib (see note on Isa 37:29; cf. Eze 38:4; Am 4:2).
19:29 *This year you will eat what grows by itself.* Sennacherib had apparently either destroyed or confiscated the entire harvest that had been sown the previous fall. The people would only have use of the later, second growth that came from seeds dropped from the previous year's harvest (see Lev 25:5). This suggests that Sennacherib came to Judah in March or April, about the time of harvest. *the second year what springs from that.* Sennacherib's departure would be too late in the fall

But in the third year sow and reap,
    plant vineyards *m* and eat their fruit.
³⁰Once more a remnant *n* of the house of Judah
    will take root *o* below and bear fruit above.
³¹For out of Jerusalem will come a remnant, *p*
    and out of Mount Zion a band of survivors. *q*

"The zeal *r* of the LORD Almighty will accomplish this.

³²"Therefore this is what the LORD says concerning the king of Assyria:

" 'He will not enter this city
    or shoot an arrow here.
He will not come before it with shield
    or build a siege ramp against it.
³³By the way that he came he will return; *s*
    he will not enter this city,

                         declares the LORD.

³⁴I will defend *t* this city and save it,
    for my sake and for the sake of David *u* my servant.' "

³⁵That night the angel of the LORD *v* went out and put to death a hundred and eighty-five thousand in the Assyrian camp. When the people got up the next morning—there were all the dead bodies! *w* ³⁶So Sennacherib king of Assyria broke camp and withdrew. *x* He returned to Nineveh *y* and stayed there.

³⁷One day, while he was worshiping in the temple of his god Nisrok, his sons Adrammelek *z* and Sharezer killed him with the sword, *a* and they escaped to the land of Ararat. *b* And Esarhaddon *c* his son succeeded him as king.

HEZEKIAH'S ILLNESS
20:1–11pp — 2Ch 32:24–26; Isa 38:1–8

20 In those days Hezekiah became ill and was at the point of death. The prophet Isaiah son of Amoz went to him and said, "This is what the LORD says: Put your house in order, because you are going to die; you will not recover." ²Hezekiah turned his face to the wall and prayed to the LORD, ³"Remember, *d* LORD, how I have walked *e* before you faithfully *f* and with wholehearted devotion and have done what is good in your eyes." And Hezekiah wept bitterly.

⁴Before Isaiah had left the middle court, the word of the LORD came to him: ⁵"Go back and tell Hezekiah, the ruler of my people, 'This is what the LORD, the God of your father David, says: I have heard *g* your prayer and seen your tears; *h* I will heal you. On the third

---

19:29 *m* Ps 107:37; Isa 65:21; Am 9:14
19:30 *n* S Ge 45:7
o Isa 5:24; 11:1; 27:6; Eze 17:22; Am 2:9
19:31 *p* S Ge 45:7
q Isa 66:19; Zep 2:9; Zec 14:16 *r* Isa 9:7
19:33 *s* ver 28
19:34 *t* 2Ki 20:6
u S 2Sa 7:15
19:35 *v* S Ge 19:13; S Ex 12:23
w Job 24:24; Isa 17:14; 41:12; Na 3:3
19:36 *x* S 2Ki 12:18
y S Ge 10:11
19:37 *z* 2Ki 17:31
a S ver 7 *b* S Ge 8:4
c S 2Ki 17:24
20:3 *d* S Ge 8:1; Ne 1:8; 5:19; 13:14
e S Ge 5:22
f S 1Ki 2:4; 2Ch 31:20
20:5 *g* S 1Ki 9:3
h Ps 6:6,8; 39:12; 56:8

(October) for new crops to be planted for the coming year. In the Holy Land, crops are normally sown in September and October. *in the third year sow and reap.* The routine times for sowing and harvesting could be observed in the following year. The third year is likely a reference to the third year of harvests detrimentally affected by the Assyrian presence.

A **19:30–31** *remnant.* See note on v. 4. For use of the term "remnant" as a designation for those who will participate in the future unfolding of God's redemptive program, see Isa 11:11,16; 28:5; Mic 4:7; Ro 11:5.

19:32 *not enter this city.* Sennacherib, who was presently at Libnah (see v. 8; see also note on 8:22), would not be able to carry out his threats against Jerusalem (see note on 18:13).

19:34 *for the sake of David my servant.* See note on 1Ki 11:13.

19:35 *angel of the LORD.* See note on Ge 16:7. *a hundred and eighty-five thousand.* See Isa 37:36 and note.

19:36 *Nineveh.* The capital of the Assyrian empire.

B **19:37** *his sons Adrammelek and Sharezer.* Ancient records refer to the murder of Sennacherib by an unnamed son in the 23rd year of Sennacherib's reign. *Ararat.* See note on Ge 8:4. *Esarhaddon his son succeeded him.* And reigned 681–669 B.C. (see chart, p. 482). Assyrian inscriptions speak of a struggle among Sennacherib's sons for the right of succession to the Assyrian throne. Sennacherib's designation of Esarhaddon as heir apparent, even though he was younger than several of his brothers, may have sparked the abortive attempt at a coup by

Adrammelech and Sharezer.

B **20:1** *In those days.* Hezekiah's illness (vv. 1–11), as well as his reception of envoys from Babylon (vv. 12–19), must have preceded the Assyrian campaign in 701 B.C. (see v. 6; see also notes on vv. 12–13). Babylonian records indicate that Marduk-Baladan (v. 12) died in Elam after being expelled from Babylon in 703. *Put your house in order.* Arrangements of a testamentary nature needed to be made, especially with respect to throne succession. *you are going to die.* Assuming that Hezekiah was 25 years old in 715 when he began his sole reign (see 18:2) and that his illness occurred a little more than 15 years prior to his death (see note on v. 6), he would have been about 37 or 38 years old at this time.

A **20:3** *walked before you faithfully . . . and have done what is good.* Hezekiah's prayer is not an appeal for divine favor that is based on good works, but it expresses the realization that the Lord graciously favors those who earnestly serve him (see note on 2Sa 22:21).

A **20:5** *I will heal you.* God is the one who sovereignly ordains all that comes to pass (Ps 139:16; Eph 1:11). Hezekiah's petition and God's response demonstrate that (1) divine sovereignty does not make prayer inappropriate but, on the contrary, establishes it, and (2) both prayer and the divine response to prayer are to be included in one's conception of God's sovereign plan (see 1Ki 21:29; Eze 33:13–16).

20:6 *i* S 2Ki 19:34;
S 1Ch 17:19
20:7 *j* S Ex 9:9
20:9 *k* S Dt 13:2;
Jer 44:29
20:10 *l* S 2Ki 3:18
20:11 *m* Jos 10:13;
2Ch 32:31
20:17 *n* 2Ki 24:13;
2Ch 36:10; Jer 20:5;
27:22; 52:17-23
20:18 *o* 2Ki 24:15;
Da 1:3 *p* Mic 4:10

day from now you will go up to the temple of the Lᴏʀᴅ. ⁶I will add fifteen years to your life. And I will deliver you and this city from the hand of the king of Assyria. I will defend *i* this city for my sake and for the sake of my servant David.' "

⁷Then Isaiah said, "Prepare a poultice of figs." They did so and applied it to the boil, *j* and he recovered.

⁸Hezekiah had asked Isaiah, "What will be the sign that the Lᴏʀᴅ will heal me and that I will go up to the temple of the Lᴏʀᴅ on the third day from now?"

⁹Isaiah answered, "This is the Lᴏʀᴅ's sign *k* to you that the Lᴏʀᴅ will do what he has promised: Shall the shadow go forward ten steps, or shall it go back ten steps?"

¹⁰"It is a simple *l* matter for the shadow to go forward ten steps," said Hezekiah. "Rather, have it go back ten steps."

¹¹Then the prophet Isaiah called on the Lᴏʀᴅ, and the Lᴏʀᴅ made the shadow go back *m* the ten steps it had gone down on the stairway of Ahaz.

ENVOYS FROM BABYLON

20:12–19pp — Isa 39:1–8
20:20–21pp — 2Ch 32:32–33

¹²At that time Marduk-Baladan son of Baladan king of Babylon sent Hezekiah letters and a gift, because he had heard of Hezekiah's illness. ¹³Hezekiah received the envoys and showed them all that was in his storehouses—the silver, the gold, the spices and the fine olive oil—his armory and everything found among his treasures. There was nothing in his palace or in all his kingdom that Hezekiah did not show them.

¹⁴Then Isaiah the prophet went to King Hezekiah and asked, "What did those men say, and where did they come from?"

"From a distant land," Hezekiah replied. "They came from Babylon."

¹⁵The prophet asked, "What did they see in your palace?"

"They saw everything in my palace," Hezekiah said. "There is nothing among my treasures that I did not show them."

¹⁶Then Isaiah said to Hezekiah, "Hear the word of the Lᴏʀᴅ: ¹⁷The time will surely come when everything in your palace, and all that your predecessors have stored up until this day, will be carried off to Babylon. *n* Nothing will be left, says the Lᴏʀᴅ. ¹⁸And some of your descendants, *o* your own flesh and blood who will be born to you, will be taken away, and they will become eunuchs in the palace of the king of Babylon." *p*

¹⁹"The word of the Lᴏʀᴅ you have spoken is good," Hezekiah replied. For he thought, "Will there not be peace and security in my lifetime?"

20:6 *add fifteen years to your life.* Hezekiah died in 686 B.C. The beginning of the extension of his life is thus to be placed no later than 702. *for my sake and for the sake of my servant David.* See 19:34; see also note on 1Ki 11:13.

20:7 *poultice.* The Lord healed Hezekiah (see v. 5), but divine healing does not necessarily exclude the use of known remedies.

20:9 *steps.* See v. 11 (see also note on Isa 38:8).

20:10 *simple matter...go forward.* Because that was the natural direction of the shadow's movement. Hezekiah chose the more difficult movement to make sure the sign was from the Lord.

20:11 *stairway of Ahaz.* Possibly refers to one leading to his house or to some kind of instrument used to measure time.

20:12 *Marduk-Baladan.* Means "(The god) Marduk has given me a son." He ruled in Babylon 721–710 B.C. before being forced to submit to Assyrian domination by Sargon II of Assyria. Sometime after Sargon's death in 705, Marduk-Baladan briefly reestablished Babylonian independence and ruled in Babylon until Sennacherib forced him to flee in 703 (see note on v. 1). *sent Hezekiah letters and a gift.* It is likely that Marduk-Baladan was attempting to draw Hezekiah into an alliance against Assyria. Although Hezekiah rejected the pro-Assyrian policies of his father, Ahaz (see 16:7), and rebelled against Assyria (see 18:7), he erred in seeking to strengthen Israel's security by friendship with Babylon and Egypt (see 2Ch 32:31; Isa 30–31; see also notes on 1Sa 17:11; 1Ki 15:19).

20:13 *received the envoys and showed them all.* Hezekiah's reception of the delegation from Babylon was overly hospitable.

Perhaps it was an attempt to bolster Judah's security by impressing the Babylonians with the wealth and power of his kingdom as a basis for mutual cooperation against the Assyrians. In principle this was a denial of the covenantal nature of the royal office in Israel (see note on 2Sa 24:1). *silver...oil.* The presence of these treasures in Jerusalem is evidence that this incident occurred before the payment of tribute to Sennacherib in 701 B.C. (see 18:15–16).

20:14 *What did those men say...?* Hezekiah gave no response to Isaiah's question concerning the diplomatic purpose of the Babylonian envoys.

20:17 *carried off to Babylon.* Hezekiah's reception of the Babylonians would bring the exact opposite of what he desired and expected. Isaiah's prediction of Babylonian exile at least 115 years before it happened is all the more remarkable because, when he spoke, it appeared that Assyria rather than Babylon was the world power from whom Judah had the most to fear.

20:18 *some of your descendants...will be taken away.* Hezekiah's own son Manasseh was taken by the Assyrians and held prisoner for a while in Babylon (see 2Ch 33:11); later, many more from the house of David were to follow (see 24:15; 25:7; Da 1:3).

20:19 *word...is good.* Although it is possible to understand Hezekiah's statement as a selfish expression of relief that he himself would not experience the announced adversity, it seems better to take it as a humble acceptance of the Lord's judgment (see 2Ch 32:26) and as gratefulness for the intervening time of peace that the Lord in his mercy was granting to his people.

^{20}As for the other events of Hezekiah's reign, all his achievements and how he made the pool ^{q} and the tunnel ^{r} by which he brought water into the city, are they not written in the book of the annals of the kings of Judah? ^{21}Hezekiah rested with his ancestors. And Manasseh his son succeeded him as king.

MANASSEH KING OF JUDAH
21:1–10pp — 2Ch 33:1–10
21:17–18pp — 2Ch 33:18–20

21 Manasseh was twelve years old when he became king, and he reigned in Jerusalem fifty-five years. His mother's name was Hephzibah. $^{s\,2}$He did evil ^{t} in the eyes of the LORD, following the detestable practices ^{u} of the nations the LORD had driven out before the Israelites. ^{3}He rebuilt the high places ^{v} his father Hezekiah had destroyed; he also erected altars to Baal ^{w} and made an Asherah pole, ^{x} as Ahab king of Israel had done. He bowed down to all the starry hosts ^{y} and worshiped them. ^{4}He built altars ^{z} in the temple of the LORD, of which the LORD had said, "In Jerusalem I will put my Name." $^a\,^5$In the two courts ^{b} of the temple of the LORD, he built altars to all the starry hosts. ^{6}He sacrificed his own son ^{c} in the fire, practiced divination, ^{d} sought omens, and consulted mediums and spiritists. ^{e} He did much evil in the eyes of the LORD, arousing ^{f} his anger.

^{7}He took the carved Asherah pole ^{g} he had made and put it in the temple, ^{h} of which the LORD had said to David and to his son Solomon, "In this temple and in Jerusalem, which I have chosen out of all the tribes of Israel, I will put my Name ^{i} forever. ^{8}I will not again ^{j} make the feet of the Israelites wander from the land I gave their ancestors, if only they will be careful to do everything I commanded them and will keep the whole Law that my servant Moses ^{k} gave them." ^{9}But the people did not listen. Manasseh led them astray, so that they did more evil ^{l} than the nations ^{m} the LORD had destroyed before the Israelites.

^{10}The LORD said through his servants the prophets: ^{11}"Manasseh king of Judah has committed these detestable sins. He has done more evil ^{n} than the Amorites ^{o} who preceded him and has led Judah into sin with his idols. $^p\,^{12}$Therefore this is what the LORD, the God of Israel, says: I am going to bring such disaster ^{q} on Jerusalem and Judah that the ears of everyone who hears of it will tingle. $^r\,^{13}$I will stretch out over Jerusalem the measuring line used against Samaria and the plumb line ^{s} used against the house of Ahab. I will wipe ^{t} out Jerusalem as one wipes a dish, wiping it and turning it upside down. ^{14}I will forsake ^{u} the remnant ^{v} of my inheritance and give them into the hands of enemies. They will be looted and plundered by all their enemies; ^{15}they have done evil ^{w} in my eyes and have aroused ^{x} my anger from the day their ancestors came out of Egypt until this day."

20:20 ^{q} S 2Ki 18:17
^{r} S 2Sa 5:8
21:1 ^{s} Isa 62:4
21:2 ^{t} ver 16;
S Dt 4:25; Jer 15:4
^{u} Dt 9:4; S 18:9;
S 1Ki 14:24; 2Ki 16:3
21:3 ^{v} S 1Ki 3:3;
S 2Ki 18:4
^{w} S Jdg 6:28
^{x} S Dt 16:21
^{y} S Ge 2:1; Dt 17:3;
Jer 19:13
21:4 ^{z} Isa 66:4;
Jer 4:1; 7:30; 23:11;
32:34; Eze 23:39
^{a} S Ex 20:24;
S 2Sa 7:13
21:5 ^{b} 1Ki 7:12;
2Ki 23:12
21:6 ^{c} S Lev 18:21;
S Dt 18:10; S 2Ki 3:27
^{d} Dt 18:14
^{e} S Lev 19:31
^{f} 2Ki 23:26
21:7 ^{g} Dt 16:21;
2Ki 23:4 ^{h} S Lev 15:31
^{i} S Ex 20:24;
S 2Sa 7:13
21:8 ^{j} S 2Sa 7:10
^{k} S 2Ki 18:12
21:9 ^{l} S 1Ki 14:9;
Eze 5:7 ^{m} Dt 9:4
21:11 ^{n} S 1Ki 14:9
^{o} S Ge 15:16
^{p} Eze 18:12
21:12 ^{q} 2Ki 23:26;
24:3; Jer 15:4; Eze 7:5
^{r} S 1Sa 3:11
21:13 ^{s} Isa 28:17;
34:11; La 2:8; Am 7:7-
9 ^{t} 2Ki 23:27
21:14 ^{u} Ps 78:58-
60; Jer 12:7; 23:33
^{v} 2Ki 19:4; Ezr 9:8;
Ne 1:2; Isa 1:9; 10:21;
Jer 6:9; 40:15; 42:2;
44:7,28; 50:20;
Mic 2:12
21:15 ^{w} S Ex 32:22
^{x} Jer 25:7

B **C** **20:20** *the pool and the tunnel.* Hezekiah built a tunnel from the Gihon spring (see 1Ki 1:33,38) to a cistern (2Ch 32:30) inside the city's walls (see map No. 10 at the end of this study Bible). This greatly reduced Jerusalem's vulnerability to siege by guaranteeing a continuing water supply. In 1880 an inscription (the Siloam inscription; see chart, p. xxiv) was found in the rock wall at the entrance to this tunnel, describing the method of its construction. The tunnel, cut through solid rock, is c. 1,750 feet long; its height varies from 4 feet to 12 feet and it averages 2 feet in width. *annals of the kings of Judah.* See note on 1Ki 14:29.

20:21 *rested with his ancestors.* See note on 1Ki 1:21.

C **21:1** *twelve years old.* Manasseh was born after Hezekiah's serious illness (see 20:6). *fifty-five years.* 697–642 B.C., including a ten-year coregency (697–686) with his father, Hezekiah. This was the longest reign of any king in either Israel or Judah.

C **21:2** *detestable practices.* Manasseh reversed the religious policies of his father, Hezekiah (see 18:3–5), and reverted to those of Ahaz (see 16:3).

C **21:3** *high places . . . Hezekiah had destroyed.* See note on 18:4; see also 2Ch 31:1. *Asherah pole.* See 1Ki 14:15,23; 15:13; 16:33. *as Ahab.* Manasseh was the Ahab of Judah (see 1Ki 16:30–33). *bowed down to all the starry hosts.* See note on 17:16.

21:4 *In Jerusalem I will put my Name.* See 1Ki 8:16; 9:3 and notes.

21:6 *sacrificed his own son.* See note on 16:3; see also 17:17; cf.

3:27 and note. *practiced divination, sought omens.* See notes on 16:15; 17:17. *consulted mediums and spiritists.* See Lev 19:31; Dt 18:11; 1Sa 28:3,7–9 and notes.

21:7 *carved Asherah pole.* See note on 1Ki 14:15. *David.* See 2Sa 7:13. *Solomon.* See 1Ki 9:3. *chosen out of all the tribes.* See 1Ki 11:13,32,36.

21:9 *nations the LORD had destroyed.* See 1Ki 14:24; Dt 12:29–31; 31:3.

21:10 *his servants the prophets.* See 2Ch 33:10,18.

21:11 *more evil than the Amorites.* See note on 1Ki 21:26. *idols.* See note on Lev 26:30.

21:12 *disaster on Jerusalem.* Fulfilled in the final destruction of the city by the Babylonians in 586 B.C. (see ch. 25). *ears of everyone . . . will tingle.* See Jer 19:3 and note.

21:13 *measuring line . . . plumb line.* Instruments normally associated with construction are used here as symbols of destruction (see Isa 34:11; Am 7:7–9, 17).

21:14 *I will forsake.* In the sense of giving over to judgment (see Jer 12:7), not in the sense of abrogation of the covenant (see 1Sa 12:22; Isa 43:1–7). *remnant of my inheritance.* Upon the destruction of the northern kingdom, Judah had become the remnant of the Lord's inheritance (see 1Ki 8:51; Dt 4:20; 1Sa 10:1; Ps 28:9; see also note on 2Ki 19:4).

C **21:15** The history of Israel was a history of covenant breaking. With the reign of Manasseh the cup of God's wrath overflowed, and the judgment of exile from the land of promise (see note on 17:7–23) became inevitable (see 24:1–4).

21:16 ʸ 2Ki 24:4;
Job 22:14; Ps 10:11;
94:7; 106:38;
Isa 29:15; 47:10; 59:3,
7; Jer 2:34; 7:6; 19:4;
22:17; La 4:13;
Eze 7:23; 8:12; 9:9;
22:3-4; Hos 4:2;
Zep 1:12 ᶻ S ver 2,11
21:18 ᵃ ver 26;
Est 1:5; 7:7
21:20 ᵇ 1Ki 15:26
21:22 ᶜ S 1Sa 8:8
ᵈ 1Ki 11:33
21:23 ᵉ S 2Ki 12:20
21:24 ᶠ 2Ki 14:5
ᵍ 2Ch 33:21; Zep 1:1
21:26 ʰ S ver 18
22:1 ⁱ Jer 1:2; 25:3
ʲ Jos 15:39
22:2 ᵏ S Dt 17:19;
S 1Ki 14:8 ˡ S Dt 5:32
22:3 ᵐ 2Ch 34:20;
Jer 39:14
22:4 ⁿ Ezr 7:1
ᵒ 2Ki 12:4-5
22:5 ᵖ 2Ki 12:5,11-
14
22:6 �q 2Ki 12:11-12
22:7 ʳ S 2Ki 12:15

16Moreover, Manasseh also shed so much innocent blood ʸ that he filled Jerusalem from end to end—besides the sin that he had caused Judah ᶻ to commit, so that they did evil in the eyes of the Lord.

17As for the other events of Manasseh's reign, and all he did, including the sin he committed, are they not written in the book of the annals of the kings of Judah? 18Manasseh rested with his ancestors and was buried in his palace garden, ᵃ the garden of Uzza. And Amon his son succeeded him as king.

AMON KING OF JUDAH

21:19–24pp — 2Ch 33:21–25

19Amon was twenty-two years old when he became king, and he reigned in Jerusalem two years. His mother's name was Meshullemeth daughter of Haruz; she was from Jotbah. 20He did evil ᵇ in the eyes of the Lord, as his father Manasseh had done. 21He followed completely the ways of his father, worshiping the idols his father had worshiped, and bowing down to them. 22He forsook ᶜ the Lord, the God of his ancestors, and did not walk ᵈ in obedience to him.

23Amon's officials conspired against him and assassinated ᵉ the king in his palace. 24Then the people of the land killed ᶠ all who had plotted against King Amon, and they made Josiah ᵍ his son king in his place.

25As for the other events of Amon's reign, and what he did, are they not written in the book of the annals of the kings of Judah? 26He was buried in his tomb in the garden ʰ of Uzza. And Josiah his son succeeded him as king.

THE BOOK OF THE LAW FOUND

22:1–20pp — 2Ch 34:1–2,8–28

22 Josiah ⁱ was eight years old when he became king, and he reigned in Jerusalem thirty-one years. His mother's name was Jedidah daughter of Adaiah; she was from Bozkath. ʲ 2He did what was right ᵏ in the eyes of the Lord and followed completely the ways of his father David, not turning aside to the right ˡ or to the left.

3In the eighteenth year of his reign, King Josiah sent the secretary, Shaphan ᵐ son of Azaliah, the son of Meshullam, to the temple of the Lord. He said: 4"Go up to Hilkiah ⁿ the high priest and have him get ready the money that has been brought into the temple of the Lord, which the doorkeepers have collected ᵒ from the people. 5Have them entrust it to the men appointed to supervise the work on the temple. And have these men pay the workers who repair ᵖ the temple of the Lord— 6the carpenters, the builders and the masons. Also have them purchase timber and dressed stone to repair the temple. q 7But they need not account for the money entrusted to them, because they are honest in their dealings." ʳ

8Hilkiah the high priest said to Shaphan the secretary, "I have found the Book of the

---

21:16 *innocent blood.* A reference to godly people and perhaps even prophets who were martyred for opposition to Manasseh's evil practices (see vv. 10–11). According to a Jewish tradition (not otherwise substantiated) Isaiah was sawed in two during Manasseh's reign (see Introduction to Isaiah: Author; cf. Heb 11:37).

21:17 *other events of Manasseh's reign.* See 2Ch 33:12–19. *annals of the kings of Judah.* See note on 1Ki 14:29.

21:18 *rested with his ancestors.* See note on 1Ki 1:21. *Uzza.* Probably a shortened form of Uzziah (see TNIV text note on 14:21; see also 2Ch 26:1 and note).

21:19 *two years.* 642–640 b.c. *Jotbah.* Some identify it with the Jotbathah of Nu 33:33–34 and Dt 10:7, near Ezion Geber. Others, including the church father Jerome, have located it in Judah.

21:20 *did evil.* Amon did not share in the change of heart that characterized his father, Manasseh, in the last days of his life (see 2Ch 33:12–19). He must have restored the idolatrous practices that Manasseh abolished because these were again in existence in the time of Josiah (see 23:5–7,12).

21:23 *conspired against him.* Whether this palace revolt was motivated by religious or political considerations is not known.

21:24 *people of the land.* The citizenry in general (see 11:14,18; 14:21; 23:30).

21:25 *annals of the kings of Judah.* See note on 1Ki 14:29.

21:26 *Uzza.* See note on v. 18.

22:1 *thirty-one years.* 640–609 b.c. (see note on 21:19). *Bozkath.* Located in Judah in the vicinity of Lachish (see Jos 15:39).

22:2 *ways of his father David.* See note on 18:3. Josiah was the last godly king of the Davidic line prior to the exile. Jeremiah, who prophesied during the time of Josiah (see Jer 1:2), spoke highly of him (Jer 22:15–16). Zephaniah also prophesied in the early days of his reign (Zep 1:1).

22:3 *eighteenth year.* 622 b.c. Josiah was then 26 years old (see v. 1). He had begun to serve the Lord faithfully at the age of 16 (the 8th year of his reign, 2Ch 34:3). When he was 20 years old (the 12th year of his reign, 2Ch 34:3), he had already begun to purge the land of its idolatrous practices. *secretary, Shaphan.* See note on 2Sa 8:17. Two additional individuals are mentioned as accompanying Shaphan in 2Ch 34:8.

22:4 *Hilkiah.* Father of Azariah and grandfather of Seraiah, the high priest executed at the time of the destruction of Jerusalem by the Babylonians (see 25:18–21). It is unlikely that this Hilkiah was also the father of Jeremiah (see Jer 1:1). *money . . . the doorkeepers have collected.* Josiah used the method devised by Joash for collecting funds for the restoration of the temple (see 12:1–16; 2Ch 34:9).

22:5 *men appointed to supervise.* See 2Ch 34:12–13.

22:8 *Book of the Law.* Some interpreters hold that this refers to a copy of the entire Pentateuch, while others understand it as a reference to a copy of part or all of Deuteronomy alone (see Dt 31:24,26; 2Ch 34:14).

Law[s] in the temple of the LORD." He gave it to Shaphan, who read it. [9]Then Shaphan the secretary went to the king and reported to him: "Your officials have paid out the money that was in the temple of the LORD and have entrusted it to the workers and supervisors at the temple." [10]Then Shaphan the secretary informed the king, "Hilkiah the priest has given me a book." And Shaphan read from it in the presence of the king.[t]

[11]When the king heard the words of the Book of the Law,[u] he tore his robes. [12]He gave these orders to Hilkiah the priest, Ahikam[v] son of Shaphan, Akbor son of Micaiah, Shaphan the secretary and Asaiah the king's attendant:[w] [13]"Go and inquire[x] of the LORD for me and for the people and for all Judah about what is written in this book that has been found. Great is the LORD's anger[y] that burns against us because those who have gone before us have not obeyed the words of this book; they have not acted in accordance with all that is written there concerning us."

[14]Hilkiah the priest, Ahikam, Akbor, Shaphan and Asaiah went to speak to the prophet[z] Huldah, who was the wife of Shallum son of Tikvah, the son of Harhas, keeper of the wardrobe. She lived in Jerusalem, in the New Quarter.

[15]She said to them, "This is what the LORD, the God of Israel, says: Tell the man who sent you to me, [16]'This is what the LORD says: I am going to bring disaster[a] on this place and its people, according to everything written in the book[b] the king of Judah has read. [17]Because they have forsaken[c] me and burned incense to other gods and aroused my anger by all the idols their hands have made,[a] my anger will burn against this place and will not be quenched.' [18]Tell the king of Judah, who sent you to inquire[d] of the LORD, 'This is what the LORD, the God of Israel, says concerning the words you heard: [19]Because your heart was responsive and you humbled[e] yourself before the LORD when you heard what I have spoken against this place and its people—that they would become a curse[b f] and be laid waste[g]—and because you tore your robes and wept in my presence, I also have heard you, declares the LORD. [20]Therefore I will gather you to your ancestors, and you will be buried in peace.[h] Your eyes[i] will not see all the disaster I am going to bring on this place.' "

So they took her answer back to the king.

JOSIAH RENEWS THE COVENANT

23:1–3pp — 2Ch 34:29–32
23:4–20Ref — 2Ch 34:3–7,33
23:21–23pp — 2Ch 35:1,18–19
23:28–30pp — 2Ch 35:20—36:1

23 Then the king called together all the elders of Judah and Jerusalem. [2]He went up to the temple of the LORD with the people of Judah, the inhabitants of Jerusalem, the priests and the prophets—all the people from the least to the greatest. He read[j] in their hearing all the words of the Book of the Covenant,[k] which had been found in the temple of the LORD. [3]The king stood by the pillar[l] and renewed the covenant[m] in the presence of the LORD—to follow[n] the LORD and keep his commands, stat-

---

[a] 17 Or by everything they have done   [b] 19 That is, their names would be used in cursing (see Jer. 29:22); or, others would see that they are cursed.

22:11 *tore his robes.* See notes on 18:37; Jos 7:6; contrast Josiah's reaction with that of Jehoiakim to the words of the scroll written by Jeremiah (see Jer 36:24). Perhaps the covenant curses of Lev 26 and/or Dt 28, climaxing with the threat of exile, were the statements that especially disturbed Josiah.
22:12 *Ahikam.* Father of Gedaliah, who was later to be appointed governor of Judah by Nebuchadnezzar (see 25:22; Jer 39:14). He was also the protector of Jeremiah when his life was threatened during the reign of Jehoiakim (see Jer 26:24). *Akbor.* His son Elnathan is mentioned in 24:8; Jer 26:22; 36:12. *Shaphan the secretary.* See note on v. 3.
22:14 *prophet Huldah.* For other female prophets see notes on Ex 15:20; Jdg 4:4. *Shallum ... keeper of the wardrobe.* Perhaps the same Shallum who was the uncle of Jeremiah (see Jer 32:7). *New Quarter.* A section of the city probably located in a newly developed area between the first and second walls in the northwest part of Jerusalem (see 2Ch 34:14; 34:22; Ne 11:9 and note; Zep 1:10).
22:16 *this place.* Jerusalem.
22:19 *your heart was responsive.* See v. 11.
22:20 *gather you to your ancestors.* See note on 1Ki 1:21. *you will be buried in peace.* This prediction refers to Josi-

ah's death before God's judgment on Jerusalem through Nebuchadnezzar and so is not contradicted by his death in battle with Pharaoh Necho of Egypt (see 23:29–30). Josiah was assured that the final judgment on Judah and Jerusalem would not come in his own days.
23:1 *elders.* See note on 10:1.
23:2 *Book of the Covenant.* Although this designation is used in Ex 24:7 with reference to the contents of Ex 20–23, it is here applied to either all or part of the book of Deuteronomy or the entire Mosaic law. Whatever else the scroll contained, it clearly included the covenant curses of Lev 26 and/or Dt 28 (see notes on v. 21; 22:8,11).
23:3 *pillar.* See note on 11:14. *renewed the covenant.* Josiah carries out the function of covenant mediator; cf. Moses (Ex 24:3–8; Deuteronomy), Joshua (Jos 24), Samuel (1Sa 11:14—12:25) and Jehoiada (2Ki 11:17). *follow the LORD.* See notes on 1Sa 12:14,20. *pledged themselves to the covenant.* It is likely that some sort of ratification rite was performed, in which the people participated and pledged by oath to be loyal to their covenant obligations. Whether this was done symbolically (see Jer 34:18) or verbally (see Dt 27:11–26) is not clear.

22:8 [g]S Dt 28:61; S 31:24; Gal 3:10
22:10 [t]Jer 36:21
22:11 [u]ver 8
22:12 [v]2Ki 25:22; Jer 26:24; 39:14
[w]1Sa 8:14
22:13 [x]S Ge 25:22; S 1Sa 9:9 [y]Dt 29:24-28; S 31:17; Isa 5:25; 42:25; Am 2:4
22:14 [z]S Ex 15:20
22:16 [a]S Dt 31:29; S Jos 23:15; Jer 6:19; 11:11; 18:11; 35:17
[b]Da 9:11
22:17 [c]S 1Ki 9:9
22:18 [d]Jer 21:2; 37:3,7
22:19 [e]S Ex 10:3; Isa 57:15; 61:1; Mic 6:8 [f]Jer 24:9; 25:18; 26:6
[g]Lev 26:31
22:20 [h]Isa 47:11; 57:1; Jer 18:11
[i]S 1Ki 21:29
23:2 [j]S Dt 31:11
[k]S Ex 24:7
23:3 [l]S 1Ki 7:15
[m]S 2Ki 11:12
[n]S Dt 13:4

23:4 °2Ki 25:18;
Jer 35:4 PS 2Ki 21:7
23:5 qS 2Ki 16:4
rJer 8:2 sJer 43:13
23:6 tJer 31:40
uS Ex 32:20
vS Nu 19:16
wJer 26:23
23:7 xS Ge 38:21;
1Ki 14:24; Eze 16:16
23:8 yS Jos 18:24;
S 1Ki 15:22
23:9 zEze 44:10-14
23:10 aIsa 30:33;
Jer 7:31,32; 19:6
bS Jos 15:8
cS Lev 18:21;
S Dt 18:10
23:11 dver 5,19;
Ne 9:34; Jer 44:9
eS Dt 4:19
23:12 f2Ch 33:15
gJer 19:13; Zep 1:5
hS 2Ki 21:5
iS 2Sa 15:23
23:13 j1Ki 11:7
kS Dt 27:15 lJer 11:13
23:14 mS Ex 23:24
nS Nu 19:16;
S Ps 53:5
23:15 oS Jos 7:2;
1Ki 13:1-3
pS 1Ki 12:33
23:16 qS 1Ki 13:2

utes and decrees with all his heart and all his soul, thus confirming the words of the covenant written in this book. Then all the people pledged themselves to the covenant.

⁴The king ordered Hilkiah the high priest, the priests next in rank and the doorkeepers ᵒ to remove ᵖ from the temple of the Lᴏʀᴅ all the articles made for Baal and Asherah and all the starry hosts. He burned them outside Jerusalem in the fields of the Kidron Valley and took the ashes to Bethel. ⁵He did away with the idolatrous priests appointed by the kings of Judah to burn incense on the high places of the towns of Judah and on those around Jerusalem—those who burned incense �q to Baal, to the sun and moon, to the constellations and to all the starry hosts. ʳˢ ⁶He took the Asherah pole from the temple of the Lᴏʀᴅ to the Kidron Valley ᵗ outside Jerusalem and burned it there. He ground it to powder ᵘ and scattered the dust over the graves ᵛ of the common people. ʷ ⁷He also tore down the quarters of the male shrine prostitutes ˣ that were in the temple of the Lᴏʀᴅ, the quarters where women did weaving for Asherah.

⁸Josiah brought all the priests from the towns of Judah and desecrated the high places, from Geba ʸ to Beersheba, where the priests had burned incense. He broke down the gateway at the entrance of the Gate of Joshua, the city governor, which was on the left of the city gate. ⁹Although the priests of the high places did not serve ᶻ at the altar of the Lᴏʀᴅ in Jerusalem, they ate unleavened bread with their fellow priests.

¹⁰He desecrated Topheth, ᵃ which was in the Valley of Ben Hinnom, ᵇ so no one could use it to sacrifice their son ᶜ or daughter in the fire to Molek. ¹¹He removed from the entrance to the temple of the Lᴏʀᴅ the horses that the kings of Judah ᵈ had dedicated to the sun. They were in the court ᵉ near the room of an official named Nathan-Melek. Josiah then burned the chariots dedicated to the sun. ᵉ

¹²He pulled down ᶠ the altars the kings of Judah had erected on the roof ᵍ near the upper room of Ahaz, and the altars Manasseh had built in the two courts ʰ of the temple of the Lᴏʀᴅ. He removed them from there, smashed them to pieces and threw the rubble into the Kidron Valley. ⁱ ¹³The king also desecrated the high places that were east of Jerusalem on the south of the Hill of Corruption—the ones Solomon ʲ king of Israel had built for Ashtoreth the vile goddess of the Sidonians, for Chemosh the vile god of Moab, and for Molek the detestable ᵏ god of the people of Ammon. ˡ ¹⁴Josiah smashed ᵐ the sacred stones and cut down the Asherah poles and covered the sites with human bones. ⁿ

¹⁵Even the altar ᵒ at Bethel, the high place made by Jeroboam ᵖ son of Nebat, who had caused Israel to sin—even that altar and high place he demolished. He burned the high place and ground it to powder, and burned the Asherah pole also. ¹⁶Then Josiah �q looked around, and when he saw the tombs that were there on the hillside, he had the bones re-

---

ᵃ 11 The meaning of the Hebrew for this word is uncertain.

23:4 doorkeepers. See 12:9. Baal and Asherah. See note on 1Ki 14:15. starry hosts. See note on 17:16. Kidron Valley. See note on Isa 22:7 and map, p. 486; see also 1Ki 15:13 and note. took the ashes to Bethel. See vv. 15–16. Bethel was located just over the border between Judah and the former northern kingdom in territory nominally under Assyrian control. With a decline in Assyrian power, Josiah was able to exert his own influence in the north. He apparently deposited the ashes at Bethel in order to desecrate (see note on v. 14) the very place where golden calf worship had originally polluted the land (see notes on 1Ki 12:28–30).
23:5 idolatrous priests. See Hos 10:5; Zep 1:4. kings of Judah. A reference to Manasseh and Amon, and perhaps to Ahaz before them. high places. See note on 18:4.
23:6 Asherah pole. See note on 1Ki 14:15. The Asherah poles destroyed by Hezekiah (18:4) were reintroduced by Manasseh (21:7). When Manasseh turned to the Lord, it is likely that he too got rid of the Asherah poles (see 2Ch 33:15) and that they were then again reintroduced by Amon (2Ki 21:21; 2Ch 33:22). scattered the dust over the graves of the common people. Intended as a defilement of the goddess, not as a desecration of the graves of the poor (see Jer 26:23).
23:7 male shrine prostitutes. See note on 1Ki 14:24.
23:8 desecrated the high places. See note on 18:4. Geba to Beersheba. Geba was on the northern border of the southern kingdom (see 1Ki 15:22), and Beersheba was on its southern border (see note on 1Sa 3:20).
23:9 ate unleavened bread with their fellow priests. Although not permitted to serve at the temple altar, these priests were to

be sustained by a share of the priestly provisions (see Lev 2:10; 6:16–18). They occupied a status similar to that of priests with physical defects (see Lev 21:16–23).
23:10 Topheth ... Molek. See note on 1Ki 11:5. Topheth was an area in the Valley of Hinnom where altars used for child sacrifice were located (see Isa 30:33; Jer 7:31; 19:5–6 and notes). sacrifice their son or daughter. See 17:17; 21:6; see also note on 16:3.

B **23:11** horses ... dedicated to the sun. If live, the horses may have been used to pull chariots bearing images of a sun-god in religious processions. Small images of horses have recently been found in a pagan shrine just outside one of the ancient walls of Jerusalem. Nathan-Melek. Perhaps the official in charge of the chariots.
23:12 altars ... on the roof. Altars dedicated to the worship of all the starry hosts (see Jer 19:13; Zep 1:5)—erected by Ahaz (2Ki 16:3–4,10–16), Manasseh (21:3) and Amon (21:21–22).
23:13 high places ... Solomon ... had built. See note on 1Ki 11:5.
23:14 covered the sites with human bones. The bones would defile these sites and make them unsuitable for pagan use in the future (see Nu 19:16).
23:15 altar at Bethel. See 1Ki 12:32–33. Nothing is said of the golden calf, which undoubtedly had been sent to Assyria as tribute at the time of the captivity of the northern kingdom (see Hos 10:5–6).
23:16 tombs. Of the priests of the Bethel sanctuary (see 1Ki 13:2). burned on the altar to defile it. See notes on vv. 6,14. the man of God who foretold these things. See 1Ki 13:1–2,32.

moved from them and burned on the altar to defile it, in accordance[r] with the word of the LORD proclaimed by the man of God who foretold these things.

[17] The king asked, "What is that tombstone I see?"

The people of the city said, "It marks the tomb of the man of God who came from Judah and pronounced against the altar of Bethel the very things you have done to it."

[18] "Leave it alone," he said. "Don't let anyone disturb his bones[s]." So they spared his bones and those of the prophet[t] who had come from Samaria.

[19] Just as he had done at Bethel, Josiah removed all the shrines at the high places that the kings of Israel had built in the towns of Samaria and that had aroused the LORD's anger. [20] Josiah slaughtered[u] all the priests of those high places on the altars and burned human bones[v] on them. Then he went back to Jerusalem.

[21] The king gave this order to all the people: "Celebrate the Passover[w] to the LORD your God, as it is written in this Book of the Covenant."[x] [22] Neither in the days of the judges who led Israel nor in the days of the kings of Israel and the kings of Judah had any such Passover been observed. [23] But in the eighteenth year of King Josiah, this Passover was celebrated to the LORD in Jerusalem.[y]

[24] Furthermore, Josiah got rid of the mediums and spiritists,[z] the household gods,[a] the idols and all the other detestable[b] things seen in Judah and Jerusalem. This he did to fulfill the requirements of the law written in the book that Hilkiah the priest had discovered in the temple of the LORD. [25] Neither before nor after Josiah was there a king like him who turned[c] to the LORD as he did—with all his heart and with all his soul and with all his strength, in accordance with all the Law of Moses.[d]

[26] Nevertheless, the LORD did not turn away from the heat of his fierce anger,[e] which burned against Judah because of all that Manasseh[f] had done to arouse his anger. [27] So the LORD said, "I will remove[g] Judah also from my presence[h] as I removed Israel, and I will reject[i] Jerusalem, the city I chose, and this temple, about which I said, 'There shall my Name be.'[a]"

[28] As for the other events of Josiah's reign, and all he did, are they not written in the book of the annals of the kings of Judah?

[29] While Josiah was king, Pharaoh Necho[j] king of Egypt went up to the Euphrates River to help the king of Assyria. King Josiah marched out to meet him in battle, but Necho faced him and killed him at Megiddo.[k] [30] Josiah's servants brought his body in a chariot[l] from Megiddo to Jerusalem and buried him in his own tomb. And the people of the land took Jehoahaz son of Josiah and anointed him and made him king in place of his father.

[a] 27 1 Kings 8:29

23:16 [r] 1Ki 13:32
23:18 [s] 1Ki 13:31
[t] 1Ki 13:29
23:20 [u] S Ex 22:20; S 2Ki 11:18
[v] S 1Ki 13:2
23:21 [w] S Ex 12:11; Dt 16:1-8 [x] S Ex 24:7
23:23 [y] S Ex 12:11; S Nu 28:16
23:24 [z] S Lev 19:31; S Dt 18:11
[a] S Ge 31:19
[b] Dt 7:26; 2Ki 16:3
23:25 [c] S 1Sa 7:3
[d] Jer 22:15
23:26 [e] 2Ki 21:6; Jer 23:20; 30:24
[f] S 2Ki 21:12
23:27 [g] 2Ki 21:13
[h] S Ex 33:15; 2Ki 24:3
[i] Jer 27:10; 32:31
23:29 [j] ver 33-35; Jer 46:2 [k] 2Ki 9:27
23:30 [l] S 2Ki 9:28

23:18 *prophet who had come from Samaria.* See 1Ki 13:31–32. Samaria is here not to be understood as the city by that name since the prophet came from Bethel (see 1Ki 13:11) and the city Samaria did not yet exist (see 1Ki 16:24). Rather, it is to be taken as a designation for the entire area of the former northern kingdom (see notes on 17:24,29; 1Ki 13:32).

23:20 *slaughtered all the priests of those high places.* These were non-Levitical priests of the apostate worship practiced in the area of the former northern kingdom (see notes on 17:27–28,33–34). They were treated like the pagan priests of Judah (see v. 5) in contrast to Josiah's treatment of the priests at the high places in Judah (see vv. 8–9). Josiah's actions in this matter conformed to the requirements of Dt 13; 17:2–7.

23:21 *Celebrate the Passover.* A more complete description of this observance is found in 2Ch 35:1–19. *as it is written in this Book of the Covenant.* See note on v. 2. This appears to refer to Dt 16:1–8, where the Passover is described in a communal setting at a sanctuary (see Ex 23:15–17; 34:23–24; Lev 23:4–14) rather than in the family setting of Ex 12:1–14,43–49.

23:22 The uniqueness of Josiah's Passover celebration seems to be in the fact that all the Passover lambs were slaughtered exclusively by the Levites (see 2Ch 35:1–19; cf. 2Ch 30:2–3,17–20 for the Passover observed in the time of Hezekiah).

23:23 *eighteenth year.* See note on 22:3.

23:24 *household gods.* See note on Ge 31:19. *idols.* See Lev 26:30. *requirements of the law.* See note on v. 2; 22:8.

23:25 *was there a king like him.* See note on 18:5. *with all his heart . . . soul and . . . strength.* See Dt 6:5.

23:26 *Nevertheless, the LORD did not turn away from the heat of*

his fierce anger. The judgment against Judah and Jerusalem was postponed but not rescinded because of Josiah's reformation (see notes on 21:15; 22:20).

23:27 *as I removed Israel.* See 17:18–23. *Jerusalem, the city I chose.* See 21:4,7,13. *this temple, about which I said, 'There shall my Name be.'* See note on 1Ki 8:16.

23:28 *annals of the kings of Judah.* See note on 1Ki 14:29.

23:29 *Pharaoh Necho king of Egypt.* Ruled 610–595 B.C. *help the king of Assyria.* Pharaoh Necho intended to help Ashur-Uballit II, the last Assyrian king, in his struggle against the rising power of Babylon under Nabopolassar. The Assyrian capital, Nineveh, had already fallen to the Babylonians and Medes in 612 (see the book of Nahum). The remaining Assyrian forces had regrouped at Harran, but in 609 they were forced west of the Euphrates. It appears to be at this time that the Egyptians under Necho were coming to the Assyrians' aid. *King Josiah marched out to meet him in battle.* Perhaps Josiah opposed the passage of Necho's army through the pass at Megiddo (see 2Ch 35:20–24) because he feared that the growth of either Egyptian or Assyrian power would have adverse results for the continued independence of Judah. *Megiddo.* See note on Jdg 5:19.

23:30 *buried him in his own tomb.* See 2Ch 35:24–25. *people of the land.* See note on 21:24. *Jehoahaz son of Josiah.* Jehoahaz's name was originally Shallum (see 1Ch 3:15; Jer 22:11), which was probably changed to Jehoahaz at the time of his accession to the throne. Perhaps Jehoahaz was chosen by the people over Jehoiakim because it was known that Jehoiakim favored a pro-Egyptian policy instead of the anti-Egyptian policy of Josiah and Jehoahaz. *anointed him.* See note on 1Sa 9:16.

23:31 m 1Ch 3:15;
Jer 22:11 n 2Ki 24:18
23:32 o 1Ki 15:26
23:33 p S Nu 34:11
q 1Ki 8:65
23:34 r 2Ki 24:6;
1Ch 3:15; 2Ch 36:5-8;
Jer 1:3 s Jer 22:12
23:35 t Jer 2:16
23:36 u Jer 26:1
23:37 v 1Ki 15:26
24:1 w ver 10;
2Ki 25:11; Ezr 5:12;
Jer 4:7; 25:1,9; 39:1;
40:1; 50:17; 52:15;
Eze 32:2; Da 1:1; 7:4
x Jer 35:11 y S 2Ki 18:7
24:2 z Jer 5:15;
Hab 1:6 a Jer 35:11
b S 2Ki 5:2
c Isa 28:18-19
d Jer 12:7-9; 25:1;
26:1; 36:1; Eze 23:23;
Da 1:2
24:3 e S 2Ki 18:25
f 2Ki 13:23
g S 1Ki 14:9;
S 2Ki 21:12; Jer 15:4
24:4 h S 2Ki 21:16;
Jer 22:3 i S Ex 23:21;
La 3:42
24:5 j Jer 22:18-19

JEHOAHAZ KING OF JUDAH

23:31–34pp — 2Ch 36:2–4

[31]Jehoahaz m was twenty-three years old when he became king, and he reigned in Jerusalem three months. His mother's name was Hamutal n daughter of Jeremiah; she was from Libnah. [32]He did evil o in the eyes of the LORD, just as his predecessors had done. [33]Pharaoh Necho put him in chains at Riblah p in the land of Hamath q so that he might not reign in Jerusalem, and he imposed on Judah a levy of a hundred talents a of silver and a talent b of gold. [34]Pharaoh Necho made Eliakim r son of Josiah king in place of his father Josiah and changed Eliakim's name to Jehoiakim. But he took Jehoahaz and carried him off to Egypt, and there he died. s [35]Jehoiakim paid Pharaoh Necho the silver and gold he demanded. In order to do so, he taxed the land and exacted the silver and gold from the people of the land according to their assessments. t

JEHOIAKIM KING OF JUDAH

23:36–24:6pp — 2Ch 36:5–8

[36]Jehoiakim u was twenty-five years old when he became king, and he reigned in Jerusalem eleven years. His mother's name was Zebidah daughter of Pedaiah; she was from Rumah. [37]And he did evil v in the eyes of the LORD, just as his predecessors had done.

24 During Jehoiakim's reign, Nebuchadnezzar w king of Babylon invaded x the land, and Jehoiakim became his vassal for three years. But then he turned against Nebuchadnezzar and rebelled. y [2]The LORD sent Babylonian, c z Aramean, a Moabite and Ammonite raiders b against him to destroy c Judah, in accordance with the word of the LORD proclaimed by his servants the prophets. d [3]Surely these things happened to Judah according to the LORD's command, e in order to remove them from his presence f because of the sins of Manasseh g and all he had done, [4]including the shedding of innocent blood. h For he had filled Jerusalem with innocent blood, and the LORD was not willing to forgive. i

[5]As for the other events of Jehoiakim's reign, j and all he did, are they not written in the

---

a 33 That is, about 3 3/4 tons or about 3.4 metric tons   b 33 That is, about 75 pounds or about 34 kilograms   c 2 Or *Chaldean*

23:31 *three months.* In 609 B.C. *Jeremiah.* Not the prophet (see Jer 1:1). *Libnah.* See note on 8:22.
23:32 *evil…as his predecessors.* See 16:3; 21:2,21; Eze 19:3 and note.
23:33 *in chains at Riblah.* By either deception or overt force the Egyptians were able to take Jehoahaz captive and impose tribute on Judah (see 2Ch 36:3). Jehoahaz was imprisoned in Necho's military headquarters, established at Riblah on the Orontes River. Nebuchadnezzar was later to make his headquarters at the same place (see 25:6,20).
23:34 *Eliakim son of Josiah.* Eliakim was an older brother of Jehoahaz (see 1Ch 3:15). Perhaps he had been bypassed earlier as a successor to Josiah because of a pro-Egyptian political stance. *changed Eliakim's name to Jehoiakim.* The meaning of these two names is similar (Eliakim, "God has established"; Jehoiakim, "Yahweh has established"). Perhaps Necho wanted to use the name change to imply that his actions were sanctioned by Yahweh, the God of Judah (see 18:25; 2Ch 35:21). In any case, the change in name indicated that Jehoiakim was subject to Necho's authority. *took Jehoahaz…to Egypt, and there he died.* See 2Ch 36:4; Jer 22:10–12.
23:35 *from the people of the land.* The tribute for Necho was raised by a graduated tax placed on the very people who had supported the kingship of Jehoahaz (see v. 30 and note on 21:24). Menahem of the northern kingdom had used a similar method of raising funds for tribute (see 15:20).
23:36 *eleven years.* 609–598 B.C.
23:37 *did evil in the eyes of the LORD.* Jehoiakim was responsible for the murder of the prophet Uriah from Kiriath Jearim (Jer 26:20–24), and his rule was characterized by dishonesty, oppression and injustice (see Jer 22:13–19). He reintroduced idolatrous worship in the temple (see Eze 8:5–17) and refused to accept the word of the Lord through Jeremiah (see Jer

36). *his predecessors.* Manasseh (21:1–18) and Amon (21:19–26).
24:1 *Nebuchadnezzar.* Means "Nabu [a god], protect my son/boundary!" He was the son of Nabopolassar (see note on 23:29) and the most powerful king of the Neo-Babylonian empire (612–539 B.C.), reigning 605–562 (see Da 1–4; see also chart, p. 482). *invaded the land.* In 605 Nebuchadnezzar, the crown prince and commander of the Babylonian army, defeated Pharaoh Necho and the Egyptians at the battle of Carchemish and again at Hamath (see 23:29; Jer 46:2). These victories had far-reaching implications in the geopolitical power structure of the eastern Mediterranean world. Nebuchadnezzar went on to conquer all of the "Hatti-country," which, according to Babylonian records, included the "city of Judah." Daniel was among the Judahite hostages taken at this time (see Da 1:1). Perhaps as early as Sept. 6, 605, Nebuchadnezzar acceded to the Babylonian throne upon the death of his father. *three years.* Probably 604–602. In 604 Nebuchadnezzar returned to the west and took tribute from "all the kings of Hatti-land." It is likely that Jehoiakim was included among these kings. *turned against Nebuchadnezzar and rebelled.* In 601 Nebuchadnezzar again marched west against Egypt and was repulsed by strong Egyptian resistance. This may have encouraged Jehoiakim's rebellion, even though Jeremiah had warned against it (see Jer 27:9–11).
24:2 *Babylonian, Aramean, Moabite and Ammonite raiders against him.* Reaction to Jehoiakim's rebellion was swift. Babylonian troops, perhaps garrisoned in Aram, along with troops of other loyal vassals, were sent to put down the Judahite rebellion.
24:3 *sins of Manasseh.* See 21:11–12; 23:26–27; Jer 15:3–4.
24:4 *innocent blood.* See note on 21:16. *not willing to forgive.* See 22:17.
24:5 *annals of the kings of Judah.* See note on 1Ki 14:29.

book of the annals of the kings of Judah? [6]Jehoiakim rested [k] with his ancestors. And Jehoiachin [l] his son succeeded him as king.

[7]The king of Egypt [m] did not march out from his own country again, because the king of Babylon [n] had taken all his territory, from the Wadi of Egypt to the Euphrates River.

JEHOIACHIN KING OF JUDAH
24:8–17pp — 2Ch 36:9–10

[8]Jehoiachin [o] was eighteen years old when he became king, and he reigned in Jerusalem three months. His mother's name was Nehushta [p] daughter of Elnathan; she was from Jerusalem. [9]He did evil [q] in the eyes of the LORD, just as his father had done.

[10]At that time the officers of Nebuchadnezzar [r] king of Babylon advanced on Jerusalem and laid siege to it, [11]and Nebuchadnezzar himself came up to the city while his officers were besieging it. [12]Jehoiachin king of Judah, his mother, his attendants, his nobles and his officials all surrendered [s] to him.

In the eighth year of the reign of the king of Babylon, he took Jehoiachin prisoner. [13]As the LORD had declared, [t] Nebuchadnezzar removed the treasures [u] from the temple of the LORD and from the royal palace, and cut up the gold articles [v] that Solomon [w] king of Israel had made for the temple of the LORD. [14]He carried all Jerusalem into exile: [x] all the officers and fighting men, [y] and all the skilled workers and artisans—a total of ten thousand. Only the poorest [z] people of the land were left.

[15]Nebuchadnezzar took Jehoiachin [a] captive to Babylon. He also took from Jerusalem to Babylon the king's mother, [b] his wives, his officials and the prominent people [c] of the land. [16]The king of Babylon also deported to Babylon the entire force of seven thousand fighting men, strong and fit for war, and a thousand skilled workers and artisans. [d] [17]He made Mattaniah, Jehoiachin's uncle, king in his place and changed his name to Zedekiah. [e]

ZEDEKIAH KING OF JUDAH
24:18–20pp — 2Ch 36:11–16; Jer 52:1–3

[18]Zedekiah [f] was twenty-one years old when he became king, and he reigned in Jerusalem eleven years. His mother's name was Hamutal [g] daughter of Jeremiah; she was from Libnah. [19]He did evil [h] in the eyes of the LORD, just as Jehoiakim had done. [20]It was because of the LORD's anger that all this happened to Jerusalem and Judah, and in the end he thrust [i] them from his presence. [j]

THE FALL OF JERUSALEM
25:1–12pp — Jer 39:1–10
25:1–21pp — 2Ch 36:17–20; Jer 52:4–27
25:22–26pp — Jer 40:7–9; 41:1–3,16–18

Now Zedekiah rebelled against the king of Babylon.

24:6 [k] Jer 22:19;
36:30 [l] 1Ch 3:16;
Jer 22:24,28; Eze 19:1
24:7 [m] S Ge 15:18;
S 2Ki 18:21;
S Jer 46:25 [n] Jer 1:14;
25:9; 46:24
24:8 [o] 1Ch 3:16;
Jer 22:24; 37:1
[p] ver 15; Jer 13:18;
22:26; 29:2
24:9 [q] 1Ki 15:26
24:10 [r] S ver 1
24:12 [s] 2Ki 25:27;
Jer 13:18; 22:24-30;
24:1; 29:2
24:13 [t] 2Ki 20:17
[u] 2Ki 25:15; Isa 39:6;
42:22 [v] 2Ki 25:14;
Ezr 1:7; Isa 39:6;
Jer 15:13; 17:3; 20:5;
27:16; 28:3; Eze 7:21;
Da 1:2; 5:2,23;
Zep 1:13 [w] S 1Ki 7:51
24:14 [x] S Dt 28:36;
S 2Ch 36:20;
S Mt 1:11 [y] Isa 3:1-3
[z] Dt 15:11; 2Ki 25:12;
Job 5:16; Ps 9:18;
Jer 40:7; 52:16
24:15 [a] S 2Ki 20:18;
Eze 19:9 [b] S ver 8;
S 1Ki 2:19 [c] Est 2:6;
Isa 39:7; La 2:9;
Eze 1:2; 17:12-14;
Da 1:3
24:16 [d] Ezr 2:1;
Jer 24:1
24:17 [e] 1Ch 3:15;
2Ch 36:11; Jer 1:3;
37:1; 52:1; Eze 17:13
24:18 [f] 1Ch 3:16;
Jer 39:1 [g] 2Ki 23:31
24:19 [h] 1Ki 15:26;
Jer 37:2
24:20 [i] Dt 4:26;
29:27 [j] S Ex 33:15;
S 2Ki 13:23

24:6 *rested with his ancestors.* See note on 1Ki 1:21. Jehoiakim died shortly before Jerusalem fell to the Babylonian siege (see vv. 8–12). Whether his death was due to natural causes or political intrigue is not indicated.

24:7 *The king of Egypt did not march out from his own country again.* This was due to the Egyptian defeat at Carchemish (see Jer 46:2) in 605 B.C., and it explains why Jehoiakim received no help from Egypt in his rebellion against the Babylonians. *Wadi of Egypt.* See note on 1Ki 8:65.

24:8 *three months.* Babylonian records place this capture of Jerusalem by Nebuchadnezzar on Mar. 16, 597 B.C. This means that the three-month and ten-day reign (see 2Ch 36:9–10) of Jehoiachin began in December, 598.

24:9 *as his father.* See 23:37; Jer 22:20–30.

24:12 *eighth year.* April, 597 B.C. (see 2Ch 36:10; see also note on Jer 52:28, where a different system of dating is reflected).

24:13 *As the LORD had declared.* See 20:13,17.

24:14 *ten thousand.* This figure may include the 7,000 fighting men and 1,000 craftsmen mentioned in v. 16 (see note on Jer 52:28, where a different number of captives is mentioned).

24:15 *Jehoiachin captive to Babylon.* Fulfilling Jeremiah's prophecy (Jer 22:24–27; see 2Ki 25:27–30).

24:17 *Mattaniah, Jehoiachin's uncle.* Mattaniah was a son of Josiah (see 1Ch 3:15; Jer 1:3) and brother of Jehoiachin's father, Jehoiakim. *changed his name to Zedekiah.* Mattaniah's name (meaning "gift of Yahweh") was changed to Zedekiah ("righteousness of Yahweh"). Perhaps Nebuchadnezzar wanted to imply that his actions against Jerusalem and Jehoiachin were just. In any case, the name change signified subjection to Nebuchadnezzar (see note on 23:34).

24:18 *eleven years.* 597–586 B.C. *Jeremiah.* See note on 23:31. *Libnah.* See note on 8:22.

24:19 *did evil ... as Jehoiakim.* See note on 23:37. During Zedekiah's reign idolatrous practices continued to increase in Jerusalem (see 2Ch 36:14; Eze 8–11). He was a weak and indecisive ruler (see Jer 38:5,19) who refused to heed the word of the Lord given through Jeremiah (2Ch 36:12).

24:20 *Zedekiah rebelled.* Most interpreters link Zedekiah's revolt with the succession to the Egyptian throne in 589 B.C. of the ambitious pharaoh Hophra (see Jer 44:30 and note). Zedekiah had sworn allegiance to Nebuchadnezzar (Eze 17:13), had sent envoys to Babylon (see Jer 29:3) and had made a personal visit (see Jer 51:59). However, he seems to have capitulated to the seductive propaganda of the anti-Babylonian and pro-Egyptian faction in Jerusalem (see Jer 37:5; Eze 17:15–16) in a tragically miscalculated effort to gain independence from Babylon.

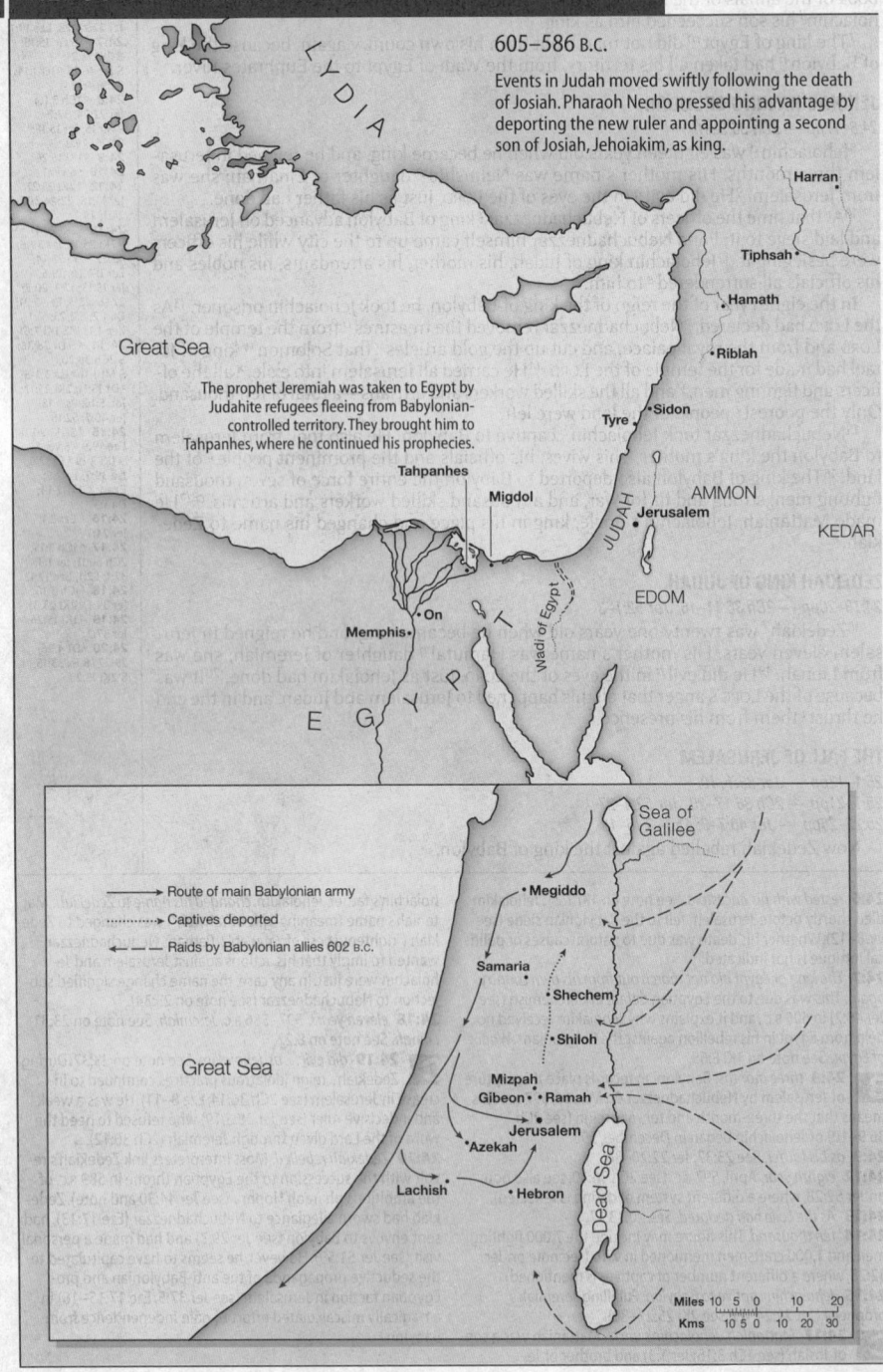

605–586 B.C.

Events in Judah moved swiftly following the death of Josiah. Pharaoh Necho pressed his advantage by deporting the new ruler and appointing a second son of Josiah, Jehoiakim, as king.

LYDIA

Harran

Tiphsah

Hamath

Great Sea

Riblah

The prophet Jeremiah was taken to Egypt by Judahite refugees fleeing from Babylonian-controlled territory. They brought him to Tahpanhes, where he continued his prophecies.

Tyre · Sidon

Tahpanhes

Migdol

JUDAH

AMMON

Jerusalem

KEDAR

On

Memphis

EDOM

Wadi of Egypt

E G Y P T

Sea of Galilee

Megiddo

→ Route of main Babylonian army

......▷ Captives deported

◄— — Raids by Babylonian allies 602 B.C.

Samaria

· Shechem

· Shiloh

Great Sea

Mizpah

Gibeon · · Ramah

· Jerusalem

· Azekah

Lachish · · Hebron

Dead Sea

Miles 10 5 0   10   20

Kms   10 5 0 10 20 30

Soon a stronger power appeared in the north in the person of Nebuchadnezzar, king of the Chaldeans (Neo-Babylonians), who determined to follow the fierce policies of his Assyrian predecessors.

The tribute of Jehoiakim was paid at a distance when he heard of Nebuchadnezzar's approach. After three years as a Babylonian vassal, he rebelled, bringing a rapid response in the form of small-scale raids from Babylonians, Arameans, Moabites and Ammonites (c. 602 B.C.). Finally, Nebuchadnezzar's forces controlled all of the coastal territory north of the Wadi of Egypt.

When 18-year-old Jehoiachin had ruled just three months (597 B.C.), the main Babylonian army struck, capturing Jerusalem and exiling the king as a captive in Babylon. Ten thousand persons were deported.

The Chaldeans (Kaldu), as the Neo-Babylonians were called, had important connections at Ur and Harran, centers of worship of the moon-god Sin. They also developed the trade routes across North Arabia, where Tema was particularly important, becoming the residence of Nabonidus during the last days of the kingdom.

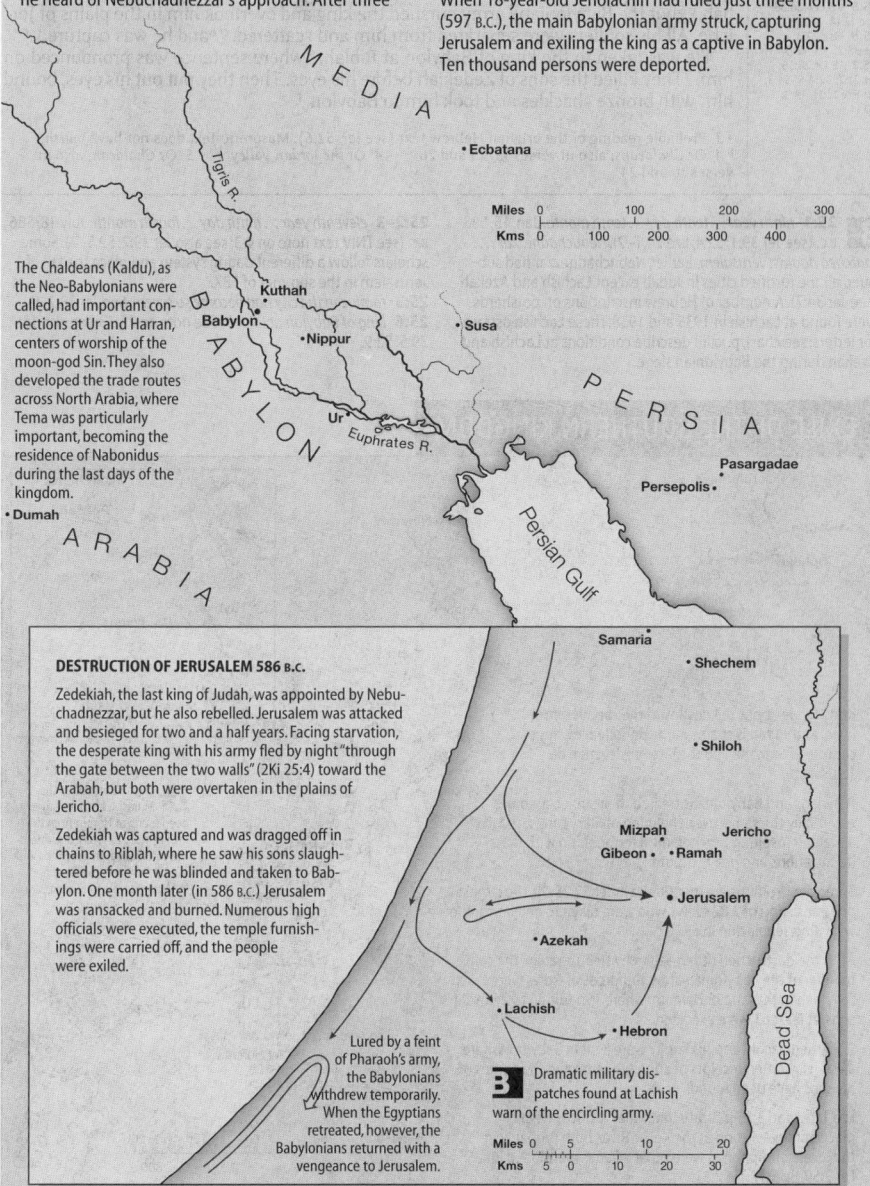

DESTRUCTION OF JERUSALEM 586 B.C.

Zedekiah, the last king of Judah, was appointed by Nebuchadnezzar, but he also rebelled. Jerusalem was attacked and besieged for two and a half years. Facing starvation, the desperate king with his army fled by night "through the gate between the two walls" (2Ki 25:4) toward the Arabah, but both were overtaken in the plains of Jericho.

Zedekiah was captured and was dragged off in chains to Riblah, where he saw his sons slaughtered before he was blinded and taken to Babylon. One month later (in 586 B.C.) Jerusalem was ransacked and burned. Numerous high officials were executed, the temple furnishings were carried off, and the people were exiled.

Lured by a feint of Pharaoh's army, the Babylonians withdrew temporarily. When the Egyptians retreated, however, the Babylonians returned with a vengeance to Jerusalem.

Dramatic military dispatches found at Lachish warn of the encircling army.

25:1 *k* Jer 32:1
l Jer 21:2; 34:1-7
m Isa 23:13; 29:3;
Jer 4:16-17; 32:2;
33:4; Eze 21:22; 24:2
25:3 *n* S Lev 26:26;
Isa 22:2; Jer 14:18;
37:21; La 2:20; 4:9
25:4 *o* Job 30:14;
Ps 144:14; Jer 50:15;
51:44,58; Eze 33:21
p Jer 4:17; 6:3
25:5 *q* S Lev 26:36;
Eze 12:14; 17:21
25:6 *r* Isa 22:3;
Jer 38:23 *s* S Nu 34:11
25:7 *t* S Dt 28:36;
Jer 21:7; 32:4-5; 34:3,
21; Eze 12:11; 19:9;
40:1

25 So in the ninth *k* year of Zedekiah's reign, on the tenth day of the tenth month, Nebuchadnezzar *l* king of Babylon marched against Jerusalem with his whole army. He encamped outside the city and built siege works *m* all around it. ²The city was kept under siege until the eleventh year of King Zedekiah.

³By the ninth day of the fourth *a* month the famine *n* in the city had become so severe that there was no food for the people to eat. ⁴Then the city wall was broken through, *o* and the whole army fled at night through the gate between the two walls near the king's garden, though the Babylonians *b* were surrounding *p* the city. They fled toward the Arabah, *c* ⁵but the Babylonian *d* army pursued the king and overtook him in the plains of Jericho. All his soldiers were separated from him and scattered, *q* ⁶and he was captured. *r*

He was taken to the king of Babylon at Riblah, *s* where sentence was pronounced on him. ⁷They killed the sons of Zedekiah before his eyes. Then they put out his eyes, bound him with bronze shackles and took him to Babylon. *t*

---

a 3 Probable reading of the original Hebrew text (see Jer. 52:6); Masoretic Text does not have *fourth*. *b 4* Or *Chaldeans;* also in verses 13, 25 and 26 *c 4* Or *the Jordan Valley* *d 5* Or *Chaldean;* also in verses 10 and 24

25:1 *ninth year ... tenth day ... tenth month.* Jan. 15, 588 B.C. (see Jer 39:1; 52:4; Eze 24:1–2). *Nebuchadnezzar ... marched against Jerusalem.* Earlier, Nebuchadnezzar had subdued all the fortified cities in Judah except Lachish and Azekah (see Jer 34:7). A number of Hebrew inscriptions on potsherds were found at Lachish in 1935 and 1938. These Lachish ostraca (or letters; see chart, p. xxiii) describe conditions at Lachish and Azekah during the Babylonian siege.

25:2–3 *eleventh year ... ninth day ... fourth month.* July 18, 586 B.C. (see TNIV text note on v. 3; see also Jer 39:2; 52:5–7). Some scholars follow a different dating system and place the fall of Jerusalem in the summer of 587.
25:3 *famine in the city had become so severe.* See Jer 38:2–9.
25:6 *king of Babylon at Riblah.* See note on 23:33; see also Jer 39:5; 52:9.

EXILE OF THE SOUTHERN KINGDOM

Knowledge about the destiny of the captives from Israel and Judah is sparse in the period following the capture of Samaria and the later destruction of Jerusalem.

Assyrians and Babylonians treated their subject peoples essentially the same: overwhelming military force used in a manner inspiring psychological terror, along with mass deportations and heavy tribute.

Three deportations are mentioned in Jer 52:28-30, the largest one consisting of 3,023 Jews who were taken to Babylon along with King Jehoiachin in 597 B.C.

After the destruction of Jerusalem by Nebuzaradan, the commander of the Babylonian army, hundreds of exiles were taken to Riblah in the land of Hamath, where, in addition to Zedekiah's sons, at least 61 others were executed.

Jehoiachin and his family were kept in Babylon, where clay ration receipts bearing his name and the names of his sons have been found.

Eze 1:1-3 and 3:15 indicate that other captives were placed at Tel Aviv and at the Kebar River, both probably in the locale of Nippur, as were other villages mentioned in Ezr 2:59; 8:15,17; Ne 7:61.

Clay tablets called the Murashu archives have been found at Nippur from the fifth century B.C. They document the commercial transactions with Jewish families who remained in Mesopotamia following Ezra's return to Jerusalem.

Locations unknown for:
Tel Aviv   Tel Harsha
Kebar River   Kerub
Ahava Canal   Addon
Kasiphia   Immer
Tel Melah

⁸On the seventh day of the fifth month, in the nineteenth year of Nebuchadnezzar king of Babylon, Nebuzaradan commander of the imperial guard, an official of the king of Babylon, came to Jerusalem. ⁹He set fire ᵘ to the temple of the LORD, the royal palace and all the houses of Jerusalem. Every important building he burned down. ᵛ ¹⁰The whole Babylonian army under the commander of the imperial guard broke down the walls ʷ around Jerusalem. ¹¹Nebuzaradan the commander of the guard carried into exile ˣ the people who remained in the city, along with the rest of the populace and those who had deserted to the king of Babylon. ʸ ¹²But the commander left behind some of the poorest people ᶻ of the land to work the vineyards and fields.

¹³The Babylonians broke ᵃ up the bronze pillars, the movable stands and the bronze Sea that were at the temple of the LORD and they carried the bronze to Babylon. ¹⁴They also took away the pots, shovels, wick trimmers, dishes ᵇ and all the bronze articles ᶜ used in the temple service. ¹⁵The commander of the imperial guard took away the censers and sprinkling bowls—all that were made of pure gold or silver. ᵈ

¹⁶The bronze from the two pillars, the Sea and the movable stands, which Solomon had made for the temple of the LORD, was more than could be weighed. ¹⁷Each pillar ᵉ was eighteen cubits ᵃ high. The bronze capital on top of one pillar was three cubits ᵇ high and was decorated with a network and pomegranates of bronze all around. The other pillar, with its network, was similar.

¹⁸The commander of the guard took as prisoners Seraiah ᶠ the chief priest, Zephaniah ᵍ the priest next in rank and the three doorkeepers. ʰ ¹⁹Of those still in the city, he took the officer in charge of the fighting men, and five royal advisers. He also took the secretary who was chief officer in charge of conscripting the people of the land and sixty of the conscripts who were found in the city. ²⁰Nebuzaradan the commander took them all and brought them to the king of Babylon at Riblah. ²¹There at Riblah, ⁱ in the land of Hamath, the king had them executed. ʲ

So Judah went into captivity, ᵏ away from her land. ˡ

²²Nebuchadnezzar king of Babylon appointed Gedaliah ᵐ son of Ahikam, ⁿ the son of Shaphan, to be over the people he had left behind in Judah. ²³When all the army officers and their men heard that the king of Babylon had appointed Gedaliah as governor, they came to Gedaliah at Mizpah—Ishmael son of Nethaniah, Johanan son of Kareah, Seraiah son of Tanhumeth the Netophathite, Jaazaniah the son of the Maakathite, and their men. ²⁴Gedaliah took an oath to reassure them and their men. "Do not be afraid of the Babylonian officials," he said. "Settle down in the land and serve the king of Babylon, and it will go well with you."

²⁵In the seventh month, however, Ishmael son of Nethaniah, the son of Elishama, who

---

ᵃ 17 That is, about 27 feet or about 8.2 meters   ᵇ 17 That is, about 4 1/2 feet or about 1.4 meters

---

25:9 ᵘIsa 60:7; 63:15,18; 64:11
ᵛS Dt 13:16; Ne 1:3; Ps 74:3-8; 79:1; Jer 2:15; 17:27; 21:10; 26:6,18; La 4:11; Am 2:5; Mic 3:12
25:10 ʷNe 1:3; Jer 50:15
25:11 ˣS Lev 26:44; 2Ki 24:14
ʸS Dt 28:36; S 2Ki 24:1
25:12 ᶻS 2Ki 24:14
25:13 ᵃS 1Ki 7:50
25:14 ᵇS Nu 7:14
ᶜS 2Ki 24:13; Ezr 1:7
25:15 ᵈS 2Ki 24:13; Jer 15:13; 20:5; 27:16-22
25:17 ᵉ1Ki 7:15-22
25:18 ᶠver 18-21; 1Ch 6:14; Ezr 7:1; Ne 11:11 ᵍJer 21:1; 29:25; 37:3
ʰS 2Ki 12:9; S 23:4
25:21 ⁱS Nu 34:11 ʲJer 34:21 ᵏS 1Ki 8:46 ˡS Ge 12:7; S Jos 23:13
25:22 ᵐJer 39:14; 40:5,7; 41:18
ⁿS 2Ki 22:12

C **25:7** *killed the sons of Zedekiah ... put out his eyes ... took him to Babylon.* See Jer 32:4–5; 34:2–3; 38:18; 39:6–7; 52:10–11. Ezekiel (12:13) had predicted that Zedekiah would be brought to Babylon but that he would not see it. Zedekiah could have spared his own life and prevented the destruction of Jerusalem if he had listened to Jeremiah (see Jer 38:14–28).
25:8 *seventh day ... fifth month ... nineteenth year.* Aug. 14, 586 B.C. (see Jer 52:12 and note).
25:9 *set fire to the temple.* See 2Ch 36:19; Jer 39:8; 52:13.
25:13 *bronze pillars.* See 1Ki 7:15–22. *movable stands.* See 1Ki 7:27–39. *bronze Sea.* See 1Ki 7:23–26.
25:14 *all the bronze articles used in the temple service.* See 1Ki 7:40,45.
25:17 *bronze capital ... was three cubits high.* See TNIV text note. In 1Ki 7:16 and Jer 52:22 the height of the capital is given as seven and a half feet (five cubits). The two-cubit difference may be due to a copyist's error.
25:18 *Seraiah the chief priest.* Seraiah was the grandson of Hilkiah (see note on 22:4; see also 22:8; 1Ch 6:13–14). His son Jehozadak was taken captive to Babylon. Ezra was one of Jehozadak's descendants (see Ezr 7:1).
25:19 *people of the land.* See note on 21:24.
25:20 *brought them to the king of Babylon at Riblah.* See v. 6 and note.
25:21 *Judah went into captivity, away from her land.* Judah's exile from Canaan fulfilled the prediction of judgment given dur-

ing the reign of Manasseh (see 23:27). Exile was the most dire of the covenant curses (see Lev 26:33; Dt 28:36; see also Jer 25:8–11).
25:22 *Gedaliah.* See note on 22:12. Gedaliah shared Jeremiah's nonresistance approach to the Babylonians (see v. 24) and won their confidence as a trustworthy governor of Judah (see Jer 41:10).

B **25:23** *Mizpah.* Had been a town of important political significance in the time just before the establishment of the monarchy (see note on 1Sa 7:5). Jeremiah found Gedaliah there (see Jer 40:1–6). *Ishmael son of Nethaniah.* Verse 25 gives a fuller genealogy. Elishama, Ishmael's grandfather, was the royal secretary under Jehoiakim (Jer 36:12). *Jaazaniah.* In 1932 an agate seal was found at Tell en-Nasbeh (Mizpah) bearing the name of Jaazaniah (perhaps the man mentioned here) with the inscription: "Belonging to Jaazaniah the servant of the king."

C **25:24** Gedaliah urged submission to the Babylonians as the judgment of God. He advocated the restoration of the normal pursuits of a peacetime society (see Jer 27). A similar message had been given by Jeremiah to the captives taken to Babylon in 597 B.C. (see Jer 29:4–7).
25:25 *seventh month.* October, 586 B.C. *assassinated Gedaliah.* A more complete account of the assassination of Gedaliah is given in Jer 40:13—41:15. Ishmael appears to have had personal designs on the throne, to have resented Gedaliah's ready submission to the Babylonians and to have been manipulated by

25:25 °S 2Ki 12:20
P Zec 7:5
25:26 9 Isa 30:2;
Jer 43:7
25:27 'S 2Ki 24:12
25:28 s S 1Ki 8:50
t Ezr 5:5; 7:6,28; 9:9;
Ne 2:1; Da 2:48
25:29 u S 2Sa 9:7
25:30 v Ge 43:34;
Est 2:9; 9:22; Jer 28:4

was of royal blood, came with ten men and assassinated ° Gedaliah and also the men of Judah and the Babylonians who were with him at Mizpah. P 26At this, all the people from the least to the greatest, together with the army officers, fled to Egypt 9 for fear of the Babylonians.

JEHOIACHIN RELEASED
25:27–30pp — Jer 52:31–34

27In the thirty-seventh year of the exile of Jehoiachin king of Judah, in the year Awel-Marduk became king of Babylon, he released Jehoiachin r king of Judah from prison. He did this on the twenty-seventh day of the twelfth month. 28He spoke kindly s to him and gave him a seat of honor t higher than those of the other kings who were with him in Babylon. 29So Jehoiachin put aside his prison clothes and for the rest of his life ate regularly at the king's table. u 30Day by day the king gave Jehoiachin a regular allowance as long as he lived. v

---

the Ammonites, who also chafed under Babylonian domination (see Jer 40:14; 41:10,15).

25:26 fled to Egypt. Pharaoh Hophra was then ruler in Egypt (see note on 24:20).

25:27 thirty-seventh year … twenty-seventh day … twelfth month. Mar. 22, 561 B.C. in the year Awel-Marduk became king of Babylon. 561 (some scholars place Awel-Marduk's succession to the throne in October, 562; see note on 24:1). His name means "man of (the god) Marduk." released Jehoiachin king of Judah from prison. Babylonian administrative

tablets (see chart, p. xxiii), recording the payment of rations in oil and barley to prisoners held in Babylon, mention Jehoiachin, king of Judah, and five of his sons (cf. 24:15). No reason is given for Jehoiachin's release. Perhaps it was part of a general amnesty proclaimed at the beginning of Awel-Marduk's reign.

25:28 spoke kindly to him and gave him a seat of honor. The book of Kings ends on a hopeful note. The judgment of exile will not destroy the people of Israel or the line of David. God's promise concerning David's house remains (see 2Sa 7:14–16).

1 CHRONICLES

The Hebrew title (*dibre hayyamim*) can be translated "the events (or annals) of the days (or years)." The same phrase occurs in references to sources used by the author or compiler of Kings (translated "annals" in, e.g., 1Ki 14:19,29; 15:7,23,31; 16:5,14,20,27; 22:45). The Septuagint (the pre-Christian Greek translation of the OT) refers to the book as "the things omitted," indicating that its translators regarded it as a supplement to Samuel and Kings. Jerome (A.D. 347–420), translator of the Latin Vulgate, suggested that a more appropriate title would be "chronicle of the whole sacred history." Luther took over this suggestion in his German version, and others have followed him. Chronicles was first divided into two books by the Septuagint translators.

AUTHOR, DATE AND SOURCES

According to ancient Jewish tradition, Ezra wrote Chronicles, Ezra and Nehemiah (see Introduction to Ezra: Literary Form and Authorship), but this cannot be established with certainty. A growing consensus dates Chronicles in the latter half of the fifth century B.C., thus possibly within Ezra's lifetime. And it must be acknowledged that the author, if not Ezra himself, at least shared many basic concerns with that reforming priest—though Chronicles is not so narrowly "priestly" in its perspective as was long affirmed.

Some believe the text contains evidence here and there of later expansions after the basic work had been composed. While editorial revisions are not unlikely, all specific proposals regarding them remain tentative.

In his recounting of history long past, the Chronicler relied on many written sources. About half his work was taken from Samuel and Kings; he also drew on the Pentateuch, Judges, Ruth, Psalms, Isaiah, Jeremiah, Lamentations and Zechariah (though he used texts of these books that varied somewhat from those that have been preserved in the later standardized Hebrew texts). And there are frequent references to still other sources: "the book of the kings of Israel" (9:1; 2Ch 20:34; cf. 2Ch 33:18), "the book of the annals of King David" (27:24), "the book of the kings of Judah and Israel" or ". . . of Israel and Judah" (2Ch 16:11; 25:26; 27:7; 28:26; 32:32; 35:27; 36:8), "the annotations on the book of the kings" (2Ch 24:27). It is unclear whether these all refer to the same source or to different sources and what their relationship is to Samuel and Kings or to the royal annals referred to in Kings. In addition, the author cites a number of prophetic writings: those of "Samuel the seer" (29:29), "Nathan the prophet" (29:29; 2Ch 9:29), "Gad the seer" (29:29), "Ahijah the Shilonite" (2Ch 9:29), "Iddo the seer" (2Ch 9:29; 12:15; 13:22), "Shemaiah the prophet" (2Ch 12:15), "the prophet Isaiah" (2Ch 26:22), "the seers" (2Ch 33:19). All these he used, often with only minor changes, to tell his own story of the past. He did not invent, but he did select, arrange and integrate his sources to compose a narrative "sermon" for postexilic Israel as she struggled to reorient herself as the people of God in a new situation.

PURPOSE AND THEMES

Just as the author of Kings had organized and interpreted the data of Israel's history to address the needs of the exiled community, so the Chronicler wrote for the restored community. The burning issue was the question of continuity with the past: Is God still interested in us? Are his covenants still in force? Now that we have no Davidic king and are subject to Persia, do God's promises to David still have meaning for us? After the great judgment (the dethroning of the house of David, the destruction of the nation, of Jerusalem and of the temple, and the exile to Babylon), what is our relationship to Israel of old? Several elements go into the Chronicler's answer:

1. Continuity with the past is signified by the temple in Jerusalem, rebuilt by the Lord's sovereign influence over a Persian imperial edict (2Ch 36:22–23). For a generation that had no independent political status and no Davidic king, the author takes great pains to show that the temple of the Lord and its service (including its book of prayer and praise, an early edition of the Psalms) are supreme gifts of God given to Israel through the Davidic dynasty. For that reason his account of the reigns of David and Solomon is largely devoted to David's preparation for and Solomon's building of the temple and to David's instructions for the temple service (with the counsel of Gad the seer and Nathan the prophet, 2Ch 29:25, and also of the Levites Asaph, Heman and Jeduthun, 2Ch 35:15). See also the Chronicler's accounts of the reigns of Asa, Jehoshaphat, Joash, Hezekiah and Josiah. The temple of the Lord in the ancient holy city and its service (including the Psalms) were the chief legacy left to the restored community by the house of David.

2. The value of this legacy is highlighted by the author's emphasis on God's furtherance of his gracious purposes toward Israel through his sovereign acts of election: (1) of the tribe of Levi to serve before the ark of the covenant (15:2; see 23:24–32), (2) of David to be king over Israel (28:4; 2Ch 6:6), (3) of Solomon his son to be king and to build the temple (28:5–6,10; 29:1), (4) of Jerusalem (2Ch 6:6,34,38; 12:13; 33:7) and (5) of the temple (2Ch 7:12,16; 33:7) to be the place where God's Name would be present among his people. These divine acts give assurance to postexilic Israel that her rebuilt temple in Jerusalem and its continuing service mark her as God's people, whose election has not been annulled.

3. In addition to the temple, Israel has the law and the prophets as a major focus of her covenant life under the leadership of the house of David. Neither the Davidic kings nor the temple had in themselves assured Israel's security and blessing. All had been conditional on Israel's and the king's faithfulness to the law (28:7; 2Ch 6:16; 7:17; 12:1; 33:8). In the Chronicler's account, a primary feature of the reign of every faithful Davidic king was his attempt to bring about compliance with the law: David (6:49; 15:13,15; 16:40; 22:11–13; 29:19), Asa (2Ch 14:4; 15:12–14), Jehoshaphat (2Ch 17:3–9; 19:8–10), Joash (2Ch 24:6,9), Hezekiah (2Ch 29:10,31; 30:15–16; 31:3–4,21), Josiah (2Ch 34:19–21,29–33; 35:6,12,26). And to heed God's prophetic word was no less crucial. The faithful kings, such as David, Asa, Jehoshaphat, Hezekiah and Josiah—and even Rehoboam (2Ch 11:4; 12:6) and Amaziah (2Ch 25:7–10)—honored it; the unfaithful kings disregarded it to their destruction (Jehoram, 2Ch 21:12–19; Joash, 2Ch 24:19–25; Amaziah, 2Ch 25:15–16,20; Manasseh, 2Ch 33:10–11; see 36:15–16). Chronicles, in fact, notes the ministries of more prophets than do Samuel and Kings. Jehoshaphat's word to Israel expresses the Chronicler's view succinctly: "Have faith in the LORD your God and you will be upheld; have faith in his prophets and you will be successful" (2Ch 20:20). In the Chronicler's account of Israel's years under the kings, her response to the law and the prophets was more decisive for her destiny than the reigns of kings.

Thus the law and the prophets, like the temple, are more crucial to Israel's continuing relationship with the Lord than the presence or absence of a king, the reigns of the Davidic kings themselves being testimony.

4. The Chronicler further underscores the importance of obedience to the law and the prophets by emphasizing the theme of immediate retribution. See the express statements of David (28:9), of the Lord (2Ch 7:14) and of the prophets (2Ch

12:5; 15:2,7; 16:7,9; 19:2–3; 21:14–15; 24:20; 25:15–16; 28:9; 34:24–28). In writing his accounts of individual reigns, the author never tires of demonstrating how sin always brings judgment in the form of disaster (usually either illness or defeat in war), whereas repentance, obedience and trust yield peace, victory and prosperity.

5. Clearly the author of Chronicles wished to sustain Israel's hope for the promised Messiah, son of David, in accordance with the Davidic covenant (2Sa 7) and the assurances of the prophets, including those near to him (Haggai, Zechariah and Malachi). He was careful to recall the Lord's pledge to David (1Ch 17) and to follow this with many references back to it (see especially his account of Solomon's reign and also 2Ch 13:5; 21:7; 23:3). But perhaps even more indicative are his idealized depictions of David, Solomon, Asa, Jehoshaphat, Hezekiah and Josiah. While not portrayed as flawless, these Davidic kings are presented as prime examples of the Messianic ideal, i.e., as royal servants of the Lord whose reigns promoted godliness and covenant faithfulness in Israel. They were crowned with God's favor toward his people in the concrete forms of victories, deliverances and prosperity. They sat, moreover, on the "throne of the LORD" (29:23; see 28:5; 2Ch 9:8) and ruled over the Lord's kingdom (17:14; 2Ch 13:8). Thus they served as types, foreshadowing the "David" to come, of whom the prophets had spoken, and their remembrance nurtured hope in the face of much discouragement (see the book of Malachi). See further the next section on "Portrait of David and Solomon."

B 6. Yet another major theme of the Chronicler's history is his concern with "all Israel" (see, e.g., 9:1; 11:1–4; 12:38–40; 16:1–3; 18:14; 21:1–5; 28:1–8; 29:21–26; 2Ch 1:1–3; 7:8–10; 9:30; 10:1–3,16; 12:1; 18:16; 28:23; 29:24; 30:1–13,23–27; 34:6–9,33). As a matter of fact, he viewed the restored community as the remnant of all Israel, both north and south (9:2–3). This was more than a theological conceit. His narrative makes frequent note of movements of godly people from Israel to Judah for specifically religious reasons. The first were Levites in the time of Rehoboam (2Ch 11:14). In the reign of Asa others followed from Ephraim and Manasseh (2Ch 15:9). Shortly after the Assyrian destruction of the northern kingdom, many from that devastated land resettled in Judah at Hezekiah's invitation (2Ch 30). Presumably not all who came for Hezekiah's great Passover remained, but archaeology has shown a sudden large increase in population in the region around Jerusalem at this time, and the Chronicler specifically mentions "people of Israel . . . who lived in the towns of Judah" (2Ch 31:6). He also speaks of "the people of Manasseh, Ephraim and the entire remnant of Israel" who joined with "the people of Judah and Benjamin and the inhabitants of Jerusalem" in restoring the temple in the days of Josiah (2Ch 34:9). These were also present at Josiah's Passover (2Ch 35:17–18). So the kingdom of "Judah" had absorbed many from the northern kingdom through the years, and the Chronicler viewed it as the remnant of all Israel from the time of Samaria's fall.

7. The genealogies also demonstrate continuity with the past. To the question "Is God still interested in us?" the Chronicler answers, "He has always been." God's grace and love for the restored community did not begin with David or the conquest or the exodus—but with creation (1:1). For the genealogies, see p. 595.

8. The Chronicler often introduces speeches not found in Samuel and Kings, using them to convey some of his main emphases. Of the 165 speeches of varying lengths in Chronicles, only 95 are found in the parallel texts of Samuel and Kings. Cf., e.g., the speeches of Abijah (2Ch 13:4–12), Asa (2Ch 14:11) and Jehoshaphat (2Ch 20:5–12).

PORTRAIT OF DAVID AND SOLOMON

The bulk of the Chronicler's history is devoted to the reigns of David (chs. 11–29) and Solomon (2Ch 1–9). His portraits of these two kings are quite distinctive and provide a key to his concerns:

1. The Chronicler has idealized David and Solomon. Anything in his source material (mainly Samuel and Kings) that might tarnish his picture of them is omitted. He makes no reference to the wars between Saul's house and David, the negotiations with Abner, or the murders of Abner and Ish-Bosheth (2Sa 1–4). The Chronicler presents David as being immediately anointed king over all Israel after the death of Saul (ch. 11) and enjoying the total support of the people (11:10—12:40; see note on 3:1–9). Subsequent difficulties for David are also not recounted. No mention is made of David's sin with Bathsheba, the crime and death of Amnon, the fratricide by Absalom and his plot against his father, the flight of David from Jerusalem, the rebellions of Sheba and Shimei, and other incidents that might diminish the glory of David's reign (2Sa 11–20). David is presented without blemish, apart from the incident of the census (the Chronicler had a special purpose for including it; see ch. 21 and notes).

The Chronicler handles Solomon similarly. Solomon is specifically named in a divine oracle as David's successor (22:7–10; 28:6). His accession to the throne is announced publicly by David and is greeted with the unanimous support of all Israel (chs. 28–29). No mention is made of the bedridden David, who must overturn the attempted coup by Adonijah at the last moment to secure the throne for Solomon. Nor is there mention that the military commander Joab and the high priest Abiathar supported Adonijah's attempt (1Ki 1). Solomon's execution of those who had wronged David (1Ki 2) is also omitted. The accession of Solomon is without competition or detracting incident. The account of his reign is devoted almost wholly to the building of the temple (2Ch 2–8), and no reference to his failures is included. No mention is made of his idolatry, his foreign wives or the rebellions against his rule (1Ki 11). Even the blame for the schism is removed from Solomon (1Ki 11:26–40; 12:1–4) and placed on the scheming of Jeroboam. Solomon's image in Chronicles is such that he can be paired with David in the most favorable light (2Ch 11:17).

The David and Solomon of the Chronicler, then, must be seen not only as the David and Solomon of history, but also as typifying the Messianic king of the Chronicler's expectation.

2. Not only is there idealization of David and Solomon, but the author also appears to consciously adopt the account of the succession of Moses and Joshua as a model for the succession of David and Solomon:

a. Both David and Moses fail to attain their goals—one to build the temple and the other to enter the promised land. In both cases the divine prohibition is related to the appointment of a successor (22:5–13; 28:2–8; Dt 1:37–38; 31:2–8).

b. Both Solomon and Joshua bring the people of God into rest (22:8–9; Jos 11:23; 21:44).

c. There are a number of verbal parallels in the appointments of Solomon and Joshua (compare 22:11–13,16; 28:7–10,20; 2Ch 1:1 with Dt 31:5–8,23; Jos 1:5,7–9).

d. There are both private and public announcements of the appointment of the successors: private (22:6; Dt 31:23); public (28:8; Dt 31:7—both "in the presence/sight of all Israel").

e. Both enjoy the immediate and wholehearted support of the people (29:23–24; Dt 34:9; Jos 1:16–18).

f. It is twice reported that God "exalted" or "made great" Solomon and Joshua (29:25; 2Ch 1:1; Jos 3:7; 4:14).

The Chronicler also uses other models from Pentateuchal history in his portrayal of David and Solomon. Like Moses, David received the plans for the temple from God (28:11–19; Ex 25:9) and called on the people to bring voluntary offerings for its construction (29:1–9; Ex 25:1–7). Solomon's relationship to Huram-Abi, the craftsman from Tyre (2Ch 2:13–14), echoes the role of Bezalel and Oholiab in the building of the tabernacle (Ex 35:30—36:7). See note on 2Ch 1:5.

GENEALOGIES

Analysis of genealogies, both inside and outside the Bible, has disclosed that they serve a variety of functions (with different principles governing the lists), that they vary in form (some being segmented, others linear) and depth (number of generations listed), and that they are often fluid (subject to change).

There are three general areas in which genealogies function: the familial or domestic, the legal-political, and the religious. In the domestic area an individual's social status, privileges and obligations may be reflected in his placement in the lineage (see 7:14–19); the rights of the firstborn son and the secondary status of the children of concubines are examples from the Bible. In the political sphere genealogies substantiate claims to hereditary office or settle competing claims when the office is contested. Land organization and territorial groupings of social units may also be determined by genealogical reckoning—e.g., the division of the land among the 12 tribes. In Israel military levies also proceeded along genealogical lines; several of the genealogies in Chronicles reflect military conscription (5:1–26; 7:1–12,30–40; 8:1–40). Genealogies function in the religious sphere primarily by establishing membership among the priests and Levites (6:1–30; 9:10–34; Ne 7:61–65).

As to form, some genealogical lists trace several lines of descent (segmented genealogies), while others are devoted to a single line (linear genealogies).

Comparison of genealogical lists of the same tribal or family line often brings to light surprising differences. This fluidity of the lists may reflect variation in function. But sometimes changes in the status or relations of social structures are reflected in genealogies by changes in the relationships of names in the genealogy (see notes on 1:35–42; 6:22,27) or by the addition of names or segments to a lineage (see notes on 5:11–22; 6:27; 7:6–12). The most common type of fluidity in Biblical materials is telescoping, the omission of names from the list. Unimportant names are left out in order to relate an individual to a prominent ancestor, or possibly to achieve the desired number of names in the genealogy. Some Biblical genealogies, for example, omit names to achieve multiples of 7: For the period from David to the exile Matthew gives 14 generations (2 times 7), while Luke gives 21 (3 times 7), and the same authors give similar multiples of 7 for the period from the exile to Jesus (Mt 1:1–17; Lk 3:23–38).

The genealogies of Chronicles show variation in all these properties; the arrangements often reflect the purpose for which the genealogies were composed prior to their being adopted by the Chronicler as part of his record.

OUTLINE

I. Genealogies: Creation to Restoration (1Ch 1–9)
   A. The Patriarchs (ch. 1)
   B. The 12 Sons of Jacob/Israel (2:1–2)
   C. The Family of Judah (2:3—4:23)
   D. The Sons of Simeon (4:24–43)
   E. Reuben, Gad and the Half-Tribe of Manasseh (ch. 5)
   F. Levi and Families (ch. 6)
   G. Issachar, Benjamin, Naphtali, Manasseh, Ephraim and Asher (chs. 7–9)
II. The Reign of David (1Ch 10–29)
   A. Death of Saul (ch. 10)
   B. Capture of Jerusalem; David's Power Base (chs. 11–12)
   C. Return of the Ark; Establishment of David's Kingdom (chs. 13–16)
   D. Dynastic Promise (ch. 17)
   E. David's Conquests (chs. 18–20)
   F. The Census (ch. 21)

G. Preparations for the Temple (ch. 22)
H. Organization of the Temple Service (chs. 23–26)
I. Administrative Structures of the Kingdom (ch. 27)
J. David's Final Preparations for Succession and the Temple (28:1—29:20)
K. Succession of Solomon; Death of David (29:21–30)

III. The Reign of Solomon (2Ch 1–9)
A. The Gift of Wisdom (ch. 1)
B. Building the Temple (2:1—5:1)
C. Dedication of the Temple (5:2—7:22)
D. Solomon's Other Activities (ch. 8)
E. Solomon's Wisdom, Splendor and Death (ch. 9)

IV. The Schism, and the History of the Kings of Judah (2Ch 10–36)
A. Rehoboam (chs. 10–12)
B. Abijah (13:1—14:1)
C. Asa (14:2—16:14)
D. Jehoshaphat (17:1—21:3)
E. Jehoram and Ahaziah (21:4—22:9)
F. Joash (22:10—24:27)
G. Amaziah (ch. 25)
H. Uzziah (ch. 26)
I. Jotham (ch. 27)
J. Ahaz (ch. 28)
K. Hezekiah (chs. 29–32)
L. Manasseh (33:1–20)
M. Amon (33:21–25)
N. Josiah (34:1—36:1)
O. Josiah's Successors (36:2–14)
P. Exile and Restoration (36:15–23)

HISTORICAL RECORDS FROM ADAM TO ABRAHAM

TO NOAH'S SONS

1 Adam, *a* Seth, Enosh, ²Kenan, *b* Mahalalel, *c* Jared, *d* ³Enoch, *e* Methuselah, *f* Lamech, *g* Noah. *h*

⁴ The sons of Noah: *a i*
Shem, Ham and Japheth. *j*

THE JAPHETHITES

1:5–7pp — Ge 10:2–5

⁵ The sons *b* of Japheth:
Gomer, Magog, Madai, Javan, Tubal, Meshek and Tiras.

⁶ The sons of Gomer:
Ashkenaz, Riphath *c* and Togarmah.

⁷ The sons of Javan:
Elishah, Tarshish, the Kittites and the Rodanites.

THE HAMITES

1:8–16pp — Ge 10:6–20

⁸ The sons of Ham:
Cush, Egypt, Put and Canaan.

⁹ The sons of Cush:
Seba, Havilah, Sabta, Raamah and Sabteka.
The sons of Raamah:
Sheba and Dedan.

¹⁰ Cush was the father *d* of
Nimrod, who became a mighty warrior on earth.

¹¹ Egypt was the father of
the Ludites, Anamites, Lehabites, Naphtuhites, ¹²Pathrusites, Kasluhites (from whom the Philistines came) and Caphtorites.

¹³ Canaan was the father of

1:1 *a* Ge 5:1-32;
Lk 3:36-38
1:2 *b* S Ge 5:9
c S Ge 5:12
d S Ge 5:15
1:3 *e* S Ge 5:18;
Jude 1:14 *f* S Ge 5:21
g S Ge 5:25
h S Ge 5:29
1:4 *i* Ge 6:10; 10:1
j S Ge 5:32

---

a 4 Septuagint; Hebrew does not have this line.   *b 5* *Sons* may mean *descendants* or *successors* or *nations*; also in verses 6-10, 17 and 20.   *c 6* Many Hebrew manuscripts and Vulgate (see also Septuagint and Gen. 10:3); most Hebrew manuscripts *Diphath*   *d 10 Father* may mean *ancestor* or *predecessor* or *founder*; also in verses 11, 13, 18 and 20.

1:1—9:44 The genealogies succinctly show the restored community's continuity with the past. The great deeds of God in Israel's behalf prior to the rise of David are passed over in silence, but the genealogies serve as a skeleton of history to show that the Israel of the restoration stands at the center of the divine purpose from the beginning (from Adam, v. 1). And the genealogies also serve the very practical purpose of legitimizing the present. They provide the framework by which the ethnic and religious purity of the people can be maintained. They also establish the continuing line of royal succession and the legitimacy of the priests for the postexilic temple service. See Introduction: Genealogies.

1:1—2:1 The Chronicler here covers the period from Adam to Jacob, and the materials are drawn almost entirely from Genesis. The subsidiary lines of descent are presented first: Japheth and Ham (vv. 5–16) are given before Shem (vv. 17–27), the sons of Shem other than those in Abraham's ancestry (vv. 17–23) before that line (vv. 24–27), the sons of Abraham's concubines (vv. 28–33) before Isaac's line (v. 34), the descendants of Esau and the Edomite ruling houses (vv. 35–54) before the sons of Israel/Jacob (2:1). In each case the elect lineage is given last. Several features of this genealogy are striking when compared with non-Biblical materials. The genealogy begins without an introduction. Two sections of the genealogy have no kinship terms and are only lists of names: the first 13 names (vv. 1–4; see note on v. 4) and vv. 24–27. In vv. 5–16 (and following v. 27) kinship terms are used. Both segmented (those

tracing several lines of descent) and linear (those tracing a single line) genealogies are included. This identical structure is found in a copy of the Assyrian King List: There is no introduction, and the scribe has drawn lines across the tablet, dividing it into four sections, two of which are lists of names without kinship terms, alternating with two lists in which relations are specified; both segmented and linear genealogies are used. This suggests that the Chronicler was following a known literary pattern for his composition.

1:1–4 From creation to the flood. This list is taken from Ge 5:1–32 (see notes there). The omission of Cain and Abel demonstrates the Chronicler's interest in the chosen line (see Ge 4:17–25).

1:4 *The sons of Noah.* Not found in the Hebrew text (see TNIV text note); this omission parallels the Assyrian King List (see note on 1:1—2:1). The Chronicler's readers would have known that these were the sons of Noah and would not have needed the kinship notice; the Septuagint (the pre-Christian Greek translation of the OT) and most modern translations insert the phrase to clarify the relationship.

1:5–23 This genealogy is drawn from the table of nations in Ge 10:2–29 (see notes there). The arrangement is primarily geographical and cultural rather than biological. Omitting the Philistines (v. 12) as a parenthesis, a total of 70 nations is achieved: Japheth, 14; Ham, 30; Shem, 26 (see note on Ge 10:2)—an example of a genealogy telescoped to attain multiples of 7 (see Introduction: Genealogies).

1:24 *k* S Ge 10:21-
25; Lk 3:34-36
1:32 *l* S Ge 22:24
m S Ge 10:7
1:34 *n* Lk 3:34
o Mt 1:2; Ac 7:8
p S Ge 17:5
1:35 *q* Ge 36:19
r S Ge 36:4

Sidon his firstborn,[a] and of the Hittites, [14]Jebusites, Amorites, Girgashites, [15]Hivites, Arkites, Sinites, [16]Arvadites, Zemarites and Hamathites.

THE SEMITES

1:17–23pp — Ge 10:21–31; 11:10–27

[17] The sons of Shem:
Elam, Ashur, Arphaxad, Lud and Aram.
The sons of Aram:[b]
Uz, Hul, Gether and Meshek.
[18] Arphaxad was the father of Shelah,
and Shelah the father of Eber.
[19] Two sons were born to Eber:
One was named Peleg,[c] because in his time the earth was divided; his brother was named Joktan.
[20] Joktan was the father of
Almodad, Sheleph, Hazarmaveth, Jerah, [21]Hadoram, Uzal, Diklah, [22]Obal,[d] Abimael, Sheba, [23]Ophir, Havilah and Jobab. All these were sons of Joktan.

[24] Shem,[k] Arphaxad,[e] Shelah,
[25] Eber, Peleg, Reu,
[26] Serug, Nahor, Terah
[27] and Abram (that is, Abraham).

THE FAMILY OF ABRAHAM

[28] The sons of Abraham:
Isaac and Ishmael.

DESCENDANTS OF HAGAR

1:29–31pp — Ge 25:12–16

[29] These were their descendants:
Nebaioth the firstborn of Ishmael, Kedar, Adbeel, Mibsam, [30]Mishma, Dumah, Massa, Hadad, Tema, [31]Jetur, Naphish and Kedemah. These were the sons of Ishmael.

DESCENDANTS OF KETURAH

1:32–33pp — Ge 25:1–4

[32] The sons born to Keturah, Abraham's concubine:[l]
Zimran, Jokshan, Medan, Midian, Ishbak and Shuah.
The sons of Jokshan:
Sheba and Dedan.[m]
[33] The sons of Midian:
Ephah, Epher, Hanok, Abida and Eldaah.
All these were descendants of Keturah.

DESCENDANTS OF SARAH

1:35–37pp — Ge 36:10–14

[34] Abraham[n] was the father of Isaac.[o]
The sons of Isaac:
Esau and Israel.[p]

ESAU'S SONS

[35] The sons of Esau:[q]
Eliphaz, Reuel,[r] Jeush, Jalam and Korah.
[36] The sons of Eliphaz:

---

a 13 Or *of the Sidonians, the foremost*   b 17 One Hebrew manuscript and some Septuagint manuscripts (see also Gen. 10:23); most Hebrew manuscripts do not have this line.   c 19 *Peleg* means *division.*
d 22 Some Hebrew manuscripts and Syriac (see also Gen. 10:28); most Hebrew manuscripts *Ebal*
e 24 Hebrew; some Septuagint manuscripts *Arphaxad, Cainan* (see also note at Gen. 11:10)

1:24–27 See notes on 1:1—2:1; Ge 11:10–26.
1:28–34 See notes on Ge 25:1–18.
1:35–42 See Ge 36:10–28 and notes.
1:36 *sons of Eliphaz.* These correspond to Ge 36:11–12, but with one difficulty: The Hebrew text of Chronicles (see second TNIV text note on this verse) lists Timna as a son of Eliphaz,

while Ge 36:12 designates Timna as the concubine of Eliphaz and mother of Amalek. The TNIV follows the Septuagint (the pre-Christian Greek translation of the OT), which regarded Timna as the mother of Amalek, not as the son of Eliphaz. According to this solution, the Hebrew text is here in error, or perhaps the Chronicler has once again omitted kinship terminology (see

Teman, Omar, Zepho,^a Gatam and Kenaz;
by Timna: Amalek.^{b s}
³⁷ The sons of Reuel:^t
Nahath, Zerah, Shammah and Mizzah.

THE PEOPLE OF SEIR IN EDOM

1:38–42pp — Ge 36:20–28
³⁸ The sons of Seir:
Lotan, Shobal, Zibeon, Anah, Dishon, Ezer and Dishan.
³⁹ The sons of Lotan:
Hori and Homam. Timna was Lotan's sister.
⁴⁰ The sons of Shobal:
Alvan,^c Manahath, Ebal, Shepho and Onam.
The sons of Zibeon:
Aiah and Anah.^u
⁴¹ The son of Anah:
Dishon.
The sons of Dishon:
Hemdan,^d Eshban, Ithran and Keran.
⁴² The sons of Ezer:
Bilhan, Zaavan and Akan.^e
The sons of Dishan^f:
Uz and Aran.

THE RULERS OF EDOM

1:43–54pp — Ge 36:31–43
⁴³ These were the kings who reigned in Edom before any Israelite king reigned:
Bela son of Beor, whose city was named Dinhabah.
⁴⁴ When Bela died, Jobab son of Zerah from Bozrah succeeded him as king.
⁴⁵ When Jobab died, Husham from the land of the Temanites^v succeeded him as king.
⁴⁶ When Husham died, Hadad son of Bedad, who defeated Midian in the country of
Moab, succeeded him as king. His city was named Avith.
⁴⁷ When Hadad died, Samlah from Masrekah succeeded him as king.
⁴⁸ When Samlah died, Shaul from Rehoboth on the river^g succeeded him as king.
⁴⁹ When Shaul died, Baal-Hanan son of Akbor succeeded him as king.
⁵⁰ When Baal-Hanan died, Hadad succeeded him as king. His city was named Pau,^h
and his wife's name was Mehetabel daughter of Matred, the daughter of Me-Za-
hab. ⁵¹Hadad also died.

The chiefs of Edom were:
Timna, Alvah, Jetheth, ⁵²Oholibamah, Elah, Pinon, ⁵³Kenaz, Teman, Mibzar,
⁵⁴Magdiel and Iram. These were the chiefs of Edom.

ISRAEL'S SONS

2:1–2pp — Ge 35:23–26

2 These were the sons of Israel:
Reuben, Simeon, Levi, Judah, Issachar, Zebulun, ²Dan, Joseph, Benjamin, Naphtali, Gad and Asher.

^a 36 Many Hebrew manuscripts, some Septuagint manuscripts and Syriac (see also Gen. 36:11); most
Hebrew manuscripts *Zephi*   ^b 36 Some Septuagint manuscripts (see also Gen. 36:12); Hebrew *Gatam,
Kenaz, Timna and Amalek*   ^c 40 Many Hebrew manuscripts and some Septuagint manuscripts (see
also Gen. 36:23); most Hebrew manuscripts *Alian*   ^d 41 Many Hebrew manuscripts and some
Septuagint manuscripts (see also Gen. 36:26); most Hebrew manuscripts *Hamran*   ^e 42 Many Hebrew
and Septuagint manuscripts (see also Gen. 36:27); most Hebrew manuscripts *Zaavan, Jaakan*   ^f 42 See
Gen. 36:28; Hebrew *Dishon*, a variant of *Dishan*   ^g 48 Possibly the Euphrates   ^h 50 Many Hebrew
manuscripts, some Septuagint manuscripts, Vulgate and Syriac (see also Gen. 36:39); most Hebrew
manuscripts *Pai*

---

notes on v. 4 and 1:1—2:1). Alternatively, some regard this as an
example of genealogical fluidity (see Introduction: Genealogies): Since the name Timna also became the name of a chief-
dom in Edom (v. 51; Ge 36:40), during the course of time Timna
was moved in the Edomite genealogies to the position of a son
of Eliphaz and brother of Amalek.
1:43–54 See Ge 36:31–43. The Chronicler continues with ex-

tensive coverage of Edom. This is striking in contrast to his omission of the line of Cain and the brief treatment of the line of Ishmael. It probably reflects the fact that the Edomites were
important in the Chronicler's own day (see 18:11–13; 2Ch 8:17;
21:8; 25:20; 28:17).
2:1–2 Although there are numerous lists of the 12 tribes in the
OT, only four are given in genealogical form: (1) Ge 29:31—

2:3 w S Ge 29:35;
38:2-10 x S Ge 38:5
y S Ge 38:2
z S Nu 26:19
2:4 a S Ge 11:31
b Ge 38:11-30
c S Ge 38:29
2:5 d S Ge 46:12
e Nu 26:21
2:7 f S Jos 7:1
g S Jos 6:18
2:9 h S Nu 26:21
2:10 i Lk 3:32-33
j S Ex 6:23 k S Nu 1:7
2:12 l S Ru 2:1
m S Ru 4:17
2:13 n S Ru 4:17
o S 1Sa 16:6

JUDAH

2:5–15pp — Ru 4:18–22; Mt 1:3–6

TO HEZRON'S SONS

3 The sons of Judah: w

Er, Onan and Shelah. x These three were born to him by a Canaanite woman, the daughter of Shua. y Er, Judah's firstborn, was wicked in the LORD's sight; so the LORD put him to death. z 4 Judah's daughter-in-law a Tamar b bore Perez c and Zerah to Judah. He had five sons in all.

5 The sons of Perez: d

Hezron e and Hamul.

6 The sons of Zerah:

Zimri, Ethan, Heman, Kalkol and Darda a—five in all.

7 The son of Karmi:

Achar, b f who brought trouble on Israel by violating the ban on taking devoted things. c g

8 The son of Ethan:

Azariah.

9 The sons born to Hezron h were:

Jerahmeel, Ram and Caleb. d

FROM RAM SON OF HEZRON

10 Ram i was the father of

Amminadab j, and Amminadab the father of Nahshon, k the leader of the people of Judah. 11 Nahshon was the father of Salmon, e Salmon the father of Boaz, 12 Boaz l the father of Obed and Obed the father of Jesse. m

13 Jesse n was the father of

Eliab o his firstborn; the second son was Abinadab, the third Shimea, 14 the fourth Nethanel, the fifth Raddai, 15 the sixth Ozem and the seventh David. 16 Their sisters

---

a 6 Many Hebrew manuscripts, some Septuagint manuscripts and Syriac (see also 1 Kings 4:31); most Hebrew manuscripts *Dara*   b 7 *Achar* means *trouble*; *Achar* is called *Achan* in Joshua.
c 7 The Hebrew term refers to the irrevocable giving over of things or persons to the LORD, often by totally destroying them.   d 9 Hebrew *Kelubai*, a variant of *Caleb*   e 11 Septuagint (see also Ruth 4:21); Hebrew *Salma*

30:24; 35:16–20; (2) Ge 35:22–26; (3) Ge 46:8–27; (4) here. Other lists of the tribes are found in 12:24–37; 27:16–22; Ex 1:2–5; Dt 27:12–13; 33; Eze 48:31–34. In other lists the tribe of Levi is omitted, and the number 12 is achieved by dividing Joseph into the tribes of Ephraim and Manasseh (Nu 1:5–15; 1:20–43; 2:3–31; 7:12–83; 10:14–28; 13:4–15; 26:5–51). In this passage the Chronicler appears to follow Ge 35:22–26 except for the position of the tribe of Dan, which is found in seventh instead of ninth place. The list here does not set the order in which the Chronicler will take up the tribes; rather, he moves immediately to his major concern with the house of David and the tribe of Judah (2:3—4:23), even though Judah is fourth in the genealogy. In the lists of these chapters, the Chronicler maintains the number 12, but with the following names: Judah, Simeon, Reuben, Gad, half of Manasseh, Levi, Issachar, Benjamin, Naphtali, Ephraim, Manasseh and Asher. Zebulun and Dan are omitted.
2:3–9 The lineage of Judah is traced to Hezron's sons (v. 9), whose descendants are given in 2:10—3:24. Of Judah's five sons, the first two (Er and Onan) died as the result of sin recorded in Ge 38. The lineage of the third son, Shelah, is taken up in 4:21; this section focuses on the remaining two (see Ge 46:12; Nu 26:19–22).
2:6 *Ethan, Heman, Kalkol and Darda.* Not immediate descendants of Zerah; rather, they are from the later period of the reign of Solomon (1Ki 4:31). A Heman and an Ethan were David's musicians (see 15:19; Ps 88–89 titles), but whether these are the same individuals is uncertain. If they are the same, the fact that in 6:33–42 and 15:19 Heman and Ethan are assigned to the tribe of Levi may be another example of genealogical fluidity,

where these men's musical skills brought them into the Levitical lineage. Or the reverse may have occurred: As Levites associated with Judah, they were brought into that lineage.
2:7 *Achar.* The change from Achan to Achar (meaning "trouble"; see TNIV text note) is probably a play on words reflecting the trouble he brought to Israel (Jos 7).
2:10—3:24 That the Chronicler's primary concern in the genealogy of Judah is with the line of David is seen in his arrangement of this section's material as an inversion:

Descendants of Ram (David's ancestry), 2:10–17
Descendants of Caleb, 2:18–24
Descendants of Jerahmeel, 2:25–33
Supplementary material on Jerahmeel, 2:34–41
Supplementary material on Caleb, 2:42–55
Supplementary material on Ram (David's descendants), ch. 3
The Chronicler has structured this central portion of the Judah genealogy to highlight the Davidic ancestry and descent, which frame this section and emphasize the position of David—in line with the Chronicler's interests in the historical portions that follow (see note on 4:1–23).
2:10–17 Verses 10–12 are a linear genealogy from Ram to Jesse; then Jesse's lineage is segmented, reminiscent of 1Sa 16:1–13. The source for most of the material is Ru 4:19–22. In 1Sa 16:10–13 David was the eighth of Jesse's sons to appear before Samuel; in this passage only seven are named, enabling David to occupy the favored place of the seventh son (v. 15; see Introduction: Genealogies). David was the half-uncle of his famous warriors Abishai, Joab, Asahel and Amasa (11:6,20,26; 2Sa 2:13,18; 17:25; 19:13).

were Zeruiah ^{p} and Abigail. Zeruiah's ^{q} three sons were Abishai, Joab ^{r} and Asahel. ^{17}Abigail was the mother of Amasa, ^{s} whose father was Jether the Ishmaelite.

CALEB SON OF HEZRON

^{18}Caleb son of Hezron had children by his wife Azubah (and by Jerioth). These were her sons: Jesher, Shobab and Ardon. ^{19}When Azubah died, Caleb ^{t} married Ephrath, who bore him Hur. ^{20}Hur was the father of Uri, and Uri the father of Bezalel. ^{u}

^{21}Later, Hezron, when he was sixty years old, married the daughter of Makir the father of Gilead. ^{v} He made love to her, and she bore him Segub. ^{22}Segub was the father of Jair, who controlled twenty-three towns in Gilead. ^{23}(But Geshur and Aram captured Havvoth Jair, $^{a\,w}$ as well as Kenath ^{x} with its surrounding settlements—sixty towns.) All these were descendants of Makir the father of Gilead.

^{24}After Hezron died in Caleb Ephrathah, Abijah the wife of Hezron bore him Ashhur ^{y} the father ^{b} of Tekoa.

JERAHMEEL SON OF HEZRON

^{25}The sons of Jerahmeel the firstborn of Hezron:
Ram his firstborn, Bunah, Oren, Ozem and ^{c} Ahijah. ^{26}Jerahmeel had another wife, whose name was Atarah; she was the mother of Onam.

^{27}The sons of Ram the firstborn of Jerahmeel:
Maaz, Jamin and Eker.

^{28}The sons of Onam:
Shammai and Jada.
The sons of Shammai:
Nadab and Abishur.

^{29}Abishur's wife was named Abihail, who bore him Ahban and Molid.

^{30}The sons of Nadab:
Seled and Appaim. Seled died without children.

^{31}The son of Appaim:
Ishi, who was the father of Sheshan.
Sheshan was the father of Ahlai.

^{32}The sons of Jada, Shammai's brother:
Jether and Jonathan. Jether died without children.

^{33}The sons of Jonathan:
Peleth and Zaza.
These were the descendants of Jerahmeel.

^{34}Sheshan had no sons—only daughters.
He had an Egyptian servant named Jarha. ^{35}Sheshan gave his daughter in marriage to his servant Jarha, and she bore him Attai.

^{36}Attai was the father of Nathan,
Nathan the father of Zabad, ^{z}
^{37}Zabad the father of Ephlal,
Ephlal the father of Obed,
^{38}Obed the father of Jehu,
Jehu the father of Azariah,
^{39}Azariah the father of Helez,
Helez the father of Eleasah,
^{40}Eleasah the father of Sismai,

---

^{a} 23 Or *captured the settlements of Jair* ^{b} 24 *Father* may mean *civic leader* or *military leader*; also in verses 42, 45, 49-52 and possibly elsewhere. ^{c} 25 Or *Oren and Ozem, by*

2:16 ^{p} 1Sa 26:6
^{q} 2Sa 2:18 ^{r} 2Sa 2:13
2:17 ^{s} 2Sa 17:25
2:19 ^{t} ver 42,50
2:20 ^{u} S Ex 31:2
2:21 ^{v} S Nu 27:1
2:23 ^{w} S Nu 32:41;
Dt 3:14 ^{x} Nu 32:42
2:24 ^{y} 1Ch 4:5
2:36 ^{z} 1Ch 11:41

2:18–24 For the Chronicler the important name in this genealogy of the Calebites is Bezalel (v. 20), the wise master craftsman who supervised the building of the tabernacle (Ex 31:1–5). He is mentioned in the Bible only in Exodus and Chronicles. The Chronicler uses Bezalel and Oholiab (Ex 31:6) as a model for his portrait of Solomon and Huram-Abi in the building of the temple (see note on 2Ch 1:5). By inserting a reference to the builder of the tabernacle next to the genealogy of David in vv. 10–17, the Chronicler characteristically juxtaposes the themes of king and temple—so important to his historical narrative.
2:25–33 This section is identified as a separate entity from the

supplementary material by its opening and closing formulas: "The sons of Jerahmeel" (v. 25) and "These were the descendants of Jerahmeel" (v. 33). Verses 25–41 are the only genealogical materials on the Jerahmeelites in the Bible. 1Sa 27:10 and 30:27–29 place their settlements in the Negev.
2:34–41 Supplementary material on the line of Sheshan (v. 31); it is a linear genealogy to a depth of 13 generations. The generation of Elishama (v. 41) would be the 23rd since Judah, if there has been no telescoping in this lineage. If no names are omitted, Elishama would likely be contemporary with David, though we know nothing of him.

2:42 ^aS ver 19
2:45 ^bS Jos 15:55
^cS Jos 15:58
2:49 ^dJos 15:31
^eJos 15:16
2:50 ^f1Ch 4:4
^gS ver 19
2:53 ^h2Sa 23:38
2:54 ⁱEzr 2:22;
Ne 7:26; 12:28
2:55 ^jS Ge 15:19;
S Jdg 4:11 ^kJos 19:35
^l2Ki 10:15,23;
Jer 35:2-19
3:1 ^m1Ch 14:3; 28:5
ⁿS 1Sa 25:43
^oS Jos 15:56
^pS 1Sa 25:42
3:2 ^q1Ki 2:22

Sismai the father of Shallum,
⁴¹Shallum the father of Jekamiah,
and Jekamiah the father of Elishama.

THE CLANS OF CALEB

⁴²The sons of Caleb *^a* the brother of Jerahmeel:
Mesha his firstborn, who was the father of Ziph, and his son Mareshah, ^a who was the father of Hebron.
⁴³The sons of Hebron:
Korah, Tappuah, Rekem and Shema. ⁴⁴Shema was the father of Raham, and Raham the father of Jorkeam. Rekem was the father of Shammai. ⁴⁵The son of Shammai was Maon ^b, and Maon was the father of Beth Zur. ^c
⁴⁶Caleb's concubine Ephah was the mother of Haran, Moza and Gazez. Haran was the father of Gazez.
⁴⁷The sons of Jahdai:
Regem, Jotham, Geshan, Pelet, Ephah and Shaaph.
⁴⁸Caleb's concubine Maakah was the mother of Sheber and Tirhanah. ⁴⁹She also gave birth to Shaaph the father of Madmannah ^d and to Sheva the father of Makbenah and Gibea. Caleb's daughter was Aksah. ^e ⁵⁰These were the descendants of Caleb.

The sons of Hur ^f the firstborn of Ephrathah:
Shobal the father of Kiriath Jearim, ^g ⁵¹Salma the father of Bethlehem, and Hareph the father of Beth Gader.
⁵²The descendants of Shobal the father of Kiriath Jearim were:
Haroeh, half the Manahathites, ⁵³and the clans of Kiriath Jearim: the Ithrites, ^h Puthites, Shumathites and Mishraites. From these descended the Zorathites and Eshtaolites.
⁵⁴The descendants of Salma:
Bethlehem, the Netophathites, ⁱ Atroth Beth Joab, half the Manahathites, the Zorites, ⁵⁵and the clans of scribes^b who lived at Jabez: the Tirathites, Shimeathites and Sucathites. These are the Kenites ^j who came from Hammath, ^k the father of the house of Rekab. ^c ^l

THE SONS OF DAVID

3:1–4pp — 2Sa 3:2–5
3:5–8pp — 2Sa 5:14–16; 1Ch 14:4–7

3 These were the sons of David ^m born to him in Hebron:
The firstborn was Amnon the son of Ahinoam ⁿ of Jezreel; ^o
the second, Daniel the son of Abigail ^p of Carmel;
²the third, Absalom the son of Maakah daughter of Talmai king of Geshur;
the fourth, Adonijah ^q the son of Haggith;
³the fifth, Shephatiah the son of Abital;
and the sixth, Ithream, by his wife Eglah.

^a 42 The meaning of the Hebrew for this phrase is uncertain.   ^b 55 Or *of the Sopherites*
^c 55 Or *father of Beth Rekab*

2:42–55 The same opening and closing formulas noted in vv. 25,33 occur in vv. 42,50a:"The sons of Caleb ...These were the descendants of Caleb."The list in this section is a mixture of personal and place-names; the phrase "father of" must often be understood as "founder of" or "leader of" a city (see TNIV text notes on 1:10; 4:4).
2:50b–55 Resumes the genealogy of Hur (v. 20). The same formulas for identifying the genealogical sections in vv. 25,33 and in vv. 42,50a are used in v. 50b and 4:4:"The sons of Hur ...These were the descendants of Hur."The presence of these formulas suggests that this section and 4:1–4 were once a unit; the Chronicler has inserted his record of the Davidic descent (ch. 3) into the middle of this other genealogy, apparently to balance the sections of his material (see notes on 2:10—3:24; 4:1–23). Otherwise the disruption of the genealogy of Hur may have already occurred in the Chronicler's sources.
2:55 *Tirathites, Shimeathites and Sucathites.* May refer to three

families, as translated here, or possibly to three different classes of scribes, perhaps those who (1) read, (2) copied and (3) checked the work. *Kenites.* Originally a foreign people, many of the Kenites were incorporated into Judah (see Nu 10:29–32; Jdg 1:16; 4:11).
3:1–24 See note on 2:10—3:24.
3:1–9 This list of David's children is largely drawn from 2Sa 3:2–5; 5:13–16; 13:1 (see notes there). The sons born in Jerusalem are repeated in 1Ch 14:3–7. The name Eliphelet occurs twice (vv. 6,8); in 14:5,7 two spellings of the name are given (only one son having this name is mentioned in 2Sa 5:14–16). The reference to David's seven-year rule in Hebron (v. 4) is repeated in 29:27, though the Chronicler does not deal with this period in his narrative. The references to Absalom, Tamar, Adonijah, Amnon and Bathsheba all recall unhappy incidents in the life of David, incidents the Chronicler has omitted from his later narrative (see 2Sa 11–15; 17–18; 1Ki 1).

3:4 ʳS 2Sa 5:4;
1Ch 29:27 ˢS 2Sa 5:5
3:5 ᵗ2Sa 11:3
3:9 ᵘS 2Sa 13:1
ᵛ1Ch 14:4
3:10 ʷ1Ki 14:21-31;
2Ch 12:16 ˣ1Ki 15:1-
8; 2Ch 13:1 ʸ1Ki 15:9-
24 ᶻ2Ch 17:1–21:3
3:11 ᵃ2Ki 8:16-24;
2Ch 21:1
ᵇ2Ki 8:25–10:14;
2Ch 22:1-10
ᶜ2Ki 11:1–12:21;
2Ch 22:11–24:27
3:12 ᵈ2Ki 14:1-22;
2Ch 25:1-28
ᵉ2Ch 26:1-23
ᶠ2Ki 15:32-38;
2Ch 27:1; Isa 1:1;
Hos 1:1; Mic 1:1
3:13 ᵍ2Ki 16:1-20;
2Ch 28:1; Isa 7:1
ʰ2Ki 18:1–20:21;
2Ch 29:1; Isa 1:1;
Jer 26:19; Hos 1:1;
Mic 1:1 ⁱ2Ki 21:1-18;
2Ch 33:1
3:14 ʲ2Ki 21:19-26;
2Ch 33:21; Zep 1:1
ᵏ2Ki 22:1; 2Ch 34:1;
Jer 1:2; 3:6; 25:3
3:15 ˡS 2Ki 23:34
ᵐJer 37:1
ⁿS 2Ki 23:31
3:16 ᵒS 2Ki 24:6,8
ᵖS 2Ki 24:18
3:17 �ۿEzr 3:2
3:18 ʳEzr 1:8; 5:14
ˢJer 22:30

⁴These six were born to David in Hebron, ʳ where he reigned seven years and six months. ˢ
David reigned in Jerusalem thirty-three years, ⁵and these were the children born to him there:

Shammua,ᵃ Shobab, Nathan and Solomon. These four were by Bathshebaᵇ ᵗ daughter of Ammiel. ⁶There were also Ibhar, Elishua,ᶜ Eliphelet, ⁷Nogah, Nepheg, Japhia, ⁸Elishama, Eliada and Eliphelet—nine in all. ⁹All these were the sons of David, besides his sons by his concubines. And Tamarᵘ was their sister. ᵛ

THE KINGS OF JUDAH

¹⁰Solomon's son was Rehoboam, ʷ
 Abijahˣ his son,
 Asaʸ his son,
 Jehoshaphatᶻ his son,
 ¹¹Jehoramᵈ ᵃ his son,
 Ahaziahᵇ his son,
 Joashᶜ his son,
 ¹²Amaziahᵈ his son,
 Azariahᵉ his son,
 Jothamᶠ his son,
 ¹³Ahazᵍ his son,
 Hezekiahʰ his son,
 Manassehⁱ his son,
 ¹⁴Amonʲ his son,
 Josiahᵏ his son.
 ¹⁵The sons of Josiah:
 Johanan the firstborn,
 Jehoiakimˡ the second son,
 Zedekiahᵐ the third,
 Shallumⁿ the fourth.
 ¹⁶The successors of Jehoiakim:
 Jehoiachinᵉ ᵒ his son,
 and Zedekiah.ᵖ

THE ROYAL LINE AFTER THE EXILE

¹⁷The descendants of Jehoiachin the captive:
 Shealtielᵠ his son, ¹⁸Malkiram, Pedaiah, Shenazzar, ʳ Jekamiah, Hoshama and Nedabiah. ˢ
¹⁹The sons of Pedaiah:

3:10 *Rehoboam.* See 2Ch 10–12 and note on 11:1–23. *Abijah.* See note on 2Ch 13:1—14:1. *Asa.* See note on 2Ch 14:2—16:14. *Jehoshaphat.* See note on 2Ch 17:1—21:3.
3:11 *Jehoram.* See 2Ch 21. *Ahaziah.* See note on 2Ch 22:1–9. *Joash.* See note on 2Ch 23:1—24:27.
3:12 *Amaziah.* See note on 2Ch 25:1–28. *Azariah.* Also called Uzziah (see note on 2Ch 26:1–23). *Jotham.* See 2Ch 27; see also 2Ki 15:32–38 and notes.
3:13 *Ahaz.* See 2Ch 28:1–27 and notes. *Hezekiah.* See note on 2Ch 29:1—32:13. *Manasseh.* See note on 2Ch 33:1–20.
3:14 *Amon.* See note on 2Ch 33:21–25. *Josiah.* See note on 2Ch 34:1—36:1.
3:15 *Johanan the firstborn.* Not mentioned elsewhere and may have died before Josiah. The genealogy is segmented at this point, instead of linear as in vv. 10–14. Since Josiah's other three sons would all occupy the throne, the succession was not uniformly father to son. Shallum/Jehoahaz (2Ch 36:2–4; 2Ki 23:30–35) was replaced by Jehoiakim (2Ch 36:5–8; 2Ki 23:34—24:6); Jehoiakim was succeeded by his son Jehoiachin (2Ch 36:9–10; 2Ki 24:8–16). After Jehoiachin was taken captive to Babylon by Nebuchadnezzar, Josiah's son Zedekiah became the

last king of Judah (2Ch 36:11–14; 2Ki 24:17—25:7).
3:17–20 Seven sons are attributed to Jehoiachin, but not one succeeded him (see notes on v. 15; Jer 22:30). Tablets found in Babylon dating from the 10th to the 35th year of Nebuchadnezzar (595–570 B.C.) and listing deliveries of rations mention Jehoiachin and five sons, as well as other Judahites held in Babylon. Jehoiachin received similar largess from Nebuchadnezzar's successor, Awel-Marduk (562–560 B.C.; see 2Ki 25:27–30).
3:18 *Shenazzar.* May be another spelling of the name Sheshbazzar. If so, the treasures of the temple were consigned to his care for return to Judah (Ezr 1:11). He also served for a short time as the first governor of the returnees and made an initial attempt at rebuilding the temple (Ezr 5:14–16). Little is known of him; he soon disappeared from the scene and was overshadowed by his nephew Zerubbabel, who assumes such importance in Ezra, Haggai and Zechariah. But see note on Ezr 1:8.
3:19 *Pedaiah.* Other texts name Shealtiel (v. 17) as Zerubbabel's father (Ezr 3:2,8; Ne 12:1; Hag 1:1,12,14; 2:2,23). Suggestions offered to resolve this difficulty are: 1. Shealtiel may have died early, and Pedaiah became the head of the family. 2. Pedaiah may have married the childless widow of Shealtiel; Zerubba-

3:19 ʳEzr 2:2; 3:2;
5:2; Ne 7:7; 12:1;
Hag 1:1; 2:2; Zec 4:6
3:22 ᵘEzr 8:2-3
4:1 ᵛS Ge 29:35;
S 1Ch 2:3 ʷNu 26:21
4:4 ˣ1Ch 2:50
ʸRu 1:19
4:5 ᶻ1Ch 2:24

Zerubbabel ᵗ and Shimei.

The sons of Zerubbabel:

Meshullam and Hananiah.

Shelomith was their sister.

²⁰ There were also five others:

Hashubah, Ohel, Berekiah, Hasadiah and Jushab-Hesed.

²¹ The descendants of Hananiah:

Pelatiah and Jeshaiah, and the sons of Rephaiah, of Arnan, of Obadiah and of Shekaniah.

²² The descendants of Shekaniah:

Shemaiah and his sons:

Hattush, ᵘ Igal, Bariah, Neariah and Shaphat—six in all.

²³ The sons of Neariah:

Elioenai, Hizkiah and Azrikam—three in all.

²⁴ The sons of Elioenai:

Hodaviah, Eliashib, Pelaiah, Akkub, Johanan, Delaiah and Anani—seven in all.

OTHER CLANS OF JUDAH

4 The descendants of Judah: ᵛ

Perez, Hezron, ʷ Karmi, Hur and Shobal.

² Reaiah son of Shobal was the father of Jahath, and Jahath the father of Ahumai and Lahad. These were the clans of the Zorathites.

³ These were the sons ᵃ of Etam:

Jezreel, Ishma and Idbash. Their sister was named Hazzelelponi. ⁴Penuel was the father of Gedor, and Ezer the father of Hushah.

These were the descendants of Hur, ˣ the firstborn of Ephrathah and father ᵇ of Bethlehem. ʸ

⁵ Ashhur ᶻ the father of Tekoa had two wives, Helah and Naarah.

⁶ Naarah bore him Ahuzzam, Hepher, Temeni and Haahashtari. These were the descendants of Naarah.

⁷ The sons of Helah:

Zereth, Zohar, Ethnan, ⁸and Koz, who was the father of Anub and Hazzobebah and of the clans of Aharhel son of Harum.

⁹ Jabez was more honorable than his brothers. His mother had named him Jabez, ᶜ saying, "I gave birth to him in pain." ¹⁰Jabez cried out to the God of Israel, "Oh, that you would

---

ᵃ 3 Some Septuagint manuscripts (see also Vulgate); Hebrew *father*   ᵇ 4 *Father* may mean *civic leader* or *military leader*; also in verses 12, 14, 17, 18 and possibly elsewhere.   ᶜ 9 *Jabez* sounds like the Hebrew for *pain*.

---

bel would then be regarded as the son of Shealtiel according to the law of levirate marriage (Dt 25:5–6). In Lk 3:27 Neri instead of Jehoiachin (v. 17) is identified as the father of Shealtiel. Suggestions similar to those above could be made in this instance as well. It is also interesting to note that the genealogies of Jesus in Mt 1 and Lk 3 both trace his descent to Zerubbabel but that none of the names subsequent to Zerubbabel (v. 19–24) is found in the NT genealogies.

3:20 *five others.* May have been sons of Zerubbabel, but no kinship terms are provided. Since the sons of Hananiah (v. 19) are specified in v. 21, they could also be the sons of Meshullam (v. 19).

3:21 *sons of Rephaiah … Shekaniah.* Probably other Davidic families at the time of Zerubbabel (v. 19) or Pelatiah and Jeshaiah. If they are understood as contemporary with Zerubbabel, his genealogy was carried only two generations (his sons and grandsons) and a date for Chronicles as early as 450 B.C. is possible (see Introduction: Author, Date and Sources).

3:22 *six.* Shemaiah appears to have five sons, but the total is given as six. Either one of the six names is missing, or Shemaiah is to be understood as the brother of the five persons named (in which case there should be a semicolon after "sons" instead of a colon)—all six then being sons of Shekaniah.

4:1–23 None of the genealogies of Judah in this section appears elsewhere in Scripture. Although the section may have

the appearance of miscellaneous notes, the careful shaping of the Chronicler is evident in light of the overall inverted structure of the genealogies of Judah:

2:3	Shelah
2:4–8	Perez
2:9—3:24	Hezron
4:1–20	Perez
4:21–23	Shelah

This balancing of the material in inverse order shows the centrality of the section of the lineage of Hezron and the house of David; the same balancing in inverse order is observed within the Hezron section (see note on 2:10—3:24). The record of Judah's oldest surviving son, Shelah, frames the entire genealogy of Judah. There are 15 fragmentary genealogies in this section, with two to six generations in each.

4:1–2 The descendants of Judah here are not brothers; rather, the genealogy is linear.

4:1 *Karmi.* Either a scribal confusion or an alternative name for Caleb (2:9); the confusion may have been induced by 2:7.

4:2 *Reaiah.* A variant of Haroeh (2:52).

4:5–8 Supplementary to 2:24.

4:9–10 The practice of inserting short historical notes into genealogical records is amply attested in non-Biblical genealogical texts from the ancient Near East, as well as in other Biblical genealogies (Ge 4:19–24; 10:8–12).

bless me and enlarge my territory! Let your hand be with me, and keep me from harm so that I will be free from pain." And God granted his request.

¹¹Kelub, Shuhah's brother, was the father of Mehir, who was the father of Eshton. ¹²Eshton was the father of Beth Rapha, Paseah and Tehinnah the father of Ir Nahash.^a These were the men of Rekah.

¹³The sons of Kenaz:
> Othniel^a and Seraiah.

The sons of Othniel:
> Hathath and Meonothai.^b ¹⁴Meonothai was the father of Ophrah.

Seraiah was the father of Joab,
> the father of Ge Harashim.^c It was called this because its people were skilled workers.

¹⁵The sons of Caleb son of Jephunneh:
> Iru, Elah and Naam.

The son of Elah:
> Kenaz.

¹⁶The sons of Jehallelel:
> Ziph, Ziphah, Tiria and Asarel.

¹⁷The sons of Ezrah:
> Jether, Mered, Epher and Jalon. One of Mered's wives gave birth to Miriam,^b Shammai and Ishbah the father of Eshtemoa. ¹⁸(His wife from the tribe of Judah gave birth to Jered the father of Gedor, Heber the father of Soko, and Jekuthiel the father of Zanoah.^c) These were the children of Pharaoh's daughter Bithiah, whom Mered had married.

¹⁹The sons of Hodiah's wife, the sister of Naham:
> the father of Keilah^d the Garmite, and Eshtemoa the Maakathite.^e

²⁰The sons of Shimon:
> Amnon, Rinnah, Ben-Hanan and Tilon.

The descendants of Ishi:
> Zoheth and Ben-Zoheth.

²¹The sons of Shelah^f son of Judah:
> Er the father of Lekah, Laadah the father of Mareshah and the clans of the linen workers at Beth Ashbea, ²²Jokim, the men of Kozeba, and Joash and Saraph, who ruled in Moab and Jashubi Lehem. (These records are from ancient times.) ²³They were the potters who lived at Netaim and Gederah; they stayed there and worked for the king.

SIMEON
4:28–33pp — Jos 19:2–10

²⁴The descendants of Simeon:^g
> Nemuel, Jamin, Jarib,^h Zerah and Shaul;
> ²⁵Shallum was Shaul's son, Mibsam his son and Mishma his son.

²⁶The descendants of Mishma:
> Hammuel his son, Zakkur his son and Shimei his son.

²⁷Shimei had sixteen sons and six daughters, but his brothers did not have many chil-

^a 12 Or *of the city of Nahash*   ^b 13 Some Septuagint manuscripts and Vulgate; Hebrew does not have *and Meonothai.*   ^c 14 *Ge Harashim* means *valley of skilled workers.*

4:13 ^a S Jos 15:17
4:17 ^b S Ex 15:20
4:18 ^c S Jos 15:34
4:19 ^d S Jos 15:44
^e S Dt 3:14
4:21 ^f S Ge 38:5
4:24 ^g S Ge 29:33
^h Nu 26:12

4:13 *Othniel.* The first of Israel's judges (Jos 15:17; Jdg 1:13; 3:9–11).

4:16–20 This portion of the genealogy is from preexilic times; several of the places named were not included in the province of Judah in the restoration period (e.g., Ziph and Eshtemoa).

4:17 *One of Mered's wives.* The pharaoh's daughter (v. 18). Mered is otherwise unknown; the fact that he married a daughter of a pharaoh suggests his prominence. The event may be associated with the fortunes of Israel in Egypt under Joseph.

4:21,23 This section accurately reflects a feature of ancient Near Eastern society. Clans were often associated not only with particular localities but also with special trades or guilds, such as linen workers (v. 21), potters (v. 23), royal patronage (v. 23) and scribes (2:55).

4:24–43 The genealogy of Simeon is also found in Ge 46:10; Ex 6:15; Nu 26:12–13. Simeon settled in part of the territory of Judah; the list of occupied towns should be compared with Jos 15:26–32,42; 19:2–7. Since Simeon occupied areas allotted to Judah, this tribe was politically incorporated into Judah and appears to have lost much of its own identity in history (see Ge 34:24–31; 49:5–7; see also notes on Ge 34:25; 49:7). Geographical and historical notes are inserted in the genealogy (see note on vv. 9–10). Apparently two genealogies are included here: vv. 24–33—ending with the formula, "they kept a genealogical record"—and vv. 34–43. Overpopulation (v. 38) caused them to expand toward Gedor and east toward Edom at the time of Hezekiah (vv. 39–43). The long hostility between Israel and Amalek surfaced once again (v. 43; cf. Ex 17:8–16; Dt 25:17–19; 1Sa 15; see Introduction to Esther: Purpose, Themes and Literary Features).

4:28 ⁱ S Ge 21:14
ʲ S Jos 15:26
4:29 ᵏ S Jos 15:29
4:30 ˡ S Nu 14:45
ᵐ S Jos 15:31
4:31 ⁿ S Jos 15:36
4:32 ᵒ S Nu 34:11
ᵖ S Jos 15:42
4:39 ᵠ S Jos 15:58
4:40 ʳ Jdg 18:7-10
4:41 ˢ 2Ch 20:1;
26:7
4:42 ᵗ S Ge 14:6
4:43 ᵘ S Ge 14:7;
Est 3:1; 9:16
5:1 ᵛ S Ge 29:32
ʷ Ge 35:22; 49:4
ˣ S Ge 48:16,22;
S 49:26 ʸ Ge 48:5
ᶻ 1Ch 26:10
5:2 ᵃ S Ge 49:10,12
ᵇ S 1Sa 9:16; S 12:12;
S 2Sa 6:21; 1Ch 11:2;
S 2Ch 7:18; Mt 2:6
ᶜ S Ge 25:31
5:3 ᵈ S Ge 29:32;
46:9; Ex 6:14;
Nu 26:5-11
ᵉ S Nu 26:5
ᶠ S Nu 26:6
5:6 ᵍ ver 26;
S 2Ki 15:19; 16:10;
2Ch 28:20
5:7 ʰ Jos 13:15-23
5:8 ⁱ S Nu 32:34;
Jdg 11:26 ʲ S Nu 32:3
ᵏ S Jos 13:17
5:9 ˡ S Ge 2:14
ᵐ S Nu 32:26
5:10 ⁿ ver 22;
1Ch 27:31

dren; so their entire clan did not become as numerous as the people of Judah. ²⁸They lived in Beersheba, ⁱ Moladah,ʲ Hazar Shual, ²⁹Bilhah, Ezem, ᵏ Tolad, ³⁰Bethuel, Hormah, ˡ Ziklag, ᵐ ³¹Beth Markaboth, Hazar Susim, Beth Biri and Shaaraim. ⁿ These were their towns until the reign of David. ³²Their surrounding villages were Etam, Ain, ᵒ Rimmon, Token and Ashanᵖ—five towns— ³³and all the villages around these towns as far as Baalath.ᵃ These were their settlements. And they kept a genealogical record.

³⁴Meshobab, Jamlech, Joshah son of Amaziah, ³⁵Joel, Jehu son of Joshibiah, the son of Seraiah, the son of Asiel, ³⁶also Elioenai, Jaakobah, Jeshohaiah, Asaiah, Adiel, Jesimiel, Benaiah, ³⁷and Ziza son of Shiphi, the son of Allon, the son of Jedaiah, the son of Shimri, the son of Shemaiah.

³⁸The men listed above by name were leaders of their clans. Their families increased greatly, ³⁹and they went to the outskirts of Gedorᵠ to the east of the valley in search of pasture for their flocks. ⁴⁰They found rich, good pasture, and the land was spacious, peaceful and quiet.ʳ Some Hamites had lived there formerly.

⁴¹The men whose names were listed came in the days of Hezekiah king of Judah. They attacked the Hamites in their dwellings and also the Meunitesˢ who were there and completely destroyedᵇ them, as is evident to this day. Then they settled in their place, because there was pasture for their flocks. ⁴²And five hundred of these Simeonites, led by Pelatiah, Neariah, Rephaiah and Uzziel, the sons of Ishi, invaded the hill country of Seir.ᵗ ⁴³They killed the remaining Amalekitesᵘ who had escaped, and they have lived there to this day.

REUBEN

5 The sons of Reubenᵛ the firstborn of Israel (he was the firstborn, but when he defiled his father's marriage bed, ʷ his rights as firstborn were given to the sons of Josephˣ son of Israel;ʸ so he could not be listed in the genealogical record in accordance with his birthright,ᶻ ²and though Judahᵃ was the strongest of his brothers and a rulerᵇ came from him, the rights of the firstbornᶜ belonged to Joseph)— ³the sons of Reubenᵈ the firstborn of Israel:

Hanok, Pallu, ᵉ Hezronᶠ and Karmi.
⁴The descendants of Joel:
Shemaiah his son, Gog his son,
Shimei his son, ⁵Micah his son,
Reaiah his son, Baal his son,
⁶and Beerah his son, whom Tiglath-Pileserᶜ ᵍ king of Assyria took into exile. Beerah was a leader of the Reubenites.
⁷Their relatives by clans, ʰ listed according to their genealogical records:
Jeiel the chief, Zechariah, ⁸and Bela son of Azaz, the son of Shema, the son of Joel. They settled in the area from Aroerⁱ to Neboʲ and Baal Meon. ᵏ ⁹To the east they occupied the land up to the edge of the desert that extends to the Euphratesˡ River, because their livestock had increased in Gilead. ᵐ
¹⁰During Saul's reign they waged war against the Hagritesⁿ, who were defeated at their hands; they occupied the dwellings of the Hagrites throughout the entire region east of Gilead.

ᵃ 33 Some Septuagint manuscripts (see also Joshua 19:8); Hebrew *Baal*   ᵇ 41 The Hebrew term refers to the irrevocable giving over of things or persons to the Lord, often by totally destroying them.
ᶜ 6 Hebrew *Tilgath-Pilneser*, a variant of *Tiglath-Pileser*; also in verse 26

5:1–26 The genealogical records of the tribes east of the Jordan: Reuben, Gad and half of Manasseh (see Nu 32:33–42). The Chronicler's concern with "all Israel" includes incorporating the genealogical records of these tribes that were no longer significant entities in Israel's life in the restoration period, having been swept away in the Assyrian conquests.
5:1–10 The necessity of explaining why the birthright of the firstborn did not remain with Reuben (see Ge 35:22; 49:4 for Reuben's sin) interrupts the initial statement (v. 1), which is then repeated after the explanation (v. 3). The parenthetical material (vv. 1–2) shows the writer's partiality for Judah, even though Joseph received the double portion (Ephraim and Manasseh) of the firstborn. The Hebrew term translated "ruler" (v. 2) is used of

David in 11:2; 17:7; 2Sa 5:2; 6:21; 7:8. The use of military titles (vv. 6–7) and a battle account (v. 10) suggest that this genealogy may have functioned in military organization (see Introduction: Genealogies). The source for some of this material on Reuben is Nu 26:5–11. The Chronicler has omitted reference to Eliab and his three sons, who perished in the rebellion of Korah (see Nu 26:8–10) and so were not relevant to his purpose.
5:6 *Tiglath-Pileser.* This Assyrian king (745–727 B.C.; see chart, p. 482) attacked Israel (v. 26; 2Ki 15:29) and also imposed tribute on Ahaz of Judah (2Ch 28:19–20; 2Ki 16:7–10).
5:10 *Hagrites.* See vv. 19–22. Named among the enemies of Israel (Ps 83:6), this tribe is apparently associated with Hagar, the mother of Ishmael (Ge 16), but see note on Ps 83:6.

GAD

[11] The Gadites[o] lived next to them in Bashan, as far as Salekah:[p]

[12] Joel was the chief, Shapham the second, then Janai and Shaphat, in Bashan.

[13] Their relatives, by families, were:

Michael, Meshullam, Sheba, Jorai, Jakan, Zia and Eber—seven in all.

[14] These were the sons of Abihail son of Huri, the son of Jaroah, the son of Gilead, the son of Michael, the son of Jeshishai, the son of Jahdo, the son of Buz.

[15] Ahi son of Abdiel, the son of Guni, was head of their family.

[16] The Gadites lived in Gilead, in Bashan and its outlying villages, and on all the pasturelands of Sharon as far as they extended.

[17] All these were entered in the genealogical records during the reigns of Jotham[q] king of Judah and Jeroboam[r] king of Israel.

[18] The Reubenites, the Gadites and the half-tribe of Manasseh had 44,760 men ready for military service[s]—able-bodied men who could handle shield and sword, who could use a bow, and who were trained for battle. [19] They waged war against the Hagrites, Jetur,[t] Naphish and Nodab. [20] They were helped[u] in fighting them, and God delivered the Hagrites and all their allies into their hands, because they cried[v] out to him during the battle. He answered their prayers, because they trusted[w] in him. [21] They seized the livestock of the Hagrites—fifty thousand camels, two hundred fifty thousand sheep and two thousand donkeys. They also took one hundred thousand people captive, [22] and many others fell slain, because the battle[x] was God's. And they occupied the land until the exile.[y]

THE HALF-TRIBE OF MANASSEH

[23] The people of the half-tribe of Manasseh[z] were numerous; they settled in the land from Bashan to Baal Hermon, that is, to Senir (Mount Hermon).[a]

[24] These were the heads of their families: Epher, Ishi, Eliel, Azriel, Jeremiah, Hodaviah and Jahdiel. They were brave warriors, famous men, and heads of their families. [25] But they were unfaithful[b] to the God of their ancestors and prostituted[c] themselves to the gods of the peoples of the land, whom God had destroyed before them. [26] So the God of Israel stirred up the spirit[d] of Pul[e] king of Assyria (that is, Tiglath-Pileser[f] king of Assyria), who took the Reubenites, the Gadites and the half-tribe of Manasseh into exile. He took them to Halah,[g] Habor, Hara and the river of Gozan, where they are to this day.

LEVI

6

[1] *The sons of Levi:[h]
Gershon, Kohath and Merari.

[2] The sons of Kohath:
Amram, Izhar, Hebron and Uzziel.[i]

[3] The children of Amram:
Aaron, Moses and Miriam.[j]

The sons of Aaron:

* 6:1-15 is numbered 5:27-41 in Hebrew texts.

5:11 °S Ge 30:11;
S Nu 1:25;
S Jos 13:24-28
ᵖS Dt 3:10
5:17 ᵠS 2Ki 15:32
ʳS 2Ki 14:23
5:18 ˢS Nu 1:3
5:19 ᵗGe 25:15
5:20 ᵘPs 37:40;
46:5; 54:4 ᵛ1Ki 8:44;
2Ch 6:34; 13:14; 14:11;
Ps 20:7-9; 22:5; 107:6
ʷPs 26:1; Isa 26:3;
Da 6:23
5:22 ˣS Dt 20:4;
2Ch 32:8 ʸS ver 10;
S 2Ki 15:29
5:23 ᶻ1Ch 7:14
ᵃS Dt 3:8,9; SS 4:8
5:25 ᵇDt 32:15-18;
1Ch 9:1; 10:13;
2Ch 12:2; 26:16;
28:19; 29:6; 30:7;
36:14 ᶜS Ex 34:15;
S Lev 18:3
5:26 ᵈIsa 37:7
ᵉS 2Ki 15:19 ᶠS ver 6;
S 2Ki 15:29 ᵍ2Ki 17:6
6:1 ʰS Ge 29:34;
S Nu 3:17
6:2 ⁱS Ex 6:18
6:3 ʲS Ex 15:20

5:11–22 The materials in this list for the tribe of Gad have no parallels in the Bible. The other genealogies of Gad are organized around his seven sons (Ge 46:16; Nu 26:15–18); here four names are given, none found in the other lists. The Chronicler states (v. 17) that these records came from the period of Jotham of Judah (750–732 B.C.) and Jeroboam of Israel (793–753). The presence of military titles and narratives (vv. 12,18–22) suggests that this genealogy originated as part of a military census. The territory of Gad is delineated in Dt 3:12.

A 5:18–22 The first example of the Chronicler's theme of immediate retribution (see Introduction: Purpose and Themes). Success in warfare is attributed to their crying out to God (v. 20; cf. 2Ch 6:24–25,34–39; 12:7–12; 13:13–16; 14:9–15; 18:31; 20:1–30; 32:1–23).

A 5:23–26 Manasseh is treated further in 7:14–19; the half-tribe that settled east of the Jordan River is dealt with here since it shared the same fate as Reuben and Gad, and possibly also so that the Chronicler could keep the total of 12 for his tribal genealogies (see note on 2:1–2). Again immediate retribution is apparent: Just as trust in God can bring victory (vv.

18–22), so also defeat comes to the unfaithful (vv. 25–26). The use of the retributive theme in these two accounts argues for the unity of the genealogies with the historical portions of Chronicles. The list of names given here is not properly a genealogy but a list of clans. Since they are described as brave warriors in connection with a battle report (vv. 24–26), this section too is likely derived from records of military conscription (see note on vv. 1–10; see also 2Ki 15:19,29; 17:6; 18:11).

5:25 *were unfaithful…prostituted themselves.* See Ex 34:15 and note.

5:26 *Pul.* Tiglath-Pileser's throne name in Babylon.

6:1–81 This chapter is devoted to a series of lists, all pertaining to the tribe of Levi. The first section (vv. 1–15) records the line of the high priests down to the exile; the clans of Levi follow (vv. 16–30). David's appointees as temple musicians came from the three clans of Levi: Gershon, Kohath and Merari (vv. 31–47). The generations between Aaron and Ahimaaz are given a separate listing (vv. 49–53), reinforcing the separate duties of priests and Levites (see note on Ex 32:26). The listing of the Levitical possessions among the tribes concludes the chapter (vv. 54–81).

6:3 ᵏS Lev 10:1;
S 10:1–20:2 ˡLev 10:6
ᵐS Ex 6:23
6:4 ⁿEzr 7:5
6:8 ᵒS 2Sa 8:17;
S 1Ch 12:28; S Ezr 7:2
6:10 ᵖS 1Ki 4:2
6:13 ᵍ2Ki 22:1–20;
2Ch 34:9; 35:8
6:14 ʳS 2Ki 25:18;
S Ezr 2:2
6:15 ˢNe 12:1;
Hag 1:1,14; 2:2,4;
Zec 6:11
6:16 ᵗS Ge 29:34;
S Nu 3:17-20
ᵘS Nu 26:57
6:17 ᵛS Ex 6:17
6:18 ʷS Ex 6:18
6:19 ˣS Ge 46:11;
1Ch 23:21; 24:26
ʸS Ex 6:19
6:22 ᶻS Ex 6:24

Nadab, Abihu, ᵏ Eleazar ˡ and Ithamar. ᵐ
⁴ Eleazar was the father of Phinehas, ⁿ
Phinehas the father of Abishua,
⁵ Abishua the father of Bukki,
Bukki the father of Uzzi,
⁶ Uzzi the father of Zerahiah,
Zerahiah the father of Meraioth,
⁷ Meraioth the father of Amariah,
Amariah the father of Ahitub,
⁸ Ahitub the father of Zadok, ᵒ
Zadok the father of Ahimaaz,
⁹ Ahimaaz the father of Azariah,
Azariah the father of Johanan,
¹⁰ Johanan the father of Azariah ᵖ (it was he who served as priest in the temple Solomon built in Jerusalem),
¹¹ Azariah the father of Amariah,
Amariah the father of Ahitub,
¹² Ahitub the father of Zadok,
Zadok the father of Shallum,
¹³ Shallum the father of Hilkiah, ᵍ
Hilkiah the father of Azariah,
¹⁴ Azariah the father of Seraiah, ʳ
and Seraiah the father of Jozadak. ᵃ

¹⁵ Jozadak ˢ was deported when the LORD sent Judah and Jerusalem into exile by the hand of Nebuchadnezzar.

*¹⁶ The sons of Levi: ᵗ
Gershon, ᵇ Kohath and Merari. ᵘ
¹⁷ These are the names of the sons of Gershon:
Libni and Shimei. ᵛ
¹⁸ The sons of Kohath:
Amram, Izhar, Hebron and Uzziel. ʷ
¹⁹ The sons of Merari: ˣ
Mahli and Mushi. ʸ
These are the clans of the Levites listed according to their fathers:
²⁰ Of Gershon:
Libni his son, Jahath his son,
Zimmah his son, ²¹ Joah his son,
Iddo his son, Zerah his son
and Jeatherai his son.
²² The descendants of Kohath:
Amminadab his son, Korah ᶻ his son,

ᵃ 14 Hebrew *Jehozadak*, a variant of *Jozadak*; also in verse 15   ᵇ 16 Hebrew *Gershom*, a variant of *Gershon*; also in verses 17, 20, 43, 62 and 71

* 6:16-81 is numbered 6:1-66 in Hebrew texts.

6:1–3 A short segmented genealogy narrows the descendants of Levi to the lineage of Eleazar, in whose line the high priests are presented in linear form (vv. 4–15). The sons of Levi (v. 1) always appear in this order, based on age (v. 16; Ge 46:11; Ex 6:16; Nu 3:17; 26:57). Of Aaron's four sons (v. 3), the first two died as a result of sacrilege (Lev 10:1–2; Nu 26:61); succeeding generations of priests would trace their lineage to either Eleazar or Ithamar.

6:4–15 This list of high priests from the time of Eleazar to the exile has been sharply telescoped. The following high priests known from the OT are not mentioned: Jehoiada (2Ki 12:2), Uriah (2Ki 16:10–16), possibly two other Azariahs (2Ch 26:17, 20; 31:10–13), Eli (1Sa 1:9; 14:3) and Abiathar (see 2Sa 8:17 and note). The list is repeated with some variation in Ezr 7:1–5 (see notes there).

6:8 *Ahitub the father of Zadok.* This Zadok was one of David's two priests (18:16; 2Sa 8:17). When David's other priest, Abiathar (see note on vv. 4–15), supported the rebellion of Adonijah, Za-

dok supported Solomon (1Ki 1). After the expulsion of Abiathar (1Ki 2:26–27), Zadok alone held the office (1Ch 29:22), which continued in his line (1Ki 4:2). The Ahitub mentioned here should not be confused with the priest who was the grandson of Eli (1Sa 14:3) and grandfather of Abiathar (1Sa 22:20); the line of Zadok replaced the line of Eli (1Sa 2:27–36; 1Ki 2:26–27). For the importance of the line of Zadok, see Eze 40:46; 43:19; 44:15; 48:11. Ezra was concerned to trace his own priestly lineage to this house (Ezr 7:1–5).

6:13 *Hilkiah.* Discovered the Book of the Law in the temple at the time of Josiah (2Ki 22; 2Ch 34).

6:14 *Seraiah.* Executed by the Babylonians after the conquest of Jerusalem in 586 B.C. (2Ki 25:18–21). *Jozadak.* See TNIV text note; father of Joshua (see note on Ezr 2:2), the high priest in the first generation of the restoration period (see Hag 1:1; 2:2; Zec 3:1 and note; 6:11; see also Ezr 3:2; 5:2; 10:18).

6:16–19a Repeated from Ex 6:16–19; Nu 3:17–20; 26:57–61.

Assir his son, ²³Elkanah his son,
Ebiasaph his son, Assir his son,
²⁴Tahath his son, Uriel ᵃ his son,
Uzziah his son and Shaul his son.
²⁵The descendants of Elkanah:
Amasai, Ahimoth,
²⁶Elkanah his son, ᵃ Zophai his son,
Nahath his son, ²⁷Eliab his son,
Jeroham his son, Elkanah ᵇ his son
and Samuel ᶜ his son. ᵇ
²⁸The sons of Samuel:
Joel ᶜ ᵈ the firstborn
and Abijah the second son.
²⁹The descendants of Merari:
Mahli, Libni his son,
Shimei his son, Uzzah his son,
³⁰Shimea his son, Haggiah his son
and Asaiah his son.

THE TEMPLE MUSICIANS

6:54–80pp — Jos 21:4–39

³¹These are the men ᵉ David put in charge of the music ᶠ in the house of the LORD after the ark came to rest there. ³²They ministered with music before the tabernacle, the tent of meeting, until Solomon built the temple of the LORD in Jerusalem. They performed their duties according to the regulations laid down for them.

³³Here are the men who served, together with their sons:
From the Kohathites:
Heman, ᵍ the musician,
the son of Joel, ʰ the son of Samuel,
³⁴the son of Elkanah, ⁱ the son of Jeroham,
the son of Eliel, the son of Toah,
³⁵the son of Zuph, the son of Elkanah,
the son of Mahath, the son of Amasai,
³⁶the son of Elkanah, the son of Joel,
the son of Azariah, the son of Zephaniah,
³⁷the son of Tahath, the son of Assir,
the son of Ebiasaph, the son of Korah, ʲ
³⁸the son of Izhar, ᵏ the son of Kohath,
the son of Levi, the son of Israel;
³⁹and Heman's associate Asaph, ˡ who served at his right hand:

ᵃ 26 Some Hebrew manuscripts, Septuagint and Syriac; most Hebrew manuscripts *Ahimoth* ²⁶*and Elkanah. The sons of Elkanah:* ᵇ 27 Some Septuagint manuscripts (see also 1 Samuel 1:19,20 and 1 Chron. 6:33,34); Hebrew does not have *and Samuel his son.* ᶜ 28 Some Septuagint manuscripts and Syriac (see also 1 Samuel 8:2 and 1 Chron. 6:33); Hebrew does not have *Joel.*

6:22–23 *Assir...Elkanah...Ebiasaph.* Ex 6:24 names these men as sons of Korah, but here they are presented in the form ordinarily used for a linear genealogy of successive generations (see vv. 20–21, 25–26, 29–30). Either this is another example of genealogical fluidity or one must understand "his son" as referring to Kohath and not to the immediately preceding name.
6:22 *Amminadab.* The almost parallel genealogy later in this chapter lists Izhar in the place of Amminadab—who is nowhere else listed as a son of Kohath, while every other list includes Izhar (vv. 2,37–38; Ex 6:18,21). Either Amminadab is an otherwise unattested alternative name of Izhar, or he is an otherwise unknown son. Or this may be another example of genealogical fluidity in which the Levites are linked with the tribe of Judah and the lineage of David (see Ru 4:18–22; see also Mt 1:4; Lk 3:33) in view of Aaron's marriage to the daughter of Amminadab of Judah (Ex 6:23; see 1Ch 2:10).
6:24 *Uriel.* Possibly the one who led the Kohathites in David's day (15:5).
6:26–27 *Zophai...Nahath...Eliab.* Apparently variant names for Zuph, Toah and Eliel (vv. 34–35).

6:27 *Samuel.* His lineage is also given in 1Sa 1:1, where his family is identified as Ephraimite (see note there). Either this is an example of genealogical fluidity, in which Samuel's involvement in the tabernacle (1Sa 3) and performance of priestly duties (9:22; 1Sa 2:18; 3:1) resulted in his incorporation into the Levites, or the term "Ephraimite" is to be understood as a place of residence, not as a statement of lineage.

B C **6:31–48** Each of the three Levitical clans contributed musicians for the temple: Heman from the family of Kohath, Asaph from Gershon, and Ethan from Merari. The Chronicler makes frequent reference to the appointment of the musical guilds by David (15:16,27; 25:1–31; 2Ch 29:25–26; see Ne 12:45–47). The frequent mention of the role of the Levites has led many to assume that the author was a member of the musicians. Non-Biblical literature also attests to guilds of singers and musicians in Canaanite temples. This genealogy appears to function as a means of legitimizing the Levites of the restoration period (Ezr 2:40–41; Ne 7:43–44; 10:9–13, 28–29; 11:15–18; 12:24–47).

6:24 ᵃ1Ch 15:5
6:27 ᵇS 1Sa 1:1
ᶜS 1Sa 1:20
6:28 ᵈver 33; 1Sa 8:2
6:31 ᵉ1Ch 25:1; 2Ch 29:25-26; Ne 12:45 ᶠ1Ch 9:33; 15:19; Ezr 3:10; Ps 68:25
6:33 ᵍ1Ki 4:31; 1Ch 15:17; 25:1 ʰS ver 28
6:34 ⁱS 1Sa 1:1
6:37 ʲS Ex 6:24
6:38 ᵏEx 6:21
6:39 ˡ1Ch 25:1,9; 2Ch 29:13; Ne 11:17

6:39 *m* 1Ch 15:17
6:44 *n* 1Ch 15:17
6:48 *o* 1Ch 23:32
6:49 *p* Ex 27:1-8
q S Ex 30:1-7,10;
2Ch 26:18
6:53 *r* S 2Sa 8:17
6:54 *s* S Nu 31:10
6:56 *t* S Jos 14:13;
S 15:13
6:57 *u* S Nu 33:20
v S Jos 15:48
6:58 *w* S Jos 10:3
6:59 *x* S Jos 15:42
6:60 *y* Jer 1:1
6:64 *z* Nu 35:1-8
6:67 *a* S Jos 10:33
6:68 *b* 1Ki 4:12
c S Jos 10:10
6:69 *d* S Jos 10:12
e S Jos 19:45

Asaph son of Berekiah, the son of Shimea, *m*
40 the son of Michael, the son of Baaseiah, *a*
the son of Malkijah, 41 the son of Ethni,
the son of Zerah, the son of Adaiah,
42 the son of Ethan, the son of Zimmah,
the son of Shimei, 43 the son of Jahath,
the son of Gershon, the son of Levi;
44 and from their associates, the Merarites, *n* at his left hand:
Ethan son of Kishi, the son of Abdi,
the son of Malluk, 45 the son of Hashabiah,
the son of Amaziah, the son of Hilkiah,
46 the son of Amzi, the son of Bani,
the son of Shemer, 47 the son of Mahli,
the son of Mushi, the son of Merari,
the son of Levi.

48 Their fellow Levites *o* were assigned to all the other duties of the tabernacle, the house of God. 49 But Aaron and his descendants were the ones who presented offerings on the altar *p* of burnt offering and on the altar of incense *q* in connection with all that was done in the Most Holy Place, making atonement for Israel, in accordance with all that Moses the servant of God had commanded.

50 These were the descendants of Aaron:
Eleazar his son, Phinehas his son,
Abishua his son, 51 Bukki his son,
Uzzi his son, Zerahiah his son,
52 Meraioth his son, Amariah his son,
Ahitub his son, 53 Zadok *r* his son
and Ahimaaz his son.

54 These were the locations of their settlements *s* allotted as their territory (they were assigned to the descendants of Aaron who were from the Kohathite clan, because the first lot was for them):
55 They were given Hebron in Judah with its surrounding pasturelands. 56 But the fields and villages around the city were given to Caleb son of Jephunneh. *t*
57 So the descendants of Aaron were given Hebron (a city of refuge), and Libnah, *b u* Jattir, *v* Eshtemoa, 58 Hilen, Debir, *w* 59 Ashan, *x* Juttah *c* and Beth Shemesh, together with their pasturelands. 60 And from the tribe of Benjamin they were given Gibeon, *d* Geba, Alemeth and Anathoth, *y* together with their pasturelands.
The total number of towns distributed among the Kohathite clans came to thirteen.
61 The rest of Kohath's descendants were allotted ten towns from the clans of half the tribe of Manasseh.
62 The descendants of Gershon, clan by clan, were allotted thirteen towns from the tribes of Issachar, Asher and Naphtali, and from the part of the tribe of Manasseh that is in Bashan.
63 The descendants of Merari, clan by clan, were allotted twelve towns from the tribes of Reuben, Gad and Zebulun.
64 So the Israelites gave the Levites these towns *z* and their pasturelands. 65 From the tribes of Judah, Simeon and Benjamin they allotted the previously named towns.
66 Some of the Kohathite clans were given as their territory towns from the tribe of Ephraim.
67 In the hill country of Ephraim they were given Shechem (a city of refuge), and Gezer, *e a* 68 Jokmeam, *b* Beth Horon, *c* 69 Aijalon *d* and Gath Rimmon, *e* together with their pasturelands.

a 40 Most Hebrew manuscripts; some Hebrew manuscripts, one Septuagint manuscript and Syriac *Maaseiah*   *b 57* See Joshua 21:13; Hebrew *given the cities of refuge: Hebron, Libnah.*   *c 59* Syriac (see also Septuagint and Joshua 21:16); Hebrew does not have *Juttah.*   *d 60* See Joshua 21:17; Hebrew does not have *Gibeon.*   *e 67* See Joshua 21:21: Hebrew *given the cities of refuge: Shechem, Gezer.*

6:49–53 Repeats vv. 4–8 but presumably serves a different function: to legitimize the line of Zadok, which is traced down to Solomon's time, as the only Levitical division authorized to offer sacrifices.

6:54–81 This list of Levitical possessions is taken from Jos 21 with only minor differences (see notes there). The Levites, who were given no block of territory of their own, were distributed throughout Israel.

6:71 *f* 1Ch 23:7
g S Jos 20:8
6:72 *h* S Jos 19:12
6:74 *i* S Jos 19:28
6:75 *j* Jos 19:34
k S Nu 13:21
6:76 *l* Jos 19:28
m S Nu 32:37
6:78 *n* S Jos 20:8
6:79 *o* S Dt 2:26
6:80 *p* Jos 20:8
q S Ge 32:2
6:81 *r* S Nu 21:32
s 2Ch 11:14
7:1 *t* S Ge 30:18
u S Ge 46:13
7:6 *v* S Nu 26:38

[70]And from half the tribe of Manasseh the Israelites gave Aner and Bileam, together with their pasturelands, to the rest of the Kohathite clans.

[71]The Gershonites *f* received the following:
From the clan of the half-tribe of Manasseh
they received Golan in Bashan *g* and also Ashtaroth, together with their pasturelands;
[72]from the tribe of Issachar
they received Kedesh, Daberath, *h* [73]Ramoth and Anem, together with their pasturelands;
[74]from the tribe of Asher
they received Mashal, Abdon, *i* [75]Hukok *j* and Rehob, *k* together with their pasturelands;
[76]and from the tribe of Naphtali
they received Kedesh in Galilee, Hammon *l* and Kiriathaim, *m* together with their pasturelands.

[77]The Merarites (the rest of the Levites) received the following:
From the tribe of Zebulun
they received Jokneam, Kartah, *a* Rimmono and Tabor, together with their pasturelands;
[78]from the tribe of Reuben across the Jordan east of Jericho
they received Bezer *n* in the wilderness, Jahzah, [79]Kedemoth *o* and Mephaath, together with their pasturelands;
[80]and from the tribe of Gad
they received Ramoth in Gilead, *p* Mahanaim, *q* [81]Heshbon and Jazer, *r* together with their pasturelands. *s*

ISSACHAR

The sons of Issachar: *t*
Tola, Puah, *u* Jashub and Shimron—four in all.
[2]The sons of Tola:
Uzzi, Rephaiah, Jeriel, Jahmai, Ibsam and Samuel—heads of their families. During the reign of David, the descendants of Tola listed as fighting men in their genealogy numbered 22,600.
[3]The son of Uzzi:
Izrahiah.
The sons of Izrahiah:
Michael, Obadiah, Joel and Ishiah. All five of them were chiefs. [4]According to their family genealogy, they had 36,000 men ready for battle, for they had many wives and children.
[5]The relatives who were fighting men belonging to all the clans of Issachar, as listed in their genealogy, were 87,000 in all.

BENJAMIN

[6]Three sons of Benjamin: *v*
Bela, Beker and Jediael.
[7]The sons of Bela:
Ezbon, Uzzi, Uzziel, Jerimoth and Iri, heads of families—five in all. Their genealogical record listed 22,034 fighting men.
[8]The sons of Beker:
Zemirah, Joash, Eliezer, Elioenai, Omri, Jeremoth, Abijah, Anathoth and Alemeth. All these were the sons of Beker. [9]Their genealogical record listed the heads of families and 20,200 fighting men.
[10]The son of Jediael:
Bilhan.

a 77 See Septuagint and Joshua 21:34; Hebrew does not have *Jokneam, Kartah.*

7:1–5 Parts of the genealogy of Issachar are taken from Ge 46:13; Nu 1:28; 26:23–25, though many of the names are otherwise unattested. This list of the clans appears to come from a military muster (vv. 2,4–5) from the time of David (v. 2), perhaps reflecting the census of ch. 21 and 2Sa 24.
7:6–12 There is considerable fluidity among the Biblical sources listing the sons of Benjamin. This list gives three sons; Ge 46:21 records ten; Nu 26:38–39 and 1Ch 8:1–2 both list five (the only name appearing in all these sources is Bela, the first-born). The variations reflect different origins and functions for these genealogies. The list here appears to function in the military sphere (vv. 7,9,11).

7:13 ʷ S Ge 30:8
7:14 ˣ S Ge 41:51;
S Jos 17:1; 1Ch 5:23
ʸ S Nu 26:30
7:15 ᶻ S Nu 26:33;
36:1-12
7:17 ᵃ S Nu 26:30
7:18 ᵇ S Jos 17:2
7:19 ᶜ Jos 17:2
7:20 ᵈ S Ge 41:52;
S Nu 1:33
7:24 ᵉ S Jos 10:10
7:28 ᶠ Jos 10:33
7:29 ᵍ S Jos 17:11

The sons of Bilhan:

Jeush, Benjamin, Ehud, Kenaanah, Zethan, Tarshish and Ahishahar. ¹¹All these sons of Jediael were heads of families. There were 17,200 fighting men ready to go out to war.

¹²The Shuppites and Huppites were the descendants of Ir, and the Hushites ᵃ the descendants of Aher.

NAPHTALI

¹³The sons of Naphtali: ʷ

Jahziel, Guni, Jezer and Shillem ᵇ—the descendants of Bilhah.

MANASSEH

¹⁴The descendants of Manasseh: ˣ

Asriel was his descendant through his Aramean concubine. She gave birth to Makir the father of Gilead. ʸ ¹⁵Makir took a wife from among the Huppites and Shuppites. His sister's name was Maakah.

Another descendant was named Zelophehad, ᶻ who had only daughters.

¹⁶Makir's wife Maakah gave birth to a son and named him Peresh. His brother was named Sheresh, and his sons were Ulam and Rakem.

¹⁷The son of Ulam:

Bedan.

These were the sons of Gilead ᵃ son of Makir, the son of Manasseh. ¹⁸His sister Hammoleketh gave birth to Ishhod, Abiezer ᵇ and Mahlah.

¹⁹The sons of Shemida ᶜ were:

Ahian, Shechem, Likhi and Aniam.

EPHRAIM

²⁰The descendants of Ephraim: ᵈ

Shuthelah, Bered his son,
Tahath his son, Eleadah his son,
Tahath his son, ²¹Zabad his son
and Shuthelah his son.

Ezer and Elead were killed by the native-born men of Gath, when they went down to seize their livestock. ²²Their father Ephraim mourned for them many days, and his relatives came to comfort him. ²³Then he made love to his wife again, and she became pregnant and gave birth to a son. He named him Beriah, ᶜ because there had been misfortune in his family. ²⁴His daughter was Sheerah, who built Lower and Upper Beth Horon ᵉ as well as Uzzen Sheerah.

²⁵Rephah was his son, Resheph his son, ᵈ
Telah his son, Tahan his son,
²⁶Ladan his son, Ammihud his son,
Elishama his son, ²⁷Nun his son
and Joshua his son.

²⁸Their lands and settlements included Bethel and its surrounding villages, Naaran to the east, Gezer ᶠ and its villages to the west, and Shechem and its villages all the way to Ayyah and its villages. ²⁹Along the borders of Manasseh were Beth Shan, ᵍ Taanach, Me-

---

ᵃ 12 Or *Ir. The sons of Dan: Hushim,* (see Gen. 46:23); Hebrew does not have *The sons of Dan.*
ᵇ 13 Some Hebrew and Septuagint manuscripts (see also Gen. 46:24 and Num. 26:49); most Hebrew manuscripts *Shallum*   ᶜ 23 *Beriah* sounds like the Hebrew for *misfortune.*   ᵈ 25 Some Septuagint manuscripts; Hebrew does not have *his son.*

7:13 Repeats Ge 46:24; Nu 26:48–50. *descendants of Bilhah.* Dan and Naphtali were the actual "sons" of Jacob's concubine Bilhah (Ge 30:3–8), so Naphtali's sons are Bilhah's "descendants."

7:14–19 See note on 5:23–26. The sources for this genealogy are Nu 26:29–34; Jos 17:1–18. The daughters of Zelophehad (v. 15) prompted the rulings on the inheritance rights of women (Nu 26:29–34; 27:1–11; 36:1–12; Jos 17:3–4). Of the 13 different clans of the tribe of Manasseh known from these genealogies, seven are mentioned in the Samaria ostraca (about 65 inscribed potsherds containing records of deliveries of wine, oil, barley and other commodities in the eighth century B.C.). The prominence of women in this genealogy is unusual;

this suggests that it may have functioned in the domestic sphere, perhaps as a statement of the social status of the various clans of Manasseh (see Introduction: Genealogies).

7:20–29 The source for part of the genealogy of Ephraim is Nu 26:35. If Rephah (v. 25) is the grandson of Ephraim, ten generations are recorded from Ephraim to Joshua, a number that fits very well the 400-year interval when Israel was in Egypt. Joshua's Ephraimite ancestry is also mentioned in Nu 13:8 (where he is called "Hoshea"; see Nu 13:16). The raid against Gath (vv. 21–22) must have taken place well before the conquest of Canaan and must have originated in Egypt. The list of settlements (vv. 28–29) summarizes Jos 16–17.

giddo and Dor,[h] together with their villages. The descendants of Joseph son of Israel lived in these towns.

ASHER

[30] The sons of Asher:[i]
Imnah, Ishvah, Ishvi and Beriah. Their sister was Serah.
[31] The sons of Beriah:
Heber and Malkiel, who was the father of Birzaith.
[32] Heber was the father of Japhlet, Shomer and Hotham and of their sister Shua.
[33] The sons of Japhlet:
Pasak, Bimhal and Ashvath.
These were Japhlet's sons.
[34] The sons of Shomer:
Ahi, Rohgah,[a] Hubbah and Aram.
[35] The sons of his brother Helem:
Zophah, Imna, Shelesh and Amal.
[36] The sons of Zophah:
Suah, Harnepher, Shual, Beri, Imrah, [37]Bezer, Hod, Shamma, Shilshah, Ithran[b] and Beera.
[38] The sons of Jether:
Jephunneh, Pispah and Ara.
[39] The sons of Ulla:
Arah, Hanniel and Rizia.
[40]All these were descendants of Asher—heads of families, choice men, brave warriors and outstanding leaders. The number of men ready for battle, as listed in their genealogy, was 26,000.

THE GENEALOGY OF SAUL THE BENJAMITE

8:28–38pp — 1Ch 9:34–44

8 Benjamin[j] was the father of Bela his firstborn,
Ashbel the second son, Aharah the third,
[2]Nohah the fourth and Rapha the fifth.
[3] The sons of Bela were:
Addar,[k] Gera, Abihud,[c] [4]Abishua, Naaman, Ahoah,[l] [5]Gera, Shephuphan and Huram.
[6] These were the descendants of Ehud,[m] who were heads of families of those living in Geba and were deported to Manahath:
[7]Naaman, Ahijah, and Gera, who deported them and who was the father of Uzza and Ahihud.
[8]Sons were born to Shaharaim in Moab after he had divorced his wives Hushim and Baara. [9]By his wife Hodesh he had Jobab, Zibia, Mesha, Malkam, [10]Jeuz, Sakia and Mirmah. These were his sons, heads of families. [11]By Hushim he had Abitub and Elpaal.
[12] The sons of Elpaal:
Eber, Misham, Shemed (who built Ono[n] and Lod with its surrounding villages), [13]and Beriah and Shema, who were heads of families of those living in Aijalon[o] and who drove out the inhabitants of Gath.[p]
[14]Ahio, Shashak, Jeremoth, [15]Zebadiah, Arad, Eder, [16]Michael, Ishpah and Joha were the sons of Beriah.
[17]Zebadiah, Meshullam, Hizki, Heber, [18]Ishmerai, Izliah and Jobab were the sons of Elpaal.

7:29 [h] S Jos 11:2
7:30 [i] S Nu 1:40
8:1 [j] S Ge 46:21
8:3 [k] S Ge 46:21
8:4 [l] 2Sa 23:9
8:6 [m] Jdg 3:12-30
8:12 [n] Ezr 2:33;
Ne 6:2; 7:37; 11:35
8:13 [o] S Jos 10:12
[p] S Jos 11:22

---

[a] 34 Or *of his brother Shomer: Rohgah*   [b] 37 Possibly a variant of *Jether*   [c] 3 Or *Gera the father of Ehud*

7:30–40 The genealogy of Asher follows Ge 46:17 for the first three generations; it is also parallel to Nu 26:44–46, except that the name Ishvah (v. 30) is missing there. This genealogy too reflects a military function (v. 40).

8:1–40 The inclusion of a second and even more extensive genealogy of Benjamin (see note on 7:6–12) reflects both the importance of this tribe and the Chronicler's interest in Saul. Judah, Simeon and part of Benjamin had composed the southern kingdom (1Ki 12:1–21), and their territory largely comprised the restoration province of Judah in the Chronicler's own time.

The genealogy of Benjamin is more extensive than that of all the other tribes except Judah and Levi. The Chronicler is also concerned with the genealogy of Saul (vv. 29–38) in order to set the stage for the historical narrative that begins with the end of his reign (ch. 10); Saul's genealogy is repeated in 9:35–44. Several references suggest that this genealogy also originated in the military sphere (vv. 6,10,13,28,40).

8:1–5 Cf. the lists in 7:6–12; Ge 46:21–22; Nu 26:38–41.

8:6–27 Unique to Chronicles.

8:29 ᑫS Jos 9:3
8:33 ʳS 1Sa 28:19
ˢ S 1Sa 9:1 ᵗ1Sa 14:49
ᵘ S 2Sa 2:8
8:34 ᵛS 2Sa 9:12
ʷ S 2Sa 4:4; S 21:7-14
8:40 ˣS Nu 26:38
9:1 ʸ1Ch 11:1,10;
12:38; 14:8; 15:3,28;
18:14; 19:17; 21:5;
28:4,8; 29:21,23;
2Ch 1:2; 5:3; 7:8;
10:3,16; 12:1; 13:4,15;
18:16; 24:5; 28:23;
29:24; 30:1
ᶻ S Dt 21:10
ᵃ S 1Ch 5:25
9:2 ᵇJos 9:27;
Ezr 2:70 ᶜEzr 2:43,
58; 8:20; Ne 7:60
9:4 ᵈ S Ge 38:29;
46:12

¹⁹ Jakim, Zikri, Zabdi, ²⁰Elienai, Zillethai, Eliel, ²¹Adaiah, Beraiah and Shimrath were the sons of Shimei.

²² Ishpan, Eber, Eliel, ²³Abdon, Zikri, Hanan, ²⁴Hananiah, Elam, Anthothijah, ²⁵Iphdeiah and Penuel were the sons of Shashak.

²⁶ Shamsherai, Shehariah, Athaliah, ²⁷Jaareshiah, Elijah and Zikri were the sons of Jeroham.

²⁸All these were heads of families, chiefs as listed in their genealogy, and they lived in Jerusalem.

²⁹ Jeielᵃ the fatherᵇ of Gibeon lived in Gibeon. ᑫ

His wife's name was Maakah, ³⁰and his firstborn son was Abdon, followed by Zur, Kish, Baal, Ner,ᶜ Nadab, ³¹Gedor, Ahio, Zeker ³²and Mikloth, who was the father of Shimeah. They too lived near their relatives in Jerusalem.

³³ Nerʳ was the father of Kish, ˢ Kish the father of Saul ᵗ, and Saul the father of Jonathan, Malki-Shua, Abinadab and Esh-Baal.ᵈ ᵘ

³⁴ The son of Jonathan: ᵛ

Merib-Baal,ᵉ ʷ who was the father of Micah.

³⁵ The sons of Micah:

Pithon, Melek, Tarea and Ahaz.

³⁶ Ahaz was the father of Jehoaddah, Jehoaddah was the father of Alemeth, Azmaveth and Zimri, and Zimri was the father of Moza. ³⁷Moza was the father of Binea; Raphah was his son, Eleasah his son and Azel his son.

³⁸ Azel had six sons, and these were their names:

Azrikam, Bokeru, Ishmael, Sheariah, Obadiah and Hanan. All these were the sons of Azel.

³⁹ The sons of his brother Eshek:

Ulam his firstborn, Jeush the second son and Eliphelet the third. ⁴⁰The sons of Ulam were brave warriors who could handle the bow. They had many sons and grandsons—150 in all.

All these were the descendants of Benjamin. ˣ

9 All Israelʸ was listed in the genealogies recorded in the book of the kings of Israel and Judah. They were taken captive to Babylonᶻ because of their unfaithfulness. ᵃ

THE PEOPLE IN JERUSALEM

9:1–17pp — Ne 11:3–19

²Now the first to resettle on their own property in their own townsᵇ were some Israelites, priests, Levites and temple servants. ᶜ

³Those from Judah, from Benjamin, and from Ephraim and Manasseh who lived in Jerusalem were:

⁴ Uthai son of Ammihud, the son of Omri, the son of Imri, the son of Bani, a descendant of Perez son of Judah. ᵈ

⁵ Of the Shelanitesᶠ:

Asaiah the firstborn and his sons.

⁶ Of the Zerahites:

ᵃ 29 Some Septuagint manuscripts (see also 1 Chron. 9:35); Hebrew does not have *Jeiel*.   ᵇ 29 *Father* may mean *civic leader* or *military leader*.   ᶜ 30 Some Septuagint manuscripts (see also 1 Chron. 9:36); Hebrew does not have *Ner*.   ᵈ 33 Also known as *Ish-Bosheth*   ᵉ 34 Also known as *Mephibosheth*   ᶠ 5 See Num. 26:20; Hebrew *Shilonites*.

8:29–38 Essentially the same as the list in 9:35–44.

C **8:33** For the sons of Saul, see 1Sa 14:49; 31:2. *Jonathan*. The firstborn and the best known of the sons of Saul, both for his military prowess and for his friendship with David (1Sa 13–14; 18:1–4; 19:1–7; 20:1–42; 23:16–18; 2Sa 21:13–14). *Esh-Baal*. See TNIV text note; see also note on 2Sa 2:8.

8:34 *Merib-Baal.* See TNIV text note; see also note on 2Sa 4:4.

9:1 *All Israel.* The Chronicler's concern with "all Israel" is one key to why he included the genealogies (see Introduction: Purpose and Themes). *book of the kings of Israel.* See Introduction: Author, Date and Sources.

B **9:2–34** This list of the members of the restored community reflects the Chronicler's concern with the institutions of his own day, especially the legitimacy of officeholders. He lists laity ("Israelites," v. 2) in vv. 3–9, priests in vv. 10–13 and Levites in vv. 14–34. He mentions a fourth class of returnees—the temple servants (v. 2)—but does not give them separate listing in the material that follows. They may originally have been foreigners who were incorporated into the Levites (Jos 9:23; Ezr 8:20) and so are not listed apart from that tribe. A similar office is known in the temple at ancient Ugarit. The list here is related to the one in Ne 11, but less than half the names are the same in the two lists.

9:3 *Ephraim and Manasseh.* Again reflecting his concern with "all Israel," the Chronicler shows that the returnees were not only from Judah and Benjamin but also from the northern tribes.

9:4–6 See 2:3–6; 4:21. The returnees of Judah are traced to Judah's sons Perez, Zerah and Shelah (see Nu 26:20).

Jeuel.

The people from Judah numbered 690.

[7] Of the Benjamites:

Sallu son of Meshullam, the son of Hodaviah, the son of Hassenuah;

[8] Ibneiah son of Jeroham; Elah son of Uzzi, the son of Mikri; and Meshullam son of Shephatiah, the son of Reuel, the son of Ibnijah.

[9] The people from Benjamin, as listed in their genealogy, numbered 956. All these men were heads of their families.

[10] Of the priests:

Jedaiah; Jehoiarib; Jakin;

[11] Azariah son of Hilkiah, the son of Meshullam, the son of Zadok, the son of Meraioth, the son of Ahitub, the official in charge of the house of God;

[12] Adaiah son of Jeroham, the son of Pashhur,[e] the son of Malkijah; and Maasai son of Adiel, the son of Jahzerah, the son of Meshullam, the son of Meshillemith, the son of Immer.

[13] The priests, who were heads of families, numbered 1,760. They were able men, responsible for ministering in the house of God.

[14] Of the Levites:

Shemaiah son of Hasshub, the son of Azrikam, the son of Hashabiah, a Merarite; [15] Bakbakkar, Heresh, Galal and Mattaniah[f] son of Mika, the son of Zikri, the son of Asaph; [16] Obadiah son of Shemaiah, the son of Galal, the son of Jeduthun; and Berekiah son of Asa, the son of Elkanah, who lived in the villages of the Netophathites.[g]

[17] The gatekeepers:[h]

Shallum, Akkub, Talmon, Ahiman and their fellow Levites, Shallum their chief [18] being stationed at the King's Gate[i] on the east, up to the present time. These were the gatekeepers belonging to the camp of the Levites. [19] Shallum[j] son of Kore, the son of Ebiasaph, the son of Korah, and his fellow gatekeepers from his family (the Korahites) were responsible for guarding the thresholds of the tent just as their ancestors had been responsible for guarding the entrance to the dwelling of the Lord. [20] In earlier times Phinehas[k] son of Eleazar was the official in charge of the gatekeepers, and the Lord was with him. [21] Zechariah[l] son of Meshelemiah was the gatekeeper at the entrance to the tent of meeting.

[22] Altogether, those chosen to be gatekeepers[m] at the thresholds numbered 212. They were registered by genealogy in their villages. The gatekeepers had been assigned to their positions of trust by David and Samuel the seer.[n] [23] They and their descendants were in charge of guarding the gates of the house of the Lord—the house called the tent of meeting. [24] The gatekeepers were on the four sides: east, west, north and south. [25] Their fellow Levites in their villages had to come from time to time and share their duties for seven-day[o] periods. [26] But the four principal gatekeepers, who were Levites, were entrusted with the responsibility for the rooms and treasuries[p] in the house of God. [27] They would spend the night stationed around the house of God,[q] because they had to guard it; and they had charge of the key[r] for opening it each morning.

[28] Some of them were in charge of the articles used in the temple service; they counted them when they were brought in and when they were taken out. [29] Others were assigned to take care of the furnishings and all the other articles of the sanctuary,[s] as well as the special flour and wine, and the oil, incense and spices. [30] But some[t] of the priests took care of mixing the spices. [31] A Levite named Mattithiah, the firstborn son of Shallum the Korahite, was entrusted with the responsibility for baking the offering bread. [32] Some of the Kohathites, their fellow Levites, were in charge of preparing for every Sabbath the bread set out on the table.[u]

9:12 *e* Ezr 2:38; 10:22; Ne 10:3; Jer 21:1; 38:1
9:15 *f* 2Ch 20:14; Ne 11:22
9:16 *g* Ne 12:28
9:17 *h* ver 22; 1Ch 26:1; 2Ch 8:14; 31:14; Ezr 2:42; Ne 7:45
9:18 *i* 1Ch 26:14; Eze 43:1; 46:1
9:19 *j* Jer 35:4
9:20 *k* Nu 25:7-13
9:21 *l* 1Ch 26:2,14
9:22 *m* S ver 17
n S 1Sa 9:9
9:25 *o* 2Ki 11:5
9:26 *p* 1Ch 26:22
9:27 *q* S Nu 3:38
r Isa 22:22
9:29 *s* S Nu 3:28; 1Ch 23:29
9:30 *t* S Ex 30:23-25
9:32 *u* Lev 24:5-8; 1Ch 23:29; 2Ch 13:11

9:10–13 The list of priests is essentially the same as that in Ne 11:10–14. Since it is tied to the list of priests earlier in the genealogies (6:1–15,50–53), contemporary Israel's continuity with her past is shown.

9:15–16 Asaph ... Jeduthun. Leaders of musical groups (6:39; 16:41). Later the Chronicler also lists the musicians (ch. 25) before the gatekeepers (ch. 26).

9:16 Netophathites. See note on Ne 12:28.

9:17–21 The Chronicler gives the names of four gatekeepers, while Ne 11:19 mentions only two. The chief of the gatekeepers had the honor of responsibility for the gate used by the king (Eze 46:1–2). The gatekeepers are also listed in ch. 26; Ezr 2:42. These officers traced their origin to Phinehas (v. 20; 6:4; Nu 3:32; 25:6–13).

9:22–27 Twenty-four guard stations were manned in three shifts around the clock; 72 men would be needed for each week. With a total of 212 men, each would have a tour of duty approximately every three weeks (26:12–18).

9:28–34 The Levites not only were responsible for the temple precincts and for opening the gates in the morning but also had charge of the chambers and supply rooms (23:28; 26:20–29), as well as the implements, supplies and furnishings (28:13–18; Ezr 1:9–11). In addition, they were responsible for the preparation of baked goods (Ex 25:30; Lev 2:5–7; 7:9). The priests alone prepared the perfumed anointing oil and spices (Ex 30:23–33).

9:33 ᵛS 1Ch 6:31;
25:1-31; S 2Ch 5:12
ʷ Ps 134:1
9:35 ˣ1Ch 8:29
9:39 ʸS 1Ch 8:33
ᶻ S 1Sa 9:1 ᵃ1Sa 13:22
ᵇ S 2Sa 2:8
9:40 ᶜS 2Sa 4:4
10:10 ᵈS Jdg 16:23
10:11 ᵉS Jdg 21:8
10:13 ᶠS 2Sa 1:1
ᵍ S 1Ch 5:25
ʰ S 1Sa 13:13
ⁱ S Lev 19:31; S 20:6;
Dt 18:9-14
10:14 ʲ1Ch 12:23
ᵏ S 1Sa 13:14

³³Those who were musicians, ᵛ heads of Levite families, stayed in the rooms of the temple and were exempt from other duties because they were responsible for the work day and night. ʷ

³⁴All these were heads of Levite families, chiefs as listed in their genealogy, and they lived in Jerusalem.

THE GENEALOGY OF SAUL

9:34–44pp — 1Ch 8:28–38

³⁵Jeiel ˣ the father ᵃ of Gibeon lived in Gibeon.

His wife's name was Maakah, ³⁶and his firstborn son was Abdon, followed by Zur, Kish, Baal, Ner, Nadab, ³⁷Gedor, Ahio, Zechariah and Mikloth. ³⁸Mikloth was the father of Shimeam. They too lived near their relatives in Jerusalem.

³⁹Ner ʸ was the father of Kish, ᶻ Kish the father of Saul, and Saul the father of Jonathan, ᵃ Malki-Shua, Abinadab and Esh-Baal. ᵇ ᵇ

⁴⁰The son of Jonathan:

Merib-Baal, ᶜ ᶜ who was the father of Micah.

⁴¹The sons of Micah:

Pithon, Melek, Tahrea and Ahaz. ᵈ

⁴²Ahaz was the father of Jadah, Jadah ᵉ was the father of Alemeth, Azmaveth and Zimri, and Zimri was the father of Moza. ⁴³Moza was the father of Binea; Rephaiah was his son, Eleasah his son and Azel his son.

⁴⁴Azel had six sons, and these were their names:

Azrikam, Bokeru, Ishmael, Sheariah, Obadiah and Hanan. These were the sons of Azel.

SAUL TAKES HIS LIFE

10:1–12pp — 1Sa 31:1–13; 2Sa 1:4–12

10 Now the Philistines fought against Israel; the Israelites fled before them, and many fell dead on Mount Gilboa. ²The Philistines were in hot pursuit of Saul and his sons, and they killed his sons Jonathan, Abinadab and Malki-Shua. ³The fighting grew fierce around Saul, and when the archers overtook him, they wounded him.

⁴Saul said to his armor-bearer, "Draw your sword and run me through, or these uncircumcised fellows will come and abuse me."

But his armor-bearer was terrified and would not do it; so Saul took his own sword and fell on it. ⁵When the armor-bearer saw that Saul was dead, he too fell on his sword and died. ⁶So Saul and his three sons died, and all his house died together.

⁷When all the Israelites in the valley saw that the army had fled and that Saul and his sons had died, they abandoned their towns and fled. And the Philistines came and occupied them.

⁸The next day, when the Philistines came to strip the dead, they found Saul and his sons fallen on Mount Gilboa. ⁹They stripped him and took his head and his armor, and sent messengers throughout the land of the Philistines to proclaim the news among their idols and their people. ¹⁰They put his armor in the temple of their gods and hung up his head in the temple of Dagon. ᵈ

¹¹When all the inhabitants of Jabesh Gilead ᵉ heard what the Philistines had done to Saul, ¹²all their valiant men went and took the bodies of Saul and his sons and brought them to Jabesh. Then they buried their bones under the great tree in Jabesh, and they fasted seven days.

¹³Saul died ᶠ because he was unfaithful ᵍ to the LORD; he did not keep ʰ the word of the LORD and even consulted a medium ⁱ for guidance, ¹⁴and did not inquire of the LORD. So the LORD put him to death and turned ʲ the kingdom ᵏ over to David son of Jesse.

ᵃ 35 *Father* may mean *civic leader* or *military leader.*   ᵇ 39 Also known as *Ish-Bosheth*   ᶜ 40 Also known as *Mephibosheth*   ᵈ 41 Vulgate and Syriac (see also Septuagint and 1 Chron. 8:35); Hebrew does not have *and Ahaz.*   ᵉ 42 Some Hebrew manuscripts and Septuagint (see also 1 Chron. 8:36); most Hebrew manuscripts *Jarah, Jarah*

9:35–44 The genealogy of Saul is duplicated here (see 8:29–38) as a transition to the short account of his reign that begins the Chronicler's narration (ch. 10).

10:1–14 This brief account of Saul's death introduces the reign of David, one of the Chronicler's major interests (see Introduction: Purpose and Themes; Portrait of David and Solomon).

10:2 For the strategy of pursuing the king in battle, see note on 1Ki 22:31.

10:6 *his three sons.* See v. 2 (Ish-Bosheth survived; see note on 1Sa 31:2). *all his house.* His three sons and his chief officials (his official "house"), not all his descendants (see 8:33–34 and notes; 1Sa 31:6).

10:13–14 These verses are not paralleled in the Samuel account; they were put here by the Chronicler in line with his concern with immediate retribution (see Introduction: Purpose and Themes). Seeking mediums was forbidden (Dt

DAVID BECOMES KING OVER ISRAEL

11:1–3pp — 2Sa 5:1–3

11 All Israel[f] came together to David at Hebron[m] and said, "We are your own flesh and blood. [2]In the past, even while Saul was king, you were the one who led Israel on their military campaigns.[n] And the LORD your God said to you, 'You will shepherd[o] my people Israel, and you will become their ruler.[p]'"

[3]When all the elders of Israel had come to King David at Hebron, he made a covenant with them at Hebron before the LORD, and they anointed[q] David king over Israel, as the LORD had promised through Samuel.

DAVID CONQUERS JERUSALEM

11:4–9pp — 2Sa 5:6–10

[4]David and all the Israelites marched to Jerusalem (that is, Jebus). The Jebusites[r] who lived there [5]said to David, "You will not get in here." Nevertheless, David captured the fortress of Zion—which is the City of David.

[6]David had said, "Whoever leads the attack on the Jebusites will become commander-in-chief." Joab[s] son of Zeruiah went up first, and so he received the command.

[7]David then took up residence in the fortress, and so it was called the City of David. [8]He built up the city around it, from the terraces[a][t] to the surrounding wall, while Joab restored the rest of the city. [9]And David became more and more powerful,[u] because the LORD Almighty was with him.

DAVID'S MIGHTY WARRIORS

11:10–41pp — 2Sa 23:8–39

[10]These were the chiefs of David's mighty warriors—they, together with all Israel,[v] gave his kingship strong support to extend it over the whole land, as the LORD had promised[w]— [11]this is the list of David's mighty warriors:[x]

Jashobeam,[b] a Hakmonite, was chief of the officers[c]; he raised his spear against three hundred men, whom he killed in one encounter.

[12]Next to him was Eleazar son of Dodai the Ahohite, one of the three mighty warriors. [13]He was with David at Pas Dammim when the Philistines gathered there for battle. At a place where there was a field full of barley, the troops fled from the Philistines. [14]But they took their stand in the middle of the field. They defended it and struck the Philistines down, and the LORD brought about a great victory.[y]

[15]Three of the thirty chiefs came down to David to the rock at the cave of Adullam, while a band of Philistines was encamped in the Valley[z] of Rephaim. [16]At that time David was in the stronghold,[a] and the Philistine garrison was at Bethlehem. [17]David longed for water and said, "Oh, that someone would get me a drink of water from the well near the gate of Bethlehem!" [18]So the Three broke through the Philistine lines, drew water from the well near the gate of Bethlehem and carried it back to David. But he refused to drink it; instead, he poured[b] it out to the LORD. [19]"God forbid that I should do this!" he said. "Should I drink the blood of these men who went at the risk of their lives?" Because they risked their lives to bring it back, David would not drink it.

Such were the exploits of the three mighty warriors.

---

[a] 8 Or *the Millo*   [b] 11 Possibly a variant of *Jashob-Baal*   [c] 11 Or *Thirty*; some Septuagint manuscripts
Three (see also 2 Samuel 23:8)

11:1 [f] S 1Ch 9:1
[m] S Ge 13:18; S 23:19
11:2 [n] S 1Sa 18:5,16
[o] Ps 78:71; Mt 2:6
[p] S 1Ch 5:2
11:3 [q] 1Sa 16:1-13
11:4 [r] S Ge 10:16;
S 15:18-21; S Jos 3:10;
S 15:8
11:6 [s] S 2Sa 2:13
11:8 [t] S 2Sa 5:9;
2Ch 32:5
11:9 [u] Est 9:4
11:10 [v] ver 1
[w] ver 3; 1Ch 12:23
11:11 [x] S 2Sa 17:10
11:14 [y] S Ex 14:30;
S 1Sa 11:13
11:15 [z] 1Ch 14:9;
Isa 17:5
11:16 [a] S 2Sa 5:17
11:18 [b] S Dt 12:16

18:9–14) and brought death to Saul. The Chronicler is obviously writing to an audience already familiar with Samuel and Kings, and he frequently assumes that knowledge. Here the consultation with the medium at Endor is alluded to (see 1Sa 28), but the Chronicler does not recount the incident.

11:1—2Ch 9:31 See Introduction: Portrait of David and Solomon.

11:1–3 The material here parallels that in 2Sa 5:1–3 but is recast by the Chronicler in accordance with his emphasis on the popular support given David by "all Israel" (v. 1). While the Chronicler twice mentions the seven-year reign at Hebron before the death of Ish-Bosheth and the covenant with the northern tribes (3:4; 29:27), these incidents are bypassed in the narrative portion of the book. Most striking is the elimination at this point of the information in 2Sa 5:4–5. Rather, the Chronicler paints a picture of immediate accession over "all Israel," followed by the immediate conquest of Jerusalem (see Introduc-

tion: Portrait of David and Solomon). The author once again assumes the reader's knowledge of the parallel account.

11:4–9 See 2Sa 5:6–10 and notes. The "all Israel" theme appears in v. 4 as a substitute for "the king and his men" (2Sa 5:6).

11:10–41a See 2Sa 23:8–39 and notes. In the Samuel account this list of David's mighty warriors is given near the end of his reign. The Chronicler has moved the list to the beginning of his reign and has greatly expanded it (11:41b—12:40), again as part of his emphasis on the broad support of "all Israel" for the kingship of David (v. 10).

11:11 *three hundred.* Actually 800 (see 2Sa 23:8), 300 here apparently being a copyist's mistake, perhaps influenced by the same number in v. 20.

11:15–19 David recognizes that he is not worthy of such devotion and makes the water a drink offering to the Lord (see Ge 35:14; 2Ki 16:13; Jer 7:18; Hos 9:4).

11:20 cS 1Sa 26:6
11:22 dS Jos 15:21
e 1Sa 17:36
11:23 fS 1Sa 17:7
11:26 gS 2Sa 2:18
11:27 hICh 27:8
11:28 iICh 27:12
11:29 jS 2Sa 21:18
11:31 kICh 27:14
jS Jdg 12:13
11:41 m 2Sa 11:6
nICh 2:36
11:44 oS Dt 1:4

20Abishai c the brother of Joab was chief of the Three. He raised his spear against three hundred men, whom he killed, and so he became as famous as the Three. 21He was doubly honored above the Three and became their commander, even though he was not included among them.

22Benaiah son of Jehoiada, a valiant fighter from Kabzeel, d performed great exploits. He struck down Moab's two mightiest warriors. He also went down into a pit on a snowy day and killed a lion. e 23And he struck down an Egyptian who was five cubits a tall. Although the Egyptian had a spear like a weaver's rod f in his hand, Benaiah went against him with a club. He snatched the spear from the Egyptian's hand and killed him with his own spear. 24Such were the exploits of Benaiah son of Jehoiada; he too was as famous as the three mighty warriors. 25He was held in greater honor than any of the Thirty, but he was not included among the Three. And David put him in charge of his bodyguard.

26 The mighty warriors were:
 Asahel g the brother of Joab,
 Elhanan son of Dodo from Bethlehem,
27 Shammoth h the Harorite,
 Helez the Pelonite,
28 Ira son of Ikkesh from Tekoa,
 Abiezer i from Anathoth,
29 Sibbekai j the Hushathite,
 Ilai the Ahohite,
30 Maharai the Netophathite,
 Heled son of Baanah the Netophathite,
31 Ithai son of Ribai from Gibeah in Benjamin,
 Benaiah k the Pirathonite, l
32 Hurai from the ravines of Gaash,
 Abiel the Arbathite,
33 Azmaveth the Baharumite,
 Eliahba the Shaalbonite,
34 the sons of Hashem the Gizonite,
 Jonathan son of Shagee the Hararite,
35 Ahiam son of Sakar the Hararite,
 Eliphal son of Ur,
36 Hepher the Mekerathite,
 Ahijah the Pelonite,
37 Hezro the Carmelite,
 Naarai son of Ezbai,
38 Joel the brother of Nathan,
 Mibhar son of Hagri,
39 Zelek the Ammonite,
 Naharai the Berothite, the armor-bearer of Joab son of Zeruiah,
40 Ira the Ithrite,
 Gareb the Ithrite,
41 Uriah m the Hittite,
 Zabad n son of Ahlai,
42 Adina son of Shiza the Reubenite, who was chief of the Reubenites, and the thirty with him,
43 Hanan son of Maakah,
 Joshaphat the Mithnite,
44 Uzzia the Ashterathite, o
 Shama and Jeiel the sons of Hotham the Aroerite,
45 Jediael son of Shimri,
 his brother Joha the Tizite,
46 Eliel the Mahavite,
 Jeribai and Joshaviah the sons of Elnaam,
 Ithmah the Moabite,
47 Eliel, Obed and Jaasiel the Mezobaite.

a 23 That is, about 7 feet or about 2.3 meters

11:41b—12:40 See note on vv. 10–41a. The list in 2Sa 23 ends with Uriah the Hittite (2Sa 11); the source for the additional names is not known. The emphasis continues to be on the support of "all Israel"—even Saul's own relatives recognized the legitimacy of David's kingship before Saul's death (12:1–7, 16–18, 23, 29).

WARRIORS JOIN DAVID

12 These were the men who came to David at Ziklag,[p] while he was banished from the presence of Saul son of Kish (they were among the warriors who helped him in battle; [2]they were armed with bows and were able to shoot arrows or to sling stones right-handed or left-handed;[q] they were relatives of Saul[r] from the tribe of Benjamin):

[3]Ahiezer their chief and Joash the sons of Shemaah the Gibeathite; Jeziel and Pelet the sons of Azmaveth; Berakah, Jehu the Anathothite, [4]and Ishmaiah the Gibeonite, a mighty warrior among the Thirty, who was a leader of the Thirty; *Jeremiah, Jahaziel, Johanan, Jozabad the Gederathite,[s] *[5]Eluzai, Jerimoth, Bealiah, Shemariah and Shephatiah the Haruphite; [6]Elkanah, Ishiah, Azarel, Joezer and Jashobeam the Korahites; [7]and Joelah and Zebadiah the sons of Jeroham from Gedor.[t]

[8]Some Gadites[u] defected to David at his stronghold in the wilderness. They were brave warriors, ready for battle and able to handle the shield and spear. Their faces were the faces of lions,[v] and they were as swift as gazelles[w] in the mountains.

[9]Ezer was the chief,
Obadiah the second in command, Eliab the third,
[10]Mishmannah the fourth, Jeremiah the fifth,
[11]Attai the sixth, Eliel the seventh,
[12]Johanan the eighth, Elzabad the ninth,
[13]Jeremiah the tenth and Makbannai the eleventh.

[14]These Gadites were army commanders; the least was a match for a hundred,[x] and the greatest for a thousand.[y] [15]It was they who crossed the Jordan in the first month when it was overflowing all its banks,[z] and they put to flight everyone living in the valleys, to the east and to the west.

[16]Other Benjamites[a] and some men from Judah also came to David in his stronghold. [17]David went out to meet them and said to them, "If you have come to me in peace to help me, I am ready for you to join me. But if you have come to betray me to my enemies when my hands are free from violence, may the God of our ancestors see it and judge you."

[18]Then the Spirit[b] came on Amasai,[c] chief of the Thirty, and he said:

"We are yours, David!
We are with you, son of Jesse!
Success,[d] success to you,
and success to those who help you,
for your God will help you."

So David received them and made them leaders of his raiding bands.

[19]Some of the tribe of Manasseh defected to David when he went with the Philistines to fight against Saul. (He and his men did not help the Philistines because, after consultation, their rulers sent him away. They said, "It will cost us our heads if he deserts to his master Saul.")[e] [20]When David went to Ziklag,[f] these were the men of Manasseh who defected to him: Adnah, Jozabad, Jediael, Michael, Jozabad, Elihu and Zillethai, leaders of units of a thousand in Manasseh. [21]They helped David against raiding bands, for all of them were brave warriors, and they were commanders in his army. [22]Day after day men came to help David, until he had a great army, like the army of God.[a]

OTHERS JOIN DAVID AT HEBRON

[23]These are the numbers of the men armed for battle who came to David at Hebron[g] to turn[h] Saul's kingdom over to him, as the LORD had said:[i]

---

[a] 22 Or a great and mighty army

* The rest of this verse (12:4b) is numbered 12:5 in Hebrew texts.   * 12:5-40 is numbered 12:6-41 in Hebrew texts.

12:1 [p]S Jos 15:31
12:2 [q]S Jdg 3:15
[r]S 2Sa 3:19
12:4 [s]Jos 15:36
12:7 [t]S Jos 15:58
12:8 [u]S Ge 30:11
[v]2Sa 17:10
[w]S 2Sa 2:18
12:14 [x]S Lev 26:8
[y]S Dt 32:30
12:15 [z]S Jos 3:15
12:16 [a]S 2Sa 3:19
12:18 [b]S Jdg 3:10;
1Ch 28:12; 2Ch 15:1;
20:14; 24:20
[c]S 2Sa 17:25
[d]1Sa 25:5-6
12:19 [e]1Sa 29:2-11
12:20 [f]S 1Sa 27:6
12:23 [g]2Sa 2:3-4
[h]1Ch 10:14
[i]S 1Sa 16:1; 1Ch 11:10

12:1 The Chronicler assumes the reader's knowledge of the events at Ziklag (1Sa 27); see vv. 19–20.
12:8–15 The warriors of Gad were from Transjordan. Melting snows to the north would have brought the Jordan to flood stage in the first month (March-April) at the time of their crossing (v. 15). The most appropriate time for this incident would have been in the period of David's wandering in the region of the Dead Sea (1Sa 23:14; 24:1; 25:1; 26:1).
12:23–37 The emphasis remains on "all Israel" (v. 38). Though

13 tribes are named, they are grouped in order to maintain the traditional number of 12 (see note on 2:1–2). The northernmost tribes and those east of the Jordan River send the largest number of men (vv. 33–37), reinforcing the degree of support that David enjoyed not only in Judah and Benjamin but throughout the other tribes as well. The numbers in this section seem quite high. Essentially two approaches are followed on this question: 1. It is possible to explain the numbers so that a lower figure is actually attained. The Hebrew word for "thousand" may repre-

12:28 /1Ch 6:8;
15:11; 16:39; 27:17
12:29 ᵏ S 2Sa 3:19
/2Sa 2:8-9
12:32 ᵐ Est 1:13
12:38 ⁿ S 1Ch 9:1
12:39 ᵒ 2Sa 3:20;
Isa 25:6-8
12:40 ᵖ S 2Sa 16:1;
17:29 ᑫ 1Sa 25:18
ʳ1Ch 29:22
13:3 ˢ1Sa 7:1-2
ᵗ2Ch 1:5
13:5 ᵘ1Ch 11:1; 15:3
ᵛ S Jos 13:3
ʷ S Nu 13:21

²⁴from Judah, carrying shield and spear—6,800 armed for battle;

²⁵from Simeon, warriors ready for battle—7,100;

²⁶from Levi—4,600, ²⁷including Jehoiada, leader of the family of Aaron, with 3,700 men, ²⁸and Zadok,ʲ a brave young warrior, with 22 officers from his family;

²⁹from Benjamin,ᵏ Saul's tribe—3,000, mostˡ of whom had remained loyal to Saul's house until then;

³⁰from Ephraim, brave warriors, famous in their own clans—20,800;

³¹from half the tribe of Manasseh, designated by name to come and make David king—18,000;

³²from Issachar, men who understood the times and knew what Israel should doᵐ—200 chiefs, with all their relatives under their command;

³³from Zebulun, experienced soldiers prepared for battle with every type of weapon, to help David with undivided loyalty—50,000;

³⁴from Naphtali—1,000 officers, together with 37,000 men carrying shields and spears;

³⁵from Dan, ready for battle—28,600;

³⁶from Asher, experienced soldiers prepared for battle—40,000;

³⁷and from east of the Jordan, from Reuben, Gad and the half-tribe of Manasseh, armed with every type of weapon—120,000.

³⁸All these were fighting men who volunteered to serve in the ranks. They came to Hebron fully determined to make David king over all Israel.ⁿ All the rest of the Israelites were also of one mind to make David king. ³⁹The men spent three days there with David, eating and drinking,ᵒ for their families had supplied provisions for them. ⁴⁰Also, their neighbors from as far away as Issachar, Zebulun and Naphtali came bringing food on donkeys, camels, mules and oxen. There were plentiful suppliesᵖ of flour, fig cakes, raisinᑫ cakes, wine, oil, cattle and sheep, for there was joyʳ in Israel.

BRINGING BACK THE ARK
13:1–14pp — 2Sa 6:1–11

13 David conferred with each of his officers, the commanders of thousands and commanders of hundreds. ²He then said to the whole assembly of Israel, "If it seems good to you and if it is the will of the Lᴏʀᴅ our God, let us send word far and wide to the rest of our people throughout the territories of Israel, and also to the priests and Levites who are with them in their towns and pasturelands, to come and join us. ³Let us bring the ark of our God back to us,ˢ for we did not inquireᵗ ofᵃ itᵇ during the reign of Saul." ⁴The whole assembly agreed to do this, because it seemed right to all the people.

⁵So David assembled all Israel,ᵘ from the Shihor Riverᵛ in Egypt to Lebo Hamath,ʷ to

---

ᵃ 3 Or *we neglected*   ᵇ 3 Or *him*

---

sent a unit of a tribe, each having its own commander (13:1; see Nu 31:14,48,52,54). In this case the numbers would be read not as a total figure, but as representative commanders. For example, the 6,800 from Judah (v. 24) would be read either as six commanders of 1,000 and eight commanders of 100 (see 13:1), or possibly as six commanders of thousands and 800 men (see Introduction to Numbers: Special Problem). Reducing the numbers in this fashion fits well with 13:1 and with the list of commanders alone found for Zadok's family (v. 28) and the tribe of Issachar (v. 32). Taking the numbers as straight totals would require the presence of 340,800 persons in Hebron for a feast at the same time. 2. Another approach is to allow the numbers to stand and to view them as hyperbole on the part of the Chronicler to achieve a number "like the army of God" (v. 22). This approach would fit well with the Chronicler's glorification of David and with the banquet scene that follows.

🅐 **12:38–40** The Chronicler's portrait of David is influenced by his Messianic expectations (see Introduction: Purpose and Themes). In the presence of a third of a million people (see note on vv. 23–37) David's coronation banquet typifies the future Messianic feast (Isa 25:6–8). The imagery of the Messianic banquet became prominent in the intertestamental literature (*Apocalypse of Baruch* 29:4–8; *Enoch* 62:14) and in the NT (see Mt 8:11–12 and Lk 13:28–30; Mt 22:1–10 and Lk 14:16–24; see also Mt 25:1–13; Lk 22:28–30; Rev 19:7–9). The

Lord's Supper anticipates that coming banquet (Mt 26:29; Mk 14:25; Lk 22:15–18; 1Co 11:23–26).

13:1–14 See 2Sa 6:1–11 and notes. The author abandons the chronological order as given in 2Sa 5–6 and puts the transfer of the ark first, delaying his account of the palace building and the Philistine campaign until later (ch. 14). This is in accordance with his portrayal of David; David's concern with the ark was expressed immediately upon his accession—his consultation with the leaders appears to be set in the context of the coronation banquet (12:38–40).

13:1–4 These verses are not found in Samuel and reflect the Chronicler's own concerns with "all Israel." The semi-military expedition to retrieve the ark in 2Sa 6:1 is here broadened by consultation with and support from the whole assembly of Israel, "throughout the territories" (v. 2), including the priests and Levites—an important point for the Chronicler since only they are allowed to move the ark (15:2,13; 23:25–27; Dt 10:8).

13:3 *we did not inquire of it during the reign of Saul.* 1Sa 14:18 may be an exception (but see note there).

13:5–6 The emphasis remains on the united action of "all Israel." Israelites came to participate in this venture all the way from Lebo Hamath in the north and from the Shihor River in the south.

13:5 *Shihor.* An Egyptian term meaning "the pool of Horus." It appears to be a part of the Nile or one of the major canals of the Nile (see Jos 13:3; Isa 23:3; Jer 2:18 and notes).

bring the ark of God from Kiriath Jearim.ˣ ⁶David and all Israel went to Baalahʸ of Judah (Kiriath Jearim) to bring up from there the ark of God the LORD, who is enthroned between the cherubimᶻ—the ark that is called by the Name.

⁷They moved the ark of God from Abinadab'sᵃ house on a new cart, with Uzzah and Ahio guiding it. ⁸David and all the Israelites were celebrating with all their might before God, with songs and with harps, lyres, timbrels, cymbals and trumpets.ᵇ

⁹When they came to the threshing floor of Kidon, Uzzah reached out his hand to steady the ark, because the oxen stumbled. ¹⁰The LORD's angerᶜ burned against Uzzah, and he struck him downᵈ because he had put his hand on the ark. So he died there before God.

¹¹Then David was angry because the LORD's wrath had broken out against Uzzah, and to this day that place is called Perez Uzzah.ᵃᵉ

¹²David was afraid of God that day and asked, "How can I ever bring the ark of God to me?" ¹³He did not take the ark to be with him in the City of David. Instead, he took it to the house of Obed-Edomᶠ the Gittite. ¹⁴The ark of God remained with the family of Obed-Edom in his house for three months, and the LORD blessed his householdᵍ and everything he had.

DAVID'S HOUSE AND FAMILY

14:1–7pp — 2Sa 5:11–16; 1Ch 3:5–8

14 Now Hiram king of Tyre sent messengers to David, along with cedar logs,ʰ stonemasons and carpenters to build a palace for him. ²And David knew that the LORD had established him as king over Israel and that his kingdom had been highly exaltedⁱ for the sake of his people Israel.

³In Jerusalem David took more wives and became the father of more sonsʲ and daughters. ⁴These are the names of the children born to him there: ᵏShammua, Shobab, Nathan, Solomon, ⁵Ibhar, Elishua, Elpelet, ⁶Nogah, Nepheg, Japhia, ⁷Elishama, Beeliadaᵇ and Eliphelet.

DAVID DEFEATS THE PHILISTINES

14:8–17pp — 2Sa 5:17–25

⁸When the Philistines heard that David had been anointed king over all Israel,ˡ they went up in full force to search for him, but David heard about it and went out to meet them. ⁹Now the Philistines had come and raided the Valleyᵐ of Rephaim; ¹⁰so David inquired of God: "Shall I go and attack the Philistines? Will you deliver them into my hands?"

The LORD answered him, "Go, I will deliver them into your hands."

¹¹So David and his men went up to Baal Perazim,ⁿ and there he defeated them. He said, "As waters break out, God has broken out against my enemies by my hand." So that place was called Baal Perazim.ᶜ ¹²The Philistines had abandoned their gods there, and David gave orders to burnᵒ them in the fire.ᵖ

ᵃ 11 *Perez Uzzah* means *outbreak against Uzzah.*   ᵇ 7 A variant of *Eliada*   ᶜ 11 *Baal Perazim* means *the lord who breaks out.*

13:5 ˣ S 1Sa 7:2
13:6 ʸ S Jos 15:9
ᶻ S Ex 25:22;
2Ki 19:15
13:7 ᵃ S 1Sa 7:1
13:8 ᵇ 1Ch 15:16,19,
24; 2Ch 5:12; Ps 92:3
13:10 ᶜ 1Ch 15:13,15
ᵈ S Lev 10:2
13:11 ᵉ 1Ch 15:13;
Ps 7:11
13:13 ᶠ 1Ch 15:18,
24; 16:38; 26:4-5,15
13:14 ᵍ S 2Sa 6:11
14:1 ʰ S 1Ki 5:6;
1Ch 17:6; 22:4;
2Ch 2:3; Ezr 3:7;
Hag 1:8
14:2 ⁱ S Nu 24:7;
S Dt 26:19
14:3 ʲ S 1Ch 3:1
14:4 ᵏ S 1Ch 3:9
14:8 ˡ 1Ch 11:1
14:9 ᵐ ver 13;
S Jos 15:8; S 1Ch 11:15
14:11 ⁿ Ps 94:16;
Isa 28:21
14:12 ᵒ S Ex 32:20
ᵖ S Jos 7:15

13:6 *Baalah.* The Canaanite name for Kiriath Jearim, also known as Kiriath Baal (Jos 18:14). The Chronicler assumes that his readers are familiar with the account of how the ark came to be at Kiriath Jearim (1Sa 6:1—7:1). *the Name.* See Ex 23:21 and note.
13:7 *Uzzah and Ahio.* Sons or descendants of Abinadab (2Sa 6:3).
13:10 *because he had put his hand on the ark.* The ark was to be moved only by Levites, who carried it with poles inserted through rings in the sides of the ark (Ex 25:12–15). None of the holy things was to be touched, on penalty of death (Nu 4:15). These strictures were observed in the second and successful attempt to move the ark to Jerusalem (15:1–15). It cannot be known whether Uzzah and Ahio were Levites—the Samuel account does not mention the presence of Levites, but the Chronicler's careful inclusion of Levites in this expedition suggests that they were present (see note on vv. 1–4). In any case, the ark should not have been moved on a cart (as done by the Philistines, 1Sa 6) or touched.
13:13 *Obed-Edom.* Perhaps the same man mentioned in 15:18,21,24. In 26:4 God's blessing on Obed-Edom included numerous sons. This reference also establishes that Obed-Edom was a Levite and that the ark was properly left in his care.
14:1–17 The Chronicler backtracks to pick up material from

2Sa 5 deferred to this point (see note on 13:1–14). The three-month period that the ark remained with Obed-Edom (13:14) was filled with incidents showing God's blessing on David: the building of his royal house (vv. 1–2), his large family (vv. 3–7) and his success in warfare (vv. 8–16)—all because of the Lord's blessing (vv. 2,17).
14:1–2 See 2Sa 5:11–12 and notes.
14:1 *Hiram.* Later provided materials and labor for building the temple (2Ch 2). His mention here implies international recognition of David as king over Israel and a treaty between David and Hiram.
14:3–7 See 3:1–9 and note; 2Sa 5:13–16. David's children born in Hebron are omitted (3:1–4; 2Sa 3:2–5; see note on 11:1–3).
14:7 *Beeliada.* Eliada (see TNIV text note) in 3:8; 2Sa 5:16.
14:8–12 See 2Sa 5:17–21 and notes.
14:11 *break out...Perazim.* The Hebrew underlying the name of this place where the Lord broke out against the Philistines is the same as that underlying the word used in 13:11 when the Lord broke out against Uzzah (see TNIV text notes there and here).
14:12 *gave orders to burn them.* 2Sa 5:21 does not mention burning but says that David and his men carried the idols away. Many have seen here an intentional change on the part of the Chronicler in order to bring David's actions into strict conformity

14:13 *q* S ver 9
14:16 *r* S Jos 9:3
s Jos 10:33
14:17 *t* S Jos 6:27
u Ex 15:14-16;
S Dt 2:25; Ps 2:1-12
15:1 *v* Ps 132:1-18
w 2Sa 6:17;
1Ch 16:1; 17:1
15:2 *x* S Nu 3:6;
4:15; Dt 10:8; 31:25;
2Ch 5:5 *y* S Dt 31:9
z 1Ch 16:4; 23:13;
2Ch 29:11; 31:2;
Ps 134:1; 135:2
15:3 *a* S 1Ch 13:5
15:4 *b* S Nu 3:17-20
15:5 *c* 1Ch 6:24
15:8 *d* S Ex 6:22
15:9 *e* Ex 6:18
15:11 *f* S 1Ch 12:28
g S 1Sa 22:20
15:12 *h* S Ex 29:1;
30:19-21,30; 40:31-
32; S Lev 11:44
15:13 *i* 1Ki 8:4
j S 1Ch 13:7-10
k S Lev 5:10
15:15 *l* S Ex 25:14
m 2Sa 6:7
15:16 *n* 1Ch 6:31
o 2Ch 7:6 *p* Ezr 2:41;
Ne 11:23; Ps 68:25
q S 1Ch 13:8; 23:5;
2Ch 29:26; Ne 12:27,
36; Job 21:12;
Ps 150:5; Am 5:5
15:17 *r* S 1Ch 6:33
s 1Ch 6:39 *t* 1Ch 6:44

[13] Once more the Philistines raided the valley; [q] [14] so David inquired of God again, and God answered him, "Do not go directly after them, but circle around them and attack them in front of the poplar trees. [15] As soon as you hear the sound of marching in the tops of the poplar trees, move out to battle, because that will mean God has gone out in front of you to strike the Philistine army." [16] So David did as God commanded him, and they struck down the Philistine army, all the way from Gibeon [r] to Gezer. [s]

[17] So David's fame [t] spread throughout every land, and the LORD made all the nations fear [u] him.

THE ARK BROUGHT TO JERUSALEM

15:25—16:3pp — 2Sa 6:12-19

15 After David had constructed buildings for himself in the City of David, he prepared [v] a place for the ark of God and pitched [w] a tent for it. [2] Then David said, "No one but the Levites [x] may carry [y] the ark of God, because the LORD chose them to carry the ark of the LORD and to minister [z] before him forever."

[3] David assembled all Israel [a] in Jerusalem to bring up the ark of the LORD to the place he had prepared for it. [4] He called together the descendants of Aaron and the Levites: [b]
[5] From the descendants of Kohath,
   Uriel [c] the leader and 120 relatives;
[6] from the descendants of Merari,
   Asaiah the leader and 220 relatives;
[7] from the descendants of Gershon, [a]
   Joel the leader and 130 relatives;
[8] from the descendants of Elizaphan, [d]
   Shemaiah the leader and 200 relatives;
[9] from the descendants of Hebron, [e]
   Eliel the leader and 80 relatives;
[10] from the descendants of Uzziel,
   Amminadab the leader and 112 relatives.

[11] Then David summoned Zadok [f] and Abiathar [g] the priests, and Uriel, Asaiah, Joel, Shemaiah, Eliel and Amminadab the Levites. [12] He said to them, "You are the heads of the Levitical families; you and your fellow Levites are to consecrate [h] yourselves and bring up the ark of the LORD, the God of Israel, to the place I have prepared for it. [13] It was because you, the Levites, [i] did not bring it up the first time that the LORD our God broke out in anger against us. [j] We did not inquire of him about how to do it in the prescribed way. [k]" [14] So the priests and Levites consecrated themselves in order to bring up the ark of the LORD, the God of Israel. [15] And the Levites carried the ark of God with the poles on their shoulders, as Moses had commanded [l] in accordance with the word of the LORD. [m]

[16] David [n] told the leaders of the Levites [o] to appoint their fellow Levites as musicians [p] to make a joyful sound with musical instruments: lyres, harps and cymbals. [q]

[17] So the Levites appointed Heman [r] son of Joel; from his relatives, Asaph [s] son of Berekiah; and from their relatives the Merarites, [t] Ethan son of Kushaiah; [18] and with them their relatives next in rank: Zechariah, [b] Jaaziel, Shemiramoth, Jehiel, Unni, Eliab, Bena-

---

a 7 Hebrew *Gershom,* a variant of *Gershon*   *b 18* Three Hebrew manuscripts and most Septuagint manuscripts (see also verse 20 and 1 Chron. 16:5); most Hebrew manuscripts *Zechariah son and* or *Zechariah, Ben and*

---

with the law, which required that pagan idols be burned (Dt 7:5,25). However, some Septuagint (the pre-Christian Greek translation of the OT) manuscripts of Samuel agree with Chronicles that David burned the idols. This would indicate that the Chronicler was not innovating for theological reasons but was carefully reproducing the Hebrew text he had before him, which differed from the Masoretic (later Hebrew) text of Samuel.
14:13–16 See 2Sa 5:22–25 and notes.
14:17 *the LORD made all the nations fear him.* Here and elsewhere the Chronicler uses an expression that refers to an incapacitating terror brought on by the sense that the awesome power of God is present in behalf of his people (see Ex 15:16). Thus David is seen by the nations as the very representative of God (similarly Asa, 2Ch 14:14; Jehoshaphat, 2Ch 17:10; 20:29).
15:1—16:3 This account of the successful attempt to move the ark to Jerusalem is greatly expanded over the material in 2 Samuel. Only 15:25—16:3 has a parallel (2Sa 6:12–19); the

rest of the material is unique to the Chronicler and reflects his own interests, especially in the Levites and worship musicians (vv. 3–24; see Introduction: Purpose and Themes). Ps 132 should also be read in connection with this account.
15:1 *constructed buildings for himself.* See 14:1–2 and note on 13:1–14.
15:2–3 See note on 13:10.
15:4–10 The three clans of Levi are represented (Kohath, Merari and Gershon), as well as three distinct subgroups within Kohath (Elizaphan, Hebron and Uzziel)—862 in all.
15:12 *consecrate yourselves.* Through ritual washings and avoidance of ceremonial defilement (Ex 29:1–37; 30:19–21; 40:31–32; Lev 8:5–35).
15:13–15 The Chronicler provides the explanation for the failure in the first attempt to move the ark, an explanation not found in the Samuel account (see note on 13:10).
15:18,21,24 *Obed-Edom.* See note on 13:13.

iah, Maaseiah, Mattithiah, Eliphelehu, Mikneiah, Obed-Edom *u* and Jeiel, *a* the gatekeepers.

¹⁹The musicians Heman, *v* Asaph and Ethan were to sound the bronze cymbals; ²⁰Zechariah, Jaaziel, *b* Shemiramoth, Jehiel, Unni, Eliab, Maaseiah and Benaiah were to play the lyres according to *alamoth*, *c* ²¹and Mattithiah, Eliphelehu, Mikneiah, Obed-Edom, Jeiel and Azaziah were to play the harps, directing according to *sheminith*.*c* ²²Kenaniah the head Levite was in charge of the singing; that was his responsibility because he was skillful at it.

²³Berekiah and Elkanah were to be doorkeepers for the ark. ²⁴Shebaniah, Joshaphat, Nethanel, Amasai, Zechariah, Benaiah and Eliezer the priests were to blow trumpets *w* before the ark of God. Obed-Edom and Jehiah were also to be doorkeepers for the ark.

²⁵So David and the elders of Israel and the commanders of units of a thousand went to bring up the ark *x* of the covenant of the LORD from the house of Obed-Edom, with rejoicing. ²⁶Because God had helped the Levites who were carrying the ark of the covenant of the LORD, seven bulls and seven rams *y* were sacrificed. ²⁷Now David was clothed in a robe of fine linen, as were all the Levites who were carrying the ark, and as were the musicians, and Kenaniah, who was in charge of the singing of the choirs. David also wore a linen ephod. *z* ²⁸So all Israel *a* brought up the ark of the covenant of the LORD with shouts, *b* with the sounding of rams' horns *c* and trumpets, and of cymbals, and the playing of lyres and harps.

²⁹As the ark of the covenant of the LORD was entering the City of David, Michal daughter of Saul watched from a window. And when she saw King David dancing and celebrating, she despised him in her heart.

MINISTERING BEFORE THE ARK
16:8–22pp — Ps 105:1–15
16:23–33pp — Ps 96:1–13
16:34–36pp — Ps 106:1,47–48

16 They brought the ark of God and set it inside the tent that David had pitched *d* for it, and they presented burnt offerings and fellowship offerings before God. ²After David had finished sacrificing the burnt offerings and fellowship offerings, he blessed *e* the people in the name of the LORD. ³Then he gave a loaf of bread, a cake of dates and a cake of raisins *f* to each Israelite man and woman.

⁴He appointed some of the Levites to minister *g* before the ark of the LORD, to extol, *d* thank, and praise the LORD, the God of Israel: ⁵Asaph was the chief, and next to him in rank were Zechariah, then Jaaziel, *e* Shemiramoth, Jehiel, Mattithiah, Eliab, Benaiah, Obed-Edom and Jeiel. They were to play the lyres and harps, Asaph was to sound the cymbals, ⁶and Benaiah and Jahaziel the priests were to blow the trumpets regularly before the ark of the covenant of God.

⁷That day David first appointed Asaph and his associates to give praise *h* to the LORD in this manner:

⁸Give praise *i* to the LORD, call on his name;

---

a 18 Hebrew; Septuagint (see also verse 21) *Jeiel and Azaziah*   *b 20* See verse 18; Hebrew *Aziel,* a variant of *Jaaziel.*   *c 20,21* Probably a musical term   *d 4* Or *petition; or invoke*   *e 5* See 15:18,20; Hebrew *Jeiel,* possibly another name for *Jaaziel.*

15:18 *u* S 2Sa 6:10;
1Ch 26:4- 5
15:19 *v* 1Ch 16:41;
25:6
15:24 *w* 2Ch 5:12;
7:6; 29:26
15:25 *x* 2Ch 1:4; 5:2;
Jer 3:16
15:26 *y* Nu 23:1-4,
29
15:27 *z* S 1Sa 2:18
15:28 *a* S 1Ch 9:1
b S 1Ki 1:39; Zec 4:7
c S Ex 19:13
16:1 *d* S 1Ch 15:1
16:2 *e* S Ex 39:43;
Nu 6:23-27
16:3 *f* Isa 16:7
16:4 *g* S 1Ch 15:2
16:7 *h* Ps 47:7
16:8 *i* ver 34;
Ps 107:1; 118:1; 136:1

15:24 *priests were to blow trumpets.* See 16:6; Nu 10:1–10.
15:27 Both 2Sa 6:14 and the Chronicler mention David's wearing a linen ephod, a garment worn by priests (1Sa 2:18; 22:18). The Chronicler adds, however, that David (as well as the rest of the Levites in the procession) was wearing a robe of fine linen, further associating him with the dress of the priestly functionaries. Apparently the Chronicler viewed David as a priest-king, a kind of Messianic figure (see Ps 110; Zec 6:9–15).
15:29 Parallel to 2Sa 6:16, but the Chronicler omits the remainder of this incident recorded there (2Sa 6:20–23). Some interpreters regard this omission as part of the Chronicler's positive view of David, so that a possibly unseemly account is omitted. On the other hand, it is equally plausible that the Chronicler here simply assumes the reader's knowledge of the other account (see notes on 10:13–14; 11:1–3; 12:1; 13:6).
16:1–3 David is further associated with the priests in his supervision of the sacrifices and his exercising the priestly prerogative of blessing the people (Nu 6:22–27; see note on 15:27).

The baked goods provided by David were for the sacrificial meal following the fellowship offerings (Lev 3:1–17; 7:11–21,28–36).
16:4 *to extol, thank, and praise the LORD.* If the TNIV text note ("petition") represents the correct translation (cf. "petition" in Ps 38 title and Ps 70 title), then the three words may refer to the three main types of psalms: (1) lament and/or petition, (2) thanksgiving and (3) praise (see Introduction to Psalms: Psalm Types; see also note on Col 3:16).
16:8–36 Similar to various parts of the book of Psalms (for vv. 8–22 see Ps 105:1–15; for vv. 23–33, Ps 96; for vv. 34–36, Ps 106:1,47–48). This psalm is not found in the Samuel account. The use of the lengthy historical portion from Ps 105 emphasizing the promises to Abraham would be particularly relevant to the Chronicler's postexilic audience, for whom the faithfulness of God was a fresh reality in their return to the land. The citation from Ps 106 would also be of immediate relevance to the Chronicler's audience as those who had been gathered and delivered from the nations (v. 35).

16:8 /S 2Ki 19:19
16:9 ᵏS Ex 15:1;
Ps 7:17
16:10 ˡPs 8:1; 29:2;
66:2
16:11 ᵐver 10;
1Ch 28:9; 2Ch 7:14;
14:4; 15:2,12; 16:12;
18:4; 20:4; 34:3;
Ps 24:6; 27:8; 105:4;
119:2,58; Pr 8:17
16:12 ⁿPs 77:11
ᵒS Dt 4:34 ᵖPs 78:43
16:14 ᵠIsa 4:4; 26:9
16:15 ʳS Ge 8:1;
Ps 98:3; 111:5; 115:12;
136:23
16:16 ˢS Ge 12:7;
S 15:18; 22:16-18
16:17 ᵗGe 35:9-12
16:18 ᵘGe 13:14-17
16:19 ᵛDt 7:7
16:20 ʷS Ge 20:13
16:21 ˣGe 12:17;
S 20:3; Ex 7:15-18;
Ps 9:5
16:22 ʸS Ge 20:7
16:24 ᶻIsa 42:12;
66:19
16:25 ᵃPs 18:3; 48:1
ᵇPs 76:7; 89:7
ᶜEx 18:11; Dt 32:39;
2Ch 2:5; Ps 135:5;
Isa 40:25
16:26 ᵈPs 8:3;
102:25
16:28 ᵉPs 29:1-2
16:29 ᶠPs 8:1
ᵍ2Ch 20:21;
Ps 29:1-2
16:30 ʰPs 2:11;
33:8; 76:8; 99:1; 114:7
ᶦPs 93:1
16:31 ʲIsa 44:23;
49:13 ᵏPs 9:7; 47:8;
93:1; 97:1; 99:1;
146:10; Isa 52:7;
La 5:19
16:32 ˡEx 20:11;
Isa 42:10
16:33 ᵐIsa 14:8;
55:12 ⁿ1Sa 2:10;
Ps 7:8; 96:10; 98:9;
110:6; Isa 2:4
16:34 ᵒS ver 8;
Ps 105:1; Isa 12:4
ᵖPs 25:7; 34:8; 100:5;
135:3; 145:9; Na 1:7

make known among the nations[j] what he has done.
⁹ Sing to him, sing praise[k] to him;
   tell of all his wonderful acts.
¹⁰ Glory in his holy name;[l]
   let the hearts of those who seek the Lᴏʀᴅ rejoice.
¹¹ Look to the Lᴏʀᴅ and his strength;
   seek[m] his face always.

¹² Remember[n] the wonders[o] he has done,
   his miracles,[p] and the judgments he pronounced,
¹³ you his servants, the descendants of Israel,
   his chosen ones, the children of Jacob.
¹⁴ He is the Lᴏʀᴅ our God;
   his judgments[q] are in all the earth.

¹⁵ He remembers[a][r] his covenant forever,
   the promise he made, for a thousand generations,
¹⁶ the covenant[s] he made with Abraham,
   the oath he swore to Isaac.
¹⁷ He confirmed it to Jacob[t] as a decree,
   to Israel as an everlasting covenant:
¹⁸ "To you I will give the land of Canaan[u]
   as the portion you will inherit."

¹⁹ When they were but few in number,[v]
   few indeed, and strangers in it,
²⁰ they[b] wandered[w] from nation to nation,
   from one kingdom to another.
²¹ He allowed no one to oppress them;
   for their sake he rebuked kings:[x]
²² "Do not touch my anointed ones;
   do my prophets[y] no harm."

²³ Sing to the Lᴏʀᴅ, all the earth;
   proclaim his salvation day after day.
²⁴ Declare his glory[z] among the nations,
   his marvelous deeds among all peoples.

²⁵ For great is the Lᴏʀᴅ and most worthy of praise;[a]
   he is to be feared[b] above all gods.[c]
²⁶ For all the gods of the nations are idols,
   but the Lᴏʀᴅ made the heavens.[d]
²⁷ Splendor and majesty are before him;
   strength and joy are in his dwelling place.

²⁸ Ascribe to the Lᴏʀᴅ, all you families of nations,
   ascribe to the Lᴏʀᴅ glory and strength.[e]
²⁹ Ascribe to the Lᴏʀᴅ the glory due his name;[f]
   bring an offering and come before him.
   Worship the Lᴏʀᴅ in the splendor of his[c] holiness.[g]
³⁰ Tremble[h] before him, all the earth!
   The world is firmly established; it cannot be moved.[i]

³¹ Let the heavens rejoice, let the earth be glad;[j]
   let them say among the nations, "The Lᴏʀᴅ reigns!"[k]
³² Let the sea resound, and all that is in it;[l]
   let the fields be jubilant, and everything in them!
³³ Let the trees[m] of the forest sing,
   let them sing for joy before the Lᴏʀᴅ,
   for he comes to judge[n] the earth.
³⁴ Give thanks[o] to the Lᴏʀᴅ, for he is good;[p]

ᵃ 15 Some Septuagint manuscripts (see also Psalm 105:8); Hebrew *Remember*   ᵇ 18-20 One Hebrew
manuscript, Septuagint and Vulgate (see also Psalm 105:12); most Hebrew manuscripts *inherit,* / ¹⁹*though
you are but few in number,* / *few indeed, and strangers in it."* / ²⁰*They*   ᶜ 29 Or *Lᴏʀᴅ with the splendor of*

16:29 *splendor of his holiness.* See 2Ch 20:21; see also Ps 29:2 and note; 96:9; 110:3.

his love endures forever. *q*

³⁵Cry out, "Save us, God our Savior; *r*
    gather us and deliver us from the nations,
that we may give thanks to your holy name,
    and glory in your praise."
³⁶Praise be to the LORD, the God of Israel, *s*
    from everlasting to everlasting.

Then all the people said "Amen" and "Praise the LORD."

³⁷David left Asaph and his associates before the ark of the covenant of the LORD to minister there regularly, according to each day's requirements. *t* ³⁸He also left Obed-Edom *u* and his sixty-eight associates to minister with them. Obed-Edom son of Jeduthun, and also Hosah, *v* were gatekeepers.

³⁹David left Zadok *w* the priest and his fellow priests before the tabernacle of the LORD at the high place in Gibeon *x* ⁴⁰to present burnt offerings to the LORD on the altar of burnt offering regularly, morning and evening, in accordance with everything written in the Law *y* of the LORD, which he had given Israel. ⁴¹With them were Heman *z* and Jeduthun and the rest of those chosen and designated by name to give thanks to the LORD, "for his love endures forever." ⁴²Heman and Jeduthun were responsible for the sounding of the trumpets and cymbals and for the playing of the other instruments for sacred song. *a* The sons of Jeduthun *b* were stationed at the gate.

⁴³Then all the people left to go to their homes, and David returned home to bless his family.

GOD'S PROMISE TO DAVID
17:1–15pp — 2Sa 7:1–17

17 After David was settled in his palace, he said to Nathan the prophet, "Here I am, living in a house of cedar, while the ark of the covenant of the LORD is under a tent. *c*"

²Nathan replied to David, "Whatever you have in mind, *d* do it, for God is with you."

³But that night the word of God came to Nathan, saying:

⁴"Go and tell my servant David, 'This is what the LORD says: You *e* are not the one to build me a house to dwell in. ⁵I have not dwelt in a house from the day I brought Israel up out of Egypt to this day. I have moved from one tent site to another, from one dwelling place to another. ⁶Wherever I have moved with all the Israelites, did I ever say to any of their leaders^a whom I commanded to shepherd my people, "Why have you not built me a house of cedar?*f*" '

⁷"Now then, tell my servant David, 'This is what the LORD Almighty says: I took you from the pasture, from tending the flock, and appointed you ruler *g* over my people Israel. ⁸I have been with you wherever you have gone, and I have cut off all your enemies from before you. Now I will make your name like the names of the greatest men on earth. ⁹And I will provide a place for my people Israel and will plant them so that they can have a home of their own and no longer be disturbed. Wicked people will not oppress them anymore, as they did at the beginning ¹⁰and have done ever since the time I appointed leaders *h* over my people Israel. I will also subdue all your enemies.

" 'I declare to you that the LORD will build a house for you: ¹¹When your days are over and you go to be with your ancestors, I will raise up your offspring to succeed you, one of your own sons, and I will establish his kingdom. ¹²He is the one who will

---

^a 6 Traditionally *judges*; also in verse 10

16:34 *q* 2Ch 5:13; 7:3; Ezr 3:11; Ps 136:1-26; Jer 33:11
16:35 *r* Dt 32:15; Ps 18:46; 38:22; Mic 7:7
16:36 *s* 1Ki 8:15; Ps 72:18-19
16:37 *t* 2Ch 8:14
16:38 *u* S 1Ch 13:13; 26:4-5 *v* 1Ch 26:10
16:39 *w* S 1Sa 2:35; S 2Sa 8:17; S 1Ch 12:28
x S Jos 9:3; 2Ch 1:3
16:40 *y* S Ex 29:38; Nu 28:1-8
16:41 *z* S 1Ch 15:19
16:42 *a* 2Ch 7:6
b 1Ch 25:3
17:1 *c* S 1Ch 15:1
17:2 *d* 1Ch 22:7; 28:2; 2Ch 6:7
17:4 *e* 1Ch 22:10; 28:3
17:6 *f* S 1Ch 14:1
17:7 *g* S 2Sa 6:21
17:10 *h* S Jdg 2:16

16:39 *tabernacle...in Gibeon.* The tabernacle remained at Gibeon until Solomon's construction of the temple in Jerusalem (2Ch 1:13; 5:5), when it was stored within the temple. The existence of these two shrines—the tabernacle and the temporary structure for the ark in Jerusalem (v. 1)—accounts for the two high priests: Zadok serving in Gibeon and Abiathar in Jerusalem (18:16; 27:34; see note on 6:8).

16:42 *sounding of the trumpets.* See Nu 10:1–10.

17:1–27 See 2Sa 7 and notes.

17:1,10 In these verses the Chronicler omits the statement that David had rest from his enemies (2Sa 7:1,11). Several factors may be at work in this omission: 1. The account of David's

major wars is yet to come (chs. 18–20). Chronologically, this passage should follow the account of the wars (v. 8), but the author has placed it here to continue his concern with the ark and the building of the temple (vv. 4–6,12). 2. The Chronicler also views David as a man of war through most of his life (22:6–8), in contrast to Solomon, who is the man of "peace and rest" (22:9) and who will build the temple (22:10). For the Chronicler, David has rest from enemies only late in his life (22:18). 3. As part of his concern to parallel David and Solomon to Moses and Joshua, Solomon (like Joshua) brings the people to rest from enemies (see Introduction: Portrait of David and Solomon).

17:12 *i* S 1Ki 5:5
j 1Ch 22:10; 2Ch 7:18;
13:5
17:13 *k* 2Co 6:18
l 1Ch 28:6; Lk 1:32;
Heb 1:5*
17:14 *m* S 1Ki 2:12;
1Ch 28:5; 29:23;
2Ch 9:8 *n* Ps 132:11;
Jer 33:17
17:19 *v* 2Sa 7:16-17;
2Ki 20:6; Isa 9:7;
37:35; 55:3
p S 2Sa 7:25
17:20 *q* S Ex 8:10;
S 9:14; S 15:11;
Isa 44:6; 46:9
17:21 *r* S Ex 6:6
17:22 *s* Ex 19:5-6
17:23 *t* S 1Ki 8:25
17:27 *u* Ps 16:11;
21:6
18:2 *v* S Nu 21:29
18:3 *w* 1Ch 19:6
x S Ge 2:14

build *i* a house for me, and I will establish his throne forever. *j* [13]I will be his father, *k* and he will be my son. *l* I will never take my love away from him, as I took it away from your predecessor. [14]I will set him over my house and my kingdom forever; his throne *m* will be established forever. *n* ' "

[15]Nathan reported to David all the words of this entire revelation.

DAVID'S PRAYER
17:16–27pp — 2Sa 7:18–29

[16]Then King David went in and sat before the LORD, and he said:

"Who am I, LORD God, and what is my family, that you have brought me this far? [17]And as if this were not enough in your sight, my God, you have spoken about the future of the house of your servant. You, LORD God, have looked on me as though I were the most exalted of men.

[18]"What more can David say to you for honoring your servant? For you know your servant, [19]LORD. For the sake *o* of your servant and according to your will, you have done this great thing and made known all these great promises. *p*

[20]"There is no one like you, LORD, and there is no God but you, *q* as we have heard with our own ears. [21]And who is like your people Israel—the one nation on earth whose God went out to redeem *r* a people for himself, and to make a name for yourself, and to perform great and awesome wonders by driving out nations from before your people, whom you redeemed from Egypt? [22]You made your people Israel your very own forever, *s* and you, LORD, have become their God.

[23]"And now, LORD, let the promise *t* you have made concerning your servant and his house be established forever. Do as you promised, [24]so that it will be established and that your name will be great forever. Then people will say, 'The LORD Almighty, the God over Israel, is Israel's God!' And the house of your servant David will be established before you.

[25]"You, my God, have revealed to your servant that you will build a house for him. So your servant has found courage to pray to you. [26]You, LORD, are God! You have promised these good things to your servant. [27]Now you have been pleased to bless the house of your servant, that it may continue forever in your sight; *u* for you, LORD, have blessed it, and it will be blessed forever."

DAVID'S VICTORIES
18:1–13pp — 2Sa 8:1–14

18 In the course of time, David defeated the Philistines and subdued them, and he took Gath and its surrounding villages from the control of the Philistines. [2]David also defeated the Moabites, *v* and they became subject to him and brought him tribute.

[3]Moreover, David defeated Hadadezer king of Zobah, *w* in the vicinity of Hamath, when he went to set up his monument at *a* the Euphrates River. *x* [4]David captured a thousand

---

a 3 Or *to restore his control over*

17:12–14 Though in this context these words refer to Solomon, the NT applies them to Jesus (Mk 1:11; Lk 1:32–33; Heb 1:5).

17:13 The Chronicler omits from his source (2Sa 7:14) any reference to "punish him with a rod" or "floggings" as discipline for Solomon. This omission reflects his idealization of Solomon as a Messianic figure, for whom such punishment would not be appropriate (see Introduction: Portrait of David and Solomon).

17:14 The Chronicler introduces his own concerns by the changes in the pronouns found in his source (2Sa 7:16); instead of "your house and your kingdom," the Chronicler reads "my house and my kingdom." This same emphasis on theocracy (God's rule) is found in several other passages unique to Chronicles (28:5–6; 29:23; 2Ch 1:11; 9:8; 13:4–8).

17:16 *sat.* Aside from its parallel in 2Sa 7:18, the only other reference in the OT to sitting as a posture for prayer is 1Ki 19:4.

17:21–22 The references to the exodus from Egypt would remind the Chronicler's audience of the second great exodus, the release of the restoration community from the period of Babylonian exile.

18:1—20:8 The accounts of David's wars serve to show the blessing of God on his reign; God keeps his promise to subdue David's enemies (17:10). These accounts are also particularly relevant to a theme developed in the postexilic prophets: that the silver and gold of the nations would flow to Jerusalem; the tribute of enemy peoples builds the temple of God (18:7–8,11; 22:2–5,14–15; cf. Hag 2:1–9,20–23; Zec 2:7–13; 6:9–15; 14:12–14). While this passage of Chronicles portrays God's blessing on David, it simultaneously explains the Chronicler's report later (22:6–8; 28:3) that David could not build the temple because he was a man of war. The material in these chapters essentially follows the Chronicler's source in 2 Samuel. The major differences are not changes the Chronicler introduces into the text, but items he chooses not to deal with—in particular 2Sa 9; 11:2—12:25, where accounts not compatible with his portrait of David occur.

18:1–13 See 2Sa 8:1–14 and notes.

18:2 The Chronicler omits the harsh treatment of the Moabites recorded in 2Sa 8:2, perhaps so that no unnecessary cruelty or brutality would tarnish his portrait of David.

of his chariots, seven thousand charioteers and twenty thousand foot soldiers. He hamstrung[y] all but a hundred of the chariot horses.

⁵When the Arameans of Damascus[z] came to help Hadadezer king of Zobah, David struck down twenty-two thousand of them. ⁶He put garrisons in the Aramean kingdom of Damascus, and the Arameans became subject to him and brought him tribute. The Lᴏʀᴅ gave David victory wherever he went.

⁷David took the gold shields carried by the officers of Hadadezer and brought them to Jerusalem. ⁸From Tebah[a] and Kun, towns that belonged to Hadadezer, David took a great quantity of bronze, which Solomon used to make the bronze Sea, [a] the pillars and various bronze articles.

⁹When Tou king of Hamath heard that David had defeated the entire army of Hadadezer king of Zobah, ¹⁰he sent his son Hadoram to King David to greet him and congratulate him on his victory in battle over Hadadezer, who had been at war with Tou. Hadoram brought all kinds of articles of gold, of silver and of bronze.

¹¹King David dedicated these articles to the Lᴏʀᴅ, as he had done with the silver and gold he had taken from all these nations: Edom[b] and Moab, the Ammonites and the Philistines, and Amalek.[c]

¹²Abishai son of Zeruiah struck down eighteen thousand Edomites[d] in the Valley of Salt. ¹³He put garrisons in Edom, and all the Edomites became subject to David. The Lᴏʀᴅ gave David victory wherever he went.

DAVID'S OFFICIALS

18:14–17pp — 2Sa 8:15–18

¹⁴David reigned[e] over all Israel, [f] doing what was just and right for all his people. ¹⁵Joab[g] son of Zeruiah was over the army; Jehoshaphat son of Ahilud was recorder; ¹⁶Zadok[h] son of Ahitub and Ahimelek[b][i] son of Abiathar were priests; Shavsha was secretary; ¹⁷Benaiah son of Jehoiada was over the Kerethites and Pelethites;[j] and David's sons were chief officials at the king's side.

DAVID DEFEATS THE AMMONITES

19:1–19pp — 2Sa 10:1–19

19 In the course of time, Nahash king of the Ammonites[k] died, and his son succeeded him as king. ²David thought, "I will show kindness to Hanun son of Nahash, because his father showed kindness to me." So David sent a delegation to express his sympathy to Hanun concerning his father.

When David's envoys came to Hanun in the land of the Ammonites to express sympathy to him, ³the Ammonite commanders said to Hanun, "Do you think David is honoring your father by sending envoys to you to express sympathy? Haven't his envoys come to

---

[a] 8 Hebrew *Tibhath*, a variant of *Tebah*   [b] 16 Some Hebrew manuscripts, Vulgate and Syriac (see also 2 Samuel 8:17); most Hebrew manuscripts *Abimelek*

18:4 ʸS Ge 49:6
18:5 ᶻ2Ki 16:9
18:8 ᵃS 1Ki 7:23; 2Ch 4:2-5
18:11 ᵇS Nu 24:18
ᶜNu 24:20
18:12 ᵈ1Ki 11:15
18:14 ᵉ1Ch 29:26
ᶠ1Ch 11:1
18:15 ᵍ2Sa 5:6-8
18:16 ʰ1Ch 6:8
ⁱ1Ch 24:6
18:17 ʲS 1Sa 30:14; S 2Sa 15:18
19:1 ᵏS Ge 19:38; Jdg 10:17–11:33; 2Ch 20:1-2; Zep 2:8-11

18:5 *Arameans.* Mentioned also among the enemies of Saul (1Sa 14:47, "Zobah"). By the time of David they were united north (Zobah) and south (Beth Rehob, 2Sa 10:6) under Hadadezer. They persisted as a foe of Israel for two centuries until they fell to Assyria shortly before the northern kingdom likewise fell (2Ki 16:7–9). See note on Dt 26:5.

18:8 *Tebah and Kun.* Located in the valley between the Lebanon and Anti-Lebanon mountain ranges. *which Solomon used to make . . . various bronze articles.* See 2Ch 4:2–5,18.

18:12 *Abishai.* 2Sa 8:13 speaks only of David (see 1Ki 11:15–16; Ps 60 title).

18:15–17 The titles and duties of these officers at David's court appear to be modeled on the organization of Egyptian functionaries serving the pharaoh.

18:15 For the account of how Joab attained his position over the army, see 11:4–6; 2Sa 5:6–8.

18:16 *Zadok . . . Ahimelek son of Abiathar.* See notes on 6:8; 16:39; 2Sa 8:17.

18:17 *Kerethites and Pelethites.* A group of foreign mercenaries who constituted part of the royal bodyguard (2Sa 8:18; 20:23; see note on 1Sa 30:14). They remained loyal to David at the time of the rebellions of Absalom (2Sa 15:18) and Sheba (2Sa 20:7) and

supported the succession of Solomon against his rival Adonijah (1Ki 1:38,44). *chief officials.* The earlier narrative at this point uses the Hebrew term ordinarily translated "priests" (see 2Sa 8:18 and note). The Chronicler has used a term for civil service instead of sacral service. Two approaches to this passage are usually followed: 1. Some interpreters see here an attempt by the Chronicler to keep the priesthood restricted to the Levitical line as part of his larger concern with legitimacy of religious institutions in his own day. 2. Others argue that the Hebrew term used in 2Sa 8:18 could earlier have had a broader meaning than "priest" and could be used of some other types of officials (cf. 2Sa 20:26; 1Ki 4:5). The Chronicler used an equivalent term, since by his day the Hebrew term for "priest" was restricted to priestly functionaries.

19:1—20:3 The Chronicler follows 2Sa 10–12 closely (see notes there), apart from his omission of the account of David's sin with Bathsheba (11:2—12:25). The Ammonites were a traditional enemy of Israel (2Ch 20:1–2,23; 27:5; Jdg 3:13; 10:7–9; 10:17—11:33; 1Sa 11:1–13; 14:47; 2Ki 10:32–33; Jer 49:1–6; Zep 2:8–11). Even during the postexilic period Tobiah the Ammonite troubled Jerusalem (Ne 2:19; 4:3,7; 6:1,12,14; 13:4–9).

19:1 *Nahash.* Possibly the same as Saul's foe (1Sa 11:1), or perhaps his descendant.

19:3 *¹* S Nu 21:32
19:6 *ᵐ* S Ge 34:30
ⁿ S 1Ch 18:3
19:7 *ᵒ* S Nu 21:30
19:11 *ᵖ* S 1Sa 26:6
19:17 *ᵩ* S 1Ch 9:1
20:1 *ʳ* S Dt 3:11
ˢ Am 1:13-15
20:3 *ᵗ* S Dt 29:11
20:4 *ᵘ* Jos 10:33

you only to explore and spy out *¹* the country and overthrow it?" *⁴* So Hanun seized David's envoys, shaved them, cut off their garments at the buttocks, and sent them away.

⁵ When someone came and told David about the men, he sent messengers to meet them, for they were greatly humiliated. The king said, "Stay at Jericho till your beards have grown, and then come back."

⁶ When the Ammonites realized that they had become obnoxious *ᵐ* to David, Hanun and the Ammonites sent a thousand talents *ᵃ* of silver to hire chariots and charioteers from Aram Naharaim, *ᵇ* Aram Maakah and Zobah. *ⁿ* *⁷* They hired thirty-two thousand chariots and charioteers, as well as the king of Maakah with his troops, who came and camped near Medeba, *ᵒ* while the Ammonites were mustered from their towns and moved out for battle.

⁸ On hearing this, David sent Joab out with the entire army of fighting men. *⁹* The Ammonites came out and drew up in battle formation at the entrance to their city, while the kings who had come were by themselves in the open country.

¹⁰ Joab saw that there were battle lines in front of him and behind him; so he selected some of the best troops in Israel and deployed them against the Arameans. *¹¹* He put the rest of the men under the command of Abishai *ᵖ* his brother, and they were deployed against the Ammonites. *¹²* Joab said, "If the Arameans are too strong for me, then you are to rescue me; but if the Ammonites are too strong for you, then I will rescue you. *¹³* Be strong, and let us fight bravely for our people and the cities of our God. The Lᴏʀᴅ will do what is good in his sight."

¹⁴ Then Joab and the troops with him advanced to fight the Arameans, and they fled before him. *¹⁵* When the Ammonites realized that the Arameans were fleeing, they too fled before his brother Abishai and went inside the city. So Joab went back to Jerusalem.

¹⁶ After the Arameans saw that they had been routed by Israel, they sent messengers and had Arameans brought from beyond the Euphrates River, with Shophak the commander of Hadadezer's army leading them.

¹⁷ When David was told of this, he gathered all Israel *ᵩ* and crossed the Jordan; he advanced against them and formed his battle lines opposite them. David formed his lines to meet the Arameans in battle, and they fought against him. *¹⁸* But they fled before Israel, and David killed seven thousand of their charioteers and forty thousand of their foot soldiers. He also killed Shophak the commander of their army.

¹⁹ When the vassals of Hadadezer saw that they had been routed by Israel, they made peace with David and became subject to him.

So the Arameans were not willing to help the Ammonites anymore.

THE CAPTURE OF RABBAH

20:1–3pp — 2Sa 11:1; 12:29–31

20 In the spring, at the time when kings go off to war, Joab led out the armed forces. He laid waste the land of the Ammonites and went to Rabbah *ʳ* and besieged it, but David remained in Jerusalem. Joab attacked Rabbah and left it in ruins. *ˢ* *²* David took the crown from the head of their king *ᶜ* —its weight was found to be a talent *ᵈ* of gold, and it was set with precious stones—and it was placed on David's head. He took a great quantity of plunder from the city *³* and brought out the people who were there, consigning them to labor with saws and with iron picks and axes. *ᵗ* David did this to all the Ammonite towns. Then David and his entire army returned to Jerusalem.

WAR WITH THE PHILISTINES

20:4–8pp — 2Sa 21:15–22

⁴ In the course of time, war broke out with the Philistines, at Gezer. *ᵘ* At that time

---

ᵃ 6 That is, about 38 tons or about 34 metric tons   *ᵇ 6* That is, Northwest Mesopotamia   *ᶜ 2* Or *of Milkom, that is, Molek*   *ᵈ 2* That is, about 75 pounds or about 34 kilograms

---

19:6 *Aram Naharaim, Aram Maakah and Zobah.* 2Sa 10:6 also mentions Beth Rehob and Tob. All these states were north and northeast of Israel and formed a solid block from the region of Lake Huleh through the Anti-Lebanon mountains to beyond the Euphrates.

19:7 *Medeba.* A town in Moab apparently in the hands of the Ammonites.

19:9 *their city.* The capital city, Rabbah, to which Joab would lay siege the following year (20:1–3).

19:18 *seven thousand.* 2Sa 10:18 has 700, which may be a copyist's mistake.

20:1 *when kings go off to war.* Immediately following the spring harvest when there was some relaxation of agricultural labors and armies on the move could live off the land. *Rabbah.* See note on 19:9. Rabbah is the site of modern Amman, Jordan.

20:2–3 The Chronicler assumes that the reader is familiar with 2Sa 12:26–29; he does not offer an explanation of how David, who had remained in Jerusalem (v. 1), came to be at Rabbah.

Sibbekai the Hushathite killed Sippai, one of the descendants of the Rephaites, *v* and the Philistines were subjugated.

5In another battle with the Philistines, Elhanan son of Jair killed Lahmi the brother of Goliath the Gittite, who had a spear with a shaft like a weaver's rod. *w*

6In still another battle, which took place at Gath, there was a huge man with six fingers on each hand and six toes on each foot—twenty-four in all. He also was descended from Rapha. 7When he taunted Israel, Jonathan son of Shimea, David's brother, killed him.

8These were descendants of Rapha in Gath, and they fell at the hands of David and his men.

DAVID COUNTS THE FIGHTING MEN

21:1–26pp — 2Sa 24:1–25

21 Satan *x* rose up against Israel and incited David to take a census *y* of Israel. 2So David said to Joab and the commanders of the troops, "Go and count *z* the Israelites from Beersheba to Dan. Then report back to me so that I may know how many there are."

3But Joab replied, "May the LORD multiply his troops a hundred times over. *a* My lord the king, are they not all my lord's subjects? Why does my lord want to do this? Why should he bring guilt on Israel?"

4The king's word, however, overruled Joab; so Joab left and went throughout Israel and then came back to Jerusalem. 5Joab reported the number of the fighting men to David: In all Israel *b* there were one million one hundred thousand men who could handle a sword, including four hundred and seventy thousand in Judah.

6But Joab did not include Levi and Benjamin in the numbering, because the king's command was repulsive to him. 7This command was also evil in the sight of God; so he punished Israel.

8Then David said to God, "I have sinned greatly by doing this. Now, I beg you, take away the guilt of your servant. I have done a very foolish thing."

9The LORD said to Gad, *c* David's seer, *d* 10"Go and tell David, 'This is what the LORD says: I am giving you three options. Choose one of them for me to carry out against you.' "

11So Gad went to David and said to him, "This is what the LORD says: 'Take your choice: 12three years of famine, *e* three months of being swept away*a* before your enemies, with their swords overtaking you, or three days of the sword *f* of the LORD *g*—days of plague in the land, with the angel of the LORD ravaging every part of Israel.' Now then, decide how I should answer the one who sent me."

13David said to Gad, "I am in deep distress. Let me fall into the hands of the LORD, for his mercy *h* is very great; but do not let me fall into human hands."

14So the LORD sent a plague on Israel, and seventy thousand men of Israel fell dead. *i* 15And God sent an angel*j* to destroy Jerusalem. *k* But as the angel was doing so, the LORD

a 12 Hebrew; Septuagint and Vulgate (see also 2 Samuel 24:13) *of fleeing*

20:4 *v* S Ge 14:5
20:5 *w* S 1Sa 17:7
21:1 *x* S 2Ch 18:21;
S Ps 109:6 *y* 2Ch 14:8;
25:5
21:2 *z* 1Ch 27:23-24
21:3 *a* S Dt 1:11
21:5 *b* S 1Ch 9:1
21:9 *c* S 1Sa 22:5
d S 1Sa 9:9
21:12 *e* S Dt 32:24
f Eze 30:25
g S Ge 19:13
21:13 *h* Ps 6:4;
86:15; 130:4,7
21:14 *i* 1Ch 27:24
21:15 *j* S Ge 32:1
k Ps 125:2

20:4 *Sibbekai.* See 11:29; 27:11. *Rephaites.* Ancient people known for their large size (see Ge 14:5; Dt 2:10–11; see also note on 2Sa 21:16).

20:5 See note on 2Sa 21:19. *weaver's rod.* See 11:23; 1Sa 17:7.

20:6 *Rapha.* See note on 2Sa 21:16.

21:1—22:1 See 2Sa 24 and notes. Although the story of David's census is quite similar in both narratives, the two accounts function differently. In Samuel the account belongs to the appendix (2Sa 21–24), which begins and ends with accounts of the Lord's anger against Israel during the reign of David because of actions by her kings (in ch. 21, an act of Saul; in ch. 24, an act of David). See note on 2Sa 21:1—24:25. The Chronicler appears to include it in order to account for the purchase of the ground on which the temple would be built. The additional material in Chronicles that is not found in Samuel (21:28—22:1) makes this interest clear. The census is the preface to David's preparations for the temple (chs. 22–29).

21:1 See note on 2Sa 24:1. *Satan.* See TNIV text notes on Job 1:6; Zec 3:1; see also notes on Mt 16:23; 2Co 4:4; 1Th 3:5; 1Jn 3:8.

21:4 The Chronicler abridges the more extensive account of Joab's itinerary found in 2Sa 24:4–8; he does not mention that the census required nine months and 20 days (2Sa 24:8).

21:5 *In all Israel . . . one million one hundred thousand men . . . including four hundred and seventy thousand in Judah.* 2Sa 24:9 has 800,000 in Israel and 500,000 (which could be a round number for 470,000) in Judah. The reason for the difference is unclear. Perhaps it is to be related to the unofficial and incomplete nature of the census (see 27:23–24), with the differing figures representing the inclusion or exclusion of certain unspecified groupings among the people (see v. 6). Or perhaps it is simply due to a copyist's mistake. The TNIV relieves the problem somewhat by translating the conjunction here as "including" instead of "and." See note on 12:23–37; see also Introduction to Numbers: Special Problem.

21:6 The Chronicler adds the note that Joab exempted Levi and Benjamin from the counting. This additional note reflects the Chronicler's concern with the Levites and with the worship of Israel. The tabernacle in Gibeon and the ark in Jerusalem both fell within the borders of Benjamin.

21:9 *Gad.* A longtime friend of David, having been with him when he was a fugitive from Saul (1Sa 22:3–5; cf. 1Ch 29:29; 2Ch 29:25).

21:12 *three years of famine.* See TNIV text note on 2Sa 24:13.

21:15 ʲS Ge 6:6;
S Ex 32:14
ᵐS Ge 19:13
21:16 ⁿS Nu 14:5;
S Jos 7:6
21:17 ᵒS 2Sa 7:8
ᵖJnh 1:12
21:18 ᑫ2Ch 3:1
21:20 ʳS Jdg 6:11
21:26 ˢS Ex 19:18;
S Jdg 6:21
21:29 ᵗS Jos 9:3
22:1 ᵘS Ge 28:17
22:2 ᵛS Ex 1:11;
S Dt 20:11; 2Ch 8:10;
S Isa 56:6 ʷ1Ki 5:17-
18; Ezr 3:7

saw it and relented ʲ concerning the disaster and said to the angel who was destroying ᵐ the people, "Enough! Withdraw your hand." The angel of the LORD was then standing at the threshing floor of Araunah ᵃ the Jebusite.

¹⁶David looked up and saw the angel of the LORD standing between heaven and earth, with a drawn sword in his hand extended over Jerusalem. Then David and the elders, clothed in sackcloth, fell facedown. ⁿ

¹⁷David said to God, "Was it not I who ordered the fighting men to be counted? I, the shepherd, ᵇ have sinned and done wrong. These are but sheep. ᵒ What have they done? LORD my God, let your hand fall on me and my family, ᵖ but do not let this plague remain on your people."

DAVID BUILDS AN ALTAR

¹⁸Then the angel of the LORD ordered Gad to tell David to go up and build an altar to the LORD on the threshing floor ᑫ of Araunah the Jebusite. ¹⁹So David went up in obedience to the word that Gad had spoken in the name of the LORD.

²⁰While Araunah was threshing wheat, ʳ he turned and saw the angel; his four sons who were with him hid themselves. ²¹Then David approached, and when Araunah looked and saw him, he left the threshing floor and bowed down before David with his face to the ground.

²²David said to him, "Let me have the site of your threshing floor so I can build an altar to the LORD, that the plague on the people may be stopped. Sell it to me at the full price."

²³Araunah said to David, "Take it! Let my lord the king do whatever pleases him. Look, I will give the oxen for the burnt offerings, the threshing sledges for the wood, and the wheat for the grain offering. I will give all this."

²⁴But King David replied to Araunah, "No, I insist on paying the full price. I will not take for the LORD what is yours, or sacrifice a burnt offering that costs me nothing."

²⁵So David paid Araunah six hundred shekels ᶜ of gold for the site. ²⁶David built an altar to the LORD there and sacrificed burnt offerings and fellowship offerings. He called on the LORD, and the LORD answered him with fire ˢ from heaven on the altar of burnt offering.

²⁷Then the LORD spoke to the angel, and he put his sword back into its sheath. ²⁸At that time, when David saw that the LORD had answered him on the threshing floor of Araunah the Jebusite, he offered sacrifices there. ²⁹The tabernacle of the LORD, which Moses had made in the wilderness, and the altar of burnt offering were at that time on the high place at Gibeon. ᵗ ³⁰But David could not go before it to inquire of God, because he was afraid of the sword of the angel of the LORD.

22

Then David said, "The house of the LORD God ᵘ is to be here, and also the altar of burnt offering for Israel."

PREPARATIONS FOR THE TEMPLE

²So David gave orders to assemble the foreigners ᵛ residing in Israel, and from among them he appointed stonecutters ʷ to prepare dressed stone for building the house of God.

ᵃ 15 Hebrew *Ornan*, a variant of *Araunah*; also in verses 18-28   ᵇ 17 Probable reading of the original Hebrew text (see 2 Samuel 24:17 and footnote); Masoretic Text does not have *the shepherd*.   ᶜ 25 That is, about 15 pounds or about 6.9 kilograms

---

21:20–21 The Chronicler reports that Araunah was threshing wheat as the king approached—information not found in 2Sa 24:20. However, Josephus and a fragmentary text of Samuel from Qumran both mention this information.

21:25 *six hundred shekels of gold.* 2Sa 24:24 says 50 shekels of silver were paid for the threshing floor and oxen. The difference has been explained by some as the Chronicler's attempt to glorify David and the temple by inflating the price. However, the difference is more likely explained by the Chronicler's statement that this was the price for the "site," i.e., for a much larger area than the threshing floor alone.

21:26 *fire from heaven.* Underscores the divine approval and the sanctity of the site (see 2Ch 7:1; Lev 9:24; 1Ki 18:37–38).

21:28—22:1 This material is not found in 2Sa 24. It reflects the Chronicler's main concern in reporting this narrative (see note on 21:1—22:1).

21:30 *it.* The tabernacle.

22:1—29:30 This material is unique to Chronicles and displays some of the Chronicler's most characteristic interests: the preparations for the building of the temple, the legitimacy of the priests and Levites, and the royal succession. The chapters portray a theocratic "Messianic" kingdom as it existed under David and Solomon.

22:1 David dedicates this property (21:18–30) as the site for the temple (see vv. 2–6; see also note on Ps 30 title).

22:2–19 Solomon's appointment to succeed David was twofold: (1) a private audience, with David and some leaders in attendance (vv. 17–19), and (2) a public announcement to the people (ch. 28), similar to when Joshua succeeded Moses (see Introduction: Portrait of David and Solomon).

22:2 *foreigners...stonecutters.* 2Sa 20:24 confirms the use of forced labor by David but does not specify that these laborers were foreigners, not Israelites. Solomon used Israelites in conscripted labor (1Ki 5:13–18; 9:15–23; 11:28), but the Chronicler mentions only his use of foreigners (2Ch 8:7–10). Though they

³He provided a large amount of iron to make nails for the doors of the gateways and for the fittings, and more bronze than could be weighed. ˣ ⁴He also provided more cedar logs ʸ than could be counted, for the Sidonians and Tyrians had brought large numbers of them to David.

⁵David said, "My son Solomon is young ᶻ and inexperienced, and the house to be built for the LORD should be of great magnificence and fame and splendor ᵃ in the sight of all the nations. Therefore I will make preparations for it." So David made extensive preparations before his death.

⁶Then he called for his son Solomon and charged him to build ᵇ a house for the LORD, the God of Israel. ⁷David said to Solomon: "My son, I had it in my heart ᶜ to build ᵈ a house for the Name ᵉ of the LORD my God. ⁸But this word of the LORD came to me: 'You have shed much blood and have fought many wars. ᶠ You are not to build a house for my Name, ᵍ because you have shed much blood on the earth in my sight. ⁹But you will have a son who will be a man of peace ʰ and rest, ⁱ and I will give him rest from all his enemies on every side. His name will be Solomon, ᵃ ʲ and I will grant Israel peace and quiet ᵏ during his reign. ¹⁰He is the one who will build a house for my Name. ˡ He will be my son, ᵐ and I will be his father. And I will establish ⁿ the throne of his kingdom over Israel forever.' ᵒ

¹¹"Now, my son, the LORD be with ᵖ you, and may you have success and build the house of the LORD your God, as he said you would. ¹²May the LORD give you discretion and understanding �q when he puts you in command over Israel, so that you may keep the law of the LORD your God. ¹³Then you will have success ʳ if you are careful to observe the decrees and laws ˢ that the LORD gave Moses for Israel. Be strong and courageous. ᵗ Do not be afraid or discouraged.

¹⁴"I have taken great pains to provide for the temple of the LORD a hundred thousand talents ᵇ of gold, a million talents ᶜ of silver, quantities of bronze and iron too great to be weighed, and wood and stone. And you may add to them. ᵘ ¹⁵You have many workers: stonecutters, masons and carpenters, ᵛ as well as those skilled in every kind of work ¹⁶in gold and silver, bronze and iron—skilled workers ʷ beyond number. Now begin the work, and the LORD be with you."

¹⁷Then David ordered ˣ all the leaders of Israel to help his son Solomon. ¹⁸He said to them, "Is not the LORD your God with you? And has he not granted you rest ʸ on every side? ᶻ For he has given the inhabitants of the land into my hands, and the land is subject to the LORD and to his people. ¹⁹Now devote your heart and soul to seeking the LORD your God. ᵃ Begin to build the sanctuary of the LORD God, so that you may bring the ark of the covenant of the LORD and the sacred articles belonging to God into the temple that will be built for the Name of the LORD."

THE LEVITES

23

When David was old and full of years, he made his son Solomon ᵇ king over Israel. ᶜ
²He also gathered together all the leaders of Israel, as well as the priests and Levites. ³The Levites thirty years old or more ᵈ were counted, ᵉ and the total number of

---

ᵃ 9 *Solomon* sounds like and may be derived from the Hebrew for *peace.* ᵇ 14 That is, about 3,750 tons or about 3,400 metric tons ᶜ 14 That is, about 37,500 tons or about 34,000 metric tons

---

22:3 ˣ S 1Ki 7:47; 1Ch 29:2-5
22:4 ʸ S 1Ki 5:6
22:5 ᶻ S 1Ki 3:7; 1Ch 29:1 ᵃ 2Ch 2:5
22:6 ᵇ Ac 7:47
22:7 ᶜ S 1Ch 17:2 ᵈ S 1Ki 8:17 ᵉ Dt 12:5, 11
22:8 ᶠ S 1Ki 5:3 ᵍ 1Ch 28:3
22:9 ʰ S Jos 14:15; S 1Ki 5:4 ⁱ ver 18; 1Ch 23:25; 2Ch 14:6, 7; 15:15; 20:30; 36:21 ʲ S 2Sa 12:24; S 1Ch 23:1 ᵏ 1Ki 4:20
22:10 ˡ S 1Ch 17:12 ᵐ S 2Sa 7:13 ⁿ 1Ki 9:5 ᵒ S 2Sa 7:14; S 1Ch 17:4; 2Ch 6:15
22:11 ᵖ S 1Sa 16:18; S 18:12
22:12 q 1Ki 3:9-12
22:13 ʳ 1Ki 2:3 ˢ 1Ch 28:7 ᵗ S Dt 31:6
22:14 ᵘ 1Ch 29:2-5, 19
22:15 ᵛ Ezr 3:7
22:16 ʷ 2Ch 2:7
22:17 ˣ 1Ch 28:1-6
22:18 ʸ S ver 9 ᶻ 2Sa 7:1
22:19 ᵃ 2Ch 7:14
23:1 ᵇ 1Ch 22:9; 28:5; 2Ch 1:8 ᶜ S 1Ki 1:30; 1Ch 29:28
23:3 ᵈ Nu 8:24 ᵉ 1Ch 21:7

---

were personally free, foreigners were without political rights and could be easily exploited. The OT frequently warns that they were not to be oppressed (Ex 22:21; 23:9; Lev 19:33; Dt 24:14; Jer 7:6; Zec 7:10). Isaiah prophesies the participation of foreigners in the building of Jerusalem's walls in the future (Isa 60:10–12).
22:3 *bronze.* See note on 18:8.
22:5 *young.* Solomon's age at the time of his accession is not known with certainty. He came to the throne in 970 B.C. and was likely born c. 991.
22:7 *house for the Name.* See 1Ki 3:2 and note.
22:8–9 See note on 17:1. In 1Ki 5:3 Solomon explains that David could not build the temple because he was too busy with wars. The Chronicler's nuance is slightly different—not just that wars took so much of his time but that David was in some sense defiled by them because of the bloodshed. A pun on Solomon's name is woven into the divine oracle (see TNIV text note on v. 9).
22:10 See note on 17:12–14.
22:12–13 See Introduction: Portrait of David and Solomon.
22:19 *bring the ark ... into the temple.* See 2Ch 5:2–7.

23:1—27:34 David's preparations for the temple were not restricted to amassing materials for the building; he also arranged for its administration and worship. Unique to Chronicles (see note on 22:1—29:30), these details of the organization of the theocracy (God's kingdom) were of vital concern in the Chronicler's own day. Characteristically for the Chronicler, details about religious and sacred matters (chs. 23–26) take precedence over those that are civil and secular (ch. 27). David's arrangements provided the basis and authority for the practices of the restored community.
23:1 *made his son Solomon king.* The account of Solomon's succession is resumed in chs. 28–29. The Chronicler omits the accounts of disputed succession and bloody consolidation recorded in 1Ki 1–2 (see note on 28:1—29:30) since these would not be in accord with his overall portrait of David and Solomon (see Introduction: Portrait of David and Solomon).
23:2–5 The Levites were not counted in the census that had provoked the wrath of God (21:6–7).
23:3 *Levites thirty years old or more.* The census of Levites was

23:3 *r* Nu 4:3-49
23:4 *g* Ezr 3:8
h 2Ch 34:13; Ne 4:10
i 1Ch 26:29; 2Ch 19:8;
Eze 44:24
23:5 *j* S 1Ch 15:16;
Ps 92:3 *k* Ne 12:45
23:6 *l* 2Ch 8:14;
23:18; 29:25
m Nu 3:17;
1Ch 24:20
23:7 *n* 1Ch 6:71
23:12 *o* S Ge 46:11;
S Ex 6:18
23:13 *p* Ex 6:20
q Ex 30:7-10
r S 1Ch 15:2
s S Nu 6:23
23:14 *t* Dt 33:1
23:15 *u* Ex 18:4
23:16 *v* 1Ch 26:24-
28
23:17 *w* 1Ch 24:21
23:18 *x* 1Ch 26:25
23:19 *y* 1Ch 24:23;
26:31
23:21 *z* S 1Ch 6:19
a S Ex 6:19
23:22 *b* Nu 36:8

men was thirty-eight thousand. [f] [4]David said, "Of these, twenty-four thousand are to be in charge[g] of the work[h] of the temple of the LORD and six thousand are to be officials and judges.[i] [5]Four thousand are to be gatekeepers and four thousand are to praise the LORD with the musical instruments[j] I have provided for that purpose."[k]

[6]David separated[l] the Levites into divisions corresponding to the sons of Levi:[m] Gershon, Kohath and Merari.

GERSHONITES

[7]Belonging to the Gershonites:[n]
Ladan and Shimei.
[8]The sons of Ladan:
Jehiel the first, Zetham and Joel—three in all.
[9]The sons of Shimei:
Shelomoth, Haziel and Haran—three in all.
These were the heads of the families of Ladan.
[10]And the sons of Shimei:
Jahath, Ziza,[a] Jeush and Beriah.
These were the sons of Shimei—four in all.
[11]Jahath was the first and Ziza the second, but Jeush and Beriah did not have many sons; so they were counted as one family with one assignment.

KOHATHITES

[12]The sons of Kohath:[o]
Amram, Izhar, Hebron and Uzziel—four in all.
[13]The sons of Amram:[p]
Aaron and Moses.
Aaron was set apart,[q] he and his descendants forever, to consecrate the most holy things, to offer sacrifices before the LORD, to minister[r] before him and to pronounce blessings[s] in his name forever. [14]The sons of Moses the man[t] of God were counted as part of the tribe of Levi.
[15]The sons of Moses:
Gershom and Eliezer.[u]
[16]The descendants of Gershom:[v]
Shubael was the first.
[17]The descendants of Eliezer:
Rehabiah[w] was the first.
Eliezer had no other sons, but the sons of Rehabiah were very numerous.
[18]The sons of Izhar:
Shelomith[x] was the first.
[19]The sons of Hebron:[y]
Jeriah the first, Amariah the second, Jahaziel the third and Jekameam the fourth.
[20]The sons of Uzziel:
Micah the first and Ishiah the second.

MERARITES

[21]The sons of Merari:[z]
Mahli and Mushi.[a]
The sons of Mahli:
Eleazar and Kish.
[22]Eleazar died without having sons: he had only daughters. Their cousins, the sons of Kish, married them.[b]
[23]The sons of Mushi:
Mahli, Eder and Jerimoth—three in all.

[24]These were the descendants of Levi by their families—the heads of families as they were registered under their names and counted individually, that is, the workers twenty

---

[a] 10 One Hebrew manuscript, Septuagint and Vulgate (see also verse 11); most Hebrew manuscripts Zina

---

made first in accordance with the Mosaic prescription (Nu 4:1–3). Apparently soon after this count, David instructed that the age be lowered to 20 years (vv. 24,27); a similar adjustment to age 25 had been made under Moses (Nu 8:23–24, but see note on 8:24).

23:6 *Gershon, Kohath and Merari.* The Levites were organized by their three clans (ch. 6; Ex 6:16–19; Nu 3). This list parallels those in 6:16–30; 24:20–30.
23:24,27 *twenty years old or more.* See note on v. 3.

years old or more ^{c} who served in the temple of the LORD. ^{25}For David had said, "Since the LORD, the God of Israel, has granted rest ^{d} to his people and has come to dwell in Jerusalem forever, ^{26}the Levites no longer need to carry the tabernacle or any of the articles used in its service." ^{e} ^{27}According to the last instructions of David, the Levites were counted from those twenty years old or more.

^{28}The duty of the Levites was to help Aaron's descendants in the service of the temple of the LORD: to be in charge of the courtyards, the side rooms, the purification ^{f} of all sacred things and the performance of other duties at the house of God. ^{29}They were in charge of the bread set out on the table, ^{g} the special flour for the grain offerings, ^{h} the thin loaves made without yeast, the baking and the mixing, and all measurements of quantity and size. ^{i} ^{30}They were also to stand every morning to thank and praise the LORD. They were to do the same in the evening ^{j} ^{31}and whenever burnt offerings were presented to the LORD on the Sabbaths, at the New Moon ^{k} feasts and at the appointed festivals. ^{l} They were to serve before the LORD regularly in the proper number and in the way prescribed for them.

^{32}And so the Levites ^{m} carried out their responsibilities for the tent of meeting, ^{n} for the Holy Place and, under their relatives the descendants of Aaron, for the service of the temple of the LORD. ^{o}

THE DIVISIONS OF PRIESTS

24 These were the divisions ^{p} of the descendants of Aaron: ^{q} ^{2}The sons of Aaron were Nadab, Abihu, Eleazar and Ithamar. ^{r} ^{2}But Nadab and Abihu died before their father did, ^{s} and they had no sons; so Eleazar and Ithamar served as the priests. ^{3}With the help of Zadok ^{t} a descendant of Eleazar and Ahimelek a descendant of Ithamar, David separated them into divisions for their appointed order of ministering. ^{4}A larger number of leaders were found among Eleazar's descendants than among Ithamar's, and they were divided accordingly: sixteen heads of families from Eleazar's descendants and eight heads of families from Ithamar's descendants. ^{5}They divided them impartially by casting lots, ^{u} for there were officials of the sanctuary and officials of God among the descendants of both Eleazar and Ithamar.

^{6}The scribe Shemaiah son of Nethanel, a Levite, recorded their names in the presence of the king and of the officials: Zadok the priest, Ahimelek ^{v} son of Abiathar and the heads of families of the priests and of the Levites—one family being taken from Eleazar and then one from Ithamar.

^{7}The first lot fell to Jehoiarib,
  the second to Jedaiah, ^{w}
^{8}the third to Harim, ^{x}
  the fourth to Seorim,
^{9}the fifth to Malkijah,
  the sixth to Mijamin,
^{10}the seventh to Hakkoz,
  the eighth to Abijah, ^{y}
^{11}the ninth to Jeshua,
  the tenth to Shekaniah,
^{12}the eleventh to Eliashib,
  the twelfth to Jakim,
^{13}the thirteenth to Huppah,
  the fourteenth to Jeshebeab,
^{14}the fifteenth to Bilgah,

23:24 ^{c} S Nu 4:3
23:25 ^{d} S 1Ch 22:9
23:26 ^{e} Nu 4:5,15; 7:9; Dt 10:8
23:28 ^{f} 2Ch 29:15; Ne 13:9; Mal 3:3
23:29 ^{g} S Ex 25:30 ^{h} Lev 2:4-7; 6:20-23 ^{i} Lev 19:35-36; S 1Ch 9:29,32
23:30 ^{j} S 1Ch 9:33; Ps 134:1
23:31 ^{k} S 2Ki 4:23 ^{l} Nu 28:9–29:39; Isa 1:13-14; Col 2:16
23:32 ^{m} 1Ch 6:48 ^{n} Nu 3:6-8,38 ^{o} 2Ch 23:18; 31:2; Eze 44:14
24:1 ^{p} 1Ch 23:6; 28:13; 2Ch 5:11; 8:14; 23:8; 31:2; 35:4,5; Ezr 6:18 ^{q} Nu 3:2-4 ^{r} S Ex 6:23
24:2 ^{s} Lev 10:1-2
24:3 ^{t} S 2Sa 8:17
24:5 ^{u} ver 31; 1Ch 25:8; 26:13
24:6 ^{v} 1Ch 18:16
24:7 ^{w} Ezr 2:36; Ne 12:6
24:8 ^{x} Ezr 2:39; 10:21; Ne 10:5
24:10 ^{y} Ne 12:4,17; Lk 1:5

23:28–32 See note on 9:28–34. The function of the Levites was to assist the priests. In addition to the care of the precincts and implements, baked goods and music (mentioned as Levitical duties in 9:22–34), the Chronicler adds details on the role of the Levites assisting in sacrifices.
23:30 *morning . . . evening.* See Ex 29:38–41; Nu 28:3–8.
24:1–19 There are several lists of priests from the postexilic period (see 6:3–15; 9:10–13; Ezr 2:36–39; Ne 10:1–8; 11:10–12; 12:1–7,12–21).
24:2 *Nadab and Abihu died.* The Chronicler alludes to the events recorded in Lev 10:1–3 (see note on 6:1–3).
24:3 *Zadok . . . Ahimelek.* Zadok and Abiathar had served as David's high priests. Here, late in David's life, Abiathar's son Ahimelek appears to have taken over some of his father's duties (see note on 6:8), but see note on 2Sa 8:17.

24:4 *sixteen . . . eight.* A total of 24 divisions were selected by lot. This would allow either for service in monthly shifts, as was done by priests in Egyptian mortuary temples, or for two-week shifts once each year as found in NT times. For the names of these divisions, see vv. 7–18. The names of the first, second, fourth, ninth and twenty-fourth divisions also occur in a Dead Sea scroll, and the name of the eighth appears in Lk 1:5. See essay, p. 1595; see also note on Ne 12:7.
24:5 *casting lots.* See notes on Ex 28:30; Jos 7:14; Ne 11:1; Pr 16:33; Jnh 1:7; Ac 1:26.
24:7 *Jehoiarib.* Mattathias, father of the Maccabees, was a member of the Jehoiarib division (in the Apocrypha see 1 Maccabees 2:1).
24:10 *Abijah.* The father of John the Baptist "belonged to the priestly division of Abijah" (Lk 1:5).

24:14 *z* Ezr 2:37;
10:20; Jer 20:1
24:15 *a* Ne 10:20
24:20 *b* S 1Ch 23:6
24:21 *c* 1Ch 23:17
24:23 *d* S 1Ch 23:19
24:26 *e* S 1Ch 6:19
24:31 *f* S ver 5
25:1 *g* S 1Ch 6:39
h S 1Ch 6:33
i 1Ch 16:41,42;
Ne 11:17 *j* S 1Sa 10:5;
2Ki 3:15 *k* S 1Ch 15:16
l S 1Ch 6:31
m 2Ch 5:12; 8:14;
34:12; 35:15; Ezr 3:10
25:3 *n* 1Ch 16:41-42

the sixteenth to Immer, *z*

¹⁵ the seventeenth to Hezir, *a*
the eighteenth to Happizzez,
¹⁶ the nineteenth to Pethahiah,
the twentieth to Jehezkel,
¹⁷ the twenty-first to Jakin,
the twenty-second to Gamul,
¹⁸ the twenty-third to Delaiah
and the twenty-fourth to Maaziah.

¹⁹ This was their appointed order of ministering when they entered the temple of the LORD, according to the regulations prescribed for them by their ancestor Aaron, as the LORD, the God of Israel, had commanded him.

THE REST OF THE LEVITES

²⁰ As for the rest of the descendants of Levi: *b*
from the sons of Amram: Shubael;
from the sons of Shubael: Jehdeiah.
²¹ As for Rehabiah, *c* from his sons:
Ishiah was the first.
²² From the Izharites: Shelomoth;
from the sons of Shelomoth: Jahath.
²³ The sons of Hebron: *d* Jeriah the first,*a* Amariah the second, Jahaziel the third and
Jekameam the fourth.
²⁴ The son of Uzziel: Micah;
from the sons of Micah: Shamir.
²⁵ The brother of Micah: Ishiah;
from the sons of Ishiah: Zechariah.
²⁶ The sons of Merari: *e* Mahli and Mushi.
The son of Jaaziah: Beno.
²⁷ The sons of Merari:
from Jaaziah: Beno, Shoham, Zakkur and Ibri.
²⁸ From Mahli: Eleazar, who had no sons.
²⁹ From Kish: the son of Kish:
Jerahmeel.
³⁰ And the sons of Mushi: Mahli, Eder and Jerimoth.

These were the Levites, according to their families. ³¹ They also cast lots, *f* just as their relatives the descendants of Aaron did, in the presence of King David and of Zadok, Ahimelek, and the heads of families of the priests and of the Levites. The families of the oldest brother were treated the same as those of the youngest.

THE MUSICIANS

25 David, together with the commanders of the army, set apart some of the sons of Asaph, *g* Heman *h* and Jeduthun *i* for the ministry of prophesying,*j* accompanied by harps, lyres and cymbals. *k* Here is the list of the men *l* who performed this service: *m*

² From the sons of Asaph:
Zakkur, Joseph, Nethaniah and Asarelah. The sons of Asaph were under the supervision of Asaph, who prophesied under the king's supervision.
³ As for Jeduthun, from his sons: *n*

a 23 Two Hebrew manuscripts and some Septuagint manuscripts (see also 1 Chron. 23:19); most Hebrew manuscripts *The sons of Jeriah:*

B **24:15** *Hezir.* The division from the family of Hezir was prominent in intertestamental times; the name appears on one of the large tombs in the Kidron Valley, east of Jerusalem.
24:20–31 This list supplements 23:7–23 by extending some of the family lines mentioned there.
25:1 *commanders of the army.* David often sought the counsel of military leaders (11:10; 12:32; 28:1), even in religious matters (13:1; 15:25). *Asaph, Heman and Jeduthun.* See notes on 6:31–48; Ps 39 title. *ministry of prophesying.* There are several passages in Chronicles, largely in portions unique to these

books, where temple personnel are designated prophets (here; 2Ch 20:14–17; 29:30; 35:15; cf. 2Ki 23:2; 2Ch 34:30). Zechariah the priest also appears to function as a prophet, though he is not so named (2Ch 24:19–22). This may reflect postexilic interest in the prophet-priest-king figure of Messianic expectation: In Chronicles not only do priests prophesy, but kings also function as priests (see notes on 15:27; 16:1–3). David's organizing of the temple musicians may reflect his overall interest in music (1Sa 16:23; 18:10; 19:9; 2Sa 1:17–27; 6:5,14).

Gedaliah, Zeri, Jeshaiah, Shimei,[a] Hashabiah and Mattithiah, six in all, under the supervision of their father Jeduthun, who prophesied, using the harp[o] in thanking and praising the LORD.

[4] As for Heman, from his sons:

Bukkiah, Mattaniah, Uzziel, Shubael and Jerimoth; Hananiah, Hanani, Eliathah, Giddalti and Romamti-Ezer; Joshbekashah, Mallothi, Hothir and Mahazioth. [5] (All these were sons of Heman the king's seer. They were given him through the promises of God to exalt him. God gave Heman fourteen sons and three daughters.)

[6] All these men were under the supervision of their father[p] for the music of the temple of the LORD, with cymbals, lyres and harps, for the ministry at the house of God.

Asaph, Jeduthun and Heman[q] were under the supervision of the king.[r] [7] Along with their relatives—all of them trained and skilled in music for the LORD—they numbered 288. [8] Young and old alike, teacher as well as student, cast lots[s] for their duties.

[9] The first lot, which was for Asaph,[t] fell to Joseph,
  his sons and relatives[b] 12[c]
the second to Gedaliah,
  him and his relatives and sons 12
[10] the third to Zakkur,
  his sons and relatives 12
[11] the fourth to Izri,[d]
  his sons and relatives 12
[12] the fifth to Nethaniah,
  his sons and relatives 12
[13] the sixth to Bukkiah,
  his sons and relatives 12
[14] the seventh to Jesarelah,[e]
  his sons and relatives 12
[15] the eighth to Jeshaiah,
  his sons and relatives 12
[16] the ninth to Mattaniah,
  his sons and relatives 12
[17] the tenth to Shimei,
  his sons and relatives 12
[18] the eleventh to Azarel,[f]
  his sons and relatives 12
[19] the twelfth to Hashabiah,
  his sons and relatives 12
[20] the thirteenth to Shubael,
  his sons and relatives 12
[21] the fourteenth to Mattithiah,
  his sons and relatives 12
[22] the fifteenth to Jerimoth,
  his sons and relatives 12
[23] the sixteenth to Hananiah,
  his sons and relatives 12
[24] the seventeenth to Joshbekashah,
  his sons and relatives 12
[25] the eighteenth to Hanani,
  his sons and relatives 12
[26] the nineteenth to Mallothi,
  his sons and relatives 12
[27] the twentieth to Eliathah,
  his sons and relatives 12
[28] the twenty-first to Hothir,
  his sons and relatives 12

25:3 [o] S Ge 4:21; Ps 33:2
25:6 [p] S 1Ch 15:16
[q] S 1Ch 15:19
[r] 2Ch 23:18; 29:25
25:8 [s] 1Ch 26:13
25:9 [t] S 1Ch 6:39

---

[a] 3 One Hebrew manuscript and some Septuagint manuscripts (see also verse 17); most Hebrew manuscripts do not have *Shimei*.   [b] 9 See Septuagint; Hebrew does not have *his sons and relatives*.
[c] 9 See the total in verse 7; Hebrew does not have *twelve*.   [d] 11 A variant of *Zeri*   [e] 14 A variant of *Asarelah*   [f] 18 A variant of *Uzziel*

25:5 *fourteen sons and three daughters.* Numerous progeny are a sign of divine blessing (see Job 1:2; 42:13). This is specifically stated for Heman as the result of the promises of God to exalt him. See 3:1–9; 14:2–7; 26:4–5; 2Ch 11:18–21; 13:21; 21:2; 24:3.

25:31 ᵘS 1Ch 9:33
26:1 ᵛS 1Ch 9:17
26:2 ʷS 1Ch 9:21
26:5 ˣS 2Sa 6:10;
S 1Ch 13:13; S 16:38
26:10 ʸDt 21:16;
1Ch 5:1
26:12 ᶻ1Ch 9:22
26:13 ᵃS 1Ch 24:5,
31; 25:8
26:14 ᵇS 1Ch 9:18
ᶜS 1Ch 9:21
26:15 ᵈS 1Ch 13:13;
2Ch 25:24

29 the twenty-second to Giddalti,
  his sons and relatives   12
30 the twenty-third to Mahazioth,
  his sons and relatives   12
31 the twenty-fourth to Romamti-Ezer,
  his sons and relatives   12. ᵘ

THE GATEKEEPERS

26

The divisions of the gatekeepers: ᵛ

From the Korahites: Meshelemiah son of Kore, one of the sons of Asaph.
2 Meshelemiah had sons:
  Zechariah ʷ the firstborn,
  Jediael the second,
  Zebadiah the third,
  Jathniel the fourth,
  3 Elam the fifth,
  Jehohanan the sixth
  and Eliehoenai the seventh.
4 Obed-Edom also had sons:
  Shemaiah the firstborn,
  Jehozabad the second,
  Joah the third,
  Sakar the fourth,
  Nethanel the fifth,
  5 Ammiel the sixth,
  Issachar the seventh
  and Peullethai the eighth.
  (For God had blessed Obed-Edom. ˣ)

6 Obed-Edom's son Shemaiah also had sons, who were leaders in their father's family because they were very capable men. 7 The sons of Shemaiah: Othni, Raphael, Obed and Elzabad; his relatives Elihu and Semakiah were also able men. 8 All these were descendants of Obed-Edom; they and their sons and their relatives were capable men with the strength to do the work—descendants of Obed-Edom, 62 in all.
9 Meshelemiah had sons and relatives, who were able men—18 in all.

10 Hosah the Merarite had sons: Shimri the first (although he was not the firstborn, his father had appointed him the first), ʸ 11 Hilkiah the second, Tabaliah the third and Zechariah the fourth. The sons and relatives of Hosah were 13 in all.

12 These divisions of the gatekeepers, through their leaders, had duties for ministering ᶻ in the temple of the LORD, just as their relatives had. 13 Lots ᵃ were cast for each gate, according to their families, young and old alike.
14 The lot for the East Gate ᵇ fell to Shelemiah. ᵃ Then lots were cast for his son Zechariah, ᶜ a wise counselor, and the lot for the North Gate fell to him. 15 The lot for the South Gate ᵈ fell to Obed-Edom, ᵈ and the lot for the storehouse fell to his sons. 16 The lots for the West Gate and the Shalleketh Gate on the upper road fell to Shuppim and Hosah.
Guard was alongside of guard: 17 There were six Levites a day on the east, four a day on the north, four a day on the south and two at a time at the storehouse. 18 As for the court ᵇ to the west, there were four at the road and two at the court ᵇ itself.

ᵃ 14 A variant of *Meshelemiah*   ᵇ 18 The meaning of the Hebrew for this word is uncertain.

26:1–19 The most extensive of the Chronicler's lists of gatekeepers (see 9:17–27; 16:37–38). A list of gatekeepers in the postexilic period is found in Ezr 2:42 (Ne 7:45).
26:1 *Asaph.* This name appears to be an abbreviation of Ebiasaph (6:23; 9:19); he should not be confused with the temple musician (25:1–2,6).
26:4–5 Numerous sons are again a sign of divine blessing (see note on 25:5).
26:4 *Obed-Edom.* Had cared for the ark when it was left at his house (see note on 13:13).
26:12 *duties.* Elaborated in 9:22–29.

26:14 *East Gate.* The main entrance; it had six guard posts, as opposed to four at the other gates (v. 17).
26:15 *South Gate.* The palaces of David and Solomon were south of the temple hill. The southern gate would be the main one used by the king, and this assignment probably reflects a particular honor for Obed-Edom (see notes on 26:4–5; see also Eze 46:1–10).
26:16 *Shalleketh Gate.* The only reference to a gate by this name; presumably it was on the western side. The Chronicler writes to an audience familiar with these topographical details.

26:19 ᵉ2Ch 35:15;
Ne 7:1; Eze 44:11
26:20 ᶠ2Ch 24:5
ᵍ1Ch 28:12
26:21 ʰ1Ch 23:7;
29:8
26:22 ⁱ1Ch 9:26
26:23 ʲS Nu 3:27
26:24 ᵏ1Ch 23:16
26:25 ˡ1Ch 23:18
26:26 ᵐS 2Sa 8:11
26:28 ⁿS 1Sa 9:9
26:29 ᵒDt 17:8-13;
S 1Ch 23:4
26:30 ᵖ1Ch 27:17
26:31 ᑫS 1Ch 23:19
ʳ2Sa 5:4
27:2 ˢ2Sa 23:8

¹⁹These were the divisions of the gatekeepers who were descendants of Korah and Me-rari.ᵉ

THE TREASURERS AND OTHER OFFICIALS

²⁰Their fellow Levitesᶠ wereᵃ in charge of the treasuries of the house of God and the treasuries for the dedicated things.ᵍ

²¹The descendants of Ladan, who were Gershonites through Ladan and who were heads of families belonging to Ladan the Gershonite,ʰ were Jehieli, ²²the sons of Jehie-li, Zetham and his brother Joel. They were in charge of the treasuriesⁱ of the temple of the LORD.

²³From the Amramites, the Izharites, the Hebronites and the Uzzielites:ʲ

²⁴Shubael,ᵏ a descendant of Gershom son of Moses, was the official in charge of the treasuries. ²⁵His relatives through Eliezer: Rehabiah his son, Jeshaiah his son, Jo-ram his son, Zikri his son and Shelomithˡ his son. ²⁶Shelomith and his relatives were in charge of all the treasuries for the things dedicatedᵐ by King David, by the heads of families who were the commanders of thousands and commanders of hundreds, and by the other army commanders. ²⁷Some of the plunder taken in battle they dedicated for the repair of the temple of the LORD. ²⁸And everything dedicated by Samuel the seerⁿ and by Saul son of Kish, Abner son of Ner and Joab son of Zeruiah, and all the other dedicated things were in the care of Shelomith and his relatives.

²⁹From the Izharites: Kenaniah and his sons were assigned duties away from the tem-ple, as officials and judgesᵒ over Israel.

³⁰From the Hebronites: Hashabiahᵖ and his relatives—seventeen hundred able men—were responsible in Israel west of the Jordan for all the work of the LORD and for the king's service. ³¹As for the Hebronites,ᑫ Jeriah was their chief according to the genealogical records of their families. In the fortiethʳ year of David's reign a search was made in the records, and capable men among the Hebronites were found at Jazer in Gilead. ³²Jeriah had twenty-seven hundred relatives, who were able men and heads of families, and King David put them in charge of the Reubenites, the Gadites and the half-tribe of Manasseh for every matter pertaining to God and for the affairs of the king.

ARMY DIVISIONS

27 This is the list of the Israelites—heads of families, commanders of thousands and commanders of hundreds, and their officers, who served the king in all that concerned the army divisions that were on duty month by month throughout the year. Each division consisted of 24,000 men.

²In charge of the first division, for the first month, was Jashobeamˢ son of Zabdiel. There

---

ᵃ 20 Septuagint; Hebrew *As for the Levites, Ahijah was*

B **26:20** *treasuries of the house of God.* The Levites in charge of these treasuries received the offerings of the people and cared for the valuable temple equipment (9:28–29). *treasuries for the dedicated things.* Contained the plunder from warfare (vv. 27–28). Texts from Mesopotamian temples confirm the pres-ence of temple officers who served as assayers to handle and re-fine the precious metals received as revenue and offerings. The procedure with reference to the offerings of the people may be seen in the reign of Joash (2Ch 24:4–14; 2Ki 12:4–16). Numerous passages reflect on the wealth collected in the temple (see, e.g., 29:1–9; 2Ch 4:1–22; 34:9–11; 36:7,10,18–19; 1Ki 14:25–28; 15:15,18; 2Ki 12:4–18; 14:14; 16:8; 25:13–17).
26:26 *things dedicated by King David.* See note on 18:1—20:8; see also 2Ch 5:1.
26:27 *plunder taken in battle they dedicated.* Cf. Ge 14:17–20.
26:29–32 These verses designate the 6,000 officials and judges (23:4) who would work outside Jerusalem; they are drawn from two sub-clans of Kohath (6:18). Dt 17:8–13 envisages a judicial function for the priests and Levites (see 2Ch 19:4–11).

A **26:30,32** *for all the work of the LORD and for the king's ser-vice … for every matter pertaining to God and for the affairs*

of the king. In the theocracy (kingdom of God) there is no divi-sion between secular and sacred, no tension in serving God and the king (cf. Mt 22:15–22; Lk 16:10–13; Ro 13:1–7; 1Ti 2:1–4; 1Pe 2:13–17).
26:31 *fortieth year.* The last year of David's reign.
27:1–15 The names of the commanders of David's army are the same as those found in the list of his mighty warriors (see 11:11–47; see also 2Sa 23:8–39 and notes). Those who had served David while he fled from Saul became commanders in the regular army.
27:1 *24,000.* See note on 12:23–37. Although a national militia consisting of 12 units of 24,000 each (a total of 288,000) is not unreasonable, the stress in this passage on unit commanders and divisions suggests that here too the Hebrew word for "1,000" should perhaps be taken as the designation of a military unit. To designate a division as "1,000" would be to give the up-per limit of the number of men in such a unit, though such units would ordinarily not have a full complement of men. If this ap-proach is followed, the figures in the following verses would be read as "24 units" instead of 24,000.
27:2 *Jashobeam.* See 11:11.

27:4 ʰS 2Sa 23:9
27:5 ᵘS 2Sa 23:20
27:7 ᵛS 2Sa 2:18
27:8 ʷ1Ch 11:27
27:9 ˣ2Sa 23:26
27:10 ʸ2Sa 23:26
27:11 ᶻS 2Sa 21:18
27:12 ᵃ2Sa 23:27
27:13 ᵇ2Sa 23:28
27:14 ᶜS 1Ch 11:31
27:15 ᵈ2Sa 23:29
ᵉS Jos 15:17
27:17 ᶠ1Ch 26:30
ᵍS 2Sa 8:17;
S 1Ch 12:28
27:23 ʰS 2Sa 24:1;
1Ch 21:2-5 ʲS Ge 12:2

were 24,000 men in his division. ³He was a descendant of Perez and chief of all the army officers for the first month.

⁴ In charge of the division for the second month was Dodai ᵗ the Ahohite; Mikloth was the leader of his division. There were 24,000 men in his division.

⁵ The third army commander, for the third month, was Benaiah ᵘ son of Jehoiada the priest. He was chief and there were 24,000 men in his division. ⁶This was the Benaiah who was a mighty warrior among the Thirty and was over the Thirty. His son Ammizabad was in charge of his division.

⁷ The fourth, for the fourth month, was Asahel ᵛ the brother of Joab; his son Zebadiah was his successor. There were 24,000 men in his division.

⁸ The fifth, for the fifth month, was the commander Shamhuth ʷ the Izrahite. There were 24,000 men in his division.

⁹ The sixth, for the sixth month, was Ira ˣ the son of Ikkesh the Tekoite. There were 24,000 men in his division.

¹⁰ The seventh, for the seventh month, was Helez ʸ the Pelonite, an Ephraimite. There were 24,000 men in his division.

¹¹ The eighth, for the eighth month, was Sibbekai ᶻ the Hushathite, a Zerahite. There were 24,000 men in his division.

¹² The ninth, for the ninth month, was Abiezer ᵃ the Anathothite, a Benjamite. There were 24,000 men in his division.

¹³ The tenth, for the tenth month, was Maharai ᵇ the Netophathite, a Zerahite. There were 24,000 men in his division.

¹⁴ The eleventh, for the eleventh month, was Benaiah ᶜ the Pirathonite, an Ephraimite. There were 24,000 men in his division.

¹⁵ The twelfth, for the twelfth month, was Heldai ᵈ the Netophathite, from the family of Othniel. ᵉ There were 24,000 men in his division.

LEADERS OF THE TRIBES

¹⁶ The leaders of the tribes of Israel:

over the Reubenites: Eliezer son of Zikri;
over the Simeonites: Shephatiah son of Maakah;
¹⁷ over Levi: Hashabiah ᶠ son of Kemuel;
over Aaron: Zadok; ᵍ
¹⁸ over Judah: Elihu, a brother of David;
over Issachar: Omri son of Michael;
¹⁹ over Zebulun: Ishmaiah son of Obadiah;
over Naphtali: Jerimoth son of Azriel;
²⁰ over the Ephraimites: Hoshea son of Azaziah;
over half the tribe of Manasseh: Joel son of Pedaiah;
²¹ over the half-tribe of Manasseh in Gilead: Iddo son of Zechariah;
over Benjamin: Jaasiel son of Abner;
²² over Dan: Azarel son of Jeroham.
These were the leaders of the tribes of Israel.

²³David did not take the number of the men twenty years old or less, ʰ because the LORD had promised to make Israel as numerous as the stars ʲ in the sky. ²⁴Joab son of Zeruiah began to count the men but did not finish. God's wrath came on Israel on account

---

27:4 *Dodai.* See 11:12.
27:5 *Benaiah.* See 11:22–25; 18:17.
27:7 *Asahel.* See 11:26; 2Sa 2:18–23.
27:9–15 The remainder of the commanders were selected from among the Thirty (see 11:25 and the names listed in 11:27–31).
27:16–22 The Chronicler's interest in "all Israel" appears in this list of officers who were over the 12 tribes (see Introduction: Purpose and Themes). The number is kept at 12 by omitting Gad and Asher (see note on 2:1–2).
27:17 *Zadok.* See note on 6:8; see also 12:28; 16:39.
27:18 *Elihu.* Not named elsewhere among the brothers of David. Perhaps he is the unnamed son from the list in 2:10–17 (see note there). Elihu could also be a variant of the name of Jesse's oldest son, Eliab, or the term "brother" could be taken in the

sense of "relative," in which case Elihu would be a more distant kinsman.
27:21 *Abner.* A relative of King Saul (see 26:28; 1Sa 14:50–51; 17:55–58; 26:5–16; 2Sa 2:8—4:1).
27:23–24 *number.* Refers to the census narrative in ch. 21 (2Sa 24).
27:23 *twenty years old or less.* The figures reported in ch. 21 and 2Sa 24 were the numbers of those older than 20 years. *promised to make Israel as numerous as the stars.* The patriarchal promises of numerous descendants (Ge 12:2; 13:16; 15:5; 22:17) appear to have been the basis for the objections of Joab (v. 24) to the taking of a census (21:3; 2Sa 24:3).
27:24 *did not finish.* Joab did not count those under age 20, nor did he include the tribes of Levi and Benjamin (21:6). *book of the annals of King David.* See Introduction: Author, Date and Sources.

of this numbering,[j] and the number was not entered in the book[a] of the annals of King David.

THE KING'S OVERSEERS

[25]Azmaveth son of Adiel was in charge of the royal storehouses.

Jonathan son of Uzziah was in charge of the storehouses in the outlying districts, in the towns, the villages and the watchtowers.

[26]Ezri son of Kelub was in charge of the workers who farmed the land.

[27]Shimei the Ramathite was in charge of the vineyards.

Zabdi the Shiphmite was in charge of the produce of the vineyards for the wine vats.

[28]Baal-Hanan the Gederite was in charge of the olive and sycamore-fig[k] trees in the western foothills.

Joash was in charge of the supplies of olive oil.

[29]Shitrai the Sharonite was in charge of the herds grazing in Sharon.[l]

Shaphat son of Adlai was in charge of the herds in the valleys.

[30]Obil the Ishmaelite was in charge of the camels.

Jehdeiah the Meronothite was in charge of the donkeys.

[31]Jaziz the Hagrite[m] was in charge of the flocks.

All these were the officials in charge of King David's property.

[32]Jonathan, David's uncle, was a counselor, a man of insight and a scribe. Jehiel son of Hakmoni took care of the king's sons.

[33]Ahithophel[n] was the king's counselor.

Hushai[o] the Arkite was the king's confidant. [34]Ahithophel was succeeded by Jehoiada son of Benaiah and by Abiathar.[p]

Joab[q] was the commander of the royal army.

DAVID'S PLANS FOR THE TEMPLE

28 David summoned[r] all the officials[s] of Israel to assemble at Jerusalem: the officers over the tribes, the commanders of the divisions in the service of the king, the commanders of thousands and commanders of hundreds, and the officials in charge of all the property and livestock belonging to the king and his sons, together with the palace officials, the mighty warriors and all the brave fighting men.

[2]King David rose to his feet and said: "Listen to me, my fellow Israelites, my people. I had it in my heart[t] to build a house as a place of rest[u] for the ark of the covenant of the LORD, for the footstool[v] of our God, and I made plans to build it.[w] [3]But God said to me,[x] 'You are not to build a house for my Name,[y] because you are a warrior and have shed blood.'[z]

[4]"Yet the LORD, the God of Israel, chose me[a] from my whole family[b] to be king over Israel forever. He chose Judah[c] as leader, and from the house of Judah he chose my family, and from my father's sons he was pleased to make me king over all Israel.[d] [5]Of all my sons—and the LORD has given me many[e]—he has chosen my son Solomon[f] to sit on the throne[g] of the kingdom of the LORD over Israel. [6]He said to me: 'Solomon your son is the one who will build[h] my house and my courts, for I have chosen him to be my son,[i] and I

[a] 24 Septuagint; Hebrew *number*

27:25–31 A list of the administrators of David's property (v. 31). The large cities of the ancient Near East had three basic economic sectors: (1) royal, (2) temple and (3) private. There is no evidence of direct taxation during the reign of David; his court appears to have been financed by extensive landholdings, commerce, plunder from his many wars, and tribute from subjugated kingdoms.

27:27 *wine vats.* See note on Hag 2:16.

27:32–34 A list of David's cabinet members, supplementary to that in 18:14–17.

27:33 *Ahithophel.* Was replaced after he committed suicide, following his support of Absalom's rebellion (2Sa 15:12,31–37; 16:20—17:23).

27:34 *Benaiah.* See v. 5.

28:1—29:30 The account of the transition from the reign of David to that of Solomon is one of the clearest demonstrations of the Chronicler's idealization of their reigns when it is compared with the succession narrative in 1Ki 1–2. The Chronicler makes no mention of the infirmities of the aged David (1Ki 1:1–4), the rebellion of Adonijah and the king's sons (1Ki 1:5–10),

the court intrigue to secure Solomon's succession (1Ki 1:11–31) or David's charge to Solomon to punish his enemies after his death (1Ki 2:1–9). His selection of material presents a transition of power that is smooth and peaceful and receives the support of "all Israel" (29:25), the officials and the people (28:1–2; 29:6–9, 21–25). Instead of the bedridden David who sends others to anoint Solomon (1Ki 1:32–35), David himself is present and in charge of the ceremonies (see 23:1 and note).

28:1 The assembly is composed largely of the groups named in ch. 27. This public announcement (v. 5) follows the private announcement of Solomon's succession in ch. 22 (see note on 22:2–19).

28:3 *you are a warrior and have shed blood.* See note on 22:8–9.

28:5 *chosen my son Solomon.* See vv. 6,10; 29:1. These are the only uses in the OT of the Hebrew verb for "chosen" with reference to any king after David (see Introduction: Purpose and Themes). The Chronicler's application of this term to Solomon is consistent with his depiction of that king. *kingdom of the LORD.* See note on 17:14.

28:6 *my son.* See 17:12–14 and note; see also 22:10.

27:24 /S 2Sa 24:15; 1Ch 21:14
27:28 *k*S 1Ki 10:27
27:29 /SS 2:1; Isa 33:9; 35:2; 65:10
27:31 *m*S 1Ch 5:10
27:33 *n*S 2Sa 15:12
°S 2Sa 15:37
27:34 *p*S 1Sa 22:20
*q*S 2Sa 2:13
28:1 *r*1Ch 22:17
*s*1Ch 27:1-31; 29:6
28:2 *t*S 1Sa 10:7;
S 1Ch 17:2 *u*2Ch 6:41
*v*Ps 99:5; 132:7;
Isa 60:13 *w*Ps 132:1-5
28:3 *x*S 2Sa 7:5
*y*1Ch 22:8 *z*S 1Ki 5:3;
S 1Ch 17:4
28:4 *a*2Ch 6:6
*b*1Sa 16:1-13
*c*S Ge 49:10;
Nu 24:17-19
*d*1Ch 11:1
28:5 *e*S 1Ch 3:1
*f*S 2Sa 12:24;
S 1Ch 23:1
*g*S 1Ch 17:14
28:6 *h*1Ki 8:20
*i*S 2Sa 7:13;
S 1Ch 17:13

28:7 ʲ1Ch 22:13
28:8 ᵏS 1Ch 9:1
ˡDt 6:1 ᵐDt 4:1;
S 17:14-20
28:9 ⁿS 1Ch 29:19
ᵒS 1Sa 2:3; 2Ch 6:30;
Ps 7:9 ᵖS 1Ch 16:11;
S Ps 40:16
ᑫS Dt 4:31;
S Jos 24:20;
S 2Ch 7:19; 15:2
ʳ1Ki 9:7; Ps 44:23;
74:1; 77:7
28:11 ˢS Ex 25:9;
Ac 7:44; Heb 8:5
28:12 ᵗS 1Ch 12:18
ᵘ1Ch 26:20
28:13 ᵛS 1Ch 24:1
28:15 ʷEx 25:31
28:16 ˣS Ex 25:23
28:17 ʸS Ex 27:3
28:18 ᶻEx 30:1-10
ᵃS Ex 25:22
ᵇS Ex 25:20
28:19 ᶜ1Ki 6:38
ᵈS Ex 25:9
28:20 ᵉS Dt 31:6;
1Ch 22:13; 2Ch 9:11;
Hag 2:4 ᶠS Dt 4:31;
S Jos 24:20
ᵍS 1Ki 6:14; 2Ch 7:11
28:21 ʰEx 35:25–
36:5
29:1 ʲ1Ki 3:7;
1Ch 22:5; 2Ch 13:7
29:2 ʲver 7,14,16;
Ezr 1:4; 6:5; Hag 2:8
ᵏIsa 54:11
ˡ1Ch 22:2-5
29:3 ᵐ2Ch 24:10;
31:3; 35:8
29:4 ⁿS Ge 10:29
ᵒ1Ch 22:14

will be his father. [7]I will establish his kingdom forever if he is unswerving in carrying out my commands and laws,ʲ as is being done at this time.'

[8]"So now I charge you in the sight of all Israelᵏ and of the assembly of the LORD, and in the hearing of our God: Be careful to follow all the commandsˡ of the LORD your God, that you may possess this good land and pass it on as an inheritance to your descendants forever.ᵐ

[9]"And you, my son Solomon, acknowledge the God of your father, and serve him with wholehearted devotionⁿ and with a willing mind, for the LORD searches every heartᵒ and understands every desire and every thought. If you seek him,ᵖ he will be found by you; but if you forsakeᑫ him, he will rejectʳ you forever. [10]Consider now, for the LORD has chosen you to build a house as the sanctuary. Be strong and do the work."

[11]Then David gave his son Solomon the plansˢ for the portico of the temple, its buildings, its storerooms, its upper parts, its inner rooms and the place of atonement. [12]He gave him the plans of all that the Spiritᵗ had put in his mind for the courts of the temple of the LORD and all the surrounding rooms, for the treasuries of the temple of God and for the treasuries for the dedicated things.ᵘ [13]He gave him instructions for the divisionsᵛ of the priests and Levites, and for all the work of serving in the temple of the LORD, as well as for all the articles to be used in its service. [14]He designated the weight of gold for all the gold articles to be used in various kinds of service, and the weight of silver for all the silver articles to be used in various kinds of service: [15]the weight of gold for the gold lampstandsʷ and their lamps, with the weight for each lampstand and its lamps; and the weight of silver for each silver lampstand and its lamps, according to the use of each lampstand; [16]the weight of gold for each tableˣ for consecrated bread; the weight of silver for the silver tables; [17]the weight of pure gold for the forks, sprinkling bowlsʸ and pitchers; the weight of gold for each gold dish; the weight of silver for each silver dish; [18]and the weight of the refined gold for the altar of incense.ᶻ He also gave him the plan for the chariot,ᵃ that is, the cherubim of gold that spread their wings and overshadowᵇ the ark of the covenant of the LORD.

[19]"All this," David said, "I have in writing as a result of the LORD's hand on me, and he enabled me to understand all the detailsᶜ of the plan.ᵈ"

[20]David also said to Solomon his son, "Be strong and courageous,ᵉ and do the work. Do not be afraid or discouraged, for the LORD God, my God, is with you. He will not fail you or forsakeᶠ you until all the work for the service of the temple of the LORD is finished.ᵍ [21]The divisions of the priests and Levites are ready for all the work on the temple of God, and every willing person skilledʰ in any craft will help you in all the work. The officials and all the people will obey your every command."

GIFTS FOR BUILDING THE TEMPLE

29 Then King David said to the whole assembly: "My son Solomon, the one whom God has chosen, is young and inexperienced.ʲ The task is great, because this palatial structure is not for human beings but for the LORD God. [2]With all my resources I have provided for the temple of my God—goldʲ for the gold work, silver for the silver, bronze for the bronze, iron for the iron and wood for the wood, as well as onyx for the settings, turquoise,ᵃᵏ stones of various colors, and all kinds of fine stone and marble—all of these in large quantities.ˡ [3]Besides, in my devotion to the temple of my God I now give my personal treasures of gold and silver for the temple of my God, over and above everything I have providedᵐ for this holy temple: [4]three thousand talentsᵇ of gold (gold of Ophir)ⁿ and seven thousand talentsᶜ of refined silver, ᵒ for the overlaying of the walls of the buildings, [5]for the gold work and the silver work, and for all the

---

ᵃ 2 The meaning of the Hebrew for this word is uncertain.   ᵇ 4 That is, about 110 tons or about 100 metric tons   ᶜ 4 That is, about 260 tons or about 235 metric tons

---

28:8–9 See Introduction: Portrait of David and Solomon.
28:11 *portico.* See diagram, p. 494.
28:12 David provides Solomon with the plans for the temple. This reflects the Chronicler's modeling David after Moses: Just as Moses received the plans for the tabernacle from God (Ex 25–30), so also David received the plans for the temple.
28:18 *chariot.* Probably God's mobile throne (see note on Ps 18:10).
28:19 *I have in writing as a result of the LORD's hand on me.* The Chronicler may intend no more than the ordinary process of inspiration whereby David wrote under divine influence. On the

other hand, he may imply a parallel with Moses, who also received documents from the hand of the Lord (Ex 25:40; 27:8; 31:18; 32:16).
28:20 See Introduction: Portrait of David and Solomon.
29:1 *chosen.* See note on 28:5. *young.* See note on 22:5.
29:2–9 After donating his personal fortune to the construction of the temple, David appeals to the people for their voluntary gifts. The Chronicler again appears to be modeling his account of David on events from the life of Moses (Ex 25:1–8; 35:4–9,20–29). The willing response of the people aided the building of both tabernacle and temple.

work to be done by the skilled workers. Now, who among you is willing to consecrate yourself to the LORD today?"

⁶Then the leaders of families, the officers of the tribes of Israel, the commanders of thousands and commanders of hundreds, and the officials ᵖ in charge of the king's work gave willingly. ⁷They ʳ gave toward the work on the temple of God five thousand talents ᵃ and ten thousand darics ᵇ of gold, ten thousand talents ᶜ of silver, eighteen thousand talents ᵈ of bronze and a hundred thousand talents ᵉ of iron. ⁸Anyone who had precious stones ˢ gave them to the treasury of the temple of the LORD in the custody of Jehiel the Gershonite. ᵗ ⁹The people rejoiced at the willing response of their leaders, for they had given freely and wholeheartedly ᵘ to the LORD. David the king also rejoiced greatly.

DAVID'S PRAYER

¹⁰David praised the LORD in the presence of the whole assembly, saying,

"Praise be to you, LORD,
    the God of our father Israel,
    from everlasting to everlasting.
¹¹Yours, LORD, is the greatness and the power ᵛ
    and the glory and the majesty and the splendor,
    for everything in heaven and earth is yours. ʷ
Yours, LORD, is the kingdom;
    you are exalted as head over all. ˣ
¹²Wealth and honor ʸ come from you;
    you are the ruler ᶻ of all things.
In your hands are strength and power
    to exalt and give strength to all.
¹³Now, our God, we give you thanks,
    and praise your glorious name.

¹⁴"But who am I, and who are my people, that we should be able to give as generously as this? ᵃ Everything comes from you, and we have given you only what comes from your hand. ᵇ ¹⁵We are foreigners and strangers ᶜ in your sight, as were all our ancestors. Our days on earth are like a shadow, ᵈ without hope. ¹⁶LORD our God, all this abundance that we have provided for building you a temple for your Holy Name comes from your hand, and all of it belongs to you. ¹⁷I know, my God, that you test the heart ᵉ and are pleased with integrity. All these things have I given willingly and with honest intent. And now I have seen with joy how willingly your people who are here have given to you. ᶠ ¹⁸LORD, the God of our fathers Abraham, Isaac and Israel, keep these desires and thoughts in the hearts of your people forever, and keep their hearts loyal to you. ¹⁹And give my son Solomon the wholehearted devotion ᵍ to keep your commands, statutes and decrees ʰ and to do everything to build the palatial structure for which I have provided." ⁱ

²⁰Then David said to the whole assembly, "Praise the LORD your God." So they all praised the LORD, the God of their fathers; they bowed down, prostrating themselves before the LORD and the king.

SOLOMON ACKNOWLEDGED AS KING
29:21–25pp — 1Ki 1:28–53

²¹The next day they made sacrifices to the LORD and presented burnt offerings to him: ʲ a thousand bulls, a thousand rams and a thousand male lambs, together with their drink offerings, and other sacrifices in abundance for all Israel. ᵏ ²²They ate and drank with great joy ˡ in the presence of the LORD that day.

ᵃ 7 That is, about 190 tons or about 170 metric tons   ᵇ 7 That is, about 185 pounds or about 84 kilograms   ᶜ 7 That is, about 375 tons or about 340 metric tons   ᵈ 7 That is, about 675 tons or about 610 metric tons   ᵉ 7 That is, about 3,750 tons or about 3,400 metric tons

---

29:7 *darics.* See TNIV text note. The daric was a Persian gold coin, apparently named for Darius I (522–486 B.C.), in whose reign it first appears (see Ezr 8:27). Since the Chronicler's readers were familiar with it, he could use it as an up-to-date standard of value for an earlier treasure of gold.
29:22 *ate and drank.* See 12:38–40 and note. The anointing of both Solomon and Zadok portrays the harmony between them (see Zec 4:14; 6:13 and notes). *second time.* Perhaps the first time was Solomon's anointing, recorded in 1Ki 1:32–36 but

omitted by the Chronicler (see note on 28:1—29:30). However, the phrase "second time" is missing in the Septuagint (the pre-Christian Greek translation of the OT), suggesting that it may have been an addition to the Hebrew text of this passage by an ancient scribe after the Septuagint had already been translated, in order to harmonize the Chronicles account with Kings. Multiple anointings are found in the cases of both Saul (1Sa 10:1,24; 11:14–15) and David (1Sa 16:13; 2Sa 2:4; 5:3).

29:6 ᵖ 1Ch 27:1; S 28:1 ᵠ ver 9; Ex 25:1-8; 35:20-29; 36:2; 2Ch 24:10; Ezr 7:15
29:7 ʳ S Ex 25:2; Ne 7:70-71
29:8 ˢ Ex 35:27 ᵗ S 1Ch 26:21
29:9 ᵘ 1Ki 8:61
29:11 ᵛ Ps 24:8; 59:17; 62:11 ʷ Ps 89:11 ˣ Rev 5:12-13
29:12 ʸ 2Ch 1:12; 32:27; Ezr 7:27; Ecc 5:19 ᶻ 2Ch 20:6
29:14 ᵃ Ps 8:4; 144:3 ᵇ S ver 2
29:15 ᶜ S Ge 17:8; S 23:4; Ps 39:12; S Heb 11:13 ᵈ Job 7:6; 8:9; 14:2; 32:7; Ps 102:11; 144:4; Ecc 6:12
29:17 ᵉ Ps 139:23; Pr 15:11; 17:3; Jer 11:20; 17:10 ᶠ 1Ch 28:9; Ps 15:1-5; Pr 11:20
29:19 ᵍ S 1Ki 8:61; 11:4; 1Ch 28:9; Isa 38:3 ʰ Ps 72:1 ⁱ S 1Ch 22:14
29:21 ʲ S 1Ki 8:62 ᵏ 1Ch 11:1
29:22 ˡ 1Ch 12:40

29:22 *m* S 1Sa 2:35
29:23 *n* S Dt 17:18
o S 1Ki 2:12;
S 1Ki 17:14
29:24 *p* 1Ki 1:9
29:25 *q* S Jos 3:7
r 1Ki 10:7; 2Ch 1:1,12
s Ecc 2:9
29:26 *t* 1Ch 18:14
u 1Ch 11:1
29:27 *v* S Ge 23:19
w 2Sa 5:4-5;
S 1Ch 3:4
29:28 *x* S Ge 15:15;
Ac 13:36 *y* S 1Ch 23:1
29:29 *z* S 1Sa 9:9
a S 2Sa 7:2
b S 1Sa 22:5

Then they acknowledged Solomon son of David as king a second time, anointing him before the Lord to be ruler and Zadok *m* to be priest. [23] So Solomon sat *n* on the throne *o* of the Lord as king in place of his father David. He prospered and all Israel obeyed him. [24] All the officers and mighty warriors, as well as all of King David's sons, *p* pledged their submission to King Solomon.

[25] The Lord highly exalted *q* Solomon in the sight of all Israel and bestowed on him royal splendor *r* such as no king over Israel ever had before. *s*

THE DEATH OF DAVID

29:26–28pp — 1Ki 2:10–12

[26] David son of Jesse was king *t* over all Israel. *u* [27] He ruled over Israel forty years—seven in Hebron *v* and thirty-three in Jerusalem. *w* [28] He died *x* at a good old age, having enjoyed long life, wealth and honor. His son Solomon succeeded him as king. *y*

[29] As for the events of King David's reign, from beginning to end, they are written in the records of Samuel the seer, *z* the records of Nathan *a* the prophet and the records of Gad *b* the seer, [30] together with the details of his reign and power, and the circumstances that surrounded him and Israel and the kingdoms of all the other lands.

29:24 *all … pledged their submission.* But compare the rebellion of Adonijah, in which the officers and sons of the king had assisted the attempted coup (1Ki 1:9,19,25). Again the Chronicler has bypassed a negative event that would tarnish his image of David and Solomon.
29:25 *all Israel.* See 11:1,10; 12:38–40; see also Introduction: Purpose and Themes.
29:27 See note on 3:1–9.

29:28 *long life, wealth and honor.* As a feature of the Chronicler's theme of immediate retribution (see Introduction: Purpose and Themes), the righteous enjoy these blessings (cf. Ps 128; Pr 3:2,4, 9–10,16,22,33–35).
29:29 See Introduction: Author, Date and Sources.
29:30 *kingdoms of all the other lands.* Those immediately surrounding David's kingdom.

See Introduction to 1 Chronicles for Outline and other introductory information.

THE BUILDING OF THE TEMPLE IN CHRONICLES

The Chronicler has used the Pentateuchal history as a model for his account of the reigns of David and Solomon. Similarly, the Pentateuchal record of the building of the tabernacle affects his account of the building of the temple:

1. The building of the tabernacle was entrusted to Bezalel and Oholiab (Ex 35:30—36:7), and they provide the Chronicler's model for the relationship of Solomon and Huram-Abi (2Ch 2:13). It is significant that the only references to Bezalel outside the book of Exodus are in Chronicles (1Ch 2:20; 2Ch 1:5).

Solomon is the new Bezalel: (1) Both Solomon and Bezalel are designated by name for their tasks by God; they are the only workers on their projects to be chosen by name (Ex 31:2; 35:30—36:2; 38:22–23; 1Ch 28:6). (2) Both are from the tribe of Judah (Ex 31:2; 35:30; 1Ch 2:20; 3:10). (3) Both receive the Spirit to endow them with wisdom (Ex 31:3; 35:30–31; 2Ch 1:1–13), and Solomon's vision at Gibeon (2Ch 1:3–13) dominates the preface to the account of the temple construction (2Ch 2–7). (4) Both build a bronze altar for the sanctuary (2Ch 1:5; 4:1; 7:7)—significantly, the bronze altar is not mentioned in the summary list of Huram-Abi's work (4:12–16). (5) Both make the sanctuary furnishings (Ex 31:1–10; 37:10–29; 2Ch 4:19–22).

Similarly, Huram-Abi becomes the new Oholiab: (1) In the account of the temple building in Kings, Huram-Abi is not mentioned until after the story of the main construction of temple and palace has been told (1Ki 7:13–45); in Chronicles he is introduced as being involved in the building work from the beginning, just as Oholiab worked on the tabernacle from the beginning (Ex 31:6; 2Ch 2:13). (2) Kings speaks only of Huram-Abi's skill in casting bronze (1Ki 7:14); in Chronicles, however, his list of skills is the same as Oholiab's (Ex 31:1–6; 35:30—36:2; 38:22–23; 2Ch 2:14). (3) Kings reports that the mother of Huram-Abi was a widow from the tribe of Naphtali (1Ki 7:14); Chronicles, however, states that she was a widow from the tribe of Dan (2Ch 2:14), thus giving Huram-Abi the same ancestry as Oholiab (Ex 31:6; 35:34; 38:23). See note on 2Ch 2:13.

2. The plans for both tabernacle and temple are given by God (Ex 25:1—30:37; see Ex 25:9,40; 27:8; see also 1Ch 28:11–19—not mentioned in Samuel and Kings).

3. The spoils of war are used as building materials for both tabernacle and temple (Ex 3:21–22; 12:35–36; see 1Ch 18:6–11—not mentioned in Samuel and Kings).

4. The people contribute willingly and generously for both structures (Ex 25:1–7; 36:3–7; see 1Ch 29:1–9—not mentioned in Samuel and Kings).

5. The glory cloud appears at the dedication of both structures (Ex 40:34–35; 2Ch 7:1–3).

1:1 ᵃS 1Ki 2:12,26;
S 2Ch 12:1
ᵇS Ge 21:22; S 39:2;
S Nu 14:43
ᶜS 1Ch 29:25
1:2 ᵈS 1Ch 9:1
1:3 ᵉS Jos 9:3
ᶠS Lev 17:4 ᵍEx 40:18
1:4 ʰS 1Ch 15:25
ⁱ2Sa 6:17
1:5 ʲEx 38:2
ᵏS Ex 31:2 ˡ1Ch 13:3
1:7 ᵐ2Ch 7:12
1:8 ⁿS 1Ch 23:1
1:9 ᵒS 2Sa 7:25;
S 1Ki 8:25 ᵖS Ge 12:2
1:10 ᵠNu 27:17;
2Sa 5:2; Pr 8:15-16
1:11 ʳS 1Ch 29:12
1:12 ˢS 1Ch 29:12
ᵗS 1Ch 29:25;
2Ch 9:22; Ne 13:26
1:14 ᵘS 1Sa 8:11;
S 1Ki 9:19
1:15 ᵛS 1Ki 9:28;
Isa 60:5
1:17 ʷSS 1:9

SOLOMON ASKS FOR WISDOM

1:2–13pp — 1Ki 3:4–15
1:14–17pp — 1Ki 10:26–29; 2Ch 9:25–28

1 Solomon son of David established ᵃ himself firmly over his kingdom, for the Lᴏʀᴅ his God was with ᵇ him and made him exceedingly great. ᶜ ²Then Solomon spoke to all Israel ᵈ—to the commanders of thousands and commanders of hundreds, to the judges and to all the leaders in Israel, the heads of families— ³and Solomon and the whole assembly went to the high place at Gibeon, ᵉ for God's tent of meeting ᶠ was there, which Moses ᵍ the Lᴏʀᴅ's servant had made in the wilderness. ⁴Now David had brought up the ark ʰ of God from Kiriath Jearim to the place he had prepared for it, because he had pitched a tent ⁱ for it in Jerusalem. ⁵But the bronze altar ʲ that Bezalel ᵏ son of Uri, the son of Hur, had made was in Gibeon in front of the tabernacle of the Lᴏʀᴅ; so Solomon and the assembly inquired ˡ of him there. ⁶Solomon went up to the bronze altar before the Lᴏʀᴅ in the tent of meeting and offered a thousand burnt offerings on it.

⁷That night God appeared ᵐ to Solomon and said to him, "Ask for whatever you want me to give you."

⁸Solomon answered God, "You have shown great kindness to David my father and have made me ⁿ king in his place. ⁹Now, Lᴏʀᴅ God, let your promise ᵒ to my father David be confirmed, for you have made me king over a people who are as numerous as the dust of the earth. ᵖ ¹⁰Give me wisdom and knowledge, that I may lead ᵠ this people, for who is able to govern this great people of yours?"

¹¹God said to Solomon, "Since this is your heart's desire and you have not asked for wealth, ʳ possessions or honor, nor for the death of your enemies, and since you have not asked for a long life but for wisdom and knowledge to govern my people over whom I have made you king, ¹²therefore wisdom and knowledge will be given you. And I will also give you wealth, possessions and honor, ˢ such as no king who was before you ever had and none after you will have. ᵗ"

¹³Then Solomon went to Jerusalem from the high place at Gibeon, from before the tent of meeting. And he reigned over Israel.

¹⁴Solomon accumulated chariots ᵘ and horses; he had fourteen hundred chariots and twelve thousand horses, ᵃ which he kept in the chariot cities and also with him in Jerusalem. ¹⁵The king made silver and gold ᵛ as common in Jerusalem as stones, and cedar as plentiful as sycamore-fig trees in the foothills. ¹⁶Solomon's horses were imported from Egypt and from Kue ᵇ—the royal merchants purchased them from Kue at the current price. ¹⁷They imported a chariot ʷ from Egypt for six hundred shekels ᶜ of silver, and a horse for a hundred and fifty. ᵈ They also exported them to all the kings of the Hittites and of the Arameans.

ᵃ 14 Or *charioteers*   ᵇ 16 Probably Cilicia   ᶜ 17 That is, about 15 pounds or about 6.9 kilograms
ᵈ 17 That is, about 3 3/4 pounds or about 1.7 kilograms

1:1—9:31 The account of the reign of Solomon is primarily devoted to his building of the temple (chs. 2–7); his endowment with wisdom is mainly to facilitate the building work. Much of the material in Kings that does not bear on building the temple is omitted by the Chronicler; e.g., he does not mention the judgment between the prostitutes (1Ki 3:16–28) or the building of the royal palace (1Ki 7:1–12).

1:1 *established himself.* This expression, or a variation of it, is common in Chronicles (12:13; 13:7–8,21; 15:8; 16:9; 17:1; 21:4; 23:1; 25:11; 27:6; 32:5; 1Ch 11:10; 19:13). Here and in 21:4 it includes the elimination of enemies and rivals to the throne (see 1Ki 2, especially v. 46).

1:2–13 See 1Ki 3:4–15 and notes. Verses 2–6 are largely unique to Chronicles and show some of the writer's concerns: 1. The support of "all Israel" (v. 2) is emphasized (see Introduction to 1 Chronicles: Purpose and Themes). 2. While the writer of Kings is somewhat apologetic about Solomon's visit to a high place (1Ki 3:3), the Chronicler adds the note that this was the location of the tabernacle made by Moses in the desert (v. 3), bringing Solomon's action into line with the provisions of the law (Lev 17:8–9).

1:5 *Bezalel.* See Introduction: The Building of the Temple in Chronicles. It is specifically in connection with his offering on the altar built by Bezalel (Ex 31:1–11; 38:1–2) that Solomon receives the wisdom from God to reign. In the account that follows, Solomon devotes his gift of wisdom primarily to building the temple, just as Bezalel had been gifted by God to serve as the master craftsman of the tabernacle.

1:9 *numerous as the dust.* In provisional fulfillment of the promise to Abraham (Ge 13:16; 22:17; see note on 1Ch 27:23; cf. Ge 28:14).

1:14–17 The Chronicler does not include the material in 1Ki 3:16—4:34. He moves rather to the account of Solomon's wealth in 1Ki 10:26–29; part of this material is repeated in 2Ch 9:25–28. Recounting Solomon's wealth at this point shows the fulfillment of God's promise (v. 12).

1:15 *sycamore-fig trees.* See note on Am 7:14.

1:16–17 *imported … exported.* See note on 1Ki 10:29.

1:17 *Hittites.* See note on Ge 10:15. *Arameans.* See notes on 1Ch 18:5; Dt 26:5.

PREPARATIONS FOR BUILDING THE TEMPLE

2:1–18pp — 1Ki 5:1–16

2 *Solomon gave orders to build a temple* ˣ *for the Name of the LORD and a royal palace for himself.* ʸ *²He conscripted 70,000 men as carriers and 80,000 as stone-cutters in the hills and 3,600 as supervisors over them.* ᶻ

³Solomon sent this message to Hiramᵃ ᵃ king of Tyre:

"Send me cedar logs ᵇ as you did for my father David when you sent him cedar to build a palace to live in. ⁴Now I am about to build a temple ᶜ for the Name of the LORD my God and to dedicate it to him for burning fragrant incense ᵈ before him, for setting out the consecrated bread ᵉ regularly, and for making burnt offerings ᶠ every morning and evening and on the Sabbaths, ᵍ at the New Moons ʰ and at the appointed festivals of the LORD our God. This is a lasting ordinance for Israel.

⁵"The temple I am going to build will be great, ⁱ because our God is greater than all other gods.ʲ ⁶But who is able to build a temple for him, since the heavens, even the highest heavens, cannot contain him? ᵏ Who then am I ˡ to build a temple for him, except as a place to burn sacrifices before him?

⁷"Send me, therefore, a man skilled to work in gold and silver, bronze and iron, and in purple, crimson and blue yarn, and experienced in the art of engraving, to work in Judah and Jerusalem with my skilled workers, ᵐ whom my father David provided.

⁸"Send me also cedar, juniper and algumᵇ logs from Lebanon, for I know that your servants are skilled in cutting timber there. My men will work with yours ⁹to provide me with plenty of lumber, because the temple I build must be large and magnificent. ¹⁰I will give your servants, those who cut the timber, twenty thousand corsᶜ of ground wheat, twenty thousand corsᵈ of barley, twenty thousand bathsᵉ of wine and twenty thousand baths of olive oil. ⁿ"

¹¹Hiram king of Tyre replied by letter to Solomon:

"Because the LORD loves ᵒ his people, he has made you their king."

¹²And Hiram added:

"Praise be to the LORD, the God of Israel, who made heaven and earth!ᵖ He has given King David a wise son, endowed with intelligence and discernment, who will build a temple for the LORD and a palace for himself.

¹³"I am sending you Huram-Abi, �q a man of great skill, ¹⁴whose mother was from Dan ʳ and whose father was from Tyre. He is trained ˢ to work in gold and silver, bronze and iron, stone and wood, and with purple and blue ᵗ and crimson yarn and fine linen. He is experienced in all kinds of engraving and can execute any design given to him. He will work with your skilled workers and with those of my lord, David your father.

¹⁵"Now let my lord send his servants the wheat and barley and the olive oil ᵘ and wine he promised, ¹⁶and we will cut all the logs from Lebanon that you need and will float them as rafts by sea down to Joppa. ᵛ You can then take them up to Jerusalem."

ᵃ 3 Hebrew *Huram*, a variant of *Hiram*; also in verses 11 and 12   ᵇ 8 Probably a variant of *almug*
ᶜ 10 That is, probably about 3,600 tons or about 3,275 metric tons   ᵈ 10 That is, probably about 3,000 tons or about 2,700 metric tons   ᵉ 10 That is, about 120,000 gallons or about 440,000 liters

*2:1 is numbered 1:18 in Hebrew texts.   *2:2-18 is numbered 2:1-17 in Hebrew texts.

2:1 *palace.* Although the Chronicler frequently mentions the palace Solomon built (7:11; 8:1; 9:11), he gives no details of its construction (see 1Ki 7:1–12).
2:2 See vv. 17–18 and note.
2:3–10 The Chronicler's theological interests appear in his handling of Solomon's correspondence with Hiram of Tyre. In the Kings account the correspondence was initiated by Hiram (1Ki 5:1). The Chronicler omits this (and also the material in 1Ki 5:3–5) but adds his own material, reflecting his concerns with the temple worship in vv. 3–7.
2:4 See 1Ch 23:28–32 and note.
2:7 See Introduction: The Building of the Temple in Chronicles. In the Kings account Solomon's request for a master craftsman is found late in the narrative (1Ki 7:13); to carry out his parallel between Oholiab and Huram-Abi, the Chronicler includes it in the initial correspondence. Furthermore, here and in vv. 13–14 the list of Huram-Abi's skills is expanded and matches that of Bezalel

and Oholiab (Kings is concerned only with casting bronze).
2:10 The payment here differs from that reported in 1Ki 5:11, but the texts speak of two different payments: In Kings the payment is an annual sum delivered to the royal household of Hiram, while Chronicles speaks of one payment to those "who cut the timber." The goods paid are also not identical; the oil specified in Kings is of a finer quality.
2:11–16 See 1Ki 5:7–9; 7:13–14 and notes.
2:13 *Huram-Abi.* See note on v. 7. Kings reports that the ancestry of Huram-Abi was through a widow of Naphtali (1Ki 7:14); Chronicles strengthens the parallel between Huram-Abi and Oholiab by assigning him Danite ancestry. These statements are not necessarily contradictory: (1) The mother's ancestry may have been Danite, though she lived in the territory of Naphtali; or (2) her parents may have been from Dan and Naphtali, allowing her descent to be reckoned to either. The Danites had been previously associated with the Phoenicians (Jdg 18:7).

2:1 ˣS Dt 12:5
ʸEcc 2:4
2:2 ᶻ2Ch 10:4
2:3 ᵃS 2Sa 5:11
ᵇS 1Ch 14:1
2:4 ᶜS Dt 12:5
ᵈS Ex 30:7 ᵉEx 25:30
ᶠEx 29:42; 2Ch 13:11;
29:28 ᵍS Lev 23:38
ʰS Nu 28:14
2:5 ⁱ1Ch 22:5
ʲS Ex 12:12;
S 1Ch 16:25
2:6 ᵏS 1Ki 8:27;
Jer 23:24 ˡS Ex 3:11
2:7 ᵐS Ex 35:31;
1Ch 22:16
2:10 ⁿEzr 3:7
2:11 ᵒ1Ki 10:9;
2Ch 9:8
2:12 ᵖNe 9:6;
Ps 8:3; 33:6; 96:5;
102:25; 146:6
2:13 �q S 1Ki 7:13
2:14 ʳS Ex 31:6
ˢS Ex 35:31 ᵗEx 35:35
2:15 ᵘEzr 3:7
2:16 ᵛS Jos 19:46;
Jnh 1:3

2:17 w 1Ch 22:2
x S 2Sa 24:2
2:18 y 1Ch 22:2;
2Ch 8:8
3:1 z Ac 7:47
a S Ge 28:17
b S 2Sa 24:18
3:2 c Ezr 5:11
3:3 d Eze 41:2
3:5 e Eze 40:16
3:7 f Ge 3:24;
Eze 41:18
3:8 g S Ex 26:33
3:9 h Ex 26:32
3:10 i Ex 25:18
3:13 j S Ex 25:18
3:14 k S Ex 26:31,33
l Ge 3:24
3:15 m S 1Ki 7:15;
Rev 3:12

¹⁷Solomon took a census of all the foreigners ʷ residing in Israel, after the census ˣ his father David had taken; and they were found to be 153,600. ¹⁸He assigned ʸ 70,000 of them to be carriers and 80,000 to be stonecutters in the hills, with 3,600 supervisors over them to keep the people working.

SOLOMON BUILDS THE TEMPLE

3:1–14pp — 1Ki 6:1–29

3 Then Solomon began to build ᶻ the temple of the LORD ᵃ in Jerusalem on Mount Moriah, where the LORD had appeared to his father David. It was on the threshing floor of Araunah ᵃ ᵇ the Jebusite, the place provided by David. ²He began building on the second day of the second month in the fourth year of his reign. ᶜ

³The foundation Solomon laid for building the temple of God was sixty cubits long and twenty cubits wide ᵇ ᵈ (using the cubit of the old standard). ⁴The portico at the front of the temple was twenty cubits ᶜ long across the width of the building and twenty cubits ᵈ high.

He overlaid the inside with pure gold. ⁵He paneled the main hall with juniper and covered it with fine gold and decorated it with palm tree ᵉ and chain designs. ⁶He adorned the temple with precious stones. And the gold he used was gold of Parvaim. ⁷He overlaid the ceiling beams, doorframes, walls and doors of the temple with gold, and he carved cherubim ᶠ on the walls.

⁸He built the Most Holy Place, ᵍ its length corresponding to the width of the temple— twenty cubits long and twenty cubits wide. He overlaid the inside with six hundred talents ᵉ of fine gold. ⁹The gold nails ʰ weighed fifty shekels. ᶠ He also overlaid the upper parts with gold.

¹⁰For the Most Holy Place he made a pair ⁱ of sculptured cherubim and overlaid them with gold. ¹¹The total wingspan of the cherubim was twenty cubits. One wing of the first cherub was five cubits ᵍ long and touched the temple wall, while its other wing, also five cubits long, touched the wing of the other cherub. ¹²Similarly one wing of the second cherub was five cubits long and touched the other temple wall, and its other wing, also five cubits long, touched the wing of the first cherub. ¹³The wings of these cherubim ʲ extended twenty cubits. They stood on their feet, facing the main hall. ʰ

¹⁴He made the curtain ᵏ of blue, purple and crimson yarn and fine linen, with cherubim ˡ worked into it.

¹⁵For the front of the temple he made two pillars, ᵐ which totaled thirty-five cubits ⁱ in

---

ᵃ 1 Hebrew *Ornan*, a variant of *Araunah*   ᵇ 3 That is, about 90 feet long and 30 feet wide or about 27 meters long and 9 meters wide   ᶜ 4 That is, about 30 feet or about 9 meters; also in verses 8, 11 and 13   ᵈ 4 Some Septuagint and Syriac manuscripts; Hebrew *and a hundred and twenty*   ᵉ 8 That is, about 23 tons or about 20 metric tons   ᶠ 9 That is, about 1 1/4 pounds or about 575 grams   ᵍ 11 That is, about 7 1/2 feet or about 2.3 meters; also in verse 15   ʰ 13 Or *facing inward*   ⁱ 15 That is, about 52 feet or about 16 meters

---

2:17–18 See 1Ki 5:13–18 and notes. The Chronicler specifies that this levy of forced laborers was from foreigners living among the Israelites, not from the Israelites themselves. This is not stated in the parallel passage in Kings, though 1Ki 9:20–22 confirms that foreign laborers were used (see 8:8).

2:18 *3,600 supervisors.* See v. 2. The number given in 1Ki 5:16 is 3,300; however, some manuscripts of the Septuagint (the pre-Christian Greek translation of the OT) also have 3,600. The Chronicler may have been following a different text of Kings from the traditional Hebrew text at this point (but see note on 1Ki 5:16).

3:1–17 The Chronicler has considerably curtailed the description of the temple's construction found in Kings, omitting completely 1Ki 6:4–20. This abridgment probably indicates that the Chronicler's audience was familiar with the details of the earlier history and that the temple of the restoration period was less elaborate than the original Solomonic structure (Hag 2:3). On the other hand, the Chronicler goes into more detail on the furnishings and implements (3:6–9; 4:1,6–9).

3:1 *Mount Moriah.* The only passage in the OT where Mount Zion is identified with Mount Moriah, the place where Abraham was commanded to offer Isaac (Ge 22:2,14). *place provided by David.* See 1Ch 21:18—22:5.

3:2 *second month in the fourth year.* In the spring of 966 B.C. (see note on 1Ki 6:1).

3:3 *cubit of the old standard.* About three inches longer than the common cubit, which was c. 18 inches (see Eze 40:5 and note).

3:4 *portico.* See diagram, p. 494. *overlaid.* Or "inlaid," which perhaps gives a more correct picture: not that the entire interior was covered with gold leaf, but that designs (palm trees, chains) were inlaid with gold leaf (v. 5).

3:6 *Parvaim.* Designates either the source of the gold (perhaps southeast Arabia) or a particular quality of fine gold.

3:7 *cherubim.* See vv. 10–14; see also notes on Ge 3:24; Eze 1:5.

3:8 *twenty cubits long and twenty cubits wide.* It was also 20 cubits high (1Ki 6:20), making the dimensions of the Most Holy Place a perfect cube, as probably also in the tabernacle. In the new Jerusalem there is no temple (Rev 21:22); rather, the whole city is in the shape of a cube (Rev 21:16), for the whole city becomes "the Most Holy Place."

3:9 *gold nails.* The fact that gold is a soft metal would make it unlikely that nails were made of this substance. It is probable that this small amount (only 1 1/4 pounds; see TNIV text note) represents gold leaf or sheeting used to gild the nail heads.

3:10–13 See 1Ki 6:23–27 and notes.

3:14 *curtain.* Also separated the two rooms of the tabernacle (Ex 26:31). Wooden doors could also be closed across the opening (4:22; 1Ki 6:31–32; cf. Mt 27:51; Heb 9:8).

3:15 *totaled thirty-five cubits in length.* The TNIV supplies the word "totaled" in an attempt to harmonize this measurement length, each with a capital[n] five cubits high. [16]He made interwoven chains[a o] and put them on top of the pillars. He also made a hundred pomegranates[p] and attached them to the chains. [17]He erected the pillars in the front of the temple, one to the south and one to the north. The one to the south he named Jakin[b] and the one to the north Boaz.[c]

THE TEMPLE'S FURNISHINGS
4:2–6,10—5:1pp — 1Ki 7:23–26,38–51

4 He made a bronze altar[q] twenty cubits long, twenty cubits wide and ten cubits high.[d] [2]He made the Sea[r] of cast metal, circular in shape, measuring ten cubits from rim to rim and five cubits[e] high. It took a line of thirty cubits[f] to measure around it. [3]Below the rim, figures of bulls encircled it—ten to a cubit.[g] The bulls were cast in two rows in one piece with the Sea.

[4]The Sea stood on twelve bulls, three facing north, three facing west, three facing south and three facing east.[s] The Sea rested on top of them, and their hindquarters were toward the center. [5]It was a handbreadth[h] in thickness, and its rim was like the rim of a cup, like a lily blossom. It held three thousand baths.[i]

[6]He then made ten basins[t] for washing and placed five on the south side and five on the north. In them the things to be used for the burnt offerings[u] were rinsed, but the Sea was to be used by the priests for washing.

[7]He made ten gold lampstands[v] according to the specifications[w] for them and placed them in the temple, five on the south side and five on the north.

[8]He made ten tables[x] and placed them in the temple, five on the south side and five on the north. He also made a hundred gold sprinkling bowls.[y]

[9]He made the courtyard[z] of the priests, and the large court and the doors for the court, and overlaid the doors with bronze. [10]He placed the Sea on the south side, at the southeast corner.

[11]And Huram also made the pots and shovels and sprinkling bowls.

So Huram finished[a] the work he had undertaken for King Solomon in the temple of God:

[12] the two pillars;

the two bowl-shaped capitals on top of the pillars;

the two sets of network decorating the two bowl-shaped capitals on top of the pillars;

[13] the four hundred pomegranates for the two sets of network (two rows of pomegranates for each network, decorating the bowl-shaped capitals on top of the pillars);

[14] the stands[b] with their basins;

[15] the Sea and the twelve bulls under it;

[16] the pots, shovels, meat forks and all related articles.

a 16 Or possibly *made chains in the inner sanctuary*; the meaning of the Hebrew for this phrase is uncertain.   b 17 *Jakin* probably means *he establishes.*   c 17 *Boaz* probably means *in him is strength.*
d 1 That is, about 30 feet long and wide and 15 feet high or about 9 meters long and wide and 4.5 meters high   e 2 That is, about 7 1/2 feet or about 2.3 meters   f 2 That is, about 45 feet or about 13.5 meters
g 3 That is, about 18 inches or about 45 centimeters   h 5 That is, about 3 inches or about 7.5 centimeters   i 5 That is, about 18,000 gallons or about 66,000 liters

3:15 [n] 1Ki 7:22
3:16 [o] 1Ki 7:17
[p] S 1Ki 7:20
4:1 [q] S Ex 20:24;
S 40:6; S 1Ki 8:64
4:2 [r] Rev 4:6; 15:2
4:4 [s] Nu 2:3-25;
Eze 48:30-34;
Rev 21:13
4:6 [t] S Ex 30:18
[u] Ne 13:5, 9;
Eze 40:38
4:7 [v] S Ex 25:31
[w] Ex 25:40
4:8 [x] S Ex 25:23
[y] S Nu 4:14
4:9 [z] 1Ki 6:36;
2Ch 33:5
4:11 [a] 1Ki 7:14
4:14 [b] 1Ki 7:27-30

---

with the 18 cubits (each) in 1Ki 7:15; 2Ki 25:17 (see note there); Jer 52:21 (though the Septuagint at Jer 52:21 has 35). Alternatively, 35 may be the result of a copyist's mistake.

3:17 *pillars.* Remains of such pillars have been found in the excavations of numerous temples in the Holy Land. Cf. Rev 3:12. *Jakin…Boaz.* See TNIV text notes.

4:1 *bronze altar.* The parallel text in Kings does not mention the main altar of the temple described here (1Ki 7:22–23), though several other passages in Kings do refer to it (1Ki 8:64; 9:25; 2Ki 16:14). The main altar of Solomon's temple was similar to the altar with steps that is described in Eze 43:13–17.

4:2 *Sea of cast metal.* A larger reservoir of water that replaced the bronze basin of the tabernacle (Ex 30:18); it was used by the priests for their ceremonial washing (v. 6; Ex 30:21). The NT views these rituals as foreshadowing the cleansing provided by Christ (Tit 3:5; Heb 9:11–14). In the temple of Ezekiel, the Sea, which was on the south side in front of the temple (v. 10), has been replaced by a life-giving river that flows from the south side of the temple (Eze 47:1–12; cf. Joel 3:18; Zec 14:8; Jn 4:9–15; Rev 22:1–2).

4:3 *bulls.* 1Ki 7:24 has "gourds." The Hebrew for the two words is very similar, so the difference may be due to a copyist's mistake.

4:4 *twelve bulls.* Possibly symbolic of the 12 tribes, which also encamped three on each side of the tabernacle during the desert journeys (Nu 2; cf. Eze 48:30–35).

4:5 *three thousand baths.* 1Ki 7:26 has 2,000 baths. The Hebrew for these figures could easily have been misread by the ancient scribes.

4:6 *ten basins.* See 1Ki 7:38–39.

4:7 *ten gold lampstands.* Instead of one, as in the tabernacle (Ex 25:31–40). *specifications.* See 1Ch 28:15. These lamps were not necessarily of the same shape as those described in Ex 25:31–40 but could have resembled the style depicted in Zec 4:2–6.

4:8 *ten tables.* Instead of one, as in the tabernacle (Ex 25:23–30; 40:4; Lev 24:5–9; 1Sa 21:1–6; Eze 41:22; Heb 9:2; cf. 2Ch 13:11; 29:18).

4:11–16 See 1Ki 7:40–45.

4:11 *sprinkling bowls.* See notes on Ex 27:3; 1Ki 7:40.

4:16 c S 1Ki 7:13
4:17 d S Ge 33:17
4:18 e S 1Ki 7:23
4:19 f S Ex 25:23,30
4:20 g Ex 25:31
4:22 h S Nu 7:14
i S Lev 10:1
5:1 j S 1Ki 6:14
k S 2Sa 8:11
5:2 l S Nu 3:31;
S 1Ch 15:25
5:3 m S 1Ch 9:1
5:5 n S Nu 3:31;
S 1Ch 15:2
5:7 o Rev 11:19
5:8 p S Ge 3:24
5:10 q Heb 9:4
r S Ex 16:34; S Dt 10:2
5:11 s S 1Ch 24:1
5:12 t 1Ki 10:12;
1Ch 9:33; S 25:1;
Ps 68:25 u S 1Ch 13:8
5:13 v S 1Ch 16:34,
41; 2Ch 7:3; 20:21;
Ezr 3:11; Ps 100:5;
106:1; 107:1; 118:1;
136:1; Jer 33:11

All the objects that Huram-Abi[c] made for King Solomon for the temple of the LORD were of polished bronze. [17]The king had them cast in clay molds in the plain of the Jordan between Sukkoth[d] and Zarethan.[a] [18]All these things that Solomon made amounted to so much that the weight of the bronze[e] could not be calculated.

[19]Solomon also made all the furnishings that were in God's temple:

the golden altar;

the tables[f] on which was the bread of the Presence;

[20]the lampstands[g] of pure gold with their lamps, to burn in front of the inner sanctuary as prescribed;

[21]the gold floral work and lamps and tongs (they were solid gold);

[22]the pure gold wick trimmers, sprinkling bowls, dishes[h] and censers;[i] and the gold doors of the temple: the inner doors to the Most Holy Place and the doors of the main hall.

5 When all the work Solomon had done for the temple of the LORD was finished,[j] he brought in the things his father David had dedicated[k]—the silver and gold and all the furnishings—and he placed them in the treasuries of God's temple.

THE ARK BROUGHT TO THE TEMPLE

5:2—6:11pp — 1Ki 8:1–21

[2]Then Solomon summoned to Jerusalem the elders of Israel, all the heads of the tribes and the chiefs of the Israelite families, to bring up the ark[l] of the LORD's covenant from Zion, the City of David. [3]And all the Israelites[m] came together to the king at the time of the festival in the seventh month.

[4]When all the elders of Israel had arrived, the Levites took up the ark, [5]and they brought up the ark and the tent of meeting and all the sacred furnishings in it. The Levitical priests[n] carried them up; [6]and King Solomon and the entire assembly of Israel that had gathered about him were before the ark, sacrificing so many sheep and cattle that they could not be recorded or counted.

[7]The priests then brought the ark[o] of the LORD's covenant to its place in the inner sanctuary of the temple, the Most Holy Place, and put it beneath the wings of the cherubim. [8]The cherubim[p] spread their wings over the place of the ark and covered the ark and its carrying poles. [9]These poles were so long that their ends, extending from the ark, could be seen from in front of the inner sanctuary, but not from outside the Holy Place; and they are still there today. [10]There was nothing in the ark except[q] the two tablets[r] that Moses had placed in it at Horeb, where the LORD made a covenant with the Israelites after they came out of Egypt.

[11]The priests then withdrew from the Holy Place. All the priests who were there had consecrated themselves, regardless of their divisions. [s] [12]All the Levites who were musicians[t]—Asaph, Heman, Jeduthun and their sons and relatives—stood on the east side of the altar, dressed in fine linen and playing cymbals, harps and lyres. They were accompanied by 120 priests sounding trumpets. [u] [13]The trumpeters and musicians joined in unison to give praise and thanks to the LORD. Accompanied by trumpets, cymbals and other instruments, the singers raised their voices in praise to the LORD and sang:

"He is good;

his love endures forever."[v]

---

a 17 Hebrew *Zeredatha*, a variant of *Zarethan*

4:17–22 See 1Ki 7:46–50 and notes.
4:17 *clay molds.* The clay of the Jordan plain was used to make molds for these bronze castings. *Sukkoth and Zarethan.* See note on 1Ki 7:46.
5:1 *things his father David had dedicated.* See notes on 1Ch 18:1—20:8; 22:2–16; 29:2–5; see also 1Ch 26:26 and note.
5:2–14 See 1Ki 8:1–11 and notes.
5:2 *ark.* Had been in a tent provided for it 40 years earlier when David brought it to Jerusalem (1Ch 15:1—16:6).
5:3 *festival in the seventh month.* The Festival of Tabernacles. The month is designated by its Canaanite name, Ethanim, in 1Ki 8:2; the Hebrew name is Tishri. According to 1Ki 6:38 the temple was completed in the eighth month of Solomon's 11th year, i.e., September–October, 959 B.C. This celebration of dedication

probably took place 11 months after the completion of the work (see note on 1Ki 8:2).
5:5 *brought up ... the tent of meeting.* The tabernacle had been at Gibeon (see 1:13; see also note on 1Ch 16:39).
5:6 Cf. David's bringing of the ark to Jerusalem (1Ch 15:26; 16:1–3).
5:9 *still there today.* See note on 1Ki 8:8; see also 8:8; 10:19; 20:26; 21:10; 35:25; 1Ch 4:41,43; 5:26; 13:11; 17:5.
5:10 *two tablets.* See Ex 31:18 and note; see also Ex 32:15–16. The ark had earlier contained also the gold jar of manna (Ex 16:32–34) and Aaron's staff (Nu 17:10–11; Heb 9:4). These items were presumably lost, perhaps while the ark was in Philistine hands.
5:12 *fine linen.* See 1Ch 15:27 and note.

Then the temple of the LORD was filled with the cloud, [w] [14]and the priests could not perform[x] their service because of the cloud, [y] for the glory[z] of the LORD filled the temple of God.

6 Then Solomon said, "The LORD has said that he would dwell in a dark cloud; [a] [2]I have built a magnificent temple for you, a place for you to dwell forever. [b]"

[3]While the whole assembly of Israel was standing there, the king turned around and blessed them. [4]Then he said:

"Praise be to the LORD, the God of Israel, who with his hands has fulfilled what he promised with his mouth to my father David. For he said, [5]'Since the day I brought my people out of Egypt, I have not chosen a city in any tribe of Israel to have a temple built so that my Name might be there, nor have I chosen anyone to be ruler over my people Israel. [6]But now I have chosen Jerusalem[c] for my Name[d] to be there, and I have chosen David[e] to rule my people Israel.'

[7]"My father David had it in his heart[f] to build a temple for the Name of the LORD, the God of Israel. [8]But the LORD said to my father David, 'You did well to have it in your heart to build a temple for my Name. [9]Nevertheless, you are not the one to build the temple, but your son, who is your own flesh and blood—he is the one who will build the temple for my Name.'

[10]"The LORD has kept the promise he made. I have succeeded David my father and now I sit on the throne of Israel, just as the LORD promised, and I have built the temple for the Name of the LORD, the God of Israel. [11]There I have placed the ark, in which is the covenant[g] of the LORD that he made with the people of Israel."

SOLOMON'S PRAYER OF DEDICATION
6:12–40pp — 1Ki 8:22–53
6:41–42pp — Ps 132:8–10

[12]Then Solomon stood before the altar of the LORD in front of the whole assembly of Israel and spread out his hands. [13]Now he had made a bronze platform,[h] five cubits long, five cubits wide and three cubits high,[a] and had placed it in the center of the outer court. He stood on the platform and then knelt down[i] before the whole assembly of Israel and spread out his hands toward heaven. [14]He said:

"LORD, the God of Israel, there is no God like you[j] in heaven or on earth—you who keep your covenant of love[k] with your servants who continue wholeheartedly in your way. [15]You have kept your promise to your servant David my father; with your mouth you have promised[l] and with your hand you have fulfilled it—as it is today.

[16]"Now LORD, the God of Israel, keep for your servant David my father the promises you made to him when you said, 'You shall never fail[m] to have a successor to sit before me on the throne of Israel, if only your descendants are careful in all they do to walk before me according to my law,[n] as you have done.' [17]And now, LORD, the God of Israel, let your word that you promised your servant David come true.

[18]"But will God really dwell[o] on earth with human beings? The heavens,[p] even the highest heavens, cannot contain you. How much less this temple I have built! [19]Yet, LORD my God, give attention to your servant's prayer and his plea for mercy. Hear the cry and the prayer that your servant is praying in your presence. [20]May your eyes[q] be open toward this temple day and night, this place of which you said you would put your Name[r] there. May you hear[s] the prayer your servant prays toward this place. [21]Hear the supplications of your servant and of your people Israel when they pray toward this place. Hear from heaven, your dwelling place; and when you hear, forgive.[t]

[22]"When anyone wrongs their neighbor and is required to take an oath[u] and they come and swear the oath before your altar in this temple, [23]then hear from heaven

---

[a] 13 That is, about 7 1/2 feet long and wide and 4 1/2 feet high or about 2.3 meters long and wide and 1.4 meters high

---

5:13 [w] S Ex 40:34
5:14 [x] Ex 40:35;
Rev 15:8 [y] Ex 19:16
[z] S Ex 29:43; S 40:35
6:1 [a] S Ex 19:9
6:2 [b] Ezr 6:12; 7:15;
Ps 135:21
6:6 [c] S Dt 12:5;
S Isa 14:1
[d] S Ex 20:24
[e] S 1Ch 28:4
6:7 [f] S 1Sa 10:7;
S 1Ch 17:2; Ac 7:46
6:11 [g] S Dt 10:2;
Ps 25:10; 50:5
6:13 [h] Ne 8:4
[i] Ps 95:6
6:14 [j] S Ex 8:10;
15:11 [k] S Dt 7:9
6:15 [l] S 1Ch 22:10
6:16 [m] S 2Sa 7:13,
15; 2Ch 23:3
[n] Ps 132:12
6:18 [o] S Rev 21:3
[p] Ps 11:4; Isa 40:22;
66:1
6:20 [q] S Ex 3:16;
Ps 34:15 [r] Dt 12:11
[s] 2Ch 7:14; 30:20
6:21 [t] Ps 51:1;
Isa 33:24; 40:2;
43:25; 44:22; 55:7;
Mic 7:18
6:22 [u] S Ex 22:11

A **5:14** *cloud … glory of the LORD.* Cf. 7:1–3. The glory cloud represented the presence of God. It had guided Israel out of Egypt and through the desert and was present above the tabernacle (Ex 13:21–22; 40:34–38; cf. Eze 43:1–5; Hag 2:9; Zec 1:16; 2:10; 8:3).
6:1–11 See notes on 1Ki 8:12–21.
6:8–9 Cf. David's speech in 1Ch 28:2–3.
6:12–21 See notes on 1Ki 8:22–30.

6:13 Not in 1Ki 8. Some think that the Chronicler may have wished to clarify the fact that Solomon was not "before the altar" (v. 12) exercising priestly duties. On the other hand, the verse may have been dropped from Kings by a copying error.
6:14 *who keep your covenant of love.* See 1Ki 8:23 and note.
6:18 Cf. 2:6.
6:22–39 See notes on 1Ki 8:31–46.
6:22–23 See Ex 22:10–11; Lev 6:3–5.

6:23 ʸ Isa 3:11; 65:6;
S Mt 16:27
6:24 ʷ S Lev 26:17
6:26 ˣ Lev 26:19;
S Dt 11:17; 28:24;
2 Sa 1:21
6:27 ʸ ver 30,39;
2Ch 7:14
6:28 ᶻ 2Ch 20:9
6:30 ᵃ S ver 27
ᵇ S 1Sa 2:3; Ps 7:9;
44:21; Pr 16:2; 17:3
6:31 ᶜ S Dt 6:13;
Ps 34:7,9; 103:11,13;
Pr 8:13
6:32 ᵈ 2Ch 9:6
ᵉ S Ex 3:19,20
6:33 ᶠ S Ex 12:43
6:34 ᵍ Dt 28:7
ʰ S 1Ch 5:20
6:36 ⁱ S 1Ki 8:46;
Job 11:12; 15:14;
Ps 143:2; Ecc 7:20;
Jer 9:5; 13:23; 17:9;
S Ro 3:9; Eph 2:3
ʲ S Lev 26:44
6:37 ᵏ 1Ki 8:48;
2Ch 7:14; 12:6,12;
30:11; 33:12,19,23;
34:27; 36:12; Isa 58:3;
Jer 24:7; 29:13
6:39 ˡ S ver 27;
2Ch 30:9
6:40 ᵐ S 1Ki 8:29,
52; 2Ch 7:15; Ne 1:6,
11; Ps 17:1,6; 116:1;
130:2; Isa 37:17
6:41 ⁿ Ps 3:7; 7:6;
59:4; Isa 33:10
ᵒ 1Ch 28:2 ᵖ Ps 132:16
�q Ps 13:6; 27:13;
116:12; 142:7
6:42 ʳ Ps 2:2
ˢ Ps 89:24,28

and act. Judge between your servants, condemning ᵛ the guilty and bringing down on their heads what they have done, and vindicating the innocent by treating them in accordance with their innocence.

²⁴"When your people Israel have been defeated ʷ by an enemy because they have sinned against you and when they turn back and give praise to your name, praying and making supplication before you in this temple, ²⁵then hear from heaven and forgive the sin of your people Israel and bring them back to the land you gave to them and their ancestors.

²⁶"When the heavens are shut up and there is no rain ˣ because your people have sinned against you, and when they pray toward this place and give praise to your name and turn from their sin because you have afflicted them, ²⁷then hear from heaven and forgive ʸ the sin of your servants, your people Israel. Teach them the right way to live, and send rain on the land you gave your people for an inheritance.

²⁸"When famine ᶻ or plague comes to the land, or blight or mildew, locusts or grasshoppers, or when enemies besiege them in any of their cities, whatever disaster or disease may come, ²⁹and when a prayer or plea is made by anyone among your people Israel—being aware of their afflictions and pains, and spreading out their hands toward this temple— ³⁰then hear from heaven, your dwelling place. Forgive, ᵃ and deal with everyone according to all they do, since you know their hearts (for you alone know the human heart), ᵇ ³¹so that they will fear you ᶜ and walk in obedience to you all the time they live in the land you gave our ancestors.

³²"As for foreigners who do not belong to your people Israel but have come ᵈ from a distant land because of your great name and your mighty hand ᵉ and your outstretched arm—when they come and pray toward this temple, ³³then hear from heaven, your dwelling place. Do whatever the foreigner ᶠ asks of you, so that all the peoples of the earth may know your name and fear you, as do your own people Israel, and may know that this house I have built bears your Name.

³⁴"When your people go to war against their enemies, ᵍ wherever you send them, and when they pray ʰ to you toward this city you have chosen and the temple I have built for your Name, ³⁵then hear from heaven their prayer and their plea, and uphold their cause.

³⁶"When they sin against you—for there is no one who does not sin ⁱ—and you become angry with them and give them over to the enemy, who takes them captive ʲ to a land far away or near; ³⁷and if they have a change of heart ᵏ in the land where they are held captive, and repent and plead with you in the land of their captivity and say, 'We have sinned, we have done wrong and acted wickedly'; ³⁸and if they turn back to you with all their heart and soul in the land of their captivity where they were taken, and pray toward the land you gave their ancestors, toward the city you have chosen and toward the temple I have built for your Name; ³⁹then from heaven, your dwelling place, hear their prayer and their pleas, and uphold their cause. And forgive ˡ your people, who have sinned against you.

⁴⁰"Now, my God, may your eyes be open and your ears attentive ᵐ to the prayers offered in this place.

⁴¹"Now arise, ⁿ Lᴏʀᴅ God, and come to your resting place, ᵒ
　you and the ark of your might.
May your priests, ᵖ Lᴏʀᴅ God, be clothed with salvation,
　may your faithful people rejoice in your goodness. q
⁴²Lᴏʀᴅ God, do not reject your anointed one. ʳ
　Remember the great love ˢ promised to David your servant."

6:24–25 See Lev 26:17,23; Dt 28:25,36–37,48–57,64; Jos 7:11–12.

6:26–27 See Lev 26:19; Dt 11:10–15; 28:18,22–24.

6:28–31 See Lev 26:16,20,25–26; Dt 28:20–22,27–28,35,42.

6:32–33 The prophets also envisaged the Gentiles coming to Jerusalem to worship the Lord (Isa 2:3; 56:6–8; Mic 4:2; Zec 8:20–23; 14:16–21; cf. Ps 87).

6:34–35 See Lev 26:7–8; Dt 28:6–7. The Chronicler repeatedly demonstrates God's answer to prayer in time of battle (ch. 13; 14:9–15; 18:31; 20:1–29; 25:5–13; 32:20–22).

6:36 no one who does not sin. See Jer 13:23; Ro 3:23. captive to a land far away. See 36:15–20; Lev 26:33,44–45; Dt 28:49–52; 2Ki 17:7–20; 25:1–21.

6:40–42 The Chronicler replaces the ending of Solomon's prayer in Kings (1Ki 8:50–53) with Ps 132:8–10, a psalm that deals with bringing the ark to the temple, the theme of this section in Chronicles (5:2–14). The prayer in Kings ends with an appeal to the exodus deliverance under Moses, while in Chronicles the appeal is on the basis of the eternal promises to David.

THE DEDICATION OF THE TEMPLE

7:1–10pp — 1Ki 8:62–66

7 When Solomon finished praying, fire[t] came down from heaven and consumed the burnt offering and the sacrifices, and the glory of the LORD filled[u] the temple.[v] ²The priests could not enter[w] the temple of the LORD because the glory[x] of the LORD filled it. ³When all the Israelites saw the fire coming down and the glory of the LORD above the temple, they knelt on the pavement with their faces to the ground, and they worshiped and gave thanks to the LORD, saying,

"He is good;
his love endures forever."[y]

⁴Then the king and all the people offered sacrifices before the LORD. ⁵And King Solomon offered a sacrifice of twenty-two thousand head of cattle and a hundred and twenty thousand sheep and goats. So the king and all the people dedicated the temple of God. ⁶The priests took their positions, as did the Levites[z] with the LORD's musical instruments,[a] which King David had made for praising the LORD and which were used when he gave thanks, saying, "His love endures forever." Opposite the Levites, the priests blew their trumpets, and all the Israelites were standing.

⁷Solomon consecrated the middle part of the courtyard in front of the temple of the LORD, and there he offered burnt offerings and the fat[b] of the fellowship offerings, because the bronze altar he had made could not hold the burnt offerings, the grain offerings and the fat portions.

⁸So Solomon observed the festival[c] at that time for seven days, and all Israel[d] with him—a vast assembly, people from Lebo Hamath[e] to the Wadi of Egypt.[f] ⁹On the eighth day they held an assembly, for they had celebrated[g] the dedication of the altar for seven days and the festival[h] for seven days more. ¹⁰On the twenty-third day of the seventh month he sent the people to their homes, joyful and glad in heart for the good things the LORD had done for David and Solomon and for his people Israel.

THE LORD APPEARS TO SOLOMON

7:11–22pp — 1Ki 9:1–9

¹¹When Solomon had finished[i] the temple of the LORD and the royal palace, and had succeeded in carrying out all he had in mind to do in the temple of the LORD and in his own palace, ¹²the LORD appeared[j] to him at night and said:

"I have heard your prayer and have chosen[k] this place for myself[l] as a temple for sacrifices.

¹³"When I shut up the heavens so that there is no rain,[m] or command locusts to devour the land or send a plague among my people, ¹⁴if my people, who are called by my name,[n] will humble[o] themselves and pray and seek my face[p] and turn[q] from their wicked ways, then I will hear[r] from heaven, and I will forgive[s] their sin and will heal[t] their land. ¹⁵Now my eyes will be open and my ears attentive to the prayers offered in this place.[u] ¹⁶I have chosen[v] and consecrated this temple so that my Name may be there forever. My eyes and my heart will always be there.

¹⁷"As for you, if you walk before me faithfully[w] as David your father did, and do all I command, and observe my decrees[x] and laws, ¹⁸I will establish your royal throne,

---

Cross-references

7:1 ʳS Ex 19:18;
S Lev 9:24;
S 1Ki 18:38
ᵘS Ex 16:10 ᵛPs 26:8
7:2 ʷS 1Ki 8:11
ˣS Ex 29:43; S 40:35
7:3 ʸS 1Ch 16:34;
2Ch 5:13; Ezr 3:11
7:6 ᶻ1Ch 15:16
ᵃS 1Ch 15:24
7:7 ᵇS Ex 29:13
7:8 ᶜ2Ch 30:26;
Ne 8:17 ᵈS 1Ch 9:1
ᵉS Nu 13:21
ᶠS Ge 15:18
7:9 ᵍ2Ch 30:23
ʰS Lev 23:36
7:11 ⁱS 1Ch 28:20
7:12 ʲ2Ch 1:7
ᵏDt 12:11 ˡS Dt 12:5
7:13 ᵐS Dt 11:17;
Am 4:7
7:14 ⁿS Nu 6:27
ᵒS Ex 10:3;
S Lev 26:41;
S 2Ch 6:37
ᵖS 1Ch 16:11
�q S 2Ki 17:13;
Isa 55:7; Eze 18:32;
Zec 1:4 ʳS 2Ch 6:20
ˢS 2Ch 6:27
ᵗS Ex 15:26;
2Ch 30:20; Ps 60:2;
Isa 30:26; 53:5; 57:18;
Jer 33:6; Mal 4:2
7:15 ᵘS 1Ki 8:29;
S 2Ch 6:40; Ne 1:6
7:16 ᵛS Dt 12:5;
2Ch 33:7
7:17 ʷS 1Ki 9:4
ˣS Lev 19:37

7:1–22 See 1Ki 8:54—9:9 and notes.

7:1–3 Not found in 1Ki 8. The addition of the fire descending from heaven to consume the sacrifices provides the same sign of divine acceptance given at the dedication of the tabernacle (Lev 9:23–24) and at David's offering on the threshing floor of Araunah the Jebusite (1Ch 21:26; cf. 1Ki 18:38). While vv. 1–3 are unique to Chronicles, the Chronicler has omitted Solomon's blessing of the congregation (1Ki 8:55–61).

7:1 *glory of the LORD.* See 5:14 and note.

7:3 *He is good . . . forever.* See v. 6; 5:13.

7:6 The verse is unique to Chronicles and reflects the author's overall interest in the Levites, especially the musicians (cf. 29:26–27; see note on 1Ch 6:31–48). *all the Israelites.* See Introduction to 1 Chronicles: Purpose and Themes.

7:8 *from Lebo Hamath to the Wadi of Egypt.* Not only were the patriarchal promises of descendants provisionally fulfilled under David and Solomon (see 1:9; 1Ch 27:23–24 and notes), but

also the promises of land (Ge 15:18–21). *Lebo Hamath.* See note on Eze 47:15. *Wadi of Egypt.* See note on Eze 47:19.

7:9 *eighth day.* The final day of the Festival of Tabernacles (see 5:3 and note; Lev 23:36; Nu 29:35). *seven days . . . seven days.* The dedication had run from the 8th to the 14th day of the month, and the Festival of Tabernacles from the 15th to the 22nd day. The Day of Atonement was on the 10th day of the 7th month (Lev 16; cf. 1Ki 8:65–66).

7:12 *appeared to him.* The second time God appeared to Solomon; the first was at Gibeon (1:3–13; 1Ki 9:2).

7:13–15 Unique to Chronicles. These verses illustrate the writer's emphasis on immediate retribution (see Introduction to 1 Chronicles: Purpose and Themes). The Chronicler subsequently portrays the kings in a way that demonstrates this principle (see v. 22).

7:14 See, e.g., 12:6–7,12.

7:17–18 See 1Ki 9:4–5. Such words as these reinforced ancient Israel's Messianic hopes.

7:18 ʸ Isa 9:7;
Jer 33:17,21
ᶻ S 1Ch 5:2; Isa 55:4;
Mic 5:2 ᵃ S 2Sa 7:13;
S 1Ch 17:12; 2Ch 13:5;
23:3
7:19 ᵇ S Dt 28:15
ᶜ S 1Ch 28:9;
2Ch 12:1; 24:18;
Jer 9:13; 11:8
7:20 ᵈ S Dt 29:28
ᵉ 1Ki 14:15; Jer 12:14;
16:13; 50:11
ᶠ S Dt 28:37
7:21 ᵍ Jer 19:8
ʰ Dt 29:24
7:22 ⁱ Jer 16:11
8:1 ʲ S 2Sa 7:2
8:4 ᵏ S 2Sa 8:9
8:5 ˡ S Jos 10:10
8:6 ᵐ S Jos 19:44
8:7 ⁿ S Ge 10:16;
S 15:18-21; Ezr 9:1
8:8 ᵒ S 2Ch 2:18
8:11 ᵖ S 1Ki 3:1
8:12 �q S 1Ki 8:64;
2Ch 15:8
8:13 ʳ S Ex 29:38
ˢ Nu 28:9 ᵗ S Nu 10:10
ᵘ S Ex 23:14
ᵛ S Ex 12:17;
Nu 28:16-25
ʷ S Ex 23:16
ˣ Nu 29:12-38;
Ne 8:17
8:14 ʸ S 1Ch 24:1
ᶻ S 1Ch 25:1
ᵃ S 1Ch 9:17
ᵇ Ne 12:24,36
ᶜ S 1Ch 23:6;
Ne 12:45

as I covenanted ʸ with David your father when I said, 'You shall never fail to have a successor ᶻ to rule over Israel.' ᵃ

¹⁹"But if you ᵃ turn away ᵇ and forsake ᶜ the decrees and commands I have given you ᵃ and go off to serve other gods and worship them, ²⁰then I will uproot ᵈ Israel from my land, ᵉ which I have given them, and will reject this temple I have consecrated for my Name. I will make it a byword and an object of ridicule ᶠ among all peoples. ²¹This temple will become a heap of rubble. All ᵇ who pass by will be appalled ᵍ and say, ʰ 'Why has the LORD done such a thing to this land and to this temple?' ²²People will answer, 'Because they have forsaken the LORD, the God of their ancestors, who brought them out of Egypt, and have embraced other gods, worshiping and serving them ⁱ—that is why he brought all this disaster on them.' "

SOLOMON'S OTHER ACTIVITIES

8:1–18pp — 1Ki 9:10–28

8 At the end of twenty years, during which Solomon built the temple of the LORD and his own palace, ʲ ²Solomon rebuilt the villages that Hiram ᶜ had given him, and settled Israelites in them. ³Solomon then went to Hamath Zobah and captured it. ⁴He also built up Tadmor in the desert and all the store cities he had built in Hamath. ᵏ ⁵He rebuilt Upper Beth Horon ˡ and Lower Beth Horon as fortified cities, with walls and with gates and bars, ⁶as well as Baalath ᵐ and all his store cities, and all the cities for his chariots and for his horses ᵈ—whatever he desired to build in Jerusalem, in Lebanon and throughout all the territory he ruled.

⁷There were still people left from the Hittites, Amorites, Perizzites, Hivites and Jebusites ⁿ (these people were not Israelites). ⁸Solomon conscripted ᵒ the descendants of all these people remaining in the land—whom the Israelites had not destroyed—to serve as slave labor, as it is to this day. ⁹But Solomon did not make slaves of the Israelites for his work; they were his fighting men, commanders of his captains, and commanders of his chariots and charioteers. ¹⁰They were also King Solomon's chief officials—two hundred and fifty officials supervising the men.

¹¹Solomon brought Pharaoh's daughter ᵖ up from the City of David to the palace he had built for her, for he said, "My wife must not live in the palace of David king of Israel, because the places the ark of the LORD has entered are holy."

¹²On the altar q of the LORD that he had built in front of the portico, Solomon sacrificed burnt offerings to the LORD, ¹³according to the daily requirement ʳ for offerings commanded by Moses for the Sabbaths, ˢ the New Moons ᵗ and the three ᵘ annual festivals—the Festival of Unleavened Bread, ᵛ the Festival of Weeks ʷ and the Festival of Tabernacles. ˣ ¹⁴In keeping with the ordinance of his father David, he appointed the divisions ʸ of the priests for their duties, and the Levites ᶻ to lead the praise and to assist the priests according to each day's requirement. He also appointed the gatekeepers ᵃ by divisions for the various gates, because this was what David the man of God ᵇ had ordered. ᶜ ¹⁵They did not deviate from the king's commands to the priests or to the Levites in any matter, including that of the treasuries.

ᵃ *19* The Hebrew is plural.   ᵇ *21* See some Septuagint manuscripts, Old Latin, Syriac, Arabic and Targum; Hebrew *And though this temple is now so imposing, all*   ᶜ *2* Hebrew *Huram*, a variant of *Hiram*; also in verse 18   ᵈ *6* Or *charioteers*

7:19–22 See 1Ki 9:6–9.
8:1–18 See 1Ki 9:10–18 and notes. Verses 13–16 are unique to Chronicles and underscore the Chronicler's concern to show continuity with the past and his association of David with Moses (see Introduction to 1 Chronicles: Purpose and Themes).
8:1–2 In 1 Ki 9:10–14 the cities were given to Hiram by Solomon, whereas in Chronicles the reverse is true. Perhaps as part of his effort to idealize Solomon, the Chronicler does not record the fact that Hiram found these cities unacceptable payment (1Ki 9:11–13); he mentions only the sequel to the story, the return of the cities to Solomon and their subsequent improvement. They may also have served as a kind of collateral against the monies owed Hiram, who returned them when the debt was satisfied (see note on 1Ki 9:11). The Chronicler also says nothing about the pharaoh's gift of Gezer to Solomon (1Ki 9:16).
8:3–4 The Chronicler records an additional military campaign to the north, not mentioned in Kings. David had also cam-

paigned in the north against Zobah (1Ch 18:3–9; 19:6; 2Sa 8:3–12; 10:6–8; cf. 1Ki 11:23–24).
8:5 The two Beth Horons were situated on a strategic road from the coastal plain to the area just north of Jerusalem.
8:7 *not Israelites.* See 2:17; 1Ch 22:2; 1Ki 9:21.
8:8 *to this day.* See note on 5:9.
8:11 *holy.* Both 1Ki 9:24 and Chronicles record the transfer of the pharaoh's daughter to special quarters, but only Chronicles adds the reason: Not only the temple but also David's palace was regarded as holy, because of the presence of the ark (see note on Lev 11:44).
8:12–16 In line with his overall interests, the Chronicler elaborates on the sacrificial and temple provisions made by Solomon. While 1Ki 9:25 mentions only the sacrifices at the three annual festivals, the Chronicler adds the offerings on Sabbaths and New Moons to conform these provisions fully to Mosaic prescription (Lev 23:1–37; Nu 28–29).

8:18 d 2Ch 9:9
9:1 e S Ge 10:7;
Eze 23:42; Mt 12:42;
Lk 11:31
9:3 f 1Ki 5:12
9:6 g 2Ch 6:32
9:8 h S 1Ki 2:12;
S 1Ch 17:14; 2Ch 13:8
i 2Ch 2:11
9:9 j 2Ch 8:18
9:10 k 2Ch 8:18
9:14 l 2Ch 17:11;
Isa 21:13; Jer 25:24;
Eze 27:21; 30:5
9:16 m 2Ch 12:9
n S 1Ki 7:2
9:17 o S 1Ki 22:39

¹⁶All Solomon's work was carried out, from the day the foundation of the temple of the LORD was laid until its completion. So the temple of the LORD was finished.

¹⁷Then Solomon went to Ezion Geber and Elath on the coast of Edom. ¹⁸And Hiram sent him ships commanded by his own officers, sailors who knew the sea. These, with Solomon's servants, sailed to Ophir and brought back four hundred and fifty talents[a] of gold, [d] which they delivered to King Solomon.

THE QUEEN OF SHEBA VISITS SOLOMON

9:1–12pp — 1Ki 10:1–13

9 When the queen of Sheba[e] heard of Solomon's fame, she came to Jerusalem to test him with hard questions. Arriving with a very great caravan—with camels carrying spices, large quantities of gold, and precious stones—she came to Solomon and talked with him about all she had on her mind. ²Solomon answered all her questions; nothing was too hard for him to explain to her. ³When the queen of Sheba saw the wisdom of Solomon, [f] as well as the palace he had built, ⁴the food on his table, the seating of his officials, the attending servants in their robes, the cupbearers in their robes and the burnt offerings he made at[b] the temple of the LORD, she was overwhelmed.

⁵She said to the king, "The report I heard in my own country about your achievements and your wisdom is true. ⁶But I did not believe what they said until I came[g] and saw with my own eyes. Indeed, not even half the greatness of your wisdom was told me; you have far exceeded the report I heard. ⁷How happy your people must be! How happy your officials, who continually stand before you and hear your wisdom! ⁸Praise be to the LORD your God, who has delighted in you and placed you on his throne[h] as king to rule for the LORD your God. Because of the love of your God for Israel and his desire to uphold them forever, he has made you king[i] over them, to maintain justice and righteousness."

⁹Then she gave the king 120 talents[c] of gold, [j] large quantities of spices, and precious stones. There had never been such spices as those the queen of Sheba gave to King Solomon.

¹⁰(The servants of Hiram and the servants of Solomon brought gold from Ophir;[k] they also brought algumwood[d] and precious stones. ¹¹The king used the algumwood to make steps for the temple of the LORD and for the royal palace, and to make harps and lyres for the musicians. Nothing like them had ever been seen in Judah.)

¹²King Solomon gave the queen of Sheba all she desired and asked for; he gave her more than she had brought to him. Then she left and returned with her retinue to her own country.

SOLOMON'S SPLENDOR

9:13–28pp — 1Ki 10:14–29; 2Ch 1:14–17

¹³The weight of the gold that Solomon received yearly was 666 talents, [e] ¹⁴not including the revenues brought in by merchants and traders. Also all the kings of Arabia[l] and the governors of the territories brought gold and silver to Solomon.

¹⁵King Solomon made two hundred large shields of hammered gold; six hundred shekels[f] of hammered gold went into each shield. ¹⁶He also made three hundred small shields[m] of hammered gold, with three hundred shekels[g] of gold in each shield. The king put them in the Palace of the Forest of Lebanon. [n]

¹⁷Then the king made a great throne inlaid with ivory[o] and overlaid with pure gold.

---

a 18 That is, about 17 tons or about 15 metric tons   b 4 Or *and the ascent by which he went up to*
c 9 That is, about 4 1/2 tons or about 4 metric tons   d 10 Probably a variant of *almugwood*   e 13 That is, about 25 tons or about 23 metric tons   f 15 That is, about 15 pounds or about 6.9 kilograms
g 16 That is, about 7 1/2 pounds or about 3.5 kilograms

8:17–18 See 1Ki 9:26–28. This joint venture between Solomon and Hiram secured for these kings the lucrative trade routes through the Mediterranean to the south Arabian peninsula; Solomon became the middleman between these economic spheres.

8:17 *Ezion Geber and Elath.* See note on Dt 2:8.

8:18 *Hiram sent him ships.* Presumably ships crafted in Phoenicia and assembled at the port of Ezion Geber after being shipped overland (see 9:21).

C **9:1–12** See 1Ki 10:1–13 and notes. The visit of the queen of Sheba portrays the fulfillment of God's promise to give Solomon wisdom and wealth (1:12). Although the themes of Solomon's wisdom and wealth are here put to the fore, a major motive for the queen's visit may have been commercial, perhaps prompted by Solomon's naval operations toward south Arabia (8:17–18).

9:1 *Sheba.* See note on 1Ki 10:1; see also Job 1:15; 6:19; Ps 72:10,15; Isa 60:6; Jer 6:20; Eze 27:22; 38:13; Joel 3:8.

9:8 *his throne.* The most significant variation from the account of the queen's visit in 1 Kings (10:9) is found here. The queen's speech becomes the vehicle for the Chronicler's conviction that the throne of Israel is the throne of God, for whom the king ruled (see 13:18; see also note on 1Ch 17:14).

9:16,20 *Palace of the Forest of Lebanon.* The royal palace in Jerusalem (cf. note on 1Ki 7:2).

9:22 *p* S 1Ki 3:13;
S 2Ch 1:12
9:23 *q* 1Ki 4:34
9:24 *r* 2Ch 32:23;
Ps 45:12; 68:29;
72:10; Isa 18:7
9:25 *s* S 1Sa 8:11
9:26 *t* S 1Ki 4:21
u Ps 72:8-9
v Ge 15:18-21
9:29 *w* S 2Sa 7:2
x S 1Ki 11:29
y 2Ch 10:2
9:31 *z* 1Ki 2:10
10:2 *a* S 2Ch 9:29
b S 1Ki 11:40
10:3 *c* S 1Ch 9:1
10:4 *d* 2Ch 2:2
10:6 *e* Job 8:8-9;
12:12; 15:10; 32:7
10:7 *f* Pr 15:1
10:8 *g* S 2Sa 17:14
h Pr 13:20

¹⁸The throne had six steps, and a footstool of gold was attached to it. On both sides of the seat were armrests, with a lion standing beside each of them. ¹⁹Twelve lions stood on the six steps, one at either end of each step. Nothing like it had ever been made for any other kingdom. ²⁰All King Solomon's goblets were gold, and all the household articles in the Palace of the Forest of Lebanon were pure gold. Nothing was made of silver, because silver was considered of little value in Solomon's day. ²¹The king had a fleet of trading ships[a] manned by Hiram's[b] servants. Once every three years it returned, carrying gold, silver and ivory, and apes and baboons.

²²King Solomon was greater in riches and wisdom than all the other kings of the earth.[p] ²³All the kings[q] of the earth sought audience with Solomon to hear the wisdom God had put in his heart. ²⁴Year after year, everyone who came brought a gift[r]—articles of silver and gold, and robes, weapons and spices, and horses and mules.

²⁵Solomon had four thousand stalls for horses and chariots,[s] and twelve thousand horses,[c] which he kept in the chariot cities and also with him in Jerusalem. ²⁶He ruled[t] over all the kings from the Euphrates River[u] to the land of the Philistines, as far as the border of Egypt.[v] ²⁷The king made silver as common in Jerusalem as stones, and cedar as plentiful as sycamore-fig trees in the foothills. ²⁸Solomon's horses were imported from Egypt and from all other countries.

SOLOMON'S DEATH

9:29-31pp — 1Ki 11:41-43

²⁹As for the other events of Solomon's reign, from beginning to end, are they not written in the records of Nathan[w] the prophet, in the prophecy of Ahijah[x] the Shilonite and in the visions of Iddo the seer concerning Jeroboam[y] son of Nebat? ³⁰Solomon reigned in Jerusalem over all Israel forty years. ³¹Then he rested with his ancestors and was buried in the city of David[z] his father. And Rehoboam his son succeeded him as king.

ISRAEL REBELS AGAINST REHOBOAM

10:1—11:4pp — 1Ki 12:1-24

10 Rehoboam went to Shechem, for all Israel had gone there to make him king. ²When Jeroboam[a] son of Nebat heard this (he was in Egypt, where he had fled[b] from King Solomon), he returned from Egypt. ³So they sent for Jeroboam, and he and all Israel[c] went to Rehoboam and said to him: ⁴"Your father put a heavy yoke on us,[d] but now lighten the harsh labor and the heavy yoke he put on us, and we will serve you."

⁵Rehoboam answered, "Come back to me in three days." So the people went away.

⁶Then King Rehoboam consulted the elders[e] who had served his father Solomon during his lifetime. "How would you advise me to answer these people?" he asked.

⁷They replied, "If you will be kind to these people and please them and give them a favorable answer,[f] they will always be your servants."

⁸But Rehoboam rejected[g] the advice the elders[h] gave him and consulted the young men who had grown up with him and were serving him. ⁹He asked them, "What is your advice? How should we answer these people who say to me, 'Lighten the yoke your father put on us'?"

¹⁰The young men who had grown up with him replied, "The people have said to you, 'Your father put a heavy yoke on us, but make our yoke lighter.' Now tell them, 'My little

---

a 21 Hebrew *of ships that could go to Tarshish*   *b 21* Hebrew *Huram,* a variant of *Hiram*
c 25 Or *charioteers*

9:26 See 7:8 and note.

9:27 See 1:15.

9:28 The Chronicler omits the accounts of Solomon's wives and the rebellions at the end of his reign (1Ki 11:1–40), both of which would detract from his uniformly positive portrayal of Solomon. *horses…Egypt.* See note on 1:16–17.

9:29–31 See 1Ki 11:41–43.

10:1—36:23 The material covering the divided monarchy in Chronicles is considerably shorter than that in Kings: 27 chapters compared to 36 (1Ki 12–2Ki 25). Moreover, about half of this material is unique to Chronicles and shows no dependence on Kings. The most obvious reason for this is that the Chronicler has written a history of the Davidic dynasty in Judah; the history of the northern kingdom is passed over in silence except where it impinges

on that of Judah. At least two considerations prompt this treatment of the divided kingdom: 1. The Chronicler is concerned to trace God's faithfulness to his promise to give David an unbroken line of descent on the throne of Israel. 2. At the time of the Chronicler the restored community was confined to the returnees of the kingdom of Judah, who were actually the remnant of all Israel (see Introduction to 1 Chronicles: Purpose and Themes).

10:1–19 See 1Ki 12:1–20 and notes. Somewhat in line with his idealization of Solomon, the Chronicler places most of the blame for the schism on the rebellious Jeroboam (cf. 13:6–7).

10:1 *Rehoboam.* Reigned 930–913 B.C.

10:2 *Jeroboam.* Reigned 930–909 B.C.; his second mention in Chronicles (see 9:29). The Chronicler assumes the reader's familiarity with 1Ki 11:26–40.

finger is thicker than my father's waist. [11]My father laid on you a heavy yoke; I will make it even heavier. My father scourged you with whips; I will scourge you with scorpions.' "

[12]Three days later Jeroboam and all the people returned to Rehoboam, as the king had said, "Come back to me in three days." [13]The king answered them harshly. Rejecting the advice of the elders, [14]he followed the advice of the young men and said, "My father made your yoke heavy; I will make it even heavier. My father scourged you with whips; I will scourge you with scorpions." [15]So the king did not listen to the people, for this turn of events was from God,[i] to fulfill the word the LORD had spoken to Jeroboam son of Nebat through Ahijah the Shilonite.[j]

[16]When all Israel[k] saw that the king refused to listen to them, they answered the king:

"What share do we have in David,[l]
    what part in Jesse's son?
To your tents, Israel!
    Look after your own house, David!"

So all the Israelites went home. [17]But as for the Israelites who were living in the towns of Judah, Rehoboam still ruled over them.

[18]King Rehoboam sent out Adoniram,[a][m] who was in charge of forced labor, but the Israelites stoned him to death. King Rehoboam, however, managed to get into his chariot and escape to Jerusalem. [19]So Israel has been in rebellion against the house of David to this day.

11 When Rehoboam arrived in Jerusalem,[n] he mustered the house of Judah and Benjamin—a hundred and eighty thousand able young men—to make war against Israel and to regain the kingdom for Rehoboam.

[2]But this word of the LORD came to Shemaiah[o] the man of God: [3]"Say to Rehoboam son of Solomon king of Judah and to all Israel in Judah and Benjamin, [4]'This is what the LORD says: Do not go up to fight against your fellow Israelites.[p] Go home, every one of you, for this is my doing.' " So they obeyed the words of the LORD and turned back from marching against Jeroboam.

REHOBOAM FORTIFIES JUDAH

[5]Rehoboam lived in Jerusalem and built up towns for defense in Judah: [6]Bethlehem, Etam, Tekoa, [7]Beth Zur, Soko, Adullam, [8]Gath, Mareshah, Ziph, [9]Adoraim, Lachish, Azekah, [10]Zorah, Aijalon and Hebron. These were fortified cities[q] in Judah and Benjamin. [11]He strengthened their defenses and put commanders in them, with supplies of food, olive oil and wine. [12]He put shields and spears in all the cities, and made them very strong. So Judah and Benjamin were his.

[13]The priests and Levites from all their districts throughout Israel sided with him. [14]The Levites[r] even abandoned their pasturelands and property[s] and came to Judah and Jerusalem, because Jeroboam and his sons had rejected them as priests of the LORD [15]when he appointed[t] his own priests[u] for the high places and for the goat[v] and calf[w] idols he had made. [16]Those from every tribe of Israel[x] who set their hearts on seeking the LORD, the God of Israel, followed the Levites to Jerusalem to offer sacrifices to the LORD, the God of their

---

[a] 18 Hebrew *Hadoram*, a variant of *Adoniram*

10:15 *i* 2Ch 11:4;
25:16-20 / S 1Ki 11:29
10:16 *k* S 1Ch 9:1
l S 2Sa 20:1
10:18 *m* S 2Sa 20:24;
S 1Ki 5:14
11:1 *n* S 1Ki 12:21
11:2 *o* S 1Ki 12:22;
2Ch 12:5-7,15
11:4 *p* 2Ch 28:8-11
11:10 *q* S Jos 10:20;
2Ch 12:4; 17:2,19;
21:3
11:14 *r* S Nu 35:2-5
s 1Ch 6:81
11:15 *t* S 1Ki 13:33
u S 1Ki 12:31
v Lev 17:7 *w* 1Ki 12:28;
2Ch 13:8
11:16 *x* 2Ch 15:9

10:15 *Ahijah.* The Chronicler assumes the reader's familiarity with 1Ki 11:29–33.
10:18 *Adoniram...in charge of forced labor.* Had held the same office under Solomon (1Ki 4:6; 5:14).
10:19 *to this day.* See note on 5:9.

11:1–23 Verses 1–4 are parallel to 1Ki 12:21–24; vv. 5–23 are largely unique to Chronicles. The Chronicler's account of Rehoboam is a good example of his emphasis on immediate retribution (see Introduction to 1 Chronicles: Purpose and Themes). Ch. 11 traces the rewards for obedience to the command of God (vv. 1–4): Rehoboam enjoys prosperity and power (vv. 5–12), popular support (vv. 13–17) and progeny (vv. 18–23). Ch. 12 demonstrates the reverse: Disobedience brings judgment.
11:2 *Shemaiah.* The function of the prophets as guardians of the theocracy (God's kingdom) is prominent in Chronicles; most of Judah's kings are portrayed as receiving advice from prophets (see Introduction to 1 Chronicles: Purpose and Themes).

11:3 *all Israel in Judah and Benjamin.* A variation from the wording found in 1Ki 12:23, in accordance with the Chronicler's interest in "all Israel."
11:4 *my doing.* See 10:15.
11:5–10 This list of cities is not found in Kings. Rehoboam fortified his eastern, western and southern borders, but not the north, perhaps demonstrating his hope of reunification of the kingdoms, as well as the threat of invasion from Egypt.
11:13–17 The Chronicler assumes the reader's familiarity with 1Ki 12:26–33. This material is unique to Chronicles and reflects the author's concern both with the temple and its personnel and with showing that the kingdom of Judah was the remnant of all Israel.
11:14 *pasturelands and property.* See 1Ch 6:54–80; Lev 25:32–34; Nu 35:1–5; see also Introduction to 1 Chronicles: Purpose and Themes.
11:15 *goat and calf idols.* The account in Kings mentions only the golden calves. For the worship of goat idols, see Lev 17:7.

11:17 y 2Ch 12:1
11:20 z S 1Ki 15:2
a 2Ch 12:16; 13:2
11:21 b S Dt 17:17
11:22 c Dt 21:15-17
11:23 d 2Ch 21:3
12:1 e ver 13;
2Ch 1:1 f 2Ch 11:17
g S 1Ch 9:1
h S 2Ch 7:19
12:2 i 1Ki 14:22-24;
S 1Ch 5:25 / 1Ki 11:40
12:3 k Da 11:43
l S Ge 10:6; 2Ch 14:9;
16:8; Isa 18:2; Am 9:7;
Na 3:9
12:4 m S 2Ch 11:10
12:5 n 2Ch 11:2
o S Dt 28:15
12:6 p S Lev 26:41;
S 2Ch 6:37 q Ex 9:27;
Ezr 9:15; Ps 11:7;
116:5; Da 9:14
12:7 r Ps 78:38
s Dt 9:19; Ps 69:24;
Jer 7:20; 42:18;
Eze 5:13
12:8 t Dt 28:48
12:9 u 2Ch 9:16

ancestors. [17]They strengthened y the kingdom of Judah and supported Rehoboam son of Solomon three years, following the ways of David and Solomon during this time.

REHOBOAM'S FAMILY

[18]Rehoboam married Mahalath, who was the daughter of David's son Jerimoth and of Abihail, the daughter of Jesse's son Eliab. [19]She bore him sons: Jeush, Shemariah and Zaham. [20]Then he married Maakah z daughter of Absalom, who bore him Abijah, a Attai, Ziza and Shelomith. [21]Rehoboam loved Maakah daughter of Absalom more than any of his other wives and concubines. In all, he had eighteen wives b and sixty concubines, twenty-eight sons and sixty daughters.

[22]Rehoboam appointed Abijah c son of Maakah as crown prince among his brothers, in order to make him king. [23]He acted wisely, dispersing some of his sons throughout the districts of Judah and Benjamin, and to all the fortified cities. He gave them abundant provisions d and took many wives for them.

SHISHAK ATTACKS JERUSALEM

12:9–16pp — 1Ki 14:21,25–31

12 After Rehoboam's position as king was established e and he had become strong, f he and all Israel a g with him abandoned h the law of the LORD. [2]Because they had been unfaithful i to the LORD, Shishak j king of Egypt attacked Jerusalem in the fifth year of King Rehoboam. [3]With twelve hundred chariots and sixty thousand horsemen and the innumerable troops of Libyans, k Sukkites and Cushites b l that came with him from Egypt, [4]he captured the fortified cities m of Judah and came as far as Jerusalem.

[5]Then the prophet Shemaiah n came to Rehoboam and to the leaders of Judah who had assembled in Jerusalem for fear of Shishak, and he said to them, "This is what the LORD says, 'You have abandoned me; therefore, I now abandon o you to Shishak.' "

[6]The leaders of Israel and the king humbled p themselves and said, "The LORD is just." q

[7]When the LORD saw that they humbled themselves, this word of the LORD came to Shemaiah: "Since they have humbled themselves, I will not destroy them but will soon give them deliverance. r My wrath s will not be poured out on Jerusalem through Shishak. [8]They will, however, become subject t to him, so that they may learn the difference between serving me and serving the kings of other lands."

[9]When Shishak king of Egypt attacked Jerusalem, he carried off the treasures of the temple of the LORD and the treasures of the royal palace. He took everything, including the gold shields u Solomon had made. [10]So King Rehoboam made bronze shields to replace

a 1 That is, Judah, as frequently in 2 Chronicles   b 3 That is, people from the upper Nile region

---

11:17 *three years.* See note on 12:2. *ways of David and Solomon.* Characteristic of the Chronicler's idealization of Solomon; contrast the portrait of Solomon in 1Ki 11:1–13.

11:18–22 The report on the size of Rehoboam's family is placed here as part of the Chronicler's effort to show God's blessing on his obedience (see note on 11:1–23). The material is not in chronological sequence with the surrounding context but summarizes events throughout his reign. The Chronicler uses numerous progeny as a sign of divine blessing (see 13:21; see also notes on 21:2; 1Ch 25:5).

11:20 *Maakah daughter of Absalom.* See note on 1Ki 15:2. She was likely the granddaughter of Absalom, through his daughter Tamar (2Sa 14:27; 18:18), who was married to Uriel (2Ch 13:2).

11:21–22 These verses explain why the eldest son was not appointed Rehoboam's successor.

11:23 *dispersing some of his sons.* Rehoboam may have sought to secure the succession of Abijah by assigning other sons to outlying posts, perhaps to avoid the difficulties faced by David, whose sons at court (Absalom and Adonijah) had attempted to seize power.

12:1–14 See note on 11:1–23. Whereas obedience to the prophetic word (11:1–4) had brought blessing (11:5–23), now the prophet comes to announce judgment for disobedience (see 1Ki 14:25–28). While the writer of Kings also reports the attack of Shishak, the Chronicler alone adds the rationale that the invasion was because of forsaking

the commands of God (vv. 1–2,5).

12:1 *all Israel.* Used in a variety of ways in 2 Chronicles: (1) of both kingdoms (9:30), (2) of the northern kingdom (10:16; 11:13) or (3) of the southern kingdom alone (as here; 11:3). See also Introduction to 1 Chronicles: Purpose and Themes, 6. *abandoned.* The opposite of "seeking the LORD" (v. 14); see v. 5; see also note on 24:18,20,24.

12:2 *Shishak.* Founder of the 22nd dynasty of Egypt, he ruled c. 945–924 B.C. The Bible mentions this invasion only as it affected Jerusalem, but Shishak's own inscription on the wall of the temple of Amun at Karnak (Thebes) indicates that his armies also swept as far north as Megiddo. *fifth year.* 925 B.C. The Chronicler often introduces chronological notes not found in Kings (e.g., 11:17; 15:10,19; 16:1,12–13; 17:7; 21:20; 24:15,17,23; 26:16; 27:5,8; 29:3; 34:3; 36:21). These become a vehicle for his emphasis on immediate retribution by dividing the reigns of individual kings into cycles of obedience-blessing and disobedience-punishment. This sequence is clear for Rehoboam: Three years of obedience and blessing (11:17) are followed by rebellion, presumably in the fourth year (12:1), and punishment in the fifth (here).

12:3 *Sukkites.* Probably a group of mercenary soldiers of Libyan origin who are known from Egyptian texts.

12:5 See notes on vv. 1–14; v. 1.

12:6–7 See v. 12. The Chronicler has in mind God's promise in 7:14.

them and assigned these to the commanders of the guard on duty at the entrance to the royal palace. ¹¹Whenever the king went to the Lord's temple, the guards went with him, bearing the shields, and afterward they returned them to the guardroom.

¹²Because Rehoboam humbled ᵛ himself, the Lord's anger turned from him, and he was not totally destroyed. Indeed, there was some good ʷ in Judah.

¹³King Rehoboam established ˣ himself firmly in Jerusalem and continued as king. He was forty-one years old when he became king, and he reigned seventeen years in Jerusalem, the city the Lord had chosen out of all the tribes of Israel in which to put his Name. ʸ His mother's name was Naamah; she was an Ammonite. ¹⁴He did evil because he had not set his heart on seeking the Lord.

¹⁵As for the events of Rehoboam's reign, from beginning to end, are they not written in the records of Shemaiah ᶻ the prophet and of Iddo the seer that deal with genealogies? There was continual warfare between Rehoboam and Jeroboam. ¹⁶Rehoboam ᵃ rested with his ancestors and was buried in the City of David. And Abijah ᵇ his son succeeded him as king.

ABIJAH KING OF JUDAH
13:1–2,22—14:1pp — 1Ki 15:1–2,6–8

13 In the eighteenth year of the reign of Jeroboam, Abijah became king of Judah, ²and he reigned in Jerusalem three years. His mother's name was Maakah, ᵃ ᶜ a daughter ᵇ of Uriel of Gibeah.

There was war between Abijah ᵈ and Jeroboam. ᵉ ³Abijah went into battle with an army of four hundred thousand able fighting men, and Jeroboam drew up a battle line against him with eight hundred thousand able troops.

⁴Abijah stood on Mount Zemaraim, ᶠ in the hill country of Ephraim, and said, "Jeroboam and all Israel, ᵍ listen to me! ⁵Don't you know that the Lord, the God of Israel, has given the kingship of Israel to David and his descendants forever ʰ by a covenant of salt? ⁱ ⁶Yet Jeroboam son of Nebat, an official of Solomon son of David, rebelled ʲ against his master. ⁷Some worthless scoundrels ᵏ gathered around him and opposed Rehoboam son of Solomon when he was young and indecisive ˡ and not strong enough to resist them.

⁸"And now you plan to resist the kingdom of the Lord, which is in the hands of David's descendants. ᵐ You are indeed a vast army and have with you ⁿ the golden calves ᵒ that Jeroboam made to be your gods. ⁹But didn't you drive out the priests ᵖ of the Lord, ᑫ the sons of Aaron, and the Levites, and make priests of your own as the peoples of other lands do? Whoever comes to consecrate himself with a young bull ʳ and seven rams ˢ may become a priest of what are not gods. ᵗ

¹⁰"As for us, the Lord is our God, and we have not forsaken him. The priests who serve the Lord are sons of Aaron, and the Levites assist them. ¹¹Every morning and evening ᵘ they present burnt offerings and fragrant incense ᵛ to the Lord. They set out the bread on the ceremonially clean table ʷ and light the lamps ˣ on the gold lampstand every evening. We are observing the requirements of the Lord our God. But you have forsaken him. ¹²God is with us; he is our leader. His priests with their trumpets will sound the battle cry against you. ʸ People of Israel, do not fight against the Lord, ᶻ the God of your ancestors, for you will not succeed." ᵃ

ᵃ 2 Most Septuagint manuscripts and Syriac (see also 2 Chron. 11:20 and 1 Kings 15:2); Hebrew *Micaiah*
ᵇ 2 Or *granddaughter*

12:12 ᵛ 2Ch 6:37
ʷ S 1Ki 14:13;
2Ch 19:3
12:13 ˣ S ver 1;
S 1Ki 2:12
ʸ S Ex 20:24; Dt 12:5
12:15 ᶻ S 2Ch 11:2
12:16 ᵃ S 1Ch 3:10
ᵇ S 2Ch 11:20
13:2 ᶜ 2Ch 15:16
ᵈ S 2Ch 11:20
ᵉ 1Ki 15:6
13:4 ᶠ Jos 18:22
ᵍ 1Ch 11:1
13:5 ʰ S 2Sa 7:13;
S 1Ch 17:12
ⁱ S Lev 2:13
13:6 ʲ 1Ki 11:26
13:7 ᵏ S Jdg 9:4
ˡ S 1Ch 29:1
13:8 ᵐ S 2Ch 9:8
ⁿ 1Sa 4:3 ᵒ S Ex 32:4;
S 2Ch 11:15
13:9 ᵖ S 1Ki 12:31
ᑫ 2Ch 11:14-15
ʳ Ex 29:35-36
ˢ S Ex 29:31 ᵗ Jer 2:11;
Gal 4:8
13:11 ᵘ S Ex 29:39;
S 2Ch 2:4 ᵛ S Ex 25:6
ʷ S 1Ch 9:32
ˣ S Ex 25:37
13:12 ʸ S Nu 10:8-9
ᶻ S Jdg 2:15; Ac 5:39
ᵃ Job 9:4; Pr 21:30;
29:1

12:13 *seventeen years.* See note on 10:1.
12:15–16 See 1Ki 14:29–31.

13:1—14:1 The Chronicler's account of Abijah's reign is about three times longer than that in 1Ki 15:1–8, largely due to Abijah's lengthy speech (13:4–12; see note on 28:1–27). The most striking difference in the accounts of Abijah's reign in Kings and in Chronicles is the evaluation given in each: Kings offers a negative evaluation (1Ki 15:3), for which there was no doubt warrant, while the assessment in Chronicles is positive, in view of what the Chronicler is able to report of him. The kings' reigns, like the lives of common people, were often a mixture of good and evil.

13:2 *three years.* 913–910 B.C. *Maakah.* See note on 11:20.
13:3 *four hundred thousand ... eight hundred thousand.* Surprisingly large figures but in line with those in 1Ch 21:5 (see note there; see also Introduction to Numbers: Special Problem).
13:4 *Mount Zemaraim.* The town Zemaraim was in the territory

of Benjamin (Jos 18:22); presumably the battle was along the common border of Benjamin and Israel. *all Israel.* See note on 12:1; here and in v. 15 the reference is to the northern kingdom.
13:5 See 7:17–18; 1Ch 17:13–14. *covenant of salt.* See notes on Nu 18:19; 2Ki 2:20.
13:6 See note on 10:1–19.
13:7 Not all in the northern kingdom are rebuked, only the leadership—a subtle appeal to those in the north who had been led into rebellion. *scoundrels.* See note on Dt 13:13. *young and indecisive.* Cf. 1Ch 22:5; 29:1. Rehoboam was 41 years old at the time of the schism (12:13).
13:8 *kingdom of the Lord.* The house of David represents the kingdom of God (see 9:8 and note).
13:9 See 1Ki 12:25–33. *consecrate himself.* Cf. Ex 29:1.
13:10–12 The Chronicler's concern with acceptable worship focuses on the legitimate priests and the observance of prescribed worship (cf. 1Ch 23:28–31).

13:13 *b* Jos 8:9;
2Ch 20:22
13:14 *c* S 1Ch 5:20;
2Ch 14:11; 18:31
13:15 *d* S 1Ch 9:1
13:16 *e* 2Ch 16:8
13:18 *f* 2Ch 14:11;
16:7; Ps 22:5
14:2 *g* 2Ch 21:12
14:3 *h* S Jdg 2:2
i S Ex 23:24
j S Ex 34:13
14:4 *k* S 1Ch 16:11
14:5 *l* S 1Ki 15:14
m Isa 27:9; Eze 6:4
14:6 *n* S 1Ch 22:9
14:7 *o* S 1Ch 22:9
14:8 *p* S 1Ch 21:1
14:9 *q* S 2Ch 12:3

¹³Now Jeroboam had sent troops around to the rear, so that while he was in front of Judah the ambush *b* was behind them. ¹⁴Judah turned and saw that they were being attacked at both front and rear. Then they cried out *c* to the Lord. The priests blew their trumpets ¹⁵and the men of Judah raised the battle cry. At the sound of their battle cry, God routed Jeroboam and all Israel *d* before Abijah and Judah. ¹⁶The Israelites fled before Judah, and God delivered *e* them into their hands. ¹⁷Abijah and his troops inflicted heavy losses on them, so that there were five hundred thousand casualties among Israel's able men. ¹⁸The Israelites were subdued on that occasion, and the men of Judah were victorious because they relied *f* on the Lord, the God of their ancestors.

¹⁹Abijah pursued Jeroboam and took from him the towns of Bethel, Jeshanah and Ephron, with their surrounding villages. ²⁰Jeroboam did not regain power during the time of Abijah. And the Lord struck him down and he died.

²¹But Abijah grew in strength. He married fourteen wives and had twenty-two sons and sixteen daughters.

²²The other events of Abijah's reign, what he did and what he said, are written in the annotations of the prophet Iddo.

14

*And Abijah rested with his ancestors and was buried in the City of David. Asa his son succeeded him as king, and in his days the country was at peace for ten years.

ASA KING OF JUDAH

14:2–3pp — 1Ki 15:11–12

*²Asa did what was good and right in the eyes of the Lord his God. *g* ³He removed the foreign altars *h* and the high places, smashed the sacred stones *i* and cut down the Asherah poles. *a* *j* ⁴He commanded Judah to seek the Lord, *k* the God of their ancestors, and to obey his laws and commands. ⁵He removed the high places *l* and incense altars *m* in every town in Judah, and the kingdom was at peace under him. ⁶He built up the fortified cities of Judah, since the land was at peace. No one was at war with him during those years, for the Lord gave him rest. *n*

⁷"Let us build up these towns," he said to Judah, "and put walls around them, with towers, gates and bars. The land is still ours, because we have sought the Lord our God; we sought him and he has given us rest *o* on every side." So they built and prospered.

⁸Asa had an army of three hundred thousand *p* men from Judah, equipped with large shields and with spears, and two hundred and eighty thousand from Benjamin, armed with small shields and with bows. All these were brave fighting men.

⁹Zerah the Cushite *q* marched out against them with an army of thousands upon thou-

---

a 3 That is, wooden symbols of the goddess Asherah; here and elsewhere in 2 Chronicles
* 14:1 is numbered 13:23 in Hebrew texts.   * 14:2-15 is numbered 14:1-14 in Hebrew texts.

13:21 See note on 11:18–22.

14:1 *peace for ten years.* For the Chronicler peace and prosperity go hand in hand with righteous rule. This first decade of Asa's reign (910–900 B.C.) preceded the invasion by Zerah (14:9–15) and was followed by 20 more years of peace, from the 15th (15:10) to the 35th years (15:19). Contrast this account with the statement that there was war between Asa and Baasha throughout their reigns (see 1Ki 15:16 and note). The tensions between the two kingdoms may have accounted for Asa's fortifications (14:7–8), though actual combat was likely confined to raids until the major campaign was launched in Asa's 36th year (16:1). See 15:8 and note.

14:2—16:14 The account of Asa's reign (910–869 B.C.) here is greatly expanded over the one in 1Ki 15:9–24. The expansions characteristically express the Chronicler's view concerning the relationship between obedience and blessing, disobedience and punishment. The author introduces chronological notes into his account to divide Asa's reign into these periods (see note on 12:2): For ten years Asa did what was right and prospered (14:1–7), and an invasion by a powerful Cushite force was repulsed because he called on the Lord (14:8–15). There followed further reforms (15:1–9) and a covenant renewal in Asa's 15th year (15:10–18), and so he enjoyed peace until his 35th year (15:19). But then came a change: When confronted

by an invasion from the northern kingdom in his 36th year (16:1), he hired Aramean reinforcements, rather than trusting in the Lord (16:2–6), and imprisoned the prophet who rebuked him (16:7–10). In his 39th year he was afflicted with a disease (16:12) but still steadfastly refused to seek the Lord. In his 41st year he died (16:13).

14:3 *sacred stones.* See note on 1Ki 14:23. *Asherah poles.* See note on Ex 34:13.

14:5 *removed the high places.* 1Ki 15:14 states that Asa did not remove the high places. This difficulty is best resolved by the Chronicler's own statement in 15:17, which is properly parallel to 1Ki 15:14: Early in his reign Asa did attempt to remove the high places, but pagan worship was extremely resilient, and ultimately his efforts were unsuccessful (15:17). Statements that the high places both were and were not removed are also found in the reign of Jehoshaphat (17:6; 20:33). Cf. Dt 12:2–3.

14:7 *rest on every side.* See note on 20:30.

14:9 *Zerah.* Probably a general leading Egyptian forces in the service of Pharaoh Osorkon I. The invasion appears to have been an attempt to duplicate the attack of Shishak 30 years earlier (12:1–12), but the results against Asa were quite different. *Cushite.* See vv. 12–13. The Cushites were natives of Nubia, the region that borders Egypt on the south—not to be confused with modern Ethiopia (Abyssinia). See also note on Isa 18:1.

sands and three hundred chariots, and came as far as Mareshah. [r] [10]Asa went out to meet him, and they took up battle positions in the Valley of Zephathah near Mareshah.

[11]Then Asa called [s] to the LORD his God and said, "LORD, there is no one like you to help the powerless against the mighty. Help us, [t] LORD our God, for we rely [u] on you, and in your name [v] we have come against this vast army. LORD, you are our God; do not let mere mortals prevail [w] against you."

[12]The LORD struck down [x] the Cushites before Asa and Judah. The Cushites fled, [13]and Asa and his army pursued them as far as Gerar. [y] Such a great number of Cushites fell that they could not recover; they were crushed [z] before the LORD and his forces. The men of Judah carried off a large amount of plunder. [a] [14]They destroyed all the villages around Gerar, for the terror [b] of the LORD had fallen on them. They plundered all these villages, since there was much booty there. [15]They also attacked the camps of the herders and carried off droves of sheep and goats and camels. Then they returned to Jerusalem.

ASA'S REFORM

15:16–19pp — 1Ki 15:13–16

15 The Spirit of God came on [c] Azariah son of Oded. [2]He went out to meet Asa and said to him, "Listen to me, Asa and all Judah and Benjamin. The LORD is with you [d] when you are with him. [e] If you seek [f] him, he will be found by you, but if you forsake him, he will forsake you. [g] [3]For a long time Israel was without the true God, without a priest to teach [h] and without the law. [i] [4]But in their distress they turned to the LORD, the God of Israel, and sought him, [j] and he was found by them. [5]In those days it was not safe to travel about, [k] for all the inhabitants of the lands were in great turmoil. [6]One nation was being crushed by another and one city by another, [l] because God was troubling them with every kind of distress. [7]But as for you, be strong [m] and do not give up, for your work will be rewarded." [n]

[8]When Asa heard these words and the prophecy of Azariah son of [a] Oded the prophet, he took courage. He removed the detestable idols [o] from the whole land of Judah and Benjamin and from the towns he had captured [p] in the hills of Ephraim. He repaired the altar [q] of the LORD that was in front of the portico of the LORD's temple.

[9]Then he assembled all Judah and Benjamin and the people from Ephraim, Manasseh and Simeon who had settled among them, for large numbers [r] had come over to him from Israel when they saw that the LORD his God was with him.

[10]They assembled at Jerusalem in the third month [s] of the fifteenth year of Asa's reign. [11]At that time they sacrificed to the LORD seven hundred head of cattle and seven thousand sheep and goats from the plunder [t] they had brought back. [12]They entered into a covenant [u] to seek the LORD, [v] the God of their ancestors, with all their heart and soul. [13]All who would not seek the LORD, the God of Israel, were to be put to death, [w] whether small or great, man or woman. [14]They took an oath to the LORD with loud acclamation, with shouting and with trumpets and horns. [15]All Judah rejoiced about the oath because they had sworn it wholeheartedly. They sought God [x] eagerly, and he was found by them. So the LORD gave them rest [y] on every side.

[16]King Asa also deposed his grandmother Maakah [z] from her position as queen mother, [a] because she had made a repulsive image for the worship of Asherah. [b] Asa cut it down,

---

a 8 Vulgate and Syriac (see also Septuagint and verse 1); Hebrew does not have *Azariah son of*.

14:9 [r] S Ge 10:8-9; 2Ch 11:8; 24:24
14:11 [s] S 1Ki 8:44; S 2Ch 13:14; 25:8 [t] Ps 60:11-12; 79:9 [u] S 2Ch 13:18 [v] S 1Sa 17:45 [w] Ps 9:19
14:12 [x] 1Ki 8:45
14:13 [y] Ge 10:19 [z] 2Sa 22:38; Ne 9:24; Ps 44:2,19; 135:10 [a] 2Ch 15:11,18
14:14 [b] S Ge 35:5; S Dt 2:25; 11:25
15:1 [c] S Nu 11:25,26
15:2 [d] 2Ch 20:17 [e] Jas 4:8 [f] 2Ch 7:14; Ps 78:34; Isa 45:19; 55:6; Jer 29:13; Hos 3:5 [g] S Dt 31:17; S 1Ch 28:9
15:3 [h] S Lev 10:11 [i] La 2:9; Am 8:11
15:4 [j] S Dt 4:29
15:5 [k] S Jdg 5:6; 19:20; Zec 8:10
15:6 [l] Isa 19:2; Mt 24:7; Mk 13:8; Lk 21:10
15:7 [m] Jos 1:7,9 [n] 1Sa 24:19; Ps 18:20; 58:11; Pr 14:14; Jer 31:16
15:8 [o] 1Ki 15:12 [p] 2Ch 17:2 [q] S 1Ki 8:64; S 2Ch 8:12
15:9 [r] 2Ch 11:16-17
15:10 [s] S Lev 23:15-21
15:11 [t] S 2Ch 14:13
15:12 [u] S 2Ki 11:17 [v] S 1Ch 16:11
15:13 [w] S Ex 22:20; Dt 13:9-16
15:15 [x] Dt 4:29 [y] S 1Ch 22:9
15:16 [z] 2Ch 13:2 [a] 1Ki 2:19 [b] S Ex 34:13

14:10 *Valley of Zephathah.* Marked the entrance to a road leading to the hills of Judah and Jerusalem. *Mareshah.* Earlier fortified by Rehoboam (11:8) to protect the route mentioned here.

14:13 *Gerar.* See note on Ge 20:1. *plunder.* Much of this booty (v. 14) made its way to the storehouses of the temple (15:18; see note on 1Ch 18:1—20:8).

14:14 *terror of the LORD.* See note on 1Ch 14:17.

15:1–19 This chapter appears to recount a second stage in the reforms introduced by Asa, beginning with the victory over Zerah and encouraged by the preaching of Azariah (v. 1).

15:3 *priest to teach.* The duties of the priests were not only to officiate at the altar but also to teach the law (see 17:7–9; Lev 10:11; Dt 17:9–11).

15:8 *towns he had captured in ... Ephraim.* A tacit admission that there had been some fighting between Baasha and Asa prior to Asa's 36th year (16:1); see 17:1.

15:9 *large numbers had come over to him.* Cf. the defection

from the northern kingdom that also occurred under Rehoboam (11:13–17).

15:10 *third month of the fifteenth year.* Spring, 895 B.C., the year after Zerah's invasion (v. 19). The Festival of Weeks (or Pentecost) was held in the third month (Lev 23:15–21) and may have been the occasion for this assembly.

15:12 *covenant.* A renewal of the covenant made at Sinai, similar to the covenant renewals on the plain of Moab (Dt 29:1), at Mount Ebal (Jos 8:30–35), at Shechem (Jos 24:25) and at Gilgal (1Sa 11:14; see note there). Later the priest Jehoiada (23:16), as well as Hezekiah (29:10) and Josiah (34:31), would also lead in renewals of the covenant—events of primary significance in the view of the Chronicler.

15:13 *would not seek the LORD.* Would turn to other gods. *were to be put to death.* In accordance with basic covenant law (Ex 22:20; Dt 13:6–9).

15:15 *rest.* See note on 20:30.

15:16 *Asherah.* See note on Ex 34:13. *Kidron Valley.* Just east of

15:16 ᶜS 2Sa 15:23
15:18 ᵈS 2Ch 14:13
16:1 ᵉ2Ki 9:9;
Jer 41:9
16:2 ᶠ2Ch 19:1–
20:37; 22:1-9
16:3 ᵍ2Ch 20:35;
25:7
16:4 ʰS 2Ki 15:29
16:6 ⁱJer 41:9
16:7 ʲ1Ki 16:1
ᵏS 2Ch 13:18
16:8 ˡS Ge 10:6,8-9;
S 2Ch 12:3
ᵐ2Ch 24:24
ⁿ2Ch 13:16
16:9 ᵒJob 24:23;
Ps 33:13-15; Pr 15:3;
Jer 16:17; Zec 3:9;
4:10 ᵖ1Sa 13:13
ᵍS 1Ki 15:6; 2Ch 19:2;
25:7; 28:16-21
16:10 ʳS 1Ki 22:27
16:12 ˢ2Ch 21:18;
26:19; Ps 103:3
ᵗ2Ch 7:14 ᵘJer 17:5-6
16:14 ᵛS Ge 50:5
ʷS Ge 50:2
ˣ2Ch 21:19; Jer 34:5
17:1 ʸS 1Ki 2:12
17:2 ᶻS 2Ch 11:10
ᵃ2Ch 15:8

broke it up and burned it in the Kidron Valley. ᶜ ¹⁷Although he did not remove the high places from Israel, Asa's heart was fully committed ᴸto the LORDᴶ all his life. ¹⁸He brought into the temple of God the silver and gold and the articles that he and his father had dedicated. ᵈ

¹⁹There was no more war until the thirty-fifth year of Asa's reign.

ASA'S LAST YEARS

16:1–6pp — 1Ki 15:17–22
16:11—17:1pp — 1Ki 15:23–24

16 In the thirty-sixth year of Asa's reign Baasha ᵉ king of Israel went up against Judah and fortified Ramah to prevent anyone from leaving or entering the territory of Asa king of Judah.

²Asa then took the silver and gold out of the treasuries of the LORD's temple and of his own palace and sent it to Ben-Hadad king of Aram, who was ruling in Damascus. ᶠ ³"Let there be a treaty ᵍ between me and you," he said, "as there was between my father and your father. See, I am sending you silver and gold. Now break your treaty with Baasha king of Israel so he will withdraw from me."

⁴Ben-Hadad agreed with King Asa and sent the commanders of his forces against the towns of Israel. They conquered Ijon, Dan, Abel Maim ᵃ and all the store cities of Naphtali. ʰ ⁵When Baasha heard this, he stopped building Ramah and abandoned his work. ⁶Then King Asa brought all the men of Judah, and they carried away from Ramah the stones and timber Baasha had been using. With them he built up Geba and Mizpah. ⁱ

⁷At that time Hanani ʲ the seer came to Asa king of Judah and said to him: "Because you relied ᵏ on the king of Aram and not on the LORD your God, the army of the king of Aram has escaped from your hand. ⁸Were not the Cushites ᵇ ˡ and Libyans a mighty army with great numbers ᵐ of chariots and horsemen ᶜ? Yet when you relied on the LORD, he delivered ⁿ them into your hand. ⁹For the eyes ᵒ of the LORD range throughout the earth to strengthen those whose hearts are fully committed to him. You have done a foolish ᵖ thing, and from now on you will be at war. ᵍ"

¹⁰Asa was angry with the seer because of this; he was so enraged that he put him in prison. ʳ At the same time Asa brutally oppressed some of the people.

¹¹The events of Asa's reign, from beginning to end, are written in the book of the kings of Judah and Israel. ¹²In the thirty-ninth year of his reign Asa was afflicted ˢ with a disease in his feet. Though his disease was severe, even in his illness he did not seek ᵗ help from the LORD, ᵘ but only from the physicians. ¹³Then in the forty-first year of his reign Asa died and rested with his ancestors. ¹⁴They buried him in the tomb that he had cut out for himself ᵛ in the City of David. They laid him on a bier covered with spices and various blended perfumes, ʷ and they made a huge fire ˣ in his honor.

JEHOSHAPHAT KING OF JUDAH

17 Jehoshaphat his son succeeded him as king and strengthened ʸ himself against Israel. ²He stationed troops in all the fortified cities ᶻ of Judah and put garrisons in Judah and in the towns of Ephraim that his father Asa had captured. ᵃ

ᵃ 4 Also known as *Abel Beth Maakah*   ᵇ 8 That is, people from the upper Nile region   ᶜ 8 Or *charioteers*

Jerusalem (see note on Isa 22:7 and map, p. 486; see also 1Ki 15:13 and note).

15:17 *did not remove the high places.* See 14:5 and note.

16:1 *thirty-sixth year of Asa's reign Baasha.* According to Kings, Baasha ruled for 24 years and was succeeded by Elah in the 26th year of Asa (1Ki 15:33; 16:8). Obviously Baasha could not have been alive in the 36th year of Asa, where this passage places him—he had been dead for a decade. The action described here is not dated in 1Ki 15:17. Perhaps the Chronicler's dates here and in 15:19 are the result of a copyist's error (possibly for an original 25th and 26th).

16:2–9 Hiring foreign troops brought Asa into a foreign alliance, which showed lack of trust in the Lord. Other examples of condemned foreign alliances are found in the reigns of Jehoshaphat (20:35–37), Ahaziah (22:1–9) and Ahaz (28:16–21). By hiring Ben-Hadad to the north, Asa opened a two-front war for Baasha and forced his withdrawal.

16:3 *treaty ... between my father and your father.* See note on 1Ki 15:19.

16:9 *eyes of the LORD range throughout the earth.* Asserted also in Zec 4:10.

16:11 *book of the kings of Judah and Israel.* See Introduction to 1 Chronicles: Author, Date and Sources.

16:12 *disease in his feet.* For other examples of disease as punishment for sin, see 21:16–20; 26:16–23; Ac 12:23. Cf. 2Ki 15:5. *did not seek help from the LORD, but only from the physicians.* Contrast King Hezekiah (Isa 38); cf. Jer 17:5–8; Jas 5:14–16.

17:1—21:3 The Chronicler's account of Jehoshaphat's reign is more than twice as long as that in Kings, where the interest in Ahab and Elijah overshadows the space allotted to Jehoshaphat (1Ki 22:1–46). The Chronicler has also used Jehoshaphat's reign to emphasize immediate retribution. This theme is specifically announced in 19:10 and is illustrated in the blessing of Jehoshaphat's obedient faith and in the reproof for his wrongdoing (19:2–3; 20:35–37). Jehoshaphat reigned 872–848 B.C., from 872 to 869 likely as coregent with his father Asa (see 20:31 and note). The details of this reign may not be in chronological order; the teaching mission of 17:7–9 may have been part of the reforms noted in 19:4–11.

³The Lord was with Jehoshaphat because he followed the ways of his father David *b* before him. He did not consult the Baals ⁴but sought *c* the God of his father and followed his commands rather than the practices of Israel. ⁵The Lord established the kingdom under his control; and all Judah brought gifts *d* to Jehoshaphat, so that he had great wealth and honor. *e* ⁶His heart was devoted *f* to the ways of the Lord; furthermore, he removed the high places *g* and the Asherah poles *h* from Judah. *i*

⁷In the third year of his reign he sent his officials Ben-Hail, Obadiah, Zechariah, Nethanel and Micaiah to teach *j* in the towns of Judah. ⁸With them were certain Levites *k*—Shemaiah, Nethaniah, Zebadiah, Asahel, Shemiramoth, Jehonathan, Adonijah, Tobijah and Tob-Adonijah—and the priests Elishama and Jehoram. ⁹They taught throughout Judah, taking with them the Book of the Law *l* of the Lord; they went around to all the towns of Judah and taught the people.

¹⁰The fear *m* of the Lord fell on all the kingdoms of the lands surrounding Judah, so that they did not make war with Jehoshaphat. ¹¹Some Philistines brought Jehoshaphat gifts and silver as tribute, and the Arabs *n* brought him flocks: *o* seven thousand seven hundred rams and seven thousand seven hundred goats.

¹²Jehoshaphat became more and more powerful; he built forts and store cities in Judah ¹³and had large supplies in the towns of Judah. He also kept experienced fighting men in Jerusalem. ¹⁴Their enrollment *p* by families was as follows:

From Judah, commanders of units of 1,000:
   Adnah the commander, with 300,000 fighting men;
    ¹⁵next, Jehohanan the commander, with 280,000;
      ¹⁶next, Amasiah son of Zikri, who volunteered *q* himself for the service of the Lord, with 200,000.
   ¹⁷From Benjamin: *r*
      Eliada, a valiant soldier, with 200,000 men armed with bows and shields;
      ¹⁸next, Jehozabad, with 180,000 men armed for battle.

¹⁹These were the men who served the king, besides those he stationed in the fortified cities *s* throughout Judah. *t*

MICAIAH PROPHESIES AGAINST AHAB
18:1–27pp — 1Ki 22:1–28

18 Now Jehoshaphat had great wealth and honor, *u* and he allied *v* himself with Ahab *w* by marriage. ²Some years later he went down to see Ahab in Samaria. Ahab slaughtered many sheep and cattle for him and the people with him and urged him to attack Ramoth Gilead. ³Ahab king of Israel asked Jehoshaphat king of Judah, "Will you go with me against Ramoth Gilead?"

Jehoshaphat replied, "I am as you are, and my people as your people; we will join you in the war." ⁴But Jehoshaphat also said to the king of Israel, "First seek the counsel of the Lord."

17:3 *b* S 1Ki 22:43
17:4 *c* 2Ch 22:9
17:5 *d* S 1Sa 10:27
  e 2Ch 18:1
17:6 *f* S 1Ki 8:61
  g S 1Ki 15:14;
  2Ch 19:3; 20:33
  h S Ex 34:13
  i 2Ch 21:12
17:7 *j* S Lev 10:11;
  Dt 6:4-9; 2Ch 19:4-
  11; 35:3; Ne 8:7;
  Mal 2:7
17:8 *k* 2Ch 19:8;
  Ne 8:7-8; Hos 4:6
17:9 *l* S Dt 28:61
17:10 *m* S Ge 35:5;
  S Dt 2:25
17:11 *n* S 2Ch 9:14
  o 2Ch 21:16
17:14 *p* S 2Sa 24:2
17:16 *q* S Jdg 5:9
17:17 *r* S Nu 1:36
17:19 *s* S 2Ch 11:10
  t 2Ch 25:5
18:1 *u* 2Ch 17:5
  v 2Ch 19:1-3; 22:3
  w 2Ch 21:6

17:2 *cities of Judah...towns of Ephraim.* See note on 15:8. Abijah (13:19), Asa (15:8) and now Jehoshaphat had managed to hold these cities; they would be lost under Amaziah (25:17–24).
17:6 *removed the high places.* Just as his father Asa had attempted to remove the high places, only to have them be restored (14:5; 15:17), so also Jehoshaphat removed them initially, only to have them revive and persist (20:33; cf. 1Ki 22:43). But see notes on 1Ki 3:2; 15:14. *Asherah poles.* See TNIV text note on 14:3 and note on Ex 34:13.
17:7–9 This incident may be part of the reform more fully detailed in 19:4–11. In the theocracy, the law of the Lord was supposed to be an integral part of the law of the land; the king and his officials, as well as the priests and prophets, were representatives of the Lord's kingship over his people.
17:7 *third year.* Perhaps the first year of his sole reign after a coregency of three years with his father Asa (see 20:31 and note).
17:9 *Book of the Law of the Lord.* See 34:14–15; Jos 8:31,34; 23:6; see also notes on Jos 1:8; 2Ki 22:8; Ne 8:1.
17:10–11 See note on 1Ch 18:1—20:8.
17:10 *fear of the Lord.* See note on 1Ch 14:17.
17:14–18 *300,000...280,000...200,000...200,000... 180,000.* See notes on 1Ch 12:23–37; 27:1.

18:1—19:3 See 1Ki 22:1–40 and notes. In conformity with his interest in the southern kingdom and Jehoshaphat, the Chronicler omits elaboration on the death of Ahab and his succession (1Ki 22:36–40) and adds the material on the prophetic condemnation of Jehoshaphat's involvement (19:1–3).
18:1 Not found in 1Ki 22. The verse enhances the status of Jehoshaphat by mentioning the blessing of wealth for his fidelity, and also sets the stage for an entangling foreign alliance condemned by the prophet in 19:2–3. *allied himself with Ahab by marriage.* This marriage alliance to Athaliah, daughter of Ahab, resulted later in an attempt to exterminate the Davidic line (22:10—23:21).
18:2 The Chronicler further enhances the status of Jehoshaphat by noting the large number of animals Ahab slaughtered in his honor, a note not found in 1Ki 22. *urged him.* Also not found in the parallel text. The Hebrew for this verb is often used in the sense of "inciting to evil" (e.g., 1Ch 21:1) and may express the Chronicler's attitude toward Jehoshaphat's involvement. *Ramoth Gilead.* See notes on 22:5; 1Ki 22:3; see also map No. 7 at the end of this study Bible.
18:4 *seek the counsel of the Lord.* This request fits the Chronicler's overall positive portrait of Jehoshaphat.

18:11 ˣ 2Ch 22:5
18:13 ʸ Nu 22:18, 20, 35
18:16 ᶻ S 1Ch 9:1
ᵃ S Nu 27:17
18:18 ᵇ Da 7:9
18:21 ᶜ 1Ch 21:1; Job 1:6; Zec 3:1; Jn 8:44
18:22 ᵈ Job 12:16; Eze 14:9
18:23 ᵉ Ac 23:2
18:26 ᶠ Heb 11:36
18:29 ᵍ S 1Sa 28:8

⁵So the king of Israel brought together the prophets—four hundred men—and asked them, "Shall we go to war against Ramoth Gilead, or shall I not?"

"Go," they answered, "for God will give it into the king's hand."

⁶But Jehoshaphat asked, "Is there no longer a prophet of the LORD here whom we can inquire of?"

⁷The king of Israel answered Jehoshaphat, "There is still one through whom we can inquire of the LORD, but I hate him because he never prophesies anything good about me, but always bad. He is Micaiah son of Imlah."

"The king should not say such a thing," Jehoshaphat replied.

⁸So the king of Israel called one of his officials and said, "Bring Micaiah son of Imlah at once."

⁹Dressed in their royal robes, the king of Israel and Jehoshaphat king of Judah were sitting on their thrones at the threshing floor by the entrance of the gate of Samaria, with all the prophets prophesying before them. ¹⁰Now Zedekiah son of Kenaanah had made iron horns, and he declared, "This is what the LORD says: 'With these you will gore the Arameans until they are destroyed.' "

¹¹All the other prophets were prophesying the same thing. "Attack Ramoth Gilead ˣ and be victorious," they said, "for the LORD will give it into the king's hand."

¹²The messenger who had gone to summon Micaiah said to him, "Look, the other prophets without exception are predicting success for the king. Let your word agree with theirs, and speak favorably."

¹³But Micaiah said, "As surely as the LORD lives, I can tell him only what my God says." ʸ

¹⁴When he arrived, the king asked him, "Micaiah, shall we go to war against Ramoth Gilead, or shall I not?"

"Attack and be victorious," he answered, "for they will be given into your hand."

¹⁵The king said to him, "How many times must I make you swear to tell me nothing but the truth in the name of the LORD?"

¹⁶Then Micaiah answered, "I saw all Israel ᶻ scattered on the hills like sheep without a shepherd, ᵃ and the LORD said, 'These people have no master. Let each one go home in peace.' "

¹⁷The king of Israel said to Jehoshaphat, "Didn't I tell you that he never prophesies anything good about me, but only bad?"

¹⁸Micaiah continued, "Therefore hear the word of the LORD: I saw the LORD sitting on his throne ᵇ with all the host of heaven standing on his right and on his left. ¹⁹And the LORD said, 'Who will entice Ahab king of Israel into attacking Ramoth Gilead and going to his death there?'

"One suggested this, and another that. ²⁰Finally, a spirit came forward, stood before the LORD and said, 'I will entice him.'

" 'By what means?' the LORD asked.

²¹" 'I will go and be a lying spirit ᶜ in the mouths of all his prophets,' he said.

" 'You will succeed in enticing him,' said the LORD. 'Go and do it.'

²²"So now the LORD has put a lying spirit in the mouths of these prophets of yours. ᵈ The LORD has decreed disaster for you."

²³Then Zedekiah son of Kenaanah went up and slapped ᵉ Micaiah in the face. "Which way did the spirit from ᵃ the LORD go when he went from me to speak to you?" he asked.

²⁴Micaiah replied, "You will find out on the day you go to hide in an inner room."

²⁵The king of Israel then ordered, "Take Micaiah and send him back to Amon the ruler of the city and to Joash the king's son, ²⁶and say, 'This is what the king says: Put this fellow in prison ᶠ and give him nothing but bread and water until I return safely.' "

²⁷Micaiah declared, "If you ever return safely, the LORD has not spoken through me." Then he added, "Mark my words, all you people!"

AHAB KILLED AT RAMOTH GILEAD
18:28–34pp — 1Ki 22:29–36

²⁸So the king of Israel and Jehoshaphat king of Judah went up to Ramoth Gilead. ²⁹The king of Israel said to Jehoshaphat, "I will enter the battle in disguise, but you wear your royal robes." So the king of Israel disguised ᵍ himself and went into battle.

³⁰Now the king of Aram had ordered his chariot commanders, "Do not fight with any-

ᵃ 23 Or *Spirit of*

18:10 *Arameans.* See notes on 1Ch 18:5; Dt 26:5.
18:22 *lying spirit.* See note on 1Ki 22:23.
18:29 The fact that Ahab directs Jehoshaphat into battle in

royal regalia, thus making Jehoshaphat the logical target for attack, is consistent with Israel's dominant position at this time.

one, small or great, except the king of Israel." [31]When the chariot commanders saw Jehoshaphat, they thought, "This is the king of Israel." So they turned to attack him, but Jehoshaphat cried out,[h] and the LORD helped him. God drew them away from him, [32]for when the chariot commanders saw that he was not the king of Israel, they stopped pursuing him.

[33]But someone drew his bow at random and hit the king of Israel between the breastplate and the scale armor. The king told the chariot driver, "Wheel around and get me out of the fighting. I've been wounded." [34]All day long the battle raged, and the king of Israel propped himself up in his chariot facing the Arameans until evening. Then at sunset he died.[i]

19 When Jehoshaphat king of Judah returned safely to his palace in Jerusalem, [2]Jehu[j] the seer, the son of Hanani, went out to meet him and said to the king, "Should you help the wicked[k] and love[l] those who hate the LORD?[l] Because of this, the wrath[m] of the LORD is on you. [3]There is, however, some good[n] in you, for you have rid the land of the Asherah poles[o] and have set your heart on seeking God.[p]"

JEHOSHAPHAT APPOINTS JUDGES

[4]Jehoshaphat lived in Jerusalem, and he went out again among the people from Beersheba to the hill country of Ephraim and turned them back to the LORD, the God of their ancestors. [5]He appointed judges[q] in the land, in each of the fortified cities of Judah. [6]He told them, "Consider carefully what you do,[r] because you are not judging for mere mortals[s] but for the LORD, who is with you whenever you give a verdict. [7]Now let the fear of the LORD be on you. Judge carefully, for with the LORD our God there is no injustice[t] or partiality[u] or bribery."

[8]In Jerusalem also, Jehoshaphat appointed some of the Levites,[v] priests[w] and heads of Israelite families to administer[x] the law of the LORD and to settle disputes. And they lived in Jerusalem. [9]He gave them these orders: "You must serve faithfully and wholeheartedly in the fear of the LORD. [10]In every case that comes before you from your people who live in the cities—whether bloodshed or other concerns of the law, commands, decrees or regulations—you are to warn them not to sin against the LORD;[y] otherwise his wrath will come on you and your people. Do this, and you will not sin.

[11]"Amariah the chief priest will be over you in any matter concerning the LORD, and Zebadiah son of Ishmael, the leader of the tribe of Judah, will be over you in any matter concerning the king, and the Levites will serve as officials before you. Act with courage,[z] and may the LORD be with those who do well."

JEHOSHAPHAT DEFEATS MOAB AND AMMON

20 After this, the Moabites[a] and Ammonites with some of the Meunites[bb] came to make war on Jehoshaphat.
[2]Some people came and told Jehoshaphat, "A vast army[c] is coming against

---

[a] 2 Or *and make alliances with*   [b] 1 Some Septuagint manuscripts; Hebrew *Ammonites*

18:31 [h]S 2Ch 13:14
18:34 [i]2Ch 22:5
19:2 [j]S 1Ki 16:1
[k]S 2Ch 16:2-9
[l]Ps 139:21-22
[m]2Ch 24:18; 32:25; Ps 7:11
19:3 [n]S 1Ki 14:13
[o]S 2Ch 17:6
[p]S 2Ch 18:1; 20:35; 25:7
19:5 [q]S Ge 47:6; S Ex 18:26
19:6 [r]S Lev 19:15
19:7 [s]Dt 16:18-20; 17:8-13
[t]S Ge 18:25; S Job 8:3 [u]S Ex 18:16; Dt 10:17; Job 13:10; 32:21; 34:19
19:8 [v]S 1Ch 23:4
[w]Eze 44:24
[x]2Ch 17:8-9
19:10 [y]Dt 17:8-13
19:11 [z]S 1Ch 28:20
20:1 [a]Ps 83:6
[b]S 1Ch 4:41
20:2 [c]2Ch 24:24

19:1–3 Not found in 1Ki 22.

19:2 *Should you help the wicked…?* Jehu's father, Hanani, had earlier given Jehoshaphat's father, Asa, the same warning (see 16:7–9). Jehoshaphat later committed the same sin again and suffered for it (20:35–37).
19:3 *Asherah poles.* See TNIV text note on 14:3 and note on Ex 34:13.
19:4 *Jehoshaphat…went…among the people.* The king traveled throughout the realm personally to promote religious reformation.
19:5 *appointed judges.* The name Jehoshaphat (meaning "The LORD judges") is appropriate for the king who instituted this judicial reform. The arrangement of the courts under Jehoshaphat (vv. 5–11) would be of particular interest to the Chronicler's audience in the postexilic period, when the courts of the restored community would have their own existence and structure legitimized by this precedent.
19:6 Cf. Dt 16:18–20; 17:8–13.
19:7 *let the fear of the LORD be on you.* Let a terrifying sense of God's presence restrain you from any injustice (see note on 1Ch 14:17).
19:8 *Levites, priests…to administer the law.* See note on 1Ch 26:29–32. One effect of this judicial reform appears to be the bringing of the traditional system of justice administered by the

elders of the city under closer royal and priestly supervision.
19:11 *any matter concerning the LORD…any matter concerning the king.* This division into the affairs of religion and the affairs of the king reflects the postexilic structure of the Chronicler's day. Cf. the anointing of Solomon and Zadok (1Ch 29:22) and the administration of the postexilic community by Zerubbabel, a Davidic descendant, and Joshua, the high priest (Zec 4:14; 6:9–15).
20:1–30 This episode held special interest for the Chronicler since the restored community was being harassed by the descendants of these same peoples (see Ne 2:19; 4:1–3,7–9; 6:1–4; 13). He uses it to encourage his contemporaries to trust in the Lord and his prophets, as Jehoshaphat, son of David, had exhorted (v. 20). The account is significantly structured. Apart from the outer frame, which highlights the reversal of circumstances (vv. 1–4,28–30), it falls into three divisions: (1) Jehoshaphat's prayer (vv. 5–13), (2) the Lord's response (vv. 14–19) and (3) the great victory (vv. 20–27). At the center of each is its crucial statement, and these are all linked by a key word: v. 9, "we will *stand* in your presence before this temple"; v. 17, "*stand firm* and see the deliverance the LORD will give you"; v. 23, "The Ammonites and Moabites rose up (lit. '*stood up*') against the men from Mount Seir to destroy…them."
20:1 *Meunites.* A people from the region of Mount Seir in Edom (26:7; 1Ch 4:41; cf. 2Ch 20:10,22–23).

20:2 ᵈS Ge 14:7
ᵉS 1Sa 23:29; SS 1:14
20:3 ᶠ1Sa 7:6;
Ezr 8:23; Ne 1:4;
Est 4:16; Isa 58:6;
Jer 36:9; Da 9:3;
Joel 1:14; 2:15;
Jnh 3:5,7
20:4 ᵍJer 36:6
20:6 ʰMt 6:9
ⁱDt 4:39 / 1Ch 29:11-
12 ᵏ2Ch 25:8;
Job 25:2; 41:10; 42:2;
Isa 14:27; Jer 32:27;
49:19
20:7 ˡS Ge 12:7
ᵐIsa 41:8; Jas 2:23
20:8 ⁿ2Ch 6:20
20:9 ᵒS 2Ch 6:28
20:10 ᵖNu 20:14-
21; Dt 2:4-6,9,18-19
20:11 ᑫPs 83:1-12
20:12 ʳJdg 11:27
ˢPs 25:15; Isa 30:15;
45:22; Mic 7:7
20:14 ᵗS 1Ch 12:18
ᵘ1Ch 9:15
20:15 ᵛ2Ch 32:7
ʷS 1Sa 17:47; Ps 91:8
20:17 ˣS Ex 14:13
20:18 ʸS Ge 24:26;
2Ch 29:29
20:20 ᶻIsa 7:9
ᵃS Ge 39:3; Pr 16:3
20:21 ᵇS 1Ch 16:29
ᶜS 2Ch 5:13; Ps 136:1
20:22 ᵈS 2Ch 13:13

you from Edom,ᵃ from the other side of the Dead Sea. It is already in Hazezon Tamarᵈⁿ (that is, En Gedi).ᵉ ³Alarmed, Jehoshaphat resolved to inquire of the LORD, and he proclaimed a fastᶠ for all Judah. ⁴The people of Judahᵍ came together to seek help from the LORD; indeed, they came from every town in Judah to seek him.

⁵Then Jehoshaphat stood up in the assembly of Judah and Jerusalem at the temple of the LORD in the front of the new courtyard ⁶and said:

"LORD, the God of our ancestors,ʰ are you not the God who is in heaven?ⁱ You rule over all the kingdomsʲ of the nations. Power and might are in your hand, and no one can withstand you.ᵏ ⁷Our God, did you not drive out the inhabitants of this landˡ before your people Israel and give it forever to the descendants of Abraham your friend?ᵐ ⁸They have lived in it and have built in it a sanctuaryⁿ for your Name, saying, ⁹'If calamity comes upon us, whether the sword of judgment, or plague or famine,ᵒ we will stand in your presence before this temple that bears your Name and will cry out to you in our distress, and you will hear us and save us.'

¹⁰"But now here are men from Ammon, Moab and Mount Seir, whose territory you would not allow Israel to invade when they came from Egypt;ᵖ so they turned away from them and did not destroy them. ¹¹See how they are repaying us by coming to drive us out of the possessionᑫ you gave us as an inheritance. ¹²Our God, will you not judge them?ʳ For we have no power to face this vast army that is attacking us. We do not know what to do, but our eyes are on you.ˢ"

¹³All the men of Judah, with their wives and children and little ones, stood there before the LORD.

¹⁴Then the Spiritᵗ of the LORD came on Jahaziel son of Zechariah, the son of Benaiah, the son of Jeiel, the son of Mattaniah,ᵘ a Levite and descendant of Asaph, as he stood in the assembly.

¹⁵He said: "Listen, King Jehoshaphat and all who live in Judah and Jerusalem! This is what the LORD says to you: 'Do not be afraid or discouragedᵛ because of this vast army. For the battleʷ is not yours, but God's. ¹⁶Tomorrow march down against them. They will be climbing up by the Pass of Ziz, and you will find them at the end of the gorge in the Desert of Jeruel. ¹⁷You will not have to fight this battle. Take up your positions; stand firm and seeˣ the deliverance the LORD will give you, Judah and Jerusalem. Do not be afraid; do not be discouraged. Go out to face them tomorrow, and the LORD will be with you.'"

¹⁸Jehoshaphat bowed downʸ with his face to the ground, and all the people of Judah and Jerusalem fell down in worship before the LORD. ¹⁹Then some Levites from the Kohathites and Korahites stood up and praised the LORD, the God of Israel, with a very loud voice.

²⁰Early in the morning they left for the Desert of Tekoa. As they set out, Jehoshaphat stood and said, "Listen to me, Judah and people of Jerusalem! Have faithᶻ in the LORD your God and you will be upheld; have faith in his prophets and you will be successful.ᵃ"

²¹After consulting the people, Jehoshaphat appointed men to sing to the LORD and to praise him for the splendor of hisᵇ holinessᵇ as they went out at the head of the army, saying:

"Give thanks to the LORD,
    for his love endures forever."ᶜ

²²As they began to sing and praise, the LORD set ambushesᵈ against the men of Ammon and Moab and Mount Seir who were invading Judah, and they were defeated. ²³The

---

ᵃ 2 One Hebrew manuscript; most Hebrew manuscripts, Septuagint and Vulgate *Aram*   ᵇ 21 Or *him with the splendor of*

20:2 *Edom.* See TNIV text note. Since the Arameans are well to the north and not mentioned among the attackers named in v. 1, the TNIV has followed the reading "Edom." The difference between "Aram" and "Edom" in Hebrew is only one letter, which is very similar in shape and was often confused in the process of copying manuscripts.

A 20:5–12 Jehoshaphat's prayer shows him to be a true theocratic king, a worthy son of David and type (foreshadowing) of the awaited Messiah (see Introduction to 1 Chronicles: Purpose and Themes).

20:7 *Abraham your friend.* See Isa 41:8; Jas 2:23 and note.

20:9 An apparent reference to Solomon's prayer and the divine promise of response (6:14–42; 7:12–22).

20:15 See Ex 14:13–14 and note on 14:14.

20:16 *Pass of Ziz.* Began seven miles north of En Gedi and wound inland, emerging west of Tekoa. *Jeruel.* Southeast of Tekoa.

20:19 *Levites.* The Chronicler's interest in the priests and Levites is apparent throughout the account (vv. 14,21–22,28).

A 20:20 *Have faith in the LORD your God and … in his prophets.* A particularly apt word for the Chronicler's contemporaries to hear from this son of David—at a time when their only hope for the future lay with the Lord and the reassuring words of his prophets.

20:21 *splendor of his holiness.* See note on 1Ch 16:29.

20:22 *ambushes.* The nature of this "ambush" is indicated in v. 23: Israel's foes destroyed each other in the confusion of battle, similar to the victory under Gideon (Jdg 7:22).

Ammonites [e] and Moabites rose up against the men from Mount Seir [f] to destroy and annihilate them. After they finished slaughtering the men from Seir, they helped to destroy one another. [g]

[24] When the men of Judah came to the place that overlooks the desert and looked toward the vast army, they saw only dead bodies lying on the ground; no one had escaped. [25] So Jehoshaphat and his men went to carry off their plunder, and they found among them a great amount of equipment and clothing [a] and also articles of value—more than they could take away. There was so much plunder that it took three days to collect it. [26] On the fourth day they assembled in the Valley of Berakah, where they praised the LORD. This is why it is called the Valley of Berakah [b] to this day.

[27] Then, led by Jehoshaphat, all the men of Judah and Jerusalem returned joyfully to Jerusalem, for the LORD had given them cause to rejoice over their enemies. [28] They entered Jerusalem and went to the temple of the LORD with harps and lyres and trumpets.

[29] The fear [h] of God came on all the surrounding kingdoms when they heard how the LORD had fought [i] against the enemies of Israel. [30] And the kingdom of Jehoshaphat was at peace, for his God had given him rest [j] on every side.

THE END OF JEHOSHAPHAT'S REIGN
20:31–21:1pp — 1Ki 22:41–50

[31] So Jehoshaphat reigned over Judah. He was thirty-five years old when he became king of Judah, and he reigned in Jerusalem twenty-five years. His mother's name was Azubah daughter of Shilhi. [32] He followed the ways of his father Asa and did not stray from them; he did what was right in the eyes of the LORD. [33] The high places, [k] however, were not removed, and the people still had not set their hearts on the God of their ancestors.

[34] The other events of Jehoshaphat's reign, from beginning to end, are written in the annals of Jehu [l] son of Hanani, which are recorded in the book of the kings of Israel.

[35] Later, Jehoshaphat king of Judah made an alliance [m] with Ahaziah king of Israel, whose ways were wicked. [n] [36] He agreed with him to construct a fleet of trading ships. [c] After these were built at Ezion Geber, [37] Eliezer son of Dodavahu of Mareshah prophesied against Jehoshaphat, saying, "Because you have made an alliance with Ahaziah, the LORD will destroy what you have made." The ships [o] were wrecked and were not able to set sail to trade. [d]

21 Then Jehoshaphat rested with his ancestors and was buried with them in the City of David. And Jehoram [p] his son succeeded him as king. [2] Jehoram's brothers, the sons of Jehoshaphat, were Azariah, Jehiel, Zechariah, Azariahu, Michael and Shephatiah. All these were sons of Jehoshaphat king of Israel. [e] [3] Their father had given them many gifts [q] of silver and gold and articles of value, as well as fortified cities [r] in Judah, but he had given the kingdom to Jehoram because he was his firstborn son.

JEHORAM KING OF JUDAH
21:5–10,20pp — 2Ki 8:16–24

[4] When Jehoram established [s] himself firmly over his father's kingdom, he put all his brothers [t] to the sword along with some of the officials of Israel. [5] Jehoram was thirty-two

---

20:23 [e] S Ge 19:38
[f] 2Ch 21:8
[g] S Jdg 7:22;
1Sa 14:20; Eze 38:21
20:29 [h] S Ge 35:5;
S Dt 2:25 [i] S Ex 14:14
20:30 [j] 1Ch 22:9
20:33 [k] S 2Ch 17:6
20:34 [l] S 1Ki 16:1
20:35 [m] S 2Ch 16:3
[n] S 2Ch 19:1-3
20:37 [o] S 1Ki 9:26
21:1 [p] S 1Ch 3:11
21:3 [q] 2Ch 11:23
[r] S 2Ch 11:10
21:4 [s] S 1Ki 2:12
[t] Jdg 9:5

---

[a] 25 Some Hebrew manuscripts and Vulgate; most Hebrew manuscripts *corpses*   [b] 26 *Berakah* means *praise.*   [c] 36 Hebrew *of ships that could go to Tarshish*   [d] 37 Hebrew *sail for Tarshish*   [e] 2 That is, Judah, as frequently in 2 Chronicles

---

20:26 *to this day.* See note on 5:9.

20:29 *The fear of God.* See note on 1Ch 14:17.

20:30 *rest on every side.* Rest from enemies is part of God's blessing for obedience in Chronicles (14:5–7; 15:15; 1Ch 22:8–9,18). Righteous kings have victory in warfare (Abijah, Asa, Jehoshaphat, Uzziah, Hezekiah), while wicked rulers experience defeat (Jehoram, Ahaz, Joash, Zedekiah).

20:31 *twenty-five years.* The book of Kings reports 22 (18 in 2Ki 3:1 and 4 more in 8:16). These figures are reconciled by suggesting a coregency with his father, Asa, for three years, probably due to the severity of his father's illness and the need to arrange for a secure succession (16:10–14). The book of Kings speaks only of his years of sole reign after his father's death.

20:33 *high places ... were not removed.* See note on 17:6.

20:34 *Jehu son of Hanani.* See note on 19:2.

20:35–37 See 1Ki 22:48–49. The lucrative maritime trade through the Gulf of Aqaba no doubt tempted Jehoshaphat to enter into this improper alliance (see 19:2 and note). Solomon's

earlier alliance for the same purpose had been with a non-Israelite king (8:17–18).

20:35 *Ahaziah.* Reigned 853–852 B.C. (see 1Ki 22:51—2Ki 1:18 for the account of his reign).

21:2 *sons of Jehoshaphat.* The Chronicler shows the blessing of God on Jehoshaphat by mentioning his large family, particularly his seven sons (see 11:18–22; 1Ch 25:5 and notes). Jehoshaphat's large number of sons is in striking contrast to the wicked Jehoram who, after murdering his brothers (v. 4), is left with but one son (v. 17). Jehoram's wife, Athaliah, would later perform a similar slaughter (22:10).

21:3 Cf. the similar actions of Rehoboam (11:23).

21:4–20 See 2Ki 8:16–24 and notes.

21:4 This bloody assassination of all potential rivals is not reported in Kings, but it fits the pattern of the northern kings (see v. 6). The princes of Israel were probably leading men in the southern kingdom who opposed having a king married to a daughter of Ahab. For this use of "Israel," see note on 12:1.

21:6 *u* 1Ki 12:28-30
v 2Ch 18:1; 22:3
21:7 *w* S 2Sa 7:13
x S 2Sa 7:15; 2Ch 23:3
y S 2Sa 21:17
21:8 *z* 2Ch 20:22-23
21:10 *a* S Nu 33:20
21:12 *b* 2Ki 1:16-17
c 2Ch 17:3-6
d 2Ch 14:2
21:13 *e* 1Ki 16:29-33
f 1Ki 2:32
21:15 *g* S Nu 12:10
21:16 *h* 2Ch 17:10-11; 22:1; 26:7
21:17 *i* 2Ki 12:18; 2Ch 22:1; Joel 3:5
21:19 *j* S 2Ch 16:14
21:20 *k* 2Ch 24:25; 28:27; 33:20
22:1 *l* 2Ch 33:25; 36:1 *m* 2Ch 23:20-21; 26:1 *n* S 2Ch 21:16-17

years old when he became king, and he reigned in Jerusalem eight years. [6]He followed the ways of the kings of Israel, *u* as the house of Ahab had done, for he married a daughter of Ahab. *v* He did evil in the eyes of the LORD. [7]Nevertheless, because of the covenant the LORD had made with David, *w* the LORD was not willing to destroy the house of David. *x* He had promised to maintain a lamp *y* for him and his descendants forever.

[8]In the time of Jehoram, Edom *z* rebelled against Judah and set up its own king. [9]So Jehoram went there with his officers and all his chariots. The Edomites surrounded him and his chariot commanders, but he rose up and broke through by night. [10]To this day Edom has been in rebellion against Judah.

Libnah *a* revolted at the same time, because Jehoram had forsaken the LORD, the God of his ancestors. [11]He had also built high places on the hills of Judah and had caused the people of Jerusalem to prostitute themselves and had led Judah astray.

[12]Jehoram received a letter from Elijah *b* the prophet, which said:

"This is what the LORD, the God of your father *c* David, says: 'You have not followed the ways of your father Jehoshaphat or of Asa *d* king of Judah. [13]But you have followed the ways of the kings of Israel, and you have led Judah and the people of Jerusalem to prostitute themselves, just as the house of Ahab did. *e* You have also murdered your own brothers, members of your own family, men who were better *f* than you. [14]So now the LORD is about to strike your people, your sons, your wives and everything that is yours, with a heavy blow. [15]You yourself will be very ill with a lingering disease *g* of the bowels, until the disease causes your bowels to come out.' "

[16]The LORD aroused against Jehoram the hostility of the Philistines and of the Arabs *h* who lived near the Cushites. [17]They attacked Judah, invaded it and carried off all the goods found in the king's palace, together with his sons and wives. Not a son was left to him except Ahaziah, *a* the youngest. *i*

[18]After all this, the LORD afflicted Jehoram with an incurable disease of the bowels. [19]In the course of time, at the end of the second year, his bowels came out because of the disease, and he died in great pain. His people made no funeral fire in his honor, *j* as they had for his predecessors.

[20]Jehoram was thirty-two years old when he became king, and he reigned in Jerusalem eight years. He passed away, to no one's regret, and was buried *k* in the City of David, but not in the tombs of the kings.

AHAZIAH KING OF JUDAH

22:1–6pp — 2Ki 8:25–29
22:7–9pp — 2Ki 9:21–29

22 The people *l* of Jerusalem *m* made Ahaziah, Jehoram's youngest son, king in his place, since the raiders, *n* who came with the Arabs into the camp, had killed all the older sons. So Ahaziah son of Jehoram king of Judah began to reign.

a 17 Hebrew *Jehoahaz,* a variant of *Ahaziah*

21:5 *eight years.* 848–841 B.C. The period 853–848 was probably a coregency of Jehoram with his father, Jehoshaphat— Jehoshaphat's 18th year was also Jehoram's second year (cf. 2Ki 1:17; 3:1).
21:6 *married a daughter of Ahab.* Probably the marriage referred to in 18:1, used to cement the alliance between Jehoshaphat and Ahab. Such political marriages were common. Many of Solomon's marriages sealed international relationships (see note on 1Ki 11:1), as did Ahab's marriage to Jezebel.
21:8–10 The pious Jehoshaphat had enjoyed victory over Edom (20:1–30), while the wicked Jehoram is defeated in his attempt to keep Edom in subjection to Judah (see note on 20:30).
21:10 *To this day.* See note on 5:9. *Libnah.* Located between Judah and Philistia. *because Jehoram had forsaken the LORD.* Not found in 2Ki 8:22. The Chronicler introduces this judgment as an indication of immediate retribution (see notes on 12:1–14; 12:2; see also Introduction to 1 Chronicles: Purpose and Themes).
21:11 *prostitute themselves.* See Ex 34:15 and note.
21:12–20a Not found in the parallel text in 2Ki 8.
21:12–15 This reference to a letter from Elijah is the only mention in Chronicles of that prophet, to whom the books of Kings give so much attention (1Ki 17–2Ki 2). Elijah's letter specifically announces the immediate consequences of Jehoram's disobedi-

ence—further defeat in war, which will cost Jehoram his wives and sons; and disease, which will lead to his death (see note on 16:12). Cf. also the foot disease of Asa (16:12–14) and the leprosy of Uzziah (26:16–23). The book of Kings does not mention the nature of Jehoram's death. Some have argued that this letter could not be authentic because, they claim, Elijah was taken to heaven before Jehoram became king. But this is not a necessary conclusion (see 2Ki 1:17; see also note on 2Ki 3:11). Elijah's translation may well have taken place as late as 848 B.C.
21:16 *Cushites.* See note on 14:9; see also TNIV text note on 16:8.
21:20 *eight years.* See note on v. 5. *not in the tombs of the kings.* Only the Chronicler mentions the refusal of the people to accord Jehoram the customary burial honors of a tomb with the other kings of Judah (cf. 24:25).
C **22:1–9** The Chronicler's account of Ahaziah's reign is much shorter than the parallel in 2Ki 8:24—9:29, probably due to the fact that the Kings account focuses on the rebellion of Jehu and the downfall of the dynasty of Omri (see 2Ki 8:26; see also 1Ki 16:21–28)—events in the northern kingdom, in which the Chronicler is not interested. The Chronicler's account again shows his interest in immediate retribution: Ahaziah's personal wickedness and his involvement in a foreign

22:3 ⁰S 2Ch 18:1
ᵖS 2Ch 21:6
22:5 �q2Ch 18:11,34
22:6 ʳ1Ki 19:15;
2Ki 8:13-15
22:7 ˢ2Ki 9:16
22:8 ᵗS 2Ki 10:13
22:9 ᵘS Jdg 9:5
ᵛ2Ch 17:4

²Ahaziah was twenty-two ᵃ years old when he became king, and he reigned in Jerusalem one year. His mother's name was Athaliah, a granddaughter of Omri.

³He too followed ⁰ the ways of the house of Ahab, ᵖ for his mother encouraged him to act wickedly. ⁴He did evil in the eyes of the Lord, as the house of Ahab had done, for after his father's death they became his advisers, to his undoing. ⁵He also followed their counsel when he went with Joram ᵇ son of Ahab king of Israel to war against Hazael king of Aram at Ramoth Gilead. �q The Arameans wounded Joram; ⁶so he returned to Jezreel to recover from the wounds they had inflicted on him at Ramoth ᶜ in his battle with Hazael ʳ king of Aram.

Then Ahaziah ᵈ son of Jehoram king of Judah went down to Jezreel to see Joram son of Ahab because he had been wounded.

⁷Through Ahaziah's ˢ visit to Joram, God brought about Ahaziah's downfall. When Ahaziah arrived, he went out with Joram to meet Jehu son of Nimshi, whom the Lord had anointed to destroy the house of Ahab. ⁸While Jehu was executing judgment on the house of Ahab, ᵗ he found the officials of Judah and the sons of Ahaziah's relatives, who had been attending Ahaziah, and he killed them. ⁹He then went in search of Ahaziah, and his men captured him while he was hiding ᵘ in Samaria. He was brought to Jehu and put to death. They buried him, for they said, "He was a son of Jehoshaphat, who sought ᵛ the Lord with all his heart." So there was no one in the house of Ahaziah powerful enough to retain the kingdom.

ATHALIAH AND JOASH
22:10—23:21pp — 2Ki 11:1–21

¹⁰When Athaliah the mother of Ahaziah saw that her son was dead, she proceeded to destroy the whole royal family of the house of Judah. ¹¹But Jehosheba, ᵉ the daughter of King Jehoram, took Joash son of Ahaziah and stole him away from among the royal princes who were about to be murdered and put him and his nurse in a bedroom. Because Jehosheba, ᵉ the daughter of King Jehoram and wife of the priest Jehoiada, was Ahaziah's sister, she hid the child from Athaliah so she could not kill him. ¹²He remained hidden with them at the temple of God for six years while Athaliah ruled the land.

23 In the seventh year Jehoiada showed his strength. He made a covenant with the commanders of units of a hundred: Azariah son of Jeroham, Ishmael son of Jehohanan, Azariah son of Obed, Maaseiah son of Adaiah, and Elishaphat

---

ᵃ 2 Some Septuagint manuscripts and Syriac (see also 2 Kings 8:26); Hebrew *forty-two*   ᵇ 5 Hebrew *Jehoram*, a variant of *Joram*; also in verses 6 and 7   ᶜ 6 Hebrew *Ramah*, a variant of *Ramoth*   ᵈ 6 Some Hebrew manuscripts, Septuagint, Vulgate and Syriac (see also 2 Kings 8:29); most Hebrew manuscripts *Azariah*   ᵉ 11 Hebrew *Jehoshabeath*, a variant of *Jehosheba*

---

alliance result in immediate judgment and a reign of only one year (see note on 16:2–9; see also Introduction to 1 Chronicles: Purpose and Themes).

22:1 *had killed all the older sons.* Emphasizes divine retribution: Jehoram, who murdered all his brothers, had to watch the death of his own sons (21:4,13,16–17).

22:2 *twenty-two.* See TNIV text note. The Hebrew reading of "42" would make Ahaziah older than his father (21:20). *one year.* 841 B.C.

22:3–4 The great influence of the dynasty of Omri in Judah is indicated by the power of Athaliah and the presence of advisers from the northern kingdom (see note on 18:29).

22:5 *went with Joram…to war.* An action similar to that for which Jehoshaphat had been rebuked (see 19:2 and note). *Hazael.* Had been anointed by Elisha; he later killed his master in a coup to seize the throne (2Ki 8:13–15; cf. 1Ki 19:15 and note). *Ramoth Gilead.* Located in the Transjordan border area between Israel and Aram. More than ten years earlier Jehoshaphat had participated with Ahab in a battle there that cost Ahab his life (ch. 18; 1Ki 22).

22:6 *returned to Jezreel.* Joram apparently recovered Ramoth Gilead and left Jehu in charge (2Ki 8:28—9:28). *Jezreel.* See map, p. 527.

C 22:7 *God brought about Ahaziah's downfall.* The Chronicler assumes that the reader is familiar with the account of Jehu's anointing and the additional details of the coup, which resulted in the deaths of Joram and Ahaziah (2Ki 8:28—9:28). While the writer of Kings primarily portrays the end of the dy-

nasty of Omri as a result of the judgment of God (1Ki 21:20–29; 2Ki 9:24—10:17), the Chronicler notes that the assassination of Ahaziah was also brought about by God.

22:9 The account of Ahaziah's death appears to be somewhat different in the two histories (cf. 2Ki 9:21–27; 10:12–14). Since the writer of Chronicles presumes the reader's familiarity with the other account (see note on v. 7), it is best to take the details of Chronicles as supplementary to Kings, not contradictory, though it is difficult to know the precise sequence and location of events. Apart from the Chronicler's statement that Ahaziah received a decent burial because of his father's piety rather than his own, the apparent differences in the two accounts do not appear to be theologically motivated.

C 22:10–12 See 2Ki 11:1–3. In the history of Judah, Athaliah represents the only break in the continuity of the Davidic dynasty; she is the only queen of Judah to rule in her own name (841–835 B.C.). Her attempt to wipe out the royal family repeated the action of her husband, Jehoram (21:4). It threatened the continuity of the Davidic dynasty, and if she had succeeded, Judah may have been claimed by the dynasty of Omri in the north since Athaliah was from that dynasty and had no living son and heir.

22:11 *wife of the priest Jehoiada.* Not noted in Kings.

C 23:1—24:27 See 2Ki 11:4—12:21 and notes. The Chronicler divides the reign of Joash (835–796 B.C.) into three parts: (1) the recovery of the throne for the house of David (ch. 23); (2) Joash and Jehoiada—the good years (24:1–16); and (3) Joash alone—the bad years (24:17–27). The last section is

23:2 *w* S Nu 35:2-5
23:3 *x* S 2Ki 11:17
y S 2Sa 7:12;
S 1Ki 2:4; S 2Ch 6:16;
S 7:18; S 21:7
23:6 *z* Zec 3:7
23:8 *a* 2Ki 11:9
b S 1Ch 24:1
23:11 *c* Dt 17:18
23:13 *d* 1Ki 1:41
e S 1Ki 7:15
23:15 *f* Jer 31:40
23:16 *g* 2Ch 29:10;
34:31; Ne 9:38
23:17 *h* Dt 13:6-9
23:18 *i* S 1Ch 23:28-
32 *j* S 1Ch 23:6;
S 25:6
23:19 *k* 1Ch 9:22

son of Zikri. ²They went throughout Judah and gathered the Levites *w* and the heads of Israelite families from all the towns. When they came to Jerusalem, ³the whole assembly made a covenant *x* with the king at the temple of God.

Jehoiada said to them, "The king's son shall reign, as the LORD promised concerning the descendants of David. *y* ⁴Now this is what you are to do: A third of you priests and Levites who are going on duty on the Sabbath are to keep watch at the doors, ⁵a third of you at the royal palace and a third at the Foundation Gate, and all the others are to be in the courtyards of the temple of the LORD. ⁶No one is to enter the temple of the LORD except the priests and Levites on duty; they may enter because they are consecrated, but all the others are to observe *z* the LORD's command not to enter. *a* ⁷The Levites are to station themselves around the king, each with weapon in hand. Anyone who enters the temple is to be put to death. Stay close to the king wherever he goes."

⁸The Levites and all the men of Judah did just as Jehoiada the priest ordered. *a* Each one took his men—those who were going on duty on the Sabbath and those who were going off duty—for Jehoiada the priest had not released any of the divisions. *b* ⁹Then he gave the commanders of units of a hundred the spears and the large and small shields that had belonged to King David and that were in the temple of God. ¹⁰He stationed all the men, each with his weapon in his hand, around the king—near the altar and the temple, from the south side to the north side of the temple.

¹¹Jehoiada and his sons brought out the king's son and put the crown on him; they presented him with a copy *c* of the covenant and proclaimed him king. They anointed him and shouted, "Long live the king!"

¹²When Athaliah heard the noise of the people running and cheering the king, she went to them at the temple of the LORD. ¹³She looked, and there was the king, *d* standing by his pillar *e* at the entrance. The officers and the trumpeters were beside the king, and all the people of the land were rejoicing and blowing trumpets, and musicians with their instruments were leading the praises. Then Athaliah tore her robes and shouted, "Treason! Treason!"

¹⁴Jehoiada the priest sent out the commanders of units of a hundred, who were in charge of the troops, and said to them: "Bring her out between the ranks *b* and put to the sword anyone who follows her." For the priest had said, "Do not put her to death at the temple of the LORD." ¹⁵So they seized her as she reached the entrance of the Horse Gate *f* on the palace grounds, and there they put her to death.

¹⁶Jehoiada then made a covenant *g* that he, the people and the king *c* would be the LORD's people. ¹⁷All the people went to the temple of Baal and tore it down. They smashed the altars and idols and killed *h* Mattan the priest of Baal in front of the altars.

¹⁸Then Jehoiada placed the oversight of the temple of the LORD in the hands of the Levitical priests, *i* to whom David had made assignments in the temple, *j* to present the burnt offerings of the LORD as written in the Law of Moses, with rejoicing and singing, as David had ordered. ¹⁹He also stationed gatekeepers *k* at the gates of the LORD's temple so that no one who was in any way unclean might enter.

²⁰He took with him the commanders of hundreds, the nobles, the rulers of the people

---

a 6 Or *are to stand guard where the LORD has assigned them*   *b* 14 Or *out from the precincts*
c 16 Or *covenant between the LORD and the people and the king that they* (see 2 Kings 11:17)

---

largely unique to Chronicles and further develops the theme of immediate retribution: Once again chronological notes provide the framework for cycles of obedience and disobedience (24:15–17,23); see notes on 12:2; 14:2—16:14.
23:1–21 See 2Ki 11:4–20. The Chronicler has followed his source rather closely but has introduced material reflecting his own concerns in three areas: 1. The account in Kings has more to say about the participation of the military in the coup; the Chronicler adds material emphasizing the presence of temple officials and their role (vv. 2,6,8,13,18–19). 2. The Chronicler stresses the widespread popular support for the coup by mentioning the presence of large groups of people, such as "all the people" or "the whole assembly" (vv. 3,5–6, 8,10,16–17). 3. The Chronicler shows additional concern for the sanctity of the temple area by inserting notes showing the steps taken to ensure that only qualified personnel enter the temple precincts (vv. 5–6,19).
23:1 *Azariah … Elishaphat.* The Chronicler names the commanders, which was not done in Kings, but he does not men-

tion the Carites, mercenaries who served as a royal guard (see note on 2Ki 11:4). Verse 20 exhibits the same omission (cf. 2Ki 11:19). The Chronicler's motive may have been his concern that only authorized persons enter the temple precincts.
23:2 *the Levites and the heads of Israelite families.* Reflects both the Chronicler's concerns with the temple personnel and the widespread support for the coup against Athaliah.
23:3 *as the LORD promised.* See 2Sa 7:11–16.
23:11 *copy of the covenant.* May refer to the covenant sworn by the assembly (vv. 1,3; cf. v. 16) or to the law of God, by which the king was to rule (see Dt 17:18–20). See note on 2Ki 11:12. *Long live the king!* See note on Ps 62:4.
23:13 *musicians with their instruments.* The Chronicler adds a word (not found in 2Ki 11:14) about the presence of Levitical musicians, who were leading the praises (see note on 1Ch 6:31–48).
23:18–19 The Chronicler adds information on the temple ritual and the guards at the gates (see note on vv. 1–21).
23:20 See note on v. 1.

and all the people of the land and brought the king down from the temple of the LORD. They went into the palace through the Upper Gate *l* and seated the king on the royal throne. ²¹All the people of the land rejoiced, and the city was calm, because Athaliah had been slain with the sword. *m*

JOASH REPAIRS THE TEMPLE
24:1–14pp — 2Ki 12:1–16
24:23–27pp — 2Ki 12:17–21

24 Joash was seven years old when he became king, and he reigned in Jerusalem forty years. His mother's name was Zibiah; she was from Beersheba. ²Joash did what was right in the eyes of the LORD *n* all the years of Jehoiada the priest. ³Jehoiada chose two wives for him, and he had sons and daughters.

⁴Some time later Joash decided to restore the temple of the LORD. ⁵He called together the priests and Levites and said to them, "Go to the towns of Judah and collect the money *o* due annually from all Israel, *p* to repair the temple of your God. Do it now." But the Levites *q* did not act at once.

⁶Therefore the king summoned Jehoiada the chief priest and said to him, "Why haven't you required the Levites to bring in from Judah and Jerusalem the tax imposed by Moses the servant of the LORD and by the assembly of Israel for the tent of the covenant law?" *r*

⁷Now the sons of that wicked woman Athaliah had broken into the temple of God and had used even its sacred objects for the Baals.

⁸At the king's command, a chest was made and placed outside, at the gate of the temple of the LORD. ⁹A proclamation was then issued in Judah and Jerusalem that they should bring to the LORD the tax that Moses the servant of God had required of Israel in the wilderness. ¹⁰All the officials and all the people brought their contributions gladly, *s* dropping them into the chest until it was full. ¹¹Whenever the chest was brought in by the Levites to the king's officials and they saw that there was a large amount of money, the royal secretary and the officer of the chief priest would come and empty the chest and carry it back to its place. They did this regularly and collected a great amount of money. ¹²The king and Jehoiada gave it to those who carried out the work required for the temple of the LORD. They hired *t* masons and carpenters to restore the LORD's temple, and also workers in iron and bronze to repair the temple.

¹³The men in charge of the work were diligent, and the repairs progressed under them. They rebuilt the temple of God according to its original design and reinforced it. ¹⁴When they had finished, they brought the rest of the money to the king and Jehoiada, and with it were made articles for the LORD's temple: articles for the service and for the burnt offerings, and also dishes and other objects of gold and silver. As long as Jehoiada lived, burnt offerings were presented continually in the temple of the LORD.

¹⁵Now Jehoiada was old and full of years, and he died at the age of a hundred and thirty. ¹⁶He was buried with the kings in the City of David, because of the good he had done in Israel for God and his temple.

THE WICKEDNESS OF JOASH
¹⁷After the death of Jehoiada, the officials of Judah came and paid homage to the king, and he listened to them. ¹⁸They abandoned *u* the temple of the LORD, the God of their an-

---

23:20 *l* S 2Ki 15:35
23:21 *m* S 2Ch 22:1
24:2 *n* 2Ch 25:2; 26:5
24:5 *o* S Ex 30:16; Ne 10:32-33; Mt 17:24 *p* 1Ch 11:1 *q* S 1Ch 26:20
24:6 *r* S Ex 38:21
24:10 *s* S Ex 25:2; S 1Ch 29:3,6,9
24:12 *t* 2Ch 34:11
24:18 *u* S Jos 24:20; S 2Ch 7:19

24:1–14 See 2Ki 12:1–17 and notes.
24:1 *forty years.* 835–796 B.C.
C **24:2** Provides the outline for the Chronicler's treatment of Joash—the good years while Jehoiada was alive (vv. 1–16), and the turn to evil after his death (vv. 17–27). See note on 25:2.
24:3 Another expression of the Chronicler's conviction that large families represent the blessing of God (see v. 27; see also note on 1Ch 25:5).
24:4 *restore the temple.* The vandalism and atrocities of Athaliah (v. 7) required the refurbishing of the temple.
24:5 The writer of 2 Kings speaks of three different sources of revenue (2Ki 12:4–5), whereas the Chronicler mentions only the census tax (see Ex 30:14; 38:26; Mt 17:24). The reason for the tardiness of the priests is not stated (see 2Ki 12:6–8). The writer of Kings notes that the audience with the priests takes place in the 23rd year of Joash's reign, when he is presumably no longer the ward of Jehoiada. Resistance on the part of the priests to the re-

assignment of the temple revenues for repair work may be the underlying cause.
B **24:8** *chest.* Mesopotamian texts speak of a similar offering box placed in temples. Representatives of both the king and the temple officials administered temple revenues (see note on 1Ch 26:20).
C **24:14** See 2Ki 12:13–14. *As long as Jehoiada lived.* An additional note on the part of the Chronicler to introduce the turn to the worse in the reign of Joash upon Jehoiada's death (vv. 15–16).
A C **24:15–22** This section is unique to the Chronicler and shows his emphasis on immediate retribution (see note on 23:1—24:27). After a period of righteous rule until the death of Jehoiada, Joash turns to idolatry and murders Jehoiada's son. In the following year he is invaded and defeated by Aram because Judah, under his leadership, "had forsaken the LORD" (v. 24).
24:18,20,24 *abandoned...forsaken...forsaken...forsaken.*

24:18 ᵛS Ex 34:13;
2Ch 33:3; Jer 17:2
ᵚS 2Ch 19:2
24:19 ˣS Nu 11:29;
Jer 7:25; Zec 1:4
24:20 ʸS Jdg 3:10;
S 1Ch 12:18
ᶻMt 23:35; Lk 11:51
ᵃNu 14:41
ᵇS Dt 31:17
24:21 ᶜS Jos 7:25
ᵈJer 26:21 ᵉJer 20:2
24:22 ᶠS Ge 9:5
24:23 ᵍ2Ki 12:17-18
24:24 ʰS 2Ch 14:9;
16:8; 20:2,12
ⁱLev 26:23-25;
Dt 28:25
24:25 ʲS 2Ch 21:20
24:26 ᵏ2Ki 12:21
ˡS Ru 1:4
25:2 ᵐS 1Ki 8:61;
S 2Ch 24:2
25:4 ⁿS Dt 28:61
ᵒS Nu 26:11

cestors, and worshiped Asherah poles and idols.ᵛ Because of their guilt, God's angerᵚ came on Judah and Jerusalem. ¹⁹Although the LORD sent prophets to the people to bring them back to him, and though they testified against them, they would not listen.ˣ

²⁰Then the Spiritʸ of God came on Zechariahᶻ son of Jehoiada the priest. He stood before the people and said, "This is what God says: 'Why do you disobey the LORD's commands? You will not prosper.ᵃ Because you have forsaken the LORD, he has forsakenᵇ you.' "

²¹But they plotted against him, and by order of the king they stonedᶜ him to deathᵈ in the courtyard of the LORD's temple.ᵉ ²²King Joash did not remember the kindness Zechariah's father Jehoiada had shown him but killed his son, who said as he lay dying, "May the LORD see this and call you to account."ᶠ

²³At the turn of the year,ᵃ the army of Aram marched against Joash; it invaded Judah and Jerusalem and killed all the leaders of the people.ᵍ They sent all the plunder to their king in Damascus. ²⁴Although the Aramean army had come with only a few men,ʰ the LORD delivered into their hands a much larger army.ⁱ Because Judah had forsaken the LORD, the God of their ancestors, judgment was executed on Joash. ²⁵When the Arameans withdrew, they left Joash severely wounded. His officials conspired against him for murdering the son of Jehoiada the priest, and they killed him in his bed. So he died and was buriedʲ in the City of David, but not in the tombs of the kings.

²⁶Those who conspired against him were Zabad,ᵇ son of Shimeath an Ammonite woman, and Jehozabad, son of Shimrithᶜ ᵏ a Moabite woman.ˡ ²⁷The account of his sons, the many prophecies about him, and the record of the restoration of the temple of God are written in the annotations on the book of the kings. And Amaziah his son succeeded him as king.

AMAZIAH KING OF JUDAH

25:1–4pp — 2Ki 14:1–6
25:11–12pp — 2Ki 14:7
25:17–28pp — 2Ki 14:8–20

25 Amaziah was twenty-five years old when he became king, and he reigned in Jerusalem twenty-nine years. His mother's name was Jehoaddan; she was from Jerusalem. ²He did what was right in the eyes of the LORD, but not wholeheartedly.ᵐ ³After the kingdom was firmly in his control, he executed the officials who had murdered his father the king. ⁴Yet he did not put their children to death, but acted in accordance with what is written in the Law, in the Book of Moses,ⁿ where the LORD commanded: "Parents shall not be put to death for their children, nor children be put to death for their parents; each of you will die for your own sin."ᵈᵒ

⁵Amaziah called the people of Judah together and assigned them according to their families to commanders of thousands and commanders of hundreds for all Judah and Benja-

---

ᵃ **23** Probably in the spring   ᵇ **26** A variant of *Jozabad*   ᶜ **26** A variant of *Shomer*   ᵈ **4** Deut. 24:16

The Hebrew word is the same in these verses; it is a verb frequently used by the Chronicler to denote the reason for divine punishment (see note on 12:1; see also 7:19,22; 12:5; 13:10–11; 15:2; 21:10; 24:18,20,24; 28:6; 29:6; 34:25; 1Ch 28:9,20).

24:19 *Although the LORD sent prophets.* Israel's failure to heed the Lord's prophets ultimately led to her destruction (see 36:16; cf. 20:20; see also Introduction to 1 Chronicles: Purpose and Themes).

24:20 *Zechariah.* See note on Mt 23:35.

24:24 *only a few men.* Just as God had helped the small army of Judah against overwhelming odds when the king and people were faithful to him (14:8–9; 20:2,12), so now in their unfaithfulness they are defeated by a much smaller force of invaders (see note on 20:30).

24:25 *for murdering ... they killed him.* Only the Chronicler mentions that this assassination was revenge for the murder of Zechariah. *not in the tombs of the kings.* Burial in the tombs of the kings was an honor accorded to Jehoiada (v. 16) but withheld from his rebellious ward, Joash (see note on 21:20).

24:26 *an Ammonite ... a Moabite.* Information not given in Kings but important to the Chronicler (see note on 20:1–30).

24:27 *annotations on the book of the kings.* See Introduction to 1 Chronicles: Author, Date and Sources.

25:1–28 Typically, the Chronicler divides the reign of Amaziah into two parts: (1) the good years, marked by obedience, divine blessing and victory (vv. 1–13), and (2) the bad years of idolatry, defeat and regicide (vv. 14–28). See 2Ki 14:1–20 and notes.

25:1 *twenty-nine years.* 796–767 B.C.

25:2 The Chronicler does not indicate that Amaziah failed to remove the high places, which continued to be used as places for sacrifice by the people (see 2Ki 14:4). Also compare 24:2 with 2Ki 12:2–4, and 26:4 with 2Ki 15:3–4. The writer appears to be motivated by his outline, which covered the good years first and then the reversion to evil. Negative comments about these kings are held to the second half of the account of their reigns, whereas in Kings the summary judgment about their reigns and the high places is given immediately.

25:5–16 An expansion of 2Ki 14:7. The book of Kings mentions the successful war with Edom only as a prelude to Amaziah's challenge to Jehoash, but the Chronicler sets it in the framework of his emphasis on immediate retribution: Obedience brings victory over Edom, while the subsequent idolatry (vv. 14–16) brings defeat in the campaign against Israel. By expanding his account the Chronicler gives the theological reason for both the victory over Edom and the defeat before Israel.

min. He then mustered[p] those twenty years old[q] or more and found that there were three hundred thousand men fit for military service,[r] able to handle the spear and shield. [6]He also hired a hundred thousand fighting men from Israel for a hundred talents[a] of silver.

[7]But a man of God came to him and said, "Your Majesty, these troops from Israel[s] must not march with you, for the LORD is not with Israel—not with any of the people of Ephraim. [8]Even if you go and fight courageously in battle, God will overthrow you before the enemy, for God has the power to help or to overthrow."[t]

[9]Amaziah asked the man of God, "But what about the hundred talents I paid for these Israelite troops?"

The man of God replied, "The LORD can give you much more than that."[u]

[10]So Amaziah dismissed the troops who had come to him from Ephraim and sent them home. They were furious with Judah and left for home in a great rage.[v]

[11]Amaziah then marshaled his strength and led his army to the Valley of Salt, where he killed ten thousand men of Seir. [12]The army of Judah also captured ten thousand men alive, took them to the top of a cliff and threw them down so that all were dashed to pieces.[w]

[13]Meanwhile the troops that Amaziah had sent back and had not allowed to take part in the war raided towns belonging to Judah from Samaria to Beth Horon. They killed three thousand people and carried off great quantities of plunder.

[14]When Amaziah returned from slaughtering the Edomites, he brought back the gods of the people of Seir. He set them up as his own gods,[x] bowed down to them and burned sacrifices to them. [15]The anger of the LORD burned against Amaziah, and he sent a prophet to him, who said, "Why do you consult this people's gods, which could not save[y] their own people from your hand?"

[16]While he was still speaking, the king said to him, "Have we appointed you an adviser to the king? Stop! Why be struck down?"

So the prophet stopped but said, "I know that God has determined to destroy you, because you have done this and have not listened to my counsel."

[17]After Amaziah king of Judah consulted his advisers, he sent this challenge to Jehoash[b] son of Jehoahaz, the son of Jehu, king of Israel: "Come, meet me face to face."

[18]But Jehoash king of Israel replied to Amaziah king of Judah: "A thistle[z] in Lebanon sent a message to a cedar in Lebanon, 'Give your daughter to my son in marriage.' Then a wild beast in Lebanon came along and trampled the thistle underfoot. [19]You say to yourself that you have defeated Edom, and now you are arrogant and proud. But stay at home! Why ask for trouble and cause your own downfall and that of Judah also?"

[20]Amaziah, however, would not listen, for God so worked that he might deliver them into the hands of Jehoash, because they sought the gods of Edom.[a] [21]So Jehoash king of Israel attacked. He and Amaziah king of Judah faced each other at Beth Shemesh in Judah. [22]Judah was routed by Israel, and every man fled to his home. [23]Jehoash king of Israel captured Amaziah king of Judah, the son of Joash, the son of Ahaziah,[c] at Beth Shemesh. Then Jehoash brought him to Jerusalem and broke down the wall of Jerusalem from the Ephraim Gate[b] to the Corner Gate[c]—a section about four hundred cubits[d] long. [24]He took all the gold and silver and all the articles found in the temple of God that had been in the care of Obed-Edom,[d] together with the palace treasures and the hostages, and returned to Samaria.

[25]Amaziah son of Joash king of Judah lived for fifteen years after the death of Jehoash son of Jehoahaz king of Israel. [26]As for the other events of Amaziah's reign, from beginning to end, are they not written in the book of the kings of Judah and Israel? [27]From the time that Amaziah turned away from following the LORD, they conspired against him in Jerusa-

---

25:5 P S 2Sa 24:2
q S Ex 30:14
25:7 r S 1Ch 21:1; 2Ch 17:14-19
25:7 s S 2Ch 16:2-9; S 19:1-3
25:8 t S 2Ch 14:11; S 20:6
25:9 u Dt 8:18; Pr 10:22
25:10 v ver 13
25:12 w Ps 141:6; Ob 1:3
25:14 x Ex 20:3; 2Ch 28:23; Isa 44:15
25:15 y Isa 36:20
25:18 z Jdg 9:8-15
25:20 a S 2Ch 10:15
25:23 b 2Ki 14:13; Ne 8:16; 12:39
c 2Ch 26:9; Jer 31:38
25:24 d S 1Ch 26:15

---

[a] 6 That is, about 3 3/4 tons or about 3.4 metric tons; also in verse 9   [b] 17 Hebrew *Joash,* a variant of *Jehoash*; also in verses 18, 21, 23 and 25   [c] 23 Hebrew *Jehoahaz,* a variant of *Ahaziah*   [d] 23 That is, about 600 feet or about 180 meters

---

A **25:7** *troops from Israel must not march with you.* Another instance of the Chronicler's condemnation of alliances that imply lack of trust in the Lord (see notes on 16:2–9; 22:5). Cf. other prophetic speeches that call on the people to trust in God (20:15–17,20; 32:7–8).

25:13 This may be the inciting incident for the later war with the north. *Samaria.* A town by this name in the southern kingdom is not otherwise known. The reference may be a copyist's error.

C **25:14–25** The Chronicler's account of the war with the north is close to the parallel in 2Ki 14:8–14, except for some additions in line with his theme of immediate retribution.

The Chronicler mentions Amaziah's foolish idolatry and the prophetic speech of judgment, neither of which is found in Kings. He also adds notes in vv. 20,27 to emphasize that the idolatry of Amaziah was being punished.

25:18 Cf. the parable in Jdg 9:7–15.

25:23 *Ephraim Gate to the Corner Gate.* Both gates were located in the northern wall of the city, the Ephraim Gate at the northwest and the Corner Gate at the northeast.

25:24 The family of Obed-Edom was the Levitical family into whose care the temple storehouse had been entrusted (1Ch 26:15; cf. 2Sa 6:10 and note).

25:27 See note on vv. 14–25.

25:27 *e* S Jos 10:3
26:1 *f* S 2Ch 22:1
26:5 *g* S 2Ch 24:2
h 2Ch 27:6
26:6 *i* Isa 2:6; 11:14;
14:29; Jer 25:20
j Am 1:8; 3:9
26:7 *k* S 2Ch 21:16
l 2Ch 20:1
26:8 *m* S Ge 19:38
26:9 *n* S 2Ki 14:13;
S 2Ch 25:23
o Ne 2:13; 3:13
26:14 *p* Jer 46:4
26:16 *q* S 2Ki 14:10
r Dt 32:15

lem and he fled to Lachish *e*, but they sent men after him to Lachish and killed him there. ²⁸He was brought back by horse and was buried with his ancestors in the City of Judah. *a*

UZZIAH KING OF JUDAH

26:1–4pp — 2Ki 14:21–22; 15:1–3
26:21–23pp — 2Ki 15:5–7

26 Then all the people of Judah *f* took Uzziah, *b* who was sixteen years old, and made him king in place of his father Amaziah. ²He was the one who rebuilt Elath and restored it to Judah after Amaziah rested with his ancestors.

³Uzziah was sixteen years old when he became king, and he reigned in Jerusalem fifty-two years. His mother's name was Jekoliah; she was from Jerusalem. ⁴He did what was right in the eyes of the LORD, just as his father Amaziah had done. ⁵He sought God during the days of Zechariah, who instructed him in the fear*c* of God. *g* As long as he sought the LORD, God gave him success. *h*

⁶He went to war against the Philistines *i* and broke down the walls of Gath, Jabneh and Ashdod. *j* He then rebuilt towns near Ashdod and elsewhere among the Philistines. ⁷God helped him against the Philistines and against the Arabs *k* who lived in Gur Baal and against the Meunites. *l* ⁸The Ammonites *m* brought tribute to Uzziah, and his fame spread as far as the border of Egypt, because he had become very powerful.

⁹Uzziah built towers in Jerusalem at the Corner Gate, *n* at the Valley Gate *o* and at the angle of the wall, and he fortified them. ¹⁰He also built towers in the wilderness and dug many cisterns, because he had much livestock in the foothills and in the plain. He had people working his fields and vineyards in the hills and in the fertile lands, for he loved the soil.

¹¹Uzziah had a well-trained army, ready to go out by divisions according to their numbers as mustered by Jeiel the secretary and Maaseiah the officer under the direction of Hananiah, one of the royal officials. ¹²The total number of family leaders over the fighting men was 2,600. ¹³Under their command was an army of 307,500 men trained for war, a powerful force to support the king against his enemies. ¹⁴Uzziah provided shields, spears, helmets, coats of armor, bows and slingstones for the entire army. *p* ¹⁵In Jerusalem he made devices designed by skilled workers for use on the towers and on the corner defenses so that soldiers could shoot arrows and hurl large stones from the walls. His fame spread far and wide, for he was greatly helped until he became powerful.

¹⁶But after Uzziah became powerful, his pride *q* led to his downfall. *r* He was unfaith-

---

a 28 Most Hebrew manuscripts; some Hebrew manuscripts, Septuagint, Vulgate and Syriac (see also 2 Kings 14:20) *David*   *b 1* Also called *Azariah*   *c 5* Many Hebrew manuscripts, Septuagint and Syriac; other Hebrew manuscripts *vision*

25:28 *City of Judah.* A later name for the City of David (2Ki 14:20).

A C **26:1–23** See 2Ki 15:1–7 and notes. The Chronicler characteristically divides his account of Uzziah's reign into two parts: the good years, then the bad; cf. his treatment of Uzziah's father, Amaziah, and his grandfather Joash (see notes on 24:2; 25:1–28). The Chronicler elaborates on the blessings and divine help that flowed from Uzziah's obedience and fidelity (vv. 4–15), whereas the author of Kings only alludes to his fidelity (2Ki 15:3). Where Kings only mentions Uzziah's leprosy (2Ki 15:5), the Chronicler gives additional details to show that the disease was a result of unfaithfulness (vv. 16–21). Under Uzziah and his contemporary in the north, Jeroboam II, the borders of Israel and Judah briefly reached the extent they had attained under David and Solomon (vv. 6–8; 2Ki 14:25). In part, this flourishing of the two kingdoms was facilitated by the removal of the Aramean threat by Assyria under Adadnirari III (802 B.C.), following which Assyria herself went into a period of weakness.

26:1 *Uzziah.* See TNIV text note (see also, e.g., 2Ki 15:6–7; 1Ch 3:12). It is likely that Uzziah was a throne name, while Azariah was his personal name.

26:3 *fifty-two years.* 792–740 B.C., including a coregency with Amaziah from 792 to 767.

26:4 The Chronicler constructs his account of Uzziah's reign to give it the same outline as that for Amaziah and Joash (see note on vv. 1–23). He also once again bypasses the statement in the parallel account that the king did not remove the high places (2Ki 15:4), just as he does in the accounts of the other

two kings (see note on 25:2).

26:5 *days of Zechariah.* The author again uses chronological notes to portray the cycles of blessing and judgment associated with the individual king's response to God's commands (see note on 12:2).

26:6–8 Uzziah's conquests were toward the southeast and the southwest; Israel's powerful Jeroboam II was in control to the north of Judah.

26:7 *Meunites.* See note on 20:1.

26:9 *Corner Gate … Valley Gate.* Found at the northeast and southwest portions of the walls. *fortified.* This construction along the wall of Jerusalem may reflect, in part, repair of the damage done by Jehoash during the reign of Amaziah (25:23).

B **26:10** *towers … cisterns.* Towers and cisterns have been found in several excavations (Qumran, Gibeah, Beersheba). A seal bearing Uzziah's name has been found in a cistern at Tell Beit Mirsim.

B **26:11** *Uzziah had a well-trained army.* Tiglath-Pileser III of Assyria states that he was opposed in his advance toward the west (743 B.C.) by a coalition headed by "Azriau of Yaudi," perhaps Azariah (Uzziah) of Judah.

26:15 *devices … shoot arrows and hurl large stones.* Since the catapult was not known in the military technology of the period, and since torsion-operated devices for shooting arrows did not appear for approximately another three centuries, the devices mentioned here may refer to defensive constructions to protect those shooting arrows and hurling stones from the tops of the walls.

ful [s] to the LORD his God, and entered the temple of the LORD to burn incense [t] on the altar of incense. [17]Azariah [u] the priest with eighty other courageous priests of the LORD followed him in. [18]They confronted King Uzziah and said, "It is not right for you, Uzziah, to burn incense to the LORD. That is for the priests, [v] the descendants [w] of Aaron, [x] who have been consecrated to burn incense. [y] Leave the sanctuary, for you have been unfaithful; and you will not be honored by the LORD God."

[19]Uzziah, who had a censer in his hand ready to burn incense, became angry. While he was raging at the priests in their presence before the incense altar in the LORD's temple, leprosy [a][z] broke out on his forehead. [20]When Azariah the chief priest and all the other priests looked at him, they saw that he had leprosy on his forehead, so they hurried him out. Indeed, he himself was eager to leave, because the LORD had afflicted him.

[21]King Uzziah had leprosy until the day he died. He lived in a separate house [b][a]—leprous, and excluded from the temple of the LORD. Jotham his son had charge of the palace and governed the people of the land.

[22]The other events of Uzziah's reign, from beginning to end, are recorded by the prophet Isaiah [b] son of Amoz. [23]Uzziah [c] rested with his ancestors and was buried near them in a cemetery that belonged to the kings, for people said, "He had leprosy." And Jotham his son succeeded him as king. [d]

JOTHAM KING OF JUDAH
27:1–4,7–9pp — 2Ki 15:33–38

27 Jotham [e] was twenty-five years old when he became king, and he reigned in Jerusalem sixteen years. His mother's name was Jerusha daughter of Zadok. [2]He did what was right in the eyes of the LORD, just as his father Uzziah had done, but unlike him he did not enter the temple of the LORD. The people, however, continued their corrupt practices. [3]Jotham rebuilt the Upper Gate of the temple of the LORD and did extensive work on the wall at the hill of Ophel. [f] [4]He built towns in the hill country of Judah and forts and towers in the wooded areas.

[5]Jotham made war on the king of the Ammonites [g] and conquered them. That year the Ammonites paid him a hundred talents [c] of silver, ten thousand cors [d] of wheat and ten thousand cors [e] of barley. The Ammonites brought him the same amount also in the second and third years.

[6]Jotham grew powerful [h] because he walked steadfastly before the LORD his God.

[7]The other events in Jotham's reign, including all his wars and the other things he did, are written in the book of the kings of Israel and Judah. [8]He was twenty-five years old when he became king, and he reigned in Jerusalem sixteen years. [9]Jotham rested with his ancestors and was buried in the City of David. And Ahaz his son succeeded him as king.

AHAZ KING OF JUDAH
28:1–27pp — 2Ki 16:1–20

28 Ahaz [i] was twenty years old when he became king, and he reigned in Jerusalem sixteen years. Unlike David his father, he did not do what was right in the eyes of the LORD. [2]He followed the ways of the kings of Israel and also

---

[a] 19 The Hebrew for *leprosy* was used for various diseases affecting the skin; also in verses 20, 21 and 23. [b] 21 Or *in a house where he was relieved of responsibilities* [c] 5 That is, about 3 3/4 tons or about 3.4 metric tons [d] 5 That is, probably about 1,800 tons or about 1,600 metric tons [e] 5 That is, probably about 1,500 tons or about 1,350 metric tons

---

26:16 [s] S 1Ch 5:25
[t] 2Ki 16:12
26:17 [u] S 1Ki 4:2
26:18 [v] Nu 16:39
[w] Nu 18:1-7
[x] S Ex 30:7
[y] S 1Ch 6:49
26:19 [z] S Nu 12:10
26:21 [a] S Ex 4:6;
Lev 13:46; S 14:8;
Nu 5:2; S 19:12
26:22 [b] 2Ki 15:1;
Isa 1:1; 6:1
26:23 [c] Isa 1:1; 6:1
[d] S 2Ki 14:21; Am 1:1
27:1 [e] S 2Ki 15:5, 32;
S 1Ch 3:12
27:3 [f] 2Ch 33:14;
Ne 3:26
27:5 [g] S Ge 19:38
27:6 [h] 2Ch 26:5
28:1 [i] S 1Ch 3:13;
Isa 1:1

26:16 *after Uzziah became powerful.* See note on v. 5.
26:19 *leprosy.* See TNIV text note; see also note on Lev 13:2; for disease as a punishment for sin see notes on 16:12; 21:12–15.

B **26:21** *Uzziah ... died.* See Isa 6:1 and note. *separate house.* See TNIV text note; the same phrase in the Canaanite texts from Ugarit suggests a kind of quarantine or separation.
26:22 *recorded by ... Isaiah.* Not a reference to the canonical book but to some other work no longer in existence.
26:23 *buried ... in a cemetery that belonged to the kings.* Cf. 2Ki 15:7. Apparently due to his leprosy, Uzziah was buried in a cemetery belonging to the kings, though not in the tombs of the kings.
27:1–9 See 2Ki 15:32–38 and notes.
27:1 *sixteen years.* 750–735 B.C., including a coregency with Uzziah (750–740). His reign also overlapped that of his successor, Ahaz, from 735 to 732.
27:2 *did not enter the temple.* The Chronicler commends Jotham for not making the same error Uzziah did (26:16). *corrupt prac-*

tices. Appears to refer to the flourishing high places (2Ki 15:35).

A **27:3–6** Unique to the Chronicler and an elaboration of his thesis that fidelity to God's commands brings blessing: in construction, military victory and prosperity—all "because he walked steadfastly before the LORD" (v. 6). Judah's relationship with the Ammonites held particular interest for the Chronicler (see notes on 20:1–30; 24:26).
27:7 *all his wars.* See, e.g., 2Ki 15:37.

C **28:1–27** See 2Ki 16:1–20 and notes, though only the introduction and conclusion in the two accounts are strictly parallel. The reign of Ahaz is the only one for which the Chronicler does not mention a single redeeming feature. In his account the Chronicler appears to adopt explicit parallels from the speech of Abijah condemning the northern kingdom (ch. 13) in order to show that under Ahaz the southern kingdom had sunk to the same depths of apostasy. Judah's religious fidelity, of which Abijah had boasted, was completely overthrown under Ahaz.

28:2 / Ex 34:17
28:3 ᵏ S Jos 15:8
ˡ S Lev 18:21;
S 2Ki 3:27; Eze 20:26
ᵐ S Dt 18:9; 2Ch 33:2
28:5 ⁿ Isa 7:1
28:6 ᵒ S 2Ki 15:25,
27 ᵖ ver 8; Isa 9:21;
11:13
28:8 ᵍ Dt 28:25-41
ʳ 2Ch 29:9
28:9 ˢ Isa 10:6; 47:6;
Zec 1:15 ᵗ Ezr 9:6;
Rev 18:5
28:10 ᵘ Lev 25:39-
46
28:11 ᵛ 2Ch 11:4
28:15 ʷ 2Ki 6:22;
Pr 25:21-22
ˣ S Dt 34:3; S Jdg 1:16
ʸ Lk 10:25-37
28:16 ᶻ S 2Ki 16:7;
Eze 23:12
28:17 ᵃ Ps 137:7;
Isa 34:5; 63:1;
Jer 25:21; Eze 16:57;
25:12; Am 1:11
ᵇ 2Ch 29:9
28:18 ᶜ Isa 9:12;
11:14; Jer 25:20;
Eze 16:27,57; 25:15
ᵈ S Jos 10:12
ᵉ Jos 15:41 ᶠ S 1Sa 17:1
ᵍ S Ge 38:12
28:19 ʰ S 1Ch 5:25
28:20 ⁱ S 2Ki 15:29;
S 1Ch 5:6 ʲ Isa 7:17;
8:7; 10:5-6; 36:1
ᵏ Isa 10:20 ˡ S 2Ki 16:7

made idols ʲ for worshiping the Baals. ³He burned sacrifices in the Valley of Ben Hinnom ᵏ and sacrificed his children ˡ in the fire, engaging in the detestable ᵐ practices of the nations the LORD had driven out before the Israelites. ⁴He offered sacrifices and burned incense at the high places, on the hilltops and under every spreading tree.

⁵Therefore the LORD his God delivered him into the hands of the king of Aram. ⁿ The Arameans defeated him and took many of his people as prisoners and brought them to Damascus.

He was also given into the hands of the king of Israel, who inflicted heavy casualties on him. ⁶In one day Pekah ᵒ son of Remaliah killed a hundred and twenty thousand soldiers in Judah ᵖ—because Judah had forsaken the LORD, the God of their ancestors. ⁷Zikri, an Ephraimite warrior, killed Maaseiah the king's son, Azrikam the officer in charge of the palace, and Elkanah, second to the king. ⁸The men of Israel took captive from their fellow Israelites in Judah ᵍ two hundred thousand wives, sons and daughters. They also took a great deal of plunder, which they carried back to Samaria. ʳ

⁹But a prophet of the LORD named Oded was there, and he went out to meet the army when it returned to Samaria. He said to them, "Because the LORD, the God of your ancestors, was angry ˢ with Judah, he gave them into your hand. But you have slaughtered them in a rage that reaches to heaven. ᵗ ¹⁰And now you intend to make the men and women of Judah and Jerusalem your slaves. ᵘ But aren't you also guilty of sins against the LORD your God? ¹¹Now listen to me! Send back your fellow Israelites you have taken as prisoners, for the LORD's fierce anger rests on you. ᵛ"

¹²Then some of the leaders in Ephraim—Azariah son of Jehohanan, Berekiah son of Meshillemoth, Jehizkiah son of Shallum, and Amasa son of Hadlai—confronted those who were arriving from the war. ¹³"You must not bring those prisoners here," they said, "or we will be guilty before the LORD. Do you intend to add to our sin and guilt? For our guilt is already great, and his fierce anger rests on Israel."

¹⁴So the soldiers gave up the prisoners and plunder in the presence of the officials and all the assembly. ¹⁵The men designated by name took the prisoners, and from the plunder they clothed all who were naked. They provided them with clothes and sandals, food and drink, ʷ and healing balm. All those who were weak they put on donkeys. So they took them back to their fellow Israelites at Jericho, the City of Palms, ˣ and returned to Samaria. ʸ

¹⁶At that time King Ahaz sent to the kings ᵃ of Assyria ᶻ for help. ¹⁷The Edomites ᵃ had again come and attacked Judah and carried away prisoners, ᵇ ¹⁸while the Philistines ᶜ had raided towns in the foothills and in the Negev of Judah. They captured and occupied Beth Shemesh, Aijalon ᵈ and Gederoth, ᵉ as well as Soko, ᶠ Timnah ᵍ and Gimzo, with their surrounding villages. ¹⁹The LORD had humbled Judah because of Ahaz king of Israel, ᵇ for he had promoted wickedness in Judah and had been most unfaithful ʰ to the LORD. ²⁰Tiglath-Pileser ᶜ ⁱ king of Assyria ʲ came to him, but he gave him trouble ᵏ instead of help. ˡ

ᵃ 16 Most Hebrew manuscripts; one Hebrew manuscript, Septuagint and Vulgate (see also 2 Kings 16:7) *king*   ᵇ 19 That is, Judah, as frequently in 2 Chronicles   ᶜ 20 Hebrew *Tilgath-Pilneser*, a variant of *Tiglath-Pileser*

28:1 *sixteen years.* 732–715 B.C., not including the coregency with Jotham (735–732).

28:2 *made idols.* Cf. 13:8. *Baals.* See notes on Jdg 2:11,13.

28:3 *Valley of Ben Hinnom.* See 33:6; see also notes on Ne 11:30; Jer 7:31. Josiah put an end to the pagan practices observed there (2Ki 23:10). *sacrificed his children.* See Lev 20:1–5; Jer 7:31–32. 2Ki 16:3 has the singular "son." Some have regarded the plural as a deliberate inflation on the part of the Chronicler to heighten the wickedness of Ahaz. However, some manuscripts of the Septuagint (the pre-Christian Greek translation of the OT) also have a plural in 2Ki 16:3, suggesting that the Chronicler faithfully copied the text before him.

■ 28:5 Cf. 13:16–17. *God delivered him into the hands of.* According to the Chronicler's view on immediate retribution, defeat in war is one of the results of disobedience (see note on 20:30). *also given into the hands of the king of Israel.* 2Ki 16:5–6 and Isa 7 make it clear that Rezin (king of Aram) and Pekah acted together against Judah. The Chronicler has chosen either to treat them separately or to report on two different episodes of the Aram-Israel coalition.

28:6 *Pekah.* Reigned over the northern kingdom 752–732 B.C.

(see 2Ki 15:27–31). *had forsaken the LORD.* The same charge Abijah made against the northern kingdom (13:11).

■ 28:9–15 The kindness of the northern captors to their captives from Judah, especially as recorded in vv. 14–15, may be the background for Jesus' parable of the Good Samaritan (Lk 10:25–37). Oded's attitude to the north is shown by his willingness to call them "fellow Israelites" (v. 11). In this case, too, the record of ch. 13 has been reversed: The northern tribes are more righteous than the south.

28:17–18 *Edomites . . . attacked Judah . . . Philistines had raided.* Foreign alliances (v. 16) led to further defeats for Ahaz (see note on 16:2–9).

28:19 *The LORD had humbled Judah because of Ahaz.* The same formula used to describe the defeat of the northern tribes in 13:18, though under Ahaz it is Judah that is subdued.

28:20 *Tiglath-Pileser.* King of Assyria 745–727 B.C. (see 1Ch 5:26 and note). *trouble instead of help.* Appears on the surface to contradict the statement in 2Ki 16:9 that Tiglath-Pileser III responded to Ahaz's request by attacking and capturing Damascus, exiling its population and killing Rezin. The Chronicler assumes the reader's familiarity with the other account and knows of the

²¹Ahaz *m* took some of the things from the temple of the Lᴏʀᴅ and from the royal palace and from the officials and presented them to the king of Assyria, but that did not help him. *n*

²²In his time of trouble King Ahaz became even more unfaithful *o* to the Lᴏʀᴅ. ²³He offered sacrifices to the gods *p* of Damascus, who had defeated him; for he thought, "Since the gods of the kings of Aram have helped them, I will sacrifice to them so they will help me." *q* But they were his downfall and the downfall of all Israel. *r*

²⁴Ahaz gathered together the furnishings *s* from the temple of God *t* and cut them in pieces. He shut the doors *u* of the Lᴏʀᴅ's temple and set up altars *v* at every street corner in Jerusalem. ²⁵In every town in Judah he built high places to burn sacrifices to other gods and aroused the anger of the Lᴏʀᴅ, the God of his ancestors.

²⁶The other events of his reign and all his ways, from beginning to end, are written in the book of the kings of Judah and Israel. ²⁷Ahaz rested *w* with his ancestors and was buried *x* in the city of Jerusalem, but he was not placed in the tombs of the kings of Israel. And Hezekiah his son succeeded him as king.

HEZEKIAH PURIFIES THE TEMPLE

29:1–2pp — 2Ki 18:2–3

29 Hezekiah *y* was twenty-five years old when he became king, and he reigned in Jerusalem twenty-nine years. His mother's name was Abijah daughter of Zechariah. ²He did what was right in the eyes of the Lᴏʀᴅ, just as his father David *z* had done.

³In the first month of the first year of his reign, he opened the doors of the temple of the Lᴏʀᴅ and repaired *a* them. ⁴He brought in the priests and the Levites, assembled them in the square on the east side ⁵and said: "Listen to me, Levites! Consecrate *b* yourselves now and consecrate the temple of the Lᴏʀᴅ, the God of your ancestors. Remove all defilement from the sanctuary. ⁶Our ancestors *c* were unfaithful; *d* they did evil in the eyes of the Lᴏʀᴅ our God and forsook him. They turned their faces away from the Lᴏʀᴅ's dwelling place and turned their backs on him. ⁷They also shut the doors of the portico and put out the lamps. They did not burn incense *e* or present any burnt offerings at the sanctuary to the God of Israel. ⁸Therefore, the anger of the Lᴏʀᴅ has fallen on Judah and Jerusalem; he has made them an object of dread and horror *f* and scorn, *g* as you can see with your own eyes. ⁹This is why our ancestors have fallen by the sword and why our sons and

28:21 *m* S 2Ch 16:2-9 *n* Jer 2:36
28:22 *o* Jer 5:3; 15:7; 17:23
28:23 *p* S 2Ch 25:14 *q* Isa 10:20; Jer 44:17-18 *r* 1Ch 11:1; Jer 18:15
28:24 *s* 2Ch 29:19 *t* S 2Ki 16:18 *u* Mal 1:10 *v* 2Ch 30:14
28:27 *w* Isa 14:28-32 *x* S 2Ch 21:20
29:1 *y* S 1Ch 3:13
29:2 *z* 2Ch 34:2
29:3 *a* 2Ki 18:16
29:5 *b* S Lev 11:44; Ne 13:9
29:6 *c* Ezr 9:7; Ps 106:6-47; Jer 2:27; 18:17; Eze 23:35; Da 9:5-6 *d* S 1Ch 5:25
29:7 *e* S Ex 30:7
29:8 *f* S Dt 28:25 *g* S Lev 26:32; Jer 18:16; 19:8; 25:9, 18

---

temporary respite for Judah gained by Assyrian intervention against Damascus and the northern kingdom of Israel. But he focuses on the long-range results, in which Judah herself was reduced to vassalage to Assyria.

28:22–23 The Chronicler presumes the reader's familiarity with Ahaz's trip to Damascus and his copying of the altar and practices there (2Ki 16:10–16).

28:24–25 Additional details on Ahaz's alterations are found in 2Ki 16:17–18. The Chronicler also adds details in his description of Hezekiah's reforming activities to correct some of the abuses under Ahaz: Not only had the doors been shut, but also the lamps were put out and offerings were not made at the sanctuary (29:7); the altar and utensils were desecrated, and the table for the consecrated bread was neglected (29:18–19). It is precisely these accoutrements of proper temple service about which Abijah had boasted when he proclaimed the faithfulness of Judah, in contrast to that of the northern kingdom (13:11). Now these orthodox furnishings are lacking under Ahaz and make the southern kingdom just like the north (see note on vv. 1–27).

28:27 *not placed in the tombs of the kings.* The third king whose wickedness resulted in the loss of this honor at death. The others were Jehoram (21:20) and Joash (24:25). Uzziah's sin and leprosy brought the same result, though it is not reported in exactly the same terms (26:23). Cf. also Manasseh (33:20).

A C **29:1—32:33** The Chronicler devotes more attention to Hezekiah than to any other post-Solomonic king. Although the parallel text (2Ki 18–20) has about the same amount of material, only about a fourth of the total relates the same or similar material; only a few verses are strict literary parallels (29:1–2; 32:32–33). In Kings preeminence among the

post-Solomonic kings is given to Josiah (2Ki 22–23; cf. 1Ki 13:2), and the record of Hezekiah is primarily devoted to his confrontation with Sennacherib of Assyria. By contrast, the Chronicler highlights almost exclusively Hezekiah's religious reform and his devotion to matters of ceremony and ritual. The parallel passage (2Ki 18:1–6) touches the religious reform only briefly. The numerous parallels in these chapters with the account of Solomon's reign suggest that the Chronicler viewed Hezekiah as a second Solomon in his celebration of the Passover (30:2,5,23, 25–26), his arrangements for worship (29:7,18,35; 31:2–3), his wealth (32:27–29), the honor accorded him by the Gentiles (32:23) and the extent of his dominion (30:25).

29:1 *twenty-nine years.* 715–686 b.c. (but see note on Isa 36:1), including a 15-year extension of life granted by God (2Ki 20:6) but not mentioned by the Chronicler.

29:3—30:27 Not found in Kings.

29:3 *first year.* 715 b.c., another example of the Chronicler's practice of introducing chronological materials into his narrative (see note on 12:2). *opened the doors of the temple.* Necessary after the actions of Ahaz (28:24). *repaired them.* The repairs to the doors included new gold overlay (2Ki 18:16).

A **29:5–11** Hezekiah's speech demonstrates again the Chronicler's convictions about the coherence of action and effect: The sins of the past bring difficulty and judgment, but renewed fidelity brings relief.

29:7 Hezekiah reinstitutes these temple arrangements— following the pattern of Solomon (2:4; 4:7).

29:8 *object of dread and horror and scorn.* Echoes the language of the prophets, especially Jeremiah (see Jer 19:8; 25:9,18; 29:18; 51:37). Reference is to the Assyrian devastation of the northern kingdom and much of Judah.

29:9 *h* 2Ch 28:5-8,
17
29:10 *i* S 2Ki 11:17;
S 2Ch 23:16
j S Nu 25:4; 2Ch 30:8;
Ezr 10:14
29:11 *k* S Nu 3:6;
8:6,14 *l* S 1Ch 15:2
29:12 *m* S Nu 3:17-
20 *n* 2Ch 31:15
29:13 *o* S Ex 6:22
p S 1Ch 6:39
29:15 *q* S 1Ch 23:28;
S Isa 1:25
29:16 *r* S 2Sa 15:23
29:19 *s* 2Ch 28:24
29:21 *t* Ezr 6:17;
8:35 *u* S 1Ch 15:2
29:22 *v* S Lev 4:18;
Nu 18:17
29:23 *w* S Lev 16:5
x Lev 4:15
29:24 *y* S Ex 29:36;
Lev 4:26 *z* 1Ch 11:1;
Ezr 8:35
29:25 *a* S 1Ch 25:6;
28:19 *b* S 1Sa 22:5
29:26 *c* S 1Ch 15:16
d S 1Ch 15:24
29:27 *e* S 1Sa 16:16
29:28 *f* S 2Ch 2:4

daughters and our wives are in captivity. *h* **10**Now I intend to make a covenant *i* with the LORD, the God of Israel, so that his fierce anger *j* will turn away from us. **11**My sons, do not be negligent now, for the LORD has chosen you to stand before him and serve him, *k* to minister *l* before him and to burn incense."

12Then these Levites *m* set to work:
from the Kohathites,
Mahath son of Amasai and Joel son of Azariah;
from the Merarites,
Kish son of Abdi and Azariah son of Jehallelel;
from the Gershonites,
Joah son of Zimmah and Eden *n* son of Joah;
13from the descendants of Elizaphan, *o*
Shimri and Jeiel;
from the descendants of Asaph, *p*
Zechariah and Mattaniah;
14from the descendants of Heman,
Jehiel and Shimei;
from the descendants of Jeduthun,
Shemaiah and Uzziel.

15When they had assembled their fellow Levites and consecrated themselves, they went in to purify *q* the temple of the LORD, as the king had ordered, following the word of the LORD. **16**The priests went into the sanctuary of the LORD to purify it. They brought out to the courtyard of the LORD's temple everything unclean that they found in the temple of the LORD. The Levites took it and carried it out to the Kidron Valley. *r* **17**They began the consecration on the first day of the first month, and by the eighth day of the month they reached the portico of the LORD. For eight more days they consecrated the temple of the LORD itself, finishing on the sixteenth day of the first month.

18Then they went in to King Hezekiah and reported: "We have purified the entire temple of the LORD, the altar of burnt offering with all its utensils, and the table for setting out the consecrated bread, with all its articles. **19**We have prepared and consecrated all the articles *s* that King Ahaz removed in his unfaithfulness while he was king. They are now in front of the LORD's altar."

20Early the next morning King Hezekiah gathered the city officials together and went up to the temple of the LORD. **21**They brought seven bulls, seven rams, seven male lambs and seven male goats *t* as a sin offering *a u* for the kingdom, for the sanctuary and for Judah. The king commanded the priests, the descendants of Aaron, to offer these on the altar of the LORD. **22**So they slaughtered the bulls, and the priests took the blood and splashed it against the altar; next they slaughtered the rams and splashed their blood against the altar; then they slaughtered the lambs and splashed their blood *v* against the altar. **23**The goats *w* for the sin offering were brought before the king and the assembly, and they laid their hands *x* on them. **24**The priests then slaughtered the goats and presented their blood on the altar for a sin offering to atone *y* for all Israel, because the king had ordered the burnt offering and the sin offering for all Israel. *z*

25He stationed the Levites in the temple of the LORD with cymbals, harps and lyres in the way prescribed by David *a* and Gad *b* the king's seer and Nathan the prophet; this was commanded by the LORD through his prophets. **26**So the Levites stood ready with David's instruments, *c* and the priests with their trumpets. *d*

27Hezekiah gave the order to sacrifice the burnt offering on the altar. As the offering began, singing to the LORD began also, accompanied by trumpets and the instruments *e* of David king of Israel. **28**The whole assembly bowed in worship, while the musicians played and the trumpets sounded. All this continued until the sacrifice of the burnt offering *f* was completed.

---

a 21 Or *purification offering*; also in verses 23 and 24

29:12 *Kohathites…Merarites…Gershonites.* The three clans of Levi (1Ch 6:1).

29:13–14 *Asaph…Heman…Jeduthun.* Founders of the three families of Levitical musicians (1Ch 6:31–48; 25:1–31).

29:13 *Elizaphan.* A leader of the Kohathites (Nu 3:30), whose family had achieved status almost as a sub-clan (see 1Ch 15:8 and note on 15:4–10).

29:16 *Kidron Valley.* See note on Isa 22:7 and map, p. 486; see also 1Ki 15:13 and note.

29:18 These actions under Hezekiah mirror those of Solomon (2:4).

29:21 *sin offering.* See Lev 4:1—5:13 and chart, p. 155.

29:22 *splashed their blood.* See Lev 17:6; Nu 18:17.

29:23 *laid their hands on them.* See Lev 4:13–15; 8:14–15; Nu 8:12.

29:25 *Gad…Nathan.* See 1Sa 22:5 and note; 2Sa 7; 12.

29:26 *David's instruments.* See 1Ch 23:5.

²⁹When the offerings were finished, the king and everyone present with him knelt down and worshiped. *g* ³⁰King Hezekiah and his officials ordered the Levites to praise the LORD with the words of David and of Asaph the seer. So they sang praises with gladness and bowed down and worshiped.

³¹Then Hezekiah said, "You have now dedicated yourselves to the LORD. Come and bring sacrifices *h* and thank offerings to the temple of the LORD." So the assembly brought sacrifices and thank offerings, and all whose hearts were willing *i* brought burnt offerings.

³²The number of burnt offerings *j* the assembly brought was seventy bulls, a hundred rams and two hundred male lambs—all of them for burnt offerings to the LORD. ³³The animals consecrated as sacrifices amounted to six hundred bulls and three thousand sheep and goats. ³⁴The priests, however, were too few to skin all the burnt offerings; *k* so their relatives the Levites helped them until the task was finished and until other priests had been consecrated, *l* for the Levites had been more conscientious in consecrating themselves than the priests had been. ³⁵There were burnt offerings in abundance, together with the fat *m* of the fellowship offerings *n* and the drink offerings *o* that accompanied the burnt offerings.

So the service of the temple of the LORD was reestablished. ³⁶Hezekiah and all the people rejoiced at what God had brought about for his people, because it was done so quickly. *p*

HEZEKIAH CELEBRATES THE PASSOVER

30 Hezekiah sent word to all Israel *q* and Judah and also wrote letters to Ephraim and Manasseh, *r* inviting them to come to the temple of the LORD in Jerusalem and celebrate the Passover *s* to the LORD, the God of Israel. ²The king and his officials and the whole assembly in Jerusalem decided to celebrate *t* the Passover in the second month. ³They had not been able to celebrate it at the regular time because not enough priests had consecrated *u* themselves and the people had not assembled in Jerusalem. ⁴The plan seemed right both to the king and to the whole assembly. ⁵They decided to send a proclamation throughout Israel, from Beersheba to Dan, *v* calling the people to come to Jerusalem and celebrate the Passover to the LORD, the God of Israel. It had not been celebrated in large numbers according to what was written.

⁶At the king's command, couriers went throughout Israel and Judah with letters from the king and from his officials, which read:

"People of Israel, return to the LORD, the God of Abraham, Isaac and Israel, that he may return to you who are left, who have escaped from the hand of the kings of Assyria. ⁷Do not be like your parents *w* and your fellow Israelites, who were unfaithful *x* to the LORD, the God of their ancestors, so that he made them an object of horror, *y* as you see. ⁸Do not be stiff-necked, *z* as your parents were; submit to the LORD. Come to his sanctuary, which he has consecrated forever. Serve the LORD your God, so that his fierce anger *a* will turn away from you. ⁹If you return *b* to the LORD, then your fellow Israelites and your children will be shown compassion *c* by their captors and will

29:29 *g* S 2Ch 20:18
29:31 *h* Heb 13:15-16 *i* S Ex 25:2; 35:22
29:32 *j* Lev 1:1-17
29:34 *k* Eze 44:11 *l* 2Ch 30:3,15
29:35 *m* S Ge 4:4; S Ex 29:13 *n* Lev 7:11-21 *o* S Ge 35:14
29:36 *p* 2Ch 35:8
30:1 *q* S 1Ch 9:1 *r* S Ge 41:52 *s* S Ex 12:11; S Nu 28:16
30:2 *t* Nu 9:10
30:3 *u* Nu 9:6-13; S 2Ch 29:34
30:5 *v* S Jdg 20:1
30:7 *w* Ps 78:8,57; 106:6; Jer 11:10; Eze 20:18 *x* S 1Ch 5:25 *y* S Dt 28:25
30:8 *z* S Ex 32:9 *a* S Nu 25:4; S 2Ch 29:10
30:9 *b* Dt 30:2-5; Isa 1:16; 55:7; Jer 25:5; Eze 33:11 *c* S Ex 3:21; S 1Ki 8:50

29:35 *burnt offerings in abundance…fellowship offerings… drink offerings.* Reminiscent of the dedication of the temple under Solomon (7:4–6). For the laws regarding the fellowship offerings see Lev 3; 7:11–21; for the drink offerings see Nu 15:1–12. *service of the temple of the LORD was reestablished.* Similar to the formula used in 8:16 with reference to Solomon's work.

30:1–27 Unique to the Chronicler; cf. the famous Passover under Josiah (35:1–19; 2Ki 23:21–23). Hezekiah allowed two deviations from the law (Ex 12; Dt 16:1–8) in this observance: (1) the date in the second month (v. 2) and (2) exemption from some ritual requirements (vv. 18–19).

30:1 *all Israel and Judah.* See Introduction to 1 Chronicles: Purpose and Themes. With the northern kingdom now ended as the result of the Assyrian invasion and deportation (which surprisingly is not mentioned), the Chronicler shows "all Israel" once again united around the Davidic king and the temple (see vv. 5,18–19,25).

30:2 *second month.* After the division of the kingdom, Jeroboam deferred the sacral calendar of the northern kingdom by one month (1Ki 12:32), possibly to further wean the subjects in the north away from devotion to Jerusalem. By delaying the celebration of Passover one month, Hezekiah not only allows time for the

priests to consecrate themselves (v. 3) and for the people to gather (vv. 3,13) but also achieves unity between the kingdoms on the date of the Passover for the first time since the schism more than two centuries earlier. Delaying the date reflects Hezekiah's concern to involve "all Israel." For the first time since Solomon the entire nation observes Passover together, reflecting the Chronicler's view that Hezekiah is a second Solomon. Passover was prescribed for the 14th day of the first month (Ex 12:2,6; Dt 16:1–8), but could not be celebrated at that time due to the defilement of the temple and the purification rites under way (29:3,17). For celebration of Passover by the restored community shortly after the dedication of the rebuilt temple, see Ezr 6:16–22.

30:5 *large numbers.* Another comparison with the time of Solomon (see v. 26). At the time of its inception, Passover was primarily a family observance (Ex 12). It later became a national celebration at the temple (v. 8; see Dt 16:1–8).

30:8 *Come to his sanctuary.* Passover was one of three annual festivals requiring attendance at the temple (see Nu 28:9—29:39).

30:9 *shown compassion by their captors.* In Solomon's prayer in 6:39 the Chronicler omitted the phrase found in the parallel account (1Ki 8:50) that their conquerors would "show them mer-

30:9 ᵈS Ex 22:27;
S Dt 4:31;
S 2Ch 6:39; Mic 7:18
30:10 ᵉ2Ch 36:16
30:11 ᶠS 2Ch 6:37
ᵍver 25
30:12 ʰJer 32:39;
Eze 11:19
30:13 ʲS Nu 28:16
30:14 ʲ2Ch 28:24
ᵏS 2Sa 15:23
30:15 ˡS 2Ch 29:34
30:16 ᵐ2Ch 35:10
30:17 ⁿ2Ch 35:11;
Ezr 6:20
30:18 ᵒEx 12:43-
49; Nu 9:6-10
30:20 ᵖS 2Ch 6:20
ᵠS 2Ch 7:14; Mal 4:2
ʳJas 5:16
30:21 ˢEx 12:15,17;
13:6
30:23 ᵗ2Ch 7:9
30:24 ᵘ1Ki 8:5;
2Ch 35:7; Ezr 6:17;
8:35
30:25 ᵛver 11
30:26 ʷS 2Ch 7:8
30:27 ˣS Ex 39:43
31:1 ʸS 2Ki 18:4;
2Ch 32:12; Isa 36:7

return to this land, for the LORD your God is gracious and compassionate. ᵈ He will not turn his face from you if you return to him."

¹⁰The couriers went from town to town in Ephraim and Manasseh, as far as Zebulun, but people scorned and ridiculed ᵉ them. ¹¹Nevertheless, some from Asher, Manasseh and Zebulun humbled ᶠ themselves and went to Jerusalem. ᵍ ¹²Also in Judah the hand of God was on the people to give them unity ʰ of mind to carry out what the king and his officials had ordered, following the word of the LORD.

¹³A very large crowd of people assembled in Jerusalem to celebrate the Festival of Unleavened Bread ᶦ in the second month. ¹⁴They removed the altars ʲ in Jerusalem and cleared away the incense altars and threw them into the Kidron Valley. ᵏ

¹⁵They slaughtered the Passover lamb on the fourteenth day of the second month. The priests and the Levites were ashamed and consecrated ˡ themselves and brought burnt offerings to the temple of the LORD. ¹⁶Then they took up their regular positions ᵐ as prescribed in the Law of Moses the man of God. The priests splashed against the altar the blood handed to them by the Levites. ¹⁷Since many in the crowd had not consecrated themselves, the Levites had to kill ⁿ the Passover lambs for all those who were not ceremonially clean and could not consecrate ˌtheir lambsˌ to the LORD. ¹⁸Although most of the many people who came from Ephraim, Manasseh, Issachar and Zebulun had not purified themselves, ᵒ yet they ate the Passover, contrary to what was written. But Hezekiah prayed for them, saying, "May the LORD, who is good, pardon everyone ¹⁹who sets their heart on seeking God— the LORD, the God of their ancestors—even if they are not clean according to the rules of the sanctuary." ²⁰And the LORD heard ᵖ Hezekiah and healed ᵠ the people. ʳ

²¹The Israelites who were present in Jerusalem celebrated the Festival of Unleavened Bread ˢ for seven days with great rejoicing, while the Levites and priests praised the LORD every day with resounding instruments dedicated to the LORD. ᵃ

²²Hezekiah spoke encouragingly to all the Levites, who showed good understanding of the service of the LORD. For the seven days they ate their assigned portion and offered fellowship offerings and praised ᵇ the LORD, the God of their ancestors.

²³The whole assembly then agreed to celebrate ᵗ the festival seven more days; so for another seven days they celebrated joyfully. ²⁴Hezekiah king of Judah provided ᵘ a thousand bulls and seven thousand sheep and goats for the assembly, and the officials provided them with a thousand bulls and ten thousand sheep and goats. A great number of priests consecrated themselves. ²⁵The entire assembly of Judah rejoiced, along with the priests and Levites and all who had assembled from Israel ᵛ, including the foreigners who had come from Israel and also those who resided in Judah. ²⁶There was great joy in Jerusalem, for since the days of Solomon ʷ son of David king of Israel there had been nothing like this in Jerusalem. ²⁷The priests and the Levites stood to bless ˣ the people, and God heard them, for their prayer reached heaven, his holy dwelling place.

31 When all this had ended, the Israelites who were there went out to the towns of Judah, smashed the sacred stones and cut down ʸ the Asherah poles. They destroyed the high places and the altars throughout Judah and Benjamin and

---

ᵃ 21 Or *priests sang to the LORD every day, accompanied by the LORD's instruments of praise* ᵇ 22 Or *and confessed their sins to*

---

cy." Here the phrase is found in the speech of Hezekiah, again portraying him as a second Solomon (see Lev 26:40–42). *will return to this land.* Those who repent will have hope of return, even those from the Assyrian captivity.
30:14 *Kidron Valley.* See 29:16 and note.
30:15 *The priests and the Levites . . . consecrated themselves.* The reproach previously directed against the priests (v. 3; 29:34) is here broadened to include also the Levites—an exhortation to the priests and Levites of the restored community to be faithful.
30:17 *Levites had to kill the Passover lambs.* See Ex 12:6; Dt 16:6. According to the law the heads of families were to slay the Passover sacrifice. The Levites perhaps acted for the recent arrivals from the northern kingdom who were not ceremonially clean. Cf. Jn 11:55.
30:18–19 Faith and obedience take precedence over ritual (see note on Isa 1:11–15; cf. Mk 7:1–23; Jn 7:22–23; 9:14–16).
30:20 The response to Hezekiah's prayer recalls the prayer of Solomon (7:14).

30:23 *another seven days.* The festival was observed for two weeks, just as the observance of the dedication of Solomon's temple had been (7:8–9).
30:26 *since the days of Solomon.* An explicit indication of the Chronicler's modeling of the reign of Hezekiah after that of Solomon (see note on 29:1—32:33).
30:27 *prayer reached heaven, his holy dwelling place.* Another echo of Solomon's dedication prayer (6:21,30,33,39).
31:1–21 Apart from the first verse, which parallels 2Ki 18:4, the material of this chapter is unique to the Chronicler, whose interest in the Levites and the temple predominates. Hezekiah's efforts to ensure the material support of the Levites (v. 4) probably had relevance to the postexilic audience for whom the Chronicler wrote.
31:1 *the Israelites . . . the Israelites.* Lit."all Israel . . . all the Israelites." The Chronicler's interest in"all Israel" as united under Hezekiah is again apparent. *sacred stones.* See note on 1Ki 14:23. *Asherah poles.* See TNIV text note on 14:3 and note on Ex 34:13.

in Ephraim and Manasseh. After they had destroyed all of them, the Israelites returned to their own towns and to their own property.

CONTRIBUTIONS FOR WORSHIP
31:20–21pp — 2Ki 18:5–7

[2]Hezekiah [z] assigned the priests and Levites to divisions [a]—each of them according to their duties as priests or Levites—to offer burnt offerings and fellowship offerings, to minister, [b] to give thanks and to sing praises [c] at the gates of the LORD's dwelling. [d] [3]The king contributed [e] from his own possessions for the morning and evening burnt offerings and for the burnt offerings on the Sabbaths, at the New Moons and at the appointed festivals as written in the Law of the LORD. [f] [4]He ordered the people living in Jerusalem to give the portion [g] due the priests and Levites so they could devote themselves to the Law of the LORD. [5]As soon as the order went out, the Israelites generously gave the firstfruits [h] of their grain, new wine, [i] oil and honey and all that the fields produced. They brought a great amount, a tithe of everything. [6]The people of Israel and Judah who lived in the towns of Judah also brought a tithe [j] of their herds and flocks and a tithe of the holy things dedicated to the LORD their God, and they piled them in heaps. [k] [7]They began doing this in the third month and finished in the seventh month. [l] [8]When Hezekiah and his officials came and saw the heaps, they praised the LORD and blessed [m] his people Israel.

[9]Hezekiah asked the priests and Levites about the heaps; [10]and Azariah the chief priest, from the family of Zadok, [n] answered, "Since the people began to bring their contributions to the temple of the LORD, we have had enough to eat and plenty to spare, because the LORD has blessed his people, and this great amount is left over." [o]

[11]Hezekiah gave orders to prepare storerooms in the temple of the LORD, and this was done. [12]Then they faithfully brought in the contributions, tithes and dedicated gifts. Konaniah, [p] a Levite, was the overseer in charge of these things, and his brother Shimei was next in rank. [13]Jehiel, Azaziah, Nahath, Asahel, Jerimoth, Jozabad, [q] Eliel, Ismakiah, Mahath and Benaiah were assistants of Konaniah and Shimei his brother. All these served by appointment of King Hezekiah and Azariah the official in charge of the temple of God.

[14]Kore son of Imnah the Levite, keeper of the East Gate, was in charge of the freewill offerings given to God, distributing the contributions made to the LORD and also the consecrated gifts. [15]Eden, [r] Miniamin, Jeshua, Shemaiah, Amariah and Shekaniah assisted him faithfully in the towns [s] of the priests, distributing to their fellow priests according to their divisions, old and young alike.

[16]In addition, they distributed to the males three years old or more whose names were in the genealogical records [t]—all who would enter the temple of the LORD to perform the daily duties of their various tasks, according to their responsibilities and their divisions. [17]And they distributed to the priests enrolled by their families in the genealogical records and likewise to the Levites twenty years old or more, according to their responsibilities and their divisions. [18]They included all the little ones, the wives, and the sons and daughters of the whole community listed in these genealogical records. For they were faithful in consecrating themselves.

[19]As for the priests, the descendants of Aaron, who lived on the farm lands around their towns or in any other towns, [u] men were designated by name to distribute portions to every male among them and to all who were recorded in the genealogies of the Levites.

[20]This is what Hezekiah did throughout Judah, doing what was good and right and faithful [v] before the LORD his God. [21]In everything that he undertook in the service of God's temple and in obedience to the law and the commands, he sought his God and worked wholeheartedly. And so he prospered. [w]

31:2 [z] S 2Ch 29:9
[a] S 1Ch 24:1
[b] S 1Ch 15:2 [c] Ps 7:17; 9:2; 47:6; 71:22
[d] S 1Ch 23:28-32
31:3 [e] S 1Ch 29:3; 2Ch 35:7; Eze 45:17
[f] Nu 28:1–29:40
31:4 [g] S Nu 18:8; S Dt 18:8; Ne 13:10
31:5 [h] S Nu 18:12, 24; Ne 13:12; Eze 44:30 [i] Dt 12:17
31:6 [j] S Lev 27:30; Ne 13:10-12
[k] S Ru 3:7
31:7 [l] Ex 23:16
31:8 [m] Ps 144:13-15
31:10 [n] S 2Sa 8:17
[o] S Ex 36:5; Eze 44:30; Mal 3:10-12
31:12 [p] 2Ch 35:9
31:13 [q] 2Ch 35:9
31:15 [r] 2Ch 29:12
[s] Jos 21:9-19
31:16 [t] 1Ch 23:3
31:19 [u] S Nu 35:2-5
31:20 [v] S 2Ki 20:3
31:21 [w] S Dt 29:9

31:2 Echoes 8:14. The Chronicler continues to model Hezekiah as a second Solomon (see notes on 29:7,18).

🔺 31:3 *king contributed.* The king's giving from his own wealth prompted a generous response from the people, as it had also under David (1Ch 29:3–9).

31:5–6 See Dt 12:5–19; 14:22–27. The grain, new wine and olive oil had to be brought to the temple (Dt 12:17). Those coming from a distance, however, could bring the value of their offerings and purchase them on arrival (Dt 14:24). Only those who actually lived in Judah brought the tithe of their herds and flocks, a difficult procedure for those who lived farther away. For the restored community's commitment to bring their firstfruits, tithes and offerings, see Ne 10:35–39. For their failure to do so

see Ne 13:10–13; Mal 3:8–10.

31:7 *third month.* May–June, the time of the Festival of Pentecost and the grain harvest. *seventh month.* September–October, the time of the Festival of Tabernacles and the fruit and vine harvest (see Ex 23:16).

31:16 *three years.* Although no ancient versions or manuscripts disagree with this figure, it may represent a copyist's mistake for "30 years," the age at which duties were assigned in the temple (1Ch 23:3).

🔺 31:20–21 Another brief indication of the Chronicler's emphasis on immediate retribution: Not only does disobedience bring immediate chastening, but obedience and seeking God bring prosperity.

32:1 ˣ Isa 36:1; 37:9,
17, 37
32:2 ʸ Isa 22:7;
Jer 1:15
32:4 ᶻ S 2Ki 18:17;
Isa 22:9, 11; Na 3:14
32:5 ᵃ Isa 22:10
ᵇ S 1Ch 11:8 ᶜ Isa 22:8
32:7 ᵈ S Dt 31:6
ᵉ 2Ch 20:15
ᶠ S Nu 14:9; 2Ki 6:16
32:8 ᵍ Job 40:9;
Isa 52:10; Jer 17:5;
32:21 ʰ S Dt 3:22;
S 1Sa 17:45
ⁱ S 1Ch 5:22; Ps 20:7;
Isa 28:6
32:9 ʲ S Jos 10:3, 31
32:10 ᵏ Eze 29:16
32:11 ˡ Isa 37:10
32:12 ᵐ S 2Ch 31:1
32:13 ⁿ ver 15
32:15 ᵒ Isa 37:10
ᵖ Da 3:15 �q Ex 5:2
32:17 ʳ Isa 37:14
ˢ Ps 74:22; Isa 37:4,
17 ᵗ S 2Ki 19:12
32:19 ᵘ Ps 115:4-8;
Isa 2:8; 17:8; 37:19;
Jer 1:16
32:20 ᵛ Isa 1:15;
37:15
32:21 ʷ S Ge 19:13

SENNACHERIB THREATENS JERUSALEM

32:9–19pp — 2Ki 18:17–35; Isa 36:2–20
32:20–21pp — 2Ki 19:35–37; Isa 37:36–38

32 After all that Hezekiah had so faithfully done, Sennacheribˣ king of Assyria came and invaded Judah. He laid siege to the fortified cities, thinking to conquer them for himself. ²When Hezekiah saw that Sennacherib had come and that he intended to make war on Jerusalem,ʸ ³he consulted with his officials and military staff about blocking off the water from the springs outside the city, and they helped him. ⁴A large force assembled and blocked all the springsᶻ and the stream that flowed through the land. "Why should the kingsᵃ of Assyria come and find plenty of water?" they said. ⁵Then he worked hard repairing all the broken sections of the wallᵃ and building towers on it. He built another wall outside that one and reinforced the terracesᵇ ᵇ of the City of David. He also made large numbers of weaponsᶜ and shields.

⁶He appointed military officers over the people and assembled them before him in the square at the city gate and encouraged them with these words: ⁷"Be strong and courageous.ᵈ Do not be afraid or discouragedᵉ because of the king of Assyria and the vast army with him, for there is a greater power with us than with him.ᶠ ⁸With him is only the arm of flesh,ᵍ but with usʰ is the Lᴏʀᴅ our God to help us and to fight our battles."ⁱ And the people gained confidence from what Hezekiah the king of Judah said.

⁹Later, when Sennacherib king of Assyria and all his forces were laying siege to Lachish,ʲ he sent his officers to Jerusalem with this message for Hezekiah king of Judah and for all the people of Judah who were there:

¹⁰"This is what Sennacherib king of Assyria says: On what are you basing your confidence,ᵏ that you remain in Jerusalem under siege? ¹¹When Hezekiah says, 'The Lᴏʀᴅ our God will save us from the hand of the king of Assyria,' he is misleadingˡ you, to let you die of hunger and thirst. ¹²Did not Hezekiah himself remove this god's high places and altars, saying to Judah and Jerusalem, 'You must worship before one altarᵐ and burn sacrifices on it'?

¹³"Do you not know what I and my predecessors have done to all the peoples of the other lands? Were the gods of those nations ever able to deliver their land from my hand?ⁿ ¹⁴Who of all the gods of these nations that my predecessors destroyed has been able to save his people from me? How then can your god deliver you from my hand? ¹⁵Now do not let Hezekiah deceiveᵒ you and mislead you like this. Do not believe him, for no god of any nation or kingdom has been able to deliverᵖ his people from my hand or the hand of my predecessors. q How much less will your god deliver you from my hand!"

¹⁶Sennacherib's officers spoke further against the Lᴏʀᴅ God and against his servant Hezekiah. ¹⁷The king also wrote lettersʳ ridiculingˢ the Lᴏʀᴅ, the God of Israel, and saying this against him: "Just as the godsᵗ of the peoples of the other lands did not rescue their people from my hand, so the god of Hezekiah will not rescue his people from my hand." ¹⁸Then they called out in Hebrew to the people of Jerusalem who were on the wall, to terrify them and make them afraid in order to capture the city. ¹⁹They spoke about the God of Jerusalem as they did about the gods of the other peoples of the world—the work of human hands.ᵘ

²⁰King Hezekiah and the prophet Isaiah son of Amoz cried out in prayerᵛ to heaven about this. ²¹And the Lᴏʀᴅ sent an angel,ʷ who annihilated all the fighting men and the

---

ᵃ 4 Hebrew; Septuagint and Syriac *king*   ᵇ 5 Or *the Millo*

32:1–23 The record of Sennacherib's invasion is much more detailed in 2 Kings and Isaiah (see note on 29:1—32:33).
32:1 The Chronicler omits the date of the invasion (701 B.C., Hezekiah's 14th year; see 2Ki 18:13; Isa 36:1; see also chart, p. 482).
32:2–8 Normal preparations for invasion.
32:3–4 See v. 30.
32:9 The Chronicler omits 2Ki 18:14–16, which records Hezekiah's suit for peace with its accompanying bribe stripped from the temple treasures. These acts were apparently out of accord with the Chronicler's portrait of Hezekiah. He also omits 2Ki 18:17b–18.
32:10 The Chronicler omits 2Ki 18:20–21 (and Isa 36:5–6), containing a portion of the Assyrian commander's speech ridiculing Hezekiah and the citizens of Jerusalem for trusting in Egypt and

the pharaoh. This, too, may be theologically motivated, in light of the Chronicler's attitude toward foreign alliances (see note on 16:2–9). The same concern with foreign alliances is also likely the reason for the omission of the material in 2Ki 18:23–27 (and Isa 36:8–12), where mention is again made of the hope of Egyptian intervention (see 2Ki 19:9 for the incursion of Tirhakah).
32:16 *spoke further.* The Chronicler appears to assume his reader's familiarity with the longer account of the Assyrian taunts found in Kings and Isaiah.
32:18 *called out in Hebrew.* Assumes knowledge of the fuller story (2Ki 18:26–28; Isa 36:11–13).
32:20 This brief reference to the prayers of Hezekiah and Isaiah abridges the much longer narrative in 2Ki 19:1–34 (and Isa 37:1–35).

commanders and officers in the camp of the Assyrian king. So he withdrew to his own land in disgrace. And when he went into the temple of his god, some of his sons cut him down with the sword. *

²²So the LORD saved Hezekiah and the people of Jerusalem from the hand of Sennacherib king of Assyria and from the hand of all others. He took care of them ª on every side. ²³Many brought offerings to Jerusalem for the LORD and valuable gifts ʸ for Hezekiah king of Judah. From then on he was highly regarded by all the nations.

HEZEKIAH'S PRIDE, SUCCESS AND DEATH
32:24–33pp — 2Ki 20:1–21; Isa 37:21–38; 38:1–8

²⁴In those days Hezekiah became ill and was at the point of death. He prayed to the LORD, who answered him and gave him a miraculous sign. ᶻ ²⁵But Hezekiah's heart was proud ª and he did not respond to the kindness shown him; therefore the LORD's wrath ᵇ was on him and on Judah and Jerusalem. ²⁶Then Hezekiah repented ᶜ of the pride of his heart, as did the people of Jerusalem; therefore the LORD's wrath did not come on them during the days of Hezekiah. ᵈ

²⁷Hezekiah had very great wealth and honor, ᵉ and he made treasuries for his silver and gold and for his precious stones, spices, shields and all kinds of valuables. ²⁸He also made buildings to store the harvest of grain, new wine and olive oil; and he made stalls for various kinds of cattle, and pens for the flocks. ²⁹He built villages and acquired great numbers of flocks and herds, for God had given him very great riches. ᶠ

³⁰It was Hezekiah who blocked ᵍ the upper outlet of the Gihon ʰ spring and channeled ⁱ the water down to the west side of the City of David. He succeeded in everything he undertook. ³¹But when envoys were sent by the rulers of Babylon ʲ to ask him about the miraculous sign ᵏ that had occurred in the land, God left him to test ˡ him and to know everything that was in his heart.

³²The other events of Hezekiah's reign and his acts of devotion are written in the vision of the prophet Isaiah son of Amoz in the book of the kings of Judah and Israel. ³³Hezekiah rested with his ancestors and was buried on the hill where the tombs of David's descendants are. All Judah and the people of Jerusalem honored him when he died. And Manasseh his son succeeded him as king.

MANASSEH KING OF JUDAH
33:1–10pp — 2Ki 21:1–10
33:18–20pp — 2Ki 21:17–18

33 Manasseh ᵐ was twelve years old when he became king, and he reigned in Jerusalem fifty-five years. ²He did evil in the eyes of the LORD, ⁿ following the detestable ᵒ practices of the nations the LORD had driven out before the Israelites. ³He rebuilt the high places his father Hezekiah had demolished; he also erected altars to the Baals and made Asherah poles. ᵖ He bowed down � to all the starry hosts and worshiped them. ⁴He built altars in the temple of the LORD, of which the LORD had said,

---

ª 22 Hebrew; Septuagint and Vulgate *He gave them rest*

32:21 ˣ S 2Ki 19:7;
Isa 37:7, 38; Jer 41:2
32:23 ʸ S 1Sa 10:27;
S 2Ch 9:24; Ps 68:18,
29; 76:11; Isa 16:1;
18:7; 45:14; Zep 3:10;
Zec 14:16-17
32:24 ᶻ ver 31
32:25 ª S 2Ki 14:10
ᵇ S 2Ch 19:2
32:26 ᶜ Jer 26:18-19
ᵈ 2Ch 34:27, 28;
Isa 39:8
32:27 ᵉ S 1Ch 29:12;
S 2Ch 9:24
32:29 ᶠ Isa 39:2
32:30 ᵍ S 2Ki 18:17
ʰ S 1Ki 1:33
ⁱ S 2Sa 5:8
32:31 ʲ Isa 13:1; 39:1
ᵏ ver 24; Isa 38:7
ˡ S Ge 22:1; Dt 8:16
33:1 ᵐ S 1Ch 3:13
33:2 ⁿ Jer 15:4
ᵒ S Dt 18:9
33:3 ᵖ Dt 16:21-22;
S 2Ch 24:18 ᵠ Dt 17:3

32:21 See 2Ki 19:35–37; Isa 36:36–38. The Chronicler and the parallel accounts telescope events somewhat: Sennacherib's invasion of Judah was in 701 B.C., while his death at the hand of his sons was in 681.

32:23 *highly regarded by all the nations.* Another effort to compare Hezekiah with Solomon (see 9:23–24).

32:24 The Chronicler again abridges the narrative in 2Ki 20:1–11 (and Isa 38:1–8), assuming the reader's familiarity with the role of Isaiah and the miraculous sign of the shadow reversing ten steps.

32:25–30 Not found in the parallel texts.

32:25–26 *proud...pride.* The Chronicler does not specify the nature of Hezekiah's pride (however, see v. 31; 2Ki 20:12–13; Isa 39:1–2). Even for a second Solomon like Hezekiah, disobedience brings anger from the Lord.

32:27–29 The Chronicler likens Hezekiah to Solomon also by recounting his wealth (9:13–14).

32:30 See vv. 2–4; 2Ki 20:20.

32:31 See v. 25. The Chronicler assumes the reader's knowledge of the fuller account in 2Ki 20:12–19 (and Isa 39:1–8). The envoys from Babylon were apparently interested in joint efforts

against the Assyrians, hoping to open two fronts against them simultaneously.

33:1–20 See 2Ki 21:1–18 and notes. Manasseh had the longest reign of any of the kings of Judah, a total of 55 years (v. 1). The emphasis in the two accounts differs: While both histories report at length the evil done in Manasseh's reign, only the Chronicler mentions his journey to Babylon and his repentance and restoration to rule. For the writer of Kings, the picture is only a bad one in which Manasseh could be considered almost single-handedly the cause of the exile (2Ki 21:10–15; 23:26). Some interpreters regard the record of Manasseh's repentance in Chronicles as motivated by the author's emphasis on immediate retribution: Length of reign is viewed as a blessing for obedience, so that the Chronicler deliberately records some good in Manasseh as a ground for his long reign. However, it must be noted that length of reign is not elsewhere used by the Chronicler as an indication of divine blessing. The usual indicators for such blessing in his account are peace and prosperity, building projects, success in warfare and large families.

33:1 *fifty-five years.* 697–642 B.C.

33:3, 19 *Asherah poles.* See note on Ex 34:13.

33:4 ʳ 2Ch 7:16
33:5 ˢ S 2Ch 4:9
33:6 ᵗ S Lev 18:21;
S Dt 18:10
ᵘ S Ex 22:18;
S Lev 19:31
ᵛ S 1Sa 28:13
33:7 ʷ S 2Ch 7:16
33:8 ˣ S 2Sa 7:10
33:9 ʸ Jer 15:4;
Eze 5:7
33:11 ᶻ S Dt 28:36
ᵃ S 2Ki 19:28;
Isa 37:29; Eze 29:4;
38:4; Am 4:2
ᵇ Ps 149:8
33:12 ᶜ S 2Ch 6:37
33:14 ᵈ S 1Ki 1:33
ᵉ Ne 3:3; 12:39;
Zep 1:10 ᶠ 2Ch 27:3;
Ne 3:26
33:15 ᵍ 2Ki 23:12
33:16 ʰ Lev 7:11-18
33:19 ⁱ S 2Ch 6:37
ʲ 2Ki 21:17
33:20 ᵏ 2Ki 21:18;
S 2Ch 21:20
33:21 ˡ S 1Ch 3:14

"My Name ʳ will remain in Jerusalem forever." ⁵In both courts of the temple of the LORD, ˢ he built altars to all the starry hosts. ⁶He sacrificed his children ᵗ in the fire in the Valley of Ben Hinnom, practiced divination and witchcraft, sought omens, and consulted mediums ᵘ and spiritists. ᵛ He did much evil in the eyes of the LORD, arousing his anger.

⁷He took the image he had made and put it in God's temple, ʷ of which God had said to David and to his son Solomon, "In this temple and in Jerusalem, which I have chosen out of all the tribes of Israel, I will put my Name forever. ⁸I will not again make the feet of the Israelites leave the land ˣ I assigned to your ancestors, if only they will be careful to do everything I commanded them concerning all the laws, decrees and regulations given through Moses." ⁹But Manasseh led Judah and the people of Jerusalem astray, so that they did more evil than the nations the LORD had destroyed before the Israelites. ʸ

¹⁰The LORD spoke to Manasseh and his people, but they paid no attention. ¹¹So the LORD brought against them the army commanders of the king of Assyria, who took Manasseh prisoner, ᶻ put a hook ᵃ in his nose, bound him with bronze shackles ᵇ and took him to Babylon. ¹²In his distress he sought the favor of the LORD his God and humbled ᶜ himself greatly before the God of his ancestors. ¹³And when he prayed to him, the LORD was moved by his entreaty and listened to his plea; so he brought him back to Jerusalem and to his kingdom. Then Manasseh knew that the LORD is God.

¹⁴Afterward he rebuilt the outer wall of the City of David, west of the Gihon ᵈ spring in the valley, as far as the entrance of the Fish Gate ᵉ and encircling the hill of Ophel; ᶠ he also made it much higher. He stationed military commanders in all the fortified cities in Judah.

¹⁵He got rid of the foreign gods and removed ᵍ the image from the temple of the LORD, as well as all the altars he had built on the temple hill and in Jerusalem; and he threw them out of the city. ¹⁶Then he restored the altar of the LORD and sacrificed fellowship offerings and thank offerings ʰ on it, and told Judah to serve the LORD, the God of Israel. ¹⁷The people, however, continued to sacrifice at the high places, but only to the LORD their God.

¹⁸The other events of Manasseh's reign, including his prayer to his God and the words the seers spoke to him in the name of the LORD, the God of Israel, are written in the annals of the kings of Israel.ᵃ ¹⁹His prayer and how God was moved by his entreaty, as well as all his sins and unfaithfulness, and the sites where he built high places and set up Asherah poles and idols before he humbled ⁱ himself—all these are written in the records of the seers.ᵇʲ ²⁰Manasseh rested with his ancestors and was buried ᵏ in his palace. And Amon his son succeeded him as king.

AMON KING OF JUDAH
33:21–25pp — 2Ki 21:19–24

²¹Amon ˡ was twenty-two years old when he became king, and he reigned in Jerusalem two years. ²²He did evil in the eyes of the LORD, as his father Manasseh had done. Amon

ᵃ 18 That is, Judah, as frequently in 2 Chronicles   ᵇ 19 One Hebrew manuscript and Septuagint; most Hebrew manuscripts of Hozai

---

33:4 *My Name will remain in Jerusalem forever.* See 1Ki 3:2 and note; 9:3; Ps 132:13–14.
33:6 *sacrificed his children . . . Valley of Ben Hinnom.* See 28:3 and note.
33:10 See note on vv. 1–20. The Chronicler abridges what the Lord said to Manasseh and the people through the prophets; the fuller record is found in 2Ki 21:10–15.

A C **33:11–17** Unique to the Chronicler, showing his stress on immediate retribution: Manasseh's evil brings invasion and defeat, while his repentance brings restoration to rule.

B **33:11** *took him to Babylon.* In extant non-Biblical records there is no reference as yet to Manasseh being taken to Babylon by an Assyrian king. Esarhaddon (681–669 B.C.) lists him among 22 kings required to forward materials for his building projects, and Ashurbanipal (669–627) names him as one of a number of vassals supporting his campaign against Egypt. The fact that an Assyrian king would have him taken to Babylon suggests that this incident may have taken place during the rebellion of Shamash-Shum-Ukin against his brother and overlord Ashurbanipal. This rebellion lasted from 652 to 648, and Manasseh may have joined or at least have been suspected of assist-

ing in the Babylonian defection from Assyria. Manasseh may have been found innocent, or he may have been pardoned on the basis of a renewed pledge of loyalty. Egypt had also bolted from the Assyrian yoke under the new 26th dynasty, and the return of Manasseh to rule may reflect the Assyrian need of a vassal near the border of Egypt.
33:12 The language is reminiscent of Solomon's prayer (7:14).
33:14 *rebuilt the outer wall.* For the Chronicler such building programs are a sign of divine blessing (8:1–6; 11:5–12; 14:6–7; 26:9–10,14–15; 32:1–5, 27–30; 1Ch 11:7–9; 15:1).
33:15–16 Whatever the precise nature of Manasseh's reforms, Josiah would later still need to remove "the altars Manasseh had built in the two courts of the temple" (2Ki 23:12).
33:20 *buried in his palace.* Cf. 2Ki 21:18. His burial in the palace garden makes Manasseh the fifth king the Chronicler names who was not buried in the tombs of the kings (see note on 28:27).
33:21–25 See 2Ki 21:19–26. The Chronicler's account of the reign of Amon (642–640 B.C.) is quite similar to that in Kings, apart from (1) the additional note that Amon was not repentant like his father, Manasseh, a note based on a passage unique to the Chronicler (vv. 12–13), and (2) the absence of the death formula.

worshiped and offered sacrifices to all the idols Manasseh had made. ²³But unlike his father Manasseh, he did not humble ᵐ himself before the Lord; Amon increased his guilt.

²⁴Amon's officials conspired against him and assassinated him in his palace. ²⁵Then the people ⁿ of the land killed all who had plotted against King Amon, and they made Josiah his son king in his place.

JOSIAH'S REFORMS

34:1–2pp — 2Ki 22:1–2
34:3–7Ref — 2Ki 23:4–20
34:8–13pp — 2Ki 22:3–7

34 Josiah ᵒ was eight years old when he became king, ᵖ and he reigned in Jerusalem thirty-one years. ²He did what was right in the eyes of the Lord and followed the ways of his father David, �q not turning aside to the right or to the left.

³In the eighth year of his reign, while he was still young, he began to seek the God ʳ of his father David. In his twelfth year he began to purge Judah and Jerusalem of high places, Asherah poles and idols. ⁴Under his direction the altars of the Baals were torn down; he cut to pieces the incense altars that were above them, and smashed the Asherah poles ˢ and the idols. These he broke to pieces and scattered over the graves of those who had sacrificed to them. ᵗ ⁵He burned ᵘ the bones of the priests on their altars, and so he purged Judah and Jerusalem. ⁶In the towns of Manasseh, Ephraim and Simeon, as far as Naphtali, and in the ruins around them, ⁷he tore down the altars and the Asherah poles and crushed the idols to powder ᵛ and cut to pieces all the incense altars throughout Israel. Then he went back to Jerusalem.

⁸In the eighteenth year of Josiah's reign, to purify the land and the temple, he sent Shaphan son of Azaliah and Maaseiah the ruler of the city, with Joah son of Joahaz, the recorder, to repair the temple of the Lord his God.

⁹They went to Hilkiah ʷ the high priest and gave him the money that had been brought into the temple of God, which the Levites who were the gatekeepers had collected from the people of Manasseh, Ephraim and the entire remnant of Israel and from all the people of Judah and Benjamin and the inhabitants of Jerusalem. ¹⁰Then they entrusted it to the men appointed to supervise the work on the Lord's temple. These men paid the workers who repaired and restored the temple. ¹¹They also gave money ˣ to the carpenters and builders to purchase dressed stone, and timber for joists and beams for the buildings that the kings of Judah had allowed to fall into ruin. ʸ

¹²The workers did their work faithfully. ᶻ Over them to direct them were Jahath and Obadiah, Levites descended from Merari, and Zechariah and Meshullam, descended from

33:23 ᵐ S Ex 10:3;
2Ch 7:14; Ps 18:27;
147:6; Pr 3:34
33:25 ⁿ S 2Ch 22:1
34:1 ᵒ S 1Ch 3:14
ᵖ Zep 1:1
34:2 q 2Ch 29:2
34:3 ʳ S 1Ch 16:11
34:4 ˢ S Ex 34:13
ᵗ Ex 32:20;
S Lev 26:30;
2Ki 23:11; Mic 1:5
34:5 ᵘ S 1Ki 13:2
34:7 ᵛ S Ex 32:20
34:9 ʷ S 1Ch 6:13
34:11 ˣ 2Ch 24:12
ʸ 2Ch 33:4-7
34:12 ᶻ 2Ki 12:15

34:1—36:1 See 2Ki 22:1—23:30 and notes. Both accounts of Josiah's reign are about the same length and treat the same subjects, but with considerable variation in emphasis. Both deal with three different aspects of Josiah's reform: (1) the removal of foreign religions, (2) the finding of the Book of the Law and the covenant renewal that followed and (3) the celebration of Passover. On the second item the two histories are quite similar. On the first item the writer of Kings goes to great lengths (2Ki 23:4–20), while the Chronicler summarizes it only briefly (34:3–7,33). The account of the Passover is greatly expanded in Chronicles (35:1–19), while only alluded to in 2 Kings (23:21–23). Not only are these items treated at different lengths, but the order is also changed. In Kings the finding of the Book of the Law in the temple in Josiah's 18th year is the first incident mentioned. The writer appears to have organized his material geographically, i.e., beginning with the temple and spreading through the city, then into the rest of the nation. The Chronicler, on the other hand, has arranged the incidents in order of their occurrence and has characteristically introduced a number of chronological notes into the text: 34:3 (two notes without parallel in Kings); 34:8 (see 2Ki 22:3); 35:19 (see 2Ki 23:23; see also note on 2Ch 12:2). Chronicles makes it clear that the reform began in Josiah's 12th year (34:3), six years before the discovery of the Book of the Law.

34:1–2 See 2Ki 22:1–2.

34:1 *thirty-one years.* 640–609 B.C.

34:3–7 The writer of Kings covers this aspect of Josiah's reform

in much greater detail (2Ki 23:4–20). He also delays his account of the removal of pagan religions until after the discovery of the Book of the Law, while the Chronicler places it before.

34:3 Some interpreters have sought to tie the events of Josiah's 8th (v. 3), 12th (v. 3) and 18th (v. 8) years to stages in the progressive decline and fall of the Assyrian empire, which had dominated the area for about two centuries. The demise of Assyrian control over Aram and Israel undoubtedly facilitated and encouraged Josiah's reassertion of Davidic authority over former Assyrian provinces (vv. 6–7). However, one must not undercut religious motives in Josiah's reforms. If one does, the reform is reduced to a mere political rebellion. *Asherah poles.* See note on Ex 34:13.

34:6 *Manasseh, Ephraim and Simeon, as far as Naphtali.* The Chronicler's concern for "all Israel" (see Introduction to 1 Chronicles: Purpose and Themes) is apparent in his recording the involvement of the northern tribes in Josiah's reform (see also vv. 9,21,33). The Chronicler again shows all Israel united under a Davidic king, just as he did under Hezekiah (see note on 30:1). *Simeon.* Some Simeonites must have migrated from Judah to the north.

34:7 *throughout Israel.* Defined by the list of tribes in v. 6.

34:8–21 See 2Ki 22:3–13 and notes.

34:9 *Manasseh, Ephraim and the entire remnant of Israel.* Again as part of his concern with "all Israel," the Chronicler notes that worshipers from the north also brought gifts to the temple (not explicitly indicated in 2Ki 22:4).

34:10–13 Cf. 24:8–12.

34:12 *a* S 1Ch 25:1
34:13 *b* S 1Ch 23:4
34:15 *c* S 2Ki 22:8;
Ezr 7:6; Ne 8:1
34:19 *d* Dt 28:3-68
e Isa 36:22; 37:1
34:20 *f* S 2Ch 22:3
34:21 *g* La 2:4; 4:11;
Eze 36:18
34:22 *h* S Ex 15:20;
Ne 6:14
34:24 *i* Pr 16:4;
Isa 3:9; Jer 40:2;
42:10; 44:2,11
j 2Ch 36:14-20
k Dt 28:15-68
34:25 *l* 2Ch 33:3-6;
Jer 22:9
34:27 *m* S 2Ch 32:26
n S Ex 10:3;
S 2Ch 6:37
34:28 *o* 2Ch 35:20-
25 *p* S 2Ch 32:26
34:30 *q* S 2Ki 23:2
34:31 *r* S 1Ki 7:15
s S 2Ki 11:17;
S 2Ch 23:16
t S Dt 13:4
34:33 *u* S Dt 18:9

Kohath. The Levites—all who were skilled in playing musical instruments— *a* [13]had charge of the laborers *b* and supervised all the workers from job to job. Some of the Levites were secretaries, scribes and gatekeepers.

THE BOOK OF THE LAW FOUND

34:14–28pp — 2Ki 22:8–20
34:29–32pp — 2Ki 23:1–3

[14]While they were bringing out the money that had been taken into the temple of the Lord, Hilkiah the priest found the Book of the Law of the Lord that had been given through Moses. [15]Hilkiah said to Shaphan the secretary, "I have found the Book of the Law *c* in the temple of the Lord." He gave it to Shaphan.

[16]Then Shaphan took the book to the king and reported to him: "Your officials are doing everything that has been committed to them. [17]They have paid out the money that was in the temple of the Lord and have entrusted it to the supervisors and workers." [18]Then Shaphan the secretary informed the king, "Hilkiah the priest has given me a book." And Shaphan read from it in the presence of the king.

[19]When the king heard the words of the Law, *d* he tore *e* his robes. [20]He gave these orders to Hilkiah, Ahikam son of Shaphan *f*, Abdon son of Micah, *a* Shaphan the secretary and Asaiah the king's attendant: [21]"Go and inquire of the Lord for me and for the remnant in Israel and Judah about what is written in this book that has been found. Great is the Lord's anger that is poured out *g* on us because those who have gone before us have not kept the word of the Lord; they have not acted in accordance with all that is written in this book."

[22]Hilkiah and those the king had sent with him *b* went to speak to the prophet *h* Huldah, who was the wife of Shallum son of Tokhath, *c* the son of Hasrah, *d* keeper of the wardrobe. She lived in Jerusalem, in the New Quarter.

[23]She said to them, "This is what the Lord, the God of Israel, says: Tell the man who sent you to me, [24]'This is what the Lord says: I am going to bring disaster *i* on this place and its people *j*—all the curses *k* written in the book that has been read in the presence of the king of Judah. [25]Because they have forsaken me *l* and burned incense to other gods and aroused my anger by all that their hands have made, *e* my anger will be poured out on this place and will not be quenched.' [26]Tell the king of Judah, who sent you to inquire of the Lord, 'This is what the Lord, the God of Israel, says concerning the words you heard: [27]Because your heart was responsive *m* and you humbled *n* yourself before God when you heard what he spoke against this place and its people, and because you humbled yourself before me and tore your robes and wept in my presence, I have heard you, declares the Lord. [28]Now I will gather you to your ancestors, *o* and you will be buried in peace. Your eyes will not see all the disaster I am going to bring on this place and on those who live here.' " *p*

So they took her answer back to the king.

[29]Then the king called together all the elders of Judah and Jerusalem. [30]He went up to the temple of the Lord *q* with the people of Judah, the inhabitants of Jerusalem, the priests and the Levites—all the people from the least to the greatest. He read in their hearing all the words of the Book of the Covenant, which had been found in the temple of the Lord. [31]The king stood by his pillar *r* and renewed the covenant *s* in the presence of the Lord— to follow *t* the Lord and keep his commands, statutes and decrees with all his heart and all his soul, and to obey the words of the covenant written in this book.

[32]Then he had everyone in Jerusalem and Benjamin pledge themselves to it; the people of Jerusalem did this in accordance with the covenant of God, the God of their ancestors.

[33]Josiah removed all the detestable *u* idols from all the territory belonging to the Israelites, and he had all who were present in Israel serve the Lord their God. As long as he lived, they did not fail to follow the Lord, the God of their ancestors.

---

a 20 Also called *Akbor son of Micaiah*   *b* 22 One Hebrew manuscript, Vulgate and Syriac; most Hebrew manuscripts do not have *had sent with him*.   *c* 22 Also called *Tikvah*   *d* 22 Also called *Harhas*   *e* 25 Or *by everything they have done*

34:14 *Book of the Law of the Lord.* See note on 17:9.
34:22–28 See 2Ki 22:14–20 and notes.
34:22 *prophet Huldah.* See note on 2Ki 22:14.
34:28 *will be buried in peace.* See the death and burial account (35:20–25).

34:29–31 See 2Ki 23:1–3 and notes.
34:30 *the priests and the Levites.* Cf. 2Ki 23:2, which has "the priests and the prophets."
34:33 *all the territory belonging to the Israelites . . . all who were present in Israel.* See note on v. 6.

JOSIAH CELEBRATES THE PASSOVER
35:1,18–19pp — 2Ki 23:21–23

35 Josiah celebrated the Passover[v] to the Lord in Jerusalem, and the Passover lamb was slaughtered on the fourteenth day of the first month. [2]He appointed the priests to their duties and encouraged them in the service of the Lord's temple. [3]He said to the Levites, who instructed[w] all Israel and who had been consecrated to the Lord: "Put the sacred ark in the temple that Solomon son of David king of Israel built. It is not to be carried about on your shoulders. Now serve the Lord your God and his people Israel. [4]Prepare yourselves by families in your divisions,[x] according to the instructions written by David king of Israel and by his son Solomon.

[5]"Stand in the holy place with a group of Levites for each subdivision of the families of your fellow Israelites, the lay people. [6]Slaughter the Passover lambs, consecrate yourselves[y] and prepare the lambs for your fellow Israelites, doing what the Lord commanded through Moses."

[7]Josiah provided for all the lay people who were there a total of thirty thousand lambs and goats for the Passover offerings,[z] and also three thousand cattle—all from the king's own possessions.[a]

[8]His officials also contributed[b] voluntarily to the people and the priests and Levites. Hilkiah,[c] Zechariah and Jehiel, the officials in charge of God's temple, gave the priests twenty-six hundred Passover offerings and three hundred cattle. [9]Also Konaniah[d] along with Shemaiah and Nethanel, his brothers, and Hashabiah, Jeiel and Jozabad,[e] the leaders of the Levites, provided five thousand Passover offerings and five hundred head of cattle for the Levites.

[10]The service was arranged and the priests stood in their places with the Levites in their divisions[f] as the king had ordered.[g] [11]The Passover lambs were slaughtered,[h] and the priests splashed against the altar the blood handed to them, while the Levites skinned the animals. [12]They set aside the burnt offerings to give them to the subdivisions of the families of the people to offer to the Lord, as it is written in the Book of Moses. They did the same with the cattle. [13]They roasted the Passover animals over the fire as prescribed,[i] and boiled the holy offerings in pots, caldrons and pans and served them quickly to all the people. [14]After this, they made preparations for themselves and for the priests, because the priests, the descendants of Aaron, were sacrificing the burnt offerings and the fat portions[j] until nightfall. So the Levites made preparations for themselves and for the Aaronic priests.

[15]The musicians,[k] the descendants of Asaph, were in the places prescribed by David, Asaph, Heman and Jeduthun the king's seer. The gatekeepers at each gate did not need to leave their posts, because their fellow Levites made the preparations for them.

[16]So at that time the entire service of the Lord was carried out for the celebration of the Passover and the offering of burnt offerings on the altar of the Lord, as King Josiah had ordered. [17]The Israelites who were present celebrated the Passover at that time and observed the Festival of Unleavened Bread for seven days. [18]The Passover had not been observed like this in Israel since the days of the prophet Samuel; and none of the kings of Israel had ever celebrated such a Passover as did Josiah, with the priests, the Levites and all Judah and Israel who were there with the people of Jerusalem. [19]This Passover was celebrated in the eighteenth year of Josiah's reign.

THE DEATH OF JOSIAH
35:20—36:1pp — 2Ki 23:28–30

[20]After all this, when Josiah had set the temple in order, Necho king of Egypt went up to fight at Carchemish[l] on the Euphrates,[m] and Josiah marched out to meet him in bat-

---

35:1 v Ex 12:1-30; S Nu 28:16
35:3 w S 2Ch 17:7
35:4 x ver 10; S 1Ch 24:1; Ezr 6:18
35:6 y S Lev 11:44
35:7 z S 2Ch 30:24
a S 2Ch 31:3
35:8 b S 1Ch 29:3; 2Ch 29:31-36
c S 1Ch 6:13
35:9 d 2Ch 31:12
e 2Ch 31:13
35:10 f S ver 4
g 2Ch 30:16
35:11 h S 2Ch 30:17
35:13 i Ex 12:2-11
35:14 j S Ex 29:13
35:15 k S 1Ch 25:1; S 26:12-19; 2Ch 29:30; Ne 12:46; Ps 68:25
35:20 l Isa 10:9; Jer 46:2 m S Ge 2:14

35:1–19 The Chronicler gives much more extensive coverage to Josiah's Passover celebration than is found in the brief allusion in Kings (2Ki 23:21–23).
35:1 *first month.* The traditional month; contrast the Passover of Hezekiah (see note on 30:2).
35:3 *Put the sacred ark in the temple.* Implies that it had been removed, perhaps for protection during the evil reigns of Manasseh and Amon, who preceded Josiah.
35:4 *David … Solomon.* The Chronicler specifically parallels David and Solomon in three cases: 7:10 (contrast 1Ki 8:66, where only David is mentioned); 11:17; and here. This tendency reflects his glorification and idealization of both (see Introduction to 1 Chronicles: Portrait of David and Solomon).

35:7–9 The emphasis in Chronicles on voluntary and joyful giving (24:8–14; 29:31–36; 31:3–21; 1Ch 29:3–9) presumably had direct relevance to the postexilic readers for whom the Chronicler wrote.
35:18 *since the days of the prophet Samuel.* Instead of "in the days of the judges" (2Ki 23:22). This is the Chronicler's way of highlighting the importance of the prophets (see Introduction to 1 Chronicles: Purpose and Themes, 3).
35:19 *eighteenth year.* The same year as the discovery of the Book of the Law (34:8,14).
35:20–27 See 2Ki 23:28–30. In 609 b.c. Pharaoh Necho "went up to the Euphrates River to help the king of Assyria" (2Ki 23:29) against the Babylonians.

35:21 ⁿ S 1Ki 13:18;
S 2Ki 18:25
35:22 ᵒ S 1Sa 28:8
35:23 ᵖ S 1Ki 22:34
35:25 ᑫ S Ge 50:10;
Jer 22:10,15-16
ʳ 2Ch 34:28
36:1 ˢ S 2Ch 22:1
36:4 ᵗ Jer 22:10-12
ᵘ Eze 19:4
36:5 ᵛ Jer 22:18;
25:1; 26:1; 35:1; 36:1;
45:1; 46:2
36:6 ʷ Jer 25:9;
27:6; Eze 29:18
ˣ Eze 19:9; Da 1:1
36:7 ʸ ver 18;
Ezr 1:7; Jer 27:16;
Da 1:2

tle. ²¹But Necho sent messengers to him, saying, "What quarrel is there, king of Judah, between you and me? It is not you I am attacking at this time, but the house with which I am at war. God has told ⁿ me to hurry; so stop opposing God, who is with me, or he will destroy you."

²²Josiah, however, would not turn away from him, but disguised ᵒ himself to engage him in battle. He would not listen to what Necho had said at God's command but went to fight him on the plain of Megiddo.

²³Archers ᵖ shot King Josiah, and he told his officers, "Take me away; I am badly wounded." ²⁴So they took him out of his chariot, put him in his other chariot and brought him to Jerusalem, where he died. He was buried in the tombs of his ancestors, and all Judah and Jerusalem mourned for him.

²⁵Jeremiah composed laments for Josiah, and to this day all the male and female singers commemorate Josiah in the laments. ᑫ These became a tradition in Israel and are written in the Laments. ʳ

²⁶The other events of Josiah's reign and his acts of devotion in accordance with what is written in the Law of the LORD— ²⁷all the events, from beginning to end, are written in the book of the kings of Israel and Judah. ¹And the people ˢ of the land took Jehoahaz son of Josiah and made him king in Jerusalem in place of his father.

JEHOAHAZ KING OF JUDAH

36:2–4pp — 2Ki 23:31–34

²Jehoahaz ᵃ was twenty-three years old when he became king, and he reigned in Jerusalem three months. ³The king of Egypt dethroned him in Jerusalem and imposed on Judah a levy of a hundred talents ᵇ of silver and a talent ᶜ of gold. ⁴The king of Egypt made Eliakim, a brother of Jehoahaz, king over Judah and Jerusalem and changed Eliakim's name to Jehoiakim. But Necho ᵗ took Eliakim's brother Jehoahaz and carried him off to Egypt. ᵘ

JEHOIAKIM KING OF JUDAH

36:5–8pp — 2Ki 23:36—24:6

⁵Jehoiakim ᵛ was twenty-five years old when he became king, and he reigned in Jerusalem eleven years. He did evil in the eyes of the LORD his God. ⁶Nebuchadnezzar ʷ king of Babylon attacked him and bound him with bronze shackles to take him to Babylon. ˣ ⁷Nebuchadnezzar also took to Babylon articles from the temple of the LORD and put them in his temple ᵈ there. ʸ

⁸The other events of Jehoiakim's reign, the detestable things he did and all that was

---

ᵃ 2 Hebrew *Joahaz,* a variant of *Jehoahaz;* also in verse 4   ᵇ 3 That is, about 3 3/4 tons or about 3.4 metric tons   ᶜ 3 That is, about 75 pounds or about 34 kilograms   ᵈ 7 Or *palace*

C **35:21–22** Unique to the Chronicler, showing his view on retribution once again: Josiah's death in battle comes as a result of his disobedience to the word of God as heard even in the mouth of the pagan pharaoh.
35:21 *house with which I am at war.* A reference to the Babylonians; Nabopolassar was on the throne of Babylon, while his son Nebuchadnezzar was commanding the armies in the field. Nebuchadnezzar would succeed his father after another battle at Carchemish against Egypt in 605 B.C. Josiah may have been an ally of Babylon (see 32:31; 33:11 and notes).
35:22 *disguised himself.* Cf. Ahab and Jehoshaphat (see 18:29 and note).*plain of Megiddo.* See note on Jdg 5:19.
35:24b–25 Unique to Chronicles.
35:25 *Jeremiah composed laments for Josiah.* Jeremiah held Josiah in high esteem (Jer 22:15–16).The statement that he composed laments is one of the reasons the book of Lamentations has been traditionally associated with him.*to this day.* See note on 5:9.
36:2–14 Josiah is the only king of Judah to be succeeded by three of his sons (Jehoahaz, Jehoiakim and Zedekiah).The Chronicler's account of the reigns of the remaining kings of Judah is quite brief.
36:2 See 2Ki 23:31–35.With the death of Josiah at the hands

of Pharaoh Necho, Judah slipped into a period of Egyptian domination (vv. 3–4).*three months.* In 609 B.C. Necho's assertion of authority over Judah ended the brief 20 years of Judahite independence under Josiah.The Chronicler makes no moral judgment on this brief reign, though the author of Kings does (2Ki 23:32).
36:4 Just as Necho took Jehoahaz into captivity and replaced him with Eliakim, whose name he changed to Jehoiakim, so also Nebuchadnezzar would later take Jehoiachin to Babylon, replacing him with Mattaniah, whose name he changed to Zedekiah (2Ki 24:15–17). Each conqueror wanted to place his own man on the throne; the change of name implied authority over him.
36:5–8 See 2Ki 23:36—24:7. Jehoiakim persecuted the prophets and is the object of scathing denunciation by Jeremiah (Jer 25–26; 36). After the Egyptian defeat at Carchemish (Jer 46:2) in 605 B.C., Jehoiakim transferred allegiance to Nebuchadnezzar of Babylon.When he later rebelled and again allied himself with Egypt, Nebuchadnezzar sent a punitive army against him. But Jehoiakim died before the army arrived, and Nebuchadnezzar took his son Jehoiachin into captivity.
36:5 *eleven years.* 609–598 B.C.
36:6 *Nebuchadnezzar…attacked him.* See chart, p. 482.

found against him, are written in the book of the kings of Israel and Judah. And Jehoiachin his son succeeded him as king.

JEHOIACHIN KING OF JUDAH

36:9–10pp — 2Ki 24:8–17

[9]Jehoiachin[z] was eighteen[a] years old when he became king, and he reigned in Jerusalem three months and ten days. He did evil in the eyes of the LORD. [10]In the spring, King Nebuchadnezzar sent for him and brought him to Babylon,[a] together with articles of value from the temple of the LORD, and he made Jehoiachin's uncle,[b] Zedekiah, king over Judah and Jerusalem.

ZEDEKIAH KING OF JUDAH

36:11–16pp — 2Ki 24:18–20; Jer 52:1–3

[11]Zedekiah[b] was twenty-one years old when he became king, and he reigned in Jerusalem eleven years. [12]He did evil in the eyes of the LORD[c] his God and did not humble[d] himself before Jeremiah the prophet, who spoke the word of the LORD. [13]He also rebelled against King Nebuchadnezzar, who had made him take an oath[e] in God's name. He became stiff-necked[f] and hardened his heart and would not turn to the LORD, the God of Israel. [14]Furthermore, all the leaders of the priests and the people became more and more unfaithful,[g] following all the detestable practices of the nations and defiling the temple of the LORD, which he had consecrated in Jerusalem.

THE FALL OF JERUSALEM

36:17–20pp — 2Ki 25:1–21; Jer 52:4–27
36:22–23pp — Ezr 1:1–3

[15]The LORD, the God of their ancestors, sent word to them through his messengers[h] again and again,[i] because he had pity on his people and on his dwelling place. [16]But they mocked God's messengers, despised his words and scoffed[j] at his prophets until the wrath[k] of the LORD was aroused against his people and there was no remedy.[l] [17]He brought up against them the king of the Babylonians,[c][m] who killed their young men with the sword in the sanctuary, and spared neither young man[n] nor young woman, the elderly or the aged.[o] God gave them all into the hands of Nebuchadnezzar.[p] [18]He carried to Babylon all the articles[q] from the temple of God, both large and small, and the treasures of the LORD's temple and the treasures of the king and his officials. [19]They set fire[r] to God's temple[s] and broke down the wall[t] of Jerusalem; they burned all the palaces and destroyed[u] everything of value there.[v]

[20]He carried into exile[w] to Babylon the remnant, who escaped from the sword, and they became servants[x] to him and his successors until the kingdom of Persia came to power. [21]The land enjoyed its sabbath rests;[y] all the time of its desolation it rested,[z] until the seventy years[a] were completed in fulfillment of the word of the LORD spoken by Jeremiah.

[22]In the first year of Cyrus[b] king of Persia, in order to fulfill the word of the LORD spo-

---

[a] 9 One Hebrew manuscript, some Septuagint manuscripts and Syriac (see also 2 Kings 24:8); most Hebrew manuscripts *eight*   [b] 10 Hebrew *brother*, that is, relative (see 2 Kings 24:17)
[c] 17 Or *Chaldeans*

36:9 [z] Jer 22:24-28; 24:1; 27:20; 29:21; 52:31
36:10 [a] ver 18; S 2Ki 20:17; Ezr 1:7; Isa 30:17; Jer 14:18; 21:7; 22:25; 24:1; 27:16,20,22; 29:1; 34:21; 40:1; Eze 17:12; Da 5:2
36:11 [b] S 2Ki 24:17; Jer 27:1; 28:1; 34:2; 37:1; 39:1
36:12 [c] Jer 37:1-39:18 [d] S Dt 8:3; 2Ch 7:14; Jer 44:10
36:13 [e] Eze 17:13 [f] S Ex 32:9; S Dt 9:27
36:14 [g] S 1Ch 5:25
36:15 [h] Isa 5:4; 44:26; Jer 7:25; Hag 1:13; Zec 1:4; Mal 2:7; 3:1; S Mt 5:12 [i] Jer 7:13, 25; 11:7; 25:3-4; 35:14,15; 44:4-6
36:16 [j] S 2Ki 2:23; Job 8:2; Isa 28:14,22; 29:20; 57:4; Jer 5:13; 43:2; Mic 2:11 [k] Ezr 5:12; Pr 1:30-31; Jer 44:3 [l] Ne 9:30; Pr 29:1; Jer 7:26; 20:8; 25:4; 30:12; Da 9:6; Zec 1:2
36:17 [m] S Ge 10:10 [n] Jer 6:11; 9:21; 18:21; 44:7 [o] S Dt 32:25; Jer 51:22 [p] Ezr 5:12; Jer 32:28; La 2:21; Eze 9:6; 23:47
36:18 [q] S ver 7; S ver 10; Jer 27:20
36:19 [r] Jer 11:16; 17:27; 21:10,14; 22:7; 32:29; 39:8; La 4:11; Eze 20:47; Am 2:5; Zec 11:1 [s] 1Ki 9:8-9; La 2:6 [t] Ps 79:1-3
36:20 [w] S Lev 26:44; S 2Ki 24:14; Ezr 2:1; Ne 7:6 [x] Jer 27:7
36:21 [y] S Lev 25:4 [z] S 1Ch 22:9 [a] Jer 1:1; 25:11; 27:22; 29:10; 40:1; Da 9:2; Zec 1:12; 7:5
36:22 [b] Isa 44:28; 45:1,13; Da 1:21; 6:28; 10:1

36:9–10 See 2Ki 24:8–17; see also Jer 22:24–28; 24:1; 29:2; 52:31. Although Jehoiachin was taken into captivity (597 B.C.) with a large retinue, including the queen mother and high officials, and was succeeded by Zedekiah, the exiles continued to date in terms of his reign (Jer 52:31; Eze 1:2; cf. Est 2:5–6).
36:9 *three months and ten days.* 598–597 B.C.
36:11–14 See 2Ki 24:18–20; Jer 52:1–3. Verses 13b–14 are unique to the Chronicler (cf. Jer 1:3; 21:1–7; 24:8; 27:1–15; 32:1–5; 34:1–7,21; 37:1—39:7). Zedekiah succumbed to the temptation to look to Egypt for help and rebelled against Nebuchadnezzar. Babylonian reaction was swift. Jerusalem was besieged (Jer 21:3–7) in 588 B.C. and held out for over two years before being destroyed in the summer of 586.
36:11 *eleven years.* 597–586 B.C.
36:15–16 See 24:19 and note.
36:20–21 The conclusions of the two Biblical histories are interestingly different: 1. The author(s) of Kings had sought to show why the exile occurred and had traced the sad history of

Israel's disobedience to the exile. With the state at an end, the author(s) could still show God's faithfulness to his promises to David (2Ki 25:27–30) by reporting the favor bestowed on his descendants. 2. The Chronicler, whose vantage point was after the exile, was able to look back on the exile not only as judgment but also as containing hope for the future. For him the purified remnant had returned to a purified land (vv. 22–23), and a new era of hope was beginning. The exile was not judgment alone, but also blessing, for it allowed the land to catch up on its sabbath rests (Lev 26:40–45). And God had remembered his covenant (Lev 26:45) and restored his people to the land (see note on vv. 22–23).
36:22–23 Not found in Kings. It is repeated at the beginning of Ezra (1:1–3), which resumes the history at the point where Chronicles ends—indicating that Chronicles and Ezra may have been written by the same author. See the prophecy of Jeremiah (Jer 25:1–14; cf. Da 9). Cyrus also issued decrees for other captive peoples, allowing them to return to their

36:23 c S Jdg 4:10

ken by Jeremiah, the LORD moved the heart of Cyrus king of Persia to make a proclamation throughout his realm and also to put it in writing:

23"This is what Cyrus king of Persia says:

" 'The LORD, the God of heaven, has given me all the kingdoms of the earth and he has appointed c me to build a temple for him at Jerusalem in Judah. Any of his people among you—may the LORD their God be with them, and let them go up.' "

lands. Under God's sovereignty, this effort by a Persian king to win the favor of peoples treated harshly by the Babylonians also inaugurated the restoration period. See notes on Ezr 1:1–4.

36:22 *Cyrus king of Persia.* See chart, p. 482.
36:23 *God of heaven.* See note on Ezr 1:2.

RETURN FROM EXILE

Miles 0   100   200   300
Kms 0   100   200   300   400

PERSIAN EMPIRE

TRANS-EUPHRATES

1. RESTORATION of the exiles began under Cyrus (559–530 B.C.), who allowed them to return to Judah with the captured temple treasures.

2. THE TEMPLE was consecrated in 516 B.C. by official permission of Darius I (522–486).

3. EZRA won the approval of Artaxerxes I (465–424 B.C.) to return with additional exiles and to promote obedience to the Law; Nehemiah, to rebuild the walls of Jerusalem.

4. BABYLON and vicinity long retained a large and prosperous Jewish community, as clay tablets from the Murashu archives at Nippur testify.

Exact location of exiles' villages unknown:

Tel Melah
Tel Harsha
Kerub
Addon
Immer

Harran ·   Tiphsah ·   Tadmor ·   Byblos   Tyre   · Damascus   Samaria   Ashdod   · Rabbah   Jerusalem   · Dumah   Ecbatana ·   Babylon ·   · Nippur   · Susa

Tigris R.   Euphrates R.

EZRA AND NEHEMIAH — EZRA — INTRODUCTION

Although the caption to Ne 1:1, "The words of Nehemiah son of Hakaliah," indicates that Ezra and Nehemiah were originally two separate compositions, they were combined as one very early. Josephus (c. A.D. 37–100) and the Jewish Talmud refer to the book of Ezra but not to a separate book of Nehemiah. The oldest manuscripts of the Septuagint (the pre-Christian Greek translation of the OT) also treat Ezra and Nehemiah as one book, calling it Esdras B (Esdras A is an Apocryphal work).

Origen (c. A.D. 185–253) is the first writer known to distinguish between two books, which he called 1 Ezra and 2 Ezra. In translating the Latin Vulgate (c. A.D. 390–405), Jerome called Nehemiah the second book of Esdrae (Ezra). The English translations by Wycliffe (1382) and Coverdale (1535) called Ezra "I Esdras" and Nehemiah "II Esdras." The same separation first appeared in a Hebrew manuscript in 1448.

LITERARY FORM AND AUTHORSHIP

As in the closely related books of 1 and 2 Chronicles, one notes the prominence of various lists in Ezra and Nehemiah, which have evidently been obtained from official sources. Included are lists of (1) the temple articles (Ezr 1:9–11), (2) the returned exiles (Ezr 2, which is virtually the same as Ne 7:6–73), (3) the genealogy of Ezra (Ezr 7:1–5), (4) the heads of the clans (8:1–14), (5) those involved in mixed marriages (10:18–43), (6) those who helped rebuild the wall (Ne 3), (7) those who sealed the covenant (Ne 10:1–27), (8) residents of Jerusalem and other towns (Ne 11:3–36) and (9) priests and Levites (Ne 12:1–26).

B Also included in Ezra are seven official documents or letters (all in Aramaic except the first, which is in Hebrew): (1) the decree of Cyrus (1:2–4), (2) the accusation of Rehum and others against the Jews (4:11–16), (3) the reply of Artaxerxes I (4:17–22), (4) the report from Tattenai (5:7–17), (5) the memorandum of Cyrus's decree (6:2b–5), (6) Darius's reply to Tattenai (6:6–12) and (7) the authorization given by Artaxerxes I to Ezra (7:12–26). The documents are similar to contemporary non-Biblical documents of the Persian period.

Certain materials in Ezra are first-person extracts from his memoirs: 7:27–28; 8:1–34; 9. Other sections are written in the third person: 7:1–26; 10; see also Ne 8. Linguistic analysis has shown that the first-person and third-person extracts resemble each other, making it likely that the same author wrote both.

Most scholars conclude that the author/compiler of Ezra and Nehemiah was also the author of 1,2 Chronicles. This viewpoint is based on certain characteristics common to both Chronicles and Ezra-Nehemiah. The verses at the end of Chronicles and at the beginning of Ezra are virtually identical. Both Chronicles and Ezra-Nehemiah exhibit a fondness for lists, for the description of religious festivals and for such phrases as "heads of families" and "the house of God." Especially striking in these books is the prominence of Levites and temple personnel. The words for "singer," "gatekeeper" and "temple servants" are used almost exclusively in Ezra-Nehemiah and Chronicles. See Introduction to 1 Chronicles: Author, Date and Sources.

DATE

The Ezra memoirs (see note on 7:28) may be dated c. 440 B.C. and the Nehemiah memoirs c. 430. These were then combined with other materials somewhat later. See Introduction to 1 Chronicles: Author, Date and Sources.

THE ORDER OF EZRA AND NEHEMIAH

According to the traditional view, Ezra arrived in Jerusalem in the seventh year (Ezr 7:8) of Artaxerxes I (458 B.C.), followed by Nehemiah, who arrived in the king's 20th year (444; Ne 2:1,11).

　　Some have proposed a reverse order in which Nehemiah arrived in 444 B.C., while Ezra arrived in the seventh year of Artaxerxes II (398). By amending "seventh" (Ezr 7:8) to either "27th" or "37th," others place Ezra's arrival after Nehemiah's but still maintain that they were contemporaries.

　　These alternative views, however, present more problems than the traditional position. As the text stands, Ezra arrived before Nehemiah, and they are found together in Ne 8:9 (at the reading of the Law) and Ne 12:26,36 (at the dedication of the wall). See chart, p. 694; see also notes on Ne 1:1; 2:1.

LANGUAGES

Ezra and Nehemiah were written in a form of late Hebrew with the exception of Ezr 4:8—6:18; 7:12–26, which were written in Aramaic, the language of international diplomacy during the Persian period. Of these 67 Aramaic verses, 52 are in records or letters. Ezra evidently found these documents in Aramaic and copied them, inserting connecting verses in Aramaic.

MAJOR THEOLOGICAL THEMES

The books of Ezra and Nehemiah relate how God's covenant people were restored from Babylonian exile to the covenant land as a theocratic (kingdom of God) community, even while continuing under Gentile rule. The major theological themes of this account are:

　　1. The restoration of Israel from exile was God's doing. He moved the hearts of Persian emperors and of the repatriates and those who supported them, raised up prophets to prod and support the repatriates, protected them on the way and delivered them from their opponents, stirred up Ezra and Nehemiah to perform their separate ministries, and prospered the rebuilding of the temple and Jerusalem.

　　2. The restoration of the covenant community was complete—even though political independence was not attained. "All Israel" was repatriated through a representative remnant; the temple was rebuilt and its services (daily sacrifices, priestly ministries, Levitical praise, annual festivals) revived in accordance with the Law of Moses and the regulations instituted by David; the Law was reestablished as regulative for the life of the community; the "holy city" (Jerusalem) was rebuilt and inhabited; the people were purged; the covenant was renewed.

　　3. Just as God used the world powers to judge his people, so he used them to restore his people to their land; imperial action and authority directly and indirectly initiated, protected and sustained every aspect of the restoration.

　　4. Israel's restoration evoked fierce opposition, but that opposition was thwarted at every turn.

　　5. The restored community was a chastened people, yet they were also in

need of frequent rebuke and reformation. The Israelites remained a wayward people. They still awaited the "new covenant," of which Jeremiah had spoken (ch. 31), and the renewal to be effected by God's Spirit, as announced by Joel (ch. 2) and Ezekiel (chs. 36–37).

OUTLINE

1:1 *a* Jer 25:11-12;
29:10-14; Zec 1:12-16
b Ezr 6:22; 7:27
1:2 *c* S Jdg 4:10;
Ps 72:11; Isa 41:2,25;
44:28; 45:13; 46:11;
49:7,23; 60:3,10
d Hag 1:2
1:4 *e* Isa 10:20-22
f S Ex 3:22 *g* Nu 15:3;
Ps 50:14; 54:6; 116:17
h Ps 72:8-11;
Rev 21:24 *i* Ezr 3:7;
4:3; 5:13; 6:3,14
1:5 *j* 2Ch 11:1,3,10,
12,23; 15:2,8-9; 25:5;
31:1; 34:9; Ezr 4:1;
10:9; Ne 11:4; 12:34
k ver 1; Ex 35:20-22;
2Ch 36:22; Hag 1:14;
S Php 2:13 *l* Ps 127:1
1:6 *m* S Ex 3:22
1:7 *n* S 2Ki 24:13;
S 2Ch 36:7,10;
Ezr 5:14; 6:5;
Jer 52:17-19
1:8 *o* S 1Ch 3:18

CYRUS HELPS THE EXILES TO RETURN

1:1–3pp — 2Ch 36:22–23

In the first year of Cyrus king of Persia, in order to fulfill the word of the LORD spoken by Jeremiah, *a* the LORD moved the heart *b* of Cyrus king of Persia to make a proclamation throughout his realm and also to put it in writing:

²"This is what Cyrus king of Persia says:

" 'The LORD, the God of heaven, has given me all the kingdoms of the earth and he has appointed *c* me to build *d* a temple for him at Jerusalem in Judah. ³Any of his people among you—may their God be with them, and let them go up to Jerusalem in Judah and build the temple of the LORD, the God of Israel, the God who is in Jerusalem. ⁴And in any locality where survivors *e* may now be living, the people are to provide them with silver and gold, *f* with goods and livestock, and with freewill offerings *g* for the temple of God *h* in Jerusalem.' " *i*

⁵Then the family heads of Judah and Benjamin, *j* and the priests and Levites—everyone whose heart God had moved *k*—prepared to go up and build the house *l* of the LORD in Jerusalem. ⁶All their neighbors assisted them with articles of silver and gold, *m* with goods and livestock, and with valuable gifts, in addition to all the freewill offerings. ⁷Moreover, King Cyrus brought out the articles belonging to the temple of the LORD, which Nebuchadnezzar had carried away from Jerusalem and had placed in the temple of his god. *a* *n* ⁸Cyrus king of Persia had them brought by Mithredath the treasurer, who counted them out to Sheshbazzar *o* the prince of Judah.

⁹This was the inventory:

gold dishes	30
silver dishes	1,000

a 7 Or *gods*

1:1–3a Virtually identical with the last two verses of 2 Chronicles. This fact has been used to argue that Chronicles and Ezra-Nehemiah were written and/or edited by the same person, the so-called Chronicler. However, the repetition may have been a device of the author of Chronicles (or less probably of Ezra) to dovetail the narratives chronologically.

1:1 *first year.* Of the reign of Cyrus over Babylon, beginning in March, 538 B.C., after he captured Babylon in October, 539. Cyrus, the founder of the Persian empire, reigned over the Persians from 559 until 530 (see chart, p. 482). Isa 44:28; 45:1 speak of him as the Lord's "shepherd" and his "anointed." *to fulfill the word of the LORD spoken by Jeremiah.* Jeremiah prophesied a 70-year Babylonian exile (Jer 25:11–12; 29:10). The first deportation began in 605, the third year of Jehoiakim (see Da 1:1 and note); in 538, approximately 70 years later, the people began to return.

1:2–4 This oral proclamation of Cyrus's decree was written in Hebrew, the language of the Israelite captives, in contrast to the copy of the decree in 6:3–5, which was an Aramaic memorandum for the archives.

1:2 *God of heaven.* A Persian title for God. Of the 22 OT occurrences of the phrase, 17 occur in Ezra, Nehemiah and Daniel. *temple … at Jerusalem.* Jerusalem and the house of God are prominent subjects in Ezra and Nehemiah.

1:3 Cyrus instituted the policy of placating the gods of his subject peoples instead of carrying off their idols as the Assyrians and the Babylonians had done earlier. His generosity to the Jews was paralleled by his benevolence to the Babylonians.

1:4 *any locality where survivors may now be living, the people.* Probably designates the many Jews who did not wish to leave Mesopotamia. *freewill offerings.* A key to the restoration of God's temple and its services (see 2:68; 3:5; 8:28).

1:5 *family heads.* In ancient times families were extended families—more like clans than modern nuclear families. The authority figure was the patriarch, who was the "family head." See 10:16; see also 2:59; Ne 7:61; 10:34. *Judah and Benjamin.* The two main tribes of the kingdom of Judah, which the Babylonians had exiled. *Levites.* See Introduction to Leviticus: Title.

1:7 It was the custom for conquerors to carry off the images of

the gods of conquered cities. Since the Jews did not have an image of the Lord (see note on Ex 20:4), Nebuchadnezzar (see chart, p. 482) carried away only the temple articles.

1:8 *Mithredath.* A Persian name meaning "given by/to Mithra," a Persian god who became popular among Roman soldiers in the second century A.D. *Sheshbazzar.* A Babylonian name meaning either "Sin, protect the father" or "Shamash/Shashu, protect the father." Sin was the moon-god, and Shamash (Shashu is a variant) was the sun-god. In spite of his Babylonian name, Sheshbazzar was probably a Jewish official who served as a deputy governor of Judah under the satrap in Samaria (see 5:14). Some believe that Sheshbazzar and Zerubbabel were the same person and give the following reasons: 1. Both were governors (5:14; Hag 1:1; 2:2). 2. Both are said to have laid the foundation of the temple (3:2–8; 5:16; Hag 1:14–15; Zec 4:6–10). 3. Jews in Babylon were often given "official" Babylonian names (cf. Da 1:7). 4. Josephus (*Antiquities,* 11.1.3) seems to identify Sheshbazzar with Zerubbabel.

Others point out, however, that the Apocrypha distinguishes between the two men (1 Esdras 6:18). Furthermore, it is likely that Sheshbazzar was an elderly man at the time of the return, while Zerubbabel was probably a younger contemporary. Sheshbazzar also may have been viewed as the official governor, while Zerubbabel served as the popular leader (3:8–11). Whereas the high priest Joshua is associated with Zerubbabel, no priest is associated with Sheshbazzar. Although Sheshbazzar presided over the foundation of the temple in 536 B.C., so little was accomplished that Zerubbabel had to preside over a second foundation some 16 years later (see Hag 1:14–15; Zec 4:6–10).

Still others hold that Sheshbazzar is to be identified with Shenazzar (1Ch 3:18), the fourth son of King Jehoiachin. Zerubbabel would then have been Sheshbazzar's nephew (compare 3:2 with 1Ch 3:17–18).

1:9–11 When Assyrian and Babylonian conquerors carried off plunder, their scribes made a careful inventory of all the goods seized. The total of the figures in vv. 9–10 adds up to 2,499 rather than the 5,400 of v. 11. It may be that only the larger and more valuable vessels were specified.

silver pans[a]	29
[10] gold bowls	30
matching silver bowls	410
other articles	1,000

[11]In all, there were 5,400 articles of gold and of silver. Sheshbazzar brought all these along with the exiles when they came up from Babylon to Jerusalem.

THE LIST OF THE EXILES WHO RETURNED

2:1–70pp — Ne 7:6–73

2 Now these are the people of the province who came up from the captivity of the exiles,[p] whom Nebuchadnezzar king of Babylon[q] had taken captive to Babylon (they returned to Jerusalem and Judah, all to their own towns,[r] [2]in company with Zerubbabel,[s] Joshua,[t] Nehemiah, Seraiah,[u] Reelaiah, Mordecai, Bilshan, Mispar, Bigvai, Rehum and Baanah):

The list of the men of the people of Israel:

[3]the descendants of Parosh[v]	2,172
[4]of Shephatiah	372
[5]of Arah	775
[6]of Pahath-Moab (through the line of Jeshua and Joab)	2,812
[7]of Elam	1,254
[8]of Zattu	945
[9]of Zakkai	760
[10]of Bani	642
[11]of Bebai	623
[12]of Azgad	1,222
[13]of Adonikam[w]	666
[14]of Bigvai	2,056
[15]of Adin	454
[16]of Ater (through Hezekiah)	98
[17]of Bezai	323
[18]of Jorah	112
[19]of Hashum	223
[20]of Gibbar	95
[21]the men of Bethlehem[x]	123
[22]of Netophah	56
[23]of Anathoth	128
[24]of Azmaveth	42

[a] 9 The meaning of the Hebrew for this word is uncertain.

2:1 P S 2Ch 36:20
q S 2Ki 24:16; 25:12
r ver 70; 1Ch 9:2;
Ne 7:73; 11:3
2:2 s 1Ch 3:19;
Mt 1:12; Lk 3:27
t Ezr 3:2; 5:2; 10:18;
Ne 12:1,8; Hag 1:1,12;
2:4; Zec 3:1-10; 6:9-
15 u 1Ch 6:14;
Ne 10:2; 11:11; 12:1
2:3 v Ezr 8:3; 10:25;
Ne 3:25
2:13 w Ezr 8:13
2:21 x Mic 5:2

1:11 We are not told anything about the details of Sheshbazzar's journey, which probably took place in 537 B.C. Judging from Ezra's later journey (7:8–9), the trip took about four months. See map No. 8b at the end of this study Bible; see also map, p. 688.
2:1–70 The list of returning exiles in ch. 2 almost exactly parallels the list in Ne 7:6–73 (see also 1 Esdras 5:4–46 in the Apocrypha). The list of localities indicates that people retained the memories of their homes and that exiles from a wide background of tribes, villages and towns returned. In comparing the list here with that in Ne 7, one notes many differences in the names and numbers listed. About 20 percent of the numbers, e.g., are not the same in Ezra and Nehemiah. Many of these differences may be explained, however, by assuming that a cipher notation was used with vertical strokes for units and horizontal strokes for tens, which led to copying errors.
2:1 *province.* Probably Judah (cf. 5:8, where the Aramaic word for "province" is translated "district"; see also Ne 1:3).
2:2 *Zerubbabel.* See notes on 3:2; 5:2. *Joshua.* Means "The LORD saves." The Greek form is "Jesus" (see TNIV text note on Mt 1:21). This Joshua is the same as the Joshua of Hag 1:1, the son of the high priest Jozadak (see Ezr 3:2), who was taken into exile (1Ch 6:15). *Nehemiah.* Not the Nehemiah of the book by that name. *Mordecai.* A Babylonian name based on that of

Marduk, the god of Babylon (cf. Jer 50:2). Esther's cousin had the same name (see Est 2:5 and note).
2:3 *Parosh.* Means "flea" (Israelites were often named after insects and animals). Other members of this family, as well as of several other families named in vv. 6–14, returned with Ezra (8:3–14).
2:5 *Arah.* Probably means "wild ox." Since the name is rare in the OT and has been found in documents from Mesopotamia, it may have been adopted during the exile.
2:6 *Pahath-Moab.* Means "governor of Moab" and may have once designated an official title.
2:12 *Azgad.* Cf. 8:12; means "Gad is strong." It is a reference either to Gad (the god of fortune, referred to in Isa 65:11) or to the Transjordanian tribe of Gad.
2:16 *Ater.* Means "left-handed," as in Jdg 3:15; 20:16.
2:21–35 Whereas the names in vv. 3–20 are of families, vv. 21–35 present a series of villages and towns, many of which were in Benjamite territory north of Jerusalem. It is significant that there are no references to towns in the Negev, south of Judah. When Nebuchadnezzar overran Judah in 597 B.C. (Jer 13:19), the Edomites (see the book of Obadiah) took advantage of the situation and occupied that area.
2:23 *Anathoth.* See note on Jer 1:1.

Dates below are given according to a Nisan-to-Nisan Jewish calendar (see chart, p. 105).
Roman numerals represent months;
Arabic numerals represent days.

YEAR	MONTH	DAY	EVENT	REFERENCE
539 B.C.	Oct.	12	Capture of Babylon	Da 5:30
538	Mar.	24	Cyrus's first year	Ezr 1:1–4
537	to Mar.	11		
537(?)			Return under Sheshbazzar	Ezr 1:11
537	VII		Building of altar	Ezr 3:1
536	II		Work on temple begun	Ezr 3:8
536–530			Opposition during Cyrus's reign	Ezr 4:1–5
530–520			Work on temple ceased	Ezr 4:24
520	VI	24	Work on temple renewed under Darius	Ezr 5:2; Hag 1:14
	=Sept.	21		
516	XII	3	Temple completed	Ezr 6:15
	=Mar.	12		
458	I	1	Ezra departs from Babylon	Ezr 7:6–9
	=Apr.	8		
	V	1	Ezra arrives in Jerusalem	Ezr 7:8–9
	=Aug.	4		
	IX	20	People assemble	Ezr 10:9
	=Dec.	19		
	X	1	Committee begins investigation	Ezr 10:16
	=Dec.	29		
457	I	1	Committee ends investigation	Ezr 10:17
	=Mar.	27		
445	Apr.	13	20th year of Artaxerxes I	Ne 1:1
444	to Apr.	2		
444	I		Nehemiah approaches the king	Ne 2:1
	=Mar.–Apr.			
	Aug.(?)		Nehemiah arrives in Jerusalem	Ne 2:11
	VI	25	Completion of wall	Ne 6:15
	=Oct.	2		
	VII=Oct.	8	Public assembly	Ne 7:73—8:1
	to Nov.	5		
	VII	15–22	Festival of Tabernacles	Ne 8:14
	=Oct.	22–28		
	VII	24	Fast	Ne 9:1
	=Oct.	30		
433	Apr.	1	32nd year of Artaxerxes;	Ne 5:14; 13:6
432	to Apr.	19	Nehemiah's recall and return	

540 B.C.

530

520

510

500

490

480

470

460

450

440

430 B.C.

²⁵of Kiriath Jearim,^a Kephirah and Beeroth   743
²⁶of Ramah^y and Geba   621
²⁷of Mikmash   122
²⁸of Bethel and Ai^z   223
²⁹of Nebo   52
³⁰of Magbish   156
³¹of the other Elam   1,254
³²of Harim   320
³³of Lod, Hadid and Ono   725
³⁴of Jericho^a   345
³⁵of Senaah   3,630

³⁶The priests:

the descendants of Jedaiah^b (through the family of Jeshua)   973
³⁷of Immer^c   1,052
³⁸of Pashhur^d   1,247
³⁹of Harim^e   1,017

⁴⁰The Levites:^f

the descendants of Jeshua^g and Kadmiel (of the line of Hodaviah)   74

⁴¹The musicians:^h

the descendants of Asaph   128

⁴²The gatekeepersⁱ of the temple:

the descendants of
Shallum, Ater, Talmon,
Akkub, Hatita and Shobai   139

⁴³The temple servants:^j

the descendants of
Ziha, Hasupha, Tabbaoth,
⁴⁴Keros, Siaha, Padon,
⁴⁵Lebanah, Hagabah, Akkub,
⁴⁶Hagab, Shalmai, Hanan,
⁴⁷Giddel, Gahar, Reaiah,
⁴⁸Rezin, Nekoda, Gazzam,
⁴⁹Uzza, Paseah, Besai,
⁵⁰Asnah, Meunim, Nephusim,
⁵¹Bakbuk, Hakupha, Harhur,
⁵²Bazluth, Mehida, Harsha,
⁵³Barkos, Sisera, Temah,
⁵⁴Neziah and Hatipha

---

^a 25 See Septuagint (see also Neh. 7:29); Hebrew *Kiriath Arim.*

2:26 *y* S Jos 18:25
2:28 *z* S Ge 12:8
2:34 *a* 1Ki 16:34;
2Ch 28:15
2:36 *b* S 1Ch 24:7
2:37 *c* S 1Ch 24:14
2:38 *d* S 1Ch 9:12
2:39 *e* S 1Ch 24:8
2:40 *f* Ge 29:34;
Nu 3:9; Dt 18:6-7;
1Ch 16:4; Ezr 7:7;
8:15; Ne 12:24
g Ezr 3:9
2:41 *h* S 1Ch 15:16
2:42 *i* 1Sa 3:15;
S 1Ch 9:17
2:43 *j* S 1Ch 9:2;
Ne 11:21

B **2:28** *Bethel.* See note on Ge 12:8. Towns such as Bethel, Mizpah, Gibeon and Gibeah seem to have escaped the Babylonian assault. Bethel, however, was destroyed in the transition between the Babylonian and Persian periods. Archaeological excavations reveal that there was a small town on the site in Ezra's day. *Ai.* See note on Jos 7:2.
2:31 See v. 7.
2:33 *Lod.* Modern Lydda.
2:35 *Senaah.* The largest number of returnees—3,630 (3,930 in Ne 7:38)—is associated with Senaah. It has therefore been suggested that they did not come from a specific locality or family but represented the poorer and lower classes of people, as inferred from the meaning of the name ("the hated one").
2:36–39 Four clans of priests numbering 4,289, about a tenth of the total.
2:40 *Levites.* See Introduction to Leviticus: Title. *74.* The number of Levites who returned was relatively small (cf. 8:15). Since the Levites had been entrusted with the menial tasks of temple ser-

vice, many of them may have found a more comfortable way of life in exile.
2:41 *Asaph.* One of the three Levites appointed by David over the temple singers (1Ch 25:1; 2Ch 5:12; 35:15), whose duties are detailed in 1Ch 15:16–24.
2:42 *gatekeepers.* Usually Levites (1Ch 9:26; 2Ch 23:4; 35:15; Ne 12:25; 13:22). They are mentioned 16 times in Ezra-Nehemiah and 19 times in Chronicles. Their primary function was to tend the doors and gates of the temple (1Ch 9:17–27) and to perform other menial tasks (1Ch 9:28–32; 2Ch 31:14).
2:43–58 The temple servants and the descendants of Solomon's servants together numbered 392 (v. 58), which was more than the total of the Levites, singers and gatekeepers together (vv. 40–42).
2:46 *Hanan.* Means "(God) is gracious." The verb "to be gracious" and its derivatives are the components of numerous personal names in the OT—e.g., Johanan ("The LORD is gracious"; see 8:12), which has given us the English name John (see note on Mk 1:4).

2:58 *k* S 1Ch 9:2
2:59 *l* S Nu 1:18
2:61 *m* S 2Sa 17:27
2:62 *n* Nu 3:10;
16:39-40
2:63 *o* Lev 2:3,10
p S Ex 28:30
2:65 *q* S 2Sa 19:35
2:66 *r* Isa 66:20
2:68 *s* S Ex 25:2

⁵⁵The descendants of the servants of Solomon:

the descendants of
Sotai, Hassophereth, Peruda,
⁵⁶Jaala, Darkon, Giddel,
⁵⁷Shephatiah, Hattil,
Pokereth-Hazzebaim and Ami

⁵⁸The temple servants *k* and the descendants of the servants of
Solomon   392

⁵⁹The following came up from the towns of Tel Melah, Tel Harsha, Kerub, Addon and Immer, but they could not show that their families were descended *l* from Israel:

⁶⁰The descendants of
Delaiah, Tobiah and Nekoda   652

⁶¹And from among the priests:

The descendants of
Hobaiah, Hakkoz and Barzillai (a man who had married a daughter of Barzillai the Gileadite *m* and was called by that name).
⁶²These searched for their family records, but they could not find them and so were excluded from the priesthood *n* as unclean. ⁶³The governor ordered them not to eat any of the most sacred food *o* until there was a priest ministering with the Urim and Thummim. *p*

⁶⁴The whole company numbered 42,360, ⁶⁵besides their 7,337 male and female slaves; and they also had 200 male and female singers. *q* ⁶⁶They had 736 horses, *r* 245 mules, ⁶⁷435 camels and 6,720 donkeys.

⁶⁸When they arrived at the house of the Lᴏʀᴅ in Jerusalem, some of the heads of the families *s* gave freewill offerings toward the rebuilding of the house of God on its site. ⁶⁹According to their ability they gave to the treasury for this work 61,000 darics *a* of gold, 5,000 minas *b* of silver and 100 priestly garments.
⁷⁰The priests, the Levites, the musicians, the gatekeepers and the temple servants set-

---

a 69 That is, about 1,100 pounds or about 500 kilograms   *b* 69 That is, about 3 tons or about 2.8 metric tons

---

2:55,58 *descendants of the servants of Solomon*. The phrase occurs only here and in Ne 7:57,60; 11:3. These may be the descendants of the Canaanites whom Solomon enslaved (1Ki 9:20–21).
2:59–63 Individuals who lacked evidence of their ancestry.

2:59 *towns*. Places in Mesopotamia where the Jews were settled by their Babylonian captors. *Tel Melah*. Means "mound of salt," possibly a mound on which salt had been scattered (see Jdg 9:45 and note). The Hebrew word *tel* designates a hill-like mound (see note on Jos 11:13) formed by the remains of a ruined city. The Jewish exiles had been settled along the Kebar River (Eze 1:1), perhaps near Nippur, a city in southern Mesopotamia that was the stronghold of rebels. The Jews had probably been settled on the mounds of ruined cities that had been depopulated by the Babylonians.
2:63 *governor*. Probably either Sheshbazzar or Zerubbabel (see note on 1:8). *Urim and Thummim*. See note on Ex 28:30.
2:64 *42,360*. Considerably more than the sum of the other figures given:

Categories	Ezra	Nehemiah	1 Esdras
Men of Israel	24,144	25,406	25,947
Priests	4,289	4,289	5,288
Levites, musicians, gatekeepers	341	360	341
Temple servants, descendants of Solomon's servants	392	392	372
Men of unproven origin	652	642	652
Totals	29,818	31,089	32,600

It is difficult to account for the difference of about 10,000–12,000. The figure may refer to an unspecified 10,000–12,000 women and/or children, and it doubtless includes the priests of unproven origin referred to in vv. 61–63. Some suggest that the groups explicitly counted were returnees from Judah and Benjamin, while the remainder were from other tribes.
2:65 *male and female slaves*. The ratio of slaves to others (one to six) is relatively high. The fact that so many returned with their masters speaks highly of the benevolent treatment of servants by the Jews. *singers*. The male and female singers listed here may be secular singers who sang at social events such as weddings and funerals (2Ch 35:25), as distinct from the temple singers (or musicians) of v. 41, who were all male.
2:66 *horses*. Perhaps a donation from Cyrus for the nobility. *mules*. See 1Ki 1:33 and note.
2:67 *donkeys*. Were used to carry loads, women or children. Sheep, goats and cattle are not mentioned. They would have slowed the caravan.
2:68 *arrived ... Jerusalem*. For the route of the return from exile, see map No. 8b at the end of this study Bible; see also map, p. 688.
2:69 The parallel passage (Ne 7:70–72) gives a fuller description than the account in Ezra. In Ezra the gifts come from the heads of the families (v. 68), while in Nehemiah the gifts are credited to three sources: the governor, the heads of the families, and the rest of the people. *darics*. See note on 1Ch 29:7. Some believe that the coin intended was the Greek *drachma*, a silver coin. *minas*. In the sexagesimal system (based on the number 60) there were 60 shekels in a mina and 60 minas in a talent. A shekel, which was about two-fifths of an ounce of silver, was the average wage for a month's work. Thus a mina would be the equivalent of five years' wages, and a talent would be 300 years' wages.
2:70 Later, Nehemiah (11:1–2) would be compelled to move people by lot to reinforce the population of Jerusalem.

tled in their own towns, along with some of the other people, and the rest of the Israelites settled in their towns. [t]

REBUILDING THE ALTAR

3 When the seventh month came and the Israelites had settled in their towns, [u] the people assembled [v] with one accord in Jerusalem. [2] Then Joshua [w] son of Jozadak [x] and his fellow priests and Zerubbabel son of Shealtiel [y] and his associates began to build the altar of the God of Israel to sacrifice burnt offerings on it, in accordance with what is written in the Law of Moses [z] the man of God. [3] Despite their fear [a] of the peoples around them, they built the altar on its foundation and sacrificed burnt offerings on it to the LORD, both the morning and evening sacrifices. [b] [4] Then in accordance with what is written, they celebrated the Festival of Tabernacles [c] with the required number of burnt offerings prescribed for each day. [5] After that, they presented the regular burnt offerings, the New Moon [d] sacrifices and the sacrifices for all the appointed sacred festivals of the LORD, [e] as well as those brought as freewill offerings to the LORD. [6] On the first day of the seventh month they began to offer burnt offerings to the LORD, though the foundation of the LORD's temple had not yet been laid.

REBUILDING THE TEMPLE

[7] Then they gave money to the masons and carpenters, [f] and gave food and drink and olive oil to the people of Sidon and Tyre, so that they would bring cedar logs [g] by sea from Lebanon [h] to Joppa, as authorized by Cyrus [i] king of Persia.

[8] In the second month [j] of the second year after their arrival at the house of God in Jerusalem, Zerubbabel [k] son of Shealtiel, Joshua son of Jozadak and the rest of the people (the priests and the Levites and all who had returned from the captivity to Jerusalem) began the work, appointing Levites twenty [l] years old and older to supervise the building of the house of the LORD. [9] Joshua [m] and his sons and brothers and Kadmiel and his sons (descendants of Hodaviah[a]) and the sons of Henadad and their sons and brothers—all Levites—joined together in supervising those working on the house of God.

[10] When the builders laid [n] the foundation of the temple of the LORD, the priests in their vestments and with trumpets, [o] and the Levites (the sons of Asaph) with cymbals, took their places to praise [p] the LORD, as prescribed by David [q] king of Israel. [r] [11] With praise and thanksgiving they sang to the LORD:

> "He is good;
>   his love toward Israel endures forever." [s]

And all the people gave a great shout [t] of praise to the LORD, because the foundation [u] of the house of the LORD was laid. [12] But many of the older priests and Levites and family heads, who had seen the former temple, [v] wept [w] aloud when they saw the foundation of this temple being laid, while many others shouted for joy. [13] No one could distinguish the sound of the shouts of joy [x] from the sound of weeping, because the people made so much noise. And the sound was heard far away.

[a] 9 Hebrew *Yehudah*, a variant of *Hodaviah*

2:70 [t] S ver 1; S 1Ch 9:2; Ne 11:3- 4
3:1 [u] Ne 7:73; [v] S Lev 23:24
3:2 [w] S Ezr 2:2; [x] Hag 1:1; Zec 6:11; [y] 1Ch 3:17; [z] S Ex 20:24; Dt 12:5-6
3:3 [a] Ezr 4:4; Da 9:25 [b] S Ex 29:39; Nu 28:1-8
3:4 [c] S Ex 23:16; Nu 29:12-38; Ne 8:14-18; Zec 14:16-19
3:5 [d] S Nu 28:3,11, 14; Col 2:16; [e] Lev 23:1-44; S Nu 29:39
3:7 [f] Ch 22:15; [g] Isa 35:2; 60:13; [h] S Ezr 1:2- 4
3:8 [i] 1Ki 6:1
3:9 [m] Ezr 2:40
3:10 [n] Ezr 5:16; 6:3; Hag 2:15 [o] S Nu 10:2; S 2Sa 6:5; 1Ch 16:6; 2Ch 5:13; Ne 12:35; [p] S 1Ch 25:1; [q] S 1Ch 6:31 [r] Zec 6:12
3:11 [s] 1Ch 16:34,41; S 2Ch 7:3; Ps 30:5; 107:1; 118:1; 138:8; [t] S Ezr 6:5,10; [u] Hag 2:18; Zec 4:9; 8:9
3:12 [v] Hag 2:3,9; [w] Jer 31:9; 50:4
3:13 [x] Job 8:21; 33:26; Ps 27:6; 42:4; Isa 16:9; Jer 48:33

3:1 *seventh month.* Tishri (September-October), about three months after the arrival of the exiles in Judah (in 537 B.C.). Tishri was one of the most sacred months of the Jewish year (see Lev 23:23–43 and notes).
3:2 *Joshua…Zerubbabel.* The priest takes precedence over the civil leader in view of the nature of the occasion (contrast 3:8; 4:3; 5:2; Hag 1:1).
3:4 *Festival of Tabernacles.* See Lev 23:33–43 and notes.
3:5 *New Moon.* See note on 1Sa 20:5. *appointed sacred festivals.* See note on Lev 23:2. *freewill offerings.* See note on 1:4. It is noteworthy that the restoration of the sacrifices preceded the erection of the temple itself.
3:7 *cedar logs.* As in the case of the first temple, the Phoenicians cooperated by sending timber and workers (1Ki 5:6–12).
3:8 *second month.* The same month (April-May) in which Solomon had begun his temple (1Ki 6:1). *second year.* Since the Jews probably returned to Judah in the spring of 537 B.C., the second year would be the spring of 536. *twenty years.* In earlier times the lower age limit for Levites was 30 (Nu 4:3) or 25 years (Nu 8:24). It was later reduced to 20 (1Ch 23:24,27; 2Ch 31:17),

probably because there were so few Levites.
3:10 *trumpets.* Made of hammered silver (see Nu 10:2 and note). According to Josephus (*Antiquities*, 3.12.6), the trumpet was "in length a little short of a cubit; it is a narrow tube, slightly thicker than a flute." With the possible exception of their use at the coronation of Joash (2Ki 11:14; 2Ch 23:13), the trumpets were always blown by priests. They were most often used on joyous occasions, such as here and at the dedication of the rebuilt walls of Jerusalem (Ne 12:35; cf. 2Ch 5:13; Ps 98:6). *cymbals.* The Hebrew for this word occurs 13 times in the OT, all in Chronicles except here and Ne 12:27.
3:11 *sang.* May mean "sang responsively," referring to antiphonal singing by a choir divided into two groups. *He is good …endures forever.* See introduction to Ps 136.
3:13 *shouts of joy…sound of weeping.* The people of Israel were accustomed to showing their emotions in visible and audible ways (10:1; Ne 1:4; 8:9). The same God who had permitted judgment had now brought them back and would enable them to complete the project. A Babylonian cornerstone reads: "I started the work weeping, I finished it rejoicing." Cf. Ps 126:5–6.

4:1 ʸNe 2:20
4:2 ᶻS 2Ki 17:24
ᵃS 2Ki 17:41
4:3 ᵇEzr 1:1-4
4:4 ᶜS Ezr 3:3

| OPPOSITION TO THE REBUILDING

4 When the enemies of Judah and Benjamin heard that the exiles were building ʸ a temple for the LORD, the God of Israel, ²they came to Zerubbabel and to the heads of the families and said, "Let us help you build because, like you, we seek your God and have been sacrificing to him since the time of Esarhaddon ᶻ king of Assyria, who brought us here." ᵃ

³But Zerubbabel, Joshua and the rest of the heads of the families of Israel answered, "You have no part with us in building a temple to our God. We alone will build it for the LORD, the God of Israel, as King Cyrus, the king of Persia, commanded us." ᵇ

⁴Then the peoples around them set out to discourage the people of Judah and make them afraid to go on building. ᵃ ᶜ ⁵They bribed officials to work against them and frustrate

ᵃ 4 Or *and troubled them as they built*

4:1–23 A summary of various attempts to thwart the efforts of the Jews. In vv. 1–5 the author describes events in the reign of Cyrus (559–530 B.C.), in v. 6 the reign of Xerxes (486–465) and in vv. 7–23 the reign of Artaxerxes I (465–424). He then reverts in v. 24 to the time of Darius I (522–486), during whose reign the temple was completed (see 5:1–2; 6:13–15; Haggai; Zec 1:1–17; 4:9).
4:1 *enemies.* The people who offered their "help" (v. 2) were from Samaria. *Judah and Benjamin.* See notes on 1:5; 1Ki 12:21.
4:2 After the fall of Samaria in 722–721 B.C., the Assyrian kings

brought in people from Mesopotamia and Aram (modern Syria).These people served their own gods but also took up the worship of the Lord as the god of the land (2Ki 17:24–41). *Esarhaddon.* See note on 2Ki 19:37; see also chart, p.482.
4:4 *make them afraid.* The Hebrew for this verb often describes the fear aroused in a battle situation (Jdg 20:41; 2Sa 4:1; 2Ch 32:18).
4:5 *bribed.* Cf. the hiring of Balaam (Dt 23:4–5; Ne 13:2) and the hiring of a prophet to intimidate Nehemiah (Ne 6:12–13). *Darius king of Persia.* See chart, p.482.

ZERUBBABEL'S TEMPLE

W N S E

Movable stands of bronze

CUBITS

FEET

Altar

Sea

Construction of the second temple was started in 536 B.C. on the Solomonic foundations leveled a half-century earlier by the Babylonians. People who remembered the earlier temple wept at the comparison (Ezr 3:12). Not until 516 B.C., the 6th year of the Persian emperor Darius I (522–486), was the temple finally completed at the urging of Haggai and Zechariah (Ezr 6:13–15).

B Archaeological evidence confirms that the Persian period in the Holy Land was a comparatively impoverished one in terms of material culture. Later Aramaic documents from Elephantine in Upper Egypt illustrate the official process of gaining permission to construct a Jewish place of worship and the opposition engendered by such a project.

Of the temple and its construction, little is known. Consequently, all art reconstructions of it are tentative. Among the few contemporary buildings, the Persian palace at Lachish and the Tobiad monument at Iraq el-Amir may be compared in terms of technique.

Unlike the more famous structures razed in 586 B.C. and A.D. 70, the temple begun by Zerubbabel suffered no major hostile destruction, but was gradually repaired and reconstructed over a long period. Eventually it was replaced entirely by Herod's magnificent edifice.

©1981 Hugh Claycombe

their plans during the entire reign of Cyrus king of Persia and down to the reign of Darius king of Persia.

LATER OPPOSITION UNDER XERXES AND ARTAXERXES

⁶At the beginning of the reign of Xerxes, ᵃ ᵈ they lodged an accusation against the people of Judah and Jerusalem. ᵉ

⁷And in the days of Artaxerxes ᶠ king of Persia, Bishlam, Mithredath, Tabeel and the rest of his associates wrote a letter to Artaxerxes. The letter was written in Aramaic script and in the Aramaic ᵍ language. ᵇ,ᶜ

⁸Rehum the commanding officer and Shimshai the secretary wrote a letter against Jerusalem to Artaxerxes the king as follows:

⁹Rehum the commanding officer and Shimshai the secretary, together with the rest of their associates ʰ—the judges, officials and administrators over the people from Persia, Uruk ⁱ and Babylon, the Elamites of Susa, ʲ ¹⁰and the other people whom the great and honorable Ashurbanipal ᵏ deported and settled in the city of Samaria and elsewhere in Trans-Euphrates. ˡ

¹¹(This is a copy of the letter they sent him.)

To King Artaxerxes,

From your servants in Trans-Euphrates:

¹²The king should know that the people who came up to us from you have gone to Jerusalem and are rebuilding that rebellious and wicked city. They are restoring the walls and repairing the foundations. ᵐ

¹³Furthermore, the king should know that if this city is built and its walls are restored, no more taxes, tribute or duty ⁿ will be paid, and eventually the royal revenues will suffer. ᵈ ¹⁴Now since we are under obligation to the palace and it is not proper for us to see the king dishonored, we are sending this message to inform the king, ¹⁵so that a search may be made in the archives ᵒ of your predecessors. In these rec-

---

4:6 ᵈ Est 1:1; Da 9:1
ᵉ Est 3:13; 9:5
4:7 ᶠ Ezr 7:1; Ne 2:1
ᵍ 2Ki 18:26; Isa 36:11;
Da 1:4; 2:4
4:9 ʰ ver 23; Ezr 5:6;
6:6,13 ⁱ Ge 10:10
ʲ Ne 1:1; Est 1:2;
Da 8:2
4:10 ᵏ S 2Ki 17:24
ˡ ver 17; Ne 4:2
4:12 ᵐ Ezr 5:3,9
4:13 ⁿ Ezr 7:24;
Ne 5:4
4:15 ᵒ Ezr 5:17; 6:1

ᵃ 6 Hebrew *Ahasuerus*   ᵇ 7 Or *written in Aramaic and translated*   ᶜ 7 The text of Ezra 4:8–6:18 is in Aramaic.   ᵈ 13 The meaning of the Aramaic for this clause is uncertain.

4:6 *Xerxes.* See the book of Esther; see also chart, p. 482. When Darius died in 486 B.C., Egypt rebelled, and Xerxes, the son of Darius, had to march west to suppress the revolt.

4:7 *Artaxerxes.* Three Persian kings bore this name: Artaxerxes I (465–424 B.C.), II (404–358) and III (358–338). The king here is Artaxerxes I (see chart, p. 482). *Mithredath.* See 1:8 and note. *Tabeel.* An Aramaic name (see Isa 7:6 and note). *wrote a letter.* Near Eastern kings employed an elaborate system of informers and spies. Egyptian sources speak of the "ears and eyes" of the pharaoh. Sargon II of Assyria had agents in Urartu whom he ordered: "Write me whatever you see and hear." The King's Eye and the King's Ear were two officials who reported to the Persian monarch.

4:8—6:18 For this passage the author draws upon Aramaic documents; a further Aramaic section is 7:12–26.

4:8 *commanding officer.* An official who had the role of a chancellor or commissioner. Perhaps Rehum dictated, and Shimshai wrote the letter in Aramaic. (Alternatively, Shimshai may have been a high official rather than a scribe.) The letter would then be read in a Persian translation before the king (v. 18). According to Herodotus (3.128), royal scribes were attached to each governor to report directly to the Persian king.

4:9 *associates.* See vv. 17,23; 5:3,6; 6:6 ("other officials"); 6:13. One of the striking characteristics of Persian bureaucracy was that each responsibility was shared among colleagues. *Uruk.* See note on Ge 10:10. *Babylon.* During the reign of the Assyrian king Ashurbanipal (669–627 B.C.) a major revolt had taken place (652–648), involving Shamash-Shum-Ukin, the brother of the king and the ruler over Babylonia. After a long siege Shamash-Shum-Ukin hurled himself into the flames. Doubtless these men of Babylon and the other cities mentioned were the descendants of the rebels, whom the Assyrians deported to the west. *Susa.* See note on Est 1:2; the major city of Elam (in southwest

Iran). Because of Susa's part in the revolt, Ashurbanipal brutally destroyed it in 640 (two centuries before Rehum's letter).

4:10 *Ashurbanipal.* The last great Assyrian king (see chart, p. 482), famed for his library at Nineveh. He is not named elsewhere in the OT, but he is probably the king who freed Manasseh from exile (2Ch 33:11–13). *deported.* Ashurbanipal may be the unnamed Assyrian king who brought people to Samaria, according to 2Ki 17:24. It is characteristic of such deportations that the descendants of populations that had been removed from their homelands nearly two centuries earlier should still stress their origins. *Samaria.* The murder of Amon, king of Judah (642–640 B.C.; see 2Ki 21:23; 2Ch 33:24), was probably the result of an anti-Assyrian movement inspired by the revolt in Elam and Babylonia. The Assyrians may then have deported the rebellious Samaritans and replaced them with the rebellious Elamites and Babylonians. *Trans-Euphrates.* Lit. "beyond the River," i.e., the Euphrates River. From Israel's point of view the land "beyond the River" was Mesopotamia (Jos 24:2–3,14–15; 2Sa 10:16). From the Mesopotamian point of view the land "beyond the River" extended from the Euphrates to Gaza (1Ki 4:24).

4:12 *people.* Lit. "Jews" or "Judahites" (see note on Jer 34:9). *restoring the walls and repairing the foundations.* As Isaiah had foretold (see Isa 58:12 and note).

4:13 Most of the gold and silver coins that came into Persia's treasury were melted down to be stored as bullion. Very little of the taxes returned to benefit the provinces.

4:14 *we are under obligation to the palace.* Lit. "we eat the salt of the palace." Salt was made a royal monopoly by the Ptolemies in Egypt, and perhaps by the Persians as well.

4:15 *archives.* See 5:17; 6:1 and note; Est 2:23; 6:1–2. There were several repositories of such documents at the major capitals. These royal archives preserved documents for centuries. In the third century B.C. the Babylonian priest

4:15 *P* Est 3:8
4:17 *q* S ver 10
4:19 *r* S 2Ki 18:7
4:20 *s* Ge 15:18-21;
S Ex 23:31; S Jos 1:4;
S 1Ki 4:21; 1Ch 18:3;
Ps 72:8-11
4:22 *t* Da 6:2
4:23 *u* S ver 9
4:24 *v* Ne 2:1-8;
Da 9:25; Hag 1:1,15;
Zec 1:1
5:1 *w* Ezr 6:14;
Hag 1:1,3,12; 2:1,10,
20 *x* Zec 1:1; 7:1
y Hag 1:14-2:9;
Zec 4:9-10; 8:9
5:2 *z* S 1Ch 3:19;
Hag 1:14; 2:21;
Zec 4:6-10 *a* S Ezr 2:2
b ver 8; Hag 2:2-5
5:3 *c* Ezr 6:6
d Ezr 6:6 *e* S Ezr 4:12
5:5 *f* S 2Ki 25:28;
Ezr 7:6,9,28; 8:18,22,
31; Ne 2:8,18;
Ps 33:18; Isa 66:14

ords you will find that this city is a rebellious city, troublesome to kings and provinces, a place with a long history of sedition. That is why this city was destroyed. *P* ¹⁶We inform the king that if this city is built and its walls are restored, you will be left with nothing in Trans-Euphrates.

¹⁷The king sent this reply:

To Rehum the commanding officer, Shimshai the secretary and the rest of their associates living in Samaria and elsewhere in Trans-Euphrates: *q*

Greetings.

¹⁸The letter you sent us has been read and translated in my presence. ¹⁹I issued an order and a search was made, and it was found that this city has a long history of revolt *r* against kings and has been a place of rebellion and sedition. ²⁰Jerusalem has had powerful kings ruling over the whole of Trans-Euphrates, *s* and taxes, tribute and duty were paid to them. ²¹Now issue an order to these people to stop work, so that this city will not be rebuilt until I so order. ²²Be careful not to neglect this matter. Why let this threat grow, to the detriment of the royal interests? *t*

²³As soon as the copy of the letter of King Artaxerxes was read to Rehum and Shimshai the secretary and their associates, *u* they went immediately to the Jews in Jerusalem and compelled them by force to stop.

²⁴Thus the work on the house of God in Jerusalem came to a standstill until the second year of the reign of Darius *v* king of Persia.

TATTENAI'S LETTER TO DARIUS

5 Now Haggai *w* the prophet and Zechariah *x* the prophet, a descendant of Iddo, prophesied *y* to the Jews in Judah and Jerusalem in the name of the God of Israel, who was over them. ²Then Zerubbabel *z* son of Shealtiel and Joshua *a* son of Jozadak set to work *b* to rebuild the house of God in Jerusalem. And the prophets of God were with them, supporting them.

³At that time Tattenai, *c* governor of Trans-Euphrates, and Shethar-Bozenai *d* and their associates went to them and asked, "Who authorized you to rebuild this temple and to finish it?" *e* ⁴They *a* also asked, "What are the names of those who are constructing this building?" ⁵But the eye of their God *f* was watching over the elders of the Jews, and they were not stopped until a report could go to Darius and his written reply be received.

⁶This is a copy of the letter that Tattenai, governor of Trans-Euphrates, and Shethar-

---

a 4 See Septuagint; Aramaic *We*.

Berossus made use of the Babylonian Chronicles in his history of Babylon, which covered events from the Assyrian to the Hellenistic (beginning with Alexander's conquest of Babylon in 330 B.C.) eras.

4:18 *read.* Since the king probably could not read Aramaic, he would have had the document read to him. *translated.* From Aramaic into Persian (see TNIV text notes on v. 7; Ne 8:8).

4:19 *rebellion.* There is some truth in the accusation. Jerusalem had rebelled against the Assyrians in 701 B.C. (2Ki 18:7) and against the Babylonians in 600 and 589 (2Ki 24:1,20).

4:21–23 As a result of the intervention of the provincial authorities, Artaxerxes I (see v. 11 and note on v. 7) ordered that the Jews stop rebuilding the walls of Jerusalem (see note on Ne 1:3). The events of vv. 7–23 probably occurred prior to 444 B.C. The forcible destruction of these recently rebuilt walls rather than the destruction by Nebuchadnezzar would then be the basis of the report made to Nehemiah (Ne 1:3).

4:24 After this long digression describing the opposition to Jewish efforts, the writer returns to his original subject of the rebuilding of the temple (vv. 1–5). *second year of the reign of Darius.* According to Persian reckoning, the second regnal year of Darius I began on Nisan 1 (Apr. 3), 520 B.C., and lasted until Feb. 21, 519. In that year the prophet Haggai (Hag 1:1–5) exhorted Zerubbabel to begin rebuilding the temple on the first day of the sixth month (Aug. 29). Work began on

the temple on the 24th day of the month, Sept. 21 (Hag 1:15). During his first two years Darius had to establish his right to the throne by fighting numerous rebels, as recounted in his famous Behistun (Bisitun) inscription. It was only after the stabilization of the Persian empire that efforts to rebuild the temple could be permitted.

5:1 *Haggai … Zechariah.* Beginning on Aug. 29, 520 B.C. (see Hag 1:1 and note), and continuing until Dec. 18 (see Hag 2:1,10,20 and notes), the prophet Haggai delivered a series of messages to stir up the people to resume work on the temple. Two months after Haggai's first speech, Zechariah began to prophesy (see Zec 1:1 and note; see also Introduction to Zechariah: Dates).

5:2 *Zerubbabel.* A Babylonian name meaning "offspring of Babylon," referring to his birth in exile. He was the son of Shealtiel and the grandson of Jehoiachin (1Ch 3:17), the next-to-last king of Judah. Zerubbabel was the last of the Davidic line to be entrusted with political authority by the occupying powers. He was also an ancestor of Jesus (Mt 1:12–13; Lk 3:27). *Joshua.* See note on 2:2.

5:3 *Tattenai.* Probably a Babylonian name. *Shethar-Bozenai.* Perhaps a Persian official.

5:5 *not stopped.* The Persian governor gave the Jews the benefit of the doubt by not stopping the work while the inquiry was proceeding.

Bozenai and their associates, the officials of Trans-Euphrates, sent to King Darius. [7]The report they sent him read as follows:

To King Darius:

Cordial greetings.

[8]The king should know that we went to the district of Judah, to the temple of the great God. The people are building it with large stones and placing the timbers in the walls. The work[g] is being carried on with diligence and is making rapid progress under their direction.

[9]We questioned the elders and asked them, "Who authorized you to rebuild this temple and to finish it?"[h] [10]We also asked them their names, so that we could write down the names of their leaders for your information.

[11]This is the answer they gave us:

"We are the servants of the God of heaven and earth, and we are rebuilding the temple[i] that was built many years ago, one that a great king of Israel built and finished. [12]But because our ancestors angered[j] the God of heaven, he gave them into the hands of Nebuchadnezzar the Chaldean, king of Babylon, who destroyed this temple and deported the people to Babylon.[k]

[13]"However, in the first year of Cyrus king of Babylon, King Cyrus issued a decree[l] to rebuild this house of God. [14]He even removed from the temple[a] of Babylon the gold and silver articles of the house of God, which Nebuchadnezzar had taken from the temple in Jerusalem and brought to the temple[a] in Babylon.[m] Then King Cyrus gave them to a man named Sheshbazzar,[n] whom he had appointed governor, [15]and he told him, 'Take these articles and go and deposit them in the temple in Jerusalem. And rebuild the house of God on its site.'

[16]"So this Sheshbazzar came and laid the foundations of the house of God[o] in Jerusalem. From that day to the present it has been under construction but is not yet finished."

[17]Now if it pleases the king, let a search be made in the royal archives[p] of Babylon to see if King Cyrus did in fact issue a decree to rebuild this house of God in Jerusalem. Then let the king send us his decision in this matter.

THE DECREE OF DARIUS

6 King Darius then issued an order, and they searched in the archives[q] stored in the treasury at Babylon. [2]A scroll was found in the citadel of Ecbatana in the province of Media, and this was written on it:

Memorandum:

[3]In the first year of King Cyrus, the king issued a decree concerning the temple of God in Jerusalem:

Let the temple be rebuilt as a place to present sacrifices, and let its foundations

[a] 14 Or *palace*

5:8 [g] S ver 2
5:9 [h] S Ezr 4:12
5:11 [i] 1Ki 6:1; 2Ch 3:1-2
5:12 [j] S 2Ch 36:16
[k] S Dt 21:10; S 28:36; S 2Ki 24:1; S Jer 1:3
5:13 [l] S Ezr 1:2-4
5:14 [m] Ezr 1:7
[n] S 1Ch 3:18
5:16 [o] S Ezr 3:10
5:17 [p] S Ezr 4:15
6:1 [q] S Ezr 4:15

5:6–7 *sent to King Darius...sent him.* Texts found in the royal city of Persepolis vividly confirm that such inquiries were sent directly to the king himself, revealing the close attention he paid to minute details.
5:8 *timbers.* The Hebrew word may refer to interior paneling (1Ki 6:15–18) or to logs alternating with the brick or stone layers in the walls (see note on 6:4).
5:11 *great king of Israel.* According to 1Ki 6:1 Solomon began building the temple in the fourth year of his reign (966 B.C.). The project lasted seven years (1Ki 6:38).
5:12 *Chaldean.* The Akkadian word means "conqueror." The origin of the Chaldeans is obscure. Led by Nebuchadnezzar's father, Nabopolassar, they overthrew the Assyrians and established the Neo-Babylonian empire (612–539 B.C.).
5:14 *Sheshbazzar...governor.* See note on 1:8.
6:1 *archives...in the treasury at Babylon.* Many documents have also been found in the so-called "treasury" area of Persepolis (see map, pp. 586–587).

6:2 *Ecbatana.* One of the four capitals (along with Babylon, Persepolis and Susa) of the Persian empire. Located in what is today the Iranian city of Hamadan, its remains have not yet been excavated. This is the only reference to the site in the OT, though there are numerous references in the Apocryphal books (Judith 1:1–4; Tobit 3:7; 7:1; 14:12–14; 2 Maccabees 9:3). *Media.* The homeland of the Medes in northwestern Iran. The Medes were an Indo-European tribe related to the Persians. After the rise of Cyrus in 550 B.C., they became subordinate to the Persians. The name of the area was retained as late as the NT era (cf. Ac 2:9).
6:3–5 Compare this Aramaic memorandum of the decree of Cyrus with the Hebrew version in 1:2–4. The Aramaic is written in a more sober administrative style, without any reference to the Lord (Yahweh). A similar memorandum dealing with permission to rebuild the Jewish temple at Elephantine in Upper Egypt was found among fifth-century B.C. Aramaic papyri recovered at that site.

6:3 ʳ S Ezr 3:10;
Hag 2:3
6:4 ˢ S 1Ki 6:36
ᵗ ver 8; Ezr 7:20
6:5 ᵘ S 1Ch 29:2
ᵛ S Ezr 1:7
6:6 ʷ Ezr 5:3
ˣ Ezr 5:3
6:8 ʸ S ver 4
ᶻ S 1Sa 9:20
6:9 ᵃ Lev 1:3,10
6:10 ᵇ Ezr 7:23;
1Ti 2:1-2
6:11 ᶜ S Dt 21:22-
23; Est 2:23; 5:14;
9:14 ᵈ Ezr 7:26;
Da 2:5; 3:29
6:12 ᵉ S Ex 20:24;
S Dt 12:5; S 2Ch 6:2
ᶠ ver 14
6:13 ᵍ S Ezr 4:9
6:14 ʰ S Ezr 5:1
ⁱ S Ezr 1:1-4 ʲ ver 12

be laid. ʳ It is to be sixty cubits ᵃ high and sixty cubits wide, ⁴with three courses ˢ of large stones and one of timbers. The costs are to be paid by the royal treasury. ᵗ ⁵Also, the gold ᵘ and silver articles of the house of God, which Nebuchadnezzar took from the temple in Jerusalem and brought to Babylon, are to be returned to their places in the temple in Jerusalem; they are to be deposited in the house of God. ᵛ

⁶Now then, Tattenai, ʷ governor of Trans-Euphrates, and Shethar-Bozenai ˣ and you other officials of that province, stay away from there. ⁷Do not interfere with the work on this temple of God. Let the governor of the Jews and the Jewish elders re-build this house of God on its site.

⁸Moreover, I hereby decree what you are to do for these elders of the Jews in the construction of this house of God:

Their expenses are to be fully paid out of the royal treasury, ʸ from the revenues ᶻ of Trans-Euphrates, so that the work will not stop. ⁹Whatever is needed—young bulls, rams, male lambs for burnt offerings ᵃ to the God of heaven, and wheat, salt, wine and olive oil, as requested by the priests in Jerusalem—must be given them daily without fail, ¹⁰so that they may offer sacrifices pleasing to the God of heaven and pray for the well-being of the king and his sons. ᵇ

¹¹Furthermore, I decree that if anyone defies this edict, a beam is to be pulled from their house and they are to be impaled ᶜ on it. And for this crime their house is to be made a pile of rubble. ᵈ ¹²May God, who has caused his Name to dwell there, ᵉ over-throw any king or people who lifts a hand to change this decree or to destroy this temple in Jerusalem.

I Darius ᶠ have decreed it. Let it be carried out with diligence.

COMPLETION AND DEDICATION OF THE TEMPLE

¹³Then, because of the decree King Darius had sent, Tattenai, governor of Trans-Eu-phrates, and Shethar-Bozenai and their associates ᵍ carried it out with diligence. ¹⁴So the elders of the Jews continued to build and prosper under the preaching ʰ of Haggai the prophet and Zechariah, a descendant of Iddo. They finished building the temple accord-ing to the command of the God of Israel and the decrees of Cyrus, ⁱ Darius ʲ and Artaxer-

---

ᵃ 3 That is, about 90 feet or about 27 meters

6:3 *sixty cubits high and sixty cubits wide.* See TNIV text note. These dimensions, which differ from those of Solomon's temple (see TNIV text note on 1Ki 6:2), are probably not specifications of the temple as built but of the outer limits of a building the Persians were willing to subsidize. The second temple was not as grandiose as the first (3:12; Hag 2:3).

6:4 *large stones ... timbers.* See 5:8. The same kind of con-struction is mentioned in 1Ki 6:36; 7:12. Such a design was possibly intended to cushion the building against earth-quake shocks. *costs are to be paid by the royal treasury.* In 1973 archaeologists discovered at Xanthos in southwest Turkey a temple foundation charter from the late Persian period that provides some striking parallels with this decree of Cyrus. As in Ezra, amounts of sacrifices, names of priests and the responsibil-ity for the upkeep of the temple are specified. The Persian king seems to have known details of the temple. See also notes on v. 8; 7:20.

6:8 *paid out of the royal treasury.* It was a consistent poli-cy of Persian kings to help restore sanctuaries in their em-pire. For example, a memorandum concerning the rebuilding of the Jewish temple at Elephantine was written by the Persian governors of Judah and Samaria. Also from non-Biblical sources we learn that Cyrus repaired temples at Uruk and Ur. Cambyses, successor to Cyrus, gave funds for the temple at Sais in Egypt. The temple of Amun in the Khargah Oasis was rebuilt by order of Darius.

6:9 That the Persian monarchs were interested in the de-tails of foreign religions is shown clearly by the ordi-nances of Cambyses and Darius I, regulating the temples and priests in Egypt. On the authority of Darius II (423–404 B.C.) a letter was written to the Jews at Elephantine concerning the keeping of the Festival of Unleavened Bread.

6:10 *pray for the well-being of the king and his sons.* In the inscription on the Cyrus Cylinder (made of baked clay), the king asks: "May all the gods whom I have resettled in their sacred cities ask Bel and Nebo daily for a long life for me." The Jews of Elephantine offered to pray for the Persian gover-nor of Judah. The daily synagogue services included a prayer for the royal family (cf. 1Ti 2:1–2).

6:11 *if anyone defies this edict.* It was customary at the end of decrees and treaties to append a long list of curses against any-one who might disregard them. *impaled.* According to Herodotus (3.159), Darius I impaled 3,000 Babylonians when he took the city of Babylon. See note on Est 2:23.

6:12 *May God ... overthrow any king or people.* At the end of his famous Behistun (Bisitun) inscription Darius I warned: "If you see this inscription or these sculptures, and de-stroy them and do not protect them as long as you have strength, may Ahuramazda strike you, and may you not have a family, and what you do ... may Ahuramazda utterly destroy." *caused his Name to dwell.* See note on Dt 12:5.

6:13–14 Work on the temple had made little progress, not only because of opposition but also because of the preoccupation of the returnees with their own homes (Hag 1:2–9). Because they had placed their own interests first, God sent them famine as a judgment (Hag 1:5–6,10–11). Spurred by the preaching of Haggai and Zechariah, and under the leadership of Zerubbabel and Joshua, a new effort was begun (Hag 1:12–15).

6:14 *Artaxerxes.* The reference to him seems out of place, be-cause he did not contribute to rebuilding the temple. He may have been inserted here since he contributed to the work of the temple at a later date under Ezra (7:21–24).

xes,[k] kings of Persia. [15]The temple was completed on the third day of the month Adar, in the sixth year of the reign of King Darius.[l]

[16]Then the people of Israel—the priests, the Levites and the rest of the exiles—celebrated the dedication[m] of the house of God with joy. [17]For the dedication of this house of God they offered[n] a hundred bulls, two hundred rams, four hundred male lambs and, as a sin offering[a] for all Israel, twelve male goats, one for each of the tribes of Israel. [18]And they installed the priests in their divisions[o] and the Levites in their groups[p] for the service of God at Jerusalem, according to what is written in the Book of Moses.[q]

THE PASSOVER

[19]On the fourteenth day of the first month, the exiles celebrated the Passover.[r] [20]The priests and Levites had purified themselves and were all ceremonially clean. The Levites slaughtered[s] the Passover lamb for all the exiles, for their relatives the priests and for themselves. [21]So the Israelites who had returned from the exile ate it, together with all who had separated themselves[t] from the unclean practices[u] of their Gentile neighbors in order to seek the LORD,[v] the God of Israel. [22]For seven days they celebrated with joy the Festival of Unleavened Bread,[w] because the LORD had filled them with joy by changing the attitude[x] of the king of Assyria so that he assisted them in the work on the house of God, the God of Israel.

EZRA COMES TO JERUSALEM

7 After these things, during the reign of Artaxerxes[y] king of Persia, Ezra son of Seraiah,[z] the son of Azariah, the son of Hilkiah,[a] [2]the son of Shallum, the son of Zadok,[b] the son of Ahitub,[c] [3]the son of Amariah, the son of Azariah, the son of Meraioth, [4]the son of Zerahiah, the son of Uzzi, the son of Bukki, [5]the son of Abishua, the

---

[a] 17 Or *purification offering*

6:14 [k] Ezr 7:1; Ne 2:1
6:15 [l] Zec 1:1; 4:9
6:16 [m] S 1Ki 8:63
6:17 [n] S 2Sa 6:13; S 2Ch 29:21; S 30:24
6:18 [o] S 2Ch 35:4; Lk 1:5 [p] S 1Ch 24:1 [q] Nu 3:6-9; 8:9-11; 18:1-32
6:19 [r] S Ex 12:11; S Nu 28:16
6:20 [s] S 2Ch 30:15, 17; 35:11
6:21 [t] Ezr 9:1; Ne 9:2 [u] S Dt 18:9; Eze 36:25 [v] 1Ch 22:19; Ps 14:2
6:22 [w] S Ex 12:17 [x] S Ezr 1:1
7:1 [y] S Ezr 4:7; S 6:14 [z] S 2Ki 25:18 [a] 2Ki 22:4
7:2 [b] 1Ki 1:8; 2:35; 1Ch 6:8; Eze 40:46; 43:19; 44:15 [c] Ne 11:11

6:15 *temple was completed.* On Mar. 12, 516 B.C., almost 70 years after its destruction. The renewed work on the temple had begun on Sept. 21, 520 (Hag 1:15), and sustained effort had continued for almost three and a half years. According to Hag 2:3, the older members who could remember the splendor of Solomon's temple were disappointed when they saw the smaller size of Zerubbabel's temple (cf. Ezr 3:12). Yet in the long run the second temple, though not as grand as the first, enjoyed a much longer life. The general plan of the second temple was similar to that of Solomon's, but the Most Holy Place was left empty because the ark of the covenant had been lost through the Babylonian conquest. According to Josephus, on the Day of Atonement the high priest placed his censer on the slab of stone that marked the former location of the ark. The Holy Place was furnished with a table for the bread of the Presence, the incense altar, and one lampstand (in the Apocrypha, cf. 1 Maccabees 1:21–22; 4:49–51) instead of Solomon's ten (1Ki 7:49).
6:16 *exiles…dedication.* Cf. the dedication of Solomon's temple (1Ki 8). The leaders of those who returned from exile were responsible for the completion of the temple. "Dedication" translates the Aramaic word *hanukkah.* The Jewish holiday in December that celebrates the recapture of the temple from the Seleucids and its rededication (165 B.C.) is also known as Hanukkah.
6:17 *hundred…two hundred…four hundred.* The number of animals sacrificed was small in comparison with similar services in the reigns of Solomon (1Ki 8:5,63), Hezekiah (2Ch 30:24) and Josiah (2Ch 35:7), when thousands rather than hundreds were offered.
6:18 *divisions.* The priests were separated into 24 divisions (1Ch 24:1–19), each of which served at the temple for a week at a time (cf. Lk 1:5,8). In 1962 fragments of a synagogue inscription listing the 24 divisions were found at Caesarea. *written in the Book of Moses.* Perhaps referring to such passages as Ex 29; Lev 8; Nu 3; 8:5–26; 18.
6:19 *fourteenth day…first month…Passover.* The date would have been about Apr. 21, 516 B.C. For the origin and meaning of the Passover and the Festival of Unleavened Bread (v. 22) see Ex 12:1–30 and notes.
6:20 *purified themselves…ceremonially clean.* See note on Lev

4:12. Priests and Levites had to be ceremonially clean to fulfill their ritual functions.
6:21 *with all who had separated themselves.* The returning exiles were willing to accept those who separated themselves from the paganism of the foreigners who had been introduced into the area by the Assyrians.
6:22 *king of Assyria.* A surprising title for Darius, the Persian king. But even after the fall of Nineveh in 612 B.C., the term "Assyria" continued to be used for former territories the Assyrians had occupied. Persian kings adopted a variety of titles, including "king of Babylon" (cf. 5:13; Ne 13:6).
7:1–5 The genealogy of Ezra given here lists 16 ancestors back to Aaron, the brother of Moses.
7:1 *After these things.* The events of the preceding chapter concluded with the completion of the temple in 516 B.C. *Artaxerxes.* The identity of the king mentioned in this chapter has been disputed. If this was Artaxerxes I, which seems likely, Ezra would have arrived in Judah in 458, and there would be a gap of almost 60 years between the events of ch. 6 and those of ch. 7. The only recorded event during this interval is the opposition to the rebuilding of Jerusalem in the reign of Xerxes (486–465) in 4:6. *Ezra.* Perhaps a shortened form of Azariah ("The LORD helps"), a name that occurs twice in the list of his ancestors. The Greek form is Esdras, as in the Apocrypha. *Seraiah.* Means "The LORD is prince." The high priest under Zedekiah, he was killed by Nebuchadnezzar in 586 (2Ki 25:18–21), some 128 years before Ezra's arrival. He was therefore the ancestor rather than the father of Ezra; "son" often means "descendant" (see 1Ch 6:14–15). *Hilkiah.* Means "My portion is the LORD." He was the high priest under Josiah (2Ki 22:4).
7:2 *Zadok.* Means "righteous." He was a priest under David (2Sa 8:17). Solomon appointed Zadok as high priest in place of Abiathar, who supported the rebel Adonijah (1Ki 1:7–8; 2:35). Ezekiel regarded the Zadokites as free from idolatry (Eze 44:15). They held the office of high priest until 171 B.C. The Sadducees may have been named after Zadok, and the Qumran community (see essay, p. 1956) looked for the restoration of the Zadokite priesthood. *Ahitub.* Probably means "My (divine) brother is good." He was actually the grandfather of Zadok (Ne 11:11).

7:5 *d* 1Ch 6:4
7:6 *e* Ne 12:36
f S 2Ki 25:28
g S Ezr 5:5;
S Isa 41:20
7:7 *h* Ezr 8:1
7:9 *i* ver 6
7:10 *j* S Dt 33:10
7:12 *k* Eze 26:7;
Da 2:37
7:14 *l* Est 1:14
7:15 *m* S 1Ch 29:6
n S Dt 12:5; S 2Ch 6:2
7:16 *o* S Ex 3:22
p Zec 6:10
7:17 *q* S 2Ki 3:4
r Nu 15:5-12
s Dt 12:5-11
7:19 *t* Ezr 5:14;
Jer 27:22

son of Phinehas, *d* the son of Eleazar, the son of Aaron the chief priest— 6this Ezra *e* came up from Babylon. He was a teacher well versed in the Law of Moses, which the LORD, the God of Israel, had given. The king had granted *f* him everything he asked, for the hand of the LORD his God was on him. *g* 7Some of the Israelites, including priests, Levites, musicians, gatekeepers and temple servants, also came up to Jerusalem in the seventh year of King Artaxerxes. *h*

8Ezra arrived in Jerusalem in the fifth month of the seventh year of the king. 9He had begun his journey from Babylon on the first day of the first month, and he arrived in Jerusalem on the first day of the fifth month, for the gracious hand of his God was on him. *i* 10For Ezra had devoted himself to the study and observance of the Law of the LORD, and to teaching *j* its decrees and laws in Israel.

KING ARTAXERXES' LETTER TO EZRA

11This is a copy of the letter King Artaxerxes had given to Ezra the priest, a teacher of the Law, a man learned in matters concerning the commands and decrees of the LORD for Israel:

12 *a* Artaxerxes, king of kings, *k*

To Ezra the priest, teacher of the Law of the God of heaven:

Greetings.

13Now I decree that any of the Israelites in my kingdom, including priests and Levites, who volunteer to go to Jerusalem with you, may go. 14You are sent by the king and his seven advisers *l* to inquire about Judah and Jerusalem with regard to the Law of your God, which is in your hand. 15Moreover, you are to take with you the silver and gold that the king and his advisers have freely given *m* to the God of Israel, whose dwelling *n* is in Jerusalem, 16together with all the silver and gold *o* you may obtain from the province of Babylon, as well as the freewill offerings of the people and priests for the temple of their God in Jerusalem. *p* 17With this money be sure to buy bulls, rams and male lambs, *q* together with their grain offerings and drink offerings, *r* and sacrifice *s* them on the altar of the temple of your God in Jerusalem.

18You and your fellow Israelites may then do whatever seems best with the rest of the silver and gold, in accordance with the will of your God. 19Deliver *t* to the God of

a 12 The text of Ezra 7:12-26 is in Aramaic.

7:5 *Eleazar.* Means "God helps."
7:6 *teacher.* Lit. "scribe" (see Ne 8:1,4,9,13; 12:26,36). Earlier, scribes served kings as secretaries, such as Shaphan under Josiah (2Ki 22:3, where the Hebrew word for "scribe" is translated "secretary"). Other scribes took dictation—such as Baruch, who wrote down what Jeremiah spoke (Jer 36:32). From the exilic period on, the "scribes" were scholars who studied and taught the Scriptures ("scribes" is rendered "teachers of the law" in the NT; see notes on Mt 2:4; Lk 5:17). In the NT period they, among others, were addressed as "rabbis" (cf. Mt 23:7). *well versed.* The Hebrew for this phrase is translated "skillful" in Ps 45:1 and "skilled" in Pr 22:29. *hand of the LORD.* For this striking description of God's power and favor cf. also vv. 9,28; 8:18,22,31; Ne 2:8,18.
7:7–9 *seventh year . . . first day of the first month . . . first day of the fifth month.* Ezra began his journey on the first of Nisan (Apr. 8, 458 B.C.) and arrived in Jerusalem on the first of Ab (Aug. 4, 458). The journey took four months, including an 11-day delay indicated by the comparison of v. 9 with 8:31. The spring was the most auspicious time for such journeys; most armies went on campaigns at this time of the year (see 2Sa 11:1 and note). Although the actual distance between Babylon and Jerusalem is about 500 miles, the travelers had to cover a total of about 900 miles, going northwest along the Euphrates River and then south. The relatively slow pace was caused by the presence of the elderly and the children. See map No. 8b at the end of this study Bible; see also map, p. 688.
7:10 *study . . . observance . . . teaching.* See Ne 8.
7:11 *letter.* Many regard the letter of Artaxerxes I as the beginning point of Daniel's first 69 "sevens" (Da 9:24–27). Others regard the commission of Nehemiah by the same king as the

starting point of this prophecy (Ne 1:1,11; 2:1–8). By using either a solar calendar with the former date (458 B.C.) or a lunar calendar with the latter date (444), one can arrive remarkably close to the date of Jesus' public ministry.
7:12 See TNIV text note. *king of kings.* The phrase was originally used by Assyrian kings, since their empires incorporated many kingdoms. It was then used by the later Babylonian (Eze 26:7; Da 2:37) and Persian kings. Cf. 1Ti 6:15; Rev 17:14; 19:16.
7:13 *Israelites.* It is noteworthy that "Israel" is used rather than "Judah." It was Ezra's aim to make one Israel of all who returned. The markedly Jewish coloring of this decree may have resulted from the king's use of Jewish officials, quite possibly Ezra himself, to help him compose it.
7:14 *seven advisers.* Cf. Est 1:14, which refers to the seven nobles who "had special access to the king." This corresponds with Persian practice as reported by the early Greek historians Herodotus and Xenophon. *Law of your God.* Perhaps the complete Pentateuch (the five books of Moses; see v. 6).
7:15 *silver and gold.* Cf. Hag 2:8. *freely given.* The Persian treasury had ample funds, and benevolence was a well-attested policy of Persian kings.
7:16 *offerings of the people.* The custom of sending gifts to Jerusalem from the Jews who lived outside the Holy Land continued until the Jewish-Roman War (A.D. 66–73), when the Romans forced the Jews to send such contributions to the temple of Jupiter instead (Josephus, *Antiquities,* 18.9.1; *Wars,* 7.6.6). There are close parallels to such directives in the contemporary letters from the Jewish garrison at Elephantine in Egypt, including a papyrus in which Darius II ordered: "Let grain offering, incense and burnt offering be offered" on Yahweh's altar "in your name."

Jerusalem all the articles entrusted to you for worship in the temple of your God. [20]And anything else needed for the temple of your God that you are responsible to supply, you may provide from the royal treasury. [u]

[21]Now I, King Artaxerxes, decree that all the treasurers of Trans-Euphrates are to provide with diligence whatever Ezra the priest, the teacher of the Law of the God of heaven, may ask of you— [22]up to a hundred talents[a] of silver, a hundred cors[b] of wheat, a hundred baths[c] of wine, a hundred baths[c] of olive oil, and salt without limit. [23]Whatever the God of heaven has prescribed, let it be done with diligence for the temple of the God of heaven. Why should his wrath fall on the realm of the king and of his sons? [v] [24]You are also to know that you have no authority to impose taxes, tribute or duty [w] on any of the priests, Levites, musicians, gatekeepers, temple servants or other workers at this house of God. [x]

[25]And you, Ezra, in accordance with the wisdom of your God, which you possess, appoint [y] magistrates and judges to administer justice to all the people of Trans-Euphrates—all who know the laws of your God. And you are to teach [z] any who do not know them. [26]Whoever does not obey the law of your God and the law of the king must surely be punished by death, banishment, confiscation of property, or imprisonment. [a]

[27]Praise be to the LORD, the God of our ancestors, who has put it into the king's heart [b] to bring honor [c] to the house of the LORD in Jerusalem in this way [28]and who has extended his good favor [d] to me before the king and his advisers and all the king's powerful officials. Because the hand of the LORD my God was on me, [e] I took courage and gathered leaders from Israel to go up with me.

LIST OF THE FAMILY HEADS RETURNING WITH EZRA

8 These are the family heads and those registered with them who came up with me from Babylon during the reign of King Artaxerxes: [f]

[2] of the descendants of Phinehas, Gershom;
of the descendants of Ithamar, Daniel;
of the descendants of David, Hattush [3] of the descendants of Shekaniah; [g]

of the descendants of Parosh, [h] Zechariah, and with him were registered 150 men;

7:20 ᵘ S Ezr 6:4
7:23 ᵛ S Ezr 6:10
7:24 ʷ S Ezr 4:13
ˣ Ezr 8:36
7:25 ʸ S Ex 18:21,26
ᶻ S Lev 10:11
7:26 ᵃ S Ezr 6:11
7:27 ᵇ S Ezr 1:1
ᶜ S 1Ch 29:12
7:28 ᵈ S 2Ki 25:28
ᵉ S Ezr 5:5
8:1 ᶠ Ezr 7:7
8:3 ᵍ 1Ch 3:22
ʰ S Ezr 2:3

ᵃ 22 That is, about 3 3/4 tons or about 3.4 metric tons   ᵇ 22 That is, probably about 18 tons or about 16 metric tons   ᶜ 22 That is, about 600 gallons or about 2,200 liters

---

7:20 *provide from the royal treasury.* Texts from the treasury at Persepolis also record the disbursement of supplies and funds from the royal purse.

7:22 *hundred talents.* An enormous amount (see TNIV text note). *hundred cors.* The total was relatively small (see TNIV text note). The wheat would be used in grain offerings. *salt without limit.* See note on 4:14. A close parallel is the benefaction of Antiochus III as recorded by Josephus (*Antiquities,* 12.3.3): "In the first place we have decided, on account of their piety, to furnish for their sacrifices an allowance of sacrificial animals, wine, oil and frankincense to the value of 20,000 pieces of silver, and sacred artabae of fine flour in accordance with their native law, and 1,460 medimni of wheat and 375 medimni of salt."

7:23 *wrath fall on the realm of the king.* Egypt had revolted against the Persians in 460 B.C. and had expelled the Persians with the help of the Athenians in 459. In 458, when Ezra traveled to Jerusalem, the Persians were involved in suppressing this revolt. *his sons.* We do not know how many sons the king had at this time, but he ultimately had 18, according to Ctesias (a Greek physician who wrote an extensive history of Persia).

7:24 *no ... taxes ... or duty on any of the priests ... temple servants.* Priests and other temple personnel were often given exemptions from enforced labor or taxes. A close parallel is found in the Gadates Inscription of Darius I to a governor in western Turkey, granting exemptions to the priests of Apollo. Antiochus III granted similar exemptions to the Jews: "The priests, the scribes of the temple and the temple singers shall be relieved from the poll tax, the crown tax and the salt tax that

they pay" (Josephus, *Antiquities,* 12.3.3).

7:26 *Whoever does not obey ... must surely be punished.* The extensive powers given to Ezra are striking and extend to secular fields. Perhaps the implementation of these provisions involved Ezra in a great deal of traveling, which would explain the silence about his activities between his arrival and the arrival of Nehemiah 13 years later. A close parallel to the king's commission of Ezra may be found in an earlier commission by Darius I, who sent Udjahorresnet, a priest and scholar, back to Egypt. He ordered the codification of the Egyptian laws by the chief men of Egypt—a task that took from 518 to 503 B.C.

7:28 *me.* The first occurrence of the first person for Ezra—a trait that characterizes the Ezra memoirs, which begin in v. 27 and continue to the end of ch. 9.

8:1–21 In vv. 1–14 Ezra lists those who accompanied him in his return from Mesopotamia, including the descendants of 15 individuals. The figures of the men given total 1,496, in addition to the individuals named. There were also women and children (see note on v. 21). About 40 Levites (vv. 18–19) are also included, as are 220 "temple servants" (v. 20).

8:2 *Gershom.* For the meaning of the name see TNIV text note on Ex 2:22. *Ithamar.* Also the name of the fourth son of Aaron (Ex 6:23).

8:3 *Zechariah.* Cf. v. 11. The name means "The LORD remembers"; it was the name of about 30 individuals mentioned in the Bible, including both the OT prophet and the father of John the Baptist (Lk 1:5–67).

8:4 *i* Ezr 2:6
8:6 *j* Ezr 2:15;
Ne 7:20; 10:16
8:13 *k* Ezr 2:13
8:15 *l* ver 21,31
m S Ezr 2:40
8:17 *n* Ezr 2:43
8:18 *o* S Ezr 5:5
p ver 24
8:20 *q* S 1Ch 9:2
8:21 *r* S ver 15
s Ps 5:8; 27:11; 107:7
8:22 *t* Ne 2:9;
Jer 41:16 *u* S Ezr 5:5
v Dt 31:17
8:23 *w* S 2Ch 20:3;
Ac 14:23
8:24 *x* ver 18

⁴ of the descendants of Pahath-Moab, *i* Eliehoenai son of Zerahiah, and with him 200 men;

⁵ of the descendants of Zattu, ª Shekaniah son of Jahaziel, and with him 300 men;

⁶ of the descendants of Adin, *j* Ebed son of Jonathan, and with him 50 men;

⁷ of the descendants of Elam, Jeshaiah son of Athaliah, and with him 70 men;

⁸ of the descendants of Shephatiah, Zebadiah son of Michael, and with him 80 men;

⁹ of the descendants of Joab, Obadiah son of Jehiel, and with him 218 men;

¹⁰ of the descendants of Bani, ᵇ Shelomith son of Josiphiah, and with him 160 men;

¹¹ of the descendants of Bebai, Zechariah son of Bebai, and with him 28 men;

¹² of the descendants of Azgad, Johanan son of Hakkatan, and with him 110 men;

¹³ of the descendants of Adonikam, *k* the last ones, whose names were Eliphelet, Jeuel and Shemaiah, and with them 60 men;

¹⁴ of the descendants of Bigvai, Uthai and Zakkur, and with them 70 men.

THE RETURN TO JERUSALEM

¹⁵ I assembled them at the canal that flows toward Ahava, *l* and we camped there three days. When I checked among the people and the priests, I found no Levites *m* there. ¹⁶ So I summoned Eliezer, Ariel, Shemaiah, Elnathan, Jarib, Elnathan, Nathan, Zechariah and Meshullam, who were leaders, and Joiarib and Elnathan, who were men of learning, ¹⁷ and I ordered them to go to Iddo, the leader in Kasiphia. I told them what to say to Iddo and his associates, the temple servants *n* in Kasiphia, so that they might bring attendants to us for the house of our God. ¹⁸ Because the gracious hand of our God was on us, *o* they brought us Sherebiah, *p* a capable man, from the descendants of Mahli son of Levi, the son of Israel, and Sherebiah's sons and brothers, 18 in all; ¹⁹ and Hashabiah, together with Jeshaiah from the descendants of Merari, and his brothers and nephews, 20 in all. ²⁰ They also brought 220 of the temple servants *q*—a body that David and the officials had established to assist the Levites. All were registered by name.

²¹ There, by the Ahava Canal, *r* I proclaimed a fast, so that we might humble ourselves before our God and ask him for a safe journey *s* for us and our children, with all our possessions. ²² I was ashamed to ask the king for soldiers *t* and horsemen to protect us from enemies on the road, because we had told the king, "The gracious hand of our God is on everyone *u* who looks to him, but his great anger is against all who forsake him. *v*" ²³ So we fasted *w* and petitioned our God about this, and he answered our prayer.

²⁴ Then I set apart twelve of the leading priests, namely, Sherebiah, *x* Hashabiah and

---

ᵃ 5 Some Septuagint manuscripts (also 1 Esdras 8:32); Hebrew does not have *Zattu*.   ᵇ 10 Some Septuagint manuscripts (also 1 Esdras 8:36); Hebrew does not have *Bani*.

8:4 *Eliehoenai.* Means "On the LORD are my eyes"; the name occurs only here and in 1Ch 26:3. Cf. Ps 25:15.

8:6 *Ebed.* May be a shortened form of Obadiah (cf. v. 9), meaning "servant of the LORD." *Jonathan.* Means "The LORD gives"; it was the name of 15 OT individuals.

8:7 *Athaliah.* The father of Jeshaiah. Athaliah was also the name of a famous queen, daughter of Ahab (2Ki 11).

8:8 *Michael.* Means "Who is like God?" It was the name of ten other Biblical personages, including the archangel (Da 10:13; Jude 9; Rev 12:7).

8:10 *Shelomith.* Although it is a feminine form (see also note on SS 6:13), it is often a man's name, as here. The Greek equivalent is Salome.

8:12 *Azgad.* See note on 2:12. *Johanan.* See note on 2:46.

8:15 *canal that flows toward Ahava.* Probably flows into either the Euphrates or the Tigris at a place not far from Babylon (the Kebar "River" in Eze 1:1 was also a canal). *three days.* Perhaps from the 9th to the 12th day of Nisan; the journey began on the 12th (see v. 31). *no Levites.* Since they were entrusted with many menial tasks, they may have found a more comfortable way of life in exile. A Rabbinic midrash (comment) on Ps 137 relates the legend that Levites were in the caravan but that they were not qualified to officiate because when Nebuchadnezzar had ordered them to sing for him the songs of Zion "they refused and bit off the ends of their fingers, so that they could not play on the harps." In the Hellenistic era (following Alexander's conquest of the Holy Land in 333 B.C.) the role of the Levites declined sharply, though the Temple Scroll among

the Dead Sea Scrolls from Qumran (see essay, p. 1596) assigns important roles to them.

8:16 *Ariel.* Means "lion of God" or "altar hearth" or possibly "City of God" (see note on Isa 29:1,2,7). It occurs only here as a personal name. *Meshullam.* Some assume that he is the same as the Meshullam who opposed the marriage reforms (10:15).

8:17 *Kasiphia.* Some have located it at the site that was later to become the Parthian capital of Ctesiphon on the Tigris River, north of Babylon.

8:18–19 *18...20.* Only about 40 Levites from two families were found who were willing to join Ezra's caravan.

8:20 *temple servants.* See note on 2:43–57.

8:21 *safe journey.* Lit. "straight way"—unimpeded by obstacles and dangers (see v. 31; cf. Pr 3:6). *possessions.* The vast treasures they were carrying with them offered a tempting bait for robbers.

8:22 *I was ashamed.* Scripture speaks often of unholy shame (Jer 48:13; 49:23; Mic 3:7) and on occasion, as here, of holy shame. Ezra was quick to blush with such shame (see also 9:6). Having proclaimed his faith in God's ability to protect the caravan, he was embarrassed to ask for human protection. Grave dangers faced travelers going the great distance between Mesopotamia and the Holy Land. Some 13 years later Nehemiah was accompanied by an armed escort. The difference, however, does not mean that Nehemiah was a man of lesser faith (see note on Ne 2:9).

8:23 *fasted and petitioned.* For the association of fasting and prayer see 2Sa 12:16; Ne 1:4; Da 9:3; Mt 17:21; Ac 14:23.

ten of their brothers, ²⁵and I weighed out ʸ to them the offering of silver and gold and the articles that the king, his advisers, his officials and all Israel present there had donated for the house of our God. ²⁶I weighed out to them 650 talents ᵃ of silver, silver articles weighing 100 talents, ᵇ 100 talents ᵇ of gold, ²⁷20 bowls of gold valued at 1,000 darics, ᶜ and two fine articles of polished bronze, as precious as gold.

²⁸I said to them, "You as well as these articles are consecrated to the LORD. ᶻ The silver and gold are a freewill offering to the LORD, the God of your ancestors. ²⁹Guard them carefully until you weigh them out in the chambers of the house of the LORD in Jerusalem before the leading priests and the Levites and the family heads of Israel." ³⁰Then the priests and Levites received the silver and gold and sacred articles that had been weighed out to be taken to the house of our God in Jerusalem.

³¹On the twelfth day of the first month we set out from the Ahava Canal ᵃ to go to Jerusalem. The hand of our God was on us, ᵇ and he protected us from enemies and bandits along the way. ³²So we arrived in Jerusalem, where we rested three days. ᶜ

³³On the fourth day, in the house of our God, we weighed out ᵈ the silver and gold and the sacred articles into the hands of Meremoth ᵉ son of Uriah, the priest. Eleazar son of Phinehas was with him, and so were the Levites Jozabad ᶠ son of Jeshua and Noadiah son of Binnui. ᵍ ³⁴Everything was accounted for by number and weight, and the entire weight was recorded at that time.

³⁵Then the exiles who had returned from captivity sacrificed burnt offerings to the God of Israel: twelve bulls ʰ for all Israel, ⁱ ninety-six rams, seventy-seven male lambs and, as a sin offering, ᵈ twelve male goats. ʲ All this was a burnt offering to the LORD. ³⁶They also delivered the king's orders ᵏ to the royal satraps and to the governors of Trans-Euphrates, ˡ who then gave assistance to the people and to the house of God. ᵐ

EZRA'S PRAYER ABOUT INTERMARRIAGE

9 After these things had been done, the leaders came to me and said, "The people of Israel, including the priests and the Levites, have not kept themselves separate ⁿ from the neighboring peoples with their detestable practices, like those of the Canaanites, Hittites, Perizzites, Jebusites, ᵒ Ammonites, ᵖ Moabites, �q Egyptians and Amorites. ʳ ²They have taken some of their daughters ˢ as wives for themselves and their sons, and have mingled ᵗ the holy race ᵘ with the peoples around them. And the leaders and officials have led the way in this unfaithfulness." ᵛ

³When I heard this, I tore ʷ my tunic and cloak, pulled hair from my head and beard

---

ᵃ 26 That is, about 24 tons or about 22 metric tons   ᵇ 26 That is, about 3 3/4 tons or about 3.4 metric tons   ᶜ 27 That is, about 19 pounds or about 8.5 kilograms   ᵈ 35 Or *purification offering*

8:26 *650 talents … 100 talents.* Enormous sums, worth millions of dollars today. See also note on 7:22.
8:27 *darics.* See TNIV text note. The word occurs only here and in 2:69; 1Ch 29:7; Ne 7:70. *polished.* This kind of bronze may have been orichalc, a bright yellow (the Hebrew for "yellow" in Lev 13:30,32,36 is related to the Hebrew for "polished" here) alloy of copper, which resembles gold and was highly prized in ancient times.
8:31 *twelfth day.* See notes on v. 15; 7:7–9.
8:32 *rested three days.* Nehemiah also took a similar rest period after his arrival in Jerusalem (Ne 2:11).
8:33 *Meremoth son of Uriah.* Probably the same as the man who repaired two sections of the wall (Ne 3:4,21).
B **8:34** *recorded.* According to Babylonian practice (e.g., in the Code of Hammurapi; see chart, p. xxiii), almost every transaction, including sales and marriages, had to be recorded in writing. Ezra may have had to send back to Artaxerxes a signed certification of the delivery of the treasures.
8:35 *sacrificed.* Except for the identical number of male goats, the offerings here were far fewer than those presented by the returnees under Zerubbabel (6:17), who brought with him a far greater number of families.
B **9:1** *After these things had been done … have not kept themselves separate.* Ezra had reached Jerusalem in the fifth month (7:9). The measures dealing with the problem of intermarriage were announced in the ninth month (10:9), or four months after his arrival. Those who brought Ezra's attention to the problem were probably the ordinary members of the com-

munity rather than the leaders, who were themselves guilty (v. 2). Malachi, who prophesied about the same time as Ezra's mission, indicates that some Jews had broken their marriages to marry daughters of a foreign god (Mal 2:10–16), perhaps the daughters of influential landholders. One of the reasons for such intermarriages may have been the shortage of returning Jewish women who were available. What happened to a Jewish community that was lax concerning intermarriage can be seen in the example of the Elephantine settlement in Egypt, which was contemporary with Ezra and Nehemiah. There the Jews who married pagan spouses expressed their devotion to pagan gods in addition to the Lord. The Elephantine community was gradually assimilated and disappeared. *neighboring peoples.* The eight groups mentioned are representative of the original inhabitants of Canaan before the Israelite conquest (see note on Ex 3:8). Only the Ammonites, Moabites and Egyptians were still living there in the postexilic period (cf. 2Ch 8:7–8). *Canaanites.* See note on Ge 10:6. *Hittites.* See note on Ge 10:15. *Perizzites.* See note on Ge 13:7. *Jebusites.* See note on Ge 10:16. *Ammonites, Moabites.* See note on Ge 19:36–38. *Amorites.* See note on Ge 10:16.
A **9:2** *holy race.* The Hebrew for this phrase is translated "holy seed" in Isa 6:13. *led the way.* In the wrong direction (see 10:18). *unfaithfulness.* See 10:6; Jos 22:16; Da 9:7. Marrying those who did not belong to the Lord was an act of infidelity for the people of Israel (cf. 1Co 7:39 and note).
9:3 *tore my tunic and cloak.* A common way to express grief or distress (see v. 5; Ge 37:29,34; Jos 7:6; Jdg 11:35; 2Sa 13:19; 2Ch

---

8:25 ʸ ver 33
8:28 ᶻ S Lev 21:6; 22:2-3
8:31 ᵃ S ver 15
  ᵇ S Ezr 5:5
8:32 ᶜ S Ge 40:13
8:33 ᵈ ver 25
  ᵉ Ne 3:4,21 ᶠ Ne 11:16
  ᵍ Ne 3:24
8:35 ʰ S Lev 1:3
  ⁱ S 2Ch 29:24
  ʲ S 2Ch 29:21; S 30:24
8:36 ᵏ Ezr 7:21-24
  ˡ Ne 2:7 ᵐ Est 9:3
9:1 ⁿ S Ezr 6:21
  ᵒ S Ge 10:16;
  S Jos 15:8 ᵖ Ge 19:38
  q S Ge 19:37 ʳ Ex 13:5; 23:28; Dt 20:17;
  S Jos 3:10; S Jdg 3:5;
  1Ki 9:20; S 2Ch 8:7;
  Ne 9:8
9:2 ˢ S Ex 34:16;
  S Ru 1:4 ᵗ Ps 106:35
  ᵘ S Ex 22:31;
  S Lev 27:30;
  S Dt 14:2 ᵛ Ezr 10:2
9:3 ʷ S Nu 14:6

9:3 ˣS Ex 32:19;
S 33:4
9:4 ʸEzr 10:3;
Ps 119:120; Isa 66:2,5
ᶻNe 1:4; Ps 119:136;
Da 10:2
9:5 ªS Ex 29:41
ᵇNe 8:6; Ps 28:2;
134:2
9:6 ᶜJer 31:19
ᵈS 2Ch 28:9;
Job 42:6; Ps 38:4;
Isa 59:12; Jer 3:25;
14:20; Rev 18:5
9:7 ᵉS 2Ch 29:6
ᶠEze 21:1-32
ᵍS Dt 28:64
ʰS Dt 28:37
9:8 ⁱPs 25:16; 67:1;
119:58; Isa 33:2
ʲS Ge 45:7
ᵏEcc 12:11; Isa 22:23
ˡPs 13:3; 19:8
9:9 ᵐS Ex 1:14;
Ne 9:36
ⁿS 2Ki 25:28;
Ps 106:46 ᵒPs 69:35;
Isa 43:1; 44:26;
48:20; 52:9; 63:9;
Jer 32:44; Zec 1:16-17
9:10 ᵖDt 11:8;
Isa 1:19-20
9:11 �q Dt 4:5
ʳS Lev 18:25-28
ˢS Dt 9:4; S 18:9;
S 1Ki 14:24
9:12 ᵗS Ex 34:15
ᵘDt 11:8 ᵛS Ge 45:18
ʷPs 103:17;
Eze 37:25; Joel 3:20
9:13 ˣS Ex 32:22
ʸJob 11:6; 15:5; 22:5;
33:27; Ps 103:10
9:14 ᶻNe 13:27
ªS Dt 9:8 ᵇDt 9:14
9:15 ᶜS Ge 18:25;
S 2Ch 12:6; Ne 9:8;
Ps 51:4; 129:4; 145:17;
Isa 24:16; Jer 12:1;
23:6; 33:16; La 1:18;
Da 9:7; Zep 3:5

and sat down appalled.ˣ ⁴Then everyone who trembledʸ at the words of the God of Israel gathered around me because of this unfaithfulness of the exiles. And I sat there appalledᶻ until the evening sacrifice.

⁵Then, at the evening sacrifice,ª I rose from my self-abasement, with my tunic and cloak torn, and fell on my knees with my handsᵇ spread out to the LORD my God ⁶and prayed:

"I am too ashamedᶜ and disgraced, my God, to lift up my face to you, because our sins are higher than our heads and our guilt has reached to the heavens.ᵈ ⁷From the days of our ancestorsᵉ until now, our guilt has been great. Because of our sins, we and our kings and our priests have been subjected to the swordᶠ and captivity,ᵍ to pillage and humiliationʰ at the hand of foreign kings, as it is today.

⁸"But now, for a brief moment, the LORD our God has been graciousⁱ in leaving us a remnantʲ and giving us a firm placeªᵏ in his sanctuary, and so our God gives light to our eyesˡ and a little relief in our bondage. ⁹Though we are slaves,ᵐ our God has not forsaken us in our bondage. He has shown us kindnessⁿ in the sight of the kings of Persia: He has granted us new life to rebuild the house of our God and repair its ruins,ᵒ and he has given us a wall of protection in Judah and Jerusalem.

¹⁰"But now, our God, what can we say after this? For we have forsaken the commandsᵖ ¹¹you gave through your servants the prophets when you said: 'The land you are enteringq to possess is a land pollutedʳ by the corruption of its peoples. By their detestable practicesˢ they have filled it with their impurity from one end to the other. ¹²Therefore, do not give your daughters in marriage to their sons or take their daughters for your sons. Do not seek a treaty of friendship with themᵗ at any time, that you may be strongᵘ and eat the good thingsᵛ of the land and leave it to your children as an everlasting inheritance.'ʷ

¹³"What has happened to us is a result of our evilˣ deeds and our great guilt, and yet, our God, you have punished us less than our sins deservedʸ and have given us a remnant like this. ¹⁴Shall we then break your commands again and intermarryᶻ with the peoples who commit such detestable practices? Would you not be angry enough with us to destroy us,ª leaving us no remnantᵇ or survivor? ¹⁵LORD, the God of Israel, you are righteous!ᶜ We are left this day as a remnant. Here we are before you in our guilt, though because of it not one of us can standᵈ in your presence. ᵉ"

ª 8 Or *a foothold*

9:15 ᵈPs 76:7; 130:3; Mal 3:2 ᵉS 1Ki 8:47

34:27; Est 4:1; Job 1:20; Isa 36:22; Jer 41:5; Mt 26:65). *pulled hair from my head and beard.* Unique in the Bible. Elsewhere we read about the shaving of one's head and/or beard (Job 1:20; Jer 41:5; 47:5; Eze 7:18; Am 8:10). When Nehemiah was confronted with the same problem of intermarriage, instead of pulling out his own hair he pulled out the hair of the offending parties (Ne 13:25).

9:4 *everyone who trembled.* Cf. Ex 19:16; Isa 66:2; Heb 12:21. *appalled.* See v. 3; cf. Da 4:19; 8:27. *evening sacrifice.* See Ex 12:6. The informants had probably visited Ezra in the morning, so that he must have sat appalled for many hours. The time of the evening sacrifice, usually about 3:00 P.M., was also the appointed time for prayer and confession (Ac 3:1).

9:5–15 See similar prayers in Ne 9:5–37; Da 9:3–19 (see also notes there).

9:5 *self-abasement.* The Hebrew for this word later meant "fasting." See note on Lev 16:29,31. *fell on my knees.* Cf. 1Ki 8:54; Ps 95:6; Da 6:10. *with my hands spread out.* See note on Ne 9:29.

■ **9:6** *ashamed and disgraced.* See 8:22 and note; Lk 18:13. Ezra felt both an inner shame before God and an outward humiliation before people for his own sins and the sins of his people. The two Hebrew verbs often occur together; see Ps 35:4; Isa 45:16; Jer 31:19 ("ashamed and humiliated"). *our sins . . . our guilt.* Cf. also vv. 7,13,15; 10:10,19; 1Ch 21:3; 2Ch 24:18; Ps 38:4. *has reached to the heavens.* But God's love is more than a match for our guilt (Ps 103:11–12).

9:7 *From the days of our ancestors.* Israelites were conscious of their corporate solidarity with their ancestors. *sword.* Cf. Ne 4:13. In Eze 21 "the sword of the king of Babylon" (21:19) is described as an instrument of divine judgment. *humiliation.* Cf. Da 9:7–8; 2Ch 32:21.

9:8 *remnant.* See Ge 45:7; Isa 1:9; 10:20–22; Ro 11:5 and notes. *firm place.* Lit. "nail" or "peg," like a nail driven into a wall (see Isa 22:23 and note) or a tent peg driven into the ground (Isa 33:20; 54:2). *light to our eyes.* An increase in light means vitality and joy (Ps 13:3; 19:8; Ecc 8:1; see note on Ps 6:7; cf. also note on Ps 27:1).

■ **9:9** *kings of Persia.* The Achaemenid Persian kings were favorably disposed to the Jews: Cyrus (539–530 B.C.) gave them permission to return (ch. 1); his son Cambyses (530–522), though not named in the Bible, also favored the Jews, as we learn from Elephantine papyri; Darius I (522–486) renewed the decree of Cyrus (ch. 6); his son Xerxes (486–465) granted privileges and protection to Jews (Est 8–10); his son Artaxerxes I (465–424) gave authorizations to Ezra (ch. 7) and to Nehemiah (Ne 2). *repair its ruins.* Isaiah had prophesied that the Lord would restore Jerusalem's ruins (Isa 44:26), which would burst into singing (Isa 52:9; cf. 58:12; 61:4). *wall of protection.* Used of a city wall only in Mic 7:11. The use here is metaphorical (cf. Zec 2:4–5).

9:11–12 The references are not to a single OT passage but to several passages, such as Dt 11:8–9; Isa 1:19; Eze 37:25.

■ **9:11** *your servants the prophets.* See notes on Jer 7:25; Zec 1:6. *corruption.* Of Canaanite idolatry and the immoral practices associated with it (Lev 18:3; 2Ch 29:5; La 1:17; Eze 7:20; 36:17). The degrading practices and beliefs of the Canaanites are described in texts from ancient Ugarit (see chart, p. xxiv).

9:14 *be angry.* God's anger came upon the Israelites because they had violated his covenant with them (Dt 7:4; 11:16–17; 29:26–28; Jos 23:16; Jdg 2:20).

■ **9:15** *you are righteous.* See note on Ps 4:1. *our guilt.* A proper sense of God's holiness makes us aware of our unworthi-

10:1 ᶠ2Ch 20:9;
Da 9:20 ᵍS Nu 25:6
10:2 ʰver 26
ⁱS Ezr 9:2 ʲDt 30:8-
10
10:3 ᵏS 2Ki 11:17
ˡS Ex 34:16
10:5 ᵐNe 5:12;
13:25
10:6 ⁿS Ex 34:28;
Dt 9:18; Ps 102:4;
Jnh 3:7
10:9 ᵒS Ezr 1:5
10:10 ᵖEzr 7:21
�q2Ch 28:13
10:11 ʳS Dt 24:1;
Mal 2:10-16
10:12 ˢS Jos 6:5

THE PEOPLE'S CONFESSION OF SIN

10 While Ezra was praying and confessing, ᶠweeping ᵍand throwing himself down before the house of God, a large crowd of Israelites—men, women and children—gathered around him. They too wept bitterly. ²Then Shekaniah son of Jehiel, one of the descendants of Elam, ʰsaid to Ezra, "We have been unfaithful ⁱto our God by marrying foreign women from the peoples around us. But in spite of this, there is still hope for Israel. ʲ ³Now let us make a covenant ᵏbefore our God to send away ˡall these women and their children, in accordance with the counsel of my lord and of those who fear the commands of our God. Let it be done according to the Law. ⁴Rise up; this matter is in your hands. We will support you, so take courage and do it."

⁵So Ezra rose up and put the leading priests and Levites and all Israel under oath ᵐto do what had been suggested. And they took the oath. ⁶Then Ezra withdrew from before the house of God and went to the room of Jehohanan son of Eliashib. While he was there, he ate no food and drank no water, ⁿbecause he continued to mourn over the unfaithfulness of the exiles.

⁷A proclamation was then issued throughout Judah and Jerusalem for all the exiles to assemble in Jerusalem. ⁸Anyone who failed to appear within three days would forfeit all his property, in accordance with the decision of the officials and elders, and would himself be expelled from the assembly of the exiles.

⁹Within the three days, all the men of Judah and Benjamin ᵒhad gathered in Jerusalem. And on the twentieth day of the ninth month, all the people were sitting in the square before the house of God, greatly distressed by the occasion and because of the rain. ¹⁰Then Ezra ᵖthe priest stood up and said to them, "You have been unfaithful; you have married foreign women, adding to Israel's guilt. �q ¹¹Now honor ᵃthe LORD, the God of your ancestors, and do his will. Separate yourselves from the peoples around you and from your foreign wives." ʳ

¹²The whole assembly responded with a loud voice: ˢ "You are right! We must do as you say. ¹³But there are many people here and it is the rainy season; so we cannot stand outside. Besides, this matter cannot be taken care of in a day or two, because we have sinned greatly in this thing. ¹⁴Let our officials act for the whole assembly. Then let everyone in our towns who has married a foreign woman come at a set time, along with the elders and

---

ᵃ 11 Or *Now make confession to*

---

ness. See Isa 6:1–5; Lk 5:8. For comparable passages of national lament see Ps 44; 60; 74; 79–80; 83; 85; 90; 108; 126; 129; 137.
10:1 *weeping.* Not silently but out loud (see 3:13 and note; Ne 1:4; Joel 2:12). *throwing himself down.* The prophets and other leaders used object lessons, even bizarre actions, to attract people's attention (Isa 7:3; 8:1–4,18; Jer 13:1–11; 19; 27:2–12; Eze 4:1—5:4).
10:2 Ezra, as a wise teacher, waited for his audience to draw their own conclusions about what should be done. *Shekaniah.* Perhaps his father, Jehiel, is the Jehiel mentioned in v. 26 since he was also of the family of Elam. If so, Shekaniah was doubtless grieved that his father had married a non-Jewish woman. Six members of the clan of Elam were involved in intermarriage (v. 26).

B **10:3** *women and their children.* Mothers were given custody of their children when marriages were dissolved. When Hagar was dismissed, Ishmael was sent with her (Ge 21:14). In Babylonia divorced women were granted their children and had to wait for them to grow up before remarrying, according to the Code of Hammurapi (see chart, p. xxiii). In Greece, however, children from broken homes remained with their fathers.
10:4 *Rise up.* Cf. David's exhortation (1Ch 22:16).
10:6 *room.* Such temple chambers were used as storerooms (8:29; Ne 13:4–5). *ate no food and drank no water.* Complete fasting from both food and drink was rare. Moses did it twice (Ex 34:28; Dt 9:18), and the Ninevites also did it (Jnh 3:7). Ordinarily, fasting involved abstaining only from eating (1Sa 1:7; 2Sa 3:35). *mourn.* The Hebrew for this word often describes the reaction of those aware of the threat of deserved judgment (Ex 33:4; Nu 14:39).

A **10:7–8** While Ezra continued to fast and pray, the officials and elders ordered all the exiles to assemble in Jerusalem.

Although Ezra had been invested with great authority (7:25–26), he used it sparingly and influenced the people by his example.
10:8 *within three days.* Since the territory of Judah had been much reduced, the most distant people would not be more than 50 miles from Jerusalem. The borders were Bethel in the north, Beersheba in the south, Jericho in the east and Ono in the west (cf. Ne 7:26–38; 11:25–35). *forfeit.* The Hebrew for this word means "to ban from profane use and to devote to the Lord," either by destruction (see Ex 22:20; Dt 13:12–18 and TNIV text notes) or by giving it to the Lord's treasury (cf. Lev 27:28; Jos 6:19; 7:1–15).
10:9,16–17 See chart, p. 694.
10:9 *Judah and Benjamin.* See note on 1:5. *square.* Either the outer court of the temple or the open space before the Water Gate (Ne 8:1). *rain.* The Hebrew for this word is a plural of intensity, indicating torrential rains. The ninth month, Kislev (November-December), is in the middle of the "rainy season" (v. 13), which begins with light showers in October and lasts to mid-April. December and January are also cold months, with temperatures in the 50s and even 40s in Jerusalem. The people shivered not only because they were drenched but perhaps also because they sensed divine displeasure in the heavy rains (see 1Sa 12:17–18; Eze 13:11,13).

A **10:10** *adding to Israel's guilt.* See Ex 9:34; Jdg 3:12; 4:1; 2Ch 28:13. The sins and failures of the exiles were great enough, but they added insult to injury by marrying pagan women.
10:11 *Separate yourselves.* See Nu 16:21; 2Co 6:14.
10:12 *with a loud voice.* See Ne 9:4.
10:14 *elders and judges of each town.* See Dt 16:18; 19:12; 21:3,19; Ru 4:2.

10:14 *t* Dt 16:18
u S Nu 25:4;
S 2Ch 29:10
10:15 *v* Ne 11:16
10:18 *w* S Jdg 3:6
x S Ezr 2:2
10:19 *y* S 2Ki 10:15
z S Lev 5:15; 6:6
10:20 *a* S 1Ch 24:14
10:21 *b* S 1Ch 24:8
10:22 *c* S 1Ch 9:12
10:23 *d* Ne 8:7; 9:4
10:24 *e* Ne 3:1;
12:10; 13:7,28
10:25 *f* S Ezr 2:3
10:26 *g* S ver 2

judges *t* of each town, until the fierce anger *u* of our God in this matter is turned away from us." [15] Only Jonathan son of Asahel and Jahzeiah son of Tikvah, supported by Meshullam and Shabbethai *v* the Levite, opposed this.

[16] So the exiles did as was proposed. Ezra the priest selected men who were family heads, one from each family division, and all of them designated by name. On the first day of the tenth month they sat down to investigate the cases, [17] and by the first day of the first month they finished dealing with all the men who had married foreign women.

THOSE GUILTY OF INTERMARRIAGE

[18] Among the descendants of the priests, the following had married foreign women: *w*

From the descendants of Joshua *x* son of Jozadak, and his brothers: Maaseiah, Eliezer, Jarib and Gedaliah. [19] (They all gave their hands *y* in pledge to put away their wives, and for their guilt they each presented a ram from the flock as a guilt offering.) *z*

[20] From the descendants of Immer: *a*
Hanani and Zebadiah.

[21] From the descendants of Harim: *b*
Maaseiah, Elijah, Shemaiah, Jehiel and Uzziah.

[22] From the descendants of Pashhur: *c*
Elioenai, Maaseiah, Ishmael, Nethanel, Jozabad and Elasah.

[23] Among the Levites: *d*
Jozabad, Shimei, Kelaiah (that is, Kelita), Pethahiah, Judah and Eliezer.

[24] From the musicians:
Eliashib. *e*
From the gatekeepers:
Shallum, Telem and Uri.

[25] And among the other Israelites:
From the descendants of Parosh: *f*
Ramiah, Izziah, Malkijah, Mijamin, Eleazar, Malkijah and Benaiah.

[26] From the descendants of Elam: *g*
Mattaniah, Zechariah, Jehiel, Abdi, Jeremoth and Elijah.

[27] From the descendants of Zattu:
Elioenai, Eliashib, Mattaniah, Jeremoth, Zabad and Aziza.

[28] From the descendants of Bebai:
Jehohanan, Hananiah, Zabbai and Athlai.

[29] From the descendants of Bani:
Meshullam, Malluk, Adaiah, Jashub, Sheal and Jeremoth.

[30] From the descendants of Pahath-Moab:
Adna, Kelal, Benaiah, Maaseiah, Mattaniah, Bezalel, Binnui and Manasseh.

[31] From the descendants of Harim:
Eliezer, Ishijah, Malkijah, Shemaiah, Shimeon, [32] Benjamin, Malluk and Shema-riah.

[33] From the descendants of Hashum:
Mattenai, Mattattah, Zabad, Eliphelet, Jeremai, Manasseh and Shimei.

[34] From the descendants of Bani:
Maadai, Amram, Uel, [35] Benaiah, Bedeiah, Keluhi, [36] Vaniah, Meremoth, Eliashib, [37] Mattaniah, Mattenai and Jaasu.

[38] From the descendants of Binnui: *a*

a 37,38 See Septuagint (also 1 Esdras 9:34); Hebrew *Jaasu 38and Bani and Binnui,*

10:15 Perhaps these four men opposed the measure because they wanted to protect themselves or their relatives, or they may have viewed it as being too harsh. *Tikvah.* Means "hope" (found elsewhere only in 2Ki 22:14). *Meshullam.* See note on 8:16. If he is the Meshullam of v. 29, he himself had married a pagan wife.

10:16–17 The committee completed its work in three months, discovering that about 110 men were guilty of marrying pagan wives.

10:18–22 See 2:36–39.

10:19 *gave their hands.* For the symbolic use of the hands in making commitments or pledges, cf. notes on Ge 14:22; Pr 6:1.

ram. Guilt offerings were to be made for sins committed unintentionally (Lev 5:14–19) as well as intentionally (Lev 6:1–7), and a ram was the appropriate offering in either case (Lev 5:15; 6:6).

10:24 It is striking that only one musician and three gatekeepers were involved. No temple servants (2:43–54) or descendants of Solomon's servants (2:55–57) sinned through intermarriage.

10:25–43 See 2:3–20.

10:30 *Bezalel.* Cf. Ex 31:2.

10:31 *Shimeon.* The Hebrew for this name is the same as that for Simeon, Jacob's second son (see TNIV text note on Ge 29:33). In Greek the name became Simon (e.g., Mt 4:18).

Shimei, [39]Shelemiah, Nathan, Adaiah, [40]Maknadebai, Shashai, Sharai, [41]Azarel, Shelemiah, Shemariah, [42]Shallum, Amariah and Joseph.
[43] From the descendants of Nebo:
Jeiel, Mattithiah, Zabad, Zebina, Jaddai, Joel and Benaiah.

[44]All these had married foreign women, and some of them had children by these wives.[a]

[a] 44 Or *and they sent them away with their children*

10:43 *Nebo.* The Hebrew equivalent of the name of the Babylonian god Nabu (see Isa 46:1); found only here as a personal name.

10:44 Some of the marriages had produced children, but this was not accepted as a reason for halting the divorce proceedings. See TNIV text note.

NEHEMIAH

INTRODUCTION

OUTLINE

1:1 *a* Zec 7:1
b S Ezr 4:9; S Est 2:8
1:2 *c* Ne 7:2
d S 2Ki 21:14; Ne 7:6;
Jer 52:28
1:3 *e* S Lev 26:31;
2Ki 25:10; Ne 2:3,13,
17; Isa 22:9; Jer 39:8;
52:14; La 2:9
1:4 *f* Ps 137:1
g S 2Ch 20:3;
S Ezr 9:4; Da 9:3
1:5 *h* S Dt 7:21;
Ne 4:14 *i* S Dt 7:9;
S 1Ki 8:23; Da 9:4
1:6 *j* S 1Ki 8:29;
S 2Ch 7:15
k S 1Ki 8:30
l S 1Ki 8:47
1:7 *m* Ps 106:6
1:8 *n* S Ge 8:1;
S 2Ki 20:3; Ne 4:14;
5:19; 6:14; 13:22,29,
31 *o* S Lev 26:33
1:9 *p* S Dt 30:4;
Ps 106:47; 107:3;
Isa 11:12; 56:8;
Jer 42:12; Eze 11:17
q S 1Ki 8:48;
Jer 29:14; Eze 11:17;
20:34-38; 36:24-38;
Mic 2:12
1:10 *r* S Ex 32:11;
Isa 51:9-11
1:11 *s* S 2Ch 6:40
t S Ex 3:21 *u* S Ge 40:1

NEHEMIAH'S PRAYER

1 The words of Nehemiah son of Hakaliah:

In the month of Kislev *a* in the twentieth year, while I was in the citadel of Susa, *b* ²Hanani, *c* one of my brothers, came from Judah with some other men, and I questioned them about the Jewish remnant *d* that had survived the exile, and also about Jerusalem.

³They said to me, "Those who survived the exile and are back in the province are in great trouble and disgrace. The wall of Jerusalem is broken down, and its gates have been burned with fire. *e* "

⁴When I heard these things, I sat down and wept. *f* For some days I mourned and fasted *g* and prayed before the God of heaven. ⁵Then I said:

"LORD, the God of heaven, the great and awesome God, *h* who keeps his covenant of love *i* with those who love him and keep his commandments, ⁶let your ear be attentive *j* and your eyes open to hear *j* the prayer *k* your servant is praying before you day and night for your servants, the people of Israel. I confess *l* the sins we Israelites, including myself and my ancestral family, have committed against you. ⁷We have acted very wickedly *m* toward you. We have not obeyed the commands, decrees and laws you gave your servant Moses.

⁸"Remember *n* the instruction you gave your servant Moses, saying, 'If you are unfaithful, I will scatter *o* you among the nations, ⁹but if you return to me and obey my commands, then even if your exiled people are at the farthest horizon, I will gather *p* them from there and bring them to the place I have chosen as a dwelling for my Name.' *q*

¹⁰"They are your servants and your people, whom you redeemed by your great strength and your mighty hand. *r* ¹¹Lord, let your ear be attentive *s* to the prayer of this your servant and to the prayer of your servants who delight in revering your name. Give your servant success today by granting him favor *t* in the presence of this man."

I was cupbearer *u* to the king.

1:1 *The words of.* Originally an introduction to the title of a separate composition (see Jer 1:1; Am 1:1), though the books of Ezra and Nehemiah appear as a single work from earliest times (see Introduction to Ezra: Ezra and Nehemiah). *Nehemiah.* Means "The LORD comforts." *Kislev … twentieth year.* November-December, 445 B.C. See chart, p. 694. *Susa.* See note on Ezr 4:9.

B **1:2** *Hanani.* Probably a shortened form of Hananiah, which means "The LORD is gracious." *one of my brothers.* See 7:2. The Elephantine papyri (see chart, p. xxiii) mention a Hananiah who was the head of Jewish affairs in Jerusalem. Many believe that he is to be identified with Nehemiah's brother and that he may have governed between Nehemiah's first and second terms. *Jewish remnant.* See Ezr 9:8 and notes on Ge 45:7; 2Ki 19:30-31; Isa 1:9; 10:20-22; Zec 8:23.

B **1:3** *province.* See note on Ezr 2:1. *wall of Jerusalem is broken down.* The lack of a city wall meant that the people were defenseless against their enemies. Thucydides (1.89) describes the comparable condition of Athens after its devastation by the Persians in 480-479 B.C. Excavations at Jerusalem during 1961-67 revealed that the lack of a wall on the eastern slopes also meant the disintegration of the terraces there. When Nebuchadnezzar assaulted Jerusalem in 586, he battered and broke down the walls around it (2Ki 25:10). But most interpreters do not believe that Nehemiah's distress was caused by Nebuchadnezzar's destruction but by the episode of Ezr 4:7-23. The Jews had attempted to rebuild the walls earlier in the reign of Artaxerxes I; but after the protest of Rehum and Shimshai the king ordered the Jews to desist. See note on Ezr 4:21-23.

1:4 *sat down.* Cf. Ezr 9:3; Job 2:13. *wept.* See 8:9; Ezr 3:13 and note; 10:1; Est 8:3. *mourned.* See Ezr 10:6; Da 10:2. *fasted and prayed.* See note on Ezr 8:23. During the exile, fasting became a common practice, including solemn fasts to commemorate the fall of Jerusalem and the murder of Gedaliah (see note on Zec 8:19; see also Est 4:16; Da 9:3; 10:3; Zec 7:3-7). *God of heaven.* See note on Ezr 1:2.

1:5 *who keeps his covenant of love.* See 9:32; see also Dt 7:9,12

and note. *who love him and keep his commandments.* See Da 9:4; cf. Ex 20:6 and note.

A **1:6** *praying before you day and night.* Cf. Ps 42:3; 88:1; Jer 9:1; 14:17; La 2:18; Lk 2:37; 1Th 3:10; 1Ti 5:5; 2Ti 1:3. *sins … myself and my ancestral family.* Nehemiah does not exclude himself or members of his own family in his confession of sins. A true sense of the awesome holiness of God reveals the depths of our own sinfulness (Isa 6:1-5; Lk 5:8).

1:7 *commands, decrees and laws.* See note on Ge 26:5. *laws you gave … Moses.* For the prominence of the Law of Moses in Ezra and Nehemiah, see Ezr 3:2; 6:18; 7:6; Ne 1:8; 8:1,14; 9:14; 10:29; 13:1.

A **1:8** *Remember.* See notes on 13:31; Ge 8:1; a key word in the book (4:14; 5:19; 6:14; 13:14, 22,29,31). *unfaithful … scatter.* Dispersion was the inescapable consequence of the people's unfaithfulness. By the NT period there were still more Jews in the Diaspora (dispersion) than in the Holy Land.

1:9 *I will gather them.* See Dt 30:1-5; a frequent promise, especially in the prophets (e.g., Isa 11:12; Jer 23:3; 31:8-10; Eze 20:34,41; 36:24; Mic 2:12). *chosen as a dwelling for my Name.* See Dt 12:5 and note; Ps 132:13.

A **1:10** *your people … you redeemed.* Although they had sinned and failed, they were still God's people by virtue of his redeeming them (see Dt 4:34; 9:29).

C **1:11** *Give your servant success today.* Cf. Ge 24:12. *cupbearer.* Lit. "one who gives (someone) something to drink." The Hebrew for this word occurs 11 other times in the OT in the sense of "cupbearer" (Ge 40:1-2,5,9,13,20-21,23; 41:9; 1Ki 10:5; 2Ch 9:4). According to the Greek historian Xenophon (*Cyropaedia,* 1.3.9), one of the cupbearer's duties was to choose and taste the king's wine to make certain that it was not poisoned (see 2:1). Thus Nehemiah had to be a man who enjoyed the unreserved confidence of the king. The need for trustworthy court attendants is underscored by the intrigues that characterized the Achaemenid court of Persia. Xerxes, the father of Artaxerxes I, was killed in his own bedchamber by a courtier.

ARTAXERXES SENDS NEHEMIAH TO JERUSALEM

2 In the month of Nisan in the twentieth year of King Artaxerxes, *v* when wine was brought for him, I took the wine and gave it to the king. I had not been sad in his presence before, ²so the king asked me, "Why does your face look so sad when you are not ill? This can be nothing but sadness of heart."

I was very much afraid, ³but I said to the king, "May the king live forever! *w* Why should my face not look sad when the city *x* where my ancestors are buried lies in ruins, and its gates have been destroyed by fire? *y*"

⁴The king said to me, "What is it you want?"

Then I prayed to the God of heaven, ⁵and I answered the king, "If it pleases the king and if your servant has found favor in his sight, let him send me to the city in Judah where my ancestors are buried so that I can rebuild it."

⁶Then the king *z*, with the queen sitting beside him, asked me, "How long will your journey take, and when will you get back?" It pleased the king to send me; so I set a time.

⁷I also said to him, "If it pleases the king, may I have letters to the governors of Trans-Euphrates, *a* so that they will provide me safe-conduct until I arrive in Judah? ⁸And may I have a letter to Asaph, keeper of the royal park, so he will give me timber to make beams

2:1 *v* S Ezr 4:7;
S 6:14
2:3 *w* 1Ki 1:31;
Da 2:4; 3:9; 5:10; 6:6,
21 *x* Ps 137:6
y S Ne 1:3
2:6 *z* Ne 5:14; 13:6
2:7 *a* S Ezr 8:36

2:1 *Nisan ... twentieth year.* March-April, 444 B.C. (see chart, p. 694). *King Artaxerxes.* See chart, p. 482. *sad in his presence.* No matter what one's personal problems were, the king's servants were expected to keep their feelings to themselves and to display a cheerful disposition before him.

2:3 *May the king live forever!* A common form of address to kings (cf. note on Ps 62:4). *city.* Nehemiah does not mention Jerusalem by name (see v. 5); he may have wished to arouse the king's sympathy by stressing first the desecration of ancestral tombs.

A C **2:4** *prayed.* Before turning to answer the king, Nehemiah utters a brief, spontaneous prayer to God. One of Nehemiah's striking characteristics is his frequent recourse to prayer (1:4; 4:4,9; 5:19; 6:9,14; 13:14,22,29,31).

2:6 *queen.* The Hebrew for this word is used only here and in Ps 45:9 ("royal bride"). It is a loanword from Akkadian and means lit. "(woman) of the palace." The Aramaic equivalent is found only in Da 5:2–3,23, where it is translated "wives." Ctesias, a Greek who lived at the Achaemenid court, informs us that the

name of Artaxerxes's queen was Damaspia and that he had at least three concubines. Like Esther (Est 5), Damaspia may have used her influence with the king. The Achaemenid court was notorious for the great influence exercised by the royal women. Especially domineering was Amestris, the cruel wife of Xerxes and mother of Artaxerxes I. *How long will your journey take ...?* Nehemiah probably asked for a brief leave of absence, which he then had extended. We can infer from 5:14 that he spent 12 years on his first term as governor of Judah. In the 32nd year of Artaxerxes, Nehemiah returned to report to the king and then came back to Judah for a second term (13:6–7).

B **2:7** *letters ... provide me safe-conduct.* A contemporary document from Arsames, the satrap of Egypt who was at the Persian court, to one of his officers who was returning to Egypt orders Persian officials to provide him with food and drink on the stages of his journey. *Trans-Euphrates.* See note on Ezr 4:10.

2:8 *park.* The Hebrew for this word is *pardes,* a loanword from Old Persian meaning "enclosure," a pleasant retreat. The word

JERUSALEM OF THE RETURNING EXILES

after 458 B.C.

A smaller city was rebuilt, with new walls higher on the eastern hill. Temple worship was restored in a rebuilt temple on the former site. Rebuilding on the western hill may have begun.

©1982 Hugh Claycombe

Jerusalem is shown from above and at an angle; therefore wall shapes appear different from those on flat maps. Wall locations have been determined from limited archaeological evidence; houses are artist's concept.

2:8 *b* Ne 7:2
c S Ezr 5:5
d S Ezr 4:24
2:9 *e* S Ezr 8:22
2:10 *f* ver 19; Ne 4:1,
7; 6:1-2,5,12,14;
13:28 *g* Ne 4:3; 13:4-7
h Est 10:3
2:11 *i* S Ge 40:13
2:13 *j* S 2Ch 26:9
k Ne 3:13; 12:31
l S Ne 1:3
2:14 *m* Ne 3:15;
12:37 *n* S 2Ki 18:17

for the gates of the citadel *b* by the temple and for the city wall and for the residence I will occupy?" And because the gracious hand of my God was on me, *c* the king granted my requests. *d* ⁹So I went to the governors of Trans-Euphrates and gave them the king's letters. The king had also sent army officers and cavalry *e* with me.

¹⁰When Sanballat *f* the Horonite and Tobiah *g* the Ammonite official heard about this, they were very much disturbed that someone had come to promote the welfare of the Israelites. *h*

NEHEMIAH INSPECTS JERUSALEM'S WALLS

¹¹I went to Jerusalem, and after staying there three days *i* ¹²I set out during the night with a few others. I had not told anyone what my God had put in my heart to do for Jerusalem. There were no mounts with me except the one I was riding on.

¹³By night I went out through the Valley Gate *j* toward the Jackal *a* Well and the Dung Gate, *k* examining the walls *l* of Jerusalem, which had been broken down, and its gates, which had been destroyed by fire. ¹⁴Then I moved on toward the Fountain Gate *m* and the King's Pool, *n* but there was not enough room for my mount to get through; ¹⁵so I went up the valley by night, examining the wall. Finally, I turned back and reentered through the Valley Gate. ¹⁶The officials did not know where I had gone or what I was doing, because as yet I had said nothing to the Jews or the priests or nobles or officials or any others who would be doing the work.

¹⁷Then I said to them, "You see the trouble we are in: Jerusalem lies in ruins, and its

a 13 Or *Serpent* or *Fig*

---

occurs elsewhere in the OT only in Ecc 2:5 ("parks") and SS 4:13 ("orchard"). In the Septuagint (the pre-Christian Greek translation of the OT) the Greek transliteration *paradeisos* is used here. In the period between the OT and the NT, the word acquired the sense of the abode of the blessed dead, i.e., "paradise." It appears three times in the NT (Lk 23:43; 2Co 12:4; Rev 2:7). As to the location of the "royal park," some believe that it was in Lebanon, which was famed for its forests of cedars and other coniferous trees (see notes in Jdg 9:15; Ezr 3:7). But a more plausible suggestion is that it should be identified with Solomon's gardens at Etham, about six miles south of Jerusalem (see Josephus, *Antiquities,* 8.7.3). For city gates, costly imported cedars from Lebanon would not be used but rather indigenous oak, poplar or terebinth (Hos 4:13). *citadel.* Probably refers to the fortress north of the temple, the forerunner of the Antonia fortress built by Herod the Great (Josephus, *Antiquities,* 15.11.4; see Ac 21:34,37; 22:24).

2:9 *army officers and cavalry.* In striking contrast to Ezra (see note on Ezr 8:22), Nehemiah was accompanied by an armed escort since he was officially Judah's governor.

B C **2:10** *Sanballat.* A Babylonian name, meaning "Sin (the moon-god) has given life." *Horonite.* Identifies him as coming from (1) Hauran (Eze 47:16,18), east of the Sea of Galilee; (2) Horonaim, in Moab (Jer 48:34); or, most probably, (3) either Upper or Lower Beth Horon, two key cities about 11 miles northwest of Jerusalem (Jos 10:10; 16:3,5; 1 Maccabees 3:16; 7:39). Sanballat was the chief political opponent of Nehemiah (v. 19; 4:1,7; 6:1–2,5,12,14; 13:28). He held the position of governor over Samaria (cf. 4:1–2). An Elephantine papyrus letter of the late fifth century B.C. to Bagohi (Bigvai), governor of Judah, refers to "Delaiah and Shelemiah, the sons of Sanballat, governor of Samaria." In 1962 a fourth-century B.C. papyrus listing the name Sanballat, probably a descendant of Nehemiah's contemporary, was found in a cave north of Jericho. *Tobiah.* Means "The LORD is good." He was probably a worshiper of the Lord (Yahweh), as indicated not only by his name but also by that of his son Jehohanan (6:17–18), meaning "The LORD is gracious." Jehohanan was married to the daughter of Meshullam, son of Berekiah, the leader of one of the groups repairing the wall (3:4,30; 6:18). Tobiah also had a close relationship with Eliashib the priest (13:4–7). *Ammonite.* See Ezr 9:1; see also note on Ge 19:36–38. Tobiah was probably governor of Transjordan under the Persians. In later generations a prominent family bearing the name

of Tobiah was sometimes associated with the region of Ammon in non-Biblical texts. *very much disturbed.* The reasons for the opposition of Sanballat and Tobiah were not basically religious but political. The authority of the Samaritan governor in particular was threatened by Nehemiah's arrival.

2:11 *three days.* See note on Ezr 8:32.

2:12 Nehemiah was cautious and discreet as he inspected the city's fortifications. *one I was riding on.* Probably a mule or donkey.

B **2:13** Nehemiah did not make a complete circuit of the walls but only of the southern area (see map, p. 715). Jerusalem was always attacked from the north because it was most vulnerable there, so the walls had probably been completely destroyed in that part of the city. *Valley Gate.* See 3:13. According to 2Ch 26:9 Uzziah fortified towers in the west wall, which overlooked the central valley between the Hinnom and Kidron valleys. Excavations in 1927–28 uncovered the remains of a gate from the Persian period, which has been identified as the Valley Gate. *Jackal Well.* Many interpreters suggest that this was En Rogel (Jos 15:7–8; 18:16; 2Sa 17:17; 1Ki 1:9), a well situated at the junction of the Hinnom and Kidron valleys, 250 yards south of the southeast ridge of Jerusalem (see map on p. 715). Others suggest that it was the Pool of Siloam (see map, p. 1677). *Dung Gate.* Perhaps the gate leading to the rubbish dump in the Hinnom Valley (cf. 3:13–14; 12:31; 2Ki 23:10). It was situated about 500 yards south of the Valley Gate (3:13).

B **2:14** *Fountain Gate.* Possibly in the southeast wall facing toward En Rogel (see 3:15; 12:37). *King's Pool.* Hezekiah may have diverted the overflow from his Siloam tunnel (cf. 2Ki 20:20; 2Ch 32:30) to irrigate the royal gardens (2Ki 25:4) located outside the city walls at the junction of the Kidron and Hinnom valleys. The King's Pool was probably therefore the Pool of Siloam (3:15) or the adjacent Birket el-Hamra. *not enough room.* Possibly because of the collapse of the supporting terraces (cf. 2Sa 5:9; 1Ki 9:15,24) on the east side of the city.

2:15 *valley.* The Kidron.

2:16 *nobles.* The Hebrew root for this word means "free" (see 4:14,19; 5:7; 6:17; 7:5; 13:17; see also note on 3:5).

2:17 *ruins.* The condition of the walls and gates of the city since their destruction by Nebuchadnezzar in 586 B.C., in spite of abortive attempts to rebuild them. The leaders and people had evidently become reconciled to this sad state of affairs. It took an outsider to assess the situation and to rally them to renewed efforts.

gates have been burned with fire. ^{o} Come, let us rebuild the wall ^{p} of Jerusalem, and we will no longer be in disgrace. ^{q}" ^{18}I also told them about the gracious hand of my God on me ^{r} and what the king had said to me.

They replied, "Let us start rebuilding." So they began this good work.

^{19}But when Sanballat ^{s} the Horonite, Tobiah the Ammonite official and Geshem ^{t} the Arab heard about it, they mocked and ridiculed us. ^{u} "What is this you are doing?" they asked. "Are you rebelling against the king?"

^{20}I answered them by saying, "The God of heaven will give us success. We his servants will start rebuilding, ^{v} but as for you, you have no share ^{w} in Jerusalem or any claim or historic right to it."

BUILDERS OF THE WALL

3 Eliashib ^{x} the high priest and his fellow priests went to work and rebuilt ^{y} the Sheep Gate. ^{z} They dedicated it and set its doors in place, building as far as the Tower of the Hundred, which they dedicated, and as far as the Tower of Hananel. ^{a} ^{2}The men of Jericho ^{b} built the adjoining section, and Zakkur son of Imri built next to them.

^{3}The Fish Gate ^{c} was rebuilt by the sons of Hassenaah. They laid its beams and put its doors and bolts and bars in place. ^{4}Meremoth ^{d} son of Uriah, the son of Hakkoz, repaired the next section. Next to him Meshullam son of Berekiah, the son of Meshezabel, made repairs, and next to him Zadok son of Baana also made repairs. ^{5}The next section was repaired by the men of Tekoa, ^{e} but their nobles would not put their shoulders to the work under their supervisors. ^{a}

^{6}The Jeshanah ^{b} Gate ^{f} was repaired by Joiada son of Paseah and Meshullam son of Besodeiah. They laid its beams and put its doors with their bolts and bars in place. ^{7}Next to them, repairs were made by men from Gibeon ^{g} and Mizpah—Melatiah of Gibeon and Jadon of Meronoth—places under the authority of the governor of Trans-Euphrates. ^{8}Uzziel son of Harhaiah, one of the goldsmiths, repaired the next section; and Hananiah, one

---

^{a} 5 Or *their Lord* or *the governor* ^{b} 6 Or *Old*

2:17 ^{o} S Ne 1:3
^{p} Ps 102:16; Isa 30:13; 58:12 ^{q} Eze 5:14
2:18 ^{r} S Ezr 5:5
2:19 ^{s} S ver 10
^{t} Ne 6:1,2,6
^{u} Ps 44:13-16
2:20 ^{v} Ezr 4:1
^{w} Ezr 4:3; Ac 8:21
3:1 ^{x} S Ezr 10:24
^{y} Isa 58:12 ^{z} ver 32; Ne 12:39; Jn 5:2
^{a} Ne 12:39; Ps 48:12; Jer 31:38; Zec 14:10
3:2 ^{b} Ne 7:36
3:3 ^{c} S 2Ch 33:14
3:4 ^{d} S Ezr 8:33
3:5 ^{e} ver 27; S 2Sa 14:2
3:6 ^{f} Ne 12:39
3:7 ^{g} S Jos 9:3

C **2:18** *my God...and...the king.* Nehemiah could personally attest that God was alive and active in his behalf and that he (Nehemiah) had come with royal sanction and authority.

B **2:19** *Sanballat...Tobiah.* See note on v. 10. *Geshem.* Inscriptions from Dedan in northwest Arabia and from Tell el-Maskhutah near Ismailia in Egypt bear the name Geshem, who may have been in charge of a north Arabian confederacy that controlled vast areas from northeast Egypt to northern Arabia, including the southern part of the Holy Land. Geshem may have been opposed to Nehemiah's development of an independent kingdom because he feared that it might interfere with his lucrative spice trade. *Arab.* See Ge 21:13; Isa 21:13; Jer 25:24. Arabs became dominant in Transjordan from the Assyrian to the Persian periods. Sargon II of Assyria resettled some Arabs in Samaria in 715 B.C. Early Greek and Roman sources reveal that the Arabs enjoyed a favored status under the Persians.

3:1–32 One of the most important chapters in the OT for determining the topography of Jerusalem (see map No. 10 at the end of this study Bible; see also map, p. 715). The narrative begins at the Sheep Gate (northeast corner of the city) and proceeds in a counterclockwise direction around the wall. About 40 key men are named as participants in the reconstruction of about 45 sections. The towns listed as the homes of the builders may have represented the administrative centers of the province of Judah. Ten gates are named: (1) Sheep Gate (v. 1), (2) Fish Gate (v. 3), (3) Jeshanah Gate (v. 6), (4) Valley Gate (v. 13), (5) Dung Gate (v. 14), (6) Fountain Gate (v. 15), (7) Water Gate (v. 26), (8) Horse Gate (v. 28), (9) East Gate (v. 29), (10) Inspection Gate (v. 31). The account suggests that most of the rebuilding was concerned with the gates, where the enemy's assaults were always concentrated. Not all the sections of the walls or buildings in Jerusalem were in the same state of disrepair. A selective policy of destruction seems to be indicated by 2Ki 25:9.

B **3:1** *Eliashib the high priest.* It was fitting that the high priest should set the example. Among the ancient Sumerians the king himself would carry bricks for the building of a tem-

ple. *Sheep Gate.* See v. 32; 12:39. It was known in NT times (Jn 5:2) as located near the Bethesda Pool (in the northeast corner of Jerusalem). Even today a sheep market is held periodically near this area. The Sheep Gate may have replaced the earlier Benjamin Gate (Jer 37:13; 38:7; Zec 14:10). *Tower of the Hundred.* See 12:39. "Hundred" may refer to (1) its height (100 cubits), (2) the number of its steps or (3) a military unit (cf. Dt 1:15). *Tower of Hananel.* The towers were associated with the "citadel by the temple" (2:8) in protecting the vulnerable northern approaches to the city.

3:3 *Fish Gate.* See 12:39. During the days of the first temple, it was one of Jerusalem's main entrances (2Ch 33:14; Zep 1:10). Merchants brought fish from either Tyre or the Sea of Galilee to the fish market (13:16) through this entrance, which was located in the north wall of the city (see note on Zep 1:10).

3:4 *Meremoth.* See note on Ezr 8:33. *Meshullam.* Repaired a second section (v. 30). Nehemiah complained that Meshullam had given his daughter in marriage to a son of Tobiah (see 6:17–18 and note on 2:10).

3:5 *Tekoa.* A small town about 6 miles south of Bethlehem and 11 miles from Jerusalem. It was the hometown of the prophet Amos. *nobles.* The Hebrew for this word is different from that in 2:16 (see note there) and means "mighty" or "magnificent" (see 10:29; 2Ch 23:20; Jer 14:3). These aristocrats disdained manual labor. *shoulders.* Lit. "back of the neck." The expression is drawn from the imagery of oxen that refuse to yield to the yoke (Jer 27:12).

3:6 *Jeshanah Gate.* In the northwest corner. It may be another name for the Gate of Ephraim (see 12:39), which otherwise is not mentioned in ch. 3.

B **3:8** *goldsmiths.* See vv. 31–32. *perfume-makers.* See 1Sa 8:13. *Broad Wall.* See 12:38. In 1970–71 archaeological excavations in Jerusalem uncovered such a wall west of the temple area. It is dated to the early seventh century B.C. and was probably built by Hezekiah (2Ch 32:5). The expansion to and beyond the Broad Wall may have become necessary because of the influx of refugees fleeing from the fall of Samaria in 722–721.

3:8 *h* Ne 12:38
3:11 *i* Ne 12:38
3:13 *j* S 2Ch 26:9
k S Jos 15:34
l S Ne 2:13
3:14 *m* Jer 6:1
3:15 *n* Isa 8:6; Jn 9:7
3:16 *o* S Jos 15:58
p Ac 2:29
3:17 *q* S Jos 15:44
3:21 *r* S Ezr 8:33
3:24 *s* S Ezr 8:33
3:25 *t* Jer 32:2;
37:21; 39:14
u S Ezr 2:3
3:26 *v* Ne 7:46; 11:21
w S 2Ch 33:14

of the perfume-makers, made repairs next to that. They restored Jerusalem as far as the Broad Wall. *h* 9Rephaiah son of Hur, ruler of a half-district of Jerusalem, repaired the next section. 10Adjoining this, Jedaiah son of Harumaph made repairs opposite his house, and Hattush son of Hashabneiah made repairs next to him. 11Malkijah son of Harim and Hasshub son of Pahath-Moab repaired another section and the Tower of the Ovens. *i* 12Shallum son of Hallohesh, ruler of a half-district of Jerusalem, repaired the next section with the help of his daughters.

13The Valley Gate*j* was repaired by Hanun and the residents of Zanoah. *k* They rebuilt it and put its doors with their bolts and bars in place. They also repaired a thousand cubits*a* of the wall as far as the Dung Gate. *l*

14The Dung Gate was repaired by Malkijah son of Rekab, ruler of the district of Beth Hakkerem. *m* He rebuilt it and put its doors with their bolts and bars in place.

15The Fountain Gate was repaired by Shallun son of Kol-Hozeh, ruler of the district of Mizpah. He rebuilt it, roofing it over and putting its doors and bolts and bars in place. He also repaired the wall of the Pool of Siloam, *b n* by the King's Garden, as far as the steps going down from the City of David. 16Beyond him, Nehemiah son of Azbuk, ruler of a half-district of Beth Zur, *o* made repairs up to a point opposite the tombs*c p* of David, as far as the artificial pool and the House of the Heroes.

17Next to him, the repairs were made by the Levites under Rehum son of Bani. Beside him, Hashabiah, ruler of half the district of Keilah, *q* carried out repairs for his district. 18Next to him, the repairs were made by their neighbors under Binnui*d* son of Henadad, ruler of the other half-district of Keilah. 19Next to him, Ezer son of Jeshua, ruler of Mizpah, repaired another section, from a point facing the ascent to the armory as far as the angle of the wall. 20Next to him, Baruch son of Zabbai zealously repaired another section, from the angle to the entrance of the house of Eliashib the high priest. 21Next to him, Meremoth*r* son of Uriah, son of Hakkoz, repaired another section, from the entrance of Eliashib's house to the end of it.

22The repairs next to him were made by the priests from the surrounding region. 23Beyond them, Benjamin and Hasshub made repairs in front of their house; and next to them, Azariah son of Maaseiah, the son of Ananiah, made repairs beside his house. 24Next to him, Binnui*s* son of Henadad repaired another section, from Azariah's house to the angle and the corner, 25and Palal son of Uzai worked opposite the angle and the tower projecting from the upper palace near the court of the guard. *t* Next to him, Pedaiah son of Parosh*u* 26and the temple servants*v* living on the hill of Ophel*w* made repairs up to a point oppo-

a 13 That is, about 1,500 feet or about 450 meters   *b* 15 Hebrew *Shelah,* a variant of *Shiloah,* that is, Siloam   *c* 16 Hebrew; Septuagint, some Vulgate manuscripts and Syriac *tomb*   *d* 18 Two Hebrew manuscripts and Syriac (see also Septuagint and verse 24); most Hebrew manuscripts *Bavvai*

3:10 *Jedaiah ... made repairs opposite his house.* See vv. 23, 28–30. It made sense to have him and others repair the sections of the wall nearest their homes.

3:11 *Tower of the Ovens.* It was on the western wall, perhaps in the same location as one built by Uzziah (2Ch 26:9). The ovens may have been those situated in the "street of the bakers" (Jer 37:21).

3:12 *daughters.* A unique reference to women working on the wall. When the Athenians attempted to rebuild their walls after the Persians had destroyed them, it was decreed that "the whole population of the city—men, women and children—should take part in the wall-building" (Thucydides, 1.90.3).

3:13 *Valley Gate.* See note on 2:13. *a thousand cubits.* An extraordinary length (see TNIV text note); probably most of the section was relatively intact. *Dung Gate.* See note on 2:13.

3:14 *Beth Hakkerem.* Means "house of the vineyard." It was a fire-signal point (Jer 6:1) and is identified with Ramat Rahel, two miles south of Jerusalem. It may have been the residence of a district governor in the Persian period.

3:15 *Fountain Gate.* See note on 2:14. *Pool of Siloam.* See TNIV text note; perhaps the Lower Pool of Isa 22:9 (see note on Isa 8:6). *King's Garden.* See note on 2:14. *City of David.* See 12:37; see also 2Sa 5:7 and note.

■ 3:16 *Beth Zur.* A district capital, 13 miles south of Jerusalem. Excavations in 1931 and 1957 revealed that occupation was sparse during the early Persian period but was

resumed in the fifth century B.C. *tombs of David.* Cf. 2:5. David was buried in the city area (1Ki 2:10; 2Ch 21:20; 32:33; Ac 2:29). The so-called Tomb of David on Mount Zion, venerated today by Jewish pilgrims, is in the Coenaculum building, erected in the 14th century A.D. Such a site for David's tomb is mentioned no earlier than the ninth century A.D. *House of the Heroes.* May have been the house of David's mighty warriors (see 2Sa 23:8–39), which perhaps served later as the barracks or armory.

3:17–18 *Keilah.* Located about 15 miles southwest of Jerusalem, it played an important role in David's early history (1Sa 23:1–13).

3:19 *armory.* See note on v. 16. *angle.* See 2Ch 26:9.

3:20–21 The residences of the high priest and his fellow priests were located inside the city along the eastern wall.

3:25 *upper palace.* Perhaps the old palace of David (see 12:37). Like Solomon's palace, it would have had a guardhouse (Jer 32:2).

■ 3:26 *Ophel.* See v. 27. The word means "swelling" or "bulge," hence a (fortified) "hill" (as in Mic 4:8; see TNIV text note there), specifically the northern part of the southeastern hill of Jerusalem, which formed the original City of David, just south of the temple area (2Ch 27:3). *Water Gate.* So called because it led to the main source of Jerusalem's water, the Gihon spring. It must have opened onto a large area, for the reading of the Law took place there (8:1,3,16; 12:37). *projecting tower.* Perhaps the large tower whose ruins were discovered by archaeologists on the crest of the Ophel hill in 1923–25. Excavations at the base of the tower in 1978 revealed a level dating to the Persian era.

site the Water Gate^x toward the east and the projecting tower. ²⁷Next to them, the men of Tekoa^y repaired another section, from the great projecting tower^z to the wall of Ophel.

²⁸Above the Horse Gate, ^a the priests made repairs, each in front of his own house. ²⁹Next to them, Zadok son of Immer made repairs opposite his house. Next to him, Shemaiah son of Shekaniah, the guard at the East Gate, made repairs. ³⁰Next to him, Hananiah son of Shelemiah, and Hanun, the sixth son of Zalaph, repaired another section. Next to them, Meshullam son of Berekiah made repairs opposite his living quarters. ³¹Next to him, Malkijah, one of the goldsmiths, made repairs as far as the house of the temple servants and the merchants, opposite the Inspection Gate, and as far as the room above the corner; ³²and between the room above the corner and the Sheep Gate^b the goldsmiths and merchants made repairs.

OPPOSITION TO THE REBUILDING

4 [*]When Sanballat^c heard that we were rebuilding the wall, he became angry and was greatly incensed. He ridiculed the Jews, ²and in the presence of his associates^d and the army of Samaria, he said, "What are those feeble Jews doing? Will they restore their wall? Will they offer sacrifices? Will they finish in a day? Can they bring the stones back to life from those heaps of rubble^e—burned as they are?"

³Tobiah^f the Ammonite, who was at his side, said, "What they are building—even a fox climbing up on it would break down their wall of stones!"^g

⁴Hear us, our God, for we are despised.^h Turn their insults back on their own heads. Give them over as plunder in a land of captivity. ⁵Do not cover up their guiltⁱ or blot out their sins from your sight,^j for they have thrown insults in the face of^a the builders.

⁶So we rebuilt the wall till all of it reached half its height, for the people worked with all their heart.

^{*7}But when Sanballat, Tobiah,^k the Arabs, the Ammonites and the people of Ashdod heard that the repairs to Jerusalem's walls had gone ahead and that the gaps were being closed, they were very angry. ⁸They all plotted together^l to come and fight against Jerusalem and stir up trouble against it. ⁹But we prayed to our God and posted a guard day and night to meet this threat.

¹⁰Meanwhile, the people in Judah said, "The strength of the laborers^m is giving out, and there is so much rubble that we cannot rebuild the wall."

¹¹Also our enemies said, "Before they know it or see us, we will be right there among them and will kill them and put an end to the work."

¹²Then the Jews who lived near them came and told us ten times over, "Wherever you turn, they will attack us."

¹³Therefore I stationed some of the people behind the lowest points of the wall at the exposed places, posting them by families, with their swords, spears and bows. ¹⁴After I looked things over, I stood up and said to the nobles, the officials and the rest of the people, "Don't be afraidⁿ of them. Remember^o the Lord, who is great and awesome,^p and fight^q for your people, your sons and your daughters, your wives and your homes."

---

^a 5 Or *have aroused your anger before*

[*] 4:1-6 is numbered 3:33-38 in Hebrew texts.   [*] 4:7-23 is numbered 4:1-17 in Hebrew texts.

3:26 ^x Ne 8:1,3,16; 12:37
3:27 ^y S ver 5
^z Ps 48:12
3:28 ^a S 2Ki 11:16
3:32 ^b S ver 1; Jn 5:2
4:1 ^c S Ne 2:10
4:2 ^d S Ezr 4:9-10
^e Ps 79:1; Jer 26:18
4:3 ^f S Ne 2:10
^g Job 13:12; 15:3
4:4 ^h Ps 44:13; 123:3-4; Jer 33:24
4:5 ⁱ Isa 2:9; La 1:22
^j 2Ki 14:27; Ps 51:1; 69:27-28; 109:14; Jer 18:23
4:7 ^k S Ne 2:10
4:8 ^l Ps 2:2; 83:1-18
4:10 ^m S 1Ch 23:4
4:14 ⁿ S Ge 28:15; S Dt 1:29 ^o S Ne 1:8
^p S Ne 1:5
^q S 2Sa 10:12

3:27 *men of Tekoa.* The common people of Tekoa did double duty, whereas the nobles of Tekoa shirked their responsibility (see note on v. 5).

3:28 *Horse Gate.* Where Athaliah was slain (2Ch 23:15). It may have been the easternmost point in the city wall—a gate through which one could reach the Kidron Valley (Jer 31:40).

3:29 *East Gate.* May have been the predecessor of the present Golden Gate.

3:31 *goldsmiths.* See v. 8. *Inspection Gate.* In the northern part of the eastern wall.

3:32 *Sheep Gate.* Back to the point of departure (see v. 1).

4:1 *Jews.* See note on Jer 34:9.

4:2 *he said.* Disputes between rival Persian governors were frequent. Sanballat asked several derisive questions to taunt the Jews and to discourage them in their efforts. *burned.* Fire had damaged the stones, which were probably limestone, and had caused many of them to crack and crumble.

4:4–5 As in the so-called imprecatory psalms (see note on Ps

5:10), Nehemiah does not himself take action against his opponents but calls down on them redress from God. In v. 5 Nehemiah's prayer echoes the language of Jer 18:23.

4:7 *Ashdod.* See note on Isa 20:1. It became a district capital under Persian rule.

4:9 *prayed … posted a guard.* Prayer and watchfulness blend faith and action and also emphasize both the divine side and the human side.

4:10 *giving out.* The picture is of workers staggering under the weight of their load and ready to fall at any step.

4:11 *our enemies said.* Either Nehemiah had friendly informants, or the enemy was spreading unsettling rumors.

4:12 *ten times over.* Many times.

4:13 *lowest points … exposed places.* Nehemiah posted men conspicuously in the areas that were the most vulnerable along the wall. *spears.* Used as thrusting weapons (Nu 25:7–8; 1Ki 18:28).

4:14 *Don't be afraid of them. Remember the Lord.* See note on 1:8. The best way to dispel fear is to remember

4:15 `r` 2Sa 17:14;
Job 5:12
4:17 `s` Ps 149:6
4:18 `t` S Nu 10:2
4:20 `u` Eze 33:3
`v` S Ex 14:14;
S Dt 20:4; Jos 10:14
5:3 `w` Ps 109:11
`x` Ge 47:23
5:4 `y` S Ezr 4:13
5:5 `z` S Ge 29:14
`a` Lev 25:39-43, 47;
S 2Ki 4:1; Isa 50:1
`b` Dt 15:7-11; S 2Ki 4:1

¹⁵When our enemies heard that we were aware of their plot and that God had frustrated it,^r we all returned to the wall, each to our own work.

¹⁶From that day on, half of my men did the work, while the other half were equipped with spears, shields, bows and armor. The officers posted themselves behind all the people of Judah ¹⁷who were building the wall. Those who carried materials did their work with one hand and held a weapon^s in the other, ¹⁸and each of the builders wore his sword at his side as he worked. But the man who sounded the trumpet^t stayed with me.

¹⁹Then I said to the nobles, the officials and the rest of the people, "The work is extensive and spread out, and we are widely separated from each other along the wall. ²⁰Wherever you hear the sound of the trumpet, ^u join us there. Our God will fight^v for us!"

²¹So we continued the work with half the men holding spears, from the first light of dawn till the stars came out. ²²At that time I also said to the people, "Have every man and his helper stay inside Jerusalem at night, so they can serve us as guards by night and as workers by day." ²³Neither I nor my brothers nor my men nor the guards with me took off our clothes; each had his weapon, even when he went for water.^a

NEHEMIAH HELPS THE POOR

5 Now the men and their wives raised a great outcry against their fellow Jews. ²Some were saying, "We and our sons and daughters are numerous; in order for us to eat and stay alive, we must get grain."

³Others were saying, "We are mortgaging our fields, ^w our vineyards and our homes to get grain during the famine."^x

⁴Still others were saying, "We have had to borrow money to pay the king's tax^y on our fields and vineyards. ⁵Although we are of the same flesh and blood^z as the rest of our people and though our children are as good as theirs, yet we have to subject our sons and daughters to slavery.^a Some of our daughters have already been enslaved, but we are powerless, because our fields and our vineyards belong to others."^b

---

^a 23 The meaning of the Hebrew for this clause is uncertain.

---

the Lord, who alone is to be feared (see Dt 3:22; 20:3; 31:6; Ps 56:3–4).

4:16 *shields.* Made primarily of wood or wickerwork and therefore combustible (Eze 39:9). *armor.* The Hebrew for this word designated primarily a breastplate of metal or a coat of mail (see 2Ch 18:33).

4:17 *work with one hand … weapon in the other.* Means either that the workers carried their materials with one hand and their weapons with the other or simply that the weapons were kept close at hand.

4:18 *trumpet.* See note on Isa 18:3; see also Jos 6:4, 6,8,13.

4:20 *Our God will fight for us!* For the concept of holy war, in which God fights for his people, see Jos 10:14,42; Jdg 4:14; 20:35; 2Sa 5:24; see also essay, p. 294.

4:21 *till the stars came out.* Indicates the earnestness of their efforts, since the usual time to stop working was at sunset (Dt 24:15; Mt 20:8).

4:22 *guards by night.* Even men from outside Jerusalem stayed in the city at night so that some of them could serve as sentries.

4:23 See TNIV text note. Although the precise meaning of the end of the verse is not clear, the implication is that constant preparedness was the rule. According to Josephus (*Antiquities*, 11.5.8), Nehemiah "himself made the rounds of the city by night, never tiring either through work or lack of food and sleep, neither of which he took for pleasure but as a necessity."

5:1–19 During his major effort to rebuild the walls of Jerusalem, Nehemiah confronted a socioeconomic crisis that had deep moral implications. Since the building of the wall took only 52 days (6:15), it is surprising that Nehemiah called a "large meeting" (v. 7) in the midst of such a project. Perhaps the pressures created by the rebuilding program brought to light problems that had long been simmering and that had to be dealt with before work could proceed. Among the classes affected by the crisis were (1) the landless, who were short of food (v. 2); (2) the landowners, who were compelled to mortgage their properties (v. 3); and (3) those forced to borrow money at exor-

bitant interest rates and sell their children into slavery (vv. 4–5).

5:1 *wives.* The situation was so serious that the wives joined in the protest as they ran short of funds and supplies to feed their families. They complained not against the foreign authorities but against their own countrymen who were taking advantage of their poorer neighbors at a time when all were needed for the defense of the country.

5:2 *grain.* About six to seven bushels would be needed for a man to feed his family for a month.

5:3 *mortgaging.* Even those who had property were forced to mortgage it, benefiting the wealthy few (cf. Isa 5:8). In times of economic stress the rich got richer and the poor got poorer. *famine.* The economic situation was aggravated by the natural conditions that had produced a famine. Some 75 years earlier the prophet Haggai had referred to a time of drought, when food was insufficient (Hag 1:5–11). Such times of distress were considered to be expressions of God's judgment (Isa 51:19; Jer 14:13–18; Am 4:6). Famines were common in Canaan. They occurred in the times of Abraham (Ge 12:10), Isaac (Ge 26:1), Joseph (Ge 41:27,54), Ruth (Ru 1:1), David (2Sa 21:1), Elijah (1Ki 18:2), Elisha (2Ki 4:38) and Claudius (Ac 11:28).

5:4 *tax.* It is estimated that the Persian king collected the equivalent of 20 million darics (see TNIV text note on Ezr 8:27) a year in taxes. Little was ever returned to benefit the provinces, because most of it was melted down and stored as bullion. Alexander the Great found at Susa alone 9,000 talents (about 340 tons) of coined gold and 40,000 talents (about 1,500 tons) of silver stored as bullion. As coined money was increasingly taken out of circulation by taxes, poverty increased dramatically. The acquisition of land by the Persians and its removal from production also contributed to produce a 50 percent rise in prices during the Persian period.

5:5 *slavery.* In times of economic distress families would borrow funds, using family members as collateral. If a man could not repay the loan and its interest, his children, his wife, or even the man himself could be sold into bondage. An Israelite who fell into debt, however, would serve his creditor as a "hired

5:7 c Ex 22:25-27;
S Lev 25:35-37;
Dt 23:19-20; 24:10-13
5:8 d Lev 25:47
e Jer 34:8
5:9 f Isa 52:5
5:10 g S Ex 22:25
5:11 h Isa 58:6
5:12 i S Ezr 10:5
5:13 j S Mt 10:14
k Dt 27:15-26
5:14 l S Ne 2:6
m Ge 42:6; Ezr 6:7;
Jer 40:7; Hag 1:1
5:15 n S Ge 20:11
5:16 o 2Th 3:7-10

[6]When I heard their outcry and these charges, I was very angry. [7]I pondered them in my mind and then accused the nobles and officials. I told them, "You are charging your own people interest!" c So I called together a large meeting to deal with them [8]and said: "As far as possible, we have bought d back our fellow Jews who were sold to the Gentiles. Now you are selling your own people, only for them to be sold back to us!" They kept quiet, because they could find nothing to say. e

[9]So I continued, "What you are doing is not right. Shouldn't you walk in the fear of our God to avoid the reproach f of our Gentile enemies? [10]I and my brothers and my men are also lending the people money and grain. But let us stop charging interest! g [11]Give back to them immediately their fields, vineyards, olive groves and houses, and also the interest h you are charging them—one percent of the money, grain, new wine and olive oil."

[12]"We will give it back," they said. "And we will not demand anything more from them. We will do as you say."

Then I summoned the priests and made the nobles and officials take an oath i to do what they had promised. [13]I also shook j out the folds of my robe and said, "In this way may God shake out of their houses and possessions anyone who does not keep this promise. So may such a person be shaken out and emptied!"

At this the whole assembly said, "Amen," k and praised the LORD. And the people did as they had promised.

[14]Moreover, from the twentieth year of King Artaxerxes, l when I was appointed to be their governor m in the land of Judah, until his thirty-second year—twelve years—neither I nor my brothers ate the food allotted to the governor. [15]But the earlier governors—those preceding me—placed a heavy burden on the people and took forty shekels a of silver from them in addition to food and wine. Their assistants also lorded it over the people. But out of reverence for God n I did not act like that. [16]Instead, o I devoted myself to the work on this wall. All my men were assembled there for the work; we b did not acquire any land.

[17]Furthermore, a hundred and fifty Jews and officials ate at my table, as well as those

---

a 15 That is, about 1 pound or about 460 grams   b 16 Most Hebrew manuscripts; some Hebrew manuscripts, Septuagint, Vulgate and Syriac I

---

worker" (Lev 25:39–40). He was to be released in the seventh year (Dt 15:12–18), unless he chose to stay voluntarily. During the seven-year famine in Egypt, Joseph was approached by people who asked him to accept their land and their bodies in exchange for food (Ge 47:18–19). The irony for the Israelites was that at least as exiles in Mesopotamia their families were together, but now, because of dire economic necessity, their children were being sold into slavery.

5:6 *I was very angry.* Sometimes it becomes necessary to express righteous indignation against social injustice (cf. Mk 11:15–18; Eph 4:26).

5:7 *interest.* See notes on Ex 22:25–27; Lev 25:36; Dt 23:20. Josephus (*Antiquities,* 4.8.25) explains: "Let it not be permitted to lend upon usury to any Hebrew either meat or drink; for it is not just to draw a revenue from the misfortunes of a fellow countryman. Rather, in consoling him in his distress, you should reckon as gain the gratitude of such persons and the recompense that God has in store for an act of generosity."

5:8 *fellow Jews who were sold.* Impoverished fellow Jews could be hired as servants, but they were not to be sold as slaves (Lev 25:39–42). *to the Gentiles.* The sale of fellow Hebrews as slaves to foreigners was forbidden (Ex 21:8). *kept quiet.* Their guilt was so obvious that they had no rebuttal or excuse (cf. Jn 8:7–10).

5:9 *not right.* Failure to treat others, especially fellow believers, with compassion is an insult to our Maker and a blot on our testimony (cf. Pr 14:31; 1Pe 2:12–15).

5:10 *let us stop charging interest!* The OT condemns the greed that seeks a profit at the expense of people (Ps 119:36; Isa 56:9–12; 57:17; Jer 6:13; 8:10; 22:13–17; Eze 22:12–13; 33:31). In view of the economic crisis facing his people, Nehemiah urges the creditors to relinquish their rights to repayment with interest.

5:11 *one percent.* Perhaps one percent per month, an annual interest rate of 12 percent. *grain, new wine and olive oil.* See notes on 10:37; Dt 7:13.

5:13 *shook out the folds of my robe.* Symbolizing the solemnity

of an oath and reinforcing the attendant curses for its nonfulfillment. *Amen.* See 8:6; Nu 5:22; see also note on Dt 27:15.

5:14 *thirty-second year.* From Apr. 1, 433 B.C., to Apr. 19, 432. Nehemiah served his first term as governor for 12 years before being recalled to court (13:6), after which he returned to Jerusalem (13:7) for a second term whose length cannot be determined. *food allotted to the governor.* See v. 18. Provincial governors normally assessed the people in their provinces for their support. But Nehemiah, like Paul (1Co 9; 2Th 3:8–9), sacrificed even what was normally his in order to serve as an example to the people.

5:15 *governors.* The Hebrew for this word is used of Sheshbazzar (Ezr 5:14) and Zerubbabel (Hag 1:1, 14; 2:2), as well as of various Persian officials (Ezr 5:3,6; 6:6–7,13; 8:36; Ne 2:7,9; 3:7). Nehemiah was not referring here to men of the caliber of Zerubbabel. Some believe that Judah did not have governors before Nehemiah and that the reference here is to governors of Samaria. But new archaeological evidence, in the form of seals and seal impressions, confirms the reference to the previous governors of Judah. *heavy burden.* It was customary Persian practice to exempt temple personnel from taxation, which increased the burden on lay people. *assistants.* If the governors themselves used extortion, their underlings often proved even more oppressive (cf. Mt 18:21–35; 20:25–28). *reverence for God.* Those in high positions are in danger of abusing their authority over their subordinates if they forget that they themselves are servants of a superior "Master in heaven" (Col 4:1; cf. Ge 39:9; 2Co 5:11).

5:16 *did not acquire any land.* Nehemiah's behavior as governor was guided by principles of service rather than by opportunism.

5:17 *ate at my table.* As part of his social responsibility, a ruler or governor was expected to entertain lavishly. A text found at Nimrud has Ashurnasirpal II feeding 69,574 guests at a banquet for ten days. When Solomon dedicated the temple, he sacrificed 22,000 cattle and 120,000 sheep and goats and

5:18 *P* 1Ki 4:23
5:19 *q* S Ge 8:1;
S 2Ki 20:3; S Ne 1:8
6:1 *r* Ne 2:10
s S Ne 2:19
6:2 *t* S 1Ch 8:12
6:5 *u* S Ne 2:10
6:6 *v* S Ne 2:19
6:10 *w* Nu 18:7

who came to us from the surrounding nations. [18]Each day one ox, six choice sheep and some poultry *P* were prepared for me, and every ten days an abundant supply of wine of all kinds. In spite of all this, I never demanded the food allotted to the governor, because the demands were heavy on these people.

[19]Remember *q* me with favor, my God, for all I have done for these people.

FURTHER OPPOSITION TO THE REBUILDING

6 When word came to Sanballat, Tobiah, *r* Geshem *s* the Arab and the rest of our enemies that I had rebuilt the wall and not a gap was left in it—though up to that time I had not set the doors in the gates— [2]Sanballat and Geshem sent me this message: "Come, let us meet together in one of the villages *a* on the plain of Ono. *t*"

But they were scheming to harm me; [3]so I sent messengers to them with this reply: "I am carrying on a great project and cannot go down. Why should the work stop while I leave it and go down to you?" [4]Four times they sent me the same message, and each time I gave them the same answer.

[5]Then, the fifth time, Sanballat *u* sent his aide to me with the same message, and in his hand was an unsealed letter [6]in which was written:

"It is reported among the nations—and Geshem *b v* says it is true—that you and the Jews are plotting to revolt, and therefore you are building the wall. Moreover, according to these reports you are about to become their king [7]and have even appointed prophets to make this proclamation about you in Jerusalem: 'There is a king in Judah!' Now this report will get back to the king; so come, let us meet together."

[8]I sent him this reply: "Nothing like what you are saying is happening; you are just making it up out of your head."

[9]They were all trying to frighten us, thinking, "Their hands will get too weak for the work, and it will not be completed."

But I prayed, "Now strengthen my hands."

[10]One day I went to the house of Shemaiah son of Delaiah, the son of Mehetabel, who was shut in at his home. He said, "Let us meet in the house of God, inside the temple *w*, and let us close the temple doors, because some people are coming to kill you—by night they are coming to kill you."

[11]But I said, "Should someone like me run away? Or should one like me go into the

---

a 2 Or in *Kephirim*   *b* 6 Hebrew *Gashmu*, a variant of *Geshem*

---

held a great festival for the assembly for 14 days (1Ki 8:62–65). We are not told how many he fed (cf. 1Ki 4:27).

B **5:18** *Each day.* The meat listed here would provide one meal for 600–800 persons, including the 150 Jews and officials of v. 17. Cf. Solomon's provisions for one day (1Ki 4:22–23). *choice sheep.* Cf. Mal 1:8. *poultry.* Chickens were domesticated in the Indus River Valley by 2000 B.C. and were brought to Egypt by the time of Thutmose III (15th century B.C.). They were known in Mesopotamia and in Greece by the eighth century. The earliest inscriptional evidence of poultry in the land of Canaan is the seal of Jaazaniah (dated c. 600 B.C.), which depicts a fighting rooster.

B **5:19** *Remember me.* See note on 1:8; cf. Heb 6:10. Perhaps Nehemiah's memoirs (see Introduction to Ezra: Literary Form and Authorship) were inscribed as a memorial that was set up in the temple. A striking parallel to Nehemiah's prayer is found in a prayer of Nebuchadnezzar: "O Marduk, my lord, do remember my deeds favorably as good [deeds]; may (these) my good deeds be always before your mind."

6:1 *Sanballat, Tobiah, Geshem.* See notes on 2:10,19.

6:2 *Ono.* Located about seven miles southeast of Joppa near Lod (Lydda; see note on Ezr 2:33), in the westernmost area settled by the returning Jews (Ne 7:37; 11:35). It may have been proposed as neutral territory, but Nehemiah recognized the invitation as a trap (cf. Ge 4:8; Jer 41:1–3).

C **6:3** Nehemiah's sharp reply may seem like a haughty response to a reasonable invitation, but he correctly discerned the insincerity of his enemies. He refused to be distracted by matters that would divert his energies from rebuilding Jerusalem's wall.

6:4 *Four times.* Nehemiah's foes were persistent, but he was

equally persistent in resisting them.

B **6:5** *unsealed letter.* During this period a letter was ordinarily written on a papyrus or leather sheet, which was rolled up, tied with a string and sealed with a clay bulla (seal impression) to guarantee the letter's authenticity. Sanballat apparently wanted the contents of his letter to be made known to the public at large.

B **6:6** *their king.* The Persian kings did not tolerate the claims of pretenders to kingship, as can be seen from the Behistun (Bisitun) inscription of Darius I. In NT times the Roman emperor was likewise suspicious of any unauthorized claims to royalty (Jn 19:12; cf. Mt 2:1–13).

6:8 *Nothing.* Nehemiah does not mince words. He calls the report a lie. He may have sent his own messenger to the Persian king to assure him of his loyalty.

B **6:9** *hands will get … weak.* Figurative language to express the idea of discouragement. The Hebrew for this phrase is used also in Ezr 4:4; Jer 38:4, as well as on an ostracon from Lachish dated c. 588 B.C.

6:10 *Shemaiah … was shut in.* Perhaps as a symbolic action to indicate that his own life was in danger and to suggest that both Nehemiah and he must flee to the temple (for other symbolic actions see 1Ki 22:11; Isa 20:2–4; Jer 27:2–7; 28:10–11; Eze 4:1–17; 12:3–11; Ac 21:11). Since Shemaiah had access to the temple, he may have been a priest. He was clearly a friend of Tobiah (cf. v. 12), and therefore Nehemiah's enemy. It was at least credible for Shemaiah to propose that Nehemiah take refuge in the temple area at the altar of asylum (see Ex 21:13–14 and notes), but not in the "house of God," the temple building itself.

6:11 Even if the threat against his life was real, Nehemiah was not a coward who would run into hiding. Nor would he transtemple to save his life? I will not go!" [12] I realized that God had not sent him, but that he had prophesied against me [x] because Tobiah and Sanballat [y] had hired him. [13] He had been hired to intimidate me so that I would commit a sin by doing this, and then they would give me a bad name to discredit me. [z]

[14] Remember [a] Tobiah and Sanballat, [b] my God, because of what they have done; remember also the prophet [c] Noadiah and how she and the rest of the prophets [d] have been trying to intimidate me. [15] So the wall was completed on the twenty-fifth of Elul, in fifty-two days.

OPPOSITION TO THE COMPLETED WALL

[16] When all our enemies heard about this, all the surrounding nations were afraid and lost their self-confidence, because they realized that this work had been done with the help of our God.

[17] Also, in those days the nobles of Judah were sending many letters to Tobiah, and replies from Tobiah kept coming to them. [18] For many in Judah were under oath to him, since he was son-in-law to Shekaniah son of Arah, and his son Jehohanan had married the daughter of Meshullam son of Berekiah. [19] Moreover, they kept reporting to me his good deeds and then telling him what I said. And Tobiah sent letters to intimidate me.

7 After the wall had been rebuilt and I had set the doors in place, the gatekeepers, [e] the musicians [f] and the Levites [g] were appointed. [2] I put in charge of Jerusalem my brother Hanani, [h] along with Hananiah [i] the commander of the citadel, [j] because he was trustworthy and feared [k] God more than most people do. [3] I said to them, "The gates of Jerusalem are not to be opened until the sun is hot. While the gatekeepers are still on duty, have them shut the doors and bar them. Also appoint residents of Jerusalem as guards, some at their posts and some near their own houses."

THE LIST OF THE EXILES WHO RETURNED

7:6–73pp — Ezr 2:1–70

[4] Now the city was large and spacious, but there were few people in it, [l] and the houses had not yet been rebuilt. [5] So my God put it into my heart to assemble the nobles, the officials and the common people for registration by families. I found the genealogical record of those who had been the first to return. This is what I found written there:

[6] These are the people of the province who came up from the captivity of the exiles [m] whom Nebuchadnezzar king of Babylon had taken captive (they returned to Jerusalem and Judah, each to his own town, [7] in company with Zerubbabel, [n] Joshua, Nehemiah, Azariah, Raamiah, Nahamani, Mordecai, Bilshan, Mispereth, Bigvai, Nehum and Baanah):

The list of the men of Israel:

[8] the descendants of Parosh	2,172
[9] of Shephatiah	372
[10] of Arah	652
[11] of Pahath-Moab (through the line of Jeshua and Joab)	2,818
[12] of Elam	1,254

6:12 ˣEze 13:22-23
ʸS Ne 2:10
6:13 ᶻJer 20:10
6:14 ᵃS Ne 1:8
ᵇS Ne 2:10
ᶜS Ex 15:20;
Eze 13:17-23;
S Ac 21:9; Rev 2:20
ᵈJer 23:9-40;
Zec 13:2-3
7:1 ᵉ1Ch 9:27;
S 26:12-19 ᶠPs 68:25
ᵍNe 8:9
7:2 ʰNe 1:2
ⁱNe 10:23 ʲNe 2:8
ᵏ1Ki 18:3
7:4 ˡNe 11:1
7:6 ᵐS 2Ch 36:20;
S Ne 1:2
7:7 ⁿS 1Ch 3:19

---

gress the law to save his life. As a layman, he was not permitted to enter the sanctuary (Nu 18:7). When King Uzziah entered the temple to burn incense, he was punished by being afflicted with leprosy (2Ch 26:16–21).

A **6:12** The fact that Shemaiah proposed a course of action contrary to God's word revealed him as a false prophet (cf. Dt 18:20; Isa 8:19–20; see note on Dt 13:1–5).

A **C** **6:13** If Nehemiah had wavered in the face of the threat against him, his leadership would have been discredited and morale among the people would have plummeted.

6:14 *Remember.* See note on 1:8. *prophet.* See note on Ex 15:20.

B **6:15** *twenty-fifth of Elul.* Oct. 2, 444 B.C. *fifty-two days.* The walls that lay in ruins for nearly a century and a half were rebuilt in less than two months once the people were galvanized into action by Nehemiah's leadership. Archaeological investigations have shown that the circumference of the wall in Nehemiah's day was much reduced. Josephus states (*Antiquities,*

11.5.8) that the rebuilding of the wall took two years and four months, but he is doubtless including such additional tasks as further strengthening of various sections, embellishing and beautifying, and the like. The dedication of the wall is described in 12:27–47.

6:17–18 Tobiah was related to an influential family in Judah, since his son Jehohanan was married to the daughter of Meshullam, who had helped repair the wall of Jerusalem (3:4,30).

7:2 *in charge of Jerusalem.* Over Rephaiah and Shallum, who were over sections of the city (3:9,12). *Hanani.* See note on 1:2. *citadel.* See notes on 2:8; 3:1.

7:3 *until the sun is hot.* Normally the gates would be opened at dawn, but their opening was to be delayed until the sun was high in the heavens to prevent the enemy from making a surprise attack before most of the people were up.

7:6–73 Essentially the same as Ezr 2. See notes there for the nature of the list and the reasons for the numerous variations in names and numbers between the two lists.

7:20 *o* S Ezr 8:6
7:26 *p* S 2Sa 23:28;
S 1Ch 2:54
7:27 *q* S Jos 21:18
7:29 *r* S Jos 18:26
s S Jos 18:25
7:32 *t* S Ge 12:8
7:36 *u* Ne 3:2
7:37 *v* S 1Ch 8:12
7:44 *w* Ne 11:23
7:45 *x* S 1Ch 9:17
7:46 *y* S Ne 3:26

¹³ of Zattu	845
¹⁴ of Zakkai	760
¹⁵ of Binnui	648
¹⁶ of Bebai	628
¹⁷ of Azgad	2,322
¹⁸ of Adonikam	667
¹⁹ of Bigvai	2,067
²⁰ of Adin *o*	655
²¹ of Ater (through Hezekiah)	98
²² of Hashum	328
²³ of Bezai	324
²⁴ of Hariph	112
²⁵ of Gibeon	95
²⁶ the men of Bethlehem and Netophah *p*	188
²⁷ of Anathoth *q*	128
²⁸ of Beth Azmaveth	42
²⁹ of Kiriath Jearim, Kephirah *r* and Beeroth *s*	743
³⁰ of Ramah and Geba	621
³¹ of Mikmash	122
³² of Bethel and Ai *t*	123
³³ of the other Nebo	52
³⁴ of the other Elam	1,254
³⁵ of Harim	320
³⁶ of Jericho *u*	345
³⁷ of Lod, Hadid and Ono *v*	721
³⁸ of Senaah	3,930

³⁹ The priests:

the descendants of Jedaiah (through the family of Jeshua)	973
⁴⁰ of Immer	1,052
⁴¹ of Pashhur	1,247
⁴² of Harim	1,017

⁴³ The Levites:

the descendants of Jeshua (through Kadmiel through the line of Hodaviah)	74

⁴⁴ The musicians: *w*

the descendants of Asaph	148

⁴⁵ The gatekeepers: *x*

the descendants of Shallum, Ater, Talmon, Akkub, Hatita and Shobai	138

⁴⁶ The temple servants: *y*

the descendants of
Ziha, Hasupha, Tabbaoth,
⁴⁷ Keros, Sia, Padon,
⁴⁸ Lebana, Hagaba, Shalmai,
⁴⁹ Hanan, Giddel, Gahar,
⁵⁰ Reaiah, Rezin, Nekoda,
⁵¹ Gazzam, Uzza, Paseah,
⁵² Besai, Meunim, Nephusim,
⁵³ Bakbuk, Hakupha, Harhur,
⁵⁴ Bazluth, Mehida, Harsha,
⁵⁵ Barkos, Sisera, Temah,
⁵⁶ Neziah and Hatipha

⁵⁷ The descendants of the servants of Solomon:

the descendants of

7:43 *74.* See note on Ezr 2:40.

7:57,60 *descendants of the servants of Solomon.* See note on Ezr 2:55,58.

Sotai, Sophereth, Perida,
58 Jaala, Darkon, Giddel,
59 Shephatiah, Hattil,
Pokereth-Hazzebaim and Amon

60 The temple servants and the descendants of the servants of
Solomon[z]   392

61 The following came up from the towns of Tel Melah, Tel Harsha, Kerub, Addon and Immer, but they could not show that their families were descended from Israel:

62 the descendants of
Delaiah, Tobiah and Nekoda   642

63 And from among the priests:

the descendants of
Hobaiah, Hakkoz and Barzillai (a man who had married a daughter of Barzillai the Gileadite and was called by that name).

64 These searched for their family records, but they could not find them and so were excluded from the priesthood as unclean. 65 The governor, therefore, ordered them not to eat any of the most sacred food until there should be a priest ministering with the Urim and Thummim.[a]

66 The whole company numbered 42,360, 67 besides their 7,337 male and female slaves; and they also had 245 male and female singers. 68 There were 736 horses, 245 mules,[a] 69 435 camels and 6,720 donkeys.

70 Some of the heads of the families contributed to the work. The governor gave to the treasury 1,000 darics[b] of gold, 50 bowls and 530 garments for priests. 71 Some of the heads of the families[b] gave to the treasury for the work 20,000 darics[c] of gold and 2,200 minas[d] of silver. 72 The total given by the rest of the people was 20,000 darics of gold, 2,000 minas[e] of silver and 67 garments for priests.[c]

73 The priests, the Levites, the gatekeepers, the musicians and the temple servants,[d] along with certain of the people and the rest of the Israelites, settled in their own towns.[e]

EZRA READS THE LAW

8 When the seventh month came and the Israelites had settled in their towns,[f] 1 all the people assembled with one accord in the square before the Water Gate.[g] They told Ezra the teacher of the Law to bring out the Book of the Law of Moses,[h] which the LORD had commanded for Israel.

2 So on the first day of the seventh month[i] Ezra the priest brought the Law[j] before the assembly, which was made up of men and women and all who were able to understand. 3 He read it aloud from daybreak till noon as he faced the square before the Water Gate[k] in the presence of the men, women and others who could understand. And all the people listened attentively to the Book of the Law.

4 Ezra the teacher of the Law stood on a high wooden platform[l] built for the occasion. Beside him on his right stood Mattithiah, Shema, Anaiah, Uriah, Hilkiah and Maaseiah;

7:60 [z] S 1Ch 9:2
7:65 [a] S Ex 28:30
7:71 [b] S 1Ch 29:7
7:72 [c] S Ex 25:2
7:73 [d] Ne 1:10;
Ps 34:22; 103:21;
113:1; 135:1
[e] S Ezr 3:1; Ne 11:1
[f] Ezr 3:1
8:1 [g] S Ne 3:26
[h] S Dt 28:61;
S 2Ch 34:15
8:2 [i] Lev 23:23-25;
Nu 29:1-6 / S Dt 31:11
8:3 [k] S Ne 3:26
8:4 [l] 2Ch 6:13

---

[a] 68 Some Hebrew manuscripts (see also Ezra 2:66); most Hebrew manuscripts do not have this verse.
[b] 70 That is, about 19 pounds or about 8.5 kilograms   [c] 71 That is, about 375 pounds or about 170 kilograms; also in verse 72   [d] 71 That is, about 1 1/3 tons or about 1.2 metric tons   [e] 72 That is, about 1 1/4 tons or about 1.1 metric tons

---

7:70 *darics.* See note on Ezr 2:69.
7:73 *settled in their own towns.* See note on Ezr 2:70. *seventh month.* October-November, 444 B.C.
8:1–18 The reading of the Law of Moses by Ezra is the first reference to Ezra in almost 13 years since his arrival in 458 B.C.
8:1 *all the people assembled.* See Ezr 3:1, which also refers to an assembly called in the seventh month (Tishri), the beginning of the civil year (see chart, p. 105). *square before the Water Gate.* See vv. 3, 16; see also notes on 3:26; Ezr 10:9. Squares were normally located near a city gate (2Ch 32:6). *teacher of the Law.* See note on Ezr 7:6. *Book of the Law of Moses.* Cf. vv. 2–3, 5, 8–9, 13–15, 18. Several views have been proposed concerning the extent of this Book: (1) the laws of Exodus and Leviticus, (2) the laws of

Deuteronomy, (3) the Pentateuch. See notes on Jos 1:8; 2Ki 22:8.
8:2 *first day of the seventh month.* Oct. 8, 444 B.C.; the New Year's Day of the civil calendar (see note on Lev 23:24), celebrated as the Festival of Trumpets (Nu 29:1–6), with cessation of labor and a sacred assembly. *women.* See 10:28. Women did not usually participate in assemblies (see note on Ex 10:11) but were brought, together with children, on such solemn occasions (Dt 31:12; Jos 8:35; 2Ki 23:2).
8:3 *read it aloud.* See Ex 24:7; Ac 8:30 and note; 1Ti 4:13. *from daybreak till noon.* The people evidently stood (vv. 5, 7) for five or six hours, listening attentively to the reading and exposition (vv. 7–8, 12) of the Scriptures.

8:5 *m* Jdg 3:20
8:6 *n* S Ezr 9:5;
1Ti 2:8
8:7 *o* S Ezr 10:23
p S Lev 10:11;
S 2Ch 17:7
8:9 *q* Ne 7:1,65,70
r Dt 12:7,12; 16:14-15
8:10 *s* 1Sa 25:8;
S 2Sa 6:19; Est 9:22;
Lk 14:12-14
t S Lev 23:40;
S Dt 12:18; 16:11,14-15
8:12 *u* Est 9:22
8:14 *v* S Ex 23:16

and on his left were Pedaiah, Mishael, Malkijah, Hashum, Hashbaddanah, Zechariah and Meshullam.

⁵Ezra opened the book. All the people could see him because he was standing *m* above them; and as he opened it, the people all stood up. ⁶Ezra praised the LORD, the great God; and all the people lifted their hands *n* and responded, "Amen! Amen!" Then they bowed down and worshiped the LORD with their faces to the ground.

⁷The Levites *o*—Jeshua, Bani, Sherebiah, Jamin, Akkub, Shabbethai, Hodiah, Maaseiah, Kelita, Azariah, Jozabad, Hanan and Pelaiah—instructed *p* the people in the Law while the people were standing there. ⁸They read from the Book of the Law of God, making it clear *a* and giving the meaning so that the people understood what was being read.

⁹Then Nehemiah the governor, Ezra the priest and teacher of the Law, and the Levites *q* who were instructing the people said to them all, "This day is holy to the LORD your God. Do not mourn or weep." *r* For all the people had been weeping as they listened to the words of the Law.

¹⁰Nehemiah said, "Go and enjoy choice food and sweet drinks, and send some to those who have nothing *s* prepared. This day is holy to our Lord. Do not grieve, for the joy *t* of the LORD is your strength."

¹¹The Levites calmed all the people, saying, "Be still, for this is a holy day. Do not grieve."

¹²Then all the people went away to eat and drink, to send portions of food and to celebrate with great joy, *u* because they now understood the words that had been made known to them.

¹³On the second day of the month, the heads of all the families, along with the priests and the Levites, gathered around Ezra the teacher to give attention to the words of the Law. ¹⁴They found written in the Law, which the LORD had commanded through Moses, that the Israelites were to live in temporary shelters *v* during the festival of the seventh month ¹⁵and that they should proclaim this word and spread it throughout their towns and in Jerusalem: "Go out into the hill country and bring back branches from olive and wild olive trees, and from myrtles, palms and shade trees, to make temporary shelters"—as it is written. *b*

¹⁶So the people went out and brought back branches and built themselves temporary shelters on their own roofs, in their courtyards, in the courts of the house of God and in

---

a 8 Or *God, translating it*   *b* 15 See Lev. 23:37-40.

8:5 *book.* Scroll (see note on Ex 17:14). *people all stood up.* The rabbis deduced from this verse that the congregation should stand for the reading of the Torah. It is customary in Eastern Orthodox churches for the congregation to stand throughout the service.

8:6 *lifted their hands.* See Ex 9:29 and note; Ps 28:2; 134:2; 1Ti 2:8. *Amen! Amen!* See notes on Dt 27:15; Ro 1:25. The repetition conveys the intensity of feeling behind the affirmation (for other repetitions see Ge 22:11 and note; cf. 2Ki 11:14; Lk 23:21). *worshiped.* In its original sense the Hebrew for this verb meant "to prostrate oneself on the ground," as the frequently accompanying phrase "to the ground" indicates. Private acts of worship often involved prostration "to the ground," as in the case of Abraham's servant (Ge 24:52), Moses (Ex 34:8), Joshua (Jos 5:14) and Job (Job 1:20). There are three cases of spontaneous communal worship in Exodus (4:31; 12:27; 33:10). In 2Ch 20:18 Jehoshaphat and the people "fell down in worship before the LORD" when they heard his promise of victory.

8:7 *instructed.* See v. 8; Ezr 7:6,10 and note on 7:6.

8:8 *read.* See note on v. 3. *making it clear.* Rabbinic tradition understands the Hebrew for this expression as referring to translation from Hebrew into an Aramaic Targum (see TNIV text note). But there is no evidence of Targums (free Aramaic translations of OT books or passages) from such an early date. The earliest extensive Targum is one on Job dated c. 150–100 B.C. (from Qumran). Targums exist for every book of the OT except Daniel and Ezra-Nehemiah. *understood.* See v. 12.

8:9 *Nehemiah . . . Ezra.* An explicit reference showing that they were contemporaries (see 12:26,36). *Do not mourn.* See Ezr 10:6 and note; Est 9:22; Isa 57:18–19; Jer 31:13. *weep.* See 1:4; Ezr 3:13 and note; 10:1. *weeping as they listened.* Out of remorse for their own failures and those of their ancestors.

8:10 *choice food.* Delicious, festive food prepared with much fat. The fat of sacrificial animals was offered to God as the tastiest element of the burnt offering (Lev 1:8,12), the fellowship offering (Lev 3:9–10), the sin offering (Lev 4:8–10) and the guilt offering (Lev 7:3–4). The fat was not to be eaten in these cases. *send some to those who have nothing.* It was customary for God's people to remember the less fortunate on joyous occasions (2Sa 6:19; Est 9:22; contrast 1Co 11:20–22; Jas 2:14–16).

8:14 *temporary shelters.* See notes on Ex 23:16; Lev 23:34,42; Jn 7:37.

8:15 *myrtles.* Evergreen bushes with a pleasing odor (Isa 41:19; 55:13; Zec 1:8,10–11). *palms.* The date palm was grown around Jericho (Dt 34:3; 2Ch 28:15). *shade trees.* Cf. Eze 6:13; 20:28. Later Jewish celebrations of the Festival of Tabernacles include waving the *lulav* (made of branches of palms, myrtles and willows) with the right hand and holding branches of the *ethrog* (a citrus native to Canaan) in the left.

8:16 *courts of the house of God.* See note on 13:7. The temple that Ezekiel saw in his visions had an outer and an inner court (see diagram, p. 1427). Ezekiel's temple was to some extent patterned after Solomon's, which had an inner court of priests and an outer court (1Ki 6:36; 7:12; 2Ki 21:5; 23:12; 2Ch 4:9; 33:5). The temple of the NT era had a court of the Gentiles and an inner court, which was subdivided into courts of the women, of Israel and of the priests. The Temple Scroll from Qumran has God setting forth in detail an ideal temple. Columns 40–46 describe the outer court as follows: "On the roof of the third story are columns for the constructing of booths for the Festival of Tabernacles, to be occupied by the elders, tribal chieftains and commanders of thousands and hundreds." *Gate of Ephraim.* A gate of the oldest rampart of Jerusalem (see note on 3:6; see also 2Ki 14:13). It was restored by Nehemiah (12:39).

the square by the Water Gate ^{w} and the one by the Gate of Ephraim. ^{x} ^{17}The whole company that had returned from exile built temporary shelters and lived in them. ^{y} From the days of Joshua son of Nun until that day, the Israelites had not celebrated ^{z} it like this. And their joy was very great.

^{18}Day after day, from the first day to the last, Ezra read ^{a} from the Book of the Law ^{b} of God. They celebrated the festival for seven days, and on the eighth day, in accordance with the regulation, ^{c} there was an assembly. ^{d}

THE ISRAELITES CONFESS THEIR SINS

9 On the twenty-fourth day of the same month, the Israelites gathered together, fasting and wearing sackcloth and putting dust on their heads. ^{e} ^{2}Those of Israelite descent had separated themselves from all foreigners. ^{f} They stood in their places and confessed their sins and the sins of their ancestors. ^{g} ^{3}They stood where they were and read from the Book of the Law of the LORD their God for a quarter of the day, and spent another quarter in confession and in worshiping the LORD their God. ^{4}Standing on the stairs of the Levites ^{h} were Jeshua, Bani, Kadmiel, Shebaniah, Bunni, Sherebiah, Bani and Kenani. They cried out with loud voices to the LORD their God. ^{5}And the Levites— Jeshua, Kadmiel, Bani, Hashabneiah, Sherebiah, Hodiah, Shebaniah and Pethahiah—said: "Stand up and praise the LORD your God, ^{i} who is from everlasting to everlasting. ^{a}"

"Blessed be your glorious name, ^{j} and may it be exalted above all blessing and praise. ^{6}You alone are the LORD. ^{k} You made the heavens, ^{l} even the highest heavens, and all their starry host, ^{m} the earth ^{n} and all that is on it, the seas ^{o} and all that is in them. ^{p} You give life to everything, and the multitudes of heaven ^{q} worship you.

^{7}"You are the LORD God, who chose Abram ^{r} and brought him out of Ur of the Chaldeans ^{s} and named him Abraham. ^{t} ^{8}You found his heart faithful to you, and you made a covenant with him to give to his descendants the land of the Canaanites, Hittites, Amorites, Perizzites, Jebusites and Girgashites. ^{u} You have kept your promise ^{v} because you are righteous. ^{w}

^{9}"You saw the suffering of our ancestors in Egypt; ^{x} you heard their cry at the Red Sea. $^{b\,y}$ ^{10}You sent signs ^{z} and wonders ^{a} against Pharaoh, against all his officials and all the people of his land, for you knew how arrogantly the Egyptians treated them. You made a name ^{b} for yourself, ^{c} which remains to this day. ^{11}You divided the sea before them, ^{d} so that they passed through it on dry ground, but you hurled their pursuers into the depths, ^{e} like a stone into mighty waters. ^{f} ^{12}By day ^{g} you led ^{h} them with a pillar of cloud, ^{i} and by night with a pillar of fire to give them light on the way they were to take.

^{13}"You came down on Mount Sinai; ^{j} you spoke ^{k} to them from heaven. ^{l} You gave them regulations and laws that are just ^{m} and right, and decrees and commands that are good. ^{n} ^{14}You made known to them your holy Sabbath ^{o} and gave them commands, decrees and laws through your servant Moses. ^{15}In their hunger you gave them bread from heaven ^{p} and in their thirst you brought them water from the rock; ^{q}

---

^{a} 5 Or God for ever and ever ^{b} 9 Or the Sea of Reeds

8:16 ^{w} S Ne 3:26
^{x} S 2Ch 25:23
8:17 ^{y} Hos 12:9
^{z} S 1Ki 8:2; S 2Ch 7:8;
S 8:13
8:18 ^{a} S Dt 31:11;
S 33:10 ^{b} S Dt 28:61
^{c} S Lev 23:36,40;
S Ezr 3:4
^{d} S Lev 23:36
9:1 ^{e} Lev 26:40-45;
S Jos 7:6; 2Ch 7:14-16
9:2 ^{f} S Ezr 6:21;
Ne 10:28; 13:3,30
^{g} S Lev 26:40;
S Ezr 10:11; Ps 106:6
9:4 ^{h} S Ezr 10:23
9:5 ^{i} Ps 78:4
^{j} S 2Sa 7:26
9:6 ^{k} S Dt 6:4
^{l} S Ge 23:56
^{m} Isa 40:26; 45:12
^{n} S Ge 1:1; Isa 37:16
^{o} Ps 95:5; 146:6;
^{p} Ps 103:20; 148:2
9:7 ^{r} S Ge 11:28
^{s} S Ge 11:28
^{t} S Ge 17:5
9:8 ^{u} S Ge 15:18-21;
S Ezr 9:1 ^{v} S Jos 21:45
^{w} Ge 15:6; S Ezr 9:15
9:9 ^{x} Ex 2:23-25; 3:7
^{y} Ex 14:10-30
9:10 ^{z} S Ex 10:1;
Ps 74:9 ^{a} S Ex 3:20;
S 6:6 ^{b} Jer 32:20;
Da 9:15 ^{c} S Nu 6:27
9:11 ^{d} Ps 78:13
^{e} S Ex 14:28 ^{f} Ex 15:4-
5,10; Heb 11:29
9:12 ^{g} S Dt 1:33
^{h} S Ex 15:13
^{i} S Ex 13:21
9:13 ^{j} S Ex 19:11
^{k} S Ex 19:19
^{l} S Ex 20:22
^{m} Ps 119:137
^{n} S Ex 20:1; Dt 4:7-8
9:14 ^{o} S Ge 2:3;
Ex 20:8-11
9:15 ^{p} S Ex 16:4;
Ps 78:24-25; Jn 6:31
^{q} Ex 17:6; Nu 20:7-13

8:17 *From the days of Joshua ... until that day.* The phrase does not mean that the Festival of Tabernacles had not been celebrated since Joshua's time, because such celebrations took place after the dedication of Solomon's temple (2Ch 7:8–10) and after the return of the exiles (Ezr 3:4). What apparently is meant is that the festival had not been celebrated before with such great joy (cf. 2Ch 30:26; 35:18).

8:18 *assembly.* See Nu 29:35.

9:1–37 The ninth chapters of Ezra, Nehemiah and Daniel are devoted to confessions of national sin and to prayers for God's grace.

9:1 *twenty-fourth day.* Oct. 30, 444 B.C.; a day of penance in the spirit of the Day of Atonement, which was held on the tenth day (Lev 16:29–30). *fasting ... sackcloth ... dust.* See notes on Ge 37:34; Ezr 8:23; 10:6; Joel 1:13–14.

9:3 *quarter of the day.* About three hours.

9:5–37 One of the most beautiful prayers outside the Psalms, it reviews God's grace and power (1) in creation (v. 6), (2) in the Abrahamic covenant (vv. 7–8), (3) in Egypt and at the Red Sea (vv. 9–11), (4) in the desert and at Sinai (vv. 12–21), (5) during the conquest of Canaan (vv. 22–25), (6) through the

judges (vv. 26–28), (7) through the prophets (vv. 29–31) and (8) in the present situation (vv. 32–37). Cf. Ps 78; 105–106. See similar prayers in Ezr 9:5–15; Da 9:3–19 (see also note there).

9:6 *You alone are the LORD.* Though not in the words of Dt 6:4, which expresses the central monotheistic conviction of Israel's faith, the prayer begins with a similar affirmation (cf. 2Ki 19:15; Ps 86:10). *highest heavens.* See Dt 10:14; 1Ki 8:27; 2Ch 2:6; Ps 148:4. *multitudes of heaven worship you.* See Ps 89:5–7.

9:7 *Ur of the Chaldeans.* See note on Ge 11:28. *named him Abraham.* See note on Ge 17:5.

9:8 *faithful.* Compare Ro 4:16–22 with Jas 2:21–23. *made a covenant with him.* See note on Ge 15:18. *Canaanites ... Girgashites.* See notes on Ge 10:6,15–18; 13:7; Ex 3:8; Ezr 9:1.

9:9 *Red Sea.* See notes on Ex 13:18; 14:2.

9:11 *divided the sea.* See Ex 14:21–22; 1Co 10:1.

9:14 *holy Sabbath.* According to the rabbis, "the Sabbath outweighs all the commandments of the Torah." See 10:31–33; 13:15–22.

9:15 *bread from heaven.* See note on Ex 16:4. *water from the rock.* See note on Ex 17:6. *sworn with uplifted hand.* See Ge 14:22 and note; 22:15–17; Ex 6:8; Eze 20:6; 47:14.

9:15 ʳS Ge 14:22
ˢ Dt 1:8, 21
9:16 ᵗS Ex 32:9;
Jer 7:26; 17:23; 19:15
ᵘ Dt 1:26-33; 31:29
9:17 ᵛ Jdg 8:34;
Ps 78:42 ʷ Ps 77:11;
78:12; 105:5; 106:7
ˣ Jer 7:26; 19:15
ʸ Nu 14:1-4
ᶻ Ps 130:4; Da 9:9
ᵃ S Dt 4:31
ᵇ S Ex 34:6; Ps 103:8;
Na 1:3 ᶜS Ex 22:27;
Nu 14:17-19; Ps 86:15
ᵈ Ps 78:11; Eze 5:6
9:18 ᵉS Ex 32:4
ᶠ S Ex 20:23
9:19 ᵍ S Ge 12:2;
ʰ S Ex 13:21
9:20 ⁱ Nu 9:17; 11:17;
Isa 63:11,14; Hag 2:5;
Zec 4:6 ʲ Ps 23:3;
143:10 ᵏ S Ex 16:15
ˡ Ex 17:6
9:21 ᵐ S Ex 16:35
ⁿ S Dt 2:7 ᵒ S Dt 8:4
9:22 ᵖ S Nu 21:21
ᵠ S Nu 21:33;
Dt 2:26-3:11
9:23 ʳ S Ge 12:2;
S Lev 26:9;
S Nu 10:36
9:24 ˢ S Jos 11:23
ᵗ S Jdg 4:23;
S 2Ch 14:13
9:25 ᵘ S Dt 11:11
ᵛ S Ex 18:9 ʷ Dt 6:10-
12 ˣ 8:8-11; 32:12-15;
Ps 23:6; 25:7; 69:16
9:26 ʸ S 1Ki 14:9;
Jer 44:10 ᶻ S Jos 7:25
ᵃ Jer 2:30; 26:8;
Mt 21:35-36; 23:29-
36; Ac 7:52
ᵇ S Jdg 2:12-13
9:27 ᶜ S Nu 25:17;
S Jdg 2:14 ᵈ Ps 51:1;
103:8; 106:45; 119:156
ᵉ S Jdg 3:9
9:28 ᶠ S Ex 32:22;
S Jdg 2:17
ᵍ S 2Sa 24:14
ʰ Ps 22:4; 106:43;
136:24
9:29 ⁱ S Jdg 6:8
ʲ ver 16-17; Ps 5:5;
Isa 2:11; Jer 43:2
ᵏ S Dt 30:16
ˡ S 1Sa 8:3 ᵐ Jer 19:15
ⁿ Zec 7:11-12
9:30 ᵒ 2Ki 17:13-18;
S 2Ch 36:16

you told them to go in and take possession of the land you had sworn with uplifted hand ʳ to give them. ˢ

16"But they, our ancestors, became arrogant and stiff-necked, ᵗ and did not obey your commands. ᵘ ¹⁷They refused to listen and failed to remember ᵛ the miracles ʷ you performed among them. They became stiff-necked ˣ and in their rebellion appointed a leader in order to return to their slavery. ʸ But you are a forgiving God, ᶻ gracious and compassionate, ᵃ slow to anger ᵇ and abounding in love. ᶜ Therefore you did not desert them, ᵈ ¹⁸even when they cast for themselves an image of a calf ᵉ and said, 'This is your god, who brought you up out of Egypt,' or when they committed awful blasphemies. ᶠ

19"Because of your great compassion you did not abandon ᵍ them in the wilderness. By day the pillar of cloud ʰ did not cease to guide them on their path, nor the pillar of fire by night to shine on the way they were to take. ²⁰You gave your good Spirit ⁱ to instruct ʲ them. You did not withhold your manna ᵏ from their mouths, and you gave them water ˡ for their thirst. ²¹For forty years ᵐ you sustained them in the wilderness; they lacked nothing, ⁿ their clothes did not wear out nor did their feet become swollen. ᵒ

22"You gave them kingdoms and nations, allotting to them even the remotest frontiers. They took over the country of Sihon ᵃ ᵖ king of Heshbon and the country of Og king of Bashan. ᵠ ²³You made their children as numerous as the stars in the sky, ʳ and you brought them into the land that you told their parents to enter and possess. ²⁴Their children went in and took possession of the land. ˢ You subdued ᵗ before them the Canaanites, who lived in the land; you gave the Canaanites into their hands, along with their kings and the peoples of the land, to deal with them as they pleased. ²⁵They captured fortified cities and fertile land; ᵘ they took possession of houses filled with all kinds of good things, ᵛ wells already dug, vineyards, olive groves and fruit trees in abundance. They ate to the full and were well-nourished; ʷ they reveled in your great goodness. ˣ

26"But they were disobedient and rebelled against you; they put your law behind their backs. ʸ They killed ᶻ your prophets, ᵃ who had warned them in order to turn them back to you; they committed awful blasphemies. ᵇ ²⁷So you delivered them into the hands of their enemies, ᶜ who oppressed them. But when they were oppressed they cried out to you. From heaven you heard them, and in your great compassion ᵈ you gave them deliverers, ᵉ who rescued them from the hand of their enemies.

28"But as soon as they were at rest, they again did what was evil in your sight. ᶠ Then you abandoned them to the hand of their enemies so that they ruled over them. And when they cried out to you again, you heard from heaven, and in your compassion ᵍ you delivered them ʰ time after time.

29"You warned ⁱ them in order to turn them back to your law, but they became arrogant ʲ and disobeyed your commands. They sinned against your ordinances, of which you said, 'Whoever obeys them will live by them.' ᵏ Stubbornly they turned their backs ˡ on you, became stiff-necked ᵐ and refused to listen. ⁿ ³⁰For many years you were patient with them. By your Spirit you warned them through your prophets. ᵒ Yet they paid no attention, so you gave them into the hands of the neighboring

---

ᵃ 22 One Hebrew manuscript and Septuagint; most Hebrew manuscripts *Sihon, that is, the country of the*

9:16 *stiff-necked.* See vv. 17,29; see also notes on 3:5; Ex 32:9.

9:17 *appointed a leader.* Their intention to do so is recorded in Nu 14:4. *gracious . . . abounding in love.* See note on Ex 34:6–7.

9:18 *blasphemies.* See v. 26; Ex 32:4; Eze 35:12.

9:19 *compassion.* See vv. 27–28.

9:20 *Spirit to instruct.* See Ex 31:3.

A 9:21 *clothes did not wear out.* Evidence of the special providence of God (see Dt 8:4; 29:5; contrast Jos 9:13). *swollen.* Or "blistered"; the Hebrew for this word occurs only here and in Dt 8:4.

9:22 *Sihon . . . Og.* See Nu 21:21–35.

9:23 *numerous as the stars.* See notes on Ge 13:16; 15:5; 22:17.

B 9:25 See Dt 6:10–12 and note; Jos 24:13. *fertile.* See v. 35; cf. Nu 14:7; Dt 8:7; Jos 23:13. *wells already dug.* Because of the lack of rainfall during much of the year, almost every house had its own well or cistern in which to store water from the rainy seasons (2Ki 18:31; Pr 5:15). By 1200 B.C. the technique of

waterproofing cisterns was developed, permitting greater occupation of the central hills of Judah. *vineyards, olive groves and fruit trees.* Cf. Dt 8:8. The Egyptian story of Sinuhe (c. 2000 B.C.) describes Canaan as follows: "Figs were in it, and grapes. It had more wine than water. Plentiful was its honey, abundant its olives. Every (kind of) fruit was on its trees." *well-nourished.* Elsewhere the Hebrew for this word always implies physical fullness and spiritual insensitivity.

9:26–28 See note on Jdg 2:6—3:6.

9:26 *put your law behind their backs.* Totally disregarded God's law (cf. Ps 50:17; Jer 2:27; 32:33; Eze 23:35). *killed your prophets.* See 1Ki 18:4,13; 19:10,14; 2Ch 24:20–21; Jer 2:30; 26:20–23; cf. Lk 11:50–51; Heb 11:32,36–38.

9:27 *deliverers.* See Introduction to Judges: Title.

9:29 *Whoever obeys them will live by them.* See note on Lev 18:5. *Stubbornly they turned their backs.* See Zec 7:11; cf. the similar expressions in v. 16; 3:5; Hos 4:16.

peoples. *p* 31But in your great mercy you did not put an end *q* to them or abandon them, for you are a gracious and merciful *r* God.

32"Now therefore, our God, the great God, mighty *s* and awesome, *t* who keeps his covenant of love, *u* do not let all this hardship seem trifling in your eyes—the hardship *v* that has come on us, on our kings and leaders, on our priests and prophets, on our ancestors and all your people, from the days of the kings of Assyria until today. 33In all that has happened to us, you have remained righteous; *w* you have acted faithfully, while we acted wickedly. *x* 34Our kings, *y* our leaders, our priests and our ancestors *z* did not follow your law; they did not pay attention to your commands or the statutes you warned them to keep. 35Even while they were in their kingdom, enjoying your great goodness *a* to them in the spacious and fertile land you gave them, they did not serve you *b* or turn from their evil ways.

36"But see, we are slaves *c* today, slaves in the land you gave our ancestors so they could eat its fruit and the other good things it produces. 37Because of our sins, its abundant harvest goes to the kings you have placed over us. They rule over our bodies and our cattle as they please. We are in great distress. *d*

THE AGREEMENT OF THE PEOPLE

*38"In view of all this, we are making a binding agreement, *e* putting it in writing, *f* and our leaders, our Levites and our priests are affixing their seals to it."

10

*Those who sealed it were:

Nehemiah the governor, the son of Hakaliah.

Zedekiah, 2Seraiah, *g* Azariah, Jeremiah,
3Pashhur, *h* Amariah, Malkijah,
4Hattush, Shebaniah, Malluk,
5Harim, *i* Meremoth, Obadiah,
6Daniel, Ginnethon, Baruch,
7Meshullam, Abijah, Mijamin,
8Maaziah, Bilgai and Shemaiah.
These were the priests. *j*

9The Levites: *k*

Jeshua son of Azaniah, Binnui of the sons of Henadad, Kadmiel,
10and their associates: Shebaniah,
Hodiah, Kelita, Pelaiah, Hanan,
11Mika, Rehob, Hashabiah,
12Zakkur, Sherebiah, Shebaniah,
13Hodiah, Bani and Beninu.

14The leaders of the people:

Parosh, Pahath-Moab, Elam, Zattu, Bani,
15Bunni, Azgad, Bebai,
16Adonijah, Bigvai, Adin, *l*
17Ater, Hezekiah, Azzur,
18Hodiah, Hashum, Bezai,
19Hariph, Anathoth, Nebai,
20Magpiash, Meshullam, Hezir, *m*
21Meshezabel, Zadok, Jaddua,
22Pelatiah, Hanan, Anaiah,
23Hoshea, Hananiah, *n* Hasshub,
24Hallohesh, Pilha, Shobek,

* 9:38 is numbered 10:1 in Hebrew texts.   * 10:1–39 is numbered 10:2–40 in Hebrew texts.

Cross references

9:30 *p* Jer 16:11; Zec 7:12
9:31 *q* Isa 48:9; 65:9 *r* S Dt 4:31
9:32 *s* Job 9:19; Ps 24:8; 89:8; 93:4 *t* S Dt 7:21 *u* S Dt 7:9; S 1Ki 8:23; Da 9:4 *v* S Ex 18:8
9:33 *w* S Ge 18:25 *x* Jer 44:3; Da 9:7-8, 14
9:34 *y* S 2Ki 23:11 *z* Jer 44:17
9:35 *a* Isa 63:7 *b* Dt 28:45-48
9:36 *c* S Ezr 9:9
9:37 *d* Dt 28:33; La 5:5
9:38 *e* S 2Ch 23:16 *f* Isa 44:5
10:2 *g* S Ezr 2:2
10:3 *h* S 1Ch 9:12
10:5 *i* S 1Ch 24:8
10:8 *j* Ne 12:1
10:9 *k* Ne 12:1
10:16 *l* S Ezr 8:6
10:20 *m* 1Ch 24:15
10:23 *n* S Ne 7:2

9:32 *who keeps his covenant of love.* See 1:5; see also Dt 7:9,12 and note. *kings of Assyria.* Including Tiglath-Pileser III, also known as Pul (1Ch 5:26); Shalmaneser V (2Ki 18:9); Sargon II (Isa 20:1); Sennacherib (2Ki 18:13); Esarhaddon (Ezr 4:2); and Ashurbanipal (Ezr 4:10). See chart, p. 482.
9:37 *rule over our bodies.* See 1Sa 8:11–13. The Persian rulers drafted their subjects into military service. Some Jews may have accompanied Xerxes on his invasion of Greece in 480 B.C.

10:1–27 A legal list, bearing the official seal and containing a roster of 84 names.
10:2–8 About half of these names occur again in 12:1–7.
10:9–13 Most of these names appear also in the lists of Levites in 8:7; 9:4–5.
10:14–27 Almost half of the names in this category are also found in the lists of 7:6–63; Ezr 2:1–61.

10:28 ° Ps 135:1
P 2Ch 6:26; S Ne 9:2
10:29 ª S Nu 5:21;
Ps 119:106
10:30 ʳ S Ex 34:16;
Ne 13:23
10:31 ª Ne 13:16,18;
Jer 17:27; Eze 23:38;
Am 8:5 ᵗ S Ex 23:11;
Lev 25:1-7 ᵘ S Dt 15:1
10:33 ᵛ Lev 24:6
ʷ Nu 10:10; Ps 81:3;
Isa 1:14 ˣ S 2Ch 24:5
10:34 ʸ S Lev 16:8
ᶻ Ne 13:31
10:35 ª S Ex 22:29;
S Nu 18:12 ᵇ Dt 26:1-
11
10:36 ᶜ S Ex 13:2;
S Nu 18:14-16
ᵈ Ne 13:31
10:37 ᵉ S Nu 18:12
ᶠ S Lev 27:30;
S Nu 18:21
ᵍ Dt 14:22-29
ʰ Eze 44:30
10:38 ⁱ Nu 18:26

²⁵Rehum, Hashabnah, Maaseiah, ²⁶Ahiah, Hanan, Anan, ²⁷Malluk, Harim and Baanah.

²⁸"The rest of the people—priests, Levites, gatekeepers, musicians, temple servants ° and all who separated themselves from the neighboring peoples ᵖ for the sake of the Law of God, together with their wives and all their sons and daughters who are able to understand— ²⁹all these now join their fellow Israelites the nobles, and bind themselves with a curse and an oath �q to follow the Law of God given through Moses the servant of God and to obey carefully all the commands, regulations and decrees of the Lᴏʀᴅ our Lord.

³⁰"We promise not to give our daughters in marriage to the peoples around us or take their daughters for our sons. ʳ

³¹"When the neighboring peoples bring merchandise or grain to sell on the Sabbath, ˢ we will not buy from them on the Sabbath or on any holy day. Every seventh year we will forgo working the land ᵗ and will cancel all debts. ᵘ

³²"We assume the responsibility for carrying out the commands to give a third of a shekel ª each year for the service of the house of our God: ³³for the bread set out on the table; ᵛ for the regular grain offerings and burnt offerings; for the offerings on the Sabbaths, at the New Moon ʷ feasts and at the appointed festivals; for the holy offerings; for sin offerings ᵇ to make atonement for Israel; and for all the duties of the house of our God. ˣ

³⁴"We—the priests, the Levites and the people—have cast lots ʸ to determine when each of our families is to bring to the house of our God at set times each year a contribution of wood ᶻ to burn on the altar of the Lᴏʀᴅ our God, as it is written in the Law.

³⁵"We also assume responsibility for bringing to the house of the Lᴏʀᴅ each year the firstfruits ª of our crops and of every fruit tree. ᵇ

³⁶"As it is also written in the Law, we will bring the firstborn ᶜ of our sons and of our cattle, of our herds and of our flocks to the house of our God, to the priests ministering there. ᵈ

³⁷"Moreover, we will bring to the storerooms of the house of our God, to the priests, the first of our ground meal, of our ⌊grain⌋ offerings, of the fruit of all our trees and of our new wine and olive oil. ᵉ And we will bring a tithe ᶠ of our crops to the Levites, ᵍ for it is the Levites who collect the tithes in all the towns where we work. ʰ ³⁸A priest descended from Aaron is to accompany the Levites when they receive the tithes, and the Levites are to bring a tenth of the tithes ⁱ up to the house of our God, to the storerooms of the treasury. ³⁹The people of Israel, including the Levites, are to bring their contributions of grain, new wine and olive oil to the storerooms, where the articles

ª 32 That is, about 1/8 ounce or about 4 grams   ᵇ 33 Or *purification offerings*

10:28 *The rest of the people.* Those who did not affix their seals to the agreement (cf. 9:38—10:1). *Levites.* See Introduction to Leviticus: Title. *gatekeepers.* See note on Ezr 2:42. *wives ... sons and daughters.* See note on 8:2.
10:31–33 Perhaps a code drawn up by Nehemiah to correct the abuses listed in 13:15–22.
10:31 *sell on the Sabbath.* Though Ex 20:8–11; Dt 5:12–15 do not explicitly prohibit trading on the Sabbath, see Jer 17:19–27; Am 8:5 and note. *seventh year ... forgo working the land ... cancel all debts.* See note on Lev 25:4. The Romans misrepresented the Sabbath and the sabbath year as caused by laziness. According to Tacitus, the Jews "were led by the charms of indolence to give over the seventh year as well to inactivity."
10:32 *third of a shekel.* Ex 30:13–14 speaks of a "half shekel" as "an offering to the Lᴏʀᴅ" from each man who was 20 years old or more as a symbolic ransom. Later Joash used the annual contributions for the repair of the temple (2Ch 24:4–14). In the NT period Jewish men from everywhere sent an offering of a half shekel (actually two drachmas, its equivalent; see Josephus, *Antiquities,* 3.8.2) for the temple in Jerusalem (Mt 17:24). The pledge of a third of a shekel in Nehemiah's time may have been due to economic circumstances.
10:33 *bread.* See note on Lev 24:8.

10:34 *cast lots.* See notes on 11:1; Jnh 1:7. *contribution of wood.* Though there is no specific reference to a wood offering in the Pentateuch, the perpetual burning of fire on the sanctuary altar (Lev 6:12–13) would have required a continual supply of wood. Josephus mentions "the festival of wood offering" on the 14th day of the fifth month (Ab). The Jewish Mishnah (Rabbinic interpretations and applications of Pentateuchal laws) lists nine times when certain families brought wood and stipulates that all kinds of wood were suitable, except the vine and the olive. The Temple Scroll from Qumran describes the celebration of a wood offering festival for six days following a new oil festival.
10:35 *firstfruits.* Brought to the sanctuary to support the priests and Levites (see Ex 23:19 and note; Nu 18:13; Dt 26:1–11; Eze 44:30).
10:36 *firstborn.* See note on Ex 13:13.
10:37 *storerooms.* Chambers in the courts of the temple were used as storage rooms for silver, gold and sacred articles (cf. vv. 38–39; 12:44; 13:4–5,9; Ezr 8:28–30). *new wine.* See note on Dt 7:13. Though the Hebrew for this term can refer to freshly pressed grape juice (Isa 65:8; Mic 6:15), it can also be used of intoxicating wine (Hos 4:11). *tithe.* See notes on Ge 14:20; 28:22; Lev 27:30; Am 4:4. *Levites.* Tithes were meant for their support (13:12–13; Nu 18:21–32).

for the sanctuary and for the ministering priests, the gatekeepers and the musicians are also kept.

"We will not neglect the house of our God."[j]

THE NEW RESIDENTS OF JERUSALEM
11:3–19pp — 1Ch 9:1–17

11 Now the leaders of the people settled in Jerusalem. The rest of the people cast lots to bring one out of every ten of them to live in Jerusalem,[k] the holy city,[l] while the remaining nine were to stay in their own towns.[m] [2]The people commended all who volunteered to live in Jerusalem.

[3]These are the provincial leaders who settled in Jerusalem (now some Israelites, priests, Levites, temple servants and descendants of Solomon's servants lived in the towns of Judah, each of them on their own property in the various towns,[n] [4]while other people from both Judah and Benjamin[o] lived in Jerusalem):[p]

From the descendants of Judah:

Athaiah son of Uzziah, the son of Zechariah, the son of Amariah, the son of Shephatiah, the son of Mahalalel, a descendant of Perez; [5]and Maaseiah son of Baruch, the son of Kol-Hozeh, the son of Hazaiah, the son of Adaiah, the son of Joiarib, the son of Zechariah, a descendant of Shelah. [6]The descendants of Perez who lived in Jerusalem totaled 468 men of standing.

[7]From the descendants of Benjamin:

Sallu son of Meshullam, the son of Joed, the son of Pedaiah, the son of Kolaiah, the son of Maaseiah, the son of Ithiel, the son of Jeshaiah, [8]and his followers, Gabbai and Sallai—928 men. [9]Joel son of Zikri was their chief officer, and Judah son of Hassenuah was over the New Quarter of the city.

[10]From the priests:

Jedaiah; the son of Joiarib; Jakin; [11]Seraiah[q] son of Hilkiah, the son of Meshullam, the son of Zadok, the son of Meraioth, the son of Ahitub,[r] the official in charge of the house of God, [12]and their associates, who carried on work for the temple—822 men; Adaiah son of Jeroham, the son of Pelaliah, the son of Amzi, the son of Zechariah, the son of Pashhur, the son of Malkijah, [13]and his associates, who were heads of families—242 men; Amashsai son of Azarel, the son of Ahzai, the son of Meshillemoth, the son of Immer, [14]and his[a] associates, who were men of standing—128. Their chief officer was Zabdiel son of Haggedolim.

[15]From the Levites:

Shemaiah son of Hasshub, the son of Azrikam, the son of Hashabiah, the son of Bunni; [16]Shabbethai[s] and Jozabad,[t] two of the heads of the Levites, who had charge of the outside work of the house of God; [17]Mattaniah[u] son of Mika, the son of Zabdi, the son of Asaph,[v] the director who led in thanksgiving and prayer; Bakbukiah, second

---

[a] *14 Most Septuagint manuscripts; Hebrew their*

10:39 / Ne 13:11,12
11:1 [k] Ne 7:4
[l] Isa 48:2; 52:1; 64:10; Zec 14:20-21
[m] S Ne 7:73
11:3 [n] S Ezr 2:1
11:4 [o] S Ezr 1:5
[p] S Ezr 2:70
11:11 [q] S 2Ki 25:18; S Ezr 2:2 [r] S Ezr 7:2
11:16 [s] Ezr 10:15
[t] S Ezr 8:33
11:17 [u] S 1Ch 9:15; Ne 12:8 [v] 2Ch 5:12

A **10:39** See 13:11. *We will not neglect.* Haggai (Hag 1:4–9) had accused the people of neglecting the temple.

11:1 *cast lots.* See 10:34. Lots were usually made out of small stones or pieces of wood. Sometimes arrows were used (Eze 21:21). *one out of every ten of them to live in Jerusalem.* Josephus (*Antiquities,* 11.5.8) asserts: "But Nehemiah, seeing that the city had a small population, urged the priests and Levites to leave the countryside and move to the city and remain there, for he had prepared houses for them at his own expense." The practice of redistributing populations was also used to establish Greek and Hellenistic cities. It involved the forcible transfer from rural settlements to urban centers. Tiberias on the Sea of Galilee was populated with Gentiles by such a process by Herod Antipas in A.D. 18. *holy city.* See Isa 48:2 and note; Da 9:24; Mt 4:5; 27:53; Rev 11:2; cf. Joel 3:17.

11:2 In addition to those chosen by lot (v. 1), some volunteered out of a sense of duty. But evidently most preferred to stay in their hometowns.

11:3–19 A census roster that parallels 1Ch 9:2–21, a list of the first residents in Jerusalem after the return from Babylonia. About half the names in the two lists are the same.

11:8 *928.* The men of Benjamin provided twice as many men as Judah (v. 6) to live in and protect the city of Jerusalem.

B **11:9** *New Quarter.* See 2Ki 22:14 and note; 2Ch 34:22; Zep 1:10. Like the "market district" (Zep 1:11), which was probably the Tyropoeon Valley area, the New Quarter was a new suburb. Excavations indicate that the city had spread outside the walls in this direction by the late eighth century B.C. before the so-called Broad Wall was built c. 700 by Hezekiah (see note on 3:8).

11:16 *outside work.* Duties outside the temple (cf. 1Ch 26:29) but connected with it.

11:17 *Asaph.* See note on Ezr 2:41; see also titles of Ps 50; 73–83. *Jeduthun.* See 1Ch 16:42; 25:1,3; 2Ch 5:12; titles of Ps 39; 62; 77.

11:17 *w* S 1Ch 25:1
11:18 *x* S Rev 21:2
11:21 *y* S Ezr 2:43;
S Ne 3:26
11:22 *z* S 1Ch 9:15
11:23 *a* S 1Ch 15:16;
Ne 7:44
11:24 *b* S Ge 38:30
11:25 *c* S Ge 35:27
d S Nu 21:30
11:26 *e* Jos 15:26
f Jos 15:27
11:27 *g* Jos 15:28
h S Ge 21:14
11:28 *i* S 1Sa 27:6
11:29 *j* Jos 15:33
k S Jos 10:3; S 15:35
11:30 *l* Jos 15:34
m Jos 15:35
n S Jos 10:3; S 15:39
o S Jos 10:10
p Jos 15:28
11:31 *q* Jos 21:17;
Isa 10:29 *r* S 1Sa 13:2
s S Jos 12:9
11:32 *t* Jos 21:18;
Isa 10:30; Jer 1:1
u S 1Sa 21:1
11:33 *v* S Jos 11:1
w S Jos 18:25
x 2Sa 4:3
11:34 *y* 1Sa 13:18
11:35 *z* S 1Ch 8:12
12:1 *a* Ne 10:1-8
b Ne 10:9
c S 1Ch 3:19; Ezr 3:2;
Zec 4:6-10 *d* Ezr 3:2
e S Ezr 2:2 *f* S Ezr 2:2

among his associates; and Abda son of Shammua, the son of Galal, the son of Jeduthun. *w* ¹⁸The Levites in the holy city *x* totaled 284.

¹⁹The gatekeepers:

Akkub, Talmon and their associates, who kept watch at the gates—172 men.

²⁰The rest of the Israelites, with the priests and Levites, were in all the towns of Judah, each of them on their ancestral property.

²¹The temple servants *y* lived on the hill of Ophel, and Ziha and Gishpa were in charge of them.

²²The chief officer of the Levites in Jerusalem was Uzzi son of Bani, the son of Hashabiah, the son of Mattaniah, *z* the son of Mika. Uzzi was one of Asaph's descendants, who were the musicians responsible for the service of the house of God. ²³The musicians *a* were under the king's orders, which regulated their daily activity.

²⁴Pethahiah son of Meshezabel, one of the descendants of Zerah *b* son of Judah, was the king's agent in all affairs relating to the people.

²⁵As for the villages with their fields, some of the people of Judah lived in Kiriath Arba *c* and its surrounding settlements, in Dibon *d* and its settlements, in Jekabzeel and its villages, ²⁶in Jeshua, in Moladah, *e* in Beth Pelet, *f* ²⁷in Hazar Shual, *g* in Beersheba *h* and its settlements, ²⁸in Ziklag, *i* in Mekonah and its settlements, ²⁹in En Rimmon, in Zorah, *j* in Jarmuth, *k* ³⁰Zanoah, *l* Adullam *m* and their villages, in Lachish *n* and its fields, and in Azekah *o* and its settlements. So they were living all the way from Beersheba *p* to the Valley of Hinnom.

³¹The descendants of the Benjamites from Geba *q* lived in Mikmash, *r* Aija, Bethel *s* and its settlements, ³²in Anathoth, *t* Nob *u* and Ananiah, ³³in Hazor, *v* Ramah *w* and Gittaim, *x* ³⁴in Hadid, Zeboim *y* and Neballat, ³⁵in Lod and Ono, *z* and in Ge Harashim.

³⁶Some of the divisions of the Levites of Judah settled in Benjamin.

PRIESTS AND LEVITES

12 These were the priests *a* and Levites *b* who returned with Zerubbabel *c* son of Shealtiel *d* and with Joshua: *e*
Seraiah, *f* Jeremiah, Ezra,

11:18 *284.* The relatively small number of Levites, compared with 1,192 priests (the total of 822, 242 and 128 in vv. 12–13), is striking (see note on Ezr 2:40).
11:20 *ancestral property.* Inalienable hereditary possessions—including land, buildings and movable goods—acquired by either conquest or inheritance (Ge 31:14; Nu 18:21; 27:7; 34:2; 36:3; 1Ki 21:1–4).
11:21 *Ophel.* See note on 3:26.
11:23 *king's orders…regulated.* David had regulated the services of the Levites, including the musicians (1Ch 25). The Persian king, Darius I, gave a royal stipend so that the Jewish elders might "pray for the well-being of the king and his sons" (Ezr 6:10). Artaxerxes I may have done much the same for the Levite choir.
11:25–30 An important list, corresponding to earlier lists of towns in Judah. All these names also appear in Jos 15 with the exception of Dibon, Jekabzeel (but see Kabzeel in Jos 15:21), Jeshua, Meconah and En Rimmon (but see Ain and Rimmon in Jos 15:32). The list, however, is not comprehensive, since a number of towns listed in ch. 3; Ezr 2:21–22 are lacking. No Judean coins have been found outside the area designated by vv. 25–30.
11:25 *Kiriath Arba.* See note on Ge 23:2. In the Hellenistic era it fell to the Idumeans, together with other Judean towns.
11:26 *Moladah.* Near Beersheba; later occupied by the Idumeans. *Beth Pelet.* Means "house of refuge," a site near Beersheba.
11:27 *Beersheba.* See note and NIV text note on Ge 21:31. Archaeological excavations reveal that the city was destroyed by Sennacherib in 701 B.C. and only resettled in the Persian period.
11:28 *Ziklag.* Given to David by Achish, king of Gath (1Sa 27:6), and taken by the Amalekites (1Sa 30:1); see Jos 15:31.
11:29 *En Rimmon.* Means "spring of the pomegranate," probably Khirbet Umm er-Ramamin, nine miles northeast of Beersheba (see Jos 15:32). *Zorah.* See note on Jdg

13:2. *Jarmuth.* Eight miles north-northeast of Eleutheropolis (Beit Jibrin), it was one of five Canaanite cities in the south that attempted to halt Joshua's invasion (Jos 10:3–5).
11:30 *Zanoah.* A village in the Shephelah district of low hills between Judah and Philistia. The residents of Zanoah repaired the Valley Gate (3:13). The site has been identified with Khirbet Zanu, three miles south-southeast of Beth Shemesh. *Adullam.* See note on Ge 38:1. *Lachish.* See Jos 10:3; see also notes on Isa 36:2; Mic 1:13. *Azekah.* See note on Jer 34:7. *Hinnom.* The valley west and south of Jerusalem; Gehenna in the NT.
11:31–35 Most of the Benjamite towns listed here appear also in 7:26–38; Ezr 2:23–35.
11:31 *Geba.* See 12:29; see also note on 1Sa 13:3. *Mikmash.* See note on 1Sa 13:2. *Aija.* An alternative name for Ai (see note on Jos 7:2). *Bethel.* See notes on Ge 12:8; Jos 7:2; Ezr 2:28; Am 4:4.
11:32 *Anathoth.* See note on Jer 1:1. *Nob.* See note on 1Sa 21:1. *Ananiah.* Probably Bethany, meaning "house of Ananiah" (see note on Mt 21:17).
11:33 *Gittaim.* Its location is not known.
11:34 *Hadid.* Three to four miles northeast of Lod (see 7:37; Ezr 2:33).
11:35 *Lod.* See note on Ezr 2:33. *Ono.* See note on 6:2. *Ge Harashim.* See 1Ch 4:14 and TNIV text note; the broad valley between Lod and Ono. The name may preserve the ancient memory that the Philistines in that area were blacksmiths (1Sa 13:19–20).
12:1 *Zerubbabel son of Shealtiel.* See Ezr 3:2,8; 5:2; see also note on Hag 1:1. *Joshua.* Returned from Babylonian exile in 538/537 B.C. (see vv. 10,26; 7:7; Ezr 2:2 and note; Hag 1:1; Zec 3:1 and note). *Ezra.* Not the Ezra of the book, who was the leader of the exiles who returned 80 years later.

² Amariah, Malluk, Hattush,

³ Shekaniah, Rehum, Meremoth,

⁴ Iddo, ^g Ginnethon,ª Abijah, ^h

⁵ Mijamin, ^b Moadiah, Bilgah,

⁶ Shemaiah, Joiarib, Jedaiah, ⁱ

⁷ Sallu, Amok, Hilkiah and Jedaiah.

These were the leaders of the priests and their associates in the days of Joshua.

⁸ The Levites were Jeshua, ^j Binnui, Kadmiel, Sherebiah, Judah, and also Mattaniah, ^k who, together with his associates, was in charge of the songs of thanksgiving. ⁹ Bakbukiah and Unni, their associates, stood opposite them in the services.

¹⁰ Joshua was the father of Joiakim, Joiakim the father of Eliashib, ^l Eliashib the father of Joiada, ¹¹ Joiada the father of Jonathan, and Jonathan the father of Jaddua.

¹² In the days of Joiakim, these were the heads of the priestly families:

of Seraiah's family, Meraiah;

of Jeremiah's, Hananiah;

¹³ of Ezra's, Meshullam;

of Amariah's, Jehohanan;

¹⁴ of Malluk's, Jonathan;

of Shekaniah's, ^c Joseph;

¹⁵ of Harim's, Adna;

of Meremoth's, ^d Helkai;

¹⁶ of Iddo's, ^m Zechariah;

of Ginnethon's, Meshullam;

¹⁷ of Abijah's, ⁿ Zikri;

of Miniamin's and of Moadiah's, Piltai;

¹⁸ of Bilgah's, Shammua;

of Shemaiah's, Jehonathan;

¹⁹ of Joiarib's, Mattenai;

of Jedaiah's, Uzzi;

²⁰ of Sallu's, Kallai;

of Amok's, Eber;

²¹ of Hilkiah's, Hashabiah;

of Jedaiah's, Nethanel.

²² The family heads of the Levites in the days of Eliashib, Joiada, Johanan and Jaddua, as well as those of the priests, were recorded in the reign of Darius the Persian. ²³ The family heads among the descendants of Levi up to the time of Johanan son of Eliashib were recorded in the book of the annals. ²⁴ And the leaders of the Levites ^o were Hashabiah, Sherebiah, Jeshua son of Kadmiel, and their associates, who stood opposite them to give praise and thanksgiving, one section responding to the other, as prescribed by David the man of God. ^p

ª 4 Many Hebrew manuscripts and Vulgate (see also Neh. 12:16); most Hebrew manuscripts *Ginnethoi* b 5 A variant of *Miniamin* c 14 Very many Hebrew manuscripts, some Septuagint manuscripts and Syriac (see also Neh. 12:3); most Hebrew manuscripts *Shebaniah's* d 15 Some Septuagint manuscripts (see also Neh. 12:3); Hebrew *Meraioth's*

12:4 ^g ver 16; Zec 1:1
^h S 1Ch 24:10; Lk 1:5
12:6 ⁱ S 1Ch 24:7
12:8 ^j S Ezr 2:2
^k Ne 11:17
12:10 ^l S Ezr 10:24; Ne 3:20
12:16 ^m S ver 4
12:17 ⁿ S 1Ch 24:10
12:24 ^o S Ezr 2:40
^p S 2Ch 8:14

12:7 *leaders of the priests.* The rotation of 24 priestly divisions was established at the time of David (see 1Ch 24:3,7–19 and note on 24:4). Twenty-four heads of priestly houses are mentioned in vv. 1–7. Inscriptions listing the 24 divisions of the priests probably hung in many synagogues in the Holy Land. So far, only fragments of two such inscriptions have been recovered—from Ashkelon in the 1920s and from Caesarea in the 1960s (dated to the third and fourth centuries A.D.).

12:9 *opposite them.* See v. 24; Ezr 3:11 and note; cf. 2Ch 7:6. The singing was antiphonal, with two sections of the choir standing opposite each other. *services.* The Hebrew for this word (*Mishmarot*) is the title of a work from Qumran, which discusses in detail the rotation of the priestly families' service in the temple according to the sect's solar calendar and synchronized with the conventional lunar calendar.

12:10 *Joshua.* See note on v. 1. *Joiakim.* See vv. 12,26. *Eliashib.* See vv. 22–23; the high priest who assisted in rebuilding the wall (3:1,20–21; 13:28). A priest named Eliashib was guilty of defiling the temple by assigning rooms to Tobiah the Ammonite (13:4,7). It is not known whether this Eliashib was the same as the high priest.

12:11 *Jonathan.* Since v. 22 mentions a Johanan after Joiada and before Jaddua, and v. 23 identifies Johanan as "son" of Eliashib, some believe that "Jonathan" is an error for "Johanan." Further complicating the identification are attempts to identify this high priest with a "Johanan" mentioned in the Elephantine papyri and in Josephus (*Antiquities*, 11.7.1). Such an identification, however, is disputable.

12:12–21 All but one (Hattush, v. 2) of the 22 priestly families listed in vv. 1–7 are repeated (Rehum, v. 3, is a variant of Harim, v. 15; Mijamin, v. 5, is a variant of Miniamin, v. 17) in this later list, which dates to the time of Joiakim (v. 12), high priest in the late sixth and/or early fifth centuries B.C.

12:22 *Darius the Persian.* Either Darius II Nothus (423–404 B.C.) or Darius III Codomannus (336–331).

12:23 *book of the annals.* Cf. 7:5. This may have been the official temple chronicle, containing various lists and records. Cf. the annals of the Persian kings (Ezr 4:15; Est 2:23; 6:1; 10:2); cf. also the "book of the annals of the kings," mentioned frequently in 1, 2 Kings.

12:27 *q* Dt 20:5
r S 2Sa 6:5
s S 1Ch 15:16,28;
25:6; Ps 92:3
12:28 *t* S 1Ch 2:54;
9:16
12:30 *u* Ex 19:10;
Job 1:5
12:31 *v* Ne 2:13
12:34 *w* S Ezr 1:5
12:35 *x* S Ezr 3:10
12:36 *y* S 1Ch 15:16
z S 2Ch 8:14 *a* Ezr 7:6
12:37 *b* S Ne 2:14
c S Ne 3:26
12:38 *d* Ne 3:11
e Ne 3:8
12:39 *f* S 2Ki 14:13
g Ne 3:6
h S 2Ch 33:14
i S Ne 3:1 *j* Ne 3:1
k S Ne 3:1
12:44 *l* Ne 13:4,13

25Mattaniah, Bakbukiah, Obadiah, Meshullam, Talmon and Akkub were gatekeepers who guarded the storerooms at the gates. 26They served in the days of Joiakim son of Joshua, the son of Jozadak, and in the days of Nehemiah the governor and of Ezra the priest, the teacher of the Law.

DEDICATION OF THE WALL OF JERUSALEM

27At the dedication *q* of the wall of Jerusalem, the Levites were sought out from where they lived and were brought to Jerusalem to celebrate joyfully the dedication with songs of thanksgiving and with the music of cymbals, *r* harps and lyres. *s* 28The musicians also were brought together from the region around Jerusalem—from the villages of the Netophathites, *t* 29from Beth Gilgal, and from the area of Geba and Azmaveth, for the musicians had built villages for themselves around Jerusalem. 30When the priests and Levites had purified themselves ceremonially, they purified the people, *u* the gates and the wall.

31I had the leaders of Judah go up on top of *a* the wall. I also assigned two large choirs to give thanks. One was to proceed on top of *b* the wall to the right, toward the Dung Gate. *v* 32Hoshaiah and half the leaders of Judah followed them, 33along with Azariah, Ezra, Meshullam, 34Judah, Benjamin, *w* Shemaiah, Jeremiah, 35as well as some priests with trumpets, *x* and also Zechariah son of Jonathan, the son of Shemaiah, the son of Mattaniah, the son of Micaiah, the son of Zakkur, the son of Asaph, 36and his associates— Shemaiah, Azarel, Milalai, Gilalai, Maai, Nethanel, Judah and Hanani—with musical instruments *y* ⌊prescribed by⌋ David the man of God. *z* Ezra *a* the teacher of the Law led the procession. 37At the Fountain Gate *b* they continued directly up the steps of the City of David on the ascent to the wall and passed above the site of David's palace to the Water Gate *c* on the east.

38The second choir proceeded in the opposite direction. I followed them on top of *c* the wall, together with half the people—past the Tower of the Ovens *d* to the Broad Wall, *e* 39over the Gate of Ephraim, *f* the Jeshanah *d* Gate, *g* the Fish Gate, *h* the Tower of Hananel *i* and the Tower of the Hundred, *j* as far as the Sheep Gate. *k* At the Gate of the Guard they stopped.

40The two choirs that gave thanks then took their places in the house of God; so did I, together with half the officials, 41as well as the priests—Eliakim, Maaseiah, Miniamin, Micaiah, Elioenai, Zechariah and Hananiah with their trumpets— 42and also Maaseiah, Shemaiah, Eleazar, Uzzi, Jehohanan, Malkijah, Elam and Ezer. The choirs sang under the direction of Jezrahiah. 43And on that day they offered great sacrifices, rejoicing because God had given them great joy. The women and children also rejoiced. The sound of rejoicing in Jerusalem could be heard far away.

44At that time men were appointed to be in charge of the storerooms *l* for the contri-

---

a 31 Or *go alongside*   *b 31* Or *proceed alongside*   *c 38* Or *them alongside*   *d 39* Or *Old*

12:26 *Nehemiah ... Ezra.* See note on 8:9.

12:27 *dedication.* See note on Ezr 6:16. *cymbals.* See note on Ezr 3:10. Cymbals were used in religious ceremonies (1Ch 16:42; 25:1; 2Ch 5:12; 29:25). Ancient examples have been found at Beth Shemesh and Tell Abu Hawam. *harps.* See note on Ge 31:27; used mainly in religious ceremonies (1Sa 10:5; 2Sa 6:5; Ps 150:3). Ancient harps have been reconstructed from information derived from the remains of harps at Ur, pictures of harps, and cuneiform texts describing in detail the tuning of harps. *lyres.* Had strings of the same length but of different diameters and tensions (see 1Ch 15:16; Da 3:5).

12:28 *Netophathites.* From Netophah, a town near Bethlehem (7:26).

12:29 *Beth Gilgal.* Perhaps the Gilgal near Jericho (see note on Jos 4:19), or the Gilgal of Elijah (2Ki 2:1), about seven miles north of Bethel.

12:30 *purified.* See note on Lev 4:12. The Levites are said to have purified all that was sacred in the temple (1Ch 23:28) and the temple itself (2Ch 29:15) during times of revival. Ritual purity was intended to teach God's holiness and moral purity (Lev 16:30).

12:31 *two large choirs.* See note on v. 38. The two great processions probably started from the area of the Valley Gate (2:13,15; 3:13) near the center of the western section of the wall. The first

procession, led by Ezra (v. 36), moved in a counterclockwise direction upon the wall; the second, with Nehemiah (v. 38), moved in a clockwise direction. Both met between the Water Gate (v. 37) and the Gate of the Guard (v. 39), then entered the temple area. Cf. Ps 48:12–13. *to the right.* Or "to the south." Semites oriented themselves facing east, so the right hand represented the south (see Jos 17:7; 1Sa 23:24; Job 23:9). *Dung Gate.* See note on 2:13.

12:35 *trumpets.* See note on Ezr 3:10. Each choir had priests blowing trumpets, as well as Levites playing other musical instruments. *Asaph.* See note on 11:17.

12:36 *Ezra the teacher of the Law.* See notes on Ezr 7:1,6.

12:37 *Fountain Gate.* See note on 2:14. *City of David.* See 3:15; see also note on 2Sa 5:7. *Water Gate.* See note on 3:26.

12:38 *choir.* Lit. "thanks," i.e., "thanksgiving choir" (see v. 40). *Tower of the Ovens.* See note on 3:11. *Broad Wall.* See note on 3:8.

12:39 *Gate of Ephraim.* See notes on 3:6; 8:16. *Jeshanah Gate.* See note on 3:6. *Fish Gate.* See note on 3:3. *Tower of Hananel ... Tower of the Hundred ... Sheep Gate.* See note on 3:1. *Gate of the Guard.* Cf. Jer 32:2.

12:43 *God had given them great joy.* See 1Ch 29:9. *women.* See 8:2; Ex 15:20 and notes. *heard far away.* See note on Ezr 3:13; cf. 1Ki 1:40; 2Ki 11:13.

butions, firstfruits and tithes. ^{m} From the fields around the towns they were to bring into the storerooms the portions required by the Law for the priests and the Levites, for Judah was pleased with the ministering priests and Levites. ^{n} ^{45}They performed the service of their God and the service of purification, as did also the musicians and gatekeepers, according to the commands of David ^{o} and his son Solomon. ^{p} ^{46}For long ago, in the days of David and Asaph, ^{q} there had been directors for the musicians and for the songs of praise ^{r} and thanksgiving to God. ^{47}So in the days of Zerubbabel and of Nehemiah, all Israel contributed the daily portions for the musicians and the gatekeepers. They also set aside the portion for the other Levites, and the Levites set aside the portion for the descendants of Aaron. ^{s}

NEHEMIAH'S FINAL REFORMS

13 On that day the Book of Moses was read aloud in the hearing of the people and there it was found written that no Ammonite or Moabite should ever be admitted into the assembly of God, ^{t} ^{2}because they had not met the Israelites with food and water but had hired Balaam ^{u} to call a curse down on them. ^{v} (Our God, however, turned the curse into a blessing.) ^{w} ^{3}When the people heard this law, they excluded from Israel all who were of foreign descent. ^{x}

^{4}Before this, Eliashib the priest had been put in charge of the storerooms ^{y} of the house of our God. He was closely associated with Tobiah, ^{z} ^{5}and he had provided him with a large room formerly used to store the grain offerings and incense and temple articles, and also the tithes ^{a} of grain, new wine and olive oil prescribed for the Levites, musicians and gatekeepers, as well as the contributions for the priests.

^{6}But while all this was going on, I was not in Jerusalem, for in the thirty-second year of Artaxerxes ^{b} king of Babylon I had returned to the king. Some time later I asked his permission ^{7}and came back to Jerusalem. Here I learned about the evil thing Eliashib ^{c} had done in providing Tobiah ^{d} a room in the courts of the house of God. ^{8}I was greatly displeased and threw all Tobiah's household goods out of the room. ^{e} ^{9}I gave orders to purify the rooms, ^{f} and then I put back into them the equipment of the house of God, with the grain offerings and the incense. ^{g}

^{10}I also learned that the portions assigned to the Levites had not been given to them, ^{h} and that all the Levites and musicians responsible for the service had gone back to their own fields. ^{i} ^{11}So I rebuked the officials and asked them, "Why is the house of God neglected?" ^{j} Then I called them together and stationed them at their posts.

^{12}All Judah brought the tithes ^{k} of grain, new wine and olive oil into the storerooms. ^{l} ^{13}I put Shelemiah the priest, Zadok the scribe, and a Levite named Pedaiah in charge of the

12:44 ^{m} S Lev 27:30
^{n} S Dt 18:8
12:45 ^{o} S 2Ch 8:14
^{p} S 1Ch 6:31; 23:5
12:46 ^{q} S 2Ch 35:15
^{r} 2Ch 29:27; Ps 137:4
12:47 ^{s} S Dt 18:8
13:1 ^{t} ver 23;
Dt 23:3
13:2 ^{u} Nu 22:3-11
^{v} S Nu 23:7; S Dt 23:3
^{w} S Nu 23:11;
Dt 23:4-5
13:3 ^{x} ver 23;
S Ne 9:2
13:4 ^{y} S Ne 12:44
^{z} Ne 2:10
13:5 ^{a} S Lev 27:30;
S Nu 18:21
13:6 ^{b} S Ne 2:6
13:7 ^{c} S Ezr 10:24
^{d} S Ne 2:10
13:8 ^{e} Mt 21:12-13;
Mk 11:15-17;
Lk 19:45-46; Jn 2:13-16
13:9 ^{f} S 1Ch 23:28;
S 2Ch 29:5
^{g} S Lev 2:1
13:10 ^{h} S Dt 12:19
^{i} S 2Ch 31:4
13:11 ^{j} S Ne 10:37-39; Hag 1:1-9;
Mal 3:8-9
13:12 ^{k} S 2Ch 31:6
^{l} S Dt 18:8; 1Ki 7:51;
S 2Ch 31:5;
S Ne 10:37-39;
Mal 3:10

12:44 *Judah was pleased.* The people cheerfully contributed their offerings to support the priests and Levites (cf. 2Co 9:7). *ministering.* See Dt 10:8.
12:46 *Asaph.* See note on 11:17.
12:47 *Zerubbabel.* See Ezr 1:2 and note. *contributed.* The Hebrew for this verb implies continued giving.
13:1–2 See Dt 23:3–6.
13:2 *Balaam.* See notes on Nu 22:5,8.
13:4 *Eliashib.* See note on 12:10. *Tobiah.* See note on 2:10.
13:5 *provided him with a large room.* During Nehemiah's absence from the city to return to the Persian king's court, Tobiah, one of his archenemies, had used his influence with Eliashib to gain entrance into a chamber ordinarily set aside for the storage of tithes and other offerings (see 10:37 and note; cf. Nu 18:21–32; Dt 14:28–29; 26:12–15). Elsewhere we read of the chamber of Meshullam (3:30) and of Jehohanan (Ezr 10:6).
13:6 *thirty-second year of Artaxerxes.* See note on 5:14. *king of Babylon.* The title was assumed by Cyrus after his conquest of Babylon (see Ezr 5:13) and was adopted by subsequent Achaemenid (Persian) kings.
13:7 *came back to Jerusalem.* Nehemiah's second term must have ended before 407 B.C., when Bagohi (Bigvai) was governor of Judah according to the Elephantine papyri. Some have suggested that after Nehemiah's first term he was succeeded by his brother Hanani (see note on 1:2). *courts.* See note on 8:16. Zerubbabel's temple had two courtyards (Zec 3:7; cf. Isa 62:9).

A C **13:8** *displeased … threw.* Nehemiah expressed his indignation by taking action (cf. vv. 24–25; 5:6–7). Contrast the reaction of Ezra, who "sat down appalled" (Ezr 9:3). Nehemiah's action reminds us of Christ's expulsion of the money changers from the temple area (Mt 21:12–13).
B **13:9** *rooms.* Though only a single chamber was mentioned in vv. 5–8, additional rooms were involved. A parallel to the occupation and desecration of the temple by Tobiah comes from a century earlier in Egypt, where Greek mercenaries had occupied the temple of Neith at Sais. Upon the appeal of the Egyptian priest, Udjahorresnet, the Persian king had the squatters driven out and the temple's ceremonies, processions and revenues restored: "And His Majesty commanded that all the foreigners who had settled in the temple of Neith should be driven out and that all their houses and all their superfluities that were in this temple should be thrown down, and that all their own baggage should be carried for them outside the wall of this temple."
13:10 Nehemiah was apparently correcting an abuse of long standing. Strictly speaking, the Levites had no holdings (Nu 18:20,23–24; Dt 14:29; 18:1), but some may have had private income (Dt 18:8). Therefore the Levites were dependent on the faithful support of the people. This may explain the reluctance of great numbers of Levites to return from exile (see Ezr 8:15–20). For the complaints of those who found little material advantage in serving the Lord, see Mal 2:17; 3:13–15.
13:11 *neglected.* See note on 10:39.
B **13:12** *tithes.* See 12:44. Temples in Mesopotamia also levied tithes for the support of their personnel.

13:13 *m* S Ne 12:44;
Ac 6:1-5
13:14 *n* S Ge 8:1;
S 2Ki 20:3
13:15 *o* Ex 20:8-11;
S 34:21; Dt 5:12-15
13:16 *p* S Ne 10:31
13:18 *q* Jer 44:23
r S Ne 10:31
13:19 *s* Lev 23:32
13:22 *t* S Ge 8:1;
S Ne 1:8
13:23 *u* Ezr 9:1-2;
Mal 2:11 *v* ver 1;
S ver 1, S 3; Ex 34:16;
S Ru 1:4; S Ne 10:30
13:24 *w* Est 1:22;
3:12; 8:9
13:25 *x* S Ezr 10:5
y S Ex 34:16
13:26 *z* S 1Ki 3:13;
S 2Ch 1:12 *a* 2Sa 12:25
b S Ex 34:16;
S 1Ki 11:3
13:27 *c* Ezr 9:14

storerooms and made Hanan son of Zakkur, the son of Mattaniah, their assistant, because they were considered trustworthy. They were made responsible for distributing the supplies to their fellow Levites. *m*

[14]Remember *n* me for this, my God, and do not blot out what I have so faithfully done for the house of my God and its services.

[15]In those days I saw people in Judah treading winepresses on the Sabbath and bringing in grain and loading it on donkeys, together with wine, grapes, figs and all other kinds of loads. And they were bringing all this into Jerusalem on the Sabbath. *o* Therefore I warned them against selling food on that day. [16]People from Tyre who lived in Jerusalem were bringing in fish and all kinds of merchandise and selling them in Jerusalem on the Sabbath *p* to the people of Judah. [17]I rebuked the nobles of Judah and said to them, "What is this wicked thing you are doing—desecrating the Sabbath day? [18]Didn't your ancestors do the same things, so that our God brought all this calamity on us and on this city? *q* Now you are stirring up more wrath against Israel by desecrating the Sabbath." *r*

[19]When evening shadows fell on the gates of Jerusalem before the Sabbath, *s* I ordered the doors to be shut and not opened until the Sabbath was over. I stationed some of my own men at the gates so that no load could be brought in on the Sabbath day. [20]Once or twice the merchants and sellers of all kinds of goods spent the night outside Jerusalem. [21]But I warned them and said, "Why do you spend the night by the wall? If you do this again, I will lay hands on you." From that time on they no longer came on the Sabbath. [22]Then I commanded the Levites to purify themselves and go and guard the gates in order to keep the Sabbath day holy.

Remember *t* me for this also, my God, and show mercy to me according to your great love.

[23]Moreover, in those days I saw men of Judah who had married *u* women from Ashdod, Ammon and Moab. *v* [24]Half of their children spoke the language of Ashdod or the language of one of the other peoples, and did not know how to speak the language *w* of Judah. [25]I rebuked them and called curses down on them. I beat some of them and pulled out their hair. I made them take an oath *x* in God's name and said: "You are not to give your daughters in marriage to their sons, nor are you to take their daughters in marriage for your sons or for yourselves. *y* [26]Was it not because of marriages like these that Solomon king of Israel sinned? Among the many nations there was no king like him. *z* He was loved by his God, *a* and God made him king over all Israel, but even he was led into sin by foreign women. *b* [27]Must we hear now that you too are doing all this terrible wickedness and are being unfaithful to our God by marrying *c* foreign women?"

A **13:13** Of the four treasurers, one was a priest, one a Levite, one a scribe and one a layman of rank. *trustworthy.* Nehemiah appointed honest men to make sure that supplies were distributed equitably, just as the church appointed deacons for this purpose (Ac 6:1–5).

13:15 *treading winepresses.* See notes on Isa 5:2; 16:10. *Sabbath.* The temptation to violate the Sabbath rest was especially characteristic of non-Jewish merchants (see 10:31; Isa 56:1–8). On the other hand, the high regard that many had for the Sabbath was expressed by parents who called their children Shabbethai (see 8:7; 11:16; Ezr 10:15).

13:16 *Tyre.* See note on Isa 23:1. *fish.* Most of the fish exported by the Tyrians (Eze 26:4–5,14) was dried, smoked or salted. Fish, much of it from the Sea of Galilee, was an important part of the Israelites' diet (Lev 11:9; Nu 11:5; Mt 15:34; Lk 24:42; Jn 21:5–13). It was sold at the market near the Fish Gate (see note on 3:3).

C **13:17–18** *desecrating the Sabbath.* Cf. Ex 16:28–29; Nu 15:32–36; Isa 58:13–14; Jer 17:19–27; Am 8:5,7–8. "Desecrating" means turning what is sacred into common use and so profaning it (see Mal 2:10–11).

13:17 *rebuked the nobles.* Because they were the leaders.

B **13:19** *When evening shadows fell on the gates.* Before sunset, when the Sabbath began. The Israelites, like the Babylonians, counted their days from sunset to sunset (the Egyptians reckoned theirs from dawn to dawn). The precise moment when the Sabbath began was heralded by the blowing of a trumpet by a priest. According to the Jewish Mishnah, "On the eve of Sabbath

they used to blow six more blasts, three to cause the people to cease from work and three to mark the break between the sacred and the profane." Josephus (*Wars,* 4.9.12) speaks of the location on the parapet of the temple where the priests "gave a signal beforehand, with a trumpet, at the beginning of every seventh day, in the evening twilight, and also at the evening when that day was finished, announcing to the people the respective hours for ceasing work and for resuming their labors." Excavators at the temple mount recovered a stone from the southwest corner of the parapet, which had fallen to the ground in Titus's siege, with the inscription "for the place of the blowing (of the trumpet)."

13:22 *Remember me.* See note on 1:8.

13:23 Ezra had dealt with the same problem of intermarriage some 25 years before (see note on Ezr 9:1). *Ashdod.* See 4:7; Isa 20:1 and notes. *Ammon and Moab.* See note on Ge 19:36–38.

13:24 The Israelites recognized other people as foreigners by their languages (see Dt 3:9; Jdg 12:6; Ps 114:1; Isa 33:19; Eze 3:5–6).

13:25 *pulled out their hair.* See Ezr 9:3; Isa 50:6 and notes. *You are not to give.* Nehemiah's action was designed to prevent future intermarriages, whereas Ezra dissolved the existing unions.

A C **13:26** *Solomon.* Israel's outstanding king in terms of wealth and political achievements (1Ki 3:13; 2Ch 1:12). Solomon began his reign by humbly asking for wisdom from the Lord (1Ki 3:5–9). *he was led into sin.* In later years his foreign wives led him to worship other gods, so that he built a high place for Chemosh, the god of the Moabites (1Ki 11:7).

13:28 *d* S Ezr 10:24
e S Ne 2:10
13:29 *f* S Ne 1:8
g S Nu 3:12
13:30 *h* S Ne 9:2
13:31 *i* Ne 10:34
j Ne 10:35-36
k S Ge 8:1; S Ne 1:8

²⁸One of the sons of Joiada son of Eliashib *d* the high priest was son-in-law to Sanballat *e* the Horonite. And I drove him away from me.

²⁹Remember *f* them, my God, because they defiled the priestly office and the covenant of the priesthood and of the Levites. *g*

³⁰So I purified the priests and the Levites of everything foreign, *h* and assigned them duties, each to his own task. ³¹I also made provision for contributions of wood *i* at designated times, and for the firstfruits. *j*

Remember *k* me with favor, my God.

13:28 *son-in-law to Sanballat.* According to Lev 21:14 the high priest was not to marry a foreigner. The expulsion of Joiada's son followed either this special ban or the general prohibition against intermarriage. The union described in this verse was especially rankling to Nehemiah in the light of Sanballat's enmity (see 2:10). Josephus (*Antiquities,* 11.7.2) records that an almost identical episode, involving a marriage between the daughter of a Sanballat of Samaria and the brother of the Jewish high priest, took place a little over a century later in the time of Alexander the Great.

13:30 *duties.* Or "divisions," referring to the assignment of particular duties to groups of priests and Levites, possibly on a rotating basis (see note on 12:9).

13:31 *wood.* See 10:34 and note. *Remember me with favor.* The last recorded words of Nehemiah recapitulate a theme running through the final chapter (vv. 14,22; see note on 1:8). His motive throughout his ministry was to please and to serve his divine Sovereign.

ESTHER

AUTHOR AND DATE   INTRODUCTION

Although we do not know who wrote the book of Esther, from internal evidence it is possible to make some inferences about the author and the date of composition. It is clear that the author was a Jew, both from his emphasis on the origin of a Jewish festival and from the Jewish nationalism that permeates the story. The author's knowledge of Persian customs, the setting of the story in the city of Susa and the absence of any reference to conditions or circumstances in the land of Judah suggest that he was a resident of a Persian city. The earliest date for the book would be shortly after the events narrated, i.e., c. 460 B.C. (before Ezra's return to Jerusalem; see note on 8:12). Internal evidence also suggests that the festival of Purim had been observed for some time prior to the actual writing of the book (9:19) and that Xerxes had already died (see 10:2 and note). Several scholars have dated the book later than 330 B.C.; the absence of Greek words and the style of the author's Hebrew dialect, however, suggest that the book must have been written before the Persian empire fell to Greece in 331.

PURPOSE, THEMES AND LITERARY FEATURES

The author's central purpose was to record the institution of the annual festival of Purim and to keep alive for later generations the memory of the great deliverance of the Jewish people during the reign of Xerxes. The book accounts for both the initiation of that observance and the obligation for its perpetual commemoration (see 3:7; 9:26–32; see also chart, pp. 180–181).

Throughout much of the story the author calls to mind the ongoing conflict between Israel and the Amalekites (see notes on 2:5; 3:1–6; 9:5–10), a conflict that began during the exodus (Ex 17:8–16; Dt 25:17–19) and continued through Israel's history (1Sa 15; 1Ch 4:43; and, of course, Esther). As the first to attack Israel after its deliverance from Egypt, the Amalekites were viewed—and the author of Esther views them—as the epitome of all the powers of the world arrayed against God's people (see Nu 24:20; 1Sa 15:2–3; 28:18). Now that Israel has been released from captivity, Haman's edict is the final major effort in the OT period to destroy them.

Closely associated with the conflict with the Amalekites is the rest that is promised to the people of God (see Dt 25:19). With Haman's defeat the Jews enjoy rest from their enemies (9:16,22).

The author also draws upon the remnant motif that recurs throughout the Bible (natural disasters, disease, warfare or other calamities threaten God's people; those who survive constitute a remnant). Events in the Persian city of Susa threatened the continuity of God's purposes in redemptive history. The future existence of God's chosen people, and ultimately the appearance of the Redeemer-Messiah, were jeopardized by Haman's edict to destroy the Jews. The author of Esther patterned much of his material on the events of the Joseph story (see notes on 2:3–4,9,21–23; 3:4; 4:14; 6:1,8,14; 8:6), in which the remnant motif is also central to the narrative (see Ge 45:7 and note).

Feasting is another prominent theme in Esther, as shown in the outline below. Banquets provide the setting for important plot developments. There are ten banquets: (1) 1:3–4, (2) 1:5–8, (3) 1:9, (4) 2:18, (5) 3:15, (6) 5:5–6, (7) 7:1–10, (8) 8:17, (9) 9:17 and (10) 9:18. The three pairs of banquets that mark the beginning, middle

KEY   **A** APPLICATION FOR LIVING   **B** BACKGROUND NOTES   **C** CHARACTER INFORMATION

and end of the story are particularly prominent: the two banquets given by Xerxes, the two prepared by Esther and the double celebration of Purim.

Recording duplications appears to be one of the favorite compositional techniques of the writer. In addition to the three groups of banquets that come in pairs, there are two lists of the king's servants (1:10,14), two reports that Esther concealed her identity (2:10,20), two gatherings of women (2:8,19), two fasts (4:3,16), two consultations of Haman with his wife and friends (5:14; 6:13), two unscheduled appearances of Esther before the king (5:2; 8:3), two investitures for Mordecai (6:10–11; 8:15), two coverings of Haman's face (6:12; 7:8), two royal edicts (3:12–15; 8:1–14), two references to the subsiding of the king's anger (2:1; 7:10), two references to the irrevocability of the Persian laws (1:19; 8:8), two days for the Jews to take vengeance (9:5–12,13–15) and two letters instituting the commemoration of Purim (9:20–28,29–32).

An outstanding feature of this book—one that has given rise to considerable discussion—is the complete absence of any explicit reference to God, worship, prayer or sacrifice. This "secularity" has produced many detractors who have judged the book to be of little religious value. However, it appears that the author has deliberately refrained from mentioning God or any religious activity as a literary device to heighten the fact that it is God who controls and directs all the seemingly insignificant coincidences (see, e.g., note on 6:1) that make up the plot and issue in deliverance for the Jews. God's sovereign rule is assumed at every point (see note on 4:12–16), an assumption made all the more effective by the total absence of reference to him. It becomes clear to the careful reader that Israel's Great King exercises his providential and sovereign control over all the vicissitudes of his beleaguered covenant people.

OUTLINE

1:1 *a* S Ezr 4:6
b Est 9:30; Da 3:2; 6:1
c Est 8:9
1:2 *d* S Ezr 4:9;
S Est 2:8
1:3 *e* S 1Ki 3:15
1:5 *f* Jdg 14:17
g S 2Ki 21:18
1:6 *h* Est 7:8;
Eze 23:41; Am 3:12;
6:4
1:7 *i* Est 2:18; Da 5:2
1:9 *j* S 1Ki 3:15
1:10 *k* S Jdg 16:25;
S Ru 3:7 *l* S Ge 14:18;
Est 3:15; 5:6; 7:2;
Pr 31:4-7; Da 5:1-4
m Est 7:9
1:11 *n* SS 2:4
o Ps 45:11; Eze 16:14
1:12 *p* Ge 39:19;
Est 2:21; 7:7; Pr 19:12
1:13 *q* 1Ch 12:32
1:14 *r* Ezr 7:14
1:18 *s* Pr 19:13;
27:15
1:19 *t* Ecc 8:4
u Est 8:8; Da 6:8,12

QUEEN VASHTI DEPOSED

1 This is what happened during the time of Xerxes,[a] *a* the Xerxes who ruled over 127 provinces[b] stretching from India to Cush[b]: *c* ²At that time King Xerxes reigned from his royal throne in the citadel of Susa, *d* ³and in the third year of his reign he gave a banquet *e* for all his nobles and officials. The military leaders of Persia and Media, the princes, and the nobles of the provinces were present.

⁴For a full 180 days he displayed the vast wealth of his kingdom and the splendor and glory of his majesty. ⁵When these days were over, the king gave a banquet, lasting seven days, *f* in the enclosed garden *g* of the king's palace, for all the people from the least to the greatest who were in the citadel of Susa. ⁶The garden had hangings of white and blue linen, fastened with cords of white linen and purple material to silver rings on marble pillars. There were couches *h* of gold and silver on a mosaic pavement of porphyry, marble, mother-of-pearl and other costly stones. ⁷Wine was served in goblets of gold, each one different from the other, and the royal wine was abundant, in keeping with the king's liberality. *i* ⁸By the king's command each guest was allowed to drink with no restrictions, for the king instructed all the wine stewards to serve each man what he wished.

⁹Queen Vashti also gave a banquet *j* for the women in the royal palace of King Xerxes.

¹⁰On the seventh day, when King Xerxes was in high spirits *k* from wine, *l* he commanded the seven eunuchs who served him—Mehuman, Biztha, Harbona, *m* Bigtha, Abagtha, Zethar and Karkas— ¹¹to bring *n* before him Queen Vashti, wearing her royal crown, in order to display her beauty *o* to the people and nobles, for she was lovely to look at. ¹²But when the attendants delivered the king's command, Queen Vashti refused to come. Then the king became furious and burned with anger. *p*

¹³Since it was customary for the king to consult experts in matters of law and justice, he spoke with the wise men who understood the times *q* ¹⁴and were closest to the king—Karshena, Shethar, Admatha, Tarshish, Meres, Marsena and Memukan, the seven nobles *r* of Persia and Media who had special access to the king and were highest in the kingdom.

¹⁵"According to law, what must be done to Queen Vashti?" he asked. "She has not obeyed the command of King Xerxes that the eunuchs have taken to her."

¹⁶Then Memukan replied in the presence of the king and the nobles, "Queen Vashti has done wrong, not only against the king but also against all the nobles and the peoples of all the provinces of King Xerxes. ¹⁷For the queen's conduct will become known to all the women, and so they will despise their husbands and say, 'King Xerxes commanded Queen Vashti to be brought before him, but she would not come.' ¹⁸This very day the Persian and Median women of the nobility who have heard about the queen's conduct will respond to all the king's nobles in the same way. There will be no end of disrespect and discord. *s*

¹⁹"Therefore, if it pleases the king, *t* let him issue a royal decree and let it be written in the laws of Persia and Media, which cannot be repealed, *u* that Vashti is never again to enter the presence of King Xerxes. Also let the king give her royal position to someone

---

a 1 Hebrew *Ahasuerus*; here and throughout Esther   *b 1* That is, the upper Nile region

---

1:1 *Xerxes.* A transliteration of the Greek form of the Persian name Khshayarshan (see TNIV text note). Xerxes succeeded his father Darius and ruled 486–465 B.C. (see chart, p. 482). *127 provinces.* See 8:9. The Greek historian Herodotus (3.89) records that Xerxes's father Darius had organized the empire into 20 satrapies. (Satraps, the rulers of the satrapies, are mentioned in 3:12; 8:9; 9:3.) The provinces were smaller administrative units.

1:2 *citadel of Susa.* The fortified acropolis and palace complex; it is distinguished from the surrounding city in 3:15; 8:14–15. Several archaeological investigations have been made at the site since the mid–19th century. Xerxes had made extensive renovations in the palace structures. *Susa.* The winter residence of the Persian kings (see note on Ezr 4:9). The three other capitals were Ecbatana (see Ezr 6:2 and note), Babylon and Persepolis. One of Daniel's visions was set in Susa (Da 8:2); Nehemiah also served there (Ne 1:1).

1:3–4 The year (483–482 B.C.), the persons in attendance and the length of the meeting suggest that the purpose of the gathering may have been to plan for the disastrous campaigns of 482–479 against Greece. Herodotus (7.8) possibly describes this assembly.

1:3 *banquet.* Feasting is a prominent theme in Esther (see Introduction: Purpose, Themes and Literary Features).

1:5–6 The excavations at Susa have unearthed a text in which Xerxes's father Darius describes in some detail the building of his palace. Xerxes continued the work his father had begun.

1:9 *Queen Vashti.* Deposed in 484/483 B.C.; Esther became queen in 479/478 (2:16–17). The Greek historians call Xerxes' queen Amestris; they record her influence during the early part of his reign and as queen mother during the following reign of her son Artaxerxes (Ezr 7:1,7,11–12,21; 8:1; Ne 2:1; 5:14; 13:6) until the time of her own death c. 424. Artaxerxes came to the throne when he was 18 years old; therefore he was born c. 484/483, approximately at the time when Vashti was deposed. Since he was the third son of Amestris, the name Amestris cannot be identified with Esther and must be viewed as a Greek version of the name Vashti. Comparatively little is known of the late portions of Xerxes' reign, nor is it possible to determine the subsequent events of the life of Esther. Apparently after Esther's death or her fall from favor, Vashti was able to reassert her power and to exercise a controlling influence over her son.

1:12 *refused to come.* We are not told why.

1:13–14 Ezr 7:14 and the Greek historian Herodotus indicate that seven men functioned as the immediate advisers to the king.

1:19 *cannot be repealed.* The irrevocability of Persian laws is mentioned in 8:8 and Da 6:8,12. *never again to enter.* The punishment corresponds to the crime: Since Vashti refused to appear before the king, it is decreed that she never appear before

1:22 ᵛS Ne 13:24
2:1 ʷEst 7:10
2:5 ˣS 1Sa 9:1
2:6 ʸS 2Ki 24:6,15
ᶻDa 1:1-5; 5:13
2:7 ᵃGe 41:45
ᵇS Ge 39:6
2:8 ᶜNe 1:1; Est 1:2;
Da 8:2
2:9 ᵈS Ge 39:21
ᵉS Ge 37:3; 1Sa 9:22-
24; S 2Ki 25:30;
Est 9:19; Eze 16:9-13;
Da 1:5

else who is better than she. ²⁰Then when the king's edict is proclaimed throughout all his vast realm, all the women will respect their husbands, from the least to the greatest."

²¹The king and his nobles were pleased with this advice, so the king did as Memukan proposed. ²²He sent dispatches to all parts of the kingdom, to each province in its own script and to each people in their own language, ᵛ proclaiming that every man should be ruler over his own household, using his native tongue.

ESTHER MADE QUEEN

2 Later when King Xerxes' fury had subsided, ʷ he remembered Vashti and what she had done and what he had decreed about her. ²Then the king's personal attendants proposed, "Let a search be made for beautiful young virgins for the king. ³Let the king appoint commissioners in every province of his realm to bring all these beautiful young women into the harem at the citadel of Susa. Let them be placed under the care of Hegai, the king's eunuch, who is in charge of the women; and let beauty treatments be given to them. ⁴Then let the young woman who pleases the king be queen instead of Vashti." This advice appealed to the king, and he followed it.

⁵Now there was in the citadel of Susa a Jew of the tribe of Benjamin, named Mordecai son of Jair, the son of Shimei, the son of Kish, ˣ ⁶who had been carried into exile from Jerusalem by Nebuchadnezzar king of Babylon, among those taken captive with Jehoiachinᵃ ʸ king of Judah. ᶻ ⁷Mordecai had a cousin named Hadassah, whom he had brought up because she had neither father nor mother. This young woman, who was also known as Esther, ᵃ had a lovely figure ᵇ and was beautiful. Mordecai had taken her as his own daughter when her father and mother died.

⁸When the king's order and edict had been proclaimed, many young women were brought to the citadel of Susa ᶜ and put under the care of Hegai. Esther also was taken to the king's palace and entrusted to Hegai, who had charge of the harem. ⁹She pleased him and won his favor. ᵈ Immediately he provided her with her beauty treatments and special food. ᵉ He assigned to her seven female attendants selected from the king's palace and moved her and her attendants into the best place in the harem.

ᵃ 6 Hebrew *Jeconiah*, a variant of *Jehoiachin*

---

him again. Furthermore, from this point on she is no longer given the title "Queen" in the book of Esther.

1:22 *proclaiming ... tongue.* Referring to the practice in ethnically mixed marriages of using the husband's native language as a sign of his rule in the home (see Ne 13:23–25).

2:1 *Later.* Esther was taken to Xerxes "in the seventh year of his reign" (v. 16), i.e., in December, 479 B.C., or January, 478. The Greek wars intervened before a new queen was sought (see note on 1:3–4).

2:2 *virgins for the king.* To add to his harem.

2:3–4 The phraseology here is similar to that in Ge 41:34–37. This and numerous other parallels suggest that the author of Esther modeled his work after the Joseph story (see Introduction: Purpose, Themes and Literary Features). Both accounts are set in the courts of foreign monarchs and portray Israelite heroes who rise to prominence and provide the means by which their people are saved (see notes on vv. 9,21–23; 3:4; 4:14; 6:1,8,14; 8:6).

2:5 *in the citadel of Susa a Jew.* As far back as the fall of the northern kingdom in 722–721 B.C. Israelites had been exiled among the cities of the Medes (2Ki 17:6). After the conquest of Babylon by King Cyrus of Persia in 539, some of the Jewish population taken there by the Babylonians (605–586) probably moved eastward into the cities of Medo-Persia. Only 50,000 returned to Israel in the restoration of 538/537 (Ezr 2:64–65). The presence of a large Jewish population in Medo-Persia is confirmed by the discovery of an archive of texts in Nippur (southern Mesopotamia) from the period of Artaxerxes I (465–424) and Darius II (424–405). This archive contains the names of about 100 Jews who lived in that city. Some had attained positions of importance and wealth. Similar Jewish populations are probable in many other Medo-Persian cities. *Mordecai.* The name is derived from that of the Babylonian deity Marduk. There are numerous examples in the Bible of Israelites having double names—a Hebrew name and a "Gentile" name. Mordecai likely had a Hebrew name, as did Esther (v. 7), Daniel and his friends (Da 1:6–7), Joseph (Ge 41:45) and others, but the text does not mention Mordecai's Hebrew name. A cuneiform tablet from Borsippa near Babylon mentions a scribe by the name of Mardukaya; he was an accountant or minister at the court of Susa in the early years of Xerxes. Many interpreters identify him with Mordecai. *son of Jair, the son of Shimei, the son of Kish.* The persons named could be immediate ancestors, in which case Mordecai would be the great-grandson of a Kish who was among the exiles with Jehoiachin in 597 B.C. It is more likely, however, that the names refer to remote ancestors in the tribe of Benjamin (see 2Sa 16:5 for Shimei, 1Sa 9:1 for Kish). This association with the tribe and family of King Saul sets the stage for the ongoing conflict between Israel and the Amalekites (see notes on 3:1–6). If the names are those of remote ancestors, the clause "who had been carried into exile" (v. 6) would not apply to Mordecai, who would have been over 100 years old in that case; rather, it would have to be taken as an elliptical construction in the sense of "whose family had been carried into exile."

2:6 *carried into exile.* In 597 B.C. *Jehoiachin king of Judah.* See 2Ki 24:8–17; 2Ch 36:9–10.

2:7 *Hadassah.* Esther's Hebrew name, meaning "myrtle." The name Esther is likely derived from the Persian word for "star," though some derive it from the name of the Babylonian goddess Ishtar (see note on Jer 7:18).

2:8 *Esther also was taken.* Neither she nor Mordecai would have had any choice in the matter (cf. 2Sa 11:4).

2:9 *special food.* Unlike Daniel and his friends (Da 1:5–10), Esther does not observe the dietary laws, perhaps in part to conceal her Jewish identity (vv. 10,20). Giving such portions is a sign of special favor (1Sa 9:22–24; 2Ki 25:29–30; Da 1:5–10; negatively, Jer 13:25); in the Joseph narrative cf. Ge 43:34 and note. The motif of giving portions appears later as a practice in observing Purim (9:19,22).

2:10 ^fver 20
2:12 ^gPr 27:9;
SS 1:3; Isa 3:24
2:14 ^h1Ki 11:3;
SS 6:8; Da 5:2
ⁱEst 4:11
2:15 ^jEst 9:29
^kPs 45:14 ^lS Ge 18:3;
S 30:27; Est 5:8; 7:3;
8:5
2:17 ^mEze 16:9-13
2:18 ⁿS 1Ki 3:15
^oS Ge 40:20
^pS Est 1:7
2:19 ^qEst 4:2; 5:13
2:20 ^rver 10
2:21 ^sS Ge 40:2
^tS Est 1:12; 3:5; 5:9;
7:7
2:23 ^uS Ge 40:19;
S Dt 21:22-23;
Ps 7:14-16; Pr 26:27;
Ecc 10:8 ^vEst 6:1;
10:2 ^wEst 6:2
3:1 ^xS Ex 17:8-16;
S Nu 24:7; Dt 25:17-
19; 1Sa 14:48

¹⁰Esther had not revealed her nationality and family background, because Mordecai had forbidden her to do so. ^f ¹¹Every day he walked back and forth near the courtyard of the harem to find out how Esther was and what was happening to her.

¹²Before a young woman's turn came to go in to King Xerxes, she had to complete twelve months of beauty treatments prescribed for the women, six months with oil of myrrh and six with perfumes ^g and cosmetics. ¹³And this is how she would go to the king: Anything she wanted was given her to take with her from the harem to the king's palace. ¹⁴In the evening she would go there and in the morning return to another part of the harem to the care of Shaashgaz, the king's eunuch who was in charge of the concubines. ^h She would not return to the king unless he was pleased with her and summoned her by name. ⁱ

¹⁵When the turn came for Esther (the young woman Mordecai had adopted, the daughter of his uncle Abihail^j) to go to the king, ^k she asked for nothing other than what Hegai, the king's eunuch who was in charge of the harem, suggested. And Esther won the favor^l of everyone who saw her. ¹⁶She was taken to King Xerxes in the royal residence in the tenth month, the month of Tebeth, in the seventh year of his reign.

¹⁷Now the king was attracted to Esther more than to any of the other women, and she won his favor and approval more than any of the other virgins. So he set a royal crown on her head and made her queen ^m instead of Vashti. ¹⁸And the king gave a great banquet, ⁿ Esther's banquet, for all his nobles and officials. ^o He proclaimed a holiday throughout the provinces and distributed gifts with royal liberality. ^p

MORDECAI UNCOVERS A CONSPIRACY

¹⁹When the virgins were assembled a second time, Mordecai was sitting at the king's gate. ^q ²⁰But Esther had kept secret her family background and nationality just as Mordecai had told her to do, for she continued to follow Mordecai's instructions as she had done when he was bringing her up. ^r

²¹During the time Mordecai was sitting at the king's gate, Bigthana^a and Teresh, two of the king's officers ^s who guarded the doorway, became angry ^t and conspired to assassinate King Xerxes. ²²But Mordecai found out about the plot and told Queen Esther, who in turn reported it to the king, giving credit to Mordecai. ²³And when the report was investigated and found to be true, the two officials were impaled ^u on poles. All this was recorded in the book of the annals ^v in the presence of the king. ^w

HAMAN'S PLOT TO DESTROY THE JEWS

3 After these events, King Xerxes honored Haman son of Hammedatha, the Agagite, ^x elevating him and giving him a seat of honor higher than that of all the other nobles. ²All the royal officials at the king's gate knelt down and paid honor to

---

^a 21 Hebrew *Bigthan,* a variant of *Bigthana*

2:10 The fact that Esther concealed her identity is reported twice—here and in v. 20 (for the author's use of duplications, see Introduction: Purpose, Themes and Literary Features).
2:14 *to another part of the harem.* To the chambers of the concubines.

2:16 *tenth month … seventh year.* December, 479 B.C., or January, 478 (see notes on 1:3–4; 2:1). Esther's tenure as queen continued through the events of the book, i.e., through 473 (see 3:7 and note; see also 8:9–13; 9:1). She may have died or fallen from favor shortly thereafter (see note on 1:9).
2:18 *holiday.* The Hebrew for this word, unique to this verse, may imply a remission of taxes, an emancipation of slaves, a cancellation of debts or a remission of obligatory military service.

2:19 See Introduction: Purpose, Themes and Literary Features. The enlargement of the harem apparently continued unabated. Perhaps there is a causal connection between the second gathering of women and the assassination plot (vv. 21–23); some have suggested that it reflects palace intrigue in support of the deposed Vashti. *king's gate.* The gateway of an ancient city was its major commercial and legal center. Markets were held in the gateway; the court sat there to transact its business (see Dt 21:18–20; Jos 20:4; Ru 4:1–11; Ps 69:12). A king might hold an audience at the gate (see 2Sa 19:8; 1Ki 22:10). Daniel was at the king's gate (TNIV "royal court") as ruler over all Babylon (Da 2:48–49). Mordecai's sitting at the king's gate confirms his holding a high po-

sition in the civil service of the empire (see note on v. 5). From this vantage point he might overhear plans for the murder of the king.
2:21–23 Another point of comparison with the Joseph narrative is the involvement of two chamberlains (Ge 40:1–3; see note on vv. 3–4).

2:23 *impaled on poles.* The Persian form of execution, as is confirmed in pictures and statues from the ancient Near East and in the comments of the Greek historian Herodotus (3.125,129; 4.43). According to Herodotus (3.159) Darius I impaled 3,000 Babylonians when he took Babylon, an act that Darius himself recorded in his Behistun (Bisitun) inscription. In Israelite and Canaanite practice, hanging was an exhibition of the corpse and not the means of execution itself (Dt 21:22–23; Jos 8:29; 10:26; 1Sa 31:8–10; 2Sa 4:12). The sons of Haman were killed by the sword, and then their corpses were displayed on poles (9:5–14). The execution of the pharaoh's chief baker in the Joseph narrative was similar (Ge 40:19). *annals.* The concern of the author of Esther with rhetorical symmetry is seen in the fact that the annals are mentioned in the beginning (here), middle (6:1) and end (10:2) of the narrative. The episode dealing with the plot of Bigthana and Teresh is a good example of the many "coincidences" in the book that later take on crucial significance for the story, showing God's providence at work.

3:1 *After these events.* Four years have elapsed since Esther's selection as queen (v. 7; 2:16–17). *son of Hamme-*

Haman, for the king had commanded this concerning him. But Mordecai would not kneel down or pay him honor.

³Then the royal officials at the king's gate asked Mordecai, "Why do you disobey the king's command?" ʸ ⁴Day after day they spoke to him but he refused to comply. ᶻ Therefore they told Haman about it to see whether Mordecai's behavior would be tolerated, for he had told them he was a Jew.

⁵When Haman saw that Mordecai would not kneel down or pay him honor, he was enraged. ᵃ ⁶Yet having learned who Mordecai's people were, he scorned the idea of killing only Mordecai. Instead Haman looked for a way ᵇ to destroy ᶜ all Mordecai's people, the Jews, ᵈ throughout the whole kingdom of Xerxes.

⁷In the twelfth year of King Xerxes, in the first month, the month of Nisan, the *pur* ᵉ (that is, the lot ᶠ) was cast in the presence of Haman to select a day and month. And the lot fell on ᵃ the twelfth month, the month of Adar. ᵍ

⁸Then Haman said to King Xerxes, "There is a certain people dispersed among the peoples in all the provinces of your kingdom who keep themselves separate. Their customs ʰ are different from those of all other people, and they do not obey ᶦ the king's laws; it is not in the king's best interest to tolerate them. ʲ ⁹If it pleases the king, let a decree be issued to destroy them, and I will give ten thousand talents ᵇ of silver to the king's administrators for the royal treasury." ᵏ

¹⁰So the king took his signet ring ᶦ from his finger and gave it to Haman son of Hammedatha, the Agagite, the enemy of the Jews. ¹¹"Keep the money," the king said to Haman, "and do with the people as you please."

¹²Then on the thirteenth day of the first month the royal secretaries were summoned. They wrote out in the script of each province and in the language ᵐ of each people all Haman's orders to the king's satraps, the governors of the various provinces and the nobles of the various peoples. These were written in the name of King Xerxes himself and sealed ⁿ with his own ring. ¹³Dispatches were sent by couriers to all the king's provinces with the order to destroy, kill and annihilate all the Jews ᵒ—young and old, women and children—

ᵃ 7 Septuagint; Hebrew does not have *And the lot fell on.*   ᵇ 9 That is, about 375 tons or about 335 metric tons

3:3 ʸ Est 5:9;
Da 3:12
3:4 ᶻ Ge 39:10
3:5 ᵃ S Est 2:21
3:6 ᵇ Pr 16:25
ᶜ Ps 74:8; 83:4
ᵈ Est 9:24
3:7 ᵉ Est 9:24,26
ᶠ S Lev 16:8;
S 1Sa 10:21 ᵍ ver 13;
Est 9:19
3:8 ʰ Ac 16:20-21
ᶦ Jer 29:7; Da 6:13
ʲ Ezr 4:15
3:9 ᵏ Est 7:4
3:10 ᶦ S Ge 41:42
3:12 ᵐ S Ne 13:24
ⁿ S Ge 38:18
3:13 ᵒ S 1Sa 15:3;
S Ezr 4:6

---

datha, the Agagite. There is some debate about the ancestry of Haman. The name Hammedatha appears to be Persian and probably refers to an immediate ancestor. The title "Agagite" could refer to some other immediate ancestor or to an unknown place; however, it is far more likely that it refers to Agag, king of Amalek (1Sa 15:20). The Amalekites had attacked Israel after she fled from Egypt (Ex 17:8–16; 1Sa 15:2); for this reason the Lord would "be at war against the Amalekites from generation to generation" (Ex 17:16). Israel was not to forget but must "blot out the name of Amalek from under heaven" (Dt 25:19). Saul's attack on Amalek (1Sa 15) resulted in the death of most, though not all (1Ch 4:42–43), of King Agag's people and later in the death of the king himself. Centuries after the battle led by the Benjamite Saul, the Benjamite Mordecai (see note on 2:5) continues the war with the Amalekites. *elevating him.* The fact that no reason is given for the promotion of Haman provides an ironic contrast between the unrewarded merit of Mordecai (2:21–23; see 6:3) and the unmerited reward of Haman.

3:2–6 Obedience to the second commandment (Ex 20:4–5) is not the issue in Mordecai's refusal to bow down to Haman, for Israelites were willing to bow down to kings (see 1Sa 24:8; 2Sa 14:4; 1Ki 1:16) and to other persons (see Ge 23:7; 33:3; 44:14). Only the long-standing enmity between Israel and Amalek accounts both for Mordecai's refusal and for Haman's intent to destroy all the Jews (vv. 5–6). The threat against the Jews "throughout the whole kingdom" (v. 6) is a threat against the ultimate issue of redemptive history (see Introduction: Purpose, Themes and Literary Features).

3:4 Compare the phraseology with that in the Joseph story (Ge 39:10).

B **3:7** *twelfth year … first month.* April or May, 474 B.C., the fifth year of Esther's reign. *pur.* See 9:24,26. This word is found in Akkadian texts with the meaning "lot" (as here). The

celebration known as Purim takes its name from the plural of this noun (see 9:26). There is irony in the fact that the month of the Jews' celebration of the Passover deliverance from Egypt is also the month that Haman begins plotting their destruction (Ex 12:2–11). *twelfth month.* An 11-month delay is contemplated between the securing of the decree and the execution of it in the month Adar (February-March).

3:8 *a certain people.* The name of the people Haman wishes to destroy is slyly omitted in this blend of the true and the false: The Jews did have their own customs and laws, but they were not disobedient to the king (Jer 29:7). *dispersed.* See 8:11,17; 9:2,12,16,19–20,28.

3:9 *ten thousand talents.* Herodotus (3.95) records that the annual income of the Persian empire was 15,000 talents. If this figure is correct, Haman offers two-thirds of that amount—a huge sum. Presumably the money would have come from the plundered wealth of the victims of the decree. Verse 13 implies that those who would take part in the massacre were to be allowed to keep the plunder, perhaps adding financial incentive to the execution of the decree since Xerxes disavows taking the money (v. 11). On the other hand, 4:7 may imply that the king had planned on collecting some of the money (see also 7:4 and note). *king's administrators.* This phrase may represent the title of revenue officers who would bring the money to the treasury, or it could refer to those who carry out the decree. The Amalekites had once before plundered Israel (1Sa 14:48); Haman plans a recurrence.

3:10 *took his signet ring … and gave it to Haman.* Authorizing Haman to put the king's seal on the royal decree (v. 12). *enemy of the Jews.* An epithet also applied to Haman later in the book (8:1; 9:10; cf. also 7:6; 9:24).

3:12 *thirteenth day … first month.* In the 12th year of Xerxes' reign (v. 7), i.e., Apr. 17, 474 B.C.

3:13 Haman's decree against Israel mandates virtually the same

3:13 ᵖS ver 7
�q Est 8:11; 9:10
3:14 ʳEst 8:8; 9:1
3:15 ˢEst 8:14
ʳS Est 1:10 ᵘEst 8:15
4:1 ᵛS Nu 14:6
ʷS 2Sa 13:19;
Eze 27:30-31
ˣS Ex 11:6; Ps 30:11
4:2 ʸS Est 2:19
4:7 ᶻEst 7:4
4:11 ᵃEst 2:14
ᵇDa 2:9 ᶜEst 5:1,2;
8:4; Ps 125:3
4:14 ᵈJob 34:29;
Ps 28:1; 35:22;
Ecc 3:7; Isa 42:14;
57:11; 62:1; 64:12;
Am 5:13 ᵉEst 9:16,22
ᶠS Ge 45:7;
S Dt 28:29
ᵍS Ge 50:20
4:16 ʰS 2Ch 20:3;
Est 9:31 ⁱS Ge 43:14

on a single day, the thirteenth day of the twelfth month, the month of Adar, ᵖ and to plunder �q their goods. ¹⁴A copy of the text of the edict was to be issued as law in every province and made known to the people of every nationality so they would be ready for that day. ʳ

¹⁵The couriers went out, spurred on by the king's command, and the edict was issued in the citadel of Susa. ˢ The king and Haman sat down to drink, ᵗ but the city of Susa was bewildered. ᵘ

MORDECAI PERSUADES ESTHER TO HELP

4 When Mordecai learned of all that had been done, he tore his clothes, ᵛ put on sackcloth and ashes, ʷ and went out into the city, wailing ˣ loudly and bitterly. ²But he went only as far as the king's gate, ʸ because no one clothed in sackcloth was allowed to enter it. ³In every province to which the edict and order of the king came, there was great mourning among the Jews, with fasting, weeping and wailing. Many lay in sackcloth and ashes.

⁴When Esther's eunuchs and female attendants came and told her about Mordecai, she was in great distress. She sent clothes for him to put on instead of his sackcloth, but he would not accept them. ⁵Then Esther summoned Hathak, one of the king's eunuchs assigned to attend her, and ordered him to find out what was troubling Mordecai and why.

⁶So Hathak went out to Mordecai in the open square of the city in front of the king's gate. ⁷Mordecai told him everything that had happened to him, including the exact amount of money Haman had promised to pay into the royal treasury for the destruction of the Jews. ᶻ ⁸He also gave him a copy of the text of the edict for their annihilation, which had been published in Susa, to show to Esther and explain it to her, and he told him to instruct her to go into the king's presence to beg for mercy and plead with him for her people.

⁹Hathak went back and reported to Esther what Mordecai had said. ¹⁰Then she instructed him to say to Mordecai, ¹¹"All the king's officials and the people of the royal provinces know that for any man or woman who approaches the king in the inner court without being summoned ᵃ the king has but one law: ᵇ that they be put to death unless the king extends the gold scepter ᶜ to them and spares their lives. But thirty days have passed since I was called to go to the king."

¹²When Esther's words were reported to Mordecai, ¹³he sent back this answer: "Do not think that because you are in the king's house you alone of all the Jews will escape. ¹⁴For if you remain silent ᵈ at this time, relief ᵉ and deliverance ᶠ for the Jews will arise from another place, but you and your father's family will perish. And who knows but that you have come to royal position for such a time as this?" ᵍ

¹⁵Then Esther sent this reply to Mordecai: ¹⁶"Go, gather together all the Jews who are in Susa, and fast ʰ for me. Do not eat or drink for three days, night or day. I and my attendants will fast as you do. When this is done, I will go to the king, even though it is against the law. And if I perish, I perish." ⁱ

¹⁷So Mordecai went away and carried out all of Esther's instructions.

---

destruction that had earlier been decreed against Amalek (1Sa 15:3). *thirteenth day...twelfth month.* Mar. 7, 473 B.C. (see 8:12).

3:15 Haman and the king will drink together again in the story when the fate of the Jews is once again being decided (7:1–2), but then it will be at the dissolution of their relationship and the reversal of the decree here celebrated. The celebration here is in sharp contrast to the fasting and mourning of the Jews (4:1–3,16).

4:2 *king's gate.* See note on 2:19.

4:3 See note on 3:15. The prominence of feasting throughout the book of Esther sets the fasts of vv. 3,16 in sharp relief; a pair of fasts matches the prominent pairs of banquets (see Introduction: Purpose, Themes and Literary Features; see also note on 9:31).

4:5–15 The fact that the dialogue of Esther and Mordecai is mediated by Hathach reflects the prohibition against Mordecai's entering the royal citadel dressed in mourning (v. 2).

4:7 See note on 3:9. That Mordecai is aware of the amount Haman promised to the king is a reminder of his high position in the bureaucracy at Susa (2:21–23; see also note on 2:5).

4:11 Herodotus (3.118,140) also notes that anyone approaching the Persian king unsummoned would be killed unless the king gave immediate pardon.

4:12–16 The themes of the book of Esther are most clearly expressed in this passage. Mordecai's confidence

that the Jews would be delivered is based on God's sovereignty in working out his purposes and fulfilling his promises. Their deliverance will come, even if through some means other than Esther. Yet that sovereignty is not fatalistic: Unless Esther exercises her individual responsibility, she and her family will perish. Cf. Mt 26:24; Ac 2:23 for similar treatments of the relationship between divine sovereignty and human responsibility.

4:14 *from another place.* As close as the book comes to an explicit reference to God (see Introduction: Purpose, Themes and Literary Features). In Jewish tradition, "the Place" is one of the surrogates used for God's name. *such a time as this.* Cf. Ge 45:5–7 in the Joseph narrative.

4:16 *fast.* See note on v. 3. Prayer, which usually accompanied such fasting, was presumably a part of this fast as well (see Jdg 20:26–27; 1Sa 7:6; 2Sa 12:16; Ezr 8:21–23; Ne 9:1–3; Isa 58:3–4; Jer 14:12; Joel 1:14; 2:12–17; Jnh 3:7–8). The omission of any reference to prayer or to God is consistent with the author's intention; absence of any distinctively religious concepts or vocabulary is a rhetorical device used to heighten the fact that it is indeed God who has been active in the whole narrative (see Introduction: Purpose, Themes and Literary Features). *if I perish.* Cf. the similar formulation in the Joseph narrative (Ge 43:14).

ESTHER'S REQUEST TO THE KING

5 On the third day Esther put on her royal robes[j] and stood in the inner court of the palace, in front of the king's[k] hall. The king was sitting on his royal throne in the hall, facing the entrance. ²When he saw Queen Esther standing in the court, he was pleased with her and held out to her the gold scepter that was in his hand. So Esther approached and touched the tip of the scepter.[l]

³Then the king asked, "What is it, Queen Esther? What is your request? Even up to half the kingdom,[m] it will be given you."

⁴"If it pleases the king," replied Esther, "let the king, together with Haman, come today to a banquet I have prepared for him."

⁵"Bring Haman at once," the king said, "so that we may do what Esther asks."

So the king and Haman went to the banquet Esther had prepared. ⁶As they were drinking wine,[n] the king again asked Esther, "Now what is your petition? It will be given you. And what is your request? Even up to half the kingdom,[o] it will be granted."[p]

⁷Esther replied, "My petition and my request is this: ⁸If the king regards me with favor[q] and if it pleases the king to grant my petition and fulfill my request, let the king and Haman come tomorrow to the banquet[r] I will prepare for them. Then I will answer the king's question."

HAMAN'S RAGE AGAINST MORDECAI

⁹Haman went out that day happy and in high spirits. But when he saw Mordecai at the king's gate and observed that he neither rose nor showed fear in his presence, he was filled with rage[s] against Mordecai.[t] ¹⁰Nevertheless, Haman restrained himself and went home. Calling together his friends and Zeresh,[u] his wife, ¹¹Haman boasted[v] to them about his vast wealth, his many sons,[w] and all the ways the king had honored him and how he had elevated him above the other nobles and officials. ¹²"And that's not all," Haman added. "I'm the only person[x] Queen Esther invited to accompany the king to the banquet she gave. And she has invited me along with the king tomorrow. ¹³But all this gives me no satisfaction as long as I see that Jew Mordecai sitting at the king's gate.[y]"

¹⁴His wife Zeresh and all his friends said to him, "Have a pole set up, reaching to a height of fifty cubits,[a][z] and ask the king in the morning to have Mordecai impaled[a] on it. Then go with the king to the banquet and enjoy yourself." This suggestion delighted Haman, and he had the pole set up.

MORDECAI HONORED

6 That night the king could not sleep;[b] so he ordered the book of the chronicles,[c] the record of his reign, to be brought in and read to him. ²It was found recorded there that Mordecai had exposed Bigthana and Teresh, two of the king's officers who guarded the doorway, who had conspired to assassinate King Xerxes.[d]

³"What honor and recognition has Mordecai received for this?" the king asked.

"Nothing has been done for him," [e] his attendants answered.

⁴The king said, "Who is in the court?" Now Haman had just entered the outer court of the palace to speak to the king about impaling Mordecai on the pole he had set up for him.

---

a 14 That is, about 75 feet or about 22.5 meters

**Cross references (right margin):**

5:1 *j* Eze 16:13
k Pr 21:1
5:2 *l* S Est 4:11
5:3 *m* Est 7:2; Da 5:16; Mk 6:23
5:6 *n* S Est 1:10
o Da 5:16; Mk 6:23
p Est 9:12
5:8 *q* S Est 2:15
r S 1Ki 3:15
5:9 *s* S Est 2:21; Pr 14:17 *t* S Est 3:3,5
5:10 *u* Est 6:13
5:11 *v* Pr 13:16
w Est 9:7-10,13
5:12 *x* Job 22:29; Pr 16:18; 29:23
5:13 *y* S Est 2:19
5:14 *z* Est 7:9
a S Ezr 6:11
6:1 *b* Da 2:1; 6:18
c S Est 2:23
6:2 *d* Est 2:21-23
6:3 *e* Ecc 9:13-16

5:2 An example of divine providence influencing a king, as in Pr 21:1.

5:6–7 One can only speculate regarding Esther's reasons for delaying her answer to the king's question until he had asked it a third time (vv. 3,6; 7:2). The author uses these delays as plot retardation devices that sustain the tension and permit the introduction of new material on Haman's self-aggrandizement (vv. 11–12) and Mordecai's reward (6:6–11).

5:9 Haman's rage is kindled when Mordecai does not rise in his presence—an ironic contrast to his earlier refusal to bow (3:2–5).

5:11 *many sons.* Haman had ten sons (9:7–10). Herodotus (1.136) reports that the Persians prized a large number of sons second only to valor in battle; the Persian king sent gifts to the subject with the most sons (cf. Ps 127:3–5).

5:12–13 See Pr 16:18; 29:23.

5:13 *that Jew Mordecai.* See notes on 6:10; 7:6.

5:14 *height of fifty cubits.* Perhaps hyperbolic (see TNIV text note). Some, however, suggest that the pole (see 2:23 and note) was set up atop another structure to achieve this height, e.g.,

the city wall (see 1Sa 31:10). *impaled.* See note on 2:23.

6:1 This verse marks the literary center of the narrative. When things could not look worse, a series of seemingly trivial coincidences marks a critical turn that brings resolution to the story. The king's inability to sleep, his requesting the reading of the annals, the reading of the passage reporting Mordecai's past kindness (v. 2), Haman's preparations in the early hours of the morning (5:14), his sudden entry into the outer court (6:5) and his assumption that he was the man the king wished to honor (v. 6)—all are events testifying to the sovereignty of God over the events of the narrative. Circumstances that seemed incidental earlier in the narrative take on crucial significance later. Just as in the Joseph story (Ge 41:1–45), the hero's personal fortunes are reversed because of the monarch's disturbed sleep (cf. Da 2:1; 6:18).

6:2 The scribe was reading from the annals that recorded events five years earlier (compare 3:7 with 2:16).

6:4–6 Again, the irony is evident: Just as Haman had withheld from the king the identity of the "certain people" (see 3:8 and

6:8 ^{f} S Ge 41:42;
S Isa 52:1 ^{g} 1Ki 1:33
6:9 ^{h} Ge 41:43
6:11 ^{i} S Ge 41:42
6:12 ^{j} 2Sa 15:30;
Est 7:8; Jer 14:3,4;
Mic 3:7
6:13 ^{k} Est 5:10
^{l} Ps 57:6; Pr 26:27;
28:18 ^{m} Est 7:7
6:14 ^{n} S 1Ki 3:15
7:1 ^{o} Ge 40:20-22;
Mt 22:1-14
7:2 ^{p} S Est 1:10
^{q} S Est 5:3 ^{r} Est 9:12
7:3 ^{s} S Est 2:15
7:4 ^{t} Est 3:9; S 4:7
7:7 ^{u} S Ge 34:7;
S Est 1:12; Pr 19:12;
20:1-2 ^{v} S 2Ki 21:18
^{w} Est 6:13
7:8 ^{x} S Est 1:6
^{y} Ge 39:14; Jn 13:23

^{5}His attendants answered, "Haman is standing in the court."

"Bring him in," the king ordered.

^{6}When Haman entered, the king asked him, "What should be done for the man the king delights to honor?"

Now Haman thought to himself, "Who is there that the king would rather honor than me?" ^{7}So he answered the king, "For the man the king delights to honor, ^{8}have them bring a royal robe ^{f} the king has worn and a horse ^{g} the king has ridden, one with a royal crest placed on its head. ^{9}Then let the robe and horse be entrusted to one of the king's most noble princes. Let them robe the man the king delights to honor, and lead him on the horse through the city streets, proclaiming before him, 'This is what is done for the man the king delights to honor!^{h}'"

^{10}"Go at once," the king commanded Haman. "Get the robe and the horse and do just as you have suggested for Mordecai the Jew, who sits at the king's gate. Do not neglect anything you have recommended."

^{11}So Haman got ^{i} the robe and the horse. He robed Mordecai, and led him on horseback through the city streets, proclaiming before him, "This is what is done for the man the king delights to honor!"

^{12}Afterward Mordecai returned to the king's gate. But Haman rushed home, with his head covered ^{j} in grief, ^{13}and told Zeresh ^{k} his wife and all his friends everything that had happened to him.

His advisers and his wife Zeresh said to him, "Since Mordecai, before whom your downfall ^{l} has started, is of Jewish origin, you cannot stand against him—you will surely come to ruin!" ^{m} ^{14}While they were still talking with him, the king's eunuchs arrived and hurried Haman away to the banquet ^{n} Esther had prepared.

HAMAN IMPALED

7 So the king and Haman went to Queen Esther's banquet, ^{o} ^{2}and as they were drinking wine ^{p} on the second day, the king again asked, "Queen Esther, what is your petition? It will be given you. What is your request? Even up to half the kingdom, ^{q} it will be granted.^{r}"

^{3}Then Queen Esther answered, "If I have found favor ^{s} with you, Your Majesty, and if it pleases you, grant me my life—this is my petition. And spare my people—this is my request. ^{4}For I and my people have been sold to be destroyed, killed and annihilated. ^{t} If we had merely been sold as male and female slaves, I would have kept quiet, because no such distress would justify disturbing the king.^{a}"

^{5}King Xerxes asked Queen Esther, "Who is he? Where is he—the man who has dared to do such a thing?"

^{6}Esther said, "An adversary and enemy! This vile Haman!"

Then Haman was terrified before the king and queen. ^{7}The king got up in a rage, ^{u} left his wine and went out into the palace garden. ^{v} But Haman, realizing that the king had already decided his fate, ^{w} stayed behind to beg Queen Esther for his life.

^{8}Just as the king returned from the palace garden to the banquet hall, Haman was falling on the couch ^{x} where Esther was reclining. ^{y}

---

^{a} 4 Or *quiet, but the compensation our adversary offers cannot be compared with the loss the king would suffer*

---

note), so now the king unintentionally keeps from Haman the identity of the "man the king delights to honor" (v. 6).
6:8 *royal robe the king has worn.* See 8:15; see also Introduction: Purpose, Themes and Literary Features. Cf. in the Joseph story Ge 41:41–43. Great significance was attached to the king's garment in ancient times; wearing his garments was a sign of unique favor (1Sa 18:4). To wear another's garments was to partake of his power, stature, honor or sanctity (2Ki 2:13–14; Isa 61:3,10; Zec 3:3–7; cf. Mk 5:27–28). Haman's suggestion is not only a great honor to the recipient but is also considerably flattering to the king: Wearing his garment was chosen instead of wealth.
6:10 *Mordecai the Jew.* An ironic echo of Haman's sarcastic epithet "that Jew Mordecai" (5:13; see also note on 7:6).
6:13 *his wife and all his friends.* See 5:14; see also Introduction: Purpose, Themes and Literary Features.
6:14 Guests were usually escorted to feasts (see in the Joseph narrative Ge 43:15–26; cf. Mt 22:1–14).
7:2 See 5:3,6; see also note on 5:6–7.

7:3 *found favor with you.* See 2:15,17.
7:4 *sold.* Esther refers to the bribe Haman offered to the king (3:9; 4:7); she also paraphrases Haman's edict (3:13). *because no such distress ... king.* See TNIV text note. The statement probably means either (1) that the affliction of the Jews would be less injurious to the king if slavery was all that was involved, or (2) that Esther would not trouble the king if slavery was the only issue.
7:6 *This vile Haman!* Esther's biting words are a rhetorical counterpoint to Haman's sneering characterization of Mordecai as "that Jew Mordecai" (5:13; see also note on 6:10).
7:7 *went out.* The king's leaving the room sets the stage for the final twist that would seal Haman's fate.
7:8 *falling on the couch where Esther was reclining.* Meals were customarily taken reclining on a couch (see Am 6:4,7; Jn 13:23 and note). It is ironic that Haman, who became angry when the Jew Mordecai would not bow down (which set the whole story in motion), now falls before the Jewess Esther (see 6:10). *covered Haman's face.* See 6:12; see also Introduction: Purpose, Themes and Literary Features.

The king exclaimed, "Will he even molest the queen while she is with me in the house?"[z]

As soon as the word left the king's mouth, they covered Haman's face. [a] [9]Then Harbona, [b] one of the eunuchs attending the king, said, "A pole reaching to a height of fifty cubits[a][c] stands by Haman's house. He had it set up for Mordecai, who spoke up to help the king."

The king said, "Impale him on it!"[d] [10]So they impaled[e] Haman[f] on the pole[g] he had set up for Mordecai.[h] Then the king's fury subsided.[i]

THE KING'S EDICT IN BEHALF OF THE JEWS

8 That same day King Xerxes gave Queen Esther the estate of Haman,[j] the enemy of the Jews. And Mordecai came into the presence of the king, for Esther had told how he was related to her. [2]The king took off his signet ring,[k] which he had reclaimed from Haman, and presented it to Mordecai. And Esther appointed him over Haman's estate.[l]

[3]Esther again pleaded with the king, falling at his feet and weeping. She begged him to put an end to the evil plan of Haman the Agagite,[m] which he had devised against the Jews. [4]Then the king extended the gold scepter[n] to Esther and she arose and stood before him.

[5]"If it pleases the king," she said, "and if he regards me with favor[o] and thinks it the right thing to do, and if he is pleased with me, let an order be written overruling the dispatches that Haman son of Hammedatha, the Agagite, devised and wrote to destroy the Jews in all the king's provinces. [6]For how can I bear to see disaster fall on my people? How can I bear to see the destruction of my family?"[p]

[7]King Xerxes replied to Queen Esther and to Mordecai the Jew, "Because Haman attacked the Jews, I have given his estate to Esther, and they have impaled[q] him on the pole he set up. [8]Now write another decree[r] in the king's name in behalf of the Jews as seems best to you, and seal[s] it with the king's signet ring[t]—for no document written in the king's name and sealed with his ring can be revoked."[u]

[9]At once the royal secretaries were summoned—on the twenty-third day of the third month, the month of Sivan. They wrote out all Mordecai's orders to the Jews, and to the satraps, governors and nobles of the 127 provinces stretching from India to Cush.[b][v] These orders were written in the script of each province and the language of each people and also to the Jews in their own script and language.[w] [10]Mordecai wrote in the name of King Xerxes, sealed the dispatches with the king's signet ring, and sent them by mounted couriers, who rode fast horses especially bred for the king.

[11]The king's edict granted the Jews in every city the right to assemble and protect themselves; to destroy, kill and annihilate the armed men of any nationality or province who might attack them and their women and children,[c] and to plunder[x] the property of their enemies. [12]The day appointed for the Jews to do this in all the provinces of King Xerxes was the thirteenth day of the twelfth month, the month of Adar.[y] [13]A copy of the text of the edict was to be issued as law in every province and made known to the people of ev-

---

[a] 9 That is, about 75 feet or about 22.5 meters   [b] 9 That is, the upper Nile region   [c] 11 Or *province, together with their women and children, who might attack them;*

7:8 [z] S Ge 34:7
[a] S Est 6:12
7:9 [b] Est 1:10
[c] Est 5:14
[d] S Dt 21:22-23;
Ps 7:14-16; 9:16;
Pr 11:5-6; S 26:27;
S Mt 7:2
7:10 [e] Ge 40:22
[f] Pr 10:28 [g] Est 9:25
[h] Da 6:24 [i] Est 2:1
8:1 [j] Pr 22:22-23
8:2 [k] S Ge 24:22;
S 41:42 [l] S Ge 41:41;
Pr 13:22; 14:35;
Da 2:48
8:3 [m] S Ex 17:8-16
8:4 [n] S Est 4:11
8:5 [o] S Est 2:15
8:6 [p] Ge 44:34
8:7 [q] S Dt 21:22-23
8:8 [r] S Est 3:12-14
[s] S Ge 38:18
[t] S Ge 41:42
[u] S Est 1:19; Da 6:15
8:9 [v] Est 1:1
[w] S Ne 13:24
8:11 [x] S Ge 14:23;
S Est 3:13; 9:10,15,16
8:12 [y] Est 3:13; 9:1

7:9 Before this moment there is no evidence that Esther had known of Mordecai's triumph earlier in the day (6:1–11); she has pleaded for the life of her people. Harbona's reference to the pole (see 2:23 and note) in effect introduces a second charge against Haman—his attempt to kill the king's benefactor.
7:10 *subsided.* See 2:1; see also Introduction: Purpose, Themes and Literary Features.
8:1–17 By echoing much of the phraseology of 3:1—4:3, the author emphasizes how the tables were turned.
8:1 *gave Queen Esther the estate of Haman.* Herodotus (3.128–129) and Josephus (*Antiquities,* 11.17) confirm that the property of a traitor reverted to the crown; Xerxes presents Haman's wealth (5:11) to Esther.
8:2 Cf. 3:10–11, where the king's offer of his ring includes Haman's keeping the money; here Mordecai receives the office and the estate of Haman.
8:3–6 Esther and Mordecai are secure (7:4—8:2), but the irrevocable decree is still a threat to the rest of the Jews.

8:3 *Agagite.* See note on 3:1.
8:5 *favor.* See 4:11; 5:2.
8:6 Cf. the Joseph story (Ge 44:34).
8:8 *write another decree.* See 1:19 and note; see also Introduction: Purpose, Themes and Literary Features. The dilemma is the same as the one that confronted Darius the Mede in Daniel (Da 6:8,12,15). The solution is to issue another decree (cf. Da 6:25–27) that in effect counters the original decree of Haman (3:12; cf. Da 6:7–9) without formally revoking it (see note on 9:2–3).
8:9–13 The phraseology is taken from the parallel in 3:12–14. The extent of the destruction mandated is virtually the same as that earlier decreed against Amalek (see note on 3:13).
8:9 *twenty-third day…third month.* In Xerxes' 12th year, i.e., June 25, 474 B.C., two months and ten days after the proclamation of Haman's edict (see note on 3:12).
8:12 *thirteenth day…twelfth month.* Mar. 7, 473 B.C. (see 3:13 and note). Some 15 years after this first Purim, Ezra would lead his expedition to Jerusalem in 458 B.C. (Ezr 7:9).

8:13 *z* Est 3:14
8:14 *a* Est 3:15
8:15 *b* Est 9:4; 10:2
c 2Sa 12:30
d S Ge 41:42
e Est 3:15
8:16 *f* Ps 97:10-12
g Est 4:1-3; Ps 112:4;
Jer 29:4-7
8:17 *h* Ps 35:27;
45:15; 51:8; Pr 11:10
i S Ex 15:14,16;
Dt 11:25; Da 6:26
j Est 9:3
9:1 *k* S Est 8:12
l Jer 29:4-7
m S Est 3:12-14;
Pr 22:22-23
9:2 *n* S Ge 22:17
o Ps 35:26; 40:14;
70:2; 71:13,24
9:3 *p* S Ezr 8:36
q Est 8:17
9:4 *r* S Est 8:15
s S Ex 11:3 *t* S 2Sa 3:1;
1Ch 11:9
9:5 *u* Dt 25:17-19;
S 1Sa 15:3; S Ezr 4:6
9:10 *v* S Est 5:11;
Ps 127:3-5
w S 1Sa 15:33
x S Ge 14:23;
S 1Sa 14:32;
S Est 3:13
9:12 *y* Est 5:6; 7:2
9:13 *z* S Est 5:11
a S Dt 21:22-23
9:14 *b* S Ezr 6:11
9:15 *c* S Ge 14:23;
S Est 8:11
9:16 *d* S Est 4:14
e Dt 25:19
f S 1Ch 4:43
g S Est 8:11
9:17 *h* S 1Ki 3:15

ery nationality so that the Jews would be ready on that day *z* to avenge themselves on their enemies.

¹⁴The couriers, riding the royal horses, went out, spurred on by the king's command, and the edict was issued in the citadel of Susa. *a*

THE TRIUMPH OF THE JEWS

¹⁵When Mordecai *b* left the king's presence, he was wearing royal garments of blue and white, a large crown of gold *c* and a purple robe of fine linen. *d* And the city of Susa held a joyous celebration. *e* ¹⁶For the Jews it was a time of happiness and joy, *f* gladness and honor. *g* ¹⁷In every province and in every city to which the edict of the king came, there was joy *h* and gladness among the Jews, with feasting and celebrating. And many people of other nationalities became Jews because fear *i* of the Jews had seized them. *j*

9 On the thirteenth day of the twelfth month, the month of Adar, *k* the edict commanded by the king was to be carried out. On this day the enemies of the Jews had hoped to overpower them, but now the tables were turned and the Jews got the upper hand *l* over those who hated them. *m* ²The Jews assembled in their cities *n* in all the provinces of King Xerxes to attack those seeking their destruction. No one could stand against them, *o* because the people of all the other nationalities were afraid of them. ³And all the nobles of the provinces, the satraps, the governors and the king's administrators helped the Jews, *p* because fear of Mordecai had seized them. *q* ⁴Mordecai *r* was prominent *s* in the palace; his reputation spread throughout the provinces, and he became more and more powerful. *t*

⁵The Jews struck down all their enemies with the sword, killing and destroying them, *u* and they did what they pleased to those who hated them. *t* ⁶In the citadel of Susa, the Jews killed and destroyed five hundred men. ⁷They also killed Parshandatha, Dalphon, Aspatha, ⁸Poratha, Adalia, Aridatha, ⁹Parmashta, Arisai, Aridai and Vaizatha, ¹⁰the ten sons *v* of Haman son of Hammedatha, the enemy of the Jews. *w* But they did not lay their hands on the plunder. *x*

¹¹The number of those killed in the citadel of Susa was reported to the king that same day. ¹²The king said to Queen Esther, "The Jews have killed and destroyed five hundred men and the ten sons of Haman in the citadel of Susa. What have they done in the rest of the king's provinces? Now what is your petition? It will be given you. What is your request? It will also be granted." *y*

¹³"If it pleases the king," Esther answered, "give the Jews in Susa permission to carry out this day's edict tomorrow also, and let Haman's ten sons *z* be impaled *a* on poles."

¹⁴So the king commanded that this be done. An edict was issued in Susa, and they impaled *b* the ten sons of Haman. ¹⁵The Jews in Susa came together on the fourteenth day of the month of Adar, and they put to death in Susa three hundred men, but they did not lay their hands on the plunder. *c*

¹⁶Meanwhile, the remainder of the Jews who were in the king's provinces also assembled to protect themselves and get relief *d* from their enemies. *e* They killed seventy-five thousand of them *f* but did not lay their hands on the plunder. *g* ¹⁷This happened on the thirteenth day of the month of Adar, and on the fourteenth they rested and made it a day of feasting *h* and joy.

8:14–17 The phraseology is taken from 3:15—4:3.
8:15 *royal garments.* See note on 6:8; Mordecai's second investiture (see 6:7–11; see also Introduction: Purpose, Themes and Literary Features).
9:1 The Jews carry out the edict of Mordecai eight months and 20 days later (see 8:9). *tables were turned.* The statement that the opposite happened points to the author's concern with literary symmetry: He balances most of the details from the first half of the story with their explicit reversal in the second half.
9:2–3 An illustration of Ge 12:3. Confronted with two conflicting edicts issued in the king's name—the edict of Haman (see 3:12) and the edict of Mordecai (see 8:7–14)—the governors follow the edict of the current regime.
9:3 Just as "people of other nationalities" were seized by "fear of the Jews" (8:17), so also the government officials of Persia were seized by "fear of Mordecai."
9:5–10 The Jews attend to the unfinished business of blotting out the name and memory of the Amalekites (Ex 17:14–16; Dt

25:17–19; see notes on 3:1–6). This incident is presented as the antithesis of 1Sa 15: The narrator is emphatic that the Jews did not take plunder, in spite of the king's permission to do so (8:11). Seizing the plunder centuries earlier in the battle against Amalek had cost Saul his kingship (1Sa 15:17–19,23); here, not taking the plunder brings royal power to Mordecai, as well as grateful recognition by his people (vv. 20–23). See vv. 15–16; cf. Ge 14:22—15:1.
9:12 See 5:3,6; 7:2.
9:13–14 *impaled ... impaled.* See vv. 7–10 and note on 2:23.
9:13 *Susa.* The city, not the citadel (vv. 11–12; see note on 1:2).
9:15–16 See note on vv. 5–10.
9:16,22 *relief from their enemies.* Closely associated with the vengeance on its enemies is the rest promised to Israel (Dt 25:19). The defeat of Haman brings rest to the Jews (see Introduction: Purpose, Themes and Literary Features; cf. 1Ch 22:6–10; Ps 95:7–11; Isa 32:18; Heb 3:7–4:11).

¹⁸The Jews in Susa, however, had assembled on the thirteenth and fourteenth, and then on the fifteenth they rested and made it a day of feasting and joy.

¹⁹That is why rural Jews—those living in villages—observe the fourteenth of the month of Adarⁱ as a day of joy and feasting, a day for giving presents to each other.^j

PURIM ESTABLISHED

²⁰Mordecai recorded these events, and he sent letters to all the Jews throughout the provinces of King Xerxes, near and far, ²¹to have them celebrate annually the fourteenth and fifteenth days of the month of Adar ²²as the time when the Jews got relief^k from their enemies, and as the month when their sorrow was turned into joy and their mourning into a day of celebration.^l He wrote them to observe the days as days of feasting and joy and giving presents of food^m to one another and gifts to the poor.ⁿ

²³So the Jews agreed to continue the celebration they had begun, doing what Mordecai had written to them. ²⁴For Haman son of Hammedatha, the Agagite,^o the enemy of all the Jews, had plotted against the Jews to destroy them and had cast the *pur*^p (that is, the lot^q) for their ruin and destruction.^r ²⁵But when the plot came to the king's attention,^a he issued written orders that the evil scheme Haman had devised against the Jews should come back onto his own head,^s and that he and his sons should be impaled^t on poles.^u ²⁶(Therefore these days were called Purim, from the word *pur*.^v) Because of everything written in this letter and because of what they had seen and what had happened to them, ²⁷the Jews took it on themselves to establish the custom that they and their descendants and all who join them should without fail observe these two days every year, in the way prescribed and at the time appointed. ²⁸These days should be remembered and observed in every generation by every family, and in every province and in every city. And these days of Purim should never cease to be celebrated by the Jews, nor should the memory of them die out among their descendants.

²⁹So Queen Esther, daughter of Abihail,^w along with Mordecai the Jew, wrote with full authority to confirm this second letter concerning Purim. ³⁰And Mordecai sent letters to all the Jews in the 127 provinces^x of Xerxes' kingdom—words of goodwill and assurance— ³¹to establish these days of Purim at their designated times, as Mordecai the Jew and Queen Esther had decreed for them, and as they had established for themselves and their descendants in regard to their times of fasting^y and lamentation.^z ³²Esther's decree confirmed these regulations about Purim, and it was written down in the records.

THE GREATNESS OF MORDECAI

10 King Xerxes imposed tribute throughout the empire, to its distant shores.^a ²And all his acts of power and might, together with a full account of the greatness of Mordecai^b to which the king had raised him,^c are they not written in the book of the annals^d of the kings of Media and Persia? ³Mordecai the Jew was second^e in rank^f to King Xerxes,^g preeminent among the Jews, and held in high esteem by his many fellow Jews, because he worked for the good of his people and spoke up for the welfare of all the Jews.^h

^a 25 Or *when Esther came before the king*

9:19 ⁱS Est 3:7
^jDt 16:11,14;
S Est 2:9; Rev 11:10
9:22 ^kS Est 4:14
^lNe 8:12; Ps 30:11-12
^mS 2Ki 25:30
ⁿS Ne 8:10
9:24 ^oS Ex 17:8-16
^pS Est 3:7
9:25 ^qS Lev 16:8 ^rEst 3:6
^sS Ps 7:16
^tS Dt 21:22-23
^uEst 7:10
9:26 ^vS Est 3:7
9:29 ^wEst 2:15
9:30 ^xS Est 1:1
9:31 ^yS Est 4:16
^zEst 4:1-3
10:1 ^aPs 72:10; 97:1
10:2 ^bS Est 8:15
^cS Ge 41:44
^dS Est 2:23
10:3 ^eDa 5:7
^fGe 41:43 ^gGe 41:40
^hNe 2:10; Jer 29:4-7;
Da 6:3

9:18–19 The author accounts for the tradition of observing Purim on two different days: It is observed on the 14th in most towns, but the Jews of Susa observed it on the 15th. Today it is observed on the 14th except in Jerusalem, where it is observed on the 15th.

9:20 *Mordecai recorded these events.* Some take this as indicating that Mordecai wrote the book of Esther; however, the more natural understanding is that he recorded the events in the letters he sent.

9:22 *presents of food.* See note on 2:9; cf. Ne 8:10,12.

9:24,26 *pur.* See note on 3:7.

9:25 *come back onto his own head.* See note on v. 1.

9:31 *fasting.* See notes on 4:3,16. No date is assigned for this fast. Jews traditionally observe the 13th of Adar, Haman's propitious day (see 3:7,13), as a fast ("the fast of Esther") before the celebration of Purim. These three days of victory celebration on the 13th–15th days of Adar rhetorically balance the three days of Esther's fasting prior to interceding with the king (4:16).

10:1–2 The reference to this taxation may represent material in the author's source, to which he directs the reader for additional information and confirmation (see note on 2:23).

10:2 This verse indicates that the book of Esther was written after the death of Xerxes (cf. 1Ki 11:41; 14:19,29 and often in 1,2 Kings).

An ancient tradition among the Jews divided the collection of their holy books into three major divisions: the Law (Pentateuch), the Prophets (Former and Latter) and the Writings. Included within the third division are Psalms and wisdom materials such as Job, Proverbs and Ecclesiastes (also some psalms and probably the Song of Songs—see introduction to that book: Interpretation).

This wisdom literature is usually associated with the sages, who are mentioned along with priests and prophets as an important force in Israelite society (see, e.g., Jer 18:18 and note). These gifted persons were recognized as possessing wide knowledge of the created world (see 1Ki 4:29–34), special insight into human affairs (as exemplified by proverbs) and exceptionally good judgment regarding courses of action to be followed to attain success in various enterprises (see 2Sa 16:15–23). In general, priests and prophets dealt with religious and moral concerns (proclaiming, teaching, interpreting and applying God's word to his people), whereas the sages generally focused more on the practical aspects of how life should be guided in the created order of things (Proverbs) and on the intellectual challenges that arise from the ambiguities of human experience (Job, Ecclesiastes).

Israel's sages reflected on life in light of God's special revelations to his people, but for their unique contribution to understanding how people ought to live in God's world they drew heavily on human experience of the created order. In this they learned much from the sages and wisdom traditions of other peoples. Comparison of their writings with those of their neighbors discloses their acquaintance with the larger intellectual world of the ancient Near East but also the distinctive perspective they brought to their reflections on the human condition.

AUTHOR

JOB

INTRODUCTION

Although most of the book consists of the words of Job and his friends, Job himself was not the author. We may be sure that the author was an Israelite, since he (not Job or his friends) frequently uses the Israelite covenant name for God (Yahweh; TNIV "the LORD"). In the prologue (chs. 1–2), divine discourses (38:1—42:6) and epilogue (42:7–17) "LORD" occurs a total of 25 times, while in the rest of the book (chs. 3–37) it appears only once (12:9).

This unknown author probably had access to a tradition (oral or written) about an ancient righteous man who endured great suffering with remarkable "perseverance" (Jas 5:11; see note there) and without turning against God (see Eze 14:14,20), a tradition he put to use for his own purposes. While the author preserves much of the archaic and non-Israelite flavor in the language of Job and his friends, he also reveals his own style as a writer of wisdom literature. The book's profound insights, its literary structures and the quality of its rhetoric display the author's genius.

DATE

Two dates are involved: (1) that of Job himself and (2) that of the composition of the book. The latter could be dated anytime from the reign of Solomon to the time of Israel's exile in Babylonia. Although the author was an Israelite, he mentions nothing of Israel's history. He had an account of a non-Israelite sage, Job (1:1), who probably lived in the second millennium B.C. (2000–1000). Like the Hebrew patriarchs, Job lived more than 100 years (42:16). Like them, his wealth was measured in livestock and servants (1:3), and like them he acted as priest for his family (1:5). The raiding of Sabean (1:15) and Chaldean (1:17) tribes fits the second millennium, as does the mention of the *kesitah,* "a piece of silver," in 42:11 (see Ge 33:19; Jos 24:32). The discovery of a Targum (Aramaic paraphrase) on Job dating to the first or second century B.C. (the earliest written Targum yet discovered) makes a very late date for composition highly unlikely.

LANGUAGE AND TEXT

In many places Job is difficult to translate because of its many unusual words and its style. For that reason, modern translations frequently differ widely. Even the pre-Christian translator(s) of Job into Greek (the Septuagint) seem(s) often to have been perplexed. The Septuagint of Job is about 400 lines shorter than the accepted Hebrew text, and it may be that the translator(s) simply omitted lines he (they) did not understand. The early Syriac (Peshitta), Aramaic (Targum) and Latin (Vulgate) translators had similar difficulties.

SETTING AND PERSPECTIVE

While it may be that the author intended his book to be a contribution to an ongoing high-level discussion of major theological issues in an exclusive company of learned men, it seems more likely that he intended his story to be told to godly sufferers who, like Job, were struggling with the crisis of faith brought on by prolonged, bitter suffering. He seems to sit too close to the suffering—to be more the sympathetic and compassionate pastor than the detached theologian or philosopher. He has heard what the learned theologians of his day have been saying about the ways of God and what brings on suffering, and he lets their voices be heard. And he knows that the godly sufferers of his day have also heard the "wisdom" of the learned and have internalized it as the wisdom of the ages. But he also knows what "miserable comfort" (cf. 16:2) that so-called wisdom gives—that it ony rubs salt in the wounds and creates a stumbling-block for faith. Against that wisdom he has no rational arguments to marshal. But he has a story to tell that challenges it at its very roots and speaks to the struggling faith of the sufferer. In effect he says to the godly sufferer, "Forget the logical arguments spun out by those who sit together at their ease and discuss the ways of God, and forget those voices in your own heart that are little more than echoes of their pronouncements. Let me tell you a story."

THEOLOGICAL THEME AND MESSAGE

When good people (those who "fear God and shun evil," 1:1) suffer, the human spirit struggles to understand. Throughout recorded history people have asked: How can this be? If God is almighty and "holds the whole world in his hands," and if he is truly good, how can he allow such an outrage? The way this question has often been put leaves open three possibilities: (1) God is not almighty after all; (2) God is not just (is not wholly good but has a demonic streak in him); (3) humans may be innocent. In ancient Israel, however, it was indisputable that God is almighty, that he is perfectly just and that no human is pure in his sight. These three assumptions were also fundamental to the theology of Job and his friends. Simple logic then dictated the conclusion: Every person's suffering is indicative of the measure of their guilt in the eyes of God. In the abstract, this conclusion appeared inescapable, logically imperative and theologically satisfying.

But what thus appeared to be theologically self-evident and unassailable in the abstract was often in radical tension with actual human experience. There were those whose godliness was genuine, whose moral character was upright and who had kept themselves from great transgression, but who nonetheless were made to suffer bitterly (see, e.g., Ps 73). For these the self-evident theology brought no consolation and offered no guidance. It only gave rise to a great enigma. And the God to whom the sufferer was accustomed to turn in moments of need himself became the overwhelming enigma. This theology left innocent sufferers imprisoned in windowless cells to agonize over their crisis of faith. In the speeches of chs. 3–37, we hear on the one hand the flawless logic but wounding thrusts of those who insisted on the traditional theology and on the other hand the writhing of soul of the righteous sufferer struggling with the great enigma even while being wounded by his well-intended, theologically orthodox friends (see note on 5:27). Their learned theology had no helpful, encouraging or comforting word for a truly godly sufferer.

The author of the book of Job broke out of the tight, logical mold of the traditional orthodox theology of his day. He saw that it led to a dead end, that it had no way to cope with the suffering of godly people. It could only deny the reality of the experienced anomaly and add to the pain and inner turmoil of the sufferer. Instead of logical arguments, he tells a story. And in his story he shifts the angle of perspective. All around him, among theologians and common people alike, were those who attempted to solve the "God problem" in the face of human suffering (are the ways of God just?) at the expense of humans (they must all deserve what they get). Even those who were suffering were told they must see matters in that light. The author of Job, on the other hand, gave encouragement to godly sufferers by showing them that their suffering provided an occasion like no other for exemplifying what true godliness is for human beings.

He begins by introducing a third party into the equation. The relationship between God and humans is not exclusive and closed. Among God's creatures there is the great adversary (see chs. 1–2). Incapable of contending with God hand to hand, power pitted against power, he is bent on frustrating God's creation enterprise centered on God's relationship with the creature that bears his image. As tempter he seeks to alienate humans from God (see Ge 3; Mt 4:1); as accuser (one of the names by which he is called, *satan*, means "accuser" or "adversary" [see note on 1:6]) he seeks to alienate God from humans (see Zec 3:1; Rev 12:9–10). His all-consuming purpose is to drive an irremovable wedge between God and humans to effect an alienation that cannot be reconciled.

In his story, the author portrays this adversary in his boldest and most radical assault on God and godly people in the special and intimate relationship that is dearest to them both. When God calls up the name of Job before the accuser and testifies to his righteousness—this creature in whom God takes special delight—Satan attempts with one crafty thrust both to assail God's beloved and to show up God as a fool. True to one of his modes of operation, he accuses Job before God. He charges that Job's godliness is evil. The very godliness in which God takes such delight lacks all integrity; it is a terrible sin. Job's godliness is mere self-serving; he is righteous only because it pays. If God will only let Satan tempt Job by breaking the link between righteousness and blessing, he will expose this man and all righteous people as the frauds they are.

It is the adversary's ultimate challenge. He is sure he has found an opening to accomplish his purpose in the very structure of creation. Humans are totally dependent on God for their very lives and well-being. That fact can occasion one of humankind's greatest temptations: to love the gifts rather than the Giver, to try to please God merely for the sake of his benefits, to be "religious" and "good" only because it pays. Satan's accusation of Job is that this is the deep truth concerning his apparently godly and upright conduct—that this is, in fact, the deep truth about the godliness of all righteous people. If he is right, if the godliness of the righteous in whom God delights can be shown to be evil, then a chasm of alienation stands between God and human beings that cannot be bridged. Then even the redemption of human beings is unthinkable, for the godliest among them would be shown to be the most ungodly. God's whole enterprise in creation and redemption would be shown to be radically flawed, and God can only sweep it all away in awful judgment.

The accusation, once raised, cannot be ignored, and it cannot be silenced—not even by destroying the accuser; it strikes too deeply into the very structure of creation and is rooted too deeply in the human condition within that structure. So God lets the adversary have his way with Job (within specified limits), so that God and righteous Job may be vindicated and the great accuser silenced. From this comes Job's profound anguish, robbed as he is of every sign of God's favor so that God becomes for him the great enigma. And his righteousness is also assailed on earth through the logic of the orthodox theology of his friends. Alone he agonizes. But he knows in the depths of his heart that his godliness has been authentic and that someday he will be vindicated (see 13:18; 14:13–17; 16:19; 19:25–27). And in spite of all, though he may curse the day of his birth (ch. 3) and chide God for treating him unjustly (9:28–35)—the uncalculated outcry of a distraught spirit—he will not curse God (as his wife, the human nearest his heart, proposed; see 2:9). In fact, what pains him most is God's apparent alienation from him.

So the adversary is silenced, and God's delight in the godly is vindicated. Robbed of every sign of God's favor, Job refuses to repudiate his Maker. He faces toward God with anguish, puzzlement, anger and bitter complaints, but never turns his back on him to march off—godless—into the dark night. His whole being yearns, not for God's gifts as such, but for a sign of God's favor (cf. Ps 42). Godly Job, dependent creature that he is, passes the supreme test occasioned by his creaturely condition and the adversary's accusation.

This first test of Job's godliness inescapably involves a second that challenges his godliness at a level no less deep than the first. For the test that sprang from Satan's accusation to be real, Job has to be kept in the dark about the goings-on in God's council chamber. But Job belongs to a race of creatures endowed with wisdom, understanding and insight (something of their godlikeness) that cannot rest until it knows and understands all it can about the creation and the ways of God. For that reason, Job's sudden loss of all that makes life good—every good gift from God—cries out for explanation and puts human wisdom to a supreme test. Job's friends confidently assume that the logic of their theology can account for all God's ways. However, Job's experience makes bitterly clear to him that their "wisdom" cannot fathom the truth of his situation. Yet Job's wisdom is also at a loss to understand. Still, he demands an explanation from God; he wants to reason matters out with God as his equal. When the dialogue between Job and his three wise friends finally stalemates, and before Job's last defense (chs. 29–31), the vain attempt of a brash younger voice to explain Job's plight, and Yahweh's own breaking-in on the scene, the author introduces a poetic essay on wisdom (ch. 28) that exposes the limits of all human wisdom. The wisdom God has given human beings can indeed understand creaturely things, but from these things humans cannot learn all of God's ways. For them the supreme wisdom is to "fear...the Lord...and to shun evil" (28:28)—the very wisdom that had marked Job's life all the while (see 1:1,8; 2:3). Standing as it does at a major juncture between the dialogue and the final, major speeches, this authorial commentary on what has been going on in the stalemated dialogue anticipates God's final word to Job, which silences his arguments and defenses. In the end Job passes the second supreme test of his godliness—of all true godliness—namely, to live by the wisdom God gave him (28:28), even while acknowledging the limits of human wisdom. But that insight and Job's acceptance of it came only after the long night of suffering and a new hearing of the voice of the Creator speaking from behind the glory curtain of the creation.

In the end the adversary is silenced. Job's friends are silenced. Job is silenced. But God is not. And when he speaks, it is to the godly Job that he speaks, bringing the silence of regret for hasty words in days of suffering and the silence of repose in the ways of the Almighty (see 38:1—42:6). Furthermore, as his heavenly friend, God hears Job's intercessions for his associates (42:8–10) and restores Job's blessed state (42:10–17).

In summary, the author's pastoral word to godly sufferers is that God treasures their righteousness above all else. And Satan knows that if he is to thwart the all-encompassing purpose of God, he must assail the godly righteousness of human beings (see 1:21–22; 2:9–10; 23:8,10; cf. Ge 15:6; Hab 2:4). At stake in the suffering of the truly godly is the outcome of the titanic struggle between the great adversary and God. At the same time the author gently reminds the godly sufferer that true, godly wisdom is to reverently love God more than all his gifts and to trust the wise goodness of God even though his ways are at times past the power of human wisdom to fathom. So here is presented a profound, but painfully practical, drama that wrestles with the wisdom and justice of the Great King's rule (a "theodicy"). Righteous sufferers must trust in, acknowledge, serve and submit to the omniscient and omnipotent Sovereign, realizing that some suffering is the result of unseen, spiritual conflicts between the kingdom of God and the kingdom of Satan—between the kingdom of light and the kingdom of darkness (cf. Eph 6:10–18; Col 1:12–13 and notes).

LITERARY FORM AND STRUCTURE

Like some other ancient compositions (cf., e.g., the Code of Hammurapi; see chart, p. xxiii), the book of Job has a sandwich literary structure: prologue (prose), main body (poetry), and epilogue (prose), revealing a creative composition, not an arbitrary compilation. Some of Job's words are lament (cf. ch. 3 and many shorter poems in his speeches), but the form of lament is unique to Job and often unlike the regular format of most lament psalms (except Ps 88). Much of the book takes the form of legal disputation. Although the friends come to console him, they end up arguing over the reason for Job's suffering. The argument breaks down in ch. 27, and Job then proceeds to make his final appeal to God for vindication (chs. 29–31). The wisdom poem in ch. 28 appears to be the words of the author, who sees the failure of the dispute as evidence of a lack of wisdom. So in praise of true wisdom he centers his structural apex between the three cycles of dialogue-dispute (chs. 3–27) and the three monologues: Job's (chs. 29–31), Elihu's (chs. 32–37) and God's (38:1—42:6). Job's monologue turns directly to God for a legal decision: that he is innocent of the charges his counselors have leveled against him. Elihu's monologue—another human perspective on why people suffer—rebukes Job but moves beyond the punishment theme to the value of divine chastening and God's redemptive purpose in it. God's monologue gives the divine perspective: Job is not condemned, but neither is a logical or legal answer given to why Job has suffered. That remains a mystery to Job, though the readers are ready for Job's restoration in the epilogue because they have had the heavenly vantage point of the prologue all along. So the literary structure and the theological significance of the book are beautifully tied together.

OUTLINE

I. Prologue (chs. 1–2)
  A. Job's Happiness (1:1–5)
  B. Job's Testing (1:6—2:13)
    1. Satan's first accusation (1:6–12)
    2. Job's faith despite loss of family and property (1:13–22)
    3. Satan's second accusation (2:1–6)
    4. Job's faith during personal suffering (2:7–10)
    5. The coming of the three friends (2:11–13)
II. Dialogue-Dispute (chs. 3–27)
  A. Job's Opening Lament (ch. 3)
  B. First Cycle of Speeches (chs. 4–14)
    1. Eliphaz (chs. 4–5)
    2. Job's reply (chs. 6–7)
    3. Bildad (ch. 8)
    4. Job's reply (chs. 9–10)
    5. Zophar (ch. 11)
    6. Job's reply (chs. 12–14)
  C. Second Cycle of Speeches (chs. 15–21)
    1. Eliphaz (ch. 15)
    2. Job's reply (chs. 16–17)
    3. Bildad (ch. 18)
    4. Job's reply (ch. 19)
    5. Zophar (ch. 20)
    6. Job's reply (ch. 21)
  D. Third Cycle of Speeches (chs. 22–26)
    1. Eliphaz (ch. 22)
    2. Job's reply (chs. 23–24)

PROLOGUE

1 In the land of Uz[a] there lived a man whose name was Job.[b] This man was blameless[c] and upright;[d] he feared God[e] and shunned evil.[f] [2]He had seven sons[g] and three daughters,[h] [3]and he owned seven thousand sheep, three thousand camels, five hundred yoke of oxen and five hundred donkeys,[i] and had a large number of servants.[j] He was the greatest man[k] among all the people of the East.[l]

[4]His sons used to hold feasts[m] in their homes on their birthdays, and they would invite their three sisters to eat and drink with them. [5]When a period of feasting had run its course, Job would make arrangements for them to be purified.[n] Early in the morning he would sacrifice a burnt offering[o] for each of them, thinking, "Perhaps my children have sinned[p] and cursed God[q] in their hearts." This was Job's regular custom.

[6]One day the angels[a] [r] came to present themselves before the LORD, and Satan[b] [s] also came with them. [7]The LORD said to Satan, "Where have you come from?"

Satan answered the LORD, "From roaming through the earth and going back and forth in it."[u]

[8]Then the LORD said to Satan, "Have you considered my servant Job?[v] There is no one on earth like him; he is blameless and upright, a man who fears God[w] and shuns evil."[x]

[9]"Does Job fear God for nothing?"[y] Satan replied. [10]"Have you not put a hedge[z] around him and his household and everything he has?[a] You have blessed the work of his hands, so that his flocks and herds are spread throughout the land.[b] [11]But now stretch out your hand and strike everything he has,[c] and he will surely curse you to your face."[d]

[12]The LORD said to Satan, "Very well, then, everything he has[e] is in your power, but on the man himself do not lay a finger."[f]

Then Satan went out from the presence of the LORD.

[13]One day when Job's sons and daughters[g] were feasting[h] and drinking wine at the oldest brother's house, [14]a messenger came to Job and said, "The oxen were plowing and the donkeys were grazing[i] nearby, [15]and the Sabeans[j] attacked and made off with them. They put the servants to the sword, and I am the only one who has escaped to tell you!"

[16]While he was still speaking, another messenger came and said, "The fire of God fell from the sky[k] and burned up the sheep and the servants,[l] and I am the only one who has escaped to tell you!"

---

[a] 6 Hebrew *the sons of God*   [b] 6 Hebrew *satan* means *adversary*.

1:16 2Ki 1:12; Job 20:26 [l] S Ge 18:17; [l] S Lev 10:2; S Nu 11:1-3

1:1 [a] S Ge 10:23
[b] Eze 14:14,20;
Jas 5:11 [c] S Ge 6:9;
S Job 23:10
[d] Job 23:7; Ps 11:7;
107:42; Pr 21:29;
Mic 7:2 [e] S Ge 22:12
[f] ver 8; S Dt 4:6;
Job 2:3; 1Th 5:22
1:2 [g] S Ru 4:15
[h] ver 13,18; Job 42:13;
Ps 127:3; 144:12
1:3 [i] S Ge 13:2
[j] S Ge 12:16 [k] ver 8;
Job 29:25 [l] S Ge 25:6;
Job 42:10; Ps 103:10
1:4 [m] ver 13,18
1:5 [n] S Ne 12:30
[o] S Ge 8:20 [p] Job 8:4
[q] 1Ki 21:10,13;
Ps 10:3; 74:10
1:6 [r] S 1Ki 22:19;
fn Ge 6:2
[s] S 2Sa 24:1;
S 2Ch 18:21;
S Ps 109:6; Lk 22:31
[t] Job 2:1
1:7 [u] S Ge 3:1;
1Pe 5:8
1:8 [v] S Jos 1:7
[w] Ps 25:12; 112:1;
128:4 [x] S ver 1;
S Ex 20:20
1:9 [y] 1Ti 6:5
1:10 [z] S 1Sa 25:16
[a] ver 12; Job 2:4;
Ps 34:7 [b] ver 3;
Job 8:7; 29:6; 42:12,17
1:11 [c] Job 19:21;
Lk 22:31 [d] Lev 24:11;
Job 2:5; Isa 3:8; 65:3;
Rev 12:9-10
1:12 [e] S ver 10
[f] Job 2:6; 1Co 10:13
1:13 [g] S ver 2
[h] S ver 4
1:14 [i] Ge 36:24
1:15 [j] S Ge 10:7;
S Job 9:24
1:16 [k] S 1Ki 18:38;

A C 1:1 *land of Uz.* A large territory east of the Jordan Valley (see v. 3), which included Edom in the south (see Ge 36:28; La 4:21) and Aram in the north (see Ge 10:23; 22:21; see also note on 1Ch 18:5). *blameless and upright.* Spiritually and morally upright (see note on Ps 26:1). This does not mean that Job was sinless. He later defends his moral integrity but also admits he is a sinner (see 6:24; 7:21 and note). *feared God.* See 28:28; Pr 3:7 and note; see also note on Ge 20:11.
1:2 *seven sons.* An ideal number, signifying completeness (see notes on 42:13; Ru 4:15).
1:3 *seven thousand sheep.* See note on 42:12. Job's enormous wealth was in livestock, not land (see Ge 12:16 and note; 13:2; 26:14). *camels.* See note on Ge 12:16. *donkeys.* The Hebrew for this word is feminine in form. Donkeys that produced offspring were very valuable. *people of the East.* The Hebrew for this phrase is translated "eastern peoples" in Ge 29:1; Jdg 6:3 (see note there).
1:5 *period of feasting.* On special occasions, feasts might last a week (see Ge 29:27; Jdg 14:12). *purified.* Made ceremonially clean in preparation for the sacrifices he offered for his children (see Ex 19:10,14, where the Hebrew for this verb is translated "consecrate"). *he would sacrifice.* Before the ceremonial laws of Moses were introduced, the father of the household acted as priest (see Ge 15:9-10).
1:6 *angels came to present themselves.* See TNIV text note here and on 2:1; 38:7. They came as members of the heavenly council who stand in the presence of God (see 1Ki 22:19 and note; Ps 89:5-7; Jer 23:18,22 and note on 23:18). *Satan.* Lit. "the accuser" or "the adversary" (see TNIV text note; see also Rev 12:10 and note). In Job the Hebrew for this word is always preceded by the definite article. In the Hebrew of 1Ch 21:1 the article is not used, because by then "Satan" had become a proper name.

1:7 *The LORD.* That is, Yahweh, the Israelite covenant name for God (see Introduction: Author; see also note on Ge 2:4).
C 1:8 *Have you considered . . . Job?* The Lord, not Satan, initiates the dialogue that leads to the testing of Job. He holds up Job as one against whom "the accuser" can lodge no accusation. *my servant.* See 42:7-8 and note; a designation for one who stands in a special relationship with God and is loyal in service (e.g., Moses, Nu 12:7; David, 2Sa 7:5; see Isa 42:1 and note; 52:13; 53:11).
1:9 "The accuser" boldly accuses the man God commends: He says Job's righteousness, in which God delights, is self-serving—the heart of Satan's attack on God and his faithful servant in the book of Job.
1:10 *hedge.* Symbolizes protection (see Isa 5:5; contrast Job 3:23).
1:11 *stretch out your hand and strike.* See 4:5.
A 1:12 Satan, the accuser, is given power to afflict (v. 12a) but is kept on a leash (v. 12b). In all the evil he effects among human beings (vv. 15,17) or in nature (vv. 16,19), Satan is under God's power (compare 1Ch 21:1 with 2Sa 24:1; see 1Sa 16:14 and note; 2Sa 24:16; 1Co 5:5 and note; 2Co 12:7; Heb 2:14). The contest, however, is not a sham. Will Job curse God to his face? If Job does not, the accuser will be proven false and God's delight in Job will be vindicated.
1:15 *Sabeans.* Probably south Arabians from Sheba, whose descendants became wealthy traders in spices, gold and precious stones (see the account of the queen of Sheba in 1Ki 10:1-13; see also Ps 72:10,15; Isa 60:6; Jer 6:20; Eze 27:22; Joel 3:8). Job 6:19 calls the Sabeans "traveling merchants" and associates them with Tema (about 350 miles southeast of Jerusalem).
1:16 *fire of God.* Lightning (see Nu 11:1 and note; 1Ki 18:38; 2Ki 1:12).

1:17 *m* S Ge 11:28, 31; S Job 9:24
1:18 *n* S ver 2
o S ver 4
1:19 *p* Ps 11:6;
Isa 5:28; 21:1; Jer 4:11;
13:24; 18:17;
Eze 17:10; Hos 13:15;
Mt 7:25 *q* Job 16:7;
19:13-15 *r* Eze 24:26
1:20 *s* S Ge 37:29;
S Mk 14:63 *t* Isa 3:24;
15:2; 22:12; Jer 7:29;
16:6; Eze 27:31; 29:18;
Mic 1:16 *u* 1Pe 5:6
1:21 *v* Ecc 5:15;
1Ti 6:7 *w* Ru 1:21;
1Sa 2:7 *x* S Jdg 10:15;
Job 2:10; Ecc 7:14;
Jer 40:2; S Eph 5:20;
1Th 5:18; Jas 5:11
1:22 *y* Job 2:10;
Ps 39:1; Pr 10:19;
13:3; Isa 53:7;
Ro 9:20
2:1 *z* Jn Ge 6:2
a S Job 1:6
2:2 *b* S Ge 3:1
2:3 *c* S Ex 20:20;
S Job 1:1,8 *d* Job 6:29;
13:18; 27:6; 31:6; 32:1;
40:8 *e* Job 9:17;
Ps 44:17
2:4 *f* S Job 1:10
2:5 *g* Job 16:8; 19:20;
33:21; Ps 102:5;
La 4:8 *h* S Ex 20:7;
S Job 1:11
2:6 *i* 2Co 12:7
j S Job 1:12
2:7 *k* S Dt 28:35;
S Job 16:16
2:8 *l* Ge 18:27;
Est 4:3; Job 16:15;
19:9; 30:19; 42:6;
Ps 7:5; Isa 58:5; 61:3;
Jer 6:26; La 3:29;
Eze 26:16; Jnh 3:5-8,
6; Mt 11:21
2:9 *m* Job 6:29;
13:15; 27:5; 33:9;
35:2; 1Th 5:8
n S Ex 20:7;
S 2Ki 6:33
2:10 *o* S Job 1:21;
S Ecc 2:24; La 3:38
p S Job 1:22; S 6:24;
Jas 1:12; 5:11

¹⁷While he was still speaking, another messenger came and said, "The Chaldeans *m* formed three raiding parties and swept down on your camels and made off with them. They put the servants to the sword, and I am the only one who has escaped to tell you!"

¹⁸While he was still speaking, yet another messenger came and said, "Your sons and daughters *n* were feasting *o* and drinking wine at the oldest brother's house, ¹⁹when suddenly a mighty wind *p* swept in from the desert and struck the four corners of the house. It collapsed on them and they are dead, *q* and I am the only one who has escaped to tell you! *r*"

²⁰At this, Job got up and tore his robe *s* and shaved his head. *t* Then he fell to the ground in worship *u* ²¹and said:

"Naked I came from my mother's womb,
    and naked I will depart. *a v*
The LORD gave and the LORD has taken away; *w*
    may the name of the LORD be praised." *x*

²²In all this, Job did not sin by charging God with wrongdoing. *y*

2 On another day the angels *b z* came to present themselves before the LORD, and Satan also came with them *a* to present himself before him. ²And the LORD said to Satan, "Where have you come from?"

Satan answered the LORD, "From roaming through the earth and going back and forth in it." *b*

³Then the LORD said to Satan, "Have you considered my servant Job? There is no one on earth like him; he is blameless and upright, a man who fears God and shuns evil. *c* And he still maintains his integrity, *d* though you incited me against him to ruin him without any reason." *e*

⁴"Skin for skin!" Satan replied. "A man will give all he has *f* for his own life. ⁵But now stretch out your hand and strike his flesh and bones, *g* and he will surely curse you to your face." *h*

⁶The LORD said to Satan, "Very well, then, he is in your hands; *i* but you must spare his life." *j*

⁷So Satan went out from the presence of the LORD and afflicted Job with painful sores from the soles of his feet to the crown of his head. *k* ⁸Then Job took a piece of broken pottery and scraped himself with it as he sat among the ashes. *l*

⁹His wife said to him, "Are you still maintaining your integrity? *m* Curse God and die!" *n*

¹⁰He replied, "You are talking like a foolish *c* woman. Shall we accept good from God, and not trouble?" *o*

In all this, Job did not sin in what he said. *p*

a 21 Or *will return there*   *b 1* Hebrew *the sons of God*   *c 10* The Hebrew word rendered *foolish* denotes moral deficiency.

1:17 *Chaldeans.* A people who were nomadic until c. 1000 B.C., when they settled in southern Mesopotamia and later became the nucleus of Nebuchadnezzar's Neo-Babylonian empire (see note on Ezr 5:12).
1:19 *mighty wind.* Tornado.
1:20 *At this, Job got up.* He is silent until his children are killed. *tore his robe and shaved his head.* In mourning (see notes on Ge 37:34; Isa 15:2).
1:21 *depart.* See TNIV text note; see also Ge 2:7; 3:19 and note. *The LORD gave and the LORD has taken away.* Job's faith leads him to see the sovereign God's hand at work, and that gives him repose even in the face of calamity.
2:1-3 Except for the final sentence, this passage is almost identical to 1:6-8. He who accused Job of having a deceitful motive is now shown to have a deceitful motive himself: to discredit the Lord through Job.
2:3 *you incited me.* God cannot be stirred up to do things against his will. Though it is not always clear how, everything that happens is part of his divine purpose (see 42:2 and note).
2:4 *Skin for skin!* Probably a proverbial statement equivalent to our "quid pro quo" (this for that).
2:5 *strike his flesh and bones.* See 1:11-12; cf. Ge 2:23; Lk 24:39.
2:6 *spare his life.* Satan is still limited by God. If Job should die, neither God nor Job could be vindicated.

2:7 The precise nature of Job's sickness is uncertain, but its symptoms were painful, festering sores over the whole body (7:5), nightmares (7:14), scabs that peeled and became black (30:28,30), disfigurement and a revolting appearance (2:12; 19:19), bad breath (19:17), excessive thinness (17:7; 19:20), fever (30:30) and pain day and night (30:17). *sores.* The Hebrew for this word is translated "boils" in Ex 9:9; Lev 13:18; 2Ki 20:7.
2:8 *ashes.* Symbolic of mourning (see 42:6; Est 4:3; cf. Jnh 3:6, which speaks of sitting in dust).
2:9 *Curse God.* The Hebrew for this expression here and in 1:5 employs a euphemism (lit. "Bless God"). Satan is using Job's wife to tempt Job as he used Eve to tempt Adam. *and die.* Since nothing but death is left for Job, his wife wants him to provoke God to administer the final stroke due to all who curse him (Lev 24:10-16).
2:10 *Shall we accept good from God, and not trouble?* A key theme of the book: Trouble and suffering are not merely punishment for sin; for God's people they may serve as a trial (as here) or as a discipline that culminates in spiritual gain (see note on 5:17-26; see also Dt 8:5; 2Sa 7:14; Ps 94:12; Pr 3:11-12; 1Co 11:32; Heb 12:5-11 and notes). Job's reply to his wife silences the accuser, who is not heard from again. And true to his word here, Job refuses to turn his back on God throughout the long struggle that follows. He faces God with questions, complaints, accusations and appeals, but he continues to face him.

¹¹When Job's three friends, Eliphaz the Temanite, �q Bildad the Shuhite ʳ and Zophar the Naamathite, ˢ heard about all the troubles that had come upon him, they set out from their homes and met together by agreement to go and sympathize with him and comfort him. ᵗ ¹²When they saw him from a distance, they could hardly recognize him; ᵘ they began to weep aloud, ᵛ and they tore their robes ʷ and sprinkled dust on their heads. ˣ ¹³Then they sat on the ground ʸ with him for seven days and seven nights. ᶻ No one said a word to him, ᵃ because they saw how great his suffering was.

JOB SPEAKS

3 After this, Job opened his mouth and cursed the day of his birth. ᵇ ²He said:

³ "May the day of my birth perish,
    and the night that said, 'A boy is conceived!' ᶜ
⁴ That day—may it turn to darkness;
    may God above not care about it;
    may no light shine on it.
⁵ May gloom and utter darkness ᵈ claim it once more;
    may a cloud settle over it;
    may blackness overwhelm it.
⁶ That night—may thick darkness ᵉ seize it;
    may it not be included among the days of the year
    nor be entered in any of the months.
⁷ May that night be barren;
    may no shout of joy ᶠ be heard in it.
⁸ May those who curse days ᵃ curse that day, ᵍ
    those who are ready to rouse Leviathan. ʰ
⁹ May its morning stars become dark;
    may it wait for daylight in vain
    and not see the first rays of dawn, ⁱ
¹⁰ for it did not shut the doors of the womb on me
    to hide trouble from my eyes.

¹¹ "Why did I not perish at birth,
    and die as I came from the womb? ʲ
¹² Why were there knees to receive me ᵏ
    and breasts that I might be nursed?
¹³ For now I would be lying down ˡ in peace;
    I would be asleep and at rest ᵐ
¹⁴ with kings and rulers of the earth, ⁿ
    who built for themselves places now lying in ruins, ᵒ
¹⁵ with princes ᵖ who had gold,
    who filled their houses with silver. �q
¹⁶ Or why was I not hidden away in the ground like a stillborn child, ʳ
    like an infant who never saw the light of day? ˢ

ᵃ 8 Or *the sea*

2:11 q S Ge 36:11
ʳ S Ge 25:2 ˢ Job 11:1;
20:1 ᵗ S Ge 37:35;
S Job 6:10; Jn 11:19
2:12 ᵘ Job 17:7;
Isa 52:14
ᵛ 2Sa 15:23
ʷ S Ge 37:29;
S Mk 14:63
ˣ S Jos 7:6; S 2Sa 1:2
2:13 ʸ Isa 3:26; 47:1;
Jer 48:18; La 2:10;
Eze 26:16; Jnh 3:6;
Hag 2:22 ᶻ S Ge 50:10
ᵃ Pr 17:28; Isa 23:2;
47:5
3:1 ᵇ Jer 15:10; 20:14
3:3 ᶜ ver 11,16;
Job 10:18-19; Ecc 4:2;
6:3; Jer 20:14-18;
Mt 26:24
3:5 ᵈ Job 10:21,22;
34:22; 38:17; Ps 23:4;
44:19; 88:12; Jer 2:6;
13:16
3:6 ᵉ Job 23:17;
30:26
3:7 ᶠ Ps 20:5; 33:3;
65:13; Isa 26:19;
Jer 51:48
3:8 ᵍ Job 10:18;
Jer 20:14 ʰ S Ge 1:21;
Job 41:1,8,10,25;
Ps 74:14; 104:26
3:9 ⁱ Job 41:18;
Hab 3:4
3:11 ʲ S ver 3
3:12 ᵏ S Ge 48:12;
Isa 66:12
3:13 ˡ Job 17:13;
30:23 ᵐ ver 17;
Job 7:8-10,21; 10:22;
13:19; 14:10-12; 19:27;
21:13,23; 27:19;
Ps 139:11; Isa 8:22
3:14 ⁿ Job 9:24;
12:17; Isa 14:9;
Eze 32:28-32
ᵒ Job 15:28; Jer 51:37;
Na 3:7
3:15 ᵖ Job 12:21;
Isa 45:1 q Job 15:29;
20:10; 27:17;
Ps 49:16-17; Pr 13:22;
28:8; Ecc 2:26;
Isa 2:7; Zep 1:11
3:16 ʳ Ps 58:8;
Ecc 4:3; 6:3 ˢ S ver 3;
Ps 71:6

C **2:11** *three friends.* Older than Job (see 15:10). *Eliphaz.* An Edomite name (see note on Ge 36:11). *Temanite.* Teman was a village in Edom, south of the Dead Sea (see Ge 36:11; Jer 49:7; Eze 25:13; Am 1:12; Ob 9 and notes). *Shuhite.* Bildad may have been a descendant of Shuah, the youngest son of Abraham and Keturah (Ge 25:2).
2:12 *could hardly recognize him.* Cf. Isa 52:14; 53:3. *tore their robes and sprinkled dust on their heads.* Visible signs of mourning (see note on 1:20).

A **2:13** *sat on the ground with him.* See Eze 3:15; possibly an expression of sympathy or shock. *seven.* The number of completeness (see 1:2; Ge 50:10; 1Sa 31:13 and note; see also note on Ru 4:15). *No one said a word to him.* A wiser response than their later speeches would prove to be (see 16:2-3).
3:1-26 Job's first speech is addressed to no one in particular. In it he simply gives expression to the depths of his suffering.

C **3:3** *May the day of my birth perish.* Job's very existence, which has been a joy to him because of God's favor, is now

his intolerable burden. He is as close as he will ever come to cursing God, but he does not do it (see Jer 20:14–18 and note).
3:4 *may it turn to darkness.* God had said in Ge 1:3, "Let there be light." Job, using similar language, would negate God's creative act.
3:8 *those who curse days.* Eastern soothsayers, like Balaam (see Nu 22–24), who pronounced curses on people, objects and days. *Leviathan.* Using vivid, figurative language, Job wishes that "those who curse days" would arouse the sea monster Leviathan (see note on Isa 27:1) to swallow the day and night of his birth (see v. 3).
3:11–12,16,20–23 A series of rhetorical questions.
3:16 Since in fact his birth had taken place, the next possibility would have been a stillbirth. He would then have lived only in the grave (or Sheol), which he envisions as a place of peace and rest (vv. 13–19; see note on Ge 37:35). Such a situation would be much better than his present intolerable condition, in which he can find neither peace nor rest (v. 26).

3:17 *t* ver 26;
Job 30:26; Ecc 4:2;
Isa 14:3 *u* S ver 13
3:18 *v* Isa 51:14
w S Ge 15:13 *x* Job 39:7
3:19 *y* Job 9:22;
17:16; 21:33; 24:24;
30:23; Ecc 12:5
3:20 *z* S 1Sa 1:10;
Eze 27:30-31
3:21 *a* Rev 9:6
b Ps 119:127; Pr 2:4
3:22 *c* Job 7:16;
Ecc 4:3; Jer 8:3
3:23 *d* Pr 4:19;
Isa 59:10; Jer 13:16;
23:12 *e* Job 6:4; 16:13;
19:6, 8, 12; Ps 88:8;
La 2:4; 3:7; Hos 2:6
3:24 *f* Ps 5:1; 38:9;
Isa 35:10 *g* Job 6:7;
33:20; Ps 107:18
h Ps 22:1; 32:3; 38:8
i 1Sa 1:15; Job 30:16;
Ps 6:6; 22:14; 42:3, 4;
80:5; Isa 53:12; La 2:12
3:25 *j* Job 7:9; 9:28;
30:15; Hos 13:3
k S Ge 42:36
3:26 *l* Isa 48:22;
Jn 14:27 *m* Job 7:4, 14;
Ps 6:6; Da 4:5;
Mt 11:28 *n* S ver 17;
S Job 10:18; S 19:8
4:1 *o* S Ge 36:11;
Job 15:1; 22:1
4:2 *p* Job 32:20;
Jer 4:19; 20:9
4:3 *q* Dt 32:2;
Job 29:23; Hos 6:3
r Job 26:2; Ps 71:9;
Isa 13:7; 35:3;
Zep 3:16; Heb 12:12
4:4 *s* Job 16:5; 29:16,
25; Isa 1:17 *t* Job 29:11,
15; Isa 35:3; Jer 31:8;
Heb 12:12
4:5 *u* S Jos 1:9
v Ru 1:13; Job 1:11;
19:21; 30:21; Ps 38:2;
Isa 53:4 *w* Job 6:14;
Pr 24:10
4:6 *x* 2Ki 18:19;
Ps 27:3; 71:5; Pr 3:26
y S Ge 6:9
4:7 *z* Job 5:11; 36:7;
Ps 41:2; 2Pe 2:9
a Job 8:20; Ps 37:25;
91:9-10; Pr 12:21; 19:23
4:8 *b* Job 5:3; 15:17
c Jdg 14:18; Job 5:6;
15:35; Ps 7:14;
Isa 59:4 *d* Ps 7:15;
9:15; Pr 11:18; 22:8;
Isa 17:11; Hos 8:7;
10:13; Gal 6:7-8
4:9 *e* S Ex 15:10;
S Job 41:21; 2Th 2:8
f S Lev 26:38;
Job 40:13; Isa 25:7
4:10 *g* Ps 22:13
h Ps 17:12; 22:21;
Pr 28:15 *i* Job 5:15;
29:17; 36:6; 38:15;
Ps 35:10; 58:6

¹⁷ There the wicked cease from turmoil, *t*
  and there the weary are at rest. *u*
¹⁸ Captives *v* also enjoy their ease;
  they no longer hear the slave driver's *w* shout. *x*
¹⁹ The small and the great are there, *y*
  and the slaves are freed from their owners.

²⁰ "Why is light given to those in misery,
  and life to the bitter of soul, *z*
²¹ to those who long for death that does not come, *a*
  who search for it more than for hidden treasure, *b*
²² who are filled with gladness
  and rejoice when they reach the grave? *c*
²³ Why is life given to a man
  whose way is hidden, *d*
  whom God has hedged in? *e*
²⁴ For sighing *f* has become my daily food; *g*
  my groans *h* pour out like water. *i*
²⁵ What I feared has come upon me;
  what I dreaded *j* has happened to me. *k*
²⁶ I have no peace, *l* no quietness;
  I have no rest, *m* but only turmoil." *n*

ELIPHAZ

4 Then Eliphaz the Temanite *o* replied:

² "If someone ventures a word with you, will you be impatient?
  But who can keep from speaking? *p*
³ Think how you have instructed many, *q*
  how you have strengthened feeble hands. *r*
⁴ Your words have supported those who stumbled; *s*
  you have strengthened faltering knees. *t*
⁵ But now trouble comes to you, and you are discouraged; *u*
  it strikes *v* you, and you are dismayed. *w*
⁶ Should not your piety be your confidence *x*
  and your blameless *y* ways your hope?

⁷ "Consider now: Who, being innocent, has ever perished? *z*
  Where were the upright ever destroyed? *a*
⁸ As I have observed, *b* those who plow evil *c*
  and those who sow trouble reap it. *d*
⁹ At the breath of God *e* they perish;
  at the blast of his anger they are no more. *f*
¹⁰ The lions may roar *g* and growl,
  yet the teeth of the great lions *h* are broken. *i*
¹¹ The lion perishes for lack of prey, *j*
  and the cubs of the lioness are scattered. *k*

¹² "A word *l* was secretly brought to me,
  my ears caught a whisper *m* of it. *n*

4:11 *j* Dt 28:41; Job 27:14; 29:17; Ps 34:10; 58:6; Pr 30:14 *k* Job 5:4 **4:12** *l* ver 17-21; Job 32:13; Jer 9:23 *m* Job 26:14 *n* Job 33:14

3:18 *slave driver's shout.* As in Egypt (see Ex 5:13–14).
3:23 *whom God has hedged in.* God, who had put a hedge of protection around him (see 1:10 and note), has now, he feels, hemmed him in with turmoil (see v. 26).

A C **4:1** *Eliphaz the Temanite.* See note on 2:11. Teman was an Edomite town noted for wisdom (see Jer 49:7). The speeches of Job's three friends contain elements of truth, but they must be carefully interpreted in context. The problem is not so much with what the friends knew but with what they did not know: God's high purpose in allowing Satan to buffet Job.
4:2 *ventures a word.* Eliphaz seems to be genuinely concerned with Job's well-being and offers a complimentary word (vv. 3–4). *impatient.* See note on 9:2–3.

4:5 *strikes you.* See 1:11; 2:5; 19:21.
4:6–7 Eliphaz counsels Job to be confident that his piety will count with God, that though God is now chastening him for some sin, it is to a good end (see v. 17; 5:17), and he can be assured that God will not destroy him along with the wicked.
4:6 *piety.* Lit. "fear (of God)" (see note on 1:1). The word is used only by Eliphaz (see 15:4; 22:4).
4:7–9 If Job is truly innocent, he will not be destroyed.
4:8–11 Just as the strongest lions eventually die (vv. 10–11), so the wicked are eventually destroyed (vv. 8–9).
4:9 *blast of his anger.* See Ex 15:7–8. God's judgment is fearfully severe.
4:12–21 Eliphaz tells of a hair-raising (see v. 15), mystical ex-

¹³ Amid disquieting dreams in the night,
  when deep sleep falls on people, ᵒ
¹⁴ fear and trembling ᵖ seized me
  and made all my bones shake. �q
¹⁵ A spirit glided past my face,
  and the hair on my body stood on end. ʳ
¹⁶ It stopped,
  but I could not tell what it was.
  A form stood before my eyes,
  and I heard a hushed voice: ˢ
¹⁷ 'Can a mortal be more righteous than God? ᵗ
  Can human beings be more pure than their Maker? ᵘ
¹⁸ If God places no trust in his servants, ᵛ
  if he charges his angels with error, ʷ
¹⁹ how much more those who live in houses of clay, ˣ
  whose foundations ʸ are in the dust, ᶻ
  who are crushed ᵃ more readily than a moth! ᵇ
²⁰ Between dawn and dusk they are broken to pieces;
  unnoticed, they perish forever. ᶜ
²¹ Are not the cords of their tent pulled up, ᵈ
  so that they die ᵉ without wisdom?' ᶠ

  "Call if you will, but who will answer you? ᵍ
  To which of the holy ones ʰ will you turn?
² Resentment ⁱ kills a fool,
  and envy slays the simple. ʲ
³ I myself have seen ᵏ a fool taking root, ˡ
  but suddenly ᵐ his house was cursed. ⁿ
⁴ His children ᵒ are far from safety, ᵖ
  crushed in court q without a defender. ʳ
⁵ The hungry consume his harvest, ˢ
  taking it even from among thorns,
  and the thirsty pant after his wealth.
⁶ For hardship does not spring from the soil,
  nor does trouble sprout from the ground. ᵗ
⁷ Yet human beings are born to trouble ᵘ
  as surely as sparks fly upward.

⁸ "But if I were you, I would appeal to God;
  I would lay my cause before him. ᵛ
⁹ He performs wonders ʷ that cannot be fathomed, ˣ
  miracles that cannot be counted. ʸ

4:13 ᵒJob 33:15
4:14 ᵖJob 21:6;
Ps 48:6; 55:5;
119:120,161; Jer 5:22;
Hab 3:16; S 2Co 7:15
qJer 23:9; Da 10:8;
Hab 3:16
4:15 ʳDa 5:6; 7:15,
28; 10:8; Mt 14:26
4:16 ˢS 1Ki 19:12
4:17 ᵗJob 9:2; 13:18;
Ps 143:2 ᵘJob 8:3;
10:3; 14:4; 15:14;
21:14; 25:4; 31:15;
32:22; 35:10; 36:3,13;
37:23; 40:19; Ps 18:26;
51:5; 119:73; Pr 20:9;
Ecc 7:20; Isa 51:13;
Mal 2:10; Ac 17:24
4:18 ᵛHeb 1:14
ʷJob 15:15; 21:22; 25:5
4:19 ˣJob 10:9;
33:6; Isa 64:8;
Ro 9:21; 2Co 4:7; 5:1
ʸJob 22:16 ᶻS Ge 2:7
ᵃJob 5:4 ᵇJob 7:17;
15:16; 17:14; 25:6;
Ps 22:6; Isa 41:14
4:20 ᶜJob 14:2,20;
15:33; 20:7; 24:24;
Ps 89:47; 90:5-6;
Jas 4:14
4:21 ᵈJob 8:22;
Isa 38:12 ᵉJn 8:24
ᶠJob 18:21; 36:12;
Pr 5:23; Jer 9:3
5:1 ᵍHab 1:2
ʰJob 15:15; Ps 89:5,7
5:2 ⁱJob 21:15; 36:13
ʲPr 12:16; Gal 5:26
5:3 ᵏS Job 4:8
ˡPs 37:35; Isa 40:24;
Jer 12:2; Eze 17:6
ᵐPr 6:15 ⁿJob 24:18;
Ps 37:22,35-36;
109:9-10; Pr 3:33
5:4 ᵒJob 20:10; 27:14
ᵖS Job 4:11 qJob 4:19;
Am 5:12 ʳPs 109:12;
Isa 9:17; 1Jn 2:1
5:5 ˢLev 26:16;
S Jdg 2:15; Job 20:18;
31:8; Mic 6:15
5:6 ᵗS Job 4:8
5:7 ᵘS Ge 3:17;
Job 10:17; 15:35;
Ps 51:5; 58:3; 90:10;
Pr 22:8
5:8 ᵛJob 8:5; 11:13;
13:3,15; 23:4; 40:1;
Ps 35:23; 50:15;
Jer 12:1; 1Co 4:4
5:9 ʷPs 78:4; 111:2
ˣDt 29:29; Job 9:4; 10;

5:9 11:7; 25:2; 26:14; 33:12; 36:5,22,26; 37:5,14,16,23; 42:3; Ps 40:5; 71:17; 72:18; 86:10; 131:1; 139:6,17; 145:3; Isa 40:28; Ro 11:33 ʸPs 71:15

perience mediated through a dream (see v. 13), through which he claims to have received divine revelation and on which he bases his advice to Job.

4:13 *Amid ... dreams ... when deep sleep falls on people.* Eliphaz's words are echoed by Elihu in 33:15.

4:14 *all my bones shake.* A sign of great distress (see Jer 23:9; Hab 3:16).

4:17–21 All mortals are sinful; therefore God has a right to punish them. Job should be thankful for the correction God is giving him (see 5:17–26 and note).

4:18–19 See 15:15–16.

4:18 *servants.* Angels.

4:19 *houses of clay.* Bodies made of dust (see 10:9; 33:6; see also note on Ge 2:7). *moth.* A symbol of fragility (cf. 27:18).

4:20 *Between dawn and dusk.* A vivid picture of the shortness of life.

4:21 *tent.* A temporary home, like the human body (see 2Co 5:1,4; 2Pe 1:13 and notes). *without wisdom.* Needlessly and senselessly (see v. 20).

A **5:1** *To which ... will you turn?* To plead your case with God. The idea of a mediator, someone to arbitrate be-

tween God and Job, is an important motif in the book (see 9:33; 16:19–20 and notes; see also note and TNIV text note on 19:25). *holy ones.* Holy angels, the "sons of God" in the prologue (see TNIV text notes on 1:6; 2:1).

5:2 Without mentioning him, Eliphaz implies that Job is resentful against God and that harm will follow. *fool.* One who pays no attention to God (see TNIV text notes on 2:10; Pr 1:7).

5:3 *A fool taking root.* A wicked man prospering like a tree taking root (see Ps 1:3).

5:6 Unlike a weed, trouble must be sown and cultivated.

B **5:7** *human beings are born to trouble.* Proof that no one is righteous in the eyes of God (see notes on 4:17–21; 13:28—14:1). Job should stop behaving like a fool (see vv. 1–6) and should humble himself. Then God would bless, and injustice would shut its mouth (see v. 16). *sparks.* Lit. "sons of Resheph." In Canaanite mythology, Resheph was a god of plague and destruction. "(Sons of) Resheph" is used as a poetic image in the OT for fire (SS 8:6), bolts of lightning (Ps 78:48) and pestilence (Dt 32:24; Hab 3:5).

5:9 Repeated in 9:10.

5:10 z Mt 5:45
a S Lev 26:4;
Job 36:28; 37:6,13;
38:28,34; Ps 135:7;
Jer 14:22
5:11 b S 1Sa 2:7-8;
S Job 4:7; Ps 75:7;
113:7-8 c Isa 61:2;
Mt 5:4; Ro 12:15
d S Mt 23:12; Jas 4:10
5:12 e Ne 4:15;
Ps 33:10; Isa 8:10;
19:3; Jer 19:7
f Job 12:23; Ps 78:59;
140:8
5:13 g Job 37:24;
Isa 29:14; 44:25;
Jer 8:8; 18:18; 51:57
h Job 15:5; Ps 18:26;
Lk 20:23; 1Co 3:19*;
2Co 11:3; Eph 4:14
i Job 9:4; 18:7;
Pr 21:30; 29:6; Jer 8:9
5:14 j Job 15:22,30;
18:6,18; 20:26; 22:11;
27:20; Isa 8:22;
Jn 12:35 k S Dt 28:29;
S Job 18:5; Am 8:9
5:15 l S Ex 22:23;
Job 8:6; 22:27; 33:26;
36:15 m S Job 4:10;
S 31:22
5:16 n Job 20:19;
31:16; Pr 17:5; 22:22;
Isa 11:4; 41:17; 61:1
o Ps 63:11; 107:42;
Ro 3:19
5:17 p Dt 8:5;
Job 33:19; 36:10;
Zep 3:7; Jas 1:12
q Ps 94:12; Pr 3:11;
Jer 31:18 r S Ge 17:1;
S Job 15:11; Heb
12:5-11
5:18 s Ps 147:3;
Isa 57:15; 61:1;
Hos 6:1 t S Dt 32:39
5:19 u Da 3:17; 6:16
v Ps 34:19; 91:10;
Pr 3:25-26; 24:15-16
5:20 w ver 22;
Ps 33:19; 37:19
x Ps 22:20; 91:7;
140:7; 144:10;
Jer 39:18
5:21 y Ps 12:2-4;
31:20 z Ps 23:4; 27:1;
91:5 a ver 15
5:22 b Job 8:21; 39:7,
18,22; 41:29 c S ver 20
d S Lev 25:18; Ps 91:13;
Hos 2:18; Mk 1:13
5:23 e Isa 28:15;
Hos 2:18 f 2Ki 3:19,
25; Ps 91:12; Mt 13:8
g Job 40:20; Isa 11:6-
9; 65:25; Eze 34:25
5:24 h Job 12:6; 21:9
i Job 8:6; 22:23
5:25 j Dt 28:4;
Ps 112:2

¹⁰He bestows rain on the earth;ᶻ
   he sends water on the countryside.ᵃ
¹¹The lowly he sets on high,ᵇ
   and those who mournᶜ are liftedᵈ to safety.
¹²He thwarts the plansᵉ of the crafty,
   so that their hands achieve no success.ᶠ
¹³He catches the wiseᵍ in their craftiness,ʰ
   and the schemes of the wily are swept away.ⁱ
¹⁴Darknessʲ comes upon them in the daytime;
   at noon they grope as in the night.ᵏ
¹⁵He saves the needyˡ from the sword in their mouth;
   he saves them from the clutches of the powerful.ᵐ
¹⁶So the poorⁿ have hope,
   and injustice shuts its mouth.ᵒ

¹⁷"Blessed are those whom God corrects;ᵖ
   so do not despise the disciplineᑫ of the Almighty.ᵃ ʳ
¹⁸For he wounds, but he also binds up;ˢ
   he injures, but his hands also heal.ᵗ
¹⁹From six calamities he will rescueᵘ you;
   in seven no harm will touch you.ᵛ
²⁰In famineʷ he will deliver you from death,
   and in battle from the stroke of the sword.ˣ
²¹You will be protected from the lash of the tongue,ʸ
   and need not fearᶻ when destruction comes.ᵃ
²²You will laughᵇ at destruction and famine,ᶜ
   and need not fear the wild animals.ᵈ
²³For you will have a covenantᵉ with the stonesᶠ of the field,
   and the wild animals will be at peace with you.ᵍ
²⁴You will know that your tent is secure;ʰ
   you will take stock of your property and find nothing missing.ⁱ
²⁵You will know that your children will be many,ʲ
   and your descendants like the grass of the earth.ᵏ
²⁶You will come to the grave in full vigor,ˡ
   like sheaves gathered in season.ᵐ

²⁷"We have examined this, and it is true.
   So hear itⁿ and apply it to yourself."ᵒ

JOB 6

Then Job replied:

²"If only my anguish could be weighed
   and all my misery be placed on the scales!ᵖ
³It would surely outweigh the sandᑫ of the seas—

ᵃ 17 Hebrew *Shaddai*; here and throughout Job

5:25 k Ps 72:16; Isa 44:3-4; 48:19 **5:26** l S Ge 15:15; S Dt 11:21; S Ecc 8:13 m Pr 3:21-26 **5:27** n Job 32:10,17 o Job 8:5; 11:13; 22:27
6:2 p Job 31:6; Pr 11:1; Da 5:27 **6:3** q 1Ki 4:29; Pr 27:3

5:13 Quoted in part in 1Co 3:19 (the only clear quotation of Job in the NT).

5:17–26 While the preceding hymn (vv. 8–16) spoke of God's goodness and justice, this poem celebrates the blessedness of the one whom God disciplines (see Pr 1:2,7; 3:11–12 and note; 5:12 and note; 23:13,23). Eliphaz believed that discipline is temporary and is followed by healing (v. 18), and that those who are good will always be rescued. But with Job's wealth gone and his children dead, these words about security (v. 24) and children (v. 25) must have seemed cruel and hollow to him.

5:17 *Almighty.* The first of 31 times that the Hebrew word *Shaddai* is used in Job (see note on Ge 17:1).

5:18–19 See Hos 6:1–2.

5:19 *six…seven.* See 33:29; 40:5; Pr 6:16 and note; 30:15, 18,21,29; Ecc 11:2; Am 1:3 and note,6,9,11,13; 2:1,4,6; Mic 5:5 and note. Normally, such number patterns are not to be taken

literally but are a poetic way of saying "many."

5:23 *covenant with the stones.* A figurative way of saying that stones will "be at peace with you" and will not ruin the crops (see 2Ki 3:19; Isa 5:2; Mt 13:5).

5:25 *like the grass of the earth.* As numerous as blades of grass (see note on Ge 13:16).

5:26 Eliphaz's prediction was more accurate than he realized (see 42:16–17).

A **5:27** *apply it to yourself.* Eliphaz's conclusion: Job must turn from unrighteousness (4:7) and resentment against God (v. 2) to humility (v. 11) and the acceptance of God's righteous discipline (v. 17). Eliphaz's purpose is to offer theological comfort and counsel to Job (2:11), but instead he wounds him with false accusation.

6:2–3 Job appeals for a sympathetic understanding of the harsh words he spoke in ch. 3.

no wonder my words have been impetuous. *r*

4 The arrows *s* of the Almighty *t* are in me, *u*
　　my spirit drinks *v* in their poison; *w*
　　God's terrors *x* are marshaled against me. *y*
5 Does a wild donkey *z* bray *a* when it has grass,
　　or an ox bellow when it has fodder? *b*
6 Is tasteless food eaten without salt,
　　or is there flavor in the sap of the mallow*a*? *c*
7 I refuse to touch it;
　　such food makes me ill. *d*

8 "Oh, that I might have my request,
　　that God would grant what I hope for, *e*
9 that God would be willing to crush *f* me,
　　to let loose his hand and cut off my life! *g*
10 Then I would still have this consolation *h*—
　　my joy in unrelenting pain *i*—
　　that I had not denied the words *j* of the Holy One. *k*

11 "What strength do I have, that I should still hope?
　　What prospects, that I should be patient? *l*
12 Do I have the strength of stone?
　　Is my flesh bronze? *m*
13 Do I have any power to help myself, *n*
　　now that success has been driven from me?

14 "Anyone who withholds kindness from a friend *o*
　　forsakes the fear of the Almighty. *p*
15 But my brothers are as undependable as intermittent streams, *q*
　　as the streams that overflow
16 when darkened by thawing ice
　　and swollen with melting snow, *r*
17 but that cease to flow in the dry season,
　　and in the heat *s* vanish from their channels.
18 Caravans turn aside from their routes;
　　they go off into the wasteland and perish.
19 The caravans of Tema *t* look for water,
　　the traveling merchants of Sheba *u* look in hope.
20 They are distressed, because they had been confident;
　　they arrive there, only to be disappointed. *v*
21 Now you too have proved to be of no help;
　　you see something dreadful and are afraid. *w*
22 Have I ever said, 'Give something on my behalf,
　　pay a ransom *x* for me from your wealth, *y*
23 deliver me from the hand of the enemy,
　　rescue me from the clutches of the ruthless'? *z*

24 "Teach me, and I will be quiet; *a*
　　show me where I have been wrong. *b*
25 How painful are honest words! *c*
　　But what do your arguments prove?
26 Do you mean to correct what I say,
　　and treat my desperate words as wind? *d*

a 6 The meaning of the Hebrew for this phrase is uncertain.

6:4 *arrows of the Almighty.* Job shares Eliphaz's "orthodox" theology and believes that God is aiming his arrows of judgment at him—though he does not know why (see 7:20 and note; 16:12–13; see also La 3:12; cf. Dt 32:23; Ps 7:13; 38:2).
6:5–6 Job claims the right to bray and bellow, since he has been wounded by God and offered tasteless food (words) by his friends.
6:8–9 Job repeats the anguished thoughts of 3:20–26.
6:10 *Then.* In the afterlife, Job would have the joy of knowing that he had remained true to God.
6:11–13 With no human resources left, Job considers his condition hopeless.

6:11 *patient.* See note on 9:2–3.
6:14–17 Job needs spiritual help, but his friends are proving to be undependable (cf. Gal 6:1).
6:15 *brothers.* By calling his friends his "brothers," Job makes their callousness stand out more sharply.
6:19 *Tema.* See note on Isa 21:14. *Sheba.* See note on 1:15.
6:22–23 Job has not asked them for anything except what will cost them nothing: their friendship and counsel.
6:25 *honest words.* Job is referring to his own words.
6:26 *wind.* See 8:2.

6:3 *r* ver 11,26; Job 7:11; 16:6; 21:4; 23:2
6:4 *s* S Dt 32:23; Ps 38:2 *t* S Ge 17:1 *u* Job 7:20; 16:12,13; 19:12; La 3:12 *v* Job 21:20 *w* S Dt 32:32; Job 30:21; 34:6; Jer 15:18; 30:12 *x* Job 9:34; 13:21; 18:11; 23:6; 27:20; 30:15; 33:16 *y* S Job 3:23; Ps 88:15-18
6:5 *z* S Ge 16:12 *a* Job 30:7 *b* Job 24:6; Isa 30:24
6:6 *c* Job 33:20; Ps 107:18
6:7 *d* S Job 3:24
6:8 *e* Job 14:13
6:9 *f* Job 19:2 *g* S Nu 11:15; S Ps 31:22
6:10 *h* S Job 2:11; 15:11; Ps 94:19 *i* Ps 38:17; Jer 4:19; 45:3 *j* Job 22:22; 23:12; Ps 119:102; Mk 8:38 *k* S Lev 11:44; S 2Ki 19:22; S Isa 31:1
6:11 *l* S ver 3
6:12 *m* Job 26:2
6:13 *n* Job 26:2
6:14 *o* Job 12:4; 17:2, 6; 19:19,21; 21:3; 30:1, 10; Ps 38:11; 69:20; 1Jn 3:17 *p* S Ge 17:1
6:15 *q* Job 13:4; 16:2; 21:34; Ps 22:1; 38:11; Jer 15:18
6:16 *r* Ps 147:18
6:17 *s* Job 24:19
6:19 *t* S Ge 25:15 *u* S Ge 10:7,28
6:20 *v* Jer 14:3; Joel 1:11
6:21 *w* Ps 38:11
6:22 *x* S Nu 35:31; Job 33:24; Ps 49:7 *y* Jer 15:10
6:23 *z* S 2Ki 19:19
6:24 *a* S Job 2:10; 33:33; Ps 39:1; 141:3; Pr 10:19; Ni 11:12; 17:27; Ecc 5:2 *b* Job 19:4
6:25 *c* Ecc 12:11; Isa 22:23
6:26 *d* S ver 3; S Ge 41:6; Job 8:2; 15:3; 16:3; Jer 5:13

6:27 *e* Eze 24:6;
Joel 3:3; Ob 1:11;
Na 3:10 *f* S Ex 22:22,
24; Job 31:17, 21;
Isa 10:2
6:28 *g* Job 9:15;
24:25; 27:4; 32:10;
33:1, 3; 34:6; 36:3, 4
6:29 *h* Job 19:6;
27:2; 40:8; Isa 40:27
i S Job 2:3 *j* Job 9:21;
10:7; 11:2; 12:4; 23:7,
10; 33:9, 32; 34:5, 36;
35:2; 42:6; Ps 66:10;
Zec 13:9
6:30 *k* Job 27:4
l Job 12:11
7:1 *m* Job 14:14;
Isa 40:2 *n* S Job 5:7
o S Lev 25:50
7:2 *p* Job 14:1;
Ecc 2:23 *q* S Lev 19:13;
S Job 14:6
7:3 *r* Job 16:7;
Ps 6:6; 42:3; 56:8;
Ecc 4:1; Isa 16:9;
Jer 9:1; La 1:2, 16
7:4 *s* Dt 28:67
t ver 13-14
7:5 *u* Job 17:14;
21:26; 24:5; 25:6;
Isa 14:11 *v* S Dt 28:35
7:6 *w* Job 9:25;
Ps 39:5; Isa 38:12
x Job 13:15; 14:19; 17:11,
15; 19:10; Ps 37:4; 52:9
7:7 *y* ver 16;
Ge 27:46; Ps 39:4, 5,
11; 62:9; 78:39; 89:47;
144:4; Ecc 7:15;
S Jas 4:14 *z* Job 10:20
7:8 *a* S Job 3:13;
8:18; 15:29; 20:7, 9, 21;
27:17; Ps 37:36;
103:16; Isa 41:12;
Jn 16:16; Ac 20:25
7:9 *b* S Job 3:25
c S Job 3:13; 11:8; 14:13;
17:16; 26:6; 38:17;
Am 9:2 *d* 2Sa 12:23
7:10 *e* Job 18:21;
21:18; 27:21, 23;
Ps 58:9; Jer 18:17;
19:8 *f* S ver 8;
Ps 37:10; 104:35
7:11 *g* Job 9:35;
13:13; Ps 22:2; 40:9
h Job 10:1; Ps 6:3;
Isa 38:15, 17 *i* ver 13;
Job 9:27; 21:4; 23:2
j S 1Sa 1:10; S Job 6:3
7:12 *k* Job 38:8-11
l S Ge 1:21 *m* ver 20;
Isa 1:14
7:13 *n* S ver 11
7:14 *o* Job 9:34
p S Job 4:13; S Job 3:26
7:15 *q* 1Ki 19:4;
Jnh 4:3

27 You would even cast lots *e* for the fatherless *f*
  and barter away your friend.

28 "But now be so kind as to look at me.
  Would I lie to your face? *g*
29 Relent, do not be unjust; *h*
  reconsider, for my integrity *i* is at stake. *a j*
30 Is there any wickedness on my lips? *k*
  Can my mouth not discern *l* malice?

"Do not mortals have hard service *m* on earth? *n*
  Are not their days like those of hired laborers? *o*
2 Like a slave longing for the evening shadows, *p*
  or a hired laborer waiting to be paid, *q*
3 so I have been allotted months of futility,
  and nights of misery have been assigned to me. *r*
4 When I lie down I think, 'How long before I get up?' *s*
  The night drags on, and I toss and turn until dawn. *t*
5 My body is clothed with worms *u* and scabs,
  my skin is broken and festering. *v*

6 "My days are swifter than a weaver's shuttle, *w*
  and they come to an end without hope. *x*
7 Remember, O God, that my life is but a breath; *y*
  my eyes will never see happiness again. *z*
8 The eye that now sees me will see me no longer;
  you will look for me, but I will be no more. *a*
9 As a cloud vanishes *b* and is gone,
  so those who go down to the grave *c* do not return. *d*
10 They will never come to their homes again;
  their places *e* will know them no more. *f*

11 "Therefore I will not keep silent; *g*
  I will speak out in the anguish *h* of my spirit,
  I will complain *i* in the bitterness of my soul. *j*
12 Am I the sea, *k* or the monster of the deep, *l*
  that you put me under guard? *m*
13 When I think my bed will comfort me
  and my couch will ease my complaint, *n*
14 even then you frighten me with dreams
  and terrify *o* me with visions, *p*
15 so that I prefer strangling and death, *q*
  rather than this body of mine. *r*
16 I despise my life; *s* I would not live forever. *t*
  Let me alone; *u* my days have no meaning. *v*

17 "What are human beings that you make so much of them,

a 29 Or *my righteousness still stands*

7:15 *r* Job 6:9; Rev 9:6 **7:16** *s* S 1Ki 19:4; Job 9:21 *t* S Job 3:22 *u* ver 19; Job 10:20; Ps 39:13 *v* S ver 7

6:27 In addition to dishonesty, Job accuses his friends of heartless cruelty.
6:29 Job softens his tone, pleading that his friends take back their false accusations.
7:1–21 Having replied to Eliphaz, Job now addresses his complaint toward God.
7:1 *hard service.* See 14:14. The Hebrew for this expression sometimes implies military service. It is also used in reference to the Babylonian exile (see Isa 40:2 and note).
7:2 *evening shadows.* End of the workday.
7:5 See note on 2:7.
7:7 *my life is but a breath.* As a chronic sufferer he has lost all sense of purpose in life (see v. 3; see also Ps 144:3–4). He does not anticipate healing and sees death as his only escape.
7:8 *you will look . . . no more.* See v. 21.
7:9 *those who go down to the grave do not return.* Such statements are based on common observation and are

not meant to dogmatize about what happens after death. Mesopotamian descriptions of the netherworld refer to it similarly as the "land of no return" (see note on v. 21). For the OT perspective on life after death, see Ps 6:5 and note.
7:11 *not keep silent.* Job is determined to cry out against the apparent injustice of God, who, it seems, will not leave him alone (vv. 17–20). *speak out in . . . anguish.* See Jer 4:19. *bitterness of . . . soul.* See 10:1 and note; 21:25; 27:2.
7:12 *the sea, or the monster of the deep.* See 3:8 and TNIV text note. The boisterous sea monster was a symbol of chaos (see Ps 74:13–14 and note; Isa 27:1 and note; 51:9), and Job objects to being treated like it.
7:13–15 Job thinks that even the nightmares that disturb his sleep are from God.
7:16 *I despise my life.* See note on 9:21.
7:17 *What are human beings that you make so much of them . . . ?* See Ps 144:3; cf. Ps 8:4–8, where the answer is

that you give them so much attention, [w]
[18] that you examine them every morning [x]
and test them [y] every moment? [z]
[19] Will you never look away from me, [a]
or let me alone even for an instant? [b]
[20] If I have sinned, what have I done to you, [c]
you who watch over us all?
Why have you made me your target? [d]
Have I become a burden to you? [a] [e]
[21] Why do you not pardon my offenses
and forgive my sins? [f]
For I will soon lie down in the dust; [g]
you will search for me, but I will be no more." [h]

BILDAD

8 Then Bildad the Shuhite [i] replied:

[2] "How long will you say such things? [j]
Your words are a blustering wind. [k]
[3] Does God pervert justice? [l]
Does the Almighty pervert what is right? [m]
[4] When your children sinned against him,
he gave them over to the penalty of their sin. [n]
[5] But if you will seek God earnestly
and plead [o] with the Almighty, [p]
[6] if you are pure and upright,
even now he will rouse himself on your behalf [q]
and restore you to your prosperous state. [r]
[7] Your beginnings will seem humble,
so prosperous [s] will your future be. [t]

[8] "Ask the former generation [u]
and find out what their ancestors learned,
[9] for we were born only yesterday and know nothing, [v]
and our days on earth are but a shadow. [w]
[10] Will they not instruct [x] you and tell you?
Will they not bring forth words from their understanding? [y]
[11] Can papyrus grow tall where there is no marsh? [z]
Can reeds [a] thrive without water?
[12] While still growing and uncut,
they wither more quickly than grass. [b]

---

[a] 20 A few manuscripts of the Masoretic Text, an ancient Hebrew scribal tradition and Septuagint; most manuscripts of the Masoretic Text *I have become a burden to myself.*

---

given that humanity is created in God's image to have dominion over the world (see notes on Ge 1:26–28; Ps 8:6–8). Job's words (vv. 18–21) are a parody on this theme—as if God's only interest in people is to scrutinize them unmercifully and take quick offense at their slightest fault.

7:19 *even for an instant.* Lit. "long enough for me to swallow my saliva."

7:20 *If I have sinned, what have I done to you …?* I have not been perfect, but what terrible sin have I committed that deserves this kind of suffering? *you who watch over.* The Hebrew for this phrase is used in a favorable sense in Isa 27:3, but here Job complains that God is too critical (cf. v. 12). *made me your target.* See note on 6:4. *burden to you.* See TNIV text note. Ancient Hebrew scribes report that a change in the text had been made from "you" to "myself" because the reading "you" involved too presumptuous a questioning of God's justice.

7:21 *offenses … sins.* Job confesses that he is a sinner, but he cannot understand why God refuses to forgive him. *lie down in the dust.* Of the netherworld, as in Mesopotamian descriptions of it (see note on v. 9).

8:2 *How long …?* See 18:2. In contrast to the older Eliphaz,

Bildad is impatient.

8:3 *Does God pervert justice?* But Job has not yet blatantly accused God of injustice.

C **8:5–6** Bildad reasons as follows: God cannot be unjust, so Job and his family must be suffering as a result of sinfulness. Job should plead for mercy, and if he has been upright, God will restore him.

8:6 *if you are pure and upright.* We know God's verdict about Job (see 1:8; 2:3), but Bildad is confident that Job is a hypocrite (see v. 13).

8:7 See v. 21. Bildad spoke more accurately than he realized (see 42:10–17).

8:8 *Ask the former generation.* Eliphaz appealed to revelation from the spirit world (see 4:12–21), while Bildad appeals to the accumulated wisdom of tradition.

A **8:9** *our days … are but a shadow.* A common motif in wisdom literature (see 14:2 and note; 1Ch 29:15; Ps 102:11; 144:4; Ecc 6:12; 8:13).

8:11–19 A practical wisdom poem, giving words of instruction learned from the "former generation" and "their ancestors" (v. 8). It is introduced in v. 10 and applied to Job in vv. 20–22.

7:17 [w] S Job 4:19; 22:2; Ps 8:4; 144:3; Heb 2:6
7:18 [x] Ps 73:14
[y] Job 23:10; Ps 139:23
[z] Job 14:3; Ps 17:3; 26:2; 66:10; 139:1-6; 143:2
7:19 [a] S ver 16
[b] Job 9:18; 13:26; 14:6; 27:2; Ps 139:7
7:20 [c] Job 35:6; Jer 7:19 [d] S Job 6:4
[e] S ver 12
7:21 [f] Job 9:28; 10:14; 16:6; Ps 119:120; Isa 43:25; Jer 31:34; Heb 1:3
[g] S Ge 3:19; Job 10:9; 34:15; Ps 7:5; 22:15; 90:3; 104:29
[h] S ver 8; S Job 3:13
8:1 [i] S Ge 25:2; Job 18:1; 25:1
8:2 [j] Job 11:2; 18:2
[k] S 2Ch 36:16; S Job 6:26
8:3 [l] S Job 4:17; 34:12; Isa 29:15; Ro 3:5 [m] S Ge 18:25; S Jer 12:1
8:4 [n] Job 1:19
8:5 [o] Job 9:15
[p] S Job 5:8,27
8:6 [q] S Job 5:15; 22:27; 33:26; 34:28; Isa 58:9; 65:24
[r] S Job 5:24
8:7 [s] Job 21:13; 22:21; 36:11; Ps 25:13
[t] S Job 1:10; Jer 29:11; 31:17
8:8 [u] S Dt 32:7; S Ps 71:18
8:9 [v] S Ge 47:9
[w] S 1Ch 29:15; S 2Ch 10:6; S Ps 39:6
8:10 [x] Pr 1:8
[y] Pr 2:1-2; 4:1
8:11 [z] Job 40:21
[a] S Ex 2:3; Isa 19:6; 35:7
8:12 [b] ver 19; S 2Ki 19:26; Job 18:16; 20:5; Ps 90:5-6; 102:11; Isa 34:4; 40:7, 24

8:13 c Ps 37:38;
73:17 d Ps 9:17; 50:22;
Isa 51:13; Jer 17:6
e Job 6:9; 11:20; 13:16;
15:34; 20:5; 27:8;
34:30; Ps 37:1-2;
112:10; Pr 10:28; 11:7;
Jer 15:9
8:14 f ver 15;
Job 27:18; Isa 59:5
8:15 g S ver 14
h Ps 49:11; Mt 7:26-27
8:16 i Ps 80:11;
Isa 16:8 / Ps 37:35;
Jer 11:16
8:18 k Job 20:9;
Ps 103:16 / S Job 7:8;
S 14:20
8:19 m S ver 12;
S Job 15:30
n Ps 119:90; Ecc 1:4
8:20 o Job 1:1
p S Ge 18:25
8:21 q S Job 5:22
r S Ezr 3:13; Job 35:10;
Ps 47:5; 107:22; 118:15;
126:2; Job 33:16; Isa 35:6
8:22 s Job 27:7;
Ps 6:10; 35:26; 44:7;
53:5; 71:13; 86:17;
109:29; 132:18;
Eze 7:27; 26:16
t S Job 4:21 u S 1Sa 8:3;
Job 18:6,14,21; 21:28;
27:8,18; 34:26; 36:6;
38:13; Ps 52:5; Pr 14:11
9:2 v S Job 4:17;
Ro 3:20
9:3 w ver 32;
Job 40:5 x ver 12,14,
29,32; Job 10:2; 12:14;
13:9,14; 22:4; 23:7,13;
37:19; 40:2; Ps 44:21;
Isa 14:24
9:4 y Job 11:6; 28:12,
20,23; 38:36; Ps 51:6;
Pr 2:6; Ecc 2:26
z ver 19; S Job 5:9;
12:13,16; 23:6; 24:22;
26:12; 30:18; Ps 93:4;
95:3; Pr 8:14;
Isa 40:26; 63:1;
Da 2:20; 4:35
a Jer 50:24
b S 2Ch 13:12;
S Job 5:13
9:5 c Mt 17:20
d Ps 18:7; 46:2-3;
Isa 13:13; Mic 1:4
9:6 e S Ex 19:18;
Isa 2:21; 13:13; 24:18-
20; Am 8:8;
Heb 12:26
f S 2Sa 22:8;
Job 26:14; 36:29;
37:4-5; Ps 75:3;
Hab 3:4

[13] Such is the destiny [c] of all who forget God; [d]
  so perishes the hope of the godless. [e]
[14] What they trust in is fragile [a];
  what they rely on is a spider's web. [f]
[15] They lean on the web, [g] but it gives way;
  they cling to it, but it does not hold. [h]
[16] They are like a well-watered plant in the sunshine,
  spreading its shoots [i] over the garden; [j]
[17] it entwines its roots around a pile of rocks
  and looks for a place among the stones.
[18] But when it is torn from its spot,
  that place disowns [k] it and says, 'I never saw you.' [l]
[19] Surely its life withers [m] away,
  and [b] from the soil other plants grow. [n]

[20] "Surely God does not reject the blameless [o]
  or strengthen the hands of evildoers. [p]
[21] He will yet fill your mouth with laughter [q]
  and your lips with shouts of joy. [r]
[22] Your enemies will be clothed in shame, [s]
  and the tents [t] of the wicked will be no more." [u]

JOB 9

Then Job replied:

[2] "Indeed, I know that this is true.
  But how can mere mortals prove their innocence before God? [v]
[3] Though they wished to dispute with him, [w]
  they could not answer him one time out of a thousand. [x]
[4] His wisdom [y] is profound, his power is vast. [z]
  Who has resisted [a] him and come out unscathed? [b]
[5] He moves mountains [c] without their knowing it
  and overturns them in his anger. [d]
[6] He shakes the earth [e] from its place
  and makes its pillars tremble. [f]
[7] He speaks to the sun and it does not shine; [g]
  he seals off the light of the stars. [h]
[8] He alone stretches out the heavens [i]
  and treads on the waves of the sea. [j]
[9] He is the Maker [k] of the Bear [c] and Orion,
  the Pleiades and the constellations of the south. [l]

a 14 The meaning of the Hebrew for this word is uncertain.   b 19 Or *Surely all the joy it has / is that*   c 9 Or *of Leo*

9:7 g Isa 34:4; Jer 4:28; Joel 2:2,10,31; 3:15; Zep 1:15; Zec 14:6 h Isa 13:10; Jer 4:23; Eze 32:8   9:8 i S Ge 1:1,8; S Isa 48:13 j Job 38:16;
Ps 77:19; Pr 8:28; Hab 3:15; Mt 14:25; Mk 6:48; Jn 6:19   9:9 k Job 32:22; 40:15,19 l S Ge 1:16

8:20 Bildad is blunt about Job's being an evildoer, whereas Eliphaz had resorted to insinuation (see 4:7–9).
8:21 See note on v. 7.
8:22 *clothed in.* See note on Ps 109:29.

A C 9:2–3 Job does not believe he is sinless (see note on 1:1), but he wishes to have his day in court so he can prove he is innocent of the kind of sin that deserves the suffering he endures. In his despair he voices awful complaints against God (see vv. 16–20,22–24,29–35; 10:1–7,13–17). Yet he does not abandon God or curse him (see 10:2,8–12; see also Introduction: Theological Theme and Message), as Satan said he would (see 1:11; 2:5; cf. 2:9). Ch. 42 implies that Job persevered, but chs. 9–10 show that he did so with impatience (see 4:2; 6:11; 21:4). Cf. Jas 5:11, which speaks of Job's perseverance, not (as traditionally) his patience.
9:3 *dispute.* See v. 14. Job's speech is filled with the imagery of the courtroom: "answer him" (vv. 3,15,32), "argue with him" (v. 14), "innocent . . . plead . . . Judge" (v. 15), "summoned" (v. 16), "pronounce me guilty" (v. 20), "judges" (v. 24), "court" (v. 32), "charges . . .

against me" (10:2), "witnesses" (10:17). Job argues his innocence, but he feels that because God is so great there is no use in contending with him (v. 14). Job's innocence does him no good (v. 15).

A 9:5–10 A beautiful hymn about God's greatness. But Job is not blessed by it, for he does not see that God's power is controlled by goodness and justice.
9:6 For the metaphor of the earth resting on a foundation, see 38:6; 1Sa 2:8 and note; Ps 24:2 and note; 75:3; 104:5.
B 9:8 *stretches out the heavens.* Either (1) creates the heavens (see Isa 44:24), or perhaps (2) causes the dawn to spread, like someone stretching out a tent (see Ps 104:2). *treads on the waves.* Canaanite texts describe the goddess Asherah as walking on the sea (or sea-god) to subdue it. Similarly, God "treads on the waves" to control the boisterous sea.
9:9 *Bear . . . Orion . . . Pleiades.* These three constellations are mentioned again in 38:31–32, and the last two are mentioned in Am 5:8 (see note there). Despite their limited knowledge of astronomy, the ancient Israelites were awed by the fact that God had created the constellations.

[10] He performs wonders *m* that cannot be fathomed,
  miracles that cannot be counted. *n*
[11] When he passes me, I cannot see him;
  when he goes by, I cannot perceive him. *o*
[12] If he snatches away, who can stop him? *p*
  Who can say to him, 'What are you doing?' *q*
[13] God does not restrain his anger; *r*
  even the cohorts of Rahab *s* cowered at his feet.

[14] "How then can I dispute with him?
  How can I find words to argue with him? *t*
[15] Though I were innocent, I could not answer him; *u*
  I could only plead *v* with my Judge *w* for mercy. *x*
[16] Even if I summoned him and he responded,
  I do not believe he would give me a hearing. *y*
[17] He would crush me *z* with a storm *a*
  and multiply *b* my wounds for no reason. *c*
[18] He would not let me catch my breath
  but would overwhelm me with misery. *d*
[19] If it is a matter of strength, he is mighty! *e*
  And if it is a matter of justice, who can challenge him *a*? *f*
[20] Even if I were innocent, my mouth would condemn me;
  if I were blameless, it would pronounce me guilty. *g*

[21] "Although I am blameless, *h*
  I have no concern for myself; *i*
  I despise my own life. *j*
[22] It is all the same; that is why I say,
  'He destroys both the blameless and the wicked.' *k*
[23] When a scourge *l* brings sudden death,
  he mocks the despair of the innocent. *m*
[24] When a land falls into the hands of the wicked, *n*
  he blindfolds its judges. *o*
  If it is not he, then who is it? *p*

[25] "My days are swifter than a runner; *q*
  they fly away without a glimpse of joy. *r*
[26] They skim past *s* like boats of papyrus, *t*
  like eagles swooping down on their prey. *u*
[27] If I say, 'I will forget my complaint, *v*
  I will change my expression, and smile,'
[28] I still dread *w* all my sufferings,
  for I know you will not hold me innocent. *x*
[29] Since I am already found guilty,
  why should I struggle in vain? *y*
[30] Even if I washed myself with soap *z*

a 19 See Septuagint; Hebrew *me*.

9:10 The same words are spoken by Eliphaz in 5:9.
9:12 *who can stop him?* Job argues that God has an unchallengeable, sovereign freedom that works to accomplish everything he pleases.
9:13 *Rahab.* A mythical sea monster (see 26:12), elsewhere used as symbolic of Egypt (see Isa 30:7 and note). See 3:8; 7:12 and notes. The name Rahab in Jos 2 is from a different Hebrew root.
9:15 Job believes that his only recourse before the lofty majesty of God is to throw himself on God's mercy.
9:17 Job does not know that God has allowed Satan to crush him for a high purpose.
9:20 *my mouth would condemn me.* See 15:6.
9:21 *I despise my own life.* See 7:16; words of despairing resignation that would be partially echoed in Job's final outpouring of repentance (see 42:6 and note).

9:22–24 God has become Job's great enigma. Job describes a phantom God—one who does not exist, except in Job's mind. The God of the Bible is not morally indifferent (cf. God's words in 38:2; 40:2 and Job's response in 42:3).
9:24 *blindfolds its judges.* Statues of Lady Justice are blindfolded, implying that she will judge impartially. But Job's accusation against God is that he has blindfolded the judges so that they see neither crimes nor innocence.
9:26 *boats of papyrus.* See note on Ex 2:3.
9:28 *you will not hold me innocent.* Job wants to stand before God as an innocent man—not sinless, but innocent of any sin commensurate with his suffering.
9:29 *already found guilty.* As appears from the bitter suffering he is enduring.
9:30 *cleansing powder.* A vegetable alkali used as a cleansing agent (see Jer 2:22). The Hebrew underlying this word is translated "soap" in Mal 3:2.

9:10 *m* Dt 6:22;
Ps 72:18; 136:4;
Jer 32:20 *n* S Job 5:9
9:11 *o* Job 23:8-9;
35:14
9:12 *p* Nu 23:20;
Job 11:10; Isa 14:27;
43:13 *q* S ver 3;
S Dt 32:39; Isa 29:16;
45:9; Da 2:21; 4:32;
Ro 9:20
9:13 *r* Nu 14:18;
Job 10:15; Ps 78:38;
Isa 3:11; 6:5; 48:9
s Job 26:12; Ps 87:4;
89:10; Isa 30:7; 51:9
9:14 *t* S ver 3
9:15 *u* Job 10:15;
13:19; 34:5-6; 40:5;
42:7 *v* Job 8:5
w S Ge 18:25;
1Sa 24:12; Ps 50:6;
96:13 *x* ver 20, 29;
Job 15:6; 23:4; 40:2
9:16 *y* Job 13:22;
Ro 9:20-21
9:17 *z* Job 16:12;
30:16; Ps 10:10;
Isa 38:13 *a* Job 30:22;
Ps 83:15; Jnh 1:4
b Job 16:14 *c* S Job 2:3
9:18 *d* S Job 7:19;
S 10:1
9:19 *e* S ver 4;
S Ne 9:32 *f* ver 33;
Jer 49:19
9:20 *g* S ver 15
9:21 *h* S Ge 6:9;
Job 34:6, 7 *i* ver 14;
S Job 6:29; 10:1; 13:13
j S Nu 11:15;
S Job 7:16
9:22 *k* S Job 3:19;
10:8; Ecc 9:2, 3;
Eze 21:3
9:23 *l* Heb 11:36
m Job 24:1, 12; Ps 64:4;
Hab 1:3; 1Pe 1:7
9:24 *n* Job 1:15, 17;
10:3; 16:11; 21:16;
22:18; 27:2; 40:8;
Ps 73:3 *o* S Job 3:14;
12:6; 19:7; 21:7; 24:23;
31:35; 35:15; Ps 73:12;
Ecc 8:11; Jer 12:1;
La 3:9 *p* Job 12:9; 13:1;
24:12; Isa 41:20
9:25 *q* S Job 7:6
r Job 7:7; 10:20
9:26 *s* Job 24:18;
Ps 46:3 *t* Isa 18:2
u Job 39:29; Hab 1:8
9:27 *v* S Job 7:11
9:28 *w* S Job 3:25
x S Ex 34:7; S Job 7:21
9:29 *y* S ver 3, S 15;
Ps 37:33
9:30 *z* Mal 3:2

9:30 *a* Job 17:9; 31:7;
Isa 1:15 *b* Job 14:4,17;
33:9; Isa 1:18;
Jer 2:22; Hos 13:12
9:31 *c* Ps 35:7; 40:2;
51:9; Jer 2:22; Na 3:6;
Mal 2:3 *d* S Job 7:20;
34:9; 35:3; Ps 73:13
9:32 *e* S Nu 23:19
f S ver 3; Ro 9:20
g Ps 143:2; Ecc 6:10
9:33 *h* S 1Sa 2:25
i S ver 19
9:34 *j* Job 21:9;
Ps 39:10; 73:5
k S Job 6:4; 7:14; 33:7;
Ps 32:4
9:35 *l* S Job 7:11
m Job 13:21
10:1 *n* S Nu 11:15;
S 1Ki 19:4
o S 1Sa 1:10;
S Job 7:11; 9:18,21
10:2 *p* Job 13:3; 40:1
q Isa 3:13; Hos 4:1;
5:1; 12:2; Mic 6:2;
Ro 8:33 *r* S Job 9:3
10:3 *s* S Job 9:22;
16:9,14; 19:6,21;
22:10; 30:13,21; 31:23;
34:6 *t* ver 8; Ge 1:26;
S Job 4:17; 14:15;
34:19; Ps 8:6; 95:6;
100:3; 138:8; 149:2;
Isa 60:21; 64:8
u S Job 9:24
10:4 *v* 1Sa 16:7;
Job 11:11; 14:16; 24:23;
28:24; 31:4; 34:21;
41:11; Ps 11:4; 33:15;
119:168; 139:12;
Pr 5:21; 15:3;
Jer 11:20-23; 16:17
10:5 *w* Job 36:26;
Ps 39:5; 90:2,4;
102:24; 2Pe 3:8
10:6 *x* Job 14:16
10:7 *y* ver 15;
S Job 6:29; 11:4;
16:17; 27:5,6; 31:6;
32:1 *z* S Dt 32:39
10:8 *a* Ge 2:7
b S ver 3; S 2Sa 14:14;
S Job 30:15
10:9 *c* S Job 4:19;
Isa 29:16 *d* S Ge 2:7;
S Job 7:21
10:11 *e* Ps 139:13,15
10:12 *f* S Ge 2:7
g S Ge 24:12
h S Ge 45:5 *i* 1Pe 2:25
10:13 *j* Job 23:13;
Ps 115:3
10:14 *k* Job 13:27
l S Ex 34:7; S Job 7:21
10:15 *m* S ver 7
n S Job 9:13
o S Job 9:15 *p* Ps 25:16

and my hands *a* with cleansing powder, *b*
³¹ you would plunge me into a slime pit *c*
   so that even my clothes would detest me. *d*

³² "He is not a mere mortal *e* like me that I might answer him, *f*
   that we might confront each other in court. *g*
³³ If only there were someone to arbitrate between us, *h*
   to lay a hand on us both, *i*
³⁴ someone to remove God's rod from me, *j*
   so that his terror would frighten me no more. *k*
³⁵ Then I would speak up without fear of him, *l*
   but as it now stands with me, I cannot. *m*

10

"I loathe my very life; *n*
   therefore I will give free rein to my complaint
   and speak out in the bitterness of my soul. *o*
² I say to God: *p* Do not declare me guilty,
   but tell me what charges *q* you have against me. *r*
³ Does it please you to oppress me, *s*
   to spurn the work of your hands, *t*
   while you smile on the plans of the wicked? *u*
⁴ Do you have eyes of flesh?
   Do you see as a mortal sees? *v*
⁵ Are your days like those of a mortal
   or your years like those of a human being, *w*
⁶ that you must search out my faults
   and probe after my sin *x*—
⁷ though you know that I am not guilty *y*
   and that no one can rescue me from your hand? *z*

⁸ "Your hands shaped *a* me and made me.
   Will you now turn and destroy me? *b*
⁹ Remember that you molded me like clay. *c*
   Will you now turn me to dust again? *d*
¹⁰ Did you not pour me out like milk
   and curdle me like cheese,
¹¹ clothe me with skin and flesh
   and knit me together *e* with bones and sinews?
¹² You gave me life *f* and showed me kindness, *g*
   and in your providence *h* watched over *i* my spirit.

¹³ "But this is what you concealed in your heart,
   and I know that this was in your mind: *j*
¹⁴ If I sinned, you would be watching me *k*
   and would not let my offense go unpunished. *l*
¹⁵ If I am guilty *m*—woe to me! *n*
   Even if I am innocent, I cannot lift my head, *o*
  for I am full of shame
   and drowned in *a* my affliction. *p*

---

a 15 Or *and aware of*

9:33 *someone to arbitrate between us.* See note on 5:1. God is so immense that Job feels he needs someone who can help him, someone who can argue his case in court. Job's call is not directly predicting the mediatorship of Christ, for Job is not looking for one to forgive him but for one who can testify to his innocence (see 16:18–21; 19:25–26 and notes).

9:34 See 13:21. *God's rod.* Symbolic of divine judgment and wrath (see, e.g., Ps 89:30–37; La 3:1 and notes).

10:1 *I loathe my very life.* See note on 9:21. *bitterness of my soul.* Because Job is so bitter, his mind has conjured up a false picture of God.

10:3 Job imagines that God is angry with him, an innocent man (see 9:28 and note), and that he takes delight in the wicked. Such words are a reminder that the sickroom is not the place to argue theology; in times of severe suffering, people may

say things that require a response of love and understanding. Job himself will eventually repent, and God will forgive (42:1–6).

10:8–17 Job continues to question God as if he were his adversary in court. He wants to know how God, who so wonderfully formed him in the womb, could all the while have planned (see v. 13) to punish him—even though he may be innocent.

10:8–11 A poetic description of God making a baby in the womb (see Ps 139:13–16 and notes).

10:8 See Ps 119:73.

10:9 *molded me like clay.* See note on 4:19. *turn me to dust.* See note on Ge 3:19.

10:10 *like milk…like cheese.* As semen poured into the womb produces an embryo.

10:15–16 Job says that whether he is guilty or innocent, the all-powerful God will not treat him justly.

¹⁶ If I hold my head high, you stalk me like a lion ^q
  and again display your awesome power against me. ^r
¹⁷ You bring new witnesses against me ^s
  and increase your anger toward me; ^t
  your forces come against me wave upon wave. ^u
¹⁸ "Why then did you bring me out of the womb? ^v
  I wish I had died before any eye saw me. ^w
¹⁹ If only I had never come into being,
  or had been carried straight from the womb to the grave! ^x
²⁰ Are not my few days ^y almost over? ^z
  Turn away from me ^a so I can have a moment's joy ^b
²¹ before I go to the place of no return, ^c
  to the land of gloom and utter darkness, ^d
²² to the land of deepest night,
  of utter darkness ^e and disorder,
  where even the light is like darkness." ^f

ZOPHAR

11 Then Zophar the Naamathite ^g replied:

² "Are all these words to go unanswered? ^h
  Is this talker to be vindicated? ⁱ
³ Will your idle talk ^j reduce others to silence?
  Will no one rebuke you when you mock? ^k
⁴ You say to God, 'My beliefs are flawless ^l
  and I am pure ^m in your sight.'
⁵ Oh, how I wish that God would speak, ⁿ
  that he would open his lips against you
⁶ and disclose to you the secrets of wisdom, ^o
  for true wisdom has two sides.
  Know this: God has even forgotten some of your sin. ^p

⁷ "Can you fathom ^q the mysteries of God?
  Can you probe the limits of the Almighty?
⁸ They are higher ^r than the heavens ^s above—what can you do?
  They are deeper than the depths below ^t—what can you know? ^u
⁹ Their measure ^v is longer than the earth
  and wider than the sea. ^w

¹⁰ "If he comes along and confines you in prison
  and convenes a court, who can oppose him? ^x
¹¹ Surely he recognizes deceivers;
  and when he sees evil, does he not take note? ^y
¹² But the witless can no more become wise
  than a wild donkey's colt ^z can be born a human being. ^{a a}

^a 12 Or *wild donkey can be born tame*

10:16 ^q S 1Sa 17:34;
Ps 7:2; Isa 38:13;
Jer 5:6; 25:38;
La 3:10; ^r Job 5:9;
Isa 28:21; 29:14; 65:7
10:17 ^s 1Ki 21:10;
Job 16:8 ^t Ru 1:21
^u S Job 5:7
10:18 ^v S Job 3:8;
S Ps 22:9 ^w Job 3:26;
Ecc 4:2; 7:1
10:19 ^x S Job 3:3;
Jer 15:10
10:20 ^y Job 14:1;
Ecc 6:12 ^z S Job 7:7
^a S Job 7:16
^b S Job 9:25
10:21 ^c S 2Sa 12:23;
S Job 3:13; 16:22;
Ps 39:13; Ecc 12:5
^d S Job 3:5
10:22 ^e S Job 3:5
^f S 1Sa 2:9; S Job 3:13
11:1 ^g S Job 2:11
11:2 ^h S Job 8:2;
S 16:3 ⁱ S Ge 41:6;
S Job 6:29
11:3 ^j Eph 4:29; 5:4
^k Job 12:4; 16:10; 17:2;
21:3; 30:1; Ps 1:1
11:4 ^l Job 9:21
^m S Job 10:7
11:5 ⁿ Ex 20:19;
Job 23:5; 32:13; 38:1
11:6 ^o S Job 9:4;
1Co 2:10 ^p S Ezr 9:13;
S Job 15:5
11:7 ^q S Job 5:9;
Ecc 3:11
11:8 ^r Eph 3:18
^s S Ge 15:5; Job 22:12;
25:2; Ps 57:10;
Isa 55:9 ^t S Job 7:9
^u Job 15:13, 25; 33:13;
40:2; Ps 139:8
11:9 ^v Eph 3:19-20
^w Job 22:12; 35:5;
36:26; 37:5, 23;
Isa 40:26
11:10 ^x S Job 9:12;
Rev 3:7
11:11 ^y S Job 10:4;
31:37; 34:11, 25; 36:7;
Ps 10:14
11:12 ^z S Ge 16:12
^a S 2Ch 6:36

10:17 *witnesses against me.* See note on 9:3.
10:18–22 See notes on ch. 3.

10:21 *place of no return.* See note on 7:9. *land of gloom and utter darkness.* See 38:17. Ancient Mesopotamian documents refer to the netherworld as the "house of darkness" (see note on Ecc 12:5).

11:1–20 Like Eliphaz (see 4:7–11) and Bildad (see 8:3–6), Zophar claims that Job's sins have caused his troubles.

11:2–3 Zophar's failure to put himself in Job's place before condemning him shows a lack of compassion. Job has sincerely challenged what he perceives to be God's unjust actions (see 9:14–24), but he has not mocked God, as Zophar accuses him of having done.

11:4 *I am pure.* In 10:7,15 Job had disclaimed being guilty, and in 9:21 he said he was "blameless," the word God used to describe him in 1:8; 2:3. Zophar, however, implies that Job was claiming purity, but Job nowhere makes such a claim.

11:5 Zophar thought God should speak against Job, but eventually God spoke against Zophar himself (see 42:7–9 and notes).

11:6 *true wisdom has two sides.* OT wisdom literature (especially Proverbs) makes abundant use of the term *mashal* ("proverb," "riddle," "parable"), which often had a hidden as well as an obvious meaning. Zophar thinks Job is shallow and lacks an understanding of the true nature of God (see vv. 7–9).

11:7 Unwittingly, Zophar anticipates the Lord's discourses in 38:1—42:6.

11:8–9 In the same way that Zophar speaks of the height, depth, length and width of God's knowledge, Paul speaks of Christ's love (see Eph 3:18).

11:8 *what can you do?* Can you climb into the heavens and explore God's knowledge?

11:11–12 *deceivers … the witless.* Zophar claims that it would take a miracle to change Job.

11:12 The TNIV text note contrasts two related but utterly dif-

11:13 *b* 1Sa 7:3;
Ps 78:8 *c* S Ex 9:29
d S Job 5:8,27
11:14 *e* S Jos 24:14
f Ps 101:4 *g* Job 22:23
11:15 *h* Job 22:26
i 1Sa 2:9; Ps 20:8;
37:23; 40:2; 119:5;
Eph 6:14 *j* S Ge 4:7;
S Ps 3:6
11:16 *k* Isa 26:16;
37:3; 65:16 *l* Jos 7:5;
Job 22:11; Ps 58:7;
112:10; Eze 21:7
11:17 *m* Job 22:28;
Ps 37:6; Isa 58:8,10;
62:1 *n* Job 17:12; 18:6;
29:3; Ps 18:28; 112:4;
119:105; Isa 5:20;
Jn 8:12
11:18 *o* Ps 3:5; 4:8;
127:2; Ecc 5:12
p S Lev 26:6; Pr 3:24;
Isa 11:10; 14:3; 28:12;
30:15; 32:18; Zec 3:10
11:19 *q* S Lev 26:6
r Isa 45:14
11:20 *s* Dt 28:65;
Job 17:5 *t* Job 12:10;
18:18; 27:22; 34:22;
36:6; Ps 139:11-12;
Jer 11:11; 23:24; 25:35;
Am 2:14; 9:2-3
u S Job 8:13
12:2 *v* Job 15:8;
17:10
12:3 *w* Job 13:2; 15:9
12:4 *x* S Ge 38:23
y S Job 6:14; S 11:3;
S 16:10; S 19:14
z Ps 91:15 *a* S Ge 6:9;
S Job 6:29; S 15:16
12:5 *b* Ps 123:4
c Ps 17:5; 37:31; 38:16;
66:9; 73:2; 94:18
12:6 *d* S Job 5:24
e S Job 9:24
12:7 *f* Job 35:11 fn
g Mt 6:26 *h* Job 18:3;
Ro 1:20
12:9 *i* Isa 1:3
j S Job 9:24
12:10 *k* Da 5:23
l S Ge 2:7;
S Nu 16:22;
S Job 11:20; Ac 17:28

13 "Yet if you devote your heart *b* to him
    and stretch out your hands *c* to him, *d*
14 if you put away *e* the sin that is in your hand
    and allow no evil *f* to dwell in your tent, *g*
15 then, free of fault, you will lift up your face; *h*
    you will stand firm *i* and without fear. *j*
16 You will surely forget your trouble, *k*
    recalling it only as waters gone by. *l*
17 Life will be brighter than noonday, *m*
    and darkness will become like morning. *n*
18 You will be secure, because there is hope;
    you will look about you and take your rest *o* in safety. *p*
19 You will lie down, with no one to make you afraid, *q*
    and many will court your favor. *r*
20 But the eyes of the wicked will fail, *s*
    and escape will elude them; *t*
    their hope will become a dying gasp." *u*

JOB

12

Then Job replied:

2 "Doubtless you are the people,
    and wisdom will die with you! *v*
3 But I have a mind as well as you;
    I am not inferior to you.
    Who does not know all these things? *w*

4 "I have become a laughingstock *x* to my friends, *y*
    though I called on God and he answered *z*—
    a mere laughingstock, though righteous and blameless! *a*
5 Those who are at ease have contempt *b* for misfortune
    as the fate of those whose feet are slipping. *c*
6 The tents of marauders are undisturbed, *d*
    and those who provoke God are secure *e*—
    those God has in his hand. *a*

7 "But ask the animals, and they will teach you, *f*
    or the birds in the sky, *g* and they will tell you; *h*
8 or speak to the earth, and it will teach you,
    or let the fish in the sea inform you.
9 Which of all these does not know
    that the hand of the LORD has done this? *i*
10 In his hand is the life *k* of every creature
    and the breath of every human being. *l*
11 Does not the ear test words

---

a 6 Or *those whose god is in their own hand*

---

ferent Biblical animals—the wild donkey and the domestic donkey. Then the point would be that a witless man can no more become wise than a wild donkey can be born as a domestic one.

A C **11:13–20** Zophar assumes that Job's problems are rooted in his sin; all Job has to do is to repent, and then his life will become blessed and happy. But God nowhere guarantees a life "brighter than noonday" (v. 17) simply because we are his children. He has higher purposes for us than our physical prosperity, or people courting our favor (v. 19). Zophar's philosophy is in conflict with Ps 73.
11:13 *stretch out your hands to him.* To pray for help (see Ex 9:29; 17:11 and notes; Ps 28:2; 44:20; 77:2; 88:9; 141:2; 143:6; Isa 1:15; 1Ti 2:8).
11:15 *free of fault, you will lift up your face.* Zophar echoes Job's thought in 10:15.
11:20 Bildad ended his speech in a similar way (see 8:22).
12:1—14:22 As before, Job's reply is divided into two parts:

He speaks to his three friends (12:2—13:19), then to God (13:20—14:22).
12:2 For the first time, Job reacts with sarcasm to the harshness of his counselors (see v. 20).
12:3 *Who does not know …?* See v. 9. The advice of Job's friends is trivial and commonplace.
12:4 *God … answered.* In the days before his suffering began (contrast 9:16).
12:5 The prosperous despise those who, like Job, have trouble.
12:6 Such statements (see 9:21–24) irked the counselors and made them brand Job as a man whose feet were slipping (see v. 5).
12:7–12 Job appeals to all creation to testify that God does what he pleases.
12:9 *LORD.* The only place in Job's and his friends' speeches (chs. 3–37) where the divine name "LORD" (Hebrew *Yahweh*) is used (see Introduction: Author).
12:11 Echoed by Elihu in 34:3. Cf. 6:6, where Job says that Eliphaz's words are like "tasteless food."

as the tongue tastes food? *m*

¹² Is not wisdom found among the aged? *n*
   Does not long life bring understanding? *o*

¹³ "To God belong wisdom *p* and power; *q*
   counsel and understanding are his. *r*
¹⁴ What he tears down *s* cannot be rebuilt; *t*
   those he imprisons cannot be released. *u*
¹⁵ If he holds back the waters, *v* there is drought; *w*
   if he lets them loose, they devastate the land. *x*
¹⁶ To him belong strength and insight; *y*
   both deceived and deceiver are his. *z*
¹⁷ He leads rulers away stripped *a*
   and makes fools of judges. *b*
¹⁸ He takes off the shackles *c* put on by kings
   and ties a loincloth *a* around their waist. *d*
¹⁹ He leads priests away stripped *e*
   and overthrows officials long established. *f*
²⁰ He silences the lips of trusted advisers
   and takes away the discernment of elders. *g*
²¹ He pours contempt on nobles *h*
   and disarms the mighty. *i*
²² He reveals the deep things of darkness *j*
   and brings utter darkness *k* into the light. *l*
²³ He makes nations great, and destroys them; *m*
   he enlarges nations, *n* and disperses them. *o*
²⁴ He deprives the leaders of the earth of their reason; *p*
   he makes them wander in a trackless waste. *q*
²⁵ They grope in darkness with no light; *r*
   he makes them stagger like drunkards. *s*

13 "My eyes have seen all this, *t*
   my ears have heard and understood it.
² What you know, I also know;
   I am not inferior to you. *u*
³ But I desire to speak to the Almighty *v*
   and to argue my case with God. *w*
⁴ You, however, smear me with lies; *x*
   you are worthless physicians, *y* all of you! *z*
⁵ If only you would be altogether silent! *a*
   For you, that would be wisdom. *b*
⁶ Hear now my argument;
   listen to the pleas of my lips. *c*
⁷ Will you speak wickedly on God's behalf?
   Will you speak deceitfully for him? *d*
⁸ Will you show him partiality? *a*
   Will you argue the case for God?
⁹ Would it turn out well if he examined you? *f*
   Could you deceive him as you might deceive mortals? *g*

---

a 18 Or *shackles of kings / and ties a belt*

12:11 *m* Job 34:3
12:12 *n* S 1Ki 4:2;
Job 15:10 *o* ver 20;
Job 17:4; 32:7,9;
34:4,10
12:13 *p* Pr 21:30;
Isa 45:9 *q* S Job 9:4;
S Jer 32:19; 1Co 1:24
r S Nu 23:19; 1Ki 3:12;
Job 32:8; 38:36; Pr 2:6;
Isa 40:13-14; Da 1:17
12:14 *s* Job 16:9;
19:10 *t* Dt 13:16;
Ps 127:1; Isa 24:20;
25:2; Eze 26:14
u S Job 9:3; Isa 22:22;
Rev 3:7
12:15 *v* Job 28:25;
Isa 40:12
w S Dt 28:22;
S 1Ki 17:1 *x* S Ge 7:24
12:16 *y* S Job 9:4
z 2Ch 18:22; Job 13:7,
9; 27:4; Ro 2:11
12:17 *a* ver 19;
Job 19:9; Isa 20:4
b S Job 3:14; 1Co 1:20
12:18 *c* Ps 107:14;
116:16; Na 1:13
d ver 21; Job 34:18;
Ps 107:40; Isa 5:27;
40:23
12:19 *e* S ver 17
f S Dt 24:15;
S Job 9:24; 14:20;
22:8; 24:12,22; 34:20,
28; 35:9; Isa 2:22;
31:8; 40:17,23;
Jer 25:18; Da 2:21,34;
Lk 1:52
12:20 *g* S ver 12,24;
Da 4:33-34
12:21 *h* S ver 18;
S Isa 34:12
i S Job 3:15
12:22 *j* 1Co 4:5
k Job 3:5 *l* Ps 139:12;
Da 2:22
12:23 *m* Ps 2:1;
46:6; Isa 13:4;
Jer 25:9 *n* S Ex 34:24;
Ps 107:38; Isa 9:3;
26:15; 54:3
o S Job 5:12; Ac 17:26
12:24 *p* S ver 20
q Ps 107:40
12:25 *r* S Dt 28:29;
Job 18:6; 21:17; 29:3
s Ps 107:27; Isa 24:20
13:1 *t* S Job 9:24
13:2 *u* S Job 12:3
13:3 *v* Job 5:17; 40:2
w S Job 5:8; 9:14-20;
S 10:2
13:4 *x* Ps 119:69;
Isa 9:15; Jer 23:32
y Jer 8:22 *z* S Job 6:15
13:5 *a* ver 13;
S Jdg 18:19 *b* Pr 17:28
13:6 *c* Job 33:1; 36:4
13:7 *d* S Job 12:16;
S 16:2
13:8 *e* S Lev 19:15
13:9 *f* S Job 9:3
g S Job 12:16; Gal 6:7

12:12 Job sarcastically chides his counselors for being elders and yet lacking in true wisdom.
12:13–25 The theme of this section is stated in v. 13: God is sovereign in the created world, and especially in history. The rest of the poem dwells on the negative aspects of God's power and wisdom—e.g., the destructive forces of nature (vv. 14–15), how judges become fools (v. 17), how priests become humiliated (v. 19), how trusted advisers are silenced and elders deprived of good sense (v. 20). Contrast the claim of Eliphaz that God always uses his power in ways that make sense (5:10–16).
12:20 See note on v. 2.
12:21a,24b The Hebrew text of these lines is repeated verbatim in Ps 107:40 (see note there).

12:22 God knows even secret, evil plans.
12:25 *grope in darkness.* Job concludes this section with a parody of Eliphaz's confident assertion in 5:14.
13:1–12 Job feels that his counselors have become completely untrustworthy (see v. 12). He calls them quacks (see v. 4; see also 16:2 and note) and accuses them of showing partiality to God through their false accusations (see vv. 7–8). Someday God will examine them and punish them (see vv. 9–11).
13:1 *all this.* God's sovereign actions as described in ch. 12.
13:2 See 15:9. *I am not inferior to you.* See 12:3 and note.
13:5 See v. 13. The friends' earlier silence may have ministered to Job (see 2:13 and note); his current retort is intended as sarcasm (cf. Pr 17:28).

13:10 ʰ S Lev 19:15;
S 2Ch 19:7
13:11 ʲ Job 31:23
ʲ S Ex 3:6
13:12 ᵏ S Ne 4:2-3
13:13 ˡ S ver 5
ᵐ S Job 7:11
ⁿ S Job 9:21
13:14 ᵒ S Jdg 9:17
13:15 ᵖ S Job 7:6
ᵠ Ps 23:4; 27:1;
Pr 14:32; Isa 12:2;
Da 3:28 ʳ S Job 5:8;
27:5
13:16 ˢ Ps 30:5;
Isa 12:1; 54:7-8;
Hos 14:4; Php 1:19
ᵗ S Job 8:13 ᵘ S Ge 3:8
13:17 ᵛ Job 21:2
13:18 ʷ S ver 3;
Job 23:4; 37:19
ˣ S Job 2:3; S 9:21
13:19 ʸ Job 40:4;
Isa 50:8; Ro 8:33
ᶻ S Job 9:15
ᵃ S Job 3:13; 10:8
13:21 ᵇ S Ex 9:3;
Heb 10:31 ᶜ S Job 6:4
13:22 ᵈ Job 9:35;
14:15 ᵉ S Job 9:16
13:23 ᶠ S 1Sa 26:18
ᵍ Job 7:21; 9:21; 14:17;
33:9
13:24 ʰ S Dt 32:20
ⁱ Job 16:9; 19:11;
33:10; Ps 88:14-15;
Jer 30:14; La 2:5
13:25 ⁱ Job 19:2
ᵏ Lev 26:36
ˡ Job 19:22,28
ᵐ Job 21:18; Ps 1:4;
35:5; 83:13; Isa 17:13;
42:3; 43:17; Hos 13:3
13:26 ⁿ Job 18:7;
20:11; 21:23; Ps 25:7
13:27 ᵒ S Ge 40:15;
Job 33:11; Jer 20:2;
Ac 16:24 ᵖ Job 10:14
13:28 ᵠ Ps 102:26;
Mk 2:21 ʳ S Dt 28:35;
Ps 39:11; Isa 50:9;
51:8; Hos 5:12; Jas 5:2
14:1 ˢ Job 15:14;
Mt 11:11 ᵗ S Job 10:20
ᵘ S Ge 3:17; S Job 7:2
14:2 ᵛ Ps 103:15;
S Jas 1:10 ʷ Ps 37:2;
90:5-6; Isa 40:6-8

10 He would surely call you to account
    if you secretly showed partiality. ʰ
11 Would not his splendor ⁱ terrify you?
    Would not the dread of him fall on you? ʲ
12 Your maxims are proverbs of ashes;
    your defenses are defenses of clay. ᵏ

13 "Keep silent ˡ and let me speak; ᵐ
    then let come to me what may. ⁿ
14 Why do I put myself in jeopardy
    and take my life in my hands? ᵒ
15 Though he slay me, yet will I hope ᵖ in him; ᵠ
    I will surely ᵃ defend my ways to his face. ʳ
16 Indeed, this will turn out for my deliverance, ˢ
    for no godless ᵗ person would dare come before him! ᵘ
17 Listen carefully to what I say; ᵛ
    let my words ring in your ears.
18 Now that I have prepared my case, ʷ
    I know I will be vindicated. ˣ
19 Can anyone bring charges against me? ʸ
    If so, I will be silent ᶻ and die. ᵃ

20 "Only grant me these two things, God,
    and then I will not hide from you:
21 Withdraw your hand ᵇ far from me,
    and stop frightening me with your terrors. ᶜ
22 Then summon me and I will answer, ᵈ
    or let me speak, and you reply to me. ᵉ
23 How many wrongs and sins have I committed? ᶠ
    Show me my offense and my sin. ᵍ
24 Why do you hide your face ʰ
    and consider me your enemy? ⁱ
25 Will you torment ʲ a windblown leaf? ᵏ
    Will you chase ˡ after dry chaff? ᵐ
26 For you write down bitter things against me
    and make me reap the sins of my youth. ⁿ
27 You fasten my feet in shackles; ᵒ
    you keep close watch on all my paths ᵖ
    by putting marks on the soles of my feet.

28 "So humans waste away like something rotten,
    like a garment ᵠ eaten by moths. ʳ

14 "Mortals, born of woman, ˢ
    are of few days ᵗ and full of trouble. ᵘ
2 They spring up like flowers ᵛ and wither away; ʷ

ᵃ 15 Or *He will surely slay me; I have no hope — / yet I will*

13:12 *defenses.* Arguments in their defense of God's judgment.

A **13:15** See TNIV text note. Both readings state that no matter what happens, Job intends to seek vindication from God and believes that he will receive it (see v. 18).

A **13:16** *turn out for my deliverance.* See Php 1:19 (perhaps Paul was reflecting on Job's experience).

13:17 Job asks his friends to listen to what he is going to say to God in 13:20—14:22.

13:20 *two things.* Job wants God to (1) withdraw his hand of punishment (v. 21), and (2) to start communicating with him (v. 22).

13:21 See 9:34.

A **13:23** Job's words are based on the counselors' point that suffering always implies sinfulness. He does not yet understand that God has a higher purpose in his suffering. *wrongs . . . sins . . . offense.* The three most important Hebrew terms for sin lie behind these translations (see Ex 34:7; see also notes on Ps 32:5; 51:1–2; Isa 59:12).

13:24 *hide your face.* Withhold your blessing (see note on Ps 13:1).
13:25 *windblown leaf . . . dry chaff.* See note on Ps 1:4.
13:26 *write down . . . things against me.* See Ps 130:3; Hos 13:12; contrast 1Co 13:5. *sins of my youth.* Since Job feels that he is not presently guilty of a sinful life, God must still be holding the sins of his youth against him.

B **13:27** *You fasten . . . my paths.* Elihu later quotes Job's words (see 33:11). *marks on the soles of my feet.* The Babylonian Code of Hammurapi (see chart, p. xxiii) attests to the practice of putting marks on slaves. Job feels that he is being harassed by a God who has taken him captive and is tormenting him (see v. 25).

13:28—14:1 The introduction to ch. 14, expressing the pessimistic theme that the legacy of human beings is trouble and their destiny is death.

13:28 *garment eaten by moths.* See Mt 6:19–20 and notes; Lk 12:33.

14:1 See 5:7 and note.

14:2–6 A symmetrical poem centered around v. 4 (v. 2 correlike fleeting shadows, ˣ they do not endure. ʸ

³ Do you fix your eye on such as these? ᶻ
  Will you bring them ᵃ before you for judgment? ᵃ
⁴ Who can bring what is pure ᵇ from the impure? ᶜ
  No one! ᵈ
⁵ The days of mortals are determined; ᵉ
  you have decreed the number of their months ᶠ
  and have set limits they cannot exceed. ᵍ
⁶ So look away from us and leave us alone, ʰ
  till we have put in our time like hired laborers. ⁱ

⁷ "At least there is hope for a tree: ʲ
  If it is cut down, it will sprout again,
  and its new shoots ᵏ will not fail. ˡ
⁸ Its roots may grow old in the ground
  and its stump ᵐ die in the soil,
⁹ yet at the scent of water ⁿ it will bud
  and put forth shoots like a plant. ᵒ
¹⁰ But human beings die and are laid low; ᵖ
  they breathe their last and are no more. �q
¹¹ As the water of a lake dries up
  or a riverbed becomes parched and dry, ʳ
¹² so they lie down and do not rise; ˢ
  till the heavens are no more, ᵗ they will not awake
  or be roused from their sleep. ᵘ

¹³ "If only you would hide me in the grave ᵛ
  and conceal me till your anger has passed! ʷ
  If only you would set me a time
  and then remember ˣ me! ʸ
¹⁴ If someone dies, will they live again?
  All the days of my hard service ᶻ
  I will wait for my renewal ᵇ ᵃ to come.
¹⁵ You will call and I will answer you; ᵇ
  you will long for the creature your hands have made. ᶜ
¹⁶ Surely then you will count my steps ᵈ
  but not keep track of my sin. ᵉ
¹⁷ My offenses will be sealed ᶠ up in a bag; ᵍ
  you will cover over my sin. ʰ

¹⁸ "But as a mountain erodes and crumbles ⁱ
  and as a rock is moved from its place, ʲ
¹⁹ as water wears away stones
  and torrents ᵏ wash away the soil, ˡ
  so you destroy everyone's hope. ᵐ
²⁰ You overpower them once for all, and they are gone; ⁿ
  you change their countenance and send them away. ᵒ
²¹ If their children are honored, they do not know it;
  if their offspring are brought low, they do not see it. ᵖ
²² They feel but the pain of their own bodies q
  and mourn only for themselves. ʳ "

ᵃ 3 Septuagint, Vulgate and Syriac; Hebrew *me*   ᵇ 14 Or *release*

14:2 ˣ Job 8:9;
Ps 39:4; 102:11;
109:23; 144:4;
Ecc 6:12 ʸ S Job 4:20;
Ps 49:12
14:3 ᶻ Ps 8:4; 144:3
ᵃ S Job 7:18
14:4 ᵇ Ps 51:10
ᶜ S Job 4:17; Eph 2:1-
3 ᵈ S Job 9:30; Jn 3:6;
Ro 5:12; 7:14
14:5 ᵉ Job 24:1;
Ps 31:15; 139:16
ᶠ Job 21:21; Ps 39:4;
90:12 ᵍ Ac 17:26
14:6 ʰ S Job 7:19
ⁱ Job 7:1,2; Ps 39:13;
Isa 16:14; 21:16
14:7 ʲ Job 19:10;
24:20; Ps 52:5
ᵏ Isa 11:1; 53:2; 60:21
ˡ Isa 6:13
14:8 ᵐ Isa 6:13; 11:1;
53:2
14:9 ⁿ Job 29:19;
Ps 1:3; Jer 17:8;
Eze 31:7 ᵒ Lev 26:4;
Eze 34:27; Zec 10:1
14:10 ᵖ ver 12
q S Job 10:21; 13:19
14:11 ʳ S 2Sa 14:14
14:12 ˢ ver 10
ᵗ Ps 102:26; Rev 20:11;
21:1 ᵘ Ac 3:21
14:13 ᵛ S Job 7:9
ʷ Ps 30:5; Isa 26:20;
54:7 ˣ S Ge 8:1
ʸ Job 6:8
14:14 ᶻ S Job 7:1
ᵃ S 2Ki 6:33
14:15 ᵇ S Job 13:22
ᶜ S Job 10:3
14:16 ᵈ S Job 10:4;
Ps 139:1-3; Pr 5:21;
Jer 16:17; 32:19
ᵉ Job 10:6; 1Co 13:5
14:17 ᶠ Jer 32:10
ᵍ S Dt 32:34
ʰ S Job 9:30; S 13:23
14:18 ⁱ Eze 38:20
ʲ Job 18:4
14:19 ᵏ Eze 13:13
ˡ S Ge 7:23
ᵐ S Job 7:6
14:20 ⁿ S Job 4:20
ᵒ S Job 7:10; 8:18;
S 12:19; 27:19;
Jas 1:10
14:21 ᵖ Job 21:21;
Ecc 9:5; Isa 63:16
14:22 q Ps 38:7;
Isa 21:3; Jer 4:19
ʳ Job 21:21

---

sponds to v. 5, and v. 3 to v. 6). Job complains to God: Given the insignificance of humans and their inherent impurity, why do you take them so seriously (see 13:25)?

14:2 *They . . . wither away.* Life at best is brief and fragile (see 8:9; Ps 37:2; Isa 40:7,24; cf. Jas 1:10). *like fleeting shadows.* See note on 8:9.

14:7-12 People are like a flower that lives its short life and is gone (v. 2), not like a tree that revives even after it has been cut down.

14:7 *sprout.* The Hebrew root underlying this word is translated "renewal" in v. 14.

14:13-17 Job's spirit now appears to rise above the despair engendered by his rotting body. Although resurrection in the fullest sense is not taught here, Job is saying that if God so desires he is able to hide Job in the grave, then raise him back to life at a time when the divine anger is past.

14:14 *hard service.* See note on 7:1.

14:18-22 Job's pessimism arises not from skepticism about the possibility of resurrection from the dead but rather from God's apparent unwillingness to do something immediately for a person like him, whose life has become a nightmare of pain and mourning.

15:1 ᵍ S Job 4:1
15:2 ᵗ S Ge 41:6
15:3 ᵘ S Ne 4:2-3; S Job 6:26
15:4 ᵛ Job 25:6
15:5 ʷ Job 11:6; 22:5 ˣ Pr 16:23 ʸ S Job 5:13
15:6 ᶻ S Job 9:15; 18:7; Ps 10:2; S Mt 12:37; Lk 19:22
15:7 ᵃ Job 38:21 ᵇ S 1Sa 2:8; Ps 90:2; Pr 8:25
15:8 ᶜ Job 29:4; Isa 9:6; 40:13; 41:28; Jer 23:18; Ro 11:34; 1Co 2:11 ᵈ S Job 12:2
15:9 ᵉ S Job 12:3
15:10 ᶠ S Job 12:12 ᵍ S 2Ch 10:6
15:11 ʰ S Ge 37:35; S Job 6:10; 2Co 1:3-4 ⁱ Zec 1:13 ʲ S Dt 8:3; S 32:39; S Job 5:17; 22:22; 23:12; 36:16; Ps 119:11,72; Jer 15:16
15:12 ᵏ Job 11:13; 36:13
15:13 ˡ Pr 29:11; Da 11:30 ᵐ Ps 94:4 ⁿ S Job 11:8; 22:5; 32:3
15:14 ᵒ S Job 14:1 ᵖ S 2Ch 6:36; S Job 4:17
15:15 �q S Job 5:1 ʳ Job 4:18
15:16 ˢ S Lev 5:2; S Job 4:19; Ps 14:1 ᵗ Job 20:12 ᵘ Job 12:4; 34:7; Pr 19:28
15:17 ᵛ S Job 4:8
15:18 ʷ S Dt 32:7
15:19 ˣ Ge 12:1; Job 22:8
15:20 ʸ ver 24; Isa 8:22; 50:11; 66:24 ᶻ Job 24:1; 27:13-23; Isa 2:12; Jer 46:10; Ob 1:15; Zep 1:7

ELIPHAZ

15

Then Eliphaz the Temanite ˢ replied:

2 "Would the wise answer with empty notions
  or fill their bellies with the hot east wind? ᵗ
3 Would they argue with useless words,
  with speeches that have no value? ᵘ
4 But you even undermine piety
  and hinder devotion to God. ᵛ
5 Your sin ʷ prompts your mouth; ˣ
  you adopt the tongue of the crafty. ʸ
6 Your own mouth condemns you, not mine;
  your own lips testify against you. ᶻ

7 "Are you the first man ever born? ᵃ
  Were you brought forth before the hills? ᵇ
8 Do you listen in on God's council? ᶜ
  Do you have a monopoly on wisdom? ᵈ
9 What do you know that we do not know?
  What insights do you have that we do not have? ᵉ
10 The gray-haired and the aged ᶠ are on our side,
  men even older than your father. ᵍ
11 Are God's consolations ʰ not enough for you,
  words ⁱ spoken gently to you? ʲ
12 Why has your heart ᵏ carried you away,
  and why do your eyes flash,
13 so that you vent your rage ˡ against God
  and pour out such words ᵐ from your mouth? ⁿ

14 "What are mortals, that they could be pure,
  or those born of woman, ᵒ that they could be righteous? ᵖ
15 If God places no trust in his holy ones, q
  if even the heavens are not pure in his eyes, ʳ
16 how much less mortals, who are vile and corrupt, ˢ
  who drink up evil ᵗ like water! ᵘ

17 "Listen to me and I will explain to you;
  let me tell you what I have seen, ᵛ
18 what the wise have declared,
  hiding nothing received from their ancestors ʷ
19 (to whom alone the land ˣ was given
  when no foreigners moved among them):
20 All their days the wicked suffer torment, ʸ
  the ruthless through all the years stored up for them. ᶻ

15:1–6 Up to this point Eliphaz has been the most sympathetic of the three counselors, but now he has run out of patience with Job and denounces him more severely than before.

15:2 *empty.* The Hebrew for this word is translated "long-winded" in 16:3, where Job hurls Eliphaz's charges back at him. *hot east wind.* The sirocco that blows in from the desert (see 27:21; 38:24; see also notes on Ge 41:6; Jer 4:11).

15:4 *piety.* See note on 4:6.

15:5 See Mt 15:11,17–18.

15:6 *mouth condemns you.* See 9:20.

15:7–10 Job, says Eliphaz, presumes to be wise enough to sit among the members of God's council in heaven (see note on 1:6), when in reality he is no wiser than ordinary elders and sages on earth.

15:10 In ancient times, wisdom was associated with advanced age (cf. 32:6–9).

15:11–13 Eliphaz chides Job for replying in rage to his friends' attempts to console him with gentle words, which Eliphaz believes come from God himself (v. 11). But Eliphaz has been guilty of cruel insinuation (ch. 5), and the other two counselors have been even more malicious. Genuine words of comfort for Job have been few indeed (see 4:2–6).

15:14–16 See 25:4–6. Eliphaz repeats what he had already said in 4:17–19, perhaps because he thought the earlier words had come to him through divine revelation (see note on 4:12–21).

15:14 *born of woman.* An echo of Job's words in 14:1.

15:15 *holy ones.* Angels (see note on 5:1).

15:16 *drink up evil like water.* See Elihu's description of Job in 34:7.

15:17–26 Eliphaz now bolsters his earlier advice with traditional wisdom: The wicked can never escape the suffering they deserve.

15:19 *no foreigners moved among them.* Corrupting the community's traditions.

15:20–35 A poem on the fate of the wicked (see 8:11–19). Eliphaz continues with a variety of figures: belligerent sinners who attack God (vv. 24–26); fat, rich wicked people who finally get what they deserve (vv. 27–32); grapevines stripped before the fruit is ripe (v. 33a); olive trees shedding their blossoms (v. 33b). As long as Eliphaz rejects Job's insistence that the wicked go on prospering, he does not have to wrestle with the disturbing corollary: the mystery of why the innocent sometimes suffer.

²¹ Terrifying sounds fill their ears;^a
　　when all seems well, marauders attack them.^b
²² They despair of escaping the realm of darkness;^c
　　they are marked for the sword.^d
²³ They wander about^e for food like vultures;^f
　　they know the day of darkness^g is at hand.^h
²⁴ Distress and anguishⁱ fill them with terror;^j
　　troubles overwhelm them, like a king^k poised to attack,
²⁵ because they shake their fists^l at God
　　and vaunt themselves against the Almighty,^m
²⁶ defiantly charging against him
　　with thick, strong shields.ⁿ

²⁷ "Though their faces are covered with fat
　　and their waists bulge with flesh,^o
²⁸ they will inhabit ruined towns
　　and houses where no one lives,^p
　　houses crumbling to rubble.^q
²⁹ They will no longer be rich and their wealth will not endure,^r
　　nor will their possessions spread over the land.^s
³⁰ They will not escape the darkness;^t
　　a flame^u will wither their shoots,^v
　　and the breath of God's mouth^w will carry them away.^x
³¹ Let them not deceive^y themselves by trusting what is worthless,^z
　　for they will get nothing in return.^a
³² Before their time^b they will wither,^c
　　and their branches will not flourish.^d
³³ They will be like a vine stripped of its unripe grapes,^e
　　like an olive tree shedding its blossoms.^f
³⁴ For the company of the godless^g will be barren,
　　and fire will consume^h the tents of those who love bribes.ⁱ
³⁵ They conceive trouble^j and give birth to evil;^k
　　their womb fashions deceit."

JOB
16

Then Job replied:

² "I have heard many things like these;
　　you are miserable comforters,^l all of you!^m
³ Will your long-winded speeches never end?ⁿ
　　What ails you that you keep on arguing?^o
⁴ I also could speak like you,
　　if you were in my place;
　I could make fine speeches against you
　　and shake my head^p at you.
⁵ But my mouth would encourage you;
　　comfort^q from my lips would bring you relief.^r

⁶ "Yet if I speak, my pain is not relieved;
　　and if I refrain, it does not go away.^s
⁷ Surely, God, you have worn me out;^t
　　you have devastated my entire household.^u
⁸ You have shriveled me up—and it has become a witness;
　　my gauntness^v rises up and testifies against me.^w
⁹ God assails me and tears^x me in his anger^y

16:9 ^x S Job 12:14; Hos 6:1 ^y S Job 9:5; 18:4; 19:11

15:21 ^a ver 24;
S 1Sa 3:11; Job 18:11;
20:25; Jer 6:25; 20:3
^b Job 22:10; 27:20;
Isa 13:3; Jer 51:25,53,
56; 1Th 5:3
15:22 ^c ver 23;
S Job 5:14; 24:17;
38:15; Ps 91:5; SS 3:8
^d Job 16:13; 18:19;
19:29; 20:24; 27:14;
33:18; 36:12; Pr 7:23;
Isa 1:20; Jer 44:27;
Hos 9:13; Am 5:19
15:23 ^e Ps 109:10
^f Pr 30:17; Eze 39:17;
Mt 24:28; Lk 17:37
^g S ver 22 ^h Job 18:12
15:24 ⁱ Isa 8:22; 9:1
^j ver 20 ^k Job 18:14
15:25 ^l Ps 44:16;
Isa 10:32; 37:23
^m S Job 11:8; 35:12;
36:9; 40:8; Ps 2:2-3;
73:9; 75:5; Pr 21:30;
Isa 3:16; 45:9
15:26 ⁿ Jer 44:16
15:27 ^o S Jdg 3:17
15:28 ^p Isa 5:9
^q S Job 3:14
15:29 ^r S Job 3:15;
S 7:8 ^s Isa 5:8
15:30 ^t S Job 5:14
^u ver 34; Job 16:7;
20:26; 22:20; 31:12
^v ver 32; Job 8:19;
18:16; 29:19; Hos 9:1-
16; Mal 4:1
^w S Ex 15:10
^x Isa 40:23-24
15:31 ^y Job 31:5;
Pr 1:16; 6:18;
Isa 44:20; 59:7;
Mic 2:11; S Mk 13:5;
Jas 1:16 ^z Isa 30:12;
47:10; 59:4; Jer 7:4,8;
S Mt 6:19 ^a Job 20:7;
22:13; 27:9; 35:13;
Pr 15:29; Isa 1:15;
Jer 11:11; Mic 3:4
15:32 ^b Ecc 7:17
^c Job 22:16; 36:14;
Ps 55:23; 109:8;
Pr 10:27 ^d S ver 30
15:33 ^e Hab 3:17
^f S Job 4:20
15:34 ^g S Job 8:13
^h S ver 30; Heb 10:27
ⁱ S Ex 23:8; S 1Sa 8:3
15:35 ^j S Job 5:7
^k S Job 4:8;
S Isa 29:20; Gal 6:7;
Jas 1:15
16:2 ^l Ps 69:20
^m S Job 6:15
16:3 ⁿ Job 11:2; 18:2
^o S Job 6:26
16:4 ^p S 2Ki 19:21;
Ps 22:7; Isa 37:22;
Jer 48:27; La 2:15;
Zep 2:15; S Mt 27:39
16:5 ^q Job 29:25
^r S Ge 37:35
16:6 ^s S Job 6:3;
S 7:21
16:7 ^t S Jdg 8:5;
S Job 7:3 ^u S Job 1:19
16:8 ^v Job 17:7;
19:20; 33:21; Ps 6:7;
22:17; 88:9; 102:5;
109:24; La 5:17
^w S Job 10:17

15:23,30 *darkness.* Death, characterized by the journey to the netherworld (see note on 10:21).

　15:35 *They conceive trouble and give birth to evil.* See Isa 59:4 and note. Once initiated, sinful thoughts develop quickly into evil acts (cf. Jas 1:15 and note).

　16:2–5 Helpful advice is usually brief and encouraging, not lengthy and judgmental.

16:2 *miserable comforters.* See note on 13:1–12. Job would eventually be comforted, but not by his three friends (see 42:11).

16:3 *long-winded.* See note on 15:2.

16:4 *shake . . . head.* A gesture of insult and scorn (see Ps 22:7; Jer 48:27; Mt 27:39).

16:9 *z* Job 30:21;
Ps 35:16; 37:12;
112:10; La 2:16;
Ac 7:54 *a* S Job 13:24
16:10 *b* Ps 22:13;
35:21 *c* Job 12:4;
19:18; 21:3; 30:1,9;
Ps 22:13; 69:12; 119:51
d Isa 50:6; La 3:30;
Mic 5:1; Ac 23:2
e ver 7; S Job 11:3;
19:12; 30:12; Ps 27:3;
35:15; Ac 7:57
16:11 *f* S Job 9:24
16:12 *g* S Job 9:17
h S Job 6:4; La 3:12
16:13 *i* S Job 3:23
j Job 20:24; Pr 7:23;
La 3:13
16:14 *k* Job 9:17
l S Job 10:3; Joel 2:7
16:15 *m* S Ge 37:34
n S Job 2:8
16:16 *o* ver 20;
Ps 6:6 *p* Job 2:7; 17:7;
30:17,30; 33:19;
Isa 52:14
16:17 *q* Isa 55:7;
59:6; Jer 18:11;
Jnh 3:8 *r* S Job 6:28;
S 10:7; 13:7; Isa 53:9;
Zep 3:13
16:18 *s* S Ge 4:10;
Isa 26:21 *t* Ps 5:2;
18:6; 102:1; 119:169
u Job 19:24; Ps 66:18-
19; Heb 11:4
16:19 *v* S Ge 31:50;
S Ro 1:9; 1Th 2:5
w Job 22:12; 42:2
x Job 19:27; 21:17;
25:2; 27:13; 31:2;
Ps 113:5; Isa 33:5;
57:15; 58:4; 66:1;
Mk 11:10
16:20 *y* S Ro 8:34
z Jn 15:15 *a* La 2:19
b S ver 16
16:21 *c* 1Ki 8:45;
Ps 9:4; 140:12
16:22 *d* S Job 10:21
17:1 *e* Ps 143:4
f Isa 38:12 *g* Ps 88:3-
4; Ecc 12:1-7
17:2 *h* S Job 11:3
i S Job 6:14; Ps 22:7;
119:51; Jer 20:7;
La 3:14
17:3 *j* Ps 35:27;
119:122 *k* Pr 6:1
l Ps 35:2; 40:17;
Isa 38:14
17:4 *m* S Job 12:12
17:5 *n* S Ex 22:15
o S Job 11:20
17:6 *p* 1Ki 9:7;
Job 30:9; Jer 15:4
q S ver 2

and gnashes his teeth at me;*z*
my opponent fastens on me his piercing eyes. *a*
¹⁰ People open their mouths *b* to jeer at me; *c*
they strike my cheek *d* in scorn
and unite together against me. *e*
¹¹ God has turned me over to the ungodly
and thrown me into the clutches of the wicked. *f*
¹² All was well with me, but he shattered me;
he seized me by the neck and crushed me. *g*
He has made me his target; *h*
¹³   his archers surround me. *i*
Without pity, he pierces*j* my kidneys
and spills my gall on the ground.
¹⁴ Again and again *k* he bursts upon me;
he rushes at me like a warrior. *l*

¹⁵ "I have sewed sackcloth *m* over my skin
and buried my brow in the dust. *n*
¹⁶ My face is red with weeping, *o*
dark shadows ring my eyes; *p*
¹⁷ yet my hands have been free of violence *q*
and my prayer is pure. *r*

¹⁸ "Earth, do not cover my blood; *s*
may my cry *t* never be laid to rest! *u*
¹⁹ Even now my witness *v* is in heaven; *w*
my advocate is on high. *x*
²⁰ My intercessor *y* is my friend *a z*
as my eyes pour out *a* tears *b* to God;
²¹ on behalf of a human being he pleads *c* with God
as one pleads for a friend.

²² "Only a few years will pass
before I take the path of no return. *d*

17 ¹ My spirit *e* is broken,
my days are cut short, *f*
the grave awaits me. *g*
² Surely mockers *h* surround me; *i*
my eyes must dwell on their hostility.

³ "Give me, O God, the pledge you demand.*j*
Who else will put up security *k* for me? *l*
⁴ You have closed their minds to understanding; *m*
therefore you will not let them triumph.
⁵ If people denounce their friends for reward, *n*
the eyes of their children will fail. *o*

⁶ "God has made me a byword *p* to everyone, *q*

a 20 Or *My friends treat me with scorn*

16:9 The figure here is graphic and disturbing: God, like a ferocious lion (see 10:16), attacks and tears at Job's flesh.
16:10–14 Job sees himself as God's target and views his situation as the reverse of Eliphaz's description in 15:25–26.
16:12 *All was well ... but he shattered me.* See 2:3 and note. *made me his target.* See note on 6:4.
16:15–17 Job summarizes his misery: Though innocent, he continues to suffer.
16:15 *sackcloth ... dust.* Signs of mourning (see notes on Ge 37:34; Jnh 3:5–6).

16:18–21 Verse 18 (see v. 22; 17:1) indicates that Job does not think he will live long enough to be vindicated before his peers. His only hope is that in heaven he has a friend (v. 20), a holy one (see 5:1), who will be his "witness," his "advocate," his "intercessor," one who will plead with God on his behalf (v. 21; see 5:1; 9:33 and notes).

16:18 *blood ... cry.* Job felt that his blood, like Abel's (see Ge 4:10 and note), was innocent and would therefore cry out from the ground after his death.
16:20 *intercessor.* The Hebrew for this word is translated "messenger" in 33:23 (see note on 33:23–28).
16:22 *Only a few years will pass.* Job does not expect his death immediately. *path of no return.* Path to the netherworld (see notes on 7:9; 10:21; see also 17:1).
17:1 *the grave awaits me.* See note on vv. 10–16.
17:3 *Give me ... the pledge you demand.* Job is asking God for a guarantee that he is right, that he is not guilty of sins that deserve punishment (as his counselors have said).
17:4 *their minds.* Those of his three friends.
17:5 Job quotes a proverb to counter the false accusations of his friends.
17:6–9 The guarantee Job asked for (v. 3) is not provided, so he

a man in whose face people spit. *r*
⁷ My eyes have grown dim with grief; *s*
   my whole frame is but a shadow. *t*
⁸ The upright are appalled at this;
   the innocent are aroused *u* against the ungodly.
⁹ Nevertheless, the righteous *v* will hold to their ways,
   and those with clean hands *w* will grow stronger. *x*

¹⁰ "But come on, all of you, try again!
   I will not find a wise man among you. *y*
¹¹ My days have passed, *z* my plans are shattered.
   Yet the desires of my heart *a*
¹² turn night into day; *b*
   in the face of the darkness light is near. *c*
¹³ If the only home I hope for is the grave, *d*
   if I spread out my bed *e* in the realm of darkness, *f*
¹⁴ if I say to corruption, *g* 'You are my father,'
   and to the worm, *h* 'My mother' or 'My sister,'
¹⁵ where then is my hope— *i*
   who can see any hope for me? *j*
¹⁶ Will it go down to the gates of death? *k*
   Will we descend together into the dust?" *l*

BILDAD

18

Then Bildad the Shuhite *m* replied:

² "When will you end these speeches? *n*
   Be sensible, and then we can talk.
³ Why are we regarded as cattle *o*
   and considered stupid in your sight? *p*
⁴ You who tear yourself *q* to pieces in your anger, *r*
   is the earth to be abandoned for your sake?
   Or must the rocks be moved from their place? *s*

⁵ "The lamp of a wicked man is snuffed out; *t*
   the flame of his fire stops burning. *u*
⁶ The light in his tent *v* becomes dark; *w*
   the lamp beside him goes out. *x*
⁷ The vigor *y* of his step is weakened; *z*
   his own schemes *a* throw him down. *b*
⁸ His feet thrust him into a net; *c*
   he wanders into its mesh.
⁹ A trap seizes him by the heel;
   a snare *d* holds him fast. *e*
¹⁰ A noose *f* is hidden for him on the ground;
   a trap *g* lies in his path. *h*
¹¹ Terrors *i* startle him on every side *j*
   and dog *k* his every step.

17:6 *r* S Nu 12:14
17:7 *s* S Job 16:8
 t S Job 2:12; S 16:16
17:8 *u* S Ex 4:14
17:9 *v* Pr 4:18
 w S 2Sa 22:21;
S Job 9:30
 x S 1Sa 2:4; Ps 84:7
17:10 *y* S Job 12:2
17:11 *z* ver 15;
Isa 38:10; *a* S Job 7:6
17:12 *b* Isa 50:11
 c Job 5:17-26; S 11:17
17:13 *d* S 2Sa 14:14;
S Job 3:13 *e* Ps 139:8
 f Ps 88:18
17:14 *g* Job 13:28;
30:28,30; Ps 16:10;
49:9 *h* S Job 4:19;
S 7:5
17:15 *i* S Job 7:6
 j Ps 31:22; La 3:18;
Eze 37:11
17:16 *k* S Job 7:9;
33:28; Ps 9:13; 30:3;
107:18; Isa 38:10,17;
Jnh 2:6 *l* S Ge 2:7;
S Job 3:19; 20:11;
21:26
18:1 *m* S Job 8:1
18:2 *n* S Job 8:2;
S 16:3
18:3 *o* S Job 12:7
 p Ps 73:22
18:4 *q* Job 13:14
 r S Job 16:9
 s Job 14:18
18:5 *t* Job 21:17;
35:15; Pr 13:9; 20:20;
24:20; Jer 25:10;
Mt 25:8; Jn 8:12
 u S Job 5:14; 12:25;
24:17; 38:15
18:6 *v* S Job 8:22
 w S Job 5:14
 x S Job 11:17; S 12:25
18:7 *y* S Job 13:26
 z Ps 18:36; Pr 4:12
 a S Job 5:13
 b S Job 15:6
18:8 *c* Job 19:6;
Ps 9:15; 10:9; 35:7;
57:6; 66:11; 140:5;
La 3:19; *d* Job 22:10;
Hab 1:15
18:9 *d* Job 22:10;
30:12; Isa 24:18;
Jer 48:44; Am 5:19
 e Pr 5:22
18:10 *f* Pr 7:22;
Isa 51:20 *g* S 1Sa 28:9
 h Ps 140:5
18:11 *i* ver 14;
S Job 6:4; 20:25;
24:17; Ps 55:4; 88:15;
Isa 28:19; Jer 15:8;
La 2:22 *j* S Job 15:21;
Ps 31:13 *k* ver 18;
Job 20:8; Isa 22:18

17:15 *where ... is my hope ...?* See 14:19.

B **17:16** *gates of death.* See 38:17; Mt 16:18. In Mesopotamian literature, all who entered the netherworld passed through a series of seven gates. *dust.* See note on 7:21.

18:1–4 Bildad resents what he perceives to be a belittling attitude. He considers Job's emotional reaction as self-centered and irrational.

C **18:5–21** Another poem on the fate of the wicked (see 8:11–19; 15:20–35). Bildad wants to convince Job that he is wrong when he claims that the righteous suffer and the wicked prosper. Bildad is absolutely certain that every wicked person gets paid in full, in this life, for his wicked deeds.

18:5 *The lamp of a wicked man is snuffed out.* See 21:17; Pr 13:9 and note. Life, symbolized by light, is extinguished.

feels that God is responsible for making him an object of scorn. If the tone of vv. 8–9 is intended as sarcastic (as v. 10 would seem to indicate), the so-called "upright" and "innocent" (v. 8) are the three counselors.

17:6 *byword.* See 30:9; an object of scorn and ridicule (see the covenant curse in Dt 28:37). *in whose face people spit.* See 30:10; see also Isa 50:6 and note; Mt 27:30.

17:7 *frame is but a shadow.* See note on 2:7.

17:10–16 Zophar had promised that Job's repentance would turn his darkness into light (11:17). Job now makes a parody on such advice (vv. 12–16). His only hope is the grave (see v. 1), which will not be as his home had been (vv. 13–15).

17:13 *home.* See Ecc 12:5 and note. *darkness.* The netherworld (see 10:21; 18:18 and notes).

17:14 In the grave, one's family consists only of decomposition and maggots.

18:12 *l* Job 21:17
m Isa 8:21; 9:20; 65:13
n Job 31:3 *o* Job 15:23
18:13 *p* Nu 12:12
q Zec 14:12
18:14 *r* S Job 8:22
s Job 15:24 *t* S ver 11
18:15 *u* ver 18;
Job 20:26
v S Ge 19:24
18:16 *w* Isa 5:24;
Hos 5:12; Am 2:9
x S Ge 27:28;
S Job 8:12; S 15:30
18:17 *y* S Dt 32:26
z Dt 9:14; Ps 9:5;
69:28; Pr 10:7;
Isa 14:22 *a* Job 24:20;
Ps 34:16; Pr 2:22;
10:7; Isa 49:15
18:18 *b* S Job 5:14
c S ver 11
d S Job 11:20; 30:8
18:19 *e* Ps 37:28;
Isa 1:4; 14:20;
Jer 22:30 *f* Ps 21:10;
109:13; Isa 14:22
g S 2Ki 10:11;
S Eze 17:8
h Job 27:14-15
18:20 *i* Ps 22:6-7;
Isa 52:14; 53:2-3;
Eze 27:35 *j* Ps 37:13;
Jer 46:21; 50:27,31;
Eze 7:7
18:21 *k* Job 21:28
l Isa 57:20 *m* S Job 7:10
n S Job 4:21; 1Th 4:5
19:2 *o* Job 13:25
p Job 6:9
19:3 *q* S Ge 31:7
r Job 20:3
19:4 *s* Job 6:24
19:5 *t* Ps 35:26;
38:16; 55:12
19:6 *u* S Job 6:29
v S Job 18:8
w S Job 10:3
19:7 *x* Job 30:20;
Ps 22:2 *y* Job 30:24,
28; 31:35; Ps 5:2
z S Job 9:24; Hab 1:2-4
19:8 *a* La 3:7;
Hos 2:6 *b* Job 3:26;
23:17; 30:26; Ecc 6:4;
Isa 59:9; Jer 8:15;
14:19; La 3:2
19:9 *c* S Job 12:17
d Ge 43:28; Ex 12:42;
Ps 15:4; 50:23;
Pr 14:31 *e* S Job 2:8;
29:14; Ps 89:39,44;
La 5:16
19:10 *f* S Job 12:14
g S Job 7:6
h S Job 14:7

^{12}Calamity ^{l} is hungry ^{m} for him;
   disaster ^{n} is ready for him when he falls. ^{o}
^{13}It eats away parts of his skin; ^{p}
   death's firstborn devours his limbs. ^{q}
^{14}He is torn from the security of his tent ^{r}
   and marched off to the king ^{s} of terrors. ^{t}
^{15}Fire resides ^{a} in his tent; ^{u}
   burning sulfur ^{v} is scattered over his dwelling.
^{16}His roots dry up below ^{w}
   and his branches wither above. ^{x}
^{17}The memory of him perishes from the earth; ^{y}
   he has no name ^{z} in the land. ^{a}
^{18}He is driven from light into the realm of darkness ^{b}
   and is banished ^{c} from the world. ^{d}
^{19}He has no offspring ^{e} or descendants ^{f} among his people,
   no survivor ^{g} where once he lived. ^{h}
^{20}People of the west are appalled ^{i} at his fate; ^{j}
   those of the east are seized with horror.
^{21}Surely such is the dwelling ^{k} of an evil man; ^{l}
   such is the place ^{m} of one who knows not God." ^{n}

JOB 19

Then Job replied:

^{2}"How long will you torment ^{o} me
   and crush ^{p} me with words?
^{3}Ten times ^{q} now you have reproached ^{r} me;
   shamelessly you attack me.
^{4}If it is true that I have gone astray,
   my error ^{s} remains my concern alone.
^{5}If indeed you would exalt yourselves above me ^{t}
   and use my humiliation against me,
^{6}then know that God has wronged me ^{u}
   and drawn his net ^{v} around me. ^{w}

^{7}"Though I cry, 'Violence!' I get no response; ^{x}
   though I call for help, ^{y} there is no justice. ^{z}
^{8}He has blocked my way so I cannot pass; ^{a}
   he has shrouded my paths in darkness. ^{b}
^{9}He has stripped ^{c} me of my honor ^{d}
   and removed the crown from my head. ^{e}
^{10}He tears me down ^{f} on every side till I am gone;
   he uproots my hope ^{g} like a tree. ^{h}

---

^{a} 15 Or *Nothing he had remains*

18:13 *death's firstborn.* Probably a deadly disease (cf. 5:7 and note).

18:14 *king of terrors.* A vivid figure of speech referring to death, which is personified in v. 13. Canaanite literature pictured death as the devouring god Mot. Isaiah reverses the figure and envisions the Lord as swallowing up death forever (see Isa 25:8 and note; see also 1Co 15:54).

18:15 *burning sulfur.* Reminiscent of the destruction of Sodom and Gomorrah (see Ge 19:24 and note).

18:16 *roots … and … branches.* Figurative for descendants (see, e.g., Isa 11:1,10) and/or ancestors (see, e.g., Jdg 5:14; Isa 14:29). See also Am 2:9 and note.

18:17 *memory of him perishes.* Apparently, for Bildad, the only retribution beyond death is having one's memory (name) cut off by not leaving any heirs (see v. 19).

18:18 *darkness.* The netherworld (see 10:21 and note; 17:13).

18:21 *evil man … knows not God.* Having no intimate knowledge of God is synonymous with being wicked (see Hos 4:1–2,6).

19:3 *Ten times.* Several times. Ten is often used as a round number (see, e.g., Ge 31:41; 1Sa 1:8).

19:4 *my concern alone.* Job's friends have no right to interfere or to behave as if they were God (see v. 22).

19:6 *wronged.* Cf. 40:8 and note. The Hebrew for this verb is twice translated "pervert" in 8:3 (see note there), where Bildad denied that God perverts justice. But Job, struggling with the enigma of his suffering, can only conclude that God is his enemy, though in fact he is his friend who delights in him (see 1:8; 2:3). Job's true enemy, of course, is Satan, the accuser (see notes on 1:6,12). *drawn his net.* The wicked may get themselves into trouble, as Bildad had pointed out (see 18:8–10), but Job here attributes his suffering to God.

19:7 *I cry, 'Violence!'* See Hab 1:2–4 and notes.

19:8–12 In Job's mind, God is at war with him (see 16:10–14 and note).

19:10 *uproots my hope like a tree.* Unlike 14:7–9, where Job had used as a symbol of hope a tree that is cut down but later sprouts again. See also 24:20.

11 His anger *i* burns against me;
   he counts me among his enemies. *j*
12 His troops advance in force; *k*
   they build a siege ramp *l* against me
   and encamp around my tent. *m*

13 "He has alienated my family *n* from me;
   my acquaintances are completely estranged from me. *o*
14 My relatives have gone away;
   my friends *p* have forgotten me.
15 My guests *q* and my female servants *r* count me a foreigner;
   they look on me as on a stranger.
16 I summon my servant, but he does not answer,
   though I beg him with my own mouth.
17 My breath is offensive to my wife;
   I am loathsome *s* to my own family.
18 Even the little boys *t* scorn me;
   when I appear, they ridicule me. *u*
19 All my intimate friends *v* detest me; *w*
   those I love have turned against me. *x*
20 I am nothing but skin and bones; *y*
   I have escaped only by the skin of my teeth. *a*

21 "Have pity on me, my friends, *z* have pity,
   for the hand of God has struck *a* me.
22 Why do you pursue *b* me as God does? *c*
   Will you never get enough of my flesh? *d*

23 "Oh, that my words were recorded,
   that they were written on a scroll, *e*
24 that they were inscribed with an iron tool *f* on *b* lead,
   or engraved in rock forever! *g*
25 I know that my redeemer *c h* lives,
   and that in the end he will stand on the earth. *d*
26 And after my skin has been destroyed,
   yet *e* in *f* my flesh I will see God; *i*
27 I myself will see him
   with my own eyes *k*—I, and not another.
   How my heart yearns *l* within me!

---

a 20 Or *only by my gums*   *b 24* Or *and*   *c 25* Or *vindicator*   *d 25* Or *on my grave*   *e 26* Or *And
after I awake, / though this body, has been destroyed, / then*   *f 26* Or *destroyed, / apart from*

19:11 *i* Job 16:9
j S Job 13:24
19:12 *k* S Job 16:13
l S Job 16:10
m S Job 3:23
19:13 *n* Ps 69:8
o ver 19; Job 16:7;
42:11; Ps 31:11; 38:11;
88:8
19:14 *p* ver 19;
S 2Sa 15:12; Job 12:4;
16:20; Ps 88:18;
Jer 20:10; 38:22
19:15 *q* Ge 14:14
r Ecc 2:7
19:17 *s* Ps 38:5
19:18 *t* S 2Ki 2:23
u S Job 16:10
19:19 *v* S ver 14;
S Job 6:14; Ps 55:12-
13 *w* Job 30:10
x S ver 13; Jn 13:18
19:20 *y* S Job 2:5
19:21 *z* S Job 6:14
a S Jdg 2:15;
S Job 4:5; S 10:3;
La 3:1
19:22 *b* S Job 13:25
c ver 6 *d* S 2Ch 28:9;
Ps 14:4; 27:2; 69:26;
Pr 30:14; Isa 53:4
19:23 *e* S Ex 17:14;
S Ps 40:7; S Isa 8:1
19:24 *f* Jer 17:1
g S Job 16:18
19:25 *h* S Ex 6:6;
S Lev 25:25; Ps 68:5;
78:35; Pr 23:11;
Isa 41:14; 43:14; 44:6,
24; 47:4; 48:17;
49:26; 54:5; 59:20;
60:16 *i* S 1Sa 14:39;
Job 16:19
19:26 *j* S Nu 12:8;
S Mt 5:8; 1Co 13:12;
1Jn 3:2
19:27 *l* Lk 2:30
l Ps 42:1; 63:1; 84:2

19:12 *siege ramp.* See 30:12.

A C **19:13–19** See Jer 12:6 and note. Very little in life hurts more than rejection by one's family and friends. Job's children are gone, and his wife, brothers, friends and servants find him repulsive.

19:17 *breath is offensive.* See note on 2:7.

19:18 *little boys scorn me.* An intolerable insult in a patriarchal society, where one's elders were to be honored and respected (see Ex 20:12 and note).

19:20 *skin and bones.* See note on 2:7. *skin of my teeth.* The TNIV text note understands the phrase to imply that even Job's teeth are gone.

19:21 *hand of God has struck me.* See note on v. 6; see also 1:11; 2:4–6.

A **19:23–27** Probably the best-known and most-loved passage in the book of Job, reaching a high point in Job's understanding of his own situation and of his relationship to God. Its position between two sections in which Job pleads with (vv. 21–22) and then warns (vv. 28–29) his friends causes it to stand out even more boldly.

19:23 *my words.* Job wishes that his complaint and defense were recorded, so that even after his death they would endure until he is finally vindicated. *scroll.* See note on Ex 17:14.

B **19:24** *iron.* See also 20:24; 28:2; 40:18; 41:27. Iron did not come into common use in the ancient Near East until the 12th century B.C., though limited use of iron in the region is attested at least as early as 2000 B.C.

A C **19:25** *I know that my redeemer lives.* This staunch confession of faith has been appropriated by generations of Christians, especially through the medium of Handel's *The Messiah.* But these celebrate redemption from guilt and judgment; Job had something else in mind. Although in other contexts he desires a "vindicator" (see TNIV text note; see also Pr 23:11 and note) as an advocate in heaven who would plead with God on his behalf (see 9:33–34; 16:18–21 and notes; see also note on 5:1), here the Redeemer seems to be none other than God himself (see note on Ru 2:20). Job expresses confidence that ultimately God will vindicate his faithful servants in the face of all false accusations. *in the end.* Lit. "afterward" (after Job's life has ended). *he will stand.* To defend and vindicate me (see 42:7–10 and notes).

A **19:26** *my skin has been destroyed.* Job senses that the ravages of his disease will eventually bring about his death. *I will see God.* He is absolutely certain, however, that death is not the end of existence and that someday he will stand in the presence of his Redeemer and see him with his own eyes (see v. 27; see also Mt 5:8; 1Jn 3:2). See note on 42:5.

19:28 *m* S Job 13:25
19:29 *n* Job 15:22
o Job 27:13-23; Ps 1:5;
9:7; 58:11; Ecc 3:17;
11:9; 12:14
20:1 *p* S Job 2:11
20:2 *q* Ps 42:5;
La 1:20
20:3 *r* Job 19:3
20:4 *s* Dt 4:32;
S 32:7
20:5 *t* Ps 94:3
u S Job 8:13
v S Job 8:12;
Ps 37:35-36; 73:19
20:6 *w* Job 33:17;
Isa 16:6 *x* S Ge 11:4
y Isa 14:13-14;
Ob 1:3-4
20:7 *z* S Job 4:20
a S Job 7:8; S 14:20
20:8 *b* Ps 73:20;
Ecc 5:3 *c* Ps 90:10;
Ecc 6:12; 12:7
d S Job 18:11
e Job 27:20; 34:20;
Ps 90:5; Isa 17:14;
29:7
20:9 *f* S Job 7:8
20:10 *g* S Job 5:4
h ver 15,18,20;
S Job 3:15; 31:8
20:11 *i* S Job 13:26
j Job 21:24
k S Job 17:16
20:12 *l* S Job 15:16
m Ps 10:7; 140:3
20:13 *n* S Nu 11:18-
20
20:14 *o* Pr 20:17;
Jer 2:19; 4:18;
Rev 10:9 *p* S Nu 21:6
20:15 *q* S ver 10
r S Lev 18:25
20:16 *s* S Dt 32:32
t Dt 32:24
20:17 *u* Ps 36:8
v Dt 32:13 *w* Dt 32:14;
Job 29:6
20:18 *x* S ver 10;
S Job 5:5 *y* Ps 109:11
20:19 *z* S Job 5:16;
Ps 10:2; 94:6; 109:16
a S Dt 15:11; 24:14;
Job 24:4,14; 35:9;
Pr 14:31; 28:28;
Am 8:4 *b* Isa 5:8

28 "If you say, 'How we will hound *m* him,
    since the root of the trouble lies in him,*a*'
29 you should fear the sword yourselves;
    for wrath will bring punishment by the sword, *n*
    and then you will know that there is judgment.*b* *o*

ZOPHAR

20

Then Zophar the Naamathite*p* replied:

2 "My troubled thoughts prompt me to answer
    because I am greatly disturbed. *q*
3 I hear a rebuke *r* that dishonors me,
    and my understanding inspires me to reply.

4 "Surely you know how it has been from of old, *s*
    ever since people were*c* placed on the earth,
5 that the mirth of the wicked *t* is brief,
    the joy of the godless *u* lasts but a moment. *v*
6 Though his pride *w* reaches to the heavens *x*
    and his head touches the clouds, *y*
7 he will perish forever, *z* like his own dung;
    those who have seen him will say, 'Where is he?' *a*
8 Like a dream *b* he flies away, *c* no more to be found,
    banished *d* like a vision of the night. *e*
9 The eye that saw him will not see him again;
    his place will look on him no more. *f*
10 His children *g* must make amends to the poor;
    his own hands must give back his wealth. *h*
11 The youthful vigor*i* that fills his bones*j*
    will lie with him in the dust. *k*

12 "Though evil *l* is sweet in his mouth
    and he hides it under his tongue, *m*
13 though he cannot bear to let it go
    and lets it linger in his mouth, *n*
14 yet his food will turn sour in his stomach; *o*
    it will become the venom of serpents*p* within him.
15 He will spit out the riches *q* he swallowed;
    God will make his stomach vomit *r* them up.
16 He will suck the poison *s* of serpents;
    the fangs of an adder will kill him. *t*
17 He will not enjoy the streams,
    the rivers *u* flowing with honey *v* and cream. *w*
18 What he toiled for he must give back uneaten; *x*
    he will not enjoy the profit from his trading. *y*
19 For he has oppressed the poor*z* and left them destitute; *a*
    he has seized houses *b* he did not build.

---

a 28 Many Hebrew manuscripts, Septuagint and Vulgate; most Hebrew manuscripts *me*
b 29 Or *sword,* / *that you may come to know the Almighty*   *c* 4 Or *since Adam was*

19:28 *hound.* The Hebrew for this verb is translated "pursue" in v. 22. It serves as a clue that Job's tirade against the counselors is being resumed after the intervening section (vv. 23–27).
20:1–29 Yet another poem on the fate of the wicked as held by the traditional theology of Job's friends (see 8:11–19; 15:20–35; 18:5–21).
20:2–3 Zophar takes Job's words, especially his closing words in 19:28–29, as a personal affront. Job has dared to assert that on Zophar's theory of retribution Zophar himself is due for punishment.
20:4–11 Zophar is proud that he is a healthy and prosperous man, for in his view, that in itself is proof of his goodness and righteousness. But the joy and vigor of the wicked will always be brief and elusive (see Ps 73:18–20 and note).
20:6 *pride reaches to the heavens.* See Ge 11:4 and note.

20:7 *dung.* A symbol of what is temporary and worthless (see 1Ki 14:10).
20:10,19 Oppression of the poor is the mark of the truly wicked (see, e.g., Am 2:6–8 and notes; 8:4–8). On this subject, Job had no quarrel with Zophar (see 31:16–23).
20:11 *dust.* See note on 7:21.
20:12–15 The wicked deeds of evil people are like tasty food that pleases their palates but turns sour in their stomachs.
20:15 *riches he swallowed.* After taking what belonged to the poor (see note on vv. 10,19).
20:17 *honey and cream.* See 29:6 and note; cf. Dt 6:3 and note.
20:18 *What he toiled for . . . he will not enjoy.* A common theme in wisdom literature (see, e.g., Ecc 2:18–23).

20 "Surely he will have no respite from his craving; *c*
    he cannot save himself by his treasure. *d*
21 Nothing is left for him to devour;
    his prosperity will not endure. *e*
22 In the midst of his plenty, distress will overtake him; *f*
    the full force of misery will come upon him. *g*
23 When he has filled his belly, *h*
    God will vent his burning anger *i* against him
    and rain down his blows on him. *j*
24 Though he flees *k* from an iron weapon,
    a bronze-tipped arrow pierces him. *l*
25 He pulls it out of his back,
    the gleaming point out of his liver.
    Terrors *m* will come over him; *n*
26   total darkness *o* lies in wait for his treasures.
    A fire *p* unfanned will consume him *q*
    and devour what is left in his tent. *r*
27 The heavens will expose his guilt;
    the earth will rise up against him. *s*
28 A flood will carry off his house, *t*
    rushing waters *a* on the day of God's wrath. *u*
29 Such is the fate God allots the wicked,
    the heritage appointed for them by God." *v*

JOB
21

Then Job replied:

2 "Listen carefully to my words; *w*
    let this be the consolation you give me. *x*
3 Bear with me while I speak,
    and after I have spoken, mock on. *y*

4 "Is my complaint *z* directed to a human being?
    Why should I not be impatient? *a*
5 Look at me and be appalled;
    clap your hand over your mouth. *b*
6 When I think about this, I am terrified; *c*
    trembling seizes my body. *d*
7 Why do the wicked live on,
    growing old and increasing in power? *e*
8 They see their children established around them,
    their offspring before their eyes. *f*
9 Their homes are safe and free from fear; *g*
    the rod of God is not on them. *h*
10 Their bulls never fail to breed;
    their cows calve and do not miscarry. *i*

---

a 28 Or *The possessions in his house will be carried off, / washed away*

20:20 *c* Ecc 5:12-14
d S ver 10; Pr 11:4;
Zep 1:18; Lk 12:15
20:21 *e* S Job 7:8
20:22 *f* S Jdg 2:15;
Lk 12:16-20 *g* ver 29;
Job 21:17,30; 31:2-3
20:23 *h* S Nu 11:18-
20 *i* La 4:11; Eze 5:13;
6:12 *j* ver 14;
Ps 78:30-31
20:24 *k* Isa 24:18;
Jer 46:21; 48:44
l S Job 15:22
20:25 *m* S Job 18:11
n S Job 15:21;
Ps 88:15-16
20:26 *o* S Job 5:14
p S Job 1:16
q Job 15:34; 26:6;
28:22; 31:12; Ps 21:9
r S Job 18:15
20:27 *s* S Dt 31:28
20:28 *t* Dt 28:31;
Mt 7:26-27 *u* ver 29;
Nu 14:28-32;
Job 21:17,20,30;
40:11; Ps 60:3; 75:8;
Pr 16:4; Isa 24:18;
51:17; Am 5:18;
Jn 3:36; Ro 1:18;
Eph 5:6
20:29 *v* S ver 22;
S Job 15:20; 22:5;
31:2; 36:17; Jer 13:25;
Rev 21:8
21:2 *w* S Job 13:17
x ver 34
21:3 *y* S Job 6:14;
S 11:3; S 16:10
21:4 *z* S Job 7:11
a S Job 6:3
21:5 *b* S Jdg 18:19;
Job 29:9; 40:4
21:6 *c* S Ge 45:3
d S Job 4:14
21:7 *e* ver 13;
S Job 9:24; 12:19;
Ps 37:1; 73:3;
Ecc 7:15; 8:14;
Hab 1:13; Mal 3:15
21:8 *f* Ps 17:14;
Mal 3:15
21:9 *g* S Job 5:24
h S Job 9:34
21:10 *i* Ex 23:26

20:20–25 Although the wicked may fill their bellies, when God vents his anger against them there will be nothing for them to eat.
20:24 *iron.* See note on 19:24.
20:26 *darkness.* See note on 10:21.
20:27 See Dt 30:19 and note.
20:28 *flood…rushing waters.* Caused by intermittent streams that can overflow and cause extensive damage during the rainy season (see 6:15–16).
20:29 Like Bildad in 18:21 (see note there), Zophar concludes his speech with a summary statement in which he claims that all he has said is in accord with God's plans for judging sinners. *Such is the fate God allots the wicked.* Repeated almost verbatim by Job in 27:13.
21:2 *consolation you give me.* See v. 34 ("you console me"), which, with v. 2, frames Job's reply to Zophar.

21:4 *Is my complaint directed to a human being?* No, says Job, I am complaining to God, because he is responsible for my condition—at least Job so perceived it. *impatient.* See note on 9:2–3.
21:5 *Look at me.* Job addresses his three friends.
21:6 *this.* His complaint to God. *I am terrified.* To contemplate the morally upside-down situation in which the wicked flourish.
21:7–15 Job's counselors have elaborated on the fate of the wicked (see 8:11–19; 15:20–35; 18:5–21; ch. 20), but Job insists that experience shows just the reverse of what his friends have said. The wicked, who want to know nothing of God's ways and who even consider prayer a useless exercise (vv. 14–15), flourish in all they do. Far from dying prematurely, as Zophar assumed concerning them (see 20:11), they live long and increase in power (v. 7). Bildad's claim that the wicked have no offspring or descendants (see 18:19) Job flatly denies (vv. 8,11).
21:9 *rod of God.* See note on 9:34.

21:11 j Ps 78:52; 107:41
21:12 k Ps 33:2
l S Ge 4:21; S 1Ch 15:16; Ps 71:22; 81:2; 108:2; Isa 5:12; Mt 11:17
21:13 m S ver 7; S Job 8:7; Ps 10:1-12; 94:3 n Job 24:19; Ps 49:14; Isa 14:15 o S Job 3:13
21:14 p S Job 4:17; 22:17; Isa 30:11 q S Dt 32:15; S 1Sa 15:11; Ps 95:10; Pr 1:29; Jer 2:20,31
21:15 r S Job 5:2; 34:9; 35:3; Ps 73:13; 139:20; Isa 48:5; Jer 9:6; 44:17
21:16 s Job 22:18; Ps 1:1; 26:5; 36:1
21:17 t S Job 18:5 u Job 18:12 v S Job 20:22,28
21:18 w S Job 13:25 x S Ge 19:15 y S Job 7:10; Pr 10:25 z S Ge 7:23
21:19 a Ex 20:5; Jer 31:29; Eze 18:2; Jn 9:2 b Jer 25:14; 50:29; 51:6,24,56
21:20 c S Ex 32:33; Nu 16:22; S 2Ki 14:6; Jer 42:16 d Job 6:4 e S Job 20:28; Jer 25:15; Rev 14:10
21:21 f Job 14:22 g S Job 14:5 h S Job 14:21; Ecc 9:5-6
21:22 i Job 35:11; 36:22; 39:17; Ps 94:12; Isa 40:13-14; Jer 32:33; Ro 11:34 j S Job 4:18; Ps 82:1; 86:8; 135:5
21:23 k S Ge 15:15; S Job 13:26 l S Job 3:13
21:24 m Ps 73:4 n Job 20:11 o Pr 3:8
21:25 p S Job 10:1
21:26 q S Job 17:16 r S Job 7:5 s Job 24:20; Ecc 9:2-3; Isa 14:11
21:28 t Job 1:3; 12:21; 29:25; 31:37 u S Job 8:22
21:30 v Job 31:3 w S Job 20:22,28; S Isa 5:30; Ro 2:5; 2Pe 2:9
21:31 x Job 34:11; Ps 62:12; Pr 24:11-12; Isa 59:18
21:32 y Isa 14:18
21:33 z Job 3:22 a S Job 3:19
21:34 b ver 2 c S Job 6:15; 8:20

[11] They send forth their children as a flock;[j]
　　their little ones dance about.
[12] They sing to the music of timbrel and lyre;[k]
　　they make merry to the sound of the pipe.[l]
[13] They spend their years in prosperity[m]
　　and go down to the grave[n] in peace.[a][o]
[14] Yet they say to God, 'Leave us alone![p]
　　We have no desire to know your ways.[q]
[15] Who is the Almighty, that we should serve him?
　　What would we gain by praying to him?'[r]
[16] But their prosperity is not in their own hands,
　　so I stand aloof from the counsel of the wicked.[s]

[17] "Yet how often is the lamp of the wicked snuffed out?[t]
　　How often does calamity[u] come upon them,
　　the fate God allots in his anger?[v]
[18] How often are they like straw before the wind,
　　like chaff[w] swept away[x][y] by a gale?[z]
[19] ⌊It is said,⌋ 'God stores up the punishment of the wicked for their
　　children.'[a]
　　Let him repay the wicked, so that they themselves will experience it![b]
[20] Let their own eyes see their destruction;[c]
　　let them drink[d] of the wrath of the Almighty.[e]
[21] For what do they care about the families they leave behind[f]
　　when their allotted months[g] come to an end?[h]

[22] "Can anyone teach knowledge to God,[i]
　　since he judges even the highest?[j]
[23] One person dies in full vigor,[k]
　　completely secure and at ease,[l]
[24] well nourished[m] in body,[b]
　　bones[n] rich with marrow.[o]
[25] Another dies in bitterness of soul,[p]
　　never having enjoyed anything good.
[26] Side by side they lie in the dust,[q]
　　and worms[r] cover them both.[s]

[27] "I know full well what you are thinking,
　　the schemes by which you would wrong me.
[28] You say, 'Where now is the house of the great,[t]
　　the tents where the wicked lived?'[u]
[29] Have you never questioned those who travel?
　　Have you paid no regard to their accounts—
[30] that the wicked are spared from the day of calamity,[v]
　　that they are delivered from[c] the day of wrath?[w]
[31] Who denounces their conduct to their face?
　　Who repays them for what they have done?[x]
[32] They are carried to the grave,
　　and watch is kept over their tombs.[y]
[33] The soil in the valley is sweet to them;[z]
　　everyone follows after them,
　　and a countless throng goes[d] before them.[a]

[34] "So how can you console me[b] with your nonsense?
　　Nothing is left of your answers but falsehood!"[c]

---

[a] 13 Or *in an instant*　　[b] 24 The meaning of the Hebrew for this word is uncertain.　　[c] 30 Or *are reserved for the day of calamity, / that they are brought forth to*　　[d] 33 Or *them, / as a countless throng went*

21:13 *peace.* The Hebrew root underlying this word is translated "those who live quietly" in Ps 35:20.
21:16 See 22:18. Job disavows the unholy counsel of the wicked and knows that God is in control (see v. 17), but such knowledge makes God all the more an enigma to him.
21:17 *lamp of the wicked snuffed out.* See 18:5 and note.
21:18 *straw...chaff.* See 13:25; see also note on Ps 1:4.

21:20 *drink...wrath of the Almighty.* See note on Isa 51:17.
21:22 *Can anyone teach...God...?* See Isa 40:14. On the contrary, God is the one who does the teaching (see 35:11; 36:22; chs. 38–41).
21:26 *dust.* See note on 7:21.
21:34 *how can you console me...?* See 16:2 and note.

ELIPHAZ

22

Then Eliphaz the Temanite *d* replied:

2 "Can a human being be of benefit to God? *e*
Can even the wise benefit him? *f*
3 What pleasure *g* would it give the Almighty if you were righteous? *h*
What would he gain if your ways were blameless? *i*

4 "Is it for your piety that he rebukes you
and brings charges against you? *j*
5 Is not your wickedness great?
Are not your sins *k* endless? *l*
6 You demanded security *m* from your relatives for no reason; *n*
you stripped people of their clothing, leaving them naked. *o*
7 You gave no water *p* to the weary
and you withheld food from the hungry, *q*
8 though you were a powerful man, owning land *r*—
an honored man, *s* living on it. *t*
9 And you sent widows *u* away empty-handed *v*
and broke the strength of the fatherless. *w*
10 That is why snares *x* are all around you, *y*
why sudden peril terrifies you, *z*
11 why it is so dark *a* you cannot see,
and why a flood of water covers you. *b*

12 "Is not God in the heights of heaven? *c*
And see how lofty are the highest stars!
13 Yet you say, 'What does God know? *d*
Does he judge through such darkness? *e*
14 Thick clouds *f* veil him, so he does not see us *g*
as he goes about in the vaulted heavens.' *h*
15 Will you keep to the old path
that the wicked *i* have trod? *j*
16 They were carried off before their time, *k*
their foundations *l* washed away by a flood. *m*
17 They said to God, 'Leave us alone!
What can the Almighty do to us?' *n*
18 Yet it was he who filled their houses with good things, *o*
so I stand aloof from the counsel of the wicked. *p*
19 The righteous see their ruin and rejoice; *q*
the innocent mock *r* them, saying,
20 'Surely our foes are destroyed, *s*
and fire *t* devours their wealth.'

21 "Submit to God and be at peace *u* with him; *v*

22:20 *s* Ps 18:39 *t* S Job 15:30   **22:21** *u* Isa 26:3,12; 27:5; Ro 5:1 *v* S Ge 17:1; Jer 9:24

22:1 *d* S Job 4:1
22:2 *e* Lk 17:10
f S Job 7:17
22:3 *g* Isa 1:11;
Hag 1:8 *h* Ps 143:2
i Job 35:7; Pr 9:12
22:4 *j* S Job 9:3;
19:29; Ps 143:2;
Isa 3:14; Eze 20:35
22:5 *k* S Ezr 9:13;
S Job 15:5
l S Job 15:13; S 20:29;
29:17
22:6 *m* S Ex 22:26
n S 2Ki 4:1
o S Ex 22:27;
Dt 24:12-13
22:7 *p* Mt 10:42
q ver 9; Job 29:12;
31:17,21,31; Isa 58:7,
10; Eze 18:7;
Mt 25:42
22:8 *r* S Job 15:19
s Isa 3:3; 5:13; 9:15
t S Job 12:19
22:9 *u* Job 29:13;
31:16; Ps 146:9
v Job 24:3,21;
Isa 10:2; Lk 1:53
w S ver 7; S Job 6:27;
S Isa 1:17
22:10 *x* S Job 18:9
y S Job 10:3
z S Job 15:21
22:11 *a* S Job 5:14
b S Ge 7:23;
Job 36:28; 38:34,37;
Ps 69:1-2; 124:4-5;
Isa 58:10-11; La 3:54
22:12 *c* S Job 11:8;
S 16:19
22:13 *d* ver 14;
Ps 10:11; 59:7; 64:5;
73:11; 94:7; Isa 29:15;
Eze 9:9; Zep 1:12
e Ps 139:11; Eze 8:12;
Eph 6:12
22:14 *f* Job 26:9;
Ps 97:2; 105:39
g S ver 13; S 2Ki 21:16
h Job 37:18; Ps 18:11;
Pr 8:27; Isa 40:22;
Jer 23:23-24
22:15 *i* Job 23:10;
34:36 *j* Job 34:8;
Ps 1:1; 50:18
22:16 *k* S Job 15:32
l S Job 4:19
m S Ge 7:23; Mt 7:26-27
22:17 *n* Job 21:15
22:18 *o* S Job 12:6
p S Job 21:16
22:19 *q* Ps 5:11; 9:2;
32:11; 58:10; 64:10;
97:12; 107:42
r Job 21:3; Ps 52:6

22:1—26:14 The third cycle of speeches, unlike the first (chs. 4–14) and second (chs. 15–21), is truncated and abbreviated. Bildad's speech is very brief (25:1–6), and Zophar does not speak at all. The dialogue between Job and his friends comes to an end because the friends cannot convince Job of his guilt—Job cannot acknowledge what is not true.

22:2–4 Eliphaz's odd reasoning is as follows: All things have their origin in God. So when people give back what God has given them, that does not enhance God in any way. Indeed, God is indifferent to human goodness, because goodness is expected of them. It is when people become wicked that God is aroused (v. 4).

22:4 *piety.* See note on 4:6. *brings charges against.* See note on 9:3.

22:5–11 In his earlier speeches, Eliphaz was the least caustic and at first even offered consolation (4:6; 5:17). But despite what he said in 4:3–4, Eliphaz now reprimands Job for gross social sins against the needy, who are naked and hun-

gry (vv. 6–7), and against widows and the fatherless (v. 9). The only proof Eliphaz has for Job's alleged wickedness is his present suffering (vv. 10–11). In ch. 29 Job emphatically denies the kind of behavior of which Eliphaz accuses him.

22:6 *demanded security…stripped people of their clothing.* Sins condemned by the prophets (see, e.g., Am 2:8 and note).
22:9 *widows…fatherless.* See 24:3; Isa 1:17 and note; Jas 1:27. *strength.* Lit."arms" (as in 38:15).
22:10 *snares.* See 19:6 and note.
22:11 *dark…flood of water.* Two common figures of trouble and distress (see Ps 42:7 and note; Isa 8:7–8 and notes; 8:22; 43:2).

22:12–20 Eliphaz finally appears to support the argument of Bildad and Zophar, who were fully convinced that Job was a wicked man. Eliphaz makes a severe accusation: Job follows the path of the ungodly (v. 15), who defy God's power and say, "What can the Almighty do to us?" (v. 17; see vv. 13–14). They even have contempt for God's goodness (v. 18).
22:18 See 21:16 and note.

22:21 ʷ S Job 8:7;
Ps 34:8-10; Pr 3:10;
1Pe 5:6
22:22 ˣ S Dt 8:3
ʸ S Job 6:10
ᶻ S Job 15:11; 28:23;
Ps 37:31; 40:8; Pr 2:6;
Eze 3:10
22:23 ᵃ Isa 31:6;
44:22; 55:7; 59:20;
Jer 3:14,22;
Eze 18:32; Zec 1:3;
Mal 3:7 ᵇ S Job 5:24;
Isa 19:22; Ac 20:32
ᶜ Job 11:14
22:24 ᵈ Job 28:6
ᵉ Ps 19:10
ᶠ S Ge 10:29
ᵍ S Job 1:10; 31:25;
Isa 2:20; 30:22; 31:7;
40:19-20; Mt 6:19
22:25 ʰ Job 31:24;
Ps 49:6; 52:7; Pr 11:28
ⁱ 2Ki 18:7; Isa 33:6;
Mt 6:20-21
22:26 ʲ Job 27:10;
Ps 2:8; 16:6; 37:4;
Isa 58:14; 61:10
ᵏ Job 11:15 ˡ Job 11:17;
33:26; Ps 27:6; 100:1
22:27 ᵐ S Job 5:27
ⁿ S Job 5:15;
S Ps 86:7; S Isa 30:19
ᵒ S Nu 30:2
22:28 ᵖ Ps 103:11;
145:19 ᵍ Job 33:28;
Ps 97:11; Pr 4:18
ʳ S Job 11:17
22:29 ˢ S Est 5:12
ᵗ Ps 18:27; S Mt 23:12
22:30 ᵘ Isa 1:18;
Ro 4:5; ᵛ S 2Sa 22:21
23:2 ʷ S Job 7:11
ˣ S 1Sa 1:10; S Job 6:3
ʸ Ps 6:6; 32:4;
Jer 45:3; Eze 21:7
23:3 ᶻ Dt 4:29
23:4 ᵃ S Job 13:18
ᵇ S Job 9:15
23:5 ᶜ S Job 11:5
23:6 ᵈ S Job 9:4
ᵉ S Job 6:4
23:7 ᶠ S Job 1:1
ᵍ S Ge 3:8; S Job 9:3;
13:3 ʰ S Job 6:29
23:9 ⁱ S Job 9:11
23:10 ʲ Job 1:1; 27:6;
31:6; 36:7; Ps 7:9;
11:5; 34:15; 37:18;
94:11; 119:168; 146:8
ᵏ S Job 7:18; Ps 139:1-
3 ˡ S Job 6:29;
S 22:15; S Ps 12:6;
1Pe 1:7
23:11 ᵐ Ps 17:5

in this way prosperity will come to you. ʷ
22 Accept instruction from his mouth ˣ
    and lay up his words ʸ in your heart. ᶻ
23 If you return ᵃ to the Almighty, you will be restored: ᵇ
    If you remove wickedness far from your tent ᶜ
24 and assign your nuggets ᵈ to the dust,
    your gold ᵉ of Ophir ᶠ to the rocks in the ravines, ᵍ
25 then the Almighty will be your gold, ʰ
    the choicest silver for you. ⁱ
26 Surely then you will find delight in the Almighty ʲ
    and will lift up your face ᵏ to God. ˡ
27 You will pray to him, ᵐ and he will hear you, ⁿ
    and you will fulfill your vows. ᵒ
28 What you decide on will be done, ᵖ
    and light ᵍ will shine on your ways. ʳ
29 When people are brought low ˢ and you say, 'Lift them up!'
    then he will save the downcast. ᵗ
30 He will deliver even one who is not innocent, ᵘ
    who will be delivered through the cleanness of your hands." ᵛ

JOB 23

Then Job replied:

2 "Even today my complaint ʷ is bitter; ˣ
    his hand ᵃ is heavy in spite of ᵇ my groaning. ʸ
3 If only I knew where to find him;
    if only I could go to his dwelling! ᶻ
4 I would state my case ᵃ before him
    and fill my mouth with arguments. ᵇ
5 I would find out what he would answer me, ᶜ
    and consider what he would say to me.
6 Would he vigorously oppose me? ᵈ
    No, he would not press charges against me. ᵉ
7 There the upright ᶠ can establish their innocence before him, ᵍ
    and there I would be delivered forever from my judge. ʰ

8 "But if I go to the east, he is not there;
    if I go to the west, I do not find him.
9 When he is at work in the north, I do not see him;
    when he turns to the south, I catch no glimpse of him. ⁱ
10 But he knows the way that I take; ʲ
    when he has tested me, ᵏ I will come forth as gold. ˡ
11 My feet have closely followed his steps; ᵐ

ᵃ 2 Septuagint and Syriac; Hebrew / *the hand on me*   ᵇ 2 Or *heavy on me in*

22:21–30 Eliphaz makes one last attempt to reach Job. In many ways it is a commendable call to repentance: Submit to God (v. 21), lay up God's words in your heart (v. 22), return to the Almighty and forsake wickedness (v. 23), find your delight in God rather than in gold (vv. 24–26), pray and obey (v. 27) and become concerned about sinners (vv. 29–30). But Eliphaz's advice assumes (1) that Job is a very wicked man and (2) that Job's major concern is the return of his prosperity (see v. 21). Job had already made it clear in 19:25–27 that he deeply yearned to see God and be his friend.
22:22 See Job's response in 23:12. *lay up his words in your heart.* The author of Ps 119 speaks similarly about the written word God gave Israel (Ps 119:11; see Pr 2:1 and note).
22:24 *gold of Ophir.* The finest gold (see 28:16; see also notes on 1Ki 9:28; 10:11; Ps 45:9; Isa 13:12).
22:28 *light will shine on your ways.* Through obedience to the word of God (see vv. 22,27; 29:3; cf. Ps 119:105).
22:30 *cleanness of your hands.* See note on Ps 24:4.

23:2 *my complaint.* See 21:4 and note. *his hand is heavy.* See TNIV text notes; 33:7 and note; see also note on 1Sa 5:6.
23:3 *where to find him.* See note on vv. 8–9.
23:6 *not press charges against me.* Job is seeking a fair trial. In 9:14–20 Job was fearful he could not find words to argue with God. Now he is confident that if God would give him a hearing, he would be acquitted (see 13:13–19; see also Ps 17:1–3; 26:1–3 and notes).
23:8–9 *east…west…north…south.* Whatever direction Job went, he could not find God (contrast Ps 139:7–10).
23:8,10 *I do not find him…But he knows the way that I take.* Job is frustrated over his apparent inability to have an audience with God, who knows that he is an upright man. Job is here answering Eliphaz's admonition beginning in 22:21: "Submit to God and …prosperity will come." Job replies that this is what he has always done (vv. 11–12). He treasures God's words more than his daily food. He admits that God is testing him—not to purge away his sinful dross but to show that Job is pure gold (see Ps 119:11,101,168; 1Pe 1:7 and note).

I have kept to his way without turning aside. [n]
[12] I have not departed from the commands of his lips; [o]
I have treasured the words of his mouth more than my daily bread. [p]

[13] "But he stands alone, and who can oppose him? [q]
He does whatever he pleases.
[14] He carries out his decree against me,
and many such plans he still has in store. [s]
[15] That is why I am terrified before him; [t]
when I think of all this, I fear him. [u]
[16] God has made my heart faint; [v]
the Almighty [w] has terrified me. [x]
[17] Yet I am not silenced by the darkness, [y]
by the thick darkness that covers my face.

24 "Why does the Almighty not set times [z] for judgment? [a]
Why must those who know him look in vain for such days? [b]
[2] There are those who move boundary stones; [c]
they pasture flocks they have stolen. [d]
[3] They drive away the orphan's donkey
and take the widow's ox in pledge. [e]
[4] They thrust the needy [f] from the path
and force all the poor [g] of the land into hiding. [h]
[5] Like wild donkeys [i] in the desert,
the poor go about their labor [j] of foraging food;
the wasteland [k] provides food for their children.
[6] They gather fodder [l] in the fields
and glean in the vineyards [m] of the wicked. [n]
[7] Lacking clothes, they spend the night naked;
they have nothing to cover themselves in the cold. [o]
[8] They are drenched [p] by mountain rains
and hug [q] the rocks for lack of shelter. [r]
[9] The fatherless [s] child is snatched [t] from the breast;
the infant of the poor is seized [u] for a debt. [v]
[10] Lacking clothes, they go about naked; [w]
they carry the sheaves, [x] but still go hungry.
[11] They crush olives among the terraces[a];
they tread the winepresses, [y] yet suffer thirst. [z]
[12] The groans of the dying rise from the city,
and the souls of the wounded cry out for help. [a]
But God charges no one with wrongdoing. [b]

[13] "There are those who rebel against the light, [c]
who do not know its ways
or stay in its paths. [d]

a 11 The meaning of the Hebrew for this word is uncertain.

23:11 [n] Job 31:7; Ps 40:4; 44:18; 119:51,59,157; 125:5; Jer 11:20
23:12 [o] S Job 6:10 [p] S Job 15:11; Mt 4:4; Jn 4:32,34
23:13 [q] S Job 9:3 [r] S Job 10:13; Isa 55:11
23:14 [s] 1Th 3:3; 1Pe 4:12
23:15 [t] S Ge 45:3 [u] S Jos 24:14; Ps 34:9; 36:1; 111:10; Pr 1:7; Ecc 3:14; 12:13; 2Co 5:11
23:16 [v] S Dt 20:3 [w] Job 27:2 [x] S Ex 3:6; Rev 6:16
23:17 [y] S Job 3:6; S 19:8
24:1 [z] S Job 14:5 [a] S Job 9:23; 2Pe 3:7 [b] S Job 15:20; Ac 1:7
24:2 [c] S Dt 19:14 [d] Ex 20:15; Dt 28:31
24:3 [e] S Job 6:27; S 22:9
24:4 [f] Job 29:16; 31:19 [g] Job 29:12; 30:25; Ps 12:5; 41:1; 82:3,4; Isa 11:4 [h] S Job 20:19; S Pr 28:12
24:5 [i] S Ge 16:12 [j] Ps 104:23 [k] Job 30:3
24:6 [l] S Job 6:5
24:6 [m] ver 18 [n] Ru 2:22; S 1Ki 21:19
24:7 [o] S Ex 22:27
24:8 [p] Da 4:25,33 [q] La 4:5 [r] S Jdg 6:2
24:9 [s] S Dt 24:17 [t] Job 29:17 [u] Ps 14:4; Pr 30:14; Isa 3:14; 10:1-2; Eze 18:12 [v] S Lev 25:47; S 2Ki 4:1
24:10 [w] Dt 24:12-13 [x] S Lev 19:9
24:11 [y] Isa 5:2; 16:10; Hag 2:16 [z] Mic 6:15
24:12 [a] S Job 12:19; 30:28; Ps 5:2; 22:24; 39:12; 119:147; Isa 30:19; Jer 50:46; 51:52,54; Eze 26:15; Rev 6:10 [b] S Job 9:23
24:13 [c] ver 16; Job 38:15; Jn 3:19-20; 1Th 5:4-5 [d] Job 17:12; 38:20; Ps 18:28; Isa 5:20; Eph 5:8-14

23:12 Job's response to the advice offered by Eliphaz in 22:22. *words ... more than my daily bread.* See Dt 8:3; Mt 4:4 and notes.
23:13 *he stands alone.* Lit."he is one (unique)."Though Job is not an Israelite, he worships the one true God—there is no other (see Dt 6:4 and note). *He does whatever he pleases.* He is sovereign (see Ps 115:3; 135:6 and notes; see also Lk 10:21).
23:15 *I am terrified.* See note on 21:6. A part of Job's faith is the recognition that God does what he pleases. By contrast, the counselors tried to make God predictable.
23:17 *I am not silenced by the darkness.* Job responds to Eliphaz's accusation in 22:11 (see note there).
24:1–12 Job describes the terrible injustice that often exists in the world. Robbery of both the haves (see v. 2) and the have-nots (see vv. 3–4) is equally obnoxious to him. But perhaps his suffering has enabled him to empathize with the poor, who must forage food (v. 5) and "glean in the vineyards of the wicked" (v. 6). The scene he depicts is heartrending: The naked shiver in the cold of night (vv. 7–8), fatherless infants are "snatched from the breast" (v. 9), field hands harvest food but

go hungry (v. 10), vineyard workers make wine but suffer thirst (v. 11), groans rise from the dying and wounded (v. 12). Job cannot understand why God is silent and indifferent (vv. 1,12) in the face of such misery, but the fact that God waits disproves the counselors' theory of suffering. Job is no more out of God's favor as one of the victims than the criminal in vv. 13–17 is in God's favor because of God's inaction.
24:1 See note on vv. 21–24.
24:2 *move boundary stones.* A serious crime in ancient times (see note on Dt 19:14).
24:3 *orphan's ... widow's.* See 22:9; Isa 1:17 and note; Jas 1:27.
24:5 *wild donkeys.* See 39:5–8.
24:6 *glean.* See note on Ru 1:22.
24:7,10 Job implicitly denies the accusation of Eliphaz (see 22:6).
24:13–17 A description of those who cause the suffering depicted in vv. 2–12: the murderer (v. 14), the adulterer (v. 15), the robber (v. 16). Darkness is their element, the medium in which they thrive (see vv. 14–17; Jn 3:19; Ro 1:21).

24:14 *e* Isa 3:15;
Mic 3:3 *f* S Job 20:19;
Ps 37:32 *g* Ps 10:9
24:15 *h* Job 31:9,27;
Pr 1:10 *i* Pr 7:8-9
j Ps 10:11
24:16 *k* S Ex 22:2;
Mt 6:19 *l* S ver 13
24:17 *m* S Job 18:11
n S Job 15:22; S 18:5
24:18 *o* S Job 9:26;
Jude 1:13 *p* Job 22:16;
Isa 57:20 *q* S Job 5:3
r ver 6
24:19 *s* Job 6:17
t S Job 21:13
24:20 *u* S Job 7:5
v S Job 21:26
w S Job 18:17
x S Job 14:7; Ps 31:12;
Da 4:14
24:21 *y* S Job 22:9
24:22 *z* S Job 9:4
a S Job 12:19
b Dt 28:66; Mt 6:27;
Jas 4:14
24:23 *c* S Job 9:24;
Am 6:1 *d* S 2Ch 16:9
e S Job 10:4
24:24 *f* S 2Ki 19:35;
S Job 4:20; Ps 37:10;
83:13; Isa 5:24; 17:13;
40:24; 41:2,15
g S Job 3:19 *h* Isa 17:5
24:25 *i* S Job 6:28;
S 16:17
25:1 *j* S Job 8:1
25:2 *k* S Job 9:4;
Ps 47:9; 89:18;
Zec 9:7; Rev 1:6
l S 2Ch 20:6;
S Job 11:8; S 16:19
25:3 *m* Mt 5:45;
Jas 1:17
25:4 *n* S Job 4:17
25:5 *o* Job 31:26
p S Job 4:18
25:6 *q* Ps 80:17;
144:3; Eze 2:1
r S Job 4:19; S 7:5
26:2 *s* Job 6:12

¹⁴ When daylight is gone, the murderer rises up,
  kills *e* the poor and needy, *f*
  and in the night steals forth like a thief. *g*
¹⁵ The eye of the adulterer *h* watches for dusk; *i*
  he thinks, 'No eye will see me,' *j*
  and he keeps his face concealed.
¹⁶ In the dark, thieves break into houses, *k*
  but by day they shut themselves in;
  they want nothing to do with the light. *l*
¹⁷ For all of them, midnight is their morning;
  they make friends with the terrors *m* of darkness. *n*

¹⁸ "Yet they are foam *o* on the surface of the water; *p*
  their portion of the land is cursed, *q*
  so that no one goes to the vineyards. *r*
¹⁹ As heat and drought snatch away the melted snow, *s*
  so the grave *t* snatches away those who have sinned.
²⁰ The womb forgets them,
  the worm *u* feasts on them; *v*
  the wicked are no longer remembered *w*
  but are broken like a tree. *x*
²¹ They prey on the barren and childless woman,
  and to the widow show no kindness. *y*
²² But God drags away the mighty by his power; *z*
  though they become established, *a* they have no assurance of life. *b*
²³ He may let them rest in a feeling of security, *c*
  but his eyes *d* are on their ways. *e*
²⁴ For a little while they are exalted, and then they are gone; *f*
  they are brought low and gathered up like all others; *g*
  they are cut off like heads of grain. *h*

²⁵ "If this is not so, who can prove me false
  and reduce my words to nothing?" *i*

BILDAD

25

Then Bildad the Shuhite *j* replied:

² "Dominion and awe belong to God; *k*
  he establishes order in the heights of heaven. *l*
³ Can his forces be numbered?
  On whom does his light not rise? *m*
⁴ How then can a mortal be righteous before God?
  How can one born of woman be pure? *n*
⁵ If even the moon *o* is not bright
  and the stars are not pure in his eyes, *p*
⁶ how much less a mortal, who is but a maggot—
  a human being, *q* who is only a worm!" *r*

JOB

26

Then Job replied:

² "How you have helped the powerless! *s*

24:18–20 Job seems to agree with the counselors here. But it is also legitimate to translate the verses as Job's call for redress against evildoers: "May their portion of the land be cursed … / may the grave snatch away … / May the womb forget them, / may the worm feast on them; / may the wicked be no longer remembered / but be broken like a tree."
24:20 *worm feasts on them.* See 21:26; Isa 14:11; 66:24 and note; Mk 9:48 and note. *broken like a tree.* See note on 19:10.
24:21–24 By way of summary, Job says that God judges the wicked, but he does so in his own good time. Job wishes, however, that God would give the righteous the satisfaction of seeing it happen (v. 1).

25:1–6 See note on 22:1—26:14. Bildad adds nothing new here, and Zophar, who has already admitted how disturbed he was (see 20:2), does not even comment.
25:2 *establishes order in the heights of heaven.* He who establishes order in heaven is sovereign over all creation.
25:3 *his forces.* Angels. *his light.* The sun.
25:4–6 Bildad echoes Eliphaz's earlier statements about human depravity (4:17–19; 15:14–16).
26:2–4 With biting sarcasm, Job responds to Bildad alone (the Hebrew for the words "you" and "your" in these verses is singular rather than plural), indicating that Eliphaz and Zophar have already been silenced.

How you have saved the arm that is feeble! [t]

³ What advice you have offered to one without wisdom!
    And what great insight [u] you have displayed!

⁴ Who has helped you utter these words?
    And whose spirit spoke from your mouth? [v]

⁵ "The dead are in deep anguish, [w]
    those beneath the waters and all that live in them.

⁶ Death [x] is naked before God;
    Destruction [a][y] lies uncovered. [z]

⁷ He spreads out the northern ˌskiesˌ [a] over empty space;
    he suspends the earth over nothing. [b]

⁸ He wraps up the waters [c] in his clouds, [d]
    yet the clouds do not burst under their weight.

⁹ He covers the face of the full moon,
    spreading his clouds [e] over it.

¹⁰ He marks out the horizon on the face of the waters [f]
    for a boundary between light and darkness. [g]

¹¹ The pillars of the heavens quake, [h]
    aghast at his rebuke.

¹² By his power he churned up the sea; [i]
    by his wisdom [j] he cut Rahab [k] to pieces.

¹³ By his breath the skies [l] became fair;
    his hand pierced the gliding serpent. [m]

¹⁴ And these are but the outer fringe of his works;
    how faint the whisper [n] we hear of him! [o]
    Who then can understand the thunder of his power?" [p]

JOB'S FINAL WORD TO HIS FRIENDS

27 And Job continued his discourse: [q]

² "As surely as God lives, who has denied me justice, [r]
    the Almighty, [s] who has made my life bitter, [t]

³ as long as I have life within me,
    the breath of God [u] in my nostrils,

⁴ my lips will not say anything wicked,
    and my tongue will not utter lies. [v]

⁵ I will never admit you are in the right;
    till I die, I will not deny my integrity. [w]

⁶ I will maintain my innocence [x] and never let go of it;
    my conscience [y] will not reproach me as long as I live. [z]

---

[a] 6 Hebrew *Abaddon*

26:2 [s] S Job 4:3
26:3 [u] Job 34:35
26:4 [v] 1Ki 22:24
26:5 [w] Ps 88:10;
Isa 14:9; 26:14
26:6 [x] Ps 139:8
[y] S Job 20:26;
S Rev 9:11 [z] Job 10:22;
11:8; 38:17; 41:11;
Ps 139:11-12; Pr 15:11;
S Heb 4:13
26:7 [a] Job 9:8
[b] Job 38:6; Ps 104:5;
Pr 3:19-20; 8:27;
Isa 40:22
26:8 [c] Pr 30:4
[d] S Ge 1:2; Job 36:27;
37:11; Ps 147:8
26:9 [e] S 2Sa 22:10;
S Job 22:14
26:10 [f] Pr 8:27,29;
Isa 40:22 [g] S Ge 1:4;
S Job 28:3; 38:8-11
26:11 [h] S 2Sa 22:8
26:12 [i] S Ex 14:21
[j] Job 12:13 [k] S Job 9:13
26:13 [l] Job 9:8
[m] Isa 27:1
26:14 [n] Job 4:12
[o] Job 42:5; Hab 3:2;
1Co 13:12 [p] S Job 9:6
27:1 [q] Job 29:1
27:2 [r] S Job 6:29;
S 9:24; Isa 45:9;
49:4,14 [s] Job 23:16
[t] S 1Sa 1:10;
S Job 7:19; S 10:1
27:3 [u] S Ge 2:7;
Job 32:8; 33:4; 34:14;
S Ps 144:4
27:4 [v] S Job 6:28;
S 12:16; S 16:17
27:5 [w] S Job 2:9;
S 10:7; S 32:2
27:6 [x] Job 29:14;
Ps 119:121; 132:9;
Isa 59:17; 61:10
[y] S Ac 23:1; Ro 2:15
[z] S Job 2:3; S 10:7;
S 23:10; S 34:17

26:2 *saved the arm that is feeble.* See 4:3–4; Isa 35:3; Heb 12:12.
26:5–14 Job's highly figurative description of the vast power of God—the theme also of Bildad's final speech (ch. 25).
26:5 *The dead.* The Hebrew for this expression is translated "spirits of the dead" in Pr 2:18, "spirits of the departed" in Isa 14:9 and "spirits" in Isa 26:14. The term is used figuratively of the deceased who inhabit the netherworld (see 3:13–15,17–19; see also note on 3:16). *waters.* Part of the world inhabited by living beings, and therefore above the netherworld.
26:6 *Death.* Personified elsewhere as the "king of terrors" (18:14; see note there). *Destruction.* See TNIV text note; see also 28:22; 31:12; Pr 15:11 and TNIV text notes. In Rev 9:11, Abaddon is the name of the "angel of the Abyss."
26:7 See 37:18. *He.* God. *suspends the earth over nothing.* Perhaps Job's way of acknowledging that the landmasses are made secure only by God's sustaining power.
26:12 *churned up the sea.* See Isa 51:15; Jer 31:35. *Rahab.* See note on 9:13.
26:13 *gliding serpent.* A description of the sea monster Leviathan (see note on 3:8; Isa 27:1).
26:14 *these are but the outer fringe of his works.* What God has revealed of his dominion over natural and super-

natural forces amounts to no more than a whisper. Job is impressed with the severely limited character of human understanding. Zophar had chided Job about his inability to fathom the mysteries of God (11:7–9), but the knowledge possessed by Job's friends was not superior to that of Job himself (see 12:3; 13:2). *thunder of his power.* If it is difficult for us to comprehend the little that we know about God, how much more impossible it would be to understand the full extent of his might!
27:1–23 The dialogue-dispute section of the book begins with Job's opening lament (ch. 3), continues with the three cycles of speeches (chs. 4–14; 15–21; 22–26) and concludes with Job's closing discourse (ch. 27), in which he reasserts his own innocence (vv. 2–6) and eloquently describes the ultimate fate of the wicked (vv. 13–23).
27:2 *As surely as God lives.* The most solemn of oaths (see note on Ge 42:15). Job's faith in God continued despite his perception of denied justice.
27:5 *you.* The Hebrew for this word is plural. In his summary statement, Job once again speaks to his three friends as a group.
27:6 *maintain my innocence.* God had spoken similarly of Job (see 2:3).

[7] "May my enemies be like the wicked, *a*
my adversaries *b* like the unjust!
[8] For what hope have the godless *c* when they are cut off,
when God takes away their life? *d*
[9] Does God listen to their cry
when distress comes upon them? *e*
[10] Will they find delight in the Almighty? *f*
Will they call on God at all times?

[11] "I will teach you about the power of God;
the ways *g* of the Almighty I will not conceal. *h*
[12] You have all seen this yourselves.
Why then this meaningless talk?

[13] "Here is the fate God allots to the wicked,
the heritage a ruthless man receives from the Almighty: *i*
[14] However many his children, *j* their fate is the sword; *k*
his offspring will never have enough to eat. *l*
[15] The plague will bury those who survive him,
and their widows will not weep for them. *m*
[16] Though he heaps up silver like dust *n*
and clothes like piles of clay, *o*
[17] what he lays up *p* the righteous will wear, *q*
and the innocent will divide his silver. *r*
[18] The house *s* he builds is like a moth's cocoon, *t*
like a hut *u* made by a watchman.
[19] He lies down wealthy, but will do so no more; *v*
when he opens his eyes, all is gone. *w*
[20] Terrors *x* overtake him like a flood; *y*
a tempest snatches him away in the night. *z*
[21] The east wind *a* carries him off, and he is gone; *b*
it sweeps him out of his place. *c*
[22] It hurls itself against him without mercy *d*
as he flees headlong *e* from its power. *f*
[23] It claps its hands *g* in derision
and hisses them out of their place." *h*

INTERLUDE: WHERE WISDOM IS FOUND

28

There is a mine for silver
and a place where gold is refined. *i*
[2] Iron is taken from the earth,
and copper is smelted from ore. *j*
[3] Miners put an end to the darkness; *k*
they search out the farthest recesses
for ore in the blackest darkness. *l*
[4] Far from human dwellings they cut a shaft, *m*
in places untouched by human feet;

27:7 *May my enemies be like the wicked.* Job calls for his friends, who had falsely accused him of being wicked, to be treated as though they themselves were wicked (cf. Ps 109:6–15; 137:8–9).
27:11 *I will teach you.* Job is about to remind his counselors about an issue on which they all agree: that the truly wicked deserve God's wrath (vv. 13–23). The three friends had falsely put Job in that category.
27:13–23 A poem that dramatizes the effect of Job's earlier call for redress (v. 7).
27:13 Job echoes the words of Zophar in 20:29 (see note there).
27:18 *cocoon ... hut.* Symbols of fragility (see note on 4:19; Isa 1:8 and note; 24:20).
27:21 *east wind.* See note on 15:2.

28:1–28 Job's friends' application of traditional wisdom to human suffering has been even more unsatisfactory than Job's untraditional response. Both attempts to penetrate the mystery have failed, and the dialogue has come to a stale-

mate. Therefore the author of the book inserts a striking wisdom poem that answers the question, "Where can wisdom be found?" (v. 12; see v. 20). The poem consists of three parts: (1) precious stones and metals are found in the deepest mines (vv. 1–11); (2) wisdom is not found in mines, nor can it be bought with precious stones or metals (vv. 12–19); (3) wisdom is found only in God (vv. 20–27). And God tells human beings that true wisdom is to "fear ... the Lord ... and to shun evil" (see v. 28). This chapter, then, anticipates the theme of God's speeches (38:1—42:6) and echoes the assessment of Job that God had given at the beginning.
28:1–11 A fascinating, lyrical description of ancient mining techniques.
28:2 *Iron.* See note on 19:24.
28:3 *put an end to the darkness.* By using an artificial source of light, such as a torch or lamp.

far from other people they dangle and sway.
5 The earth, from which food comes, [n]
  is transformed below as by fire;
6 lapis lazuli [o] comes from its rocks,
  and its dust contains nuggets of gold. [p]
7 No bird of prey knows that hidden path,
  no falcon's eye has seen it. [q]
8 Proud beasts [r] do not set foot on it,
  and no lion prowls there. [s]
9 The miners' hands assault the flinty rock [t]
  and lay bare the roots of the mountains. [u]
10 They tunnel through the rock; [v]
  their eyes see all its treasures. [w]
11 They search [a] the sources of the rivers [x]
  and bring hidden things [y] to light.

12 But where can wisdom be found? [z]
  Where does understanding dwell? [a]
13 No mortal comprehends its worth; [b]
  it cannot be found in the land of the living. [c]
14 The deep [d] says, "It is not in me";
  the sea [e] says, "It is not with me."
15 It cannot be bought with the finest gold,
  nor can its price be weighed out in silver. [f]
16 It cannot be bought with the gold of Ophir, [g]
  with precious onyx or lapis lazuli. [h]
17 Neither gold nor crystal can compare with it, [i]
  nor can it be had for jewels of gold. [j]
18 Coral [k] and jasper [l] are not worthy of mention;
  the price of wisdom is beyond rubies. [m]
19 The topaz [n] of Cush [o] cannot compare with it;
  it cannot be bought with pure gold. [p]

20 Where then does wisdom come from?
  Where does understanding dwell? [q]
21 It is hidden from the eyes of every living thing,
  concealed even from the birds in the sky. [r]
22 Destruction [b][s] and Death [t] say,
  "Only a rumor of it has reached our ears."
23 God understands the way to it
  and he alone [u] knows where it dwells, [v]
24 for he views the ends of the earth [w]
  and sees everything under the heavens. [x]
25 When he established the force of the wind
  and measured out the waters, [y]
26 when he made a decree for the rain [z]
  and a path for the thunderstorm, [a]
27 then he looked at wisdom and appraised it;
  he confirmed it and tested it. [b]
28 And he said to the human race,
  "The fear of the Lord—that is wisdom,
  and to shun evil [c] is understanding." [d]

---

[a] 11 Septuagint, Aquila and Vulgate; Hebrew *They dam up*   [b] 22 Hebrew *Abaddon*

28:5 [n] Ge 1:29;
Ps 104:14; 145:15
28:6 [o] ver 16;
SS 5:14; Isa 54:11
[p] S Job 22:24
28:7 [q] ver 21
28:8 [r] Job 41:34
[s] Isa 35:9
28:9 [t] S Dt 8:15
[u] Jnh 2:6
28:10 [v] S ver 4
[w] Pr 2:4
28:11 [x] S Ge 7:11
[y] Isa 48:6; Jer 33:3
28:12 [z] ver 28;
Pr 1:20; 3:13-20; 8:1;
9:1-3; Ecc 7:24
[a] ver 20, 23
28:13 [b] Pr 3:15;
Mt 13:44-46
[c] Dt 29:29; Ps 27:13;
52:5; 116:9; 142:5;
Isa 38:11; Jer 11:19;
Eze 26:20; 32:24
28:14 [d] Ps 42:7;
Ro 10:7 [e] Dt 30:13
28:15 [f] ver 17;
Pr 3:13-14; 8:10-11;
16:16; Ac 8:20
28:16 [g] S Ge 10:29
[h] S ver 6; S Ex 24:10
28:17 [i] Ps 119:72;
Pr 8:10 / S ver 15
28:18 [k] Eze 27:16
[l] Rev 21:11 [m] Pr 3:15;
8:11
28:19 [n] Ex 28:17
[o] Isa 11:11 [p] Pr 3:14-
15; 8:10-11,19
28:20 [q] S Job 9:4
28:21 [r] ver 7
28:22 [s] S Job 20:26;
S Rev 9:11 [t] Pr 8:32-
36
28:23 [u] Ecc 3:11;
8:17 [v] S Job 9:4;
S 22:22; Pr 8:22-31
28:24 [w] Job 36:32;
37:3; 38:18,24,35;
Ps 33:13-14; 66:7;
Isa 11:12 [x] S Jos 3:11;
S Job 10:4;
S Heb 4:13
28:25 [y] S Job 12:15;
38:8-11
28:26 [z] Job 36:28;
37:6; Jer 51:16
[a] Job 36:33; 37:3,8,11;
38:25,27; Ps 65:12;
104:14; 147:8;
Isa 35:7
28:27 [b] Pr 3:19;
8:22-31
28:28 [c] Ps 11:5;
97:10; Pr 3:7; 8:13
[d] S Ex 20:20;
S Dt 4:6; S Job 37:24

28:4 *dangle and sway.* Mining, then as now, is difficult and dangerous work. People will hazard everything to dig the earth's treasures.
28:6 *lapis lazuli.* See v. 16; see also notes on SS 5:14; Isa 54:11.
28:9 *roots of the mountains.* A poetic expression emphasizing great depth (cf. Jnh 2:6).

B **28:10** *tunnel through the rock.* An eighth-century B.C. inscription found at Jerusalem's Pool of Siloam testifies to the sophistication of ancient tunneling technology.
28:12 The questions, repeated almost verbatim in v. 20, are answered in v. 28.
28:16 *gold of Ophir.* See 22:24 and note.

A **28:18** *the price of wisdom is beyond rubies.* Cf. the value of a "wife of noble character" (Pr 31:10), who fears the Lord (Pr 31:30) and is therefore wise (see v. 28).
28:19 *Cush.* The upper Nile region, south of Egypt.
28:21 *hidden . . . from the birds.* As are precious stones and metals (see v. 7).
28:22 *Destruction and Death.* See note on 26:6.

A **28:25-27** Wisdom has been with God from the time of creation itself (see Pr 8:22-31 and notes).

A **28:28** *fear of the Lord . . . shun evil.* See the description of Job's character in 1:1,8; 2:3. *that is wisdom.* "The fear of the Lord is the beginning of wisdom" (Ps 111:10; Pr 9:10; see Pr 1:7).

29:1 ᵉJob 27:1
29:2 ᶠS Ge 31:30
ᵍJer 1:12; 31:28;
44:27
29:3 ʰS Job 11:17;
S 12:25
29:4 ⁱS Job 15:8
ʲPs 25:14; Pr 3:32
29:5 ᵏPs 127:3-5;
128:3 ˡRu 4:1
29:6 ᵐS Job 20:17
ⁿPs 81:16 ᵒGe 49:20;
S Dt 32:13
29:7 ᵖver 21;
Job 5:4; 31:21;
Jer 20:2; 38:7
29:8 �q1Ti 5:1
ʳS Lev 19:32
29:9 ˢver 21;
Job 31:21 ᵗS Jdg 18:19;
Job 40:4; Pr 30:32
29:10 ᵘver 22
ᵛPs 137:6
29:11 ʷS Job 4:4;
Heb 11:4
29:12 ˣS Job 24:4
ʸS Dt 24:17;
Job 31:17,21
ᶻPs 72:12; Pr 21:13
29:13 ᵃJob 31:20
ᵇS Dt 10:18;
S Job 22:9
29:14 ᶜS 2Sa 8:15;
S Job 27:6; Eph 4:24;
6:14 ᵈS Job 19:9
29:15 ᵉNu 10:31
ᶠS Job 4:4
29:16 ᵍS Job 24:4
ʰEx 18:26 ⁱS Job 4:4;
Pr 22:22-23
29:17 ʲJob 24:9
ᵏS Job 4:10,11;
S Ps 3:7
29:18 ˡPs 1:1-3;
15:5; 16:8; 30:6; 62:2;
139:18; Pr 3:1-2
29:19 ᵐS Nu 24:6;
S Job 14:9
ⁿS Ge 27:8;
S Job 15:30;
S Ps 133:3
29:20 ᵒPs 92:14
ᵖJob 30:11; Ps 18:34;
Isa 38:12 qGe 49:24
29:21 ʳS ver 7, S 9

JOB'S FINAL DEFENSE

29

Job continued his discourse: ᵉ

2 "How I long for the months gone by, ᶠ
  for the days when God watched over me, ᵍ
3 when his lamp shone on my head
  and by his light I walked through darkness! ʰ
4 Oh, for the days when I was in my prime,
  when God's intimate friendship ⁱ blessed my house, ʲ
5 when the Almighty was still with me
  and my children ᵏ were around me, ˡ
6 when my path was drenched with cream ᵐ
  and the rock ⁿ poured out for me streams of olive oil. ᵒ

7 "When I went to the gate ᵖ of the city
  and took my seat in the public square,
8 the young men saw me and stepped aside q
  and the old men rose to their feet; ʳ
9 the chief men refrained from speaking ˢ
  and covered their mouths with their hands; ᵗ
10 the voices of the nobles were hushed, ᵘ
  and their tongues stuck to the roof of their mouths. ᵛ
11 Whoever heard me spoke well of me,
  and those who saw me commended me, ʷ
12 because I rescued the poor ˣ who cried for help,
  and the fatherless ʸ who had none to assist them. ᶻ
13 Those who were dying blessed me; ᵃ
  I made the widow's ᵇ heart sing.
14 I put on righteousness ᶜ as my clothing;
  justice was my robe and my turban. ᵈ
15 I was eyes ᵉ to the blind
  and feet to the lame. ᶠ
16 I was a father to the needy; ᵍ
  I took up the case ʰ of the stranger. ⁱ
17 I broke the fangs of the wicked
  and snatched the victims ʲ from their teeth. ᵏ

18 "I thought, 'I will die in my own house,
  my days as numerous as the grains of sand. ˡ
19 My roots will reach to the water, ᵐ
  and the dew will lie all night on my branches. ⁿ
20 My glory will remain fresh ᵒ in me,
  the bow ᵖ ever new in my hand.' q

21 "People listened to me expectantly,
  waiting in silence for my counsel. ʳ

29:1—31:40 Job submits his final defense in a three-part summation: Part one (ch. 29) is a nostalgic review of his former happiness, wealth and honor; part two (ch. 30) is a lament over the loss of everything, especially his honor; part three (ch. 31) is a final protestation of his innocence.

29:1–25 A classic example of Semitic rhetoric, using the following symmetrical pattern: blessing (vv. 2–6), honor (vv. 7–10), benevolence (vv. 11–17), blessing (vv. 18–20), honor (vv. 21–25).

29:2–6 Words charged with emotion. In earlier days, God had been Job's friend and companion.

29:3 *by his light I walked.* See note on 22:28.

29:4 *when God's intimate friendship blessed my house.* Lit. "when God's council was by my tent," or "when God was an intimate in my tent." The clause evokes a situation similar to that in Ge 18, where God and two members of his heavenly council eat and drink at Abraham's tent—and there God discloses to his friend the imminent birth of the promised son and God's intentions concerning Sodom and Gomorrah.

29:5 *my children were around me.* See 1:2 and note.

29:6 *cream...olive oil.* Symbols of richness and luxury (see 20:17; Eze 16:19).

29:7 *gate of the city.* Where the most important business was conducted and the most significant legal cases were tried (see note on Ru 4:1). *took my seat.* As a city elder, a member of the ruling council (see note on Ge 19:1).

29:12–13 *I rescued...the fatherless...I made the widow's heart sing.* Implicitly responding to Eliphaz's accusation in 22:9, Job expresses his concern for the helpless and unfortunate (see 24:9; 31:16–18, 21).

29:14 *I put on righteousness...justice was my robe.* For similar imagery see Ps 132:9,16; Isa 59:17; 61:10; Ro 13:14; Eph 4:24; 6:14,17 and notes; see also note on Ps 109:29.

29:18 *I thought.* Job muses on what might have been the course of his life.

29:21–25 Job's counsel was valued (vv. 21– 23), his approval sought (v. 24) and his civic leadership accepted with gratitude (v. 25).

²² After I had spoken, they spoke no more; ^s
  my words fell gently on their ears. ^t
²³ They waited for me as for showers
  and drank in my words as the spring rain. ^u
²⁴ When I smiled at them, they scarcely believed it;
  the light of my face ^v was precious to them. ^{a w}
²⁵ I chose the way for them and sat as their chief; ^x
  I dwelt as a king ^y among his troops;
  I was like one who comforts mourners. ^z

30

¹ "But now they mock me, ^a
  men younger than I,
  whose fathers I would have disdained
  to put with my sheep dogs. ^b
² Of what use was the strength of their hands to me,
  since their vigor had gone from them?
³ Haggard from want and hunger,
  they roamed ^b the parched land ^c
  in desolate wastelands ^d at night. ^e
⁴ In the brush they gathered salt herbs, ^f
  and their food ^c was the root of the broom bush. ^g
⁵ They were banished from human society,
  shouted at as if they were thieves.
⁶ They were forced to live in the dry stream beds,
  among the rocks and in holes in the ground. ^h
⁷ They brayed ⁱ among the bushes ^j
  and huddled in the undergrowth.
⁸ A base and nameless brood, ^k
  they were driven out of the land. ^l

⁹ "And now their young men mock me ^m in song; ⁿ
  I have become a byword ^o among them.
¹⁰ They detest me ^p and keep their distance;
  they do not hesitate to spit in my face. ^q
¹¹ Now that God has unstrung my bow ^r and afflicted me, ^s
  they throw off restraint ^t in my presence.
¹² On my right ^u the tribe ^d attacks;
  they lay snares ^v for my feet, ^w
  they build their siege ramps against me. ^x
¹³ They break up my road; ^y
  they succeed in destroying me. ^z
  'No one can help him,' they say.
¹⁴ They advance as through a gaping breach; ^a
  amid the ruins they come rolling in.
¹⁵ Terrors ^b overwhelm me; ^c
  my dignity is driven away as by the wind,
  my safety vanishes like a cloud. ^d

¹⁶ "And now my life ebbs away; ^e
  days of suffering grip me. ^f
¹⁷ Night pierces my bones;
  my gnawing pains never rest. ^g

---

^a *24* The meaning of the Hebrew for this clause is uncertain.   ^b *3* Or *gnawed*   ^c *4* Or *fuel*
^d *12* The meaning of the Hebrew for this word is uncertain.

29:22 ^s ver 10
^t Dt 32:2
29:23 ^u S Job 4:3
29:24 ^v S Nu 6:25
^w Pr 16:14,15
29:25 ^x S Job 21:28
^y S Job 1:3 ^z S Job 4:4
30:1 ^a S Job 6:14;
S 11:3; S Ps 119:21
^b Isa 56:10
30:3 ^c Isa 8:21
^d Job 24:5 ^e Jer 17:6
30:4 ^f Job 39:6
^g S 1Ki 19:4
30:6 ^h Isa 2:19;
Hos 10:8
30:7 ⁱ Job 6:5
^j Job 39:5-6
30:8 ^k S Jdg 9:4
^l S Job 18:18
30:9 ^m S Job 16:10;
Ps 69:11 ⁿ Job 12:4;
La 3:14,63
^o S Job 17:6
30:10 ^p Job 19:19
^q S Dt 25:9; Mt 26:67
30:11 ^r S Job 29:20
^s S Ge 12:17; S Ru 1:21
^t Job 41:13; Ps 32:9
30:12 ^u S Ps 109:6;
Zec 3:1 ^v S Job 18:9
^w Ps 140:4-5
^x S Job 16:10
30:13 ^y Isa 3:12
^z S Job 10:3
30:14 ^a S 2Ki 25:4
30:15 ^b S Job 6:4
^c S Ex 3:6; Job 10:8;
31:2,3,23; Ps 55:4-5
^d S Job 3:25
30:16 ^e S Job 3:24
^f ver 27; S Job 9:17
30:17 ^g S Dt 28:35;
S Job 16:16

30:1–31 In contrast to the positive notes of blessing and honor sounded in ch. 29, Job now bemoans the suffering and dishonor he has been forced to undergo. God has heaped overwhelming terrors on him (v. 15). His final, forlorn lament (see v. 31) over his condition shows that his rage has not yet subsided.
30:1,9 *now…mock me.* Earlier both young and old had deferred to him (see 29:8–11,21–25).
30:4 *salt herbs.* Probably saltwort, which grows in otherwise infertile areas, including the regions where Job and his friends lived. Cf. 39:6. *broom bush.* A large shrub that grows in the deserts of the Middle East (see 1Ki 19:4; Ps 120:4 and notes).
30:9 *byword.* See note on 17:6.
30:11 *God has unstrung my bow.* In contrast to 29:20, where Job was confident that his bow would be new and strong.
30:12 *siege ramps.* See 19:12.
30:14 *breach.* In a city wall.
30:15 *driven…as by the wind.* See v. 22.
30:17 *gnawing pains.* See note on 2:7.

30:18 *h* S Job 9:4
30:19 *i* Ps 40:2;
69:2,14; 130:1;
Jer 38:6,22
j S Ge 3:19; S Job 2:8
30:20 *k* S 1Ki 8:52;
Ps 34:17; Pr 2:3;
Mic 4:9 *l* S Job 19:7;
La 3:8
30:21 *m* Jer 6:23;
30:14; 50:42
n Isa 9:12; 14:26; 31:3;
Eze 6:14 *o* S Job 4:5;
S 6:4; S 10:3
30:22 *p* Job 27:21;
Jude 1:12 *q* S Job 9:17
30:23 *r* S 2Sa 14:14;
S Job 3:13; S 10:3
s S Job 3:19
30:24 *t* Ps 145:14;
Isa 42:3; 57:15
u S Job 19:7
30:25 *v* Lk 19:41;
Php 3:18
w S Job 24:4;
Ps 35:13-14; Ro 12:15
30:26 *x* S Job 3:6,17;
S 19:8; S Ps 82:5;
S Jer 4:23
30:27 *y* Ps 38:8;
La 2:11 *z* S ver 16
30:28 *a* S Job 17:14;
La 4:8 *b* S Job 19:7;
S 24:12
30:29 *c* Ps 44:19;
Isa 34:13; Jer 9:11
d Ps 102:6; Mic 1:8
30:30 *e* S Job 17:14
f La 3:4; 4:8
g S Dt 28:35;
S Job 16:16; Ps 102:3;
La 1:13; 5:10
30:31 *h* S Ge 8:8;
Ps 137:2; Isa 16:11;
24:8; Eze 26:13
i S Ge 4:21
31:1 *j* Pr 4:25; 17:24;
2Pe 2:14 *k* Ex 20:14,
17; Dt 5:18; Mt 5:28
31:2 *l* Nu 26:55;
Ps 11:6; 16:5; 50:18;
Ecc 3:22; 5:19; 9:9
m S Job 16:19; S 20:29
31:3 *n* S Job 21:30
o Job 18:12
p Job 34:22; Ro 2:9
31:4 *q* 2Ch 16:9;
Ps 139:3; Da 4:37;
5:23 *r* S ver 14;
S Job 10:4
31:5 *s* S Job 15:31
31:6 *t* Ps 139:23
u S Lev 19:36;
S Job 6:2 *v* S Ge 6:9;
S Job 2:3; S 23:10
31:7 *w* S Job 23:11

18 In his great power *h* ⌊God⌋ becomes like clothing to me *a*;
　　he binds me like the neck of my garment.
19 He throws me into the mud, *i*
　　and I am reduced to dust and ashes. *j*

20 "I cry out to you, *k* God, but you do not answer; *l*
　　I stand up, but you merely look at me.
21 You turn on me ruthlessly; *m*
　　with the might of your hand *n* you attack me. *o*
22 You snatch me up and drive me before the wind; *p*
　　you toss me about in the storm. *q*
23 I know you will bring me down to death, *r*
　　to the place appointed for all the living. *s*

24 "Surely no one lays a hand on those who are crushed *t*
　　when they cry for help in their distress. *u*
25 Have I not wept for those in trouble? *v*
　　Has not my soul grieved for the poor? *w*
26 Yet when I hoped for good, evil came;
　　when I looked for light, then came darkness. *x*
27 The churning inside me never stops; *y*
　　days of suffering confront me. *z*
28 I go about blackened, *a* but not by the sun;
　　I stand up in the assembly and cry for help. *b*
29 I have become a brother of jackals, *c*
　　a companion of owls. *d*
30 My skin grows black *e* and peels; *f*
　　my body burns with fever. *g*
31 My lyre is tuned to mourning, *h*
　　and my pipe *i* to the sound of wailing.

31 "I made a covenant with my eyes *j*
　　not to look lustfully at a virgin. *k*
2 For what is our lot *l* from God above,
　　our heritage from the Almighty on high? *m*
3 Is it not ruin *n* for the wicked,
　　disaster *o* for those who do wrong? *p*
4 Does he not see my ways *q*
　　and count my every step? *r*

5 "If I have walked with falsehood
　　or my foot has hurried after deceit *s*—
6 let God weigh me *t* in honest scales *u*
　　and he will know that I am blameless *v*—
7 if my steps have turned from the path, *w*

---

a 18 Hebrew; Septuagint ⌊God⌋ *grasps my clothing*

30:18 *neck of my garment.* Tight-fitting collar.
30:19 *dust and ashes.* Symbolic of humiliation and insignificance (see note on Ge 18:27). Job would someday use "dust and ashes" to symbolize repentance (42:6).
30:20–23 Job now shifts his thoughts away from human beings and toward God. He accuses God of abusing his power by attacking him despite his pleas for mercy.
30:24 Job feels that he has been treated unjustly, whether by God or by humans.
30:26 Cf. Isa 5:2,7.
30:28 *blackened.* See v. 30; see also note on 2:7.
30:29 *brother of jackals . . . companion of owls.* The prophet Micah uses similar imagery of himself in Mic 1:8.
30:30 *fever.* See note on 2:7.
31:1–40 The climactic section of Job's three-part summation (see note on 29:1—31:40). It is negative in the sense that Job denies all the sins listed, but it has the positive purpose of attesting loyalty to God as his sovereign Lord. In the strongest legal terms, using a series of self-maledictory oaths,

Job completes his defense. No more can be said (v. 40). He now affixes his signature to the document (v. 35), and the burden of proof that he is a wretched sinner rests with God. Job's call for vindication had reached a climax in 27:2–6. Now he amplifies that statement with the details of his godly life. Each disavowal (vv. 5–7,9,13,16–21,24–27,29–34,38–39) is accompanied by an oath that calls for the punishment the offense deserves (vv. 8,10–12,14–15,22–23,28,40). The principle at work is the so-called law of retaliation (see Ex 21:23–25; Lev 24:20 and notes).
31:1–12 Job begins with sins of the heart, especially sexual lust (vv. 1–4), cheating in business (vv. 5–8) and marital infidelity (vv. 9–12).
31:1 *look lustfully at a virgin.* To do so is to sin (see Mt 5:28 and note).
31:4 Echoed by Elihu in 34:21.
31:6 *God weigh me in honest scales.* See 6:2; Pr 16:11 and note; 21:2; 24:12; Am 8:5; Mic 6:11. *blameless.* Does not imply sinless perfection (see note on 1:1).

if my heart has been led by my eyes,
    or if my hands[x] have been defiled,[y]
[8]then may others eat what I have sown,[z]
    and may my crops be uprooted. [a]

[9]"If my heart has been enticed[b] by a woman,[c]
    or if I have lurked at my neighbor's door,
[10]then may my wife grind[d] another man's grain,
    and may other men sleep with her. [e]
[11]For that would have been wicked,[f]
    a sin to be judged.[g]
[12]It is a fire[h] that burns to Destruction[a];[i]
    it would have uprooted my harvest.[j]

[13]"If I have denied justice to any of my servants,[k]
    whether male or female,
    when they had a grievance against me,[l]
[14]what will I do when God confronts me?[m]
    What will I answer when called to account?[n]
[15]Did not he who made me in the womb make them?[o]
    Did not the same one form us both within our mothers?[p]

[16]"If I have denied the desires of the poor[q]
    or let the eyes of the widow[r] grow weary,[s]
[17]if I have kept my bread to myself,
    not sharing it with the fatherless[t]—
[18]but from my youth I reared them as a father would,
    and from my birth I guided the widow[u]—
[19]if I have seen anyone perishing for lack of clothing,[v]
    or the needy[w] without garments,
[20]and their hearts did not bless me[x]
    for warming them with the fleece[y] from my sheep,
[21]if I have raised my hand against the fatherless,[z]
    knowing that I had influence in court,[a]
[22]then let my arm fall from the shoulder,
    let it be broken off at the joint.[b]
[23]For I dreaded destruction from God,[c]
    and for fear of his splendor[d] I could not do such things.[e]

[24]"If I have put my trust in gold[f]
    or said to pure gold, 'You are my security,'[g]
[25]if I have rejoiced over my great wealth,[h]
    the fortune my hands had gained,[i]
[26]if I have regarded the sun[j] in its radiance
    or the moon[k] moving in splendor,
[27]so that my heart was secretly enticed[l]
    and my hand offered them a kiss of homage,[m]
[28]then these also would be sins to be judged,[n]
    for I would have been unfaithful to God on high.[o]

[29]"If I have rejoiced at my enemies' misfortune[p]
    or gloated over the trouble that came to them[q]—
[30]I have not allowed my mouth to sin
    by invoking a curse against their life[r]—
[31]if those of my household have never said,

---

[a] 12 Hebrew *Abaddon*

31:7 [x] S Job 9:30
[y] Ps 7:3
31:8 [z] S Job 5:5;
S 20:10; Jn 4:37
[a] ver 12; Mic 6:15
31:9 [b] S Dt 11:16;
S Job 24:15; Jas 1:14
[c] Pr 5:3; 7:5
31:10 [d] S Jdg 16:21
[e] Dt 28:30
31:11 [f] Pr 6:32-33
[g] S Ge 38:24;
S Ex 21:12; Jn 8:4-5
31:12 [h] S Job 15:30
[i] S Job 26:6 / S ver 8
31:13 [k] S Dt 5:14
[l] Ex 21:2-11;
Lev 25:39-46;
Dt 24:14-15
31:14 [m] Job 33:5
[n] ver 4,37; Ps 10:13,
15; 94:7; Isa 10:3;
Jer 5:31; Hos 9:7;
Mic 7:4; Col 4:1
31:15 [o] S Job 4:17;
Pr 22:2 [p] S Job 10:3;
Eph 6:9
31:16 [q] S Lev 25:17;
S Job 5:16
[r] S Job 22:9; Jas 1:27
[s] Job 22:7
31:17 [t] S Job 6:27;
S 22:7
31:18 [u] Isa 51:18
31:19 [v] Job 22:6;
Isa 58:7 [w] S Job 24:4
31:20 [x] Job 29:13
[y] Jdg 6:37
31:21 [z] S Job 22:7;
Jas 1:27 [a] S Job 29:7,9
31:22 [b] Nu 15:30;
Ps 10:15; 37:17; 137:5
31:23 [c] S Job 10:3;
S 30:15 [d] Job 13:11
[e] S Ge 20:11
31:24 [f] S Job 22:25
[g] Mt 6:24; Lk 12:15
31:25 [h] S Ge 12:16;
Ps 49:6; 52:7; 62:10;
Isa 10:14
[i] S Job 22:24;
Eze 28:5; Lk 12:20-21
31:26 [j] S Ge 1:16
[k] Job 25:5
31:27 [l] S Dt 11:16;
S Job 24:15; Jas 1:14
[m] Jer 8:2; 16:11
31:28 [n] S Ge 38:24;
Dt 17:2-7
[o] S Nu 11:20; Eze 8:16
31:29 [p] S Nu 14:1;
Ps 35:15; Ob 1:12;
Mt 5:44 [q] Pr 17:5;
24:17-18
31:30 [r] Job 5:3;
Ro 12:14

31:12 *Destruction*. See note on 26:6.

▲ **31:13–23** Job reveals genuine understanding concerning matters of social justice: Human equality is based on creation (vv. 13–15), compassion toward those in need is essential (vv. 16–20), and power and influence must not be abused (vv. 21–23).

31:16–17 *widow…fatherless*. See note on 29:12–13.

▲ **31:24–28** Covetous greed (vv. 24–25) and idolatry (vv. 26–27) are equally reprehensible in the eyes of God (v. 28;

see Mt 6:19–21 and notes; Col 3:5).

31:25 *my great wealth*. See 1:3 and note; see also 1:10.

31:26–28 The sun and moon are not to be objects of worship (see note on Ge 1:16; see also Dt 4:19; 17:3; Eze 8:16–17).

31:27 *kiss*. An ancient gesture of worship (see 1Ki 19:18; Hos 13:2 and note).

▲ **31:29–32** The sin of gloating over one's enemy was condemned by Moses (see Ex 23:4–5 and note) and by Christ (see Mt 5:43–47).

31:31 *S Job 22:7
31:32 †Ge 19:2-3;
Jdg 19:20; Mt 25:35;
S Ro 12:13
31:33 uPs 32:5;
Pr 28:13 vS Ge 3:8
31:34 wEx 23:2
xPs 32:3; 39:2
31:35 yS Job 9:24;
30:28 zJob 27:7
31:36 aS Ex 28:12
bJob 29:14
31:37 cS ver 14;
S Job 11:11
dS Job 21:28
31:38 eS Ge 4:10
fPs 65:10
31:39 gS 1Ki 21:19
hS Lev 19:13; Jas 5:4
31:40 iS Ge 3:18;
Mt 13:7 jZep 2:9;
Mt 13:26 kPs 72:20;
Jer 51:64
32:1 lver 15
mS Job 2:3; S 10:7
32:2 nS Ge 22:21
over 1 pS Job 13:19;
27:5; 30:21; 35:2
32:3 qJob 42:7
rver 12-13
sS Job 15:13
32:4 tS Lev 19:32
32:6 uJob 15:10

'Who has not been filled with Job's meat?'*—
32 but no stranger had to spend the night in the street,
     for my door was always open to the traveler†—
33 if I have concealed u my sin as people do, a
     by hiding v my guilt in my heart
34 because I so feared the crowd w
     and so dreaded the contempt of the clans
     that I kept silent x and would not go outside—

35 ("Oh, that I had someone to hear me! y
     I sign now my defense—let the Almighty answer me;
     let my accuser z put his indictment in writing.
36 Surely I would wear it on my shoulder, a
     I would put it on like a crown. b
37 I would give him an account of my every step; c
     I would present it to him as to a ruler. d)—

38 "if my land cries out against me e
     and all its furrows are wet f with tears,
39 if I have devoured its yield without payment g
     or broken the spirit of its tenants, h
40 then let briers i come up instead of wheat
     and stinkweed j instead of barley."

The words of Job are ended. k

ELIHU

32 So these three men stopped answering Job, l because he was righteous in his own eyes. m 2 But Elihu son of Barakel the Buzite, n of the family of Ram, became very angry with Job for justifying himself o rather than God. p 3 He was also angry with the three friends, q because they had found no way to refute Job, r and yet had condemned him. b 4 Now Elihu had waited before speaking to Job because they were older than he. t 5 But when he saw that the three men had nothing more to say, his anger was aroused.

6 So Elihu son of Barakel the Buzite said:

"I am young in years,
     and you are old; u
that is why I was fearful,
     not daring to tell you what I know.
7 I thought, 'Age should speak;

---

a 33 Or as Adam did   b 3 Masoretic Text; an ancient Hebrew scribal tradition Job, and so had condemned God

---

31:33-34 A strong denial of hypocrisy.
31:33 as people do. See TNIV text note and Ge 3:8–10; Hos 6:7 and note.
31:35-37 Job's final call for justice. His signature endorses every word of the oaths he has just taken.
31:35 someone to hear me. See notes on 5:1; 9:33; 16:18–21; 19:25. let the Almighty answer me. See note on 38:1. accuser. The Hebrew for this word is not the same as that for "Satan" (see note on 1:6). Here Job's accuser is either (1) a human adversary (perhaps one of the three friends) or (2) God himself. In any event, Job assumes that accusations have been lodged against him before the court of heaven to which God has responded with judgments.
31:36 shoulder. Inscriptions were sometimes worn on the shoulder as a perpetual reminder of their importance (see Ex 28:12).
31:38-40 A climactic oath that completes an earlier theme and creates a unique emphasis. Job calls for a curse on his land if he has not been fully committed to social justice (see also vv. 13–15).
31:40 The words of Job are ended. His complaints and arguments are now over. He will make only brief statements of contrition (see 40:3–5; 42:1–6 and notes) following the divine discourses.

32:1—37:24 A fourth counselor, named Elihu and younger than the other three (32:4,6–7,9), has been standing on the sidelines, giving deference to age and listening to the dialogue-dispute. But now he declares himself ready to show that both Job and the three other counselors are in the wrong. The author introduces Elihu's four poetic speeches (32:5—33:33; ch. 34; ch. 35; chs. 36–37) with a short prose preface (32:1–4).
32:1 righteous in his own eyes. He insisted on his innocence in spite of the terrible suffering that he was experiencing.
32:2-3 angry. Elihu considers Job's emphasis on vindicating himself rather than God reprehensible, but he also believes that the friends' inability to refute Job was tantamount to condemning God (see TNIV text note on v. 3).
32:2 Elihu. Means "He is my God." Elihu's speeches in some ways anticipate the divine word out of the storm (38:1—42:6). Buzite. An inhabitant of Buz, a desert region in the east (see Jer 25:23).
32:6,10,17 tell . . . what I know. Elihu is eager to share his knowledge and assumes that he can communicate it effectively (see note on 36:4).
32:6 young . . . fearful. See Jer 1:6–8; 1Ti 4:12; 2Ti 1:7 and notes.

advanced years should teach wisdom.' [v]
[8] But it is the spirit [a][w] in mortals,
 the breath of the Almighty, [x] that gives them understanding. [y]
[9] It is not only the old [b] who are wise, [z]
 not only the aged [a] who understand what is right. [b]

[10] "Therefore I say: Listen to me; [c]
 I too will tell you what I know. [d]
[11] I waited while you spoke,
 I listened to your reasoning;
while you were searching for words,
[12] I gave you my full attention.
But not one of you has proved Job wrong;
 none of you has answered his arguments. [e]
[13] Do not say, 'We have found wisdom; [f]
 let God refute [g] him, not a mere mortal.'
[14] But Job has not marshaled his words against me, [h]
 and I will not answer him with your arguments.

[15] "They are dismayed and have no more to say;
 words have failed them. [i]
[16] Must I wait, now that they are silent,
 now that they stand there with no reply?
[17] I too will have my say;
 I too will tell what I know. [j]
[18] For I am full of words,
 and the spirit [k] within me compels me; [l]
[19] inside I am like bottled-up wine,
 like new wineskins ready to burst. [m]
[20] I must speak and find relief;
 I must open my lips and reply. [n]
[21] I will show no partiality, [o]
 nor will I flatter anyone; [p]
[22] for if I were skilled in flattery,
 my Maker [q] would soon take me away. [r]

33 "But now, Job, listen [s] to my words;
 pay attention to everything I say. [t]
[2] I am about to open my mouth;
 my words are on the tip of my tongue.
[3] My words come from an upright heart; [u]
 my lips sincerely speak what I know. [v]
[4] The Spirit [w] of God has made me; [x]
 the breath of the Almighty [y] gives me life. [z]
[5] Answer me [a] then, if you can;
 stand up [b] and argue your case before me. [c]

[a] 8 Or *Spirit*; also in verse 18 [b] 9 Or *many*; or *great*

32:7 [v] S 1Ch 29:15;
S 2Ch 10:6
32:8 [w] ver 18
[x] S Job 27:3
[y] S Job 12:13;
S Ps 119:34; Jas 1:5
32:9 [z] 1Co 1:26
[a] Ps 119:100
[b] S Job 12:12,20;
Lk 2:47; 1Ti 4:12
32:10 [c] Job 33:1,31,
33; 34:2,16; 37:2,14;
Ps 34:11 [d] S Job 5:27
32:12 [e] ver 3
32:13 [f] S Job 4:12;
S Ecc 9:11 [g] S Job 11:5
32:14 [h] Job 23:4
32:15 [i] ver 1
32:17 [j] S Job 5:27;
33:3; 36:4
32:18 [k] ver 8
[l] Ac 4:20; 1Co 9:16;
2Co 5:14
32:19 [m] Jer 20:9;
Am 3:8; Mt 9:17
32:20 [n] S Job 4:2;
S Jer 6:11
32:21 [o] S Lev 19:15;
S 2Ch 19:7;
S Job 13:10; Mt 22:16
[p] Pr 29:5; 1Th 2:5
32:22 [q] S Job 4:17;
S 9:9 [r] Ps 12:2-4
33:1 [s] Job 32:10
[t] S Job 6:28; S 13:6
33:3 [u] 1Ki 3:6;
Ps 7:10; 11:2; 64:10
[v] S Job 6:28
33:4 [w] S Ge 1:2
[x] Job 10:3 [y] S Job 27:3
[z] S Nu 16:22;
S Job 12:10
33:5 [a] ver 32
[b] Job 13:18
[c] S Job 31:14

32:8 *breath of the Almighty.* See 33:4.

C **32:14** *I will not answer him with your arguments.* Elihu feels that something important has been left out and, where the wisdom of age has failed, he by the Spirit of God (see TNIV text note on v. 8) has the understanding to supply the right answers.

32:15–22 Elihu delivers a soliloquy to himself, but it is also for the benefit of those who may be listening.

32:15–16 *words have failed them … they stand there with no reply.* See v. 5. The breakdown of the third cycle in the dialogue-dispute cut short Bildad's last word and left Zophar without a third speech (see note on 22:1—26:14).

C **32:18** *I am full of words.* Elihu's speeches continue unabated through ch. 37. He has a genuine contribution to make, however, to the problems Job is facing. At the same time, he does not stoop to false accusation about Job's earlier life but usually confines his criticism of Job to quotations from Job himself. This is perhaps the reason that God, in the epilogue, does not condemn Elihu along with Job's three friends (see 42:7–9 and note).

32:19 *new wineskins ready to burst.* Old wineskins might be expected to crack or break (see Mt 9:17 and note), but not new ones. Elihu is obviously eager to speak.

33:1–33 Elihu turns to Job and speaks directly to him. Unlike the three friends, he addresses Job by name (vv. 1,31; 37:14).

33:1 *pay attention to everything I say.* He is thoroughly convinced of the importance and wisdom of the advice he is about to give (see vv. 31,33).

33:4 *Spirit of God has made me.* See Ge 1:2 and note. *breath of the Almighty.* See 32:8. *gives me life.* See 27:3; see also Ge 2:7 and note.

C **33:5** *Answer me.* He opens and closes his speech (see v. 32) with the same plea. *if you can.* His attitude of superiority shows through.

33:6 d Ac 14:15;
Jas 5:17 e S Job 4:19
33:7 f S Job 9:34;
2Co 2:4
33:9 g S Job 10:7
h S Job 9:30; S 13:23
i S Job 2:9
33:10 j S Job 13:24
33:11 k S Job 13:27
l Job 14:16; Pr 3:6;
Isa 30:21
33:12 m S Job 5:9;
Ps 8:4; 50:21;
Ecc 7:20; Isa 55:8-9
33:13 n Job 40:2;
Isa 45:9 o S Job 11:8
33:14 p Ps 62:11
q ver 29 r Job 4:12
33:15 s Ge 20:3;
Job 4:13; S Mt 27:19
t Ac 16:9 u S Ge 15:1;
Da 2:19 v S Ge 2:21
33:16 w Job 36:10,
15 x S Job 6:4
y Ps 88:15-16
33:17 z S Job 20:6
33:18 a ver 22,24,
28, 30; Ps 28:1; 30:9;
69:15; 88:6; 103:4;
Pr 1:12; Isa 14:15;
38:17; Jnh 2:6;
Zec 9:11 b S Job 15:22;
Mt 26:52
33:19 c S Job 5:17
d S Ge 17:1; S Dt 8:5;
2Co 12:7-10; Jas 1:3
e S Job 16:16; Ps 6:2;
38:3; Isa 38:13
33:20 f Ps 102:4;
107:18 g S Job 3:24;
S 6:6
33:21 h S Job 2:5
i S Job 16:8
33:22 j S ver 18
k Job 38:17; Ps 9:13;
88:3; 107:18; 116:3
33:23 l Gal 3:19;
Heb 8:6; 9:15

⁶ I am the same as you in God's sight; d
   I too am a piece of clay. e
⁷ No fear of me should alarm you,
   nor should my hand be heavy on you. f

⁸ "But you have said in my hearing—
   I heard the very words—
⁹ 'I am pure, g I have done no wrong; h
   I am clean and free from sin. i
¹⁰ Yet God has found fault with me;
   he considers me his enemy. j
¹¹ He fastens my feet in shackles; k
   he keeps close watch on all my paths.' l

¹² "But I tell you, in this you are not right,
   for God is greater than any mortal. m
¹³ Why do you complain to him n
   that he responds to no one's words a? o
¹⁴ For God does speak p—now one way, now another q—
   though no one perceives it. r
¹⁵ In a dream, s in a vision t of the night, u
   when deep sleep v falls on people
   as they slumber in their beds,
¹⁶ he may speak w in their ears
   and terrify them x with warnings, y
¹⁷ to turn them from wrongdoing
   and keep them from pride, z
¹⁸ to preserve them from the pit, a
   their lives from perishing by the sword. b b

¹⁹ "Or they may be chastened c on a bed of pain d
   with constant distress in their bones, e
²⁰ so that their bodies find food f repulsive
   and their souls loathe the choicest meal. g
²¹ Their flesh wastes away to nothing,
   and their bones, h once hidden, now stick out. i
²² They draw near to the pit, j
   and their lives to the messengers of death. c k
²³ Yet if there is an angel at their side,
   a messenger, l one out of a thousand,

---

a 13 Or *that he does not answer for any of his actions*   b 18 Or *from crossing the river*   c 22 Or *to the place of the dead*

33:6 *I…am a piece of clay.* See note on 4:19.
33:7 *hand…heavy on.* The idiom is elsewhere used only of God (see 23:2 and TNIV text notes; see also note on 1Sa 5:6).
33:8 *But you have said.* Elihu's method is to quote Job (vv. 9–11; 34:5–6,9; 35:2–3) and then show him where and how he is wrong. The quotations are not always verbatim, which indicates that Elihu is content simply to repeat the substance of Job's arguments.
33:11 Elihu quotes Job's words almost verbatim here (see 13:27).
33:12 *you are not right.* Elihu feels that Job needs to be corrected. Certainly Job's perception of God as his enemy (see v. 10; 13:24; 19:11) is wrong, but Elihu is also offended by what he considers Job's claim to purity (see v. 9). Job, however, had never claimed to be "pure …and free from sin," though some of his words were also understood that way by Eliphaz (see 15:14–16). Job admits being a sinner (7:21; 13:26) but disclaims the outrageous sins for which he thinks he is being punished. His complaints about God's silence (see v. 13) are also an offense to Elihu. He imputes to Job the blanket statement that God never speaks to human beings, whereas Job's point is that God is silent in his present experience.
33:15 *In a dream…when deep sleep falls on people.* Elihu echoes Eliphaz (see 4:13).
33:18 *pit.* A metaphor for the grave (see vv. 22,24,28,30), as of-

ten in the Psalms. *perishing by the sword.* See 36:12. The reading in the TNIV text note on both verses refers to the figurative waterway between the land of the living and the realm of the dead. The Hebrew for "River" here is *shelah* (from a root that means "to send") and sometimes means "water channel" (see Ne 3:15 and TNIV text note), a conduit through which water is "sent" (see Jn 9:7 and note) by a spring. The "River" therefore is the figurative means of passage between this world and the next.
33:19 *they may be chastened on a bed of pain.* Dreams and visions (see v. 15) are not the only ways in which God speaks. He can talk to us in ways that we do not perceive (see v. 14). Elihu rightly states that God speaks to humans in order to turn them from sin. But he overlooks Job's reason for wanting an audience with God: to find out what sins he is being accused of (see 13:22–23).
33:23–28 Having emphasized the importance of the chastening aspect of suffering, a point mentioned only briefly by Eliphaz (see 5:17; see also note on 5:17–26), Elihu now moves on to the possibility of deliverance and restoration based on a mediator (see note on 5:1). He further allows for God's gracious response of forgiveness whenever sincere repentance is present (vv. 27–28). But Elihu is still ignorant of the true nature of Job's relationship to God, known only in the divine council (chs. 1–2).

sent to tell them how to be upright, *m*
24 and he is gracious to them and says to God,
  'Spare them from going down to the pit; *n*
  I have found a ransom for them *o*—
25 let their flesh be renewed *p* like a child's;
  let them be restored as in the days of their youth' *q*—
26 then they can pray to God and find favor with him, *r*
  they will see God's face and shout for joy; *s*
  he will restore them to full well-being. *t*
27 And they will go to others and say,
  'We have sinned, *u* we have perverted what is right, *v*
  but we did not get what we deserved. *w*
28 God has delivered *x* us from going down to the pit, *y*
  and we shall live to enjoy the light of life.' *z*

29 "God does all these things to people *a*—
  twice, even three times *b*—
30 to turn them back *c* from the pit, *d*
  that the light of life *e* may shine on them. *f*

31 "Pay attention, Job, and listen *g* to me; *h*
  be silent, *i* and I will speak.
32 If you have anything to say, answer me; *j*
  speak up, for I want to vindicate you. *k*
33 But if not, then listen to me; *l*
  be silent, *m* and I will teach you wisdom. *n*"

34

Then Elihu said:

2 "Hear my words, you wise men;
  listen to me, *o* you men of learning.
3 For the ear tests words
  as the tongue tastes food. *p*
4 Let us discern for ourselves what is right; *q*
  let us learn together what is good. *r*

5 "Job says, 'I am innocent, *s*
  but God denies me justice. *t*
6 Although I am right,
  I am considered a liar; *u*
although I am guiltless, *v*
  his arrow inflicts an incurable wound.' *w*
7 Is there anyone like Job,
  who drinks scorn like water? *x*
8 He keeps company with evildoers;

33:23 *m* Job 36:9-10; Mic 6:8
33:24 *n* S ver 18
  o S Job 6:22
33:25 *p* Ps 103:5
  q 2Ki 5:14
33:26 *r* S Job 5:15; Pr 8:35; 12:2; 18:22; Lk 2:52 *s* S Ezr 3:13; S Job 22:26 *t* Ps 13:5; 50:15; 51:12; 1Jn 1:9
33:27 *u* S Nu 22:34
  v Lk 15:21
  w S Ezr 9:13; Ps 22:27; 51:13; Ro 6:21; Jas 2:13
33:28 *x* S Ex 15:13; Ps 34:22; 107:20
  y S ver 18; S Job 17:16
  z S Job 22:28
33:29 *a* Ps 139:16; Pr 16:9; 20:24; Jer 10:23; 1Co 12:6; Eph 1:11; Php 2:13
  b ver 14
33:30 *c* Jas 5:19
  d S ver 18 *e* Ps 49:19; 56:13; 116:9; Isa 53:11
  f Isa 60:1; Eph 5:14
33:31 *g* Jer 23:18
  h S Job 32:10 *i* ver 33
33:32 *j* ver 5
  k S Job 6:29; 35:2
33:33 *l* S Job 32:10
  m ver 31 *n* S Job 6:24; Pr 10:8,10,19
34:2 *o* S Job 32:10
34:3 *p* Job 12:11
34:4 *q* S Job 12:12; Heb 5:14 *r* 1Th 5:21
34:5 *s* S Job 10:7
  t S Job 6:29
34:6 *u* S Job 6:28
  v S Job 9:21
  w S Job 6:4; S 10:3; S Jer 10:19
34:7 *x* S Job 9:21; S 15:16

33:24 *Spare them from going down to the pit.* See Isa 38:17 and note. *ransom.* See Ps 49:7–9 and note.
33:25 *flesh be renewed like a child's . . . restored.* Similar phrases are used in 2Ki 5:14 with reference to healing from leprosy.
33:26 *see God's face.* Not literally (see note on Ge 16:13).
33:29 *twice . . . three times.* See note on 5:19.
C **33:30** *to turn them back from the pit.* Elihu teaches that God's apparent harshness in chastening human beings is in reality an act of love, since they are never punished in this life in keeping with what they fully deserve (see v. 27). *light of life.* Spiritual well-being (see Ps 49:19; see also Ps 27:1 and note). In some contexts, the phrase refers to resurrection (see note on Isa 53:11).
33:32 *I want to vindicate you.* But this will happen, Elihu insists, only if Job repents.
C **34:1–37** The second of Elihu's four speeches (see note on 32:1—37:24), divided into three sections: (1) addressed to a group of wise men (vv. 2–15), doubtless including the three friends; (2) addressed to Job (vv. 16–33); (3) addressed to himself (vv. 34–37), as in 32:15–22 (see note there).
34:2,10 *listen to me.* Although it is possible that Elihu is overly

impressed with his own wisdom, it is more likely that he considered himself a messenger of God (see 32:8,18 and TNIV text note on 32:8), especially in the light of his humble attitude in v. 4.
34:2 *wise men . . . men of learning.* Also referred to as "men of understanding" (vv. 10,34).
34:3 Elihu echoes the words of Job in 12:11 (see note there).
34:5,9 *Job says . . . For he says.* Elihu again quotes Job and then goes on to defend God's justice against what he considers to be Job's false theology (e.g., 9:14–24; 16:11–17; 19:7; 21:17–18; 24:1–12; 27:2). The substance of the quotation in v. 5 is accurate (cf. 12:4; 13:18; 27:6), and much of v. 6 represents Job fairly (see 21:34; 27:5; see also 6:4 and note)— though Job had never claimed to be completely guiltless. Verse 9 is not a direct quotation from Job, who had only imagined the wicked saying something similar (see 21:15). But perhaps Elihu derives it from Job's repeated statement that God treats the righteous and the wicked in the same way (cf. 9:22; 21:17; 24:1–12), leading to the conclusion that it does not pay to please God.
34:7 *drinks scorn like water.* See Eliphaz's description of humans in 15:16.

34:8 ʸ S Job 22:15
34:9 ᶻ S Job 9:29-31;
S 21:15
34:10 ᵃ Job 32:10
ᵇ ver 16; S Job 12:12
ᶜ S Ge 18:25 ᵈ ver 12;
Dt 32:4; Job 8:3;
36:23; Ps 92:15;
Ro 3:5; 9:14
34:11 ᵉ S Job 21:31;
S Mt 16:27 ᶠ Jer 17:10;
32:19; Eze 33:20
34:12 ᵍ S ver 10;
Tit 1:2; Heb 6:18
ʰ S Job 8:3; Ps 9:16;
Col 3:25; 2Th 1:6
34:13 ⁱ Heb 1:2
ʲ Job 36:23; 38:4,6;
Isa 40:14
34:14 ᵏ S Ge 6:3
ˡ S Nu 16:22;
S Job 27:3
34:15 ᵐ S Ge 6:13;
La 3:22; Mal 3:6;
Jn 3:16 ⁿ S Ge 2:7;
S Job 7:21; 9:22;
Ps 90:10
34:16 ᵒ S ver 10
ᵖ S Job 32:10
34:17 �q ver 30;
2Sa 23:3-4; Pr 20:8,
26; 24:23-25; 28:28
ʳ ver 29; S Job 10:7;
40:8; Ro 3:5-6
34:18 ˢ S Job 12:18
ᵗ Ex 22:28; Isa 40:24
34:19 ᵘ S Job 13:10;
S Ac 10:34
ᵛ S Lev 19:15; Jas 2:5
ʷ S Job 10:3
34:20 ˣ ver 25;
S Ex 11:4; S Job 20:8
ʸ S Job 12:19
34:21 ᶻ Jer 32:19
ᵃ S Job 14:16; Pr 15:3;
S Heb 4:13
34:22 ᵇ S Job 3:5
ᶜ Ps 74:20 ᵈ S Ge 3:8;
S Job 11:20
34:23 ᵉ Ps 11:4
ᶠ Job 11:11
34:24 ᵍ Isa 8:9; 9:4;
Jer 51:20; Da 2:34
ʰ Job 12:19 ⁱ Da 2:21
34:25 ʲ S Job 11:11
ᵏ S ver 20 ˡ Pr 5:21-23
34:26 ᵐ S Ge 6:5;
S Job 8:22; S 28:24;
Ps 9:5; Jer 44:5
34:27 ⁿ Ps 14:3
ᵒ S 1Sa 15:11
34:28 ᵖ S Ex 22:23;
S Job 5:15; S 12:19
34:29 q Ps 28:1;
83:1; 109:1 ʳ S ver 17;
Ro 8:34 ˢ Ps 13:1
ᵗ Ps 83:18; 97:9

he associates with the wicked. ʸ
⁹ For he says, 'There is no profit
    in trying to please God.' ᶻ

¹⁰ "So listen to me, ᵃ you men of understanding. ᵇ
    Far be it from God to do evil, ᶜ
    from the Almighty to do wrong. ᵈ
¹¹ He repays everyone for what they have done; ᵉ
    he brings on them what their conduct deserves. ᶠ
¹² It is unthinkable that God would do wrong, ᵍ
    that the Almighty would pervert justice. ʰ
¹³ Who appointed ⁱ him over the earth?
    Who put him in charge of the whole world? ʲ
¹⁴ If it were his intention
    and he withdrew his spiritᵃ ᵏ and breath, ˡ
¹⁵ all people would perish ᵐ together
    and would return to the dust. ⁿ

¹⁶ "If you have understanding, ᵒ hear this;
    listen to what I say. ᵖ
¹⁷ Can one who hates justice govern? q
    Will you condemn the just and mighty One? ʳ
¹⁸ Is he not the One who says to kings, 'You are worthless,'
    and to nobles, ˢ 'You are wicked,' ᵗ
¹⁹ who shows no partiality ᵘ to princes
    and does not favor the rich over the poor, ᵛ
    for they are all the work of his hands? ʷ
²⁰ They die in an instant, in the middle of the night; ˣ
    the people are shaken and they pass away;
    the mighty are removed without human hand. ʸ

²¹ "His eyes are on the ways of mortals; ᶻ
    he sees their every step. ᵃ
²² There is no deep shadow, ᵇ no utter darkness, ᶜ
    where evildoers can hide. ᵈ
²³ God has no need to examine people further, ᵉ
    that they should come before him for judgment. ᶠ
²⁴ Without inquiry he shatters ᵍ the mighty ʰ
    and sets up others in their place. ⁱ
²⁵ Because he takes note of their deeds, ʲ
    he overthrows them in the night ᵏ and they are crushed. ˡ
²⁶ He punishes them for their wickedness ᵐ
    where everyone can see them,
²⁷ because they turned from following him ⁿ
    and had no regard for any of his ways. ᵒ
²⁸ They caused the cry of the poor to come before him,
    so that he heard the cry of the needy. ᵖ
²⁹ But if he remains silent, q who can condemn him? ʳ
    If he hides his face, ˢ who can see him?
    Yet he is over individual and nation alike, ᵗ

ᵃ 14 Or Spirit

34:10 *Far be it from God to do evil.* See Ge 18:25 and
note. Elihu's concern that Job was making God the author
of evil is commendable. Job, in his frustration, has come per-
ilously close to charging God with wrongdoing (12:4–6;
24:1–12). He has suggested that this is the only conclusion he
can reach on the basis of his knowledge and experience (9:24).
34:11 See Ecc 12:14; Ro 2:6–11; 2Co 5:10 and notes.
34:13–15 Elihu is zealous for God's glory as the sovereign Sustainer who demonstrates his grace every moment by granting life and breath to human beings.
34:15 *return to the dust.* See Ecc 12:7; see also Ge 3:19 and note.
34:16 *hear…listen.* The Hebrew for these verbs is singular, addressed to Job. Elihu is concerned that Job's attitude

about God's justice be corrected (see v. 17), so he stresses God's
impartial rule as Lord of all, especially in meting out justice to
the wicked in high places (see vv. 18–20).
34:18 *worthless.* See note on Dt 13:13.
34:21–28 God's omniscience guarantees that he will
not make any mistakes when he punishes evildoers. It is
not necessary for him to set times to examine people for judgment (see v. 23; contrast 24:1).
34:21 Elihu echoes the words of Job in 31:4.
34:29 *if he remains silent, who can condemn him?* Elihu attempts to answer Job's complaint about God's silence (ch. 23).
God watches over people and nations to see that right is done
(vv. 29–30).

³⁰ to keep the godless ^u from ruling, ^v
　　from laying snares for the people. ^w

³¹ "Suppose someone says to God,
　　'I am guilty ^x but will offend no more.
³² Teach me what I cannot see; ^y
　　if I have done wrong, I will not do so again.' ^z
³³ Should God then reward you on your terms,
　　when you refuse to repent? ^a
　　You must decide, not I;
　　so tell me what you know.

³⁴ "Men of understanding declare,
　　wise men who hear me say to me,
³⁵ 'Job speaks without knowledge; ^b
　　his words lack insight.' ^c
³⁶ Oh, that Job might be tested to the utmost
　　for answering like a wicked man! ^d
³⁷ To his sin he adds rebellion;
　　scornfully he claps his hands ^e among us
　　and multiplies his words ^f against God." ^g

35

Then Elihu said:

² "Do you think this is just?
　　You say, 'I am in the right, ^h not God.' ⁱ
³ Yet you ask him, 'What profit is it to me, ^a
　　and what do I gain by not sinning?' ^j

⁴ "I would like to reply to you
　　and to your friends with you.
⁵ Look up at the heavens ^k and see;
　　gaze at the clouds so high above you. ^l
⁶ If you sin, how does that affect him?
　　If your sins are many, what does that do to him? ^m
⁷ If you are righteous, what do you give to him, ⁿ
　　or what does he receive ^o from your hand? ^p
⁸ Your wickedness only affects human beings like yourself, ^q
　　and your righteousness only members of the human race. ^r

⁹ "People cry out ^s under a load of oppression; ^t
　　they plead for relief from the arm of the powerful. ^u
¹⁰ But no one says, 'Where is God my Maker, ^v
　　who gives songs ^w in the night, ^x
¹¹ who teaches ^y us ^z more than he teaches ^b the beasts of the earth
　　and makes us wiser than ^c the birds in the sky?'
¹² He does not answer ^a when people cry out
　　because of the arrogance ^b of the wicked. ^c

^a 3 Or you　^b 10,11 Or night, / ¹¹who teaches us by　^c 11 Or us wise by

---

34:31–33 First indirectly (vv. 31–32) and then more directly (v. 33), Elihu condemns Job and calls for his repentance.
34:35 *Job speaks without knowledge.* A motif in the first discourse of the Lord (see 38:2 and note) and the final response of Job (see 42:3).
35:1–16 Elihu's third speech (see note on 32:1—37:24), addressed to Job.

🅰 **35:2** *in the right.* The Hebrew for this phrase is translated "vindicated" in Job's statement in 13:18. Elihu thinks that it is unjust and inconsistent for Job to expect vindication from God and at the same time imply that God does not care whether we are righteous (see v. 3). But allowance must be made for a person to express his feelings. The psalmist who thirsted for God (Ps 42:1–2) also questioned why God had forgotten him (Ps 42:9) and rejected him (Ps 43:2).
35:5 *Look up at the heavens and see.* Elihu asserts that God is so

far above human beings that there is really nothing they can do, good or bad, that will affect God's essential nature (see v. 6).
35:9 *People cry out … they plead for relief.* Elihu states that those like Job who pray for help when suffering innocently never seem to get around to trusting the justice and goodness of their Maker, who is also the author of wisdom and joy (see vv. 10–11). Such failure is a sign of arrogance (see v. 12), so Job's complaint against God's justice and about God's silence is meaningless talk (see vv. 13–16).
🅰 **35:10–11** *God … gives songs … teaches … makes us wiser.* God chooses to condescend, to reach out to people in love.
35:12 The verse is difficult. A comma after the first line would change the meaning and make more sense of the verse in context: Since the wicked are arrogant, God does not listen (see v. 13). Job himself shares their arrogance. He too receives no answer, because he does not ask rightly (see v. 14).

34:30 ^u S Job 8:13 ^v S ver 17 ^w Ps 25:15; 31:4; 91:3; 124:7; 140:5; Pr 29:2-12 **34:31** ^x Ps 51:5; Lk 15:21; Ro 7:24; 1Jn 1:8,10 **34:32** ^y Ex 33:13; Job 35:11; 38:36; Ps 15:2; 25:4; 27:11; 51:6; 86:11; 139:23-24; 143:8 ^z Job 33:27; S Lk 19:8 **34:33** ^a S 2Ki 17:13; Job 33:23; 36:10,15, 18,21; 41:11; 42:6; Pr 17:23; Jnh 3:8 **34:35** ^b Job 35:16; 38:2; 42:3 ^c Job 26:3 **34:36** ^d S Job 6:29; S 22:15 **34:37** ^e S Job 27:23 ^f Job 35:16 ^g Job 23:2 **35:2** ^h S Job 33:32 ⁱ S Job 2:9; S 32:2 **35:3** ^j S Job 9:29-31; S 21:15 **35:5** ^k S Ge 15:5; S Dt 10:14 ^l S Job 11:7-9; Ps 19:1-4 **35:6** ^m S Job 7:20 **35:7** ⁿ Ro 11:35 ^o 1Co 4:7 ^p S Job 22:2-3; Lk 17:10 **35:8** ^q Eze 18:24 ^r Eze 18:5-9; Zec 7:9-10 **35:9** ^s Ex 2:23 ^t S Job 20:19 ^u S Job 5:15; S 12:19 **35:10** ^v S Job 4:17 ^w S Job 8:21 ^x Ps 42:8; 77:6; 119:62; 149:5; Ac 16:25 **35:11** ^y S Job 21:22; Lk 12:24 ^z Job 12:7 **35:12** ^a S 1Sa 8:18 ^b S Job 15:25 ^c Ps 66:18

35:13 *d* S Dt 1:45;
S 1Sa 8:18;
S Job 15:31; S Pr 15:8
35:14 *e* S Job 9:11
f Ps 37:6 *g* Job 31:35
35:15 *h* S Job 9:24
i S Job 18:5; Ps 10:11;
Hos 7:2; Am 8:7
35:16 *j* Tit 1:10
k S Job 34:35,37;
1Co 4:20; Jude 1:10
36:3 *l* S Job 6:28
m S Job 4:17
36:4 *n* S Job 6:28;
S 13:6 *o* Job 37:5,16,
23 *p* S Job 32:17
36:5 *q* S Job 9:4
r Ps 5:2; 22:24; 31:22;
69:33; 102:17; 103:10
s S Nu 23:19; Ro 11:29
36:6 *t* S Job 34:26
u S Job 4:10
36:7 *v* S Job 11:11;
Ps 11:5; 33:18; 34:15;
Mt 6:18 *w* Ps 113:8;
Isa 22:23 *x* S 1Sa 2:7-
8; S Job 4:7
36:8 *y* S 2Sa 3:34;
2Ki 23:33; Ps 107:10,
14 *z* ver 10,15,21;
Ps 119:67,71
36:9 *a* S Job 15:25
36:10 *b* S Job 33:16
c S Job 5:17 *d* S ver 8;
S Jdg 6:8;
S Job 34:33; 1Th 5:22
36:11 *e* S Lev 26:33;
Dt 28:1; Isa 1:19;
Hag 1:12 *f* S Dt 30:15;
S Job 8:7 *g* S Ex 8:22;
S Dt 8:1; Jn 14:21;
1Ti 4:8
36:12 *h* S Lev 26:38;
S Job 15:22
i S Job 4:21; Eph 4:18
36:13 *j* S Job 15:12;
Ro 2:5 *k* S Job 5:2
l S Job 4:17; Am 4:11
36:14 *m* S Job 15:32
n S Dt 23:17
36:15 *o* S Job 5:15
p 2Co 12:10
q S Job 33:16 *r* S ver 8;
S Job 34:33

13 Indeed, God does not listen to their empty plea;
　the Almighty pays no attention to it. *d*
14 How much less, then, will he listen
　when you say that you do not see him, *e*
that your case *f* is before him
　and you must wait for him, *g*
15 and further, that his anger never punishes *h*
　and he does not take the least notice of wickedness. *a i*
16 So Job opens his mouth with empty talk; *j*
　without knowledge he multiplies words." *k*

36

Elihu continued:

2 "Bear with me a little longer and I will show you
　that there is more to be said in God's behalf.
3 I get my knowledge from afar; *l*
　I will ascribe justice to my Maker. *m*
4 Be assured that my words are not false; *n*
　one who has perfect knowledge *o* is with you. *p*

5 "God is mighty, *q* but despises no one; *r*
　he is mighty, and firm in his purpose. *s*
6 He does not keep the wicked alive *t*
　but gives the afflicted their rights. *u*
7 He does not take his eyes off the righteous; *v*
　he enthrones them with kings *w*
　and exalts them forever. *x*
8 But if people are bound in chains, *y*
　held fast by cords of affliction, *z*
9 he tells them what they have done—
　that they have sinned arrogantly. *a*
10 He makes them listen *b* to correction *c*
　and commands them to repent of their evil. *d*
11 If they obey and serve him, *e*
　they will spend the rest of their days in prosperity *f*
　and their years in contentment. *g*
12 But if they do not listen,
　they will perish by the sword *b h*
　and die without knowledge. *i*

13 "The godless in heart *j* harbor resentment; *k*
　even when he fetters them, they do not cry for help. *l*
14 They die in their youth, *m*
　among male prostitutes of the shrines. *n*
15 But those who suffer *o* he delivers in their suffering; *p*
　he speaks *q* to them in their affliction. *r*

---

a 15 Symmachus, Theodotion and Vulgate; the meaning of the Hebrew for this word is uncertain.
b 12 Or *will cross the river*

35:16 *without knowledge.* See 38:2 and note. *multiplies words.* Against God (see 34:37).
36:1—37:24 Elihu's fourth and final (see 36:2) speech (see note on 32:1—37:24), addressed for the most part to Job (but see note on 37:2).
36:2–4 Elihu desires to strengthen the case for God's goodness and justice.

C **36:4** *perfect knowledge.* Here Elihu applies the phrase to himself, while in 37:16 he applies it to God—thus appearing to make himself equal to God. But the Hebrew for "knowledge" is not quite the same here as in 37:16. Elihu is probably referring to his ability as a communicator; i.e., he claims perfection in the knowledge of speech (see note on 32:6,10,17).

A **36:5** God's power assures the fulfillment of his purpose.

36:6–9 A classic statement of God's justice in rewarding the righteous and punishing sinners (in contrast to what Job has been claiming). In v. 7 Elihu perhaps has in mind Job's complaint that God will not leave him alone (see 7:17–19), and in v. 9 he may be thinking of Job's charge that God will not present his indictment against him (see 31:35–36).
36:10 *makes them listen to correction.* Elihu states that God uses trouble to gain people's attention.
36:12 See TNIV text note (see also note on 33:18).
36:13–15 Elihu understands that the basic spiritual need of human beings stems from their hardness of heart—their refusal to yield to God, to cry out to God in their distress (see Ps 107:6 and note), or to hear the voice of God in their suffering.
36:14 *male prostitutes of the shrines.* See note on 1Ki 14:24.

¹⁶ "He is wooing ^s you from the jaws of distress
    to a spacious place ^t free from restriction, ^u
    to the comfort of your table ^v laden with choice food. ^w
¹⁷ But now you are laden with the judgment due the wicked; ^x
    judgment and justice have taken hold of you. ^y
¹⁸ Be careful that no one entices you by riches;
    do not let a large bribe ^z turn you aside. ^a
¹⁹ Would your wealth ^b or even all your mighty efforts
    sustain you so you would not be in distress?
²⁰ Do not long for the night, ^c
    to drag people away from their homes. ^a
²¹ Beware of turning to evil, ^d
    which you seem to prefer to affliction. ^e

²² "God is exalted in his power. ^f
    Who is a teacher like him? ^g
²³ Who has prescribed his ways ^h for him, ⁱ
    or said to him, 'You have done wrong'? ^j
²⁴ Remember to extol his work, ^k
    which people have praised in song. ^l
²⁵ All human beings have seen it; ^m
    mortals gaze on it from afar.
²⁶ How great is God—beyond our understanding! ⁿ
    The number of his years is past finding out. ^o

²⁷ "He draws up the drops of water, ^p
    which distill as rain to the streams ^b; ^q
²⁸ the clouds pour down their moisture
    and abundant showers ^r fall on the human race. ^s
²⁹ Who can understand how he spreads out the clouds,
    how he thunders ^t from his pavilion? ^u
³⁰ See how he scatters his lightning ^v about him,
    bathing the depths of the sea. ^w
³¹ This is the way he governs ^c the nations ^x
    and provides food ^y in abundance. ^z
³² He fills his hands with lightning
    and commands it to strike its mark. ^a
³³ His thunder announces the coming storm; ^b
    even the cattle make known its approach. ^{d c}

37 "At this my heart pounds ^d
    and leaps from its place.
² Listen! ^e Listen to the roar of his voice, ^f
    to the rumbling that comes from his mouth. ^g
³ He unleashes his lightning ^h beneath the whole heaven
    and sends it to the ends of the earth. ⁱ
⁴ After that comes the sound of his roar;

---

^a 20 The meaning of the Hebrew for verses 18-20 is uncertain.   ^b 27 Or distill from the mist as rain
^c 31 Or nourishes   ^d 33 Or announces his coming— / the One zealous against evil

36:16 ^s Hos 2:14
^t 2Sa 22:20;
Ps 18:19 ^u Ps 118:5
^v Ps 23:5; 78:19
^w S Ge 17:1;
S Job 15:11
36:17 ^x S Job 20:29
^y Job 22:11
36:18 ^z S Ex 23:8;
Am 5:12 ^a S Job 34:33
36:19 ^b Ps 49:6;
Jer 9:23
36:20 ^c Job 34:20,25
36:21 ^d S Job 34:33;
Ps 66:18 ^e S ver 8;
Heb 11:25
36:22 ^f S Job 5:9;
S 9:4 ^g S Job 21:22;
S Ro 11:34
36:23 ^h Job 27:11
ⁱ S Job 34:13; Ro 11:33
^j S Ge 18:25;
S Job 34:10
36:24 ^k 1Ch 16:24;
Ps 35:27; 92:5; 111:2;
138:5; 145:10
^l S Ex 15:1; Rev 15:3
36:25 ^m Ro 1:20
36:26 ⁿ S Job 5:9;
1Co 13:12
^o S Ge 21:33;
S Job 10:5; Heb 1:12
36:27 ^p S Job 26:8
^q S 2Sa 1:21;
Job 28:26; 38:28;
Isa 55:10
36:28 ^r Ps 65:10;
72:6; Joel 2:23
^s S Job 5:10; S 22:11;
S 28:26; Mt 5:45
36:29 ^t Ps 29:3;
Jer 10:13 ^u S Job 9:6;
37:16; Ps 18:7-15;
19:4,5; 104:2; Pr 8:28;
Isa 40:22
36:30 ^v Ex 19:16;
Job 37:11,15; Ps 18:12,
14; 97:4; Jer 10:13;
Hab 3:11 ^w Ps 68:22;
Isa 51:10
36:31 ^x Dt 28:23-
24; 1Ki 17:1;
Job 37:13; Am 4:7-8
^y Ps 145:15
^z Ps 104:14,15,27-28;
Isa 30:23; Ac 14:17
36:32 ^a S Job 28:24;
37:12,15; Ps 18:14;
29:7-9
36:33 ^b Job 37:5;
40:9 ^c S Job 28:26
37:1 ^d Ps 38:10;
Isa 15:5; Jer 4:19;
Hab 3:16
37:2 ^e S Job 32:10
^f ver 5 ^g Ps 18:13;
29:3-9
37:3 ^h S 2Sa 22:13;
Ps 18:14 ⁱ S Job 36:32;
Mt 24:27; Lk 17:24

36:16–21 Elihu warns Job to respond to God's discipline by turning away from evil (see v. 21). Verse 16 shows that he still views Job as a man for whom there is hope.

36:16 *He is wooing you.* With tender compassion, God brings his people back to himself (see Hos 2:14 and note).
36:21 *Beware of turning to evil.* Elihu's evaluation of Job is the opposite of God's (see 1:8 and note; 2:3).
36:22–33 Elihu anticipates some of God's statements in the discourses of chs. 38–41.
36:24 *his work, which people have praised in song.* See, e.g., notes on Ex 15:1–18; Jdg 5:1–31.

36:26 *beyond our understanding.* See 37:5. That God's ways and thoughts are infinitely higher than ours is an important theme in chs. 38–41 (see also Isa 55:8–9; Ro 11:33–36).
36:30 *bathing.* That is, in light.
36:31 *governs.* The TNIV text note understands the verse to

mean that the Lord "nourishes" the nations with the showers mentioned in vv. 27–30.
37:1–13 A continuation of Elihu's hymnic description of God's marvels exhibited in the earth's atmosphere, beginning in 36:27. His heart pounds at the awesome display (see v. 1). The passage reveals a sophisticated observation of atmospheric conditions and their effects: the evaporation and distillation of water for rain (see 36:27 and TNIV text note), the clouds as holders of moisture (see 36:28; 37:11) and the cyclonic behavior of clouds (see v. 12). Such forces originate from God's command and always perform his will for humankind, whether for good or for ill (v. 13).
37:2 *Listen.* The Hebrew for this verb is plural, indicating that others (including the three friends) besides Job are being addressed here (see note on 36:1—37:24). *roar of his voice ... rumbling.* Thunder (see v. 4).

37:4 /S 1Sa 2:10
k S Ex 20:19
37:5 /S 1Sa 2:10;
Jn 12:29
m S Job 36:33
n S Job 5:9; S 11:7-9;
S 36:4
37:6 oDt 28:12;
Job 38:22 P S Ge 7:4;
S Job 5:10; S 28:26
37:7 q Ps 109:27
r Ps 104:19-23; 111:2
37:8 s S Job 28:26
t Job 38:40; Ps 104:22
37:9 u Ps 50:3
v Ps 147:17
37:10 w Job 38:29-
30; Ps 147:17
37:11 x S Job 26:8
y S Job 36:30
z S Job 28:26
37:12 a S ver 3;
Ps 147:16; 148:8
37:13 b S Ge 7:4;
Ex 9:22-23;
S 1Sa 12:17
c S 1Ki 18:45;
S Job 5:10; S 36:31;
38:27
37:14 d S Job 32:10
e S Job 5:9
37:15 f S Job 36:30
g S Job 8:3
37:16 h S Job 36:29
i S Job 5:9; S 36:4
37:17 j Ac 27:13
37:18 k S Ge 1:1,8;
S Job 22:14 l Dt 28:23
37:19 m Ro 8:26
n S Job 13:18
o S Job 9:3
37:21 p S Jdg 5:31;
Ac 22:11; 26:13
37:22 q Ps 19:5
r Ex 24:17
37:23 s S Job 5:9;
S 36:4; Ro 11:33;
1Ti 6:16 t S Job 8:3
u S Job 4:17; Ps 44:1;
Isa 63:9; Jer 25:5;
La 3:33; Eze 18:23,32
37:24 v S Ge 22:12;
Job 28:28; Ecc 12:13;
Mic 6:8; Mt 10:28
w S Job 5:13; Eph 5:15
38:1 x S Job 11:5
y S Ex 14:21;
S 1Sa 2:10; Job 40:6;
Isa 21:1; Eze 1:4
38:2 z S 1Ki 22:5;
Isa 40:13

he thunders[j] with his majestic voice.[k]
When his voice resounds,
  he holds nothing back.
[5] God's voice thunders[l] in marvelous ways;[m]
  he does great things beyond our understanding.[n]
[6] He says to the snow,[o] 'Fall on the earth,'
  and to the rain shower, 'Be a mighty downpour.'[p]
[7] So that everyone he has made may know his work,[q]
  he stops all mortals from their labor.[a][r]
[8] The animals take cover;[s]
  they remain in their dens.[t]
[9] The tempest comes out from its chamber,[u]
  the cold from the driving winds.[v]
[10] The breath of God produces ice,
  and the broad waters become frozen.[w]
[11] He loads the clouds with moisture;[x]
  he scatters his lightning[y] through them.[z]
[12] At his direction they swirl around
  over the face of the whole earth
  to do whatever he commands them.[a]
[13] He brings the clouds to punish people,[b]
  or to water his earth and show his love.[c]

[14] "Listen[d] to this, Job;
  stop and consider God's wonders.[e]
[15] Do you know how God controls the clouds
  and makes his lightning[f] flash?[g]
[16] Do you know how the clouds hang poised,[h]
  those wonders of him who has perfect knowledge?[i]
[17] You who swelter in your clothes
  when the land lies hushed under the south wind,[j]
[18] can you join him in spreading out the skies,[k]
  hard as a mirror of cast bronze?[l]

[19] "Tell us what we should say to him;[m]
  we cannot draw up our case[n] because of our darkness.[o]
[20] Should he be told that I want to speak?
  Would anyone ask to be swallowed up?
[21] Now no one can look at the sun,[p]
  bright as it is in the skies
  after the wind has swept them clean.
[22] Out of the north he comes in golden splendor;[q]
  God comes in awesome majesty.[r]
[23] The Almighty is beyond our reach and exalted in power;[s]
  in his justice[t] and great righteousness, he does not oppress.[u]
[24] Therefore, people revere him,[v]
  for does he not have regard for all the wise[w] in heart?[b]

THE LORD SPEAKS

38 Then the LORD spoke to Job[x] out of the storm.[y] He said:

[2] "Who is this that obscures my plans[z]

a 7 Or *work, / he fills all mortals with fear by his power*   b 24 Or *for he does not have regard for any who think they are wise.*

37:5 *beyond our understanding.* See note on 36:26.
37:10 *breath of God.* Here a metaphor for a chilling wind.
37:14–18 Elihu challenges Job to ponder God's power over the elements. The question format is also used in the divine discourses (chs. 38–41).
37:16 *perfect knowledge.* See note on 36:4.
37:18 See 26:7.
37:19 *we cannot draw up our case.* Job had dared to sign his defense and call for an audience with God (see 31:35). For this Elihu seeks to shame him. But he softens his tone by including

himself as one equally vulnerable to God's majesty.
37:22 *Out of the north he comes.* See note on Ps 48:2. *God comes.* Elihu prepares Job for the appearance of God in the storm (chs. 38–41).
37:24 *revere.* Fear (see 28:28; Ge 20:11 and notes).
38:1—42:6 The theophany (appearance of God) to Job, consisting of two discourses by the Lord (38:1—40:2; 40:6—41:34), each of which receives a brief response from Job (40:3–5; 42:1–6).
 38:1 *the LORD.* The Israelite covenant name for God (see Introduction: Author). *storm.* See 40:6. Elihu

with words without knowledge?[a]
3 Prepare to defend yourself;
  I will question you,
    and you shall answer me. [b]

4 "Where were you when I laid the earth's foundation? [c]
  Tell me, if you understand. [d]
5 Who marked off its dimensions? [e] Surely you know!
  Who stretched a measuring line [f] across it?
6 On what were its footings set, [g]
  or who laid its cornerstone [h]—
7 while the morning stars [i] sang together [j]
  and all the angels [a][k] shouted for joy? [l]

8 "Who shut up the sea behind doors [m]
  when it burst forth from the womb, [n]
9 when I made the clouds its garment
  and wrapped it in thick darkness, [o]
10 when I fixed limits for it [p]
  and set its doors and bars in place, [q]
11 when I said, 'This far you may come and no farther; [r]
  here is where your proud waves halt'? [s]

12 "Have you ever given orders to the morning, [t]
  or shown the dawn its place, [u]
13 that it might take the earth by the edges
  and shake the wicked [v] out of it? [w]
14 The earth takes shape like clay under a seal; [x]
  its features stand out like those of a garment.
15 The wicked are denied their light, [y]
  and their upraised arm is broken. [z]

16 "Have you journeyed to the springs of the sea
  or walked in the recesses of the deep? [a]
17 Have the gates of death [b] been shown to you?
  Have you seen the gates of the deepest darkness? [c]
18 Have you comprehended the vast expanses of the earth? [d]
  Tell me, if you know all this. [e]

a 7 Hebrew *the sons of God*

38:2 a S Job 34:35; Mk 10:38; 1Ti 1:7
38:3 b Job 40:7; 42:4; Mk 11:29
38:4 c S ver 5; S Ge 1:1; S 1Sa 2:8; d ver 18; S Job 34:13; Pr 30:4
38:5 e ver 4; Ps 102:25; Pr 8:29; Isa 40:12; 48:13; Jer 31:37 f Jer 31:39; Zec 1:16; 4:9-10
38:6 g Pr 8:25; h S Job 26:7
38:7 i S Ge 1:16; j Ps 19:1-4; 148:2-3; k 1Ki 22:19; l S Dt 16:15
38:8 m ver 11; Ps 33:7; Pr 8:29; Jer 5:22 n S Ge 1:9-10
38:9 o S Ge 1:2
38:10 p S Job 28:25; Ps 33:7; 104:9; Isa 40:12 q Ne 3:3; Job 7:12; 26:10
38:11 r S ver 8; s Ps 65:7; 89:9; 104:6-9
38:12 t Ps 57:8; u Ps 74:16; Am 5:8
38:13 v Ps 104:35; w S Job 8:22
38:14 x Ex 28:11
38:15 y S Dt 28:29; S Job 15:22; S 18:5; z S Ge 17:14; S Job 4:10; S 31:22
38:16 a S Ge 1:7; S Job 9:8
38:17 b S Job 33:22; Mt 16:18; Rev 1:18; c S Job 7:9
38:18 d S Job 28:24; Isa 40:12 e S ver 4

had imagined the appearance of the divine presence as a display of "golden splendor" and "awesome majesty" (37:22). He also had anticipated the storm or whirlwind (see note on 37:22), from which Job would hear the voice of God. Job had said, "let the Almighty answer me" (31:35). Now God speaks to Job, but not to give Job the justification of his ways that Job had been demanding. Out of the awesome majesty of the thunderstorm, he reminds Job that the wisdom that directs the Creator's ways is beyond the reach of human understanding—that humanity's almost godlike wisdom should not presume to match God's wisdom or take its measure.

38:2 See 35:16. In 42:3 Job echoes the Lord's words. God states that Job's complaining and raging against him are unjustified and proceed from limited understanding.

38:3 Repeated in 40:7 (see also 42:4). The format of God's response is to ply Job with rhetorical questions, to each of which Job must plead ignorance. God says nothing about Job's suffering, nor does he address Job's problem about divine justice. Job gets neither a bill of indictment nor a verdict of innocence. But, more importantly, God does not humiliate or condemn him—which surely would have been the case if the counselors had been right. So by implication Job is vindicated, and later his vindication is directly affirmed (see 42:7-9 and note). The divine discourses, then, succeed in bringing Job to complete faith in God's wisdom and goodness without his receiving a direct answer to his questions.

38:4-38 Inanimate creation testifies to God's sovereignty and power (the earth, vv. 4-7,18; the sea, vv. 8-11,16; the sun, vv. 12-15; the netherworld, v. 17; light and darkness, vv. 19-20; the weather, vv. 22-30,34-38; the constellations, vv. 31-33). See note on 38:39—39:30.

38:4-5 See the similar questions of Agur and the similar irony in his demand for a response (see Pr 30:4; Isa 40:12 and note).

38:7 See Ps 148:2-3 and note on Ps 65:13. When the earth was created, the angels were there to sing the praises of the Creator, but Job was not (see vv. 4-5). He should therefore not expect to be able to understand even lesser aspects of God's plans for the world and for humankind. *angels.* See TNIV text notes here and on 1:6; 2:1.

38:10-11 See Ps 33:7 and note; Jer 5:22.

38:11 *when I said.* God the Father controls the sea by speaking to it, as does God the Son (see Mk 4:41 and note; Lk 8:24-25).

38:12-13 The arrival of the dawn sends the wicked scurrying for cover.

38:14 *clay under a seal.* Either a cylinder seal (see note on Ge 38:18) or a stamp seal.

38:15 *their light.* The night is when the wicked are active (see Jn 3:19; for the imagery cf. Lk 11:35). *upraised arm is broken.* See 22:9 and note.

38:16 *springs of the sea.* See Ge 7:11; 8:2.

38:17 *gates of death.* See note on 17:16; see also 26:5-6.

38:19 ᶠS Ge 1:4;
S Job 28:3; Ps 139:11-
12
38:20 ᵍS Job 24:13
38:21 ʰJob 15:7
38:22 ⁱS Job 37:6
ʲS Dt 28:12
ᵏPs 105:32; 147:17
38:23 ˡPs 27:5;
Isa 28:17; 30:30;
Eze 13:11 ᵐEx 9:26;
Jos 10:11; Eze 13:13;
Rev 16:21
38:24 ⁿS Job 28:24
ᵒS Job 27:21
ᵖJer 10:13; 51:16
38:25 �q Job 28:26
38:26 ʳJob 36:27
ˢPs 84:6; 107:35;
Isa 41:18
38:27 ᵗS Job 28:26;
S 37:13; S Ps 104:14
38:28 ᵘS 2Sa 1:21;
S Job 5:10
38:29 ᵛPs 147:16-17
38:30 ʷJob 37:10
38:31 ˣJob 9:9;
Am 5:8
38:32 ʸ2Ki 23:5;
Isa 13:10; 40:26;
45:12; Jer 19:13
ᶻS Ge 1:16
38:33 ᵃPs 148:6;
Jer 31:36 ᵇS Ge 1:16
38:34 ᶜS Job 5:10;
S 22:11
38:35 ᵈS Job 36:32
38:36 ᵉS Job 9:4;
S 34:32; Jas 1:5
ᶠS Job 12:13
38:37 ᵍS Jos 3:16
ʰS Job 22:11
38:38 ⁱS Lev 26:19
ʲ1Ki 18:45
38:39 ᵏS Ge 49:9
38:40 ˡS Job 37:8
ᵐS Ge 49:9
38:41 ⁿS Ge 1:30
ᵒS Ge 8:7; Lk 12:24
ᵖPs 147:9; S Mt 6:26
39:1 �q S Dt 14:5
ʳGe 49:21

¹⁹ "What is the way to the abode of light?
And where does darkness reside? ᶠ
²⁰ Can you take them to their places?
Do you know the paths ᵍ to their dwellings?
²¹ Surely you know, for you were already born! ʰ
You have lived so many years!

²² "Have you entered the storehouses of the snow ⁱ
or seen the storehouses ʲ of the hail, ᵏ
²³ which I reserve for times of trouble, ˡ
for days of war and battle? ᵐ
²⁴ What is the way to the place where the lightning is dispersed, ⁿ
or the place where the east winds ᵒ are scattered over the earth? ᵖ
²⁵ Who cuts a channel for the torrents of rain,
and a path for the thunderstorm, q
²⁶ to water ʳ a land where no one lives,
an uninhabited desert, ˢ
²⁷ to satisfy a desolate wasteland
and make it sprout with grass? ᵗ
²⁸ Does the rain have a father? ᵘ
Who fathers the drops of dew?
²⁹ From whose womb comes the ice?
Who gives birth to the frost from the heavens ᵛ
³⁰ when the waters become hard as stone,
when the surface of the deep is frozen? ʷ

³¹ "Can you bind the chains ᵃ of the Pleiades?
Can you loosen Orion's belt? ˣ
³² Can you bring forth the constellations ʸ in their seasons ᵇ
or lead out the Bear ᶜ with its cubs? ᶻ
³³ Do you know the laws ᵃ of the heavens? ᵇ
Can you set up ⌊God's ᵈ⌋ dominion over the earth?

³⁴ "Can you raise your voice to the clouds
and cover yourself with a flood of water? ᶜ
³⁵ Do you send the lightning bolts on their way? ᵈ
Do they report to you, 'Here we are'?
³⁶ Who gives the ibis wisdom ᵉ ⌊about the flooding of the Nile⌋,
or gives the rooster understanding ᶠ ⌊of when to crow⌋? ᵉ
³⁷ Who has the wisdom to count the clouds?
Who can tip over the water jars ᵍ of the heavens ʰ
³⁸ when the dust becomes hard ⁱ
and the clods of earth stick together? ʲ

³⁹ "Do you hunt the prey for the lioness
and satisfy the hunger of the lions ᵏ
⁴⁰ when they crouch in their dens ˡ
or lie in wait in a thicket? ᵐ
⁴¹ Who provides food ⁿ for the raven ᵒ
when its young cry out to God
and wander about for lack of food? ᵖ

39

"Do you know when the mountain goats q give birth?
Do you watch when the doe bears her fawn? ʳ
² Do you count the months till they bear?

ᵃ 31 Septuagint; Hebrew *beauty*   ᵇ 32 Or *the morning star in its season*   ᶜ 32 Or *out Leo*
ᵈ 33 Or *his; or their*   ᵉ 36 The meaning of the Hebrew for this verse is uncertain.

38:22–23 *hail … for days of war.* See, e.g., Jos 10:11; Isa 28:2 and notes.
38:24 *east winds.* See note on 15:2.
38:31–32 *Pleiades … Orion's … Bear.* See note on 9:9.
38:36 *ibis … rooster.* Two birds whose habits were sometimes observed by people who wished to forecast the weather. The words serve as a transition to the next major section of the first divine discourse.

38:39—39:30 Animate creation testifies to God's sovereignty, power and loving care (the lion, 38:39–40; the raven, 38:41; the mountain goat, 39:1–4; the wild donkey, vv. 5–8; the wild ox, vv. 9–12; the ostrich, vv. 13–18; the horse, vv. 19–25; the hawk, v. 26; the eagle, vv. 27–30). See note on 38:4–38.
38:41 *provides food for the raven.* God cares for and feeds all the birds, of which the raven is representative (e.g., compare Lk 12:24 with Mt 6:26).

Do you know the time they give birth?[s]

[3] They crouch down and bring forth their young;
    their labor pains are ended.

[4] Their young thrive and grow strong in the wilds;
    they leave and do not return.

[5] "Who let the wild donkey[t] go free?
    Who untied its ropes?

[6] I gave it the wasteland[u] as its home,
    the salt flats[v] as its habitat.[w]

[7] It laughs[x] at the commotion in the town;
    it does not hear a driver's shout.[y]

[8] It ranges the hills[z] for its pasture
    and searches for any green thing.

[9] "Will the wild ox[a] consent to serve you?[b]
    Will it stay by your manger[c] at night?

[10] Can you hold it to the furrow with a harness?[d]
    Will it till the valleys behind you?

[11] Will you rely on it for its great strength?[e]
    Will you leave your heavy work to it?

[12] Can you trust it to haul in your grain
    and bring it to your threshing floor?

[13] "The wings of the ostrich flap joyfully,
    though they cannot compare
    with the wings and feathers of the stork.[f]

[14] She lays her eggs on the ground
    and lets them warm in the sand,

[15] unmindful that a foot may crush them,
    that some wild animal may trample them.[g]

[16] She treats her young harshly,[h] as if they were not hers;
    she cares not that her labor was in vain,

[17] for God did not endow her with wisdom
    or give her a share of good sense.[i]

[18] Yet when she spreads her feathers to run,
    she laughs[j] at horse and rider.

[19] "Do you give the horse its strength[k]
    or clothe its neck with a flowing mane?

[20] Do you make it leap like a locust,[l]
    striking terror[m] with its proud snorting?[n]

[21] It paws fiercely, rejoicing in its strength,[o]
    and charges into the fray.[p]

[22] It laughs[q] at fear, afraid of nothing;
    it does not shy away from the sword.

[23] The quiver[r] rattles against its side,
    along with the flashing spear[s] and lance.

[24] In frenzied excitement it eats up the ground;
    it cannot stand still when the trumpet sounds.[t]

[25] At the blast of the trumpet[u] it snorts, 'Aha!'
    It catches the scent of battle from afar,
    the shout of commanders and the battle cry.[v]

39:2 ⁸ S Ge 31:7-9
39:5 ᵗ S Ge 16:12
39:6 ᵘ Job 24:5;
Ps 107:34; Jer 2:24
ᵛ Job 30:4 ʷ Job 30:7;
Jer 14:6; 17:6
39:7 ˣ S Job 5:22
ʸ Job 3:18
39:8 ᶻ Isa 32:20
39:9 ᵃ S Nu 23:22
ᵇ S Ex 21:6
ᶜ S Ge 42:27
39:10 ᵈ Job 41:13;
Ps 32:9
39:11 ᵉ ver 19;
Job 40:16; 41:12,22;
Ps 147:10
39:13 ᶠ Zec 5:9
39:15 ᵍ 2Ki 14:9
39:16 ʰ ver 17;
La 4:3
39:17 ⁱ S ver 16;
S Job 21:22
39:18 ʲ S Job 5:22
39:19 ᵏ S ver 11
39:20 ˡ Joel 2:4-5;
Rev 9:7 ᵐ Job 41:25
ⁿ Jer 8:16
39:21 ᵒ ver 11
ᵖ Jer 8:6
39:22 �q S Job 5:22
39:23 ʳ Isa 5:28;
Jer 5:16 ˢ Na 3:3
39:24 ᵗ Nu 10:9;
Jer 4:5,19; Eze 7:14;
Am 3:6
39:25 ᵘ Jos 6:5
ᵛ Jer 8:6; Am 1:14; 2:2

39:5 *wild donkey.* See 24:5; see also the description of Ishmael in Ge 16:12 and note there.

39:9–12 As there was an implied contrast between the wild donkey and the domestic donkey (see v. 7), here there is a more explicit contrast between the wild ox and the domestic ox.

39:11 *great strength.* In the OT, the wild ox (the now virtually extinct aurochs) often symbolizes strength (see, e.g., Nu 23:22 and note; 24:8; Dt 33:17; Ps 22:21 and note; 29:6). Next to the elephant and rhinoceros, the wild ox was the largest and most powerful land animal of the OT world.

39:13–18 This stanza is unique in the discourses, because in

it the Lord asks Job no questions.

39:13 *wings and feathers of the stork.* A stork's wings were particularly impressive (see Zec 5:9).

39:18 *horse and rider.* Forms a transition to the next paragraph.

39:19–25 The horse is the only domestic animal in the discourses. This fact, though unexpected, serves the Lord's purpose, since it is specifically the war horse that is in view.

39:20 *like a locust.* Horses and locusts are compared also in Jer 51:27; Rev 9:7; cf. Joel 2:4 and note.

39:26 w Jer 8:7
39:27 x Jer 49:16;
Ob 1:4; Hab 2:9
39:28 y Jer 49:16;
Ob 1:3
39:29 z S Job 9:26
39:30 a Mt 24:28;
Lk 17:37
40:1 b S Job 5:8;
S 10:2
40:2 c S Job 13:3
d S Job 9:15; S 11:8;
S 33:13; Ro 9:20
e S Job 9:3
40:4 f Job 42:6
g S Jdg 18:19;
S Job 29:9
40:5 h S Job 9:3
i S Job 9:15
40:6 j S Ex 14:21;
S Job 38:1
40:7 k S Job 38:3
40:8 l S Job 15:25;
S 27:2; Ro 3:3
m S Job 2:3; S 34:17
40:9 n S 2Ch 32:8;
S Ps 98:1 o Isa 6:8;
Eze 10:5 p S Ex 20:19;
S Job 36:33
40:10 q Ps 29:1-2;
45:3; 93:1; 96:6;
104:1; 145:5
40:11 r S Job 20:28;
Ps 7:11; Isa 5:25; 9:12,
19; 10:5; 13:3,5;
30:27; 42:25; 51:20;
Jer 7:20; Na 1:6;
Zep 1:18 s Ps 18:27;
Isa 2:11,12,17; 23:9;
24:10; 25:12; 26:5;
32:19
40:12 t Ps 10:4;
Isa 25:11; Jer 48:29;
49:16; Zep 2:10
u S 1Sa 2:7; S Ps 52:5;
1Pe 5:5 v Ps 60:12;
Isa 22:5; 28:3; 63:2-3,
6; Da 5:20; Mic 5:8;
7:10; Zec 10:5;
Mal 4:3
40:13 w Nu 16:31-
34 x S Job 4:9
40:14 y Ex 15:6,12;
Ps 18:35; 20:6; 48:10;
60:5; 108:6; Isa 41:10;
63:5
40:15 z S Job 9:9

26 "Does the hawk take flight by your wisdom
  and spread its wings toward the south? w
27 Does the eagle soar at your command
  and build its nest on high? x
28 It dwells on a cliff and stays there at night;
  a rocky crag y is its stronghold.
29 From there it looks for food; z
  its eyes detect it from afar.
30 Its young ones feast on blood,
  and where the slain are, there it is." a

40 The LORD said to Job: b

2 "Will the one who contends with the Almighty c correct him? d
  Let him who accuses God answer him!" e

3 Then Job answered the LORD:

4 "I am unworthy f—how can I reply to you?
  I put my hand over my mouth. g
5 I spoke once, but I have no answer h—
  twice, but I will say no more." i

6 Then the LORD spoke to Job out of the storm: j

7 "Prepare to defend yourself;
  I will question you,
  and you shall answer me. k

8 "Would you discredit my justice? l
  Would you condemn me to justify yourself? m
9 Do you have an arm like God's, n
  and can your voice o thunder like his? p
10 Then adorn yourself with glory and splendor,
  and clothe yourself in honor and majesty. q
11 Unleash the fury of your wrath, r
  look at all who are proud and bring them low, s
12 look at all who are proud t and humble them, u
  crush v the wicked where they stand.
13 Bury them all in the dust together; w
  shroud their faces in the grave. x
14 Then I myself will admit to you
  that your own right hand can save you. y

15 "Look at the behemoth, a
  which I made z along with you

a 15 Possibly the hippopotamus or the elephant

39:26 *hawk.* The sparrow hawk, though not resident to the Holy Land, stops there in its migration south for the winter.
39:27 *eagle.* Or possibly "vulture" (see v. 30).
40:1–2 The conclusion of the first divine discourse. Once again, God challenges Job to answer him.
40:3–5 Job, duly chastened, is unwilling to speak another word of complaint.
40:4 *unworthy.* The Hebrew for this word can also mean "small" or "insignificant."
40:5 *once … twice.* See note on 5:19.
40:6 See 38:1 and note.
40:7 Repeated from 38:3 (see note there).
40:8–14 The second divine discourse, which ends at 41:34. Unlike the first discourse, God here addresses the issues of his own justice and Job's futile attempt at self-justification. In chs. 21 and 24 Job had complained about God's indifference toward the evil actions of the wicked. Here the Lord asserts his ability and determination to administer justice—a matter over which Job has no control. Therefore by implication Job is

admonished to leave all this, including his own vindication (see v. 14), under God's control (see v. 9).
40:8 *Would you condemn me to justify yourself?* In 19:6, Job had said, "God has wronged me."
40:10 *clothe yourself in honor and majesty.* The same Hebrew underlying this clause describes God in Ps 104:1: "you are clothed with splendor and majesty." The Lord here challenges Job to take on the appearance of deity—if he can. *clothe yourself in.* See note on Ps 109:29.
40:11–12 See Isa 13:11, where the Lord describes himself as doing these things.
40:13 *dust.* See note on 7:21.
40:14 *your own right hand can save you.* Contrast Ps 49:7–9 (see note there).
40:15–24 The first of two poems (ch. 41 constitutes the second) in this discourse, each describing a huge beast and resuming the animal theme of ch. 39.
40:15 *behemoth.* The word is Hebrew and means "beast par excellence," referring to a large land animal (for possible identi-

and which feeds on grass like an ox. *a*

16 What strength *b* it has in its loins,
   what power in the muscles of its belly! *c*

17 Its tail sways like a cedar;
   the sinews of its thighs are close-knit. *d*

18 Its bones are tubes of bronze,
   its limbs *e* like rods of iron. *f*

19 It ranks first among the works of God, *g*
   yet its Maker *h* can approach it with his sword. *i*

20 The hills bring it their produce, *j*
   and all the wild animals play *k* nearby. *l*

21 Under the lotus plants it lies,
   hidden among the reeds *m* in the marsh. *n*

22 The lotuses conceal it in their shadow;
   the poplars by the stream *o* surround it.

23 A raging river *p* does not alarm it;
   it is secure, though the Jordan *q* should surge against its mouth.

24 Can anyone capture it by the eyes,
   or trap it and pierce its nose? *r*

41

*1 "Can you pull in the leviathan *a* *s* with a fishhook *t*
   or tie down its tongue with a rope?

2 Can you put a cord through its nose *u*
   or pierce its jaw with a hook? *v*

3 Will it keep begging you for mercy? *w*
   Will it speak to you with gentle words?

4 Will it make an agreement with you
   for you to take it as your slave for life? *x*

5 Can you make a pet of it like a bird
   or put it on a leash for the young women in your house?

6 Will traders barter for it?
   Will they divide it up among the merchants?

7 Can you fill its hide with harpoons
   or its head with fishing spears? *y*

8 If you lay a hand on it,
   you will remember the struggle and never do it again! *z*

*9 Any hope of subduing it is false;
   the mere sight of it is overpowering. *a*

10 No one is fierce enough to rouse it. *b*
   Who then is able to stand against me? *c*

11 Who has a claim against me that I must pay? *d*
   Everything under heaven belongs to me. *e*

12 "I will not fail to speak of Leviathan's limbs, *f*
   its strength *g* and its graceful form.

13 Who can strip off its outer coat?
   Who can penetrate its double coat of armor? *b* *h*

14 Who dares open the doors of its mouth, *i*
   ringed about with fearsome teeth?

15 Its back has *c* rows of shields

---

a 1 Possibly the crocodile   *b 13* Septuagint; Hebrew *double bridle*   *c 15* Or *Its pride is its*

* 41:1-8 is numbered 40:25-32 in Hebrew texts.   * 41:9-34 is numbered 41:1-26 in Hebrew texts.

40:15 *a* Isa 11:7;
65:25
40:16 *b* S Job 39:11
c Job 41:9
40:17 *d* Job 41:15
40:18 *e* Job 41:12
f Isa 11:4; 49:2
40:19 *g* Job 41:33;
Ps 40:5; 139:14;
Isa 27:1 *h* S Job 4:17;
S 9:9 *i* S Ge 3:24
40:20 *j* Ps 104:14
k Ps 104:26
l S Job 5:23
40:21 *m* S Ge 41:2;
Ps 68:30; Isa 35:7
n Job 8:11
40:22 *o* Ps 1:3;
Isa 44:4
40:23 *p* Isa 8:7;
11:15 *q* S Jos 3:1
40:24 *r* 2Ki 19:28;
Job 41:2,7,26;
Isa 37:29
41:1 *s* S Job 3:8
t Am 4:2
41:2 *u* S Job 40:24
v Eze 19:4
41:3 *w* 1Ki 20:31
41:4 *x* S Ex 21:6
41:7 *y* S Job 40:24
41:8 *z* S Job 3:8
41:9 *a* Job 40:16
41:10 *b* S Job 3:8
c 2Ch 20:6;
S Isa 46:5; Jer 50:44;
Rev 6:17
41:11 *d* S Job 34:33;
Ro 11:35 *e* Ps 24:1;
50:12; S Jos 3:11;
S Job 10:4; Ac 4:24;
1Co 10:26
41:12 *f* Job 40:18
g S Job 39:11
41:13 *h* S Job 30:11;
S 39:10
41:14 *i* Ps 22:13

---

fications, see TNIV text note). Much of the language used to describe him in vv. 16–24 is highly poetic and hyperbolic. *which I made.* He is one of God's creatures, not a mythical being.
40:18 *iron.* See note on 19:24.
40:19 *first among the works of God.* The Hebrew underlying this phrase is translated "first of his works" in Pr 8:22 with reference to the creation of wisdom (see Pr 8:12). Here the descriptive phrase stresses the importance of the behemoth as an example of a huge animal under the control of a sovereign God.
40:21–23 *reeds in the marsh . . . poplars . . . Jordan.* The area described is probably the Huleh region, north of the Sea of Galilee.

40:24 The proposal to capture the behemoth forms a transition to the similar proposal concerning the leviathan in 41:1.
41:1–34 The second of two poems in the Lord's final discourse (see note on 40:15–24).
41:1 *leviathan.* Its description in this chapter indicates that it is even more terrifying than the behemoth in ch. 40.
41:10 The leviathan is mighty, but God is infinitely more powerful.
41:11 Alluded to by Paul in Ro 11:35.
41:14–15 *doors of its mouth . . . fearsome teeth . . . back has rows of shields.* Characteristic of the crocodile (see TNIV text note on v. 1).

41:15 *i* Job 40:17
41:18 *k* S Job 3:9
41:19 *l* Da 10:6
41:20 *m* Ps 18:8
41:21 *n* S Job 4:9;
Isa 11:4; 40:7
o Ps 18:8; Isa 10:17;
30:27; 33:14; 66:14-
16; Jer 4:4
41:22 *p* S Job 39:11
41:24 *q* Mt 18:6
41:25 *r* Job 39:20
s S Job 3:8
41:26 *t* S Job 8:18
u S Job 40:24
41:27 *v* ver 29
41:28 *w* Ps 91:5
41:29 *y* ver 27
y S Job 5:22
41:30 *z* Isa 28:27;
41:15; Am 1:3
41:31 *a* 1Sa 2:14
b Eze 32:2
41:33 *c* S Job 40:19
41:34 *d* Ps 18:27;
101:5; 131:1; Pr 6:17;
21:4; 30:13 *e* Job 28:8
42:2 *f* S Ge 18:14;
S Mt 19:26
g S 2Ch 20:6;
S Job 16:19; Ac 4:28;
Eph 1:11
42:3 *h* S Job 34:35
i S Job 5:9
42:4 *j* S Job 38:3
42:5 *k* S Job 26:14;
Ro 10:17

tightly sealed together; *j*
16 each is so close to the next
    that no air can pass between.
17 They are joined fast to one another;
    they cling together and cannot be parted.
18 Its snorting throws out flashes of light;
    its eyes are like the rays of dawn. *k*
19 Flames *l* stream from its mouth;
    sparks of fire shoot out.
20 Smoke pours from its nostrils *m*
    as from a boiling pot over burning reeds.
21 Its breath *n* sets coals ablaze,
    and flames dart from its mouth. *o*
22 Strength *p* resides in its neck;
    dismay goes before it.
23 The folds of its flesh are tightly joined;
    they are firm and immovable.
24 Its chest is hard as rock,
    hard as a lower millstone. *q*
25 When it rises up, the mighty are terrified; *r*
    they retreat before its thrashing. *s*
26 The sword that reaches it has no effect,
    nor does the spear or the dart or the javelin. *t u*
27 Iron it treats like straw *v*
    and bronze like rotten wood.
28 Arrows do not make it flee; *w*
    slingstones are like chaff to it.
29 A club seems to it but a piece of straw; *x*
    it laughs *y* at the rattling of the lance.
30 Its undersides are jagged potsherds,
    leaving a trail in the mud like a threshing sledge. *z*
31 It makes the depths churn like a boiling caldron *a*
    and stirs up the sea like a pot of ointment. *b*
32 It leaves a glistening wake behind it;
    one would think the deep had white hair.
33 Nothing on earth is its equal *c*—
    a creature without fear.
34 It looks down on all that are haughty; *d*
    it is king over all that are proud. *e*"

JOB

42

Then Job replied to the LORD:

2 "I know that you can do all things; *f*
    no purpose of yours can be thwarted. *g*
3 You asked, 'Who is this that obscures my plans without knowledge?' *h*
    Surely I spoke of things I did not understand,
    things too wonderful for me to know. *i*

4 "You said, 'Listen now, and I will speak;
    I will question you,
    and you shall answer me.' *j*
5 My ears had heard of you *k*

41:18–21 *Exaggerated poetic imagery.*
41:27 *Iron.* See note on 19:24.
41:30 *jagged potsherds.* Broken pottery fragments.
41:34 *king over all that are proud.* The Lord alone can humble such creatures. Job cannot be expected to do so, though God challenges him to attempt it—if he so desires (see 40:11–12 and note).
42:1–6 Job's last words are his response to the Lord's second discourse.

42:2 Job finally sees that God and his purposes are supreme.
42:3 *You asked.* Job quotes the Lord's words in 38:2.
42:4 *You said.* Job quotes the Lord's words in 38:3; 40:7.
42:5 Job—and his three friends and Elihu—had only heard about God, but now Job has seen God (see Isa 6:5) with the eyes of faith and spiritual understanding. He can therefore accept God's ways with him (see v. 2)—which include suffering. *my eyes have seen you.* A down payment on the hope expressed in 19:26 (see note there).

but now my eyes have seen you. *l*
⁶ Therefore I despise myself *m*
and repent *n* in dust and ashes." *o*

EPILOGUE

⁷After the LORD had said these things to Job *p*, he said to Eliphaz the Temanite, "I am angry with you and your two friends, *q* because you have not spoken of me what is right, as my servant Job has. *r* ⁸So now take seven bulls and seven rams *s* and go to my servant Job *t* and sacrifice a burnt offering *u* for yourselves. My servant Job will pray for you, and I will accept his prayer *v* and not deal with you according to your folly. *w* You have not spoken of me what is right, as my servant Job has." *x* ⁹So Eliphaz the Temanite, Bildad the Shuhite and Zophar the Naamathite *y* did what the LORD told them; and the LORD accepted Job's prayer. *z*

¹⁰After Job had prayed for his friends, the LORD restored his fortunes *a* and gave him twice as much as he had before. *b* ¹¹All his brothers and sisters and everyone who had known him before *c* came and ate with him in his house. They comforted and consoled him over all the trouble the LORD had brought on him, *d* and each one gave him a piece of silver *a* and a gold ring.

¹²The LORD blessed the latter part of Job's life more than the former part. He had fourteen thousand sheep, six thousand camels, a thousand yoke of oxen and a thousand donkeys. ¹³And he also had seven sons and three daughters. ¹⁴The first daughter he named Jemimah, the second Keziah and the third Keren-Happuch. ¹⁵Nowhere in all the land were there found women as beautiful as Job's daughters, and their father granted them an inheritance along with their brothers.

¹⁶After this, Job lived a hundred and forty years; he saw his children and their children to the fourth generation. ¹⁷And so he died, old and full of years. *e*

---

a 11 Hebrew *him a kesitah*; a kesitah was a unit of money of unknown weight and value.

42:5 *l* Jdg 13:22;
Isa 6:5; S Mt 5:8;
Lk 2:30; Eph 1:17-18
42:6 *m* Job 40:4;
Eze 6:9; Ro 12:3
n S Job 34:33
o S Ex 10:3; S Ezr 9:6;
S Job 2:8; S 6:29
42:7 *p* S Jos 1:7
q Job 32:3 *r* ver 8;
S Job 9:15
42:8 *s* Nu 23:1,29;
Eze 45:23 *t* Job 1:8
u S Ge 8:20
v Jas 5:15-16; 1Jn 5:16
w Ge 20:7; Job 22:30
x S ver 7
42:9 *y* Job 2:11
z S Ge 19:21; S 20:17;
Eze 14:14
42:10 *a* Dt 30:3;
Ps 14:7 *b* S Job 1:3;
Ps 85:1-3; 126:5-6;
Php 2:8-9; Jas 5:11
42:11 *c* S Job 19:13
d S Ge 37:35
42:17 *e* S Ge 15:15

42:6 *I despise myself.* See note on 9:21. To his humility (see 40:4–5) Job adds repentance for the presumptuous words he had spoken to God. *dust and ashes.* See 30:19 and note.

42:7–9 Despite Job's mistakes in word and attitude while he suffered, he is now commended and the counselors are rebuked. Why? Because even in his rage, even when he challenged God, he was determined to speak honestly before him. The counselors, on the other hand, mouthed many correct theological statements, but without living knowledge of the God they claimed to honor. Job spoke *to* God; they only spoke *about* God. Even worse, their spiritual arrogance caused them to claim knowledge they did not possess. They presumed to know why Job was suffering.

42:7–8 *my servant Job.* The phrase is used four times in these two verses (see note on 1:8).

42:10 Job's prayer for those who had abused him is a touching OT illustration of the high Christian virtue our Lord taught in Mt 5:44 (see note on Ps 35:13–14). Job's prayer marked the turning point back to prosperity for him. *restored his fortunes.* See Ps 14:7.

42:11 Contrast 16:2; 19:13. *piece of silver.* The Hebrew for this phrase (see TNIV text note) is found elsewhere in the OT only in Ge 33:19 (see note there); Jos 24:32.

42:12–16 The cosmic contest with Satan, the accuser, is now over, and Job is restored. No longer is there a reason for Job to experience suffering—unless he was sinful and deserved it, which is not the case. God does not allow us to suffer for no reason, and even though the reason may be hidden in the mystery of his divine purpose (see Isa 55:8–9)—never for us to know in this life—we must trust in him as the God who does only what is right (see Ge 18:25; Ps 119:121; Eze 18:5 and notes).

42:12 The number of animals is in each case twice as many (see v. 10) as Job had owned before (see 1:3).

42:13 *seven sons and three daughters.* To replace the children he had lost earlier (see 1:2,18–19).

42:14 Strikingly, only the names of the daughters are given. *Jemimah.* Means "dove." *Keziah.* Means "cinnamon." *Keren-Happuch.* Means "container of antimony," a highly prized eyeshadow (see note on Jer 4:30).

42:15 *granted them an inheritance along with their brothers.* Cf. Nu 27:1–11; 36:1–13 and notes.

42:16 *lived a hundred and forty years.* The longevity of a true patriarch (see note on Ex 6:16). *he saw … to the fourth generation.* See Ge 50:23 and note.

42:17 *old and full of years.* See 5:26; Ge 25:8 and notes.

PSALMS

INTRODUCTION

The titles "Psalms" and "Psalter" come from the Septuagint (the pre-Christian Greek translation of the OT), where they originally referred to stringed instruments (such as harp, lyre and lute), then to songs sung with their accompaniment. The traditional Hebrew title is *tehillim* (meaning "praises"; see note on Ps 145 title), even though many of the psalms are *tephilloth* (meaning "prayers"). In fact, one of the first collections included in the book is titled "the prayers of David son of Jesse" (72:20).

COLLECTION, ARRANGEMENT AND DATE

The Psalter is a collection of collections and represents the final stage in a process that spanned centuries. It was put into its final form by postexilic temple personnel, who completed it probably in the third century B.C. As such, it has often been called the prayer book of the "second" (Zerubbabel's and Herod's) temple and was used in the synagogues as well. But it is more than a treasury of prayers and hymns for liturgical and private use on chosen occasions. Both the scope of its subject matter and the arrangement of the whole collection strongly suggest that this collection was viewed by its final editors as a book of instruction in the faith and in full-orbed godliness—thus a guide for the life of faith in accordance with the Law, the Prophets and the canonical wisdom literature (see chart, pp. 819–822). By the first century A.D. it was referred to as the "Book of Psalms" (Lk 20:42; Ac 1:20). At that time Psalms appears also to have been used as a title for the entire section of the Hebrew OT canon more commonly known as the "Writings" (see Lk 24:44 and note).

Many collections preceded this final compilation of the Psalms. In fact, the formation of psalters probably goes back to the early days of the first (Solomon's) temple (or even to the time of David), when the temple liturgy began to take shape. Reference has already been made to "the prayers of David." Additional collections expressly referred to in the present Psalter titles are: (1) the songs and/or psalms "of the Sons of Korah" (Ps 42–49; 84–85; 87–88), (2) the psalms and/or songs "of Asaph" (Ps 50; 73–83) and (3) the songs "of ascents" (Ps 120–134).

Other evidence points to further compilations. Ps 1–41 (Book I) make frequent use of the divine name Yahweh ("the LORD"), while Ps 42–72 (Book II) make frequent use of Elohim ("God"). The reason for the Elohim collection in distinction from the Yahweh collection remains a matter of speculation. Moreover, Ps 93–100 appear to be a traditional collection (see "The LORD reigns" in 93:1; 96:10; 97:1; 99:1). Other apparent groupings include Ps 111–118 (a series of Hallelujah psalms; see introduction to Ps 113–118), Ps 138–145 (all of which include "of David" in their titles) and Ps 146–150 (with their frequent "Praise the LORD"; see TNIV text note on 111:1). Whether the "Great Hallel" (Ps 120–136) was already a recognized unit is not known.

In its final edition, the Psalter contained 150 psalms. On this the Septuagint (the pre-Christian Greek translation of the OT) and Hebrew texts agree, though they arrive at this number differently. The Septuagint has an extra psalm at the end (but not numbered separately as Ps 151); it also unites Ps 9–10 (see TNIV text note on Ps 9) and Ps 114–115 and divides Ps 116 and Ps 147 each into two psalms. Strangely, both the Septuagint and Hebrew texts number Ps 42–43 as two psalms, though they were evidently originally one (see TNIV text note on Ps 42).

KEY   **A** APPLICATION FOR LIVING   **B** BACKGROUND NOTES   **C** CHARACTER INFORMATION

In its final form the Psalter was divided into five Books (Ps 1–41; 42–72; 73–89; 90–106; 107–150), each of which was provided with a concluding doxology (see 41:13; 72:18–19; 89:52; 106:48; 150). The first two of these Books, as already noted, were probably preexilic. The division of the remaining psalms into three Books, thus attaining the number five, was possibly in imitation of the five books of Moses (otherwise known simply as the Law). At least one of these divisions (between Ps 106–107) seems arbitrary (see introduction to Ps 107). In spite of this five-book division, the Psalter was clearly thought of as a whole, with an introduction (Ps 1–2) and a conclusion (Ps 146–150). Notes throughout the Psalms give additional indications of conscious arrangement (see also chart, pp. 819–822).

AUTHORSHIP AND TITLES (OR SUPERSCRIPTIONS)

Of the 150 psalms, only 34 lack superscriptions of any kind (only 17 in the Septuagint, the pre-Christian Greek translation of the OT). These so-called "orphan" psalms are found mainly in Books III–V, where they tend to occur in clusters: Ps 91; 93–97; 99; 104–107; 111–119; 135–137; 146–150. (In Books I–II, only Ps 1–2; 10; 33; 43; 71 lack titles, and Ps 10 and 43 are actually continuations of the preceding psalms.)

The contents of the superscriptions vary but fall into a few broad categories: (1) author, (2) name of collection, (3) type of psalm, (4) musical notations, (5) liturgical notations and (6) brief indications of occasion for composition. For details, see notes on the titles of the various psalms.

Students of the Psalms are not agreed on the antiquity and reliability of these superscriptions. That many of them are at least preexilic appears evident from the fact that the Septuagint translators were sometimes unclear as to their meaning. Furthermore, the practice of attaching titles, including the name of the author, is ancient. On the other hand, comparison between the Septuagint and the Hebrew texts shows that the content of some titles was still subject to change well into the postexilic period. Most discussion centers on categories 1 and 6, above.

As for the superscriptions regarding occasion of composition, many of these brief notations of events read as if they had been taken from 1,2 Samuel. Moreover, they are sometimes not easily correlated with the content of the psalms they head. The suspicion therefore arises that they are later attempts to fit the psalms into the real-life events of history. But then why the limited number of such notations, and why the apparent mismatches? The arguments cut both ways.

Regarding authorship, opinions are even more divided. The notations themselves are ambiguous since the Hebrew phraseology used, meaning in general "belonging to," can also be taken in the sense of "concerning" or "for the use of" or "dedicated to." The name may refer to the title of a collection of psalms that had been gathered under a certain name (as "Of Asaph" or "Of the Sons of Korah"). To complicate matters, there is evidence within the Psalter that at least some of the psalms were subjected to editorial revision in the course of their transmission. As for Davidic authorship, there can be little doubt that the Psalter contains psalms composed by that noted singer and musician and that there was at one time a "Davidic" psalter. This, however, may have also included psalms written concerning David, or concerning one of the later Davidic kings, or even psalms written in the manner of those he authored. It is also true that the tradition as to which psalms are "Davidic" remains somewhat indefinite, and some "Davidic" psalms seem clearly to reflect later situations (see, e.g., Ps 30 title—but see also note there; and see introduction to Ps 69 and note on Ps 122 title). Moreover, "David" is sometimes used elsewhere as a collective for the kings of his dynasty, and this could also be true in the psalm titles.

The word *Selah* is found in 39 psalms, all but two of which (Ps 140; 143, both "Davidic") are in Books I–III. It is also found in Hab 3, a psalm-like poem. Suggestions as to its meaning abound, but honesty must confess ignorance. Most likely it is a liturgical notation. The common suggestions that it calls for a brief musical interlude or for a brief liturgical response by the congregation are plausible but unproven (the former may be supported by the Septuagint rendering). In some instances its present placement in the Hebrew text is highly questionable. It is found in the TNIV only in TNIV text notes.

PSALM TYPES

Hebrew superscriptions to the Psalms acquaint us with an ancient system of classification: (1) *mizmor* ("psalm"); (2) *shiggaion* (see note on Ps 7 title); (3) *miktam* (see note on Ps 16 title); (4) *shir* ("song"); (5) *maskil* (see note on Ps 32 title); (6) *tephillah* ("prayer"); (7) *tehillah* ("praise"); (8) *lehazkir* ("for being remembered"—i.e., before God, a petition); (9) *letodah* ("for praising" or "for giving thanks"); (10) *lelammed* ("for teaching"); and (11) *shir yedidoth* ("song of loves"—i.e., a wedding song). The meaning of many of these terms, however, is uncertain. In addition, some titles contain two of these (especially *mizmor* and *shir*), indicating that the types are diversely based and overlapping.

Analysis of content has given rise to a different classification that has proven useful for study of the Psalms. The main types that can be identified are: (1) prayers of the individual (e.g., Ps 3–7); (2) praise from the individual for God's saving help (e.g., Ps 30; 34); (3) prayers of the community (e.g., Ps 12; 44; 79); (4) praise from the community for God's saving help (e.g., Ps 66; 75); (5) confessions of confidence in the Lord (e.g., Ps 11; 16; 52); (6) hymns in praise of God's majesty and virtues (e.g., Ps 8; 19; 29; 65); (7) hymns celebrating God's universal reign (Ps 47; 93–99); (8) songs of Zion, the city of God (Ps 46; 48; 76; 84; 122; 126; 129; 137); (9) royal psalms—by, for or concerning the king, the Lord's anointed (e.g., Ps 2; 18; 20; 45; 72; 89; 110); (10) pilgrimage songs (Ps 120–134); (11) liturgical songs (e.g., Ps 15; 24; 68); (12) didactic (instructional) songs (e.g., Ps 1; 34; 37; 73; 112; 119; 128; 133).

This classification also involves some overlapping. For example, "prayers of the individual" may include prayers of the king (in his special capacity as king) or even prayers of the community speaking in the collective first person singular. Nevertheless, it is helpful to study a psalm in conjunction with others of the same type. Attempts to fix specific liturgical settings for each type have not been very convincing. For those psalms about which something can be said in this regard, see introductions to the individual psalms.

Of all these psalm types, the prayers (both of the individual and of the community) are the most complex. Several speech functions are combined to form these appeals to God: (1) address to God: "Lord," "my God," "my deliverer"; (2) initial appeal: "Arise," "Answer me," "Help," "Save me"; (3) description of distress: "Many are rising against me," "The wicked attack," "I am in distress"; (4) complaint against God: "Why have you forsaken me?" "How long will you hide your face from me?"; (5) petition: "Do not be far from me," "Vindicate me"; (6) motivation for God to hear: "for I take refuge in you," "for your name's sake"; (7) accusation against the adversary: "There is no truth in their mouths," "Ruthless people seek my life" ("the wicked" are often quoted); (8) call for judicial redress: "Let them be put to shame," "Call them to account for their wickedness"; (9) claims of innocence: "I have walked in my integrity," "They hate me without cause"; (10) confessions of sin: "I have sinned against you," "I confess my iniquity"; (11) professions of trust: "You are a shield about me," "You will answer me"; (12) vows to praise for deliverance: "I will sing your might," "My lips will praise you"; (13) calls to praise: "Glorify the Lord with me," "Sing praise to the Lord"; (14) motivations for praise: "for you have delivered me," "for the Lord hears the needy."

Though not all these appear in every prayer, they all belong to the conventions of prayer in the Psalter, with petition itself being only one (usually brief) element among the rest. On the whole they reflect the then-current conventions of a court trial, the psalmists presenting their cases before the heavenly King/Judge. When beset by wicked adversaries, the petitioners appeal to God for a hearing, describe their situation, plead their innocence ("righteousness"), lodge their accusations against their adversaries, and appeal for deliverance and judicial redress. When suffering at the hands of God (when God is their adversary), they confess their guilt and plead for mercy. Attention to these various speech functions and their role in the psalmists' judicial appeals to the heavenly Judge will significantly aid the reader's understanding of these psalms.

It should be noted that reference to "penitential" and "imprecatory" psalms as distinct psalm "types" has no basis in the Psalter collection itself. The former ("penitential") refers to an early Christian selection of seven psalms (6; 32; 38; 51; 102; 130; 143) for liturgical expressions of penitence; the latter ("imprecatory") is based on a misconstrual of one of the speech functions found in the prayers. What are actually appeals to the heavenly Judge for judicial redress (function 8 noted on p. 812) are taken to be curses ("imprecation" means "curse") pronounced by the psalmists on their adversaries. See note on 5:10.

LITERARY FEATURES

The Psalter is poetry from first to last, even though it contains many prayers and not all OT prayers were poetic (see 1Ki 8:23–53; Ezr 9:6–15; Ne 9:5–37; Da 9:4–19)—nor, for that matter, was all praise poetic (see 1Ki 8:15–21). The Psalms are impassioned, vivid and concrete; they are rich in images, in simile and metaphor. Assonance, alliteration and wordplays abound in the Hebrew text. Effective use of repetition and the piling up of synonyms and complements to fill out the picture are characteristic. Key words frequently highlight major themes in prayer or song. Enclosure (repetition of a significant word or phrase from the beginning that recurs at the end) frequently wraps up a composition or a unit within it. The notes on the structure of the individual psalms often call attention to literary frames within which the psalm has been set.

Hebrew poetry lacks rhyme and regular meter. Its most distinctive and pervasive feature is parallelism. Most poetic lines are composed of two (sometimes three) balanced segments (the balance is often loose, with the second segment commonly somewhat shorter than the first). The second segment either echoes (synonymous parallelism), contrasts (antithetic parallelism) or syntactically completes (synthetic parallelism) the first. These three types are generalizations and are not wholly adequate to describe the rich variety that the creativity of the poets has achieved within the basic two-segment line structure. When the second or third segment of a poetic line repeats, echoes or overlaps the content of the preceding segment, it usually intensifies or more sharply focuses the thought or its expression. They can serve, however, as rough distinctions that will assist the reader. In the TNIV the second and third segments of a line are slightly indented relative to the first.

Determining where the Hebrew poetic lines or line segments begin or end (scanning) is sometimes an uncertain matter. Even the Septuagint (the pre-Christian Greek translation of the OT) at times scans the lines differently from the way the Hebrew texts now available to us do. It is therefore not surprising that modern translations occasionally differ.

A related problem is the extremely concise, often elliptical writing style of the Hebrew poets. The syntactical connection of words must at times be inferred simply from context. Where more than one possibility presents itself, translators are confronted with ambiguity. They are not always sure with which line segment a border word or phrase is to be read.

The stanza structure of Hebrew poetry is also a matter of dispute. Occasionally, recurring refrains mark off stanzas, as in Ps 42–43; 57. In Ps 110 two balanced stanzas are divided by their introductory oracles (see also introduction to Ps 132), while Ps 119 devotes eight lines to each letter of the Hebrew alphabet. For the most part, however, no such obvious indicators are present. The TNIV has used spaces to mark off poetic paragraphs (called "stanzas" in the notes). Usually this could be done with some confidence, and the reader is advised to be guided by them. But there are a few places where these divisions are questionable—and are challenged in the notes.

Close study of the Psalms discloses that the authors often composed with an overall design in mind. This is true of the alphabetic acrostics, in which the poet devoted to each letter of the Hebrew alphabet one line segment (as in Ps 111–112), a single line (as in Ps 25; 34; 145), two lines (as in Ps 37) or eight lines (as in Ps 119). In addition Ps 33; 38; 103 each has 22 lines, no doubt because of the number of letters in the Hebrew alphabet (see Introduction to Lamentations: Literary Features). The oft-voiced notion that this device was used as a memory aid seems culturally prejudiced and probably unwarranted. Actually, people of that time were able to memorize far more readily than most people today. It is much more likely that the alphabet—which was invented relatively recently as a simple system of symbols capable of representing in writing the rich and complex patterns of human speech and therefore of inscribing all that can be put into words (one of the greatest intellectual achievements of all time)—commended itself as a framework on which to hang significant phrases.

Other forms were also used. Ps 44 is a prayer fashioned after the design of a ziggurat (a Babylonian stepped pyramid; see note on Ge 11:4). A sense of symmetry is pervasive. There are psalms that devote the same number of lines to each stanza (e.g., Ps 12; 41), or do so with variation only in the introductory or concluding stanza (e.g., Ps 38; 83; 94). Others match the opening and closing stanzas and balance those between (e.g., Ps 33; 86). A particularly interesting device is to place a key thematic line at the very center, sometimes constructing the whole or part of the poem around that center (see note on 6:6). Still other design features are pointed out in the notes. The authors of the psalms crafted their compositions very carefully. They were heirs of an ancient art (in many details showing that they had inherited a poetic tradition that goes back hundreds of years), and they developed it to a state of high sophistication. Their works are best appreciated when carefully studied and pondered.

THEOLOGY: INTRODUCTION

The Psalter is for the most part a book of prayer and praise. In it faith speaks to God in prayer and about God in praise. But there are also psalms that are explicitly didactic (instructional) in form and purpose (teaching the way of godliness). As noted above (Collection, Arrangement and Date), the manner in which the whole collection has been arranged suggests that one of its main purposes was instruction in the life of faith, a faith formed and nurtured by the Law, the Prophets and the canonical wisdom literature. Accordingly, the Psalter is theologically rich. Its theology is, however, not abstract or systematic but doxological, confessional and practical. So a summation of that "theology" impoverishes it by translating it into an objective mode.

Furthermore, any summation faces a still greater problem. The Psalter is a large collection of independent pieces of many kinds, serving different purposes and composed over the course of many centuries. Not only must a brief summary of its "theology" be selective and incomplete; it will also of necessity be somewhat artificial. It will suggest that each psalm reflects or at least presupposes the "theology" outlined, that there is no "theological" tension or progression within the Psalter. Manifestly this is not so.

Still, the final editors of the Psalter were obviously not eclectic in their selection. They knew that many voices from many times spoke here, but none that in their judgment was incompatible with the Law and the Prophets. No doubt they also assumed that each psalm was to be understood in the light of the collection as a whole. That assumption we may share. Hence something, after all, can be said concerning seven major theological themes that, while admittedly a bit artificial, need not seriously distort and can be helpful to the student of the Psalms.

THEOLOGY: MAJOR THEMES

1. At the core of the theology of the Psalter is the conviction that the gravitational center of life (of right human understanding, trust, hope, service, morality, adoration), but also of history and of the whole creation (heaven and earth), is *God* (Yahweh, "the LORD"; see Dt 6:4 and note). He is *the Great King* over all, the One to whom all things are subject. He created all things and preserves them; they are the robe of glory with which he has clothed himself. Because he ordered them, they have a well-defined and "true" identity (no chaos there). Because he maintains them, they are sustained and kept secure from disruption, confusion or annihilation. Because he alone is the sovereign God, they are governed by one hand and held in the service of one divine purpose. Under God creation is a cosmos—an orderly and systematic whole. What we distinguish as "nature" and history had for the psalmists one Lord, under whose rule all things worked together. Through the creation the Great King's majestic glory is displayed. He is good (wise, righteous, faithful, amazingly benevolent and merciful—evoking trust), and he is great (his knowledge, thoughts and works are beyond human comprehension—evoking reverent awe). By his good and lordly rule he is shown to be the Holy One.

2. As the Great King by right of creation and enduring, absolute sovereignty, *he ultimately will not tolerate any worldly power that opposes, denies or ignores him.* He will come to rule the nations so that all will be compelled to acknowledge him. This expectation is no doubt the root and broadest scope of the psalmists' long view of the future. Because the Lord is the Great King beyond all challenge, *his righteous and peaceable kingdom will come, overwhelming all opposition* and purging the creation of all rebellion against his rule—such will be the ultimate outcome of history.

3. As the Great King on whom all creatures depend, *he opposes the "proud,"* those who rely on their own resources (and/or the gods they have contrived) to work out their own destiny. These are the ones who ruthlessly wield whatever power they possess to attain worldly wealth, status and security; who are a law to themselves and exploit others as they will. In the Psalter, this kind of "pride" is the root of all evil. Those who embrace it, though they may seem to prosper, will be brought down to death, their final end. The "humble," the "poor and needy," those who acknowledge their dependence on the Lord in all things—these are the ones in whom God delights. Hence the "fear of the LORD"—i.e., humble trust in and obedience to the Lord—is the "beginning" of all wisdom (111:10). Ultimately, those who embrace it will inherit the earth. Not even death can hinder their seeing the face of God.

The psalmists' hope for the future—the future of God and his kingdom and the future of the godly—was firm, though somewhat generalized. None of the psalmists gives expression to a two-age vision of the future (the present evil age giving way to a new age of righteousness and peace on the other side of a great eschatological divide). Such a view began to appear in the intertestamental literature—a view that had been foreshadowed by Daniel (see especially 12:2–3) and by Isaiah (see 65:17–25; 66:22–24)—and it later received full expression in the teaching of Jesus and the apostles. But this revelation was only a fuller development consistent with the hopes the psalmists lived by.

4. Because God is the Great King, *he is the ultimate Executor of justice among humans (to avenge oneself is an act of the "proud").* God is the court of appeal when persons are threatened or wronged—especially when no earthly court that he has established has jurisdiction (as in the case of international conflicts) or is able to judge (as when one is wronged by public slander) or is willing to act (out of fear or corruption). *He is the mighty and faithful Defender of the defenseless and the wronged.* He knows every deed and the secrets of every heart. There is no escaping his scrutiny. No false testimony will mislead him in judgment. And he hears the pleas brought to him. As the good and faithful Judge, he delivers those who are oppressed or wrongfully attacked and redresses the wrongs committed against them (see note on 5:10). This is the unwavering conviction that accounts for the psalmists' impatient complaints when they boldly, yet as "poor and needy," cry to him, "Why, LORD (have you not yet delivered me)?" "How long, LORD (before you act)?"

5. As the Great King over all the earth, *the Lord has chosen the Israelites to be his servant people, his "inheritance" among the nations.* He has delivered them by mighty acts out of the hands of the world powers, has given them a land of their own (territory that he took from other nations to be his own "inheritance" in the earth) *and has united them with himself in covenant as the initial embodiment of his redeemed kingdom.* Thus both their destiny and his honor came to be bound up with this relationship. *To them he also gave his word of revelation,* which testified of him, made specific his promises and proclaimed his will. By God's covenant, Israel was to live among the nations, loyal only to her heavenly King. She was to trust solely in his protection, hope in his promises, live in accordance with his will and worship him exclusively. She was to sing his praises to the whole world—which in a special sense revealed Israel's anticipatory role in the evangelization of the nations.

6. As the Great King, Israel's covenant Lord, *God chose David to be his royal representative on earth.* In this capacity, David was the Lord's "servant"—i.e., a member of the Great King's administration. The Lord himself anointed him and adopted him as his royal "son" to rule in his name. Through him God made his people secure in the promised land and subdued all the powers that threatened them. What is more, *he covenanted to preserve the Davidic dynasty.* Henceforth the kingdom of God on earth, while not dependent on the house of David, was linked to it by God's decision and commitment. In its continuity and strength lay Israel's security and hope as she faced a hostile world. And since the Davidic kings were God's royal representatives in the earth, in concept seated at God's right hand (110:1), the scope of their rule was potentially worldwide (see Ps 2).

The Lord's anointed, however, was more than a warrior king. He was to be endowed by God to govern his people with godlike righteousness: to deliver the oppressed, defend the defenseless, suppress the wicked and thus bless the nation with internal peace and prosperity. He was also an intercessor with God in behalf of the nation, the builder and maintainer of the temple (as God's earthly palace and the nation's house of prayer) and the foremost voice calling the nation to worship the Lord. It is perhaps with a view to these last duties that he is declared to be not only king, but also "priest" (see Ps 110 and notes).

7. As the Great King, Israel's covenant Lord, *God* (who had chosen David and his dynasty to be his royal representatives) *also chose Jerusalem (the City of David) as his own royal city, the earthly seat of his throne. Thus Jerusalem (Zion) became the earthly capital (and symbol) of the kingdom of God. There in his palace (the temple) he sat enthroned among his people.* There his people could meet with him to bring their prayers and praise and to see his power and glory. From there he brought salvation, dispensed blessings and judged the nations. And with him as the city's great Defender, Jerusalem was the secure citadel of the kingdom of God, the hope and joy of God's people.

God's goodwill and faithfulness toward his people were most strikingly symbolized by his pledged presence among them at his temple in Jerusalem, the "city of the Great King" (48:2). But no manifestation of his benevolence was greater than his readiness to forgive the sins of those who humbly confessed them and whose hearts showed him that their repentance was genuine and their professions of loyalty to him had integrity. As they anguished over their own sinfulness, the psalmists remembered the ancient testimony of their covenant Lord: I am Yahweh ("the LORD"), "the compassionate and gracious God, slow to anger, abounding in love and faithfulness, maintaining love to thousands and forgiving wickedness, rebellion and sin" (Ex 34:6–7). Only so did they dare to submit to him as his people, to "fear" him (see 130:3–4).

THEOLOGY: SUMMARY, MESSIANIC IMPORT AND CONCLUSION

Unquestionably the supreme kingship of Yahweh (in which he displays his transcendent greatness and goodness) is the most basic metaphor and most pervasive theological concept in the Psalter—as in the OT generally. It provides the fundamental perspective in which people are to view themselves, the whole creation, events in "nature" and history, and the future. All creation is Yahweh's one kingdom. To be a creature in the world is to be a part of his kingdom and under his rule. To be a human being in the world is to be dependent on and responsible to him. To proudly deny that fact is the root of all wickedness—the wickedness that now pervades the world.

God's election of Israel and subsequently of David and Zion, together with the giving of his word, represent the renewed inbreaking of God's righteous kingdom into this world of rebellion and evil. It initiates the great divide between the righteous nation and the wicked nations, and on a deeper level between the righteous and the wicked, a more significant distinction that cuts even through Israel. In the end this divine enterprise will triumph. Human pride will be humbled, and wrongs will be redressed. The humble will be given the whole earth to possess, and the righteous and peaceable kingdom of God will come to full realization. These theological themes, of course, have profound religious and moral implications. Of these, too, the psalmists spoke.

One question that ought yet to be addressed is: Do the Psalms speak of the Christ? Yes, in a variety of ways—but not as the prophets do. The Psalter was never numbered among the "prophetic" books. On the other hand, when the Psalter was being given its final form, what the psalms said about the Lord and his ways with his people, about the Lord and his ways with the nations, about the Lord and his ways with the righteous and the wicked, and what the psalmists said about the Lord's anointed, his temple and his holy city—all this was understood in light of the prophetic literature (both Former and Latter Prophets). Relative to these matters, the Psalter and the Prophets were mutually reinforcing and interpretive.

When the Psalms speak of the king on David's throne, they speak of the king who is being crowned (as in Ps 2; 72; 110—though some think 110 is an exception) or is reigning (as in Ps 45) at the time. They proclaim his status as the Lord's anointed and declare what the Lord will accomplish through him and his dynasty. Thus they also speak of the sons of David to come—and in the exile and the postexilic era, when there was no reigning king, they spoke to Israel only of the great Son of David whom the prophets had announced as the one in whom God's covenant with David would yet be fulfilled. So the NT quotes these psalms as testimonies to Christ, which in their unique way they are. In him they are truly fulfilled.

When in the Psalms righteous sufferers—who are "righteous" because they are innocent, not having provoked or wronged their adversaries, and because they are among the "humble" who trust in the Lord—cry out to God in their distress (as in

Ps 22; 69), they give voice to the sufferings of God's servants in a hostile and evil world.

These cries became the prayers of God's oppressed people, and as such they were taken up into Israel's book of prayers. When Christ came in the flesh, he identified himself with God's "humble" people in the world. He became for them God's righteous servant par excellence, and he shared their sufferings at the hands of the wicked. Thus these prayers became his prayers also—uniquely his prayers. In him the suffering and deliverance of which these prayers speak are fulfilled (though they continue to be the prayers also of those who take up their cross and follow him).

Similarly, in speaking of God's covenant people, of the city of God and of the temple in which God dwells, the Psalms ultimately speak of Christ's church. The Psalter is not only the prayer book of the second temple; it is also the enduring prayer book of the people of God. Now, however, it must be used in the light of the new era of redemption that dawned with the first coming of the Messiah and that will be consummated at his second coming.

Instruction in the Godly Life under the Reign of God

BOOK I

Ps 1–2 Introduction, framed by two 'ashre ("Blessed is/are") declarations

1 Evokes instructions of Torah [Law] and Hokmah [Wisdom]

2 Evokes Former and Latter Prophets (Yahweh and his anointed, Israel's only hope in the turmoil of history)

Thus 1. The Psalter must be read in the context of the rest of the OT canon.

2. As portal to the temple of the Psalter, these two psalms teach that those who would appropriate the prayers and praises of the Psalter must fit the profile of the framing declarations; their lives must be shaped by Law and godly Wisdom, and they must "take refuge" in Yahweh and his anointed—the two components of "the fear of Yahweh."

Ps 3–14

3 Plea for deliverance from foes	9 Plea for deliverance from hostile nations
4 Plea for relief in time of drought	10 Plea for deliverance from the wicked
5 Plea for deliverance from foes	11 Trust in Yahweh's righteous rule
6 Plea for healing	12 Plea for help in an ungodly time
7 Plea for deliverance from foes	13 Plea for deliverance from serious illness and enemies
8 Praise of the Creator (the glory of God bestowed on humans)	**14 The folly of humankind ("The Lord looks down ... to see ... All have turned aside")**

Ps 15–24

15 Who has access to the temple?   **24 Who may ascend the holy hill?**

16 Confession of trust in Yahweh   23 Confession of trust in Yahweh

17 Plea for deliverance from foes   22 Plea for deliverance from foes

18 Royal praise for deliverance   20–21 Prayer for king's victory; praise for victory

19 Yahweh's glory in Creation and Torah

(The summer sun moving across the face of the sky from east to west)

Ps 25–33

25 Twenty-two verses (alphabetic acrostic)   **33 Twenty-two verses (not alphabetic)**

Prayer for covenant mercies   **Praise for God's good rule**

26 Prayer of a "blameless" one   32 Blessedness of a penitent

27 Appeal against false accusers   31 Appeal against false accusers

"Be strong and take heart,   "Be strong and take heart,

and wait for the Lord."   all you who hope in the Lord."

28 Prayer of one "going down to the pit"   30 Praise of one spared from "going down

"strength ... strength," vv. 7-8   into the pit" / "stand firm" (strong), v. 7

29 Praise of the King of creation

(The winter thunderstorm moving across the face of the sky from west to east)

Ps 34–37

34 Alphabetic acrostic   **37 Alphabetic acrostic**

Instruction in godly wisdom   **Instruction in godly wisdom**

35 Appeal against malicious slanderers   36 Appeal against threats of godless wicked

Ps 38–41

38 Prayer for relief from serious illness and enemies: a confession of sin

39 Prayer for relief from serious illness and enemies: a confession of sin

40 Prayer for relief from troubles (serious illness?) and enemies: a confession of sin

41 Prayer for relief from serious illness and enemies: a confession of sin

40:4 'Ashre [Blessed are...] those who "make the Lord their trust."

41:1 'Ashre [Blessed are...] those who "have regard for the weak."

BOOK II

Ps 42–45 Three prayers with a royal psalm attached (see Ps 69–72)
42 Prayer of individual ("Why have you forgotten me" in the face of the "oppression" of enemies?)
43 Continuation of Ps 42
44 Prayer of the community ("Why do you hide your face and forget our . . . oppression?")
45 Song in praise of the king in a day of his glory (wedding to a foreign princess)
    (" . . . ride forth . . . in behalf of truth, humility and righteousness")
    ("Your throne . . . will last for ever and ever")

Ps 46–48 In celebration of the security of Zion
46 Zion's security
        47 Zion's Great King triumphant over all nations
48 Zion's security

Ps 49–53 The proper posture before God
49 The folly of those who "trust in their wealth" / "boast of their great riches"
        50 God calls his people to account
        51 Humble prayer for forgiveness and cleansing
52 The folly of the one who "trusted in his great wealth" / "boasted" in his evil ways
53 The folly of those who live as if there is no God (repeat of Ps 14)

Ps 54–60 Seven prayers at the center of Book II (main weapon in Ps 54–59 is the mouth)
54 Prayer of individual for help against enemies (formally paradigmatic)
        55 Prayer for help: a conspiracy in Jerusalem ("they prowl about on its walls")
            ("words . . . are drawn **swords**")
            56 Prayer for help against enemies
                57 Prayer for deliverance from enemies (May "God Most High" "be exalted")
                    ("tongues are sharp **swords**")
            58 Prayer for the heavenly Judge to set right what human rulers have not
        59 Prayer for help: enemies surround Jerusalem ("they . . . prowl about the city")
            ("spew out **swords** from their lips")
60 Prayer of community for help after suffering devastating defeat (cf. Ps 44)
    ("you . . . have rejected us and no longer go out with our armies")

Ps 61–64 Four royal prayers with interweaving themes
61 Appeal for restoration to God's presence ("rock," "refuge," "strong tower," "in the shelter of your wings")
62 Appeal for deliverance from arrogant foes ("rock," "fortress," "mighty rock," "refuge"; "You reward
    everyone according to what they have done")
63 Appeal for God's refreshing presence when threatened by enemies ("sing in the shadow of your wings";
    "Those who seek my life . . . will go down to the depths of the earth")
64 Appeal for God's protection against conspirators ("they shoot . . . suddenly . . . / God will shoot
    them . . . suddenly")

Ps 65–68 God's "awesome deeds" evoke the praise of "all . . . the earth"
65 God's blessing the earth into fruitfulness is highlighted ("the hope of all the ends of the earth")
66 God's saving acts on behalf of Israel are highlighted ("Shout with joy to God, all the earth!")
67 God's blessing the earth into fruitfulness is highlighted ("all the peoples praise . . . all the ends
    of the earth . . . fear")
68 God's saving acts in behalf of Israel are highlighted ("kings . . . bring you gifts . . . Sing to God,
    kingdoms of the earth")

Ps 69–72 Three prayers with a royal psalm attached (see Ps 42–45)
69 A king's prayer for deliverance when under vicious attack
70 A short prayer (repeat of Ps 40; see introduction to Ps 71)
71 A king's prayer for God's help in old age when under attack
72 A prayer that the king be specially gifted to rule justly
    (" . . . endure . . . through all generations")
    (" . . . all nations . . . be blessed through him")

BOOK III

Made up of three groups of six psalms (73–78), five psalms (79–83), six psalms (84–89)

Ps 73–78

73 Instruction based on individual experience

74 Communal prayer: God has "rejected" his people

75 Thanks to God: His "Name is near," and he
   "cuts off" the horns of the wicked but
   causes the "horns of the righteous"
   to be "lifted up"

78 Instruction based on communal experience

77 Individual prayer: God has "rejected" him

76 Celebration: God's "name is great in Israel";
   he "breaks the spirit of the [enemy] rulers"

Ps 79–83

79 Communal prayer:
   when invaded by fierce enemies

80 Prayer for God to restore his people after
   they have been ravaged by enemies

83 Communal prayer:
   when attacked by coalition of enemies

82 Prayer for God to judge the wicked
   rulers of the earth

**81 Exhortation to Israel:
"If Israel would follow my ways,
how quickly would I subdue their enemies."**

Ps 84–89

84 Expression of yearning for "the courts of the LORD"
   and prayer for God to "look with favor" on "our shield," "your anointed"

85 Prayer for God to "restore" his people
   from some situation of distress

86 Individual prayer for God's help
   when under attack by enemies

89 Prayer for God to rescue his people,
   to remember his covenant with David

88 Individual prayer for God to remove
   his wrath and deliver from death

**87 Song celebrating God's special
love for Zion and care for its citizens**

BOOKS IV AND V

Ps 90–100 Eleven psalms framed by "Adonai . . . our dwelling place throughout all generations" (90:1) and "Yahweh . . . his love . . . faithfulness continues through all generations" (100:5)

90 Plaintive prayer concerning the mortality of those who have long had the Lord as their "dwelling place"

91 Assurances for those who make the Most High their "dwelling" place (v. 9; cf. v. 1): "With long life will I satisfy" them (v. 16).

92 Celebration of Yahweh's righteous rule and its result (what the "senseless" do not know): "Evildoers . . . will be forever destroyed" but "the righteous . . . will still bear fruit in old age."

93 Celebration of the invincible reign of Yahweh

94 Appeal to Yahweh to deal judicially with those who perpetrate injustices and oppression: "Take notice, you senseless ones among the people."

95 Call for the delivered covenant community to joyfully worship Yahweh, their God (and warning not to repeat earlier rebelliousness)

96 Call to all nations to worshipfully celebrate the universal reign of Yahweh—and its "coming"

97 Joyful celebration of Yahweh's universal reign—whose throne is founded on "righteousness and justice"

98 Call to all nations to worshipfully praise Yahweh for his saving acts in behalf of Israel—his reign is "coming"

99 Joyful celebration of Yahweh's universal reign, especially for what he has done for Israel

100 Concluding exhortation to worshipfully praise Yahweh, Israel's Maker and "good" Shepherd-King

BOOKS IV AND V, cont.

Ps 101–110 A "little psalter" framed by two royal psalms

101 A royal pledge to reign righteously
    102 Individual lament
       103 Praise of Yahweh for his "great love"
          104 Praise of Yahweh the Creator
             105 Recital of Israel's saving history

                   110 Oracles concerning the Messianic
                               King-Priest
                 109 Individual lament
             108 Praise of Yahweh for his "great love"
          107 Call for praise of Yahweh, who hears cries of distress
       106 Recital of Israel's history of rebellion

Ps 111–119 The "Egyptian Hallel" framed by 111/112 and 119

111/112 Formal and thematic twins: "Righteous" God and God-fearing people, "who find great delight in his
        (God's) commands" (112:1)

	113	Psalms used
Egyptian Hallel	114	in Israel's
	115	
	116	great annual
	117	festivals
	118	

119 Prayer of one who "find(s) delight" in God's "commands" (v. 35)

Ps 120–137 Songs of Ascents plus two appendices

120–134 The "Songs of Ascents"
       135–136 Hymns traditionally associated by the Jews with the Songs of Ascents
           137 Song of love for Zion by one returned from Babylonian exile
              (brings closure to the preceding collection)

Ps 138–145 Eight psalms assigned to David: prayers framed by praise

138 Praise of Yahweh: "When I called, you answered"; "May all the kings … praise you … for (your) glory"
    139 Acknowledgment of total nakedness before the omniscient and omnipresent God
        140–144 Five prayers for deliverance from:
               140: evil men, men of violence, the wicked
               141: evildoers
               142: pursuers who "are too strong for me"
               143: enemies
               144: foreigners
    145 (Alphabetic acrostic) Praise of Yahweh, "the King": who "is near to all who call on him";
        "All you have made will … tell of the glory of your kingdom … so that all … may know of …
           the glorious splendor of your kingdom."

Ps 146–150 Five Hallelujah psalms that conclude the Psalter

BOOK I

Psalms 1–41

PSALM 1

[1] Blessed are those[a]
 who do not walk[b] in step with the wicked[c]
or stand in the way[d] that sinners take[e]
 or sit[f] in the company of mockers,[g]
[2] but who delight[h] in the law of the LORD[i]
 and meditate[j] on his law day and night.
[3] They are like a tree[k] planted by streams[l] of water,[m]
 which yields its fruit[n] in season
and whose leaf[o] does not wither—
 whatever they do prospers.[p]

[4] Not so the wicked!
 They are like chaff[q]
 that the wind blows away.
[5] Therefore the wicked will not stand[r] in the judgment,[s]
 nor sinners in the assembly[t] of the righteous.

[6] For the LORD watches over[u] the way of the righteous,
 but the way of the wicked will be destroyed.[v]

PSALM 2

[1] Why do the nations conspire[a]
 and the peoples plot[w] in vain?

---

[a] 1 Hebrew; Septuagint *rage*

1:1 [a] S Dt 33:29;
Ps 40:4; 128:4
[b] Ps 89:15
[c] S Ps 21:16; Ps 10:2-
11 [d] S Ge 49:6
[e] Ps 26:9; 37:38;
51:13; 104:35 [f] Ps 26:4
[g] S Job 11:3; Pr 1:22;
Isa 28:14; Hos 7:5
1:2 [h] Ps 112:1; 119:16,
35; Ro 7:22 [i] Ps 19:7;
119:1; Eze 11:20; 18:17
[j] S Ge 24:63
1:3 [k] Ps 52:8; 92:12;
128:3; Jer 11:16;
Zec 4:3 [l] Ps 46:4;
65:9; Isa 33:21;
Jer 31:9 [m] S Nu 24:6;
S Job 14:9; S Eze 17:5
[n] Ps 92:14; Eze 47:12
[o] Isa 1:30; 64:6
[p] S Ge 39:3
1:4 [q] S Job 13:25;
Isa 40:24; Jer 13:24
1:5 [r] Ps 5:5
[s] S Job 19:29
[t] Ps 26:12; 35:18; 82:1;
89:5; 107:32; 111:1;
149:1
1:6 [u] Ps 37:18; 121:5;
145:20; Na 1:7
[v] S Lev 26:38; Ps 9:6
2:1 [w] Ps 21:11; 83:5;
Pr 24:2

Ps 1–2 These two "orphan" psalms (having no title) are bound together by framing clauses ("Blessed are those …who delight in the law of the LORD";"Blessed are all who take refuge in him") that highlight their function as the introduction to the whole Psalter. Together they point on the one hand to God's law and to the instruction of the wisdom teachers (Ps 1) and on the other hand to a central theme in the Prophets, both Former and Latter, namely, what Yahweh has committed himself to accomplish for and through his anointed king from the house of David (Ps 2). In this way these two psalms link the Psalter with the rest of the literature and alert those who take it in hand that to hear these psalms aright they must be understood within that larger frame of reference. At the same time, as the port of entry into the Psalter, they make clear that those who would find their own voice in the psalms and so would appropriate them as testimonies to their own faith must fit the profile of those called "blessed" here. See also note on Ps 40–41.
Ps 1 Author and date unknown. Godly wisdom here declares the final outcome of the two "ways":"the way that sinners take" (v. 1) and "the way of the righteous" (v. 6). See 34:19–22; 37. As part of the introduction to the Psalter, this psalm reminds the reader (1) that those of whom the Psalms speak (using various terms) as the people of God, those whom he receives in his presence and favors with his salvation and blessing, must be characterized by delight in God's revealed will—those who stubbornly choose the way of sinners have no place among them (v. 5; see Ps 15; 24)—and (2) that the godly piety that speaks in the Psalms is a faithful response to God's revealed (and written) directives for life—which is the path that leads to blessedness. For a prime indicator of the psalm's central theme cf. the first and last words, which frame the whole ("Blessed …destroyed").
1:1 Speaks progressively of association with the ungodly and participation in their ungodly ways. *Blessed.* The happy condition of those who revere the Lord and do his will (see 94:12; 112:1; 119:1–2; 128:1; Pr 29:18; cf. Ps 41:1; 106:3; Pr 14:21; Isa 56:2) and who put their trust in him (see 40:4; 84:5,12; 144:15; 146:5; Pr 16:20; Isa 30:18; Jer 17:7; cf. Ps 2:12; 34:8). Reference is not first of

all to health and wealth but to the assurance and experience that they live under the guardianship and faithful care of the gracious Lord of life. The Psalter begins by proclaiming the blessedness of the godly and ends by calling all living things to praise God in his earthly and heavenly sanctuaries (Ps 150). *walk in step with the wicked.* Order one's life according to the deliberations and advice of the wicked (see Pr 1:10–19). *stand.* Position oneself. *sinners.* Those for whom wickedness is habitual—a way of life (see v. 5). *sit.* Settle oneself. *mockers.* Those who ridicule God and defiantly reject his law (see Pr 1:22 and note).
1:2 *meditate on his law.* Seeking guidance for life in God's law rather than in the deliberations of the wicked. *day and night.* See Jos 1:8.
1:3 *like a tree …does not wither.* See Jer 17:8; a simile of the blessedness of the righteous. Such a tree withstands the buffeting of the winds and, flourishing, it blesses people, animals and birds with its unfailing fruit and shade.
1:4 *like chaff … blows away.* A simile of the wretchedness of the wicked. Chaff is carried away by the lightest wind, and its removal brings about cleansing by extracting what is utterly useless (see note on Ru 1:22).
1:5 *will not stand in the judgment.* Will not be able to withstand God's wrath when he judges (see 76:7; 130:3; Ezr 9:15; Na 1:6 and note; Mal 3:2; Mt 25:31–46; Rev 6:17). *assembly.* The worshiping assembly at God's sanctuary (as in 22:25; 26:12; 35:18; 40:9–10; 111:1; 149:1; see Ps 15; 24). *righteous.* One of several terms in the OT for God's people; it presents them as those who honor God and order their lives in all things according to his will. In every human relationship they faithfully fulfill the obligations that the relationship entails, remembering that power and authority (of whatever sort: domestic, social, political, economic, religious, intellectual) are to be used to bless, not to exploit.
1:6 *way … way.* What is here said of the two "ways" applies by implication also to those who choose them (see 37:20).
Ps 2 Author and date unknown (Peter and John ascribed it to David in Ac 4:25—possibly in accordance with the

2:2 ˣ Ps 48:4
ʸ S 1Sa 9:16; Jn 1:41;
Ac 4:25-26*
2:3 ᶻ S Job 36:8
ᵃ S 2Sa 3:34
2:4 ᵇ Isa 37:16;
40:22; 66:1 ᶜ Ps 37:13;
Pr 1:26
2:5 ᵈ Ps 6:1; 27:9;
38:1 ᵉ Ps 21:9; 79:6;
90:7; 110:5
2:6 ᶠ Ps 10:16; 24:10
ᵍ 2Ki 19:31; Ps 9:11;
48:2,11; 78:68; 110:2;
133:3 ʰ S Ex 15:17
2:7 ⁱ S Mt 3:17; S 4:3
ʲ S 2Sa 7:14;
Ac 13:33*; Heb 1:5*;
5:5*
2:8 ᵏ Rev 2:26
ˡ S Job 22:26;
Mt 21:38 ᵐ Ps 22:27;
67:7
2:9 ⁿ S Ge 49:10;
Rev 12:5 ᵒ S Ex 15:6
ᵖ Isa 30:14; Jer 19:10;
Rev 2:27*; 19:15
2:10 �q Pr 27:11
ʳ Ps 141:6; Pr 8:15;
Am 2:3
2:11 ˢ Ps 103:11
ᵗ Ps 9:2; 35:9; 104:34;
Isa 61:10
ᵘ S 1Ch 16:30
2:12 ᵛ ver 7
ʷ S Dt 9:8; Rev 6:16
ˣ Ps 84:12 ʸ Ps 5:11;
34:8; 64:10

2 The kings ˣ of the earth rise up
　　and the rulers band together
　against the Lᴏʀᴅ and against his anointed, ʸ saying,
3 "Let us break their chains ᶻ
　　and throw off their shackles." ᵃ

4 The One enthroned ᵇ in heaven laughs; ᶜ
　　the Lord scoffs at them.
5 He rebukes them in his anger ᵈ
　　and terrifies them in his wrath, ᵉ saying,
6 "I have installed my king ᶠ
　　on Zion, ᵍ my holy mountain. ʰ"

7 I will proclaim the Lᴏʀᴅ's decree:

　He said to me, "You are my son; ⁱ
　　today I have become your father. ʲ
8 Ask me,
　　and I will make the nations ᵏ your inheritance, ˡ
　　the ends of the earth ᵐ your possession.
9 You will break them with a rod of iron ᵃ; ⁿ
　　you will dash them to pieces ᵒ like pottery. ᵖ"

10 Therefore, you kings, be wise; q
　　be warned, you rulers ʳ of the earth.
11 Serve the Lᴏʀᴅ with fear ˢ
　　and celebrate his rule ᵗ with trembling. ᵘ
12 Kiss his son, ᵛ or he will be angry
　　and you and your ways will be destroyed,
　for his wrath ʷ can flare up in a moment.
　Blessed ˣ are all who take refuge ʸ in him.

ᵃ 9 Or *will rule them with an iron scepter* (see Septuagint and Syriac)

Jewish practice of honoring David as the primary author of the Psalter). A royal psalm, it was originally composed for the coronation of Davidic kings in light of the Lord's covenant with David (see 2Sa 7). Later, prophetic words of judgment against the house of David and announcements of God's future redemption of his people through an exalted, royal son of David highlighted the Messianic import of this psalm. As the second half of a two-part introduction to the Psalms, it proclaims the blessedness of all who acknowledge the lordship of God and his anointed and "take refuge in him" (v. 12; see introductions to Ps 1–2 and Ps 1; see also note on 1:1)—as does the godly piety that speaks in the Psalms. This psalm is frequently quoted in the NT, where it is applied to Christ as the great Son of David and God's Anointed.
2:1–3 The nations rebel. In the ancient Near East the coronation of a new king was often the occasion for the revolt of peoples and kings who had been subject to the crown. The newly anointed king is here pictured as ruler over an empire.
2:1–2 For a NT application, see Ac 4:25–28.
2:1 *Why . . . ?* A rhetorical question that implies "How dare they!"
Ⓐ **2:2** *Lᴏʀᴅ . . . his anointed.* To rebel against the Lord's anointed is also to rebel against the One who anointed him. *anointed.* Refers to the Davidic king and is ultimately fulfilled in Christ. The English word "Messiah" comes from the Hebrew word for "anointed one," and the English word "Christ" from the Greek word for "anointed one" (see TNIV text note on Mt 1:1).
2:4–6 The Lord mocks the rebels. With derisive laughter the Lord meets the confederacy of rebellious world powers with the sovereign declaration that it is he who has established the Davidic king in his own royal city of Zion (Jerusalem).
2:4 See 59:8.
2:5 *anger . . . wrath.* God's anger is always an expression of his

righteousness (see 7:11; see also note on 4:1).
2:6 *holy mountain.* The site of the Jerusalem temple (see 2Ch 33:15); see also 3:4; 15:1; 43:3; 99:9.
Ⓐ **2:7–9** The Lord's anointed proclaims the Lord's coronation decree. For NT application to Jesus' resurrection, see Ac 13:33; to his superiority over angels, see Heb 1:5; to his appointment as high priest, see Heb 5:5.
2:7 *son . . . father.* In the ancient Near East the relationship between a great king and one of his subject kings, who ruled by his authority and owed him allegiance, was expressed not only by the words "lord" and "servant" but also by "father" and "son." The Davidic king was the Lord's "servant" and his "son" (2Sa 7:5,14; cf. chart, p. 20).
2:8 *your inheritance.* Your domain—just as the promised land was the Lord's "inheritance" (Ex 15:17; see Jos 22:19; Ps 28:9; 79:1; 82:8). *ends of the earth.* Ultimately the rule of the Lord's anointed will extend as far as the rule of God himself.
Ⓐ **2:9** According to Rev 12:5; 19:15–16 this word will be fulfilled in the triumphant reign of Christ; in Rev 2:26–27 Christ declares that he will appoint those who remain faithful to him to share in his subjugating rule over the nations. *dash them to pieces like pottery.* See Jer 19:11.
2:10–12 The rebellious rulers are warned.
2:11 *celebrate his rule.* Hail the Lord as King with joy. *trembling.* Awe and reverence.
Ⓐ **2:12** *Kiss.* As a sign of submission (see 1Sa 10:1; 1Ki 19:18; Hos 13:2; see also note on Ge 41:40). Submission to an Assyrian king was expressed by kissing his feet. *he . . . his . . . him.* Most likely the reference is to "the Lᴏʀᴅ" (v. 11), who anointed "his son." *you and your ways will be destroyed.* See 1:6 and note. *Blessed.* See 1:1 and note. *take refuge.* See 5:11; 34:8; 64:10; cf. 104:18.

PSALM 3

A psalm of David. When he fled from his son Absalom. z

*¹ LORD, how many are my foes!
How many rise up against me!
² Many are saying of me,
"God will not deliver him. a" a

³ But you, LORD, are a shield b around me,
my glory, the one who lifts my head high. c
⁴ I call out to the LORD, d
and he answers me from his holy mountain. e

⁵ I lie down and sleep; f
I wake again, g because the LORD sustains me.
⁶ I will not fear h though tens of thousands
assail me on every side. i

⁷ Arise, j LORD!
Deliver me, k my God!
Strike l all my enemies on the jaw;
break the teeth m of the wicked.

⁸ From the LORD comes deliverance. n
May your blessing o be on your people.

PSALM 4

For the director of music. With stringed instruments. A psalm of David.

*¹ Answer me p when I call to you,
my righteous God.

a 2 The Hebrew has *Selah* (a word of uncertain meaning) here and at the end of verses 4 and 8.

* 3:1-8 is numbered 3:2-9 in Hebrew texts.   * 4:1-8 is numbered 4:2-9 in Hebrew texts.

Title z 2Sa 15:14
3:2 a Ps 22:8; 71:11;
Isa 36:15; 37:20
3:3 b S Ge 15:1
c Ps 27:6
3:4 d S Job 30:20
e Ps 2:6
3:5 f S Lev 26:6
g Ps 17:15; 139:18
3:6 h Job 11:15;
Ps 23:4; 27:3
i Ps 118:11
3:7 j S 2Ch 6:41
k Ps 6:4; 7:1; 59:1;
109:21; 119:153;
Isa 25:9; 33:22; 35:4;
36:15; 37:20;
Jer 42:11; Mt 6:13
l Job 16:10
m Job 29:17; Ps 57:4;
Pr 30:14; La 3:16
3:8 n Ps 27:1; 37:39;
62:1; Isa 43:3,11;
44:6,8; 45:21;
Hos 13:4; Jnh 2:9;
Rev 7:10 o Nu 6:23;
Ps 29:11; 129:8
4:1 p Ps 13:3; 27:7;
69:16; 86:7; 102:2

Ps 3–14 A group of 12 psalms composed of ten prayers (but see introduction to Ps 11), divided into two groups of five (Ps 3–7; 9–13), each of which has appended to it a sixth that characterizes the human condition (Ps 8; 14). For the sharp contrast between these two characterizations and how their complementary depictions of humankind bear on the collection of prayers to which they have been attached, see introductions to Ps 8; 14.

Ps 3 Though threatened by many foes, the psalmist prays confidently to the Lord. Ps 3 and 4 are linked by references to glory (see v. 3; 4:2) and to David's sleep at night (see v. 5; 4:8). In v. 5 David speaks of the assurance of his waking in the morning because the Lord will keep him while he sleeps; in 4:8 he speaks of the inner quietness with which he goes to sleep because of the Lord's care. This juxtaposition of prayers with references to waking (morning) and sleeping (evening) at the beginning of the Psalter suggests that God's faithful care sustains the godly day and night whatever the need or circumstances.

3 title *When he fled.* See 2Sa 15:13—17:22. References to events in David's life stand in the superscriptions of 13 psalms (3; 7; 18; 34; 51–52; 54; 56–57; 59–60; 63; 142), all but one (Ps 142) in Books I and II. See Introduction: Authorship and Titles (or Superscriptions).

3:1–2 David's need: threatened by many foes.

3:2 See 22:7–8; 71:10–11. The psalmists frequently quote their wicked oppressors in order to portray how they mock (see note on 1:1) God and his servants (see note on 10:11). For *Selah,* see TNIV text note; see also Introduction: Authorship and Titles (or Superscriptions), last paragraph.

3:3–4 David's confidence in God, who does not fail to answer his prayers.

3:3 *shield.* That the king is a shield (protector) of his people was a common concept in ancient Israel (see TNIV text notes on 7:10; 47:9; 59:11; 84:9; 89:18; Ge 15:1). That the Lord is the shield

of his people is frequently asserted (see 84:11; 91:4; 115:9–11; Dt 33:29; Pr 30:5) or claimed (see 18:2,30; 28:7; 33:20; 119:114; 144:2). *my glory.* David rejoices in the Lord as his provider and protector, who has raised him to a position of honor. *lifts my head high.* In victory over his enemies (see 110:7).

3:4 *I call out ... he answers.* See note on 118:5. *holy mountain.* The place of the Lord's sanctuary, the earthly counterpart of his heavenly throne room (see note on 2:6).

3:5–6 David's sense of security.

3:5 Even while David's own watchfulness is surrendered to sleep, the watchful Lord preserves him (see 4:8).

3:7–8 David's prayer.

3:7 *Arise ... Deliver.* Hebrew idiom frequently prefaces an imperative calling for immediate action with a call to "arise" (see Ex 12:31, "Up!"; Dt 2:13; Jdg 7:9, "Get up"). In poetry the two imperatives of the idiom are often distributed between the two halves of the Hebrew poetic line. Hence David's prayer is: "Arise (and) deliver me." *LORD ... my God.* That is, LORD my God; the two elements of a compound divine name are also frequently distributed between the two halves of a poetic line. *break the teeth.* Probably likening the enemies to wild animals (see note on 7:2).

3:8 *From the LORD comes deliverance.* A common feature in the prayers of the Psalter is a concluding expression of confidence that the prayer will be or has been heard (as in 6:8–10; 7:10–17; 10:16–18; 12:7; 13:5–6 and often elsewhere; see note on 12:5–6). Here David's confidence becomes a testimony to God's people. *May your blessing be on your people.* See 25:22; 28:8–9; 51:18. Those anointed by God to rule in Israel stood before the heavenly King as his servants, responsible for the well-being of his people.

Ps 4 A prayer for relief from the threat of slanderers who falsely blame the king for some calamity (possibly a drought; see v. 7) that has stricken the nation, thereby undermining his public standing (his "glory," v. 2) and endangering the very security of

4:1 *q* S Ge 32:7;
S Jdg 2:15 *r* Ps 30:10
s Ps 17:6; 54:2; 84:8;
88:2
4:2 *t* Ex 16:7;
1Sa 4:21 *u* 2Ki 19:26;
Job 8:22; Ps 35:26
v Jdg 2:17; Ps 31:6;
40:4; Jer 13:25; 16:19;
Am 2:4
4:3 *w* Ps 12:1; 30:4;
31:23; 79:2; Mic 7:2;
1Ti 4:7; 2Pe 3:11
x Ps 6:8; Mic 7:7
4:4 *y* Eph 4:26*
z Ps 63:6; Da 2:28
4:5 *a* Ps 31:6; 115:9;
Pr 3:5; 28:26;
Isa 26:4; Jn 14:1
4:6 *b* Nu 6:25
4:7 *c* Ac 14:17
d Isa 9:3; 35:10;
65:14,18 *e* S Ge 27:28;
S Dt 28:51
4:8 *f* S Nu 6:26;
S Job 11:18
g S Lev 26:6
h S Dt 33:28;
S Jer 32:37
5:1 *i* S 1Ki 8:29;
Ps 17:1; 40:1; 116:2;
Da 9:18 *j* Ps 38:9;
Isa 35:10; 51:11

Give me relief from my distress; *q*
　　have mercy *r* on me and hear my prayer. *s*

2 How long will you men turn my glory *t* into shame? *u*
　　How long will you love delusions and seek false gods a? *b v*
3 Know that the LORD has set apart his faithful servant *w* for himself;
　　the LORD hears *x* when I call to him.

4 Tremble and *c* do not sin; *y*
　　when you are on your beds, *z*
　　search your hearts and be silent.
5 Offer the sacrifices of the righteous
　　and trust in the LORD. *a*

6 Many, LORD, are asking, "Who will bring us prosperity?"
　　Let the light of your face shine on us. *b*
7 Fill my heart *c* with joy *d*
　　when their grain and new wine *e* abound.

8 In peace *f* I will lie down and sleep, *g*
　　for you alone, LORD,
　　make me dwell in safety. *h*

PSALM 5

For the director of music. For pipes. A psalm of David.

**1 Listen *i* to my words, LORD,
　　consider my lament. *j*

---

a 2 Or *seek lies*　　b 2 The Hebrew has *Selah* (a word of uncertain meaning) here and at the end of
verse 4.　　c 4 Or *In your anger* (see Septuagint)

* 5:1-12 is numbered 5:2-13 in Hebrew texts.

---

his throne. Those spreading falsehoods (see v. 2 and note) appear to have looked to the king, rather than to the Lord, to preserve the nation from all disasters. See introductions to Ps 3 and 5 for links with those psalms.
4 title See Hab 3:19. *For the director of music.* Probably a liturgical notation, indicating either that the psalm was to be added to the collection of works to be used by the director of music in Israel's worship services or that when the psalm was used in the temple worship it was to be spoken by the leader of the Levitical choir—or by the choir itself (see 1Ch 23:5,30; 25; Ne 11:17). In this liturgical activity the Levites functioned as representatives of the worshiping congregation. Following their lead, the people probably responded with "Amen" and "Praise the LORD" (Hallelujah); see 1Ch 16:36; Ne 5:13; cf. 1Co 14:16; Rev 5:14; 7:12; 19:4. *With stringed instruments.* See Ps 6; 54; 55; 61; 67; 76 titles (cf. Hab 3:19 and note). This is a liturgical notation, indicating that the Levites were to accompany the psalm with harp and lyre (see 1Ch 23:5; 25:1,3,6; cf. Ps 33:2; 43:4; 71:22; see also notes on Ps 39; 42 titles).
A C **4:1** Initial request to be heard. *Answer me when I call.* See note on 118:5. *righteous.* Very often the "righteousness" of God in the Psalms (and frequently elsewhere in the OT) refers to the faithfulness with which he acts. This faithfulness is in full accordance with his commitments to his people and with his status as the divine King—to whom the powerless may look for protection, the oppressed for redress and the needy for help. *Give me relief.* Lit. "Make a spacious place for me" (see 18:19 and note). *my distress.* The threat of being publicly discredited by the slander of those who blame him for the nation's troubles.
4:2–3 David challenges those who have turned on him and warns them that the Lord will hear his prayer for deliverance from their attacks (see note on 5:9).
4:2 *How long . . . ?* See Introduction: Major Themes, 4; see also note on 6:3. *turn my glory into shame.* That is, through slander rob David of the public honor he had enjoyed under the Lord's blessing and care (see 3:3 and note) and bring him into public

disrepute. *delusions.* Rumors and accusations that were void of any truth. *false gods.* Or, more likely here, "lies," as indicated in the TNIV text note (see 5:6 and note on 5:9). For *Selah,* see TNIV text note and note on 3:2.
A C **4:3** *his faithful servant.* Hebrew *hasid,* which occurs 26 times in the Psalms (once of God: 145:17, "faithful"; cf. 18:25) and is usually rendered (in the plural) in the TNIV as "faithful (servants/people)." It is one of several Hebrew words for God's people, referring to them as people who are or should be devoted to God and faithful to him (see note on 1Sa 2:9).
A **4:4–5** An exhortation not to give way to anger or fear and go looking for some scapegoat (the king) on whom to lay blame for the present troubles, but to search their own hearts and put their trust in the Lord.
4:4 *Tremble and do not sin.* Paul uses these words in a different context (see Eph 4:26 and TNIV text note here).
4:6 In the face of widespread uncertainty, David prays for the Lord to bless. *Who . . . ?* Because of the slanders being spread, many are looking for another leader to replace the king. *will bring us prosperity.* See 34:10; 84:11; 85:12; 103:5; 107:9; cf. 16:2; Jas 1:17. *Let . . . your face shine on.* David appeals to the Lord to restore the well-being of the nation—employing a common expression for favor (see note on 13:1), reminiscent of the Aaronic benediction (see Nu 6:25–26).
4:7–8 David's confidence (see note on 3:8).
A **4:7** *heart.* In Biblical language the center of the human spirit, from which spring emotions, thoughts, motivations, courage and action—"everything you do flows from it" (Pr 4:23).
4:8 *In peace.* Without anxiety. *I will lie down and sleep.* See 3:5 and note.
Ps 5 This morning prayer, perhaps offered at the time of the morning sacrifice, is the psalmist's cry for help when his enemies spread malicious lies to destroy him.
5 title *For the director of music.* See note on Ps 4 title. *pipes.* The Hebrew for this word occurs only here; meaning uncertain.

² Hear my cry for help,ᵏ ˡ
   my King and my God,ˡ
   for to you I pray.

³ In the morning,ᵐ Lᴏʀᴅ, you hear my voice;
   in the morning I lay my requests before you
   and wait expectantly.ⁿ

⁴ For you are not a God who is pleased with wickedness;
   with you, evil peopleᵒ are not welcome.

⁵ The arrogantᵖ cannot stand�q
   in your presence.
You hateʳ all who do wrong;
⁶ you destroy those who tell lies.ˢ
The bloodthirsty and deceitful
   you, Lᴏʀᴅ, detest.

⁷ But I, by your great love,
   can come into your house;
in reverenceᵗ I bow downᵘ
   toward your holy temple.ᵛ

⁸ Lead me, Lᴏʀᴅ, in your righteousnessʷ
   because of my enemies—
make your way straightˣ before me.

⁹ Not a word from their mouth can be trusted;
   their heart is filled with malice.
Their throat is an open grave;ʸ
   with their tongues they tell lies.ᶻ

¹⁰ Declare them guilty, O God!
   Let their intrigues be their downfall.
Banish them for their many sins,ᵃ
   for they have rebelledᵇ against you.

¹¹ But let all who take refuge in you be glad;

5:2 ᵏ S Job 19:7;
S 24:12; S 36:5
ˡ Ps 44:4; 68:24; 84:3
5:3 ᵐ Isa 28:19;
50:4; Jer 21:12;
Eze 46:13; Zep 3:5
ⁿ Ps 62:1; 119:81;
130:5; Hab 2:1;
Ro 8:19
5:4 ᵒ Ps 1:5; 11:5;
104:35; Pr 2:22
5:5 ᵖ 2Ki 19:32;
Ps 73:3; 75:4;
Isa 33:19; 37:33
q Ps 1:5 ʳ Ps 45:7;
101:3; 119:104; Pr 8:13
5:6 ˢ Pr 19:22;
S Jn 8:44; Ac 5:3;
Rev 21:8
5:7 ᵗ Dt 13:4;
Jer 44:10; Da 6:26
ᵘ S 2Sa 12:16;
Ps 138:2 ᵛ S 1Ki 8:48
5:8 ʷ Ps 23:3; 31:1;
71:2; 85:13; 89:16;
Pr 8:20 ˣ S 1Ki 8:36;
Jn 1:23
5:9 ʸ Jer 5:16;
Lk 11:44 ᶻ Ps 12:2;
28:3; 36:3; Pr 15:4;
Jer 9:8; Ro 3:13*
5:10 ᵃ La 1:5
ᵇ Ps 78:40; 106:7;
107:11; La 3:42

5:1–3 Initial appeal to be heard.
5:2 *King.* See Introduction: Theology: Major Themes.
5:3 *In the morning.* See introduction to Ps 57; cf. Jer 21:12 and note.
5:4–6 An appeal to the righteousness of God's rule over humankind.
5:5 *The arrogant.* See note on 31:23.
5:6 *tell lies.* Destroy others by slander or false testimony (see v. 9 and note).

5:7–8 The psalmist presents his plea to the Lord in humble reverence (v. 7), trusting in the Lord's "great love" (v. 7) and "righteousness" (v. 8).
5:7 *great love.* See note on 6:4.
5:8 *Lead me.* As a shepherd (see 23:3). *righteousness.* See note on 4:1. *make your way straight.* May the way down which you lead me be straight, level and smooth, free from obstacles and temptations. The psalmist prays that God will so direct him that his enemies will have no grounds for their malicious accusations (see 25:4; 27:11; 139:24; 143:8–10).
5:9–10 Accusation and call for judicial action (both are common elements in the prayers of the Psalter when the psalmist is under threat or attack from human adversaries).

5:9 *word from their mouth.* The most frequent weapon used against the psalmists is the tongue (for a striking example, see Ps 12; see also note on 10:7). The psalmists experienced that the tongue is as deadly as swords and arrows (see 55:21; 57:4; 59:7; 64:3–4; cf. Pr 12:18; 25:18). Perhaps appeals to God against those who maliciously wield the tongue are frequent in the Psalms because only in God's courtroom can a person experience redress for such attacks. *heart.* See note on 4:7. *throat . . . grave.* See note on 49:14. *they tell lies.* For the plots and intrigues of enemies, usually involving lies to discredit the king and bring him down, see Ps 17; 25; 27–28; 31; 35; 41; 52; 54–57; 59; 63–64; 71; 86; 109; 140–141—all psalms ascribed to David.

Frequently such attacks came when the king was "low" and seemingly abandoned by God (as in Ps 25; 35; 41; 71; 86; 109). In that case he was viewed as no longer fit to be king—God was no longer with him (and so he could no longer secure the safety of the nation; see 1Sa 8:20; 11:12; 12:12; 25:28; 2Sa 3:18; 7:9–11). In any event, he was an easy prey (see 3:2; 22:7–8; 71:11). See note on 86:17. See also Paul's use of this verse in Ro 3:13.

5:10 The presence of so-called imprecations (curses) in the Psalms has occasioned endless discussion and has caused many Christians to wince, in view of Jesus' instructions to turn the other cheek and to pray for one's enemies (see Mt 5:39,44), and his own example on the cross (see Lk 23:34). Actually, these "imprecations" are not that at all; rather, they are appeals to God to redress wrongs perpetrated against the psalmists by imposing penalties commensurate with the violence done (see 28:4)—in accordance also with God's norm for judicial action in human courts (see Dt 25:1–3; see also 2Th 1:6; Rev 6:10; 19:2). The psalmists knew that those who have been wronged are not to avenge that wrong by their own hand but are to leave redress to the Lord, who says, "It is mine to avenge; I will repay" (Dt 32:35; see Pr 20:22; Ro 12:19). Therefore they appeal their cases to the divine Judge (see Jer 15:15). *Banish them.* From God's presence, thus from the source of blessing and life (see Ge 3:23). *rebelled against you.* By their attacks on the psalmist.

5:11 The psalmist expands his prayer to include all the godly (see note on 3:8). *your name.* The name of the Lord is the manifestation of his character (see notes on Ex 3:14–15; 34:6–7). It has no separate existence apart from the Lord but is synonymous with the Lord himself in his gracious manifestation and accessibility to his people. Hence the Jerusalem temple is the earthly residence of his name among his people (see 74:7; Dt 12:5,11; 2Sa 7:13), and his people can pray to him by calling on his name (see 79:6; 80:18; 99:6; 105:1; 116:4,13,17). The name of the Lord protects (see 20:1; Pr 18:10); the Lord saves by his name

5:11 c Ps 33:1; 81:1;
90:14; 92:4; 95:1;
145:7 d Ps 69:36;
119:132 e S Job 22:19
5:12 f Ps 112:2
g Ps 32:7 h S Ge 15:1
6:1 i S Ps 2:5
6:2 j Ps 4:1; 26:11;
Jer 3:12; 12:15; 31:20
k Ps 61:2; 77:3; 142:3;
Isa 40:31; Jer 8:18;
Eze 21:7 l S Nu 12:13
m Ps 22:14; 31:10;
32:3; 38:3; 42:10;
102:3
6:3 n S Job 7:11;
Ps 31:7; 38:8; 55:4;
S Jn 12:27; Ro 9:2;
2Co 2:4 o 1Sa 1:14;
1Ki 18:21; Ps 4:2;
89:46; Isa 6:11;
Jer 4:14; Hab 1:2;
Zec 1:12
6:4 p Ps 25:16; 31:2;
69:16; 71:2; 86:16;
88:2; 102:2; 119:132
q Ps 13:5; 31:16; 77:8;
85:7; 119:41; Isa 54:8,
10
6:5 r Ps 30:9; 88:10-
12; 115:17; Ecc 9:10;
Isa 38:18
6:6 s S Jdg 8:5
t S Job 3:24; S 23:2;
Ps 12:5; 77:3; 102:5;
La 1:8,11,21,22
u S Job 16:16

let them ever sing for joy. c
Spread your protection over them,
   that those who love your name d may rejoice in you. e

12 Surely, Lord, you bless the righteous; f
   you surround them g with your favor as with a shield. h

PSALM 6

*For the director of music. With stringed instruments. According
to sheminith. a A psalm of David.*

*1 Lord, do not rebuke me in your anger i
   or discipline me in your wrath.
2 Have mercy on me, j Lord, for I am faint; k
   heal me, l Lord, for my bones are in agony. m
3 My soul is in deep anguish. n
   How long, o Lord, how long?

4 Turn, p Lord, and deliver me;
   save me because of your unfailing love. q
5 Among the dead no one proclaims your name.
   Who praises you from the grave? r

6 I am worn out s from my groaning. t

All night long I flood my bed with weeping u

---

a Title: Probably a musical term

* 6:1-10 is numbered 6:2-11 in Hebrew texts.

(see 54:1); and his saving acts testify that his name is near (see 52:9). Accordingly, the godly "trust in" his name (20:7; 33:21), "hope" in his name (52:9), "sing the praises" of his name (7:17; 9:2; 18:49) and "rejoice in" his name (89:16). Both the "love" and the "fear" that belong alone to God are similarly directed toward his name (love: 69:36; 119:132; fear: 61:5; 86:11; 102:15).

5:12 See note on 3:8. *righteous.* See note on 1:5.

Ps 6 A prayer in time of severe illness, an occasion seized upon by David's enemies to vent their animosity. In early Christian liturgical tradition it was numbered with the seven penitential psalms (the others: Ps 32; 38; 51; 102; 130; 143).

6 title See note on Ps 4 title. *According to.* Represents a Hebrew preposition of varied usage (also found in the titles of Ps 8; 12; 46; 53; 81; 84; 88). *sheminith.* Occurs also in Ps 12 title and in 1Ch 15:21. It perhaps refers to an eight-stringed instrument (see TNIV text note).

6:1–3 Initial appeal for mercy. Though the Lord has sent him illness to chasten him for his sin (see 32:3–5; 38:1–8,17–18), David asks that God would not in anger impose the full measure of the penalty for sin, for then death must come (see v. 5; see also 130:3).

6:1 Ps 38 begins similarly. *rebuke . . . discipline.* That is, rebuke-and-discipline (see 39:11; see also note on 3:7). *anger . . . wrath.* See note on 2:5.

6:2 *bones.* As the inner skeleton, they here represent the whole body.

6:3 *soul.* Not a spiritual aspect in distinction from the physical, nor the psalmist's "inner" being in distinction from his "outer" being, but his very self as a living, conscious, personal being. Its use in conjunction with "bones" (also in 35:9–10: "soul" and "whole being") did not for the Hebrew writer involve reference to two distinct entities but constituted for him two ways of referring to himself, as is the case also in the combination "soul" and "body" (31:9; 63:1). *How long . . . how long?* See Introduction: Theology: Major Themes, 4. Such language of impatience and complaint is found frequently in the prayers of the Psalter (usually "how long?" or "when?" or "why?"). It expresses the anguish of relief not (yet) granted and exhibits the boldness with which the psalmists wrestled with God on the basis of

their relationship with him and their conviction concerning his righteousness (see note on 4:1).

6:4–5 Earnest prayer for deliverance from death.

6:4 *unfailing love.* The Hebrew for this phrase denotes a strong sense of goodwill, especially such as can be relied upon in times of need. Appeal to God's "(unfailing) love" (sometimes rendered "kindness" or "mercy") is frequent in the OT since it summarizes all that the Lord covenanted to show to Israel (see Dt 7:9,12), as well as to David and his dynasty (see 89:24,28,33,49; 2Sa 7:15; Isa 55:3).

6:5 David urges that God's praise is at stake. It is the living, not the dead, who remember God's mercies and celebrate his deliverances. The Israelites usually viewed death as they saw it—the very opposite of life. And resurrection was not yet a part of their communal experience with God. The grave brought no escape from God (see 139:8), but just how they viewed the condition of the godly dead is not clear. (Non-Biblical documents from the ancient Near East indicate a general conception that immortality was reserved for the gods but that the dead continued to have some kind of shadowy existence in the dismal netherworld.) The OT writers knew that human beings were created for life, that God's will for his people was life and that he had power over death. They also knew that death was everyone's lot, and at its proper time the godly rested in God and accepted it with equanimity (see Ge 15:15; 25:8; 47:30; 49:33; 1Ki 2:2). Death could even be a blessing for the righteous, affording escape from the greater evil that would overtake the living (see 2Ki 22:20; Isa 57:1–2). Furthermore, the death of the righteous was reputedly better than that of the wicked (see Nu 23:10). It seems clear that there was even an awareness that death (as observed) was not the end of hope for the righteous, that God had more in store for them (see especially 16:9–11; 17:15; 49:14–15; 73:24; see also note on Ge 5:24). But when the psalmists wrestled with God for the preservation of life, it was death as they saw it, in its radical contradiction to life, that they prayed to be delivered from.

6:6–7 Anguish at night because of the prolongation of the illness and the barbs of the enemies.

6:6 *I am worn out from my groaning.* The very center of the

and drench my couch with tears. [v]
[7] My eyes grow weak [w] with sorrow;
 they fail because of all my foes.

[8] Away from me, [x] all you who do evil, [y]
 for the LORD has heard my weeping.
[9] The LORD has heard my cry for mercy; [z]
 the LORD accepts my prayer.
[10] All my enemies will be overwhelmed with shame and anguish; [a]
 they will turn back and suddenly be put to shame. [b]

PSALM 7

A shiggaion [a] [c] *of David, which he sang to the LORD concerning Cush,
a Benjamite.*

[*][1] LORD my God, I take refuge [d] in you;
 save and deliver me [e] from all who pursue me, [f]
[2] or they will tear me apart like a lion [g]
 and rip me to pieces with no one to rescue [h] me.

[3] LORD my God, if I have done this
 and there is guilt on my hands [i]—
[4] if I have repaid my ally with evil
 or without cause [j] have robbed my foe—
[5] then let my enemy pursue and overtake [k] me;
 let him trample my life to the ground [l]
 and make me sleep in the dust. [b] [m]

[6] Arise, [n] LORD, in your anger;
 rise up against the rage of my enemies. [o]
 Awake, [p] my God; decree justice.
[7] Let the assembled peoples gather around you,
 while you sit enthroned over them on high. [q]
[8] Let the LORD judge [r] the peoples.
 Vindicate me, LORD, according to my righteousness, [s]
 according to my integrity, [t] O Most High. [u]
[9] Bring to an end the violence of the wicked
 and make the righteous secure— [v]

[a] Title: Probably a literary or musical term   [b] 5 The Hebrew has *Selah* (a word of uncertain meaning)
here.
[*] 7:1-17 is numbered 7:2-18 in Hebrew texts.

6:6 [v] S Job 7:3;
Lk 7:38; Ac 20:19
6:7 [w] S Job 16:8;
Ps 31:9; 69:3; 119:82;
Isa 38:14
6:8 [x] S Ps 119:115;
139:19 [y] Ps 5:5;
S Mt 7:23
6:9 [z] Ps 28:6; 116:1
6:10 [a] S 2Ki 19:26
[b] Ps 40:14
7:1 [c] Hab 3:1
[d] Ps 2:12; 11:1; 31:1
[e] S Ps 3:7 [f] Ps 31:15;
119:86,157,161
7:2 [g] S Ge 49:9;
Rev 4:7 [h] Ps 3:2; 71:11
7:3 [i] Isa 59:3
7:4 [j] Ps 35:7,19;
Pr 24:28
7:5 [k] S Ex 15:9
[l] S 2Sa 22:43;
2Ki 9:33; Isa 10:6;
La 3:16 [m] S Job 7:21
7:6 [n] S 2Ch 6:41
[o] Ps 138:7 [p] Ps 35:23;
44:23
7:7 [q] Ps 68:18
7:8 [r] S 1Ch 16:33
[s] S 1Sa 26:23;
Ps 18:20 [t] S Ge 20:5
[u] S Ge 3:5;
S Nu 24:16; S Mk 5:7
7:9 [v] Ps 37:23; 40:2

poem—thus underscoring the pathos of this prayer. This literary device—of placing a key thematic line at the very center of the psalm—was frequently used (see notes on 8:4; 21:7; 23:4; 34:8–14; 42:8; 47:5–6; 48:8; 54:4; 71:14; 74:12; 76:7; 82:5a; 86:9; 92:8; 97:7; 113:5; 138:4–5; 141:5; see also Introduction: Literary Features).
6:7 *eyes grow weak . . . fail.* In the vivid language of the OT the eyes are dimmed by failing strength (see 38:10; 1Sa 14:27,29 and TNIV text notes; Jer 14:6), by grief (often associated with affliction: 31:9; 88:9; Job 17:7; La 2:11) and by longings unsatisfied or hope deferred (see 69:3; 119:82,123; Dt 28:32; Isa 38:14). *because of all my foes.* See note on 5:9.
6:8–10 Concluding expression of buoyant confidence (see note on 3:8).
6:10 At David's restoration, his enemies will be disgraced.
Ps 7 An appeal to the Lord's court of justice when enemies attack.
7 title *shiggaion.* See TNIV text note. The word occurs only here (but see its plural in Hab 3:1). *Cush.* Not otherwise known, but as a Benjamite he was probably a supporter of Saul. Hence the title evokes Saul's determined attempts on David's life. See Introduction: Authorship and Titles (or Superscriptions).
7:1–2 Initial summation of David's appeal.
7:2 *like a lion.* As a young shepherd, David had been attacked by lions (see 1Sa 17:34–35). But it is also a convention in the

Psalms to liken the attack of enemies to that of ferocious animals, especially the lion (see 10:9; 17:12; 22:12–13,16, 20–21; 35:17; 57:4; 58:6; 124:6).
7:3–5 David pleads his own innocence; he has given his enemy no cause to attack him.
7:5 *me.* Lit. "my glory," a way of referring to the core of one's being (see 16:9; 30:12; 57:8; 108:1 and notes). For *Selah,* see TNIV text note and note on 3:2.
7:6–9 An appeal to the Judge of all the earth to execute his judgment over all peoples, and particularly to adjudicate David's cause.
7:6 *Arise . . . rise up.* See note on 3:7. *anger.* See v. 11 and note on 2:5. *Awake.* The Lord does not sleep (see 121:4) while evil triumphs and the oppressed cry to him in vain (as they do to Baal; see 1Ki 18:27). But the psalmists' language of urgent prayer vividly expresses their anguished impatience with God's inaction in the face of their great need (see 80:2; see also 78:65; Isa 51:9).
7:8 *my righteousness.* See vv. 3–5. *my integrity.* See note on 15:2.
7:9 *the righteous.* See note on 1:5. *righteous God.* See note on 4:1. *minds and hearts.* Lit. "hearts and kidneys." The Israelites used the words as virtual synonyms (but "heart" most often) to refer to the innermost center of one's conscious life (see note on 4:7). To "search mind and heart" was a conventional expression for God's examination of one's hidden character and motives (see Jer 11:20; 17:10; 20:12).

7:9 w Jer 11:20
x S 1Ch 28:9; Ps 26:2;
Rev 2:23
7:10 y Ps 3:3
z S Job 33:3
7:11 a S Ge 18:25;
Ps 9:8; 67:4; 75:2;
96:13; 98:9; Isa 11:4;
Jer 11:20 b S Dt 9:8
7:12 c Eze 3:19; 33:9
d S Dt 32:41
e S 2Sa 22:35;
Ps 21:12; Isa 5:28;
13:18
7:13 f Ps 11:2; 18:14;
64:3
7:14 g Isa 59:4;
Jas 1:15
7:15 h Ps 35:7,8;
40:2; 94:13; Pr 26:27
i S Job 4:8
7:17 j Ps 5:8
k S 2Ch 31:2; Ro 15:11;
Heb 2:12 l S Ge 14:18
8:1 m S 1Ch 16:10
n S Ex 15:11; Lk 2:9
o Ps 57:5; 108:5;
113:4; 148:13; Hab 3:3
8:2 p Mt 21:16*
q Ps 143:12

you, the righteous God [w]
  who probes minds and hearts. [x]

[10] My shield [a] [y] is God Most High,
  who saves the upright in heart. [z]
[11] God is a righteous judge, [a]
  a God who displays his wrath [b] every day.
[12] If he does not relent, [c]
  he [b] will sharpen his sword; [d]
  he will bend and string his bow. [e]
[13] He has prepared his deadly weapons;
  he makes ready his flaming arrows. [f]

[14] Those who are pregnant with evil
  conceive trouble and give birth [g] to disillusionment.
[15] Those who dig a hole and scoop it out
  fall into the pit [h] they have made. [i]
[16] The trouble they cause recoils on them;
  their violence comes down on their own heads.

[17] I will give thanks to the LORD because of his righteousness; [j]
  I will sing the praises [k] of the name of the LORD Most High. [l]

PSALM 8

For the director of music. According to gittith. [c] *A psalm of David.*

*[1] LORD, our Lord,
  how majestic is your name [m] in all the earth!

You have set your glory [n]
  above the heavens. [o]
[2] Through the praise of children and infants
  you have established a stronghold [p] against your enemies,
  to silence the foe [q] and the avenger.

---

a 10 Or *sovereign*   b 12 Or *If anyone does not repent, / God*   c Title: Probably a musical term
* 8:1-9 is numbered 8:2-10 in Hebrew texts.

7:10–13 David's confidence that his prayer will be heard (see note on 3:8).
7:10 *shield.* See note on 3:3. *heart.* See note on 4:7.
7:11 *every day.* God's judgments are not all kept in store for some future day.
7:12–13 *sword ... bow ... flaming arrows.* The weapons of the heavenly Warrior King used in defense of his people (see Ex 15:3 and note) but also in judgment.
7:12 *his bow.* See note on Ge 9:13.

7:14–16 David comforts himself with the common wisdom that under God's rule "crime does not pay."
7:15 *dig a hole.* A metaphor from the hunt; pits were used to trap animals (see 9:15 and note).

7:17 A vow to praise. Many prayers in the Psalter include such vows in anticipation of the expected answer to prayer. They reflect Israel's religious consciousness that praise must follow deliverance as surely as prayer springs from need —if God is to be truly honored. Such praise was usually offered with thank offerings and involved celebrating God's saving act in the presence of those assembled at the temple (see 50:14–15,23; see also note on 9:1). *name of the LORD.* See note on 5:11. *Most High.* See note on Ge 14:19.

Ps 8 In praise of the Creator (not of human beings—as is evident from the doxology that encloses it, vv. 1,9; see also note on 9:1) out of wonder over his sovereign ordering of the creation. Ge 1 (particularly vv. 26–28) clearly provides the lenses, but David speaks out of his present experience of reality (perhaps on a bright, clear night when the vast host of the heavenly lights, stretching from horizon to horizon, erased from his musings small everyday affairs and engaged his mind with deeper thoughts). Two matters especially impressed him: (1) the glory of God reflected in the starry heavens, and (2) the astonishing condescension of God to be mindful of puny mortals, to crown them with glory almost godlike and to grant them lordly power over his other creatures. At this juncture in the Psalter this psalm surprises. After five psalms (and 64 Hebrew poetic lines—following the introduction to the Psalter; see introduction to Ps 1–2) in which the psalmists have called on Yahweh to deal with human perversity, this psalm's praise of Yahweh for his astounding endowment of the human race with royal "glory and honor" (v. 5) serves as a striking and unexpected counterpoint. Its placement here highlights the glory (God's gift) and disgrace (humanity's own doing) that characterize human beings and the corresponding range of differences in God's dealings with them. And after five more psalms (and 64 poetic lines), this psalm in turn receives a counterpoint (see introduction to Ps 14; see also chart, p. 819, and introduction to Ps 3–14).
8 title *For the director of music.* See note on Ps 4 title. *According to.* See note on Ps 6 title. *gittith.* See Ps 81; 84 titles. The Hebrew word perhaps refers to either a winepress ("song of the winepress") or the Philistine city of Gath ("Gittite lyre or music"; see 2Sa 15:18).
8:1a *name.* See note on 5:11.

8:1b–2 The mighty God, whose glory is displayed across the face of the heavens, appoints (and evokes) the praise of little children to silence the dark powers arrayed against him (for a NT application see Mt 21:16).
8:2 *avenger.* See 44:16; one who strikes back in malicious revenge (not as in 9:12).

³When I consider your heavens, ʳ
　　the work of your fingers, ˢ
the moon and the stars, ᵗ
　　which you have set in place,
⁴what are mere mortals that you are mindful of them,
　　human beings that you care for them?ᵃ ᵘ
⁵You have made themᵇ a little lower than the heavenly beingsᶜ ᵛ
　　and crowned themᵇ with glory and honor. ʷ
⁶You made them rulersˣ over the works of your hands;ʸ
　　you put everything under theirᵈ feet:ᶻ ᵃ
⁷all flocks and herds, ᵇ
　　and the animals of the wild, ᶜ
⁸the birds in the sky,
　　and the fish in the sea, ᵈ
all that swim the paths of the seas.

⁹Lᴏʀᴅ, our Lord,
　　how majestic is your name in all the earth!ᵉ

PSALM 9ᵉ

For the director of music. To the tune of "The Death of the Son." A psalm of David.

*¹I will praise you, Lᴏʀᴅ, with all my heart;ᶠ
　　I will tell of all your wonderful deeds. ᵍ

ᵃ 4 Or *what is a human being that you are mindful of him, / a son of man that you care for him?*
ᵇ 5 Or *him*　　ᶜ 5 Or *than God*　　ᵈ 6 Or *made him ruler . . . ; / . . . his*　　ᵉ Psalms 9 and 10 may originally
have been a single acrostic poem in which alternating lines began with the successive letters of the
Hebrew alphabet. In the Septuagint they constitute one psalm.
* 9:1-20 is numbered 9:2-21 in Hebrew texts.

8:3 ʳ S Ge 15:5;
S Dt 10:14 ˢ S Ex 8:19;
S 1Ch 16:26;
S 2Ch 2:12; Ps 102:25
ᵗ S Ge 1:16; 1Co 15:41
8:4 ᵘ S 1Ch 29:14
8:5 ᵛ S Ge 1:26
ʷ Ps 21:5; 103:4
8:6 ˣ S Ge 1:28
ʸ S Job 10:3; Ps 19:1;
102:25; 145:10;
Isa 26:12; 29:23;
45:11; Heb 1:10
ᶻ Heb 2:6-8*
ᵃ S 1Ki 5:3; 1Co 15:25,
27*; Eph 1:22
8:7 ᵇ Ge 13:5; 26:14
ᶜ S Ge 2:19
8:8 ᵈ Ge 1:26
8:9 ᵉ ver 1
9:1 ᶠ Ps 86:12; 111:1;
119:2,10,145; 138:1
ᵍ S Dt 4:34

8:3–5 The vastness and majesty of the heavens as the handiwork of God (see 19:1–6; 104:19–23) evoke wonder for what their Maker has done for human beings, who are here today and gone tomorrow (see 144:3–4). (See Job 7:17–21 for Job's complaint that God takes humans too seriously.)
8:3 *fingers.* See note on Ex 8:19.

🔺 **8:4–6** Heb 2:6–8, quoting the Septuagint (the pre-Christian Greek translation of the OT), applies these verses to Jesus, who as the incarnate Son of God is both the representative human being and the one in whom humanity's appointed destiny will be fully realized. The author of Hebrews thus makes use of the eschatological implications of these words in his testimony to Christ. Paul does the same with v. 6 in 1Co 15:27 (see also Eph 1:22).
8:4 *what . . . ?* The Hebrew for this word is translated "how" in vv. 1,9 and begins the line that serves as the center of the psalm (see note on 6:6). *are mindful of.* Lit. "remember" (see note on Ge 8:1). *human beings.* See TNIV text note. "Son of man" is a literal translation of a Hebrew phrase commonly used to refer to a human being (see 80:17; 144:3; see also note on Eze 2:1 and TNIV text note there).
8:5 *heavenly beings.* The exalted angelic creatures that surround God in his heavenly realm (as, e.g., in Isa 6:2); but see TNIV text note.

🔺 **8:6–8** See Ge 1:26–27. The power to exercise rule over some of God's creatures is even now a part of humanity's "glory and honor" (v. 5). The full realization of that potential—and vocation—belongs to humanity's appointed destiny (the eschatological import drawn upon by Paul and the author of Hebrews; see note on vv. 4–6). But this power—and vocation—to rule is not absolute or independent. It is participation, but not as an equal, in God's rule; and it is a gift, not a right.
8:9 Repeated verbatim from v. 1a (see note there).
Ps 9 That Ps 9 and 10 were sometimes viewed (or used) as one psalm is known from the Septuagint (the pre-Christian Greek

translation of the OT; see TNIV text note). Whether they were originally composed as one psalm is not known, though a number of indicators point in that direction. Ps 10 is the only psalm from Ps 3 to 32 that has no superscription, and the Hebrew text of the two psalms together appears to reflect an incomplete (or broken) acrostic structure. The first letter of each verse or pair of verses tends to follow the order of the Hebrew alphabet near the beginning of Ps 9 and again near the end of Ps 10. The thoughts also tend to be developed in two-verse units throughout. Ps 9 is predominantly praise (by the king) for God's deliverance from hostile nations (the specific occasion is unknown, but since there is no reference to victories on the part of Israel, God's destruction of the nations may have come by other means). It concludes with a short prayer for God's continuing righteous judgments (see v. 4) on the haughty nations. Ps 10 is predominantly prayer against the rapacity of unscrupulous people within the realm—as arrogant and wicked in their dealings with the "weak" (v. 2) as the nations were in their attacks on Israel (vv. 2–11 can serve equally as a description of both). The conjunction of these two within a single psalm is not unthinkable since the attacks of "the wicked" (9:5; 10:4), whether from within or from without, on the godly community are equally threatening to true Israel. Praise of God's past deliverances is often an integral part of prayer in the Psalter (see 3:3–4,8 and notes; 25:6; 40:1–5), as also in other ancient Near Eastern prayers. Such praise expressed the basis of the psalmist's hope that his present prayer would be heard, and it also functioned to motivate the Lord to act once more in his people's (or his servant's) behalf. For other lengthy prefaces to prayer, see Ps 40; 44; 89. Probably Ps 9–10 came to be separated for the purpose of separate liturgical use, as did Ps 42–43 (see introduction there).
9 title *For the director of music.* See note on Ps 4 title. *To the tune of.* See titles of Ps 22; 45; 56–60; 69; 75; 80; see also TNIV text note on Ps 88 title. Nothing more is known of the apparent tune titles.

9:2 ʰ S Job 22:19;
Ps 14:7; 31:7; 70:4;
97:8; 126:3; Pr 23:15;
Isa 25:9; Jer 30:19;
Joel 2:21; Zep 3:14;
S Mt 5:12; Rev 19:7
ⁱ S 2Ch 31:2 ʲ Ps 92:1
9:4 ᵏ S 1Ki 8:45
ˡ S Job 16:21 ᵐ Ps 11:4;
47:8; Isa 6:1 ⁿ Ps 7:11;
67:4; 98:9; 1Pe 2:23
9:5 ᵒ Ge 20:7;
S 37:10; S 1Ch 16:21;
Ps 59:5; 105:14;
Isa 26:14; 66:15
ᵖ S Job 18:17
9:6 �q S Dt 29:28;
Jer 2:3; 46:1–51:58;
Zep 2:8-10 ʳ Ps 34:16;
109:15; Ecc 9:5;
Isa 14:22; 26:14
9:7 ˢ S 1Ch 16:31;
Rev 19:6 ᵗ Ps 11:4;
47:8; 93:2; Isa 6:1; 66:1
9:8 ᵘ S ver 4; Ps 7:11
ᵛ Ps 11:7; 45:6; 72:2
9:9 ʷ S Dt 33:27;
S 2Sa 22:3 ˣ Ps 10:18;
74:21 ʸ Ps 32:7; 121:7
9:10 ᶻ Ps 91:14
ᵃ S Ge 28:15; S Dt 4:31;
Ps 22:1; 37:25; 71:11;
Isa 49:14; Jer 15:18;
Heb 13:5 ᵇ Ps 70:4
9:11 ᶜ Ps 7:17
ᵈ S Ps 2:6 ᵉ Ps 18:49;
44:11; 57:9; 106:27;
Isa 24:13; Eze 20:23;
1Ti 3:16 ᶠ Ps 105:1
9:12 ᵍ S 2Sa 4:11
ʰ ver 18; Ps 10:17;
22:24; 72:4; Isa 49:13
9:13 ⁱ Nu 10:9;
Ps 3:7; 18:3 ʲ Ps 6:2;
41:4; 51:1; 86:3,16;
119:132 ᵏ S Job 17:16;
Mt 16:18
9:14 ˡ Ps 51:15;
1Pe 2:9 ᵐ 2Ki 19:21;
Isa 1:8; 10:32; 37:22;

² I will be glad and rejoice ʰ in you;
　　I will sing the praises ⁱ of your name, ʲ O Most High.

³ My enemies turn back;
　　they stumble and perish before you.
⁴ For you have upheld my right ᵏ and my cause, ˡ
　　sitting enthroned ᵐ as the righteous judge. ⁿ
⁵ You have rebuked the nations ᵒ and destroyed the wicked;
　　you have blotted out their name ᵖ for ever and ever.
⁶ Endless ruin has overtaken my enemies,
　　you have uprooted their cities; q
　　even the memory of them ʳ has perished.

⁷ The LORD reigns forever; ˢ
　　he has established his throne ᵗ for judgment.
⁸ He rules the world in righteousness ᵘ
　　and judges the peoples with equity. ᵛ
⁹ The LORD is a refuge ʷ for the oppressed, ˣ
　　a stronghold in times of trouble. ʸ
¹⁰ Those who know your name ᶻ trust in you,
　　for you, LORD, have never forsaken ᵃ those who seek you. ᵇ

¹¹ Sing the praises ᶜ of the LORD, enthroned in Zion; ᵈ
　　proclaim among the nations ᵉ what he has done. ᶠ
¹² For he who avenges blood ᵍ remembers;
　　he does not ignore the cries of the afflicted. ʰ

¹³ LORD, see how my enemies ⁱ persecute me!
　　Have mercy ʲ and lift me up from the gates of death, ᵏ
¹⁴ that I may declare your praises ˡ
　　in the gates of Daughter Zion, ᵐ
　　and there rejoice in your salvation. ⁿ

¹⁵ The nations have fallen into the pit they have dug; ᵒ

9:14 62:11; Jer 4:31; 6:2; La 1:6; Mic 1:13; Zep 3:14; Zec 2:10; Mt 21:5; Jn 12:15 ⁿ Ps 13:5; 35:9; 50:23; 51:12   **9:15** ᵒ S Job 4:8; Ps 35:7

9:1–2 Initial announcement of praise.

A **9:1** *heart.* See note on 4:7. *tell of.* The Hebrew for this phrase is translated "declare" in v. 14. The praise of God in the Psalter is rarely a private matter between the psalmist and the Lord. It is usually a public (at the temple) celebration of God's holy virtues or of his saving acts or gracious bestowal of blessings. In his praise the psalmist proclaims to the assembled throng God's glorious attributes or his righteous (see note on 4:1) deeds (see, e.g., 22:22–31; 56:12–13; 61:8; 65:1; 69:30–33). To this is usually added a call to praise, summoning all who hear to take up the praise—to acknowledge and joyfully celebrate God's glory, his goodness and all his righteous acts. This aspect of praise in the Psalms has rightly been called the OT anticipation of NT evangelism. *wonderful deeds.* God's saving acts, sometimes involving miracles—as in the exodus from Egypt, the desert wanderings and the entrance into the promised land—and sometimes not, but always involving the manifestation of God's sovereign lordship over events. Here reference is to the destruction of the enemies celebrated in this psalm.

9:2,10 *your name.* See note on 5:11.

9:2 *Most High.* See note on Ge 14:19.

9:3–6 In destroying the enemies, God has redressed the wrongs committed by them against David (and Israel).

9:4 *enthroned.* See note on v. 7.

9:5 *blotted out their name.* As if from a register of all living persons written on a papyrus scroll (see Nu 5:23; see also Dt 9:14; 25:19; 29:20; 2Ki 14:27).

A **9:7–10** Celebration of the righteous rule of God (see note on 4:1; see also Ps 93; 96–99), which evokes trust on the part of those who look to the Lord.

9:7 *his throne.* In heaven (see 11:4). See also v. 4.

9:8 See Ac 17:31.

9:10 *Those who know your name.* Those who acknowledge in their hearts who the Lord is and also live out that acknowledgment (see 91:14; see also note on 5:11).

9:11–12 A call to the assembly at the temple to take up the praise of God for his righteous judgments (see note on v. 1).

9:11 *enthroned in Zion.* God's heavenly throne (see v. 7) has its counterpart on earth in his temple at Jerusalem, from which center he rules the world (see 2:6; 3:4 and notes; 20:2). For God's election of Zion as the seat of his rule, see 132:13; see also Introduction: Theology: Major Themes, 7.

9:12 *he who avenges blood.* See Dt 32:41,43.

9:13–14 Perhaps a recollection of David's prayer ("the cries of the afflicted," v. 12), which the Lord has now answered.

9:13 *gates of death.* See Job 17:16 and note.

9:14 *declare.* See notes on v. 1; 7:17. *gates.* Having been thrust down by the attacks of his enemies to "the gates of death" (v. 13), David prayed to be lifted up so he could celebrate his deliverance (see note on v. 1) in "the gates of … Zion." *Daughter Zion.* A personification of Jerusalem (see note on 2Ki 19:21).

A **9:15–18** Under the Lord's just rule, those who wickedly attack others bring destruction on themselves (see 7:14–16 and note), and their end will be the grave. But those who are attacked ("the needy," v. 18) will not trust in the Lord in vain.

9:15 *pit … dug … net … hidden.* In the Psalter, imagery drawn from the hunt is frequently (in 14 psalms) employed to depict the cunning attacks of enemies who sought to destroy by hidden means or surprise attacks, the tongue being the most common weapon (see 5:9 and note). In ancient times hunters used snares, traps, nets and pits, often in combination, and always involving concealment.

their feet are caught in the net they have hidden. *p*

16 The LORD is known by his acts of justice;
  the wicked are ensnared by the work of their hands. *a q*

17 The wicked go down to the realm of the dead, *r*
  all the nations that forget God. *s*

18 But God will never forget the needy;
  the hope *t* of the afflicted *u* will never perish.

19 Arise, *v* LORD, do not let mortals triumph; *w*
  let the nations be judged *x* in your presence.

20 Strike them with terror, *v* LORD;
  let the nations know they are only mortals. *z*

PSALM 10 *b*

1 Why, LORD, do you stand far off? *a*
  Why do you hide yourself *b* in times of trouble?

2 In their arrogance the wicked hunt down the weak, *c*
  catching them in the schemes they devise.

3 They boast *d* about the cravings of their hearts;
  they bless the greedy and revile the LORD. *e*

4 In their pride the wicked do not seek him;
  in all their thoughts there is no room for God. *f*

5 Their ways are always prosperous;
  your laws are rejected by *c* them;
  they sneer at all their enemies.

6 They say to themselves, "Nothing will ever shake us."
  They swear, "No one will ever do us harm." *g*

7 Their mouths are full *h* of lies and threats; *i*
  trouble and evil are under their tongues. *j*

8 They lie in wait *k* near the villages;
  from ambush they murder the innocent. *l*
  Their eyes watch in secret for their victims;

9   like a lion in cover they lie in wait.
  They lie in wait to catch the helpless; *m*
  they catch the helpless and drag them off in their nets. *n*

10 L The innocent J are crushed, *o* they collapse;
  they fall victim to superior strength.

11 The wicked say to themselves, "God will never notice; *p*
  he covers his face and never sees." *q*

---

a 16 The Hebrew has *Higgaion* and *Selah* (words of uncertain meaning) here; *Selah* occurs also at the end of verse 20.   b Psalms 9 and 10 may originally have been a single acrostic poem in which alternating lines began with the successive letters of the Hebrew alphabet. In the Septuagint they constitute one psalm.   c 5 See Septuagint; Hebrew / *they are haughty, and your laws are far from*

9:15 *p* Ps 35:8; 57:6
9:16 *q* Pr 5:22
9:17 *r* S Nu 16:30;
Pr 5:5 *s* S Job 8:13
9:18 *t* Ps 25:3; 39:7;
71:5; Pr 23:18; Jer 14:8
u ver 12; Ps 74:19
9:19 *v* Ps 3:7
w 2Ch 14:11
x Ps 110:6; Isa 2:4;
Joel 3:12
9:20 *v* S Ge 35:5;
Ps 31:13; Isa 13:8;
Lk 21:26 *z* Ps 62:9;
Isa 31:3; Eze 28:2
10:1 *a* Ps 22:1,11;
35:22; 38:21; 71:12
b Ps 13:1
10:2 *c* ver 9;
S Job 20:19
10:3 *d* Ps 49:6;
94:4; Jer 48:30
e S Job 1:5
10:4 *f* Ps 36:1
10:6 *g* Rev 18:7
10:7 *h* Ro 3:14*
i Ps 73:8; 119:134;
Ecc 4:1; Isa 30:12
j S Job 20:12
10:8 *k* Ps 37:32;
59:3; 71:10; Pr 1:11;
Jer 5:26; Mic 7:2
l Hos 6:9
10:9 *m* S ver 2
n S Job 18:8
10:10 *o* S Job 9:17
10:11 *p* Job 22:13;
Ps 42:9; 77:9
q S Job 22:14

9:16 For *Selah*, see TNIV text note and note on 3:2.

9:17 *forget.* Take no account of.

9:18 *God will never forget.* Those who forget God will come to nothing, but the needy and afflicted will not be forgotten by God (see v. 12). *needy ... afflicted.* In this psalm David and Israel are counted among them because of the threat from the enemies.

9:19–20 A prayer at the conclusion of praise, asking that the Lord may ever rule over the nations as he has done in the event here celebrated—that those who "forget God" (v. 17) may know that they are only weak mortals, not gods, and cannot withstand the God of Israel (see 10:18).

9:19 *Arise.* See note on 3:7.

Ps 10 A prayer for rescue from the attacks of unscrupulous people—containing a classic OT portrayal of "the wicked" (v. 4). See introduction to Ps 9.

10:1 See note on 3:7.

10:2–11 Accusation lodged against the oppressors (see note on 5:9–10). Here the psalmist launches into a characterization of oppressors in general. Their deeds betray the ar-

rogance (see vv. 2–5—so long as they prosper, v. 5) with which they defy God (see vv. 3–4,13; see especially their words in vv. 6,11,13). They greedily seek to glut their unrestrained appetites (see v. 3) by victimizing others, taking account of neither God (see v. 4) nor his law (see v. 5).

10:2 *hunt ... catching.* The psalmists often use imagery from the hunt (see vv. 8–9 and note on v. 9).

10:3 *hearts.* See note on 4:7.

10:4 The wicked do not consider that they have God to contend with (see note on v. 11; see also 14:1; 36:1; 53:1).

10:6 See vv. 11,13 and note on 3:2. *to themselves.* Lit. "in their hearts" (also in vv. 11,13); see note on 4:7. *shake us.* Take away our well-being, destroy our security.

10:7 *lies and threats.* The two most common weapons of the tongue in Israel's experience (see note on 5:9). *lies.* Slander and false testimony for malicious purposes (see, e.g., 1Ki 21:8–15).

10:9 See note on 7:2. *lie in wait.* The imagery shifts from the lion to the hunter (see note on 9:15).

10:11 See note on 3:2. The arrogance with which the wicked speak (see 17:10), especially their easy dismissal of God's knowl-

10:12 ʳPs 3:7
ˢPs 17:7; 20:6;
106:26; Isa 26:11;
Mic 5:9 ᵗPs 9:12
10:13 ᵘver 3
ᵛS Job 31:14
10:14 ʷver 7;
Ps 22:11 ˣPs 37:5
ʸS Dt 33:29
10:15 ᶻS Job 31:22
10:16 ᵃS Ex 15:18
ᵇS Dt 8:20
10:17 ᶜS Ps 9:12
ᵈS Ex 22:23
10:18 ᵉS Dt 24:17;
Ps 146:9 ᶠS Ps 9:9
11:1 ᵍS Ps 7:1
ʰS Ge 14:10 ⁱPs 50:11
11:2 ʲS 2Sa 22:35
ᵏS Ps 7:13; S 58:7
ˡPs 10:8 ᵐS Job 33:3;
Ps 7:10
11:3 ⁿPs 18:15;
82:5; Isa 24:18
11:4 ᵒS 1Ki 8:48;
Ps 18:6; 27:4; Jnh 2:7;
Mic 1:2; Hab 2:20
ᵖS 2Ch 6:18;
S Ps 9:7; Mt 5:34;
23:22; S Rev 4:2
ᑫPs 15:3 ʳPs 33:18;
66:7
11:5 ˢS Dt 7:13;
S Job 23:10
ᵗS Job 28:28; Ps 5:5;
45:7; Isa 1:14

¹² Arise,ʳ Lᴏʀᴅ! Lift up your hand,ˢ O God.
 Do not forget the helpless.ᵗ
¹³ Why do the wicked revile God?ᵘ
 Why do they say to themselves,
 "He won't call us to account"?ᵛ
¹⁴ But you, God, see the troubleʷ of the afflicted;
 you consider their grief and take it in hand.
 The victims commit themselves to you;ˣ
 you are the helperʸ of the fatherless.
¹⁵ Break the arms of the wicked and the evildoers;ᶻ
 call them to account for their wickedness
 that would not otherwise be found out.

¹⁶ The Lᴏʀᴅ is King for ever and ever;ᵃ
 the nations ᵇ will perish from his land.
¹⁷ You, Lᴏʀᴅ, hear the desire of the afflicted;ᶜ
 you encourage them, and you listen to their cry,ᵈ
¹⁸ defending the fatherlessᵉ and the oppressed,ᶠ
 so that mere earthly mortals
 will never again strike terror.

PSALM 11

For the director of music. Of David.

¹ In the Lᴏʀᴅ I take refuge.ᵍ
 How then can you say to me:
 "Fleeʰ like a bird to your mountain.ⁱ
² For look, the wicked bend their bows;ʲ
 they set their arrowsᵏ against the strings
 to shoot from the shadowsˡ
 at the upright in heart.ᵐ
³ When the foundations ⁿ are being destroyed,
 what can the righteous do?"

⁴ The Lᴏʀᴅ is in his holy temple;ᵒ
 the Lᴏʀᴅ is on his heavenly throne.ᵖ
 He observes everyone on earth;ᑫ
 his eyes examineʳ them.
⁵ The Lᴏʀᴅ examines the righteous,ˢ
 but the wicked, those who love violence,
 he hates with a passion.ᵗ
⁶ On the wicked he will rain

---

edge of their evil acts and his unfailing prosecution of their malicious deeds, is frequently noted by the psalmists (see v. 13; 12:4; 42:3,10; 59:7; 64:5; 71:11; 73:11; 94:7; 115:2; see also Isa 29:15; Eze 8:12).

10:12–15 Prayer that God will call the wicked to account.
10:12 *Arise.* See note on 3:7. *forget.* See 9:18. *helpless.* Those at the mercy of the oppressors (see v. 9).
10:13 *Why...?Why...?* See note on 6:3.
10:14 Appeal to God's righteous rule (see 5:4–6).
10:15 *Break the arms.* Destroy the power to oppress. *call them to account.* Humble such arrogance (see v. 13) with your righteous judgment.
10:16–18 The psalmist's confidence in the righteous reign of the Lord (see note on 3:8). Reference to the nations (v. 16) and to the humbling of proud humans (see v. 18; see also 9:19–20) suggests links with Ps 9. As the conclusion to Ps 10, this stanza expands the vision of God's just rule to its universal scope and sets the purging of the Lord's land of all nations that do not acknowledge him (see v. 16) alongside God's judicial dealing with the wicked oppressors. Both belong to God's assertion of his righteous rule in the face of arrogant denial of it.
10:18 *mere earthly mortals.* Who are not God and so constitute no ultimate threat (see 49:12,20; 56:4,11; 62:9; 78:39; 103:14–16;

118:6,8–9; 144:4; Isa 31:3; Jer 17:5).
Ps 11 A confession of confident trust in the Lord's righteous rule, at a time when wicked adversaries seem to have the upper hand.
11 title *For the director of music.* See note on Ps 4 title.
11:1–3 David testifies of his unshakable trust in the Lord (his refuge) to apprehensive people around him. These people, seeing the power and underhandedness of the enemy (they "shoot from the shadows," v. 2), fear that the foundations (v. 3) are crumbling and that flight to a mountain refuge is the only recourse. He dismisses their fearful advice with disdain.
11:2 It is not clear whether those who wield the bows and arrows are archers or false accusers (see 57:4; 64:3–4; see also note on 5:9). *heart.* See note on 4:7.
11:3 *foundations.* Of the world order (see 82:5). To those who counsel flight, the powerful upsurge of evil appears to indicate that the righteous can no longer count on a world order in which good triumphs over evil. *righteous.* See note on 1:5.
11:4–7 Reply to the fearful: The Lord is still securely on his heavenly throne. And the righteous Lord (see v. 7) discerns the righteous (see v. 5) to give them a place in his presence (see v. 7), while his judgment will "rain" (v. 6) on the wicked.
11:4 *The Lᴏʀᴅ is in his holy temple.* Repeated verbatim in Hab 2:20. Here reference is to his heavenly temple.

fiery coals and burning sulfur; *u*
a scorching wind *v* will be their lot.

[7] For the LORD is righteous, *w*
he loves justice; *x*
the upright *y* will see his face. *z*

PSALM 12

For the director of music. According to sheminith. *a A psalm of David.*

*[1] Help, LORD, for no one is faithful anymore; *a*
those who are loyal have vanished from the human race.

[2] Everyone lies *b* to their neighbor;
they flatter with their lips
but harbor deception in their hearts. *c*

[3] May the LORD silence all flattering lips *d*
and every boastful tongue— *e*

[4] those who say,
"By our tongues we will prevail; *f*
our own lips will defend us—who is lord over us?"

[5] "Because the poor are plundered *g* and the needy groan, *h*
I will now arise, *i*" says the LORD.
"I will protect them *j* from those who malign them."

[6] And the words of the LORD are flawless, *k*
like silver purified *l* in a crucible, *m*
like gold *b* refined seven times.

[7] You, LORD, will keep the needy safe *n*
and will protect us forever from the wicked, *o*

[8] who freely strut *p* about
while depravity is honored by the human race.

---

a Title: Probably a musical term   *b* 6 Probable reading of the original Hebrew text; Masoretic Text *earth*
* 12:1-8 is numbered 12:2-9 in Hebrew texts.

11:6 *u* S Ge 19:24; S Rev 9:17
v S Ge 41:6; S Job 1:19
11:7 *w* S 2Ch 12:6; S Ezr 9:15; 2Ti 4:8
x S Ps 9:8; 33:5; 99:4; Isa 28:17; 30:18; 56:1; 61:8; Jer 9:24
y S Job 1:1; Lk 23:50
z Ps 17:15; 140:13
12:1 *a* Isa 57:1; Mic 7:2
12:2 *b* Ps 5:6; 34:13; 141:3; Pr 6:19; 12:17; 13:3; Isa 32:7
c S Ps 5:9; Ro 16:18
12:3 *d* Pr 26:28; 28:23 *e* Ps 73:9; Da 7:8; Jas 3:5; Rev 13:5
12:4 *f* Pr 18:21; Jas 3:6
12:5 *g* Ps 44:24; 62:10; 72:14; 73:8; Ecc 4:1; 5:8; Isa 3:15; 5:7; 30:12; 59:13; Ac 7:34 *h* S Ps 6:6
i Ps 3:7 *j* Ps 34:6; 35:10
12:6 *k* S 2Sa 22:31; Ps 18:30 *l* S Job 23:10; S 28:1; Isa 48:10; Zec 13:9 *m* Ps 119:140
12:7 *n* Ps 16:1; 27:5 *o* Ps 37:28; Jn 17:12
12:8 *p* Ps 55:10-11

13:1 ^qPs 6:3
^rPs 42:9; La 5:20
^sS Dt 31:17;
S Ps 22:24; S Isa 8:17;
S 54:9
13:2 ^tPs 42:4; 55:2;
139:23; Isa 33:18;
Da 7:28 ^uPs 94:3
13:3 ^vPs 9:12;
25:18; 31:7; 35:23;
59:4; 80:14; 107:41;
119:50,153 ^wS Ps 4:1
^xS Ezr 9:8 ^yPs 76:5;
90:5; Jer 51:39
13:4 ^zS 1Ki 19:2;
Ps 25:2 ^aPs 38:16;
118:13
13:5 ^bS Ps 6:4
^cS Job 33:26; Ps 9:14;
Isa 25:9; 33:2
13:6 ^dS Ex 15:1;
Ps 7:17
14:1 ^ePs 10:4
14:2 ^fJob 41:34;
Ps 85:11; 102:19;
La 3:50 ^gPs 92:6
^hS Ezr 6:21
14:3 ⁱS 1Sa 8:3;
1Ti 5:15 ^j2Pe 2:7

PSALM 13

For the director of music. A psalm of David.

*1 How long, ^q LORD? Will you forget me ^r forever?
　　How long will you hide your face ^s from me?
2 How long must I wrestle with my thoughts ^t
　　and day after day have sorrow in my heart?
　　How long will my enemy triumph over me? ^u

3 Look on me ^v and answer, ^w LORD my God.
　　Give light to my eyes, ^x or I will sleep in death, ^y
4 and my enemy will say, "I have overcome him, ^z"
　　and my foes will rejoice when I fall. ^a

5 But I trust in your unfailing love; ^b
　　my heart rejoices in your salvation. ^c
6 I will sing ^d the LORD's praise,
　　for he has been good to me.

PSALM 14

14:1–7pp — Ps 53:1–6

For the director of music. Of David.

1 Fools ^a say in their hearts,
　　"There is no God." ^e
They are corrupt, their deeds are vile;
　　there is no one who does good.

2 The LORD looks down from heaven ^f
　　on the human race
to see if there are any who understand, ^g
　　any who seek God. ^h

3 All have turned away, ⁱ all have become corrupt; ^j

---

^a *1* The Hebrew words rendered *fool* in Psalms denote one who is morally deficient.

[*] 13:1-6 is numbered 13:2-6 in Hebrew texts.

Ps 13 A cry to the Lord for deliverance from a serious illness that threatens to be fatal (see v. 3), which would give David's enemies just what they wanted. See introduction to Ps 6.
13 title *For the director of music.* See note on Ps 4 title.
13:1–2 An anguished complaint concerning a prolonged, serious illness.
13:1 *How long . . . ?* See note on 6:3. *forget.* Ignore. *hide your face.* For use in combination with "forget," see 44:24. In moments of need the psalmists frequently ask God why he hides his face (see 30:7; 44:24; 88:14), or they plead with him not to do so (see 27:9; 69:17; 102:2; 143:7). When he does hide his face, those who depend on him can only despair (see 30:7; 104:29). When his face shines on a person, blessing and deliverance come (see 4:6 and note; 31:16; 44:3; 67:1; 80:3,7,19; 119:135; see also Nu 6:25 and note).
13:2 *heart.* See note on 4:7.
13:3–4 Appeal for deliverance from death.
13:3 *Give light to my eyes.* Restore me (see note on 6:7).
13:4 See notes on 3:2; 5:9. *fall.* Referring to death (as in 18:38; 82:7; 106:26; Jdg 5:27; 2Sa 1:19; Job 18:12).
13:5–6 Concluding expression of confidence (see note on 3:8).
13:5 *unfailing love.* See note on 6:4. *heart.* See note on 4:7. *rejoices.* It is David who will rejoice, not his enemies.
13:6 See note on 7:17.

Ps 14 A testimony concerning the moral folly of those who live as if there were no God and therefore feel free to cruelly prey on others who are at their mercy (Ps 53 is a somewhat revised duplicate). In its depiction of their godless arrogance, it has links with Ps 10; 12 (see also 28:3–5). And it shares with Ps 11 the conviction that the righteous Lord is on his heav-

enly throne. This psalm brings to closure the collection of prayers that began with Ps 3 (for the next grouping of psalms, see introduction to Ps 15–24). Five psalms (and 64 Hebrew poetic lines) after Ps 8's surprising evocation of humanity's "glory and honor" (8:5), this psalm highlights people's disgrace (see introduction to Ps 8). In this it serves as a counterpoint to that earlier recollection of humanity's high dignity and thereby exposes more sharply the depth of human disgrace—from which the petitioners in this and the preceding psalms have suffered.
14 title *For the director of music.* See note on Ps 4 title.
14:1–3 Characterization of the wicked. For Paul's use of these verses in a different context, see Ro 3:10–12.
14:1 *Fools.* See TNIV text note. The Hebrew word is *nabal;* for its meaning, see 1Sa 25:25; 2Sa 13:13; Isa 32:5–7 (in Proverbs "fool" renders two other Hebrew words; see TNIV text notes on Pr 1:4,7). *say.* See note on 3:2. *hearts.* See note on 4:7. *no God.* A practical atheism (see 10:4,6,11,13; 36:1; see also note on 10:4). *no one who does good.* Context limits the scope of this assertion—and the assertion in v. 3—to the "fools" who take no account of God and do not hesitate to show their malice toward "the company of the righteous" (v. 5)—as in 9:19–20; 10:2–11,13,18; 12:1–4,7–8 (this is also the situation that Ps 11 describes). In other psalms the psalmists do include themselves among those who are not righteous in God's eyes (see 130:3; 143:2; see also 1Ki 8:46; Job 9:2; Ecc 7:20).
14:2 *The LORD.* Emphatically contrasted with "Fools" (v. 1). *looks down from heaven.* See 33:13–14. *who seek God.* To "seek God" authentically is to "seek" what is morally "good" (Am 5:14–15); it is to "seek justice" in all human relationships (Isa 1:17). See also Ps 15.
14:3 *turned away.* From God and goodness.

there is no one who does good, [k]
not even one. [l]

[4] Do all these evildoers know nothing? [m]

They devour my people [n] as though eating bread;
they never call on the LORD. [o]
[5] But there they are, overwhelmed with dread,
for God is present in the company of the righteous.

[6] You evildoers frustrate the plans of the poor,
but the LORD is their refuge. [p]

[7] Oh, that salvation for Israel would come out of Zion! [q]
When the LORD restores [r] his people,
let Jacob rejoice and Israel be glad!

PSALM 15

A psalm of David.

[1] LORD, who may dwell [s] in your sanctuary? [t]
Who may live on your holy mountain? [u]

[2] Those whose walk is blameless, [v]
who do what is righteous,
who speak the truth [w] from their hearts;
[3] who have no slander [x] on their tongues,
who do their neighbors no wrong,
who cast no slur on others;
[4] who despise those whose ways are vile
but honor [y] whoever fears the LORD;
who keep their oaths [z] even when it hurts;
[5] who lend money to the poor without interest [a]
and do not accept bribes [b] against the innocent.

Whoever does these things
will never be shaken. [c]

14:3 [k]1Ki 8:46;
Ps 143:2; Ecc 7:20
[l] Ro 3:10-12*
14:4 [m] Ps 82:5;
Jer 4:22 [n] Ps 27:2;
Mic 3:3 [o] Ps 79:6;
Isa 64:7; 65:1;
Jer 10:25; Hos 7:7
14:6 [p] S 2Sa 22:3
14:7 [q] Ps 2:6
[r] S Dt 30:3;
S Jer 48:47
15:1 [s] Ex 29:46;
Ps 23:6; 27:4; 61:4
[t] Ex 25:8; 1Ch 22:19;
Ps 20:2; 78:69; 150:1
[u] S Ex 15:17
15:2 [v] S Ge 6:9;
S Ps 18:32; Eph 1:4;
S 1Th 3:13; Tit 1:6
[w] Pr 16:13; Isa 45:19;
Jer 7:28; 9:5; Zec 8:3,
16; Ro 9:1; S Eph 4:25
15:3 [x] S Lev 19:16
15:4 [y] S Job 19:9;
Ac 28:10 [z] S Dt 23:21;
S Jos 9:18; Mt 5:33
15:5 [a] S Ex 22:25
[b] S Ex 18:21;
S 1Sa 8:3; Ac 24:26
[c] S Job 29:18; Ps 21:7;
112:6; Ac 2:25;
Heb 12:28; 2Pe 1:10

14:4–6 The folly of the wicked exposed.

14:4 *devour . . . never call on the LORD.* Renewed characterization of the wicked: They live by the violence of their own hands and do not rely on the Lord (see 10:2–4).
14:5 Even God's mighty defense of the righteous teaches the wicked nothing. *righteous.* See note on 1:5.
14:6 *poor.* Those who lack the resources to defend themselves. The same Hebrew word is rendered "weak" in 10:2 and "helpless" in 10:9,12. *refuge.* See note on 2:12.
14:7 The psalmist longs for Israel's complete deliverance from her enemies—which will come when God deals with the wicked in defense of their victims. For a similar expansion of scope, see 10:16–18 and note. *Zion.* See note on 9:11. *Jacob . . . Israel.* Synonyms (see Ge 32:28).
Ps 15–24 Ps 15 and its distinctive counterpart, Ps 24, frame a cluster of psalms that have been arranged in a concentric pattern with Ps 19 serving as the hinge (for the thematic links between Ps 16 and 23, Ps 17 and 22, and Ps 18 and 20–21, see introductions to those psalms). The framing psalms (15; 24) are thematically linked by their evocation of the high majesty of God and their insistence on moral purity "without [which] no one will see the Lord" (Heb 12:14). At the center, Ps 19 uniquely combines a celebration of the divine majesty as displayed in the creation and an exposition of how moral purity is attained through God's law, forgiveness and shepherding care. Together, these three psalms (15; 19; 24) provide instructive words concerning the petitioners heard in the enclosed psalms, offer a counterpoint to Ps 14, and reinforce the instruction of Ps 1.

Ps 15 Instruction concerning those who wish to have access to God at his temple (see 24:3–6; Isa 33:14–16). See also introduction to Ps 15–24.
15:1 *dwell . . . live on.* Not as a priest but as God's welcome guest in his holy, royal house, the temple (see 23:6; 27:4–6; 61:4; 84:10; 2Sa 12:20). *holy mountain.* See note on 2:6.

15:2–5 Not sacrifices or ritual purity (as among the religions of the ancient Near East) but moral righteousness gives access to the Lord, the God of Israel (see the basic covenantal law: Ex 20:1–17; see also Isa 1:10–17; 33:14–16; 58:6–10; Jer 7:2–7; Eze 18:5–9; Hos 6:6; Am 5:14–15,21–24; Mic 6:6–8; Zec 7:9–10; 8:16–17).
15:2 *Those . . . righteous.* A summary introduction to the list that follows. *blameless.* That is, uniting loyalty to God and faithfulness to his covenant directives. See Ge 17:1 and note; see also how the Hebrew word is used in 18:23; 37:18; 84:1; 101:2,6; 119:1,80; Jos 24:14 ("all faithfulness"); Jdg 9:16,19 ("honorably") and how a closely related word is used in Ps 7:8 ("integrity"). *righteous.* See note on 1:5. *hearts.* See note on 4:7.
15:3 *tongues.* See note on 5:9.

15:4 *despise those . . . vile.* Or "despise those repudiated by God—because they have become an offense to him. *whoever fears the LORD.* Those who honor God and order their lives in accordance with his will (see note on Ge 20:11) because of their reverence for him.
15:5 *interest.* See note on Ex 22:25–27. *be shaken.* See note on 10:6.

16:1 *d* S Ps 12:7
e Ps 2:12
16:2 *f* Ps 31:14;
118:28; 140:6
g Ps 73:25
16:3 *h* Dt 33:3;
Ps 30:4; 85:8;
Da 7:18; Ac 9:13;
Ro 1:7 *i* Ps 101:6
16:4 *j* Ex 18:11; 20:3;
S Dt 8:19; S 31:20
k Ps 32:10; Pr 23:29
l S Ex 23:13
16:5 *m* S Lev 2:2
n Ps 23:5; 75:8;
116:13; Isa 51:17;
La 4:21; Eze 23:32-
34; Hab 2:16
o Ps 31:2
16:6 *p* S Dt 19:14;
Ps 104:9; Pr 8:29;
Jer 5:22 *q* S Job 22:26
16:7 *r* Ps 73:24;
Pr 15:22; Isa 11:2
s Job 35:10; Ps 42:8;
77:6
16:8 *t* 1Ki 2:19;
1Ch 6:39; Ps 73:23
u Ps 15:5
16:9 *v* Ps 4:7; 13:5;
28:7; 30:11
w S Dt 33:28
16:10 *x* S Nu 16:30;
Ps 30:3; 31:17; 86:13;
Hos 13:14
y S 2Ki 19:22
z S Job 17:14; Ac 2:31;
13:35*
16:11 *a* Ps 139:24;
Mt 7:14 *b* Ac 2:25-
28* *c* Ps 21:6
d Ps 80:17

PSALM 16

A miktam *a* *of David.*

1 Keep me safe, *d* my God,
  for in you I take refuge. *e*

2 I say to the LORD, "You are my Lord; *f*
  apart from you I have no good thing." *g*

3 I say of the godly *h* who are in the land, *i*
  "They are the noble people
  in whom is all my delight."

4 Those who run after other gods *j*
  will suffer *k* more and more.
  I will not pour out their libations of blood
  or take up their names *l* on my lips.

5 LORD, you have assigned me my portion *m* and my cup; *n*
  you have made my lot *o* secure.

6 The boundary lines *p* have fallen for me in pleasant places;
  surely I have a delightful inheritance. *q*

7 I will praise the LORD, who counsels me; *r*
  even at night *s* my heart instructs me.

8 I keep my eyes always on the LORD.
  With him at my right hand, *t* I will not be shaken. *u*

9 Therefore my heart is glad *v* and my tongue rejoices;
  my body also will rest secure, *w*

10 because you will not abandon me to the realm of the dead, *x*
  nor will you let your faithful *b* one *y* see decay. *z*

11 You make known to me the path of life; *a*
  you will fill me with joy in your presence, *b*
  with eternal pleasures *c* at your right hand. *d*

---

a Title: Probably a literary or musical term   *b* 10 Or *holy*

Ps 16 A prayer for safekeeping (the petition element in prayer psalms is often relatively short; see 3:7; 22:19–21; 44:23–26), pleading for the Lord's protection against the threat of death. In accordance with its dominant theme, it could also be called a psalm of trust. In this regard it has close thematic links with Ps 23 (compare 16:2 with 23:1; 16:5 with 23:5; 16:7–8 with 23:4; 16:11 with 23:6). Together these two psalms underscore faith/trust as the second essential characteristic (alongside conformity to God's law; see introduction to Ps 15–24) of those who bring their prayers to God (see introduction to Ps 1–2; see also note on 34:8–14).

16 title *miktam.* The term remains unexplained, though it always stands in the superscription of Davidic prayers occasioned by great danger (see Ps 56–60).

16:1 The petition and the basis for it. The rest of the psalm elaborates on the latter element.

16:2–4 The Lord is David's one and only good thing (see 73:25,28); David will have nothing to do with the counterfeit gods to whom others pour out their libations (see 4:2).

16:3 See Ps 101.

16:4 *suffer more and more.* In contrast with David's good "portion" (v. 5; see note on 11:6), which affords him much joy (see 73:18–26). *libations of blood.* Blood of sacrifices poured on altars. *take up their names.* Appeal to or worship them (see Jos 23:7).

16:5–6 Joy over the inheritance received from the Lord. David refers to what the Lord bestowed on his people in the promised land, either to the gift of fields there (see Nu 16:14) or to the Lord himself (as in 73:26; 119:57; 142:5; La 3:24), who was the inheritance of the priests (see Nu 18:20) and the Levites (see Dt 10:9).

16:5 *cup.* A metaphor referring to what the host offers his guests to drink. To the godly Lord offers a cup of

blessing (see 23:5) or salvation (see 116:13); he makes the wicked drink from a cup of wrath (see Jer 25:15; Rev 14:10; 16:19). *secure.* Just as each Israelite's family inheritance in the promised land was to be secure (see Lev 25; Nu 36:7).

16:7–8 Praise of the Lord who counsels and keeps.

16:7 *counsels.* Shows the way that leads to life (see v. 11). *heart.* Lit. "kidneys" (see note on 7:9). The reference here is probably to conscience.

16:8 *With him at my right hand.* As sustainer and protector (see 73:23; 109:31; 110:5; 121:5); complemented by the reference to the Lord's right hand in v. 11. *not be shaken.* See note on 10:6.

16:9–11 Describes the joy of the total security that God's faithful care provides. David speaks of himself and of the life he enjoys by the gracious provision and care of God. The Lord, in whom the psalmist takes refuge, wills life for him (hence he made known to him the path of life, v. 11) and will not abandon him to the grave, even though "flesh and . . . heart . . . fail" (73:26). But implicit in these words of assurance (if not actually explicit) is the confidence that, with the Lord as his refuge, even the grave cannot rob him of life (see 17:15; 73:24; see also note in 11:7). If this could be said of David— and of all those godly Israelites who made David's prayer their own— how much more of his promised Son! So Peter quotes vv. 8–11 and declares that with these words David prophesied of Christ and his resurrection (Ac 2:25–28; see Paul's similar use of v. 10b in Ac 13:35). See also note on 6:5.

16:9 *heart.* See note on 4:7. *tongue.* Lit. "glory" (see note on 7:5).

16:10 *faithful one.* Hebrew *hasid* (see note on 4:3). Reference is first of all to David, but the psalm is ultimately fulfilled in Christ (see note on vv. 9–11).

16:11 *path of life.* See Pr 15:24. *your right hand.* See note on v. 8.

PSALM 17

A prayer of David.

¹ Hear me, *e* LORD, my plea is just;
    listen to my cry. *f*
Hear *g* my prayer—
    it does not rise from deceitful lips. *h*
² Let my vindication *i* come from you;
    may your eyes see what is right. *j*

³ Though you probe my heart, *k*
    though you examine me at night and test me, *l*
you will find that I have planned no evil; *m*
    my mouth has not transgressed. *n*
⁴ Though people tried to bribe me,
    I have kept myself from the ways of the violent
    through what your lips have commanded.
⁵ My steps have held to your paths; *o*
    my feet have not stumbled. *p*

⁶ I call on you, my God, for you will answer me; *q*
    turn your ear to me *r* and hear my prayer. *s*
⁷ Show me the wonders of your great love, *t*
    you who save by your right hand *u*
    those who take refuge *v* in you from their foes.
⁸ Keep me *w* as the apple of your eye; *x*
    hide me *y* in the shadow of your wings *z*
⁹ from the wicked who are out to destroy me,
    from my mortal enemies who surround me. *a*

¹⁰ They close up their callous hearts, *b*
    and their mouths speak with arrogance. *c*
¹¹ They have tracked me down, they now surround me, *d*
    with eyes alert, to throw me to the ground.
¹² They are like a lion *e* hungry for prey, *f*
    like a fierce lion crouching in cover.

¹³ Rise up, *g* LORD, confront them, bring them down; *h*
    with your sword rescue me from the wicked.
¹⁴ By your hand save me from such people, LORD,
    from those of this world *i* whose reward is in this life. *j*
May what you have stored up for the wicked fill their bellies;
    may their children gorge themselves on it,
    may there be leftovers *k* for their little ones.

17:1 *e* Ps 30:10;
64:1; 80:1; 140:6
f Ps 5:2; 39:12; 142:6;
143:1 *g* S Ps 5:1
h Isa 29:13
17:2 *i* Ps 24:5; 26:1;
Isa 46:13; 50:8-9;
54:17 *j* Ps 99:4
17:3 *k* Ps 139:1;
Jer 12:3 *l* S Job 7:18
m Job 23:10; Jer 50:20
n Ps 39:1
17:5 *o* Job 23:11;
Ps 44:18; 119:133
p Dt 32:35; Ps 73:2;
121:3
17:6 *q* Ps 86:7
r Ps 116:2 *s* Ps 4:1
17:7 *t* Ps 31:21;
69:13; 106:45; 107:43;
117:2 *u* S Ps 10:12
v Ps 2:12
17:8 *w* S Nu 6:24
x S Dt 32:10; Pr 7:2
y Ps 27:5; 31:20; 32:7
z Ru 2:12; Ps 36:7;
63:7; Isa 34:15
17:9 *a* Ps 109:3
17:10 *b* Ps 73:7;
119:70; Isa 6:10
c S 1Sa 2:3
17:11 *d* Ps 88:17
17:12 *e* Ps 7:2;
Jer 5:6; 12:8; La 3:10
f S Ge 49:9
17:13 *g* S Nu 10:35
h Ps 35:8; 55:23;
73:18
17:14 *i* Lk 16:8
j Ps 49:17; Lk 16:25
k Isa 2:7; 57:17

Ps 17 David appeals to the Lord as Judge when he is under attack by ungodly foes. The circumstances evoked and the petition to which they gave rise show considerable affinity with Ps 22 (see introduction to Ps 15–24). The psalm reflects many of the Hebrew conventions of lodging a judicial appeal before the king.
17 title *A prayer.* See titles of Ps 86; 90; 102; 142; see also 72:20.
17:1–2 The initial appeal for justice.
17:1 *plea.* For justice. His case is truly "just," not a clever misrepresentation by deceitful lips (for a similar situation see 1Sa 24:15).
17:3–5 David's claim of innocence in support of the rightness of his case. He is not guilty of the ungodly ways of his attackers—let God examine him (cf. 139:23–24).
17:3 *heart.* See note on 4:7.
17:4 *what your lips have commanded.* God's revealed will, by which he has made known the "paths" (v. 5) that people are to walk.
17:6–9 The petition: what David wants the Lord to do for him—motivated by David's trust in him ("for you will answer me," v. 6) and the Lord's unfailing righteousness (see v. 7).
17:6 *I call ... you will answer.* See note on 118:5.

17:7 *wonders.* See note on 9:1. *great love.* See note on 6:4.
17:8 *apple of your eye.* See note on Dt 32:10. *shadow.* A conventional Hebrew metaphor for protection against oppression—as shade protects from the oppressive heat of the hot desert sun. Kings were spoken of as the "shade" of those dependent on them for protection (as in Nu 14:9, "protection"—lit. "shade"; La 4:20; Eze 31:6,12,17). Similarly, the Lord is the protective "shade" of his people (see 91:1; 121:5; Isa 25:4; 49:2; 51:16). *wings.* Metaphor for the protective outreach of God's power (see 36:7; 57:1; 61:4; 63:7; 91:4; Ru 2:12; see also Mt 23:37).
17:10–12 The accusation lodged against the vicious adversaries (see note on 5:9–10).
17:10 *mouths.* See note on 5:9. *speak with arrogance.* See note on 10:11.
17:12 *lion.* See note on 7:2.
17:13–14 Petition: how David wants the Lord to deal with the two parties in the conflict.
17:13 *Rise up.* See note on 3:7. *bring them down.* See note on 5:10. *your sword.* See 7:12–13 and note.
17:14 *such people.* See 9:19–20; 10:18; 12:1–4,8; 14:1–3.

17:15 /S Ps 3:5
m Nu 12:8;
S Mt 5:8; 1Jn 3:2
18:1 *n* S Ex 15:2;
S Dt 33:29;
S 1Sa 2:10; Ps 22:19;
28:7; 59:9; 81:1;
Isa 12:2; 49:5;
Jer 16:19
18:2 *o* S Ex 33:22
p Ps 28:8; 31:2,3;
Isa 17:10; Jer 16:19
q Ps 40:17 *r* Ps 2:12;
9:9; 94:22 *s* S Ge 15:1;
Ps 28:7; 84:9; 119:114;
144:2 *t* S 1Sa 2:1;
S Lk 1:69
18:3 *u* S 1Ch 16:25
v S Ps 9:13
18:4 *w* Ps 116:3
x Ps 93:4; 124:4;
Isa 5:30; 17:12;
Jer 6:23; 51:42,55;
Eze 43:2
18:5 *y* Pr 13:14
18:6 *z* S Dt 4:30
a Ps 30:2; 99:6; 102:2;
120:1 *b* Ps 66:19; 116:1
c S Job 16:18
18:7 *d* Ps 97:4;
Isa 5:25; 64:3
e S Jdg 5:4 *f* S Jdg 5:5
g S Job 9:5; Jer 10:10
18:8 *h* S Job 41:20
i S Ex 15:7; S 19:18;
S Job 41:21; Ps 50:3;
97:3; Da 7:10
j Pr 25:22; Ro 12:20
18:9 *k* S Ge 11:5;
S Ps 57:3 *l* S Ex 20:21;
S Dt 33:26;
S Ps 104:3

15 As for me, I will be vindicated and will see your face;
   when I awake, *l* I will be satisfied with seeing your likeness. *m*

PSALM 18

18:Title–50pp — 2Sa 22:1–51

*For the director of music. Of David the servant of the LORD. He sang to the
LORD the words of this song when the LORD delivered him from the hand
of all his enemies and from the hand of Saul. He said:*

**1 I love you, LORD, my strength. *n*

2 The LORD is my rock, *o* my fortress *p* and my deliverer; *q*
   my God is my rock, in whom I take refuge, *r*
   my shield*a s* and the horn*b* of my salvation, *t* my stronghold.

3 I called to the LORD, who is worthy of praise, *u*
   and I have been saved from my enemies. *v*
4 The cords of death *w* entangled me;
   the torrents *x* of destruction overwhelmed me.
5 The cords of the grave coiled around me;
   the snares of death *y* confronted me.

6 In my distress *z* I called to the LORD; *a*
   I cried to my God for help.
 From his temple he heard my voice; *b*
   my cry came *c* before him, into his ears.
7 The earth trembled *d* and quaked, *e*
   and the foundations of the mountains shook; *f*
   they trembled because he was angry. *g*
8 Smoke rose from his nostrils; *h*
   consuming fire *i* came from his mouth,
   burning coals *j* blazed out of it.
9 He parted the heavens and came down; *k*
   dark clouds *l* were under his feet.

---

a 2 Or *sovereign*   *b 2* *Horn* here symbolizes strength.

* 18:1-50 is numbered 18:2-51 in Hebrew texts.

17:15 Concluding confession of confidence (see note on 3:8). *will
be vindicated.* The righteous Judge (see note on 4:1) will acknowledge and vindicate the innocence (righteousness) of the petitioner. *see your face.* See note on 11:7. *when I awake.* From the night of
death (see note on 11:7)—in radical contrast to the destiny of
"those of this world" (v. 14; see notes on 6:5; 16:9–11). *seeing your
likeness.* As Moses the servant of the Lord had seen it (see Nu 12:8).
Ps 18 This song of David occurs also (with minor variations) in
2Sa 22 (see notes there). In its structure, apart from the introduction (vv. 1–3) and the conclusion (vv. 46–50), the song is
composed of three major divisions: (1) the Lord's deliverance of
David from his mortal enemies in answer to his cry for help (vv.
4–19); (2) the moral grounds for the Lord's saving help (vv.
20–29); (3) the Lord's help recounted (vv. 30–45). David's celebration of God's saving help in answer to prayer when under
threat from powerful enemies receives its counterpart in the
two closely related psalms (Ps 20–21; see introductions to those
psalms and introduction to Ps 15–24).
18 title *For the director of music.* See note on Ps 4 title. *servant of
the LORD.* See 78:70; 89:3,20,39; 132:10; 144:10. The title designates
David in his royal office as, in effect, an official in the Lord's own
kingly rule over his people (see 2Sa 7:5)—as were Moses (see Ex
14:31 and note), Joshua (see Jos 24:29) and the prophets (Elijah,
2Ki 9:36; Jonah, 2Ki 14:25; Isaiah, Isa 20:3; Daniel, Da 6:20). *song.*
See note on Ps 30 title. *when the LORD delivered him.* It is possible
that David composed his song shortly after his victories over his
foreign enemies (2Sa 8:1–14), but it may have been later in his life.
18:1–3 A prelude of praise.
18:1 Does not occur in 2Sa 22. *I love you.* From an unusual He-

brew expression that emphasizes the fervor of David's love.
18:2 *rock . . . rock.* The translation of two different Hebrew
words. "Rock" is a common poetic figure for God (or the gods:
Dt 32:31,37; Isa 44:8), symbolizing his unfailing (see Isa 26:4)
strength as a fortress refuge (see vv. 31,46; 31:2–3; 42:9; 62:7;
71:3; 94:22; Isa 17:10) or as deliverer (see 19:14; 62:2; 78:35;
89:26; 95:1; Dt 32:15). It is a figure particularly appropriate for
David's experience (see 1Sa 23:14,25; 24:2,22; 26:20), for the
Lord was his true security. *fortress.* See note on 2Sa 22:2. *shield.*
See note on 3:3. *horn.* See TNIV text note; Dt 33:17; Jer 48:25.
18:4–6 God heard his cry for help.
18:4–5 David depicts his experiences in poetic figures of mortal danger.
18:4 *cords.* 2Sa 22:5 has "waves." *torrents of destruction.* See
note on 30:1.
18:5 *cords of the grave . . . snares of death.* See 116:3. He had, as
it were, been snared by death (personified) and bound as a prisoner of the grave (see Job 36:8).
18:6 *temple.* God's heavenly abode, where he sits enthroned
(see 11:4; 113:5; Isa 6:1; 40:22).
18:7–15 The Lord came to the aid of his servant—depicted as
a fearful theophany (divine manifestation) of the heavenly Warrior descending in wrathful attack upon David's enemies (see
5:4–5; 68:1–8; 77:16–19; Mic 1:3–4; Na 1:2–6; Hab 3:3–15). He
sweeps down upon them like a fierce thunderstorm (see Jos
10:11; Jdg 5:20–22; 1Sa 2:10; 7:10; 2Sa 5:24; Isa 29:6).
18:8 God's fierce majesty is portrayed in terms similar to those
applied to the awesome leviathan (Job 41:19–21).
18:9 *parted the heavens and came down.* See Isa 64:1 and note.

¹⁰ He mounted the cherubim ^m and flew;
   he soared ⁿ on the wings of the wind. ^o
¹¹ He made darkness his covering, ^p his canopy ^q around him—
   the dark rain clouds of the sky.
¹² Out of the brightness of his presence ^r clouds advanced,
   with hailstones ^s and bolts of lightning. ^t
¹³ The LORD thundered ^u from heaven;
   the voice of the Most High resounded. ^a
¹⁴ He shot his arrows ^v and scattered the enemy,
   with great bolts of lightning ^w he routed them. ^x
¹⁵ The valleys of the sea were exposed
   and the foundations ^y of the earth laid bare
at your rebuke, ^z LORD,
   at the blast of breath from your nostrils. ^a

¹⁶ He reached down from on high and took hold of me;
   he drew me out of deep waters. ^b
¹⁷ He rescued me from my powerful enemy, ^c
   from my foes, who were too strong for me. ^d
¹⁸ They confronted me in the day of my disaster, ^e
   but the LORD was my support. ^f
¹⁹ He brought me out into a spacious place; ^g
   he rescued me because he delighted in me. ^h

²⁰ The LORD has dealt with me according to my righteousness; ⁱ
   according to the cleanness of my hands ^j he has rewarded me. ^k
²¹ For I have kept the ways of the LORD; ^l
   I am not guilty of turning ^m from my God.
²² All his laws are before me; ⁿ
   I have not turned away from his decrees.
²³ I have been blameless ^o before him
   and have kept myself from sin.
²⁴ The LORD has rewarded me according to my righteousness, ^p
   according to the cleanness of my hands in his sight.

²⁵ To the faithful ^q you show yourself faithful, ^r
   to the blameless you show yourself blameless,
²⁶ to the pure ^s you show yourself pure,
   but to the devious you show yourself shrewd. ^t
²⁷ You save the humble ^u
   but bring low those whose eyes are haughty. ^v

---

^a *13* Some Hebrew manuscripts and Septuagint (see also 2 Samuel 22:14); most Hebrew manuscripts *resounded, / amid hailstones and bolts of lightning*

18:10 ^m S Ge 3:24; Eze 10:18 ⁿ S Dt 33:26 ^o Ps 104:3
18:11 ^p S Ex 19:9; S Dt 4:11 ^q S Job 22:14; Isa 4:5; Jer 43:10
18:12 ^r Ps 104:2 ^s S Jos 10:11 ^t S Job 36:30
18:13 ^u S Ex 9:23; S 1Sa 2:10
18:14 ^v S Dt 32:23 ^w S Job 36:30; Rev 4:5 ^x S Jdg 4:15
18:15 ^y S Ps 11:3 ^z Ps 76:6; 104:7; 106:9; Isa 50:2 ^a S Ex 15:8
18:16 ^b Ex 15:5; Ps 69:2; Pr 18:4; 20:5
18:17 ^c ver 48; Ps 38:19; 59:1; 143:9 ^d S Jdg 18:26
18:18 ^e Pr 1:27; 16:4; Jer 17:17; 40:2; Ob 1:13 ^f Ps 20:2; Isa 3:1
18:19 ^g Ps 31:8 ^h Nu 14:8
18:20 ⁱ S 1Sa 26:23 ^j Job 22:30; Ps 24:4 ^k S Ru 2:12; S 2Ch 15:7; 1Co 3:8
18:21 ^l 2Ch 34:33; Ps 37:34; 119:2; Pr 8:32; 23:26 ^m Ps 119:102
18:22 ⁿ Ps 119:30
18:23 ^o S Ge 6:9
18:24 ^p S 1Sa 26:23
18:25 ^q Ps 31:23; 37:28; 50:5; Pr 2:8 ^r Ps 25:10; 40:11; 89:24; 146:6
18:26 ^s Pr 15:26; Mt 5:8; Php 1:10; 1Ti 5:22; Tit 1:15; 1Jn 3:3 ^t Pr 3:34; Mt 10:16; Lk 16:8
18:27 ^u S 2Ch 33:23; S Mt 23:12 ^v S Job 41:34; S Ps 10:5; Pr 3:33-34

18:10 *cherubim.* Symbols of royalty (see 80:1; 99:1; see also notes on Ge 3:24; Ex 25:18). In Eze 1 and 10, cherubim appear as the bearers of the throne-chariot of God.
18:13 *voice.* For thunder as the voice of God, see Ps 29; Job 37:2–5. *Most High.* See note on Ge 14:19.
18:14 *arrows.* For shafts of lightning as the arrows of God, see 77:17; 144:6; Hab 3:11; see also note on Ge 9:13.
18:15 Perhaps recalls the great deed of the heavenly Warrior when he defeated Israel's enemy at the Red Sea (see Ex 15:1–12).
18:16–19 The deliverance.
18:16 *deep waters.* See note on 32:6.
18:19 *spacious place.* See 4:1 note; where he is free to roam unconfined by the threats and dangers that had hemmed him in (vv. 4–6,16–18). To be afflicted or oppressed is like being bound by fetters (Job 36:8,13). To be delivered is to be set free (Job 36:16). *delighted in me.* God was pleased with David as "a man after his own heart" (1Sa 13:14; see also 1Sa 15:28; 1Ki 14:8; 15:5; Ac 13:22), a man with whom he had made a covenant assuring him of an enduring dynasty (2Sa 7). The thought is further elaborated in vv. 20–29.

 18:20–24 David's righteousness rewarded. David's assertion of his righteousness (like that of Samuel,

1Sa 12:3; Hezekiah, 2Ki 20:3; Job, Job 13:23; 27:6; 31; see also Ps 17:3–5; 26; 44:17–18; 101) is not a pretentious boast of sinless perfection (see 51:5). Rather, it is a claim that, in contrast to his enemies, he has devoted himself heart and life to the service of the Lord, that his has been a godliness with integrity—itself the fruit of God's gracious working in his heart (see 51:10–12).
18:20,24 *my righteousness.* See note on 1:5. *rewarded me.* As a king benevolently rewards those who loyally serve him.
18:21 *ways of the LORD.* See 25:4 and note.
18:23 *blameless.* See note on 15:2.

 18:25–29 Because God responds to people in accordance with their ways (see Job 34:11; Pr 3:34), David has experienced the Lord's favor.
18:26 *devious.* Deviating from the straight path of truth and righteousness. *shrewd.* God responds to their perverse dealings thrust for thrust, like a wrestler countering his opponent (see 2Ki 22:23 and note; see also note on Jdg 11:35).
18:27 The thought of this verse fits well with David's and Saul's reversals of status. It also echoes the central theme of Hannah's song (1Sa 2:1–10), which the author of Samuel uses to highlight a major thesis of his account of the ways of God as he brings about his kingdom.

18:28 w 1Ki 11:36;
Ps 132:17 x Job 29:3;
Ps 97:11; 112:4; Jn 1:5;
S Ac 26:18; 2Co 4:6;
2Pe 1:19
18:29 y ver 32,39;
Isa 45:5; Heb 11:34
18:30 z S Dt 32:4
a S Ps 12:6; Pr 30:5
b Ps 3:3 c Ps 2:12
18:31 d S Dt 4:35;
32:39; Ps 35:10; 86:8;
89:6; Isa 44:6,8;
45:5,6,14,18,21; 46:9
e S Ge 49:24
18:32 f S ver 29;
1Pe 5:10 g S Ps 15:2;
19:13; Heb 10:14;
Jas 3:2
18:33 h Ps 42:1;
Pr 5:19; Isa 35:6;
Hab 3:19 i S Dt 32:13
18:34 j Ps 144:1
18:35 k Ps 3:5; 37:5,
17; 41:3; 51:12; 54:4;
55:22; 119:116;
Isa 41:4,10,13; 43:2;
46:4
18:36 l Ps 31:8
m S Job 18:7; Ps 66:9
18:37 n S Lev 26:7
18:38 o Ps 68:21;
110:6 p Ps 36:12;
140:10; Isa 26:14
q Ps 47:3
18:39 r ver 32;
Isa 45:5,24 s ver 47;
Ps 47:3; 144:2
18:40 t S Jos 7:12
u ver 37
18:41 v S 2Ki 14:26;
Ps 50:22 w S 1Sa 8:18;
S 14:37; Jer 11:11
18:42 x S Dt 9:21;
S Isa 2:22
18:43 y 2Sa 8:1-14
z Isa 55:5
18:44 a Ps 54:3;
144:7,11; Isa 25:5
18:45 b S 1Sa 17:32;
2Co 4:1; Heb 12:3
c Isa 66:2; Hos 3:5;
11:10 d Ps 9:9;
Mic 7:17
18:46 e S Jos 3:10;
S 1Sa 14:39; 2Co 13:4
f ver 31; Ex 33:22
g Ps 21:13; 35:27;
40:16; 108:5
h S 1Ch 16:35;
S Lk 1:47
18:47 i S Ge 4:24
j S ver 39; S Jdg 4:23
18:48 k Ps 7:10;
37:40; Da 3:17
l S ver 17 m Ps 140:1
18:49 n Ps 9:11
o Ps 7:17; 9:2; 101:1;
108:1; 146:2
p Ro 15:9*

28 You, LORD, keep my lamp w burning;
  my God turns my darkness into light. x
29 With your help y I can advance against a troop a;
  with my God I can scale a wall.

30 As for God, his way is perfect: z
  The LORD's word is flawless; a
  he shields b all who take refuge c in him.
31 For who is God besides the LORD? d
  And who is the Rock e except our God?
32 It is God who arms me with strength f
  and keeps my way secure. g
33 He makes my feet like the feet of a deer; h
  he causes me to stand on the heights. i
34 He trains my hands for battle; j
  my arms can bend a bow of bronze.
35 You make your saving help my shield,
  and your right hand sustains k me;
  your help has made me great.
36 You provide a broad path l for my feet,
  so that my ankles do not give way. m

37 I pursued my enemies n and overtook them;
  I did not turn back till they were destroyed.
38 I crushed them o so that they could not rise; p
  they fell beneath my feet. q
39 You armed me with strength r for battle;
  you humbled my adversaries s before me.
40 You made my enemies turn their backs t in flight,
  and I destroyed u my foes.
41 They cried for help, but there was no one to save them v—
  to the LORD, but he did not answer. w
42 I beat them as fine as windblown dust; x
  I trampled them b like mud in the streets.
43 You have delivered me from the attacks of the people;
  you have made me the head of nations. y
  People I did not know z now serve me,
44   foreigners a cower before me;
  as soon as they hear of me, they obey me.
45 They all lose heart; b
  they come trembling c from their strongholds. d

46 The LORD lives! e Praise be to my Rock! f
  Exalted be God g my Savior! h
47 He is the God who avenges i me,
  who subdues nations j under me,
48   who saves k me from my enemies. l
  You exalted me above my foes;
  from violent people m you rescued me.
49 Therefore I will praise you, LORD, among the nations; n
  I will sing o the praises of your name. p

---

a 29 Or *can run through a barricade* b 42 Many Hebrew manuscripts, Septuagint, Syriac and Targum (see also 2 Samuel 22:43); Masoretic Text *I poured them out*

18:28 *keep my lamp burning.* God causes his life, his undertakings and his dynasty to flourish (see especially Job 18:5–6; 21:17). *light.* See note on 27:1.
18:30–36 By God's blessing David the king has thrived.
18:30 *is perfect.* Does not fail—and so, because of his blessing, David's way has not failed (see v. 32). *The LORD's word.* While the reference is general, it applies especially to God's promise to David (see 2Sa 7:8–16). *flawless.* See note on 12:6. *shields.* See note on 3:3.
18:37–42 With God's help David has crushed all his foes.
18:43–45 God has made David the head of nations (see 2Sa 5; 8; 10)—he who had been, it seemed, on the brink of death (see

vv. 4–5), sinking into the depths (see v. 16).
18:43 *attacks of the people.* All the threats he had endured from his own people in the days of Saul, and perhaps also in the time of Absalom's rebellion. *People I did not know.* Those with whom he had had no previous relationship.
18:46–50 Concluding doxology.
■ **18:46** *The LORD lives!* God's interventions and blessings in David's behalf have shown him to be the living God (see Dt 5:26).
18:47 *avenges me.* Redresses the wrongs committed against me (see Dt 32:41).

18:50 9 S 2Sa 23:1
r Ps 144:10 s Ps 89:4
19:1 t Ps 89:5;
Isa 40:22 u Ps 50:6;
148:3; Ro 1:19
v Ps 4:2; 8:1; 97:6;
Isa 6:3 w S Ge 1:8
x S Ps 8:6; S 103:22
19:2 y Ps 74:16
19:4 z Ro 10:18*
a S Job 36:29;
Ps 104:2 b S Jdg 5:31
19:5 c Joel 2:16
d S Job 36:29
e 1Sa 17:4
19:6 f Dt 30:4
g Ps 113:3; Ecc 1:5
19:7 h S Ps 1:2
i Ps 119:142; Jas 1:25
j Ps 23:3 k Ps 93:5;
111:7; 119:138,144
l S Dt 4:6; Ps 119:130
19:8 m Ps 33:4;
119:128 n Ps 119:14
o S Ezr 9:8; Ps 38:10
19:9 p Ps 34:11;
111:10; Pr 1:7;
Ecc 12:13; Isa 33:6

50 He gives his king great victories;
 he shows unfailing love to his anointed, q
 to David r and to his descendants forever. s

PSALM 19

For the director of music. A psalm of David.

*1 The heavens t declare u the glory of God; v
 the skies w proclaim the work of his hands. x
2 Day after day they pour forth speech;
 night after night they display knowledge. y
3 They have no speech, they use no words;
 no sound is heard from them.
4 Yet their voice a goes out into all the earth,
 their words to the ends of the world. z
 In the heavens he has pitched a tent a for the sun, b
5 which is like a bridegroom c coming out of his chamber, d
 like a champion e rejoicing to run his course.
6 It rises at one end of the heavens f
 and makes its circuit to the other; g
 nothing is deprived of its warmth.

7 The law of the LORD h is perfect, i
 refreshing the soul. j
 The statutes of the LORD are trustworthy, k
 making wise the simple. l
8 The precepts of the LORD are right, m
 giving joy n to the heart.
 The commands of the LORD are radiant,
 giving light to the eyes. o
9 The fear of the LORD p is pure,
 enduring forever.

---

a 4 Septuagint, Jerome and Syriac; Hebrew *line*

* 19:1-14 is numbered 19:2-15 in Hebrew texts.

18:49 David vows to praise the Lord among the nations (see note on 9:1). *name.* See note on 5:11.

18:50 *his king … his anointed.* David views himself as the Lord's chosen and anointed king (see 1Sa 16:13; see also notes on 1Sa 10:25; 12:14–15). *shows unfailing love.* David's final words recall the Lord's covenant with him (see 2Sa 7:8–16). The whole song is to be understood in the context of David's official capacity and the Lord's covenant with him. What David claims in this grand conclusion—as, indeed, in the whole psalm—has been and is being fulfilled in Jesus Christ, David's great descendant.

Ps 19 A hymn extolling the majestic "glory of God" (v. 1) as displayed in the heavens, especially in the brilliant summer sun as it moves across a cloudless sky from east to west (see vv. 1–6; see also introduction to Ps 29), and "the law of the LORD" (v. 7), which blesses the lives of those who heed it (see vv. 7–13). An attached prayer (vv. 12–13) asks God to provide what his law cannot: forgiveness for "hidden faults" and a shepherd's care that preserves from "willful sins." Placed next to Ps 18, this psalm completes the cycle of praise—for the Lord's saving acts, for his glory reflected in creation and for his life-nurturing law. Placed at the center of Ps 15–24, it powerfully reinforces the themes of the two framing psalms (see introduction to Ps 15–24) and reminds all who would enter Yahweh's presence that they must come as those who have seen with their eyes his glory on display in the creation and who have in their hearts a deep devotion to his law.

19 title *For the director of music.* See note on Ps 4 title.

19:1–4a The silent heavens speak, declaring the glory of their Maker to all who are on the earth (see 148:3). The heavenly lights are not divine (see Ge 1:16 and note; Dt 4:19; 17:3), nor do they control or disclose anyone's destiny (see Isa 47:13; Jer 10:2; Da 4:7). Their glory testifies to the righteousness and faithfulness of the Lord who created them (see 50:6; 89:5–8; 97:6; see also Ro 1:19–20).

19:4 Interpreting this heavenly proclamation eschatologically in the light of Christ, Paul applies this verse to the proclamation of the gospel in his own day (see Ro 10:18). He thus associates these two universal proclamations.

19:4b–6 The heavens are the divinely pitched "tent" for the lordly sun—widely worshiped in the ancient Near East (cf. Dt 4:19; 17:3; 2Ki 23:5,11; Jer 8:2; Eze 8:16), but here, as in 136:7–8; Ge 1:16, a mere creature of God. Of the created realm, the sun is the supreme metaphor of the glory of God (see 84:11; Isa 60:19–20), as it makes its daily triumphant sweep across the whole extent of the heavens and pours out its warmth on every creature.

19:7–9 Stately, rhythmic celebration of the life-nurturing effects of the Lord's revealed law (see Ps 119).

19:7 *trustworthy.* God's laws are "trustworthy" (see also 111:7; 119:86) or "sure" (19:9) or "true" (119:142,151,160) in the sense that they faithfully represent God's righteous will (119:138,160), they endure generation after generation (they "stand firm," 93:5; see also 119:91,152,160), and they truly fulfill their purpose in the lives of those who honor them (see the effects noted here; see also 119:43,93,98–100,165)—they can be trusted. *the simple.* The childlike, those whose understanding and judgment have not yet matured (see 119:98–100; Pr 1:4; cf. also 2Ti 3:15; Heb 5:13–14).

19:8 *heart.* See note on 4:7.

19:9 *fear of the LORD.* The sum of what the law requires (see note on 15:4).

19:9 ^qPs 119:138,
142
19:10 ^rS Job 22:24;
Ps 119:72; Pr 8:10
^sPs 119:103; SS 4:11;
Eze 3:3 ^tS 1Sa 14:27
19:12 ^uPs 51:2;
90:8; Ecc 12:14
19:13 ^vS Nu 15:30
^wPs 119:133
^xS Ge 6:9; S Ps 18:32
19:14 ^yPs 104:34
^zPs 18:31 ^aS Ex 6:6;
S Job 19:25
20:1 ^bPs 4:1
^cEx 3:6; Ps 46:7,11
^dPs 59:1; 69:29; 91:14
20:2 ^ePs 30:10;
33:20; 37:40; 40:17;
54:4; 118:7
^fS Nu 3:28
^gS Ps 18:18 ^hPs 2:6;
128:5; 134:3; 135:21
20:3 ⁱAc 10:4
^jS Dt 33:11
20:4 ^kPs 21:2; 37:4;
145:16,19; Isa 26:8;
Eze 24:25; Ro 10:1
^lPs 140:8; Pr 16:3;
Da 11:17
20:5 ^mS Job 3:7
ⁿS Nu 1:52; Ps 60:4;
Isa 5:26; 11:10,12;
13:2; 30:17; 49:22;
62:10; Jer 50:2; 51:12,
27 ^o1Sa 1:17
20:6 ^pS 2Sa 23:1;
Ps 28:8 ^qS Job 40:14;
Hab 3:13
20:7 ^rS 2Ki 19:23
^sS Dt 17:16; Ps 33:17;
147:10; Pr 21:31;
Isa 31:1; 36:8,9
^tS 2Ch 32:8
20:8 ^uPs 27:2;
Isa 40:30; Jer 46:6;
50:32 ^vMic 7:8
^wS Job 11:15;
Ps 37:23; Pr 10:25;
Isa 7:9

The ordinances of the LORD are sure,
　　and all of them are righteous. ^q

¹⁰ They are more precious than gold, ^r
　　than much pure gold;
they are sweeter than honey, ^s
　　than honey from the honeycomb. ^t
¹¹ By them your servant is warned;
　　in keeping them there is great reward.
¹² But who can discern their own errors?
　　Forgive my hidden faults. ^u
¹³ Keep your servant also from willful sins; ^v
　　may they not rule over me. ^w
Then I will be blameless, ^x
　　innocent of great transgression.

¹⁴ May these words of my mouth and this meditation of my heart
　　be pleasing ^y in your sight,
　LORD, my Rock ^z and my Redeemer. ^a

PSALM 20

For the director of music. A psalm of David.

^{*1} May the LORD answer you when you are in distress; ^b
　　may the name of the God of Jacob ^c protect you. ^d
² May he send you help ^e from the sanctuary ^f
　　and grant you support ^g from Zion. ^h
³ May he remember ⁱ all your sacrifices
　　and accept your burnt offerings. ^{aj}
⁴ May he give you the desire of your heart ^k
　　and make all your plans succeed. ^l
⁵ May we shout for joy ^m over your victory
　　and lift up our banners ⁿ in the name of our God.

May the LORD grant all your requests. ^o

⁶ Now this I know:
　　The LORD gives victory to his anointed. ^p
He answers him from his heavenly sanctuary
　　with the victorious power of his right hand. ^q
⁷ Some trust in chariots ^r and some in horses, ^s
　　but we trust in the name of the LORD our God. ^t
⁸ They are brought to their knees and fall, ^u
　　but we rise up ^v and stand firm. ^w

---

^a 3 The Hebrew has *Selah* (a word of uncertain meaning) here.
[*] 20:1-9 is numbered 20:2-10 in Hebrew texts.

19:10–11 The matchless worth of God's law and its rich value for life (see Dt 5:33).
19:10 *sweeter than honey.* By contrast, those who abandon the law turn justice into bitterness (see Am 5:7; 6:12).
19:12–13 Humanity's moral consciousness remains flawed; hence people err without realizing it and have reason to seek pardon for "hidden faults" (v. 12; see Lev 5:2–4). "Willful sins" (v. 13), however, are open rebellion; they are the "great transgression" (v. 13) that leads to being cut off from God's people (see Nu 15:30–31).
19:14 The psalmist presents this hymn as a praise offering to the Lord. *heart.* See note on 4:7. *Redeemer.* See 78:35. *Rock.* See notes on 18:2; Ge 49:24. *Redeemer.* See notes on Ex 6:6; Isa 41:14.
Ps 20 A liturgy of prayer for the king just before he goes out to battle against a threatening force (see 2Ch 20:1–30). Ps 20–21 serve as the counterpart of Ps 18 in the arrangement of Ps 15–24 (see introduction to Ps 15–24); in Ps 18 we hear the voice of the king, while in Ps 20–21 we hear the voices of the people.
20 title *For the director of music.* See note on Ps 4 title.

20:1–5 The people (perhaps his assembled army) address the king, adding their prayers to his prayer for victory.
20:1 *answer you.* Hear your prayers, offered in the present distress, accompanied by "sacrifices" (v. 3); see v. 9. *name.* See vv. 5,7; see also note on 5:11. *Jacob.* See note on 14:7. *protect you.* Lit. "raise you to a high, secure place."
20:2 *Zion.* See note on 9:11.
20:3 For *Selah,* see TNIV text note and note on 3:2.
20:4 *heart.* See note on 4:7.
20:5 *May we shout . . . name of our God.* See note on 5:11. *banners.* Probably the troop standards around which the units rallied.
20:6 A participant in the liturgy (perhaps a Levite; see 2Ch 20:14) announces assurance that the king's prayer will be heard. *his anointed.* The king appointed by the Lord to rule in his name (see 2:2 and note).

A **20:7–8** The army's confession of trust in the Lord rather than in a chariot corps (cf. 33:16–17)—the enemy perhaps came reinforced by such a prized corps. See David's similar confession of confidence when he faced Goliath (1Sa 17:45–47).

9 LORD, give victory to the king!
  Answer us[x] when we call!

PSALM 21

For the director of music. A psalm of David.

[*]1 The king rejoices in your strength, LORD.[y]
  How great is his joy in the victories you give![z]

2 You have granted him his heart's desire[a]
  and have not withheld the request of his lips.[a]
3 You came to greet him with rich blessings
  and placed a crown of pure gold[b] on his head.[c]
4 He asked you for life, and you gave it to him—
  length of days, for ever and ever.[d]
5 Through the victories[e] you gave, his glory is great;
  you have bestowed on him splendor and majesty.[f]
6 Surely you have granted him unending blessings
  and made him glad with the joy[g] of your presence.[h]
7 For the king trusts in the LORD;[i]
  through the unfailing love[j] of the Most High[k]
  he will not be shaken.[l]

8 Your hand will lay hold[m] on all your enemies;
  your right hand will seize your foes.
9 When you appear for battle,
  you will burn them up as in a blazing furnace.
  The LORD will swallow them up in his wrath,
  and his fire will consume them.[n]
10 You will destroy their descendants from the earth,
  their posterity from the human race.[o]
11 Though they plot evil[p] against you
  and devise wicked schemes,[q] they cannot succeed.
12 You will make them turn their backs[r]
  when you aim at them with drawn bow.

13 Be exalted[s] in your strength, LORD;[t]
  we will sing and praise your might.

---

[a] *2* The Hebrew has *Selah* (a word of uncertain meaning) here.
[*] 21:1-13 is numbered 21:2-14 in Hebrew texts.

20:9 ˣ Ps 17:6
21:1 ʸ S 1Sa 2:10
  ᶻ S 2Sa 22:51
21:2 ᵃ S Ps 20:4
21:3 ᵇ S 2Sa 12:30;
  Rev 14:14 ᶜ Zec 6:11
21:4 ᵈ Ps 10:16;
  45:17; 48:14; 133:3
21:5 ᵉ ver 1;
  Ps 18:50; 44:4
  ᶠ S Ps 8:5; 45:3; 93:1;
  96:6; 104:1
21:6 ᵍ Ps 43:4;
  126:3 ʰ S 1Ch 17:27
21:7 ⁱ S 2Ki 18:5
  ʲ Ps 6:4 ᵏ Ge 14:18
  ˡ S Ps 15:5; S 55:22
21:8 ᵐ Isa 10:10
21:9 ⁿ S Dt 32:22;
  Ps 50:3; Jer 15:14
21:10 ᵒ Dt 28:18
21:11 ᵖ Ps 2:1
  ᵠ Job 10:3; Ps 10:2;
  26:10; 37:7
21:12 ʳ S Ex 23:27
21:13 ˢ S Ps 18:46
  ᵗ Ps 18:1

20:9 The army's concluding petition. *Answer…when.* See note on v. 1. The psalm ends as it began.
Ps 21 A psalm of praise for victories granted to the king. It is thus linked with Ps 20, but whether both were occasioned by the same events is unknown. Here the people's praise follows that of the king (see v. 1); there (Ps 20) the people's prayer was added to the king's. In its structure, the psalm is framed by vv. 1,13 ("in your strength, LORD" is in both verses) and is centered around v. 7, which proclaims the king's trust in the Lord and the security afforded him by God's unfailing love (see Introduction: Literary Features). See introduction to Ps 20; see also introduction to Ps 15–24.
21 title *For the director of music.* See note on Ps 4 title.
21:2–6 The people celebrate the Lord's many favors to the king: all "his heart's desire" (v. 2). Verse 2 announces the theme; vv. 3–5 develop the theme; v. 6 climactically summarizes the theme.
21:2 *heart's.* See note on 4:7. For *Selah,* see TNIV text note and note on 3:2.
21:3 *came to greet him.* Back from the battles. *placed a crown …on his head.* Exchanged the warrior's helmet for the ceremonial emblem of royalty—possibly the captured crown of the defeated king (see 2Sa 12:30).
21:4 The king's life has been spared—to live "for ever and

ever" (see 1Ki 1:31; Da 2:4; 3:9; see also 1Sa 10:24; 1Ki 1:25, 34,39).
21:5 *glory…splendor and majesty.* See 45:3; like that of his heavenly Overlord (see 96:3).
21:6 *unending blessings.* Either (1) blessings of enduring value or (2) an unending flow of blessings. *your presence.* Your favor, which is the supreme cause of joy because it is the greatest blessing and the wellspring of all other blessings.
21:7 The center of the psalm (see note on 6:6). A participant in the liturgy (perhaps a priest or Levite) proclaims the reasons for the king's security. *LORD…Most High.* That is, LORD Most High (see 7:17; see also note on 3:7). *unfailing love.* See note on 6:4. *Most High.* See note on Ge 14:19. *shaken.* See note on 10:6.
21:8–12 The people hail the future victories of their triumphant king. Verse 8 announces the theme; vv. 9–11 develop the theme; v. 12 summarizes the theme.
21:9 *The LORD…in his wrath.* Credits the king's victories to the Lord's wrath (see note on 2:5).
21:10 The king's royal enemies will be left no descendants to rise up against him again.
21:12 *with drawn bow.* See note on Ge 9:13.
21:13 Conclusion—and return to the beginning: Lord, assert your strength, in which "the king rejoices" (v. 1; see also v. 7), and we will ever praise your might.

22:1 ᵘ S Job 6:15;
S Ps 9:10; Mt 27:46*;
Mk 15:34* ᵛ Ps 10:1
ʷ S Job 3:24
22:2 ˣ S Job 19:7
ʸ Ps 42:3; 88:1
22:3 ᶻ 2Ki 19:22;
Ps 71:22; S Mt 1:24
ᵃ S Ex 15:2; Ps 148:14
22:4 ᵇ Ps 78:53;
107:6
22:5 ᶜ S 1Ch 5:20
ᵈ Isa 8:17; 25:9; 26:3;
30:18 ᵉ S 2Ch 13:18;
Ps 25:3; 31:17; 71:1;
Isa 49:23; Ro 9:33
22:6 ᶠ S Job 4:19
ᵍ S 2Sa 12:14;
Ps 31:11; 64:8; 69:19;
109:25 ʰ Ps 119:141;
Isa 49:7; 53:3; 60:14;
Mal 2:9; Mt 16:21
22:7 ⁱ S Job 17:2;
Ps 35:16; 69:12; 74:18;
Mt 27:41; Mk 15:31;
Lk 23:36 ʲ Mt 27:39,
44; Mk 15:32;
Lk 23:39 ᵏ Mk 15:29
22:8 ˡ Ps 91:14
ᵐ S Ps 3:2
ⁿ S 2Sa 22:20;
S Mt 3:17; 27:43
22:9 ᵒ Job 10:18;
Ps 71:6 ᵖ Ps 78:7;
Na 1:7
22:10 ᑫ Ps 71:6;
Isa 46:3; 49:1
22:11 ʳ ver 19;
S Ps 10:1 ˢ S Ps 10:14
ᵗ S 2Ki 14:26;
S Isa 41:28
22:12 ᵘ Ps 68:30
ᵛ Ps 17:9; 27:6; 49:5;
109:3; 140:9
ʷ Dt 32:14; Isa 2:13;
Eze 27:6; 39:18;
Am 4:1
22:13 ˣ ver 21;
Eze 22:25; Zep 3:3
ʸ S Ge 49:9 ᶻ La 3:46
22:14 ᵃ S Ps 6:2
ᵇ Job 23:16; Ps 68:2;
97:5; Mic 1:4
ᶜ Jos 7:5; Ps 107:26;
Da 5:6

PSALM 22

For the director of music. To the tune of "The Doe of the Morning." A psalm of David.

¹ My God, my God, why have you forsaken me? ᵘ
　Why are you so far ᵛ from saving me,
　so far from the words of my groaning? ʷ
² My God, I cry out by day, but you do not answer, ˣ
　by night, ʸ but I find no rest. ᵃ

³ Yet you are enthroned as the Holy One; ᶻ
　you are the praise ᵇ ᵃ of Israel.
⁴ In you our ancestors put their trust;
　they trusted and you delivered them. ᵇ
⁵ They cried to you ᶜ and were saved;
　in you they trusted ᵈ and were not disappointed. ᵉ

⁶ But I am a worm, ᶠ not a human being;
　I am scorned by everyone, ᵍ despised ʰ by the people.
⁷ All who see me mock me; ⁱ
　they hurl insults, ʲ shaking their heads. ᵏ
⁸ "He trusts in the LORD," they say,
　"let the LORD rescue him. ˡ
Let him deliver him, ᵐ
　since he delights ⁿ in him."

⁹ Yet you brought me out of the womb; ᵒ
　you made me feel secure ᵖ on my mother's breast.
¹⁰ From birth ᑫ I was cast on you;
　from my mother's womb you have been my God.
¹¹ Do not be far from me, ʳ
　for trouble is near ˢ
　and there is no one to help. ᵗ

¹² Many bulls ᵘ surround me; ᵛ
　strong bulls of Bashan ʷ encircle me.
¹³ Roaring lions ˣ that tear their prey ʸ
　open their mouths wide ᶻ against me.
¹⁴ I am poured out like water,
　and all my bones are out of joint. ᵃ
My heart has turned to wax; ᵇ
　it has melted ᶜ within me.

ᵃ 2 Or *night, and am not silent*　　ᵇ 3 Or *Yet you are holy, / enthroned on the praises*

* 22:1-31 is numbered 22:2-32 in Hebrew texts.

Ps 22 The anguished prayer of David as a godly sufferer victimized by the vicious and prolonged attacks of enemies whom he has not provoked and from whom the Lord has not (yet) delivered him. In the arrangement of Ps 15–24, this psalm serves as the counterpart of Ps 17 (see introduction to Ps 17; see also introduction to Ps 15–24). The prayer is in many ways similar to Ps 69, but it contains no calls for redress (see note on 5:10) such as are found in 69:22–28. No other psalm fitted quite so aptly the circumstances of Jesus at his crucifixion. Hence on the cross he took it to his lips (see Mt 27:46 and parallels), and the Gospel writers, especially Matthew and John, frequently alluded to it (as they did to Ps 69) in their accounts of Christ's passion (Mt 27:35,39,43; Jn 19:23–24,28). They saw in the passion of Jesus the fulfillment of this cry of the righteous sufferer. The author of Hebrews placed the words of v. 22 on Jesus' lips (see Heb 2:12 and note). No psalm is quoted more frequently in the NT.

22 title See notes on Ps 4; 9 titles.
22:1 *why . . . ? Why . . . ?* See note on 6:3.
22:1a Quoted by Jesus in Mt 27:46; Mk 15:34.
22:2 *I cry . . . you do not answer.* See note on 118:5.

22:3–5 Recollection of what the Lord has been for Israel (see note on vv. 9–10).
22:3 *enthroned.* See note on 9:11. *Holy One.* See Lev 11:44 and note. *praise of Israel.* The one Israel praises for his saving acts in her behalf (see 148:14; Dt 10:21; Jer 17:14).
22:6 *a worm, not a human being.* See Job 25:6; Isa 41:14.
22:7 *hurl insults, shaking their heads.* See Mt 27:39; Mk 15:29; see also note on 5:9.
22:8 Quoted in part in Mt 27:43; see note on 3:2.
22:9–10 Recollection of what the Lord has been for him (see note on vv. 3–5).
22:12–18 The psalmist's deep distress. In vv. 12–13,16–18 he uses four figures to portray the attacks of his enemies; in vv. 14–15 he describes his inner sense of powerlessness under their fierce attacks.
22:12–13,16 *bulls . . . lions . . . Dogs.* Metaphors for the enemies (see note on 7:2).
22:12 *Bashan.* Noted for its good pasturage, and hence for the size and vigor of its animals (see Dt 32:14; Eze 39:18 and note; Am 4:1).
22:14 *bones . . . heart.* See note on 102:4. *heart.* See note on 4:7.

¹⁵ My mouth[a] is dried up like a potsherd,[d]
and my tongue sticks to the roof of my mouth;[e]
you lay me[b] in the dust[f] of death.
¹⁶ Dogs[g] surround me,
a pack of villains encircles me;
they pierce[c][h] my hands and my feet.
¹⁷ All my bones are on display;
people stare[i] and gloat over me.[j]
¹⁸ They divide my clothes among them
and cast lots[k] for my garment.[l]

¹⁹ But you, LORD, do not be far from me.[m]
You are my strength;[n] come quickly[o] to help me.[p]
²⁰ Deliver me from the sword,[q]
my precious life[r] from the power of the dogs.[s]
²¹ Rescue me from the mouth of the lions;[t]
save me from the horns of the wild oxen.[u]

²² I will declare your name to my people;
in the assembly[v] I will praise you.[w]
²³ You who fear the LORD, praise him![x]
All you descendants of Jacob, honor him![y]
Revere him,[z]
all you descendants of Israel!
²⁴ For he has not despised[a] or scorned
the suffering of the afflicted one;[b]
he has not hidden his face[c] from him
but has listened to his cry for help.[d]

²⁵ From you comes the theme of my praise in the great assembly;[e]
before those who fear you[d] I will fulfill my vows.[f]
²⁶ The poor will eat[g] and be satisfied;
those who seek the LORD will praise him—[h]
may your hearts live forever!
²⁷ All the ends of the earth[i]
will remember and turn to the LORD,
and all the families of the nations
will bow down before him,[j]
²⁸ for dominion belongs to the LORD[k]
and he rules over the nations.

²⁹ All the rich[l] of the earth will feast and worship;[m]

---

a 15 Probable reading of the original Hebrew text; Masoretic Text *strength*   b 15 Or *mouth; / I am laid*
c 16 Some Hebrew manuscripts, Septuagint and Syriac; most Hebrew manuscripts *me, / like a lion*
d 25 Hebrew *him*

22:15 d Isa 45:9
e Ps 137:6; La 4:4;
Eze 3:26; Jn 19:28
f S Job 7:21; Ps 104:29
22:16 g Php 3:2
h Isa 51:9; 53:5;
Zec 12:10; Jn 20:25
22:17 i Lk 23:35
j Ps 25:2; 30:1; 35:19;
38:16; La 2:17;
Mic 7:8
22:18 k S Lev 16:8;
Mt 27:35*; Mk 15:24;
Lk 23:34; Jn 19:24*
l Mk 9:12
22:19 m S ver 11
n S Ps 18:1 o Ps 38:22;
70:5; 141:1 p Ps 40:13
22:20 q S Job 5:20;
Ps 37:14 r Ps 35:17
s Php 3:2
22:21 t S ver 13;
S Job 4:10 u ver 12;
S Nu 23:22
22:22 v Ps 26:12;
40:9,10; 68:26
w Ps 35:18; Heb 2:12*
22:23 x Ps 33:2;
66:8; 86:12; 103:1;
106:1; 113:1; 117:1;
135:19 y Ps 50:15;
Isa 24:15; 25:3;
49:23; 60:9; Jer 3:17
z Dt 14:23; Ps 33:8
22:24 a Ps 102:17
b S Ps 9:12 c Ps 13:1;
27:9; 69:17; 102:2;
143:7 d S Job 24:12;
S 36:5; Heb 5:7
22:25 e Ps 26:12;
35:18; 40:9; 82:1
f S Nu 30:2
22:26 g Ps 107:9
h Ps 40:16
22:27 i S Ps 2:8
j Ps 86:9; 102:22;
Da 7:27; Mic 4:1
22:28 k Ps 47:7-8;
Zec 14:9
22:29 l Ps 45:12
m S Ps 96:6; 96:9; 99:5;
Isa 27:13; 49:7; 66:23;
Zec 14:16

22:15 See Jn 19:28 and note. *dust of death.* See v. 29; see also Job 7:21 and note.
22:16 *pierce my hands and my feet.* The "dogs" wound his limbs as he seeks to ward off their attacks. But see also Isa 53:5; Zec 12:10; Jn 19:34,37.
22:17 *All my bones are on display.* The figure is probably that of one attacked by highway robbers or enemy soldiers, who strip him of his garments (see v. 18; see also note on vv. 20–21).
22:18 See introduction to this psalm; see also Jn 19:23–24.
22:20–21 The psalmist's prayer recalls in reverse order the four figures by which he portrayed his attackers in vv. 12–13, 16–18: "sword," "dogs," "lions," "wild oxen." Here "sword" refers back to the scene described in vv. 16–18, and thus many interpret it as an attack by robbers or enemy soldiers, though "sword" is often used figuratively of any violent death.
22:21 *wild oxen.* Aurochs, wild ancestors of domestic cattle.
22:22–31 Vows to praise the Lord when the Lord's sure deliverance comes (see note on 7:17). The vows proper appear in vv. 22,25. Verses 23–24 anticipate the calls to praise that will accompany the psalmist's praise (see note on 9:1). Verses 26–31 de-

scribe the expanding company of those who will take up the praise—a worldwide company of persons from every station in life and continuing through the generations. No psalm or prophecy contains a grander vision of the scope of the throng of worshipers who will join in the praise of God's saving acts.
22:22 See Heb 2:12 and note. *name.* See note on 5:11.
22:23 *fear the LORD.* See v. 25; see also note on 15:4.
22:25 *assembly.* See note on 1:5.
22:26 *will eat and be satisfied.* As they share in the ceremonial festival of praise (see Lev 7:11–27).
22:27 *All the ends of the earth.* They too will be told of God's saving acts (see 18:49 and note on 9:1). The good news that the God of Israel hears the prayers of his people and saves them will move them to turn from their idols to the true God (cf. 1Th 1:9).
22:28 The rule of the God of Israel is universal, and the nations will come to recognize that fact through what he does in behalf of his people (see Ps 47; Ge 12:2–3; see also Dt 32:21; Ro 10:19; 11:13–14).
22:29 *All the rich … all who go down.* The most prosperous and

22:29 *n* Isa 26:19
o Ps 89:48
22:30 *p* Isa 53:10;
54:3; 61:9; 66:22
q Ps 102:18
22:31 *r* Ps 5:8;
40:9 *s* Ps 71:18; 78:6;
102:18 *t* Lk 18:31;
24:44
23:1 *u* S Ge 48:15;
S Ps 28:9; S Jn 10:11
v Ps 34:9,10; 84:11;
107:9; Php 4:19
23:2 *w* Ps 36:8;
46:4; Rev 7:17
23:3 *x* S Ps 19:7
y Ps 25:9; 73:24;
Isa 42:16 *z* S Ps 5:8
a Ps 25:11; 31:3; 79:9;
106:8; 109:21; 143:11
23:4 *b* S Job 3:5;
Ps 107:14 *c* Ps 3:6;
27:1 *d* Ps 16:8;
Isa 43:2
23:5 *e* S Job 36:16
f Ps 45:7; 92:10;
Lk 7:46 *g* S Ps 16:5
23:6 *h* S Ne 9:25

all who go down to the dust *n* will kneel before him—
those who cannot keep themselves alive. *o*
³⁰ Posterity *p* will serve him;
future generations *q* will be told about the Lord.
³¹ They will proclaim his righteousness, *r*
declaring to a people yet unborn: *s*
He has done it! *t*

PSALM 23

A psalm of David.

¹ The LORD is my shepherd, *u* I lack nothing. *v*
²   He makes me lie down in green pastures,
he leads me beside quiet waters, *w*
³   he refreshes my soul. *x*
He guides me *y* along the right paths *z*
for his name's sake. *a*
⁴ Even though I walk
through the darkest valley, *a* *b*
I will fear no evil, *c*
for you are with me; *d*
your rod and your staff,
they comfort me.

⁵ You prepare a table *e* before me
in the presence of my enemies.
You anoint my head with oil; *f*
my cup *g* overflows.
⁶ Surely your goodness and love *h* will follow me
all the days of my life,

---

a 4 Or the valley of the shadow of death

---

those on the brink of death, and all those whose life situation falls in between these two extremes. *dust.* See v. 15; see also Job 7:21 and note.

22:31 *righteousness.* See note on 4:1.

Ps 23 A profession of joyful trust in the Lord as the good Shepherd-King. In the arrangement of Ps 15–24 it serves as the counterpart of Ps 16, with which it is thematically linked (see introduction to Ps 16; see also introduction to Ps 15–24). The psalm may have accompanied a festival of praise at "the house of the LORD" (v. 6) following a deliverance, such as is contemplated in 22:25–31 (see note on 7:17). The basic theme of the psalm is announced in v. 1. Verses 2–3 develop the theme by affirming the psalmist's total security under the Shepherd-King's care. Verse 4 elaborates on this theme by focusing on the Shepherd's protection in times of great danger and distress. Verse 5 describes the psalmist's privileged position as the recipient of the Shepherd's provision of every need. In v. 6 the psalmist professes his full confidence for the future—a confidence grounded in the Shepherd-King's faithful covenant love. The psalm is framed by its first and last lines, in each of which "the LORD" is expressly named.

23:1 *shepherd.* A widely used metaphor for kings in the ancient Near East, and also in Israel (see 78:70–72; 2Sa 5:2; Isa 44:28; Jer 3:15; 23:1–4; Mic 5:4; see also Jer 2:8 and note). For the Lord as the shepherd of Israel, see 28:9; 79:13; 80:1; 95:7; 100:3; Ge 48:15; Isa 40:11; Jer 17:16; 31:10; 50:19; Eze 34:11–16. Here David the king acknowledges that the Lord is his Shepherd-King. For Jesus as the shepherd of his people, see Jn 10:11,14; Heb 13:20; 1Pe 5:4; Rev 7:17. *lack nothing.* On the contrary, he will enjoy "goodness" all his life (v. 6).

23:2 *lie down.* For flocks lying down in contented and secure rest, see Isa 14:30; 17:2; Jer 33:12; Eze 34:14–15; Zep 2:7; 3:13. *green pastures.* Metaphor for all that makes life flourish (see Eze 34:14; Jn 10:9). *leads me.* Like a shepherd (see Isa 40:11). *quiet waters.* Lit. "waters of resting places," i.e., restful waters—waters

that provide refreshment and well-being (see Isa 49:10).

23:3 *refreshes my soul.* Revives me, refreshes my spirit (see 19:7; Ru 4:15; Pr 25:13; La 1:16). *guides me along the right paths.* As a shepherd leads his sheep (see 77:20; 78:72) in paths that offer safety and well-being, so David's Shepherd-King guides him in ways that cause him to be secure and prosperous. For this meaning of "right," see Pr 8:18 ("prosperity"); 21:21 ("prosperity"); Isa 48:18; see also Pr 8:20–21. It is possible that "right paths" intentionally bears a double meaning, namely, that it also refers to paths that conform the psalmist's life to God's moral will (cf. Pr 4:11 and note). *for his name's sake.* The prosperity of the Lord's servant brings honor to the Lord's name (see 1Ki 8:41–42; Isa 48:9; Jer 14:21; Eze 20:9,14,22).

23:4 *the darkest valley.* A metaphor for circumstances of greatest peril (see 107:10 and note). See also TNIV text note. *with me.* See 16:8 and note; see also Dt 31:6,8; Mt 28:20. *rod.* Instrument of authority (as in 2:9; 45:6; Ex 21:20; 2Sa 7:14; Job 9:34); used also by shepherds for counting, guiding, rescuing and protecting sheep (see Lev 27:32; Eze 20:37). *staff.* Instrument of support (as in Ex 21:19; Jdg 6:21; 2Ki 4:29; Zec 8:4). *comfort me.* Reassure me (as in 71:21; 86:17; Ru 2:13; Isa 12:1; 40:1; 49:13).

23:5 The heavenly Shepherd-King receives David at his table as his vassal king and takes him under his protection. In the ancient Near East, covenants were often concluded with a meal expressive of the bond of friendship (see 41:9; Ge 31:54; Ob 7); in the case of vassal treaties or covenants, the vassal was present as the guest of the overlord (see Ex 24:8–12). *anoint my head with oil.* Customary treatment of an honored guest at a banquet (see Lk 7:46; see also 2Sa 12:20; Ecc 9:8; Da 10:3). *cup.* Of the Lord's banquet (see note on 16:5).

23:6 *goodness and love.* Both frequently refer to covenant benefits (see note on 6:4); here they are personified (see 25:21; 43:3; 79:8; 89:14). *follow.* Lit. "pursue"—usually with hostile intent. Rather than having enemies ever in pursuit of him (see 1Sa

and I will dwell in the house of the LORD
forever.

PSALM 24

Of David. A psalm.

¹ The earth is the LORD's, *i* and everything in it,
the world, and all who live in it; *j*
² for he founded it on the seas
and established it on the waters. *k*

³ Who may ascend the mountain *l* of the LORD?
Who may stand in his holy place? *m*
⁴ Those who have clean hands *n* and a pure heart, *o*
who do not put their trust in an idol *p*
or swear by a false god. *a*

⁵ They will receive blessing *q* from the LORD
and vindication *r* from God their Savior.
⁶ Such is the generation of those who seek him,
who seek your face, *s* God of Jacob. *b, c*

⁷ Lift up your heads, you gates; *t*
be lifted up, you ancient doors,
that the King *u* of glory *v* may come in. *w*
⁸ Who is this King of glory?
The LORD strong and mighty, *x*
the LORD mighty in battle. *y*
⁹ Lift up your heads, you gates;
lift them up, you ancient doors,
that the King of glory may come in.
¹⁰ Who is he, this King of glory?

---

a 4 Or *swear falsely*   *b* 6 Two Hebrew manuscripts and Syriac (see also Septuagint); most Hebrew
manuscripts *face, Jacob*   *c* 6 The Hebrew has *Selah* (a word of uncertain meaning) here and at the end
of verse 10.

24:1 *i* S Ex 9:29;
Job 41:11 / 1Co 10:26*
24:2 *k* S Ge 1:6;
Ps 104:3; 2Pe 3:5
24:3 *l* Ps 2:6
m Ps 15:1; 65:4
24:4 *n* S 2Sa 22:21
o Ps 51:10; 73:1;
Mt 5:8 *p* Eze 18:15
24:5 *q* Dt 11:26
r Ps 17:2
24:6 *s* Ps 27:8;
105:4; 119:58;
Hos 5:15
24:7 *t* Ps 118:19,20;
Isa 26:2; 60:11,18;
62:10 *u* Ps 44:4; 74:12
v Ps 29:3; Ac 7:2;
1Co 2:8 *w* Zec 9:9;
Mt 21:5
24:8 *x* S 1Ch 29:11;
Ps 89:13; Jer 50:34;
Eph 6:10 *y* Ex 15:3,6;
Dt 4:34

23:25; 24:14; 26:18,20), David will have the goodness and unfailing love of his Shepherd-King attending him. *dwell in the house
of the LORD.* See note on 15:1. *forever.* The Hebrew for this word
suggests "throughout the years," as in Pr 28:16 ("enjoy a long
reign"). But see also notes on 11:7; 16:9–11.
Ps 24 A processional liturgy (see Ps 47; 68; 118; 132) celebrating the Lord's entrance into Zion—composed either for the occasion when David brought the ark to Jerusalem (see 2Sa 6) or
for a festival commemorating the event. Together with Ps 15 it
frames the intervening collection of psalms and with that psalm
sharply delineates those who may approach God in prayer and
"dwell in the house of the LORD" (23:6; see introduction to Ps
15–24). The church has long used this psalm in celebration of
Christ's ascension into the heavenly Jerusalem—and into the
sanctuary on high (see introduction to Ps 47).
24:1–2 The prelude (perhaps spoken by a Levite), proclaiming
the Lord as the Creator, Sustainer and Possessor of the whole
world (see 19:1–4) and therefore worthy of worship and reverent loyalty as "the King of glory" (vv. 7–10; see Ps 29; 33:6–11;
89:5–18; 93; 95:3–5; 96; 104).
24:1 *The earth . . . everything in it.* For Paul's use of this declaration, see 1Co 10:25–26.
24:2 An echo of Ge 1:1–10. *founded . . . established.* A metaphor
taken from the founding of a city (see Jos 6:26; 1Ki 16:24; Isa
14:32) or of a temple (see 1Ki 5:17; 6:37; Ezr 3:6–12; Isa 44:28; Hag
2:18; Zec 4:9; 8:9). Like a temple, the earth was depicted as having
foundations (see 18:15; 82:5; 1Sa 2:8; Pr 8:29; Isa 24:18) and pillars
(see 75:3; Job 9:6). In the ancient Near East temples were thought
of as microcosms of the created world, so language applicable to a
temple could readily be applied to the earth (see note on Ex 26:1).
on. Or "above" (see 104:5–9; Ge 1:9; 7:11; 49:25; Ex 20:4; Dt 33:13).

24:3–6 Instruction concerning those who may enter the sanctuary (probably spoken by a priest).
24:3 *mountain of the LORD.* See 2:6 and note.
24:4 *clean hands.* Guiltless actions. *pure heart.* Right attitudes
and motives (see 51:10; 73:1). Jesus said that the "pure in heart
. . . will see God" (Mt 5:8). *heart.* See note on 4:7. *put their trust in.*
Or "worship" (see 25:1–2; 86:4; 143:8). *by a false god.* Cf. Isa
19:18; Jer 7:9; Zep 1:5. But see TNIV text note. If the latter is the
sense, reference is probably to perjury (for the same concern
see Ex 20:16 and note; Lev 19:12; Jer 5:2; 7:9; Zec 5:4; Mal 3:5).
24:5 *vindication.* That is, the fruits of vindication, such as righteous treatment from a faithful God; hence, here a synonym of
"blessing" (see 23:3 and note).
24:6 *generation.* Or "company," as in 14:5 (those who share a
common characteristic); see also 112:2; Pr 30:11–14 and notes
on Ps 73:15; 78:8. *Jacob.* See note on 14:7. For *Selah,* see TNIV
text note and note on 3:2.
24:7–10 Heralding the approach of the King of glory (perhaps
spoken by the king at the head of the assembled Israelites, with
responses by the keepers of the gates). The Lord's arrival at his
sanctuary in Zion completes his march from Egypt. "The LORD
Almighty" (v. 10), "the LORD mighty in battle" (v. 8; see Ex 15:1–18),
has triumphed over all his enemies and comes now in victory to
his own city (see Ps 46; 48; 76; 87), his "resting place" (132:8,14; see
68:7–8; Jdg 5:4–5; Hab 3:3–7). Henceforth Jerusalem is the royal
city of the kingdom of God (see note on 9:11).
24:7 *Lift up your heads . . . be lifted up.* In jubilant reception of
the victorious King of glory (see 3:3; 27:6; 110:7). *gates.* Reference could be to the gates of either the city or the sanctuary.
doors. A synonym for "gates," not in this case the doors of the
gates (as in Jdg 16:3; 1Sa 21:13). The gates are personified for

24:10 ᶻ S 1Sa 1:11
25:1 ᵃ Ps 86:4; 143:8
25:2 ᵇ Ps 31:6; 143:8
25:3 ᶜ S Ps 22:5;
S Isa 29:22
ᵈ Isa 24:16; Hab 1:13;
Zep 3:4; 2Ti 3:4
25:4 ᵉ S Job 34:32
25:5 ᶠ Ps 31:3; 43:3;
Jn 16:13 ᵍ Ps 24:5
ʰ ver 3; Ps 33:20;
39:7; 42:5; 71:5;
130:7; 131:3
25:6 ⁱ Ps 5:7; 98:3;
Isa 63:7,15; Jer 31:20;
Hos 11:8
25:7 ʲ Job 13:26;
Isa 54:4; Jer 3:25;
31:19; 33:9;
Eze 16:22,60; 23:3;
2Ti 2:22 ᵏ S Ex 23:21;
Ps 107:17 ˡ Ps 6:4;
51:1; 69:16; 109:26;
119:124
ᵐ S 1Ch 16:34;
Ps 34:8; 73:1
25:8 ⁿ Ps 92:15;
Isa 26:7 ᵒ Ps 32:8;
Isa 28:26

The Lᴏʀᴅ Almighty ᶻ—
    he is the King of glory.

PSALM 25 ᵃ

Of David.

¹ In you, Lᴏʀᴅ my God,
    I put my trust. ᵃ

² I trust in you; ᵇ
    do not let me be put to shame,
    nor let my enemies triumph over me.
³ No one who hopes in you
    will ever be put to shame, ᶜ
but shame will come on those
    who are treacherous ᵈ without cause.

⁴ Show me your ways, Lᴏʀᴅ,
    teach me your paths. ᵉ
⁵ Guide me in your truth ᶠ and teach me,
    for you are God my Savior, ᵍ
    and my hope is in you ʰ all day long.
⁶ Remember, Lᴏʀᴅ, your great mercy and love, ⁱ
    for they are from of old.
⁷ Do not remember the sins of my youth ʲ
    and my rebellious ways; ᵏ
according to your love ˡ remember me,
    for you, Lᴏʀᴅ, are good. ᵐ

⁸ Good and upright ⁿ is the Lᴏʀᴅ;
    therefore he instructs ᵒ sinners in his ways.

ᵃ This psalm is an acrostic poem, the verses of which begin with the successive letters of the Hebrew alphabet.

---

dramatic effect, as in Isa 14:31.
24:10 Lᴏʀᴅ *Almighty.* See note on 1Sa 1:3. Here it stands in climactic position.
Ps 25–33 A group of nine psalms containing an unusual (even for the Psalter) concentration of pleas for "mercy" or "grace" (25:16; 26:11; 27:7; 28:2; 30:8,10; 31:9) accompanied by professions of "trust" (25:2; 26:1; 27:3; 28:7; 31:6,14; 32:10; 33:21) and appeals to or celebrations of Yahweh's "(unfailing) love" (25:6–7, 10; 26:3; 31:7,16,21; 32:10; 33:5,18,22). The series begins with an alphabetical acrostic prayer for God's saving help (Ps 25) and culminates in a 22-verse (the number of letters in the Hebrew alphabet) hymn of praise for Yahweh's sovereign rule and saving help (Ps 33). (For thematic links between these two psalms, see notes on 25:3,6). This prayer and hymn frame a concentrically arranged cluster that hinges on Ps 29 (for thematic links between Ps 26 and 32, 27 and 31, and 28 and 30, see introductions to those psalms). For the significance of Ps 29 as hinge, see introduction to that psalm.

A Ps 25 David prays for God's covenant mercies when suffering affliction for sins and when enemies seize the occasion to attack, perhaps by trying to discredit the king through false accusations (see note on 5:9). Appealing to God's covenant benevolence (his mercy, love, goodness, uprightness, faithfulness and grace; see vv. 6–8,10,16) and to his own reliance on the Lord (see vv. 1,5,15,20–21), he prays for deliverance from his enemies (see vv. 2,19), for guidance in God's will (see vv. 4–5,21; see also vv. 8–10,12), for the forgiveness of his sins (see vv. 7,11,18) and for relief from his affliction (see vv. 2,16–18,20). These are related: God's forgiveness will express itself in removing his affliction, and then his enemies will no longer have occasion to slander him. And with God guiding him in "his way" (v. 9)—i.e., in "the demands of his covenant" (v. 10)—he will no longer wander into "rebellious ways" (v. 7). This psalm is linked

with Ps 24 by its reference to putting one's trust in the true "God" (v. 1) instead of a "false god" (24:4). Structurally, the psalm is an alphabetic acrostic (somewhat irregular, with an additional, concluding verse that extends the lines beyond the alphabet). It is composed of four unequal stanzas (of three, four, eight and six verses). The first and fourth stanzas are thematically related, as are the second and third (an *a-b/b-a* pattern).
25:1–3 Prayer for relief from distress or illness and the slander of David's enemies that it occasions.
25:3 *hopes.* The three references to hoping in God occurring here (vv. 3,5,21) are echoed by three references to "hope" in 33:18,20,22 (by means of closely related Hebrew synonyms). *without cause.* David has given no cause for the hostility of his adversaries.
25:4–7 Prayer for guidance and pardon.
25:4 *your ways . . . your paths.* Metaphors for "the demands of his covenant" (v. 10; see Dt 8:6; 10:12–13; 26:17; 30:16; Jos 22:5; see also vv. 8–9; 18:21; 51:13; 81:13; 95:10; 119:3,15; 128:1 and note on 119:29).
25:5 *your truth.* Here synonymous for "your ways" and "your paths" (see note on v. 4; see also note on 19:7).

A 25:6–7 *Remember . . . Do not remember.* Remember your long-standing ("from of old") "mercy and love," but do not remember my long-standing sins (those "of my youth").
25:7 *love.* See v. 10 and note on 6:4.

A 25:8–15 Confidence in the Lord's covenant favors. In this context of prayer for pardon, David implicitly identifies himself with "sinners" (v. 8), as well as with the "humble" (v. 9)—those who keep God's covenant (see vv. 10,14) and those who fear the Lord (see vv. 12,14). As sinner he is in need of forgiveness; as humble servant of the Lord he hopefully awaits God's pardon and guidance in covenant faithfulness.

⁹ He guides^p the humble in what is right
and teaches them^q his way.
¹⁰ All the ways of the LORD are loving and faithful^r
toward those who keep the demands of his covenant.^s
¹¹ For the sake of your name,^t LORD,
forgive^u my iniquity,^v though it is great.

¹² Who, then, are those who fear the LORD?^w
He will instruct them in the ways^x they should choose.
¹³ They will spend their days in prosperity,^y
and their descendants will inherit the land.^z
¹⁴ The LORD confides^a in those who fear him;
he makes his covenant known^b to them.
¹⁵ My eyes are ever on the LORD,^c
for only he will release my feet from the snare.^d

¹⁶ Turn to me^e and be gracious to me,^f
for I am lonely^g and afflicted.
¹⁷ Relieve the troubles^h of my heart
and free me from my anguish.ⁱ
¹⁸ Look on my affliction^j and my distress^k
and take away all my sins.^l

¹⁹ See how numerous are my enemies^m
and how fiercely they hate me!ⁿ

²⁰ Guard my life^o and rescue me;^p
do not let me be put to shame,^q
for I take refuge^r in you.
²¹ May integrity^s and uprightness^t protect me,
because my hope, LORD,^a is in you.^u

²² Redeem Israel,^v O God,
from all their troubles!

PSALM 26

Of David.

¹ Vindicate me,^w LORD,
for I have led a blameless life;^x

^a 21 Septuagint; Hebrew does not have LORD.

25:9 ^p S Ps 23:3
^q ver 4; Ps 27:11
25:10 ^r S Ps 18:25
^s Ps 103:18; 132:12
25:11 ^t S Ex 9:16; Ps 31:3; 79:9; Jer 14:7
^u S Ex 34:9
^v S Ex 32:30; S Ps 78:38
25:12 ^w S Job 1:8
^x ver 8
25:13 ^y S Dt 30:15; S 1Ki 3:14; S Job 8:7
^z S Nu 14:24; Mt 5:5
25:14 ^a Pr 3:32
^b Ge 17:2; Jn 7:17
25:15 ^c S 2Ch 20:12; Ps 123:2; Heb 12:2
^d S Job 34:30; S Ps 119:110
25:16 ^e S Ps 6:4
^f S Nu 6:25 ^g Ps 68:6
25:17 ^h 1Ki 1:29; Ps 34:6,17; 40:12; 54:7; 116:3 ⁱ Ps 6:3; 39:2
25:18 ^j S Ps 13:3; Ro 12:12 ^k S 2Sa 16:12
^l Ps 103:3
25:19 ^m Ps 3:1; 9:13
ⁿ Ps 35:19; 38:19; 69:4
25:20 ^o Ps 86:2
^p Ps 17:13; 22:21; 43:1; 71:2; 116:4; 140:1; 142:6; 144:11 ^q ver 3
^r Ps 2:12
25:21 ^s S Ge 20:5; Pr 10:9 ^t 1Ki 9:4; Ps 85:10; 111:8; Isa 60:17; Mal 2:6
^u ver 3
25:22 ^v Ps 130:8; Lk 24:21
26:1 ^w S 1Sa 24:15
^x Ps 15:2; Pr 20:7

25:9 *humble.* Those who acknowledge that they are without resources.
25:10 *ways of the LORD.* The Lord's benevolent dealings (see 103:7; 138:5) with those who are true to his ways (see note on v. 4).
25:11 *For the sake of your name.* See note on 23:3; see also 1Jn 2:12. *name.* See note on 5:11.
25:12 *fear the LORD.* See notes on 34:8–14; Pr 1:7; Lk 12:5.
25:13 *inherit the land.* Retain their family portion in the promised land (see 37:9,11,18,22,29,34; 69:36; Isa 60:21).
25:14 *confides.* Takes them into his confidence, as friends (see Ge 18:17–19; Job 29:4). *fear.* See note on 15:4.
25:15 *snare.* Set by the enemies (v. 2; see note on 9:15).
25:16–21 Prayer for relief from distress (probably illness) and related attacks of his enemies.
25:17 *heart.* See note on 4:7.
25:21 *integrity and uprightness.* Personified virtues (see 23:6 and note). Pardon is not enough; David prays that God will enable him to live a life of unmarred moral rectitude—even as God is "good and upright" (v. 8; see 51:10–12). *integrity.* See note on 15:2.
25:22 A concluding prayer in behalf of all God's people (see 3:8 and note). *Redeem.* Here, as often, a synonym for "deliver."
Ps 26 A prayer for God's discerning mercies—to spare his faithful and godly servant from the death that overtakes the

wicked and ungodly. This prayer for vindication (v. 1) because the psalmist has led "a blameless life" (v. 11) and has refused "to sit with the wicked" (v. 5) has its counterpart (in the concentric arrangement of Ps 25–33; see introduction to Ps 25–33) in Ps 32, which celebrates the blessedness of those who have confessed their sins and been forgiven. The king's prayer for vindication suggests that he is threatened by the "deceitful" (v. 4) and "bloodthirsty" (v. 9) to whom he refers (as in Ps 23; 25; 27–28). This psalm is linked with Ps 27–28 (see also Ps 23–24) by the theme of the Lord's house: Here David's "love" (v. 8) for the temple (or tabernacle) testifies to the authenticity of his piety; in Ps 27 the Lord's temple is David's sanctuary from his enemies; in Ps 28 David directs his cry for help to the Lord's throne room ("your Most Holy Place," 28:2) in the temple. Three thematically important verbs ("lived," v. 3; "sit," vv. 4–5; "stand," v. 12) recall the three thematic verbs of 1:1.
26:1–8 An appeal for God to take account of David's moral integrity, his unwavering trust and his genuine delight in the Lord—not a boast of self-righteousness, such as that of the Pharisee (Lk 18:9–14).
26:1 *blameless life.* A claim of moral integrity (see vv. 2–5; see also note on 15:2). *trusted.* Obedience and trust are the two sides of godliness, as the Abraham story exemplifies (see Ge 12:4 and note; 22:12; see also Ps 34:8–14 and note).

26:1 ʸ Ps 22:4; 40:4;
Isa 12:2; 25:9;
Jer 17:7; Da 3:28
ᶻ 2Ki 20:3; Heb 10:23
26:2 ᵃ Ps 66:10
ᵇ S Dt 6:6; S Ps 7:9;
Jer 11:20; 20:12;
Eze 11:5
26:3 ᶜ Ps 6:4
ᵈ S 1Ki 2:4 ᵉ Ps 40:11;
43:3; 86:11; 119:30
26:4 ᶠ Ps 1:1
ᵍ Ps 28:3; Mt 6:2
26:5 ʰ Ps 139:21
26:6 ⁱ Ps 73:13;
Mt 27:24
26:7 ʲ Isa 42:12;
60:6 ᵏ S Jos 3:5;
Ps 9:1
26:8 ˡ Ps 122:6;
Isa 66:10
ᵐ S Ex 29:43;
2Ch 7:1; Ps 96:6
26:9 ⁿ Ps 5:6; 28:3;
55:23; 139:19;
Pr 29:10
26:10 ᵒ Ps 21:11
ᵖ Job 36:18;
S Isa 1:23;
S Eze 22:12
26:11 �q Ps 31:5;
69:18; 119:134;
Tit 2:14
26:12 ʳ Ps 27:11;
40:2; 143:10; Isa 26:7;
40:3-4; 45:13;
Zec 4:7; Lk 6:17
ˢ S Ps 22:25
27:1 ᵗ S 2Sa 22:29
ᵘ S Ex 15:2; S Ps 3:8
ᵛ Ps 9:9 ʷ S Job 13:15;
Ps 56:4,11; 118:6

I have trusted ʸ in the LORD
   and have not faltered. ᶻ
2 Test me, ᵃ LORD, and try me,
   examine my heart and my mind; ᵇ
3 for I have always been mindful of your unfailing love ᶜ
   and have lived ᵈ in reliance on your faithfulness. ᵉ

4 I do not sit ᶠ with the deceitful,
   nor do I associate with hypocrites. ᵍ
5 I abhor ʰ the assembly of evildoers
   and refuse to sit with the wicked.
6 I wash my hands in innocence, ⁱ
   and go about your altar, LORD,
7 proclaiming aloud your praise ʲ
   and telling of all your wonderful deeds. ᵏ

8 LORD, I love ˡ the house where you live,
   the place where your glory dwells. ᵐ
9 Do not take away my soul along with sinners,
   my life with those who are bloodthirsty, ⁿ
10 in whose hands are wicked schemes, ᵒ
   whose right hands are full of bribes. ᵖ
11 I lead a blameless life;
   redeem me q and be merciful to me.

12 My feet stand on level ground; ʳ
   in the great congregation ˢ I will praise the LORD.

PSALM 27

Of David.

1 The LORD is my light ᵗ and my salvation ᵘ—
   whom shall I fear?
The LORD is the stronghold ᵛ of my life—
   of whom shall I be afraid? ʷ

26:2 *heart … mind.* See note on 7:9.

26:3 *your unfailing love … your faithfulness.* That is, your unfailing love-and-faithfulness (see 40:10). David keeps his eye steadfastly on the Lord's great love (see note on 6:4) and faithfulness (see 25:10), which are pledged to those "who keep the demands of his covenant" (25:10). *lived in reliance on.* In order to receive the covenant benefits.

26:4–5 *sit with.* David refuses to settle in or associate himself with that company he describes as "deceitful," "hypocrites," "evildoers," "wicked" (see 1:1 and note; see also Ps 101).

26:4 *hypocrites.* Context may suggest those who deal fraudulently—or people like those described in Pr 6:12–14.

A   **26:6** *wash my hands in innocence.* Reference appears to be to a ritual claiming innocence. "Clean hands and a pure heart" are requisite for those who come to God (see 24:4 and note). *go about your altar.* To vocally celebrate God's saving acts beside his altar was a public act of devotion in which one also invited all the assembled worshipers to praise the Lord (see 43:3–4).

26:7 *your praise.* See note on 9:1.

A   **26:8** *where your glory dwells.* Cf. note on Eze 1:1–28. The presence of God's glory signaled the presence of God himself (see Ex 24:16; 33:22). His glory dwelling in the tabernacle (see Ex 40:34 and note) and later the temple (see 1Ki 8:11) assured Israel of the Lord's holy, yet gracious, presence among them. Jn 1:14 announces that same presence in the Word who became flesh and who "made his dwelling among us."

26:9–11 An appeal that God will not bring on David the end (death) that awaits the wicked.

26:9 *soul.* See note on 6:3.

26:11 *lead a blameless life.* A return to the appeal with which David began (see v. 1). *redeem.* See note on 25:22.

26:12 A concluding confession of confidence (see note on 3:8) and a vow to praise (see note on 7:17). *level ground.* Where the going is smooth and free from the danger of falling (see 143:10; Isa 40:4; 42:16). *congregation.* See note on 1:5 ("assembly"). *praise.* See note on 9:1.

A   **Ps 27** David's triumphantly confident prayer to God to deliver him from all those who conspire to bring him down. The prayer presupposes the Lord's covenant with David (see 2Sa 7). Faith's soliloquy (in two stanzas: vv. 1–3,4–6), which publicly testifies to the king's confident reliance on the Lord, introduces the prayer of vv. 7–12. The conclusion (vv. 13–14) echoes the confidence of vv. 1–6 and adds faith's dialogue with itself—faith exhorting faith to wait patiently for that which is sure, though not yet seen (see Ps 42–43; Heb 11:1). See further the introduction to Ps 26. In the concentric arrangement of Ps 25–33 (see introduction to Ps 25–33), Ps 27 stands in counterpoint with Ps 31, a similar confident prayer for Yahweh's saving help as the psalmist's refuge when under attack. In both, the adversaries try to destroy the psalmist by spreading lies. Both psalms speak of keeping "safe" in Yahweh's "dwelling" (27:5; 31:20) and of hiding in the "shelter" of Yahweh's "tabernacle" (27:5) or "presence" (31:20). Both conclude with an exhortation to "be strong and take heart" out of hope in the Lord. In addition, they share other significant vocabulary—e.g., reference to the "goodness" of Yahweh (27:13; 31:19).

27:1–3 The king's security in the Lord in the face of all that his enemies can do (see Ps 2).

A   **27:1** *light.* Often symbolizes well-being (see 97:11; Job 18:5–6; 22:28; 29:3; Pr 13:9; La 3:2) or life and salvation (see 18:28; Isa 9:2; 49:6; 58:8; 59:9; Jer 13:16; Am 5:18–20). To say "The LORD is my light" is to confess confidence in him as the source of these benefits (see Isa 10:17; 60:1–2,19–20; Mic 7:8–9;

² When the wicked advance against me
　　to devour[a] me,
　it is my enemies and my foes
　　who will stumble and fall. ˣ
³ Though an army besiege me,
　　my heart will not fear; ʸ
　though war break out against me,
　　even then I will be confident. ᶻ

⁴ One thing[a] I ask from the Lᴏʀᴅ,
　　this only do I seek:
　that I may dwell in the house of the Lᴏʀᴅ
　　all the days of my life, ᵇ
　to gaze on the beauty of the Lᴏʀᴅ
　　and to seek him in his temple.
⁵ For in the day of trouble ᶜ
　　he will keep me safe ᵈ in his dwelling;
　he will hide me ᵉ in the shelter of his tabernacle
　　and set me high upon a rock. ᶠ
⁶ Then my head will be exalted ᵍ
　　above the enemies who surround me; ʰ
　at his tabernacle I will sacrifice ⁱ with shouts of joy; ʲ
　　I will sing ᵏ and make music ˡ to the Lᴏʀᴅ.

⁷ Hear my voice ᵐ when I call, Lᴏʀᴅ;
　　be merciful to me and answer me. ⁿ
⁸ My heart says of you, "Seek his face! ᵒ"
　　Your face, Lᴏʀᴅ, I will seek.
⁹ Do not hide your face ᵖ from me,
　　do not turn your servant away in anger; �q
　　you have been my helper. ʳ
　Do not reject me or forsake ˢ me,
　　God my Savior. ᵗ
¹⁰ Though my father and mother forsake me,
　　the Lᴏʀᴅ will receive me.
¹¹ Teach me your way, ᵘ Lᴏʀᴅ;
　　lead me in a straight path ᵛ
　　because of my oppressors. ʷ
¹² Do not turn me over to the desire of my foes,
　　for false witnesses ˣ rise up against me,
　　spouting malicious accusations.

¹³ I remain confident of this:
　　I will see the goodness of the Lᴏʀᴅ ʸ
　　in the land of the living. ᶻ
¹⁴ Wait[a] for the Lᴏʀᴅ;
　　be strong ᵇ and take heart
　　and wait for the Lᴏʀᴅ.

ᵃ 2 Or slander

27:2 ˣPs 9:3;
S 20:8; 37:24;
Da 11:19; Ro 11:11
27:3 ʸS Ge 4:7;
S Ps 3:6 ᶻS Job 4:6
27:4 ᵃLk 10:42
ᵇPs 23:6; 61:4
27:5 ᶜS Job 38:23
ᵈPs 12:7 ᵉS Ps 17:8
ᶠPs 40:2
27:6 ᵍ2Sa 22:49;
Ps 3:3; 18:48
ʰS Ps 22:12
ⁱPs 50:14; 54:6;
107:22; 116:17
ʲS Ezr 3:13;
S Job 22:26
ᵏS Ex 15:1 ˡPs 33:2;
92:1; 147:7;
S Eph 5:19
27:7 ᵐPs 5:3; 18:6;
55:17; 119:149; 130:2;
Isa 28:23 ⁿS Ps 4:1
27:8 ᵒS 1Ch 16:11
27:9 ᵖS Dt 31:17;
S Ps 22:24 �q S Ps 2:5
ʳS Ge 49:25;
S Dt 33:29
ˢS Dt 4:31; Ps 37:28;
119:8; Isa 41:17; 62:12;
Jer 14:9 ᵗPs 18:46
27:11 ᵘS Ex 33:13
ᵛS Ezr 8:21; Ps 5:8
ʷPs 72:4; 78:42;
106:10; Jer 21:12
27:12 ˣS Dt 19:16;
S Mt 26:60; Ac 6:13;
1Co 15:15
27:13 ʸS Ex 33:19;
S 2Ch 6:41; Ps 23:6;
31:19; 145:7
ᶻS Job 28:13
27:14 ᵃPs 33:20;
130:5,6; Isa 8:17;
30:18; Hab 2:3;
Zep 3:8; Ac 1:4
ᵇS Dt 1:21;
S Jdg 5:21; S Eph 6:10

---

cf. also note on Col 1:12). *my salvation.* "My Savior" (v. 9).
27:2 *devour me.* See 7:2 and note.
27:3 *heart.* See note on 4:7.
27:4–6 The Lord's temple (or tabernacle) is the king's stronghold—because the Lord himself is his "stronghold" (v. 1; see notes on 9:11; 18:2).
27:4 *dwell in.* See note on 15:1. *beauty of the Lord.* His unfailing benevolence (see 90:17: "favor of the Lord").
27:5 *shelter of his tabernacle.* See 31:20; 32:7; 61:4; 91:1.
27:6 *I will sacrifice.* See note on 7:17. *I will sing.* See note on 9:1.
27:7–12 Prayer for deliverance from treacherous enemies. These remain unspecified, whether from inside or outside the kingdom or both. Their chief weapon is false charges intent on discrediting the king (see note on 5:9).

27:7 *I call ... answer me.* See note on 118:5.
27:9 *hide your face.* See note on 13:1. *anger.* See note on 2:5. *you have been my helper.* Or "be my helper."
27:10 *the Lord will receive me.* Or "may the Lord receive me."
　27:11 *Teach me your way.* Only those who know and do the Lord's will can expect to receive favorable response to their prayers (see Ps 24–26; see also 2Sa 7:14). *lead me in a straight path.* See 5:8 and note.
27:13–14 Concluding note of confidence (see note on 3:8).
27:13 *goodness of the Lord.* The "good" things promised in the Lord's covenant with David (see 2Sa 7:28; see also 31:19 and note). *land of the living.* This life.
　27:14 *Wait for the Lord.* Faith encouraging faith (see 42:5,11; 43:5; 62:5).

28:1 ^{c} S Dt 1:45
^{d} Est 4:14
^{e} S Job 33:18
28:2 ^{f} Ps 17:1; 61:1;
116:1; 130:2; 142:1;
143:1 ^{g} S Ezr 9:5;
Ps 63:4; 141:2;
La 2:19; 1Ti 2:8
^{h} Ps 5:7; 11:4
28:3 ^{i} Ps 12:2;
S 26:4; 55:21; Jer 9:8
28:4 ^{j} Ps 62:12;
2Ti 4:14; Rev 22:12
^{k} La 3:64; Rev 18:6
28:5 ^{l} Isa 5:12
28:6 ^{m} S Ge 24:27;
2Co 1:3; Eph 1:3;
1Pe 1:3 ^{n} ve. 2
28:7 ^{o} S Ps 18:1
^{p} Ps 13:5; 112:7;
Isa 26:3 ^{q} S Dt 16:15;
S Ps 16:9 ^{r} Ps 33:3;
40:3; 69:30; 144:9;
149:1
28:8 ^{s} Ps 18:1
^{t} S Ex 15:2; Ps 27:1;
Hab 3:13 ^{u} S Ps 20:6
28:9 ^{v} 1Ch 16:35;
Ps 106:47; 118:25
^{w} S Ex 34:9
^{x} 1Ch 11:2; S Ps 23:1;
78:52, 71; 80:1;
Isa 40:11; Jer 31:10;
Eze 34:12-16, 23, 31;
Mic 7:14 ^{y} S Dt 1:31;
32:11; Isa 46:3; 63:9

PSALM 28

Of David.

1 To you, LORD, I call;
  you are my Rock,
    do not turn a deaf ear ^{c} to me.
  For if you remain silent, ^{d}
    I will be like those who go down to the pit. ^{e}
2 Hear my cry for mercy ^{f}
  as I call to you for help,
  as I lift up my hands ^{g}
    toward your Most Holy Place. ^{h}

3 Do not drag me away with the wicked,
  with those who do evil,
  who speak cordially with their neighbors
    but harbor malice in their hearts. ^{i}
4 Repay them for their deeds
  and for their evil work;
  repay them for what their hands have done ^{j}
    and bring back on them what they deserve. ^{k}

5 Because they have no regard for the deeds of the LORD
    and what his hands have done, ^{l}
  he will tear them down
    and never build them up again.

6 Praise be to the LORD, ^{m}
    for he has heard my cry for mercy. ^{n}
7 The LORD is my strength ^{o} and my shield;
    my heart trusts ^{p} in him, and he helps me.
  My heart leaps for joy, ^{q}
    and with my song I praise him. ^{r}

8 The LORD is the strength ^{s} of his people,
    a fortress of salvation ^{t} for his anointed one. ^{u}
9 Save your people ^{v} and bless your inheritance; ^{w}
    be their shepherd ^{x} and carry them ^{y} forever.

Ps 28 A prayer for deliverance from deadly peril at the hands of malicious and God-defying enemies. As with Ps 25, the prayer ends with intercession for all the people of the Lord (see 3:8 and note). Reference in the last verse to the Lord as the shepherd of his people connects this psalm with Ps 23. However, in the concentric arrangement of Ps 25–33 (see introduction to Ps 25–33) it is linked more closely with Ps 30. In Ps 28 the psalmist cries to Yahweh "for mercy" (vv. 2,6) when about to go "down to the pit" (v. 1); in Ps 30 the psalmist praises Yahweh for having heard his cry "for mercy" (vv. 8,11) and sparing him from going "down to the pit" (v. 3). These two psalms are also linked by other significant language: cf. 28:1 and 30:8 ("To you, LORD, I call[ed]"); 28:2 and 30:2 ("call[ed] to you for help"); 28:7 ("he helps me") and 30:10 ("be my help").

28:1–2 Initial appeal to be heard.
28:1 *Rock.* See note on 18:2. *remain silent.* Do not act in my behalf. *pit.* Metaphor for the grave (see note on 30:1).
28:2 *lift up my hands.* In worship and prayer (see 63:4; 134:2; 141:2). *Most Holy Place.* The inner sanctuary of the temple (see 1Ki 6:5), where the ark of the covenant stood (see 1Ki 8:6–8); it was God's throne room on earth.
28:3–5 Prayer for the Lord, enthroned in the temple, to deliver his servant and deal in judgment with those who harbor malice toward the king and God's people and defy God himself.

28:3 *harbor malice.* See note on 5:9. *hearts.* See note on 4:7.
28:4 *Repay them.* See note on 5:10; see also Mt 16:27; 2Ti 4:14; Rev 20:12–13; 22:12.
28:5 *deeds of the LORD.* His redemption of Israel, the establishment of Israel as his kingdom (by covenant, Ex 19–24), and the appointment of the house of David (also by covenant, 2Sa 7) as his earthly regent over his people. *what his hands have done.* By "what his hands have done" (v. 4), "the wicked" (v. 3) show that they do not acknowledge Israel and David's regency as the work of God's hands. *he will tear.* Or "may he tear."
28:6–7 Joyful praise, in confidence of being heard (see note on 3:8).
28:7 *shield.* See note on 3:3. *heart.* See note on 4:7.
28:8–9 The Lord and his people (see note on 3:8).
28:8 *people ... anointed one.* These constitute a unity (see note on 2:2).

28:9 *Save ... bless.* God's two primary acts by which he effects his people's well-being: He saves from time to time as circumstances require; he blesses day by day to make their lives and labors fruitful. *your inheritance.* See Dt 9:29. *shepherd.* See introduction; see also 80:1; Isa 40:11; Jer 31:10; Eze 34; Mic 5:4 and note on Ps 23:1. The answer to this prayer—the last, full answer—has come in the ministry of the "good shepherd" (Jn 10:11,14).

PSALM 29

A psalm of David.

[1] Ascribe to the LORD, [z] you heavenly beings, [a]
 ascribe to the LORD glory [b] and strength.
[2] Ascribe to the LORD the glory due his name;
 worship the LORD in the splendor of his[a] holiness. [c]

[3] The voice [d] of the LORD is over the waters;
 the God of glory [e] thunders, [f]
 the LORD thunders over the mighty waters. [g]
[4] The voice of the LORD is powerful; [h]
 the voice of the LORD is majestic.
[5] The voice of the LORD breaks the cedars;
 the LORD breaks in pieces the cedars of Lebanon. [i]
[6] He makes Lebanon leap[j] like a calf,
 Sirion[b][k] like a young wild ox. [l]
[7] The voice of the LORD strikes
 with flashes of lightning. [m]
[8] The voice of the LORD shakes the desert;
 the LORD shakes the Desert of Kadesh. [n]
[9] The voice of the LORD twists the oaks[c][o]
 and strips the forests bare.
 And in his temple all cry, "Glory!" [p]

[10] The LORD sits enthroned over the flood; [q]
 the LORD is enthroned as King forever. [r]
[11] The LORD gives strength to his people; [s]
 the LORD blesses his people with peace. [t]

---

[a] 2 Or *LORD with the splendor of*   [b] 6 That is, Mount Hermon   [c] 9 Or *LORD makes the deer give birth*

29:1 [z] ver 2;
1Ch 16:28
[a] S 2Sa 1:19;
Ps 103:20; Isa 10:13
[b] Ps 8:1
29:2 [c] S 1Ch 16:29;
Ps 96:7-9
29:3 [d] Job 37:5
[e] S Ps 24:7; Ac 7:2
[f] S 1Sa 2:10; Ps 18:13;
46:6; 68:33; 77:17;
Jer 10:13; 25:30;
Joel 2:11; Am 1:2
[g] S Ex 15:10
29:4 [h] Ps 68:33
29:5 [i] S Jdg 9:15
29:6 [j] Ps 114:4
[k] Dt 3:9 [l] S Nu 23:22;
Job 39:9; Ps 92:10
29:7 [m] Eze 1:14;
Rev 8:5
29:8 [n] Nu 13:26;
S 20:1
29:9 [o] Isa 2:13;
Eze 27:6; Am 2:9
[p] Ps 26:8
29:10 [q] Ge 6:17
[r] S Ex 15:18
29:11 [s] S Ps 18:1;
28:8; 68:35
[t] S Lev 26:6;
S Nu 6:26

Ps 29 A hymn in praise of the King of creation, whose glory is trumpeted by the thunderclaps that rumble through the cloudy mass of winter's rainstorms as they rise above the Mediterranean ("the mighty waters," v. 3), and move from west to east across the face of the sky, sweeping over the Lebanon range (vv. 5–6) and reaching the wilds of (northern) Kadesh on the upper reaches of the Orontes River (v. 8). The glory of the Lord is not only visible in the creation (19:1–6; see introduction to that psalm; see also Ps 104); it is also audible in creation's most awesome voice. (The most powerful forces experienced by the ancients were earthquakes, the raging sea, and heavy thunderstorms.) This hymn to Yahweh ("the LORD") served also as a testimony and protest against the worship of the Canaanite god Baal, who was thought to be the divine power present in the thunderstorm (cf. 31:6). Its placement marks it as the hinge psalm in the concentric arrangement of Ps 25–33 (see introduction to Ps 25–33), a placement and function similar to that of Ps 19 (see introduction to Ps 15–24). In the midst of prayer and praise, it reminds those who meditate on the psalms and use them as their own that the One with whom they have to do is the mighty Lord over all that is. All creation displays his power and glory, evoking awe and praise (vv. 1–2), but his gracious ways with his people (v. 11) also invite confident prayer in every need.

In its structure a two-verse introduction and a two-verse conclusion enclose a seven-verse stanza. In both the introduction and the conclusion the name Yahweh ("the LORD") is sounded four times; in the body of the psalm it is heard ten times. "The voice of the LORD" is repeated seven times—the seven thunders of God. (The numbers four, seven and ten often signified completeness in OT number symbolism.)

29:1–2 A summons to all beings in the divine realm (see note on v. 1) to worship the Lord—adapted from a conventional call to praise in the liturgy of the temple (see 96:7–9; 1Ch 16:28–29).
29:1 *heavenly beings.* Lit. "sons of god(s)." Perhaps reference is to the angelic host (see 103:20; 148:2; Job 1:6 and TNIV text note; 2:1 and TNIV text note; Isa 6:2) or possibly to all those foolishly thought to be gods—as in Ps 97 (see 97:7), which has several thematic links with this psalm. The Lord alone must be acknowledged as the divine King.
29:2 *name.* See note on 5:11. *in the splendor of his holiness.* A rather literal translation of a difficult Hebrew phrase (see TNIV text note; see also 96:9; 110:3; 1Ch 16:29; 2Ch 20:21). It is uncertain whether it describes God himself or the sanctuary or the (priestly) garb the worshipers are to wear when they approach God. The use of an almost identical Hebrew phrase in 110:3 (translated "in holy splendor") seems to support the last alternative, but the Hebrew text and the context of 2Ch 20:21 favor "in the splendor of his holiness."
29:3–9 Praise of the Lord, whose voice is the crashing thunder (see 68:4,33). The sound and fury of creation's awesome displays of power proclaim the glory of Israel's God.
29:5 *cedars of Lebanon.* The most majestic and highly prized trees of the Middle East (see SS 5:15 and note).
29:6 *leap.* See 114:4 and note.
29:9 *temple.* A primary thematic link with Ps 23–28. Reference may be to the temple in Jerusalem or to God's heavenly temple, where he sits enthroned (see 2:4; 11:4; 113:5; Isa 6:1; 40:22) as the Lord of all creation. But perhaps it is the creation itself that here is named God's temple (see note on 24:2). Then the "all" (those who cry "Glory!") is absolutely all—all creation shouts his praise (cf. 150:6). *Glory!* See note on 26:8.

29:10–11 The Lord's absolute and everlasting rule is committed to his people's complete salvation and unmixed blessedness—the crowning comfort in a world where threatening tides seem to make everything uncertain.
29:10 *enthroned over the flood.* As the One who by his word brought the ordered creation out of the formless "deep" (Ge 1:2,6–10).

30:1 ^u S Ex 15:2
^v Job 11:8; Ps 63:9;
107:26; Pr 9:18;
Isa 14:15 ^w S Ps 22:17
30:2 ^x Ps 5:2; 88:13
^y S Nu 12:13
30:3 ^z S Ps 16:10;
S 56:13 ^a Ps 28:1;
55:23; 69:15; 86:13;
143:7; Pr 1:12;
Isa 38:17; Jnh 2:6
30:4 ^b Ps 33:1; 47:7;
68:4 ^c S Ps 16:3
^d Ex 3:15; Ps 33:21;
103:1; 145:21
30:5 ^e Ps 103:9
^f S Job 14:13
^g S Ezr 3:11
^h 2Sa 15:30; Ps 6:6;
126:6; Jer 31:16
ⁱ 2Co 4:17
30:6 ^j S Job 29:18
30:7 ^k S Dt 31:17
30:9 ^l S Job 33:18;
Isa 38:18 ^m S Ps 6:5;
88:11

PSALM 30

A psalm. A song. For the dedication of the temple. ^a *Of David.*

^{*1} I will exalt ^u you, Lord,
    for you lifted me out of the depths ^v
    and did not let my enemies gloat over me. ^w
² Lord my God, I called to you for help, ^x
    and you healed me. ^y
³ You, Lord, brought me up from the realm of the dead; ^z
    you spared me from going down to the pit. ^a

⁴ Sing ^b the praises of the Lord, you his faithful people; ^c
    praise his holy name. ^d
⁵ For his anger ^e lasts only a moment, ^f
    but his favor lasts a lifetime; ^g
weeping ^h may remain for a night,
    but rejoicing comes in the morning. ⁱ

⁶ When I felt secure, I said,
    "I will never be shaken." ^j
⁷ Lord, when you favored me,
    you made my royal mountain ^b stand firm;
but when you hid your face, ^k
    I was dismayed.

⁸ To you, Lord, I called;
    to the Lord I cried for mercy:
⁹ "What is gained if I am silenced,
    if I go down to the pit? ^l
Will the dust praise you?
    Will it proclaim your faithfulness? ^m

^a Title: Or *palace*   ^b 7 That is, Mount Zion

* 30:1-12 is numbered 30:2-13 in Hebrew texts.

Ps 30 A song of praise publicly celebrating the Lord's deliverance from the threat of death, probably brought on by illness ("you healed me," v. 2; see note on 7:17). For its relationship to Ps 28, see introduction to that psalm. The psalm is framed by commitments to praise (see vv. 1,12).
30 title *A song.* See titles of Ps 18; 45–46; 48; 65–68; 75–76; 83; 87–88; 92; 108—all psalms of praise except 83; 88. In addition there are the songs "of ascents" (Ps 120–134). *For the dedication of the temple. Of David.* If "Of David" indicates authorship, the most probable occasion for the psalm is recorded in 1Ch 21:1—22:6. In 1Ch 22:1–6 David dedicated both property and building materials for the temple, and he may well have intended that Ps 30 be used at the dedication of the temple itself. If this is the case, vv. 2–3 would refer to David's predicament in 1Ch 21:17–30. The "favor" of v. 5 would be an echo of the "mercy" of 1Ch 21:13, and v. 6 would refer to his sin of misplaced trust in a large, superior army (see 1Ch 21:1–8). Later, the psalm came to be applied to the exile experience of Israel. In Jewish liturgical practice dating from Talmudic times it is chanted at Hanukkah, the feast that celebrates the rededication of the temple by Judas Maccabeus (165 B.C.) after its desecration by Antiochus Epiphanes (168). In such communal use, the "I" of the psalm becomes the collective "person" of Israel—a common mode of speaking in the OT.
30:1–3 Introductory announcement of the occasion for praise.
30:1 *lifted me out of the depths.* The vivid imagery that associates distress with "the depths"—so expressive of universal human experience—is common in OT poetry (see 69:2,15; 71:20; 88:6; 130:1; La 3:55; Jnh 2:2). The depths are often linked, as here, with Sheol ("the realm of the dead," v. 3) and "the pit" (v. 3), together with a cluster of related associations: silence (see 31:17; 94:17; 115:17; 1Sa 2:9), darkness (see 88:6,12; 143:3; Job 10:21–22; 17:13; Ecc 6:4; La 3:6), destruction (see v. 9; 18:4; 55:23,

"decay"; 88:11; Isa 38:17; Hos 13:14), dust (see v. 9; 7:5; 22:15,29; Job 17:16; 40:13; Isa 26:19; 29:4), mire (see 40:2; 69:2,14), slime (see 40:2) and mud (see 40:2; Job 30:19). See also note on 49:14. *my enemies gloat over me.* See introduction to Ps 6.
30:3 *realm of the dead.* Figurative of a "brink-of-death" experience, as in 18:5; Jnh 2:2. *pit.* See note on 28:1.
30:4–5 Call to the gathered worshipers to take up the praise of God (see note on 9:1).
30:4 *faithful people.* See note on 4:3. *name.* Lit. "memorial" or "name of renown" (see 97:12; 135:13; Isa 26:8; Hos 12:5). The Hebrew evokes Ex 3:15 and refers to the name around which clustered memories of all that God had done, especially in Israel's history.
30:5 *anger.* See note on 2:5. *lasts only a moment.* See Isa 54:7. *remain for a night.* Lit. "come in at evening to lodge." The figure is that of a guest lodging for only one night.
30:6–10 Expanded recollection of the Lord's gracious deliverance.
30:6–7 In his security he had grown arrogant, forgetful of who had made his "mountain stand firm," but the Lord reminded him.
30:6 *never be shaken.* He spoke as do the wicked (see 10:6), hence lost the blessing of the righteous (see 15:5). *shaken.* See note on 10:6.
30:7 *made my royal mountain stand firm.* Reference may be to David's security in his mountain fortress, Zion; or that mountain fortress may here serve as a metaphor for David's state as a vigorous and victorious king, the "mountain" on which he sat with such secure confidence in God. *hid your face.* See note on 13:1.
30:8–10 Shattered strength swept away all self-reliance; at the brink of death his cries for God's mercy rose.
30:9 See note on 6:5. *your faithfulness.* To your covenant.

¹⁰ Hear, ⁿ LORD, and be merciful to me; ^o
LORD, be my help. ^p”

¹¹ You turned my wailing ^q into dancing; ^r
you removed my sackcloth ^s and clothed me with joy, ^t
¹² that my heart may sing your praises and not be silent.
LORD my God, I will praise ^u you forever. ^v

PSALM 31

31:1–4pp — Ps 71:1–3

For the director of music. A psalm of David.

^{*1} In you, LORD, I have taken refuge; ^w
let me never be put to shame;
deliver me in your righteousness. ^x
² Turn your ear to me, ^y
come quickly to my rescue; ^z
be my rock of refuge, ^a
a strong fortress to save me.
³ Since you are my rock and my fortress, ^b
for the sake of your name ^c lead and guide me.
⁴ Keep me free from the trap ^d that is set for me,
for you are my refuge. ^e
⁵ Into your hands I commit my spirit; ^f
redeem me, LORD, my faithful God. ^g

⁶ I hate those who cling to worthless idols; ^h
as for me, I trust in the LORD. ⁱ
⁷ I will be glad and rejoice in your love,
for you saw my affliction ^j
and knew the anguish ^k of my soul.
⁸ You have not given me into the hands ^l of the enemy
but have set my feet in a spacious place. ^m

⁹ Be merciful to me, LORD, for I am in distress; ⁿ
my eyes grow weak with sorrow, ^o
my soul and body ^p with grief.

---

* 31:1-24 is numbered 31:2-25 in Hebrew texts.

30:10 ⁿ S Ps 17:1
^o Ps 4:1 ^p S Ps 20:2
30:11 ^q S Est 4:1
^r S Ex 15:20
^s S 2Sa 3:31;
S Ps 35:13
^t S Dt 16:15; S Ps 16:9
30:12 ^u Ps 35:18;
75:1; 118:21; Rev 11:17
^v Ps 44:8; 52:9
31:1 ^w S Ps 7:1
^x Ps 5:8
31:2 ^y S Ps 6:4
^z S Ex 2:17
^a S 2Sa 22:3;
S Ps 18:2
31:3 ^b S Ps 18:2
^c S Ps 23:3
31:4 ^d S 1Sa 28:9;
S Job 18:10 ^e Ps 9:9
31:5 ^f Lk 23:46;
Ac 7:59 ^g Isa 45:19;
65:16
31:6 ^h S Dt 32:21
ⁱ S Ps 4:5
31:7 ^j S Ps 13:3
^k S Ps 25:17; Lk 22:44
31:8 ^l S Dt 32:30
^m S 2Sa 22:20
31:9 ⁿ Ps 4:1
^o Ps 6:7 ^p Ps 63:1

30:11–12 God answered—and David vows to prolong his praise forever (see note on 7:17). Dancing and joy replace wailing and sackcloth, so that songs of praise, not silence, may attend the acts of God.

30:11 *sackcloth.* A coarse, black fabric (see Isa 50:3; Rev 11:3 and note) woven of goat hair and commonly used for making sacks. It was worn as a symbol of mourning (see 35:13; 69:11 and note on Ge 37:34).

30:12 *heart.* Lit. "glory" (see note on 7:5).

Ps 31 A prayer for deliverance when confronted by a conspiracy so powerful and open that all David's friends abandoned him. According to Lk 23:46, Jesus on the cross applied Ps 31:5 to his own circumstances; thus those who share in his sufferings at the hands of anti-Christian forces are encouraged to hear and use this psalm in a new light (see Ac 7:59; 1Pe 4:19). No psalm expresses a more sturdy trust in the Lord when powerful human forces threaten. The heart of the prayer itself is found in vv. 9–18, which are both preceded and followed by nine Hebrew poetic lines—stanzas that resound with the theme of trust (see v. 14). Verse 13, at the center of the psalm, expresses most clearly the prayer's occasion. For the linkage of this psalm with Ps 27, see introduction to that psalm.

31 title *For the director of music.* See note on Ps 4 title.

31:1–5 Initial appeal to the Lord, the faithful refuge.

31:1 *righteousness.* See note on 4:1.

31:2 *rock.* See note on 18:2.

31:3 *for the sake of your name.* God's honor is at stake in the safety of his servant now under attack (see note on 23:3). *name.* See note on 5:11. *lead and guide.* As a shepherd (see 23:2–3 and notes).

31:4 *trap that is set for me.* By his enemies (see v. 11; see also note on 9:15).

31:5 *Into your hands I commit my spirit.* The climactic expression of trust in the Lord—echoed by Jesus in Lk 23:46. *commit.* Lit. "deposit" (as in Jer 36:20, "put"), here in the very hands of God, thus entrusting to God's care (see Lev 6:4; 1Ki 14:27). *my spirit.* His very life. *redeem.* See note on 25:22. *faithful God.* The trustworthy God (see note on 30:9).

31:6–8 Confession of loyal trust in the Lord, whose past mercies to David when enemies threatened are joyfully recalled.

31:6 *hate.* Refuse to be associated with. *who cling to worthless idols.* See Jnh 2:8. *cling to.* Literally "watch" (expectantly for the help of; see 59:9 and note).

31:7 *love.* See vv. 16,21; see also note on 6:4. *soul.* See note on 6:3.

31:8 *spacious place.* See note on 18:19.

31:9–13 The distress described: He is utterly drained physically and emotionally (see vv. 9–10; see also 22:14–15); all his friends have abandoned him like a piece of broken pottery (see vv. 11–12); and all this because the conspiracy against him is so strong (v. 13).

31:9 *eyes grow weak.* See note on 13:3. *soul.* See note on 6:3.

31:10 *q* ver 7
r Ps 6:6 *s* Ps 22:15;
32:4; 38:10; 73:26
t Ps 25:18 *u* Ps 6:2
31:11 *v* Dt 30:7;
Ps 3:7; 25:19; 102:8
w S Ps 22:6 *x* Ps 38:11
31:12 *y* Ps 28:1;
88:4
31:13 *z* S Lev 19:16;
Ps 50:20 *a* S Job 18:11;
Isa 13:8; Jer 6:25;
20:3,10; 46:5; 49:5;
La 2:22 *b* Ps 41:7;
56:6; 71:10; 83:3
c S Ge 37:18;
S Mt 12:14
31:14 *d* Ps 4:5
31:15 *e* S Job 14:5
31:16 *f* S Nu 6:25
g S Ps 6:4
31:17 *h* S Ps 22:5
i 1Sa 2:9; Ps 94:17;
115:17
31:18 *j* Ps 120:2;
Pr 10:18; 26:24
k 1Sa 2:3; Jude 1:15
31:19 *l* S Ps 27:13;
Ro 11:22 *m* Ps 23:5
n Ps 2:12
31:20 *o* Ps 55:8
p S Ps 17:8
q S Ge 37:18
31:21 *r* Ps 28:6
s S Ps 17:7 *t* 1Sa 23:7
31:22 *u* Ps 116:11
v Job 6:9; 17:1;
Ps 37:9; 88:5;
Isa 38:12 *w* Ps 6:9;
66:19; 116:1; 145:19

¹⁰ My life is consumed by anguish *q*
    and my years by groaning; *r*
my strength fails *s* because of my affliction, *a t*
    and my bones grow weak. *u*
¹¹ Because of all my enemies, *v*
    I am the utter contempt *w* of my neighbors; *x*
I am a dread to my friends—
    those who see me on the street flee from me.
¹² I am forgotten as though I were dead; *y*
    I have become like broken pottery.
¹³ For I hear many whispering, *z*
    "Terror on every side!" *a*
They conspire against me *b*
    and plot to take my life. *c*

¹⁴ But I trust *d* in you, LORD;
    I say, "You are my God."
¹⁵ My times *e* are in your hands;
    deliver me from the hands of my enemies,
    from those who pursue me.
¹⁶ Let your face shine *f* on your servant;
    save me in your unfailing love. *g*
¹⁷ Let me not be put to shame, *h* LORD,
    for I have cried out to you;
but let the wicked be put to shame
    and be silent *i* in the realm of the dead.
¹⁸ Let their lying lips *j* be silenced,
    for with pride and contempt
    they speak arrogantly *k* against the righteous.

¹⁹ How great is your goodness, *l*
    which you have stored up for those who fear you,
which you bestow in the sight of all *m*
    on those who take refuge *n* in you.
²⁰ In the shelter *o* of your presence you hide *p* them
    from all human intrigues; *q*
you keep them safe in your dwelling
    from accusing tongues.

²¹ Praise be to the LORD, *r*
    for he showed me the wonders of his love *s*
    when I was in a city under siege. *t*
²² In my alarm *u* I said,
    "I am cut off *v* from your sight!"
Yet you heard my cry *w* for mercy
    when I called to you for help.

a 10 Or *guilt*

31:10 *bones.* See note on 6:2.
31:11–12 Abandonment by friends was a common experience at a time when God seemed to have withdrawn his favor (see 38:11; 41:9; 69:8; 88:8,18; Job 19:13–19; Jer 12:6; 15:17).
31:13 *many whispering.* See note on 5:9. *Terror on every side!* See notes on Jer 6:25; 20:3.

    31:14–18 His trust in the Lord is unwavering; his defense against his powerful enemies is his reliance on God's faithfulness and discerning judgment.
31:14 Cf. v. 22.

    31:15 *My times are in your hands.* All the events and circumstances of life are in the hands of the Lord, "my God" (v. 14).
31:16 *face shine.* See note on 13:1.
31:17–18 *but let the wicked … be silent.* See note on 5:10.
31:18 *lying lips.* See note on 5:9. *righteous.* See note on 1:5.

31:19–20 Confident anticipation of God's saving help (see note on 3:8).

    31:19 *stored up.* David deposits his life in the hands of God to share in the covenant benefits that God has stored up for his faithful servants ("goodness"; see 27:13; Ex 18:9; Nu 10:29,32; Dt 26:11; Jos 21:45; 23:14–15; 2Ch 6:41; Ne 9:25,35; Isa 63:7; Jer 33:9; see also Jer 31:12,14, "bounty"). *fear.* See note on 15:4. *bestow in the sight of all.* Thus showing the Lord's approval of and his standing with his faithful servants, in contrast to the accusations of their adversaries (see 86:17).
31:20 *shelter of your presence.* See note on 27:5. *accusing tongues.* See "whispering" (v. 13) and "lying lips" (v. 18).
31:21–22 Praise anticipating deliverance (see note on 12:5–6).
31:21 *city under siege.* Metaphor for the threat he had experienced.
31:22 *cut off from your sight.* See note on 13:1.

²³ Love the LORD, all his faithful people!ˣ
    The LORD preserves those who are true to him,ʸ
    but the proud he pays backᶻ in full.
²⁴ Be strong and take heart,ᵃ
    all you who hope in the LORD.

PSALM 32

*Of David. A maskil.*ᵃ

¹ Blessed are those
    whose transgressions are forgiven,
    whose sins are covered.ᵇ
² Blessed are those
    whose sin the LORD does not count against themᶜ
    and in whose spirit is no deceit.ᵈ

³ When I kept silent,ᵉ
    my bones wasted awayᶠ
    through my groaningᵍ all day long.
⁴ For day and night
    your hand was heavyʰ on me;
    my strength was sappedⁱ
    as in the heat of summer.ᵇ

⁵ Then I acknowledged my sin to you
    and did not cover up my iniquity.ʲ
    I said, "I will confessᵏ
    my transgressionsˡ to the LORD."
And you forgave
    the guilt of my sin.ᵐ

⁶ Therefore let all the faithful pray to you

31:23 ˣS Ps 4:3
ʸS Ps 18:25; Rev 2:10
ᶻDt 32:41; Ps 94:2
31:24 ᵃPs 27:14
32:1 ᵇPs 85:2; 103:3
32:2 ᶜS Ro 4:7-8*
ᵈJn 1:47; Rev 14:5
32:3 ᵉS Job 31:34
ᶠPs 31:10
ᵍS Job 3:24; Ps 6:6
32:4 ʰ1Sa 5:6;
S Job 9:34; Ps 38:2;
39:10 ⁱPs 22:15
32:5 ʲJob 31:33
ᵏPr 28:13 ˡPs 103:12
ᵐS Lev 26:40; 1Jn 1:9

ᵃ Title: Probably a literary or musical term   ᵇ 4 The Hebrew has *Selah* (a word of uncertain meaning)
here and at the end of verses 5 and 7.

31:23–24 Praise culminates by encouraging the saints (see 62:8). **31:23** *faithful people.* See note on 4:3. *those ... true to him.* Those who maintain moral integrity and faithfulness to the Lord. *the proud.* Those who refuse to live in humble reliance on the Lord. They arrogantly try to make their way in the world either as a law to themselves (see, e.g., v. 18; 10:2–11; 73:6; 94:2–7; Dt 8:14; Isa 2:17; Eze 28:2,5; Hos 13:6) or by relying on false gods (see Jer 13:9–10). Hence "the proud" is often equivalent to "the wicked."

Ps 32 A grateful testimony of joy for God's gift of forgiveness toward those who with integrity confess their sins and are receptive to God's rule in their lives. The psalm appears to be a liturgical dialogue between David and God in the presence of the worshipers at the sanctuary. In vv. 1–2 and again in v. 11 David speaks to the assembly; in vv. 3–7 he speaks to God (in their hearing); in vv. 8–10 he is addressed by one of the Lord's priests (but see note on vv. 8–10). In traditional Christian usage, the psalm has been numbered among the penitential psalms (see introduction to Ps 6). Its placement in the concentric arrangement of Ps 25–33 (see introduction to Ps 25–33) suggests that the editors of the Psalter intended it to stand in counterpoint to Ps 26 (see introduction to that psalm). **32 title** *maskil.* Occurs also in the titles of Ps 42; 44–45; 52–55; 74; 78; 88–89; 142. The Hebrew word perhaps indicates that these psalms contain instruction in godliness (see 14:2; 41:1, "those who have regard"; 53:2, "any who understand"; but see also 47:7, where it is rendered "psalm").

32:1–2 Exuberant proclamation of the happy state of those who experience God's forgiveness. *Blessed ... Blessed.* See note on 1:1. Repetition underscores. *are forgiven ... are covered ... does not count against them.* Repetition with variation emphasizes and illumines. For Paul's use of these verses, see Ro 4:6–8.

32:2 *in whose spirit is no deceit.* Only those honest with God receive pardon.

32:3–5 Testimony to a personal experience of God's pardon. God's heavy hand, pressing down "day and night" on the stubborn silence of unacknowledged sin, filled life with groaning, but full confession brought blessed relief. Neither the sin nor the form of suffering is identified, other than that the latter was physically and psychologically devastating. But it would be uncharacteristic of the Psalms to speak of mere emotional disturbance brought on by suppressed guilt. Some affliction, perhaps illness, was most likely the instrument of God's discipline (see Ps 38). **32:4** *strength was sapped.* Under God's heavy hand he wilted like a plant in the heat of summer. For *Selah,* see TNIV text note and note on 3:2. **32:5** Again repetition is used (see note on vv. 1–2). *sin ... iniquity ... transgressions.* See 51:1–2; the three most common OT words for evil thoughts and actions (see Isa 59:12). *confess.* See Ps 51; 2Sa 12:13.

32:6–7 A chastened confession that life is secure only with God. **32:6** Though addressed to God as confession, it is also intended for the ears of the fellow worshipers. He admonishes them to "seek the LORD while he may be found ... while he is near" (Isa 55:6) and not to foolishly provoke his withdrawal—and the coming near of his heavy hand—as David had done. A God who forgives is a God to whom one can entrust and devote one's life (see 130:4). *faithful.* See note on 4:3. *mighty waters.* Powerful imagery for threatening forces or circumstances. This and related imagery was borrowed from ancient Near Eastern creation myths. In many of these a primal mass of chaotic waters (their threatening and destructive forces were often depicted as a many-headed monster of the deep; see 74:13–14 and note) had to be subdued

32:6 *n* Ps 69:13;
Isa 55:6 *o* Ps 69:1
p S Ex 15:10 *q* Isa 43:2
32:7 *r* S Ps 9:35
s S Ps 9:9 *t* S Jdg 5:1
32:8 *u* S Ps 25:8
v Ps 34:11 *w* Ps 33:18
32:9 *x* S Job 30:11;
S 39:10; Jas 3:3
32:10 *y* Ro 2:9
z Ps 4:5; Pr 16:20
32:11 *a* Ps 64:10
33:1 *b* S Ps 5:11;
S 101:1 *c* Ps 147:1
d Ps 11:7
33:2 *e* S Ge 4:21;
1Co 14:7; Rev 5:8
f Ps 92:3; 144:9
33:3 *g* Ps 40:3;
Isa 42:10; S Rev 5:9
h S Job 3:7; Ps 35:27;
47:1
33:4 *i* S Ps 19:8
j Ps 119:142; Rev 19:9;
22:6 *k* Ps 18:25; 25:10

while you may be found; *n*
surely the rising *o* of the mighty waters *p*
    will not reach them. *q*
[7] You are my hiding place; *r*
you will protect me from trouble *s*
and surround me with songs of deliverance. *t*

[8] I will instruct *u* you and teach you *v* in the way you should go;
I will counsel you with my loving eye on *w* you.
[9] Do not be like the horse or the mule,
which have no understanding
but must be controlled by bit and bridle *x*
or they will not come to you.
[10] Many are the woes of the wicked, *y*
but the LORD's unfailing love
surrounds those who trust *z* in him.

[11] Rejoice in the LORD *a* and be glad, you righteous;
sing, all you who are upright in heart!

PSALM 33

[1] Sing joyfully *b* to the LORD, you righteous;
it is fitting *c* for the upright *d* to praise him.
[2] Praise the LORD with the harp; *e*
make music to him on the ten-stringed lyre. *f*
[3] Sing to him a new song; *g*
play skillfully, and shout for joy. *h*

[4] For the word of the LORD is right *i* and true; *j*
he is faithful *k* in all he does.

---

by the creator-god before he could fashion the world and/or rule as the divine king over the earth. Though in these myths the chaotic waters were subdued when the present world was created, they remained a constant threat to the security and well-being of the present order in the earth (the realm of dry land that is the normal habitat for people and animals). Hence by association they were linked with anything that in human experience endangered or troubled that order. They were also associated with the sea, whose angry waves seemed determined at times to engulf the land. Since in Canaanite mythology Sea and Death were the two great enemies of Baal ("lord" of earth), imagery drawn from both realms was used by OT poets, sometimes side by side, to depict threats and distress (see 18:4–5,16; 42:7; 65:7; 74:12–14; 77:16,19; 89:9–10; 93:3–4; 124:4–5; 144:7–8; Job 7:12; 26:12; 38:8–11; Isa 5:30; 8:7–8; 17:12–14; 51:9–10; Jer 5:22; 47:2; 51:55; Hab 3:8–10; see also note on SS 8:7). For imagery associated with the realm of death, see notes on 30:1; 49:14.

32:7 *surround me with songs of deliverance.* Because of your help, I will be surrounded by people celebrating your acts of deliverance, as I bring my thank offerings to you (see notes on 7:17; 9:1; see also 35:27; 51:8).

32:8–10 A priestly word of godly instruction, either to David (do not be foolish toward God again) or to those who have just been exhorted to trust in the Lord (to trust add obedience). Some believe that the psalmist himself here turns to others to warn them against the ways in which he has fallen (see 51:13).

32:9 God's servants must be wiser than beasts, more open to God's will than horses and mules are to the will of their masters (see Isa 1:3).

32:10 *unfailing love.* See note on 6:4.

32:11 A final word to the assembled worshipers—let the praise of God resound (see note on 9:1). See also note on 1:5. *heart.* See note on 4:7.

Ps 33 A liturgy in praise of the Lord, the sovereign God of Israel—a counterpoint to the acrostic prayer of Ps 25. These two psalms frame the intervening psalms (see introduction to Ps

25–33). In the Psalms, calls to praise (as in vv. 1–3) and motivations for praise (as in vv. 4–19) belong to the language of praise (see note on 9:1). Most likely the voices of the Levitical choir (see 1Ch 16:7–36; 25:1) are heard in this psalm. Perhaps the choir leader spoke vv. 1–3, the choir vv. 4–19, and the people responded with the words of vv. 20–22. The original occasion is unknown, but reference to a "new song" (see note on v. 3) suggests a national deliverance, such as Judah experienced in the time of Jehoshaphat (see 2Ch 20) or Hezekiah (see 2Ki 19); see vv. 10–11,16–17. Along with Ps 1–2; 10 (but see introduction to Ps 9), this is one of only four psalms in Book I without a superscription.

Although structurally not an alphabetic acrostic like the psalm that follows it, the length of the psalm (22 verses) has been determined by the length of the Hebrew alphabet (22 letters); see Ps 38; 103; La 5. The body of the psalm is framed by a three-verse introduction (call to praise) and a three-verse conclusion (response to praise). In vv. 4–19 are heard the praise of the Lord, developed in two parts of eight verses each (vv. 4–11,12–19). In the first of these a four-verse stanza (vv. 6–9) has been inserted between the two halves of the main stanza (vv. 4–5,10–11) to reinforce its theme. A similar use of this poetic device can be found in Ps 77 (see introduction to that psalm and note on 77:16–19).

33:1–3 The call to praise. Cf. Eph 5:19.

33:1 *righteous.* The assembly of worshipers (see note on 1:5).

33:3 *new song.* Celebrating God's saving act, as in 40:3; 96:1; 98:1; 144:9; 149:1; see Isa 42:10; Rev 5:9; 14:3; see also note on 7:17.

33:4–19 The praise, in two eight-verse parts.

33:4–11 Under the Lord's rule by his sovereign "word" (v. 4) his "plans" for his people "stand firm" (v. 11), even as the creation order "stood firm" (v. 9) because it was ordered by his sovereign "word" (v. 6). Hence his chosen people are the blessed nation (see vv. 12–19).

33:4 *word.* God's royal word, by which he governs all things (see 107:20; 147:15,18). *right and true.* Not chaotic, devious or erratic. Under the Lord's rule, order and goodness are present in the creation.

⁵ The Lord loves righteousness and justice;ᶦ
  the earth is full of his unfailing love.ᵐ

⁶ By the wordⁿ of the Lord the heavens were made,ᵒ
  their starry hostᵖ by the breath of his mouth.

⁷ He gathers the waters�q of the sea into jarsª;ʳ
  he puts the deep into storehouses.

⁸ Let all the earth fear the Lord;ˢ
  let all the people of the worldᵗ revere him.ᵘ

⁹ For he spoke, and it came to be;
  he commanded,ᵛ and it stood firm.

¹⁰ The Lord foilsʷ the plansˣ of the nations;ʸ
   he thwarts the purposes of the peoples.

¹¹ But the plans of the Lord stand firmᶻ forever,
   the purposesª of his heart through all generations.

¹² Blessed is the nation whose God is the Lord,ᵇ
   the people he choseᶜ for his inheritance.ᵈ

¹³ From heaven the Lord looks downᵉ
   and sees all humankind;

¹⁴ from his dwelling placeᵍ he watches
   all who live on earth—

¹⁵ he who formsʰ the hearts of all,
   who considers everything they do.ᶦ

¹⁶ No king is saved by the size of his army;ʲ
   no warrior escapes by his great strength.

¹⁷ A horseᵏ is a vain hope for deliverance;
   despite all its great strength it cannot save.

¹⁸ But the eyesᶦ of the Lord are on those who fear him,
   on those whose hope is in his unfailing love,ᵐ

¹⁹ to deliver them from deathⁿ
   and keep them alive in famine.ᵒ

²⁰ We waitᵖ in hope for the Lord;
   he is our help and our shield.

²¹ In him our hearts rejoice,q
   for we trust in his holy name.ʳ

²² May your unfailing loveˢ be with us, Lord,
   even as we put our hope in you.

PSALM 34ᵇ

*Of David. When he pretended to be insane before Abimelek, who drove him
away, and he left.*

*¹ I will extol the Lord at all times;ᵗ
  his praise will always be on my lips.

ª 7 Or *sea as into a heap*   ᵇ This psalm is an acrostic poem, the verses of which begin with the
successive letters of the Hebrew alphabet.

* 34:1-22 is numbered 34:2-23 in Hebrew texts.

33:5 ᦦPs 11:7
ᵐ Ps 6:4
33:6 ⁿS Ge 1:3;
Heb 11:3 ᵒS Ex 8:19;
S 2Ch 2:12 ᵖS Ge 1:16
33:7 qS Ge 1:10
ʳS Jos 3:16
33:8 ˢS Dt 6:13;
Ps 2:11 ᵗPs 49:1;
Isa 18:3; Mic 1:2
ᵘS Dt 14:23
33:9 ᵛPs 148:5
33:10 ʷIsa 44:25
ˣS Job 5:12 ʸPs 2:1
33:11 ᶻS Nu 23:19
ªJer 51:12,29
33:12 ᵇPs 144:15
ᶜS Ex 8:22; Dt 7:6;
Ps 4:3; 65:4; 84:4
ᵈS Ex 34:9
33:13 ᵉPs 53:2;
102:19 ᶠJob 28:24;
Ps 11:4; 14:2;
S Heb 4:13
33:14 ᵍS Lev 15:31;
1Ki 8:39
33:15 ʰJob 10:8;
Ps 119:73 ᦦS Job 10:4;
Jer 32:19
33:16 ᦦIsa 14:6
33:17 ᵏS Ps 20:7
33:18 ᦦS Ex 3:16;
S Ps 11:4; 1Pe 3:12
ᵐS Ps 6:4
33:19 ⁿPs 56:13;
Ac 12:11 ᵒS Job 5:20
33:20 ᵖS Ps 27:14
33:21 qS 1Sa 2:1;
S Joel 2:23
ʳS Ps 30:4; S 99:3
33:22 ˢPs 6:4
34:1 ᵗPs 71:6;
S Eph 5:20; 1Th 5:18

33:5 *loves.* Delights in doing. *righteousness and justice.* See
note on 4:1. *his unfailing love.* Here, his goodness to all his creatures (see 36:5–9; 104:27–28; see also note on 6:4).
33:6 *word.* God's creating word (see v. 9; 104:7; 119:89; Ge 1;
Job 38:8–11; Heb 11:3).
33:7 *into jars…storehouses.* Like a householder storing up olive
oil and grain (see 104:9; Ge 1:9–10; Job 38:8–11; Pr 8:29; Jer 5:22).
33:8 *all the earth…all the people.* Not only Israel, but all humankind, for all experience the goodness of his sovereign rule
(see note on 9:1)—but he foils all their contrary designs (vv.
10–11). *fear the Lord.* See v. 18; see also note on 15:4.
33:11 *heart.* See note on 4:7.
33:12–19 Israel is safe and secure under God's protective rule.

33:12 *Blessed.* See note on 1:1. *people he chose for his inheritance.* Israel (see Dt 9:29).
33:16 *king.* Nation (see v. 12) and king constitute an organic
social unit (see 28:8 and note).
33:18–19 This concluding couplet of the second eight-verse
unit of praise contrasts with the concluding couplet of the first
(vv. 10–11); both are climactic, and together they voice the
heart of the praise.
33:18,22 *unfailing love.* Here, his covenant favor toward Israel
(see note on 6:4).
33:20–22 The people's response: faith's commitment
expressed in confession (vv. 20–21) and petition (v. 22).
33:20 *shield.* See note on 3:3.
33:21 *hearts.* See note on 4:7. *name.* See note on 5:11.

34:2 *u* Ps 44:8;
Jer 9:24; 1Co 1:31
v Ps 69:32; 107:42;
119:74
34:3 *w* Ps 63:3;
86:12; Da 4:37;
Jn 17:1; Ro 15:6
x S Ex 15:2
34:4 *y* S Ex 32:11;
Ps 77:2 *z* ver 17;
Ps 18:43; 22:4; 56:13;
86:13
34:5 *a* S Ex 34:29
b Ps 25:3; 44:15; 69:7;
83:16
34:6 *c* Ps 25:17
34:7 *d* S Ge 32:1;
S Da 3:28; S Mt 18:10
e Ps 22:4; 37:40; 41:1;
97:10; Isa 31:5;
Ac 12:11
34:8 *f* Heb 6:5;
1Pe 2:3 *g* S Ps 2:12
34:9 *h* S Dt 6:13;
Rev 14:7 *i* S Ps 23:1
34:10 *j* S Ps 23:1
34:11 *k* Ps 66:16
l S Ps 32:8
m S Ps 19:9
34:12 *n* Ecc 3:13
34:13 *o* Ps 39:1;
141:3; Pr 13:3; 21:23;
Jas 1:26 *p* S Ps 12:2;
1Pe 2:22
34:14 *q* Ps 37:27;
Isa 1:17; 3Jn 1:11
r S Ro 14:19
34:15 *s* Ps 33:18
t S Job 23:10; S 36:7

² I will glory *u* in the LORD;
    let the afflicted hear and rejoice. *v*
³ Glorify the LORD *w* with me;
    let us exalt *x* his name together.

⁴ I sought the LORD, *y* and he answered me;
    he delivered *z* me from all my fears.
⁵ Those who look to him are radiant; *a*
    their faces are never covered with shame. *b*
⁶ This poor man called, and the LORD heard him;
    he saved him out of all his troubles. *c*
⁷ The angel of the LORD *d* encamps around those who fear him,
    and he delivers *e* them.

⁸ Taste and see that the LORD is good; *f*
    blessed are those who take refuge *g* in him.
⁹ Fear the LORD, *h* you his holy people,
    for those who fear him lack nothing. *i*
¹⁰ The lions may grow weak and hungry,
    but those who seek the LORD lack no good thing. *j*
¹¹ Come, my children, listen *k* to me;
    I will teach you *l* the fear of the LORD. *m*
¹² Whoever of you loves life *n*
    and desires to see many good days,
¹³ keep your tongue *o* from evil
    and your lips from telling lies. *p*
¹⁴ Turn from evil and do good; *q*
    seek peace *r* and pursue it.

¹⁵ The eyes of the LORD *s* are on the righteous *t*

Ps 34–37 This small grouping of four psalms is framed by two alphabetic acrostics that contain wisdom-like instruction (see essay, p. 750) in godliness and related warnings concerning the fate of the wicked—instruction and warnings that reinforce key themes in the two enclosed prayers (Ps 35–36).
Ps 34 An alphabetic acrostic that begins with praise of the Lord for deliverance in answer to prayer (vv. 1–7), then shifts to wisdom-like instruction. This shift is unusual in the Psalter (but see also Ps 92); more commonly, praise of the Lord leads to a call to praise, as in v. 3 (see note on 9:1). Together with Ps 37 it frames the two intervening psalms (see introduction to Ps 34–37). The structure of Ps 34 is somewhat complex, yet it is strikingly effective. Following an introduction of three verses, the poem's themes are developed in stanzas of four verses (4–7), seven verses (8–14), four verses (15–18) and four verses (19–22). For further details, see following notes.
34 title The superscription assigns this psalm to the occasion in David's life (see note on Ps 3 title) narrated in 1Sa 21:10–15—but note "Abimelek" rather than "Achish" (perhaps Abimelek was a traditional dynastic name or title for Philistine kings; see Ge 20; 21:22–34; 26). Not all agree with this tradition, however; some feel that it is more likely that early Hebrew editors of the Psalms linked 1Sa 21 with Ps 34 on the basis of word association (the Hebrew for "pretended to be insane," 1Sa 21:13, comes from the same root as the Hebrew used here for "Taste," v. 8).
34:1–7 Praise for the Lord's deliverance in answer to prayer.
34:1–3 Commitment to continual praise of the Lord—so that the godly who are afflicted may be encouraged (v. 2; see also the instruction that follows in vv. 8–22).
34:2 *glory in the LORD.* That is, give the Lord all the praise.
34:3 *name.* See note on 5:11.
34:4–7 The occasion: God's saving answer to prayer. The theme is developed in alternating lines—an *a-b/a-b* pattern (note the shift from first-person singular references to third-person plural references—what Yahweh has done for the psalmist he will do for all those who "fear him," v. 7). For thematic links with vv.

15–18, see note on those verses.
34:5 *radiant.* With joy (see Isa 60:5).
A **34:6** *poor.* Here, as often in the Psalms, "poor" characterizes not necessarily one who has no possessions but one who is (and recognizes that he is) without resources to effect his own deliverance (or secure his own life, safety or well-being)—and so is dependent upon God.
34:7 *angel of the LORD.* God's heavenly representative, his "messenger," sent to effect his will on earth (see 35:5–6; see also note on Ge 16:7). *encamps around.* The line speaks of the security with which the Lord surrounds his people, individually and collectively; it does not necessarily teach a doctrine of individual "guardian angels." *those who fear him.* Those described in vv. 8–14 (see note on 25:12).
A C **34:8–14** Instruction in "the fear of the LORD." These verses are thematically linked, with a title line (v. 11) at the center—Hebrew authors often centered key lines (see note on 6:6). Note the pattern of the imperatives: "Taste" (v. 8), "Fear" (v. 9), "Come" (v. 11), "keep" (v. 13), "Turn" (v. 14). A symmetrical development of the theme "good" dominates the stanza: Because the Lord is "good" (v. 8), those who trust in him will lack nothing "good" (v. 10); but in order to experience "good days" (v. 12) they must shun evil and "do good" (v. 14). To trust and obey—that is "the fear of the LORD." On the instruction of this stanza, see Ps 37. For Peter's use of vv. 12–16, see 1Pe 3:8–12.
34:8 *blessed.* See note on 1:1.
34:9 *Fear the LORD.* See v. 11; see also note on 15:4. *holy people.* See notes on Ex 3:5; Lev 11:44; Ro 6:22; 1Co 1:2; 1Pe 1:16.
34:11 *Come, my children.* Conventional language of the wisdom teachers (see Introduction to Proverbs: Purpose and Teaching).
34:13 See 15:2–3; Jas 3:5–10. For the tongue as a weapon, see note on 5:9.
34:14 *Turn from evil and do good.* A key link with Ps 37 (see 37:27). *seek peace.* See 37:37; 120:7; Pr 12:20; Zec 8:19 (also Zec 8:16–17); Mt 5:9; Ro 12:18; 1Co 7:15; 2Co 13:11; 1Th 5:13; Heb 12:14; Jas 3:17–18.

and his ears are attentive [u] to their cry.
[16] The face of the LORD is against [v] those who do evil, [w]
to blot out their name [x] from the earth.

[17] The righteous cry out, and the LORD hears [y] them;
he delivers them from all their troubles.
[18] The LORD is close [z] to the brokenhearted [a]
and saves those who are crushed in spirit.

[19] The righteous may have many troubles, [b]
but the LORD delivers them from them all; [c]
[20] he protects all their bones,
not one of them will be broken. [d]

[21] Evil will slay the wicked; [e]
the foes of the righteous will be condemned.
[22] The LORD redeems [f] his servants;
no one who takes refuge [g] in him will be condemned.

PSALM 35

Of David.

[1] Contend, [h] LORD, with those who contend with me;
fight [i] against those who fight against me.
[2] Take up shield [j] and armor;
arise [k] and come to my aid. [l]
[3] Brandish spear [m] and javelin [a][n]
against those who pursue me.
Say to me,
"I am your salvation. [o]"

[4] May those who seek my life [p]
be disgraced [q] and put to shame; [r]
may those who plot my ruin

---

[a] 3 Or *and block the way*

34:15 [u] Mal 3:16;
S Jn 9:31
34:16 [v] Lev 17:10;
Jer 23:30 [w] 1Pe 3:10-
12* [x] S Ex 17:14;
Ps 9:6
34:17 [y] Ps 145:19
34:18 [z] Dt 4:7;
Ps 119:151; 145:18;
Isa 50:8 [a] Ps 51:17;
109:16; 147:3; Isa 61:1
34:19 [b] ver 17;
Ps 25:17 [c] S Job 5:19;
2Ti 3:11
34:20 [d] Jn 19:36*
34:21 [e] Ps 7:9; 9:16;
11:5; 37:20; 73:27;
94:23; 106:43; 112:10;
140:11; Pr 14:32; 24:16
34:22 [f] S Ex 6:6;
S 15:13; Lk 1:68;
Rev 14:3 [g] Ps 2:12
35:1 [h] S 1Sa 24:15
[i] S Ex 14:14
35:2 [j] Ps 3:3 [k] Ps 3:7
[l] S Ge 50:24;
S Job 17:3
35:3 [m] S Nu 25:7
[n] S Jos 8:18 [o] Ps 27:1
35:4 [p] Ps 38:12;
40:14; Jer 4:30
[q] Ps 69:6,19; 70:2;
83:17; Isa 45:16;
Mal 2:9 [r] Ps 25:3

34:15–18 Assurance that the Lord hears the prayers of the righteous. He so thoroughly thwarts those who do evil that they are forgotten (v. 16). As in vv. 4–7, which these verses structurally balance, the theme is developed in alternating lines (in an a-b/a-b pattern). Furthermore, the corresponding lines of these two balanced stanzas are thematically, and sometimes even verbally, linked (cf. vv. 4 and 15, vv. 5 and 16, vv. 6 and 17, vv. 7 and 18); godly instruction is patterned after the praise. And these two stanzas, each of which has four Hebrew poetic lines, frame the intervening seven-line stanza (vv. 8–14).
34:15 *righteous.* See vv. 8–14; see also note on 1:5.
34:16 *face of the LORD.* See note on 13:1.
34:17–18 See especially 51:17.
34:19–22 Assurance that the Lord is the unfailing deliverer of the righteous—and that he holds the wicked accountable for their hostility toward the righteous (see v. 21). Here, too, an a-b/a-b thematic pattern appears to be employed (note the contrast expressed in vv. 19,21 and the reinforcement of v. 20 found in v. 22).

A **34:20** *all their bones.* Their whole being (see note on 6:2). *not one of them will be broken.* Perhaps John's Gospel applies this word to Jesus (see TNIV text note on Jn 19:36)—as the one above all others who could be called "righteous" (v. 19).
34:21–22 *condemned.* Dealt with as guilty (cf. Jer 2:3; Hos 10:2).
34:22 *redeems.* See note on 25:22. *who takes refuge in him.* See 2:12.
Ps 35 An appeal to the heavenly King, as divine Warrior and Judge, to come to the defense of "his servant" (v. 27) who is being maliciously slandered by those toward whom he had shown only the most tender friendship. The attack seems to have been occasioned by some "distress" (v. 26) that had overtaken the king (see vv. 15,19,21,25), perhaps an illness (see v. 13; see also

introduction to Ps 6). Ps 35 exemplifies such a "cry" (34:15) to the Lord in expectation of vindication as that spoken of in 34:15–22—except that here the author does not expressly identify himself as one of the "righteous" (34:21); he appeals to the Lord rather as innocent victim of an unmotivated attack. This psalm has been paired with Ps 36 and placed between the two acrostic wisdom psalms (34 and 37; see introduction to Ps 34–37). Together they evoke the terrors of life in the midst of people who have "no fear of God before their eyes" (36:1) but also testify to the security of those who fear the Lord (cf. 34:7) and trust him (cf. 37:3,5), relying on his love (36:5,7,11) and righteousness (35:24,28; 36:6,10).

Regarding structure, two stanzas at the beginning, having four Hebrew poetic lines each (vv. 1–3,4–6), are balanced by two four-line stanzas at the end (vv. 22–25,26–27—for thematic links between the beginning and the end, see notes on these stanzas). At the center a seven-line stanza (vv. 11–16) sets forth the psalmist's chief indictment against his adversaries. A final line (v. 28) brings the psalm to a close with a vow to praise (see note on 7:17).
35:1–3 Appeal for help to the Lord as Warrior-King (see Ex 15:1–18), David's Overlord. For links with vv. 22–25, see note on those verses.
35:2 *shield and armor.* For defense. For the Lord himself as the psalmists' "shield," see 3:3; 7:10; 18:2,30; 28:7; 33:20; 59:11; 84:9,11; 89:18; 115:9–11; 119:114; 144:2. *arise.* See note on 3:7.
35:3 *spear and javelin.* For attack (but see TNIV text note on "javelin"). For the Lord wielding a spear, see Hab 3:11.
35:4–6 Appeal to the Lord to deal with the attackers by frustrating all their efforts and totally disabling them. For links with vv. 26–27, see note on those verses.
35:4 *plot my ruin.* See note on 5:9.

35:4 *s* Ps 129:5
35:5 *t* S Job 13:25;
Ps 1:4 *u* Ps 34:7
35:7 *v* S Job 18:8
w S Ps 7:4
x S Job 9:31;
S Ps 7:15; S 55:23
35:8 *y* Isa 47:11;
1Th 5:3 *z* S Ps 7:15
35:9 *a* S Ps 2:11;
S Lk 1:47 *b* Ps 9:14;
13:5; 27:1
35:10 *c* S Ex 9:14;
S Ps 18:31; 113:5
d Ps 18:17 *e* Ps 12:5;
37:14; 74:21; 86:1;
109:16; 140:12;
Isa 41:17
35:11 *f* S Ex 23:1;
S Mt 26:60
35:12 *g* Ps 38:20;
109:5; Pr 17:13;
Jer 18:20
35:13 *h* S 2Sa 3:31;
1Ki 20:31; Ps 30:11;
69:11 *i* Job 30:25;
Ps 69:10; 109:24
35:14 *j* Ps 38:6;
42:9; 43:2
35:15 *k* S Job 31:29
l S Job 16:10
35:16 *m* S Ps 22:7;
Mk 10:34 *n* S Job 16:9;
Mk 9:18; Ac 7:54
35:17 *o* Ps 6:3
p Ps 22:20 *q* Ps 22:21;
57:4; 58:6
35:18 *r* S Ps 22:25
s Ps 42:4; 109:30
t S Ps 22:22
35:19 *u* Ps 9:13
v ver 7; Ps 38:19;
69:4; Jn 15:25*
w Pr 6:13; 10:10
35:20 *x* Ps 38:12;
55:21; Jer 9:8;
Mic 6:12

be turned back *s* in dismay.
5 May they be like chaff *t* before the wind,
 with the angel of the LORD *u* driving them away;
6 may their path be dark and slippery,
 with the angel of the LORD pursuing them.

7 Since they hid their net *v* for me without cause *w*
 and without cause dug a pit *x* for me,
8 may ruin overtake them by surprise— *y*
 may the net they hid entangle them,
 may they fall into the pit, *z* to their ruin.
9 Then my soul will rejoice *a* in the LORD
 and delight in his salvation. *b*
10 My whole being will exclaim,
 "Who is like you, *c* LORD?
You rescue the poor from those too strong *d* for them,
 the poor and needy *e* from those who rob them."

11 Ruthless witnesses *f* come forward;
 they question me on things I know nothing about.
12 They repay me evil for good *g*
 and leave me like one bereaved.
13 Yet when they were ill, I put on sackcloth *h*
 and humbled myself with fasting. *i*
When my prayers returned to me unanswered,
14   I went about mourning *j*
 as though for my friend or brother.
I bowed my head in grief
 as though weeping for my mother.
15 But when I stumbled, they gathered in glee; *k*
 assailants gathered against me without my knowledge.
 They slandered *l* me without ceasing.
16 Like the ungodly they maliciously mocked; *a m*
 they gnashed their teeth *n* at me.

17 How long, *o* Lord, will you look on?
 Rescue me from their ravages,
 my precious life *p* from these lions. *q*
18 I will give you thanks in the great assembly; *r*
 among the throngs *s* I will praise you. *t*
19 Do not let those gloat over me
 who are my enemies *u* without cause;
do not let those who hate me without reason *v*
 maliciously wink the eye. *w*
20 They do not speak peaceably,
 but devise false accusations *x*
 against those who live quietly in the land.

a 16 Septuagint; Hebrew may mean *Like an ungodly circle of mockers,*

35:5–6 *angel of the LORD.* See 34:7 and note.
35:5 *like chaff.* See note on 1:4.
35:7–10 Appeal to the Lord to match the attackers' violent intent with his saving act (see note on 5:10)—which the psalmist will celebrate with praise (see note on 7:17).
35:7–8 *hid their net … dug a pit … net they hid … fall into the pit.* See 9:15 and note.
35:9 *soul.* See note on 6:3.
35:10 *poor and needy.* See 34:6 and note.
35:11–16 The accusation: They repaid my friendship with malicious slander. This accusation stands at the center of the psalm (see note on 6:6).

A **35:13–14** The psalmist provides a living example of Jesus' later command to "pray for those who persecute you" (Mt 5:44)—as do Job (Job 42:7–10; see note on 42:10) and Jesus himself (Lk 23:34).

35:13 *sackcloth.* See note on 30:11. *fasting.* An act of mourning (see 69:10).
35:15 *stumbled.* Not morally. He was brought low by circumstances (see 9:3; 27:2; 37:24; 56:13; 119:165).
35:16 *gnashed their teeth.* In malice (see 37:12; La 2:16).
35:17–21 Renewed appeal for God's saving help, accompanied by a vow to praise (v. 18; see note on 7:17). This five-line stanza and the five-line stanza in vv. 7–10 frame the central accusation.
35:17 *How long …?* See note on 6:3. *lions.* See note on 7:2.
35:18 *assembly.* See note on 1:5.

A **35:19** *enemies without cause.* See vv. 11–17; an experience frequently reflected also elsewhere in the Psalter (see 38:19; 69:4; 109:3; 119:78,86,161). See also La 3:52. *hate me without reason.* See 69:4. It is not known which of these passages is referred to in Jn 15:25. Both psalms reflect circumstances applicable also to Jesus' experience (but see introduction to Ps 69).

21 They sneer[y] at me and say, "Aha! Aha![z]
  With our own eyes we have seen it."

22 LORD, you have seen[a] this; do not be silent.
  Do not be far[b] from me, Lord.
23 Awake,[c] and rise[d] to my defense!
  Contend[e] for me, my God and Lord.
24 Vindicate me in your righteousness, LORD my God;
  do not let them gloat[f] over me.
25 Do not let them think, "Aha,[g] just what we wanted!"
  or say, "We have swallowed him up."[h]

26 May all who gloat[i] over my distress[j]
  be put to shame[k] and confusion;
  may all who exalt themselves over me[l]
  be clothed with shame and disgrace.
27 May those who delight in my vindication[m]
  shout for joy[n] and gladness;
  may they always say, "The LORD be exalted,
  who delights[o] in the well-being of his servant."[p]

28 My tongue will proclaim your righteousness,[q]
  your praises all day long.[r]

PSALM 36

For the director of music. Of David the servant of the LORD.

*[*]1 I have a message from God in my heart
  concerning the sinfulness of the wicked:[a][s]
There is no fear[t] of God
  before their eyes.[u]

2 In their own eyes they flatter themselves
  too much to detect or hate their sin.[v]
3 The words of their mouths[w] are wicked and deceitful;[x]
  they have ceased to be wise[y] and to do good.[z]
4 Even on their beds they plot evil;[a]

---

[a] 1 Or *A message from God: The transgression of the wicked / resides in their hearts.*
[*] 36:1-12 is numbered 36:2-13 in Hebrew texts.

35:21 [y] S Job 16:10
[z] Ps 40:15; 70:3;
Eze 25:3
35:22 [a] Ex 3:7;
Ps 10:14 [b] S Ps 10:1
35:23 [c] S Ps 7:6;
80:2 [d] Ps 17:13
[e] S 1Sa 24:15
35:24 [f] Ps 22:17
35:25 [g] ver 21
[h] Ps 124:3; Pr 1:12;
La 2:16
35:26 [i] Ps 22:17
[j] Ps 4:1 [k] S Job 8:22;
Ps 109:29; Mic 7:10
[l] Job 19:5; Ps 38:16
35:27 [m] Ps 9:4
[n] Ps 20:5; S 33:3
[o] Ps 147:11; 149:4
[p] S Job 17:3
35:28 [q] Ps 5:8; 51:14
[r] Ps 71:15,24; 72:15
36:1 [s] S Job 21:16
[t] Jer 2:19; 36:16,24
[u] S Job 23:15;
Ro 3:18*
36:2 [v] Dt 29:19
36:3 [w] Ps 10:7
[x] S Job 5:13; Ps 5:6,9;
43:1; 144:8,11;
Isa 44:20 [y] Ps 94:8
[z] Jer 4:22; 13:23;
Am 3:10
36:4 [a] Pr 4:16

35:21 *Aha! Aha!* See v. 25; see also note on 3:2.
35:22–25 A return to the opening appeal (vv. 1–3) for God to arouse himself, take up the psalmist's cause and "contend" (v. 23) with those attacking him.
35:22 *do not be silent.* Do not remain inactive (see 28:1 and note; 83:1; 109:1).
35:23 *Awake.* See note on 7:6. *rise.* See note on 3:7.
35:24 *righteousness.* See note on 4:1.
35:25 *swallowed.* See 124:3.
35:26–27 Again (see vv. 4–6) an appeal for God to bring "shame" and "disgrace" on the adversaries. For both form and substance, cf. 40:14–16.
35:26 *who gloat over my distress.* In Hebrew, a verbal echo of "who plot my ruin" (v. 4). *clothed with.* See note on 109:29.
35:27 May all who are faithful supporters of the Lord's "servant" (here no doubt equivalent to his "anointed"; see note on 2:2) have reason to rejoice and praise the Lord.
35:28 A concluding vow to praise (see note on 7:17). *righteousness.* See note on 4:1.
Ps 36 A prayer for God's unfailing protection, as the psalmist reflects on the godlessness of the wicked and the goodness of God. For this psalm's relationship with Ps 35, see introduction to Ps 35. Structurally, a short couplet (v. 1) introduces a series of four stanzas of three Hebrew poetic lines each (vv. 2–4, 5–7a,7b–9,10–12). In later Jewish practice, vv. 7–10 became part of the morning prayer.

36 title *For the director of music.* See note on Ps 4 title. *servant of the LORD.* His royal servant (see notes on Ps 18 title; 35:27; see also 2Sa 7:20).

A 36:1 *message from God.* Usually reserved for words of revelation from God, such as those spoken by the prophets. Here reference is to an insight, perhaps coming like a flash, into the true character of the wicked. *heart.* See note on 4:7. *no fear of God.* Such as the psalmist calls for in Ps 34 and (implicitly) in Ps 37. See 55:19; Ge 20:11 and note. They take no account of his all-seeing eye, his righteous judgment and his power to deal with them (see note on 10:11). For Paul's use of this verse, see Ro 3:18.

C 36:2–4 The wicked characterized (see also 10:2–11).

36:2 *flatter themselves.* Not in self-righteousness but out of the smug, conceited notion that they are accountable to no one.
36:3 *words of their mouths.* See note on 5:9. *are ... deceitful.* See 35:20. *ceased to be wise.* See 94:8–11; Pr 2:9–11. *ceased ... to do good.* In contrast to the wise and godly person (see 34:14; 37:3,27; see also note on 34:8–14).

A 36:4 *on their beds.* Where one's thoughts are free to range and to set the course for the activities of the day. The wicked do not meditate on God's law "day and night" (1:2; see 119:55); let a godly heart instruct them at night (see 16:7). Commune at night with God (see 42:8), think of him (see 63:6) and reflect on his promises (see 119:148). *plot evil.* See 34:14; 37:27; cf. Mic 2:1.

36:4 ^b Isa 65:2
^c Ps 52:3; Ro 12:9
36:5 ^d Ps 89:1;
119:90 ^e Ps 57:10;
71:19; 89:2; 103:11;
108:4
36:6 ^f Ps 5:8
^g Ps 68:15 ^h S Ge 1:2;
S 7:11 ⁱ Ne 9:6;
Ps 104:14; 145:16
36:7 ^j Ps 6:4
^k S Ru 2:12; S Ps 17:8;
57:1; 91:4
36:8 ^l Ps 65:4;
Isa 25:6; Jer 31:12,14
^m Job 20:17; Rev 22:1
ⁿ S Ps 23:2; 63:5
36:9 ^o Ps 87:7;
Pr 10:11; 16:22;
Jer 2:13 ^p Ps 4:6; 27:1;
76:4; 104:2; Isa 2:5;
9:2; 60:1,19; Jn 1:4;
1Pe 2:9
36:10 ^q Jer 31:3
^r Jer 9:24; 22:16
^s Ps 7:10; 11:2; 94:15;
125:4
36:11 ^t Ps 71:4;
140:4
36:12 ^u S Ps 18:38
37:1 ^v Pr 3:31;
23:17-18 ^w Ps 73:3;
Pr 24:19

they commit themselves to a sinful course ^b
and do not reject what is wrong. ^c

⁵ Your love, LORD, reaches to the heavens,
your faithfulness ^d to the skies. ^e
⁶ Your righteousness ^f is like the highest mountains, ^g
your justice like the great deep. ^h
You, LORD, preserve both people and animals. ⁱ
⁷ How priceless is your unfailing love, O God! ^j
People take refuge in the shadow of your wings. ^k
⁸ They feast on the abundance of your house; ^l
you give them drink from your river ^m of delights. ⁿ
⁹ For with you is the fountain of life; ^o
in your light ^p we see light.

¹⁰ Continue your love ^q to those who know you, ^r
your righteousness to the upright in heart. ^s
¹¹ May the foot of the proud not come against me,
nor the hand of the wicked ^t drive me away.
¹² See how the evildoers lie fallen—
thrown down, not able to rise! ^u

PSALM 37 ^a

Of David.

¹ Do not fret because of those who are evil
or be envious ^v of those who do wrong; ^w

^a This psalm is an acrostic poem, the stanzas of which begin with the successive letters of the Hebrew alphabet.

36:5–7a The trustworthiness of the Lord.
36:5 *love…faithfulness.* That is, love-and-faithfulness (as in 57:3; 61:7; 85:10; 86:15; 89:14; 115:1; 138:2; Pr 3:3; 14:22; 16:6; 20:28; see note on 3:7). *reaches to the heavens…to the skies.* Encompasses all the realms of creaturely existence (see 57:10; 108:4).
36:6 *righteousness…justice.* That is, righteousness-and-justice (as in 33:5; 37:6; 89:14; 97:2; Hos 2:19; see also Isa 9:7; 33:5; Jer 9:24). *righteousness.* See note on 4:1. *like the highest mountains …great deep.* As high as the mountains, as deep as the sea.
36:7a *unfailing love.* See v. 5; see also note on 6:4.
36:7b–9 The Lord's benevolence toward all his creatures (see 33:4–5).
36:7b *shadow of your wings.* See 17:8 and note.

36:8 *feast…drink.* Life-giving food and water. *house.* Here, God's whole estate or realm—i.e., the earth, from which springs the abundance of food for all living things (see note on 24:2). *river.* The "channel" (Job 38:25) by which God brings forth the rain out of his "storehouses" (33:7; see Job 38:8–11,22,37; Jer 10:13) in his "upper chambers" (104:13; see 65:9; Isa 30:25 and the references to "blessings" from heaven in Ge 49:25; Dt 33:23). This vivid imagery, depicting God's control over, and gift of, the waters from heaven, which feed the rivers and streams of earth to give life and health wherever they flow, is the source of the symbol of "the river of the water of life" that flows from the temple of God (Rev 22:1–2; see also Eze 47:1–12). *of delights.* Furnishing many sources of joy.

36:9 The climax and summation of vv. 5–9. *fountain of life.* See Jer 2:13; 17:13. Ultimately, for sinners, God provides the water of life through Jesus Christ (Jn 4:10,14). *your light.* See 27:1 and note. *see.* Experience, have, enjoy, as in 16:10; 27:13; 34:8,12; 49:9,19; 89:48; 90:15; 106:5 ("enjoy"); Job 9:25 ("glimpse"); 42:5; Ecc 1:16 ("experienced"); 3:13 ("find"); 6:6 ("enjoy"); 8:16; Isa 53:10; La 3:1. *light.* Life in its fullness as it was created to be. For the association of light with life, see 49:19; 56:13; Job 3:20; 33:28,30; Isa 53:11.

36:10–12 The prayer: Your "love" (v. 5) and "righteousness" (v. 6), which you display in all creation—show these

to all who know (acknowledge) you and are upright (the people of God). But keep the wicked, "foot" and "hand," from success against me (the king; see note on 33:16).
36:10 *love.* See note on 6:4. *those who know you.* See 9:10 and note. *righteousness.* See note on 4:1.
36:11 *proud.* See note on 31:23.
36:12 Confidence (see note on 3:8). *lie fallen.* Perhaps in death (see note on 13:4).

Ps 37 Instruction in godly wisdom. (For other "wisdom" psalms, see 34:8–22; 49; 112; others closely related are Ps 1; 73; 91; 92:6–9,12–15; 111; 119; 127–128; 133; see also essay, p. 750.) This psalm's dominant theme is related to the contrast between the wicked and the righteous reflected in Ps 36. The central issue addressed is: Who will "inherit the land" (vv. 9,11,22,29), i.e., live on to enjoy the blessings of the Lord in the promised land? Will the wicked, who plot (v. 12), scheme (vv. 7,32), default on debts (v. 21), use raw power to gain advantage (v. 14) and seem thereby to flourish (vv. 7,16,35)? Or will the righteous, who trust in the Lord (vv. 3,5,7,34) and are humble (v. 11), blameless (vv. 18,37), generous (vv. 21,26), upright (v. 37) and peaceable (v. 37), and from whose mouth is heard the moral wisdom that reflects meditation on God's law (vv. 30–31)? For a similar characterization of the wicked, see 10:2–11; 73:4–12. For a similar characterization of the righteous see Ps 112. For a similar statement concerning the transitoriness of the wicked see Ps 49; 73:18–20.

Structurally, in this alphabetic acrostic, two verses are devoted to each letter of the alphabet, though with some irregularity. The main theme is developed in vv. 1–11, then further elaborated in the rest of the psalm. The whole is framed by statements contrasting the brief career of the wicked (vv. 1–2) and the Lord's sustaining help of the righteous (vv. 39–40). For this psalm's relationship to Ps 34–36, see introduction to Ps 34–37.
37:1–2 See v. 7; Ps 73.
37:1 Almost identical to Pr 24:19.

2 for like the grass they will soon wither,[x]
  like green plants they will soon die away.[y]

3 Trust in the LORD and do good;
  dwell in the land[z] and enjoy safe pasture.[a]

4 Take delight[b] in the LORD
  and he will give you the desires of your heart.[c]

5 Commit your way to the LORD;
  trust in him[d] and he will do this:

6 He will make your righteous reward[e] shine like the dawn,[f]
  your vindication like the noonday sun.

7 Be still[g] before the LORD
  and wait patiently[h] for him;
do not fret[i] when people succeed in their ways,[j]
  when they carry out their wicked schemes.[k]

8 Refrain from anger[l] and turn from wrath;
  do not fret[m]—it leads only to evil.

9 For those who are evil will be destroyed,[n]
  but those who hope[o] in the LORD will inherit the land.[p]

10 A little while, and the wicked will be no more;[q]
  though you look for them, they will not be found.

11 But the meek will inherit the land[r]
  and enjoy peace and prosperity.[s]

12 The wicked plot[t] against the righteous
  and gnash their teeth[u] at them;

13 but the Lord laughs at the wicked,
  for he knows their day is coming.[v]

14 The wicked draw the sword[w]
  and bend the bow[x]
to bring down the poor and needy,[y]
  to slay those whose ways are upright.

15 But their swords will pierce their own hearts,[z]
  and their bows will be broken.[a]

16 Better the little that the righteous have
  than the wealth[b] of many wicked;

37:2 [x] S 2Ki 19:26; Job 14:2; Ps 102:4; Isa 40:7 [y] ver 38; Ps 90:6; 92:7; Jas 1:10
37:3 [z] Dt 30:20 [a] Eze 34:14; Jn 10:9
37:4 [b] S Job 27:10 [c] S Job 7:6; Ps 21:2; 145:19; Mt 6:33
37:5 [d] Ps 4:5
37:6 [e] Ps 18:24; 103:17; 112:3 [f] S Job 11:17
37:7 [g] S Ex 14:14; S Isa 41:1 [h] S Ps 27:14; 40:1; 130:5; Isa 38:13; Hab 3:16; Ro 8:25 [i] ver 1 / Jer 12:1 [k] Ps 21:11; 26:10; 119:150
37:8 [l] Eph 4:31; Col 3:8 [m] ver 1
37:9 [n] S Ps 31:22; 101:8; 118:10; Pr 2:22 [o] Isa 25:9; 26:8; 40:31; 49:23; 51:5 [p] ver 22; Ps 25:13; Isa 49:8; 57:13; Mt 5:5
37:10 [q] S Job 7:10; Eze 27:36
37:11 [r] S Nu 14:24; Mt 5:5 [s] S Lev 26:6; S Nu 6:26
37:12 [t] Ps 2:1; 31:13 [u] S Job 16:9; Ps 35:16; 112:10
37:13 [v] S Isa 26:10; Eze 12:23
37:14 [w] S Ps 22:20 [x] Ps 11:2 [y] S Ps 35:10
37:15 [z] S Ps 9:16 [a] S Isa 2:4; Ps 46:9; Jer 49:35
37:16 [b] Pr 15:16; 16:8

37:2 See note on v. 20.
37:3 See 34:8–14 and note.
37:4 *heart.* See note on 4:7.
37:5 *Commit.* See 1Pe 5:7.
37:6 *your righteous reward.* That is, the prosperity and well-being that God will bestow in accordance with "your" faithful reliance on him (cf. v. 9; see Pr 8:18; 21:21 ["prosperity"] for this sense of the Hebrew word; see also Isa 48:18). *righteous reward . . . vindication.* That is, righteous reward-and-vindication (see note on 36:6). *your vindication.* See 35:27 and note; see also Isa 54:17. The close Hebrew synonyms here rendered "righteous reward" and "vindication" both refer to manifestations of God's favor on those he pleases to bless or deliver, as in Isa 59:9 (where these terms are linked with "light") and 59:11 (where "justice" [or "vindication"] is linked with "deliverance"). Accordingly, "your righteous reward" and "your vindication" in this verse have direct links with "your (God's) righteousness" and "your (God's) justice" in 36:6. It is God's "righteousness" and "justice" that secure the "righteous reward" and "vindication" of those who "trust in him" (v. 5).
37:8 *anger . . . wrath.* Evidence of fretting over the wicked's prosperity, gained to the disadvantage of and even at the expense of the righteous.

A **37:9** *hope in.* See v. 34. *inherit the land.* Receive from the Lord secure entitlement (for them and their children) in the promised land as the created and redeemed sphere and bountiful source of provision for the life of God's people. Those

who hope in the Lord—i.e., trustfully look to him to bestow life and its blessings as a gift—will inherit the land, not those who apart from God and by evil means try to take possession of it and its wealth (see vv. 11,22,29; cf. Jos 7).
37:10 *A little while.* Shortness of time is here a figure for certainty of event (see 58:9; Job 20:5–11; Hag 2:6).

A **37:11** See Mt 5:5. *meek.* Those who humbly acknowledge their dependence on the goodness and grace of God and betray no arrogance toward others. *peace and prosperity.* Unmixed blessedness.
37:12 *righteous.* See note on 1:5. *gnash their teeth.* See 35:16 and note.
37:13 *Lord laughs.* See 2:4. *knows their day is coming.* Strikingly, the psalmist nowhere speaks of God's active involvement in bringing the wicked down—though he hints at it in v. 22. The certainty that the life of the wicked will be "destroyed" is frequently asserted (vv. 9,22,28,34,38; cf. vv. 2,8,10,15,17,20,36, 38)—and the Lord also knows it—but God's positive action is here reserved for his care for and protection of the righteous. *their day.* The time when each will be "destroyed," as in 1Sa 26:10 ("his time," lit. "his day"); Job 18:20 ("his fate").
37:14–15 *sword . . . bow . . . swords . . . bows.* See 64:3–4,7–8; Pr 30:14 and note on Ps 5:9.
37:14 *poor and needy.* See 34:6 and note.
37:15 *pierce . . . hearts.* See 45:5.
37:16–17 *righteous.* See note on 1:5.

37:17 c Job 38:15;
Ps 10:15 d Ps 41:12;
140:12; 145:14; 146:7
37:18 e S Job 23:10;
Ps 44:21 f ver 27,29
37:20 g S Ps 34:21
h Ps 68:2; 102:3;
Isa 51:6
37:21 i S Lev 25:35;
Ps 112:5
37:22 j S Job 5:3
k ver 9
37:23 l S Job 11:15;
S Ps 7:9; 66:9
m S Nu 14:8; Ps 147:11
37:24 n S Ps 13:4;
27:2; 38:17; 55:22;
119:165; Pr 3:23; 10:9
o 2Ch 9:8; Ps 41:12;
145:14
37:25 p ver 28;
S Ge 15:1; Heb 13:5
q Ps 111:5; 145:15;
Mk 10:46
37:26 r S Lev 25:35
s Dt 28:4; Ps 112:2
37:27 t Ps 34:14;
3Jn 1:11 u S Nu 24:21
37:28 v S Dt 7:6;
S Ps 18:25; S 97:10
w S Ge 17:14;
S Dt 32:26; Pr 2:22
37:29 x ver 9;
Pr 2:21 y Isa 34:17
37:30 z Ps 49:3;
Pr 10:13
37:31 a S Dt 6:6;
S Job 22:22
b S Dt 32:35
37:32 c S Ps 10:8
d Ps 11:5
37:33 e Job 32:3;
Ps 34:22; 79:11
f 2Pe 2:9
37:34 g S Ps 27:14
h S Ps 18:21 i ver 9
j Ps 52:6
37:35 k S Job 5:3

17 for the power of the wicked will be broken, c
   but the LORD upholds d the righteous.

18 The blameless spend their days under the LORD's care, e
   and their inheritance will endure forever. f

19 In times of disaster they will not wither;
   in days of famine they will enjoy plenty.

20 But the wicked will perish: g
   Though the LORD's enemies are like the flowers of the field,
   they will be consumed, they will go up in smoke. h

21 The wicked borrow and do not repay,
   but the righteous give generously; i

22 those the LORD blesses will inherit the land,
   but those he curses j will be destroyed. k

23 The LORD makes firm the steps l
   of those who delight m in him;

24 though they stumble, they will not fall, n
   for the LORD upholds o them with his hand.

25 I was young and now I am old,
   yet I have never seen the righteous forsaken p
   or their children begging q bread.

26 They are always generous and lend freely; r
   their children will be a blessing. a s

27 Turn from evil and do good; t
   then you will dwell in the land forever. u

28 For the LORD loves the just
   and will not forsake his faithful ones. v

   Wrongdoers will be completely destroyed b;
   the offspring of the wicked will perish. w

29 The righteous will inherit the land x
   and dwell in it forever. y

30 The mouths of the righteous utter wisdom, z
   and their tongues speak what is just.

31 The law of their God is in their hearts; a
   their feet do not slip. b

32 The wicked lie in wait c for the righteous, d
   seeking their very lives;

33 but the LORD will not leave them in their power
   or let them be condemned e when brought to trial. f

34 Hope in the LORD g
   and keep his way. h
   He will exalt you to inherit the land;
   when the wicked are destroyed, i you will see j it.

35 I have seen the wicked and ruthless
   flourishing k like a luxuriant native tree,

---

a 26 Or freely; / the names of their children will be used in blessings (see Gen. 48:20); or freely; / others will
see that their children are blessed   b 28 See Septuagint; Hebrew They will be protected forever

---

37:18 blameless. See v. 37; see also 15:2 and note. under the
LORD's care. See 1:6 ("the LORD watches over").
37:20 flowers. Cf. v. 2; 90:5–6; 92:7; 102:11; 103:15–16; Job 14:2
and note; Isa 40:6–7; see Jas 1:10–11.
37:21 Or "The wicked must borrow and cannot repay,/but the
righteous are able to give generously" (see Dt 15:6; 28:12,44).
37:24 See Pr 24:16.
37:26 See note on v. 21.
37:27 Turn from evil and do good. See 34:14 and note.
37:28 faithful ones. See note on 4:3.

37:29 forever. They and their children and children's children,
in contrast to the wicked (see v. 28).
37:30 wisdom. See 119:98,130; Dt 4:6.
37:31 hearts. See note on 4:7. do not slip. From the right path
(see 17:5).
37:32 lie in wait. See 10:8–9; see also note on 7:2. seeking their
very lives. Attempting to seize by false charges at court (see v.
33) the very livelihood of their intended victims.
37:34 See v. 9.
37:35–36 Cf. vv. 25–26.

³⁶ but they soon passed away and were no more;
  though I looked for them, they could not be found. [l]

³⁷ Consider the blameless, [m] observe the upright; [n]
  a future awaits those who seek peace. [a][o]
³⁸ But all sinners [p] will be destroyed; [q]
  there will be no future [b] for the wicked. [r]

³⁹ The salvation [s] of the righteous comes from the LORD;
  he is their stronghold in time of trouble. [t]
⁴⁰ The LORD helps [u] them and delivers [v] them;
  he delivers them from the wicked and saves [w] them,
  because they take refuge [x] in him.

PSALM 38

A psalm of David. A petition.

^{*1} LORD, do not rebuke me in your anger
  or discipline me in your wrath. [y]
² Your arrows [z] have pierced me,
  and your hand has come down on me.
³ Because of your wrath there is no health [a] in my body;
  there is no soundness in my bones [b] because of my sin.
⁴ My guilt has overwhelmed [c] me
  like a burden too heavy to bear. [d]

⁵ My wounds [e] fester and are loathsome [f]
  because of my sinful folly. [g]
⁶ I am bowed down [h] and brought very low;
  all day long I go about mourning. [i]
⁷ My back is filled with searing pain; [j]
  there is no health [k] in my body.
⁸ I am feeble and utterly crushed; [l]
  I groan [m] in anguish of heart. [n]

⁹ All my longings [o] lie open before you, Lord;
  my sighing [p] is not hidden from you.
¹⁰ My heart pounds, [q] my strength fails [r] me;
  even the light has gone from my eyes. [s]
¹¹ My friends and companions avoid me because of my wounds; [t]
  my neighbors stay far away.
¹² Those who seek my life set their traps, [u]

---

^a 37 Or / *those who seek peace will have posterity*   ^b 38 Or *posterity*

[*] 38:1-22 is numbered 38:2-23 in Hebrew texts.

37:36 [l] ver 10;
Pr 12:7; Isa 41:12;
Da 11:19
37:37 [m] ver 18;
S Ge 6:9; Ps 18:25
[n] Ps 11:7 [o] Isa 57:1-2
37:38 [p] S Ps 1:1
[q] S ver 2; Ps 73:19
[r] ver 9
37:39 [s] S Ps 3:8
[t] S Ps 9:9
37:40 [u] S 1Ch 5:20;
S Ps 20:2 [v] S Ps 34:7
[w] S Ps 18:48 [x] Ps 2:12
38:1 [y] Ps 6:1
38:2 [z] S Job 6:4
38:3 [a] Pr 3:8; 4:22
[b] S Job 33:19
38:4 [c] Ps 40:12; 65:3
[d] S Nu 11:14;
S Ezr 9:6; Lk 11:46
38:5 [e] ver 11;
Ps 147:3 [f] Job 19:17
[g] Ps 69:5; Pr 5:23;
12:23; 13:16; Ecc 10:3
38:6 [h] Ps 57:6;
145:14; 146:8
[i] S Ps 35:14
38:7 [j] S Job 14:22
[k] ver 3
38:8 [l] Ps 34:18;
Pr 17:22 [m] S Ps 6:6;
22:1; Pr 5:11 [n] S Ps 6:3
38:9 [o] Ps 119:20;
143:7 [p] S Job 3:24
38:10 [q] S Job 37:1
[r] S Ps 31:10 [s] S Ps 6:7;
S 19:8; 88:9
38:11 [t] S ver 5
38:12 [u] Ps 31:4;
140:5; 141:9

37:37–38 *The great contrast: hope for the "upright," no hope for the "wicked."*

37:39–40 *the righteous . . . them.* They are not at the mercy of the wicked: The Lord is their refuge, and in spite of all that the wicked do the Lord makes secure their inheritance in the promised land.

Ps 38–41 The final four psalms of Book I are all linked by common central themes (see introductions to these psalms). One of these themes is confession of sin, which is found elsewhere in Book I only in Ps 25; 32 (see introductions to those psalms). Significantly, following a wisdom psalm (37), the first reference to sin here characterizes it as "folly" (38:5).

Ps 38 An urgent appeal for relief from a severe and painful illness, God's "rebuke" for a sin David has committed. Neither the specific occasion nor the illness can be identified. David's suffering is aggravated by the withdrawal of his friends (see v. 11) and the unwarranted efforts of his enemies to seize this opportunity to bring him down (vv. 12,16,19–20). In traditional Christian usage, this is one of seven penitential psalms (see introduction to Ps 6). Like Ps 33 (see introductory note on its structure), its length (22 verses) is based on the number of letters in the He-

brew alphabet. The psalm is composed of five stanzas of four verses each, with a two-verse conclusion.

38 title *A petition.* Occurs elsewhere only in the title of Ps 70.

38:1–4 Plea for relief from the Lord's rebuke.

38:1 *rebuke . . . discipline.* That is, rebuke-and-discipline (see 39:11; see also note on 3:7). *anger . . . wrath.* See note on 2:5.

38:2 *arrows.* A vivid metaphor for God's blows (see Job 6:4; 34:6; La 3:12; Eze 5:16; see also note on Ge 9:13). *your hand has come down on me.* See 32:4 and note on 32:3–5.

38:3 *bones.* See note on 6:2.

38:4 *burden.* Not only a psychological "burden of guilt" but the heavy burden of suffering described in vv. 5–8.

38:5–8 The devastating physical and psychological effects of his illness.

38:8 *heart.* See note on 4:7.

38:9–12 Renewed appeal, with further elaboration of his troubles: his illness (v. 10), abandonment by his friends (v. 11) and the hostility of his enemies (v. 12).

38:10 *light has gone from my eyes.* See note on 13:3.

38:11 See note on 31:11–12.

38:12 See note on 5:9. *set their traps.* See note on 9:15.

38:12 ᵛ Ps 35:4;
41:5 ʷ S Ps 35:20
38:13 ˣ Ps 115:6;
135:17; Isa 43:8;
Mk 7:37
38:15 ʸ Ps 27:14
ᶻ Ps 17:6
38:16 ᵃ S Ps 22:17
ᵇ S Dt 32:35
38:17 ᶜ S Ps 37:24
ᵈ ver 7; S Job 6:10
38:18 ᵉ S Lev 26:40
38:19 ᶠ S Ps 18:17
ᵍ S Ps 25:19
ʰ S Ps 35:19
38:20 ⁱ S Ge 44:4;
1Jn 3:12 ʲ Ps 54:5;
59:10; 119:23
38:21 ᵏ Ps 27:9;
71:18; 119:8
ˡ S Ps 10:1; S 22:11;
35:22; 71:12
38:22 ᵐ S Ps 22:19
ⁿ Ps 40:13
ᵒ S 1Ch 16:35
39:1 ᵖ 1Ki 2:4;
Ps 119:9,59; Pr 20:11
��q S Job 1:22; Ps 34:13;
Jas 3:2 ʳ S Job 6:24;
Jas 1:26
39:2 ˢ ver 9;
S Job 31:34; Ps 77:4
ᵗ Ps 6:3; S 25:17; 31:10
39:3 ᵘ Lk 24:32
ᵛ Ps 1:2; 48:9; 77:12;
119:15 ʷ Jer 5:14;
20:9; 23:29

those who would harm me talk of my ruin;ᵛ
   all day long they scheme and lie.ʷ

13 I am like the deaf, who cannot hear,ˣ
   like the mute, who cannot speak;
14 I have become like one who does not hear,
   whose mouth can offer no reply.
15 Lᴏʀᴅ, I waitʸ for you;
   you will answer,ᶻ Lord my God.
16 For I said, "Do not let them gloatᵃ
   or exalt themselves over me when my feet slip."ᵇ

17 For I am about to fall,ᶜ
   and my painᵈ is ever with me.
18 I confess my iniquity;ᵉ
   I am troubled by my sin.
19 Many have become my enemiesᶠ without causeᵃ;
   those who hate meᵍ without reasonʰ are numerous.
20 Those who repay my good with evilⁱ
   lodge accusationsʲ against me,
   though I seek only to do what is good.

21 Lᴏʀᴅ, do not forsake me;ᵏ
   do not be farˡ from me, my God.
22 Come quicklyᵐ to help me,ⁿ
   my Lord and my Savior.ᵒ

PSALM 39

For the director of music. For Jeduthun. A psalm of David.

*1 I said, "I will watch my waysᵖ
   and keep my tongue from sin;ᵠ
I will put a muzzle on my mouthʳ
   while in the presence of the wicked."
2 So I remained utterly silent,ˢ
   not even saying anything good.
But my anguishᵗ increased;
3   my heart grew hotᵘ within me.
While I meditated,ᵛ the fireʷ burned;
   then I spoke with my tongue:

ᵃ 19 One Dead Sea Scrolls manuscript; Masoretic Text *my vigorous enemies*

* 39:1-13 is numbered 39:2-14 in Hebrew texts.

38:13–16 Let the Lord answer (v. 15) my enemies. Like a deaf-mute, David will not reply to his enemies (vv. 13–14); he waits for the Lord to act in his behalf (vv. 15–16). See 1Sa 25:32–39; 2Sa 16:10,12.

38:16 *when my feet slip.* When he experiences a personal blow to health or circumstance—here referring to his illness (see 66:9; 94:18; 121:3).

38:17–20 As health declines, the vigor of his many enemies increases.

38:17 *about to fall.* Death seems near (see note on 13:4). *fall.* In Hebrew, a verbal link with 35:15 ("stumbled").

38:18 See vv. 3–4; Ps 32.

38:19–20 He has sinned against the Lord, but he is innocent of any wrong against those attacking him (see note on 35:19).

38:20 *repay my good.* See 35:12–14. *lodge accusations against.* Accuse (falsely), as in 71:13; 109:4,20,29; Zec 3:1. *good.* Morally good (see 34:14).

38:21–22 In conclusion, a renewed appeal.

Ps 39 David's poignant prayer when deeply troubled by the fragility of human life. He is reminded of this by the present illness through which God is rebuking him (vv. 10–11) for his "transgressions" (v. 8). Ps 38 speaks of silence before the enemy, Ps 39 of silence before God. Both are prayers in times of illness (God's "rebuke," v. 11; 38:1); both acknowledge sin, and both express deep trust in God. See introduction to Ps 40. In addition, this psalm has many links with Ps 90; see also Ps 49. The psalm's structure is symmetrical: The first two stanzas of five and three Hebrew poetic lines are balanced by the last two stanzas of five and three lines. At the center (v. 6; see note on 6:6) stands a wisdom observation that places David's situation in the broader context of a widespread human condition (see note on v. 6).

39 title *For the director of music.* See note on Ps 4 title. *Jeduthun.* One of David's three choir leaders (1Ch 16:41–42; 25:1,6; 2Ch 5:12; called his "seer" in 2Ch 35:15). Jeduthun is probably also the Ethan of 1Ch 6:44; 15:19; if so, he represented the family of Merari, even as Asaph did the family of Gershon and Heman the family of Kohath, the three sons of Levi (see 1Ch 6:16,33, 39,43–44). See titles of Ps 62; 77; 89.

39:1–3 Introduction: Having determined to keep silent, he could finally no longer suppress his anguish.

39:1 He had kept a muzzle on his mouth for fear that rebellious words would escape in the hearing of the wicked (see Ps 73).

39:2–3 Suppressed anguish only intensified the agony (see Jer 20:9).

⁴ "Show me, LORD, my life's end
  and the number of my days; *ˣ*
  let me know how fleeting *ʸ* my life is. *ᶻ*
⁵ You have made my days *ª* a mere handbreadth;
  the span of my years is as nothing before you.
  Everyone is but a breath, *ᵇ*
  even those who seem secure. *ª*

⁶ "Surely everyone goes around *ᶜ* like a mere phantom; *ᵈ*
  in vain they rush about, *ᵉ* heaping up wealth *ᶠ*
  without knowing whose it will finally be. *ᵍ*

⁷ "But now, Lord, what do I look for?
  My hope is in you. *ʰ*
⁸ Save me *ⁱ* from all my transgressions; *ʲ*
  do not make me the scorn *ᵏ* of fools.
⁹ I was silent; *ˡ* I would not open my mouth, *ᵐ*
  for you are the one who has done this. *ⁿ*
¹⁰ Remove your scourge from me;
  I am overcome by the blow *ᵒ* of your hand. *ᵖ*
¹¹ When you rebuke *�q* and discipline *ʳ* people for their sins,
  you consume *ˢ* their wealth like a moth *ᵗ*—
  surely everyone is but a breath. *ᵘ*

¹² "Hear my prayer, LORD,
  listen to my cry for help; *ᵛ*
  do not be deaf *ʷ* to my weeping. *ˣ*
  I dwell with you as a foreigner, *ʸ*
  a stranger, *ᶻ* as all my ancestors were. *ª*
¹³ Look away from me, that I may enjoy life again
  before I depart and am no more." *ᵇ*

PSALM 40

40:13–17pp — Ps 70:1–5

For the director of music. Of David. A psalm.

*¹ I waited patiently *ᶜ* for the LORD;
  he turned to me and heard my cry. *ᵈ*

ª 5 The Hebrew has *Selah* (a word of uncertain meaning) here and at the end of verse 11.
* 40:1-17 is numbered 40:2-18 in Hebrew texts.

39:4 ˣ S Job 14:5
ʸ Job 14:2
ᶻ Ge 47:9; S Job 7:7
39:5 ª S Job 10:20;
Ps 89:45; 102:23
ᵇ S Job 7:7; Ps 62:9
39:6 ᶜ Jas 1:11
ᵈ Job 8:9; Ps 102:11;
Ecc 6:12; S Jas 4:14
ᵉ Ps 127:2
ᶠ S Job 27:17
ᵍ Lk 12:20
39:7 ʰ S Ps 9:18;
S 25:5
39:8 ⁱ Ps 6:4; 51:14
ʲ Ps 32:1; 51:1;
Isa 53:5,8,10
ᵏ S Dt 28:37; Ps 69:7;
79:4; Isa 43:28;
Da 9:16
39:9 ˡ S ver 2
ᵐ Ps 38:13 ⁿ Isa 38:15
39:10 ᵒ 2Ch 21:14;
Eze 7:9; 24:16
ᵖ S Ex 9:3
39:11 q S Dt 28:20;
Isa 66:15; Eze 5:15;
2Pe 2:16 ʳ Ps 94:10;
Isa 26:16 ˢ Ps 90:7
ᵗ S Job 13:28;
S Isa 51:8; Lk 12:33;
S Jas 5:2 ᵘ S Job 7:7
39:12 ᵛ S Ps 17:1
ʷ S Dt 1:45
ˣ S 2Ki 20:5
ʸ Lev 25:23
ᶻ S Ge 23:4;
S Heb 11:13
ª S Ge 47:9;
S 1Ch 29:15
39:13 ᵇ S Job 10:21
40:1 ᶜ S Ps 37:7
ᵈ Ps 6:9; S 31:22;
34:15; 116:1; 145:19

39:4–5 A prayer for understanding and patient acceptance of the brief span of human life.
39:4 *how fleeting my life is.* See 78:39 and note on 37:20.
39:5 *as nothing before you.* See 90:4. *but a breath.* See v. 11; 62:9; 144:4. For *Selah,* see TNIV text note and note on 3:2.
39:6 Could almost serve as a summary of Ecclesiastes.
39:7–11 A modest prayer: Only grant me relief from your present rebuke.
39:8 *Save me.* As from an enemy. *scorn of fools.* If the Lord does not restore him, he will be mocked (see 22:7–8; 69:6–12) by godless fools (see 14:1).
39:10 *blow of your hand.* See 32:4; 38:2.
39:11 *rebuke and discipline.* See 6:1; 38:1. *but a breath.* See note on v. 5.
39:12–13 The modest prayer repeated even more modestly.
39:12 *a foreigner, a stranger.* He lives this life before God only as a pilgrim passing through (cf. Heb 11:13 and note).
39:13 *Look away from me.* See Job 7:17–19; 10:20–21; 14:6. *enjoy life again.* See Job 9:27; 10:20. *am no more.* Here there is no glimpse of what lies beyond the horizon of death (see note on 6:5).

Ps 40–41 Book I of the Psalter closes with two psalms containing "Blessed are those who" statements (40:4; 41:1), thus balancing the two psalms with which the Book begins (1:1; 2:12). In this way, the whole of Book I is framed by dec-

larations of the blessedness of those who "delight in the law of the LORD" (1:2), who "take refuge in him" (2:12), who "do not look to the proud" but make the Lord their "trust" (40:4) and who have "regard for the weak" (41:1)—a concise instruction in godliness. See introduction to Ps 1–2.

Ps 40 A prayer for help when troubles abound. The causes of distress are not specified, but David acknowledges that they are occasioned by his sin (see v. 12), as in Ps 38–39; 41 (see introductions to Ps 39; 41). They are aggravated by the gloating of his enemies, a theme also present in Ps 38–39; 41 (see introduction to Ps 38). The prayer begins with praise of God for his past mercies (vv. 1–5: two stanzas of five Hebrew poetic lines each) and a testimony to the king's own faithfulness to the Lord (vv. 6–10: two three-line stanzas). These form the grounds for his present appeal for help (vv. 11–17: two five-line stanzas and a concluding couplet; note the structural centering of vv. 6–10). For other lengthy prefaces to prayer, see Ps 44; 89. Ps 70 is a somewhat revised duplicate of vv. 13–17 of this psalm.
40 title *For the director of music.* See note on Ps 4 title.
40:1–5 Praise of the Lord for past mercies (see introduction to Ps 9).

40:1–3 David's experience of God's past help in time of trouble, which moved him to praise and others to faith (see notes on 7:17; 9:1).

40:2 ᵉS Job 9:31;
S Ps 7:15 ᶠS Job 30:19
ᵍ Ps 69:14 ʰ Ps 31:8
ⁱ Ps 27:5
40:3 ʲ S Ps 28:7;
S 96:1; Rev 5:9
ᵏ Ps 52:6; 64:9
ˡ S Ex 14:31
40:4 ᵐ Ps 34:8
ⁿ Ps 84:12 ᵒ Ps 101:5;
138:6; Pr 3:34; 16:5;
Isa 65:5; 1Pe 5:5
ᵖ S Dt 31:20; S Ps 4:2;
S 26:1
40:5 �q S Dt 4:34;
Ps 75:1; 105:5; 136:4
ʳ Ps 139:18 ˢ Ps 71:15;
139:17
40:6 ᵗ S 1Sa 15:22;
Jer 6:20; Am 5:22
ᵘ Ex 21:6 ᵛ Ps 50:8;
51:16; Isa 1:11;
Hos 6:6
40:7 ʷ Job 19:23;
Jer 36:2; 45:1;
Eze 2:9; Zec 5:1
40:8 ˣ S Mt 26:39
ʸ Heb 10:5-7*
ᶻ S Dt 6:6;
S Job 22:22; Ro 7:22
40:9 ᵃ S Ps 22:31
ᵇ S Ps 22:25
ᶜ S Jos 22:22
40:10 ᵈ Ps 89:1
ᵉ S Ps 22:22
40:11 ᶠ Zec 1:12
ᵍ Pr 20:28 ʰ S Ps 26:3
ⁱ Ps 61:7
40:12 ʲ S Ps 25:17
ᵏ Ps 38:4; 65:3

² He lifted me out of the slimy pit, ᵉ
  out of the mud ᶠ and mire; ᵍ
he set my feet ʰ on a rock ⁱ
  and gave me a firm place to stand.
³ He put a new song ʲ in my mouth,
  a hymn of praise to our God.
Many will see and fear the LORD ᵏ
  and put their trust ˡ in him.

⁴ Blessed are those ᵐ
  who make the LORD their trust, ⁿ
who do not look to the proud, ᵒ
  to those who turn aside to false gods. ᵃ ᵖ
⁵ Many, LORD my God,
  are the wonders �q you have done,
  the things you planned for us.
None can compare ʳ with you;
  were I to speak and tell of your deeds,
  they would be too many ˢ to declare.

⁶ Sacrifice and offering you did not desire— ᵗ
  but my ears you have opened ᵇ— ᵘ
  burnt offerings ᵛ and sin offerings ᶜ you did not require.
⁷ Then I said, "Here I am, I have come—
  it is written about me in the scroll. ᵈ ʷ
⁸ I desire to do your will, ˣ my God; ʸ
  your law is within my heart." ᶻ

⁹ I proclaim your saving acts ᵃ in the great assembly; ᵇ
  I do not seal my lips, LORD,
  as you know. ᶜ
¹⁰ I do not hide your righteousness in my heart;
  I speak of your faithfulness ᵈ and your saving help.
I do not conceal your love and your faithfulness
  from the great assembly. ᵉ

¹¹ Do not withhold your mercy ᶠ from me, LORD;
  may your love ᵍ and faithfulness ʰ always protect ⁱ me.
¹² For troubles ʲ without number surround me;
  my sins have overtaken me, and I cannot see. ᵏ

ᵃ 4 Or *to lies*   ᵇ 6 Hebrew; some Septuagint manuscripts *but a body you have prepared for me*
ᶜ 6 Or *purification offerings*   ᵈ 7 Or *come / with the scroll written for me*

40:2 See 30:1 and note.

40:3 *new song.* See note on 33:3. *Many will see.* As a result of David's praise (see 18:49; 22:22–31; see also note on 9:1). *fear.* See notes on 15:4; 25:12; 34:8–14; Pr 1:7; Lk 12:5.

40:4–5 The Lord's benevolence to others: to all who trust in the Lord (v. 4), and to his people Israel (v. 5).

40:4 See Jer 17:7; praise of the Lord for the blessedness of those who trust in him (see 32:1–2; 146:5). *Blessed.* See note on 1:1. *proud.* See note on 31:23.

🔺 40:5 *wonders.* See note on 9:1. *planned.* God's actions in behalf of Israel are according to his predetermined purpose (see Isa 25:1; 46:10–11).

🔺 40:6–8 David's commitment to God's will. Heb 10:5–10 applies these verses to Christ (see notes there).

🔺 40:6 *did not desire ... not require.* More important is obedience (see 1Sa 15:22), especially to God's moral law (see Isa 1:10–17; Am 5:21–24; Mic 6:6–8)—i.e., the ten basic commandments of his covenant (see Ex 20:3–17; Dt 5:7–21). *ears ... opened.* Ears made able and eager to hear God's law (see Pr 28:9; Isa 48:8; 50:4–5).

🔺 40:7 *Here I am, I have come.* Probably refers to David's commitment to the Lord at the time of his enthronement. *it is written about me in the scroll.* Some take this to be a reference to a prophecy, perhaps Dt 17:14–15. The context, however,

strongly suggests that the "scroll" refers to the personal copy of the law that the king is to take at the time of his enthronement to serve as the covenant charter of his administration (see Dt 17:18–20; 2Ki 11:12; cf. 1Ki 2:3; see also TNIV text note).

40:8 *I desire.* Whatever is in full accord with God's "desire" (v. 6)—a claim that frames the stanza.

🔺 40:9–10 David's life is filled with praise, proclaiming God's faithful and loving acts in behalf of his people (cf. 85:10–11). This, too, God desires more than animal sacrifices (see 50:7–15,23).

40:9 *proclaim.* See 68:11; 96:2; as good tidings (see 1Ki 1:42; Isa 40:9; 41:27; 52:7; 61:1). *in the great assembly.* See notes on 1:5; 9:1. *not seal my lips.* He is not silent about God's praise (see 38:13–16; 39:1 and notes).

40:10 *heart.* See note on 4:7. *your love and your faithfulness.* See note on 26:3.

40:11–17 The prayer for help.

40:11–13 David's plea for deliverance from his troubles.

40:11 *your love and faithfulness.* Which he has been proclaiming to all at the temple (see v. 10 and note).

40:12 *sins have overtaken me.* In the form of the "troubles without number" that burden him (see Ps 38–39 and their introductions). *cannot see.* See note on 13:3. *more than the hairs of my head.* See Mt 10:30; Lk 12:7. *heart.* See note on 4:7.

They are more than the hairs of my head, *l*
  and my heart fails *m* within me.
¹³ Be pleased to save me, Lord;
  come quickly, Lord, to help me. *n*

¹⁴ May all who seek to take my life *o*
  be put to shame and confusion; *p*
may all who desire my ruin *q*
  be turned back in disgrace.
¹⁵ May those who say to me, "Aha! Aha!" *r*
  be appalled at their own shame.
¹⁶ But may all who seek you *s*
  rejoice and be glad *t* in you;
may those who long for your saving help always say,
  "The Lord is great!" *u*

¹⁷ But as for me, I am poor and needy; *v*
  may the Lord think *w* of me.
You are my help *x* and my deliverer; *y*
  you are my God, do not delay. *z*

PSALM 41

For the director of music. A psalm of David.

^{*1} Blessed *a* are those who have regard for the weak; *b*
  the Lord delivers them in times of trouble. *c*
² The Lord protects *d* and preserves them— *e*
  they are counted among the blessed in the land— *f*
  he does not give them over to the desire of their foes. *g*

³ The Lord sustains them on their sickbed *h*
  and restores them from their bed of illness. *i*

⁴ I said, "Have mercy *j* on me, Lord;
  heal *k* me, for I have sinned *l* against you."
⁵ My enemies say of me in malice,
  "When will he die and his name perish? *m*"
⁶ Whenever they come to see me,
  they speak falsely, *n* while their hearts gather slander; *o*
  then they go out and spread *p* it abroad.

⁷ All my enemies whisper together *q* against me;
  they imagine the worst for me, saying,
⁸ "A vile disease has beset him;
  he will never get up *r* from the place where he lies."
⁹ Even my close friend, *s*

* 41:1-13 is numbered 41:2-14 in Hebrew texts.

40:12 *l* Ps 69:4
m Ps 73:26
40:13 *n* Ps 22:19; 38:22
40:14 *o* S 1Sa 20:1
P S Est 9:2; Ps 35:26
q S Ps 35:4
40:15 *r* S Ps 35:21
40:16 *s* Dt 4:29; 1Ch 28:9; Ps 9:10; 119:2 *t* Ps 9:2
u Ps 35:27
40:17 *v* Ps 86:1; 109:22 *w* Ps 144:3
x S Ps 20:2 *y* S Ps 18:2
z Ps 119:60
41:1 *a* S Dt 14:29
b S Job 24:4
c Ps 25:17
41:2 *d* Ps 12:5; 32:7
e Ezr 9:9; Ps 71:20; 119:88,159; 138:7; 143:11 *f* Ps 37:22
g S Dt 6:24
41:3 *h* Ps 6:6
i 2Sa 13:5; 2Ki 1:4
41:4 *j* Ps 6:2; S 9:13
k Dt 32:39 *l* Ps 51:4
41:5 *m* S Ps 38:12
41:6 *n* Ps 12:2; 101:7; Mt 5:11 *o* Pr 26:24
P Lev 19:16
41:7 *q* Ps 71:10
41:8 *r* S 2Ki 1:4
41:9 *s* S 2Sa 15:12; S Job 19:14

40:14–16 Prayer for God's saving help to confound David's adversaries and move the godly to praise. For harassment by enemies in times of trouble, see 38:12; 39:8; 41:5,7 and often in the Psalms (see note on 5:9). For both form and substance, see 35:26–27.
40:14 *shame . . . confusion . . . disgrace.* David asks that those who have wished to put him to public shame be put to shame themselves (see note on 5:10).
40:15 *Aha! Aha!* See note on 3:2.
40:17 *poor and needy.* In need of God's help (see note on 34:6).
Ps 41 David's prayer for mercy when seriously ill. He acknowledges that his illness is related to his sin (v. 4). See introductions to Ps 38–40. His enemies greet the prospect of his death with malicious glee (see note on 5:9), and even his "close friend" (v. 9) betrays his friendship (see note on 31:11–12). This psalm concludes a collection of four psalms connected by common themes and together with Ps 40 forms the conclusion to Book I (see introduction to Ps 40–41). (Book I begins and ends with a "Blessed" psalm.) In its structure, the psalm is very symmetrical, composed

of four stanzas of three verses each. The first and fourth stanzas frame the prayer with expressions of confidence; stanzas two and three elaborate the prayer. Verse 13 is actually not part of the psalm but the doxology that closes Book I (see note on v. 13).
41 title *For the director of music.* See note on Ps 4 title.
41:1–3 Confidence that the Lord will restore.
41:1 *Blessed are those who have regard for the weak.* True of all, but especially of a king, whose duty it is to defend the powerless (see 72:2,4,12–14; 82:3–4; Pr 29:14; 31:8–9; Isa 11:4; Jer 22:16). *Blessed.* See note on 1:1.
41:4–6 Prayer for God to show mercy and to heal.
41:4 *sinned.* See note on 32:3–5.
41:5 *When will he die . . . ?* See note on 3:2. *his name perish.* See note on 9:5.
41:6 *see me.* Visit him in his sickness. *speak falsely.* Speak as if they were his friends. *hearts.* See note on 4:7.
41:7–9 His enemies and his friend.

A   **41:9** *close friend . . . who shared my bread.* One who shared the king's table—i.e., was an honored, as well as

41:9 ᵗNu 30:2;
Job 19:19; Ps 55:20;
89:34; Mt 26:23;
Lk 22:21; Jn 13:18*
41:10 ᵘver 4
ᵛPs 3:3; 9:13
ʷS 2Sa 3:39
41:11 ˣS Nu 14:8
ʸPs 25:2
41:12 ᶻS Ps 25:21
ᵃPs 18:35; S 37:17;
63:8 ᵇS Job 4:7;
Ps 21:6; 61:7
41:13 ᶜS Ge 24:27
ᵈPs 72:18 ᵉPs 72:19;
89:52; 106:48
42:1 ᶠS Ps 18:33
ᵍS Dt 10:7
ʰS Job 19:27;
Ps 119:131; Joel 1:20

someone I trusted,
one who shared my bread,
has lifted up his heel against me. ᵗ

¹⁰ But may you have mercy ᵘ on me, Lᴏʀᴅ;
raise me up, ᵛ that I may repay ʷ them.
¹¹ I know that you are pleased with me, ˣ
for my enemy does not triumph over me. ʸ
¹² In my integrity ᶻ you uphold me ᵃ
and set me in your presence forever. ᵇ
¹³ Praise ᶜ be to the Lᴏʀᴅ, the God of Israel, ᵈ
from everlasting to everlasting.
Amen and Amen. ᵉ

BOOK II

Psalms 42–72

PSALM 42 ᵃ

For the director of music. A maskil ᵇ *of the Sons of Korah.*

*¹ As the deer ᶠ pants for streams of water, ᵍ
so my soul pants ʰ for you, my God.

ᵃ In many Hebrew manuscripts Psalms 42 and 43 constitute one psalm.   ᵇ Title: Probably a literary or musical term
* 42:1-11 is numbered 42:2-12 in Hebrew texts.

---

trusted, friend (see note on 31:11–12). Reference may be to one who had sealed his friendship by a covenant (see note on 23:5). For Jesus' use of this verse in application to himself, see Jn 13:18. In fulfilling the role of his royal ancestor as God's anointed king over Israel, the great Son of David also experienced the hostility of others and the betrayal of a trusted associate and thus fulfilled his forefather's lament.

41:10–12 Prayer, with confidence.

41:10 *that I may repay them.* That I (as king) may call them to account.

41:12 *my integrity.* See note on 15:2.*set.* Establish.*in your presence.* As the royal servant of Israel's heavenly King. (For the idiom see 101:7; 1Sa 16:22, "in my service"; 1Ki 10:8, "before you"; 17:1, "whom I serve.") *forever.* Never to be rejected (see 2Sa 7:15–16).

41:13 The doxology with which the worshiping community is to respond to the contents of Book I (see 72:18–19; 89:52; 106:48; 150).

Ps 42–45 Book II of the Psalter begins with three prayers (but see introduction to Ps 42–43) and an attached royal psalm in perfect balance with the ending of Book II (see introduction to Ps 69–72). These prayers contain certain key words found elsewhere in Book II only in Ps 69–71—and in the cluster of seven psalms placed at the center of this Book (see introduction to Ps 54–60). Although Ps 42–43 is the prayer of an individual and Ps 44 a prayer of the community, the two have much in common. Central to both is the cry, "Why, God?" (42:9; 43:2; 44:23–24)— why have you forgotten me/us (42:9; 44:24) and rejected me/us (43:2; 44:23) in the face of the oppression of our enemies (42:9; 44:24)? But that "Why?" (see note on 6:3), so expressive of the tension faith experiences in the face of such circumstances as the psalmists describe, is not faith's last word. Just here—and that in the first of these two introductory psalms—faith responds with its own reassuring refrain, "Hope in God" (42:5,11; 43:5), because his "love" will not fail (42:8; 44:26).

Following the communal cry of anguish over God's apparently unprovoked abandonment of his people to the pillage and ridicule of foreign peoples (Ps 44), the editors of the Psalter have pointed its readers to the Lᴏʀᴅ's anointed as he is depicted in an honorific song on one of the high days of his reign. In this song two relevant themes loom large: (1) the king's responsibility to uphold justice

within the realm and to protect the people from external enemies and (2) the assurance of his enjoying God's favor so that his kingdom flourishes under his rule and his dynasty is stable and enduring—of which the glory of his wedding to a foreign princess is a token. This placement of Ps 45 hints at a Messianic reading of the psalm on the part of the Psalter's editors. See further the introduction to Ps 45 and the introduction to Ps 69–72.

Ps 42–43 A prayer for deliverance from being "oppressed by the enemy" (42:9; 43:2) and for restoration to the presence of God at his temple. That these two psalms form a single prayer (though they are counted as two psalms also in the Septuagint, the pre-Christian Greek translation of the OT [but see TNIV text note]) is evident from its unique structure (see below) and the development of common themes. Ps 43 may have come to be separated from Ps 42 for a particular liturgical purpose (see introduction to Ps 9). The speaker may have been a leading member of the Korahites, whose normal duties involved him in the liturgical activities of the temple (see especially 42:4 and note on Ps 42 title). It may be that the "unfaithful nation" (43:1) referred to was the Arameans of Damascus and that the author had been taken captive by the Arameans during one of their incursions into Judah, such as that of Hazael (see 2Ki 12:17–18). (This attack by Hazael affected especially the area in which the Korahites, descendants of Kohath, had been assigned cities; see Jos 21:4,9–19.) See also notes below. This psalm begins Book II of the Psalter (see introduction to Ps 42–45), a collection that is distinguished from Book I primarily by the fact that the Hebrew word for "God" (*Elohim*) predominates, whereas in the first book the Hebrew word for "the Lᴏʀᴅ" (*Yahweh*) predominates.

Structurally, the three stanzas of this psalm are symmetrical (each contains four verses), and each is followed by the same refrain (42:5,11; 43:5). The middle stanza, however, has at its center (see note on 6:6) an additional verse (42:8) that interrupts the developing thought and injects a note of confidence, such as comes to expression also in the threefold refrain. Apart from the refrains, the prayer is framed by an expression of longing for God's presence (42:1) and a vow to praise God at his altar (43:4; see note there). For other psalms with recurring refrains, see Ps 46; 49; 59; 80; 107.

42 title *For the director of music.* See note on Ps 4 title.*maskil.*

² My soul thirsts *i* for God, for the living God. *j*
    When can I go *k* and meet with God?
³ My tears *l* have been my food
    day and night,
while people say to me all day long,
    "Where is your God?" *m*
⁴ These things I remember
    as I pour out my soul: *n*
how I used to go to the house of God *o*
    under the protection of the Mighty One *a*
with shouts of joy *p* and praise *q*
    among the festive throng. *r*

⁵ Why, my soul, are you downcast? *s*
    Why so disturbed *t* within me?
Put your hope in God, *u*
    for I will yet praise *v* him,
    my Savior *w* and my God. *x*

⁶ My soul is downcast within me;
    therefore I will remember *y* you
from the land of the Jordan, *z*
    the heights of Hermon *a*—from Mount Mizar.
⁷ Deep calls to deep *b*
    in the roar of your waterfalls;
all your waves and breakers
    have swept over me. *c*

⁸ By day the Lᴏʀᴅ directs his love, *d*
    at night *e* his song *f* is with me—
    a prayer to the God of my life. *g*

---

a 4 See Septuagint and Syriac; the meaning of the Hebrew for this line is uncertain.

42:2 *i* Ps 63:1; 143:6
j S Jos 3:10;
S 1Sa 14:39;
S Mt 16:16; Ro 9:26
k Ps 43:4; 84:7
42:3 *l* S Job 3:24
m ver 10; Ps 79:10;
115:2; Joel 2:17;
Mic 7:10
42:4 *n* S 1Sa 1:15
o Ps 55:14; 122:1;
Isa 2:2; 30:29
p Ezr 3:13
q S Jos 6:5; Ps 95:2;
100:4; 147:7; Jnh 2:9
r Ps 35:18; 109:30
42:5 *s* Ps 38:6; 77:3;
La 3:20; Mt 26:38
t S Job 20:2
u Ps 25:5; S 71:14
v Ps 9:1 *w* Ps 18:46
x ver 11; Ps 43:5
42:6 *y* Ps 63:6; 77:11
z Ge 13:10; S Nu 13:29
a S Dt 3:8; S 4:48
42:7 *b* S Ge 1:2;
S 7:11 *c* Ps 69:2;
Jnh 2:3
42:8 *d* Ps 57:3
e S Ps 16:7 *f* Ps 77:6
g Ps 133:3; Ecc 5:18;
8:15

See note on Ps 32 title. *of the Sons of Korah.* Or "for the Sons of Korah"; see "For Jeduthun" in Ps 39 title. "Sons of Korah" refers to the Levitical choir made up of the descendants of Korah appointed by David to serve in the temple liturgy. The Korahites represented the Levitical family of Kohath, son of Levi. Their leader in the days of David was Heman (see Ps 88 title)—just as Asaph led the choir of the Gershonites and Jeduthun (Ethan) the choir of the Merarites (see 1Ch 6:31–47 and note on Ps 39 title). This is the first of a collection of seven psalms ascribed to the "Sons of Korah" (Ps 42–49); four more occur in Book III (Ps 84–85; 87–88).

42:1–4 Longing to be with God at the temple.
42:1 *deer pants for … water.* Because its life depends on water—especially when being pressed by hunters, as the psalmist was by his oppressors. *soul.* See note on 6:3.
42:2 *living God.* See Dt 5:26. *When … ?* Circumstances (see v. 9; 43:1–2) now prevent him from being at the temple. *meet with God.* His presence to commune with him (see Ex 19:17; 29:42–43; 30:6,36).
42:3 *day and night.* See vv. 8, 10. *Where is your God?* See note on 10:11.
42:4 *soul.* See note on 6:3.
42:5 The refrain: faith encouraging faith (see 27:13–14 and introduction to Ps 27). *praise him.* For his saving help (see notes on 7:17; 9:1; see also 43:4).
42:6–10 The cause and depth of the trouble of his soul.
42:6 *soul is downcast.* See vv. 5,11; 43:5. *therefore I will remember you.* As he remembers (v. 4) in his exile the joy of his past intimacy with God, so now in his exile he remembers God and painfully wonders (vv. 7,9–10), yet not without hope (v. 8). (But some believe that the clause should be rendered "because I remember you.") *from the land … from Mount Mizar.* Probably indicating that the author speaks from exile outside the contemporary boundaries of Israel and Judah. Some think the author locates himself at

Mount Mizar (a small peak or village, not otherwise known) on the flanks of Mount Hermon somewhere near the headwaters of the Jordan. Others translate the Hebrew for "from" as "far from" and understand "the land of the Jordan" to refer to the promised land (which lies along the Jordan and from which the author was separated). The mention of "the heights of Hermon" may then be a reference to the high peak that marked the northern border of the land (see Dt 3:8; Jos 11:17; 13:11; 1Ch 5:23) and looked down upon it (see 133:3; SS 4:8). Some have suggested that "Mount Mizar" is an additional reference to "the heights of Hermon," calling that high peak the "little mountain" (literal translation) in comparison with Mount Zion (see 68:15–16).
42:7 *Deep calls … your waterfalls.* Often taken to be an allusion to the cascading waters of the upper Jordan as they rush down from Mount Hermon. It is more likely, however, that this is a literary allusion to the "waterfalls" by which the waters from God's storehouse of water above (see note on 36:8)—the "deep" above—pour down into the streams and rivers that empty into the seas—the "deep" below. It pictures the great distress the author suffers, and the imagery is continued in the following reference to God's "waves and breakers" sweeping over him (see 69:1–2; 88:7; Jnh 2:3,5; see also note on 32:6). God's hand is involved in the psalmist's suffering, at least to the extent that he has allowed this catastrophe. He seems to the psalmist to have "forgotten" (v. 9)—to have "rejected" (43:2)—him. But he makes no link between this and any sin in his life (see Ps 44; 77).
42:8 The center: confession of hope in all the trouble. That is, "Day-and-night [cf. v. 3] the Lᴏʀᴅ directs his love, and his song is with me" (see note on 3:7). *the Lᴏʀᴅ.* Only here at the center in this psalm (see introduction). *directs his love.* Sends forth his love, like a messenger to do his will (see 43:3). *love.* See note on 6:4. *his song.* A song concerning him. *prayer.* Praise and prayer belong together in the thought of the psalmist.

42:9 ʰ Ps 18:31
ⁱ S Ps 10:11
ʲ S Ps 35:14
ᵏ Job 20:19; Ps 43:2;
106:42 ˡ Ps 9:13; 43:2
42:10 ᵐ S Ps 6:2
ⁿ Dt 32:27; Ps 44:16;
89:51; 102:8; 119:42
º S ver 3
42:11 ᵖ ver 5;
Ps 43:5
43:1 ᵠ S Jdg 6:31
ʳ S Ps 25:20
ˢ S Ps 36:3; 109:2
43:2 ᵗ Ps 44:9; 74:1;
88:14; 89:38
ᵘ S Ps 35:14
ᵛ S Ps 42:9
43:3 ʷ Ps 27:1
ˣ S Ps 26:3 ʸ S Ps 25:5
ᶻ Ps 2:6 ª S 2Sa 15:25
43:4 ᵇ S Ps 42:2
ᶜ Ps 26:6; 84:3
ᵈ S Ps 21:6 ᵉ Ps 16:3
ᶠ S Ge 4:21
43:5 ᵍ S Ps 42:6
44:1 ʰ 2Sa 7:22;
1Ch 17:20; Jer 26:11
ⁱ S Jdg 6:13
ʲ S Dt 32:7;
S Job 37:23

⁹ I say to God my Rock, ʰ
   "Why have you forgotten ⁱ me?
Why must I go about mourning, ʲ
   oppressed ᵏ by the enemy?" ˡ
¹⁰ My bones suffer mortal agony ᵐ
   as my foes taunt ⁿ me,
saying to me all day long,
   "Where is your God?" º

¹¹ Why, my soul, are you downcast?
   Why so disturbed within me?
Put your hope in God,
   for I will yet praise him,
   my Savior and my God. ᵖ

PSALM 43 ª

¹ Vindicate me, my God,
   and plead my cause ᵠ
   against an unfaithful nation.
Rescue me ʳ from those who are
   deceitful and wicked. ˢ
² You are God my stronghold.
   Why have you rejected ᵗ me?
Why must I go about mourning, ᵘ
   oppressed by the enemy? ᵛ
³ Send me your light ʷ and your faithful care, ˣ
   let them lead me; ʸ
let them bring me to your holy mountain, ᶻ
   to the place where you dwell. ª
⁴ Then I will go ᵇ to the altar ᶜ of God,
   to God, my joy ᵈ and my delight. ᵉ
I will praise you with the lyre, ᶠ
   O God, my God.

⁵ Why, my soul, are you downcast?
   Why so disturbed within me?
Put your hope in God,
   for I will yet praise him,
   my Savior and my God. ᵍ

PSALM 44

For the director of music. Of the Sons of Korah. A maskil. ᵇ

*¹ We have heard it with our ears, ʰ O God;
   our ancestors have told us ⁱ
what you did in their days,
   in days long ago. ʲ

ª In many Hebrew manuscripts Psalms 42 and 43 constitute one psalm.   ᵇ Title: Probably a literary or
musical term

* 44:1-26 is numbered 44:2-27 in Hebrew texts.

42:9 Echoed in 43:2. *Rock.* See note on 18:2. *Why … ? Why … ?*
See note on 6:3 and introduction to Ps 42–45.
42:10 See v. 3. *bones.* See note on 6:2.
43:1–4 Prayer for deliverance from the enemy and for restoration to God's presence.
43:1 A plea in the language of the court (see introduction to Ps 17).
43:2 Echoes 42:9.
43:3 *your light and your faithful care.* Personified as God's messengers who work out (1) his salvation (light; see note on 27:1) and (2) his faithful care in behalf of his own (see 26:3; 30:9; 40:10). May these guide me back to your temple. *holy mountain.* See note on 2:6.

43:4 See note on 7:17. *to the altar.* See 26:6 and note.
Ps 44 Israel's cry for help after suffering a devastating defeat at the hand of an enemy. In the light of vv. 17–22, it is difficult to associate this psalm with any of those defeats announced by the prophets as judgments on Israel's covenant unfaithfulness. It probably relates to an experience of the kingdom of Judah (which as a nation did not break covenant with the Lord until late in her history), perhaps during the reign of Jehoshaphat or Hezekiah.

Structurally, three thematic developments rise one upon the other as the psalm advances to the prayer in the closing verses. Its structure is like the stages of a ziggurat (a stepped pyramidal structure that the Babylonians built as a mountain-like base for some of their temples; see Ge 11:4 and note) leading to the tem-

² With your hand you drove out ^k the nations
  and planted ^l our ancestors;
you crushed ^m the peoples
  and made our ancestors flourish. ⁿ
³ It was not by their sword ^o that they won the land,
  nor did their arm bring them victory;
it was your right hand, ^p your arm, ^q
  and the light ^r of your face, for you loved ^s them.

⁴ You are my King ^t and my God, ^u
  who decrees ^a victories ^v for Jacob.
⁵ Through you we push back ^w our enemies;
  through your name we trample ^x our foes.
⁶ I put no trust in my bow, ^y
  my sword does not bring me victory;
⁷ but you give us victory ^z over our enemies,
  you put our adversaries to shame. ^a
⁸ In God we make our boast ^b all day long, ^c
  and we will praise your name forever. ^{b d}

⁹ But now you have rejected ^e and humbled us; ^f
  you no longer go out with our armies. ^g
¹⁰ You made us retreat ^h before the enemy,
  and our adversaries have plundered ⁱ us.
¹¹ You gave us up to be devoured like sheep ^j
  and have scattered us among the nations. ^k
¹² You sold your people for a pittance, ^l
  gaining nothing from their sale.

¹³ You have made us a reproach ^m to our neighbors, ⁿ
  the scorn ^o and derision ^p of those around us.
¹⁴ You have made us a byword ^q among the nations;
  the peoples shake their heads ^r at us.
¹⁵ I live in disgrace ^s all day long,
  and my face is covered with shame ^t
¹⁶ at the taunts ^u of those who reproach and revile ^v me,
  because of the enemy, who is bent on revenge. ^w

¹⁷ All this came upon us,
  though we had not forgotten ^x you;
  we had not been false to your covenant.
¹⁸ Our hearts had not turned ^y back;
  our feet had not strayed from your path.

---

^a 4 Septuagint, Aquila and Syriac; Hebrew *King, O God; / command*   ^b 8 The Hebrew has *Selah* (a word of uncertain meaning) here.

44:2 ^kS Jos 3:10;
Ac 7:45 ^lS Ex 15:17;
S Isa 60:21
^mS Jdg 4:23;
S 2Ch 14:13 ⁿPs 80:9;
Jer 32:23
44:3 ^oJos 24:12
^pPs 78:54 ^qEx 15:16;
Ps 77:15; 79:11; 89:10;
98:1; Isa 40:10; 52:10;
63:5 ^rPs 89:15
^sS Dt 4:37
44:4 ^tS Ps 24:7
^uPs 5:2 ^vS Ps 21:5
44:5 ^wS Jos 23:5
^xPs 60:12; 108:13
44:6 ^yGe 48:22;
Hos 1:7
44:7 ^zS Dt 20:4
^aS Job 8:22
44:8 ^bS Ps 34:2;
1Co 1:31; 2Co 10:17
^cPs 52:1 ^dS Ps 30:12
44:9 ^eS Ps 43:2
^fS Dt 8:3; S 31:17;
Ps 107:39; Isa 5:15
^gS Jos 7:12; Ps 108:11
44:10 ^hS Lev 26:17
ⁱS Jdg 2:14
44:11 ^jver 22;
Jer 12:3 ^kS Lev 26:33;
S Ps 9:11; Eze 6:8;
Zec 2:6
44:12 ^lS Dt 32:30;
Isa 52:3; Jer 15:13;
50:1; 52:3
44:13 ^mS 2Ch 29:8;
Isa 30:3; Jer 25:9;
42:18; 44:8 ⁿPs 79:4;
80:6; 89:41
^oS Dt 28:37;
S Mic 2:6 ^pEze 23:32
44:14 ^qS 1Ki 9:7
^rS 2Ki 19:21
44:15 ^sGe 30:23;
2Ch 32:21; Ps 35:26
^tS Ps 34:5
44:16 ^uS Ps 42:10
^vPs 10:13; 55:3; 74:10
^wS 1Sa 18:25;
S Jer 11:19; Ro 12:19
44:17 ^xS Dt 6:12;
S 32:18; Ps 119:16, 61,
153, 176; Pr 3:1
44:18 ^yPs 119:51,
157

---

ple that crowns it. First there is praise of the Lord for past victories (vv. 1–8), second a description of the present defeat and its consequences (vv. 9–16), third a plea of innocence (vv. 17–22), then finally the prayer (vv. 23–26). Each of the themes (recalling of past mercies, description of the present distress and claim of covenant loyalty) in its own way functions as a ground for the appeal for help (see Ps 40 and its introduction; see also the lengthy prefaces to prayer in Ps 40; 89). For the thematic links between Ps 44 and 42–43 and the function of these psalms in the arrangement of Book II, see introduction to Ps 42–45.

44 title See note on Ps 42 title.

44:1–8 Praise to God for past victories: (1) those by which Israel became established in the land (vv. 1–3) and (2) those by which Israel has been kept secure in the land (vv. 4–8).

44:1 See 78:3.

44:3 *light of your face.* See notes on 4:6; 13:1.

44:4 *my.* Here and elsewhere in this psalm the first-person singular pronoun refers to the nation corporately (see note on Ps 30 title). *Jacob.* See note on 14:7.

44:5,8 *your name.* See v. 20; see also note on 5:11.

44:8 *In God we make our boast.* That is, we give God all the praise. For *Selah,* see TNIV text note and note on 3:2.

44:9–16 But now you have forsaken us: (1) You have caused us to suffer defeat (vv. 9–12); (2) you have shamed us before our enemies (vv. 13–16).

44:11 *gave us up to be devoured like sheep.* Have not protected us as our Shepherd-King (see v. 4 and note on 23:1).

44:12 *sold your people.* Like chattel no longer valued (see Dt 32:30; Jdg 2:14). *for a pittance.* For nothing of value (see Isa 52:3; Jer 15:13; cf. Isa 43:3–4).

44:14 *shake their heads.* In scorn (see 64:8).

44:16 *bent on revenge.* See 8:2 and note.

44:17–22 And we have not been disloyal to you: (1) We have not been untrue to your covenant (vv. 17–19); (2) you are our witness that we have not turned to another god (vv. 20–22).

44:17 *your covenant.* See Ex 19–24.

44:18 *hearts.* See note on 4:7. *your path.* The way marked out in God's covenant (see note on 5:8).

44:19 z S 2Ch 14:13;
Ps 51:8 a S Job 30:29;
S Isa 34:13 b S Job 3:5
44:20 c S Dt 32:18;
S Jdg 3:7 d S Ex 20:3;
Isa 43:12; Jer 5:19
44:21 e S 1Sa 16:7;
1Ki 8:39; Pr 15:11;
Jer 12:3; 17:10
44:22 f S ver 11
g Isa 53:7; Jer 11:19;
12:3; Ro 8:36*
44:23 h S Ps 7:6
i Ps 78:65 j Ps 59:5
k Ps 74:1; 77:7
44:24 l S Dt 32:20;
Ps 13:1 m La 5:20
n S Dt 26:7
44:25 o Ps 119:25
44:26 p S Nu 10:35;
S Ps 12:5; 102:13
q Ps 26:11 r Ps 6:4
45:1 s SS 1:1
45:2 t Lk 4:22
u Ps 21:6

¹⁹ But you crushed ᶻ us and made us a haunt for jackals; ᵃ
  you covered us over with deep darkness. ᵇ

²⁰ If we had forgotten ᶜ the name of our God
  or spread out our hands to a foreign god, ᵈ
²¹ would not God have discovered it,
  since he knows the secrets of the heart? ᵉ
²² Yet for your sake we face death all day long;
  we are considered as sheep ᶠ to be slaughtered. ᵍ

²³ Awake, ʰ Lord! Why do you sleep? ⁱ
  Rouse yourself! ʲ Do not reject us forever. ᵏ
²⁴ Why do you hide your face ˡ
  and forget ᵐ our misery and oppression? ⁿ

²⁵ We are brought down to the dust; ᵒ
  our bodies cling to the ground.
²⁶ Rise up ᵖ and help us;
  redeem ᑫ us because of your unfailing love. ʳ

PSALM 45

For the director of music. To the tune of "Lilies." Of the Sons of Korah. A maskil. ᵃ *A wedding song.* ˢ

*¹ My heart is stirred by a noble theme
  as I recite my verses for the king;
  my tongue is the pen of a skillful writer.

² You are the most excellent of men
  and your lips have been anointed with grace, ᵗ
  since God has blessed you forever. ᵘ

ᵃ Title: Probably a literary or musical term
* 45:1-17 is numbered 45:2-18 in Hebrew texts.

44:19 *you crushed us.* But that cannot be used as evidence that we have been disloyal. *haunt for jackals.* A desolate place, uninhabited by people (see Isa 13:22; Jer 9:11). *deep darkness.* The absence of all that was associated with the metaphor "light" (see notes on 30:1; 36:9).
44:20 *spread out our hands.* Prayed (see Ex 9:29 and note).

⚫ 44:22 *Yet.* Or "As a matter of fact" or "As you, God, know." From the time of her stay in Egypt (see Ex 1), Israel has suffered the hostility of the nations because of her relationship with the Lord (see Mt 10:34). For Paul's application of this verse to the Christian community in the light of Christ's death and resurrection, see Ro 8:36.
44:23–26 The appeal for help: (1) Awake to our need (vv. 23–24); (2) arise to our help (vv. 25–26; see introduction to Ps 16).
44:23 *Awake.* See note on 7:6. *Why . . . ?* See note on 6:3 and introduction to Ps 42–45.
44:24 *hide your face.* See note on 13:1.
44:25 *We are brought down to the dust.* About to sink into death (see 22:29 and note; see also note on 30:1). In Hebrew there is a verbal link with the refrain, "Why, my soul, are you downcast?" in Ps 42–43.
44:26 *Rise up and help.* See 46:1,5; see also note on 3:7. *redeem.* See note on 25:22. *unfailing love.* See note on 6:4; see also 42:8 and note.

⚫ Ps 45 A song in praise of the king on his wedding day (see title; see also introduction to Ps 42–45). He undoubtedly belonged to David's dynasty, and the song was probably used at more than one royal wedding. Since the bride is a foreign princess (see vv. 10,12), the wedding reflects the king's standing as a figure of international significance (see note on v. 9). Accordingly he is addressed as one whose reign is to be characterized by victories over the nations (vv. 3–5; cf. Ps 2; 110). As a royal son of David, he is a type (foreshadowing) of Christ. After the exile

this psalm was applied to the Messiah, the promised Son of David who would sit on David's throne (for the application of vv. 6–7 to Christ, see Heb 1:8–9). The superscription implies that it was composed and sung by a member of the Levitical temple choir, a fact not surprising in view of the close link between the temple (housing the earthly throne room of Israel's heavenly King) and the Davidic dynasty (the Lord's appointed regents over his people, described throughout the books of Samuel, Kings and Chronicles). As a word from one of the temple personnel, the song was no doubt received as a word from the temple—and from the One who sat enthroned there.

In its structure, the song is framed by vv. 1,17, while vv. 2,16 constitute a secondary frame within them—all addressed to the king. The body of the song falls into two parts: (1) words addressed to the king (vv. 3–9) and (2) words addressed to the royal bride (vv. 10–15). These in turn each contain two parts, reflecting a similar pattern: (1) (a) exhortations to the king (vv. 3–5), (b) the glory of the king (vv. 6–9); (2) (a) exhortations to the bride (vv. 10–12), (b) the glory of the bride (vv. 13–15).
45 title *For the director of music.* See note on Ps 4 title. *To the tune of.* See note on Ps 9 title. *Lilies.* See Ps 69 title. "Lilies" may be an abbreviated form of "The Lily (Lilies) of the Covenant" found in the titles of Ps 60; 80. *Of the Sons of Korah.* See note on Ps 42 title. *maskil.* See note on Ps 32 title. *song.* See note on Ps 30 title.
45:1 See v. 17, where the speaker pledges (perhaps by means of this song) to perpetuate the king's memory throughout the generations and awaken the praise of the nations. *heart.* See note on 4:7.
45:2 *most excellent of men.* One who excels in manly traits and beauty, as a king should (see 1Sa 9:2; 16:18)—but he is so beyond ordinary men as to be almost Godlike (see note on v. 6). *lips . . . anointed with grace.* See Pr 22:11; Ecc 10:12; cf. Isa 50:4; Lk 4:22; see also v. 16, where it is suggested that such a king will be perpetuated in his sons. *forever.* See note on v. 6.

³ Gird your sword ᵛ on your side, you mighty one; ʷ
   clothe yourself with splendor and majesty. ˣ
⁴ In your majesty ride forth victoriously ʸ
   in the cause of truth, humility and justice; ᶻ
   let your right hand ᵃ achieve awesome deeds. ᵇ
⁵ Let your sharp arrows ᶜ pierce the hearts ᵈ of the king's enemies; ᵉ
   let the nations fall beneath your feet.
⁶ Your throne, O God, ᵃ will last for ever and ever; ᶠ
   a scepter of justice will be the scepter of your kingdom.
⁷ You love righteousness ᵍ and hate wickedness; ʰ
   therefore God, your God, has set you above your companions
   by anointing ⁱ you with the oil of joy. ʲ
⁸ All your robes are fragrant ᵏ with myrrh ˡ and aloes ᵐ and cassia; ⁿ
   from palaces adorned with ivory ᵒ
   the music of the strings ᵖ makes you glad.
⁹ Daughters of kings �𐞥 are among your honored women;
   at your right hand ʳ is the royal bride ˢ in gold of Ophir. ᵗ

¹⁰ Listen, daughter, ᵘ and pay careful attention: ᵛ
   Forget your people ʷ and your father's house.
¹¹ Let the king be enthralled by your beauty; ˣ
   honor ʸ him, for he is your lord. ᶻ
¹² The city of Tyre ᵃ will come with a gift, ᵇ ᵇ
   people of wealth will seek your favor.
¹³ All glorious ᶜ is the princess within her chamber;
   her gown is interwoven with gold. ᵈ
¹⁴ In embroidered garments ᵉ she is led to the king; ᶠ
   her virgin companions ᵍ follow her—
   those brought to be with her.
¹⁵ Led in with joy and gladness, ʰ
   they enter the palace of the king.

¹⁶ Your sons will take the place of your fathers;
   you will make them princes ⁱ throughout the land.

ᵃ 6 Here the king is addressed as God's representative.   ᵇ 12 Or *A Tyrian robe is among the gifts*

45:3 ᵛ S Dt 32:41;
Ps 149:6; Rev 1:16
ʷ S 2Sa 1:19
ˣ S Job 40:10;
S Ps 21:5
45:4 ʸ Rev 6:2
ᶻ Zep 2:3 ᵃ Ps 21:8
ᵇ S Dt 4:34; Ps 65:5;
66:3
45:5 ᶜ S Dt 32:23
ᵈ Nu 24:8 ᵉ Ps 9:13;
92:9
45:6 ᶠ S Ge 21:33;
La 5:19
45:7 ᵍ Ps 33:5
ʰ S Ps 11:5 ⁱ Ps 2:2;
Isa 45:1; 61:1;
Zec 4:14 / S Ps 23:5;
Heb 1:8-9*
45:8 ᵏ Pr 27:9;
SS 1:3; 4:10
ˡ S Ge 37:25
ᵐ S Nu 24:6; Jn 19:39
ⁿ S Ex 30:24
ᵒ S 1Ki 22:39
ᵖ Ps 144:9; 150:4;
Isa 38:20
45:9 𐞥 SS 6:8
ʳ 1Ki 2:19 ˢ Isa 62:5
ᵗ S Ge 10:29
45:10 ᵘ Ru 1:11
ᵛ Jer 5:1 ʷ Ru 1:16
45:11 ˣ S Est 1:11;
S La 2:15 ʸ Eph 5:33
ᶻ 1Pe 3:6
45:12 ᵃ S Jos 19:29
ᵇ S Ps 9:16;
S 2Ch 9:24
45:13 ᶜ Isa 61:10
ᵈ Ex 39:3
45:14 ᵉ S Jdg 5:30
ᶠ Est 2:15 ᵍ SS 1:3
45:15 ʰ S Est 8:17
45:16 ⁱ 1Sa 2:8;
Ps 68:27; 113:8

45:3–5 Go forth with your sword victoriously in the service of all that is right, and clothe yourself thereby with glory—make your reign adorn you more truly than the wedding garb with which you are now arrayed (v. 8).
45:3 *clothe yourself with.* See note on 109:29. *splendor and majesty.* See 21:5 and note.
45:4 *justice.* See notes on 37:6; Zec 7:9; see also Introduction to Amos: Theological Theme and Message. *awesome deeds.* See 66:5; 106:22; 145:6.
45:5 *nations fall beneath your feet.* See 2:8–9; 110:1–2, 5–6.
45:6–9 The glory of the king's reign: justice and righteousness (see Ps 72).

B A 45:6 *O God.* Possibly the king's throne is called God's throne because he is God's appointed regent. But it is also possible that the king himself is addressed as "god." The Davidic king (the "LORD's anointed," 2Sa 19:21), because of his special relationship with God, was called at his enthronement the "son" of God (see 2:7; 2Sa 7:14; 1Ch 28:6; cf. Ps 89:27). In this psalm, which praises the king and especially extols his "splendor and majesty" (v. 3), it is not unthinkable that he was called "god" as a title of honor (cf. Isa 9:6). Such a description of the Davidic king attains its fullest meaning when applied to Christ, as the author of Hebrews does (Heb 1:8–9). (The pharaohs of Egypt were sometimes addressed as "my god" by their vassal kings in Canaan, as evidenced by the Amarna letters; see chart, p. xxiii.) *for ever and ever.* See vv. 2, 17. Such was the language used with respect to kings (see note on 21:4). It here gains added significance in the light of God's covenant with David (see 89:4, 29, 36; 132:12; 2Sa 7:16). In Christ, the Son of David, it is fulfilled.
45:7 *companions.* The noble guests of the king, perhaps from

other lands. *oil of joy.* God has anointed him with a more delightful oil than the aromatic oils with which his head and body were anointed on his wedding day—namely, with joy (see 23:5; Isa 61:3).
45:8–9 The glory of the king's wedding.
45:8 *myrrh.* See notes on Ge 37:25; SS 1:13. *aloes.* See note on SS 4:14. *cassia.* See note on Ex 25:6. *palaces adorned with ivory.* See 1Ki 22:39; Am 3:15; 6:4.
45:9 *Daughters of kings.* Whether members of his royal harem (see 1Ki 11:1–3) or guests at his wedding, they represent international recognition of the king. *in gold of Ophir.* Adorned with jewels of finest gold (see notes on Ge 10:29; 1Ki 9:28) and all the finery associated with it.
45:10–12 The word to the royal bride.
45:10–11 Be totally loyal to your adoring king.
45:12 *city of Tyre.* Lit. "Daughter (of) Tyre," a personification of the city of Tyre (see note on 2Ki 19:21). The king of Tyre was the first foreign ruler to recognize the Davidic dynasty (see 2Sa 5:11), and Solomon maintained close relations with that city-state (see 1Ki 5; 9:10–14, 26–28). As a great trading center on the Mediterranean coast, Tyre was world-renowned for its wealth (see Isa 23; Eze 26:1—28:19). *people of wealth.* Such as those from your homeland. *seek your favor.* Desire to be in your good graces as the wife of this king. These honors will be yours if you faithfully honor your royal husband.
45:13–15 The royal bride's glory.
45:14 *virgin companions.* She too has "companions" (see v. 7), perhaps her permanent attendants. *to you.* To the king.
45:16 *Your.* The king's. *take the place of your fathers.* As the family line continues (dynastic succession). Perhaps it is also

45:17 /S Ex 3:15;
Ps 33:11; 119:90;
135:13 k Ps 138:4
/S Ps 21:4; Rev 22:5
46:1 m Ps 9:9;
37:39; 61:3; 73:26;
91:2,9; 142:5;
Isa 33:16; Jer 16:19;
17:17; Joel 3:16;
Na 1:7 n Ps 18:1
o Ps 34:18; La 3:57
p Ps 18:6; Lk 1:54
q S Dt 4:30; Ps 25:17
46:2 r S Ge 4:7;
Ps 3:6 s Ps 82:5;
Isa 13:13; 24:1,19,20;
Jer 4:23; Da 11:19;
Am 8:14; S Rev 6:14
t ver 6; Ps 18:7; 97:5;
Isa 54:10; Am 9:5;
Mic 1:4; Na 1:5;
Hab 3:6 u Ex 15:8
46:3 v Ps 93:3;
Isa 17:13; Jer 5:22;
Eze 1:24; Rev 19:6
w S Job 9:26
x S Jdg 5:5
46:4 y S Ge 2:10;
Rev 22:1 z S Ps 1:3
a Ps 48:1,8; 87:3;
101:8; Rev 3:12
b Ge 14:18
c S 2Sa 15:25
46:5 d Dt 23:14;
S Ps 26:8; Isa 12:6;
Zec 2:5 e Ps 125:1
f S 1Ch 5:20
46:6 g S Job 12:23
h Ps 74:23; Isa 5:30;
17:12 i Ps 68:32;
102:22; Isa 13:4,13;
23:11; Eze 26:18;
Mt 4:8 j S Ps 29:3;
Isa 33:3 k S ver 2

17 I will perpetuate your memory through all generations;[j]
      therefore the nations will praise you [k] for ever and ever. [l]

PSALM 46

For the director of music. Of the Sons of Korah. According to alamoth. [a]
A song.

*1 God is our refuge [m] and strength, [n]
      an ever-present [o] help [p] in trouble. [q]
2 Therefore we will not fear, [r] though the earth give way [s]
      and the mountains fall [t] into the heart of the sea, [u]
3 though its waters roar [v] and foam [w]
      and the mountains quake [x] with their surging. [b]

4 There is a river [y] whose streams [z] make glad the city of God, [a]
      the holy place where the Most High [b] dwells. [c]
5 God is within her, [d] she will not fall; [e]
      God will help [f] her at break of day.
6 Nations [g] are in uproar, [h] kingdoms [i] fall;
      he lifts his voice, [j] the earth melts. [k]

7 The Lord Almighty [l] is with us; [m]
      the God of Jacob [n] is our fortress. [o]

8 Come and see what the Lord has done, [p]
      the desolations [q] he has brought on the earth.

---

a Title: Probably a musical term   b 3 The Hebrew has *Selah* (a word of uncertain meaning) here and at
the end of verses 7 and 11.

* 46:1-11 is numbered 46:2-12 in Hebrew texts.

46:7 l S 1Sa 1:11 m S Ge 21:22 n S Ps 20:1 o ver 11; Ps 18:2   **46:8** p Ps 66:5 q Isa 17:9; 64:10; Da 9:26; Lk 21:20

---

hinted that they will surpass the fathers in honor (see note on v.
2). *land.* Or "earth."

45:17 See note on v. 1. *for ever and ever.* See note on v.6.

Ps 46–48 Following the cluster of psalms that introduce Book
II of the Psalter (see introduction to Ps 42–45), the next thematically related cluster of psalms all express confidence in the security of God's people in the midst of a threatening world. Ps 46
and 48 focus on the security of Jerusalem, "the city of [our] God"
(46:4; 48:1), and Ps 47 on the worldwide reign of "the great
King" (47:2), whose royal city Jerusalem is (48:2).

■ **Ps 46** A celebration of the security of Jerusalem as the
city of God (the inspiration of Martin Luther's great hymn
"A Mighty Fortress Is Our God"; see vv. 7,11). Thematically, this
psalm is closely related to Ps 48 (see also Ps 76; 87), while Ps 47
celebrates God's victorious reign over all the earth (see introduction to Ps 46–48). It probably predates the exile. However,
as a song concerning the "city of God" (v. 4), the royal city of his
kingdom on earth (see Ps 48), it remained for Israel a song of
hope celebrating the certain triumph of God's kingdom. It was
originally liturgical and sung at the temple: The citizens of
Jerusalem (or the Levitical choir in their stead) apparently sang
the opening stanza (vv. 1–3) and the responses (vv. 7,11), while
the Levitical leader of the liturgy probably sang the second and
third stanzas (vv. 4–6,8–10). In its structure, apart from the refrains (vv. 7,11), the psalm is composed of three symmetrical
stanzas, each containing three verses. For other psalms with recurring refrains, see introduction to Ps 42–43.

46 title *For the director of music.* See note on Ps 4 title. *Of the
Sons of Korah.* See note on Ps 42 title. *According to.* See note on
Ps 6 title. *alamoth.* See TNIV text note. Since the Hebrew word
appears to mean "young women," the phrase "According to *alamoth*" may refer to the "young women playing the timbrels"
who accompanied the singers as the liturgical procession made
its way to the temple (68:25). *A song.* See note on Ps 30 title.

■ **46:1–3** A triumphant confession of fearless trust in God,
though the continents break up and sink beneath the
surging waters of the seas—i.e., though the creation itself may
seem to become uncreated (see 104:6–9; Ge 1:9–10) and all
may appear to be going down before the onslaught of the
primeval deep. The described upheaval is probably imagery for
great threats to Israel's existence (see note on 32:6), especially
from her enemies (see vv. 6,8–10; 65:5–8).
46:3 For *Selah,* see TNIV text note and note on 3:2.

■ **46:4–6** A description of blessed Zion—a comforting
declaration of God's mighty, sustaining presence in his city.

■ **46:4** *river.* Jerusalem had no river, unlike Thebes (Na 3:8),
Damascus (2Ki 5:12), Nineveh (Na 2:6,8) or Babylon
(137:1)—yet she had a "river." Here the "river" of 36:8 (see note
there) serves as a metaphor for the continual outpouring of the
sustaining and refreshing blessings of God, which make the city
of God like the Garden of Eden (see v. 5; Ge 2:10; Isa 33:21; 51:3;
cf. also Eze 31:4–9). *city of God.* See v. 5; see especially Ps 48. *God
...Most High.* That is, God Most High (see 57:2; see also note on
3:7). *Most High.* See note on Ge 14:19. *dwells.* See note on 9:11.

■ **46:5** *at break of day.* Or "as dawn approaches"—i.e.,
when attacks against cities were likely to be launched. His
help brings on the dawn of deliverance, dispelling the night of
danger (see 44:19 and note; cf. Isa 37:36 for an example).
46:6 *Nations...fall.* Because of God's victory (see vv. 8–9;
48:4–7). *in uproar.* See v. 3 and note on vv. 1–3; see also 2:1–3;
Rev 11:18. *lifts his voice.* See 2:5; 9:5; Jer 25:30; Am 1:2; see also
104:7. God's thunder is evoked (see introduction to Ps 29), the
thunder of his wrath (see 18:13; Isa 2:10). *earth melts.* As though
struck by lightning (see 97:4–5).
46:7 The people's glad response (also v. 11). *Lord Almighty.* See
note on 1Sa 1:3. *Jacob.* See note on 14:7.
46:8–10 A declaration of the blessed effects of God's triumph
over the nations.
46:8 *Come and see.* An invitation to see God's victories in the

⁹ He makes wars ʳ cease
    to the ends of the earth.
He breaks the bow ˢ and shatters the spear;
    he burns the shields ᵃ with fire. ᵗ
¹⁰ "Be still, and know that I am God; ᵘ
    I will be exalted ᵛ among the nations,
    I will be exalted in the earth."

¹¹ The Lᴏʀᴅ Almighty is with us;
    the God of Jacob ʷ is our fortress. ˣ

PSALM 47

For the director of music. Of the Sons of Korah. A psalm.

*¹ Clap your hands, ʸ all you nations;
    shout to God with cries of joy. ᶻ

² For the Lᴏʀᴅ Most High ᵃ is awesome, ᵇ
    the great King ᶜ over all the earth.
³ He subdued ᵈ nations under us,
    peoples under our feet.
⁴ He chose our inheritance ᵉ for us,
    the pride of Jacob, ᶠ whom he loved. ᵇ

⁵ God has ascended ᵍ amid shouts of joy, ʰ
    the Lᴏʀᴅ amid the sounding of trumpets. ⁱ
⁶ Sing praises ʲ to God, sing praises;
    sing praises to our King, sing praises.
⁷ For God is the King of all the earth; ᵏ
    sing to him a psalm ˡ of praise.

ᵃ 9 Or *chariots*   ᵇ 4 The Hebrew has *Selah* (a word of uncertain meaning) here.
* 47:1-9 is numbered 47:2-10 in Hebrew texts.

46:9 ʳ Isa 2:4
ˢ S Ps 37:15;
S Isa 22:6 ᵗ Isa 9:5;
Eze 39:9; Hos 2:18
46:10 ᵘ Dt 4:35;
1Ki 18:36,39;
Ps 100:3; Isa 37:16,
20; 43:11; 45:21;
Eze 36:23 ᵛ Ps 18:46;
Isa 2:11
46:11 ʷ S Ps 20:1
ˣ S ver 7
47:1 ʸ S 2Ki 11:12
ᶻ S Ps 33:3
47:2 ᵃ Ge 14:18
ᵇ S Dt 7:21 ᶜ Ps 2:6;
48:2; 95:3; Mt 5:35
47:3 ᵈ Ps 18:39,47;
Isa 14:6
47:4 ᵉ Ps 2:8; 16:6;
78:55; 1Pe 1:4
ᶠ Am 6:8; 8:7
47:5 ᵍ Ps 68:18;
Eph 4:8 ʰ S Job 8:21;
S Ps 106:5
ⁱ S Nu 10:2;
S 2Sa 6:15
47:6 ʲ S 2Sa 22:50
47:7 ᵏ Zec 14:9
ˡ 1Ch 16:7; Col 3:16

---

world (see 48:8 and note). *the Lᴏʀᴅ.* Emphatic because of its rare use in Book II of the Psalter. *on the earth.* Among the hostile nations.

46:9 No more attacks against his city. The verse probably speaks of universal peace (see note on 65:6–7). *breaks . . . shatters . . . burns.* See 76:3; see also 1Sa 2:4. For the Messiah's universal victory over Israel's enemies, see Isa 9:2–7.

46:10 God's voice breaks through as he addresses the nations (see v. 6)—the climax. *Be still.* Here, the Hebrew for this phrase probably means "Enough!" as in 1Sa 15:16. *know.* Acknowledge. *I will be exalted . . . in the earth.* God's mighty acts in behalf of his people will bring him universal recognition, a major theme in the Psalter (see 22:27; 47:9; 57:5,11; 64:9; 65:8; 66:1–7; 67:2–5,7; 77:14; 86:9; 98:2–3; 99:2–3; 102:15) and elsewhere in the OT (see Ex 7:5; 14:4,18; Lev 26:45; Nu 14:15; 1Sa 17:46; 1Ki 8:41–43; 2Ki 19:19; Isa 2:2–3; 11:10; 25:3; 49:6–7; 51:5; 52:10; 60:1–14; 62:1–2; Jer 16:19; Eze 20:41; 28:25; 36:23; Hab 2:14). This has proven to be supremely true of God's climactic saving act in the birth, life, death, resurrection and glorification of Jesus Christ—yet to be brought to complete fruition at his return.

46:11 See note on v. 7.

Ps 47 Celebration of the universal reign of Israel's God: a testimony to the nations. This psalm belongs to a group of hymns to the Great King found elsewhere clustered in Ps 92–100. Here it serves to link Ps 46 and 48, identifying the God who reigns in Zion as "the great King over all the earth" (v. 2; see v. 7; 48:2; see also introduction to Ps 46–48). It dates from the period of the monarchy and was composed for use in the temple liturgy on one of the high festival days. The specific setting was perhaps the Festival of Tabernacles (see Lev 23:34), which was also the festival for which Solomon waited to dedicate the temple (see 1Ki 8:2). A liturgical procession is presupposed (v. 5), similar to that indicated in Ps 24; 68. Later Jewish usage employed this

psalm in the synagogue liturgy for *Rosh Hashanah* (the New Year festival). The Christian church has appropriately employed it in the celebration of Christ's ascension (see v. 5). Structurally, an introductory call to praise (v. 1) is followed by three stanzas of three Hebrew poetic lines each (vv. 2–4,5–7,8–9) devoted to the praise of which God is worthy as "the King of all the earth" (v. 7).

47 title See note on Ps 42 title.

47:1–4 The nations are called to rejoice in the God of Israel, the Lord over all the earth—OT anticipation of the evangelization of the nations (see notes on v. 9; 9:1).

47:1 *Clap your hands.* As at the enthronement of a king (see 2Ki 11:12; see also 98:8) or at other times of rejoicing (see Isa 55:12). *cries of joy.* See 1Ki 1:40; 2Ki 11:14.

47:2–3 The Lord of all the earth has shaped the destiny of his people Israel (see 105:6; 135:4; Ex 9:29; 15:1–18; 19:5–6; Dt 7:6; 14:2; Isa 41:8).

47:2 *Lᴏʀᴅ Most High is awesome.* See 68:35; 89:7; 99:3; 111:9; cf. note on 45:4. *Most High.* See note on Ge 14:19. *great King.* A title often used by the imperial rulers of Assyria (see note on 2Ki 18:19).

47:3 See 2Sa 5:17–25; 8:1–14; 10.

47:4 *inheritance.* The promised land (see Ge 12:7; 17:8; Ex 3:8; Dt 1:8; Jer 3:18). *pride.* That in which Jacob took supreme delight. *Jacob.* See note on 14:7. For *Selah,* see TNIV text note and note on 3:2.

47:5–6 The center of the poem (see note on 6:6). These verses portray the liturgical ascension of God to the temple—perhaps represented by the processional bearing of the ark into the temple. The ark is symbolic of God's throne; the temple is the earthly symbol of his heavenly palace (see Ps 24; 68).

47:5 *shouts of joy . . . sounding of trumpets.* See note on v. 1. *trumpets.* The ram's horn, here announcing the presence of God as King (see 98:6; Ex 19:16,19; Jos 6:4).

47:7–9 The liturgical enthronement of God as world ruler.

47:8 *m* S 1Ch 16:31
n S 1Ki 22:19;
S Ps 9:4; Rev 4:9
47:9 *o* S Job 25:2
p Ps 46:10; 97:9
48:1 *q* Ps 86:10;
96:4; 99:2; 135:5;
147:5; Jer 10:6
r S 2Sa 22:4;
S 1Ch 16:25; Ps 18:3
s S Ps 46:4
t S Dt 33:19; Ps 2:6;
87:1; Isa 11:9; 32:16;
Jer 31:23; Da 9:16;
Mic 4:1; Zec 8:3
48:2 *u* Ps 50:2;
La 2:15; Eze 16:14
v S Jos 13:27
w S Ps 2:6 *x* Mt 5:35
48:3 *y* ver 13;
Ps 122:7 *z* Ps 18:2
48:4 *a* 2Sa 10:1-19
48:5 *b* Ex 15:16;
Isa 13:8; Jer 46:5;
Da 5:9
48:6 *c* S Job 4:14
d Ge 3:16
48:7 *e* S Ge 10:4;
S 1Ki 10:22; 22:48
f S Ge 41:6

⁸God reigns *m* over the nations;
  God is seated on his holy throne. *n*
⁹The nobles of the nations assemble
  as the people of the God of Abraham,
for the kings*a* of the earth belong to God; *o*
  he is greatly exalted. *p*

PSALM 48

A song. A psalm of the Sons of Korah.

*1Great is the LORD, *q* and most worthy of praise, *r*
  in the city of our God, *s* his holy mountain. *t*

²Beautiful *u* in its loftiness,
  the joy of the whole earth,
like the heights of Zaphon*b v* is Mount Zion, *w*
  the city of the Great King. *x*
³God is in her citadels; *y*
  he has shown himself to be her fortress. *z*

⁴When the kings joined forces,
  when they advanced together, *a*
⁵they saw her and were astounded;
  they fled in terror. *b*
⁶Trembling seized *c* them there,
  pain like that of a woman in labor. *d*
⁷You destroyed them like ships of Tarshish *e*
  shattered by an east wind. *f*

⁸As we have heard,
  so we have seen
in the city of the LORD Almighty,
  in the city of our God:

---

a 9 Or *shields*   *b* 2 *Zaphon* was the most sacred mountain of the Canaanites.

* 48:1-14 is numbered 48:2-15 in Hebrew texts.

47:7 *God is the King of all the earth.* See 2Sa 15:10; 2Ki 9:13; Isa 52:7. *psalm.* Hebrew *maskil;* see note on Ps 32 title.

A **47:8** *seated on his holy throne.* In the Most Holy Place of the temple, where he takes the reins of world rule into his hands (see Jer 17:12). This verse is frequently echoed in Revelation (see Rev 4:9,10; 5:1,7,13; 6:16; 7:10,15; 19:4).

A **47:9** The nations acknowledge the God of Israel to be the Great King—anticipated as the final effect of God's rule (see note on 46:10). *as the people of the God of Abraham.* Thus the promises to Abraham will be fulfilled (see Ge 12:2–3; 17:4–6; 22:17–18). *kings.* See TNIV text note; see also note on 3:3; cf. Isa 2:2; 56:7.

Ps 48 A celebration of the security of Zion (as viewed with the eyes of faith) in that it is the city of the Great King (see introductions to Ps 46–47; see also introduction to Ps 46–48). It may have been sung by the Levitical choir on behalf of the assembled worshipers at the temple. Structure and theme are beautifully matched. The first and last verses combine to frame the whole with a comforting confession concerning Zion's God. The center, v. 8 (see note on 6:6), summarizes the main theme of the body of the psalm. Four stanzas (having a symmetrical pattern in Hebrew: three lines, four lines, four lines, three lines) develop the theme: (1) the beauty of Zion as God's impregnable citadel (vv. 2–3); (2) the futility of all enemy attacks (vv. 4–7); (3) Zion's joy over God's saving acts (vv. 9–11)—related to the second stanza; (4) Zion as impregnable citadel (vv. 12–13)—related to the first stanza. Regularly distributed between the four main stanzas are allusions to the four primary directions (see notes on vv. 2,7,10,13)—suggesting that the city is secure from all points of attack.

48 title *song.* See note on Ps 30 title. *of the Sons of Korah.* See note on Ps 42 title.

48:1 *in the city of our God, his holy mountain.* See 46:4. *our God.* Occurs in this psalm only here, in the center (v. 8) and at the end (v. 14). *holy mountain.* See 43:3; see also note on 2:6.

48:2–3 Describes the lofty impregnability of Mount Zion.

B **48:2** *Beautiful.* Its loftiness and secure position are its beauty (see note on 27:4). *loftiness.* Although not the highest ridge in its environment, in its significance as the mountain of God it is the "highest" mountain in the world (see 68:15–16 and note; Isa 2:2). *joy of the whole earth.* Perhaps referring to admiration from other nations, like that expressed by the queen of Sheba (see 1Ki 10:1–13). *Zaphon.* See TNIV text note. Mount Zaphon in the far north was for the Phoenicians the sacred residence of El, the chief of their gods—as Mount Olympus was the mountain citadel of Zeus for the Greeks. *Great King.* See note on 47:2.

A **48:3** God himself, not her walls, was Zion's defense, a fact on which the next stanza elaborates (see note on vv. 12–13). *her citadels.* See v. 13.

48:4–7 The futile attacks of hostile nations—they fled in panic when they saw that the Great King was in Zion. Such events as the destruction of the confederacy in the days of Jehoshaphat (see 2Ch 20) or the slaughter of the Assyrians in the time of Hezekiah (see 2Ki 19:35–36) may have been in the psalmist's mind.

48:7 *ships of Tarshish.* Great merchant ships of the Mediterranean (see 1Ki 10:22 and note). *shattered by an east wind.* See Ac 27:14; see also 1Ki 22:48. *east.* See introduction above.

48:8 The central verse and theme (see note on 6:6). *heard ... seen.* "Seen" is climactic, as in Job 42:5. They had heard because "our ancestors have told us what you did in their days" (44:1; see

God makes her secure
    forever.[a][g]

[9] Within your temple, O God,
    we meditate[h] on your unfailing love.[i]
[10] Like your name,[j] O God,
    your praise reaches to the ends of the earth;[k]
    your right hand is filled with righteousness.
[11] Mount Zion rejoices,
    the villages of Judah are glad
    because of your judgments.[l]

[12] Walk about Zion, go around her,
    count her towers,[m]
[13] consider well her ramparts,[n]
    view her citadels,[o]
that you may tell of them
    to the next generation.[p]

[14] For this God is our God for ever and ever;
    he will be our guide[q] even to the end.

PSALM 49

For the director of music. Of the Sons of Korah. A psalm.

[*1] Hear[r] this, all you peoples;[s]
    listen, all who live in this world,[t]
[2] both low and high,[u]
    rich and poor alike:

[a] 8   The Hebrew has *Selah* (a word of uncertain meaning) here.
[*] 49:1-20 is numbered 49:2-21 in Hebrew texts.

48:8 ᵍJer 23:6; Zec 8:13; 14:11
48:9 ʰS Ps 39:3; ⁱPs 6:4
48:10 ʲS Ex 6:3; S Jos 7:9 ᵏ1Sa 2:10; Ps 22:27; 65:5; 98:3; 100:1; Isa 11:12; 24:16; 42:10; 49:6
48:11 ˡPs 97:8
48:12 ᵐS Ne 3:1
48:13 ⁿ2Sa 20:15; Isa 26:1; La 2:8; Hab 2:1 ᵒS ver 3 ᵖPs 71:18; 78:6; 109:13
48:14 �q Ps 25:5; 73:24; Pr 6:22; Isa 49:10; 57:18; 58:11
49:1 ʳIsa 1:2 ˢPs 78:1 ᵗPs 33:8
49:2 ᵘPs 62:9

78:3), but now in the liturgical experience of God at his temple they have "seen" how secure the city of God is. *Lord Almighty.* See note on 1Sa 1:3. *our God.* See note on v. 1. For *Selah,* see TNIV text note and note on 3:2.

48:9–11 The worshipers meditate at the temple with joy because of God's mighty acts in Zion's behalf.

48:9 *Within your temple.* In the temple courts. *unfailing love.* See note on 6:4. As is clear from vv. 10–11, reference here is to God's saving acts by which he has expressed his covenant love for his people (see 31:21; 40:9–10).

48:10 *name.* See note on 5:11. *reaches.* From the temple to the ends of the earth (see 9:11; 22:27). *right hand.* In Hebrew idiom a subtle reference to the south. *righteousness.* Righteous acts (see 40:9–10 and note; see also note on 4:1).

48:11 *judgments.* God's righteous judgments, by which he has acted in defense of Zion.

48:12–13 The people contemplate Zion's defense, viewed from the perspective of what they have "seen" (v. 8) at the temple. The strength of Zion's "towers," "ramparts" and "citadels" is the presence of God.

48:13 *next generation.* Lit. "the generation behind"; in Hebrew idiom "behind" is a subtle reference to the west.

48:14 *our God.* See note on v. 1. *guide.* The great Shepherd-King (see notes on 23:1,3). *the end.* Lit. "death."

Ps 49–53 This cluster of psalms presents a striking contrast that brings the Psalter's call for godliness into sharp focus. On the one hand, we meet two psalms that face each other: (1) as God's summons to his people to come before him and hear his verdict concerning their lives (Ps 50) and (2) as a penitent's humble prayer for forgiveness and cleansing (Ps 51). On the other hand, these are bracketed by two psalms (49; 52) that denounce those who trust in their wealth (49:6; 52:7) and make their "boast" either in that wealth (49:6) or in the "evil" practices by which they obtained it (52:1). These descriptions of the ungodly are found nowhere else in the Psalter. In the first of these

framing psalms, such people are characterized as "foolish" and "senseless" (49:10). So it is appropriate that this four-psalm segment of the Psalter has appended to it in climax a somewhat revised repetition of Ps 14 with its denunciation of the fools whose thoughts and ways are God-less. Placed immediately after Ps 46–48, these five psalms serve as a stern reminder that only those who put their trust in the Lord have reason to celebrate the security of "the city of our God" (48:1,8; see introduction to Ps 46–48).

Ps 49 A wisdom word concerning rich fools who proudly rely on their great wealth and on themselves to assure their welfare and security in the world (see Ps 52 and introduction to Ps 49–53). The Levitical author knows what it is to be without wealth (see Nu 18:21–24; Dt 14:27–29) and has observed the attitudes of many of the rich (see vv. 5–6). He has seen through their folly, however, and offers his wisdom for all to hear (vv. 1–2), so that those who are awed by the rich may be freed from their spell. Inescapable death is the destiny and undoing of such "foolish and . . . senseless" (49:10) people, and in the end the "upright will prevail over them" (v. 14). As elsewhere (see note on structure in the introduction to Ps 33), the author has composed a poem of 22 Hebrew lines, in accordance with the number of letters in the Hebrew alphabet. The thematic structure is symmetrical: Following a four-line introduction (vv. 1–4), the instruction proper is developed in two balanced stanzas of eight lines each (vv. 5–11,13–19) with appended refrains (vv. 12,20). For other psalms with recurring refrains, see introduction to Ps 42–43. The date of this psalm may well be postexilic. See introduction to Ps 37.

49 title See note on Ps 42 title.

49:1–4 Introduction.

49:1–2 More like the address of the prophets (see 1Ki 22:28; Isa 34:1; Mic 1:2) than that of the wisdom teachers (see 34:11; Pr 1:8,10; 2:1).

49:3 ᵛS Ps 37:30
ʷPs 119:130
49:4 ˣPs 78:2;
Pr 1:6; Eze 12:22;
16:44; 18:2-3; Lk 4:23
ʸS 1Sa 16:16; Ps 33:2
ᶻNu 12:8
49:5 ᵃPs 23:4; 27:1
49:6 ᵇS Job 22:25;
Ps 73:12; Jer 48:7
ᶜS Ps 10:3
ᵈS Job 36:19
49:8 ᵉS Nu 35:31
ᶠMt 16:26
49:9 ᵍPs 22:29;
89:48 ʰPs 16:10
49:10 ʲEcc 2:16
ʲPs 92:6; 94:8
ᵏS Job 27:17
ˡEcc 2:18,21; Lk 12:20
49:11 ᵐMk 5:3;
Lk 8:27 ⁿPs 106:31
ᵒDt 3:14
49:12 ᵖS Job 14:2
�q ver 20; 2Pe 2:12
49:13 ʳLk 12:20
49:14 ˢJer 43:11;
Eze 31:14 ᵗNu 16:30;
S Job 31:13; Ps 9:17;
55:15 ᵘ Isa 14:2;
Da 7:18; 1Co 6:2
49:15 ᵛPs 56:13;
Hos 13:14

3 My mouth will speak words of wisdom; ᵛ
  the meditation of my heart will give you understanding. ʷ
4 I will turn my ear to a proverb; ˣ
  with the harp ʸ I will expound my riddle: ᶻ

5 Why should I fear ᵃ when evil days come,
  when wicked deceivers surround me—
6 those who trust in their wealth ᵇ
  and boast ᶜ of their great riches? ᵈ
7 No one can redeem the life of another
  or give to God a sufficient ransom—
8 the ransom ᵉ for a life is costly,
  no payment is ever enough— ᶠ
9 so that someone should live on ᵍ forever
  and not see decay. ʰ
10 For all can see that the wise die, ʲ
  that the foolish and the senseless ʲ also perish,
  leaving their wealth ᵏ to others. ˡ
11 Their tombs ᵐ will remain their houses ᵃ forever,
  their dwellings for endless generations, ⁿ
  though they had ᵇ named ᵒ lands after themselves.

12 Human beings, despite their wealth, do not endure; ᵖ
  they are like the beasts that perish. q

13 This is the fate of those who trust in themselves, ʳ
  and of their followers, who approve their sayings. ᶜ
14 They are like sheep and are destined ˢ to die; ᵗ
  death will be their shepherd
  (but the upright will prevail ᵘ over them in the morning).
  Their forms will decay in the grave,
  far from their princely mansions.
15 But God will redeem me from the realm of the dead; ᵛ

ᵃ 11 Septuagint and Syriac; Hebrew *In their thoughts their houses will remain* ᵇ 11 Or *generations, / they have* ᶜ 13 The Hebrew has *Selah* (a word of uncertain meaning) here and at the end of verse 15.

49:3 See Mt 12:34. *wisdom.* See essay, p. 750. *heart.* See note on 4:7.
49:4 *turn my ear.* The wisdom he is about to speak first had to be "heard" by him—all true wisdom is from God (see Job 28). *proverb ... riddle.* The two Hebrew words for these nouns were used to refer to insightful pieces of instruction that were artfully crafted (see 78:2 ["parable," "lessons from the past"]; Pr 1:6 ["proverbs," "riddles"]; Eze 17:2 ["allegory," "parable"]). *with the harp.* Another hint of the author's sense of inspiration (see 1Sa 10:5–6; 2Ki 3:15).

A 49:5–11 Those of little means or power need not be unsettled when surrounded by rich fools who threaten and strut; death is their destiny.

49:6 *who trust in their wealth.* See 52:7. *boast of.* Or "boast in," i.e., openly proclaim that they rely on their wealth to preserve them in a happy condition (see 52:1 and note).

A 49:7–9 Wealth cannot buy escape from death—not even one's family "redeemer" can accomplish it (cf. Ex 21:30; Lev 25:47–49). Only God himself can redeem a life from the grave (see v. 15 and note).

A 49:10 Any who have "eyes in their heads" (Ecc 2:14) can see that even the wise die (see Ecc 7:2; 9:5) and leave their wealth to others (see Ecc 2:18,21). How much more the fool (see 73:18–20; 92:6–7)! See also 52:5; 89:48; Job 30:23; Ecc 2:14–16. *wise ... foolish ... senseless.* Essentially the "righteous" and the "wicked" of Ps 37. *wealth.* Often gotten by devious means that their foolish "wisdom" had contrived (vv. 5,12; see also 52:1–4,7). *to others.* But not to their children (see note on 37:29; see also 39:6; Lk 12:20–21).

49:11 Though they lavish wealth on their tombs and try at least to perpetuate their memory by putting their names to their large landholdings (see Nu 32:41) as an enduring memorial, they only suffer the bitter irony of having their graves as their "eternal home" (Ecc 12:5). Cf. the psalmist's hope in v. 15.

49:12 Their epitaph (see note on 10:18; see also Ecc 3:19; 7:2) and the psalm's refrain.

49:13–19 The final end of these rich fools and of the righteous—so why should any stand in awe of the rich?

49:13 *in themselves.* As those who have "succeeded" (see v. 6). For *Selah,* see TNIV text note and note on 3:2.

B 49:14 *like sheep.* Death is already their shepherd, "guiding" them to the grave. *death will be their shepherd.* For the imagery of death (or the grave) as an insatiable monster feeding on its victims, see 69:15; 141:7; Pr 1:12; 27:20; 30:15–16; Isa 5:14; Jnh 2:2 ("deep"; lit. "belly"); Hab 2:5. The imagery is borrowed from Canaanite mythology, which so depicts the god Mot (death). As one Canaanite document reads, "Do not approach divine Mot, or he will put you like a lamb into his mouth." *prevail over.* See Lev 26:17; Isa 14:2; in contrast to the situation referred to in v. 5. *in the morning.* See vv. 15,19 and notes on 6:5; 11:7; 16:9–11; 17:15. But see also introduction to Ps 57.

A 49:15 See note on vv. 7–9. *redeem ... from the realm of the dead.* Cf. v. 11. While the psalmist may here refer to saving (for a while) from the universal prospect of death (as in Job 5:20; see 116:8), the context strongly suggests that he, as one of the upright, speaks of his final destiny. Perhaps the thought is of being conveyed into the presence of God in his heavenly temple, analogous to the later Jewish thought of being conveyed to "Abraham's side" (Lk 16:22; see notes on 6:5; 11:7; 16:9–11; 17:15). *take me to himself.* See 73:24; Ge 5:24 and notes.

he will surely take me to himself. [w]
16 Do not be overawed when others grow rich,
     when the splendor of their houses increases;
17 for they will take nothing [x] with them when they die,
     their splendor will not descend with them. [y]
18 Though while they live they count themselves blessed— [z]
     and people praise you when you prosper—
19 they will join those who have gone before them, [a]
     who will never again see the light [b] of life.

20 Human beings who have wealth but lack understanding [c]
     are like the beasts that perish. [d]

PSALM 50

A psalm of Asaph.

1 The Mighty One, God, the LORD, [e]
     speaks and summons the earth
     from the rising of the sun to where it sets. [f]
2 From Zion, [g] perfect in beauty, [h]
     God shines forth. [i]
3 Our God comes [j]
     and will not be silent; [k]
   a fire devours [l] before him, [m]
     and around him a tempest [n] rages.
4 He summons the heavens above,
     and the earth, [o] that he may judge his people: [p]
5 "Gather to me this consecrated people, [q]
     who made a covenant [r] with me by sacrifice."
6 And the heavens proclaim [s] his righteousness,
     for he is a God of justice. [a, b] [t]

49:15 [w] S Ge 5:24
49:17 [x] 1Ti 6:7
[y] S Ps 17:14
49:18 [z] Ps 10:6;
Lk 12:19
49:19 [a] S Ge 15:15
[b] S Job 33:30
49:20 [c] Pr 16:16
[d] S ver 12
50:1 [e] Jos 22:22
[f] Ps 113:3
50:2 [g] Ps 2:6
[h] S Ps 48:2; S La 2:15
[i] S Dt 33:2
50:3 [j] Ps 96:13
[k] ver 21; Isa 42:14;
64:12; 65:6
[l] S Lev 10:2
[m] S Ps 18:8
[n] Job 37:9; Ps 83:15;
107:25; 147:18;
Isa 29:6; 30:28;
Jnh 1:4; Na 1:3
50:4 [o] Dt 4:26;
31:28; Isa 1:2
[p] Heb 10:30
50:5 [q] S Dt 7:6;
S Ps 18:25 / Ex 24:7;
S 2Ch 6:11
50:6 [s] S Ps 19:1
[t] S Ge 16:5; S Job 9:15

---

[a] 6 With a different word division of the Hebrew; Masoretic Text *for God himself is judge*   [b] 6 The
Hebrew has *Selah* (a word of uncertain meaning) here.

49:16 *their houses.* Their whole estates (see Ex 20:17).
49:17 *take nothing with them when they die.* See 1Ti 6:7.
49:19 *light of life.* See notes on 27:1; 36:9; see also Isa 53:11.
49:20 The last word. See note on v. 12.
Ps 50 The Lord calls his covenant people to account. For this psalm's place in the arrangement of the Psalter, see introduction to Ps 49–53. The psalm appears to have been composed for a temple liturgy in which Israel reaffirms her commitment to God's covenant. A leader of the Levitical choir addresses Israel on behalf of the Lord (see Ps 15; 24, either of which may have been spoken earlier in the same liturgy). This liturgy was possibly related to the Festival of Tabernacles (see Dt 31:9–13; see also introduction to Ps 47). In its rebuke of a false understanding of sacrifice, the psalm has affinity with the prophecies of Amos, Micah and Isaiah and so may date from the late eighth and/or early seventh centuries B.C. Others find a closer relationship with the reformation of Josiah (2Ki 22:1—23:25) and the ministry of Jeremiah. Structurally, the psalm has three parts: (1) the announcement of the "coming" of Israel's covenant Lord to call his people to account (vv. 1–6); (2) the Lord's words of correction for those of honest intent (vv. 7–15); (3) his sharp rebuke of "the wicked" among them (vv. 16–23).
50 title A traditional ascription of the psalm to Asaph; or it may mean "for Asaph" (see "For Jeduthun" in Ps 39 title) or for the descendants of Asaph who functioned in his place. This psalm may have been separated from the other psalms of Asaph (73–83) in order to be paired with Ps 51 in the cluster of Ps 49–53. Asaph was one of David's three choir leaders (see note on Ps 39 title).
50:1–6 The Lord comes (v. 3) in the temple worship to correct and rebuke his people: Israel must know that the God of Zion is the God of Sinai (see Ex 19:16–20).
50:1 *The Mighty One, God, the LORD.* A sequence found else-

where only in Jos 22:22 (see note there). Ps 50 is noteworthy for its use of numerous names and titles for God (seven in all: three in v. 1, four in the rest of the psalm; see notes on vv. 6,14,21–22). *the earth.* See "the heavens . . . the earth" (v. 4) and "the heavens" (v. 6). When Moses renewed the covenant between the Lord and Israel on the plains of Moab, he called upon the heavens and the earth to serve as third-party witnesses to the covenant (Dt 30:19; 31:28). The Lord now summons these (vv. 1–4) to testify that his present word to his people is in complete accord with that covenant (see Isa 1:2). God's relationship with his people has the whole creation as its context, and for that reason the whole creation is a party of interest to that relationship (see Ge 1–3; see also Jer 12:4; Ro 8:22 and notes).
50:2 *perfect in beauty.* Because God resides there (cf. Eze 27:3–4,11; 28:12). *shines forth.* Manifests his glory as he comes to act (see 80:1; 94:1; Dt 33:2; cf. Eze 28:7,17), now calling his people to account but not yet announcing judgment as in Isa 1 or Mic 1.
50:3 *comes.* From his enthronement between the cherubim (see 80:1; 99:1; see also 1Sa 4:4; 2Sa 6:2; 2Ki 19:15) in the Most Holy Place of the temple (see note on 28:2; see also Isa 26:21; Mic 1:3). *will not be silent.* No longer (see v. 21) will he let their sins go unrebuked. *fire . . . tempest.* See Ex 19:16,18.
50:4 *judge.* Call them to account in accordance with his covenant.
50:5 *consecrated people.* See note on 4:3. *by sacrifice.* Sacrifices were a part of the ritual that sealed the covenant (see Ex 24:4–8) and continued to be an integral part of Israel's expression of covenant commitment to the Lord.
50:6 *proclaim.* See note on v. 1. *righteousness.* See note on 4:1. *God of justice.* See notes on 89:14; Ge 18:25; Zec 7:9; see also Introduction to Amos: Theological Theme and Message. For *Selah,* see TNIV text note and note on 3:2.

50:7 *u* Heb 2:4
v Ex 20:2; Ps 48:14
50:8 *w* S 2Sa 22:16
x S Ps 40:6
50:9 *y* S Lev 1:5
z S Lev 16:5
a S Nu 32:16
50:10 *b* Ps 104:20;
Isa 56:9; Mic 5:8
c Ps 104:24
50:11 *d* Mt 6:26
e Ps 8:7; 80:13
50:12 *f* Ex 19:5
g Dt 10:14; S Jos 3:11;
Ps 24:1; 1Co 10:26
50:14 *h* S Ezr 1:4;
S Ps 27:6 *i* S Nu 30:2;
S Ps 66:13; 76:11
j Ps 7:8
50:15 *k* Ps 4:1; 81:7;
Isa 55:6; 58:9;
Zec 13:9 *l* Ps 69:17;
86:7; 107:6; 142:2;
Jas 5:13 *m* Ps 3:7
n S Ps 22:23
50:16 *o* Ps 25:10
p Isa 29:13
50:17 *q* Pr 1:22
r 1Ki 14:9
50:18 *s* Ro 1:32;
1Ti 5:22 *t* S Job 22:15
50:19 *u* Ps 10:7;
36:3; 52:2; 101:7
50:20 *v* Mt 10:21
50:21 *w* Isa 42:14;
57:11; 62:1; 64:12
x Ps 6:1; S 18:15; 76:6;
104:7; Isa 50:2
y Ps 85:5; Isa 57:16
50:22 *z* S Job 8:13;
S Isa 17:10
a S Dt 32:39; Mic 5:8
50:23 *b* S Ps 9:14;
91:16; 98:3; Isa 52:10

7 "Listen, my people, and I will speak;
   I will testify *u* against you, Israel:
   I am God, your God. *v*
8 I bring no charges *w* against you concerning your sacrifices
   or concerning your burnt offerings, *x* which are ever before me.
9 I have no need of a bull *y* from your stall
   or of goats *z* from your pens, *a*
10 for every animal of the forest *b* is mine,
   and the cattle on a thousand hills. *c*
11 I know every bird *d* in the mountains,
   and the creatures of the field *e* are mine.
12 If I were hungry I would not tell you,
   for the world *f* is mine, and all that is in it. *g*
13 Do I eat the flesh of bulls
   or drink the blood of goats?

14 "Sacrifice thank offerings *h* to God,
   fulfill your vows *i* to the Most High, *j*
15 and call *k* on me in the day of trouble; *l*
   I will deliver *m* you, and you will honor *n* me."

16 But to the wicked, God says:

   "What right have you to recite my laws
   or take my covenant *o* on your lips? *p*
17 You hate *q* my instruction
   and cast my words behind *r* you.
18 When you see thieves, you join *s* with them;
   you throw in your lot with adulterers. *t*
19 You use your mouth for evil
   and harness your tongue to deceit. *u*
20 You sit and testify against your brother *v*
   and slander your own mother's son.
21 When you did these things and I kept silent, *w*
   you thought I was exactly *a* like you.
   But I now arraign *x* you
   and set my accusations *y* before you.

22 "Consider this, you who forget God, *z*
   or I will tear you to pieces, with no one to rescue: *a*
23 Those who sacrifice thank offerings honor me,
   and to the blameless *b* I will show my salvation. *b* "

a 21 Or *thought the 'I AM' was*   *b* 23 Probable reading of the original Hebrew text; the meaning of the
Masoretic Text for this phrase is uncertain.

50:7–15 The Lord corrects his people.
50:7 *my people.* "Our God" (v. 3) and "your God" (here) reflect the covenant bond (see Zec 8:8 and note). *I am God, your God.* See Ex 19:3–6; Lev 19:2–4,10,25,31,34,36; 20:7,24; 22:33; 23:22.

A **50:8–13** Israel had not failed to bring enough sacrifices (v. 8), but she was ever tempted to think that sacrifices were of first importance to God, as though he were dependent on them. This notion was widespread among Israel's pagan neighbors. See note on 40:6.
50:10 *thousand.* Used here figuratively for a very large number.
50:12 *the world . . . in it.* See 24:1 and note.

A **50:14–15** God wants Israel to acknowledge her dependence on him by giving thank offerings for his mercies (v. 14) and by praying to him in times of need (v. 15; see 116:17–19). Those who do so may expect God's gracious answer to their prayers (stated more directly in v. 23). God also desires obedience to his moral law (see vv. 16–21 and note on 40:6).

A **50:14** *thank offerings.* See Lev 7:12–13 and note on Ps 7:17. *God . . . Most High.* That is, God Most High (see 57:2 and note on 3:7). *your vows.* Vows that accompanied prayer in times of need, usually involving thank offerings (see 66:13–15),

always involving praise of the Lord for his answer to prayer (see note on 7:17). See also Heb 13:15. *Most High.* See note on v. 1; see also note on Ge 14:19.

A **50:15** *honor me.* With praise in the fulfillment of the vows (see v. 23)—and, implicitly, with obedience to his covenant law (see following verses).
50:16–23 The Lord's rebuke of the wicked.
50:16 *recite my laws.* Apparently a part of the liturgy of covenant commitment.

A **50:17** *You hate my instruction.* They formally participate in the holy ritual but reject God's law as the rule for life outside the ritual.
50:19 *use your mouth for evil.* See note on 5:9.
50:21 God's merciful and patient "silence" is distorted by the wicked into bad and self-serving theology (see Ecc 8:11; Isa 42:14; 57:11). *thought I was exactly.* See TNIV text note; Ex 3:14 and note (see also note on v. 1). *set my accusations before you.* Confront you with the particulars of my indictment.
50:22 *God.* A relatively rare word for "God" (Hebrew *Eloah*), though common in Job. See note on v. 1.
50:23 See note on vv. 14–15.

PSALM 51

For the director of music. A psalm of David. When the prophet Nathan came to him after David had committed adultery with Bathsheba. c

*[1] Have mercy d on me, O God,
  according to your unfailing love; e
  according to your great compassion f
  blot out g my transgressions. h
2 Wash away i all my iniquity
  and cleanse j me from my sin.

3 For I know my transgressions,
  and my sin is always before me. k
4 Against you, you only, have I sinned l
  and done what is evil in your sight; m
so you are right in your verdict
  and justified when you judge. n
5 Surely I was sinful o at birth, p
  sinful from the time my mother conceived me.
6 Yet you desired faithfulness even in the womb;
  you taught me wisdom q in that secret place. r

7 Cleanse s me with hyssop, t and I will be clean;
  wash me, and I will be whiter than snow. u
8 Let me hear joy and gladness; v
  let the bones w you have crushed rejoice.
9 Hide your face from my sins x
  and blot out y all my iniquity.

10 Create in me a pure heart, z O God,
  and renew a steadfast spirit within me. a

* 51:1-19 is numbered 51:3-21 in Hebrew texts.

51:1 c 2Sa 11:4; 12:1
d 2Sa 24:14;
S Ps 9:13 e S Ps 25:7;
S 119:88 f S Ne 9:27;
Ps 86:15; Isa 63:7
g S 2Sa 12:13;
S 2Ch 6:21; S Ne 4:5;
Ac 3:19 h S Ps 39:8
51:2 i S Ru 3:3;
Jer 2:22; 13:27;
Ac 22:16; 1Jn 1:9
j Pr 20:30; Isa 4:4;
Eze 36:25; Zec 13:1;
Mt 23:25-26;
Heb 9:14
51:3 k Isa 59:12
51:4 l S 1Sa 15:24
m S Ge 20:6; Lk 15:21
n Ro 3:4*
51:5 o S Lev 5:2
p S Job 5:7
51:6 q Ps 119:66;
143:10 r S Job 9:4;
S 34:32
51:7 s Isa 4:4;
Eze 36:25; Zec 13:1
t S Ex 12:22;
S Nu 19:6; Heb 9:19
u Isa 1:18; 43:25;
44:22
51:8 v Isa 35:10;
Jer 33:11; Joel 1:16
w S Ex 12:46
51:9 x Jer 16:17;
Zec 4:10 y S 2Sa 12:13
51:10 z S Ps 24:4;
78:37; Mt 5:8; Ac 15:9
a Eze 18:31; 36:26

Ps 51 David's humble prayer for forgiveness and cleansing. As the prayer of a contrite sinner, it represents a proper response to the Lord's confrontation of his people in Ps 50 (compare v. 16 with 50:8–15; see also introduction to Ps 49–53). This psalm has many points of contact with Ps 25. In traditional Christian usage it is one of seven penitential psalms (see introduction to Ps 6). The psalm is constructed symmetrically: A two-verse introduction balances a two-verse conclusion, and the enclosed four stanzas in Hebrew consist of five lines, three lines, three lines and five lines, respectively. The whole is framed by David's prayer for himself (vv. 1–2) and for Zion (vv. 18–19). The well-being of the king and the city stand and fall together (see 28:8 and note on 3:8).

51 title *For the director of music.* See note on Ps 4 title. *When.* For the event referred to, see 2Sa 11:1—12:25; see also note on Ps 3 title.

51:1–2 In mercy grant pardon (see Lk 18:13). Note the piling up of synonyms: mercy, unfailing love, great compassion; blot out, wash, cleanse; transgressions, iniquity, sin (for this last triad, see note on 32:5).

51:1 *unfailing love.* See note on 6:4. *blot out.* See v. 9. The image is that of a papyrus scroll (see note on 9:5) on which God had recorded David's deeds. The "blotting out" of sins pictures forgiveness (Jer 18:23; see Isa 43:25). For the imagery of God's keeping records of the events in his realm in the way that earthly kings do, see 56:8 and note; 87:6; 130:3; 139:16 and note; Ne 13:14; Da 7:10; see also Ex 32:32–33.

51:2 See v. 7. *Wash.* As a filthy garment. *cleanse me.* Make me clean in your sight (see Lev 11:32).

51:3–6 Confession of sin (cf. Pr 28:13; 1Jn 1:9).

51:3 *before me.* On my mind.

51:4 *Against you ... only.* David acknowledges that his sin was preeminently against God (see 2Sa 12:13; cf. Ge 20:6; 39:9; Lk 15:18). He had violated specific covenant stipulations (Ex 20:13–14,17). *when you judge.* As the Lord did through Nathan

the prophet (2Sa 12:7–12). For a NT application, see Ro 3:4.

51:5 He cannot plead that this sin was a rare aberration in his life; it sprang from what he is and has been from birth (see 58:3; Ge 8:21; cf. Jn 9:34; Eph 2:3). The apparently similar statements in Job 14:4; 15:14; 25:4–6 rise from a different motivation.

51:6 The great contrast: He has acted absolutely contrary to what God desires and to what God has been teaching him. But it is just this "desire" of God and this "teaching" of God that are his hope—what he pleads for in vv. 7,10. *faithfulness.* Moral integrity. *womb.* See 139:13–16 and notes. *wisdom.* Those who give themselves over to sin are fools; those who have God's law in their hearts are wise (see 37:30–31).

51:7–9 Renewed prayer for pardon.

51:7 *Cleanse me.* Lit. "Un-sin me." *hyssop.* Used in ritual cleansing; see note on Ex 12:22. *be clean.* The Hebrew root for this phrase is the same as that for "cleanse" in v. 2. *whiter than snow.* Like a filthy garment, he needs washing (see note on v. 2); but if God washes him, he will be so pure that there is no figurative word that can describe him (see Isa 1:18; Da 7:9; Rev 7:14; 19:14).

51:8 *Let me hear joy.* Let me be surrounded by joy (see 32:7 and note; see also 35:27), or let me hear a prophetic oracle of forgiveness that will result in joy—from the assurance of sins forgiven (see 2Sa 12:13). *bones.* See note on 6:2.

51:9 *Hide your face.* From what is "always before me" (v. 3). *blot out.* See note on v. 1.

51:10–12 Prayer for purity—for a pure heart, a steadfast spirit of faithfulness and a willing spirit of service. These can be his only if God does not reject him and take his Holy Spirit from him. If granted, the joy of God's salvation will return to gladden his troubled soul.

51:10 *Create.* As something new, which cannot emerge from what now is (see v. 5) and which only God can fashion (see Ge 1:1 and note; Isa 65:17; Jer 31:22). *heart.* See note on 4:7.

51:11 *b* Ps 27:9;
71:9; 138:8
c S Ge 4:14;
S Ex 33:15
d Ps 106:33; Isa 63:10;
Eph 4:30
51:12 *e* S Job 33:26
f Ps 110:3 *g* S Ps 18:35
51:13 *h* S Ex 33:13;
Ac 9:21-22 *i* S Ps 1:1
j S Job 33:27
51:14 *k* S Ps 39:8
l S 2Sa 12:9
m Ps 25:5; 68:20; 88:1
n S Ps 5:8; 35:28;
71:15
51:15 *o* Ex 4:15
51:16 *p* S 1Sa 15:22
51:17 *q* Pr 15:8;
Hag 2:14 *r* Mt 11:29
51:18 *s* Ps 102:16;
147:2; Isa 14:32; 51:3;
Zec 1:16-17
t Ps 69:35; Isa 44:26
51:19 *u* Dt 33:19
v Ps 66:13; 96:8;
Jer 17:26 *w* Ps 66:15
52:1 *x* 1Sa 21:7; 22:9
y Ps 10:3; 94:4
z Ps 44:8
52:2 *a* S Ps 50:19
b Ps 5:9 *c* S Nu 6:5
52:3 *d* Ex 10:10;
1Sa 12:25; Am 5:14-
15; Jn 3:20

[11] Do not cast me *b* from your presence *c*
  or take your Holy Spirit *d* from me.
[12] Restore to me the joy of your salvation *e*
  and grant me a willing spirit, *f* to sustain me. *g*

[13] Then I will teach transgressors your ways, *h*
  and sinners *i* will turn back to you. *j*
[14] Deliver me *k* from bloodguilt, *l* O God,
  you who are God my Savior, *m*
  and my tongue will sing of your righteousness. *n*
[15] Open my lips, Lord, *o*
  and my mouth will declare your praise.
[16] You do not delight in sacrifice, *p* or I would bring it;
  you do not take pleasure in burnt offerings.
[17] My sacrifice, *q* O God, is *a* a broken spirit;
  a broken and contrite heart *r*
  you, God, will not despise.

[18] May it please you to prosper Zion, *s*
  to build up the walls of Jerusalem. *t*
[19] Then you will delight in the sacrifices of the righteous, *u*
  in burnt offerings *v* offered whole;
  then bulls *w* will be offered on your altar.

PSALM 52

For the director of music. A maskil *b* *of David. When Doeg the Edomite* *x*
had gone to Saul and told him: "David has gone to the house of Ahimelek."

*[1] Why do you boast of evil, you mighty hero?
  Why do you boast* *y* *all day long,* *z*
  you who are a disgrace in the eyes of God?
[2] You who practice deceit, *a*
  your tongue plots destruction; *b*
  it is like a sharpened razor. *c*
[3] You love evil *d* rather than good,

---

a 17 Or *The sacrifices of God are*   *b* Title: Probably a literary or musical term
* 52:1-9 is numbered 52:3-11 in Hebrew texts.

51:11 The two requests are essentially one (see 139:7;
Eze 39:29). David's prayer recalls the rejection of Saul (see
1Sa 16:1,14; 2Sa 7:15) and pleads for God not to take away his
Spirit, by which he had equipped and qualified him for his royal
office (see 1Sa 16:13; cf. 2Sa 23:1–2). *Holy Spirit.* The phrase is
found elsewhere in the OT only in Isa 63:10–11. By his Spirit,
God effected his purposes in creation (see 104:30; Ge 1:2; Job
33:4) and redemption (see Isa 32:15; 44:3; 63:11,14; Hag 2:5),
equipped his servants for their appointed tasks (see Ex 31:3; Nu
11:29; Jdg 3:10; 1Sa 10:6; 16:13; Isa 11:2; 42:1), inspired his
prophets (see Nu 24:2–3; 2Sa 23:2; Ne 9:30; Isa 59:21; 61:1; Eze
11:5; Mic 3:8; Zec 7:12) and directed their ministries (see 1Ki
18:12; 2Ki 2:16; Isa 48:16; Eze 2:2; 3:14). And it is by his Spirit that
God gives his people a "new heart and . . . a new spirit" to live by
his will (see Eze 36:26–27; see also Jer 24:7; 32:39; Eze 11:19;
18:31).
51:13–17 The vow to praise (see note on 7:17).
51:13 His praise for God's forgiveness and purification will be
accompanied by instruction for "transgressors" and "sinners,"
whose waywardness he himself had been guilty of (see v. 3). He
commits himself to go from praise of God to instruction of others, as did the author of Ps 34 (see also note on 32:8–10). *your
ways.* See 25:4 and note.
51:14 If God will only forgive, praise will follow. *righteousness.*
See note on 4:1.
51:15 *Open my lips.* By granting the forgiveness and cleansing
I seek.

51:16 See note on 40:6.
51:17 *broken spirit; a broken and contrite heart.* What
pleases God more than sacrifices is a humble heart that
looks to him when troubles crush and penitently pleads for
mercy when sin has been committed (see 50:7–15 and notes;
see also 34:17–18).
51:18–19 Prayer for Zion (see note on 3:8).
51:19 *sacrifices of the righteous.* Such as are pleasing to God;
here, sacrifices accompanied by praise for God's mercies (see
50:14–15 and notes).
Ps 52 Fearless confidence in God when under attack by an
arrogant and evil enemy. David stands in the presence of God
and from the high tower of that refuge hurls his denunciation
(much like the prophetic denunciation in Isa 22:15–19) into the
face of his attacker. Though not a wisdom psalm, it has much in
common with Ps 49 (see introduction to Ps 49–53; see also introduction to Ps 49). The extended depiction of David's enemy
forms a sharp contrast with the spirit of Ps 51. See also David's
denunciation of Goliath (1Sa 17:45–47).
52 title *For the director of music.* See note on Ps 4 title. *maskil.*
See note on Ps 32 title. *When.* See note on Ps 3 title. For the
event referred to, see 1Sa 22:9–10.
52:1–4 The enemy castigated.
52:1 *Why . . . ?* By what right? See 50:16; Isa 3:15. *boast.* By act
as well as by word (see 75:4–5). *mighty hero.* In his own estimation (see Isa 22:17).
52:2 *your tongue.* See v. 4; see also note on 5:9.

falsehood *e* rather than speaking the truth. *a*
⁴ You love every harmful word,
you deceitful tongue! *f*

⁵ Surely God will bring you down to everlasting ruin:
He will snatch you up and pluck *g* you from your tent;
he will uproot *h* you from the land of the living. *i*
⁶ The righteous will see and fear;
they will laugh *j* at you, saying,
⁷ "Here now is the one
who did not make God his stronghold *k*
but trusted in his great wealth *l*
and grew strong by destroying others!"

⁸ But I am like an olive tree *m*
flourishing in the house of God;
I trust *n* in God's unfailing love
for ever and ever.
⁹ For what you have done I will always praise you *o*
in the presence of your faithful people. *p*
And I will hope in your name, *q*
for your name is good. *r*

PSALM 53

53:1–6pp — Ps 14:1–7

For the director of music. According to mahalath. *b A maskil c of David.*

*1 Fools *s* say in their hearts,
"There is no God." *t*
They are corrupt, and their ways are vile;
there is no one who does good.

² God looks down from heaven *u*
on the human race
to see if there are any who understand, *v*
any who seek God. *w*
³ Everyone has turned away, all have become corrupt;
there is no one who does good,
not even one. *x*

⁴ Do all these evildoers know nothing?

They devour my people as though eating bread;

a 3 The Hebrew has *Selah* (a word of uncertain meaning) here and at the end of verse 5.   *b* Title: Probably a musical term   *c* Title: Probably a literary or musical term
* 53:1-6 is numbered 53:2-7 in Hebrew texts.

52:3 *p* Ps 58:3; Jer 9:5; Rev 21:8
52:4 *r* Ps 5:9; 10:7; 109:2; 120:2,3; Pr 10:31; 12:19
52:5 *g* S Dt 29:28; S Job 40:12; Isa 22:19; Eze 17:24 *h* S Dt 28:63 *i* S Job 28:13
52:6 *j* S Job 22:19
52:7 *k* S 2Sa 22:3 *l* S Ps 49:6; S Pr 11:28; Mk 10:23
52:8 *m* S Ps 1:3; S Rev 11:4 *n* Ps 6:4; 13:5
52:9 *o* S Ps 30:12 *p* S Dt 7:6; Ps 16:3 *q* S Job 7:6; Ps 25:3 *r* Ps 54:6
53:1 *s* Ps 74:22; 107:17; Pr 10:23 *t* Ps 10:4
53:2 *u* S Ps 33:13 *v* Ps 82:5; Jer 4:22; 8:8 *w* 2Ch 15:2
53:3 *x* Ro 3:10-12*

52:3 Your whole moral sense is perverted. *love.* Prefer. For *Selah,* see TNIV text note and note on 3:2.
52:4 *tongue.* See note on v. 2.
52:5–7 The enemy's end announced (implicitly a prayer): God will slay you, and the righteous will mock you.
52:5 Note the triple imagery: "bring you down," "snatch you up," "uproot you." The arrogant enemy will meet the same end as the rich fools of Ps 49. *from your tent.* See Job 18:14. *uproot you.* Contrast v. 8.
52:6 *righteous.* See note on 1:5. *fear.* Learn from your downfall (see 40:3 and note).
52:7 See Ps 49.
52:8–9 David's security is God.
52:8 *like an olive tree.* Which lives for hundreds of years. *flourishing.* See 1:3. It will not be uprooted (see v. 5). *in the house of God.* Olive trees were not planted in the temple courts, but David had access to God's temple as his refuge (see 15:1; 23:6; 27:4; 61:4 and note), where he was kept safe (see 27:5 and note). *unfailing love.* See note on 6:4.

52:9 A vow to praise (see note on 7:17). *faithful people.* See note on 4:3. *name.* See note on 5:11.
Ps 53 A testimony concerning the folly of the wicked, a somewhat revised duplicate of Ps 14; see introduction there. (The main difference between the two psalms is that here the word "God" is used instead of "the LORD"; see also note on v. 5.) The original psalm may have been revised in the light of an event such as is narrated in 2Ch 20. Here it also serves as a further commentary on the kind of arrogant fool denounced in Ps 49; 52 (see introduction to Ps 49–53).
53 title *For the director of music.* See note on Ps 4 title. *According to.* See note on Ps 6 title. *mahalath.* Possibly the name of a tune (see note on Ps 9 title). The Hebrew appears to be the word for "suffering" or "sickness" (see Ps 88 title and TNIV text note there). Perhaps the Hebrew phrase indicates here that the psalm is to be used in a time of affliction, when the godless mock (see Ps 102; see also note on 5:9). *maskil.* See note on Ps 32 title.
53:1–4 See notes on 14:1–4.

53:5 ʸ S Lev 26:17
ᶻ 2Ki 23:14; Ps 141:7;
Jer 8:1; Eze 6:5
ᵃ 2Ki 17:20
ᵇ S Job 8:22
ᶜ Jer 6:30; 14:19;
La 5:22
54:1 ᵈ 1Sa 23:19;
26:1 ᵉ S 1Sa 24:15
ᶠ Ps 20:1 ᵍ 2Ch 20:6
54:2 ʰ S Ps 4:1; 5:1;
55:1
54:3 ⁱ Ps 86:14
ʲ Ps 18:48; 140:1,4,11
ᵏ S 1Sa 20:1 ˡ Ps 36:1
54:4 ᵐ S 1Ch 5:20;
S Ps 20:2 ⁿ S Ps 18:35
54:5 ᵒ S Dt 32:35;
Ps 94:23; Pr 24:12
ᵖ Ps 89:49; Isa 42:3
54:6 ᑫ S Lev 7:12,16;
S Ezr 1:4; S Ps 27:6
ʳ Ps 44:8; 69:30;
138:2; 142:7; 145:1
ˢ Ps 52:9
54:7 ᵗ Ps 34:6
ᵘ Ps 59:10; 92:11;
112:8; 118:7
55:1 ᵛ Ps 27:9;
La 3:56

they never call on God.
⁵ But there they are, overwhelmed with dread,
where there was nothing to dread. ʸ
God scattered the bones ᶻ of those who attacked you; ᵃ
you put them to shame, ᵇ for God despised them. ᶜ

⁶ Oh, that salvation for Israel would come out of Zion!
When God restores his people,
let Jacob rejoice and Israel be glad!

PSALM 54

For the director of music. With stringed instruments. A maskil ᵃ *of David.
When the Ziphites* ᵈ *had gone to Saul and said, "Is not David hiding
among us?"*

*¹ Save me ᵉ, O God, by your name; ᶠ
vindicate me by your might. ᵍ
² Hear my prayer, O God; ʰ
listen to the words of my mouth.

³ Arrogant foes are attacking me; ⁱ
ruthless people ʲ seek my life ᵏ—
people without regard for God. ᵇ ˡ

⁴ Surely God is my help; ᵐ
the Lord is the one who sustains me. ⁿ

⁵ Let evil recoil ᵒ on those who slander me;
in your faithfulness ᵖ destroy them.

⁶ I will sacrifice a freewill offering ᑫ to you;
I will praise ʳ your name, Lᴏʀᴅ, for it is good. ˢ
⁷ You have delivered me ᵗ from all my troubles,
and my eyes have looked in triumph on my foes. ᵘ

PSALM 55

For the director of music. With stringed instruments. A maskil ᵃ *of David.*

**¹ Listen to my prayer, O God,
do not ignore my plea;* ᵛ

ᵃ Title: Probably a literary or musical term   ᵇ 3 The Hebrew has *Selah* (a word of uncertain meaning) here.
* 54:1-7 is numbered 54:3-9 in Hebrew texts.   * 55:1-23 is numbered 55:2-24 in Hebrew texts.

53:5 Differs considerably from 14:5–6, though the basic thought
remains the same: God overwhelms the godless who attack his
people. Here the verbs are in the past tense (perhaps to express
the certainty of their downfall). *where there was nothing to dread.*
They fell victim to fear when, humanly speaking, they were not
even threatened. God's curse fell on them rather than on Israel
(see Lev 26:36–37; see also Jdg 7:21; 2Ki 3:22–23; 7:6–7; Pr 28:1).
scattered the bones. Over the battlefield of their defeat, their bodies left unburied like something loathsome (see Isa 14:18–20; Jer
8:2 and note). *God despised them.* As they had despised him.
53:6 See note on 14:7.
Ps 54–60 A cluster of seven prayers framed by a prayer of an individual (Ps 54) and a prayer of the community (Ps 60; see introduction to Ps 42–45). The psalm that introduces this cluster (Ps 54)
is a seven-verse poem that is paradigmatic in its structure (see introduction to this psalm, below). The psalm that concludes it echoes the key complaint of Ps 44, namely, that God has "rejected" his
people and no longer goes out "with our armies" (44:9; 60:10). At
the center is Ps 57, a prayer of 14 Hebrew lines—structurally a
double seven—with a refrain that appeals to God to "be exalted"
(vv. 5,11) above all creation through his saving acts. For the links
between Ps 55 and 59, see introductions to those psalms; for the
contrast between Ps 56 and 58 see introductions to those psalms.
Ps 54 A prayer for deliverance from enemies who want to have

David killed. The prayer is short, like those of Ps 3; 4; 13; yet it is
one of the most typical prayers of the Psalter, containing the main
speech functions found in these prayers (see Introduction: Psalm
Types). Completely symmetrical, the prayer is framed by David's
cry for vindication (v. 1) and his statement of assurance that he
will look in triumph on his foes (v. 7). A confession of confidence
(v. 4) centers the prayer (see 42:8 and note on 6:6). The opening
stanza has two verses, like the conclusion (and both refer to "your
name"), while vv. 3,5 each form a separate element in the prayer.
On the seven-verse structure, see introduction to Ps 29.
54 title *For the director of music.* See note on Ps 4 title. *With
stringed instruments.* See note on Ps 4 title. *maskil.* See note on
Ps 32 title. *When.* For the event referred to, see 1Sa 23:19; see
also note on Ps 3 title.
54:1–2 Prayer for God to judge his case (see Ps 17).
54:1 *name.* See v. 6; see also note on 5:11.
54:3 The case against his enemies. *without regard for God.* Like
those of Ps 53. For *Selah,* see TNIV text note and note on 3:2.
54:4 A confession of confidence at the center of the prayer
(see 42:8 and note).
54:5 The call for redress (see note on 5:10).
54:6 The vow to praise (see note on 7:17). *name.* See v. 1 and
note.
54:7 Assurance of being heard (see note on 3:8).

2 hear me and answer me. [w]
  My thoughts trouble me and I am distraught [x]
3 because of what my enemy is saying,
    because of the threats of the wicked;
  for they bring down suffering on me [y]
    and assail [z] me in their anger. [a]

4 My heart is in anguish [b] within me;
    the terrors [c] of death have fallen on me.
5 Fear and trembling [d] have beset me;
    horror [e] has overwhelmed me.
6 I said, "Oh, that I had the wings of a dove!
    I would fly away and be at rest.
7 I would flee far away
    and stay in the desert; [a][f]
8 I would hurry to my place of shelter, [g]
    far from the tempest and storm. [h]"

9 Lord, confuse the wicked, confound their words, [i]
    for I see violence and strife [j] in the city. [k]
10 Day and night they prowl [l] about on its walls;
    malice and abuse are within it.
11 Destructive forces [m] are at work in the city;
    threats and lies [n] never leave its streets.

12 If an enemy were insulting me,
    I could endure it;
  if a foe were rising against me,
    I could hide.
13 But it is you, one like myself,
    my companion, my close friend, [o]
14 with whom I once enjoyed sweet fellowship [p]
    at the house of God, [q]
  as we walked about
    among the worshipers.

15 Let death take my enemies by surprise; [r]
    let them go down alive to the realm of the dead, [s]
  for evil finds lodging among them.

[a] 7 The Hebrew has *Selah* (a word of uncertain meaning) here and in the middle of verse 19.

55:2 [w] Ps 4:1
[x] 1Sa 1:15-16; Ps 77:3; 86:6-7; 142:2
55:3 [y] S 2Sa 16:6-8; Ps 17:9; 143:3
[z] S Ps 44:16 [a] Ps 71:11
55:4 [b] S Ps 6:3
[c] S Job 18:11
55:5 [d] S Job 4:14; S 2Co 7:15 [e] Dt 28:67; Isa 21:4; Jer 46:5; 49:5; Eze 7:18
55:7 [f] 1Sa 23:14
55:8 [g] Ps 31:20
[h] Ps 77:18; Isa 4:6; 25:4; 28:2; 29:6; 32:2
55:9 [i] Ge 11:9; Ac 2:4 [j] Ps 11:5; Isa 59:6; Jer 6:7; Eze 7:11; Hab 1:3
[k] Ge 4:17
55:10 [l] 1Pe 5:8
55:11 [m] Ps 5:9
[n] Ps 10:7
55:13 [o] S 2Sa 15:12
55:14 [p] Ac 1:16-17
[q] Ps 42:4
55:15 [r] Ps 64:7; Pr 6:15; Isa 29:5; 47:9,11; 1Th 5:3
[s] S Ps 49:14

Ps 55 A prayer for God's help when threatened by a powerful conspiracy in Jerusalem under the leadership of a former friend. (Ps 59 is also a prayer for God's help against powerful foes who "prowl about" [55:10; 59:6,14] the city to achieve their evil ends and whose primary weapon is the mouth; see introduction to Ps 54–60.) The situation described is like that of Absalom's conspiracy against the king (see 25:15–17). The city is in turmoil; danger is everywhere; there is uncertainty as to who can be trusted; rumors, false reports and slander are circulating freely. Under such circumstances David longs for a quiet retreat to escape it all (vv. 6–8). That being out of the question, he casts his cares on the Lord, whom he knows he can trust. In its structure, the prayer is framed by a plea for help (v. 1) and a simple confession of faith: "I trust in you" (v. 23); at the center (v. 15) stands the heart of the prayer. On either side of the center, 12 Hebrew lines link it with introduction and conclusion, and each of these dozen lines is divided into a similar stanza pattern: five lines, three lines, four lines.
55 title *For the director of music. With stringed instruments.* See note on Ps 4 title. *maskil.* See note on Ps 32 title.
55:1–3 Initial appeal for God to hear.
55:4–8 His heart's anguish.
55:4–5 Danger is everywhere (see 31:13), a danger so great that it is as if death itself were stalking him (see 18:4–5; 116:3).

55:4 *heart.* See note on 4:7. *terrors of death.* See 1Sa 5:11; 15:32; 28:5; Job 18:14.
55:6–8 He longs for a quiet retreat, away from treacherous and conniving people (see similarly Jer 9:2–6).
55:7 For *Selah*, see TNIV text note and note on 3:2.
55:9–11 Prayer for God to foil the plots of his enemies.
55:9 *confuse . . . confound their words.* Paralyze the conspirators with conflicting designs, as at Babel (Ge 11:5–9; see 2Sa 17:1–14). *the city.* See v. 11; Jerusalem.
55:10 *malice and abuse.* Like watchmen on the walls (see 127:1; 130:6; SS 5:7).
55:11 *threats and lies.* Like watchmen who patrol the city streets (see SS 3:3).
55:12–14 The insults and plots of an enemy can be endured—but those of a treacherous friend?
55:13 *my companion, my close friend.* See v. 20; see also 41:9 and note.
55:14 *at the house of God.* Their ties of friendship had been a bond hallowed by common commitment to the Lord and sealed by its public display in the presence of God and the worshipers at the temple.
55:15 Prayer for redress (see note on 5:10). *Let death take my enemies.* The conspirators were seeking his death. *alive to the realm of the dead.* May they go to the grave before life has run its normal course (see v. 23; Nu 16:29–33; Pr 1:12; Isa 5:14).

55:17 *t* Ps 141:2;
Ac 3:1; 10:3, 30
u Ps 5:3; 88:13; 92:2
v Ac 10:9
55:19 *w* S Ex 15:18;
Dt 33:27; Ps 29:10
x Ps 78:59 *y* Ps 36:1;
64:4
55:20 *z* Ps 7:4
a Ps 41:9
55:21 *b* Ps 12:2
c Pr 5:3; 6:24
d Ps 57:4; 59:7; 64:3;
Pr 12:18; Rev 1:16
55:22 *e* S Ps 18:35;
Mt 6:25-34; 1Pe 5:7
f Ps 15:5; 21:7; 37:24;
112:6
55:23 *g* Ps 9:15;
S 30:3; 73:18; 94:13;
Isa 14:15; Eze 28:8;
S Lk 8:31 *h* Ps 5:6
i S Job 15:32 *j* Ps 11:1;
25:2; 56:3
56:1 *k* Ps 6:2
l Ps 57:1-3 *m* Ps 17:9
56:2 *n* Ps 35:25;
124:3 *o* Ps 35:1
56:3 *p* Ps 55:4-5
q S Ps 55:23
56:4 *r* ver 10

16 As for me, I call to God,
   and the LORD saves me.
17 Evening, *t* morning *u* and noon *v*
   I cry out in distress,
   and he hears my voice.
18 He rescues me unharmed
   from the battle waged against me,
   even though many oppose me.
19 God, who is enthroned from of old, *w*
   who does not change—
   he will hear *x* them and humble them,
   because they have no fear of God. *y*

20 My companion attacks his friends; *z*
   he violates his covenant. *a*
21 His talk is smooth as butter, *b*
   yet war is in his heart;
   his words are more soothing than oil, *c*
   yet they are drawn swords. *d*

22 Cast your cares on the LORD
   and he will sustain you; *e*
   he will never let
   the righteous be shaken. *f*
23 But you, God, will bring down the wicked
   into the pit *g* of decay;
   the bloodthirsty and deceitful *h*
   will not live out half their days. *i*

   But as for me, I trust in you. *j*

PSALM 56

For the director of music. To the tune of "A Dove on Distant Oaks."
Of David. A miktam. a When the Philistines had seized him in Gath.

*1 Be merciful to me, *k* my God,
   for my enemies are in hot pursuit; *l*
   all day long they press their attack. *m*
2 My adversaries pursue me all day long; *n*
   in their pride many are attacking me. *o*

3 When I am afraid, *p* I put my trust in you. *q*
4   In God, whose word I praise— *r*

---

a Title: Probably a literary or musical term
* 56:1-13 is numbered 56:2-14 in Hebrew texts.

55:16–19 Assurance of being heard (see note on 3:8).
55:17 *Evening, morning and noon I cry out.* Cf. Da 6:10.
55:18 *rescues.* See Isa 50:2; Jer 31:11 and note.
A **55:19** He who is the eternal King will deal with those who never change in their ways and show "no fear of God" (see 36:1 and note; see also Ps 14; 53).
55:20–21 Further sorrowful (or angry) reflection over the treachery of his former friend.
55:20 *his friends.* Lit. "those at peace with him" (see 7:4).
55:21 See 28:3; Pr 5:3–4; see also note on 5:9. *heart.* See note on 4:7.
55:22–23 Once more, assurance of being heard.
A **55:22** A testimony that all who are assembled at the temple. 1Pe 5:7 echoes this assurance. *righteous.* See note on 1:5.
55:23 *pit of decay.* The grave (see note on 30:1). *not live out half their days.* See note on v. 15.
A **Ps 56** A prayer for help when the psalmist is attacked by enemies and his very life is threatened. It is marked by consoling trust in the face of unsettling fear. Structurally, the prayer

falls into two balanced halves of seven Hebrew lines each, as does Ps 57 (see introduction to that psalm). The structure of each half is the same (two lines, two lines, three lines) with a refrain at the center of each (on the use of refrains see introduction to Ps 42–43). The whole is framed by an urgent appeal to God (vv. 1–2) and a word of confident assurance (vv. 12–13). This confidence in God's defense and deliverance stands in sharp contrast to the failure of wicked earthly rulers referred to in Ps 58.
56 title *For the director of music.* See note on Ps 4 title. *To the tune of.* See note on Ps 9 title. *miktam.* See note on Ps 16 title. *When.* See note on Ps 3 title. For the event referred to, see 1Sa 21:10–15; see also Ps 34 title and note. *had seized.* Or "were about to seize."
56:1–2 Initial appeal for God's help.
56:2 *their pride.* Confident in their position of strength, David's enemies take no account of his God (see notes on 3:2; 5:9; 10:11).
56:3–4 See vv. 10–11; confession of trust in the face of fear.
A **56:4** *word.* God's reassuring promise that he will be the God of his people and will come to their aid when they

in God I trust and am not afraid. [s]
 What can mere mortals do to me? [t]

5 All day long they twist my words; [u]
 all their schemes are for my ruin.
6 They conspire, [v] they lurk,
 they watch my steps, [w]
 hoping to take my life. [x]
7 Because of their wickedness do not[a] let them escape; [y]
 in your anger, God, bring the nations down. [z]

8 Record my misery;
 list my tears on your scroll[b] [a]—
 are they not in your record? [b]
9 Then my enemies will turn back[c]
 when I call for help. [d]
 By this I will know that God is for me. [e]

10 In God, whose word I praise,
 in the LORD, whose word I praise—
11 in God I trust and am not afraid.
 What can mere human beings do to me?

12 I am under vows [f] to you, my God;
 I will present my thank offerings to you.
13 For you have delivered me from death [g]
 and my feet from stumbling,
 that I may walk before God
 in the light of life. [h]

PSALM 57

57:7–11pp — Ps 108:1–5

For the director of music. To the tune of "Do Not Destroy." Of David.
A miktam. [c] *When he had fled from Saul into the cave.* [i]

*1 Have mercy on me, my God, have mercy on me,
 for in you I take refuge. [j]
 I will take refuge in the shadow of your wings [k]
 until the disaster has passed. [l]

2 I cry out to God Most High,
 to God, who vindicates me. [m]

---

[a] 7 Probable reading of the original Hebrew text; Masoretic Text does not have *do not*.   [b] 8 Or *misery; / put my tears in your wineskin*   [c] Title: Probably a literary or musical term

* 57:1-11 is numbered 57:2-12 in Hebrew texts.

56:4 [s] S Ps 27:1
[t] Ps 118:6; Mt 10:28;
Heb 13:6
56:5 [u] Ps 41:7;
2Pe 3:16
56:6 [v] Ps 59:3;
94:21; Mk 3:6
[w] Ps 17:11 [x] Ps 71:10
56:7 [y] Pr 19:5;
Eze 17:15; Ro 2:3;
Heb 12:25 [z] Ps 36:12;
55:23
56:8 [a] S 2Ki 20:5
[b] Isa 4:3; Da 7:10;
12:1; Mal 3:16
56:9 [c] Ps 9:3
[d] Ps 102:2
[e] S Nu 14:8;
S Dt 31:6; Ro 8:31
56:12 [f] Ps 50:14
56:13 [g] Ps 30:3;
33:19; 49:15; 86:13;
107:20; 116:8
[h] S Job 33:30
57:1 [i] 1Sa 22:1; 24:3;
Ps 142 Title [j] Ps 2:12;
9:9; 34:22
[k] Ru 2:12;
S Mt 23:37 [l] Isa 26:20
57:2 [m] Ps 138:8

---

appeal to him (see 50:15; 91:15; see also 119:74,81; 130:5). *mortals*. Lit. "flesh"—i.e., human feebleness compared with God's power (see note on 10:18).
56:5–7 Accusation and call for redress (see note on 5:9–10).
56:5 *twist my words*. See notes on 3:2; 5:9; 10:11.
56:7 See note on 5:10. *anger*. See note on 2:5.
56:8–9 Appeal for God to take special note of the psalmist's troubles.
56:8 *Record . . . list . . . on your scroll*. Record my troubles in your heavenly royal records as matters calling for your action (see note on 51:1).
56:9 If God takes such note of his tears that he records them in his book, he will surely respond to David's call for help.
56:10–11 Renewed confession of trust in the face of fear (see vv. 3–4).
56:12–13 Assurance of being heard (see note on 3:8).
A 56:12 *I am under vows*. Speaking as if his prayer has already been heard, David acknowledges that now he must keep the vows he made to God when he was in trouble (see 66:14 and note on 7:17).

56:13 *stumbling*. See note on 35:15. *before God*. See note on 11:7. *light of life*. The full blessedness of life (see note on 36:9).
A Ps 57 A prayer for deliverance when threatened by fierce enemies (it has many links with Ps 56). The psalm appears to reflect the imagery of the night of danger followed by the morning of salvation (v. 8: "I will awaken the dawn"). For other instances of these associations, see 30:5; 46:5; 59:6,14,16; 63:1,6; 90:14. Verses 7–11 are used again in 108:1–5. Structurally, the prayer is made up of two balanced halves, each having seven Hebrew lines and each composed of three couplets and a refrain (see introduction to Ps 56; see also introduction to Ps 54). For the placement of this psalm in the arrangement of Book II of the Psalter, see introduction to Ps 42–45; see also introduction to Ps 54–60.
57 title See note on Ps 56 title. *Do Not Destroy*. See Ps 58; 59; 75 titles. *When*. For the event referred to, see 1Sa 24:1–3; see also Ps 142 title.
57:1–5 The prayer.
57:1 Initial cry for God's merciful help. *shadow of your wings*. See note on 17:8.
57:2–3 Confidence of being heard.

57:3 ⁿ Ps 18:9,16;
69:14; 142:6; 144:5,7
ᵒ Ps 56:1 ᵖ Ps 25:10;
40:11; 115:1
57:4 �q S Ps 35:17
ʳ S Ps 55:21; Pr 30:14
57:5 ˢ ver 11;
Ps 108:5
57:6 ᵗ Ps 10:9; 31:4;
140:5 ᵘ S Ps 38:6;
145:14 ᵛ S Ps 9:15
ʷ S Est 6:13; Ps 7:15;
Pr 28:10; Ecc 10:8
57:7 ˣ Ps 112:7
57:8 ʸ Ps 33:2;
149:3; 150:3
57:10 ᶻ S Ps 36:5
57:11 ᵃ S Ps 8:1;
113:4 ᵇ S ver 5
58:1 ᶜ Ps 82:2

3 He sends from heaven and saves me, ⁿ
    rebuking those who hotly pursue me— ᵃᵒ
    God sends forth his love and his faithfulness. ᵖ

4 I am in the midst of lions; �q
    I am forced to dwell among man-eating beasts,
whose teeth are spears and arrows,
    whose tongues are sharp swords. ʳ

5 Be exalted, O God, above the heavens;
    let your glory be over all the earth. ˢ

6 They spread a net for my feet ᵗ—
    I was bowed down ᵘ in distress.
They dug a pit ᵛ in my path—
    but they have fallen into it themselves. ʷ

7 My heart, O God, is steadfast,
    my heart is steadfast; ˣ
    I will sing and make music.
8 Awake, my soul!
    Awake, harp and lyre! ʸ
    I will awaken the dawn.

9 I will praise you, Lord, among the nations;
    I will sing of you among the peoples.
10 For great is your love, reaching to the heavens;
    your faithfulness reaches to the skies. ᶻ

11 Be exalted, O God, above the heavens; ᵃ
    let your glory be over all the earth. ᵇ

PSALM 58

*For the director of music. To the tune of "Do Not Destroy." Of David.
A miktam.* ᵇ

*1 Do you rulers indeed speak justly? ᶜ
    Do you judge people with equity?

ᵃ 3 The Hebrew has *Selah* (a word of uncertain meaning) here and at the end of verse 6.   ᵇ Title:
Probably a literary or musical term
* 58:1-11 is numbered 58:2-12 in Hebrew texts.

57:2 *Most High.* See note on Ge 14:19. *who vindicates me.* See
138:8. But the Hebrew can also be translated "who makes an
end ιof troublesℐ for me" (see 7:9).
57:3 *He sends.* God sends his love and faithfulness (here personified) as his messengers from heaven to save his servant (see
note on 43:3). *his love and his faithfulness.* See note on 26:3. *love.*
See note on 6:4.
57:4 The threatening situation. *I am forced to dwell.* Like a
sheep among lions. *man-eating beasts.* The psalmists often
compare their enemies to ferocious beasts (see note on 7:2).
(The use of the metaphor here has no connection with the description of Saul and Jonathan in 2Sa 1:23.) *tongues.* See note
on 5:9.
57:5 A prayer for God to show his exalted power and glory
throughout his creation by coming to his servant's rescue (see
7:6–7; 21:13; 46:10; 59:5,8; 113:4–9; cf. Ex 14:4; Isa 26:15; 44:23;
59:19; see also note on Ps 46:10).
A   **57:6–11** Praise for God's saving help—confidently an-
    ticipating the desired deliverance. For such a sudden tran-
sition from prayer to assurance, see note on 3:8.
57:6 The threat and its outcome: The enemies suffer the calamity they plotted. *net . . . pit.* They hunted him as if he were a wild
beast, but the "lions" themselves were caught (see 7:15; 9:15 and
notes).
57:7 All cause for fear has been removed. *heart.* See note on
4:7. *is steadfast.* Feels secure (see 112:7).

B   **57:8** *Awake . . . Awake.* Greet with joy the dawn of the
    day of deliverance (see Isa 51:9,17; 52:1). *soul.* Lit. "glory."
(see note on 7:5). *harp and lyre.* Instruments (here personified)
to accompany the praise of the Lord at his temple in celebration
of deliverance (see 71:22; 81:2 and note on Ps 4 title). *awaken
the dawn.* With joyful cries proclaiming God's saving act. (Dawn,
too, is here personified—the Canaanites even deified it.)
57:9–10 The vow to praise (see notes on 7:17; 9:1).
57:10 *love.* See note on 6:4. *love . . . faithfulness.* That is, love-
and-faithfulness (see v. 3 and note on 36:5; see also note on
3:7). *reaching to the heavens . . . to the skies.* See note on 36:5.
57:11 The refrain (see v. 5), but now as praise (see 18:46; 30:1;
34:3; 35:27; 40:16; 70:4; 92:8; 97:9; 99:2; 113:4; 148:13).
A   **Ps 58** A prayer for God, the supreme Judge, to set right
    human affairs, judging those rulers who corrupt justice
and championing the cause of the righteous. (The psalm was
applied by the early church to Jesus' trial before the Sanhedrin;
see Mt 26:57–68 and parallels.) Concern for the just use of judicial power is pervasive throughout the OT. This was the primary
agency in the administrative structures of the ancient Near East
for the protection of the innocent (usually the poor and powerless) against the assaults of unscrupulous people (usually the
rich and powerful). Israelite society was troubled with the corruption of this judicial power from the days of Samuel to the
end of the monarchy (see, e.g., 1Sa 8:3; Isa 1:23; 5:23; 10:1–2;
Eze 22:6,12; Am 5:7,10–13; Mic 3:1–3,9–11; 7:2). Even in David's

2 No, in your heart you devise injustice, *d*
    and your hands mete out violence on the earth. *e*

3 Even from birth the wicked go astray;
    from the womb they are wayward, spreading lies.
4 Their venom is like the venom of a snake, *f*
    like that of a cobra that has stopped its ears,
5 that will not heed *g* the tune of the charmer, *h*
    however skillful the enchanter may be.

6 Break the teeth in their mouths, O God; *i*
    LORD, tear out the fangs of those lions! *j*
7 Let them vanish like water that flows away; *k*
    when they draw the bow, let their arrows fall short. *l*
8 May they be like a slug that melts away as it moves along, *m*
    like a stillborn child *n* that never sees the sun.

9 Before your pots can feel the heat of the thorns *o*—
    whether they be green or dry—the wicked will be swept
        away. *a p*
10 The righteous will be glad *q* when they are avenged, *r*
    when they dip their feet in the blood of the wicked. *s*
11 Then people will say,
    "Surely the righteous still are rewarded; *t*
    surely there is a God who judges the earth." *u*

---

a 9 The meaning of the Hebrew for this verse is uncertain.

58:2 *d* Mt 15:19
e Ps 94:20; Isa 10:1;
Lk 6:38
58:4 *f* S Nu 21:6
58:5 *g* Ps 81:11
h Ecc 10:11; Jer 8:17
58:6 *i* Ps 3:7
j S Job 4:10
58:7 *k* S Lev 26:36;
S Job 11:16 *l* Ps 11:2;
57:4; 64:3
58:8 *m* Isa 13:7
n S Job 3:16
58:9 *o* Ps 118:12;
Ecc 7:6 *p* S Job 7:10;
S 21:18
58:10 *q* S Job 22:19
r Dt 32:35; Ps 7:9;
91:8; Jer 11:20;
Ro 12:17-21 *s* Ps 68:23
58:11 *t* S Ge 15:1;
S Ps 128:2; Lk 6:23
u S Ge 18:25

---

time all was not well (see 2Sa 15:1–4). For the central concern of this psalm, see Ps 82. In the arrangement of the Psalter, Ps 58 stands in counterpoint to Ps 56 (see introduction to that psalm).

Structurally, the psalm is framed by a rhetorical address to the wicked judges (vv. 1–2) and by a reassuring word to "the righteous" (vv. 9–11). The frame emphasizes the fact that those who do not judge uprightly (v. 1) will be judged by God (v. 11). Between the framing verses, two three-verse stanzas flesh out the theme: Verses 3–5 elaborate on the ways of the wicked rulers, and vv. 6–8 call for their disablement and removal.

58 title *For the director of music.* See note on Ps 4 title. *To the tune of.* See note on Ps 9 title. *Do Not Destroy.* See Ps 57; 59; 75 titles. *miktam.* See note on Ps 16 title.

58:1–5 Accusation against the wicked judges.

58:1–2 Direct challenge to the wicked rulers: Their mouths, hearts and hands are united in the pursuit of injustice.

58:1 *rulers.* Lit. "gods" (see Ps 82:1 and note; see also introduction to Ps 82), a title applied to those whose administrative positions called upon them to act as earthly representatives of God's heavenly court (see TNIV text notes on Ex 21:6; 22:8–9; see also Dt 1:17; 2Ch 19:6 and note on Ps 45:6). *speak justly.* Make just judicial pronouncements.

58:2 *heart.* See note on 4:7. *mete out violence.* Issue decisions that result in cruel injustice.

58:3–5 The depth and stubbornness of the rulers' wickedness.

58:3 *from birth … from the womb.* Their corrupt ways are not sporadic; they act in accordance with their nature (see 51:5). Here reference is to "the wicked"; the author does not make a general statement about all people, as is the case in Ge 6:5; 8:21; Job 14:4; 15:14–16; 25:4–6. *the wicked.* Most probably a characterization of the wicked rulers. For a description of the wicked in general, see Ps 10. *spreading lies.* They have never been concerned for the truth (see Jn 8:44).

58:4 *venom.* What issues from their mouths is as cruel and

deadly as the venom of snakes (see 140:3; Mt 23:33; Jas 3:8). *stopped its ears.* They are incorrigible; nothing—neither appeals nor threats—will move them.

58:6–8 Appeal for God to defang the wicked rulers and purge the land of such perverse judges. The author uses imagery drawn from conventional curses of the ancient Near East (see notes on 5:10; Ge 12:3).

58:6 Let the weapons of their mouths (see 57:4) be broken and torn out. *lions.* See note on 7:2.

58:7 *water that flows away.* And is absorbed by the ground. *arrows.* Malicious pronouncements (see 57:4—but the Hebrew of the whole clause is obscure).

58:8 *slug.* That appears to dry up to nothing as it moves over a stone in the hot sun.

58:9–11 Assurance that God will surely judge them (see note on 3:8).

58:9 See TNIV text note. The verse may be speaking picturesquely of the speed of God's judgment—speed probably signifying here the inescapable certainty of his judgment (see note on 37:10; see also Lk 18:7–8). *thorns.* Twigs from wild thornbushes were used as fuel for quick heat (see 118:12; Ecc 7:6). *swept away.* As by a storm—God's storm (see Job 27:21).

58:10 *righteous.* Here a judicial term for those who are in the right but who have been wronged (see note on 1:5). *when they are avenged.* When the wrongs committed against them are redressed. *dip their feet in the blood.* Vivid imagery borrowed from the literary conventions of the ancient Near East (see 68:23). Its origin is the exaggerated language of triumphant reports of victory on the battlefield.

58:11 The climax: When God has judged the unjust "gods" (see note on v. 1), all people will see that right ultimately triumphs under God's just rule (see note on 46:10; see also Ps 93; 96–99). No more will people despair, like those in Mal 3:15.

59:1 ᵛ1Sa 19:11
ʷPs 143:9 ˣS Ps 20:1
59:2 ʸPs 14:4;
36:12; 53:4; 92:7;
94:16 ᶻS Ps 26:9;
139:19; Pr 29:10
59:3 ᵃS Ps 56:6
59:4 ᵇPs 119:3
ᶜMt 5:11 ᵈS Ps 13:3
59:5 ᵉPs 69:6; 80:4;
84:8 ᶠS Ps 44:23
ᵍS Ps 9:5; S Isa 10:3
ʰJer 18:23
59:6 ᶦver 14;
Ps 22:16
59:7 ʲPs 94:4;
Pr 10:32; 12:23; 15:2,
28 ᵏS Ps 55:21
ˡS Job 22:13
59:8 ᵐPs 37:13;
Pr 1:26 ⁿPs 2:4
59:9 ᵒS Ps 18:1
ᵖPs 9:9; 18:2; 62:2;
71:3

PSALM 59

*For the director of music. To the tune of "Do Not Destroy." Of David.
A miktam.* ᵃ *When Saul had sent men to watch David's house* ᵛ *in order to
kill him.*

*¹Deliver me from my enemies, O God; ʷ
   be my fortress against those who are attacking me. ˣ
² Deliver me from evildoers ʸ
   and save me from those who are after my blood. ᶻ

³ See how they lie in wait for me!
   Powerful people conspire ᵃ against me
   for no offense or sin of mine, Lᴏʀᴅ.
⁴ I have done no wrong, ᵇ yet they are ready to attack me. ᶜ
   Arise to help me; look on my plight! ᵈ
⁵ You, Lᴏʀᴅ God Almighty,
   you who are the God of Israel, ᵉ
rouse yourself ᶠ to punish all the nations; ᵍ
   show no mercy to wicked traitors. ᵇ ʰ

⁶ They return at evening,
   snarling like dogs, ᶦ
   and prowl about the city.
⁷ See what they spew from their mouths ʲ—
   the words from their lips are sharp as swords, ᵏ
   and they think, "Who can hear us?" ˡ
⁸ But you laugh at them, Lᴏʀᴅ; ᵐ
   you scoff at all those nations. ⁿ

⁹ You are my strength, ᵒ I watch for you;
   you, God, are my fortress, ᵖ
¹⁰   my God on whom I can rely.

ᵃ Title: Probably a literary or musical term   ᵇ 5 The Hebrew has *Selah* (a word of uncertain meaning)
here and at the end of verse 13.

* 59:1-17 is numbered 59:2-18 in Hebrew texts.

Ps 59 A prayer for deliverance when endangered by enemy attacks (for links with Ps 55, see introduction to that
psalm; see also introduction to Ps 54–60). If originally composed
by David under the circumstances noted in the superscription, it
must have been revised for use by one of David's royal sons when
Jerusalem was under siege by a hostile force made up of troops
from many nations—as when Hezekiah was besieged by the Assyrians (see 2Ki 18:19). (Some, however, ascribe it to Nehemiah; see
Ne 4.) The enemy weapon most prominent is the tongue, attacking with slander and curses (see note on 5:9). In this psalm, too, the
imagery of the night of danger (vv. 6,14), followed by the morning
of deliverance (v. 16), is evoked (see introduction to Ps 57).

Regarding the structure, the two closely balanced halves of
the psalm (vv. 1–9,10–17) each concludes with an almost identical refrain (vv. 9,17), preceded by a stanza that begins with a
like characterization of the enemies (vv. 6,14). The first half of
the psalm is predominantly prayer, the second half predominantly assurance of deliverance. The whole is framed by a cry for
God to be the psalmist's "fortress" (v. 1) and a joyful confession
that God is indeed his "fortress" (v. 17).

59 title See note on Ps 56 title. *Do Not Destroy.* See Ps 57; 58;
75 titles. *When.* For the event referred to, see 1Sa 19:11.
59:1–2 The cry for deliverance.
59:1 *be my fortress.* Lit. "raise me to a high, secure place."
59:2 *evildoers . . . those who are after my blood.* Common
characterizations of those who attack the psalmists out of
malice.
59:3–5 By slander (v. 10) and lies (v. 12) the enemies seek to
justify their attacks, but the psalmist protests his innocence and
pleads with God to judge those who wrong him (see 58:11).

59:3 *lie in wait.* See 10:8–9 and note on 7:2.
59:4 *Arise.* See note on 3:7.
59:5 *Lᴏʀᴅ God Almighty.* See note on 1Sa 1:3. *God of Israel.* This
appeal to the Lord as the God of Israel to punish the nations
makes clear that the attack on the psalmist involves an attack
by the nations on Israel. *rouse yourself.* See note on 7:6. *punish
. . . show no mercy.* See note on 5:10. *traitors.* Whether Israelites
had joined in the attack is not clear; the Hebrew indicates only
that the enemies were treacherous. For *Selah,* see TNIV text note
and note on 3:2.
59:6–8 Confidence: Surely God mocks such a pack of dogs (see
22:16–17).
59:6 *about the city.* The enemies besiege the city like dogs at
night on the prowl for food (see vv. 14–15).
59:7 *words from their lips are sharp as swords.* Their "curses and
lies" (v. 12). For the imagery, see 57:4; see also note on 5:9. *they
think.* See note on 3:2.
59:9 *watch.* Hebrew *shamar* (see note on v. 17). This verb is used
similarly in 31:6; Jnh 2:8 ("cling to"); the basic idea appears to be
to "look to expectantly" for help. The psalmist watches as one who
longingly waits for the morning (of salvation); see 130:6.
59:10–13 The prayer renewed. Confident that the Lord will
hear his prayer (v. 10) and will punish the nations (v. 5), the
psalmist prays that God will not sweep them away suddenly but
will prolong their punishment so that Israel ("my people," v. 11)
will not forget God's acts of salvation, as they had done so often
before (see 78:11; 106:13). Nevertheless, the psalmist asks God
not to allow the enemies to escape the full consequences of
their malice (vv. 12–13).
59:10 *rely.* See note on 6:4. *slander.* See note on 5:9.

God will go before me
and will let me gloat over those who slander me.
[11] But do not kill them, Lord our shield,[a][q]
or my people will forget.[r]
In your might uproot them
and bring them down.[s]
[12] For the sins of their mouths,[t]
for the words of their lips,[u]
let them be caught in their pride.[v]
For the curses and lies they utter,
[13]   consume them in wrath,
consume them till they are no more.[w]
Then it will be known to the ends of the earth
that God rules over Jacob.[x]

[14] They return at evening,
snarling like dogs,
and prowl about the city.
[15] They wander about for food[y]
and howl if not satisfied.
[16] But I will sing[z] of your strength,[a]
in the morning[b] I will sing of your love;[c]
for you are my fortress,[d]
my refuge in times of trouble.[e]

[17] You are my strength, I sing praise to you;
you, God, are my fortress,
my God on whom I can rely.[f]

PSALM 60

60:5–12pp — Ps 108:6–13

For the director of music. To the tune of "The Lily of the Covenant."
A miktam[b] of David. For teaching. When he fought Aram Naharaim[c] and
Aram Zobah,[d] and when Joab returned and struck down twelve thousand
Edomites in the Valley of Salt.[g]

[*][1] You have rejected us,[h] God, and burst upon us;
you have been angry[i]—now restore us![j]

---

[a] 11 Or *sovereign*   [b] Title: Probably a literary or musical term
Mesopotamia   [d] Title: That is, Arameans of central Syria   [c] Title: That is, Arameans of Northwest

[*] 60:1-12 is numbered 60:3-14 in Hebrew texts.

59:11 *shield.* See note on 3:3. *uproot them.* Like vagabonds, with no place to settle (see Ge 4:12; 2Sa 15:20; La 4:15) and having to hunt for food (like dogs, v. 15; see 109:10; Am 4:8).
59:12 See note on v. 7. *caught in their pride.* Let the pride with which they treacherously attack the Lord's servant and his people be the trap that catches them. *curses and lies.* See 10:7; Ge 12:3 and notes.
59:13 *Then it will be known.* When God has thus dealt with Israel's enemies, all the world will acknowledge that the Judge of all the earth (see 58:11) is the God of Israel. *Jacob.* See note on 14:7.
59:14–16 Assurance of being heard (see note on 3:8). Just as God mocks the defiant pack of dogs (vv. 6–8), so the psalmist will sing for joy at God's triumph over them.
59:16 *strength . . . love . . . fortress.* See the refrain (vv. 9,17). *morning.* See introduction.

A **59:17** The vow to praise (see note on 7:17). *sing.* Hebrew *zamar* (see note on v. 7). The play on words in the refrain marks an advance from looking to God for help in the night of danger to singing in the morning of salvation (cf. 57:8 and note; cf. also 30:5).
Ps 60 A national prayer for God's help after suffering a severe blow by a foreign nation, presumably Edom (see v. 9). The prayer leader may have been the king (the "me" in v. 9), as in 2Ch 20.

The lament that God has "rejected" (vv. 1,10) his people and no longer goes out "with our armies" (v. 10) links the psalm with Ps 44 (see 44:9; see also introduction to Ps 54–60). Verses 5–12 appear again in 108:6–13. As for its structure, the prayer is framed by three verses lamenting God's rejection of his people (vv. 1–3) and three verses expressing confidence that the God who has rejected them will yet give them victory (vv. 10–12). This transition from lament to confidence constitutes the overarching movement of the prayer. Verses 4–8 contain the plea for help (v. 5) and the grounds for confidence (vv. 4,6–8).
60 title See note on Ps 56 title. *The Lily of the Covenant.* See Ps 80 title and note on Ps 45 title. *For teaching.* Only here in the psalm titles. For other songs that Israel was to learn, see Dt 31:19,21; 2Sa 1:18. That it was intended for a variety of uses, especially to convey confidence in times of national threat, is illustrated by its use in Ps 108. *When.* For the events referred to, see 2Sa 8; 1Ch 18 (perhaps also 2Sa 10). If the tradition that assigns the prayer to these events is correct, it must be supposed that our knowledge of the events is incomplete, since these accounts do not mention Edom. The Israelite war against Edom at this time of great northern battles may have been occasioned by an attack on the part of Edom trying to take advantage of Israel's preoccupation elsewhere, an attack in which Edom suc-

59:11 [q] Ps 3:3; 84:9
[r] Dt 4:9; 6:12
[s] Ps 89:10; 106:27; 144:6; Isa 33:3
59:12 [t] Ps 10:7
[u] Ps 64:8; Pr 10:14; 12:13 [v] Isa 2:12; 5:15; Zep 3:11
59:13 [w] Ps 104:35
[x] Ps 83:18
59:15 [y] Job 15:23
59:16 [z] Ps 108:1
[a] S 1Sa 2:10 [b] Ps 5:3; 88:13 [c] Ps 101:1
[d] S 2Sa 22:3
[e] S Dt 4:30
59:17 [f] ver 10
60:1 [g] 2Sa 8:13
[h] 2Sa 5:20; Ps 44:9
[i] Ps 79:5 [j] Ps 80:3

60:2 *k* Ps 18:7
l S 2Ch 7:14
60:3 *m* Ps 71:20
n Ps 75:8; Isa 29:9;
51:17; 63:6; Jer 25:16;
Zec 12:2; Rev 14:10
60:4 *o* Isa 5:26;
11:10,12; 18:3
60:5 *p* S Job 40:14
q S Dt 33:12
60:6 *r* S Ge 12:6
s S Ge 33:17
60:7 *t* Jos 13:31
u S Ge 41:52
v S Nu 34:19
w S Ge 49:10
60:8 *x* S 2Sa 8:1
60:10 *y* S Jos 7:12
60:11 *z* Ps 146:3;
Pr 3:5
60:12 *a* S Job 40:12;
Ps 44:5

2 You have shaken the land *k* and torn it open;
　　mend its fractures, *l* for it is quaking.
3 You have shown your people desperate times; *m*
　　you have given us wine that makes us stagger. *n*
4 But for those who fear you, you have raised a banner *o*
　　to be unfurled against the bow. *a*

5 Save us and help us with your right hand, *p*
　　that those you love *q* may be delivered.
6 God has spoken from his sanctuary:
　　"In triumph I will parcel out Shechem *r*
　　and measure off the Valley of Sukkoth. *s*
7 Gilead *t* is mine, and Manasseh is mine;
　　Ephraim *u* is my helmet,
　　Judah *v* is my scepter. *w*
8 Moab is my washbasin,
　　on Edom I toss my sandal;
　　over Philistia I shout in triumph. *x*"

9 Who will bring me to the fortified city?
　　Who will lead me to Edom?
10 Is it not you, God, you who have now rejected us
　　and no longer go out with our armies? *y*
11 Give us aid against the enemy,
　　for human help is worthless. *z*
12 With God we will gain the victory,
　　and he will trample down our enemies. *a*

a 4 The Hebrew has *Selah* (a word of uncertain meaning) here.

---

ceeded in overrunning the garrisons that guarded Judah's southern borders.

60:1–3 Lament over God's rejection of his people (see 44:9–16; 89:38–45) and prayer for restoration.

60:1 *rejected us.* At least momentarily (see 30:5). Defeat by the enemy is interpreted as a sign of God's anger (though no reason for that anger is noted, and the bond between Israel and God is not broken). *burst upon.* Like a flood (see 2Sa 5:20).

60:2 *shaken the land.* As by a devastating earthquake—such as was occasionally experienced in ancient Canaan.

60:3 *wine that makes us stagger.* God has made them drink from the cup of his wrath rather than from his cup of blessing and salvation (see note on 16:5).

60:4–8 A plea for help, grounded in reasons for confidence.

60:4 *those who fear you.* Your people, in distinction from the nations (see 61:5; see also note on Ge 20:11). *banner.* Possibly the reassuring word from God recited in vv. 6–8 (see Ex 17:15). *bow.* The enemy armed with bows. For *Selah,* see TNIV text note and note on 3:2.

A **60:5–8** The petition (v. 5) followed by a reassuring oracle from the Lord (vv. 6–8)—perhaps recalling an already ancient word from the time of the conquest. If so, it may have been preserved in the "Book of the Wars of the LORD" (Nu 21:14). In any event, the Lord is depicted as Israel's triumphant Warrior-King (see Ex 15:3,13–18).

60:5 *those you love.* The Hebrew for this expression is here a word of special endearment, as in 127:2; 2Sa 12:25; Jer 11:15.

60:6 *parcel out ... measure off.* Divide his conquered territory among his servant people who were with him in the battles. *Shechem ... Sukkoth.* Places representative of the territory west and east of the Jordan taken over by the Lord and Israel (see Ge 33:17–18; 1Ki 12:25).

60:7 Israel is the Lord's kingdom—the land conquered and his people established within it. *Gilead ... Manasseh.* Half of Manasseh was established in Gilead, east of the Jordan, and half of it

west of the Jordan, just north of Ephraim (see Jos 13:29–31; 17:5–11). This once again showed that the Lord's kingdom included territory both east and west of the Jordan. *Ephraim ... Judah.* The two leading tribes of Israel, the one representative of the Rachel tribes (Ephraim) in the north, the other of the Leah tribes (Judah) in the south; see Ge 48:13–20; 49:8–12; Nu 2:3,18; Jos 15–16. Together they represented all Israel (Isa 11:13; Zec 9:13). *helmet.* As a powerful and aggressive tribe (Dt 33:17; Jdg 7:24—8:3; 12:1), Ephraim figuratively represents the Lord's helmet. *scepter.* Called such because from Judah would come (Ge 49:10)—and had now come (1Sa 16:1–13)—the Lord's chosen earthly regent over his people (see 2Sa 7).

60:8 *Moab ... Edom ... Philistia.* Perpetual enemies on Israel's eastern, southern and western borders, respectively (see Ex 15:14–15; see also Ex 13:17; Nu 20:14–21; 22–24). *is my washbasin.* Is reduced to a household vessel in which the Lord washes his feet (Ge 18:4). The metaphor is perhaps suggested by the fact that Moab lay along the east shore of the Dead Sea. *toss my sandal.* Perhaps refers to the conventional symbolic act by which one claimed possession of land (cf. Ru 4:7 and note).

60:9–12 The closing stanza, expressing confidence of victory (see note on 3:8).

60:9 *me ... me.* Possibly referring to the king (see introduction), though the praying community may be referring to itself collectively (see note on Ps 30 title). *lead me.* As God went before his people into battle in the desert (Ex 13:21) and during the conquest (Ex 23:27–28; 33:2; Dt 9:3; 31:8).

60:10 *rejected.* See v. 1.

60:11 *human help.* See 108:12–13; 121:1–2; Isa 30:1–5. *help.* Lit. "salvation" (see v. 5, "Save").

60:12 *gain the victory.* Lit. "do mighty things." With God's help Israel will achieve in a manner similar to that of the Lord himself (see 118:15–16) and will triumph over Edom (see Nu 24:18, "grow strong"). *trample down.* Like a victorious warrior (see Isa 14:19,25; Jer 12:10; Zec 10:5).

PSALM 61

For the director of music. With stringed instruments. Of David.

*[1] Hear my cry, O God; [b]
　listen to my prayer. [c]

[2] From the ends of the earth I call to you,
　I call as my heart grows faint; [d]
　lead me to the rock [e] that is higher than I.
[3] For you have been my refuge, [f]
　a strong tower against the foe. [g]

[4] I long to dwell [h] in your tent forever
　and take refuge in the shelter of your wings. [a][i]
[5] For you, God, have heard my vows; [j]
　you have given me the heritage of those who fear your name. [k]

[6] Increase the days of the king's life, [l]
　his years for many generations. [m]
[7] May he be enthroned in God's presence forever; [n]
　appoint your love and faithfulness to protect him. [o]

[8] Then I will ever sing in praise of your name [p]
　and fulfill my vows day after day. [q]

PSALM 62

For the director of music. For Jeduthun. A psalm of David.

*[1] Truly my soul finds rest [r] in God; [s]
　my salvation comes from him.
[2] Truly he is my rock [t] and my salvation; [u]
　he is my fortress, [v] I will never be shaken. [w]

---

a 4 The Hebrew has *Selah* (a word of uncertain meaning) here.
* 61:1-8 is numbered 61:2-9 in Hebrew texts.　　* 62:1-12 is numbered 62:2-13 in Hebrew texts.

61:1 [b] Ps 64:1
[c] Ps 4:1; 86:6
61:2 [d] S Ps 6:2
[e] Ps 18:2; 31:2; 94:22
61:3 [f] Ps 9:9; S 46:1;
62:7 [g] Ps 59:9;
Pr 18:10
61:4 [h] S Ps 15:1
[i] S Dt 32:11;
S Mt 23:37
61:5 [j] S Nu 30:2;
Ps 56:12 [k] S Ex 6:3;
S Dt 33:9; Ne 1:11;
Ps 102:15; Isa 59:19;
Mt 6:9
61:6 [l] 1Ki 3:14
[m] S Ps 21:4
61:7 [n] S Ps 41:12;
Lk 22:69; Eph 1:20;
Col 3:1 [o] Ps 40:11
61:8 [p] S Ex 15:1;
Ps 7:17; 30:4
[q] S Nu 30:2;
S Dt 23:21
62:1 [r] S Ps 5:3
[s] ver 5
62:2 [t] Ps 18:31;
89:26 [u] S Ex 15:2
[v] S Ps 59:9
[w] S Job 29:18

Ps 61–64 A series of four psalms linked together by the common theme of strong reliance on God for deliverance in the face of great—perhaps mortal—danger. Two make explicit reference to the king (Ps 61; 63), and the other two (62; 64) may also represent a royal voice, though this is disputed. All have been crafted with considerable care.

Ps 61 A prayer for restoration to God's presence. The circumstances appear to be similar to those referred to in Ps 42–43. Here, however, a king is involved (v. 6), and if the author was David, he may have composed this prayer at the time of his flight from Absalom (see 2Sa 17:21–29). For another possibility, see note on v. 2. Structurally, the prayer is framed by a cry to God (v. 1) and a vow to praise (v. 8). The body of the psalm is composed of three couplets: vv. 2–3, 4–5, 6–7.

61 title See note on Ps 4 title.
61:1 Initial plea for God to hear.
61:2–3 The prayer.

61:2 *ends of the earth.* So it seemed (see 42:6). Possibly the phrase here refers to the brink of the netherworld, i.e., the grave (see 63:9); the psalmist feels himself near death. *heart.* See note on 4:7. *lead me.* See 23:2. *rock.* Secure place (see 27:5; 40:2). *higher than I.* The place of security that he seeks is beyond his reach; only God can bring him to it. Since God is often confessed by the psalmists to be their "rock of refuge" (31:2; see also 18:2; 62:2, 6–7; 71:3; 94:22), it may be that God himself is that higher "rock" (the secure refuge) that the psalmist pleads for (see v. 3). Or it may be the secure refuge of God's sanctuary (see v. 4; see also 27:5).

61:3 The reason he appeals to God: God has never failed him as a refuge. *foe.* If this is a prayer when faced with death, death is the present foe (see 68:20; 141:8; Job 33:22; Isa 25:8; 28:15; Jer 9:21; Hos 13:14; see also 1Co 15:26). See note on 49:14.

61:4–5 Longing for the security of God's sanctuary (see 27:5 and note).
61:4 *dwell in.* See note on 15:1. *tent.* Residence (see 2Sa 6:17; 7:2; 1Ki 1:39; 2:28–30). *shelter of your wings.* See note on 17:8. For *Selah,* see TNIV text note and note on 3:2.
61:5 The reason for his longing: Either (1) because God has been so responsive to him in the past or (2) confidence that his longing is about to be satisfied. *my vows.* The vows that accompanied his prayers (see 50:14; 66:14; see also note on 7:17). *heritage.* A place with God's people in the promised land, together with all that the Lord had promised to give and to be to his people (see 16:6; 37:18; 135:12; 136:21–22). *those who fear.* See 60:4 and note. *your name.* See note on 5:11.

61:6–7 Prayer for the king's long life. The king himself may have made this prayer—such transitions to the third person are known from the literature of the ancient Near East— or it may be the prayer of the people, perhaps voiced by a priest or Levite. Later Jewish interpretations applied these verses to the Messiah. They are fulfilled in Christ, David's great Son.
61:6 May the king live forever (see note on 45:6).
61:7 *enthroned in God's presence.* See note on 41:12. *love and faithfulness.* Personified as God's agents (see notes on 23:6; 43:3; see also note on 26:3).
61:8 The vow to praise (see note on 7:17).

Ps 62 The psalmist commits himself to God when threatened by the assaults of conspirators who wish to "topple me from my lofty place" (v. 4). The author may have been a king. If it was David, the circumstances could well have been the efforts of the family of Saul to topple him. Verse 3 suggests a time of weakness and may indicate advanced age. Implicitly the psalm is an appeal to God to uphold him. No psalm surpasses it in its expression

62:3 ˣ Isa 30:13
62:4 ʸ Ps 28:3; 55:21
62:5 ᶻ ver 1
62:7 ᵃ S Ps 61:3
62:8 ᵇ Ps 37:5;
Isa 26:4 ᶜ Isa 1:15;
Ps 42:4; Mt 26:36-46
62:9 ᵈ Ps 49:2
ᵉ S Job 7:7 ᶠ Isa 40:15
62:10 ᵍ S Ps 12:5;
1Ti 6:17 ʰ Isa 61:8;
Eze 22:29; Na 3:1
ⁱ S Job 31:25;
Mt 19:23-24; 1Ti 6:6-10
62:11 ʲ S 1Ch 29:11;
Rev 19:1
62:12 ᵏ Ps 86:5;
103:8; 130:7
ˡ S Job 21:31; Ps 28:4;
S Mt 16:27; Ro 2:6*;
1Co 3:8; Col 3:25

³ How long will you assault me?
 Would all of you throw me down—
 this leaning wall, ˣ this tottering fence?
⁴ Surely they intend to topple me
 from my lofty place;
 they take delight in lies.
With their mouths they bless,
 but in their hearts they curse. ᵃ ʸ

⁵ Yes, my soul, find rest in God; ᶻ
 my hope comes from him.
⁶ Truly he is my rock and my salvation;
 he is my fortress, I will not be shaken.
⁷ My salvation and my honor depend on God ᵇ;
 he is my mighty rock, my refuge. ᵃ
⁸ Trust in him at all times, you people; ᵇ
 pour out your hearts to him, ᶜ
 for God is our refuge.

⁹ Surely the lowborn ᵈ are but a breath, ᵉ
 the highborn are but a lie.
If weighed on a balance, ᶠ they are nothing;
 together they are only a breath.
¹⁰ Do not trust in extortion ᵍ
 or put vain hope in stolen goods; ʰ
though your riches increase,
 do not set your heart on them. ⁱ

¹¹ One thing God has spoken,
 two things I have heard:
 "Power belongs to you, God, ʲ
¹² and with you, Lord, is unfailing love"; ᵏ
and, "You reward everyone
 according to what they have done." ˡ

PSALM 63

A psalm of David. When he was in the Desert of Judah.

*¹ You, God, are my God,
 earnestly I seek you;

ᵃ 4 The Hebrew has *Selah* (a word of uncertain meaning) here and at the end of verse 8.   ᵇ 7 Or / *God Most High is my salvation and my honor*
* 63:1-11 is numbered 63:2-12 in Hebrew texts.

---

of simple trust in God (see Ps 31 and introduction to Ps 61). The psalm is composed of three parts (vv. 3–4,5–8,9–10), framed by a confession of tranquil resting in God (vv. 1–2) and the reason for such trust (vv. 11–12). The middle stanza constitutes a thematic hinge: Its first two verses (vv. 5–6) echo the opening couplet, while the last two verses (vv. 7–8) anticipate the closing couplet. The other two stanzas (vv. 3–4,9–10) speak of those who threaten.
62 title See note on Ps 39 title.
62:1–2 Profession of complete trust in God for protection.
62:1 *my soul.* See note on 6:3. *finds rest.* Lit. "is silence," i.e., is in repose.
62:2,6 *shaken.* See note on 10:6.
62:3–4 The threatening activities of the enemies.
62:3 Question to the assailants: Will you never give up? *leaning wall . . . tottering fence.* A metaphor for the psalmist's fragile condition: either (1) a confession that he has no strength in himself, (2) an acknowledgment that he is in a weakened condition or, perhaps, (3) a reflection on how his enemies perceive him, as a "pushover."
62:4 *lofty place.* Possibly the throne. *lies.* See note on 10:7. *bless.* For example, "Long live the king" (1Sa 10:24; 2Sa 16:16; see also 1Ki 1:25,34,39). *curse.* Call down curses (see note on Ge

12:3). For *Selah*, see TNIV text note and note on 3:2.
62:5–8 Trust in God: an exhortation to himself (v. 5) and to the people (v. 8).
62:5 *find rest.* See note on v. 1; faith encouraging faith (see 27:13–14; 42:5,11; 43:5).
62:8 Exhortation to God's people (see 31:23–24). *pour out your hearts.* In earnest prayer (see La 2:19). *hearts.* See note on 4:7.
62:9–10 Humans, as a threat, are nothing (see note on 10:18).
62:9 *lowborn . . . highborn.* Persons of every condition. *breath . . . lie.* People appear to be much more than they really are (see 37:2,20; 39:5 and notes), especially the rich and powerful.
62:10 A warning to those (including those conspiring against him) who trust in their own devices to get what they want (by fair means or foul) rather than trusting in God to sustain them—a virtual summary of Ps 49. *heart.* See note on 4:7.
62:11–12 The climax: recollection of God's reassuring word to his people. *Power . . . unfailing love.* He is able to do all that he has promised and is committed to his people's salvation and blessedness.
62:11 *One thing . . . two things.* See note on Am 1:3.
62:12 *unfailing love.* See note on 6:4. *reward . . . according to.* See notes on Jer 17:10; 32:19.

I thirst for you, *m*
   my whole being longs for you,
in a dry and parched land
   where there is no water. *n*

² I have seen you in the sanctuary *o*
   and beheld your power and your glory. *p*
³ Because your love is better than life, *q*
   my lips will glorify you.
⁴ I will praise you as long as I live, *r*
   and in your name I will lift up my hands. *s*
⁵ I will be fully satisfied as with the richest of foods; *t*
   with singing lips my mouth will praise you.

⁶ On my bed I remember you;
   I think of you through the watches of the night. *u*
⁷ Because you are my help, *v*
   I sing in the shadow of your wings. *w*
⁸ I cling to you; *x*
   your right hand upholds me. *y*

⁹ Those who seek my life will be destroyed; *z*
   they will go down to the depths of the earth. *a*
¹⁰ They will be given over to the sword *b*
   and become food for jackals. *c*

¹¹ But the king will rejoice in God;
   all who swear by God will glory in him, *d*
   while the mouths of liars will be silenced. *e*

63:1 *m* Ps 42:2; 84:2
n Ps 143:6
63:2 *o* S Ps 15:1;
27:4; 68:24
p S Ex 16:7
63:3 *q* Ps 36:7;
69:16; 106:45; 109:21
63:4 *r* Ps 104:33;
146:2; Isa 38:20
s S Ps 28:2; 1Ti 2:8
63:5 *t* S Ps 36:8;
Mt 5:6
63:6 *u* Dt 6:4-9;
Ps 16:7; 119:148;
Mt 14:25
63:7 *v* Ps 27:9; 118:7
w S Ru 2:12
63:8 *x* S Nu 32:12;
Hos 6:3 *y* S Ps 41:12
63:9 *z* Ps 40:14
a Ps 55:15; 71:20;
95:4; 139:15
63:10 *b* Jer 18:21;
Eze 35:5; Am 1:11
c La 5:18
63:11 *d* Ps 21:1;
Isa 19:18; 45:23; 65:16
e S Job 5:16; Ro 3:19

Ps 63 A confession of longing for God and for the security his presence offers when deadly enemies threaten. That longing is vividly described by the metaphor of thirst (v. 1) and hunger (v. 5; see 42:1–2). Like Ps 62 this psalm is an implicit prayer. It is linked to that psalm also by the advancement from hearing (62:11) to seeing (v. 2; see 48:8 and note). The imagery of the night of danger (v. 6) and the morning of salvation (see note on v. 1) once more occurs (see introduction to Ps 57). In the early church this psalm was prescribed for daily public prayers. In its structure, the initial expression of longing (v. 1) gives way at the end to the expectation of joy (v. 11)—the literary frame of the psalm. Verse 6 provides the key thematic link connecting vv. 1 and 11. It stands at the center between two precisely balanced stanzas (vv. 2–5, 7–10), each having four verses and each made up of 27 Hebrew words. The psalmist's night meditations (v. 6) nurture his longing for God (v. 1; cf. 143:5–6) and reinforce his expectations (v. 11). For the thematic links between the two major stanzas, see following notes.

63 title See note on Ps 3 title. *When.* If this tradition is correct, the reference is probably to 2Sa 15:23–28; 16:2,14; 17:16,29 since the psalmist is referred to as king (see v. 11).

63:1 Intense longing for God in a time of need. *earnestly.* Lit. "at dawn," "in the morning." *dry and parched land.* A metaphor (see 143:6; Isa 32:2) for his situation of need, in which he does not taste "the richest of foods" (v. 5) supplied by the "river whose streams make glad the city of God" (46:4; see note there).

63:2–5 Comforting reflection on what he had seen in the sanctuary; it awakens joyful expectations.

63:2 See 27:4; 48:8 and notes.

63:3 *love.* See note on 6:4.

63:4 *name.* See note on 5:11. *lift up my hands.* While lifting the hands to God usually signifies prayer, it also—though rarely in Biblical reference—accompanied praise (see 134:2).

63:5 *richest of foods.* Lit. "fat and fatness" (for a similar idea, see Isa 25:6).

63:6 A centering line (see introduction to this psalm): night reflections, remembering what he had seen "in the sanctuary" (v. 2). *On my bed.* At night as he expectantly awaits the dawning of the morning of deliverance. *watches of the night.* See note on Jdg 7:19; see also 119:148; La 2:19.

63:7–10 The great contrast between "my" prospects (vv. 7–8) and theirs (vv. 9–10). As will be noted, each of these four verses has some kind of thematic link with the corresponding verse in the four-verse stanza with which it is balanced (see introduction to this psalm).

63:7 *shadow of your wings.* See note on 17:8. God's saving help brings the psalmist back to the sanctuary (see v. 2) with songs of praise.

63:8 He has experienced God's "love," which is "better than life" (v. 3).

63:9 His enemies will get what they deserve; in seeking his life they forfeit their own (see Ge 9:5; Ex 21:23; Dt 19:21; see also note on Ps 5:10). The final end of the enemies stands in sharp contrast with the psalmist's prospects, as anticipated in vv. 7–8 —but also as voiced in v. 4: "I will praise," but "they will go down" to the place of silence (see v. 11). *depths.* See note on 30:1. *earth.* Here, the netherworld or grave (see note on 61:2).

63:10 *food for jackals.* Like bodies of enemies left unburied on the battlefield to add to their disgrace (see note on 53:5). Note the vivid portrayal of the contrast between the two prospects: I "will be fully satisfied as with the richest of foods" (v. 5); "they will . . . become food for jackals."

63:11 The closing frame (see introduction to this psalm), in which the speaker is finally identified as the king. *all who swear by God.* Those who revere and trust God (see Dt 6:13). *mouths of liars.* Those who live by falsehood (see 5:6; 58:3; 101:7 and note on 5:9).

64:1 *f* Ps 142:2
g Ps 140:1
64:2 *h* S Ex 1:10
i Ps 56:6; 59:2
64:3 *j* S Ps 55:21;
Isa 49:2 *k* S Ps 7:13;
S 58:7
64:4 *l* S Job 9:23;
Ps 10:8; 11:2
m S Ps 55:19
64:5 *n* Ps 91:3;
119:110; 140:5; 141:9
o S Job 22:13
64:8 *p* S Ps 59:12;
Pr 18:7 *q* S 2Ki 19:21;
Ps 109:25
r S Dt 28:37
64:9 *s* S Ps 40:3
t Jer 51:10
64:10 *u* S Job 22:19
v Ps 11:1; 25:20; 31:2
w Ps 32:11
65:1 *x* Ps 2:6
y S Dt 23:21; Ps 116:18

PSALM 64

For the director of music. A psalm of David.

¹ Hear me, my God, as I voice my complaint; *f*
　protect my life from the threat of the enemy. *g*

² Hide me from the conspiracy *h* of the wicked, *i*
　from the plots of evildoers.
³ They sharpen their tongues like swords *j*
　and aim cruel words like deadly arrows. *k*
⁴ They shoot from ambush at the innocent; *l*
　they shoot suddenly, without fear. *m*

⁵ They encourage each other in evil plans,
　they talk about hiding their snares; *n*
　they say, "Who will see it *a* ?" *o*
⁶ They plot injustice and say,
　"We have devised a perfect plan!"
　Surely the human mind and heart are cunning.

⁷ But God will shoot them with his arrows;
　they will suddenly be struck down.
⁸ He will turn their own tongues against them *p*
　and bring them to ruin;
　all who see them will shake their heads *q* in scorn. *r*
⁹ All people will fear; *s*
　they will proclaim the works of God
　and ponder what he has done. *t*

¹⁰ The righteous will rejoice in the LORD *u*
　and take refuge in him; *v*
　all the upright in heart will glory in him! *w*

PSALM 65

For the director of music. A psalm of David. A song.

¹ Praise awaits *b* you, our God, in Zion; *x*
　to you our vows will be fulfilled. *y*

---

a 5 Or *us*　　*b* 1 Or *befits*; the meaning of the Hebrew for this word is uncertain.

*** 64:1-10 is numbered 64:2-11 in Hebrew texts.　　*** 65:1-13 is numbered 65:2-14 in Hebrew texts.

Ps 64 Confident prayer to God for protection when threatened by a conspiracy (see introduction to Ps 61–64). The circumstances may be similar to those reflected in Ps 62 (see introduction to that psalm), but here there is no allusion to the king's weakened condition, and it is not clear whether the conspirators come from within or outside Israel (see note on v. 2). As so often in the prayers of the Psalter, the enemy's tongue is his main weapon (see note on 5:9). The prayer is framed by an initial plea for protection from an enemy (v. 1) and a concluding call to rejoicing and praise (v. 10)—linked by a wordplay (see notes on these verses). Two carefully balanced stanzas spell out David's prayer and the adversaries' threat (vv. 2–4) and God's anticipated counteraction and its effect on all who hear about it (vv. 7–9). The point-counterpoint relationship of these two stanzas is highlighted by the use of key words that occur in corresponding positions in the Hebrew poetic lines—in reverse order: "-doers" (v. 2), "tongues" (v. 3), "shoot … suddenly" (v. 4), "shoot … suddenly" (v. 7), "tongues" (v. 8), "works" (v. 9: in Hebrew the same word as for "-doers" in v. 2). At the center, vv. 5–6 describe the disdainful confidence of the conspirators.
64 title See note on Ps 4 title.
64:1 Initial appeal for God to hear. *Hear.* In Hebrew a wordplay on the word for "rejoice" in v. 10 (see note there).
64:2–4 The petition and the threat.
64:2 *plots.* The Hebrew root underlying this word is the same as that for "conspire" in 2:1.

64:3 *tongues.* See note on 5:9. *swords … deadly arrows.* See 59:7 and note.
64:4 *without fear.* They feel themselves secure from exposure and retaliation (see Ps 10 and notes on 10:6,11), but see vv. 7–8.
64:5–6 The enemies' contemptuous self-confidence.
64:5 *hiding their snares.* See note on 9:15.
64:6 *heart.* See note on 4:7. *cunning.* Lit. "deep" (see Pr 18:4; 20:5).
64:7–9 Confidence in God's righteous judgment—he will do to the adversaries what they had intended to do to David (see vv. 3–4)—and its effect on those who hear about it. For the links between this stanza and vv. 2–4, see introduction to this psalm.
64:7 *shoot … arrows.* See note on Ge 9:13.
64:8 *shake their heads.* See 44:14.
64:9 All people will fear, proclaim and ponder how God's "works" undo and judge the doings of the "evildoers" (v. 2; see note on 46:10; see also 40:3; 58:11; 65:8).
64:10 Framing conclusion (see v. 1): The righteous will rejoice, take refuge and praise. *righteous.* See note on 1:5. *rejoice.* In Hebrew this is the first word of the line and is a wordplay on the Hebrew for "Hear," which is the first word of the first verse.
Ps 65–68 Four psalms dominated by the theme of praise and linked by the shared recognition that God's "awesome" deeds evoke the wonder of "all the ends of the earth" and move (or should move) "all the earth" to join Israel in singing the praise of her God (see note on 46:10). In these four psalms, the occa-

² You who answer prayer,
  to you all people will come. ^z
³ When we were overwhelmed by sins, ^a
  you forgave^a our transgressions. ^b
⁴ Blessed are those you choose^c
  and bring near^d to live in your courts!
We are filled with the good things of your house, ^e
  of your holy temple.

⁵ You answer us with awesome and righteous deeds, ^f
  God our Savior, ^g
the hope of all the ends of the earth ^h
  and of the farthest seas, ⁱ
⁶ who formed the mountains^j by your power,
  having armed yourself with strength, ^k
⁷ who stilled the roaring of the seas, ^l
  the roaring of their waves,
  and the turmoil of the nations. ^m
⁸ The whole earth is filled with awe at your wonders;
  where morning dawns, where evening fades,
  you call forth songs of joy. ⁿ

⁹ You care for the land and water it; ^o
  you enrich it abundantly. ^p
The streams of God are filled with water
  to provide the people with grain, ^q
  for so you have ordained it. ^b

---

^a 3 Or *made atonement for*   ^b 9 Or *for that is how you prepare the land*

65:2 ^z Ps 86:9;
Isa 66:23
65:3 ^a S Ps 40:12
^b Ps 79:9; Ro 3:25;
Heb 9:14
65:4 ^c S Ps 33:12
^d S Nu 16:5
^e S Ps 36:8
65:5 ^f S Dt 4:34;
S Ps 45:4; 106:22;
Isa 64:3 ^g Ps 18:46;
68:19; 85:4
^h S Ps 48:10
ⁱ Ps 107:23
65:6 ^j Am 4:13
^k S Ps 18:1; 93:1;
Isa 51:9
65:7 ^l Ps 89:9; 93:3-
4; 107:29; S Mt 8:26
^m Dt 32:41; Ps 2:1;
74:23; 139:20;
Isa 17:12-13
65:8 ⁿ Ps 100:2;
107:22; 126:2;
Isa 24:16; 52:9
65:9 ^o S Lev 26:4
^p Ps 104:24
^q S Ge 27:28;
S Dt 32:14; Ps 104:14

---

sions—and reasons—for this universal praise include (1) God's mighty acts in maintaining the creation order and making it fruitful so that humans are richly blessed, and (2) God's saving acts in behalf of his people. These are significantly brought together here by alternating the focus; Ps 65 and 67 speak of the former, and Ps 66 and 68 speak of the latter. Thus in this short series all of God's benevolent acts are brought into purview, and the whole human race is encompassed in the community of praise.

Ps 65 A hymn in praise of God's great goodness to his people. In answer to their prayers (1) he pardons their sins so that they continue to enjoy the "good things" that accompany their fellowship with him at his temple (vv. 1–4); (2) as the One who established the secure order of the creation, he also orders the affairs of the world so that international turbulence is put to rest and Israel is secure in her land (vv. 5–8); and (3) he turns the promised land into a veritable Garden of Eden (vv. 9–13). In all this he is hailed as "the hope" of all humankind. His wondrous deeds evoke their "fear" and move them to "songs of joy."
65 title See notes on Ps 4; 30 titles.
65:1–2 Introductory commitment to praise.
65:1 *awaits.* Or "is silent before" (see note on 62:1; see also TNIV text note here). Perhaps the imagery is that of praise personified as a permanent resident of the temple, lying quietly at rest, whom the people will awaken when they come to make good their vows (see 57:8). *our vows.* Those made in conjunction with their prayers in time of need (see 66:14 and note on 7:17).
65:2 *all people.* Lit. "all flesh," perhaps referring to all God's people, as in Joel 2:28. Most interpreters believe (in light of vv. 5,8) that the reference is more universal, as in 64:9; 66:1,4,8; 67:3–5 and elsewhere. *will come.* To praise God as the (only) God who hears and graciously answers prayers.
65:3–4 The crucial act of divine mercy that opens the way for the benefits spelled out in the two remaining stanzas.

65:3 *forgave our transgressions.* Accepted the atonement sacrifices you appointed and so forgave our sins (see TNIV text note; see also 32:1–2; 78:38; 79:9 and notes on Lev 16:20–22; 17:11; Heb 2:17; 9:5,7).
65:4 *Blessed.* See note on 1:1. *those you choose and bring near.*

Everyone belonging to Israel as God's chosen people (see, e.g., 33:12; Dt 4:37) and whom God accepts at his temple. *live in your courts.* See note on 15:1; see also 23:6. *good things of your house.* All the blessings that flow from God's presence (see 36:8 and note).
65:5–8 God, who continues to uphold the creation order, stills the nations and makes Israel secure in answer to her prayers.
65:5 *awesome . . . deeds.* Acts of God such as were associated with his deliverance of Israel from Egypt and the conquest of Canaan, acts of power that made Israel's enemies cringe (see 66:3; see also 106:22; 145:6; Dt 10:21; 2Sa 7:23; Isa 64:3). *righteous deeds.* Saving acts by which God kept his covenanted promises to Israel (see note on 4:1). *hope of all.* Even if the nations of the world did not yet fully realize it.

65:6–7 The God of creation, who by his power brought order to the world out of the earlier chaos (see Ge 1), similarly in the redemption of his people establishes a peaceful order among nations (see Isa 2:4; 11:6–9; Mic 4:3–4) so that Israel may be at rest in the promised land (see also Ps 33; 46). God's mighty acts in redemption are often compared by OT poets with his mighty acts in creation (see 74:12–17; 89:9–18; Isa 27:1; 40:6–14,21–31; 51:9–11), since his power as Creator guaranteed his power as Redeemer. *formed the mountains . . . stilled . . . the seas.* Gave order to the whole creation (see 95:4–5).
65:7 *turmoil of the nations.* God's stilling the turbulence of the nations—which often threatened Israel—is compared to his taming the turbulence of the primeval waters of chaos (see notes on 32:6; 33:7).

65:8 All peoples will (ultimately) see God's saving acts in behalf of his people and will be moved to fear (see note on 46:10). And all creation will rejoice (see v. 13). *wonders.* Or "signs," referring to God's great saving acts, such as those he performed when he delivered Israel out of Egypt (Dt 4:34; see Ps 78:43; 105:27; 135:9). As "signs" they indicated that God was at work (see Jn 2:11 and note).
65:9–13 God blesses the promised land with all good things in answer to Israel's prayers.
65:9 *streams of God.* See note on 36:8.

65:10 ʳ S Dt 32:2;
S 2Sa 1:21;
S Job 36:28; Ac 14:17
65:11 ˢ S Dt 28:12;
Ps 104:28; Jn 10:10
ᵗ Job 36:28; Ps 147:14;
Lk 6:38
65:12 ᵘ S Job 28:26;
Joel 2:22 ᵛ Ps 98:8
65:13 ʷ Ps 144:13;
Isa 30:23; Zec 8:12
ˣ Ps 72:16 ʸ Ps 98:8;
Isa 14:8; 44:23; 49:13;
55:12
66:1 ᶻ Ps 81:1; 84:8;
95:1; 98:4; 100:1
66:2 ᵃ Ps 79:9; 86:9
ᵇ Isa 42:8,12; 43:21
66:3 ᶜ S Dt 7:21;
S 10:21; Ps 65:5;
106:22; 111:6; 145:6
ᵈ S 2Sa 22:45
66:4 ᵉ Ps 22:27
ᶠ Ps 7:17; 67:3
66:5 ᵍ ver 3;
Ps 106:22
66:6 ʰ S Ge 8:1;
S Ex 14:22 ᶦ 1Co 10:1
ʲ S Lev 23:40
66:7 ᵏ S Ex 15:18;
Ps 145:13 ˡ S Ex 3:16;
S Ps 11:4
ᵐ S Nu 17:10;
Ps 112:10; 140:8
66:8 ⁿ S Ps 22:23
66:9 ᵒ Ps 30:3
ᵖ S Dt 32:35;
S Job 12:5

¹⁰ You drench its furrows and level its ridges;
    you soften it with showers ʳ and bless its crops.
¹¹ You crown the year with your bounty, ˢ
    and your carts overflow with abundance. ᵗ
¹² The grasslands of the wilderness overflow; ᵘ
    the hills are clothed with gladness. ᵛ
¹³ The meadows are covered with flocks ʷ
    and the valleys are mantled with grain; ˣ
    they shout for joy and sing. ʸ

PSALM 66

For the director of music. A song. A psalm.

¹ Shout for joy to God, all the earth! ᶻ
²   Sing the glory of his name; ᵃ
    make his praise glorious. ᵇ
³ Say to God, "How awesome are your deeds! ᶜ
   So great is your power
    that your enemies cringe ᵈ before you.
⁴ All the earth bows down ᵉ to you;
    they sing praise ᶠ to you,
    they sing the praises of your name." ᵃ

⁵ Come and see what God has done,
    his awesome deeds ᵍ for humankind!
⁶ He turned the sea into dry land, ʰ
    they passed through ᶦ the waters on foot—
    come, let us rejoice ʲ in him.
⁷ He rules forever ᵏ by his power,
    his eyes watch ˡ the nations—
    let not the rebellious ᵐ rise up against him.

⁸ Praise ⁿ our God, all peoples,
    let the sound of his praise be heard;
⁹ he has preserved our lives ᵒ
    and kept our feet from slipping. ᵖ

ᵃ 4   The Hebrew has *Selah* (a word of uncertain meaning) here and at the end of verses 7 and 15.

65:11 *bounty.* Lit."goodness" (see 68:10; see also 31:19 and note).
65:13 *they shout for joy and sing.* In the exuberant language of
the psalmists, all creation—even its inanimate elements—joins
the human chorus to celebrate the goodness of God in creation,
blessing and redemption (see 89:12; 96:11–13; 98:8–9; 103:22;
145:10; 148:3–4,7–10; see also Job 38:7; Isa 44:23; 49:13; 55:12).
Ps 66 A psalm of praise for God's answer to prayer—probably
delivering the psalmist from an enemy threat. It has often been
suggested that the psalm speaks of Judah's remarkable deliverance from the Assyrians (see 2Ki 19). But the occasion may have
been a more private crisis, which comes specifically into focus in
vv. 13–20. If that is the case, the psalmist has set his personal experience of God's saving help as one of God's people in the larger
context of God's help of Israel in the exodus. The praise is offered
at the temple in fulfillment of a vow (vv. 13–14; see note on 7:17).
Such praise was often climaxed by a call for others to take up the
praise (see note on 9:1). Here the psalmist exuberantly begins
with that call and, as often elsewhere (e.g., 67:3–5; 68:32; 98:4;
99:1–3; 100:1; 117:1), addresses it even to the far corners of the
earth. This psalm is the second in a series of four (see introduction
to Ps 65–68). It is framed by a call to praise (vv. 1–2) and a declaration of the present occasion for praise (vv. 19–20, in Hebrew involving a play on words—the Hebrew for "praise" and "prayer"
sound very much alike). The opening stanza (vv. 1–4) is followed
by two thematic sequences having the same structure: a three-
verse stanza (vv. 5–7,13–15) followed by a five-verse stanza (vv.
8–12,16–20). The first line of the first stanza of the first sequence
(v. 5) begins with "Come and see"; the first line of the second stan-

za of the second sequence (v. 16) begins with "Come and hear."
66 title See notes on Ps 4; 30 titles.
66:1–4 Calling all the earth to joyful praise.
66:1 *all the earth.* See note on 65:2.
66:2 *name.* See note on 5:11.
66:3 *awesome.* See v. 5; see also note on 65:5. *cringe.* See 18:44;
cf. Jos 5:1; 2Ch 20:29.
66:4 See note on 46:10. For *Selah,* see TNIV text note and note
on 3:2.

🅰   **66:5–7** Recollection of God's deliverance of Israel at the
    Red Sea as a sign of his power to rule over the nations.
The psalmist portrays his deliverance (see introduction above)
both as similar to this Red Sea rescue in its manifestation of
God's saving power (see 65:5–7 for a comparison of God's
mighty saving acts with his mighty acts of creation) and as a
continuation of God's same saving purposes.
66:5 *Come and see.* See introduction to this psalm. God's saving acts of old can still be "seen" at his temple, where they are
continually celebrated (see 46:8; 48:8–9 and notes). *for humankind.* Specifically for his people.
66:6 *waters.* Possibly the Jordan, but more likely a parallel reference to the Red Sea.
66:7 *rebellious.* Nations that are in revolt against God's rule
(see 68:6).
66:8–12 Praise of God's deliverance of his people.
66:8 *peoples.* Here probably the grateful throng of worshipers
(see 2Ch 20:27–28).
66:9 *from slipping.* See note on 38:16.

¹⁰ For you, God, tested ^q us;
      you refined us like silver. ^r
¹¹ You brought us into prison ^s
      and laid burdens ^t on our backs.
¹² You let people ride over our heads; ^u
      we went through fire and water,
      but you brought us to a place of abundance. ^v

¹³ I will come to your temple with burnt offerings ^w
      and fulfill my vows ^x to you—
¹⁴ vows my lips promised and my mouth spoke
      when I was in trouble.
¹⁵ I will sacrifice fat animals to you
      and an offering of rams;
      I will offer bulls and goats. ^y

¹⁶ Come and hear, ^z all you who fear God;
      let me tell ^a you what he has done for me.
¹⁷ I cried out to him with my mouth;
      his praise was on my tongue.
¹⁸ If I had cherished sin in my heart,
      the Lord would not have listened; ^b
¹⁹ but God has surely listened
      and has heard ^c my prayer.
²⁰ Praise be to God,
      who has not rejected ^d my prayer
      or withheld his love from me!

PSALM 67

For the director of music. With stringed instruments. A psalm. A song.

^{*1} May God be gracious to us and bless us
      and make his face shine on us— ^{a e}
² so that your ways may be known on earth,
      your salvation ^f among all nations. ^g

³ May the peoples praise you, God;
      may all the peoples praise you. ^h

^a *1* The Hebrew has *Selah* (a word of uncertain meaning) here and at the end of verse 4.
[*] 67:1-7 are numbered 67:2-8 in Hebrew texts.

66:10 ^q S Ex 15:25
^r S Job 6:29; S 28:1;
S Ps 12:6
66:11 ^s Ps 142:7;
146:7; Isa 42:7,22;
61:1 ^t S Ge 3:17;
S Ex 1:14; Ps 38:4;
Isa 10:27
66:12 ^u Isa 51:23
^v Ps 18:19
66:13 ^w S Ps 51:19
^x Ps 22:25; 50:14;
116:14; Ecc 5:4;
Jnh 2:9
66:15 ^y S Lev 16:5;
Ps 51:19
66:16 ^z Ps 34:11
^a Ps 71:15,24
66:18 ^b S Dt 1:45;
S 1Sa 8:18; Jas 4:3
66:19 ^c S Ps 18:6
66:20 ^d Ps 22:24
67:1 ^e Nu 6:24-26
67:2 ^f Isa 40:5;
52:10; 62:1 ^g Ps 98:2;
Isa 62:2; Ac 10:35;
Tit 2:11
67:3 ^h ver 5

66:10 *tested … refined.* From one point of view, times of distress constitute a testing of God's people as to their trust in and loyalty to God. The metaphor is borrowed from the technology of refining precious metals, which included heating the metals in a crucible to see if all impurities had been removed (see 12:6 and note; 17:3).

66:11–12 *You … You.* God's rule is all-pervasive; even when enemies maliciously oppress his people, God is not a mere passive observer but has his own holy purposes in it (see Isa 45:7; Am 3:6). *prison … burdens … ride over.* Probably recalling the Egyptian oppression from which the exodus brought relief. **66:12** *fire and water.* Conventional metaphors for severe trials (see Isa 43:2). *to a place of abundance.* Lit. "to an overflowing" (see 23:5). God's people were brought out of a situation of distress into a situation of overflowing blessings: the promised land.

66:13–15 Announcement of fulfillment of vows: addressed to God (see note on 7:17; see also 50:14; 116:17–19).

66:13 *I.* The king.

66:16–20 Proclamation of what God has done for the psalmist—in praise of God and addressed to the worshiping congregation (cf. 34:1–7).

66:16 *Come and hear.* See introduction. *fear God.* See notes on 15:4; Ge 20:11; Pr 1:7; Lk 12:5.

66:17 *his praise.* Prayer and praise belonged together in the OT (see also Php 4:6; 1Ti 2:1).

66:20 *Praise be to God.* See v. 8. *love.* See note on 6:4.

Ps 67 A communal prayer for God's blessing. Its content, form and brevity suggest that it served as a liturgical prayer of the people at the conclusion of worship, perhaps just prior to (or immediately after) the priestly benediction (see note on v. 1). God's blessing of his people (as well as his saving acts in their behalf) will catch the attention of the nations and move them to praise (see 65:2). This psalm is the third in a series of four having special thematic links with Ps 65 (see introduction to Ps 65–68). It has a completely symmetrical structure: Two verses at the beginning contain the prayer, while the two verses of the concluding stanza speak of the effects of God's answer. In the intervening stanza, framed by a refrain (vv. 3,5), the people seek to motivate God's answer by referring to the worldwide praise that his mercies to his people will awaken.

67 title See notes on Ps 4; 30 titles.

67:1–2 The prayer.

67:1 The heart of the prayer, anticipating (or echoing) the priestly benediction (see Nu 6:24–26). *make his face shine.* See notes on 4:6; 13:1. For *Selah,* see TNIV text note and note on 3:2.

67:2 May God's favors to his people be so obvious that all the world takes notice (see note on 46:10).

67:3–5 The motivation. Elaborating on v. 2, the people speak of the worldwide praise that will resound to God when he graciously blesses his people. Their wish is twofold:

67:4 *i* Ps 100:1-2
j S Ps 9:4; 96:10-13
k Ps 68:32
67:6 *l* S Ge 8:22;
S Lev 26:4; Ps 85:12;
Isa 55:10; Eze 34:27;
Zec 8:12 *m* S Ge 12:2
67:7 *n* S Ps 2:8
o Ps 33:8
68:1 *p* Ps 12:5; 132:8
q Ps 18:14; 89:10;
92:9; 144:6
r Nu 10:35; Isa 17:13;
21:15; 33:3
68:2 *s* S Ps 37:20
t S Ps 22:14
u S Nu 10:35; Ps 9:3;
80:16
68:3 *v* Ps 64:10;
97:12
68:4 *w* S 2Sa 22:50;
Ps 7:17; S 30:4; 66:2;
96:2; 100:4; 135:3
x ver 33; S Ex 20:21;
S Dt 33:26 *y* S Ex 6:3;
Ps 83:18
68:5 *z* Ps 10:14
a S Ex 22:22;
S Dt 10:18
b S Dt 26:15;
Jer 25:30
68:6 *c* Ps 25:16
d Ps 113:9

⁴May the nations be glad and sing for joy,*i*
  for you rule the peoples with equity*j*
  and guide the nations of the earth.*k*
⁵May the peoples praise you, God;
  may all the peoples praise you.

⁶The land yields its harvest;*l*
  God, our God, blesses us.*m*
⁷May God bless us still,
  so that all the ends of the earth*n* will fear him.*o*

PSALM 68

For the director of music. Of David. A psalm. A song.

*¹May God arise,*p* may his enemies be scattered;*q*
  may his foes flee*r* before him.
²May you blow them away like smoke—*s*
  as wax melts*t* before the fire,
  may the wicked perish*u* before God.
³But may the righteous be glad
  and rejoice*v* before God;
  may they be happy and joyful.

⁴Sing to God, sing in praise of his name,*w*
  extol him who rides on the clouds*a x*;
  rejoice before him—his name is the LORD.*y*
⁵A father to the fatherless,*z* a defender of widows,*a*
  is God in his holy dwelling.*b*
⁶God sets the lonely*c* in families,*b d*

---

a 4 Or *name, / prepare the way for him who rides through the deserts*   *b* 6 Or *the desolate in a homeland*

* 68:1-35 is numbered 68:2-36 in Hebrew texts.

---

(1) that God's blessings may be so abundant that the people will be moved to praise, and (2) that the nations may indeed add their praise to that of Israel—an appropriate expression at this climax of the liturgy of worship.

▲ **67:4** May the nations rejoice in the Lord when they see how benevolent the rule of God is (see 65:7–8; 98:4–6; 100:1).

67:6–7 The effects of God's blessing his people.
67:6 The promised land will yield its abundance (see 65:9–13).
67:7 *all the ... earth will fear him.* See 65:8; 66:16 and note.
Ps 68 A hymn celebrating the triumphal march of Israel's God from Mount Sinai to Mount Zion. Interwoven in it is a prayer that this mighty display of God's power be continued until all God's people are rescued and secure and all kingdoms of the earth bring tribute to and sing the praises of the God of Israel. The voice heard here is that of the worshiping community, and the psalm may originally have accompanied a liturgical procession of the people up to the temple in Jerusalem (see introductions to Ps 24; 47; 118; 132). The first half of the psalm (vv. 1–18:19 Hebrew poetic lines) contains many clear references to God's triumphal march from Mount Sinai (in the days of Moses) to Mount Zion (in the days of David). The events at Mount Sinai marked the birth of the kingdom of God among his people Israel; the placement of the ark of the covenant (symbol of God's throne) in the temple in Jerusalem marked the establishment of God's redemptive kingdom among the nations of the earth, with Jerusalem as its royal city. The second half of the psalm (vv. 19–35:19 Hebrew poetic lines) is framed by the cry "Praise be to the Lord/God" and looks forward with expectations of God's continuing triumphs until the redemption of his people is complete and his kingly rule is universally acknowledged with songs of praise. The early church, taking its cue from Eph 4:8–13, understood this psalm to foreshadow the resurrection, ascension and present rule of Christ and the final triumph of his church over the hostile world. Ps 68 is the

last in a series of four (see introduction to Ps 65–68).

The psalm is composed of nine stanzas (vv. 19–20 should probably be joined with vv. 21–23), with a concluding doxology. The first stanza (vv. 1–3) suggests the beginning of a liturgical procession, and the last (vv. 32–35) its conclusion, with God enthroned in his sanctuary. The seventh (vv. 24–27) speaks expressly of a procession coming into view and entering the sanctuary. In light of these clear references, the third stanza (vv. 7–10) suggests a stage in the procession recalling the desert journey from Sinai to the promised land, while the fifth (vv. 15–18) marks that stage in which the Lord ascends Mount Zion. On the other hand, the second stanza (vv. 4–6) reflects on the benevolence of God's rule; the fourth (vv. 11–14) recalls his victories over the kings of Canaan; the sixth (vv. 19–23) speaks reassuringly of God's future victories; and the eighth (vv. 28–31) contains prayers that God may muster his power to subdue the enemy as he had done before.

68 title See notes on Ps 4; 30 titles.
68:1–3 The start of the procession, liturgically recalling the beginning of God's march with his people in army formation from Sinai (see Nu 10:33–35).
68:1 *enemies be scattered.* See note on v. 30.

▲ **68:3** *righteous.* Israel as the committed people of God in distinction from those opposed to the coming of God's kingdom (the "wicked" of v. 2); see 1:5 and note.
68:4–6 A call to praise God for the benevolence of his rule.

▣ **68:4** *name.* See note on 5:11. *who rides on the clouds.* An epithet of Baal found in Canaanite literature is used to make the point that the Lord (Yahweh, not Baal) is the exalted One who truly makes the storm cloud his chariot (see v. 33; 18:9; 104:3; Dt 33:26; Isa 19:1; Mt 26:64).
68:5–6 God is the defender of the powerless (see 10:14; 146:7–9; 147:6; Dt 10:18).
68:6 *sets the lonely in families.* See Ex 1:21; Ru 4:14–17; 1Sa 2:5.

he leads out the prisoners *e* with singing;
but the rebellious live in a sun-scorched land. *f*

[7] When you, God, went out *g* before your people,
when you marched through the wilderness, *a h*
[8] the earth shook, *i* the heavens poured down rain, *j*
before God, the One of Sinai, *k*
before God, the God of Israel. *l*
[9] You gave abundant showers, *m* O God;
you refreshed your weary inheritance.
[10] Your people settled in it,
and from your bounty, *n* God, you provided *o* for the poor.

[11] The Lord announced the word,
and great was the company *p* of those who proclaimed it:
[12] "Kings and armies flee *q* in haste;
every household shares in the plunder. *r*
[13] Even while you sleep among the sheep pens, *b s*
the wings of my dove are sheathed with silver,
its feathers with shining gold."
[14] When the Almighty *c* scattered *t* the kings in the land,
it was like snow fallen on Mount Zalmon. *u*

[15] Mount Bashan, *v* majestic mountain, *w*
Mount Bashan, rugged mountain,
[16] why gaze in envy, you rugged mountain,
at the mountain where God chooses *x* to reign,
where the Lord himself will dwell forever? *y*
[17] The chariots *z* of God are tens of thousands
and thousands of thousands; *a*
the Lord has come from Sinai into his sanctuary. *d*
[18] When you ascended *b* on high, *c*
you took many captives; *d*

a 7 The Hebrew has *Selah* (a word of uncertain meaning) here and at the end of verses 19 and 32.
b 13 Or *the campfires;* or *the saddlebags*   *c 14* Hebrew *Shaddai*   *d 17* Probable reading of the original
Hebrew text; Masoretic Text *Lord is among them at Sinai in holiness*

68:6 *e* Ps 79:11;
102:20; 146:7;
Isa 61:1; Lk 4:18
f Isa 35:7; 49:10; 58:11
68:7 *g* S Ex 13:21
h Ps 78:40; 106:14
68:8 *i* S 2Sa 22:8
j S Jdg 5:4; 2Sa 21:10;
Ecc 11:3 *k* S Dt 33:2
l S Jdg 5:5
68:9 *m* S Dt 32:2;
S Job 36:28;
S Eze 34:26
68:10 *n* S Dt 28:12
o Ps 65:9
68:11 *p* Lk 2:13
68:12 *q* Jos 10:16
r S Jdg 5:30
68:13 *s* S Ge 49:14
68:14 *t* 2Sa 22:15
u Jdg 9:48
68:15 *v* ver 22;
Nu 21:33; Jer 22:20
w S Ps 36:6
68:16 *x* Dt 12:5;
S Ps 2:6; 132:13
y Ps 132:14
68:17 *z* S 2Ki 2:11;
Isa 66:15; Hab 3:8
a Da 7:10
68:18 *b* S Ps 47:5
c Ps 7:7 *d* Jdg 5:12

leads out the prisoners. As he led Israel out of Egypt (see 69:33; 107:10,14). *rebellious.* See notes on v. 18; 66:7. *sun-scorched land.* A place utterly barren, lacking even soil for vegetation (see Eze 26:4,14).

68:7–10 Recollection of God's march through the desert from Sinai into the promised land (see Jdg 5:4–5; Hab 3:3–6).
68:7 For *Selah,* see TNIV text note and note on 3:2.
68:8 *earth shook.* A reference to the quaking of Mount Sinai (Ex 19:18). *heavens poured down rain.* The Pentateuch preserves no tradition of rain during the desert wanderings, but here (and in Jdg 5:4) rain is closely associated with the quaking of the earth as a manifestation of the majesty of God. Perhaps the "thunder and lightning, with a thick cloud" over Mount Sinai (Ex 19:16) were accompanied by rain. But see also v. 9, which suggests rains that refreshed the people on their journey.
68:9 *your…inheritance.* The people of Israel (see Dt 9:29).
68:10 *it.* Probably refers to the promised land. *bounty.* Lit. "goodness" (see 65:11 and note). *provided.* From the produce of Canaan (see Jos 5:11–12). *poor.* Israel as a people dependent on God.
68:11–14 Recollection of God's victories over the kings of Canaan.
68:11 *announced the word.* God declared beforehand that he would be victorious over the Canaanite kings (see Ex 23:22–23, 27–28,31; Dt 7:10–24; 11:23–25; Jos 1:2–6). *proclaimed it.* Celebrated God's victories (see Ex 15:1–21; 1Sa 18:6–7; 2Ch 20:26–28). *proclaimed.* See 40:9 and note.
68:13 *sleep among the sheep pens.* Rest in camp (see Jdg 5:16; see also TNIV text note). *wings of my dove are sheathed.* Israel, God's "dove" (see 74:19 and note; cf. Hos 7:11), is enriched with the silver and gold of plunder from the kings of Canaan even

though she still remains in camp. This poetic hyperbole (a figure of speech that uses exaggeration for emphasis) celebrates the fact that God had defeated the kings even before Israel met them in battle (see Jos 2:8–11; 5:1; 6:16; see also 2Sa 5:24; 2Ki 7:5–7; 19:35; 2Ch 20:22–30).
68:14 *Almighty.* See TNIV text note; see also note on Ge 17:1. *like snow fallen on Mount Zalmon.* A mountain near Shechem bore this name (see Jdg 9:46–48), but some identify the mountain referred to here as Jebel Druze, a dark volcanic mountain east of Bashan. Its name appears to mean "the dark one"—in distinction from the Lebanon ("the white one") range, composed of limestone—and the figure may involve the contrast of white snow scattered on "Dark Mountain." The reference may then be to abandoned weapons littering the field from which the kings have fled headlong (see 2Ki 7:15).
68:15–18 Celebration of God's ascent to Mount Zion.
68:15–16 The mountains surrounding Bashan, including the towering Mount Hermon, are portrayed as being jealous because God has chosen Mount Zion as the seat of his rule, making it the "highest" of mountains (see 48:2 and note).

A **68:17** *chariots of God.* God's great heavenly host, here likened to a vast chariot force (see 2Ki 6:17; Hab 3:8,15). In the time of the Roman empire Jesus referred to God's host in terms of "legions" (Mt 26:53).

A **68:18** *ascended on high.* Went up to your place of enthronement on Mount Zion (see 47:5–6 and note; see also 7:7). *took many captives…received gifts.* Like a victorious king after triumphs on the field of battle. *rebellious.* Those who had opposed the kingdom of God (see v. 6 and note on 66:7) are compelled to submit to him and bring tribute. *that you…might*

68:18 *e* Eph 4:8*
f S Nu 17:10
68:19 *g* S Ps 65:5
h Ps 81:6
68:20 *i* S 1Sa 10:19
j Ps 56:13; Jer 45:5;
Eze 6:8
68:21 *k* Ps 74:14;
110:5; Hab 3:13
68:22 *l* S Job 36:30;
Mt 18:6
68:23 *m* Ps 58:10
n S 1Ki 21:19;
S 2Ki 9:36
68:24 *o* S Ps 63:2
68:25 *p* S 1Ch 15:16
q S 1Ch 6:31;
S 2Ch 5:12; Rev 18:22
r S Ge 31:27;
S Isa 5:12
68:26 *s* S Ps 22:22;
Heb 2:12 *t* S Lev 19:2
68:27 *u* S 1Sa 9:21
v S Nu 34:21
w S Jdg 5:18
68:28 *x* S Ex 9:16
y Ps 29:11 *z* Isa 26:12;
29:23; 45:11; 60:21;
64:8
68:29 *a* S 2Ch 9:24;
S 32:23
68:30 *b* Isa 27:1;
51:9; Eze 29:3
c S Job 40:21
d Ps 22:12; Isa 34:7;
Jer 50:27 *e* Ps 18:14;
89:10 *f* Ps 120:7;
140:2
68:31 *g* Isa 19:19;
43:3; 45:14 *h* Isa 11:11;
18:1; Zep 3:10
68:32 *i* S Ps 46:6;
67:4 *j* Ps 7:17

you received gifts from people, *e*
even from *a* the rebellious *f*—
    that you, *b* LORD God, might dwell there.

19 Praise be to the Lord, to God our Savior, *g*
    who daily bears our burdens. *h*
20 Our God is a God who saves; *i*
    from the Sovereign LORD comes escape from death. *j*
21 Surely God will crush the heads *k* of his enemies,
    the hairy crowns of those who go on in their sins.
22 The Lord says, "I will bring them from Bashan;
    I will bring them from the depths of the sea, *l*
23 that your feet may wade in the blood of your foes, *m*
    while the tongues of your dogs *n* have their share."

24 Your procession, God, has come into view,
    the procession of my God and King into the sanctuary. *o*
25 In front are the singers, *p* after them the musicians; *q*
    with them are the young women playing the timbrels. *r*
26 Praise God in the great congregation; *s*
    praise the LORD in the assembly of Israel. *t*
27 There is the little tribe *u* of Benjamin, *v* leading them,
    there the great throng of Judah's princes,
    and there the princes of Zebulun and of Naphtali. *w*

28 Summon your power, *x* God *c*;
    show us your strength, *y* our God, as you have done *z* before.
29 Because of your temple at Jerusalem
    kings will bring you gifts. *a*
30 Rebuke the beast *b* among the reeds, *c*
    the herd of bulls *d* among the calves of the nations.
    Humbled, may it bring bars of silver.
    Scatter the nations *e* who delight in war. *f*
31 Envoys will come from Egypt; *g*
    Cush *d h* will submit herself to God.

32 Sing to God, you kingdoms of the earth, *i*
    sing praise *j* to the Lord,

---

a 18 Or *gifts for people, / even*   *b* 18 Or *they*   *c* 28 Many Hebrew manuscripts, Septuagint and Syriac;
most Hebrew manuscripts *Your God has summoned power for you*   *d* 31 That is, the upper Nile region

---

dwell there. Grammatically completes the clause, "When you ascended on high." Paul applies this verse (as translated in the Septuagint, the pre-Christian Greek translation of the OT) to the ascended Christ (Eph 4:8–13; see notes on Eph 4:8–9,11), thereby implying that Christ's ascension was a continuation of, and a fulfillment of, God's establishment of his kingdom in his royal city, Jerusalem (see introduction to this psalm).
68:19–23 Joyous confession of hope that God's victorious campaigns will continue until the salvation of his people is complete.
68:19 *bears our burdens.* Releases us from bearing the burdens that enslavement to our enemies would impose on us (see 81:6; Isa 9:4; 10:27). But some associate this line with such passages as 55:22; Isa 46:4.
68:20 *escape from death.* At the hand of our enemies—implicitly, perhaps, also from death itself as the last great enemy (see notes on 6:5; 11:7; 16:9–11; 17:15; 49:14–15).
68:21 As God assures the life of his people (see v. 20), so he will crush those who oppose him. *crush the heads.* See Nu 24:17; Jer 48:45–46 and note.
68:22 *them.* The enemies who fled at the victorious onward march of God and his host (see vv. 12,17). *Bashan ... depths of the sea.* The former (see also v. 15) was the high plateau east of the Jordan, the latter the Mediterranean Sea—none of the enemies will escape (see Am 9:1–4).
68:23 See note on 58:10.

68:24–27 The liturgical procession approaches the temple (see Ps 24; 47).
68:25 *young women playing the timbrels.* See note on Jer 31:4.
68:27 All Israel is represented, from little Benjamin to powerful Judah, and tribes from the north as well as the south. *Benjamin, leading.* Perhaps reflecting the fact that from the tribe of Benjamin came the first king (Saul), who began the royal victories over Israel's enemies (see 1Sa 11:11; 14:20–23).
68:28–31 Prayer for God to continue his conquest of the threatening powers.
68:28 *Summon your power.* Or, perhaps, "Command your power to act."
68:29 *Because of your temple.* Because your earthly royal house has been established in Jerusalem. *bring you gifts.* Acknowledge you by bringing tribute, as subjected kings brought tribute to their conquerers (see 2Sa 8:2,6,10; 2Ki 3:4).
68:30 *Rebuke.* See note on 76:6. *beast among the reeds.* The pharaoh (see Eze 29:3). *herd of bulls among the calves.* Powerful princes supporting the pharaoh, and the lesser princes of other nations. Egypt is singled out here as representative of the hostile nations—because of Israel's past experiences with that world power. It may also be that at the time the psalm was composed Egypt was the one great empire on Israel's immediate horizons. *Scatter the nations.* See v. 1; so that Israel may have peace (see 46:9; 48:4–7; 65:7; 76:3).

33 to him who rides ^k the ancient skies above,
    who thunders ^l with mighty voice. ^m
34 Proclaim the power ⁿ of God,
    whose majesty ^o is over Israel,
    whose power is in the skies.
35 You, God, are awesome ^p in your sanctuary; ^q
    the God of Israel gives power and strength ^r to his people. ^s

Praise be to God! ^t

PSALM 69

For the director of music. To the tune of "Lilies." Of David.

*¹ Save me, O God,
    for the waters ^u have come up to my neck. ^v
2 I sink in the miry depths, ^w
    where there is no foothold.
I have come into the deep waters;
    the floods engulf me.
3 I am worn out calling for help; ^x
    my throat is parched.
My eyes fail, ^y
    looking for my God.
4 Those who hate me ^z without reason ^a
    outnumber the hairs of my head;
many are my enemies without cause, ^b
    those who seek to destroy me. ^c
I am forced to restore
    what I did not steal.

* 69:1-36 is numbered 69:2-37 in Hebrew texts.

68:33 ^kS Dt 33:26
^lS Ex 9:23; S Ps 29:3
^mPs 29:4; Isa 30:30; 33:3; 66:6
68:34 ⁿver 28
^oPs 45:3
68:35 ^pS Dt 7:21
^qS Ge 28:17 ^rPs 18:1; Isa 40:29; 41:10; 50:2
^sS Ps 29:11 ^rPs 28:6; 66:20; 2Co 1:3
69:1 ^uS Ps 42:7
^vPs 32:6; Jnh 2:5
69:2 ^wS Job 30:19
69:3 ^xPs 6:6
^yPs 119:82
69:4 ^zS Ps 25:19
^aJn 15:25*
^bS Ps 35:19; 38:19
^cPs 40:14; 119:95; Isa 32:7

68:32–35 Climax of the liturgical procession: a call for all kingdoms to hail with praise the God of Israel as the God who reigns in heaven and has established his earthly throne in the temple in Jerusalem (see Ps 47).

68:33 See v. 4 and note. *thunders with mighty voice.* See note on 29:3–9.

68:35 *awesome.* See 45:4 and note. *gives power and strength to his people.* The Lord of all has made Israel his people (his "kingdom"; see Ex 19:5–6), and his rule among them makes them participants in his victorious power (see 29:10–11). **Ps 69–72** Book II of the Psalter closes with a cluster of three prayers and an attached royal psalm—in perfect balance with its beginning (see note on Ps 42–45). These three prayers were originally all pleas of a king in Israel for deliverance from enemies (apparently internal) determined to do away with him. They all contain certain key words that are found elsewhere in Book II only in Ps 42–44 and in the seven psalms (54–60) placed at the center of the Book. Another link between Ps 69–71 and 42–44 is the placement of a short psalm at the center of each triad. These placements have the appearance of deliberate editorial design. In the former cluster Ps 43 has been artificially separated from 42 (see introduction to Ps 42–43), while in the latter cluster Ps 70 repeats (with some revision) Ps 40:13–17 and was probably intended to serve as an introduction to Ps 71. The attached prayer for the king (Ps 72) stands in similar relationship to Ps 69–71 as Ps 45 stands to Ps 42–44 and brings Book II to its conclusion. Thus, as with Ps 45, its placement hints at a Messianic reading of the psalm already by the editors of the Psalter (see also introduction to Ps 72). It should be further noted that in Ps 65–68 all peoples on earth are drawn into the community of those praising God (see note on Ps 65–68). Here in Ps 69 all creation is called to join that chorus (v. 34), and Ps 72 envisions that all peoples and kings will submit to the son of David (vv. 8–11) and be blessed through his reign (v. 17).

Ps 69 A plea for God to have mercy and to save from a host of enemies: the prayer of a godly king when under vicious attack by a widespread conspiracy at a time when God had "wounded" him (see v. 26) for some sin in his life (see v. 5). If, as tradition claims, David authored the original psalm (see title), the occasion is unknown. In its present form the prayer suggests a later son of David who ruled over the southern kingdom of Judah (see v. 35). That king may have been Hezekiah (see 2Ki 18–20; 2Ch 29–32). This psalm begins a series of three prayers for deliverance when threatened by enemies (see introduction to Ps 69–72). Structurally, this psalm is composed of two halves of 22 lines each (a double [blank] alphabetic acrostic; see introduction to Ps 33). The first half (vv. 1–15) ends with petitions that echo the descriptions of distress at the beginning. It should also be noted that v. 5 stands at the center of vv. 1–15 and v. 29 stands at the center of vv. 22–36. The "centering" of these two verses accounts for why they both stand thematically somewhat apart from their immediate contexts (for this literary device, see note on 6:6; for the thematic relationship of these two verses, see notes below). The authors of the NT viewed this cry of a godly sufferer as foreshadowing the sufferings of Christ; no other psalm, except Ps 22, is quoted more frequently in the NT. **69 title** *For the director of music.* See note on Ps 4 title. *To the tune of.* See note on Ps 9 title. *Lilies.* See note on Ps 45 title. **69:1–15** Description of the dire distress that evokes the psalmist's prayer.

69:1–2 *waters…miry depths…deep waters…floods.* Conventional imagery for great distress (see notes on 30:1; 32:6)—here the results of God's "wounding" (see v. 26), but especially of the attacks of the enemies (see vv. 14–15,29).

69:3 *throat is parched.* See 22:15. *eyes fail.* See 6:7 and note. **69:4** *without reason…without cause.* Those whom he has not wronged are pitted against him (see 35:19 and note). *outnumber the hairs of my head.* See note on 40:12. *I am forced.* An illustrative way of saying that his enemies are spreading false accusations about him (see 5:9 and note).

69:5 *d* Ps 38:5
e S Ps 44:21
69:7 *f* S Ps 39:8
g Jer 15:15 *h* Ps 44:15
69:8 *i* Job 19:13-15;
Ps 31:11; 38:11;
Isa 53:3; Jn 7:5
69:9 *j* Jn 2:17*
k Ps 89:50-51;
Ro 15:3*
69:10 *l* S Ps 35:13
69:11 *m* S 2Sa 3:31;
S Ps 35:13
69:12 *n* S Ge 18:1;
S 23:10 *o* Job 30:9
69:13 *p* Isa 49:8;
2Co 6:2 *q* S Ps 17:7;
51:1
69:14 *r* ver 2;
Ps 144:7
69:15 *s* Ps 124:4-5
t Nu 16:33 *u* Ps 28:1
69:16 *v* S Ps 63:3
69:17 *w* S Ps 22:24
x Ps 143:7
y S Ps 50:15; 66:14
69:18 *z* Ps 49:15
69:19 *a* S Ps 22:6

5 You, God, know my folly; *d*
  my guilt is not hidden from you. *e*

6 Lord, the LORD Almighty,
  may those who hope in you
  not be disgraced because of me;
  God of Israel,
  may those who seek you
  not be put to shame because of me.
7 For I endure scorn *f* for your sake, *g*
  and shame covers my face. *h*
8 I am a foreigner to my own family,
  a stranger to my own mother's children; *i*
9 for zeal for your house consumes me, *j*
  and the insults of those who insult you fall on me. *k*
10 When I weep and fast, *l*
  I must endure scorn;
11 when I put on sackcloth, *m*
  people make sport of me.
12 Those who sit at the gate *n* mock me,
  and I am the song of the drunkards. *o*

13 But I pray to you, LORD,
  in the time of your favor; *p*
  in your great love, *q* O God,
  answer me with your sure salvation.
14 Rescue me from the mire,
  do not let me sink;
  deliver me from those who hate me,
  from the deep waters. *r*
15 Do not let the floodwaters *s* engulf me
  or the depths swallow me up *t*
  or the pit close its mouth over me. *u*

16 Answer me, LORD, out of the goodness of your love; *v*
  in your great mercy turn to me.
17 Do not hide your face *w* from your servant;
  answer me quickly, *x* for I am in trouble. *y*
18 Come near and rescue me;
  redeem *z* me because of my foes.

19 You know how I am scorned, *a* disgraced and shamed;
  all my enemies are before you.
20 Scorn has broken my heart
  and has left me helpless;

69:5 A confession of personal guilt—the reason why God has "wounded" him (v. 26) and why he is "in pain and distress" (v. 29). *folly.* See TNIV text note on 14:1.

69:6–12 Prayer that God's discipline of his godly servant may not bring disgrace on all those who trustingly look to the Lord. The author acknowledges that God's "wounding" of him has been occasioned by some sin in his life (but he has not sinned against those who have become his enemies). Because of his present suffering, his enemies mock his deep commitment to the Lord (see 22:6–8; 42:3; 79:10; 115:2; Job 2:9). Implicitly he prays that God will restore him again and vindicate his trust in him.

69:8 Even those nearest him dissociate themselves from him (see 31:11–12 and note).

A 69:9 *zeal for your house.* What was true of the author was even more true of Jesus (see Jn 2:17). *insults of those who insult you.* Those who mock God also mock his servant who trusts in him (see 74:18,22–23; 2Ki 18:31–35), as Christ experienced (see Ro 15:3).

69:10–11 *weep and fast ... put on sackcloth.* As tokens of humbling himself before the Lord in repentance as he prays for God

to have mercy and restore him (see 35:13 and note; see also Ge 37:34; 2Sa 12:16–17; Joel 1:13–14; 2:15–17; Jnh 3:5).

69:12 *Those who sit at the gate ... drunkards.* Everyone, from the elders of the city to the town drunks.

69:13–15 Though they mock, I pray to you.

69:13 *time of your favor.* When God is near to save (see 32:6 and note; see also Isa 49:8; 61:2; 2Co 6:2). *great love.* See note on 6:4.

69:14–15 *mire ... deep waters ... floodwaters ... depths.* See note on vv. 1–2. The psalmists' petitions commonly echo their earlier descriptions of the distress that occasions the prayer. Here the return to the beginning marks the end of the first half of the psalmist's appeal to God.

69:15 *swallow me.* See note on 49:14. *pit.* See note on 30:1.

69:16–18 An appeal for God to hear—such as commonly begins the prayers brought together in the Psalter.

69:16 *love.* See note on 6:4.

69:17 *hide your face.* See note on 13:1.

69:18 *redeem.* See note on 25:22.

69:19–21 In my trouble they heaped on scorn instead of bringing comfort (see 35:11–16; see also 142:4; Job 13:4; 16:2; 21:34).

69:20 *heart.* See note on 4:7.

I looked for sympathy, but there was none,
  for comforters, *b* but I found none. *c*
21 They put gall in my food
  and gave me vinegar *d* for my thirst. *e*

22 May the table set before them become a snare;
  may it become retribution and *a* a trap. *f*
23 May their eyes be darkened so they cannot see,
  and their backs be bent forever. *g*
24 Pour out your wrath *h* on them;
  let your fierce anger overtake them.
25 May their place be deserted; *i*
  let there be no one to dwell in their tents. *j*
26 For they persecute those you wound
  and talk about the pain of those you hurt. *k*
27 Charge them with crime upon crime; *l*
  do not let them share in your salvation. *m*
28 May they be blotted out of the book of life *n*
  and not be listed with the righteous. *o*

29 But as for me, afflicted and in pain—
  may your salvation, God, protect me. *p*

30 I will praise God's name in song *r*
  and glorify him *r* with thanksgiving.
31 This will please the LORD more than an ox,
  more than a bull with its horns and hooves. *s*
32 The poor will see and be glad *t*—
  you who seek God, may your hearts live! *u*
33 The LORD hears the needy *v*
  and does not despise his captive people.

34 Let heaven and earth praise him,
  the seas and all that move in them, *w*
35 for God will save Zion *x*
  and rebuild the cities of Judah. *y*

a 22 Or snare / and their fellowship become

69:20 *b* Job 16:2
c Ps 142:4; Isa 63:5
69:21 *d* S Nu 6:3;
Mt 27:48; Mk 15:36;
Lk 23:36 *e* Mt 27:34;
Mk 15:23; Jn 19:28-30
69:22 *f* S 1Sa 28:9;
S Job 18:10
69:23 *g* Ro 11:9-10*
69:24 *h* Ps 79:6;
Jer 10:25
69:25 *i* S Lev 26:43;
Mt 23:38 *j* Ac 1:20*
69:26 *k* S Job 19:22;
Zec 1:15
69:27 *l* Ne 4:5
m Ps 109:14
69:28 *n* Ex 32:32-
33; S Lk 10:20
o Eze 13:9
69:29 *p* S Ps 20:1
69:30 *q* Ps 28:7
r Ps 34:3
69:31 *s* Ps 50:9-13;
51:16
69:32 *t* S Ps 34:2
u Ps 22:26
69:33 *v* Ps 12:5
69:34 *w* Ps 96:11;
98:7; Isa 44:23
69:35 *x* Ob 1:17
y S Ezr 9:9; S Ps 51:18

69:21 *gall in my food ... vinegar for my thirst.* Vivid metaphors for the bitter scorn they made him eat and drink when his whole being craved the nourishment and refreshment of comfort. The authors of the Gospels, especially Matthew, suggest that the suffering expressed in this verse foreshadowed Christ's suffering on the cross (see Mt 27:34,48; Mk 15:23,36; Lk 23:36; Jn 19:29).

69:22–28 Prayer for God to redress the wrongs committed (see note on 5:10).

69:22–23 For Paul's application of these verses to the Jews who rejected the Christ, see Ro 11:9–10.

69:22 They had set his table with "gall" and "vinegar" (v. 21). *table set before them.* Reference may be to the meal accompanying the sealing of a covenant (see note on 23:5). In that case, this verse alludes to a pact uniting the enemies and calls on God to turn it against them. *become a snare ... a trap.* Note the unusual use of this imagery (see note on 9:15).

69:23 They mocked him for his "wound" (v. 26); now may they experience the same failing of the eyes (see v. 3 and note on 6:7) and bending of the back (from weakness and pain; see 38:5–8). *May ... their backs be bent.* Lit. "May ... their loins give way." "Loins" refers to the belly and lower part of the back; they were viewed as the back's center of strength (see 66:11; see also Job 40:16).

69:24 *wrath ... anger.* See note on 2:5. *overtake them.* Like a flash flood.

69:25 They sought to remove him from his place; may they be removed. Cf. Peter's application of this judgment to Judas (Ac 1:20).

69:26 The great wrong committed by his enemies against him

and to which reference has repeatedly been made.

69:27 They have falsely charged him with crimes (v. 4); may their real crimes all be charged against them.

69:28 They had plotted his death; may death be their destiny. *book of life.* God's royal list of the righteous, whom he blesses with life (see 1:3; 7:9; 11:7; 34:12; 37:17,29; 55:22; 75:10; 92:12–14; 140:13). For other references to God's books see notes on 9:5; 51:1. In the NT the "book of life" refers to God's list of those destined for eternal life (see Php 4:3; Rev 3:5 and note; 13:8; 17:8; 20:12,15; 21:27; cf. Lk 10:20; Heb 12:23 and notes).

69:29 A summary renewal of the prayer just prior to the vow to praise (see note on v. 5). *pain.* An echo of v. 26. *your salvation.* Cf. vv. 13,27. *protect me.* Lit. "raise me to a high, secure place."

69:30–33 A vow to praise (see note on 7:17) out of assurance that the prayer will be heard (see note on 3:8).

69:30 *God's name.* See v. 36 and note on 5:11.

69:32 *poor.* See note on 34:6. *see and be glad.* See 22:26 and note. *hearts.* See note on 4:7. *live.* Bubble over with the joy of life, because the Lord does hear the prayers of his people in need—contrary to the mocking of scoffers.

69:34–36 A call for all creation to take up the praise of the Lord (see note on 9:1), a call that confidently anticipates that God will restore Judah and assure his people's inheritance in the promised land. This stanza appears to indicate that in its final form this royal prayer was used at a time when not only the king was in trouble but the kingdom of Judah had also suffered devastating defeat.

69:34 See 148:1–13; Isa 49:13.

69:36 *z* Ps 25:13
a S Ps 37:29
70:1 *b* Ps 22:19;
71:12
70:2 *c* Ps 35:4
d Ps 6:10; 35:26;
71:13; 109:29; 129:5
70:3 *e* S Ps 35:21
70:4 *f* Ps 9:10
g Ps 31:6-7; 32:11;
118:24 *h* Ps 35:27
70:5 *i* Ps 86:1;
109:22 *j* Ps 141:1
k Ps 30:10; 33:20
l Ps 18:2 *m* Ps 119:60
71:1 *n* S Dt 23:15;
Ru 2:12 *o* S Ps 22:5
71:2 *p* S 2Ki 19:16
71:3 *q* Ps 18:2

Then people will settle there and possess it;
36 the children of his servants will inherit it, *z*
and those who love his name will dwell there. *a*

PSALM 70

70:1–5pp — Ps 40:13–17

For the director of music. Of David. A petition.

*1 Hasten, O God, to save me;
come quickly, LORD, to help me. *b*

2 May those who seek my life *c*
be put to shame and confusion;
may all who desire my ruin
be turned back in disgrace. *d*
3 May those who say to me, "Aha! Aha!" *e*
turn back because of their shame.
4 But may all who seek you *f*
rejoice and be glad *g* in you;
may those who long for your saving help always say,
"The LORD is great!" *h*

5 But as for me, I am poor and needy; *i*
come quickly to me, *j* O God.
You are my help *k* and my deliverer; *l*
LORD, do not delay. *m*

PSALM 71

71:1–3pp — Ps 31:1–4

1 In you, LORD, I have taken refuge; *n*
let me never be put to shame. *o*
2 In your righteousness, rescue me and deliver me;
turn your ear *p* to me and save me.
3 Be my rock of refuge,
to which I can always go;
give the command to save me,
for you are my rock and my fortress. *q*

* 70:1-5 is numbered 70:2-6 in Hebrew texts.

69:35–36 *people ... children.* God's people and their children through the generations, specifically "those who love his name."
69:35 *Zion.* See note on 9:11.
Ps 70 An urgent prayer for God's help when threatened by enemies—a somewhat revised duplicate of 40:13–17 (see notes there). This is the second in a series of three such prayers; its language has many links with that of Ps 71. For this psalm's placement in the Psalter, see introduction to Ps 69–72; for its special relationship to Ps 71 see introduction to that psalm. The prayer is framed by pleas for God to "come quickly" with his help (vv. 1,5). The rest of the prayer focuses on the effects of God's saving help: (1) upon those "who seek my life" (vv. 2–3) and (2) for those "who seek you" (v. 4).
70 title See note on Ps 4 title. *A petition.* See note on Ps 38 title.
70:4 God's deliverance of his servant will give joy to all who trust in the Lord, because they see in it the assurance of their own salvation. *The LORD is great!* Because his saving help is sure and effective (contrast v. 3).
70:5 This verse echoes most of the language of v. 1: "God," "LORD," "come quickly," "(my) help (me)."
Ps 71 A prayer for God's help in old age when enemies threaten because they see that the king's strength is waning (see note on 5:9). The psalm bears no title, but it may well be that Ps 70 was viewed by the editors of the Psalms as the introduction to Ps 71 (compare vv. 1,12–13 with 70:1–2,5), in which case the

psalm is ascribed to David (in his old age; see vv. 9,18). This suggestion gains support from the fact that Ps 72 is identified as a prayer by and/or for King Solomon (see introduction to that psalm). This is the third in a series of three prayers (see introduction to Ps 69–72); its dominant theme is hope (see v. 14). Formally symmetrical, the psalm is composed of six stanzas, having a five-four-five, five-four-five (in Hebrew) line pattern: vv. 1–4 (five lines), vv. 5–8 (four lines), vv. 9–13 (five lines), vv. 15–18 (five lines), vv. 19–21 (four lines), vv. 22–24 (five lines). Thus each half is made up of 14 lines. At the center (v. 14; see note on 6:6) stands a confident confession of hope. The whole is framed by an appeal for help (vv. 1–4) and a vow to praise in anticipation of deliverance (vv. 22–24). The second and fifth stanzas are linked by references to the troubles the king has experienced; stanzas three and four are linked by references to old age. This psalm appears to contain an unusual number of echoes of other psalms, though these alleged "echoes" may simply reflect a well-established prayer tradition (for particulars see notes below).
71:1–4 The initial appeal for God's help. Verses 1–3 differ only a little from 31:1–3a.
71:2 *your righteousness.* See vv. 15–16,19,24; see also note on 4:1.
71:3 *give the command to save.* In Hebrew a noteworthy verbal link with 44:4 ("who decrees victories"). The Hebrew phraseology occurs only in these two places in the OT.

⁴ Deliver ʳ me, my God, from the hand of the wicked, ˢ
  from the grasp of those who are evil and cruel. ᵗ

⁵ For you have been my hope, ᵘ Sovereign LORD,
  my confidence ᵛ since my youth.
⁶ From birth ʷ I have relied on you;
  you brought me forth from my mother's womb. ˣ
  I will ever praise ʸ you.
⁷ I have become like a portent ᶻ to many,
  but you are my strong refuge. ᵃ
⁸ My mouth ᵇ is filled with your praise,
  declaring your splendor ᶜ all day long.

⁹ Do not cast ᵈ me away when I am old; ᵉ
  do not forsake ᶠ me when my strength is gone.
¹⁰ For my enemies ᵍ speak against me;
  those who wait to kill ʰ me conspire ⁱ together.
¹¹ They say, "God has forsaken ʲ him;
  pursue him and seize him,
  for no one will rescue ᵏ him."
¹² Do not be far ˡ from me, my God;
  come quickly, God, to help ᵐ me.
¹³ May my accusers ⁿ perish in shame; ᵒ
  may those who want to harm me
  be covered with scorn and disgrace. ᵖ

¹⁴ As for me, I will always have hope; �q
  I will praise you more and more.

¹⁵ My mouth will tell ʳ of your righteous deeds, ˢ
  of your saving acts all day long—
  though I know not how to relate them all.
¹⁶ I will come and proclaim your mighty acts, ᵗ Sovereign LORD;
  I will proclaim your righteous deeds, yours alone.
¹⁷ Since my youth, God, you have taught ᵘ me,
  and to this day I declare your marvelous deeds. ᵛ
¹⁸ Even when I am old and gray, ʷ
  do not forsake me, my God,
  till I declare your power ˣ to the next generation,
  your mighty acts to all who are to come. ʸ

¹⁹ Your righteousness, God, reaches to the skies, ᶻ
  you who have done great things. ᵃ
  Who is like you, God? ᵇ
²⁰ Though you have made me see troubles, ᶜ

71:4 ʳ S 2Ki 19:19
ˢ Ps 140:4
ᵗ S Ge 48:16
71:5 ᵘ S Ps 9:18;
S 25:5 ᵛ S Job 4:6;
Jer 17:7
71:6 ʷ S Ps 22:10
ˣ S Job 3:16; S Ps 22:9
ʸ Ps 9:1; 34:1; 52:9;
119:164; 145:2
71:7 ᶻ S Dt 28:46;
Isa 8:18; 1Co 4:9
ᵃ S 2Sa 22:3; Ps 61:3
71:8 ᵇ ver 15;
Ps 51:15; 63:5
ᶜ Ps 96:6; 104:1
71:9 ᵈ S Ps 51:11
ᵉ Ps 92:14; Isa 46:4
ᶠ S Dt 4:31; S 31:6
71:10 ᵍ Ps 3:7
ʰ S Ps 10:8; 59:3;
Pr 1:18 ⁱ S Ex 1:10;
S Ps 31:13; S Mt 12:14
71:11 ʲ S Ps 9:10;
Isa 40:27; 54:7;
La 5:20; Mt 27:46
ᵏ S Ps 7:2
71:12 ˡ S Ps 38:21
ᵐ Ps 22:19; 38:22
71:13 ⁿ Jer 18:19
ᵒ S Job 8:22; Ps 25:3
ᵖ S Ps 70:2
71:14 q Ps 25:3;
42:5; 130:7; 131:3
71:15 ʳ S ver 8;
S Ps 66:16
ˢ S Ps 51:14
71:16 ᵗ Ps 9:1;
77:12; 106:2; 118:15;
145:4
71:17 ᵘ S Dt 4:5;
S Jer 7:13 ᵛ S Job 5:9;
Ps 26:7; 86:10; 96:3
71:18 ʷ Isa 46:4
ˣ S Ex 9:16 ʸ Job 8:8;
Ps 22:30,31; 78:4;
145:4; Joel 1:3
71:19 ᶻ S Ps 36:5
ᵃ Ps 126:2; Lk 1:49
ᵇ Ps 35:10; 77:13;
89:8
71:20 ᶜ Ps 25:17

71:5–8 A confession that the Lord has always been his hope (see vv. 14,19–21).
71:5–6 Cf. 22:10–11.
71:7 *like a portent.* The troubles of his life (see v. 20) have been viewed by others as holding some special significance—especially since the Lord has been his "strong refuge" through them all.
71:8 *My mouth is filled with your praise ... your splendor.* Because of the Lord's faithful care, the psalmist has been moved to fulfill in his life the high purpose of God in saving and blessing his people (see Jer 13:11; 33:9).
71:9–13 A prayer for God's continuing help in the waning years of the psalmist's life.
71:10 *enemies speak against me.* See notes on 3:2; 5:9.
71:12 *Do not be far from me.* Cf. 22:11,19; 35:22; 38:21. *come quickly ... to help me.* Cf. 22:19; 38:22; 40:13; 70:1; cf. also 70:5; 141:1.
71:13 A plea for redress (see note on 5:10). Key words in this closing verse of the first half of the psalm are echoed in the last verse of the second half. Similar language is found in 35:4,26; 40:14–15; 70:2–3; 83:17; 109:28–29.
71:14 A centered confession of unfaltering hope—providing a

striking link with Ps 42–43 (see 42:8 and note; see also note on 6:6).
71:15–18 A vow to praise, accompanying the renewal of his prayer (v. 18); see note on 7:17.
71:15 *tell ... righteous deeds ... saving acts.* Here one of the "righteous deeds" the psalmist vows to "tell," i.e., to recount, is God's act of deliverance in answer to the psalmist's prayer (see notes on vv. 16–17; 4:1).
71:16–17 *mighty acts ... righteous deeds ... marvelous deeds.* God's "mighty (marvelous) acts" in behalf of his people are expressions of his righteousness; see also his "righteous acts" (v. 24).
71:16 *come.* To the temple, where God's people assemble for worship.

71:19–21 A confession that the Lord is still his hope, in the face of all his troubles (see vv. 5–8,14).
71:19 *reaches to the skies.* Is as expansive as all space above the earth (see also 36:5 and note). *Who is like you, God?* See Mic 7:18 and note.

71:20 *you have made me see troubles.* The "troubles" referred to are not specified. That God is somehow involved the psalmist does not question; he shares the mature and ro-

71:20 *d* Ps 80:3,19;
85:4; Hos 6:2
e S Ps 63:9
71:21 *f* Ps 18:35
g Ps 23:4; 86:17;
Isa 12:1; 40:1-2;
49:13; 54:10
71:22 *h* Ps 33:2
i S Job 21:12; Ps 92:3;
144:9 *j* S 2Ki 19:22
71:23 *k* Ps 20:5
l S Ex 15:13
71:24 *m* S Ps 35:28
n ver 13 *o* S Est 9:2
72:1 *p* S Dt 1:16;
S Ps 9:8
72:2 *q* Isa 9:7; 11:4-
5; 16:5; 32:1; 59:17;
63:1; Jer 23:5; 33:15
72:4 *r* S Ps 9:12;
76:9; Isa 49:13
s ver 13; Isa 11:4;
29:19; 32:7
t S Ps 27:11
72:5 *u* 1Sa 13:13
v Ps 33:11
72:6 *w* S Dt 32:2
72:7 *x* Ps 92:12;
Pr 14:11

many and bitter,
 you will restore *d* my life again;
from the depths of the earth *e*
 you will again bring me up.
21 You will increase my honor *f*
 and comfort *g* me once more.

22 I will praise you with the harp *h*
 for your faithfulness, my God;
I will sing praise to you with the lyre, *i*
 Holy One of Israel. *j*
23 My lips will shout for joy *k*
 when I sing praise to you—
 I, whom you have redeemed. *l*
24 My tongue will tell of your righteous acts
 all day long, *m*
for those who wanted to harm me *n*
 have been put to shame and confusion. *o*

PSALM 72

Of Solomon.

1 Endow the king with your justice, *p* O God,
 the royal son with your righteousness.
2 May he judge your people in righteousness, *q*
 your afflicted ones with justice.

3 May the mountains bring prosperity to the people,
 the hills the fruit of righteousness.
4 May he defend the afflicted *r* among the people
 and save the children of the needy; *s*
 may he crush the oppressor. *t*
5 May he endure *a u* as long as the sun,
 as long as the moon, through all generations. *v*
6 May he be like rain *w* falling on a mown field,
 like showers watering the earth.
7 In his days may the righteous flourish *x*
 and prosperity abound till the moon is no more.

a 5 Septuagint; Hebrew You will be feared

---

bust faith that all things are in the hands of the one sovereign God (see 1Sa 16:11–12; Isa 45:5–7; Am 3:6). *restore my life again.* He who gave him life (see v. 6) will renew his life. *depths of the earth.* The realm of the dead, of which the grave is the portal (see note on 30:1).

71:22–24 A vow to praise in confident anticipation of God's saving help (see notes on 3:8; 7:17).

71:22 *harp . . . lyre.* See note on 57:8. *Holy One of Israel.* See 78:41; 89:18; see also 2Ki 19:22 and note.

71:23 *redeemed.* Here, as often, a synonym for "delivered."

71:24 *righteous acts.* God's saving acts in behalf of his people according to his covenant promises (see 88:12; Jdg 5:11; 1Sa 12:7 and note; Da 9:16; Mic 6:5; Rev 15:4).

Ps 72 A prayer for the king, a son of David who rules on David's throne as God's earthly regent over his people. It may have been used at the time of the king's coronation (as were Ps 2; 110). These verses express the desire of the nation that the king's reign will, as a consequence of God's endowment of his servant, be characterized by justice and righteousness, the supreme virtues of kingship. The prayer reflects the ideal concept of the king and the glorious effects of his reign. See Jeremiah's indictment of some of the last Davidic kings (e.g., Jer 22:2–3,13,15) and the prophetic announcement of the Messiah's righteous rule (see Isa 9:7; 11:4–5; Jer 23:5–6; 33:15–16; Zec 9:9). Later Jewish tradition saw in this psalm a

description of the Messiah, as did the early church. The last three verses do not belong to the prayer (see notes there). For this psalm's function within Book II of the Psalter, see introduction to Ps 69–72.

72 title *Of Solomon.* Either by him or for him—of course, both may be true. Undoubtedly it was also used by Israel (Judah) as a prayer for later Davidic kings.

72:1 The basic prayer. *justice . . . righteousness.* May the king be endowed with the gift for and the love of justice and righteousness so that his reign reflects the rule of God himself. Solomon asked for the necessary wisdom so he could govern God's people justly (see 1Ki 3:9,11–12; see also Pr 16:12). *righteousness.* See note on 4:1.

72:2–7 The quality of his reign: May it be righteous, prosperous and enduring.

72:3 Righteousness in the realm will be like fertilizing rain on the land, for then the Lord will bless his people with abundance (see vv. 6–7; 5:12; 65:9–13; 133:3; Lev 25:19; Dt 28:8).

72:5 *endure as long as the sun.* See 21:4 and note.

72:6 See v. 3 and note; see also v. 7. For another vivid metaphor expressive of the significance of the Lord's anointed for the realm, see La 4:20.

72:7 *righteous.* See note on 1:5. *flourish.* Because the king supports and protects them but uses all his royal power to suppress the wicked (see Ps 101).

⁸May he rule from sea to sea
   and from the River[a][y] to the ends of the earth.[z]
⁹May the desert tribes bow before him
   and his enemies lick the dust.
¹⁰May the kings of Tarshish[a] and of distant shores[b]
      bring tribute to him.
   May the kings of Sheba[c] and Seba
      present him gifts.[d]
¹¹May all kings bow down[e] to him
   and all nations serve[f] him.

¹²For he will deliver the needy who cry out,
   the afflicted who have no one to help.
¹³He will take pity[g] on the weak and the needy
   and save the needy from death.
¹⁴He will rescue[h] them from oppression and violence,
   for precious[i] is their blood in his sight.

¹⁵Long may he live!
   May gold from Sheba[j] be given him.
   May people ever pray for him
   and bless him all day long.[k]
¹⁶May grain[l] abound throughout the land;
   on the tops of the hills may it sway.
   May the crops[m] flourish like Lebanon[n]
   and thrive[b] like the grass of the field.[o]

¹⁷May his name endure forever;[p]
   may it continue as long as the sun.[q]

   Then all nations will be blessed through him,[c]
   and they will call him blessed.[r]

¹⁸Praise be to the LORD God, the God of Israel,[s]
   who alone does marvelous deeds.[t]
¹⁹Praise be to his glorious name[u] forever;
   may the whole earth be filled with his glory.[v]
      Amen and Amen.[w]

²⁰This concludes the prayers of David son of Jesse.[x]

BOOK III

Psalms 73–89

PSALM 73

A psalm of Asaph.

¹Surely God is good to Israel,
   to those who are pure in heart.[y]

---

a 8 That is, the Euphrates   *b 16* Probable reading of the original Hebrew text; Masoretic Text *Lebanon,*
/ from the city   *c 17* Or *will use his name in blessings* (see Gen. 48:20)

72:8–14 The extent of his domain (vv. 8–11) as the result of his righteous rule (vv. 12–14).
72:8 May his kingdom and authority extend to all the world (see vv. 9–11; cf. 110:2 and note). Ideally and potentially, as God's earthly regent, he possesses royal authority that extends on earth as far as God's—an expectation that is fulfilled in Christ. See Zec 9:10 and note.
72:9 May the tribes of the Arabian Desert to the east yield to him. *lick the dust.* See Mic 7:17 and note.
72:10 May the kings whose lands border the Mediterranean Sea to the west acknowledge him as overlord, as well as those who rule in south Arabia and along the eastern African coast. *Tarshish.* A distant Mediterranean seaport, perhaps as far west as modern Spain. *Sheba.* See notes on Ge 10:28; 1Ki 10:1; Joel 3:8. *Seba.* Elsewhere in the OT associated with Cush (Ge 10:7; Isa

43:3); it may refer to a region in modern Sudan, south of Egypt.
72:15–17 Concluding summation: May the king enjoy a long, prosperous, world-renowned reign—one that blesses all the nations.
72:17 *all nations.* The language recalls the promise to Abraham (see Ge 12:3; 22:18) and suggests that it will be fulfilled through the royal son of David—ultimately the Messiah.
72:18–19 A doxology at the conclusion of Book II of the Psalter (see 41:13 and note). It is the people's response, their "Amen," to the contents of Book II (see note on Ps 4 title).
72:19 *filled with his glory.* See note on 85:9.
72:20 An editorial notation probably carried over from an earlier collection of psalms ascribed exclusively to David. *prayers of David.* See titles of Ps 86; 142.
Ps 73–78 Book III consists of three groupings of psalms, having

72:8 *y* Ex 23:31;
S 1Ki 4:21 *z* Zec 9:10
72:10 *a* S Ge 10:4
b S Est 10:1
c S Ge 10:7
d S 1Ki 9:16;
S 2Ch 9:24
72:11 *e* S Ge 27:29
f S Ezr 1:2
72:13 *g* Isa 60:10;
Joel 2:18; Lk 10:33
72:14 *h* Ps 69:18;
Eze 13:23; 34:10
i Isa 26:21
72:15 *j* S Ge 10:7
k Ps 35:28
72:16 *l* S Ge 27:28;
Ps 4:7 *m* Isa 4:2; 27:6;
Eze 34:27 *n* Ps 92:12;
104:16 *o* S Nu 22:4;
Isa 44:4; 58:11; 66:14
72:17 *p* S Ex 3:15
q Ps 89:36 *r* S Ge 12:3;
Lk 1:48
72:18 *s* 1Ch 29:10;
Ps 41:13; 106:48;
Lk 1:68 *t* S Job 5:9
72:19 *u* S 2Sa 7:26
v Nu 14:21
w Ps 41:13
72:20 *x* S Ru 4:17
73:1 *y* S Ps 24:4;
Mt 5:8

73:2 ᶻ S Dt 32:35
ᵃ Ps 69:2; Eph 4:27
73:3 ᵇ Pr 3:31; 23:17;
24:1-2 ᶜ S Job 9:24;
S 21:7; Jer 12:1;
Mal 3:15
73:5 ᵈ ver 12;
Eze 23:42
73:6 ᵉ S Lev 26:19
ᶠ S Ge 41:42; SS 4:9;
Eze 16:11 ᵍ S Ge 6:11;
S Pr 4:17
73:7 ʰ S Ps 17:10
73:8 ⁱ Ps 41:5;
Eze 25:15; Col 3:8
ʲ Ps 17:10 ᵏ S Ps 10:7;
S 12:5
73:12 ˡ S ver 5
ᵐ S Ps 49:6

² But as for me, my feet had almost slipped; ᶻ
   I had nearly lost my foothold. ᵃ
³ For I envied ᵇ the arrogant
   when I saw the prosperity of the wicked. ᶜ

⁴ They have no struggles;
   their bodies are healthy and strong. ᵃ
⁵ They are free ᵈ from common human burdens;
   they are not plagued by human ills.
⁶ Therefore pride ᵉ is their necklace; ᶠ
   they clothe themselves with violence. ᵍ
⁷ From their callous hearts ʰ comes iniquity ᵇ;
   the evil conceits of their minds know no limits.
⁸ They scoff, and speak with malice; ⁱ
   with arrogance ʲ they threaten oppression. ᵏ
⁹ Their mouths lay claim to heaven,
   and their tongues take possession of the earth.
¹⁰ Therefore their people turn to them
   and drink up waters in abundance. ᶜ
¹¹ They say, "How would God know?
   Does the Most High know anything?"

¹² This is what the wicked are like—
   always free of care, ˡ they go on amassing wealth. ᵐ

ᵃ 4 With a different word division of the Hebrew; Masoretic Text *struggles at their death; / their bodies are healthy*   ᵇ 7 Syriac (see also Septuagint); Hebrew *Their eyes bulge with fat*   ᶜ 10 The meaning of the Hebrew for this verse is uncertain.

---

an overall symmetrical pattern (six psalms [73–78], five psalms [79–83], six psalms [84–89]) and at its center (Ps 81) an urgent exhortation to fundamental covenant loyalty to the Lord (see introduction to Ps 79–83, introduction to Ps 84–89 and introduction to Ps 81). The first group is framed by psalms of instruction. Ps 73 is a word of godly wisdom based on an individual's life experience, while Ps 78 is a psalm of instruction based on Israel's communal experience in its historical pilgrimage with God. Within this frame, Ps 74 (a communal prayer) is linked with Ps 77 (a prayer of an individual) by the common experience of seeming to be rejected by God (see 74:1; 77:7) and by an extended evocation of God's saving act in Israel's exodus from Egypt (see 74:13–15; 77:16–19). At the center, two psalms (75; 76) express joyful assurance that Israel's God (his "Name is near," 75:1; "in Israel his name is great," 76:1) calls the arrogant wicked to account and rescues their victims; he cuts off "the horns of all the wicked" (75:10) and breaks "the spirit of rulers" (76:12).

A Ps 73 A word of godly wisdom concerning the destinies of the righteous and the wicked (see introduction to Ps 73–78). Placed at the beginning of Book III, this psalm voices the faith (confessed [v. 1], tested [vv. 2–26] and reaffirmed [vv. 27–28]) that undergirds the following collection. It serves in Book III as Ps 1–2 serve in Book I (see introduction to Ps 1–2). Here the psalmist addresses one of the most disturbing problems of the OT saints: How is it that the wicked so often prosper while the godly suffer so much? Thematically the psalm has many links with Ps 49 (see introduction to that psalm; see also Ps 37). Its date may be as late as the postexilic era. Thematic development divides the psalm's structure into two halves of 14 verses each. Apart from the opening profession of faith (v. 1), the first half is framed by two couplets (vv. 2–3, 13–14) that focus on the psalmist's condition—which is sharply contrasted with the perceived condition of the wicked (vv. 4–12). The psalm as a whole is framed by the equally sharp contrast between v. 1 and v. 27.

73 title The psalm is ascribed to Asaph, leader of one of David's three Levitical choirs (the other two leaders were Heman and Jeduthun/Ethan; these three represented the families and descendants of the three sons of Levi; see notes on Ps 39; 42; 50 titles). It

begins a collection of 11 Asaphite psalms (Ps 73–83), to which Ps 50 at one time probably belonged. In view of the fact that the collection clearly contains prayers from a later date (e.g., Ps 74; 79; 83), references to Asaph in these titles must sometimes include descendants of Asaph who functioned in his place (see note on Ps 50 title). The Asaphite psalms are dominated by the theme of God's rule over his people and the nations. Apart from an introductory word of instruction (Ps 73), the collection is bracketed by prayers for God to rescue his people from foreign oppression (Ps 74; 83). The rest of the collection (Ps 75–82) appears to reflect thematic pairing: 1. The God who brings down the wicked and exalts the righteous (Ps 75) is the God and Savior of Israel (Ps 76). 2. God's saving acts in behalf of his people are remembered (Ps 77–78). 3. God is petitioned for help against the devastating attacks of Israel's enemies (Ps 79–80). 4. God is portrayed as presiding in judgment over his people (Ps 81) and over the world powers (Ps 82). This pairing, however, as is true of the whole Asaph collection, has been subsumed under another ordering principle (see introduction to Ps 73–78).

A 73:1–14 An almost fatal trial of faith: In the midst of many troubles a godly Israelite lets his eyes become fixed on the prosperity of the wicked.

73:1 *pure in heart.* See v. 13; see also note on 24:4. *heart.* See note on 4:7.

73:2 *feet had almost slipped.* From the path of truth and godliness (see 37:31 and note).

73:4–12 A description of the prosperous state of the wicked and the haughty self-reliance such prosperity engenders—hardly an objective account; it is rather the exaggerated picture that envious and troubled eyes perceived (see the description of the wicked in 10:2–11; cf. Job's anguished portrayal of the prosperity of the wicked in Job 21).

73:6 *pride is their necklace.* Contrast Pr 1:9; 3:3,22. *clothe themselves with.* See note on 109:29.

73:11 *They say.* Their speech, as well as their actions, shows that they live "far from" God (v. 27). *God . . . Most High.* That is, God Most High (see 57:2; see also note on 3:7). *Most High.* See note on Ge 14:19.

¹³ Surely in vain ⁿ I have kept my heart pure
and have washed my hands in innocence. ᵒ
¹⁴ All day long I have been afflicted, ᵖ
and every morning brings new punishments.

¹⁵ If I had spoken out like that,
I would have betrayed your children.
¹⁶ When I tried to understand �q all this,
it troubled me deeply
¹⁷ till I entered the sanctuary ʳ of God;
then I understood their final destiny. ˢ

¹⁸ Surely you place them on slippery ground; ᵗ
you cast them down to ruin. ᵘ
¹⁹ How suddenly ᵛ are they destroyed,
completely swept away ʷ by terrors!
²⁰ They are like a dream ˣ when one awakes; ʸ
when you arise, Lord,
you will despise them as fantasies. ᶻ

²¹ When my heart was grieved
and my spirit embittered,
²² I was senseless ᵃ and ignorant;
I was a brute beast ᵇ before you.

²³ Yet I am always with you;
you hold me by my right hand. ᶜ
²⁴ You guide ᵈ me with your counsel, ᵉ
and afterward you will take me into glory.
²⁵ Whom have I in heaven but you? ᶠ
And earth has nothing I desire besides you. ᵍ
²⁶ My flesh and my heart ʰ may fail, ⁱ
but God is the strength ʲ of my heart
and my portion ᵏ forever.

²⁷ Those who are far from you will perish; ˡ
you destroy all who are unfaithful ᵐ to you.
²⁸ But as for me, it is good to be near God. ⁿ
I have made the Sovereign Lord my refuge; ᵒ
I will tell of all your deeds. ᵖ

73:13 ⁿ S Job 9:29-31; S 21:15
ᵒ S Ge 44:16
73:14 ᵖ ver 5
73:16 q Ecc 8:17
73:17 ʳ Ex 15:17; Ps 15:1 ˢ S Job 8:13; Php 3:19
73:18 ᵗ S Dt 32:35; Ps 35:6 ᵘ S Ps 17:13
73:19 ᵛ Dt 28:20; Pr 24:22; Isa 47:11 ʷ S Ge 19:15
73:20 ˣ S Job 20:8 ʸ Ps 78:65; Isa 29:8 ᶻ Pr 12:11; 28:19
73:22 ᵃ Ps 49:10; 92:6; 94:8 ᵇ Ps 49:12, 20; Ecc 3:18; 9:12
73:23 ᶜ S Ge 48:13
73:24 ᵈ S Ps 48:14 ᵉ S Ge 48:13
73:25 ᶠ Ps 16:2 ᵍ Php 3:8
73:26 ʰ Ps 84:2 ⁱ S Ps 31:10; 40:12 ʲ Ps 18:1 ᵏ S Dt 32:9
73:27 ˡ S Ps 34:21 ᵐ S Lev 6:2; Jer 5:11; Hos 4:12; 9:1
73:28 ⁿ Zep 3:2; Heb 10:22; Jas 4:8 ᵒ Ps 9:9 ᵖ Ps 26:7; 40:5

73:13–14 The thoughts that plagued the psalmist when he compared the state of the wicked with his own troubled lot.
73:13 *heart pure.* See note on v. 1.
73:14 *punishments.* As children are punished by their parents to keep them in the right way (see Pr 3:12; 23:13–14).

73:15–28 The renewal of faith: In the temple, where God's ways are celebrated and taught, the psalmist sees the destiny God has appointed for the wicked.
73:15 *If I had spoken out like that.* If the psalmist had given public expression to his thoughts as embodying true insight. *your children.* Those characterized by a humble reliance on and commitment to God.
73:18–20 Though the wicked seem to prosper, God has made their position precarious; without warning they are swept away. The psalmist does not reflect on their state after death but leaves it as his final word that the wicked fall utterly and inevitably from their state of proud prosperity (see Ps 49; cf. the final state of the godly in v. 24).
73:20 When God arouses himself as from sleep (see note on 7:6) and deals with the wicked, they vanish like the shadowy characters of a dream.
73:21 *heart.* See note on 4:7. *spirit.* Lit. "kidneys" (see note on 7:9).
73:22 *a brute beast.* As stupid as a beast (see Job 18:3).

73:23–26 Although the psalmist had (almost) fallen to the level of beastly stupidity, God has not, will not, let him go—ever!

73:24 God's counsel has overcome the psalmist's folly and will guide him through all the pitfalls of life (see 16:7; 32:8; 107:11). *take me into glory.* At the end of the believer's pilgrimage (see 49:15 and note).

73:25 Though he has envied the prosperity of the wicked, he now confesses that nothing in heaven or earth is more desirable than God.

73:26 *My flesh … heart.* My whole being (see 84:2). *heart.* See note on 4:7. *portion.* Since the psalmist was a Levite, the Lord was his portion in the promised land in that he lived by the people's tithes dedicated to the Lord (see Nu 18:21–24; Dt 10:9; 18:1–2). But here he confesses more—what every godly Israelite could confess: The Lord himself is the sustainer and preserver of the life of those who put their trust in him (see note on 16:5–6).
73:27–28 See 34:21–22; 37:18–20; Pr 24:16.
73:27 *all who are unfaithful.* Lit. "all who commit (spiritual) prostitution/adultery." Although this expression elsewhere refers to blatant idolatry (as, e.g., in Dt 31:16; Jer 2:20; Hos 2:5 [see note there]) or to political alliance with any world power rather than relying on the Lord for security (as, e.g., in Eze 16:26–29), here it refers to the reliance of the wicked on their predatory economic and political practices, the "violence" with which they accumulated their wealth at the expense of others (vv. 6–11). See Isa 1:21 and note.

73:28 *I will tell of all your deeds.* A concluding vow to praise God for all his mercies to him (see note on 7:17).

74:1 ^q S Ps 43:2
^r S Ps 44:23
^s Ps 79:13; 95:7; 100:3
74:2 ^t S Ex 15:16;
S 1Co 6:20
^u S Dt 32:7
^v S Ex 34:9
^w S Ex 15:13;
S Isa 48:20 ^x Ps 2:6
^y Ps 43:3; 68:16;
Isa 46:13; Joel 3:17,
21; Ob 1:17
74:3 ^z Isa 44:26;
52:9
74:4 ^a La 2:7
^b S Nu 2:2; S Jer 4:6
74:5 ^c Jer 46:22
74:6 ^d S 1Ki 6:18
74:7 ^e S Lev 20:3;
Ac 21:28 ^f S Lev 15:31
^g Ps 75:1
74:8 ^h Ps 94:5
ⁱ 2Ki 25:9; 2Ch 36:19;
Jer 21:10; 34:22; 52:13
74:9 ^j S Ex 4:17;
S 10:1 ^k S 1Sa 3:1
74:10 ^l Ps 63:3; 79:5;
80:4 ^m ver 22
ⁿ S Ps 44:16
74:11 ^o S Ex 15:6
^p Ne 5:13; Eze 5:3
74:12 ^q Ps 2:6;
S 24:7; 68:24 ^r Ps 27:1

PSALM 74

A maskil ^a of Asaph.

¹ O God, why have you rejected ^q us forever? ^r
　Why does your anger smolder against the sheep of your
　　pasture? ^s
² Remember the people you purchased ^t long ago, ^u
　the tribe of your inheritance, ^v whom you redeemed ^w—
　Mount Zion, ^x where you dwelt. ^y
³ Turn your steps toward these everlasting ruins, ^z
　all this destruction the enemy has brought on the sanctuary.

⁴ Your foes roared ^a in the place where you met with us;
　they set up their standards ^b as signs.
⁵ They behaved like men wielding axes
　to cut through a thicket of trees. ^c
⁶ They smashed all the carved ^d paneling
　with their axes and hatchets.
⁷ They burned your sanctuary to the ground;
　they defiled ^e the dwelling place ^f of your Name. ^g
⁸ They said in their hearts, "We will crush ^h them completely!"
　They burned ⁱ every place where God was worshiped in the
　　land.

⁹ We are given no signs from God; ^j
　no prophets ^k are left,
　and none of us knows how long this will be.
¹⁰ How long ^l will the enemy mock ^m you, God?
　Will the foe revile ⁿ your name forever?
¹¹ Why do you hold back your hand, your right hand? ^o
　Take it from the folds of your garment ^p and destroy them!

¹² But God is my King ^q from long ago;
　he brings salvation ^r on the earth.

---

^a Title: Probably a literary or musical term

Ps 74 A prayer for God to come to the aid of his people and defend his cause in the face of the mocking of the enemies—the Lord's relation to his people is like that of a king to his nation. The psalm dates from the time of the exile, when Israel had been destroyed as a nation, the promised land devastated and the temple reduced to ruins (see Ps 79; La 2). Its relationship to the ministries of Jeremiah and Ezekiel is uncertain (see note on v. 9). Thematically the psalm divides into two halves of 11 verses each, with v. 12 (the center line; see note there) highlighting the primary thematic element that unifies the prayer. Verses 1–11 are framed by the "Why's" of the people's complaint (vv. 1,11); the whole psalm is framed by pleas for God to "remember" (vv. 2,22). Note also that the "theys" of vv. 4–8 have their counterpoint in the "yous" of vv. 13–17 (highlighted in the Hebrew by seven emphatic pronouns) —the mighty acts of God are appealed to against the destructive and haughty deeds of the enemies. For the placement of this psalm in the Psalter and its relationship to the psalms around it, see introduction to Ps 73–78.
74 title *maskil.* See note on Ps 32 title. *Asaph.* See note on Ps 73 title.
74:1–2 Initial complaint and appeal.
74:1 *why ... ? Why ... ?* Cf. "How long ... ?" (v. 10) and "Why ... ?" (v. 11). See note on 6:3. *forever.* So it seemed, since no relief was in sight. *anger.* See note on 2:5. *sheep ... pasture.* Metaphors related to the basic figure of a king as the shepherd of his realm (see notes on 23:1; 95:7; see also 79:13; 100:3).
74:2 *purchased.* Or "acquired" or "created." *tribe.* Here referring to all Israel. *your inheritance.* See Dt 9:29. *redeemed.* Here, as often, a synonym for "delivered" (see note on 71:23). *Mount Zion.* See note on 9:11. This verse recalls the victory song of Ex 15 (see

especially vv. 13–17, and compare the center verse of this psalm, v. 12, with the last verse of the song, Ex 15:18) and thus sets the stage for the other exodus recollections that follow. The Babylonian destruction of Zion seems to be the undoing of God's great victory over Egypt when he redeemed his people.
74:3–8 The Babylonians' high-handed destruction of the Lord's temple.
74:3 *Turn your steps toward.* Hurry to restore.
74:4 *standards.* Probably troop standards (see Nu 1:52; Isa 31:9; Jer 4:21). *as signs.* Signifying their triumph.
74:6 *carved paneling.* See 1Ki 6:15.
74:7 *your Name.* See note on 5:11. The TNIV capitalizes "Name" when it stands for God's presence at the sanctuary (see Dt 12:5).
74:8 *They said.* See note on 10:11. *every place where God was worshiped.* Lit. "all the meeting places of God" (see v. 4). The reference is uncertain. At the time of the Babylonian attacks there may have been a number of (illegitimate) places in Judah where people went to worship God (see notes on 1Ki 3:2; 2Ki 18:4).
74:9–11 The complaint and prayer renewed (see vv. 1–2).
74:9 *no signs.* As there were at the time of the exodus (see vv. 13–15; 78:43). *no prophets.* Jeremiah had been taken to Egypt (see Jer 43:6–7), but whether Ezekiel was no longer prophesying is unknown. Perhaps this psalm was composed by an Asaphite who remained in Israel, part of a small group overlooked by Johanan when that army officer led the remnant to Egypt (see Jer 43:4–7).
74:10 *mock you ... revile your name.* See v. 18; see also v. 22; 2Ki 18:32–35; Isa 37:6,23.
74:12 The center verse (center line in the Hebrew text; see note on 6:6). The whole psalm presupposes the truth

¹³ It was you who split open the sea ˢ by your power;
　　you broke the heads of the monster ᵗ in the waters.
¹⁴ It was you who crushed the heads of Leviathan ᵘ
　　and gave it as food to the creatures of the desert. ᵛ
¹⁵ It was you who opened up springs ʷ and streams;
　　you dried up ˣ the ever-flowing rivers.
¹⁶ The day is yours, and yours also the night;
　　you established the sun and moon. ʸ
¹⁷ It was you who set all the boundaries ᶻ of the earth;
　　you made both summer and winter. ᵃ

¹⁸ Remember how the enemy has mocked you, LORD,
　　how foolish people ᵇ have reviled your name.
¹⁹ Do not hand over the life of your dove ᶜ to wild beasts;
　　do not forget the lives of your afflicted ᵈ people forever.
²⁰ Have regard for your covenant, ᵉ
　　because haunts of violence fill the dark places ᶠ of the land.
²¹ Do not let the oppressed ᵍ retreat in disgrace;
　　may the poor and needy ʰ praise your name.
²² Rise up, ⁱ O God, and defend your cause;
　　remember how fools ʲ mock you all day long.
²³ Do not ignore the clamor ᵏ of your adversaries, ˡ
　　the uproar ᵐ of your enemies, ⁿ which rises continually.

PSALM 75

*For the director of music. To the tune of "Do Not Destroy." A psalm
of Asaph. A song.*

*¹ We praise you, God,
　　we praise you, for your Name is near; ᵒ
　　people tell of your wonderful deeds. ᵖ

* 75:1-10 is numbered 75:2-11 in Hebrew texts.

74:13 ˢ S Ex 14:21
ᵗ Isa 27:1; 51:9;
Eze 29:3; 32:2
74:14 ᵘ S Job 3:8
ᵛ Isa 13:21; 23:13;
34:14; Jer 50:39
74:15 ʷ S Ex 17:6;
S Nu 20:11
ˣ S Ex 14:29;
S Jos 2:10
74:16 ʸ S Ge 1:16;
Ps 136:7-9
74:17 ᶻ Dt 32:8;
Ac 17:26 ᵃ S Ge 8:22
74:18 ᵇ Dt 32:6
74:19 ᶜ S Ge 8:8;
S Isa 59:11 ᵈ S Ps 9:18
74:20 ᵉ S Ge 6:18
ᶠ Job 34:22
74:21 ᵍ Ps 9:9;
10:18; 103:6; Isa 58:10
ʰ S Ps 35:10
74:22 ⁱ Ps 17:13
ʲ Ps 53:1
74:23 ᵏ Isa 31:4
ˡ S Ps 65:7
ᵐ S Ps 46:6
ⁿ S Nu 25:17
75:1 ᵒ Ps 145:18
ᵖ S Jos 3:5; Ps 44:1;
S 71:16; 77:12; 105:2;
107:8,15; 145:5,12

---

confessed here: God is Israel's King, her hope and Savior; Israel is God's people (kingdom). This accounts for both the complaint and the prayer, and why the destruction of Israel brings with it the mocking of God. *my.* Communal use of the singular pronoun (see note on Ps 30 title). *from long ago.* From the days of the exodus (see Ex 3:7; 19:5–6).

74:13–17 The Lord is the mighty God of salvation and creation (see 65:6–7 and note).

74:13–14 Recollection of God's mighty acts when he delivered his people from Egypt. The imagery is borrowed from ancient Near Eastern creation myths, in which the primeval chaotic waters were depicted as a many-headed monster that the creator-god overcame, after which he established the world order (see note on 32:6). The poet here interweaves creation and salvation themes to celebrate the fact that the God of Israel has shown by his saving acts (his opening of the Red Sea for his people and his destruction of the Egyptians) that he is able to overcome all hostile powers to redeem his people and establish his new order in the world. For poetic use of this imagery (1) to celebrate God's creation works, see 89:10; Job 9:13; 26:12–13; (2) to celebrate the deliverance from Egypt, see Isa 51:9; (3) to announce a future deliverance of Israel, see Isa 27:1. Echoes of the same imagery are present in the judgment announced against Egypt in Eze 29:3–5; 32:2–6.

74:15 Recollection of God's water miracles at the Red Sea, in the wilderness and at the Jordan.

74:16–17 God is the One who established the orders of creation; he (alone) is able to effect redemption and establish his kingdom in the world against all creaturely opposition.

74:18–23 A prayer for God to defend his cause and restore his people.

74:18 See vv. 2,10. *foolish people.* The foes of v. 10 ("foe" is col-

lective) are here called "foolish" for their contempt of God (see v. 22; see also TNIV text note on 14:1).

74:19 *your dove.* Israel—probably a figure of endearment (see SS 2:14; 5:2; 6:9; see also Ps 68:13 and note). *wild beasts.* See note on 7:2.

74:20 *your covenant.* God's covenant to be the God of Israel, the one who makes his people secure and richly blessed in the promised land (see Ex 19:5–6; 23:27–31; 34:10–11; Lev 26:11–12,42,44–45; Dt 28:1–14; see also Ps 105:8–11; 106:45; 111:5,9; Isa 54:10; Jer 14:21; Eze 16:60).

74:21 *poor and needy.* See note on 34:6. *praise your name.* May they have cause to do so.

74:22 *Rise up.* See note on 3:7.

74:23 *clamor . . . uproar.* See 64:2.

Ps 75 A song of reassurance when arrogant worldly powers threaten Israel's security. The psalm may date from the time of the Assyrian menace (see 2Ki 18:13—19:37). See also Ps 11; 76. Thematic parallels to the song of Hannah (1Sa 2:1–10) are numerous. The worshiping congregation speaks (v. 1), perhaps led in its praise by one of the descendants of Asaph (v. 9). The psalm is framed by thanksgiving (v. 1) and praise (vv. 9–10). Two stanzas of four (Hebrew) lines each form the body of the psalm, and each stanza is composed of two couplets. The first stanza contains a reassuring word from heaven; the second contains a triumphant response from earth. For this psalm's relationship to those around it, especially to Ps 76, see introduction to Ps 73–78.

75 title *For the director of music.* See note on Ps 4 title. *To the tune of.* See note on Ps 9 title. *Do Not Destroy.* See Ps 57; 58; 59 titles. *Asaph.* See note on Ps 73 title. *song.* See note on Ps 30 title.

75:1 The congregation begins with thanksgiving in the form of praise (see 7:17; 28:7; 30:12; 35:18). *Name.* See notes on 5:11; 74:7. *wonderful deeds.* See note on 9:1.

75:2 *q* S Ex 13:10
r S Ps 7:11
75:3 *s* Isa 24:19
t 1Sa 2:8; S 2Sa 22:8
75:4 *u* S Ps 5:5
v 1Sa 2:3 *w* Zec 1:21
75:5 *x* S Job 15:25
75:7 *y* S Ge 16:5;
Ps 50:6; 58:11;
Rev 18:8 *z* Isa 2:7;
S Job 5:11; Ps 147:6;
Eze 21:26; Da 2:21
75:8 *a* Pr 23:30
b Isa 51:17; Jer 25:15;
Zec 12:2
75:9 *c* Ps 40:10
d Ps 108:1
e S Ge 24:12; Ps 76:6
75:10 *f* Ps 89:17;
92:10; 112:9; 148:14
76:1 *g* Ps 99:3
76:2 *h* S Ge 14:18;
Heb 7:1 *i* S 2Sa 5:7;
Ps 2:6

2 You say, "I choose the appointed time; *q*
 it is I who judge with equity. *r*
3 When the earth and all its people quake, *s*
 it is I who hold its pillars *t* firm. *a*
4 To the arrogant *u* I say, 'Boast no more,' *v*
 and to the wicked, 'Do not lift up your horns. *b* *w*
5 Do not lift your horns against heaven;
 do not speak with outstretched neck. *x* '"

6 No one from the east or the west
 or from the desert can exalt themselves.
7 It is God who judges: *y*
 He brings one down, he exalts another. *z*
8 In the hand of the LORD is a cup
 full of foaming wine mixed *a* with spices;
 he pours it out, and all the wicked of the earth
 drink it down to its very dregs. *b*

9 As for me, I will declare *c* this forever;
 I will sing *d* praise to the God of Jacob, *e*
10 who says, "I will cut off the horns of all the wicked,
 but the horns of the righteous will be lifted up." *f*

PSALM 76

*For the director of music. With stringed instruments. A psalm of Asaph.
A song.*

*1 God is renowned in Judah;
 in Israel his name is great. *g*
2 His tent is in Salem, *h*
 his dwelling place in Zion. *i*

---

a 3 The Hebrew has *Selah* (a word of uncertain meaning) here. *b 4* *Horns* here symbolize strength;
also in verses 5 and 10.

* 76:1-12 is numbered 76:2-13 in Hebrew texts.

75:2–5 A reassuring word from above: God will not fail to call the arrogant to account. It is not clear whether a new word from the Lord is heard or whether these verses recall (and perhaps summarize) earlier prophetic words (such as those of Isaiah in 2Ki 19:21–34; see notes there).

75:2 God will not fail to judge (see Ps 96; 98 and notes on 96:13; 98:9)—but in his own time.

75:3 When, because of the upsurge of evil powers, the whole moral order of the world seems to have crumbled, God still guarantees its stability (see note on 11:3). *pillars.* A figure for that which stabilizes the world order (see note on 24:2). For *Selah,* see TNIV text note and note on 3:2.

75:4 *arrogant . . . wicked.* To the psalmists the wicked are both arrogant (see especially Ps 10 and note on 10:2–11; 73:4–12 and note; 94:4; see also note on 31:23) and foolish (see introduction to Ps 14 and note on 14:1; 74:18,22 and note on 74:18; 92:6; 94:8 and note on 94:8–11). *lift up your horns.* A figure for defiant opposition, based on the action of attacking bulls. "Horn" (see also v. 10) is a common Biblical metaphor for vigor or strength (see TNIV text notes here and on 18:2).

75:5 *outstretched neck.* A sign of defiance.

75:6–8 Triumphant echo from earth: perhaps spoken by the Levitical song leader in elaboration of the comforting word from God.

75:8 *cup.* See note on 16:5. *mixed with spices.* The spices used increased the intoxicating effect (see Pr 9:2,5 and note on 9:2; 23:29–30 and note on 23:30; SS 8:2; Isa 65:11). *drink it down.* Because God pours it out, they have no choice.

75:9 Concluding vow to praise God forever (see note on 7:17)

for his righteous judgments. *me.* Probably the Levitical song leader speaking representatively for the people, but the pronoun may be a communal use of the singular, as in 74:12 (see note on Ps 30 title). *Jacob.* A synonym for Israel (see Ge 32:28 and note).

75:10 *righteous.* See notes on 1:5; Ge 7:1; Dt 6:25; 2Sa 22:21,25. *lifted up.* See v. 7; see also note on v. 4.

Ps 76 A celebration of the Lord's invincible power in defense of Jerusalem, his royal city. The psalm is thematically related to Ps 46; 48; 87 (see introduction to Ps 46). The ancient tradition may well be correct that the psalm was composed after the Lord's destruction of Sennacherib's army when it threatened Jerusalem (see 2Ki 19:35). Structurally, the opening (vv. 1–3) and closing (vv. 11–12) stanzas contain the main theme. Between them, two four-line (in Hebrew) stanzas of praise addressed to God (vv. 4–6,7–10) celebrate his awesome act of judgment. For this psalm's relationship to those around it, especially to Ps 75, see introduction to Ps 73–78.

76 title *For the director of music.* See note on Ps 4 title. *With stringed instruments.* See note on Ps 4 title. *Asaph.* See note on Ps 73 title. *song.* See note on Ps 30 title.

76:1–3 God's crushing defeat of the enemy in defense of Zion.

76:1 *is renowned.* Now especially—as a result of his marvelous act. *Israel.* The poet probably does not intend to distinguish between the two kingdoms (Judah and Israel) but only, by joining their names together, to refer to the whole of God's covenant people. Moreover, as a result of the Assyrian invasions, many displaced Israelites from the northern kingdom now resided in and around Jerusalem.

76:2 *tent . . . dwelling place.* Since the two Hebrew words for

³ There he broke the flashing arrows, [j]
the shields and the swords, the weapons of war. [a][k]

⁴ You are resplendent with light, [l]
more majestic than mountains rich with game.
⁵ The valiant [m] lie plundered,
they sleep their last sleep; [n]
not one of the warriors
can lift his hands.
⁶ At your rebuke, [o] God of Jacob,
both horse and chariot [p] lie still.

⁷ It is you alone who are to be feared. [q]
Who can stand [r] before you when you are angry? [s]
⁸ From heaven you pronounced judgment,
and the land feared [t] and was quiet—
⁹ when you, God, rose up to judge, [u]
to save all the afflicted [v] of the land.
¹⁰ Surely your wrath against human beings brings you praise, [w]
and the survivors of your wrath are restrained. [b]

¹¹ Make vows to the LORD your God and fulfill them; [x]
let all the neighboring lands
bring gifts [y] to the One to be feared.
¹² He breaks the spirit of rulers;
he is feared by the kings of the earth.

PSALM 77

For the director of music. For Jeduthun. Of Asaph. A psalm.

[*][1] I cried out to God [z] for help;
I cried out to God to hear me.
² When I was in distress, [a] I sought the Lord;

---

a 3 The Hebrew has *Selah* (a word of uncertain meaning) here and at the end of verse 9.
b 10 Or *Surely human wrath brings you praise, / and with the remainder of wrath you arm yourself*

* 77:1-20 is numbered 77:2-21 in Hebrew texts.

76:3 j Eze 39:9
k Ps 46:9
76:4 l S Ps 36:9
76:5 m S Jdg 20:44
n S Ps 13:3; S Mt 9:24
76:6 o S Ps 50:21
p S Ex 15:1
76:7 q S 1Ch 16:25
r S Ezr 9:15; Rev 6:17
s Ps 2:5; Na 1:6
76:8 t S 1Ch 16:30;
Eze 38:20
76:9 u S Ps 9:8;
58:11; 74:22; 82:8;
96:13 v S Ps 72:4
76:10 w Ex 9:16;
Ro 9:17
76:11 x S Lev 22:18;
S Ps 50:14; Ecc 5:4-5
y S 2Ch 32:23
77:1 z S 1Ki 8:52
77:2 a S Ge 32:7;
S 2Sa 22:7; S Ps 118:5

---

these nouns frequently refer to a lion's den, covert or lair (see 10:9; 104:22; Job 38:40; Jer 25:38; Am 3:4), it may be that the psalmist is here depicting Israel's God as a lion overpowering its prey. In that case, an alternative rendering of v. 4 should be considered (see note on that verse). *Salem.* Jerusalem, as the parallelism makes clear (see note on Ge 14:18). *Zion.* See note on 9:11.
76:3 For *Selah,* see TNIV text note and note on 3:2.
76:4–10 Praise of the awesome majesty of God, whose mighty judgment evokes fearful reverence (see introduction).
76:4 *more majestic . . . with game.* If the nouns in v. 2 refer to a lion's den (see note there), this line should be rendered something like "the majestic One from the mountains rich with game."
76:5–6 Perhaps echoes also God's victory over the Egyptians at the Red Sea (see Ex 14:28,30; 15:4–5,10).
76:6 *rebuke.* This word, when predicated of God, usually refers to either (1) the thunder of his fierce majesty, by which he wields his sovereign control over cosmic entities (see 18:15; 104:7; 106:9; Job 26:11; Isa 50:2; Na 1:4) or repulses his enemies (as here; see also 9:5; 68:30; Isa 17:13); or (2) the thunder of his wrath (see 80:16; Isa 51:20; 54:9; 66:15; Mal 2:3). *God of Jacob.* A link with Ps 75 (see 75:9 and note).
76:7 *you alone . . . you.* This first line of the second four-line stanza echoes the emphatic "You" with which the first four-line stanza begins (v. 4).
76:8 *From heaven.* Though God is present in Zion (see v. 2), he sovereignly rules from heaven.
76:10 *wrath.* See note on 2:5. *brings you praise.* When his judgments bring deliverance, those rescued praise him. If the alternative translation in the TNIV text note is taken, "human wrath brings you praise" would mean that when people rise up against God's kingdom he crushes them in wrath, to his own praise as Victor and Deliverer. And "the remainder of wrath" would indicate that particular judgments do not exhaust his wrath; a remainder is left to deal with other hostile powers.
76:11–12 Let Israel acknowledge God's help with grateful vows; let the nations acknowledge his sovereign rule with tribute.
76:11 *Make vows.* See note on 50:14.
76:12 *spirit of rulers.* Their bold rebelliousness.
Ps 77 Comforting reflections in a time of great distress. For the relationship of this psalm to Ps 74, see introduction to Ps 73–78. The interplay of verb forms in vv. 1–6 makes it uncertain whether the psalm is a prayer (in which case the verbs of these verses would have to be rendered in the present tense) or the recollection of a past experience (as the TNIV understands it). The "distress" (v. 2) appears to be personal rather than national. Comparison of vv. 16–19 with Hab 3:8–10 suggests, but does not prove, a time late in the monarchy. The poetic development advances from anguished bewilderment (vv. 1–9) to comforting recollection (vv. 10–20). A striking and dramatic feature is the insertion of a four-verse stanza (vv. 16–19) between the third and fourth verses of another four-verse stanza (vv. 13–15,20).
77 title *For the director of music.* See note on Ps 4 title. *Jeduthun.* See note on Ps 39 title. *Asaph.* See note on Ps 73 title.
77:1–9 Anguished perplexity over God's apparent inaction, when he seemingly fails to respond to unceasing and urgent prayers.

77:2 *b* Ps 6:6; 22:2;
88:1 *c* S Ex 9:29;
S Job 11:13
d S Ge 37:35; Mt 2:18
77:3 *e* Ps 78:35
f Ex 2:23; S Ps 6:6;
Jer 45:3 *g* S Ps 6:2
77:4 *h* S Ps 39:2
77:5 *i* Dt 32:7;
Ps 44:1; 143:5;
Ecc 7:10
77:7 *j* S 1Ch 28:9
k Ps 85:1; 102:13;
106:4
77:8 *l* S Ps 6:4;
90:14 *m* 2Pe 3:9
77:9 *n* Ps 25:6;
40:11; 51:1 *o* Isa 49:15
77:10 *p* S Ex 15:6
77:11 *q* S Ne 9:17
77:12 *r* S Ge 24:63
s Ps 143:5
77:13 *t* S Ex 15:11;
S Ps 71:19; 86:8
77:14 *u* S Ex 3:20;
S 34:10
77:15 *v* S Ex 6:6
77:16 *w* Ex 14:21,28;
Isa 50:2; Hab 3:8
x Ps 114:4; Hab 3:10
77:17 *y* S Jdg 5:4
z S Ex 9:23; S Ps 29:3
a S Dt 32:23
77:18 *b* S Ps 55:8
c S 2Sa 22:13
d S Jdg 5:4

at night *b* I stretched out untiring hands, *c*
and I would not be comforted. *d*

³ I remembered *e* you, God, and I groaned; *f*
  I meditated, and my spirit grew faint. *a g*
⁴ You kept my eyes from closing;
  I was too troubled to speak. *h*
⁵ I thought about the former days, *i*
  the years of long ago;
⁶ I remembered my songs in the night.
  My heart meditated and my spirit asked:

⁷ "Will the Lord reject forever?*j*
  Will he never show his favor *k* again?
⁸ Has his unfailing love *l* vanished forever?
  Has his promise *m* failed for all time?
⁹ Has God forgotten to be merciful? *n*
  Has he in anger withheld his compassion? *o*"

¹⁰ Then I thought, "To this I will appeal:
  the years when the Most High stretched out his right hand. *p*
¹¹ I will remember the deeds of the LORD;
  yes, I will remember your miracles *q* of long ago.
¹² I will consider *r* all your works
  and meditate on all your mighty deeds." *s*

¹³ Your ways, God, are holy.
  What god is as great as our God? *t*
¹⁴ You are the God who performs miracles; *u*
  you display your power among the peoples.
¹⁵ With your mighty arm you redeemed your people, *v*
  the descendants of Jacob and Joseph.

¹⁶ The waters *w* saw you, God,
  the waters saw you and writhed; *x*
  the very depths were convulsed.
¹⁷ The clouds poured down water, *y*
  the heavens resounded with thunder; *z*
  your arrows *a* flashed back and forth.
¹⁸ Your thunder was heard in the whirlwind, *b*
  your lightning *c* lit up the world;
  the earth trembled and quaked. *d*

---

a 3 The Hebrew has *Selah* (a word of uncertain meaning) here and at the end of verses 9 and 15.

77:3–6 Remembrance of God's past mercies intensifies the present perplexity (as also in 22:1–11). God's failure to act now is so troubling that the psalmist cannot sleep (cf. 3:5; 4:8) and words fail (but see vv. 10–20).
77:3 For *Selah,* see TNIV text note and note on 3:2.
77:6 *heart.* See note on 4:7.
77:7–9 Though words fail (v. 4), troubled thoughts will not go away.
77:8 *unfailing love.* See note on 6:4.
77:9 *anger.* See note on 2:5.
77:10–20 Reassuring recollection of God's mighty acts in behalf of Israel in the exodus.
77:10–12 Faith's decision to look beyond the present troubles—and God's bewildering inactivity—to draw hope anew from God's saving acts of old.
77:10 *Most High.* See note on Ge 14:19.
77:11,14 *miracles.* See note on 9:1 ("wonderful deeds").
77:13–20 God's mighty acts in the exodus recalled.
77:13 Appears to echo Ex 15:11. *are holy.* Or "have seen you in the sanctuary" (see 63:2).
77:15 *redeemed.* Here, as often, a synonym for "delivered" (see note on 71:23). *Joseph.* OT authors sometimes refer to the northern kingdom as "Joseph" (or "Ephraim," Joseph's son) in

distinction from the southern kingdom of Judah (see 78:67; 2Sa 19:20; 1Ki 11:28; Eze 37:16,19; Am 5:6,15; 6:6; Zec 10:6). However, here and elsewhere (see 80:1; 81:5; Ob 18) Joseph—the one elevated to the position of firstborn (see Ge 48:5 and note; Jos 16:1–4; 1Ch 5:2; Eze 47:13)—represents the whole of his generation and thus also all the descendants of Jacob.
77:16–19 A poetically heightened description of the majesty of God displayed when he opened a way through the Red Sea (see 74:13–15). Verses 16,19 speak expressly of that event; the intervening verses (vv. 17–18) evoke the majesty of God displayed in the thunderstorm and earthquake. Ex 14:19 speaks only of God's cloud, not of a thunderstorm or earthquake, but the Hebrew poets often associated either or both with the Lord's coming to effect redemption or judgment—no doubt because these were the two most fearsome displays of power known to them (see 18:12–14; 68:8; Jdg 5:4–5; Hab 3:6, 10). Here the psalmist declares that it was the God of thunderstorm and earthquake who made his majestic way through the mighty waters of the sea to bring his people out of bondage. For Christians, the display of God's power in behalf of his people now includes the resurrection of Jesus Christ from the dead (see Mt 28:2; cf. Eph 1:18–23).
77:17 *arrows.* Lightning bolts (see note on Ge 9:13).

77:19 *e* S Ex 14:22
f S Job 9:8
77:20 *g* S Ex 13:21
h Ps 78:52; Isa 63:11
i S Ex 4:16; S Nu 33:1
78:1 *j* Isa 51:4; 55:3
78:2 *k* S Ps 49:4;
S Mt 13:35*
78:3 *l* S Jdg 6:13
78:4 *m* S Dt 11:19
n S Dt 32:7;
S Ps 71:18 *o* Ps 26:7;
71:17 *p* S Job 5:9
78:5 *q* Ps 19:7; 81:5
r Ps 147:19
78:6 *s* S Ps 22:31
78:7 *t* S Dt 6:12
u S Dt 5:29

¹⁹ Your path *e* led through the sea, *f*
    your way through the mighty waters,
    though your footprints were not seen.

²⁰ You led your people *g* like a flock *h*
    by the hand of Moses and Aaron. *i*

PSALM 78

A maskil *a* *of Asaph.*

¹ My people, hear my teaching; *j*
    listen to the words of my mouth.
² I will open my mouth with a parable; *k*
    I will teach you lessons from the past—
³ things we have heard and known,
    things our ancestors have told us. *l*
⁴ We will not hide them from their descendants; *m*
    we will tell the next generation *n*
the praiseworthy deeds *o* of the LORD,
    his power, and the wonders *p* he has done.
⁵ He decreed statutes *q* for Jacob *r*
    and established the law in Israel,
which he commanded our ancestors
    to teach their children,
⁶ so the next generation would know them,
    even the children yet to be born, *s*
    and they in turn would tell their children.
⁷ Then they would put their trust in God
    and would not forget *t* his deeds
    but would keep his commands. *u*

---

a Title: Probably a literary or musical term

77:20 Completes the thought of v. 15 (see introduction). *led your people.* Through the Desert of Sinai. *like a flock.* See 23:1; 74:1 and notes.

Ps 78 A psalm of instruction—of warnings not to repeat Israel's sins of the past but to remember God's saving acts and marvelously persistent grace and, remembering, to keep faith with him and his covenant. Here, as elsewhere (pervasively in the OT), trust in and loyalty to God on the part of God's people are covenant matters. They do not spring from abstract principles (such as the formal structure of the God-human relationship) or from general human consciousness (such as feelings of dependence on "God" or a sense of awe in the presence of the "holy"), but they result from remembering God's mighty saving acts. Correspondingly, unfaithfulness is the more blameworthy because it contemptuously disregards all God's wonderful acts in his people's behalf (see Ps 105–106).

The psalm probably dates from the period of the divided monarchy and may have been composed about the time of the prophet Hosea (both Hosea and Isaiah speak frequently of the northern kingdom as Ephraim since it was the dominant tribe of that realm). Israel's unfaithfulness is here epitomized in the sin of Ephraim (v. 9); the psalm concludes by recalling the rejection of "Israel" (v. 59) and the abandonment of Shiloh (v. 60) but the election of Judah and Mount Zion (v. 68). Coming, as may be assumed, from the pen of an Asaphite, the psalm was no doubt a warning to worshipers at Jerusalem not to fall away after the manner of the Israelites to the north.

By placing this psalm next to Ps 77, the editors of the Psalter ranked David alongside Moses (and Aaron) as the Lord's shepherd over his people (see vv. 70–72; 77:20), who brought the exodus to its (provisionally) climactic fruition by completing the conquest of the promised land—a perspective apparently shared by the author of the psalm.

The psalm is composed of 77 (Hebrew) lines (72 numbered verses) and seven stanzas—with an 11-line introduction. After the introduction, the structure of the stanzas is symmetrical: 8 lines, 16 lines, 9 lines, 16 lines, 9 lines, 8 lines. The two sequences of 16 lines–9 lines constitute a thematic cycle, while the two 8-line stanzas frame the double cycle and underscore the contrast between the sin of Israel ("Ephraim," vv. 9–16) and the unending mercy of God to his people—mercy that is evidenced in his victory over his enemies and his election of Zion (in Judah) and David (vv. 65–72). For this psalm's relationship to Ps 73 in the arrangement of the Psalter, see introduction to Ps 73–78.

78 title *maskil.* See note on Ps 32 title. *Asaph.* See note on Ps 73 title.

78:1–8 Our children must hear what our fathers have told us, so that they may be faithful to the Lord.

78:1–2 This introduction is written in the style of a wisdom writer (see essay, p. 750; see also Ps 49:1–4).

78:2 *parable…lessons.* While both terms had specialized uses, they apparently also became conventionalized more generally for instruction in a wide variety of forms (see note on 49:14). Mt 13:35 refers to this verse as a prophecy of Jesus' parabolic teaching. Matthew apparently perceived in this psalm a prophetic voice anticipating that of the great Prophet. The "parable" of the psalm is, however, more like the teaching of Stephen (Ac 7) than that of Jesus.

78:4–5 The Lord's saving acts and his covenant statutes—both must be taught, and in relationship, for together they remain the focal point for faith and obedience down through the generations (see vv. 7–8).

78:4 *not hide them.* See Job 15:18.

78:5 *teach their children.* See, e.g., Ex 10:2; 12:26–27; 13:8,14; Dt 4:9; 6:20–21.

78:8 ᵛ S 2Ch 30:7
ʷ S Ex 32:9
ˣ S Ex 23:21;
S Dt 21:18; Isa 30:9;
65:2
78:9 ʸ ver 57;
1Ch 12:2; Hos 7:16
ᶻ S Jdg 20:39
78:10 ᵃ S Jos 7:11;
S 2Ki 17:15
ᵇ S Ex 16:28;
S Jer 11:8
78:11 ᶜ Ps 106:13
78:12 ᵈ S Ne 9:17;
Ps 106:22 ᵉ Ex 11:9
ᶠ S Nu 13:22
78:13 ᵍ S Ex 14:21;
Ps 66:6; 136:13
ʰ S Ex 14:22; S 15:8
78:14 ᶦ Ex 13:21;
Ps 105:39
78:15 ʲ S Nu 20:11;
1Co 10:4
78:17 ᵏ ver 32,40;
Dt 9:22; Isa 30:1;
63:10; Heb 3:16
78:18 ˡ S Ex 17:2;
1Co 10:9
ᵐ S Ex 15:24; Nu 11:4
78:19 ⁿ Nu 21:5
78:20 ᵒ S Nu 20:11;
S Isa 35:6 ᵖ Nu 11:18
78:21 �q S Nu 11:1
78:22 ʳ S Dt 1:32;
Heb 3:19
78:23 ˢ Ge 7:11;
S 2Ki 7:2
78:24 ᵗ Ex 16:4;
Jn 6:31*

8 They would not be like their ancestors ᵛ—
    a stubborn ʷ and rebellious ˣ generation,
    whose hearts were not loyal to God,
    whose spirits were not faithful to him.

9 The men of Ephraim, though armed with bows, ʸ
    turned back on the day of battle; ᶻ
10 they did not keep God's covenant ᵃ
    and refused to live by his law. ᵇ
11 They forgot what he had done, ᶜ
    the wonders he had shown them.
12 He did miracles ᵈ in the sight of their ancestors
    in the land of Egypt, ᵉ in the region of Zoan. ᶠ
13 He divided the sea ᵍ and led them through;
    he made the water stand up like a wall. ʰ
14 He guided them with the cloud by day
    and with light from the fire all night. ᶦ
15 He split the rocks ʲ in the wilderness
    and gave them water as abundant as the seas;
16 he brought streams out of a rocky crag
    and made water flow down like rivers.

17 But they continued to sin ᵏ against him,
    rebelling in the wilderness against the Most High.
18 They willfully put God to the test ˡ
    by demanding the food they craved. ᵐ
19 They spoke against God; ⁿ
    they said, "Can God really
    spread a table in the wilderness?
20 True, he struck the rock,
    and water gushed out, ᵒ
    streams flowed abundantly,
    but can he also give us bread?
    Can he supply meat ᵖ for his people?"
21 When the Lᴏʀᴅ heard them, he was furious;
    his fire broke out q against Jacob,
    and his wrath rose against Israel,
22 for they did not believe in God
    or trust ʳ in his deliverance.
23 Yet he gave a command to the skies above
    and opened the doors of the heavens; ˢ
24 he rained down manna ᵗ for the people to eat,
    he gave them the grain of heaven.

78:8 *stubborn and rebellious.* Like a rebellious son (see Dt 9:6–7,24; 31:27). *generation.* Reference here is to a people with certain shared characteristics (see 24:6; Dt 32:5,20), thus not limited to the exodus generation (see vv. 9–11,56–64). *hearts.* See note on 4:7.

🅰 🅲 **78:9–16** The northern kingdom has violated God's covenant, not remembering his saving acts (a message emphasized by the prophets Amos and Hosea). Israel's history with God has been a long series of rebellions on her part (vv. 9–16,32–39,56–64), beginning already in the desert (vv. 17–31,40–55).

78:9 *men of Ephraim.* The northern kingdom, dominated by the tribe of Ephraim (see introduction). *turned back.* Neither the tribe of Ephraim nor the northern kingdom had a reputation for cowardice or ineffectiveness in battle (see, e.g., Dt 33:17). This verse is best understood as a metaphor for Israel's betrayal of God's covenant (see v. 10), related to the figure of the "faulty bow" (v. 57).

78:12–16 A summary reference to the plagues in Egypt and to the water miracles at the Red Sea and in the desert. In the two cycles that follow (vv. 17–39,40–64), further elaboration intensifies the indictment.

78:12 See Ex 7–12. *Zoan.* A city in the northeast part of the Nile delta (see v. 43; see also Nu 13:22 and note).

78:13 See Ex 14:1—15:21.

78:15–16 See v. 20; Ex 17:6; Nu 20:8,10–11.

78:17–31 Israel's rebelliousness in the desert; God's marvelous provision of food—and his anger.

78:17 *continued.* Although no sin in the desert has yet been mentioned, the poet probably expected his readers to recall (in conjunction with the miraculous provisions of water just mentioned) how the people grumbled at Marah because of lack of water (see Ex 15:24). *Most High.* See vv. 35,56; see also note on Ge 14:19.

78:18 See Ex 16:2–3. *put God to the test.* See vv. 41,56; see also note on Ex 17:2.

78:19 *Can God really spread a table…?* For a different use of the same imagery, see 23:5.

78:20 *bread…meat.* The poet is probably combining and compressing two episodes (Ex 16:2–3; Nu 11:4).

78:21 *wrath.* See vv. 31,49–50,58–59,62; see also note on 2:5.

78:23 *opened the doors of the heavens.* For this imagery, see Ge 7:11; 2Ki 7:2; Mal 3:10.

25 Human beings ate the bread of angels;
 he sent them all the food they could eat.
26 He let loose the east wind *u* from the heavens
 and by his power made the south wind blow.
27 He rained meat down on them like dust,
 birds *v* like sand on the seashore.
28 He made them come down inside their camp,
 all around their tents.
29 They ate till they were gorged— *w*
 he had given them what they craved.
30 But before they turned from what they craved,
 even while the food was still in their mouths, *x*
31 God's anger rose against them;
 he put to death the sturdiest *y* among them,
 cutting down the young men of Israel.

32 In spite of all this, they kept on sinning; *z*
 in spite of his wonders, *a* they did not believe. *b*
33 So he ended their days in futility *c*
 and their years in terror.
34 Whenever God slew them, they would seek *d* him;
 they eagerly turned to him again.
35 They remembered that God was their Rock, *e*
 that God Most High was their Redeemer. *f*
36 But then they would flatter him with their mouths, *g*
 lying to him with their tongues;
37 their hearts were not loyal *h* to him,
 they were not faithful to his covenant.
38 Yet he was merciful; *i*
 he forgave *j* their iniquities *k*
 and did not destroy them.
 Time after time he restrained his anger *l*
 and did not stir up his full wrath.
39 He remembered that they were but flesh, *m*
 a passing breeze *n* that does not return.

40 How often they rebelled *o* against him in the wilderness *p*
 and grieved him *q* in the wasteland!
41 Again and again they put God to the test; *r*
 they vexed the Holy One of Israel. *s*
42 They did not remember *t* his power—
 the day he redeemed them from the oppressor, *u*
43 the day he displayed his signs *v* in Egypt,
 his wonders *w* in the region of Zoan.
44 He turned their river into blood; *x*
 they could not drink from their streams.

78:26 *u* S Nu 11:31
78:27 *v* S Ex 16:13;
Nu 11:31
78:29 *w* S Nu 11:20
78:30 *x* S Nu 11:33
78:31 *y* Isa 10:16
78:32 *z* S ver 17
a ver 11 *b* ver 22
78:33 *c* Nu 14:29,35
78:34 *d* S Dt 4:29;
Hos 5:15
78:35 *e* S Ge 49:24
f S Dt 9:26
78:36 *g* Eze 33:31
78:37 *h* ver 8;
Ac 8:21
78:38 *i* S Ex 34:6
j Isa 1:25; 27:9; 48:10;
Da 11:35 *k* Ps 25:11;
85:2 *l* S Job 9:13;
S Isa 30:18
78:39 *m* S Ge 6:3;
S Isa 29:5 *n* S Job 7:7;
Jas 4:14
78:40 *o* S Ex 23:21
p Ps 95:8; 106:14
q Eph 4:30
78:41 *r* S Ex 17:2
s S 2Ki 19:22;
Ps 71:22; 89:18
78:42 *t* S Jdg 3:7;
S Ne 9:17 *u* S Ps 25:11
78:43 *v* Ex 10:1
w S Ex 3:20
78:44 *x* Ex 7:20-21;
Ps 105:29

78:25 *bread of angels.* So called because it came down from heaven. *angels.* Lit. "mighty ones." The Hebrew word is used only here of the angels, but reference is clearly to heavenly beings (see 103:20).
78:26–28 See Ex 16:13; Nu 11:31.
78:26 *east wind … south wind.* Since the quail were migrating from Egypt at this time, the south wind may have carried them north and the east wind may have diverted them to the desert area occupied by the Israelites (the book of Numbers does not provide wind directions).
78:27 *like dust … like sand.* Similes for a huge number (see note on Ge 13:16).
78:30–31 See Nu 11:33.
78:32–39 Rebelliousness, which became Israel's way of life, showed itself early in the desert wandering (vv. 17–31) and continued throughout that journey.
78:32 *did not believe.* That God could give them victory over the Canaanites (see Nu 14:11).
78:33 The exodus generation was condemned to die in the

desert (see Nu 14:22–23,28–35).
78:34–37 A cycle repeated frequently during the period of the judges.
78:35 *Rock.* See note on 18:2. *Redeemer.* Deliverer (see note on 71:23).
78:36 See Isa 29:13.
78:37 *hearts.* See note on 4:7.
78:38 See Ex 32:14; Nu 14:20. *forgave.* See note on 65:3.
78:39 See 103:14; see also 39:5; 62:9; 144:4 and notes.
78:40–64 The second cycle (the first is vv. 17–39).
78:40–55 Israel's rebelliousness began in the desert; she did not remember how she had been delivered from oppression by God's plagues upon Egypt (see v. 12). Yet he brought his people through the sea and the desert and established them in the promised land.
78:41 *Holy One of Israel.* See 71:22; 89:18; see also 2Ki 19:22 and note.
78:44–51 The plagues upon Egypt (see Ex 7–12): The sequence in Exodus is followed only in the first and last; the third, fifth, sixth and ninth plagues are not mentioned.

78:45 ʸ Ex 8:24;
Ps 105:31 ᶻ S Ex 8:2,6
78:46 ᵃ Na 3:15
ᵇ S Ex 10:13
78:47 ᶜ Ex 9:23;
Ps 105:32; 147:17
78:48 ᵈ Ex 9:25
78:49 ᵉ Ex 15:7
ᶠ S Ge 19:13;
1Co 10:10
78:51 ᵍ S Ex 12:12;
Ps 135:8 ʰ Ps 105:23;
106:22
78:52 ⁱ S Job 21:11;
S Ps 28:9; 77:20
78:53 ʲ S Ex 14:28
ᵏ Ex 15:7; Ps 106:10
78:54 ˡ Ps 44:3
78:55 ᵐ Ps 44:2
ⁿ S Dt 1:38;
S Jos 13:7; Ac 13:19
78:57 ᵒ S 2Ch 30:7;
Eze 20:27 ᵖ S ver 9
78:58 �q S Jdg 2:12
ʳ S Lev 26:30
ˢ Ex 20:4; S Dt 5:8;
32:21
78:59 ᵗ Ps 55:19
ᵘ S Lev 26:28;
S Nu 32:14
ᵛ S Dt 32:19
78:60 ʷ S Jos 18:1
ˣ Eze 8:6
78:61 ʸ Ps 132:8
ᶻ S 1Sa 4:17
78:62 ᵃ S Dt 28:25
ᵇ S 1Sa 10:1
78:63 ᶜ S Nu 11:1
ᵈ S 1Ki 4:32; Jer 7:34;
16:9; 25:10
78:64 ᵉ 1Sa 4:17

45 He sent swarms of flies ʸ that devoured them,
  and frogs ᶻ that devastated them.
46 He gave their crops to the grasshopper, ᵃ
  their produce to the locust. ᵇ
47 He destroyed their vines with hail ᶜ
  and their sycamore-figs with sleet.
48 He gave over their cattle to the hail,
  their livestock ᵈ to bolts of lightning.
49 He unleashed against them his hot anger, ᵉ
  his wrath, indignation and hostility—
  a band of destroying angels. ᶠ
50 He prepared a path for his anger;
  he did not spare them from death
  but gave them over to the plague.
51 He struck down all the firstborn of Egypt, ᵍ
  the firstfruits of manhood in the tents of Ham. ʰ
52 But he brought his people out like a flock; ⁱ
  he led them like sheep through the wilderness.
53 He guided them safely, so they were unafraid;
  but the sea engulfed ʲ their enemies. ᵏ
54 And so he brought them to the border of his holy land,
  to the hill country his right hand ˡ had taken.
55 He drove out nations ᵐ before them
  and allotted their lands to them as an inheritance; ⁿ
  he settled the tribes of Israel in their homes.

56 But they put God to the test
  and rebelled against the Most High;
  they did not keep his statutes.
57 Like their ancestors ᵒ they were disloyal and faithless,
  as unreliable as a faulty bow. ᵖ
58 They angered him q with their high places; ʳ
  they aroused his jealousy with their idols. ˢ
59 When God heard ᵗ them, he was furious; ᵘ
  he rejected Israel ᵛ completely.
60 He abandoned the tabernacle of Shiloh, ʷ
  the tent he had set up among mortals. ˣ
61 He sent the ark of his might ʸ into captivity, ᶻ
  his splendor into the hands of the enemy.
62 He gave his people over to the sword; ᵃ
  he was furious with his inheritance. ᵇ
63 Fire consumed ᶜ their young men,
  and their young women had no wedding songs; ᵈ
64 their priests were put to the sword, ᵉ
  and their widows could not weep.

78:47 *sycamore-figs.* See note on Am 7:14.
78:49 *destroying angels.* The poet personifies God's wrath, indignation and hostility as agents of his anger.
78:51 *tents.* Dwellings. *Ham.* For the association of Ham with Egypt, see 105:23,27; 106:21—22; Ge 10:6 and note.
78:52 *like a flock.* See 77:20 and note.
78:53 *sea.* Red Sea (see Ex 15:1—21 and notes).
78:54 *holy land.* See note on Zec 2:12.
78:55 Summarizes the story told in Joshua.

■ **A** ■ **C** 78:56—64 Rebelliousness continued to be Israel's way of life in the promised land (a recurring theme of Judges; see also 1Sa 2:12—7:2), so God rejected Israel (v. 59; see Jer 7:15).
78:57 *faulty bow.* See note on v. 9.
78:58 *high places.* See note on 1Sa 9:12. *jealousy.* God's intense reaction to disloyalty to him (see note on Ex 20:5).

■ **A** ■ 78:59 *rejected Israel completely.* Abandoned her to her enemies. The psalmist does not speak of a permanent

casting off of Israel, not even of the ten northern tribes (cf. Ro 11:1 and note).
78:60 *Shiloh.* The center of worship since the time of Joshua (see Jos 18:1,8; 21:1–2; Jdg 18:31; 1Sa 1:3; Jer 7:12), it was located in Ephraim between Bethel and Shechem (see Jdg 21:19; see also map No. 6 at the end of this study Bible). Apparently it was destroyed by the Philistines when they captured the ark or shortly afterward (see note on Jer 7:12).

■ **A** ■ 78:61 *his might ... his splendor.* The ark is here so called because it was the sign of God's kingship in Israel and the focal point for the display of his power and glory (see 26:8; 63:2; 1Sa 4:3,21–22).
78:62,71 *his inheritance.* See Dt 9:29.
78:63 *Fire.* Often associated with the sword (see vv. 62,64) as the two primary instruments of destruction in ancient warfare. *no wedding songs.* So great was the catastrophe that both the wedding songs of the brides and the wailing of the widows (see v. 64) were silenced in the land.
78:64 *priests were put to the sword.* See 1Sa 4:11.

65 Then the Lord awoke as from sleep, *f*
   as a warrior wakes from the stupor of wine.
66 He beat back his enemies;
   he put them to everlasting shame. *g*
67 Then he rejected the tents of Joseph,
   he did not choose the tribe of Ephraim; *h*
68 but he chose the tribe of Judah, *i*
   Mount Zion, *j* which he loved.
69 He built his sanctuary *k* like the heights,
   like the earth that he established forever.
70 He chose David *l* his servant
   and took him from the sheep pens;
71 from tending the sheep *m* he brought him
   to be the shepherd *n* of his people Jacob,
   of Israel his inheritance.
72 And David shepherded them with integrity of heart; *o*
   with skillful hands he led them.

PSALM 79

A psalm of Asaph.

1 O God, the nations have invaded your inheritance; *p*
   they have defiled *q* your holy temple,
   they have reduced Jerusalem to rubble. *r*

78:65 *f* Ps 44:23
78:66 *g* 1Sa 5:6
78:67 *h* Jer 7:15;
Hos 9:13; 12:1
78:68 *i* S Nu 1:7;
Ps 108:8 *j* S Ex 15:17;
S Ps 68:16
78:69 *k* S Ps 15:1
78:70 *l* S 1Sa 16:1
78:71 *m* S Ge 37:2
n S Ps 28:9
78:72 *o* S Ge 17:1
79:1 *p* S Ex 34:9
q S Lev 20:3
r S 2Ki 25:9;
S Ne 4:2; S Isa 6:11

78:65–72 The Lord's election of Judah (instead of Ephraim) as the leading tribe in Israel (anticipated in Jacob's deathbed blessing of his sons, Ge 49:8–12), of Mount Zion (instead of Shiloh) as the place of his sanctuary (royal seat) and of David as his regent to shepherd his people. By these acts the Lord established his people securely as his kingdom in the promised land, following the long period of Israel's troubles from the death of Joshua to the death of Saul—by then God's salvation of Israel begun in the exodus reached its climactic (if provisional) fulfillment (see introduction to Ps 68 and the combination of echoes of God's saving act in the exodus and through David in Isaiah's prophecy of Israel's future deliverance, Isa 11:11–16).
78:65 *awoke as from sleep.* Poetic hyperbole to highlight the contrast between God's action in behalf of his people in the days of David and the preceding time of Israel's troubles (see note on 7:6).
78:66–72 The saving events noted have two focal points: (1) God's decisive victory over his enemies (thus securing his realm) and the establishment of Zion as his royal city, and (2) the appointment of David to be the shepherd of his people.
78:67 *tents of Joseph.* A figure for the tribe of Ephraim (for the figurative use of "tents," see v. 51; see also 69:25; 83:6; 84:10; 120:5; Ge 9:27; Dt 33:18; 1Ki 12:16; Job 8:22; 12:6; Hab 3:7; Mal 2:12).
78:68,70 *he chose ... Mount Zion ... He chose David.* See Ps 132.
78:69 *heights ... earth.* The verse is subject to two interpretations: (1) The Lord built his sanctuary as impregnable as a mountain fortress and as enduring and immovable as the age-old earth, or (2) the Lord built his sanctuary as secure and enduring as the heavens and the earth (see note on 24:2) and there manifests himself as the Lord of glory (see 24:7–10; 26:8; 63:2; 96:6), even as he does in the creation (see 19:1; 29:9; 97:6).
78:70–71 See 1Sa 16:11–13; 2Sa 7:8.
78:70 *his servant.* Here an official title marking David as a member of God's royal administration (see notes on Ex 14:31; Ps 18 title; Isa 41:8–9; 42:1). For David as God's "servant," see also 89:3,20,39; 132:10; 144:20.
78:71 *shepherd.* See v. 72; see also note on 23:1.

A **78:72** Israel under the care of the Lord's royal shepherd from the house of David was for the prophets the hope of God's people (see Eze 34:23; 37:24; Mic 5:4—fulfilled in Jesus Christ, Mt 2:6; Jn 10:11; Rev 7:17). *shepherded.* See note on 23:1.

Ps 79–83 A group of five psalms at the center of Book III that are framed by two urgent prayers of the community when the nation has been invaded by powerful enemies (for the different events alluded to, see introduction to Ps 79; 83). These two prayers share four thematic links: 1. In 79:4 the Israelites complain that they have become "objects of contempt ... scorn and derision" to their enemies, while in 83:17 they pray that their enemies may "ever be ashamed and dismayed" and "perish in disgrace." 2. In 79:11 they appeal to God to effect deliverance by his strong "arm," while in 83:8 they charge that Assyria is the strong "arm" assisting the invaders. 3. In 79:5 they express anguish over the fact that they continue to feel God's anger "burn like fire," while in 83:14 they pray that God will pursue their enemies like a "fire" that "consumes" a forest. 4. Most significantly, in 79:6 they pray that God will pour out his wrath on "the nations that do not acknowledge [know] you, on the kingdoms that do not call on your name," while in 83:16,18 they pray that God will so overwhelm the foreign invaders that they will "seek your name" and will "know" that the Lord is "the Most High over all the earth."
In the center of this group (Ps 81)—thus also at the center of Book III—stands an urgent admonition to wayward Israel, reminding God's people that only if they are faithful to the Lord, who brought them out of Egypt, will he preserve them or rescue them from the ravaging of their enemies.
Bracketing this center on one side is a communal prayer for God to "restore" his "flock" and revive his once thriving "vine" that has been decimated by enemies (Ps 80) and on the other a prayer that the God who judges all kings and possesses all nations will arouse himself to "judge the earth" (Ps 82). Notably, Ps 80 is linked with Ps 79 by a shared use of the shepherd-sheep metaphor (see 79:13; 80:1), and Ps 82 is linked with Ps 83 by their shared references to "the Most High" (82:6; 83:18).
Ps 79 Israel's prayer for God's forgiveness and help and for his judgment on the nations that have so cruelly destroyed her, showing utter contempt for both the Lord and his people. For the relationship of this psalm to Ps 80–83 in the arrangement of the Psalter, see introduction to Ps 79–83. Like Ps 74, with which it has many thematic links, Ps 79 dates from the time of the exile. The poignancy of its appeal is heightened by its juxtaposition to Ps 77 (recalling God's saving acts under Moses) and Ps 78

79:2 *s* Rev 19:17-18
t S Dt 28:26; Jer 7:33
79:3 *u* Jer 25:33;
Rev 11:9 *v* Jer 16:4
79:4 *w* S Ps 39:8;
S Eze 5:14 *x* Ps 44:13;
80:6
79:5 *y* S Ps 74:10
z Ps 74:1; 85:5
a S Dt 29:20;
Ps 89:46; Zep 3:8
79:6 *b* S Ps 2:5;
69:24; 110:5; Rev 16:1
c Ps 147:20; Jer 10:25
d S Ps 14:4
79:7 *e* Isa 9:12;
Jer 10:25
79:8 *f* S Ge 9:25;
Jer 44:21 *g* Ps 116:6;
142:6
79:9 *h* S 2Ch 14:11
i Ps 25:11; 31:3;
Jer 14:7
79:10 *j* S Ps 42:3
k Ps 94:1; S Rev 6:10
l ver 3
79:12 *m* Isa 65:6;
Jer 32:18 *n* S Ge 4:15

² They have left the dead bodies of your servants
  as food for the birds of the sky, *s*
  the flesh of your own people for the animals of the wild. *t*
³ They have poured out blood like water
  all around Jerusalem,
  and there is no one to bury *u* the dead. *v*
⁴ We are objects of contempt to our neighbors,
  of scorn *w* and derision to those around us. *x*

⁵ How long, *y* LORD? Will you be angry *z* forever?
  How long will your jealousy burn like fire? *a*
⁶ Pour out your wrath *b* on the nations
  that do not acknowledge *c* you,
 on the kingdoms
  that do not call on your name; *d*
⁷ for they have devoured *e* Jacob
  and devastated his homeland.

⁸ Do not hold against us the sins of past generations; *f*
  may your mercy come quickly to meet us,
  for we are in desperate need. *g*
⁹ Help us, *h* God our Savior,
  for the glory of your name;
deliver us and forgive our sins
  for your name's sake. *i*
¹⁰ Why should the nations say,
  "Where is their God?" *j*

Before our eyes, make known among the nations
  that you avenge *k* the outpoured blood *l* of your servants.
¹¹ May the groans of the prisoners come before you;
  with your strong arm preserve those condemned to die.
¹² Pay back into the laps *m* of our neighbors seven times *n*
  the contempt they have hurled at you, Lord.

(recalling God's saving acts under David), two psalms with which
it is significantly linked by the shepherd-sheep figure and other
thematic elements. Israel acknowledges that the Lord has used
the nations to punish her for her sins, so she pleads for pardon.
But she knows too that the nations have acted out of their hostility to and disdain for God and his people; that warrants her
plea for God's judgment on them (see Isa 10:5–11; 47:6–7). Daniel's prayer (Da 9:4–19) contains much that is similar to the elements of penitence in this psalm.
79 title *Asaph.* See note on Ps 73 title.

79:1–4 What the nations have done: They have attacked
God's own special domain, violated his temple, destroyed
his royal city, slaughtered his people, degraded them in death
(by withholding burial—see note on 53:5—and leaving their
bodies as carrion for birds and beasts) and reduced them to the
scorn of the world.
79:1 *your inheritance.* Cf. 78:62,71. Here reference is to Israel's
homeland as the Lord's domain (see note on 2:8; cf. 114:2 and
note). *holy temple.* See note on 78:69.
79:2 *your servants.* Though banished from the Lord's land for
sins that cannot be denied, the exiles plead their special covenant relationship with God (see "your own people," here, and
"your own people, the sheep of your pasture," v. 13). *your own people.*
See note on 4:3.
79:3 *poured out blood ... all around Jerusalem.* Cf. 2Ki 21:16.
79:5–8 A prayer for God to relent and deal with the nations
who do not acknowledge him.
79:5 *How long ... ?* See note on 6:3. *angry.* See v. 6 ("wrath");
see also note on 2:5. *jealousy.* See note on 78:58. *burn like fire.*
See Dt 4:24; 6:15; Zep 1:18; 3:8.
79:6–7 See Jer 10:25 and note. Perhaps the psalmist is quoting
Jeremiah here.

79:6 *Pour out your wrath.* As they "poured out" (v. 3) the blood
of your people. The exiles plead with God to redress the wrongs
committed against them (see note on 5:10).
79:7 *devoured.* Like wild beasts (see 44:11; 74:19 and note on
7:2). *Jacob.* A synonym for Israel (see Ge 32:28).
79:8 *sins of past generations.* Israel suffered exile because of
the accumulated sins of the nation (see 2Ki 17:7–23; 23:26–27;
24:3–4; Da 9:4–14), from which she did not repent until the
judgment of God had fallen on her. The exiles here pray that
God will take notice of their penitence and not continue to hold
the sins of past generations against his now repentant people.
mercy. Here personified as God's agent sent to bring relief (see
notes on 23:6; 43:3).
79:9–11 A prayer for God to help and forgive his people and
to redress the violent acts of the enemies.

79:9 *for the glory of your name.* As the desolation of
God's people brings reproach to God (see v. 10), so their
salvation and prosperity bring him glory (see note on 23:3). *forgive.* See note on 65:3.
79:10 *Where is their God?* See note on 3:2. *avenge.* Redress (see
Dt 32:35,43).
79:11 *prisoners ... those condemned to die.* The exiles, as imperial captives in Babylonia (see 102:20)—not actually in prisons,
but under threat of death should they seek to return to their
homeland.
79:12–13 Concluding prayer and vow to praise.
79:12 *Pay back into the laps.* See note on Jer 32:18. *seven times.*
In full measure; the number seven symbolized completeness.
contempt ... at you. The enemies' violent action against Israel
was above all a high-handed reviling of God (see vv. 1,10; 2Ki
19:10–12,22–23; Isa 52:5).

¹³ Then we your people, the sheep of your pasture, ᵒ
      will praise you forever; ᵖ
   from generation to generation
      we will proclaim your praise.

PSALM 80

For the director of music. To the tune of "The Lilies of the Covenant."
Of Asaph. A psalm.

*¹ Hear us, Shepherd of Israel,
      you who lead Joseph like a flock. �q
   You who sit enthroned between the cherubim, ʳ
      shine forth ²before Ephraim, Benjamin and Manasseh. ˢ
   Awaken ᵗ your might;
      come and save us. ᵘ

³ Restore ᵛ us, ʷ O God;
      make your face shine on us,
      that we may be saved. ˣ

⁴ How long, ʸ Lᴏʀᴅ God Almighty,
      will your anger smolder ᶻ
      against the prayers of your people?
⁵ You have fed them with the bread of tears; ᵃ
      you have made them drink tears by the bowlful. ᵇ
⁶ You have made us an object of derision ᵃ to our neighbors,
      and our enemies mock us. ᶜ

⁷ Restore us, God Almighty;
      make your face shine on us,
      that we may be saved. ᵈ

⁸ You transplanted a vine ᵉ from Egypt;

ᵃ 6 Probable reading of the original Hebrew text; Masoretic Text *contention*
* 80:1-19 is numbered 80:2-20 in Hebrew texts.

79:13 *sheep of your pasture.* See 23:2; 74:1 and notes; see also 77:20; 78:72; 80:1. *will praise you forever.* See note on 7:17. *from generation to generation.* See 78:4.

Ps 80 Israel's prayer for restoration when she had been ravaged by a foreign power. For the relationship of this psalm to the others in its group, see introduction to Ps 79–83. It seems likely that "Ephraim, Benjamin and Manasseh" (v. 2) here represent the northern kingdom. If Jeroboam was indeed given ten tribes (see 1Ki 11:29–36), leaving only one to Rehoboam—Judah (see 1Ki 12:20), which was actually two tribes because Simeon was located within Judah (see Jos 19:1–9)—then Benjamin belonged to the northern kingdom. However, part of Benjamin must always have remained with the southern kingdom since its territory actually bordered on Jerusalem itself, and the southern kingdom continued to control Jerusalem's environs (see 1Ki 12:21). This suggests that the disaster suffered was the Assyrian campaign that swept the northern kingdom away (see 2Ki 17:1–6). Recent archaeological surveys of the Holy Land have shown that Jerusalem and the surrounding countryside experienced a dramatic increase of population at this time, no doubt the result of a massive influx of displaced persons from the north fleeing the Assyrian beast. This could account for the presence of "Ephraim, Benjamin and Manasseh" at the Jerusalem sanctuary, and for a national prayer for restoration with special focus on these tribes (see notes below). The prayer has five stanzas of four (Hebrew) lines each. A recurring petition climaxes the first, second and last (for other refrains, see introduction to Ps 42–43), with a progressing urgency of appeal: "God" (v. 3); "God Almighty" (v. 7); "Lᴏʀᴅ God Almighty" (v. 19).
80 title *For the director of music.* See note on Ps 4 title. *To the tune of.* See note on Ps 9 title. *Lilies.* See note on Ps 45 title.

Asaph. See note on Ps 73 title.
80:1–3 An appeal for God to arouse himself and go before his people again with all his glory and might as he did of old in the desert.
80:1 See the shepherd-flock motif in 74:1; 77:20; 78:52,71–72; 79:13; see also 23:1–2 and notes. *Joseph.* See note on 77:15. *enthroned between the cherubim.* See note on Ex 25:18. *shine forth.* Let your glory be seen again, as in the desert journey (see Ex 24:16–17; 40:34–35), but now especially through your new saving act (see 102:15–16; Ex 14:4,17–18; Nu 14:22; Isa 40:5; 44:23; 60:1–2).
80:2 *before Ephraim, Benjamin and Manasseh.* March against the nations as you marched in the midst of your army from Sinai into the promised land (in that march the ark of the covenant advanced in front of the troops of these three tribes; see Nu 10:21–24; see also introduction to Ps 68). *Awaken.* See note on 7:6.
80:3 *make your face shine.* See vv. 7,19; an echo of the priestly benediction (see Nu 6:25; see also notes on 4:6; 13:1).
80:4–7 A lament over the Lord's severe punishment of his people.
80:4 *How long . . . ?* See note on 6:3. *Lᴏʀᴅ . . . Almighty.* See vv. 7,14,19; see also note on 1Sa 1:3. *anger.* See note on 2:5.
80:5 God has now given them tears to eat and tears to drink rather than "the bread of angels" and water from the rock (see 78:20,25).
80:8–16 This use of the vine-vineyard metaphor (here to describe Israel's changed condition) is found also in the prophets (see Isa 3:14; 5:1–7; 27:2; Jer 2:21; 12:10; Eze 17:6–8; 19:10–14; Hos 10:1; 14:7; Mic 7:1; see also Ge 49:22; Mt 20:1–16; Mk 12:1–9; Lk 20:9–16; Jn 15:1–5).
80:8–11 Israel was once God's flourishing, transplanted vine.

79:13 ᵒ S Ps 74:1
ᵖ Ps 44:8
80:1 q Ps 77:20
ʳ S Ex 25:22
80:2 ˢ Nu 2:18-24
ᵗ S Ps 35:23 ᵘ Ps 54:1; 69:1; 71:2; 109:26; 116:4; 119:94
80:3 ᵛ S Ps 71:20; 85:4; Jer 31:18; La 5:21 ʷ S Nu 6:25 ˣ ver 7,19
80:4 ʸ S Ps 74:10 ᶻ Dt 29:20
80:5 ᵃ S Job 3:24 ᵇ Isa 30:20
80:6 ᶜ S Ps 79:4
80:7 ᵈ ver 3
80:8 ᵉ Isa 5:1-2; Jer 2:21; Mt 21:33-41

80:8 *f* Ex 23:28-30;
S Jos 13:6; Ac 7:45
g S Ex 15:17
80:11 *h* Ps 72:8
80:12 *i* Ps 89:40;
Isa 5:5; 30:13;
Jer 39:8
80:13 *j* Jer 5:6
80:14 *k* S Dt 26:15
80:16 *l* Ps 79:1
m S Dt 28:20
80:17 *n* S Job 25:6
80:18 *o* Ps 85:6;
Isa 57:15; Hos 6:2
81:1 *p* S Ps 66:1

you drove out *f* the nations and planted *g* it.
⁹ You cleared the ground for it,
and it took root and filled the land.
¹⁰ The mountains were covered with its shade,
the mighty cedars with its branches.
¹¹ Its branches reached as far as the Sea, *a*
its shoots as far as the River. *b h*

¹² Why have you broken down its walls *i*
so that all who pass by pick its grapes?
¹³ Boars from the forest ravage *j* it
and wild animals feed on it.
¹⁴ Return to us, God Almighty!
Look down from heaven and see! *k*
Watch over this vine,
¹⁵   the root your right hand has planted,
the son *c* you have raised up for yourself.

¹⁶ Your vine is cut down, it is burned with fire; *l*
at your rebuke *m* your people perish.
¹⁷ Let your hand rest on the man at your right hand,
the son of man *n* you have raised up for yourself.
¹⁸ Then we will not turn away from you;
revive *o* us, and we will call on your name.

¹⁹ Restore us, LORD God Almighty;
make your face shine on us,
that we may be saved.

PSALM 81

For the director of music. According to gittith. *d Of Asaph.*

*¹ Sing for joy to God our strength;
shout aloud to the God of Jacob! *p*

---

a 11 Probably the Mediterranean   *b 11* That is, the Euphrates   *c 15* Or *branch*   *d* Title: Probably a
musical term

* 81:1-16 is numbered 81:2-17 in Hebrew texts.

80:8 *transplanted... from Egypt.* See 78:52. *drove out the nations and planted.* See 44:2.
80:9 *cleared the ground.* See Isa 5:2.
80:10 *mighty cedars.* Lit. "cedars of God" (the Hebrew word for "God" is sometimes used in the sense of "mighty"; see, e.g., note on 29:1).
80:11 *Sea...River.* See TNIV text notes; see also Ex 23:31 and note.
80:12–15 A prayer for God to renew his care for his ravaged vine.
80:12 *Why...?* Israel's anguished perplexity over God's abandonment (see note on 6:3). *broken down its walls.* Taken away its defenses.
80:14 *Watch over.* See Ex 3:16. But the Hebrew for this phrase may have the sense here that it has in Ru 1:6: "Come to the aid of."
80:15 *son.* Israel (see Ex 4:22–23; Hos 11:1). But "son" may sometimes be used also to refer to a vine branch (see TNIV text note; see also note on Ge 49:22). That may be the case here, thus, yielding the conventional pair "root and branch," a figure for the whole vine (see Job 18:16; 29:19; Eze 17:7; Mal 4:1; see also Isa 5:24; 27:6; 37:31; Eze 17:9; 31:7; Hos 9:16; Am 2:9; Ro 11:16). *raised up.* See v. 17; lit. "made vigorous."
80:16–19 Concluding prayer for restoration.
80:16 *rebuke.* See 9:5 and note on 76:6.
80:17 *Let your hand rest on.* Show your favor to (see Ezr 7:6,9, 28; 8:18,22,31; Ne 2:8,18). *at.* Lit. "of." *your right hand.* Reference may be to the Davidic king as the Lord's anointed, seated in the place of honor in God's presence (see 110:1) and the one in whom the hope of the nation rested (see 2:7–9; 72:8–11;

89:21–25). But v. 15 strongly suggests another sense: that "the man" is Jacob/Israel and that he is "of" God's "right hand" in that he has been "planted" and "raised up" by him.
80:18 A vow to be loyal to God and to trust in him alone. It occurs in a place where it would be more common to find a vow to praise (see note on 7:17).
Ps 81 A festival song. But it is unclear whether the festival is Passover/Unleavened Bread (v. 5; see Ex 12:14–17) or the Jewish New Year (v. 3; see Lev 23:24; Nu 29:1) or the Festival of Tabernacles (v. 3; see Lev 23:34; Nu 29:12). It may have been used at all three. But more likely it was composed for use at both New Year (the first day of the month, "New Moon") and the beginning of Tabernacles (the 15th day of the month, full moon); see notes below. Whether the psalm is preexilic or postexilic cannot be determined, but it clearly shows the grand significance of Israel's annual religious festivals (see chart, pp. 180–181). As memorials of God's saving acts, they called Israel to celebration, remembrance and recommitment (see Ps 95). For the significant placement of this psalm within Book III of the Psalter, see introduction to Ps 73–78 and introduction to Ps 79–83.
Though the psalm falls into two main parts (vv. 1–5, 6–16), thematic development follows a symmetrical pattern: two verses, three verses; two verses, three verses; two verses, four verses. Note also the contrast between vv. 6–7 and vv. 11–12 and the thematic link between v. 10c and v. 16.
81 title *For the director of music.* See note on Ps 4 title. *According to.* See note on Ps 6 title. *gittith.* See note on Ps 8 title. *Asaph.* See note on Ps 73 title.

2 Begin the music, strike the timbrel, *q*
   play the melodious harp *r* and lyre. *s*

3 Sound the ram's horn *t* at the New Moon, *u*
   and when the moon is full, on the day of our festival;
4 this is a decree for Israel,
   an ordinance of the God of Jacob. *v*
5 When God went out against Egypt, *w*
   he established it as a statute for Joseph.

   I heard an unknown voice say: *x*

6 "I removed the burden *y* from their shoulders; *z*
   their hands were set free from the basket.
7 In your distress you called *a* and I rescued you,
   I answered *b* you out of a thundercloud;
   I tested you at the waters of Meribah. *a c*
8 Hear me, my people, *d* and I will warn you—
   if you would only listen to me, Israel!
9 You shall have no foreign god *e* among you;
   you shall not worship any god other than me.
10 I am the LORD your God,
   who brought you up out of Egypt. *f*
   Open *g* wide your mouth and I will fill *h* it.

11 "But my people would not listen to me;
   Israel would not submit to me. *i*
12 So I gave them over *j* to their stubborn hearts
   to follow their own devices.

13 "If my people would only listen to me, *k*
   if Israel would only follow my ways,
14 how quickly I would subdue *l* their enemies
   and turn my hand against *m* their foes!
15 Those who hate the LORD would cringe *n* before him,
   and their punishment would last forever.

---

a 7   The Hebrew has *Selah* (a word of uncertain meaning) here.

81:2 *q* S Ex 15:20
r Ps 92:3 *s* Job 21:12
81:3 *t* S Ex 19:13
u S Ne 10:33
81:4 *v* ver 1
81:5 *w* S Ex 11:4
x Ps 114:1
81:6 *y* S Ex 1:14
z Isa 9:4; 52:2
81:7 *a* S Ex 2:23
b Ex 19:19 *c* S Ex 17:7;
S Dt 33:8
81:8 *d* Ps 50:7; 78:1
81:9 *e* S Ex 20:3
81:10 *f* S Ex 6:6;
S 13:3; S 29:46
g Eze 2:8 *h* Ps 107:9
81:11 *i* Ex 32:1-6
81:12 *j* Eze 20:25;
Ac 7:42; Ro 1:24
81:13 *k* S Dt 5:29
81:14 *l* Ps 47:3
m Am 1:8
81:15 *n* S 2Sa 22:45

81:1–5 A summons to celebrate the appointed sacred feast.
81:1 *Jacob.* A synonym for Israel (see Ge 32:28).
81:2 *timbrel.* See note on Jer 31:4. *harp and lyre.* See note on 57:8.
81:3 *ram's horn.* The ram's horn trumpet (see Ex 19:13). *our festival.* Probably the Festival of Tabernacles, often called simply "the festival" (see 1Ki 8:2,65; 12:32; 2Ch 5:3; 7:8; Ne 8:14,18; Eze 45:25; see also Dt 16:14). As the great seven-day autumn festival, beginning on the 15th of the month (full moon), it followed shortly after the Day of Atonement (observed on the tenth of the month, Lev 16:29), recalled God's care for his people during the desert journey (see Lev 23:43), served as a festival of thanksgiving for the harvest (see Lev 23:39–40; Dt 16:13–15) and marked the conclusion of the annual cycle of religious festivals that began with Passover and Unleavened Bread six months earlier (see Ex 23:14–17; Lev 23; Dt 16:16; see also note on Zec 14:16). Every seventh year at this festival the covenant law was to be read to all the people (see Dt 31:9–13; Ne 8:2,15). The first day of this month (New Moon) was commemorated with trumpets (see Lev 23:24). It later came to be known as New Year since the seventh month marked the end of harvest and the beginning of the rainy season, when the new crops were planted.
81:4–5 *decree … ordinance … statute.* See the passages referred to in note on v. 3.
81:5 *When God went out against Egypt.* Some believe this indicates that the festival referred to is Passover and Unleavened Bread (see Ex 12:14,42). More likely it serves as a reference to the whole exodus period, while highlighting especially God's triumph over Egypt by which he had set his people free (see vv. 6–7). *Joseph.* See note on 77:15. *heard an unknown voice.* The

"voice" is the "thunder" of God's judgment against Egypt (see v. 7), which the Levitical author then proceeds to interpret as to its present reference for the celebrating congregation (vv. 6–16).

81:6–10 God heard and delivered and now summons his people to loyalty.
81:6 *burden … basket.* The forced labor to which the Israelites were subjected in Egypt (see Ex 1:11–14).
81:7 *you called and I rescued.* See Ex 3:7–10. *out of a thundercloud.* See 106:9; Ex 14:21,24; 15:8,10; see also note on 76:6. *I tested you.* See Ex 17:1–7. For *Selah,* see TNIV text note and note on 3:2.
81:8–10 God heard his people in their distress (vv. 6–7); now they must listen to him.
81:9–10 See Ex 19:4–5; 20:2–4; Dt 4:15–20.

81:10 *Open wide your mouth.* Trust in the Lord alone for all of life's needs. *I will fill it.* See v. 16; as he did in the desert (see 78:23–29; see also 37:3–4; Dt 11:13–15; 28:1–4).
81:11–16 Israel has not listened—if only God's people would! See Eze 18:23,32; 33:11.
81:11 See 78:10,17,32,40,56; Dt 9:7,24; Jer 7:24–26.
81:12 It is God who "circumcises" the heart (see Dt 30:6; see also 1Ki 8:58; Jer 31:33; Eze 11:19; 36:26). Thus for God to abandon his people to their sins is the most fearful of punishments (see 78:29; Isa 6:9–10; 29:10; 63:17; cf. Ro 1:24,26,28).
81:13–16 See the promised covenant blessings outlined in Ex 23:22–27; Lev 26:3–13; Dt 7:12–26; 28:1–14.
81:13 *my ways.* See 25:4 and note.

81:16 °S Dt 32:14
82:1 °Ps 7:8; 58:11;
Isa 3:13; 66:16;
Joel 3:12 °S Job 21:22
82:2 °Dt 1:17
°Ps 58:1-2; Pr 18:5
82:3 °S Dt 24:17
°Ps 140:12; Jer 5:28;
22:16
82:5 °S Ps 14:4;
S 53:2 °Job 30:26;
Isa 5:30; 8:21-22; 9:2;
59:9; 60:2; Jer 13:16;
23:12; La 3:2
°S Jdg 5:4; S Ps 11:3
82:6 °Jn 10:34*
82:7 °Ps 49:12;
Eze 31:14
82:8 °Ps 12:5
°S Ps 76:9 °Ps 2:8
83:1 °Ps 28:1;
35:22; Isa 42:14;
57:11; 62:1; 64:12

16 But you would be fed with the finest of wheat; °
   with honey from the rock I would satisfy you."

PSALM 82

A psalm of Asaph.

1 God presides in the great assembly;
   he gives judgment ᵖ among the "gods": ᵠ

2 "How long will you ᵃ defend the unjust
   and show partiality ʳ to the wicked? ᵇ ˢ
3 Defend the weak and the fatherless; ᵗ
   uphold the cause of the poor ᵘ and the oppressed.
4 Rescue the weak and the needy;
   deliver them from the hand of the wicked.

5 "The 'gods' know nothing, they understand nothing. ᵛ
   They walk about in darkness; ʷ
   all the foundations ˣ of the earth are shaken.

6 "I said, 'You are gods'; ʸ
   you are all sons of the Most High.'
7 But you will die ᶻ like mere mortals;
   you will fall like every other ruler."

8 Rise up, ᵃ O God, judge ᵇ the earth,
   for all the nations are your inheritance. ᶜ

PSALM 83

A song. A psalm of Asaph.

*1 O God, do not remain silent; ᵈ
   do not turn a deaf ear,
   do not stand aloof, O God.

ᵃ 2 The Hebrew is plural.   ᵇ 2 The Hebrew has *Selah* (a word of uncertain meaning) here.
* 83:1-18 is numbered 83:2-19 in Hebrew texts.

81:16 *honey from the rock.* See note on Dt 32:13.

🔺 **Ps 82** A word of judgment on unjust rulers and judges. The Levitical author of this psalm evokes a vision of God presiding over his heavenly court—analogous to the experiences of the prophets (see 1Ki 22:19–22; Isa 6:1–7; Jer 23:18, 22; see also Job 15:8). As the Great King (see introduction to Ps 47) and the Judge of all the earth (see 94:2; Ge 18:25; 1Sa 2:10) who "loves justice" (99:4) and judges the nations in righteousness (see 9:8; 96:13; 98:9), he is seen calling to account those responsible for defending the weak and oppressed on earth. An early Rabbinic interpretation (see Jn 10:34–35) understood the "gods" (vv. 1,6) to be unjust rulers and judges in Israel, of whom there were many (see 1Sa 8:3; Isa 1:16–17; 3:13–15; Jer 21:12; 22:3; Eze 34:4,21; Mic 3:1–3; 7:3). Today many identify the "gods" as the kings of surrounding nations who encouraged the conceit that they were actually or virtually divine beings but who ruled with lofty disregard for justice—though honoring it as a royal ideal. Others hold that the "gods" are the divine beings in whose names the kings claimed to rule (see 95:3). In any event, rulers and judges here are confronted by their King and Judge (see Ps 58). Structurally, the words of the Levite (vv. 1,6) frame the words of God. At the very center (see note on v. 5) stands the most devastating judgment of all. For this psalm's placement in Book III of the Psalter, see introduction to Ps 79–83.
82 title See note on Ps 73 title.

🔺 **82:1** *great assembly.* The assembly in the great Hall of Justice (cf. 1Ki 7:7) in heaven (see 89:5; 1Ki 22:19; Job 1:6; 2:1; Isa 6:1–4). As if in a vision, the psalmist sees the rulers and judges gathered before the Great King to give account of their administration of justice. *gods.* See v. 6. In the language of the OT—and in

accordance with the conceptual world of the ancient Near East—rulers and judges, as deputies of the heavenly King, could be given the honorific title "god" (see note on 45:6; see also TNIV text notes on Ex 21:6; 22:8) or be called "son of God" (see 2:7 and note).
82:2 For *Selah,* see TNIV text note and note on 3:2.

🔺 **82:3–4** In the OT a first-order task of kings and judges was to protect the powerless against all who would exploit or oppress them (see 72:2,4, 12–14; Pr 31:8–9; Isa 11:4; Jer 22:3,16).

🔺 **82:5** *The 'gods' know ... nothing.* The center of the poem (see note on 6:6). They ought to have shared in the wisdom of God (see 1Ki 3:9; Pr 8:14–16; Isa 11:2), but they are utterly devoid of true understanding of moral issues or of the moral order that God's rule sustains (see Isa 44:18; Jer 3:15; 9:24). *foundations ... are shaken.* When such people are the wardens of justice, the whole world order crumbles (see 11:3; 75:3 and notes).
82:6 *I said.* Those who rule (or judge) do so by God's appointment (see 2:7; Isa 44:28) and thus are his representatives—whether they acknowledge him or not (see Ex 9:16; Jer 27:6; Da 2:21; 4:17,32; 5:18; Jn 19:11; Ro 13:1). *gods.* See notes on v. 1; Jn 10:34. *sons of.* See note on v. 1. *Most High.* See note on Ge 14:19.
82:7 However exalted their position, these corrupt "gods" will be brought low by the same judgment as other human beings. *fall.* See note on 13:4.
82:8 Having seen the prospect in store, the psalmist prays for God's judgment to hasten and for the perfect reign of God to come quickly to the whole world. *Rise up.* See note on 3:7. *inheritance.* Domain (see note on 79:1).
Ps 83 Israel's prayer for God to crush his enemies when the whole world—or so it seemed—was arrayed against his peo-

² See how your enemies growl, ^e
    how your foes rear their heads. ^f
³ With cunning they conspire ^g against your people;
    they plot against those you cherish. ^h
⁴ "Come," they say, "let us destroy ⁱ them as a nation, ^j
    so that Israel's name is remembered ^k no more."

⁵ With one mind they plot together; ^l
    they form an alliance against you—
⁶ the tents of Edom ^m and the Ishmaelites,
    of Moab ⁿ and the Hagrites, ^o
⁷ Byblos, ^p Ammon ^q and Amalek, ^r
    Philistia, ^s with the people of Tyre. ^t
⁸ Even Assyria ^u has joined them
    to reinforce Lot's descendants. ^a ^v

⁹ Do to them as you did to Midian, ^w
    as you did to Sisera ^x and Jabin ^y at the river Kishon, ^z
¹⁰ who perished at Endor ^a
    and became like dung ^b on the ground.
¹¹ Make their nobles like Oreb and Zeeb, ^c
    all their princes like Zebah and Zalmunna, ^d
¹² who said, "Let us take possession ^e
    of the pasturelands of God."

¹³ Make them like tumbleweed, my God,
    like chaff ^f before the wind.
¹⁴ As fire consumes the forest
    or a flame sets the mountains ablaze, ^g
¹⁵ so pursue them with your tempest ^h
    and terrify them with your storm. ⁱ
¹⁶ Cover their faces with shame, ^j LORD,
    so that they will seek your name.

¹⁷ May they ever be ashamed and dismayed; ^k
    may they perish in disgrace. ^l

^a 8 The Hebrew has *Selah* (a word of uncertain meaning) here.

83:2 ^e Ps 2:1;
Isa 17:12 ^f Jdg 8:28
83:3 ^g S Ex 1:10;
S Ps 31:13 ^h Ps 17:14
83:4 ⁱ S 1Sa 15:3
^j Jer 33:24 ^k Jer 11:19
83:5 ^l Ps 2:2
83:6 ^m Ps 137:7;
Isa 34:5; Jer 49:7;
Am 1:11 ⁿ 2Ch 20:1
^o S Ge 25:16
83:7 ^p S Jos 13:5
^q Ge 19:38
^r S Ge 14:7; S Ex 17:14
^s Ex 15:14 ^t Isa 23:3;
Eze 27:3
83:8 ^u S Ge 10:11
^v S Dt 2:9
83:9 ^w S Ge 25:2;
Jdg 7:1-23 ^x S Jdg 4:2
^y S Jos 11:1
^z S Jdg 4:23-24
83:10 ^a S 1Sa 28:7
^b S 2Ki 9:37; Isa 5:25;
Jer 8:2; 9:22; 16:4;
25:33; Zep 1:17
83:11 ^c Jdg 7:25
^d S Jdg 8:5
83:12 ^e 2Ch 20:11;
Eze 35:10
83:13 ^f S Job 13:25
83:14 ^g Dt 32:22;
Isa 9:18
83:15 ^h S Ps 50:3
ⁱ S Job 9:17
83:16 ^j S Ps 34:5;
109:29; 132:18
83:17 ^k S 2Ki 19:26
^l S Ps 34:4

---

ple. For this psalm's relationship to those around it, see introduction to Ps 79–83. Neither Kings nor Chronicles tells of a confederacy as extensive as that described here. Perhaps only some of the nations mentioned were actually attacking, while the rest of Israel's historic enemies were more passively supporting the campaign. If so, the occasion may have been that reported in 2Ch 20, when Moab, Ammon, Edom and their allies were invading Judah. In any event, the psalm must date from sometime after the reign of Solomon and before the great thrust of Assyria in the time of King Menahem (see 2Ki 15:19).

Each of the two main divisions (vv. 1–8, 9–18) consists of two four-verse stanzas, with the latter division being extended by a two-verse stanza that brings the prayer to its climactic conclusion.

83 title *song.* See note on Ps 30 title. *Asaph.* See note on Ps 73 title.
83:1–4 An appeal to God to act in the face of Israel's imminent danger.
83:1 *do not remain silent.* Do not remain inactive (see 35:22; 109:1).
83:2 *growl.* In Hebrew the same verb as for "are in uproar" in 46:6 and for "snarling" in 59:6,14.
83:4 *they say.* See note on 3:2. *let us destroy them.* Israel's very existence is at stake (see v. 12).
83:5–8 The array of nations allied against Israel—threat from every quarter.
83:6 *Hagrites.* Either Ishmaelites (descendants of Hagar) or a group mentioned in Assyrian inscriptions as an Aramean confederacy (see 1Ch 5:10,18–22; 27:31).

83:7 *Byblos.* See 1Ki 5:18; Eze 27:9; an important Phoenician city.
83:8 *Assyria.* Since it is mentioned only as an ally of Moab and Ammon (the descendants of Lot; see note on Ge 19:36–38), Assyria, though distantly active in the region, must not yet have become a major threat in its own right. For *Selah,* see TNIV text note and note on 3:2.
83:9–12 A plea for God to destroy his enemies as he did in the time of the judges. Those who hurl themselves against the kingdom of God to destroy it from the earth—so that the godless powers are left to shape the destiny of the world as they will—must be crushed if God's kingdom of righteousness and peace is to come and be at rest (see note on 5:10).
83:9 *as you did to Midian.* In Gideon's great victory (see Jdg 7). *as you did to Sisera and Jabin.* In Barak's defeat of the Canaanite coalition (see Jdg 4).
83:10 *Endor.* See Jos 17:11 and note; northeast of where the main battle was fought—apparently where much of the fleeing army was overtaken and decimated.
83:11 *Oreb and Zeeb . . . Zebah and Zalmunna.* Leaders of the Midianite host destroyed by Gideon.
83:12 See v. 4.
83:13–16 Imagery of fleeing armies and of God's fearsome power.
83:15 Imagery of the heavenly Warrior attacking his enemies out of the thunderstorm (see 18:7–15; 68:33; 77:17–18; Ex 15:7–10; Jos 10:11; Jdg 5:4,20–21; 1Sa 2:10; 7:10; Isa 29:5–6; 33:3). For the storm cloud as God's chariot, see 68:4 and note.
83:16 *will seek.* See note on v. 18. *name.* See note on 5:11.
83:17–18 The prayer's climactic conclusion.

83:18 ᵐ S Ps 68:4
ⁿ Ps 7:8; 18:13
ᵒ S Job 34:29
84:1 ᵖ S Dt 33:27;
Ps 27:4; 43:3; 90:1;
132:5
84:2 �q S Job 19:27
ʳ Jos 3:10
84:3 ˢ S Ps 43:4
ᵗ Jer 44:11 ᵘ Ps 2:6
ᵛ Ps 5:2
84:5 ʷ Ps 81:1
ˣ Jer 31:6

¹⁸ Let them know that you, whose name is the LORD ᵐ—
  that you alone are the Most High ⁿ over all the earth. ᵒ

PSALM 84

For the director of music. According to gittith. ᵃ *Of the Sons of Korah.*
A psalm.

*¹ How lovely is your dwelling place, ᵖ
  LORD Almighty!
² My soul yearns, �q even faints,
  for the courts of the LORD;
my heart and my flesh cry out
  for the living God. ʳ
³ Even the sparrow has found a home,
  and the swallow a nest for herself,
  where she may have her young—
a place near your altar, ˢ
  LORD Almighty, ᵗ my King ᵘ and my God. ᵛ
⁴ Blessed are those who dwell in your house;
  they are ever praising you. ᵇ

⁵ Blessed are those whose strength ʷ is in you,
  whose hearts are set on pilgrimage. ˣ
⁶ As they pass through the Valley of Baka,

ᵃ Title: Probably a musical term   ᵇ 4 The Hebrew has *Selah* (a word of uncertain meaning) here and at
the end of verse 8.

* 84:1-12 is numbered 84:2-13 in Hebrew texts.

83:18 The ultimate goal of God's warfare is not merely the security of Israel and the destruction of Israel's (and God's) enemies but the worldwide acknowledgment of the true God and of his rule, even to the point of seeking him as his people do (see v. 16; see also 40:9; 47:9; 58:11; 59:13 and notes). *Most High.* See note on Ge 14:19.

Ps 84–89 The first of the six psalms that make up the final group of Book III (see introduction to Ps 73–78) expresses yearning for fellowship with God, who dwells in his temple in Zion and from whom alone come security and blessing. References to God as "LORD Almighty" and a prayer for "our shield," the Lord's "anointed," form distinctive links with the final psalm of the group (for the former, see 84:1,3,8,12 and 89:8; for the latter see 84:9 and 89:18,38,51). The five psalms thus introduced are four cries out of distress arranged around a central song (Ps 87) that celebrates God's special love of Zion and the care he has for all its citizens. Of these four, the first (Ps 85) and the last (Ps 89) are communal prayers, and the remaining two (Ps 86; 88) are prayers of individuals. They all make much of God's "love and faithfulness" (see 85:7,10–11; 86:5,13,15; 88:11; 89:1–2,5,8,14,24, 28,33,49) and his "saving" help (see 85:4,7,9; 86:2,16; 88:1; 89:26). And three of them share another key concept, "righteousness" (see 85:10–11,13; 88:12; 89:14). The two final prayers (Ps 88; 89) both end unrelieved by the usual expression of confidence that God will hear and act (see note on 3:8). However, the editors of Book III have placed them under the near shadow of Ps 87, the more distant shadow of Ps 84 and the still more distant shadow of Ps 82. From these psalms they should not be disassociated.

Ps 84 A prayer of longing for the house of the Lord. In tone and perspective it stands close to Ps 42 and may reflect similar circumstances. If so, the author (presumably a Levite who normally functioned in the temple service), now barred from access to God's house (perhaps when Sennacherib was ravaging Judah; see 2Ki 18:13–16), gives voice to his longing for the sweet nearness to God in his temple that he had known in the past. Reference to God and his temple and to the "blessedness" (see vv. 4–5,12) of those having free access to both dominates the prayer and highlights its central themes. For its placement in the arrangement of

the Psalter, see introduction to Ps 84–89. Whatever its origin, the psalm now voices the devotion to and reliance on God that motivate the remaining prayers of the group it introduces.

The psalm has three main divisions and a conclusion (v. 12). In the Hebrew text, a six-line unit (vv. 1–4) precedes and another six-line unit (vv. 8–11) follows a three-line reflection (vv. 5–7) on the blessedness of those free to make pilgrimage to Zion. Each of these six-line divisions contains three references to the "LORD," while the seventh reference (symbolizing completeness or perfection) appears in the conclusion.

84 title *For the director of music.* See note on Ps 4 title. *According to.* See note on Ps 6 title. *gittith.* See note on Ps 8 title. *Of the Sons of Korah.* See note on Ps 42 title.

84:1–4 A confession of deep longing for the house of the Lord.

84:1 *lovely.* The traditional rendering of the Hebrew here, but perhaps better translated "beloved" or "loved." *LORD Almighty.* See vv. 3,8,12; see also note on 1Sa 1:3.

84:2 *My soul.* I (see note on 6:3). *courts.* Of the temple (see v. 10; 2Ki 21:5; 23:11–12). *my heart . . . flesh.* My whole being (see 73:26). *heart.* See note on 4:7. *living God.* See Dt 5:26.

84:3 The psalmist is jealous of the small birds that have such unhindered access to the temple and the altar. They are able even to build their nests for their young there—the place where Israel was to have communion with God.

84:4–5,12 *Blessed.* See note on 1:1.

84:4 *who dwell in your house.* See note on 15:1. For *Selah,* see TNIV text note and note on 3:2.

84:5–7 The joyful blessedness of those who are free to make pilgrimage to Zion—them too the psalmist envies.

84:5 *those whose strength is in you.* Those who have come to know the Lord as their deliverer and the sustainer of their lives. *whose hearts are set on pilgrimage.* Lit. "in whose hearts are (the) highways," i.e., the highways the Israelites took to observe the religious festivals at Jerusalem (Zion, v. 7). *hearts.* See note on 4:7.

84:6 *As they pass.* On their way to the temple. *Baka.* Means either "weeping" or "balsam trees" (common in arid valleys). The place is unknown and may be figurative (see 23:4)

they make it a place of springs;^{y}
the autumn^z rains also cover it with pools.^{a}
^{7} They go from strength to strength,^{a}
till each appears^b before God in Zion.^{c}

^{8} Hear my prayer,^{d} LORD God Almighty;
listen to me, God of Jacob.
^{9} Look on our shield,^{b}^{e} O God;
look with favor on your anointed one.^{f}

^{10} Better is one day in your courts
than a thousand elsewhere;
I would rather be a doorkeeper^g in the house of my God
than dwell in the tents of the wicked.
^{11} For the LORD God is a sun^h and shield;^{i}
the LORD bestows favor and honor;
no good thing does he withhold^j
from those whose walk is blameless.

^{12} LORD Almighty,
blessed^k are those who trust in you.

PSALM 85

For the director of music. Of the Sons of Korah. A psalm.

*^{1} You, LORD, showed favor to your land;
you restored the fortunes^l of Jacob.
^{2} You forgave^m the iniquity^n of your people
and covered all their sins.^{c}

^{a} 6 Or *blessings* ^{b} 9 Or *sovereign* ^{c} 2 The Hebrew has *Selah* (a word of uncertain meaning) here.

* 85:1-13 is numbered 85:2-14 in Hebrew texts.

84:6 ^{y} S Job 38:26
^{z} Joel 2:23
84:7 ^{a} S Job 17:9
^{b} S Dt 16:16 ^{c} 1Ki 8:1
84:8 ^{d} Ps 4:1
84:9 ^{e} S Ps 59:11
^{f} Isa 16:6; Ps 2:2;
18:50; 132:17
84:10 ^{g} 1Ch 23:5
84:11 ^{h} Isa 60:19;
Jer 43:13; Rev 21:23
^{i} S Ge 15:1 / Ps 34:10
84:12 ^{k} Ps 2:12
85:1 ^{l} S Dt 30:3;
Ps 14:7
85:2 ^{m} S Nu 14:19
^{n} S Ex 32:30;
S Ps 78:38

for arid stretches the pilgrims had to traverse. *place of springs.*
The joyful expectations of the pilgrims transform the difficult
ways into places of refreshment. *autumn rains.* These gentle early
showers were greeted as harbingers of the winter rains that covered Israel's sun-scorched hills once more with flourishing vegetation (104:13–15) and mantled the valleys with grain (65:9–13;
see also Joel 2:23–24). Reference to these rains suggests that the
psalmist had in mind especially the pilgrimage to observe the
Festival of Tabernacles (see chart, pp. 180–181). *pools.* The Hebrew for this word may refer to "blessings" or to "pools" (see TNIV
text note); it is likely that both are intended. By God's benevolent
care over his pilgrims, the vale of weeping (or balsam trees), already transformed by the glad hearts of the expectant wayfar-
ers, is turned into a valley of praise (see 2Ch 20:26). God's people
on their hopeful way to Zion experience anew the bountiful
hand of God as their ancestors did on their way through the
Desert of Sinai to the promised land (see 78:15–16; 105:41;
114:8)—and as their descendants would on their return to Zion
from Babylonian exile (see Isa 41:17–20; 43:19–20; 49:10).
84:7 *from strength to strength.* Whatever the toils and hardships of the journey (see Isa 40:31). *Zion.* See 9:11 and note.
84:8–11 A prayer for the king, and its motivation: Only as God
blesses the king in Jerusalem will the psalmist once more realize his great desire to return to his accustomed service in the
temple (see introduction).
84:8 *LORD God Almighty ... God of Jacob.* That is, LORD God Almighty, the God of Jacob (see 59:5; see also note on 3:7). *Jacob.*
A synonym for Israel (see Ge 32:28).
84:9 *our shield.* The king in Jerusalem (see TNIV text note; see
also note on 3:3). *anointed one.* God's earthly regent over his
people (from David's line—perhaps Hezekiah [see introduction
to this psalm]); see note on 2:2.
84:10 *doorkeeper.* Probably the psalmist's normal (and humble) service at the temple (see 2Ki 22:4). *dwell in the tents of the
wicked.* Share in the life of those who do not honor the God of

Zion. Perhaps reference is to the peoples imported by Sargon II
(see 2Ki 17:24–33), among whom the psalmist was forced at the
time to live.
84:11 *sun.* The glorious source of the light of life (see note on
27:1). *shield.* See note on 3:3. *blameless.* See 15:2; Ge 17:1 and
notes.
84:12 The sum of it all (see 40:4).

Ps 85 A communal prayer for the renewal of God's mercies
to his people at a time when they are once more suffering
distress. Many believe that vv. 1–3 refer to the return from exile
and that the troubles experienced are those alluded to by Nehemiah and Malachi. Verse 12 suggests that a drought has ravaged
the land and may reflect the drought with which the Lord chastened his people in the time of Haggai (see Hag 1:5–11). For this
prayer's placement in the Psalter and its relationship to the psalms
of its group, see introduction to Ps 84–89. Christian liturgical usage
has often employed this psalm in the Christmas season. The psalm
has two main divisions of seven (Hebrew) lines each: (1) the prayer
(vv. 1–7); (2) a reassuring word (vv. 8–13). Each division contains a
three-line stanza followed by a four-line stanza, with the corresponding stanzas of the second half answering to those of the
first: Verses 1–3 speak of mercies granted, while vv. 8–9 speak of
mercies soon to come; vv. 4–7 voice the prayer, and vv. 10–13 offer
the blessed reassurance that the prayer will be heard. Each of the
four stanzas contains one reference to the "LORD."
85 title *For the director of music.* See note on Ps 4 title. *Of the
Sons of Korah.* See note on Ps 42 title.
85:1–7 Prayer for the renewal of God's favor.

85:1–3 Israel begins her prayer by appealing to the Lord's
past mercies, recalling how he has forgiven and restored his
people before (perhaps a reference to the restoration from exile).
85:1 *restored the fortunes of Jacob.* Or "brought Jacob back
from exile" (see Jer 29:14 and TNIV text note there). *Jacob.* A synonym for Israel (see Ge 32:28).
85:2 For *Selah,* see TNIV text note and note on 3:2.

85:3 o Ps 106:23;
Da 9:16 p Ex 32:12;
Dt 13:17; Ps 78:38;
Jnh 3:9
85:4 q S Ps 71:20
r S Ps 65:5
85:5 s S Ps 50:21
85:6 t S Ps 80:18
u Php 3:1
85:7 v S Ps 6:4
w Ps 27:1
85:8 x S Lev 26:6;
S Isa 60:17;
S Jn 14:27; 2Th 3:16
y Pr 26:11; 27:22
85:9 z Ps 27:1;
Isa 43:3; 45:8; 46:13;
51:5; 56:1; 62:11
a S Ps 29:43;
Isa 60:19; Hag 2:9;
Zec 2:5
85:10 b Ps 89:14;
115:1; Pr 3:3
c Ps 72:2-3; Isa 32:17
85:11 d Isa 45:8
85:12 e Ps 84:11;
Jas 1:17 f Lev 26:4;
S Ps 67:6; Zec 8:12
86:1 g Ps 17:6

³ You set aside all your wrath ᵒ
  and turned from your fierce anger. ᵖ

⁴ Restore �q us again, God our Savior, ʳ
  and put away your displeasure toward us.
⁵ Will you be angry with us forever? ˢ
  Will you prolong your anger through all generations?
⁶ Will you not revive ᵗ us again,
  that your people may rejoice ᵘ in you?
⁷ Show us your unfailing love, ᵛ LORD,
  and grant us your salvation. ʷ

⁸ I will listen to what God the LORD says;
  he promises peace ˣ to his people, his faithful servants—
  but let them not turn to folly. ʸ
⁹ Surely his salvation ᶻ is near those who fear him,
  that his glory ᵃ may dwell in our land.

¹⁰ Love and faithfulness ᵇ meet together;
  righteousness ᶜ and peace kiss each other.
¹¹ Faithfulness springs forth from the earth,
  and righteousness ᵈ looks down from heaven.
¹² The LORD will indeed give what is good, ᵉ
  and our land will yield ᶠ its harvest.
¹³ Righteousness goes before him
  and prepares the way for his steps.

PSALM 86

A prayer of David.

¹ Hear me, LORD, and answer �g me,
  for I am poor and needy.

85:3 *wrath … anger.* See v. 5; see also note on 2:5.
85:4–7 The prayer acknowledges that the present troubles are indicative of God's displeasure. No confession of sin is expressed, but in the light of v. 3 (and possibly v. 8; see below) it is probably implicit.
85:7 *unfailing love.* See v. 10; see also note on 6:4.
85:8–13 God's reassuring answer to the prayer, conveyed through a priest or Levite, perhaps one of the Korahites (see note on 12:5–6; see also 2Ch 20:14).
85:8–9 The assurance that God will again bless his people.
85:8 *I will listen.* The speaker awaits the word from the Lord. *promises peace.* The word from the Lord perhaps takes the form of the priestly benediction (see Nu 6:22–26). *faithful servants.* See note on 4:3. *but let them not return to folly.* And so provoke God's displeasure again. But it is also possible to translate the clause: "and to those who turn from folly." *folly.* See TNIV text note on 14:1.
85:9 *glory.* Wherever God's saving power is displayed his glory is revealed (see 57:5 and note; 72:18–19; Ex 14:4, 17–18; Nu 14:22; Isa 6:3 and note; 40:5 and note; 44:23; 66:19; Eze 39:21).
85:10–13 God's sure mercies to his people spring from his covenant love, to which in his faithfulness and righteousness he remains true, and that assures his people's welfare (peace). Cf. 40:9–10.
85:10 *Love and faithfulness … righteousness and peace.* These expressions of God's favor toward his people are here personified (see note on 23:6), and the vivid portrayal of their meeting and embracing offers one of the most beautiful images in all Scripture of God's gracious dealings with his covenant people. *righteousness.* See vv. 11,13; see also note on 4:1. *peace.* See note on Nu 6:26.
85:11 *Faithfulness springs forth.* As new growth springs from the earth to bless all living things with plenty. *righteousness looks down.* It shines down benevolently. (With "disaster" as sub-

ject, the Hebrew for "looks down" indicates the opposite effect: Jer 6:1, "looms.") From heaven and from earth God's covenant blessings will abound till Israel's cup overflows.
85:12 *what is good.* See 4:6 and note. *will yield its harvest.* See 67:6 and note.
85:13 *Righteousness goes before.* Again the psalmist personifies. Acting either as herald or guide, righteousness leads the way and marks the course for God's engagement in his people's behalf—and righteousness is God's perfect faithfulness to all his covenant commitments (see note on 4:1).
Ps 86 The prayer of an individual for God's help when attacked by enemies, whose fierce onslaughts betray their disdain for the Lord. Whether or not David was the author (see Introduction: Authorship and Titles), the psalmist's identification of himself as God's "servant" (v. 2) suggests his royal status and thus his special relationship with the Lord (see 2Sa 7:5,8 and note on Ps 18 title). The enemies may then be either those within the kingdom who refuse to acknowledge him as the Lord's anointed, or foreign powers that are attempting to remove him from the international scene. For the placement of this psalm in the arrangement of the Psalter, see introduction to Ps 84–89.
  This carefully designed poetic prayer is composed of five stanzas, having a symmetrical verse pattern (four, three, three, three, four). The author identifies himself as the Lord's servant in the first and last stanzas, which also contain the prayer for God's mercy and deliverance from the enemy threat. The second stanza (vv. 5–7) adds a profession of assurance; the fourth stanza (vv. 11–13) adds a vow to praise. These are linked by references to God's "love" (see note on 6:4) in vv. 5,13. The center stanza (vv. 8–10) hails the Lord as the incomparable, the only God, whom all the nations will someday worship. Verse 9 is the center verse (see note on 6:6). Yahweh ("LORD") occurs four times (once each in stanzas 1,2,4, 5), Elohim ("God") occurs four times, and Adonai ("Lord") occurs seven times. Here and elsewhere such numbers appear to be deliberate.

2 Guard my life, for I am faithful to you;
　save your servant who trusts in you. *h*
You are my God; 3 have mercy *i* on me, Lord,
　for I call *j* to you all day long.
4 Bring joy to your servant, Lord,
　for I put my trust *k* in you.

5 You, Lord, are forgiving and good,
　abounding in love *l* to all who call to you.
6 Hear my prayer, LORD;
　listen to my cry *m* for mercy.
7 When I am in distress, *n* I call *o* to you,
　because you answer *p* me.

8 Among the gods *q* there is none like you, *r* Lord;
　no deeds can compare with yours.
9 All the nations you have made
　will come *s* and worship *t* before you, Lord;
　they will bring glory *u* to your name.
10 For you are great *v* and do marvelous deeds; *w*
　you alone *x* are God.

11 Teach me your way, *y* LORD,
　that I may rely on your faithfulness; *z*
give me an undivided *a* heart,
　that I may fear *b* your name.
12 I will praise you, Lord my God, with all my heart; *c*
　I will glorify your name forever.
13 For great is your love toward me;
　you have delivered me *d* from the depths,
　from the realm of the dead. *e*

14 Arrogant foes are attacking me, O God;
　a band of ruthless people seeks my life—
　they have no regard for you. *f*
15 But you, Lord, are a compassionate and gracious *g* God,
　slow to anger, *h* abounding *i* in love and faithfulness. *j*
16 Turn to me *k* and have mercy *l* on me;
　show your strength *m* in behalf of your servant

86:2 *h* Ps 25:2; 31:14
86:3 *i* Ps 4:1; S 9:13;
57:1 / Ps 88:9
86:4 *k* Ps 46:5; 143:8
86:5 *l* Ex 34:6;
Ne 9:17; Ps 103:8;
145:8; Joel 2:13;
Jnh 4:2
86:6 *m* Ps 5:2; 17:1
86:7 *n* Ps 27:5;
S 50:15; 94:13;
Hab 3:16 *o* Job 22:27;
Ps 4:3; 80:18; 91:15;
Isa 30:19; 58:9;
65:24; Zec 13:9
p Ps 3:4
86:8 *q* S Ex 8:10;
S Job 21:22
r S Ps 18:31
86:9 *s* S Ps 65:2
t Ps 66:4; Isa 19:21;
27:13; 49:7; Zec 8:20-
22; 14:16; Rev 15:4
u Isa 43:7; 44:23
86:10 *v* S 2Sa 7:22;
S Ps 48:1 *w* S Ex 3:20;
S Ps 71:17; 72:18
x S Dt 6:4;
S Isa 43:10; Mk 12:29;
1Co 8:4
86:11 *y* S Ex 33:13;
S 1Sa 12:23; Ps 25:5
z S Ps 26:3 *a* Jer 24:7;
32:39; Eze 11:19;
1Co 7:35 *b* S Dt 6:2
86:12 *c* S Ps 9:1
86:13 *d* S Ps 34:4;
49:15; 116:8
e S Ps 16:10; S 56:13
86:14 *f* Ps 54:3
86:15 *g* S Ps 51:1;
103:8; 111:4; 116:5;
145:8 *h* Nu 14:18
i ver 5 / S Ex 34:6;
S Ne 9:17; Joel 2:13
86:16 *k* S Ps 6:4
l S Ps 9:13 *m* Ps 18:1

---

86 title *prayer.* See note on Ps 17 title; see also note on 72:20.
of David. This is the only psalm in Book III (Ps 73–89) that is ascribed to David. Perhaps its placement among the Korahite
psalms is in part because those who arranged the Psalter perceived a thematic link between v. 9 and 87:4.
86:1–4 Initial prayer for God to have mercy and protect the life
of his servant.
86:1 *poor and needy.* See 35:10; see also 34:6 and note.

86:2 *faithful to you.* The Hebrew for this phrase is *hasid*
(see note on 4:3). *your servant.* See vv. 4, 16; see also introduction. *You are my God.* Not that David has chosen him, but
that he has chosen David to be his servant (see 1Sa 13:14; 15:28;
16:12; 2Sa 7:8). David's faithfulness to God and God's commitment to him are deliberately juxtaposed.

86:5–7 In his need David prays to the Lord because he is
confident that, out of his kindness and love, God answers
prayer.
86:5 *love.* See vv. 13, 15; see also note on 6:4.
86:7 *I call ... you answer.* See note on 118:5.

86:8–10 At the center of his prayer David gives expression to his fundamental belief (see also 115:3–7;
135:13–17 and related notes) and makes clear why he appeals
to Yahweh in the surrounding stanzas.

86:9 *All the nations.* See note on 46:10. This is the center
verse of the psalm (see note on 6:6) and contains the
psalm's most exalted confession of faith concerning God's sovereign and universal rule. *they will bring glory.* As David vows to

do (v. 12). *your name.* See vv. 11–12; see also note on 5:11.
86:10 *marvelous deeds.* See note on 9:1.
86:11–13 A prayer for godliness and a vow to praise.

86:11 *Teach me ... give me.* What would be the
benefit if God were to save him from his enemies
but abandon him to his own waywardness? David's dependence on God is complete, and so is his devotion to God—save
me from the enemy outside but also from my frailty within (see
25:5; 51:7, 10 and notes). Only one who is thus devoted to God
may expect God's help and will truly fulfill the vow (v. 12). *undivided heart.* See Eze 11:19 and note; see also 1Ch 12:33; 1Co
7:35. *heart.* See note on 4:7.

86:12 Vow to praise (see note on 7:17).
86:13 David anticipates the answer to his prayer (see note on
3:8). *depths.* See note on 30:1.
86:14–17 Conclusion: the prayer renewed.
86:14 *ruthless.* The Hebrew for this word suggests also ferocity.
they have no regard for you. In their arrogance they dismiss the
heavenly Warrior, who is David's defender (see note on 10:11;
see also Jer 20:11).
86:15 Echoes v. 5, but is even more similar to Ex 34:6 (see note
on Ex 34:6–7).
86:16 *show your strength.* Exert your power in my behalf. *son of
a woman who served you.* That is, one born and raised in the
household—and thus the Lord's servant from infancy (see
116:16).

86:16 ⁿPs 116:16
86:17 ᵒS Ex 3:12;
Mt 24:3; S Jn 2:11
87:1 ᵖS Ps 48:1
87:2 ᑫPs 2:6
87:3 ʳS Ps 46:4
87:4 ˢS Job 9:13
ᵗS 2Sa 8:1; Ps 83:7
ᵘPs 45:12; Joel 3:4
ᵛIsa 19:25
87:6 ʷEx 32:32;
Ps 69:28; Isa 4:3;
Mal 3:16
87:7 ˣPs 149:3
ʸS Ps 36:9

and save the son of a woman
  who served you before me. ⁿ
¹⁷ Give me a sign ᵒ of your goodness,
  that my enemies may see it and be put to shame,
  for you, Lᴏʀᴅ, have helped me and comforted me.

PSALM 87

Of the Sons of Korah. A psalm. A song.

¹ He has founded his city on the holy mountain. ᵖ
² The Lᴏʀᴅ loves the gates of Zion ᑫ
  more than all the other dwellings of Jacob.

³ Glorious things are said of you,
  city of God: ᵃ ʳ
⁴ "I will record Rahab ᵇ ˢ and Babylon
  among those who acknowledge me—
Philistia ᵗ too, and Tyre ᵘ, along with Cush ᶜ—
  and will say, 'This one was born in Zion.' " ᵈ ᵛ
⁵ Indeed, of Zion it will be said,
  "This one and that one were born in her,
  and the Most High himself will establish her."
⁶ The Lᴏʀᴅ will write in the register ʷ of the peoples:
  "This one was born in Zion."

⁷ As they make music ˣ they will sing,
  "All my fountains ʸ are in you."

ᵃ 3 The Hebrew has *Selah* (a word of uncertain meaning) here and at the end of verse 6.   ᵇ 4 A poetic name for Egypt   ᶜ 4 That is, the upper Nile region   ᵈ 4 Or "I will record concerning those who acknowledge me: / 'This one was born in Zion.' / Hear this, Rahab and Babylon, / and you too, Philistia, Tyre and Cush."

86:17 *goodness.* Covenanted favors (see 27:13 and note). *may see it.* May see that you stand with me and help me (see 31:19 and note).

🄰 **Ps 87** A celebration of Zion as the "city of God" (v. 3), the special object of his love and the royal city of his kingdom (see introductions to Ps 46; 48; 76). According to the ancient and consistent interpretation of Jewish and Christian interpreters alike, this psalm stands in lonely isolation in the Psalter (but see 47:9) in that it foresees the ingathering of the nations into Zion as fellow citizens with Israel in the kingdom of God—after the manner of such prophetic visions as Isa 2:2–4; 19:19–25; 25:6; 45:14,22–24; 56:6–8; 60:3; 66:23; Da 7:14; Mic 4:1–3; Zec 8:23; 14:16. (Accordingly, some have assigned it to the time of Isaiah and Micah, while others have thought it to be postexilic.) So interpreted, this psalm stands in sharpest possible contrast to the other Zion songs of the Psalter (see Ps 46; 48; 76; 125; 129; 137). The key to its main thrust lies in v. 4. It may be that its historic interpretation has sprung from the failure of tradition to preserve memory of the Hebrew poetic device of interrupted syntax (which occurs elsewhere) and that the references to foreign nations should be read as vocatives (see TNIV text note on v. 4). With this reading, the psalm stands in thematic accord with the other Zion songs, celebrating God's special love for Zion—which is thrown into the teeth of Zion's historic enemies (see note on v. 4). Placed at the center of four prayers arising from deep crises—two of individuals (Ps 86; 88) and two of the community (Ps 85:89)—it offers reassurance that God will surely answer such prayers (see introduction to Ps 84–89).

87 title *Of the Sons of Korah.* See note on Ps 42 title. *song.* See note on Ps 30 title.

87:1 *He has founded his city.* The Lord himself has laid the foundations of Zion (see Isa 14:32) and of the temple as his royal house. *mountain.* The Hebrew for this word is plural, emphasizing the majesty of the holy mountain on which God's throne has been set (see 48:2; 121:1 and notes).

87:2 *loves ... more than.* As the city of his founding, his chosen seat of rule over his people, Zion is the Lord's most cherished city, even among the towns of Israel (see 9:11 and note; 78:68; 132:13–14). *Jacob.* A synonym for Israel (see Ge 32:28).

87:3 For *Selah*, see TNIV text note and note on 3:2.

87:4 *I will record ... This one was born in Zion.* God will list them in his royal register (see notes on 9:5; 51:1; 69:28) as those who are native (born) citizens of his royal city, having all the privileges and enjoying all the benefits and security of such citizenship. *Rahab.* Whereas elsewhere this name is applied to the mythical monster of the deep (see 89:10; see also notes on 32:6; Job 9:13), here the reference is to Egypt (see TNIV text note), as in Isa 30:7 (see note there); 51:9. The nations listed are representative of all Gentile peoples. As usually interpreted, the psalm here foresees a widespread conversion to the Lord from the peoples who from time immemorial had been hostile to him and to his kingdom (see Isa 19:21; 26:18 and note). But if the TNIV text note is correct (see also v. 5), the Lord is here portrayed as carefully recording the names of all his people, those who acknowledge him as their covenant Lord (Hos 6:3), so as to take them under his protection as the citizens of his royal city. Ominously he warns the nations (as in Isa 14:28–32) that he has carefully registered his people one and all and will hold the nations accountable for the harm they do to any one of them (see 105:15). *Philistia too.* See Zec 9:7 and note.

87:5 *This one and that one.* Wherever they may be dispersed among the nations. *Most High.* See note on Ge 14:19.

87:7 *All my fountains.* All that refreshes them is found in the city of God, a possible allusion to God's "river of delights" (36:8) "whose streams make glad the city of God" (46:4); see notes on those passages. Alternatively, "fountains" may be a metaphor for sources; the sense of the line would then be: We all spring from you. *my.* Communal use of the singular pronoun (see note on Ps 30 title).

PSALM 88

A song. A psalm of the Sons of Korah. For the director of music. According to mahalath leannoth.[a] A maskil[b] of Heman the Ezrahite.

[*1] LORD, you are the God who saves me;[z]
    day and night I cry out[a] to you.
[2] May my prayer come before you;
    turn your ear to my cry.

[3] I am overwhelmed with troubles[b]
    and my life draws near to death.[c]
[4] I am counted among those who go down to the pit;[d]
    I am like one without strength.[e]
[5] I am set apart with the dead,
    like the slain who lie in the grave,
    whom you remember no more,
    who are cut off[f] from your care.

[6] You have put me in the lowest pit,
    in the darkest depths.[g]
[7] Your wrath[h] lies heavily on me;
    you have overwhelmed me with all your waves.[c][i]
[8] You have taken from me my closest friends[j]
    and have made me repulsive to them.
    I am confined[k] and cannot escape;[l]
[9]   my eyes[m] are dim with grief.

I call[n] to you, LORD, every day;
    I spread out my hands[o] to you.
[10] Do you show your wonders to the dead?
    Do their spirits rise up and praise you?[p]

---

a Title: Possibly a tune, "The Suffering of Affliction"   b Title: Probably a literary or musical term
c 7 The Hebrew has *Selah* (a word of uncertain meaning) here and at the end of verse 10.

* 88:1-18 is numbered 88:2-19 in Hebrew texts.

88:1 z S Ps 51:14
a Ps 3:4; 22:2; Lk 18:7
88:3 b Ps 6:3; 25:17
c S Job 33:22
88:4 d S Ps 31:12
e Ps 18:1
88:5 f S Ps 31:22
88:6 g Ps 30:1;
S 69:15; La 3:55;
Jnh 2:3
88:7 h Ps 7:11
i S Ps 42:7
88:8 j S Job 19:13;
Ps 31:11 k Jer 32:2;
33:1 l S Job 3:23
88:9 m S Ps 38:10
n Ps 5:2 o Job 11:13;
Ps 143:6
88:10 p S Ps 6:5

A **Ps 88** A cry out of the depths, the prayer of one on the edge of death, whose whole life has been lived, as it were, in the near vicinity of the grave (see also Ps 90). So troubled have been his years that he seems to have known only the back of God's hand (God's "wrath," v. 7), and even those nearest him have withdrawn themselves as from one with a defiling skin disease (see v. 8). No expressions of hopeful expectation (as in most prayers of the Psalter; but see Ps 44; 89) burst from these lips; the last word speaks of darkness as "my closest friend." And yet the prayer begins, "LORD, you are the God who saves me." The psalm recalls the fact that although sometimes godly persons live lives of unremitting trouble (see 73:14) they can still grasp the hope that God is Savior (see also Ps 87 and introduction to Ps 84–89). Many early church leaders interpreted this psalm as a prayer of the suffering Christ (as they did Ps 22); for that reason it became part of the Good Friday liturgy.

Structurally, the prayer ends (vv. 13–18) as it began (vv. 1–5), each section with two Hebrew poetic lines of petition (vv. 1–2, 13–14) followed by four lines describing the psalmist's distress (vv. 3–5, 15–18). Between the beginning and the end are two stanzas of four lines each (vv. 6–9a, 9b–12). In the first of these the psalmist expresses his recognition that what has happened to him is God's doing. In the second he appeals to God to consider the consequences if he does not deliver the petitioner from death.

88 title The psalm bears a double title, perhaps representing two different traditions. *song.* See note on Ps 30 title. *of the Sons of Korah.* See note on Ps 42 title. *For the director of music.* See note on Ps 4 title. *According to.* See note on Ps 6 title. *maskil.* See note on Ps 32 title. *Heman.* See note on Ps 39 title. *Ezrahite.* The reference appears to be to Zerah, one of Judah's sons, who is recorded as having a Heman and an Ethan (see Ps 89 title) among his sons

(see 1Ch 2:6). If so, the title here represents a confusion in the tradition, arising from the similarity between these two Judahite names and those of two famous Korahite choir leaders, Heman and Ethan (Jeduthun; see note on Ps 39 title).

88:1–2 Opening appeal to the Lord as "the God who saves me."
88:3–5 Living on the brink of death. Whether the psalmist lies mortally ill or experiences some analogous trouble or peril cannot be known.
88:4 *pit.* See 28:1; 30:3,9; 143:7.
88:5 *remember no more.* From the perspective of this life, death cuts off from God's care; there is no remembering by God of the needy sufferer to rescue and restore (see 25:7; 74:2; 106:4). In his dark mood the author portrays his situation in bleakest colors (see note on 6:5).

A **88:6–9a** You, God, have done this! The psalmist knows no reason for it (see v. 14; cf. Ps 44), but he knows God's hand is in it (see Ru 1:20–21; Am 3:6). That his Savior-God shows him the face of wrath deepens his anguish and helplessness. But he does not try to resolve the dark enigma; he simply pleads his case—and it is to his Savior-God that he can appeal (see v. 1).
88:6 *lowest pit . . . darkest depths.* See note on 30:1.
88:7 *wrath.* See v. 16; see also note on 2:5. *all your waves.* See note on 32:6. For *Selah,* see TNIV text note and note on 3:2.
88:8 *my closest friends.* See v. 18 and note on 31:11–12.
88:9 *eyes are dim.* See note on 6:7.
88:9b–12 Appeal to God to help before the psalmist sinks into "the land of oblivion" (see note on v. 5).
88:10,12 *wonders.* God's saving acts in behalf of his people (see note on 9:1).
88:10 *rise up.* In the realm of the dead (not in the resurrection); see Isa 14:9. *praise you.* See 6:5; 30:9; 115:17 and notes.

88:11 *q* S Ps 30:9
88:13 *r* S Ps 30:2
s Ps 5:3; S 55:17
t Ps 119:147
88:14 *u* S Ps 43:2
v Ps 13:1
88:15 *w* Ps 129:1;
Jer 22:21; Eze 16:22;
Hos 2:15 *x* Ps 9:12
y Job 6:4; S 18:11
z 2Co 4:8
88:16 *a* Ps 7:11
b Job 6:4
88:17 *c* Ps 124:4
88:18 *d* ver 8;
Ps 38:11
89:1 *e* Ps 59:16
f S Ps 36:5; 40:10
89:2 *g* S Ps 36:5
89:4 *h* 2Sa 7:12-16;
1Ki 8:16; Ps 132:11-12;
Isa 9:7; Eze 37:24-
25; S Mt 1:1; S Lk 1:33
89:5 *i* S Ps 19:1

¹¹ Is your love declared in the grave,
  your faithfulness *q* in Destruction *a*?
¹² Are your wonders known in the place of darkness,
  or your righteous deeds in the land of oblivion?

¹³ But I cry to you for help, *r* Lᴏʀᴅ,
  in the morning *s* my prayer comes before you. *t*
¹⁴ Why, Lᴏʀᴅ, do you reject *u* me
  and hide your face *v* from me?

¹⁵ From my youth *w* I have suffered *x* and been close to death;
  I have borne your terrors *y* and am in despair. *z*
¹⁶ Your wrath *a* has swept over me;
  your terrors *b* have destroyed me.
¹⁷ All day long they surround me like a flood; *c*
  they have completely engulfed me.
¹⁸ You have taken from me friend *d* and neighbor—
  darkness is my closest friend.

PSALM 89

*A maskil *b* of Ethan the Ezrahite.*

*¹ I will sing *e* of the Lᴏʀᴅ's great love forever;
  with my mouth I will make your faithfulness known *f*
  through all generations.
² I will declare that your love stands firm forever,
  that you have established your faithfulness in heaven itself. *g*
³ You said, "I have made a covenant with my chosen one,
  I have sworn to David my servant,
⁴ 'I will establish your line forever
  and make your throne firm through all generations.' " *c h*

⁵ The heavens *i* praise your wonders, Lᴏʀᴅ,

---

a 11 Hebrew *Abaddon*   *b* Title: Probably a literary or musical term   *c* 4 The Hebrew has *Selah* (a word
of uncertain meaning) here and at the end of verses 37, 45 and 48.
* 89:1-52 is numbered 89:2-53 in Hebrew texts.

88:11 *love ... faithfulness.* That is, love-and-faithfulness (see note on 36:5; see also note on 3:7). *love.* See note on 6:4.
88:12 *righteous deeds.* See 71:24 and note.
88:13–14 Concluding prayer—with echoes of the initial petition in vv. 1–2.
88:13 *in the morning.* See 101:8 and note.
88:14 *Why ... ?* See note on 6:3. *hide your face.* See note on 13:1.
88:15–18 The psalmist has been no stranger to trouble; all his life he has suffered the terrors of God (cf. Ps 90).
88:17 *like a flood.* See v. 7; see also note on 32:6.

Ps 89 A prayer that mourns the downfall of the Davidic dynasty and pleads for its restoration. The bitter shock of that event (reflected in the sudden transition at v. 38) is almost unbearable—that God, the faithful and almighty One, has abandoned his anointed and made him the mockery of the nations, in seeming violation of his firm covenant with David—and it evokes from the psalmist a lament that borders on reproach (vv. 38–45). The event may have been the attack on Jerusalem by Nebuchadnezzar and the exile of King Jehoiachin in 597 B.C. (see 2Ki 24:8–17). Although like Ps 44 and 88 this prayer ends in unrelieved perplexity and lamentation over the deep crisis God's "rejection" has brought about (see v. 38; cf. 44:9; 88:14), in the arrangement of the Psalter it has been brought into relationship with the reassuring themes of Ps 84; 87 (see introduction to Ps 84–89).

As with Ps 44 (see introduction to that psalm), a massive foundation is laid for the prayer with which the psalm concludes. An introduction (vv. 1–4) sings of God's love and faithfulness (vv. 1–2) and his covenant with David (vv. 3–4). These two themes are then jubilantly expanded in order: vv. 5–18, God's love and faithfulness; vv. 19–37, his covenant with David. Suddenly jubilation turns to lament, and the psalmist recounts in detail how God has rejected his anointed (vv. 38–45). Thus he comes to his prayer, impatient and urgent, that God will remember once more his covenant with David (vv. 46–51). (Verse 52 concludes not the psalm but Book III of the Psalter.)
89 title *maskil.* See note on Ps 32 title. *Ethan.* Jeduthun (see note on Ps 39 title). The author was no doubt a Levite (perhaps a descendant of Jeduthun) who voiced this agonizing prayer as spokesman for the nation. *Ezrahite.* See note on Ps 88 title.
89:1–2 God's love and faithfulness celebrated.
89:1 *love ... faithfulness.* See vv. 2,33,49; that is, love-and-faithfulness (see v. 14); see note on 36:5. *love.* See vv. 2,14,24,28,33, 49; see also note on 6:4. It is God's love and faithfulness that appear to have failed in his rejection (see vv. 38–45) of the Davidic king. The author repeats each of these words precisely seven times (in v. 14 the Hebrew uses a different—but related—word for "faithfulness").

89:2 *in heaven itself.* God's love and faithfulness have been made sure in the highest seat of power and authority (see vv. 5–8).
89:3–4 God's covenant with David celebrated (see 2Sa 7:8–16).
89:3 *servant.* See vv. 20,39,50; here an official title (see note on 78:70).
89:4 For *Selah,* see TNIV text note and note on 3:2.

89:5–8 The Lord's faithfulness and awesome power set him apart among all the powers in the heavenly realm, and they acknowledge him with praise and reverence.

your faithfulness too, in the assembly[j] of the holy ones.
⁶ For who in the skies above can compare with the Lord?
  Who is like the Lord among the heavenly beings?[k]
⁷ In the council[l] of the holy ones[m] God is greatly feared;
  he is more awesome than all who surround him.[n]
⁸ Who is like you,[o] Lord God Almighty?[p]
  You, Lord, are mighty, and your faithfulness surrounds you.

⁹ You rule over the surging sea;
  when its waves mount up, you still them.[q]
¹⁰ You crushed Rahab[r] like one of the slain;
  with your strong arm you scattered[s] your enemies.
¹¹ The heavens are yours,[t] and yours also the earth;[u]
  you founded the world and all that is in it.[v]
¹² You created the north and the south;
  Tabor[w] and Hermon[x] sing for joy[y] at your name.
¹³ Your arm is endued with power;
  your hand is strong, your right hand exalted.[z]

¹⁴ Righteousness and justice are the foundation of your throne;[a]
  love and faithfulness go before you.[b]
¹⁵ Blessed are those who have learned to acclaim you,
  who walk[c] in the light[d] of your presence, Lord.
¹⁶ They rejoice in your name[e] all day long;
  they exult in your righteousness.
¹⁷ For you are their glory and strength,[f]
  and by your favor you exalt our horn.[a][g]
¹⁸ Indeed, our shield[b][h] belongs to the Lord,
  our king[i] to the Holy One of Israel.

¹⁹ Once you spoke in a vision,
  to your faithful people you said:
  "I have bestowed strength on a warrior;
  I have raised up a young man from among the people.
²⁰ I have found David[j] my servant;[k]
  with my sacred oil[l] I have anointed[m] him.
²¹ My hand will sustain him;
  surely my arm will strengthen him.[n]
²² No enemy will get the better of him;[o]
  no wicked person will oppress[p] him.
²³ I will crush his foes before him[q]
  and strike down his adversaries.[r]
²⁴ My faithful love will be with him,[s]

---

[a] 17 *Horn* here symbolizes strong one.   [b] 18 Or *sovereign*

**Cross references (right margin):**

89:5 [i] S Ps 1:5
89:6 [k] S Ge 1:26; S Ex 9:14; S Ps 18:31; 113:5
89:7 [l] Ps 111:1 [m] S Job 5:1 [n] Ps 47:2
89:8 [o] S Ps 71:19 [p] Isa 6:3
89:9 [q] S Ps 65:7
89:10 [r] S Job 9:13 [s] S Ps 59:11; S 68:1; 92:9
89:11 [t] S Dt 10:14; Ps 115:16 [u] 1Ch 29:11; S Ps 24:1 [v] S Ge 1:1
89:12 [w] S Jos 19:22 [x] S Dt 3:8; S 4:48 [y] Ps 98:8
89:13 [z] S Jos 4:24
89:14 [a] Ps 97:2 [b] Ps 85:10-11
89:15 [c] Ps 1:1 [d] Ps 44:3
89:16 [e] Ps 30:4; 105:3
89:17 [f] Ps 18:1 [g] ver 24; Ps 75:10; 92:10; 112:9; 148:14
89:18 [h] Ps 18:2 [i] Ps 47:9; Isa 16:5; 33:17,22
89:20 [j] Ac 13:22 [k] Ps 78:70 [l] S Ex 29:7; S 1Ki 1:39 [m] S 1Sa 2:35; S 2Sa 22:51
89:21 [n] ver 13; Ps 18:35
89:22 [o] S Jdg 3:15 [p] 2Sa 7:10
89:23 [q] Ps 18:40 [r] 2Sa 7:9
89:24 [s] S 2Sa 7:15

89:5 *The heavens.* All beings belonging to the divine realm in the heavens. *wonders.* God's mighty acts in creation and redemption (see note on 9:1). *assembly of the holy ones.* The divine council in heaven (see v. 7; see also note on 82:1).
89:6 *heavenly beings.* Lit. "sons of god(s)" (see 29:1 and note).
89:8 *Lord ... Almighty.* See note on 1Sa 1:3. *your faithfulness surrounds you.* It also surrounds this stanza (see v. 5).
89:9–13 The Lord's power as Creator—and creation's joy in him.

89:9–10 Poetic imagery borrowed from ancient Near Eastern myths of creation, here celebrating God's power in ordering the primeval chaotic waters so that the creation order could be established (see Ge 1:6–10; see also notes on 65:6–7; 74:13–14).
89:10 *Rahab.* Mythical monster of the deep (see notes on 32:6; 87:4), probably another name for Leviathan (see 74:14; 104:26). The last half of this verse is probably echoed in Lk 1:51.
89:12 *the north and the south.* Reference may be to two mountains, here parallel to Tabor and Hermon: "Mount North" (Zaphon; see 48:2 and note) and Mount Amana (see SS 4:8). *Tabor.* See note on Jdg 4:6. *Hermon.* See note on Dt 3:8. *sing for joy.* See note on 65:13. *name.* See vv. 16,24; see also note on 5:11.

89:14–18 The Lord's righteousness and faithfulness in his rule in behalf of his people—and their joy in him.
89:14 Righteousness and justice are the foundation stones of God's throne (see Pr 16:12; 25:5; 29:14). Love and faithfulness are personified as throne attendants that herald his royal movements (see note on 23:6). *Righteousness.* See v. 16; see also note on 4:1.
89:17 *horn.* King (see TNIV text note; see also v. 18).
89:18 *Holy One of Israel.* See 71:22; 78:41; 2Ki 19:22 and note.

89:19–29 The Lord's election of David to be his regent over his people, and his everlasting covenant with him. The thought is developed by couplets: (1) introduction (v. 19); (2) I have anointed David as my servant and will sustain him (vv. 20–21); (3) I will crush all his foes (vv. 22–23); (4) I will extend his realm (vv. 24–25); (5) I will make him first among the kings (vv. 26–27); (6) I will cause his dynasty to endure forever (vv. 28–29)—a promise fulfilled in the eternal reign of Jesus Christ (see Jn 12:34).
89:19 *vision.* Reference is to the revelation to Samuel (see 1Sa 16:12) and/or to Nathan (see 2Sa 7:4–16). *faithful people.* See note on 4:3.

89:25 ᵗ Ps 72:8
89:26 ᵘ S 2Sa 7:14;
S Jer 3:4; Heb 1:5
ᵛ S Ps 62:2
ʷ S 2Sa 22:47
89:27 ˣ S Col 1:18
ʸ S Nu 24:7 ᶻ Ps 2:6;
Rev 1:5; 19:16
89:28 ᵃ ver 33-34;
Isa 55:3
89:29 ᵇ ver 4,36
89:32 ᶜ 2Sa 7:14
89:33 ᵈ S 2Sa 7:15
89:34 ᵉ S Nu 23:19
89:36 ᶠ ver 4
89:37 ᵍ Jer 33:20-21
89:38 ʰ 1Ch 28:9;
Ps 44:9; 78:59
89:39 ⁱ La 5:16
89:40 ʲ S Ps 80:12
ᵏ Isa 22:5; La 2:2
89:41 ˡ S Jdg 2:14
ᵐ S Ps 44:13
89:42 ⁿ Ps 13:2;
80:6
89:43 ᵒ Ps 44:10
89:45 ᵖ S Ps 39:5
ᵍ Ps 44:15; 109:29
89:46 ʳ Ps 79:5
89:47 ˢ S Ge 47:9;
S Job 7:7; Ps 39:5;
1Pe 1:24

and through my name his horn ᵃ will be exalted.

²⁵ I will set his hand over the sea,
    his right hand over the rivers. ᵗ
²⁶ He will call out to me, 'You are my Father, ᵘ
    my God, the Rock ᵛ my Savior.' ʷ
²⁷ And I will appoint him to be my firstborn, ˣ
    the most exalted ʸ of the kings ᶻ of the earth.
²⁸ I will maintain my love to him forever,
    and my covenant with him will never fail. ᵃ
²⁹ I will establish his line forever,
    his throne as long as the heavens endure. ᵇ

³⁰ "If his sons forsake my law
    and do not follow my statutes,
³¹ if they violate my decrees
    and fail to keep my commands,
³² I will punish their sin with the rod,
    their iniquity with flogging; ᶜ
³³ but I will not take my love from him, ᵈ
    nor will I ever betray my faithfulness.
³⁴ I will not violate my covenant
    or alter what my lips have uttered. ᵉ
³⁵ Once for all, I have sworn by my holiness—
    and I will not lie to David—
³⁶ that his line will continue forever
    and his throne endure before me like the sun; ᶠ
³⁷ it will be established forever like the moon,
    the faithful witness in the sky." ᵍ

³⁸ But you have rejected, ʰ you have spurned,
    you have been very angry with your anointed one.
³⁹ You have renounced the covenant with your servant
    and have defiled his crown in the dust. ⁱ
⁴⁰ You have broken through all his walls ʲ
    and reduced his strongholds ᵏ to ruins.
⁴¹ All who pass by have plundered ˡ him;
    he has become the scorn of his neighbors. ᵐ
⁴² You have exalted the right hand of his foes;
    you have made all his enemies rejoice. ⁿ
⁴³ Indeed, you have turned back the edge of his sword
    and have not supported him in battle. ᵒ
⁴⁴ You have put an end to his splendor
    and cast his throne to the ground.
⁴⁵ You have cut short ᵖ the days of his youth;
    you have covered him with a mantle of shame. ᵍ

⁴⁶ How long, LORD? Will you hide yourself forever?
    How long will your wrath burn like fire? ʳ
⁴⁷ Remember how fleeting is my life. ˢ
    For what futility you have created all humanity!

ᵃ 24 Horn here symbolizes strength.

89:25 *sea . . . rivers.* David's rule will reach from the Mediterranean Sea to the Euphrates River (see 72:8; 80:11 and note on Ex 23:31). But the author uses imagery that underscores the fact that, as his royal "son" (see v. 26) and regent, David's rule will be a reflection of God's (see vv. 9–10 and notes; also compare v. 23 with v. 10).
89:27 *firstborn.* The royal son of highest privilege and position in the kingdom of God (see 2:7–12; 45:6–9; 72:8–11; 110), thus "the most exalted of the kings of the earth" (see Rev 1:5). So the words may speak of universal rule—ultimately fulfilled in Christ.
89:29 *as long as the heavens endure.* See vv. 36–37.
89:30–37 The Lord's covenant with David and his dynasty (see note on 2Sa 7:1–29; see also chart, p. 20) was everlasting (see vv. 28–29) and unconditional—though if any of

his royal descendants is unfaithful he will individually suffer under God's rod (to the detriment of the entire nation).
89:38–45 God's present rejection of David's son, and all its fearful consequences—the undoing of all that had been promised and assured by covenant (see especially vv. 19–29). To fully appreciate the poignancy of this lament, cf. Ps 18.
89:46–51 The prayer, an appeal—in spite of all—to God's faithfulness to his covenant with David. In this dark hour that remains the psalmist's hope.
89:46 *How long . . . ?* See note on 6:3. *wrath.* See note on 2:5.
89:47 *how fleeting is my life.* See 37:20; 39:4–6 and notes. The shortness of human life adds urgency to the prayer. *futility.* Because humans have limited powers and are subject to death,

89:48 ᵗ S Ge 5:24;
Ps 22:29
89:50 ᵘ Ps 69:19
89:51 ᵛ Ps 74:10
89:52 ʷ S Ps 41:13;
S 72:19
90:1 ˣ S Dt 33:27;
Eph 2:22; Rev 21:3
90:2 ʸ S Job 15:7
ᶻ Isa 9:6; 57:15
ᵃ S Ge 21:33;
S Job 10:5; Ps 102:24-
27; Pr 8:23-26
90:3 ᵇ S Ge 2:7;
S Job 7:21; 34:15;
1Co 15:47

48 Who can live and not see death,
   or who can escape the power of the grave? ᵗ
49 Lord, where is your former great love,
   which in your faithfulness you swore to David?
50 Remember, Lord, how your servant has ᵃ been mocked, ᵘ
   how I bear in my heart the taunts of all the nations,
51 the taunts with which your enemies, LORD, have mocked,
   with which they have mocked every step of your anointed one. ᵛ

52 Praise be to the LORD forever!
   Amen and Amen. ʷ

BOOK IV

Psalms 90–106

PSALM 90

A prayer of Moses the man of God.

1 Lord, you have been our dwelling place ˣ
   throughout all generations.
2 Before the mountains were born ʸ
   or you brought forth the whole world,
   from everlasting to everlasting ᶻ you are God. ᵃ

3 You turn people back to dust,
   saying, "Return to dust, you mortals." ᵇ
4 A thousand years in your sight
   are like a day that has just gone by,

ᵃ 50 Or *your servants have*

---

they are dependent on God's involvement in the world (see 60:11; 90:5–6 and note; 108:12; 127:1–2; see also Job 7:1–3; Ecc 1:2 and note).

89:49 *former great love.* The love referred to in v. 1.

89:50 *Remember.* See v. 47.

89:52 A brief doxology with which the final editors concluded Book III of the Psalter (see note on 41:13).

Ps 90–100 A series of 11 psalms arranged within the frame "you have been our dwelling place throughout all generations" (90:1) and "his faithfulness continues through all generations" (100:5)—a series that begins with prayer and ends with praise. The first two of these psalms (90–91) are thematically connected (point and counterpoint); the next three (92–94) form a trilogy that serves as a transition to the final thematic cluster (95–99). At the very middle, Ps 95 anticipates the four following psalms and adds a warning for the celebrants of Yahweh's reign that echoes the warning of Moses in Dt 6:13–18. Evidently the editors of the Psalter intended readers of this group of psalms to hear echoes of the voice of Moses as interceder (Ps 90) and as admonisher (95:8–11), through which ministries (shared also by Aaron and Samuel) Israel had been blessed under the reign of the Great King, Yahweh (see 99:6–8). See further the introductions to the several psalms of this group.

Ps 90 A prayer to the everlasting God to have compassion on his servants, who through the ages have known him to be their safe haven (v. 1; see also 91:9) but who also painfully experience his wrath because of their sin and his sentence of death that cuts short their lives—a plea that through this long night of his displeasure God will teach them true wisdom (see v. 12 and note) and, in the morning after, bless them in equal measure with expressions of his love so that joy may yet fill their days and the days of their children and their daily labors may be blessed. This psalm has many links with Ps 39.

So that the melancholy depiction of the human state found here might not stand alone, the editors of the Psalter have followed it immediately with a psalm that speaks in counterpoint of the happy condition of those who dwell "in the shelter of the Most High" (91:1) and "make the Most High [their] dwelling" (91:9; see also 92:13). To isolate Ps 90 from this context is to distort its intended function in the Psalter collection. See also Ps 103.

Two stanzas descriptive of the human condition under God's aggrieved anger (vv. 3–6, 7–10) are framed by two couplets (vv. 1–2, 11–12) that, by their implicit contrasts, highlight the major polarities over which the intervening stanzas brood: 1. The Lord, who has ever been our "dwelling place" (v. 1), has shown us the power of his wrath (v. 7). 2. God is the Everlasting One (v. 2), while we must come to terms with the small number of our days (v. 12). These reflections lead to the prayer with which the psalm concludes (vv. 13–17).

90 title *A prayer.* See note on Ps 17 title. *Moses.* Tradition has assigned this psalm to Moses—perhaps because (1) it shares some language with Dt 32–33; (2) as an intercessory prayer it fits well on the lips of Moses, the great intercessor for Israel (see Ex 32:11–13; 34:9; Nu 14:13–19; Dt 9:25–29; Ps 106:23; Jer 15:1; see also Ps 99:6); and (3) elsewhere only Moses asks God directly to "relent" from his anger toward Israel (v. 13; see Ex 32:12). *man of God.* A phrase normally applied in the OT to prophets (see note on 1Sa 2:27), including Moses (see, e.g., Jos 14:6).

90:1 *dwelling place.* See 91:9. The Hebrew for this phrase is translated "refuge" in 71:3. Here and in 91:9 it has the connotation of "home" or "safe haven."

90:3–6 Human beings live under God's sentence of death—"dust . . . to dust" (Ge 3:19).

90:4–5 *A . . . Yet.* Though for God 1,000 years are like a mere watch in the night (three–four hours), he cuts human life short like new grass that shows itself at dawn's light but is withered away by the hot Canaanite sun before evening falls.

90:4 *A thousand years . . . are like a day.* Cf. 2Pe 3:8 and note. *watch in the night.* See note on Jdg 7:19.

90:4 *c* S Job 10:5;
2Pe 3:8
90:5 *d* S Ge 19:15
90:6 *e* Isa 40:6-8;
Mt 6:30; Jas 1:10
90:8 *f* S Ps 19:12;
2Co 4:2; Eph 5:12
g S Heb 4:13
90:9 *h* Ps 78:33
90:10 *i* Isa 23:15,17;
Jer 25:11 / 2Sa 19:35
k S Job 5:7
l S Job 20:8; S 34:15
90:11 *m* Ps 7:11
n Ps 76:7
90:12 *o* Ps 39:4;
139:16; Pr 16:9; 20:24
p Dt 32:29
90:13 *q* Ps 6:3
r S Dt 32:36
90:14 *s* Ps 103:5;
107:9; 145:16,19
t S Ps 77:8; 143:8
u S Ps 5:11 *v* Ps 31:7
90:16 *w* Ps 44:1;
Hab 3:2
90:17 *x* Isa 26:12
91:1 *y* S Ex 33:22
z Ps 63:7; Isa 49:2;
La 4:20

or like a watch in the night. *c*

[5] Yet you sweep people away *d* in the sleep of death—
 they are like the new grass of the morning:
[6] In the morning it springs up new,
 but by evening it is dry and withered. *e*

[7] We are consumed by your anger
 and terrified by your indignation.
[8] You have set our iniquities before you,
 our secret sins *f* in the light of your presence. *g*
[9] All our days pass away under your wrath;
 we finish our years with a moan. *h*
[10] Our days may come to seventy years, *i*
 or eighty, *j* if our strength endures;
 yet the best of them are but trouble and sorrow, *k*
 for they quickly pass, and we fly away. *l*
[11] If only we knew the power of your anger!
 Your wrath *m* is as great as the fear that is your due. *n*
[12] Teach us to number our days, *o*
 that we may gain a heart of wisdom. *p*

[13] Relent, LORD! How long *q* will it be?
 Have compassion on your servants. *r*
[14] Satisfy *s* us in the morning with your unfailing love, *t*
 that we may sing for joy *u* and be glad all our days. *v*
[15] Make us glad for as many days as you have afflicted us,
 for as many years as we have seen trouble.
[16] May your deeds be shown to your servants,
 your splendor to their children. *w*

[17] May the favor *a* of the Lord our God rest on us;
 establish the work of our hands for us—
 yes, establish the work of our hands. *x*

PSALM 91

[1] Whoever dwells in the shelter *y* of the Most High
 will rest in the shadow *z* of the Almighty. *b*

a 17 Or *beauty*   *b 1* Hebrew *Shaddai*

90:5–6 The shortness of human life frequently occupied the thoughts of Biblical writers (see 37:2,20,36; 39:5,11; 62:9; 78:39; 89:47; 102:3,11; 103:15–16; 109:23; 144:4; Job 8:9; 14:1–2; Ecc 6:12; Isa 40:6–8; Jas 1:10–11; 1Pe 1:24–25).
90:7–10 Even life's short span is filled with trouble, as God ferrets out every sin and makes the sinner feel his righteous anger.
90:7 *anger . . . indignation.* See vv. 9,11; see also note on 2:5.
90:8 *light of your presence.* The holy light of God that illumines the hidden corners of the heart and exposes its dark secrets.
90:10 *eighty.* Hebrew poetic convention called for 80 following 70 in parallel construction (see note on Am 1:3). *the best of them.* Reference is either to the best of the days or to what people prize most in their years—these are all soured by trouble and sorrow (or disappointment).
[A] **90:11–12** *If only we knew . . . Teach us.* No one has taken the measure of God's anger. But everyone ought to know the measure of their (few) days or they will play the arrogant fool, with no thought of their mortality or of their accountability to God (see Ps 10; 30:6; 49; 73:4–12; see also Dt 8).
90:11 *fear that is your due.* See note on Ge 20:11.
90:12 *gain a heart of wisdom.* God's discipline humbles arrogant sinners and teaches them true wisdom (see 39; 94:12; Pr 3:1–12; Heb 12:7–11; cf. Ps 92:6–7; 94:8–10).
90:13–17 Prayer for God to be compassionate and restore the joys of life. The good hope with which such a prayer may be uttered comes to expression in Ps 91; 92; see also 94:12–14.
90:13 *Relent.* Lit. "Turn" (cf. v. 3). *How long . . . ?* See note on 6:3.

[A] **90:14** *in the morning.* Let there be for us a dawning of your love to relieve this long, dark night of your anger (see introduction to Ps 57). The final answer to this prayer comes with the resurrection (see Ro 5:2–5; 8:18; 2Co 4:16–18). *unfailing love.* See note on 6:4.
90:16 *deeds . . . splendor.* That is, deeds-of-splendor (see 111:3; see also note on 3:7). For a fuller description of such deeds, see the whole of Ps 111. *to their children.* As to past generations (v. 1).
90:17 *favor.* See TNIV text note; see also 27:4 and note. *establish.* As you only have been our security in the world (see v. 1), so also make our labors to be effective and enduring—though we are so transient.

[A] **Ps 91** A glowing testimony to the security of those who trust in God—set beside Ps 90 as a counterpoint to the dismal depiction of the human condition found there (see introduction to that psalm). It was probably written by one of the temple personnel (a priest or Levite) as a word of assurance to godly worshipers. Because the "you" of vv. 3–13 applies to any who "make the Most High your dwelling" (v. 9; see 90:1), the devil applied vv. 11–12 to Jesus (see Mt 4:6; Lk 4:10–11).
 Structurally, the psalm is divided into two halves of eight verses each, with the opening couplet of the second half (vv. 9–10) echoing the theme of vv. 1–2. In the first half, the godly are assured of security from four threats (vv. 5–6)—though thousands fall (v. 7). In the second half, they are assured of triumphing over four menacing beasts (v. 13). The oracle of vv. 14–16 offers climactic assurance.

2 They say of the LORD, "He is my refuge *a* and my fortress, *b*
  my God, in whom I trust."

3 Surely he will save you
  from the fowler's snare *c*
  and from the deadly pestilence. *d*
4 He will cover you with his feathers,
  and under his wings you will find refuge; *e*
  his faithfulness will be your shield *f* and rampart.
5 You will not fear *g* the terror of night,
  nor the arrow that flies by day,
6 nor the pestilence that stalks in the darkness,
  nor the plague that destroys at midday.
7 A thousand may fall at your side,
  ten thousand at your right hand,
  but it will not come near you.
8 You will only observe with your eyes
  and see the punishment of the wicked. *h*

9 If you say, "The LORD is my refuge,"
  and you make the Most High your dwelling,
10 no harm *i* will overtake you,
  no disaster will come near your tent.
11 For he will command his angels *j* concerning you
  to guard you in all your ways; *k*
12 they will lift you up in their hands,
  so that you will not strike your foot against a stone. *l*
13 You will tread on the lion and the cobra;
  you will trample the great lion and the serpent. *m*

14 "Because they love me," says the LORD, "I will rescue them;
  I will protect them, for they acknowledge my name.
15 They will call on me, and I will answer them;
  I will be with them in trouble,
  I will deliver them and honor them. *n*
16 With long life *o* I will satisfy them
  and show them my salvation. *p*"

PSALM 92

A psalm. A song. For the Sabbath day.

*1 It is good to praise the LORD
  and make music *q* to your name, *r* O Most High, *s*

* 92:1-15 is numbered 92:2-16 in Hebrew texts.

91:2 *a* ver 9;
S 2Sa 22:3; Ps 9:9
b S 2Sa 22:2
91:3 *c* Ps 124:7;
Pr 6:5 *d* 1Ki 8:37
91:4 *e* S Ru 2:12;
Ps 17:8 *f* S Dt 32:10;
Ps 35:2; Isa 27:3;
31:5; Zec 12:8
91:5 *g* S Job 5:21
91:8 *h* Ps 37:34;
S 58:10
91:10 *i* Pr 12:21
91:11 *j* S Ge 32:1;
Heb 1:14 *k* Ps 34:7
91:12 *l* Mt 4:6*;
Lk 4:10-11*
91:13 *m* Da 6:22;
Lk 10:19
91:15 *n* S 1Sa 2:30;
Jn 12:26
91:16 *o* Dt 6:2;
S Ps 21:4 *p* S Ps 50:23
92:1 *q* S Ps 27:6
r S Ps 9:2; 147:1
s Ps 135:3

91:1 *shelter.* The temple (as in 27:5; 31:20; see also 23:6; 27:4), where the godly find safety under the protective wings of the Lord (see v. 4; 61:4). *Most High.* See v. 9; see also note on Ge 14:19. *shadow.* See note on 17:8. *Almighty.* See TNIV text note and note on Ge 17:1.
91:3 *fowler's snare.* Metaphor for danger from human enemies (see 124:7; see also note on 9:15). *pestilence.* Danger to life from disease. These two threats are further elaborated in vv. 5–6.
91:4 *with his feathers . . . wings.* See note on 17:8.
91:5 *terror.* As in 64:1 ("threat"), reference is to attack by enemies; thus it is paired with "arrow." These two references to threats from war are arrayed alongside "pestilence" and "plague" (v. 6), two references to mortal diseases that often reached epidemic proportions. *night . . . day.* At whatever time of day or night the threat may come, you will be kept safe—the time references are not specific to their respective phrases (see also v. 6).
91:7 *ten thousand.* Hebrew poetic convention called for 10,000 following 1,000 in parallel construction (see notes on 90:10; 1Sa 18:7; Am 1:3).
91:9 *dwelling.* See 90:1 and note.
91:11–12 Quoted by Satan in Mt 4:6; Lk 4:10–11.

91:11 *his angels.* See note on 34:7.
91:12 *against a stone.* On the stony trails of Canaan (see Pr 3:23).
91:13 *lion . . . cobra . . . great lion . . . serpent.* These double references to lions and to poisonous snakes balance the double references of vv. 5–6 and complete the illustrative roster of mortal threats (see Am 5:19).
91:14–16 Employing the form of a prophetic oracle, the author (see introduction) supports his testimony by assuring the godly that it is confirmed by all the promises of God to those who truly love and trust him.
91:14 *protect them.* Lit. "raise them to a high, secure place." *acknowledge my name.* See 9:10 ("know your name") and note. *my name.* See note on 5:11.
91:15 *They will call . . . I will answer.* See note on 118:5.
91:16 *With long life.* The climactic counterpoint to Ps 90.
Ps 92 A joyful celebration of the righteous rule of God. Its testimony to the prosperity of the righteous, "planted in the house of the LORD" (v. 13), links it thematically with Ps 91 (see introduction to that psalm), while its joy over God's righteous reign relates it to the cluster of psalms that follow (Ps 93–100; see especially Ps 94). There are, in fact, reasons to be-

92:2 ʳS Ps 55:17
92:3 ᵘS Ps 71:22
ᵛS 1Sa 10:5;
S Ne 12:27; S Ps 33:2;
81:2
92:4 ʷS Ps 5:11;
27:6 ˣS Ps 8:6; 111:7;
143:5
92:5 ʸS Job 36:24;
Rev 15:3 ᶻPs 40:5;
139:17; Isa 28:29;
31:2; Ro 11:33
92:6 ᵃS Ps 73:22
92:7 ᵇS Ps 37:2
92:9 ᶜS Ps 45:5
ᵈS Ps 68:1; S 89:10
92:10 ᵉS Ps 89:17
ᶠS Ps 29:6 ᵍS Ps 23:5
92:11 ʰS Ps 54:7;
91:8
92:12 ⁱS Ps 72:7
ʲS Ps 1:3; 52:8;
Jer 17:8; Hos 14:6
92:13 ᵏPs 135:2
92:14 ˡS Ps 1:3;
S Jn 15:2
92:15 ᵐS Job 34:10
93:1 ⁿS 1Ch 16:31;
S Ps 97:1
ᵒS Job 40:10;
S Ps 21:5 ᵖS Ps 65:6

² proclaiming your love in the morning ᵗ
  and your faithfulness at night,
³ to the music of the ten-stringed lyre ᵘ
  and the melody of the harp. ᵛ

⁴ For you make me glad by your deeds, LORD;
  I sing for joy ʷ at what your hands have done. ˣ
⁵ How great are your works, ʸ LORD,
  how profound your thoughts! ᶻ
⁶ Senseless people ᵃ do not know,
  fools do not understand,
⁷ that though the wicked spring up like grass
  and all evildoers flourish,
  they will be destroyed forever. ᵇ

⁸ But you, LORD, are forever exalted.

⁹ For surely your enemies ᶜ, LORD,
  surely your enemies will perish;
  all evildoers will be scattered. ᵈ
¹⁰ You have exalted my horn ᵃ ᵉ like that of a wild ox; ᶠ
  fine oils ᵍ have been poured on me.
¹¹ My eyes have seen the defeat of my adversaries;
  my ears have heard the rout of my wicked foes. ʰ

¹² The righteous will flourish ⁱ like a palm tree,
  they will grow like a cedar of Lebanon; ʲ
¹³ planted in the house of the LORD,
  they will flourish in the courts of our God. ᵏ
¹⁴ They will still bear fruit ˡ in old age,
  they will stay fresh and green,
¹⁵ proclaiming, "The LORD is upright;
  he is my Rock, and there is no wickedness in him. ᵐ"

PSALM 93

¹ The LORD reigns, ⁿ he is robed in majesty; ᵒ
  the LORD is robed in majesty and armed with strength; ᵖ

ᵃ 10 *Horn* here symbolizes strength.

---

lieve that the editors of the Psalter brought together Ps 92–94 as a trilogy that serves as a bridge between Ps 90–91 and 95–99 (see introductions to Ps 93; 94). Notably, God's name Yahweh ("LORD") occurs seven times in this psalm. Verses 10–11 suggest that the author may have been one of Israel's kings.

Following the introduction on praise (vv. 1–3), vv. 4–5 offer the motivation for the praise ("me," "I"), which is picked up again in vv. 10–11 ("my," "me," "My," "my," "my," "my"). Verses 6–9 expound the folly and destiny of evildoers, while vv. 12–15 expound the prosperity of the righteous. Notice also the link between v. 7 and v. 13. The TNIV text offers a different analysis of the psalm's structure.

A **92 title** *A song.* See note on Ps 30 title. *For the Sabbath day.* In the postexilic liturgy of the temple, this psalm came to be sung at the time of the morning sacrifice on the Sabbath. (The rest of the weekly schedule was: first day, Ps 24; second day, Ps 48; third day, Ps 82; fourth day, Ps 94; fifth day, Ps 81; sixth day, Ps 93.)

92:1–3 Hymnic introduction.
92:1 *LORD... Most High.* That is, LORD Most High (see 7:17; see also note on 3:7). *name.* See note on 5:11. *Most High.* A link with Ps 91 (see vv. 1,9 of that psalm). For the name, see note on Ge 14:19.
92:2 *love... faithfulness.* That is, love-and-faithfulness (see note on 36:5; see also note on 3:7). *love.* See note on 6:4. *morning... night.* Continuously.
92:3 *lyre... harp.* See note on 57:8. *harp.* See note on Ge 31:27.
92:4–5 Joy over God's saving acts (see vv. 10–11).
92:5 *profound.* Lit. "deep." *your thoughts.* As shown by your deeds.

92:6–9 The fatal folly of evildoers (contrast vv. 12–15).
C **92:6** *Senseless... fools.* See TNIV text note on 14:1; see also 49:10—and note especially 94:8–11. They do not know that the Lord rules righteously. They see the wicked flourishing but do not see the Lord or foresee the end he has appointed for them. The author thus characterizes his "wicked foes" (v. 11), whom the Lord has routed.
92:7 A condensed statement of what is expounded more fully in Ps 73 (see also 37:2; 62:9; 90:5–6 and notes).
92:8 *exalted forever.* God's eternal exaltation assures the destruction of his enemies.
92:9 *enemies.* Here the evildoers, referred to also in v. 7.
A **92:10–11** Joy over God's favors (see vv. 4–5): God has made him triumphant (see 89:24) and anointed him with "the oil of joy" (45:7; see also 23:5) by giving him victory over all his enemies.
92:12–15 The secure prosperity of the righteous (contrast vv. 6–9).
92:13 *planted in the house of the LORD.* Though the wicked may "spring up like grass," their end is sure (see v. 7). But the righteous are planted in a secure place (see Ps 91) and so retain the vigor of youth into old age, rejoicing in God's just discrimination (see v. 15). *courts.* Of the temple (see 84:2,10; 2Ki 21:5; 23:11–12).
92:15 *upright... Rock... no wickedness in him.* See Dt 32:4 and note.

A **Ps 93** A hymn to the eternal, universal and invincible reign of the Lord, a theme it shares with Ps 47; 95–99.

indeed, the world is established, �q firm and secure. ʳ
² Your throne was established ˢ long ago;
you are from all eternity. ᵗ

³ The seas ᵘ have lifted up, Lᴏʀᴅ,
the seas have lifted up their voice; ᵛ
the seas have lifted up their pounding waves. ʷ
⁴ Mightier than the thunder ˣ of the great waters,
mightier than the breakers ʸ of the sea—
the Lᴏʀᴅ on high is mighty. ᶻ

⁵ Your statutes, Lᴏʀᴅ, stand firm;
holiness ᵃ adorns your house ᵇ
for endless days.

PSALM 94

¹ The Lᴏʀᴅ is a God who avenges. ᶜ
O God who avenges, shine forth. ᵈ
² Rise up, ᵉ Judge ᶠ of the earth;
pay back ᵍ to the proud what they deserve.
³ How long, Lᴏʀᴅ, will the wicked,
how long will the wicked be jubilant? ʰ

⁴ They pour out arrogant ⁱ words;
all the evildoers are full of boasting. ʲ
⁵ They crush your people, ᵏ Lᴏʀᴅ;
they oppress your inheritance. ˡ
⁶ They slay the widow ᵐ and the foreigner;
they murder the fatherless. ⁿ
⁷ They say, "The Lᴏʀᴅ does not see; ᵒ
the God of Jacob ᵖ takes no notice."

93:1 �q Ps 24:2;
78:69; 119:90
ʳ 1Ch 16:30; Ps 96:10
93:2 ˢ S 2Sa 7:16
ᵗ S Ge 21:33
93:3 ᵘ Ps 96:11;
98:7; Isa 5:30; 17:12-
13; Jer 6:23
ᵛ S Ps 46:3 ʷ Job 9:8;
Ps 107:25,29;
Isa 51:15; Jer 31:35;
Hab 3:10
93:4 ˣ Ps 65:7;
Jer 6:23 ʸ S Ps 18:4;
Jnh 1:15 ᶻ S Ne 9:32;
S Job 9:4
93:5 ᵃ Ps 29:2; 96:9
ᵇ Ps 5:7; 23:6
94:1 ᶜ S Ge 4:24;
Ro 12:19 ᵈ S Dt 33:2;
Ps 80:1
94:2 ᵉ S Nu 10:35
ᶠ S Ge 18:25;
Heb 12:23; S Jas 5:9
ᵍ S Ps 31:23
94:3 ʰ Ps 13:2
94:4 ⁱ Jer 43:2
ʲ S Ps 52:1
94:5 ᵏ Ps 44:2; 74:8;
Isa 3:15; Jer 8:21
ˡ Ps 28:9
94:6 ᵐ S Dt 10:18;
S Isa 1:17 ⁿ Dt 24:19
94:7 ᵒ S Job 22:14
ᵖ S Ge 24:12

Together these hymns offer a majestic confession of faith in and hope for the kingdom of God on earth. They were probably composed for the liturgy of a high religious festival in which the kingship of the Lord—over the cosmic order, over the nations and in a special sense over Israel—was annually celebrated (see introduction to Ps 47). And implicitly, where not explicitly, the Lord's kingship is hailed in contrast to the claims of all other gods; he is "the great King above all gods" (95:3). These hymns may all have been composed by temple personnel and spoken by them in the liturgy. They probably date from the preexilic era. Ps 93 appears to have been separated from Ps 95–99 to serve as a thematic pivot between Ps 92 and 94 (as Ps 47 was used as a pivot between Ps 46 and 48). It celebrates Yahweh's secure cosmic rule that grounds his righteous and effective rule over human affairs—which is the joy (Ps 92) and the hope (Ps 94) of those who rely on him for protection against the assaults of the godless fools who live by violence. Structurally, the psalm has two short stanzas (vv. 1–2,3–4) and a conclusion (v. 5).

A **93:1–2** The Lord's reign, by which the creation order has been and will be secure throughout the ages, is from eternity (see Ge 1:1). Though Israel as a nation has come late on the scene, her God has been King since before the creation of the world.

A **93:1** *The Lᴏʀᴅ reigns.* The ultimate truth, and first article, in Israel's creed (see 96:10; 97:1; 99:1; see also Zec 14:9 and note).

93:3–4 Both at and since his founding of the world, the Lord has shown himself to be mightier than all the forces of disorder that threaten his kingdom.

93:3 *seas.* Reference is to the primeval chaotic waters, tamed and assigned a place by the Lord's creative word (see 33:7; 104:7–9; Ge 1:6–10; Job 38:8–11). Implicitly they symbolize all that opposes the coming of the Lord's kingdom (see 65:6–7; 74:13–14 and notes).

93:4 The thunder of the chaotic waters is no match for the thunder of the Lord's ordering word (see 104:7).

A **93:5** *statutes.* He whose indisputable rule has made the world secure has given his people life directives that are stable and reliable (see 19:7)—and that they must honor (see 95:8–11). *your house.* His earthly temple—but also the heavenly. *for endless days.* Qualifies both clauses.

Ps 94 An appeal to the Lord, as "Judge of the earth" (v. 2), to redress the wrongs perpetrated against the weak by arrogant and wicked persons who occupy seats of power. The psalm has links with Ps 92 (see introductions to Ps 92; 93), but is the voice of the oppressed within Israel, seeking redress at God's throne for injustices done them by the "fools" smugly established in the power structures of the nation. Thus it is unique within the Ps 90–100 group of psalms and stands here as representative of the many cries of the oppressed found in Books I–III of the Psalter. Following a three-verse introduction, the thought advances regularly in five stanzas of four verses each, with the main thematic shift coming at v. 12.

94:1–3 Initial appeal to God, the Judge.

94:1 *avenges.* Redresses wrongs (see Dt 32:35,41 and note on 32:35). To avenge is the function of a king in his role as chief executive of the realm. Thus a direct conceptual link with Ps 47; 93; 95–99 is established at the outset. *shine forth.* Cf. notes on 50:2; 80:1.

94:2 *the proud.* See vv. 4–7 for a description of them.

94:3 *How long . . . ?* See note on 6:3.

94:4–7 Indictment of the wicked.

C **94:4** *arrogant words . . . boasting.* For similar expressions of the arrogance of the wicked, see 10:2–11 and notes.

94:5 *your people . . . your inheritance.* Those among them who are vulnerable (see v. 6).

94:7 *They say.* See note on 3:2. *Jacob.* A synonym for Israel (see Ge 32:28).

94:8 q S Dt 32:6;
S Ps 73:22
94:9 r Ex 4:11;
Pr 20:12
94:10 s S Ps 39:11
t S Ex 35:34;
Job 35:11; Isa 28:26
94:11 u Ps 139:2;
Pr 15:26; S Mt 9:4
v 1Co 3:20*
94:12 w S Job 5:17;
1Co 11:32; Heb 12:5
x S Dt 8:3;
S 1Sa 12:23
94:13 y S Ps 86:7
z S Ps 7:15; S 55:23
94:14 a S Dt 31:6;
Ps 37:28; Ro 11:2
94:15 b Ps 97:2
c Ps 7:10; 11:2; S 36:10
94:16 d Nu 10:35;
Ps 17:13; Isa 14:22
e S Ps 59:2
94:17 f Ps 124:2
g S Ps 31:17
94:18 h S Dt 32:35;
S Job 12:5
94:19 i Ecc 11:10
j S Job 6:10
94:20 k Jer 22:30;
36:30 l S Ps 58:2
94:21 m S Ps 56:6
n Ps 106:38; Pr 17:15,
26; 28:21; Isa 5:20,
23; Mt 27:4
o S Ge 18:23
94:22 p Ps 61:2
q S 2Sa 22:3;
S Ps 18:2
94:23 r S Ex 32:34;
S Ps 54:5 s Ps 9:5;
37:38; 145:20
95:1 t Ps 34:11; 80:2
u S Ps 5:11 v Ps 81:1;
Isa 44:23; Zep 3:14
w S 2Sa 22:47

8 Take notice, you senseless ones q among the people;
you fools, when will you become wise?
9 Does he who fashioned the ear not hear?
Does he who formed the eye not see? r
10 Does he who disciplines s nations not punish?
Does he who teaches t human beings lack knowledge?
11 The LORD knows all human plans; u
he knows that they are futile. v

12 Blessed are those you discipline, w LORD,
those you teach x from your law;
13 you grant them relief from days of trouble, y
till a pit z is dug for the wicked.
14 For the LORD will not reject his people; a
he will never forsake his inheritance.
15 Judgment will again be founded on righteousness, b
and all the upright in heart c will follow it.

16 Who will rise up d for me against the wicked?
Who will take a stand for me against evildoers? e
17 Unless the LORD had given me help, f
I would soon have dwelt in the silence of death. g
18 When I said, "My foot is slipping," h
your unfailing love, LORD, supported me.
19 When anxiety i was great within me,
your consolation j brought me joy.

20 Can a corrupt throne k be allied with you—
a throne that brings on misery by its decrees? l
21 The wicked band together m against the righteous
and condemn the innocent n to death. o
22 But the LORD has become my fortress,
and my God the rock p in whom I take refuge. q
23 He will repay r them for their sins
and destroy s them for their wickedness;
the LORD our God will destroy them.

PSALM 95

1 Come, t let us sing for joy u to the LORD;
let us shout aloud v to the Rock w of our salvation.

94:8–11 Warning to the wicked—those "senseless ... fools" (see 92:6–9; see also TNIV text note on 14:1).
94:10 *disciplines.* Keeps them in line by means of punishment (see Lev 26:18; Jer 31:18). *teaches.* Gives human beings some knowledge of the creation order (see Isa 28:26).
94:11 *The LORD knows.* Contrary to their foolish supposition (see v. 7).
94:12–15 Here the focus shifts from the arrogance and folly of the wicked to the happy state of those who count themselves among the Lord's people and who live under his discipline and rely on his royal protection.
94:12 *Blessed.* See note on 1:1. *discipline ... teach.* See v. 10. Here the author speaks of God's correcting and teaching his people in the ways of his law.
94:14 *people ... inheritance.* See v. 5. The Lord will not abandon the powerless among his people to the injustice of their oppressors. Paul may be echoing this verse in Ro 11:1–2.
94:15 However this difficult verse is to be translated, the author appears to say that God's righteous rule will restore justice for those who have been wrongly treated while being themselves innocent—described as "the upright in heart" (see also v. 21). *heart.* See note on 4:7.
94:16–19 The Lord is the only sure court of appeal.
94:17 *silence of death.* See note on 30:1. Without God's help the wicked would have silenced the psalmist in the grave, but

now it is the wicked for whom the pit will be dug (see v. 13).
94:18 *When I said.* When feeling about to be overwhelmed by the wicked (see note on 38:16). *love.* See note on 6:4.
94:20–23 Confidence that the Lord's justice will prevail.
94:20 *corrupt throne.* A seat of authority that works mischief. The author speaks of injustice at the center of power.
94:21 *righteous.* Here referring to those who have not wronged anyone—i.e., "the innocent" (see note on v. 15). For the basic concept, see note on 1:5.
Ps 95 A call to worship the Lord, spoken by a priest or Levite to the assembled Israelites at the temple. (See introduction to Ps 93.) Placed at the center of its group (Ps 90–100) and at the beginning of a series of psalms celebrating the universal reign of Israel's God (Ps 95–99), Ps 95 contains a sharp reminder that Israel's sense of security under Yahweh's rule— from which spring both her prayers (as in Ps 90; 94) and her praise (as in Ps 91–93; 95–100)—is warranted only if she shows herself to be Yahweh's loyal and obedient servant. Its function in context is similar to that of Ps 81 (see introduction to Ps 79–83).
The psalm is composed of two parts: (1) a call to praise the Lord of all the earth (vv. 1–5); (2) a call to acknowledge by submissive attitude and obedient heart the Lord's kingship over his people (vv. 6–11). Each part also has two subdivisions, the latter of which forms the climax. Cf. the structure of Ps 96.

[2] Let us come before him [x] with thanksgiving [y]
  and extol him with music [z] and song.

[3] For the LORD is the great God, [a]
  the great King [b] above all gods. [c]
[4] In his hand are the depths of the earth, [d]
  and the mountain peaks belong to him.
[5] The sea is his, for he made it,
  and his hands formed the dry land. [e]

[6] Come, let us bow down [f] in worship, [g]
  let us kneel [h] before the LORD our Maker; [i]
[7] for he is our God
  and we are the people of his pasture, [j]
  the flock under his care.

Today, if only you would hear his voice,
[8] "Do not harden your hearts [k] as you did at Meribah, [a] [l]
  as you did that day at Massah [b] in the wilderness, [m]
[9] where your ancestors tested [n] me;
  they tried me, though they had seen what I did.
[10] For forty years [o] I was angry with that generation;
  I said, 'They are a people whose hearts go astray, [p]
  and they have not known my ways.' [q]
[11] So I declared on oath [r] in my anger,
  'They shall never enter my rest.' " [s]

PSALM 96

96:1–13pp — 1Ch 16:23–33

[1] Sing to the LORD [t] a new song; [u]
  sing to the LORD, all the earth.

---

[a] *8 Meribah means quarreling.*   [b] *8 Massah means testing.*

95:2 [x] Ps 100:2; Mic 6:6 [y] S Ps 42:4 [z] Ps 81:2; S Eph 5:19
95:3 [a] Ps 48:1; 86:10; 145:3; 147:5 [b] S Ps 47:2 [c] Ps 96:4; 97:9
95:4 [d] S Ps 63:9
95:5 [e] S Ge 1:9; Ps 146:6
95:6 [f] S 2Sa 12:16; Php 2:10 [g] S Ps 22:29 [h] 2Ch 6:13 [i] Ps 100:3; 149:2; Isa 17:7; 54:5; Da 6:10-11; Hos 8:14
95:7 [j] S Ps 74:1
95:8 [k] Mk 10:5; Heb 3:8 [l] S Ex 17:7; S Dt 33:8; Heb 3:15*; 4:7 [m] S Ps 78:40
95:9 [n] S Nu 14:22; 1Co 10:9
95:10 [o] S Ex 16:35; S Nu 14:34; Ac 7:36; Heb 3:17 [p] Ps 58:3; 119:67,176; Pr 12:26; 16:29; Isa 53:6; Jer 31:19; 50:6; Eze 34:6 [q] S Dt 8:6
95:11 [r] S Nu 14:23 [s] Dt 1:35; Heb 3:7-11*; 4:3*
96:1 [t] Ps 30:4 [u] Ps 33:3; S 40:3; 98:1; 144:9; 149:1; Isa 42:10; S Rev 5:9

95:1–2 The call to praise.
95:1 *Rock of our salvation.* See note on 18:2.
95:3–5 Why Israel is to praise the Lord—because he is above all gods, and there is no corner of the universe that is not in his hand. The ancient pagan world had different gods for different peoples, different geographical areas, different cosmic regions (heaven, earth, netherworld) and different aspects of life (e.g., war, fertility, crafts).
95:4–5 *depths . . . mountain peaks . . . sea . . . dry land.* All the world—the extremes and all that lies between and all that is in them.
95:6–11 The exhortation to submit to the Lord with obedient hearts—a bent knee is not enough. For a NT reflection on these verses in the light of the advent of Christ, see Heb 3:7—4:13.
95:6–7 The call to confess submission to the Lord by kneeling before him.
95:6 *our Maker.* Both as Creator of all things (see Ge 1) and as Israel's Redeemer, he has "made" them what they are: the people of the Lord in the earth (see Isa 45:9–13; 51:12–16).
95:7 *people of his pasture.* See 100:3; Jer 23:1; Eze 34:17–23. Since kings were commonly called the "shepherds" of their people (see notes on 23:1; 74:1), their realms could be referred to as their "pastures" (see 23:2; Jer 25:36; 49:20; 50:45). *if only you would hear his voice.* In the liturgy of the religious festival, possibly in some such manner as Ps 50 and/or 78. The concern expressed in what follows echoes that of Moses in Dt 6:16–19.
95:8 *Meribah . . . Massah.* See TNIV text notes. The leader of the liturgy reminds Israel of times of her rebellion in the desert (see Ex 17:7; Nu 20:13).
95:9 *me.* Official representatives of the Lord, when speaking for him, could shift to first person (see 50:5,7–15; see also note on

Ge 16:7). *had seen what I did.* In Egypt and at the Red Sea—and his provision of food in the desert (see Ex 16; see also Nu 14:11).
95:10 *forty years.* The climax of Israel's rebellion came when God's people faithlessly refused to undertake the conquest of Canaan and considered returning to Egypt (see Nu 14:1–4). It was then that God condemned them to a 40-year stay in the desert (see Nu 14:34). *angry.* See note on 2:5. *that generation.* The (adult) Israelites who came out of Egypt and covenanted with God at Sinai (see Nu 32:13). *They are a people . . . my ways.* A restatement of the Lord's word in Nu 14:11. *hearts.* See note on 4:7. *my ways.* See 25:4 and note.
95:11 *on oath.* See Nu 14:28; Dt 1:34–35. *never enter my rest.* The language of Nu 14:30 is "not one of you will enter the land," but since the promised land was also called the place where God will give his people "rest" (Jos 1:13,15; see Ex 33:14; Dt 12:10; 25:19), the two statements are equivalent. *rest.* A rich concept indicating the Israelites' possession of a place with God in the earth where they are secure from all external threats and internal calamities (see Dt 3:20; 1Ki 5:4 and notes).
Ps 96 A call to all nations to praise the Lord as the only God and to proclaim the glory of his reign throughout the world—an OT anticipation of the world mission of the NT people of God (see Mt 28:16–20). (See introductions to Ps 93; 95.) This psalm appears in slightly altered form in 1Ch 16:23–33. Here in the Psalter it is paired with Ps 98, with which it shares much in form, language and theme (compare especially their opening and closing stanzas). Each of these in turn is followed by a hymn that celebrates Yahweh's reign (cf. 97:1; 99:1) and its special benefits for Israel (cf. 97:8–12; 99:4–9). This arrangement suggests that Ps 97 has been linked with 96 and Ps 99 with 98 to form a pair of thematic couplets—introduced by Ps 95.
The psalm is composed of two parts: (1) The first begins with a threefold call to all nations to "sing to the LORD" in praise of his

96:2 ᵛ S Ps 68:4
ʷ Ps 27:1; 71:15
96:3 ˣ Ps 8:1
ʸ S Ps 71:17; Rev 15:3
96:4 ᶻ S Ps 48:1
ᵃ S Dt 28:58;
S 1Ch 16:25; Ps 89:7
ᵇ S Ps 95:3
96:5 ᶜ S Lev 19:4
ᵈ S Ge 1:1; S 2Ch 2:12
96:6 ᵉ S Ps 21:5
ᶠ Ps 29:1; 89:17
96:7 ᵍ Ps 29:1
ʰ Ps 22:27
96:8 ⁱ Ps 45:12;
S 51:19; 72:10
ʲ Ps 65:4; 84:10;
92:13; 100:4
96:9 ᵏ Ex 23:25;
Jnh 1:9 ˡ S Ps 93:5
ᵐ S Ex 15:14; Ps 114:7
ⁿ Ps 33:8
96:10 ᵒ Ps 97:1
ᵖ Ps 24:2; 78:69;
119:90 �q S Ps 93:1
ʳ Ps 58:11 ˢ Ps 67:4;
98:9
96:11 ᵗ S Rev 12:12
ᵘ Ps 97:1; Isa 49:13
96:12 ᵛ Isa 44:23;
55:12; Eze 17:24
ʷ Ps 65:13
96:13 ˣ Rev 19:11
ʸ Ps 7:11; Ac 17:31
ᶻ Ps 86:11

² Sing to the LORD, praise his name;ᵛ
  proclaim his salvation ʷ day after day.
³ Declare his glory ˣ among the nations,
  his marvelous deeds ʸ among all peoples.

⁴ For great is the LORD and most worthy of praise;ᶻ
  he is to be feared ᵃ above all gods. ᵇ
⁵ For all the gods of the nations are idols, ᶜ
  but the LORD made the heavens. ᵈ
⁶ Splendor and majesty ᵉ are before him;
  strength and glory ᶠ are in his sanctuary.

⁷ Ascribe to the LORD, ᵍ all you families of nations, ʰ
  ascribe to the LORD glory and strength.
⁸ Ascribe to the LORD the glory due his name;
  bring an offering ⁱ and come into his courts.ʲ
⁹ Worship the LORD ᵏ in the splendor of his ᵃ holiness; ˡ
  tremble ᵐ before him, all the earth. ⁿ
¹⁰ Say among the nations, "The LORD reigns. ᵒ"
  The world is firmly established, ᵖ it cannot be moved; q
  he will judge ʳ the peoples with equity. ˢ

¹¹ Let the heavens rejoice, ᵗ let the earth be glad; ᵘ
  let the sea resound, and all that is in it.
¹² Let the fields be jubilant, and everything in them;
  let all the trees of the forest ᵛ sing for joy. ʷ
¹³ Let all creation rejoice before the LORD, for he comes,
  he comes to judge ˣ the earth.
  He will judge the world in righteousness ʸ
  and the peoples in his faithfulness. ᶻ

ᵃ 9 Or LORD with the splendor of

"name" (vv. 1–6); (2) the second begins with a threefold call to all nations to "ascribe to the LORD glory … the glory due his name" (vv. 7–13). Each part has two subdivisions, the last of which forms the climax to the whole psalm. Cf. the structure of Ps 95.

A **96:1–3** The call to all the earth to sing the praise of the Lord among the nations. Triple repetition ("Sing … sing … Sing") was a common feature in OT liturgical calls to worship (see vv. 7–9 and note; see also 103:20–22; 118:2–4; 135:1; 136:1–3).
96:1 *new song.* See note on 33:3. *all the earth.* See v. 9; or "all the land," in which case the call is addressed to all Israel. However, the worldwide perspective of this psalm (see especially v. 7) suggests that here the psalmist has in view broader horizons (see 97:1; 100:1 and note; 117:1; see also note on 9:1).
96:2 *name.* See v. 8; see also note on 5:11. *proclaim his salvation.* Proclaim as good news (see 40:9 and note) the Lord's saving acts in Israel's behalf (see 3:8; see also 85:9).
96:3 *glory.* See note on 85:9. *marvelous deeds.* See note on 71:16–17.
A **96:4–6** Why "all the earth" (v. 1) is to praise the Lord: He alone is God (see Ps 115).
96:4 *feared.* See note on Ge 20:11.
96:5 *made the heavens.* As the Maker of the heavenly realm, in pagan eyes the abode of the gods, the Lord is greater than all the gods (see 97:7).
96:6 *Splendor and majesty … strength and glory.* Two pairs of divine attributes personified as throne attendants whose presence before the Lord heralds the exalted nature of the one, universal King. For similar personifications, see 23:6 and note. *glory.* The Hebrew for this word here connotes radiant beauty.
96:7–9 The call to all nations to worship the Lord (see 29:1–2 and note). The two half-sentences of 29:2 have been expanded in this psalm.

96:8 *courts.* Of the temple (see 84:2,10; 2Ki 21:5; 23:11–12).
96:9 *splendor of his holiness.* See note on 29:2. *tremble.* In reverent awe, equivalent to "fear" (see v. 4).
96:10–13 The call to all nations to proclaim among the nations the righteous reign of the Lord.
A **96:10** *The LORD reigns.* See 93:1 and note. *The world … with equity.* In OT perspective, the world order is one, embracing both its physical and moral aspects because both have been established by God as aspects of his one kingdom and both are upheld by his one rule. Therefore God's rule over creation and over human affairs (also his acts of creation and redemption) is often spoken of in one breath, and righteousness, faithfulness and love are equally ascribable to both. And since the creation order is secure in its goodness (see Ge 1), it often serves in OT poetry (as it does here) as a manifest assurance that God's rule over human affairs will also be "with equity," "in righteousness" and "in … faithfulness" (v. 13; see also 9:7–8; 11:3; 33:4–11; 36:5–9; 57:10; 58:11; 65:6–7; 71:19; 74:13–14, 16–17; 75:2; 82:5; 93:3–4; 98:9; 99:4; 119:89–91 and notes). *will judge.* See v. 13 and note.
A **96:11–12** Because God's kingdom is one (see v. 10 and note), all his creatures will rejoice when God's rule over humankind brings righteousness to full expression in his cosmic kingdom (see note on 65:13; see also 97:7–9). For the present state of the creation as it awaits the fullness of redemption, see Ro 8:21–22 and notes.
A **96:13** *comes … comes … will judge.* Because God reigns over all things and is the Lord of history, Israel lived in hope (as the prophets announced) of the "coming" of God—his future acts by which he would decisively deal with all wickedness and establish his righteousness in the earth. *righteousness.* See note on 4:1.

PSALM 97

¹ The Lord reigns,ᵃ let the earth be glad;ᵇ
    let the distant shoresᶜ rejoice.
² Cloudsᵈ and thick darknessᵉ surround him;
    righteousness and justice are the foundation of his throne. ᶠ
³ Fireᵍ goes beforeʰ him
    and consumesⁱ his foes on every side.
⁴ His lightningʲ lights up the world;
    the earthᵏ sees and trembles. ˡ
⁵ The mountains meltᵐ like waxⁿ before the Lord,
    before the Lord of all the earth. ᵒ
⁶ The heavens proclaim his righteousness,ᵖ
    and all peoples see his glory. �q

⁷ All who worship imagesʳ are put to shame, ˢ
    those who boast in idolsᵗ—
    worship him, ᵘ all you gods! ᵛ

⁸ Zion hears and rejoices
    and the villages of Judah are gladʷ
    because of your judgments, ˣ Lord.
⁹ For you, Lord, are the Most Highʸ over all the earth; ᶻ
    you are exaltedᵃ far above all gods.
¹⁰ Let those who love the Lord hate evil, ᵇ
    for he guardsᶜ the lives of his faithful onesᵈ
    and deliversᵉ them from the hand of the wicked. ᶠ
¹¹ Light shinesᵃ ᵍ on the righteousʰ
    and joy on the upright in heart. ⁱ
¹² Rejoice in the Lord, ʲ you who are righteous,
    and praise his holy name. ᵏ

ᵃ 11 One Hebrew manuscript and ancient versions (see also 112:4); most Hebrew manuscripts *Light is sown*

97:1 ᵃ Ex 15:18; Ps 93:1; 96:10; 99:1; Isa 24:23; 52:7 ᵇ S Ps 96:11 ᶜ S Est 10:1
97:2 ᵈ S Job 22:14 ᵉ S Ex 19:9 ᶠ Ps 89:14
97:3 ᵍ S Isa 9:19; Da 7:10; Joel 1:19; 2:3 ʰ Hab 3:5 ⁱ S 2Sa 22:9
97:4 ʲ S Job 36:30 ᵏ S 2Sa 22:8 ˡ Ps 18:7; 104:32; S Rev 6:12
97:5 ᵐ S Ps 46:2,6 ⁿ S Ps 22:14 ᵒ S Jos 3:11
97:6 ᵖ Ps 50:6; 98:2 q S Ps 19:1
97:7 ʳ S Lev 26:1 ˢ Isa 42:17; Jer 10:14 ᵗ Dt 5:8 ᵘ Heb 1:6 ᵛ Ex 12:12; Ps 16:4
97:8 ʷ S Ps 9:2 ˣ Ps 48:11
97:9 ʸ Ps 7:8 ᶻ S Job 34:29 ᵃ S Ps 47:9
97:10 ᵇ S Job 28:28; Am 5:15; Ro 12:9 ᶜ Ps 145:20 ᵈ Pr 31:23; 37:28; Pr 2:8 ᵉ S Ps 34:7; Da 3:28; 6:16 ᶠ Ps 37:40; Jer 15:21; 20:13
97:11 ᵍ S Job 22:28 ʰ Ps 11:5 ⁱ Ps 7:10
97:12 ʲ S Job 22:19; Ps 104:34; Isa 41:16; Php 4:4 ᵏ S Ex 3:15; S Ps 99:3

Ps 97 A joyful celebration of the Lord's righteous reign over all the earth (see introductions to Ps 93; 95), with special attention to the benefits of the Lord's reign enjoyed by Israel (see introduction to Ps 96). The psalm's two main divisions (vv. 1–6,8–12 —closely balanced, having 42 and 43 Hebrew words, respectively) are joined by a centered verse (v. 7; see note on 6:6) that serves as a counterpoint to the main theme. The opening verses of the two main divisions are thematically linked: v. 1, "be glad … rejoice"; v. 8, "rejoices … are glad"— in reverse order, a frequent stylistic device in OT poetry. The first major division is framed by references to "earth" (v. 1) and "the heavens" (v. 6), the second by references to "Zion … the villages of Judah" (v. 8) and the "righteous" (v. 12).

97:1–6 A testimony to the nations—that they too have seen God's majesty displayed (vv. 2–6) and ought to rejoice with Israel that the Lord reigns supreme.
97:1 *The Lord reigns.* See 93:1 and note. *earth.* See 96:1; 99:1; 117:1; see also note on 9:1. *distant shores.* Even distant lands reached by the far-ranging ships that sail the seas (see 1Ki 9:26–28; 10:22; Isa 60:9; Jnh 1:3).
97:2–6 The Lord's majestic glory revealed in the sky's awesome displays, especially in the thunderstorm (see 18:7–15 and note; see also introduction to Ps 29).
97:2 *Clouds and thick darkness.* The dark storm clouds that hide the sun and cast a veil across the sky are dramatic visual reminders that the fierce heat and brilliance (also metaphors) of God's naked glory must be veiled from creaturely eyes (see Ex 19:9; 1Ki 8:12). Thus also a curtain closed off the Most Holy Place in the tabernacle and temple (see Ex 26:33; 2Ch 3:14), veiling in darkness. *righteousness.* See v. 6; see also note on 4:1. *foundation of his throne.* God rules by his power (see 66:7), but his reign is founded on righteousness and justice,

which also the heavens proclaim (see v. 6 and note). That a throne was established by righteousness and justice was proverbial in Israel (see Pr 16:32; 25:5; 29:14; cf. Ps 9:7–8; 103:6,19 and notes).
97:3 *Fire.* Manifested in the storm cloud's lightning bolts (see v. 4), fire often signified God's judicial wrath (see, e.g., 21:9; 50:3; 83:14; Dt 4:24; 9:3; 32:22; 1Ki 19:12; Isa 10:17; 30:27,30; see also note on La 1:13).
97:4 *earth.* Here the land realm (the continents) personified.
97:6 *proclaim his righteousness.* The stable order of the heaven's vast array "speaks" (see 19:1–4); it declares that God's reign similarly upholds the moral order (see note on 96:10). *all peoples see.* Verses 2–6 have spoken of general revelation (cf. 19:1–6).

97:7 The center verse (see note on 6:6) and counterpoint of the psalm: joy to all who acknowledge the Lord; shame and disgrace to those who trust in false gods. *worship him.* With biting irony the psalm calls on all the gods that people foolishly worship to bow in worship before the Lord (see v. 9; see also 29:1 and note).

97:8–12 A declaration of Zion's joy that the Lord reigns (vv. 8–9), and a reminder that only those who hate evil have real cause to rejoice in his righteous rule (vv. 10–12).
97:8 *Zion hears.* That "the Lord reigns" (v. 1) in "righteousness" (v. 6). *judgments.* The executive and judicial acts of the Lord who reigns (v. 1) over all human affairs (see 105:7; Isa 26:9), especially his saving acts in Israel's behalf (see 48:11; 105:5; Dt 33:21).
97:9 *Most High.* See note on Ge 14:19.
97:10 *faithful ones.* See note on 4:3.
97:11 *Light.* See 27:1 and note; see also 36:9. *righteous.* See v. 12; see also note on 1:5. *heart.* See note on 4:7.
97:12 *name.* See note on 30:4.

98:1 *l* Ps 30:4
m S Ps 96:1 *n* Ex 15:1;
Ps 96:3; Isa 12:5;
Lk 1:51 *o* S Ex 15:6
p S Jos 4:24; Job 40:9;
Isa 51:9; 52:10; 53:1;
63:5 *q* S Ps 44:3;
Isa 59:16
98:2 *r* Isa 52:10;
Lk 3:6 *s* S Ps 97:6
t S Ps 67:2
98:3 *u* S 1Ch 16:15
v S Ge 49:10;
S Ps 48:10
w S Ps 50:23
98:4 *x* Ps 20:5;
Isa 12:6; 44:23; 52:9;
54:1; 55:12
98:5 *y* Ps 33:2; 92:3;
147:7 *z* Isa 51:3
98:6 *a* S Nu 10:2;
2 Sa 6:15
b S Ex 19:13 *c* Ps 20:5;
100:1; Isa 12:6
d Ps 2:6; 47:7
98:7 *e* S Ps 93:3
f S Ps 24:1
98:8 *g* S 2Ki 11:12
h Ps 148:9; Isa 44:23;
55:12
98:9 *i* S Ps 96:10
99:1 *j* S 1Ch 16:31;
S Ps 97:1 *k* S Ex 15:14;
S 1Ch 16:30
l S 2Sa 6:2
m S Ex 25:22

PSALM 98

A psalm.

[1] Sing to the LORD *l* a new song, *m*
　　for he has done marvelous things; *n*
　his right hand *o* and his holy arm *p*
　　have worked salvation *q* for him.
[2] The LORD has made his salvation known *r*
　　and revealed his righteousness *s* to the nations. *t*
[3] He has remembered *u* his love
　　and his faithfulness to the house of Israel;
　all the ends of the earth *v* have seen
　　the salvation of our God. *w*

[4] Shout for joy *x* to the LORD, all the earth,
　　burst into jubilant song with music;
[5] make music to the LORD with the harp, *y*
　　with the harp and the sound of singing, *z*
[6] with trumpets *a* and the blast of the ram's horn *b*—
　　shout for joy *c* before the LORD, the King. *d*

[7] Let the sea *e* resound, and everything in it,
　　the world, and all who live in it. *f*
[8] Let the rivers clap their hands, *g*
　　let the mountains *h* sing together for joy;
[9] let them sing before the LORD,
　　for he comes to judge the earth.
　He will judge the world in righteousness
　　and the peoples with equity. *i*

PSALM 99

[1] The LORD reigns, *j*
　　let the nations tremble; *k*
　he sits enthroned *l* between the cherubim, *m*
　　let the earth shake.

Ps 98 A call to celebrate with joy the righteous reign of the Lord (see introductions to Ps 93; 95). Its beginning and end echo Ps 96, with which it has been paired (see introduction to Ps 96). The three stanzas progressively extend the call to ever wider circles: (1) the worshiping congregation at the temple; (2) all the peoples of the earth; (3) the whole creation. The first stanza recalls God's revelation of his righteousness (v. 2) in the past; the last stanza speaks confidently of his coming rule "in righteousness" (v. 9); the middle stanza is enclosed by the jubilant cry "Shout for joy" (vv. 4,6).

98:1–3 The call to celebrate in song God's saving acts in behalf of his people.
98:1 *new song.* See note on 33:3. *marvelous things.* See note on 9:1 ("wonderful deeds").
98:2 *made ... known ... revealed ... to the nations.* God's saving acts in behalf of his people are also his self-revelation to the nations; in this sense God is his own evangelist (see 77:14 and note on 46:10; see also Isa 52:10). *salvation ... righteousness.* God's saving acts reveal his righteousness (see notes on 4:1; 71:24).
98:3 *love ... faithfulness.* That is, love-and-faithfulness (see note on 36:5; see also note on 3:7). This compound expression often sums up God's covenant commitment to his people (see note on 6:4).
98:4–6 The call to all the earth to join in the celebration.
98:4 See 100:1. *all the earth.* The peoples of the earth (see 96:1 and note; see also 99:1).
98:5 *harp.* See note on Ge 31:27.
98:6 *trumpets.* The special long, straight trumpets of the sanctuary (referred to only here in Psalms; see notes on Nu 10:2–3, 10). *ram's horn.* The more common trumpet (referred to also in

47:5; 81:3; 150:3; see note on Joel 2:1).
98:7–9 The call to the whole creation to celebrate (see note on 96:11–12).
98:7 *sea ... world.* The two great regions of creaturely life.
98:8 *rivers ... mountains.* From the rivers to the mountains, let every feature of the whole earth clap and sing (see note on 65:13).
98:9 *comes to judge.* See 96:13 and note. Israel in faith lived between the past (see vv. 1–3) and the future righteous (saving) acts of God. *righteousness ... equity.* See 96:10 and note.
Ps 99 A hymn celebrating the Lord as the great and holy King in Zion—with special emphasis on the benefits of the Lord's reign for Israel, a feature it shares with Ps 97 (see introduction to Ps 96). In developing his theme, the poet makes striking use of the symbolic significance (completeness) of the number seven: Seven times he speaks of the "LORD," and seven times he refers to him by means of independent personal pronouns (Hebrew). (See introduction to Ps 93.)
　The form is symmetrical, with four stanzas of three Hebrew poetic lines each and two main divisions (marked by a refrain) that are closely balanced, having 42 and 41 Hebrew words, respectively—a formal feature it shares with Ps 97 (see introduction to that psalm). The lesser refrain, "he is holy" (vv. 3,5, and expanded in v. 9), probably reflects a traditional, threefold liturgical rubric (see Isa 6:3; Rev 4:8; see also Ps 96:1–3,7–9 and notes for further evidence of a liturgical penchant for triple repetition). The second half of the psalm develops the theme introduced in the second stanza.

99:1–3 The God enthroned in Zion is ruler over all the nations—let them acknowledge him.

² Great is the Lord ⁿ in Zion; ᵒ
⠀⠀he is exalted ᵖ over all the nations.
³ Let them praise �q your great and awesome name ʳ—
⠀⠀he is holy. ˢ

⁴ The King ᵗ is mighty, he loves justice ᵘ—
⠀⠀you have established equity; ᵛ
⠀in Jacob you have done
⠀⠀what is just and right. ʷ
⁵ Exalt ˣ the Lord our God
⠀⠀and worship at his footstool;
⠀⠀he is holy.

⁶ Moses ʸ and Aaron ᶻ were among his priests,
⠀⠀Samuel ᵃ was among those who called on his name;
⠀they called on the Lord
⠀⠀and he answered ᵇ them.
⁷ He spoke to them from the pillar of cloud; ᶜ
⠀⠀they kept his statutes and the decrees he gave them.

⁸ Lord our God,
⠀⠀you answered them;
⠀you were to Israel a forgiving God, ᵈ
⠀⠀though you punished ᵉ their misdeeds. ᵃ
⁹ Exalt the Lord our God
⠀⠀and worship at his holy mountain,
⠀⠀for the Lord our God is holy.

PSALM 100

A psalm. For giving grateful praise.

¹ Shout for joy ᶠ to the Lord, all the earth.
²⠀⠀Worship the Lord ᵍ with gladness;
⠀⠀come before him ʰ with joyful songs.

ᵃ 8 Or *God, / an avenger of the wrongs done to them*

99:2 ⁿ S Ps 48:1
ᵒ Ps 2:6 ᵖ Ex 15:1;
Ps 46:10; 97:9; 113:4;
148:13
99:3 q Ps 30:4;
33:21; 97:12; 103:1;
106:47; 111:9; 145:21;
148:5 ʳ Ps 76:1
ˢ Ex 15:11;
S Lev 11:44; Rev 4:8
99:4 ᵗ Ps 2:6
ᵘ S 1Ki 10:9 ᵛ Ps 98:9
ʷ S Ge 18:19; Rev 15:3
99:5 ˣ S Ex 15:2
99:6 ʸ S Ex 24:6
ᶻ S Ex 28:1 ᵃ 1Sa 7:5
ᵇ Ps 4:3; 91:15
99:7 ᶜ S Ex 13:21;
S 19:9; S Nu 11:25
99:8 ᵈ S Ex 22:27;
S Nu 14:20
ᵉ S Lev 26:18
100:1 ᶠ S Ps 98:6
100:2 ᵍ S Dt 10:12
ʰ S Ps 95:2

99:1 *The Lord reigns.* See 93:1 and note. *tremble … shake.* In reverent awe before God. *cherubim.* See 80:1; see also notes on Ex 25:18; Eze 1:5.

99:3 *Let them praise.* As the Great King, he ought to be shown the fear (v. 1) and honor that are his due. *name.* See v. 6; see also note on 5:11. *holy.* See vv. 5,9; see also Introduction to Leviticus: Theological Themes and note on Lev 11:44.
99:4–5 The Lord has shown the quality of his rule by what he has done for Israel.
99:4 *is mighty … loves justice.* Two chief characteristics of God's reign. *established equity.* That is, created conditions in the world that embody equity—especially for Israel (see 96:10 and note). *Jacob.* A synonym for Israel (see Ge 32:28). *just and right.* Justice and righteousness, as in 97:2 (see note on 119:121). Though even the heavens proclaim God's righteousness (see 97:6 and note), it is in the whole complex of his saving acts in and for Israel that the "righteousness" of God's reign is especially disclosed (see 98:2 and note).
99:5 See also v. 9. For other refrains in the Psalms, see introduction to Ps 42–43. *footstool.* God's royal footstool (see 2Ch 9:18), here a metaphor linking the heavenly throne with the earthly; when God sits on his heavenly throne, his earthly throne is his footstool (here "his holy mountain," v. 9; see 132:7; 1Ch 28:2; La 2:1).
99:6–7 In Israel the Lord provided priestly intermediaries, who (1) were appointed to intercede with him on behalf of his faltering people (v. 6), and (2) were given knowledge of his will so they could instruct Israel (v. 7).
99:6 *Moses … Aaron … Samuel.* These three no doubt serve here as representatives of all those the Lord used as intermedi-

aries with his people in times of great crises. *priests … who called on his name.* The priestly function of intercession is highlighted (see Ex 17:11 and note; 32:11–13,31–32; Nu 14:13–19; 21:7; 1Sa 7:5,8–9; 12:19,23; Jer 15:1). *they called … he answered.* See note on 118:5. *answered them.* See v. 8; see also the Lord's responses to the intercessions referred to in note on vv. 6–7.
99:7 *spoke to them from the pillar of cloud.* Though reference may be to all Israel ("them"), more likely the hymn recalls God's speaking with Moses (see Ex 33:9) and Aaron (see Nu 12:5–6). But that special mode of revelation in the desert may also be generalized here to include God's revelations to Samuel, who was called to his prophetic ministry at the sanctuary, "where the ark of God was" (1Sa 3:3; see also 1Sa 12:23). *they kept.* However imperfectly, it was in Israel that God's righteous statutes and decrees were kept because only in Israel had they been made known (see 147:19–20; Dt 4:5–8).
99:8–9 The justice and righteousness of God's rule in Israel (see v. 4) have been especially shown in the manner in which he has dealt with the nation's sins (see Ex 34:6–7; see also note on 4:1).
99:9 *holy mountain.* See v. 5 and note. *the Lord our God is holy.* Climactic expansion of the secondary refrain.
Ps 100 A call to praise the Lord. Whether or not it was composed for that purpose, the final editors of the Psalter used it to close the series that begins with Ps 90. It has special affinity with 95:1–2,6–7; see also Ps 117. (See introduction to Ps 93.) The second main division (vv. 4–5) parallels the structure of the first (vv. 1–3), namely, a call to praise followed by a declaration of why the Lord is worthy of praise—the corresponding elements of the two divisions are complementary.
100 title *grateful praise.* See v. 4; see also note on 75:1. Per-

100:3 *j* S 1Ki 18:21;
S Ps 46:10 *i* S Job 10:3
k Ps 79:13; Isa 19:25;
63:8,17-19; 64:9
l S 2Sa 24:17;
S Ps 74:1
100:4 *m* S Ps 42:4
n S Ps 96:8 *o* Ps 116:17
100:5 *p* S 1Ch 16:34
q S Ezr 3:11; Ps 106:1
r Ps 108:4; 119:90
101:1 *j* Ps 33:1;
51:14; 89:1; 145:7
101:2 *t* S Ge 17:1;
Php 1:10 *u* S 1Ki 3:14
101:3 *v* Jer 16:18;
Eze 11:21; Hos 9:10
w S Ps 5:5
101:4 *x* Pr 3:32;
6:16-19; 11:20

³ Know that the LORD is God. *i*
　　It is he who made us, *j* and we are his ª;
　　we are his people, *k* the sheep of his pasture. *l*

⁴ Enter his gates with thanksgiving *m*
　　and his courts *n* with praise;
　　give thanks to him and praise his name. *o*
⁵ For the LORD is good *p* and his love endures forever; *q*
　　his faithfulness *r* continues through all generations.

PSALM 101

Of David. A psalm.

¹ I will sing of your love *s* and justice;
　　to you, LORD, I will sing praise.
² I will be careful to lead a blameless life *t*—
　　when will you come to me?

　　I will conduct the affairs *u* of my house
　　with a blameless heart.
³ I will not look with approval
　　on anything that is vile. *v*

　　I hate what faithless people do; *w*
　　I will have no part in it.
⁴ The perverse of heart *x* shall be far from me;
　　I will have nothing to do with what is evil.

ª 3 Or *and not we ourselves*

---

haps it indicates that the psalm was to accompany a thank offering (see note on 7:17; see also Lev 7:12).

100:1 *all the earth.* Though vv. 3,5 clearly speak of God's special relationship with Israel, the call to worship goes out to the whole world, which ought to acknowledge the Lord because of what he has done for his people (see also Ps 98–99; 117).
100:3 *Know.* Acknowledge. *made us.* See 95:6 and note. *sheep of his pasture.* See 95:7 and note; see also note on 23:1.
100:4 *his gates.* The gates of the temple (see 24:7 and note). *courts.* Of the temple (see 84:2,10; 2Ki 21:5; 23:11–12).
100:5 *the LORD is good.* In that his love-and-faithfulness (see note on 36:5) are unfailing through all time (see 98:3 and note). *love.* See note on 6:4.
Ps 101–110 A collection of ten psalms located between two other groups (see introductions to Ps 90–100; 111–119) and framed by two psalms that pertain to the king (the first the king's vow to pattern his reign after God's righteous rule; the last God's commitment to maintain the king—his anointed—and give him victories over all his enemies). This little psalter-within-the-Psalter is concentrically arranged. Inside the frame, Ps 102 and 109 are prayers of individuals in times of intense distress; Ps 103 and 108 praise the Lord for his "great . . . love" that reaches to the heavens (103:11; 108:4); Ps 104 and 107 are complements, with 104 celebrating God's many wise and benevolent acts in creation and 107 celebrating God's "wonderful deeds" (vv. 8,15,21,24,31) for people through his lordship over creation. The remaining two are also complements, with Ps 105 reciting the history of Israel's redemption and 106 reciting the same history as a history of Israel's rebellion. This little psalter includes most of the forms and themes found in the rest of the Psalter. Its outer frame is devoted to royal psalms and its center pair to recitals of Israel's history with God. Meanwhile, its themes range from creation and God's eternal enthronement to the covenant with Abraham, Isaac and Jacob, Israel's exodus from Egypt and entrance into Canaan, her exile and restoration, and finally the ultimate triumph of the Lord's anointed. As a collection it bears a distinctively redemption-history stamp and evokes recollection of all the salient elements of the OT mes-

sage. (For the problem of the Book division at Ps 107, see introduction to that psalm.)

Ps 101 A king's pledge to reign righteously (see 2Ki 23:3), after the pattern of God's rule. For its relationship to Ps 110, see introduction to Ps 101–110. If authored by David (see title), it may have been composed before the ark of God was successfully brought into Jerusalem (see note on v. 2a; see also 2Sa 6). Only Christ, the great Son of David, has perfectly fulfilled these commitments.

Composed of seven couplets (the number of completeness), the psalm begins with a twofold introduction (vv. 1–3a; see notes below), followed by a five-stanza (vv. 3b–8) elaboration of the theme of the second stanza. Of these five stanzas, the middle one (v. 6) speaks of the king's commitment to the "faithful" and "blameless," while the other four (vv. 3b–4,5,7,8) declare his repudiation of all the "faithless" and "wicked" in the land. (For the parallel relationship of stanzas six and seven with three and four, see notes below.) The middle stanza is linked with stanzas one and two also by the catchword "blameless." (For centering in the Psalms, see note on 6:6.) The whole psalm is framed by references to the "LORD" in the first and last stanzas (see vv. 1,8). The second stanza from the end echoes two phrases found in the second stanza from the beginning ("of/in my house" [vv. 2,7] and "in my presence" [v. 7]—in Hebrew the same as for "look with approval" [v. 3]), thus forming an inner frame. For other doublets, see notes below.
101:1–2a Celebration of the pattern of God's reign, which the king makes the model for his own.
101:1 *love and justice.* Two of the chief qualities of God's rule (see 6:4; 99:4 and notes). For this particular combination, see Hos 12:6; Mic 6:8; cf. Zec 7:9. The present phrase is probably a shortened form of "love and faithfulness" combined with "righteousness and justice" (as in 89:14; cf. 33:5; 36:5–6; 48:9–11; Isa 16:5; Hos 2:19).
101:2a *blameless.* See vv. 2b,6; see also note on Ge 17:1. *when . . . ?* Perhaps expressive of David's yearning for the presence of the ark of the Lord in his royal city as the sign of God's readiness to be with him and sustain him in his pledge to reign as he ought (see 2Sa 6 and note on 6:2). For later kings it would be a

⁵Whoever slanders their neighbor ʸ in secret,
I will put to silence;
whoever has haughty eyes ᶻ and a proud heart,
I will not endure.

⁶My eyes will be on the faithful in the land,
that they may dwell with me;
those whose walk is blameless ᵃ
will minister to me.

⁷No one who practices deceit
will dwell in my house;
no one who speaks falsely
will stand in my presence.

⁸Every morning ᵇ I will put to silence
all the wicked ᶜ in the land;
I will cut off every evildoer ᵈ
from the city of the LORD. ᵉ

PSALM 102

*A prayer of an afflicted person who has grown weak and pours out a lament
before the LORD.*

*¹Hear my prayer, ᶠ LORD;
let my cry for help ᵍ come to you.

* 102:1-28 is numbered 102:2-29 in Hebrew texts.

101:5 ʸ S Ex 20:16;
S Lev 19:16
ᶻ S Ps 10:5
101:6 ᵃ ver 2;
Ps 119:1
101:8 ᵇ Ps 5:3;
Jer 21:12 ᶜ Ps 75:10
ᵈ S 2Sa 3:39;
Ps 118:10-12
ᵉ S Ps 46:4
102:1 ᶠ Ps 4:1
ᵍ S Ex 2:23

---

plea for divine enablement relative to the pledge given in vv. 1–2 (cf. Ps 72; 1Ki 3:7–9).
101:2b–3a The essential commitment. *heart... look.* In OT understanding, a person follows the dictates of the heart—the inmost being (see note on 4:7)—and/or the attractions of the eye—external influences (see 119:37; Jdg 14:1–2; 2Sa 11:2; 2Ki 16:10; Job 31:1; Pr 4:25; 17:24). For the combination heart-eyes, see v. 5; Nu 15:39; Job 31:7; Pr 21:4; Ecc 2:10; Jer 22:17.
101:2b *house.* Royal administration (also in v. 7).
101:3a *vile.* "Belial" (2Co 6:15) is derived from the Hebrew for this word (see note on Dt 13:13).
101:3b–4 A repudiation of evil deeds and those who promote them (see v. 7).
101:3b *faithless.* Those who rebel against what is right (see Hos 5:2, "rebels").
101:4 *perverse.* The opposite of "blameless" (see 18:26, "devious"; see also Pr 11:20; 19:1; 28:6). A perverse heart and a deceitful tongue (see v. 7) are root and fruit (see Pr 17:20).
101:5 A pledge to remove from his presence all slanderous and all arrogant persons (see v. 8). *put to silence.* Destroy (as in 54:5; 94:23). See v. 8. *haughty eyes ... proud heart.* See vv. 2b–3a and note; called "the unplowed field of the wicked" in Pr 21:4; cf. Ps 131:1; Isa 10:12. The arrogant tend to be ruthless (see Isa 10:12) and are a law to themselves (see note on 31:23).
101:6 A pledge to surround himself in his reign with the faithful and blameless. *My eyes will be on.* I will look with favor on (see 33:18; 34:15). *the faithful.* Those who maintain moral integrity. *minister to me.* Serve as my aide (see Ex 24:13), attendant (see Ge 39:4; 1Ki 19:21), personal servant (see 2Ki 4:43), commander and official (see 1Ch 27:1; 2Ch 17:19; Pr 29:12).
101:7 A repudiation of all who make their way by doubledealing (see vv. 3b–4).
101:8 A pledge to remove all the wicked from the Lord's kingdom (see v. 5). *Every morning.* With diligence and persistence (see Jer 21:12; Zep 3:5). It appears to have been customary for kings to hear judicial cases in the morning—when the mind is fresh and the air cool. That is when victims looked for deliverance from those oppressing them (cf. 88:13; 143:8; Isa 33:2). *city of the LORD.* See Ps 46; 48; 87; see also note on 3:4.

Ps 102 The prayer of an individual in a time of great distress. For its relationship to Ps 109 in the arrangement of the Psalter, see introduction to Ps 101–110. The author may have been someone caught up in a great national calamity (see note on title). If this is the case, the voice heard here would be like one of the "we/us" of Ps 90 speaking for himself (for thematic links between these two psalms, see notes below). Some interpreters believe that the "I" of vv. 1–11, 23–24 is a communal "I" (see the latter part of the note on Ps 30 title), but that does not seem necessary. In early Christian worship this psalm came to be used as a penitential prayer (see introduction to Ps 6), even though it contains no explicit confession of sin.
The main body of the psalm (vv. 1–22) is developed in four stanzas (initial appeal for God to hear, vv. 1–2; description of distress, vv. 3–11; assurance that the Lord will surely hear, vv. 12–17; call for the Lord's certain deliverance to be recorded for his enduring praise, vv. 18–22), followed by a concluding recapitulation (vv. 23–28).
102 title Unique in the Psalter (no author named and no liturgical or historical notes), the title identifies only the life situation in which the prayer is to be used, and in accordance with vv. 1–11, 23–24 it designates the prayer as that of an individual. But vv. 12–22, 28 clearly indicate national involvement in the calamity. It may be that the distress suffered by the individual, while its description suggests physical illness, is the result of his sharing in a national disaster such as the exile—a suggestion supported by references to the restoration of Zion. Because of the close relationship of the fortunes of king and nation and because of the many themes shared by this and some of the royal psalms, it has been plausibly suggested that the prayer was originally that of a Davidic king, or of a member of the Davidic royal house, while in Babylonian exile. *prayer.* See vv. 1, 17. *weak.* See 61:2; 77:3; 142:3; 143:4; see also 107:5; Jnh 2:7. *lament.* The Hebrew for this word is translated "complaint" in 64:1; 142:2; Job 7:13; 9:27; 10:1; 21:4. See Introduction: Psalm Types; Introduction to Lamentations: Themes and Theology.
102:1–2 Initial appeal for God to hear.
102:2 *hide your face.* See note on 13:1. *when I call, answer me.* See note on 118:5.

102:2 *h* S Ps 22:24
i 2Ki 19:16; Ps 31:2;
88:2
102:3 *j* S Ps 37:20;
S Jas 4:14 *k* La 1:13
102:4 *l* S Ps 37:2;
90:5-6 *m* S 1Sa 1:7;
S Ezr 10:6;
S Job 33:20
102:5 *n* S Ps 6:6
102:6 *o* S Dt 14:15-
17; Ps 30:29;
Isa 34:11; Zep 2:14
102:7 *p* Ps 77:4
q Ps 38:11
102:8 *r* S Ps 31:11
s S Ps 42:10;
Lk 22:63-65; 23:35-
37 *t* S Ex 22:28;
Isa 65:15; Jer 24:9;
25:18; 42:18; 44:12;
Eze 14:8; Zec 8:13
102:9 *u* Isa 44:20
v Ps 6:6; 42:3; 80:5
102:10 *w* Ps 7:11;
38:3
102:11 *x* S 1Ch 29:15;
S Job 14:2; S Ps 39:6
y S Job 8:12; Jas 1:10
102:12 *z* S Ex 15:18
a Ps 135:13; Isa 55:13;
63:12 *b* S Ex 3:15
102:13 *c* S Ps 44:26
d S Dt 32:36;
S 1Ki 3:26; Isa 54:8;
60:10; Zec 10:6
e Ps 119:126
f S Ps 77:7
g S Ex 13:10; Da 8:19;
Ac 1:7
102:15 *h* 1Ki 8:43;
Ps 67:7; Isa 2:2
i Ps 76:12; 138:4;
148:11
102:16 *j* S Ps 51:18
k Ps 8:1; Isa 60:1-2
102:17 *l* S 1Ki 8:29;
Ps 4:1; 6:9

² Do not hide your face *h* from me
  when I am in distress.
 Turn your ear *i* to me;
  when I call, answer me quickly.

³ For my days vanish like smoke; *j*
  my bones *k* burn like glowing embers.
⁴ My heart is blighted and withered like grass; *l*
  I forget to eat my food. *m*
⁵ In my distress I groan aloud *n*
  and am reduced to skin and bones.
⁶ I am like a desert owl, *o*
  like an owl among the ruins.
⁷ I lie awake; *p* I have become
  like a bird alone *q* on a roof.
⁸ All day long my enemies *r* taunt me; *s*
  those who rail against me use my name as a curse. *t*
⁹ For I eat ashes *u* as my food
  and mingle my drink with tears *v*
¹⁰ because of your great wrath, *w*
  for you have taken me up and thrown me aside.
¹¹ My days are like the evening shadow; *x*
  I wither *y* away like grass.

¹² But you, LORD, sit enthroned forever; *z*
  your renown endures *a* through all generations. *b*
¹³ You will arise *c* and have compassion *d* on Zion,
  for it is time *e* to show favor *f* to her;
  the appointed time *g* has come.
¹⁴ For her stones are dear to your servants;
  her very dust moves them to pity.
¹⁵ The nations will fear *h* the name of the LORD,
  all the kings *i* of the earth will revere your glory.
¹⁶ For the LORD will rebuild Zion *j*
  and appear in his glory. *k*
¹⁷ He will respond to the prayer *l* of the destitute;
  he will not despise their plea.

102:3–11 The description of distress—a suffering so great that it withers body and spirit—brought on by a visitation of God's wrath (v. 10) and making him the mockery of his enemies (v. 8). For the framing imagery that binds this section together, see vv. 3–4 and v. 11.
102:3 *my days vanish like smoke.* See also vv. 11, 23. *bones burn.* As if a fire is consuming his physical frame (see 31:10; 32:3; 42:10).
102:4 *heart.* See note on 4:7. Here "heart" is used in combination with "bones" (v. 3) to refer to the whole person (body and spirit); see 22:14; Pr 14:30; 15:30; Isa 66:14 ("and you" represents the Hebrew for "and your bones"); Jer 20:9; 23:9. *blighted.* Or "scorched" (by the hot sun); see 121:6. *withered like grass.* See v. 11; see also note on 90:5–6.
102:6 *owl . . . owl.* Translations of two different Hebrew words (cf. Lev 11:16–18). The owl was associated with desert areas and ruins (see Isa 34:11,15; Jer 50:39; Zep 2:14).
102:8 *enemies taunt me.* See 109:25; see also notes on 5:9; 39:8. *use my name as a curse.* They say, "May you become like that one (the one named) is."
102:9 *drink . . . tears.* For tears as food and drink, see 42:3; 80:5.
102:10 *wrath.* See note on 2:5.
102:11 An echo of vv. 3–4. *shadow.* See 109:23; 144:4; Job 8:9; 14:2; Ecc 6:12. *grass.* See 37:20; 90:5–6 and notes.

102:12–17 Assurance that heaven's eternal King will surely hear the prayer of the destitute (v. 17) and restore Zion. For such expressions of assurance in the prayers of the Psalter, see note on 3:8. This six-verse stanza weaves its themes

in a balanced *a-b-c/a-b-c* pattern (see notes on vv. 15–17).
102:12 *sit enthroned forever.* A central theme of the preceding collection (Ps 90–100). Because God reigns forever and remains the same (see v. 27), his mercies to those who look to him for salvation will not fail. *renown.* See note on 30:4 ("name"). For elaborate celebrations of the Lord's renown, see Ps 111; 135; 145.
102:13 This verse and v. 16 (see also v. 14) suggest that the psalmist's distress was occasioned by the Babylonian exile. *arise.* See note on 3:7. *appointed time.* The time set by God for judgment and deliverance (see 75:2; Ex 9:5; 2Sa 24:15; Da 11:27,35). Perhaps the psalmist is referring to a time announced by a prophet.
102:14 *dear to your servants.* If Zion, the city of God (see 46:4; 48:1–2,8; 87:3; 101:8; 132:13), is so loved by the Lord's servants (see Ps 126; 137), how much more is she cherished by the Lord!
102:15 *nations will fear.* See notes on 25:12; 46:10. *the name of the LORD.* An echo of reference to the "LORD's" "renown" (see note on 30:4 ["name"]). Yahweh's "renown" that "endures through all generations" (v. 12) will evoke the awe of earth's most powerful inhabitants. *name.* See note on 5:11.
102:16 *will rebuild Zion.* Yahweh will "have compassion" on Zion (v. 13) by rebuilding her. *and appear in his glory.* Or "and thus appear in his glory" (see v. 15 and note on 46:10; see also Isa 40:1–5). This hope will find its fullest expression in the "new Jerusalem" (see Rev 21).
102:17 *the destitute.* Reference is to "your servants" (v. 14). *their plea.* Expressive of the pity they feel for their beloved Zion now lying in ruins (v. 14).

¹⁸ Let this be written ^m for a future generation,
    that a people not yet created ⁿ may praise the LORD:
¹⁹ "The LORD looked down ^o from his sanctuary on high,
    from heaven he viewed the earth,
²⁰ to hear the groans of the prisoners ^p
    and release those condemned to death."
²¹ So the name of the LORD will be declared ^q in Zion
    and his praise ^r in Jerusalem
²² when the peoples and the kingdoms
    assemble to worship ^s the LORD.

²³ In the course of my life ^a he broke my strength;
    he cut short my days. ^t
²⁴ So I said:
"Do not take me away, my God, in the midst of my days;
    your years go on ^u through all generations.
²⁵ In the beginning ^v you laid the foundations of the earth,
    and the heavens ^w are the work of your hands. ^x
²⁶ They will perish, ^y but you remain;
    they will all wear out like a garment.
Like clothing you will change them
    and they will be discarded.
²⁷ But you remain the same, ^z
    and your years will never end. ^a
²⁸ The children of your servants ^b will live in your presence;
    their descendants ^c will be established before you."

PSALM 103

Of David.

¹ Praise the LORD, ^d my soul; ^e
    all my inmost being, praise his holy name. ^f
² Praise the LORD, ^g my soul,
    and forget not ^h all his benefits—

a 23 Or *By his power*

102:18 ^m S Ro 4:24
ⁿ S Ps 22:31
102:19 ^o Ps 53:2
102:20 ^p S Ps 68:6; S Lk 4:19
102:21 ^q Ps 22:22
^r Ps 9:14
102:22 ^s S Ps 22:27; Isa 49:22-23; Zec 8:20-23
102:23 ^t S Ps 39:5
102:24 ^u S Ge 21:33; Job 36:26; Ps 90:2
102:25 ^v S Ge 1:1; Heb 1:10-12*
^w S 2Ch 2:12
^x S Ps 8:3
102:26 ^y Isa 13:10, 13; 34:4; 51:6; Eze 32:8; Joel 2:10; Mt 24:35; 2Pe 3:7-10; Rev 20:11
102:27 ^z S Nu 23:19; Heb 13:8; Jas 1:17
^a Ps 9:7
102:28 ^b Ps 69:36
^c Ps 25:13; 89:4
103:1 ^d Ps 28:6
^e Ps 104:1 ^f S Ps 30:4
103:2 ^g Ps 106:1; 117:1 ^h S Dt 6:12; Ps 77:11

102:18–22 Let God's certain deliverance of his people be recorded for his continual praise (v. 8)—until that great day when the worshiping community celebrating Zion's redemption has expanded to include representatives of the "peoples" and "kingdoms" of the world (v. 22). See introduction to Ps 117; see also Rev 15:4; 21:24,26.
102:18 *written.* Only here does a psalmist call for memory to be sustained by a written record of God's saving act; usually oral transmission suffices (see 22:30; 44:1; 78:1–4). *created.* Brought into being by God's sovereign act (see 51:10; 104:30; 139:13).
102:20 *prisoners . . . those condemned to death.* Perhaps prisoners of war, but more likely the exiles in Babylon (see 79:11 and note).
102:21 *praise.* See note on 9:1.
102:22 See note on 46:10; see also 47:9 and note; 96; 98; 100. The expectation here expressed may also be influenced by such prophecies as Isa 2:2–4; Mic 4:1–3.
102:23–28 Concluding recapitulation. The stanza is framed by the radical contrast expressed in vv. 23,28. That human life is cut short (v. 23) by the One whose own being spans all ages (vv. 25–27) adds to the psalmist's sense of loss on the one hand but also to his hope on the other (v. 28) and thus to the urgency of his prayer—as in 90:1–6 (see note on 90:4–5).
102:23–24a See vv. 3–11.
102:24b–27 See v. 12 and note. For a NT application of vv. 25–27 to Christ see Heb 1:10–12 and note on 1:10.
102:26 *Like clothing.* With his first creation God clothed himself with the manifestation of his glory (see 8:1,3–4; 19:1; 29:3–9; 104:1,31; Isa 6:3; see also Job 38–41, especially 40:10).

But he is more enduring than what he has made—and the first creation will give way to a new creation (see Isa 65:17; 66:22).
102:28 Because the Lord does not change (see v. 27), Israel's future is secure (see Mal 3:6). *live in your presence.* Or "dwell in the (promised) land" (see 37:3,29; see also 69:36; Isa 65:9). *established before you.* See 2Sa 7:24.
Ps 103 A hymn to God's love and compassion toward his people. For its relationship to Ps 108 in the arrangement of the Psalter, see introduction to Ps 101–110. Calls to praise frame the body of the hymn (vv. 1–2,20–22) and set its tone. The recital of praise falls into two unequal parts: (1) a three-verse celebration of personal benefits received (vv. 3–5) and (2) a 14-verse recollection of God's mercies to his people Israel (vv. 6–19). The major division (vv. 6–19) is composed of six couplets framed by the breakup of a seventh couplet (vv. 6,19) that describe the general character of God's reign. Thematic development divides the six framed couplets into two equal parts (vv. 7–12,13–18), of which the first celebrates God's compassion on his people as sinners, while the second sings of his compassion on them as frail mortals (see also 78:38–39). The concluding couplets of these two parts proclaim the vastness of his love (vv. 11–12) and its unending perseverance (vv. 17–18). As with the hymn found in Ps 33, the length of the psalm has been determined by the number of letters in the Hebrew alphabet (see introduction to Ps 33).
103:1–2 Call to praise, directed inward (cf. vv. 20–22).
103:1–2,22 *my soul.* A conventional Hebrew way of addressing oneself (see 104:1,35; 116:7). *soul.* See note on 6:3.

103:3 ⁱ S Ex 34:7
ʲ S Ex 15:26; Col 3:13;
1Pe 2:24; 1Jn 1:9
103:4 ᵏ Ps 34:22;
56:13; Isa 43:1
ˡ S Ps 8:5; 23:6
103:5 ᵐ S Ps 90:14;
S 104:28 ⁿ Job 33:25;
Ps 119:25,93;
2Co 4:16 ᵒ S Ee 19:4
103:6 ᵖ Ps 9:8; 65:5;
Isa 9:7 ᵠ S Ps 74:21;
S Lk 4:19
103:7 ʳ Ps 99:7;
147:19 ˢ S Ee 33:13
ᵗ Ps 106:22
103:8 ᵘ S Ex 22:27;
S Ps 86:15; Mic 7:18-
19; Jas 5:11
103:9 ᵛ Ps 30:5;
79:5; Jer 3:5,12; Mic 7:18
103:10 ʷ S Ezr 9:13
; Ro 6:23
103:11 ˣ Ps 13:5;
57:10; 100:5; 106:45;
117:2; La 3:22;
Eph 3:18 ʸ S 2Ch 6:31
103:12 ᶻ S 2Sa 12:13;
Ro 4:7; Eph 2:5
103:13 ᵃ Mal 3:17;
1Jn 3:1
103:14 ᵇ Ps 119:73;
139:13-15; Isa 29:16
ᶜ S Ge 2:7; S Ps 146:4
103:15 ᵈ Ps 37:2;
90:5; 102:11; Isa 40:6
ᵉ S Job 14:2; Jas 1:10
103:16 ᶠ Isa 40:7;
Hag 1:9 ᵍ S Job 7:8
103:17 ʰ S Ge 48:11;
S Ezr 9:12
103:18 ⁱ S Dt 29:9
ʲ Ps 119:52
ᵏ S Nu 15:40; Jn 14:15
103:19 ˡ Ps 47:8;
80:1; 113:5
ᵐ Ps 22:28; 66:7;
Da 4:17
103:20 ⁿ Ps 28:6
ᵒ S Ne 9:6; Lk 2:13;
Heb 1:14 ᵖ S Ps 29:1
ᵠ Ps 107:25; 135:7;
148:8

³ who forgives all your sins ⁱ
    and heals ʲ all your diseases,
⁴ who redeems your life ᵏ from the pit
    and crowns you with love and compassion, ˡ
⁵ who satisfies ᵐ your desires with good things
    so that your youth is renewed ⁿ like the eagle's. ᵒ

⁶ The LORD works righteousness ᵖ
    and justice for all the oppressed. ᵠ

⁷ He made known ʳ his ways ˢ to Moses,
    his deeds ᵗ to the people of Israel:
⁸ The LORD is compassionate and gracious, ᵘ
    slow to anger, abounding in love.
⁹ He will not always accuse,
    nor will he harbor his anger forever; ᵛ
¹⁰ he does not treat us as our sins deserve ʷ
    or repay us according to our iniquities.
¹¹ For as high as the heavens are above the earth,
    so great is his love ˣ for those who fear him; ʸ
¹² as far as the east is from the west,
    so far has he removed our transgressions ᶻ from us.

¹³ As a father has compassion ᵃ on his children,
    so the LORD has compassion on those who fear him;
¹⁴ for he knows how we are formed, ᵇ
    he remembers that we are dust. ᶜ
¹⁵ As for mortals, their days are like grass, ᵈ
    they flourish like a flower ᵉ of the field;
¹⁶ the wind blows ᶠ over it and it is gone,
    and its place ᵍ remembers it no more.
¹⁷ But from everlasting to everlasting
    the LORD's love is with those who fear him,
    and his righteousness with their children's children ʰ—
¹⁸ with those who keep his covenant ⁱ
    and remember ʲ to obey his precepts. ᵏ

¹⁹ The LORD has established his throne ˡ in heaven,
    and his kingdom rules ᵐ over all.

²⁰ Praise the LORD, ⁿ you his angels, ᵒ
    you mighty ones ᵖ who do his bidding, ᵠ
    who obey his word.

103:3–5 Recital of personal blessings received.
103:3 *forgives … heals.* See Mt 9:2,5 and parallels.
103:4 *redeems.* A synonym for "delivers" (see note on 71:23). *pit.* A metaphor for the grave (see note on 30:1). *love and compassion.* The key words of the hymn (see vv. 8,11,13,17). *love.* See vv. 8,11,17; see also note on 6:4.
103:5 *like the eagle's.* The vigor of youth is restored to match the proverbial, unflagging strength of the eagle (see Isa 40:30–31).
103:6–19 God's love and compassion toward his people.
103:6 Together with v. 19 (the second verse of a split couplet, providing the other side of the literary frame) it characterizes the reign of God, under which Israel has been so graciously blessed. *righteousness.* See v. 17; see also note on 4:1.
103:7–12 God's compassion on his people as sinners.
103:7–8 See Ex 33:13; see also note on Ex 34:6–7.
103:7 *his ways.* See 25:10 and note.
103:9 *anger.* See note on 2:5.
103:11–12 The vastness of God's love (note the spatial imagery) is supremely shown in his forgiving Israel's sins.
103:11 See 36:5–9. *so great is.* So prevails. *those who fear him.* See vv. 13,17–18; see also note on 66:16.
103:12 See Isa 1:18; 38:17; 43:25; Jer 31:34; 50:20; Mic 7:18–19.

103:13–18 God's compassion on his people as frail mortals (see 78:39).
103:13–14 In Hebrew the initial words of these two verses strikingly echo the sounds of the initial words of vv. 11–12, thereby effecting a tight literary bond between vv. 13–18 and vv. 7,12.
103:14 *we are dust.* See Ge 2:7; 3:19.
103:15–16 See note on 90:5–6.
103:17–18 The infinite temporal span of God's love (cf. the spatial imagery in vv. 11–12).
103:17 *everlasting to everlasting … their children's children.* God's love outlasts anyone's little time in this life (cf. note on 109:12).
103:18 *who keep his covenant … obey his precepts.* See 25:10; Ex 19:5 and note; 20:6 and note; Dt 4:40; 29:9.
103:19 See v. 6 and note; see also 9:4,7; 11:4; 47:2,7–8; 123:1.
103:20–22 Concluding call to praise, directed to all creatures—from the psalmist's inner self (vv. 1–2) to the creatures who serve God in heaven. A call to praise is often the climax of praise in the Psalter (as also of the whole collection; see Ps 148–150). See note on 9:1. *Praise … Praise … Praise.* See note on 96:1–3. (The final line was probably added by the editors of the Psalter; see 104:1,35.)
103:20 *who do his bidding.* See 91:11; Heb 1:14.

²¹ Praise the LORD, all his heavenly hosts,^r
  you his servants ^s who do his will.
²² Praise the LORD, all his works ^t
  everywhere in his dominion.

Praise the LORD, my soul. ^u

PSALM 104

¹ Praise the LORD, my soul. ^v

LORD my God, you are very great;
  you are clothed with splendor and majesty. ^w

² The LORD wraps ^x himself in light ^y as with a garment;
  he stretches ^z out the heavens ^a like a tent ^b
³   and lays the beams ^c of his upper chambers on their waters. ^d
He makes the clouds ^e his chariot ^f
  and rides on the wings of the wind. ^g
⁴ He makes winds his messengers,^{a h}
  flames of fire ⁱ his servants.

⁵ He set the earth ^j on its foundations; ^k
  it can never be moved.
⁶ You covered it ^l with the deep ^m as with a garment;
  the waters stood ⁿ above the mountains.
⁷ But at your rebuke ^o the waters fled,
  at the sound of your thunder ^p they took to flight;
⁸ they flowed over the mountains,
  they went down into the valleys,
  to the place you assigned ^q for them.
⁹ You set a boundary ^r they cannot cross;
  never again will they cover the earth.

---

^a 4 Or *angels*

103:21 *heavenly hosts.* Uniquely here and in 148:2 the Hebrew for "hosts" is masculine, and in both places the "hosts" are associated with "angels." *servants.* Translates the participle of the Hebrew verb for "minister" in 101:6 (see note there; see also note on 104:4).
103:22 *all his works.* See 65:13; 96:11–12 and notes.
Ps 104 A hymn to the Creator. For its relationship to Ps 108 in the arrangement of the Psalter, see introduction to Ps 101–110. The preexilic author has adapted Ge 1 to his own quite different purpose and has subordinated its sequence somewhat to his own design (see next paragraph). Ge 1 recounts God's acts of creation as his first work at the beginning, but the poet views the created world displayed before his eyes and sings the glory of its Maker and Sustainer. Surprisingly, he only hints at the angelic world (v. 4) and mentions humans only in passing (vv. 14,23); his theme is the visible creation, which he views as the radiant and stately robe with which the invisible Creator has clothed himself to display his glory.

Following the one-verse introduction, the poet designed the main body of his poem concentrically, with stanzas of three-five-nine-five-three verses. The first stanza speaks of the celestial realm above (vv. 2–4) and the fifth of the nautical realm below (vv. 24–26)—the two realms that bracket the "earth" (see note on v. 5). The second sings of the earth's solid foundations and secure boundaries (vv. 5–9) and the fourth of the orderly cycles of life on earth, governed by sun and moon (vv. 19–23). At the center a nine-verse stanza (composed of three triplets) celebrates the luxuriation of life in the earth (vv. 10–18). To the poem's main body he added a four-verse stanza that recites how God maintains life on earth (vv. 27–30), a two-verse conclusion (vv. 31–32—which together with v. 1 frames the whole), and a three-verse epilogue (vv. 33–35). The outer frame ("Praise

the LORD, my soul") was probably added by the editors of the Psalter when they inserted the Book division after Ps 106—thus concluding Book IV with doxologies (see the liturgical frames added to Ps 105–106 and the similar conclusion to Book V: Ps 146–150).
104:1–2 *clothed with ... wraps himself in.* See note on 109:29.
104:1 Introduction: the theme of the hymn.
104:2–4 The celestial realm above.
104:2 *light.* Cf. the first day of creation (Ge 1:3–5). *heavens.* Cf. the second day of creation (Ge 1:6–8). *like a tent.* Over the earth and the luminaries that give it light.
104:3 *upper chambers.* Vivid imagery for the heavenly abode of God (see v. 13). In the singular, the Hebrew for this phrase usually refers to the upper-level room of a house (as in 1Ki 17:19; 2Ki 1:2). *their waters.* The waters above the "tent" (v. 2; see Ge 1:7), from which, in the imagery of the OT, God gives the rain (see v. 13; see also 36:8 and note). *clouds his chariot.* See 18:7–15; 68:4; 77:16–19 and notes.
104:4 *winds ... flames of fire.* The winds and lightning bolts of the thunderstorm, here personified as the agents of God's purposes (see 148:8; cf. 103:21; see also Heb 1:7 and note).
104:5–9 The earth realm (the spatial element) made secure. Verses 5,9 frame the stanza, highlighting its two main themes.
104:5 *earth.* Land in distinction from sky and seas, not the earth as a planet (see Ge 1:10). *foundations.* See 24:2 and note. *can never be moved.* Firmly founded (see 93:1; 96:10), it will not give way (cf. v. 9).
104:7 *rebuke.* See note on 76:6. *waters fled.* Cf. the third day of creation (Ge 1:9–13).
104:9 *set a boundary.* So that the land ("earth") will never be overwhelmed by the sea (cf. v. 5; see 33:7 and note; see also Ge 9:15).

104:10 s Ps 107:33;
Isa 41:18
104:11 t ver 13
u S Ge 16:12;
Isa 32:14; Jer 14:6
104:12 v ver 17;
Mt 8:20 w Mt 13:32
104:13 x Ps 135:7;
147:8; Jer 10:13;
Zec 10:1 y S Lev 26:4
z Am 9:6
104:14 a S Job 38:27;
Ps 147:8 b S Ge 1:30;
S Job 28:5
104:15 c S Ge 14:18;
S Jdg 9:13 d Ps 23:5;
92:10; Lk 7:46
e S Dt 8:3; Mt 6:11
104:16 f Ge 1:11
g S Ps 72:16
104:17 h ver 12
104:18 i S Dt 14:5
j Pr 30:26
104:19 k S Ge 1:14
l Ps 19:6
104:20 m Isa 45:7;
Am 5:8 n Ps 74:16
o S Ps 50:10
104:21 p Am 3:4
q Ps 145:15; Joel 1:20;
S Mt 6:26
104:22 r S Job 37:8
104:23 s S Ge 3:19
t Jdg 19:16
104:24 u Ps 40:5
v S Ge 1:31 w Ps 24:1;
50:10-11
104:25 x Ps 69:34
y Eze 47:10
104:26 z Ps 107:23;
Eze 27:9; Jnh 1:3
a S Job 3:8; 41:1
b Job 40:20
c S Ge 1:21
104:27 d Job 36:31;
Ps 145:15; 147:9
104:28 e Ps 103:5;
145:16; Isa 58:11
104:29 f S Dt 31:17

¹⁰ He makes springs ^s pour water into the ravines;
  it flows between the mountains.
¹¹ They give water ^t to all the beasts of the field;
  the wild donkeys ^u quench their thirst.
¹² The birds of the sky ^v nest by the waters;
  they sing among the branches. ^w
¹³ He waters the mountains ^x from his upper chambers; ^y
  the land is satisfied by the fruit of his work. ^z
¹⁴ He makes grass grow ^a for the cattle,
  and plants for people to cultivate—
  bringing forth food ^b from the earth:
¹⁵ wine ^c that gladdens human hearts,
  oil ^d to make their faces shine,
  and bread that sustains ^e their hearts.
¹⁶ The trees of the Lord ^f are well watered,
  the cedars of Lebanon ^g that he planted.
¹⁷ There the birds ^h make their nests;
  the stork has its home in the junipers.
¹⁸ The high mountains belong to the wild goats; ⁱ
  the crags are a refuge for the hyrax. ^j

¹⁹ He made the moon to mark the seasons, ^k
  and the sun ^l knows when to go down.
²⁰ You bring darkness, ^m it becomes night, ⁿ
  and all the beasts of the forest ^o prowl.
²¹ The lions roar for their prey ^p
  and seek their food from God. ^q
²² The sun rises, and they steal away;
  they return and lie down in their dens. ^r
²³ Then people go out to their work, ^s
  to their labor until evening. ^t

²⁴ How many are your works, ^u Lord!
  In wisdom you made ^v them all;
  the earth is full of your creatures. ^w
²⁵ There is the sea, ^x vast and spacious,
  teeming with creatures beyond number—
  living things both large and small. ^y
²⁶ There the ships ^z go to and fro,
  and the leviathan, ^a which you formed to frolic ^b there. ^c

²⁷ All creatures look to you
  to give them their food ^d at the proper time.
²⁸ When you give it to them,
  they gather it up;
  when you open your hand,
  they are satisfied ^e with good things.
²⁹ When you hide your face, ^f

104:10–18 The earth a flourishing garden of life—the center of the psalm and the focal point of the author's contemplation of the creation (the earth, bounded by sky, vv. 2–4, and sea, vv. 24–26). Cf. the third and sixth days of creation (Ge 1:9–13, 24–31).
104:10–12 The gift of water from below—watering the ravines of the Negev, south of Israel's heartland.
104:13–15 The gift of water from above—watering the uplands of Israel's heartland with its cultivated fields.
104:13 *upper chambers.* See v. 3 and note.
104:15 *hearts…hearts.* See note on 4:7. *oil.* Olive oil. *make their faces shine.* As food (see 1Ki 17:12), causing a person's face to glow with health, and/or as cosmetic (Est 2:12).
104:16–18 Well-watered Lebanon (north of Israel's heartland), with its great trees, its hordes of birds and its alpine animals, the very epitome of God's earthly parkland (see 72:16; 2Ki 14:9; 19:23; Isa 10:34; 35:2; 40:16; 60:13; Jer 22:6; Hos 14:7).
104:19–23 The orderly cycles of life (the temporal element;

see notes on vv. 2–4,5–9; see also introduction) on earth, governed by the moon and sun. Cf. the fourth day of creation (Ge 1:14–19).
104:21,23 *lions…people.* The one (representing the animal world) lord of the night; the other lord of the day.
104:24–26 The nautical realm below (see note on vv. 19–23). Cf. the fifth day of creation (Ge 1:20–23). The realm of the sea is structurally balanced with the celestial realm (vv. 2–4) as the other boundary to the realm of earth.
104:24 A pause to recapitulate before treating the sea.
104:25 *teeming.* See Ge 1:20–21.
104:26 *leviathan.* That fearsome mythological monster of the deep (see Job 3:8 and note) is here portrayed as nothing more than God's harmless pet playing in the ocean.
104:27–30 By God's benevolent care this zoological garden flourishes. Cf. the sixth day of creation (Ge 1:24–31).
104:29 *hide your face.* See note on 13:1.

they are terrified;
when you take away their breath,
    they die and return to the dust. *g*
³⁰When you send your Spirit, *h*
    they are created,
and you renew the face of the ground.

³¹May the glory of the Lord *i* endure forever;
    may the Lord rejoice in his works*j*—
³²he who looks at the earth, and it trembles, *k*
    who touches the mountains, *l* and they smoke. *m*

³³I will sing *n* to the Lord all my life;
    I will sing praise to my God as long as I live.
³⁴May my meditation be pleasing to him,
    as I rejoice *o* in the Lord.
³⁵But may sinners vanish *p* from the earth
    and the wicked be no more. *q*

Praise the Lord, my soul.

Praise the Lord. *a r*

PSALM 105

105:1–15pp — 1Ch 16:8–22

¹Give praise to the Lord, *s* call on his name; *t*
    make known among the nations what he has done.
²Sing of him, *u* sing his praises; *v*
    tell of all his wonderful acts. *w*
³Glory in his holy name; *x*
    let the hearts of those who seek the Lord rejoice.
⁴Look to the Lord and his strength;
    seek his face *y* always.
⁵Remember the wonders *z* he has done,
    his miracles, and the judgments he pronounced, *a*

^a 35 Hebrew *Hallelu Yah*; in the Septuagint this line stands at the beginning of Psalm 105.

104:30 *your Spirit.* See note on 51:11. *created.* See note on 102:18.
104:31 *glory of the Lord.* Such as is displayed in his creation (see 19:1–4a and note).
104:32 He is so much greater than his creation that with a look or a touch he could undo it.
104:33–35 A concluding expression of the psalmist's devotion to Yahweh (cf. TNIV text note on v. 35).
104:33 A vow to praise—here attached to a hymn of praise (see note on 7:17).
104:34 *my meditation.* The preceding hymn (see 19:14 and note).
104:35 May the earth be purged of that which alone mars it (cf. Rev 21:27). *Praise the Lord* (last occurrence). Probably belonged originally to Ps 105 (see TNIV text note and 105:45; 106:1,48).

Ps 105 An exhortation to Israel to worship and trust in the Lord because of all his saving acts in fulfillment of his covenant with Abraham to give his descendants the land of Canaan. It was composed to be addressed to Israel by a Levite (see 1Ch 16:7 and compare vv. 1–15 with 1Ch 16:8–22) on one of Israel's annual religious festivals (see chart, pp. 180–181), possibly the Festival of Tabernacles (see Lev 23:34) but more likely the Festival of Weeks or Pentecost (see Ex 23:16; Lev 23:15–21; Nu 28:26; Dt 16:9–12; see also Dt 26:1–11). For other recitals of the same history (but for different purposes), see Ps 78; 106; Jos 24:2–13; Ne 9:7–25. For the relationship of this psalm to Ps 106 in the arrangement of the Psalter, see introduction to Ps 101–110.

The introduction is composed of seven verses in two parts: (1) an exhortation (with ten imperatives) to worship the Lord (vv. 1–4); (2) a call to remember what the Lord has done (vv. 5–7). The main body that follows is framed by two four-verse stanzas (vv. 8–11, 42–45) that summarize—as introduction and conclusion—its main theme: The Lord has remembered his covenant with Abraham (see chart, p. 20). The editors of the Psalter have added an outer frame of "Hallelujahs" (see introduction to Ps 104; see also note on 104:35).
105:1–4 The exhortation to worship and trust.
105:1 *Give praise.* See note on Ps 100 title. *call on.* In prayer (see v. 4). The first two imperatives highlight the two themes of the ten imperatives of the exhortation: praise and prayer as expressions of devotion to the Lord (celebration of his past saving acts; trust in him for future deliverance and blessing). *his name.* See v. 3; see also note on 5:11. *make known among the nations.* As an integral part of praise (see note on 9:1).
105:2 *wonderful acts.* See v. 5 ("wonders"); see also note on 9:1.
105:3,25 *hearts.* See note on 4:7.
105:5–7 Exhortation to remember God's saving acts.
105:5 *Remember.* As a motivation for and focus of worship and the basis for trust—remember how the Lord has remembered (see vv. 8–11). *judgments.* See v. 7; see also notes on 48:11; 97:8. *pronounced.* As Lord, he commands and it is done (see 7:6 ["decree justice"]; 33:9; 71:3; 78:23; 147:15,18; 148:5; Isa 5:6; 55:11; Jer 1:12; Am 9:3–4).

104:29 *g* S Job 7:21
104:30 *h* S Ge 1:2
104:31 *i* Ex 40:35;
Ps 8:1; S Ro 11:36
j S Ge 1:4
104:32 *k* S Ps 97:4
l S Ex 19:18
m Ps 144:5
104:33 *n* S Ex 15:1;
Ps 108:1
104:34 *o* Ps 2:11;
9:2; 32:11
104:35 *p* Ps 37:38
q S Job 7:10 *r* Ps 28:6;
105:45; 106:48
105:1 *s* S 1Ch 16:34
t Ps 80:18; 99:6;
116:13; Joel 2:32;
Ac 2:21
105:2 *u* Ps 30:4;
33:3; 96:1 *v* Ps 7:17;
18:49; 27:6; 59:17;
71:22; 146:2
w S Ps 75:1
105:3 *x* S Ps 89:16
105:4 *y* S Ps 24:6
105:5 *z* S Ps 40:5
a S Dt 7:18

105:6 *b* ver 42
c S Dt 10:15; Ps 106:5
105:8 *d* S Ge 9:15;
Ps 106:45; 111:5;
Eze 16:60; S Lk 1:72
105:9 *e* Ge 12:7;
S 15:18; S 22:16-18;
Lk 1:73; Gal 3:15-18
105:10 *f* Ge 28:13-
15 *g* Isa 55:3
105:11 *h* S Ge 12:7
i S Nu 34:2
105:12 *j* Dt 7:7
k Ge 23:4; Heb 11:9
105:13 *l* Ge 15:13-
16; Nu 32:13; 33:3-49
105:14 *m* Ge 35:5
n Ge 12:17-20; S 20:3;
S Ps 9:5
105:15 *o* S Ge 26:11;
S 1Sa 12:3 *p* S Ge 20:7
105:16 *q* S Ge 12:10
; S Lev 26:26; Isa 3:1;
Eze 4:16
105:17 *r* S Ge 37:28
; Ac 7:9
105:18 *s* S Ge 40:15
105:19 *t* S Ge 12:10;
40:20-22 *u* Ge 41:40
105:20 *v* Ge 41:14
105:22 *w* Ge 41:43-
44 *x* S Ge 41:40
105:23 *y* Ge 46:6;
Ac 7:15; 13:17
z Ge 47:28
a S Ps 78:51
105:24 *b* Ex 1:7,9;
Ac 7:17
105:25 *c* S Ex 4:21
d Ex 1:6-10; Ac 7:19
105:26 *e* S Ge 3:10
f S Ex 4:16; S Nu 33:1
g S Nu 16:5; 17:5-8
105:27 *h* ver 28-37;
Ex 7:8-12:51
i S Ex 4:17; S 10:1

⁶ you his servants, the descendants of Abraham, *b*
    his chosen *c* ones, the children of Jacob.
⁷ He is the Lord our God;
    his judgments are in all the earth.

⁸ He remembers his covenant *d* forever,
    the promise he made, for a thousand generations,
⁹ the covenant he made with Abraham, *e*
    the oath he swore to Isaac.
¹⁰ He confirmed it *f* to Jacob as a decree,
    to Israel as an everlasting covenant: *g*
¹¹ "To you I will give the land of Canaan *h*
    as the portion you will inherit." *i*

¹² When they were but few in number, *j*
    few indeed, and strangers in it, *k*
¹³ they wandered from nation to nation, *l*
    from one kingdom to another.
¹⁴ He allowed no one to oppress *m* them;
    for their sake he rebuked kings: *n*
¹⁵ "Do not touch *o* my anointed ones;
    do my prophets *p* no harm."

¹⁶ He called down famine *q* on the land
    and destroyed all their supplies of food;
¹⁷ and he sent a man before them—
    Joseph, sold as a slave. *r*
¹⁸ They bruised his feet with shackles, *s*
    his neck was put in irons,
¹⁹ till what he foretold *t* came to pass,
    till the word *u* of the Lord proved him true.
²⁰ The king sent and released him,
    the ruler of peoples set him free. *v*
²¹ He made him master of his household,
    ruler over all he possessed,
²² to instruct his princes *w* as he pleased
    and teach his elders wisdom. *x*

²³ Then Israel entered Egypt; *y*
    Jacob resided *z* as a foreigner in the land of Ham. *a*
²⁴ The Lord made his people very fruitful;
    he made them too numerous *b* for their foes,
²⁵ whose hearts he turned *c* to hate his people,
    to conspire *d* against his servants.
²⁶ He sent Moses *e* his servant,
    and Aaron, *f* whom he had chosen. *g*
²⁷ They performed *h* his signs *i* among them,

105:6,9 *Abraham ... Jacob ... Isaac.* While "Jacob" occurs 34 times in the Psalter, Abraham is recalled by name in Psalms only here (see also v. 42) and in 47:9. Reference to Isaac occurs in Psalms only here.
105:8–11 The Lord remembers his covenant with Abraham (see vv. 42–45).
105:8 *covenant.* The promissory covenant of Ge 15:9–21 (see chart, p. 20). This verse and v. 9 may be echoed in Lk 1:72–73. *thousand generations.* See Ge 20:6; Dt 7:9; 1Ch 16:15.
105:10 *as a decree.* As a fixed policy governing his future actions (see note on v. 45).
105:12–41 A recital of God's saving acts in Israel's behalf from the granting of the covenant (see v. 11; Ge 15:9–21) to its fulfillment (see v. 44; Jos 21:43). Cf. the recital prescribed by Moses in conjunction with the offering of firstfruits (Dt 26:1–11).
105:14–15 See Ge 20:2–7 and note on 20:7.
105:18 *shackles ... irons.* That is, shackles of iron (see 149:8; see also note on 3:7). The poet takes the freedom to use a later con-

ventional description of prisoners (see Job 13:27; 33:11). (Shackles are not spoken of in Ge 39:20–23, and iron came into common use for them at a later time—earlier shackles were made of bronze; see Jdg 16:21.)
105:22 *instruct.* Lit. "bind," i.e., govern or control. He whose "neck" (v. 18; Hebrew *nephesh*) had been shackled was given authority to "bind" the pharaoh's princes "as he pleased" (Hebrew "with his *nephesh*"—here meaning his will). *elders.* The pharaoh's counselors, conventionally older men of wide experience and learning (see note on Ex 3:16).
105:23,27 *land of Ham.* See 78:51 and note.
105:25 *turned.* In OT perspective God's sovereign control over Israel's destiny is so complete that it governs—mysteriously—even the evil that others commit against them; hence the bold language used here (see Ex 4:21; 7:3; Jos 11:20; 2Sa 24:1; Isa 10:5–7; 37:26–27; Jer 34:22).
105:26,42 *servant.* See 78:70 and note.

his wonders[j] in the land of Ham.
28 He sent darkness[k] and made the land dark—
for had they not rebelled against[l] his words?
29 He turned their waters into blood,[m]
causing their fish to die.[n]
30 Their land teemed with frogs,[o]
which went up into the bedrooms of their rulers.
31 He spoke,[p] and there came swarms of flies,[q]
and gnats[r] throughout their country.
32 He turned their rain into hail,[s]
with lightning throughout their land;
33 he struck down their vines[t] and fig trees[u]
and shattered the trees of their country.
34 He spoke,[v] and the locusts came,[w]
grasshoppers[x] without number;[y]
35 they ate up every green thing in their land,
ate up the produce of their soil.
36 Then he struck down all the firstborn[z] in their land,
the firstfruits of all their manhood.
37 He brought out Israel, laden with silver and gold,[a]
and from among their tribes no one faltered.
38 Egypt was glad when they left,
because dread of Israel[b] had fallen on them.

39 He spread out a cloud[c] as a covering,
and a fire to give light at night.[d]
40 They asked,[e] and he brought them quail;[f]
he fed them well with the bread of heaven.[g]
41 He opened the rock,[h] and water gushed out;
it flowed like a river in the desert.

42 For he remembered his holy promise[i]
given to his servant Abraham.
43 He brought out his people with rejoicing,[j]
his chosen ones with shouts of joy;
44 he gave them the lands of the nations,[k]
and they fell heir to what others had toiled[l] for—
45 that they might keep his precepts
and observe his laws.[m]

Praise the LORD.[a][n]

---

[a] 45 Hebrew *Hallelu Yah*

105:27 [j] S Ex 3:20; Da 4:3
105:28 [k] S Ge 1:4; S Ex 10:22 [l] S Ex 7:22
105:29 [m] S Ps 78:44 [n] Ex 7:21
105:30 [o] S Ex 8:2,6
105:31 [p] Ps 107:25; 148:8 [q] Ex 8:21-24; S Ps 78:45 [r] Ex 8:16-18
105:32 [s] Ex 9:22-25; S Job 38:22; S Ps 78:47
105:33 [t] Ps 78:47 [u] Ex 10:5,12
105:34 [v] Ps 107:25 [w] S Ex 10:4,12-15 [x] S 1Ki 8:37 [y] Joel 1:6
105:36 [z] S Ex 4:23; S 12:12
105:37 [a] S Ex 3:21, 22
105:38 [b] Ex 15:16
105:39 [c] S Ex 13:21; 1Co 10:1 [d] S Ps 78:14
105:40 [e] Ps 78:18, 24 [f] S Ex 16:13 [g] S Ex 16:4; Jn 6:31
105:41 [h] S Nu 20:11; 1Co 10:4
105:42 [i] Ge 12:1-3; 13:14-17; 15:13-16
105:43 [j] Ex 15:1-18; Ps 106:12
105:44 [k] Ex 32:13; Jos 11:16-23; 12:8; 13:6-7; Ps 111:6 [l] Dt 6:10-11; Ps 78:55
105:45 [m] S Dt 4:40; 6:21-24; Ps 78:5-7 [n] S Ps 104:35

105:28–36 Recital of the plagues against Egypt. In this poetic recollection seven plagues (symbolizing completeness) represent the ten plagues of Ex 7–11. Apart from omissions (the plagues of livestock disease and boils) the poet follows the order of Exodus, except that he combines the third and fourth plagues (gnats and flies)—in reverse order—to stay within the number seven. He also places the ninth plague (darkness) first in order to frame his recital with mention of the two plagues that climaxed the series.

105:37 *laden with silver and gold.* See Ex 3:22 and note; 12:35–36.

105:39 *as a covering.* Elsewhere it is said that the cloud (symbolic of God's presence) served (1) as a guide for Israel in her desert journeys (see 78:14; Ex 13:21; Nu 9:17; Ne 9:12,19), (2) as a shield of darkness to protect Israel from the pursuing Egyptians (see Ex 14:19–20) and (3) as a covering for the fiery manifestations of God's glorious presence (see Ex 16:10; 24:16; 34:5; 40:34–35,38; Nu 11:25; 12:5; 16:42; Dt 31:15; 1Ki 8:11). The psalmist appears to highlight yet another function: God's protective cover over his people in the desert, per-

haps as his shading "wings" (17:8; see note there), so that the sun would not harm them by day (see 121:5–6).

105:40 *bread of heaven.* See 78:24–25 and note on 78:25.

105:41 *like a river.* Poetically heightened imagery to evoke due wonder for the event. This miracle of the desert wanderings concludes the recital and has been placed in climactic position as one of the most striking manifestations of God's redeeming power and benevolence (see 114:8; Isa 43:19–20; cf. Isa 50:2).

105:42–45 Concluding summary (balancing the introduction to the recital: vv. 8–11).

105:44 *gave them the lands.* See v. 11.

105:45 *precepts.* God has kept his "decree" (v. 10) so that Israel might keep his "precepts"—the Hebrew word is the same (see note on v. 5: "remember"). God's redemptive working in fulfillment of his covenant promise has as its goal the creating of a people in the earth who conform their lives to his holy will (see Isa 5:1–7). Thus the list of appropriate responses begun in v. 1—praise and prayer (trust)—is completed by the third: obedience (see Ge 18:19).

106:1 ° S Ps 22:23;
S 103:2 ᵖ S Ps 119:68
ᵍ S Ezr 3:11; Ps 136:1-
26; Jer 33:11
106:2 ʳ S Ps 71:16
106:3 ˢ Ps 112:5;
Hos 12:6 ᵗ Ps 15:2
106:4 ᵘ Ps 25:6,7
ᵛ S Ps 77:7
ʷ S Ge 50:24
106:5 ˣ S Dt 30:15;
Ps 1:3 ʸ S Ps 105:6
ᶻ Ps 20:5; 27:6; 47:5;
118:15 ᵃ S Ex 34:9
106:6 ᵇ S 1Ki 8:47;
S Ro 3:9 ᶜ S 2Ch 30:7
ᵈ Ne 1:7
106:7 ᵉ S Jdg 3:7
ᶠ Ps 78:11,42
ᵍ Ex 14:11-12
106:8 ʰ Ex 14:30;
S Ps 80:3; 107:13;
Isa 25:9; Joel 2:32
ⁱ S Ex 9:16; S Ps 23:3
ʲ S Ex 14:31
106:9 ᵏ Ps 18:15;
Isa 50:2 ˡ S Ex 14:21;
Na 1:4 ᵐ Ps 78:13;
Isa 63:11-14
106:10 ⁿ Ex 14:30;
Ps 107:13 ° S Ps 78:53
ᵖ Ps 78:42; 107:2;
Isa 35:9; 62:12
106:11 ᵍ S Ex 14:28

PSALM 106

106:1,47–48pp — 1Ch 16:34–36

¹ Praise the LORD.ᵃ °

Give thanks to the LORD, for he is good; ᵖ
   his love endures forever. ᵍ

² Who can proclaim the mighty acts ʳ of the LORD
   or fully declare his praise?
³ Blessed are those who act justly, ˢ
   who always do what is right. ᵗ

⁴ Remember me, ᵘ LORD, when you show favor ᵛ to your people,
   come to my aid ʷ when you save them,
⁵ that I may enjoy the prosperity ˣ of your chosen ones, ʸ
   that I may share in the joy ᶻ of your nation
   and join your inheritance ᵃ in giving praise.

⁶ We have sinned, ᵇ even as our ancestors ᶜ did;
   we have done wrong and acted wickedly. ᵈ
⁷ When our ancestors were in Egypt,
   they gave no thought ᵉ to your miracles;
   they did not remember ᶠ your many kindnesses,
   and they rebelled by the sea, ᵍ the Red Sea. ᵇ
⁸ Yet he saved them ʰ for his name's sake, ⁱ
   to make his mighty power ʲ known.
⁹ He rebuked ᵏ the Red Sea, and it dried up; ˡ
   he led them through ᵐ the depths as through a desert.
¹⁰ He saved them ⁿ from the hand of the foe; °
   from the hand of the enemy he redeemed them. ᵖ
¹¹ The waters covered ᵍ their adversaries;

ᵃ 1 Hebrew *Hallelu Yah*; also in verse 48   ᵇ 7 Or *the Sea of Reeds*; also in verses 9 and 22

Ps 106 A confession of Israel's long history of rebellion and a prayer for God to once again save his people. In length, poetic style and shared themes it has much affinity with Ps 105, even while it contrasts with it by reciting the past as a history of rebellion (see Ps 78; Ne 9:5–37). It was most likely authored by a Levite in Jerusalem sometime after the return of some of the exiles. The first verse and the last two verses seem to have been taken over from an earlier composition (see 1Ch 16:34–36). These may have been added (along with the "Hallelujah"; see TNIV text note on v.1) by the editors of the Psalter (borrowing from an earlier Davidic psalter) when they set the Book divisions between Ps 106 and 107. See further the introduction to Ps 101–110.

In the final edited form of the Psalter, the psalm is set between two liturgical calls to praise ("Hallelujah!"). Within this outer frame stands another, also drawn from the liturgical language of praise (vv. 1b,48a; see notes there). And still a third frame (formed by two couplets devoted to prayer [vv. 4–5,47; see notes there]) encloses the main body of the psalm. Verses 2–3 are transitional. While the recital character of the central theme (as in Ps 105; see also Ps 78) controls the basic outline, attention to symmetry brings to light the carefully designed pattern of thematic development. The recital begins with 14 Hebrew poetic lines devoted to the period of the exodus and the desert wanderings (vv. 6–18) and ends with 14 Hebrew lines devoted to Israel's time in the promised land (34–46). The intervening verses (19–33) make up three stanzas with a six-four-six line pattern. In the two six-line stanzas, instances of Israel's engagement in idolatry in the desert period are recalled (the golden calf at Mt. Horeb [vv. 19–23]; the Baal of Peor in the plains of Moab [vv. 28–33]). These stanzas each end with a word about Moses: In the first, Moses intercedes for Israel and wards off God's wrath; in the second, Israel so vexes Moses that he acts rashly and loses his opportunity to enter the promised land—a most poignant contrast. At the center, a four-

line stanza recalls Israel's refusal to take over the promised land and Yahweh's condemnation of that generation to die in the desert (see Nu 14:1–23; cf. Heb 3:16–19 and note).
106:1–5 Introduction.
106:1 *Give thanks.* With praise (see note on Ps 100 title); a conventional, liturgical call to praise (see 107:1; 118:1,29; 136:1). *love.* See note on 6:4.
106:2–3 Transition to the main body of the psalm—question and answer.
106:2 *Who can … ?* With integrity. *his praise.* Praise for his mighty acts (see v. 47; see also note on 9:1).
106:3 *Blessed.* See note on 1:1. *act justly … do what is right.* See note on 119:121. This verse answers the question posed in v. 2.
106:4–5 A poetic couplet, voicing the prayer of an individual (cf. v. 47).
106:4 *Remember me.* As one committed to the way of life described in v. 3. *when you show favor.* Or "with the favor you show" (see vv. 44–46). *when you save them.* Or "with your salvation." The psalmist prays that God will include him in all the mercies of his "great love" (v. 45), which he shows to his people. Thus the inner logic of the prayer seems to be completed at v. 46.
106:5 *prosperity … joy … praise.* A progressive sequence of cause and effect. *your inheritance.* See v. 40.
106:6–12 Israel's rebelliousness and the Lord's mercy in the exodus event.
106:6 A general confession of sin introducing the recital. *We.* The author identifies himself with Israel in her rebellion, even as he prays for inclusion in God's mercies toward his people (see Ezr 9:6–7).
106:7,22 *miracles.* For example, the plagues against Egypt (see note on 9:1, "wonderful deeds").
106:10 *redeemed.* Here, as often, a synonym for "delivered" (see note on 71:23).

not one of them survived.
[12] Then they believed his promises
and sang his praise.[r]

[13] But they soon forgot[s] what he had done
and did not wait for his plan to unfold.[t]
[14] In the desert[u] they gave in to their craving;
in the wilderness[v] they put God to the test.[w]
[15] So he gave them[x] what they asked for,
but sent a wasting disease[y] among them.

[16] In the camp they grew envious[z] of Moses
and of Aaron, who was consecrated to the LORD.
[17] The earth opened[a] up and swallowed Dathan;[b]
it buried the company of Abiram.[c]
[18] Fire blazed[d] among their followers;
a flame consumed the wicked.
[19] At Horeb they made a calf[e]
and worshiped an idol cast from metal.
[20] They exchanged their glorious God[f]
for an image of a bull, which eats grass.
[21] They forgot the God[g] who saved them,
who had done great things[h] in Egypt,
[22] miracles in the land of Ham[i]
and awesome deeds[j] by the Red Sea.
[23] So he said he would destroy[k] them—
had not Moses, his chosen one,
stood in the breach[l] before him
to keep his wrath from destroying them.

[24] Then they despised[m] the pleasant land;[n]
they did not believe[o] his promise.
[25] They grumbled[p] in their tents
and did not obey the LORD.
[26] So he swore[q] to them with uplifted hand
that he would make them fall in the wilderness,[r]
[27] make their descendants fall among the nations
and scatter[s] them throughout the lands.

[28] They yoked themselves to the Baal of Peor[t]
and ate sacrifices offered to lifeless gods;
[29] they aroused the LORD's anger[u] by their wicked deeds,[v]
and a plague[w] broke out among them.
[30] But Phinehas[x] stood up and intervened,
and the plague was checked.[y]
[31] This was credited to him[z] as righteousness
for endless generations[a] to come.
[32] By the waters of Meribah[b] they angered the LORD,

106:12 [r] Ex 15:1-21; S Ps 105:43
106:13 [s] S Ex 15:24 [t] S Ex 16:28; S Nu 27:21
106:14 [u] S Ps 78:40 [v] S Ps 68:7 [w] S Ex 17:2; 1Co 10:9
106:15 [x] S Ex 16:13; Ps 78:29 [y] S Nu 11:33
106:16 [z] Nu 16:1-3
106:17 [a] Dt 11:6 [b] S Ex 15:12 [c] S Nu 16:1
106:18 [d] S Lev 10:2
106:19 [e] S Ex 32:4; Ac 7:41
106:20 [f] Jer 2:11; Ro 1:23
106:21 [g] Ps 78:11 [h] Dt 10:21; Ps 75:1
106:22 [i] S Ps 78:51 [j] S Ex 3:20; S Dt 4:34
106:23 [k] S Ex 32:10 [l] Ex 32:11-14; S Nu 11:2; S Dt 9:19
106:24 [m] Nu 14:30-31 [n] S Dt 8:7; S Jer 3:19 [o] S Nu 14:11; Heb 3:18-19
106:25 [p] S Ex 15:24; Dt 1:27; 1Co 10:10
106:26 [q] S Nu 14:23; Heb 4:3 [r] S Dt 2:14; Heb 3:17
106:27 [s] S Lev 26:33
106:28 [t] S Nu 23:28
106:29 [u] Nu 25:3 [v] S Ps 64:2; 141:4 [w] S Nu 16:46; 25:8
106:30 [x] S Ex 6:25 [y] Nu 25:8
106:31 [z] S Ge 15:6; S Nu 25:11-13 [a] Ps 49:11
106:32 [b] S Ex 17:7; Nu 20:2-13

106:12 *sang his praise.* See Ex 15:1–21.
106:13–18 Israel's discontent and the Lord's judgments.
106:13–15 Discontent with the Lord's provisions (see Ex 16; Nu 11).
106:16–18 Discontent with the Lord's leadership arrangements (see Nu 16:1–35).
106:19–23 Idolatry at Mt. Horeb and Moses' intercession.
106:19 *Horeb.* See note on Ex 3:1.
106:20 *glorious God.* See 1Sa 15:29; Jer 2:11 and notes; Hos 4:7.
106:22 *land of Ham.* See 78:51 and note.
106:23 *stood in the breach.* See Ex 32:11–14,31–32. *wrath.* See note on 2:5.
106:24–27 Israel's lack of faith at the border of the promised land and the Lord's judgment (see Nu 14:1–23).
106:24–27 As described in Jer 3:19; 12:10; Zec 7:14; see also Dt 8:7–9; Eze 20:6.
106:26–27 *fall.* See note on 13:4.

106:27 *scatter them throughout the lands.* See Lev 26:33; Dt 28:36–37,64 and note; Eze 20:23.
106:28–33 Idolatry at Peor—and Moses' loss.
106:28 *yoked themselves to.* See Nu 25:3,5.
106:31 *credited … to him as righteousness.* As Abram's faith was "credited to him as righteousness" (Ge 15:6), so, says the psalmist, was Phinehas's priestly zeal for the Lord (see Nu 25:7–8). *for endless generations.* The psalmist refers to the "covenant of a lasting priesthood" (Nu 25:13) that the Lord granted Phinehas as a gracious reward for his zealous act. It was the granting of this promissory covenant that warranted the statement about crediting righteousness, for God's granting of a promissory covenant to Abram had followed upon his crediting Abram's faith to him as righteousness (see Ge 15:9–21). Similarly, God's promissory covenants with Noah (see Ge 9:9–17) and with David (see 2Sa 7:5–16) followed upon God's testimony to their righteousness (see Ge 7:1; 1Sa 13:14). See chart, p. 20.
106:32 *Meribah.* See note on Ex 17:7.

106:33 ^cS Ex 23:21;
Ps 107:11 ^dS Ps 51:11;
Isa 63:10 ^eEx 17:4-7;
Nu 20:8-12
106:34 ^fS Jos 9:15;
Jdg 1:27-36
^gEx 23:24; S Dt 2:34;
7:16; 20:17
106:35 ^hJdg 3:5-6;
Ezr 9:1-2
106:36 ⁱS Dt 7:16
^jS Ex 10:7
106:37 ^kS Lev 18:21;
S Dt 12:31; Eze 16:20-
21 ^lS Ex 22:20;
S Dt 32:17; 1Co 10:20
106:38 ^mS Lev 18:21;
S Dt 18:10; S 2Ki 3:27
106:39 ⁿS Ge 3:17;
Lev 18:24; Eze 20:18
^oS Nu 15:39
106:40 ^pS Lev 26:2
8 ^qS Ex 34:9;
S Dt 9:29
106:41 ^rS Jdg 2:14
106:42 ^sS Jdg 4:3
106:43 ^tS Jos 10:14;
Jdg 7:1-25; S Ne 9:28;
Ps 81:13-14
^uS Jdg 2:16-19; 6:1-7
106:44 ^vS Jdg 3:9
106:45 ^wS Ge 9:15;
Ps 105:8; S Lk 1:72
^xS Ps 17:7; S 103:11
^yS Ex 32:14
106:46 ^zS Ex 3:21;
S 1Ki 8:50
106:47 ^aS Ps 28:9
^bPs 107:3; 147:2;
Isa 11:12; 27:13; 56:8;
66:20; Jer 31:8;
Eze 20:34; Mic 4:6
^cPs 105:1 ^dPs 30:4;
S 99:3
106:48 ^eS Ps 41:13;
S 72:19

and trouble came to Moses because of them;
³³ for they rebelled^c against the Spirit^d of God,
  and rash words came from Moses' lips.^{a e}

³⁴ They did not destroy^f the peoples
  as the LORD had commanded^g them,
³⁵ but they mingled^h with the nations
  and adopted their customs.
³⁶ They worshiped their idols,ⁱ
  which became a snare^j to them.
³⁷ They sacrificed their sons^k
  and their daughters to demons.^l
³⁸ They shed innocent blood,
  the blood of their sons^m and daughters,
whom they sacrificed to the idols of Canaan,
  and the land was desecrated by their blood.
³⁹ They defiled themselvesⁿ by what they did;
  by their deeds they prostituted^o themselves.

⁴⁰ Therefore the LORD was angry^p with his people
  and abhorred his inheritance.^q
⁴¹ He gave them into the hands^r of the nations,
  and their foes ruled over them.
⁴² Their enemies oppressed^s them
  and subjected them to their power.
⁴³ Many times he delivered them,^t
  but they were bent on rebellion^u
  and they wasted away in their sin.
⁴⁴ Yet he took note of their distress
  when he heard their cry;^v
⁴⁵ for their sake he remembered his covenant^w
  and out of his great love^x he relented.^y
⁴⁶ He caused all who held them captive
  to show them mercy.^z

⁴⁷ Save us,^a LORD our God,
  and gather us^b from the nations,
that we may give thanks^c to your holy name^d
  and glory in your praise.

⁴⁸ Praise be to the LORD, the God of Israel,
  from everlasting to everlasting.

Let all the people say, "Amen!"^e

Praise the LORD.

---

^a 33 Or *against his spirit, / and rash words came from his lips*

106:33 *against the Spirit of God.* For a literal rendering of the Hebrew, see TNIV text note. The interpretation embodied in the TNIV text appears warranted by Isa 63:10 (see also Ps 78:40). For the Spirit of God present and at work in the desert wanderings, see Ex 31:3; Nu 11:17; 24:2; Ne 9:20; Isa 63:10–14. See also note on 51:11.
106:34–39 A general description of Israel's rebelliousness in the promised land, applicable from the time of the judges to the Babylonian exile.
106:36 *became a snare to them.* See Ex 23:33; Dt 7:16; Jdg 2:3; 8:27; cf. Lk 10:7; 34:12; 1Sa 18:21; cf. also note on 9:15.
106:37 *demons.* The Hebrew for this word occurs elsewhere in the OT only in Dt 32:17, where it refers to false gods. It is related to a Babylonian word referring to (pagan) protective spirits.
106:38 Cf. Jer 19:4–5. *innocent blood.* The blood of anyone not guilty of a capital crime. *desecrated.* The very land itself is defiled by the slaughter of innocents (see Nu 35:33; Jer 3:2,9).
106:39 *defiled.* See Lev 18:24; Jer 2:23; Eze 20:30–31; 22:3–4. *prostituted themselves.* See Ex 34:15 and note.
106:40–46 God's stern measures against his rebellious people (vv. 40–43), but at the same time his gracious remembering of

his covenant (vv. 44–46). The judgments here recalled focus particularly on God's most severe covenant sanctions (see Lev 26:25–26,33,38–39; Dt 28:25,36–37,48–57,64–68).
106:40 *angry.* See note on 2:5. *abhorred.* See 5:6.
106:44 *heard their cry.* See Ex 2:23; 3:7–9; Nu 20:16; Jdg 3:9,15; 4:3; 6:6–7; 10:10; 1Sa 9:16; 2Ch 20:6–12; Ne 9:27–28.
106:45 *remembered his covenant.* See 105:8,42; Ex 2:24; Lev 26:42,45. *love.* See note on 6:4.
106:46 Makes clear that the author's recital includes the Babylonian captivity (see 1Ki 8:50; 2Ch 30:9; Ezr 9:9; Jer 42:12). Although there were earlier captivities of Israelite communities, no other captive group was said to have been shown "mercy."
106:47 A communal prayer for deliverance and restoration from dispersion (see introduction and note on v. 4). *name.* See note on 5:11. *glory in.* Triumphantly celebrate. The Hebrew for this phrase is found elsewhere only in the parallel in 1Ch 16:35. *praise.* See note on 9:1.
106:48a A conventional word of praise, serving as the doxology to close the psalm and Book IV (see 41:13 and note; see also introduction to this psalm and note on v. 1).

BOOK V

Psalms 107–150

PSALM 107

[1] Give thanks to the LORD, [f] for he is good; [g]
  his love endures forever.

[2] Let the redeemed [h] of the LORD tell their story—
  those he redeemed from the hand of the foe,
[3] those he gathered [i] from the lands,
  from east and west, from north and south. [a]

[4] Some wandered in desert [j] wastelands,
  finding no way to a city [k] where they could settle.
[5] They were hungry [l] and thirsty, [m]
  and their lives ebbed away.
[6] Then they cried out [n] to the LORD in their trouble,
  and he delivered them from their distress.
[7] He led them by a straight way [o]
  to a city [p] where they could settle.
[8] Let them give thanks [q] to the LORD for his unfailing love [r]
  and his wonderful deeds [s] for humankind,
[9] for he satisfies [t] the thirsty
  and fills the hungry with good things. [u]

---

[a] 3 Hebrew *north and the sea*

107:1 [f] S 1Ch 16:8;
S 2Ch 5:13
[g] S 2Ch 7:3
107:2 [h] S Ps 106:10;
S Isa 35:9
107:3 [i] S Ne 1:9
107:4 [j] S Jos 5:6
[k] ver 36
107:5 [l] Ex 16:3
[m] S Ex 15:22; S 17:2
107:6 [n] S Ex 14:10
107:7 [o] S Ezr 8:21
[p] ver 36
107:8 [q] Ps 105:1
[r] Ps 6:4 [s] S Ps 75:1
107:9 [t] Ps 22:26;
63:5; Isa 58:11;
Mt 5:6; Lk 1:53
[u] S Ps 23:1; Jer 31:25

106:48b *Let all the people say.* 1Ch 16:36 sets off the closing exclamations somewhat differently. *Amen!* See Dt 27:15 and note; 1Ch 16:36; Ne 5:13; Jer 11:5; Rom 1:25 and note; 1Co 14:16.

A **Ps 107** An exhortation to praise the Lord for his unfailing love in that he hears the prayers of those in need and saves them (see next paragraph—on structure). It was composed for liturgical use at one of Israel's annual religious festivals. Interpretations vary widely, but the following is most likely: Having experienced anew God's mercies in her return from Babylonian exile (v. 3; see Jer 33:11), Israel is led by a Levite in celebrating God's unfailing benevolence toward those who have cried out to him in the crises of their lives. In its recitational style the psalm is closely related to Ps 104–106, and in its language to Ps 105–106. For that reason it has been seriously proposed that with these last two psalms it forms a trilogy from the same author. Whether or not this is so, its affinity with the preceding psalms strongly suggests that it was associated with them before the insertion of a Book division between Ps 106 and 107 and that it was intended to conclude the little series, Ps 104–107. Its recital of God's "wonderful deeds for humankind" (v. 8)—which climaxes Ps 105–106—balances the recital of his many wise works in creation (see 104:2–26) and his benevolent care over the animal world (see 104:27–30). The editors may have inserted a Book division between Ps 106 and 107 with a view to a fivefold division of the Psalter (see Introduction: Collection, Arrangement and Date). See further the introduction to Ps 101–110.

The introduction (vv. 1–3) and conclusion (v. 43) enclose six stanzas, of which the last two (vv. 33–38, 39–42) stand apart as an instructive supplement focusing in a more general way on reversals in fortunes—which, however, end up with God restoring the "hungry" (v. 36) and the "needy" (v. 41). Of the four remaining stanzas (marked by recurring refrains: vv. 6,13,19,28; vv. 8,15,21,31), the first and last refer to God's deliverance of those lost in the trackless desert (vv. 4–9) and those imperiled on the boisterous sea (vv. 23–32). The two central stanzas celebrate deliverance from the punishment of foreign bondage (vv. 10–16) and from the punishment of disease (vv. 17–22). Of the concluding lines to these four stanzas, the first two (vv. 9,16) and the

last two (vv. 22,32) are similar. The verse pattern of these four stanzas (six-seven-six-ten) makes deliberate use of the significant numbers seven and ten.

107:1–3 Introductory call to praise.
107:1 A conventional, liturgical call to praise (see 106:1; 118:1,29; 136:1; Jer 33:11). *Give thanks.* See vv. 8,15,21,31; see also note on Ps 100 title. *love.* See vv. 8,15,21,31,43; see also note on 6:4.
107:2 *redeemed.* Here, as often, a synonym for "delivered" (see note on 71:23).
107:3 *from the lands.* From the dispersion resulting from the Assyrian (see 2Ki 17:6) and Babylonian captivities (see 2Ki 24:14,16; 25:11,26; Jer 52:28–30; see also Ne 1:8; Est 8:5,9,13; Isa 11:12; 43:5–6; Eze 11:17; 20:34). *south.* Lit. "(the) sea" (see TNIV text note), i.e., the west, as in Isa 49:12. But perhaps the final letter of the Hebrew word has been lost, which if supplied yields "south."
107:4–9 Deliverance for those lost in the trackless desert. No reference is made to rebellion (as in the third and fourth stanzas), but since Israel had journeyed through the desert on her way to Canaan she had firsthand experience of the terrors of the desert. She was, moreover, bounded on the east by the great Arabian Desert (as on the west by the Mediterranean Sea; see vv. 23–32), across which her merchant caravans traveled.
107:4,7,36 *city where they could settle.* Lit. "city of habitation," i.e., where people live and where a steady supply of food and water makes human life secure.
107:6 *they cried out.* The author uses the same Hebrew verb in v. 28, thus linking the fifth stanza with the second. In vv. 13,19 he uses a different (but similar-sounding) Hebrew verb, linking the third and fourth stanzas. Just as Israel's history was a history of divine deliverance (see Ps 105) and a history of rebellion (see Ps 106), so also it was a history of crying out to the Lord in distress (see references in note on 106:44).
107:7 *straight way.* Direct route, clear of dangerous and difficult obstacles.
107:8 For other refrains, see introduction to Ps 42–43. *wonderful deeds.* See vv. 15,21,24,31; see also note on 9:1.
107:9 *satisfies the thirsty ... fills the hungry.* See v. 5; see also 105:40–41.

107:10 ᵛver 14;
Ps 88:6; 143:3;
Isa 9:2; 42:7,16; 49:9;
Mic 7:9 ʷPs 102:20;
Isa 61:1 ˣS Job 36:8
107:11 ʸS Ps 5:10
ᶻS Nu 14:11
ᵃS 1Ki 22:5;
2Ch 36:16
107:12 ᵇS 2Ki 14:26;
Ps 72:12
107:13 ᶜS Ps 106:8
107:14 ᵈS ver 10;
Isa 9:2; 42:7; 50:10;
59:9; 60:2; S Lk 1:79
ᵉPs 86:13; Isa 29:18
ᶠS Job 36:8; Ps 116:16;
Ac 12:7
107:15 ᵍver 8,21,
31; Ps 105:1 ʰPs 6:4
ⁱS Ps 75:1
107:17 ʲS Ps 53:1
ᵏS Ps 25:7
ˡS Lev 26:16;
Isa 65:6-7; Jer 30:14-
15; Gal 6:7-8
107:18 ᵐS Job 3:24;
S 6:6 ⁿS Job 17:16;
S 33:22
107:19 ᵒver 28;
Ps 5:2 ᵖver 13;
Ps 34:4
107:20 �ۥS Dt 32:2;
Ps 147:15; Mt 8:8;
Lk 7:7 ʳS Ex 15:26
ˢS Job 33:28
ᵗPs 16:10; 30:3;
S 56:13
107:21 ᵘS ver 15
ᵛPs 6:4 ʷPs 75:1
107:22 ˣS Lev 7:12
ʸPs 9:11; 73:28;
118:17 ᶻS Job 8:21;
S Ps 65:8
107:23 ᵃIsa 42:10
ᵇS Ps 104:26
107:24 ᶜPs 64:9;
111:2; 143:5
107:25 ᵈS Ps 105:31
ᵉS Ps 50:3 ᶠS Ps 93:3
107:26 ᵍLk 8:23
ʰS Jos 2:11
107:27 ⁱIsa 19:14;
24:20; 28:7

¹⁰ Some sat in darkness, ᵛ in utter darkness,
　　prisoners suffering ʷ in iron chains, ˣ
¹¹ because they rebelled ʸ against God's commands
　　and despised ᶻ the plans ᵃ of the Most High.
¹² So he subjected them to bitter labor;
　　they stumbled, and there was no one to help. ᵇ
¹³ Then they cried to the Lᴏʀᴅ in their trouble,
　　and he saved them ᶜ from their distress.
¹⁴ He brought them out of darkness, ᵈ the utter darkness, ᵉ
　　and broke away their chains. ᶠ
¹⁵ Let them give thanks ᵍ to the Lᴏʀᴅ for his unfailing love ʰ
　　and his wonderful deeds ⁱ for humankind,
¹⁶ for he breaks down gates of bronze
　　and cuts through bars of iron.

¹⁷ Some became fools ʲ through their rebellious ways ᵏ
　　and suffered affliction ˡ because of their iniquities.
¹⁸ They loathed all food ᵐ
　　and drew near the gates of death. ⁿ
¹⁹ Then they cried ᵒ to the Lᴏʀᴅ in their trouble,
　　and he saved them ᵖ from their distress.
²⁰ He sent out his word ۥ and healed them; ʳ
　　he rescued ˢ them from the grave. ᵗ
²¹ Let them give thanks ᵘ to the Lᴏʀᴅ for his unfailing love ᵛ
　　and his wonderful deeds ʷ for humankind.
²² Let them sacrifice thank offerings ˣ
　　and tell of his works ʸ with songs of joy. ᶻ

²³ Some went out on the sea ᵃ in ships; ᵇ
　　they were merchants on the mighty waters.
²⁴ They saw the works of the Lᴏʀᴅ, ᶜ
　　his wonderful deeds in the deep.
²⁵ For he spoke ᵈ and stirred up a tempest ᵉ
　　that lifted high the waves. ᶠ
²⁶ They mounted up to the heavens and went down to the depths;
　　in their peril ᵍ their courage melted ʰ away.
²⁷ They reeled ⁱ and staggered like drunkards;
　　they were at their wits' end.

107:10–16 Deliverance from the punishment of foreign bondage. God even delivers those who cry out to him when their distress is a result of his discipline for their sins (see vv. 17–20, 33–41).
107:10 *sat in darkness … utter darkness.* Vivid imagery for distress (see 18:28; Isa 5:30; 8:22; 59:9; see also note on 44:19). *prisoners.* While reference is no doubt to foreign bondage, the imagery of being bound was also used by OT poets to refer to other forms of distress (see Job 36:8; Isa 28:22; La 3:7); so the reference may be deliberately ambiguous.
107:11 *God … Most High.* That is, God Most High (see Ge 14:19 and note; see also note on 3:7). *plans.* God's wise directives embodied in his words (see 73:24 and note).
107:12 *subjected them to bitter labor.* Lit. "brought down their heart with labor," i.e., a labor so burdensome it broke their spirit. *stumbled.* Their strength failed (see 31:10; 109:24; Ne 4:10; Isa 40:30; Zec 12:8).
107:13 *cried to.* See note on v. 6.
107:16 Either this verse is quoted from Isa 45:2 or both verses quote an established saying. *gates of bronze.* City gates—normally of wood; here proverbially of bronze, the strongest gates then imaginable (see 1Ki 4:13; cf. Jer 1:18). *bars of iron.* Bars that secured city gates (see Dt 3:5; Jer 51:30). "Can anyone break iron … or bronze?" was a proverb of the time (see Jer 15:12).
107:17–22 Deliverance from the punishment of wasting disease (see note on vv. 10–16).
107:17 *fools.* See Jer 4:22; see also TNIV text note on 14:1. "Fools

despise wisdom and instruction" (Pr 1:7; see v. 43). *affliction because of their iniquities.* See Lev 26:16,25; Dt 28:20–22,35,58–61.

B **107:18** *gates of death.* The realm of the dead was sometimes depicted as a netherworld city with a series of concentric walls and gates (seven, each inside the other, according to ancient Near Eastern mythology) to keep those descending there from returning to the land of the living (see 9:13 and note on Job 38:17; see also Mt 16:18).
107:19 *cried to.* See note on v. 6. *saved.* See v. 13 (another link between the second and third stanzas); cf. vv. 6,28.
107:20 *his word.* His command, here personified as the agent of his purpose (see 147:15,18; see note on 23:6).
107:22 *thank offerings.* See Lev 7:12–15; 22:29–30. *tell of his works.* See note on 7:17. In their concluding lines, stanzas four and five are linked, as are stanzas two and three. *songs of joy.* See, e.g., Ps 116.
107:23–32 Deliverance from the perils of the sea (see note on vv. 4–9). Israel's merchants also braved the sea in pursuit of trade (see Ge 49:13; Jdg 5:17; 1Ki 9:26–28; 10:22).
107:23 *mighty waters.* See 29:3.
107:24 *wonderful deeds in the deep.* Since the peoples of the eastern Mediterranean coastlands associated the "mighty waters" (v. 23) of the sea with the primeval chaotic waters (see note on 32:6), the Lord's total control of them was always for Israel a cause of wonder and a sense of security. Therefore the terrifying storms that sometimes swept the Mediterranean (see Jnh 1; Ac 27) are here included among his wonderful deeds.

²⁸ Then they cried[j] out to the LORD in their trouble,
  and he brought them out of their distress.[k]
²⁹ He stilled the storm[l] to a whisper;
  the waves[m] of the sea[a] were hushed.[n]
³⁰ They were glad when it grew calm,
  and he guided them[o] to their desired haven.
³¹ Let them give thanks[p] to the LORD for his unfailing love[q]
  and his wonderful deeds[r] for humankind.
³² Let them exalt[s] him in the assembly[t] of the people
  and praise him in the council of the elders.

³³ He turned rivers into a desert,[u]
  flowing springs[v] into thirsty ground,
³⁴ and fruitful land into a salt waste,[w]
  because of the wickedness of those who lived there.
³⁵ He turned the desert into pools of water[x]
  and the parched ground into flowing springs;[y]
³⁶ there he brought the hungry to live,
  and they founded a city where they could settle.
³⁷ They sowed fields and planted vineyards[z]
  that yielded a fruitful harvest;
³⁸ he blessed them, and their numbers greatly increased,[a]
  and he did not let their herds diminish.[b]

³⁹ Then their numbers decreased,[c] and they were humbled[d]
  by oppression, calamity and sorrow;
⁴⁰ he who pours contempt on nobles[e]
  made them wander in a trackless waste.[f]
⁴¹ But he lifted the needy[g] out of their affliction
  and increased their families like flocks.[h]

⁴² The upright see and rejoice,[i]
  but all the wicked shut their mouths.[j]

⁴³ Let all who are wise[k] heed these things
  and ponder the loving deeds[l] of the LORD.

PSALM 108

108:1–5pp — Ps 57:7–11
108:6–13pp — Ps 60:5–12

A song. A psalm of David.

*[*]1 My heart, O God, is steadfast;[m]
  I will sing[n] and make music with all my soul.

ª 29 Dead Sea Scrolls; Masoretic Text / *their waves*

* 108:1-13 is numbered 108:2-14 in Hebrew texts.

**Cross references (right margin):**

107:28 ʲS ver 19
ᵏPs 4:1; Jnh 1:6
107:29 ˡLk 8:24
ᵐS Ps 93:3
ⁿS Ps 65:7; Jnh 1:15
107:30 ᵒver 7
107:31 ᵖS ver 15
ᑫPs 6:4; ʳPs 75:1; 106:2
107:32 ˢPs 30:1; 34:3; 99:5; ᵗS Ps 1:5; 22:22,25; 26:12; 35:18
107:33 ᵘ1Ki 17:1; Ps 74:15; Isa 41:15; 42:15; 50:2
ᵛS Ps 104:10
107:34 ʷS Ge 13:10
107:35 ˣS 2Ki 3:17; Ps 105:41; 126:4; Isa 43:19; 51:3
ʸS Job 38:26; S Isa 35:7
107:37 ᶻS 2Ki 19:29; S Isa 37:30
107:38 ᵃS Ge 12:2; S Dt 7:13
ᵇS Ge 49:25
107:39 ᶜS 2Ki 10:32; Eze 5:12 ᵈS Ps 44:9
107:40 ᵉS Job 12:18
ᶠS Dt 32:10
107:41 ᵍS 1Sa 2:8; Ps 113:7-9
ʰS Job 21:11
107:42 ⁱS Job 22:19; Ps 97:10-12
ʲS Job 5:16; Ro 3:19
107:43 ᵏJer 9:12; Hos 14:9 ˡPs 103:11
108:1 ᵐPs 112:7; 119:30,112
ⁿS Ps 18:49

Footnotes (bottom)

107:27 *they were at their wits' end.* Lit. "all their wisdom/skill was swallowed up."
107:30 *haven.* Perhaps trading center.
107:32 See v. 22. *elders.* See note on Ex 3:16.
107:33–42 A twofold instructive supplement recalling how the Lord sometimes disciplined his people by turning the fruitful land (v. 34) into a virtual desert (see 1Ki 17:1–7; 2Ki 8:1) but then restored the land again (see Ru 1:6; 1Ki 18:44–45), so that the hungry (v. 36) could live there and prosper in the midst of plenty. But then he sent powerful armies against them (such as the Assyrians, 2Ki 17:3–6, and the Babylonians, 2Ki 24:10–17; 25:1–26) that devastated the land once more and deported its people; yet afterward he restored the needy (v. 41). But the poet generalizes upon these experiences in the manner of the wisdom teachers.
107:33–35 The imagery is similar to that found in Isa 35:6–7; 41:18; 42:15; 43:19–20; 50:2 and may indicate that the author has been influenced by Isaiah.
107:40 Perhaps quoted from Job 12:21,24. In their prosperity the people, led by their nobles, grow proud and turn

their backs on the God who has blessed them (see Dt 31:20; 32:15), so he returns them to the desert (see Dt 32:10; Hos 2:3,14).
107:41 *needy.* Those in need of help (see v. 39; see also 9:18 and note).
107:42 Conclusion to the instruction (vv. 33–41); perhaps an echo of Job 5:16. *upright ... wicked.* A frequent contrast in OT wisdom literature (see Pr 2:21–22; 11:6–7; 12:6; 14:11; 15:8; 21:18,29; 29:27—but the Hebrew for "wicked" here is shared more often with Job).
107:43 Conclusion to the psalm. *all who are wise.* See Dt 32:29; Hos 14:9. *these things.* The instruction in vv. 33–42. *ponder the loving deeds of the LORD.* The theme of vv. 4–32, emphatically reiterated.
Ps 108 Praise of God's love, and prayer for his help against the enemies—a combination (with very slight modifications) of 57:7–11 and 60:5–12. For a similar composition of a new psalm by combination of portions from several psalms, see 1Ch 16:8–36. The celebration of the greatness of God's love (v. 4) links this psalm thematically with Ps 103 (see 103:11). See introduction to Ps 101–110.

108:2 °S Job 21:12
108:4 PNu 14:18;
Ps 106:45 ªS Ex 34:6
ʳS Ps 36:5
108:5 ˢS Ps 8:1
ᵗS Ps 57:5
108:6 ᵘS Job 40:14
108:7 ᵛPs 89:35
ʷPs 68:35; 102:19
ˣGe 12:6
ʸGe 33:17
108:8 ᶻS Ps 78:68
108:9 ªS Ge 19:37
ᵇS 2Sa 8:13-14
ᶜS 2Sa 8:1
108:11 ᵈS Ps 44:9
108:12 ᵉPs 118:8;
146:3; Isa 10:3; 30:5;
31:3; Jer 2:36; 17:5
108:13 ᶠPs 44:5;
Isa 22:5; 63:3,6
109:1 ᵍS Ex 15:2;
Jer 17:14
ʰS Job 34:29
109:2 ⁱS Ps 43:1
ʲS Ps 52:4
109:3 ᵏPs 69:4
ˡPs 35:7; Jn 15:25
109:4 ᵐPs 69:13;
141:5
109:5 ⁿS Ge 44:4

² Awake, harp and lyre! °
   I will awaken the dawn.
³ I will praise you, LORD, among the nations;
   I will sing of you among the peoples.
⁴ For great is your love, ᵖ higher than the heavens;
   your faithfulness �q reaches to the skies. ʳ
⁵ Be exalted, O God, above the heavens; ˢ
   let your glory be over all the earth. ᵗ

⁶ Save us and help us with your right hand, ᵘ
   that those you love may be delivered.
⁷ God has spoken ᵛ from his sanctuary: ʷ
   "In triumph I will parcel out Shechem ˣ
   and measure off the Valley of Sukkoth. ʸ
⁸ Gilead is mine, Manasseh is mine;
   Ephraim is my helmet,
   Judah ᶻ is my scepter.
⁹ Moab ª is my washbasin,
   on Edom ᵇ I toss my sandal;
   over Philistia ᶜ I shout in triumph."

¹⁰ Who will bring me to the fortified city?
   Who will lead me to Edom?
¹¹ Is it not you, God, you who have rejected us
   and no longer go out with our armies? ᵈ
¹² Give us aid against the enemy,
   for human help is worthless. ᵉ
¹³ With God we will gain the victory,
   and he will trample down ᶠ our enemies.

PSALM 109

For the director of music. Of David. A psalm.

¹ My God, whom I praise, ᵍ
   do not remain silent, ʰ
² for people who are wicked and deceitful ⁱ
   have opened their mouths against me;
   they have spoken against me with lying tongues. ʲ
³ With words of hatred ᵏ they surround me;
   they attack me without cause. ˡ
⁴ In return for my friendship they accuse me,
   but I am a man of prayer. ᵐ
⁵ They repay me evil for good, ⁿ
   and hatred for my friendship.

---

108 title *song.* See note on Ps 30 title. *of David.* Both sources
(Ps 57; 60) were credited to him.
108:1–5 Praise of God's love, possibly intended to function
here as an expression of trust in God (the God of vv. 7–9,11), to
whom appeal is to be made (vv. 6,12); see 109:1 and note. For
this stanza see notes on 57:7–11.
108:1 *soul.* Lit. "glory" (see note on 7:5).
108:6–13 Prayer for God's help against enemies (see notes on
60:5–12).

A Ps 109 A prayer for God to deliver from false accusers.
The author speaks of his enemies in the singular in vv.
6–19 but in the plural elsewhere. Either (1) the author shifts here
to a collective mode of speaking, or (2) the enemies are united
under a leader whose personal animosity toward the psalmist
has fired the antagonism of others and so is singled out for special attention. Traditional attempts to isolate a distinct class of
psalms called "imprecatory" (and then identify Ps 109 as the climax of the series) are mistaken (see note on vv. 6–15). Thematically, this prayer has much affinity with Ps 35. Within the cluster
in which it stands, its affinity is with Ps 102 (see introduction to

Ps 101–110)—and it is only one line longer than that psalm.
   Two (Hebrew) four-line stanzas of petition frame the whole
(vv. 1–5,26–29), followed by a two-line conclusion (vv. 30–31).
The remaining 20 lines fall into two main divisions of ten lines
each (vv. 6–15,16–25). Of these, the second is thematically divided into two parts of five lines each, the first of which (vv.
16–20) catalogues what "he" has done, while the second (vv.
21–25) describes how "I" am suffering.
109 title See note on Ps 4 title.
109:1–5 Appeal to God to deliver David from false accusers.
109:1 *whom I praise.* The one he publicly praises as his trustworthy deliverer and defender (see 22:3 and note; see also
35:18; 74:21; 76:10; 79:13; 102:18). *silent.* (Judicially) inactive
(see 28:1; 35:22; 50:3,21; 83:1).
109:2–5 The particulars of his case, which he presents before
the heavenly bar of justice (see 35:11–16).
109:2 *opened their mouths against me.* See note on 5:9.

A 109:4 *but I am a man of prayer.* In contrast to the enemy
(see vv. 16–18). The intent may be: But I have prayed for
them (as in 35:13–14).

⁶ Appoint someone evil to oppose my enemy;
  let an accuser ᵒ stand at his right hand.
⁷ When he is tried, let him be found guilty, ᵖ
  and may his prayers condemn ��q him.
⁸ May his days be few; ʳ
  may another take his place ˢ of leadership.
⁹ May his children be fatherless
  and his wife a widow. ᵗ
¹⁰ May his children be wandering beggars; ᵘ
  may they be driven ᵃ from their ruined homes.
¹¹ May a creditor ᵛ seize all he has;
  may strangers plunder ʷ the fruits of his labor. ˣ
¹² May no one extend kindness to him
  or take pity ʸ on his fatherless children.
¹³ May his descendants be cut off, ᶻ
  their names blotted out ᵃ from the next generation.
¹⁴ May the iniquity of his fathers ᵇ be remembered before the Lᴏʀᴅ;
  may the sin of his mother never be blotted out.
¹⁵ May their sins always remain before ᶜ the Lᴏʀᴅ,
  that he may blot out their name ᵈ from the earth.

¹⁶ For he never thought of doing a kindness,
  but hounded to death the poor
  and the needy ᵉ and the brokenhearted. ᶠ
¹⁷ He loved to pronounce a curse—
  may it come on him. ᵍ
  He found no pleasure in blessing—
  may it be far from him.
¹⁸ He wore cursing ʰ as his garment;
  it entered into his body like water, ⁱ
  into his bones like oil.
¹⁹ May it be like a cloak wrapped ʲ about him,
  like a belt tied forever around him.
²⁰ May this be the Lᴏʀᴅ's payment ᵏ to my accusers,
  to those who speak evil ˡ of me.

²¹ But you, Sovereign Lᴏʀᴅ,
  help me for your name's sake; ᵐ
  out of the goodness of your love, ⁿ deliver me. ᵒ

ᵃ 10 Septuagint; Hebrew *sought*

109:6 ᵒ1Ch 21:1;
Job 1:6; Zec 3:1
109:7 ᵖ Ps 1:5
ᵠ Pr 28:9; Isa 41:24
109:8 ʳS Job 15:32
ˢ Ac 1:20*
109:9 ᵗ Ex 22:24;
Jer 18:21
109:10 ᵘ S Ge 4:12
109:11 ᵛ Ne 5:3
ʷ S Ne 14:3; Isa 1:7;
6:11; 36:1; La 5:2
ˣ Job 20:18
109:12 ʸ S Job 5:4
109:13 ᶻ Job 18:19;
Ps 21:10 ᵃ S Nu 14:12;
Ps 9:5; Pr 10:7
109:14 ᵇ Ex 20:5;
Nu 14:18; Isa 65:6-7;
Jer 32:18
109:15 ᶜ Ps 90:8
ᵈ S Ex 17:14;
S Dt 32:26
109:16 ᵉ S Job 20:19;
S Ps 35:10 ᶠ S Ps 34:18
109:17 ᵍ Pr 28:27;
S Mt 7:2
109:18 ʰ Ps 10:7
ⁱ Nu 5:22
109:19 ʲ ver 29;
Ps 73:6; Eze 7:27
109:20 ᵏ S Ex 32:34;
Ps 54:5; 94:23;
Isa 3:11; 2Ti 4:14
ˡ Ps 71:10
109:21 ᵐ S Ex 9:16;
S Ps 23:3 ⁿ Ps 69:16
ᵒ S Ps 3:7

109:6–15 Appeal for judicial redress—that the Lord will deal with them in accordance with their malicious intent against him, matching punishment with crime (see note on 5:10; see also 35:4–10 and note).
109:6 *someone evil...accuser.* The psalmist's enemy falsely accused him in order to bring him down; now let the enemy be confronted by an accuser.
109:7 *his prayers.* The petitions he offers in his defense.
109:8 *days be few.* The false accuser was no doubt seeking to effect David's death (see 1Ki 21:8–15). *another take his place of leadership.* The enemy held some official position and was perhaps plotting a coup. For a NT application of these words to Judas, see Ac 1:20.
109:10–11 May he also be deprived of all his property so that he has no inheritance to pass on to his children.
109:12 *no one extend kindness.* See v. 16. *his...children.* The close identity of a man with his children and of children with their parents, resulting from the tightly bonded unity of the three- or four-generation households of that ancient society, is alien to the modern reader, whose sense of self is highly individualistic. But that deep, profoundly human bond accounts for the ancient legal principle of "punishing the children for the sin of the parents to the third and fourth generation" (see Ex 20:5; but see also 103:17; Ge 18:19).

109:13 Since a man lived on in his children (see previous note), the focus of judgment remains on the false accuser (see 21:10; 37:28). *names blotted out.* See note on 9:5.
109:14–15 *iniquity of his fathers...sin of his mother...their sins.* These verses return to the theme of vv. 7–8 (and thus form a frame around the stanza): May the indictment the accuser lodges against him include the sins of his parents (see note on v. 12).
109:15 *blot out their name.* May this slanderer be the last of his family line.
109:16–20 The ruthless character of the enemy—may he be made to suffer the due consequences (see 10:2–15; 59:12–13). Accusation of the adversary is a common feature in psalms that are appeals to the heavenly Judge (see, e.g., 5:9–10; 10:2–11; 17:10–12).
109:17 *pronounce a curse.* The enemy added curses to lies (see note on Ge 12:3).
109:18–19 *garment...cloak wrapped.* See note on v. 29.
109:18 *into his body like water, into his bones like oil.* Pronouncing curses on others was his food and drink, as well as his clothing; he lived by such cursing (cf. Pr 4:17 and note).
109:20 *the Lᴏʀᴅ's payment.* See 54:5; 94:23; Isa 3:11; 2Ti 4:14.
109:21–25 The intensity of "my" suffering—Lord, deliver me!
109:21 *for your name's sake.* See notes on 5:11; 23:3. *love.* See v. 26; see also note on 6:4.

109:23 ᵖ S Job 14:2
109:24 ᵠ Heb 12:12
ʳ S Ps 35:13
ˢ S Job 16:8
109:25 ᵗ S Ps 22:6
ᵘ S Job 16:4;
S Mt 27:39; Mk 15:29
109:26 ᵛ Ps 12:1;
119:86
109:27 ʷ S Job 37:7
109:28 ˣ S 2Sa 16:12
ʸ Ps 66:4; Isa 35:10;
51:11; 54:1; 65:14
109:29 ᶻ S Ps 35:26
109:30 ᵃ S Ps 35:18
109:31 ᵇ Ps 16:8;
108:6
110:1 ᶜ Mt 22:44*;
Mk 12:36*;
Lk 20:42*; Ac 2:34*
ᵈ S Mk 16:19;
Heb 1:13*; 12:2
ᵉ S Jos 10:24;
S 1Ki 5:3; 1Co 15:25
110:2 ᶠ S Ge 49:10;
Ps 45:6; Isa 14:5;
Jer 48:17 ᵍ S Ps 2:6
ʰ Ps 72:8

²²For I am poor and needy,
and my heart is wounded within me.
²³I fade away like an evening shadow; ᵖ
I am shaken off like a locust.
²⁴My knees give ᵠ way from fasting; ʳ
my body is thin and gaunt. ˢ
²⁵I am an object of scorn ᵗ to my accusers;
when they see me, they shake their heads. ᵘ

²⁶Help me, ᵛ LORD my God;
save me according to your unfailing love.
²⁷Let them know ʷ that it is your hand,
that you, LORD, have done it.
²⁸While they curse, ˣ may you bless;
may those who attack me be put to shame,
but may your servant rejoice. ʸ
²⁹May my accusers be clothed with disgrace
and wrapped in shame ᶻ as in a cloak.

³⁰With my mouth I will greatly extol the LORD;
in the great throng ᵃ of worshipers I will praise him.
³¹For he stands at the right hand ᵇ of the needy,
to save their lives from those who would condemn them.

PSALM 110

Of David. A psalm.

¹The LORD says ᶜ to my lord: ᵃ
"Sit at my right hand ᵈ
until I make your enemies
a footstool for your feet." ᵉ

²The LORD will extend your mighty scepter ᶠ from Zion, ᵍ saying,
"Rule ʰ in the midst of your enemies."

ᵃ 1 Or *Lord*

109:22 The psalmist's description of his situation echoes the words of v. 16. *poor and needy.* Dependent on the Lord (see note on 34:6). *heart.* See note on 4:7. *is wounded.* The Hebrew for this phrase sounds like the Hebrew for "curse" in vv. 17–18, a deliberate wordplay—while he lives by cursing, I live with deep inward pain.
109:23 *I fade away.* Apparently the psalmist suffers a life-sapping affliction, which is the occasion for his enemies to turn on him (see vv. 24–25; see also note on 5:9). *like an evening shadow.* See 102:11. *shaken off.* See Ne 5:13; Job 38:13.
109:26–29 Concluding petition, with many echoes of preceding themes.
109:28 *servant.* Perhaps identifies the psalmist as the Lord's anointed (see title; see also 78:70 and note).
109:29 *clothed with … wrapped in.* For other uses of this imagery, see vv. 18–19; 35:26; 45:3; 73:6; 104:1–2; 132:9,16,18; Job 8:22; 29:14; 40:10; Pr 31:25; Isa 59:17; 61:3,10; Eze 7:27; 26:16; 31:15; Zec 6:13; Lk 24:19; Ro 13:14; 1Co 15:53–54; Gal 3:27; Col 3:12; 1Pe 5:5.
109:30–31 A vow to praise the Lord for his deliverance (see note on 7:17).

Ps 110 Oracles concerning the Messianic King-Priest. This psalm (specifically its two brief oracles, vv. 1,4) is frequently referred to in the NT testimony to Christ. Like Ps 2, it has the marks of a coronation psalm, composed for use at the enthronement of a new Davidic king. Before the Christian era Jews already viewed it as Messianic. Because of the manner in which it has been interpreted in the NT—especially by Jesus (see Mt 22:43–45; Mk 12:36–37; Lk 20:42–44) but also by Peter (see Ac 2:34–36) and the author of Hebrews (see especially Heb 1:13; 5:6–10; 7:11–28)—Christians have generally held that this is the most directly "prophetic" of all the psalms. If so, David,

speaking prophetically (see 2Sa 23:2), composed a coronation psalm for his great future Son, of whom the prophets did not speak until later. It may be, however, that David composed the psalm for the coronation of his son Solomon, that he called him "my lord" (v. 1; but see TNIV text note) in view of his new status, which placed him above the aged David, and that in so doing he spoke a word that had far larger meaning than he knew. This would seem to be in more accord with what we know of David from Samuel, Kings and Chronicles. For this psalm's setting in the Psalter, see introduction to Ps 101–110.
The psalm falls into two precisely balanced halves (vv. 1–3, 4–7). Each of the two brief oracles (vv. 1,4) is followed by thematically and structurally similar elaboration: As v. 4 is to v. 1, so v. 5 is to v. 2 and vv. 6–7 are to v. 3 (a poetic couplet).
110:1–3 The Lord's decree, establishing his anointed as his regent in the face of all opposition (see 2:7–12).

110:1 The first oracle (see note on v. 4). *my lord.* My sovereign, therefore superior to David (see Mt 22:44–45; Mk 12:36–37; Lk 20:42–44; Ac 2:34–35; Heb 1:13 and their contexts). *Sit.* Sit enthroned. *right hand.* The place of honor beside a king (see 45:9; 1Ki 2:19); thus he is made second in authority to God himself. NT references to Jesus' exaltation to this position are many (see Mt 26:64; Mk 14:62; 16:19; Lk 22:69; Ac 2:33; 5:31; 7:55–56; Ro 8:34; Eph 1:20; Col 3:1; Heb 1:3; 8:1; 10:12; 12:2). *enemies.* See note on 2:1–3. *footstool for your feet.* See Heb 10:12–13. Ancient kings often had themselves portrayed as placing their feet on vanquished enemies (see Jos 10:24). For a royal footstool as part of the throne, see 2Ch 9:18. For the thought here, see 1Ki 5:3. Paul applies this word to Christ in 1Co 15:25; Eph 1:22.
110:2 *extend your mighty scepter.* Expand your reign in ever

3 Your troops will be willing
 on your day of battle.
 Arrayed in holy splendor, [i]
 your young men will come to you
 like dew from the morning's womb. [a][j]

4 The LORD has sworn
 and will not change his mind: [k]
 "You are a priest forever, [l]
 in the order of Melchizedek. [m]"

5 The Lord is at your right hand [b]; [n]
 he will crush kings [o] on the day of his wrath. [p]
6 He will judge the nations, [q] heaping up the dead [r]
 and crushing the rulers [s] of the whole earth.
7 He will drink from a brook along the way, [c]
 and so he will lift up his head. [t]

PSALM 111 [d]

1 Praise the LORD. [e]

 I will extol the LORD [u] with all my heart [v]
 in the council [w] of the upright and in the assembly. [x]

110:3 [i] S Ex 15:11
[j] Mic 5:7
110:4 [k] S Nu 23:19
[l] Zec 6:13; Heb 5:6*;
7:21* [m] S Ge 14:18;
Heb 5:10; 7:15-17*
110:5 [n] Ps 16:8
[o] S Dt 7:24; Ps 2:12;
68:21; 76:12;
Isa 60:12; Da 2:44
[p] Ps 2:5; Ro 2:5;
Rev 6:17; 11:18
110:6 [q] S Ps 9:19
[r] Isa 5:25; 34:3; 66:24
[s] S Ps 18:38
110:7 [t] Ps 3:3; 27:6
111:1 [u] Ps 34:1;
109:30; 115:18; 145:10
[v] S Ps 9:1 [w] Ps 89:7
[x] S Ps 1:5

---

[a] 3 The meaning of the Hebrew for this sentence is uncertain.   [b] 5 Or My lord is at your right hand,
LORD   [c] 7 The meaning of the Hebrew for this clause is uncertain.   [d] This psalm is an acrostic poem,
the lines of which begin with the successive letters of the Hebrew alphabet.   [e] 1 Hebrew Hallelu Yah

---

widening circles until no foe remains to oppose your rule. *Zion.* David's royal city (see 2Sa 5:7,9), but also God's (see 9:11 and note), where he rules as the Great King (see Ps 46; 48; 132:13–18). The Lord's anointed is his regent over his emerging kingdom in the world.

A **110:3** *willing.* Lit. "freewill offerings," i.e., they will offer themselves as dedicated warriors to support you on the battlefield (see Jdg 5:2)—as the Israelites offered of their treasures for the building of the tabernacle in the desert (see Ex 35:29; 36:3; see also Ezr 1:4; 2:68). Accordingly, Paul speaks of Christ's followers offering their bodies "as a living sacrifice" (Ro 12:1) and of himself as a "drink offering" (Php 2:17; see also 2Co 8:5. *Arrayed in holy splendor.* If the phrase is descriptive of the Lord's anointed, it depicts him as clothed in royal majesty and glory. If it speaks of the young warriors who flock to him, it apparently describes them as dressed in priestly garb, ready for participation in a holy war (see 1Sa 21:4–5; 25:28; 2Ch 13:8,12; 20:15,21; Isa 13:3–4; Jer 6:4; 51:27) and pouring into his camp morning by morning as copious as the dew (see 2Sa 17:11–12). *holy splendor.* See note on 29:2.

110:4–7 The Lord's oath, establishing his anointed as king-priest in Zion and assuring him victory over all powers that oppose him.

A **110:4** The second oracle (see note on v. 1). *has sworn.* In accordance also with his sworn covenant to maintain David's royal line forever (see 89:35–37). The force of this oath is elaborated by the author of Hebrews (Heb 6:16–18; 7:20–22). *priest . . . in the order of Melchizedek.* David and his royal sons, as chief representatives of the rule of God, performed many worship-focused activities, such as overseeing the ark of the covenant (see 2Sa 6:1–15, especially v. 14; 1Ki 8:1), building and overseeing the temple (see 1Ki 5–7; 2Ki 12:4–7; 22:3–7; 23:4–7; 2Ch 15:8; 24:4–12; 29:3–11; 34:8) and overseeing the work of the priests and Levites and the temple liturgy (see 1Ch 6:31; 15:11–16; 16:4–42; 23:3–31; 25:1; 2Ch 17:7–9; 19:8–11; 29:25, 30; 31:2; 35:15–16; Ezr 3:10; 8:20; Ne 12:24, 36,45). In all these duties they exercised authority even over the high priest. But they could not engage in those specifically priestly functions that had been assigned to the Aaronic priesthood (see 2Ch 26:16–18). In the present oracle the son of David is installed by God as king-priest in Zion after the manner of Melchizedek, the king-priest of God Most High at Jerusalem in the days of Abraham (see Ge 14:18). As such a king-priest, he was appointed to a higher order of priesthood than that of Aaron and his sons. (For the union of king and priest in one person, see Zec 6:13 and note.) What this means for Christ's priesthood is the main theme of Heb 7. *forever.* Permanently and irrevocably; perhaps alluded to in Jn 12:34.

110:5 *The Lord is at your right hand.* God is near to assist you in your warfare (see v. 2; cf. 109:31). Some take these words as an address to God (see TNIV text note): The Lord (David's superior son) is at your (God's) right hand (as in v. 1). *on the day of his wrath.* See 2:5 and note.

110:6 *He.* The Lord's anointed. *heaping up the dead.* Battlefield imagery (borrowed from David's victories) that depicts the victory of the Lord's anointed over all powers that oppose the kingdom of God (see 2:9; Rev 19:11–21).

110:7 *drink from a brook.* Even in the heat of battle he will find refreshment and lift up his head with undiminished vigor (see note on v. 3).

Ps 111–119 A cluster of nine psalms framed by unusual alphabetic acrostics (see introductions to Ps 111; 119) that enclose the "Egyptian Hallel" (see introduction to Ps 113–118). The framing psalms that enclose the celebration of redemption contained in the Hallel offer instruction in the piety that must characterize those who join in the celebration of God's saving acts in behalf of his people.

A **Ps 111** Praise of God for his unfailing righteousness. The psalm combines hymnic praise with wisdom instruction, as its first and last verses indicate. Close comparison with Ps 112 shows that these two psalms, probably written by the same author and intended to be kept together. The two psalms are most likely postexilic. For the relationship of these psalms with those that follow, see introduction to Ps 111–119.

Structurally, both Ps 111 and Ps 112 are alphabetic acrostics (see TNIV text note), but unique in that each (Hebrew) half-line advances the alphabet. Both psalms are framed by first and last verses that highlight their primary themes, and in both psalms the main body develops the theme introduced by the first verse, while the closing verse adds a counterpoint. In both

111:2 ʸ S Job 36:24;
Ps 143:5; Rev 15:3
ᶻ Ps 64:9
111:3 ᵃ Ps 112:3,9;
119:142
111:4 ᵇ S Dt 4:31;
S Ps 86:15
111:5 ᶜ S Ge 1:30;
S Ps 37:25; Mt 6:26,
31-33 ᵈ Ps 103:11
ᵉ S 1Ch 16:15;
S Ps 105:8
111:6 ᶠ Ps 64:9;
S 66:3,5
ᵍ S Ps 105:44
111:7 ʰ S Ps 92:4
ⁱ Ps 19:7; 119:128
111:8 ʲ Ps 119:89,
152,160; Isa 40:8;
S Mt 5:18
111:9 ᵏ Ps 34:22;
S 103:4; 130:7;
Lk 1:68 ˡ Ps 30:4;
99:3; Lk 1:49
111:10 ᵐ S Job 23:15;
S Ps 19:9 ⁿ Dt 4:6
ᵒ S Dt 4:6; Ps 119:98,
104,130 ᵖ Ps 28:6;
89:52
112:1 ᵠ Ps 33:2;
103:1; 150:1 ʳ Ps 1:1-2
ˢ S Job 1:8; Ps 103:11;
115:13; 128:1
ᵗ S Ps 1:2; 119:14,16,
47,92
112:2 ᵘ Ps 25:13;
37:26; 128:2-4
112:3 ᵛ S Dt 8:18
ʷ S Ps 37:6; S 111:3

² Great are the works ʸ of the LORD;
  they are pondered by all ᶻ who delight in them.
³ Glorious and majestic are his deeds,
  and his righteousness endures ᵃ forever.
⁴ He has caused his wonders to be remembered;
  the LORD is gracious and compassionate. ᵇ
⁵ He provides food ᶜ for those who fear him; ᵈ
  he remembers his covenant ᵉ forever.

⁶ He has shown his people the power of his works, ᶠ
  giving them the lands of other nations. ᵍ
⁷ The works of his hands ʰ are faithful and just;
  all his precepts are trustworthy. ⁱ
⁸ They are established for ever ʲ and ever,
  enacted in faithfulness and uprightness.
⁹ He provided redemption ᵏ for his people;
  he ordained his covenant forever—
  holy and awesome ˡ is his name.

¹⁰ The fear of the LORD ᵐ is the beginning of wisdom; ⁿ
  all who follow his precepts have good understanding. ᵒ
  To him belongs eternal praise. ᵖ

PSALM 112 ᵃ

¹ Praise the LORD. ᵇ ᵠ

Blessed are those ʳ who fear the LORD, ˢ
  who find great delight ᵗ in his commands.

² Their children ᵘ will be mighty in the land;
  the generation of the upright will be blessed.
³ Wealth and riches ᵛ are in their houses,
  and their righteousness endures ʷ forever.

ᵃ This psalm is an acrostic poem, the lines of which begin with the successive letters of the Hebrew alphabet.   ᵇ 1 Hebrew *Hallelu Yah*

---

psalms the main body of eight verses thematically into two halves of four verses each, with the corresponding verses of each half containing certain thematic links (compare, e.g., 111:2 and 111:6; also vv. 5 and 9). Corresponding verses of the two psalms also tend to share common themes (compare, e.g., 111:3–5 with 112:3–5). These twin psalms are composed of the same number of Hebrew syllables.

111:1 *I will extol.* Introductory to the praise that follows in vv. 2–9. *with all my heart.* A verbal link with a recurring phrase in Ps 119 (see vv. 2,10,34,58,69,145). *council of the upright.* Probably a more intimate circle than the assembly (see 107:32 for a similar distinction) and referring to those who are truly godly—such as the "upright" of 112:2,4 (see 11:7; 33:1; 49:14; 97:11; 107:42; 140:13). *in the assembly.* See note on 9:1.

111:2–5 The stanza is framed by references to the Lord's "works" and "his covenant" (see vv. 6–9 and note).

111:2 *works of the LORD.* The hymn focuses especially on what God has done for his people. Verses 5,9 sum it up. *pondered.* Reflectively examined (see Ezr 10:16, "investigate"; Ecc 1:13, "study").

111:3 *righteousness.* As embodied in his deeds (see note on 4:1).

111:4 *wonders.* See note on 9:1. *gracious and compassionate.* See Ex 34:6–7 and note.

🅰 **111:5** *provides food.* Illustrative of his bountiful provisions for the daily needs of his people (as in the Lord's prayer: "Give us today our daily bread," Mt 6:11). *fear.* See v. 10 and note. *his covenant.* The Lord remembers "forever" the covenant he "ordained ... forever" (v. 9; see also 105:8–11).

111:6–9 The stanza is framed by references to the Lord's "works" and "his covenant" (see vv. 2–5 and note).

111:7 *faithful and just.* Cf. "Glorious and majestic" (v. 3). *pre-*

cepts are trustworthy. See note on 93:5.

111:8 *They.* "The works of his hands" (v. 7). *faithfulness and uprightness.* Cf. "gracious and compassionate" (v. 4).

111:9 *provided redemption.* The other great benefit of God's deeds in behalf of his people (cf. "provides food," v. 5). *holy and awesome.* As shown by his works. *name.* See note on 5:11.

🅰 **111:10** Concluding word of godly wisdom. *The fear of the LORD is the beginning of wisdom.* The classic OT statement concerning the religious basis of what it means to be wise (see Job 28:28; Pr 1:7; 9:10; see also note on 66:16). *who follow his precepts.* Lit. "who do them." The plural Hebrew pronoun refers back to "precepts" in v. 7 (see 19:7–9, where "The fear of the LORD" stands parallel to "statutes," "precepts," "commands," "ordinances"; see also 112:1).

Ps 112 A eulogy to the godly—in the spirit of Ps 1 but formed after the pattern of Ps 111 and likely intended as its complement (see introduction to Ps 111).

112:1 The basic theme, developed more fully in vv. 2–9. Verse 10 states its converse. See 1:1–2; 128:1. *Blessed.* See note on 1:1. *fear the LORD.* See 66:16 and note. *delight ... commands.* A verbal and conceptual link with Ps 119 (see 119:35).

112:2–5 The stanza is framed by references to godly people's children and their generosity (see vv. 6–9 and note).

🅰 **112:2** *children.* The godly bring blessing to their children and to themselves—not least in the fact that through their children they are "remembered" in the community (see v. 6; see also Dt 25:6; Ru 4:10; see further Ps 37:26; 127:3–5; 128:3 and note on 109:12). *will be mighty.* Will be persons of influence and reputation.

112:3 Cf. 111:3. *Wealth and riches.* See 1:3; 128:2. *righteousness.*

⁴ Even in darkness light dawns ˣ for the upright,
 for those who are gracious and compassionate and righteous. ʸ
⁵ Good will come to those who are generous and lend freely, ᶻ
 who conduct their affairs with justice.

⁶ Surely the righteous will never be shaken; ᵃ
 they will be remembered ᵇ forever.
⁷ They will have no fear of bad news;
 their hearts are steadfast, ᶜ trusting in the Lord. ᵈ
⁸ Their hearts are secure, they will have no fear; ᵉ
 in the end they will look in triumph on their foes. ᶠ
⁹ They have scattered abroad their gifts to the poor, ᵍ
 their righteousness endures ʰ forever;
 their horn ᵃ will be lifted ⁱ high in honor.

¹⁰ The wicked will see ʲ and be vexed,
 they will gnash their teeth ᵏ and waste away; ˡ
 the longings of the wicked will come to nothing. ᵐ

PSALM 113

¹ Praise the Lord. ᵇ ⁿ

 Praise the Lord, you his servants; ᵒ
 praise the name of the Lord.
² Let the name of the Lord be praised, ᵖ
 both now and forevermore. �q
³ From the rising of the sun ʳ to the place where it sets,
 the name of the Lord is to be praised.

⁴ The Lord is exalted ˢ over all the nations,

ᵃ 9 *Horn* here symbolizes dignity. ᵇ 1 Hebrew *Hallelu Yah*; also in verse 9

112:4 ˣ S Ps 18:28
ʸ Ps 5:12
112:5 ᶻ S Ps 37:21,
26; Lk 6:35
112:6 ᵃ S Ps 15:5;
S 55:22 ᵇ Pr 10:7;
Ecc 2:16
112:7 ᶜ Ps 57:7;
108:1 ᵈ S Ps 28:7;
56:3-4; S Isa 12:2
112:8 ᵉ Ps 3:6; 27:1;
56:11; Pr 1:33; Isa 12:2
ᶠ S Ps 54:7
112:9 ᵍ Lk 19:8;
Ac 9:36; 2Co 9:9*
ʰ S Ps 111:3
ⁱ S Ps 75:10
112:10 ʲ Ps 86:17
ᵏ S Ps 37:12;
S Mt 8:12 ˡ S Ps 34:21
ᵐ S Job 8:13
113:1 ⁿ S Ps 22:23
ᵒ Ps 34:22; S 103:21;
134:1
113:2 ᵖ S Ps 30:4;
48:10; 145:21; 148:13;
149:3; Isa 12:4
q Ps 115:18; 131:3;
Da 2:20
113:3 ʳ Isa 24:15;
45:6; 59:19; Mal 1:11
113:4 ˢ S Ps 99:2

See v. 9; see also note on 1:5. *endures.* It is not an occasional characteristic of his actions (see "steadfast," v. 7).
112:4 *darkness.* A metaphor for calamitous times (see 107:10 and note). *light.* See note on 27:1. *gracious and compassionate.* See 111:4; cf. Ex 34:6–7 and note. *righteous.* Cf. what is said of the Lord in 116:5; 145:8,17.
112:5 *Good.* Well-being and prosperity (see 34:8–14 and note). *are generous and lend freely.* See v. 9; see also 111:5.
112:6–9 The stanza is framed by reference to the righteous being "remembered" (see note on v. 2) and their generosity (see note on vv. 2–5).
112:6 *shaken.* See note on 10:6.

 A **112:7** Shares with 111:7 the basic theme of reliability. *hearts.* See v. 8; see also note on 4:7. *trusting.* Their trust in God will be as steadfast as their righteousness is enduring (see v. 3). For trust and obedience to God's righteous will as the sum of true godliness, see 34:8–14 and note.
112:8 *secure.* In Hebrew a verbal echo of "established" in 111:8. *will look in triumph.* "Even in darkness light dawns" (v. 4).
112:9 See 2Co 9:9 and note. *gifts to the poor.* See v. 5. *their righteousness.* Just as the Lord remembers his covenant (111:5,9), so the righteous act according to "justice" (v. 5) and "righteousness" (v. 9), two of the prime moral virtues the Lord requires of his covenant servant (see Ge 18:19; Ps 106:3; Isa 5:7; 56:1; Eze 18:5,21; 33:14,16,19; 45:9; Am 5:24; 6:12; see also 2Sa 8:15; Pr 1:3; 21:3; Jer 22:15; 32:15—sometimes rendered "just" and "right"). *lifted high in honor.* As God's name is held in holy awe (see 111:9), so the godly will be held in honor.
112:10 The counterpoint—like 111:10. *see and be vexed.* Godliness is the way to blessedness, whereas the way the wicked have chosen leads to a dead end (see 10:2–11; 107:42). *come to nothing.* See 1:4–6; see also Ps 37; Pr 10:28.
Ps 113–118 The "Egyptian Hallel," which came to be used in Jewish liturgy at the great religious festivals (Passover, Weeks, Tabernacles, Dedication, New Moon; see Lev 23; Nu 10:10; Jn

10:22; see also chart, pp. 180–181). At Passover, Ps 113 and 114 were sung before the meal (before the second cup was passed) and Ps 115–118 after the meal (when the fourth cup had been filled). For the frame within which the "Hallel" has been set, see introduction to Ps 111–119.
Ps 113 A hymn to the Lord celebrating his high majesty and his mercies to the lowly (see 138:6). It was probably composed originally for the temple liturgy. Thematically, the psalm has strong links with the song of Hannah (1Sa 2:1–15) and the song of Mary (Lk 1:46–55).
 Three precisely balanced stanzas (each having three verses) give the psalm a pleasing symmetry. With seven (the number of completeness) verbs the author celebrates God's praise in stanzas two and three ("is exalted," "sits … on high," "stoops down," "raises," "lifts," "seats," "settles")—and note the fourfold praise in the first stanza. At the center (v. 5; see note on 6:6) a rhetorical question focuses and heightens the hymnic theme.
113:1b–3 The fourfold call to praise.
113:1 *name of the Lord.* See vv. 2–3. Triple repetition was a common liturgical convention (see note on 96:1–3). *name.* See note on 5:11.
113:2 *now and forevermore.* The praise of those who truly praise the Lord cannot rest content until it fills all time—and space (v. 3).

 B **113:3** The psalmist employs an ancient formula for indicating universal space. Canaanite Amarna letter No. 288 reads as follows: "Behold, the king, my lord, has set his name at the rising of the sun and at the setting of the sun" (see chart, p. xxiii; cf. Ps 139:9 and note).
113:4–6 The Lord is enthroned on high, exalted over all creation.
113:4 See the refrain in 57:5,11. *exalted over all the nations.* And implicitly over all their gods (see 95:3; 96:4–5; 97:9; see also 47:2,7–8). Accordingly, those who receive his saving help "exalt" him in grateful praise (118:28)—a thematic frame to the "Hallel." *above the heavens.* Above even the most exalted aspect of the creation (see v. 6; 148:13).

113:4 ^r S Ps 8:1;
S 57:11
113:5 ^u S Ex 8:10;
S Ps 35:10
^v S Ps 103:19
^w S Job 16:19
113:6 ^x Ps 11:4;
138:6; Isa 57:15
113:7 ^y 1Sa 2:8;
Ps 35:10; 68:10;
140:12 ^z Ps 107:41
113:8 ^a S 2Sa 9:11
113:9 ^b S 1Sa 2:5
114:1 ^c S Ex 13:3;
S 29:46
114:2 ^d Ps 76:1
^e S Ex 15:17;
Ps 78:68-69
114:3 ^f Ex 14:21;
Ps 77:16 ^g S Ex 15:8;
S Jos 3:16
114:4 ^h S Jdg 5:5
114:5 ⁱ S Ex 14:21
114:7 ^j S Ex 15:14;
S 1Ch 16:30
114:8 ^k S Ex 17:6;
S Nu 20:11

his glory above the heavens. ^t
⁵ Who is like the LORD our God, ^u
   the One who sits enthroned ^v on high, ^w
⁶ who stoops down to look ^x
   on the heavens and the earth?

⁷ He raises the poor ^y from the dust
   and lifts the needy ^z from the ash heap;
⁸ he seats them ^a with princes,
   with the princes of his people.
⁹ He settles the childless ^b woman in her home
   as a happy mother of children.

Praise the LORD.

PSALM 114

¹ When Israel came out of Egypt, ^c
   the house of Jacob from a people of foreign tongue,
² Judah ^d became God's sanctuary, ^e
   Israel his dominion.

³ The sea looked and fled, ^f
   the Jordan turned back; ^g
⁴ the mountains leaped ^h like rams,
   the hills like lambs.

⁵ Why was it, sea, that you fled? ⁱ
   Why, Jordan, did you turn back?
⁶ Why, mountains, did you leap like rams,
   you hills, like lambs?

⁷ Tremble, earth, ^j at the presence of the Lord,
   at the presence of the God of Jacob,
⁸ who turned the rock into a pool,
   the hard rock into springs of water. ^k

113:5 The rhetorical center (see note on 6:6). *Who is like the LORD … ?* See note on Mic 1:1. *our God.* What grace, that he has covenanted to be "our" God (see Ge 17:7; Ex 19:5–6; 20:2)!

113:7–9 The Lord exalts the lowly—the God of highest majesty does not ally himself with the high and mighty of the earth but stands with and raises up the poor and needy (see 1Sa 2:3–8; Lk 1:46–55). Cf. the deliverance celebrated in Ps 118.

113:7–8 Repeated almost verbatim from 1Sa 2:8.

113:7 *poor … needy.* See 9:18; 34:6 and notes. *dust … ash heap.* Symbolic of a humble status (see Ge 18:27; 1Ki 16:2), but here probably also of extreme distress and need (see Job 30:19; 42:6; Isa 47:1; Jer 25:34).

113:9 *childless woman.* In that ancient society barrenness was the greatest disgrace and the deepest tragedy for a woman (see Ge 30:1; 1Sa 1:6–7,10); in her old age she would be as desolate as Naomi because she would have no one to sustain her (see Ru 1:11–13; see also 2Ki 4:14). *home.* Family circle. *happy mother.* Because of God's gracious provision, as in the case of Sarah (see Ge 21:2), Rebekah (see Ge 25:21), Rachel (see Ge 30:23), Hannah (see 1Sa 1:20), the Shunammite (see 2Ki 4:17) and others.

Ps 114 A hymnic celebration of the exodus, the second psalm in the "Egyptian Hallel" (see introduction to Ps 113–118). It is one of the most exquisitely fashioned songs of the Psalter. It probably dates from the period of the monarchy sometime after the division of the kingdom (see v. 2). No doubt it was composed for liturgical use at the temple during one of the annual religious festivals (see introduction to Ps 113). The theme is progressively developed through four balanced stanzas, reaching its climax in the fourth. The first two stanzas (vv. 1–4) recall the great events of the exodus; the last two (vv. 5–8) celebrate their continuing significance.

114:1–2 The great OT redemptive event.

114:1 *Israel … house of Jacob.* Synonyms (see Ex 19:3). *came out of Egypt.* Recalls the exodus and all the great events of the wilderness journey.

114:2 *Judah … Israel.* The southern and northern kingdoms, viewed here as the one people of God. *became.* The crucial event was the establishment of the covenant at Sinai, where Israel became bound to the Lord as a "kingdom of priests and a holy nation" (Ex 19:3–6). *God's.* Lit. "his." The antecedent is not expressed until the climax (v. 7). *sanctuary.* His temple, in which he took up his residence in the world—symbolized by the tabernacle, later the temple. In Ex 15:17 the promised land is similarly called God's sanctuary. *dominion.* The special realm over which he ruled as King. This, rather than the exodus itself, was the great wonder of God's grace.

114:3–4 The author evokes a fearsome scene, such as that portrayed by other poets (see 18:7–15; 68:7–8; 77:16–19; Jdg 5:4–5; Hab 3:3–10).

114:3 *sea … Jordan.* The Red Sea and the Jordan River, through which the Lord brought his people—here they are personified. *looked and fled.* Saw the mighty God approach in his awesome pillar of cloud and fled.

114:4 *leaped.* The mountains and hills quaked at God's approach (see 29:6).

114:7–8 The Lord of yesterday (vv. 5–6)—the God of Jacob—is still with us.

114:7 *Tremble.* In awesome recognition. *earth.* All creation. *Jacob.* A synonym for Israel (see Ge 32:28).

114:8 *turned the rock into a pool.* Thus sustaining and refreshing life (see Ex 17:6; Nu 20:11).

PSALM 115

115:4–11pp — Ps 135:15–20

[1] Not to us, LORD, not to us
  but to your name be the glory,[l]
  because of your love and faithfulness.[m]

[2] Why do the nations say,
  "Where is their God?"[n]
[3] Our God is in heaven;[o]
  he does whatever pleases him.[p]
[4] But their idols are silver and gold,[q]
  made by human hands.[r]
[5] They have mouths, but cannot speak,[s]
  eyes, but cannot see.
[6] They have ears, but cannot hear,
  noses, but cannot smell.
[7] They have hands, but cannot feel,
  feet, but cannot walk,
  nor can they utter a sound with their throats.
[8] Those who make them will be like them,
  and so will all who trust in them.

[9] House of Israel, trust[t] in the LORD—
  he is their help and shield.
[10] House of Aaron,[u] trust in the LORD—
  he is their help and shield.
[11] You who fear him,[v] trust in the LORD—
  he is their help and shield.

[12] The LORD remembers[w] us and will bless us:[x]
  He will bless the house of Israel,
  he will bless the house of Aaron,
[13] he will bless those who fear[y] the LORD—
  small and great alike.

[14] May the LORD cause you to increase,[z]
  both you and your children.
[15] May you be blessed by the LORD,
  the Maker of heaven[a] and earth.

[16] The highest heavens belong to the LORD,[b]
  but the earth he has given[c] to humankind.

115:1 [l] Ps 29:2; 66:2; 96:8
[m] S Ex 34:6
115:2 [n] S Ps 42:3
115:3 [o] Ezr 5:11; Ne 1:4; Ps 103:19; 136:26; Mt 6:9
[p] Ps 135:6
115:4 [q] Rev 9:20
[r] S 2Ki 19:18; S 2Ch 32:19; Jer 10:3-5; Ac 19:26
115:5 [s] Jer 10:5
115:9 [t] Ps 37:3; 62:8
115:10 [u] Ex 30:30; Ps 118:3
115:11 [v] Ps 22:23; 103:11; 118:4
115:12 [w] S 1Ch 16:15
[x] S Ge 12:2
115:13 [y] S Ps 112:1
115:14 [z] Dt 1:11
115:15 [a] S Ge 1:1; Ac 14:15; S Rev 10:6
115:16 [b] S Ps 89:11
[c] S Ge 1:28; Ps 8:6-8

Ps 115 This third psalm in the "Egyptian Hallel" (see introduction to Ps 113–118) offers praise to the Lord, the one true God, for his love and faithfulness toward his people. It was composed as a liturgy of praise for the temple worship. It may have been written for use at the dedication of the second temple (see Ezr 6:16) when Israel was beginning to revive after the disruption of the exile. See introduction to Ps 113. Structurally, the song advances in five movements, involving a liturgical exchange between the people and temple personnel: (1) vv. 1–8: the people; (2) vv. 9–11: Levitical choir leader (the refrain perhaps spoken by the Levitical choir); (3) vv. 12–13: the people; (4) vv. 14–15: the priests; (5) vv. 16–18: the people.
115:1–8 Praise of God's love and faithfulness toward his people, which silences the taunts of the nations.
115:1 *Not to us . . . not to us.* The introductory confession of faith. Israel's existence, and now her revival, is not her own achievement. *name.* See note on 5:11. *love and faithfulness.* The most common OT expression for God's covenant benefits (see note on 26:3). *love.* See note on 6:4.
115:2 *Where is their God?* The taunt of the nations when Israel is decimated by natural disasters (see Joel 2:17) or crushed by enemies, especially when Judah is destroyed and the temple of God razed (see 3:2; 10:11 and notes; 79:10; Mic 7:10).

115:3 *is in heaven.* Sits enthroned (see 113:5) in the "highest heavens" (v. 16). *whatever pleases him.* If Israel is decimated or destroyed, it is God's doing; it is not his failure or inability to act, nor is it the achievement of the idols the nations worship. When Israel is revived, that is also God's doing, and no other god can oppose him.
115:4–7 Whatever glory and power the false gods are thought to have (as symbolized in the images made to represent them), they are mere figments of human imagination and utterly worthless (see 135:15–18; Isa 46:1–7).
115:8 *Those who make them.* The taunting nations (cf. v. 2). *like them.* Powerless and ineffectual. For a graphic elaboration of this truth, see Isa 44:9–20.
115:9–11 The call to trust in the Lord, not in idols (see v. 8). For triple repetition as a liturgical convention, see note on 96:1–3. For the same groupings, see 118:2–4; see also 135:19–20.
115:11 *You who fear him.* Perhaps proselytes (see 1Ki 8:41–43; Ezr 6:21; Ne 10:28).
115:12–13 The people's confession of trust.
115:14–15 The priestly blessing.
115:14 *cause you to increase.* In numbers, wealth and strength (cf. Ecc 2:9: "became greater by far than"—lit. "increased more than").
115:16–18 The people's concluding doxology.

115:17 *d* Ps 88:10-12
115:18 *e* S Ps 111:1
f S Ps 113:2; *g* Ps 28:6; 33:2; 103:1
116:1 *h* Ps 18:1
i S Ps 31:22; S 40:1
j S Ps 6:9; S 28:2
116:2 *k* S Ps 5:1
116:3 *l* S 2Sa 22:6; Ps 18:4-5
116:4 *m* Ps 80:18; 118:5 *n* S Ps 80:2
116:5 *o* S Ex 9:27; S 2Ch 12:6; S Ezr 9:15
p S Ex 22:27; S Ps 86:15
116:6 *q* S Ps 79:8
r Ps 18:3; 22:5; 107:13
116:7 *s* Ps 46:10; 62:1; 131:2; Mt 11:29
t Ps 13:6; 106:1; 142:7
116:8 *u* S Ps 86:13
116:9 *v* S Ge 5:22; Ps 56:13; 89:15
w S Job 28:13; Ps 27:13; Isa 38:11; Jer 11:19
116:10 *x* 2Co 4:13*
y Ps 9:18; 72:2; S 107:17; 119:67,71,75

¹⁷ It is not the dead *d* who praise the LORD,
　　those who go down to the place of silence;
¹⁸ it is we who extol the LORD, *e*
　　both now and forevermore. *f*

　　Praise the LORD. *a g*

PSALM 116

¹ I love the LORD, *h* for he heard my voice;
　　he heard my cry *i* for mercy. *j*
² Because he turned his ear *k* to me,
　　I will call on him as long as I live.

³ The cords of death *l* entangled me,
　　the anguish of the grave came over me;
　　I was overcome by distress and sorrow.
⁴ Then I called on the name *m* of the LORD:
　　"LORD, save me! *n*"

⁵ The LORD is gracious and righteous; *o*
　　our God is full of compassion. *p*
⁶ The LORD protects the unwary;
　　when I was brought low, *q* he saved me. *r*

⁷ Return to your rest, *s* my soul,
　　for the LORD has been good *t* to you.

⁸ For you, LORD, have delivered me *u* from death,
　　my eyes from tears,
　　my feet from stumbling,
⁹ that I may walk before the LORD *v*
　　in the land of the living. *w*

¹⁰ I trusted *x* in the LORD when I said,
　　"I am greatly afflicted"; *y*

a 18 Hebrew *Hallelu Yah*

115:16 *highest heavens … earth.* The one the exclusive realm of the exalted, all-sovereign God; the other the divinely appointed place for human beings, where they live under God's rule and care, enjoy his abundant blessings (vv. 12–13) and celebrate his praise (v. 18).

115:17 *not the dead.* The dead no longer live in "the earth" (v. 16) but have descended to the silent realm below, where blessings are no longer enjoyed and hence praise is absent (see notes on 6:5; 30:1).

Ps 116 Praise of the Lord for deliverance from death. It may have been written by a king (see v. 16 and note; cf. also Hezekiah's thanksgiving, Isa 38:10–20); its language echoes many of the psalms of David. In Jewish liturgy (see introduction to Ps 113–118), the singular personal pronoun must have been used corporately (see note on Ps 30 title), and the references to "death" may have been understood as alluding to the Egyptian bondage and/or the exile.

Structurally, the psalm is so designed that the second half (vv. 10–19) mirrors the first half (vv. 1–9)—which may be why the Septuagint (the pre-Christian Greek translation of the OT) divides the psalm into two. Basically the theme is developed in a series of couplets (vv. 1–2,3–4,5–6,8–9//10–11,13–14,15–16, 17–19—the final couplet being expanded into a triplet). Verse 7 (between the last two couplets of the first half) and v. 12 (between the first two couplets of the second half) have striking verbal and thematic links (see notes on those verses). Further, the divine name Yahweh ("LORD") occurs seven times in each half of the psalm (in v. 8 "LORD" has been supplied by the translators for clarity; in v. 19 the second instance belongs to the appended liturgical formula).

116:1–2 I love the Lord because he has heard and saved me.

116:2 *I will call on him.* In him I will trust, and my prayers will ever be to him. "I will call/I called" is a key thematic phrase (in Hebrew one word, and always in the same form as here), occurring twice in each half of the psalm (vv. 2,4,13,17).

116:3–4 The deadly threat (see 18:4–6).

116:3 *cords of death.* See note on 18:5.

116:5–6 Testimony to God's goodness—echoing Ex 34:6.

116:5 *gracious … righteous … compassion.* See 145:8,17; cf. 112:4. *our God.* The author is conscious of those about him; he is praising the Lord "in the presence of all his people" (vv. 14,18).

116:6 *unwary.* Those who are childlike in their sense of dependence on and trust in the Lord (see note on 19:7).

116:7 *rest.* A state of unthreatened well-being (cf. Jer 6:16; see 1Ki 5:4; see also note on 23:2,"quiet waters"). *my soul.* See note on 103:1–2,22. *has been good.* See v. 12 and note.

116:8–9 The deliverance experienced—a return to the theme of vv. 3–4.

116:10–11 Introduction to the second half of the psalm, an elaboration on the introduction to the first half (vv. 1–2).

116:10 *I trusted in the LORD.* The author speaks of his faith that moved him to call on the Lord when he was threatened. *I am greatly afflicted.* This and the quotation in v. 11 should perhaps be taken, together with the one in v. 4, as a brief recollection of the prayer offered when the psalmist was in distress. The threat of death from which he had been delivered was brought on by the false accusations of enemies, as in Ps 109 (see notes on 5:9; 10:7). (For another interpretation, see following note.)

¹¹ in my alarm I said,
  "Everyone is a liar."^z

¹² What shall I return to the Lord
  for all his goodness^a to me?
¹³ I will lift up the cup of salvation
  and call on the name^b of the Lord.
¹⁴ I will fulfill my vows^c to the Lord
  in the presence of all his people.

¹⁵ Precious in the sight^d of the Lord
  is the death of those faithful to him.^e
¹⁶ Truly I am your servant, Lord;^f
  I am your servant, as was my mother before me;^g
  you have loosed my bonds of affliction.^h

¹⁷ I will sacrifice a thank offeringⁱ to you
  and call on the name of the Lord.
¹⁸ I will fulfill my vows^j to the Lord
  in the presence of all his people,
¹⁹ in the courts^k of the house of the Lord—
  in your midst, Jerusalem.^l

  Praise the Lord.^a

PSALM 117

¹ Praise the Lord, ^m all you nations; ⁿ
  extol him, all you peoples.
² For great is his love^o toward us,
  and the faithfulness of the Lord^p endures forever.

  Praise the Lord.^a

PSALM 118

¹ Give thanks to the Lord, ^q for he is good; ^r
  his love endures forever. ^s

^a 19,2 Hebrew *Hallelu Yah*

116:11 *Everyone is a liar.* The heart of the accusation he had lodged against his false accusers (for examples of similar accusations, see 5:9–10; 35:11,15; 109:2–4). Others interpret these words as a declaration that all people offer but a false hope for deliverance (see 60:11; 118:8–9)—therefore the psalmist called on the Lord.
116:12 *goodness.* The Hebrew for this word occurs only here in the OT but represents the same basic root as "has been good" in v. 7. Verses 7,12, taken together, concisely focus the central movement of the psalm's theme.
116:13–14 Answer to the question in v. 12: By offering to the Lord those expressions of devotion he desires (compare vv. 13–14,17–18 with 50:14–15,23).
116:13 *cup of salvation.* Often thought to be related to the cup of the Passover meal referred to in Mt 26:27 and parallels, but far more likely the cup of wine drunk at the festal meal that climaxed a thank offering (cf. 22:26,29; Lev 7:11–21)—called the "cup of salvation" because the thank offering and its meal celebrated deliverance by the Lord. See the parallel with "sacrifice a thank offering" in the corresponding series in vv. 17–18.
116:14 *vows.* To praise the Lord (see note on 7:17).
116:15–16 Elaboration on vv. 3–4. Note the references to "death" in vv. 3,15; cf. vv. 8–9.
116:15 *Precious ... is the death.* Not in the sense of highly valued but of that which is carefully watched over; cf. the analogous expression, "precious is their blood in his sight" (72:14). *those faithful to him.* See note on 4:3.
116:16 *your servant.* This may identify the psalmist as the Lord's

anointed (see 78:70), but in any event as one devoted to the Lord (see 19:11,13). *your servant, as ... my mother.* See 86:16 and note.
116:17–19 Reiteration of the vows of vv. 13–14.
116:17 *sacrifice a thank offering.* See note on v. 13.
116:19 *courts.* Of the temple (see 84:2,10; 2Ki 21:5; 23:11–12).

Ps 117 The shortest psalm in the Psalter—and the shortest chapter in the Bible—Ps 117 is an expanded Hallelujah (sometimes joined with Ps 118). It may originally have served as the conclusion to the preceding collection of Hallelujah psalms (Ps 111–116)—of which it is the seventh. All nations and peoples are called on to praise the Lord (as in 47:1; 67:3–5; 96:7; 98:4; 100:1; see note on 9:1) for his great love and enduring faithfulness toward Israel (see Isa 12:4–6). Thus the Hallelujahs of the OT Psalter, when fully expounded, express that great truth, so often emphasized in the OT, that the destiny of all peoples is involved in what God was doing in and for his people Israel (see, e.g., 2:8–12; 47:9; 67:2; 72:17; 102:15; 110; Ge 12:3; Dt 32:43; 1Ki 8:41–43; Isa 2:2–4; 11:10; 14:2; 25:6–7; 52:15; 56:7; 60:3; 66:18–24; Jer 3:17; 16:19–21; 33:9; Am 9:11–12; Mic 5:7–9; Zep 3:8–9; Hag 2:7; Zec 2:10–11; 8:20–23; 9:9–10; 14:2–3; Mal 3:12). See introduction to Ps 113–118.

117:1 Quoted in Ro 15:11 as proof that the salvation of Gentiles and the glorifying of God by Gentiles was not a divine afterthought.
117:2 The reason for the praise. *love ... faithfulness.* That is, love-and-faithfulness (see 36:5 and note; see also note on 3:7). *love.* See note on 6:4.

Ps 118 A hymn of thanksgiving for deliverance from enemies. Of the many interpretations of this psalm, three have

---

Cross references (right column):
116:11 ^z Jer 9:3-5; Hos 7:13; Mic 6:12; Ro 3:4
116:12 ^a Ps 103:2; 106:1
116:13 ^b Ps 105:1
116:14 ^c S Nu 30:2; S Ps 66:13
116:15 ^d Ps 72:14 ^e S Nu 23:10
116:16 ^f Ps 119:125; 143:12 ^g S Ps 86:16 ^h S Job 12:18
116:17 ⁱ S Lev 7:12; S Ezr 1:4
116:18 ^j ver 14; S Lev 22:18
116:19 ^k Ps 92:13; 96:8; 100:4; 135:2 ^l Ps 102:21
117:1 ^m S Ps 22:23; S 103:2 ⁿ Ro 15:11*
117:2 ^o S Ps 17:7; S 103:11 ^p Ps 119:90; 146:6
118:1 ^q S 1Ch 16:8 ^r S 2Ch 5:13; S 7:3 ^s S Ezr 3:11

118:2 *t* Ps 115:9
u Ps 106:1; 136:1-26
118:3 *v* Ex 30:30;
Ps 115:10
118:4 *w* S Ps 115:11
118:5 *x* Ps 18:6;
31:7; 77:2; 120:1
y ver 21; Ps 34:4;
86:7; 116:1; 138:3
118:6 *z* S Dt 31:6;
Heb 13:6* *a* S Ps 56:4
118:7 *b* S Dt 33:29
c S Ps 54:7
118:8 *d* Ps 2:12;
5:11; 9:9; 37:3; 40:4;
Isa 25:4; 57:13
e 2Ch 32:7-8;
S Ps 108:12;
S Isa 2:22
118:9 *f* Ps 146:3
118:10 *g* S Ps 37:9
118:11 *h* Ps 88:17
i Ps 3:6
118:12 *j* Dt 1:44
k S Ps 58:9 *l* Ps 37:9
118:13 *m* ver 7;
2Ch 18:31; Ps 86:17
118:14 *n* S Ex 15:2
o Ps 62:2
118:15 *p* S Job 8:21;
S Ps 106:5

2 Let Israel say: *t*
　"His love endures forever." *u*
3 Let the house of Aaron say: *v*
　"His love endures forever."
4 Let those who fear the LORD *w* say:
　"His love endures forever."

5 When hard pressed, *x* I cried to the LORD;
　he brought me into a spacious place. *y*
6 The LORD is with me; *z* I will not be afraid.
　What can human beings do to me? *a*
7 The LORD is with me; he is my helper. *b*
　I look in triumph on my enemies. *c*

8 It is better to take refuge in the LORD *d*
　than to trust in human beings. *e*
9 It is better to take refuge in the LORD
　than to trust in princes. *f*
10 All the nations surrounded me,
　but in the name of the LORD I cut them down. *g*
11 They surrounded me *h* on every side, *i*
　but in the name of the LORD I cut them down.
12 They swarmed around me like bees, *j*
　but they were consumed as quickly as burning thorns; *k*
　in the name of the LORD I cut them down. *l*
13 I was pushed back and about to fall,
　but the LORD helped me. *m*
14 The LORD is my strength *n* and my defense[a];
　he has become my salvation. *o*

15 Shouts of joy *p* and victory
　resound in the tents of the righteous:

---

a 14 Or *song*

---

gained the most adherents (but with much variation in detail): 1. A Davidic king leads the nation in a liturgy of thanksgiving for deliverance and victory after a hard-fought battle with a powerful confederacy of nations (cf. 2Ch 20:27–28; see note on v. 19). 2. Israel celebrates—probably at the Festival of Tabernacles—her deliverance from Egypt and victory over the Canaanites. 3. The postexilic Jews celebrate deliverance from their enemies, either at the dedication of the second temple (see Ezr 6:16) or at the dedication of the rebuilt walls of Jerusalem (see Ne 12:37–43). According to the first interpretation, the speaker in vv. 5–21 is the king; according to the second and third, the speaker is the Levitical (or priestly) leader of the liturgy, speaking (representatively) on behalf of the people. As the notes that follow assume the first interpretation. In the postexilic liturgy developed for the annual festivals (see introduction to Ps 113), the song was used as a thanksgiving for national deliverance. As the last song of that liturgy, it may have been the hymn sung by Jesus and his disciples at the conclusion of the Last Supper (see Mt 26:30).

Following a liturgical call to praise (vv. 1–4), the king offers a song of thanksgiving for deliverance and victory in battle (vv. 5–21). A three-verse stanza (vv. 5–7) summarizing the main theme is followed by two seven-verse composite stanzas (vv. 8–14, 15–21) of elaboration, each closing with the refrain: "has/have become my salvation." In vv. 22–27 the people rejoice over what the Lord has done. Thereafter, the king speaks his final word of praise (v. 28) and a liturgical conclusion (v. 29) repeats the opening call to praise, thus framing the whole. In the two seven-verse stanzas (vv. 8–14, 15–21) the divine name Yahweh (or its shortened form, Yah) occurs seven times in the six-verse stanza (vv. 22–27), and in the remaining verses (1–7, 28–29) it again occurs seven times.

118:1–4 The liturgical call to praise.

118:1 A conventional call to praise (shared in whole or in part

with Ps 105–107; 136; 1Ch 16:8,34; 2Ch 20:21). *Give thanks.* See note on Ps 100 title. This, together with vv. 2–4 (except for the refrain) and 29, may have been by the same voice that speaks in vv. 5–21. *love.* See vv. 2–4,29; see also note on 6:4.

118:2–4 *Israel … house of Aaron … those who fear the LORD.* See 115:9–11 and note. Triple repetition is a common feature in this psalm (see note on 96:1–3).

118:4 *fear the LORD.* See note on 66:16.

118:5–21 The king's song of thanksgiving for deliverance and victory.

118:5–7 The introduction: I cried to the Lord; he answered; I need fear no one.

118:5 *I cried … he brought me.* For the conjunction of this appeal and response elsewhere, see 3:4; 4:1; 17:6; 22:2; 27:7; 86:7; 91:15; 99:6; 102:2; 120:1; 138:3; 1Ki 18:24; Pr 21:13; Isa 65:24; Jer 33:3; Jnh 2:2—all these passages share the same Hebrew terms. *into a spacious place.* See 18:19 and note.

118:8–14 Reflection on the experience of the Lord's saving help—framed by vv. 8–9 and v. 14.

118:8–9 See 33:16–19; see also Ps 62; 146.

118:10 *in the name of the LORD.* See 1Sa 17:45. *name.* See vv. 11–12,26; see also note on 5:11.

118:12 *as burning thorns.* See 58:9 and note.

118:13 *fall.* Be killed (see vv. 17–18; see also note on 13:4).

118:14 Perhaps recalls the triumph song of Ex 15, but more likely the verse had become a widely used testimony of praise (see Isa 12:2).

118:15–21 Celebration of the Lord's deliverance—framed by vv. 15–16 and v. 21.

118:15 *tents.* Dwellings. *righteous.* Israel as the people (ideally) committed in heart and life to the Lord (see v. 20; see also 68:3 and note). Cf. "the tents of the wicked" (84:10).

"The Lord's right hand *q* has done mighty things! *r*
¹⁶   The Lord's right hand is lifted high;
the Lord's right hand has done mighty things!"
¹⁷ I will not die *s* but live,
and will proclaim *t* what the Lord has done.
¹⁸ The Lord has chastened *u* me severely,
but he has not given me over to death. *v*
¹⁹ Open for me the gates *w* of the righteous;
I will enter *x* and give thanks to the Lord.
²⁰ This is the gate of the Lord *y*
through which the righteous may enter. *z*
²¹ I will give you thanks, for you answered me; *a*
you have become my salvation. *b*

²² The stone *c* the builders rejected
has become the cornerstone; *d*
²³ the Lord has done this,
and it is marvelous *e* in our eyes.
²⁴ The Lord has done it this very day;
let us rejoice today and be glad. *f*

²⁵ Lord, save us! *g*
Lord, grant us success!

²⁶ Blessed is he who comes *h* in the name of the Lord.
From the house of the Lord we bless you. *a i*
²⁷ The Lord is God, *j*
and he has made his light shine *k* on us.
With boughs in hand, *l* join in the festal procession
up *b* to the horns of the altar. *m*

²⁸ You are my God, and I will praise you;
you are my God, *n* and I will exalt *o* you.

²⁹ Give thanks to the Lord, for he is good;
his love endures forever.

---

^a 26 The Hebrew is plural.   ^b 27 Or *Bind the festal sacrifice with ropes / and take it*

118:15 *q* S Ex 15:6; Ps 89:13; 108:6 *r* Lk 1:51
118:17 *s* Hab 1:12 *t* S Dt 32:3; Ps 64:9; 71:16; 73:28
118:18 *u* Jer 31:18; 1Co 11:32; Heb 12:5 *v* Ps 86:13
118:19 *w* S Ps 24:7 *x* Ps 100:4
118:20 *y* Ps 122:1-2 *z* Ps 15:1-2; 24:3-4; Rev 22:14
118:21 *a* S ver 5 *b* Ps 27:1
118:22 *c* Isa 8:14 *d* Isa 17:10; 19:13; 28:16; Zec 4:7; 10:4; Mt 21:42; Mk 12:10; Lk 20:17*; S Ac 4:11*; 1Pe 2:7*
118:23 *e* Mt 21:42*; Mk 12:11*
118:24 *f* S Ps 70:4
118:25 *g* S Ps 28:9; 116:4
118:26 *h* S Mt 11:3; 21:9*; 23:39*; Mk 11:9*; Lk 13:35*; 19:38*; Jn 12:13* *i* Ps 129:8
118:27 *j* S 1Ki 18:21 *k* Ps 27:1; Isa 58:10; 60:1,19,20; Mal 4:2; 1Pe 2:9 *l* S Lev 23:40 *m* Ex 27:2
118:28 *n* S Ge 28:21; S Ps 16:2; 63:1; Isa 25:1 *o* S Ex 15:2

118:17 *live, and … proclaim.* See 115:17–18; see also note on 6:5.

⬛ **118:18** *chastened me.* The king acknowledges that the grave threat through which he has passed has also served God's purpose—to discipline him and teach him humble godliness (see 6:1; 38:1; 94:12; Dt 4:36; 8:5).

118:19 *Open for me.* This line suggests a liturgical procession (see v. 27) in which the king approaches the inner court of the temple at the head of the jubilant worshipers (see Ps 24; 68). *gates.* Those leading to the inner temple court. *of the righteous.* Often thought to be the name of a particular gateway, but more likely only descriptive here of the gate "through which the righteous may enter" (v. 20). It is possible that the procession began outside the city and that "the gates of the righteous" are the gates of Jerusalem, the city of God (see note on 24:7; see also Isa 26:2).

118:21 This closing verse of the thanksgiving song echoes the "Give thanks" of v. 1, the "brought me" of v. 5 and the testimony of v. 14.

118:22–27 The people's exultation.

⬛ **118:22** *The stone the builders rejected.* Most likely a reference to the king (whose deliverance and victory are being celebrated), who had been looked on with disdain by the kings invading his realm—the builders of worldly empires. Others suppose that the stone refers to Israel, a nation held in contempt by the world powers. *cornerstone.* Lit. "head of the corner"—either a capstone over a door (a large stone used as a lintel), a large stone used to anchor and align the corner of a wall or the keystone of an arch (see Zec 4:7; 10:4). By a wordplay (pun) the author hints at "chief ruler" (the Hebrew word for "corner" is sometimes used as a metaphor for leader/ruler; see Isa 19:13; see also Jdg 20:2; 1Sa 14:38). This stone, dis-

dained by the worldly powers, has become the most important stone in the structure of the new world order that God is bringing about through Israel. Jesus applied this verse (and v. 23) to himself (see Mt 21:42; Mk 12:10–11; Lk 20:17; see also Ac 4:11; Eph 2:20; 1Pe 2:7).

118:24 *The Lord has done it this very day … rejoice.* This day of rejoicing was made possible by God's deliverance in the victory being celebrated. Others suppose a reference to Passover or the Festival of Tabernacles. *has done it.* Has made the "stone" the "cornerstone" (v. 22; see also vv. 15–17, 23).

118:25 Prayer for the Lord to continue to save and sustain his people.

⬛ **118:26** *who comes in the name of the Lord.* The one who with God's help had defeated the enemies "in the name of the Lord" (see vv. 10–12). *From the house of the Lord.* From God's very presence (see 134:3). *you.* The plural (see TNIV text note) may have been used to exalt the king (the plural was often used with reference to God), whom God had so singularly blessed (see TNIV text note on 1Ki 9:6). Alternatively, it may refer to those who have come with the king victoriously from the battle. The crowds who greeted Jesus at his entrance into Jerusalem as King used the words of vv. 25–26 (see Jn 12:13).

118:27 *made his light shine on us.* An echo of the priestly benediction (see Nu 6:25). *With boughs … up.* Apparently a call to complete the climax of the liturgy of a thank offering (see Lev 7:11–21), though others suggest the liturgy of the Festival of Tabernacles.

118:28 The king's closing reiteration of his vow in v. 21.

118:29 Renewal of the opening call to grateful praise (see v. 1 and note).

119:1 ᵖS Ge 17:1;
S Dt 18:13; Pr 11:20
�q Ps 128:1 ʳ S Ps 1:2
119:2 ˢ Ps 112:1;
Isa 56:2 ᵗ ver 146;
Ps 99:7 ᵘ S 1Ch 16:11;
S Ps 40:16
ᵛ S Dt 10:12
119:3 ʷ S Ps 59:4;
1Jn 3:9; 5:18
ˣ Ps 128:1; Jer 6:16;
7:23
119:4 ʸ Ps 103:18
ᶻ S ver 56; S Dt 6:17
119:5 ᵃ S Lev 19:37
119:6 ᵇ ver 46,80
ᶜ ver 117

PSALM 119 ᵃ

א Aleph

¹Blessed are those whose ways are blameless,ᵖ
  who walk �q according to the law of the LORD. ʳ
²Blessed ˢ are those who keep his statutes ᵗ
  and seek him ᵘ with all their heart— ᵛ
³they do no wrong ʷ
  but follow his ways. ˣ
⁴You have laid down precepts ʸ
  that are to be fully obeyed. ᶻ
⁵Oh, that my ways were steadfast
  in obeying your decrees! ᵃ
⁶Then I would not be put to shame ᵇ
  when I consider all your commands. ᶜ

ᵃ This psalm is an acrostic poem; the verses of each stanza begin with the same letter of the Hebrew alphabet.

Ps 119 A devotional on the word of God. The author was an Israelite of exemplary piety (probably postexilic) who (1) was passionately devoted to the word of God as the word of life; (2) humbly acknowledged, nevertheless, the errant ways of his heart and life; (3) knew the pain—but also the fruits—of God's corrective discipline; and (4) had suffered much at the hands of those who arrogantly disregarded God's word and made him the target of their hostility, ridicule and slander. It is possible that he was a priest (see notes on vv. 23,57)—and the psalm might well be a vehicle for priestly instruction in godliness. He elaborated on the themes of 19:7–13 and interwove with them many prayers for deliverance, composing a massive alphabetic acrostic (see TNIV text note) that demands patient, meditative reading. In regard to length, form and type it stands alone in the Psalter. And of all the psalms, this one is the most likely to have been composed originally in writing and intended to be read rather than sung or recited. Most of its lines are addressed to God, mingling prayers with professions of devotion to God's law. Yet, as the opening verses (and perhaps also its elaborate acrostic form) make clear, it was intended for godly instruction (in the manner of Ps 1; see v. 9 and note). It was included in the Psalter no doubt as a model of piety. For its placement in the Psalter, see introduction to Ps 111–119. See also notes on 111:1; 112:1.

Whereas elsewhere in the Psalter the focus falls primarily on God's mighty acts of creation and redemption and his rule over all the world, here devotion to the word of God (and the God of the word) is the dominant theme. The author highlights two aspects of that word: (1) God's directives for life and (2) God's promises—the one calling for obedience, the other for faith (the two elements of true godliness; see 34:8–14 and note). In referring to these, he makes use of eight Hebrew terms supplied him by OT traditions: *torah*, "law"; *'edot*, "statutes"; *piqqudim*, "precepts"; *miswot*, "commands, commandments"; *mishpatim*, "laws" (all shared with 19:7–9; *mishpatim* is translated "ordinances" in 19:9); *huqqim*, "decrees"; *dabar*, "word" (sometimes in the sense of "law," sometimes in the sense of "promise"); *'imrah*, "word," but more often "promise." These terms he distributes throughout the 22 stanzas (using all eight in *He, Waw, Heth, Yodh, Kaph, Pe*—never using less than six), employing a different order in each stanza. It may be that the availability of these eight terms determined (in large part) for the author the decision to devote eight verses to each letter of the alphabet. The alphabetic acrostic form, especially one as elaborate as this, may appear arbitrary and artificial to a modern reader (as if the author merely selected a traditional form from the poet's workshop and then labored to fill it with pious sentences), but a sympathetic and reflective reading of this devotional will compel a more favorable judgment. The author had a theme that filled his soul, a theme as big as life, that ranged the length and breadth and height and depth of a person's walk with God. Nothing less than the use of the full power of language would suffice, and of that the alphabet was a most apt symbol.

Apart from the obvious formal structure dictated by the chosen acrostic form, little need (or can) be said. It must be noted, however, that the first three and the last three verses were designed as introduction and conclusion to the whole. The former sets the tone of instruction in godly wisdom; the latter succinctly restates and summarizes the main ideas. It may also be observed that the middle of the psalm has been marked by a similar three-verse introduction to the second half (see note on vv. 89–91). For the rest, the thought meanders, turns back upon itself and repeats (with varied nuances). The following notes point out continuities of thought and possible structure within stanzas.

119:1–3 General introduction.

119:1–2 *Blessed.* See note on 1:1.

119:1 *whose ways are blameless.* This opening general description is further elaborated in the rest of the introduction, which concludes with an equally general statement: "follow his ways" (v. 3). See Ge 17:1; cf. Ge 26:5 and note. *law.* Hebrew *torah,* a collective term for God's covenant directives for his people (see Dt 4:44 and note). "Law" often came, especially later, to have a broader reference—the whole Pentateuch (see Lk 24:44 and note) or even the whole OT (see Jn 10:34; 12:34; 15:25; 1Co 14:21 and notes)—but here it is limited by the synonyms with which it is used interchangeably.

119:2 *statutes.* Hebrew *'edot,* a specifically covenantal term referring to stipulations laid down by the covenant Lord (see 25:10, "demands"; Dt 4:45, "stipulations"). *seek him with all their heart.* See Dt 4:29 and note. *heart.* See v. 7; see also note on 4:7.

119:3 *ways.* The Hebrew for this word occurs only rarely in this psalm but is common in Deuteronomy and elsewhere as a general reference to God's covenant requirements (see note on 25:4)—used here to balance "ways" in v. 1.

119:4–8 Those who obey God's law (see vv. 4–5,8) can hope for God's help (see vv. 6–8).

119:4 *precepts.* Hebrew *piqqudim,* covenant regulations laid down by the Lord (see 19:8; 111:7).

119:5 *decrees.* Hebrew *huqqim,* covenant directives (see Dt 6:2; 28:15,45; 30:10,16; 1Ki 11:11), emphasizing their fixed character.

119:6 *not be put to shame.* The psalmist would not suffer poverty, sickness or humiliation at the hands of his enemies and so become the object of sneers (see vv. 31,46,80; 25:2–3,20; see also introduction to this psalm), but he would have reason to praise the Lord (see v. 7) for blessings received and deliverances granted because the Lord does not forsake him (see v. 8). *consider.* Respect, have regard for (see v. 15; 74:20). *commands.*

⁷ I will praise you with an upright heart
  as I learn your righteous laws.
⁸ I will obey your decrees;
  do not utterly forsake me. *d*

⊐ Beth

⁹ How can those who are young keep their way pure? *e*
  By living according to your word. *f*
¹⁰ I seek you with all my heart; *g*
  do not let me stray from your commands. *h*
¹¹ I have hidden your word in my heart *i*
  that I might not sin *j* against you.
¹² Praise be *k* to you, LORD;
  teach me *l* your decrees. *m*
¹³ With my lips I recount
  all the laws that come from your mouth. *n*
¹⁴ I rejoice in following your statutes *o*
  as one rejoices in great riches.
¹⁵ I meditate on your precepts *p*
  and consider your ways.
¹⁶ I delight *q* in your decrees;
  I will not neglect your word.

⊃ Gimel

¹⁷ Be good to your servant *r* while I live,
  that I may obey your word. *s*
¹⁸ Open my eyes that I may see
  wonderful things in your law.
¹⁹ I am a stranger on earth; *t*
  do not hide your commands from me.
²⁰ My soul is consumed *u* with longing
  for your laws *v* at all times.
²¹ You rebuke the arrogant, *w* who are accursed, *x*
  those who stray *y* from your commands.
²² Remove from me their scorn *z* and contempt,
  for I keep your statutes. *a*
²³ Though rulers sit together and slander me,

119:8 *d* S Ps 38:21
119:9 *e* S Ps 39:1
  f ver 65,169
119:10 *g* S Ps 9:1
  h ver 21,118
119:11 *i* S Dt 6:6;
S Job 22:22 *j* ver 133,
165; Ps 18:22-23;
19:13; Pr 3:23;
Isa 63:13
119:12 *k* Ps 28:6
  l Ps 143:8,10
  m S Ex 18:20
119:13 *n* ver 72
119:14 *o* ver 111
119:15 *p* ver 97,
148; Ps 1:2
119:16 *q* S Ps 112:1
119:17 *r* Ps 13:6;
116:7 *ver 67;
Ps 103:20
119:19 *t* S Ge 23:4;
Heb 11:13
119:20 *u* Ps 42:2;
84:2 *v* ver 131;
S Ps 63:1; Isa 26:9
119:21 *w* ver 51;
Job 30:1; Ps 5:5;
Jer 20:7; 50:32;
Da 4:37; Mal 3:15
  x Dt 27:26 *y* S ver 10
119:22 *z* Ps 39:8
  a ver 2

Hebrew *miṣwot*, covenant directives (see Ex 20:6; 24:12; Dt 4:2) designated specifically as that which God has commanded.
119:7 *righteous.* One of the author's favorite characterizations of God's law (see vv. 62,75,106,123,138, 144,160,164,172; see also 19:9). *laws.* Hebrew *mishpaṭim*, covenant directives (see Ex 21:1; 24:3; Dt 4:1), as the laws laid down by a ruler (king).
119:8 *not ... forsake me.* To poverty, sickness or my enemies (cf. 9:10; 22:1; 27:9–10; 38:21; 71:9,11,18).
119:9 *those who are young.* Indicates instruction addressed to the young after the manner of the wisdom teachers (see 34:11; Pr 1:4; Ecc 11:9; 12:1; see also the first paragraph of Introduction to Proverbs: Purpose and Teaching). *pure.* Free from all moral taint (see 73:13). *word.* Hebrew *dabar*, a general designation for God's (word) revelation but here used with special reference to his law (sometimes promises).

▲ **119:10** *I seek you.* The author's devotion is first of all to the God of the law and the promises; they have meaning for him only because they are God's word of life for him. *heart.* See v. 11; see also note on 4:7.
119:11 *word.* Hebrew *'imrah,* a synonym of *dabar* ("word"; see note on v. 9; see also Dt 33:9; Pr 30:5). Except where noted, as here, "word" in this psalm is *dabar ; 'imrah* is usually translated "promise."
119:13 *recount.* Either in meditation or in liturgies of covenant commitment to the Lord (see 50:16, "recite").
119:14 *as one rejoices in great riches.* See vv. 72,111,162.

119:15 *ways.* The Hebrew for this word is a synonym of the Hebrew for "ways" in v. 3 (see 25:4 and note).

▲ **119:17–24** Devotion to God's law marks the Lord's servant but alienates him from the arrogant (v. 21) of the world.

▲ **119:17** *that I may obey.* Out of gratitude for God's care and blessing.

▲ **119:18** *wonderful things.* Usually ascribed to God's redeeming acts (see 9:1 and note)—but God's law also contains wonders (see v. 27) to contemplate, if only God opens a person's eyes.

▲ **119:19** *stranger on earth.* As a servant of the Lord, i.e., a citizen of his kingdom, the psalmist is not at home in any of the kingdoms of the world (see 39:12 and note; see also note on v. 54).
119:20 *My soul is.* I am (see vv. 28,81; see also note on 6:3).

▲ **C** **119:21** *the arrogant.* Those who are a law to themselves, most fully described in 10:2–11 (see vv. 51,69,78,85,122; see also note on 31:23). The author has suffered much from their hostility because of his zeal for God and his law, as the next two verses and many others indicate. *accursed.* Ripe for God's judgment.
119:22 *scorn and contempt.* Of the arrogant.

▲ **119:23** *rulers.* Because the author mentions also speaking "before kings" (v. 46) and being persecuted by "rulers" (v. 161), it may be that he held some official position, such as

119:25 *b* Ps 44:25
c ver 50,107;
Ps 143:11 *d* ver 9
119:26 *e* Ps 25:4;
27:11; 86:11
119:27 *f* Ps 105:2;
145:5
119:28 *g* Ps 6:7;
116:3; Isa 51:11;
Jer 45:3 *h* Ps 18:1;
Isa 40:29; 41:10
i ver 9
119:29 *j* Ps 26:4
k S Nu 6:25
119:30 *l* S Jos 24:22
m S Ps 26:3
n S Ps 108:1
119:31 *o* S Dt 10:20
119:33 *p* ver 12
119:34 *q* ver 27,73,
144,169; S Job 32:8;
Pr 2:6; Da 2:21;
Jas 1:5 *r* S Dt 6:25
s ver 69
119:35 *t* Ps 25:4-5
u ver 32 *v* S Ps 1:2
119:36 *w* S Jos 24:23
x Eze 33:31
119:37 *y* ver 25;
Ps 71:20 *z* ver 9
119:38 *a* S Nu 23:19
119:39 *b* ver 22;
Ps 69:9; 89:51;
Isa 25:8; 51:7; 54:4
119:40 *c* ver 20
d ver 25,149,154

your servant will meditate on your decrees.
24 Your statutes are my delight;
     they are my counselors.

ד Daleth

25 I am laid low in the dust; *b*
     preserve my life *c* according to your word. *d*
26 I gave an account of my ways and you answered me;
     teach me your decrees. *e*
27 Cause me to understand the way of your precepts,
     that I may meditate on your wonderful deeds. *f*
28 My soul is weary with sorrow; *g*
     strengthen me *h* according to your word. *i*
29 Keep me from deceitful ways; *j*
     be gracious to me *k* and teach me your law.
30 I have chosen *l* the way of faithfulness; *m*
     I have set my heart *n* on your laws.
31 I hold fast *o* to your statutes, Lord;
     do not let me be put to shame.
32 I run in the path of your commands,
     for you have set my heart free.

ה He

33 Teach me, *p* Lord, the way of your decrees,
     that I may follow it to the end. *a*
34 Give me understanding, *q* so that I may keep your law *r*
     and obey it with all my heart. *s*
35 Direct me *t* in the path of your commands, *u*
     for there I find delight. *v*
36 Turn my heart *w* toward your statutes
     and not toward selfish gain. *x*
37 Turn my eyes away from worthless things;
     preserve my life *y* according to your word. *b z*
38 Fulfill your promise *a* to your servant,
     so that you may be feared.
39 Take away the disgrace *b* I dread,
     for your laws are good.
40 How I long *c* for your precepts!
     In your righteousness preserve my life. *d*

---

a 33 Or *follow it for its reward* *b 37* Two manuscripts of the Masoretic Text and Dead Sea Scrolls; most manuscripts of the Masoretic Text *life in your way*

---

priest (one of whose functions it would have been to teach God's law; see Lev 10:11; Ezr 7:6; Ne 8:2–8; Jer 2:8; 18:18; Mal 2:7; see also note on v. 57). The kings and rulers referred to may have been Israelite in the time of the monarchy but more likely were local rulers in the postexilic Persian imperial system. *sit.* As those securely settled in the world—not as strangers (cf. v. 19). *together and slander.* As they share their worldly counsels, they speak derisively of the one who stands apart because he delights in God's statutes and makes them his "counselors" (v. 24).
119:25–32 Whether "laid low" (v. 25) or "set ... free" (v. 32), he is determined to "hold fast" (v. 31) to God's word.
[A] [C] **119:25** *laid low.* The author speaks much of his sorrow, suffering and affliction (see vv. 28,50,67,71, 75,83,92,107,143,153). It is likely that the ridicule, slander and persecution from his adversaries are usually occasioned by this suffering of God's devoted servant, who makes God's word (his law and promises) the hope of his life (see vv. 42,51,65,69,78, 85,95,110,134,141,150,154,157,161; see also notes on v. 6; 5:9; 31:11–12). *in the dust.* See 44:25 and note. *word.* Especially its promises, as also in vv. 28,37,42,49,65,74,81,107,114,147.
119:27 *wonderful deeds.* See note on v. 18.

[A] **119:29** *deceitful ways.* Ways that seem right but lead to death (see Pr 14:12 and note)—in contrast to the ways prescribed by God's law, which are trustworthy (see vv. 86,138) and true (see vv. 142,151,160). *teach me your law.* By keeping me true to your law, let me enjoy your blessings.
119:30 *way of faithfulness.* See note on v. 29.
119:31 *put to shame.* See note on v. 6.
[A] **119:32** *set my heart free.* Lit. "enlarged my heart," i.e., expanded it with joy (see Isa 60:5, "swell with joy"). Others translate it "increased my understanding" (see 1Ki 4:29, "breadth of understanding"). *heart.* See note on 4:7.
119:33–40 Prayer for instruction in God's will as he longs for his precepts.
119:34 *heart.* See v. 36; see also note on 4:7.
119:36–37 *heart ... eyes.* See 101:2b–3a and note.
[A] **119:38** *that you may be feared.* The Lord's saving acts in fulfillment of his promises contribute to the recognition that he is the true God (see 130:4; 2Sa 7:25–26; 1Ki 8:39–40; Jer 33:8–9).
119:39 *disgrace I dread.* See notes on vv. 6,25.
119:40 *righteousness.* See note on 4:1.

ɪ Waw

41 May your unfailing love *e* come to me, Lord,
  your salvation, according to your promise; *f*
42 then I can answer *g* anyone who taunts me, *h*
  for I trust in your word.
43 Never take your word of truth from my mouth, *i*
  for I have put my hope *j* in your laws.
44 I will always obey your law, *k*
  for ever and ever.
45 I will walk about in freedom,
  for I have sought out your precepts. *l*
46 I will speak of your statutes before kings *m*
  and will not be put to shame, *n*
47 for I delight *o* in your commands
  because I love them. *p*
48 I reach out for your commands, which I love,
  that I may meditate *q* on your decrees.

ɪ Zayin

49 Remember your word *r* to your servant,
  for you have given me hope. *s*
50 My comfort in my suffering is this:
  Your promise preserves my life. *t*
51 The arrogant mock me *u* unmercifully,
  but I do not turn *v* from your law.
52 I remember, *w* Lord, your ancient laws,
  and I find comfort in them.
53 Indignation grips me *x* because of the wicked,
  who have forsaken your law. *y*
54 Your decrees are the theme of my song *z*
  wherever I lodge.
55 In the night, Lord, I remember *a* your name,
  that I may keep your law. *b*
56 This has been my practice:
  I obey your precepts. *c*

ח Heth

57 You are my portion, *d* Lord;
  I have promised to obey your words. *e*
58 I have sought *f* your face with all my heart;
  be gracious to me *g* according to your promise. *h*
59 I have considered my ways *i*
  and have turned my steps to your statutes.

119:41 *e* S Ps 6:4
f ver 76,116,154,170
119:42 *g* Pr 27:11
h S Ps 42:10
119:43 *i* S 1Ki 17:24
j ver 74,81,114,147
119:44 *k* ver 33,34,
55; S Dt 6:25
119:45 *l* ver 94,155
119:46 *m* Mt 10:18;
Ac 26:1-2 *n* S ver 6
119:47 *o* ver 77,
143; S Ps 112:1
p ver 97,127,159,163,
165
119:48 *q* S Ge 24:63
119:49 *r* ver 9
s ver 43
119:50 *t* S ver 25
119:51 *u* S ver 21;
S Job 16:10; S 17:2
v S Job 23:11
119:52 *w* Ps 103:18
119:53 *x* S Ex 32:19;
S 33:4 *y* Ps 89:30
119:54 *z* ver 172;
Ps 101:1; 138:5
119:55 *a* ver 62,72;
Ps 1:2; 42:8; S 63:6;
77:2; Isa 26:9;
Ac 16:25 *b* S ver 44
119:56 *c* ver 4,100,
134,168; S Nu 15:40
119:57 *d* S Dt 32:9;
Jer 51:19; La 3:24
e ver 17,67,101
119:58 *f* S Dt 4:29;
S 1Ch 16:11; Ps 34:4
g S Ge 43:29;
S Ezr 9:8 *h* ver 41
119:59 *i* Jos 24:14-
15; S Ps 39:1

119:41–48 May the Lord deliver me and not take his truth from my mouth; then I will honor his law in my life and speak of it before kings, for I love his commands.
119:41 *love.* See vv. 64,76,88,124,149,159; see also note on 6:4.
119:42 *anyone who taunts me.* See note on v. 25 ("laid low"). *word.* See note on v. 25.
119:43 *word of truth from my mouth.* See v. 13 and note; see also v. 46.
119:45 *freedom.* Lit. "a wide space," i.e., unconfined by affliction or oppression (see 18:19 and note).
119:46 *before kings.* Such will be his boldness (see note on v. 23).
119:48 *I reach out for.* An act accompanying praise (as in 63:4; 134:2); so the sense may be: I praise.
119:49–56 God's word is my comfort and my guide, whatever my circumstances.
119:49 *word.* See note on v. 25.
119:50–51 *in my suffering…The arrogant mock.* See note on v. 25 ("laid low").
119:51 *arrogant.* See note on v. 21.

119:52 *ancient.* God's law is not fickle but is grounded firmly in his unchanging moral character. This is a major source of the author's comfort and one of the main reasons he cherishes the law so highly (see vv. 89,144,152,160).
119:53 *Indignation grips me.* Zeal for God's law (see vv. 136,139) awakens righteous anger against those who reject it (see vv. 113,115,158) and brings abhorrence of all that is contrary to it (see vv. 104,128,163), but it draws together those who honor it (see v. 63).
119:54 *wherever I lodge.* Lit. "in my temporary house." The sense may be that of v. 19 (see note there).
119:55 *name.* See note on 5:11.
119:57–64 The Lord is the psalmist's true homestead because it is God's law that fills the earth with all that makes life secure and joyous. So God's promises are his hope and God's righteous laws his delight.
119:57 *portion.* May identify the author as a priest or Levite (see 73:26 and note).
119:58 *heart.* See note on 4:7.

119:60 *j* ver 115
119:61 *k* ver 83,109,
153,176
119:62 *l* S ver 55;
Ac 16:25 *m* ver 7
119:63 *n* Ps 15:4;
101:6-7; 103:11
o ver 56; Ps 111:10
119:64 *p* Ps 33:5
q ver 12,108
119:65 *r* ver 17;
Ps 125:4; Isa 50:2;
59:1; Mic 2:7 *s* S ver 9
119:66 *t* S Ps 51:6
119:67 *u* S Ps 116:10
v S Ps 95:10; S Jer 8:4
w S ver 17
119:68 *x* Ps 100:5;
106:1; 107:1; 135:3
y S Ex 18:20
119:69 *z* Job 13:4;
Ps 109:2
119:70 *a* S Ps 17:10;
Isa 29:13; Ac 28:27
119:71 *b* ver 67,75
119:72 *c* S Job 28:17;
S Ps 19:10
119:73 *d* S Ge 1:27;
S Job 4:17; 10:8;
Ps 138:8; 139:13-16
119:74 *e* S Ps 34:2
f ver 9; Ps 130:5
119:75 *g* ver 7,138,
172 *h* Heb 12:5-11
119:76 *i* Ps 6:4
j S ver 41
119:77 *k* Ps 90:13;
103:13 *l* S ver 47
119:78 *m* ver 51;
Jer 50:32 *n* ver 86,161;
Ps 35:19

60 I will hasten and not delay
  to obey your commands. *j*
61 Though the wicked bind me with ropes,
  I will not forget *k* your law.
62 At midnight *l* I rise to give you thanks
  for your righteous laws. *m*
63 I am a friend to all who fear you, *n*
  to all who follow your precepts. *o*
64 The earth is filled with your love, *p* LORD;
  teach me your decrees. *q*

ט Teth

65 Do good *r* to your servant
  according to your word, *s* LORD.
66 Teach me knowledge *t* and good judgment,
  for I trust your commands.
67 Before I was afflicted *u* I went astray, *v*
  but now I obey your word. *w*
68 You are good, *x* and what you do is good;
  teach me your decrees. *y*
69 Though the arrogant have smeared me with lies, *z*
  I keep your precepts with all my heart.
70 Their hearts are callous *a* and unfeeling,
  but I delight in your law.
71 It was good for me to be afflicted *b*
  so that I might learn your decrees.
72 The law from your mouth is more precious to me
  than thousands of pieces of silver and gold. *c*

י Yodh

73 Your hands made me *d* and formed me;
  give me understanding to learn your commands.
74 May those who fear you rejoice *e* when they see me,
  for I have put my hope in your word. *f*
75 I know, LORD, that your laws are righteous, *g*
  and that in faithfulness *h* you have afflicted me.
76 May your unfailing love *i* be my comfort,
  according to your promise *j* to your servant.
77 Let your compassion *k* come to me that I may live,
  for your law is my delight. *l*
78 May the arrogant *m* be put to shame for wronging me without
    cause; *n*
  but I will meditate on your precepts.

119:61 *bind me with ropes.* Oppress me.
119:62 *give you thanks.* See note on Ps 100 title. *righteous.* See note on v. 7.
119:63 *friend.* See note on v. 53.

A **119:65–72** Do good to me in accordance with your goodness, even if that means affliction, because your affliction is good for me; it teaches me knowledge and good judgment from your law.
119:65 *Do good.* Cf. v. 68; see 31:19; 86:17 and notes. *word.* See note on v. 25.
119:66 *trust.* Have confidence in; God's commands are not deceitful (see note on v. 29) or fickle (see note on v. 52).
119:67 *afflicted.* At the hands of God (see v. 71; see also note on v. 25, "laid low"). *word.* See note on v. 11.
119:69 *arrogant.* See note on v. 21.
119:70 *callous and unfeeling.* Lit. "fat as grease." Similar expressions occur also in Isa 6:10; Jer 5:28 (see also 17:10).
119:72 *than thousands...of silver and gold.* See vv. 14,57,111, 162.

A **119:73–80** Complete your forming of me by helping me to conform to your righteous laws so that the arrogant may be put to shame and those who fear you may rejoice with me. (The stanza has a concentric structure; compare vv. 73 and 80, 74 and 79, 75 and 78, 76 and 77.)
119:73 *give me understanding.* What I need to perfect the work you began when you formed me.
119:74 *fear you.* See v. 79; see also note on 34:8–14. *when they see me.* When I am perfectly formed and enjoying the blessings of the godly. *word.* See note on v. 25.
119:75 *laws.* Here the Hebrew for this word (*mishpatim*) may refer to God's just decisions in dealing with his servant, as the rest of the verse implies (see v. 84 and note). *you have afflicted me.* See vv. 67,71.
119:76 *unfailing love.* See note on 6:4. *my comfort.* In my affliction.
119:77 *that I may live.* And not perish in my affliction.
119:78 *the arrogant.* See note on v. 21. *be put to shame.* As they have subjected me to shame (see note on 5:10). *for wronging me.* See note on v. 25 ("laid low").

119:79 °ver 27,125
119:80 °ver 1;
S 1Ki 8:61 °S Ge 26:5
′S ver 6
119:81 °ver 20;
Ps 84:2 ′ver 123
°S ver 43
119:82 °S Ps 6:7;
69:3; La 2:11 °ver 41,
123
119:83 °S ver 61
119:84 ′Ps 6:3;
Rev 6:10 °ver 51;
Jer 12:3; 15:15; 20:11
119:85 °ver 51
°Ps 35:7; 57:6;
Jer 18:20,22
119:86 °ver 138
°S Ps 109:26
°S Ps 7:1 ′S ver 78
119:87 °ver 150;
Isa 1:4,28; 58:2; 59:13
119:88 °ver 124;
Ps 51:1; 109:26
′S Ps 41:2 °ver 2,100,
129,134,168
119:89 °ver 111,
144; S Ps 111:8;
Isa 51:6; S Mt 5:18;
1Pe 1:25
119:90 °S Ps 36:5
°S Ps 45:17
°S Job 8:19; Ps 148:6
119:91 °Jer 33:25
°Ps 104:2-4;
Jer 31:35
119:92 °Ps 37:4;
S 112:1 ′ver 50,67
119:93 °ver 83
′S Ps 103:5
119:94 °ver 146;
Ps 54:1; 116:4;
Jer 17:14; 31:18; 42:11
°S ver 45
119:95 °S Ps 69:4
°ver 99
119:96 °Ps 19:7

79 May those who fear you turn to me,
   those who understand your statutes. °
80 May my heart be blameless ° toward your decrees, °
   that I may not be put to shame. ′

כ Kaph

81 My soul faints ° with longing for your salvation, ′
   but I have put my hope ° in your word.
82 My eyes fail, ° looking for your promise; °
   I say, "When will you comfort me?"
83 Though I am like a wineskin in the smoke,
   I do not forget ° your decrees.
84 How long ° must your servant wait?
   When will you punish my persecutors? °
85 The arrogant ° dig pits ° to trap me,
   contrary to your law.
86 All your commands are trustworthy; °
   help me, ° for I am being persecuted ° without cause. ′
87 They almost wiped me from the earth,
   but I have not forsaken ° your precepts.
88 In your unfailing love ° preserve my life, ′
   that I may obey the statutes ′ of your mouth.

ל Lamedh

89 Your word, LORD, is eternal; °
   it stands firm in the heavens.
90 Your faithfulness ′ continues through all generations; °
   you established the earth, and it endures. °
91 Your laws endure ° to this day,
   for all things serve you. °
92 If your law had not been my delight, °
   I would have perished in my affliction. ′
93 I will never forget ° your precepts,
   for by them you have preserved my life. ′
94 Save me, ° for I am yours;
   I have sought out your precepts. °
95 The wicked are waiting to destroy me, °
   but I will ponder your statutes. °
96 To all perfection I see a limit,
   but your commands are boundless. °

119:79 *turn to me.* See v. 63 and note on v. 53.
119:80 *heart.* See note on 4:7. *not be put to shame.* See note on v. 6.

Λ **119:81–88** Save me from my affliction and my persecutors, according to your promises, and I will obey your statutes. This last stanza of the first half of the psalm, like the closing stanza, is dominated by prayer for God's help (see note on v. 25).
119:81 *soul.* See note on 6:3.
119:82 *My eyes fail.* See note on 6:7.
119:83 *like a wineskin in the smoke.* As a wineskin hanging in the smoke and heat above a fire becomes smudged and shriveled, so the psalmist bears the marks of his affliction.
119:84 *How long … wait?* Lit. "How (many are) the days of your servant?" That is, do not delay the punishment of my persecutors, because my life is short. *punish.* Lit. "effect justice upon" (the Hebrew for "justice" is *mishpat*; see note on v. 7, "laws"; see also note on 5:10).
119:85 *The arrogant.* See note on v. 21. *dig pits.* Probably referring to slander—public accusations that the psalmist must be guilty of vile sins or he would not be suffering such affliction (see notes on 5:9; 9:15). *contrary to your law.* See Ex 20:16.
119:86 *trustworthy.* See note on v. 29 ("deceitful ways").

119:88 *love.* See note on 6:4.

Λ **119:89** God's sovereign and unchanging word governs and maintains all creation. (These first three verses of the second half of the psalm teach a general truth; cf. vv. 1–3.)

Λ **119:89** *Your word.* Here God's word by which he created, maintains and governs all things (see 33:4,6; 107:20; 147:15,18). *stands firm in the heavens.* The secure order of the heavens and the earth (v. 90) declares (19:1–4) the reassuring truth that God's word (his "laws," v. 91), by which he upholds and governs all things, is enduring (eternal) and trustworthy ("Your faithfulness," v. 90). And that is the larger truth that confirms the confidence of the godly in the trustworthiness of God's word (his laws and promises) of special revelation (see notes on 93:5; 96:10; see also note on v. 29, "deceitful ways").
119:90 *Your faithfulness.* An indirect reference to God's word (see v. 89 and note).
119:92 *would have perished in my affliction.* Would not have learned the way of life (see v. 93) from your law (see vv. 67,71 and note on vv. 65–72).
119:95 *The wicked.* See note on v. 21 ("the arrogant"). *waiting to destroy me.* See note on v. 25 ("laid low").
119:96 *perfection.* Probably that which has been perfected in

119:97 ² S ver 47
ª S ver 15
119:98 ᵇ ver 130;
S Dt 4:6; Ps 19:7;
2Ti 3:15
119:99 ᶜ ver 15
119:100 ᵈ S ver 56;
S Dt 6:17
119:101 ᵉ Pr 1:15
ᶠ S ver 57
119:102 ᵍ S Dt 17:20
ʰ S Dt 4:5
119:103 ⁱ S Ps 19:10
ʲ Pr 24:13-14
119:104 ᵏ S Ps 111:10
ˡ ver 128
119:105 ᵐ Pr 20:27;
2Pe 1:19 ⁿ ver 130;
Pr 6:23
119:106 ᵒ S Ne 10:29
ᵖ ver 7
119:107 ᑫ S ver 25
119:108 ʳ Ps 51:15;
63:5; 71:8; 109:30
ˢ S ver 64
119:109 ᵗ S Jdg 12:3
ᵘ S ver 61
119:110 ᵛ Ps 25:15;
S 64:5; Isa 8:14;
Am 3:5 ʷ ver 10
119:111 ˣ ver 14,
162
119:112 ʸ S Ps 108:1
ᶻ ver 33
119:113 ª S 1Ki 18:21;
Jas 1:8; 4:8 ᵇ ver 47
119:114 ᶜ S Ge 15:1;
S Ps 18:2 ᵈ S ver 43
119:115 ᵉ S Ps 6:8
119:116 ᶠ S Ps 18:35;
41:3; 55:22; Isa 46:4
ᵍ S ver 41

⊏ Mem

97 Oh, how I love your law! ᶻ
   I meditate ª on it all day long.
98 Your commands are always with me
   and make me wiser ᵇ than my enemies.
99 I have more insight than all my teachers,
   for I meditate on your statutes. ᶜ
100 I have more understanding than the elders,
   for I obey your precepts. ᵈ
101 I have kept my feet ᵉ from every evil path
   so that I might obey your word. ᶠ
102 I have not departed from your laws, ᵍ
   for you yourself have taught ʰ me.
103 How sweet are your words to my taste,
   sweeter than honey ⁱ to my mouth! ʲ
104 I gain understanding ᵏ from your precepts;
   therefore I hate every wrong path. ˡ

⊃ Nun

105 Your word is a lamp ᵐ to my feet
   and a light ⁿ for my path.
106 I have taken an oath ᵒ and confirmed it,
   that I will follow your righteous laws. ᵖ
107 I have suffered much;
   preserve my life, ᑫ Lᴏʀᴅ, according to your word.
108 Accept, Lᴏʀᴅ, the willing praise of my mouth, ʳ
   and teach me your laws. ˢ
109 Though I constantly take my life in my hands, ᵗ
   I will not forget ᵘ your law.
110 The wicked have set a snare ᵛ for me,
   but I have not strayed ʷ from your precepts.
111 Your statutes are my heritage forever;
   they are the joy of my heart. ˣ
112 My heart is set ʸ on keeping your decrees
   to the very end. ª ᶻ

⊃ Samekh

113 I hate double-minded people, ª
   but I love your law. ᵇ
114 You are my refuge and my shield; ᶜ
   I have put my hope ᵈ in your word.
115 Away from me, ᵉ you evildoers,
   that I may keep the commands of my God!
116 Sustain me ᶠ according to your promise, ᵍ and I will live;

ª 112 Or / for their enduring reward

---

the sense of completed, given fixed bounds so that it is no longer open-ended. *boundless.* Lit. "very broad," i.e., an inexhaustible source of wise counsel for life (see vv. 97–100).

A **119:97–104** Meditation on God's law yields the highest wisdom.

119:98 *my enemies.* Those arrogant ones (see note on v. 21) who place confidence in worldly wisdom.

119:99 *teachers.* Merely human teachers.

119:100 *elders.* Old men, taught by experience (see note on Ex 3:16).

119:102 *you…have taught me.* Through your laws.

119:103 *words.* Perhaps better understood here as "laws" (see vv. 67,133,158,172 and note on v. 11).

119:104 *hate every wrong path.* See note on v. 53.

A **119:105** *lamp…light.* Apart from which I could only grope about in the darkness.

119:106 *have taken an oath and confirmed it.* Have covenanted (see Ne 10:29).

119:107 See v. 25 and note.

119:109 *take my life in my hands.* By publicly honoring God's law even in the face of threats and hostility (see especially vv. 23,46,161).

119:110 *set a snare.* See v. 85 and note.

119:111–112 *heart.* See note on 4:7.

119:111 *my heritage.* The possession I have received from God as my homestead and that from which I draw the provisions for my life (see note on vv. 57–64).

A **119:113** *hate double-minded people.* See v. 115; see also note on v. 53. Double-minded people are unstable in all they do (Jas 1:8).

119:114 *word.* See note on v. 25.

do not let my hopes be dashed. *h*
117 Uphold me, *i* and I will be delivered; *j*
    I will always have regard for your decrees. *k*
118 You reject all who stray *l* from your decrees,
    for their delusions come to nothing.
119 All the wicked of the earth you discard like dross; *m*
    therefore I love your statutes. *n*
120 My flesh trembles *o* in fear of you; *p*
    I stand in awe *q* of your laws.

ע Ayin

121 I have done what is righteous and just; *r*
    do not leave me to my oppressors.
122 Ensure your servant's well-being; *s*
    do not let the arrogant oppress me. *t*
123 My eyes fail, *u* looking for your salvation, *v*
    looking for your righteous promise. *w*
124 Deal with your servant according to your love *x*
    and teach me your decrees. *y*
125 I am your servant; *z* give me discernment
    that I may understand your statutes. *a*
126 It is time for you to act, LORD;
    your law is being broken. *b*
127 Because I love your commands *c*
    more than gold, *d* more than pure gold, *e*
128 and because I consider all your precepts right, *f*
    I hate every wrong path. *g*

פ Pe

129 Your statutes are wonderful; *h*
    therefore I obey them. *i*
130 The unfolding of your words gives light; *j*
    it gives understanding to the simple. *k*
131 I open my mouth and pant, *l*
    longing for your commands. *m*
132 Turn to me *n* and have mercy *o* on me,
    as you always do to those who love your name. *p*
133 Direct my footsteps according to your word; *q*
    let no sin rule *r* over me.
134 Redeem me from human oppression, *s*
    that I may obey your precepts. *t*
135 Make your face shine *u* on your servant
    and teach me your decrees. *v*

119:116 *h* Ro 5:5
119:117 *i* Isa 41:10; 46:4 *j* Ps 34:4 *k* ver 6
119:118 *l* S ver 10
119:119 *m* Isa 1:22, 25; Eze 22:18,19 *n* ver 47
119:120 *o* S Job 4:14; S Isa 64:2 *p* S Jos 24:14 *q* Jer 10:7; Hab 3:2
119:121 *r* S 2Sa 8:15; S Job 27:6
119:122 *s* S Job 17:3 *t* ver 21,121,134; Ps 106:42
119:123 *u* Isa 38:14 *v* ver 81 *w* S ver 82
119:124 *x* S ver 88; S Ps 25:7 *y* ver 12
119:125 *z* S Ps 116:16 *a* S ver 79
119:126 *b* S Nu 15:31
119:127 *c* S ver 47 *d* Ps 19:10 *e* S Job 3:21
119:128 *f* S Ps 19:8 *g* ver 104,163; Ps 31:6; Pr 13:5
119:129 *h* ver 18 *i* ver 22, S 88
119:130 *j* S ver 105 *k* S Ps 19:7
119:131 *l* Ps 42:1 *m* S ver 20
119:132 *n* S Ps 6:4 *o* S 2Sa 24:14; S Ps 9:13 *p* S Ps 5:11
119:133 *q* ver 9 *r* S ver 11; S Ro 6:16
119:134 *s* S ver 122 *t* S ver 56, S 88
119:135 *u* S Nu 6:25; Ps 4:6; 67:1; 80:3 *v* ver 12

119:118 *reject.* Or "shake off" or "make light of." *their delusions.* Probably their ways, which are deceitful (see note on v. 29).
119:119 *dross.* Scum removed from molten ore or metal. The Hebrew for this word is a pun on the word for "stray" in v. 118: Those who stray are treated like dross.
119:120 *My flesh trembles.* He quivers out of his deep reverence for God.
119:121–128 As your faithful servant, I pray for deliverance from my oppressors—another stanza in which prayer for deliverance is dominant (see vv. 81–88 and note; see also note on v. 25, "laid low").
▲ **119:121** *what is righteous and just.* A phrase commonly used to sum up the whole will of God for moral action (see 106:3; Ge 18:19; 2Sa 8:15; Pr 1:3; 21:3; Isa 56:1; Jer 22:15; 33:15; Eze 18:5,19,21,17; 33:14,16,19; 45:9).
119:122 The only verse in this psalm that does not have either a direct or an indirect (as in vv. 90,121,132; see note on v. 75) reference to God's word. *the arrogant.* See note on v. 21.

119:123 *My eyes fail.* See note on 6:7.
119:124 *love.* See note on 6:4.
119:126 *act.* Either in defense of his servant or in judgment on the lawbreakers or both.
119:127 *more than gold.* See vv. 14,57,72,111.
119:128 *I hate every wrong path.* See note on v. 53.
119:129 *wonderful.* See v. 18 and note.
▲ **119:130** *unfolding.* Lit. "opening," here meaning (1) the revelation of your words, (2) the interpretation (see "expound," 49:4) of your words or (3) the entering of your words into the heart. *the simple.* See 19:7 and note.
119:132 *as you always do.* Lit. "as is (your) manner" (the Hebrew for "manner" is *mishpat*); hence an indirect reference (see note on v. 122) to God's law (see note on v. 7).
119:134,154 *Redeem.* Here, as often, a synonym for "deliver."
119:134 *oppression.* See note on v. 25 ("laid low").
119:135 *your face shine.* See note on 13:1 ("hide your face").

119:136 ʷPs 6:6; Isa 22:4; Jer 9:1;18; 13:17; 14:17; La 1:16; 3:48 ˣver 158; Ps 106:25; Isa 42:24; Eze 9:4
119:137 ʸS Ex 9:27; S Ezr 9:15 ᶻS Ne 9:13
119:138 ᵃS ver 75; S Ps 19:7 ᵇver 86
119:139 ᶜPs 69:9; Jn 2:17
119:140 ᵈS Jos 23:14 ᵉPs 12:6 ᶠver 47
119:141 ᵍS Ps 22:6 ʰver 61,134
119:142 ⁱver 151, 160; Ps 19:7
119:143 ʲver 24, S 47
119:144 ᵏS ver 34
119:145 ˡver 10 ᵐver 22,55
119:146 ⁿS ver 94
119:147 ᵒPs 5:3; 57:8; 108:2
119:148 ᵖS Ps 63:6
119:149 �q S Ps 27:7 ʳver 124 ˢS ver 40
119:150 ᵗS Ps 37:7
119:151 ᵘS Ps 34:18; Php 4:5 ᵛS ver 142
119:152 ʷver 7,73 ˣS ver 89; S Ps 111:8; Lk 21:33
119:153 ʸS Ps 13:3 ᶻS Ps 3:7 ᵃS Ps 44:17
119:154 ᵇPs 35:1; Jer 50:34; Mic 7:9 ᶜS 1Sa 24:15 ᵈver 25 ᵉS ver 41
119:155 ᶠver 94, 118
119:156 ᵍS Ne 9:27; Jas 5:11 ʰver 25 ⁱver 149
119:157 ʲS Ps 7:1

136 Streams of tears ʷ flow from my eyes,
for your law is not obeyed. ˣ

צ Tsadhe

137 You are righteous, ʸ LORD,
and your laws are right. ᶻ
138 The statutes you have laid down are righteous; ᵃ
they are fully trustworthy. ᵇ
139 My zeal wears me out, ᶜ
for my enemies ignore your words.
140 Your promises ᵈ have been thoroughly tested, ᵉ
and your servant loves them. ᶠ
141 Though I am lowly and despised, ᵍ
I do not forget your precepts. ʰ
142 Your righteousness is everlasting
and your law is true. ⁱ
143 Trouble and distress have come upon me,
but your commands give me delight. ʲ
144 Your statutes are always righteous;
give me understanding ᵏ that I may live.

ק Qoph

145 I call with all my heart; ˡ answer me, LORD,
and I will obey your decrees. ᵐ
146 I call out to you; save me ⁿ
and I will keep your statutes.
147 I rise before dawn ᵒ and cry for help;
I have put my hope in your word.
148 My eyes stay open through the watches of the night, ᵖ
that I may meditate on your promises.
149 Hear my voice q in accordance with your love; ʳ
preserve my life, ˢ LORD, according to your laws.
150 Those who devise wicked schemes ᵗ are near,
but they are far from your law.
151 Yet you are near, ᵘ LORD,
and all your commands are true. ᵛ
152 Long ago I learned from your statutes ʷ
that you established them to last forever. ˣ

ר Resh

153 Look on my suffering ʸ and deliver me, ᶻ
for I have not forgotten ᵃ your law.
154 Defend my cause ᵇ and redeem me; ᶜ
preserve my life ᵈ according to your promise. ᵉ
155 Salvation is far from the wicked,
for they do not seek out ᶠ your decrees.
156 Your compassion, LORD, is great; ᵍ
preserve my life ʰ according to your laws. ⁱ
157 Many are the foes who persecute me, ʲ

119:136 See v. 53 and note.
119:137–144 The Lord and his laws are righteous.
119:137 *righteous.* See note on 4:1.
119:138 *trustworthy.* See v. 142; see also note on v. 29 ("deceitful ways").
119:139 *My zeal.* See note on v. 53.
119:140 *promises.* Hebrew *'imrah;* perhaps better rendered "word" here (see note on v. 11). *tested.* Lit. "refined," i.e., God's word contains nothing worthless or useless.
119:141 *lowly and despised.* Cf. v. 143; see also note on v. 25.
119:145–152 Save me, Lord, and I will keep your law. As the psalm draws to a close, prayer for deliverance becomes more

dominant (see note on v. 25, "laid low").
119:148 *watches of the night.* See note on Jdg 7:19; see also La 2:19.
119:149 *love.* See note on 6:4. *your laws.* Or "your justice" (complementing "your love"); Hebrew *mishpat* (see note on v.75).
119:150 *far from your law.* See vv. 21,53,85,118,126,139,155, 158.
119:151 *are true.* See note on v. 29 ("deceitful ways").
119:152 *last forever.* See note on v. 52.
119:153–160 See note on vv. 145–152.
119:155 *the wicked.* See note on v. 21 ("the arrogant").
119:156 *your laws.* See v. 149 and note.

but I have not turned [k] from your statutes.
158 I look on the faithless with loathing, [l]
   for they do not obey your word. [m]
159 See how I love your precepts;
   preserve my life, [n] LORD, in accordance with your love.
160 All your words are true;
   all your righteous laws are eternal. [o]

ש Sin and Shin

161 Rulers persecute me [p] without cause,
   but my heart trembles [q] at your word.
162 I rejoice [r] in your promise
   like one who finds great spoil. [s]
163 I hate and detest [t] falsehood
   but I love your law. [u]
164 Seven times a day I praise you
   for your righteous laws. [v]
165 Great peace [w] have those who love your law,
   and nothing can make them stumble. [x]
166 I wait for your salvation, [y] LORD,
   and I follow your commands.
167 I obey your statutes,
   for I love them [z] greatly.
168 I obey your precepts [a] and your statutes, [b]
   for all my ways are known [c] to you.

ת Taw

169 May my cry come [d] before you, LORD;
   give me understanding [e] according to your word. [f]
170 May my supplication come [g] before you;
   deliver me [h] according to your promise. [i]
171 May my lips overflow with praise, [j]
   for you teach me [k] your decrees.
172 May my tongue sing [l] of your word,
   for all your commands are righteous. [m]
173 May your hand be ready to help [n] me,
   for I have chosen [o] your precepts.
174 I long for your salvation, [p] LORD,
   and your law gives me delight. [q]
175 Let me live [r] that I may praise you,
   and may your laws sustain me.
176 I have strayed like a lost sheep. [s]
   Seek your servant,
   for I have not forgotten [t] your commands.

PSALM 120

A song of ascents.

1 I call on the LORD [u] in my distress, [v]
   and he answers me.

119:157 [k] Ps 44:18
119:158 [l] ver 104;
S Ex 32:19
[m] S ver 136
119:159 [n] ver 25;
S Ps 41:2
119:160 [o] S ver 89;
S Ps 111:8
119:161 [p] ver 23,
122,157; 1Sa 24:14-15
[q] ver 120
119:162 [r] S ver 111
[s] 1Sa 30:16; Isa 9:3;
53:12
119:163 [t] S ver 128
[u] ver 47
119:164 [v] ver 7,160
119:165 [w] Ps 37:11;
Isa 26:3,12; 27:5;
32:17; 57:19; 66:12
[x] S ver 11; S Ps 37:24;
1Jn 2:10
119:166 [y] ver 81
119:167 [z] ver 47
119:168 [a] S ver 56,
S 88 [b] ver 2,22
[c] Job 10:4; S 23:10;
Ps 139:3; Pr 5:21
119:169 [d] S Job 16:18
[e] S ver 34 [f] S ver 9
119:170 [g] 1Ki 8:30;
2Ch 6:24; Ps 28:2;
140:6; 143:1 [h] Ps 3:7;
22:20; 59:1 [i] S ver 41
119:171 [j] Ps 51:15;
63:3 [k] Ps 94:12;
Isa 2:3; Mic 4:2
119:172 [l] Ps 51:14
[m] ver 7, S 75
119:173 [n] Ps 37:24;
73:23; Isa 41:10
[o] S Jos 24:22
119:174 [p] ver 166
[q] ver 16,24
119:175 [r] ver 116,
159; Isa 55:3
119:176 [s] ver 10;
S Ps 95:10; Jer 50:17;
Eze 34:11; S Lk 15:4
[t] S Ps 44:17
120:1 [u] S Ps 18:6
[v] S 2Sa 22:7;
S Ps 118:5

119:158 *word.* Hebrew *'imrah* (see note on v. 11).
119:160 *All.* Lit. "The sum of" (as in 139:17). *true.* See note on v. 29 ("deceitful ways"). *eternal.* See note on v. 52.
119:161–168 See note on vv. 145–152.
119:161 *Rulers.* See note on v. 23. *heart.* See note on 4:7.
119:162 *great spoil.* See vv. 14,72,111.
119:163 *I hate.* See note on v. 53. *falsehood.* Or "that which is (ways that are) deceitful" (see v. 29 and note).

119:164 *Seven.* A number signifying completeness—he praises God throughout the day.

119:165 *Great peace.* Complete security and well-being.

119:169–176 See note on vv. 145–152.
119:171 *overflow with praise.* Because you have delivered me.
119:172 *righteous.* See note on v. 7.
119:174–176 The conclusion to the psalm.

119:176 *I have strayed.* See Isa 53:6; the clearest expression of the author's acknowledgment that, for all his devotion to God's law, he has again and again wandered into other (deceitful) ways and, like a lost sheep, must be brought back by his heavenly Shepherd. For one who has made God's law the guide and dearest treasure of his life, the last word can only be such a confession—and such a prayer.

Ps 120–137 A collection of 15 psalms (120–134), each bearing

120:2 ʷ S Ps 31:18
ˣ S Ps 52:4
120:4 ʸ S Dt 32:23
120:5 ᶻ S Ge 25:13;
Jer 2:10
121:2 ª S Ge 1:1
ᵇ S Ps 104:5; Ps 115:15

² Save me, LORD,
from lying lips ʷ
and from deceitful tongues. ˣ

³ What will he do to you,
and what more besides,
you deceitful tongue?
⁴ He will punish you with a warrior's sharp arrows, ʸ
with burning coals of the broom bush.

⁵ Woe to me that I dwell in Meshek,
that I live among the tents of Kedar! ᶻ
⁶ Too long have I lived
among those who hate peace.
⁷ I am for peace;
but when I speak, they are for war.

PSALM 121

A song of ascents.

¹ I lift up my eyes to the mountains—
where does my help come from?
² My help comes from the LORD,
the Maker of heaven ª and earth. ᵇ

³ He will not let your foot slip—
he who watches over you will not slumber;

---

the title "song of ascents," to which has been attached Ps 135–137. Ps 120–136 have been referred to in some Jewish traditions as the "Great Hallel" (in distinction from the "Egyptian Hallel"; see introduction to Ps 113–118). Ps 137, expressive of deep devotion to Zion/Jerusalem, the city containing the great symbols of the Lord's presence with his people, brings the collection to its close. Some have thought that the Hebrew for "ascents" refers to 15 steps leading up to the temple, so that the title means "A song of the stairs" and indicates that these songs were to be used in a liturgical procession up to the temple (probably at the Festival of Tabernacles). Most, however, believe that it refers to the annual religious pilgrimages to Jerusalem (see 84:5–7; Ex 23:14–17; Dt 16:16; Mic 4:2; Zec 14:16 and note), which brought the worshipers singing to Mount Zion (Isa 30:29)—a view that does not exclude the use of these psalms also in the temple liturgy. The title no doubt reflects postexilic usage rather than the original purpose of the composition of each of the several psalms bearing it. The spirit of Ps 84 pervades the collection (see also Ps 42–43).

Whether an overall thematic (or some other) scheme controls the arrangement of the "ascents" psalms is unclear, though it is probably not coincidental that they begin with a prayer that evokes the experience of being far from home and beset by barbarians and end with a call to praise in the sanctuary. It has been pointed out that in the main Hebrew text tradition the middle psalm (127) is ascribed to Solomon, while four of the others (122; 124; 131; 133), two on each side of the middle, are ascribed to David. But little can be made of this since the Septuagint (the pre-Christian Greek translation of the OT) reflects a text tradition in which none of the "ascents" psalms is ascribed to a named author. For further observations relative to arrangement within this collection, see introductions to the individual psalms.

Ps 120 The prayer of an individual for deliverance from false accusers (see 5:9 and note). The reference to "war" (v. 7) is probably metaphorical. The theme is developed in three short stanzas: The prayer uttered (vv. 1–2), the adversaries addressed (vv. 3–4), the circumstances lamented (vv. 5–7).
120 title See introduction to Ps 120–137.
120:1–2 The prayer.
120:1 *I call . . . he answers.* See note on 118:5.
120:2,6 *me . . . I.* Lit. "my soul" (see note on 6:3).

120:2 *lying lips . . . deceitful tongues.* See note on 5:9.
120:3–4 Assurance that God will act (see 6:8–10 and note on 3:8).
120:3 *he.* The Lord. *what more besides.* An echo of a common oath formula (see 1Sa 3:17 and note), thus suggesting the certainty and severity of God's judgment on the enemies.
120:4 *sharp arrows . . . burning coals.* As a weapon, the tongue is a sharp arrow (see Pr 25:18; Jer 9:8; see also 57:4; 64:3) and a searing fire (see Pr 16:27; Jas 3:6), and God's judgment will answer in kind (see 7:11–13; 11:6; 64:7). For judgment in kind, see 63:9–10; 64:7–8 and notes. *broom bush.* A desert shrub, sometimes large enough to provide shade. Charcoal made from its wood produced an especially hot and durable fire.
120:5–7 Complaint over prolonged harassment.
120:5 *Meshek . . . Kedar.* The former was in central Asia Minor (see note on Ge 10:2), the latter in Arabia (see note on Isa 21:16). Besieged by slanderers, the psalmist feels as though he is far from home, surrounded by barbarians.
Ps 121 A dialogue (perhaps liturgical) of confession and assurance. Its use as a pilgrimage song provides the key to its understanding. Whether the dialogue takes place in a single heart (cf. the refrain in Ps 42–43) or between individuals in the caravan is of no great consequence since all would share the same convictions. The comforting assurance expressed (see Ps 33) is equally appropriate for the pilgrimage to Jerusalem and for the pilgrimage of life to the "glory" into which the faithful will be received (see notes on 49:15; 73:24). The psalm is composed of four couplets, each having an introductory line, which the rest of the couplet develops. Key terms are "the LORD" and "watch over," each occurring five times.
121 title See introduction to Ps 120–137.
121:1–2 Confession of trust in the Lord.
121:1 *mountains.* Those in the vicinity of Jerusalem, of which Mount Zion is one (125:2), or, if the plural indicates majesty (as in the Hebrew in 87:1; 133:3), Mount Zion itself.
121:2 *Maker of heaven and earth.* The one true God, the King of all creation (see 124:8; 134:3; see also 33:6; 89:11–13; 96:4–5; 104:2–9; 136:4–9).
121:3–4 Assurance concerning the unsleeping guardian over Israel.
121:3 *not let your foot slip.* Not even where the way is treacher-

121:4 c Ps 127:1
121:5 d S Ps 1:6
121:6 e Isa 49:10
121:7 f S Ps 9:9
121:8 g Dt 28:6
122:6 h S Ps 26:8
122:7 i S 1Sa 25:6
j S Ps 48:3

⁴ indeed, he who watches ᶜ over Israel
 will neither slumber nor sleep.

⁵ The Lᴏʀᴅ watches over ᵈ you—
 the Lᴏʀᴅ is your shade at your right hand;
⁶ the sun ᵉ will not harm you by day,
 nor the moon by night.

⁷ The Lᴏʀᴅ will keep you from all harm ᶠ—
 he will watch over your life;
⁸ the Lᴏʀᴅ will watch over your coming and going
 both now and forevermore. ᵍ

PSALM 122

A song of ascents. Of David.

¹ I rejoiced with those who said to me,
 "Let us go to the house of the Lᴏʀᴅ."
² Our feet are standing
 in your gates, Jerusalem.

³ Jerusalem is built like a city
 that is closely compacted together.
⁴ That is where the tribes go up—
 the tribes of the Lᴏʀᴅ—
 to praise the name of the Lᴏʀᴅ
 according to the statute given to Israel.
⁵ There stand the thrones for judgment,
 the thrones of the house of David.

⁶ Pray for the peace of Jerusalem:
 "May those who love ʰ you be secure.
⁷ May there be peace ⁱ within your walls
 and security within your citadels. ʲ"
⁸ For the sake of my friends and of all the people,

---

ous. *not slumber.* Like the pagan god Baal (see 1Ki 18:27)—though sometimes he seemed to (see 44:23; 78:65).

121:4 *he who watches over Israel.* The Lord of all creation and the guardian over Israel—the One in whom the faithful may put unfaltering trust.

121:5–6 Assurance concerning unfailing protection.

121:5 *shade.* See 91:1 ("shadow") and note on 17:8. *at your right hand.* See Isa 4:6; 25:4–5; 49:10; Jnh 4:8).

121:6 *sun ... moon.* Here, in agreement with the "shade" metaphor, these serve as figures for all that distresses or threatens, day or night (see Isa 4:6; 25:4–5; 49:10; Jnh 4:8).

121:7–8 Assurance concerning all of life.

121:8 *your coming and going.* Lit. "your going and coming." Although the Hebrew order is like that in such military contexts as 1Sa 29:6 ("to have you serve"); 2Sa 3:25 ("your movements"), the sense here is similar to that in Dt 28:6.

Ps 122 A hymn of joy over Jerusalem (see Ps 42–43; 46; 48; 84; 87; 137 and the introductions to those psalms). Sung by a pilgrim in Jerusalem (very likely at one of the three annual festivals, Dt 16:16), it expresses deep joy over the city and offers a prayer for its welfare. As the third of the pilgrimage psalms (see introduction to Ps 120–137), it shares many dominant themes with Ps 132, the third from the end of this collection—possibly a deliberate arrangement. Structurally, a two-verse introduction locates the worshiper with the festival throng in the city of his joy, and the major themes are developed in two closely balanced stanzas of four verses each (in Hebrew the first has a total of 57 syllables, the second 60 syllables; see also introductions to Ps 127; 128; 129). References to "the house of the Lᴏʀᴅ" (vv. 1,9) frame the song.

122 title *ascents.* See introduction to Ps 120–137. *Of David.* This element is not present in all ancient witnesses to the text,

and the content suggests a later date (see note on v. 1).

122:1–2 Joy for having joined the pilgrimage to Jerusalem.

122:1 *the house of the Lᴏʀᴅ.* The temple (2Sa 7:5,13; 1Ki 5:3,5; 8:10, "temple"). That Jerusalem became the city of pilgrimage before the dedication of the temple is doubtful in light of 1Ki 3:4; 8:1–11.

122:2 *gates.* Gateways.

122:3–5 Jerusalem's significance for the faithful.

122:3 *closely compacted together.* Perhaps refers to the city's well-knit construction (see Ps 48) and probably echoes the account of the construction of the tabernacle (cf. Ex 26:11, "fasten ...together as a unit"). If so, Jerusalem is being celebrated as the earthly residence of God (see note on 9:11; see also Isa 4:5).

122:4 *to praise.* For God's saving acts in behalf of Israel and his blessings on the nation. *name.* See note on 5:11. *statute given to Israel.* See 81:3–5; Dt 16:1–17.

122:5 *There ... the thrones of the house of David.* Jerusalem is both the city of the Lord and the royal city of his chosen dynasty, through which he (ideally) protects and governs the nation (see 2:2,6–7; 89:3–4,19–37; 110; 2Sa 7:8–16 and notes). In postexilic times it remained, though now in Messianic hope, the city of David.

122:6–9 Prayers for Jerusalem's peace.

122:6 In Hebrew a beautiful wordplay tightly binds together "Pray," "peace," "Jerusalem" and "be secure." *peace.* See vv. 7–8; includes both security and prosperity. *those who love you.* The psalmist, those referred to in vv. 1,8 and all who love Jerusalem because they are devoted to the Lord and his chosen king. These constitute a loving fellowship of those who worship together, pray together and seek each other's welfare as the people of God (see Ps 133).

122:7 *walls ... citadels.* See 48:13 ("ramparts ...citadels").

122:9 *k* Ps 128:5
123:1 *l* S Ps 68:5;
Isa 6:1; 63:15
123:2 *m* S Ps 25:15
124:1 *n* Ps 129:1
124:4 *o* Ps 88:17
p Ps 18:4
124:7 *q* S Ps 91:3
r Ps 25:15

I will say, "Peace be within you."
⁹ For the sake of the house of the Lord our God,
     I will seek your prosperity. *k*

PSALM 123

A song of ascents.

¹ I lift up my eyes to you,
     to you who sit enthroned *l* in heaven.
² As the eyes of slaves look to the hand of their master,
     as the eyes of a female slave look to the hand of her mistress,
so our eyes look to the Lord *m* our God,
     till he shows us his mercy.

³ Have mercy on us, Lord, have mercy on us,
     for we have endured no end of contempt.
⁴ We have endured no end
     of ridicule from the arrogant,
     of contempt from the proud.

PSALM 124

A song of ascents. Of David.

¹ If the Lord had not been on our side—
     let Israel say *n*—
² if the Lord had not been on our side
     when people attacked us,
³ they would have swallowed us alive
     when their anger flared against us;
⁴ the flood *o* would have engulfed us,
     the torrent *p* would have swept over us,
⁵ the raging waters
     would have swept us away.

⁶ Praise be to the Lord,
     who has not let us be torn by their teeth.
⁷ We have escaped like a bird
     from the fowler's snare; *q*
the snare has been broken, *r*
     and we have escaped.

122:8–9 *For the sake of ... For the sake of.* Because Jerusalem is the place supreme where God and his people meet together in fruitful communion, the psalmist vows to seek the city's peace.
122:9 *the house of the Lord.* See v. 1 and note; the phrase provides a literary frame for the psalm.
Ps 123 A prayer of God's humble people for him to show mercy and so foil the contempt of the proud. See introduction to Ps 124. As to its structure, a one-verse introduction is followed by two brief stanzas, each developing its own theme.
123 title See introduction to Ps 120–137.
123:1 *I lift up my eyes.* The psalmist speaks as a representative member of or as spokesperson for the community—see the first-person plurals that follow. *who sit enthroned in heaven.* The same God whose earthly throne is in the temple on Mount Zion (see 122:5 and note; see also 2:4; 9:11; 11:4; 80:1; 99:1; 113:5; 132:14).
123:2 With the use of two similes drawn from domestic life, the faithful (men and women alike) present themselves as dependent and confidently reliant on God.
123:4 *the arrogant ... the proud.* Those who live by their own wits and strength (see notes on 10:2–11; 31:23) and pour contempt on those who humbly rely on the Lord. For examples, see those with whom King Hezekiah (2Ki 18:17—19:19) or Governor Nehemiah (Ne 4; 6:1–4) had to contend.
Ps 124 Israel's praise of the Lord for deliverance from powerful

enemies—an appropriate sequel to Ps 123. Very likely a Levite speaks in vv. 1–5, while the worshipers answer in vv. 6–8. That it shares with Ps 129 a similar introduction and a theme focused on Zion's deliverance from powerful enemies suggests that these two psalms were arranged to frame the intervening four (see note on 125:5).
124 title *ascents.* See introduction to Ps 120–137. *Of David.* Not all ancient witnesses to the text contain this element, and both language and theme suggest a postexilic date (see note on Ps 122 title). It may have been assigned to David because of supposed echoes of Ps 18; 69.
124:1–5 Let Israel acknowledge that the Lord alone has saved her from extinction (see 20:7; 94:17).
124:2 *people attacked.* Proud and arrogant people (123:4) may attack, but the Lord is Israel's help (v. 8).
124:3 *swallowed us.* Like death (see note on 49:14). But see 69:15.
124:4–5 *flood ... torrent ... raging waters.* See 18:16; see also 32:6; 69:1–2 and notes.
124:6–8 Response of praise for deliverance—with a vivid enrichment of the imagery.
124:6 *torn by their teeth.* As by wild beasts (see note on 7:2).
124:7 *escaped like a bird from the fowler's snare.* A most apt figure for Israel's release from Babylonian captivity (cf. note on 9:15).

8 Our help is in the name *s* of the L<small>ORD</small>,
  the Maker of heaven *t* and earth.

PSALM 125

A song of ascents.

1 Those who trust in the L<small>ORD</small> are like Mount Zion, *u*
  which cannot be shaken *v* but endures forever.
2 As the mountains surround Jerusalem, *w*
  so the L<small>ORD</small> surrounds *x* his people
  both now and forevermore.

3 The scepter *y* of the wicked will not remain *z*
  over the land allotted to the righteous,
for then the righteous might use
  their hands to do evil. *a*

4 L<small>ORD</small>, do good *b* to those who are good,
  to those who are upright in heart. *c*
5 But those who turn *d* to crooked ways *e*
  the L<small>ORD</small> will banish *f* with the evildoers.

  Peace be on Israel. *g*

PSALM 126

A song of ascents.

1 When the L<small>ORD</small> restored *h* the fortunes of *a* Zion,
  we were like those who dreamed. *b*
2 Our mouths were filled with laughter, *i*
  our tongues with songs of joy. *j*
Then it was said among the nations,
  "The L<small>ORD</small> has done great things *k* for them."
3 The L<small>ORD</small> has done great things *l* for us,
  and we are filled with joy. *m*

4 Restore our fortunes, *c n* L<small>ORD</small>,

---

a 1 Or L<small>ORD</small> *brought back the captives to* *b* 1 Or *those restored to health* *c* 4 Or *Bring back our captives*

Right margin cross-references

124:8 *s* 1Sa 17:45
t Ge 1:1; Ps 115:15;
121:2; 134:3
125:1 *u* Ps 48:12;
Isa 33:20 *v* Ps 46:5;
48:2-5
125:2 *w* S 1Ch 21:15
x Ps 32:10; Zec 2:4-5
125:3 *y* S Est 4:11
z Ps 89:22; Pr 22:8;
Isa 13:11; 14:5
a 1Sa 24:10
125:4 *b* S Ps 119:65
c S Ps 36:10
125:5 *d* S Job 23:11
e Pr 2:15; Isa 59:8
f Ps 92:7 *g* Ps 128:6;
Gal 6:16
126:1 *h* Ezr 1:1-3;
Ps 85:1; Hos 6:11
126:2 *i* S Ge 21:6
j S Job 8:21; S Ps 65:8
k S Dt 10:21; Ps 71:19;
Lk 1:49
126:3 *l* Ps 106:21;
Joel 2:21,26
m S Ps 9:2; 16:11
126:4 *n* S Dt 30:3

124:8 In climax, the great confession (see 121:2 and note).
Ps 125 Israel's security celebrated in testimony, prayer and benediction. The psalm is most likely postexilic and was probably spoken in the temple liturgy by a Levite. Ps 125 and 126 are thematically linked and precisely balanced, each being composed (in Hebrew) of 116 syllables. Their juxtaposition was no doubt deliberate.
125 title See introduction to Ps 120–137.
125:1–2 The solid security of God's people.
125:1 *Those who trust in the* L<small>ORD</small>. God's "people" (v. 2) are also characterized as "the righteous" (v. 3) and "those who are good," "who are upright in heart" (v. 4). For a similar description of the "righteous," see 34:8–14 and note. *like Mount Zion.* In their security (see Ps 46; 48).
125:2 *mountains surround Jerusalem.* Though Jerusalem is not surrounded by a ring of peaks, the city is located in what OT writers called a mountainous region. *so the* L<small>ORD</small> *surrounds his people.* As surely, as substantially and as immovably (see 2Ki 6:17; Zec 2:5).
125:3 Wicked rulers, whether by example or by oppression, tend to corrupt even the righteous, but the Lord will preserve his people also from this corrosive threat. *scepter of the wicked.* Probably referring to Persian rule (see Ne 9:36–37) and its invidious underlings, such as those Nehemiah had to contend with (see Ne 2:19; 4:1–3,7–8; 6:1–14,17–19; 13:7–8,28). *land allotted to the righteous.* The promised land (see 78:55).
125:4–5 To everyone as they are and do—that is God's way (see 18:25–27); thus the confident prayer (v. 4) and the equally confident assertion (v. 5).

125:4 *heart.* See note on 4:7.
125:5 *Peace be on Israel.* Perhaps a concise form of the priestly benediction (Nu 6:24–26). This benediction has its counterpart in the prayer of 126:4–6. Its repetition at the end of Ps 128 suggests a frame around the four closely balanced psalms (made up of two pairs: 125–126; 127–128).
Ps 126 A song of joy for restoration to Zion. If not composed for those who returned from Babylonian exile (see Ezra and Nehemiah)—the place of exile is not named—it surely served to voice the joy of that restored community (cf. Ps 42–43; 84; 137). The psalm divides into two stanzas of four (Hebrew) lines each, with their initial lines sharing a common theme. Thematic unity is further served by repetition (cf. vv. 2–3) and other key words ("the L<small>ORD</small>," "songs of joy," "carrying"). References to God's action (vv. 1,3) frame the first stanza, while v. 2 offers exposition. For this psalm's relationship to Ps 125, see introduction to that psalm.
126 title See introduction to Ps 120–137.
126:1–3 Joy over restoration experienced.
126:1 *restored the fortunes of.* This translation and its alternative (see TNIV text note here and on v. 4) have essentially the same result. *dreamed.* The wonder and joy of the reality were so marvelous that they hardly dared believe it. It seemed more like the dreams with which they had so long been tantalized.
126:2 The twofold effect: joy for those who returned and honor for God among the nations (see note on 46:10).
126:4–6 Prayer for restoration to be completed.
126:4 *Restore our fortunes.* Either complete the repatriation of exiles or fully restore the security and prosperity of former

126:4 °S Ps 107:35;
Isa 43:19; 51:3
126:5 ᵖPs 6:6; 80:5;
Jer 50:4 ᵍGal 6:9
ʳPs 16:11; 20:5; 23:6;
Isa 35:10; 51:11; 60:15;
61:7; Jer 31:6-7,12
126:6 ˢS Nu 25:6;
S Ps 30:5
127:1 ᵗPs 78:69
ᵘPs 121:4
127:2 ᵛS Ge 3:17
ʷS Nu 6:26;
S Job 11:18
ˣS Dt 33:12; Ecc 2:25
127:3 ʸS Ge 1:28
127:4 ᶻPs 112:2
127:5 ᵃPs 128:2-3
ᵇS Ge 24:60
ᶜS Ge 23:10
128:1 ᵈPs 103:11;
S 112:1 ᵉPs 119:1-3
128:2 ᶠS Ps 58:11;
109:11; Isa 3:10
ᵍS Ge 39:3; Pr 10:22
128:3 ʰS Ge 49:22

like streams in the Negev. °
⁵ Those who sow with tears ᵖ
   will reap ᵍ with songs of joy. ʳ
⁶ Those who go out weeping, ˢ
   carrying seed to sow,
will return with songs of joy,
   carrying sheaves with them.

PSALM 127

A song of ascents. Of Solomon.

¹ Unless the LORD builds ᵗ the house,
   the builders labor in vain.
Unless the LORD watches ᵘ over the city,
   the guards stand watch in vain.
² In vain you rise early
   and stay up late,
toiling for food ᵛ to eat—
   for he grants sleep ʷ to ᵃ those he loves. ˣ

³ Children are a heritage from the LORD,
   offspring a reward ʸ from him.
⁴ Like arrows ᶻ in the hands of a warrior
   are children born in one's youth.
⁵ Blessed is the man
   whose quiver is full of them. ᵃ
They will not be put to shame
   when they contend with their opponents ᵇ in court. ᶜ

PSALM 128

A song of ascents.

¹ Blessed are all who fear the LORD, ᵈ
   who walk in obedience to him. ᵉ
² You will eat the fruit of your labor; ᶠ
   blessings and prosperity ᵍ will be yours.
³ Your wife will be like a fruitful vine ʰ

ᵃ 2 Or *eat— / for while they sleep he provides for*

---

times. *like streams in the Negev.* Which are bone-dry in summer, until the winter rains renew their flow.
126:5–6 An apt metaphorical portrayal of the joy already experienced and the joy anticipated. *with tears … weeping.* Even when sowing is accompanied by trouble or sorrow, harvest brings joy. For a related figure, see 20:5.

A Ps 127 Godly wisdom concerning home and hearth. Its theme is timeless; it reminded the pilgrims on their way to Jerusalem that all of life's securities and blessings are gifts from God rather than their own achievements (see Dt 28:1–14). Two precisely balanced stanzas (in Hebrew having four poetic lines each, and each composed of 57 syllables) develop, respectively, two distinct but related themes. Since this psalm shares with Ps 128 the theme of domestic happiness and is structurally very similar to it, their juxtaposition appears to be deliberate.
127 title *ascents.* See introduction to Ps 120–137. *Of Solomon.* If Solomon was not the author (not all witnesses to the text ascribe it to him), it is easy to see why some thought him so.

A 127:1–2 It is the Lord who provides shelter, security and sustenance.
127:1 *house.* Domestic shelter. *builders.* The Hebrew for this word is a pun on that for "Children" in v. 3. *watches over.* See 121:3–8. *city.* The center of power, the refuge when enemies invade the land. *guards stand watch.* See 2Sa 13:34; 18:24–27; SS 3:3; 5:7.
127:2 *he grants sleep.* A good harvest is not the achievement of endless toil but the result of God's blessing (see Pr 10:22; Mt

6:25–34; 1Pe 5:7). *those he loves.* See especially Dt 33:12; Jer 11:15.
127:3–5 Children are God's gift and a sign of his favor.
127:3 *Children.* See note on v. 1. Children too are a gift—not the mere product of virility and fertility (see 113:9 and note; Ge 30:2). *heritage.* Emphasis here is on gift rather than possession. But perhaps more is implied. In the OT economy an Israelite's "inheritance" from the Lord was first of all property in the promised land (Nu 26:53; Jos 11:23; Jdg 2:6), which provided a sure place in the life and "rest" (Jos 1:13) of the Lord's kingdom. But without children the inheritance in the land would be lost (Nu 27:8–11), so that offspring were a heritage in a double sense. *reward from him.* Bestowed by God on one who stands in his favor because he has been faithful.
127:5 *when they contend with their opponents.* Fathers with many children have many defenders when falsely accused in court. Moreover, the very fact that they have many children as God's "reward" (v. 3) testifies to God's favor toward them (in effect, they are God-provided character witnesses; see 128:3–4). *in court.* Lit. "in the gate." For "(city) gate" as court, see Dt 17:5; 21:19; 22:15,24; 25:7; Ru 4:1; Isa 29:21 ("court"); Am 5:12 ("courts").

Ps 128 The blessedness of the godly man; another word of wisdom concerning hearth and home (see introduction to Ps 127). The concluding benediction suggests that the psalm originally served as a Levitical (or priestly) word of instruction to those assembled from their homes to worship in Jerusalem. Its date may

within your house;
    your children *i* will be like olive shoots *j*
        around your table.
⁴ Yes, this will be the blessing *k*
    for the man who fears the Lord. *l*

⁵ May the Lord bless you from Zion; *m*
    may you see the prosperity of Jerusalem *n*
    all the days of your life.
⁶ May you live to see your children's children— *o*
    peace be on Israel. *p*

PSALM 129

A song of ascents.

¹ "They have greatly oppressed *q* me from my youth," *r*
    let Israel say; *s*
² "they have greatly oppressed me from my youth,
    but they have not gained the victory *t* over me.
³ Plowmen have plowed my back
    and made their furrows long.
⁴ But the Lord is righteous; *u*
    he has cut me free *v* from the cords of the wicked." *w*

⁵ May all who hate Zion *x*
    be turned back in shame. *y*
⁶ May they be like grass on the roof, *z*
    which withers *a* before it can grow;
⁷ reapers cannot fill their hands with it, *b*
    nor those who gather fill their arms.
⁸ May those who pass by not say to them,
    "The blessing of the Lord be on you;
    we bless you *c* in the name of the Lord."

PSALM 130

A song of ascents.

¹ Out of the depths *d* I cry to you, *e* Lord;
²   Lord, hear my voice. *f*

128:3 *i* S Job 29:5
j Ps 52:8; 144:12
128:4 *k* S Ps 1:1
l Ps 112:1
128:5 *m* S Ps 20:2
n Ps 122:9
128:6 *o* S Ge 48:11
p S Ps 125:5
129:1 *q* S Ex 1:13
r S Ps 88:15 *s* Ps 124:1
129:2 *t* Jer 1:19;
15:20; 20:11; Mt 16:18
129:4 *u* S Ex 9:27
v Ps 37:9 *w* Ps 140:5
129:5 *x* Mic 4:11
y S Ps 70:2
129:6 *z* Isa 37:27
a S 2Ki 19:26;
Ps 102:11
129:7 *b* S Dt 28:38;
Ps 79:12
129:8 *c* Ps 118:26
130:1 *d* S Job 30:19;
Ps 42:7; La 3:55
e Ps 22:2; 55:17; 142:5
130:2 *f* S Ps 27:7;
28:2

---

well be preexilic. Structurally, the frame ("who fear[s] the Lord") around vv. 1–4 sets off those verses as the main body of the psalm.
128 title See introduction to Ps 120–137.
128:1–4 Blessedness affirmed.
128:1 *Blessed.* See note on 1:1. *fear the Lord.* See v. 4; see also note on 66:16.
128:2 Blessings upon labor.
128:3 A faithful and fruitful wife. *vine.* Symbol of fruitfulness (Ge 49:22)—and perhaps also of sexual charms (SS 7:8–12) and festivity (Jdg 9:13). *within your house.* She is not like the faithless wife whose "feet never stay at home" (Pr 7:11). *olive shoots.* Ever green and with the promises of both long life and productivity (of staples: wood, fruit, oil). The vine and the olive tree are frequently paired in the OT (as, e.g., in Ex 23:11). Both were especially long-lived, and they produced the wine and the oil that played such a central role in the lives of the people. *around your table.* Converting each family meal into a banquet of domestic joys.
128:5–6 The benediction pronounced—completing the scope of true blessedness: unbroken prosperity, secure relationship with God and secure national existence (the prosperity of Jerusalem entailed both), and long life.
128:5 *from Zion.* See 9:11 and note; 20:2; 135:21.
128:6 *peace be on Israel.* See 125:5 and note.
Ps 129 Israel's prayer for the continued withering of all her powerful enemies. The rescue celebrated (v. 4) is probably from Bab-

ylonian exile. Against the background of Ps 124–128, this prayer for the withholding of God's blessing (v. 8) is set in sharp relief. Like Ps 127, its two main stanzas (vv. 1–4, 5–8a) are perfectly balanced, having a total of 59 Hebrew syllables each. Its total syllable count (127) closely matches that of Ps 130 (128 syllables). For its apparent link with Ps 124, see introduction to that psalm.
129 title See introduction to Ps 120–137.
129:1–4 The wicked oppressors have not prevailed.
129:1 *from my youth.* From the time Israel was enslaved in Egypt, she has suffered much at the hands of hostile powers.
129:2 *have not gained the victory.* Have not succeeded in their efforts to destroy Israel totally or to hold her permanently in bondage.
129:4 *righteous.* See note on 4:1.
129:5–8 May all those oppressors who have shown hatred toward Zion wither away (see Ps 137).
129:5 See note on 5:10.
129:6 *like grass on the roof.* May those who would "plow" the backs of Israel (see v. 3) wither like grass that sprouts on the flat, sunbaked housetops, where no plow can prepare a nurturing soil to sustain the young shoots—and so there is no harvest (v. 7).
129:8 *those who pass by.* Whoever may pass by the harvesters in the fields will exchange no joyful greetings (Ru 2:4) because the hands of the harvesters will be empty.
Ps 130 A testimony of trust in the Lord—by one who knows that even though he is a sinner, the Lord hears his cry

130:2 *g* S 2Ch 6:40
h S Ps 28:6; 31:22;
86:6; 140:6
130:3 *i* S 1Sa 6:20;
S Ezr 9:15; Ps 143:2;
Na 1:6; Rev 6:17
130:4 *j* S Ex 34:7;
S 2Sa 24:14;
S Jer 31:34
k S 1Ki 8:40
130:5 *l* S Ps 27:14;
Isa 8:17; 26:8; 30:18;
49:23 *m* S Ps 5:3
n S Ps 119:74
130:6 *o* Ps 63:6
p S Ps 23:4
130:7 *q* S Ps 25:5;
S 71:14 *r* S 1Ch 21:13
s S Ps 111:9; S Ro 3:24
130:8 *t* Lk 1:68
u S Ex 34:7; S Mt 1:21
131:1 *v* Ps 101:5;
Isa 2:12; Ro 12:16
w S 2Sa 22:28;
S Job 41:34 *x* Jer 45:5
y S Job 5:9; Ps 139:6
131:2 *z* S Ps 116:7
a Mt 18:3; 1Co 13:11;
14:20
131:3 *b* S Ps 25:5;
119:43; 130:7
c S Ps 113:2
132:1 *d* 1Sa 18:11;
S 2Sa 15:14

Let your ears be attentive *g*
    to my cry for mercy. *h*

3 If you, LORD, kept a record of sins,
    Lord, who could stand? *i*
4 But with you there is forgiveness, *j*
    so that we can, with reverence, serve you. *k*

5 I wait for the LORD, *l* my whole being waits, *m*
    and in his word *n* I put my hope.
6 I wait for the Lord
    more than watchmen *o* wait for the morning,
    more than watchmen wait for the morning. *p*

7 Israel, put your hope *q* in the LORD,
    for with the LORD is unfailing love *r*
    and with him is full redemption. *s*
8 He himself will redeem *t* Israel
    from all their sins. *u*

PSALM 131

A song of ascents. Of David.

1 My heart is not proud, *v* LORD,
    my eyes are not haughty; *w*
I do not concern myself with great matters *x*
    or things too wonderful for me. *y*
2 But I have calmed myself *z*
    and quieted my ambitions.
I am like a weaned child with its mother;
    like a weaned child I am content. *a*

3 Israel, put your hope *b* in the LORD
    both now and forevermore. *c*

PSALM 132

132:8–10pp — 2Ch 6:41–42

A song of ascents.

1 LORD, remember David
    and all his self-denial. *d*

---

out of the depths. The language of the psalm suggests a postexilic date. This is the sixth of seven penitential psalms (see introduction to Ps 6). Composed of four couplets, the psalm further divides into two halves of two couplets each. Its total syllable count closely matches that of Ps 129 (see introduction to that psalm).
130 title See introduction to Ps 120–137.
130:1–4 A prayer for mercy and grounds for assurance.
130:1 *the depths.* As in 69:2 (see notes on 30:1; 32:6; cf. 121:1; 123:1).
🔲 **130:4** *there is forgiveness.* No doubt recalling such reassuring words as Ex 34:6–7. *with reverence, serve you.* Honor, worship, trust and serve you as the one true God (see Ps 34:8–14 and note). If God were not forgiving, people could only flee from him in terror.
130:5–8 Trust in the Lord: a personal testimony, expanding into a reassuring invitation (see 131:3).
130:5 *I wait.* In hopeful expectation. *his word.* Especially his covenant promises (see 119:25,28,37,42,49,65,74,81,107,114, 147).
130:6 *watchmen.* See 127:1; 2Sa 13:34; 18:24–27; SS 3:3; 5:7. *the morning.* See introduction to Ps 57; see also note on 59:9.
130:7 See 131:3. *unfailing love.* See note on 6:4.
🔲 **130:8** *from all their sins.* From the root of trouble—but also from all its consequences. This greatest of all hopes

has been fulfilled in Christ.
Ps 131 A confession of humble trust in the Lord—appropriately placed next to Ps 130.
131 title *ascents.* See introduction to Ps 120–137. *Of David.* Not all ancient witnesses to the text contain this element (see notes on the titles of Ps 122; 134; 127; 133). It may have been assigned to David because its tone matches the traditional view of David the psalmist.
🔲 **131:1** *heart.* See note on 4:7. *proud … haughty.* Pride in humanity's presumed ability to master the whole creation, design its own moral world and control its own destiny (of which Babel is the prime Biblical example; see Ge 11:1–9) is that which, more than all else, alienates humans from God (see note on 31:23). *concern myself with.* (Presume to) walk among, live among, be party to. *great matters … too wonderful for me.* Heroic exploits or achievements to rival, if not substitute for, the mighty works of God. The focus seems to be on not claiming Godlike powers (thus trusting in God for deliverance and blessing) rather than on seeking (or claiming) Godlike understanding.
131:2 *weaned child.* A child of four or five who walks trustingly beside its mother.
131:3 As the psalmist, so ought all Israel (see 130:7)—for all time.
Ps 132 A prayer for God's favor on the reigning son of David and

² He swore an oath to the LORD
　　and made a vow to the Mighty One of Jacob: ᵉ
³ "I will not enter my house ᶠ
　　or go to my bed,
⁴ I will allow no sleep to my eyes
　　or slumber to my eyelids,
⁵ till I find a place ᵍ for the LORD,
　　a dwelling for the Mighty One of Jacob."

⁶ We heard it in Ephrathah, ʰ
　　we came upon it in the fields of Jaar: ᵃ ⁱ
⁷ "Let us go to his dwelling place, ʲ
　　let us worship at his footstool, ᵏ saying,
⁸ 'Arise, LORD, ˡ and come to your resting place,
　　you and the ark of your might.
⁹ May your priests be clothed with your righteousness; ᵐ
　　may your faithful people ⁿ sing for joy.' "

¹⁰ For the sake of your servant David,
　　do not reject your anointed one.

¹¹ The LORD swore an oath to David, ᵒ
　　a sure oath that he will not revoke:
"One of your own descendants ᵖ
　　I will place on your throne.

ᵃ 6 Or *heard of it in Ephrathah, / we found it in the fields of Jearim.* (See 1 Chron. 13:5,6) (And no quotation marks around verses 7-9)

132:2 ᵉ S Ge 49:24; Isa 49:26; 60:16
132:3 ᶠ S 2Sa 7:2,27
132:5 ᵍ S 1Ki 8:17; Ac 7:46
132:6 ʰ S 1Sa 17:12
ⁱ S Jos 9:17; S 1Sa 7:2
132:7 ʲ S 2Sa 15:25; Ps 5:7; 122:1
ᵏ S 1Ch 28:2
132:8 ˡ S Nu 10:35
132:9 ᵐ S Job 27:6; Isa 61:3,10; Zec 3:4; Mal 3:3; Eph 6:14
ⁿ Ps 16:3; 30:4; 149:5
132:11 ᵒ S Ps 89:3-4,35 ᵖ S 1Ch 7:11-14; S Mt 1:1; Lk 3:31

---

on the regime that David founded—as the structure makes clear (and see note on v. 10). Its language suggests a date early in the monarchy. The venerable belief that it was composed for the dedication of the temple may be correct (compare vv. 8–10 with 2Ch 6:41–42), but the possibility cannot be ruled out that it was used in the coronation ritual (cf. Ps 2; 72; 110). The author of Chronicles places the prayer (or a portion of it) on the lips of the king himself. As used in postexilic liturgies, it had Messianic implications.

Two verses of petition (vv. 1,10) are each followed (in Hebrew) by two four-line stanzas, all having an identical form: an introductory line followed by a three-line quotation (see the structure of these quotations). A final couplet brings the prayer to its climactic conclusion. The four stanzas, together with the final couplet, ground the prayer made in vv. 1,10. Verses 2–9 appeal to David's oath to the Lord to find a "place" for the Lord and to bring the ark to its "resting place," while vv. 11–18 appeal to the Lord's oath to David and to his election of Zion as his "resting place" (but see note on v. 10).

132 title See introduction to Ps 120–137.
132:1 The initial petition (see v. 10). *remember.* See 20:3; see also 1Ki 11:12–13; 15:4–5. *self-denial.* What David took on himself in his vow (vv. 2–5; see Nu 30:13, where the same technical term for a self-denying oath is used).
132:2–5 David's oath concerning a temple for the Lord is recalled.
132:2 *He swore an oath.* This prayer for David's son is grounded in the special relationship between David and the Lord, as epitomized in their mutual oaths (see vv. 11–12). In 2Sa 6–7, which narrates the events here recalled, David's oath is not mentioned. *LORD . . . Mighty One of Jacob.* See v. 5; Isa 1:24; see also note on 3:7. *Jacob.* A synonym for Israel (see Ge 32:28).
132:6–9 Moments in the people's procession to the temple for worship are recalled.
132:6 *it . . . it.* Often thought to refer to the ark (see TNIV text note), but more likely it refers to the call to worship that follows (in Hebrew the pronoun is feminine, but the Hebrew for "ark" is masculine). *Ephrathah.* The region around Bethlehem, David's hometown (see Ru 4:11; Mic 5:2). *fields of Jaar.* See TNIV text note; see also 2Sa 6:2 and first TNIV text note there. The call to worship is depicted as emanating from David's city and the city

where the ark had been since the days of Samuel (see 1Sa 7:1). The call appears to come from a time after the temple had been built—thus involving a poetic compression of events.
132:7 *footstool.* See 99:5 and note.
132:8 *Arise.* Although (in accordance with a common feature in Hebrew poetry) the TNIV omits an introductory word, such as "saying" (which the TNIV supplies at the end of v. 7 for clarity), vv. 8–9 are probably words on the lips of the worshipers. See introduction to Ps 24. *resting place.* As the promised land was Israel's place of rest at the end of her wanderings (see Nu 10:33; Jos 1:13; Mic 2:10), so the temple was the Lord's resting place after he had been moving about in a tent (see 2Sa 7:6; see also 1Ch 28:2). The expression may suggest that the temple was the place of God's throne (v. 14). *ark of your might.* See note on 78:61.
132:9 *clothed with.* Beyond their normal priestly garb—may their ministry be characterized by, i.e., result in. See note on 109:29. *righteousness.* Since the corresponding word in v. 16 is "salvation," the same word used by the author of Chronicles when quoting this verse (2Ch 6:41), and since "righteousness" and "salvation" are often paralleled (40:10; 51:14; 71:15; 98:2; Isa 45:8; 46:13; 51:5–6; 56:1; 59:17; 60:17–18; 61:10; 62:1), the reference is clearly to God's righteousness that effects the salvation of his people (see note on 4:1). *faithful people.* See note on 4:3.
132:10 The second petition (see v. 1). *your servant.* See note on Ps 18 title. *do not reject.* Do not refuse his petitions (as in 1Ki 2:16–17,20; see 1Ki 8:59; 2Ch 6:41–42). If, as some have proposed, the petitions in vv. 1,10 form a frame around the first half of the psalm, the second half offers assurance that the prayer will be heard (perhaps spoken by a priest or Levite). In any event, David's vow to provide the Lord a dwelling place, which would be for his royal sons and for Israel a house of prayer (see 1Ki 8:27–53; 9:3; 2Ch 7:15–16; Isa 56:7), is made the basis for the appeal that God will hear his anointed's prayer. *your anointed one.* See note on 2:2.
132:11–12 The Lord's covenant with David is recalled, as grounds for the prayer. These and vv. 13–18 are a poetic recollection of 1Ki 9:1–5 (see 2Ch 7:11–18).
132:11 *swore an oath.* See v. 2 and note. 2Sa 7 does not mention an oath, but elsewhere God's promise to David is called a covenant (89:3,28,34,39; 2Sa 23:5; Isa 55:3), and covenants were made on oath. *will not revoke.* See 110:4.

132:12 q 2Ch 6:16;
S Ps 25:10 r Lk 1:32;
Ac 2:30
132:13 s S Ex 15:17;
Ps 48:1-2; S 68:16
t S 1Ki 8:13
132:14 u ver 8;
Ps 68:16 v S 2Sa 6:2;
Ps 80:1
132:15 w Ps 107:9;
147:14
132:16 x S 2Ch 6:41
y S Job 8:21; Ps 149:5
132:17 z S 1Sa 2:10;
Ps 92:10; Eze 29:21;
S Lk 1:69 a 1Ki 11:36;
2Ki 8:19; 2Ch 21:7;
Ps 18:28 b S Ps 84:9
132:18 c S Job 8:22
d S 2Sa 12:30
133:1 e S Ge 13:8;
S Ro 12:10 f Jn 17:11
133:2 g S Ex 29:7
133:3 h Job 29:19;
Pr 19:12; Isa 18:4;
26:19; 45:8; Hos 14:5;
Mic 5:7 i S Dt 3:8;
S 4:48 j S Ex 15:17;
S Ps 2:6; 74:2
k S Lev 25:21
l S Ps 21:4
134:1 m S Ps 113:1;
135:1-2; Rev 19:5
n S Nu 16:9;
S 1Ch 15:2
o S 1Ch 23:30

12 If your sons keep my covenant q
　　and the statutes I teach them,
then their sons will sit
　　on your throne r for ever and ever."

13 For the LORD has chosen Zion, s
　　he has desired it for his dwelling, t saying,
14 "This is my resting place for ever and ever; u
　　here I will sit enthroned, v for I have desired it.
15 I will bless her with abundant provisions;
　　her poor I will satisfy with food. w
16 I will clothe her priests x with salvation,
　　and her faithful people will ever sing for joy. y

17 "Here I will make a horn a grow z for David
　　and set up a lamp a for my anointed one. b
18 I will clothe his enemies with shame, c
　　but his head will be adorned with a resplendent crown." d

PSALM 133

A song of ascents. Of David.

1 How good and pleasant it is
　　when God's people live together e in unity! f

2 It is like precious oil poured on the head, g
　　running down on the beard,
running down on Aaron's beard,
　　down on the collar of his robe.
3 It is as if the dew h of Hermon i
　　were falling on Mount Zion. j
For there the LORD bestows his blessing, k
　　even life forevermore. l

PSALM 134

A song of ascents.

1 Praise the LORD, all you servants m of the LORD
　　who minister n by night o in the house of the LORD.

---

a 17 *Horn* here symbolizes strong one, that is, king.

132:12 *covenant…statutes.* The stipulations of the Sinai covenant, which all Israelites were to keep (see 1Sa 10:25 and note; see also 1Ki 2:3–4).
132:13–16 The Lord's election of Zion recalled, as grounds for the prayer (see Introduction: Theology: Major Themes, 7).
132:13 *desired it for his dwelling.* David's and the Lord's desires harmonize (see Dt 12:5–14).
132:15 The Lord, enthroned in his resting place (see vv. 8,14), will bless the land, making it a place of rest for his people (see Dt 12:9; Jos 1:13; 1Ki 5:4).
132:16 See note on v. 9.
132:17–18 Concluding word of assurance, which addresses the petition (vv. 1,10) directly and climactically.
132:17 *horn.* The Lord's anointed (see TNIV text note). *grow.* Like a plant or branch. *set up a lamp for.* See note on 1Ki 11:36.
132:18 *clothe…with…adorned with.* See note on 109:29. *clothe …with shame.* In contrast with v. 16. *be adorned with.* Lit. "blossom"—subtly evoking the imagery: "grow" (v. 17) and blossom.
Ps 133 A song in praise of unity among the people of God. If David was the author (but see note on title), he may have been moved to write it by some such occasion as when, after many years of conflict, all Israel came to Hebron to make him king (2Sa 5:1–3). Other historical possibilities are after the influx of many refugees from the northern tribes into the kingdom of Judah during the great Assyrian invasions (see introduction to Ps

80) or the postexilic regathering of representatives of "all Israel," as reflected in Ezra and Nehemiah (see Ezr 8:25; Ne 12:47). The first and last (Hebrew) lines (vv. 1,3b) frame the whole with the song's main theme. Next to these an inner frame (lines 2,4) elaborates with two striking, complementary similes (vv. 2a,3a). The center line (v. 2b) extends the first simile.
133 title *ascents.* See introduction to Ps 120–137. *Of David.* Not all ancient textual sources ascribe the psalm to David (see notes on titles of Ps 122; 124; 127; 131).
133:1 *good and pleasant.* See 135:3; 147:1.

A **133:2** *like precious oil…on Aaron's beard…on the collar of his robe.* The oil of Aaron's anointing (Ex 29:7; Lev 21:10) saturated all the hair of his beard and ran down on his priestly robe, signifying his total consecration to holy service. Similarly, communal harmony sanctifies God's people.

A **133:3** *dew of Hermon…on Mount Zion.* A dew as profuse as that of Mount Hermon would make Mount Zion (or the mountains of Zion) richly fruitful (see Ge 27:28; Hag 1:10; Zec 8:12). So would communal unity make Israel richly fruitful. The two similes (vv. 2–3) are well chosen: God's blessings flowed to Israel through the priestly ministrations at the sanctuary (Ex 29:44–46; Lev 9:22–24; Nu 6:24– 26)—epitomizing God's redemptive mercies—and through heaven's dew that sustained life in the fields—epitomizing God's providential mercies in the creation order. *life.* The great covenant blessing (see Dt 30:15,19–20; 32:47).

2 Lift up your hands[p] in the sanctuary[q]
  and praise the Lord. [r]

3 May the Lord bless you from Zion, [s]
  he who is the Maker of heaven[t] and earth.

PSALM 135

135:15–20pp — Ps 115:4–11

1 Praise the Lord. [a]

  Praise the name of the Lord;
    praise him, you servants[u] of the Lord,
2 you who minister in the house[v] of the Lord,
    in the courts[w] of the house of our God.

3 Praise the Lord, for the Lord is good;[x]
    sing praise to his name,[y] for that is pleasant. [z]
4 For the Lord has chosen Jacob[a] to be his own,
    Israel to be his treasured possession. [b]

5 I know that the Lord is great, [c]
    that our Lord is greater than all gods. [d]
6 The Lord does whatever pleases him, [e]
    in the heavens and on the earth, [f]
    in the seas and all their depths.
7 He makes clouds rise from the ends of the earth;
    he sends lightning with the rain[g]
    and brings out the wind[h] from his storehouses. [i]

8 He struck down the firstborn[j] of Egypt,
    the firstborn of people and animals.
9 He sent his signs[k] and wonders into your midst, Egypt,
    against Pharaoh and all his servants. [l]
10 He struck down many[m] nations
    and killed mighty kings—
11 Sihon[n] king of the Amorites, [o]
    Og king of Bashan, [p]
    and all the kings of Canaan[q]—

---

a 1 Hebrew *Hallelu Yah*; also in verses 3 and 21

134:2 p S Ps 28:2;
1Ti 2:8 q Ps 15:1
r Ps 33:2; 103:1
134:3 s S Lev 25:21;
S Ps 20:2 t S Ps 124:8
135:1 u Ne 7:73
135:2 v S 1Ch 15:2;
Lk 2:37 w S Ps 116:19
135:3 x S 1Ch 16:34;
S Ps 119:68
y S Ps 68:4
z S Ps 92:1; 147:1
135:4 a S Dt 10:15
b Ex 19:5; Dt 7:6;
Mal 3:17; S Tit 2:14
135:5 c S Ps 48:1;
145:3 d S Ex 12:12;
S 1Ch 16:25;
S Job 21:22
135:6 e Ps 115:3;
Da 4:35 f Mt 6:10
135:7 g S Job 5:10;
Ps 68:9; Isa 30:23;
Jer 10:13; 51:16;
Joel 2:23; Zec 10:1
h Am 4:13 i S Dt 28:12
135:8 j S Ex 4:23;
S 12:12
135:9 k S Ex 7:9
l Ps 136:10-15
135:10 m Nu 21:21-
25; Jos 24:8-11;
Ps 44:2; 78:55;
136:17-21
135:11 n S Nu 21:21
o S Nu 21:26
p S Nu 21:33
q S Jos 12:7-24; 24:12

Ps 134 A liturgy of praise—a brief exchange between the worshipers, as they are about to leave the temple after the evening service, and the Levites, who kept the temple watch through the night. In the Psalter it concludes the "songs of ascent," as Ps 117 concludes a collection of Hallelujah psalms (Ps 111–117). Its date is probably postexilic.

134 title See introduction to Ps 120–137.

134:1–2 The departing worshipers call on the Levites to continue the praise of the Lord through the night (see 1Ch 9:33).

134:2 *Lift up your hands.* See 63:4 and note.

134:3 One of the Levites responds with a benediction on the worshipers (see note on 121:2; see also 124:8; 128:5).

Ps 135 A call to praise the Lord—the one true God: Lord of all creation, Lord over all the nations, Israel's Redeemer. No doubt postexilic, it echoes many lines found elsewhere in the OT. It was clearly composed for the temple liturgy. For its place in the Great Hallel, see introduction to Ps 120–137. Framed with "Hallelujahs" (as are also Ps 146–150), its first and last stanzas are also calls to praise. Recital of God's saving acts for Israel in Egypt and Canaan (vv. 8–12) makes up the middle of seven stanzas, while the remaining four constitute two pairs related to each other by theme and language (vv. 3–4, 13–14; vv. 5–7, 15–18).

135:1–2 Initial call to praise, addressed to priests and Levites (see 134:1–2).

135:1,3,13 *name.* See note on 5:11.

135:3–4 A central reason for Israel to praise the Lord (see vv. 13–14).

135:3 *that is pleasant.* See 133:1.

135:4 *Jacob.* A synonym for Israel (see Ge 32:28). *his treasured possession.* See Ex 19:5 and note.

135:5–7 The Lord is great, as well as good (v. 3); he is the absolute Lord in all creation (cf. the word about idols in vv. 15–18; see Jer 10:11–16; see also 115:3 and 96:5; 97:7 and notes).

135:6 *does whatever pleases him.* The idols can do nothing (vv. 16–17); they are themselves "done" (made) by their worshipers (v. 18). *heavens . . . earth . . . seas.* The three great domains of the visible creation, as the ancients viewed it (see Ge 1:8–10 and introduction to Ps 104).

135:7 *He makes clouds.* The Lord, not Baal or any other god, brings the life-giving rains (see Ps 29 and its introduction; see also Jer 14:22; Zec 10:1 and notes). *wind.* See 104:4; 148:8. The idols do not even have any "wind" (breath) in their mouths (v. 17). *storehouses.* See 33:7 and note; Job 38:22.

135:8–12 The Lord's triumph over Egypt and over the kings whose lands became Israel's inheritance, a concise recollection of Ex 7–14; Nu 21:21–35; Joshua.

135:12 ʳS Dt 29:8
135:13 ˢS Ex 3:15
ᵗS Ps 102:12
135:14 ᵘS 1Sa 24:15;
Heb 10:30*
ᵛS Dt 32:36
135:15 ʷPs 96:5;
Rev 9:20 ˣIsa 2:8;
31:7; 37:19; 40:19;
Jer 1:16; 10:5
135:16 ʸS 1Ki 18:26
135:17 ᶻJer 10:14;
Hab 2:19
135:19 ᵃS Ps 22:23
135:21 ᵇPs 128:5;
134:3 ᶜS 1Ki 8:13;
S 2Ch 6:2
136:1 ᵈPs 105:1
ᵉPs 100:5; 106:1;
145:9; Jer 33:11;
Na 1:7 ᶠver 2-26;
S 2Ch 5:13;
S Ezr 3:11; Ps 118:1-4
136:2 ᵍPs 105:1
ʰS Dt 10:17
136:3 ⁱPs 105:1
ʲS Dt 10:17; S 1Ti 6:15
136:4 ᵏS Ex 3:20;
S Job 9:10
136:5 ˡPr 3:19;
Jer 51:15 ᵐS Ge 1:1
136:6 ⁿS Ge 1:1;
Isa 42:5; Jer 10:12;
33:2 ᵒS Ge 1:6
136:7 ᵖGe 1:14,16;
Ps 74:16; Jas 1:17
136:8 ᵠS Ge 1:16
136:10 ʳS Ex 4:23;
S 12:12

¹² and he gave their land as an inheritance,ʳ
an inheritance to his people Israel.

¹³ Your name, Lᴏʀᴅ, endures forever,ˢ
your renown,ᵗ Lᴏʀᴅ, through all generations.
¹⁴ For the Lᴏʀᴅ will vindicate his peopleᵘ
and relent concerning his servants.ᵛ

¹⁵ The idols of the nationsʷ are silver and gold,
made by human hands.ˣ
¹⁶ They have mouths, but cannot speak,ʸ
eyes, but cannot see.
¹⁷ They have ears, but cannot hear,
nor is there breathᶻ in their mouths.
¹⁸ Those who make them will be like them,
and so will all who trust in them.

¹⁹ House of Israel, praise the Lᴏʀᴅ;ᵃ
house of Aaron, praise the Lᴏʀᴅ;
²⁰ house of Levi, praise the Lᴏʀᴅ;
you who fear him, praise the Lᴏʀᴅ.
²¹ Praise be to the Lᴏʀᴅ from Zion,ᵇ
to him who dwells in Jerusalem.ᶜ

Praise the Lᴏʀᴅ.

PSALM 136

¹ Give thanksᵈ to the Lᴏʀᴅ, for he is good.ᵉ

*His love endures forever.*ᶠ

² Give thanksᵍ to the God of gods.ʰ

His love endures forever.

³ Give thanksⁱ to the Lord of lords:ʲ

His love endures forever.

⁴ to him who alone does great wonders,ᵏ

His love endures forever.

⁵ who by his understandingˡ made the heavens,ᵐ

His love endures forever.

⁶ who spread out the earthⁿ upon the waters,ᵒ

His love endures forever.

⁷ who made the great lightsᵖ—

His love endures forever.

⁸ the sun to governᵠ the day,

His love endures forever.

⁹ the moon and stars to govern the night;

His love endures forever.

¹⁰ to him who struck down the firstbornʳ of Egypt

His love endures forever.

135:13–14 See vv. 3–4 and note.
135:14 *vindicate.* Uphold against all attacks by the world powers both Israel's cause and her claim that the Lord is the only true God. *relent concerning.* See Ex 34:6–7 and note. *his servants.* His covenant people.
135:15–18 The powerlessness of the false gods and of those who trust in them (see vv. 5–7 and note; see also 115:4–8 and notes).
135:19–21 Concluding call to praise, addressed to all who are assembled at the temple (see 115:9–11; 118:2–4).
135:20 *house of Levi.* Mentioned expressly only here in the Psalter (cf. 1Ch 23:4,30–31; 25:1; 2Ch 20:19,21).
135:21 *from Zion.* Not only in Zion but also from Zion—to the ends of the earth (see notes on 9:1; 22:22–31).
Ps 136 A liturgy of praise to the Lord as Creator and as Israel's Redeemer. Its theme and many of its verses parallel much of Ps 135. Most likely a Levitical song leader led the recital, while the Levitical choir (1Ch 16:41; 2Ch 5:13; Ezr 3:11) or the worshipers

(2Ch 7:3,6; 20:21) responded with the refrain (see 106:1; 107:1; 118:1–4,29). This liturgy concludes the Great Hallel (see introduction to Ps 120–137).
Following the initial call to praise (vv. 1–3), the recital devotes six verses to God's creation acts (vv. 4–9), six to his deliverance of Israel out of Egypt (vv. 10–15), one to the desert journey (v. 16) and six to the conquest (vv. 17–22). The four concluding verses return to the same basic themes in reverse order: God's action in history in behalf of his people (vv. 23–24), God's action in the creation order (v. 25) and a closing call to praise (v. 26). The echoing response (*"His love endures forever"*) occurs 26 times, the numerical value of the divine name Yahweh (when the Hebrew letters were used as numbers).
136:1–3,26 *Give thanks to.* Or "Praise" (see 7:17 and note).
136:2 *the God of gods.* See Dt 10:17; see also 135:5.
136:5 *by his understanding.* See Pr 3:19; Jer 10:12.
136:6 *upon the waters.* See 24:2 and note.
136:7–9 Direct echoes of Ge 1:16.

¹¹ and brought Israel out ^s from among them
His love endures forever.

¹² with a mighty hand ^t and outstretched arm; ^u
His love endures forever.

¹³ to him who divided the Red Sea ^{a v} asunder
His love endures forever.

¹⁴ and brought Israel through ^w the midst of it,
His love endures forever.

¹⁵ but swept Pharaoh and his army into the Red Sea; ^x
His love endures forever.

¹⁶ to him who led his people through the wilderness; ^y
His love endures forever.

¹⁷ to him who struck down great kings, ^z
His love endures forever.

¹⁸ and killed mighty kings ^a—
His love endures forever.

¹⁹ Sihon king of the Amorites ^b
His love endures forever.

²⁰ and Og king of Bashan ^c—
His love endures forever.

²¹ and gave their land ^d as an inheritance, ^e
His love endures forever.

²² an inheritance ^f to his servant Israel. ^g
His love endures forever.

²³ He remembered us ^h in our low estate
His love endures forever.

²⁴ and freed us ⁱ from our enemies. ^j
His love endures forever.

²⁵ He gives food ^k to every creature.
His love endures forever.

²⁶ Give thanks ^l to the God of heaven. ^m
His love endures forever. ⁿ

PSALM 137

¹ By the rivers of Babylon ^o we sat and wept ^p
when we remembered Zion. ^q
² There on the poplars ^r
we hung our harps, ^s
³ for there our captors ^t asked us for songs,
our tormentors demanded ^u songs of joy;
they said, "Sing us one of the songs of Zion!" ^v

⁴ How can we sing the songs of the LORD ^w
while in a foreign land?

^a 13 Or *the Sea of Reeds*; also in verse 15

136:11 ^s S Ex 6:6;
13:3; Ps 105:43
136:12 ^t S Ex 3:20;
S Dt 5:15 ^u S Dt 9:29
136:13 ^v S Ps 78:13
136:14 ^w Ex 14:22;
Ps 106:9
136:15 ^x S Ex 14:27
136:16 ^y S Ex 13:18;
Ps 78:52
136:17 ^z Nu 21:23-
25; Jos 24:8-11;
Ps 78:55; 135:9-12
136:18 ^a Dt 29:7;
S Jos 12:7-24
136:19 ^b Nu 21:21-
25
136:20 ^c Nu 21:33-
35
136:21 ^d Jos 12:1
^e S Dt 1:38; S Jos 14:1
136:22 ^f S Dt 29:8;
Ps 78:55 ^g Isa 20:3;
41:8; 42:19; 43:10;
44:1,21; 45:4; 49:5- 7
136:23 ^h Ps 78:39;
103:14; 115:12
136:24 ⁱ S Jos 10:14;
S Ne 9:28 ^j S Dt 6:19
136:25 ^k S Ge 1:30;
S Mt 6:26
136:26 ^l Ps 105:1
^m S Ps 115:3
ⁿ S Ezr 3:11
137:1 ^o Eze 1:1,3;
3:15; 10:15 ^p Ne 1:4
^q Isa 3:26; La 1:4
137:2 ^r S Lev 23:40
^s Job 30:31; Isa 24:8;
Eze 26:13; Am 6:5
137:3 ^t Ps 79:1-4;
La 1:5 ^u S Job 30:9;
Ps 80:6 ^v Eze 16:57;
22:4; 34:29
137:4 ^w S Ne 12:46

136:23–24 Probably a concluding summary of the deliverance recalled above, but may allude also to the deliverances experienced during the period of the judges and the reign of David.

136:26 *the God of heaven.* A Persian title for God (see note on Ezr 1:2) found frequently in Ezra, Nehemiah and Daniel. Its intent is similar to that of the language of vv. 2–3.

Ps 137 A plaintive song of the exile—of one who has recently returned from Babylon but in whose soul there lingers the bitter memory of the years in a foreign land and of the cruel events that led to that enforced stay. Here speaks the same deep love of Zion as that found in Ps 42–43; 46; 48; 84; 122; 126. The editors of the Psalter attached this song to the Great Hallel as a closing expression of supreme devotion to the city at the center of Israel's worship of the Lord (see introduction to Ps 120–137). The 12 poetic lines of the Hebrew song divide symmetrically into three

stanzas of four lines each: the remembered sorrow and torment (vv. 1–3), an oath of total commitment to Jerusalem (vv. 4–6), a call for retribution on Edom and Babylon (vv. 7–9).

137:1 *rivers.* The Tigris and Euphrates and the many canals associated with them. *we sat.* Again and again the thought of their forced separation from Zion brought them down to the posture of mourning (see Job 2:8,13; La 2:10).

137:2 *we hung our harps.* "The joyful harp is silent" (Isa 24:8) because the callous Babylonians demanded exotic entertainment with the joyful songs of distant Zion, while the exiles' instruments were only "tuned to mourning" (Job 30:31).

137:4–6 Only someone whose heart had disowned the Lord and his holy city, Jerusalem, could play the puppet on a Babylonian stage. But may I never play the harp again or sing another syllable if I am untrue to that beloved city!

137:5 ˣ Isa 2:3;
56:7; 55:11; 66:20
137:6 ʸ S Ps 22:15
ᶻ Ne 2:3 ᵃ S Dt 4:29;
Jer 51:50; Eze 6:9
137:7 ᵇ S Ge 25:30;
S 2Ch 28:17;
S Ps 83:6; La 4:21-22
ᶜ 2Ki 25:1-10; Ob 1:11
ᵈ Ps 74:8
137:8 ᵉ Isa 13:1,19;
47:1-15; Jer 25:12,26;
50:1; 50:2-51:58
137:9 ᶠ S 2Ki 8:12;
S Isa 13:16; Lk 19:44
138:1 ᵍ Ps 95:3;
96:4 ʰ Ps 27:6; 108:1
138:2 ⁱ S 1Ki 8:29;
S Ps 5:7 / Ps 74:21;
97:12; 140:13
ᵏ Ps 108:4; 115:1
ˡ Ps 119:9
138:3 ᵐ Ps 18:6;
30:2; 99:6; 116:4
ⁿ S Ps 118:5 ᵒ Pr 28:1;
S Ac 4:29

⁵ If I forget you, ˣ Jerusalem,
  may my right hand forget its skill.
⁶ May my tongue cling to the roof ʸ of my mouth
  if I do not remember ᶻ you,
  if I do not consider Jerusalem ᵃ
  my highest joy.

⁷ Remember, Lᴏʀᴅ, what the Edomites ᵇ did
  on the day Jerusalem fell. ᶜ
  "Tear it down," they cried,
  "tear it down to its foundations!" ᵈ
⁸ Daughter Babylon, doomed to destruction, ᵉ
  happy are those who repay you
  according to what you have done to us.
⁹ Happy are those who seize your infants
  and dash them ᶠ against the rocks.

PSALM 138

Of David.

¹ I will praise you, Lᴏʀᴅ, with all my heart;
  before the "gods" ᵍ I will sing ʰ your praise.
² I will bow down toward your holy temple ⁱ
  and will praise your name ʲ
  for your unfailing love and your faithfulness, ᵏ
  for you have so exalted your solemn decree
  that it surpasses your fame. ˡ
³ When I called, ᵐ you answered me; ⁿ
  you greatly emboldened ᵒ me.

137:7–9 Lord, remember Edom; and as for you, Babylon, I bless whoever does to you what you did to Jerusalem: a passionate call for redress from a loyal son of the ravaged city (see note on 5:10).
137:7 *Edomites.* The agelong animosity of Edom— descendants of Esau, Jacob's brother—showed its most dastardly face in Jerusalem's darkest hour. No doubt the author knew the Lord's judgments against that nation announced by the prophets (Isa 63:1–4; Jer 49:7–22; Eze 25:8,12–14; 35; Obadiah). *Tear it down.* Lit. "Strip her"—cities were conventionally portrayed as women. La 4:21 anticipates that Edom will be punished by suffering the same humiliation.
137:8 *Daughter Babylon.* A personification of Babylon (see note on 2Ki 19:21). *doomed to destruction.* The author and those who took up this psalm surely knew of the Lord's announced judgments on this cruel destroyer (Isa 13; 47; Jer 50–51). In the day of the Lord's judgment Babylon was to receive what she had done to others (see Jer 50:15,29; 51:24,35,49; cf. Rev 18:5–6). For the principle involved, see note on Eze 16:43. *happy are those.* Because a cruel international predator has been removed from the earth (see Isa 14:3–8 and notes; cf. Jer 51:47–48; Rev 19:1–3).
137:9 *your infants.* War was as cruel then as now; women and children were not spared (see 2Ki 8:12; 15:16; Isa 13:16,18; Hos 10:14; 13:16; Am 1:13; Na 3:10). For the final announcement of the destruction of the "Babylon" that persists in its warfare against the City of God, and the joy with which that announcement is greeted, see Rev 18:1—19:4.
Ps 138–145 A final collection of eight "Davidic" psalms brings the Psalter toward its close. While much in some of these psalms point to a later, even postexilic, date, they clearly stand in the tradition of psalmody of which David was the reputed father and echo the language and concerns of the earlier Davidic psalms. The collection is framed by songs of praise (Ps 138; 145). The first of these extols the greatness of the Lord's glory as displayed in his answering the prayer ("call") of the "lowly" when suffering at the hands of the "proud." The last, employing a grand and intricately woven alphabetic acrostic design, extols the "glorious majesty" of the Lord as displayed in his benevolent care over all his creatures—especially those who "call" on him (look to him in every need). Within this frame have been placed six prayers—with certain interlocking themes that will be pointed out in the notes on the individual psalms.

This final "Davidic" collection contains the Psalter's two most magnificent expositions of the greatness and goodness of God, one of them (Ps 139) focusing on his relationship with an individual, the other (Ps 145) on his relationship with his whole creation.
Ps 138 A song of praise for God's saving help against threatening foes—understood by many to have been originally on the lips of a king. In some respects it is like Ps 18, though in style and scope much less grand. Two (Hebrew) four-line stanzas (vv. 1–3,6–8) develop the main theme; at the center a two-line stanza (vv. 4–5) expands the company of those who praise the Lord to "all the kings of the earth." The psalm shares nearly a third of its vocabulary with Ps 145.
138 title See introduction to Ps 138–145.

138:1–3 Praise for God's faithful love shown in answer to prayers for help.
138:1 *heart.* See note on 4:7. *gods.* Either pagan kings (see vv. 4–5) or the gods they claimed to represent (see introduction to Ps 82; see also note on 82:1).

138:2 *your holy temple.* If David is in fact the author, reference is to the tent he set up for the ark (2Sa 6:17)—many psalms ascribed to David refer to the "temple" (see, e.g., 5:7; 11:4; 18:6; 27:4; see also Ps 30 title). *name.* See note on 5:11. *love and ... faithfulness.* See note on 36:5. *love.* See v. 8; see also note on 6:4. *your solemn decree.* Perhaps God's command that effects his purposes in the world (see 147:15), but more likely his promises (see v. 4 and note). God's display of his love and faithfulness in his answers to prayer (v. 3) has made his name ("fame") and promises more magnificent than anything else that even kings may prize.
138:3 *I called, you answered.* See note on 118:5.

⁴ May all the kings of the earth ^p praise you, Lᴏʀᴅ,
    when they hear what you have decreed.
⁵ May they sing ^q of the ways of the Lᴏʀᴅ,
    for the glory of the Lᴏʀᴅ ^r is great.

⁶ Though the Lᴏʀᴅ is exalted, he looks kindly on the lowly, ^s
    but he takes notice of the proud ^t from afar.
⁷ Though I walk ^u in the midst of trouble,
    you preserve my life. ^v
  You stretch out your hand ^w against the anger of my foes; ^x
    with your right hand ^y you save me. ^z
⁸ The Lᴏʀᴅ will vindicate ^a me;
    your love, Lᴏʀᴅ, endures forever ^b—
    do not abandon ^c the works of your hands. ^d

PSALM 139

For the director of music. Of David. A psalm.

¹ You have searched me, ^e Lᴏʀᴅ,
    and you know ^f me.
² You know when I sit and when I rise; ^g
    you perceive my thoughts ^h from afar.
³ You discern my going out ⁱ and my lying down;
    you are familiar with all my ways. ^j
⁴ Before a word is on my tongue
    you, Lᴏʀᴅ, know it completely. ^k
⁵ You hem me in ^l behind and before,
    and you lay your hand upon me.
⁶ Such knowledge is too wonderful for me, ^m
    too lofty ⁿ for me to attain.

⁷ Where can I go from your Spirit?
    Where can I flee ^o from your presence?
⁸ If I go up to the heavens, ^p you are there;
    if I make my bed ^q in the depths, you are there.
⁹ If I rise on the wings of the dawn,

138:4 ^p Ps 72:11; 102:15
138:5 ^q S Ps 51:14; 71:16; 145:7 ^r Ps 21:5
138:6 ^s S Ps 113:6 ^t S Ps 40:4; S Mt 23:12
138:7 ^u Ps 23:4 ^v S Ps 41:2 ^w S Ex 7:5 ^x Ps 7:6 ^y Ps 20:6; 60:5; 108:6 ^z Ps 17:7, 14
138:8 ^a Php 1:6 ^b S Ezr 3:11; Ps 100:5 ^c S Ps 51:11 ^d S Job 10:3,8
139:1 ^e S Ps 17:3; Ro 8:27 ^f Ps 44:21
139:2 ^g 2Ki 19:27 ^h Ps 94:11; Pr 24:12; Jer 12:3
139:3 ⁱ 2Ki 19:27 ^j S Job 31:4
139:4 ^k S Heb 4:13
139:5 ^l S 1Sa 25:16; Ps 32:10; 34:7; 125:2
139:6 ^m S Ps 131:1 ⁿ Ro 11:33
139:7 ^o Jer 23:24; Jnh 1:3
139:8 ^p Dt 30:12-15; Am 9:2-3 ^q Job 17:13

138:4–5 The center of the poem (see note on 6:6): a wish that all the kings of earth may come to join in the praise of the Lord (see note on 9:1). The verbs, however, could be read as simple futures. In that case, these verses voice a confident expectation.
138:4 *what you have decreed.* God's grand commitments either to his people or to the royal house of David (see 18:30 and note; there, too, God's word and "ways" [v. 5] are linked).
138:5 *ways of the Lᴏʀᴅ.* See 25:10 and note. God's words and his ways are in harmony, and together they display his great glory (cf. Ps 145).
138:6–8 A testimony to God's condescending and faithful love, concluded with a prayer.
138:6 See 113:4–9 and notes. *takes notice of the proud from afar.* Already from a great distance recognizes them for what they are and so does not let them "see his face" (see note on 11:7). Cf. the acknowledgment of the psalmist in 139:2. *the proud.* See notes on 31:23; 101:5; 131:1.
138:8 *will vindicate me.* See 57:2 and note. *do not abandon the works of your hands.* A concluding prayer that the faithfulness of God celebrated here will truly "endure forever."

Ps 139 A prayer for God to examine the heart and see its true devotion. Like Job, the psalmist firmly claims his loyalty to the Lord. Nowhere (outside Job) does one find expressed such profound awareness of how awesome it is to ask God to examine not only one's life but also one's soul—God, who knows every thought, word and deed, from whom there is no hiding, who has been privy even to one's formation in the dark concealment of the womb. The thought progresses steadily in four poetic paragraphs of six verses each (vv. 1–6,7–12,13–18,19–24), and each paragraph is conclud-

ed with a couplet that elaborates on the unit's central theme. References to God's searching and knowing begin and end the prayer.
139 title *For the director of music.* See note on Ps 4 title. *Of David.* See introduction to Ps 138–145.

139:1–6 God, you know me perfectly, far beyond my knowledge of myself: my every action (v. 2a), my every undertaking (v. 3a) and the manner in which I pursue it (v. 3b), even my thoughts before they are fully crystallized (v. 2b) and my words before they are uttered (v. 4). See also v. 23.
139:2 *perceive . . . from afar.* See the contrast in 138:8 (see also note there). *my thoughts.* Those that pertain to my wishes, desires and/or plans.
139:5–6 The psalmist's response to the fact that God knows him so well.
139:5 *You hem me in.* To keep me under scrutiny. *lay your hand upon me.* So that I do not escape you. The figures are different in Job 13:27, but the thought is much the same. *hand.* Or "hands."
139:6 *too wonderful for me.* Yours is a "wonder" knowledge, beyond my human capacity—the Hebrew term regularly applies to God's wondrous acts (see 77:11,14, "miracles"; Ex 15:11).

139:7–12 There is no hiding from you—here no abstract doctrine of divine omnipresence but an awed confession that God cannot be escaped (see Jer 23:23–24).
139:7 *your Spirit . . . your presence.* See 51:11 and note; Isa 63:9–10; Eze 39:29 ("face . . . Spirit").
139:8 *the heavens . . . the depths.* The two vertical extremes.
139:9 *wings of the dawn . . . far side of the sea.* The two horizontal extremes: east and west (the sea is the Mediterranean). Using a literary figure in which the totality is denoted by referring

139:10 ^r Ps 23:3
^s Ps 108:6; Isa 41:10
139:12 ^t Job 34:22;
Da 2:22
139:13 ^u Ps 119:73
^v S Job 10:11
^w Isa 44:2,24; 46:3;
49:5; Jer 1:5
139:14 ^x Ps 119:164;
145:10 ^y S Job 40:19
139:15 ^z Ecc 11:5
^a S Job 10:11
^b S Ps 63:9
139:16 ^c S Job 33:29;
S Ps 90:12
139:17 ^d S Ps 92:5
^e S Job 5:9
139:18 ^f Ps 40:5
^g S Job 29:18
^h S Ps 3:5
139:19 ⁱ Ps 5:6;
Isa 11:4 ^j S Ps 6:8
^k S Ps 59:2
139:20 ^l S Ps 65:7
^m S Dt 5:11
139:21 ⁿ 2Ch 19:2;
Ps 31:6; 119:113
^o S Ps 26:5
139:22 ^p Mt 5:43

if I settle on the far side of the sea,
¹⁰ even there your hand will guide me, ^r
    your right hand ^s will hold me fast.
¹¹ If I say, "Surely the darkness will hide me
    and the light become night around me,"
¹² even the darkness will not be dark ^t to you;
    the night will shine like the day,
    for darkness is as light to you.

¹³ For you created my inmost being; ^u
    you knit me together ^v in my mother's womb. ^w
¹⁴ I praise you ^x because I am fearfully and wonderfully made;
    your works are wonderful, ^y
    I know that full well.
¹⁵ My frame was not hidden from you
    when I was made ^z in the secret place.
    When I was woven together ^a in the depths of the earth, ^b
¹⁶   your eyes saw my unformed body.
    All the days ordained ^c for me
    were written in your book
    before one of them came to be.
¹⁷ How precious to me are your thoughts, ^a ^d God! ^e
    How vast is the sum of them!
¹⁸ Were I to count them, ^f
    they would outnumber the grains of sand ^g—
    when I awake, ^h I am still with you.

¹⁹ If only you, God, would slay the wicked! ⁱ
    Away from me, ^j you who are bloodthirsty! ^k
²⁰ They speak of you with evil intent;
    your adversaries ^l misuse your name. ^m
²¹ Do I not hate those ⁿ who hate you, Lord,
    and abhor ^o those who are in rebellion against you?
²² I have nothing but hatred for them;
    I count them my enemies. ^p

---

^a 17 Or *precious are your thoughts concerning me*

---

to its two extremes (merism), vv. 8–9 specify all spatial reality, the whole creation.

A **139:10** *guide me…hold me fast.* Though this language occurs in 73:23–24 to indicate God's solicitous care, it here denotes God's inescapable supervision, not unlike the thought of v. 5.
139:11–12 Just as the whole creation offers no hiding place (vv. 8–9), neither does the darkness of night (see Job 34:22).

A **139:13–18** You yourself put me together in the womb and ordained the span of my life before I was born. You know me so thoroughly because you made me.
139:13 *created.* The Hebrew for this verb is the same as in Ge 14:19,22; Pr 8:22 ("brought…forth"), not as in Ge 1:1,21,27. *inmost being.* Lit. "kidneys"—in Hebrew idiom, the innermost center of emotions and of moral sensitivity—that which God tests and examines when he searches (vv. 1,23) a person (see note on 7:9).

A **139:14** *fearfully…wonderfully…wonderful.* You know me as the One who formed me (see vv. 15–16), but I cannot begin to comprehend this creature you have fashioned. I can only look upon him with awe and wonder (see note on v. 6)—and praise you (see Ecc 11:5).
139:15 *secret place…depths of the earth.* Reference is to the womb: called "the secret place" because it normally conceals (see 2Sa 12:12), and it shares with "the depths of the earth" (see note on 30:1) associations with darkness, dampness and separation from the visible realm of life. Moreover, both phrases refer to the place of the dead (63:9; Job 14:13; Isa 44:23; 45:19), with which on one level the womb appears to have been associated: Humans come from the dust and return to the dust (90:3; Ge 3:19; Ecc 3:20; 12:7), and the womb is the "depth"-like place

where they are formed (see Isa 44:2,24; 49:5; Jer 1:5).
139:16 *All the days ordained.* The span of life sovereignly determined. *your book.* The heavenly royal register of God's decisions (see note on 56:8).
139:17–18 The psalmist's response: God's thoughts of him are vast and precious.
139:17 *your thoughts.* As expressed in his works—and in contrast with "my thoughts" (v. 2; see note there).

A **139:18** *when I awake.* The sleep of exhaustion overcomes every attempt to count God's thoughts/works (see 63:6; 119:148), and waking only floods my soul once more with the sense of the presence of this God. On the other hand, reference may be to "awaking" from the sleep of death, as in Ps 17:15 (see also 2Ki 4:31; Job 14:12; Isa 26:9; Jer 51:39,57; Da 12:2). If so, the psalmist extends the sphere of God's presence to beyond the "gates of death."
139:19–24 My zeal for you and loyalty to you set me against all your adversaries.
139:19 *If only.* Jealous impatience with God's patience toward the wicked—whose end will come (Isa 11:4). But the psalmist leaves it to God (cf. note on 5:10).
139:20 *misuse your name.* Perhaps by calling down curses on those trying to be the faithful servants of God (see note on Ge 12:3).

B **139:21–22** A declaration of loyalty that echoes the pledge required by ancient Near Eastern kings of their vassals (e.g., "With my friend you shall be friend, and with my enemy you shall be enemy," from a treaty between Mursilis II, a Hittite king, and Tette of Nuhassi, 14th century B.C.).

²³ Search me,*q* God, and know my heart;*r*
    test me and know my anxious thoughts.
²⁴ See if there is any offensive way*s* in me,
    and lead me*t* in the way everlasting.

PSALM 140

For the director of music. A psalm of David.

*¹ Rescue me,*u* LORD, from evildoers;
    protect me from the violent,*v*
² who devise evil plans*w* in their hearts
    and stir up war*x* every day.
³ They make their tongues as sharp as*y* a serpent's;
    the poison of vipers*z* is on their lips.*ᵃ*

⁴ Keep me safe,*ᵃ* LORD, from the hands of the wicked;*b*
    protect me from the violent,
    who devise ways to trip my feet.
⁵ The arrogant have hidden a snare*c* for me;
    they have spread out the cords of their net*d*
    and have set traps*e* for me along my path.

⁶ I say to the LORD, "You are my God."*f*
    Hear, LORD, my cry for mercy.*g*
⁷ Sovereign LORD,*h* my strong deliverer,
    you shield my head in the day of battle.
⁸ Do not grant the wicked*i* their desires, LORD;
    do not let their plans succeed.

⁹ Those who surround me proudly rear their heads;
    may the mischief of their lips engulf them.*j*
¹⁰ May burning coals fall on them;
    may they be thrown into the fire,*k*
    into miry pits, never to rise.
¹¹ May slanderers not be established in the land;
    may disaster hunt down the violent.*l*

¹² I know that the LORD secures justice for the poor*m*
    and upholds the cause*n* of the needy.*o*
¹³ Surely the righteous will praise your name,*p*
    and the upright will live*q* in your presence.*r*

ᵃ 3 The Hebrew has *Selah* (a word of uncertain meaning) here and at the end of verses 5 and 8.
* 140:1-13 is numbered 140:2-14 in Hebrew texts.

139:23 *q* Job 31:6
r S 1Sa 16:7;
S 1Ch 29:17; S Ps 7:9;
Pr 17:3; Jer 11:20;
S Rev 2:23
139:24 *s* Jer 25:5;
36:3 *t* Ps 5:8; 23:2;
143:10
140:1 *u* Ps 17:13;
S 25:20; 59:2; 71:4;
142:6; 143:9 *v* ver 11;
Ps 86:14
140:2 *w* Ps 36:4;
52:2; Pr 6:14; 16:27;
Isa 59:4; Hos 7:15
x S Ps 68:30
140:3 *y* Ps 57:4
z Ps 58:4; Ro 3:13*;
Jas 3:8
140:4 *a* Ps 141:9
b S Ps 36:11
140:5 *c* S Job 34:30;
S Ps 119:110
d S Job 18:8
e Job 18:9; Ps 31:4;
S 38:12
140:6 *f* S Ps 16:2
g S Ps 28:2,6
140:7 *h* Ps 68:20
140:8 *i* Ps 10:2-3;
S 66:7
140:9 *j* Pr 18:7
140:10 *k* Ps 11:6;
21:9; S Mt 3:10;
Lk 12:49; Rev 20:15
140:11 *l* S Ps 34:21
140:12 *m* S Ps 82:3
n S 1Ki 8:45
o S Ps 35:10
140:13 *p* S Ps 138:2
q S Ps 11:7 *r* Ps 16:11

139:23–24 Examine me, see the integrity of my devotion and keep me true (see 17:3–5 and note). Cf. vv. 1–2.
139:23 *heart.* See note on 4:7. *anxious thoughts.* See 94:19. It is
no light matter to be examined by God.
139:24 *the way everlasting.* See note on 16:9–11.
Ps 140 A prayer for deliverance from the plots and slander of
unscrupulous enemies. It recalls Ps 58 and 64 but employs a
number of words found nowhere else in the OT. Four well-bal-
anced stanzas are followed by a two-verse conclusion. The
prayer is strikingly rich in physiological allusions: heart, head,
tongue, lips, hands, feet—also ears (lit. "Give ear to," v. 6) and
teeth (by a wordplay on the Hebrew for "make . . . sharp," v. 3).
See introduction to Ps 141; see also introduction to Ps 138–145.
140 title *For the director of music.* See note on Ps 4 title. *of David.* See note on Ps 138 title.
140:1–3 Rescue me from those "vipers."
140:1 *LORD.* Hebrew *Yahweh;* this divine name occurs seven
times in this psalm.
140:2 *hearts.* See note on 4:7.
140:3 *tongues.* See note on 5:9. *poison of vipers.* See 58:4 and
note. For *Selah,* see TNIV text note and note on 3:2.
140:4–5 Protect me from those proud and wicked hunters

(see 10:2–11 and notes).
140:5 *The arrogant.* See note on 31:23. *snare . . . net . . . traps.*
See 141:9–10.
140:6–8 Do not let these wicked men attain their evil designs
against me.
140:6 *Hear, LORD, my cry for mercy.* A thematic and verbal link
with 141:1; 142:1; 143:1.
140:9–11 Let the harm they plot against me recoil on their
heads (see note on 5:10).
140:10 *burning coals.* For the reference, see Lev. 16:12; Job
41:21; Pr 6:28; Isa 47:14; Eze 24:11. Other examples of this imagery for divine judgment may be found in Ps 18:8; 120:4; Eze
10:2. *fire . . . miry pits.* This combination, together with the conjunction of fire and darkness in Job 15:30; 20:26, suggests the
idea that the fire of God's judgment (see, e.g., 21:9; 97:3; Isa 1:31;
26:11; 33:14) reaches even into the realm of the dead (see Job
31:12 and note on Ps 30:1). *never to rise.* See 36:12; Isa 26:14.
140:11 *hunt down.* May the ruin these hunters (vv. 4–5) intended to bring on me hunt them down.
140:12–13 Confidence in God's just judgment (see note on 3:8).
140:12 *poor . . . needy.* See notes on 9:18; 34:6.
140:13 *the righteous.* See note on 1:5. *will praise.* Having experi-

141:1 *s* S Ps 22:19
t S Ps 4:1; 5:1-2; 27:7;
143:1
141:2 *u* S Lk 1:9;
Rev 5:8; 8:3
v S Ps 28:2; 63:4;
1Ti 2:8 *w* S Ex 29:39,
41; 30:8
141:3 *x* S Ps 34:13;
Jas 1:26; 3:8
y S Ps 12:2
141:4 *z* S Jos 24:23
a S Ps 106:29
b Pr 23:1-3
141:5 *c* Pr 9:8;
19:25; 25:12; Ecc 7:5
d S Ex 29:7; Ps 23:5
141:6 *e* S 2Ch 25:12
141:7 *f* Ps 129:3
g Nu 16:32-33
h Nu 16:30
141:8 *i* Ps 123:2
j Ps 2:12; 11:1
141:9 *k* Ps 140:4
l S Ps 64:5
m S Ps 38:12
141:10 *n* Ps 7:15;
35:8; 57:6 *o* Ps 124:7
142:1 *p* 1Sa 22:1;
24:3; Ps 57 Title
q S 1Ki 8:52; Ps 3:4
r Ps 30:8

PSALM 141

A psalm of David.

¹ I call to you, L ORD, come quickly*s* to me;
    hear me*t* when I call to you.
² May my prayer be set before you like incense;*u*
    may the lifting up of my hands*v* be like the evening sacrifice.*w*

³ Set a guard over my mouth,*x* L ORD;
    keep watch over the door of my lips.*y*
⁴ Do not let my heart*z* be drawn to what is evil
    so that I take part in wicked deeds*a*
along with those who are evildoers;
    do not let me eat of their delicacies.*b*

⁵ Let a righteous man strike me—that is a kindness;
    let him rebuke me*c*—that is oil on my head.*d*
My head will not refuse it,
    for my prayer will still be against the deeds of evildoers.

⁶ Their rulers will be thrown down from the cliffs,*e*
    and the wicked will learn that my words were well spoken.
⁷ They will say, "As one plows*f* and breaks up the earth,*g*
    so our bones have been scattered at the mouth*h* of the grave."

⁸ But my eyes are fixed*i* on you, Sovereign L ORD;
    in you I take refuge*j*—do not give me over to death.
⁹ Keep me safe*k* from the traps set by evildoers,*l*
    from the snares*m* they have laid for me.
¹⁰ Let the wicked fall*n* into their own nets,
    while I pass by in safety.*o*

PSALM 142

A maskil[a] *of David. When he was in the cave.*[p] *A prayer.*

*¹ I cry aloud*q* to the L ORD;
    I lift up my voice to the L ORD for mercy.*r*

---

[a] Title: Probably a literary or musical term
* 142:1-7 is numbered 142:2-8 in Hebrew texts.

---

enced God's help (see notes on 7:17; 9:1). *will live in your presence.* In contrast to the wicked (v. 10; see notes on 11:7; 16:9–11).
Ps 141 A prayer for deliverance from the wicked and their evil ways. The stanza structure of the first half (two Hebrew lines plus three lines) is repeated in the second half, while at the center a couplet develops a complementary theme (see note on v. 5). Like Ps 140, the prayer is profuse in its physiological allusions: hands, mouth, lips, heart, head, bones, eyes (see introduction to that psalm).
141 title See introduction to Ps 138–145.
141:1–2 Initial appeal for God to hear.
141:1 *hear me when I call.* See 140:6 and note.
141:2 *my prayer . . . like incense.* See notes on Ex 30:1; Lk 1:9; Rev 5:8. *like the evening sacrifice.* See Ex 29:38–41; Nu 28:3–8. These sacrifices are frequently mentioned (see 1Ki 18:29; 2Ki 16:15; 1Ch 16:40; 2Ch 13:11; 31:3; Ezr 3:3; 9:4–5; Da 9:21).

A **141:3–4** A plea that God will keep him from speaking, desiring or doing what is evil.
141:4 *Do not let my heart.* Keep me from yielding to the example and urgings of the wicked (see Pr 1:10–16). *heart.* See note on 4:7. *their delicacies.* Usually taken to refer to the luxuriant tables the wicked set from their unjust gains—thus a prayer that the psalmist be kept from acquiring an appetite for such unholy dainties. But the noun occurs only here, and it may refer to the pleasant sounding, but deceptive and evil, words of the wicked—thus a prayer that the psalmist be kept from taking into his mouth the

talk of the wicked that corresponds with their evil way of life (cf. v. 6 and note). Words related to this noun are elsewhere used to characterize words/thoughts (see Pr 15:26; 16:21; 23:8).
141:5 The center of the poem (see note on 6:6). *Let a righteous man strike me.* The disciplining blows and rebukes of the righteous are the true "kindness" (Hebrew *hesed,* meaning "love" or "acts of authentic friendship"; see Pr 27:6; see also note on Ps 6:4). *oil on my head.* See note on 23:5. *My head . . . deeds of evildoers.* Perhaps better: "Let my head not refuse it (this 'oil' from the righteous), for my prayer is still against their (the wicked's) evil deeds."
141:6–7 The destiny of the wicked. *Their rulers will be thrown down . . . the wicked will learn . . . They will say.* Perhaps better: "Let their rulers be thrown down . . . let the wicked learn . . . Let them say."
141:6 *my words.* Of commitment to righteousness, as in vv. 3–5. *well spoken.* Good and right.
141:8–10 A plea that God will deliver from the designs of the wicked.
141:8 *do not give me over to death.* As you do the wicked (see v. 7; see also 73:18–20, 23–26 and notes).
141:9 *traps . . . snares.* Perhaps, as usual, the plots of enemies to bring him down (as in 38:12; 64:5; 91:3; 140:5; 142:3; see note on 9:15)—note this link with Ps 140; 142.
141:10 *Let the wicked fall.* See note on 5:10. *fall into their own nets.* In Hebrew a verbal echo of 140:10 ("thrown into . . . miry pits").

² I pour out before him my complaint; ^s
  before him I tell my trouble. ^t

³ When my spirit grows faint ^u within me,
  it is you who watch over my way.
 In the path where I walk
  people have hidden a snare for me.
⁴ Look and see, there is no one at my right hand;
  no one is concerned for me.
 I have no refuge; ^v
  no one cares ^w for my life.

⁵ I cry to you, LORD;
  I say, "You are my refuge, ^x
  my portion ^y in the land of the living." ^z

⁶ Listen to my cry, ^a
  for I am in desperate need; ^b
 rescue me ^c from those who pursue me,
  for they are too strong ^d for me.
⁷ Set me free from my prison, ^e
  that I may praise your name. ^f
 Then the righteous will gather about me
  because of your goodness to me. ^g

PSALM 143

A psalm of David.

¹ LORD, hear my prayer, ^h
  listen to my cry for mercy; ⁱ
 in your faithfulness ^j and righteousness ^k
  come to my relief.
² Do not bring your servant into judgment,
  for no one living is righteous ^l before you.
³ The enemy pursues me,

142:2 ^s Ps 64:1
^t S Ps 50:15
142:3 ^u S Ps 6:2; 77:3;
84:2; 88:4; 143:4, 7;
Jer 8:18; La 1:22
142:4 ^v Jer 25:35
^w Jer 30:17
142:5 ^x S Ps 46:1
^y S Dt 32:9; Ps 16:5
^z S Job 28:13; Ps 27:13
142:6 ^a S Ps 17:1
^b S Ps 79:8
^c S Ps 25:20
^d Jer 31:11
142:7 ^e S Ps 66:11
^f Ps 7:17; 9:2
^g S 2Ch 6:41
143:1 ^h S Ps 141:1
ⁱ S Ps 28:2; 130:2
^j S Ex 34:6; Ps 89:1-2
^k Ps 71:2
143:2 ^l S Ps 14:3;
Ro 3:10

Ps 142 A plaintive prayer for deliverance from powerful enemies—when powerless, alone and without refuge. Much of its language echoes that of other psalms (see notes below). Apart from the introduction (vv. 1–2) and conclusion (v. 7b), the prayer (in Hebrew) is composed of two four-line stanzas (vv. 3–7a).
142 title *maskil.* See note on Ps 32 title. *of David.* See introduction to Ps 57 title. *When . . . cave.* See note on Ps 57 title. *A prayer.* See note on Ps 17 title.
142:1–2 Initial appeal—using the formal third person (as was often done when addressing kings), equivalent to: "I cry aloud to you, LORD."
142:1 Very similar to 77:1. *lift up my voice to the LORD for mercy.* See 140:6 and note.
142:2 *I pour out before him my complaint.* Very similar to language found in the title of Ps 102.
142:3–4 Description of his "desperate need" (v. 6).
142:3 *When my spirit grows faint.* Because he is overwhelmed by his situation (see 22:14–15)—a thematic and verbal link with 143:6 (see also 77:3; Ps 102 title; Jnh 2:7). *you who watch over.* And are concerned about (cf. v. 4). *hidden a snare for me.* A thematic and verbal link with 140:5; 141:9–10 (see note on 9:15).
142:4 *right hand.* Where one's helper or defender stands (see 16:8 and note). *is concerned.* In Hebrew a less common synonym of "know" (v. 3, "watch over"); see Ru 2:10,19 ("notice"). *cares for.* See Dt 11:12.
142:5–7 Prayer for rescue.
142:5 *You are my refuge.* See 71:7; Jer 17:17. *portion.* The sustainer and preserver of his life (see 73:26 and note). *in the land of the living.* See 27:13 and note; 52:5; 116:9.
142:6 *Listen to my cry.* See 17:1. *rescue me.* See 143:9; 144:7.
142:7 *prison.* Metaphor for the sense of being fettered by afflic-

tion (see note on 18:19; see also Job 36:8). *that I may praise.* In celebration of God's saving help (see note on 7:17). *name.* See note on 5:11. *righteous.* See note on 1:5. *will gather about me.* He will no longer be alone. The conclusion expresses an expectant word of confidence (see note on 3:8). *your goodness to me.* See 13:6; 116:7.
Ps 143 A prayer for deliverance from enemies and for divine leading. This is the seventh and final penitential psalm (see introduction to Ps 6). The psalm is composed of two balanced divisions of seven Hebrew lines each (vv. 1–6, 7–10) and a two-line concluding reiteration of the basic appeal of the prayer (vv. 11–12). The three middle lines (vv. 3–4) of the first division describe the psalmist's distress, while the three middle lines (vv. 8–9) of the second division express the psalmist's trust in the Lord to deliver him from his distress. Appeal to God's righteousness (vv. 1,11) and the author's self-identification as "your servant" (vv. 2,12) enclose the prayer. See also his appeal to God's faithfulness (v. 1) and unfailing love (v. 12), which together form a frequent pair (see note on 36:5). For another enclosure, see note on v. 7.
143 title See introduction to Ps 138–145.
143:1–2 Initial appeal.
143:1 *my cry for mercy.* See 140:6 and note. *righteousness.* See note on 4:1.
143:2 As he begins his prayer, he pleads that God not sit in judgment over his servant (he knows his own failings; see also v. 10) but that he focus his judicial attention on the enemy's harsh and unwarranted attacks. *your servant.* A verbal link with 144:10—which suggests why this psalm was traditionally ascribed to David (see also 78:70; 132:10 and notes).
143:3–4 The distress he suffers.
143:3 The last half of this verse appears almost verbatim in

143:3 *m* S Ps 107:10
n La 3:6
143:4 *o* Ps 30:7
143:5 *p* Ps 77:6
q S Ge 24:63
143:6 *r* S Ex 9:29;
S Job 11:13
143:7 *s* S Ps 69:17
t S Ps 142:3
u S Ps 22:24; 27:9;
30:7
143:8 *v* Ps 6:4;
90:14 *w* S Ex 33:13;
S Job 34:32; Ps 27:11;
32:8 *x* Ps 25:1-2;
S 86:4
143:9 *y* S Ps 140:1
z S Ps 18:17; 31:15
143:10 *a* S Ps 107:10
b Ps 31:14 *c* S Ne 9:20;
Ps 25:4-5 *d* Ps 26:12
143:11 *e* Ps 25:11
f S Ps 41:2 *g* Ps 31:1;
71:2
143:12 *h* Ps 8:2
i Ps 54:5 *j* S Ps 116:16
144:1 *k* S Ge 49:24

he crushes me to the ground;
he makes me dwell in the darkness *m*
  like those long dead. *n*
⁴ So my spirit grows faint within me;
  my heart within me is dismayed. *o*
⁵ I remember *p* the days of long ago;
  I meditate *q* on all your works
  and consider what your hands have done.
⁶ I spread out my hands *r* to you;
  I thirst for you like a parched land. *a*

⁷ Answer me quickly, *s* Lord;
  my spirit fails. *t*
Do not hide your face *u* from me
  or I will be like those who go down to the pit.
⁸ Let the morning bring me word of your unfailing love, *v*
  for I have put my trust in you.
Show me the way *w* I should go,
  for to you I entrust my life. *x*
⁹ Rescue me *y* from my enemies, *z* Lord,
  for I hide myself in you.
¹⁰ Teach me *a* to do your will,
  for you are my God; *b*
may your good Spirit
  lead *c* me on level ground. *d*

¹¹ For your name's sake, *e* Lord, preserve my life; *f*
  in your righteousness, *g* bring me out of trouble.
¹² In your unfailing love, silence my enemies; *h*
  destroy all my foes, *i*
  for I am your servant. *j*

PSALM 144

Of David.

¹ Praise be to the Lord my Rock, *k*
  who trains my hands for war,
  my fingers for battle.

---

a 6 The Hebrew has *Selah* (a word of uncertain meaning) here.

La 3:6. *in the darkness.* As one cut off from the enjoyments of life (see v. 7; see also notes on 27:1; 30:1).

143:4 *my spirit grows faint.* See note on 142:3. *heart.* See note on 4:7.

143:5–6 Remembrance of God's past acts of deliverance encourages him in his appeal.

143:6 *spread out my hands.* In prayer (see 44:20; 88:9; Ex 9:29). *thirst for you.* See note on 63:1. For *Selah,* see TNIV text note and note on 3:2.

143:7–10 The prayer.

143:7 *my spirit fails.* Or perhaps:"my spirit faints with longing," which parallels the construction in 119:81; in view of the next line the thought appears closer to that of 104:29 (where "breath" translates the same Hebrew word as that for "spirit" here). Ultimately, the failing of "my spirit" will be healed by the leading of "your good Spirit" (v. 10)—the two references enclose the prayer. *hide your face.* See note on 13:1. *the pit.* See v. 3 and note on 30:1.

143:8 *the morning.* Of salvation from the present "darkness" (v. 3; see introduction to Ps 57; see also note on 101:8). *unfailing love.* See v. 12; see also note on 6:4. *I have put my trust in you ... to you I entrust my life.* See 25:1–2; see also 24:4 and note. *Show me the way.* See v. 10. Deliverance from the enemy is not enough—either for God's "servant" (vv. 2, 12) or for entrance into life.

143:10 *level ground.* See note on 26:12.

143:11–12 Concluding reiteration of the prayer (see introduction). Note how "your righteousness,""your unfailing love" and "your servant" all establish links with vv. 1–2.

143:11 *For your name's sake.* See note on 23:3.

143:12 *destroy all my foes.* See note on 5:10.

Ps 144 A prayer for deliverance from treacherous enemies, composed in the mode of a royal prayer. Verses 1–10 show much affinity to Ps 18, with vv. 5–7 all appearing to be variations on lines found there (see notes below). The remaining lines of this section contain similar echoes of other psalms, and the author may have drawn directly on them. This first part of the psalm is fairly typical of the prayers of the Psalter. What follows is clearly composite: Verse 11 recapitulates the prayer of vv. 5–8; vv. 12–14 describe a people enjoying ideal conditions; v. 15 closes the psalm with an echo of 33:12. For thematic continuities, see notes below.

144 title See introduction to Ps 138–145.

144:1–2 Praise of the Lord. As the opening words of a prayer, it seems to function both as an initial appeal (see 143:1–2) and as a confession of confidence that the prayer will be heard. The unusual piling up of epithets for God echoes Ps 18 (see note on 18:2).

144:2 *my loving God.* Lit."my unfailing love" (see note on 6:4); so called because God is the source of benevolent acts of love that David can count on—just as God can be called "my salvation" because he is the source of salvation (see 27:1; 35:3; 62:2).

² He is my loving God and my fortress, *l*
　　my stronghold *m* and my deliverer,
　　my shield, *n* in whom I take refuge,
　　who subdues peoples *a o* under me.

³ LORD, what are human beings *p* that you care for them,
　　mere mortals that you think of them?
⁴ They are like a breath; *q*
　　their days are like a fleeting shadow. *r*

⁵ Part your heavens, *s* LORD, and come down; *t*
　　touch the mountains, so that they smoke. *u*
⁶ Send forth lightning *v* and scatter *w* the enemy;
　　shoot your arrows *x* and rout them.
⁷ Reach down your hand from on high; *y*
　　deliver me and rescue me *z*
　　from the mighty waters, *a*
　　from the hands of foreigners *b*
⁸ whose mouths are full of lies, *c*
　　whose right hands *d* are deceitful. *e*

⁹ I will sing a new song *f* to you, my God;
　　on the ten-stringed lyre *g* I will make music to you,
¹⁰ to the One who gives victory to kings, *h*
　　who delivers his servant David. *i*

　　From the deadly sword; *j* ¹¹deliver me;
　　rescue me *k* from the hands of foreigners *l*
　　whose mouths are full of lies, *m*
　　whose right hands are deceitful. *n*

¹² Then our sons in their youth
　　will be like well-nurtured plants, *o*
　　and our daughters will be like pillars *p*
　　carved to adorn a palace.
¹³ Our barns will be filled *q*
　　with every kind of provision.
　　Our sheep will increase by thousands,
　　by tens of thousands in our fields;
¹⁴　our oxen *r* will draw heavy loads. *b*
　　There will be no breaching of walls, *s*
　　no going into captivity,
　　no cry of distress in our streets. *t*
¹⁵ Blessed is the people *u* of whom this is true;
　　blessed is the people whose God is the LORD.

a 2 Many manuscripts of the Masoretic Text, Dead Sea Scrolls, Aquila, Jerome and Syriac; most
manuscripts of the Masoretic Text *subdues my people*　　*b* 14 Or *our chieftains will be firmly established*

144:2 *l* Ps 59:9; 91:2
m Ps 27:1; 37:39; 43:2
n S Ge 15:1; S Ps 18:2
o S Jdg 4:23;
S Ps 18:39
144:3 *p* Heb 2:6
144:4 *q* S Job 7:7;
27:3; Isa 2:22
r S 1Ch 29:15;
S Job 14:2; S Jas 4:14
144:5 *s* Ps 18:9;
Isa 64:1 *t* S Ge 11:5;
S Ps 57:3 *u* Ps 104:32
144:6 *v* Hab 3:11;
Zec 9:14 *w* S Ps 59:11;
S 68:1 *x* Ps 7:12-13;
18:14
144:7 *y* S 2Sa 22:17
z Ps 3:7; S 57:3
a Ps 69:2 *b* S Ps 18:44
144:8 *c* Ps 12:2; 41:6
d Ge 14:22; Dt 32:40
e S Ps 36:3
144:9 *f* S Ps 28:7;
S 96:1 *g* Ps 33:2-3;
S 71:22
144:10 *h* S 2Sa 8:14
i Ps 18:50 *j* S Job 5:20
144:11 *k* Ps 3:7;
S 25:20 *l* S Ps 18:44
m Ps 41:6-7 *n* Ps 12:2;
S 36:3; 106:26;
Isa 44:20
144:12 *o* Ps 92:12-
14; S 128:3 *p* SS 4:4;
7:4
144:13 *q* Pr 3:10
144:14 *r* Pr 14:4
s 2Ki 25:11 *t* Isa 24:11;
Jer 14:2-3
144:15 *u* Dt 28:3

144:3-4 Acknowlegment of the relative insignificance of human beings and an expression of wonder that God cares for them.
144:3 A variation of 8:4.
144:4 *breath.* See 39:4-6 and notes. *shadow.* See 102:11 and note.
144:5-8 Prayer for deliverance.
144:5 See 18:9 and note on 18:7-15; see also Isa 64:1 and note.
144:6 See 18:14 and note.
144:7 See 18:16-17 and note on 32:6.
144:8 *mouths.* See note on 5:9. *right hands.* Hands raised to swear covenant oaths of allegiance or submission (see 106:26; Ex 6:8; Dt 32:40).
144:9-10 Vow to praise (see note on 7:17).
144:9 *new song.* See note on 33:3.

144:10 *his servant David.* See 143:2 and note.
144:11 Repetition of the prayer in vv. 7-8, apparently to serve as transition to what follows: If God will deliver his servant David, the realm will prosper and be secure.
144:12-15 Many believe this to be a separate prayer ("May our sons ..."), unrelated to vv. 1-11, but the apparently transitional function of v. 11 supports the TNIV rendering.
144:12-14 Possibly a postexilic echo of Dt 28:3-8.
144:12 *daughters ... like pillars carved.* Temple columns in the shape of women were not uncommon (e.g., on the Acropolis in Athens).
144:14 *our oxen will draw heavy loads.* Or "our oxen will be heavy with flesh" or "our oxen will be heavy with young" (see also TNIV text note).
144:15 *Blessed.* See note on 1:1. *the people of whom this is true.* Cf. 33:12; see Dt 28:3-8; 1Ki 5:4 and note.

145:1 ᵛPs 30:1; 34:1
ʷPs 2:6; 5:2
ˣS Ps 54:6
145:2 ʸS Ps 71:6
ᶻPs 34:1; Isa 25:1;
26:8
145:3 ᵃS Ps 95:3
ᵇS 2Sa 22:4; Ps 96:4
ᶜS Job 5:9
145:4 ᵈPs 22:30
ᵉS Dt 11:19
ᶠS Ps 71:16
145:5 ᵍPs 96:6;
148:13 ʰS Ps 75:1
145:6 ⁱPs 78:4
ʲS Ps 66:3; ᵏS Dt 32:3
ˡPs 75:1; 106:22
145:7 ᵐS Ex 18:9;
S Ps 27:13 ⁿS Ps 5:11;
S 101:1 ᵒS Ps 138:5
145:8 ᵖS Ps 86:15;
103:8 �q S Ps 86:5
145:9 ʳS 1Ch 16:34;
S Ps 136:1; Mt 19:17;
Mk 10:18 ˢS Ps 103:13-
14
145:10 ᵗS Ps 8:6;
S 103:22; S 139:14
ᵘPs 30:4; 148:14;
149:9 ᵛS Ps 115:17-18
145:11 ʷver 12-13;
S Ex 15:2; Mt 6:33
ˣPs 21:13
145:12 ʸS Ps 75:1;
105:1 ᶻver 11;
Ps 103:19; Isa 2:10,19,
21
145:13 ᵃS Ex 15:18;
1Ti 1:17; 2Pe 1:11;
Rev 11:15 ᵇS Dt 7:9;
S 1Co 1:9 ᶜS Jos 23:14
145:14 ᵈS Ps 37:17
ᵉS 1Sa 2:8; Ps 146:8
ᶠS Ps 38:6
145:15 ᵍS Ge 1:30;
S Job 28:5;
S Ps 37:25; S Mt 6:26
145:16 ʰS Ps 90:14;
S 104:28

PSALM 145ᵃ

A psalm of praise. Of David.

¹ I will exalt you, ᵛ my God the King; ʷ
    I will praise your name ˣ for ever and ever.
² Every day I will praise ʸ you
    and extol your name ᶻ for ever and ever.

³ Great ᵃ is the Lᴏʀᴅ and most worthy of praise; ᵇ
    his greatness no one can fathom. ᶜ
⁴ One generation ᵈ commends your works to another;
    they tell ᵉ of your mighty acts. ᶠ
⁵ They speak of the glorious splendor ᵍ of your majesty—
    and I will meditate on your wonderful works. ᵇ ʰ
⁶ They tell ⁱ of the power of your awesome works— ʲ
    and I will proclaim ᵏ your great deeds. ˡ
⁷ They celebrate your abundant goodness ᵐ
    and joyfully sing ⁿ of your righteousness. ᵒ

⁸ The Lᴏʀᴅ is gracious and compassionate, ᵖ
    slow to anger and rich in love. q

⁹ The Lᴏʀᴅ is good ʳ to all;
    he has compassion ˢ on all he has made.
¹⁰ All your works praise you, ᵗ Lᴏʀᴅ;
    your faithful people extol ᵘ you. ᵛ
¹¹ They tell of the glory of your kingdom ʷ
    and speak of your might, ˣ
¹² so that all people may know of your mighty acts ʸ
    and the glorious splendor of your kingdom. ᶻ
¹³ Your kingdom is an everlasting kingdom, ᵃ
    and your dominion endures through all generations.

The Lᴏʀᴅ is trustworthy ᵇ in all he promises ᶜ
    and faithful in all he does. ᶜ
¹⁴ The Lᴏʀᴅ upholds ᵈ all who fall
    and lifts up all ᵉ who are bowed down. ᶠ
¹⁵ The eyes of all look to you,
    and you give them their food ᵍ at the proper time.
¹⁶ You open your hand
    and satisfy the desires ʰ of every living thing.

ᵃ This psalm is an acrostic poem, the verses of which (including verse 13b) begin with the successive letters of the Hebrew alphabet.   ᵇ 5 Dead Sea Scrolls and Syriac (see also Septuagint); Masoretic Text *On the glorious splendor of your majesty / and on your wonderful works I will meditate*   ᶜ *13* One manuscript of the Masoretic Text, Dead Sea Scrolls and Syriac (see also Septuagint); most manuscripts of the Masoretic Text do not have the last two lines of verse 13.

Ps 145 A magnificent hymn to the Lord, the Great King, for his mighty acts and benevolent virtues, which are the glory of his kingly rule. It exploits to the full the traditional language of praise and, as an alphabetic acrostic, reflects the care of studied composition. This care can be seen also in the manner in which the whole is structured. Between the two-line introduction (vv. 1–2) and one-line conclusion (v. 21), four main stanzas (vv. 3–7,9–13a, 13b–16,17–20) develop as many themes, each introduced by a thematic line. The first two of these stanzas are each composed of five poetic lines, the last two of four lines. Centered between the first two is an additional thematic line (v. 8) echoing Ex 34:6–7. This significant theme is centered (see note on 6:6) and not elaborated here (but see 86:15; 103:8–12; 111:4–5; 116:5–6) to allow the author to remain within the 22-line limits of the Hebrew alphabet. Further, the first two stanzas (vv. 3–13a) highlight the commending, telling, celebrating, singing and extolling of the glory of the Lord's reign, while the last two (vv. 13b–20) focus on what it is he does that is worthy of praise.

145 title *praise.* Hebrew *tehillah,* occurring only here in the psalm titles, but from a plural form (*tehillim*) has come the traditional Hebrew name of the Psalter. *Of David.* See introduction to Ps 138–145.

145:1–2 Initial commitment to praise. *name.* See v. 21, thus framing the psalm (see note on 5:11).

145:3–7 Praise of God's mighty acts, which display his greatness (v. 3) and his goodness (v. 7)—as the author underscores by framing the paragraph with these two references. For the same combination, see 86:10,17; 135:3,5.

145:4 *commends . . . tell.* See vv. 5–7,10–12,21; see also note on 9:1. *your works.* In creation, providence and redemption.

145:7 *righteousness.* See v. 17; see also note on 4:1.

145:8 This centered line (see introduction above) is equal in thematic importance to vv. 3,9,13b,17.

145:9–13a Praise of God's benevolent virtues, which move all creatures to celebrate the glory of his kingdom.

145:10 *All your works praise you.* See v. 21; see also note on 65:13. *faithful people.* See note on 4:3.

145:13b–16 Praise God's faithfulness.

145:13b,17 *faithful.* See note on 6:4.

¹⁷ The LORD is righteous ⁱ in all his ways
and faithful in all he does. ^j
¹⁸ The LORD is near ^k to all who call on him, ^l
to all who call on him in truth.
¹⁹ He fulfills the desires ^m of those who fear him; ⁿ
he hears their cry ^o and saves them. ^p
²⁰ The LORD watches over ^q all who love him, ^r
but all the wicked he will destroy. ^s

²¹ My mouth will speak ^t in praise of the LORD.
Let every creature ^u praise his holy name ^v
for ever and ever.

PSALM 146

¹ Praise the LORD. ^a

Praise the LORD, ^w my soul.

² I will praise the LORD all my life; ^x
I will sing praise ^y to my God as long as I live. ^z
³ Do not put your trust in princes, ^a
in human beings, ^b who cannot save.
⁴ When their spirit departs, they return to the ground; ^c
on that very day their plans come to nothing. ^d
⁵ Blessed are those ^e whose help ^f is the God of Jacob,
whose hope is in the LORD their God.

⁶ He is the Maker of heaven ^g and earth,
the sea, and everything in them—
he remains faithful ^h forever.
⁷ He upholds ⁱ the cause of the oppressed ^j
and gives food to the hungry. ^k
The LORD sets prisoners free, ^l
⁸ the LORD gives sight ^m to the blind, ⁿ
the LORD lifts up those who are bowed down, ^o
the LORD loves the righteous. ^p
⁹ The LORD watches over the foreigner ^q
and sustains the fatherless ^r and the widow, ^s
but he frustrates the ways of the wicked.

^a 1 Hebrew *Hallelu Yah*; also in verse 10

145:17 ⁱ S Ex 9:27;
S Ezr 9:15 ^j ver 13
145:18 ^k S Nu 23:21;
S Ps 46:1; Php 4:5
^l Ps 18:6; 80:18
145:19 ^m S Ps 20:4
ⁿ S Job 22:28
^o S Ps 31:22; S 40:1
^p S 1Sa 10:19; Ps 7:10;
34:18
145:20 ^q S Ps 1:6
^r Ps 31:23; 91:14;
97:10 ^s S Ps 94:23
145:21 ^t Ps 71:8
^u Ps 65:2; 150:6
^v S Ex 3:15; S Ps 30:4;
S 99:3
146:1 ^w Ps 103:1;
104:1
146:2 ^x Ps 104:33
^y S Ps 105:2
^z S Ps 63:4
146:3 ^a Ps 118:9
^b Ps 60:11; S 108:12;
Isa 2:22
146:4 ^c S Ge 3:19;
S Job 7:21; Ps 103:14;
Ecc 12:7 ^d Ps 33:10;
1Co 2:6
146:5 ^e Ps 33:18;
37:9; 119:43; 144:15;
Jer 17:7 ^f Ps 70:5;
71:5; 121:2
146:6 ^g S 2Ch 2:12;
Ps 115:15; Ac 14:15;
S Rev 10:6 ^h S Dt 7:9;
S Ps 18:25; 108:4;
117:2
146:7 ⁱ S Ps 37:17
^j Ps 103:6 ^k Ps 107:9;
145:15 ^l S Ps 66:11;
S 68:6
146:8 ^m Pr 20:12;
Isa 29:18; 32:3; 35:5;
42:7,18-19; 43:8;
Mt 11:5 ⁿ S Ex 4:11
^o S Ps 38:6
^p S Dt 7:13;
S Job 23:10
146:9 ^q S Lev 19:34
^r S Ps 10:18
^s S Ex 22:22; Jas 1:27

145:17–20 Praise of God's righteousness.
145:18 *in truth.* With godly integrity.
145:21 The praise of God must continue, and every creature take it up—forever. *every creature.* Or perhaps "every human" (lit. "all flesh"; see 65:2, "all people"; but see also 150:6).
Ps 146–150 A final cluster of five hymns (probably postexilic) all bracketed by shouts of Hallelujah! ("Praise Yahweh!")—which may have been added by the final editors (see introductions to Ps 105–106; see also Ps 111–117). The Psalter collection begins with two psalms that address the reader and whose function is to identify those to whom the collections specifically belong (see introduction to Ps 1–2). Here, at the collection's end, that congregation gives voice to its final themes. They are the themes of praise—and calls to praise—of Zion's heavenly King (see 146:10; 147:12; 149:2), the Maker, Sustainer and Lord over all creation (see 146:6; 147:4,8–9,15–18; 148:5–6); the one sure hope of those who in their need and vulnerability look to him for help (see 146:5–9; 147:2–3,6,11,13–14; 149:4); the Lord of history whose commitment to his people is their security and the guarantee that, as his kingdom people (see especially 147:19–20), they will ultimately triumph over all the forces of this world arrayed against them (see 146:3,10; 147:2,6,10,13–14; 148:14; 149:4–9).
Ps 146 A hymn in praise of Zion's heavenly King, with special focus on his powerful and trustworthy care for Zion's citizens

who look to him when oppressed, broken or vulnerable. It has many thematic links with Ps 33; 62; 145. For its placement, see introduction to Ps 146–150.
146:1–2 Initial vow to praise—as long as life continues (see 145:21 and note on 7:17).
146:1 *Praise the LORD, my soul.* See the frames around Ps 103–104. *soul.* See note on 6:3.
146:3–4 A call to trust ultimately in the Lord rather than in any human help (see 118:10–11 and note; 147:10–11).
146:5–9 Encouragement to trust in the covenant God of Jacob (see note on 14:7), who as Creator is Lord over all, as the Faithful One defends the defenseless and provides for the needy, and as the Righteous One shows favor to the righteous but checks the wicked in their pursuits.
146:6 *Maker of heaven and earth.* See note on 121:2.
146:7 *upholds the cause of the oppressed.* See 9:9; 10:18; 103:6. *gives food to the hungry.* See 17:14; 34:10; 107:9; cf. Isa 49:10. *sets prisoners free.* See 68:6; 79:11; 102:20; 107:10,14; cf. Isa 42:7 and note; 61:1.
146:8 *gives sight to the blind.* See Isa 29:18; 35:5; cf. Isa 42:7; 43:8. *lifts up those who are bowed down.* See 145:14. *righteous.* See note on 1:5.
146:9 *watches over the foreigner … fatherless … widow.* See Dt 10:18; cf. Isa 1:17; 9:17 and notes; cf. also Jer 22:16; Jas 1:17. *frustrates the ways of the wicked.* Cf. 104:35; 145:20.

146:10 ʳS Ge 21:33;
S 1Ch 16:31; Ps 93:1;
99:1; Rev 11:15
147:1 ᵘS Ps 135:3
ᵛPs 33:1
147:2 ʷS Ps 51:18
ˣS Ps 106:47
147:3 ʸS Ps 34:18
ᶻS Nu 12:13;
S Job 5:18; Isa 1:6;
Eze 34:16
147:4 ᵃS Ge 15:5
147:5 ᵇS Ps 48:1
ᶜS Ex 14:31
ᵈPs 145:3; Isa 40:28
147:6 ᵉS 2Ch 33:23;
Ps 146:8-9 ᶠPs 37:9-
10; 145:20
147:7 ᵍPs 30:4;
33:3 ʰS Ps 42:4
ⁱS Ps 27:6 ʲS Ps 98:5
147:8 ᵏS Job 26:8
ˡS Dt 11:14; S 32:2;
S 2Sa 1:21; S Job 5:10
ᵐS Job 28:26;
S Ps 104:14
147:9 ⁿS Ge 1:30;
Ps 104:27-28;
S Mt 6:26 ᵒS Ge 8:7
147:10 ᵖS 1Sa 16:7
ᵠS Job 39:11;
Ps 33:16-17
147:11 ʳS Ps 35:27
ˢPs 33:18; 103:11
ᵗPs 119:43 ᵘPs 6:4
147:12 ᵛPs 48:1
147:13 ʷS Dt 33:25
ˣS Lev 25:21;
Ps 128:5; 134:3

¹⁰ The Lord reigns ᵗ forever,
your God, O Zion, for all generations.

Praise the Lord.

PSALM 147

¹ Praise the Lord. ᵃ

How good it is to sing praises to our God,
how pleasant ᵘ and fitting to praise him! ᵛ

² The Lord builds up Jerusalem; ʷ
he gathers the exiles ˣ of Israel.
³ He heals the brokenhearted ʸ
and binds up their wounds. ᶻ
⁴ He determines the number of the stars ᵃ
and calls them each by name.
⁵ Great is our Lord ᵇ and mighty in power; ᶜ
his understanding has no limit. ᵈ
⁶ The Lord sustains the humble ᵉ
but casts the wicked ᶠ to the ground.

⁷ Sing to the Lord ᵍ with grateful praise; ʰ
make music ⁱ to our God on the harp. ʲ
⁸ He covers the sky with clouds; ᵏ
he supplies the earth with rain ˡ
and makes grass grow ᵐ on the hills.
⁹ He provides food ⁿ for the cattle
and for the young ravens ᵒ when they call.

¹⁰ His pleasure is not in the strength ᵖ of the horse, ᵠ
nor his delight in the power of human legs;
¹¹ the Lord delights ʳ in those who fear him, ˢ
who put their hope ᵗ in his unfailing love. ᵘ

¹² Extol the Lord, Jerusalem; ᵛ
praise your God, Zion.
¹³ He strengthens the bars of your gates ʷ
and blesses your people ˣ within you.

ᵃ 1 Hebrew *Hallelu Yah*; also in verse 20

146:10 Concluding exultant testimony to the citizens of God's royal city. *The Lord reigns forever.* See 93:1 and note. *Zion.* See note on 9:11.

Ps 147 Praise of God, the Creator and Lord over all, for his special mercies to Israel—possibly composed for the Levitical choirs on the joyous occasion of the dedication of the rebuilt walls of Jerusalem (see Ne 12:27–43). The Septuagint (the pre-Christian Greek translation of the OT) plausibly divides the work into two separate psalms (vv. 1–11,12–20). However, the form of the psalm as handed down in the Hebrew text tradition also has the appearance of a rhetorical whole. Following the introduction (v. 1), two couplets in which the Lord's unique favors to Israel are celebrated (vv. 2–3,19–20) frame its main body, while at the center another couplet (vv. 10–11) highlights the Lord's special pleasure in those who rely finally on him rather than on any of his creatures. In the balanced stanzas that intervene (vv. 4–9, 12–18), this thematic core is placed in the larger context of God's works and ways. See introduction to Ps 146–150.

147:1 See note on 135:3.

147:2 *builds up.* Refers to the postexilic rebuilding of Jerusalem. *exiles.* Translates an unusual Hebrew word found also in Isa 11:10; 56:8—all of which speak of gathering (restoring) "the exiles of Israel."

147:3 *brokenhearted.* Such as the exiles (see Ps 137; cf. Ps 126) and those who struggled in the face of great opposition to re-

build Jerusalem's walls (Ne 2:17–20; 4:1–23).

147:4–6 He whose power and understanding are such that he fixes the number of (or counts) the stars and names them is able to sustain his humble ones and bring the wicked down (see 20:8; 146:9; see also Isa 40:26–29).

147:6 *humble.* Those who acknowledge that they are without resources to deliver or maintain themselves—those who, as God's people, put their trust in him (see 149:4; see also 22:26, "The poor"; 37:11, "the meek," and note; 69:32, "The poor"). *ground.* Probably the grave (see note on 61:2).

147:7–9 Israel's God is Lord of creation, the one who provides for all living things.

147:10–11 The central couplet (see note on 6:6), thematically linked with vv. 2–3 and vv. 19–20 (see introduction, above). Israel's God is not particularly impressed by the creaturely capacities that humans are prone to rely on (cf. 146:3–4 and note); it gives him delight when his people rely on him (cf. 146:5–9).

147:11 *fear.* See note on 34:8–14. *unfailing love.* See note on 6:4.

147:12–18 The Lord of all creation, Zion's God, secures his people's defenses and prosperity, their peace and abundant provision. The verses mention clouds and rain (v. 8); snow, frost and hail (vv. 16–17); icy winds and warm breezes (vv. 17–18)—the whole range of weather.

¹⁴ He grants peace ᵛ to your borders
　　and satisfies you ᶻ with the finest of wheat. ᵃ

¹⁵ He sends his command ᵇ to the earth;
　　his word runs ᶜ swiftly.
¹⁶ He spreads the snow ᵈ like wool
　　and scatters the frost ᵉ like ashes.
¹⁷ He hurls down his hail ᶠ like pebbles.
　　Who can withstand his icy blast?
¹⁸ He sends his word ᵍ and melts them;
　　he stirs up his breezes, ʰ and the waters flow.

¹⁹ He has revealed his word ⁱ to Jacob, ʲ
　　his laws and decrees ᵏ to Israel.
²⁰ He has done this for no other nation; ˡ
　　they do not know ᵐ his laws. ᵃ

　Praise the LORD. ⁿ

PSALM 148

¹ Praise the LORD. ᵇ ᵒ

Praise the LORD from the heavens; ᵖ
　　praise him in the heights above.
² Praise him, all his angels; �q
　　praise him, all his heavenly hosts. ʳ
³ Praise him, sun ˢ and moon;
　　praise him, all you shining stars.
⁴ Praise him, you highest heavens ᵗ
　　and you waters above the skies. ᵘ

⁵ Let them praise the name ᵛ of the LORD,
　　for at his command ʷ they were created,
⁶ and he established them for ever and ever—
　　he issued a decree ˣ that will never pass away.

⁷ Praise the LORD ʸ from the earth,
　　you great sea creatures ᶻ and all ocean depths, ᵃ
⁸ lightning and hail, ᵇ snow and clouds,
　　stormy winds that do his bidding, ᶜ
⁹ you mountains and all hills, ᵈ
　　fruit trees and all cedars,
¹⁰ wild animals ᵉ and all cattle,
　　small creatures and flying birds,
¹¹ kings ᶠ of the earth and all nations,

147:14 ᵛ S Lev 26:6;
S 2Sa 7:10;
S Isa 48:18
ᶻ S Ps 132:15
ᵃ S Dt 32:14
147:15 ᵇ Job 37:12;
Ps 33:9; 148:5
ᶜ Isa 55:11
147:16 ᵈ Ps 148:8
ᵉ S Job 37:12; 38:29
147:17 ᶠ Ex 9:22-
23; S Job 38:22;
S Ps 78:47
147:18 ᵍ ver 15;
Ps 33:9; 107:20
ʰ S Ps 50:3
147:19 ⁱ S Ex 20:1;
Ro 3:2 ʲ Ps 78:5
ᵏ S Dt 33:4; Jos 1:8;
2Ki 22:8; Mal 4:4;
Ro 9:4
147:20 ˡ Dt 4:7-8,
32-34 ᵐ S Ps 79:6
ⁿ Ps 33:2; 103:1
148:1 ᵒ Ps 33:2;
103:1 ᵖ Ps 19:1; 69:34;
150:1
148:2 q Ps 103:20
ʳ S 1Ki 22:19
148:3 ˢ S Ps 19:1
148:4 ᵗ S Dt 10:14
ᵘ S Ge 1:7
148:5 ᵛ Ps 145:21
ʷ S Ps 147:15
148:6 ˣ Jer 31:35-
36; 33:25
148:7 ʸ Ps 33:2
ᶻ S Ge 1:21; Ps 74:13-
14 ᵃ S Dt 33:13
148:8 ᵇ S Ex 9:18;
S Jos 10:11
ᶜ Job 37:11-12;
S Ps 103:20; 147:15-
18
148:9 ᵈ Isa 44:23;
49:13; 55:12
148:10 ᵉ Isa 43:20;
Hos 2:18
148:11 ᶠ S Ps 102:15

ᵃ 20 Masoretic Text; Dead Sea Scrolls and Septuagint / he has not made his laws known to them
ᵇ 1 Hebrew Hallelu Yah; also in verse 14

147:15 *his command … his word.* Personified as messengers commissioned to carry out a divine order (see v. 18; see also notes on 23:6; 33:4; 104:4).

147:19–20 God's most unique gift to Israel: his other word, his redemptive word, by which he makes known his program of salvation and his holy will. These verses constitute the end frame, thematically linked with vv. 2–3 and vv. 10–11 (see introduction above and note on vv. 10–11).

Ps 148 A call to all things in all creation to praise the Lord. Whatever its original liturgical purpose, its placement here at the center of the five concluding hymns serves to complete the scope of the calls to praise with which the Psalter closes (see introduction to Ps 146–150). Two similarly constructed stanzas call on all creatures in the heavens (vv. 1–6) and all creatures beneath the heavens (vv. 7–14) to join in the chorus of praise (see 103:20–22 and note). Both stanzas end with a couplet setting forth the motivation for praise. The second of these (vv. 12–14), made up of extended lines, clearly constitutes the climax.

148:1–6 Let all creatures in the heavens praise the Lord.

148:2 *heavenly hosts.* See 103:21 and note.
148:3 *sun and moon … shining stars.* See note on 65:13.
148:4 *waters above the skies.* The "deep" above (see Ge 1:7; cf. "ocean depths" in v. 7; see also note on 42:7).
148:5–6 Motivation ("for," v. 5) for the heavenly creatures to praise the Lord (cf. vv. 13–14 and "for," v. 13).
148:5,13 *name of the LORD.* See note on 5:11. They are to praise the Lord because he has created them and made their existence secure.
148:7–14 Let all creatures of earth praise the Lord ("the earth and the heavens" [v. 13] are the sum of all creation; see 89:11; 113:6; 136:5–6; Ge 2:1,4).
148:7 *sea creatures and all ocean depths.* Likely with Ge 1 in mind (see Ge 1:7,10,21), the call begins with these and moves toward the human components. This and the pairs that follow employ a figure of speech that refers to all reality pertaining to the sphere to which they belong—here, all creatures great and small that belong to the realm of lakes and seas.
148:8 *his bidding.* Lit. "his word" (see 147:15 and note).

148:13 9 S Ps 113:2;
138:4 h S Ps 145:5
i S Ps 8:1
148:14 j S 1Sa 2:1
k Ex 15:2; Ps 22:3
l S Ps 145:10
m S Dt 26:19
149:1 n Ps 33:2;
103:1 o S Ps 28:7;
S 96:1; Rev 5:9
p S Ps 1:5
149:2 q Isa 13:3;
Jer 51:48 r S Job 10:3;
Ps 95:6; Isa 44:2;
45:11; 54:5 s Ps 10:16;
47:6; Isa 32:1; Zec 9:9
149:3 t S Ex 15:20
u S Ps 57:8
149:4 v Ps 35:27;
147:11 w Ps 132:16
149:5 x S Ps 132:16
y Job 35:10; Ps 42:8
149:6 z Ps 66:17
a Heb 4:12; Rev 1:16
b Ne 4:17
149:7 c S Nu 31:3;
S Dt 32:41 d Ps 81:15
149:8 e S 2Sa 3:34;
S Isa 14:1-2
f 2Ch 33:11
149:9 g Dt 7:1;
Eze 28:26
h S Ps 145:10

you princes and all rulers on earth,
12 young men and women,
old men and children.

13 Let them praise the name of the Lord, g
for his name alone is exalted;
his splendor h is above the earth and the heavens. i
14 And he has raised up for his people a horn, a j
the praise k of all his faithful servants, l
of Israel, the people close to his heart. m

Praise the Lord.

PSALM 149

1 Praise the Lord. b n

Sing to the Lord a new song, o
his praise in the assembly p of his faithful people.

2 Let Israel rejoice q in their Maker; r
let the people of Zion be glad in their King. s
3 Let them praise his name with dancing t
and make music to him with timbrel and harp. u
4 For the Lord takes delight v in his people;
he crowns the humble with victory. w
5 Let his faithful people rejoice x in this honor
and sing for joy on their beds. y

6 May the praise of God be in their mouths z
and a double-edged a sword in their hands, b
7 to inflict vengeance c on the nations
and punishment d on the peoples,
8 to bind their kings with fetters, e
their nobles with shackles of iron, f
9 to carry out the sentence written against them— g
this is the glory of all his faithful people. h

Praise the Lord.

---

a 14 *Horn* here symbolizes strength.   b 1 Hebrew *Hallelu Yah*; also in verse 9

148:13–14 Climactic conclusion, with focus again on motivation for praise (cf. vv. 5–6 and note).
148:13 *his name ... his splendor.* As shown in the glory of his creation. *is above.* The glory of the Creator is greater than the glory of the creation.
148:14 *horn.* The Lord's anointed (see TNIV text note; see also notes on 2:2; Ps 18 title). It may be, however, that "horn" here represents the strength and vigor of God's people (see 92:10; 1Sa 2:1; Jer 48:25; La 2:17). In any event, reference is to God's saving acts for Israel—God is to be praised for his works in creation and redemption (see note on 65:6–7). *praise.* See 22:3 and note. *faithful servants.* See note on 4:3.
Ps 149 Praise of God for the high honor bestowed on his people Israel. Israel's unique honor has two sides: She was granted salvation (in fact and in promise) and, under the particular administration of the emerging kingdom of God put in place in the inauguration of the Sinai covenant (see chart, p. 20), she was armed to execute God's sentence of judgment on the world powers that have launched attacks against the kingdom of God. Under that arrangement, she served as the earthly contingent of the armies of the King of heaven (see 68:17 and note; see also Jos 5:14; 2Sa 5:23–24; 2Ch 20:15–17,22; Hab 3:3–15). This next-to-last psalm should be read in the light of the second psalm (see introduction to Ps 2; see also introduction to Ps 146–150).

Following an introductory verse, the two main themes are developed in two balanced stanzas of four verses each. References to God's "faithful people" enclose the song (see also v. 5). The common

pair of synonyms, "honor" (v. 5) and "glory" (v. 9), effectively link the two stanzas (see 8:5; 21:5, "glory ... majesty"; 104:1,31, "majesty ... glory"; 145:5,12, "glorious splendor"; Isa 35:2, "glory ... splendor").
149:1 *new song.* See note on 33:3. *in the assembly.* See note on 9:1. *his faithful people.* See vv. 5,9; see also note on 4:3.
149:2–5 Let Israel rejoice in their King, who has crowned them with the honor of salvation.
149:3 *his name.* See note on 5:11.
149:4 *crowns.* Endows with splendor (see Isa 55:5; 60:9; 61:3). *humble.* Those who acknowledge that they are without resources (see 147:6).
149:5 *on their beds.* The salvation (v. 4) so tangible in the daytime evokes songs in the night (see 42:8; 63:6; 77:6).
149:6–9 Let Israel praise their God, who has given them the glory of bearing the sword as his army in service (cf. Ps 137; 139:19–22; Am 9:12; Eze 38–39; Da 2:44; 7:22,26–27).
149:7 *vengeance.* God's just retribution on those who have attacked his kingdom. Of this divine retribution the OT speaks often: 58:10; 79:10; 94:1; Nu 31:2; Dt 32:35,41,43; 2Ki 9:7; Isa 34:8; 35:4; 47:3; 59:17; 61:2; 63:4; Jer 46:10; 50:15, 28; 51:6,11,36; Eze 25:14,17; Na 1:2. In the NT age, however, God's people are armed with the "sword of the Spirit" for overcoming the powers arrayed against God's kingdom (see 2Co 6:7; 10:4; Eph 6:12,17; Heb 4:12); their participation in God's retribution on the world awaits the final judgment (see 1Co 6:2–3).
149:9 *sentence written.* God's firmly determined judgment (see 139:16 and note).

PSALM 150

150:1 /S Ps 112:1
/ Ps 68:24-26; 73:17;
102:19 *S Ps 148:1
150:2 /S Dt 3:24
m S Ex 15:7
150:3 *n* S Nu 10:2
o S Ps 57:8
150:4 *p* S Ex 15:20
q S Ps 45:8
r S Ge 4:21
150:5 *s* S 2Sa 6:5
150:6 *t* S Ps 103:22

[1] Praise the LORD.[a] [i]

Praise God in his sanctuary; [j]
 praise him in his mighty heavens. [k]
[2] Praise him for his acts of power; [l]
 praise him for his surpassing greatness. [m]
[3] Praise him with the sounding of the trumpet, [n]
 praise him with the harp and lyre, [o]
[4] praise him with timbrel and dancing, [p]
 praise him with the strings [q] and pipe, [r]
[5] praise him with the clash of cymbals, [s]
 praise him with resounding cymbals.

[6] Let everything [t] that has breath praise the LORD.

Praise the LORD.

[a] 1 Hebrew *Hallelu Yah*; also in verse 6

Ps 150 The final great Hallelujah—perhaps composed specifically to close the Psalter. See the conclusions to the first four Books: 41:13; 72:18–19; 89:52; 106:48. This final call to praise moves powerfully by stages from place to themes to orchestra to choir, framed with Hallelujahs. See introduction to Ps 146–150.
150:1 *Where* God should be praised. *his sanctuary.* At Jerusalem. *his mighty heavens.* Lit. "the vault of his power" (see 19:1, "skies"; Ge 1:6), i.e., the vault that displays or symbolizes his power or in which his power resides. Usually thought to refer to

God's heavenly temple (see 11:4), it may signify the vaulted ceiling of the visible universe viewed as a cosmic temple.
150:2 *Why* God should be praised. *his acts of power.* What he does (in creation and redemption). *his surpassing greatness.* Who he is.
150:3–5 *How* God should be praised—with the whole orchestra (eight instruments: wind, string, percussion), with dancing aptly placed at the middle.
150:6 *Who* should praise God. The choir, with articulate expression, celebrates God's mighty acts and surpassing greatness.

PROVERBS

INTRODUCTION

Although the book begins with a title ascribing the proverbs to Solomon, it is clear from later chapters that he was not the only author of the book. Pr 22:17 refers to the "sayings of the wise," and 24:23 mentions additional "sayings of the wise." The presence of an introduction in 22:17–21 further indicates that these sections stem from a circle of wise men, not from Solomon himself. Ch. 30 is attributed to Agur, son of Jakeh, and 31:1–9 to King Lemuel, neither of whom is mentioned elsewhere. Lemuel's sayings contain several Aramaic spellings that may point to a non-Israelite background.

Most of the book, however, is closely linked with Solomon. The headings in 10:1 and 25:1 again include his name, though 25:1 states that these proverbs were "compiled by the men of Hezekiah king of Judah." This indicates that a group of wise men or scribes compiled these proverbs as editors and added chs. 25–29 to the earlier collections. Solomon's ability to produce proverbs is specified in 1Ki 4:32, where 3,000 proverbs are attributed to him. In light of statements about his unparalleled wisdom (1Ki 4:29–31,34; 10:1–13, 23–24), it is quite likely that he was the source of most of Proverbs. The book contains a short prologue (1:1–7) and a longer epilogue (31:10–31), which may have been added to the other materials. It is possible that the discourses in the large opening section (1:8—9:18) were the work of a compiler or editor, but the similarities of ch. 6 in this section with other chapters (compare 6:1 with 11:15; 17:18; 20:16; 27:13; compare 6:14,19 with 10:12; 15:18; 16:28; 28:25; 29:22; compare 6:19 with 14:5,25; 19:5) fit a Solomonic origin equally well. The emphasis on the "fear of the LORD" (1:7) throughout the book ties the various segments together.

DATE

B If Solomon is granted a prominent role in the book, most of Proverbs would stem from the tenth century B.C., during the time of Israel's united kingdom. The peace and prosperity that characterized that era accord well with the development of reflective wisdom and the production of literary works. Moreover, several interpreters have noted that the 30 sayings of the wise in 22:17—24:22 (especially the first ten) contain similarities to the 30 sections of the Egyptian "Wisdom of Amenemope," an instructional piece that is roughly contemporary with the time of Solomon (see chart, p. xxiii). Likewise, the personification of wisdom so prominent in chs. 1–9 (see 1:20 and note; 3:15–18; 8:1–36; 9:1–12) can be compared with the personification of abstract ideas in both Mesopotamian and Egyptian writings of the second millennium B.C.

The role of Hezekiah's men (see 25:1) indicates that important sections of Proverbs were compiled and edited from 715 to 686 B.C. This was a time of spiritual renewal led by the king, who also showed great interest in the writings of David and Asaph (see 2Ch 29:30). Perhaps it was also at this time that the sayings of Agur (ch. 30) and Lemuel (31:1–9) and the other "sayings of the wise" (22:17—24:22; 24:23–34) were added to the Solomonic collections, though it is possible that the task of compilation was not completed until after the reign of Hezekiah.

KEY **A** APPLICATION FOR LIVING   **B** BACKGROUND NOTES   **C** CHARACTER INFORMATION

THE NATURE OF A PROVERB

The proverbs contained in this book are not to be interpreted as prophecies or their statements about effects and results as promises. For instance, 10:27 says that the years of the wicked are cut short, while the righteous live long and prosperous lives (see 3:2 and note). The righteous have abundant food (10:3), but the wicked will go hungry (13:25). While such statements are generally true, there are enough exceptions to indicate that sometimes the righteous suffer and the wicked prosper (see note on 3:2). Normally the righteous and wicked "receive their due on earth" (11:31), but at other times reward and punishment lie beyond the grave.

The Hebrew word translated "proverb" is also translated "message" (Nu 23:7,18), "taunt" (Isa 14:4) and "parable" (Eze 17:2), so its meaning is considerably broader than the English term. This may help explain the presence of the longer discourse sections in chs. 1–9. Most proverbs are short, compact statements that express truths about human behavior. Often there is repetition of a word or sound that aids memorization. In 30:33, e.g., the same Hebrew verb is translated "churning," "twisting" and "stirring up."

In the longest section of the book (10:1—22:16) most of the proverbs are two lines long, and those in chs. 10–15 almost always express a contrast. Sometimes the writer simply makes a general observation, such as "A bribe is seen as a charm by those who give it" (17:8; cf. 14:20), but usually he evaluates conduct: "those who hate bribes will live" (15:27). Many proverbs, in fact, describe the consequences of a particular action or character trait: "Wise children bring joy to their father" (10:1). Since the proverbs were written primarily for instruction, they are often given in the form of commands: "Do not love sleep or you will grow poor" (20:13). Even where the imperative form is not used, the desired action is quite clear (see 14:5).

A common feature of the proverbs is the use of figurative language: "Like cold water to a weary soul / is good news from a distant land" (25:25). In ch. 25 alone there are 12 verses that begin with "Like" or "As." These similes make the proverbs more vivid and powerful. Occasionally the simile is used in a humorous or sarcastic way: "Like a gold ring in a pig's snout / is a beautiful woman who shows no discretion" (11:22; cf. 26:9), or, "As a door turns on its hinges, / so a sluggard turns on the bed" (26:14). Equally effective is the use of metaphors: "The teaching of the wise is a fountain of life" (13:14), and "The soothing tongue is a tree of life" (15:4). According to 16:24, "Gracious words are a honeycomb." The figure of sowing and reaping is used in both a positive and a negative way (cf. 11:18; 22:8).

In order to develop a proper set of values, a number of proverbs use direct comparisons: "Better the poor whose walk is blameless / than the rich whose ways are perverse" (28:6). This "better . . . than" pattern can be seen also in 15:16–17; 16:19,32; 17:1,12; a modified form occurs in 22:1. Another pattern found in the book is the so-called numerical proverb. Used for the first time in 6:16 (see note there), this type of saying normally has the number three in the first line and four in the second (cf. 30:15,18,21,29).

The repetition of entire proverbs (compare 6:10–11 with 24:33–34; 14:12 with 16:25; 18:8 with 26:22; 20:16 with 27:13; 21:19 with 25:24) or parts of proverbs may serve a poetic purpose. A slight variation allows the writer(s) to use the same image to make a related point (as in 17:3; 27:21) or to substitute a word or two to achieve greater clarity or a different emphasis (cf. 19:1; 28:6). In 26:4–5 the same line is repeated in a seemingly contradictory way, but this was designed to make two different points (see notes there).

At times the book of Proverbs is very direct and earthy (cf. 6:6; 21:9; 25:16; 26:3). This is the nature of wisdom literature as it seeks pedagogically effective ways to illumine life situations and to guide the unwise (or not yet wise) into wise choices concerning how to shape their lives as members of the human community that lives under the scrutiny and the providential rule and care of the Creator (see essay, p. 750).

PURPOSE AND TEACHING

According to the purpose and theme of the book (1:1–7), Proverbs was written to give "prudence to those who are simple, knowledge and discretion to the young" (1:4), and to make the wise even wiser (1:5). The frequent references to "my son(s)" (1:8,10; 2:1; 3:1; 4:1; 5:1) emphasize instructing the young and guiding them in a way of life that yields rewarding ends. Acquiring wisdom and knowing how to avoid the pitfalls of folly lead to personal well-being, happy family relationships, fruitful labors and good standing in the community (see chart, p. 1023). Although Proverbs is a practical book dealing with the art of living, it bases its practical wisdom solidly on the fear of the Lord (1:7; see Ps 34:8–14 and note). Throughout the book reverence for God and reliance on him are set forth as the path to life, prosperity and security (cf. 3:5–10; 9:10–12; 14:26–27; 16:3,6–7; 18:10; 19:23; 20:22; 22:4; 28:25; 29:25). Such godly wisdom is a virtual "tree of life" (3:18; 11:30; 13:12; 15:4) that yields the happy life that God fashioned the creation to produce.

In the initial cycle of instruction (1:8—9:18) the writer urges the young man to choose the way of wisdom (that leads to life) and shun the ways of folly (that, however tempting they may be, lead to death). The author chooses two prime exemplifications of folly to give concreteness to his exhortations: (1) to get ahead in the world by exploiting (even oppressing) others, rather than by diligent and honest labor, and (2) to find sexual pleasure outside the bonds and responsibilities of marriage. Temptation to the one comes from the young man's male peers (1:10-19); temptation to the other comes from the adulterous woman (2:16–19; ch. 5; 6:20–35; ch. 7). Together, these two temptations illustrate the pervasiveness and power of the allurements to folly that the young man will face in life and must be prepared to resist (see also Literary Structure below).

The major collections of proverbs that follow range widely across the broad spectrum of human situations, relationships and responsibilities, offering insights, warnings, instructions and counsel, along with frequent motivations to heed them. The range and variety of these defy summation. However, an illustrative section can convey the general character, moral tone and scope of the collections. In a variety of situations and relationships the reader is exhorted to honesty, integrity, diligence, kindness, generosity, readiness to forgive, truthfulness, patience, humility, cheerfulness, loyalty, temperance, self-control and the prudent consideration of consequences that flow from attitudes, choices and/or actions. Anger is to be held in check, violence and quarrelsomeness shunned, gossip avoided, arrogance repudiated. Drunkenness, gluttony, envy and greed are all to be renounced. The poor are not to be exploited, the courts are not to be unjustly manipulated, legitimate authorities are to be honored. Parents are responsible to care for the proper instruction and discipline of their children, and children are to duly honor their parents and bring no disgrace on them. Human observation and experience have taught the wise that a certain order is in place in God's creation. To honor it leads to known positive effects; to defy it leads only to unhappy consequences. All of life is to be lived in conscious awareness of the unfailing scrutiny of the Lord of creation and in reliance on his generous providence.

Although Proverbs is more practical than theological, God's work as Creator is especially highlighted. The role of wisdom in creation is the subject of 8:22–31 (see notes there), where wisdom as an attribute of God is personified. God is called the Maker of the poor (14:31; 17:5; 22:2). He sovereignly directs the steps of people (cf. 16:9; 20:24)—even the actions of kings (21:1)—and his eyes observe all that humans do (cf. 5:21; 15:3). All history moves forward under his control (see 16:4,33 and notes).

In summary, Proverbs provides instruction on how to live wisely and successfully in the "fear of the Lord" (1:7; 9:10) within the theocratic arrangement. The fear of the Lord includes reverence for, trust in and commitment to the Lord and his will, as disclosed in his creation and as revealed in his word. Wisdom in this context, then, is basically following the benevolent King's design for human happiness within the creation order—resulting in quality of mind (1:2) and quality of life (1:3).

LITERARY STRUCTURE

The sectional headings found in the TNIV text itself divide the book into well-defined units. A short statement of the purpose and theme (1:1–7) opens the book, and a longer epilogue (identifiable by its subject matter and its alphabetic form, 31:10–31) closes it. The first nine chapters contain a series of discourses that contrast the way and benefits of wisdom with the way of the fool. Except for the sections where personified wisdom speaks (1:20; 8:1; 9:1), each discourse begins with "my son" or "my sons."

A key feature in the introductory discourses of Proverbs is the personification of both wisdom and folly as women, each of whom (by appeals and warnings on the part of Lady Wisdom, by enticements on the part of Lady Folly) seeks to persuade "simple" youths to follow her ways. These discourses are strikingly organized. Beginning (1:8–33) and ending (chs. 8–9) with direct enticements and appeals, the main body of the discourses is made up of two nicely balanced sections, one devoted to the commendation of wisdom (chs. 2–4) and the other to warnings against folly (chs. 5–7). In these discourses the young man is depicted as being enticed to folly by men who try to get ahead in the world by exploiting others (1:10–19) and by women who seek sexual pleasure outside the bond of marriage (ch. 5; 6:20–35; ch. 7). In the social structures of that day, these were the two great temptations for young men. The second especially functions here as illustrative and emblematic of the appeal of Lady Folly.

The main collection of Solomon's proverbs in 10:1—22:16 consists of individual couplets, many of which express a contrast. On the surface, there does not seem to be any discernible arrangement, though occasionally two or three proverbs deal with the same subject. For example, 11:24–25 deals with generosity, 16:12–15 mentions kings, and 19:4,6–7 talks about friendship. However, there is growing evidence that arrangements of larger units were deliberate. Further study of this possibility is necessary. The second Solomonic collection (chs. 25–29) continues the pattern of two-line verses, but there are also examples of proverbs with three (25:13; 27:10,22,27) or four (25:4–5,21–22; 26:18–19) lines. The last five verses of ch. 27 (vv. 23–27) present a short discourse on the benefits of raising flocks and herds.

In the "thirty sayings" (22:20) of the wise (22:17—24:22) and the further sayings of 24:23–34, there is a prevalence of two- or three-verse units and something of a return to the style of chs. 1–9 (see especially 23:29–35). These sections have been appended to the preceding and contain some proverbs similar to those included in the foregoing collections (compare 24:6 with 11:14; 24:16 with 11:5). One finds even stronger links with chs. 1–9 (compare 23:27 with 2:16; 24:33–34 with 6:10–11).

At the end of the book the editor(s) has (have) attached three additional pieces, diverse in form and content: the "sayings of Agur," the "sayings of King Lemuel" and a description of "a wife of noble character." The first of these (ch. 30) is dominated by numerical proverbs (30:15,18,21,24,29; see note on 6:16). The second (31:1–9) is devoted exclusively to instruction for kings. The third (31:10–31), effectively an epilogue to the whole, is an impressive acrostic poem honoring the wife of noble character (cf. Ru 3:11 and note). She demonstrates, and thus epitomizes, many of the qualities and values identified with wisdom throughout the book. In view of the fact that Proverbs is primarily addressed to young men on the threshold of mature life, this focus on the ideal wife appears surprising. But its purpose may be twofold: (1) to offer counsel on the kind of wife a young man ought to seek, and (2) in a subtle way to advise the young man (again) to marry Lady Wisdom, thus returning to the theme of chs. 1–9 (as climaxed in ch. 9; compare the description of Lady Wisdom in 9:1–2 with the virtues of the wife in 31:10–31). In any event, the concluding epitomizing of wisdom in the wife of noble character forms a literary frame with the opening discourses, where wisdom is personified as a woman.

THE WISE MAN ACCORDING TO PROVERBS: AN OUTLINE

I. His Character
- A. He Is Teachable, Not Intractable
  - 1. He receives and loves instruction (18:15; 19:20)
  - 2. He grows in wisdom (1:5; 9:9; 10:14)
- B. He Is Righteous, Not Wicked
  - 1. He fears the Lord (1:7; 14:16; see below under relationship to the Lord)
  - 2. He hates what is false (13:5)
  - 3. He shuns evil (3:7; 14:16; 16:6)
  - 4. He does what is righteous (2:20)
  - 5. He speaks the truth (22:21)
- C. He Is Humble, Not Proud (15:33)
- D. He Is Self-controlled, Not Rash
  - 1. His temperament
    - a. He is self-controlled (29:11)
    - b. He has a calm spirit (17:27)
    - c. He is slow to become angry (29:8,11)
  - 2. His actions
    - a. He is cautious, not hasty (19:2)
    - b. He thinks before he acts (13:16; 14:8)
    - c. He thinks before he speaks (12:23; 15:2)
- E. He Is Forgiving, Not Vindictive
  - 1. He is patient (19:11)
  - 2. He is concerned about goodwill/peace (14:9)
  - 3. He forgives those who wrong him (10:12; 17:9)
  - 4. He is not vindictive (20:22; 24:29)

II. His Relationships
- A. To the Lord
  - 1. He fears the Lord (9:10; 14:16; 15:33)
  - 2. He trusts in the Lord (3:5; 16:3,20)
  - 3. He is ever mindful of the Lord (3:6)
  - 4. He chooses the Lord's way/wisdom (8:10–11; 17:24)
  - 5. He submits to the Lord's discipline (1:2–3; 3:11)
  - 6. He confesses his sin (28:13)
- B. To His Family
  - 1. To his parents
    - a. Respects them (17:6; contrast 30:17)
    - b. Listens to them (23:22; cf. 1:8; 4:1)
    - c. Seeks to bring them honor and joy
      - 1) By being wise (10:1; 15:20; 29:3)
      - 2) By being righteous (23:24)
      - 3) By being diligent (10:5)
  - 2. To his wife
    - a. He appreciates her
      - 1) As a gift from the Lord (18:22; 19:14)
      - 2) As his crowning glory (12:4; 31:10–31)
    - b. He praises her (31:28)
    - c. He trusts her (31:11)
    - d. He is faithful to her (5:15–20)
  - 3. To his children
    - a. He loves them (3:12; 13:24)
    - b. He is concerned about them (1:8—9:18)
    - c. He trains them (22:6)
      - 1) Reasons for training them
        - a) Own peace of mind and joy (29:17)
        - b) Child's honor and well-being (1:8–9; 4:9; 19:18; 23:13–14)
      - 2) By teaching/instructing them (1:10; chs. 5–7; 28:7; cf. 4:1–9)
      - 3) By disciplining them
        - a) By verbal correction (13:1)
        - b) By physical discipline (13:24; 23:13–14)
    - d. He provides for their
      - 1) Physical needs (21:20; cf. 27:23–27)
      - 2) Spiritual heritage (14:26; 20:7)
- C. To His Friends and Neighbors
  - 1. To his friends
    - a. He values them (27:10)
    - b. He is constant to them (17:17; 18:24)
    - c. He gives them counsel (27:9,17; cf. 27:6; 28:23)
  - 2. To his neighbors
    - a. He fulfills his obligations (3:27–28)
    - b. He strives for peace (3:29–30)
    - c. He does not outstay his welcome (25:17)
    - d. He does not deceive or mislead them (16:29; 26:18–19)

III. His Words
- A. The Power of His Words
  - 1. Their power
    - a. The power of life and death (12:6; 13:14; 15:4; 18:21)
    - b. The power to heal or to wound (11:9,11; 12:18; 15:4,30; 16:24)
  - 2. Their limitation
    - a. No substitute for deeds (14:23)
    - b. Cannot alter the facts (26:23–26)
    - c. Cannot compel response (29:19)
- B. The Character of His Words
  - 1. They are honest, not false (12:22; 16:13)
  - 2. They are few, not many (10:19)
    - a. Not boastful (27:2)
    - b. Not argumentative (17:14)
    - c. Not contentious (29:9)
    - d. Not a gossip
      - 1) Revealing secrets (11:13; 20:19)
      - 2) Spreading slander (10:18; 26:20–22)
  - 3. They are calm, not emotional
    - a. Rational (15:28; 17:27)
    - b. Gentle and peaceable (15:1,18)
    - c. Yet persuasive (25:15)
  - 4. They are apt, not untimely (15:23; 25:11)
- C. The Source of His Words
  - 1. His heart/character (compare 4:23 with Mt 12:33–35)
    - a. Positively, he is righteous (cf. 10:11; 13:14)
    - b. Negatively, he is not
      - 1) Proud (13:10; cf. 6:16–19)
      - 2) Hateful (26:24,28)
  - 2. His companions (13:20; 27:17)
  - 3. Reflections (15:28)

1:1 *a* Mt 13:3
b 1Ki 4:29-34
c Pr 10:1; 25:1; Ecc 1:1
1:4 *d* Pr 8:5 *e* Pr 8:12
1:5 *f* Pr 9:9
1:6 *g* Ps 49:4;
Mt 13:10-17
h S Nu 12:8;
S Jdg 14:12 *i* Pr 22:17;
24:23
1:7 *j* S Ex 20:20;
S Job 23:15; Ps 34:4-
22; S 112:1; Pr 9:10;
15:33; Isa 33:6; 50:10;
59:19 *k* S Dt 4:6;
Jer 8:9 *l* Pr 8:33-36;
9:7-9; 12:1; 13:18;
15:32
1:8 *m* ver 8-9; Pr 2:1;
3:1; 4:1; 5:1; 6:1; 7:1;
19:27; 22:17; 23:26-
28 *n* Jer 35:8
o S Dt 21:18; Pr 6:20
1:9 *p* Pr 3:21-22;
4:1-9
1:10 *q* S Job 24:15
r Dt 13:8 *s* ver 15;
Ps 1:1; Pr 16:29
1:11 *t* S Ps 10:8
1:12 *u* S Ps 35:25
v ver 16-18;
S Job 33:18; S Ps 30:3

PURPOSE AND THEME

1

The proverbs *a* of Solomon *b* son of David, king of Israel: *c*

2 for gaining wisdom and instruction;
    for understanding words of insight;
3 for receiving instruction in prudent behavior,
    doing what is right and just and fair;
4 for giving prudence to those who are simple, *a d*
    knowledge and discretion *e* to the young—
5 let the wise listen and add to their learning, *f*
    and let the discerning get guidance—
6 for understanding proverbs and parables, *g*
    the sayings and riddles *h* of the wise. *b i*

7 The fear of the LORD *j* is the beginning of knowledge,
    but fools *c* despise wisdom *k* and instruction. *l*

PROLOGUE: EXHORTATIONS TO EMBRACE WISDOM

WARNING AGAINST THE INVITATION OF SINFUL MEN

8 Listen, my son, *m* to your father's *n* instruction
    and do not forsake your mother's teaching. *o*
9 They are a garland to grace your head
    and a chain to adorn your neck. *p*

10 My son, if sinful men entice *q* you,
    do not give in *r* to them. *s*
11 If they say, "Come along with us;
    let's lie in wait *t* for innocent blood,
    let's ambush some harmless soul;
12 let's swallow *u* them alive, like the grave,
    and whole, like those who go down to the pit; *v*
13 we will get all sorts of valuable things

a 4 The Hebrew word rendered *simple* in Proverbs denotes a person who is gullible, without moral direction and inclined to evil.   *b 6* Or *understanding a proverb, namely, a parable, / and the sayings of the wise, their riddles*   *c 7* The Hebrew words rendered *fool* in Proverbs, and often elsewhere in the Old Testament, denote a person who is morally deficient.

1:1 *Solomon*. His wisdom and prolific production of proverbs and songs are mentioned in 1Ki 4:29–34 (see notes there). His name occurs again in the headings of 10:1 and 25:1. Cf. SS 1:1. **1:2–4** Verses 2–3 apply to the son (or student); v. 4 refers to the father (or teacher).

▲ ◪ **1:2** *wisdom and instruction*. The two primary virtues in the long list that articulates the purpose of the book (vv. 2–6). Repeated at the end of v. 7, the phrase thus frames the entire prologue (vv. 2–7). *wisdom*. This key term occurs more than 40 times in the book. It includes skill in living— following God's design and thus avoiding moral pitfalls. A craftsman can be called a wise (skillful) man (Ex 31:3). Proverbs urges people to get wisdom (4:5; cf. Jas 1:5 and note), for it is worth more than silver or gold (3:13–14). The NT refers to Christ as "wisdom from God" (1Co 1:30; cf. Col 2:3).
1:3 *right and just and fair*. See 2:9; Ps 119:121 and note; Php 4:8.
1:4 *prudence*. Good judgment or good sense (see 15:5; 19:25). Outside Proverbs the Hebrew word is used in the negative sense of "crafty" (Ge 3:1; Job 5:13). *simple*. Another key word in Proverbs, occurring about 15 times. It denotes those who are easily persuaded and who "have no sense" (9:4,16), who are immature, inexperienced and naive (cf. Ps 19:7 and note). See TNIV text note on 1:4.
1:6 *riddles*. The Hebrew for this word can sometimes refer to allegories (cf. Eze 17:2).

▲ ◪ **1:7** The theme of the book (see 9:10; 31:30; cf. Job 28:28; Ps 111:10 and note). *fear of the LORD*. A loving reverence for God that includes submission to his lordship and to the commands of his word (see Ecc 12:13 and note; see also Intro-

duction: Purpose and Teaching). See note on Ge 20:11. *fools*. See TNIV text note. "Fools" are those who "hate knowledge" (v. 22) and correction of any kind (12:1), who are "quick to quarrel" (20:3) and "give full vent" to their anger (29:11), who are complacent (1:32) and who trust in themselves (28:26) rather than in God (Ps 14:1). *despise wisdom and instruction*. See 1:2; 5:12 and notes.
1:8 A typical introduction to an instruction speech in Proverbs, evoking a domestic situation of a father preparing his son for life in the world. Here and in 6:20 the mother is also depicted as teacher.

◪ **1:9** *to grace … to adorn*. See 6:21. Those who follow wisdom add beauty and honor to their lives.
1:10 *entice*. The Hebrew word is related to the Hebrew noun translated "simple" (see v. 4 and note). One who is "simple" is easily enticed. See Ps 19:7 and note.

▲ **1:11** *Come along*. But the father wisely advises, "Come, do not go along" (v. 15). Cf. Lady Wisdom's appeal in 9:4–6. *lie in wait for … blood*. Their goal is personal enrichment by theft or oppression (vv. 13,19), even if they have to commit murder. The author uses two major enticements that confronted the young man (in that culture) as examples of the way of folly: (1) to get rich by exploiting others (here) and (2) to be drawn into illicit sexual pleasure by immoral women who fail to honor their marriage vows (5:1–6; 6:24; 7:5; cf. 2:12–19).
1:12 *swallow … like the grave*. Vivid poetic imagery for shamelessly victimizing others (cf. Ps 49:14 and note).

▲ **1:13** *valuable things*. By contrast, the book of Proverbs teaches that wisdom brings the greatest riches people could ever gain (3:13–16; 16:16; see also Job 28:12–19).

and fill our houses with plunder;
¹⁴ cast lots with us;
we will all share the loot ʷ"—
¹⁵ my son, do not go along with them,
do not set foot ˣ on their paths; ʸ
¹⁶ for their feet rush into evil, ᶻ
they are swift to shed blood. ᵃ
¹⁷ How useless to spread a net
where every bird can see it!
¹⁸ These men lie in wait ᵇ for their own blood;
they ambush only themselves! ᶜ
¹⁹ Such are the paths of all who go after ill-gotten gain;
it takes away the life of those who get it. ᵈ

WISDOM'S REBUKE

²⁰ Out in the open wisdom calls aloud, ᵉ
she raises her voice in the public square;
²¹ on top of the wall ᵃ she cries out,
at the city gate she makes her speech:

²² "How long will you who are simple ᶠ love your simple ways?
How long will mockers delight in mockery
and fools hate ᵍ knowledge?
²³ Repent at my rebuke!
Then I will pour out my thoughts to you,
I will make known to you my teachings.
²⁴ But since you refuse ʰ to listen when I call ⁱ
and no one pays attention ʲ when I stretch out my hand,
²⁵ since you disregard all my advice
and do not accept my rebuke,
²⁶ I in turn will laugh ᵏ when disaster ˡ strikes you;
I will mock ᵐ when calamity overtakes you ⁿ—
²⁷ when calamity overtakes you like a storm,
when disaster ᵒ sweeps over you like a whirlwind,
when distress and trouble overwhelm you.

ᵃ 21 Septuagint; Hebrew / *at noisy street corners*

1:14 ʷ ver 19
1:15 ˣ S Ps 119:101
ʸ S Ge 49:6; Pr 4:14
1:16 ᶻ S Job 15:31
ᵃ Pr 6:18; Isa 59:7
1:18 ᵇ S Ps 71:10
ᶜ S ver 11-12
1:19 ᵈ S ver 13-14;
Pr 4:14-17; 11:19
1:20 ᵉ S Job 28:12;
Pr 7:10-13; 9:1-3, 13-
15
1:22 ᶠ Pr 6:32; 7:7;
8:5; 9:4,16 ᵍ Ps 50:17
1:24 ʰ Jer 26:5;
35:17; 36:31
ⁱ Isa 65:12; 66:4;
Jer 7:13 / S 1Sa 8:19
1:26 ᵏ S Ps 2:4
ˡ ver 33; S Ps 59:8
ᵐ S 2Ki 19:21
ⁿ Dt 28:63
1:27 ᵒ S Ps 18:18;
Pr 5:12-14

1:15 *paths.* Cf. the destructive paths of the adulteress in 2:18 (see note there); 7:25.
1:16 The same as the first two lines of Isa 59:7 and partially quoted in Ro 3:15. Cf. Pr 6:17–18.
1:17 *net.* Nets were used to catch birds and animals (see 6:5; 7:23; Ecc 9:12; Isa 51:20; Jer 5:26).
1:18 *ambush only themselves.* See v. 11. The wicked unintentionally spread a net for their own feet (29:6; Ps 35:8), so they are less intelligent than birds (see 7:22–23).
1:19 According to Isa 17:14, destruction is the fate of those who plunder God's people. Contrast the long life enjoyed by the one who "hates ill-gotten gain" (28:16).
1:20 *wisdom calls aloud.* Personified wisdom also calls out to the simple in 8:1–5; 9:4–6 (see note on 8:1–36). *public square.* Open area inside the gate of a fortified city (see 8:3).
1:21 *city gate.* Where the leaders of the city met to hold court (see 31:23; see also Ge 19:1; Ru 4:1; Job 29:7 and notes) and where the marketplace was located (2Ki 7:1). As a young man confronts life in its social context, two voices lure him, appeal for his allegiance and seek to shape his life: (1) the voice of wisdom (as exemplified in the instructions of the teachers of wisdom) and (2) the voice of folly (as exemplified in the sinners of vv. 10–19 and in the adulteress of 5:3; 6:24; 7:5). Thus in the midst of life the youth must learn to exercise discretion. Here and in chs. 8–9 wisdom makes her appeal. She speaks neither out of heaven (by special revelation, as do the prophets) nor out of the earth (through voices from the dead—necromancy; see Lev 19:31; Dt 18:11; 1Sa 28:7–19), but out of the center of the life of the city,

where communal experience of the creation order (established by God's wisdom, 8:22–31) is concentrated (see, e.g., 11:10 and note). And it is there also that the godly, the truly wise, test human experience in the crucible of faith and afterward give divine wisdom a human voice in their wise instructions—as in Proverbs.
1:22 *mockers.* Those who are "proud and arrogant" (21:24); who are full of insults, hatred and strife (9:7–8; 22:10; 29:8); who resist correction (13:1; 15:12) even though they deserve flogging (19:25; 21:11).
1:23 *pour out my thoughts.* Wisdom is like a fountain. Her words constantly refresh and strengthen (see 18:4 and note).
1:24 *refuse to listen.* As Israel rejected the Lord (see Isa 1:4; 5:24; Hos 2:13; 11:2), who brought forth wisdom "as the first of his works" (8:22), and as the people of Jerusalem rejected Jesus (see Mt 23:37), the embodiment and supreme manifestation of God's wisdom (see Jn 1:1–14; 1Co 1:24; Col 1:15–17; 2:3; Heb 1:1–4 and notes). *stretch out my hand.* Cf. Isa 65:2, where God held out his hands all day long to "an obstinate people."
1:25 *disregard ... advice.* Cf. 8:33.
1:26 *laugh when disaster strikes you.* Not an expression of heartlessness but a reaction to the absurdity of fools, who laugh at wisdom, choose folly and bring disaster on themselves. Cf. the Lord's response to kings who think they can rebel against him (Ps 2:4). *calamity overtakes you.* Also the fate of "troublemakers and villains" (6:12–15).
1:27 *like a storm.* See 10:25 and note. *distress and trouble.* See Isa 8:22.

1:28 *p* S Dt 1:45;
S 1Sa 8:18; S Jer 11:11
q S Job 27:9; Pr 8:17;
Eze 8:18; Hos 5:6;
Zec 7:13
1:29 *r* S Job 21:14
1:30 *s* ver 25
1:31 *t* S 2Ch 36:16;
Pr 14:14; Jer 6:19;
14:16; 21:14; 30:15
1:32 *u* Pr 5:22;
15:10; Isa 66:4
1:33 *v* S Nu 24:21;
S Dt 33:28; Pr 3:23
w S ver 21-26;
S Ps 112:8
2:1 *x* S Pr 1:8
2:2 *y* Pr 22:17; 23:12
2:3 *z* Jas 1:5
2:4 *a* S Job 3:21;
Mt 13:44
2:5 *b* S Dt 4:6
2:6 *c* S Job 12:13;
S Ps 119:34
d S Job 9:4; S 22:22
2:7 *e* S Ge 15:1;
Pr 30:5-6 *f* S Ge 6:9;
Ps 84:11
2:8 *g* 1Sa 2:9;
S Ps 18:25; S 97:10
2:9 *h* S Dt 1:16
2:10 *i* Pr 14:33
2:11 *j* Pr 4:6
2:12 *k* ver 16;
Pr 3:13-18; 4:5
2:13 *l* Pr 4:19

28 "Then they will call to me but I will not answer; *p*
  they will look for me but will not find me, *q*
29 since they hated knowledge
  and did not choose to fear the LORD. *r*
30 Since they would not accept my advice
  and spurned my rebuke, *s*
31 they will eat the fruit of their ways
  and be filled with the fruit of their schemes. *t*
32 For the waywardness of the simple will kill them,
  and the complacency of fools will destroy them; *u*
33 but whoever listens to me will live in safety *v*
  and be at ease, without fear of harm." *w*

MORAL BENEFITS OF WISDOM

2 My son, *x* if you accept my words
  and store up my commands within you,
2 turning your ear to wisdom
  and applying your heart to understanding *y*—
3 indeed, if you call out for insight *z*
  and cry aloud for understanding,
4 and if you look for it as for silver
  and search for it as for hidden treasure, *a*
5 then you will understand the fear of the LORD
  and find the knowledge of God. *b*
6 For the LORD gives wisdom; *c*
  from his mouth come knowledge and understanding. *d*
7 He holds success in store for the upright,
  he is a shield *e* to those whose walk is blameless, *f*
8 for he guards the course of the just
  and protects the way of his faithful ones. *g*

9 Then you will understand *h* what is right and just
  and fair—every good path.
10 For wisdom will enter your heart, *i*
  and knowledge will be pleasant to your soul.
11 Discretion will protect you,
  and understanding will guard you. *j*

12 Wisdom will save *k* you from the ways of wicked men,
  from men whose words are perverse,
13 who have left the straight paths
  to walk in dark ways, *l*

1:28 *I will not answer.* Just as God refused to listen to Israel when the people sinned (see Dt 1:45; Isa 1:15 and note). *find me.* Those who find wisdom find life and blessing (see v. 33; 3:13; 8:17,35).
1:29 *fear the LORD.* See v. 7 and note.

A **1:31** *eat . . . be filled with the fruit.* The consequences depend on their actions (see 12:14 and note; 18:20; 31:31; Isa 3:10). People reap what they sow (Gal 6:7). *schemes.* To refuse wisdom's "advice" (v. 30) is to suffer the consequences of one's own foolish "schemes" (the Hebrew for "advice" and "schemes" is the same).

1:32 *complacency.* A false sense of security (see Isa 32:9; Am 6:1 and notes; Zep 1:12).
1:33 *in safety . . . at ease.* Words used of places that enjoy God's protection (see Isa 32:18; Eze 34:27).

A **2:1** *store up . . . within you.* Just as the psalmist hid God's word in his heart to avoid sin (Ps 119:11).

2:2 *turning your ear.* Listening implies attentiveness and obedience (Isa 55:3; Jer 13:15). *heart.* See note on Ps 4:7.
2:4 *silver . . . hidden treasure.* Job 28:1–11 describes ancient mining techniques, comparing mining with the search for wisdom (see Job 28:12,20).

A **2:5** *fear of the LORD.* See note on 1:7. *knowledge of God.* Involves having a personal relationship with God (cf. Php

3:10 and note) and knowing what he is teaching us (v. 6).
2:7 *holds . . . in store.* For those who "store up" his commands (v. 1). *shield.* Associated with victory also in Ps 18:2,35; cf. Pr 30:5. See Ps 3:3 and note. *blameless.* Having spiritual and moral integrity. This does not imply sinlessness (see 19:1). See v. 21; see also Ps 15:2 and note.
2:8 *guards . . . protects.* See Ps 91:3–7,11–12.

A **2:9–11** Those who know the Lord and the wisdom he gives will know what course of action to follow (cf. Heb 5:11–14).

2:9 *right and just and fair.* See 1:3 and note. *good path.* Cf. "right paths" in Ps 23:3 (and see note there).
2:10 *pleasant to your soul.* Just as the words of the wise are "sweet to the soul" of another (see 16:24 and note; cf. 3:17).
2:11 *protect . . . guard.* As God guards the faithful (v. 8).

A **2:12–19** Wisdom will save from the enticements of men to follow perverse ways (vv. 12–15) and from the "seductive words" of the adulteress (vv. 16–19). See note on 1:11.

2:12 *words are perverse.* Cf. v. 14. The deceitfulness of human speech is also mentioned in 6:12,17; 8:13; 10:31–32; 17:20; 19:28.

A **2:13** *straight paths.* See 3:6 and note. *dark ways.* People love darkness instead of light (see Jn 3:19–21; see also Job 24:14–17; Isa 29:15; Ro 13:12).

¹⁴ who delight in doing wrong
    and rejoice in the perverseness of evil, ^m
¹⁵ whose paths are crooked ⁿ
    and who are devious in their ways. ^o

¹⁶ Wisdom will save you also from the adulterous woman, ^p
    from the wayward woman with her seductive words,
¹⁷ who has left the partner of her youth
    and ignored the covenant she made before God. ^{a q}
¹⁸ Surely her house leads down to death
    and her paths to the spirits of the dead. ^r
¹⁹ None who go to her return
    or attain the paths of life. ^s

²⁰ Thus you will walk in the ways of the just
    and keep to the paths of the righteous.
²¹ For the upright will live in the land, ^t
    and the blameless will remain in it;
²² but the wicked ^u will be cut off from the land, ^v
    and the unfaithful will be torn from it. ^w

WISDOM BESTOWS WELL-BEING

My son, ^x do not forget my teaching, ^y
    but keep my commands in your heart,
² for they will prolong your life many years ^z
    and bring you peace and prosperity. ^a

³ Let love and faithfulness ^b never leave you;
    bind them around your neck,
    write them on the tablet of your heart. ^c
⁴ Then you will win favor and a good name
    in the sight of God and humankind. ^d

⁵ Trust in the LORD ^e with all your heart
    and lean not on your own understanding;
⁶ in all your ways submit to him,
    and he will make your paths ^f straight. ^{b g}

---

^a 17 Or *covenant of her God*   ^b 6 Or *will direct your paths*

### Cross-references (right margin)

2:14 ^m Pr 10:23; 15:21
2:15 ⁿ S Ps 125:5 ^o Pr 21:8
2:16 ^p Pr 5:1-6; 6:20-29; 7:5-27
2:17 ^q Mal 2:14
2:18 ^r Pr 5:5; 7:27; 9:18
2:19 ^s Pr 3:16-18; 5:8; Ecc 7:26
2:21 ^t S Ps 37:29
2:22 ^u S Ps 5:4
^v S Job 18:17
^w Dt 28:63; S 29:28; Ps 37:9,28-29; Pr 10:30
3:1 ^x S Pr 1:8
^y S Ps 44:17
3:2 ^z S Dt 11:21
^a S Dt 5:16; S 30:15, 16; S 1Ki 3:13,14; Pr 9:6,10-11
3:3 ^b S Ps 85:10
^c S Ex 13:9; S Dt 6:6; Pr 6:21; 7:3; S 2Co 3:3
3:4 ^d S 1Sa 2:26; Lk 2:52
3:5 ^e S Ps 4:5
3:6 ^f S Job 33:11; S Isa 30:11 ^g Ps 5:8; Pr 16:3; Isa 40:3; Jer 42:3

2:14 *delight ... rejoice in ... evil.* Like the sinners of 1:10–19.

2:15 *paths are crooked.* See Isa 59:7–8.

2:16 *adulterous woman ... wayward woman.* The Hebrew for these terms occurs again in 5:20 and 7:5. The terms mean lit. "stranger" and "foreigner" (cf. 5:10) because anyone other than one's own wife was to be considered off limits, like a foreigner who worshiped another god (cf. 1Ki 11:1–2). "Wayward woman/wife" is parallel to "neighbor's wife" in 6:24 and "adulterous woman" in 23:27. *seductive words.* Equal to the "smooth talk" of 6:24; 7:21. Cf. 5:3 and note.

2:17 *partner of her youth.* Her husband, whom she married when she was a young woman (cf. Isa 54:6). *covenant ... before God.* Probably the marriage covenant, spoken in God's presence (see Eze 16:8; Mal 2:14). Alternatively, the breaking of the seventh commandment (Ex 20:14) may be indicated (see TNIV text note).

2:18 *leads down to death.* According to 7:27, "Her house is a highway to the grave." A life of immorality leads to the destruction and death of all who are involved (cf. 5:5; 9:18). *spirits of the dead.* See Job 26:5 and note. The deceased are in the grave (or Sheol), "the chambers of death" (7:27).

2:21 *live in the land.* Abraham's descendants had been promised the land of Canaan (Ge 12:7; 17:8; Dt 4:1), and Ps 37:29 says, "The righteous will inherit the land" (see Ps 37:9,11; Mt 5:5). *blameless.* See note on v. 7.

2:22 *cut off from the land ... torn from it.* In Dt 28:63 God warned that if the people refuse to obey him, they "will be uprooted from the land." The wicked and their offspring will be cut off (Ps 37:9,28).

3:2 *prolong your life.* Fear of the Lord (19:23) brings health to the body (v. 8) and "adds length to life" (10:27; see also 9:10–11). *prosperity.* When Solomon prayed for wisdom (1Ki 3:9), God promised him riches as well as long life if he obeyed God's commands (1Ki 3:13–14). Normally the righteous are prosperous and happy (12:21), but sometimes it is the wicked who are strong and prosperous (Ps 73:3,12), temporary though that may be (Ps 37:10,20,35–36; 73:17–19). Job 1–2 also shows how disaster and death can strike a godly person (see note on vv. 11–12).

3:3 *love and faithfulness.* See Ps 26:3 and note. *bind ... neck.* Like a beautiful necklace (cf. v. 22; 1:9; 3:22). *write them on the tablet of your heart.* See 7:3; cf. Jer 31:33 and note. These instructions are not to be taken literally (see Ex 13:9; Dt 6:8–9 and notes).

3:4 *favor.* See 8:35; 12:2; Ge 6:8. *God and humankind.* See 1Sa 2:26; Lk 2:52; Ro 12:17 and note; 2Co 8:21.

3:5 *Trust in the LORD.* "Commit your way to the LORD" (Ps 37:5), like Israel's ancestors, who trusted in God and were rescued (Ps 22:4–5). *with all your heart.* Like Caleb (Nu 14:24; Dt 1:36; Jos 14:6–14) or the godly King Hezekiah (Isa 38:3). David challenged Solomon to serve God "with whole-hearted devotion" (1Ch 28:9).

3:6 *submit to him.* Be ever mindful of God and serve him with a willing, faithful and obedient heart (see 1Ch 28:9; Hos 4:1; 6:3,6). *make your paths straight.* He will remove the obstacles from your pathway and bring you to your appointed goal (see 11:5; Isa 45:13).

3:7 ʰ Pr 26:5,12;
Isa 5:21 / Ps 111:10
ʲ S Ex 20:20; S Dt 4:6;
S Job 1:1
3:8 ᵏ S Ps 38:3;
Pr 4:22 ˡ Job 21:24
3:9 ᵐ S Ex 22:29;
Dt 26:1-15
3:10 ⁿ Ps 144:13
ᵒ S Job 22:21;
Joel 2:24; Mal 3:10-12
3:11 ᵖ Pr 1:8-9
�q S Job 5:17
3:12 ʳ Pr 13:24;
Rev 3:19 ˢ S Dt 8:5;
S Job 5:17; Heb 12:5-
6*
3:14 ᵗ S Job 28:15;
Pr 8:19; 16:16
3:15 ᵘ S Job 28:18
ᵛ S Job 28:17-19
3:16 ʷ S Ge 15:15
ˣ S 1Ki 3:13,14
3:17 ʸ Mt 11:28-30
3:18 ᶻ S Ge 2:9;
S Pr 10:11; S Rev 2:7
ᵃ S Pr 2:12; 4:3-9,8;
8:17-21
3:19 ᵇ S Ge 1:31;
Ps 136:5-9
ᶜ S Job 28:25-27
ᵈ Pr 8:27-29
3:21 ᵉ Pr 1:8-9; 6:20
ᶠ Pr 4:20-22
3:22 ᵍ S Dt 30:20;
Pr 4:13 ʰ S Pr 1:8-9
3:23 ʲ S Pr 1:33
ʲ S Ps 37:24; S 119:11;
Pr 4:12

⁷ Do not be wise in your own eyes; ʰ
  fear the Lord ʲ and shun evil. ʲ
⁸ This will bring health to your body ᵏ
  and nourishment to your bones. ˡ

⁹ Honor the Lord with your wealth,
  with the firstfruits ᵐ of all your crops;
¹⁰ then your barns will be filled ⁿ to overflowing,
  and your vats will brim over with new wine. ᵒ

¹¹ My son, ᵖ do not despise the Lord's discipline, q
  and do not resent his rebuke,
¹² because the Lord disciplines those he loves, ʳ
  as a father the son he delights in. ᵃ ˢ

¹³ Blessed are those who find wisdom,
  those who gain understanding,
¹⁴ for she is more profitable than silver
  and yields better returns than gold. ᵗ
¹⁵ She is more precious than rubies; ᵘ
  nothing you desire can compare with her. ᵛ
¹⁶ Long life is in her right hand; ʷ
  in her left hand are riches and honor. ˣ
¹⁷ Her ways are pleasant ways,
  and all her paths are peace. ʸ
¹⁸ She is a tree of life ᶻ to those who take hold of her;
  those who hold her fast will be blessed. ᵃ

¹⁹ By wisdom ᵇ the Lord laid the earth's foundations, ᶜ
  by understanding he set the heavens ᵈ in place;
²⁰ by his knowledge the deeps were divided,
  and the clouds let drop the dew.

²¹ My son, ᵉ do not let wisdom and understanding out of your sight, ᶠ
  preserve sound judgment and discretion;
²² they will be life for you, ᵍ
  an ornament to grace your neck. ʰ
²³ Then you will go on your way in safety, ʲ
  and your foot will not stumble. ʲ

ᵃ 12 Hebrew; Septuagint / *and he chastens everyone he accepts as his child*

3:7 *fear the Lord and shun evil.* Cf. Job, who was "blameless and upright" (Job 1:1). See note on 1:7.
3:8 *bones.* The whole body. Elsewhere, good news and pleasant words bring health to the bones (15:30; 16:24; cf. 12:4; 14:30; 17:22).
3:9 *firstfruits.* The Israelites were required to give to the priests the first part of the olive oil, wine and grain produced each year (see Lev 23:10; Nu 18:12-13).
3:10 *filled to overflowing.* For those who bring to the Lord his tithes and offerings, God promises to pour out more blessing than they have room for (see Mal 3:10; see also Dt 28:8,12; 2Co 9:6-11). *vats.* See note on Hag 2:16.
3:11-12 A warning that the righteous are not always prosperous (see v. 2 and note). Through times of testing and affliction, God is teaching them (see 12:1; Ps 119:71). Heb 12:5-6 quotes both of these verses to encourage believers to endure hardship (Heb 12:7). "God disciplines us for our good" (Heb 12:10).
3:12 *as a father.* God disciplined his son Israel by testing the nation in the desert 40 years (Dt 8:2-5).
3:13-18 A poem praising wisdom that begins and ends with the word "blessed" (cf. Job 5:17).
3:14 *more profitable than silver . . . gold.* The psalmist makes the same claim for the commands and precepts of the Lord (Ps 19:10; 119:72,127).
3:15-18 Wisdom is personified.
3:15 *rubies.* See 8:11; 20:15. Although rubies were the most

priceless jewels in the ancient world, they are considered of less value than wisdom also in Job 28:18. The "wife of noble character" is "worth far more than rubies" (31:10; see note on 31:10-31).
3:16 *Long life.* See note on v. 2. *riches and honor.* See 8:18; 22:4.
3:17 *peace.* Hebrew *shalom,* translated "peace and prosperity" in v. 2 (see 16:7; Ps 119:165).
3:18 *tree of life.* Source of life. This figure of speech (see also 11:30; 13:12; 15:4) may recall the tree in the Garden of Eden (see Ge 2:9 and note; see also Introduction: Purpose and Teaching).
3:19-20 The role of wisdom in creation is described more fully in 8:22-31 (see notes there). Divine wisdom guided the Creator and now permeates the whole creation. To live by wisdom is to imitate the Lord and conform to the divinely appointed creation order.
3:19 *earth's foundations.* See 8:29. God's work in creation is compared to the construction of a building (see 1Ki 5:17; 6:37; see also Job 38:4-6; Ps 24:2 and note; 104:5; Zec 12:1). *set the heavens in place.* See Isa 42:5; 48:13 and note; 51:16.
3:20 *divided.* Or "broken open." God opened up springs and streams (see Ge 7:11; 49:25; Ps 74:15). Alternatively, though perhaps less likely, reference is to the dividing of the waters above from the waters below (see Ge 1:7; Ps 42:7 and note). *dew.* Probably also includes rain (see Dt 33:13; 2Sa 1:21).
3:22 *ornament to grace your neck.* Like a beautiful necklace (see v. 3 and note).
3:23 *in safety, and your foot will not stumble.* See v. 26; cf. 10:9.

²⁴ When you lie down,ᵏ you will not be afraid;ˡ
    when you lie down, your sleep ᵐ will be sweet.
²⁵ Have no fear of sudden disaster
    or of the ruin that overtakes the wicked,
²⁶ for the LORD will be at your side ⁿ
    and will keep your foot ᵒ from being snared. ᵖ

²⁷ Do not withhold good from those to whom it is due,
    when it is in your power to act.
²⁸ Do not say to your neighbor,
    "Come back tomorrow and I'll give it to you"—
    when you already have it with you. ۹
²⁹ Do not plot harm against your neighbor,
    who lives trustfully near you. ʳ
³⁰ Do not accuse anyone for no reason—
    when they have done you no harm.

³¹ Do not envyˢ the violent
    or choose any of their ways.
³² For the LORD detests the perverseᵗ
    but takes the upright into his confidence. ᵘ
³³ The LORD's curseᵛ is on the house of the wicked,ʷ
    but he blesses the home of the righteous. ˣ
³⁴ He mocksʸ proud mockersᶻ
    but shows favor to the humbleᵃ and oppressed.
³⁵ The wise inherit honor,
    but fools get only shame.

GET WISDOM AT ANY COST

4 Listen, my sons,ᵇ to a father's instruction;ᶜ
    pay attention and gain understanding. ᵈ
² I give you sound learning,
    so do not forsake my teaching.
³ For I too was a son to my father,
    still tender, and cherished by my mother.
⁴ Then he taught me, and he said to me,
    "Take holdᵉ of my words with all your heart;
    keep my commands, and you will live. ᶠ
⁵ Get wisdom,ᵍ get understanding;
    do not forget my words or turn away from them.
⁶ Do not forsake wisdom, and she will protect you;ʰ
    love her, and she will watch over you. ⁱ
⁷ The beginning of wisdom is this: Getᵃ wisdom.
    Though it cost allʲ you have,ᵇ get understanding. ᵏ

ᵃ 7 Or *Wisdom is supreme; therefore get*   ᵇ 7 Or *Whatever else you get*

3:24 S Lev 26:6
ˡ Ps 91:5; 112:8
ᵐ S Job 11:18;
Jer 31:26
3:26 ⁿ S 2Ki 18:5;
S Job 4:6 ᵒ S 1Sa 2:9
ᵖ S Job 5:19
3:28 ۹ Lev 19:13;
Dt 24:15; Lk 10:25-37
3:29 ʳ Zec 8:17
3:31 ˢ S Ps 37:1;
Pr 24:1-2
3:32 ᵗ S Ps 101:4
ᵘ S Job 29:4
3:33 ᵛ S Job 5:3
ʷ Zec 5:4 ˣ Ps 37:22;
Pr 14:11
3:34 ʸ S 2Ki 19:21
ᶻ S Ps 40:4
ᵃ S Ps 18:25-27;
S Mt 23:12; Jas 4:6*;
1Pe 5:5*
4:1 ᵇ S Pr 1:8
ᶜ Pr 19:20 ᵈ S Job 8:10
4:4 ᵉ S 1Ki 9:4
ᶠ Pr 7:2
4:5 ᵍ S Pr 2:12; 3:13-18
4:6 ʰ 2Th 2:10
ⁱ S Pr 2:11
4:7 ʲ Mt 13:44-46
ᵏ Pr 23:23

3:24 *When you lie down, you will not be afraid.* Also listed among the covenant blessings (see Lev 26:6; Job 11:18–19; Mic 4:4; Zep 3:13; see also Pr 1:33). *your sleep will be sweet.* See 6:22; Ps 4:8.
3:25 *disaster…ruin.* The Lord shields the godly from deadly arrows and plagues (see 10:25; Ps 91:3–8; Job 5:21).
3:26 *will keep your foot from being snared.* Contrast the fate of the fool in 1:18; 7:22–23.
3:27 *withhold good.* See Ac 9:36; Gal 6:10; 1Jn 3:17–18. *those to whom it is due.* Especially the poor and needy.
3:28 See Lk 11:5–8; Jas 2:15–16.
3:30 *Do not accuse…for no reason.* See Job 2:3.
3:31 *Do not envy.* See 23:17; 24:19; Ps 37:1,7. *the violent.* Like the sinners of 1:10–19 (cf. 16:29).
3:32 *detests.* A word that elsewhere expresses abhorrence of pagan practices (see Dt 18:9,12) and moral abuses. It is common in Proverbs (e.g., 6:16; 8:7; 11:20). *takes the upright into his confidence.* See Ge 18:17 and note; Job 29:4; Ps 25:14; Am 3:7; Jn 15:15.

3:33 This contrast is seen also in Dt 11:26–28. *The LORD's curse is on the house of the wicked.* See Jos 7:24–25; Zec 5:3–4. *blesses the home of the righteous.* See Job 42:12–14.
3:34 *mocks proud mockers.* See note on 1:26. *shows favor.* See v. 4. James and Peter both quote this verse (Jas 4:6; 1Pe 5:5).
4:3 *still tender.* Cf. David's words about Solomon, who was "young and inexperienced" (1Ch 22:5; 29:1). This is part of an autobiographical statement, such as was sometimes used by the wisdom teachers (see 24:30–34; see also the book of Ecclesiastes). *cherished.* Deeply loved (cf. Ge 37:3; Jer 6:26 and note; Zec 12:10).
4:4 *with all your heart.* See note on 3:5.

4:6 *protect…watch over.* The Hebrew words for these two verbs occur together also in 2:8,11. *love her.* To love wisdom is to prosper (8:21); to hate wisdom is to "love death" (8:36).
4:7 *beginning of wisdom.* See 1:7; see also TNIV text note. *Though it cost all you have.* Cf. the parables of the hidden treasure and the pearl in Mt 13:44–46 (see note there).

4:8 *l* S Pr 3:18
4:9 *m* S Pr 1:8-9
4:10 *n* Ps 34:11-16;
Pr 1:8-9 *o* S Dt 11:21
4:11 *p* S 1Sa 12:23
q 2Sa 22:37; Ps 5:8
4:12 *r* S Job 18:7;
Pr 3:23
4:13 *s* S Pr 3:22
4:14 *t* Ps 1:1;
S Pr 1:15
4:16 *u* Ps 36:4;
Mic 7:3
4:17 *v* Ge 49:5;
Ps 73:6; Pr 1:10-19;
14:22; Isa 59:6;
Jer 22:3; Hab 1:2;
Mal 2:16
4:18 *w* Job 17:9
x S Job 22:28
y S 2Sa 23:4; Da 12:3;
Mt 5:14; Jn 8:12;
Php 2:15
4:19 *z* S Pr 2:13
a S Dt 32:35;
S Job 3:23; Pr 13:9;
S Isa 8:15
4:20 *b* Ps 34:11-16;
Pr 1:8-9 *c* Pr 5:1
4:21 *d* Pr 3:21
4:22 *e* S Pr 3:8
4:23 *f* S 2Ki 10:31
g Pr 10:11; Lk 6:45
4:25 *h* S Job 31:1
4:26 *i* Heb 12:13*
4:27 *j* S Lev 10:11;
S Dt 5:32

8 Cherish her, and she will exalt you;
    embrace her, and she will honor you. *l*
9 She will give you a garland to grace your head
    and present you with a glorious crown. *m*

10 Listen, my son, *n* accept what I say,
    and the years of your life will be many. *o*
11 I instruct *p* you in the way of wisdom
    and lead you along straight paths. *q*
12 When you walk, your steps will not be hampered;
    when you run, you will not stumble. *r*
13 Hold on to instruction, do not let it go;
    guard it well, for it is your life. *s*
14 Do not set foot on the path of the wicked
    or walk in the way of evildoers. *t*
15 Avoid it, do not travel on it;
    turn from it and go on your way.
16 For they cannot rest until they do evil; *u*
    they are robbed of sleep till they make someone stumble.
17 They eat the bread of wickedness
    and drink the wine of violence. *v*

18 The path of the righteous *w* is like the morning sun, *x*
    shining ever brighter till the full light of day. *y*
19 But the way of the wicked is like deep darkness; *z*
    they do not know what makes them stumble. *a*

20 My son, *b* pay attention to what I say;
    turn your ear to my words. *c*
21 Do not let them out of your sight, *d*
    keep them within your heart;
22 for they are life to those who find them
    and health to one's whole body. *e*
23 Above all else, guard *f* your heart,
    for everything you do flows from it. *g*
24 Keep your mouth free of perversity;
    keep corrupt talk far from your lips.
25 Let your eyes *h* look straight ahead;
    fix your gaze directly before you.
26 Give careful thought to the *a* paths for your feet *i*
    and be steadfast in all your ways.
27 Do not turn to the right or the left; *j*
    keep your foot from evil.

a 26 Or *Make level*

4:9 *glorious crown.* Wreaths or crowns were worn at joyous oc-casions, such as weddings or feasts (see SS 3:11; Eze 16:12; 23:42; cf. 1Pe 5:4).
4:10 *years … will be many.* See note on 3:2.
4:11 *straight paths.* Right paths (see notes on 3:6; Ps 23:3).
4:12 *you will not stumble.* Because of some obstacle or lack of light (see v. 19; 3:23; 10:9; Ps 18:36; Isa 5:27; 40:30–31).
4:14 *path of the wicked.* Cf. the destructive paths of the adul-teress in 2:18; 7:25; see Ps 1:1; 17:4–5.
4:16 *cannot rest until they do evil.* See Ps 36:4 and note; Mic 2:1. Contrast the attitude of David, who would not sleep until he found a permanent place for God's house (Ps 132:3–5).
4:17 *eat the bread … drink the wine.* They thrive on wickedness and violence (see 13:2; Job 15:16; cf. Ps 109:18 and note).
4:18 *path of the righteous is … shining ever brighter.* The godly have all the guidance and protection they need (see vv. 11–12) and are able to lead others to righteousness (Da 12:3).
4:19 *deep darkness.* A dangerous path that leads to destruc-

tion (see note on 2:13; see also Isa 59:9–10; Jer 23:12; Jn 11:10; 12:35).
4:21 *heart.* See 3:1,3; see also note on Ps 4:7.
4:22 *health.* Physical, psychological and spiritual (see 3:8 and note).
4:23 *everything you do flows from it.* If we store up good things (2:1) in our hearts, our words and actions will be good. "Out of the overflow of the heart the mouth speaks" (Mt 12:34; cf. Mk 7:21).
4:24 *Keep your mouth free of perversity.* See note on 2:12; see also 19:1. *corrupt talk.* See 6:12; 19:28; Eph 4:29 and note; Jas 3:6.
4:25 *look straight ahead.* Not at "worthless things" (Ps 119:37).
4:26 Heb 12:13 quotes the first half of this verse (see note there and see TNIV text note here).
4:27 *Do not turn to the right or the left.* A warning found also in Dt 5:32–33; 28:14; Jos 1:7. *foot from evil.* See 1:15.

WARNING AGAINST ADULTERY

My son, [k] pay attention to my wisdom,
 turn your ear to my words [l] of insight,
[2] that you may maintain discretion
 and your lips may preserve knowledge.
[3] For the lips of the adulterous woman drip honey,
 and her speech is smoother than oil; [m]
[4] but in the end she is bitter as gall, [n]
 sharp as a double-edged sword.
[5] Her feet go down to death;
 her steps lead straight to the grave. [o]
[6] She gives no thought to the way of life;
 her paths wander aimlessly, but she does not know it. [p]

[7] Now then, my sons, listen [q] to me;
 do not turn aside from what I say.
[8] Keep to a path far from her, [r]
 do not go near the door of her house,
[9] lest you lose your honor to others
 and your dignity [a] to one who is cruel,
[10] lest strangers feast on your wealth
 and your toil enrich the house of another. [s]
[11] At the end of your life you will groan,
 when your flesh and body are spent.
[12] You will say, "How I hated discipline!
 How my heart spurned correction! [t]
[13] I would not obey my teachers
 or turn my ear to my instructors.
[14] And I was soon in serious trouble [u]
 in the assembly of God's people." [v]

[15] Drink water from your own cistern,
 running water from your own well.
[16] Should your springs overflow in the streets,
 your streams of water in the public squares?
[17] Let them be yours alone,
 never to be shared with strangers.
[18] May your fountain [w] be blessed,
 and may you rejoice in the wife of your youth. [x]
[19] A loving doe, a graceful deer [y] —

---

[a] 9 Or *years*

5:1 [k] S Pr 1:8
[l] Pr 4:20
5:3 [m] S Ps 55:21;
Pr 7:5
5:4 [n] Ecc 7:26
5:5 [o] S Ps 9:17;
S Pr 2:18; 7:26-27
5:6 [p] Pr 9:13; 30:20
5:7 [q] Pr 1:8-9
5:8 [r] S Pr 2:16-19;
6:20-29; 7:1-27
5:10 [s] Pr 29:3
5:12 [t] Pr 12:1
5:14 [u] Pr 1:24-27;
6:33 [v] Pr 31:3
5:18 [w] SS 4:12-15
[x] S Dt 20:7; Pr 2:17;
Ecc 9:9; Mal 2:14
5:19 [y] SS 4:5; 8:14

5:2 *lips may preserve knowledge.* Applied to a priest in Mal 2:7.

5:3 *lips . . . drip honey.* Probably a reference to the pleasant-sounding talk (cf. 16:24) of the adulterous woman, though some explain it as kisses (cf. SS 4:11; 5:13; 7:9). *adulterous woman.* See note on 2:16. *smoother than oil.* See 2:16. Her words are soothing (see Ps 55:21) but full of flattery (Pr 26:28) and hypocrisy (see Ps 5:9 and note).

5:4 *gall.* A bitter herb (see Dt 29:18; La 3:15,19; Am 6:12). *double-edged sword.* A lethal weapon (see Jdg 3:16; see also Ps 55:21; 149:6; Heb 4:12; cf. Rev 1:16 and note).

5:5 *down to death.* Her immorality hastens her end (see note on 2:18).

5:6 *paths wander aimlessly.* See 2:15; 10:9. *does not know it.* Or "does not acknowledge it."

5:7–14 The father (teacher) warns the son (student) about the high cost of immorality.

5:8 *far from her.* See Ge 39:12; 2Ti 2:22. *door of her house.* Cf. 7:27; 9:14.

5:9 *one who is cruel.* Possibly the vengeful husband (see 6:34–35).

5:10 *strangers feast on your wealth.* Contrast the riches and honor that come to those who embrace wisdom (3:16–18). Immorality eventually reduces one "to a loaf of bread" (6:26; see note there).

5:11 *flesh and body are spent.* Possibly because of the debilitating effects of immorality (see 1Co 6:18; cf. Pr 3:8; 4:22), but more likely referring to the loss of vigor that accompanies old age.

5:12 *hated discipline . . . spurned correction.* In old age he will look back and sadly acknowledge that he has played the fool (see 1:7 and note; see also 1:22,29–30).

5:13 *would not obey.* In spite of the repeated urging to "listen" or "pay attention" to their instruction (cf. v. 7; 1:8; 4:1; 5:1).

5:14 *serious trouble.* Physical, financial and social. *in the assembly of God's people.* The offender was subject to "blows and disgrace" (6:33) or even death (see Lev 20:10; Dt 22:22).

5:15 *your own cistern . . . your own well.* Your own wife (see SS 4:12,15). Let your own wife be your source of pleasure, as water refreshes a thirsty man. Wells and cisterns were privately owned (Jer 38:6) and of great value (2Ki 18:31).

5:16 *springs . . . streams of water.* Like "cistern" and "well" in v. 15 and "fountain" in v. 18, these also refer to the wife (see SS 4:12,15). *in the public squares.* The wife may become promiscuous if the husband is unfaithful.

5:18 *wife of your youth.* Chosen by you when you were young.

5:19 *doe . . . deer.* Descriptive of the wife, perhaps because of the delicate beauty of the doe's limbs (see SS 2:9). *may her breasts satisfy you always.* See SS 7:7–8. *intoxicated.* Marital love is portrayed as better than wine in SS 4:10 (cf. SS 7:9).

5:21 ᶻS Ps 119:168
ᵃ Jer 29:23
ᵇ S Job 10:4; S 14:16;
Pr 15:3; Jer 32:19;
S Heb 4:13
5:22 ᶜPs 9:16
ᵈNu 32:23;
S Job 18:9; Ps 7:15-16;
S Pr 1:31-32
5:23 ᵉS Job 4:21;
Pr 10:21 ᶠJob 34:21-
25; Pr 11:5
6:1 ᵍS Pr 1:8
ʰJob 17:3 ⁱPr 17:18
ʲPr 11:15; 22:26-27
6:4 ᵏPs 132:4
6:5 ˡS 2Sa 2:18
ᵐIsa 13:14 ⁿS Ps 91:3
6:6 ᵒver 6-11;
Pr 20:4
6:8 ᵖPr 30:24-25
�۹Pr 10:4
6:9 ʳPr 24:30-34;
26:13-16
6:10 ˢPr 24:33;
Ecc 4:5
6:11 ᵗver 10-11;
Pr 20:13; 24:30-34

may her breasts satisfy you always,
may you ever be intoxicated with her love.
²⁰ Why, my son, be intoxicated with another man's wife?
Why embrace the bosom of a wayward woman?

²¹ For your ways are in full view ᶻ of the LORD,
and he examines ᵃ all your paths. ᵇ
²² The evil deeds of the wicked ensnare them; ᶜ
the cords of their sins hold them fast. ᵈ
²³ For lack of discipline they will die, ᵉ
led astray by their own great folly. ᶠ

WARNINGS AGAINST FOLLY

6
My son, ᵍ if you have put up security ʰ for your neighbor, ⁱ
if you have shaken hands in pledge ʲ for a stranger,
² you have been trapped by what you said,
ensnared by the words of your mouth.
³ So do this, my son, to free yourself,
since you have fallen into your neighbor's hands:
Go—to the point of exhaustion— ᵃ
and give your neighbor no rest!
⁴ Allow no sleep to your eyes,
no slumber to your eyelids. ᵏ
⁵ Free yourself, like a gazelle ˡ from the hand of the hunter, ᵐ
like a bird from the snare of the fowler. ⁿ

⁶ Go to the ant, you sluggard; ᵒ
consider its ways and be wise!
⁷ It has no commander,
no overseer or ruler,
⁸ yet it stores its provisions in summer ᵖ
and gathers its food at harvest. ۹

⁹ How long will you lie there, you sluggard? ʳ
When will you get up from your sleep?
¹⁰ A little sleep, a little slumber,
a little folding of the hands to rest ˢ—
¹¹ and poverty ᵗ will come on you like a thief
and scarcity like an armed man.

¹² Troublemakers and villains,
who go about with corrupt mouths,

ᵃ 3 Or *Go and humble yourself,*

A **5:20** *Why …?* In light of the sheer joy found within the bonds of marriage and the "serious trouble" (v. 14) outside it, why commit adultery? *another man's wife.* See v. 3; 2:16 and note.
5:21 *in full view of the LORD.* See 15:3; Job 31:4; 34:21; Jer 16:17; 32:19. *examines all your paths.* See Job 7:18; 34:23; Ps 11:4; 26:2; 139:23; Jer 11:20; 12:3; 17:10.
5:22 *ensnare them.* See 1:18 and note; Dt 7:25; 12:30. In Ecc 7:26 the sinner is ensnared by a woman "whose heart is a trap." *cords of their sins.* See Job 36:8; Ecc 4:12; Isa 5:18; cf. Hos 11:4 and note.
5:23 The death of the fool is described in similar terms in 1:29–32; 7:21–27; cf. Job 36:12. *discipline.* See v. 12 and note.
6:1 *put up security … shaken hands in pledge.* Refers to responsibility for someone else's debt (cf. 22:26) or for some other obligation. It can end in abject poverty (cf. 22:27) or even slavery if you cannot pay. For example, Judah volunteered to personally guarantee the safe return of Benjamin to Jacob (Ge 43:9), and when this seemed impossible, he had to offer himself to Joseph as a slave (Ge 44:32–33). Such an arrangement was sealed by "striking hands," equivalent to our handshake (see 11:15; 17:18; 20:16; 22:26; cf. Job 17:3).
6:2 *trapped … ensnared.* Cf. v. 5; see also 1:18; 5:22 and notes.
6:3 *to free yourself.* To gain release from the obligation. *fallen*

into your neighbor's hands. Assumed responsibility for the neighbor's obligation. *give your neighbor no rest.* Be as persistent as the person in Lk 11:8.
6:4 *no sleep … no slumber.* Like David in Ps 132:4.
6:5 *snare of the fowler.* See Ps 124:7.

B **6:6** *ant.* A creature referred to elsewhere in the Bible only in 30:25, where it stores up its food in the summer (as here; see v. 8). The ant is mentioned also in Canaanite Amarna letter 252.15–19, again in a proverbial context (see chart, p. xxiii). *sluggard.* A lazy individual who refuses to work and whose desires are not met (see 10:26; 13:4; 15:19; 19:24; 20:4; 21:25; 22:13; 24:30; 26:13–16).
6:7 *no commander.* Cf. the locust in 30:27.
6:9 *How long will you lie there, you sluggard?* The sluggard's love for sleep is described also in 26:14 (see note there).
6:10–11 Repeated in 24:33–34.
6:11 *poverty … scarcity.* Connected with too much sleep also in 10:5; 19:15; 20:13. Hard work is an antidote to poverty (see 12:11; 14:23; 28:19). *like a thief … an armed man.* Poverty will come when it is too late to do anything about it (cf. Mt 24:43).

A **6:12–14** A vivid description of one who uses mouth, eyes, feet and fingers (all a person's means of communi-

13 who wink maliciously with their eyes, ^u
    signal with their feet
    and motion with their fingers, ^v
14 who plot evil ^w with deceit in their hearts—
    they always stir up dissension. ^x

15 Therefore disaster will overtake them in an instant; ^y
    they will suddenly ^z be destroyed—without remedy. ^a

16 There are six things the LORD hates, ^b
    seven that are detestable to him:
17   haughty eyes, ^c
    a lying tongue, ^d
    hands that shed innocent blood, ^e
18   a heart that devises wicked schemes,
    feet that are quick to rush into evil, ^f
19   a false witness ^g who pours out lies ^h
    and a person who stirs up dissension in the community. ⁱ

WARNING AGAINST ADULTERY

20 My son, ^j keep your father's command
    and do not forsake your mother's teaching. ^k
21 Bind them always on your heart;
    fasten them around your neck. ^l
22 When you walk, they will guide you;
    when you sleep, they will watch over you;
    when you awake, they will speak to you.
23 For this command is a lamp,
    this teaching is a light, ^m
    and correction and instruction
    are the way to life, ⁿ

24 keeping you from your neighbor's wife,
    from the smooth talk of a wayward woman. ^o

25 Do not lust in your heart after her beauty
    or let her captivate you with her eyes.

26 For a prostitute can be had for a loaf of bread,
    but another man's wife preys on your very life. ^p
27 Can a man scoop fire into his lap
    without his clothes being burned?
28 Can a man walk on hot coals

6:13 ^u S Ps 35:19;
Pr 16:30 ^v Isa 58:9
6:14 ^w S Ps 140:2
^x ver 16-19
6:15 ^y S Ps 55:15
^z Job 5:3 ^a Pr 14:32;
29:1
6:16 ^b ver 16-19;
Pr 3:32; 8:13; 15:8,9,
26; 16:5
6:17 ^c S Job 41:34;
S Ps 10:5 ^d Pr 12:22
^e S Dt 19:10; Pr 1:16;
Isa 1:21; 59:7;
Jer 2:34; Mic 7:2
6:18 ^f S Job 15:31
6:19 ^g S Dt 19:16
^h S Ps 12:2 ⁱ ver 12-15;
Pr 15:18; Zec 8:17
6:20 ^j S Pr 3:21
^k Pr 1:8
6:21 ^l Dt 6:8;
S Pr 3:3; 7:1-3
6:23 ^m S Ps 119:105
ⁿ Pr 10:17
6:24 ^o Ge 39:8;
S Ps 55:21; Pr 2:16;
7:5
6:26 ^p Pr 7:22-23

cation) in devious ways to achieve the deceitful plots of the
heart—here especially to spread slander to destroy someone.
6:12 *Troublemakers.* Worthless, wicked persons (16:27; Jdg
19:22; 1Sa 25:25; Job 34:18). See note on Dt 13:13. *corrupt
mouths.* See 2:12 and note; 19:28.
6:13 *wink ... with their eyes.* To make insinuations (see 10:10;
16:30).
6:14 *plot evil.* See v. 18; 3:29; Mic 2:1. *stir up dissension.* Through
slander such people create distrust (see v. 19; 10:12; 15:18; 16:28; 28:25; 29:22).
6:15 *disaster will overtake them in an instant.* Usually a sign of
God's judgment (see 1:26; 24:22 and note; Job 34:20). *suddenly
be destroyed—without remedy.* Such scoundrels will suffer the
same fate they thought to bring upon others—their punishment will fit their crime (cf. Gal 6:7–8). *without remedy.* See 29:1
and note.
6:16–19 A further elaboration on the theme of vv. 12–15, explaining why "disaster will overtake" (v. 15) the scoundrel described here.
6:16 *six ... seven.* A way of handling numbers in synonymous
parallelism in Hebrew poetry (see Introduction: The Nature of a
Proverb). Such catalogues of items are frequent in the wisdom
literature of the OT (see 30:15,18,21,29; see also Job 5:19 and
note). In all such cases in Proverbs, the higher number is the op-
erational one. *detestable.* See 3:32 and note.

6:17 *haughty eyes.* They reflect a proud heart, and God will
judge them (see 21:4; 30:13; Ps 18:27; 101:5). *lying tongue.* See
2:12 and note; 12:19; 17:7; 21:6. *hands that shed innocent blood.*
See 1:11 and note; see also 1:16; 28:17.
6:18 *heart that devises wicked schemes.* See 1:31; 24:2; Ge 6:5.
feet that ... rush into evil. See 1:16 and note.
6:19 *false witness.* See Ex 20:16; Dt 19:16–19. Proverbs emphasizes the damage done by false witnesses (12:17–18; 25:18; see
note on Ps 5:9) and the punishment they receive (see note on v.
15; see also 19:5,9; 21:28). *pours out lies.* See 14:5,25. *stirs up dissension.* See note on v. 14.
6:20 See 1:8 and note.
6:21 See 1:9 and note.
6:22 *walk.* Cf. 4:11. *when you sleep.* See note on 3:24. *watch
over you.* See 4:6.
6:23 *lamp ... light.* Just as the word of God "is a lamp to my feet
and a light for my path" (Ps 119:105; cf. Ps 19:8). *way to life.* See
3:22; 4:22; 10:17. Contrast the way to death for the one who
hates discipline (see 5:23 and note).
6:24 See notes on 2:16; 5:3.
6:25 *Do not lust.* Jesus shows the close connection between
lust and adultery (Mt 5:28; cf. Ex 20:14,17 and notes). *captivate
you.* See 5:20.
6:26 *another man's wife preys on your very life.* See 2:16–18 and
notes; 5:5; 7:27.

6:29 *q* S Ex 20:14
r Pr 2:16-19; S 5:8
6:31 *s* Ex 22:1-14
6:32 *t* S Ex 20:14
u Pr 7:7; 9:4,16
6:33 *v* Pr 5:9-14
6:34 *w* S Nu 5:14
x S Ge 34:7
6:35 *y* Job 31:9-11;
SS 8:7
7:1 *z* S Pr 1:8
7:2 *a* Pr 4:4
7:3 *b* S Pr 3:3
7:5 *c* ver 21;
S Job 31:9; S Pr 2:16;
6:24
7:7 *d* S Pr 1:22;
S 6:32
7:9 *e* Job 24:15
7:11 *f* Pr 9:13
7:12 *g* Pr 8:1-36;
23:26-28
7:13 *h* S Ge 39:12
i S Pr 1:20
7:14 *j* S Lev 7:11-18

without his feet being scorched?
²⁹ So is he who sleeps *q* with another man's wife; *r*
   no one who touches her will go unpunished.

³⁰ People do not despise a thief if he steals
   to satisfy his hunger when he is starving.
³¹ Yet if he is caught, he must pay sevenfold, *s*
   though it costs him all the wealth of his house.
³² But a man who commits adultery *t* has no sense; *u*
   whoever does so destroys himself.
³³ Blows and disgrace are his lot,
   and his shame will never *v* be wiped away.

³⁴ For jealousy *w* arouses a husband's fury, *x*
   and he will show no mercy when he takes revenge.
³⁵ He will not accept any compensation;
   he will refuse a bribe, however great it is. *y*

WARNING AGAINST THE ADULTEROUS WOMAN

7 My son, *z* keep my words
   and store up my commands within you.
² Keep my commands and you will live; *a*
   guard my teachings as the apple of your eye.
³ Bind them on your fingers;
   write them on the tablet of your heart. *b*
⁴ Say to wisdom, "You are my sister,"
   and to insight, "You are my relative."
⁵ They will keep you from the adulterous woman,
   from the wayward woman with her seductive words. *c*

⁶ At the window of my house
   I looked down through the lattice.
⁷ I saw among the simple,
   I noticed among the young men,
   a youth who had no sense. *d*
⁸ He was going down the street near her corner,
   walking along in the direction of her house
⁹ at twilight, *e* as the day was fading,
   as the dark of night set in.

¹⁰ Then out came a woman to meet him,
   dressed like a prostitute and with crafty intent.
¹¹ (She is unruly *f* and defiant,
   her feet never stay at home;
¹² now in the street, now in the squares,
   at every corner she lurks.) *g*
¹³ She took hold of him *h* and kissed him
   and with a brazen face she said: *i*

¹⁴ "Today I fulfilled my vows,
   and I have food from my fellowship offering *j* at home.

6:29 *no one ... will go unpunished.* See vv. 33–34; see also note on 5:14.
6:31 *sevenfold.* Hebrew law demanded no more than fivefold payment as a penalty for any theft (Ex 22:1–9). The number seven is here symbolic—the thief will pay in full.
6:32 *destroys himself.* See 5:14; 7:22–23 and notes.
6:33 *disgrace.* Followed Amnon's rape of Tamar (2Sa 13:13,22).
6:34 *jealousy.* Its strength is also illustrated in 27:4; SS 8:6.
7:1 See Ps. 119:11.
7:2 *apple of your eye.* See Dt 32:10 and note.
7:3 *Bind them on your fingers.* As a reminder (see 6:21; Dt 6:8). *tablet of your heart.* See 3:3; Jer 31:33 and note.
7:4 *wisdom.* As embodied in the instructions of the wisdom teacher (vv. 1–3). *my sister ... relative.* Make wisdom your most intimate companion. "Sister" may be used here in the sense of

"bride" (see SS 4:9–10,12; 5:1–2).
7:5 See notes on 2:16; 5:3.
7:7 *simple.* See note on 1:4. *who had no sense.* See 6:32; 9:4,16.
7:8 *in the direction of her house.* See 5:8.
7:9 *dark of night.* He was hoping no one would see him (see 2:13 and note).
7:10 *dressed like a prostitute.* Perhaps in a gaudy manner (see Eze 16:16) and heavily veiled (see Ge 38:14–15).
7:11 *unruly.* Applied to the woman "Folly" in 9:13 (see note there).
7:12 *she lurks.* Ready to catch her prey (see vv. 22–33).
7:13 *kissed him.* A bold greeting (see Ge 29:11).
7:14 *Today I fulfilled my vows.* An offering made as the result of a vow was one of the fellowship offerings, and the meat had to be eaten on the first or second day (see Lev 7:15–16). So the young man had an opportunity to enjoy a sumptuous feast, one that

¹⁵ So I came out to meet you;
 I looked for you and have found you!
¹⁶ I have covered my bed
 with colored linens from Egypt.
¹⁷ I have perfumed my bed ^k
 with myrrh, ^l aloes and cinnamon.
¹⁸ Come, let's drink deep of love till morning;
 let's enjoy ourselves with love! ^m
¹⁹ My husband is not at home;
 he has gone on a long journey.
²⁰ He took his purse filled with money
 and will not be home till full moon."

²¹ With persuasive words she led him astray;
 she seduced him with her smooth talk. ⁿ
²² All at once he followed her
 like an ox going to the slaughter,
 like a deer^a stepping into a noose^b ^o
²³   till an arrow pierces^p his liver,
 like a bird darting into a snare,
 little knowing it will cost him his life. ^q

²⁴ Now then, my sons, listen ^r to me;
 pay attention to what I say.
²⁵ Do not let your heart turn to her ways
 or stray into her paths. ^s
²⁶ Many are the victims she has brought down;
 her slain are a mighty throng.
²⁷ Her house is a highway to the grave,
 leading down to the chambers of death. ^t

WISDOM'S CALL

Does not wisdom call out? ^u
 Does not understanding raise her voice?
² At the highest point along the way,
 where the paths meet, she takes her stand;
³ beside the gate leading into the city,
 at the entrance, she cries aloud: ^v
⁴ "To you, O people, I call out; ^w
 I raise my voice to all humankind.
⁵ You who are simple, ^x gain prudence; ^y
 you who are foolish, set your hearts on it. ^c
⁶ Listen, for I have trustworthy things to say;

^a 22 Syriac (see also Septuagint); Hebrew *fool*   ^b 22 The meaning of the Hebrew for this line is uncertain.   ^c 5 Septuagint; Hebrew *foolish, instruct your minds*

7:17 ^k S Est 1:6;
Isa 57:7; Eze 23:41;
Am 6:4 ^l S Ge 37:25
7:18 ^m S Ge 39:7
7:21 ⁿ S ver 5
7:22 ^o S Job 18:10
7:23 ^p S Job 15:22;
S 16:13 ^q S Pr 6:26;
Ecc 7:26
7:24 ^r Pr 1:8-9; 8:32
7:25 ^s Pr 5:7-8
7:27 ^t Jdg 16:19;
S Pr 2:18; Rev 22:15
8:1 ^u S Job 28:12
8:3 ^v Pr 7:6-13
8:4 ^w Isa 42:2
8:5 ^x S Pr 1:22
^y Pr 1:4

---

ironically had a religious significance (cf. 1Sa 1:21 and note). *fellowship offering.* Part of the meat could be eaten by the one who brought the offering and by his (or her) family (Lev 7:12–15).
7:16 *colored linens from Egypt.* Linen is associated with the wealthy in 31:22. Egyptian linen was of great value (see Isa 19:9 and note; Eze 27:7).
7:17 *myrrh, aloes and cinnamon.* Fragrant perfumes that are linked with making love (see SS 1:3; 4:14; 5:5 and notes; see also Ps 45:8).
7:18 *drink deep of love.* Making love is compared to eating and drinking also in 9:17; 30:20; SS 4:16; 5:1. *enjoy ourselves.* See SS 4:10.
7:19 *not at home.* So he will never know (cf. 6:34–35). *long journey.* Perhaps he was a wealthy merchant.
7:20 *money.* Pieces of silver of various weights were a common medium of exchange, but not in the form of coins until a later period (see note on Ge 20:16).
7:21 *persuasive words . . . smooth talk.* See notes on 2:16; 5:3; see also 6:24; 7:5. *led him astray.* Cf. 5:23.

7:22 *like an ox going to the slaughter.* Totally oblivious of the fate that awaits him. *noose.* Cf. Isa 51:20.
7:23 *pierces his liver.* The terrible fate of the wicked is similarly described in Job 20:24–25. *darting into a snare.* See notes on 1:17–18; 5:22.
7:24 See 5:7.
7:25 *her paths.* See 1:15.
7:26 *Many are the victims.* See 9:18; 23:28; Isa 5:14 and note.
7:27 *highway to the grave.* See notes on 2:18; 5:5; see also 14:12; 16:25; Mt 7:13; cf. 1Co 6:9–10.
8:1–36 Wisdom is personified (see note on 1:20) as she addresses humankind in preparation for the final plea from both "Wisdom" and "Folly" in ch. 9.
8:1 *call out . . . raise her voice.* See 1:20 and note.
8:2–3 See notes on 1:20–21.
8:4 *humankind.* See v. 31 and note.
8:5 *simple . . . foolish.* Both are addressed in wisdom's speech in 1:22, 32. *simple, gain prudence.* See note on 1:4.
8:6 *trustworthy things . . . what is right.* See Php 4:8.

I open my lips to speak what is right.
[7] My mouth speaks what is true, *z*
    for my lips detest wickedness.
[8] All the words of my mouth are just;
    none of them is crooked or perverse.
[9] To the discerning all of them are right;
    they are upright to those who have found knowledge.
[10] Choose my instruction instead of silver,
    knowledge rather than choice gold, *a*
[11] for wisdom is more precious *b* than rubies,
    and nothing you desire can compare with her. *c*

[12] "I, wisdom, dwell together with prudence;
    I possess knowledge and discretion. *d*
[13] To fear the LORD *e* is to hate evil; *f*
    I hate *g* pride and arrogance,
    evil behavior and perverse speech.
[14] Counsel and sound judgment are mine;
    I have insight, I have power. *h*
[15] By me kings reign
    and rulers *i* issue decrees that are just;
[16] by me princes govern, *j*
    and nobles—all who rule on earth. *a*
[17] I love those who love me, *k*
    and those who seek me find me. *l*
[18] With me are riches and honor, *m*
    enduring wealth and prosperity. *n*
[19] My fruit is better than fine gold; *o*
    what I yield surpasses choice silver. *p*
[20] I walk in the way of righteousness, *q*
    along the paths of justice,
[21] bestowing a rich inheritance on those who love me
    and making their treasuries full. *r*

[22] "The LORD brought me forth as the first of his works, *b,c*
    before his deeds of old;
[23] I was formed long ages ago,
    at the very beginning, when the world came to be.
[24] When there were no oceans, I was given birth,
    when there were no springs abounding with water; *s*

---

a 16 Some Hebrew manuscripts and Septuagint; other Hebrew manuscripts *all righteous rulers*
b 22 Or *way*; or *dominion*   *c 22* Or *The LORD possessed me at the beginning of his work*; or *The LORD brought me forth at the beginning of his work*

8:7 *my lips detest wickedness.* See 3:32 and note; 12:22.
8:8 *crooked or perverse.* See Php 2:15; cf. Pr 2:15.
8:9 *To the discerning.* The wiser they are the more they appreciate words of wisdom. *who have found knowledge.* Especially the knowledge of God (see note on 2:5).
8:10 *silver...gold.* See v. 19; 2:4; 3:14 and note.
8:11 Almost identical with 3:15 (see note there).
8:12 *dwell together with prudence.* Cf. Job 28:20. *prudence...knowledge and discretion.* See 1:4 and note.
8:13 *To fear the LORD is to hate evil.* See 3:7 and note; 16:6. *I hate pride and arrogance.* See 16:18; 1Sa 2:3; Isa 13:11; see also Ps 10:2–11 and note. *evil behavior and perverse speech.* See note on 2:12; see also 6:12–19.
8:14 *Counsel and sound judgment...insight...power.* These characterize the Lord (2:6–7; Job 12:13,16; Isa 40:13–14; Ro 16:27) and the Spirit of the Lord (Isa 11:2). *Counsel.* See 1:25; 19:20. *power.* Cf. Ecc 9:16.
8:15 *By me kings reign.* See 29:4. Solomon prayed for wisdom to govern Israel (see 1Ki 3:9; 2Ch 1:10).
8:17 *I love.* I pour out my benefits on (see 4:6 and note; see also Jn 14:21). *those who seek me find me.* See 2:4–5; Isa 55:6; Jas 1:5. Verse 35 completes the thought: "those who find me find life."

8:18 *riches and honor.* See v. 21; 3:16; 22:4. *prosperity.* See note on 3:2; see also 21:21.
8:19 *My fruit.* Wisdom is called a "tree of life" in 3:18 (see note there). *fine gold...choice silver.* See v. 10; Job 28:15; see also 3:14 and note.
8:20 *walk in the way.* See introduction to Ps 1; see also note on Ps 1:6. *way...paths.* See 3:17. *justice.* See v. 15.
8:21 *bestowing a rich inheritance.* See v. 18; Zec 8:12 and note. *making their treasuries full.* See 3:10; 24:4 and notes.
8:22–31 A hymn describing wisdom's role in creation. Wisdom is here personified, as in 1:20–33; 3:13–18; 9:1–12. Therefore these verses should not be interpreted as a direct description of Christ. Yet they provide part of the background for the NT portrayal of Christ as the divine Word (Jn 1:1–5) and as the wisdom of God (see note on 1:24). Here, wisdom is an attribute of God involved with him in creation.
8:22 *brought...forth.* The Hebrew for this verb is also used in Ge 4:1; 14:19,22 ("Creator"); Dt 32:6 ("Creator"). *me.* Wisdom (see 3:19 and note; Ps 104:24). *as the first of his works.* Cf. Job 40:19 and note.
8:23 *when the world came to be.* Wisdom was already there when God began to create the world (cf. Jn 1:1 and Christ's statement in Jn 17:5).

²⁵ before the mountains were settled in place,^{*t*}
  before the hills, I was given birth,^{*u*}
²⁶ before he made the world or its fields
  or any of the dust of the earth.^{*v*}
²⁷ I was there when he set the heavens in place,^{*w*}
  when he marked out the horizon^{*x*} on the face of the deep,
²⁸ when he established the clouds above^{*y*}
  and fixed securely the fountains of the deep,^{*z*}
²⁹ when he gave the sea its boundary^{*a*}
  so the waters would not overstep his command,^{*b*}
  and when he marked out the foundations of the earth.^{*c*}
³⁰   Then I was constantly^{*a*} at his side.^{*d*}
  I was filled with delight day after day,
  rejoicing always in his presence,
³¹ rejoicing in his whole world
  and delighting in humankind.^{*e*}

³² "Now then, my children, listen^{*f*} to me;
  blessed are^{*g*} those who keep my ways.^{*h*}
³³ Listen to my instruction and be wise;
  do not disregard it.
³⁴ Blessed are those who listen^{*i*} to me,
  watching daily at my doors,
  waiting at my doorway.
³⁵ For those who find me^{*j*} find life^{*k*}
  and receive favor from the Lord.^{*l*}
³⁶ But those who fail to find me harm themselves;^{*m*}
  all who hate me love death."^{*n*}

INVITATIONS OF WISDOM AND FOLLY

9 Wisdom has built^{*o*} her house;
  she has set up^{*b*} its seven pillars.
² She has prepared her meat and mixed her wine;^{*p*}
  she has also set her table.^{*q*}
³ She has sent out her servants, and she calls^{*r*}
  from the highest point of the city,^{*s*}
⁴   "Let all who are simple^{*t*} come to my house!"
  To those who have no sense^{*u*} she says,
⁵   "Come,^{*v*} eat my food
  and drink the wine I have mixed.^{*w*}
⁶ Leave your simple ways and you will live;^{*x*}
  walk in the way of insight."^{*y*}

---

^a 30 Or *was the artisan*; or *was a little child*   ^b 1 Septuagint, Syriac and Targum; Hebrew *has hewn out*

8:25 ^t S Job 38:6
^u S Job 15:7
8:26 ^v S Ps 90:2
8:27 ^w S Job 26:7
^x S Job 22:14
8:28 ^y S Job 36:29
^z S Ge 1:7; S Job 9:8; S 26:10
8:29 ^a S Ge 1:9; S Ps 16:6 ^b S Job 38:8
^c S 1Sa 2:8; S Job 38:5
8:30 ^d Pr 3:19-20; Rev 3:14
8:31 ^e S Job 28:25-27; 38:4-38; Ps 104:1-30; Pr 30:4; Jn 1:1-4; Col 1:15-20
8:32 ^f S Pr 7:24
^g Lk 11:28
^h S 2Sa 22:22; S Ps 18:21
8:34 ⁱ 1Ki 10:8
8:35 ^j Pr 3:13-18
^k Pr 9:6; Jn 5:39-40
^l S Job 33:26
8:36 ^m Pr 15:32; Isa 3:9; Jer 40:2
ⁿ S Job 28:22
9:1 ^o Eph 2:20-22; 1Pe 2:5
9:2 ^p Isa 25:6; 62:8
^q Lk 14:16-23
9:3 ^r S Pr 1:20; 8:1-3
^s ver 14
9:4 ^t S Pr 1:22
^u ver 16; S Pr 6:32
9:5 ^v Jn 7:37-38
^w S Ps 42:2; 63:1; 143:6; Isa 44:3; 55:1
9:6 ^x S Pr 8:35
^y S Pr 3:1-2

8:24 *I was given birth.* Elsewhere it is the sea (Job 38:8–9) and the mountains and earth that are "brought forth" (Ps 90:2; Job 15:7). *springs abounding with water.* See Ps 104:10.
8:27 *set the heavens in place.* See 3:19 and note. *when he marked out the horizon on the face of the deep.* See Job 26:10.
8:28 *fountains of the deep.* Earth's springs and streams (see note on 3:20; cf. Ge 7:11).
8:29 *the sea its boundary.* See Ge 1:9 and note; Job 38:10–11; Ps 104:9. *foundations of the earth.* See note on 3:19.
8:30 *filled with delight . . . rejoicing.* Cf. the joyful shouts of the angels at the time of creation (Job 38:7).
8:31 *delighting in humankind.* Cf. v. 4. Humans, made in the image of God, represented the climax of creation (see Ge 1:26–28 and notes).
8:32 *blessed.* The blessings associated with gaining wisdom are given in 3:13–18; see Ps 1:1–3 and notes; 119:1–2; 128:1.
8:34 *watching daily at my doors.* Contrast the warning not to go near the door of the adulteress's house (5:8).
8:35 *find life.* See 1:28; 3:2; 4:22 and notes. Cf. Jn 1:4. *favor.* See 3:4; 12:2; 18:22 and note.

8:36 *all who hate me love death.* See 1:28–33; 5:12,23; 7:27 and notes.
9:1 *has built her house.* See 14:1 and note; cf. 24:3 and note; 31:10–27. Both wisdom and folly have a house to which humans are invited (see v. 14; 5:8; 7:8; 8:34). *seven pillars.* Perhaps "seven" refers symbolically to the perfection of wisdom's work.
9:2 See v. 17 and note. The banquet prepared by wisdom contrasts with the perfumed bed made ready by the adulteress in 7:17. *mixed her wine.* With spices, to make it tastier (see SS 8:2).
9:3 *she calls from the highest point of the city.* See the description of Folly in v. 14; see also 8:1–3.
9:4 The same invitation is given by Folly in v. 16. *simple.* See 1:4; 8:5 and notes. *have no sense.* See 6:32; 7:7.
9:5 *Come.* Wisdom's invitation counters the enticements of sinners in 1:10–11 (see note on 1:11). *eat . . . drink.* As in v. 2, wisdom's gifts are described symbolically as a great banquet (see Isa 55:1–2 and notes; cf. Jn 6:27,35,51,55).
9:6 *Leave your simple ways.* See 1:22; see also 1:10–11 and notes. *you will live.* See v. 11; 8:35; see also note on 3:2; cf. 3:18 and note.

9:7 z Pr 23:9; Mt 7:6
9:8 a Pr 15:12
b Ps 141:5
9:9 c Pr 1:5,7; 12:15;
13:10; 14:6; 15:31;
19:25
9:10 d S Pr 1:7
e Ps 22:3; Pr 30:3
f S Dt 4:6
9:11 g S Ge 15:15;
S Dt 11:21; S Pr 3:1-2;
10:27
9:13 h Pr 7:11
i S Pr 5:6
9:14 j ver 3;
Eze 16:25
9:15 k S Pr 1:20
9:16 l S Pr 1:22
9:17 m Pr 20:17
9:18 n S Pr 2:18;
7:26-27
10:1 o S 1Ki 4:32
p S Pr 1:1 q Pr 15:20;
17:21; 19:13; 23:22-
25; 27:11; 29:3
10:2 r Pr 13:11; 21:6
s ver 16; Pr 11:4,19;
12:28
10:3 t Mt 6:25-34
u Pr 13:25

7 Whoever corrects a mocker invites insults;
   whoever rebukes the wicked incurs abuse. z
8 Do not rebuke mockers a or they will hate you;
   rebuke the wise and they will love you. b
9 Instruct the wise and they will be wiser still;
   teach the righteous and they will add to their learning. c

10 The fear of the LORD d is the beginning of wisdom,
   and knowledge of the Holy One e is understanding. f
11 For through wisdom a your days will be many,
   and years will be added to your life. g
12 If you are wise, your wisdom will reward you;
   if you are a mocker, you alone will suffer.

13 Folly is an unruly woman; h
   she is simple and knows nothing. i
14 She sits at the door of her house,
   on a seat at the highest point of the city, j
15 calling out k to those who pass by,
   who go straight on their way,
16   "Let all who are simple come to my house!"
   To those who have no sense l she says,
17   "Stolen water is sweet;
   food eaten in secret is delicious! m"
18 But little do they know that the dead are there,
   that her guests are deep in the realm of the dead. n

PROVERBS OF SOLOMON

10 The proverbs o of Solomon: p

Wise children bring joy to their father, q
   but foolish children bring grief to their mother.

2 Ill-gotten treasures have no lasting value, r
   but righteousness delivers from death. s

3 The LORD does not let the righteous go hungry, t
   but he thwarts the craving of the wicked. u

a 11 Septuagint, Syriac and Targum; Hebrew me

9:7 *Whoever corrects a mocker invites insults.* See 1:22 and note; cf. 1:30. *incurs abuse.* Cf. 1Pe 4:4.
9:8 *they will hate you.* See 15:12,32. *rebuke the wise and they will love you.* See 10:8; 17:10.
9:9 *they will be wiser still.* See 18:15; 21:11.
9:10–12 Wisdom's final words summarize the heart of the message in chs. 1–9.
9:10 *The fear of the LORD is the beginning of wisdom.* See 1:7 and note. *knowledge of the Holy One.* See 30:3; see also note on 2:5. *Holy One.* Occurs elsewhere in Proverbs only in 30:3. See note on Lev 11:44.
9:11 *years will be added to your life.* See note on 3:2; see also 3:16; 10:27; 14:27; 19:23.
9:12 *your wisdom will reward you.* Some of wisdom's rewards are given in 3:16–18; 4:22; 8:35; 14:14. *mocker.* See v. 7; see also note on 1:22. *will suffer.* See 1:26 and note; 19:29.
9:13 *Folly is an unruly woman.* "Unruly" links the personified "Folly" with the adulterous woman, the wayward wife of 2:16; 7:11. *simple and knows nothing.* She lacks good judgment, prudence and the fear of the Lord (see 1:3–4,22,29; 5:6).
9:14 *sits.* Cf. wisdom's building her house (v. 1). *at the door of her house.* See v. 1 and note. *at the highest point of the city.* Cf. the position of wisdom in v. 3; 8:2.
9:15 *calling out.* Cf. the appeal of Lady Wisdom in v. 3; 8:1,4.
9:16 Her invitation is identical to wisdom's (v. 4; see note on 1:21).

9:17 *Stolen water ... food eaten in secret.* The "banquet" prepared by Lady Folly seems poorer than the wine and meat of wisdom (v. 2). And it was stolen at that! This "meal" refers to stolen pleasures, exemplified by the illicit sex offered by the adulteress (see 7:18 and note; cf. 5:15–16). *sweet.* But see Job 20:12–15 and note.
9:18 *the dead are there ... her guests are deep in the realm of the dead.* Similar to 2:18; 5:5; 7:27 (see notes there).
10:1 *The proverbs of Solomon.* See note on 1:1; the title of a collection of individual proverbs that extends through 22:16. The numerical values of the consonants in the Hebrew word for "Solomon" total 375—the exact number of verses in 10:1—22:16; 375 of Solomon's proverbs were selected from a much larger number (cf. 1Ki 4:32). At the very center of this section is a verse that highlights one of its dominant themes (see 16:4 and note). *Wise children.* See v. 5; 15:20; 17:21,25. In later collections they are described as "righteous" (23:24) and as those "who heed instruction" (28:7).
10:2 *Ill-gotten treasures have no lasting value.* They are fleeting (21:6) and result in God's judgment (see v. 16; 1:19 and note; Eze 7:19). *righteousness delivers from death.* Repeated in 11:4 (see also 2:16–18; 3:2; 13:21; cf. 12:28; 21:21; Ps 1:5 and note).
10:3 *not let the righteous go hungry.* See 13:25; 28:25 and note; Ps 34:9–10; 37:19,25–26. But see note on Pr 3:2. *thwarts the craving of the wicked.* See Nu 11:34; Ps 112:10 and note.

⁴ Lazy hands make for poverty, ᵛ
    but diligent hands bring wealth. ʷ

⁵ He who gathers crops in summer is a prudent son,
    but he who sleeps during harvest is a disgraceful son. ˣ

⁶ Blessings crown the head of the righteous,
    but violence overwhelms the mouth of the wicked. ᵃ ʸ

⁷ The name of the righteous ᶻ is used in blessings, ᵇ
    but the name of the wicked ᵃ will rot. ᵇ

⁸ The wise in heart accept commands,
    but a chattering fool comes to ruin. ᶜ

⁹ Whoever walks in integrity ᵈ walks securely, ᵉ
    but whoever takes crooked paths will be found out. ᶠ

¹⁰ Whoever winks maliciously ᵍ causes grief,
    and a chattering fool comes to ruin.

¹¹ The mouth of the righteous is a fountain of life, ʰ
    but the mouth of the wicked conceals violence. ⁱ

¹² Hatred stirs up dissension,
    but love covers over all wrongs. ʲ

¹³ Wisdom is found on the lips of the discerning, ᵏ
    but a rod is for the back of one who has no sense. ˡ

¹⁴ The wise store up knowledge, ᵐ
    but the mouth of a fool invites ruin. ⁿ

¹⁵ The wealth of the rich is their fortified city, ᵒ
    but poverty is the ruin of the poor. ᵖ

¹⁶ The wages of the righteous is life, �q
    but the earnings of the wicked are sin and death. ʳ

¹⁷ Whoever heeds discipline shows the way to life, ˢ
    but whoever ignores correction leads others astray.

¹⁸ Whoever conceals hatred with lying lips ᵗ
    and spreads slander is a fool.

¹⁹ Sin is not ended by multiplying words,
    but the prudent hold their tongues. ᵘ

ᵃ 6 Or *but the mouth of the wicked conceals violence*   ᵇ 7 See Gen. 48:20.

**Cross references (right margin):**

10:4 ᵛ Pr 6:6-8; 19:15; 24:30-34
ʷ Pr 12:24; 21:5
10:5 ˣ Pr 24:30-34
10:6 ʸ ver 8,11,14; Pr 12:13; 13:3; Ecc 10:12
10:7 ᶻ S Ps 112:6
ᵃ S Job 18:17; S Ps 109:13
ᵇ S Job 18:17; Ps 9:6
10:8 ᶜ ver 14; S Job 33:33; Mt 7:24-27
10:9 ᵈ S Ps 25:21
ᵉ S Ps 37:24 ᶠ Pr 28:18
10:10 ᵍ S Ps 35:19
10:11 ʰ ver 27; S Pr 3:18; S 4:23; 11:30; 13:12,14,19; 14:27; 15:4; 16:22
ⁱ S ver 6
10:12 ʲ Pr 17:9; 1Co 13:4-7; 1Pe 4:8
10:13 ᵏ ver 31; S Ps 37:30; Pr 15:7
ˡ Dt 25:2; Pr 14:3; 26:3
10:14 ᵐ Pr 11:13; 12:23 ⁿ S ver 6; S Ps 59:12; S Pr 14:3; 18:6,7; S Mt 12:37
10:15 ᵒ Pr 18:11
ᵖ Pr 19:7
10:16 q S Dt 30:15
ʳ Pr 11:18-19; 15:6; S Ro 6:23
10:17 ˢ Pr 6:23; 15:5
10:18 ᵗ S Ps 31:18
10:19 ᵘ S Job 1:22; S 6:24; Pr 17:28; S 20:25; 21:23; Jas 1:19; 3:2-12

10:4 Many proverbs praise diligence and the profit it brings, and they condemn laziness as a cause of hunger and poverty (see 6:6–11 and notes; 12:11,24,27; 13:4; 14:23; 18:9; 27:23–27; 28:19).

10:5 *sleeps during harvest.* Sleeping when there is work to be done is condemned also in 6:9–11; 19:15; 20:13. *disgraceful son.* See 17:2; 19:26; 28:7; 29:15.

10:6 *Blessings.* God's gifts and favors (see 3:13–18; 28:20; Ge 49:26; Dt 33:16). *crown.* See 11:26. *violence overwhelms the mouth of the wicked.* The trouble caused by their lips will eventually ruin them (see v. 11 and note; see also Ps 140:9; Hab 2:17; but cf. Pr 2:11).

10:7 *name of the righteous.* Their name is remembered and is "used in blessings" (see Ge 48:20; cf. 22:1 and note).

10:8 *The wise ... accept commands.* See 9:8–9. *chattering fool comes to ruin.* See vv. 10,14,18,19.

10:9 *Whoever walks in integrity walks securely.* See 2:7; 3:23; 13:6; Ps 23:4; Isa 33:15–16. *whoever takes crooked paths will be found out.* See 26:26; Lk 8:17; 1Ti 5:24–25; 2Ti 3:9.

10:10 *winks maliciously.* See note on 6:13. *chattering fool.* See v.8.

10:11 *fountain of life.* A source of life-giving wisdom (see 13:14; 14:27; 16:22; see also Ps 37:30). *mouth of the wicked conceals violence.* Perhaps the meaning is that violence controls the mouth of the wicked (but see note on v.6).

10:12 *stirs up dissension.* See note on 6:14. *covers over all wrongs.* Promotes forgiveness (see 17:9). This line is quoted in Jas 5:20; 1Pe 4:8.

10:13 *rod is for the back.* See 14:3; 19:29; 26:3.

10:14 *store up knowledge.* Rather than babbling folly—and so the wise prosper. See 2:1 and note. Quick with his mouth, the fool only brings ruin on himself (see vv. 8,10; 13:3).

10:15 *wealth ... is their fortified city.* Repeated in 18:11. Wealth brings friends (14:20; 19:4) and power (18:23; 22:7)—but ultimate security is found only in God (Ps 52:7–8). *poverty is the ruin of the poor.* Poverty has no security—as it has no influence (18:23), or friends (19:4,7). See v. 4 and note.

10:16 *wages of the righteous is life.* Not wealth (v. 15) but righteousness assures life (see note on 3:2; see also 3:16; 4:22). *earnings of the wicked are sin and death.* See 15:6; see also 1:13,31 and notes. "The wages of sin is death" (Ro 6:23).

10:17 *way to life.* See 6:23; 12:28 and notes. *whoever ignores correction.* See 5:12; 15:10.

10:18 *conceals hatred.* By pretending friendliness (see 26:24,26,28).

10:19 *hold their tongues.* See 11:12; 21:23; see also 13:3; Ps 5:9; 10:7; 120:4; Jas 3:2 and notes.

10:21 ᵛPr 5:22-23;
Isa 5:13; Jer 5:4;
Hos 4:1,6,14
10:22 ʷS Ps 128:2
ˣS Ge 13:2; S 49:25;
S Dt 8:18
ʸS 2Ch 25:9
10:23 ᶻS Pr 2:14
10:24 ᵃIsa 65:7;
66:4 ᵇS Ge 42:36
ᶜS Ps 37:4; 145:17-
19; Eze 11:8
10:25 ᵈS Ps 20:8
ᵉPr 12:3,7; Mt 7:24-
27
10:26 ᶠIsa 65:5
ᵍPr 13:17; 25:13; 26:6
10:27 ʰS ver 11;
Dt 11:9; Pr 9:10-11;
19:23; 22:4
ⁱS Job 15:32
10:28 ʲEst 7:10;
S Job 8:13; Ps 112:10;
Pr 11:7
10:29 ᵏPr 21:15;
Hos 14:9
10:30 ˡPs 37:9,28-
29; S Pr 2:20-22
10:31 ᵐS ver 13;
S Pr 15:2; 31:26
ⁿS Ps 52:4
10:32 ᵒEcc 10:12
ᵖS Ps 59:7
11:1 �q S Lev 19:36;
Dt 25:13-16;
S Job 6:2; Pr 20:10,23
ʳPr 16:11; Eze 45:10
11:2 ˢPr 16:18
ᵗPr 18:12; 29:23
11:3 ᵘver 5; Pr 13:6

²⁰ The tongue of the righteous is choice silver,
   but the heart of the wicked is of little value.

²¹ The lips of the righteous nourish many,
   but fools die for lack of sense. ᵛ

²² The blessing of the Lᴏʀᴅ ʷ brings wealth, ˣ
   without painful toil for it. ʸ

²³ Fools find pleasure in wicked schemes, ᶻ
   but those who have understanding delight in wisdom.

²⁴ What the wicked dread ᵃ will overtake them; ᵇ
   what the righteous desire will be granted. ᶜ

²⁵ When the storm has swept by, the wicked are gone,
   but the righteous stand firm ᵈ forever. ᵉ

²⁶ As vinegar to the teeth and smoke ᶠ to the eyes,
   so are sluggards to those who send them. ᵍ

²⁷ The fear of the Lᴏʀᴅ adds length to life, ʰ
   but the years of the wicked are cut short. ⁱ

²⁸ The prospect of the righteous is joy,
   but the hopes of the wicked come to nothing. ʲ

²⁹ The way of the Lᴏʀᴅ is a refuge for the blameless,
   but it is the ruin of those who do evil. ᵏ

³⁰ The righteous will never be uprooted,
   but the wicked will not remain in the land. ˡ

³¹ From the mouth of the righteous comes the fruit of wisdom, ᵐ
   but a perverse tongue ⁿ will be silenced.

³² The lips of the righteous know what finds favor, ᵒ
   but the mouth of the wicked only what is perverse. ᵖ

11 The Lᴏʀᴅ detests dishonest scales, �q
   but accurate weights find favor with him. ʳ

² When pride comes, then comes disgrace, ˢ
   but with humility comes wisdom. ᵗ

³ The integrity of the upright guides them,
   but the unfaithful are destroyed by their duplicity. ᵘ

10:20 *choice silver.* What the righteous say has great value (see 3:14; 8:10; 25:11). *heart of the wicked.* Their thoughts and schemes (see 6:14,18).
10:21 *nourish many.* See v. 11 and note. *die for lack of sense.* See 5:23 and note; 7:7; 9:16.
10:22 *blessing of the Lᴏʀᴅ brings wealth.* Wealth is a gift from God, not a product of human attainment (see notes on v. 6; 3:10; see also 8:21; Ge 24:35; 26:12). *without painful toil for it.* Unlike the "ill-gotten treasures" of v. 2 (see note there); cf. 15:6.
10:23 *find pleasure in wicked schemes.* See 2:14; 15:21; 26:19.
10:24 *What the wicked dread.* Calamity and distress (see 1:26–27 and notes; 3:25; Job 15:21; Isa 66:4). *what the righteous desire.* See Ps 9:18; 37:4; 145:19; Mt 5:6; 1Jn 5:14–15.
10:25 Cf. the wise man who built his house on a rock, and the foolish man who built his on the sand (Mt 7:24–27). *the wicked are gone.* See Ps 37:10; Isa 28:18. *the righteous stand firm.* Unshakable, immovable (see 3:25 and note; see also 12:3,7; 14:11; Ps 10:6 and note; 15:5; 1Co 15:58).
10:26 *sluggards.* See note on 6:6. *who send them.* As messengers (cf. 13:17 and note; 25:13; 26:6 and note) or workers.
10:27 *fear of the Lᴏʀᴅ.* See note on 1:7. *adds length to life.* See note on 3:2. *years ... are cut short.* See Job 22:16; Ps 37:36; 55:23.
10:28 *prospect of the righteous.* See v. 24 and note. *joy.* Of ful-

fillment (cf. 11:23). *hopes of the wicked come to nothing.* See 11:7,23.
10:29 *way of the Lᴏʀᴅ.* The way he prescribes, the life of wisdom (see Ps 27:11; 143:8; Mt 22:16; Ac 18:25). *ruin of those who do evil.* Since judgment comes to those who refuse God's way (see 21:15; 2Co 2:15–16; 2Pe 2:21 and note).
10:30 *never be uprooted.* See v. 25; 2:21 and note; 12:3; Ps 125:1. *not remain in the land.* See note on 2:22.
10:31 *perverse tongue.* See note on 2:12. *silenced.* See Ps 12:3; cf. Mt 5:29–30 and notes.
11:1 *detests dishonest scales.* Similar denunciation is found in the Law (see Lev 19:35 and note) and the Prophets (Hos 12:7; Am 8:5; Mic 6:11). See also 16:11; 20:10,23. *accurate weights.* See note on 16:11. Silver was weighed on scales balanced against a stone weight. Weights with dishonest labels were used for cheating.
11:2 *When pride comes, then comes disgrace.* Along with destruction (see 16:18; cf. the humbling of proud Assyria in Isa 10:12; cf. also Isa 14:13–15). *with humility comes wisdom.* Along with honor (see note on 15:33).
11:3 *integrity ... guides them.* Cf. the actions of Joseph in Ge 39:6–12. *unfaithful are destroyed.* See v. 6; 2:22 and note; 19:3. *duplicity.* Cf. Lk 20:23.

⁴ Wealth ᵛ is worthless in the day of wrath, ʷ
  but righteousness delivers from death. ˣ

⁵ The righteousness of the blameless makes their paths straight, ʸ
  but the wicked are brought down by their own wickedness. ᶻ

⁶ The righteousness of the upright delivers them,
  but the unfaithful are trapped by evil desires. ᵃ

⁷ Hopes placed in mortals die with them; ᵇ
  all the promise ofᵃ their power comes to nothing. ᶜ

⁸ The righteous are rescued from trouble,
  and it falls on the wicked instead. ᵈ

⁹ With their mouths the godless destroy their neighbors,
  but through knowledge the righteous escape. ᵉ

¹⁰ When the righteous prosper, the city rejoices; ᶠ
  when the wicked perish, there are shouts of joy. ᵍ

¹¹ Through the blessing of the upright a city is exalted, ʰ
  but by the mouth of the wicked it is destroyed. ⁱ

¹² Those who have no sense deride their neighbors, ʲ
  but those who have understanding hold their tongues. ᵏ

¹³ Gossips betray a confidence, ˡ
  but the trustworthy keep a secret. ᵐ

¹⁴ For lack of guidance a nation falls, ⁿ
  but victory is won through many advisers. ᵒ

¹⁵ Whoever puts up securityᵖ for a stranger will surely suffer,
  but whoever refuses to shake hands in pledge is safe. �q

¹⁶ A kindhearted woman gains honor, ʳ
  but ruthless men gain only wealth.

¹⁷ Those who are kind benefit themselves,
  but the cruel bring ruin on themselves.

¹⁸ The wicked earn deceptive wages,
  but those who sow righteousness reap a sure reward. ˢ

¹⁹ Truly the righteous attain life, ᵗ
  but those who pursue evil go to their death. ᵘ

²⁰ The Lᴏʀᴅ detests those whose hearts are perverse, ᵛ
  but he delights ʷ in those whose ways are blameless. ˣ

ᵃ 7 Two Hebrew manuscripts; most Hebrew manuscripts, Vulgate, Syriac and Targum *When the wicked die, their hope perishes; / all they expected from*

11:4 ᵛ Eze 27:27
ʷ S Job 20:20;
S Eze 7:19 ˣ S Pr 10:2
11:5 ʸ S 1Ki 8:36
ᶻ S ver 3; Pr 5:21-23;
13:6; 21:7
11:6 ᵃ S Est 7:9
11:7 ᵇ S Job 8:13
ᶜ S Pr 10:28
11:8 ᵈ Pr 21:18
11:9 ᵉ Pr 12:6;
Jer 45:5
11:10 ᶠ S 2Ki 11:20
ᵍ S Est 8:17
11:11 ʰ Pr 14:34
ⁱ Pr 29:8
11:12 ʲ Pr 14:21
ᵏ S Job 6:24
11:13 ˡ Pr 20:19
ᵐ S Pr 10:14
11:14 ⁿ Pr 20:18
ᵒ S 2Sa 15:34;
Pr 15:22; 24:6
11:15 ᵖ S Pr 6:1
q Pr 17:18; 22:26-27
11:16 ʳ Pr 31:31
11:18 ˢ S Ex 1:20;
S Job 4:8; Hos 10:12-
13
11:19 ᵗ S Dt 30:15;
S Pr 10:2 ᵘ 1Sa 2:6;
Ps 89:48; Pr 1:18-19;
Ecc 7:2; Jer 43:11
11:20 ᵛ Pr 3:32
ʷ S Nu 14:8
ˣ S 1Ch 29:17;
S Ps 15:2; 101:1-4;
S 119:1; Pr 12:2,22;
15:9

11:4 *day of wrath.* The day of judgment (see Isa 10:3; Zep 1:18). *righteousness delivers from death.* See 2:16–18; 3:2; 10:2; 13:21.
11:5 *blameless.* See note on 2:7. *makes their paths straight.* Enables them to reach their goals (see v. 3; 3:6 and note; 10:9).
11:6 *righteousness . . . delivers them.* See vv. 3–4. *trapped.* See 5:22 and note.
11:7 For the thought in the TNIV text note, see v. 23; 10:28.
11:8 Cf. the rescue of Mordecai and the execution of Haman in Est 5:14; 7:10.
11:9 *destroy their neighbors.* By spreading slander (cf. 10:18). *through knowledge.* Perhaps the knowledge of the schemes and distortions of the godless (cf. Jn 2:25).
11:10 *city rejoices.* See 28:12; 29:2. Thus life in the city is itself a teacher of wisdom (see note on 1:21). *shouts of joy.* Cf. the joy at the fall of Assyria (see Isa 30:32 and note; Na 3:19; cf. 2Ch 21:20).
11:11 *blessing of the upright.* Their good influence and desire for justice, as well as their prosperity (v. 10), bring honor to the city. *mouth of the wicked.* Their deceit, dishonesty and sowing of discord (see v. 9; 6:12–14 and notes).

11:12 *deride their neighbors.* Show their contempt openly (see 10:18; 14:21). *hold their tongues.* See 10:19 and note.
11:14 See the close parallels in 15:22; 20:18; 24:6. *advisers.* See 2Sa 16:23; Isa 1:26.
11:15 See note on 6:1.
🅰 **11:16** Assumes that "a good name is more desirable than great riches" (22:1) and insightfully observes that a woman, if she is kindhearted, will be accorded more respect than wealthy men if they are ruthless. *kindhearted woman.* See 31:28,30.
11:17 *benefit themselves.* See Mt 5:7. *bring ruin on themselves.* See Ge 34:25–30; 49:7.
11:18 *deceptive wages.* Because they do not last (see notes on 10:2,16; see also Hag 1:6). *reap a sure reward.* See 10:24; Gal 6:8–9; Jas 3:18.
11:19 *attain life.* See 10:16 and note; 12:28; 19:23. *go to their death.* See 5:23; 21:16; Ro 6:23; Jas 1:15.
11:20 *detests those whose hearts are perverse.* See 3:32 and note; 16:5. *blameless.* See note on 2:7.

11:21 *y* Pr 16:5
11:25 *z* 1Ch 29:17;
Isa 32:8 *a* Pr 22:9;
2Co 9:6-9
11:27 *b* Ps 7:15-16
11:28 *c* Job 31:24-
28; S Ps 49:6; S 52:7;
62:10; Jer 9:23; 48:7
d Ps 52:8; 92:12-14
11:29 *e* Pr 14:19
11:30 *f* S Ge 2:9;
S Pr 10:11
11:31 *g* Jer 25:29;
49:12; 1Pe 4:18
12:1 *h* Pr 5:11-14;
S 9:7-9; 13:1,18; 15:5,
10,12,32
12:2 *i* Job 33:26;
Ps 84:11 *j* 2Sa 15:3;
S Pr 11:20
12:3 *k* S Pr 10:25
12:4 *l* S Ru 3:11;
Pr 31:10-11 *m* Pr 18:22

²¹ Be sure of this: The wicked will not go unpunished,
  but those who are righteous will go free. *y*

²² Like a gold ring in a pig's snout
  is a beautiful woman who shows no discretion.

²³ The desire of the righteous ends only in good,
  but the hope of the wicked only in wrath.

²⁴ One person gives freely, yet gains even more;
  another withholds unduly, but comes to poverty.

²⁵ A generous *z* person will prosper;
  whoever refreshes others will be refreshed. *a*

²⁶ People curse those who hoard grain,
  but they pray God's blessing on those who are willing to sell.

²⁷ Whoever seeks good finds favor,
  but evil comes to those who search for it. *b*

²⁸ Those who trust in their riches will fall, *c*
  but the righteous will thrive like a green leaf. *d*

²⁹ Those who bring ruin on their families will inherit only wind,
  and the fool will be servant to the wise. *e*

³⁰ The fruit of the righteous is a tree of life, *f*
  and those who win souls are wise.

³¹ If the righteous receive their due *g* on earth,
  how much more the ungodly and the sinner!

12 Whoever loves discipline loves knowledge,
  but whoever hates correction is stupid. *h*

² Good people obtain favor from the LORD, *i*
  but he condemns those who devise wicked schemes. *j*

³ No one can be established through wickedness,
  but the righteous cannot be uprooted. *k*

⁴ A wife of noble character *l* is her husband's crown,
  but a disgraceful wife is like decay in his bones. *m*

⁵ The plans of the righteous are just,
  but the advice of the wicked is deceitful.

11:21 *will not go unpunished.* See 6:29. *will go free.* See Ps 118:5.
11:22 *gold ring.* Commonly worn by women on their noses (see Ge 24:47; Eze 16:12 and note). *shows no discretion.* Abigail was praised by David for her display of "good judgment" (1Sa 25:33).
11:23 See 10:24,28. *wrath.* Judgment (see v. 4; Isa 10:3; Zep 1:18; Ro 2:8–9).
11:24 Generosity is the path to blessing and further prosperity (see 3:9–10; Ecc 11:1–2 and notes; Ps 112:9; 2Co 9:6–9). By contrast, the stingy do not make friends and hurt themselves in the long run (21:13; cf. 23:6–8 and notes; see also TNIV text note on 23:7).
11:25 *generous person will prosper.* "For they share their food with the poor" (22:9). "Whoever sows generously will also reap generously" (2Co 9:6; cf. Lk 6:38). *be refreshed.* See Ro 1:12 and note; 15:32.
11:26 *hoard grain.* Probably in times of scarcity to raise the price. *pray God's blessing on.* Cf. 10:6.
11:27 *Whoever seeks good finds favor.* Like the person in v. 25 (cf. Mt 7:12). *evil comes to those who search for it.* Their wicked schemes will backfire (see v. 8; 1:18 and notes).
11:28 *Those who trust in their riches.* Usually said of the wicked (see Ps 49:6; 62:10 and note; cf. 1Ti 6:17). *like a green leaf.* See Ps 1:3 and note; Ge 49:22; Jer 17:8.

11:29 *Those who bring ruin on their families will inherit only wind.* The inheritance of Levi and Simeon was affected because of their cruelty against Shechem (Ge 34:25–30; 49:5–7). See 15:27 and note. *servant to the wise.* As those who are evil serve the good (14:19; cf. 17:2).
11:30 *fruit of the righteous.* What the wise produce (8:18–19). *tree of life.* See note on 3:18. *win souls.* Win people over to wisdom and righteousness (see Da 12:3; 1Co 9:19–22; Jas 5:20). However, the Hebrew for this expression is unusual so that its translation is somewhat uncertain.
11:31 *the righteous receive their due.* Even Moses and David were punished for their sins (see Nu 20:11–12; 2Sa 12:10 and notes). *how much more the ungodly and the sinner!* See 1:18,31 and notes; Ps 11:6; 73:18–19.
12:1 *loves discipline loves knowledge.* See 1:7; 10:17; see also 6:23 and note. *hates correction is stupid.* See 1:22; 5:12 and note.
12:2 *obtain favor.* See 3:4; 8:35. *condemns those who devise wicked schemes.* Cf. 14:17; Job 5:12–13; 1Co 3:19.
12:3 *No one can be established.* See 11:5. *righteous cannot be uprooted.* See 2:21; 10:25,30 and notes.
12:4 *wife of noble character.* Someone like Ruth (Ru 3:11). Such a woman is fully described in 31:10–31. *her husband's crown.* She brings him honor and joy (see 4:9 and note). *decay.* See Hab 3:16 and note. *his bones.* See note on 3:8.

⁶ The words of the wicked lie in wait for blood,
　　but the speech of the upright rescues them. ⁿ

⁷ The wicked are overthrown and are no more, ᵒ
　　but the house of the righteous stands firm. ᵖ

⁸ People are praised according to their prudence,
　　and those with warped ᑫ minds are despised.

⁹ Better to be a nobody and yet have a servant
　　than pretend to be somebody and have no food.

¹⁰ The righteous care for the needs of their animals, ʳ
　　but the kindest acts of the wicked are cruel.

¹¹ Those who work their land will have abundant food,
　　but those who chase fantasies have no sense. ˢ

¹² The wicked desire the plunderᵃ of evildoers,
　　but the root of the righteous flourishes.

¹³ Evildoers are trapped by their sinful talk, ᵗ
　　and so the innocent escape trouble. ᵘ

¹⁴ From the fruit of their lips people are filled with good things, ᵛ
　　and the work of their hands brings them reward. ʷ

¹⁵ The way of fools seems right to them, ˣ
　　but the wise listen to advice. ʸ

¹⁶ Fools ᶻ show their annoyance at once, ᵃ
　　but the prudent overlook an insult. ᵇ

¹⁷ An honest witness tells the truth,
　　but a false witness tells lies. ᶜ

¹⁸ The words of the reckless pierce like swords, ᵈ
　　but the tongue of the wise brings healing. ᵉ

¹⁹ Truthful lips endure forever,
　　but a lying tongue lasts only a moment.

²⁰ Deceit is in the hearts of those who plot evil,
　　but those who promote peace have joy. ᶠ

²¹ No harm overtakes the righteous, ᵍ
　　but the wicked have their fill of trouble.

²² The LORD detests lying lips, ʰ
　　but he delights ⁱ in people who are trustworthy. ʲ

ᵃ 12 Or *stronghold*

12:6 ⁿ S Pr 11:9; 14:3
12:7 ᵒ S Ps 37:36
ᵖ S Pr 10:25; 14:11; 15:25
12:8 ᑫ Isa 19:14; 29:24
12:10 ʳ S Nu 22:29
12:11 ˢ Pr 28:19
12:13 ᵗ S Ps 59:12; S Pr 10:6; 18:7
ᵘ Pr 21:23
12:14 ᵛ Pr 13:2; 15:23; 18:20
ʷ Pr 14:14
12:15 ˣ Pr 14:12; 16:2,25 ʸ S Pr 9:7-9; 19:20
12:16 ᶻ S 1Sa 25:25
ᵃ S Job 5:2 ᵇ Pr 29:11
12:17 ᶜ S Pr 12:2; Pr 14:5,25
12:18 ᵈ S Ps 55:21; Pr 25:18 ᵉ Pr 15:4
12:20 ᶠ S Ro 14:19
12:21 ᵍ S Job 4:7
12:22 ʰ 1Ki 13:18; Pr 6:17 ⁱ Ps 18:19
ʲ S Pr 11:20

12:5 *advice of the wicked is deceitful.* See 1:10–19 and notes; Ps 1:1.
12:6 *lie in wait for blood.* See note on 1:11; see also 1:16. *speech of the upright rescues them.* See 11:3–4,6,9.
12:7 See 10:25 and note.
12:8 *praised according to their prudence.* See 3:4 and note. *those with warped minds are despised.* See Dt 32:5; Tit 3:11 and note.
12:9 *yet have a servant.* Even people of moderate means had servants (see Jdg 6:15,27). *pretend to be somebody.* Cf. 13:7.
12:10 *care for the needs of their animals.* See 27:23; Dt 25:4; Mt 12:11; see also chart, p. 275. *kindest acts of the wicked are cruel.* Probably to both people and animals.
12:11 Repeated with slight variation in 28:19. *chase fantasies.* Scheme for making easy money.
12:12 *desire the plunder of evildoers.* See 1:13 and note; 21:10. *root of the righteous flourishes.* They bear fruit, like firmly rooted trees (see vv. 3,7; 11:30; Ps 1:3; see also 10:25 and note).
12:13 *trapped by their sinful talk.* See 1:18 and note; 29:6. *the innocent escape trouble.* See 11:8–9 and notes; 21:23; 2Pe 2:9.

12:14 Those who speak wisely will reap a harvest from their words, just as farmers enjoy the harvest of their crops (see 1:31 and note; Job 34:11).
12:15 *seems right.* But ends in death (see 1:25,30; 14:12; 16:25).
12:16 *overlook an insult.* Have good self-control (see 29:11; 2Sa 16:11–12).
12:17 *false witness tells lies.* See note on 6:19.
12:18 *The words of the reckless.* Cf. Ps 106:33. *pierce like swords.* See note on Ps 5:9. *tongue of the wise brings healing.* With soothing, comforting words (see 4:20–22; 15:4).
12:19 *lasts only a moment.* The lies will be refuted and the liar punished (see 19:9; Ps 52:4–5).
12:20 *Deceit is in the hearts.* See 6:14 and note; see also 1:31; 24:2; Ge 6:5. *hearts.* See note on Ps 4:7. *those who promote peace have joy.* "Blessed are the peacemakers" (Mt 5:9).
12:21 *No harm.* See 1:33 and note; 2:8; Ps 91:9–13; 121:7. *their fill of trouble.* See 1:31 and note; 11:5,8; 22:8; Job 4:8.
12:22 Compare the structure of this verse with that of 11:1,20. *detests.* See note on 3:32. *people who are trustworthy.* See 16:13.

12:23 ᵏ S Pr 10:14
ˡ S Ps 38:5; S 59:7;
Pr 18:2
12:24 ᵐ S Pr 10:4
12:25 ⁿ Pr 15:13
12:26 ° S Ps 95:10
12:28 ᵖ S Dt 30:15;
S Pr 10:2
13:1 ᑫ S Pr 12:1; 15:5
13:2 ʳ S Pr 12:14
13:3 ˢ S Ps 12:2;
S 34:13 ᵗ S Pr 10:6;
21:23 ᵘ S Job 1:22;
Pr 18:7,20-21
13:4 ᵛ Pr 21:25-26
13:5 ʷ S Ps 119:128
13:6 ˣ S Pr 11:3,5;
Jer 44:5
13:7 ʸ Rev 3:17
ᶻ 2Co 6:10
13:8 ᵃ Pr 15:16
13:9 ᵇ S Job 18:5;
S Pr 4:18-19
13:10 ᶜ S Jdg 19:30;
S Pr 9:9

²³ The prudent keep their knowledge to themselves, ᵏ
　　but a fool's heart blurts out folly. ˡ

²⁴ Diligent hands will rule,
　　but laziness ends in forced labor. ᵐ

²⁵ Anxiety weighs down the heart, ⁿ
　　but a kind word cheers it up.

²⁶ The righteous choose their friends carefully,
　　but the way of the wicked leads them astray. °

²⁷ The lazy do not roastᵃ any game,
　　but the diligent feed on the riches of the hunt.

²⁸ In the way of righteousness there is life; ᵖ
　　along that path is immortality.

13

A wise child heeds a parent's instruction,
　　but a mocker does not respond to rebukes. ᑫ

² From the fruit of their lips people enjoy good things, ʳ
　　but the unfaithful have an appetite for violence.

³ Those who guard their lips ˢ preserve their lives, ᵗ
　　but those who speak rashly will come to ruin. ᵘ

⁴ A sluggard's appetite is never filled, ᵛ
　　but the desires of the diligent are fully satisfied.

⁵ The righteous hate what is false, ʷ
　　but the wicked make themselves a stench
　　and are filled with shame.

⁶ Righteousness guards the person of integrity,
　　but wickedness overthrows the sinner. ˣ

⁷ One person pretends to be rich, yet has nothing; ʸ
　　another pretends to be poor, yet has great wealth. ᶻ

⁸ The rich may be able to ransom their lives,
　　but the poor cannot respond to threatening rebukes. ᵃ

⁹ The light of the righteous shines brightly,
　　but the lamp of the wicked is snuffed out. ᵇ

¹⁰ Where there is strife, there is pride,
　　but wisdom is found in those who take advice. ᶜ

ᵃ 27 The meaning of the Hebrew for this word is uncertain.

12:23 *keep their knowledge to themselves.* Store up knowledge (see 10:14 and note). *blurts out folly.* See v. 16; 13:16; 15:2,7,28; 29:11.

12:24 *Diligent hands … laziness.* Contrasted also in 10:4 (see note there). *will rule.* Cf. 17:2. *forced labor.* See Jdg 1:28; see also note on 2Sa 20:24.

12:25 *Anxiety weighs down the heart.* See Ps 94:19. *kind word cheers it up.* See 15:23.

12:26 *choose their friends carefully.* See 13:20; 18:24; 22:24. *leads them astray.* See 5:23; 14:22.

12:27 *do not roast any game.* And are too lazy to lift the food from the dish to their mouths (19:24). *feed on the riches of the hunt.* Cf. Ecc 5:19.

12:28 See 10:2 and note. *there is life.* Cf. 3:2 and note; 11:4. *immortality.* Lit. "no death." The way or path of righteousness does not lead to death. Cf. the identification of wisdom with the "tree of life" (3:18 [see note there]; cf. 14:32).

13:1 *heeds a parent's instruction.* See 1:8 and note; 4:1. *mocker does not respond to rebukes.* See 1:22; 9:7–8 and notes.

13:2 See 12:14 and note. *have an appetite for violence.* See 4:17 and note.

13:3 *Those who guard their lips preserve their lives.* "The tongue has the power of life and death" (18:21). The ability to control the tongue is one of the clearest marks of wisdom. See 10:19 and note. *those who speak rashly will come to ruin.* See 10:14; 12:18 and note; 18:7.

13:4 *sluggard's.* See 6:6 and note. *appetite is never filled.* Is never satisfied, yet the sluggard refuses to work (see 21:25–26). *desires of the diligent are fully satisfied.* Diligence yields a profit (see 6:6; see also notes on 10:4,24).

13:5 *filled with shame.* Like a lazy son (10:5; cf. 19:26).

13:6 This contrast repeats the thought of 2:21–22; 10:9; 11:3,5 (see notes there); cf. 21:12; Ps 25:21.

13:7 Both pretenses are folly and lead to folly (see 14:8 and note; see also 11:24 and note; 12:9).

13:8 *be able to ransom their lives.* Have the means to pay off robbers or enemies (see 10:15 and note; Jer 41:8).

13:9 *light … lamp.* Symbols of life (cf. Job 3:20). *shines brightly.* There is joy and prosperity (see note on 4:18). *lamp of the wicked is snuffed out.* Their lives will end (see 20:20; 24:20; Job 18:5; 21:17).

13:10 *pride.* See 11:2 and note.

¹¹ Dishonest money dwindles away, ^d
    but whoever gathers money little by little makes it grow.

¹² Hope deferred makes the heart sick,
    but a longing fulfilled is a tree of life. ^e

¹³ Whoever scorns instruction will pay for it, ^f
    but whoever respects ^g a command is rewarded. ^h

¹⁴ The teaching of the wise is a fountain of life, ⁱ
    turning a person from the snares of death. ^j

¹⁵ Good judgment wins favor,
    but the way of the unfaithful leads to their destruction. ^a

¹⁶ All who are prudent act with ^b knowledge,
    but fools expose ^k their folly. ^l

¹⁷ A wicked messenger falls into trouble, ^m
    but a trustworthy envoy brings healing. ⁿ

¹⁸ Whoever disregards discipline comes to poverty and shame, ^o
    but whoever heeds correction is honored. ^p

¹⁹ A longing fulfilled is sweet to the soul, ^q
    but fools detest turning from evil.

²⁰ Walk with the wise and become wise,
    for a companion of fools suffers harm. ^r

²¹ Trouble pursues the sinner, ^s
    but the righteous ^t are rewarded with good things. ^u

²² Good people leave an inheritance for their children's children,
    but a sinner's wealth is stored up for the righteous. ^v

²³ An unplowed field produces food for the poor,
    but injustice sweeps it away.

²⁴ Those who spare the rod ^w hate their children,
    but those who love them are careful to discipline ^x them. ^y

²⁵ The righteous eat to their hearts' content,
    but the stomach of the wicked goes hungry. ^z

14

The wise woman builds her house, ^a
    but with her own hands the foolish one tears hers down.

---

^a 15 Septuagint and Syriac; the meaning of the Hebrew for this phrase is uncertain.   ^b 16 Or *prudent protect themselves through*

13:11 *Dishonest money dwindles away.* Such as wealth gained by extortion (Ps 62:10) or deceit (Pr 21:6). See note on 10:2; see also Jer 17:11. *makes it grow.* See note on 10:4.
13:12 *Hope deferred makes the heart sick.* Cf. Ge 30:1. *longing fulfilled is a tree of life.* It revives and strengthens (see note on 3:18; see also 10:28; 13:19).
13:13 *Whoever scorns instruction will pay for it.* See 1:29–31; 5:12 and note. *whoever respects a command is rewarded.* With the benefits wisdom gives (see 3:2 and note; 3:16–18; 16:20; cf. 13:21).
13:14 *fountain of life.* See note on 10:11. *from the snares of death.* See notes on 1:17; 5:22; see also 7:23; 22:5.
13:15 *wins favor.* See 3:4; 8:35. *leads to their destruction.* See v. 13 and note.
13:16 See 12:23 and note.
13:17 *falls into trouble.* Perhaps by misrepresenting the sender. *brings healing.* A tactful, honest approach benefits both parties (see 25:13; cf. 12:18; 15:4).
13:18 *comes to poverty and shame.* See 5:10–12 and notes. *whoever heeds correction is honored.* See v. 1; 3:16–18; 8:35; 10:17.
13:19 *longing fulfilled.* See v. 12. *fools detest turning from evil.*

Cf. their hatred of correction in 5:12.
13:20 *Walk with the wise and become wise.* Choose your friends with care (see 2:20; 12:26). *companion of fools suffers harm.* See 1:10,18; 2:12; 16:29; 22:24–25.
13:21 See v. 13 and note.
13:22 *is stored up for the righteous.* Job agrees that this is often what happens to the possessions of the wicked (Job 27:16–17; cf. Pr 28:8; Ecc 2:18–21).
13:23 *injustice sweeps it away.* Probably a case of the rich and powerful oppressing the poor (see Am 2:6–7 and notes; cf. Ps 35:10).
13:24 *who spare the rod hate their children.* Parents are encouraged to apply the rod of punishment to drive out folly (22:15) so that the child will not follow a path of destruction (19:18; 23:13–14). The rod and a reprimand "impart wisdom" (29:15) and promote a healthy and happy family life (29:17). Discipline is rooted in love (see 3:11–12 and note). *rod.* Probably a figure of speech for caring discipline of any kind.
13:25 States more specifically the teaching of vv. 13,18,21; see 10:3 and note.
14:1 *wise woman builds her house.* She is a source of strength

---

13:11 ^d S Pr 10:2
13:12 ^e S Pr 10:11
13:13 ^f S Nu 15:31
  ^g Ex 9:20 ^h Pr 16:20
13:14 ⁱ S Pr 10:11
  ^j Pr 14:27
13:16 ^k Ecc 10:3
  ^l Est 5:11; S Ps 38:5
13:17 ^m S Pr 10:26
  ⁿ Pr 25:13
13:18 ^o S Pr 1:7;
S 12:1 ^p Ps 141:5;
Pr 25:12; Ecc 7:5
13:19 ^q S Pr 10:11
13:20 ^r 2Ch 10:8
13:21 ^s 2Sa 3:39;
Jer 40:3; 50:7;
Eze 14:13; 18:4
  ^t Ps 32:10 ^u Ps 25:13
13:22 ^v S Est 8:2;
S Job 27:17; Ecc 2:26
13:24 ^w S 2Sa 7:14
  ^x S Pr 3:12 ^y Pr 19:18;
22:15; 23:13-14;
29:15,17; Eph 6:4;
Heb 12:7
13:25 ^z Pr 10:3
14:1 ^a S Ru 3:11;
Pr 24:3

14:3 b S Pr 10:14;
Ecc 10:12 c S Pr 10:13;
S 12:6
14:4 d Ps 144:14
14:5 e S Ps 12:2;
S Pr 12:17
14:6 f S Pr 9:9
14:8 g ver 15;
Pr 15:28; 21:29
h ver 24
14:11 i S Job 8:22;
Pr 21:12 j S Ps 72:7;
S Pr 3:33; S 12:7
14:12 k S Pr 12:15
l Pr 16:25
14:13 m Ecc 2:2;
7:3,6
14:14 n S Pr 1:31
o 2Ch 15:7; Pr 12:14
14:15 p S ver 8
14:16 q S Ex 20:20;
Pr 22:3 r S 1Sa 25:25
14:17 s S 2Ki 5:12
t ver 29; Pr 15:18;
16:28; 26:21; 28:25;
29:22 u S Est 5:9
14:19 v Pr 11:29

² Whoever fears the LORD walks uprightly,
    but those who despise him are devious in their ways.

³ A fool's mouth lashes out with pride, b
    but the lips of the wise protect them. c

⁴ Where there are no oxen, the manger is empty,
    but from the strength of an ox d come abundant harvests.

⁵ An honest witness does not deceive,
    but a false witness pours out lies. e

⁶ The mocker seeks wisdom and finds none,
    but knowledge comes easily to the discerning. f

⁷ Stay away from the foolish,
    for you will not find knowledge on their lips.

⁸ The wisdom of the prudent is to give thought to their ways, g
    but the folly of fools is deception. h

⁹ Fools mock at making amends for sin,
    but goodwill is found among the upright.

¹⁰ Each heart knows its own bitterness,
    and no one else can share its joy.

¹¹ The house of the wicked will be destroyed, i
    but the tent of the upright will flourish. j

¹² There is a way that appears to be right, k
    but in the end it leads to death. l

¹³ Even in laughter m the heart may ache,
    and rejoicing may end in grief.

¹⁴ The faithless will be fully repaid for their ways, n
    and the good rewarded for theirs. o

¹⁵ The simple believe anything,
    but the prudent give thought to their steps. p

¹⁶ The wise fear the LORD and shun evil, q
    but a fool r is hotheaded and yet feels secure.

¹⁷ The quick-tempered s do foolish things, t
    and those who devise evil schemes are hated. u

¹⁸ The simple inherit folly,
    but the prudent are crowned with knowledge.

¹⁹ Evildoers will bow down in the presence of the good,
    and the wicked at the gates of the righteous. v

---

and an example of diligence for her family (see 31:10–31). Cf. the house built by wisdom in 9:1.
14:2 *fears the LORD.* See note on 1:7.
14:3 *lips of the wise protect them.* Cf. Ecc 9:13–18.
14:4 Perhaps the thought is that people need to take good care of their oxen (the means of production) if they expect an abundant harvest (see 12:10 and note).
14:5 See note on 6:19.
14:6 *mocker.* See 1:22 and note. *seeks wisdom and finds none.* Because of refusal to fear the Lord or accept any correction.
14:8 *folly of fools is deception.* What fools believe to be prudent (but is really folly) does not bring success; instead, it tends toward their ruin.
14:9 *mock at making amends for sin.* Cf. 19:28. *goodwill ... among the upright.* See 11:27.
14:10 *knows its own bitterness.* See 1Ki 8:38. Cf. the experience of Hannah (1Sa 1:10) and Peter (Mt 26:75). *can share its joy.* Cf. Mt 13:44; 1Pe 1:8.
14:11 See 10:25 and note.

14:12 Repeated in 16:25. *in the end it leads to death.* See 5:4,23; 7:21–27; Mt 7:13–14.
14:13 *in laughter the heart may ache.* Cf. Ezr 3:11–12. *rejoicing may end in grief.* As the death of Rachel in childbirth (Ge 35:16–18).
14:14 See 1:31; 12:14 and notes; see also 11:5,8; 18:20; 22:8; Job 4:8.
14:15 *simple.* See note on 1:4. *give thought to their steps.* See 4:26 and note; 21:29.
14:16 *fear the LORD and shun evil.* See notes on 1:7; 3:7. *hotheaded.* Cf. 21:24. *yet feels secure.* But people and nations can have a false sense of security (cf. 27:24; Jdg 18:7; Isa 32:9–13; 47:8–11; Jer 22:21; Da 8:25; 11:21,24; Am 6:1; Zec 1:15 and note).
14:17 *quick-tempered.* See v. 29; Tit 1:7. *who devise evil schemes.* Cf. 12:2; Job 5:12–13; 1Co 3:19.
14:18 *crowned with knowledge.* Adorned and blessed with knowledge (see note on 4:9; see also v. 24; 12:4; Ps 103:4).
14:19 *Evildoers will bow down.* Cf. 17:2. *at the gates of the righteous.* Perhaps to beg for a favor (cf. 1Sa 2:36).

20 The poor are shunned even by their neighbors,
   but the rich have many friends. *w*

21 It is a sin to despise one's neighbor, *x*
   but blessed are those who are kind to the needy. *y*

22 Do not those who plot evil go astray? *z*
   But those who plan what is good find *a* love and faithfulness.

23 All hard work brings a profit,
   but mere talk leads only to poverty.

24 The wealth of the wise is their crown,
   but the folly of fools yields folly. *a*

25 A truthful witness saves lives,
   but a false witness is deceitful. *b*

26 Those who fear the LORD have a secure fortress, *c*
   and for their children it will be a refuge. *d*

27 The fear of the LORD is a fountain of life, *e*
   turning a person from the snares of death. *f*

28 A large population is a king's glory,
   but without subjects a prince is ruined. *g*

29 Those who are patient have great understanding, *h*
   but the quick-tempered display folly. *i*

30 A heart at peace gives life to the body,
   but envy rots the bones. *j*

31 Whoever oppresses the poor shows contempt for their Maker, *k*
   but whoever is kind to the needy honors God. *l*

32 When calamity comes, the wicked are brought down, *m*
   but even in death the righteous seek refuge in God. *n*

33 Wisdom reposes in the heart of the discerning *o*
   and even among fools she lets herself be known. *b*

34 Righteousness exalts a nation, *p*
   but sin condemns any people.

35 A king delights in a wise servant,
   but a shameful servant arouses his fury. *q*

a 22 Or *show*   *b* 33 Hebrew; Septuagint and Syriac / *but in the heart of fools she is not known*

14:20 *w* Pr 19:4, 7
14:21 *x* Pr 11:12
y Pr 19:17
14:22 *z* Pr 4:16-17
14:24 *a* ver 8
14:25 *b* S Pr 12:17
14:26 *c* Pr 18:10
d Ps 9:9
14:27 *e* S Pr 10:11
f Ps 18:5; Pr 13:14
14:28 *g* S 2Sa 19:7
14:29 *h* S 2Ki 5:12;
Pr 17:27 *i* S ver 17;
Ecc 7:8-9
14:30 *j* Pr 17:22
14:31 *k* Pr 17:5
l S Dt 24:14;
S Job 20:19;
S Mt 10:42
14:32 *m* S Ps 34:21;
S Pr 6:15 *n* S Job 13:15
14:33 *o* Pr 2:6-10
14:34 *p* Pr 11:11
14:35 *q* S Est 8:2;
Mt 24:45-51; 25:14-30

14:20 *shunned even by their neighbors.* And sometimes by their relatives (see 19:7).

14:21 *blessed are those who are kind to the needy.* Sharing food (22:9), lending money (28:8) and defending rights (31:9) are ways one can show kindness. Such a person "honors God" (v. 31; cf. 17:5) and "will lack nothing" (28:27). Cf. 21:13; Ps 41:1.

14:22 *plot evil.* See 3:29; 6:14, 18; Mic 2:1. *go astray.* See 5:23; 12:26. *find love and faithfulness.* Receive the support and care of faithful friends (cf. 3:3; 16:6; 20:28)—perhaps God's support and care are also implied here. *love and faithfulness.* See Ps 26:3 and note.

14:23 *hard work brings a profit.* See note on 10:4; see also 21:5.

14:24 *wealth … is their crown.* The wise obtain wealth, and it adorns them like a crown (see 10:22 and note). *yields folly.* An empty inheritance (see v. 18; 3:35).

14:25 See v. 5; 12:17; see also note on 6:19.

14:26 *fear the LORD.* See 1:7; 3:7 and notes. *secure fortress … refuge.* Means either that the godliness of parents will result in blessing for themselves and their children (see 20:7) or that the "fear of the LORD" will be a strong tower where the children also can find refuge (see 18:10; Ps 71:7; Isa 33:6).

14:27 See note on 10:11; see also 13:14.

14:29 *patient.* See 15:18; 16:32; 19:11; Jas 1:19. *quick-tempered.* See v. 17; cf. Eph 4:26.

14:30 *gives life to the body.* Cf. the healthy effects of fearing the Lord and walking in wisdom in 3:7–8, 16–18. *envy rots the bones.* See note on 3:8; see also 12:4; Ps 37:7–8.

14:31 *shows contempt for their Maker.* Because God created both the rich and the poor in his image (see 17:5; 22:2; Ge 1:26 and note; Job 31:15; Jas 3:9). *kind to the needy.* See note on v. 21. *honors God.* Does God's will, and in a sense gives to God himself (see 19:17 and note; Mt 25:40).

14:32 *wicked are brought down.* See 1:26 and note; 11:5; 24:16. *even in death the righteous seek refuge in God.* Their faith in God gives them hope beyond the grave (see 12:28; Ps 49:15 and notes).

14:33 *even among fools she lets herself be known.* Perhaps means that even from fools occasionally display a bit of wisdom (cf. Ac 17:27–28; Ro 1:19–20), but see TNIV text note.

14:34 *Righteousness exalts a nation.* See note on 11:11. Israel was promised prosperity and prestige if she obeyed God's laws (see Dt 28:1–14). *sin condemns any people.* The Canaanites were driven out because of their terrible sin (Lev 18:24–25), and Israel later received the same curse (Dt 28:15–68; cf. 2Sa 12:10).

14:35 *arouses his fury.* See 16:14 and note; 19:12; Da 2:12.

15:1 ʳ1Ki 12:7;
2Ch 10:7 ˢ Pr 25:15
15:2 ᵗ ver 7;
S Pr 10:31 ᵘ S Ps 59:7;
Ecc 10:12
15:3 ᵛ S 2Ch 16:9
ʷ S Job 10:4; S 31:4;
S Heb 4:13
ˣ S Job 34:21; Pr 5:21;
Jer 16:17
15:4 ʸ S Ps 5:9
ᶻ S Pr 10:11 ᵃ Pr 12:18
15:5 ᵇ S Pr 10:17;
S 12:1; S 13:1
15:6 ᶜ S Pr 8:21
ᵈ S Pr 10:16
15:7 ᵉ S ver 2;
S Pr 10:13
15:8 ᶠ S Ps 51:17;
S Isa 1:13 ᵍ S Pr 6:16;
21:27 ʰ ver 29;
Job 35:13; Pr 28:9;
S Jn 9:31
15:9 ⁱ S Pr 6:16
ʲ S Dt 7:13; S Pr 11:20
15:10 ᵏ S Pr 1:31-32;
S 12:1
15:11 ˡ S Job 26:6
ᵐ S 1Sa 2:3;
S 2Ch 6:30;
S Ps 44:21;
S Rev 2:23
15:12 ⁿ S Pr 9:8;
S 12:1
15:13 ᵒ ver 15
ᵖ S Pr 12:25; 17:22;
18:14
15:14 �q Pr 18:15
15:15 ʳ ver 13
15:16 ˢ ver 17;
Ps 37:16-17; Pr 13:8;
16:8; 17:1
15:17 ᵗ S ver 16;
Pr 17:1; Ecc 4:6
15:18 ᵘ S Pr 6:16-
19; S 14:17 ᵛ S Ge 13:8

15

A gentle answer ʳ turns away wrath, ˢ
  but a harsh word stirs up anger.

2 The tongue of the wise adorns knowledge, ᵗ
  but the mouth of the fool gushes folly. ᵘ

3 The eyes ᵛ of the Lᴏʀᴅ are everywhere, ʷ
  keeping watch on the wicked and the good. ˣ

4 The soothing tongue ʸ is a tree of life, ᶻ
  but a perverse tongue crushes the spirit. ᵃ

5 A fool spurns a parent's discipline,
  but whoever heeds correction shows prudence. ᵇ

6 The house of the righteous contains great treasure, ᶜ
  but the income of the wicked brings ruin. ᵈ

7 The lips of the wise spread knowledge, ᵉ
  but the hearts of fools are not upright.

8 The Lᴏʀᴅ detests the sacrifice ᶠ of the wicked, ᵍ
  but the prayer of the upright pleases him. ʰ

9 The Lᴏʀᴅ detests the way of the wicked, ⁱ
  but he loves those who pursue righteousness. ʲ

10 Stern discipline awaits those who leave the path;
  those who hate correction will die. ᵏ

11 Death and Destruction ᵃ lie open before the Lᴏʀᴅ ˡ—
  how much more do human hearts! ᵐ

12 Mockers resent correction, ⁿ
  so they avoid the wise.

13 A happy heart makes the face cheerful, ᵒ
  but heartache crushes the spirit. ᵖ

14 The discerning heart seeks knowledge, q
  but the mouth of a fool feeds on folly.

15 All the days of the oppressed are wretched,
  but the cheerful heart has a continual feast. ʳ

16 Better a little with the fear of the Lᴏʀᴅ
  than great wealth with turmoil. ˢ

17 Better a small serving of vegetables with love
  than a fattened calf with hatred. ᵗ

18 The hot-tempered stir up dissension, ᵘ
  but those who are patient calm a quarrel. ᵛ

ᵃ 11 Hebrew *Abaddon*

15:1 *gentle answer turns away wrath.* Cf. the way Gideon calmed the anger of the men of Ephraim in Jdg 8:1–3 (cf. also Pr 15:18; Ecc 10:4). *harsh word stirs up anger.* Nabal's sarcastic response put David in a fighting mood (1Sa 25:10–13).
15:2 *gushes folly.* See vv. 7,28; 12:23; 13:16.
15:3 *eyes of the Lᴏʀᴅ are everywhere.* See 5:21; Job 31:4; 34:21; Jer 16:17; 32:19.
15:4 *soothing tongue.* See note on 12:18. *tree of life.* See note on 3:18. *perverse tongue crushes the spirit.* Especially false testimony in court (see 6:19 and note; 22:22), or slander in the community.
15:6 See 10:2,16,22 and notes. *great treasure.* See 8:18,21; 24:4; Zec 8:12 and note; see also note on 3:10.
15:8 *detests the sacrifice of the wicked.* Those whose hearts are not right with God gain nothing by offering sacrifices (see Ecc 5:1; see also Pr 21:3; Isa 1:11–15; Jer 6:20 and notes). *prayer of the upright.* See 3:32.

15:9 *who pursue righteousness.* See 21:21; 1Ti 6:11.
15:10 *the path.* The right (or "straight") path (see 2:13). *who hate correction will die.* See 5:12,23 and notes.
15:11 *Death and Destruction.* See 27:20. *lie open before the Lᴏʀᴅ.* Not even the grave, the netherworld, is inaccessible to God (see Job 26:6 and note; Ps 139:8). Therefore he knows the secrets of everyone's inmost being (cf. 1Sa 16:7 and note).
15:12 See 1:30; 10:8; 13:1; 17:10. *Mockers.* See note on 1:22.
15:13 *happy heart makes the face cheerful.* Cf. 14:30. *heartache crushes the spirit.* Cf. the great sorrow of Job (Job 3) and David (Ps 51:8,10).
15:15 *cheerful heart has a continual feast.* Life is as joyful and satisfying as the days of a festival (see v. 13; 14:30; cf. Lev 23:39–41).
15:16 *fear of the Lᴏʀᴅ.* See 1:7 and note. *great wealth with turmoil.* The "ill-gotten treasures" of 10:2 (see note there).
15:17 *fattened calf.* Such meat was something of a luxury, reserved for special occasions (cf. 7:14; Mt 22:4; Lk 15:23).

15:19 ʷ Pr 22:5
15:20 ˣ S Pr 10:1
15:21 ʸ S Pr 2:14
15:22 ᶻ S Pr 16:7
ᵃ 1Ki 1:12; Pr 24:6
ᵇ S Pr 11:14
15:23 ᶜ S Pr 12:14
ᵈ Pr 25:11
15:25 ᵉ S Pr 12:7
ᶠ S Dt 19:14; Pr 23:10-11
15:26 ᵍ S Ps 94:11
ʰ S Pr 6:16
ⁱ S Ps 18:26
15:27 ʲ S Ex 23:8;
S Ps 15:5; Isa 1:23; 33:15
15:28 ᵏ S Pr 14:8
ˡ S Ps 59:7
15:29 ᵐ S ver 8;
S Job 15:31;
Ps 145:18-19;
Isa 59:2; S Jn 9:31
15:30 ⁿ Pr 25:25
15:31 ᵒ S Pr 9:7-9;
S 12:1
15:32 ᵖ S Pr 1:7;
S 12:1 ᵍ S Pr 9:7-9;
S 12:1; Ecc 7:5
15:33 ʳ S Pr 1:7
ˢ Pr 16:18; 18:12; 22:4;
29:23; Isa 66:2
16:1 ᵗ ver 9; Pr 19:21
16:2 ᵘ S Pr 12:15;
30:12 ᵛ S 1Sa 2:3
ʷ 2Ch 6:30;
Pr 20:27; 21:2;
Lk 16:15

¹⁹ The way of the sluggard is blocked with thorns, ʷ
  but the path of the upright is a highway.

²⁰ Wise children bring joy to their father, ˣ
  but foolish children despise their mother.

²¹ Folly brings joy to those who have no sense, ʸ
  but those who have understanding keep a straight course.

²² Plans fail for lack of counsel, ᶻ
  but with many advisers ᵃ they succeed. ᵇ

²³ A person finds joy in giving an apt reply ᶜ—
  and how good is a timely word! ᵈ

²⁴ The path of life leads upward for the prudent
  to keep them from going down to the realm of the dead.

²⁵ The LORD tears down the house of the proud, ᵉ
  but he sets the widow's boundary stones in place. ᶠ

²⁶ The LORD detests the thoughts ᵍ of the wicked, ʰ
  but gracious words are pure ⁱ in his sight.

²⁷ The greedy bring ruin to their households,
  but those who hate bribes will live. ʲ

²⁸ The heart of the righteous weighs its answers, ᵏ
  but the mouth of the wicked gushes evil. ˡ

²⁹ The LORD is far from the wicked,
  but he hears the prayer of the righteous. ᵐ

³⁰ Light in a messenger's eyes brings joy to the heart,
  and good news gives health to the bones. ⁿ

³¹ Whoever heeds life-giving correction
  will be at home among the wise. ᵒ

³² Those who disregard discipline despise themselves, ᵖ
  but those who heed correction gain understanding. ᵍ

³³ Wisdom's instruction is to fear the LORD, ʳ
  and humility comes before honor. ˢ

16 To human beings belong the plans of the heart,
  but from the LORD comes the proper answer of the tongue. ᵗ

² People may think all their ways are pure, ᵘ
  but motives are weighed ᵛ by the LORD. ʷ

15:18 *stir up dissension.* See note on 6:14. *patient.* See 14:29; 16:32; 19:11; Jas 1:19.
15:19 *sluggard.* See note on 6:6. *blocked with thorns.* Mainly because he was too lazy to remove them (see 24:30–31; Hos 2:6). *highway.* The upright can make progress and reach their goals (see note on 3:6).
15:20 See 10:1 and note.
15:21 A variation of 10:23.
15:22 See the close parallels in 11:14; 20:18; 24:6.
15:23 *apt reply.* Cf. Isa 50:4. *how good is a timely word!* Cf. 24:26.
15:24 *leads upward.* Along the "highway" (v. 19), the "straight course" (v. 21) that leads to life. *to keep them from going down to the realm of the dead.* See note on 2:18.
15:25 *tears down the house of the proud.* See 2:22; 14:11; see also 10:25 and note. *sets the widow's boundary stones in place.* In ancient times boundary stones marked a person's property. Anyone who moved such a stone was, in effect, stealing land (see 22:28; 23:10; Job 24:2; Dt 19:14 and note).
15:26 *detests the thoughts of the wicked.* Cf. vv. 8–9. *gracious words are pure.* See 22:11; Ps 24:4 and note.
15:27 *The greedy bring ruin to their households.* See 1:19; 11:29;

28:25. Achan's whole family perished because of his greed at Jericho (see Jos 7:24 and note). *those who hate bribes will live.* See 17:8 and note; 28:16.
15:28 *weighs its answers.* Cf. 10:32; 1Pe 3:15. *gushes evil.* See v. 2; see also v. 7; 12:23.
15:29 *far from the wicked.* See 1:28 and note.
15:30 *Light in a messenger's eyes brings joy.* Cf. v. 13; 16:15; Job 29:24. *good news gives health to the bones.* See 3:8 and note; see also Php 2:19.
15:31 *Whoever heeds life-giving correction.* See 1:23; 6:23 and note.
15:32 *Those who disregard discipline despise themselves.* See note on 5:12; see also 1:7; 5:23; 8:36. *those who heed correction.* Cf. vv. 5, 31.
15:33 *fear the LORD.* See note on 1:7. *humility comes before honor.* See 18:12; 25:6–7; Mt 23:12; Lk 14:11 and note; 18:14; 1Pe 5:6. Wisdom also comes with humility (11:2; 13:10).
16:1 *from the LORD comes the proper answer of the tongue.* God must give the ability to articulate and accomplish those plans (cf. 19:21).
16:2 *think all their ways are pure.* See 14:12. *motives are*

16:3 ˣS 2Ch 20:20;
S Ps 20:4; 37:5-6;
S Pr 3:5-6
16:4 ʸEx 9:16
ᶻS 2Ch 34:24;
S Ps 18:18; Ro 9:22
16:5 ᵃS Ps 40:4;
S Pr 6:16 ᵇPr 11:20-21
16:6 ᶜS Ge 20:11;
S Ex 1:17 ᵈS Ex 20:20
16:7 ᵉS Ge 39:21
ᶠPs 105:15; Jer 39:12;
40:1; 42:12; Da 1:9
16:8 ᵍS Ps 37:16
ʰS Pr 15:16; 17:1;
Ecc 4:6
16:9 ⁱS ver 1;
S Job 33:29;
S Ps 90:12
16:10 ʲPr 17:7
16:11 ᵏS Pr 11:1;
Eze 45:10
16:12 ˡPr 26:28;
25:5; 29:14; 31:5
16:13 ᵐPr 22:11
16:14 ⁿS Ge 40:2;
S Job 29:24; Pr 20:2
ᵒPr 25:15; 29:8;
Ecc 10:4
16:15 ᵖS Ge 40:2;
S Job 29:24
�q Pr 19:12; 25:2-7
16:16 ʳPs 49:20
ˢS Job 28:15;
S Pr 3:13-14

³ Commit to the Lᴏʀᴅ whatever you do,
  and he will establish your plans. ˣ

⁴ The Lᴏʀᴅ works out everything to its proper end ʸ—
  even the wicked for a day of disaster. ᶻ

⁵ The Lᴏʀᴅ detests all the proud of heart. ᵃ
  Be sure of this: They will not go unpunished. ᵇ

⁶ Through love and faithfulness sin is atoned for;
  through the fear of the Lᴏʀᴅ ᶜ evil is avoided. ᵈ

⁷ When the Lᴏʀᴅ takes pleasure in anyone's way,
  he causes their enemies to make peace ᵉ with them. ᶠ

⁸ Better a little with righteousness
  than much gain ᵍ with injustice. ʰ

⁹ In their hearts human beings plan their course,
  but the Lᴏʀᴅ establishes their steps. ⁱ

¹⁰ The lips of a king speak as an oracle,
   and his mouth does not betray justice. ʲ

¹¹ Honest scales and balances belong to the Lᴏʀᴅ;
   all the weights in the bag are of his making. ᵏ

¹² Kings detest wrongdoing,
   for a throne is established through righteousness. ˡ

¹³ Kings take pleasure in honest lips;
   they value persons who speak what is right. ᵐ

¹⁴ A king's wrath is a messenger of death, ⁿ
   but the wise will appease it. ᵒ

¹⁵ When a king's face brightens, it means life; ᵖ
   his favor is like a rain cloud in spring. q

¹⁶ How much better to get wisdom than gold,
   to get insight ʳ rather than silver! ˢ

---

weighed by the Lᴏʀᴅ. See 21:2; 24:12 and notes; Ps 139:23; 1Co 4:4–5; Heb 4:12.

16:3 *Commit.* See 1Pe 5:7. *he will establish your plans.* Your goals will be reached (see 3:5–6 and notes; Ps 1:3; 55:22; 90:17).

16:4 The middle verse of this section of Proverbs (10:1—22:16), aptly summarizing the Lord's sovereignty over every human thought and action. The verse also occupies the central position in a series of seven verses (1–7) at the beginning of ch. 16—the middle chapter in the book of Proverbs. Each of the seven verses features the name Yahweh, again stressing his supreme position as Lord over all. *works out everything to its proper end.* God is sovereign in every life and in all of history (see Job 7:14–18; Ro 8:28). *the wicked for a day of disaster.* God displays his power even through the wicked (cf. Ex 9:16), and all evil will be judged (cf. Eze 38:22–23; Ro 2:5–11).

16:5 See 11:20–21.

16:6 *Through love and faithfulness sin is atoned for.* The moral quality of conduct that God desires is sometimes summed up as "love and faithfulness" (3:3; see Pr 26:3; Hos 4:1 and notes). When his people repent of sin and bring their lives into accord with his will, God forgives and withdraws his judgment (see Isa 1:18–19; 55:7; Jer 3:22; 18:7–10 and note; Eze 18:23,30–32; 33:11–12,14–16; Hos 14:1–2, 4). Thus it can be said that love and faithfulness, in a manner of speaking, "atone for" sin, i.e., they turn away God's wrath against it. *fear of the Lᴏʀᴅ.* See note on 1:7. *evil is avoided.* See 3:7 and note.

16:7 *causes their enemies to make peace with them.* As in the reigns of godly Asa and Jehoshaphat (2Ch 14:6–7; 17:10). *peace.* See 3:17; Ro 12:18 and notes; Heb 12:14.

16:8 See 10:2 and note.

16:9 *the Lᴏʀᴅ establishes their steps.* Verses 1,3–4 (see notes) also emphasize God's control of people's lives (see 19:21; 20:24; Ps 37:23; Jer 10:23).

16:10 *speak as an oracle.* In judging cases brought before him, a king functioned as God's representative (see Dt 1:17). Therefore he needed the divine gift of wisdom to discern between right and wrong in order to render God's judgment (see 1Ki 3:9). When he did so, his judgment was tantamount to a divine oracle for the people (see 2Sa 14:17; 1Ki 3:28 and notes).

16:11 See note on 11:1. *Honest scales … belong to the Lᴏʀᴅ.* Cf. 21:2; 24:12; Job 6:2; 31:6. *all the weights in the bag.* Merchants carried stones of different sizes with them to weigh and measure quantities of silver for payment (cf. Mic 6:11).

16:12–15 A series of four proverbs highlighting the rule of the king as chief political executive in the life of the community (cf. v. 10).

16:12 *throne is established through righteousness.* When the king "judges the poor with fairness" (29:14), refuses to take bribes (29:4) and removes any wicked advisers (25:5). See 14:34; Dt 17:19–20; Isa 16:5; Ro 13:3–4.

16:13 *in honest lips.* Rather than in flattering lips (cf. 26:28).

16:14 *messenger of death.* Any angry king can pronounce death quickly and effectively (see 19:12; Est 7:7–10; Mt 22:7; Lk 19:27). *the wise will appease it.* Cf. Daniel's response to the rage of Nebuchadnezzar (Da 2:12–16).

16:15 *face brightens.* Cf. Nu 6:25 and note; La 4:20. *his favor is like a rain cloud in spring.* The spring rain was essential for the full development of barley and wheat; it was therefore a sign of good things to come. Cf. the "dew" of 19:12; see Ps 72:6.

16:16 See 1:13; 3:14 and notes; 8:10,19.

¹⁷ The highway of the upright avoids evil;
     those who guard their ways preserve their lives. *t*

¹⁸ Pride *u* goes before destruction,
     a haughty spirit *v* before a fall. *w*

¹⁹ Better to be lowly in spirit along with the oppressed
     than to share plunder with the proud.

²⁰ Those who give heed to instruction prosper, *a x*
     and blessed are those who trust in the Lord. *y*

²¹ The wise in heart are called discerning,
     and gracious words promote instruction. *b z*

²² Prudence is a fountain of life to the prudent, *a*
     but folly brings punishment to fools.

²³ The hearts of the wise make their mouths prudent, *b*
     and their lips promote instruction. *c c*

²⁴ Gracious words are a honeycomb, *d*
     sweet to the soul and healing to the bones. *e*

²⁵ There is a way that appears to be right, *f*
     but in the end it leads to death. *g*

²⁶ The appetite of laborers works for them;
     their hunger drives them on.

²⁷ Scoundrels *h* plot evil,
     and on their lips it is like a scorching fire. *i*

²⁸ The perverse stir up dissension, *j*
     and gossips separate close friends. *k*

²⁹ The violent entice their neighbors
     and lead them down a path that is not good. *l*

³⁰ Those who wink *m* with their eyes are plotting perversity;
     those who purse their lips are bent on evil.

³¹ Gray hair is a crown of splendor; *n*
     it is attained in the way of righteousness.

³² Better a patient person than a warrior,
     those with self-control than those who take a city.

³³ The lot is cast *o* into the lap,
     but its every decision *p* is from the Lord. *q*

---

^a 20 Or *who speak prudently find what is good*   ^b 21 Or *words make a person persuasive*
^c 23 Or *prudent / and make their lips persuasive*

16:17 *t* Pr 19:16
16:18 *u* S 1Sa 17:42
v Ps 18:27; Isa 13:11;
Jer 48:29
w S Est 5:12; Pr 11:2;
S 15:33; 18:12; 29:23
16:20 *x* Pr 13:13
y S Ps 32:10; 40:4;
Pr 19:8; 29:25;
Jer 17:7
16:21 *z* ver 23
16:22 *a* S Pr 10:11
16:23 *b* Job 15:5
c ver 21
16:24 *d* S 1Sa 14:27
e Pr 24:13-14
16:25 *f* S Pr 12:15
g Est 3:6; Pr 14:12
16:27 *h* S Ps 140:2
i Jas 3:6
16:28 *j* S Pr 14:17
k Pr 17:9
16:29 *l* S Pr 1:10;
12:26
16:30 *m* S Pr 6:13
16:31 *n* Pr 20:29
16:33 *o* S Lev 16:8;
S 1Sa 10:21; Eze 21:21
p 1Sa 14:41 *q* Jos 7:14;
Pr 18:18; 29:26;
Jnh 1:7

16:17 *highway of the upright.* See notes on 3:6; 15:19. *avoids evil.* Cf. the thorns and snares in the paths of the wicked (22:5).
16:18 See 11:2 and note; cf. 1Co 10:12.
16:19 *Better to be lowly in spirit.* See 3:34; Isa 57:15; Mt 5:3 and note. *share plunder with the proud.* See 1:13–14; Jdg 5:30.
16:20 *prosper.* See 13:13; 28:25 and notes. *blessed are those who trust in the Lord.* See v. 3; 3:5–6; Ps 34:8; 37:4–5; 84:12.
16:21 *gracious words promote instruction.* Cf. the last line of v. 23. "Gracious" (lit. "sweet") is expanded in the last line of v. 24. Cf. the persuasive but destructive words of the adulteress in 7:21.
16:22 *fountain of life.* See note on 10:11. *punishment to fools.* See 13:13 and note; see also 7:22; 13:15; 15:10.
16:23 *make their mouths prudent.* See 22:17–18.
16:24 *Gracious words are a honeycomb.* They are good for you (see 24:13–14), and they taste good (cf. 2:10; Ps 19:10). *healing to the bones.* See note on 4:22; 12:18; 15:30. *bones.* See note on 3:8.
16:25 See 14:12 and note.
16:26 Cf. 2Th 3:10: "Anyone who is unwilling to work shall not eat"; see also Ecc 6:7; Eph 4:28.

16:27 *Scoundrels.* See 6:12 and note. *plot evil.* See 3:29; 6:14; Mic 2:1. *scorching fire.* Their speech is inflammatory and destructive (see Jas 3:6).
16:28 *stir up dissension.* See note on 6:14. *gossips.* See 11:13.
16:29 See 1:10–19 and notes; cf. Ro 1:32.
16:30 *wink with their eyes.* See note on 6:13. *purse their lips.* Thereby making insinuations (see note on 6:12–14).
16:31 *Gray hair is a crown of splendor.* The elderly were to receive deep respect (see Lev 19:32). *in the way of righteousness.* See 3:1–2, 16.
16:32 *patient . . . warrior.* See 14:29; 15:18; 19:11; Jas 1:19. "Wisdom is better than weapons of war" (Ecc 9:18). *those with self-control than those who take a city.* Although those who practice patience and self-control receive far less attention and acclaim than a warrior who takes a city, they accomplish better things.
16:33 *The lot is cast into the lap.* Here the lot may have been several pebbles held in the fold of a garment and then drawn out or shaken to the ground. It was commonly used to make decisions (see notes on Ex 28:30; Nu 26:53; Ne 11:1; Jnh 1:7; Ac

17:1 ʳS Pr 15:16,17;
S 16:8
17:3 ˢPr 27:21
ᵗS 1Ch 29:17; Ps 26:2;
S 139:23; 1Pe 1:7
17:5 ᵘS Job 5:16
ᵛPr 14:31
ʷS Job 31:29
ˣEze 25:3; Ob 1:12
17:6 ʸS Ps 128:5-6
17:7 ᶻPr 16:10
17:8 ᵃS Ex 23:8;
Pr 19:6
17:9 ᵇS Pr 10:12
ᶜPr 16:28
17:12 ᵈS 1Sa 25:25
17:13 ᵉS 1Sa 19:4
ᶠS Ge 44:4;
S Ps 35:12
17:14 ᵍMt 5:25-26
17:15 ʰS Ps 94:21;
S Pr 18:5 ʲEx 23:6-7;
Isa 5:23; La 3:34-36
17:16 ʲPr 23:23
17:17 ᵏS 2Sa 15:21;
Pr 27:10

17 Better a dry crust with peace and quiet
  than a house full of feasting, with strife. ʳ

2 A prudent servant will rule over a disgraceful son
  and will share the inheritance as one of the family.

3 The crucible for silver and the furnace for gold, ˢ
  but the Lᴏʀᴅ tests the heart. ᵗ

4 A wicked person listens to deceitful lips;
  a liar pays attention to a destructive tongue.

5 Whoever mocks the poor ᵘ shows contempt for their Maker; ᵛ
  whoever gloats over disaster ʷ will not go unpunished. ˣ

6 Children's children ʸ are a crown to the aged,
  and parents are the pride of their children.

7 Eloquent lips are unsuited to a godless fool—
  how much worse lying lips to a ruler! ᶻ

8 A bribe is seen as a charm by those who give it;
  they think success will come at every turn. ᵃ

9 Whoever would foster love covers over an offense, ᵇ
  but whoever repeats the matter separates close friends. ᶜ

10 A rebuke impresses a discerning person
  more than a hundred lashes a fool.

11 Evildoers foster rebellion against God;
  the messenger of death will be sent against them.

12 Better to meet a bear robbed of her cubs
  than a fool bent on folly. ᵈ

13 Evil will never leave the house
  of one who pays back evil ᵉ for good. ᶠ

14 Starting a quarrel is like breaching a dam;
  so drop the matter before a dispute breaks out. ᵍ

15 Acquitting the guilty and condemning the innocent ʰ—
  the Lᴏʀᴅ detests them both. ⁱ

16 Why should fools have money in hand to buy wisdom,
  when they are not able to understand it? ʲ

17 A friend loves at all times,
  and a brother is born for a time of adversity. ᵏ

1:26; see also Ps 22:18). *every decision is from the Lᴏʀᴅ.* God, not chance, is in control (see vv. 1,3–4,9).
17:2 *A prudent servant will rule over a disgraceful son.* See 11:29 and note. *disgraceful son.* See 10:5; 19:26; 28:7; 29:15.
17:3 The first line of this verse is repeated in 27:21. *The crucible ... the furnace.* Silver and gold were refined to remove their impurities (see Ps 12:6 and note). *tests the heart.* See 15:11; 16:2 and notes; Jer 17:10. *heart.* See note on Ps 4:7.
17:5 *Whoever mocks the poor shows contempt for their Maker.* See 14:31 and note. *whoever gloats over disaster will not go unpunished.* The people of Edom in particular were condemned for gloating over the collapse of "brother" Jacob/Israel (Ob 10; see Eze 35:12,15; see also Pr 24:17).
17:6 *crown to the aged.* Cf. the "gray hair" of 16:31. To live to see one's grandchildren was considered a great blessing (see Ge 48:11; Ps 128:5–6). *parents are the pride of their children.* See Ge 47:7.
17:7 For the structure of this verse cf. 15:11; 19:7,10; 21:27. *lying lips to a ruler.* The right to rule depends on honesty and justice (see 12:22; 16:12–13).
17:8 *A bribe is seen as a charm.* A sad commentary on human behavior (see 18:16; 21:14; Ecc 10:19). Elsewhere,

bribes are condemned (see v. 23; 15:27; 28:16; Ex 23:8; Dt 16:19; 1Sa 12:3; Ecc 7:7; Isa 1:23; Am 5:12; 1Ti 6:10).
17:9 *Whoever would foster love covers over an offense.* See 10:12 and note.
17:10 *rebuke impresses a discerning person.* See 9:8–9. *a hundred lashes a fool.* Fools deserved and received flogging (cf. 10:13; 19:25,29; 26:3; Dt 25:2–3).
17:11 *messenger of death.* See 16:14 and note; cf. the dispatching of Abishai and Joab to end Sheba's rebellion against David (2Sa 20:1–22; see 1Ki 2:25,29,46).
17:12 *bear robbed of her cubs.* Sure to attack you and rip you open (see 2Sa 17:8; Hos 13:8; cf. the raging of the fool in 29:9).
17:13 *Evil will never leave the house.* The fate of David's family after his affair with Bathsheba and the murder of Uriah (see 2Sa 12:10 and note; cf. Jer 18:20–23). *one who pays back evil for good.* Like Nabal, who refused to reward David's men (1Sa 25:21; see Ps 109:5; Ro 12:17–21).
17:15 *Acquitting the guilty.* Perhaps because of a bribe (see v. 8; 24:24).
17:16 *fools have money in hand.* Perhaps to pay the fee for their schooling.

¹⁸ One who has no sense shakes hands in pledge
   and puts up security for a neighbor. ^l

¹⁹ Whoever loves a quarrel loves sin;
   whoever builds a high gate invites destruction.

²⁰ One whose heart is corrupt does not prosper;
   one whose tongue is perverse falls into trouble.

²¹ To have a fool for a child brings grief;
   there is no joy for the parent of a godless fool. ^m

²² A cheerful heart is good medicine,
   but a crushed ⁿ spirit dries up the bones. ^o

²³ The wicked accept bribes ^p in secret
   to pervert the course of justice. ^q

²⁴ A discerning person keeps wisdom in view,
   but a fool's eyes ^r wander to the ends of the earth.

²⁵ Foolish children bring grief to their father
   and bitterness to the mother who bore them. ^s

²⁶ If imposing a fine on the innocent is not good, ^t
   surely to flog honest officials is not right.

²⁷ Those who have knowledge use words with restraint, ^u
   and those who have understanding are even-tempered. ^v

²⁸ Even fools are thought wise if they keep silent,
   and discerning if they hold their tongues. ^w

18

An unfriendly person pursues selfish ends
   and against all sound judgment starts quarrels.

² Fools find no pleasure in understanding
   but delight in airing their own opinions. ^x

³ When wickedness comes, so does contempt,
   and with shame comes reproach.

⁴ The words of the mouth are deep waters, ^y
   but the fountain of wisdom is a rushing stream.

⁵ It is not good to be partial to the wicked ^z
   and so deprive the innocent of justice. ^a

⁶ The lips of fools bring them strife,
   and their mouths invite a beating. ^b

⁷ The mouths of fools are their undoing,
   and their lips are a snare ^c to their very lives. ^d

17:18 ^l Pr 6:1-5;
S 11:15; 22:26-27
17:21 ^m S Pr 10:1
17:22 ⁿ S Ps 38:8
^o S Ex 12:46; Pr 14:30;
S 15:13; 18:14
17:23 ^p S Ex 18:21;
S 23:8; S 1Sa 8:3
^q S Job 34:33
17:24 ^r S Job 31:1
17:25 ^s S Pr 10:1
17:26 ^t S Ps 94:21
17:27 ^u S Job 6:24
^v S Pr 14:29
17:28 ^w S Job 2:13;
13:5; S Pr 10:19
18:2 ^x S Pr 12:23
18:4 ^y S Ps 18:16
18:5 ^z Pr 24:23-25;
28:21 ^a S Ps 82:2;
S Pr 17:15
18:6 ^b S Pr 10:14
18:7 ^c Ps 140:9
^d S Ps 64:8;
S Pr 10:14; S 12:13;
S 13:3; Ecc 10:12

17:17 *friend loves at all times.* See 18:24; cf. David's friendship with Jonathan (2Sa 1:26; see Lev 19:18 and note; Ru 1:16; 1Co 13:4–7).
17:18 See 6:1 and note.
17:19 *Whoever loves a quarrel loves sin.* A hot-tempered person "commits many sins" (29:22). *builds a high gate.* Or "opens his mouth wide," meaning "brags too much" and so "invites destruction," including his own (cf. 16:18; 29:23).
17:20 *does not prosper.* Contrast 16:20. *whose tongue is perverse.* See note on 2:12.
17:21 *grief . . . no joy.* See v. 25; 19:13.
17:22 *cheerful heart.* See 14:30; 15:13,30; 16:15. *crushed spirit dries up the bones.* See notes on 3:8; 14:30; see also 12:4; Ps 32:3.
17:23 *accept bribes.* See note on v. 8.
17:24 *wander to the ends of the earth.* Fools "chase fantasies" (12:11) and are interested in everything except wisdom (cf. Dt 30:11–14).
17:25 See v. 21. *bitterness.* See 14:10 and note.
17:26 *imposing a fine on the innocent.* See v. 15. *flog honest offi-*

cials. See v. 10 and note; cf. the beating and disgrace endured by Jeremiah (Jer 20:2; 38:1–6).
17:27 *use words with restraint.* See 10:19. *even-tempered.* See 16:32 and note.
17:28 *fools are thought wise if they keep silent.* Cf. Job's sarcastic comment in Job 13:5 (see note there).
18:1 *pursues selfish ends.* He is quarrelsome and hot-tempered (cf. 17:14).
18:2 *airing their own opinions.* See Ecc 10:3.
18:3 *shame . . . reproach.* Cf. 3:35; 6:33; 10:5; 11:2; Ps 31:17.
A 18:4 *deep waters.* Profound or obscure (cf. 20:5). *fountain of wisdom is a rushing stream.* A wise person's words are refreshing and a source of life (see 1:23; 10:11 and notes).
A 18:5 *partial to the wicked.* See 17:15 and note. Favoritism of any kind was condemned in the law (see Lev 19:15; Dt 1:17; 16:19). *deprive the innocent of justice.* See 17:26; 31:5; Mal 3:5.
18:6 *bring them strife.* Fools are quick to quarrel (see 17:14,19; 20:3). *invite a beating.* By a rod on their backs (see 10:13; 19:29).

18:8 *e* Pr 26:22
18:9 *f* Pr 28:24
18:10 *g* S Ps 61:3
h S Ps 20:1; Pr 14:26
18:11 *i* Pr 10:15
18:12 *j* S Pr 11:2;
15:33; S 16:18
18:13 *k* Pr 20:25
18:14 *l* S Pr 15:13;
S 17:22
18:15 *m* S Pr 15:14
18:16 *n* S Ge 32:13;
S 1Sa 10:4; Pr 19:6
18:18 *o* S Pr 16:33
18:19 *p* S 1Sa 17:28
18:20 *q* S Pr 12:14
18:21 *r* S Ps 12:4
s Pr 13:2-3;
S Mt 12:37
18:22 *t* S Pr 12:4
u S Job 33:26;
Pr 19:14; 31:10
18:24 *v* S 1Sa 20:42;
Jn 15:13-15
19:1 *w* Pr 28:6
19:2 *x* Pr 29:20

⁸ The words of a gossip are like choice morsels;
  they go down to the inmost parts. *e*

⁹ One who is slack in his work
  is a close relative of one who destroys. *f*

¹⁰ The name of the LORD is a fortified tower; *g*
  the righteous run to it and are safe. *h*

¹¹ The wealth of the rich is their fortified city; *i*
  they imagine it a wall too high to scale.

¹² Before a downfall the heart is haughty,
  but humility comes before honor. *j*

¹³ To answer before listening—
  that is folly and shame. *k*

¹⁴ The human spirit can endure in sickness,
  but a crushed spirit who can bear? *l*

¹⁵ The heart of the discerning acquires knowledge, *m*
  for the ears of the wise seek it out.

¹⁶ A gift *n* opens the way
  and ushers the giver into the presence of the great.

¹⁷ In a lawsuit the first to speak seems right,
  until someone comes forward and cross-examines.

¹⁸ Casting the lot settles disputes *o*
  and keeps strong opponents apart.

¹⁹ A brother wronged *p* is more unyielding than a fortified city;
  disputes are like the barred gates of a citadel.

²⁰ From the fruit of their mouths people's stomachs are filled;
  with the harvest of their lips they are satisfied. *q*

²¹ The tongue has the power of life and death, *r*
  and those who love it will eat its fruit. *s*

²² He who finds a wife finds what is good *t*
  and receives favor from the LORD. *u*

²³ The poor plead for mercy,
  but the rich answer harshly.

²⁴ One who has unreliable friends soon comes to ruin,
  but there is a friend who sticks closer than a brother. *v*

19 Better the poor whose walk is blameless
  than a fool whose lips are perverse. *w*

² Desire without knowledge is not good—
  how much more will hasty feet miss the way! *x*

18:7 See 10:14 and note.
18:8 Repeated in 26:22. *words of a gossip are like choice morsels.* They are as pleasant as words of wisdom (cf. 16:21,23), but they promote dissension (see 11:13; 26:20). *they go down to the inmost parts.* Where they are thoroughly digested and so are carried about and live on and on.
18:9 *who is slack in his work.* See 10:4 and note.
18:10 *name of the LORD.* His "name" often equals his "person," since it expresses his nature and qualities (see Ex 3:14–15 and notes). *fortified tower.* See Ps 18:2 and note; 91:2; 144:2. *safe.* See 29:25; Ps 27:5.
18:11 *wealth … is their fortified city.* Identical to the first line in 10:15 (see note there). *wall too high to scale.* But God can bring it down (see Isa 25:12).
18:12 *humility comes before honor.* Identical to the second line in 15:33 (see note there).

18:14 See 15:13; 17:22 and notes.
18:17 A warning to judges to hear both sides of a case (cf. Dt 1:16), but applicable to many situations.
18:18 *Casting the lot settles disputes.* See 16:33 and note.
18:19 *A brother wronged.* Cf. Esau's anger because of the blessing Jacob received from Isaac (Ge 27:41).
18:20 See 12:14 and note.
18:21 *tongue has the power of life and death.* See notes on 10:19; 13:3. *its fruit.* See v. 20.
18:22 *who finds a wife finds what is good.* See 12:4 and note; 19:14; 31:10. *receives favor from the LORD.* Identical to the second line in 8:35—where finding wisdom brings the Lord's favor.
18:24 *One who has unreliable friends soon comes to ruin.* One must choose friends carefully (see 12:26 and note; 17:17).
19:1 Almost identical to 28:6. *blameless.* See note on 2:7. *than a fool.* Even if the fool becomes rich (see 28:6).

³One's own folly ʸ leads to ruin,
  yet the heart rages against the LORD. ᶻ

⁴Wealth attracts many friends,
  but even the closest friends of the poor desert them. ᵃ

⁵A false witness ᵇ will not go unpunished, ᶜ
  and whoever pours out lies will not go free. ᵈ

⁶Many curry favor with a ruler, ᵉ
  and everyone is the friend of one who gives gifts. ᶠ

⁷The poor are shunned by all their relatives—
  how much more do their friends avoid them! ᵍ
Though they pursue them with pleading,
  they are nowhere to be found. ᵃ ʰ

⁸Those who get wisdom love their own lives;
  those who cherish understanding will soon prosper. ⁱ

⁹A false witness will not go unpunished,
  and whoever pours out lies will perish. ʲ

¹⁰It is not fitting for a fool ᵏ to live in luxury—
  how much worse for a slave to rule over princes! ˡ

¹¹A person's wisdom yields patience; ᵐ
  it is to one's glory to overlook an offense.

¹²A king's rage is like the roar of a lion, ⁿ
  but his favor is like dew ᵒ on the grass. ᵖ

¹³A foolish child is a father's ruin, ۹
  and a quarrelsome wife is like
  the constant dripping of a leaky roof. ʳ

¹⁴Houses and wealth are inherited from parents, ˢ
  but a prudent wife is from the LORD. ᵗ

¹⁵Laziness brings on deep sleep,
  and the shiftless go hungry. ᵘ

¹⁶Those who obey instructions preserve their lives,
  but those who are contemptuous of their ways will die. ᵛ

¹⁷Those who are kind to the poor lend to the LORD, ʷ
  and he will reward them for what they have done. ˣ

¹⁸Discipline your children, for in that there is hope;
  do not be a willing party to their death. ʸ

¹⁹The hot-tempered must pay the penalty;
  rescue them, and you will have to do it again.

²⁰Listen to advice and accept discipline, ᶻ
  and at the end you will be counted among the wise. ᵃ

ᵃ 7 The meaning of the Hebrew for this sentence is uncertain.

19:3 ʸ Ps 14:1;
Pr 9:13; 24:9; Isa 32:6
ᶻ Jas 1:13-15
19:4 ᵃ ver 7;
Pr 14:20
19:5 ᵇ S Ex 23:1
ᶜ S Ps 56:7 ᵈ ver 9;
S Dt 19:19; Pr 21:28
19:6 ᵉ Pr 29:26
ᶠ S Pr 17:8; S 18:16
19:7 ᵍ Pr 10:15
ʰ S ver 4
19:8 ⁱ S Pr 16:20
19:9 ʲ S ver 5;
S Dt 19:19
19:10 ᵏ Pr 26:1
ˡ Pr 30:21-23;
Ecc 10:5-7
19:11 ᵐ S 2Ki 5:12
19:12 ⁿ Pr 20:2
ᵒ S Ps 133:3
ᵖ S Est 1:12; S 7:7;
Ps 72:5-6; Pr 16:14-15
19:13 ۹ S Pr 10:1
ʳ S Est 1:18; Pr 21:9
19:14 ˢ 2Co 12:14
ᵗ S Pr 18:22
19:15 ᵘ S Pr 10:4;
20:13
19:16 ᵛ S Pr 16:17;
S Ro 10:5
19:17 ʷ S Dt 24:14
ˣ S Dt 24:19; Pr 14:21;
22:9; S Mt 10:42
19:18 ʸ S Pr 13:24;
23:13-14
19:20 ᶻ Pr 4:1
ᵃ S Pr 12:15

19:2 *Desire without knowledge.* Cf. Ro 10:2. *hasty.* Haste can lead to poverty (21:5) or folly (29:20). *miss the way.* Fail to achieve one's goal.
19:3 *the heart rages against the LORD.* God is blamed for one's troubles (see Ge 4:5; Isa 8:21; cf. La 3:39).
19:4 See v. 7; 14:20.
19:5,9 See 6:19 and note.
19:6 *curry favor.* Cf. Job 11:19. *friend of one who gives gifts.* Generosity (v. 4) or bribery (17:8) could be in view.
19:7 *The poor are shunned.* See v. 4; 14:20.
19:8 *love their own lives.* Cf. 8:35–36. *prosper.* See 13:13 and note.
19:10 *not fitting for a fool to live in luxury.* Or to have honor (26:1).
19:11 *patience.* See 14:29; 15:18; 16:32; Ecc 7:9; Jas 1:19. *over-*

look an offense. See 12:16; 29:11; 2Sa 16:11–12.
19:12 See 16:14–15 and notes. *A king's rage is like the roar of a lion.* Almost identical to the first line of 20:2.
19:13 *foolish child.* See 17:21,25. *quarrelsome wife.* Also denounced in 21:9,19; 25:24; 27:15. Stirring up dissension is condemned throughout Proverbs (see 6:14 and note).
19:14 *prudent wife.* See 12:4 and note; see also 18:22.
19:15 See 6:11; 10:4 and notes.
19:16 See 13:13; 15:10; 16:17 and notes.
19:17 *kind to the poor.* See note on 14:21; see also 14:31. *lend to the LORD.* The Lord regards it as a gift to him (cf. Mt 25:40).
19:18 *Discipline your children ... not ... to their death.* See note on 13:24.
19:19 *hot-tempered.* Cf. 14:16–17,29; 15:18.

19:21 *b* Ps 33:11;
Pr 16:9; 20:24;
Isa 8:10; 14:24,27;
31:2; 40:8; 46:10;
48:14; 55:11;
Jer 44:29; La 3:37
19:23 *c* S Job 4:7;
S Pr 10:27
19:24 *d* Pr 26:15
19:25 *e* S Ps 141:5
f S Pr 9:9; 21:11
19:26 *g* Pr 28:24
19:27 *h* S Pr 1:8
19:28 *i* S Job 15:16
19:29 *j* S Dt 25:2
20:1 *k* S Lev 10:9;
Hab 2:5 *l* S 1Sa 25:36
m 1Ki 20:16 *n* Pr 31:4
20:2 *o* S Pr 19:12
p S Est 7:7; S Pr 16:14
20:3 *q* S Isa 25:25
r S Ge 13:8
20:4 *s* S Pr 6:6
t Ecc 10:18
20:5 *u* S Ps 18:16
20:6 *v* Ps 12:1
20:7 *w* S Ps 26:1
x Ps 37:25-26; 112:2
20:8 *y* S 1Ki 7:7
z ver 26; Pr 25:4-5

²¹ Many are the plans in a human heart,
   but it is the Lord's purpose that prevails. *b*

²² What a person desires is unfailing love *a*;
   better to be poor than a liar.

²³ The fear of the Lord leads to life;
   then one rests content, untouched by trouble. *c*

²⁴ Sluggards bury their hands in the dish
   and will not even bring them back to their mouths! *d*

²⁵ Flog a mocker, and the simple will learn prudence;
   rebuke the discerning, *e* and they will gain knowledge. *f*

²⁶ Whoever robs their father and drives out their mother *g*
   is a child who brings shame and disgrace.

²⁷ Stop listening to instruction, my child, *h*
   and you will stray from the words of knowledge.

²⁸ A corrupt witness mocks at justice,
   and the mouth of the wicked gulps down evil. *i*

²⁹ Penalties are prepared for mockers,
   and beatings for the backs of fools. *j*

20 Wine *k* is a mocker *l* and beer a brawler;
   whoever is led astray *m* by them is not wise. *n*

² A king's wrath strikes terror like the roar of a lion; *o*
   those who anger him forfeit their lives. *p*

³ It is to one's honor to avoid strife,
   but every fool *q* is quick to quarrel. *r*

⁴ Sluggards *s* do not plow in season;
   so at harvest time they look but find nothing. *t*

⁵ The purposes of the human heart are deep waters, *u*
   but those who have insight draw them out.

⁶ Many claim to have unfailing love,
   but a faithful person who can find? *v*

⁷ The righteous lead blameless lives; *w*
   blessed are their children after them. *x*

⁸ When a king sits on his throne to judge, *y*
   he winnows out all evil with his eyes. *z*

---

a 22 Or Greed is a person's shame

19:21 See 16:1,4,9 and notes.
19:22 *desires ... unfailing love.* But such loyalty is difficult to find (cf. 14:22; 20:6). *better to be poor than a liar.* See vv. 1,28; 6:12.
19:23 *fear of the Lord.* See note on 1:7. *leads to life.* See note on 10:11. *untouched by trouble.* See 3:2; 14:26 and notes.
19:24 Almost identical to 26:15. *Sluggards.* See note on 6:6.
19:25 *Flog a mocker.* See v. 29; 14:3; 21:11; see also notes on 1:22; 17:10; 21:24. *the simple.* Not to be confused with the mocker (see note on 1:4).

A 19:26 *robs ... father and drives out ... mother.* Children were expected to take care of their parents when they were sick or elderly (cf. Isa 51:18). Robbing them (cf. Jdg 17:1-2) and attacking or calling down curses on them (Ex 21:15,17) were serious crimes (see note on Ex 21:17). *shame and disgrace.* See 10:5; 13:5.
19:27 See 5:1-2.
19:28 *corrupt witness.* See v. 5; see also note on 6:19. *gulps down evil.* Cf. the description of those "who drink up evil like water" (Job 15:16; see Job 34:7).

19:29 *Penalties ... for mockers.* See v. 25. *beatings for the backs of fools.* See 10:13; 14:3; 26:3.
A 20:1 *Wine is a mocker and beer a brawler.* Those who overindulge become mockers and brawlers (see Hos 7:5 and note). Proverbs associates drunkenness with poverty (see 23:20-21 and note), strife (23:29-30) and injustice (31:4-5). *led astray.* See Ge 9:21 and note; Isa 28:7.
20:2 See 16:14; 19:12 and notes.
20:3 *quick to quarrel.* See 6:14; 17:14,19; 18:6.
20:4 *Sluggards.* See note on 6:6. *but find nothing.* See 13:4; 21:25-26.
20:5 *purposes.* Or "motives" (cf. 16:1-2). *deep waters.* Cf. 18:4. *draw them out.* As if from a well.
20:6 *unfailing love.* See notes on 19:22; Ps 6:4. *a faithful person who can find?* Cf. Ecc 7:28-29.
20:7 *blameless lives.* See note on 2:7. *blessed are their children.* See 13:22; see also note on 14:26.
20:8 See v. 26 and note. *winnows out all evil.* See 16:10; Ps 11:4.

⁹ Who can say, "I have kept my heart pure;*ᵃ*
   I am clean and without sin"?*ᵇ*

¹⁰ Differing weights and differing measures—
   the Lᴏʀᴅ detests them both.*ᶜ*

¹¹ Even small children are known by their actions,
   so is their conduct really pure*ᵈ* and upright?

¹² Ears that hear and eyes that see—
   the Lᴏʀᴅ has made them both.*ᵉ*

¹³ Do not love sleep or you will grow poor;*ᶠ*
   stay awake and you will have food to spare.

¹⁴ "It's no good, it's no good!" says the buyer—
   then goes off and boasts about the purchase.

¹⁵ Gold there is, and rubies in abundance,
   but lips that speak knowledge are a rare jewel.

¹⁶ Take the garment of one who puts up security for a stranger;
   hold it in pledge*ᵍ* if it is done for an outsider.*ʰ*

¹⁷ Food gained by fraud tastes sweet,*ⁱ*
   but one ends up with a mouth full of gravel.*ʲ*

¹⁸ Plans are established by seeking advice;
   so if you wage war, obtain guidance.*ᵏ*

¹⁹ A gossip betrays a confidence;*ˡ*
   so avoid anyone who talks too much.

²⁰ If you curse your father or mother,*ᵐ*
   your lamp will be snuffed out in pitch darkness.*ⁿ*

²¹ An inheritance claimed too soon
   will not be blessed at the end.

²² Do not say, "I'll pay you back for this wrong!"*ᵒ*
   Wait for the Lᴏʀᴅ, and he will avenge you.*ᵖ*

²³ The Lᴏʀᴅ detests differing weights,
   and dishonest scales do not please him.*ᵍ*

²⁴ A person's steps are directed*ʳ* by the Lᴏʀᴅ.*ˢ*
   How then can anyone understand their own way?*ᵗ*

²⁵ It is a trap to dedicate something rashly
   and only later to consider one's vows.*ᵘ*

20:9 *ᵃ*S Job 15:14
*ᵇ*1Ki 8:46; Ecc 7:20;
1Jn 1:8
20:10 *ᶜ*ver 23;
S Pr 11:1
20:11 *ᵈ*S Ps 39:1
20:12 *ᵉ*S Ps 94:9
20:13 *ᶠ*S Pr 6:11;
S 19:15
20:16 *ᵍ*S Ex 22:26
*ʰ*Pr 27:13
20:17 *ⁱ*Pr 9:17
*ʲ*Job 20:14; La 3:16
20:18 *ᵏ*Pr 11:14;
24:6
20:19 *ˡ*Pr 11:13
20:20 *ᵐ*Pr 30:11
*ⁿ*Ex 21:17; S Job 18:5
20:22 *ᵒ*Pr 24:29
*ᵖ*Isa 37:20; Jer 1:19;
42:11; Ro 12:19
20:23 *ᵍ*S ver 10;
S Dt 25:13
20:24 *ʳ*S Ps 90:12
*ˢ*S Job 33:29
*ᵗ*S Pr 19:21; Jer 10:23
20:25 *ᵘ*S Pr 10:19;
18:13; Ecc 5:2, 4-5;
Jer 44:25

20:9 *pure … clean … without sin.* No one is without sin (cf. Job 14:4; Ro 3:23)—but those whose sins have been forgiven have "clean hands and a pure heart" (Ps 24:4; see also 51:1–2, 9–10).
20:10 See note on 11:1; cf. 16:11.
20:12 See Ex 4:11; Ps 94:8–9.
20:13 *sleep … grow poor.* See 24:33–34.
20:14 *It's no good, it's no good!* Prices were often agreed upon by bargaining, so the buyer is questioning the quality of the article in order to buy it more cheaply.
20:15 *Gold … rubies.* Wisdom is valued more highly than gold or rubies (3:14–15; 8:10–11).
20:16 Repeated in 27:13. See note on 6:1. *Take the garment.* A garment could be taken as security for a debt (Dt 24:10–13). Anyone who foolishly assumes responsibility for the debt of a stranger, whose reliability is unknown, or of a wayward woman, whose unreliability is known, ought to be held accountable, even to the degree of taking their garment as a pledge.
20:17 *tastes sweet.* Cf. the sweet "food" prepared by the adulteress in 9:17. Zophar observes that evil is sweet in the mouth of

the wicked but turns sour in their stomachs (Job 20:12–18). See note on 10:2.
20:18 *advice … guidance.* See 15:22; Lk 14:31.
20:20 *curse your father or mother.* Punishable by death (see Ex 21:17 and note; Lev 20:9; cf. Pr 30:11, 17). *your lamp … snuffed out.* You will die (see note on 13:9).
20:21 *inheritance claimed too soon will not be blessed.* Cf. 19:26; see the sad experience of the son who "squandered his wealth in wild living" (see Lk 15:12–13 and notes).
20:22 *I'll pay you back.* Vengeance was God's prerogative. He would repay the wicked for their actions (see 24:12, 29; Dt 32:35; Ps 94:1 and notes). *Wait for the Lᴏʀᴅ.* See Ps 27:14 and note; 37:34.
20:23 See v. 10 and note.
20:24 See notes on 3:5–6; 16:9.
20:25 *dedicate something.* Promise to make a special gift to the Lord if he answers an earnest request (see Lev 27:1–25; 1Sa 1:11). *rashly.* See Dt 23:21; Jdg 11:30–31, 34–35 and note on 11:30. When a vow was made hastily, it was sometimes not carried out (cf. Ecc 5:4–6).

20:26 ᵛS ver 8
20:27 ʷS Ps 119:10
5 ˣS Pr 16:2
20:28 ʸPs 40:11
ᶻS Pr 16:12; Isa 16:5
20:29 ᵃPr 16:31
20:30 ᵇS Ps 51:2;
Pr 22:15 ᶜIsa 1:5
21:1 ᵈEst 5:1;
Jer 39:11-12
21:2 ᵉS Pr 16:2
21:3 ᶠS 1Sa 15:22;
Isa 1:11; Mic 6:6-8
21:4 ᵍS Job 41:34
21:5 ʰS Pr 10:4
21:6 ⁱS Pr 10:2
21:7 ʲS Pr 11:5
21:8 ᵏS Pr 2:15
21:9 ˡver 19;
Pr 19:13; 25:24
21:11 ᵐS Pr 19:25

²⁶ A wise king winnows out the wicked;
　　he drives the threshing wheel over them. ᵛ

²⁷ The human spirit is ᵃ the lamp of the LORD ʷ
　　that sheds light on one's inmost being. ˣ

²⁸ Love and faithfulness keep a king safe;
　　through love ʸ his throne is made secure. ᶻ

²⁹ The glory of young men is their strength,
　　gray hair the splendor of the old. ᵃ

³⁰ Blows and wounds cleanse ᵇ away evil,
　　and beatings ᶜ purge the inmost being.

21 In the LORD's hand the king's heart is a stream of water
　　that he channels toward all who please him. ᵈ

² People may think all their ways are right,
　　but the LORD weighs the heart. ᵉ

³ To do what is right and just
　　is more acceptable to the LORD than sacrifice. ᶠ

⁴ Haughty eyes ᵍ and a proud heart—
　　the unplowed field of the wicked—produce sin.

⁵ The plans of the diligent lead to profit ʰ
　　as surely as haste leads to poverty.

⁶ A fortune made by a lying tongue
　　is a fleeting vapor and a deadly snare. ᵇⁱ

⁷ The violence of the wicked will drag them away, ʲ
　　for they refuse to do what is right.

⁸ The way of the guilty is devious, ᵏ
　　but the conduct of the innocent is upright.

⁹ Better to live on a corner of the roof
　　than share a house with a quarrelsome wife. ˡ

¹⁰ The wicked crave evil;
　　their neighbors get no mercy from them.

¹¹ When a mocker is punished, the simple gain wisdom;
　　by paying attention to the wise they get knowledge. ᵐ

ᵃ 27 Or *A person's words are*　　ᵇ 6 Some Hebrew manuscripts, Septuagint and Vulgate; most Hebrew
manuscripts *vapor for those who seek death*

20:26 See v. 8. *winnows.* See note on Ru 1:22. *threshing wheel.*
The wheel of the threshing cart that separated the grain from
the husk (cf. Isa 28:27–28). The wicked will be separated from the
righteous and duly punished.
20:27 Cf. 15:11; Heb 4:12–13 and notes.
20:28 *Love and faithfulness.* See 3:3; 14:22; Ps 26:3 and
note. *keep a king safe ... secure.* Benevolence and kindness
endear a king to his people and encourage them to be loyal
subjects (cf. 16:12 and note).
20:29 *their strength.* Cf. Jer 9:23. *gray hair the splendor of the
old.* See 16:31 and note.
20:30 *Blows and wounds cleanse away evil.* Stern punishment
is necessary to restrain evil. Proverbs often refers to fools whose
backs are beaten (10:13; 14:3; 19:29; 26:3), but even then, because they are fools, they may not change their ways (cf. 17:10;
see 27:22 and note).
21:1 *In the LORD's hand the king's heart.* God controls the
lives and actions even of kings, such as Nebuchadnezzar
(Da 4:31–32,35) and Cyrus (Isa 45:1–7; cf. Ezr 6:22; cf. also Ro
13:1–6 and notes). *channels toward all who please him.* Cf.
16:1,4,9 and notes.

21:2 *think all their ways are right.* See 14:12; 16:2. *weighs
the heart.* See 16:2; 24:12; Job 31:6 and notes. Ancient Egyptian paintings depict a deity weighing a human heart on scales to
determine whether the weight of its sins is heavier than a feather.
21:3 *what is right and just.* See note on Ps 119:121. *more acceptable ... than sacrifice.* A theme also found in the prophets
(see Isa 1:11–15 and note). See v. 27; see also note on 15:8.
21:4 *Haughty eyes.* See note on 6:17. *proud heart.* See 16:5,18.
21:5 *plans of the diligent lead to profit.* See note on 10:4. *haste.*
Either rash actions (see 19:2 and note) or a desire to get rich
quick (see 13:11 and note; 20:21; 28:20).
21:6 *fortune made by a lying tongue.* See note on 10:2; cf. 19:1.
fleeting vapor. See 13:11; Ecc 1:14 and notes. *deadly snare.* Cf.
5:22; 7:23.
21:7 *violence of the wicked will drag them away.* See 1:18–19
and notes.
21:9 Repeated in 25:24. *corner of the roof.* Roofs were flat, and
small rooms could be built there (see 2Ki 4:10). *quarrelsome
wife.* See 19:13 and note.
21:10 *crave evil.* See 4:16; 10:23. *their neighbors get no mercy.*
Cf. 14:21.

¹² The Righteous One[a] takes note of the house of the wicked
  and brings the wicked to ruin.[n]

¹³ Those who shut their ears to the cry of the poor
  will also cry out[o] and not be answered.[p]

¹⁴ A gift given in secret soothes anger,
  and a bribe concealed in the cloak pacifies great wrath.[q]

¹⁵ When justice is done, it brings joy to the righteous
  but terror to evildoers.[r]

¹⁶ Whoever strays from the path of prudence
  comes to rest in the company of the dead.[s]

¹⁷ Whoever loves pleasure will become poor;
  whoever loves wine and olive oil will never be rich.[t]

¹⁸ The wicked become a ransom[u] for the righteous,
  and the unfaithful for the upright.

¹⁹ Better to live in a desert
  than with a quarrelsome and nagging wife.[v]

²⁰ The wise store up choice food and olive oil,
  but fools gulp theirs down.

²¹ Whoever pursues righteousness and love
  finds life, prosperity[b w] and honor.[x]

²² One who is wise can go up against the city of the mighty[y]
  and pull down the stronghold in which they trust.

²³ Those who guard their mouths[z] and their tongues
  keep themselves from calamity.[a]

²⁴ The proud and arrogant[b]—"Mocker" is their name;
  they behave with insolent fury.

²⁵ The craving of sluggards will be the death of them,[c]
  because their hands refuse to work.

²⁶ All day long they crave for more,
  but the righteous[d] give without sparing.[e]

²⁷ The sacrifice of the wicked is detestable[f]—
  how much more so when brought with evil intent![g]

²⁸ Those who give false witness[h] will perish,[i]
  but a careful listener will testify successfully.

[a] 12 Or *The righteous person*   [b] 21 Or *righteousness*

21:12 ⁿS Pr 14:11
21:13 ᵒS Ex 11:6; ᵖS Job 29:12
21:14 ᵍS Ge 32:20
21:15 ʳS Pr 10:29
21:16 ˢEze 18:24
21:17 ᵗPr 23:20-21, 29-35
21:18 ᵘPr 11:8; Isa 43:3
21:19 ᵛS ver 9
21:21 ʷPs 25:13; ˣMt 5:6
21:22 ʸS Pr 8:14
21:23 ᶻS Ps 34:13; ᵃS Pr 10:19; 12:13; 13:3
21:24 ᵇJer 43:2
21:25 ᶜPr 13:4
21:26 ᵈS 2Sa 17:27; ᵉS Lev 25:35
21:27 ᶠS 1Ki 14:24; ᵍS Pr 15:8
21:28 ʰIsa 29:21; ⁱS Pr 19:5

21:11 See 19:25 and note.
21:12 Cf. Job 34:17. *house of the wicked ... to ruin.* See 10:25 and note; 14:11.
21:13 *cry of the poor.* See note on 14:21; see also 28:27. *also cry out and not be answered.* See note on 1:28. Cf. the fate of the rich man (Lk 16:19–31) and the unmerciful servant (Mt 18:23–35). Contrast Ps 118:5 (see note there).
21:14 *gift ... bribe.* See note on 17:8; see also 18:16; 19:6. *soothes anger ... wrath.* Perhaps that of an offended party (see 6:34–35).
21:15 *joy to the righteous.* See 11:10 and note. *terror to evildoers.* See 10:29 and note; Ro 13:3.
21:16 Graphically illustrated by the man who succumbs to the adulteress (see 2:18 and note; 5:23; 7:22–23; 9:18).
21:17 *wine and olive oil.* Both were associated with lavish feasting (see 23:20–21; Am 6:6). Olive oil was also used in various lotions or perfumes, some of which were very expensive (Jn 12:5).
21:18 *The wicked become a ransom for the righteous.* Close to the thought of 11:8. In Isa 43:3–4 God gave three nations to Persia in exchange for Persia's willingness to release the exiles of Judah (see note on Isa 43:3).

21:19 See 19:13 and note.
21:20 *store up choice food.* See 3:10 and note; 8:21. *olive oil.* See note on v. 17; see also Dt 7:13.
21:21 *pursues righteousness.* See 15:9 and note. *finds life.* See 10:2 and note. *life, prosperity and honor.* Benefits for those who seek wisdom (see note on 3:2; see also 3:16; 8:18; cf. 22:4).
21:22 *wise ... pull down the stronghold.* Probably another way of saying, "Wisdom is better than strength" (Ecc 9:16). Cf. 24:5; cf. also 2Co 10:4, where spiritual weapons "have divine power to demolish strongholds."
21:23 See 13:3 and note; 18:21.
21:24 *"Mocker" is their name.* See note on 1:22. God mocks and punishes them for their "insolent fury" (cf. v. 11; 3:34; 19:25,29).
21:25 *craving of sluggards.* See notes on 6:6; 13:4.
21:26 *give without sparing.* The righteous are prosperous, so they can share with those in need (see Ps 37:25–26; 112:9; cf. Eph 4:28).
21:27 *The sacrifice of the wicked is detestable.* See notes on v. 3; 15:8.
21:28 *false witness will perish.* See 19:5,9; see also note on 6:19.

21:29 *i* S Pr 14:8
21:30 *k* S Job 12:13;
S 15:25 *l* S 2Ch 13:12;
S Job 5:13; Isa 8:10
21:31 *m* Ps 33:12-
19; Isa 31:1
22:1 *n* Ecc 7:1
22:2 *o* S Job 31:15;
Pr 29:13; Mt 5:45
22:3 *p* S Pr 14:16
q Pr 27:12
22:4 *r* S Pr 15:33
s S Pr 10:27; Da 4:36
22:5 *t* Pr 15:19
22:6 *u* S Ge 14:14
v Eph 6:4 *w* S Dt 6:7
22:8 *x* S Ex 1:20;
S Job 4:8; Gal 6:7-8
y Hos 8:7
22:9 *z* S Dt 14:29
a S Pr 11:25; S 19:17;
28:27
22:10 *b* Ps 26:20
22:11 *c* Pr 16:13;
Mt 5:8
22:13 *d* Pr 26:13

²⁹ The wicked put up a bold front,
    but the upright give thought to their ways. *j*

³⁰ There is no wisdom, *k* no insight, no plan
    that can succeed against the Lord. *l*

³¹ The horse is made ready for the day of battle,
    but victory rests with the Lord. *m*

22 A good name is more desirable than great riches;
    to be esteemed is better than silver or gold. *n*

² Rich and poor have this in common:
    The Lord is the Maker of them all. *o*

³ The prudent see danger and take refuge, *p*
    but the simple keep going and pay the penalty. *q*

⁴ Humility is the fear of the Lord;
    its wages are riches and honor *r* and life. *s*

⁵ In the paths of the wicked are snares and pitfalls, *t*
    but those who would preserve their life stay far from them.

⁶ Start *u* children off on the way they should go, *v*
    and even when they are old they will not turn from it. *w*

⁷ The rich rule over the poor,
    and the borrower is slave to the lender.

⁸ Those who sow injustice reap calamity, *x*
    and the rod they wield in fury will be broken. *y*

⁹ The generous will themselves be blessed, *z*
    for they share their food with the poor. *a*

¹⁰ Drive out the mocker, and out goes strife;
    quarrels and insults are ended. *b*

¹¹ One who loves a pure heart and who speaks with grace
    will have the king for a friend. *c*

¹² The eyes of the Lord keep watch over knowledge,
    but he frustrates the words of the unfaithful.

¹³ The sluggard says, "There's a lion outside! *d*
    I'll be killed in the public square!"

21:29 *bold front.* Cf. the behavior of the adulteress in 7:13.

21:30 *no plan that can succeed against the Lord.* Because he is sovereign and controls people and nations (see v. 1; 16:4,9 and notes; 19:21; 1Co 3:19–20).

21:31 *horse.* God often cautions against trusting in horses and chariots for victory (e.g., Ps 20:7; Hos 1:7; cf. Dt 17:16). *victory rests with the Lord.* See 1Sa 17:47; Ps 3:8 and notes.

22:1 *good name.* Its value is recognized also in 3:4; 10:7; Ecc 7:1. *better than silver or gold.* Like the possession of wisdom (see 3:14 and note; 16:16).

22:2 *Maker of them all.* See 14:31 and note.

22:3 *prudent … take refuge.* Cf. 14:8. *simple.* See note on 1:4; see also 9:16.

22:4 See 18:12. *Humility is the fear of the Lord.* Associated also in 15:33 (see note on 1:7). *riches and honor and life.* Benefits for those who seek wisdom (see note on 3:2; see also 3:16; 8:18; cf. 21:21).

22:5 *snares and pitfalls.* Evil (cf. 15:19). *stay far from them.* By taking the "highway of the upright" (16:17).

22:6 A proverb, not a prophecy or promise (see Introduction: The Nature of a Proverb). *Start children off.* Cf. Ge 18:19. Instruction (1:8) and discipline (22:15) are primarily in-

volved. *way they should go.* The right way, the way of wisdom (see 4:11 and note). *old.* Or "grown."

22:7 *The rich.* See note on 10:15. *the borrower is slave to the lender.* One of the reasons why putting up security for someone else (v. 26) was frowned upon (cf. Ne 5:4–5).

22:8 *who sow injustice reap calamity.* See 12:21. "People reap what they sow" (Gal 6:7; see also Hos 8:7 and note). *rod they wield in fury.* Their ability to oppress others (see Ps 125:3 and note; Isa 14:5–6).

22:9 *The generous will … be blessed.* See note on 11:25. *share their food.* See 14:21 and note; see also Dt 15:7–11.

22:10 *Drive out the mocker.* See note on 1:22; cf. Ge 21:9–10. *out goes strife … insults.* Cf. 17:14; 18:3; 20:3.

22:11 *pure heart.* Cf. Ps 24:4. *speaks with grace.* Characteristic of the wise in Ecc 10:12. *king for a friend.* Cf. v. 29.

22:12 *The eyes of the Lord keep watch.* See 5:21; 15:3; Job 31:4; 34:21; Ps 121:3–8; Jer 16:17; Heb 4:13. *over knowledge.* God protects those who have knowledge (cf. Ps 1:6; 34:15). *frustrates … the unfaithful.* Overrules their plans and desires (see 16:9; 21:30 and notes).

22:13 The sluggard (see note on 6:6) creates excuses to avoid work (see 26:13).

¹⁴ The mouth of an adulterous woman is a deep pit; ^e
　　a man who is under the Lᴏʀᴅ's wrath falls into it. ^f

¹⁵ Folly is bound up in the heart of a child,
　　but the rod of discipline will drive it far away. ^g

¹⁶ Those who oppress the poor to increase their wealth
　　and those who give gifts to the rich—both come to poverty.

THIRTY SAYINGS OF THE WISE

Saying 1

¹⁷ Pay attention ^h and turn your ear to the sayings of the wise; ⁱ
　　apply your heart to what I teach, ^j
¹⁸ for it is pleasing when you keep them in your heart
　　and have all of them ready on your lips.
¹⁹ So that your trust may be in the Lᴏʀᴅ,
　　I teach you today, even you.
²⁰ Have I not written thirty sayings for you,
　　sayings of counsel and knowledge,
²¹ teaching you to be honest and to speak the truth, ^k
　　so that you bring back truthful reports
　　　to those you serve?

Saying 2

²² Do not exploit the poor ^l because they are poor
　　and do not crush the needy in court, ^m
²³ for the Lᴏʀᴅ will take up their case ⁿ
　　and will exact life for life. ^o

Saying 3

²⁴ Do not make friends with the hot-tempered,
　　do not associate with those who are easily angered,
²⁵ or you may learn their ways
　　and get yourself ensnared. ^p

Saying 4

²⁶ Do not be one who shakes hands in pledge ^q
　　or puts up security for debts;
²⁷ if you lack the means to pay,
　　your very bed will be snatched from under you. ^r

Saying 5

²⁸ Do not move an ancient boundary stone ^s
　　set up by your ancestors.

22:14 ^e S Pr 5:3-5;
23:27 ^f Ecc 7:26
22:15 ^g S Pr 13:24;
S 20:30
22:17 ^h S Pr 1:8
ⁱ S Pr 1:6; 30:1; 31:1
^j S Pr 2:2
22:21 ^k Ecc 12:10
22:22 ^l S Lev 25:17;
S Job 5:16 ^m S Ex 23:6
22:23 ⁿ S Job 29:16;
Ps 140:12 ^o Est 8:1;
S 9:1; Pr 23:10-11
22:25 ^p 1Co 15:33
22:26 ^q Pr 6:1-5
22:27 ^r S Pr 11:15;
S 17:18
22:28 ^s S Dt 19:14

22:14 *mouth of an adulterous woman.* Her seductive words (see note on 5:3; see also 2:16; 7:5). *deep pit.* Perhaps a well or a hunter's trap (see 5:22 and note; 7:22; 23:27).

22:15 *rod of discipline.* See note on 13:24.

22:16 *oppress the poor.* Condemned also in 14:31; 28:3. *give gifts to the rich.* Perhaps bribes (see 17:8 and note; 18:16; 19:6). *poverty.* See 21:5; 28:22 and note.

22:17—24:22 A new section that returns more to the style of chs. 1–9. For its relationship to the Egyptian "Wisdom of Amenemope," see Introduction: Date. Pr 22:17–21 forms the introduction to this section and is also to be numbered as the first "Saying." It emphasizes the importance of wisdom (v. 17) and "knowledge" (v. 20): "teach" (vv. 17,19) and "teaching" (v. 21) are derived from the same Hebrew root as "knowledge".

B **22:17** *Pay attention and turn your ear to.* See 4:20; 5:1. *sayings of the wise.* See 24:23; a title, like "proverbs of Solomon" in 10:1. *apply your heart to.* See 23:12; Ps 4:7 and notes; Pr 24:32. The opening saying of Amenemope begins similarly: "Give your ears, hear . . . give your heart to understand."

22:18 *it is pleasing.* See 2:10; 16:24 and notes.

22:19 *that your trust may be in the Lᴏʀᴅ.* See note on 3:5.

B **22:20** *thirty sayings.* There are 30 units in 22:17—24:22. The separate units are marked off by numbered sayings in the TNIV text. Most of them are two or three verses long, but see 22:17–21 and 23:29–35. The Egyptian "Wisdom of Amenemope" also contains 30 sections.

22:21 *those you serve.* Possibly parents or guardians.

22:22 *Do not exploit the poor.* See v. 16; 14:31. *do not crush the needy in court.* See Isa 1:17 and note.

22:23 *the Lᴏʀᴅ will take up their case.* See 23:11 and note; Ps 12:5; 140:12; Isa 3:13–15; Mal 3:5. *will exact life for life.* See Ex 22:21–27 and note.

C **22:24** *Do not make friends.* Cf. 12:26. *the hot-tempered.* Their characteristics are given in 14:16–17; 15:18; 29:22.

A **22:25** *may learn their ways.* "Bad company corrupts good character" (1Co 15:33). *ensnared.* See note on 5:22; see also 12:13; 13:14; 29:6.

22:26 See note on 6:1.

22:27 *your very bed will be snatched.* You will be reduced to poverty.

22:28 *ancient boundary stone.* See 15:25 and note.

22:29 ʳS 1Ki 11:28
ᵘS Ge 41:46
ᵛS Ge 39:4
23:3 ʷver 6-8;
Ps 141:4
23:5 ˣS Mt 6:19
ʸPr 27:24
23:6 ᶻver 1-3;
Ps 141:4
23:9 ᵃS Pr 9:7
23:10 ᵇS Dt 19:14
23:11 ᶜS Job 19:25
ᵈPs 24:8 ᵉEx 22:22-
24; Pr 15:25; 22:22-
23
23:12 ᶠS Pr 2:2
23:14 ᵍS Pr 13:24;
S 19:18

Saying 6

29 Do you see those who are skilled ᵗ in their work?
   They will serve ᵘ before kings; ᵛ
   they will not serve before officials of low rank.

Saying 7

23

When you sit to dine with a ruler,
   note well what ᵃ is before you,
2 and put a knife to your throat
   if you are given to gluttony.
3 Do not crave his delicacies, ʷ
   for that food is deceptive.

Saying 8

4 Do not wear yourself out to get rich;
   do not trust your own cleverness.
5 Cast but a glance at riches, and they are gone, ˣ
   for they will surely sprout wings
   and fly off to the sky like an eagle. ʸ

Saying 9

6 Do not eat the food of a begrudging host,
   do not crave his delicacies; ᶻ
7 for he is the kind of person
   who is always thinking about the cost. ᵇ
"Eat and drink," he says to you,
   but his heart is not with you.
8 You will vomit up the little you have eaten
   and will have wasted your compliments.

Saying 10

9 Do not speak to fools,
   for they will scorn your prudent words. ᵃ

Saying 11

10 Do not move an ancient boundary stone ᵇ
   or encroach on the fields of the fatherless,
11 for their Defender ᶜ is strong; ᵈ
   he will take up their case against you. ᵉ

Saying 12

12 Apply your heart to instruction ᶠ
   and your ears to words of knowledge.

Saying 13

13 Do not withhold discipline from children;
   if you punish them with the rod, they will not die.
14 Punish them with the rod
   and save them from death. ᵍ

ᵃ 1 Or *who*   ᵇ 7 Or *for as he thinks within himself, / so he is; or for as he puts on a feast, / so he is*

22:29 *skilled in their work.* Artisans were considered to be wise (see note on 8:30; see also Ex 35:30—36:2). *serve before kings.* Like Joseph, an administrator (Ge 41:46); David, a musician (1Sa 16:21–23); and Huram, a worker in bronze (1Ki 7:13–14).
23:2 *gluttony.* Cf. the similar warning in vv. 20–21.
23:3 *Do not crave his delicacies.* Repeated in a different context in v. 6. *deceptive.* Perhaps the meaning is that the ruler wants to obligate you in some way, even to influence you to support a wicked scheme (cf. Ps 141:4).
23:4 *Do not wear yourself out to get rich.* The desire to get rich can ruin a person physically and spiritually. "For the love of money is a root of all kinds of evil" (1Ti 6:10; cf. 15:27; 28:20; Heb 13:5).
23:5 *riches … are gone.* Our trust must be in God, not in riches (see Jer 17:11; Lk 12:20–21; 1Ti 6:17).
23:6 *begrudging host.* One "eager to get rich" (28:22).

23:7 *his heart is not with you.* Cf. 26:24–25. *heart.* See vv. 12,15,17,19,26; Ps 4:7 and note.
23:8 *vomit.* Out of disgust at the attitude of the host.
23:9 *scorn your prudent words.* Fools "despise wisdom" (1:7) and hate knowledge and correction (1:22; 12:1). They heap abuse on one who rebukes them (9:7).
23:10 *ancient boundary stone.* See note on 15:25; see also 22:28. *fatherless.* Oppressing the widow and the fatherless is strongly denounced (see Isa 10:2; Jer 22:3; Zec 7:10 and note).
23:11 *Defender.* Family Guardian or Protector, someone who helped close relatives regain land (see Lev 25:25 and note) or who avenged their death (Nu 35:12,19). God is a "father to the fatherless, a defender of widows" (Ps 68:5). See notes on Ru 2:20; Jer 31:11; see also Jer 50:34. *will take up their case.* See Ps 12:5; 140:12; Isa 3:13–15; Mal 3:5.
23:12 *Apply your heart to.* An echo of 22:17.

Saying 14

> ¹⁵ My son, if your heart is wise,
> then my heart will be glad indeed;
> ¹⁶ my inmost being will rejoice
> when your lips speak what is right. ^h

Saying 15

> ¹⁷ Do not let your heart envy ⁱ sinners,
> but always be zealous for the fear of the LORD.
> ¹⁸ There is surely a future hope for you,
> and your hope will not be cut off. ^j

Saying 16

> ¹⁹ Listen, my son, ^k and be wise,
> and set your heart on the right path:
> ²⁰ Do not join those who drink too much wine ^l
> or gorge themselves on meat,
> ²¹ for drunkards and gluttons become poor, ^m
> and drowsiness clothes them in rags.

Saying 17

> ²² Listen to your father, who gave you life,
> and do not despise your mother when she is old. ⁿ
> ²³ Buy the truth and do not sell it—
> wisdom, instruction and insight as well. ^o
> ²⁴ The father of a righteous child has great joy;
> a man who fathers a wise son rejoices in him. ^p
> ²⁵ May your father and mother rejoice;
> may she who gave you birth be joyful! ^q

Saying 18

> ²⁶ My son, ^r give me your heart
> and let your eyes delight in my ways, ^s
> ²⁷ for an adulterous woman is a deep pit ^t
> and a wayward wife is a narrow well.
> ²⁸ Like a bandit she lies in wait, ^u
> and multiplies the unfaithful among men.

Saying 19

> ²⁹ Who has woe? Who has sorrow?
> Who has strife? Who has complaints?
> Who has needless bruises? Who has bloodshot eyes?
> ³⁰ Those who linger over wine, ^v
> who go to sample bowls of mixed wine.
> ³¹ Do not gaze at wine when it is red,
> when it sparkles in the cup,
> when it goes down smoothly!
> ³² In the end it bites like a snake
> and poisons like a viper.

23:16 ^h ver 24;
Pr 27:11; 29:3
23:17 ⁱ S Ps 37:1;
S 73:3
23:18 ^j S Ps 9:18;
37:1-4; Pr 24:14,19-
20
23:19 ^k Dt 4:9;
Pr 28:7
23:20 ^l Isa 5:11,22;
56:12; Hab 2:15
23:21 ^m S Pr 21:17
23:22 ⁿ S Lev 19:32
23:23 ^o Pr 4:7; 17:16
23:24 ^p S ver 15-16
23:25 ^q S Pr 10:1
23:26 ^r Pr 5:1-6
^s S Ps 18:21
23:27 ^t S Pr 22:14
23:28 ^u Pr 7:11-12
23:30 ^v ver 20-21;
Isa 5:11

23:13–14 See 13:24 and note.

23:15 See 10:1 and note; see also v. 24; 27:11; 29:3. *My son.* See 1:8 and note.

23:16 *what is right.* The Hebrew word for this phrase is translated "smoothly" in v. 31. The same lips can be blessed by producing "right" speech or cursed by savoring wine that goes down "smoothly."

23:17 *Do not . . . envy sinners.* See 3:31; 24:1,19. *fear of the LORD.* See notes on 1:7; 3:7.

23:18 *future hope.* See 24:14,20; Ps 37:37; Jer 29:11.

23:19 *right path.* Cf. 4:25–26.

A **23:20** *Do not join.* See 1:15; 12:26 and note. *those who drink too much wine.* Drunkenness is also condemned in vv. 29–35; 20:1 (see note there); cf. Dt 21:20; Mt 24:49; Lk 21:34; Ro 13:13; Eph 5:18; 1Ti 3:3.

23:21 *gluttons.* See v. 2; 28:7; cf. Mt 11:19. *become poor.* See 21:17. *drowsiness.* Cf. the poverty that overtakes the sluggard in 6:9–11 (see notes there).

23:22 *do not despise your mother.* Cf. 1:8; 10:1; 15:20; 30:17.

23:23 *Buy the truth . . . wisdom . . . insight.* See 4:5; see also 4:7 and note.

23:24–25 See v. 15; 27:11; see also 10:1 and note.

B **23:27** *deep pit . . . narrow well.* From which it is difficult to escape. *deep pit.* See note on 22:14. *wayward wife.* See note on 2:16; see also 5:20; 7:18–20. *well.* The same metaphor is used of women in general in the Akkadian "Pessimistic Dialogue" (see chart, p. xxiv).

23:28 *lies in wait.* See 6:26; 7:12; Ecc 7:26. *multiplies the unfaithful.* Cf. 7:26.

A **23:29–35** A vivid description of the physical and psychological effects of drunkenness.

23:29 *Who has woe?* Cf. the woes pronounced on drunkards in Isa 5:11,22. *strife.* See 20:1 and note. *bruises.* Cf. the "beatings for the backs of fools" in 19:29.

23:30 *linger over wine.* See 1Sa 25:36. *mixed wine.* Wine mixed with spices (see 9:2; Ps 75:8; Isa 5:22 and notes).

23:35 ʷ Pr 20:1
24:1 ˣ Pr 3:31-32;
23:17-18
24:2 ʸ S Ps 2:1;
Isa 32:6; 55:7-8; 59:7;
65:2; 66:18; Hos 4:1
ᶻ Ps 10:7
24:3 ᵃ S Pr 14:1
24:4 ᵇ S Pr 8:21
24:6 ᶜ S Pr 11:14;
S 20:18; Lk 14:31
24:10 ᵈ S Job 4:5
24:11 ᵉ Ps 82:4
24:12 ᶠ S Ps 139:2
ᵍ S 1Sa 2:3
ʰ S Ps 54:5
ⁱ Job 34:11; Ps 62:12;
S Mt 16:27; Ro 2:6*

33 Your eyes will see strange sights
  and your mind imagine confusing things.
34 You will be like one sleeping on the high seas,
  lying on top of the rigging.
35 "They hit me," you will say, "but I'm not hurt!
  They beat me, but I don't feel it!
  When will I wake up
  so I can find another drink?" ʷ

Saying 20

24 Do not envy ˣ the wicked,
  do not desire their company;
2 for their hearts plot violence, ʸ
  and their lips talk about making trouble. ᶻ

Saying 21

3 By wisdom a house is built, ᵃ
  and through understanding it is established;
4 through knowledge its rooms are filled
  with rare and beautiful treasures. ᵇ

Saying 22

5 The wise prevail through great power,
  and those who have knowledge muster their strength.
6 Surely you need guidance to wage war,
  and victory is won through many advisers. ᶜ

Saying 23

7 Wisdom is too high for fools;
  in the assembly at the gate they must not open their mouths.

Saying 24

8 Whoever plots evil
  will be known as a schemer.
9 The schemes of folly are sin,
  and people detest a mocker.

Saying 25

10 If you falter in a time of trouble,
  how small is your strength! ᵈ
11 Rescue those being led away to death;
  hold back those staggering toward slaughter. ᵉ
12 If you say, "But we knew nothing about this,"
  does not he who weighs ᶠᵍ the heart perceive it?
  Does not he who guards your life know it?
  Will he not repay ʰ everyone according to what they have done? ⁱ

Saying 26

13 Eat honey, my son, for it is good;
  honey from the comb is sweet to your taste.

23:32 *bites like a snake.* Death will be the result (cf. Nu 21:6).
23:33 *see strange sights . . . imagine confusing things.* Perhaps a reference to the delirium that afflicts the alcoholic.
23:34 *You will be like one sleeping on the high seas.* Your head will be spinning.
23:35 *They beat me, but I don't feel it!* Cf. the condition of Israel in Jer 5:3. *so I can find another drink.* Pain and misery do not prevent drunkards from repeating their folly (cf. 26:11; 27:22; Isa 56:12; Am 4:1).
24:1 *Do not envy.* See v. 19; Ps 37:1. *do not desire their company.* See 1:15; 12:26 and note; 23:20.
24:2 *plot violence.* See 1:11; 6:14; Job 15:35; Ps 5:9 and notes; 38:12.
24:3 *house.* Symbolic of the life of an individual or a family. *is built.* Cf. the similar expression in 9:1.
24:4 *rare and beautiful treasures.* Wisdom promises to bestow wealth on those who love her (8:21).

24:5 *wise . . . knowledge.* An echo of 22:17–21. *prevail through great power.* See note on 21:22.
24:7 *gate.* See note on 1:21.
24:8 *plots evil.* See v. 2 and note. *schemer.* Cf. "those who devise wicked schemes" (12:2; cf. also 14:17).
C **24:9** *schemes of folly are sin.* Cf. 1:10–19; 9:13–18. *people detest a mocker.* Because mockers are proud, insulting (9:7) and quarrelsome (22:10). See note on 1:22.
24:10 Cf. Jer 12:5; Gal 6:9.
24:11 *those being led away to death.* Perhaps the innocent condemned to die (cf. 17:15; Isa 58:6–7).
A **24:12** *we knew nothing about this.* See Jas 4:17. *does not he who weighs the heart perceive it?* God knows even our thoughts and motives (see 16:2; 21:2 and note; Ps 94:9–11). *repay everyone.* See v. 29; 20:22; Ps 5:10 and notes. *according to what they have done.* See Mt 16:27 and note.

¹⁴ Know also that wisdom is like honey for you:
  If you find it, there is a future hope for you,
    and your hope will not be cut off. [j][k]

Saying 27

¹⁵ Do not lurk like a thief near the house of the righteous,
  do not plunder their dwelling place;
¹⁶ for though the righteous fall seven times, they rise again,
  but the wicked stumble when calamity strikes. [l]

Saying 28

¹⁷ Do not gloat [m] when your enemies fall;
  when they stumble, do not let your heart rejoice, [n]
¹⁸ or the LORD will see and disapprove
  and turn his wrath away from them. [o]

Saying 29

¹⁹ Do not fret [p] because of evildoers
  or be envious of the wicked,
²⁰ for the evildoer has no future hope,
  and the lamp of the wicked will be snuffed out. [q]

Saying 30

²¹ Fear the LORD and the king, [r] my son,
  and do not join with rebellious officials,
²² for those two will send sudden destruction [s] on them,
  and who knows what calamities they can bring?

FURTHER SAYINGS OF THE WISE

²³ These also are sayings of the wise: [t]

  To show partiality [u] in judging is not good: [v]
²⁴ Whoever says to the guilty, "You are innocent," [w]
  will be cursed by peoples and denounced by nations.
²⁵ But it will go well with those who convict the guilty,
  and rich blessing will come on them.

²⁶ An honest answer
  is like a kiss on the lips.

²⁷ Put your outdoor work in order
  and get your fields ready;
    after that, build your house.

²⁸ Do not testify against your neighbor without cause [x]—
  would you use your lips to mislead?
²⁹ Do not say, "I'll do to them as they have done to me;
  I'll pay them back for what they did." [y]

24:14 [j] Ps 119:103;
Pr 16:24 [k] Pr 23:18
24:16 [l] S Job 5:19;
S Ps 34:21
24:17 [m] Ob 1:12
[n] S 2Sa 3:32; Mic 7:8
24:18 [o] S Job 31:29
24:19 [p] Ps 37:1
24:20 [q] S Job 18:5;
S Pr 23:17-18
24:21 [r] Ro 13:1-5
24:22 [s] S Ps 73:19
24:23 [t] S Pr 1:6
[u] S Ex 18:16;
S Lev 19:15 [v] Ps 72:2;
Pr 28:21; 31:8-9;
Jer 22:16
24:24 [w] S Pr 17:15
24:28 [x] S Ps 7:4
24:29 [y] Pr 20:22;
Mt 5:38-41

24:14 *wisdom is like honey for you.* It nourishes and brings healing (see 16:24 and note). *future hope.* Contrast v. 20; see Ps 9:18; 37:37; Jer 29:11.

24:15 *lurk.* See 1:11 and note; 12:6; Ps 10:9–10.

24:16 *seven times.* Many times (see 6:16; Job 5:19 and note; cf. Pr 26:16). *rise again.* God promises to uphold and rescue the righteous (cf. Ps 34:19; 37:24; Mic 7:8). *wicked stumble.* See v. 22; 4:19; 6:15 and note; 11:3,5.

24:17 *Do not gloat.* See 17:5 and note.

24:18 *turn his wrath away from them.* Edom was made desolate because she rejoiced over Israel's destruction (see Ps 137:7 and note; Eze 35:15).

24:19 Almost identical to Ps 37:1; see v. 1; 3:31; 23:17.

24:20 *no future hope.* For himself or his posterity (contrast v. 14; 23:18; see Ps 37:2,28,38). *lamp ... will be snuffed out.* See note on 13:9.

△ 24:21 *Fear the LORD and the king.* Submission to civil authority is also commanded in Ecc 8:2–5. 1Pe 2:17 says, "fear God, honor the emperor," and Ro 13:1–7 urges the same obedience (see notes there). These passages all view the king as

a terror to the wicked (cf. 20:8,26).

24:22 *those two.* God and the king. *sudden destruction ... calamities.* God's judgment is more common (see 6:15; 11:3,5), but the power of the king is seen in 20:8,26.

24:23–34 An appendix to 22:17—24:22, giving five additional sayings of the wise.

24:23 *partiality in judging is not good.* See 18:5 and note.

24:24 *You are innocent.* See 17:15 and note. *will be cursed by peoples.* Just as they "curse those who hoard grain" (11:26).

24:25 *rich blessing.* See 10:6 and note; Dt 16:20.

24:26 *honest answer.* Cf. 16:13. *like a kiss.* Cf. the "gracious words" that are "sweet to the soul" in 16:24.

24:27 *get your fields ready.* Plan carefully and acquire the means as you build your house. *build your house.* See v. 3 and note.

24:28 *testify ... without cause.* See 3:30; Job 2:3. *use your lips to mislead.* See note; 12:17; 25:18.

24:29 *I'll pay them back.* See v. 12. A spirit of revenge is discouraged also in 20:22 (see note there); cf. 25:21–22; Mt 5:43–45; Ro 12:17.

24:30 *z* Pr 6:6-11;
26:13-16
24:33 *a* S Pr 6:10
24:34 *b* S Pr 10:4;
Ecc 10:18
25:1 *c* S 1Ki 4:32
d S Pr 1:1
25:2 *e* Pr 16:10-15
25:5 *f* S Pr 20:8
g 2Sa 7:13
h S Pr 16:12; 29:14
25:7 *i* Lk 14:7-10
25:8 *j* Mt 5:25-26
25:11 *k* ver 12;
Pr 15:23

³⁰ I went past the field of a sluggard, *z*
    past the vineyard of someone who has no sense;
³¹ thorns had come up everywhere,
    the ground was covered with weeds,
    and the stone wall was in ruins.
³² I applied my heart to what I observed
    and learned a lesson from what I saw:
³³ A little sleep, a little slumber,
    a little folding of the hands to rest *a*—
³⁴ and poverty will come on you like a thief
    and scarcity like an armed man. *b*

MORE PROVERBS OF SOLOMON

25 These are more proverbs *c* of Solomon, compiled by the men of Hezekiah king of Judah: *d*

² It is the glory of God to conceal a matter;
    to search out a matter is the glory of kings. *e*
³ As the heavens are high and the earth is deep,
    so the hearts of kings are unsearchable.

⁴ Remove the dross from the silver,
    and a silversmith can produce a vessel;
⁵ remove wicked officials from the king's presence, *f*
    and his throne will be established *g* through righteousness. *h*

⁶ Do not exalt yourself in the king's presence,
    and do not claim a place among his great men;
⁷ it is better for him to say to you, "Come up here," *i*
    than for him to humiliate you before his nobles.

What you have seen with your eyes
⁸   do not bring*a* hastily to court,
for what will you do in the end
    if your neighbor puts you to shame? *j*

⁹ If you take your neighbor to court,
    do not betray another's confidence,
¹⁰ or the one who hears it may shame you
    and the charge against you will stand.

¹¹ Like apples *b* of gold in settings of silver *k*
    is a ruling rightly given.

---

a 7,8 Or *nobles / on whom you had set your eyes.* / *⁸Do not go*   *b* 11 Or possibly *apricots*

24:30 *sluggard.* See note on 6:6.
24:31 *thorns ... weeds.* See 15:19 and note; cf. Isa 34:13.
24:32 *I applied my heart to.* See 22:17; 23:12 and note; Ps 4:7 and note.
24:33–34 See 6:10–11 and note on 6:11.
25:1—29:27 Another collection of Solomon's proverbs, similar to 10:1—22:16.
25:1 *proverbs of Solomon.* See notes on 1:1; 10:1. *compiled by the men of Hezekiah.* There was a great revival in the reign of Hezekiah (c. 715–686 B.C.), who restored the singing of hymns to its proper place (2Ch 29:30). His interest in "the words of David" corresponds to his support of this compilation of Solomon's proverbs. Solomon was the last king to rule over all Israel during the united monarchy; Hezekiah was the first king to rule over all Israel (now restricted to the southern kingdom) after the destruction of the divided monarchy's northern kingdom.
25:2–7 Appropriately enough, kings are the subject of this initial series of proverbs compiled by King Hezekiah's men to honor King Solomon.
25:2 *to conceal a matter.* God gets glory because humans cannot fully understand his universe or the way he rules it (see Dt 29:29; Job 26:14 and note; Isa 40:12–24; Ro

11:33–36). *to search out a matter.* A king gets glory if he can uncover the truth and administer justice (see 1Ki 3:9; 4:34).
25:3 *are unsearchable.* Cannot be understood—like the four things in 30:18–19. Yet God controls the hearts of kings (see note on 21:1).
25:4 *Remove the dross from the silver.* A process compared to the purification of society in general and rulers in particular in Isa 1:22–25; Eze 22:18; Zec 13:8–9; Mal 3:2–3.
25:5 *his throne will be established through righteousness.* See note on 16:12; see also 20:26.
25:6 *in the king's presence.* Probably at a feast (cf. 23:1). Jesus spoke about the place of honor at a wedding feast (Lk 14:7–11).
25:7 *Come up here.* Cf. "Friend, move up to a better place" (Lk 14:10); contrast Isa 22:15–19.
25:8 *do not bring hastily to court.* A warning about the seriousness of disputes (see 17:14) and the need to exercise caution (see 24:28).
25:9 *do not betray another's confidence.* If you do, you are a gossip (see 11:13; 20:19).
25:10 *shame you ... charge against you will stand.* A good name is one of life's most valuable possessions (see 22:1 and note).

¹² Like an earring of gold or an ornament of fine gold
    is the rebuke of a wise judge to a listening ear. ^l

¹³ Like a snow-cooled drink at harvest time
    is a trustworthy messenger to the one who sends him;
    he refreshes the spirit of his master. ^m

¹⁴ Like clouds and wind without rain
    is one who boasts of gifts never given.

¹⁵ Through patience a ruler can be persuaded, ⁿ
    and a gentle tongue can break a bone. ^o

¹⁶ If you find honey, eat just enough—
    too much of it, and you will vomit. ^p

¹⁷ Seldom set foot in your neighbor's house—
    too much of you, and you will be hated.

¹⁸ Like a club or a sword or a sharp arrow
    is one who gives false testimony against a neighbor. ^q

¹⁹ Like a broken tooth or a lame foot
    is reliance on the unfaithful in a time of trouble.

²⁰ Like one who takes away a garment on a cold day,
    or like vinegar poured on a wound,
    is one who sings songs to a heavy heart.

²¹ If your enemy is hungry, give him food to eat;
    if he is thirsty, give him water to drink.

²² In doing this, you will heap burning coals ^r on his head,
    and the LORD will reward you. ^s

²³ Like a north wind that brings unexpected rain
    is a sly tongue—which provokes a horrified look.

²⁴ Better to live on a corner of the roof
    than share a house with a quarrelsome wife. ^t

²⁵ Like cold water to a weary soul
    is good news from a distant land. ^u

²⁶ Like a muddied spring or a polluted well
    are the righteous who give way to the wicked.

²⁷ It is not good to eat too much honey, ^v
    nor is it honorable to search out matters that are too deep. ^w

²⁸ Like a city whose walls are broken through
    is a person who lacks self-control.

25:12 ^l S ver 11; Ps 141:5; S Pr 13:18
25:13 ^m S Pr 10:26; 13:17
25:15 ⁿ Ecc 10:4 ^o Pr 15:1
25:16 ^p ver 27
25:18 ^q S Pr 12:18
25:22 ^r S Ps 18:8 ^s S 2Ch 28:15; Mt 5:44; Ro 12:20*
25:24 ^t S Pr 21:9
25:25 ^u Pr 15:30
25:27 ^v ver 16 ^w Pr 27:2; S Mt 23:12

25:11 *gold . . . silver.* Cf. the fruit of wisdom in 8:19.

25:12 *earring of gold.* Comparable to the beautiful wreath and necklace that represent the adornment of wisdom and sound teaching (see 1:9; 3:22; 4:9). *rebuke of a wise judge.* Cf. the "life-giving correction" of 15:31.

25:13 *snow-cooled drink at harvest time.* Probably a drink cooled by snow from the mountains; it did not snow at harvest time. See 26:1; contrast 10:26. *trustworthy messenger.* See 13:17 and note.

25:14 *clouds . . . without rain.* An image applied to false teachers in Jude 12.

25:15 *Through patience a ruler can be persuaded.* Cf. 14:29. *gentle tongue.* See note on 15:1.

25:16 *honey.* See v. 27.

25:18 *club . . . sword . . . arrow.* Cf. Ps 57:4; Jer 9:8. *false testimony.* See note on 6:19; see also 24:28; Ex 20:16.

25:19 *broken tooth . . . lame foot.* Relying on Egypt was like leaning on a splintered reed (Isa 36:6).

25:20 *sings songs to a heavy heart.* The exiles were reluctant to sing the songs of Zion (Ps 137:3–4).

25:21–22 Quoted in Ro 12:20.

A **25:21** Kindness to one's enemy is encouraged in 20:22; Ex 23:4–5 (see note there). *give him food . . . water.* At Eli-

sha's request, a trapped Aramean army was given a great feast and then sent home (2Ki 6:21–23; cf. 2Ch 28:15).

B A **25:22** *heap burning coals on his head.* Horrible punishment reserved for the wicked (see Ps 140:10). Here, however, it is kindness that will hurt the enemy (cf. the broken bone of v. 15) but perhaps win him over. Alternatively, the expression may reflect an Egyptian expiation ritual, in which a guilty person, as a sign of his repentance, carried a basin of glowing coals on his head. The meaning here, then, would be that in returning good for evil—and so being kind to your enemy (see Ro 12:20)—you may cause him to repent or change. *the LORD will reward you.* Even if the enemy remains hostile (cf. 11:18; 19:17).

25:23 *north.* Perhaps northwest (cf. Lk 12:54). *sly tongue.* One that spreads slander (cf. 10:18).

25:24 Echoed from 21:9 (see note there).

25:25 *good news from a distant land.* See Ge 45:25–28.

25:26 *muddied spring.* Cf. Eze 34:18–19. *the righteous who give way.* Perhaps through bribery (cf. 17:8; 29:4; Isa 1:21–23).

25:27 *too much honey.* See v. 16.

25:28 *city whose walls are broken through.* Defenseless and disgraced (cf. Ne 1:3 and note). *person who lacks self-control.* See 16:32 and note.

26:1 ˣS 1Sa 12:17
ʸ ver 8; Pr 19:10
26:2 ᶻS Dt 23:5
26:3 ᵃPs 32:9
ᵇS Pr 10:13
26:4 ᶜver 5;
Isa 36:21
26:5 ᵈver 4;
S Pr 3:7
26:6 ᵉS Pr 10:26
26:7 ᶠver 9
26:8 ᵍS ver 1
26:9 ʰver 7
26:11 ⁱ2Pe 2:22*
ʲS Ps 85:8
26:12 ᵏS Pr 3:7
ˡPr 29:20
26:13 ᵐPr 6:6-11;
24:30-34 ⁿPr 22:13
26:14 ᵒS Pr 6:9
26:15 ᵖPr 19:24

26

Like snow in summer or rain ˣ in harvest,
  honor is not fitting for a fool. ʸ
² Like a fluttering sparrow or a darting swallow,
  an undeserved curse does not come to rest. ᶻ
³ A whip for the horse, a bridle for the donkey, ᵃ
  and a rod for the backs of fools! ᵇ
⁴ Do not answer fools according to their folly,
  or you yourself will be just like them. ᶜ
⁵ Answer fools according to their folly,
  or they will be wise in their own eyes. ᵈ
⁶ To send a message by the hands of a fool ᵉ
  is like cutting off one's feet or drinking poison.
⁷ Like the useless legs of one who is lame
  is a proverb in the mouth of a fool. ᶠ
⁸ Like tying a stone in a sling
  is the giving of honor to a fool. ᵍ
⁹ Like a thornbush in a drunkard's hand
  is a proverb in the mouth of a fool. ʰ
¹⁰ Like an archer who wounds at random
  is one who hires a fool or any passer-by.
¹¹ As a dog returns to its vomit, ⁱ
  so fools repeat their folly. ʲ
¹² Do you see people who are wise in their own eyes? ᵏ
  There is more hope for fools than for them. ˡ

¹³ A sluggard says, ᵐ "There's a lion in the road,
  a fierce lion roaming the streets!" ⁿ
¹⁴ As a door turns on its hinges,
  so a sluggard turns on the bed. ᵒ
¹⁵ Sluggards bury their hands in the dish
  and are too lazy to bring them back to their mouths. ᵖ
¹⁶ Sluggards are wiser in their own eyes
  than seven people who answer discreetly.

¹⁷ Like one who grabs a stray dog by the ears
  is someone who rushes into a quarrel not their own.

¹⁸ Like a maniac shooting
  flaming arrows of death
¹⁹ is one who deceives a neighbor
  and says, "I was only joking!"

26:1–12 As kings are the subject of the series of proverbs that begin ch. 25 (see note on 25:2–7), so fools are the subject at the beginning of ch. 26.
26:1 *rain in harvest.* It rarely rains in the Holy Land from June through September, but see 1Sa 12:17–18. *honor is not fitting for a fool.* See v. 8.
26:2 *undeserved curse does not come to rest.* When David was cursed by Shimei, he realized that the curse would not take effect because he was innocent of the charge of murdering members of Saul's family (2Sa 16:8,12).
26:3 *rod for the backs of fools.* See 14:3; 19:29.

▲ **26:4** *Do not answer fools according to their folly.* Do not stoop to their level (see 23:9; Mt 7:6 and notes).

▲ **26:5** *Answer fools according to their folly.* Sometimes folly must be plainly exposed and denounced. Thus vv. 4–5 do not contradict each other, as is often thought.
26:6 *To send a message by the hands of a fool.* He will likely misrepresent the one who sends him, or in some other manner frustrate the sender's purpose (see 13:17 and note).
26:8 *Like tying a stone in a sling.* A fool with authority wields a formidable weapon, but it is useless in his hands—as useless as a stone that is tied, not placed, in a sling. *honor to a fool.* See v. 1.
26:9 Fools reciting proverbs will do as much damage to themselves and others as a drunkard wielding a thornbush.

26:10 *one who hires a fool or any passer-by.* Abimelek hired "reckless scoundrels" to help him murder his half brothers and set up a brief and ill-fated rule (Jdg 9:4–6).
26:11 *As a dog returns to its vomit.* Quoted in 2Pe 2:22 with reference to false teachers (see note there). *fools repeat their folly.* Drunkards return to their drinks (see 23:35 and note).
26:12 *wise in their own eyes.* This conceit is applied to the sluggard in v. 16 and the rich in 28:11; cf. 26:5. *There is more hope … for them.* Repeated in 29:20.
26:13–16 A series of proverbs that focuses on the sluggard (see notes on 25:2–7; 26:1–12).
26:13 See 22:13 and note.
26:14 Sluggards love to sleep and seem to be attached to their beds as a door is to its hinges.
26:15 See 19:24 and note.
26:16 *wiser in their own eyes.* See v. 12 and note. *seven.* Many (see note on 24:16).
26:17 *grabs a stray dog by the ears.* To do so is to immediately create a disturbance.
26:18 *Like a maniac shooting.* Cf. the archer in v. 10. *flaming arrows.* Could easily ignite sheaves of grain (cf. Zec 12:6).
26:19 *I was only joking!* Explaining it as a prank is a poor excuse.

²⁰ Without wood a fire goes out;
    without a gossip a quarrel dies down. ^q
²¹ As charcoal to embers and as wood to fire,
    so is a quarrelsome person for kindling strife. ^r
²² The words of a gossip are like choice morsels;
    they go down to the inmost parts. ^s
²³ Like a coating of silver dross on earthenware
    are fervent ^a lips with an evil heart.
²⁴ Enemies disguise themselves with their lips, ^t
    but in their hearts they harbor deceit. ^u
²⁵ Though their speech is charming, ^v do not believe them,
    for seven abominations fill their hearts. ^w
²⁶ Their malice may be concealed by deception,
    but their wickedness will be exposed in the assembly.
²⁷ If anyone digs a pit, ^x they themselves will fall into it; ^y
    if anyone rolls a stone, it will roll back on them. ^z
²⁸ A lying tongue hates those it hurts,
    and a flattering mouth ^a works ruin.

27

Do not boast ^b about tomorrow,
    for you do not know what a day may bring. ^c

² Let someone else praise you, and not your own mouth;
    an outsider, and not your own lips. ^d

³ Stone is heavy and sand ^e a burden,
    but a fool's provocation is heavier than both.

⁴ Anger is cruel and fury overwhelming,
    but who can stand before jealousy? ^f

⁵ Better is open rebuke
    than hidden love.

⁶ Wounds from a friend can be trusted,
    but an enemy multiplies kisses. ^g

⁷ One who is full loathes honey from the comb,
    but to the hungry even what is bitter tastes sweet.

⁸ Like a bird that flees its nest ^h
    is anyone who flees from home.

⁹ Perfume ⁱ and incense bring joy to the heart,
    and the pleasantness of a friend
    springs from their heartfelt advice.

¹⁰ Do not forsake your friend or a friend of your family,
    and do not go to your relative's house when disaster ^j strikes you—
    better a neighbor nearby than a relative far away.

^a 23 Hebrew; Septuagint *smooth*

26:20 ^q Pr 22:10
26:21 ^r S Pr 14:17
26:22 ^s Pr 18:8
26:24 ^t S Ps 31:18
    ^u Ps 41:6
26:25 ^v Ps 28:3
    ^w Jer 9:4-8
26:27 ^x S Ps 7:15
    ^y S Est 6:13
    ^z S Est 2:23; S 7:9;
    Ps 35:8; 141:10;
    Pr 28:10; 29:6;
    Isa 50:11
26:28 ^a S Ps 12:3;
    Pr 29:5
27:1 ^b S 1Ki 20:11
    ^c Mt 6:34; Jas 4:13-16
27:2 ^d S Pr 25:27
27:3 ^e S Job 6:3
27:4 ^f S Nu 5:14
27:6 ^g Ps 141:5;
    Pr 28:23
27:8 ^h Isa 16:2
27:9 ⁱ S Est 2:12;
    S Ps 45:8
27:10 ^j S Pr 17:17

26:21 *kindling strife.* See 6:14 and note.
26:22 Identical to 18:8 (see note there).
26:23 *coating of silver dross on earthenware.* Silver dross was a cheap substance used to make pottery look different from the clay it actually was. This fits the analogy in the simile very well (a false and deceptive exterior). Cf. the clean outside of the cup and dish (Lk 11:39; cf. Mt 23:27). *fervent lips with an evil heart.* The speech of the adulteress is seductive (see 2:16; 5:3 and notes).
26:24 *in their hearts they harbor deceit.* See 12:20.
26:25 *their speech is charming.* See Jer 9:8. *seven.* See note on v. 16. For seven things the Lord detests, see 6:16–19.
26:26 *exposed in the assembly.* See 5:14; Lk 8:17.
26:27 *If anyone digs a pit, they themselves will fall into it.* "The trouble they cause recoils on them" (Ps 7:16). See 1:18 and note; 28:10; 29:6; Est 7:10; Ps 7:15; Ecc 10:8–9.
26:28 *lying tongue hates those it hurts.* See 10:18. *flattering*

mouth works ruin. See 29:5; cf. 16:13.
27:1 Cf. the words of the rich fool and God's response in Lk 12:19–20; cf. also Pr 16:9; Isa 56:12; Jas 4:13–16.
27:2 *Let someone else praise you.* See 2Co 10:12,18.
27:4 *who can stand before jealousy?* See 6:34; SS 8:6.
27:5 *open rebuke.* Called "life-giving correction" in 15:31; cf. Gal 2:14.
27:6 See 28:23. *Wounds from a friend.* Called a "kindness" in Ps 141:5 (see note there). *enemy multiplies kisses.* See 5:3 and note; Mt 26:49.
27:7 *loathes honey.* Cf. 25:16,27.
27:8 *anyone who flees from home.* They have lost their security and may be vulnerable to temptation (cf. 7:21–23).
27:9 *Perfume.* See note on 21:17. *incense.* Cf. the one "perfumed with myrrh and incense" (SS 3:6). *bring joy to the heart.* See v. 11. *pleasantness of a friend.* See 16:21,24 and notes.

27:11 *k* S Pr 10:1;
S 23:15-16
l S Ge 24:60
27:12 *m* Pr 22:3
27:13 *n* Pr 20:16
27:15 *o* S Est 1:18
27:18 *p* 1Co 9:7
q Lk 19:12-27
27:20 *r* Pr 30:15-16;
Hab 2:5 *s* Ecc 1:8; 6:7
27:21 *t* S Pr 17:3
27:23 *u* Pr 12:10
27:24 *v* Pr 23:5

¹¹ Be wise, my child, and bring joy to my heart; *k*
   then I can answer anyone who treats me with contempt. *l*

¹² The prudent see danger and take refuge,
   but the simple keep going and pay the penalty. *m*

¹³ Take the garment of one who puts up security for a stranger;
   hold it in pledge if it is done for an outsider. *n*

¹⁴ If anyone loudly blesses a neighbor early in the morning,
   it will be taken as a curse.

¹⁵ A quarrelsome wife is like the dripping *o*
   of a leaky roof in a rainstorm;
¹⁶ restraining her is like restraining the wind
   or grasping oil with the hand.

¹⁷ As iron sharpens iron,
   so one person sharpens another.

¹⁸ Those who guard a fig tree will eat its fruit, *p*
   and those who protect their masters will be honored. *q*

¹⁹ As water reflects the face,
   so one's life reflects the heart. *a*

²⁰ Death and Destruction *b* are never satisfied, *r*
   and neither are human eyes. *s*

²¹ The crucible for silver and the furnace for gold, *t*
   but people are tested by their praise.

²² Though you grind fools in a mortar,
   grinding them like grain with a pestle,
   you will not remove their folly from them.

²³ Be sure you know the condition of your flocks, *u*
   give careful attention to your herds;
²⁴ for riches do not endure forever, *v*
   and a crown is not secure for all generations.
²⁵ When the hay is removed and new growth appears
   and the grass from the hills is gathered in,
²⁶ the lambs will provide you with clothing,
   and the goats with the price of a field.
²⁷ You will have plenty of goats' milk to feed your family
   and to nourish your women servants.

---

a 19 Or *so others reflect your heart back to you*   *b* 20 Hebrew *Abaddon*

27:10 Do not fail a friend in need; when in need rely on friendship rather than on mere family relationships. *relative far away.* Either physically or emotionally.

27:11 *Be wise, my child.* See 10:1 and note. *then I can answer anyone who treats me with contempt.* Wise children (or students) serve as a powerful testimony that the parents (or teachers) who have shaped them have shown themselves to be people of worth.

27:12 *the simple.* See note on 1:4. *keep going and pay the penalty.* See 7:22–23; 9:16–18.

27:13 Identical to 20:16 (see note there).

27:14 *blesses a neighbor.* Perhaps to win the neighbor's favor (cf. Ps 12:2).

27:15 See 19:13 and note.

27:17 *sharpens another.* Develops and molds the other's character.

27:18 *will eat its fruit.* Cf. 2Ti 2:6. *will be honored.* See Ge 39:4; Mt 25:21; Lk 12:42–44; Jn 12:26.

27:19 *one's life reflects the heart.* And the condition of one's heart indicates one's true character (see Mt 5:8).

27:20 *Death and Destruction.* See note on Job 26:6; see also Pr

15:11. *are never satisfied.* Their appetite is insatiable (see 30:15–16; Isa 5:14; Hab 2:5). *neither are human eyes.* See Ecc 4:8.

27:21 *crucible . . . gold.* See 17:3; Ps 12:6 and note. *people are tested by their praise.* People must not become proud, and they must be wary of flattery (cf. 12:8; Lk 6:26).

27:22 *mortar.* A bowl (see Nu 11:8). *pestle.* A club-like tool for pounding grain in a mortar. *you will not remove their folly.* In spite of severe punishment, fools refuse to change (see note on 20:30; see also 26:11; Jer 5:3 and note).

27:23–27 A section praising the basic security afforded by agricultural pursuits—reflecting the agricultural base of the ancient economy.

27:23 *give careful attention to your herds.* Like Jacob, with Laban's flocks (Ge 31:38–40).

27:24 *riches do not endure.* See notes on 23:5; Mt 6:19. *crown is not secure.* Cf. 29:14. Even kings may lose their wealth and power (see Job 19:9; La 5:16).

27:25 *hay is removed.* This began in March or April.

27:26 *price of a field.* See 31:16.

27:27 *goats' milk.* Drunk as commonly as cows' milk (see Isa 7:21–22). *women servants.* See 31:15.

28

The wicked flee [w] though no one pursues, [x]
but the righteous are as bold as a lion. [y]

² When a country is rebellious, it has many rulers,
but a ruler with discernment and knowledge maintains order.

³ A ruler [a] who oppresses the poor
is like a driving rain that leaves no crops.

⁴ Those who forsake instruction praise the wicked,
but those who heed it resist them.

⁵ Evildoers do not understand what is right,
but those who seek the LORD understand it fully.

⁶ Better the poor whose walk is blameless
than the rich whose ways are perverse. [z]

⁷ Those who heed instruction are discerning children,
but companions of gluttons disgrace their parents. [a]

⁸ Whoever increases wealth by taking interest [b] or profit from the poor
amasses it for another, [c] who will be kind to the poor. [d]

⁹ If anyone turns a deaf ear to my instruction,
even their prayers are detestable. [e]

¹⁰ Those who lead the upright along an evil path
will fall into their own trap, [f]
but the blameless will receive a good inheritance.

¹¹ The rich are wise in their own eyes;
one who is poor and discerning sees how deluded they are.

¹² When the righteous triumph, there is great elation; [g]
but when the wicked rise to power, people go into hiding. [h]

¹³ Those who conceal their sins [i] do not prosper,
but those who confess [j] and renounce them find mercy. [k]

¹⁴ Blessed are those who always tremble before God,
but those who harden their hearts fall into trouble.

¹⁵ Like a roaring lion or a charging bear
is a wicked ruler over a helpless people.

---

a 3 Or A poor person

28:1 ʷ S 2Ki 7:7
ˣ S Lev 26:17
ʸ S Ps 138:3
28:6 ᶻ Pr 19:1
28:7 ᵃ Pr 23:19-21
28:8 ᵇ S Ex 18:21;
Eze 18:8 ᶜ S Job 27:17
ᵈ S Job 3:15; Ps 112:9;
Lk 14:12-14
28:9 ᵉ S Ps 109:7;
S Pr 15:8; S Isa 1:13
28:10 ᶠ S Ps 57:6;
S Pr 26:27
28:12 ᵍ S 2Ki 11:20
ʰ ver 28; Job 24:4;
Pr 29:2
28:13 ⁱ S 2Sa 12:13;
S Job 31:33 ʲ S Lev 5:5
ᵏ Ps 32:1-5; Da 4:27;
1Jn 1:9

28:1 *The wicked flee.* See Lev 26:17; Ps 53:5 and notes. *bold as a lion.* Like David in 1Sa 17:46; cf. 2Sa 22:33–37.

A **28:2** *it has many rulers.* Israel's rebellion often brought frequent and rapid change in leadership (see 1Ki 16:8–28; 2Ki 15:8–14; 23:29—24:17). *ruler with discernment ... maintains order.* A wise ruler will be successful (see 8:15–16; 16:12 and note; 24:5; 29:4).

28:3 *who oppresses the poor.* See 14:31 and note. *driving rain.* Describes the destructive power of Assyria's king in Isa 28:2 (see note there). The gentle rain is compared to a righteous king in Ps 72:6–7.

28:4 *instruction.* Either the teachings of wisdom (3:1; 7:2) or the law of Moses (Ps 119:53). *praise the wicked.* Cf. Ro 1:32 and note. *who heed it.* See v. 7; 29:18; cf. v. 9. *resist them.* See Eph 5:7,11.

28:5 *who seek the LORD.* Who fear him (see note on 1:7). *understand it fully.* They know "what is right and just and fair" (2:9).

28:6 *blameless.* See v. 18; 2:7; Ps 15:2 and notes.

28:7 *who heed instruction.* See note on v. 4. *companions of gluttons.* See 23:20–21 and notes.

28:8 *interest or profit from the poor.* Prohibited in Ex 22:25 (see notes on Ex 22:25–27; Lev 25:36; Eze 18:8). *amasses it for another.* See 13:22 and note; cf. Lk 12:20. *kind to the poor.* See 14:31 and note.

28:9 *my instruction.* See note on v. 4. *their prayers are detestable.* Like the sacrifice of the wicked in 15:8 (see note there; see 3:32 and note; see also Ps 66:18; Isa 1:15; 59:1–2; Jer 11:14).

28:10 *into their own trap.* See note on 26:27. *blameless.* See note on 2:7. *good inheritance.* See 3:35; Heb 6:12; 1Pe 3:9.

28:11 *The rich are wise in their own eyes.* Like the fool (26:5) or the sluggard (26:16).

28:12 *there is great elation.* See 11:10 and note. *people go into hiding.* See v. 28. Obadiah hid 100 prophets during the reign of Ahab (1Ki 18:3–4), and Joash was hidden for six years while the wicked Athaliah ruled (2Ki 11:2–3).

A **28:13** *Those who conceal their sins do not prosper.* Note the physical and psychological pain referred to in 3:7–8; Ps 32:3–5 and note. *those who confess and renounce them find mercy.* Note the joy of forgiveness in Ps 32:5,10–11 (cf. 1Jn 1:9 and note).

28:14 *who harden their hearts.* Like the pharaoh (Ex 7:13), and like the Israelites who tested the Lord at Meribah and Massah (see Ps 95:8 and note; Ro 2:5).

28:15 *roaring lion.* Full of rage and murderous intent (cf. 19:12; Mt 2:16; 1Pe 5:8). *charging bear.* See 17:12 and note. *wicked ruler.* See v. 12.

28:17 *l* 1Sa 30:17;
1Ki 20:20; Jer 41:15;
44:14
28:18 *m* Jer 39:18
n S Est 6:13; Pr 10:9
28:19 *o* Pr 12:11
28:20 *p* ver 22
28:21 *q* S Lev 19:15
r S Ps 94:21; S Pr 18:5
s Eze 13:19
28:22 *t* ver 20
28:23 *u* Pr 27:5-6
28:24 *v* Pr 19:26
w S Pr 18:9
28:25 *x* S Pr 14:17
y Pr 29:25
28:26 *z* S Ps 4:5;
Pr 3:5 *a* 1Co 3:18
28:27 *b* S Dt 24:19;
S Pr 22:9
c S Ps 109:17
28:28 *d* S ver 12;
S Job 20:19
29:1 *e* S Ex 32:9;
S Dt 9:27 *f* Jer 19:15;
36:31; Hab 2:7
g S 2Ch 36:16; Pr 6:15
29:2 *h* S 2Ki 11:20
i Pr 30:22; Ecc 10:6
j S Pr 28:12
29:3 *k* S Pr 10:1;
S 23:15-16 *l* Pr 5:8-10;
Lk 15:11-32

¹⁶ A tyrannical ruler practices extortion,
  but one who hates ill-gotten gain will enjoy a long reign.

¹⁷ Anyone tormented by the guilt of murder
  will seek refuge *l* in the grave;
  let no one hold them back.

¹⁸ Those whose walk is blameless are kept safe, *m*
  but those whose ways are perverse will fall *n* into the pit. *a*

¹⁹ Those who work their land will have abundant food,
  but those who chase fantasies will have their fill of poverty. *o*

²⁰ A faithful person will be richly blessed,
  but one eager to get rich will not go unpunished. *p*

²¹ To show partiality *q* is not good *r*—
  yet a person will do wrong for a piece of bread. *s*

²² The stingy are eager to get rich
  and are unaware that poverty awaits them. *t*

²³ Whoever rebukes a person will in the end gain favor
  rather than one who has a flattering tongue. *u*

²⁴ Whoever robs their father or mother *v*
  and says, "It's not wrong,"
  is partner to one who destroys. *w*

²⁵ The greedy stir up dissension, *x*
  but those who trust in the LORD *y* will prosper.

²⁶ Those who trust in themselves are fools, *z*
  but those who walk in wisdom are kept safe. *a*

²⁷ Those who give to the poor will lack nothing, *b*
  but those who close their eyes to them receive many curses. *c*

²⁸ When the wicked rise to power, people go into hiding; *d*
  but when the wicked perish, the righteous thrive.

29 Whoever remains stiff-necked *e* after many rebukes
  will suddenly be destroyed *f*—without remedy. *g*

² When the righteous thrive, the people rejoice; *h*
  when the wicked rule, *i* the people groan. *j*

³ A man who loves wisdom brings joy to his father, *k*
  but a companion of prostitutes squanders his wealth. *l*

---

a 18 Syriac (see Septuagint); Hebrew *into one*

28:16 *one who hates ill-gotten gain will enjoy a long reign.* Unlike those who love such gain (see 1:19 and note).
28:17 *will seek refuge in the grave.* Perhaps the sense is that the murderer is so tormented by a guilty conscience that he tries to commit suicide.
28:18 *blameless…perverse.* Contrasted also in v. 6; 19:1. *will fall into the pit.* Cf. 11:5.
28:19 *chase fantasies.* See 12:11 and note.
28:20 *richly blessed.* With God's gifts and favors (see 3:13–18; 10:6; Ge 49:26; Dt 33:16). *one eager to get rich will not go unpunished.* Cf. similar warnings in 20:21; 23:4 (see notes there).
28:21 *To show partiality is not good.* See 18:5 and note; 24:23. *will do wrong for a piece of bread.* Perhaps a reference to a bribe, however small (cf. Eze 13:19 and note).
28:22 *stingy.* See 23:6. *eager to get rich.* A warning to him is given in v. 20; cf. similar warnings in 20:21; 23:4 (see note there). *poverty awaits them.* Because it is the generous who prosper (see note on 11:25).
28:23 *Whoever rebukes a person.* See Gal 2:14; cf. 15:31; 25:12. *who has a flattering tongue.* See 26:28; 29:5; cf. 16:13.

28:24 *Whoever robs their father or mother.* See note on 19:26; cf. Mt 15:4–6; Mk 7:10–12.
28:25 *stir up dissension.* See note on 6:14. *will prosper.* As does also the generous person (see 11:25 and note) and the one who is diligent (13:4, lit. "the desires of the diligent prosper").
28:26 *who walk in wisdom.* Equals "whoever trusts in the LORD" in 29:25; cf. 3:5–6.
28:27 *give to the poor.* See note on 14:21. *will lack nothing.* Generosity is the path to blessing (see 11:24; 14:21 and notes; 19:17). *close their eyes to them.* See 21:13.
28:28 *people go into hiding.* See v. 12 and note. *righteous thrive.* See 11:10; 29:2.
29:1 *stiff-necked after many rebukes.* See note on Ex 32:9. Eli's sons died because of their stubbornness (see 1Sa 2:25 and note). *will suddenly be destroyed—without remedy.* Identical to 6:15. Cf. the fate of the mockers in 1:22–27.
29:2 *When the righteous thrive, the people rejoice.* See 11:10 and note. *when the wicked rule, the people groan.* See 28:12; Jdg 2:18 and notes.
29:3 *man who loves wisdom brings joy to his father.* See 10:1

⁴ By justice a king gives a country stability, *m*
　　but those who are greedy for ᵃ bribes tear it down.

⁵ Those who flatter their neighbors
　　are spreading nets for their feet. *n*

⁶ Evildoers are snared by their own sin, *o*
　　but the righteous shout for joy and are glad.

⁷ The righteous care about justice for the poor, *p*
　　but the wicked have no such concern.

⁸ Mockers stir up a city,
　　but the wise turn away anger. *q*

⁹ If a wise person goes to court with a fool,
　　the fool rages and scoffs, and there is no peace.

¹⁰ The bloodthirsty hate people of integrity
　　and seek to kill the upright. *r*

¹¹ Fools give full vent to their rage, *s*
　　but the wise bring calm in the end. *t*

¹² If a ruler *u* listens to lies,
　　all his officials become wicked. *v*

¹³ The poor and the oppressor have this in common:
　　The Lᴏʀᴅ gives sight to the eyes of both. *w*

¹⁴ If a king judges the poor with fairness,
　　his throne will be established forever. *x*

¹⁵ A rod and a reprimand impart wisdom,
　　but children left to themselves disgrace their mother. *y*

¹⁶ When the wicked thrive, so does sin,
　　but the righteous will see their downfall. *z*

¹⁷ Discipline your children, and they will give you peace;
　　they will bring you the delights you desire. *a*

¹⁸ Where there is no revelation, people cast off restraint;
　　but blessed are those who heed wisdom's instruction. *b*

¹⁹ Servants cannot be corrected by mere words;
　　though they understand, they will not respond.

²⁰ Do you see someone who speaks in haste?
　　There is more hope for a fool than for them. *c*

²¹ A servant pampered from youth
　　will turn out to be insolent.

ᵃ 4 Or *who give*

---

and note. *companion of prostitutes squanders his wealth.* See 5:10; 6:26; Lk 15:13 and notes.
29:4 *By justice a king gives a country stability.* See 16:12 and note. *bribes.* See 17:8 and note.
29:5 *Those who flatter their neighbors.* See 28:23.
29:6 *snared by their own sin.* See 1:18 and note; 22:5.
29:7 *The righteous care about justice for the poor.* As Job did (Job 29:16); see Jer 22:16 and note; Jas 1:27; cf. Pr 19:17; 22:22; 29:14.
29:8 *Mockers stir up a city.* See notes on 6:14; 11:11; see also 26:21. *Mockers.* See 1:22 and note. *the wise turn away anger.* See Jas 3:17–18.
29:9 *the fool rages and scoffs.* Like an angry bear (17:12) or the tossing sea (Isa 57:20–21).
29:10 *The bloodthirsty hate people of integrity.* Their schemes are described in 1:11–16; cf. Ps 5:6.
29:11 *give full vent to their rage.* See v. 9 and note; 14:16–17. *bring calm in the end.* See 16:32 and note.
29:12 *all his officials become wicked.* Cf. Isa 1:23.

29:13 *The Lᴏʀᴅ gives sight.* See Ex 4:11; Ps 94:9.
29:14 See Isa 9:7; cf. Pr 27:24.
29:15 *A rod and a reprimand.* See note on 13:24.
29:16 *When the wicked thrive.* See v. 2; 11:11 and note; 28:12,28. *righteous will see their downfall.* See 10:25 and note; 14:11; 21:12.
29:17 *Discipline your children.* Teach them and train them (see 13:24 and note; 22:6).
29:18 *revelation.* A message from God given through a prophet; a prophetic vision (see 1Sa 3:1; Isa 1:1; Ob 1). *people cast off restraint.* Possibly an allusion to the sinful actions of the Israelites while Moses was on Mount Sinai (see Ex 32:25 and note). *blessed are those who heed wisdom's instruction.* See 28:4 and note; see also 8:32.
29:19 *cannot be corrected by mere words.* Servants, like children (vv. 15,17), must be disciplined (see note on 22:6).
29:20 *who speaks in haste.* See 10:19; 17:27–28; Jas 1:19,26. *There is more hope . . . for them.* Identical to 26:12.
29:21 *A servant pampered.* See v. 19 and note.

29:22 ᵈ S Pr 14:17
29:23 ᵉ S Est 5:12
ᶠ S Pr 11:2; S 15:33;
S 16:18
29:24 ᵍ S Lev 5:1
29:25 ʰ S 1Sa 15:24
ⁱ Pr 28:25 ʲ S Pr 16:20
29:26 ᵏ Pr 19:6
ˡ S Pr 16:33
29:27 ᵐ S ver 10
30:1 ⁿ S Pr 22:17
30:3 ᵒ S Pr 9:10
30:4 ᵖ Dt 30:12;
Ps 24:1-2; S Pr 8:22-
31; Jn 3:13; Eph 4:7-
10 �q Isa 40:12
ʳ Job 26:8 ˢ S Ge 1:2
ᵗ Rev 19:12
30:5 ᵘ S Ps 12:6;
S 18:30 ᵛ S Ge 15:1
30:6 ʷ S Dt 4:2

²² An angry person stirs up dissension,
  and a hot-tempered person commits many sins. ᵈ

²³ Pride brings a person low, ᵉ
  but the lowly in spirit gain honor. ᶠ

²⁴ The accomplices of thieves are their own enemies;
  they are put under oath and dare not testify. ᵍ

²⁵ To fear ʰ anyone will prove to be a snare,
  but whoever trusts in the LORD ⁱ is kept safe. ʲ

²⁶ Many seek an audience with a ruler, ᵏ
  but it is from the LORD that one gets justice. ˡ

²⁷ The righteous detest the dishonest;
  the wicked detest the upright. ᵐ

SAYINGS OF AGUR

30 The sayings ⁿ of Agur son of Jakeh—an inspired utterance.

This man's utterance to Ithiel:

"I am weary, God,
  but I can prevail. ᵃ
² Surely I am only a brute, not a man;
  I do not have human understanding.
³ I have not learned wisdom,
  nor have I attained to the knowledge of the Holy One. ᵒ
⁴ Who has gone up ᵖ to heaven and come down?
  Whose hands �q have gathered up the wind?
Who has wrapped up the waters ʳ in a cloak? ˢ
  Who has established all the ends of the earth?
What is his name, ᵗ and what is the name of his son?
  Surely you know!

⁵ "Every word of God is flawless; ᵘ
  he is a shield ᵛ to those who take refuge in him.
⁶ Do not add ʷ to his words,
  or he will rebuke you and prove you a liar.

⁷ "Two things I ask of you, LORD;
  do not refuse me before I die:
⁸ Keep falsehood and lies far from me;
  give me neither poverty nor riches,

ᵃ 1 With a different word division of the Hebrew; Masoretic Text *utterance to Ithiel, / to Ithiel and Ukal:*

29:22 *angry person stirs up dissension.* See note on 6:14; see also 15:18.

29:23 See 15:33 and note; see also 18:12.

29:24 *they are put under oath.* They will be held responsible for failing to testify (cf. Lev 5:1).

29:25 *To fear anyone.* Cf. 1Sa 15:24; Isa 51:12; Jn 12:42–43. *whoever trusts in the LORD is kept safe.* See 18:10; 28:26 and notes; cf. 3:5–6.

29:26 *Many seek an audience.* See 1Ki 10:24. *it is from the LORD that one gets justice.* God controls a king's actions (see note on 21:1) and defends the cause of the poor and the just (cf. Job 36:6).

29:27 The final proverb in this second Solomonic collection (chs. 25–29) highlights in the starkest terms the opposing perspectives that characterize the righteous and the wicked (cf. Ps 1:6 and note).

30:1–33 The first of two chapters that serve as an appendix to Proverbs.

30:1 *sayings.* See 22:17 and note; 24:23. Fourteen of Agur's sayings are recorded in this chapter. *Agur son of Jakeh.* Probably a non-Israelite wise man like Job and his friends. *inspired utter-*

ance. Usually the message of a prophet (see note on Isa 13:1 ["prophecy"]).

30:2 *I am only a brute, not a man.* Paul described himself as the "worst of sinners" (1Ti 1:16).

30:3 *knowledge of the Holy One.* See 9:10 and note.

30:4 The use of rhetorical questions to express God's greatness as Creator occurs also in Job 38:4—39:30; Isa 40:12–31 (see note there). *gathered up the wind.* Cf. Ps 135:7. *wrapped up the waters in a cloak.* See Job 26:8; 38:8–9. *What is . . . the name of his son?* This question has been understood in several different ways, but its meaning remains obscure. *Surely you know!* God similarly challenged Job (see Job 38:4–5 and note).

30:5 Almost identical to Ps 18:30. *shield.* See notes on 2:7; Ps 3:3. *those who take refuge in him.* See 14:32; 18:10.

30:6 *Do not add to his words.* Cf. Moses' warning to the Israelites in Dt 4:2 (see note there); cf. also Rev 22:18–19 and note.

30:7 *Two things.* The use of lists characterizes Agur's sayings (see vv. 15,18,21,24,29).

30:8 *my daily bread.* Cf. Job 23:12 and the Lord's Prayer (see Mt 6:11 and note).

but give me only my daily bread. [x]

[9] Otherwise, I may have too much and disown [y] you
and say, 'Who is the LORD?' [z]
Or I may become poor and steal,
and so dishonor the name of my God. [a]

[10] "Do not slander servants to their master,
or they will curse you, and you will pay for it.

[11] "There are those who curse their fathers
and do not bless their mothers; [b]
[12] those who are pure in their own eyes [c]
and yet are not cleansed with their filth; [d]
[13] those whose eyes are ever so haughty, [e]
whose glances are so disdainful;
[14] those whose teeth [f] are swords
and whose jaws are set with knives [g]
to devour [h] the poor [i] from the earth
and the needy from among humankind. [j]

[15] "The leech has two daughters.
'Give! Give!' they cry.

"There are three things that are never satisfied, [k]
four that never say, 'Enough!':
[16] the grave, [l] the barren womb,
land, which is never satisfied with water,
and fire, which never says, 'Enough!'

[17] "The eye that mocks [m] a father,
that scorns an aged mother,
will be pecked out by the ravens of the valley,
will be eaten by the vultures. [n]

[18] "There are three things that are too amazing for me,
four that I do not understand:
[19] the way of an eagle in the sky,
the way of a snake on a rock,
the way of a ship on the high seas,
and the way of a man with a young woman.

[20] "This is the way of an adulterous woman:
She eats and wipes her mouth
and says, 'I've done nothing wrong.' [o]

[21] "Under three things the earth trembles,
under four it cannot bear up:

30:8 [x] Mt 6:11
30:9 [y] Jos 24:27;
Isa 1:4; 59:13
[z] Dt 6:12; 8:10-14;
Hos 13:6 [a] S Dt 8:12
30:11 [b] S Pr 20:20
30:12 [c] S Pr 16:2
[d] Jer 2:23, 35
30:13 [e] S 2Sa 22:28;
S Job 41:34
30:14 [f] S Job 4:11;
S Ps 3:7 [g] Ps 57:4
[h] S Job 24:9 [i] Am 8:4;
Mic 2:2 [j] S Job 19:22
30:15 [k] Pr 27:20
30:16 [l] Isa 5:14;
14:9,11; Hab 2:5
30:17 [m] Dt 21:18-21
[n] S Job 15:23
30:20 [o] Pr 5:6

30:9 *I may have too much and disown you.* Moses predicted that the Israelites would forget God when their food was plentiful and their herds large (Dt 8:12–17; 31:20). *Who is the LORD?* Or, Why should I serve him (see Job 21:14–15)? *become poor and steal.* Cf. 6:30.

30:10 *you will pay for it.* Since the accusation is false, the servant's curse will be effective (cf. 26:2 and note)—so do not suppose you can take advantage of a servant's lowly position.

30:11 *curse their fathers.* Cf. v. 17; see 20:20 and note.

30:12 *those who are pure in their own eyes.* Like the Pharisee in Lk 18:11 (cf. Isa 65:5 and note).

30:13 *whose eyes are . . . haughty.* See note on 6:17; see also Isa 3:16.

30:14 *whose teeth are swords . . . whose jaws are . . . knives.* The wicked are like ravenous beasts that devour the prey (see Job 29:17). *to devour the poor . . . the needy.* Cf. Ps 14:4; Mic 3:2–3 and notes.

30:15,18,21,29 *three . . . four.* See note on 6:16.

30:15 *leech has two daughters.* The "two daughters" are the two suckers with which this parasite draws blood from its victims.

30:16 *grave.* Its appetite is never satisfied (Isa 5:14; Hab 2:5). *barren womb.* In ancient Israel, a wife without children was desolate, even desperate (cf. Ge 16:2 and note; 30:1; Ru 1:11–13, 20–21; 1Sa 1:6,10–11; 2Ki 4:14 and note).

30:17 *The eye.* Haughty and disdainful (see v. 13). *mocks a father . . . an aged mother.* See v. 11 and note; 15:20. *will be pecked out by the ravens . . . the vultures.* The loss of an eye was a terrible curse (see the story of Samson in Jdg 16:21). Since vultures normally devoured the dead (see Jer 7:33 and note; Mt 24:28), the meaning may be that the body of a disgraceful son will lie unburied and exposed.

30:18–19 These four "ways" are difficult to understand because none of them leaves a track that can be readily followed. **30:19** *way of an eagle.* Soaring and swooping majestically (cf. Job 39:27; Jer 48:40; 49:22). *way of a man with a young woman.* Probably a reference to the mystery of courting and how it leads to consummation.

30:20 *adulterous woman.* See 2:16 and note. *She eats and wipes her mouth.* Eating food is used as a metaphor for making love also in 9:17 (see note there; see also 7:18 and note).

30:22 ᵖ S Pr 19:10;
S 29:2
30:25 ᑫ Pr 6:6-8
30:26 ʳ Ps 104:18
30:27 ˢ S Ex 10:4
30:32 ᵗ S Job 29:9
31:1 ᵘ S Pr 22:17
31:2 ᵛ S Jdg 11:30
31:3 ʷ S Dt 17:17;
S 1Ki 11:3; Pr 5:1-14
31:4 ˣ S Pr 20:1;
Ecc 10:16-17; Isa 5:22
31:5 ʸ S 1Ki 16:9
ᶻ S Pr 16:12

²² a servant who becomes king, ᵖ
    a godless fool who gets plenty to eat,
²³ a contemptible woman who gets married,
    and a servant who displaces her mistress.

²⁴ "Four things on earth are small,
    yet they are extremely wise:
²⁵ Ants are creatures of little strength,
    yet they store up their food in the summer; ᑫ
²⁶ hyraxes ʳ are creatures of little power,
    yet they make their home in the crags;
²⁷ locusts ˢ have no king,
    yet they advance together in ranks;
²⁸ a lizard can be caught with the hand,
    yet it is found in kings' palaces.

²⁹ "There are three things that are stately in their stride,
    four that move with stately bearing:
³⁰ a lion, mighty among beasts,
    who retreats before nothing;
³¹ a strutting rooster, a he-goat,
    and a king secure against revolt. ᵃ

³² "If you play the fool and exalt yourself,
    or if you plan evil,
    clap your hand over your mouth! ᵗ
³³ For as churning cream produces butter,
    and as twisting the nose produces blood,
    so stirring up anger produces strife."

SAYINGS OF KING LEMUEL

31 The sayings ᵘ of King Lemuel—an inspired utterance his mother taught him.

² Listen, my son! Listen, son of my womb!
    Listen, my son, the answer to my prayers! ᵛ
³ Do not spend your strength ᵇ on women,
    your vigor on those who ruin kings. ʷ

⁴ It is not for kings, Lemuel—
    it is not for kings to drink wine, ˣ
    not for rulers to crave beer,
⁵ lest they drink ʸ and forget what has been decreed, ᶻ
    and deprive all the oppressed of their rights.

ᵃ 31 The meaning of the Hebrew for this phrase is uncertain.   ᵇ 3 Or *wealth*

30:22 *servant who becomes king.* See 19:10.
30:23 *servant who displaces her mistress.* Perhaps because she was able to bear a child, whereas the wife was barren (cf. Hagar and Sarah in Ge 16:1–6).
30:25 *Ants.* See note on 6:6.
30:26 *in the crags.* Which provide a refuge for them (see Ps 104:18).
30:27 *locusts have no king.* Cf. the ant in 6:6–7. *advance together in ranks.* Locusts are portrayed as a mighty army in Joel 2:2–9 (see note on Joel 2:2).
30:28 *found in kings' palaces.* Lizards climb stone walls easily.
30:30 *lion, mighty among beasts.* See 2Sa 1:23; Mic 5:8.
30:31 *he-goat.* Goats were used to lead flocks of sheep (see Jer 50:8).
30:32 *exalt yourself.* Pride is condemned in 8:13; 11:2; 16:18. *plan evil.* Cf. 6:14; 16:27. *clap your hand over your mouth.* Stop your plotting immediately (cf. Job 21:5; 40:4).
30:33 *churning . . . twisting . . . stirring up.* See Introduction: The Nature of a Proverb. *stirring up anger produces strife.* See notes on 6:14; 15:1; see also 29:22.
31:1–9 This brief section, consisting of three proverbs, is also

of non-Israelite origin (see note on 30:1). King Lemuel is otherwise unknown. The threefold advice Lemuel's mother gives him highlights two major temptations of royalty (sexual promiscuity [vv. 2–3] and drunkenness [vv. 4–7]), as well as one of its primary obligations (defending the poor and needy [vv. 8–9; see Jer 22:15–16 and notes]).
31:1 *inspired utterance.* See note on 30:1. *his mother.* This entire chapter emphasizes the role and significance of wise women. In the ancient Near East, the queen mother was often an influential figure (see 1Ki 1:11–13 and note on 1:11).
31:2 *answer to my prayers.* Hannah also prayed for a son (see 1Sa 1:11 and note).
31:3 *your strength on women.* A warning against accumulating a large harem and engaging in sexual indulgence (see 5:9–11; 1Ki 11:1; Ne 13:26 and notes).
31:4 *It is not for kings . . . to drink wine.* Woe to the land whose rulers are drunkards (Ecc 10:16–17; cf. Pr 20:1 and note; see Hos 7:5 and note).
31:5 *deprive all the oppressed of their rights.* See 30:14 and note; see also 17:15; Isa 5:23; 10:2.

31:6 ᵃ S Ge 14:18
31:7 ᵇ S Est 1:10
31:8 ᶜ S 1Sa 19:4
31:9 ᵈ S Pr 24:23;
29:7
31:10 ᵉ S Ru 3:11;
S Pr 18:22 ᶠ Pr 8:35
31:11 ᵍ S Ge 2:18
ʰ S Pr 12:4
31:13 ⁱ 1Ti 2:9-10
31:20 ʲ Dt 15:11
31:23 ᵏ S Ex 3:16

⁶ Let beer be for those who are perishing,
   wine ᵃ for those who are in anguish!
⁷ Let them drink ᵇ and forget their poverty
   and remember their misery no more.

⁸ Speak ᶜ up for those who cannot speak for themselves,
   for the rights of all who are destitute.
⁹ Speak up and judge fairly;
   defend the rights of the poor and needy. ᵈ

EPILOGUE: THE WIFE OF NOBLE CHARACTER

¹⁰ ᵃ A wife of noble character ᵉ who can find? ᶠ
   She is worth far more than rubies.
¹¹ Her husband ᵍ has full confidence in her
   and lacks nothing of value. ʰ
¹² She brings him good, not harm,
   all the days of her life.
¹³ She selects wool and flax
   and works with eager hands. ⁱ
¹⁴ She is like the merchant ships,
   bringing her food from afar.
¹⁵ She gets up while it is still night;
   she provides food for her family
   and portions for her women servants.
¹⁶ She considers a field and buys it;
   out of her earnings she plants a vineyard.
¹⁷ She sets about her work vigorously;
   her arms are strong for her tasks.
¹⁸ She sees that her trading is profitable,
   and her lamp does not go out at night.
¹⁹ In her hand she holds the distaff
   and grasps the spindle with her fingers.
²⁰ She opens her arms to the poor
   and extends her hands to the needy. ʲ
²¹ When it snows, she has no fear for her household;
   for all of them are clothed in scarlet.
²² She makes coverings for her bed;
   she is clothed in fine linen and purple.
²³ Her husband is respected at the city gate,
   where he takes his seat among the elders ᵏ of the land.
²⁴ She makes linen garments and sells them,
   and supplies the merchants with sashes.

ᵃ 10 Verses 10-31 are an acrostic poem, the verses of which begin with the successive letters of the Hebrew alphabet.

31:8–9 The king represents God as the defender of the poor and needy (see 16:10 and note; Ps 82:3; cf. Lev 19:15; Job 29:12–17; Isa 1:17 and note).

31:10–31 The epilogue: an acrostic poem (see TNIV text note) praising the "wife of noble character" (v. 10). It corresponds to 1:1–7 as it describes a "woman who fears the LORD" (v. 30; see note on 1:7). Such a wife is almost a personification of wisdom. Like wisdom, she is "worth far more than rubies" (v. 10; 3:15; 8:11), and those who find her "receive favor from the LORD" (8:35; 18:22). See Introduction: Literary Structure.

31:10 *wife of noble character.* Like Ruth (Ru 3:11). She is "her husband's crown" (12:4; see note there).

31:12 *She brings him good.* See 18:22; 19:14.

31:13 *flax.* Its fibers were made into linen (see note on Ex 25:4; see also Pr 31:19,22,24; Isa 19:9).

31:14 *like the merchant ships.* She is an enterprising person (see v. 18).

31:15 *She gets up while it is still night.* She is the opposite of the sluggard (see 6:9–10; 26:14 and note). *portions for her*

women servants. See 27:27; Lk 12:42.

31:16 *considers a field . . . plants a vineyard.* She shows good judgment—unlike the sluggard, whose vineyard is overgrown with thorns and weeds (24:30–31).

31:17 *sets about her work vigorously.* See 10:4 and note.

31:18 *her trading is profitable.* Like wisdom, she is "worth far more than rubies" (v. 10; see note there). Wisdom "is more profitable than silver" (3:14; see note there).

31:19 *distaff . . . spindle.* Spinning thread was women's work.

31:20 *opens her arms to the poor.* See note on 14:21; see also 22:9; Job 31:16–22.

31:21 *clothed in scarlet.* Of high quality, probably made of wool (cf. 2Sa 1:24; Rev 18:16).

31:22 *fine linen.* Associated with nobility (see notes on 7:16; Ex 25:4; see also Ge 41:42). *purple.* Linked with kings (Jdg 8:26; SS 3:10) or the rich (Lk 16:19; Rev 18:16).

31:23 *city gate.* The court (see note on 1:21).

31:24 *linen garments.* See Jdg 14:12 and note; Isa 3:23. *merchants.* Cf. v. 18.

25 She is clothed with strength and dignity;
　　she can laugh at the days to come.
26 She speaks with wisdom,
　　and faithful instruction is on her tongue. ˡ
27 She watches over the affairs of her household
　　and does not eat the bread of idleness.
28 Her children arise and call her blessed;
　　her husband also, and he praises her:
29 "Many women do noble things,
　　but you surpass them all."
30 Charm is deceptive, and beauty is fleeting;
　　but a woman who fears the Lᴏʀᴅ is to be praised.
31 Honor her for all that her hands have done,
　　and let her works bring her praise ᵐ at the city gate.

31:25 *clothed with strength and dignity.* See Ps 109:29 and note; Isa 52:1; 1Ti 2:9–10. The opposite is to be "clothed with shame and disgrace" (Ps 35:26). *she can laugh at the days to come.* She is free of anxiety and worry (cf. Job 39:7).
31:26 *faithful instruction.* Given to her children and friends. She is a wise and loving counselor (see 1:8; 6:20).
31:28 *blessed.* That is, one who enjoys happy circumstances and from whom joy radiates to others. See Ge 30:13; Ps 72:17; SS 6:9; Mal 3:12; cf. Ru 4:14–15.

C **31:29** *do noble things.* The husband's reference to his wife's "noble" deeds climaxes the main body of the poem (vv. 10–29) that celebrates her "noble" character (v. 10). He fur-

ther asserts that she surpasses all other women—she is, indeed, "worth far more than rubies" (v. 10). Cf. Isa 32:8.
31:30–31 A concluding reflection on the main body of the poem.
31:30 *Charm is deceptive.* Cf. 5:3 and note. *beauty is fleeting.* See 1Pe 3:3–5 and notes; cf. Job 14:2. *who fears the Lᴏʀᴅ.* See note on 1:7.

A **31:31** *Honor her for all that her hands have done.* See v. 16; 12:14 and notes. *bring her praise.* Honor comes through "humility" and "the fear of the Lᴏʀᴅ" (22:4). *city gate.* See v. 23 and note.

ECCLESIASTES

AUTHOR AND DATE | **INTRODUCTION**

No time period or writer's name is mentioned in the book, but several passages suggest that King Solomon may be the author (1:1,12,16; 2:4–9; 7:26–29; 12:9; cf. 1Ki 2:9; 3:12; 4:29–34; 5:12; 10:1–8). On the other hand, the writer's title ("Teacher," Hebrew *qoheleth;* see note on 1:1), his unique style of Hebrew and his attitude toward rulers (suggesting that of a subject rather than a monarch—see, e.g., 4:1–2; 5:8–9; 8:2–4; 10:20) may point to another person and a later period (see note on 1:1).

PURPOSE AND TEACHING

A The author of Ecclesiastes puts his powers of wisdom to work to examine the human experience and assess the human situation. His perspective is limited to what happens "under the sun" (as is that of all the wisdom teachers). He considers life as he has experienced and observed it between the horizons of birth and death—life within the boundaries of this visible world. His wisdom cannot penetrate beyond that last horizon; he can only observe the phenomenon of death and perceive the limits it places on human beings. Within the limits of human experience and observation, he is concerned to spell out what is "good" for people to do. And he represents a devout wisdom. Life in the world is under God—for all its enigmas. Hence what begins with "Meaningless! Meaningless!" (1:2) ends with "Remember your Creator" (12:1) and "Fear God and keep his commandments" (12:13).

With a wisdom matured by many years, he takes the measure of human beings, examining their limits and their lot. He has attempted to see what human wisdom can do (1:13,16–18; 7:24; 8:16), and he has discovered that human wisdom, even when it has its beginning in "the fear of the LORD" (Pr 1:7), has limits to its powers when it attempts to go it alone—limits that circumscribe its perspectives and relativize its counsel. Most significantly, it cannot find out the larger purposes of God or the ultimate meaning of human existence. With respect to these, it can only pose questions.

Nevertheless, he does take a hard look at the human enterprise—an enterprise in which he himself has fully participated. He sees a busy, busy human ant hill in mad pursuit of many things, trying now this, now that, laboring away as if by dint of effort humans could master the world, lay bare its deepest secrets, change its fundamental structures, somehow burst through the bounds of human limitations, build for themselves enduring monuments, control their destiny, achieve a state of secure and lasting happiness—people laboring at life with an overblown conception of human powers and consequently pursuing unrealistic hopes and aspirations.

He takes a hard look and concludes that human life in this mode is "meaningless," its efforts all futile.

What, then, does wisdom teach him?

1. Humans cannot by all their striving achieve anything of ultimate or enduring significance. Nothing appears to be going anywhere (1:5–11), and people cannot by all their efforts break out of this caged treadmill (1:2–4; 2:1–11); they cannot fundamentally change anything (1:12–15; 6:10; 7:13). Hence they often toil foolishly (4:4,7–8; 5:10–17; 6:7–9). All their striving "under the sun" (1:3) after unreal goals leads only to disillusionment.

2. Wisdom is better than folly (2:13–14; 7:1–6,11–12,19; 8:1,5; 9:17–18;

10:1–3,12–15; 12:11)—it is God's gift to those who please him (2:26). But it is unwarranted to expect too much even from such wisdom—to expect that human wisdom is capable of solving all problems (1:16–18) or of securing for itself enduring rewards or advantages (2:12–17; 4:13–16; 9:13–16).

3. Experience confronts humans with many apparent disharmonies and anomalies that wisdom cannot unravel. Of these the greatest of all is this: Human life comes to the same end as that of the animals—death (2:15; 3:16–17; 7:15; 8:14; 9:1–3; 10:5–7).

4. Although God made humankind upright, people have gone in search of many "schemes" (for getting ahead by taking advantage of others; see 7:29; cf. Ps 10:2; 36:4; 140:2). So even humans are a disappointment (7:24–29).

5. People cannot know or control what will come after them, or even what lies in the more immediate future; therefore all their efforts remain balanced on the razor's edge of uncertainty (2:18; 6:12; 7:14; 9:2).

6. God keeps humans in their place (3:16–22).

7. God has ordered all things (3:1–15; 5:19; 6:1–6; 9:1), and a human being cannot change God's appointments or fully understand them or anticipate them (3:1; 7; 11:1–6). But the world is not fundamentally chaotic or irrational. It is ordered by God, and it is for humans to accept matters as they are by God's appointments, including their own limitations. Everything has its "time" and is good in its time (ch. 3).

Therefore, wisdom counsels:

1. Accept the human state as it is, shaped by God's appointments, and enjoy the life you have been given as fully as you can.

2. Don't trouble yourself with unrealistic goals—know the measure of human capabilities.

3. Be prudent in all your ways—follow wisdom's leading.

4. "Fear God and keep his commandments" (12:13), beginning already in your youth before the fleeting days of life's enjoyments are gone and "the days of trouble" (12:1) come when the infirmities of advanced age vex you and hinder you from tasting, seeing and feeling the good things of life.

To sum up, Ecclesiastes provides instruction on how to live meaningfully, purposefully and joyfully within the theocratic arrangement—primarily by placing God at the center of one's life work and activities, by contentedly accepting one's divinely appointed lot in life and by reverently trusting in and obeying the Creator-King. Note particularly 2:24–26; 3:11–14,22; 5:18–20; 8:15; 9:7–10; 11:7—12:1; 12:9–14 (see also any pertinent notes on these passages).

LITERARY FEATURES

The argument of Ecclesiastes does not flow smoothly. It meanders, with jumps and starts, through the general messiness of human experience, to which it is a response. There is also an intermingling of poetry and prose. Nevertheless, the following outline seeks to reflect, at least in a general way, the structure of the book and its main discourses. The announced theme of "meaninglessness" (futility) provides a literary frame around the whole (1:2; 12:8). And the movement from the unrelieved disillusionment of chs. 1–2 to the more serene tone and sober instructions for life in chs. 11–12 marks a development in matured wisdom's coming to terms with the human situation.

A striking feature of the book is its frequent use of key words and phrases: e.g., "meaningless" (see notes on 1:2; 2:24–25), "work/labor/toil" (see note on 2:10), "good/better" (see note on 2:1), "gift/give" (see note on 5:19), "under the sun" (see note on 1:3), "chasing after the wind" (see note on 1:14). Also to be noted is the presence of passages interwoven throughout the book that serve as key indicators of the author's theme and purpose: 1:2–3,14,17; 2:10–11,17,24–26; 3:12–13,22; 4:4,6,16; 5:18–20; 6:9,12; 7:14,24; 8:7,15,17; 9:7,12; 10:14; 11:2,5–6,8–9; 12:1,8,13–14 (see notes on these passages where present). The enjoyment of life as God gives it is a key concept in the book (see 2:24–26 and note on 2:24–25; 3:12–13,22 and note on 3:12–13; 5:18–20; 7:14; 8:15 and note; 9:7–9; 11:8–9).

1:1 *a* ver 12;
Ecc 7:27; 12:10
b S Pr 1:1
1:2 *c* Ps 39:5-6;
62:9; Ecc 12:8;
Ro 8:20-21
1:3 *d* Ecc 2:11,22;
3:9; 5:15-16
1:4 *e* S Job 8:19
1:5 *f* Ps 19:5-6
1:7 *g* Job 36:28
1:8 *h* Pr 27:20
1:9 *i* Ecc 2:12; 3:15
1:11 *j* Ge 40:23;
Ecc 9:15 *k* Ps 88:12;
Ecc 2:16; 8:10; 9:5
1:12 *l* S ver 1
m Ecc 2:9
1:13 *n* S Job 28:3

EVERYTHING IS MEANINGLESS

1 The words of the Teacher,*a a* son of David, king in Jerusalem:*b*

2 "Meaningless! Meaningless!"
　　says the Teacher.
"Utterly meaningless!
　　Everything is meaningless." *c*

3 What does anyone gain from all their labors
　　at which they toil under the sun? *d*
4 Generations come and generations go,
　　but the earth remains forever. *e*
5 The sun rises and the sun sets,
　　and hurries back to where it rises. *f*
6 The wind blows to the south
　　and turns to the north;
round and round it goes,
　　ever returning on its course.
7 All streams flow into the sea,
　　yet the sea is never full.
To the place the streams come from,
　　there they return again. *g*
8 All things are wearisome,
　　more than one can say.
The eye never has enough of seeing, *h*
　　nor the ear its fill of hearing.
9 What has been will be again,
　　what has been done will be done again; *i*
there is nothing new under the sun.
10 Is there anything of which one can say,
　　"Look! This is something new"?
It was here already, long ago;
　　it was here before our time.
11 There is no remembrance of people of old, *j*
　　and even those who are yet to come
will not be remembered
　　by those who follow them. *k*

WISDOM IS MEANINGLESS

12 I, the Teacher, *l* was king over Israel in Jerusalem. *m* 13 I applied my mind to study and
to explore by wisdom all that is done under the heavens. *n* What a heavy burden God has

---

a 1 Or *the leader of the assembly*; also in verses 2 and 12

1:1 *Teacher.* The teacher of wisdom (12:9). The Hebrew term for "Teacher" (*qoheleth*) is related to that for "assembly" (see TNIV text note; Ex 16:3; Nu 16:3). Perhaps the Teacher, whose work is described in 12:9–10, also held an office in the assembly. The Septuagint (the pre-Christian Greek translation of the OT) word for "Teacher" is *ekklesiastes,* from which most English titles of the book are taken, and from which such English words as "ecclesiastical" are derived. *son of David.* Suggests Solomon, though his name occurs nowhere in the book. The Hebrew word for "son" can refer to a descendant (even many generations removed)—or even to someone who follows in the footsteps of another (see Ge 4:21; see also Introduction: Author and Date).

1:2 Briefly states the author's theme (see 12:8 and note). *Meaningless!* This key term occurs about 35 times in the book and only once elsewhere (Job 27:12). The Hebrew for it originally meant "breath" (see Ps 39:5,11; 62:9; 144:4). The basic thrust of Ecclesiastes is that all of life is meaningless (useless, hollow, futile, vain) if it is not rightly related to God. Only when based on God and his word is life worthwhile. *Everything.* See v. 8; whatever human beings undertake apart from God.

1:3–11 The author elaborates his theme that human effort ap-

pears to be without benefit or purpose—and therefore without meaning.

1:3 Jesus expands on this question in Mk 8:36–38. *under the sun.* Another key expression (used 29 times), which refers to this present world and the limits of what it offers. "Under the heavens," though it occurs less frequently (v. 13; 2:3; 3:1), is used synonymously.

1:4–9 Toiling is profitless (v. 3) because humans live in a world of repetitiveness and sameness—one without apparent progress and meaning. This is seen in the endless succession and impermanence of human generations (v. 4) and in the behavior patterns of the sun (v. 5), the wind (v. 6) and the streams (v. 7). Hence the conclusion that "all things are wearisome" (v. 8) and "there is nothing new under the sun" (v. 9).

1:4 *earth remains forever.* By contrast, human life is fleeting.

1:8 *All things.* Everything mentioned in vv. 4–7 (see note on v. 2).

1:10 *something new.* Many things seem to be new simply because the past is easily and quickly forgotten. The old ways reappear in new guises.

1:12–18 Having set forth his theme that all human striving seems futile (see especially vv. 3,11, which frame laid on the human race! [o] [14] I have seen all the things that are done under the sun; all of them are meaningless, a chasing after the wind. [p]

> [15] What is crooked cannot be straightened; [q]
> what is lacking cannot be counted.

[16] I said to myself, "Look, I have grown and increased in wisdom more than anyone who has ruled over Jerusalem before me; [r] I have experienced much of wisdom and knowledge." [17] Then I applied myself to the understanding of wisdom, [s] and also of madness and folly, [t] but I learned that this, too, is a chasing after the wind.

> [18] For with much wisdom comes much sorrow; [u]
> the more knowledge, the more grief. [v]

PLEASURES ARE MEANINGLESS

2 I said to myself, "Come now, I will test you with pleasure [w] to find out what is good." But that also proved to be meaningless. [2] "Laughter," [x] I said, "is madness. And what does pleasure accomplish?" [3] I tried cheering myself with wine, [y] and embracing folly [z] —my mind still guiding me with wisdom. I wanted to see what was good for people to do under the heavens during the few days of their lives.

[4] I undertook great projects: I built houses for myself [a] and planted vineyards. [b] [5] I made gardens and parks and planted all kinds of fruit trees in them. [6] I made reservoirs to water groves of flourishing trees. [7] I bought male and female slaves and had other slaves [c] who were born in my house. I also owned more herds and flocks than anyone in Jerusalem before me. [8] I amassed silver and gold [d] for myself, and the treasure of kings and provinces. [e] I acquired male and female singers, [f] and a harem[a] as well—the delights of a man's heart. [9] I became greater by far than anyone in Jerusalem [g] before me. [h] In all this my wisdom stayed with me.

> [10] I denied myself nothing my eyes desired;
> I refused my heart no pleasure.
> My heart took delight in all my labor,
> and this was the reward for all my toil.
> [11] Yet when I surveyed all that my hands had done
> and what I had toiled to achieve,
> everything was meaningless, a chasing after the wind; [i]
> nothing was gained under the sun. [j]

a 8 The meaning of the Hebrew for this phrase is uncertain.

1:13 [o] S Ge 3:17; Ecc 3:10
1:14 [p] Ecc 2:11,17; 4:4; 6:9
1:15 [q] Ecc 7:13
1:16 [r] S 1Ki 3:12
1:17 [s] Ecc 7:23; 8:16
[t] Ecc 2:3,12; 7:25
1:18 [u] Jer 45:3
[v] Ecc 2:23; 12:12
2:1 [w] ver 24; Ecc 7:4; 8:15
2:2 [x] S Pr 14:13
2:3 [y] ver 24-25; S Jdg 9:13; Ru 3:3; Ecc 3:12-13; 5:18; 8:15 [z] S Ecc 1:17
2:4 [a] 2Ch 2:1; 8:1-6
[b] SS 8:11
2:7 [c] 2Ch 8:7-8
2:8 [d] S 1Ki 9:28
[e] S Jdg 3:15
[f] S 2Sa 19:35
2:9 [g] Ecc 1:12
[h] 1Ch 29:25
2:11 [i] S Ecc 1:14
[j] S Ecc 1:3

---

that section), the Teacher now shows that both human endeavor (vv. 12–15; cf. 2:1–11) and the pursuit of human wisdom (vv. 16–18; cf. 2:12–17) are futile and meaningless.

1:12 *I.* The author shifts to the first person, returning to the third person only in the conclusion (12:9–14).

1:13 *under the heavens.* See note on v. 3. *God.* The only Hebrew word the writer uses for God is *Elohim* (used almost 30 times), which emphasizes his absolute sovereignty. He does not use the covenant name, *Yahweh* (translated "LORD"; see notes on Ge 2:4; Ex 3:14–15).

1:14 *chasing after the wind.* A graphic illustration of futility and meaninglessness (see Introduction: Purpose and Teaching). These words are used nine times in the first half of the discourse (here; v. 17; 2:11,17,26; 4:4,6,16; 6:9; see also 5:16).

[A] 1:15 See 7:13 and note. Because of the unalterableness of events, human effort is meaningless and hopeless. We should therefore learn to happily accept things the way they are and to accept our divinely appointed lot in life, as the Teacher later counsels.

[B] 1:16 *anyone who has ruled over Jerusalem before me.* See 2:7,9. This does not necessarily exclude Solomon as the Teacher. The reference could include kings prior to David, such as Melchizedek (Ge 14:18); Adoni-Zedek (Jos 10:1) and Abdi-Khepa (mentioned in the Amarna letters from Egypt; see chart, p. xxiii).

[A] 1:18 Wisdom without God leads to grief and sorrow.

[A] 2:1–11 The Teacher now shows that mere pleasure cannot give meaning or satisfaction (see 1:12–15; see also note on 1:12–18).

[A] 2:1–3 The pursuit of pleasure does not bring the fulfillment that human beings seek.

2:1 *I said to myself.* See v. 15; 1:16. *good.* A key term in the book ("good" and "better" occur about 40 times).

2:3 *my mind still guiding me with wisdom.* From first to last (v. 9) the author used wisdom to discover the good (v. 1) and the worthwhile (v. 3). *under the heavens.* See note on 1:3.

2:4–9 See 1Ki 4–11, which tells of Solomon's splendor and of his wives.

2:8 *provinces.* Probably the neighboring territories from which tribute was collected. *harem.* The Hebrew for this word occurs only here in Scripture (see TNIV text note). The meaning seems to be indicated in an early Egyptian letter that uses a similar Canaanite term for concubines. It fits the situation of Solomon, who had 300 concubines in addition to 700 wives (1Ki 11:3).

2:9 See 1:16.

2:10 *labor...toil.* A key thought in Ecclesiastes is the meaninglessness (v. 11), apart from God, of toil, labor, work—words that occur almost 40 times.

2:12 *k* S Ecc 1:17
l S Ecc 1:9
2:13 *m* Ecc 7:19;
9:18 *n* Ecc 7:11-12
2:14 *o* Ps 49:10;
Ecc 3:19; 6:6; 7:2; 9:3,
11-12
2:15 *p* ver 19;
Ecc 6:8
2:16 *q* S Ps 112:6
r S Ecc 1:11 *s* Ps 49:10
2:17 *t* S Ecc 1:14
2:18 *u* Ps 39:6;
49:10
2:19 *v* S ver 15
2:22 *w* S Ecc 1:3
2:23 *x* S Ecc 1:18
y S Ge 3:17; S Job 7:2
2:24 *z* ver 3;
1Co 15:32 *a* S ver 1;
Ecc 3:22 *b* S Job 2:10;
Ecc 3:12-13; 5:17-19;
7:14; 9:7-10; 11:7-10
2:25 *c* S Ps 127:2
2:26 *d* S Job 9:4
e S Job 27:17
f S Pr 13:22
3:1 *g* ver 11,17;
Ecc 8:6
3:2 *h* Isa 28:24
3:3 *i* S Dt 5:17

WISDOM AND FOLLY ARE MEANINGLESS

¹²Then I turned my thoughts to consider wisdom,
  and also madness and folly. *k*
What more can the king's successor do
  than what has already been done? *l*
¹³I saw that wisdom *m* is better than folly, *n*
  just as light is better than darkness.
¹⁴The wise have eyes in their heads,
  while fools walk in the darkness;
but I came to realize
  that the same fate overtakes them both. *o*

¹⁵Then I said to myself,

"The fate of the fool will overtake me also.
  What then do I gain by being wise?" *p*
I said to myself,
  "This too is meaningless."
¹⁶For the wise, like the fool, will not be long remembered; *q*
  the days have already come when both have been forgotten. *r*
Like the fool, the wise too must die! *s*

TOIL IS MEANINGLESS

¹⁷So I hated life, because the work that is done under the sun was grievous to me. All of it is meaningless, a chasing after the wind. *t* ¹⁸I hated all the things I had toiled for under the sun, because I must leave them to the one who comes after me. *u* ¹⁹And who knows whether that person will be wise or foolish? *v* Yet they will have control over all the toil into which I have poured my effort and skill under the sun. This too is meaningless. ²⁰So my heart began to despair over all my toilsome labor under the sun. ²¹For people may labor with wisdom, knowledge and skill, and then they must leave all they own to others who have not toiled for it. This too is meaningless and a great misfortune. ²²What do people get for all the toil and anxious striving with which they labor under the sun? *w* ²³All their days their work is grief and pain; *x* even at night their minds do not rest. *y* This too is meaningless.

²⁴People can do nothing better than to eat and drink *z* and find satisfaction in their toil. *a* This too, I see, is from the hand of God, *b* ²⁵for without him, who can eat or find enjoyment? *c* ²⁶To the person who pleases him, God gives wisdom, *d* knowledge and happiness, but to the sinner he gives the task of gathering and storing up wealth *e* to hand it over to the one who pleases God. *f* This too is meaningless, a chasing after the wind.

A TIME FOR EVERYTHING

3 There is a time *g* for everything,
  and a season for every activity under the heavens:

² a time to be born and a time to die,
   a time to plant and a time to uproot, *h*
³ a time to kill *i* and a time to heal,

2:12–17 The Teacher returns to the folly of trying to find satisfaction in merely human wisdom (see 1:16–18; see also note on 1:12–18).

2:12 *king's successor.* Either the Teacher himself (see 1:1) or one who would come after him (cf. 4:15–16).

2:13 *wisdom is better than folly.* Even secular wisdom is better than folly, but in the end it is of no value, since "the same fate overtakes them both" (i.e., overtakes both the wise believer and the foolish unbeliever, v. 14; see Ps 49:10). *better.* See note on 2:1.

2:14 *eyes.* Understanding.

2:16 People tend to soon forget even the greatest leaders and heroes (see 1:11).

2:17–23 To pursue human fulfillment through work done "under the sun" (vv. 17–20,22; see 1:3 and note) is grievous and meaningless and leads to despair; its fruits must be left to others, whose character one cannot predict.

2:18 *leave them to the one who comes after me.* See v. 21; Ps 39:6; Lk 12:20.

2:19 *who knows ...?* For a more searching "Who knows ...?" for secular people, see 3:21.

2:24–25 The heart of Ecclesiastes, a theme repeated in 3:12–13,22; 5:18–20; 8:15; 9:7 and climaxed in 12:13. Only in God does life have meaning and true pleasure. Without him nothing satisfies, but with him we find satisfaction and enjoyment. True pleasure comes only when we acknowledge and revere God (12:13).

2:26 *but to the sinner.* For exceptions to this general principle, see 8:14; Ps 73:1–12.

3:1–22 Humans have little or no control over times and changes. The eternal God sovereignly determines all of life's activities (e.g., the 14 opposites of vv. 2–8).

3:1 Cf. 8:6. *under the heavens.* See note on 1:3.

3:2 *a time.* Divinely appointed (see Ps 31:15; Pr 16:1–9).

a time to tear down and a time to build,
4   a time to weep and a time to laugh,
    a time to mourn and a time to dance,
5   a time to scatter stones and a time to gather them,
    a time to embrace and a time to refrain,
6   a time to search and a time to give up,
    a time to keep and a time to throw away,
7   a time to tear and a time to mend,
    a time to be silent^j and a time to speak,
8   a time to love and a time to hate,
    a time for war and a time for peace.

⁹What do workers gain from their toil? ^k ¹⁰I have seen the burden God has laid on the human race. ^l ¹¹He has made everything beautiful in its time. ^m He has also set eternity in the human heart; yet no one can fathom ⁿ what God has done from beginning to end. ^o ¹²I know that there is nothing better for people than to be happy and to do good while they live. ¹³That each of them may eat and drink, ^p and find satisfaction ^q in all their toil—this is the gift of God. ^r ¹⁴I know that everything God does will endure forever; nothing can be added to it and nothing taken from it. God does it so that people will fear him. ^s

¹⁵Whatever is has already been, ^t
    and what will be has been before; ^u
    and God will call the past to account. ^a

¹⁶And I saw something else under the sun:

In the place of judgment—wickedness was there,
    in the place of justice—wickedness was there.

¹⁷I said to myself,

"God will bring into judgment ^v
    both the righteous and the wicked,
for there will be a time for every activity,
    a time to judge every deed." ^w

¹⁸I also said to myself, "As for human beings, God tests them so that they may see that they are like the animals. ^x ¹⁹Surely the fate of human beings ^y is like that of the animals; the same fate awaits them both: As one dies, so dies the other. All have the same breath^b; humans have no advantage over animals. Everything is meaningless. ²⁰All go to the same place; all come from dust, and to dust all return. ^z ²¹Who knows if the human spirit rises upward ^a and if the spirit of the animal goes down into the earth?"

²²So I saw that there is nothing better for people than to enjoy their work, ^b because that is their lot. ^c For who can bring them to see what will happen after them?

---

^a 15 Or *God calls back the past*   ^b 19 Or *spirit*

3:9 See note on 2:17–23.
3:11 The chapter summarized: God's beautiful but tantalizing world is too big for us, yet its satisfactions are too small. Since we were made for eternity, the things of time cannot fully and permanently satisfy.
3:12–13 A pointer to the book's conclusion. God's people find meaning in life when they cheerfully accept it from the hand of God.
3:14 *so that people will fear him.* Sums up the message of the book (cf. 12:13).
3:15 See 1:9.
3:17 *judgment.* God's true judgments are the answer to cynicism about human injustices. "The past" (v. 15) is not meaningless (as people dismiss it as being, 1:11), and God will override the perverse judgments (v. 16) of people (see 12:14). *the righteous and the wicked.* No one will escape divine judgment (cf. Ro 14:10; 2Co 5:10 and notes; cf. also Rev 20:12–13).

3:18 *like the animals.* Humans "under the sun" are as mortal as any animal; but, unlike animals, they must be made to see this condition and, through their dim awareness of eternity (v. 11), be distressed.
3:19 *same breath.* See Ps 104:29–30.
3:20 *to the same place.* Not heaven or hell but humankind's observable destination, which is a return to dust, just like the animals. Death is the great leveler of all living things (see Ge 3:19; Ps 103:14).
3:21 *Who knows . . . ?* See 2:19 and note; cf. 12:7. On their own, human beings cannot know; they can only guess. The answer, revealed at first in glimpses (see e.g., Ps 16:9–11; 49:15; 73:23–26; Isa 26:19; Da 12:2 and note), was brought fully "to light through the gospel" (2Ti 1:10; see also Jn 5:24–29).
3:22 *nothing better.* As an end in itself, work too is meaningless (see 4:4; 9:9). Only receiving it as a gift from God (v. 13) gives it enduring worth (v. 14).

4:1 *d* S Ps 12:5
e La 1:16
4:2 *f* Jer 20:17-18;
22:10 *g* S Job 3:17;
S 10:18
4:3 *h* S Job 3:16
i S Job 3:22
4:4 *j* S Ecc 1:14
4:5 *k* S Pr 6:10
4:6 *l* Pr 15:16-17;
S 16:8
4:8 *m* Pr 27:20

OPPRESSION, TOIL, FRIENDLESSNESS

4 Again I looked and saw all the oppression *d* that was taking place under the sun:

I saw the tears of the oppressed—
and they have no comforter;
power was on the side of their oppressors—
and they have no comforter. *e*

2 And I declared that the dead, *f*
who had already died,
are happier than the living,
who are still alive. *g*

3 But better than both
is the one who has not yet been, *h*
who has not seen the evil
that is done under the sun. *i*

4 And I saw that all toil and all achievement spring from one person's envy of another. This too is meaningless, a chasing after the wind. *j*

5 Fools fold their hands *k*
and ruin themselves.

6 Better one handful with tranquillity
than two handfuls with toil *l*
and chasing after the wind.

7 Again I saw something meaningless under the sun:

8 There was a man all alone;
he had neither son nor brother.
There was no end to his toil,
yet his eyes were not content *m* with his wealth.
"For whom am I toiling," he asked,
"and why am I depriving myself of enjoyment?"
This too is meaningless—
a miserable business!

9 Two are better than one,
because they have a good return for their labor:

10 If they fall down,
they can help each other up.
But pity those who fall
and have no one to help them up!

11 Also, if two lie down together, they will keep warm.
But how can one keep warm alone?

12 Though one may be overpowered,
two can defend themselves.
A cord of three strands is not quickly broken.

ADVANCEMENT IS MEANINGLESS

13 Better a poor but wise youth than an old but foolish king who no longer knows how to heed a warning. 14 The youth may have come from prison to the kingship, or he may have been born in poverty within his kingdom. 15 I saw that all who lived and walked under the sun followed the youth, the king's successor. 16 There was no end to all the people who were before them. But those who came later were not pleased with the successor. This too is meaningless, a chasing after the wind.

■ 4:1 *oppression.* A theme already touched on (3:16) and another ingredient in the human tragedy. To find life meaningless is sad enough, but to taste its cruelty is bitter beyond words.

■ 4:2 *happier than the living.* See Job 3; Jer 20:14–18. For faith that sees a bigger picture, see Ro 8:35–39.

4:4–6 Neither hard work (motivated by envy) nor idleness brings happiness, meaning or fulfillment.

4:4 *all toil and all achievement.* This too is meaningless unless done with God's blessing (see 3:13; cf. the selfless success of Joseph, Ge 39).

4:5 The ruin of the idle person is vividly pictured in 10:18; Pr 6:6–11; 24:30–34.

■ 4:6 *tranquillity.* See Pr 30:7–9. Paul says the last word on this subject (Php 4:11–13).

4:7–12 Those who toil only for themselves—for whatever reason—lead meaningless and difficult lives.

4:12 *two … three.* A climactic construction.

■ 4:13–16 Advancement without God is another example of the meaninglessness of secularism.

FULFILL YOUR VOW TO GOD

5 *Guard your steps when you go to the house of God. Go near to listen rather than to offer the sacrifice of fools, who do not know that they do wrong.

*2 Do not be quick with your mouth,
　　do not be hasty in your heart
　　to utter anything before God. *n*
　God is in heaven
　　and you are on earth,
　　so let your words be few. *o*
³ A dream *p* comes when there are many cares,
　　and many words mark the speech of a fool. *q*

⁴When you make a vow to God, do not delay to fulfill it. *r* He has no pleasure in fools; fulfill your vow. *s* ⁵It is better not to make a vow than to make one and not fulfill it. *t* ⁶Do not let your mouth lead you into sin. And do not protest to the ⌊temple⌋ messenger, "My vow was a mistake." Why should God be angry at what you say and destroy the work of your hands? ⁷Much dreaming and many words are meaningless. Therefore fear God. *u*

RICHES ARE MEANINGLESS

⁸If you see the poor oppressed *v* in a district, and justice and rights denied, do not be surprised at such things; for one official is eyed by a higher one, and over them both are others higher still. ⁹The increase from the land is taken by all; the king himself profits from the fields.

¹⁰ Those who love money never have enough;
　　those who love wealth are never satisfied with their income.
　This too is meaningless.

¹¹ As goods increase,
　　so do those who consume them.
　And what benefit are they to the owners
　　except to feast their eyes on them?

¹² The sleep of laborers is sweet,
　　whether they eat little or much,
　but the abundance of the rich
　　permits them no sleep. *w*

¹³I have seen a grievous evil under the sun: *x*

　wealth hoarded to the harm of its owners,
¹⁴　or wealth lost through some misfortune,
　so that when they have children
　　there is nothing left for them to inherit.
¹⁵ Everyone comes naked from their mother's womb,
　　and as everyone comes, so they depart. *y*

* 5:1 is numbered 4:17 in Hebrew texts. 　** 5:2-20 is numbered 5:1-19 in Hebrew texts.*

5:2 *n* S Jdg 11:35
o S Job 6:24;
S Pr 20:25
5:3 *p* S Job 20:8
q Ecc 10:14
5:4 *r* S Dt 23:21;
S Jdg 11:35; Ps 119:60
s S Nu 30:2; Ps 66:13-14
5:5 *t* Nu 30:2-4;
Jnh 2:9
5:7 *u* Ecc 3:14
5:8 *v* S Ps 12:5
5:12 *w* Job 20:20
5:13 *x* Ecc 6:1-2
5:15 *y* S Job 1:21

4:16 *were before them.* Stood before them and served them. *those who came later.* The next generation.

　5:1–7 The theme of this section is the meaninglessness of superficial religion, as reflected in making rash vows.

　5:1 *Guard your steps.* Think about what you ought to say and do. *house of God.* Here probably a reference to Solomon's temple. *listen.* Obey. 1Sa 15:22 uses the same Hebrew verb and makes the same contrast between real and superficial worship. *sacrifice.* Probably connected with the vow of vv. 4–6.
5:2 *quick with your mouth.* As in a rash vow. *God ... heaven ... you ... earth.* Highlights the contrast between God and humankind.
5:3 A proverb. In context it suggests that in the midst of cares one dreams of bliss (as a starving person dreams of a banquet), and in anticipation may offer rash vows ("many words") to God (see v. 7).

　5:4 *vow.* See Dt 23:21–23; 1Sa 1:11, 24–28. *no pleasure in fools.* In Scripture the fool is not one who cannot learn

but one who refuses to learn (see Pr 1:20–27; see also TNIV text note on Pr 1:7).
5:6 ⌊*temple*⌋ *messenger.* Probably the priest (see Mal 2:7 and note). *Why should God be angry ... ?* To break a vow is a serious matter (see Nu 30:2 and note on 30:1–16) and can have disastrous consequences (see Dt 23:21–23).

　5:8 *do not be surprised.* For other frank appraisals of human society, see 4:1–3. This teacher, like Jesus, who "knew what was in" people (Jn 2:25), had no illusions or utopian schemes.
5:9 *king ... profits from the fields.* See note on Am 7:1.

　5:10 Greater wealth does not bring satisfaction (see 1Ti 6:9–10).

　5:11–12 Greater wealth brings greater anxiety.

5:11 *those who consume them.* Human parasites.
5:13 *harm.* Including worry about one's possessions.

5:15 z Ps 49:17;
1Ti 6:7 a Ecc 1:3
5:16 b S Ecc 1:3
5:18 c S Ecc 2:3
d Ecc 2:10,24
5:19 e S 1Ch 29:12
f Ecc 6:2 g S Job 31:2
h S Ecc 2:24
5:20 i S Dt 12:7,18
6:2 j Ecc 5:19
k Ecc 5:13
6:3 l S Job 3:16
m S Job 3:3
6:6 n Ecc 2:14
6:7 o S Pr 27:20
6:8 p S Ecc 2:15
6:9 q S Ecc 1:14
6:10 r Ecc 3:15
6:12 s S Job 10:20;
S 20:8 t S 1Ch 29:15;
S Job 14:2; S Ps 39:6

> They take nothing from their toil z
> > that they can carry in their hands. a

16 This too is a grievous evil:

> As everyone comes, so they depart,
> > and what do they gain,
> > since they toil for the wind? b
> 17 All their days they eat in darkness,
> > with great frustration, affliction and anger.

18 This is what I have observed to be good: that it is appropriate for people to eat, to drink c and to find satisfaction in their toilsome labor d under the sun during the few days of life God has given them—for this is their lot. 19 Moreover, when God gives people wealth and possessions, e and the ability to enjoy them, f to accept their lot g and be happy in their toil—this is a gift of God. h 20 They seldom reflect on the days of their lives, because God keeps them occupied with gladness of heart. i

6 I have seen another evil under the sun, and it weighs heavily on the human race: 2 God gives some people wealth, possessions and honor, so that they lack nothing their hearts desire, but God does not grant the ability to enjoy them, j and strangers enjoy them instead. This is meaningless, a grievous evil. k

3 A man may have a hundred children and live many years; yet no matter how long he lives, if he cannot enjoy his prosperity and does not receive proper burial, I say that a stillborn l child is better off than he. m 4 It comes without meaning, it departs in darkness, and in darkness its name is shrouded. 5 Though it never saw the sun or knew anything, it has more rest than does that man— 6 even if he lives a thousand years twice over but fails to enjoy his prosperity. Do not all go to the same place? n

> 7 Everyone's toil is for the mouth,
> > yet the appetite is never satisfied. o
> 8 What advantage have the wise over fools? p
> What do the poor gain
> > by knowing how to conduct themselves before others?
> 9 Better what the eye sees
> > than the roving of the appetite.
> This too is meaningless,
> > a chasing after the wind. q

> 10 Whatever exists has already been named, r
> > and what humanity is has been known;
> no one can contend
> > with someone who is stronger.
> 11 The more the words,
> > the less the meaning,
> > and how does that profit anyone?

12 For who knows what is good for people in life, during the few and meaningless days s they pass through like a shadow? t Who can tell them what will happen under the sun after they are gone?

5:15 *They take nothing.* See Lk 12:13–21.

5:18–20 See note on 2:24–25.

▲ 6:2–3,6 *enjoy.* Comparing v. 2 with 5:19 demonstrates that the ability to enjoy God's blessings is a bonus—a gift of God, not a right or guarantee. God calls the person who forgets this truth a "fool" (Lk 12:20).

6:2 *strangers enjoy them instead.* For example, when people are robbed of their wealth or die without heirs.

6:3 *does not receive proper burial.* Dies unlamented or dishonored, like King Jehoiakim (Jer 22:18–19). *stillborn child.* For the secularist, life is a pointless journey to extinction, to which being stillborn is the quickest and easiest route (cf. Job 3:16; Ps 58:8).

6:6 *to the same place.* Still talking in terms of what we can ob-

serve (that all people die), not of what lies beyond death (see v. 12; 3:20 and note).

▲ 6:7–12 In confronting complacency, the Teacher gives several causes for concern: the short-lived (v. 7), debatable (v. 8) and elusive (v. 9) rewards of life; the limits of our creativity, power and wisdom (vv. 10–11); and the unreliability of merely human values and predictions (v. 12).

▲ 6:9 It is better to be content with what one has than to nurture unrestrained desires (cf. Php 4:11–12 and note on 4:12; 1Ti 6:6,8).

6:10 *named.* Predetermined by God. *known.* Foreknown by God. *someone who is stronger.* God.

6:12 *like a shadow.* See Job 8:9 and note.

WISDOM

A good name is better than fine perfume, [u]
 and the day of death better than the day of birth. [v]

[2] It is better to go to a house of mourning
 than to go to a house of feasting,
for death [w] is the destiny [x] of everyone;
 the living should take this to heart.

[3] Frustration is better than laughter, [y]
 because a sad face is good for the heart.

[4] The heart of the wise is in the house of mourning,
 but the heart of fools is in the house of pleasure. [z]

[5] It is better to heed the rebuke [a] of a wise person
 than to listen to the song of fools.

[6] Like the crackling of thorns [b] under the pot,
 so is the laughter [c] of fools.
 This too is meaningless.

[7] Extortion turns the wise into fools,
 and a bribe [d] corrupts the heart.

[8] The end of a matter is better than its beginning,
 and patience [e] is better than pride.

[9] Do not be quickly provoked [f] in your spirit,
 for anger resides in the lap of fools. [g]

[10] Do not say, "Why were the old days [h] better than these?"
 For it is not wise to ask such questions.

[11] Wisdom, like an inheritance, is a good thing [i]
 and benefits those who see the sun. [j]

[12] Wisdom is a shelter
 as money is a shelter,
but the advantage of knowledge is this:
 Wisdom preserves the life of its possessor.

[13] Consider what God has done: [k]

Who can straighten
 what he has made crooked? [l]

[14] When times are good, be happy;
 but when times are bad, consider:
God has made the one
 as well as the other. [m]
Therefore, you cannot discover
 anything about your future.

[15] In this meaningless life [n] of mine I have seen both of these:

the righteous perishing in their righteousness,
 and the wicked living long in their wickedness. [o]

[16] Do not be overrighteous,
 neither be overwise—
 why destroy yourself?

[17] Do not be overwicked,
 and do not be a fool—

7:1 [u] Pr 22:1; SS 1:3
[v] S Job 10:18
7:2 [w] S Pr 11:19
[x] Ecc 2:14
7:3 [y] S Pr 14:13
7:4 [z] S Ecc 2:1;
Jer 16:8
7:5 [a] S Pr 13:18;
15:31-32
7:6 [b] S Ps 58:9
[c] S Pr 14:13
7:7 [d] S Ex 18:21;
S 23:8
7:8 [e] Pr 14:29
7:9 [f] S Mt 5:22
[g] S Pr 14:29
7:10 [h] S Ps 77:5
7:11 [i] Ecc 2:13
[j] Ecc 11:7
7:13 [k] Ecc 2:24
[l] Ecc 1:15
7:14 [m] S Job 1:21;
S Ecc 2:24
7:15 [n] S Job 7:7
[o] S Job 21:7; Ecc 8:12-
14; Jer 12:1

A 7:1 *day of death better.* The Christian has ample reason to say this (2Co 5:1–10; Php 1:21–23). But the Teacher's point is valid, as explained in vv. 2–6; namely, that happy times generally teach us less than hard times.

7:6 *crackling of thorns.* The "laughter of fools" is likened to a noisy, but short-lived, fire (see Ps 58:9 and note).

7:7 *bribe.* See Mt 28:11–15; Lk 22:4–6.

7:9 *anger.* See, e.g., Pr 16:32; 17:14; 1Co 13:4–5.

7:11 *see the sun.* Are alive.

7:12 *preserves the life.* The Hebrew for this expression can also mean "gives life" or "renews life" (cf. Pr 3:13–18; 13:14).

A 7:13 *Who can straighten … ?* Not fatalism, but a reminder that mere mortals cannot change what God determines (see note on 1:15; cf. also note on 3:1–22).

7:14 *God has made the one* [bad times] *as well as the other* [good times]. Cf. Ro 8:28–29.

A 7:15 *the righteous perishing.* Righteousness is no sure protection against hard times or an early death.

A 7:16 *not … overrighteous … overwise.* If true righteousness and wisdom do not necessarily prevent ruin, then extreme, legalistic righteousness and wisdom will surely not help.

A 7:17 *not … overwicked.* Extreme wickedness is even more foolhardy.

7:17 P Job 15:32
7:18 q S Ecc 3:14
7:19 r S Ecc 2:13
s S Pr 8:14
7:20 t S Ps 14:3
u S 2Ch 6:36;
S Job 4:17; S Pr 20:9;
Ro 3:12
7:21 v Pr 30:10
7:23 w S Ecc 1:17
7:24 x S Job 28:12
7:25 y S Job 28:3
z S Ecc 1:17
7:26 a S Ex 10:7;
S Jdg 14:15
b S Pr 2:16-19; 5:3-5;
S 7:23; 22:14
7:27 c S Ecc 1:1
7:28 d 1Ki 11:3
8:3 e Ecc 10:4
8:4 f Est 1:19

why die before your time? P

18 It is good to grasp the one
and not let go of the other.
Whoever fears God q will avoid all ⌊extremes⌋. a

19 Wisdom r makes one wise person more powerful s
than ten rulers in a city.

20 Indeed, there is no one on earth who is righteous, t
no one who does what is right and never sins. u

21 Do not pay attention to every word people say,
or you v may hear your servant cursing you—
22 for you know in your heart
that many times you yourself have cursed others.

23 All this I tested by wisdom and I said,

"I am determined to be wise" w—
but this was beyond me.
24 Whatever exists is far off and most profound—
who can discover it? x
25 So I turned my mind to understand,
to investigate and to search out wisdom and the scheme of things y
and to understand the stupidity of wickedness
and the madness of folly. z

26 I find more bitter than death
the woman who is a snare, a
whose heart is a trap
and whose hands are chains.
The man who pleases God will escape her,
but the sinner she will ensnare. b

27 "Look," says the Teacher, b c "this is what I have discovered:

"Adding one thing to another to discover the scheme of things—
28 while I was still searching
but not finding—
I found one ⌊upright⌋ man among a thousand,
but not one ⌊upright⌋ woman d among them all.
29 This only have I found:
God created humankind upright,
but they have gone in search of many schemes."

8

Who is like the wise?
Who knows the explanation of things?
Wisdom brightens the face
and changes its hard appearance.

OBEY THE KING

2 Obey the king's command, I say, because you took an oath before God. 3 Do not be in a hurry to leave the king's presence. e Do not stand up for a bad cause, for he will do whatever he pleases. 4 Since a king's word is supreme, who can say to him, "What are you doing? f"

---

a 18 Or *will follow them both*   b 27 Or *the leader of the assembly*

A **7:18** *the one ... the other.* The God-fearing person will avoid both extremes (legalism and libertinism) and lead a balanced—truly righteous and wise—life (cf. Ro 6:14).

A **7:20** *no one on earth ... righteous.* A sober Biblical truth (see note on Ro 3:10–20,23).

7:24 See Job 28:12–28; 1Co 2:9–16.

7:26 See Pr 7:6–27.

A **7:27** *Teacher.* See note on 1:1. *Adding one thing to another to discover the scheme of things.* This inductive method can never be complete, nor can we reliably interpret all that we manage to observe (3:11b). Human wisdom and understanding

must always yield to revealed truth.

7:28 *one ⌊upright⌋ man ... but not one ⌊upright⌋ woman.* According to the Teacher's experience, Scripture nowhere declares that women are morally inferior.

7:29 *God created humankind upright, but.* See Ge 3:1–6; Ro 5:12.

8:2 *king's command.* Both principle (v. 2) and prudence (vv. 3–6) set limits on our freedom. *took an oath.* Of loyalty to the king (as seen, e.g., in 1Ch 29:24).

8:3 *Do not ... hurry to leave the king's presence.* To do so would show lack of respect—even disloyalty—to him.

8:4 *who can say ..., "What are you doing?"* Cf. Isa 45:9; Ro 9:20.

⁵ Whoever obeys his command will come to no harm,
   and the wise heart will know the proper time and procedure.
⁶ For there is a proper time and procedure for every matter, ^g
   though a person may be weighed down by misery.

⁷ Since no one knows the future,
   who can say what is to come?
⁸ As no one has power over the wind to contain it,
   so^a no one has power over the time of their death.
As no one is discharged in time of war,
   so wickedness will not release those who practice it.

⁹ All this I saw, as I applied my mind to everything done under the sun. There is a time when a man lords it over others to his own^b hurt. ¹⁰ Then too, I saw the wicked buried ^h—those who used to come and go from the holy place and receive praise^c in the city where they did this. This too is meaningless.
¹¹ When the sentence for a crime is not quickly carried out, people's hearts are filled with schemes to do wrong. ¹² Although a wicked person who commits a hundred crimes may live a long time, I know that it will go better ⁱ with those who fear God, ^j who are reverent before him. ^k ¹³ Yet because the wicked do not fear God, ^l it will not go well with them, and their days ^m will not lengthen like a shadow.
¹⁴ There is something else meaningless that occurs on earth: the righteous who get what the wicked deserve, and the wicked who get what the righteous deserve. ⁿ This too, I say, is meaningless. ^o ¹⁵ So I commend the enjoyment of life ^p, because there is nothing better for people under the sun than to eat and drink ^q and be glad. ^r Then joy will accompany them in their toil all the days of the life God has given them under the sun.
¹⁶ When I applied my mind to know wisdom ^s and to observe the labor that is done on earth ^t—people getting no sleep day or night— ¹⁷ then I saw all that God has done. ^u No one can comprehend what goes on under the sun. People toil to search it out, but no one can discover its meaning. Even if the wise claim they know, they cannot really comprehend it. ^v

A COMMON DESTINY FOR ALL

9 So I reflected on all this and concluded that the righteous and the wise and what they do are in God's hands, but no one knows whether love or hate awaits them. ^w
² All share a common destiny—the righteous and the wicked, the good and the bad,^d the clean and the unclean, those who offer sacrifices and those who do not.

As it is with the good,
   so with the sinful;
as it is with those who take oaths,
   so with those who are afraid to take them. ^x

³ This is the evil in everything that happens under the sun: The same destiny overtakes all. ^y The hearts of people, moreover, are full of evil and there is madness in their hearts while they live, ^z and afterward they join the dead. ^a ⁴ Anyone who is among the living has hope^e—even a live dog is better off than a dead lion!

^a 8 Or *over the human spirit to retain it, / and so*   ^b 9 Or *to their*   ^c 10 Some Hebrew manuscripts and Septuagint (Aquila); most Hebrew manuscripts *and are forgotten*   ^d 2 Septuagint (Aquila), Vulgate and Syriac; Hebrew does not have *and the bad.*   ^e 4 Or *What then is to be chosen? With all who live, there is hope*

8:6 ^g Ecc 3:1
8:10 ^h S Ecc 1:11
8:12 ⁱ S Dt 12:28
^j S Ex 1:20 ^k Ecc 3:14
8:13 ^l Ecc 3:14
^m Dt 4:40; Job 5:26;
Ps 34:12; Isa 65:20
8:14 ⁿ S Job 21:7
^o S Ecc 7:15
8:15 ^p S Ps 42:8
^q S Ex 32:6; S Ecc 2:3
^r S Ecc 2:1
8:16 ^s S Ecc 1:17
^t Ecc 1:13
8:17 ^u S Job 28:3
^v S Job 28:23;
Ro 11:33
9:1 ^w Ecc 10:14
9:2 ^x Job 9:22;
Ecc 2:14
9:3 ^y S Job 9:22;
S Ecc 2:14 ^z Jer 11:8;
13:10; 16:12; 17:9
^a S Job 21:26

8:5 *Whoever obeys...will come to no harm.* See Ro 13:3–5 and notes.
8:6 *though a person may be weighed down by misery.* People should put the king's command above their own misery.
8:7–8 *no one knows...no one has power.* See Ps 31:15; 2Cor 5:1–10; Jas 4:13–16.
🔺 **8:8** *wickedness will not release.* Moral evil has great power to enslave (see Ro 7:15–24 and note on 7:17). But see Ro 7:25 and note.
8:10 *the wicked buried.* In this context implies undeserved respect (see note on 6:3; cf. Job 21:28–33; Lk 16:22).
🔺 **8:11** Delayed punishment tends to induce more wrongdoing.
8:12 *I know.* Here the Teacher speaks from mature faith, not as one "still searching but not finding" (7:28). For similar declarations, see 3:17; 11:9; 12:14.

8:14 Job 21–24 enlarges on this; Ps 73 draws the sting of it; and Jn 5:28–29 gives the final explanation.
🔺 **8:15** *eat...drink...be glad.* Spoken gratefully (see 5:19; 9:7; Dt 8). For such words spoken arrogantly, see Lk 12:19–20; 1Co 15:32.
🔺 **8:17** *No one can comprehend.* Dt 29:29 sums up what we are allowed and not allowed to know (cf. Ro 11:33).
🔺 **9:1** *whether love or hate.* The future is under God's control, and no one knows whether that future will be good or bad.
🔺 **9:2** *common destiny.* Not only the wise and foolish (2:14) but also the good and the bad are seen leveled, in the sense noted at 3:20. For the Teacher's conviction (beyond mere observation) that God ultimately will see justice done, see note on 8:12.
9:3 *evil...evil.* The apparently common destiny (both the righteous and the wicked die) encourages some people to sin.

9:5 *b* S Job 14:21
c S Ps 9:6 *d* S Ecc 1:11
9:6 *e* S Job 21:21
9:7 *f* S Nu 6:20
g S Ecc 2:24
9:8 *h* S Rev 3:4
9:9 *i* S Pr 5:18
j S Job 31:2
9:10 *k* S 1Sa 10:7
l Ecc 11:6 *m* Nu 16:33;
S Ps 6:5; Isa 38:18
n S Ecc 2:24
9:11 *o* Am 2:14-15
p Job 32:13; Isa 47:10;
Jer 9:23 *q* Ecc 2:14
r S Dt 8:18
9:12 *s* S Pr 29:6
t S Ps 73:22;
S Ecc 2:14
9:13 *u* S 2Sa 20:22
9:15 *v* S Ge 40:14;
S Ecc 1:11
9:16 *w* Est 6:3
9:18 *x* S Ecc 2:13
10:1 *y* Pr 13:16; 18:2
10:3 *z* Pr 13:16

⁵For the living know that they will die,
 but the dead know nothing;*b*
they have no further reward,
 and even their name*c* is forgotten.*d*
⁶Their love, their hate
 and their jealousy have long since vanished;
never again will they have a part
 in anything that happens under the sun.*e*

⁷Go, eat your food with gladness, and drink your wine*f* with a joyful heart,*g* for God has already approved what you do. ⁸Always be clothed in white,*h* and always anoint your head with oil. ⁹Enjoy life with your wife,*i* whom you love, all the days of this meaningless life that God has given you under the sun—all your meaningless days. For this is your lot*j* in life and in your toilsome labor under the sun. ¹⁰Whatever*k* your hand finds to do, do it with all your might,*l* for in the realm of the dead,*m* where you are going, there is neither working nor planning nor knowledge nor wisdom.*n*

¹¹I have seen something else under the sun:

The race is not to the swift
 or the battle to the strong,*o*
nor does food come to the wise*p*
 or wealth to the brilliant
 or favor to the learned;
but time and chance*q* happen to them all.*r*

¹²Moreover, no one knows when their hour will come:

As fish are caught in a cruel net,
 or birds are taken in a snare,
so people are trapped by evil times*s*
 that fall unexpectedly upon them.*t*

WISDOM BETTER THAN FOLLY

¹³I also saw under the sun this example of wisdom*u* that greatly impressed me: ¹⁴There was once a small city with only a few people in it. And a powerful king came against it, surrounded it and built huge siege works against it. ¹⁵Now there lived in that city a man poor but wise, and he saved the city by his wisdom. But nobody remembered that poor man.*v* ¹⁶So I said, "Wisdom is better than strength." But the poor man's wisdom is despised, and his words are no longer heeded.*w*

¹⁷The quiet words of the wise are more to be heeded
 than the shouts of a ruler of fools.
¹⁸Wisdom*x* is better than weapons of war,
 but one sinner destroys much good.

10 As dead flies give perfume a bad smell,
 so a little folly*y* outweighs wisdom and honor.
²The heart of the wise inclines to the right,
 but the heart of the fool to the left.
³Even as fools walk along the road,
 they lack sense
 and show everyone*z* how stupid they are.
⁴If a ruler's anger rises against you,

9:5 *no further reward.* The dead have lost all opportunity in this life for enjoyment and reward from labor (see v. 6).

B **9:7–9** The Babylonian *Epic of Gilgamesh* contains a section (10.3.6–14) remarkably similar to this passage, illustrating the international flavor of ancient wisdom literature (see chart, p. xxiii, and essay, p. 750).

9:7 See note on 8:15.

9:8 *be clothed in white…anoint your head with oil.* Expressions of joy (cf. Ps 45:7 and note).

9:10 Cf. Col 3:23.

A **9:11** *time and chance.* Success is uncertain—more evidence that humans do not ultimately control events.

9:12 *hour.* Of disaster. *people are trapped.* Success is unpredictable, because people are not wise enough to know when misfortune may overtake them.

9:15 *But nobody remembered.* Further warning against placing too high hopes on one's wisdom. Its reputation fades, its good is soon undone (v. 18b) and it has no answer to death (2:15–16).

10:1 *a little folly outweighs.* 2Ki 20:12–19 presents a striking example.

10:2 *to the right…to the left.* These can stand for the greater and the lesser good (cf. Ge 48:13–20); or perhaps here, as in some later Jewish writings, for good and evil (cf. Mt 25:33–34,41).

do not leave your post; *a*
  calmness can lay great offenses to rest. *b*

⁵ There is an evil I have seen under the sun,
  the sort of error that arises from a ruler:
⁶ Fools are put in many high positions, *c*
  while the rich occupy the low ones.
⁷ I have seen slaves on horseback,
  while princes go on foot like slaves. *d*

⁸ Whoever digs a pit may fall into it; *e*
  whoever breaks through a wall may be bitten by a snake. *f*
⁹ Whoever quarries stones may be injured by them;
  whoever splits logs may be endangered by them. *g*

¹⁰ If the ax is dull
  and its edge unsharpened,
more strength is needed,
  but skill will bring success.

¹¹ If a snake bites before it is charmed,
  the charmer receives no fee. *h*

¹² Words from the mouth of the wise are gracious, *i*
  but fools are consumed by their own lips. *j*
¹³ At the beginning their words are folly;
  at the end they are wicked madness—
¹⁴   and fools multiply words. *k*

No one knows what is coming—
  who can tell them what will happen after them? *l*

¹⁵ The toil of fools wearies them;
  they do not know the way to town.

¹⁶ Woe to the land whose king was a servant *a m*
  and whose princes feast in the morning.
¹⁷ Blessed is the land whose king is of noble birth
  and whose princes eat at a proper time—
  for strength and not for drunkenness. *n*

¹⁸ Through laziness, the rafters sag;
  because of idle hands, the house leaks. *o*

¹⁹ A feast is made for laughter,
  wine *p* makes life merry,
and money is the answer for everything.

²⁰ Do not revile the king *q* even in your thoughts,
  or curse the rich in your bedroom,
because a bird in the sky may carry your words,
  and a bird on the wing may report what you say.

INVEST IN MANY VENTURES

11 Ship *r* your grain across the sea;
  after many days you may receive a return. *s*
² Invest in seven ventures, yes, in eight;
  you do not know what disaster may come upon the land.

a 16 Or king is a child

Cross-references

10:4 *a* Ecc 8:3
b S Pr 16:14
10:6 *c* S Pr 29:2
10:7 *d* Pr 19:10
10:8 *e* S Ps 57:6
f S Est 2:23; Ps 9:16;
Am 5:19
10:9 *g* S Pr 26:27
10:11 *h* S Ps 58:5;
S Isa 3:3
10:12 *i* Pr 10:32
j S Pr 10:6; S 14:3;
S 15:2; S 18:7
10:14 *k* Ecc 5:3
l Ecc 9:1
10:16 *m* Isa 3:4-5,
12
10:17 *n* S Dt 14:26;
S 1Sa 25:36; S Pr 31:4
10:18 *o* Pr 20:4;
S 24:30-34
10:19 *p* S Ge 14:18;
S Jdg 9:13
10:20 *q* S Ex 22:28
11:1 *r* ver 6;
Isa 32:20; Hos 10:12
s S Dt 24:19

10:5 *error . . . from a ruler.* For the Teacher's observations on human regimes, see vv. 4,6–7,16–17,20; 3:16; 4:1–3,13–16; 5:8–9; 8:2–6,10–11; 9:17.

10:6–7 See Pr 19:10 and note; 30:21–22.

10:12 *Words.* A favorite topic in wisdom literature (see, e.g., Pr 15; Jas 3:2–12).

A **10:15** *fools . . . do not know the way to town.* Since in Scripture a fool is one who refuses God's teaching (see note on 5:4), this caustic saying (probably proverbial) refers to more than mere stupidity.

10:16 *whose king was a servant.* A small-minded upstart, not a "poor but wise youth" as in 4:13. See 2Ki 15:8–25; Hos 7:3–7, which portray some of the short-lived usurpers and vicious courtiers who hastened the downfall of Israel.

10:18 *laziness . . . idle.* See note on 4:5.

10:19 *money is the answer for everything.* Can be read at various levels—as a wry comment on human values, as sober advice to earn a good living rather than have a good time (see the first two lines) or as stating the great versatility of money (cf. Lk 16:9 and note).

11:5 ᵗ Jn 3:8-10
ᵘ Ps 139:14-16
11:6 ᵛ S Ecc 9:10
11:7 ʷ Ecc 7:11
11:8 ˣ Ecc 12:1
11:9 ʸ S Job 19:29;
S Ecc 2:24; S 3:17
11:10 ᶻ Ps 94:19
ᵃ S Ecc 2:24
12:1 ᵇ Ecc 11:8
ᶜ S 2Sa 19:35

³ If clouds are full of water,
    they pour rain on the earth.
Whether a tree falls to the south or to the north,
    in the place where it falls, there it will lie.
⁴ Whoever watches the wind will not plant;
    whoever looks at the clouds will not reap.

⁵ As you do not know the path of the wind, ᵗ
    or how the body is formed ᵃ in a mother's womb, ᵘ
so you cannot understand the work of God,
    the Maker of all things.

⁶ Sow your seed in the morning,
    and at evening let your hands not be idle, ᵛ
for you do not know which will succeed,
    whether this or that,
    or whether both will do equally well.

REMEMBER YOUR CREATOR WHILE YOUNG

⁷ Light is sweet,
    and it pleases the eyes to see the sun. ʷ
⁸ However many years anyone may live,
    let them enjoy them all.
But let them remember ˣ the days of darkness,
    for there will be many.
Everything to come is meaningless.

⁹ You who are young, be happy while you are young,
    and let your hearts give you joy in the days of your youth.
Follow the ways of your heart
    and whatever your eyes see,
but know that for all these things
    God will bring you into judgment. ʸ
¹⁰ So then, banish anxiety ᶻ from your heart
    and cast off the troubles of your body,
for youth and vigor are meaningless. ᵃ

12 Remember ᵇ your Creator
    in the days of your youth,
before the days of trouble ᶜ come
    and the years approach when you will say,
    "I find no pleasure in them"—
² before the sun and the light
    and the moon and the stars grow dark,
    and the clouds return after the rain;
³ when the keepers of the house tremble,
    and the strong men stoop,
when the grinders cease because they are few,
    and those looking through the windows grow dim;

ᵃ 5 Or *know how life* (or *the spirit*) / *enters the body being formed*

11:1 Be adventurous, like those who accept the risks and reap the benefits of seaborne trade. Do not always play it safe (see Pr 11:24 and note).
11:2 Diversify your efforts because you never know which ventures may fail. "Don't put all your eggs in one basket." Diversify your undertakings and reduce the risks.
11:3–6 *clouds . . . tree . . . wind . . . seed.* Do not toy with maybes and might-have-beens. Start where you can, and recognize how limited your role (or knowledge) is.
11:5 *wind.* See TNIV text note; cf. Jn 3:8 ("wind" and "spirit" translate the same word in the original in both verses).
11:7–10 Live life to the fullest (cf. Jn 10:10 and note).
11:8,10 *meaningless.* Warns against letting the wonderful gifts mentioned in vv. 7–10 dazzle and distract us.

Verse 9 sets us on the true course.
11:9 *judgment.* See 12:14 and note. The prospect of divine praise or blame makes every detail of life significant rather than meaningless. To know this gives direction to our hearts and discrimination to our eyes. The stage is set for ch. 12.
12:1 *days of your youth.* Cf. La 3:27.
12:2–5 A graphic description of progressive deterioration; an allegory about aging.
12:3 *keepers of the house.* This and the other metaphors may refer to parts of the body (hands, legs, etc.). But the imagery should not be pressed to the extent that it destroys the poetry, which moves freely between figures such as darkness, storm, a house in decline and a deserted well, and such literal descriptions as in v. 5a.

4 when the doors to the street are closed
  and the sound of grinding fades;
when people rise up at the sound of birds,
  but all their songs grow faint; *d*
5 when people are afraid of heights
  and of dangers in the streets;
when the almond tree blossoms
  and the grasshopper drags itself along
  and desire no longer is stirred.
Then people go to their eternal home *e*
  and mourners *f* go about the streets.

6 Remember him—before the silver cord is severed,
  and the golden bowl is broken;
before the pitcher is shattered at the spring,
  and the wheel broken at the well,
7 and the dust returns *g* to the ground it came from,
  and the spirit returns to God *h* who gave it. *i*

8 "Meaningless! Meaningless!" says the Teacher. *a j*
  "Everything is meaningless! *k*"

THE CONCLUSION OF THE MATTER

9 Not only was the Teacher wise, but he also imparted knowledge to the people. He pondered and searched out and set in order many proverbs. *l* 10 The Teacher *m* searched to find just the right words, and what he wrote was upright and true. *n*
11 The words of the wise are like goads, their collected sayings like firmly embedded nails *o*—given by one shepherd. *b* 12 Be warned, my son, of anything in addition to them. Of making many books there is no end, and much study wearies the body. *p*

13 Now all has been heard;
  here is the conclusion of the matter:
Fear God *q* and keep his commandments, *r*
  for this is the ⌊duty⌋ of every human being. *s*
14 For God will bring every deed into judgment, *t*
  including every hidden thing, *u*
  whether it is good or evil.

a 8 Or *the leader of the assembly*; also in verses 9 and 10   *b* 11 Or *Shepherd*

12:5 *almond tree.* Its pale blossom possibly suggests the white hair of age. *grasshopper.* Normally agile, its slow movements on a cold morning (cf. Na 3:17) recall the stiffness of old age. *eternal home.* In context, probably points simply to the grave, not beyond it (see Job 10:21 and note; 17:13).
12:6 *silver cord . . . golden bowl.* A hanging lamp suspended by a silver chain. If only one link snaps, this light and beauty will perish, suggesting how fragile life is.
12:8 *Meaningless!* See 1:2 and note; see also Introduction: Literary Features. Such is life "under the sun" (on earth, apart from God), ending in brokenness. But with a relationship to our Creator already demanded (v. 1), and with the fact of his judgment affirmed (11:9), meaninglessness is not the last word. *Teacher.* See note on 1:1.

12:9 *pondered and searched.* A rigorous process, with no pains spared in seeking truth and comprehension.
12:11 *given by one shepherd.* See TNIV text note; the other side of the matter, recognizing that Scripture is in a class of its own, as v. 12 insists.
12:13 *Fear God.* Loving reverence is the foundation of wisdom (see Ps 111:10; Pr 1:7 and notes), as well as its content (Job 28:28) and its goal and conclusion. *the ⌊duty⌋ of every human being.* Here is our fulfillment, our all—a far cry from "meaninglessness."
12:14 *every deed into judgment.* Glimpses of this truth are given at intervals in the book: See 3:17; 8:12–13; 11:9 and note; see also Mt 12:36; 1Co 3:12–15 and notes; 2Co 5:9–10; Heb 4:12–13. *every hidden thing.* See Ro 2:16.

12:4 *d* Jer 25:10
12:5 *e* S Job 10:21
f Jer 9:17; Am 5:16
12:7 *g* S Ge 2:7;
S Ps 146:4 *h* Ecc 3:21
i S Job 20:8
12:8 *j* Ecc 1:1
k S Ecc 1:2
12:9 *l* 1Ki 4:32
12:10 *m* S Ecc 1:1
n Pr 22:20-21
12:11 *o* S Ezr 9:8;
S Job 6:25
12:12 *p* S Ecc 1:18
12:13 *q* S Ex 20:20;
S 1Sa 12:24;
S Job 23:15; S Ps 19:9
r S Dt 4:2 *s* S Dt 4:6;
S Job 37:24
12:14 *t* S Job 19:29;
u S Job 34:21;
S Ps 19:12; Jer 16:17;
23:24

TITLE   SONG OF SONGS   INTRODUCTION

The title in the Hebrew text is "Solomon's Song of Songs," meaning a song by, for, or about Solomon. The phrase "Song of Songs" means the greatest of songs (cf. Dt 10:17, "God of gods and Lord of lords"; 1Ti 6:15, "King of kings").

AUTHOR AND DATE

Verse 1 appears to ascribe authorship to Solomon (see note on 1:1; but see also Title, above). Solomon is referred to seven times (1:1,5; 3:7,9,11; 8:11–12), and several verses speak of the "king" (1:4,12; 7:5), but whether he was the author remains an open question.

To date the Song in the tenth century B.C. during Solomon's reign is not impossible. In fact, mention of Tirzah and Jerusalem in one breath (6:4; see note there) has been used to prove a date prior to King Omri (885–874 B.C.; see 1Ki 16:23–24), though the reason for Tirzah's mention is not clear. On the other hand, many have appealed to the language of the Song as proof of a much later date, but on present evidence the linguistic data are ambiguous.

Consistency of language, style, tone, perspective and recurring refrains seems to argue for a single author. However, many who have doubted that the Song came from one pen, or even from one time or place, explain this consistency by ascribing all the Song's parts to a single literary tradition, since Near Eastern traditions were very careful to maintain stylistic uniformity.

INTERPRETATION

B To find the key for unlocking the Song, interpreters have looked to prophetic, wisdom and apocalyptic passages of Scripture, as well as to ancient Egyptian and Babylonian love songs, traditional Semitic wedding songs, and songs related to ancient Mesopotamian fertility religions. The closest parallels appear to be those found in Proverbs (see Pr 5:15–20; 6:24–29; 7:6–23). The description of love in 8:6–7 (cf. the descriptions of wisdom found in Pr 1–9 and Job 28) seems to confirm that the Song belongs to Biblical wisdom literature and that it is wisdom's description of an amorous relationship. The Bible speaks of both wisdom and love as gifts of God, to be received with gratitude and celebration.

This understanding of the Song contrasts with the long-held view that the Song is an allegory of the love relationship between God and Israel, or between Christ and the church, or between Christ and the soul (the NT nowhere quotes from or even alludes to the Song). It is also distinct from more modern interpretations of the Song, such as that which sees it as a poetic drama celebrating the triumph of a maiden's pure, spontaneous love for her rustic shepherd lover over the courtly blandishments of Solomon, who sought to win her for his royal harem. Rather, it views the Song as a linked chain of lyrics depicting love in all its spontaneity, beauty, power and exclusiveness—experienced in its varied moments of separation and intimacy, anguish and ecstasy, tension and contentment. The Song shares with the love poetry of many cultures its extensive use of highly sensuous and suggestive imagery drawn from nature.

THEME AND THEOLOGY

In ancient Israel everything human came to expression in words: reverence, gratitude, anger, sorrow, suffering, trust, friendship, commitment, loyalty, hope, wisdom, moral outrage, repentance. In the Song, it is love that finds words—inspired words that disclose its exquisite charm and beauty as one of God's choicest gifts. The voice of love in the Song, like that of wisdom in Pr 8:1—9:12, is most often a woman's voice, suggesting that love and wisdom draw men powerfully with the subtlety and mystery of a woman's allurements.

This feminine voice speaks profoundly of love. She portrays its beauty and delights. She claims its exclusiveness ("My beloved is mine and I am his," 2:16) and insists on the necessity of its pure spontaneity ("Do not arouse or awaken love until it so desires," 2:7). She also proclaims its overwhelming power—it rivals that of the fearsome enemy, death; it burns with the intensity of a blazing fire; it is unquench-able even by the ocean depths (8:6–7a). She affirms its preciousness: All that one possesses cannot purchase it, nor (alternatively) should it be exchanged for it (8:7b). She hints, without saying so explicitly (see the last TNIV text note on 8:6), that it is the Lord's gift.

God intends that such love—grossly distorted and abused by both ancient and modern people—be a normal part of marital life in his good creation (see Ge 1:26–31; 2:24). Indeed, in the Song the faithful Israelite could ascertain how to live lovingly within the theocratic arrangement. Such marital love is designed by the Cre-ator-King to come to natural expression within his realm.

LITERARY FEATURES

No one who reads the Song with care can question the artistry of the poet. The sub-tle delicacy with which he evokes intense sensuous awareness while avoiding crude titillation is one of the chief marks of his achievement. This he accomplishes largely by indirection, by analogy and by bringing to the foreground the sensuous in the world of nature (or in food, drink, cosmetics and jewelry). To liken a "beloved's" (1:13) enjoyment of his "darling" (1:9) to a gazelle "browsing among the lilies" (2:16), or her breasts to "twin fawns of a gazelle that browse among the lilies" (4:5), or his darling herself to a garden filled with choice fruits inviting the beloved to feast (4:12–16)—these combine exquisite artistry and fine sensitivity.

Whether the Song has the unity of a single dramatic line linking all the sub-units into a continuing story is a matter of ongoing debate among interpreters. There do appear to be connected scenes in the love relationship (see Outline).

Virtually all agree that the literary climax of the Song is found in 8:5–7, where the unsurpassed power and value of love—the love that draws man and woman together—are finally expressly asserted. Literary relaxation follows the intenseness of that declaration. A final expression of mutual desire between the lovers brings the Song to an end, suggesting that love goes on. This last segment (8:8–14) is in some sense also a return to the beginning, as references to the darling's brothers, to her vineyard and to Solomon (the king) link 8:8–12 with 1:2–6. In this song of love the voice of the darling is dominant. It is her experience of love, both as the one who loves and as the one who is loved, that is most clearly expressed. The Song begins with her wish for the beloved's kiss and ends with her urgent invitation to him for love's intimacy.

OUTLINE

1:1 *a* S 1Ki 4:32;
Ps 45 Title
1:2 *b* ver 4; SS 4:10;
8:6 *c* S Ge 14:18;
S Jdg 9:13
1:3 *d* S Est 2:12;
S Ps 45:8 *e* S Ecc 7:1
f Ps 45:14
1:4 *g* Ps 45:15
h SS 2:3 *i* S ver 2
1:5 *j* SS 2:14; 4:3
k SS 5:16 *l* S Ge 25:13
1:6 *m* SS 2:15; 7:12;
8:12
1:7 *n* Isa 13:20
o Ge 24:65
1:8 *p* SS 5:9; 6:1

Solomon's Song of Songs. *a*

SHE *a*

² Let him kiss me with the kisses of his mouth—
  for your love *b* is more delightful than wine. *c*
³ Pleasing is the fragrance of your perfumes; *d*
  your name *e* is like perfume poured out.
  No wonder the young women *f* love you!
⁴ Take me away with you—let us hurry!
  Let the king bring me into his chambers. *g*

FRIENDS

We rejoice and delight *h* in you *b*;
  we will praise your love *i* more than wine.

SHE

How right they are to adore you!

⁵ Dark am I, yet lovely, *j*
  daughters of Jerusalem, *k*
dark like the tents of Kedar, *l*
  like the tent curtains of Solomon. *c*
⁶ Do not stare at me because I am dark,
  because I am darkened by the sun.
My mother's sons were angry with me
  and made me take care of the vineyards; *m*
  my own vineyard I had to neglect.
⁷ Tell me, you whom I love,
  where you graze your flock
  and where you rest your sheep *n* at midday.
Why should I be like a veiled *o* woman
  beside the flocks of your friends?

FRIENDS

⁸ If you do not know, most beautiful of women, *p*
  follow the tracks of the sheep

a The main male and female speakers (identified primarily on the basis of the gender of the relevant Hebrew forms) are indicated by the captions *He* and *She* respectively. The words of others are marked *Friends*. In some instances the divisions and their captions are debatable.   *b* 4 The Hebrew is masculine singular.   *c* 5 Or *Salma*

1:1 *Solomon's.* See Introduction: Title; Author and Date. *Song of Songs.* Greatest of songs (see Introduction: Title). 1Ki 4:32 says that Solomon wrote 1,005 songs.
1:2–3 *kisses ... your love ... your perfumes.* Cf. 4:10–11, "your love ... your perfume ... Your lips."
1:2 See TNIV text note on the caption *She. him ... his ... your.* These pronouns all refer to the same person, the beloved (Solomon). *love.* Expressions of love—caresses, embraces and consummation (see v. 4; 4:10; 7:12; see also Pr 7:18; Eze 16:8; 23:17). *more delightful than wine.* See v. 4. In 4:10 the beloved speaks similarly of his darling's love.
1:3 *perfumes.* Aromatic spices and gums blended in cosmetic oil. *your name.* The very mention of the beloved's name fills the air as with a pleasant aroma. The Hebrew words for "name" and "perfume" sound alike. *young women.* Probably young women of the court or of the royal city (see 6:8–9).
1:4 *king.* Solomon. *his chambers.* The king's private quarters. *We.* Probably the young women of v. 3. *praise your love more than wine.* For the reason given in v. 2.
1:5 *Dark.* Deeply browned by the sun (see v. 6); not considered desirable. *daughters of Jerusalem.* Probably the young women of v. 3 and usually the "Friends" in the sectional headings. *tents ...*

tent curtains. Handwoven from black goat hair. *Kedar.* See note on Isa 21:16.
1:6 *mother's.* Mothers are referred to seven times in the Song (here; 3:4,11; 6:9; 8:1–2,5); fathers are never mentioned. *my own vineyard.* Her body, as in 8:12 (see 2:15). Vineyard is an apt metaphor since it yields wine, and the excitements of love are compared with those produced by wine (see note on v. 2). The darling is also compared to a garden, yielding precious fruits for the lover (see note on 4:12).
1:7 *whom I love.* See 3:1. *where you graze your flock.* The beloved is portrayed as a shepherd. In v. 8 his darling is depicted as a shepherd girl. *midday.* A time of rest in warm climates. *veiled woman.* Prostitute (see Ge 38:14–15). The darling does not wish to look for her beloved among the shepherds, appearing as though she were a prostitute.
1:8 *beautiful.* The darling; also in v. 15; 2:10,13; 4:1,7; 5:9; 6:1,4,10 ("fair"). The beloved is called "handsome" in v. 16 (in Hebrew the same word as that for "beautiful"). *your young goats.* The darling is pictured as a shepherd (see v. 7). *by the tents of the shepherds.* The darling is instructed to learn where her beloved is by joining the shepherds in the fields.

and graze your young goats
   by the tents of the shepherds.

HE

⁹ I liken you, my darling, to a mare
   among Pharaoh's chariot horses. *q*
¹⁰ Your cheeks *r* are beautiful with earrings,
   your neck with strings of jewels. *s*
¹¹ We will make you earrings of gold,
   studded with silver.

SHE

¹² While the king was at his table,
   my perfume spread its fragrance. *t*
¹³ My beloved is to me a sachet of myrrh *u*
   resting between my breasts.
¹⁴ My beloved *v* is to me a cluster of henna *w* blossoms
   from the vineyards of En Gedi. *x*

HE

¹⁵ How beautiful *y* you are, my darling!
   Oh, how beautiful!
   Your eyes are doves. *z*

SHE

¹⁶ How handsome you are, my beloved! *a*
   Oh, how charming!
   And our bed is verdant.

HE

¹⁷ The beams of our house are cedars; *b*
   our rafters are firs.

SHE *a*

2 I am a rose *b c* of Sharon, *d*
   a lily *e* of the valleys.

HE

² Like a lily among thorns
   is my darling among the young women.

SHE

³ Like an apple *c* tree among the trees of the forest
   is my beloved *f* among the young men.

ᵃ Or *He*   ᵇ 1 Probably a member of the crocus family   ᶜ 3 Or possibly *apricot*; here and elsewhere in Song of Songs

---

Cross-references (right column):

1:9 *q* 2Ch 1:17
1:10 *r* SS 5:13
  s Isa 61:10
1:12 *t* SS 4:11-14
1:13 *u* S Ge 37:25
1:14 *v* ver 16;
  SS 2:3,17; 5:8
  w SS 4:13
  x S 1Sa 23:29;
  S 2Ch 20:2
1:15 *y* SS 4:7; 7:6
  z Ps 74:19; SS 2:14;
  4:1; 5:2,12; 6:9;
  Jer 48:28
1:16 *a* S ver 14
1:17 *b* 1Ki 6:9
2:1 *c* Isa 35:1
  d S 1Ch 27:29
  e SS 5:13; Hos 14:5
2:3 *f* S SS 1:14

1:9 *my darling.* Used only of *She* (see v. 15; 2:2,10,13; 4:1,7; 5:2; 6:4; see also note on v. 13). *mare.* A flattering comparison, similar to Theocritus's praise of the beautiful Helen of Troy (*Idyl,* 18.30–31). *among Pharaoh's chariot horses.* Her beauty attracts attention the way a mare would among the Egyptian chariot stallions. According to 1Ki 10:28, Solomon imported horses from Egypt.
1:11 *We.* Perhaps the "daughters of Jerusalem" (v. 5).
1:12 *king.* Solomon. *at his table.* Reclining on his couch at the table. *my perfume.* Nard, an aromatic oil extracted from the roots of a perennial herb that grows in India (see 4:13–14; Mk 14:3; Jn 12:3).
1:13 *My beloved.* Used only of *He* (see v. 14,16; 2:3,8,9,10,16,17; 4:16; 5:2,4,5,6,8,9,10,16; 6:1,2,3; 7:9,10,11,13; 8:5,14; see also note on v. 9). *myrrh.* An aromatic gum exuding from the bark of a balsam tree that grows in Arabia, Ethiopia and India. It was commonly used as an alluring feminine perfume (Est 2:12; Pr 7:17). It

was also used to perfume royal nuptial robes (Ps 45:8) and as an ingredient in the holy anointing oil (Ex 30:23). The Magi brought myrrh to the young Jesus as a gift fit for a king (Mt 2:2,11).
1:14 *henna.* A shrub (perhaps the cypress) with tightly clustered, aromatic blossoms. *En Gedi.* An oasis watered by a spring, located on the west side of the Dead Sea (see map, p. 427). David sought refuge there from King Saul (1Sa 24:1).
1:15 *How beautiful … darling!* See 4:1; 6:4; cf. v. 16. *my darling.* See note on v. 9. *doves.* Probably refers to the shape and cosmetic highlighting of her eyes (see 4:1).
1:16 *handsome.* See note on v. 8 ("beautiful"). *verdant.* The lovers lie together in the field under the trees.
2:1 *rose.* See TNIV text note and Isa 35:1–2. *Sharon.* The fertile coastal plain south of Mount Carmel (see map No. 2 at the end of this study Bible). *lily.* Probably either lotus or anemone.
2:2 *my darling.* See note on 1:9. *young women.* See note on 1:3.

2:3 *g* SS 1:4
h SS 4:16
2:4 *i* Est 1:11
j S Nu 1:52
2:5 *k* SS 7:8 *l* SS 5:8
2:6 *m* SS 8:3
2:7 *n* SS 5:8
o SS 3:5; 8:4
2:8 *p* ver 17; SS 8:14
2:9 *q* S 2Sa 2:18
r ver 17; SS 8:14
2:13 *s* Isa 28:4;
Jer 24:2; Hos 9:10;
Mic 7:1; Na 3:12
t SS 7:12
2:14 *u* S Ge 8:8;
S SS 1:15 *v* S SS 1:5
2:15 *w* Jdg 15:4
x S SS 1:6 *y* SS 7:12

I delight *g* to sit in his shade,
   and his fruit is sweet to my taste. *h*
  ⁴ Let him lead me to the banquet hall, *i*
   and let his banner *j* over me be love.
  ⁵ Strengthen me with raisins,
   refresh me with apples, *k*
   for I am faint with love. *l*
  ⁶ His left arm is under my head,
   and his right arm embraces me. *m*
  ⁷ Daughters of Jerusalem, I charge you *n*
   by the gazelles and by the does of the field:
Do not arouse or awaken love
   until it so desires. *o*

  ⁸ Listen! My beloved!
   Look! Here he comes,
leaping across the mountains,
   bounding over the hills. *p*
  ⁹ My beloved is like a gazelle *q* or a young stag. *r*
   Look! There he stands behind our wall,
gazing through the windows,
   peering through the lattice.
  ¹⁰ My beloved spoke and said to me,
   "Arise, my darling,
my beautiful one, come with me.
  ¹¹ See! The winter is past;
   the rains are over and gone.
  ¹² Flowers appear on the earth;
   the season of singing has come,
the cooing of doves
   is heard in our land.
  ¹³ The fig tree forms its early fruit; *s*
   the blossoming *t* vines spread their fragrance.
Arise, come, my darling;
   my beautiful one, come with me."

HE

  ¹⁴ My dove *u* in the clefts of the rock,
   in the hiding places on the mountainside,
show me your face,
   let me hear your voice;
for your voice is sweet,
   and your face is lovely. *v*
  ¹⁵ Catch for us the foxes, *w*
   the little foxes
that ruin the vineyards, *x*
   our vineyards that are in bloom. *y*

2:3 *apple tree.* The precise nature of this fruit tree is uncertain (see TNIV text note). *his fruit.* Probably a metaphor for the beloved's intimacies (see v. 5 and note).
2:4 *banner.* See 6:4; Nu 2:2; Ps 20:5. The king's love for her is displayed for all to see, like a large military banner.
2:5 *raisins ... apples.* Probably metaphors for love's caresses and embraces.
2:7 A recurring refrain in the Song (see 3:5; 8:4; cf. 5:8). It is always spoken by the darling and always in a context of physical intimacy with her beloved. *Daughters of Jerusalem.* See note on 1:5. *charge.* Place under oath. *gazelles ... does.* Perhaps in the imaginative language of love the gazelles and does are portrayed as witnesses to the oath. This would be in harmony with the author's frequent reference to nature. *until it so desires.* Out of the darling's experience of love comes wise admonition that love is not to be artificially stimulated; utter spontaneity is es-

sential to its genuine truth and beauty.
2:9 *gazelle.* Celebrated for its form and beauty. *young stag.* An apt simile for youthful vigor (cf. Isa 35:6). *gazing ... lattice.* The eager beloved tries to catch sight of his darling while she is still preparing herself for their meeting.
2:10 *Arise ... with me.* See v. 13; cf. 7:11–13. *my beautiful one.* See note on 1:8.
2:11–13 The first signs of spring appear (see 6:11; 7:12)—the time of love.
2:14 *dove ... on the mountainside.* Cf. Ps 55:6–8; Jer 48:28.
2:15 Perhaps spoken by *She. vineyards.* As in 1:6 ("my own vineyard"), probably a metaphor for the lovers' physical beauty. Thus the desire is expressed that the lovers be kept safe from whatever ("foxes") might mar their mutual attractiveness. *in bloom.* Their attractiveness is in its prime.

SHE

¹⁶ My beloved is mine and I am his;*z*
    he browses among the lilies. *a*
¹⁷ Until the day breaks
    and the shadows flee, *b*
turn, my beloved, *c*
    and be like a gazelle
or like a young stag *d*
    on the rugged hills. *a e*

3

All night long on my bed
    I looked *f* for the one my heart loves;
    I looked for him but did not find him.
² I will get up now and go about the city,
    through its streets and squares;
I will search for the one my heart loves.
    So I looked for him but did not find him.
³ The watchmen found me
    as they made their rounds in the city. *g*
    "Have you seen the one my heart loves?"
⁴ Scarcely had I passed them
    when I found the one my heart loves.
I held him and would not let him go
    till I had brought him to my mother's house, *h*
    to the room of the one who conceived me. *i*
⁵ Daughters of Jerusalem, I charge you*j*
    by the gazelles and by the does of the field:
Do not arouse or awaken love
    until it so desires. *k*

⁶ Who is this coming up from the wilderness *l*
    like a column of smoke,
perfumed with myrrh *m* and incense
    made from all the spices *n* of the merchant?
⁷ Look! It is Solomon's carriage,
    escorted by sixty warriors, *o*
    the noblest of Israel,
⁸ all of them wearing the sword,
    all experienced in battle,
each with his sword at his side,
    prepared for the terrors of the night. *p*
⁹ King Solomon made for himself the carriage;
    he made it of wood from Lebanon.
¹⁰ Its posts he made of silver,
    its base of gold.
Its seat was upholstered with purple,
    its interior inlaid with love.
Daughters of Jerusalem, ¹¹ come out,

a 17 Or the hills of Bether

2:16 *z* SS 7:10
a SS 4:5; 6:3
2:17 *b* SS 4:6
c S SS 1:14 *d* S ver 9
e S ver 8
3:1 *f* SS 5:6
3:3 *g* SS 5:7
3:4 *h* SS 8:2 *i* SS 6:9;
8:5
3:5 *j* S SS 2:7
k SS 8:4
3:6 *l* SS 8:5
m SS 4:6,14
n Ex 30:34
3:7 *o* S 1Sa 8:11
3:8 *p* S Job 15:22;
Ps 91:5

2:16 *My beloved is mine and I am his.* See 6:3; 7:10. They belong to each other exclusively in a relationship that allows no intrusion. *browses among the lilies.* The beloved is compared to a gazelle (see v. 17). The browsing is a metaphor for the beloved's intimate enjoyment of her charms (see 6:2–3).
3:1 This verse begins a new moment in love's experience. *All night long.* Night, with its freedom from the distractions of the day, allows the heart to be filled with its own preoccupations.
3:3 *watchmen.* Were stationed at the city gates (see Ne 3:29; 11:19; 13:22) and on the walls (see 5:7; 2Sa 13:34; 18:24–27; 2Ki 9:17–20; Ps 127:1; Isa 52:8; 62:6). Apparently they also patrolled the streets at night (see 5:7).
3:4 *mother's.* See note on 1:6.
3:5 See note on 2:7. Once again the charge occurs at the moment of intimacy.

3:6–11 Perhaps spoken by the friends (see 8:5). If so, this section probably portrays the wedding procession of Solomon and his bride approaching the city.
3:6 This verse begins a new moment in the relationship. *Who … wilderness.* See 8:5, where the reference is to the darling. *wilderness.* Uncultivated seasonal grasslands. *smoke.* Incense (see note on Ex 30:34). *of the merchant.* Imported.
3:7 *carriage.* A richly adorned royal conveyance, a palanquin (see vv. 9–10).
3:8 *terrors of the night.* See Ps 91:5.
3:9 *wood from Lebanon.* See 5:15 and note.
3:10 *posts.* Supporting the canopy. *silver … gold.* Probably metals that overlay the Lebanon wood. *purple.* See notes on 7:5; Ex 25:4.

3:11 q Isa 3:16; 4:4;
32:9-13 r Isa 54:5;
62:5; Jer 3:14
4:1 s S Ge 24:65
t SS 1:15 u Ge 37:25;
Nu 32:1; SS 6:5;
Jer 22:6; Mic 7:14
4:2 v SS 6:6
4:3 w SS 5:16
x SS 1:5 y SS 6:7
4:4 z S Ps 144:12
a Eze 27:10
4:5 b SS 7:3
c Pr 5:19 d SS 2:16
4:6 e SS 2:17
f SS 3:6
4:7 g SS 1:15
h SS 5:2
4:8 i ver 9,12; SS 5:1
j S Dt 3:9 k 1Ch 5:23
4:9 l ver 8
m S Ge 41:42;
S Ps 73:6

and look, you daughters of Zion. q
Look a on King Solomon wearing a crown,
    the crown with which his mother crowned him
on the day of his wedding,
    the day his heart rejoiced. r

HE

4

How beautiful you are, my darling!
    Oh, how beautiful!
    Your eyes behind your veil s are doves. t
Your hair is like a flock of goats
    descending from the hills of Gilead. u
² Your teeth are like a flock of sheep just shorn,
    coming up from the washing.
Each has its twin;
    not one of them is alone. v
³ Your lips are like a scarlet ribbon;
    your mouth w is lovely. x
Your temples behind your veil
    are like the halves of a pomegranate. y
⁴ Your neck is like the tower z of David,
    built with courses of stone b;
on it hang a thousand shields, a
    all of them shields of warriors.
⁵ Your breasts b are like two fawns,
    like twin fawns of a gazelle c
    that browse among the lilies. d
⁶ Until the day breaks
    and the shadows flee, e
I will go to the mountain of myrrh f
    and to the hill of incense.
⁷ All beautiful g you are, my darling;
    there is no flaw h in you.

⁸ Come with me from Lebanon, my bride, i
    come with me from Lebanon.
Descend from the crest of Amana,
    from the top of Senir, j the summit of Hermon, k
from the lions' dens
    and the mountain haunts of leopards.
⁹ You have stolen my heart, my sister, my bride; l
    you have stolen my heart
with one glance of your eyes,
    with one jewel of your necklace. m

---

a 10,11 Or *interior lovingly inlaid / by the daughters of Jerusalem. / ¹¹Come out, you daughters of Zion, / and look*   b 4 The meaning of the Hebrew for this phrase is uncertain.

3:11 *daughters of Zion.* Elsewhere "daughters of Jerusalem" (see note on 1:5). *crown.* A wedding wreath (see Isa 61:10). *mother.* Bathsheba.
4:1–7 For other exuberant descriptions of the darling's beauty, see 6:4–9; 7:1–7.
4:1b–2 See 6:5b–6.
4:1 *How beautiful … darling!* See 1:15 and note. *eyes behind your veil.* With the rest of her face concealed, the beloved's attention is focused on his darling's eyes. *doves.* See 1:15 and note. *flock of goats.* The goats of Canaan were usually black (see note on 1:5). The beloved's hair was also black (5:11). *descending from the hills of Gilead.* The darling's black tresses flowing from her head remind her beloved of a flock of sleek black goats streaming down one of the hills of Gilead (noted for its good pasturage).
4:2 *just shorn.* Clean and white. *coming up from the washing.* Still wet, like moistened teeth.
4:3 *Your lips … scarlet.* Perhaps the darling painted her lips, like

Egyptian women. *temples behind … veil.* See note on v. 1. *halves of a pomegranate.* Round and blushed with red.
4:4 The darling's erect, bespangled neck is like a tower on the city wall adorned with warriors' shields (cf. 7:4).
4:5 See 7:3. *fawns.* Representing tender, delicate beauty, and promise rather than full growth (cf. 8:8). *gazelle.* See note on 2:9. Elsewhere the simile is used of the beloved. *browse among the lilies.* For a different use of this phrase, see 2:16 and note.
4:6 *Until … shadows flee.* See 2:17. *mountain of myrrh … hill of incense.* Metaphors for lovers' intimacy.
4:8 To the beloved, his darling seems to have withdrawn as if to a remote mountain. *Lebanon … Amana … Hermon.* Mountain peaks on the northern horizon. *Senir.* Name for Mount Hermon found in Assyrian sources (Dt 3:9).
4:9 *my sister.* For lovers to address each other as "brother" and "sister" was common in the love poetry of the ancient Near East (see vv. 10,12; 5:1). *one glance of your eyes.* See 6:5 and note.

[10] How delightful [n] is your love [o], my sister, my bride!
How much more pleasing is your love than wine, [p]
and the fragrance of your perfume [q]
more than any spice!

[11] Your lips drop sweetness as the honeycomb, my bride;
milk and honey are under your tongue. [r]
The fragrance of your garments
is like the fragrance of Lebanon. [s]

[12] You are a garden [t] locked up, my sister, my bride; [u]
you are a spring enclosed, a sealed fountain. [v]

[13] Your plants are an orchard of pomegranates [w]
with choice fruits,
with henna [x] and nard,

[14] nard and saffron,
calamus and cinnamon, [y]
with every kind of incense tree,
with myrrh [z] and aloes [a]
and all the finest spices. [b]

[15] You are [a] a garden [c] fountain, [d]
a well of flowing water
streaming down from Lebanon.

SHE

[16] Awake, north wind,
and come, south wind!
Blow on my garden, [e]
that its fragrance [f] may spread abroad.
Let my beloved [g] come into his garden
and taste its choice fruits. [h]

HE

5

I have come into my garden, [i] my sister, my bride; [j]
I have gathered my myrrh with my spice.
I have eaten my honeycomb and my honey;
I have drunk my wine and my milk. [k]

FRIENDS

Eat, friends, and drink;
drink your fill of love.

[a] 15 Or *I am* (spoken by *She*)

4:10 [n] SS 7:6
[o] S SS 1:2 [p] S Jdg 9:13
[q] ver 16; S Ps 45:8;
Isa 57:9
4:11 [r] S Ps 19:10;
SS 5:1 [s] Hos 14:6
4:12 [t] ver 16; SS 5:1;
6:2; Isa 5:7 [u] S ver 8
[v] Pr 5:15-18
4:13 [w] SS 7:12
[x] SS 1:14
4:14 [y] S Ex 30:23
[z] S SS 3:6 [a] S Nu 24:6
[b] SS 1:12
4:15 [c] Isa 27:2;
58:11; Jer 31:12
[d] Pr 5:18
4:16 [e] S ver 12
[f] S ver 10 [g] SS 7:13
[h] SS 2:3
5:1 [i] S SS 4:12
[j] S SS 4:8 [k] S SS 4:11;
Isa 55:1; Joel 3:18

4:10 *more pleasing...than wine.* See note on 1:2. *fragrance of your perfume.* See 1:3. *spice.* See v. 14; 5:1,13; 6:2; 8:14. Spice was an imported luxury item (see 1Ki 10:2,10,25; Eze 27:22). Spices were used for fragrance in the holy anointing oil (Ex 25:6; 30:23–25; 35:8) and for fragrant incense (Ex 25:6; 35:8), as well as for perfume.
4:11 *Your lips drop sweetness.* The darling speaks to him of love (cf. Pr 5:3; 16:24). People in the ancient Near East associated sweetness with the delights of love. *milk and honey.* Perhaps reminiscent of the description of the promised land (see note on Ex 3:8). *under your tongue.* See Job 20:12; Ps 10:7.
4:12 *garden.* A place of sensual delights (see v. 16; 5:1; 6:2; see also note on 1:6). *locked up...enclosed...sealed.* Metaphors for the darling's virginity—or perhaps for the fact that she keeps herself exclusively for her husband. *spring...fountain.* Sources of refreshment; metaphors for the darling as a sexual partner, as in Pr 5:15–20.
4:13–15 Verses 13–14 elaborate on the garden metaphor of v. 12a, and v. 15 elaborates on the fountain metaphor of v. 12b. The trees and spices in vv. 13–14 are mostly exotic, referring to the darling's charms.
4:13 *Your plants.* All the darling's features that delight the

beloved. *orchard.* Hebrew *pardes* (from which the English word *paradise* comes), a loanword from Old Persian meaning "enclosure" or "park." In Ne 2:8 and Ecc 2:5 it refers to royal parks and forests. *henna.* See note on 1:14. *nard.* See note on 1:12.
4:14 *saffron.* A plant of the crocus family bearing purple or white flowers, parts of which, when dried, were used as a cooking spice. *calamus.* An imported (see Jer 6:20 and note), aromatic spice cane, used also in the holy anointing oil (Ex 30:23,25) and in incense (Isa 43:23–24). *cinnamon.* Used in the holy anointing oil (Ex 30:23,25). *myrrh.* See note on 1:13. *aloes.* Aromatic aloes, used to perfume royal nuptial robes (Ps 45:8). Pr 7:17 says the adulterous woman perfumed her bed "with myrrh, aloes and cinnamon."
4:15 *flowing.* Fresh, not stagnant. *streaming...from Lebanon.* Fresh, cool, sparkling water from the snowfields on the Lebanon mountains.
4:16 May the fragrance of my charms be wafted about to draw my beloved to me so that we may enjoy love's intimacies. *his garden.* She belongs to him and yields herself to her beloved (see 6:2).
5:1 The beloved claims his darling as his garden and enjoys all her delights. *my sister.* See note on 4:9. *Eat...love.* The friends of the lovers applaud their enjoyment of love.

5:2 /S SS 1:15
m SS 4:7 n SS 6:9
5:5 o ver 13
5:6 p SS 6:1 q SS 6:2
r SS 3:1
5:7 s SS 3:3
5:8 t SS 2:7
u SS 1:14 v SS 2:5
5:9 w SS 1:8
5:10 x Ps 45:2
5:12 y SS 1:15
z Ge 49:12
5:13 a SS 1:10
b SS 6:2

SHE

2 I slept but my heart was awake.
    Listen! My beloved is knocking:
"Open to me, my sister, my darling,
    my dove, l my flawless m one. n
My head is drenched with dew,
    my hair with the dampness of the night."
3 I have taken off my robe—
    must I put it on again?
I have washed my feet—
    must I soil them again?
4 My beloved thrust his hand through the latch-opening;
    my heart began to pound for him.
5 I arose to open for my beloved,
    and my hands dripped with myrrh, o
my fingers with flowing myrrh,
    on the handles of the bolt.
6 I opened for my beloved, p
    but my beloved had left; he was gone. q
My heart sank at his departure. a
I looked r for him but did not find him.
    I called him but he did not answer.
7 The watchmen found me
    as they made their rounds in the city. s
They beat me, they bruised me;
    they took away my cloak,
    those watchmen of the walls!
8 Daughters of Jerusalem, I charge you t—
    if you find my beloved, u
what will you tell him?
    Tell him I am faint with love. v

FRIENDS

9 How is your beloved better than others,
    most beautiful of women? w
How is your beloved better than others,
    that you so charge us?

SHE

10 My beloved is radiant and ruddy,
    outstanding among ten thousand. x
11 His head is purest gold;
    his hair is wavy
    and black as a raven.
12 His eyes are like doves y
    by the water streams,
    washed in milk, z
    mounted like jewels.
13 His cheeks a are like beds of spice b
    yielding perfume.

---

a 6 Or *heart had gone out to him when he spoke*

5:2–8 See 3:1–5 and note on 3:1.
5:2 *I slept ... was awake.* Love holds sway even in sleep—just as a new mother sleeps with an ear open to her baby's slightest whimper.
5:3 Instinctive reaction raises a foolish complaint before the language of love takes over.
5:5 *my hands ... flowing myrrh.* Love's eager imagination extravagantly lotioned the darling's hands with perfume.
5:9 The friends' question provides an opportunity for the darling to describe the beauty of her beloved—which she does only here.

5:10 *ruddy.* See 1Sa 16:12.
5:11 *black.* The darling's hair was also black (see note on 4:1).
5:12 *doves.* See note on 1:15. *by the water streams.* The beloved's eyes sparkle. *washed in milk.* Describing the white of the eye.
5:13 *spice ... lilies.* These similes probably compare sensuous effects rather than appearances, as do the following similes and metaphors, at least in part. *lilies.* See note on 2:1. *dripping with myrrh.* Love's pleasant excitements are aroused by the beloved's lips.

His lips are like lilies[c]
    dripping with myrrh. [d]
[14] His arms are rods of gold
    set with topaz.
His body is like polished ivory
    decorated with lapis lazuli. [e]
[15] His legs are pillars of marble
    set on bases of pure gold.
His appearance is like Lebanon, [f]
    choice as its cedars.
[16] His mouth[g] is sweetness itself;
    he is altogether lovely.
This is my beloved, [h] this is my friend,
    daughters of Jerusalem. [i]

FRIENDS

Where has your beloved[j] gone,
    most beautiful of women? [k]
Which way did your beloved turn,
    that we may look for him with you?

SHE

[2] My beloved has gone[l] down to his garden, [m]
    to the beds of spices, [n]
to browse in the gardens
    and to gather lilies.
[3] I am my beloved's and my beloved is mine; [o]
    he browses among the lilies. [p]

HE

[4] You are as beautiful as Tirzah, [q] my darling,
    as lovely as Jerusalem, [r]
    as majestic as troops with banners. [s]
[5] Turn your eyes from me;
    they overwhelm me.
Your hair is like a flock of goats
    descending from Gilead. [t]
[6] Your teeth are like a flock of sheep
    coming up from the washing.
Each has its twin,
    not one of them is missing. [u]
[7] Your temples behind your veil[v]
    are like the halves of a pomegranate. [w]
[8] Sixty queens[x] there may be,
    and eighty concubines, [y]
    and virgins beyond number;

5:13 [c] S SS 2:1
[d] ver 5
5:14 [e] S Job 28:6
5:15 [f] 1Ki 4:33;
SS 7:4
5:16 [g] SS 4:3
[h] SS 7:9 [i] SS 1:5
6:1 [j] SS 5:6
[k] S SS 1:8
6:2 [l] SS 5:6
[m] S SS 4:12 [n] SS 5:13
6:3 [o] SS 7:10
[p] S SS 2:16
6:4 [q] S Jos 12:24;
S 1Ki 15:33 [r] Ps 48:2;
50:2 [s] S Nu 1:52
6:5 [t] S SS 4:1
6:6 [u] S SS 4:2
6:7 [v] S Ge 24:65
[w] SS 4:3
6:8 [x] S Ge 22:24;
[y] S Ge 22:24;
S Est 2:14

5:14 *topaz.* See note on Eze 1:16. *lapis lazuli.* Hebrew *sappir* (from which the English word *sapphire* comes).

5:15 *appearance is like Lebanon.* Awesome and majestic. *choice as its cedars.* The cedars of Lebanon were renowned throughout the ancient Near East, and their wood was desired for adorning temples and palaces (see 3:9; 1Ki 5:16 and note).

5:16 *mouth.* The beloved's kisses and loving speech. *daughters of Jerusalem.* See note on 1:5.

6:1 The question asked by the friends forms a transition from the darling's description of her beloved to her delighted acknowledgment of his intimacy with her and the exclusiveness of their relationship.

6:2 *his garden.* His darling. *beds of spices.* Her sensuous attractions (cf. 5:13). *browse.* Enjoy (see note on 2:16). *gather lilies.* See note on 2:1. The beloved, enjoying intimacies with his darling, is compared to a graceful gazelle (see notes on 2:7,9) nibbling from lily to lily in undisturbed enjoyment of exotic delicacies.

6:3 *I... mine.* See note on 2:16. Notice the reversal; here her

yielding to her beloved is emphasized.

6:4 *Tirzah.* An old Canaanite city in the middle of the land (see Jos 12:24). It was chosen by Jeroboam I (930–909 B.C.) as the first royal city of the northern kingdom (see 1Ki 14:17; see also 1Ki 15:21; 16:23–24). The meaning of its name ("pleasure, beauty") suggests that it was a beautiful site, perhaps explaining why the author here sets it alongside Jerusalem (though what constituted the beauty of Tirzah is not known). Comparison of the darling's beauty to that of cities was perhaps not so unusual in the ancient Near East, since cities were regularly depicted as women (see note on 2Ki 19:21). *majestic.* See v. 10. *as troops with banners.* The darling's noble beauty evoked in her beloved emotions like those aroused by a troop marching under its banners.

6:5–7 See 4:1–3 and notes.

6:5 *your eyes... overwhelm me.* The darling's eyes awaken in her beloved such intensity of love that he is held captive (see 4:9).

6:8 *queens... concubines... virgins.* The reference is either to Solomon's harem or to all the beautiful women of the realm.

6:9 z S SS 1:15
a SS 5:2 b SS 3:4
6:11 c SS 7:12
6:13 d S Ex 15:20
7:1 e Ps 45:13
7:3 f SS 4:5
7:4 g S Ps 144:12
h Nu 21:26 i S SS 5:15
7:5 j Isa 35:2

9 but my dove, z my perfect one, a is unique,
   the only daughter of her mother,
   the favorite of the one who bore her. b
The young women saw her and called her blessed;
   the queens and concubines praised her.

FRIENDS

10 Who is this that appears like the dawn,
   fair as the moon, bright as the sun,
   majestic as the stars in procession?

HE

11 I went down to the grove of nut trees
   to look at the new growth in the valley,
to see if the vines had budded
   or the pomegranates were in bloom. c
12 Before I realized it,
   my desire set me among the royal chariots of my people. a

FRIENDS

*13 Come back, come back, O Shulammite;
   come back, come back, that we may gaze on you!

HE

Why would you gaze on the Shulammite
   as on the dance d of Mahanaim?

*How beautiful your sandaled feet,
   O prince's e daughter!
Your graceful legs are like jewels,
   the work of an artist's hands.
2 Your navel is a rounded goblet
   that never lacks blended wine.
Your waist is a mound of wheat
   encircled by lilies.
3 Your breasts f are like two fawns,
   like twin fawns of a gazelle.
4 Your neck is like an ivory tower. g
Your eyes are the pools of Heshbon h
   by the gate of Bath Rabbim.
Your nose is like the tower of Lebanon i
   looking toward Damascus.
5 Your head crowns you like Mount Carmel. j

---

a 12 Or *among the chariots of Amminadab; or among the chariots of the people of the prince*
* 6:13 is numbered 7:1 in Hebrew texts.   * 7:1-13 is numbered 7:2-14 in Hebrew texts.

6:9 *perfect one.* Cf. "flawless one" in 5:2. *only daughter.* Not literally, but the one uniquely loved (cf. Ge 22:2 and note; Jdg 11:34; Pr 4:3). *young women…praised her.* All the other women praised her beauty (see 1:8; 5:9; 6:1).
6:10 See 5:9; 6:1.
6:11 *nut.* Perhaps walnut. *look…in the valley.* For the first signs of spring (see note on 2:11–13).
6:12 The most obscure verse in the Song. See TNIV text note for other possible translations. *chariots.* Solomon was famous for his chariots (1Ki 10:26).
6:13 *Shulammite.* The darling. It is either a variant of "Shunammite" (see 1Ki 1:3), i.e., a young woman from Shunem (see Jos 19:18), or a feminine form of the word "Solomon," meaning "Solomon's girl." In ancient Semitic languages the letters *l* and *n* were sometimes interchanged. *Mahanaim.* Perhaps the town in Gilead (see note on 2Sa 2:8).
7:1–7 Here the description moves up from the feet rather than down from the head (cf. 5:11–15).

7:1 Cf. v. 6. *prince's daughter.* Alludes to the nobility of her beauty (see Ps 45:13). *graceful.* The Hebrew for this word suggests "curvaceous."
7:2 *goblet.* A large, two-handled, ring-based bowl (see Ex 24:6; Isa 22:24; see also Am 6:6). *encircled by lilies.* The darling perhaps wore a loose garland of flowers around her waist.
7:3 See note on 4:5.
7:4 *ivory tower.* Mixed imagery, referring to shape as well as to color and texture. *pools.* The darling's eyes reflect like the surface of a pool; or the imagery may depict serenity and gentleness. *Heshbon.* Once the royal city of King Sihon (Nu 21:26), it was blessed with an abundant supply of spring water. *Bath Rabbim.* Means "daughter of many"; perhaps a popular name for Heshbon. *tower of Lebanon.* Perhaps a military tower on the northern frontier of Solomon's kingdom, but more likely the beautiful, towering Lebanon mountain range.
7:5 *Mount Carmel.* A promontory midway along the western coast of the kingdom, with a wooded top and known for its

Your hair is like royal tapestry;
 the king is held captive by its tresses.
[6] How beautiful [k] you are and how pleasing,
 my love, with your delights! [l]
[7] Your stature is like that of the palm,
 and your breasts [m] like clusters of fruit.
[8] I said, "I will climb the palm tree;
 I will take hold of its fruit."
May your breasts be like clusters of grapes on the vine,
 the fragrance of your breath like apples, [n]
[9] and your mouth like the best wine.

SHE

May the wine go straight to my beloved, [o]
 flowing gently over lips and teeth. [a]
[10] I belong to my beloved,
 and his desire [p] is for me. [q]
[11] Come, my beloved, let us go to the countryside,
 let us spend the night in the villages. [b]
[12] Let us go early to the vineyards [r]
 to see if the vines have budded, [s]
if their blossoms [t] have opened,
 and if the pomegranates [u] are in bloom [v]—
there I will give you my love.
[13] The mandrakes [w] send out their fragrance,
 and at our door is every delicacy,
both new and old,
 that I have stored up for you, my beloved. [x]

8

If only you were to me like a brother,
 who was nursed at my mother's breasts!
Then, if I found you outside,
 I would kiss you,
 and no one would despise me.
[2] I would lead you
 and bring you to my mother's house [y]—
 she who has taught me.
I would give you spiced wine to drink,
 the nectar of my pomegranates.
[3] His left arm is under my head
 and his right arm embraces me. [z]
[4] Daughters of Jerusalem, I charge you:
 Do not arouse or awaken love
 until it so desires. [a]

FRIENDS

[5] Who is this coming up from the wilderness [b]
 leaning on her beloved?

7:6 [k] S SS 1:15
[l] SS 4:10
7:7 [m] SS 4:5
7:8 [n] SS 2:5
7:9 [o] SS 5:16
7:10 [p] Ps 45:11
[q] SS 2:16; 6:3
7:12 [r] S SS 1:6
[s] SS 2:15 [t] SS 2:13
[u] S SS 4:13 [v] SS 6:11
7:13 [w] S Ge 30:14
[x] SS 4:16
8:2 [y] SS 3:4
8:3 [z] SS 2:6
8:4 [a] SS 2:7; 3:5
8:5 [b] SS 3:6

---

[a] 9 Septuagint, Aquila, Vulgate and Syriac; Hebrew *lips of sleepers*   [b] 11 Or *the henna bushes*

---

beauty. *royal tapestry.* A reference to purple, royal cloth, as in 3:10 (see note on Ex 25:4). *king.* Solomon. *tresses.* The Hebrew for this word suggests a similarity to flowing water (cf. 4:1; 6:5).
7:7 *palm.* The stately date palm.
7:8 *I said.* To myself. *I will climb.* The darling's beauty draws him irresistibly. *vine.* Grape. *apples.* Perhaps the fragrance of apple blossoms (but see note on 2:3).
7:9 *May the wine … to my beloved.* The darling offers the wine (see 5:1) of her love to her beloved.
7:10 *I belong.* See notes on 2:16; 6:3. *desire.* Cf. Ge 3:16.
7:11–12 In 2:10–13 the darling reports a similar invitation from her beloved.
7:12 *I will give you my love.* She offers herself completely to her beloved.

7:13 *mandrakes.* Short-stemmed herbs associated with fertility (see note on Ge 30:14). The odor of its blossom is pungent. *at our door.* Where the lovers meet. *every delicacy.* Metaphor for the delights the darling has for her beloved from her "garden" (cf. 4:13–14). *both new and old.* Those already shared and those still to be enjoyed.
8:1 *no one would despise me.* The darling could openly show affection without any public disgrace.
8:2 *I would give you.* She would offer her beloved the delights of her love. *nectar.* The Hebrew for this word refers to intoxicating juices.
8:4 See 2:7 and note.
8:5 *Who … wilderness.* See 3:6 and note. *Under the apple tree.* In

8:5 ᶜS SS 3:4
8:6 ᵈS SS 1:2
ᵉS Nu 5:14
8:7 ᶠS Pr 6:35
8:11 ᵍEcc 2:4
ʰIsa 7:23
8:12 ⁱS SS 1:6

SHE

Under the apple tree I roused you;
there your mother conceived ᶜ you,
there she who was in labor gave you birth.
⁶ Place me like a seal over your heart,
like a seal on your arm;
for love ᵈ is as strong as death,
its jealousy ᵃ ᵉ unyielding as the grave.
It burns like blazing fire,
like a mighty flame. ᵇ
⁷ Many waters cannot quench love;
rivers cannot sweep it away.
If one were to give
all the wealth of one's house for love,
it ᶜ would be utterly scorned. ᶠ

FRIENDS

⁸ We have a little sister,
and her breasts are not yet grown.
What shall we do for our sister
on the day she is spoken for?
⁹ If she is a wall,
we will build towers of silver on her.
If she is a door,
we will enclose her with panels of cedar.

SHE

¹⁰ I am a wall,
and my breasts are like towers.
Thus I have become in his eyes
like one bringing contentment.
¹¹ Solomon had a vineyard ᵍ in Baal Hamon;
he let out his vineyard to tenants.
Each was to bring for its fruit
a thousand shekels ᵈ ʰ of silver.
¹² But my own vineyard ⁱ is mine to give;

ᵃ 6 Or *ardor*   ᵇ 6 Or *fire, / like the very flame of the* L ORD   ᶜ 7 Or *he*   ᵈ 11 That is, about 25 pounds or about 11.5 kilograms; also in verse 12

---

the ancient world, sexual union and birth were often associated with fruit trees.

8:6–7 *love is … grave. It burns … flame. Many waters … away.* These three wisdom statements (see essay, p. 750) characterize marital love as the strongest, most unyielding and invincible force in human experience. With these statements the Song reaches its literary climax and discloses its purpose.

8:6 *seal.* Seals were precious to their owners, as personal as their names (see note on Ge 38:18). *arm.* Probably a poetic synonym for "hand." *unyielding as the grave.* As the grave will not give up the dead, so love will not surrender the loved one. *mighty flame.* The Hebrew expression conveys the idea of a most intense flame, hinting that it has been kindled by the Lord (see TNIV text note).

8:7 *Many waters.* Words that suggest not only the ocean depths (see Ps 107:23) but also the primeval waters that the people of the ancient Near East regarded as a permanent threat to the world (see note on Ps 32:6). The waters were also associated with the realm of the dead (see note on Ps 30:1). *If one … scorned.* A fourth wisdom statement (see note on vv. 6–7), declaring love's unsurpassed worth.

8:8–14 In the closing lines of the Song, the words of the brothers (vv. 8–9), the darling's reference to her own vineyard (v. 12) and her final reference to Solomon (vv. 11–12) suggest a return to the beginning of the Song (see 1:2–7; see also Introduction:

Literary Features). The lines may recall the darling's development into the age for love and marriage and the blossoming of her relationship with her beloved.

8:8 In the ancient Near East, brothers were often guardians of their sisters, especially in matters pertaining to marriage (see Ge 24:50–60; 34:13–27). *the day she is spoken for.* Marriage was often contracted at an early age.

8:9 This imaginative verse probably expresses the brothers' determination to defend their young sister (the darling) until her proper time for love and marriage has come. Or it may mean that the brothers are concerned to see that she is properly adorned for marriage before she is spoken for.

8:10 *I … like towers.* In contrast to the time when she was watched over by her brothers, the darling rejoices in her maturity (cf. Eze 16:7–8). *his.* The beloved's.

8:11–12 *thousand shekels … two hundred.* Whether these figures are to be taken literally (see Isa 7:23) is uncertain.

8:11 *Baal Hamon.* Location unknown. The Hebrew *hamon* sometimes means "wealth" or "abundance"; hence Baal (i.e., "lord") Hamon could mean "lord of abundance," bringing to mind Solomon's great wealth.

8:12 *my own vineyard.* Her body (see note on 1:6). *mine to give.* As Solomon is master of his vineyard, so the darling is mistress of her attractions to dispense as she will. She offers Solomon the owner's portion of her vineyard.

the thousand shekels are for you, Solomon,
and two hundred[a] are for those who tend its fruit.

8:14 /S Pr 5:19
k SS 2:9 /S SS 2:8,
17

HE

¹³ You who dwell in the gardens
with friends in attendance,
let me hear your voice!

SHE

¹⁴ Come away, my beloved,
and be like a gazelle[j]
or like a young stag[k]
on the spice-laden mountains.[l]

---

[a] 12 That is, about 5 pounds or about 2.3 kilograms

8:13 *in the gardens.* In 7:11–12 the darling invites her beloved to accompany her to the countryside and the vineyards. Here the imagery places her appropriately in a garden. *friends.* Male; perhaps the companions of the beloved (see 1:7). *let me hear* *your voice.* See 2:14.

8:14 *be like a gazelle or … stag.* Display your virile strength and agility for my delight (see note on 2:9). *on the spice-laden mountains.* Cf. 2:17.

ISAIAH | INTRODUCTION

In the Hebrew Bible the book of Isaiah initiates a division called the Latter Prophets (for the Former Prophets, see Introduction to Joshua: Title and Theological Theme), including also Jeremiah, Ezekiel and the Twelve Minor Prophets (so called because of their small size by comparison with the major prophetic books of Isaiah, Jeremiah and Ezekiel, and not at all suggesting that they are of minor importance; see essay, p. 1465). Thus Isaiah occupies pride of place among the Latter Prophets. This is fitting since he is sometimes referred to as the prince of the prophets.

AUTHOR

C Isaiah, son of Amoz, is often thought of as the greatest of the writing prophets. His name means "The LORD saves." He was a contemporary of Amos, Hosea and Micah, beginning his ministry in 740 B.C., the year King Uzziah died (see note on 6:1). According to an unsubstantiated Jewish tradition (*The Ascension of Isaiah*), he was sawed in half during the reign of Manasseh (cf. Heb 11:37). Isaiah was married and had at least two sons, Shear-Jashub (7:3) and Maher-Shalal-Hash-Baz (8:3). He probably spent most of his life in Jerusalem, enjoying his greatest influence under King Hezekiah (see 37:1–2). Isaiah is also credited with writing a history of the reign of King Uzziah (2Ch 26:22).

Many scholars today challenge the claim that Isaiah wrote the entire book that bears his name. Yet his is the only name attached to it (see 1:1; 2:1; 13:1). The strongest argument for the unity of Isaiah is the expression "the Holy One of Israel," a title for God that occurs 12 times in chs. 1–39 and 14 times in chs. 40–66. Outside Isaiah it appears in the OT only 6 times. There are other striking verbal parallels between chs. 1–39 and chs. 40–66. Compare the following verses:

1:2	66:24
1:5–6	53:4–5
5:27	40:30
6:1	52:13; 57:15
6:11–12	62:4
11:1	53:2
11:6–9	65:25
11:12	49:22
35:10	51:11

Altogether, there are at least 25 Hebrew words or forms found in Isaiah (i.e., in both major divisions of the book) that occur in no other prophetic writing.

Isaiah's use of fire as a figure of punishment (see 1:31; 10:17; 26:11; 33:11–14; 34:9–10; 66:24), his references to the "holy mountain" of Jerusalem (see note on 2:2–4) and his mention of the highway to Jerusalem (see note on 11:16) are themes that recur throughout the book.

The structure of Isaiah also argues for its unity. Chs. 36–39 constitute a historical interlude that concludes chs. 1–35 and introduces chs. 40–66 (see note on 36:1).

Several NT verses refer to the prophet Isaiah in connection with various parts of the book: Mt 12:17–21 (Isa 42:1–4); Mt 3:3 and Lk 3:4 (Isa 40:3); Ro 10:16,20 (Isa 53:1; 65:1); see especially Jn 12:38–41 (Isa 53:1; 6:10).

DATE

Most of the events referred to in chs. 1–39 occurred during Isaiah's ministry (see 6:1; 14:28; 36:1), so these chapters may have been completed not long after 701 B.C., the year the Assyrian army was destroyed (see note on 10:16). The prophet lived until at least 681 (see note on 37:38) and may have written chs. 40–66 during his later years. In his message to the exiles of the sixth century B.C., Isaiah was projected into the future, just as Ezekiel was in Eze 40–48.

BACKGROUND

Isaiah wrote during the stormy period marking the expansion of the Assyrian empire and the decline of Israel. Under King Tiglath-Pileser III (745–727 B.C.) the Assyrians swept westward into Aram (Syria) and Canaan. In about 733 the kings of Aram and Israel tried to pressure Ahaz, king of Judah, into joining a coalition against Assyria. Ahaz chose instead to ask Tiglath-Pileser for help, a decision condemned by Isaiah (see note on 7:1). Assyria did assist Judah and conquered the northern kingdom in 722–721. This made Judah even more vulnerable, and in 701 King Sennacherib of Assyria threatened Jerusalem itself (see 36:1 and note). The godly King Hezekiah prayed earnestly, and Isaiah predicted that God would force the Assyrians to withdraw from the city (37:6–7).

Nevertheless, Isaiah warned Judah that her sin would bring captivity at the hands of Babylon. The visit of the Babylonian king's envoys to Hezekiah set the stage for this prediction (see 39:1,6 and notes). Although the fall of Jerusalem would not take place until 586 B.C., Isaiah assumes the destruction of Judah and proceeds to predict the restoration of the people from captivity (see 40:2–3 and notes). God would redeem his people from Babylon, just as he had rescued them from Egypt (see notes on 35:9; 41:14). Isaiah predicts the rise of Cyrus the Persian, who would unite the Medes and Persians and conquer Babylon in 539 (see 41:2 and note). The decree of Cyrus would allow the Jews to return home in 538/537, a deliverance that prefigured the greater salvation from sin through Christ (see 52:7 and note).

THEMES AND THEOLOGY

C Isaiah is a book that unveils the full dimensions of God's judgment and salvation. God is "the Holy One of Israel" (see 1:4; 6:1 and notes) who must punish his rebellious people (1:2) but will afterward redeem them (41:14,16). Israel is a nation blind and deaf (6:9–10; 42:7), a vineyard that will be trampled (5:1–7), a people devoid of justice or righteousness (5:7; 10:1–2). The awful judgment that will be unleashed upon Israel and all the nations that defy God is called "the day of the LORD." Although Israel has a foretaste of that day (5:30; 42:25), the nations bear its full power (see 2:11,17,20 and note). It is a day associated in the NT with Christ's second coming and the accompanying judgment (see 24:1,21; 34:1–2 and notes). Throughout the book God's judgment is referred to as "fire" (see 1:31; 30:33 and notes). He is the "Sovereign LORD" (see note on 25:8), far above all nations and rulers (40:15–24).

Yet God will have compassion on his people (14:1–2) and will rescue them from both political and spiritual oppression. Their restoration is like a new exodus (43:2,16–19; 52:10–12) as God redeems them (see 35:9; 41:14 and notes) and saves them (see 43:3; 49:8 and notes). Israel's mighty Creator (40:21–22; 48:13) will make streams spring up in the desert (32:2) as he graciously leads them home. The theme of a highway for the return of exiles is a prominent one (see 11:16; 40:3 and notes) in both major parts of the book. The Lord raises a banner to summon the nations to bring Israel home (see 5:26 and note).

Peace and safety mark this new Messianic age (11:6–9). A king descended from David will reign in righteousness (9:7; 32:1), and all nations will stream to the holy mountain of Jerusalem (see 2:2–4 and note). God's people will no longer be oppressed by wicked rulers (11:14; 45:14), and Jerusalem will truly be the "City of the LORD" (60:14).

The Lord calls the Messianic King "my servant" in chs. 42–53, a term also applied to Israel as a nation (see 41:8–9; 42:1 and notes). It is through the suffering of the servant that salvation in its fullest sense is achieved. Cyrus was God's instrument to deliver Israel from Babylon (41:2), but Christ delivered humankind from the prison of sin (52:13—53:12). He became a "light for the Gentiles" (42:6), so that those nations that faced judgment (chs. 13–23) could find salvation (55:4–5). These Gentiles also became "servants of the LORD" (see 54:17 and note).

The Lord's kingdom on earth, with its righteous Ruler and his righteous subjects, is the goal toward which the book of Isaiah steadily moves. The restored earth and the restored people will then conform to the divine ideal, and all will result in the praise and glory of the Holy One of Israel for what he has accomplished.

LITERARY FEATURES

Isaiah contains both prose and poetry; the beauty of its poetry is unsurpassed in the OT. The main prose material is found in chs. 36–39, the historical interlude that unites the two parts of the book (see Author). The poetic material includes a series of oracles in chs. 13–23. A taunting song against the king of Babylon is found in 14:4–23. Chs. 24–27 comprise an apocalyptic section stressing the last days (see note on 24:1—27:13). A wisdom poem is found in 28:23–29 (also cf. 32:5–8). The song of the vineyard (5:1–7) begins as a love song as Isaiah describes God's relationship with Israel. Hymns of praise are given in 12:1–6 and 38:10–20, and a national lament occurs in 63:7—64:12. The poetry is indeed rich and varied, as is the prophet's vocabulary (he uses a larger vocabulary of Hebrew words than any other OT writer).

One of Isaiah's favorite techniques is personification. The sun and moon are ashamed (24:23), while the desert and parched land rejoice (see 35:1 and note) and the mountains and forests burst into song (44:23). The trees "clap their hands" (55:12). A favorite figure is the vineyard, which represents Israel (5:7). Treading the winepress is a picture of judgment (see 63:3 and note), and to drink God's "cup of wrath" is to stagger under his punishment (see 51:17 and note). Isaiah uses the name "Rock" to describe God (17:10), and animals such as Leviathan and Rahab represent nations (see 27:1; 30:7; 51:9).

The power of Isaiah's imagery is seen in 30:27–33, and he makes full use of sarcasm in his denunciation of idols in 44:9–20. A forceful example of wordplay appears in 5:7 (see note there), and one finds inversion in 6:10 (see note there; see also note on 16:7) and alliteration and assonance in 24:16-17 (see note there). The "overwhelming scourge" of 28:15,18 is an illustration of mixed metaphor.

Isaiah often alludes to earlier events in Israel's history, especially the exodus from Egypt. The crossing of the Red Sea forms the background for 11:15 and 43:2, 16–17, and other allusions occur in 4:5–6; 31:5; 37:36 (see notes on these verses). The overthrow of Sodom and Gomorrah is referred to in 1:9, and Gideon's victory over Midian is mentioned in 9:4; 10:26 (see also 28:21). Several times Isaiah draws upon the song of Moses in Dt 32 (compare 1:2 with Dt 32:1; 30:17 with Dt 32:30; and 43:11,13 with Dt 32:39). Isaiah, like Moses, called the nation to repentance and to faith in a holy, all-powerful God. See also note on 49:8.

The refrain in 48:22 and 57:21 divides the last 27 chapters into three sections of nine chapters each (40–48; 49–57; 58–66; see Outline).

1 The vision *a* concerning Judah and Jerusalem *b* that Isaiah son of Amoz saw *c* during the reigns of Uzziah, *d* Jotham, *e* Ahaz *f* and Hezekiah, *g* kings of Judah.

A REBELLIOUS NATION

² Hear me, you heavens! Listen, earth! *h*
  For the LORD has spoken: *i*
"I reared children *j* and brought them up,
  but they have rebelled *k* against me.
³ The ox knows *l* its master,
  the donkey its owner's manger, *m*
but Israel does not know, *n*
  my people do not understand. *o*"

⁴ Ah, sinful nation,
  a people whose guilt is great, *p*
a brood of evildoers, *q*
  children given to corruption! *r*
They have forsaken *s* the LORD;
  they have spurned the Holy One *t* of Israel
  and turned their backs *u* on him.

⁵ Why should you be beaten *v* anymore?
  Why do you persist *w* in rebellion? *x*
Your whole head is injured,
  your whole heart *y* afflicted. *z*
⁶ From the sole of your foot to the top of your head *a*
  there is no soundness *b*—
only wounds and welts *c*
  and open sores,
not cleansed or bandaged *d*
  or soothed with olive oil. *e*

⁷ Your country is desolate, *f*
  your cities burned with fire; *g*
your fields are being stripped by foreigners *h*
  right before you,
  laid waste as when overthrown by strangers. *i*
⁸ Daughter Zion *j* is left *k*
  like a shelter in a vineyard,
like a hut *l* in a field of melons,
  like a city under siege.
⁹ Unless the LORD Almighty
  had left us some survivors, *m*

1:1 *a* 1Sa 3:1;
Isa 22:1,5; Ob 1:1;
Na 1:1 *b* Isa 40:9;
44:26 *c* Isa 2:1; 13:1
d 2Ki 14:21;
S 2Ch 26:22
e S 1Ch 3:12
f S 2Ki 16:1
g S 1Ch 3:13
1:2 *h* S Dt 4:26
i Jdg 11:10; Jer 42:5;
Mic 1:2 *j* Isa 23:4;
63:16 *k* ver 4, 23;
Isa 24:5, 20; 30:1, 9;
46:8; 48:8; 57:4; 65:2;
66:24; Eze 24:3;
Hag 1:12; Mal 1:6; 3:5
1:3 *l* Job 12:9
m S Ge 42:27
n Jer 4:22; 5:4; 9:3, 6;
Hos 2:8; 4:1
o S Dt 32:28;
Isa 42:25; 48:8;
Hos 4:6; 7:9
1:4 *p* Isa 5:18
q S ver 2; Isa 9:17;
14:20; 31:2; Jer 23:14
r Ps 14:3 *s* S Dt 32:15;
S Ps 119:87
t S 2Ki 19:22; Isa 5:19,
24; 31:1; 37:23; 41:14;
43:14; 45:11; 47:4;
Eze 39:7 *u* S Pr 30:9;
Isa 59:13
1:5 *v* Pr 20:30
w Jer 2:30; 5:3; 8:5
x S ver 2; Isa 31:6;
Jer 44:16-17;
Heb 3:16 *y* La 2:11;
5:17 *z* Isa 30:26; 33:6,
24; 58:8; Jer 30:17
1:6 *a* S Dt 28:35
b Ps 38:3 *c* Isa 53:5
d S Ps 147:3;
Isa 30:26; Jer 8:22;
14:19; 30:17; La 2:13;
Eze 34:4 *e* 2Sa 14:2;
Ps 23:5; 45:7; 104:15;
Isa 61:3; Lk 10:34
1:7 *f* S Lev 26:34
g S Lev 26:31;
S Dt 29:23
h Lev 26:16; Jdg 6:3-
6; Isa 62:8; Jer 5:17
i S 2Ki 18:13;
S Ps 109:11
1:8 *j* S Ps 9:14;
S Isa 10:32 *k* Isa 30:17;
49:21 *l* S Job 27:18
1:9 *m* S Ge 45:7;
S 2Ki 21:14; Isa 4:2;
6:13; 27:12; 28:5; 37:4,
31-32; 45:25; 56:8;
Jer 23:3; Joel 2:32

1:1—6:13 The first section of Isaiah's prophecies, dominated by oracles of judgment and climaxing in Isaiah's commission, found in ch. 6 (cf. note on 7:1—12:6).
1:1—31 Compare the indictment of ch. 1 with that of ch. 5; the two enclose the first series of oracles. Ch. 1 also serves as an introduction to the whole book.
1:1 The title of the book. Other headings occur in 2:1; 13:1; 14:28; 15:1; 17:1; 19:1; 21:1,11,13; 22:1; 23:1. *vision.* In the sense of "revelation" or "prophecy" (see Pr 29:18; Ob 1 and notes; see also 1Sa 3:1). *Amoz.* Not to be confused with the prophet Amos. *Uzziah, Jotham, Ahaz and Hezekiah.* These kings reigned from 792 to 686 B.C. None of the kings of Israel is mentioned since Isaiah ministered primarily to the southern kingdom (Judah).

A **1:2** Isaiah begins and ends (66:24) with a condemnation of those who rebel against God. The prophet calls on the heavens and the earth to testify to the truth of God's accusation against Israel and the rightness of his judgment—since they were witnesses of his covenant (see Dt 30:19 and note; 31:28; 32:1; Ps 50:1 and note).

A **1:3** *manger.* Feeding trough. *does not know.* Refusal to know and understand God later resulted in Judah's exile

from her land (5:13).
1:4 *Holy One of Israel.* Occurs 26 times in Isaiah (see especially 5:24) and only 6 times elsewhere in the OT (see Introduction: Author). *Holy One.* See Ex 3:5; Lev 11:44 and notes.
1:5—6 The pitiable moral and spiritual condition of Israel is transferred to the suffering servant in 53:4–5. The Hebrew words for "beaten," "injured" and "welts" correspond to those for "stricken," "pain" and "wounds."
1:6 The disease ravages the entire body, as with Job (2:7). *oil.* Commonly used for treating wounds (see Lk 10:34).
1:7—9 The desolation of the land of Judah is the result of foreign invasion: e.g., by Aram, the northern kingdom of Israel, Edom and Philistia (2Ch 28:5–18); later (701 B.C.) by King Sennacherib and the Assyrian army (36:1–2); still later (605–586) by King Nebuchadnezzar and the Neo-Babylonian army.
1:8 *Daughter Zion.* A personification of Jerusalem (see note on 2Ki 19:21). *shelter ... hut.* Temporary structures used by watchmen (Job 27:18), who were on the lookout for thieves and intruders. Thus Jerusalem was not very defensible. *melons.* Or possibly "cucumbers."

1:9 ⁿ S Ge 19:24;
Ro 9:29*
1:10 ⁿ Isa 28:14
ᴾ S Ge 13:13; S 18:20;
Eze 16:49; Ro 9:29;
Rev 11:8 �q Isa 5:24;
8:20; 30:9 ʳ Isa 13:19
1:11 ˢ Ps 50:8;
Am 6:4 ᵗ S Job 22:3
ᵘ Isa 66:3; Jer 6:20
ᵛ 1Sa 15:22;
S Ps 40:6; Mal 1:10;
Heb 10:4
1:12 ʷ Ex 23:17;
Dt 31:11
1:13 ˣ Pr 15:8;
Isa 66:3; Hag 2:14
ʸ Jer 7:9; 18:15; 44:8
ᶻ S 1Ki 14:24;
Ps 115:8; Pr 28:9;
Isa 41:24; Mal 2:11
ᵃ S Nu 10:10
ᵇ 1Ch 23:31
1:14 ᶜ S Ne 10:33
ᵈ Ex 12:16; Lev 23:1-
44; Nu 28:11-29:39;
Dt 16:1-17; Isa 5:12;
29:1; Hos 2:11
ᵉ S Ps 11:5 ᶠ S Job 7:12
ᵍ Ps 69:3; Isa 7:13;
43:22,24; Jer 44:22;
Mal 2:17; 3:14
1:15 ʰ S Ex 9:29
ⁱ S Dt 31:17; Isa 57:17;
59:2 ʲ S Dt 1:45;
S 1Sa 8:18;
S Job 15:31; S Jn 9:31
ᵏ S Job 9:30 ˡ Isa 4:4;
59:3; Jer 2:34;
Eze 7:23; Hos 4:2;
Joel 3:21
1:16 ᵐ S Ru 3:3;
Mt 27:24; Jas 4:8
ⁿ Nu 19:11,16;
Isa 52:11 ⁿ Isa 55:7;
Jer 25:5
1:17 ⁿ S Ps 34:14
ᵠ S Ps 72:1; Isa 11:4;
33:5; 56:1; 61:8;
Am 5:14-15; Mic 6:8;
Zep 2:3 ʳ S Dt 14:29
ˢ ver 23; Job 22:9;
Ps 82:3; 94:6; Isa 10:2
ᵗ S Ex 22:22;
Eze 18:31; 22:7;
Lk 18:3; Jas 1:27
1:18 ᵘ S 1Sa 2:25;
Isa 41:1; 43:9,26
ᵛ S Ps 51:7; Rev 7:14
ʷ Isa 55:7
1:19 ˣ S Job 36:11;
S Isa 50:10
ʸ Dt 30:15-16;
Ezr 9:12; Isa 34:10;
Isa 30:23; 55:2; 58:14;
62:9; 65:13,21-22

we would have become like Sodom,
   we would have been like Gomorrah. ⁿ

10 Hear the word of the Lᴏʀᴅ, ᵒ
   you rulers of Sodom; ᵖ
listen to the instruction ᵠ of our God,
   you people of Gomorrah! ʳ
11 "The multitude of your sacrifices—
   what are they to me?" says the Lᴏʀᴅ.
"I have more than enough of burnt offerings,
   of rams and the fat of fattened animals; ˢ
I have no pleasure ᵗ
   in the blood of bulls ᵘ and lambs and goats. ᵛ
12 When you come to appear before me,
   who has asked this of you, ʷ
   this trampling of my courts?
13 Stop bringing meaningless offerings! ˣ
   Your incense ʸ is detestable ᶻ to me.
New Moons, ᵃ Sabbaths and convocations ᵇ—
   I cannot bear your evil assemblies.
14 Your New Moon ᶜ feasts and your appointed festivals ᵈ
   I hate with all my being. ᵉ
They have become a burden to me; ᶠ
   I am weary ᵍ of bearing them.
15 When you spread out your hands ʰ in prayer,
   I will hide ⁱ my eyes from you;
even if you offer many prayers,
   I will not listen. ʲ
Your hands ᵏ are full of blood; ˡ
16   wash ᵐ and make yourselves clean.
Take your evil deeds
   out of my sight! ⁿ
Stop doing wrong, ᵒ
17   learn to do right! ᵖ
Seek justice, ᵠ
   encourage the oppressed. ᵃ ʳ
Defend the cause of the fatherless, ˢ
   plead the case of the widow. ᵗ

18 "Come now, let us reason together," ᵘ
   says the Lᴏʀᴅ.
"Though your sins are like scarlet,
   they shall be as white as snow; ᵛ
though they are red as crimson,
   they shall be like wool. ʷ
19 If you are willing and obedient, ˣ
   you will eat the best from the land; ʸ

ᵃ 17 Or justice, / rebuke the oppressor

1:9–10 *Sodom . . . Gomorrah.* Classic examples of sinful cities that were completely destroyed (see 3:9; Ge 13:13; 18:20–21; 19:5,24–25). Just as Jesus addressed Peter as though he were Satan (Mt 16:23), so Isaiah addresses his fellow Israelites as though they were the rulers of Sodom and the people of Gomorrah.
1:9 Quoted in Ro 9:29, where it is linked with Isa 10:22–23. Isaiah often refers to the remnant that will survive God's judgment on the nation and take possession of the land (see 4:3; 10:20–23; 11:11,16; 46:3).
1:11–15 The moral character and conduct of the worshipers, not the number of their religious activities, are most important (see 66:3; Jer 7:21–26; Hos 6:6; Am 5:21–24; Mic 6:6–8 and notes).
1:11 *fattened animals.* Those kept in confinement for special feeding.

1:14 *New Moon feasts.* Celebrated on the first day of each Hebrew month. Special sacrifices and feasts were part of the observance (see Nu 28:11–15). *appointed festivals.* Included the annual festivals, such as Passover, Weeks (Pentecost) and Tabernacles (Ex 23:14–17; 34:18–25; Lev 23; Dt 16:1–17).
1:15 *hide my eyes.* In 8:17; 59:2 God hides his face from Israel (see also Mic 3:4 and note).
1:17 See Jer 22:16 and note; Jas 1:27. *fatherless . . . widow.* Represented the weak and often oppressed part of society. Rulers were warned not to take advantage of them (see v. 23; 10:2; Jer 22:3).
1:18 *scarlet . . . crimson.* Refers to the blood that has stained the hands of murderers (see vv. 15,21). *white as snow.* A powerful figurative description of the result of forgiveness (see Ps 51:7 and note). This offer of forgiveness is conditioned on the reformation of life called for in v. 19.

²⁰ but if you resist and rebel, ^z
    you will be devoured by the sword." ^a
        For the mouth of the LORD has spoken. ^b

²¹ See how the faithful city
    has become a prostitute! ^c
She once was full of justice;
    righteousness ^d used to dwell in her—
    but now murderers! ^e
²² Your silver has become dross, ^f
    your choice wine is diluted with water.
²³ Your rulers are rebels, ^g
    companions of thieves; ^h
they all love bribes ⁱ
    and chase after gifts.
They do not defend the cause of the fatherless;
    the widow's case does not come before them. ^j
²⁴ Therefore the Lord, the LORD Almighty,
    the Mighty One ^k of Israel, declares:
"Ah, I will vent my wrath on my foes
    and avenge ^l myself on my enemies. ^m
²⁵ I will turn my hand against you; ⁿ
    I will thoroughly purge ^o away your dross ^p
    and remove all your impurities. ^q
²⁶ I will restore your judges as in days of old, ^r
    your rulers as at the beginning.
Afterward you will be called ^s
    the City of Righteousness, ^t
    the Faithful City. ^u"

²⁷ Zion will be delivered with justice,
    her penitent ^v ones with righteousness. ^w
²⁸ But rebels and sinners ^x will both be broken,
    and those who forsake ^y the LORD will perish. ^z

²⁹ "You will be ashamed ^a because of the sacred oaks ^b
    in which you have delighted;
you will be disgraced because of the gardens ^c
    that you have chosen.
³⁰ You will be like an oak with fading leaves, ^d
    like a garden without water.
³¹ The mighty man will become tinder
    and his work a spark;
both will burn together,
    with no one to quench the fire. ^e"

THE MOUNTAIN OF THE LORD

2:1–4pp — Mic 4:1–3

2 This is what Isaiah son of Amoz saw concerning Judah and Jerusalem: ^f

² In the last days ^g

1:19–20 *eat … be devoured.* The vivid contrast is stressed by the use of the same Hebrew verb.

🄰 **1:21** *become a prostitute.* Jerusalem (representing all Judah) has been unfaithful to the Lord. Here her unfaithfulness is specified as social abuse, exploitation of the powerless, and violence against one's neighbor—violating the Lord's moral order for the community of his people (see note on Ps 73:27; cf. note on Ex 34:15).

1:22 *Your silver has become dross.* See Ps 12:6 and note.

1:24 *The Lord, the LORD Almighty, the Mighty One of Israel.* Stressing God's sovereign authority as Judge (cf. Ps 50:1,6; cf. also Jos 22:22 and note). *the LORD Almighty.* See note on 1Sa 1:3.

1:25–26 *turn … restore.* The use of the same Hebrew verb em-

phasizes the contrast (see note on vv. 19–20).

1:25 *purge away your dross.* Purifying fire is also mentioned in 4:4; 48:10.

1:26 *Faithful City.* See v. 21. Using a related Hebrew noun, Zec 8:3 similarly refers to the future Jerusalem as the "City of Truth."

🄰 **1:27–28** This contrast between the redemption of Zion (Jerusalem) as a whole and the perishing of individuals who refuse to repent is developed in 65:8–16.

1:29 *sacred oaks … gardens.* Pagan sacrifices were offered and sexual immorality occurred at such places (see 65:3; 66:17).

1:31 *fire.* A figure of punishment (see 33:11–14; 34:9–10; see also note on La 1:13).

1:20 ^z S 1Sa 12:15
^a S Job 15:22;
Isa 3:25; 27:1; 65:12;
66:16; Jer 17:27
^b Nu 23:19; Isa 21:17;
34:16; 40:5; 58:14;
Jer 49:13; Mic 4:4;
Zec 1:6; Rev 1:16
1:21 ^c Isa 57:3-9;
Jer 2:20; 3:2,9; 13:27;
Eze 23:3; Hos 2:1-13
^d Isa 5:7; 46:13;
59:14; Am 6:12
^e S Pr 6:17
1:22 ^f S Ps 119:119
1:23 ^g S ver 2
^h S Dt 19:14; Mic 2:1-
2; 6:12 ⁱ S Ex 23:8;
Am 5:12 ^j Isa 10:2;
Jer 5:28; Eze 22:6-7;
Mic 3:9; Hab 1:4
1:24 ^k S Ge 49:24
^l Isa 34:2,8; 35:4;
47:3; 59:17; 61:2;
63:4; Jer 51:6;
Eze 5:13
^m S Dt 32:43;
S Isa 10:3
1:25 ⁿ Dt 28:63
^o S Ps 78:38
^p S Ps 119:119
^q 2Ch 29:15;
Isa 48:10; Jer 6:29;
9:7; Eze 22:22;
Mal 3:3
1:26 ^r Jer 33:7,11;
Mic 4:8 ^s S Ge 32:28
^t Isa 32:16; 33:5;
46:13; 48:18; 61:11;
62:1; Jer 31:23;
Zec 8:3 ^u Isa 4:3;
48:2; 52:1; 60:14;
62:2; 64:10; Da 9:24
1:27 ^v Isa 30:15;
31:6; 59:20; Eze 18:30
^w Isa 35:10; 41:14;
43:1; 52:3; 62:12;
63:4; Hos 2:19
1:28 ^x Isa 33:14;
43:27; 48:8; 50:1;
59:2; Jer 4:18
^y S Dt 32:15 ^z Ps 9:5;
Isa 24:20; 66:24;
Jer 16:4; 42:22; 44:12;
2Th 1:8-9
1:29 ^a Ps 97:7;
Isa 42:17; 44:9,11;
45:16; Jer 10:14
^b Isa 57:5; Eze 6:13;
Hos 4:13 ^c Isa 65:3;
66:17
1:30 ^d S Ps 1:3
1:31 ^e Isa 4:4; 5:24;
9:18-19; 10:17; 24:6;
26:11; 30:27,33;
33:14; 34:10; 66:15-
16,24; Jer 5:14; 7:20;
21:12; Ob 1:18;
Mal 3:2; 4:1;
S Mt 25:41
2:1 ^f Isa 1:1
2:2 ^g Ac 2:17;
Heb 1:2

2:2 *h* Isa 11:9; 24:23;
25:6,10; 27:13; 56:7;
57:13; 65:25; 66:20;
Jer 31:23; Da 11:45;
Joel 3:17; Mic 4:7
i Isa 65:9 *j* Zec 14:10
k Ps 102:15;
Jer 16:19
2:3 *l* Isa 45:23; 49:1;
60:3-6,14; 66:18;
Jer 3:17; Joel 3:2;
Zep 3:8; Zec 14:2
m Isa 45:14; 49:12,23;
55:5 *n* Dt 33:19;
S Ps 137:5
o S Isa 1:10; 33:22;
51:4,7 *p* Lk 24:47;
S Jn 4:22
2:4 *q* Ps 7:6; S 9:19;
96:13; 98:9; Isa 1:27;
3:13; 9:7; 42:4; 51:4;
Joel 3:14 *r* S Ge 49:10
s Joel 3:10 *t* Ps 46:9;
Isa 9:5; 11:6-9; 32:18;
57:19; 65:25;
Jer 30:10; Da 11:45;
Hos 2:18; Mic 4:3;
Zec 9:10
2:5 *u* Isa 58:1
v Isa 60:19-20;
1Jn 1:5,7
2:6 *w* S Dt 31:17
x Jer 12:7 *y* S Dt 18:10;
S Isa 44:25
z S 2Ki 1:2;
S 2Ch 26:6 *a* Pr 6:1
b S 2Ki 16:7; Mic 5:12
2:7 *c* S Dt 17:17
d S Ps 17:14
e S Dt 17:16
f S Ge 41:43; Isa 31:1;
Mic 5:10
2:8 *g* Isa 10:9-11;
Rev 9:20 *h* Isa 44:17
i S 2Ch 32:19;
S Ps 135:15; Mic 5:13
j Isa 17:8
2:9 *k* Ps 62:9 *l* ver 11,
17; Isa 5:15; 13:11
m S Ne 4:5
2:10 *n* ver 19;
Na 3:11 *o* S Ps 145:12;
2Th 1:9; Rev 6:15-16
2:11 *p* S Ne 9:29;
Hab 2:5 *q* S ver 9

the mountain *h* of the LORD's temple will be established
    as the highest of the mountains; *i*
it will be exalted *j* above the hills,
    and all nations will stream to it. *k*

³Many peoples *l* will come and say,

"Come, let us go *m* up to the mountain *n* of the LORD,
    to the house of the God of Jacob.
He will teach us his ways,
    so that we may walk in his paths."
The law *o* will go out from Zion,
    the word of the LORD from Jerusalem. *p*
⁴He will judge *q* between the nations
    and will settle disputes *r* for many peoples.
They will beat their swords into plowshares
    and their spears into pruning hooks. *s*
Nation will not take up sword against nation, *t*
    nor will they train for war anymore.

⁵Come, house of Jacob, *u*
    let us walk in the light *v* of the LORD.

THE DAY OF THE LORD

⁶You have abandoned *w* your people,
    the house of Jacob. *x*
They are full of superstitions from the East;
    they practice divination *y* like the Philistines *z*
    and clasp hands *a* with pagans. *b*
⁷Their land is full of silver and gold; *c*
    there is no end to their treasures. *d*
Their land is full of horses; *e*
    there is no end to their chariots. *f*
⁸Their land is full of idols; *g*
    they bow down *h* to the work of their hands, *i*
    to what their fingers *j* have made.
⁹So people will be brought low *k*
    and everyone humbled *l*—
    do not forgive them. *a m*

¹⁰Go into the rocks, hide *n* in the ground
    from the fearful presence of the LORD
    and the splendor of his majesty! *o*
¹¹The eyes of the arrogant *p* will be humbled *q*

a 9 Or *not raise them up*

2:1 A second introduction, probably relating to chs. 2–4 or to chs. 2–12 (see 13:1).
2:2–5 See note on 4:2–6.

  A 2:2–4 Almost identical to Mic 4:1–3. The theme of the "mountain of the LORD" (Mount Zion) is common in Isaiah; it occurs in passages that depict the coming of both Jews and Gentiles to Jerusalem (Zion) in the last days (see 11:9; 27:13; 56:7; 57:13; 65:25; 66:20; see also 60:3–5; Zec 14:16 and note). Some believe that the peace described in this passage has been inaugurated through the coming of Christ and the preaching of the gospel and will be consummated at the return of Christ. Others maintain that it is solely a prophecy of conditions during a future reign of Christ on the earth.

  A 2:2 *the last days.* Can refer to the future generally (see Ge 49:1), but usually it seems to have in view the Messianic era. In a real sense the last days began with the first coming of Christ (see Ac 2:17; Heb 1:1–2 and notes) and will be completely fulfilled at his second coming.
2:4 *swords into plowshares.* The reverse process occurs in Joel 3:10. What is here called a plowshare was actually an iron point

mounted on a wooden beam. Ancient plows did not have a plowshare proper.
2:6 *East.* Probably means Aram (Syria) and Mesopotamia. *divination like the Philistines.* See 1Sa 6:2 and note; for a description of such practices, see also Dt 18:10–11 and note on 18:9.

  A 2:7 *silver and gold ... horses.* Accumulating large quantities of these was forbidden to the king (see Dt 17:16–17 and note). They usually led to a failure to trust in God (see 31:1).
2:10,19,21 These verses contain a refrain that builds to a climax in v. 21.
2:10 *rocks ... ground.* During times of severe oppression the Israelites took refuge in caves and holes in the ground (see Jdg 6:1–2; 1Sa 13:6). *majesty.* The Hebrew for this word is translated "pride" when used of people. Pride is their attempt to be their own gods (see 14:13–14).

  A 2:11,17,20 *in that day.* The phrase, which refers to the day of the Lord, occurs seven times in chs. 2–4 (see 3:7,18; 4:1–2) and in chs. 24–27 (see note on 24:21). The day of the Lord (see also v. 12) is a time of judgment and/or blessing, as God intervenes decisively in the affairs of the nations (see Joel 1:15; Am

and human pride^r brought low;^s
the LORD alone will be exalted^t in that day.^u

¹² The LORD Almighty has a day^v in store
for all the proud^w and lofty,^x
for all that is exalted^y
(and they will be humbled),^z
¹³ for all the cedars of Lebanon,^a tall and lofty,^b
and all the oaks of Bashan,^c
¹⁴ for all the towering mountains
and all the high hills,^d
¹⁵ for every lofty tower^e
and every fortified wall,^f
¹⁶ for every trading ship^{a g}
and every stately vessel.
¹⁷ The arrogance of all people will be brought low^h
and human pride humbled;ⁱ
the LORD alone will be exalted in that day,^j
¹⁸ and the idols^k will totally disappear.^l

¹⁹ People will flee to caves^m in the rocks
and to holes in the groundⁿ
from the fearful presence^o of the LORD
and the splendor of his majesty,^p
when he rises to shake the earth.^q
²⁰ In that day^r people will throw away
to the moles and bats^s
their idols of silver and idols of gold,^t
which they made to worship.^u
²¹ They will flee to caverns in the rocks^v
and to the overhanging crags
from the fearful presence of the LORD
and the splendor of his majesty,^w
when he rises^x to shake the earth.^y

²² Stop trusting in human beings,^z
who have but a breath^a in their nostrils.
Why hold them in esteem?^b

JUDGMENT ON JERUSALEM AND JUDAH

3 See now, the Lord,
the LORD Almighty,
is about to take from Jerusalem and Judah
both supply and support:^c
all supplies of food^d and all supplies of water,^e
² the hero and the warrior,^f
the judge and the prophet,
the diviner^g and the elder,^h

---

^a 16 Hebrew *every ship of Tarshish*

Cross references

2:11 ^r Isa 5:15;
10:12; 37:23;
Eze 31:10
^s S Job 40:11
^t S Ps 46:10 ^u ver 17,
20; Isa 3:7,18; 4:1,2;
5:30; 7:18; 17:4,7;
24:21; 25:9; 26:1; 27:1
2:12 ^v Isa 13:6,9;
22:5,8,12; 34:8; 61:2;
Jer 30:7; La 1:12;
Eze 7:7; 30:3;
Joel 1:15; 2:11;
Am 5:18; Zep 1:14
^w S Ps 59:12
^x S 2Sa 22:28
2:13 ^a S Jdg 9:15;
Isa 10:34; 29:17;
Eze 27:5 ^b Isa 10:33
^c S Ps 22:12; Zec 11:2
2:14 ^d Isa 30:25;
40:4
2:15 ^e Isa 30:25;
32:14; 33:18 ^f Isa 25:2,
12; Zep 1:16
2:16 ^{a fn} S Ge 10:4;
S 1Ki 9:26
2:17 ^h S 2Sa 22:28;
S Job 40:11 ⁱ S ver 9
^j S ver 11
2:18 ^k S 1Sa 5:2;
Eze 36:25 ^l S Dt 9:21;
Isa 21:9; Jer 10:11;
Mic 5:13
2:19 ^m S Jdg 6:2;
Isa 7:19 ⁿ S Jdg 6:2;
S Job 30:6; Lk 23:30;
Rev 6:15 ^o S Dt 2:25
^p S Ps 145:12 ^q ver 21;
S Job 9:6; S Isa 14:16;
Heb 12:26
2:20 ^r S ver 11
^s Lev 11:19
^t S Job 22:24;
Eze 36:25; Rev 9:20
^u Eze 7:19-20; 14:6
2:21 ^v S Ex 33:22
^w S Ps 145:12
^x Isa 33:10 ^y S ver 19
2:22 ^z Ps 118:6,8;
146:3; Isa 51:12;
Jer 17:5 ^a S Ge 2:7;
S Ps 144:4
^b S Job 12:19; Ps 8:4;
18:42; 144:3;
Isa 17:13; 29:5; 40:15;
S Jas 4:14
3:1 ^c S Ps 18:18
^d S Lev 26:26; Am 4:6
^e Isa 5:13; 65:13;
Eze 4:16
3:2 ^f Eze 17:13
^g Dt 18:10 ^h Isa 9:14-
15

5:18; Zep 1:14—2:3 and notes). Assyria and Babylon would bring the terror of judgment upon Judah in Isaiah's day (5:30).
2:13 *cedars of Lebanon.* Even inanimate things that people stand in awe of will be humbled so that "the LORD alone will be exalted" (v. 11). *Bashan.* A region east of the Jordan River and north of Gilead. It was famous for its oaks (Eze 27:6) and its animals (Eze 39:18).
2:16 *trading ship.* These "ships of Tarshish" (see TNIV text note) were large vessels such as those used by Solomon (1Ki 10:22) and the Phoenicians (Isa 23:1,14) to ply the sea in far-flung commercial ventures. For the location of Tarshish, see notes on 23:6; Eze 27:12.
2:20 The futility of worshiping idols is repeatedly noted by Isaiah (see, e.g., 30:22; 31:7; 40:19–20; 44:9–20). See

also note on 40:18–20.
2:22 *Stop trusting in.* Lit. "Cease from" or "Give up on." The verb is used to describe the rejection of the Messiah in 53:3. Ironically, people "rejected," "gave up on," the one Man who should have been trusted and "held ... in ... esteem" (equals "hold ... in esteem" here). He alone was worthy of the esteem wrongly given to frail leaders.
3:1–3 Leaders would be taken away by either death or deportation (see 2Ki 24:14; 25:18–21).
3:2–3 *diviner ... enchanter.* Occult practitioners and snake charmers (see Dt 18:10 and note on 18:9; Jer 8:17), whose activities were condemned. Both legitimate and illegitimate kinds of assistance would be removed or deported (see 2Ki 24:14–16; Hos 3:4).

3:3 *i* S 2Ki 1:9
j S Job 22:8
k 2Ki 24:14
l S Ecc 10:11; Jer 8:17
3:4 *m* ver 12;
Ecc 10:16 fn
3:5 *n* Ps 28:3;
Isa 9:19; Jer 9:8;
Mic 7:2,6
3:7 *o* S Isa 2:11
p Jer 30:12; Eze 34:4;
Hos 5:13 *q* Joel 1:16
r Isa 24:2
3:8 *s* Isa 1:7
t Isa 9:15,17; 28:15;
30:9; 59:3,13
u 2Ch 33:6
v S Job 1:11; Ps 73:9,
11; Isa 65:7
3:9 *w* Nu 32:23;
Isa 59:12; Jer 14:7;
Hos 5:5 *x* S Ge 13:13
y S 2Ch 34:24;
S Pr 8:36; Ro 6:23
3:10 *z* S Dt 5:33;
S 12:28; 28:1-14;
Ps 37:17; Jer 22:15
a S Ge 15:1; S Ps 128:2
3:11 *b* S Job 9:13;
Isa 57:20 *c* Dt 28:15-
68 *d* S 2Ch 6:23
e Jer 21:14; La 5:16;
Eze 24:14
3:12 *f* S ver 4
g Isa 9:16; 19:14; 28:7;
29:9; Jer 23:13; 25:16;
Mic 3:5
3:13 *h* S Job 10:2
i S Ps 82:1; S Isa 2:4
3:14 *j* S 1Sa 12:7;
S Job 22:4
k S Job 24:9; Jas 2:6
l Isa 11:4; 25:4
3:15 *m* S Ps 94:5
n S Job 24:14
o Isa 10:6; 11:4; 26:6;
29:19; 32:6; 51:23
p Isa 5:7
3:16 *q* S SS 3:11
r S Job 15:25

³ the captain of fifty *i* and the person of rank,*j*
　　the counselor, skilled worker *k* and clever enchanter. *l*

⁴ I will make mere youths their officials;
　　children will govern them. *m*
⁵ People will oppress each other—
　　one against another, neighbor against neighbor. *n*
　The young will rise up against the old,
　　the nobody against the honored.

⁶ A man will seize one of his brothers
　　in his father's house, and say,
　"You have a cloak, you be our leader;
　　take charge of this heap of ruins!"
⁷ But in that day *o* he will cry out,
　　"I have no remedy. *p*
　I have no food *q* or clothing in my house;
　　do not make me the leader of the people." *r*

⁸ Jerusalem staggers,
　　Judah is falling; *s*
　their words *t* and deeds *u* are against the Lord,
　　defying *v* his glorious presence.
⁹ The look on their faces testifies *w* against them;
　　they parade their sin like Sodom; *x*
　　they do not hide it.
　Woe to them!
　　They have brought disaster *y* upon themselves.

¹⁰ Tell the righteous it will be well *z* with them,
　　for they will enjoy the fruit of their deeds. *a*
¹¹ Woe to the wicked! *b*
　　Disaster *c* is upon them!
　They will be paid back *d*
　　for what their hands have done. *e*

¹² Youths *f* oppress my people,
　　women rule over them.
　My people, your guides lead you astray; *g*
　　they turn you from the path.

¹³ The Lord takes his place in court; *h*
　　he rises to judge *i* the people.
¹⁴ The Lord enters into judgment *j*
　　against the elders and leaders of his people:
　"It is you who have ruined my vineyard;
　　the plunder *k* from the poor *l* is in your houses.
¹⁵ What do you mean by crushing my people *m*
　　and grinding *n* the faces of the poor?" *o*
　　　　　　　declares the Lord, the Lord Almighty. *p*

¹⁶ The Lord says,
　　"The women of Zion *q* are haughty,
　walking along with outstretched necks, *r*
　　flirting with their eyes,
　tripping along with mincing steps,
　　with ornaments jingling on their ankles.

3:3 *captain of fifty.* A company of 50 was a common military unit (see 2Ki 1:9). It was also used for civil groupings (Ex 18:25).
3:6 Normally it was unnecessary to force anyone to be a leader. In 4:1 the same social upheaval is seen as seven women "take hold of" one man. *You have a cloak.* Perhaps the one brother was not as poor as the others. *heap of ruins.* Probably Jerusalem (v. 8).
3:7,18 *in that day.* See note on 2:11,17,20.
3:8 *Judah is falling.* Fulfilled almost 150 years later in 586 B.C.
3:9 *Sodom.* See note on 1:9–10.

3:12 In the Near East, neither the rule of the young nor that of women was looked on with favor.
3:14 *vineyard.* Represents Israel (see 5:1 and note).
3:15 The leaders were grinding the poor, as women grind grain between two millstones (see note on Jdg 9:53).
3:16–24 For NT warnings against overemphasis on outward adornment, see 1Ti 2:9–10; 1Pe 3:3–5 and notes.
3:16 *walking … tripping along.* Ornaments on ankles made short steps necessary.

¹⁷ Therefore the Lord will bring sores on the heads of the women of Zion;
    the LORD will make their scalps bald. *ˢ*

¹⁸In that day *ᵗ* the Lord will snatch away their finery: the bangles and headbands and crescent necklaces, *ᵘ* ¹⁹the earrings and bracelets *ᵛ* and veils, *ʷ* ²⁰the headdresses *ˣ* and ankle chains and sashes, the perfume bottles and charms, ²¹the signet rings and nose rings, *ʸ* ²²the fine robes and the capes and cloaks, *ᶻ* the purses ²³and mirrors, and the linen garments *ᵃ* and tiaras *ᵇ* and shawls.

²⁴ Instead of fragrance *ᶜ* there will be a stench; *ᵈ*
    instead of a sash, *ᵉ* a rope;
    instead of well-dressed hair, baldness; *ᶠ*
    instead of fine clothing, sackcloth; *ᵍ*
    instead of beauty, *ʰ* branding. *ⁱ*
²⁵ Your men will fall by the sword, *ʲ*
    your warriors in battle. *ᵏ*
²⁶ The gates *ˡ* of Zion will lament and mourn; *ᵐ*
    destitute, *ⁿ* she will sit on the ground. *ᵒ*

¹ In that day *ᵖ* seven women
    will take hold of one man *�q*
and say, "We will eat our own food *ʳ*
    and provide our own clothes;
only let us be called by your name.
    Take away our disgrace!" *ˢ*

THE BRANCH OF THE LORD

²In that day *ᵗ* the Branch of the LORD *ᵘ* will be beautiful *ᵛ* and glorious, and the fruit *ʷ* of the land will be the pride and glory *ˣ* of the survivors *ʸ* in Israel. ³Those who are left in Zion, *ᶻ* who remain *ᵃ* in Jerusalem, will be called holy, *ᵇ* all who are recorded *ᶜ* among the living in Jerusalem. ⁴The Lord will wash away the filth *ᵈ* of the women of Zion; *ᵉ* he will cleanse *ᶠ* the bloodstains *ᵍ* from Jerusalem by a spirit *ᵃ* of judgment *ʰ* and a spirit *ᵃ* of fire. *ⁱ* ⁵Then the LORD will create *ʲ* over all of Mount Zion *ᵏ* and over those who assemble there a cloud of smoke by day and a glow of flaming fire by night; *ˡ* over everything the glory *ᵇ ᵐ* will be a canopy. *ⁿ* ⁶It will be a shelter *ᵒ* and shade from the heat of the day, and a refuge *ᵖ* and hiding place from the storm *q* and rain.

ᵃ 4 Or *the Spirit*   *ᵇ* 5 Or *over all the glory there*

4:5 *ᵏ* Rev 14:1 *ˡ* S Ex 13:21 *ᵐ* Isa 35:2; 58:8; 60:1 *ⁿ* S Ps 18:11; Rev 7:15   **4:6** *ᵒ* Lev 23:34-43; Ps 27:5; Isa 8:14; 25:4; Eze 11:16 *ᵖ* Isa 14:32; 25:4; 30:2; 57:13 *q* S Ps 55:8

4:5 *ʲ* Isa 41:20; 65:18

Cross-reference column

3:17 *ˢ* ver 24;
Eze 27:31; Am 8:10
3:18 *ᵗ* S Isa 2:11
ᵘ Ge 41:42; S Jdg 8:21
3:19 *ᵛ* S Ge 24:47
ʷ Eze 16:11-12
3:20 *ˣ* Ex 39:28;
Eze 24:17,23; 44:18
3:21 *ʸ* S Ge 24:22
3:22 *ᶻ* Ru 3:15
3:23 *ᵃ* Eze 16:10;
23:26 *ᵇ* S Ex 29:6;
SS 3:11; Isa 61:3; 62:3
3:24 *ᶜ* S Est 2:12
ᵈ Isa 4:4 *ᵉ* Pr 31:24
ᶠ S ver 17;
S Lev 13:40;
S Job 1:20
ᵍ S Ge 37:34;
Job 16:15; Isa 20:2;
Jer 4:8; La 2:10;
Eze 27:30-31;
Jnh 3:5-8 *ʰ* 1Pe 3:3
ⁱ S 2Sa 10:4; Isa 20:4
3:25 *ʲ* S Isa 1:20
ᵏ Jer 15:8
3:26 *ˡ* Isa 14:31;
24:12; 45:2
ᵐ S Ps 137:1; Isa 24:4,
7; 29:2; 33:9;
Jer 4:28; 14:2
ⁿ S Lev 26:31
ᵒ S Job 2:13; La 4:5
4:1 *ᵖ* S Isa 2:11
q Isa 13:12; 32:9
ʳ 2Th 3:12
ˢ S Ge 30:23
4:2 *ᵗ* S Isa 2:11
ᵘ Isa 11:1-5; 52:13;
53:2; Jer 23:5-6;
33:15-16; Eze 17:22;
Zec 3:8; 6:12
ᵛ Isa 33:17; 53:2
ʷ S Ps 72:16; Eze 36:8
ˣ Isa 60:15; Eze 34:29
ʸ S Isa 1:9
4:3 *ᶻ* S Isa 1:26
ᵃ Isa 1:9; Ro 11:5
ᵇ S Ex 19:6; Isa 26:2;
45:25; 52:1; 60:21;
Joel 3:17; Ob 1:17;
Zep 3:13 *ᶜ* S Ps 56:8;
S 87:6; S Lk 10:20
4:4 *ᵈ* Isa 3:24
ᵉ S SS 3:11 *ᶠ* S Ps 51:2
ᵍ S Isa 1:15 *ʰ* Isa 28:6
ⁱ S Isa 1:31; S 30:30;
S Zec 13:9; Mt 3:11;
Lk 3:17

3:17 *bald.* Baldness was associated with mourning over catastrophe (see v. 24; 15:2 and note).
3:18 *crescent necklaces.* Probably moon-shaped; they implied veneration of the moon-god.
3:20 *headdresses.* Perhaps a kind of turban (see Eze 24:17,23).
3:21 *signet rings.* Contained a seal and were a mark of authority (see Ge 41:42; Hag 2:23 and note). *nose rings.* Made of gold and worn by brides (see Ge 24:22,53).
3:24 *rope...branding.* Captives were led away by ropes (see notes on 37:29; 2Ki 19:28; Am 4:2) and sometimes branded.
3:26 *gates of Zion.* The gates are personified, as in Ps 24:7,9. They will lament because the crowds that used to assemble there are gone.
4:1–2 *In that day.* See notes on 2:2 and 2:11,17,20. After judgment comes salvation.
4:1 See note on 3:6. War will decimate the male population (3:25; see 13:12 and note), leaving many women with the double disgrace of being widows and childless. See 54:4.
4:2–6 An oracle of redemption just before the long message of indictment and judgment in ch. 5. It balances that found in 2:2–5, which immediately follows the long message of indictment and judgment in ch. 1 (see note on 1:1–31). These two oracles of redemption were intended to complement each other.

4:2–3 *survivors...are left.* See note on 1:9.
4:2 *Branch.* A Messianic title related to the "shoot" and "Branch" (11:1; 53:2) descended from David (see Jer 23:5 and note; 33:15; Zec 3:8; 6:12 and note)—but some believe that here "branch" refers to Judah. *pride.* A legitimate pride in the fruitfulness of the land that will characterize the Messiah's reign (see Ps 72:3,6,16 and note on 72:3). Contrast the pride of 2:11,17. *glory.* Here the fruitfulness of the land will be Israel's glory; in 46:13 God's salvation will be her glory ("splendor"); in 60:19 God himself will be her glory.
4:3 *holy.* Means "set apart" to God. See 1:26; 6:13 and note; see also Zec 14:20–21 and notes.
4:4 *judgment...fire.* Purifying fire is also mentioned in 1:25 (see also 48:10 and note).
4:5–6 *cloud...fire...shelter.* These words recall Israel's wilderness wanderings, when the pillar of cloud and fire guided and protected the people (see Ex 13:21 and note; 14:21–22). Isaiah often refers to the time of the exodus (see 11:15–16; 31:5; 51:10 and notes).
4:5 *the glory.* The manifestation of God's presence, represented by a glow of flaming fire (see Ex 16:10; 24:17; 40:34–35). *canopy.* The cloud of smoke.
4:6 God's presence in cloud and fire will protect and preserve redeemed Zion (cf. Ps 121:5–6).

5:1 *r* Ps 80:8-9;
Isa 27:2; Jn 15:1
5:2 *s* S Ex 15:17;
Isa 16:8 *t* 1Sa 2:9;
Isa 27:3; 31:5; 49:8;
Mt 21:33 *u* S Job 24:11
v Mt 21:19; Mk 11:13;
Lk 13:6
5:3 *w* Mt 21:40
5:4 *x* S 2Ch 36:15;
Jer 2:5-7; Mic 6:3-4;
Mt 23:37 *y* Jer 2:21;
24:2; 29:17
5:5 *z* 2Ch 36:21;
Isa 6:12; 27:10
a S Ps 80:12;
S Isa 22:5 *b* Isa 10:6;
26:6; 28:3,18; 41:25;
63:3; Jer 12:10; 34:22;
La 1:15; Hos 2:12;
Mic 7:10; Mal 4:3;
S Lk 21:24
5:6 *c* S Ge 6:13;
S Lev 26:32; Isa 6:13;
49:17,19; 51:3;
Joel 1:10 *d* ver 10,17;
S 2Sa 23:6; Isa 7:23,
24; 32:13; 34:13;
55:13; Eze 28:24;
Hos 2:12; Heb 6:8
e S Dt 28:24;
S 2Sa 1:21; Am 4:7
5:7 *f* Ps 80:8;
Isa 17:10; 18:5; 37:30
g Isa 10:2; 29:21; 32:7;
59:15; 61:8; Eze 9:9;
22:29 *h* S Isa 1:21
i S Ps 12:5
5:8 *j* ver 11,18,20;
Isa 6:5; 10:1; 24:16;
Jer 22:13 *k* Joh 20:19;
Mic 2:2; Hab 2:9-12
5:9 *l* Jer 44:11
m Isa 22:14 *n* Isa 6:11-
12; Mt 23:38
5:10 *o* S ver 6;
Lev 26:26;
S Dt 28:38; Zec 8:10

THE SONG OF THE VINEYARD

5 I will sing for the one I love
 a song about his vineyard: *r*
My loved one had a vineyard
 on a fertile hillside.
² He dug it up and cleared it of stones
 and planted it with the choicest vines. *s*
He built a watchtower *t* in it
 and cut out a winepress *u* as well.
Then he looked for a crop of good grapes,
 but it yielded only bad fruit. *v*

³ "Now you dwellers in Jerusalem and people of Judah,
 judge between me and my vineyard. *w*
⁴ What more could have been done for my vineyard
 than I have done for it? *x*
When I looked for good grapes,
 why did it yield only bad? *y*
⁵ Now I will tell you
 what I am going to do to my vineyard:
I will take away its hedge,
 and it will be destroyed; *z*
I will break down its wall, *a*
 and it will be trampled. *b*
⁶ I will make it a wasteland, *c*
 neither pruned nor cultivated,
 and briers and thorns *d* will grow there.
I will command the clouds
 not to rain *e* on it."

⁷ The vineyard *f* of the Lᴏʀᴅ Almighty
 is the house of Israel,
and the people of Judah
 are the vines he delighted in.
And he looked for justice, *g* but saw bloodshed;
 for righteousness, *h* but heard cries of distress. *i*

WOES AND JUDGMENTS

⁸ Woe *j* to you who add house to house
 and join field to field *k*
till no space is left
 and you live alone in the land.

⁹ The Lᴏʀᴅ Almighty *l* has declared in my hearing: *m*

"Surely the great houses will become desolate, *n*
 the fine mansions left without occupants.
¹⁰ A ten-acre vineyard will produce only a bath *a* of wine,
 a homer *b* of seed only an ephah *c* of grain." *o*

---

a 10 That is, about 6 gallons or about 22 liters   *b 10* That is, probably about 360 pounds or about 160
kilograms   *c 10* That is, probably about 36 pounds or about 16 kilograms

---

5:1–30 See note on 1:1–31.
5:1 *loved one.* God. *vineyard.* Israel (see v. 7; 3:14; Ps 80:8–16).
Jesus' parable of the tenants (Mt 21:33–44; Mk 12:1–11; Lk
20:9–18) is probably based on this song. See Jn 15:1–17.
5:2 *watchtower.* Contrast the more modest "shelter" of 1:8.
God's vineyard had every advantage (see Mt 21:33 and note).
winepress. Or "wine vat," a trough into which the grape juice
flowed (see 16:10; Hag 2:16 and notes). *he looked for . . . but.* The
interpretation (v. 7) uses the same expression (cf. also 59:9,11).
5:6 *briers and thorns.* This pair occurs five more times (7:23–25;
9:18; 27:4). *not to rain.* The withholding of rain constituted a
curse on the land. See Dt 28:23–24; 2Sa 1:21; 1Ki 17:1.
5:7 The song of the vineyard (vv. 1–6) is now interpreted. A
powerful play on words makes the point: The words for "justice"

and "bloodshed" (*mishpat* and *mispah*) sound alike, as do those
for "righteousness" (*sedaqah*) and "distress" (*se'aqah*).
5:8–23 Six woes are pronounced on God's covenant-breaking
people (vv. 8,11–12,18–19,20,21,22–23), followed by three
judgment sections (vv. 9–10, 13–15,24–25).
5:8 *house to house . . . field to field.* Land in Israel could only be
leased, never sold, because parcels had been permanently assigned to individual families (see Nu 27:7–11; 1Ki 21:1–3 and
note on 21:3).
5:10 *ephah.* A tenth of a homer (see Eze 45:11). Meager crops
often accompanied national sin (Dt 28:38–39; Hag 2:16–17).
The amount of wine and grain is only a tiny fraction of what a
"ten-acre vineyard" and a "homer of seed" would normally produce.

11 Woe[p] to those who rise early in the morning
 to run after their drinks,
who stay up late at night
 till they are inflamed with wine. [q]
12 They have harps and lyres at their banquets,
 pipes[r] and timbrels[s] and wine,
but they have no regard[t] for the deeds of the LORD,
 no respect for the work of his hands. [u]
13 Therefore my people will go into exile[v]
 for lack of understanding; [w]
those of high rank[x] will die of hunger
 and the common people will be parched with thirst. [y]
14 Therefore the grave[z] enlarges its appetite
 and opens wide its mouth; [a]
into it will descend their nobles and masses
 with all their brawlers and revelers. [b]
15 So people will be brought low[c]
 and everyone humbled, [d]
 the eyes of the arrogant[e] humbled.
16 But the LORD Almighty will be exalted[f] by his justice, [g]
 and the holy God will be proved holy[h] by his righteous acts.
17 Then sheep will graze as in their own pasture; [i]
 lambs will feed[a] among the ruins of the rich.

18 Woe[j] to those who draw sin along with cords[k] of deceit,
 and wickedness[l] as with cart ropes,
19 to those who say, "Let God hurry;
 let him hasten[m] his work
 so we may see it.
The plan of the Holy One[n] of Israel—
 let it approach, let it come into view,
 so we may know it." [o]

20 Woe[p] to those who call evil good[q]
 and good evil, [r]
who put darkness for light
 and light for darkness, [s]
who put bitter for sweet
 and sweet for bitter. [t]

21 Woe to those who are wise in their own eyes[u]
 and clever in their own sight.

22 Woe to those who are heroes at drinking wine[v]
 and champions at mixing drinks, [w]
23 who acquit the guilty for a bribe, [x]
 but deny justice[y] to the innocent. [z]
24 Therefore, as tongues of fire[a] lick up straw[b]
 and as dry grass sinks down in the flames,
so their roots will decay[c]
 and their flowers blow away like dust; [d]
for they have rejected the law of the LORD Almighty
 and spurned the word[e] of the Holy One[f] of Israel.
25 Therefore the LORD's anger[g] burns against his people;

---

[a] 17 Septuagint; Hebrew / *strangers will eat*

5:11 [p] S ver 8
[q] S 1Sa 25:36;
S Pr 23:29-30
5:12 [r] S Job 21:12
[s] Ps 68:25; Isa 24:8
[t] S 1Sa 12:24
[u] Ps 28:5; Eze 26:13
5:13 [v] Isa 49:21
[w] S Pr 10:21; S Isa 1:3;
Hos 4:6 [x] S Job 22:8
[y] S Isa 3:1
5:14 [z] S Pr 30:16
[a] S Nu 16:30
[b] Isa 22:2,13; 23:7;
24:8
5:15 [c] Isa 10:33
[d] S Isa 2:9 [e] S Isa 2:11
5:16 [f] Ps 97:9;
Isa 33:10 [g] Isa 28:17;
30:18; 33:5; 61:8
[h] S Lev 10:3;
Isa 29:23; Eze 36:23
5:17 [i] Isa 7:25; 17:2;
32:14; Zep 2:6,14
5:18 [j] S ver 8
[k] Hos 11:4 [l] Isa 59:4-
8; Jer 23:14
5:19 [m] Isa 60:22
[n] Isa 1:4; 29:23;
30:11,12 [o] Jer 17:15;
Eze 12:22; 2Pe 3:4
5:20 [p] S ver 8
[q] S Ge 18:25;
S 1Ki 22:8
[r] S Ps 94:21
[s] S Job 24:13;
Mt 6:22-23; Lk 11:34-
35 [t] Am 5:7
5:21 [u] S Pr 3:7;
Isa 47:10; Ro 12:16;
1Co 3:18-20
5:22 [v] S 1Sa 25:36;
S Pr 23:20;
S Isa 22:13
[w] S Pr 31:4; Isa 65:11;
Jer 7:18
5:23 [x] S Ex 23:8;
S Eze 22:12 [y] ver 7;
S Isa 1:17; 10:2; 29:21;
59:4,13-15
[z] S Ps 94:21; Am 5:12;
Jas 5:6
5:24 [a] S Isa 1:31
[b] Isa 47:14; Na 1:10
[c] S 2Ki 19:30;
S Job 18:16
[d] S Job 24:24;
Isa 40:8 [e] Ps 107:11;
Isa 8:6; 30:9,12
[f] Job 6:10; Isa 1:4;
10:20; 12:6
5:25 [g] S 2Ki 22:13;
S Job 40:11; Isa 10:17;
26:11; 31:9; 66:15;
S Jer 6:12

5:11–13 See Am 4:1–3; 6:4–7, where a lifestyle characterized by drunkenness and revelry is likewise condemned.
5:14 *grave.* See note on Ge 37:35. The grave has an insatiable appetite (see Ps 49:14 and note).
5:16 *be proved holy.* See Lev 10:3 and note.
5:18 *cords of deceit.* See Pr 5:22 and note.
5:19 The Hebrew for the words "hurry" and "hasten" corresponds to that of the first and third elements of the name Maher-Shalal-Hash-Baz (see 8:1 and TNIV text note). When Isaiah

named his son (8:3), he may have been responding to the sarcastic taunts of these sinners. God did bring swift judgment, according to 5:26. *Holy One of Israel.* See 1:4 and note.
5:22 *mixing drinks.* Spices were added to beer and wine (see Pr 23:30 and note).
5:23 See 1:23; 10:1–2.
5:24 *spurned ... the Holy One of Israel.* See v. 19; see also 1:4 and note.

5:25 *h* S Ex 19:18
i Ps 110:6
j S 2Ki 9:37
k S 2Sa 22:43
l Jer 4:8; Da 9:16
m Isa 9:12,17,21; 10:4
5:26 *n* S Ps 20:5
o Isa 7:18; Zec 10:8
p Dt 28:49; Isa 13:5;
18:3
5:27 *q* Isa 14:31;
40:29-31 *r* Isa 22:21;
Eze 23:15
s S Job 12:18
t Joel 2:7-8
5:28 *u* S Job 39:23;
Ps 45:5 *v* S Ps 7:12
w Eze 26:11
x S 2Ki 2:1; S Job 1:19
5:29 *y* S 2Ki 17:25;
Jer 51:38; Zep 3:3;
Zec 11:3 *z* Isa 10:6;
49:24-25 *a* Isa 42:22;
Mic 5:8
5:30 *b* S Isa 2:11
c S Ps 93:3; Jer 50:42;
Lk 21:25 *d* S 1Sa 2:9;
S Job 21:30; Ps 18:28;
44:19; S 82:5
e S Jdg 6:2; Isa 22:5;
33:2; Jer 4:23-28
f Isa 13:10; 50:3;
Joel 2:10
6:1 *g* S 2Ch 26:22,
23 *h* S 2Ki 15:7
i S Ex 24:10;
S Nu 12:8; Jn 12:41
j S 1Ki 22:19;
S Ps 9:4; S 123:1;
S Rev 4:2 *k* Isa 52:13;
53:12 *l* Rev 1:13
6:2 *m* Eze 1:5; 10:15;
Rev 4:8 *n* Eze 1:11
6:3 *o* S Ex 15:11
p Ps 89:8 *q* Isa 11:9;
54:5; Mal 1:11
r S Ex 16:7; Nu 14:21;
Ps 72:19; Rev 4:8

his hand is raised and he strikes them down.
The mountains shake, *h*
and the dead bodies *i* are like refuse *j* in the streets. *k*

Yet for all this, his anger is not turned away, *l*
his hand is still upraised. *m*

26 He lifts up a banner *n* for the distant nations,
he whistles *o* for those at the ends of the earth. *p*
Here they come,
swiftly and speedily!
27 Not one of them grows tired *q* or stumbles,
not one slumbers or sleeps;
not a belt *r* is loosened at the waist, *s*
not a sandal thong is broken. *t*
28 Their arrows are sharp, *u*
all their bows *v* are strung;
their horses' hooves *w* seem like flint,
their chariot wheels like a whirlwind. *x*
29 Their roar is like that of the lion, *y*
they roar like young lions;
they growl as they seize *z* their prey
and carry it off with no one to rescue. *a*
30 In that day *b* they will roar over it
like the roaring of the sea. *c*
And if one looks at the land,
there is only darkness *d* and distress; *e*
even the sun will be darkened *f* by clouds.

ISAIAH'S COMMISSION

6 In the year that King Uzziah *g* died, *h* I saw the Lord *i* seated on a throne, *j* high and exalted, *k* and the train of his robe *l* filled the temple. 2Above him were seraphs, *m* each with six wings: With two wings they covered their faces, with two they covered their feet, *n* and with two they were flying. 3And they were calling to one another:

"Holy, holy *o*, holy is the LORD Almighty; *p*
the whole earth *q* is full of his glory." *r*

5:25 *The mountains shake.* When God takes action, even the mountains tremble (see 64:3; Ps 18:7; Jer 4:24–26; Mic 1:4; Na 1:15; Hab 3:6,10). *Yet…upraised.* A refrain repeated in 9:12,17,21; 10:4.
5:26 *lifts up a banner.* A pole with a banner was often placed on a hill as a signal for gathering troops (13:2) or for summoning the nations to bring Israel back home (11:10,12; 49:22; 62:10). *distant nations.* Such as Assyria, whose armies struck Israel and Judah in 722 and 701 B.C., and Babylon, which began its invasions in 605. *those at the ends of the earth.* Nations like Egypt and Assyria.
5:27 *Not one…grows tired or stumbles.* Cf. the use of these terms in 40:29–31.
5:30 *In that day.* See note on 2:11,17,20. *darkness and distress.* Similar words describe the horrors of war in 8:22.

A C **6:1–13** Isaiah's commission, the climax of the first major section of his prophecies (see note on 1:1—6:13). In vv. 1–4 he sees the Lord in all his glory (v. 1); in vv. 5–7 he then sees himself in all his uncleanness (v. 5); in vv. 8–13 the prophet, now cleansed and forgiven (v. 7), sees the rebellious people to whom God is sending him to proclaim the divine message of judgment.
6:1 *the year that King Uzziah died.* 740 B.C. (cf. 14:28 and note). Isaiah's commission probably preceded his preaching ministry; the account was postponed to serve as a climax to the opening series of oracles and to provide warrant for the shocking announcements of judgment they contain. The people had mocked the "Holy One of Israel" (5:19), and now he has commis-

sioned Isaiah to call them to account. Uzziah reigned from 792 to 740 and was a godly and powerful king. When he insisted on burning incense in the temple, however, he was struck with "leprosy" and remained "leprous" until his death (see 2Ch 26:16–21 and TNIV text note on 26:19). He was also called Azariah (2Ki 14:21; 2Ch 26:1). *I saw.* Probably in a vision in the temple. *the Lord.* The true King (see v. 5). *high and exalted.* The same Hebrew words are applied to God also in 57:15, and similar terms are used of the suffering servant in 52:13. *train of his robe.* A long, flowing garment. Cf. the robe of the "son of man" in Rev 1:13. *temple.* Probably the heavenly temple, with which the earthly temple was closely associated. John's vision of God on his throne is similar (Rev 4:1–8).
6:2 *seraphs.* See v. 6; heavenly beings not mentioned elsewhere. Their actions correspond to those of the "living creatures" of Rev 4:6–9, each of whom also had six wings. *covered their faces.* Apparently they could not gaze directly at the glory of God.
6:3 *Holy, holy, holy.* See Lev 11:44 and note; Rev 4:8. The triple repetition underscores God's infinite holiness. Note the triple use of "the temple of the LORD" in Jer 7:4 to stress the people's confidence in the security of Jerusalem because of the presence of that sanctuary. *LORD Almighty.* See note on 1Sa 1:3. *full of his glory.* In Nu 14:21–22; Ps 72:18–19 the worldwide glory of God is linked with his miraculous signs (cf. note on Eze 1:1–28).
6:4 *doorposts…shook…filled with smoke.* Similarly, the power of God's voice terrified the Israelites at Mount Sinai, and the mountain was covered with smoke (see Ex 19:18–19; 20:18–19).

[4]At the sound of their voices the doorposts and thresholds shook and the temple was filled with smoke. [s]

[5]"Woe [t] to me!" I cried. "I am ruined! [u] For I am a man of unclean lips, [v w] and I live among a people of unclean lips, [x] and my eyes have seen [y] the King, [z] the LORD Almighty." [a]

[6]Then one of the seraphs flew to me with a live coal [b] in his hand, which he had taken with tongs from the altar. [7]With it he touched my mouth and said, "See, this has touched your lips; [c] your guilt is taken away and your sin atoned for. [d]"

[8]Then I heard the voice [e] of the Lord saying, "Whom shall I send? [f] And who will go for us? [g]"

And I said, "Here am I. [h] Send me!"

[9]He said, "Go [i] and tell this people:

" 'Be ever hearing, but never understanding;
be ever seeing, but never perceiving.' [j]
[10]Make the heart of this people calloused; [k]
make their ears dull
and close their eyes. [a l]
Otherwise they might see with their eyes,
hear with their ears, [m]
understand with their hearts,
and turn and be healed." [n]

[11]Then I said, "For how long, Lord?" [o]

And he answered:

"Until the cities lie ruined [p]
and without inhabitant,
until the houses are left deserted [q]
and the fields ruined and ravaged, [r]
[12]until the LORD has sent everyone far away [s]
and the land is utterly forsaken. [t]
[13]And though a tenth remains [u] in the land,
it will again be laid waste. [v]
But as the terebinth and oak
leave stumps [w] when they are cut down,
so the holy [x] seed will be the stump in the land." [y]

THE SIGN OF IMMANUEL

7 When Ahaz [z] son of Jotham, the son of Uzziah, was king of Judah, King Rezin [a] of Aram [b] and Pekah [c] son of Remaliah [d] king of Israel marched up to fight against Jerusalem, but they could not overpower it.

[a] 9,10 Hebrew; Septuagint 'You will be ever hearing, but never understanding; / you will be ever seeing, but never perceiving.' / [10]This people's heart has become calloused; / they hardly hear with their ears, / and they have closed their eyes

Cross-references

6:4 [s] S Ex 19:18; S 40:34; Eze 43:5; 44:4; Rev 15:8
6:5 [t] S Isa 5:8; [u] S Nu 17:12; S Dt 5:26 [v] Lk 5:8; [w] Ex 6:12 [x] Isa 59:3; Jer 9:3-8 [y] S Ex 24:10; [z] Ps 45:3; Isa 24:23; 32:1; 33:17; Jer 51:57 [a] S Job 42:5
6:6 [b] S Lev 10:1; Eze 10:2
6:7 [c] Jer 1:9; Da 10:16; [d] S Lev 26:41; Isa 45:25; Da 12:3; 1Jn 1:7
6:8 [e] S Job 40:9; Ac 9:4 [f] Jer 26:12,15; [g] S Ge 1:26; [h] S Ge 22:1; S Ex 3:4
6:9 [i] Eze 3:11; Am 7:15; Mt 28:19 [j] Jer 5:21; S Mt 13:15*; Lk 8:10*
6:10 [k] S Ex 4:21; Dt 32:15; Ps 119:70 [l] Isa 29:9; 42:18-20; 43:8; 44:18 [m] S Dt 29:4; Eze 12:2; Mk 8:18 [n] S Dt 32:39; Mt 13:13-15; Mk 4:12*; Jn 12:40*
6:11 [o] Ps 79:5 [p] S Lev 26:31; S Jer 4:13 [q] S Lev 26:43; Isa 24:10 [r] Ps 79:1; S 109:11; Jer 35:17
6:12 [s] S Dt 28:64 [t] Isa 5:5,9; 60:15; 62:4; Jer 4:29; 30:17
6:13 [u] S Isa 1:9; 10:22 [v] S Isa 5:6 [w] S Job 14:8 [x] S Lev 27:30; S Dt 14:2 [y] S Job 14:7
7:1 [z] S 1Ch 3:13 [a] S ver 8; S 2Ki 15:37 [b] 2Ch 28:5 [c] S 2Ki 15:25 [d] ver 5, 9; Isa 8:6

Study notes

6:5 *eyes have seen the King.* Isaiah was dismayed because anyone who saw God expected to die immediately (see Ge 16:13; 32:30 and notes; Ex 33:20).

6:6 *live coal.* Coals of fire were taken inside the Most Holy Place on the Day of Atonement (Lev 16:12), when sacrifice was made to atone for sin. See note on 1:25.

6:7 *touched my mouth.* When God commissioned Jeremiah, his hand touched the prophet's mouth (Jer 1:9).

6:8–10 Isaiah's prophetic commission will have the ironic but justly deserved effect of hardening the callous hearts of rebellious Israel—and so rendering the warnings of judgment sure (see vv. 11–13). See also Jer 1:8,19; Eze 2:3–4.

6:8 *for us.* The heavenly King speaks in the divine council (see Ge 1:26; Ps 82:1 and notes). As a true prophet, Isaiah is made privy to that council, as were Micaiah (1Ki 22:19–20) and Jeremiah (23:18,22). Cf. Am 3:7. *Here am I.* See note on Ge 22:1.

6:9–10 Quoted by Jesus in the parable of the sower (Mt 13:14–15; Mk 4:12; Lk 8:10). See also Ro 11:7–10, 25 and notes. *this people.* In 1:3; 3:15; 5:13 the Lord refers to Israel as "my people." That their persistent and pervasive rebellion (1:1; 66:24) has begun to alienate them from him is indicated by numerous

references to them as "this/these people" (e.g., 8:6,12; 29:13–14; cf. Ex 17:4 and note).

6:10 *heart … ears … eyes … eyes … ears … hearts.* The a-b-c/c-b-a inversion is a common literary device in the OT. *ears dull … close their eyes.* Israel's deafness and blindness are also mentioned in 29:9; 42:18; 43:8. One day, however, the nation will be able to see and hear (29:18; 35:5).

6:12 *far away.* See 5:13.

6:13 *a tenth.* A remnant—even it will be laid waste. *holy seed.* The few who are faithful in Israel (cf. 1Ki 19:18; see note on 1:9). *stump.* Out of which the nation will grow again. For a similar use of this imagery, see 11:1 and note.

7:1—12:6 The second section of Isaiah's prophecies, climaxing in the songs of praise found in ch. 12 (cf. note on 1:1—6:13).

7:1 The invasion of Rezin and Pekah (probably in 735/734 B.C.) is known as the Syro-Ephraimite War. Aram (Syria) and Israel (Ephraim; see note on v. 2) were trying unsuccessfully to persuade Ahaz to join a coalition against Assyria, which had strong designs on lands to the west. Isaiah was trying to keep Ahaz from forming a counteralliance with Assyria (see 2Ki 16:5–18; 2Ch 28:16–21). *Pekah.* Ruled 752–732 B.C. (see 2Ki 15:27–31).

7:2 *e* ver 13;
S 2Sa 7:11; Isa 16:5;
22:22; Jer 21:12;
Am 9:11 *f* Isa 9:9;
Hos 5:3 *g* Isa 6:4;
Da 5:6
7:3 *h* Isa 10:21-22
i 2Ki 18:17; Isa 36:2
7:4 *j* Isa 30:15;
La 3:26 *k* S Ge 15:1;
S Dt 3:2; Isa 8:12;
12:2; 35:4; 37:6;
Mt 24:6 *l* S Dt 20:3;
S Isa 21:4 *m* Am 4:11;
Zec 3:2 *n* Isa 10:24;
51:13; 54:8 *o* S 2Ki 15:27
7:5 *p* S ver 1 *q* ver 2
7:7 *r* Isa 24:3; 25:8;
28:16 *s* Ps 2:1;
Isa 8:10; 14:24; 28:18;
40:8; 46:10; Ac 4:25
7:8 *t* S Ge 14:15
u ver 1; Isa 9:11
v 2Ki 17:24; Isa 8:4;
17:1-3
7:9 *w* S 2Ki 15:29;
Isa 9:9; 28:1,3
x S Ps 20:8; Isa 8:10;
40:8 *y* 2Ch 20:20
z Isa 8:6-8; 30:12-14
7:11 *a* S Ex 7:9;
S Dt 13:2 *b* Ps 139:8
7:12 *c* Dt 4:34
7:13 *d* S ver 2
e S Ge 30:15
f S Isa 1:14 *g* Ps 63:1;
118:28; Isa 25:1; 49:4;
61:10
7:14 *h* S Ex 3:12;
S Lk 2:12 *i* S Ge 24:43
j S Ge 3:15; Lk 1:31
k S Ge 21:22; Isa 8:8,
10; Mt 1:23*
7:15 *l* S Ge 18:8
m ver 22
7:16 *n* Isa 8:4
o Dt 1:39 *p* S Dt 13:16;
Isa 17:3; Jer 7:15;
Hos 5:9,13; Am 1:3-5

²Now the house of David *e* was told, "Aram has allied itself with *a* Ephraim *f*"; so the hearts of Ahaz and his people were shaken, *g* as the trees of the forest are shaken by the wind.

³Then the LORD said to Isaiah, "Go out, you and your son Shear-Jashub, *b h* to meet Ahaz at the end of the aqueduct of the Upper Pool, on the road to the Launderer's Field. *i* ⁴Say to him, 'Be careful, keep calm *j* and don't be afraid. *k* Do not lose heart *l* because of these two smoldering stubs *m* of firewood—because of the fierce anger *n* of Rezin and Aram and of the son of Remaliah. *o* ⁵Aram, Ephraim and Remaliah's *p* son have plotted *q* your ruin, saying, ⁶"Let us invade Judah; let us tear it apart and divide it among ourselves, and make the son of Tabeel king over it." ⁷Yet this is what the Sovereign LORD says: *r*

> " 'It will not take place,
>   it will not happen, *s*
> ⁸for the head of Aram is Damascus, *t*
>   and the head of Damascus is only Rezin. *u*
> Within sixty-five years
>   Ephraim will be too shattered *v* to be a people.
> ⁹The head of Ephraim is Samaria, *w*
>   and the head of Samaria is only Remaliah's son.
> If you do not stand *x* firm in your faith, *y*
>   you will not stand at all.' " *z*

¹⁰Again the LORD spoke to Ahaz, ¹¹"Ask the LORD your God for a sign, *a* whether in the deepest depths or in the highest heights. *b*"

¹²But Ahaz said, "I will not ask; I will not put the LORD to the test. *c*"

¹³Then Isaiah said, "Hear now, you house of David! *d* Is it not enough *e* to try the patience of human beings? Will you try the patience *f* of my God *g* also? ¹⁴Therefore the Lord himself will give you *c* a sign: *h* The virgin *d i* will conceive and give birth to a son, *j* and *e* will call him Immanuel. *f k* ¹⁵He will be eating curds *l* and honey *m* when he knows enough to reject the wrong and choose the right, ¹⁶for before the boy knows *n* enough to reject the wrong and choose the right, *o* the land of the two kings you dread will be laid waste. *p*

---

a 2 Or *has set up camp in*   *b* 3 *Shear-Jashub* means *a remnant will return.*   *c* 14 The Hebrew is plural.
d 14 Or *young woman*   *e* 14 Masoretic Text; Dead Sea Scrolls *and he* or *and they*   *f* 14 *Immanuel* means *God with us.*

7:2 *house of David.* A reference to Ahaz, who belonged to David's dynasty (see 2Sa 7:8–11). *Ephraim.* Another name for Israel, the northern kingdom. *hearts . . . were shaken.* Ahaz had defeated earlier by Aram and Israel (2Ch 28:5–8).
7:3 *Shear-Jashub.* See TNIV text note; see also 10:20–22 and note. Isaiah gave each of his sons symbolic names (see 8:1,3,18). *aqueduct of the Upper Pool.* See 36:2 and note. Ahaz was probably inspecting the city's water supply. *Launderer's Field.* Clothes were cleaned by trampling on them in cold water and using a kind of soap or cleansing powder (see Mal 3:2 and note; Mk 9:3).
7:4 *two smoldering stubs.* Damascus (Aram's capital; see v. 8) was crushed by Tiglath-Pileser III in 732 B.C., and Israel was soundly defeated the same year.
7:6 *Tabeel.* An Aramaic name sometimes associated with the "land of Tob" east of the Jordan River (see Jdg 11:3 and note).
7:8 *Within sixty-five years.* By c. 670 B.C. Esarhaddon (and, shortly after him, Ashurbanipal), king of Assyria, settled foreign colonists in Israel. Their intermarriage with the few Israelites who had not been deported resulted in the "Samaritans" (see 2Ki 17:24–34 and note on 17:29) and marked the end of Ephraim as a separate nation.
7:9 *only Remaliah's son.* Pekah was a usurper and hardly worthy to challenge Ahaz, a son of David. Aram (v. 8) and Israel (v. 9) had human heads. Judah had a divine head; God was with her (v. 14; 8:8,10). *stand firm . . . stand.* The use of the same Hebrew verb emphasizes the seriousness of the Lord's warning (see 1:19–20,25–26 and notes).
7:11 *sign.* God was willing to strengthen the faith of Ahaz through a sign (see Ex 3:12 and note).
7:13 *house of David.* See note on v. 2.

7:14 *sign.* A sign was normally fulfilled within a few years (see 20:3; 37:30; cf. 8:18). *The virgin.* May refer to a young woman betrothed to Isaiah (8:3), who was to become his second wife (his first wife presumably having died after Shear-Jashub was born). In Ge 24:43 the same Hebrew word (*'almah*) refers to a woman about to be married (see also Pr 30:19). Mt 1:23 apparently understood the woman mentioned here to be a type (a foreshadowing) of the Virgin Mary. *Immanuel.* The name "God is with us" was meant to convince Ahaz that God could rescue him from his enemies. See Nu 14:9; 2Ch 13:12; Ps 46:7. The Hebrew for "Immanuel" is used again in 8:8,10, and it may be another name for Maher-Shalal-Hash-Baz (8:3). If so, the boy's names had complementary significance (see note on 8:3). Jesus was the final fulfillment of this prophecy, for he was "God with us" in the fullest sense (Mt 1:23; cf. Isa 9:6–7).
7:15 *curds and honey.* Curds (a kind of yogurt) and honey meant a return to the simple diet of those who lived off the land. The Assyrian invasion would devastate the countryside and make farming impossible. (See vv. 22–25 for the significance of the expression.) *when he knows . . . wrong . . . right.* Suggests the age of moral determination and responsibility under the law—most likely 12 or 13 years of age. Thus, "when" this boy is 12 or 13 (722/721 B.C.), he will be eating curds and honey instead of agricultural products—due to the devastation of Israel by Assyria. Some believe that this expression involves a shorter period of time, identical to that in v. 16 and 8:4.
7:16 *before the boy knows . . . land . . . laid waste.* See note on v. 4; cf. 8:4. "Before" the boy is 12 or 13 years old, Aram and Israel will be plundered. This happened in 732 B.C., when the boy was about two years old.

¹⁷The LORD will bring on you and on your people and on the house of your father a time unlike any since Ephraim broke away ^q from Judah—he will bring the king of Assyria. ^r"

ASSYRIA, THE LORD'S INSTRUMENT

¹⁸In that day ^s the LORD will whistle ^t for flies from the Nile delta in Egypt and for bees from the land of Assyria. ^u ¹⁹They will all come and settle in the steep ravines and in the crevices ^v in the rocks, on all the thornbushes ^w and at all the water holes. ²⁰In that day ^x the Lord will use ^y a razor hired from beyond the Euphrates River ^z—the king of Assyria ^a—to shave your head and the hair of your legs, and to take off your beards ^b also. ^c ²¹In that day, ^d a person will keep alive a young cow and two goats. ^e ²²And because of the abundance of the milk they give, there will be curds to eat. All who remain in the land will eat curds ^f and honey. ^g ²³In that day, ^h in every place where there were a thousand vines worth a thousand silver shekels, ^a ⁱ there will be only briers and thorns. ^j ²⁴Hunters will go there with bow and arrow, for the land will be covered with briers ^k and thorns. ²⁵As for all the hills ^l once cultivated by the hoe, you will no longer go there for fear of the briers and thorns; ^m they will become places where cattle are turned loose and where sheep run. ⁿ

ISAIAH AND HIS CHILDREN AS SIGNS

8 The LORD said to me, "Take a large scroll ^o and write on it with an ordinary pen: Maher-Shalal-Hash-Baz." ^b ^p ²So I called in Uriah ^q the priest and Zechariah son of Jeberekiah as reliable witnesses ^r for me. ³Then I made love to the prophetess, ^s and she conceived and gave birth to a son. ^t And the LORD said to me, "Name him Maher-Shal-al-Hash-Baz. ^u ⁴Before the boy knows ^v how to say 'My father' or 'My mother,' the wealth of Damascus ^w and the plunder of Samaria will be carried off by the king of Assyria. ^x"

⁵The LORD spoke to me again:

⁶"Because this people has rejected ^y
    the gently flowing waters of Shiloah ^z
and rejoices over Rezin
    and the son of Remaliah, ^a
⁷therefore the Lord is about to bring against them
    the mighty floodwaters ^b of the Euphrates—
    the king of Assyria ^c with all his pomp. ^d
It will overflow all its channels,
    run over all its banks ^e
⁸and sweep on into Judah, swirling over it, ^f
    passing through it and reaching up to the neck.
Its outspread wings ^g will cover the breadth of your land,
    Immanuel ^c!" ^h

---

^a 23 That is, about 25 pounds or about 11.5 kilograms   ^b 1 Maher-Shalal-Hash-Baz means quick to the plunder, swift to the spoil; also in verse 3.   ^c 8 Immanuel means God with us.

7:17 Ephraim broke away from Judah. Almost two centuries earlier (see 1Ki 12:19–20). king of Assyria. Ahaz's appeal to Assyria would bring temporary relief (2Ki 16:8–9), but eventually Assyria would attack Judah (see 8:7–8; 36:1 and notes).
7:18,20,23 In that day. Their difficulties will be a foretaste of the "day of the LORD." See note on 2:11, 17,20.
7:18 flies . . . bees. See Ex 23:28 and note.
7:19 crevices in the rocks. See note on 2:10. It will be impossible to escape from the invaders.
7:20 shave . . . head . . . legs . . . beards. Such forcible shaving was considered a great insult (see 2Sa 10:4 and note). hair of your legs. Pubic hair.
7:23 briers and thorns. See note on 5:6. The destruction of the vineyards and the farmlands would fulfill 5:5–6.
8:1–2 scroll . . . witnesses. The witnesses would attest to a legal transaction, either the marriage of Isaiah (see note on 7:14) or a symbolic deed connected with Maher-Shalal-Hash-Baz. The Hebrew word for "scroll" is related to the word for "unsealed copy" in Jer 32:11.
8:2 Uriah the priest. Served under King Ahaz (see 2Ki 16:10–11).
8:3–10 See 7:14–17 and notes.
8:3 prophetess . . . son. Probably the initial fulfillment of 7:14. Note

the repetition of "conceive," "give birth to," "son" and "call/name" from 7:14. The young woman may be called a prophetess here because she had become the wife of a prophet (Isaiah). Maher-Shal-al-Hash-Baz. This symbolic name (see TNIV text note on v. 1) meant that Samaria would be plundered (see v. 4 and note on 7:4), but it also implied that Judah would suffer (see vv. 7–8).
8:4 knows how to say. At about age two. The time period is identical to that in 7:16 (see notes on 7:4,16). plunder of Samaria will be carried off. The first stage of the destruction of the northern kingdom (see note on 7:4), which was not completed until 722–721 B.C. (see note on 7:15).
8:6 waters of Shiloah. See TNIV text note on Ne 3:15. The water in Jerusalem that flows from the Gihon spring (see 2Ch 32:30) to the Pool of Siloam (see Jn 9:7 and note) may be intended (see Ne 3:15 and note). Here it symbolizes the sustaining power of the Lord. Rezin and the son of Remaliah. Rezin and Pekah both died in 732 B.C. (see 2Ki 16:9; see note on Isa 7:1).
8:7–8 floodwaters . . . sweep on. Mighty rivers were often used to symbolize a powerful invading army (see 17:12 and note; 28:17–19).
8:8 up to the neck. See 30:28 and note. Sennacherib's invasion in 701 B.C. overwhelmed all the cities of Judah except Jerusalem

7:17 ^q1Ki 12:16
^rS ver 20;
S 2Ch 28:20
7:18 ^sver 20,21;
S Isa 2:11 ^tS Isa 5:26
^uIsa 13:5
7:19 ^vS Isa 2:19
^wver 25; Isa 17:9;
34:13; 55:13
7:20 ^xS ver 18
^yIsa 10:15; 29:16
^zIsa 11:15; Jer 2:18
^aver 17; 2Ki 18:16;
Isa 8:7; 10:5
^bS 2Sa 10:4
^cS Dt 28:49
7:21 ^dver 23;
Isa 2:17; Jer 39:10
7:22 ^fS Ge 18:8
^gver 15; Isa 14:30
7:23 ^hver 21
ⁱSS 8:11 / S Isa 5:6;
Hos 2:12
7:24 ^kS Isa 5:6
7:25 ^lHag 1:11
^mS ver 19 ⁿS Isa 5:17
8:1 ^oS Dt 27:8;
Job 19:23; Isa 30:8;
Jer 51:60 ^pver 3;
Hab 2:2; Jer 20:3;
Hos 1:4
8:2 ^qS 2Ki 16:10
^rver 16; S Jos 24:22;
S Ru 4:9; Jer 32:10,
12,25,44
8:3 ^sS Ex 15:20
^tS Ge 3:15 ^uS ver 1
8:4 ^vIsa 7:16
^wS Ge 14:15
^xS Isa 7:8
8:6 ^yS Isa 5:24
^zNe 3:15; Jn 9:7
^aS Isa 7:1
8:7 ^bIsa 17:12-13;
28:2,17; 30:28; 43:2;
Da 11:40; Na 1:8
^cS 2Ch 28:20;
S Isa 7:20 ^dIsa 10:16
^eS Jos 3:15
8:8 ^fIsa 28:15
^gIsa 18:6; 46:11;
Jer 4:13; 48:40
^hS Isa 7:14

8:9 ʲS Jos 6:5;
Isa 17:12-13
ʲS Job 34:24 ᵏJer 6:4;
46:3; 51:12,27-28;
Eze 38:7; Joel 3:9;
Zec 14:2-3
8:10 ˡS Job 5:12
ᵐS Pr 19:21; S 21:30;
S Isa 7:7 ⁿS Isa 7:14;
Mt 1:23; Ro 8:31
8:11 ᵒEze 1:3; 3:14
ᵖEze 2:8
8:12 ᵠIsa 7:2; 20:5;
30:1; 36:6 ʳS Isa 7:4;
Mt 10:28 ˢ1Pe 3:14*
8:13 ʳS Nu 20:12
ᵘS Ex 20:20
ᵛIsa 29:23
8:14 ʷS Isa 4:6
ˣS Ps 118:22
ʸJer 6:21; Eze 3:20;
14:3,7; Lk 20:18
ᶻS Lk 2:34; Ro 9:33*;
1Pe 2:8*
ᵃS Ps 119:110;
Isa 24:17-18
8:15 ᵇPr 4:19;
Isa 28:13; 59:10;
Ro 9:32
8:16 ᶜS Ru 4:7
ᵈIsa 29:11-12;
Jer 32:14; Da 8:26;
12:4
8:17 ᵉS Ps 27:14
ᶠS Dt 31:17
ᵍS Ps 22:5;
Heb 2:13*
8:18 ʰS Ge 33:5;
Heb 2:13* ⁱS Ex 3:12;
Eze 4:3; 12:6; 24:24;
Lk 2:34 ʲS Dt 28:46;
S Eze 12:11 ᵏPs 9:11
8:19 ˡS 1Sa 28:8
ᵐS Lev 19:31
ⁿIsa 29:4
ᵒS Nu 27:21
8:20 ᵖS Isa 1:10;
Lk 16:29 ᵠS Ru 4:7
ʳver 22; Isa 9:2; 59:9;
60:2; Mic 3:6
8:21 ˢS Job 18:12
ᵗJob 30:3

⁹ Raise the war cry,ᵃ ⁱ you nations, and be shattered!ʲ
    Listen, all you distant lands.
    Prepareᵏ for battle, and be shattered!
    Prepare for battle, and be shattered!
¹⁰ Devise your strategy, but it will be thwarted;ˡ
    propose your plan, but it will not stand,ᵐ
    for God is with us.ᵇ ⁿ

¹¹This is what the Lᴏʀᴅ says to me with his strong hand upon me,ᵒ warning me not to followᵖ the way of this people:

¹² "Do not call conspiracyᵠ
    everything this people calls a conspiracy;
    do not fear what they fear,ʳ
    and do not dread it.ˢ
¹³ The Lᴏʀᴅ Almighty is the one you are to regard as holy,ᵗ
    he is the one you are to fear,ᵘ
    he is the one you are to dread.ᵛ
¹⁴ He will be a holy place;ʷ
    for both houses of Israel he will be
a stoneˣ that causes people to stumbleʸ
    and a rock that makes them fall.ᶻ
And for the people of Jerusalem he will be
    a trap and a snare.ᵃ
¹⁵ Many of them will stumble;ᵇ
    they will fall and be broken,
    they will be snared and captured."

¹⁶ Bind up this testimony of warningᶜ
    and sealᵈ up God's instruction among my disciples.
¹⁷ I will waitᵉ for the Lᴏʀᴅ,
    who is hidingᶠ his face from the house of Jacob.
    I will put my trust in him.ᵍ

¹⁸Here am I, and the children the Lᴏʀᴅ has given me.ʰ We are signsⁱ and symbolsʲ in Israel from the Lᴏʀᴅ Almighty, who dwells on Mount Zion.ᵏ

THE DARKNESS TURNS TO LIGHT

¹⁹When someone tells you to consultˡ mediums and spiritists,ᵐ who whisper and mutter,ⁿ should not a people inquireᵒ of their God? Why consult the dead on behalf of the living? ²⁰Consult God's instructionᵖ and the testimony of warning.ᵠ If anyone does not speak according to this word, they have no lightʳ of dawn. ²¹Distressed and hungry,ˢ they will roam through the land;ᵗ when they are famished, they will become enraged and, looking

---

ᵃ 9 Or *Do your worst*   ᵇ 10 Hebrew *Immanuel*

(see 1:7–9 and note), the head of Judah (cf. the initial references to Damascus and Samaria in 7:8–9). *outspread wings.* The figure changes to a powerful bird of prey. *Immanuel.* All seems lost, but "God is with us" (v. 10) and defeats the enemy (see note on 7:14).
8:9 *nations…be shattered.* Just as Aram and Israel would be shattered (7:7–9), so Assyria and Babylon would eventually fall.
△ 8:10 *it will not stand.* Only God's plans and purposes will last. *God is with us.* See TNIV text note; see also 2Ch 13:12.
8:11 *his strong hand upon me.* See Eze 1:3 and note; 37:1; 40:1. The prophets were conscious of God's presence in and control over their lives.
8:12 The Lord warns the people not to rely on Assyria (see note on 7:1).
8:13 *the one you are to fear.* See 7:2; Pr 1:7 and note.
△ 8:14 *holy place…stone…fall.* Either the Lord is the cornerstone of our lives (see 28:16) or he is a rock over which we fall. See Ro 9:33; 1Pe 2:6 and note for an application to Christ. *both houses.* The northern and southern kingdoms, Israel and Judah.
8:16 Perhaps a reference to the legal transaction connected with vv. 1–2 (see note there). *testimony of warning.* See v. 20. This term occurs elsewhere only in Ru 4:7 ("method of legalizing

transactions"). *God's instruction.* See v. 20. The Hebrew for this phrase can also mean "law." The legal document containing Isaiah's teaching about Assyria's invasion was tied and sealed and then given to the prophet's followers, who were to preserve it until the time of its fulfillment, when God would authenticate it by the events of history (see Jer 32:12–14,44).
8:17–18 *I will put…given me.* In Heb 2:13 these words are put on Jesus' lips.
8:17 *hiding his face.* See 1:15 and note; 59:2; Mic 3:4 and note.
8:18 *signs and symbols.* See notes on 7:3,14; cf. 20:3.
8:19 *mediums and spiritists.* See Dt 18:9–12 and note on 18:9. In the present crisis, people were turning to the spirits of the dead, as King Saul did when he went to a medium to contact the spirit of Samuel (1Sa 28:8–11) and learn about the future. See note on 3:2–3.
△ 8:20 *God's instruction…testimony of warning.* See v. 16 and note. Only by heeding the Lord's word through Isaiah—reinforced by the "signs and symbols" (v. 18) that Isaiah and his sons represented—would the light dawn for Israel.
8:21–22 The Assyrian invasion would bring deep distress on all Israel.

upward, will curse [u] their king and their God. [22]Then they will look toward the earth and see only distress and darkness and fearful gloom, [v] and they will be thrust into utter darkness. [w]

9 *Nevertheless, there will be no more gloom [x] for those who were in distress. In the past he humbled the land of Zebulun and the land of Naphtali, [y] but in the future he will honor Galilee of the nations, by the Way of the Sea, beyond the Jordan—

*[2] The people walking in darkness [z]
  have seen a great light; [a]
on those living in the land of deep darkness [b]
  a light has dawned. [c]
[3] You have enlarged the nation [d]
  and increased their joy; [e]
they rejoice before you
  as people rejoice at the harvest,
as soldiers rejoice
  when dividing the plunder. [f]
[4] For as in the day of Midian's defeat, [g]
you have shattered [h]
the yoke [i] that burdens them,
  the bar across their shoulders, [j]
  the rod of their oppressor. [k]
[5] Every warrior's boot used in battle
  and every garment rolled in blood
will be destined for burning, [l]
  will be fuel for the fire.
[6] For to us a child is born, [m]
  to us a son is given, [n]
and the government [o] will be on his shoulders. [p]
And he will be called
  Wonderful Counselor, [q] Mighty God, [r]
  Everlasting [s] Father, [t] Prince of Peace. [u]
[7] Of the increase of his government [v] and peace [w]
  there will be no end. [x]
He will reign [y] on David's throne
  and over his kingdom,
establishing and upholding it
  with justice [z] and righteousness [a]
  from that time on and forever. [b]
The zeal [c] of the LORD Almighty
  will accomplish this.

* 9:1 is numbered 8:23 in Hebrew texts.   * 9:2-21 is numbered 9:1-20 in Hebrew texts.

8:21 [u] S Ex 22:28; Rev 16:11
8:22 [v] S Job 15:24 [w] S ver 20; S Job 3:13; S Isa 5:30; S Joel 2:2; Mt 25:30; Rev 16:10
9:1 [x] S Job 15:24 [y] S 2Ki 15:29
9:2 [z] S Ps 82:5; S 107:10, 14; S Isa 8:20 [a] S Ps 36:9; Isa 42:6; 49:6; 60:19; Mal 4:2; Eph 5:8 [b] S Isa 1:79 [c] Isa 58:8; Mt 4:15-16*
9:3 [d] S Job 12:23 [e] S Ps 4:7; S Isa 25:9 [f] S Ex 15:9; S Jos 22:8; S Ps 119:162
9:4 [g] S Jdg 7:25 [h] S Job 34:24; Isa 37:36-38 [i] Isa 14:25; 58:6, 9; Jer 2:20; 30:8; Eze 30:18; Na 1:13; Mt 11:30 [j] S Ps 81:6; S Isa 10:27 [k] Isa 14:4; 16:4; 29:5, 20; 49:26; 51:13; 54:14; 60:18
9:5 [l] S Isa 2:4
9:6 [m] S Ge 3:15; Isa 53:2; Lk 2:11 [n] Jn 3:16 [o] S Mt 28:18 [p] Isa 22:21 [q] S Job 15:8; Isa 28:29 [r] S Dt 7:21; Ps 24:8; Isa 10:21; 11:2; 42:13 [s] S Ps 90:2 [t] S Ex 4:22; Isa 64:8; Jn 14:9-10 [u] Isa 26:3, 12; 53:5; 66:12; Jer 33:6; Mic 5:5; S Lk 2:14
9:7 [v] S Isa 2:4 [w] S Ps 85:8; 119:165; Isa 11:9; 26:3, 12; 32:17; 48:18 [x] Da 2:44; 4:3; S Lk 1:33; Jn 12:34 [y] Isa 1:26; 32:1; 60:17; 1Co 15:25 [z] Isa 11:4; 16:5; 32:1, 16; 33:5; 42:1; Jer 23:5; 33:14 [a] S Ps 72:2 [b] S 2Sa 7:13 [c] 2Ki 19:31; Isa 26:11; 37:32; 42:13; 59:17; 63:15

8:21 *curse...king and...God.* Because of their terrible suffering (cf. Pr 19:3)—but severe punishment awaited anyone who cursed God or a ruler (Ex 22:28; Lev 24:15–16).

A 9:1 *Naphtali.* This tribe in northern Israel suffered greatly when the Assyrian Tiglath-Pileser III attacked in 734 and 732 B.C. (2Ki 15:29). *will honor Galilee.* Fulfilled when Jesus ministered in Capernaum—near the major highway from Egypt to Damascus, called "the Way of the Sea" (Mt 4:13–15).

A 9:2 *great light.* Jesus and his salvation would be a "light for the Gentiles" (42:6; 49:6; cf. Mt. 4:15–16 and note; Lk 2:32).
9:4 *Midian's defeat.* Gideon defeated the hordes of Midian and broke their domination over Israel (Jdg 7:22–25). *yoke.* In 10:26–27 Isaiah predicts that God will destroy the Assyrian army and their oppressive yoke. This was fulfilled in 701 B.C. (see 37:36–38 and notes).
9:5 *boot...garment.* Military equipment will no longer be needed. See notes on 2:2–4; Mic 5:10–15.

A 9:6 *son.* A royal son, a son of David (see v. 7; see also 2Sa 7:14; Ps 2:7; Mt 1:1; 3:17; Lk 1:32; Jn 3:16 and notes). *Wonderful Counselor.* In Hebrew each of the four throne names of

the Messiah consists of two elements. "Counselor" points to the Messiah as a king (see Mic 4:9) who determines upon and carries out a program of action (see 14:27, "purposed"; Ps 20:4, "plans"). As Wonderful Counselor, the coming Son of David will carry out a royal program that will cause all the world to marvel. What that program will be is spelled out in ch. 11, and more fully in chs. 24–27 (see 25:1—"wonderful things, planned [counseled] long ago"). In 28:29 the same two Hebrew words underlying "Wonderful Counselor" describe the Lord "whose plan is wonderful" (see also Jdg 13:18 and note). *Mighty God.* See 10:21. His divine power as a warrior is stressed. *Everlasting Father.* He will be an enduring, compassionate provider and protector (cf. 40:9–11). *Prince of Peace.* His rule will bring wholeness and well-being to individuals and to society (see 11:6–9).

A 9:7 *David's throne...righteousness...forever.* In spite of the sins of kings like Ahaz, Christ will be a descendant of David who will rule in righteousness forever (see 11:3–5; 2Sa 7:12–13, 16; Jer 33:15, 20–22). *The zeal...this.* Repeated in 37:32. God is like a jealous lover who will not abandon his people.

9:8 *d* S Dt 32:2
9:9 *e* S Isa 7:2
f S Isa 7:9 *g* Isa 46:12;
48:4; Eze 2:4;
Zec 7:11
9:10 *h* S Ge 11:3
i Am 7:14; Lk 19:4
j 1Ki 7:2-3
9:11 *k* S Isa 7:8
9:12 *l* 2Ki 16:6
m S 2Ch 28:18
n S Ps 79:7
o S Job 40:11
p S Isa 5:25
9:13 *q* S 2Ch 28:22;
Am 4:9; Zep 3:7;
Hag 2:17 *r* Jer 5:3;
Eze 7:9 *s* Isa 2:3; 17:7;
31:1; 55:6; Jer 50:4;
Da 9:13; Hos 3:5; 7:7,
10; Am 4:6,10;
Zep 1:6
9:14 *t* ver 14-15;
Isa 19:15 *u* Rev 18:8
9:15 *v* Isa 3:2-3
w S Isa 5:13
x Isa 28:7; Eze 13:2
y S Job 13:4; S Isa 3:8;
44:20; Eze 13:22;
Mt 24:24
9:16 *z* Mt 15:14;
23:16,24 *a* S Isa 3:12
9:17 *b* Jer 9:21;
11:22; 18:21; 48:15;
49:26; Am 4:10; 8:13
c S Job 5:4; Isa 27:11;
Jer 13:14 *d* Isa 10:6;
32:6; Mic 7:2
e S Isa 1:4 *f* S Isa 3:8;
Mt 12:34; Ro 3:13-14
g S Isa 5:25
9:18 *h* S Dt 29:23;
S Isa 1:31 *i* S Isa 5:6
j S Ps 83:14
9:19 *k* S Job 40:11;
Isa 13:9,13 *l* Jer 17:27
m S Ps 97:3; S Isa 1:31
n S Isa 3:5
9:20 *o* S Lev 26:26;
S Job 18:12
p Isa 49:26; Zec 11:9
9:21 *q* S Jdg 7:22;
S 12:4 *r* S 2Ch 28:6

THE LORD'S ANGER AGAINST ISRAEL

8 The Lord has sent a message *d* against Jacob;
    it will fall on Israel.
9 All the people will know it—
    Ephraim *e* and the inhabitants of Samaria *f*—
  who say with pride
    and arrogance *g* of heart,
10 "The bricks have fallen down,
    but we will rebuild with dressed stone; *h*
  the fig *i* trees have been felled,
    but we will replace them with cedars. *j*"
11 But the LORD has strengthened Rezin's *k* foes against them
    and has spurred their enemies on.
12 Arameans *l* from the east and Philistines *m* from the west
    have devoured *n* Israel with open mouth.

  Yet for all this, his anger *o* is not turned away,
    his hand is still upraised. *p*

13 But the people have not returned *q* to him who struck *r* them,
    nor have they sought *s* the LORD Almighty.
14 So the LORD will cut off from Israel both head and tail,
    both palm branch and reed *t* in a single day; *u*
15 the elders *v* and dignitaries *w* are the head,
    the prophets *x* who teach lies *y* are the tail.
16 Those who guide *z* this people mislead them,
    and those who are guided are led astray. *a*
17 Therefore the Lord will take no pleasure in the young men, *b*
    nor will he pity *c* the fatherless and widows,
  for everyone is ungodly *d* and wicked, *e*
    every mouth speaks folly. *f*

  Yet for all this, his anger is not turned away,
    his hand is still upraised. *g*

18 Surely wickedness burns like a fire; *h*
    it consumes briers and thorns, *i*
  it sets the forest thickets ablaze, *j*
    so that it rolls upward in a column of smoke.
19 By the wrath *k* of the LORD Almighty
    the land will be scorched *l*
  and the people will be fuel for the fire; *m*
    they will not spare each other. *n*
20 On the right they will devour,
    but still be hungry; *o*
  on the left they will eat, *p*
    but not be satisfied.
  They will all feed on the flesh of their own offspring*a*:
21   Manasseh will feed on Ephraim, and Ephraim on Manasseh; *q*
    together they will turn against Judah. *r*

a 20 Or arm

9:8—10:4 Although Isaiah's prophetic message was primarily "concerning Judah and Jerusalem" (1:1), he also occasionally mediated Yahweh's word to "Ephraim and the inhabitants of Samaria" (9:9). This section is an oracle of divine judgment against the northern kingdom. It consists of four balanced stanzas (vv. 8–12, 13–17, 18–21; 10:1–4), each of which ends with the same refrain (see note on 9:12,17,21).
9:9 *Ephraim.* See note on 7:2.
9:10 *bricks have fallen down.* Bricks made of clay and dried by the sun crumbled easily. *dressed stone.* Amos denounces the stone mansions of the wicked (Am 5:11). *cedars.* The cedars of Lebanon provided the most valuable wood in the ancient Near East (see 1Ki 7:2–3).

9:11 *Rezin's foes.* The Assyrians (see note on 7:1).
9:12,17,21 *Yet . . . upraised.* See 5:25. This refrain is repeated in 10:4, where the anger of the Lord reaches a climax in the captivity of his people.
9:14 *head and tail . . . palm branch and reed.* The leaders of Israel (see also 3:1–3). These two pairs refer to Egyptian leaders in 19:15.
9:17 *fatherless and widows.* They often suffered at the hands of the powerful (see note on 1:17), but now they are even wicked.
9:18 *briers and thorns.* See note on 5:6.
9:19 *fuel for the fire.* Contrast v. 5.
9:21 *Manasseh . . . Ephraim.* These two prominent tribes in the northern kingdom were descended from the two sons of Jo-

Yet for all this, his anger is not turned away,
  his hand is still upraised. [s]

10

Woe [t] to those who make unjust laws,
  to those who issue oppressive decrees, [u]
[2] to deprive [v] the poor of their rights
  and withhold justice from the oppressed of my people, [w]
making widows their prey
  and robbing the fatherless. [x]

[3] What will you do on the day of reckoning, [y]
  when disaster [z] comes from afar?
To whom will you run for help? [a]
  Where will you leave your riches?
[4] Nothing will remain but to cringe among the captives [b]
  or fall among the slain. [c]

Yet for all this, his anger is not turned away, [d]
  his hand is still upraised.

GOD'S JUDGMENT ON ASSYRIA

[5] "Woe [e] to the Assyrian, [f] the rod [g] of my anger,
  in whose hand is the club [h] of my wrath! [i]
[6] I send him against a godless [j] nation,
  I dispatch [k] him against a people who anger me, [l]
to seize loot and snatch plunder, [m]
  and to trample [n] them down like mud in the streets.
[7] But this is not what he intends, [o]
  this is not what he has in mind;
his purpose is to destroy,
  to put an end to many nations.
[8] 'Are not my commanders [p] all kings?' he says.
[9] 'Has not Kalno [q] fared like Carchemish? [r]
  Is not Hamath [s] like Arpad, [t]
  and Samaria [u] like Damascus? [v]
[10] As my hand seized the kingdoms of the idols, [w]
  kingdoms whose images excelled those of Jerusalem and Samaria—
[11] shall I not deal with Jerusalem and her images
  as I dealt with Samaria and her idols? [x]' "

[12] When the Lord has finished all his work [y] against Mount Zion [z] and Jerusalem, he will say, "I will punish the king of Assyria [a] for the willful pride [b] of his heart and the haughty look [c] in his eyes. [13] For he says:

" 'By the strength of my hand [d] I have done this, [e]
  and by my wisdom, because I have understanding.
I removed the boundaries of nations,
  I plundered their treasures; [f]
like a mighty one I subdued [a] their kings. [g]

[a] 13 Or *treasures; / I subdued the mighty,*

9:21 [s] S Isa 5:25
10:1 [t] S Isa 5:8
[u] S Ps 58:2
10:2 [v] Isa 3:14
[w] S Isa 5:23
[x] Dt 10:18;
S Job 6:27; S Isa 1:17
10:3 [y] S Job 31:14
[z] ver 25; S Ps 59:5;
Isa 1:24; 13:6; 14:23;
24:6; 26:14; 47:11;
Jer 5:9; 9:9; 50:15;
Lk 19:44
[a] S Ps 108:12;
Isa 20:6; 30:7; 31:3
10:4 [b] Isa 24:22;
Zec 9:11 [c] Isa 22:2;
34:3; 66:16; Jer 39:6;
Na 3:3 [d] S Isa 5:25;
12:1; 63:10; 64:5;
Jer 4:8; 30:24; La 1:12
10:5 [e] S 2Ki 19:21;
S Isa 28:1 [f] ver 12,18;
S Isa 7:20; 14:25;
31:8; 37:7; Zep 2:13
[g] Isa 14:5; 54:16
[h] ver 15,24; Isa 30:31;
41:15; 45:1; Jer 50:23;
51:20 [i] Isa 9:4; 13:3,5,
13; 26:20; 30:30;
34:2; 63:6; 66:14;
Eze 30:24-25
10:6 [j] S Isa 9:17
[k] Hab 1:12
[l] 2Ch 28:9; Isa 9:19
[m] S Jdg 6:4;
S Isa 5:29; 8:1
[n] S 2Sa 22:43;
S Ps 7:5; S Isa 5:5;
37:26-27
10:7 [o] S Ge 50:20;
Ac 4:23-28
10:8 [p] 2Ki 18:24
10:9 [q] S Ge 10:10
[r] S 2Ch 35:20
[s] Nu 34:8; 2Ch 8:4;
Isa 11:11 [t] 2Ki 18:34
[u] 2Ki 17:6
[v] S Ge 14:15; 2Ki 16:9;
Jer 49:24
10:10 [w] 2Ki 19:18
10:11 [x] S 2Ki 19:13;
S Isa 2:8; 36:18-20;
37:10-13
10:12 [y] Isa 28:21-
22; 65:7; 66:4;
Jer 5:29 [z] 2Ki 19:31
[a] S ver 5; S 2Ki 19:7;
Isa 30:31-33; 37:36-
38; Jer 50:18
[b] S Isa 2:11;
S Eze 28:17 [c] Ps 18:27
10:13 [d] S Dt 8:17
[e] S Dt 32:26-27;
Isa 47:7; Da 4:30
[f] Eze 28:4 [g] Isa 14:13-
14

seph (see Ge 46:20; see also Ge 48:5–6 and notes). They had fought each other centuries earlier (Jdg 12:4).
10:1 *Woe.* Cf. the series of woes in 5:8–23.
10:2 *the poor.* See note on Ex 22:21–27; cf. Jer 22:15–16. *widows...fatherless.* See notes on 1:17; 9:17.
10:4 *captives...slain.* Jer 39:6–7 similarly describes the plight of Judah's rulers when Nebuchadnezzar captured Jerusalem in 586 B.C. *Yet...upraised.* See note on 9:12,17,21.
10:5 *Woe.* See v. 1 and note. *rod...club.* See 9:4 and note. Babylonia also was a hammer or club used by God to punish other nations (Jer 50:23; 51:21; Hab 1:6).
10:6 *godless nation.* Judah (see v. 10). *loot...plunder.* The last part of the fulfillment symbolized by Maher-Shalal-Hash-Baz ("loot" here is the translation of Hebrew *shalal,* and "plunder" is the translation of *baz*). See 8:1–4 and note on 8:3.
10:9 *Kalno.* A region in northern Aram (Syria). See Kalneh in Am

6:2 (see also note there). *Carchemish.* The great fortress on the Euphrates River east of Kalno (see Jer 46:2 and note). *Hamath.* A city on the Orontes River that marked the northern extent of Solomon's rule (2Ch 8:4). See note on 2Ki 17:24. *Arpad.* A city near Hamath and just south of Kalno. All these areas submitted to Assyria by c. 717 B.C. (see 36:19).
10:10,14 *my hand seized...my hand reached.* The Hebrew verb is the same in both verses. The repetition of the phrase underscores the unquenchable greed of the Assyrian king.
10:10 *images...of Jerusalem and Samaria.* No Israelite was supposed to worship idols (see Ex 20:4 and note), but the land was full of them (2:8). Samaria fell to Shalmaneser V (2Ki 17:3–6) and Sargon II in 722–721 B.C.
10:12 The Lord's instruments of judgment are not themselves exempt from his judgment. *pride.* Judgment against the proud was announced in 2:11,17.

10:14 ʰ Jer 49:16;
Ob 1:4; Hab 2:6-11
ⁱ S Job 31:25 / Isa 14:6
ᵏ 2Ki 19:22-24;
Isa 37:24-25
10:15 ˡ S Isa 7:20;
45:9; Ro 9:20-21
ᵐ S ver 5
10:16 ⁿ ver 18;
S Nu 11:33; Isa 17:4
ᵒ Ps 78:31 ᵖ S Isa 8:7
�q Jer 21:14
10:17 ʳ S Job 41:21;
S Isa 1:31; 31:9;
Zec 2:5 ˢ Isa 37:23
ᵗ S Nu 11:1-3;
S 2Sa 23:6
ᵘ S Isa 9:18
10:18 ᵛ S 2Ki 19:23
ʷ S ver 5
10:19 ˣ ver 33-34;
Isa 32:19 ʸ Isa 17:6;
21:17; 27:13; Jer 44:28
10:20 ᶻ ver 27;
Isa 11:10,11; 12:1,4;
19:18,19; 24:21; 28:5;
52:6; Zec 9:16
ᵃ S Isa 1:9; Eze 7:16
ᵇ S 2Ki 16:7
ᶜ 2Ch 28:20
ᵈ 2Ch 14:11; Isa 17:7;
48:2; 50:10; Jer 21:2;
Hos 3:5; 6:1; Mic 3:11;
7:7 ᵉ S Isa 5:24
10:21 ᶠ S Ge 45:7;
Isa 6:13; Zep 3:13
g Isa 7:3 ʰ S Isa 9:6
10:22 ⁱ S Ge 12:2;
Isa 48:19; Jer 33:22
ʲ Ezr 1:4; Isa 11:11;
46:3 ᵏ ver 23;
Isa 28:22; Jer 40:2;
Da 9:27
10:23 ˡ S ver 22
ᵐ Isa 6:12; 28:22;
Ro 9:27-28*
10:24 ⁿ Ps 87:5-6
ᵒ S Isa 7:4 ᵖ S Ex 5:14
q S ver 5

¹⁴ As one reaches into a nest,ʰ
  so my hand reached for the wealthⁱ of the nations;
as people gather abandoned eggs,
  so I gathered all the countries;ʲ
not one flapped a wing,
  or opened its mouth to chirp.ᵏ ”

¹⁵ Does the ax raise itself above the one who swings it,
  or the saw boast against the one who uses it?ˡ
As if a rod were to wield the person who lifts it up,
  or a clubᵐ brandish one who is not wood!
¹⁶ Therefore, the Lord, the Lᴏʀᴅ Almighty,
  will send a wasting diseaseⁿ upon his sturdy warriors;ᵒ
under his pompᵖ a fireq will be kindled
  like a blazing flame.
¹⁷ The Light of Israel will become a fire,ʳ
  their Holy Oneˢ a flame;
in a single day it will burn and consume
  his thornsᵗ and his briers.ᵘ
¹⁸ The splendor of his forestsᵛ and fertile fields
  it will completely destroy,ʷ
  as when sick people waste away.
¹⁹ And the remaining trees of his forestsˣ will be so fewʸ
  that a child could write them down.

THE REMNANT OF ISRAEL

²⁰ In that dayᶻ the remnant of Israel,
  the survivorsᵃ of the house of Jacob,
will no longer relyᵇ on him
  who struck them downᶜ
but will truly relyᵈ on the Lᴏʀᴅ,
  the Holy One of Israel.ᵉ
²¹ A remnantᶠ will return,ᵃ g a remnant of Jacob
  will return to the Mighty God.ʰ
²² Though your people be like the sandⁱ by the sea, Israel,
  only a remnant will return.ʲ
Destruction has been decreed,ᵏ
  overwhelming and righteous.
²³ The Lord, the Lᴏʀᴅ Almighty, will carry out
  the destruction decreedˡ upon the whole land.ᵐ

²⁴ Therefore, this is what the Lord, the Lᴏʀᴅ Almighty, says:

"My people who live in Zion,ⁿ
  do not be afraidᵒ of the Assyrians,
who beatᵖ you with a rodq
  and lift up a club against you, as Egypt did.

ᵃ 21 Hebrew *shear-jashub*; also in verse 22

10:13–14 *my . . . l.* The king of Assyria boastfully refers to himself nine times. Cf. 14:13–14; Eze 28:2–5.
10:15 *ax . . . saw . . . rod . . . club.* See v. 5; 9:4 and notes.
10:16 *the Lord, the Lᴏʀᴅ Almighty.* See 1:24 and note. *wasting disease.* When the angel put to death 185,000 soldiers of the Assyrian king Sennacherib in 701 B.C., he may have used a rapidly spreading plague (see note on 37:36; see also 2Sa 24:15–16; 1Ch 21:22,27).
10:17,20 *Holy One.* See note on 1:4.
10:18–19 *forests.* A reference to the Assyrian army. See vv. 33–34 and note on v. 33.
10:19 Probably fulfilled between 612 B.C. (fall of Nineveh) and 605 (battle of Carchemish).

A **10:20,27** *In that day.* The day of victory and joy, the positive aspect of the "day of the Lᴏʀᴅ" (see notes on 2:11,17,20; 9:4). Israel is restored and the people praise God. Ch.

11 connects this "day" with the Messianic age (see 11:10–11 and notes; see also 12:1,4).
10:20–22 *remnant.* See note on 1:9. "A remnant will return" was the name of Isaiah's first son (see TNIV text note on 7:3). A faithful remnant led by Hezekiah survived the Assyrian invasion of 701 B.C. (see 37:4 and note). Later, a remnant returned from Babylonian exile.
10:20 *him who struck them.* The king of Assyria (see note on 7:17).
10:21 *Mighty God.* See note on 9:6.
10:22 *the sand by the sea.* See notes on Ge 13:16; 22:17. *Destruction . . . decreed.* Because of Israel's sin, God would punish the nation through foreign invaders.
10:23–24 *The Lord, the Lᴏʀᴅ Almighty.* See 1:24 and note.
10:24 *rod . . . club.* See v. 5; 9:4 and notes.

²⁵ Very soon ^r my anger against you will end
and my wrath ^s will be directed to their destruction. ^t"

²⁶ The Lord Almighty will lash ^u them with a whip,
as when he struck down Midian ^v at the rock of Oreb;
and he will raise his staff ^w over the waters, ^x
as he did in Egypt.

²⁷ In that day ^y their burden ^z will be lifted from your shoulders,
their yoke ^a from your neck; ^b
the yoke ^c will be broken
because you have grown so fat. ^a

²⁸ They enter Aiath;
they pass through Migron; ^d
they store supplies ^e at Mikmash. ^f

²⁹ They go over the pass, and say,
"We will camp overnight at Geba. ^g"
Ramah ^h trembles;
Gibeah ⁱ of Saul flees. ^j

³⁰ Cry out, Daughter Gallim! ^k
Listen, Laishah!
Poor Anathoth! ^l

³¹ Madmenah is in flight;
the people of Gebim take cover.

³² This day they will halt at Nob; ^m
they will shake their fist ⁿ
at the mount of Daughter Zion, ^o
at the hill of Jerusalem.

³³ See, the Lord, the Lord Almighty,
will lop off ^p the boughs with great power.
The lofty trees will be felled, ^q
the tall ^r ones will be brought low. ^s

³⁴ He will cut down ^t the forest thickets with an ax;
Lebanon ^u will fall before the Mighty One. ^v

THE BRANCH FROM JESSE

11 A shoot ^w will come up from the stump ^x of Jesse; ^y
from his roots a Branch ^z will bear fruit. ^a
² The Spirit ^b of the Lord will rest on him—
the Spirit of wisdom ^c and of understanding,
the Spirit of counsel and of might, ^d
the Spirit of the knowledge and fear of the Lord—
³ and he will delight in the fear ^e of the Lord.

---

^a 27 Hebrew; Septuagint *broken / from your shoulders*

10:25 ^r Isa 17:14; 29:17; Hag 2:6
^s ver 5; Ps 30:5; Isa 13:5; 24:21; 26:20; 30:30; 34:2; 66:14; Da 8:19; 11:36
^t S ver 3; Mic 5:6
10:26 ^u Isa 37:36-38 ^v S Isa 9:4
^w Isa 30:32
^x S Ex 14:16
10:27 ^y S ver 20
^z S Ps 66:11
^a S Lev 26:13;
S Isa 9:4 ^b Isa 14:25; 47:6; 52:2 ^c Jer 30:8
10:28 ^d S 1Sa 14:2
^e S Jos 1:11 ^f 1Sa 13:2
10:29 ^g S Jos 18:24; S Ne 11:31
^h S Jos 18:25
ⁱ S Jdg 19:14 / Isa 15:5
10:30 ^k 1Sa 25:44
^l S Ne 11:32
10:32 ^m S 1Sa 21:1
ⁿ S Job 15:25
^o S Ps 9:14; Isa 16:1; Jer 6:23
10:33 ^p Isa 18:5; 27:11; Eze 17:4
^q S Ex 12:12 ^r Isa 2:13; Am 2:9 ^s Isa 5:15
10:34 ^t Na 1:12; Zec 11:2 ^u S 2Ki 19:23
^v S Ge 49:24; Ps 93:4; Isa 33:21
11:1 ^w S 2Ki 19:26; S Job 14:7 ^x S Job 14:8
^y ver 10; Isa 9:7; S Mt 1:1; S Rev 5:5
^z S Isa 4:2
^a S 2Ki 19:30; S Isa 27:6
11:2 ^b S Jdg 3:10; Isa 32:15; 42:1; 44:3; 48:16; 59:21; 61:1; Eze 37:14; 39:29; Joel 2:28; Mt 3:16; Jn 1:32-33; 16:13
^c S Ex 28:3; S Eph 1:17; S Col 2:3
^d S Isa 9:6; 2Ti 1:7
11:3 ^e Isa 33:6

10:26–27 *Midian ... burden ... yoke.* See note on 9:4.
10:26 *Oreb.* One of the Midianite leaders (Jdg 7:25). *the waters ... in Egypt.* When Moses stretched out his hand over the Red Sea, the waters engulfed the chariots of the pharaoh (see Ex 14:26–28).
10:27 *fat.* Like a sturdy animal, Israel is able to break the yoke.
10:28–32 As if seeing a vision, Isaiah describes the approach of the Assyrian army to Jerusalem from about ten miles north of the city.
10:28 *Mikmash.* Located about seven miles north of Jerusalem.
10:29 *Ramah.* The home of Samuel. It was about five miles from Jerusalem (1Sa 7:17; see note on 1Sa 1:1). *Gibeah of Saul.* About three miles from Jerusalem. It had been the capital of Israel's first king (see 1Sa 10:26).
10:30 *Daughter Gallim.* A personification of a Benjamite town of Saulide association (see 1Sa 25:44; see also note on 2Ki 19:21). *Poor Anathoth.* Jeremiah's hometown (see Jer 1:1 and note). The Hebrew for "poor" sounds like the word "Anathoth"; thus a wordplay.
10:32 *Nob.* Perhaps on Mount Scopus, on the outskirts of

Jerusalem. *Daughter Zion.* A personification of Jerusalem (see note on 2Ki 19:21).
10:33 *the Lord, the Lord Almighty.* See 1:24 and note. *boughs ... trees.* Sennacherib and his armies will fall (see vv. 16–19 and notes).
10:34 *Lebanon.* Refers to the famed cedars of Lebanon (see notes on 2:13; 9:10; 14:8).
11:1 *shoot ... stump.* The Assyrians all but destroyed Judah, but it was the Babylonian exile that brought the kingdom of Judah to an end in 586 B.C. The Messiah will grow as a shoot from that stump of David's dynasty. See 6:13 and note. *Jesse.* David's father (see 1Sa 16:10–13). *Branch.* See notes on 4:2; Mt 2:23.
11:2 *The Spirit ... will rest on him.* The Messiah, like David (1Sa 16:13), will be empowered by the Holy Spirit (see 61:1 and note). *counsel ... might.* The Spirit will endow him with the wisdom to undertake wise purposes and with the power to carry them out (see note on 9:6). *fear of the Lord.* See Pr 1:7 and note.
11:3 *delight in the fear of the Lord.* See Jn 8:29.

11:3 *f* Jn 7:24
g Jn 2:25
11:4 *h* S Ps 72:2
i S Ps 72:4; S Isa 14:30
j S Isa 9:7; Rev 19:11
k S Job 5:16; S Isa 3:14
l Isa 27:7; 30:31;
Zec 14:12; Mal 4:6
m S Job 40:18; Ps 2:9;
Rev 19:15 *n* S Job 4:9;
Ps 18:8; Isa 30:28,33;
40:24; 59:19;
Eze 21:31; 2Th 2:8
o S Ps 139:19
11:5 *p* Ex 12:11;
1Ki 18:46 *q* Isa 25:1
r Eph 6:14
11:6 *s* Isa 65:25
11:7 *t* S Job 40:15
11:8 *u* Isa 65:20
v Isa 14:29; 30:6; 59:5
11:9 *w* S Nu 25:12;
S Isa 2:4; S 9:7
x S Ps 48:1; S Isa 2:2
y Isa 17:46; Ps 98:2-
3; Isa 45:22; 48:20;
52:10 *z* Ex 7:5;
Isa 19:21; 45:6,14;
49:26; Jer 24:7; 31:34;
Hab 2:14
11:10 *a* S Isa 10:20
b S ver 1 *c* S Ps 20:5;
Isa 18:3; Jer 4:6;
Jn 12:32 *d* Isa 2:4;
14:1; 49:23; 56:3,6;
60:5,10; Isa 2:2;
Ac 11:18 *e* Ro 15:12*
f S Ps 116:7; Isa 14:3;
28:12; 32:17-18; 40:2;
Jer 6:16; 30:10; 46:27
g Hag 2:9; Zec 2:5
11:11 *h* S Isa 10:20
i S Dt 30:4; S Isa 1:9
j Isa 19:24; Hos 11:11;
Mic 7:12; Zec 10:10
k Jer 44:1,15;
Eze 29:14; 30:14
l S Ge 10:6; Ac 8:27
m S Ge 10:22
n S Isa 10:9
o Isa 24:15; 41:1,5;
42:4,10,12; 49:1; 51:5;
59:18; 60:9; 66:19
p Isa 49:12; Jer 16:15;
46:27; Eze 38:8;
Zec 8:7
11:12 *q* S Ps 20:5
r Isa 14:2; 43:5; 49:22;
54:7; Jer 16:15; 31:10;
32:37 *s* S Ne 1:9;
S Ps 106:47; Isa 14:1;
41:14; 49:5
t Eze 28:25; Zep 3:10
u S Ps 48:10; 67:7;
Isa 41:5; Rev 7:1

He will not judge by what he sees with his eyes, *f*
　　or decide by what he hears with his ears; *g*
⁴but with righteousness *h* he will judge the needy, *i*
　　with justice *j* he will give decisions for the poor *k* of the earth.
He will strike *l* the earth with the rod of his mouth; *m*
　　with the breath *n* of his lips he will slay the wicked. *o*
⁵Righteousness will be his belt *p*
　　and faithfulness *q* the sash around his waist. *r*

⁶The wolf will live with the lamb, *s*
　　the leopard will lie down with the goat,
the calf and the lion and the yearling *a* together;
　　and a little child will lead them.
⁷The cow will feed with the bear,
　　their young will lie down together,
and the lion will eat straw like the ox. *t*
⁸Infants *u* will play near the hole of the cobra;
　　young children will put their hands into the viper's *v* nest.
⁹They will neither harm nor destroy *w*
　　on all my holy mountain, *x*
for the earth *y* will be filled with the knowledge *z* of the Lord
　　as the waters cover the sea.

¹⁰In that day *a* the Root of Jesse *b* will stand as a banner *c* for the peoples; the nations *d* will rally to him, *e* and his resting place *f* will be glorious. *g* ¹¹In that day *h* the Lord will reach out his hand a second time to reclaim the surviving remnant *i* of his people from Assyria, *j* from Lower Egypt, from Upper Egypt, *k* from Cush, *b, l* from Elam, *m* from Babylonia, *c* from Hamath *n* and from the islands *o* of the Mediterranean. *p*

¹²He will raise a banner *q* for the nations
　　and gather *r* the exiles of Israel; *s*
he will assemble the scattered people *t* of Judah
　　from the four quarters of the earth. *u*
¹³Ephraim's jealousy will vanish,
　　and Judah's enemies *d* will be destroyed;
Ephraim will not be jealous of Judah,
　　nor Judah hostile toward Ephraim. *v*
¹⁴They will swoop down on the slopes of Philistia *w* to the west;
　　together they will plunder the people to the east. *x*
They will lay hands on Edom *y* and Moab, *z*
　　and the Ammonites *a* will be subject to them. *b*

a 6 Hebrew; Septuagint *lion will feed*　　*b 11* That is, the upper Nile region　　*c 11* Hebrew *Shinar*
d 13 Or *hostility*

11:13 *v* S 2Ch 28:6; Jer 3:18; Eze 37:16-17,22; Hos 1:11　　**11:14** *w* S 2Ch 26:6; S 28:18 *x* S Jdg 6:3 *y* S Nu 24:18; S Ps 137:7; Isa 34:5-6; 63:1;
Jer 49:22; Eze 25:12; Da 11:41; Joel 3:19; Ob 1:1; Mal 1:4 *z* Isa 15:1; 16:14; 25:10; Jer 48:40; Zep 2:8-11 *a* Jdg 11:14-18 *b* Isa 25:3; 60:12

11:4 *righteousness ... justice.* The rulers of Isaiah's day lacked these qualities (see 1:17; 5:7; see also note on 9:7). *rod of his mouth.* Assyria was God's rod in 10:5,24, but the Messiah will rule the nations with an iron scepter (see Ps 2:9; Rev 2:27 and notes; 19:15).
11:5 *belt.* When a man prepared for vigorous action, he tied up his loose, flowing garments with a belt (see 5:27).

11:6–9 The peace and safety of the Messianic age are reflected in the fact that little children will be unharmed as they play with formerly ferocious animals. Such conditions are a description of the future consummation of the Messianic kingdom. See 2:2–4; 35:9; 65:20–25 and notes; Eze 34:25–29.
11:9 *my holy mountain.* See 2:2–4 and note. *filled with the knowledge.* See 2:3, where the word of the Lord is taught in Jerusalem (see also Hab 2:14 and note).
11:10 *In that day.* See note on 10:20,27. *Root of Jesse.* A Messianic title closely connected with v. 1 (see also 53:2; Ro 15:12; Rev 5:5; 22:16 and notes). *banner.* See 5:26 and note.
11:11 *second time.* The first time was the exodus from Egypt (see v. 16). The second is probably the return from Assyrian and

Babylonian exile, though some interpreters, who believe that the passage refers to the dispersion after the destruction of Jerusalem in A.D. 70, place the regathering at Christ's second coming. *remnant.* See notes on 1:9; 10:20–22. *Lower Egypt.* The delta region of the Nile, in the north. *Upper Egypt.* Southern Egypt, upstream from the delta. *Elam.* The land northeast of the lower Tigris Valley (see 21:2 and note; Jer 49:34–39; Da 8:2). *Hamath.* See note on 10:9. *islands of the Mediterranean.* The coastlands are probably also intended (see 41:1,5; 42:4; Ge 10:5).
11:12 *gather the exiles.* See 27:13; 49:22; 56:8; 62:10; 66:20. *four quarters.* Lit. "four wings." "Four quarters of the earth" is equivalent to "ends of the earth" (24:16; Job 37:3).
11:13 *Ephraim's jealousy.* See note on 7:2. Prior to the exile, Ephraim and Judah were frequently fighting each other (see 9:21 and note).
11:14 *people to the east.* Perhaps the Midianites, who plundered Israel, along with other eastern peoples (see 9:4). *Edom ... Moab ... Ammonites.* After the exodus, Israel did not attack these nations (see Jdg 11:14–18). Israel's future political domination is also referred to in 14:2; 49:23; 60:12 (see also 25:10; 34:5).

¹⁵ The LORD will dry up[c]
   the gulf of the Egyptian sea;
   with a scorching wind[d] he will sweep his hand[e]
      over the Euphrates River.[f]
He will break it up into seven streams
   so that anyone can cross over in sandals.[g]
¹⁶ There will be a highway[h] for the remnant[i] of his people
      that is left from Assyria,[j]
   as there was for Israel
      when they came up from Egypt.[k]

SONGS OF PRAISE

12

In that day[l] you will say:

"I will praise[m] you, LORD.
   Although you were angry with me,
your anger has turned away[n]
   and you have comforted[o] me.
² Surely God is my salvation;[p]
   I will trust[q] and not be afraid.
The LORD, the LORD,[r] is my strength[s] and my defense[a];
   he has become my salvation.[t]"
³ With joy you will draw water[u]
   from the wells[v] of salvation.

⁴ In that day[w] you will say:

"Give praise to the LORD, call on his name;[x]
   make known among the nations[y] what he has done,
   and proclaim that his name is exalted.[z]
⁵ Sing[a] to the LORD, for he has done glorious things;[b]
   let this be known to all the world.
⁶ Shout aloud and sing for joy,[c] people of Zion,
   for great[d] is the Holy One of Israel[e] among you.[f]"

A PROPHECY AGAINST BABYLON

13

A prophecy[g] concerning Babylon[h] that Isaiah son of Amoz[i] saw:[j]

² Raise a banner[k] on a bare hilltop,
   shout to them;

---

[a] 2 Or *song*

11:15 [c] S Ex 14:22;
S Dt 11:10; Isa 37:25;
42:15; Jer 50:38;
51:36 [d] S Ge 41:6
[e] Isa 19:16; 30:32
[f] S Isa 7:20
[g] S Ex 14:29
11:16 [h] Isa 19:23;
35:8; 40:3; 49:11;
51:10; 57:14; 62:10;
Jer 50:5 [i] S Ge 45:7
[j] S ver 11 [k] Ex 14:26-
31
12:1 [l] S Isa 10:20
[m] Ps 9:1; Isa 25:1
[n] S Job 13:16
[o] S Ps 71:21
12:2 [p] Isa 17:10;
25:9; 33:6; 45:17;
51:5,6; 54:8; 59:16;
61:10; 62:11
[q] S Job 13:15;
S Ps 26:1; S 112:7;
Isa 26:3; Da 6:23
[r] Isa 26:4; 38:11
[s] S Ps 18:1 [t] S Ex 15:2
12:3 [u] S 2Ki 3:17;
Ps 36:9; Jer 2:13;
17:13; Jn 4:10,14
[v] Ex 15:25
12:4 [w] S Isa 10:20
[x] Ex 3:15; Ps 80:18;
105:1; Isa 24:15; 25:1;
26:8,13; Hos 12:5
[y] Isa 54:5; 60:3;
Jer 10:7; Zep 2:11;
Mal 1:11 [z] S Ps 113:2
12:5 [a] S Ex 15:1
[b] S Ps 98:1
12:6 [c] S Ge 21:6;
S Ps 98:4; Isa 24:14;
48:20; 52:8; Jer 20:13;
31:7; Zec 2:10 [d] Ps 48:1
[e] S Ps 78:41; 99:2;
Isa 1:24; 10:20; 17:7;
29:19; 37:23; 43:3,14;
45:11; 49:26; 55:5;
Eze 39:7 [f] S Ps 46:5;
Zep 3:14-17
13:1 [g] Isa 14:28;
15:1; 21:1; Na 1:1;
Hab 1:1; Zec 9:1; 12:1;
Mal 1:1 [h] ver 19;
S Ge 10:10; Isa 14:4;
21:9; 46:1-2; 48:14;
Jer 24:1; 25:12;
Rev 14:8 [i] Isa 20:2;
37:2 [j] S Isa 1:1
13:2 [k] S Ps 20:5;
Jer 50:2; 51:27

11:15 *dry up … the Egyptian sea.* An allusion to the drying up of the Red Sea during the exodus (see Ex 14:21–22). *gulf.* Lit. "tongue" (see "bay" in Jos 15:2,5). *Euphrates.* Rev 16:12 refers to the drying up of the Euphrates, perhaps symbolizing the removal of barriers preventing the coming of "the kings from the East."
11:16 *highway.* The removal of obstacles and the building of a highway leading to Jerusalem are also described in 57:14; 62:10 (cf. 35:8–10 and note on 35:8; 40:3–4 and note on 40:3).
12:1–6 Two short psalms of praise for deliverance (vv. 1–3,4–6) climax chs. 7–11 (see note on 7:1—12:6; see also note on 6:1).
12:1,4 *In that day.* See note on 10:20,27.
12:1 *I will praise you.* The "I" is probably the nation, praising the Lord for the deliverance he is sure to bring. *your anger has turned away.* See note on 9:12,17,21. After God punishes Israel, his anger will be directed against nations like Assyria and Babylonia.
12:2 *The LORD, the LORD.* See notes on Ex 3:15; 34:6–7; Dt 28:58. *the LORD … salvation.* These lines echo Ex 15:2, a verse commemorating the defeat of the Egyptians at the Red Sea. See also Ps 118:14 and note.
12:3 *wells.* Perhaps an allusion to God's abundant provision of water for Israel during the desert wanderings (cf. Ex 15:25,27). But here God's future saving act is itself the "well" from which Israel will draw life-giving water (see Ps 36:9; Jer 2:13; Jn 4:10 and notes).

12:6 *Shout aloud and sing for joy.* These two imperatives occur again in 54:1, where Zion rejoices over the restoration of her people. *Holy One of Israel.* See notes on 1:4; 6:1.
13:1—23:18 A series of prophecies against the nations (see also Jer 46–51; Eze 25–32; Am 1–2; Zep 2:4–15 and notes). They begin with Babylon (13:1—14:23) and Assyria (14:24–27) before moving on to smaller nations. God's judgment on his people does not mean that the pagan nations will be spared (see Jer 25:29). In fact, God's judgments on the nations are often a part of his salvation of his people (see, e.g., 10:12).
13:1—14:27 This prophecy concerns Babylon during the Assyrian empire rather than during the Neo-Babylonian empire. Thus the prophecy is actually against the Assyrian empire, Babylon being its most important city. From 729 B.C. on, the kings of Assyria also assumed the title "king of Babylon." Note that there is no new "prophecy" heading at 14:24, even though 14:24–27 clearly pertains to Assyria; so 13:1—14:27 forms a unit. (Cf. 21:1–10.) This is not to say that some elements of the prophecy against the city of Babylon did not reach beyond the period of the Assyrian empire (e.g., see notes on 13:1,20).
13:1 See note on 1:1. *prophecy.* The Hebrew for this word is related to a Hebrew verb meaning "to lift up, carry" and is possibly to be understood as either lifting up one's voice or carrying a burden. Such a "prophecy" often contains a message of doom. *Bab-*

13:2 *l* Isa 24:12;
45:2; Jer 51:58
13:3 *m* ver 17;
Isa 21:2; Jer 51:11;
Da 5:28,31; Joel 3:11
n S Job 40:11;
S Isa 10:5
o S Ps 149:2
13:4 *p* Joel 3:14
q S Ps 46:6 *r* Isa 47:4;
51:15 *s* Isa 42:13;
Jer 50:41
13:5 *t* S Isa 5:26
u Isa 45:1; 54:16;
Jer 50:25 *v* S Isa 10:25
w S Jos 6:17; Isa 24:1;
30:25; 34:2
13:6 *x* Isa 14:31;
15:2; Mic 1:8;
Eze 30:2; Jas 5:1
y S Isa 2:12
z S Isa 10:3; S 14:15
a S Ge 17:1
13:7 *b* S 2Ki 19:26;
S Job 4:3; S Jer 47:3
c S Jos 2:11; Eze 21:7
13:8 *d* S Ps 31:13;
S 48:5; S Isa 21:4
e Ex 15:14 *f* S Ge 3:16;
S Jn 16:21 *g* Joel 2:6;
Na 2:10
13:9 *h* S Isa 2:12;
Jer 51:2 *i* Jer 6:23
j S Isa 9:19
k Isa 26:21; 66:16;
Jer 25:31; Joel 3:2
13:10 *l* S Job 9:7
m Isa 24:23; Zec 14:7
n S Ex 10:22;
S Isa 5:30; Rev 8:12
o Eze 32:7; Am 5:20;
8:9; S Mt 24:29*;
Mk 13:24*
13:11 *p* Isa 3:11;
11:4; 26:21; 65:6-7;
66:16 *q* S Ps 125:3
r S Ps 10:5; S Pr 16:18;
Da 5:23 *s* S Isa 2:9;
23:9; Eze 28:2;
Da 4:37 *t* Isa 25:3,5;
29:5,20; 49:25,26
13:12 *u* S Isa 4:1
v S Ge 10:29
13:13 *w* S Ps 102:26;
Isa 34:4; 51:6
x S Job 9:6;
S Isa 14:16; Mt 24:7;
Mk 13:8

beckon to them
    to enter the gates *l* of the nobles.
³ I have commanded my holy ones;
    I have summoned my warriors *m* to carry out my wrath *n*—
    those who rejoice *o* in my triumph.

⁴ Listen, a noise on the mountains,
    like that of a great multitude! *p*
Listen, an uproar *q* among the kingdoms,
    like nations massing together!
The Lord Almighty *r* is mustering *s*
    an army for war.
⁵ They come from faraway lands,
    from the ends of the heavens *t*—
the Lord and the weapons *u* of his wrath *v*—
    to destroy *w* the whole country.

⁶ Wail, *x* for the day *y* of the Lord is near;
    it will come like destruction *z* from the Almighty. *a a*
⁷ Because of this, all hands will go limp, *b*
    every man's heart will melt. *c*
⁸ Terror *d* will seize them,
    pain and anguish will grip *e* them;
    they will writhe like a woman in labor. *f*
They will look aghast at each other,
    their faces aflame. *g*

⁹ See, the day *h* of the Lord is coming
    —a cruel *i* day, with wrath *j* and fierce anger *k*—
to make the land desolate
    and destroy the sinners within it.
¹⁰ The stars of heaven and their constellations
    will not show their light. *l*
The rising sun *m* will be darkened *n*
    and the moon will not give its light. *o*
¹¹ I will punish *p* the world for its evil,
    the wicked *q* for their sins.
I will put an end to the arrogance of the haughty *r*
    and will humble *s* the pride of the ruthless. *t*
¹² I will make people *u* scarcer than pure gold,
    more rare than the gold of Ophir. *v*
¹³ Therefore I will make the heavens tremble; *w*
    and the earth will shake *x* from its place

---

a 6 Hebrew *Shaddai*

---

ylon. See 21:1–9; 46:1–2; 47:1–15; Jer 50–51 and notes. Its judgment is announced first because of the present Assyrian threat and because Babylon would later bring about the downfall of Judah and Jerusalem between 605 and 586 B.C. Babylon was conquered by Cyrus the Persian (see 45:1; 47:1) in 539. Subsequently it came to symbolize the world powers arrayed against God's kingdom (cf. 1Pe 5:13), and its final destruction is announced in Rev 14:8; 16:19; 17–18. Here, however, Babylon is still part of the Assyrian empire (see 14:24–27; see also note on 13:1—14:27).
13:2 *Raise a banner.* See note on 5:26.
13:3 *my holy ones.* Or "my consecrated ones," those set apart to carry out God's will. Here the reference is probably to the Persians under Cyrus the Great (see note on v. 1). Cf. 10:5, where the Lord calls Assyria "the rod of my anger"; see also 45:1 and note. *wrath.* God's anger is no longer turned against Israel (see 5:25; 9:12,17,21; 10:4) but against her enemies (see vv. 5,9,13; cf. 30:27). God must punish sin, particularly arrogance (see v. 11).
13:4 *The Lord Almighty is mustering an army.* See note on 1Sa 1:3. The Hebrew for "army" is the singular form of the word for "Almighty." God is the head of the armies of Israel (1Sa 17:45), of angelic powers (1Ki 22:19; Lk 2:13) and, here, of the armies

that will destroy Babylon.
13:5 *weapons of his wrath.* Assyria was the club in God's hand during Isaiah's day, and Babylon itself would later serve as God's weapon (see 10:5 and note).
13:6,9 *day of the Lord.* See note on 2:11,17,20.
13:6 *destruction.* Hebrew *shod,* forming a wordplay on "Almighty" (Hebrew *Shaddai*)—as also in Joel 1:15. See note on 5:7. For *Shaddai,* see note on Ge 17:1.
13:7 *hands will go limp.* Courage will fail. See Jer 6:24.
13:8 *Terror.* The Lord's warfare in behalf of his people usually brings panic to the enemy (see Ex 15:14–16; Jdg 7:22 and note). *pain...labor.* The prophets often compare the suffering of judgment and war with the pain and anguish that frequently accompany childbirth (see 26:17; Jer 4:31; 6:24).
13:10 *stars...sun...moon.* Cosmic darkness is associated with the day of the Lord also in Joel 2:10,31; Rev 6:12–13. Cf. Jdg 5:20.
13:11 *arrogance...pride.* Cf. 2:9,11,17; 5:15.
13:12 *scarcer...rare.* War will reduce the male population drastically (see 4:1 and note). *Ophir.* Solomon imported large quantities of gold from this place (see 1Ki 9:28; 10:11 and notes).
13:13 *heavens tremble...earth...shake.* Thunderstorms and

at the wrath ^{y} of the LORD Almighty,
in the day of his burning anger. ^{z}

14 Like a hunted ^{a} gazelle,
like sheep without a shepherd, ^{b}
they will all return to their own people,
they will flee ^{c} to their native land. ^{d}

15 Whoever is captured will be thrust through;
all who are caught will fall ^{e} by the sword. ^{f}

16 Their infants ^{g} will be dashed to pieces before their eyes;
their houses will be looted and their wives ravished. ^{h}

17 See, I will stir up ^{i} against them the Medes, ^{j}
who do not care for silver
and have no delight in gold. ^{k}

18 Their bows ^{l} will strike down the young men; ^{m}
they will have no mercy ^{n} on infants,
nor will they look with compassion on children. ^{o}

19 Babylon, ^{p} the jewel of kingdoms, ^{q}
the pride and glory ^{r} of the Babylonians, ^{a}
will be overthrown ^{s} by God
like Sodom and Gomorrah. ^{t}

20 She will never be inhabited ^{u}
or lived in through all generations;
there no nomads ^{v} will pitch their tents,
there no shepherds will rest their flocks.

21 But desert creatures ^{w} will lie there,
jackals ^{x} will fill her houses;
there the owls ^{y} will dwell,
and there the wild goats ^{z} will leap about.

22 Hyenas ^{a} will inhabit her strongholds, ^{b}
jackals ^{c} her luxurious palaces.
Her time is at hand, ^{d}
and her days will not be prolonged. ^{e}

14 The LORD will have compassion ^{f} on Jacob;
once again he will choose ^{g} Israel
and will settle them in their own land. ^{h}
Foreigners ^{i} will join them
and unite with the house of Jacob.
2 Nations will take them

---

a 19 Or *Chaldeans*

13:13 ^{y} S Isa 9:19
^{z} S Job 9:5
13:14 ^{a} Pr 6:5
^{b} S 1Ki 22:17;
S Mt 9:36; S Jn 10:11
^{c} S Ge 11:9; Isa 17:13;
21:15; 22:3; 33:3;
Jer 4:9 ^{d} Jer 46:16;
50:16; 51:9; Na 3:7
13:15 ^{e} Jer 51:4
^{f} Isa 14:19; Jer 50:25
13:16 ^{g} ver 18;
S Nu 16:27; S 2Ki 8:12
^{h} S Ge 34:29;
S Hos 13:16
13:17 ^{i} Jer 50:9,41;
51:1 ^{j} S ver 3
^{k} 2Ki 18:14-16;
Pr 6:34-35
13:18 ^{l} S Ps 7:12;
Isa 41:2; Jer 50:9,14,
29 ^{m} S Dt 32:25;
Jer 49:26; 50:30; 51:4
^{n} Isa 47:6; Jer 6:23;
50:42 ^{o} S ver 16;
Isa 14:22; 47:9
13:19 ^{p} S ver 1
^{q} Isa 47:5; Da 2:37-
38 ^{r} Da 4:30
^{s} S Ps 137:8;
S Rev 14:8
^{t} S Ge 19:25; Isa 1:9-
10; Ro 9:29
13:20 ^{u} Isa 14:23;
34:10-15; Jer 51:29,
37-43,62 ^{v} 2Ch 17:11
13:21 ^{w} S Ps 74:14;
Rev 18:2 ^{x} Jer 14:6
^{y} S Lev 11:16-18;
S Dt 14:15-17
^{z} Lev 17:7; 2Ch 11:15
13:22 ^{a} Isa 34:14
^{b} Isa 25:2; 32:14
^{c} Isa 34:13; 35:7;
43:20; Jer 9:11; 49:33;
51:37; Mal 1:3
^{d} Dt 32:35; Jer 48:16;
51:33 ^{e} Jer 50:39
14:1 ^{f} Ps 102:13;
Isa 49:10,13; 54:7-8,
10; Jer 33:26;
Zec 10:6 ^{g} Ge 18:19;
2Ch 6:6; Isa 41:8;
42:1; 44:1; 45:4; 49:7;
65:9,22; Zec 1:17;
2:12; 3:2 ^{h} Jer 3:18;
16:15; 23:8
^{i} S Ex 12:43;
S Isa 11:10;
Eze 47:22; Zec 8:22-
23; Eph 2:12-19

---

earthquakes often accompany the powerful presence of the Lord (see notes on v. 10; 34:4; Ex 19:16). Hail may also be involved (cf. 30:30; Jos 10:11).

13:14 *flee.* From parts of the Assyrian empire.

13:16 *infants … dashed to pieces.* Invading armies often slaughtered infants and children; thus there would be no future warriors, nor would there be a remnant through which the city (or country or people) might be revived (see Ps 137:8–9; Hos 10:14 and notes; Na 3:10). *wives ravished.* Women also suffered greatly in war. With their husbands killed, they were often used as prostitutes (see note on Am 7:17).

13:17 *Medes.* Inhabited by what is today northwestern Iran. There was conflict between Assyria and Media during the eighth century B.C. Some, however, relate the fulfillment of this verse to the period when the Medes joined the Babylonians in defeating Assyria in 612–609 but later united with Cyrus to conquer Babylon in 539. See Ezr 6:2 and note; Jer 51:11,28; Da 5:31; 6:28.

13:19 *pride and glory.* Babylon with its temples and palaces became a very beautiful city (see Da 4:29–30 and note on 4:30). The hanging gardens of Nebuchadnezzar were one of the seven wonders of the ancient world. In 4:2 the Hebrew words for "glory" and "pride" were used to describe the

"Branch of the LORD." *Babylonians.* The Neo-Babylonian empire of 612–539 B.C. was led by the Chaldean people of southern Babylonia. Nabopolassar welded the tribes together c. 626, and his son Nebuchadnezzar became their most powerful ruler (605–562). *Sodom and Gomorrah.* Previously Isaiah compared Judah to these cities (see 1:9–10 and note).

13:20–22 See the similar description of the desolation of Edom in 34:10–15. Cf. Rev 18:2.

13:20 *never be inhabited.* Babylon was almost totally destroyed for the last time by the Persian king Xerxes I in 478 B.C. Then, after the time of Alexander the Great in 330, the city was basically deserted, fell into complete disrepair and ruin and has remained that way ever since.

13:21 *wild goats.* This term is connected with demons ("goat idols") in Lev 17:7; 2Ch 11:15. In Rev 18:2 fallen Babylon is described as a home for demons and evil spirits.

14:1 *will have compassion … will settle them.* Babylon's fall will be linked with Israel's restoration. God's compassion on his people is the theme of chs. 40–66 (see 40:1 and note). *in their own land.* See 2:2–4; 11:10–12 and notes. *Foreigners will join them.* See 11:10; 56:6–7; 60:3 and note.

14:2 *j* S Isa 11:12;
60:9 *k* S Ps 49:14;
Isa 26:15; 43:14; 49:7,
23; 54:3 *l* Ps 149:8;
Isa 45:14; 49:25;
60:12; Jer 40:1
m Isa 60:14; 61:5;
Jer 30:16; 49:2;
Eze 39:10; Zep 3:19;
Zec 2:9
14:3 *n* S Isa 11:10
o S Job 3:17
p S Ex 1:14
14:4 *q* Mic 2:4;
Hab 2:6 *r* S Isa 13:1
s S Isa 9:4
14:5 *t* S Isa 10:15
u S Ps 125:3
v S Ps 110:2
14:6 *w* Isa 10:14
x S Ps 47:3
y S 2Ki 15:29;
Isa 47:6; Hab 1:17
14:7 *z* S Nu 6:26;
Jer 50:34; Zec 1:11
a Ps 98:1; 126:1-3;
Isa 12:6
14:8 *b* S 1Ch 16:33;
S Ps 65:13; Eze 31:16
c S 2Ki 19:23;
Isa 37:24
14:9 *d* S Pr 30:16;
Eze 32:21 *e* S Job 26:5
f Zec 10:3 *g* S Job 3:14
14:10 *h* Eze 26:20;
32:21
14:11 *i* S Nu 16:30;
S Pr 30:16 / Isa 5:12;
Eze 26:13; Am 6:5
k S Job 7:5; 24:20;
Isa 51:8; 66:24
l S Job 21:26
14:12 *m* Lk 10:18
n 2Pe 1:19; Rev 2:28;
8:10; 9:1 *o* Eze 26:17
14:13 *p* Da 5:23;
8:10; Ob 1:4; Mt 11:23

and bring[j] them to their own place.
And the house of Israel will take possession of the nations[k]
    and make them male and female servants in the Lord's land.
They will make captives[l] of their captors
    and rule over their oppressors.[m]

3On the day the Lord gives you relief[n] from your suffering and turmoil[o] and from the harsh labor forced on you,[p] 4you will take up this taunt[q] against the king of Babylon:[r]

How the oppressor[s] has come to an end!
    How his fury[a] has ended!
5The Lord has broken the rod[t] of the wicked,[u]
    the scepter[v] of the rulers,
6which in anger struck down peoples[w]
    with unceasing blows,
and in fury subdued[x] nations
    with relentless aggression.[y]
7All the lands are at rest and at peace;[z]
    they break into singing.[a]
8Even the junipers[b] and the cedars of Lebanon
    exult over you and say,
"Now that you have been laid low,
    no one comes to cut us down."[c]

9The realm of the dead[d] below is all astir
    to meet you at your coming;
it rouses the spirits of the departed[e] to greet you—
    all those who were leaders[f] in the world;
it makes them rise from their thrones—
    all those who were kings over the nations.[g]
10They will all respond,
    they will say to you,
"You also have become weak, as we are;
    you have become like us."[h]
11All your pomp has been brought down to the grave,[i]
    along with the noise of your harps;[j]
maggots are spread out beneath you
    and worms[k] cover you.[l]

12How you have fallen[m] from heaven,
    morning star,[n] son of the dawn!
You have been cast down to the earth,
    you who once laid low the nations![o]
13You said in your heart,
    "I will ascend[p] to heaven;

---

a 4 Dead Sea Scrolls, Septuagint and Syriac; the meaning of the word in the Masoretic Text is uncertain.

14:2 *Nations … place.* See note on 5:26. *will take possession of the nations.* See note on 11:14.
14:3–21 However exalted (and almost divine) the king of Babylon may have thought himself (see vv. 12–14), he will go the way of all world rulers—down to the grave.
14:3 *suffering … harsh labor forced on you.* The Babylonian captivity was much like Israel's experience in Egypt (see Ex 1:14 and note).
14:4 *taunt.* Cf. the taunts against Babylon in Rev 18. *king of Babylon.* Another title used by the king of Assyria at this time.
14:5 *rod … scepter.* See 10:5 and note; see also 10:24.
14:7 *break into singing.* See 12:6 and note.
14:8 *junipers … cedars.* Isaiah often personified nature. The trees along with the mountains burst into song in 44:23 (cf. 55:12). *cedars of Lebanon.* These highly prized timbers were hauled away by the kings of Assyria and Babylon for centuries (see notes on 2:13; 9:10).
14:9 *leaders.* Lit. "goats"; a goat often led a flock of sheep (see Jer 50:8 and note). In Zec 10:3 the term is parallel to "shep-

herds." *rise from their thrones.* Conditions among the dead are described in terms of their roles on earth. *kings over the nations.* See v. 18. Even the greatest and most powerful must go down to the "realm of the dead below."
14:11 *brought down to the grave.* See v.15 ("brought down to the realm of the dead"; the Hebrew is virtually identical). *pomp … grave.* Cf. 5:14. *noise of your harps.* Music was sometimes a sign of luxury and pleasure (see Am 6:5–6).
14:12–15 Some believe that Isaiah is giving a description of the fall of Satan (cf. Lk 10:18—where, however, Jesus is referring to an event contemporary with himself). But the passage clearly applies to the king of Babylon, who is later used as a type (prefiguration) of the "beast" who will lead the Babylon of the last days (see Rev 13:4; 17:3). Cf. the description of the king of Tyre in Eze 28.
14:12 *morning star.* The Hebrew for this expression is translated *lucifer* (lit. "light-bearer") in the Latin Vulgate, the origin of "Lucifer" in early English translations of this verse. For the true Morning Star, see Rev 22:16 (see also 2Pe 1:19; cf. Nu 24:17 and note).

I will raise my throne[q]
  above the stars of God;
I will sit enthroned on the mount of assembly,[r]
  on the utmost heights[s] of Mount Zaphon.[a]
[14] I will ascend above the tops of the clouds;[t]
  I will make myself like the Most High."[u]

[15] But you are brought down[v] to the realm of the dead,[w]
  to the depths[x] of the pit.[y]

[16] Those who see you stare at you,
  they ponder your fate:[z]
"Is this the man who shook[a] the earth
  and made kingdoms tremble,
[17] the man who made the world a wilderness,[b]
  who overthrew[c] its cities
  and would not let his captives go home?"[d]

[18] All the kings of the nations lie in state,
  each in his own tomb.[e]
[19] But you are cast out[f] of your tomb
  like a rejected branch;
you are covered with the slain,[g]
  with those pierced by the sword,[h]
  those who descend to the stones of the pit.[i]
Like a corpse trampled underfoot,
[20] you will not join them in burial,[j]
for you have destroyed your land
  and killed your people.

Let the offspring[k] of the wicked[l]
  never be mentioned[m] again.
[21] Prepare a place to slaughter his children[n]
  for the sins of their ancestors;[o]
they are not to rise to inherit the land
  and cover the earth with their cities.

[22] "I will rise up[p] against them,"
  declares the LORD Almighty.
"I will wipe out Babylon's name[q] and survivors,
  her offspring and descendants,[r]"

                     declares the LORD.

[23] "I will turn her into a place for owls[s]
  and into swampland;
I will sweep her with the broom of destruction,[t]"
  declares the LORD Almighty.[u]

[24] The LORD Almighty has sworn,[v]

"Surely, as I have planned,[w] so it will be,
  and as I have purposed, so it will happen.[x]

---

[a] 13 Or *of the north*; Zaphon was the most sacred mountain of the Canaanites.

14:13 *q* Eze 28:2; 2Th 2:4; *r* Ps 82:1; *s* Isa 37:24
14:14 *t* S Job 20:6; *u* S Ge 3:5; S Nu 24:16; Isa 10:13; 47:8; Jer 50:29; 51:53; Da 11:36; 2Th 2:4
14:15 *v* Isa 13:6; 45:7; 47:11; Jer 51:8, 43; *w* S Job 21:13; *x* Mt 11:23; Lk 10:15; *y* S Ps 55:23; Eze 31:16; 32:23
14:16 *z* Jer 50:23; Rev 18:9; *a* S Isa 2:19; 13:13; Joel 3:16; Hag 2:6, 21
14:17 *b* Isa 15:6; Joel 2:3; *c* Ps 52:7; *d* Ex 7:14; S 2Ki 15:29; Jer 50:33; Rev 18:18
14:18 *e* Job 21:32
14:19 *f* Isa 22:16-18; Jer 8:1; 36:30; *g* Isa 34:3; *h* S Isa 13:15; *i* Jer 41:7-9
14:20 *j* S 1Ki 21:19; *k* S Job 18:19; *l* S Isa 1:4; *m* S Dt 32:26
14:21 *n* S Nu 16:27; *o* S Ge 9:25; S Lev 26:39
14:22 *p* S Ps 94:16; *q* S Job 18:17; Ps 109:13; Na 1:14; *r* 2Sa 18:18; 1Ki 14:10; Job 18:19; S Ps 9:6; S Isa 13:18
14:23 *s* S Lev 11:16-18; Isa 34:11-15; Zep 2:14; *t* S Isa 10:3; Jer 25:12; *u* Jer 50:3; 51:62
14:24 *v* Isa 45:23; 49:18; 54:9; 62:8; *w* Isa 19:12,17; 23:8-9; 25:1; Da 4:35; *x* S Job 9:3; S Isa 7:7; 46:10-11; Eze 12:25; Ac 4:28

14:13 *utmost heights.* Babylon's king is destined for the "depths" of the pit (v. 15; the Hebrew word for "utmost heights" and "depths" is the same)—though he aspires to be "like the Most High" (v. 14). *Mount Zaphon.* See TNIV text note; also called Mount Casius, located in northern Syria. The Canaanites considered it the dwelling and meeting place of the gods, much like Mount Olympus for the Greeks (see Ps 48:2 and note). Cf. Ps 82:1.
14:16—20a These verses seem to take place on earth, not in the realm of the dead (Sheol)—probably also vv. 9–10.
14:17 *captives go home.* Babylon, like Assyria, deported large segments of defeated populations to subdue the rebellious among them (see 2Ki 24:14–16).
14:18 *kings of the nations.* See note on v. 9.
14:19 *cast out of your tomb.* A proper burial was considered

important. To have one's body simply discarded was a terrible fate. *corpse trampled.* See 5:25.
14:21 *slaughter his children.* A man's children, as well as his tombstone, were his memorial (see 2Sa 18:18). The king of Babylon would have neither (cf. 47:9).
14:22—23 The taunt is extended to include Babylon itself (see note on vv. 3–21); fulfilled, at least partially, through Sennacherib's destruction of Babylon in 689 B.C.—ultimately by the Medes and Persians after they took Babylon in 539 (see also note on 13:20).
14:22 *survivors.* A remnant; Israel will survive through a remnant (see 10:20–22 and note; 11:11,16), but Babylon will not.
14:23 See 13:20–22 and notes. *swampland.* Southern Babylonia, where the Chaldean tribes (see note on Ezr 5:12) once lived, was a region of marshlands.

14:25 ʸ S Isa 10:5,
12; 37:36-38
ᶻ S Isa 9:4
ᵃ S Isa 10:27
14:26 ᵇ Isa 23:9
ᶜ Ex 15:12; S Job 30:21
14:27 ᵈ Jer 49:20
ᵉ S Ex 14:21
ᶠ S 2Ch 20:6;
Isa 43:13; Da 4:35
14:28 ᵍ S Isa 13:1
ʰ S 2Ki 15:7
ⁱ S 2Ki 16:1
14:29 ʲ S Jos 13:3;
S 2Ki 1:2; S 2Ch 26:6
ᵏ S Isa 11:8 ˡ S Dt 8:15
14:30 ᵐ Isa 3:15;
25:4 ⁿ S Isa 7:21-22
ᵒ Isa 8:21; 9:20; 51:19
ᵖ Jer 25:16; Zec 9:5-6
�q Eze 25:15-17;
Zep 2:5
14:31 ʳ S Isa 13:6
ˢ S Isa 3:26
ᵗ S Ge 10:14
ᵘ Isa 41:25; Jer 1:14;
4:6; 6:1,22; 10:22;
13:20; 25:9; 46:20,24;
47:2; 50:41;
Eze 32:30 ᵛ S Isa 5:27
14:32 ʷ Isa 37:9
ˣ S Ps 51:18; 87:2,5;
Isa 2:2; 26:1; 28:16;
31:5; 33:5,20; 44:28;
51:21; 54:11
ʸ S Isa 4:6; Jas 2:5
15:1 ᶻ S Isa 13:1
ᵃ Nu 22:3-6;
S Dt 23:6; S Isa 11:14
ᵇ S Nu 21:15
ᶜ S Nu 17:12;
Isa 25:12; 26:5;
Jer 48:24,41; 51:58
ᵈ S 2Ki 3:25
15:2 ᵉ S Nu 21:30
ᶠ 1Ki 11:7; Isa 16:12;
Jer 48:35

²⁵ I will crush the Assyrian ʸ in my land;
  on my mountains I will trample him down.
His yoke ᶻ will be taken from my people,
  and his burden removed from their shoulders. ᵃ ”

²⁶ This is the plan ᵇ determined for the whole world;
  this is the hand ᶜ stretched out over all nations.
²⁷ For the Lᴏʀᴅ Almighty has purposed, ᵈ and who can thwart him?
  His hand ᵉ is stretched out, and who can turn it back? ᶠ

A PROPHECY AGAINST THE PHILISTINES

²⁸ This prophecy ᵍ came in the year ʰ King Ahaz ⁱ died:

²⁹ Do not rejoice, all you Philistines, ʲ
  that the rod that struck you is broken;
from the root of that snake will spring up a viper, ᵏ
  its fruit will be a darting, venomous serpent. ˡ
³⁰ The poorest of the poor will find pasture,
  and the needy ᵐ will lie down in safety. ⁿ
But your root I will destroy by famine; ᵒ
  it will slay ᵖ your survivors. q

³¹ Wail, ʳ you gate! ˢ Howl, you city!
  Melt away, all you Philistines! ᵗ
A cloud of smoke comes from the north, ᵘ
  and there is not a straggler in its ranks. ᵛ
³² What answer shall be given
  to the envoys ʷ of that nation?
"The Lᴏʀᴅ has established Zion, ˣ
  and in her his afflicted people will find refuge. ʸ ”

A PROPHECY AGAINST MOAB

16:6–12pp — Jer 48:29-36

15 A prophecy ᶻ concerning Moab: ᵃ

Ar ᵇ in Moab is ruined, ᶜ
  destroyed in a night!
Kir ᵈ in Moab is ruined,
  destroyed in a night!
² Dibon ᵉ goes up to its temple,
  to its high places ᶠ to weep;

14:24—27 See Zep 2:13–15 and notes; see also note on Isa 13:1—14:27.
14:24 *it will happen.* See 8:10 and note. God's sovereign purposes regarding Assyria and Babylon will be carried out.
14:25 *yoke … burden.* See 9:4 and note.
14:26—27 *hand stretched out.* See 9:12; 12:1 and notes. God's hand was stretched out against Egypt at the Red Sea (see Ex 15:12).
14:28—32 See Jer 47; Eze 25:15–17; Am 1:6–8; Zep 2:4–7 and notes.
14:28 *prophecy.* See note on 13:1. *the year.* Perhaps 715 B.C. *King Ahaz died.* Cf. 6:1 and note. The occasion appears to be the Philistine revolt against Assyria while King Sargon (see 20:1) was too preoccupied with serious revolts elsewhere to give much attention to Canaan.
14:29 *Philistines.* See note on Ge 10:14. Philistine territory was vulnerable to attack by the great empires (Egypt and Assyria) since it lay along the main route from Egypt to Mesopotamia. *the rod.* Probably Sargon of Assyria. *is broken.* If the rod was Sargon, reference is to the threats to his empire by a series of revolts in Babylonia and Asia Minor. *root … fruit.* A figure of speech that refers to the whole (tree) by speaking of its two extremes. After Sargon will come other Assyrian kings: Sennacherib, Esarhaddon, Ashurbanipal (see chart, p. 482).

14:30 *poor … needy.* Israelites (see v. 32).
14:31 *Wail.* Cf. the similar reaction in 13:6; 15:2; 16:7; 23:1. *cloud of smoke.* The dust raised by the marching feet and the chariots of the Assyrians—who always invaded Canaan from the north. *not a straggler.* A longer description is found in 5:26–29.
14:32 *has established Zion.* God will protect Jerusalem from the Assyrians (compare 31:4–5 with 2:2).
15:1—16:14 See Jer 48; Eze 25:8–11; Am 2:1–3; Zep 2:8–11 and notes.
15:1 *prophecy.* See note on 13:1. *Moab.* A country east of the Dead Sea that was a perpetual enemy of Israel (see 25:10 and note; 2Ki 13:20). *ruined.* The same word describes Isaiah's feelings about himself in 6:5. The destruction of Moab probably resulted from an invasion by Sargon of Assyria in 715/713 B.C. Cf. Jer 48:1–17. *Kir.* Probably Kir Hareseth (see note on 2Ki 3:25). Kir means "city."
15:2 *Dibon.* Located four miles north of the Arnon River and given to the tribe of Gad at one time (see Nu 32:34). *high places.* Shrines originally built on hilltops and usually associated with pagan worship (see note on 1Ki 3:2). *Nebo.* North of the Arnon River, perhaps near Mount Nebo (Dt 34:1; cf. note on Ezr 10:43). *Medeba.* About six miles south of Heshbon (see v. 4) and once captured by Israel from Sihon (see Nu 21:26,30). *head is shaved … beard cut off.* Characteristic of intense mourning (Jer 48:37).

Moab wails *g* over Nebo *h* and Medeba.
Every head is shaved *i*
and every beard cut off. *j*
3 In the streets they wear sackcloth; *k*
on the roofs *l* and in the public squares *m*
they all wail, *n*
prostrate with weeping. *o*
4 Heshbon *p* and Elealeh *q* cry out,
their voices are heard all the way to Jahaz. *r*
Therefore the armed men of Moab cry out,
and their hearts are faint.
5 My heart cries out *s* over Moab; *t*
her fugitives *u* flee as far as Zoar, *v*
as far as Eglath Shelishiyah.
They go up the hill to Luhith,
weeping as they go;
on the road to Horonaim *w*
they lament their destruction. *x*
6 The waters of Nimrim are dried up *y*
and the grass is withered; *z*
the vegetation is gone *a*
and nothing green is left. *b*
7 So the wealth they have acquired *c* and stored up
they carry away over the Ravine of the Poplars.
8 Their outcry echoes along the border of Moab;
their wailing reaches as far as Eglaim,
their lamentation as far as Beer *d* Elim.
9 The waters of Dimon *a* are full of blood,
but I will bring still more upon Dimon *a*—
a lion *e* upon the fugitives of Moab *f*
and upon those who remain in the land.

16

Send lambs *g* as tribute *h*
to the ruler of the land,
from Sela, *i* across the desert,
to the mount of Daughter Zion. *j*
2 Like fluttering birds
pushed from the nest, *k*
so are the women of Moab *l*
at the fords *m* of the Arnon. *n*

3 "Make up your mind," Moab says.
"Render a decision.
Make your shadow like night—

---

a 9 *Dimon*, a wordplay on Dibon (see verse 2), sounds like the Hebrew for *blood*.

15:3 *sackcloth.* The coarse garb of mourners (see note on Rev 11:3). *roofs.* Perhaps chosen because incense was sometimes offered there (see Jer 19:13 and note).
15:4 *Heshbon.* Located about 18 miles east of the northern tip of the Dead Sea. See also Jer 48:34. It was King Sihon's capital before Israel captured it (see Nu 21:23–26). *Elealeh.* About a mile north of Heshbon and always mentioned with it. *Jahaz.* Just north of the Arnon River and about 20 miles from Heshbon (Nu 21:23; Jer 48:34).
15:5 *Zoar.* Probably located near the southern end of the Dead Sea. Lot fled there from Sodom (see Ge 14:2; 19:23,30).
15:6 *waters of Nimrim.* Perhaps to be identified with the Wadi en-Numeirah, ten miles from the southern end of the Dead Sea (cf. Jer 48:34).
15:7 *Ravine of the Poplars.* Probably at the border between Moab and Edom (see v. 8).
15:8 *Eglaim.* Perhaps near the northern border of Moab. *Beer Elim.* Beer means "well" (cf. Nu 21:16). This site may have been

close to the southern border.
15:9 *waters of Dimon . . . blood.* The Hebrew for "blood" (*dam*) sounds like "Dimon." This is probably also a wordplay on the name "Dibon" (v. 2), close to the Arnon River. Many Moabites will die in the conflict. *lion.* A reference to either the Assyrian army (cf. 5:29; Jer 50:17) or actual lions (cf. 13:21–22).
16:1 *lambs as tribute.* As King Mesha sent 100,000 lambs to King Ahab of Israel each year (see 2Ki 3:4 and note), so now proud Moab, which has often oppressed Israel, is advised in her crisis to submit to the king in Jerusalem. *Sela.* The naturally fortified capital of the Edomites, south of the Dead Sea, situated on a rocky plateau that towers 1,000 feet above the nearby Petra (cf. 42:11). The name means "cliff." The tribute would be sent around the southern end of the Dead Sea. *Daughter Zion.* A personification of Jerusalem (see note on 2Ki 19:21).
16:2 *fords of the Arnon.* The women were fleeing south (see note on Jos 12:1), away from the northern invader.
16:3 *Hide the fugitives.* The Moabites are asking Judah for

15:2 *g* S Isa 13:6; 65:14 *h* S Nu 22:38 *i* S Lev 13:40; S Job 1:20 / S 2Sa 10:4
15:3 *k* S Isa 3:24 *l* S Jos 2:8 *m* Jer 48:38 *n* Isa 14:31; Jer 47:2 *o* ver 5; Isa 16:9; 22:4; La 2:11; Eze 7:18; Mic 1:8
15:4 *p* S Nu 21:25; S Jos 13:26 *q* S Nu 32:3 *r* S Nu 21:23
15:5 *s* S ver 3 *t* Isa 16:11; Jer 48:31 *u* S Nu 21:29 *v* S Ge 13:10 *w* Jer 48:3,34 *x* Jer 4:20; 48:5
15:6 *y* Isa 19:5-7; Jer 48:34 *z* Ps 37:2; Isa 16:8; 24:4,7,11; 33:9; 34:4; 37:27; 40:7; 51:6,12; Hos 4:3; Joel 1:12 *a* S Isa 14:17 *b* Jer 14:5
15:7 *c* Isa 30:6; Jer 48:36
15:8 *d* S Nu 21:16
15:9 *e* S 2Ki 17:25 *f* Eze 25:8-11
16:1 *g* S 2Ki 3:4 *h* S 2Ch 32:23 *i* S Jdg 1:36; Ob 3 *fn* *j* S Isa 10:32
16:2 *k* Pr 27:8 *l* Nu 21:29 *m* Jdg 12:5 *n* Nu 21:13-14; Jer 48:20

16:3 °S 1Ki 18:4
16:4 ᵖ Isa 58:7
�q S Isa 9:4 ʳ Isa 2:2-4
16:5 ˢ S 1Sa 13:14;
Da 7:14; Mic 4:7
ᵗ S Pr 20:28
ᵘ Isa 7:2; Lk 1:32
ᵛ S Isa 9:7
16:6 ʷ Jer 25:21;
Eze 25:8; Am 2:1;
Zep 2:8 ˣ S Lev 26:19;
S Job 20:6; Jer 49:16;
Ob 1:3; Zep 2:10
16:7 ʸ S Isa 13:6;
Jer 48:20; 49:3
ᶻ S 1Ch 16:3
ᵃ S 2Ki 3:25
16:8 ᵇ S Nu 21:25
ᶜ Isa 15:6
ᵈ Nu 32:3
ᵉ S Isa 5:2
ᶠ S Nu 21:32
ᵍ S Job 8:16 ʰ Ps 80:11
16:9 ⁱ S Isa 15:3;
Eze 27:31 ʲ S Nu 32:3
ᵏ S Job 7:3 ˡ S Ezr 3:13
ᵐ Jer 40:12
16:10 ⁿ Isa 24:7-8
°Jer 25:30
ᵖ S Jdg 9:27
�q S Job 24:11;
S Isa 5:2
16:11 ʳ S Isa 15:5
ˢ S Job 30:31
ᵗ Isa 63:15; Hos 11:8;
Php 2:1
16:12 ᵘ 1Ki 11:7
ᵛ S Isa 15:2
ʷ S 1Ki 18:29;
Ps 115:4-7; Isa 44:17-
18; 1Co 8:4

at high noon.
Hide the fugitives, °
    do not betray the refugees.
⁴ Let the Moabite fugitives stay with you;
    be their shelter ᵖ from the destroyer."

The oppressor q will come to an end,
    and destruction will cease; ʳ
    the aggressor will vanish from the land.
⁵ In love a throne ˢ will be established; ᵗ
    in faithfulness a man will sit on it—
    one from the house ᵃ of David ᵘ—
one who in judging seeks justice ᵛ
    and speeds the cause of righteousness.

⁶ We have heard of Moab's ʷ pride ˣ—
    her overweening pride and conceit,
    her pride and her insolence—
    but her boasts are empty.
⁷ Therefore the Moabites wail, ʸ
    they wail together for Moab.
Lament and grieve
    for the raisin cakes ᶻ of Kir Hareseth. ᵃ
⁸ The fields of Heshbon ᵇ wither, ᶜ
    the vines of Sibmah ᵈ also.
The rulers of the nations
    have trampled down the choicest vines, ᵉ
which once reached Jazer ᶠ
    and spread toward the desert.
Their shoots spread out ᵍ
    and went as far as the sea. ᵇ ʰ
⁹ So I weep, ⁱ as Jazer weeps,
    for the vines of Sibmah.
Heshbon and Elealeh, ʲ
    I drench you with tears! ᵏ
The shouts of joy ˡ over your ripened fruit
    and over your harvests ᵐ have been stilled.
¹⁰ Joy and gladness are taken away from the orchards; ⁿ
    no one sings or shouts ° in the vineyards;
no one treads ᵖ out wine at the presses, q
    for I have put an end to the shouting.
¹¹ My heart laments for Moab ʳ like a harp, ˢ
    my inmost being ᵗ for Kir Hareseth.
¹² When Moab appears at her high place, ᵘ
    she only wears herself out;
when she goes to her shrine ᵛ to pray,
    it is to no avail. ʷ

ᵃ 5 Hebrew *tent*   ᵇ 8 Probably the Dead Sea

---

refuge (contrast Ru 1:1; 1Sa 22:3–4 and note on 22:3). See map,
p. 375.
16:4 *destroyer.* Probably Assyria (see notes on 15:1; 33:1). *oppressor.* Moab.
16:5 *house of David.* See 9:7; 2Sa 7:11–16; 1Ki 12:19; Am 9:11
and notes. "House" equals "dynasty" (see note on 7:2). *in judging
seeks justice.* See 11:2–4 and notes. The Messiah is again in view.
16:6 *Moab's pride.* Though a small nation, Moab is proud and
defiant like Assyria and Babylon. Cf. 10:12; 14:13; 25:11; Jer
48:42.
16:7 *Kir Hareseth.* See note on 15:1. The four cities in vv. 7–8
appear in inverted (*a-b/b-a*) order in vv. 9–11.
16:8 *Heshbon.* See note on 15:4. *Sibmah.* Perhaps three miles
west of Heshbon. See Jer 48:32. *choicest vines.* The poet shifts to
a metaphor, comparing Moab to a vineyard (cf. 5:1–7 and
notes). He returns to a literal description again in v. 10. *Jazer.*

Possibly located about 15 miles north of the Dead Sea. *desert.*
On the eastern edge of Moab. *shoots spread out.* This is figurative language, as in Ps 80:11, where Israel is the vine. *sea.* See
TNIV text note.
16:9–11 *I...I...I...My...my.* The Lord (and/or Isaiah) weeps
and laments over the destruction brought on proud Moab to
humble her.
16:9 *Elealeh.* See note on 15:4.
16:10 *treads out wine.* The grapes were trampled on, and the
juice flowed into the wine vat (see note on 5:2; cf. Jer 48:33; Am
9:13).
16:11 Cf. Jer 48:36.
16:12 *high place.* See 15:2 and note. *pray...to no avail.* Moab's
god, Chemosh, was a mere idol (see 44:17–20 and notes; 1Ki
11:7).

¹³This is the word the LORD has already spoken concerning Moab. ¹⁴But now the LORD says: "Within three years,^x as a servant bound by contract^y would count them,^z Moab's splendor and all her many people will be despised,^a and her survivors will be very few and feeble."^b

A PROPHECY AGAINST DAMASCUS

17

A prophecy^c concerning Damascus:^d

"See, Damascus will no longer be a city
　　but will become a heap of ruins.^e
²The cities of Aroer^f will be deserted
　　and left to flocks,^g which will lie down,^h
　　with no one to make them afraid.ⁱ
³The fortified^j city will disappear from Ephraim,
　　and royal power from Damascus;
　　the remnant of Aram will be
　　like the glory^k of the Israelites,"^l
　　　　　　　　　declares the LORD Almighty.

⁴"In that day^m the gloryⁿ of Jacob will fade;
　　the fat of his body will waste^o away.
⁵It will be as when reapers harvest the standing grain,
　　gathering^p the grain in their arms—
　　as when someone gleans heads of grain^q
　　in the Valley of Rephaim.^r
⁶Yet some gleanings will remain,^s
　　as when an olive tree is beaten,^t
　　leaving two or three olives on the topmost branches,
　　four or five on the fruitful boughs,"
　　　　　　　　　declares the LORD, the God of Israel.

⁷In that day^u people will look^v to their Maker^w
　　and turn their eyes to the Holy One^x of Israel.
⁸They will not look to the altars,^y
　　the work of their hands,^z
　　and they will have no regard for the Asherah poles^{a a}
　　and the incense altars their fingers^b have made.

⁹In that day their strong cities, which they left because of the Israelites, will be like places abandoned to thickets and undergrowth.^c And all will be desolation.

¹⁰You have forgotten^d God your Savior;^e
　　you have not remembered the Rock,^f your fortress.^g
　　Therefore, though you set out the finest plants

---

^a 8 That is, wooden symbols of the goddess Asherah

16:14 ^x Isa 20:3; 37:30 ^y S Lev 25:50 ^z S Lev 19:13 ^a Isa 25:10; Jer 48:42 ^b Isa 21:17
17:1 ^c Isa 13:1 ^d S Ge 14:15; Ac 9:2 ^e S Dt 13:16; S Isa 25:2
17:2 ^f S 2Ki 10:33 ^g S Isa 5:17; 7:21; Eze 25:5 ^h Isa 27:10 ⁱ Lev 26:6; Jer 7:33; Mic 4:4
17:3 ^j Isa 25:2,12; Hos 10:14 ^k ver 4; Isa 21:16; Hos 9:11 ^l Isa 7:8,16; 8:4
17:4 ^m S Isa 2:11 ⁿ S ver 3 ^o S Isa 10:16
17:5 ^p ver 11; Isa 33:4; Jer 51:33; Joel 3:13; Mt 13:30 ^q Job 24:24 ^r S Jos 17:15; S 1Ch 11:15
17:6 ^s S Dt 4:27; S Isa 10:19; S 24:13 ^t ver 11; Isa 27:12
17:7 ^u S Isa 2:11 ^v S Isa 9:13; S 10:20 ^w S Ps 95:6 ^x S Isa 12:6
17:8 ^y S Lev 26:30 ^z S 2Ch 32:19; Isa 2:18,20; 30:22; 46:6; Rev 9:20 ^a S Jdg 3:7; S 2Ki 17:10 ^b Isa 2:8
17:9 ^c S Isa 7:19
17:10 ^d S Dt 6:12; 8:11; Ps 50:22; 106:21; Isa 51:13; 57:11; Jer 2:32; 3:21; 13:25; 18:15; Eze 22:12; 23:35; Hos 8:14; 13:6 ^e S Isa 12:2; S Lk 1:47 ^f S Ge 49:24 ^g S Ps 18:2

16:13–14 An epilogue to 15:1—16:12.

16:14 *Within three years.* Other signs that have a three-year limit are given in 20:3; 37:30; see also notes on 7:14,16. Moab's three years were over by c. 715 B.C. (see note on 15:1). *servant bound by contract.* Cf. 21:16–17, where the prophecy against Kedar follows the pattern of this verse.

17:1–14 See Jer 49:23–27; Am 1:3–5 and notes.

17:1 *prophecy.* See note on 13:1. *Damascus.* The capital of Aram (Syria), located northeast of Mount Hermon on strategic trade routes between Mesopotamia, Egypt and Arabia. Since the time of David, the Arameans of Damascus were frequent enemies of Israel (see 2Sa 8:5; 1Ki 22:31).

17:2 *Aroer.* About 14 miles east of the Dead Sea on the Arnon River. It marked the southern boundary of Aram's sphere of control (see 2Ki 10:32–33 and notes).

17:3 *Ephraim.* The northern kingdom (see note on 7:2) is mentioned here because of its alliance with Damascus against Assyria (see note on 7:1). *royal power.* In 732 B.C. Tiglath-Pileser III captured Damascus and made it an Assyrian province. Many of the cities of Israel were also captured (see note on 9:1). *remnant*

of Aram... like the glory of the Israelites. Like Israel, Aram will be reduced to a remnant.

17:4–11 The prophet shifts from Damascus to Israel (likely the northern kingdom)—a shift prepared for at the end of v. 3. This association of judgment on Damascus and Israel reflects the same linkage as that in ch. 7.

17:4,7,9 *In that day.* See notes on 2:11,17,20; 10:20,27.

17:5 *harvest the standing grain.* Harvest here signifies a time of judgment (see Joel 3:13 and note). *Valley of Rephaim.* A fertile area west and southwest of Jerusalem (Jos 15:8) and the scene of Philistine raids (1Ch 14:9).

17:7–8 Cf. 2:20; 10:20.

17:7 *Holy One of Israel.* See note on 1:4.

17:8 *altars.* Probably altars for Baal (cf. 1Ki 16:32). *Asherah poles.* See notes on Ex 34:13; Jdg 2:13; see also TNIV text note here. *incense altars.* Associated with high places in Lev 26:30 and with altars for Baal in 2Ch 34:4.

17:9 *they.* Perhaps the Canaanites, whose religious practices are referred to in v. 8. *thickets and undergrowth.* Cf. 7:23–25.

17:10 *Rock.* See 26:4; 30:29; 44:8; Ge 49:24 and note; Dt

17:10 ʰ S Isa 5:7
17:11 ⁱ Ps 90:6
ʲ S ver 5
ᵏ S Lev 26:20;
Hos 8:7; Joel 1:11;
Hag 1:6 ˡ Jer 10:19;
30:12 ᵐ S Dt 28:39;
S Job 4:8
17:12 ⁿ ver 13;
Isa 41:11 ᵒ S Ps 18:4;
Lk 21:25 ᵖ S Ps 46:6;
Isa 8:9 ᵠ Isa 8:7
17:13 ʳ S Ps 46:3
ˢ S Dt 28:20; S Ps 9:5
ᵗ S Ps 68:1; S Isa 13:14
ᵘ S Job 13:25;
S Isa 2:22; 41:2,15-16;
Da 2:35 ᵛ Job 21:18;
S Ps 65:7
17:14 ʷ Isa 29:5;
30:13; 47:11; 48:3
ˣ Isa 33:18; 54:14
ʸ S 2Ki 19:35
18:1 ᶻ Isa 5:8
ᵃ Ge 10:6;
S Ps 68:31;
S Eze 29:10
18:2 ᵇ Ob 1:1
ᶜ Ex 2:3; Job 9:26
ᵈ S Ge 41:14
ᵉ S Ge 10:8-9;
S 2Ch 12:3 ᶠ ver 7
18:3 ᵍ S Ps 33:8
ʰ S Ps 60:4; Isa 5:26;
11:10; 13:2; 31:9;
Jer 4:21 ⁱ S Jos 6:20;
S Jdg 3:27
18:4 ʲ Isa 62:1; 64:12
ᵏ Isa 26:21; Hos 5:15;
Mic 1:3 ˡ S Jdg 5:31;
S Ps 18:12; Hab 3:4
ᵐ 2Sa 1:21;
S Ps 133:3; Isa 26:19;
Hos 14:5
18:5 ⁿ S Isa 10:33
ᵒ Isa 17:10-11;
Eze 17:6

and plant imported vines, ʰ
¹¹though on the day you set them out, you make them grow,
 and on the morning ⁱ when you plant them, you bring them to bud,
yet the harvest ʲ will be as nothing ᵏ
 in the day of disease and incurable ˡ pain. ᵐ

¹²Woe to the many nations that rage ⁿ—
 they rage like the raging sea! ᵒ
Woe to the peoples who roar ᵖ—
 they roar like the roaring of great waters! ᵠ
¹³Although the peoples roar ʳ like the roar of surging waters,
 when he rebukes ˢ them they flee ᵗ far away,
driven before the wind like chaff ᵘ on the hills,
 like tumbleweed before a gale. ᵛ
¹⁴In the evening, sudden ʷ terror! ˣ
 Before the morning, they are gone! ʸ
This is the portion of those who loot us,
 the lot of those who plunder us.

A PROPHECY AGAINST CUSH

18 Woe ᶻ to the land of whirring wings ᵃ ᵃ
 along the rivers of Cush, ᵇ ᵃ
²which sends envoys ᵇ by sea
 in papyrus ᶜ boats over the water.

Go, swift messengers,
to a people tall and smooth-skinned, ᵈ
 to a people feared far and wide,
an aggressive ᵉ nation of strange speech,
 whose land is divided by rivers. ᶠ

³All you people of the world, ᵍ
 you who live on the earth,
when a banner ʰ is raised on the mountains,
 you will see it,
and when a trumpet ⁱ sounds,
 you will hear it.
⁴This is what the Lᴏʀᴅ says to me:
 "I will remain quiet ʲ and will look on from my dwelling place, ᵏ
like shimmering heat in the sunshine, ˡ
 like a cloud of dew ᵐ in the heat of harvest."
⁵For, before the harvest, when the blossom is gone
 and the flower becomes a ripening grape,
he will cut off ⁿ the shoots with pruning knives,
 and cut down and take away the spreading branches. ᵒ

ᵃ 1 Or of locusts   ᵇ 1 That is, the upper Nile region

32:4,15,18; Ps 18:2 and note; 19:14. *vines.* Probably representing the people of Israel (see 5:7; 18:5; 37:30–31; see also notes on Ps 80:8–16 and 80:8–11).
17:11 *disease and incurable pain.* Brought by the Assyrian invasions.
17:12–14 The same sequence of a powerful invader that is quickly cut down occurs in 10:28–34. Both passages may refer to Sennacherib's invasion of 701 B.C. (see 37:36–37 and notes). But it is more likely that the prophet here speaks more generally of Israel's experience of the world of nations as a perpetual threat to her existence.
17:12 *raging sea.* Assyria is called "floodwaters" in 8:7 (see notes on 8:7–8).
17:13 *chaff … tumbleweed.* Symbolic of the enemy also in 29:5; 41:15–16; Ps 83:13.
18:1–7 See Zep 2:12 and note.
18:1 *whirring wings.* Either a reference to insects (perhaps locusts) or a figurative description of the armies of Cush (see

7:18–19). *Cush.* Nubia or ancient Ethiopia (not to be confused with modern Ethiopia, which is located farther to the southeast), south of Egypt. In 715 B.C. a Cushite named Shabako gained control of Egypt and founded the 25th dynasty.
18:2 *sea.* Perhaps the Nile River (cf. 19:5; Na 3:8, where the same Hebrew word is translated "river"). *papyrus boats.* See note on Ex 2:3. *Go, swift messengers.* With the message contained in vv. 3–6. *people tall and smooth-skinned.* See v. 7; probably the peoples of Cush and Egypt. Unlike Semites, they were cleanshaven (see note on Ge 41:14). *rivers.* The Nile and its tributaries.
18:3 *All you people of the world.* All the nations arrayed against God's people Israel (see 17:12–14 and note). *banner.* See 5:26 and note. *trumpet.* Used to summon troops (see, e.g., Jdg 3:27; 6:34; 2Sa 2:28).
18:4 *remain quiet.* In the face of the hostility of the nations, the Lord will not act immediately; but when they are in the full growth of summer (v. 5), he will cut them down.

⁶They will all be left to the mountain birds of prey ᵖ
    and to the wild animals; �q
the birds will feed on them all summer,
    the wild animals all winter.

⁷At that time gifts ʳ will be brought to the Lᴏʀᴅ Almighty

from a people tall and smooth-skinned, ˢ
    from a people feared ᵗ far and wide,
an aggressive nation of strange speech,
    whose land is divided by rivers ᵘ—

the gifts will be brought to Mount Zion, the place of the Name of the Lᴏʀᴅ Almighty. ᵛ

A PROPHECY AGAINST EGYPT

19

A prophecy ʷ concerning Egypt: ˣ ʸ

See, the Lᴏʀᴅ rides on a swift cloud ᶻ
    and is coming to Egypt.
The idols of Egypt tremble before him,
    and the hearts of the Egyptians melt ᵃ within them.

²"I will stir up Egyptian against Egyptian—
    brother will fight against brother, ᵇ
    neighbor against neighbor,
    city against city,
    kingdom against kingdom. ᶜ
³The Egyptians will lose heart, ᵈ
    and I will bring their plans ᵉ to nothing; ᶠ
they will consult the idols and the spirits of the dead,
    the mediums and the spiritists. ᵍ
⁴I will hand the Egyptians over
    to the power of a cruel master,
and a fierce king ʰ will rule over them,"
    declares the Lord, the Lᴏʀᴅ Almighty.

⁵The waters of the river will dry up, ⁱ
    and the riverbed will be parched and dry. ʲ
⁶The canals will stink; ᵏ
    the streams of Egypt will dwindle and dry up. ˡ
The reeds ᵐ and rushes will wither, ⁿ
⁷   also the plants ᵒ along the Nile,
    at the mouth of the river.
Every sown field ᵖ along the Nile
    will become parched, will blow away and be no more. q
⁸Those who fish ʳ will groan and lament,
    all who cast hooks ˢ into the Nile;
those who throw nets on the water
    will pine away.
⁹Those who work with combed flax ᵗ will despair,
    the weavers of fine linen ᵘ will lose hope.

18:6 ᵖ S Isa 8:8
q Isa 37:36; 56:9;
Jer 7:33; Eze 32:4;
39:17
18:7 ʳ S 2Ch 9:24;
S Isa 60:7
ˢ S Ge 41:14 ᵗ Hab 1:7
ᵘ ver 2 ᵛ Ps 68:31
19:1 ʷ Isa 13:1
ˣ Isa 20:3; Joel 3:19
ʸ S Ex 12:12;
S Jer 44:3
ᶻ S Dt 10:14;
S 2Sa 22:10; S Rev 1:7
ᵃ S Jos 2:11
19:2 ᵇ S Jdg 7:22;
S 12:4; Mt 10:21,36
ᶜ S 2Ch 15:6; 20:23;
Mt 24:7; Mk 13:8;
Lk 21:10
19:3 ᵈ Ps 18:45
ᵉ ver 11; S Job 5:12
ᶠ 1Ch 10:13
ᵍ S Lev 19:31;
Isa 47:13; Da 2:2,10;
3:8; 5:7
19:4 ʰ Isa 20:4;
Jer 46:26; Eze 29:19;
32:11
19:5 ⁱ Isa 44:27;
50:2; Jer 50:38; 51:36
ʲ S 2Sa 14:14
19:6 ᵏ Ex 7:18
ˡ Isa 37:25; Eze 30:12
ᵐ S Ge 41:2;
S Job 8:11 ⁿ Isa 15:6
19:7 ᵒ Nu 11:5
ᵖ Dt 29:23; Isa 23:3
q Zec 10:11
19:8 ʳ Nu 11:5;
Eze 47:10 ˢ Am 4:2;
Hab 1:15
19:9 ᵗ S Jos 2:6
ᵘ Pr 7:16; Eze 16:10;
27:7

18:6 *birds of prey … wild animals.* Cf. 56:9; see Jer 7:33; Eze 32:4; 39:17–20; Rev 19:17 and notes.
18:7 See v. 2 and note. *gifts.* According to 2Ch 32:23 gifts were brought to Hezekiah after Sennacherib's death. The Moabites were asked to send tribute to Mount Zion in 16:1 (cf. 45:14; Zep 3:10). *place of the Name.* See Dt 12:5 and note.
19:1—20:6 See Jer 46; Eze 29–32 and notes.
19:1 *prophecy.* See note on 13:1. *rides on a swift cloud.* A metaphor used also in Ps 68:4 (see note there); 104:3; cf. Mt 26:64. *idols … tremble.* See Jer 50:2 and note. God had also previously judged Egypt's idols during the ten plagues (see Ex 12:12 and note). *hearts … melt.* See 13:7.
19:2 *Egyptian against Egyptian.* Cf. 9:21. The Libyan dynasty clashed with the "Ethiopians" (Cushites; see note on 18:1) and with the Saites of Dynasty 24.

19:3 *consult … spiritists.* Israel also did so in desperate times (see 8:19 and note).
19:4 *cruel master.* The king of Assyria (see 20:4). Esarhaddon conquered Egypt in 670 B.C.
19:5 *river will dry up.* The Nile was the lifeline of Egypt; its annual flooding provided essential water and produced the only fertile soil there.
19:6 *canals.* For irrigation.
19:7 *sown field.* Egypt's crops were normally abundant, and some were exported.
19:8 *Those who fish.* Fish were usually plentiful (see Nu 11:5 and note).
19:9 *work with … flax.* Large amounts of water were needed to process flax. *fine linen.* A well-known Egyptian export.

19:11 ᵛS Nu 13:22
ʷS Ge 41:37 ˣS ver 3
ʸS 1Ki 4:30; Ac 7:22
19:12 ᶻ1Co 1:20
ᵃS Isa 14:24; Ro 9:17
19:13 ᵇS Nu 13:22
ᶜJer 2:16; 44:1; 46:14,
19; Eze 30:13,16;
Hos 9:6 ᵈS Ps 118:22
19:14 ᵉS Pr 12:8;
Mt 17:17 ᶠS Ps 107:27
19:15 ᵍS Isa 9:14
19:16 ʰIsa 2:17;
11:10 ⁱJer 50:37;
51:30; Na 3:13
ʲS Dt 2:25; Heb 10:31
ᵏS Isa 11:15
19:17 ˡS Ge 35:5
ᵐS Isa 14:24
19:18 ⁿS Isa 10:20
ᵒJer 44:1 ᵖPs 22:27;
S 63:11; Isa 48:1;
Jer 4:2; Zep 3:9
�q Isa 17:1; 24:12;
32:19; fn Jer 43:13
19:19 ʳS Isa 10:20
ˢS Jos 22:10
ᵗS Ps 68:31
ᵘS Ge 28:18
19:20 ᵛS Ge 21:30
ʷS Dt 28:29;
S Jdg 2:18; S Isa 25:9
ˣIsa 49:24-26
19:21 ʸS Isa 11:9;
S 43:10 ᶻ ver 19;
S Ge 27:29;
S Ps 86:9; Isa 56:7;
60:7; Mal 1:11
ᵃS Nu 30:2;
S Dt 23:21

¹⁰ The workers in cloth will be dejected,
and all the wage earners will be sick at heart.

¹¹ The officials of Zoan ᵛ are nothing but fools;
the wise counselors ʷ of Pharaoh give senseless advice. ˣ
How can you say to Pharaoh,
"I am one of the wise men, ʸ
a disciple of the ancient kings"?

¹² Where are your wise men ᶻ now?
Let them show you and make known
what the Lᴏʀᴅ Almighty
has planned ᵃ against Egypt.

¹³ The officials of Zoan ᵇ have become fools,
the leaders of Memphis ᶜ are deceived;
the cornerstones ᵈ of her peoples
have led Egypt astray.

¹⁴ The Lᴏʀᴅ has poured into them
a spirit of dizziness; ᵉ
they make Egypt stagger in all that she does,
as drunkards stagger ᶠ around in their vomit.

¹⁵ There is nothing Egypt can do—
head or tail, palm branch or reed. ᵍ

¹⁶ In that day ʰ the Egyptians will become weaklings. ⁱ They will shudder with fear ʲ at the uplifted hand ᵏ that the Lᴏʀᴅ Almighty raises against them. ¹⁷ And the land of Judah will bring terror to the Egyptians; everyone to whom Judah is mentioned will be terrified, ˡ because of what the Lᴏʀᴅ Almighty is planning ᵐ against them.

¹⁸ In that day ⁿ five cities ᵒ in Egypt will speak the language of Canaan and swear allegiance ᵖ to the Lᴏʀᴅ Almighty. One of them will be called the City of the Sun. ᵃ �q

¹⁹ In that day ʳ there will be an altar ˢ to the Lᴏʀᴅ in the heart of Egypt, ᵗ and a monument ᵘ to the Lᴏʀᴅ at its border. ²⁰ It will be a sign and witness ᵛ to the Lᴏʀᴅ Almighty in the land of Egypt. When they cry out to the Lᴏʀᴅ because of their oppressors, he will send them a savior ʷ and defender, and he will rescue ˣ them. ²¹ So the Lᴏʀᴅ will make himself known to the Egyptians, and in that day they will acknowledge ʸ the Lᴏʀᴅ. They will worship ᶻ with sacrifices and grain offerings; they will make vows to the Lᴏʀᴅ and keep them. ᵃ

ᵃ 18 Some manuscripts of the Masoretic Text, Dead Sea Scrolls, Symmachus and Vulgate; most manuscripts of the Masoretic Text *City of Destruction*

19:11 *Zoan.* A city (possibly Tanis) in the northeastern part of the Nile delta, familiar to the Israelites during their years in Egypt (see Nu 13:22; Ps 78:12,43). It was the northern capital for the 25th dynasty (see note on 18:1). *wise men.* See v. 12. Egypt was famous for its wise men (see 1Ki 4:30 and note).
19:13 *Memphis.* An important city 15 miles south of the delta that was the capital during the Old Kingdom (c. 2686–2160 B.C.). *cornerstones.* Prophets and priests, as well as political leaders (see 9:15–16 and note).
19:14 *drunkards stagger.* Israel's leaders stagger in 28:7–8.
19:15 *head or tail, palm branch or reed.* Egypt's leaders. The same two pairs are used of Israel's leaders in 9:14–15 (see note on 9:14).
19:16–25 A chain of four announcements of coming events associated with "that day": 1. An act of divine judgment will cause Egypt to "shudder with fear" (v. 16) and be in terror of Judah (vv. 16–17). 2. "Five cities" in Egypt will "swear allegiance" to the Lord (v. 18). 3. Because of a divine act of deliverance and healing in Egypt, an altar will be erected in Egypt where Egyptians will offer sacrifices to the Lord (vv. 19–22). 4. Egypt, Assyria and Israel will be linked into one people of the Lord (vv. 23–25). The prophet looks well beyond the present realities in which the world powers do not acknowledge the true God and proudly pursue their own destinies, running roughshod over the people of the Lord. He foresees a series of divine acts that will bring about the conversion of the nations.

19:16,18–19,23–24 *In that day.* The coming day of the Lord (see 10:20,27 and note; cf. 11:10–11).
19:16 *shudder with fear.* Like the people of Jericho (Jos 2:9,11). *hand . . . the Lᴏʀᴅ . . . raises.* See 14:26–27 and note.
19:17 *land of Judah.* The Egyptians will somehow recognize (perhaps through court contacts with Hezekiah) that it is the God of Judah who has brought judgment upon them.
19:18 *five.* Perhaps in the sense of "many." *speak the language of Canaan.* Either a symbolic reference to Egypt's allegiance to the Lord (see vv. 21–22,25) or a literal reference to Jews living in Egypt. After the fall of Jerusalem in 586 B.C., many Jews fled to Egypt (see Jer 44:1 and note). *City of the Sun.* Heliopolis, city of the sun-god; it was destroyed by Nebuchadnezzar (see Jer 43:13 and note; see also TNIV text note here).
19:19 *altar.* Some relate this to the temple built in Egypt by the Jewish high priest Onias IV, who fled to Egypt in the second century B.C., but the reference appears to be to a conversion to the Lord of a significant number of Egyptians.
19:20 *sign and witness.* Cf. the purpose of the altar built near the Jordan River by the Transjordan tribes in Jos 22:26–27. *oppressors . . . savior.* The language of the book of Judges (see Jdg 2:18 and note). It is uncertain who this savior and defender is, but the prophet may well have in mind the promised Son of the house of David (see 11:1–10 and notes).
19:21 *make himself known.* Cf. Ex 7:5. *worship with sacrifices.* Offerings of foreigners are also mentioned in 56:7; 60:7 (cf. Zec 14:16–19 and note on 14:16).

²²The Lord will strike *b* Egypt with a plague; *c* he will strike them and heal them. They will turn *d* to the Lord, and he will respond to their pleas and heal *e* them.
²³In that day *f* there will be a highway *g* from Egypt to Assyria. *h* The Assyrians will go to Egypt and the Egyptians to Assyria. The Egyptians and Assyrians will worship *i* together. ²⁴In that day *j* Israel will be the third, along with Egypt and Assyria, *k* a blessing *a l* on the earth. ²⁵The Lord Almighty will bless *m* them, saying, "Blessed be Egypt my people, *n* Assyria my handiwork, *o* and Israel my inheritance. *p*"

A PROPHECY AGAINST EGYPT AND CUSH

20 In the year that the supreme commander, *q* sent by Sargon king of Assyria, came to Ashdod *r* and attacked and captured it— ²at that time the Lord spoke through Isaiah son of Amoz. *s* He said to him, "Take off the sackcloth *t* from your body and the sandals *u* from your feet." And he did so, going around stripped *v* and barefoot. *w*

³Then the Lord said, "Just as my servant *x* Isaiah has gone stripped and barefoot for three years, *y* as a sign *z* and portent *a* against Egypt *b* and Cush, *b c 4*so the king *d* of Assyria will lead away stripped *e* and barefoot the Egyptian captives *f* and Cushite *g* exiles, young and old, with buttocks bared *h*—to Egypt's shame. *i* ⁵Those who trusted *j* in Cush *k* and boasted in Egypt *l* will be dismayed and put to shame. *m* ⁶In that day *n* the people who live on this coast will say, 'See what has happened *o* to those we relied on, *p* those we fled to for help *q* and deliverance from the king of Assyria! How then can we escape? *r*' "

A PROPHECY AGAINST BABYLON

21 A prophecy *s* concerning the Desert *t* by the Sea:

Like whirlwinds *u* sweeping through the southland, *v*
    an invader comes from the desert,
    from a land of terror.

²A dire *w* vision has been shown to me:
    The traitor betrays, *x* the looter takes loot.
    Elam, *y* attack! Media, *z* lay siege!
    I will bring to an end all the groaning she caused.

---

a 24 Or Assyria, whose names will be used in blessings (see Gen. 48:20); or Assyria, who will be seen by others as blessed   *b 3 That is, the upper Nile region; also in verse 5*

21:1 *s* S Isa 13:1 *t* Isa 13:21; Jer 50:12; 51:43 *u* S Job 1:19 *v* Da 11:40; Zec 9:14   **21:2** *w* Ps 60:3 *x* Isa 24:16; 33:1 *y* S Ge 10:22; Isa 22:6 *z* S Isa 13:3; Jer 25:25; 51:28

19:22 *b* Ex 12:23; Heb 12:11 *c* Ex 11:10
d Isa 45:14; Eze 33:11; Hos 6:1; 10:12; 12:6; 14:1; Joel 2:13
e S Dt 32:39
19:23 *f* S ver 16,24; *g* S Isa 11:16
h Mic 7:12
i S Ge 27:29; Isa 2:3; 27:13; 66:23
19:24 *j* S ver 23
k S Isa 11:11 *l* S Ge 12:2
19:25 *m* S Ge 12:3; Eph 2:11-14 *n* Ps 87:4; S 100:3 *o* Isa 29:23; 43:7; 45:11; 60:21; 64:8; Eph 2:10
p S Ex 34:9; Jer 30:22; Hos 2:3
20:1 *q* 2Ki 18:17
r S Jos 11:22; S 13:3
20:2 *s* S Isa 13:1
t 2Ki 1:8; S Isa 3:24; Zec 13:4; Mt 3:4
u Eze 24:17,23
v S 1Sa 19:24
w Eze 4:1-12; Mic 1:8
20:3 *x* Isa 22:20; 41:8-9; 42:1; 43:10; 49:3,5-7; 50:10; 52:13; 53:11; Jer 7:25; Hag 2:23; Zec 4:14
y S Isa 16:14
z S Ex 3:12; S Isa 8:18; 37:30; 38:7; Ac 21:11
a S Dt 28:46
b S Isa 19:1 *c* ver 5; S Ge 10:6; Isa 37:9; 43:3
20:4 *d* S Isa 19:4
e S Job 12:17
f Jer 46:19; Na 3:10
g Isa 18:1; Zep 2:12
h S Isa 3:24 *i* Isa 47:3; Jer 13:22,26; Na 3:5
20:5 *j* S Isa 8:12
k S ver 3 *l* S 2Ki 18:21; S Isa 30:5
m Eze 29:16
20:6 *n* Isa 2:11; S 19:23 *o* S 2Ki 18:21
p Jer 46:25
q S Isa 10:3
r Jer 30:15-17; 31:2; Mt 23:33; 1Th 5:3; Heb 2:3

19:22 *strike Egypt with a plague.* Oppression (see v. 20) and plague were two common forms of divine affliction. Contrast the results of the plague on the firstborn in Ex 12:23. *turn ... heal.* Cf. 6:10; here parallel to sending Egypt a "savior and defender" (v. 20). Earlier a hardhearted pharaoh had not turned to the Lord (Ex 9:34–35).

19:23 *highway.* Cf. the highway to Jerusalem in 11:16; 35:8–10 (see notes there). For centuries Egyptians and Assyrians had fought each other (see 20:4), but in the future they would be linked in a bond of friendship sealed by their common allegiance to the Lord (cf. 25:3). *worship together.* This description of peace and unity in worship is similar to 2:2–4 (see note there; see also note on 19:21).

19:25 *will bless them.* A fulfillment of Ge 12:3 (see note on Ge 12:2–3). *Egypt my people.* Such a universal vision seems possible for Isaiah only in the light of what has been said about the "shoot ... from the stump of Jesse" (11:1; see 11:1–10). Cf. 45:14; Eph 2:11–13.

20:1–6 An epilogue to chs. 18–19, as 16:13–14 is to 15:1—16:12.

20:1 *the year.* Probably 712 B.C. *Sargon.* Sargon II, who reigned 721–705 B.C. (see chart, p. 482). He is mentioned by name only here in the OT. *Ashdod.* One of the five Philistine cities (see map, p. 338), Ashdod was located near the Mediterranean Sea about 18 miles northeast of Gaza. The city had rebelled against Assyria in 713 under King Azuri. In 1963 three fragments of an Assyrian monument commemorating Sargon's victory and

mentioning Sargon by name were discovered at Ashdod.
20:2 *sackcloth.* Normally the garment of mourners (see note on Rev 11:3); sometimes the garb of prophets (see 2Ki 1:8; Zec 13:4–6 and notes). *stripped and barefoot.* See vv. 3–4; cf. 2Ch 28:15; Mic 1:8 and note.
20:3 *my servant.* See note on 41:8–9. *three years.* See 16:14 and note. *sign and portent.* See 8:18; see also 7:3,14 and notes. The prophet Ezekiel's behavior also had symbolic significance (Eze 24:24,27; cf. Zec 3:8). *Egypt and Cush.* See 18:1; 19:1 and notes.
20:5 *trusted in Cush ... Egypt.* After Assyria conquered the northern kingdom of Israel in 722–721 B.C., King Hezekiah of Judah was under great pressure to make an alliance with Egypt. Isaiah urgently warned against such a policy (cf. 30:1–2; 31:1 and notes).
21:1 *prophecy.* See note on 13:1. *Desert.* The coming judgment would eventually turn Babylon (see v. 9) into a wasteland (cf. 13:20–22). *the Sea.* Refers either to the Persian Gulf, which lies southeast of Babylon, or to the plain laid down by the Euphrates and Tigris rivers and their tributaries. *whirlwinds ... desert.* The desert sometimes spawns powerful winds (see Hos 13:15). *an invader.* Lit. "it"; it is not clear whether "comes from the desert, from a land of terror" is ascribed to an invader or continues the description of the whirlwinds.
21:2 *Elam.* See note on 11:11; see also Jer 49:34–39. The Elamites were perpetual enemies of Assyria and Babylon. Much later, they were part of the Persian army that conquered Babylon under Cyrus in 539 B.C. *Media.* See note on 13:17. *she.* Babylon.

21:3 ᵃ S Job 14:22
ᵇ S Ge 3:16; Ps 48:6;
Isa 26:17; 37:3;
Jer 30:6; 48:41;
49:22; Jn 16:21
ᶜ Da 7:28; 8:27; 10:16
21:4 ᵈ Isa 7:4; 35:4
ᵉ S Isa 13:8; Da 5:9
ᶠ S Ps 55:5
21:5 ᵍ Isa 5:12; 22:2,
13; 23:7; 24:8; 32:13;
Jer 25:16,27; 51:39,
57; Da 5:2 ʰ 2Sa 1:21;
1Ki 10:16-17; Jer 46:3;
51:11
21:6 ⁱ S 2Ki 9:17
21:7 ʲ ver 9
ᵏ S Jdg 6:5
21:8 ˡ Mic 7:7;
Hab 2:1
21:9 ᵐ ver 7
ⁿ S Isa 13:1; 47:1,5;
S Rev 14:8 ᵒ Isa 47:11;
Jer 51:8; Da 5:30
ᵖ S Lev 26:30;
Isa 46:1; Jer 50:2;
51:44 ᑫ S Isa 2:18
21:10 ʳ Isa 27:12;
28:27,28; 41:15;
Jer 51:33; Mic 4:13;
Hab 3:12; Mt 3:12
21:11 ˢ S Ge 25:14;
S Isa 34:11 ᵗ Ge 32:3

³ At this my body is racked with pain,ᵃ
   pangs seize me, like those of a woman in labor;ᵇ
I am staggered by what I hear,
   I am bewilderedᶜ by what I see.
⁴ My heartᵈ falters,
   fear makes me tremble;ᵉ
the twilight I longed for
   has become a horrorᶠ to me.

⁵ They set the tables,
   they spread the rugs,
   they eat, they drink!ᵍ
Get up, you officers,
   oil the shields!ʰ

⁶ This is what the Lord says to me:

"Go, post a lookoutⁱ
   and have him report what he sees.
⁷ When he sees chariotsʲ
   with teams of horses,
riders on donkeys
   or riders on camels,ᵏ
let him be alert,
   fully alert."

⁸ And the lookoutᵃ ˡ shouted,

"Day after day, my lord, I stand on the watchtower;
   every night I stay at my post.
⁹ Look, here comes a man in a chariotᵐ
   with a team of horses.
And he gives back the answer:
   'Babylonⁿ has fallen,ᵒ has fallen!
All the images of its godsᵖ
   lie shatteredᑫ on the ground!' "

¹⁰ My people who are crushed on the threshing floor,ʳ
   I tell you what I have heard
from the Lord Almighty,
   from the God of Israel.

A PROPHECY AGAINST EDOM

¹¹ A prophecy concerning Dumahᵇ· ˢ

Someone calls to me from Seir,ᵗ
   "Watchman, what is left of the night?
   Watchman, what is left of the night?"
¹² The watchman replies,
   "Morning is coming, but also the night.

ᵃ 8 Dead Sea Scrolls and Syriac; Masoretic Text *A lion*   ᵇ 11 *Dumah*, a wordplay on *Edom*, means
silence or *stillness*.

21:3 *racked with pain, pangs seize me.* See note on 16:9–11; see
also Daniel's reaction to visions in Da 8:27; 10:16–17.
21:4 *twilight.* Perhaps the end of the Babylonian empire (see
note on v. 12). *a horror to me.* The devastation is beyond even
what he had desired.
21:5 *eat . . . drink.* With the kind of confident assurance reflected in Belshazzar's feast (see Da 5:1). *Get up . . . !* Rhetorically the
prophet, who has seen in a vision the coming attack on Babylon, calls on the officers of Babylon to prepare. *oil the shields.*
See note on 2Sa 1:21.
21:6 *Go, post a lookout.* Probably on the walls of Jerusalem.
21:7 *chariots . . . donkeys . . . camels.* Bearing messengers from afar.
21:9 *Babylon . . . has fallen!* See 13:19. Babylon fell in 689 B.C.
and again in 539. These words were adapted by John in Rev

14:8; 18:2. *its gods lie shattered.* The fall of a kingdom meant the
disgrace of its gods (cf. 46:1–2; 1Sa 5:3–7 and notes).
21:10 *crushed.* Judah would be punished by the Babylonians
and taken into captivity (see 39:5–7 and notes). *on the threshing
floor.* Threshing was a common metaphor for judgment or destruction from war (see Am 1:3 and note).
21:11–12 See Jer 49:7–22; Eze 25:12–14; Am 1:11–12 and
notes.
21:11 *prophecy.* See note on 13:1. *Seir.* A synonym for Edom
(Ge 32:3), homeland of Esau's descendants, south of the Dead
Sea. Edom is dealt with more extensively in 34:5–15 (see notes
there; cf. 63:1 and note).
21:12 *Morning . . . but also the night.* Perhaps meaning that the
long night of Assyrian oppression is almost over, but only a

If you would ask, then ask;
  and come back yet again."

A PROPHECY AGAINST ARABIA

¹³A prophecy ^u concerning Arabia: ^v

You caravans of Dedanites, ^w
  who camp in the thickets of Arabia,
¹⁴ bring water for the thirsty;
you who live in Tema, ^x
  bring food for the fugitives.
¹⁵They flee ^y from the sword, ^z
  from the drawn sword,
from the bent bow
  and from the heat of battle.

¹⁶This is what the Lord says to me: "Within one year, as a servant bound by contract ^a would count it, all the splendor ^b of Kedar ^c will come to an end. ¹⁷The survivors of the archers, the warriors of Kedar, will be few. ^d" The LORD, the God of Israel, has spoken. ^e

A PROPHECY ABOUT JERUSALEM

22

A prophecy ^f concerning the Valley ^g of Vision: ^h

What troubles you now,
  that you have all gone up on the roofs, ⁱ
²you town so full of commotion,
  you city of tumult ^j and revelry? ^k
Your slain ^l were not killed by the sword, ^m
  nor did they die in battle.
³All your leaders have fled ⁿ together;
  they have been captured ^o without using the bow.
All you who were caught were taken prisoner together,
  having fled while the enemy was still far away.
⁴Therefore I said, "Turn away from me;
  let me weep ^p bitterly.
Do not try to console me
  over the destruction of my people." ^q

⁵The Lord, the LORD Almighty, has a day ^r
  of tumult and trampling ^s and terror ^t
  in the Valley of Vision, ^u
a day of battering down walls ^v
  and of crying out to the mountains.
⁶Elam ^w takes up the quiver, ^x

21:13 ^u Isa 13:1
^v S 2Ch 9:14
^w S Ge 10:7; S 25:3
21:14 ^x S Ge 25:15
21:15 ^y S Isa 13:14
^z Isa 31:8
21:16 ^a S Lev 25:50
^b S Isa 17:3
^c S Ge 25:13
21:17 ^d S Dt 4:27;
S Isa 10:19
^e S Isa 1:20; 16:14
22:1 ^f Isa 13:1
^g Ps 125:2; Jer 21:13;
Joel 3:2,12,14
^h S Isa 1:1 ⁱ S Jos 2:8;
Jer 48:38
22:2 ^j Eze 22:5
^k S Isa 5:14; S 21:5
^l S Isa 10:4
^m S 2Ki 25:3
22:3 ⁿ S Isa 13:14
^o S 2Ki 25:6
22:4 ^p S Isa 15:3;
S La 1:16; Eze 21:6;
Lk 19:41 ^q Jer 9:1
22:5 ^r S Isa 2:12
^s S Job 40:12;
S Ps 103:13
^t S 2Sa 22:43;
Isa 13:3; Jer 30:7;
La 1:5; Eze 8:17-18;
9:9-10; Joel 2:31;
Am 5:18-20; Zep 1:15
^u S Isa 1:1 ^v Ne 6:15;
S Ps 89:40; Isa 5:5;
Jer 39:8; Eze 13:14
22:6 ^w S Isa 21:2
^x Ps 46:9; Jer 49:35;
51:56

short "morning" will precede Babylonian domination (see v. 4 and note).
21:13–17 See Jer 49:28–33 and notes.
21:13 *prophecy.* See note on 13:1. *Dedanites.* An Arabian tribe whose merchant activities are mentioned also in Eze 27:20; 38:13. *thickets.* The caravans had to hide from the invader (cf. Jdg 5:6). The Assyrians began to attack the Arabs in 732 B.C., and the Babylonians did the same under Nebuchadnezzar (see Jer 25:17,23–24).
21:14 *Tema.* An oasis in northern Arabia about 400 miles southwest of Babylon (cf. Job 6:19; Jer 25:23).
21:15 *sword . . . bow.* The simple bows of the Arabs were ineffective against the swords and composite bows of Assyria.
21:16 *servant bound by contract.* See 16:14 and note. *splendor.* See 14:11; 16:14. *Kedar.* The home of nomadic tribes in the Arabian Desert. Kedar was known for its flocks (60:7; Eze 27:21). Nebuchadnezzar defeated the people of Kedar (Jer 49:28–29; cf. Jer 2:10 and note).
21:17 *survivors . . . will be few.* Cf. 10:19; 16:14; 17:6.
22:1–13 The notes on this prophecy assume that it refers primarily to the final Babylonian siege of Jerusalem in 588–586 B.C.

But it is also possible that the primary reference is to the siege by the Assyrian king Sennacherib in 701.
22:1 *prophecy.* See note on 13:1. *Valley of Vision.* A valley where God revealed himself in visions, probably one of the valleys near Jerusalem (see note on v. 7). See also v. 5. *roofs.* See 15:3 and note.
22:2 *tumult and revelry.* See v. 13; 5:11–13 and note; 32:13. Jerusalem is behaving just like Babylon (see 21:5 and note; cf. 23:7). *not killed by the sword.* Perhaps a reference to death from disease and famine when the Babylonians besieged Jerusalem in 586 B.C.
22:3 *leaders have fled.* King Zedekiah and his army fled Jerusalem but were captured near Jericho (see 2Ki 25:4–6).
22:4 *my people.* Lit. "the Daughter of my people" (see note on 2Ki 19:21).
22:5 *has a day.* See 2:12 and note on 2:11,17,20. Also cf. "in that day" in v. 8 and "on that day" in v. 12. *tumult.* A fulfillment of the curse of Dt 28:20.
22:6 *Elam.* See note on 11:11; see also Jer 49:34–39. Elamites probably fought in the Babylonian army. *takes up the quiver.* See Jer 49:35. *Kir.* Perhaps another name for Media (see 21:2).

22:6 ᵛS 2Ki 16:9
22:7 ᶻJos 15:8
ᵃS 2Ch 32:1-2
22:8 ᵇS Isa 2:12
ᶜS 2Ch 32:5
ᵈS 1Ki 7:2
22:9 ᵉS Ne 1:3
ᶠS 2Ki 18:17;
S 2Ch 32:4
22:10 ᵍJer 33:4
ʰS 2Ch 32:5
22:11 ⁱ2Ki 25:4;
2Ch 32:5; Jer 39:4
ʲS 2Ch 32:4
ᵏS 1Sa 12:24
ˡ2Ki 19:25
22:12 ᵐS Isa 2:12
ⁿJoel 1:9; 2:17
ᵒS Lev 13:40;
Mic 1:16 ᵖS Isa 3:24
22:13 �q S Isa 21:5
ʳS 1Sa 25:36;
Ecc 8:15; Isa 5:22;
28:7-8; 56:12;
Lk 17:26-29
ˢ1Co 15:32ᵃ
22:14 ᵗIsa 5:9
ᵘS 1Sa 2:25; Isa 13:11;
26:21; 30:13-14;
Eze 24:13
22:15 ᵛS 2Ki 6:30;
S 18:18 ʷver 21
ˣS Ge 41:40
22:16 ʸMt 27:60
ᶻS Ge 50:5;
S Nu 32:42
22:17 ᵃJer 10:18;
13:18; 22:26
22:18 ᵇS Job 8:11;
Isa 14:19; 17:13
ᶜS Ge 41:43
22:19 ᵈS 1Sa 2:7;
S Ps 52:5 ᵉLk 16:3

with her charioteers and horses;
Kir ᵛ uncovers the shield.
⁷ Your choicest valleys ᶻ are full of chariots,
   and horsemen are posted at the city gates. ᵃ

⁸ The Lord stripped away the defenses of Judah,
   and you looked in that day ᵇ
to the weapons ᶜ in the Palace of the Forest. ᵈ
⁹ You saw that the City of David
   had many breaches ᵉ in its defenses;
you stored up water
   in the Lower Pool. ᶠ
¹⁰ You counted the buildings in Jerusalem
   and tore down houses ᵍ to strengthen the wall. ʰ
¹¹ You built a reservoir between the two walls ⁱ
   for the water of the Old Pool, ʲ
but you did not look to the One who made it,
   or have regard ᵏ for the One who planned ˡ it long ago.

¹² The Lord, the LORD Almighty,
   called you on that day ᵐ
to weep ⁿ and to wail,
   to tear out your hair ᵒ and put on sackcloth. ᵖ
¹³ But see, there is joy and revelry, q
   slaughtering of cattle and killing of sheep,
   eating of meat and drinking of wine! ʳ
"Let us eat and drink," you say,
   "for tomorrow we die!" ˢ

¹⁴The LORD Almighty has revealed this in my hearing: ᵗ "Till your dying day this sin will not be atoned ᵘ for," says the Lord, the LORD Almighty.

¹⁵This is what the Lord, the LORD Almighty, says:

"Go, say to this steward,
   to Shebna, ᵛ who is in charge ʷ of the palace: ˣ
¹⁶ What are you doing here and who gave you permission
   to cut out a grave ʸ for yourself ᶻ here,
hewing your grave on the height
   and chiseling your resting place in the rock?

¹⁷ "Beware, the LORD is about to take firm hold of you
   and hurl ᵃ you away, you mighty man.
¹⁸ He will roll you up tightly like a ball
   and throw ᵇ you into a large country.
There you will die
   and there the chariots ᶜ you were so proud of
   will become a disgrace to your master's house.
¹⁹ I will depose you from your office,
   and you will be ousted ᵈ from your position. ᵉ

22:7 *choicest valleys.* The Kidron Valley lay east of Jerusalem, the Hinnom Valley to the south and west (see map, p. 486).
22:8 *Palace of the Forest.* Built by King Solomon out of cedars from Lebanon (see 1Ki 7:2–6 and notes; 10:17,21).
22:9 *City of David.* See 2Sa 5:6–7,9 and notes; cf. Isa 29:1. *Lower Pool.* Probably the same as the "Old Pool" of v. 11. Hezekiah made a pool and a tunnel as a precaution against Sennacherib's invasion (see 2Ki 20:20 and note). The "Upper Pool" is mentioned in 7:3; 36:2.
22:10 *strengthen the wall.* Cf. Hezekiah's preparations in 2Ch 32:5.
22:11 *did not look to the One.* In 31:1 those who look to horses and chariots rather than to God are similarly condemned.
22:12 *tear out your hair.* The hair was either torn out or shaved off (cf. Jer 16:6; Eze 27:31).
22:13 *joy and revelry.* The same Hebrew phrase is translated

"gladness and joy" in 35:10; 51:11, passages depicting great hope in connection with restoration. But this was a time to mourn (Ecc 3:4). See note on v. 2. *Let us eat…we die.* Quoted by Paul in 1Co 15:32 to underscore the utter futility of life without a belief in resurrection from the dead. Cf. Lk 12:19; cf. also Ecc 8:15 and note.
22:15 *Shebna.* Apparently a foreigner, possibly Egyptian; a contemporary of King Hezekiah. *in charge of the palace.* A position second only to the king (see note on v. 21; cf. 36:3; 1Ki 4:6; 2Ki 15:5).
22:16 *cut out a grave.* One's place of burial was considered very important, and Shebna coveted a tomb worthy of a king (cf. 2Ch 16:14).
22:17 *hurl you away.* Cf. Jer 22:24–26 and notes.
22:18 *There you will die.* Apparently without an honorable burial (see note on 14:19). *chariots.* A sign of high office (see Ge 41:43).

²⁰"In that day ^f I will summon my servant, ^g Eliakim ^h son of Hilkiah. ²¹ I will clothe him with your robe and fasten your sash ⁱ around him and hand your authority ^j over to him. He will be a father to those who live in Jerusalem and to the house of Judah. ²² I will place on his shoulder ^k the key ^l to the house of David; ^m what he opens no one can shut, and what he shuts no one can open. ^{n 23} I will drive him like a peg ^o into a firm place; ^p he will become a seat ^a of honor ^q for the house of his father. ²⁴ All the glory of his family will hang on him: its offspring and offshoots—all its lesser vessels, from the bowls to all the jars.

²⁵"In that day, ^r" declares the Lord Almighty, "the peg ^s driven into the firm place will give way; it will be sheared off and will fall, and the load hanging on it will be cut down." The Lord has spoken. ^t

A PROPHECY AGAINST TYRE

23 A prophecy concerning Tyre: ^u

Wail, ^v you ships ^w of Tarshish! ^x
   For Tyre is destroyed ^y
   and left without house or harbor.
From the land of Cyprus
   word has come to them.

² Be silent, ^z you people of the island
   and you merchants ^a of Sidon, ^b
   whom the seafarers have enriched.
³ On the great waters
   came the grain of the Shihor; ^c
the harvest of the Nile ^{b d} was the revenue of Tyre, ^e
   and she became the marketplace of the nations.

⁴ Be ashamed, Sidon, ^f and you fortress of the sea,
   for the sea has spoken:
"I have neither been in labor nor given birth; ^g
   I have neither reared sons nor brought up daughters."
⁵ When word comes to Egypt,
   they will be in anguish ^h at the report from Tyre. ⁱ

⁶ Cross over to Tarshish; ^j
   wail, you people of the island.
⁷ Is this your city of revelry, ^k
   the old, old city,
whose feet have taken her
   to settle in far-off lands?

---

^a 23 Or *throne*   ^b 2,3 Masoretic Text; Dead Sea Scrolls *Sidon, / who cross over the sea; / your envoys* ³*are on the great waters. / The grain of the Shihor, / the harvest of the Nile,*

**Cross references (right margin):**

22:20 ^f ver 25; ^g S Isa 20:3; ^h S 2Ki 18:18; S Isa 36:3
22:21 ⁱ S Isa 5:27; ^j ver 15
22:22 ^k Isa 9:6; ^l 1Ch 9:27; Mt 16:19; Rev 3:7 ^m S Isa 7:2 ⁿ S Job 12:14
22:23 ^o ver 25; Eze 15:3; Zec 10:4 ^p S Ezr 9:8; S Job 6:25 ^q S 1Sa 2:7-8; S Job 36:7
22:25 ^r ver 20 ^s S ver 23 ^t Isa 46:11; Mic 4:4
23:1 ^u Jos 19:29; 1Ki 5:1; Jer 47:4; Joel 3:4-8; Am 1:9-10 ^v S Isa 13:6 ^w S 1Ki 10:22 ^x S Ge 10:4; Isa 2:16 fn ^y S Ge 1:2; Eze 26:4
23:2 ^z S Job 2:13 ^a Eze 27:5-24 ^b Jdg 1:31
23:3 ^c S Ge 41:5 ^d S Isa 19:7 ^e S Ps 83:7
23:4 ^f S Ge 10:15,19 ^g Isa 54:1
23:5 ^h Eze 30:9 ⁱ Eze 26:17-18
23:6 ^j S Ge 10:4
23:7 ^k ver 12; S Isa 5:14; S 21:5; 32:13; Eze 26:13

22:20 *In that day.* When the Lord acts in judgment (see vv. 17–19). *my servant.* See note on 20:3. *Eliakim.* See 36:3,11,22; 37:2.
22:21 *hand your authority over to him.* By 701 B.C. (see 36:3) Eliakim had replaced Shebna, who was demoted to "secretary."
22:22 Quoted in part in Rev 3:7 (see note there). The mention of "father" (v. 21) and of the responsibility "on his shoulder" recalls the words about the Messiah in 9:6. *key to the house of David.* The authority delegated to him by the king, who belongs to David's dynasty—perhaps controlling entrance into the royal palace. Cf. the "keys of the kingdom" given to Peter (Mt 16:19; see note there).
22:23 *peg.* Normally the Hebrew for this word refers to a tent peg, but here to a peg driven into wood (see Eze 15:3; Zec 10:4 and note). *seat of honor.* Cf. 1Sa 2:8.
22:25 *In that day.* Another (unspecified) day when the Lord will come in judgment. *peg … will give way.* Eliakim, like Shebna, will eventually fall from power.
23:1–18 See Eze 26:1—28:19; Am 1:9–10 and notes.
23:1 *prophecy.* See note on 13:1. *Tyre.* The main seaport along the Phoenician coast, about 35 miles north of Mount Carmel. Part of the city was built on two rocky islands about half a mile from the shore. King Hiram of Tyre supplied cedars and craftsmen for the temple (see 1Ki 5:8–9) and sailors for Solomon's

commercial fleet (1Ki 9:27). *Wail, you ships.* See v. 14. *ships of Tarshish.* Trading ships (see note on 2:16). *destroyed.* Fulfilled through Assyria, Nebuchadnezzar and Alexander. Nebuchadnezzar captured the mainland city in 572 B.C. (see Eze 26:7–11), but the island fortress was not taken until Alexander the Great destroyed it in 332 (cf. Eze 26:3–5; see Zec 9:3 and note). *Cyprus.* An island that had close ties with Tyre (see Eze 27:6 and note).
23:2,4,12 *Sidon.* See Eze 28:20–26 and notes; the other prominent Phoenician city, about 25 miles north of Tyre.
23:2 *island.* Tyre (see v. 1 and note). *merchants … seafarers.* Tyre's commercial ventures affected the entire Mediterranean world (see vv. 3,8).
23:3 *Shihor.* Probably the easternmost branch of the Nile (see TNIV text note on Jer 2:18). *harvest of the Nile.* See 19:7 and note.
23:4 *fortress of the sea.* Tyre (see note on v. 1). *labor … birth.* Contrast 54:1 (see note there).
23:6 *Tarshish.* Perhaps Tartessus in Spain (see note on Eze 27:12), an island in the western Mediterranean or a site on the coast of North Africa.
23:7 *revelry.* See note on 22:2. *old, old city.* Tyre was founded before 2000 B.C. *settle in far-off lands.* Carthage in North Africa was a colony of Tyre. Tarshish may have been another.

23:8 *l* Na 3:16
m Eze 28:5; Rev 18:23
23:9 *n* S Isa 14:24
o S Job 40:11
p S Isa 13:11
q Isa 5:13; 9:15;
Eze 27:3
23:11 *r* S Ex 14:21
s S Ps 46:6 *ver* 14;
Isa 25:2; Eze 26:4;
Zec 9:3-4
23:12 *u* S ver 7;
Rev 18:22 *v* Isa 37:22;
47:1; Jer 14:17; 46:11;
La 2:13; Zep 3:14;
Zec 2:10 *w* S Ge 10:4
23:13 *x* Isa 43:14;
Jer 51:12 *y* Isa 10:5
z S Ps 74:14; Isa 18:6
a S 2Ki 25:1 *b* Isa 10:7
23:14 *c* S 1Ki 10:22
d S Ge 10:4;
Isa 2:16 *fn* *e* S ver 11
23:15 *f* Jer 25:22
g S Ps 90:10
23:16 *h* Pr 7:10
23:17 *i* S Ps 90:10
j Dt 23:17-18;
Eze 16:26; Na 3:4;
Rev 17:1; 18:3,9
k Jer 25:26
23:18 *l* Ex 28:36;
S 39:30; Jos 6:17-19;
Ps 72:10 *m* Isa 18:7;
60:5-9; 61:6; Mic 4:13
n Am 1:9-10; Zec 14:1,
14
24:1 *o* ver 20;
Isa 2:19-21; 33:9;
Jer 25:29 *p* S Jos 6:17;
S Isa 13:5

8 Who planned this against Tyre,
the bestower of crowns,
whose merchants *l* are princes,
whose traders *m* are renowned in the earth?
9 The LORD Almighty planned *n* it,
to bring down *o* her pride in all her splendor
and to humble *p* all who are renowned *q* on the earth.

10 Till *a* your land as they do along the Nile,
Daughter Tarshish,
for you no longer have a harbor.
11 The LORD has stretched out his hand *r* over the sea
and made its kingdoms tremble. *s*
He has given an order concerning Phoenicia
that her fortresses be destroyed. *t*
12 He said, "No more of your reveling, *u*
Virgin Daughter *v* Sidon, now crushed!

"Up, cross over to Cyprus; *w*
even there you will find no rest."
13 Look at the land of the Babylonians, *b x*
this people that is now of no account!
The Assyrians *y* have made it
a place for desert creatures; *z*
they raised up their siege towers, *a*
they stripped its fortresses bare
and turned it into a ruin. *b*

14 Wail, you ships *c* of Tarshish; *d*
your fortress is destroyed! *e*

15 At that time Tyre *f* will be forgotten for seventy years, *g* the span of a king's life. But at the end of these seventy years, it will happen to Tyre as in the song of the prostitute:

16 "Take up a harp, walk through the city,
you forgotten prostitute; *h*
play the harp well, sing many a song,
so that you will be remembered."

17 At the end of seventy years, *i* the LORD will deal with Tyre. She will return to her lucrative prostitution *j* and will ply her trade with all the kingdoms on the face of the earth. *k* 18 Yet her profit and her earnings will be set apart for the LORD; *l* they will not be stored up or hoarded. Her profits will go to those who live before the LORD, *m* for abundant food and fine clothes. *n*

THE LORD'S DEVASTATION OF THE EARTH

24 See, the LORD is going to lay waste the earth *o*
and devastate *p* it;
he will ruin its face

a 10 Dead Sea Scrolls and some Septuagint manuscripts; Masoretic Text *Go through*   *b 13* Or *Chaldeans*

23:8–9 *planned.* See 14:24,26–27; 25:1 and notes.
23:8 *bestower of crowns.* Tyre crowned kings in her colonies. *traders are renowned.* See Eze 28:4–5.
23:9 *her pride in all her splendor.* See Eze 27:3–4 and notes.
23:10 *Daughter Tarshish.* A personification of Tarshish (see note on 2Ki 19:21).
23:11 *stretched out his hand.* See note on 14:26–27. *Phoenicia.* Roughly the same as modern Lebanon.
23:12 *Virgin Daughter Sidon.* A personification of Sidon (see note on 2Ki 19:21). *now crushed.* Sidon was captured by Esarhaddon in the seventh century B.C. and later by Nebuchadnezzar c. 587 (cf. Jer 25:22,26 and notes).
23:13 *Assyrians.* Sennacherib destroyed the city of Babylon in 689 B.C. Phoenicia would look like the Babylon of that time. *desert creatures.* Cf. 13:21. *siege towers.* See note on 2Ki 25:1.
23:14 See v. 1 and note.

B 23:15 *seventy years.* Also the length of the Babylonian captivity (see Jer 25:11–12; 29:10 and notes) and the length of time the Babylonian god Marduk (according to an inscription of King Esarhaddon) decreed that Babylon should remain devastated.
23:16 Cf. Pr 7:10–15.
A 23:17 *lucrative prostitution.* A "prostitute" nation was one that sought to make the highest profits, regardless of the means. Self-gratification was the key (cf. Rev 14:8; 17:5 and notes).
23:18 *set apart for the LORD.* The earnings of a prostitute could not be given to the Lord (Dt 23:18), but the silver and gold of a city that is devoted to destruction (see note on Dt 2:34) were placed in the Lord's treasury (see Jos 6:17,19 and note on 6:17; cf. Mic 4:13). *to those.* Israel will one day receive the wealth of the nations (see note on 18:7; cf. 60:5–11 and notes; 61:6).

and scatter [q] its inhabitants—
² it will be the same
for priest as for people, [r]
for master as for his servant,
for mistress as for her servant,
for seller as for buyer, [s]
for borrower as for lender,
for debtor as for creditor. [t]
³ The earth will be completely laid waste [u]
and totally plundered. [v]

The LORD has spoken [w] this word.

⁴ The earth dries up [x] and withers, [y]
the world languishes and withers,
the heavens [z] languish with the earth. [a]
⁵ The earth is defiled [b] by its people;
they have disobeyed [c] the laws,
violated the statutes
and broken the everlasting covenant. [d]
⁶ Therefore a curse [e] consumes the earth;
its people must bear their guilt.
Therefore earth's inhabitants are burned up, [f]
and very few are left.
⁷ The new wine dries up [g] and the vine withers; [h]
all the merrymakers groan. [i]
⁸ The gaiety of the timbrels [j] is stilled,
the noise [k] of the revelers [l] has stopped,
the joyful harp [m] is silent. [n]
⁹ No longer do they drink wine [o] with a song;
the beer is bitter [p] to its drinkers.
¹⁰ The ruined city [q] lies desolate; [r]
the entrance to every house is barred.
¹¹ In the streets they cry out [s] for wine; [t]
all joy turns to gloom, [u]
all gaiety is banished from the earth.
¹² The city is left in ruins, [v]
its gate [w] is battered to pieces.
¹³ So will it be on the earth
and among the nations,
as when an olive tree is beaten, [x]
or as when gleanings are left after the grape harvest. [y]

¹⁴ They raise their voices, they shout for joy; [z]
from the west [a] they acclaim the LORD's majesty.
¹⁵ Therefore in the east [b] give glory [c] to the LORD;
exalt [d] the name [e] of the LORD, the God of Israel,
in the islands [f] of the sea.
¹⁶ From the ends of the earth [g] we hear singing: [h]
"Glory [i] to the Righteous One." [j]

24:1 [q] S Ge 11:9
24:2 [r] Hos 4:9
[s] Eze 7:12; 1Co 7:29-31; [t] S Lev 25:35-37; Dt 23:19-20; Isa 3:1-7
24:3 [u] S Ge 6:13
[v] Isa 6:11-12; 10:6
[w] S Isa 7:7
24:4 [x] Jer 12:11; 14:4; Joel 1:10
[y] S Isa 15:6
[z] S Isa 2:12
[a] S Isa 3:26
24:5 [b] S Ge 3:17
[c] S Isa 1:2; 9:17; 10:6; 59:12; Jer 7:28
[d] S Ge 9:11; S Jer 11:10
24:6 [e] S Jos 23:15
[f] S Isa 1:31
24:7 [g] Jer 48:33; Joel 1:5 [h] Isa 7:23; S 15:6; 32:10
[i] S Isa 3:26; 16:8-10
24:8 [j] S Ge 31:27; S Isa 5:12 [k] Jer 7:34; 16:9; 25:10; 33:11; Hos 2:11 [l] S Isa 5:14; S 21:5 [m] S Ps 137:2; Rev 18:22 [n] La 5:14; Eze 26:13
24:9 [o] Isa 5:11,22
[p] Isa 5:20
24:10 [q] Isa 25:2; 26:5 [r] S Ge 1:2; S Isa 6:11
24:11 [s] S Ps 144:14
[t] La 2:12 [u] S Isa 15:6; 16:10; 32:13; Jer 14:3
24:12 [v] S Isa 19:18
[w] S Isa 3:26; S 13:2
24:13 [x] S Dt 30:4; S Isa 17:6 [y] Ob 1:5; Mic 7:1
24:14 [z] S Isa 12:6
[a] Isa 43:5; 49:12
24:15 [b] S Ps 113:3
[c] Isa 42:12; 66:19; 2Th 1:12 [d] S Ex 15:2; Isa 25:3; 59:19; Mal 1:11 [e] S Isa 12:4 [f] S Isa 11:11
24:16 [g] S Ps 48:10
[h] S Ps 65:8 [i] Isa 28:5; 60:1,19 [j] S Ezr 9:15

24:1—27:13 Chs. 24–27 deal with judgment and blessing in the last days, the time of God's final victory over the forces of evil. These chapters form a conclusion to chs. 13–23, just as chs. 34–35 form a conclusion to chs. 28–33.

24:1 *lay waste the earth.* Cf. 2:10,19,21; see also 13:13 and note. *scatter its inhabitants.* See Ge 11:8–9 and notes.

24:2 Social distinctions will provide no escape from the judgment (cf. 3:1–3 and notes).

24:4 *dries up and withers.* Words applied to Moab in 15:6; 16:8. Cf. 34:4.

24:5 *broken the everlasting covenant.* Reference is probably to the covenant of Ge 9:8–17 (see chart, p. 20; Ge 9:11 and note). See also v. 18 and note. Although everlasting from the divine viewpoint, God's covenants can be broken by sinful people (see Jer 31:32 and note).

24:6 *curse.* Because of the intensification of evil in the world, God's devastating curse will burn up the earth's inhabitants (cf. Ge 8:21–22; cf. also the covenant of Ge 9:8–17).

24:7 *vine withers.* See v. 4 and note.

24:8 *gaiety ... is stilled.* Cf. 22:2,13; 23:7.

24:9 *wine with a song.* Characteristic of Judah in 5:11–13 (see note there).

24:10 *ruined city.* The same idea appears in 25:2; 26:5; 27:10 (cf. 17:1; 19:18). It is probably a composite of all the cities opposed to God—such as Babylon, Tyre, Jerusalem and Rome.

24:13 Only a few olives and grapes will be left (see v. 6; 17:6, 11).

24:14 *They.* The godly remnant that survives the judgment.

24:15 *islands.* See note on 11:11.

24:16 *ends of the earth.* See note on 11:12. *l.* Probably collec-

24:16 *k* S Lev 26:39
l 1Sa 4:8; S Isa 5:8;
Jer 10:19; 45:3
m S Ps 25:3 *n* Isa 21:2;
33:1; Jer 3:6,20; 5:11;
9:2; Hos 5:7; 9:1
24:17 *o* Dt 32:23-25
p Isa 8:14; Jer 48:43
q Lk 21:35
24:18 *r* S Job 20:24
s Isa 42:22
t S Job 18:9;
S Isa 8:14; La 3:47;
Eze 12:13 *u* S Ge 7:11
v S Jdg 5:4; S Job 9:6;
S Ps 11:3; S Eze 38:19
24:19 *w* S Ps 46:2
x S Dt 11:6
24:20 *y* S Job 12:25
z S Job 27:18
a S Isa 1:2,28; 43:27;
58:1 *b* S Ps 46:2
c S Job 12:14
24:21 *d* S Isa 2:11;
S 10:20; Rev 16:14
e Isa 10:12; 13:11;
Jer 25:29 *f* 1Co 6:3;
Eph 6:11-12
g S Isa 2:12
24:22 *h* S Isa 10:4
i Isa 42:7,22; Lk 8:31;
Rev 20:7-10
j Eze 38:8
24:23 *k* S Isa 13:10
l S Ps 97:1; Rev 22:5
m S Isa 2:2;
Heb 12:22 *n* Isa 28:5;
41:16; 45:25; 60:19;
Eze 48:35; Zec 2:5;
Rev 21:23
25:1 *o* S Isa 7:13
p S Ps 145:2;
S Isa 12:1,4 *q* Isa 11:5
r Ps 40:5; 98:1;
Joel 2:21,26
s Nu 23:19;
S Isa 14:24; 37:26;
46:11; Eph 1:11
25:2 *t* Isa 17:1; 26:5;
37:26 *u* S Isa 17:3
v S Dt 13:16
w S Isa 13:22
x S Job 12:14
25:3 *y* S Ex 6:2;
S Ps 22:23; S Isa 11:14
z S Isa 13:11

But I said, "I waste away, I waste away!ᵏ
　Woeˡ to me!
The treacherousᵐ betray!
　With treachery the treacherous betray!ⁿ"
¹⁷ Terrorᵒ and pit and snareᵖ await you,
　people of the earth.�q
¹⁸ Whoever fleesʳ at the sound of terror
　will fall into a pit;ˢ
whoever climbs out of the pit
　will be caught in a snare.ᵗ

The floodgates of the heavensᵘ are opened,
　the foundations of the earth shake.ᵛ
¹⁹ The earth is broken up,ʷ
　the earth is split asunder,ˣ
　the earth is violently shaken.
²⁰ The earth reels like a drunkard,ʸ
　it sways like a hutᶻ in the wind;
so heavy upon it is the guilt of its rebellionᵃ
　that it fallsᵇ—never to rise again.ᶜ

²¹ In that dayᵈ the Lᴏʀᴅ will punishᵉ
　the powersᶠ in the heavens above
　and the kingsᵍ on the earth below.
²² They will be herded together
　like prisonersʰ bound in a dungeon;ⁱ
they will be shut up in prison
　and be punishedᵃ after many days.ʲ
²³ The moon will be dismayed,
　the sunᵏ ashamed;
for the Lᴏʀᴅ Almighty will reignˡ
　on Mount Zionᵐ and in Jerusalem,
　and before its elders—with great glory.ⁿ

PRAISE TO THE LORD

25 Lᴏʀᴅ, you are my God;ᵒ
　I will exalt you and praise your name,ᵖ
for in perfect faithfulnessq
　you have done wonderful things,ʳ
　things plannedˢ long ago.
² You have made the city a heap of rubble,ᵗ
　the fortifiedᵘ town a ruin,ᵛ
the foreigners' strongholdʷ a city no more;
　it will never be rebuilt.ˣ
³ Therefore strong peoples will honor you;ʸ
　cities of ruthlessᶻ nations will revere you.

ᵃ *22 Or released*

---

tive for the godly community that wastes away because of the
villainy of the treacherous nations that seek to crush the people
of God. *I waste away...betray!* In the Hebrew text these last four
lines of the verse (*Razi li, razi li! 'Oy li! Bogedim bagadu! Ubeged
bogedim bagadu!*) contain powerful examples of alliteration
and assonance (see 5:7 and note; see also Introduction: Literary
Features). *Woe to me!* Isaiah had the same reaction in 6:5. *The
treacherous.* The enemies of God's people.
24:17–18 Cf. Am 5:19–20 and note.
24:17 *Terror and pit and snare.* Another example (see note on
v. 16) of alliteration and assonance (see note on Jer 48:43). The
Hebrew words are *pahad, pahat and pah.*
24:18a God's judgment is inescapable (cf. Am 5:19–20; 9:2–4
and notes).
24:18b *floodgates of the heavens.* An echo of Noah's flood (Ge
7:11; 8:2). *foundations...shake.* Earthquakes and thunder (see
note on 13:13; cf. Joel 3:16).

24:20 *like a drunkard.* Cf. 19:14. *like a hut.* See 1:8 and note.
24:21 *In that day.* The phrase, which refers to the day of the
Lord (see notes on 2:11,17,20; 10:20,27), occurs seven times in
chs. 24–27 (see 25:9; 26:1; 27:1–2,12–13). *powers in the heavens
...kings.* All powers in the creation that exalt themselves
against God (see 2:6–21; Eph 6:11–12).
24:22 *shut up in prison.* Cf. Rev 20:2. *punished after many days.*
See TNIV text note; cf. Rev 20:7–10.
24:23 *The moon...dismayed, the sun ashamed.* The sun and
moon do not shine during judgment (see note on 13:10) or when
the Lord is the "everlasting light" (60:19–20; cf. Rev 21:23; 22:5).
reign on Mount Zion. See 2:2–4 and note.
25:1–5 A song of praise celebrating the deliverance brought
about by the judgments of ch. 24 (see 24:14–16; see also ch. 12).
25:1 *planned long ago.* See 14:24,26–27; 23:8–9.
25:2 *the city...a ruin.* See 24:10 and note. *never be rebuilt.* Cf.
24:20.

4 You have been a refuge [a] for the poor, [b]
a refuge for the needy [c] in their distress,
a shelter from the storm [d]
and a shade from the heat.
For the breath of the ruthless [e]
is like a storm driving against a wall
5 and like the heat of the desert.
You silence [f] the uproar of foreigners; [g]
as heat is reduced by the shadow of a cloud,
so the song of the ruthless [h] is stilled.

6 On this mountain [i] the LORD Almighty will prepare
a feast [j] of rich food for all peoples,
a banquet of aged wine—
the best of meats and the finest of wines. [k]
7 On this mountain he will destroy
the shroud [l] that enfolds all peoples, [m]
the sheet that covers all nations;
8 he will swallow up death [n] forever.
The Sovereign LORD will wipe away the tears [o]
from all faces;
he will remove his people's disgrace [p]
from all the earth.

The LORD has spoken. [q]

9 In that day [r] they will say,

"Surely this is our God; [s]
we trusted [t] in him, and he saved [u] us.
This is the LORD, we trusted in him;
let us rejoice [v] and be glad in his salvation." [w]

10 The hand of the LORD will rest on this mountain; [x]
but Moab [y] will be trampled in their land
as straw is trampled down in the manure.
11 They will stretch out their hands in it,
as swimmers stretch out their hands to swim.
God will bring down [z] their pride [a]
despite the cleverness [a] of their hands.
12 He will bring down your high fortified walls [b]
and lay them low; [c]
he will bring them down to the ground,
to the very dust.

a 11 The meaning of the Hebrew for this word is uncertain.

25:4 ª S 2Sa 22:3;
S Ps 118:8; S Isa 4:6;
17:10; 27:5; 33:16;
Joel 3:16 ᵇ S Isa 3:14
ᶜ S Isa 14:30; 29:19
ᵈ S Ps 55:8 ᵉ Isa 29:5;
49:25
25:5 ᶠ Jer 51:55
ᵍ S Ps 18:44
ʰ S Isa 13:11
25:6 ⁱ S Isa 2:2
ʲ S Ge 29:22; 1Ki 1:25;
Isa 1:19; 55:1-2; 66:11;
Joel 3:18; Mt 8:11;
22:4; Rev 19:9
ᵏ S Ps 36:8; S Pr 9:2
25:7 ˡ 2Co 3:15-16;
Eph 4:18 ᵐ S Job 4:9
25:8 ⁿ Isa 26:19;
Hos 13:14; 1Co 15:54-
55* ᵒ Isa 15:3; 30:19;
35:10; 51:11; 65:19;
Jer 31:16; Rev 7:17;
21:4 ᵖ S Ge 30:23;
S Ps 119:39; Mt 5:11;
1Pe 4:14; Rev 7:14
�q S Isa 7:7
25:9 ʳ S Isa 2:11;
S 10:20 ˢ Isa 40:9
ᵗ S Ps 22:5; S Isa 12:2
ᵘ Ps 145:19; Isa 19:20;
33:22; 35:4; 43:3,11;
45:15,21; 49:25-26;
60:16; 63:8; Jer 14:8
ᵛ S Dt 32:43;
S Ps 9:2; Isa 9:3;
35:2,10; 41:16; 51:3;
61:7,10; 66:14
ʷ S Ps 13:5; S Isa 12:2
25:10 ˣ S Isa 2:2
ʸ S Ge 19:37;
S Nu 21:29;
S Dt 23:6; S Isa 11:14;
Am 2:1-3
25:11 ᶻ Isa 5:25;
14:26; 16:14
ª S Lev 26:19;
S Job 40:12
25:12 ᵇ S Isa 2:15
ᶜ S Job 40:11;
S Isa 15:1; S Jer 51:44

25:3 strong peoples ... ruthless nations. Such as Egypt and Assyria (see 19:18–25 and notes). honor you ... revere you. See 24:15–16.
25:4–5 refuge ... shelter ... shade ... cloud. See 4:5–6 and note; cf. 32:2.
25:6–8 The eschatological feast of God (see Mt 8:11; Lk 14:15 and notes).
25:6–7,10 this mountain. Mount Zion. See 2:2–4 and note; cf. 24:23.
25:6 feast ... banquet. Associated with a coronation (1Ki 1:25) or wedding (see Jdg 14:10 and note); cf. the "wedding supper of the Lamb" (Rev 19:9). rich food. Symbolic of great spiritual blessings (see 55:2 and note). aged wine. The best wine—aged while being left on its dregs (see Jer 48:11 and note; Zep 1:12).
25:7–8 Christ has brought about the ultimate destruction of death itself (see 2Ti 1:10; cf. Heb 2:14–15 and notes).
25:7 shroud ... sheet. Or "covering ... veil," with which faces

were covered in mourning—in any event, the associations are with death.
25:8 Quoted in part in 1Co 15:54. swallow up death. Death, the great swallower (see Ps 49:14 and note), will be swallowed up. Sovereign LORD. See 7:7; 28:16; 30:15; 40:10; 49:22; 52:4; 61:11; 65:13. wipe away the tears. See Rev 7:17; 21:4. remove his people's disgrace. See 54:4.
25:9 Another brief song of praise. In that day. See 12:1,4; 24:21; see also 10:20,27 and note. we trusted ... he saved. Cf. Ps 22:4–5. rejoice and be glad. Cf. 35:10; 51:11; 66:10.
25:10–12 An elaboration on the theme of judgment.
25:10 Moab. Representative of all the enemies of God, like Edom in 34:5–17. See note on 15:1.
25:11 pride. See note on 16:6.
25:12 high fortified walls. See v. 2; 2:15; 2Ki 3:27; Jer 51:44,58 and note on 51:44.

26:1 *d* S Isa 10:20
e Isa 30:29
f S Isa 14:32
g Isa 32:18; 60:18;
Zec 2:5; 9:8
h S Ps 48:13
26:2 *i* S Ps 24:7
j Ps 24:3-4; 85:13;
S Isa 1:26; S 4:3; 9:7;
50:8; 53:11; 54:14;
58:8; 62:2
26:3 *k* S Job 22:21;
S Isa 9:6,7; Php 4:7
l S 1Ch 5:20;
S Ps 22:5; S 28:7;
S Isa 12:2
26:4 *m* S Isa 12:2;
50:10 *n* S Ps 62:8
o S Ge 49:24
26:5 *p* S Isa 25:12;
Eze 26:11 *q* S Isa 25:2
26:6 *r* S Isa 5:5
s Isa 49:26
t S Isa 3:15; S 14:30
26:7 *u* S Ps 26:12
v S Ps 25:8
w S Ex 14:19;
Isa 40:4; 42:16
26:8 *x* S Dt 18:18;
Ps 1:2; Isa 56:1; 64:5
y S Ps 37:9; S 130:5
z S Ps 145:2;
S Isa 12:4
26:9 *a* S Ps 119:55
b Ps 42:1-3; 63:1;
78:34; Isa 55:6
c S 1Ch 16:14
d Mt 6:33
26:10 *e* Mt 5:45
f Isa 32:6; 59:7,13
g S 1Sa 12:24;
Isa 22:12-13; Jer 2:19;
Hos 11:7; Jn 5:37-38;
Ro 2:4
26:11 *h* S Ps 10:12
i Isa 18:3; 44:9,18
j S Isa 9:7; Joel 2:18;
Zec 1:14 *k* Ps 7:16
l S Isa 1:31; Heb 10:27
26:12 *m* S Ps 119:16
5; S Isa 9:6
n S Ps 68:28
26:13 *o* Isa 2:8;
10:5,11 *p* S Isa 12:4
q Isa 42:8; 63:7
26:14 *r* S Dt 4:28
s S Job 26:5

A SONG OF PRAISE

26 In that day *d* this song will be sung *e* in the land of Judah:

We have a strong city; *f*
God makes salvation
its walls *g* and ramparts. *h*
² Open the gates *i*
that the righteous *j* nation may enter,
the nation that keeps faith.
³ You will keep in perfect peace *k*
those whose minds are steadfast,
because they trust *l* in you.
⁴ Trust *m* in the LORD forever, *n*
for the LORD, the LORD, is the Rock *o* eternal.
⁵ He humbles those who dwell on high,
he lays the lofty city low;
he levels it to the ground *p*
and casts it down to the dust. *q*
⁶ Feet trample *r* it down—
the feet of the oppressed, *s*
the footsteps of the poor. *t*

⁷ The path of the righteous is level; *u*
you, the Upright One, *v* make the way of the righteous smooth. *w*
⁸ Yes, LORD, walking in the way of your laws, *a x*
we wait *y* for you;
your name *z* and renown
are the desire of our hearts.
⁹ My soul yearns for you in the night; *a*
in the morning my spirit longs *b* for you.
When your judgments *c* come upon the earth,
the people of the world learn righteousness. *d*
¹⁰ But when grace is shown to the wicked, *e*
they do not learn righteousness;
even in a land of uprightness they go on doing evil *f*
and do not regard *g* the majesty of the LORD.
¹¹ LORD, your hand is lifted high, *h*
but they do not see *i* it.
Let them see your zeal *j* for your people and be put to shame; *k*
let the fire *l* reserved for your enemies consume them.

¹² LORD, you establish peace *m* for us;
all that we have accomplished you have done *n* for us.
¹³ LORD our God, other lords *o* besides you have ruled over us,
but your name *p* alone do we honor. *q*
¹⁴ They are now dead, *r* they live no more;
their spirits *s* do not rise.

---

a 8 Or *judgments*

26:1–15 Another song of praise for God's deliverance (see note on 25:1–5).
26:1 *In that day.* See 12:1,4; 24:21; 25:9; see also note on 10:20,27. *salvation its walls and ramparts.* God's saving acts are Zion's security and strength (cf. Ps 46; 48). *ramparts.* Sloping fortifications of earth or stone (cf. 2Sa 20:15).
26:3 See 30:15 and note. *minds are steadfast.* Cf. Ps 112:6–8 and notes. *trust.* Cf. 25:9.
26:4 *Rock.* See 17:10; Ps 18:2 and notes.
26:5 *lofty city.* See note on 24:10. *levels it…to the dust.* Cf. 25:2,12.
26:6 *feet of the oppressed.* The oppressors are humiliated also in 49:24–26; 51:22–23 (contrast 3:14–15).
26:7 *path…level…way…smooth.* A theme found also in 40:3–4; 42:16; 45:13 (see notes there; see also Pr 4:26 and note; contrast La 3:9).

26:8 A desire for God to reveal his power in their behalf (see Hos 12:5–6). *name and renown.* See v. 13; 24:15; 25:1.
26:9 *judgments.* Punishment (cf. 4:4).
26:10 *grace.* Such as the blessings of harvest and general prosperity (cf. Mt. 5:45 and note).
26:11 *hand is lifted high.* A sign of power. See 9:12,17,21 and note; Ps 89:13. *zeal.* See 9:7 and note; cf. 37:32; 63:15. *fire.* See note on 1:31.
26:12 *peace.* See v. 3.
26:13 *other lords.* Foreign rulers, such as those of Egypt or Assyria.
26:14 *They are now dead…their spirits do not rise.* Cf. the fate of the king of Babylon in 14:9–10—and contrast the resurrection scene in 26:19 (see note there).

You punished them and brought them to ruin;[t]
 you wiped out all memory of them.[u]
[15] You have enlarged the nation, LORD;
 you have enlarged the nation.[v]
You have gained glory for yourself;
 you have extended all the borders[w] of the land.

[16] LORD, they came to you in their distress;[x]
 when you disciplined[y] them,
 they could barely whisper[z] a prayer.[a]
[17] As a pregnant woman about to give birth[a]
 writhes and cries out in her pain,
so were we in your presence, LORD.
[18] We were with child, we writhed in pain,
 but we gave birth[b] to wind.
We have not brought salvation[c] to the earth,
 and the people of the world have not been reborn.[b][d]

[19] But your dead[e] will live, LORD;
 their bodies will rise—
let those who dwell in the dust[f]
 wake up and shout for joy—
your dew[g] is like the dew of the morning;
 you will make it fall on the spirits of the dead.[h]

[20] Go, my people, enter your rooms
 and shut the doors[i] behind you;
hide[j] yourselves for a little while
 until his wrath[k] has passed by.[l]
[21] See, the LORD is coming[m] out of his dwelling[n]
 to punish[o] the people of the earth for their sins.
The earth will disclose the blood[p] shed on it;
 the earth will conceal its slain no longer.

DELIVERANCE OF ISRAEL

27

In that day,[q]

the LORD will punish with his sword[r]—
 his fierce, great and powerful sword—
Leviathan[s] the gliding serpent,[t]
Leviathan the coiling serpent;
 he will slay the monster[u] of the sea.

[2] In that day[v]—

"Sing[w] about a fruitful vineyard:[x]

---

[a] 16 The meaning of the Hebrew for this clause is uncertain. [b] 18 Or *have not fallen*

26:14 [t] S Ps 9:5; S Isa 10:3 [u] S Ps 9:6
26:15 [v] S Job 12:23; S Isa 14:2 [w] Isa 33:17
26:16 [x] S Jdg 6:2; S Isa 5:30 [y] S Ps 39:11 [z] Isa 29:4
26:17 [a] S Isa 21:3; S Jn 16:21; Rev 12:2
26:18 [b] Isa 33:11; 59:4 [c] S Ge 49:10; Ps 17:14 [d] Isa 42:6; 49:6; 51:4; Jer 12:16
26:19 [e] S Isa 25:8; Eph 5:14 [f] Ps 22:29 [g] S Ge 27:28; S Isa 18:4 [h] Isa 66:24; Eze 37:1-14; Da 12:2
26:20 [i] Ex 12:23 [j] Ps 91:1,4 [k] S Isa 10:25; S 30:27 [l] S Job 14:13
26:21 [m] Isa 29:6; Jude 1:14 [n] S Isa 18:4 [o] S Isa 13:9,11; 30:12-14 [p] S Job 16:18; Lk 11:50-51
27:1 [q] ver 13; S Isa 2:11; 28:5 [r] S Ge 3:24; S Dt 32:41; Isa 31:8; 34:6; 65:12; 66:16; Eze 21:3; Na 3:15 [s] S Ps 3:8 [t] Job 26:13 [u] S Ps 68:30; S 74:13; Rev 12:9
27:2 [v] Isa 24:21 [w] S Isa 5:1 [x] Jer 2:21

26:15 *enlarged the nation.* Applied to the return from Babylonian exile in 54:2–3; also cf. 9:3; Zec 2:4 and note.
26:16–18 The prophet speaks to the Lord on behalf of God's people.
26:16 *distress.* Perhaps the Assyrian oppression, described in 5:30; 8:21–22 (see notes there). The period of the judges is also possible (see Jdg 6:2,6).
26:17–18 *give birth writhes…in pain.* See 13:8 and note (cf. 37:3).
26:18 *salvation to the earth.* See 49:6.
26:19–21 The prophet speaks a word of reassurance to God's people.
A **26:19** *your dead will live…bodies will rise.* A reference to the restoration of Israel (see Eze 37:11–12,14 and notes)—perhaps including the resurrection of the body (see Da 12:2 and note). Cf. 25:8; contrast 26:14. *dew.* A symbol of fruitfulness (see 2Sa 1:21; Hos 14:5 and note).
26:20–21 See 24:21–22 and note on 2:11,17,20.
26:20 *a little while…wrath.* See 10:25; 54:7–8 and notes; cf. Ps

30:5 and note. Assyrian tyranny and Babylonian exile, as well as all other oppressions, will end.
26:21 *punish.* See 66:14–16 and notes. *will disclose…will conceal…no longer.* The blood and bodies of the innocent/righteous who have been slaughtered by the oppressive powers will no longer be hidden in the ground but will be brought forth to testify against their murderers, so that God may in judgment avenge their deaths (see Ge 4:10 and note).
27:1–2,12–13 *In that day.* See 10:20,27; 24:21 and notes; see also 12:1,4; 25:9; 26:1.
B **27:1** The climactic word of judgment in 24:1—27:13 (see note there). *his sword.* See Ps 7:12–13 and note. *Leviathan…monster.* A symbol (drawn from Canaanite myths) of wicked nations, such as Egypt (see 30:7 ["Rahab"]; 51:9; Eze 29:3; 32:2 and notes). *gliding…coiling serpent.* Cf. Job 3:8; 41:1; Ps 74:13–14.
27:2–6 A second vineyard song (see 5:1–7 and notes).
27:2 *vineyard.* Israel.

27:3 ʸ Isa 58:11
ᶻ S Ps 91:4; S Isa 5:2
ᵃ S Jn 6:39
27:4 ᵇ S ver 11;
S Isa 10:17; Mt 3:12;
Heb 6:8
27:5 ᶜ S Isa 25:4
ᵈ S Job 22:21;
S Ps 119:165; Ro 5:1;
2Co 5:20
27:6 ᵉ S 2Ki 19:30;
Isa 11:10 ᶠ S Ge 40:10
ᵍ S Ps 72:16; Isa 11:1;
37:31; Eze 17:23;
36:8; Hos 14:8
27:7 ʰ Isa 10:26;
S 11:4; 37:36-38
27:8 ⁱ Isa 49:14;
50:1; 54:7 ʲ S Ge 41:6
27:9 ᵏ S Ps 78:38
ˡ Ro 11:27*
ᵐ S Ex 23:24
ⁿ S Ex 34:13
ᵒ S Lev 26:30;
S 2Ch 14:5
27:10 ᵖ S Ge 1:2;
S Dt 13:16; Isa 5:6;
32:14; Jer 10:22; 26:6;
La 1:4; 5:18 �q S Isa 5:5
ʳ S Isa 5:17 ˢ Isa 17:2
27:11 ᵗ S Isa 10:33
ᵘ S ver 4; Isa 33:12
ᵛ S Dt 32:28; S Isa 1:3
ʷ Dt 32:18; Isa 41:8;
43:1,7,15; 44:1-2,21,
24 ˣ S Isa 9:17;
Jer 11:16
27:12 ʸ S Isa 21:10;
Mt 3:12 ᶻ S Ge 15:18
ᵃ S Dt 30:4; S Isa 1:9;
S 11:12; S 17:6
27:13 ᵇ S ver 1
ᶜ S Lev 25:9;
S Jdg 3:27;
S Mt 24:31
ᵈ S Ps 106:47
ᵉ S Isa 10:19; 19:21,25
ᶠ S Ge 27:29;
S Ps 22:29; S 86:9
ᵍ S Isa 2:2

3 I, the LORD, watch over it;
  I water ʸ it continually.
 I guard ᶻ it day and night
  so that no one may harm ᵃ it.
4 I am not angry.
 If only there were briers and thorns confronting me!
  I would march against them in battle;
  I would set them all on fire. ᵇ
5 Or else let them come to me for refuge; ᶜ
  let them make peace ᵈ with me,
  yes, let them make peace with me."

6 In days to come Jacob will take root, ᵉ
  Israel will bud and blossom ᶠ
  and fill all the world with fruit. ᵍ

7 Has ʟthe LORDʟ struck her
  as he struck ʰ down those who struck her?
 Has she been killed
  as those were killed who killed her?
8 By warfare ᵃ and exile ⁱ you contend with her—
  with his fierce blast he drives her out,
  as on a day the east wind ʲ blows.
9 By this, then, will Jacob's guilt be atoned ᵏ for,
  and this will be the full fruit of the removal of his sin: ˡ
 When he makes all the altar stones ᵐ
  to be like limestone crushed to pieces,
  no Asherah poles ᵇ ⁿ or incense altars ᵒ
  will be left standing.
10 The fortified city stands desolate, ᵖ
  an abandoned settlement, forsaken �q like the wilderness;
 there the calves graze, ʳ
  there they lie down; ˢ
  they strip its branches bare.
11 When its twigs are dry, they are broken off ᵗ
  and women come and make fires ᵘ with them.
 For this is a people without understanding; ᵛ
  so their Maker has no compassion on them,
  and their Creator ʷ shows them no favor. ˣ

12 In that day the LORD will thresh ʸ from the flowing Euphrates to the Wadi of Egypt, ᶻ
and you, Israel, will be gathered ᵃ up one by one. 13 And in that day ᵇ a great trumpet ᶜ will
sound. Those who were perishing in Assyria and those who were exiled ᵈ in Egypt ᵉ will
come and worship ᶠ the LORD on the holy mountain ᵍ in Jerusalem.

ᵃ 8 See Septuagint; the meaning of the Hebrew for this word is uncertain. ᵇ 9 That is, wooden
symbols of the goddess Asherah

27:4–5 A picture of Israel's lukewarmness toward the Lord—
not "briers and thorns" (v. 4) like the other nations, but not fully
trusting in the Lord either (see 29:13 and note).
27:4 *briers and thorns.* See 5:6 and note.
27:6 *take root.* See 11:1,10 and notes. *bud and blossom.* See 4:2
and note. The Messianic age is in view. *fill all the world.* Contrast
26:18.
27:7–11 What the Lord is going to do with Israel in the judgments that are about to overtake her in Isaiah's day.
27:7 *struck her.* Cf. 10:24–26.
27:8 *exile.* Probably the Babylonian captivity. *east wind.* A hot
wind from the desert (see Jer 4:11 and note; Eze 19:12).
27:9 *atoned for.* Israel (Jacob) will have to atone for her guilt
through the coming judgment. *altar . . . Asherah poles . . . incense*

altars. See 17:8 and note. *crushed to pieces.* See Ex 34:13 and note.
27:10 *fortified city.* Jerusalem. *desolate . . . forsaken.* Cf. 6:11–12.
calves graze. Cf. 5:5; 7:25.
27:12–13 The redemption that lies beyond the coming judgment.
27:12 *will thresh.* Judgment on the nations into which Israel
has been dispersed (see note on 21:10). The threshing will separate Israelites from Gentiles. *Wadi of Egypt.* Probably the Wadi el-
Arish, the southern border of the promised land (the Euphrates
is the northern border). See Ge 15:18; 1Ki 4:21; 8:65 and notes.
27:13 *great trumpet.* Used especially to summon troops (see
1Sa 13:3). *Assyria . . . Egypt.* See 11:11–12 and notes. *holy mountain.* Mount Zion (see 2:2–4 and note; see also 11:6–9; 24:23;
25:6–7,10 and note; 65:25).

WOE TO THE LEADERS OF EPHRAIM AND JUDAH

28

Woe [h] to that wreath, the pride of Ephraim's [i] drunkards,
　　to the fading flower, his glorious beauty,
set on the head of a fertile valley[j]—
　　to that city, the pride of those laid low by wine! [k]
[2] See, the Lord has one who is powerful [l] and strong.
　　Like a hailstorm [m] and a destructive wind, [n]
like a driving rain and a flooding [o] downpour,
　　he will throw it forcefully to the ground.
[3] That wreath, the pride of Ephraim's [p] drunkards,
　　will be trampled [q] underfoot.
[4] That fading flower, his glorious beauty,
　　set on the head of a fertile valley, [r]
will be like figs [s] ripe before harvest—
　　as soon as people see them and take them in hand,
　　they swallow them.

[5] In that day [t] the LORD Almighty
　　will be a glorious [u] crown, [v]
a beautiful wreath
　　for the remnant [w] of his people.
[6] He will be a spirit of justice [x]
　　to those who sit in judgment, [y]
a source of strength
　　to those who turn back the battle [z] at the gate.

[7] And these also stagger [a] from wine [b]
　　and reel [c] from beer:
Priests [d] and prophets [e] stagger from beer
　　and are befuddled with wine;
they reel from beer,
　　they stagger when seeing visions, [f]
　　they stumble when rendering decisions.
[8] All the tables are covered with vomit [g]
　　and there is not a spot without filth.

[9] "Who is it he is trying to teach? [h]
　　To whom is he explaining his message? [i]
To children weaned [j] from their milk, [k]
　　to those just taken from the breast?
[10] For it is:
　　Do this, do that,
　　a rule for this, a rule for that [a];
　　a little here, a little there. [l]"

[11] Very well then, with foreign lips and strange tongues [m]
　　God will speak to this people, [n]
[12] to whom he said,
　　"This is the resting place, let the weary rest"; [o]

---

[a] 10 Hebrew / *sav lasav sav lasav* / *kav lakav kav lakav* (probably meaningless sounds mimicking the prophet's words); also in verse 13

28:1 [h] Isa 10:5; 29:1; 30:1; 31:1; 33:1 [i] ver 3; Isa 7:2; 9:9 [j] ver 4 [k] S Lev 10:9; Isa 5:11; Hos 7:5; Am 6:6
28:2 [l] Isa 40:10 [m] S Jos 10:11 [n] Isa 29:6 [o] S Isa 8:7; S Da 9:26
28:3 [p] S ver 1 [q] S Job 40:12; S Isa 5:5
28:4 [r] ver 1 [s] S S 2:13; Hos 9:10; Na 3:12
28:5 [t] S Isa 10:20; S 27:1; 29:18; 30:23 [u] S Isa 24:16,23 [v] Isa 62:3; Jer 13:18; Eze 16:12; 21:26; Zec 9:16 [w] S Isa 1:9
28:6 [x] S 2Sa 14:20; Isa 11:2-4; 32:1,16; 33:5 [y] Isa 4:4; Jn 5:30 [z] Jdg 9:44-45; S 2Ch 32:8
28:7 [a] S Isa 3:12 [b] S Lev 10:9; S Isa 22:13; S Eph 5:18 [c] S Ps 107:27 [d] Isa 24:2 [e] S Isa 9:15 [f] S Isa 1:1; 29:11
28:8 [g] Jer 48:26
28:9 [h] ver 26; Ps 32:8; Isa 2:3; 30:20; 48:17; 50:4; 54:13; Jer 31:34; 32:33 [i] Isa 52:7; 53:1 [j] Ps 131:2 [k] Heb 5:12-13; 1Pe 2:2
28:10 [l] ver 13
28:11 [m] S Ge 11:7; Isa 33:19; Jer 5:15 [n] Eze 3:5; 1Co 14:21*
28:12 [o] S Ex 14:14; S Jos 1:13; S Job 11:18; S Isa 11:10; Mt 11:28-29

28:1—35:10 A series of six woes (28:1; 29:1; 29:15; 30:1; 31:1; 33:1), ending with an announcement of judgment on the nations (ch. 34) and a song celebrating the joy of the redeemed (ch. 35). Cf. the six woes in ch. 5 (see note on 5:8–23).
28:1 *wreath.* Samaria, the capital of the northern kingdom, was a beautiful city on a prominent hill (see note on 1Ki 16:24). *pride.* See v. 3 and note on 16:6. *Ephraim's.* See note on 7:2. *drunkards.* In the eighth century B.C. Samaria was a city of luxury and indulgence. See 5:11–13; Am 3:12 and notes; 6:4–7. *fertile valley.* Cf. 5:1.
28:2 *one who is powerful.* The king of Assyria. *hailstorm ... flooding downpour.* See v. 17; 8:7–8 and note; 17:12 and note. Cf. 30:30; 32:19.
28:5 *In that day.* See 4:1–2; 10:20,27 and note; 12:1,4; 24:21;

25:9; 26:1; 27:1–2,12–13. *glorious ... beautiful.* See 4:2 and note. *remnant.* See note on 1:9.
28:6 *spirit of justice.* See 11:2–4 and notes. *gate.* The most vulnerable part of a city.

A **28:7** *wine ... beer.* The religious leaders should have been filled with the Spirit, not with wine. See Lev 10:9; see also Nu 11:29; Eph 5:18 and notes.
28:8 *vomit.* Cf. Jer 25:16,27.
28:9–10 The mocking response of Isaiah's hearers (see TNIV text note on v. 10). Cf. the mocking tones of 5:19.
28:11–12 Quoted in part in 1Co 14:21 (see note on 1Co 14:21–22).
28:11 *foreign lips.* The language of the Assyrians.
28:12 *resting place.* The land given to them by the Lord, in

28:13 ᵖ ver 10
ᵠ Mt 21:44; ʳ S Isa 8:15
28:14 ˢ S Isa 1:10
ᵗ 2Ch 36:16
28:15 ᵘ S Job 5:23;
Isa 8:19; ᵛ ver 2,18;
Isa 8:7-8; 10:26; 29:6;
30:28; Da 11:22
ʷ S Isa 9:15
ˣ S Jdg 9:35;
Isa 29:15; Jer 23:24
28:16 ʸ S Isa 14:32
ᶻ Ps 118:22; Isa 8:14-
15; Da 2:34-35,45;
Zec 12:3; S Ac 4:11
ᵃ Jer 51:26; 1Co 3:11;
2Ti 2:19; ᵇ Isa 29:22;
45:17; 50:7; 54:4;
Ro 9:33*; 10:11*;
1Pe 2:6*
28:17 ᶜ S Ps 11:7;
S Isa 5:16
ᵈ S 2Ki 21:13
ᵉ S Jos 10:11
ᶠ S Isa 8:7
28:18 ᵍ S Isa 7:7
ʰ ver 15; ⁱ S Isa 5:5;
63:18; Da 8:13
28:19 ʲ 2Ki 24:2
ᵏ S Ps 5:3; ⁱ S Job 18:11
28:20 ᵐ Isa 59:6
28:21 ⁿ S Ge 38:29;
S 1Ch 14:11; ᵒ S Jos 9:3
ᵖ Isa 10:12; 65:7;
Lk 19:41-44
28:22 ᵠ S 2Ch 36:16
; Jer 29:18; La 2:15;
Zep 2:15; ʳ S Isa 10:22
ˢ S Isa 10:23
28:23 ᵗ Isa 32:9

and, "This is the place of repose"—
but they would not listen.
¹³ So then, the word of the Lᴏʀᴅ to them will become:
Do this, do that,
a rule for this, a rule for that;
a little here, a little there ᵖ—
so that as they go they will fall backward;
they will be injured ᵠ and snared and captured. ʳ

¹⁴ Therefore hear the word of the Lᴏʀᴅ, ˢ you scoffers ᵗ
who rule this people in Jerusalem.
¹⁵ You boast, "We have entered into a covenant with death, ᵘ
with the realm of the dead we have made an agreement.
When an overwhelming scourge sweeps by, ᵛ
it cannot touch us,
for we have made a lie ʷ our refuge
and falsehood ᵃ our hiding place. ˣ"

¹⁶ So this is what the Sovereign Lᴏʀᴅ says:

"See, I lay a stone in Zion, ʸ a tested stone, ᶻ
a precious cornerstone for a sure foundation; ᵃ
the one who relies on it
will never be stricken with panic. ᵇ
¹⁷ I will make justice ᶜ the measuring line
and righteousness the plumb line; ᵈ
hail ᵉ will sweep away your refuge, the lie,
and water will overflow ᶠ your hiding place.
¹⁸ Your covenant with death will be annulled;
your agreement with the realm of the dead will not stand. ᵍ
When the overwhelming scourge sweeps by, ʰ
you will be beaten down ⁱ by it.
¹⁹ As often as it comes it will carry you away; ʲ
morning after morning, ᵏ by day and by night,
it will sweep through."

The understanding of this message
will bring sheer terror. ⁱ
²⁰ The bed is too short to stretch out on,
the blanket too narrow to wrap around you. ᵐ
²¹ The Lᴏʀᴅ will rise up as he did at Mount Perazim, ⁿ
he will rouse himself as in the Valley of Gibeon ᵒ—
to do his work, ᵖ his strange work,
and perform his task, his alien task.
²² Now stop your mocking, ᵠ
or your chains will become heavier;
the Lord, the Lᴏʀᴅ Almighty, has told me
of the destruction decreed ʳ against the whole land. ˢ

²³ Listen ᵗ and hear my voice;
pay attention and hear what I say.

ᵃ 15 Or *false gods*

---

whom they were to trust (see 26:3; 30:15; 40:31; Jos 1:13 and notes). *would not listen.* Cf. Jer 6:16 and note.
28:13 *will become.* They say the prophet is speaking nonsense (vv. 9–10), so the word of the Lord that he speaks will remain nonsense to them (see 6:9–10 and notes).
28:15,18 *covenant with death.* By using a vivid figure of speech, Isaiah mocks their sense of assurance against national calamity, placing on their lips a claim to have a covenant with death that it will not harm them (cf. Hos 2:18 and note). *overwhelming scourge.* A mixed metaphor referring to the armies of Assyria and Babylonia. "Overwhelming" pictures an army as a flooding river (see 8:7–8 and note); a "scourge" is a whip (10:26).
28:16 *stone.* The Lord (see 8:14; 17:10 and notes). *cornerstone.*

Cf. Ps 118:22 (see note there). *sure foundation.* See 1Co 3:11; cf. 1Pe 2:4–8 and notes.
28:17 *measuring line ... plumb line.* The standards and tests the Lord will apply are his "justice" and "righteousness" (cf. 34:11 and note). *hail.* See v. 2; 30:30; 32:19.
28:20 *too short ... too narrow.* Israel was unprepared both militarily and spiritually.
28:21 *Mount Perazim.* Where God "broke out" against the Philistines (see 2Sa 5:20 and note). *Valley of Gibeon.* Where God sent hail to demolish the Amorites (see Jos 10:10–13 and notes). *strange work ... alien task.* This time God would fight against Israel.
28:22 *destruction decreed.* See 10:22–23 and note on 10:22.

²⁴When farmers plow for planting, ^u do they plow continually?
Do they keep on breaking up and working the soil?
²⁵When they have leveled the surface,
do they not sow caraway and scatter cumin? ^v
Do they not plant wheat in its place, ^a
barley ^w in its plot, ^a
and spelt ^x in its field?
²⁶Their God instructs them
and teaches ^y them the right way.

²⁷Caraway is not threshed ^z with a sledge, ^a
nor is a cartwheel rolled over cumin;
caraway is beaten out with a rod, ^b
and cumin with a stick.
²⁸Grain must be ground to make bread;
so one does not go on threshing it forever.
The wheels of a threshing cart ^c may be rolled over it,
but one does not use horses to grind grain.
²⁹All this also comes from the LORD Almighty,
whose plan is wonderful, ^d
whose wisdom is magnificent. ^e

WOE TO DAVID'S CITY

29 Woe ^f to you, Ariel, Ariel, ^g
the city ^h where David settled!
Add year to year
and let your cycle of festivals ⁱ go on.
²Yet I will besiege Ariel; ^j
she will mourn and lament, ^k
she will be to me like an altar hearth. ^{b l}
³I will encamp against you on all sides;
I will encircle ^m you with towers
and set up my siege works ⁿ against you.
⁴Brought low, you will speak from the ground;
your speech will mumble ^o out of the dust. ^p
Your voice will come ghostlike ^q from the earth;
out of the dust your speech will whisper. ^r

⁵But your many enemies will become like fine dust, ^s
the ruthless ^t hordes like blown chaff. ^u
Suddenly, ^v in an instant,
⁶ the LORD Almighty will come ^w
with thunder ^x and earthquake ^y and great noise,
with windstorm and tempest ^z and flames of a devouring fire. ^a
⁷Then the hordes of all the nations ^b that fight against Ariel, ^c
that attack her and her fortress and besiege her,
will be as it is with a dream, ^d

^a 25 The meaning of the Hebrew for this word is uncertain.   ^b 2 The Hebrew for *altar hearth* sounds like the Hebrew for *Ariel*.

28:23–29 A wisdom poem (a poetic parable) in two stanzas, each ending in a verse that praises the wisdom of God. In the context, and since "threshing" is emphasized (vv. 27–28), the point may be that though God must punish Israel, his actions will be as measured and as well-timed as a farmer's. See 27:12 and note.
28:25 *cumin*. This word is derived from the Akkadian; an herb for seasoning (see Mt 23:23 and note). *spelt*. A kind of wheat (see note on Ex 9:32).
28:27 *rod*. See 10:5 and note.
28:29 *plan is wonderful*. See 9:6 and note.
29:1–2,7 *Ariel*. Jerusalem (Ariel may mean "City of God"). Fighting and bloodshed will turn the city into a virtual "altar hearth" (Hebrew *'ari'el;* see TNIV text note on v. 2).
29:1 *Woe*. See note on 28:1. *city where David settled*. See 2Sa 5:6–9 and notes; cf. Isa 22:9. *cycle of festivals*. See 1:13–14 and

note on 1:14.
29:3 *towers*. Pushed up to the city wall by attackers so they could fight the defenders on the same level.
29:4 *whisper*. Used of mediums and spiritists in 8:19. Judah speaks as from the realm of the dead ("ground … dust … earth")—so much for their covenant with death (see 28:15,18 and note).
29:5–8 In God's time, those nations that devastate Jerusalem will be devastated (see 10:5–19; 27:1; cf. Ge 12:2–3 and note). The sudden destruction of the enemy resembles that of Assyria's army in 701 B.C. (see 10:16 and note).
29:5 *chaff*. See 17:13; Ps 1:4 and notes.
29:6 *thunder and earthquake … windstorm and tempest*. As in Jdg 5:4–5; Ps 18:7–15; Hab 3:3–7; see also 28:2; Ps 83:13–15 and notes.

(Cross-references column: 28:24 u Ecc 3:2; 28:25 w Mt 23:23, w Ex 9:31, x Ex 9:32, Eze 4:9; 28:26 y S Ps 94:10; 28:27 z S Isa 21:10, a S Job 41:30, b Isa 10:5; 28:28 c S Isa 21:10; 28:29 d S Isa 9:6, e S Ps 92:5, Ro 11:33; 29:1 f Isa 22:12-13, S 28:1, g ver 2,7, h S 2Sa 5:7, i S Isa 1:14; 29:2 j S ver 1, k S Isa 3:26, La 2:5, l Eze 43:15; 29:3 m Lk 19:43-44, n S 2Ki 25:1; 29:4 o Isa 8:19, p Isa 47:1, 52:2, q S Lev 19:31, r Isa 26:16; 29:5 s S Dt 9:21, Ps 78:39, 103:15, S Isa 2:22, 37:27, 40:6, 51:12, t S Isa 13:11, u S Isa 17:13, v S Ps 55:15, S Isa 17:14, 1Th 5:3; 29:6 w S Isa 26:21, Zec 14:1-5, x S Ex 19:16, y Mt 24:7, Mk 13:8, Lk 21:11, S Rev 6:12, 11:19, z S Ps 50:3, S 55:8, S Isa 28:15, a S Lev 10:2, Ps 83:13-15; 29:7 b Mic 4:11-12, Zec 12:9, c S ver 1, d S Job 20:8)

29:8 *e* S Ps 73:20
f ver 5,7; Isa 41:11,15;
Jer 30:16; Zec 12:3
g Isa 17:12-14; 54:17
29:9 *h* ver 14;
Jer 4:9; Hab 1:5
i S Isa 6:10 *j* Isa 51:17;
63:6; Jer 13:13; 25:27
k S Lev 10:9; Isa 28:1;
51:21-22 *l* S Ps 60:3;
S Isa 3:12
29:10 *m* S Jdg 4:21;
Jnh 1:5 *n* Ps 69:23;
S Isa 6:9-10; 44:18;
Ro 11:8* ; 2Th 2:9-11
o Mic 3:6 *p* S 1Sa 9:9
29:11 *q* S Isa 28:7
r S Isa 8:16; Da 8:26;
12:9; Mt 13:11;
Rev 5:1-2
29:13 *s* Jer 14:11;
Hag 1:2; 2:14
t S Ps 50:16
u S Ps 119:70;
Isa 58:2; Jer 12:2;
Eze 33:31 *v* Mt 15:8-
9*; Mk 7:6-7*;
Col 2:22
29:14 *w* S Job 10:16
x S Job 5:13; Jer 8:9;
49:7 *y* Isa 6:9-10;
1Co 1:19*
29:15 *z* S Ge 3:8;
S Isa 28:15
a S Job 8:3; Ps 10:11-
13; 94:7; Isa 47:10;
57:12; Eze 8:12; 9:9
b S 2Ki 21:16;
S Job 22:13
29:16 *c* S Job 10:9;
S Isa 10:15 *d* S Ge 2:7
e Isa 45:9; 64:8;
Jer 18:6; Ro 9:20-21*
f S Job 9:12
29:17 *g* S Isa 10:25
h S Isa 2:13 *i* Ps 84:6;
107:33 *j* Isa 32:15
29:18 *k* S Isa 28:5
l Mk 7:37
m S Ps 107:14
n S Ps 146:8;
S Isa 32:3; Mt 11:5;
Lk 7:22

with a vision in the night—
[8] as when hungry people dream they are eating,
    but they awaken, *e* and their hunger remains;
as when thirsty people dream they are drinking,
    but they awaken faint, with their thirst unquenched. *f*
So will it be with the hordes of all the nations
    that fight against Mount Zion. *g*

[9] Be stunned and amazed, *h*
    blind yourselves and be sightless; *i*
be drunk, *j* but not from wine, *k*
    stagger, *l* but not from beer.
[10] The LORD has brought over you a deep sleep: *m*
    He has sealed your eyes *n* (the prophets); *o*
    he has covered your heads (the seers). *p*

[11] For you this whole vision *q* is nothing but words sealed *r* in a scroll. And if you give the scroll to someone who can read, and say, "Read this, please," they will answer, "I can't; it is sealed." [12] Or if you give the scroll to someone who cannot read, and say, "Read this, please," they will answer, "I don't know how to read."

[13] The Lord says:

"These people *s* come near to me with their mouth
    and honor me with their lips, *t*
but their hearts are far from me. *u*
Their worship of me
    is based on merely human rules they have been taught. *a* *v*
[14] Therefore once more I will astound these people
    with wonder upon wonder; *w*
the wisdom of the wise *x* will perish,
    the intelligence of the intelligent will vanish. *y*"

[15] Woe to those who go to great depths
    to hide *z* their plans from the LORD,
who do their work in darkness and think,
    "Who sees us? *a* Who will know?" *b*
[16] You turn things upside down,
    as if the potter were thought to be like the clay! *c*
Shall what is formed say to the one who formed *d* it,
    "You did not make me"?
Can the pot say to the potter, *e*
    "You know nothing"? *f*

[17] In a very short time, *g* will not Lebanon *h* be turned into a fertile field *i*
    and the fertile field seem like a forest? *j*
[18] In that day *k* the deaf *l* will hear the words of the scroll,
    and out of gloom and darkness *m*
    the eyes of the blind will see. *n*

---

a 13 Hebrew; Septuagint *They worship me in vain; / their teachings are merely human rules*

29:9–14 Isaiah speaks again of Israel's spiritual state and warns of the Lord's impending judgment.
29:9 *blind yourselves . . . be drunk.* Refers to spiritual stupor (see 6:10 and note; cf. 28:1,7 and note).
29:10 Quoted in part in Ro 11:8 (see note there). *seers.* See 1Sa 9:9 and note; 2Ki 17:13.
29:11–12 God's revelation to Isaiah here is a closed book ("sealed," v. 11) to all the people.
29:13 Quoted in part by Jesus to show the hypocrisy of the Pharisees (see Mk 7:6 and note). *These people.* Not "my people" (cf. 6:9; 8:6,11–12; cf. also Ex 17:4; Jer 14:10–11; Hag 1:2 and notes).
29:14 Quoted in part in 1Co 1:19 (see note there). *wonder upon wonder.* He who showed them wonders in the exodus (see Ex 15:11; Ps 78:12–16 and note) will now show them wonders in judgment. *wisdom . . . will perish.* Cf. 44:25; Jer 8:9.

29:15 *Woe.* A new woe begins (see note on 28:1—35:10). *their plans.* Perhaps the alliance between Ahaz and Assyria or between Hezekiah and Egypt (see 30:1–2 and notes). *Who sees us?* See note on Ps 10:11.
29:16 See 45:9; 64:8; see also notes on Jer 18:1–6. This verse is quoted in part in Ro 9:20 (see notes on Ro 9:20–21). Cf. the creation of Adam in Ge 2:7 (see note there); also cf. Isa 10:15; Ps 139.
29:17–24 Another sudden shift to the theme of redemption, as in 28:5–8.
29:17 *Lebanon.* Perhaps symbolic of Assyria (see 10:34). The forests of Lebanon were unequaled (see 2:13 and note), so "fertile field" represents a lesser status (see 32:15 and note).
29:18 *In that day.* See notes on 10:20,27; 26:1. Beyond the day of Assyria's destruction lies the day of Israel's restoration. *deaf will hear . . . blind will see.* The opposite of 6:9; linked with the Messianic age in 35:5.

¹⁹ Once more the humble ^o will rejoice in the LORD;
  the needy ^p will rejoice in the Holy One ^q of Israel.
²⁰ The ruthless ^r will vanish, ^s
  the mockers ^t will disappear,
  and all who have an eye for evil ^u will be cut down—
²¹ those who with a word make someone out to be guilty,
  who ensnare the defender in court ^v
  and with false testimony ^w deprive the innocent of justice. ^x

²²Therefore this is what the LORD, who redeemed ^y Abraham, ^z says to the house of Jacob:

  "No longer will Jacob be ashamed; ^a
    no longer will their faces grow pale. ^b
²³ When they see among them their children, ^c
    the work of my hands, ^d
  they will keep my name holy; ^e
    they will acknowledge the holiness of the Holy One ^f of Jacob,
    and will stand in awe of the God of Israel.
²⁴ Those who are wayward ^g in spirit will gain understanding; ^h
    those who complain will accept instruction." ⁱ

WOE TO THE OBSTINATE NATION

30 "Woe ^j to the obstinate children," ^k
  declares the LORD,
"to those who carry out plans that are not mine,
  forming an alliance, ^l but not by my Spirit,
  heaping sin upon sin;
² who go down to Egypt ^m
  without consulting ⁿ me;
who look for help to Pharaoh's protection, ^o
  to Egypt's shade for refuge. ^p
³ But Pharaoh's protection will be to your shame,
  Egypt's shade ^q will bring you disgrace. ^r
⁴ Though they have officials in Zoan ^s
  and their envoys have arrived in Hanes,
⁵ everyone will be put to shame
  because of a people ^t useless ^u to them,
who bring neither help ^v nor advantage,
  but only shame and disgrace. ^w"

⁶A prophecy ^x concerning the animals of the Negev: ^y

  Through a land of hardship and distress, ^z
    of lions ^a and lionesses,
    of adders and darting snakes, ^b

29:19 *o* Ps 25:9; 37:11; Isa 61:1; Mt 5:5; 11:29 *p* S Ps 72:4; S Isa 3:15; S 14:30; Mt 11:5; Lk 7:22; Jas 1:9; 2:5 *q* ver 23; Isa 1:4; S 5:19; S 12:6; 30:11
29:20 *r* S Isa 9:4; S 13:11 *s* Isa 34:12 *t* S 2Ch 36:16; Isa 28:22 *u* S Job 15:35; Ps 7:14; Isa 32:7; 33:11; 59:4; Eze 11:2; Mic 2:1; Na 1:11
29:21 *v* Am 5:10,15 *w* Pr 21:28 *x* S Isa 5:23; 32:7; Hab 1:4
29:22 *y* S Ex 6:6 *z* Ge 17:16; Isa 41:8; 51:2; 63:16 *a* Ps 22:5; 25:3; S Isa 28:16; 49:23; 61:7; Joel 2:26; Zep 3:11 *b* Jer 30:6,10; Joel 2:6,21; Na 2:10
29:23 *c* Isa 49:20-26; 53:10; 54:1-3 *d* S Ps 8:6; S Isa 19:25 *e* Mt 6:9 *f* S ver 19; S Isa 5:19
29:24 *g* Ps 95:10; S Pr 12:8; Isa 28:7; Heb 5:2 *h* Isa 1:3; 32:4; 41:20; 60:16 *i* Isa 30:21; 42:16
30:1 *j* S Isa 28:1 *k* Dt 21:18; S Isa 1:2 *l* S 2Ki 17:4; S Isa 8:12
30:2 *m* 2Ki 25:26; Isa 31:1; 36:6; Jer 2:18,36; 42:14; Eze 17:15; 29:16 *n* S Ge 25:22; S Nu 27:21 *o* Isa 36:9 *p* S Isa 4:6
30:3 *q* Jdg 9:8-15 *r* ver 5; S Ps 44:13; Isa 20:4-5; 36:6
30:4 *s* S Nu 13:22
30:5 *t* ver 7; Isa 20:5; 31:1; 36:6 *u* S 2Ki 18:21 *v* S Ps 108:12; Jer 37:3-5 *w* S ver 3; S 2Ki 18:21; Eze 17:15
30:6 *x* Isa 13:1 *y* S Jdg 1:9 *z* S Ex 1:13; 5:10,21; Isa 5:30; 8:22; Jer 11:4 *a* Isa 5:29; 35:9 *b* Dt 8:15

29:19 *needy.* See 11:4. *Holy One of Israel.* See Introduction: Author; see also note on 1:4.
29:20 *ruthless.* See v. 21. *mockers.* Cf. 28:14,22.
29:21 *deprive … of justice.* See 1:17; 9:17 and notes; see also 10:2; Am 5:10,12,24 and note.
29:22 *redeemed.* Normally used of the deliverance of Israel from Egypt (see Ex 6:6 and note; 15:13). Cf. 43:1,3,14. But Abraham also had an "exodus" out of a pagan world (see Ge 12:1; Jos 24:2–3,14–15 and notes). *be ashamed.* Cf. 45:17; 50:7; 54:4. *grow pale.* From fear of the enemy.
29:23 *see … their children.* Cf. 49:20–21; 54:1–2 and notes. Restoration from exile may be in view. See also 53:10 and note. *children, the work of my hands.* See 45:11 (cf. Eph 2:10 and note). *acknowledge the holiness … stand in awe.* See 8:13. Isaiah's contemporaries showed little respect for the Lord. *Holy One of Jacob.* Cf. v. 19; see note on 1:4.
29:24 *wayward in spirit.* See 19:14. *gain understanding.* Contrast 1:3 (see also note there).
30:1 *Woe.* See note on 28:1—35:10. *obstinate children.* See 1:2

and note. *plans … not mine.* See 29:15 and note. *alliance.* After Shabako became pharaoh in 715 B.C., the smaller nations in Aram (Syria) and Canaan sought his help against Assyria. Judah apparently joined them (see 20:5 and note). *my Spirit.* Who spoke through his prophet.
30:2 *Hezekiah did this* (see 2Ki 18:21 and note). *shade.* A metaphor for a king as one who provides protection (see Jdg 9:15; La 4:20 and notes). The Lord should have been Israel's "shade" (cf. 49:2; 51:16; see Ps 91:1; 121:5 and notes).
30:4 *Zoan.* Ironically, where the Israelites once served as slaves; see 19:11 and note. *Hanes.* Possibly Heracleopolis Magna, about 50 miles south of Cairo, or perhaps a city in the Nile delta, close to Zoan.
30:6 *prophecy.* See 13:1 and note. *Negev.* The dry region in the southern part of the Holy Land (see Ge 12:9 and note; cf. Jdg 1:9). *hardship and distress.* Perhaps it was necessary to use back roads because the Assyrians had control of the main coastal road (see Dt 8:15; Jdg 5:6 and note). *darting snakes.* See 14:29.

30:6 ^cS Ge 42:26;
S 1Sa 25:18
^dS Isa 15:7
30:7 ^eS 2Ki 18:21;
S Jer 2:36 ^fS Job 9:13
30:8 ^gS Dt 27:8
^hS Ex 17:14; S Isa 8:1;
Jer 25:13; 30:2; 36:28;
Hab 2:2 ⁱJos 24:26-
27
30:9 ^jS Ps 78:8;
S Isa 1:2; S Eze 2:6
^kIsa 28:15; 59:3-4
^lS Isa 1:10
30:10 ^mS 1Sa 9:9
ⁿJer 11:21; 32:3;
Am 7:13 ^oS 1Ki 22:8;
S Jer 4:10 ^pJer 23:26;
25:9; 26:9; 36:29;
Eze 13:7; Ro 16:18;
2Ti 4:3-4
30:11 ^qver 21;
Pr 3:6; Isa 35:8-9;
48:17 ^rS Job 21:14
^sS Isa 29:19
30:12 ^tver 15;
S Isa 5:19; 31:1
^uS Isa 5:24
^vS Ps 10:7; S 12:5;
S Isa 5:7
30:13 ^wS Ne 2:17;
Ps 62:3; S 80:12
^xS 1Ki 20:30
^yS Isa 17:14
30:14 ^zS Ps 2:9
30:15 ^aJer 7:20;
Eze 3:11 ^bS ver 12
^cS Ex 14:14; S Jos 1:13
^dS 2Ch 20:12;
Isa 32:17 ^eIsa 8:6;
42:24; 57:17
30:16 ^fJer 46:6
^gS Dt 17:16;
1Ki 10:28-29;
S Ps 20:7; Isa 31:1,3;
36:8
30:17 ^hS Lev 26:8
ⁱLev 26:36; Dt 28:25;
S 2Ki 7:7 ^jS Isa 1:8
^kS Ps 20:5

the envoys carry their riches on donkeys'^c backs,
    their treasures^d on the humps of camels,
to that unprofitable nation,
7   to Egypt, whose help is utterly useless.^e
Therefore I call her
    Rahab^f the Do-Nothing.

⁸Go now, write it on a tablet^g for them,
    inscribe it on a scroll,^h
that for the days to come
    it may be an everlasting witness.ⁱ
⁹For these are rebellious^j people, deceitful^k children,
    children unwilling to listen to the LORD's instruction.^l
¹⁰They say to the seers,^m
    "See no more visionsⁿ!"
and to the prophets,
    "Give us no more visions of what is right!
Tell us pleasant things,^o
    prophesy illusions.^p
¹¹Leave this way,^q
    get off this path,
and stop confronting^r us
    with the Holy One^s of Israel!"

¹²Therefore, this is what the Holy One^t of Israel says:

"Because you have rejected this message,^u
    relied on oppression^v
    and depended on deceit,
¹³this sin will become for you
    like a high wall,^w cracked and bulging,
    that collapses^x suddenly,^y in an instant.
¹⁴It will break in pieces like pottery,^z
    shattered so mercilessly
that among its pieces not a fragment will be found
    for taking coals from a hearth
    or scooping water out of a cistern."

¹⁵This is what the Sovereign^a LORD, the Holy One^b of Israel, says:

"In repentance and rest^c is your salvation,
    in quietness and trust^d is your strength,
    but you would have none of it.^e
¹⁶You said, 'No, we will flee^f on horses.'^g
    Therefore you will flee!
You said, 'We will ride off on swift horses.'
    Therefore your pursuers will be swift!
¹⁷A thousand will flee
    at the threat of one;
at the threat of five^h
    you will all fleeⁱ away,
till you are left^j
    like a flagstaff on a mountaintop,
    like a banner^k on a hill."

30:7 *Rahab.* A mythical sea monster, here symbolic of Egypt. The name itself means "storm," and also "arrogance." See 27:1 ("Leviathan") and note.
30:8 *write it.* Probably the name "Rahab the Do-Nothing" (v.7).
30:9 *rebellious people.* See v. 1; see also 1:2 and note.
30:10 *seers.* See 1Sa 9:9 and note; 2Ki 17:13. *See no more visions.* Cf. Am 2:12; 7:13,16; Mic 2:6. *Tell us pleasant things.* As false prophets do (see 1Ki 22:13; Jer 6:14; 8:11; 23:16–17,26; Mic 2:11; 3:5,11 and notes).
30:11-12,15 *Holy One of Israel.* See 1:4 and note.
30:12 *oppression.* Especially in their domestic policy (see 1:15–17,23; 5:7; 29:21; 58:3–4; 59:3,6–8,13). *deceit.* Especially in their foreign policy (see vv. 1–2; 29:15).
30:13 *like a high wall.* Oppression and deceit (v. 12) had been the "wall" they built to assure their safety and prosperity, but it will be shattered to pieces.
30:15 See 26:3. *repentance and rest.* The true way to salvation and security.
30:16 *horses.* See Ps 20:7–8 and note; 33:17; Pr 21:31 and note.
30:17 *A thousand will flee.* A fulfillment of the curse of Dt 32:30. *flagstaff … banner.* See 5:26 and note (see also 1:8 and note).

[18] Yet the LORD longs [l] to be gracious to you;
　　therefore he will rise up to show you compassion. [m]
　For the LORD is a God of justice. [n]
　　Blessed are all who wait for him! [o]

[19] People of Zion, who live in Jerusalem, you will weep no more. [p] How gracious he will be when you cry for help! [q] As soon as he hears, he will answer [r] you. [20] Although the Lord gives you the bread [s] of adversity and the water of affliction, your teachers [t] will be hidden [u] no more; with your own eyes you will see them. [21] Whether you turn to the right or to the left, your ears will hear a voice [v] behind you, saying, "This is the way; [w] walk in it." [22] Then you will desecrate your idols [x] overlaid with silver and your images covered with gold; [y] you will throw them away like a menstrual [z] cloth and say to them, "Away with you! [a]"

[23] He will also send you rain [b] for the seed you sow in the ground, and the food that comes from the land will be rich [c] and plentiful. [d] In that day [e] your cattle will graze in broad meadows. [f] [24] The oxen [g] and donkeys that work the soil will eat fodder [h] and mash, spread out with fork [i] and shovel. [25] In the day of great slaughter, [j] when the towers [k] fall, streams of water will flow [l] on every high mountain and every lofty hill. [26] The moon will shine like the sun, [m] and the sunlight will be seven times brighter, like the light of seven full days, when the LORD binds up the bruises of his people and heals [n] the wounds he inflicted.

[27] See, the Name [o] of the LORD comes from afar,
　　with burning anger [p] and dense clouds of smoke;
　his lips are full of wrath, [q]
　　and his tongue is a consuming fire. [r]
[28] His breath [s] is like a rushing torrent, [t]
　　rising up to the neck. [u]
　He shakes the nations in the sieve [v] of destruction;
　　he places in the jaws of the peoples
　　a bit [w] that leads them astray.
[29] And you will sing
　　as on the night you celebrate a holy festival; [x]
　your hearts will rejoice [y]
　　as when people playing pipes [z] go up
　to the mountain [a] of the LORD,
　　to the Rock [b] of Israel.
[30] The LORD will cause people to hear his majestic voice [c]
　　and will make them see his arm [d] coming down
　with raging anger [e] and consuming fire, [f]
　　with cloudburst, thunderstorm [g] and hail. [h]
[31] The voice of the LORD will shatter Assyria; [i]
　　with his rod he will strike [j] them down.

30:30 [d] Isa 9:12; 40:10; 51:9; 52:10; 53:1; 59:16; 62:8; 63:12 [e] S ver 27; S Isa 10:25 [f] S Isa 4:4; 47:14 [g] Ex 20:18; Ps 29:3 [h] S Ex 9:18
30:31 [i] S Isa 10:5,12 [j] S Isa 11:4

30:18 [l] S Ge 43:31; Isa 42:14; 2Pe 3:9,15 [m] Ps 78:38; Isa 48:9; Jnh 3:10 [n] S Ps 11:7; S Isa 5:16 [o] S Ps 27:14; Isa 25:9; 33:2; 40:31; 64:4; La 3:25; Da 12:12
30:19 [p] S Isa 25:8; 60:20; 61:3 [q] S Job 24:12 [r] Job 22:27; Ps 50:15; S 86:7; Isa 41:17; 58:9; 65:24; Zec 13:9; Mt 7:7-11
30:20 [s] 1Ki 22:27 [t] S Isa 30:9 [u] Ps 74:9; Am 8:11
30:21 [v] S Isa 29:24 [w] S ver 11; S Job 33:11
30:22 [x] S Ex 32:4; S Isa 17:8 [y] S Dt 22:24; Isa 31:7 [z] Lev 15:19-23 [a] Eze 7:19-20
30:23 [b] S Dt 28:12; Isa 65:21-22 [c] Isa 25:6; 55:2; Jer 31:14 [d] S Job 36:31; Isa 62:8 [e] S Isa 28:5 [f] S Ps 65:13
30:24 [g] Isa 32:14,20 [h] S Job 6:5 [i] Mt 3:12; Lk 3:17
30:25 [j] S Isa 13:5; 34:6; 65:12; Jer 25:32; 50:27 [k] S Isa 2:15 [l] Ex 17:6; Isa 32:2; 41:18; Joel 3:18; Zec 14:8
30:26 [m] Isa 24:23; 60:19-20; Zec 14:7; Rev 21:23; 22:5 [n] S Dt 32:39; S 2Ch 7:14; Ps 107:20; S Isa 1:5; Jer 3:22; 17:14; Hos 14:4
30:27 [o] 1Ki 18:24; Ps 20:1; Isa 59:19; 64:2 [p] Isa 26:20; 66:14; Eze 22:31 [q] Isa 10:5; 13:5 [r] S ver 30; S Job 41:21
30:28 [s] S Isa 11:4 [t] S Ps 50:3; S Isa 28:15 [u] S Isa 8:8 [v] Am 9:9 [w] 2Ki 19:28
30:29 [x] Isa 25:6 [y] Isa 12:1 [z] S Isa 10:5 [a] S Ps 42:4; Mt 26:30 [b] S Ge 49:24
30:30 [c] S Ps 68:33

30:18 *longs to be gracious.* After punishing Israel, God will once again bless his people (cf. 40:2 and note).
30:19 *weep no more.* See 25:8 and note. God's response is similar to his zeal for the vineyard (Israel) in 27:2–6 (see notes there).
30:20 *bread of adversity ... water of affliction.* Prisoners' food (see 1Ki 22:27). *teachers.* Prophets, like Isaiah. Or the Hebrew for "teachers" can be rendered "Teacher" and be referred to the Lord, who will instruct them, and this time they will respond with obedience (vv. 21–22); cf. Jer 31:31–34; Eze 11:19–20; 36:25–27.
30:21 *This is the way; walk in it.* See Dt 5:32–33. Contrast the attitude shown in v. 9 (cf. 29:24; Jer 6:16 and note).
30:22 *desecrate your idols.* In repentance, not in despair, as in 2:20 (see note there).
30:23 *rain ... food ... rich and plentiful.* Part of the covenant blessings promised in Dt 28:11–12. See 5:6 and note. *In that day.* Cf. 29:18; see notes on 10:20,27; 26:1. *cattle will graze.* Cf. 32:20 and note.
30:24 *mash.* Seasoned, tasty fodder.
30:25 *day of great slaughter.* Cf. 24:1; 34:2,6 and note. Assyria's fall (v. 31) is one illustration. *streams ... on every high mountain.*

Paradise-like conditions will return to the land (see 41:18; Ps 104:13–15 and notes).
30:26 *moon ... brighter.* The darkness will be past: Night will be like the day, and day will be illumined with sevenfold light. *binds up the bruises ... heals the wounds.* The army of Assyria was similarly described in 8:8 (see note there). *bit.* Cf. 37:29.
30:27 *the Name.* The revelation of God, especially his power and glory. *anger ... clouds of smoke.* The language of theophany (a manifestation or appearance of God). God is portrayed as coming in a storm (see v. 30; see also 28:2; 29:6; Ps 18:7–15 and notes). *consuming fire.* Perhaps lightning.
30:28 *rising up to the neck.* The army of Assyria was similarly described in 8:8 (see note there). *bit.* Cf. 37:29.
30:29 *sing ... holy festival.* Perhaps the Passover, alluded to in 31:5 (cf. Mt 26:30). *mountain of the LORD.* Zion, where the temple was (see 2:2–4 and note). *Rock.* God himself (see 17:10 and note).
30:30–31 *voice.* Associated with thunder in Ex 20:18–19; Ps 29:3–9 (see note there).
30:30 *arm coming down.* See 9:12,17,21; 51:9 and notes. *cloudburst ... hail.* See 28:2.
30:31 *voice of the LORD will shatter.* Cf. 10:5; Ps 29:5–9.

30:32 *k* Isa 10:26
l S Ex 15:20
m S Isa 11:15;
Eze 32:10
30:33 *n* S 2Ki 23:10
o S Ex 15:10;
S 2Sa 22:16
p S Ge 19:24;
S Rev 9:17 *q* S Isa 1:31
31:1 *r* S Isa 28:1
s S Dt 17:16;
S Isa 30:2, 5;
S Jer 37:5
t S Isa 30:16
u S Isa 2:7 *v* Job 6:10;
S Isa 1:4; S 30:12
w S Dt 20:1;
S Pr 21:31; S Isa 9:13;
Jer 46:9; Eze 29:16
31:2 *x* S Ps 92:5;
Ro 16:27 *y* Isa 45:7;
47:11; Am 3:6
z Nu 23:19; S Pr 19:21
a S Isa 1:4; 29:15; 32:6
31:3 *b* Isa 20:5; 36:9
c S Ps 9:20; Eze 28:9;
2Th 2:4 *d* S Isa 30:16
e Ne 1:10; S Job 30:21;
Isa 9:17, 21; Jer 51:25;
Eze 20:34 *f* Isa 10:3;
30:5-7 *g* S Isa 20:6;
Jer 17:5
31:4 *h* Nu 24:9;
S 1Sa 17:34;
Hos 11:10; Am 3:8
i Jer 3:15; 23:4;
Eze 34:23; Na 3:18
j Ps 74:23 *k* Isa 42:13
31:5 *l* S Ge 1:2;
S Mt 23:37
m S Ps 91:4; S Isa 5:2;
S Zec 9:15
n S Ps 34:7; Isa 37:35;
38:6 *o* S Ex 12:23
31:6 *p* S Job 22:23;
S Isa 1:27 *q* S Isa 1:5
31:7 *r* Isa 29:18
s S Isa 30:22
t S Ps 135:15
31:8 *u* S Isa 10:12
v S Ex 12:12; Isa 10:12;
14:25; S 27:1; 33:1;
37:7; Jer 25:12;
Hab 2:8

32 Every stroke the Lord lays on them
　　with his punishing club *k*
will be to the music of timbrels *l* and harps,
　　as he fights them in battle with the blows of his arm. *m*
33 Topheth *n* has long been prepared;
　　it has been made ready for the king.
Its fire pit has been made deep and wide,
　　with an abundance of fire and wood;
the breath *o* of the Lord,
　　like a stream of burning sulfur, *p*
　　sets it ablaze. *q*

WOE TO THOSE WHO RELY ON EGYPT

31

Woe *r* to those who go down to Egypt *s* for help,
　　who rely on horses, *t*
who trust in the multitude of their chariots *u*
　　and in the great strength of their horsemen,
but do not look to the Holy One *v* of Israel,
　　or seek help from the Lord. *w*
2 Yet he too is wise *x* and can bring disaster; *y*
　　he does not take back his words. *z*
He will rise up against the house of the wicked, *a*
　　against those who help evildoers.
3 But the Egyptians *b* are mortals and not God; *c*
　　their horses *d* are flesh and not spirit.
When the Lord stretches out his hand, *e*
　　those who help will stumble,
　　those who are helped *f* will fall;
　　all will perish together. *g*

4 This is what the Lord says to me:

"As a lion *h* growls,
　　a great lion over its prey—
and though a whole band of shepherds *i*
　　is called together against it,
it is not frightened by their shouts
　　or disturbed by their clamor *j*—
so the Lord Almighty will come down *k*
　　to do battle on Mount Zion and on its heights.
5 Like birds hovering *l* overhead,
　　the Lord Almighty will shield *m* Jerusalem;
he will shield it and deliver *n* it,
　　he will 'pass over' *o* it and will rescue it."

6 Return, *p* you Israelites, to the One you have so greatly revolted *q* against. 7 For in that day *r* every one of you will reject the idols of silver and gold *s* your sinful hands have made. *t*

8 "Assyria *u* will fall by no human sword;
　　a sword, not of mortals, will devour *v* them.

30:32 *his punishing club.* See 11:4 and note. *music of timbrels.* After a great victory the women rejoiced with singing and dancing (see Ex 15:20–21 and notes; 1Sa 18:6).
30:33 *Topheth.* A region outside Jerusalem where children were sacrificed to Molek (see 2Ki 23:10; Jer 7:31–32; 19:6,11–14 and notes), the god of the Ammonites (see 1Ki 11:7). Thus it was a place of burning. *king.* Of Assyria (or perhaps a reference to Molek; see note on Jdg 10:6). *burning sulfur.* See 1:31; Ge 19:24 and notes.
31:1 See 30:1 and note. In shorter form, ch. 31 recapitulates the structure and content of ch. 30. *go down to Egypt.* See Ge 26:2. *horses…chariots.* Egypt had large numbers of horses and chariots (see 1Ki 10:28–29 and notes). *Holy One of Israel.* See 1:4 and note.
31:2 *he too is wise.* People had questioned God's wisdom in 29:14–16 (see notes there).
31:3 *Egyptians are mortals and not God.* Cf. Hos 11:9. *God…*

spirit. See Jn 4:24 and note. *stretches out his hand.* Cf. the refrain in 5:25 (see note there); 9:12,17,21; 10:4. *those who help will stumble.* Cf. 30:3,5.
31:4 *lion.* A simile, but perhaps also an allusion to the Assyrian king (see note on 15:9). *shepherds.* Perhaps an allusion to the rulers of the nations (see TNIV text note on Na 3:18).
31:5 *birds…will shield.* Cf. Dt 32:10–11. *pass over.* The technical word used of the destroying angel who "passed over" every house in Egypt that had blood on the doorposts (see Ex 12:13, 23 and notes). Cf. Isa 37:35.
31:6 *greatly revolted.* See 1:2 and note.
31:7 *reject the idols.* See 2:20 and note.
31:8 *sword, not of mortals.* The angel of the Lord struck down 185,000 soldiers (see 37:36 and note; see also Ps 7:12–13 and note). *put to forced labor.* As prisoners of war.

They will flee before the sword
and their young men will be put to forced labor. *w*
⁹ Their stronghold *x* will fall because of terror;
at the sight of the battle standard *y* their commanders will panic, *z* ”
declares the LORD,
whose fire *a* is in Zion,
whose furnace *b* is in Jerusalem.

THE KINGDOM OF RIGHTEOUSNESS

32

See, a king *c* will reign in righteousness
and rulers will rule with justice. *d*
² Each one will be like a shelter *e* from the wind
and a refuge from the storm, *f*
like streams of water *g* in the desert *h*
and the shadow of a great rock in a thirsty land.

³ Then the eyes of those who see will no longer be closed, *i*
and the ears *j* of those who hear will listen.
⁴ The fearful heart will know and understand, *k*
and the stammering tongue *l* will be fluent and clear.
⁵ No longer will the fool *m* be called noble
nor the scoundrel be highly respected.
⁶ For fools speak folly, *n*
their hearts are bent on evil: *o*
They practice ungodliness *p*
and spread error *q* concerning the LORD;
the hungry they leave empty *r*
and from the thirsty they withhold water.
⁷ Scoundrels use wicked methods, *s*
they make up evil schemes *t*
to destroy the poor with lies,
even when the plea of the needy *u* is just. *v*
⁸ But the noble make noble plans,
and by noble deeds *w* they stand. *x*

THE WOMEN OF JERUSALEM

⁹ You women *y* who are so complacent,
rise up and listen *z* to me;
you daughters who feel secure, *a*
hear what I have to say!
¹⁰ In little more than a year *b*
you who feel secure will tremble;
the grape harvest will fail, *c*
and the harvest of fruit will not come.
¹¹ Tremble, *d* you complacent women;
shudder, you daughters who feel secure! *e*
Strip off your clothes, *f*
put sackcloth *g* around your waists.

31:8 *w* S Ge 49:15;
S Dt 20:11
31:9 *x* Dt 32:31,37
y S Isa 18:3; S Jer 4:6
z Jer 51:9; Na 3:7
a S Isa 10:17 *b* Ps 21:9;
Mal 4:1
32:1 *c* S Ps 149:2;
S Isa 6:5; 55:4;
Eze 37:24 *d* Ps 72:1-
4; S Isa 9:7; S 28:6
32:2 *e* S 1Ki 18:4
f S Ps 55:8
g S Ps 23:2;
S Isa 30:25; 49:10;
Jer 31:9 *h* S Ps 107:35;
Isa 44:3
32:3 *i* S Isa 29:18;
35:5; 42:7,16
j S Dt 29:4
32:4 *k* Isa 6:10;
S 29:24 *l* Isa 35:6
32:5 *m* S 1Sa 25:25
32:6 *n* S Pr 19:3
o S Pr 24:2;
S Isa 26:10
p S Isa 9:17 *q* Isa 3:12;
9:16 *r* S Isa 3:15
32:7 *s* Jer 5:26-28;
Da 12:10
t S Isa 29:20; Mic 7:3
u S Ps 72:4; Isa 29:19;
61:1 *v* S Isa 29:21
32:8 *w* 1Ch 29:9;
S Pr 11:25 *x* Isa 14:24
32:9 *y* S Isa 4:1
z Isa 28:23 *a* ver 11;
Isa 47:8; Da 4:4;
Am 6:1; Zep 2:15
32:10 *b* Isa 37:30
c Isa 5:5-6; S 24:7
32:11 *d* Isa 33:14
e S ver 9 *f* Isa 47:2;
Mic 1:8; Na 3:5
g S Isa 3:24

31:9 *stronghold.* Nineveh was destroyed by the Medes and
Babylonians in 612 B.C. (see Na 3:7). *commanders will panic.* Cf.
Na 2:10 and note. *fire . . . furnace.* The Lord's glory resides in Zion,
and from that center of his people his fire of judgment breaks
out upon the wicked (see 10:17; 30:33 and note; cf. Lev 10:2; Joel
3:16 and note; Am 1:2 and note).
32:1 *king . . . in righteousness.* The Messianic age is again in view
(see 9:7; 11:4; 16:5 and notes). Cf. vv. 16–17; 33:17 and note.
32:2 *Each one will be like.* The Lord's redeemed, as sources of
protection and blessing, will reflect him (see the rest of this
note; see also vv. 3–8). *shelter . . . refuge . . . shadow.* Similar terms
are applied to the Lord in 25:4 (see 4:5–6 and note). *streams . . .
in the desert.* See 35:6–7; 41:18; 49:10 and notes.
32:3 *eyes . . . no longer be closed . . . ears . . . listen.* See 35:5 and
note (contrast 6:9–10; see notes there).
32:5–8 The redeemed will no longer be among the fools. The

contrast between the fool and the wise or noble is characteristic
of wisdom literature (compare Pr 9:1–6 with Pr 9:13–18).
32:6 A full explication of what the OT calls a "fool" (see Pr
1:7 and note; see also TNIV text note there). *fools speak
folly.* Cf. 9:16–17; Ps 14:1 and note; 53:1.
32:7 *plea of the needy.* See 1:17 and note.
32:8 *plans . . . stand.* See 8:10 and note.
32:9 *women.* Cf. 3:16—4:1 and notes. *complacent . . . feel secure.*
See v. 11; Am 6:1 and note. These words are used in a good
sense in v. 18 (the Hebrew for "undisturbed" is the same as that
for "complacent").
32:10 *a year.* Perhaps the invasion of Sennacherib (701 B.C.) is
in view. *grape harvest will fail.* Cf. 37:30. The armies of Assyria
would bring widespread destruction, ruining the summer fruit.
32:11 *Strip.* Cf. 47:2–3 and notes. *sackcloth.* Cf. 3:24; 22:12; see
notes on Ge 37:34; Rev 11:3.

32:12 *h* Na 2:7
i Isa 16:9
32:13 *j* S Isa 5:6;
Hos 10:8 *k* S Isa 24:11
l S Isa 23:7
32:14 *m* S Isa 13:22
n S Isa 6:11; S 27:10
o S Isa 2:15; 34:13
p S Ps 104:11
q S Isa 5:17
32:15 *r* S Isa 11:2;
S Eze 37:9
s Ps 107:35; Isa 35:1-2
t Isa 29:17
32:16 *u* S Isa 9:7;
S 28:6 *v* Isa 35:1,6;
42:11 *w* S Ps 48:1;
S Isa 1:26
32:17 *x* S Ps 85:10
y S Ps 119:165;
S Isa 9:7; Ro 14:17;
Heb 12:11; Jas 3:18
z S Isa 30:15
32:18 *a* S Isa 2:4
b S Isa 26:1; 33:20;
37:33; 65:21; 66:14;
Am 9:14 *c* S Jos 1:13;
S Job 11:18; Hos 2:18-
23
32:19 *d* Isa 28:17
e S Isa 10:19; Zec 11:2
f S Job 40:11;
S Isa 19:18; 24:10;
27:10
32:20 *g* S Ecc 11:1
h S Dt 28:12
i Job 39:8; S Isa 30:24
33:1 *j* S 2Ki 19:21;
S Isa 28:1 *k* S Isa 31:8;
S Mt 7:2 *l* S Isa 21:2;
Jer 30:16; Eze 39:10
33:2 *m* S Ge 43:29;
S Ezr 9:8 *n* S Isa 40:10;
51:9; 59:16; 63:5
o S Ps 13:5; S Isa 12:2
p S Isa 5:30
33:3 *q* S Ps 46:6;
S 68:33 *r* S Ps 68:1;
S Isa 13:14 *s* ver 10;
Nu 10:35; Ps 12:5;
Isa 59:16-18
33:4 *t* S Nu 14:3;
S 2Ki 7:16
u Isa 17:5; Joel 3:13
v Joel 1:4
33:5 *w* S Isa 5:16
x S Job 16:19
y S Isa 9:7; S 28:6
z S Isa 1:26

¹² Beat your breasts *h* for the pleasant fields,
　　for the fruitful vines *i*
¹³ and for the land of my people,
　　a land overgrown with thorns and briers *j*—
　　yes, mourn *k* for all houses of merriment
　　and for this city of revelry. *l*
¹⁴ The fortress *m* will be abandoned,
　　the noisy city deserted; *n*
　citadel and watchtower *o* will become a wasteland forever,
　　the delight of donkeys, *p* a pasture for flocks, *q*
¹⁵ till the Spirit *r* is poured on us from on high,
　　and the desert becomes a fertile field, *s*
　　and the fertile field seems like a forest. *t*
¹⁶ The LORD's justice *u* will dwell in the desert, *v*
　　his righteousness *w* live in the fertile field.
¹⁷ The fruit of that righteousness *x* will be peace; *y*
　　its effect will be quietness and confidence *z* forever.
¹⁸ My people will live in peaceful *a* dwelling places,
　　in secure homes, *b*
　　in undisturbed places of rest. *c*
¹⁹ Though hail *d* flattens the forest *e*
　　and the city is leveled *f* completely,
²⁰ how blessed you will be,
　　sowing *g* your seed by every stream, *h*
　　and letting your cattle and donkeys range free. *i*

DISTRESS AND HELP

33 Woe *j* to you, destroyer,
　　you who have not been destroyed!
　Woe to you, betrayer,
　　you who have not been betrayed!
　When you stop destroying,
　　you will be destroyed; *k*
　when you stop betraying,
　　you will be betrayed. *l*

² LORD, be gracious *m* to us;
　　we long for you.
　Be our strength *n* every morning,
　　our salvation *o* in time of distress. *p*
³ At the uproar of your army, *q* the peoples flee; *r*
　　when you rise up, *s* the nations scatter.
⁴ Their plunder *t* is harvested *u* as by young locusts; *v*
　　like a swarm of locusts people pounce on it.

⁵ The LORD is exalted, *w* for he dwells on high; *x*
　　he will fill Zion with his justice *y* and righteousness. *z*
⁶ He will be the sure foundation for your times,

32:12 *Beat your breasts.* Like the slave girls of Nineveh (Na 2:7). *for the fruitful vines.* Cf. the Lord's weeping in 16:9.
32:13 *thorns and briers.* See 5:6; 7:23 and notes. *merriment ... revelry.* See 22:2 and note; cf. Jer 16:8-9.
32:14 *fortress ... noisy city.* Assyria's invasion is a warning that Jerusalem (see 24:10 and note) will one day be destroyed. *donkeys ... flocks.* Cf. 7:25; 13:21-22; 34:13.
32:15 *till the Spirit is poured on.* The outpouring of the Spirit is linked with abundance also in 44:3 (see note there; see also 11:2; Joel 2:28-32 and notes). *fertile field ... forest.* The forest probably stands for Lebanon (see 29:17 and note; cf. 35:1-2 and notes).
32:16 *justice ... righteousness.* See v. 1 and note.
32:17 *peace.* Cf. 9:7; 11:6-9 and note. *quietness and confidence.* Contrast 30:15 ("you would have none of it").
32:18 *secure ... undisturbed.* See note on v. 9. *places of rest.* See 28:12 and note.

32:19 *hail.* Cf. 28:2. *forest.* Probably Assyria. See 10:33-34 and notes. *city.* See 24:10 and note.
32:20 The abundance of the day of the Lord is described (see 30:23-24 and notes).
33:1 *Woe.* See note on 28:1—35:10. *destroyer ... betrayer.* Probably Assyria—depicted as treacherous (see 10:5-6; 16:4; 21:2; 24:16 and notes).
33:2-9 A prayer asking the Lord to bring about the promised destruction of Assyria.
33:2 *be gracious.* See 30:18 and note; cf. Nu 6:25. *strength ... salvation.* See 12:2 and note; cf. 59:16 and note. *every morning.* See Ps 88:13; 143:8 and note; see also introduction to Ps 57. *distress.* See 37:3.
33:3 *rise up ... scatter.* An allusion to Nu 10:35-36 (see notes there); cf. Ps 68:1 and note.
33:5 *fill ... righteousness.* See 1:26; 32:1 and note.

a rich store of salvation [a] and wisdom and knowledge;
  the fear [b] of the Lord is the key to this treasure. [a c]

[7] Look, their brave men [d] cry aloud in the streets;
  the envoys [e] of peace weep bitterly.
[8] The highways are deserted,
  no travelers [f] are on the roads. [g]
The treaty is broken, [h]
  its witnesses [b] are despised,
  no one is respected.
[9] The land dries up [i] and wastes away,
  Lebanon [j] is ashamed and withers; [k]
Sharon [l] is like the Arabah,
  and Bashan [m] and Carmel [n] drop their leaves.

[10] "Now will I arise, [o]" says the Lord.
  "Now will I be exalted; [p]
  now will I be lifted up.
[11] You conceive [q] chaff,
  you give birth [r] to straw;
  your breath is a fire [s] that consumes you.
[12] The peoples will be burned as if to lime; [t]
  like cut thornbushes [u] they will be set ablaze. [v]"

[13] You who are far away, [w] hear [x] what I have done;
  you who are near, acknowledge my power!
[14] The sinners [y] in Zion are terrified;
  trembling [z] grips the godless:
"Who of us can dwell with the consuming fire? [a]
  Who of us can dwell with everlasting burning?"
[15] Those who walk righteously [b]
  and speak what is right, [c]
who reject gain from extortion [d]
  and keep their hands from accepting bribes, [e]
who stop their ears against plots of murder
  and shut their eyes [f] against contemplating evil—
[16] they are the ones who will dwell on the heights, [g]
  whose refuge [h] will be the mountain fortress. [i]
Their bread will be supplied,
  and water will not fail [j] them.

[17] Your eyes will see the king [k] in his beauty [l]
  and view a land that stretches afar. [m]
[18] In your thoughts you will ponder the former terror: [n]

---

[a] 6 Or *is a treasure from him*   [b] 8 Dead Sea Scrolls; Masoretic Text / *the cities*

33:6 [a] S Isa 12:2; 26:1; 51:6; 60:18
[b] S Pr 1:7; Isa 11:2-3; Mt 6:33 [c] S Ge 39:3; S Job 22:25
33:7 [d] Isa 10:34
[e] S 2Ki 18:37
33:8 [f] Isa 60:15; Zec 7:14 [g] S Jdg 5:6; Isa 30:21; 35:8
[h] S 2Ki 18:14
33:9 [i] S Isa 3:26
[j] S 2Ki 19:23; Isa 2:13; 35:2; 37:24; Jer 22:6
[k] S Isa 15:6
[l] S 1Ch 27:29
[m] Mic 7:14
[n] 1Ki 19:19; Isa 35:2; Na 1:4
33:10 [o] S ver 3; Isa 2:21 [p] S Isa 5:16
33:11 [q] Ps 7:14; Isa 59:4; Jas 1:15
[r] S Isa 26:18 [s] Isa 1:31
33:12 [t] Am 2:1
[u] S Isa 5:6
[v] S Isa 10:17; S 27:11
33:13 [w] Ps 48:10; 49:1 [x] Isa 34:1; 48:16; 49:1
33:14 [y] S Isa 1:28
[z] Isa 32:11
[a] S Isa 1:31; S 30:30; S Zec 13:9; Heb 12:29
33:15 [b] Isa 58:8
[c] Ps 15:2; 24:4
[d] Eze 22:13; 33:31
[e] S Pr 15:27
[f] Ps 119:37
33:16 [g] S Dt 32:13
[h] S Ps 46:1; S Isa 25:4
[i] Ps 18:1-2; Isa 26:1
[j] Isa 48:21; 49:10; 65:13
33:17 [k] S Isa 6:5
[l] S Isa 4:2
[m] S Isa 26:15
33:18 [n] S Isa 17:14

33:6 *wisdom ... knowledge ... fear of the Lord.* Terms linked with the Messiah in 11:2 (see note there). See 9:6; Pr 1:7 and notes.
33:7 *their brave men.* The men of Judah, during Sennacherib's invasion of 701 b.c. (see 10:28–34 and notes). *envoys of peace.* Perhaps the three officials who conferred with the Assyrian field commander (see 36:3,22).
33:8 *highways are deserted.* Travel and trade were impossible, creating economic hardship (see Jdg 5:6 and note). *treaty.* Perhaps the agreement made when Hezekiah paid large sums to Sennacherib (see 2Ki 18:14 and note).
33:9 *land ... wastes away.* Farmland and pastures were ruined by the invaders. See 24:4 and note. *Lebanon.* Renowned for its cedars (2:13) and animals (40:16). *Sharon.* A plain along the Mediterranean coast north of Joppa, known for its beautiful foliage and superb grazing land (see 35:2 and note; 65:10; 1Ch 27:29). *Arabah.* Desert land associated with the Jordan River and the Dead Sea (see Dt 1:1; 2:8 and notes). *Bashan.* See 2:13 and note. *Carmel.* See note on 1Ki 18:19; means "fertile field" (as in 29:17; 32:15) or "orchards" (as in 16:10) and is also associated with lush pasturelands (see 35:2 and note; Mic 7:14 and TNIV text note; Na 1:4 and note).

33:10 *be exalted.* Through the judgment he brings on his rebellious people (see v. 14 and note).
33:11 *conceive ... give birth.* Cf. 26:18. *breath is a fire.* They only produce what results in their destruction.
33:12 *to lime.* The burning will be complete (see Am 2:1). *thornbushes.* They burn very quickly (see 27:4; 2Sa 23:6–7).
33:13 *hear ... acknowledge.* Cf. 34:1.
33:14 *sinners in Zion.* See 1:27–28 and note; 4:4. *consuming fire.* The presence of the God of judgment (see 29:6; 30:27,30; Ex 24:17; Dt 4:24; 9:3; 2Sa 22:9; Ps 18:8; Heb 12:29).
33:15 Similar requirements are found in Ps 15:2–5; 24:3–6 (see notes there). *bribes.* See 1:23.
33:16 *heights ... fortress.* Symbolic of the security found in God (cf. Ps 18:2 and note). *bread ... water.* Cf. 49:10.
33:17 *king.* See 32:1 and note; cf. 6:1,5 and notes. *in his beauty.* Reflecting on the splendor and majesty of a Davidic king; probably a foreshadowing of the Messianic kingdom (cf. 4:2; Ps 45:3–5 and notes; contrast Isa 53:2–3 [see notes there]). *land ... afar.* See 26:15 and note.
33:18 *former terror.* The Assyrian invasion (see 17:12–14 and

33:18 °S Isa 2:15
33:19 ᵖS Ps 5:5
ᵍS Ge 11:7;
S Isa 28:11
33:20 ʳS Ps 125:1
ˢS Isa 32:18
ᵗS Ge 26:22 ᵘver 6;
Ps 46:5
33:21 ᵛS Isa 10:34
ʷS Ex 17:6; S Ps 1:3;
Isa 32:2; 41:18; 48:18;
49:10; 66:12; Na 3:8
ˣIsa 23:1
33:22 ʸIsa 11:4
ᶻS Isa 2:3; Jas 4:12
ᵃS Ps 89:18
ᵇS Isa 25:9
33:23 ᶜS 2Ki 7:8
ᵈS 2Ki 7:16
33:24 ᵉS Isa 30:26
ᶠS Nu 23:21;
S 2Ch 6:21; Isa 43:1;
48:20; Jer 31:34; 33:8;
1Jn 1:7-9
34:1 ᵍS Isa 33:13
ʰIsa 41:1; 43:9
ⁱS Dt 4:26; Ps 49:1
ʲPs 24:1
34:2 ᵏS Isa 10:25
ˡS Isa 13:5; S Zec 5:3
ᵐS Isa 30:25
34:3 ⁿS Isa 5:25;
S 10:4 °S Ps 110:6;
Eze 39:11 ᵖJoel 2:20;
Am 4:10 ᵍver 7;
S 2Sa 1:22; Isa 63:6;
Eze 5:17; 14:19; 32:6;
35:6; 38:22
34:4 ʳS Job 9:7;
S Isa 13:13; 2Pe 3:10
ˢIsa 38:12; Heb 1:12
ᵗS Mt 24:29*;
Mk 13:25*

"Where is that chief officer?
  Where is the one who took the revenue?
  Where is the officer in charge of the towers? °"
19 You will see those arrogant people ᵖ no more,
    people whose speech is obscure,
    whose language is strange and incomprehensible. ᵍ

20 Look on Zion, ʳ the city of our festivals;
    your eyes will see Jerusalem,
    a peaceful abode, ˢ a tent ᵗ that will not be moved; ᵘ
  its stakes will never be pulled up,
    nor any of its ropes broken.
21 There the LORD will be our Mighty ᵛ One.
    It will be like a place of broad rivers and streams. ʷ
  No galley with oars will ride them,
    no mighty ship ˣ will sail them.
22 For the LORD is our judge, ʸ
    the LORD is our lawgiver, ᶻ
  the LORD is our king; ᵃ
    it is he who will save ᵇ us.

23 Your rigging hangs loose:
    The mast is not held secure,
    the sail is not spread.
  Then an abundance of spoils will be divided
    and even the lame ᶜ will carry off plunder. ᵈ
24 No one living in Zion will say, "I am ill"; ᵉ
    and the sins of those who dwell there will be forgiven. ᶠ

JUDGMENT AGAINST THE NATIONS

34 Come near, you nations, and listen; ᵍ
    pay attention, you peoples! ʰ
  Let the earth ⁱ hear, and all that is in it,
    the world, and all that comes out of it! ʲ
2 The LORD is angry with all nations;
    his wrath ᵏ is on all their armies.
  He will totally destroy ᵃˡ them,
    he will give them over to slaughter. ᵐ
3 Their slain ⁿ will be thrown out,
    their dead bodies ° will send up a stench; ᵖ
    the mountains will be soaked with their blood. ᵍ
4 All the stars in the sky will be dissolved ʳ
    and the heavens rolled up ˢ like a scroll;
  all the starry host will fall ᵗ

ᵃ 2 The Hebrew term refers to the irrevocable giving over of things or persons to the LORD, often by totally destroying them; also in verse 5.

---

note). *revenue.* Forced tribute (see note on v. 8). *towers.* Judah's fortifications were probably under strict Assyrian control (see 2:15).
33:19 *arrogant.* Cf. 10:12 and note. *speech is obscure.* The Assyrian language was related to Hebrew but was different enough
to sound strange to Israelite ears. See 28:11; Dt 28:49.
33:20 *Look on Zion.* The redeemed city, in contrast to the city described in vv. 7–9. *festivals.* See 1:14 and note. *peaceful abode.* See
32:17–18 and notes. *tent . . . not . . . moved.* Her exile will be over.
stakes . . . ropes. Cf. the similar description of Jerusalem in 54:2.
33:21 *Mighty One.* See 10:34 (cf. Ps 93:3–4 and notes). *broad
rivers.* To prevent easy access to her borders—thus like Tyre
(23:1) or Thebes (see Na 3:8 and note).
33:22 *our judge.* See 2:4; 11:4 and note. *our lawgiver.* See 2:3;
51:4 and note. *our king.* See v. 17; 32:1 and notes; see also Ps 46;
48. *save.* See Jdg 2:16–19 and note.
33:23 *rigging.* Jerusalem is pictured as a ship, unprepared to
sail into battle against Assyria. *Then.* When God strikes down the
Assyrian army (see 10:33–34; 37:36 and notes). *plunder.* See v. 4.

33:24 Looking beyond Isaiah's own day to the physically and
spiritually whole Jerusalem of vv. 17,20–22.
34:1—35:10 Chs. 34–35 conclude chs. 28–33 and comprise
an eschatological section corresponding to chs. 24–27, which
conclude chs. 13–23 (see note on 24:1—27:13).
34:2 *angry . . . wrath.* In the day of the Lord (see 2:11,17,20;
26:20–21 and notes). See also 13:3,13 and notes. *totally destroy.*
The kind of destruction the Canaanites had deserved. See TNIV
text note; see also v. 5; Jos 6:17 and note. *slaughter.* See 30:25
and note.
34:3 *thrown out.* Not to have a proper burial was considered a
disgrace (see 14:19 and note).
34:4 *stars . . . dissolved.* Disturbances in the heavens characterize the day of the Lord (see 13:10,13 and notes; cf. Eze 32:7–8).
sky . . . scroll . . . starry host will fall. Referred to in Mk 13:25 (see
note there); Rev 6:13–14 in connection with the "great distress"
(Mt 24:21) and the second coming of Christ. *withered leaves.* Cf.
24:4; 40:7–8.

like withered [u] leaves from the vine,
like shriveled figs from the fig tree.

⁵ My sword [v] has drunk its fill in the heavens;
see, it descends in judgment on Edom, [w]
the people I have totally destroyed. [x]

⁶ The sword [y] of the Lord is bathed in blood,
it is covered with fat—
the blood of lambs and goats,
fat from the kidneys of rams.
For the Lord has a sacrifice [z] in Bozrah [a]
and a great slaughter [b] in Edom.

⁷ And the wild oxen [c] will fall with them,
the bull calves and the great bulls. [d]
Their land will be drenched with blood, [e]
and the dust will be soaked with fat.

⁸ For the Lord has a day [f] of vengeance, [g]
a year of retribution, [h] to uphold Zion's cause.

⁹ Edom's streams will be turned into pitch,
her dust into burning sulfur; [i]
her land will become blazing pitch!

¹⁰ It will not be quenched [j] night or day;
its smoke will rise forever. [k]
From generation to generation [l] it will lie desolate; [m]
no one will ever pass through it again.

¹¹ The desert owl [a] [n] and screech owl [a] will possess it;
the great owl [a] and the raven [o] will nest there.
God will stretch out over Edom [p]
the measuring line of chaos [q]
and the plumb line [r] of desolation.

¹² Her nobles will have nothing there to be called a kingdom,
all her princes [s] will vanish [t] away.

¹³ Thorns [u] will overrun her citadels,
nettles and brambles her strongholds. [v]
She will become a haunt for jackals, [w]
a home for owls. [x]

¹⁴ Desert creatures [y] will meet with hyenas, [z]
and wild goats will bleat to each other;
there the night creatures [a] will also lie down
and find for themselves places of rest.

¹⁵ The owl will nest there and lay eggs,
she will hatch them, and care for her young
under the shadow of her wings; [b]

---

[a] 11 The precise identification of these birds is uncertain.

34:4 [u] S Job 8:12;
S Isa 15:6; Mt 21:19
34:5 [v] Dt 32:41-42;
Jer 47:6; Eze 21:5;
Zec 13:7
[w] S 2Sa 8:13-14;
S 2Ch 28:17; Am 1:11-
12 [x] S Dt 13:15;
S Jos 6:17; Isa 24:6;
Am 3:14-15; 6:11
34:6 [y] S Dt 32:41;
S Isa 27:1 [z] S Lev 3:9
[a] S Ge 36:33
[b] S Isa 30:25;
S Jer 25:34; Rev 19:17
34:7 [c] S Nu 23:22
[d] S Ps 68:30
[e] S 2Sa 1:22
34:8 [f] S Isa 2:12
[g] S Isa 1:24; 35:4;
47:3; 63:4 [h] Isa 59:18;
Eze 25:12-17;
Joel 3:4; Am 1:6-8,9-
10
34:9 [i] S Ge 19:24
34:10 [j] S Isa 1:31
[k] Rev 14:10-11; 19:3
[l] ver 17 [m] Isa 13:20;
24:1; Jer 49:18;
Eze 29:12; 35:3;
Mal 1:3
34:11 [n] S Lev 11:16-
18; S Dt 14:15-17;
Rev 18:2 [o] S Ge 8:7
[p] Isa 21:11; Eze 35:15;
Joel 3:19; Ob 1:1;
Mal 1:4 [q] S Ge 1:2
[r] S 2Ki 21:13; Am 7:8
34:12 [s] Job 12:21;
Ps 107:40; Isa 40:23;
Jer 21:7; 27:20; 39:6;
Eze 24:5 [t] Isa 29:20;
41:11-12
34:13 [u] S Isa 5:6;
S 7:19 [v] S Isa 13:22
[w] Ps 44:19;
S Isa 13:22; Jer 9:11;
10:22 [x] S Lev 11:16-18
34:14 [y] S Ps 74:14
[z] Isa 13:22 [a] Rev 18:2
34:15 [b] S Ps 17:8

34:5–6 *My sword ... The sword of the Lord.* See Ps 7:12–13 and note.
34:5 *drunk its fill.* Cf. Eze 39:18–20 and notes. *Edom.* Symbolic of all the enemies of God and his people, like Moab in 25:10–12 (see note on 25:10). See note on 21:11. The Edomites were driven from their homeland by the Nabatean Arabs, perhaps as early as 500 B.C.
34:6 *fat.* Considered the best part of the meat, and therefore offered to the Lord in the sacrifices (see Lev 3:9–11,16 and note on 3:16). *lambs and goats.* Symbolizing the people. *sacrifice.* Battles are often compared to sacrifices (see Jer 46:10 and note; 50:27; Eze 39:17–19 and notes; cf. Rev 19:17–18). *Bozrah.* An important city of Edom and a sheepherding center, it was located about 25 miles southeast of the southern end of the Dead Sea. The name means "grape-gathering" (cf. 63:1–3).
34:7 *wild oxen ... great bulls.* Symbolizing the troops and/or leaders of the nations. *drenched with blood.* See v. 3.
34:8 *day of vengeance.* See 35:4; 61:2. The Edomites opposed Israel at every opportunity (see 2Sa 8:13–14) and rejoiced when Jerusalem was destroyed (see La 4:21; see also Ps 137:7; Jer 49:8

and notes). But Edom's day would come (see 63:1–4 and notes).
34:9 *burning sulfur.* Edom's destruction is compared with the overthrow of Sodom and Gomorrah (see Jer 49:17–18 and notes). See also 1:31; Ge 19:24 and notes.
34:10 *smoke ... forever.* Applied to Babylon in Rev 19:3 (see also Rev 14:10–11 and notes). *lie desolate.* See 13:20–22; Mal 1:3–4 and notes.
34:11 *desert owl ... screech owl ... great owl ... raven.* "Unclean" birds (see Dt 14:14–17). Such birds would also live in the ruins of Babylon (13:21) and Nineveh (Zep 2:14). *measuring line ... plumb line.* Cf. 28:17 and note. *chaos ... desolation.* The Hebrew for these words is used in Ge 1:2 (see note there) to describe the earth in its "formless" and "empty" state (see also Jer 4:23 and note).
34:13 *Thorns ... nettles.* Cf. 7:24–25.
34:14 *Desert creatures ... hyenas.* See 13:20–22 and note. *wild goats.* Sometimes connected with demons (see note on 13:21).
34:15 *owl ... falcons.* Ceremonially unclean (see v. 11 and note; Dt 14:13,15–17).

34:15 c Dt 14:13
34:16 d Isa 30:8
e Isa 40:26; 48:13
f Isa 1:20; 58:14
g S Isa 1:20
34:17 h Isa 17:14;
Jer 13:25 i ver 10
35:1 j Isa 27:10;
32:15,16; 41:18-19
k Isa 27:6; 51:3
l SS 2:1
35:2 m S Ge 21:6;
Ps 105:43; Isa 12:6;
S 25:9; 44:23; 51:11;
52:9; 55:12
n S Ezr 3:7; S Isa 33:9
o SS 7:5
p S 1Ch 27:29;
Isa 65:10 q S Ex 16:7;
S Isa 4:5; S 59:19
r S Isa 25:9
35:3 s S Job 4:4;
Heb 12:12
35:4 t 2Ch 32:6;
Isa 40:2; Zec 1:13
u S Dt 20:3; S Isa 21:4
v S Jos 1:9; S Isa 7:4;
Da 10:19 w Isa 40:9,
10-11; 51:5; 62:11;
Rev 22:12 x S Isa 1:24;
S 34:8 y S Isa 25:9
35:5 z S Ps 146:8;
Jn 9:6-7; Ac 26:18
a Isa 29:18; 42:18;
50:4
35:6 b Mt 15:30;
Lk 7:22; Jn 5:8-9;
Ac 3:8 c S 2Sa 22:34
d Isa 32:4; Mt 9:32-
33; 12:22; Mk 7:35;
Lk 11:14 e Ps 20:5
f S Ex 17:6; Jn 7:38
35:7 g S Ps 68:6;
Isa 41:17; 44:3; 55:1
h Ps 107:35;
Isa 49:10; 58:11
i S Isa 13:22
j S Job 8:11; S 40:21
35:8 k S Isa 11:16;
S 33:8; S Jer 31:21;
Mt 7:13-14 l Isa 4:3;
1Pe 1:15 m Isa 52:1
35:9 n S Isa 30:6

there also the falcons e will gather,
    each with its mate.

¹⁶Look in the scroll d of the LORD and read:

None of these will be missing, e
    not one will lack her mate.
For it is his mouth f that has given the order, g
    and his Spirit will gather them together.
¹⁷ He allots their portions; h
    his hand distributes them by measure.
They will possess it forever
    and dwell there from generation to generation. i

JOY OF THE REDEEMED

35 The desert j and the parched land will be glad;
    the wilderness will rejoice and blossom. k
Like the crocus, l 2it will burst into bloom;
    it will rejoice greatly and shout for joy. m
The glory of Lebanon n will be given to it,
    the splendor of Carmel o and Sharon; p
they will see the glory q of the LORD,
    the splendor of our God. r

³Strengthen the feeble hands,
    steady the knees s that give way;
⁴say t to those with fearful hearts, u
    "Be strong, do not fear; v
your God will come, w
    he will come with vengeance; x
with divine retribution
    he will come to save y you."

⁵Then will the eyes of the blind be opened z
    and the ears of the deaf a unstopped.
⁶Then will the lame b leap like a deer, c
    and the mute tongue d shout for joy. e
Water will gush forth in the wilderness
    and streams f in the desert.
⁷The burning sand will become a pool,
    the thirsty ground g bubbling springs. h
In the haunts where jackals i once lay,
    grass and reeds j and papyrus will grow.

⁸And a highway k will be there;
    it will be called the Way of Holiness; l
it will be for those who walk that Way.
    The unclean m will not journey on it;
    wicked fools will not go about on it.
⁹No lion n will be there,

34:16 *scroll.* After the destruction of Edom, people will read this prophecy given by Isaiah. *these.* The creatures just listed.
34:17 *allots their portions.* God will give the creatures of vv. 11,13–15 clear title to the land of Edom.
35:1 *desert . . . will be glad.* The personification of nature is common in Isaiah (see 33:9; 44:23; 55:12). *wilderness.* The Arabah (see note on 33:9). *crocus.* See TNIV text note on SS 2:1.
35:2 *rejoice . . . shout for joy.* See 54:1 and note. *Lebanon . . . Carmel . . . Sharon.* Fertile areas renowned for their beautiful trees and foliage (see note on 33:9). *glory of the LORD.* In the great transformation just announced. See 6:3 and note.
35:3 See Heb 12:12.
35:4 *Be strong, do not fear.* Cf. God's words of encouragement to Joshua in Jos 1:6–7,9 (see note on Jos 1:18). *God will come.* Cf. 40:9–10. Similar language is used of the coming of the Messiah (see 62:11 and note; cf. Rev 22:12,20 and notes). *vengeance . . .*

retribution. See note on 34:8.
35:5 *eyes . . . ears.* See 29:18; 32:3; 42:7 and notes. Spiritual and physical healing are also linked together in Christ's ministry (see Lk 7:22 and note).
35:6 *lame leap . . . mute tongue shout.* Signs of the Messianic age (see Mt 12:22; Ac 3:7–8). *Water . . . streams.* See 32:2 and note. Cf. God's provision of water in Ex 17:6; 2Ki 3:15–20 (see note on 2Ki 3:17).
35:7 *springs.* Cf. 41:18. *reeds and papyrus.* Plants that grow in marshes and lakes (cf. 19:6–7).
35:8 *highway.* A road built up to make travel easier (see 11:16; 40:3 and notes). *the Way of Holiness.* The way set apart for those who are holy; only the redeemed (v. 9) could use it. In ancient times, certain roads between temples were open only to those who were ceremonially pure.
35:9 *lion . . . beast.* Sometimes wild animals made travel dan-

> nor any ravenous beast;[o]
>   they will not be found there.
> But only the redeemed[p] will walk there,
> 10   and those the LORD has rescued[q] will return.
> They will enter Zion with singing;[r]
>   everlasting joy[s] will crown their heads.
> Gladness[t] and joy will overtake them,
>   and sorrow and sighing will flee away.[u]

SENNACHERIB THREATENS JERUSALEM
36:1–22pp — 2Ki 18:13,17–37; 2Ch 32:9–19

36 In the fourteenth year of King Hezekiah's[v] reign, Sennacherib[w] king of Assyria attacked all the fortified cities of Judah and captured them.[x] ²Then the king of Assyria sent his field commander with a large army from Lachish[y] to King Hezekiah at Jerusalem. When the commander stopped at the aqueduct of the Upper Pool, on the road to the Launderer's Field,[z] ³Eliakim[a] son of Hilkiah the palace administrator,[b] Shebna[c] the secretary,[d] and Joah[e] son of Asaph the recorder[f] went out to him.

⁴The field commander said to them, "Tell Hezekiah:

" 'This is what the great king, the king of Assyria, says: On what are you basing this confidence of yours? ⁵You say you have counsel and might for war—but you speak only empty words. On whom are you depending, that you rebel[g] against me? ⁶Look, I know you are depending[h] on Egypt,[ij] that splintered reed[k] of a staff, which pierces the hand of anyone who leans on it! Such is Pharaoh king of Egypt to all who depend on him. ⁷But if you say to me, "We are depending[l] on the LORD our God"— isn't he the one whose high places and altars Hezekiah removed,[m] saying to Judah and Jerusalem, "You must worship before this altar"?[n]

⁸" 'Come now, make a bargain with my master, the king of Assyria: I will give you two thousand horses[o]—if you can put riders on them! ⁹How then can you repulse one officer of the least of my master's officials, even though you are depending on Egypt[p] for chariots[q] and horsemen[a]? [r] ¹⁰Furthermore, have I come to attack and destroy this land without the LORD? The LORD himself told[s] me to march against this country and destroy it.' "

¹¹Then Eliakim, Shebna and Joah[t] said to the field commander, "Please speak to your servants in Aramaic,[u] since we understand it. Don't speak to us in Hebrew in the hearing of the people on the wall."

---

[a] 9 Or *charioteers*

Right margin cross-references

35:9 [o] Isa 11:6;
13:22; 34:14
[p] S Ex 6:6; Lev 25:47-
55; Isa 51:11; 62:12;
63:4
35:10 [q] S Job 19:25;
S Isa 1:27 [r] Isa 30:29
[s] S Ps 4:7; S 126:5;
S Isa 25:9 [t] S Ps 51:8;
S Isa 51:3
[u] S Isa 30:19;
Rev 7:17; 21:4
36:1 [v] S 2Ki 18:9
[w] S 2Ch 32:1
[x] S Ps 109:11
36:2 [y] S Jos 10:3
[z] S Isa 7:3
36:3 [a] Isa 22:20-21;
37:2 [b] S Ge 41:40
[c] S 2Ki 18:18
[d] S 2Sa 8:17 [e] ver 11
[f] S 2Sa 8:16
36:5 [g] S 2Ki 18:7
36:6 [h] S 2Ki 17:4;
S Isa 8:12 [i] Eze 17:17
[j] S Isa 30:2,5
[k] Isa 42:3; 58:5;
Eze 29:6-7
36:7 [l] Ps 22:8;
Mt 27:43 [m] S 2Ki 18:4
[n] Dt 12:2-5;
S 2Ch 31:1
36:8 [o] S Ps 20:7;
S Isa 30:16
36:9 [p] S Isa 31:3
[q] Isa 37:24
[r] S Ps 20:7; Isa 30:2-5
36:10 [s] S 1Ki 13:18;
Isa 10:5-7
36:11 [t] ver 3
[u] S Ezr 4:7

Bottom notes

gerous (see Dt 8:15; Jdg 14:5 and note). *redeemed.* Those the Lord has delivered from bondage (cf. 1:27; 51:10; 62:12; Ex 6:6–8 and notes; Lev 25:47–48; Dt 7:8).

35:10 Repeated in 51:11. *enter Zion with singing.* As the Israelites did when they returned from Babylonian exile (see introduction to Ps 126). *overtake them.* They will be pursued, not by wild animals (v. 9), but by gladness and joy (cf. Ps 23:6 and note). *sorrow … will flee.* Cf. 25:8; 65:19.

36:1—39:8 Much of chs. 36–39 is paralleled, sometimes verbatim, in 2Ki 18:13—20:19 (see notes there). The compiler of 2 Kings may have used Isa 36–39 as one of his sources, or both may have drawn on a common source. Chs. 36–37 describe the fulfillment of many predictions about Assyria's collapse, while chs. 38–39 point toward the Babylonian context of chs. 40–66.

36:1 *fourteenth year of … Hezekiah's reign.* 701 B.C., the 14th year of his sole reign. Hezekiah ruled as sole king from 715 to 686 but was a coregent from c. 729 (see note on 2Ki 18:1). *Sennacherib.* Reigned over Assyria from 705 to 681 (see chart, p. 482). *all the … cities.* In his annals Sennacherib lists 46 such cities (see note on 2Ki 18:13).

36:2 *large army.* Cf. 37:36 and note. *Lachish.* An important city about 30 miles southwest of Jerusalem that guarded the main approach to Judah's capital from that quarter (see Jer 34:7 and note). *aqueduct … Field.* See 7:3 and note; see also note on 2Ki 18:17.

36:3 *Eliakim.* See 22:20–21 and notes. *palace administrator.* In charge of the palace (see 22:15 and note). *Shebna.* See 22:15

and note. *secretary.* Perhaps equivalent to secretary of state (see Jer 36:12; see also note on 2Sa 8:17). *recorder.* An official position also associated elsewhere with "secretary" (see 1Ki 4:3). See also note on 2Sa 8:16.

36:4,13 *great king.* See note on 2Ki 18:19.

36:5 *rebel.* By refusing to pay the expected tribute (see 2Ki 17:4; 18:7 and note).

36:6,9 *depending on Egypt.* Cf. 10:20.

36:6 *Egypt.* Hezekiah had been under pressure to make an alliance with Egypt since 715 B.C. or earlier (see 20:5; 30:1 and notes). *splintered reed.* Egypt is compared to a reed again in Eze 29:6–7 (see note on 29:6). *Such is Pharaoh.* Cf. 30:3,7.

36:7 *high places and altars.* Hezekiah had destroyed these popular shrines often dedicated to Baal worship (see note on 2Ki 18:4; see also 2Ch 31:1). *this altar.* In Solomon's temple.

36:8 *two thousand horses.* A sizable number for any army. Horses and chariots were highly prized (see note on 30:16). *if you can put riders on them!* See note on 2Ki 18:23. *riders.* Probably charioteers, since cavalry was not employed by these nations this early (see v. 9).

36:10 *The LORD … told me.* The Lord had used Assyria to punish Israel (see 10:5–6), but now it was Assyria's turn to be judged. Pharaoh Necho claimed God's approval on his mission according to 2Ch 35:21.

36:11 *Eliakim … Joah.* See v. 3 and note. *Aramaic.* The diplomatic language of that day (see note on 2Ki 18:26). *Don't speak*

36:12 ʸ 2Ki 6:25;
Eze 4:12
36:13 ʷ S 2Ch 32:18
ˣ Isa 37:4
36:14 ʸ S 2Ch 32:15
36:15 ᶻ S Ps 3:2,7
ᵃ Isa 37:10
36:16 ᵇ S 1Ki 4:25
ᶜ Pr 5:15
36:17 ᵈ S 2Ki 15:29
ᵉ S Ge 27:28;
S Dt 28:51
36:19 ᶠ S 2Ki 18:34
ᵍ S 2Ki 17:24
ʰ S 2Ki 15:29
36:20 ⁱ S 1Ki 20:23
/ Ex 5:2; 2Ch 25:15;
Isa 10:8-11; 37:10-13,
18-20; 40:18; Da 3:15
36:21 ᵏ Pr 9:7-8;
S 26:4
36:22 ˡ S 2Ki 18:18
ᵐ S 2Sa 8:16
ⁿ S Ge 37:29;
S 2Ch 34:19
37:1 ᵒ S Ge 37:29;
S 2Ch 34:19
ᵖ S Ge 37:34
ᑫ S ver 14; S 1Ki 8:33;
Mt 21:13
37:2 ʳ S 2Ki 18:18;
S Isa 36:3
ˢ S 2Ki 18:18 ᵗver 21;
Isa 1:1; S 13:1; 38:1
37:3 ᵘ S Jdg 6:2;
S Isa 5:30 ᵛ Isa 26:18;
66:9; Hos 13:13
37:4 ʷ ver 23-24;
S 2Ch 32:17
ˣ S Jos 3:10
ʸ Isa 36:13,18-20
ᶻ S 1Sa 7:8 ᵃ S Isa 1:9;
Am 7:2
37:6 ᵇ S Jos 1:9;
S Isa 7:4 ᶜ S Nu 15:30
37:7 ᵈ ver 9
ᵉ 1Ch 5:26 ᶠ S Isa 31:8
37:8 ᵍ S Jos 10:3
ʰ S Nu 33:20

¹²But the commander replied, "Was it only to your master and you that my master sent me to say these things, and not to the people sitting on the wall—who, like you, will have to eat their own excrement and drink their own urine? ᵛ"

¹³Then the commander stood and called out in Hebrew, ʷ "Hear the words of the great king, the king of Assyria! ˣ ¹⁴This is what the king says: Do not let Hezekiah deceive ʸ you. He cannot deliver you! ¹⁵Do not let Hezekiah persuade you to trust in the Lᴏʀᴅ when he says, 'The Lᴏʀᴅ will surely deliver ᶻ us; this city will not be given into the hand of the king of Assyria.' ᵃ

¹⁶"Do not listen to Hezekiah. This is what the king of Assyria says: Make peace with me and come out to me. Then every one of you will eat from your own vine and fig tree ᵇ and drink water from your own cistern, ᶜ ¹⁷until I come and take you to a land like your own ᵈ— a land of grain and new wine, ᵉ a land of bread and vineyards.

¹⁸"Do not let Hezekiah mislead you when he says, 'The Lᴏʀᴅ will deliver us.' Have the gods of any nations ever delivered their lands from the hand of the king of Assyria? ¹⁹Where are the gods of Hamath and Arpad? ᶠ Where are the gods of Sepharvaim? ᵍ Have they rescued Samaria ʰ from my hand? ²⁰Who of all the gods ⁱ of these countries have been able to save their lands from me? How then can the Lᴏʀᴅ deliver Jerusalem from my hand?" ʲ

²¹But the people remained silent and said nothing in reply, because the king had commanded, "Do not answer him." ᵏ

²²Then Eliakim ˡ son of Hilkiah the palace administrator, Shebna the secretary and Joah son of Asaph the recorder ᵐ went to Hezekiah, with their clothes torn, ⁿ and told him what the field commander had said.

JERUSALEM'S DELIVERANCE FORETOLD

37:1–13pp — 2Ki 19:1–13

37

When King Hezekiah heard this, he tore his clothes ᵒ and put on sackcloth ᵖ and went into the temple ᑫ of the Lᴏʀᴅ. ²He sent Eliakim ʳ the palace administrator, Shebna ˢ the secretary, and the leading priests, all wearing sackcloth, to the prophet Isaiah son of Amoz. ᵗ ³They told him, "This is what Hezekiah says: This day is a day of distress ᵘ and rebuke and disgrace, as when children come to the moment of birth ᵛ and there is no strength to deliver them. ⁴It may be that the Lᴏʀᴅ your God will hear the words of the field commander, whom his master, the king of Assyria, has sent to ridicule ʷ the living God, ˣ and that he will rebuke him for the words the Lᴏʀᴅ your God has heard. ʸ Therefore pray ᶻ for the remnant ᵃ that still survives."

⁵When King Hezekiah's officials came to Isaiah, ⁶Isaiah said to them, "Tell your master, 'This is what the Lᴏʀᴅ says: Do not be afraid ᵇ of what you have heard—those words with which the underlings of the king of Assyria have blasphemed ᶜ me. ⁷Listen! When he hears a certain report, ᵈ I will make him want ᵉ to return to his own country, and there I will have him cut down ᶠ with the sword.' "

⁸When the field commander heard that the king of Assyria had left Lachish, ᵍ he withdrew and found the king fighting against Libnah. ʰ

… *in Hebrew.* The officials feared that the commander's speech might damage the people's morale.

36:12 *eat…excrement…drink…urine.* A crude way of describing the horrors of famine if Jerusalem were to be besieged (cf. 2Ki 6:25 and note). Contrast v. 16 (see note there).

36:14 *deceive you.* Cf. 37:10 and note.

36:16 *own vine and fig tree.* Symbols of security and prosperity in the best of times (see 1Ki 4:25; Mic 4:4 and note; Zec 3:10 and note).

36:17 *come and take you.* The Assyrians deported rebellious peoples to reduce their will to revolt (see 2Ki 15:29; 17:6 and notes). *grain and new wine.* Two of the staples of Israel (cf. Dt 28:51; Hag 1:11 and note).

36:18–20 The commander's words echo the boasts of the proud Assyrians in 10:8–11. See note on 2Ki 18:33–35.

36:19 *Hamath and Arpad.* See 10:9 and note. *Sepharvaim.* Probably located in northern Aram (Syria) not far from Hamath. Residents of Sepharvaim were deported to Samaria, though they still worshiped the gods Adrammelek and Anammelek. See 2Ki 17:24,31 and note on 17:24. *Samaria.* The Assyrians assumed that each people had its own gods and so did not associate the God of Judah with that of Samaria.

36:21 *people remained silent.* The Assyrians had hoped that the masterful psychology of vv. 4–20 would produce panic.

36:22 See v. 3 and note. *clothes torn.* See note on 2Ki 18:37.

37:1 *clothes…sackcloth.* See Ge 37:34 and note; see also note on 2Ki 18:37. *temple.* Designated as a place of prayer by Solomon (see 1Ki 8:33). The Assyrian references to Hezekiah's dependence on the Lord (36:7,15,18) were true (see note on 36:7).

37:2 *Eliakim…Shebna.* See note on 36:3. *leading priests.* See note on 2Ki 19:2. *Isaiah son of Amoz.* See note on 1:1. Prophet, priests and king join in supplication.

37:3 *day of distress.* See 5:30; 26:16; 33:2 and notes. *moment of birth.* An even more vivid description than that of the pains of childbirth (see 13:8 and note).

37:4 *ridicule.* See vv. 17,23–24. *pray.* See note on 2Ki 19:4. *remnant.* Jerusalem was left almost alone (see 36:1 and notes on 1:9; 2Ki 19:4; see also 10:20–22 and note).

37:6 *Do not be afraid.* Cf. 7:4; see 35:4 and note.

37:7 *report.* See note on 2Ki 19:7. *return…cut down with the sword.* See vv. 37–38 and note on v. 38.

37:8 *Lachish.* See note on 36:2. *Libnah.* See note on 2Ki 8:22; see also Jos 10:31.

⁹Now Sennacherib[i] received a report[j] that Tirhakah, the king of Cush,[a][k] was marching out to fight against him. When he heard it, he sent messengers to Hezekiah with this word: ¹⁰"Say to Hezekiah king of Judah: Do not let the god you depend on deceive[l] you when he says, 'Jerusalem will not be given into the hands of the king of Assyria.'[m] ¹¹Surely you have heard what the kings of Assyria have done to all the countries, destroying them completely. And will you be delivered?[n] ¹²Did the gods of the nations that were destroyed by my ancestors[o] deliver them—the gods of Gozan, Harran,[p] Rezeph and the people of Eden[q] who were in Tel Assar? ¹³Where is the king of Hamath or the king of Arpad?[r] Where are the kings of Lair, Sepharvaim,[s] Hena and Ivvah?"[t]

HEZEKIAH'S PRAYER

37:14–20pp — 2Ki 19:14–19

¹⁴Hezekiah received the letter[u] from the messengers and read it. Then he went up to the temple[v] of the LORD and spread it out before the LORD. ¹⁵And Hezekiah prayed[w] to the LORD: ¹⁶"LORD Almighty, the God of Israel, enthroned[x] between the cherubim,[y] you alone are God[z] over all the kingdoms[a] of the earth. You have made heaven and earth.[b] ¹⁷Give ear, LORD, and hear;[c] open your eyes, LORD, and see;[d] listen to all the words Sennacherib[e] has sent to ridicule[f] the living God.[g]

¹⁸"It is true, LORD, that the Assyrian kings have laid waste all these peoples and their lands.[h] ¹⁹They have thrown their gods into the fire[i] and destroyed them,[j] for they were not gods[k] but only wood and stone, fashioned by human hands.[l] ²⁰Now, LORD our God, deliver[m] us from his hand, so that all the kingdoms of the earth[n] may know that you, LORD, are the only God.[b][o]"

SENNACHERIB'S FALL

37:21–38pp — 2Ki 19:20–37; 2Ch 32:20–21

²¹Then Isaiah son of Amoz[p] sent a message to Hezekiah: "This is what the LORD, the God of Israel, says: Because you have prayed to me concerning Sennacherib king of Assyria, ²²this is the word the LORD has spoken against him:

"Virgin Daughter[q] Zion[r]
  despises and mocks you.
Daughter Jerusalem
  tosses her head[s] as you flee.
²³Who is it you have ridiculed and blasphemed?[t]
  Against whom have you raised your voice[u]
and lifted your eyes in pride?[v]
  Against the Holy One[w] of Israel!
²⁴By your messengers
  you have ridiculed the Lord.
And you have said,
  'With my many chariots[x]

---

[a] 9 That is, the upper Nile region   [b] 20 Dead Sea Scrolls (see also 2 Kings 19:19); Masoretic Text *you alone are the LORD*

37:9 [i] S 2Ch 32:1
/ ver 7 [k] S Isa 20:3
37:10 [l] 2Ch 32:11,15
[m] Isa 36:15
37:11 [n] Isa 36:18-20
37:12 [o] 2Ki 18:11
[p] Ge 11:31; 12:1-4;
Ac 7:2 [q] Eze 27:23;
Am 1:5
37:13 [r] Isa 10:9
[s] 2Ki 17:24
[t] S Isa 36:20
37:14 [u] 2Ch 32:17
[v] ver 1,38; S 1Ki 8:33
37:15 [w] S 2Ch 32:20
37:16 [x] S Ps 2:4
[y] S Ge 3:24 [z] Dt 10:17;
136:2-3 [a] Da 4:34
[b] S Ge 1:1; S Isa 11:12;
41:9; 43:6; Ac 4:24
37:17 [c] S 1Ki 8:29;
S 2Ch 6:40
[d] Jer 25:29; Da 9:18
[e] S 2Ch 32:1
[f] S 2Ch 32:17
[g] S Jos 3:10
37:18 [h] S 2Ki 15:29;
Na 2:11-12
37:19 [i] S Jos 7:15
[j] S Jer 43:12,13
[k] 2Ch 13:9; Isa 40:17;
41:24,29; Jer 2:11;
5:7; 16:20; Gal 4:8
[l] S 2Ch 32:19;
S Ps 135:15;
Isa 40:18-20; 44:9-11
37:20 [m] S Ps 3:2,7;
S Pr 20:22
[n] S Jos 4:24
[o] S 1Sa 17:46;
S Ps 46:10
37:21 [p] S ver 2
37:22 [q] S Isa 23:12
[r] S Isa 10:32
[s] S Job 16:4
37:23 [t] ver 4;
S Nu 15:30; Isa 52:5;
Eze 36:20,23;
Da 7:25 [u] S Job 15:25
[v] S Isa 2:11
[w] S Isa 1:4; S 12:6
37:24 [x] Isa 36:9

37:9 *Tirhakah, the king of Cush.* In 701 B.C. he was actually a prince (the "lieutenant" of the new pharaoh Shebitku, who sent him with an army to help Hezekiah withstand the Assyrian invasion); he did not become king until 690. But this part of Isaiah was not written before 681 (see note on v. 38), so it was natural at that time to speak of Tirhakah as king. See 18:1 and note.
37:10 *god … deceive.* See 36:14–15. The message of vv. 10–13 is similar to that of 36:18–20 (see note there).
37:12 *Gozan.* A city in northern Mesopotamia to which some of the Israelites had been deported by the Assyrians (see 2Ki 17:6 and note). *Harran.* A city west of Gozan where Abraham lived for a number of years (see Ge 11:31 and note). *Rezeph.* A city between Harran and the Euphrates River. *Eden.* The state of Bit Adini, located between the Euphrates and Balikh rivers (see note on 2Ki 19:12).
37:13 *Hamath … Arpad.* See 10:9 and note. *Sepharvaim.* See 36:19; 2Ki 17:24 and note.
37:14 *temple.* See v. 1 and note. *spread it out.* Contrast the hypocritical spreading out of hands to pray in 1:15 (see note on 1:11–15).

37:16 *LORD Almighty.* See 13:4 and note. *enthroned … cherubim.* See notes on 1Sa 4:4; 2Sa 6:2. *all the kingdoms.* Cf. 40:17 and note. *made heaven and earth.* The role of God as Creator is emphasized also in 40:26,28; 42:5; 45:12 (see note on 40:21).
37:17 *Give ear … open your eyes.* Cf. Solomon's prayer in 1Ki 8:52; 2Ch 6:40. *ridicule the living God.* See v. 4 and note.
37:19 *not gods.* See 36:19 and note. *wood and stone.* Cf. 2:8; 44:9–20 and notes.
37:20 *that all the kingdoms of the earth may know.* See note on 2Ki 19:19. *you … are the only God.* Cf. v.16; 43:11; 45:18,21–22; see note on Ex 20:3; see also note and TNIV text note on Dt 6:4.
37:22 *Virgin Daughter Zion … Daughter Jerusalem.* A personification of Jerusalem (see note on 2Ki 19:21). *tosses her head.* A gesture of mocking (see Ps 22:7; 44:14 and notes).
37:23 *lifted … in pride.* Assyria's great pride had been condemned earlier (see 10:12 and note). *Holy One of Israel.* A designation of the God of Israel characteristic of Isaiah (see 1:4 and note).
37:24 *many chariots.* See 36:8 and note. *ascended the heights.* Cf. the words of the king of Babylon in 14:13–14. *Lebanon.* See

37:24 ʸ Isa 14:13
ᶻ S 1Ki 7:2; S Isa 14:8;
S 33:9 ᵃ 1Ki 5:8-10;
Isa 41:19; 55:13;
60:13; Hos 14:8
37:25 ᵇ S Isa 19:6;
44:27 ᶜ S Dt 11:10;
S Isa 10:14; Da 4:30
37:26 ᵈ Ac 2:23;
4:27-28; 1Pe 2:8
ᵉ Isa 10:6; S 25:1
ᶠ S Dt 13:16;
S Isa 25:2
37:27 ᵍ S Isa 15:6
ʰ Ps 129:6
37:28 ⁱ Ps 139:1-3
ʲ Ps 2:1
37:29 ᵏ Isa 10:12
ˡ S 2Ch 33:11
ᵐ S Job 40:24
ⁿ ver 34
37:30 ᵒ S Isa 20:3
ᵖ Isa 32:10
�q S Isa 16:14
ʳ S Lev 25:4
ˢ Ps 107:37; Isa 30:23;
65:21; Jer 31:5
37:31 ᵗ Isa 11:10
ᵘ S Isa 27:6
37:32 ᵛ S Isa 11:11
ʷ S Isa 1:9 ˣ S Isa 9:7
37:33 ʸ S Isa 32:18

I have ascended the heights of the mountains,
　　the utmost heights ʸ of Lebanon. ᶻ
I have cut down its tallest cedars,
　　the choicest of its junipers. ᵃ
I have reached its remotest heights,
　　the finest of its forests.
²⁵ I have dug wells in foreign lands ᵃ
　　and drunk the water there.
With the soles of my feet
　　I have dried up ᵇ all the streams of Egypt. ᶜ'

²⁶ "Have you not heard?
　　Long ago I ordained ᵈ it.
In days of old I planned ᵉ it;
　　now I have brought it to pass,
that you have turned fortified cities
　　into piles of stone. ᶠ
²⁷ Their people, drained of power,
　　are dismayed and put to shame.
They are like plants in the field,
　　like tender green shoots,
like grass ᵍ sprouting on the roof, ʰ
　　scorched ᵇ before it grows up.

²⁸ "But I know where you are
　　and when you come and go ⁱ
　　and how you rage ʲ against me.
²⁹ Because you rage against me
　　and because your insolence ᵏ has reached my ears,
I will put my hook ˡ in your nose ᵐ
　　and my bit in your mouth,
and I will make you return
　　by the way you came. ⁿ

³⁰ "This will be the sign ᵒ for you, Hezekiah:

"This year ᵖ you will eat what grows by itself,
　　and the second year what springs from that.
But in the third year q sow and reap,
　　plant vineyards ʳ and eat their fruit. ˢ
³¹ Once more a remnant of the house of Judah
　　will take root ᵗ below and bear fruit ᵘ above.
³² For out of Jerusalem will come a remnant, ᵛ
　　and out of Mount Zion a band of survivors. ʷ
The zeal ˣ of the LORD Almighty
　　will accomplish this.

³³ "Therefore this is what the LORD says concerning the king of Assyria:

"He will not enter this city ʸ
　　or shoot an arrow here.

ᵃ 25 Dead Sea Scrolls (see also 2 Kings 19:24); Masoretic Text does not have *in foreign lands.*
ᵇ 27 Some manuscripts of the Masoretic Text, Dead Sea Scrolls and some Septuagint manuscripts (see also 2 Kings 19:26); most manuscripts of the Masoretic Text *roof / and terraced fields*

33:9; 35:2 and notes. *cut down . . . cedars.* For many centuries the kings of Mesopotamia had used the cedars of Lebanon in their royal buildings (see notes on 2:13; 9:10; 14:8; cf. 1Ki 5:8–10).
37:25 *dug wells.* Desert lands could not stop him. *dried up all the streams.* The branches of the Nile were no obstacle, either. This boast was almost a claim to deity. See 11:15; 44:27 and notes.
37:26 *ordained . . . planned . . . brought it to pass.* See Ps 33:10–11. Cf. 40:21 and note. *cities into piles of stone.* Assyria had been God's tool of judgment against the nations (see 10:5–6 and note on 10:5).
37:27 See 40:6–8 and notes; Ps 37:1–2. *grass . . . on the roof.* Roofs in the Near East were flat (cf. 2Sa 11:2 and note).

37 **37:29** *hook in your nose.* The Assyrians often led away captives by tying ropes to rings placed in their noses (see note on 2Ki 19:28). *bit.* Cf. 30:28.
37:30 *sign.* See 7:11,14 and notes. *what grows by itself.* See note on 2Ki 19:29. *second . . . third year.* See note on 2Ki 19:29. Probably the second year was to begin shortly, so the total time was less than 36 months. Another three-year sign was given in 20:3. *plant vineyards and eat.* The response to Assyria's proposal in 36:16 (see note there).
37:31–32 *remnant.* See notes on v. 4; 1:9; 2Ki 19:4,30–31.
37:31 *take root . . . bear fruit.* See 4:2; 11:1,10; 27:6 and notes.
37:32 *The zeal . . . this.* See 9:7 and note.

He will not come before it with shield
    or build a siege ramp[z] against it.
[34]By the way that he came he will return;[a]
    he will not enter this city,"

        declares the LORD.

[35]"I will defend[b] this city and save it,
    for my sake[c] and for the sake of David[d] my servant!"

[36]Then the angel[e] of the LORD went out and put to death[f] a hundred and eighty-five thousand in the Assyrian[g] camp. When the people got up the next morning—there were all the dead bodies! [37]So Sennacherib[h] king of Assyria broke camp and withdrew. He returned to Nineveh[i] and stayed there.

[38]One day, while he was worshiping in the temple[j] of his god Nisrok, his sons Adrammelek and Sharezer killed him with the sword, and they escaped to the land of Ararat.[k] And Esarhaddon[l] his son succeeded him as king.[m]

HEZEKIAH'S ILLNESS
38:1–8pp — 2Ki 20:1–11; 2Ch 32:24–26

38 In those days Hezekiah became ill and was at the point of death. The prophet Isaiah son of Amoz[n] went to him and said, "This is what the LORD says: Put your house in order,[o] because you are going to die; you will not recover."[p]
[2]Hezekiah turned his face to the wall and prayed to the LORD, [3]"Remember, LORD, how I have walked[q] before you faithfully and with wholehearted devotion[r] and have done what is good in your eyes.[s]" And Hezekiah wept[t] bitterly.

[4]Then the word[u] of the LORD came to Isaiah: [5]"Go and tell Hezekiah, 'This is what the LORD, the God of your father David,[v] says: I have heard your prayer and seen your tears;[w] I will add fifteen years[x] to your life. [6]And I will deliver you and this city from the hand of the king of Assyria. I will defend[y] this city.

[7]"'This is the LORD's sign[z] to you that the LORD will do what he has promised: [8]I will make the shadow cast by the sun go back the ten steps it has gone down on the stairway of Ahaz.'" So the sunlight went back the ten steps it had gone down.[a]

[9]A writing of Hezekiah king of Judah after his illness and recovery:

[10]I said, "In the prime of my life[b]
    must I go through the gates of death[c]
    and be robbed of the rest of my years?[d]"
[11]I said, "I will not again see the LORD,
    the LORD,[e] in the land of the living;[f]
no longer will I look on my fellow mortals,
    or be with those who now dwell in this world.
[12]Like a shepherd's tent[g] my house
    has been pulled down[h] and taken from me.

37:33 [z] S 2Sa 20:15
37:34 [a] ver 29
37:35 [b] S Isa 31:5
[c] Isa 43:25; 48:9,11;
Eze 36:21-22
[d] S 1Ch 17:19
37:36 [e] S Ex 12:23
[f] S Ex 12:12
[g] S Isa 10:12
37:37 [h] S 2Ch 32:1
[i] S Ge 10:11; S Na 1:1
37:38 [j] S ver 14
[k] Ge 8:4; Jer 51:27
[l] S 2Ki 17:24
[m] S Isa 9:4; 10:26;
S 14:25
38:1 [n] S Isa 37:2
[o] 2Sa 17:23 [p] 2Ki 8:10
38:3 [q] S Ps 26:3
[r] S 1Ki 8:61;
S 1Ch 29:19
[s] S Dt 6:18; S 10:20
[t] Ps 6:8
38:4 [u] Isa 13:13;
Isa 39:5
38:5 [v] 2Ki 18:3
[w] Ps 6:6 [x] S 2Ki 18:2
38:6 [y] S Isa 31:5
[z] S Ge 24:14;
S 2Ch 32:31; Isa 7:11,
14; S 20:3
38:8 [a] Jos 10:13
38:10 [b] Ps 102:24
[c] S Job 17:16;
Ps 107:18; 2Co 1:9
[d] S Job 17:11
38:11 [e] S Isa 12:2
[f] S Job 28:13;
S Ps 116:9
38:12 [g] Isa 33:20;
2Co 5:1,4; 2Pe 1:13-
14 [h] S Job 4:21

37:33 *siege ramp.* To help the invaders bring up battering rams and scale the walls (see 2Sa 20:15).
37:35 *sake of David.* God had promised David an enduring throne in Jerusalem (see 9:7; 55:3; 2Sa 7:16 and notes). *my servant.* See note on 41:8–9.
37:36 *angel of the LORD … put to death.* The Lord often sent his angel as his agent to bring plagues. Cf. the striking down of the firstborn in Egypt (Ex 12:12–13) and the angel's sword poised against Jerusalem (see 2Sa 24:15–16 and note on 24:16; 1Ch 21:22, 27). The Greek historian Herodotus attributed this destruction to a bubonic plague. The death of these soldiers fulfills the prophecies of 10:33–34 (see notes there); 30:31; 31:8 (see note there).
37:37 *Nineveh.* The capital of Assyria (see Jnh 1:2 and note).
37:38 *in the temple.* Hezekiah had gone to the Lord's temple and gained strength (vv. 1,14). Twenty years later (681 B.C.) Sennacherib went to the temple of his god and was killed (see note on 2Ki 19:37). *Ararat.* Urartu, north of Assyria in Armenia (see note on Ge 8:4). *Esarhaddon.* Reigned 681–669 (see chart, p. 482; see also 2Ki 19:37 and note; Ezr 4:2).
38:1 *In those days.* Sometime before Sennacherib's invasion of 701 B.C. (see v. 6). *Isaiah.* He is prominent in this historical inter-

lude (chs. 36–39). *Put your house in order.* See note on 2Ki 20:1. *you are going to die.* See note on 2Ki 20:1. Elisha similarly predicted the death of Ben-Hadad (see 2Ki 8:9–10 and notes). *you will not recover.* See v. 21 and note.
38:2 *wall.* Perhaps of the nearby temple. *prayed.* Hezekiah apparently had no son and successor to the throne yet (cf. 39:7; 2Ki 21:1 and note).
38:3 *wholehearted devotion.* Like David (1Ki 11:4), Hezekiah was truly faithful (see 36:7; 2Ki 18:3–5 and notes).
38:6 *deliver … this city.* See 31:5; 37:35 and notes.
38:7 *sign.* See 7:11,14 and notes.
38:8 *stairway of Ahaz.* See note on 2Ki 20:11. *sunlight went back.* Perhaps the miracle involved the refraction of light. See 2Ki 20:9–11; Jos 10:12–14 and note on 10:13.
38:10–20 A hymn of thanksgiving in two stanzas, similar to many of the psalms. Hezekiah was deeply interested in the psalms of David and Asaph (see 2Ch 29:30).
38:10–14 Hezekiah voices his complaint about his past affliction (v. 1).
38:11 *the LORD, the LORD.* See 26:4. *land of the living.* Cf. Ps 27:13 and note.

38:12 *i* S Isa 34:4;
Heb 1:12 *j* S Nu 11:15;
S Job 7:6; S Ps 31:22
k ver 13; Ps 32:4;
73:14
38:13 *l* S Ps 37:7
m S Job 9:17; Ps 51:8
n S Job 10:16;
Jer 34:17; La 3:4;
Da 6:24 *o* S ver 12
38:14 *p* S Ge 8:8;
S Isa 59:11 *q* S Ps 6:7
r S Ge 50:24;
S Job 17:3
38:15 *s* 2Sa 7:20
t S Ps 39:9 *u* 1Ki 21:27
v S Job 7:11
38:16 *w* Ps 119:25;
Heb 12:9
38:17 *x* Ro 8:28;
Heb 12:11 *y* S Job 7:11;
Ps 119:71,75
z S Job 17:16;
S Ps 30:3 *a* Ps 103:3;
Jer 31:34
b S Ps 103:12;
Isa 43:25; Mic 7:19
38:18 *c* S Nu 16:30;
S Ecc 9:10 *d* Ps 6:5;
88:10-11; 115:17
e S Ps 30:9
38:19 *f* Ps 118:17;
119:175 *g* S Dt 11:19
38:20 *h* Ps 68:25
i S Ps 33:2; S 45:8
j Ps 23:6; S 63:4;
116:2 *k* Ps 116:17:19
38:22 *l* S 2Ch 32:31
39:1 *m* S 2Ch 32:31
39:2 *n* 2Ch 32:31

Like a weaver I have rolled *i* up my life,
  and he has cut me off from the loom; *j*
  day and night *k* you made an end of me.
[13] I waited patiently *l* till dawn,
  but like a lion he broke *m* all my bones; *n*
  day and night *o* you made an end of me.
[14] I cried like a swift or thrush,
  I moaned like a mourning dove. *p*
My eyes grew weak *q* as I looked to the heavens.
  I am being threatened; Lord, come to my aid!" *r*

[15] But what can I say? *s*
  He has spoken to me, and he himself has done this. *t*
I will walk humbly *u* all my years
  because of this anguish of my soul. *v*
[16] Lord, by such things people live;
  and my spirit finds life in them too.
You restored me to health
  and let me live. *w*
[17] Surely it was for my benefit *x*
  that I suffered such anguish. *y*
In your love you kept me
  from the pit *z* of destruction;
you have put all my sins *a*
  behind your back. *b*
[18] For the grave *c* cannot praise you,
  death cannot sing your praise; *d*
those who go down to the pit *e*
  cannot hope for your faithfulness.
[19] The living, the living—they praise *f* you,
  as I am doing today;
parents tell their children *g*
  about your faithfulness.

[20] The LORD will save me,
  and we will sing *h* with stringed instruments *i*
all the days of our lives *j*
  in the temple *k* of the LORD.

[21]Isaiah had said, "Prepare a poultice of figs and apply it to the boil, and he will recover."
[22]Hezekiah had asked, "What will be the sign *l* that I will go up to the temple of the LORD?"

ENVOYS FROM BABYLON
39:1–8pp — 2Ki 20:12–19

39 At that time Marduk-Baladan son of Baladan king of Babylon *m* sent Hezekiah letters and a gift, because he had heard of his illness and recovery. [2]Hezekiah received the envoys *n* gladly and showed them what was in his

---

38:12 *rolled up my life.* Cf. the rolling up of the sky like a scroll in 34:4 (see also Heb 1:12).
38:13 *broke all my bones.* Physical or spiritual distress is often described in terms of aching or broken bones (see Ps 6:2; 32:3).
38:15–20 Hezekiah offers praise for God's healing (see v. 5).
38:15 *what can I say?* Hezekiah wonders how he can praise God (cf. 2Sa 7:20).

38:16 *by such things.* Perhaps referring to God's promises and gracious acts, though his gracious acts can include such experiences as sickness and peril.

38:17 *pit of destruction.* The grave (see Ps 55:23 and note). *all my sins.* Physical and spiritual healing are sometimes linked together (see 53:4–5 and notes). *sins behind your back.* God not only puts our sins out of sight; he also puts them out of reach (Ps 103:12; Mic 7:19), out of mind (Jer 31:34) and out of existence (Isa 43:25; 44:22; Ps 51:1,9; Jer 50:20; Ac 3:19).

38:18 *cannot hope.* Knowledge about the afterlife was limited in the OT period, but the gospel of Christ has "brought ... immortality to light" (2Ti 1:10).
38:20 *sing with stringed instruments.* Instrumental music and hymns of praise were closely linked in worship (cf. Ps 33:1–3; 150). *all ... our lives in the temple.* Hezekiah, like David (Ps 23:6), loved God's house.

38:21 *Prepare ... apply.* The verbs are plural (probably addressed to the court physicians). *poultice of figs.* Figs were used for medicinal purposes in ancient Ugarit. *he will recover.* Contrast v. 1. God answered Hezekiah's prayer for healing (see v. 5).
38:22 *sign.* Perhaps the healing of the boil (see v. 21).
39:1 *Marduk-Baladan.* Reigned 721–710 B.C. and again later (see note on 2Ki 20:12). *Babylon.* See note on 13:1. *sent ... letters and a gift.* Marduk-Baladan probably wanted Hezekiah's support in a

storehouses—the silver, the gold, ^{o} the spices, the fine olive oil—his entire armory and everything found among his treasures. ^{p} There was nothing in his palace or in all his kingdom that Hezekiah did not show them.

³Then Isaiah the prophet went to King Hezekiah and asked, "What did those men say, and where did they come from?"

"From a distant land, ^{q}" Hezekiah replied. "They came to me from Babylon."

⁴The prophet asked, "What did they see in your palace?"

"They saw everything in my palace," Hezekiah said. "There is nothing among my treasures that I did not show them."

⁵Then Isaiah said to Hezekiah, "Hear the word ^{r} of the LORD Almighty: ⁶The time will surely come when everything in your palace, and all that your predecessors have stored up until this day, will be carried off to Babylon. ^{s} Nothing will be left, says the LORD. ⁷And some of your descendants, your own flesh and blood who will be born to you, will be taken away, and they will become eunuchs in the palace of the king of Babylon. ^{t}"

⁸"The word of the LORD you have spoken is good, ^{u}" Hezekiah replied. For he thought, "There will be peace and security in my lifetime. ^{v}"

COMFORT FOR GOD'S PEOPLE

40

Comfort, comfort ^{w} my people,
    says your God.
²Speak tenderly ^{x} to Jerusalem,
    and proclaim to her
that her hard service ^{y} has been completed, ^{z}
    that her sin has been paid for, ^{a}
that she has received from the LORD's hand
    double ^{b} for all her sins.

³A voice of one calling:
"In the wilderness prepare
    the way ^{c} for the LORD^a;
make straight ^{d} in the desert
    a highway for our God. $^{b\,e}$
⁴Every valley shall be raised up, ^{f}
    every mountain and hill ^{g} made low;
the rough ground shall become level, ^{h}
    the rugged places a plain.

^{a} 3 Or *A voice of one calling in the wilderness: / "Prepare the way for the LORD* ^{b} 3 Hebrew; Septuagint *make straight the paths of our God*

39:2 ^{o} S 2Ki 18:15
^{p} 2Ch 32:27-29
39:3 ^{q} S Dt 28:49
39:5 ^{r} S Isa 38:4
39:6 ^{s} S Jdg 6:4;
S 2Ki 24:13
39:7 ^{t} S 2Ki 24:15;
Da 1:1-7
39:8 ^{u} S Jdg 10:15;
Job 1:21; Ps 39:9
^{v} S 2Ch 32:26
40:1 ^{w} Isa 12:1;
49:13; 51:3,12; 52:9;
57:18; 61:2; 66:13;
Jer 31:13; Zep 3:14-17;
Zec 1:17; 2Co 1:3
40:2 ^{x} S Ge 34:3;
S Isa 35:4 ^{y} S Job 7:1
^{z} Isa 41:11-13; 49:25
^{a} S Lev 26:41
^{b} Isa 51:19; 61:7;
Jer 16:18; 17:18;
Zec 9:12; Rev 18:6
40:3 ^{c} S Isa 11:16;
43:19; Mal 3:1
^{d} S Pr 3:5-6
^{e} Mt 3:3*; Mk 1:3*;
Jn 1:23*
40:4 ^{f} Isa 49:11
^{g} S Isa 2:14
^{h} S Ps 26:12;
S Isa 26:7; 45:2,13;
Jer 31:9

---

campaign against Assyria. During his career he organized several revolts against his hated neighbors. See note on 2Ki 20:12.
39:2 *silver…gold…treasures.* See 2Ch 32:27–29,31 and notes. Probably Hezekiah was seeking help from the Babylonians against the Assyrian threat (see note on 2Ki 20:13). But the information gained during this ill-advised tour escorted by Hezekiah would be valuable to Marduk-Baladan's powerful successors (vv. 5–7).
39:3 *Isaiah the prophet.* Earlier God had sent Isaiah to confront Ahaz (7:3); cf. also Nathan's rebuke of David (see 2Sa 12:1,7 and note on 12:1).
39:5 *word of the LORD.* Contrast the word of hope in 38:4–6.
39:6 *carried off to Babylon.* The first mention of Babylon as Jerusalem's conqueror, though 14:3–4 implied the Babylonian exile (see notes there). The wickedness of Hezekiah's son Manasseh was a major cause of the captivity (see 2Ki 21:11–15). See also notes on 2Ki 20:17; 21:15.
39:7 *your descendants.* Such as King Jehoiachin (see 2Ki 24:15 and note). *eunuchs.* Cf. Da 1:3–6, where the Hebrew for "court officials" (Da 1:3) can also be translated "eunuchs." *king of Babylon.* Nebuchadnezzar.
39:8 *word…is good.* See note on 2Ki 20:19. *peace…in my lifetime.* See 2Ki 22:20 and note. "Peace" recurs in a refrain in 48:22; 57:21, dividing the last 27 chapters into 3 sections of 9 chapters each (40–48; 49–57; 58–66).
40:1—66:24 In chs. 1–35 Isaiah prophesied against the backdrop of the Assyrian threat against Judah and Jerusalem, in chs.

36–39 he recorded Assyria's failure and warned about the future rise of Babylon, and in chs. 40–66 he wrote as if the Babylonian exile of Judah were almost over (see Introduction: Author).
40:1 *Comfort, comfort.* That is, comfort greatly. The double imperative for emphasis is found also in 51:9,17; 52:1,11; 57:14; 62:10.
40:2 *Speak tenderly.* The Hebrew for this phrase is used also in 2Ch 32:6, where Hezekiah "encouraged" Judah to trust in God in spite of the Assyrian invasion. *hard service.* The exile in Babylon (cf. Ps 137:1–6; La 1:1–2,9,16–17,21). *sin…paid for.* By enduring the punishment of captivity (see Lev 26:41). *double.* Full (or enough) punishment. Cf. the "double calamities" of 51:19.
40:3–5 See 35:1–2 and note on 35:2.

40:3 *voice.* Three voices are mentioned (vv. 3,6,9), each showing how the comfort of v. 1 will come about. The NT links the voice of v. 3 with John the Baptist in Mt 3:3; Lk 3:4; Jn 1:23 (see notes there). *prepare the way.* Clear obstacles out of the road (cf. 57:14; 62:10). The language of vv. 3–4 has in view the ancient Near Eastern custom of sending representatives ahead to prepare the way for the visit of a monarch. The picture is that of preparing a processional highway for the Lord's coming to Jerusalem. In Mt 3:1–8 John declares that repentance is necessary to prepare the way for Christ. *make straight…a highway.* See 11:16; 35:8 and notes.
40:4 *rough ground…level.* See 26:7 and note.

40:5 *i* S Ex 16:7;
S Nu 14:21;
S Isa 59:19
j Isa 52:10; 62:2;
Lk 2:30; 3:4-6*
k S Isa 1:20; 58:14
40:6 *l* S Ge 6:3;
S Isa 29:5
40:7 *m* S Job 8:12;
S Isa 15:6
n S Ex 15:10;
S Job 41:21
o S Ps 103:16;
S Eze 22:21
40:8 *p* S Isa 5:24;
Jas 1:10 *q* Isa 55:11;
59:21 *r* S Pr 19:21;
S Isa 7:7, 9;
S Jer 39:16
s S Ps 119:89;
S Mt 5:18; 1Pe 1:24-
25*
40:9 *t* Isa 41:27;
44:28; 52:7-10; 61:1;
Na 1:15; S Ac 13:32;
Ro 10:15; 1Co 15:1-4
u S Isa 1:1 *v* Isa 25:9
40:10 *w* Isa 35:4;
59:20; Mt 21:5;
Rev 22:7 *x* Isa 28:2
y S Ps 44:3;
S Isa 30:30; S 33:2
z Isa 9:6-7
a S Isa 35:4;
Rev 22:12
40:11 *b* S Ge 48:15;
S Ps 28:9; S Mic 5:4;
S Jn 10:11 *c* S Nu 11:12
d S Dt 26:19
e Isa 49:10
f S Ge 33:13;
S Dt 30:4
40:12 *g* S Job 12:15;
S 38:10 *h* Pr 30:4
i S Job 38:5;
Heb 1:10-12
j S Job 38:18; Pr 16:11
40:13 *k* Isa 11:2; 42:1
l S Job 15:8;
Ro 11:34*; 1Co 2:16*
40:14 *m* Job 21:22;
Col 2:3 *n* S Job 12:13;
S 34:13; Isa 55:9
40:15 *o* S Ps 62:9
p S Dt 9:21; Isa 2:22

⁵And the glory *i* of the LORD will be revealed,
  and all people will see it together. *j*
          For the mouth of the LORD has spoken." *k*

⁶A voice says, "Cry out."
  And I said, "What shall I cry?"

"All people are like grass, *l*
  and all human faithfulness is like the flowers of the field.
⁷The grass withers *m* and the flowers fall,
  because the breath *n* of the LORD blows *o* on them.
  Surely the people are grass.
⁸The grass withers and the flowers *p* fall,
  but the word *q* of our God endures *r* forever. *s* "

⁹You who bring good news *t* to Zion,
  go up on a high mountain.
You who bring good news to Jerusalem, *a u*
  lift up your voice with a shout,
lift it up, do not be afraid;
  say to the towns of Judah,
  "Here is your God!" *v*
¹⁰See, the Sovereign LORD comes *w* with power, *x*
  and his arm *y* rules *z* for him.
See, his reward *a* is with him,
  and his recompense accompanies him.
¹¹He tends his flock like a shepherd: *b*
  He gathers the lambs in his arms *c*
and carries them close to his heart; *d*
  he gently leads *e* those that have young. *f*

¹²Who has measured the waters *g* in the hollow of his hand, *h*
  or with the breadth of his hand marked off the heavens? *i*
Who has held the dust of the earth in a basket,
  or weighed the mountains on the scales
  and the hills in a balance? *j*
¹³Who can fathom the Spirit *b k* of the LORD,
  or instruct the LORD as his counselor? *l*
¹⁴Whom did the LORD consult to enlighten him,
  and who taught him the right way?
Who was it that taught him knowledge, *m*
  or showed him the path of understanding? *n*

¹⁵Surely the nations are like a drop in a bucket;
  they are regarded as dust on the scales; *o*
  he weighs the islands as though they were fine dust. *p*

---

a 9 Or *Zion, bringer of good news, / go up on a high mountain. / Jerusalem, bringer of good news*
b 13 Or *mind*

40:5 *glory ... revealed.* God (through Cyrus, king of Persia) would redeem Israel from Babylon (see 35:9–10; 44:23–24), and all the nations would see the deliverance (see 52:10 and note; cf. Lk 3:6 and note). Ultimately the glory of the redeeming God would be seen in Jesus Christ (see Jn 1:14; 11:4; 17:4; Heb 1:3 and notes), especially at his return (Mt 16:27; 24:30; 25:31; Rev 1:7)—but also in the redeemed (see 1Co 10:31; 2Co 3:18; Eph 3:21 and notes). See also Isa 6:3 and note.

40:6,8 Quoted in part in 1Pe 1:24–25.

40:6 *like grass.* See 37:27 and note; 51:12. *all human faithfulness ... field.* Even the power of Assyria and Babylon would soon vanish.

40:8 *word of our God endures.* The plans and purposes of the nations will not prevail (see 8:10 and note).

40:9 *good news.* The news that God is leading his people back to Judah (vv. 10–11). He cares for his people and will redeem them (see 52:7–10; 61:1 and notes). The NT expands this "good news" or "gospel" to refer to the salvation that Christ brings

to all people (see 1Co 15:2–3 and notes). See TNIV text note for an alternative translation. *Here is your God!* The Lord is returning to Jerusalem (see v. 10). These words apply to the return from exile (see 52:7–9 and notes), the first coming of Christ (Mt 21:5) and the second coming of Christ (62:11; Rev 22:12). See 35:4 and note.

40:10 *arm rules.* Cf. 51:9; 59:16 and notes. He is characterized by both strength and gentleness (v. 11). *reward ... recompense.* His delivered people, the flock of v. 11 (see 62:11–12 and notes).

40:11 *tends his flock.* Cf. Jer 31:10; Eze 34:11–16 and notes.

40:12–31 Rhetorical questions are used to persuade the people to trust in the Lord, who has the ability to deliver, strengthen and restore his people.

40:12 *measured the waters.* See Job 28:25; 38:8. In Job 38–41 the Lord overwhelms Job with a description of his greatness. *marked off the heavens.* See 48:13 and note.

40:13 Quoted in Ro 11:34; 1Co 2:16. *counselor.* See 9:6 and note.

40:15 *nations ... a drop in a bucket.* See note on v. 6. *dust.* See 17:13 and note; 29:5.

¹⁶ Lebanon ^q is not sufficient for altar fires,
　　nor its animals ^r enough for burnt offerings.
¹⁷ Before him all the nations ^s are as nothing; ^t
　　they are regarded by him as worthless
　　and less than nothing. ^u

¹⁸ With whom, then, will you compare God? ^v
　　To what image ^w will you liken him?
¹⁹ As for an idol, ^x a metalworker casts it,
　　and a goldsmith ^y overlays it with gold ^z
　　and fashions silver chains for it.
²⁰ People too poor to present such an offering
　　select wood ^a that will not rot.
　　They look for a skilled worker
　　to set up an idol ^b that will not topple. ^c

²¹ Do you not know?
　　Have you not heard? ^d
　　Has it not been told ^e you from the beginning? ^f
　　Have you not understood ^g since the earth was founded? ^h
²² He sits enthroned ⁱ above the circle of the earth,
　　and its people are like grasshoppers. ^j
　　He stretches out the heavens ^k like a canopy, ^l
　　and spreads them out like a tent ^m to live in. ⁿ
²³ He brings princes ^o to naught
　　and reduces the rulers of this world to nothing. ^p
²⁴ No sooner are they planted,
　　no sooner are they sown,
　　no sooner do they take root ^q in the ground,
　　than he blows ^r on them and they wither, ^s
　　and a whirlwind sweeps them away like chaff. ^t

²⁵ "To whom will you compare me? ^u
　　Or who is my equal?" says the Holy One. ^v
²⁶ Lift up your eyes and look to the heavens: ^w
　　Who created ^x all these?
　　He who brings out the starry host ^y one by one,
　　and calls them each by name.
　　Because of his great power and mighty strength, ^z
　　not one of them is missing. ^a

²⁷ Why do you complain, Jacob?
　　Why do you say, Israel,
　　"My way is hidden from the LORD;
　　my cause is disregarded by my God"? ^b
²⁸ Do you not know?

40:16 ^q Isa 33:9;
37:24 ^r Ps 50:9-11;
Mic 6:7; Heb 10:5-9
40:17 ^s Isa 30:28
^t Job 12:19; Isa 29:7
^u S Isa 37:19; Da 4:35
40:18 ^v S Ex 8:10;
S 1Sa 2:2 ^w S Dt 4:15;
Ac 17:29
40:19 ^x S Ex 20:4;
Ps 115:4; S Isa 37:19;
42:17; Jer 2:8, 28;
10:8; 16:19; Hab 2:18;
Zec 10:2 ^y Isa 41:7;
46:6; Jer 10:3
^z Isa 2:20; 31:7
40:20 ^a Isa 44:19
^b S 1Sa 12:21
^c S 1Sa 5:3
40:21 ^d ver 28;
2Ki 19:25; Isa 41:22;
42:9; 44:8; 48:3, 5
^e Ps 19:1; 50:6;
Ac 14:17 ^f S Ge 1:1
^g Ro 1:19 ^h Isa 48:13;
51:13
40:22 ⁱ S 2Ch 6:18;
S Ps 2:4 ^j S Nu 13:33
^k S Ge 1:1; S Isa 48:13
^l S Ge 1:8; S Job 22:14
^m S Job 36:29
ⁿ S Job 26:7
40:23 ^o S Job 12:18;
S Isa 34:12
^p S Job 12:19; Am 2:3
40:24 ^q S Job 5:3
^r S 2Sa 22:16;
S Isa 11:4; 41:16
^s S Job 8:12; S 18:16
^t S Job 24:24;
S Isa 41:2
40:25 ^u S 1Sa 2:2;
S 1Ch 16:25 ^v Isa 1:4;
37:23
40:26 ^w Isa 51:6
^x ver 28; Ps 89:11-13;
Isa 42:5; 66:2
^y S 2Ki 17:16;
S Ne 9:6; S Job 38:32
^z S Job 9:4;
S Isa 45:24; Eph 1:19
^a S Isa 34:16
40:27 ^b S Job 6:29;
S 27:2; Lk 18:7-8

40:16 *Lebanon.* The wood of its cedar trees. *its animals.* Cf. Ps 104:16–18 and note. Sacrifices, however numerous, could never do justice to the greatness of God.

40:17 *nothing … worthless.* In spite of the temporary splendor they might possess (see 13:19 and note).

40:18–20 More than any other prophet, Isaiah shows the folly of worshiping idols. His sarcastic caricature, satire and denunciation of these false gods reach a peak in 44:9–20 (see notes there; see also 41:7,22–24; 42:17; 46:5–7; 48:5 and note).

40:18 *With whom … compare God?* See v. 25 and note; 46:5.

40:19 *metalworker … goldsmith.* See 41:7; 44:10–12. *gold … silver.* See 2:20; Hab 2:18–19 and notes.

40:20 *wood.* See 44:14–16,19 and notes. *that will not topple.* See 41:7; 46:7.

40:21 *from the beginning.* God's work as Creator is emphasized in the rest of the chapter (cf. 37:26; 41:4,26).

40:22 *sits enthroned.* Cf. 66:1; see 37:16 and note. *circle.* Or "horizon." See Job 22:14; Pr 8:27. *stretches out the heavens … like a*

tent. See 42:5; 44:24; 51:13; Ps 104:2; see also note on Ps 19:4b–6.
40:23 *princes … rulers … to nothing.* See v. 17; 2:22 and notes; cf. Jer 25:17–26; Da 2:21.
40:24 *whirlwind … like chaff.* See 17:13 and note; 41:15–16.
40:25 See v. 18. Apparently some Israelite doubters were comparing their God with the gods of their captors, and they believed that the Lord was failing the test. *Holy One.* See 1:4 and note.
40:26 *created.* See vv. 21–22 and notes. *brings out.* The Hebrew for this expression is used for bringing forth the constellations in Job 38:32. *starry host.* Also worshiped by the people (see 47:13; Jer 19:13 and note). *each by name.* See note on Ps 147:4–6. *not one … missing.* See 34:16 and note.

40:27–31 As in many psalms of praise, Isaiah now stresses the goodness of God after describing his majesty (vv. 12–26). Such a God is able to deliver and restore his distressed people if they will wait in faith for him to act. They are to trust in him and draw strength from him.
40:27 *way.* Condition. *hidden … disregarded.* Cf. 49:14; 54:8.

40:28 ^cS ver 21
^dS Dt 33:27;
S Ps 90:2 ^eS ver 26
^fS Isa 37:16
^gIsa 44:12
^hS Ps 147:5; Ro 11:33
40:29 ⁱS Ge 18:14;
S Ps 68:35; S 119:28
^jIsa 50:4; 57:19;
Jer 31:25
40:30 ^kIsa 9:17;
Jer 6:11; 9:21
^lS Ps 20:8; Isa 5:27
40:31 ^mS Ps 37:9;
40:1; S Isa 30:18;
Lk 18:1 ⁿS 1Sa 2:4;
S 2Ki 6:33;
S 2Co 4:16
^oS Ex 19:4 ^p2Co 4:1;
Heb 12:1-3
41:1 ^qS Ps 37:7;
Hab 2:20; Zep 1:7;
Zec 2:13 ^rS Isa 11:11
^sS 1Sa 2:4 ^tIsa 48:16;
57:3 ^uS Isa 1:18; 34:1;
50:8
41:2 ^vS Ezr 1:2
^wver 25; Isa 13:4,17;
44:28; 45:1,13; 48:14;
Jer 50:3; 51:11
^xIsa 45:8,13
^yIsa 44:28; Jer 25:9
^zS 2Sa 22:43 ^aPs 1:4;
Isa 40:24 ^bS Isa 13:18
41:3 ^cDa 8:4
41:4 ^dver 9;
Isa 43:7 ^ever 26;
S Ge 1:1; Isa 46:10
^fIsa 44:6; 48:12;
Rev 1:8,17
^gS Dt 32:39
41:5 ^hS Isa 11:11;
Eze 26:17-18
ⁱS Dt 30:4; S Isa 11:12
41:6 ^jS Jos 1:6
41:7 ^kIsa 44:13;
Jer 10:3-5
^lS Isa 40:19
^mS 1Sa 5:3; Isa 46:7

Have you not heard? ^c
The LORD is the everlasting ^d God,
   the Creator ^e of the ends of the earth. ^f
He will not grow tired or weary, ^g
   and his understanding no one can fathom. ^h
²⁹ He gives strength ⁱ to the weary ^j
   and increases the power of the weak.
³⁰ Even youths grow tired and weary,
   and young men ^k stumble and fall; ^l
³¹ but those who hope ^m in the LORD
   will renew their strength. ⁿ
They will soar on wings like eagles; ^o
   they will run and not grow weary,
   they will walk and not be faint. ^p

THE HELPER OF ISRAEL

41

"Be silent ^q before me, you islands! ^r
   Let the nations renew their strength! ^s
Let them come forward ^t and speak;
   let us meet together ^u at the place of judgment.

² "Who has stirred ^v up one from the east, ^w
   calling him in righteousness ^x to his service ^a? ^y
He hands nations over to him
   and subdues kings before him.
He turns them to dust ^z with his sword,
   to windblown chaff ^a with his bow. ^b
³ He pursues them and moves on unscathed, ^c
   by a path his feet have not traveled before.
⁴ Who has done this and carried it through,
   calling ^d forth the generations from the beginning? ^e
I, the LORD—with the first of them
   and with the last ^f—I am he. ^g"

⁵ The islands ^h have seen it and fear;
   the ends of the earth ⁱ tremble.
They approach and come forward;
⁶   they help each other
   and say to their companions, "Be strong! ^j"
⁷ The metalworker ^k encourages the goldsmith, ^l
   and the one who smooths with the hammer
   spurs on the one who strikes the anvil.
One says of the welding, "It is good."
   The other nails down the idol so it will not topple. ^m

^a 2 Or *east, / whom victory meets at every step*

40:28 *everlasting God.* See 9:6. *Creator.* See vv. 21–22 and notes. *ends of the earth.* See 11:12 and note; cf. 5:26; 41:9; 43:6. *not grow tired.* Contrast 44:12.
40:30 *grow tired . . . stumble.* See note on 5:27.

A **40:31** *hope in.* Trust in or look expectantly to (see 5:2; 49:23). *renew.* Lit. "exchange"; see 41:1 and note. Their weakness will give way to God's strength (v. 29). *eagles.* Known for their vigor (see Ps 103:5 and note) and speed (Jer 4:13; 48:40).
41:1,5 *islands.* Or "coastlands" (see 11:11 and note).
41:1 *renew their strength.* See 40:31 and note. The nations and their gods are challenged to display the same power and wisdom as Israel's God (see vv. 21–24).

C **41:2** *one from the east.* Cyrus the Great, king of Persia (559–530 B.C.), who conquered Babylon in 539 (see 13:17 and note) and issued the decree allowing the Jews to return to Jerusalem (see Ezr 1:1–4; 6:3–5). Cyrus is referred to also in v. 25; 44:28—45:5,13; 46:11. *calling him in righteousness.* Like the ser-

vant of the Lord in 42:6, Cyrus was chosen to carry out God's righteous purposes. *subdues kings.* Such as Croesus, king of Lydia in Asia Minor. *windblown chaff.* See 17:13 and note. *his bow.* The Persians were renowned for their ability as archers.

A **41:4** *from the beginning.* See 40:21 and note. *with the first . . . with the last.* Since the Lord was present with the first of the generations and will still be there with the last of them, he is the eternal Lord of history and nations (see Heb 13:8; Rev 1:8,17; 2:8; 21:6; 22:13).

C **41:5–7** By 546 B.C. Cyrus had fought his way victoriously to the west coast of Asia Minor, where his leading opponent was Croesus, king of Lydia. Sarcasm and satire are used in the description of the frantic efforts in vv. 6–7—all of them futile (cf. 40:19–20).
41:5 *ends of the earth.* See 11:12 and note.
41:6 *Be strong!* See 35:4 and note.
41:7 *hammer.* Cf. 44:12. *so it will not topple.* See 40:18–20 and notes.

⁸ "But you, Israel, my servant, ⁿ
  Jacob, whom I have chosen, ᵒ
  you descendants of Abrahamᵖ my friend, �q
⁹ I took you from the ends of the earth, ʳ
  from its farthest corners I calledˢ you.
I said, 'You are my servant'; ᵗ
  I have chosenᵘ you and have not rejected you.
¹⁰ So do not fear, ᵛ for I am with you; ʷ
  do not be dismayed, for I am your God.
I will strengthenˣ you and helpʸ you;
  I will uphold youᶻ with my righteous right hand. ᵃ

¹¹ "All who rageᵇ against you
  will surely be ashamed and disgraced; ᶜ
those who opposeᵈ you
  will be as nothing and perish. ᵉ
¹² Though you search for your enemies,
  you will not find them. ᶠ
Those who wage war against you
  will be as nothingᵍ at all.
¹³ For I am the Lᴏʀᴅ your God
  who takes hold of your right handʰ
and says to you, Do not fear;
  I will helpⁱ you.
¹⁴ Do not be afraid,ʲ you wormᵏ Jacob,
  little Israel, do not fear,
for I myself will helpˡ you," declares the Lᴏʀᴅ,
  your Redeemer, ᵐ the Holy Oneⁿ of Israel.
¹⁵ "See, I will make you into a threshing sledge, ᵒ
  new and sharp, with many teeth.
You will thresh the mountainsᵖ and crush them,
  and reduce the hills to chaff. q
¹⁶ You will winnowʳ them, the wind will pick them up,
  and a galeˢ will blow them away. ᵗ
But you will rejoiceᵘ in the Lᴏʀᴅ
  and gloryᵛ in the Holy Oneʷ of Israel.

¹⁷ "The poor and needy search for water, ˣ
  but there is none;
  their tongues are parched with thirst. ʸ
But I the Lᴏʀᴅ will answerᶻ them;
  I, the God of Israel, will not forsakeᵃ them.
¹⁸ I will make rivers flowᵇ on barren heights,

41:8 ⁿS Ps 136:22;
S Isa 27:11 ᵒS Isa 14:1
ᵖS Isa 29:22; 51:2;
63:16 qᵀ2Ch 20:7;
Jas 2:23
41:9 ʳIsa 11:12;
S 37:16 ˢS ver 4
ᵗS Isa 20:3 ᵘS Dt 7:6
41:10 ᵛS Ge 15:1
ʷS Dt 3:22; Jos 1:9;
Isa 43:2,5; Jer 30:10;
46:27-28; Ro 8:31
ˣS Ps 68:35; S 119:28
ʸver 13-14; Isa 44:2;
49:8; 50:7,9
ᶻS Ps 18:35; S 119:117
ᵃS Ex 3:20;
S Job 40:14
41:11 ᵇS Isa 17:12
ᶜIsa 29:22; 45:24;
54:17 ᵈS Ex 23:22
ᵉS Isa 29:8; S Jer 2:3
41:12 ᶠPs 37:35-36;
S Isa 34:12
ᵍS Job 7:8; Isa 17:14;
29:20
41:13 ʰPs 73:23;
Isa 42:6; 45:1; 51:18
ⁱver 10
41:14 ʲS Ge 15:1
ᵏS Job 4:19; S Ps 22:6
ˡS ver 10
ᵐS Ex 15:13;
S Job 19:25; S Isa 1:27
ⁿver 16,20; S Isa 1:4
41:15 ᵒS Job 41:30;
S Isa 10:5; S 21:10
ᵖS Ex 19:18;
S Ps 107:33; Jer 9:10;
Eze 33:28 qS ver 2
41:16 ʳJer 15:7; 51:2
ˢIsa 40:24 ᵗDa 2:35
ᵘS Isa 25:9
ᵛIsa 45:25; 60:19
ʷS ver 14; S Mk 1:24
41:17 ˣIsa 43:20
ʸS Isa 35:7
ᶻS Isa 30:19
ᵃS Dt 31:6; S Ps 27:9
41:18 ᵇS Isa 30:25

🅰 **41:8–9** *my servant.* A significant term in chs. 41–53, referring sometimes to the nation of Israel and other times to an individual. In these passages the title refers to one who occupies a special position in God's royal administration of his kingdom, as in "my servant Moses" (Nu 12:7), "my servant David" (2Sa 3:18; 7:5,8), "my servants the prophets" (2Ki 17:13; Jer 7:25). See note on 42:1; see also 20:3; 22:20; 42:1,19; 43:10; 44:1–2,21; 45:4; 49:3,5–7; 50:10; 52:13; 53:11.
41:8 *But.* In contrast to the nations of vv. 5–7, Israel does not need to be afraid (v. 10). *my friend.* See Ge 18:17 and note; 2Ch 20:7; Jas 2:23 and note.
41:9 *ends of the earth.* See v. 5; probably a reference to Mesopotamia and Egypt (see Ge 11:31; 12:1; 15:7; Ps 114:1–2; Jer 31:32).
41:10 *do not fear . . . be dismayed.* See vv. 13–14; 43:1,5; see also 35:4 and note. *strengthen . . . help you.* As one called to God's service (see vv. 9,15–16). See also v. 14; 40:29; 44:2; 49:8. *right hand.* A hand of power and salvation (see Ex 15:6,12; Ps 20:6; 48:10; 89:13; 98:1).
41:11 *be ashamed and disgraced.* Cf. 45:17; 50:7; 54:4. *will be as nothing.* See vv. 15–16 and notes.
41:13 *takes hold . . . right hand.* To strengthen them and keep them from stumbling. *Do not fear.* See v. 10 and note.

🅰 **41:14** *worm.* A reference to their feeble and despised condition in exile (cf. Job 25:6; Ps 22:6). *Redeemer.* Deliverer from Babylonian exile (in a new exodus). The Hebrew for this word refers to an obligated family protector and thus portrays the Lord as the family protector of Israel. He is related to Israel as father (63:16; 64:8) and husband (54:5). As Redeemer (or family protector), he redeems his people's property (for he regathers them to their land, 54:1–8), guarantees their freedom (35:9; 43:1–4; 48:20; 52:11–12), avenges them against their tormentors (47:3–4; 49:25–26; 64:4) and secures their posterity for the future (61:8–9). See note on Ru 2:20. *Holy One of Israel.* See vv. 16,20; see also 1:4 and note. The title occurs with "Redeemer" also in 43:14; 47:4; 48:17; 49:7; 54:5.
41:15 *threshing sledge.* Cf. 28:27; Am 1:3 and note; Mic 4:13; Hab 3:12. *mountains . . . hills.* Probably represent the nations. See 2:14. *reduce . . . to chaff.* See v. 2; 17:13 and note; 29:5–6.
41:16 *winnow.* A figure of judgment used also in Jer 51:2 (see note on Ru 1:22). *rejoice.* Cf. 25:9; 35:10; 51:11.
41:17 *poor and needy.* Israel in exile or on the way home (cf. v. 14; 32:7). *will answer.* See 30:19 and note.
41:18 *rivers . . . on barren heights.* See 30:25 and note. *desert into pools . . . springs.* See 32:2; 35:6–7 and notes.

41:18 ^c Isa 43:19
^d S 2Ki 3:17
^e S Job 38:26;
S Isa 35:7
41:19 ^f S Isa 35:1;
51:3 ^g S Ex 25:5,10,13
^h S Isa 37:24
ⁱ Isa 44:14 / Isa 60:13
41:20 ^k S Ex 6:7
^l S Isa 29:24
^m Ezr 7:6; 8:31;
Isa 50:2; 51:9; 59:1;
66:14; Jer 32:17
ⁿ S ver 14; Isa 43:3,14
^o S Isa 4:5
41:21 ^p S ver 1
^q Isa 43:15; 44:6
41:22 ^r ver 26;
Isa 43:9; 44:7; 45:21;
48:14 ^s Isa 43:18,26;
46:9; 48:3 ^t Isa 42:9;
43:19; 46:10; 48:6;
65:17; Jn 13:19
41:23 ^u Isa 45:3
^v Jer 10:5
^w S 2Ki 19:26
41:24 ^x S Isa 37:19;
1Co 8:4 ^y S 1Sa 12:21;
Jer 8:19; 10:5,8,15
^z S Ps 109:7;
S Isa 1:13; S 48:8
41:25 ^a S Ezr 1:2
^b S ver 2; Jer 50:9,41;
51:48 ^c S 2Sa 22:43;
S Isa 5:5; Na 3:14
41:26 ^d S ver 4
^e S ver 22; Isa 52:6
^f S 1Ki 18:26;
Hab 2:18-19
41:27 ^g Isa 48:3,16
^h S Isa 40:9
41:28 ⁱ Ps 22:11;
Isa 50:2; 59:16; 63:5;
64:7; Eze 22:30
^j Isa 40:13-14
^k S 1Ki 18:26;
Isa 65:12; 66:4;
Jer 25:4
41:29 ^l S 1Sa 12:21
^m S Isa 37:19
ⁿ Jer 5:13

and springs within the valleys.
I will turn the desert ^c into pools of water, ^d
and the parched ground into springs. ^e

¹⁹ I will put in the desert ^f
the cedar and the acacia, ^g the myrtle and the olive.
I will set junipers ^h in the wasteland,
the fir and the cypress ⁱ together, ^j

²⁰ so that people may see and know, ^k
may consider and understand, ^l
that the hand ^m of the LORD has done this,
that the Holy One ⁿ of Israel has created ^o it.

²¹ "Present your case, ^p" says the LORD.
"Set forth your arguments," says Jacob's King. ^q

²² "Tell us, you idols,
what is going to happen. ^r
Tell us what the former things ^s were,
so that we may consider them
and know their final outcome.
Or declare to us the things to come, ^t

²³ tell us what the future holds,
so we may know ^u that you are gods.
Do something, whether good or bad, ^v
so that we will be dismayed ^w and filled with fear.

²⁴ But you are less than nothing ^x
and you can do nothing; ^y
those who choose you are detestable. ^z

²⁵ "I have stirred ^a up one from the north, ^b and he comes—
one from the rising sun who calls on my name.
He treads ^c on rulers as if they were mortar,
as if he were a potter treading the clay.

²⁶ Who told of this from the beginning, ^d so we could know,
or beforehand, so we could say, 'He was right'?
No one told of this,
no one foretold ^e it,
no one heard any words ^f from you.

²⁷ I was the first to tell ^g Zion, 'Look, here they are!'
I gave to Jerusalem a messenger of good news. ^h

²⁸ I look but there is no one ⁱ—
no one among the gods to give counsel, ^j
no one to give answer ^k when I ask them.

²⁹ See, they are all false!
Their deeds amount to nothing; ^l
their images ^m are but wind ⁿ and confusion.

41:19 These trees will beautify the desert (cf. 35:1–2). Several are named in 60:13 in connection with adorning the place of God's sanctuary. Acacia wood was used for the tabernacle (see Ex 25:5,10,13 and note on 25:5). The juniper tree and myrtle replace thorns and briers in 55:13.

41:20 *created it.* These fruitful conditions are part of God's new creation in behalf of his people (see 48:7; 57:19; 65:17–18).

41:21–22 God takes the nations and their idols to court (see v. 1 and note).

41:22 *former things.* Earlier divine predictions or accomplishments (see 42:9; 43:9,18; 46:9; 48:3).

41:23 *Do something ... good or bad.* See note on 40:18–20.

41:24 *less than nothing ... can do nothing.* Like the nations that worship them. See 40:17; 44:9; Hos 9:10. *detestable.* Like those who marry idolaters (see Mal 2:11 and note).

41:25 *stirred up.* See v. 2 and note. *from the north.* Cyrus came from the east (v. 2) and conquered a number of kingdoms north of Babylon early in his reign. From the perspective of those living in Jerusalem, invasions came primarily from the north (see 14:31; Jer 1:14; 6:1,22; 10:22; 46:20; 50:3,9,41; 51:48). *calls on my name.* Cyrus used the Lord's name in his decree (Ezr 1:2) but did not acknowledge him (see 45:4–5). *treads on ... mortar ... clay.* Similar to Assyria in 10:6. Cf. Mic 7:10; Na 3:14.

41:26 *from the beginning.* Before these events began to unfold (cf. v. 4). *you.* Idols or their worshipers.

41:27 *here they are.* Words about the deliverance from Babylon. *messenger of good news.* Isaiah. See 40:9; 52:7 and notes.

41:28 *no one to give answer.* See 46:7.

41:29 *amount to nothing.* See v. 24.

THE SERVANT OF THE LORD

42 "Here is my servant,[o] whom I uphold,
my chosen one[p] in whom I delight;[q]
I will put my Spirit[r] on him,
and he will bring justice[s] to the nations.[t]
[2] He will not shout or cry out,[u]
or raise his voice in the streets.
[3] A bruised reed[v] he will not break,[w]
and a smoldering wick he will not snuff out.[x]
In faithfulness he will bring forth justice;[y]
[4]   he will not falter or be discouraged
till he establishes justice[z] on earth.
In his teaching[a] the islands[b] will put their hope."[c]

[5] This is what God the LORD says—
he who created the heavens[d] and stretched them out,
who spread out the earth[e] with all that springs from it,[f]
who gives breath[g] to its people,
and life to those who walk on it:
[6] "I, the LORD, have called[h] you in righteousness;[i]
I will take hold of your hand.[j]
I will keep[k] you and will make you
to be a covenant[l] for the people
and a light[m] for the Gentiles,[n]
[7] to open eyes that are blind,[o]
to free[p] captives from prison[q]
and to release from the dungeon those who sit in darkness.[r]

[8] "I am the LORD;[s] that is my name![t]
I will not yield my glory to another[u]
or my praise to idols.[v]
[9] See, the former things[w] have taken place,
and new things I declare;
before they spring into being
I announce[x] them to you."

SONG OF PRAISE TO THE LORD

[10] Sing[y] to the LORD a new song,[z]
his praise[a] from the ends of the earth,[b]
you who go down to the sea, and all that is in it,[c]
you islands,[d] and all who live in them.
[11] Let the wilderness[e] and its towns raise their voices;
let the settlements where Kedar[f] lives rejoice.

42:1 [o] S Isa 20:3;
S Mt 20:28
[p] S Isa 14:1; Lk 9:35;
23:35; 1Pe 2:4,6
[q] Mt 3:17 [r] S Isa 11:2;
S 44:3; Mt 3:16-17;
S Jn 3:34 [s] S Isa 9:7
[t] S Ge 49:10
42:2 [u] Pr 8:1-4
42:3 [v] S Isa 36:6
[w] S Job 30:24
[x] S Job 13:25
[y] Ps 72:2; 96:13
42:4 [z] S Isa 2:4
[a] ver 21; Ex 34:29;
Isa 51:4 [b] S Isa 11:11
[c] S Ge 49:10;
Mt 12:18-21*
42:5 [d] S Ge 1:6;
Ps 102:25; Isa 48:13
[e] S Ge 1:1 [f] Ps 24:2;
Ac 17:24 [g] S Ge 2:7;
Ac 17:25
42:6 [h] Ex 31:2;
S Jdg 4:10; Isa 41:9-
10; 43:1 [i] Isa 45:24;
Jer 23:6; Da 9:7
[j] Isa 41:13; 45:1
[k] Isa 26:3; 27:3
[l] Isa 49:8; 54:10;
59:21; 61:8; Jer 31:31;
32:40; Mal 3:1;
S Lk 22:20
[m] S Isa 9:2
[n] S Isa 26:18;
S Lk 2:32
42:7 [o] S Ps 146:8;
S Isa 32:3; Mt 11:5
[p] Isa 49:9; 51:14;
52:2; Zec 2:7
[q] S Ps 66:11;
S Isa 24:22; 48:20;
Zec 9:11; S Lk 4:19;
2Ti 2:26; Heb 2:14-15
[r] S Ps 107:10,14;
Ac 26:18
42:8 [s] Ps 81:10;
Isa 43:3,11,15; 46:9;
49:23 [t] S Ex 3:15;
S 6:3 [u] Isa 48:11
[v] S Ex 8:10; S 20:4
42:9 [w] S Isa 41:22
[x] S Isa 40:21; Eze 2:4
42:10 [y] S Ex 15:1
[z] S Ps 96:1 [a] 1Ki 10:9;
Isa 60:6 [b] S Dt 30:4;
S Ps 48:10; 65:5;
Isa 49:6
[c] S 1Ch 16:32;
Ps 96:11 [d] S Isa 11:11
42:11 [e] S Isa 32:16
[f] S Ge 25:13; Isa 60:7

42:1–4 Quoted in part in Mt 12:18–21 (see note there) with reference to Christ. There are four "servant songs" in which the servant is the Messiah: 42:1–4 (or 42:1–7 or 42:1–9); 49:1–6 (or 49:1–7 or 49:1–13); 50:4–9 (or 50:4–11); 52:13—53:12; cf. 61:1–2 and notes. He is "Israel" in its ideal form (49:3). The nation was to be a kingdom of priests (see Ex 19:6 and note), but the Messiah would be the high priest who would atone for the sins of the world (53:4–12). Cyrus was introduced in ch. 41 as a deliverer from Babylon, but the servant would deliver the world from its bondage to sin (see v. 7).
42:1 *my servant.* See 41:8–9; Zec 3:8 and notes. In the royal terminology of the ancient Near East "servant" meant something like "trusted envoy" or "confidential representative." *chosen one.* See 41:8–9 and note. *delight.* Cf. Lk 3:22. *my Spirit on him.* Like the "Branch" of 11:1–2 (see note on 11:2); cf. 61:1. *justice.* A righteous world order (see v. 4); see also 9:7; 11:4 and notes.
42:2 *not shout or cry out.* He will bring peace (see 9:6).
42:3 *bruised reed.* Someone who is weak (see Ps 72:2,4). The servant will mend broken lives.
42:4 *falter.* Cf. 40:28. *justice.* Perfect order (see v. 1 and note). *In his teaching ... hope.* As do the nations in 2:2–4. The servant will

be a new Moses (see Dt 18:15–18; Ac 3:21–23,26). *islands.* See note on 11:11.
42:5 *created the heavens ... stretched.* See 40:22 and note. *gives breath ... life.* Cf. 57:15.
42:6 *called ... righteousness.* Similar to the call of Cyrus (see 41:2 and note). *take hold of your hand.* See 41:13 and note. *covenant.* See 49:8. Through the Messiah as king, the Davidic covenant (see 2Sa 7:12–16; cf. Isa 55:3 and note) would be fulfilled (9:7), and he would institute the new covenant by his death (see Jer 31:31–34; Heb 8:6–13; 9:15 and notes). *people.* Probably the Israelites (see 49:8; Ac 26:17–18). *light for the Gentiles.* See note on 9:2. *light.* Parallel to "salvation" in 49:6 (cf. 51:4).
42:7 *open eyes.* See 29:18; 32:3; 35:5 and notes. *free ... from prison.* From the prison of Babylon and also from spiritual and moral bondage (compare 61:1 with Lk 4:18).
42:8 *my glory.* See 40:5 and note.
42:9 *former things.* See 41:22 and note. *new things.* The restoration of Israel (43:19). Cf. 48:6.
42:10 *new song.* To celebrate the "new things" of v. 9. *ends of the earth.* See 11:12 and note; 41:5. *islands.* See v. 12; 11:11 and note.
42:11 *wilderness.* See 35:1 and note. *Kedar.* See note on 21:16. *Sela.* See note on 16:1.

42:11 *g* S Jdg 1:36
h Isa 52:7; Na 1:15
42:12 *i* S 1Ch 16:24;
S Isa 24:15
j S Ps 26:7; S 66:2;
1Pe 2:9 *k* S Isa 11:11
42:13 *l* S Isa 9:6
m S Ex 14:14
n S Isa 26:11
o S Jos 6:5; Jer 25:30;
Hos 11:10; Joel 3:16;
Am 1:2; 3:4,8
p Isa 66:14
42:14 *q* S Est 4:14;
S Ps 50:21
r S Ge 43:31; Lk 18:7;
2Pe 3:9 *s* Jer 4:31
42:15 *t* Eze 38:20
u S Ps 107:33
v S Isa 11:15; 50:2;
Na 1:4-6
42:16 *w* S Isa 29:24;
40:11; 57:18; 58:11;
Jer 31:8-9; Lk 1:78-79
x S Isa 32:3
y S Ps 18:28; Isa 58:8,
10; S Ac 26:18
z S Isa 26:7; Lk 3:5
a S Dt 4:31; Heb 13:5
42:17 *b* S Ex 32:4
c S Ps 97:7; S Isa 1:29
42:18 *d* S Isa 35:5
42:19 *e* Isa 43:8;
Eze 12:2 *f* Isa 41:8-9
g Isa 44:26; Hag 1:13
h Isa 26:3
42:20 *i* Isa 6:9-10;
43:8; Jer 5:21; 6:10
42:21 *j* Isa 43:25
k S ver 4; 2Co 3:7
42:22 *l* S Jdg 6:4;
S 2Ki 24:13
m S Isa 24:18
n S Ps 66:11;
S Isa 24:22
o S Isa 5:29
42:23 *p* Dt 32:29;
Ps 81:13; Isa 47:7;
48:18; 57:11
42:24 *q* S 2Ki 17:6;
Isa 43:28; 47:6

Let the people of Sela *g* sing for joy;
    let them shout from the mountaintops. *h*
[12] Let them give glory *i* to the LORD
    and proclaim his praise *j* in the islands. *k*
[13] The LORD will march out like a champion, *l*
    like a warrior *m* he will stir up his zeal; *n*
with a shout *o* he will raise the battle cry
    and will triumph over his enemies. *p*

[14] "For a long time I have kept silent, *q*
    I have been quiet and held myself back. *r*
But now, like a woman in childbirth,
    I cry out, I gasp and pant. *s*
[15] I will lay waste *t* the mountains *u* and hills
    and dry up all their vegetation;
I will turn rivers into islands
    and dry up *v* the pools.
[16] I will lead *w* the blind *x* by ways they have not known,
    along unfamiliar paths I will guide them;
I will turn the darkness into light *y* before them
    and make the rough places smooth. *z*
These are the things I will do;
    I will not forsake *a* them.
[17] But those who trust in idols,
    who say to images, 'You are our gods,' *b*
will be turned back in utter shame. *c*

ISRAEL BLIND AND DEAF

[18] "Hear, you deaf; *d*
    look, you blind, and see!
[19] Who is blind *e* but my servant, *f*
    and deaf like the messenger *g* I send?
Who is blind like the one in covenant *h* with me,
    blind like the servant of the LORD?
[20] You have seen many things, but have paid no attention;
    your ears are open, but you hear nothing." *i*
[21] It pleased the LORD
    for the sake *j* of his righteousness
    to make his law *k* great and glorious.
[22] But this is a people plundered *l* and looted,
    all of them trapped in pits *m*
    or hidden away in prisons. *n*
They have become plunder,
    with no one to rescue them; *o*
they have been made loot,
    with no one to say, "Send them back."

[23] Which of you will listen to this
    or pay close attention *p* in time to come?
[24] Who handed Jacob over to become loot,
    and Israel to the plunderers? *q*

42:12 *give glory...praise.* See 24:14–16.
42:13 *champion.* God will fight as he did at the Red Sea (Ex 15:3); see 9:6 and note. *zeal.* Cf. 9:7; 37:32; 59:17; 63:15. *raise the battle cry.* To cause panic among the enemy (see Jos 6:5 and note; 1Sa 4:5–8).
42:14 *For a long time.* During Israel's humiliation and exile. *held myself back.* See 63:15; 64:12. The Hebrew verb is also used of Joseph, who controlled his emotions while he tested his brothers (Ge 43:31; 45:1). See 30:18 and note.
42:15 *lay waste...dry up.* The opposite of 35:1–2; 41:18. *rivers into islands.* Perhaps to make travel easier. See 37:25; 44:27.
42:16 *blind.* Israel (vv. 19–20). *rough places smooth.* See note on 26:7. *not forsake.* Cf. 40:27; 49:14; 54:8.

42:18 *deaf...blind.* See 6:10 and note.
42:19 *my servant.* Israel. See note on 41:8–9. *messenger I send.* A term associated with prophets (see Hag 1:13; cf. Isa 44:26; Mal 3:1).
42:21 *law great and glorious.* Especially the law of Moses, given in the awesome setting of Mount Sinai (see Ex 34:29).
42:22 *plundered and looted.* By the Assyrians (see 10:6 and note) and the Babylonians (see 39:6). *trapped in pits...prisons.* See v. 7 and note. Cf. Jdg 6:2–4.
42:24 *Who handed Jacob over...?* Babylon conquered Israel, not because her gods were stronger than the Lord (see 40:17–18; 1Ki 20:23 and note) but because the Lord was punishing his people.

Was it not the LORD,[r]
  against whom we have sinned?
For they would not follow[s] his ways;
  they did not obey his law.[t]
25 So he poured out on them his burning anger,[u]
  the violence of war.
It enveloped them in flames,[v] yet they did not understand;[w]
  it consumed them, but they did not take it to heart.[x]

ISRAEL'S ONLY SAVIOR

43

But now, this is what the LORD says—
  he who created[y] you, Jacob,
  he who formed[z] you, Israel:[a]
"Do not fear, for I have redeemed[b] you;
  I have summoned you by name;[c] you are mine.[d]
2 When you pass through the waters,[e]
  I will be with you;[f]
and when you pass through the rivers,
  they will not sweep over you.
When you walk through the fire,[g]
  you will not be burned;
  the flames will not set you ablaze.[h]
3 For I am the LORD your God,[i]
  the Holy One[j] of Israel, your Savior;[k]
I give Egypt[l] for your ransom,
  Cush[a][m] and Seba[n] in your stead.[o]
4 Since you are precious and honored[p] in my sight,
  and because I love[q] you,
I will give nations in exchange for you,
  and peoples in exchange for your life.
5 Do not be afraid,[r] for I am with you;[s]
  I will bring your children[t] from the east
  and gather[u] you from the west.[v]
6 I will say to the north, 'Give them up!'
  and to the south,[w] 'Do not hold them back.'
Bring my sons from afar
  and my daughters[x] from the ends of the earth[y]—
7 everyone who is called by my name,[z]
  whom I created[a] for my glory,[b]
  whom I formed and made.[c]"

8 Lead out those who have eyes but are blind,[d]
  who have ears but are deaf.[e]
9 All the nations gather together[f]

---

a 3 That is, the upper Nile region

42:24 [r] Isa 10:5-6
[s] S Isa 30:15
[t] S Jos 1:7;
S Ps 119:136; Isa 5:24;
Jer 44:10
42:25 [u] S 2Ki 22:13;
S Job 40:11;
S Isa 51:17; S Eze 7:19
[v] 2Ki 25:9; Isa 66:15;
Jer 4:4; 21:12; La 2:3;
Na 1:6 [w] S Isa 1:3
[x] Isa 29:13; 47:7; 57:1,
11; Hos 7:9
43:1 [y] S Isa 27:11
[z] S ver 7; S Ge 2:7
[a] Ge 32:28; Isa 44:21
[b] S Ex 6:6;
S Job 19:25
[c] S Isa 42:6; 45:3-4;
49:1 [d] S Dt 7:6;
Mal 3:17
43:2 [e] S Isa 8:7
[f] S Ge 26:3;
S Ex 14:22 [g] Isa 29:6;
30:27 [h] Ps 66:12;
Da 3:25-27
43:3 [i] S Ex 20:2
[j] S Isa 41:20
[k] S Ex 14:30;
S Jdg 2:18; S Ps 3:8;
S Isa 25:9
[l] S Ps 68:31; Isa 19:1;
Eze 29:20
[m] S Isa 20:3
[n] S Ge 10:7
[o] S Pr 21:18
43:4 [p] Ex 19:5;
Isa 49:5 [q] Isa 63:9;
Rev 3:9
43:5 [r] S Ge 15:1;
Isa 44:2 [s] S Ge 21:22;
S Ex 14:22; Jer 30:10-
11 [t] Isa 43:8; 54:3;
61:9; 66:22
[u] S Isa 11:12; S 49:18
[v] S Isa 24:14; Zec 8:7;
S Mt 8:11
43:6 [w] Ps 107:3
[x] Isa 60:4; Eze 16:61;
2Co 6:18 [y] S Dt 30:4;
S Isa 11:12; Jer 23:8;
Eze 36:24
43:7 [z] Isa 48:1; 56:5;
62:2; 63:19; 65:1;
Jer 15:16; Jas 2:7
[a] S Isa 27:11
[b] S Ps 86:9 [c] ver 1,21;
Ps 100:3; S Isa 19:25
43:8 [d] S Isa 6:9-10
[e] S Isa 42:20;
Eze 12:2
43:9 [f] S Isa 41:1;
45:20; 48:14

42:25 *poured out...anger.* Israel had a foretaste of the day of the Lord (see 5:25; 9:12,17,21; 13:3; 34:2 and notes; cf. Jer 10:25). **43:1** *created...formed.* God made the nation Israel as surely as he made the first man and woman (see Ge 1:27 and note; see also Isa 43:7,15,21; 44:2,24). *Do not fear.* See 41:10 and note. *redeemed you.* See notes on 35:9; 41:14. The verb is also used in 29:22; 44:22–23; 48:20 (cf. Ex 15:13). *summoned...by name.* God chose Israel to serve him in a special way. See 45:3–4 (Cyrus). In Ex 31:2; 35:30 the Hebrew underlying this expression is translated "chosen." **43:2** *waters...rivers.* Probably an allusion to crossing the Red Sea (Ex 14:21–22) and the Jordan River (Jos 3:14–17). Cf. Ps 66:6,12. *walk through the fire.* Fulfilled literally in the experience of Shadrach, Meshach and Abednego (Da 3:25–27). Contrast 42:25.

A **43:3** *Holy One of Israel.* See notes on 1:4; 41:14. *Savior.* Who delivers from the oppression of Egypt or Babylon and from the spiritual oppression of sin (see 19:20; 25:9 and notes; 33:22; 35:4 and note; 43:11–12; 45:15,21–22; 49:25; 60:16; 63:8–9). The name "Isaiah" means "The LORD saves." *ransom.* The Persians conquered Egypt, Cush and Seba, and per-

haps this was a reward or ransom for Persia's kindness to Israel (see note on 41:2; cf. Eze 29:19–20). *Cush.* See note on 18:1. *Seba.* A land near Cush (cf. 45:14) or Sheba (Ps 72:10). It was probably either in south Arabia (see Ge 10:7 and note; see also Eze 27:21–22) or in east Africa.
43:5 *Do not be afraid.* See 41:10 and note. *east.* Especially Assyria and Babylonia. See 11:11–12 and notes; cf. Ps 107:3. *west.* For example, the "islands" of 11:11 (see also 24:14–15; 49:12). **43:6** *north.* For example, Hamath (see 10:9 and note; 11:11). *south.* Egypt. *ends of the earth.* See note on 11:12 (cf. 41:5; 42:10). **43:7** *called by my name.* People belonging to God. *created... formed.* See v. 1 and note.
43:8 *blind...deaf.* Probably referring to Israel (see 6:10 and note; 42:18–20).
43:9–13 A court scene; see also 41:21–22.
43:9 *nations...peoples assemble.* See 41:1 and note. *foretold.* See 41:26 and note. *former things.* See 41:22 and note. *witnesses.* To verify the accuracy of earlier predictions by idols or their worshipers (see 41:26).

43:9 ᵍS Isa 41:26
43:10 ʰ ver 12;
S Jos 24:22
ⁱ S Isa 20:3; 41:8-9
ʲ S Ex 6:7 ᵏ ver 11;
S Ps 86:10; Isa 19:21;
44:6,8; 45:5-6,14
ˡ S Dt 4:35; S 32:39;
Jer 14:22
43:11 ᵐ S Ex 6:2;
S Isa 42:8 ⁿ S ver 10;
S Ps 3:8; S 18:31;
S Isa 25:9; 64:4
43:12 ᵒ S Dt 32:12
ᵖ S ver 10
43:13 ᵠ Ps 90:2
ʳ Dt 32:39; Isa 46:4;
48:12 ˢ Nu 23:8;
S Job 9:12
43:14 ᵗ S Ex 15:13;
S Job 19:25
ᵘ S Isa 1:4; S 41:20
ᵛ Isa 13:14-15
ʷ S Isa 23:13
43:15 ˣ S Isa 42:8
ʸ S Isa 27:11; 45:11
ᶻ S Isa 41:21
43:16 ᵃ S Ex 14:29;
S 15:8; S Isa 11:15
43:17 ᵇ Ps 118:12;
Isa 1:31 ᶜ S Ex 14:22
ᵈ S Ex 14:9 ᵉ Ps 76:5-
6 ᶠ S Job 13:25;
Jer 51:21; Eze 38:4
43:18 ᵍ S Isa 41:22
43:19 ʰ S Isa 41:22;
Jer 16:14-15; 23:7-8;
2Co 5:17; Rev 21:5
ⁱ S Isa 40:3
ʲ Ps 126:4;
S Isa 33:21; S 35:7
43:20 ᵏ S Ps 148:10
ˡ S Isa 13:22
ᵐ S Nu 20:8
43:21 ⁿ S ver 7;
S Ge 2:7 ᵒ Mal 3:17
ᵖ S Ps 66:2; 102:18;
1Pe 2:9

and the peoples assemble.
Which of their gods foretold ᵍ this
    and proclaimed to us the former things?
Let them bring in their witnesses to prove they were right,
    so that others may hear and say, "It is true."
10 "You are my witnesses," ʰ declares the LORD,
    "and my servant ⁱ whom I have chosen,
so that you may know ʲ and believe me
    and understand that I am he.
Before me no god ᵏ was formed,
    nor will there be one after me. ˡ
11 I, even I, am the LORD, ᵐ
    and apart from me there is no savior. ⁿ
12 I have revealed and saved and proclaimed—
    I, and not some foreign god ᵒ among you.
You are my witnesses," ᵖ declares the LORD, "that I am God.
13   Yes, and from ancient days ᵠ I am he. ʳ
No one can deliver out of my hand.
    When I act, who can reverse it?" ˢ

GOD'S MERCY AND ISRAEL'S UNFAITHFULNESS

14 This is what the LORD says—
    your Redeemer, ᵗ the Holy One ᵘ of Israel:
"For your sake I will send to Babylon
    and bring down as fugitives ᵛ all the Babylonians, ᵃ ʷ
    in the ships in which they took pride.
15 I am the LORD, ˣ your Holy One,
    Israel's Creator, ʸ your King. ᶻ"

16 This is what the LORD says—
    he who made a way through the sea,
    a path through the mighty waters, ᵃ
17 who drew out ᵇ the chariots and horses, ᶜ
    the army and reinforcements together, ᵈ
and they lay ᵉ there, never to rise again,
    extinguished, snuffed out like a wick: ᶠ
18 "Forget the former things; ᵍ
    do not dwell on the past.
19 See, I am doing a new thing! ʰ
    Now it springs up; do you not perceive it?
I am making a way in the wilderness ⁱ
    and streams in the wasteland. ʲ
20 The wild animals ᵏ honor me,
    the jackals ˡ and the owls,
because I provide water ᵐ in the wilderness
    and streams in the wasteland,
to give drink to my people, my chosen,
21   the people I formed ⁿ for myself ᵒ
    that they may proclaim my praise. ᵖ

ᵃ 14 Or Chaldeans

A **43:10** *You are my witnesses.* See also v. 12; 44:8. God's work in behalf of Israel is proof of his saving power. *my servant.* See 41:8–9 and note.
43:11 The main thrust is repeated in 44:6,8; 45:5–6,18,21–22; 46:9 (see also Dt 32:39). *savior.* See v. 3 and note.
43:12 *foreign god.* Cf. Dt 32:12,16. Israel repeatedly worshiped other gods (see Jdg 2:12–13 and notes). *witnesses.* See v. 10 and note.
43:13 See v. 11. *No one can deliver . . . hand.* Identical to Dt 32:39.
43:14 *Redeemer.* See 41:14 and note. *Holy One of Israel.* See 1:4; 41:14 and notes. *Babylon.* See note on 13:1. *fugitives . . . in the ships.* The Babylonians used the Persian Gulf, as well as the Tigris and Euphrates rivers, for trading purposes. But their splendid ships (cf.

2:16) would one day become their means of flight (cf. Jer 51:13).
43:15 *Creator.* See v. 1 and note. *King.* God was called "king over Jeshurun" (Israel) in Dt 33:5 (contrast 1Sa 8:7).
43:16–17 A reference to crossing the Red Sea (see v. 2 and note). The pharaoh's chariots and horsemen were destroyed as Israel's God fought against them (see 51:10; Ex 14:28; 15:4).
43:17 *snuffed out like a wick.* Contrast 42:3.
43:18–19 *former things . . . new thing.* See 41:22; 42:9 and notes.
43:19 *way in the wilderness.* See 35:8; 40:3 and notes. *streams in the wasteland.* See v. 20; 32:2 and note. Contrast 42:15 and note.
43:20 *jackals . . . owls.* Creatures of the desert (see 13:21–22; 34:13–15; 35:7).
43:21 *people . . . proclaim my praise.* Cf. 42:12.

22 "Yet you have not called on me, Jacob,
     you have not wearied [q] yourselves for [a] me, Israel. [r]
23 You have not brought me sheep for burnt offerings, [s]
     nor honored [t] me with your sacrifices. [u]
   I have not burdened [v] you with grain offerings
     nor wearied you with demands [w] for incense. [x]
24 You have not bought any fragrant calamus [y] for me,
     or lavished on me the fat [z] of your sacrifices.
   But you have burdened me with your sins
     and wearied [a] me with your offenses. [b]

25 "I, even I, am he who blots out
     your transgressions, [c] for my own sake, [d]
   and remembers your sins [e] no more. [f]
26 Review the past for me,
     let us argue the matter together; [g]
   state the case [h] for your innocence.
27 Your first father [i] sinned;
     those I sent to teach [j] you rebelled [k] against me.
28 So I disgraced the dignitaries of your temple;
     I consigned Jacob to destruction [b][l]
     and Israel to scorn. [m]

ISRAEL THE CHOSEN

44 "But now listen, Jacob, my servant, [n]
     Israel, whom I have chosen. [o]
2 This is what the LORD says—
   he who made [p] you, who formed you in the womb, [q]
     and who will help [r] you:
   Do not be afraid, [s] Jacob, my servant, [t]
     Jeshurun, [c][u] whom I have chosen.
3 For I will pour water [v] on the thirsty land,
     and streams on the dry ground; [w]
   I will pour out my Spirit [x] on your offspring,
     and my blessing [y] on your descendants. [z]
4 They will spring up like grass [a] in a meadow,
     like poplar trees [b] by flowing streams. [c]
5 Some will say, 'I belong [d] to the LORD';
     others will call themselves by the name of Jacob;
   still others will write on their hand, [e] 'The LORD's,' [f]
     and will take the name Israel.

---

[a] 22 Or *Jacob;* / *surely you have grown weary of*   [b] 28 The Hebrew term refers to the irrevocable giving over of things or persons to the LORD, often by totally destroying them.   [c] 2 *Jeshurun* means *the upright one,* that is, Israel.

43:22 [q] S Jos 22:5;
S Isa 1:14; [r] Isa 30:11
43:23 [s] S Ex 29:41
[t] Zec 7:5-6; Mal 1:6-8
[u] Am 5:25; [v] Mic 6:3;
Mal 1:12-13; [w] Jer 7:22
[x] Ex 30:35; S Lev 2:1
43:24 [y] S Ex 30:23
[z] Lev 3:9; [a] S Isa 1:14;
S 7:13; S Jer 8:21
[b] Jer 44:22; Mal 2:17
43:25 [c] S 2Sa 12:13;
S 2Ch 6:21; Mk 2:7;
Lk 5:21; Ac 3:19
[d] S Isa 37:35;
S Eze 20:44
[e] Isa 64:9; Mic 7:18
[f] S Job 7:21;
S Isa 38:17
43:26 [g] S Isa 1:18
[h] S Isa 41:1; 49:25;
50:8
43:27 [i] S Ge 12:18
[j] Isa 9:15; 28:7;
Jer 5:31 [k] S Isa 24:20;
S 48:8
43:28 [l] S Nu 5:27;
S Dt 13:15;
S Isa 42:24; S Zec 5:3
[m] S Ps 39:8; Jer 24:9;
Eze 5:15
44:1 [n] ver 21
[o] S Ge 16:11;
S Isa 14:1
44:2 [p] ver 21;
S Ps 149:2 [q] S Ge 2:7;
S Ps 139:13;
S Isa 27:11
[r] S Isa 41:10
[s] S Isa 43:5
[t] Jer 30:10; 46:27
[u] S Nu 23:21;
S Dt 32:15
44:3 [v] Joel 3:18;
Jn 4:10 [w] S Pr 9:5;
S Isa 32:2; S 35:7
[x] S Isa 11:2;
Eze 36:27; S Mk 1:8;
S Ac 2:17 [y] Mal 3:10
[z] Isa 61:9; 65:23
44:4 [a] S Job 5:25;
S Ps 72:16
[b] S Lev 23:40
[c] S Job 40:22
44:5 [d] Ps 116:16;
Isa 19:21; Jer 50:5
[e] Ex 13:9 [f] Isa 60:3;
66:23; Zec 8:20-22;
13:9; 14:16

A **43:22–24** The Israelites may have brought sacrifices (see 1:11–15 and note), but their hearts were not right with God.

A **43:22** *not called…not wearied.* Apparently their prayers were halfhearted (contrast Ps 69:3).

43:23 *not burdened…nor wearied.* God did not make excessive demands on his people.

43:24 *calamus.* Linked with incense (see v. 23) also in SS 4:14; Jer 6:20. *fat.* See note on 34:6. *burdened…wearied.* See 1:14.

43:25 *blots out…transgressions.* In spite of the punishment Israel must suffer (v. 28), God is eager to forgive his people (see 1:18; 44:22–23; see also 40:2 and note).

43:26 *state the case.* The Lord takes Israel to court, as he did the nations in 41:21–22.

43:27 *first father.* Either (1) Adam (the ultimate father; see Ge 5:3 and note; see also note on Lk 3:23–38), (2) Abraham (the more immediate father; see 51:2) or (3) Jacob (the even more immediate father; cf. vv. 22,28). All were sinners, the main point for the present sinful generation. *those I sent to teach you.* Probably the priests and prophets.

43:28 *consigned…to destruction.* See TNIV text note; see also note on 34:2. Any town of Israel that harbored idolatry was to suffer this fate (Dt 13:12–15). Jerusalem suffered destruction at the hands of the Babylonians (2Ki 25:8–9) because of idolatry (see Eze 7:15–22).

44:1–2 *my servant.* See 41:8–9 and note.

44:2 *formed you.* See 43:1 and note. *in the womb.* See v. 24. The tenderness of the Creator is shown (see also 49:5; Jer 1:5 and note). *Do not be afraid.* See v. 8; 41:10 and note. *Jeshurun.* Israel (see TNIV text note and v. 1); found elsewhere only in Dt 32:15; 33:5,26.

A **44:3** *pour water…streams.* See 30:25; 32:2; 35:6–7 and notes; see also 41:18. *pour out my Spirit.* Associated with the Messianic age in 32:15; Joel 2:28 (see notes there; see also note on Zec 12:10).

44:4 *grass.* A symbol of luxuriant growth also in 35:7 (contrast 37:27; 40:6–8).

44:5 *call…by the name.* A willingness to identify with Jacob, the Lord's people. See 43:7 and note. *write on their hand.* Perhaps a mark of ownership (cf. 49:16; Rev 13:16) or a reminder of one's allegiance (cf. Ex 13:9,16).

44:6 ᵍ S Isa 41:21
ʰ S Job 19:25; Isa 43:1
ⁱ S Isa 41:4; Rev 1:8,17
ʲ S Dt 6:4;
S 1Ch 17:20;
S Ps 18:31; S Isa 43:10
44:7 ᵏ S Dt 32:39
ˡ S Isa 41:22,26
44:8 ᵐ S Isa 40:21;
S 42:9 ⁿ S Isa 43:10
ᵒ S Ge 49:24
44:9 ᵖ S Ex 20:4;
S Lev 19:4; Isa 40:19
ᑫ S Isa 41:24
ʳ S Isa 26:11
ˢ S Isa 1:29; 65:13;
66:5; Jer 22:22
44:10 ᵗ S Isa 40:19
ᵘ Isa 41:29; Jer 10:5;
Ac 19:26
44:11 ᵛ S ver 9;
S Isa 1:29
ʷ S 2Ki 19:18;
S Isa 37:19
44:12 ˣ S Isa 40:19;
41:6-7; 54:16
ʸ Ac 17:29 ᶻ Isa 40:28
44:13 ᵃ S Isa 41:7
ᵇ Ps 115:4-7
ᶜ S Jdg 17:4-5
44:14 ᵈ S Isa 41:19
44:15 ᵉ ver 19
ᶠ S Ex 20:5; Rev 9:20
ᵍ S 2Ch 25:14

THE LORD, NOT IDOLS

6 "This is what the LORD says—
    Israel's King ᵍ and Redeemer, ʰ the LORD Almighty:
I am the first and I am the last; ⁱ
    apart from me there is no God. ʲ
7 Who then is like me? ᵏ Let them proclaim it.
    Let them declare and lay out before me
what has happened since I established my ancient people,
    and what is yet to come—
    yes, let them foretell ˡ what will come.
8 Do not tremble, do not be afraid.
    Did I not proclaim ᵐ this and foretell it long ago?
You are my witnesses. Is there any God ⁿ besides me?
    No, there is no other Rock; ᵒ I know not one."

9 All who make idols ᵖ are nothing,
    and the things they treasure are worthless. ᑫ
Those who would speak up for them are blind; ʳ
    they are ignorant, to their own shame. ˢ
10 Who shapes a god and casts an idol, ᵗ
    which can profit nothing? ᵘ
11 People like that will be put to shame; ᵛ
    skilled workers are only human beings.
Let them all come together and take their stand;
    they will be brought down to terror and shame. ʷ

12 The blacksmith ˣ takes a tool
    and works with it in the coals;
he shapes an idol with hammers,
    he forges it with the might of his arm. ʸ
He gets hungry and loses his strength;
    he drinks no water and grows faint. ᶻ
13 The carpenter ᵃ measures with a line
    and makes an outline with a marker;
he roughs it out with chisels
    and marks it with compasses.
He shapes it in human form, ᵇ
    human form in all its glory,
    that it may dwell in a shrine. ᶜ
14 He cut down cedars,
    or perhaps took a cypress or oak.
He let it grow among the trees of the forest,
    or planted a pine, ᵈ and the rain made it grow.
15 It is used as fuel ᵉ for burning;
    some of it he takes and warms himself,
    he kindles a fire and bakes bread.
But he also fashions a god and worships ᶠ it;
    he makes an idol and bows ᵍ down to it.
16 Half of the wood he burns in the fire;
    over it he prepares his meal,
    he roasts his meat and eats his fill.
He also warms himself and says,

44:6 King. See 43:15 and note. Redeemer. See v. 24; 41:14 and
note. first ... last. See 41:4 and note. apart ... God. See 43:11; Ex
20:3 and notes.
44:7 foretell. See 41:22,26 and notes.
44:8 You are my witnesses. See 43:10 and note. Rock. See 17:10
and note. As in v. 2; 43:11–13, Isaiah may be drawing on the
song of Moses, which describes God as "the Rock" (Dt 32:4,15,
30–31), but the metaphor is also common in the Psalms (see
note on Ps 18:2).
A 44:9–20 A satire on the folly of idolatry (see 40:18–20
and note).
44:9 nothing ... worthless. Like the nations and their idols (see

40:17; 41:24 and notes). shame. Cf. v. 11; 42:17; 45:16.
44:11 skilled workers. See 40:19 and note.
44:12–13 blacksmith ... carpenter. See 48:5.
44:12 grows faint. But God never gets tired (40:28).
A 44:13 human form. Human beings were made in the image of God (see Ge 1:26–27 and notes), but an idol is
made in their image (see Dt 4:16; Ro 1:23 and note).
44:14 cedars ... cypress ... oak. The most valuable kinds of
wood then known. See 2:13; 9:10; 14:8 and notes.
44:15 worships ... bows down. Repeated in vv. 17,19; see 2:8,20.
44:16 roasts his meat ... warms himself. Although wood serves
common purposes, it is also made into an idol (see v. 19).

"Ah! I am warm; I see the fire. [h]"

[17] From the rest he makes a god, his idol;
  he bows down to it and worships. [i]

He prays [j] to it and says,
  "Save [k] me! You are my god!"

[18] They know nothing, they understand [l] nothing;
  their eyes [m] are plastered over so they cannot see,
  and their minds closed so they cannot understand.

[19] No one stops to think,
  no one has the knowledge or understanding [n] to say,
"Half of it I used for fuel; [o]
  I even baked bread over its coals,
  I roasted meat and I ate.
Shall I make a detestable [p] thing from what is left?
  Shall I bow down to a block of wood?" [q]

[20] Such people feed on ashes, [r] a deluded [s] heart misleads them;
  they cannot save themselves, or say,
  "Is not this thing in my right hand a lie? [t] [u]"

[21] "Remember [v] these things, Jacob,
  for you, Israel, are my servant. [w]
I have made you, you are my servant; [x]
  Israel, I will not forget you. [y]

[22] I have swept away [z] your offenses like a cloud,
  your sins like the morning mist.
Return [a] to me,
  for I have redeemed [b] you."

[23] Sing for joy, [c] you heavens, for the LORD has done this;
  shout aloud, you earth [d] beneath.
Burst into song, you mountains, [e]
  you forests and all your trees, [f]
for the LORD has redeemed [g] Jacob,
  he displays his glory [h] in Israel.

JERUSALEM TO BE INHABITED

[24] "This is what the LORD says—
  your Redeemer, [i] who formed [j] you in the womb: [k]

I am the LORD,
  who has made all things,
  who alone stretched out the heavens, [l]
  who spread out the earth [m] by myself,

[25] who foils [n] the signs of false prophets
  and makes fools of diviners, [o]
who overthrows the learning of the wise [p]
  and turns it into nonsense, [q]

44:16 [h] Isa 47:14
44:17 [i] S Ex 20:5;
Isa 2:8; Jer 1:16
[j] S 1Ki 18:26
[k] S Jdg 10:14;
Isa 45:20; 46:7; 47:15
44:18 [l] Isa 1:3;
S 16:12; Jer 4:22; 10:8,
14,14-15 [m] S Isa 6:9-
10; S 29:10
44:19 [n] ver 18-19;
Isa 5:13; 27:11; 45:20
[o] ver 15 [p] S Dt 27:15
[q] Isa 40:20
44:20 [r] Ps 102:9
[s] S Job 15:31; Ro 1:21-
23,28, 2Th 2:11;
2Ti 3:13 [t] S Dt 4:28;
Hos 10:5; 13:2
[u] Isa 59:3,4,13;
Jer 9:3; 10:14; 51:17;
Ro 1:25
44:21 [v] Isa 46:8;
Zec 10:9 [w] S Isa 43:1
[x] S Ps 136:22;
S Isa 27:11 [y] Ps 27:10;
Isa 49:15; Jer 31:20
44:22 [z] S 2Sa 12:13;
S 2Ch 6:21; Ac 3:19
[a] S Job 22:23;
Isa 45:22; 55:7;
Jer 36:3; Mal 3:7
[b] S Isa 33:24;
S Mt 20:28; 1Co 6:20
44:23 [c] S Ps 98:4;
S Isa 12:6
[d] S 1Ch 16:31;
Ps 148:7 [e] S Ps 98:8
[f] S Ps 65:13
[g] S Ex 6:6; Isa 51:11;
62:12 [h] S Ex 16:7;
S Lev 10:3; S Isa 4:2;
43:7; 46:13; 49:3;
52:1; 55:5; 60:9,21;
61:3; Jer 30:19
44:24 [i] S Job 19:25;
Isa 43:14 [j] S Isa 27:11
[k] S Ps 139:13
[l] S Ge 2:1; S Isa 42:5
[m] S Ge 1:1
44:25 [n] Ps 33:10
[o] Lev 19:26; 1Sa 6:2;
Isa 2:6; 8:19; 47:13;
Jer 27:9; Da 2:2,10;
4:7; Mic 3:7; Zec 10:2
[p] S Job 5:13; 1Co 1:27
[q] 2Sa 15:31; 1Co 1:19-
20

44:17 *Save me.* King Amaziah was condemned for worshiping the gods of Seir (Edom), a nation he had defeated
in battle (see note on 2Ch 25:14–25). Isaiah denounces such
idolatry as totally irrational (see 45:20). Whereas those who
worshiped idols associated the god with the idol, for Isaiah
there was no god for the idol to represent, so he depicts idolatry
as worship of a mere "block of wood" (v. 19).

44:18 *eyes are plastered . . . minds closed.* Israel's condition in 6:9–10 (see note there). The description ironically
characterizes both the idols and those who worship them. See
also Ps 82:5 and note.

44:19 *detestable thing.* The Lord detests idols (see Dt
27:15). In 1Ki 11:5,7; 2Ki 23:13 Molek and Chemosh are
called detestable gods. Those who worship idols are also called
detestable (see 41:24 and note).
44:20 *feed on ashes.* Even devoted worship does not benefit
the idolater. Cf. Hos 12:1. *lie.* Or "fraud." See 2Th 2:11 and note.

44:21 *my servant.* See vv. 1–2; 41:8–9 and note.
44:22 *swept away your offenses.* As in 40:2 (see note there), the
suffering of Israel has paved the way for forgiveness and the
restoration of the nation (see 43:25 and note). *Return to me.* Cf.
Jer 31:18; Zec 1:3 and note. *redeemed.* Cf. v. 23; see notes on 35:9;
41:14; 43:1.
44:23 *Sing for joy . . . shout aloud.* Nature is called on to join in
praise (see also 35:1; 49:13). *Burst into song, you mountains.* See
49:13; 55:12. *displays his glory.* See 35:2; 40:5 and notes.
44:24 *Redeemer.* See 41:14 and note. *stretched out . . . spread
out.* See 40:22 and note; cf. 51:13.
44:25 *signs of false prophets.* See Dt 13:1–5 and notes. *diviners.*
The Hebrew for this word is used of Balaam (see Jos 13:22 and
note), the medium at Endor (1Sa 28:8) and false prophets (see
Jer 27:9 and note). It is linked with enchanting and sorcery (see
3:2–3 and note; Dt 18:9–11 and note on 18:9). *overthrows . . . the
wise.* See 29:14 and note.

44:26 *r* Isa 59:21;
Zec 1:6 *s* Isa 46:10;
55:11; Jer 23:20;
39:16; La 2:17;
Da 9:12; S Mt 5:18
t Isa 1:1 *u* S Ps 74:3;
S Isa 51:3 *v* S Ezr 9:9;
S Ps 51:18; Isa 49:8-
21; S 61:4
44:27 *w* S Isa 11:15;
S 19:5; Rev 16:12
44:28 *x* S 2Ch 36:22
; S Isa 41:2
y S Isa 14:32 *z* Ezr 1:2-
4 *a* S Isa 28:16; 58:12
45:1 *b* S Ps 45:7
c S 2Ch 36:22;
S Isa 41:2 *d* Ps 73:23;
Isa 41:13; 42:6
e Isa 48:14; Jer 50:35;
51:20,24; Mic 4:13
45:2 *f* Ex 23:20
g S Isa 40:4
h S Isa 13:2
i Ps 107:16; 147:13;
Jer 51:30; La 2:9;
Na 3:13
45:3 *j* S 2Ki 24:13;
Jer 50:37; 51:13
k Jer 41:8 *l* Isa 41:23
m S Ex 33:12;
S Isa 43:1
45:4 *n* S Isa 14:1;
41:8-9 *o* Ac 17:23
45:5 *p* S Isa 44:8
q S Dt 32:12;
S Ps 18:31; S Isa 43:10
r S Ps 18:39;
Eze 30:24-25
45:6 *s* S Ps 113:3;
Isa 43:5 *t* S Isa 11:9
u ver 5,18; Isa 14:13-
14; 47:8,10; Zep 2:15
45:7 *v* S Ge 1:4;
S Ex 10:22
w S Isa 14:15; S 31:2;
La 3:38
45:8 *x* Ps 72:6;
S 133:3; Joel 3:18
y ver 24; Ps 85:11;
S Isa 41:2; 46:13;
48:18; 60:21; 61:10,11;
62:1; Hos 10:12;
Joel 2:23; Am 5:24;
Mal 4:2

²⁶who carries out the words *r* of his servants
and fulfills *s* the predictions of his messengers,

who says of Jerusalem, *t* 'It shall be inhabited,'
of the towns of Judah, 'They shall be rebuilt,'
and of their ruins, *u* 'I will restore them,' *v*
²⁷who says to the watery deep, 'Be dry,
and I will dry up *w* your streams,'
²⁸who says of Cyrus, *x* 'He is my shepherd
and will accomplish all that I please;
he will say of Jerusalem, *y* "Let it be rebuilt,"
and of the temple, *z* "Let its foundations *a* be laid." '

45

"This is what the LORD says to his anointed, *b*
to Cyrus, *c* whose right hand I take hold *d* of
to subdue nations *e* before him
and to strip kings of their armor,
to open doors before him
so that gates will not be shut:
²I will go before you *f*
and will level *g* the mountains*a*;
I will break down gates *h* of bronze
and cut through bars of iron. *i*
³I will give you the treasures *j* of darkness,
riches stored in secret places, *k*
so that you may know *l* that I am the LORD,
the God of Israel, who summons you by name. *m*
⁴For the sake of Jacob my servant, *n*
of Israel my chosen,
I summon you by name
and bestow on you a title of honor,
though you do not acknowledge *o* me.
⁵I am the LORD, and there is no other; *p*
apart from me there is no God. *q*
I will strengthen you, *r*
though you have not acknowledged me,
⁶so that from the rising of the sun
to the place of its setting *s*
people may know *t* there is none besides me. *u*
I am the LORD, and there is no other.
⁷I form the light and create darkness, *v*
I bring prosperity and create disaster; *w*
I, the LORD, do all these things.

⁸"You heavens above, rain *x* down my righteousness; *y*
let the clouds shower it down.

---

a 2 Dead Sea Scrolls and Septuagint; the meaning of the word in the Masoretic Text is uncertain.

44:26 *servants … messengers.* The true prophets (see 42:19; Jer 7:25 and notes). *inhabited … rebuilt.* See Jer 32:15; cf. Isa 58:12; 61:4. *ruins … restore.* Contrast 6:11.
44:27 *Be dry.* A reference to the crossing of the Red Sea (see 11:15; 37:25; 43:16–17 and notes; cf. 50:2; 51:10).
44:28 *Cyrus.* See 41:2 and note; see also chart, p. 482. *shepherd.* Often applied to rulers (see 2Sa 5:2; Jer 23:2). *Jerusalem … temple.* The decree of Cyrus (Ezr 1:2–4; 6:3–5) authorized the rebuilding of the temple, which would lead to a restored Jerusalem (see 45:13).

A 45:1 *anointed.* "Messiah" comes from the Hebrew for this word. Cyrus, a foreign emperor, is called "his anointed" just as he is called "my shepherd" (44:28), because God has appointed him to carry out a divine commission in his role as king. Nebuchadnezzar is similarly called "my servant" (see Jer 25:9 and note; 27:6; 43:10). The servant—Christ (see note on 42:1–4)—is called "the Anointed One" in Da 9:25–26 (see TNIV text note on Mt 1:1).

See also Ps 2:2 and note. *right hand I … hold.* See 41:13 and note.
45:2 *gates of bronze … bars of iron.* Normally the doors of city gates were made of wood, and the bars were metal (see Jdg 16:3 and note).
45:3 *that you may know.* God's actions reveal his power (cf. Eze 6:7; 7:27). *summons you by name.* To indicate God's control of Cyrus's activities. See v. 4; see also note on 43:1.

B 45:4 *my servant.* See 41:8–9 and note. *title of honor.* Perhaps "anointed" (v. 1). *though … not acknowledge me.* See v. 5. Cyrus apparently worshiped the chief Babylonian deity, Marduk, whom he praised in his inscriptions.
45:5 *I … there is no other.* See vv. 6,14,18,21–22; 43:11 and note.
45:6 *rising … to … setting.* The whole earth (see Mal 1:11 and note).
45:7 *darkness … disaster.* Such as the darkness that plagued the Egyptians (see Ex 10:21–23; Ps 105:28; cf. Isa 47:11; Am 3:6).
45:8 *rain down … shower.* A picture of abundance (see Hos

Let the earth open wide,
    let salvation[z] spring up,
let righteousness flourish with it;
    I, the LORD, have created it.

⁹ "Woe to those who quarrel[a] with their Maker,[b]
    those who are nothing but potsherds[c]
    among the potsherds on the ground.
Does the clay say to the potter,[d]
    'What are you making?'[e]
Does your work say,
    'The potter has no hands'?[f]
¹⁰ Woe to those who say to their father,
    'What have you begotten?'
or to their mother,
    'What have you brought to birth?'

¹¹ "This is what the LORD says—
    the Holy One[g] of Israel, and its Maker:[h]
Concerning things to come,
    do you question me about my children,
    or give me orders about the work of my hands?[i]
¹² It is I who made the earth[j]
    and created human beings on it.
My own hands stretched out the heavens;[k]
    I marshaled their starry hosts.[l]
¹³ I will raise up Cyrus[a][m] in my righteousness:
    I will make all his ways straight.[n]
He will rebuild my city[o]
    and set my exiles free,
but not for a price or reward,[p]
    says the LORD Almighty."

¹⁴ This is what the LORD says:

"The products[q] of Egypt and the merchandise of Cush,[b]
    and those tall Sabeans[r]—
they will come over to you[s]
    and will be yours;
they will trudge behind you,[t]
    coming over to you in chains.[u]
They will bow down before you
    and plead[v] with you, saying,
'Surely God is with you,[w] and there is no other;
    there is no other god.[x]' "

¹⁵ Truly you are a God who has been hiding[y] himself,
    the God and Savior[z] of Israel.
¹⁶ All the makers of idols will be put to shame and disgraced;[a]
    they will go off into disgrace together.
¹⁷ But Israel will be saved[b] by the LORD

---

[a] 13 Hebrew *him*   [b] 14 That is, the upper Nile region

45:8 [z] S Ps 85:9; Isa 12:3
45:9 [a] S Job 12:13; S 15:25; S 27:2; 1Co 10:22
[b] S Job 33:13
[c] Ps 22:15
[d] S Isa 29:16; Ro 9:20-21*
[e] S Job 9:12; Da 4:35
[f] S Isa 10:15
45:11 [g] S Isa 1:4
[h] S Ps 149:2; S Isa 51:13 [i] S Ps 8:6; S Isa 19:25
45:12 [j] S Ge 1:1
[k] S Ge 2:1; S Isa 48:13
[l] S Ne 9:6; S Job 38:32
45:13 [m] S 2Ch 36:2 2; S Isa 41:2
[n] S 1Ki 8:36; S Ps 26:12; S Isa 40:4
[o] S Ezr 1:2 [p] Isa 52:3
45:14 [q] S 2Sa 8:2; Isa 18:7; 60:5
[r] S Isa 2:3; 60:11; 62:2; Zec 8:20-22
[s] S Isa 2:3
[t] S Ge 27:29
[u] S 2Sa 3:34; S Isa 14:1-2
[v] Jer 16:19; Zec 8:20-23 [w] 1Co 14:25
[x] S Ps 18:31; S Isa 11:9; S 43:10
45:15 [y] S Dt 31:17; Ps 44:24; S Isa 1:15
[z] S Isa 25:9
45:16 [a] S Ps 35:4; S Isa 1:29
45:17 [b] Jer 23:6; 33:16; Ro 11:26

10:12 and note). *righteousness.* In v. 13; 41:2 Cyrus is mentioned in connection with God's righteousness. God is "making things right" through the Persian king. *salvation spring up.* God will deliver his people. *righteousness flourish.* Peace and justice will prevail (cf. 11:4).
45:9 *clay say to the potter.* See 29:16 and note; cf. 64:8; Jer 18:6; see also Ro 9:20–21 and notes.
45:11 *Holy One of Israel.* See 1:4 and note. *children . . . work of my hands.* See 29:23 and note.
45:12 *stretched . . . heavens.* See 40:22 and note. *marshaled . . . starry hosts.* See 40:26 and note.
45:13 *Cyrus in my righteousness.* See note on 41:2. *make . . . ways straight.* Enabling him to reach his goals (see v. 2; see also

40:3 and note; cf. Pr 3:6 and note). *rebuild my city.* See note on 44:28. *not for a price.* Since God had not received a payment when he sold them (see 52:3 and note; contrast note on 43:3).

A **45:14** *products . . . merchandise.* See 18:7 and note. *Egypt . . . Cush . . . Sabeans.* See notes on 18:1; 43:3. *coming over to you . . . bow down.* See Ps 68:31. Israel's future domination over her former enemies has been mentioned in 11:14; 14:1–2 (see note on 14:1); it is also the theme of 49:23; 54:3; 60:11–14. *Surely God is with you.* One day the nations will acknowledge Israel's God (see v. 23; 19:23,25; Zec 8:20–23 and notes).
45:15 *hiding himself.* God's plans and actions are a mystery to humans (cf. 54:8; 55:8–9). *Savior.* See v. 21 and note on 43:3.
45:16 *put to shame.* See 42:17; 44:9.

45:17 ᶜS Isa 12:2
ᵈS Ge 30:23;
S Isa 29:22; S 41:11
45:18 ᵉS Ge 1:1
ᶠS Ge 1:2 ᵍS Ge 1:26
ʰver 5; Dt 4:35
45:19 ⁱIsa 48:16;
65:4 ʲJer 2:31
ᵏver 25; Isa 41:8;
65:9; Jer 31:36
ˡS Dt 4:29;
S 2Ch 15:2
ᵐS Dt 30:11
45:20 ⁿS Isa 43:9
ᵒS Isa 44:19
ᵖPs 115:7; Isa 46:1;
Jer 10:5 ᑫDt 32:37;
S Isa 44:17; Jer 1:16;
2:28
45:21 ʳS Isa 41:22
ˢIsa 46:10 ᵗver 5;
S Ps 46:10; Isa 46:9;
Mk 12:32 ᵘPs 11:7
ᵛS Ps 3:8; S Isa 25:9
45:22 ʷS Isa 44:22;
Zec 12:10 ˣNu 21:8-
9; S 2Ch 20:12
ʸS Ge 49:10;
S Isa 11:9,12; 49:6,12
ᶻHos 13:4
45:23 ᵃS Ge 22:16;
S Isa 14:24
ᵇS Dt 30:11; Heb 6:13
ᶜIsa 55:11 ᵈS ver 14
ᵉS Ps 63:11;
S Isa 19:18; Ro 14:11*;
Php 2:10-11
45:24 ᶠS ver 8;
Jer 33:16
ᵍS Dt 33:29;
S Ps 18:39;
S Isa 40:26; 63:1
ʰS Isa 41:11
45:25 ⁱS ver 19
ʲS Isa 4:3; S 49:4
ᵏS Isa 24:23; S 41:16

with an everlasting salvation; ᶜ
you will never be put to shame or disgraced, ᵈ
   to ages everlasting.

18 For this is what the LORD says—
  he who created the heavens,
    he is God;
  he who fashioned and made the earth, ᵉ
    he founded it;
  he did not create it to be empty, ᶠ
    but formed it to be inhabited ᵍ—
  he says:
  "I am the LORD,
    and there is no other. ʰ
19 I have not spoken in secret, ⁱ
    from somewhere in a land of darkness; ʲ
  I have not said to Jacob's descendants, ᵏ
    'Seek ˡ me in vain.'
  I, the LORD, speak the truth;
    I declare what is right. ᵐ

20 "Gather together ⁿ and come;
    assemble, you fugitives from the nations.
  Ignorant ᵒ are those who carry ᵖ about idols of wood,
    who pray to gods that cannot save. ᑫ
21 Declare what is to be, present it—
    let them take counsel together.
  Who foretold ʳ this long ago,
    who declared it from the distant past? ˢ
  Was it not I, the LORD?
    And there is no God apart from me, ᵗ
  a righteous God ᵘ and a Savior; ᵛ
    there is none but me.

22 "Turn ʷ to me and be saved, ˣ
    all you ends of the earth; ʸ
  for I am God, and there is no other. ᶻ
23 By myself I have sworn, ᵃ
    my mouth has uttered in all integrity ᵇ
    a word that will not be revoked: ᶜ
  Before me every knee will bow; ᵈ
    by me every tongue will swear. ᵉ
24 They will say of me, 'In the LORD alone
    are deliverance ᶠ and strength. ᵍ'"
  All who have raged against him
    will come to him and be put to shame. ʰ
25 But all the descendants ⁱ of Israel
    will find deliverance ʲ in the LORD
    and will make their boast in him. ᵏ

45:17 *everlasting salvation.* Cf. the "everlasting kindness" of 54:8. *never be put to shame.* See 29:22 and note.
45:18 *created . . . fashioned.* See 40:21–22 and notes. *empty.* Or "formless" or "chaotic" (see Ge 1:2 and note). *to be inhabited.* The Holy Land was now empty (see 6:11; Jer 4:23–26) and chaotic but would soon have inhabitants (see 44:26,28) and be orderly again.
45:19 *in secret . . . darkness.* Probably an allusion to the clandestine ways of mediums and spiritists (see 8:19–20 and notes; 29:4). *Seek me in vain.* Cf. Jer 29:13–14.
45:20 *Ignorant . . . save.* See 44:17–18 and notes.
45:21 *Declare . . . present.* See 41:21–22 and note. *foretold . . . distant past.* See 41:26 and note.

45:22 *Turn . . . be saved.* See 49:6 and note; see also the invitation of 55:7. *ends of the earth.* See 11:12 and note; 42:10.

45:23 *By myself I have sworn.* Explained in Heb 6:13 (see note there). See also 62:8. *word . . . not . . . revoked.* See 55:10–11. *every knee . . . every tongue.* See v. 14 and note. Paul quotes this portion of Isaiah in Ro 14:11 and Php 2:10–11 to describe Christ's exalted position.
45:24 *In the LORD alone . . . strength.* See v. 5 and note. This is the climax of the refrain that runs through the chapter. *All . . . put to shame.* Very similar to 41:11 except for "against you" (Israel).
45:25 *make their boast.* The Hebrew for this verb is translated "glory" in 41:16.

GODS OF BABYLON

46

Bel *l* bows down, Nebo stoops low;
　　their idols *m* are borne by beasts of burden.*a*
The images that are carried *n* about are burdensome,
　　a burden for the weary.
2 They stoop and bow down together;
　　unable to rescue the burden,
　　they themselves go off into captivity.*o*

3 "Listen *p* to me, house of Jacob,
　all the remnant *q* of the house of Israel,
you whom I have upheld since your birth,*r*
　　and have carried *s* since you were born.*t*
4 Even to your old age and gray hairs *u*
　I am he,*v* I am he who will sustain you.
I have made you and I will carry you;
　　I will sustain *w* you and I will rescue you.

5 "With whom will you compare me or count me equal?
　　To whom will you liken me that we may be compared?*x*
6 Some pour out gold from their bags
　　and weigh out silver on the scales;
they hire a goldsmith *y* to make it into a god,
　　and they bow down and worship it.*z*
7 They lift it to their shoulders and carry *a* it;
　　they set it up in its place, and there it stands.
From that spot it cannot move.*b*
Though people cry out to it, it does not answer;*c*
　　it cannot save *d* them from their troubles.

8 "Remember *e* this, keep it in mind,
　　take it to heart, you rebels.*f*
9 Remember the former things,*g* those of long ago;*h*
　I am God, and there is no other;
　I am God, and there is none like me.*i*
10 I make known the end from the beginning,*j*
　　from ancient times,*k* what is still to come.*l*
I say, 'My purpose will stand,*m*
　　and I will do all that I please.'
11 From the east I summon *n* a bird of prey;*o*
　　from a far-off land, a man to fulfill my purpose.
What I have said, that I will bring about;
　　what I have planned,*p* that I will do.*q*
12 Listen *r* to me, you stubborn-hearted,*s*
　　you who are now far from my righteousness.*t*
13 I am bringing my righteousness *u* near,
　　it is not far away;
　　and my salvation *v* will not be delayed.

---

a 1 Or *are but beasts and cattle*

46:1 *l* S Isa 21:9;
Jer 50:2; 51:44
m S 1Sa 5:2 *n* ver 7;
S Isa 45:20
46:2 *o* S Jdg 18:17-
18; S 2Sa 5:21;
Jer 51:47
46:3 *p* ver 12;
Isa 48:12; 51:1
q S Isa 1:9
r S Ps 139:13; Isa 44:2
s S Dt 1:31; S Ps 28:9
t S Ps 22:10
46:4 *u* Ps 71:18
v S Dt 32:39;
S Isa 43:13
w S Ps 18:35;
S 119:117
46:5 *x* S Ex 15:11;
Job 41:10; Isa 40:18,
25; Jer 49:19
46:6 *y* S Isa 40:19
z S Ex 20:5; Isa 44:17;
Hos 13:2
46:7 *a* S ver 1
b S 1Sa 5:3; S Isa 41:7
c S 1Ki 18:26
d S Isa 44:17; S 47:13
46:8 *e* S Isa 44:21
f S Isa 1:2
46:9 *g* S Isa 41:22
h S Dt 32:7
i S Ex 8:10; S Isa 45:5,
21; Mk 12:32
46:10 *j* S Isa 41:4
k S Isa 45:21
l S Isa 41:22
m S Pr 19:21;
S Isa 7:7, 9; S 44:26;
Ac 5:39; Eph 1:11
46:11 *n* S Jdg 4:10;
S Ezr 1:2 *o* S Isa 8:8
p S Isa 25:1
q S Ge 41:25;
Jer 44:28
46:12 *r* S ver 3
s S Ex 32:9; S Isa 9:9
t Ps 119:150; Isa 48:1;
Jer 2:5
46:13 *u* S Isa 1:26;
S 45:8; Ro 3:21
v S Ps 85:9

46:1 *Bel.* Another name for Marduk, the chief deity of Babylon.
The name "Bel" is equivalent to Canaanite "Baal" and means
"lord." *bows down . . . stoops.* In disgrace (see v. 2; 21:9 and note).
Nebo. Nabu, the god of learning and writing and the son of Marduk (see note on Ezr 10:43).
46:2 *go off into captivity.* The idols join their worshipers in exile
(see Jer 48:7 and note; 49:3; Hos 10:5; Am 1:15).
46:3 *remnant.* See 1:9 and note. *since . . . birth . . . since . . . born.*
See 44:2 and note.
46:4 *old age and gray hairs.* Cf. Ps 37:25. *sustain . . . made . . . rescue.* Unlike the helpless idols of vv. 1–2. See 41:10,13; 43:1–2
and notes.
46:5–7 See 40:18–20 and note.
46:6 *bow down and worship.* See 44:15,17,19.
46:7 *carry.* See v. 1. *cannot save.* See 44:17 and note.

46:8 *rebels.* Israel. See 1:2 and note; cf. 1:20,23,28; 30:1; 57:4.
46:9 *former things.* See 41:22 and note. *there is no other.* See
43:11 and note.
46:10–11 *My purpose.* Especially God's purposes and plans regarding Babylon and Israel (see 8:9–10; 14:24; 48:14 and notes).
Cf. Ps 33:11.
46:10 *from the beginning.* See 41:26 and note.
46:11 *east . . . bird of prey.* Cyrus, king of Persia (see 41:2 and
note). The swiftness and power of a bird of prey are in view (see
8:8 and note; Jer 49:22; cf. Da 8:4).
46:12 *stubborn-hearted.* See v. 8; 48:4; Eze 2:4.
46:13 *righteousness.* Here equivalent to salvation. See 41:2;
45:8 and notes. *salvation.* See note on 43:3. *splendor.* See 35:2;
40:5 and notes; see also 44:23; 49:3.

46:13 ʷS Ps 74:2;
Joel 2:32
ˣS Isa 44:23
47:1 ʸS Job 2:13;
S Isa 29:4
ᶻS Isa 21:9; S 23:12
ᵃPs 137:8; Jer 50:42;
51:33; Zec 2:7
ᵇDt 28:56
47:2 ᶜEx 11:5;
Mt 24:41 ᵈS Jdg 16:21
ᵉS Ge 24:65
ᶠS Isa 32:11
47:3 ᵍS Ge 2:25;
Eze 16:37; Na 3:5
ʰS Isa 20:4
ⁱS Isa 1:24; S 34:8
ʲIsa 13:18-19
47:4 ᵏS Job 19:25
ˡS Isa 13:4 ᵐIsa 48:2;
Jer 50:34; Am 4:13
ⁿS Isa 1:4; 48:17
47:5 ᵒS Job 2:13
ᵖIsa 9:2; 13:10
ᑫS Isa 21:9 ʳver 7;
La 1:1; Rev 18:7
ˢS Isa 13:19;
Rev 17:18
47:6 ᵗS 2Ch 28:9
ᵘS Dt 13:15;
S Isa 42:24; Jer 2:7;
50:11 ᵛIsa 10:13
ʷS Isa 14:6
47:7 ˣS Isa 10:13;
Da 4:30 ʸS ver 5;
Rev 18:7 ᶻS Isa 42:23,
25 ᵃS Dt 32:29
47:8 ᵇS Isa 32:9
ᶜS Isa 45:6
ᵈIsa 49:21; 54:4;
La 1:1; Rev 18:7
47:9 ᵉS Ps 55:15;
73:19; 1Th 5:3;
Rev 18:8-10
ᶠS Isa 13:18 ᵍIsa 4:1;
Jer 15:8; 18:21
ʰver 12; Na 3:4;
Mal 3:5

I will grant salvation to Zion, ʷ
  my splendor ˣ to Israel.

THE FALL OF BABYLON

47

"Go down, sit in the dust, ʸ
  Virgin Daughter ᶻ Babylon;
sit on the ground without a throne,
  queen city of the Babylonians. ᵃ ᵃ
No more will you be called
  tender or delicate. ᵇ
² Take millstones ᶜ and grind ᵈ flour;
  take off your veil. ᵉ
Lift up your skirts, ᶠ bare your legs,
  and wade through the streams.
³ Your nakedness ᵍ will be exposed
  and your shame ʰ uncovered.
I will take vengeance; ⁱ
  I will spare no one. ʲ"

⁴ Our Redeemer ᵏ—the LORD Almighty ˡ is his name ᵐ—
  is the Holy One ⁿ of Israel.

⁵ "Sit in silence, ᵒ go into darkness, ᵖ
  queen city of the Babylonians; ᑫ
no more will you be called
  queen ʳ of kingdoms. ˢ
⁶ I was angry ᵗ with my people
  and desecrated my inheritance; ᵘ
I gave them into your hand, ᵛ
  and you showed them no mercy. ʷ
Even on the aged
  you laid a very heavy yoke.
⁷ You said, 'I am forever ˣ—
  the eternal queen!' ʸ
But you did not consider these things
  or reflect ᶻ on what might happen. ᵃ

⁸ "Now then, listen, you lover of pleasure,
  lounging in your security ᵇ
and saying to yourself,
  'I am, and there is none besides me. ᶜ
I will never be a widow ᵈ
  or suffer the loss of children.'
⁹ Both of these will overtake you
  in a moment, ᵉ on a single day:
  loss of children ᶠ and widowhood. ᵍ
They will come upon you in full measure,
  in spite of your many sorceries ʰ

ᵃ 1 Or *Chaldeans*; also in verse 5

47:1 *sit in the dust…on the ground.* A sign of mourning (see 3:26). *Virgin Daughter Babylon.* A personification of Babylon (see note on 2Ki 19:21).
47:2 *millstones and grind.* A menial task performed by women (see Ex 11:5; Jdg 9:53 and notes). *through the streams.* Probably on the way to exile.
47:3 *nakedness will be exposed.* See Eze 16:36. Babylon is no longer a queen (see vv. 5,7); she is reduced to a servant girl or a prostitute (see v. 8). *take vengeance.* See 34:8 and note. *spare no one.* See 13:18–20.
47:4 *Redeemer.* See note on 41:14. *LORD Almighty.* See 13:4 and note. *Holy One of Israel.* See 1:4; 41:14 and notes.
47:5 *queen city of the Babylonians.* See v. 1. *queen of kingdoms.* Babylon was a very beautiful city (see 13:19 and note) and the power center of the empire.

47:6 *angry…desecrated my inheritance.* See 10:5–6 (where Assyria is God's tool); 42:24 and note; 43:28 and note; La 2:2. *Even on the aged.* Their suffering fulfilled Moses' curse for covenant disobedience (Dt 28:49–50).
47:7 *I am forever.* Cf. the arrogant words of Nebuchadnezzar in Da 4:30.
47:8,10 *I am…none besides me.* Almost a claim of deity (cf. the Lord's words in 43:11; 45:5–6,18,22; cf. also Ex 3:14–15; 20:3; Dt 6:4 and notes; see also Isa 14:12–15 and note).
47:8 *lounging in your security.* Similar language is used of the complacent women of Jerusalem in 32:9,11. *widow.* Deserted and distressed. See v. 9; 13:16,18; 14:22.
47:9,12 *sorceries…spells.* Magical practices to avoid danger and to inflict harm on the enemy (see 3:2–3 and note).

and all your potent spells. [i]
[10] You have trusted [j] in your wickedness
and have said, 'No one sees me.' [k]
Your wisdom [l] and knowledge mislead [m] you
when you say to yourself,
'I am, and there is none besides me.'
[11] Disaster [n] will come upon you,
and you will not know how to conjure it away.
A calamity will fall upon you
that you cannot ward off with a ransom;
a catastrophe you cannot foresee
will suddenly [o] come upon you.

[12] "Keep on, then, with your magic spells
and with your many sorceries, [p]
which you have labored at since childhood.
Perhaps you will succeed,
perhaps you will cause terror.
[13] All the counsel you have received has only worn you out! [q]
Let your astrologers [r] come forward,
those stargazers who make predictions month by month,
let them save [s] you from what is coming upon you.
[14] Surely they are like stubble; [t]
the fire [u] will burn them up.
They cannot even save themselves
from the power of the flame. [v]
Here are no coals to warm anyone;
here is no fire to sit by.
[15] That is all they can do for you—
these you have dealt with
and labored [w] with since childhood.
All of them go on in their error;
there is not one that can save [x] you.

STUBBORN ISRAEL

48

"Listen to this, house of Jacob,
you who are called by the name of Israel [y]
and come from the line of Judah, [z]
you who take oaths [a] in the name of the LORD [b]
and invoke [c] the God of Israel—
but not in truth [d] or righteousness—
[2] you who call yourselves citizens of the holy city [e]
and claim to rely [f] on the God of Israel—
the LORD Almighty is his name: [g]
[3] I foretold the former things [h] long ago,
my mouth announced [i] them and I made them known;
then suddenly [j] I acted, and they came to pass.
[4] For I knew how stubborn [k] you were;
the sinews of your neck [l] were iron,
your forehead [m] was bronze.
[5] Therefore I told you these things long ago;
before they happened I announced [n] them to you
so that you could not say,

Cross-references (right column)

47:9 [i] Dt 18:10-11; Rev 9:21; 18:23
47:10 [j] S Job 15:31; Ps 52:7; 62:10
[k] 2Ki 21:16; S Isa 29:15 [l] S Isa 5:21
[m] Isa 44:20
47:11 [n] S Isa 10:3; S 14:15; S 21:9; S 31:2; Lk 17:27
[o] Ps 55:15; S Isa 17:14; 1Th 5:3
47:12 [p] S ver 9; S Ex 7:11
47:13 [q] Isa 57:10; Jer 51:58; Hab 2:13
[r] S Isa 19:3; S 44:25
[s] ver 15; S Isa 5:29; 43:13; 46:7
47:14 [t] S Isa 5:24
[u] S Isa 30:30
[v] Isa 10:17; Jer 51:30, 32, 58
47:15 [w] Rev 18:11
[x] S ver 13; S Isa 44:17
48:1 [y] S Ge 17:5
[z] S Ge 29:35
[a] S Isa 19:18
[b] S Isa 20:42; S Isa 43:7 [c] Ex 23:13; 2Sa 14:11; Ps 50:16; Isa 58:2; Jer 7:9-10; 44:26 [d] Isa 59:14; Jer 4:2; 5:2; Da 8:12; Zec 8:3
48:2 [e] S Ne 11:1; S Isa 1:26; S Mt 4:5
[f] S Isa 10:20; Ro 2:17
[g] S Isa 47:4
48:3 [h] S Isa 41:22
[i] S Isa 40:21; 45:21
[j] S Isa 17:14; 30:13
48:4 [k] S Isa 9:9
[l] S Ex 32:9; S Dt 9:27; Ac 7:51 [m] Eze 3:9
48:5 [n] S Isa 40:21; S 42:9

Study notes (bottom)

47:10 *No one sees me.* See 29:15 and note.

47:11 *with a ransom.* The Medes and Persians would not accept any settlement short of surrender (see 13:17).

47:13 *astrologers...stargazers.* Babylon probably utilized their services more than any other nation (see Da 2:2,10).

47:14 *stubble.* This will be a rapid, powerful fire. See note on 1:31; cf. Mal 4:1 and note. *cannot...save themselves.* In contrast to the mighty Savior of Israel (see 43:3 and note), astrologers and sorcerers are as helpless as idols (see 44:17 and note). *no coals to warm anyone.* A subtle reference to firewood, a material from which pagans sometimes made idols (see 44:15).

48:1 *called by the name.* They belong to Israel (see 43:7 and note). *Israel.* See Ge 32:28 and note. *Judah.* The main tribe of the southern kingdom. See Ge 49:8 and note. *not in truth.* Contrast the oaths of 65:16 (see note there).

48:2 *holy city.* Jerusalem, where the temple was located (see 2:2–4 and note; 52:1; 56:7; 57:13; 64:10–11; 65:11). See also 1:26; 4:3 and notes; Da 9:24. *rely on...God.* Superficially (see 10:20; contrast 31:1; 36:6,9; Eze 29:6–7). *LORD Almighty.* See 13:4 and note.

48:3 *former things.* See 41:22 and note. *they came to pass.* See 42:9.

48:4 *stubborn...bronze.* See Jer 6:28; cf. Eze 3:7.

48:5 °Jer 44:15-18
48:6 ᵖS Isa 41:22;
S Ro 16:25
48:7 ᵠIsa 65:18
ʳIsa 45:21 ˢS Ex 6:7
48:8 ᵗS Isa 1:3
ᵘS Dt 29:4
ᵛIsa 41:24; Mal 2:11,
14 ʷDt 9:7,24;
Ps 58:3; S Isa 1:2;
43:27; 58:1
48:9 ˣS Isa 12:22;
S Isa 37:35
ʸS Job 9:13;
S Isa 30:18
ᶻS Ne 9:31
48:10 ᵃS Isa 1:25;
Zec 13:9; Mal 3:3;
1Pe 1:7 ᵇS Ex 15:25
ᶜS Ex 1:13; S 1Ki 8:51
48:11 ᵈS Isa 12:22;
S Isa 37:35
ᵉS Lev 18:21;
Dt 32:27; Jer 14:7,21;
Eze 20:9,14,22,44
ᶠIsa 42:8
48:12 ᵍS Isa 46:3
ʰIsa 41:8; 42:6; 43:1
ⁱS Isa 43:13
ʲS Isa 41:4; S Rev 1:17
48:13 ᵏHeb 1:10-12
ˡS Ge 2:1; Ex 20:11;
Job 9:8; Isa 40:22;
S 42:5; 45:18; 51:16;
65:17 ᵐS Isa 34:16
48:14 ⁿS Isa 43:9
°S Isa 41:22
ᵖS Isa 41:2
ᵠIsa 46:10-11
ʳS Isa 21:9; S 45:1;
Jer 50:45
48:15 ˢS Jdg 4:10;
Isa 45:1 ᵗIsa 44:28—
45:4
48:16 ᵘS Isa 41:1
ᵛS Isa 33:13
ʷS Isa 45:19

'My images brought them about; °
  my wooden image and metal god ordained them.'
6 You have heard these things; look at them all.
  Will you not admit them?

"From now on I will tell you of new things, ᵖ
  of hidden things unknown to you.
7 They are created ᵠ now, and not long ago; ʳ
  you have not heard of them before today.
So you cannot say,
  'Yes, I knew ˢ of them.'
8 You have neither heard nor understood; ᵗ
  from of old your ears ᵘ have not been open.
Well do I know how treacherous ᵛ you are;
  you were called a rebel ʷ from birth.
9 For my own name's sake ˣ I delay my wrath; ʸ
  for the sake of my praise I hold it back from you,
  so as not to destroy you completely. ᶻ
10 See, I have refined ᵃ you, though not as silver;
  I have tested ᵇ you in the furnace ᶜ of affliction.
11 For my own sake, ᵈ for my own sake, I do this.
  How can I let myself be defamed? ᵉ
  I will not yield my glory to another. ᶠ

ISRAEL FREED

12 "Listen ᵍ to me, Jacob,
  Israel, whom I have called: ʰ
I am he; ⁱ
  I am the first and I am the last. ʲ
13 My own hand laid the foundations of the earth, ᵏ
  and my right hand spread out the heavens; ˡ
when I summon them,
  they all stand up together. ᵐ

14 "Come together, ⁿ all of you, and listen:
  Which of the idols has foretold ° these things?
The LORD's chosen ally ᵖ
  will carry out his purpose ᵠ against Babylon; ʳ
  his arm will be against the Babylonians. ᵃ
15 I, even I, have spoken;
  yes, I have called ˢ him.
I will bring him,
  and he will succeed ᵗ in his mission.

16 "Come near ᵘ me and listen ᵛ to this:

"From the first announcement I have not spoken in secret; ʷ
  at the time it happens, I am there."

ᵃ 14 Or *Chaldeans*; also in verse 20

48:5 *My images brought them about.* See Isaiah's harsh words about idolatry in 44:17–20 (see notes there). *wooden image and metal god.* See note on 44:12–13.
48:6 *new things.* For example, Israel's restoration (see 42:9 and note). The Messianic age and the new heavens and new earth may also be in view (cf. 65:17). *hidden things.* Cf. Ro 16:25–26 and notes.
48:7 *created now.* Now given substance in the prophetic announcement of their coming.
48:8 *neither heard nor understood.* See 1:3. *ears ... not ... open.* See 6:10 and note. *rebel.* See 1:2; 46:8 and notes.
48:9 *delay my wrath.* Cf. Ps 78:38. *my praise.* The praise God is worthy of.
48:10 *refined ... tested.* Images of judgment (see Ps 12:6; Jer 9:7; Eze 22:18 and notes). Purifying fire is also mentioned in 1:25; 4:4. *furnace of affliction.* For Israel, Egypt had been an "iron-smelting furnace" (Dt 4:20 [see note there]; 1Ki 8:51; Jer 11:4). The fall of

Jerusalem and the Babylonian exile were a similar furnace.
48:11 *For ... defamed.* Jerusalem's fall and God's scattered people had brought dishonor to God's name (see Eze 36:20–23 and notes). *my glory.* See 40:5 and note.
48:12 *called.* To be God's servant, his chosen people. See 42:6; see also 41:2; 43:1 and notes. *first and ... last.* See 41:4 and note.
48:13 *laid the foundations ... spread out the heavens.* Isaiah often refers to God as Creator (see 40:21–22; 42:5; 51:13 and notes). Cf. Ps 102:25. *when I summon ... all stand up.* All creation does God's bidding (see 40:26 and note; Ps 103:22).
48:14 *the idols ... foretold.* See 41:21–23,26; 43:9 and notes. *chosen ally.* Cyrus the Great (see 41:2 and note). *his purpose.* See 46:10–11 and note. *Babylon.* See 13:1 and note.
48:15 *called him.* Cyrus (see 41:2 and note). *will succeed.* See 44:28; 45:1–4 and notes.
48:16 *first announcement.* The prediction about Cyrus and his

And now the Sovereign Lord[x] has sent[y] me,
　　endowed with his Spirit.[z]

[17] This is what the Lord says—
　　your Redeemer,[a] the Holy One[b] of Israel:
"I am the Lord your God,
　　who teaches[c] you what is best for you,
　　who directs[d] you in the way[e] you should go.
[18] If only you had paid attention[f] to my commands,
　　your peace[g] would have been like a river,[h]
　　your well-being[i] like the waves of the sea.
[19] Your descendants[j] would have been like the sand,[k]
　　your children like its numberless grains;[l]
　their name would never be blotted out[m]
　　nor destroyed from before me."

[20] Leave Babylon,
　　flee[n] from the Babylonians!
Announce this with shouts of joy[o]
　　and proclaim it.
Send it out to the ends of the earth;[p]
　　say, "The Lord has redeemed[q] his servant Jacob."
[21] They did not thirst[r] when he led them through the deserts;
　　he made water flow[s] for them from the rock;
　he split the rock
　　and water gushed out.[t]

[22] "There is no peace,"[u] says the Lord, "for the wicked."[v]

THE SERVANT OF THE LORD

49 Listen[w] to me, you islands;[x]
　　hear this, you distant nations:
　Before I was born[y] the Lord called[z] me;
　　from my birth he has made mention of my name.[a]
[2] He made my mouth[b] like a sharpened sword,[c]
　　in the shadow of his hand[d] he hid me;
　he made me into a polished arrow[e]
　　and concealed me in his quiver.
[3] He said to me, "You are my servant,[f]
　　Israel, in whom I will display my splendor.[g]"

48:16 [x] Isa 50:5,7,9
[y] Zec 2:9,11
[z] S Isa 11:2
48:17 [a] S Job 19:25;
Isa 49:7; 54:8
[b] S Isa 47:4
[c] S Isa 28:9; S Jer 7:13
[d] Isa 49:10; 57:18;
58:11 [e] S Isa 30:11
48:18 [f] S Isa 42:23
[g] Ps 147:14; S Isa 9:7;
54:13; 66:12
[h] S Isa 33:21
[i] S Isa 1:26; S 45:8
48:19 [j] Isa 43:5;
44:3; 61:9 [k] Ge 12:2
[l] S Job 5:25
[m] Isa 56:5; 65:23;
66:22; Jer 35:19
48:20 [n] Isa 52:11;
Jer 48:6; 50:8; 51:6;
45; Zec 2:6-7;
Rev 18:4 [o] S Isa 12:6;
49:13; 51:11
[p] S Ge 49:10;
S Dt 30:4; S Jer 25:22
[q] S Ex 6:6;
S Isa 33:24; 52:9;
63:9; Mic 4:10
48:21 [r] S Isa 33:16
[s] S Isa 30:25
[t] S Nu 20:11;
S Isa 35:6
48:22 [u] S Job 3:26
[v] S Isa 3:11; 57:21
49:1 [w] S Isa 33:13
[x] S Isa 11:11
[y] Isa 44:24; 46:3;
Mt 1:20 [z] Isa 7:14;
9:6; 44:2; Jer 1:5;
Gal 1:15 [a] S Ex 33:12;
S Isa 43:1
49:2 [b] S Job 40:18
[c] S Ps 64:3; Eph 6:17;
S Rev 1:16
[d] S Ex 33:22;
S Ps 91:1
[e] S Dt 32:23; Zec 9:13
49:3 [f] S Isa 20:3;
Zec 3:8 [g] S Lev 10:3;
S Isa 44:23

---

mission (see 41:25–27 and notes). *not spoken in secret.* See
45:19 and note. *has sent me.* A reference to either Isaiah or the
servant of the Lord. *endowed with his Spirit.* The Spirit of the
Lord comes upon the servant in 42:1 (see note there) and upon
the Messianic prophet of 61:1 (see note there).
48:17 *Redeemer, the Holy One of Israel.* See 41:14 and note.
teaches you . . . the way you should go. Through the prophets or
priests (see 30:20–21; Ps 32:8–10 and notes).
48:18 *peace . . . like a river, your well-being like the waves.* Abundant and overflowing "peace" and "well-being"; see also 45:8;
Am 5:24 and notes. Peace and "well-being" ("righteousness" in
Hebrew) are also linked in 9:7; 32:17; 54:13–14; 60:17; Ps 85:10
(see note there); Heb 7:2; Jas 3:18.
48:19 *descendants . . . like the sand.* See 10:22; see also Ge 13:16
and note; Ge 22:17; Jer 33:22 and note. *name . . . never be blotted
out.* Israel's name would not be completely obliterated (see v. 9;
54:3; Jer 31:36).
48:20 *Leave Babylon, flee.* Although the Jews did not have to flee
(see 52:12), they were encouraged to depart quickly because of
the judgment coming on Babylon (cf. Rev 18:4). This is the last
mention of Babylon by name in Isaiah. *shouts of joy.* See 44:23;
49:13; 52:9 and notes. *ends of the earth.* See 11:12; 42:10 and note.
redeemed. See 43:1 and note. *his servant.* See 41:8–9 and note.
48:21 *did not thirst . . . water . . . from the rock.* A reference to
God's provision after the exodus (see Ex 17:6 and note; Nu 20:11;

see also Isa 32:2; 35:6; 43:19; 49:10 and notes). God's people
would have water on the way home from Babylonian exile also.
48:22 Repeated almost verbatim in 57:21. *peace.* See 39:8 and
note; see also Introduction: Literary Features. *wicked.* Those who
rebel against the Lord (see note on 1:2).
49:1–6 (or **1–7** or **1–13**) The second of the four servant songs
(see note on 42:1–4).
49:1 *islands.* Or "coastlands." In 42:4 the islands "put their hope"
in the servant's teaching. *Before I was born . . . called me.* Cf. v. 5.
The language is similar to that of the call of the prophet Jeremiah (see Jer 1:5 and note) and of the apostle Paul (Gal 1:15). Cf.
41:9. *made mention of my name.* See 43:1 and note.
49:2 *my mouth . . . sharpened sword.* See Rev 1:16; 2:12,16;
19:15,21; cf. Isa 11:4; Eph 6:17; Heb 4:12. *shadow of his hand.* Descriptive of protection (see 30:2–3; 51:16). *polished arrow.* Arrows are used of God's judgment in Dt 32:23,42, of the deadly
words of the wicked in Ps 64:3–4 and of Satan's schemes and
temptations in Eph 6:11,16.
49:3 *my servant, Israel.* See notes on 41:8–9; 42:1–4;
42:1. "Servant" here cannot mean literally national Israel,
since in v. 5 this servant has a mission to Israel. Rather, the Messianic servant is the ideal Israel, through whom the Lord will be
glorified. He will succeed where national Israel failed. *display my
splendor.* Through the redemption he will accomplish (see notes
on 35:2; 40:5).

49:4 *h* S Lev 26:20;
Isa 55:2; 65:23
i Isa 45:25; 50:8;
53:10; 54:17
j S Isa 35:4
k S Job 27:2
49:5 *l* S Ps 139:13;
Gal 1:15 *m* S Dt 30:4;
S Isa 11:12
n S Isa 43:4
o S Ps 18:1
49:6 *p* S ver 3
q Isa 1:9 *r* S Isa 9:2;
Jn 1:9 *s* S Isa 26:18;
55:5; Zec 8:22;
S Lk 2:32 *t* S Dt 30:4;
S Ps 48:10;
S Mt 28:19; Jn 11:52;
Ac 13:47*
49:7 *u* S Isa 48:17
v S Ps 22:6; 69:7-9
w S Ezr 1:2; Isa 52:15
x S Ge 27:29;
S Ps 22:29; S 86:9
y S Dt 7:9; S 1Co 1:9
z S Isa 14:1
49:8 *a* Ps 69:13;
Isa 60:10; 61:2
b S Isa 41:10;
2Co 6:2* *c* S Isa 5:2;
26:3 *d* S Isa 42:6
e Lev 25:10;
S Ps 37:9; Isa 44:26;
58:12; 61:4;
Eze 36:10,33;
Am 9:11,14
f S Nu 34:13;
S Isa 60:21
49:9 *g* Isa 42:7; 61:1;
S Lk 4:19
h S Ps 107:10
i Isa 41:18
49:10 *j* S Isa 33:16

⁴But I said, "I have labored in vain; *h*
　　I have spent my strength for nothing at all.
　Yet what is due me is in the LORD's hand, *i*
　　and my reward *j* is with my God." *k*

⁵And now the LORD says—
　　he who formed me in the womb *l* to be his servant
　to bring Jacob back to him
　　and gather Israel *m* to himself,
　for I am *a* honored *n* in the eyes of the LORD
　　and my God has been my strength *o*—
⁶he says:
　"It is too small a thing for you to be my servant *p*
　　to restore the tribes of Jacob
　　and bring back those of Israel I have kept. *q*
　I will also make you a light *r* for the Gentiles, *s*
　　that my salvation may reach to the ends of the earth." *t*

⁷This is what the LORD says—
　　the Redeemer and Holy One of Israel *u*—
　to him who was despised *v* and abhorred by the nation,
　　to the servant of rulers:
　"Kings *w* will see you and stand up,
　　princes will see and bow down, *x*
　because of the LORD, who is faithful, *y*
　　the Holy One of Israel, who has chosen *z* you."

RESTORATION OF ISRAEL

⁸This is what the LORD says:

　"In the time of my favor *a* I will answer you,
　　and in the day of salvation I will help you; *b*
　I will keep *c* you and will make you
　　to be a covenant for the people, *d*
　to restore the land *e*
　　and to reassign its desolate inheritances, *f*
　⁹to say to the captives, *g* 'Come out,'
　　and to those in darkness, *h* 'Be free!'

　"They will feed beside the roads
　　and find pasture on every barren hill. *i*
　¹⁰They will neither hunger nor thirst, *j*

---

a 5 Or *him, / but Israel would not be gathered; / yet I will be*

49:4 *labored in vain . . . for nothing at all.* Just as the nation Israel had toiled in vain (see 65:23), so Christ would encounter strong opposition during his ministry and would temporarily suffer apparent failure. The "suffering servant" theme is developed in the third and fourth of the four servant songs (50:4–9 or 50:4–11; 52:13—53:12). *what is due me . . . my reward.* Perhaps referring to the spiritual offspring of the servant (see 53:10)—Jews and Gentiles alike who believe in him (vv. 5–6); see 40:10 and note. In any case, he will be vindicated and rewarded (50:8; 53:10–12; 1Ti 3:16).
49:5 *formed me in the womb.* See v. 1; 44:2 and notes. *bring Jacob back . . . gather Israel.* A prophecy of release from captivity in Babylon (see vv. 9–12,22; 41:2 and note) and from the greater captivity of sin (see 42:7 and note). *my strength.* See 12:2.
49:6 Together with Ge 12:1–3; Ex 19:5–6, this verse is sometimes called the "great commission of the OT" and is quoted in part by Paul and Barnabas in Ac 13:47. *those . . . I have kept.* Probably referring to the remnant (see 1:9 and note). *light for the Gentiles.* See 9:2; 42:6 and notes; Ac 26:23. Christ is the light of the world (Lk 2:30–32; Jn 8:12; 9:5), and Christians are to reflect his light (Mt 5:14). *ends of the earth.* See 11:12 and note; see also 41:5; 42:10; 48:20.

49:7 *Redeemer and Holy One of Israel.* See 41:14 and note. *despised.* Applied twice to the suffering servant in 53:3. In 60:14 Zion is despised by her enemies. *nation.* Refers to either Israel (1:4) or Gentiles. *Kings will see . . . bow down.* See v. 23. This reaction to the servant is similar to that of 52:15. Former oppressors bow before a restored Jerusalem in 60:14 (cf. 45:14; 60:11–12; 66:23). *chosen you.* See 41:8–9; 42:1 and notes.
49:8 Quoted in part in 2Co 6:2. *time of my favor . . . day of salvation.* The background of this verse is probably the Year of Jubilee (see 61:1–2; Lev 25:10). The return from exile will bring the same restoration of land for the people as that year of liberty did. *keep you . . . to be a covenant.* See 42:6 and note. *reassign its desolate inheritances.* See 44:26. It was under Joshua that the land had been divided among individual tribes and families (Jos 14:1–5). The Messianic servant will be a new Joshua—as well as a new Moses (see vv. 9–10, which echo Israel's deliverance from Egypt and her desert experiences under Moses during the period of the exodus).
49:9 *captives.* The exiles. See 42:7 and note. *barren hill.* See 41:18 and note.
49:10 *neither hunger nor thirst.* See 48:21 and note. *has compassion.* See 14:1 and note. *will guide them.* As a shepherd (see

nor will the desert heat or the sun beat down on them. *k*
He who has compassion *l* on them will guide *m* them
and lead them beside springs *n* of water.
¹¹ I will turn all my mountains into roads,
and my highways *o* will be raised up. *p*
¹² See, they will come from afar *q*—
some from the north, some from the west, *r*
some from the region of Aswan. *a*"

¹³ Shout for joy, *s* you heavens;
rejoice, you earth; *t*
burst into song, you mountains! *u*
For the LORD comforts *v* his people
and will have compassion *w* on his afflicted ones. *x*

¹⁴ But Zion *y* said, "The LORD has forsaken *z* me,
the Lord has forgotten me."

¹⁵ "Can a mother forget the baby at her breast
and have no compassion on the child *a* she has borne?
Though she may forget,
I will not forget you! *b*
¹⁶ See, I have engraved *c* you on the palms of my hands;
your walls *d* are ever before me.
¹⁷ Your children hasten back,
and those who laid you waste *e* depart from you.
¹⁸ Lift up your eyes and look around;
all your children gather *f* and come to you.
As surely as I live, *g*" declares the LORD,
"you will wear *h* them all as ornaments;
you will put them on, like a bride.

¹⁹ "Though you were ruined and made desolate *i*
and your land laid waste, *j*
now you will be too small for your people, *k*
and those who devoured *l* you will be far away.
²⁰ The children born during your bereavement
will yet say in your hearing,
'This place is too small for us;
give us more space to live in.' *m*
²¹ Then you will say in your heart,
'Who bore me these? *n*
I was bereaved *o* and barren;
I was exiled and rejected. *p*
Who brought these *q* up?
I was left *r* all alone, *s*
but these—where have they come from?' "

a 12 Dead Sea Scrolls; Masoretic Text *Sinim*

49:10 *k* Ps 121:6;
Rev 7:16 *l* S Isa 14:1
m S Ps 48:14;
S Isa 42:16; S 48:17
n S Isa 33:21; S 35:7
49:11 *o* S Isa 11:16
p Isa 40:4; Jer 31:9
49:12 *q* S Isa 2:3;
S 11:11; 43:5-6
r Isa 59:19; S Mt 8:11
49:13 *s* S Isa 48:20
t S Ps 96:11
u S Ps 65:12-13; 98:4;
Isa 44:23 *v* S Ps 71:21;
S Isa 40:1; S 2Co 1:4
w S Isa 14:1
x S Ps 9:12
49:14 *y* Isa 40:9
z S Ps 9:10; S 71:11;
S Isa 27:8
49:15 *a* S Isa 5:6;
10:6; 37:18
49:16 *c* S Ge 38:18;
S Ex 28:9 *d* Ps 48:12-
13; Isa 62:6
49:17 *e* S Isa 5:6;
10:6; 37:18
49:18 *f* S Isa 11:12;
14:1; 43:5; 51:3; 54:7
g S Nu 14:21;
Isa 45:23; 54:9; 62:8;
Ro 14:11 *h* Isa 52:1;
61:10; Jer 2:32
49:19 *i* S Lev 26:33;
Isa 54:1,3; 60:18; 62:4
j S Isa 5:6
k Eze 36:10-11;
Zec 10:10 *l* S Isa 1:20
49:20 *m* Isa 54:1-3;
Zec 2:4; 10:10
49:21 *n* Isa 29:23;
66:7-8 *o* S Isa 47:8;
54:1 *p* Isa 5:13; 54:6
q Isa 60:8 *r* S Isa 1:8
s S Ps 142:4;
Isa 51:18; Jer 10:20

40:11 and note). This whole verse is also a picture of heaven according to Rev 7:16–17.
49:11 *mountains into roads.* See 26:7 and note. *highways … raised up.* See 11:16; 35:8; 40:3; 62:10 and notes.
49:12 *come from afar.* See 11:11 and note; 60:4. *north … west.* See 43:5–6 and notes. *Aswan.* See Eze 29:10 and note; 30:6; located in the most southern part of Egypt.
49:13 *Shout for joy … mountains.* Nature is personified often in Isaiah. See 44:23 and note. *comforts his people.* As he redeems and saves them. Cf. 2Co 1:3–4. *will have compassion.* See v. 10 and note; 54:7–10.
49:14 *forsaken … forgotten.* See 40:27; 54:7; La 5:20–22.
49:15 *Can a mother forget … ?* Cf. Ps 27:10.
49:16 *engraved you on … my hands.* As the names of the tribes of Israel were engraved on stones and fastened to the ephod of

the high priest as a memorial before the Lord (Ex 28:9–12; cf. SS 8:6). *ever before me.* Cf. Ps 137:5–6.

B **49:17** *children.* Or "builders," following the reading of the Dead Sea Scrolls and some ancient versions (cf. note on 62:5).
49:18 *children gather.* See vv. 5,12 and notes. *ornaments.* Beautiful clothes and jewels symbolize strength and joy.
49:19–20 *too small.* The restoration of Israel will be astonishing and complete. The prophecy was partially fulfilled in the return from Babylon (see note on 11:11) and may include spiritual offspring among both Jews and Gentiles (see 54:17 and note).
49:19 *ruined … desolate.* Cf. v. 8; see 44:26 and note.
49:21 *bereaved and barren.* The concept of Israel as a barren woman is stressed in 54:1 (cf. Ps 113:9 and note).

49:22 ᵗ S Ge 15:2
ᵘ S Isa 11:10
ᵛ S Isa 11:12; S 14:2
ʷ Lk 15:5
49:23 ˣ Isa 60:3,10-
11 ʸ S Nu 11:12;
S Isa 60:16
ᶻ S Ge 27:29; Rev 3:9
ᵃ S Ge 3:14; Ps 72:9
ᵇ S Ex 6:2; S Ps
22:23; S Isa 42:8
ᶜ S Ps 37:9; S 130:5
ᵈ S Ps 22:5;
S Isa 29:22; S 41:11
49:24 ᵉ Mt 12:29;
Mk 3:27; Lk 11:21
49:25 ᶠ S Isa 14:2
ᵍ Jer 50:33-34;
Mk 3:27 ʰ S Isa 13:11;
S 25:4 ⁱ Isa 25:5;
S 43:26; 51:22;
Jer 50:34 ʲ S 1Sa 24:15
ᵏ Isa 25:9; 33:22; 35:4
49:26 ˡ S Isa 9:4;
S 13:11 ᵐ S Isa 9:20
ⁿ Nu 23:24; Jer 25:27;
Na 1:10; 3:11; Rev 16:6
ᵒ Ex 6:7; S Isa 11:9;
Eze 39:7 ᵖ S Isa 25:9
�q S Job 19:25;
S Isa 48:17
ʳ S Ge 49:24;
S Ps 132:2
50:1 ˢ S Dt 24:1;
Hos 2:2; Mt 19:7;
Mk 10:4 ᵗ S Ne 5:5;
S Mt 18:25
ᵘ S Isa 1:28
ᵛ S Dt 32:30;
S Jdg 3:8
50:2 ʷ S Isa 8:19;
S Isa 41:28
ˣ Nu 11:23; Isa 59:1
ʸ S Ge 18:14;
S Ps 68:35; Jer 14:9
ᶻ S Ps 18:15
ᵃ S Ex 14:22
ᵇ S Ps 107:33
50:3 ᶜ S Ge 10:22;
S Isa 5:30 ᵈ Rev 6:12

²²This is what the Sovereign Lord ᵗ says:

> "See, I will beckon to the nations,
>> I will lift up my banner ᵘ to the peoples;
> they will bring ᵛ your sons in their arms
>> and carry your daughters on their hips. ʷ
> ²³ Kings ˣ will be your foster fathers,
>> and their queens your nursing mothers. ʸ
> They will bow down ᶻ before you with their faces to the ground;
>> they will lick the dust ᵃ at your feet.
> Then you will know that I am the Lord; ᵇ
>> those who hope ᶜ in me will not be disappointed. ᵈ"

²⁴ Can plunder be taken from warriors, ᵉ
>> or captives be rescued from the fierce ᵃ?

²⁵But this is what the Lord says:

> "Yes, captives ᶠ will be taken from warriors, ᵍ
>> and plunder retrieved from the fierce; ʰ
> I will contend with those who contend with you, ⁱʲ
>> and your children I will save. ᵏ
> ²⁶ I will make your oppressors ˡ eat ᵐ their own flesh;
>> they will be drunk on their own blood, ⁿ as with wine.
> Then the whole human race will know ᵒ
>> that I, the Lord, am your Savior, ᵖ
>> your Redeemer, q the Mighty One of Jacob. ʳ"

ISRAEL'S SIN AND THE SERVANT'S OBEDIENCE

50 This is what the Lord says:

> "Where is your mother's certificate of divorce ˢ
>> with which I sent her away?
> Or to which of my creditors
>> did I sell ᵗ you?
> Because of your sins ᵘ you were sold; ᵛ
>> because of your transgressions your mother was sent away.
> ² When I came, why was there no one?
>> When I called, why was there no one to answer? ʷ
> Was my arm too short ˣ to deliver you?
>> Do I lack the strength ʸ to rescue you?
> By a mere rebuke ᶻ I dry up the sea, ᵃ
>> I turn rivers into a desert; ᵇ
> their fish rot for lack of water
>> and die of thirst.
> ³ I clothe the heavens with darkness ᶜ
>> and make sackcloth ᵈ its covering."

ᵃ 24 Dead Sea Scrolls, Vulgate and Syriac (see also Septuagint and verse 25); Masoretic Text *righteous*

49:22 *lift up my banner.* See 5:26 and note; 13:2. *bring your sons …daughters.* See 11:12 and note. The nations bring Israel back also in 14:2; 43:6; 60:9. *in their arms.* Cf. 60:4; see 40:11 and note. **49:23** *Kings … will bow down.* See v. 7; 11:14 and notes. *know that I am the Lord.* See v. 26; 60:16; Eze 12:20; 13:9; 36:38. *hope in me.* See 40:31 and note. *not be disappointed.* See 29:22 and note. **49:24** *warriors…fierce.* The Babylonians (see 51:13). **49:25** *captives will be taken.* See Ezr 2:1,64–65; Jer 50:33–34; 52:27–30. *I will contend.* God takes up the case of his people. He will "defend their cause" (Jer 50:34). *I will save.* See 35:4 and note. **49:26** *oppressors.* See 14:4; 16:4; 51:13. *eat their own flesh.* During the siege of Jerusalem its people were reduced to cannibalism (La 4:10; cf. Zec 11:9 and note). *drunk on their own blood.* Cf. 51:22–23. *human race will know.* See v. 23 and note. *Savior.* See 43:3 and note; 60:16. *Redeemer.* See 41:14 and note. *Mighty One of Jacob.* See 1:24 and note; 60:16.

50:1 *certificate of divorce.* A husband was required to give this

to a wife he wished to divorce (see Dt 24:1–4; Mt 19:3; Mk 10:2,5–6 and notes). According to Jer 3:8 God gave the northern kingdom of Israel her certificate of divorce, and Isa 54:6–7 indicates that God had left Judah (see 62:4). Perhaps Isaiah's point is that God did not initiate the divorce; Judah broke her relationship with him. The exile, then, was actually a temporary period of separation (see 54:7) rather than a divorce. *my creditors.* If a man's debts were not paid, his children could be sold into slavery (see 2Ki 4:1 and note). But God has no creditors. *you were sold.* Cf. 45:13; 52:3.

50:2 *I came … called.* Through his servants the prophets (see Jer 7:25 and note). *no one to answer.* Israel was deaf toward God (see 6:10 and note; 66:4). *arm too short.* The arm represented power. *dry up the sea.* A reference to crossing the Red Sea (see 43:16–17 and notes; Ps 106:9). *rivers into a desert.* See 42:15 and note. *fish rot.* Perhaps a reference to one of the plagues in Egypt (see 19:5–6,8; Ex 7:18).

⁴ The Sovereign Lord ^e has given me an instructed tongue, ^f
　　to know the word that sustains the weary. ^g
He wakens me morning by morning, ^h
　　wakens my ear to listen like one being taught. ⁱ
⁵ The Sovereign Lord ^j has opened my ears; ^k
　　I have not been rebellious, ^l
　　I have not turned away.
⁶ I offered my back to those who beat ^m me,
　　my cheeks to those who pulled out my beard; ⁿ
I did not hide my face
　　from mocking and spitting. ^o
⁷ Because the Sovereign Lord ^p helps ^q me,
　　I will not be disgraced.
Therefore have I set my face like flint, ^r
　　and I know I will not be put to shame. ^s
⁸ He who vindicates ^t me is near. ^u
　　Who then will bring charges against me? ^v
　　Let us face each other! ^w
Who are my accusers?
　　Let them confront me!
⁹ It is the Sovereign Lord ^x who helps ^y me.
　　Who will condemn ^z me?
They will all wear out like a garment;
　　the moths ^a will eat them up.

¹⁰ Who among you fears ^b the Lord
　　and obeys ^c the word of his servant? ^d
Let those who walk in the dark,
　　who have no light, ^e
trust ^f in the name of the Lord
　　and rely on their God.
¹¹ But now, all you who light fires
　　and provide yourselves with flaming torches, ^g
go, walk in the light of your fires ^h
　　and of the torches you have set ablaze.
This is what you shall receive from my hand: ⁱ
　　You will lie down in torment. ^j

EVERLASTING SALVATION FOR ZION

51 "Listen ^k to me, you who pursue righteousness ^l
　　and who seek ^m the Lord:
Look to the rock ⁿ from which you were cut

50:4 ^e ver 5; Isa 61:1
^f S Ex 4:12
^g S Isa 40:29;
Mt 11:28 ^h Ps 5:3;
88:13; 119:147; 143:8
ⁱ S Isa 28:9
50:5 ^j S Isa 48:16
^k Isa 35:5 ^l Eze 2:8;
24:3; S Mt 26:39;
Jn 8:29; 14:31; 15:10;
Ac 26:19; Heb 5:8
50:6 ^m Isa 53:5;
Mt 27:30; Mk 14:65;
15:19; Lk 22:63;
Jn 19:1 ⁿ S 2Sa 10:4
^o S Nu 12:14; La 3:30;
Mt 26:67; Mk 10:34
50:7 ^p S Isa 48:16
^q S Isa 41:10; 42:1
^r Jer 1:18; 15:20;
Eze 3:8-9
^s S Isa 28:16; S 29:22
50:8 ^t S Isa 26:2;
S 49:4 ^u S Ps 34:18
^v S Job 13:19;
S Isa 43:26; Ro 8:32-
34 ^w S Isa 41:1
50:9 ^x S Isa 48:16
^y S Isa 41:10 ^z Ro 8:1,
34 ^a S Job 13:28;
S Isa 51:8
50:10 ^b S Pr 1:7
^c Isa 1:19; Hag 1:12
^d S Isa 49:3
^e S Ps 107:14;
Ac 26:18 ^f S Isa 10:20;
S 26:4
50:11 ^g Pr 26:18
^h Isa 1:31; Jas 3:6
ⁱ S Dt 21:22-23;
S Pr 26:27
^j S Job 15:20;
Isa 65:13-15
51:1 ^k S Isa 46:3
^l ver 7; S Dt 7:13;
16:20; Ps 94:15;
Isa 63:8; Ro 9:30-31
^m Isa 55:6; 65:10
ⁿ Isa 17:10

50:3 *the heavens with darkness.* Perhaps an allusion to the plague of darkness (Ex 10:21); but see 13:10 and note.
50:4–9 (or **4–11**) The third of the four servant songs (see note on 42:1–4).
50:4–5,7,9 *Sovereign Lord.* The only uses of this title in the servant songs.

　50:4 *word that sustains the weary.* In 42:3 the servant assisted the weak (contrast 49:2). Cf. Jer 31:25. *wakens my ear.* Unlike Israel (see v. 2), the servant was responsive to God.
50:5 *opened my ears.* A sign of obedience (see 1:19; Ps 40:6 and note). *not been rebellious.* Unlike Israel (see 1:2 and note; 1:20).

　50:6 *my back to those who beat me.* Beatings were for criminals or fools (see Pr 10:13; 19:29; 26:3; Mt 27:26; Jn 19:1). *pulled out my beard.* A sign of disrespect and contempt (see 2Sa 10:4–5; Ne 13:25). *mocking and spitting.* To show hatred (Job 30:10) or to insult or disgrace (Dt 25:9; Job 17:6; Mt 27:30). This treatment of the servant anticipates his ultimate suffering in 52:13—53:12.

　50:7 *helps me.* See v. 9; 49:8. *not be disgraced ... put to shame.* See 29:22 and note. Ultimately the servant will be honored (see 49:7; 52:13; 53:10–12). *my face like flint.* Like the prophets, the servant will endure with great determination. Cf.

Lk 9:51, where Jesus "resolutely set out for Jerusalem" (lit. "resolutely set his face to go to Jerusalem").
50:8 *vindicates me.* The Lord will find him righteous (see 45:25; for its ultimate fulfillment, see 1Ti 3:16). *bring charges.* See 49:25 and note. Because Christ was sinless, he also nullifies the charges brought against any who believe in him (see Ro 8:31–34 and notes). *my accusers.* Cf. 54:17.
50:9 *Who will condemn me?* Cf. the similar language Paul uses in Ro 8:34. *wear out like a garment; the moths.* Those who falsely accuse the righteous succumb to moths in 51:8 (i.e., they will be destroyed).
50:10 *fears the Lord.* See Ge 20:11; Pr 1:7 and notes. Cf. 25:3; 59:19. *in the dark.* Perhaps trouble or distress, similar to the experience of the servant (cf. 8:22). *trust ... rely.* The Lord encouraged such trust in 12:2; 31:1.
50:11 *light fires ... flaming torches.* Perhaps a reference to wicked practices that will ultimately destroy those who engage in them. Fire is a frequent figure of punishment (see 1:31 and note; cf. 9:18; 47:14; Ps 7:13). *torment.* Cf. 66:24.
51:1 *Listen to me.* See vv. 4,7. *who pursue righteousness.* Cf. v. 7; Dt 16:20; Pr 15:9. *rock.* Abraham (v. 2). Elsewhere God is called "the Rock" (see 17:10 and note).

51:2 °S Ge 17:6;
S Isa 29:22; Ro 4:16;
Heb 11:11 ᵖ S Ge 12:2
51:3 �ۤ S Isa 40:1
ʳ S Ps 51:18; S Isa 61:4
ˢ Isa 44:26; 52:9; 61:4
ᵗ S Ge 2:8 ᵘ S Isa 5:6;
S 41:19 ᵛ S Isa 25:9;
35:10; 65:18; 66:10;
Jer 16:9 ʷ Jer 17:26;
30:19; 33:11
51:4 ˣ Ex 6:7;
Ps 50:7; Isa 3:15;
63:8; 64:9 ʸ S Ps 78:1
ᶻ S Dt 18:18
ᵃ S Isa 2:4
ᵇ S Isa 26:18; S 49:6
51:5 ᶜ S Ps 85:9;
S Isa 12:2 ᵈ S Isa 35:4
ᵉ Ps 98:1; Isa 40:10;
50:2; 52:10; 59:16;
63:1, 5 ᶠ S Isa 11:11
ᵍ S Ge 49:10;
S Ps 37:9
51:6 ʰ S Ps 37:20;
S 102:26; Mt 24:35;
Lk 21:33; 2Pe 3:10
ⁱ Ps 102:25-26;
Heb 1:10-12
ʲ S Isa 12:2 ᵏ ver 8;
S Ps 119:89
ˡ Ps 89:33; Isa 54:10
51:7 ᵐ S ver 1
ⁿ Dt 6:6; Ps 119:11
ᵒ S Ps 119:39;
Isa 50:7; 54:4;
Mt 5:11; Lk 6:22;
Ac 5:41
51:8 ᵖ S Job 13:28;
Jas 5:2 ᵍ S Isa 14:11
ʳ S ver 6
51:9 ˢ S Jdg 5:12
ᵗ S Ps 98:1;
S Isa 30:30; S 33:2
ᵘ S Ge 18:14;
S Ps 65:6; Isa 40:31;
52:1 ᵛ Ex 6:6; Dt 4:34;
S 32:7 ʷ S Job 9:13
ˣ S Ps 68:30; S 74:13
51:10 ʸ S Ex 14:22;
Zec 10:11; Rev 16:12
ᶻ Ex 15:5, 8
ᵃ S Job 36:30
ᵇ S Ex 15:13
51:11 ᶜ S Isa 35:9;
S 44:23

and to the quarry from which you were hewn;
² look to Abraham, ° your father,
  and to Sarah, who gave you birth.
When I called him he was only one man,
  and I blessed him and made him many. ᵖ
³ The LORD will surely comfort ᵍ Zion ʳ
  and will look with compassion on all her ruins; ˢ
he will make her deserts like Eden, ᵗ
  her wastelands ᵘ like the garden of the LORD.
Joy and gladness ᵛ will be found in her,
  thanksgiving ʷ and the sound of singing.

⁴ "Listen to me, my people; ˣ
  hear me, ʸ my nation:
Instruction ᶻ will go out from me;
  my justice ᵃ will become a light to the nations. ᵇ
⁵ My righteousness draws near speedily,
  my salvation ᶜ is on the way, ᵈ
and my arm ᵉ will bring justice to the nations.
The islands ᶠ will look to me
  and wait in hope ᵍ for my arm.
⁶ Lift up your eyes to the heavens,
  look at the earth beneath;
the heavens will vanish like smoke, ʰ
  the earth will wear out like a garment ⁱ
  and its inhabitants die like flies.
But my salvation ʲ will last forever, ᵏ
  my righteousness will never fail. ˡ

⁷ "Hear me, you who know what is right, ᵐ
  you people who have taken my instruction to heart: ⁿ
Do not fear the reproach of mere mortals
  or be terrified by their insults. ᵒ
⁸ For the moth will eat them up like a garment; ᵖ
  the worm ᵍ will devour them like wool.
But my righteousness will last forever, ʳ
  my salvation through all generations."

⁹ Awake, awake, ˢ arm ᵗ of the LORD,
  clothe yourself with strength! ᵘ
Awake, as in days gone by,
  as in generations of old. ᵛ
Was it not you who cut Rahab ʷ to pieces,
  who pierced that monster ˣ through?
¹⁰ Was it not you who dried up the sea, ʸ
  the waters of the great deep, ᶻ
who made a road in the depths of the sea ᵃ
  so that the redeemed ᵇ might cross over?
¹¹ Those the LORD has rescued ᶜ will return.

51:2 *was only one man.* See Ge 12:1; Eze 33:24. *blessed him and made him many.* See Ge 12:2–3; 13:16; 15:5; 17:5 and note; 22:17.
51:3 *comfort … compassion.* See 49:13 and note. *deserts like Eden.* See 35:1–2. The contrast between the lush splendor of Eden and the barrenness of the desert is found also in Joel 2:3 (see note there). Cf. Ge 2:8,10. *Joy and gladness.* See v. 11; 25:9 and note.
51:4 *Instruction … my justice.* The rule of the servant would bring justice also (see 2:2–4; 42:4 and notes). *light to the nations.* The servant is the light in 42:6; 49:6.
51:5 *righteousness draws near.* In the deliverance from exile. Ultimately, salvation through Christ will come to all nations. See 46:13 and note. *arm.* Symbolizes power. *islands.* See 11:11 and note. *look to me … hope.* See 40:31; 42:4 and notes.
51:6 *Lift … to the heavens.* See 40:26. *heavens will vanish.* See

34:4 and note. *earth will wear out like a garment.* See 24:4; Heb 1:10–11; cf. Isa 50:9. *last forever.* See v. 8; 45:17. The word of God will also endure forever (see 40:8 and note; Mt 24:35; Lk 21:33).
51:7 *who know what is right.* See v. 1 and note. *who have taken my instruction to heart.* See Ps 37:31; Jer 31:33 and note. *reproach … insults.* Such as those borne by the servant in 50:6–7.
51:8 *moth … like a garment.* See 50:9 and note; cf. 51:6.
51:9,17; 52:1 *Awake, awake … !* See 40:1 and note.
51:9 *arm of the LORD.* Symbol of God's power (cf. v. 5). See 30:30; 50:2 and notes; 52:10; 53:1; 63:12. *clothe … with strength.* Cf. 50:2; see note on 40:31. *Rahab … monster.* Egypt. See 27:1; 30:7 and notes.
51:10 *sea.* The Red Sea (see 50:2 and note). *the redeemed.* See 35:9 and note.
51:11 Identical to 35:10 (see note there).

They will enter Zion with singing;[d]
   everlasting joy will crown their heads.
Gladness and joy[e] will overtake them,
   and sorrow and sighing will flee away.[f]

[12] "I, even I, am he who comforts[g] you.
   Who are you that you fear[h] mere mortals,[i]
   human beings, who are but grass,[j]
[13] that you forget[k] the Lord your Maker,[l]
   who stretched out the heavens[m]
   and laid the foundations of the earth,
that you live in constant terror[n] every day
   because of the wrath of the oppressor,
   who is bent on destruction?
For where is the wrath of the oppressor?[o]
[14]   The cowering prisoners will soon be set free;[p]
   they will not die in their dungeon,
   nor will they lack bread.[q]
[15] For I am the Lord your God,
   who stirs up the sea[r] so that its waves roar[s]—
   the Lord Almighty[t] is his name.
[16] I have put my words in your mouth[u]
   and covered you with the shadow of my hand[v]—
I who set the heavens in place,
   who laid the foundations of the earth,[w]
   and who say to Zion, 'You are my people.'[x] "

THE CUP OF THE LORD'S WRATH

[17] Awake, awake![y]
   Rise up, Jerusalem,
you who have drunk from the hand of the Lord
   the cup[z] of his wrath,[a]
you who have drained to its dregs[b]
   the goblet that makes people stagger.[c]
[18] Among all the children[d] she bore
   there was none to guide her;[e]
among all the children she reared
   there was none to take her by the hand.[f]
[19] These double calamities[g] have come upon you—
   who can comfort you?[h]—
ruin and destruction,[i] famine[j] and sword[k]—
   who can[a] console you?
[20] Your children have fainted;
   they lie at every street corner,[l]
   like antelope caught in a net.[m]
They are filled with the wrath[n] of the Lord,
   with the rebuke[o] of your God.

[21] Therefore hear this, you afflicted[p] one,
   made drunk,[q] but not with wine.

---

[a] 19 Dead Sea Scrolls, Septuagint, Vulgate and Syriac; Masoretic Text / *how can I*

51:11 [d] Ps 109:28;
Isa 65:14; Jer 30:19;
Zep 3:14
[e] S Isa 48:20;
Jer 33:11 [f] S Isa 30:19;
Jer 31:13; S Rev 7:17
51:12 [g] S Isa 40:1;
S 2Co 1:4 [h] S 2Ki 1:15
[i] S Isa 2:22
[j] S Isa 15:6; 40:6-7;
1Pe 1:24
51:13 [k] S Job 8:13;
S Isa 17:10
[l] S Job 4:17; Isa 17:7;
45:11; 54:5 [m] S Ge 1:1;
S Isa 48:13 [n] S Isa 7:4
[o] S Isa 9:4
51:14 [p] S Isa 42:7
[q] Isa 49:10
51:15 [r] S Ps 93:3 [s] S Isa 13:4
51:16 [u] S Ex 4:12,15
[v] S Ex 33:22
[w] S Isa 48:13
[x] Jer 7:23; 11:4; 24:7;
Eze 14:11; Zec 8:8
51:17 [y] S Jdg 5:12;
Isa 52:1 [z] S ver 22;
S Ps 16:5; S Mt 20:22
[a] ver 20; Job 21:20;
Isa 42:25; 66:15;
Rev 14:10; 16:19
[b] S Ps 75:8 [c] S ver 23;
S Ps 60:3
51:18 [d] Ps 88:18
[e] S Job 31:18;
S Isa 49:21
[f] S Isa 41:13
51:19 [g] S Isa 40:2;
47:9 [h] Isa 49:13;
54:11; Jer 15:5; Na 3:7
[i] Isa 60:18; 62:4;
Jer 48:3; La 3:47
[j] S Isa 14:30
[k] Jer 14:12; 24:10
51:20 [l] Isa 5:25;
Jer 14:16; La 2:19
[m] S Job 18:10
[n] S ver 17;
S Job 40:11; Jer 44:6
[o] S Dt 28:20
51:21 [p] S Isa 14:32
[q] ver 17; S Isa 29:9

51:12 *who comforts.* See v. 3; 49:13 and note. *grass.* See 37:27; 40:6 and notes.
51:13 *stretched out the heavens and . . . earth.* See v. 16; 48:13 and note. *wrath of the oppressor.* See 49:26 and note. Babylon's wrath was insignificant beside the mighty wrath of God (cf. 13:3,5; 30:27).
51:14 *prisoners . . . set free.* The exiles in Babylon (see 42:7 and note; 49:9). *in their dungeon.* Cf. 42:7; Jer 37:16.
51:15 *stirs up the sea.* Cf. Job 26:12; Ps 107:25; Jer 31:35. *Lord Almighty.* See 13:4 and note.
51:16 *my words.* See "my instruction" (v. 7). Like the servant of 49:2, the people are responding to God's word (cf. 59:21; Jos 1:8). *shadow of my hand.* See 49:2 and note. *set the heavens . . .*

earth. See v. 13 and note.
51:17 *cup of his wrath.* See vv. 20–22; 13:3 and note. Experiencing God's judgment is often compared to becoming drunk on strong wine. It is the fate of wicked nations in particular. See 29:9; 63:6; Ps 60:3 and note; 75:8; Jer 25:15–16 and notes; La 4:21; Eze 23:31 and note; Hab 2:16 and note; Zec 12:2; cf. Jn 18:11.
🔺 51:18 Children were expected to take care of parents who were sick or unsteady (cf. 1Ti 5:8).
51:19 *who can comfort you?* A question also asked in Jer 15:5. Contrast v. 3.
51:20 *caught in a net.* Cf. Pr 7:22. *rebuke.* See 17:13; 54:9; 66:15.
51:21 *afflicted one.* Jerusalem (see 54:11). *made drunk.* On God's wrath (see v. 17 and note).

51:22 ʳS Isa 49:25
ˢS ver 17; Jer 25:15;
51:7; Hab 2:16;
S Mt 20:22
51:23 ᵗIsa 14:4;
49:26; Jer 25:15-17,
26,28; 49:12 ᵘver 17;
Zec 12:2 ᵛS Jos 10:24
ʷPs 66:12; Mic 7:10
52:1 ˣS Isa 51:17
ʸS 1Sa 2:4; S Isa 51:9
ᶻEx 28:2,40; Est 6:8;
Ps 110:3; Isa 49:18;
61:10; Zec 3:4
ᵃS Ne 11:1; S Isa 1:26;
Mt 4:5; S Rev 21:2
ᵇS Ge 34:14
ᶜS Isa 35:8
ᵈJoel 3:17; Na 1:15;
Zec 9:8; Rev 21:27
52:2 ᵉS Isa 29:4
ᶠIsa 60:1 ᵍS Ps 81:6;
S Isa 10:27 ʰPs 9:14
52:3 ⁱS Ps 44:12
ʲIsa 45:13 ᵏS Isa 1:27;
1Pe 1:18
52:4 ˡS Ge 46:6
ᵐIsa 10:24
52:5 ⁿS Isa 37:23;
Ro 2:24*
52:6 ᵒS Isa 49:23
ᵖS Ex 6:3
�۱S Isa 10:20
ʳS Isa 41:26
52:7 ˢS Isa 42:11
ᵗS 2Sa 18:26;
S Isa 40:9; Ro 10:15*
ᵘNa 1:15; Lk 2:14;
Eph 6:15

22 This is what your Sovereign LORD says,
  your God, who defends ʳ his people:
"See, I have taken out of your hand
  the cup ˢ that made you stagger;
from that cup, the goblet of my wrath,
  you will never drink again.
23 I will put it into the hands of your tormentors, ᵗ
  who said to you,
'Fall prostrate ᵘ that we may walk ᵛ on you.'
And you made your back like the ground,
  like a street to be walked on." ʷ

52

Awake, awake, ˣ Zion,
  clothe yourself with strength! ʸ
Put on your garments of splendor, ᶻ
  Jerusalem, the holy city. ᵃ
The uncircumcised ᵇ and defiled ᶜ
  will not enter you again. ᵈ
2 Shake off your dust; ᵉ
  rise up, ᶠ sit enthroned, Jerusalem.
Free yourself from the chains on your neck, ᵍ
  Daughter Zion, ʰ now a captive.

3 For this is what the LORD says:

"You were sold for nothing, ⁱ
  and without money ʲ you will be redeemed. ᵏ"

4 For this is what the Sovereign LORD says:

"At first my people went down to Egypt ˡ to live;
  lately, Assyria ᵐ has oppressed them.

5 "And now what do I have here?" declares the LORD.

"For my people have been taken away for nothing,
  and those who rule them mock,ᵃ"

                                                  declares the LORD.

"And all day long
  my name is constantly blasphemed. ⁿ
6 Therefore my people will know ᵒ my name; ᵖ
  therefore in that day ۱ they will know
that it is I who foretold ʳ it.
  Yes, it is I."

7 How beautiful on the mountains ˢ
  are the feet of those who bring good news, ᵗ
who proclaim peace, ᵘ

ᵃ 5 Dead Sea Scrolls and Vulgate; Masoretic Text *wail*

51:22 *defends his people.* See 49:25 and note. *cup…of my wrath.* See v. 17 and note.
51:23 *your tormentors.* The Babylonians. See vv. 13–14; 14:4. *your back like the ground.* Perhaps figurative, but cf. Jos 10:24 and note.
52:1 *Awake, awake.* See 51:9,17. *garments of splendor.* Perhaps the robes of the priests, which belong to Jerusalem as a "holy city." See 49:18 and note. *holy city.* See 48:2 and note. *uncircumcised and defiled.* Foreign invaders. See 35:8; Jdg 14:3 and notes.
52:2 *Shake off your dust.* Contrast the fate of Babylon in 47:1 (see note there). *Free yourself.* See 42:7 and note; 49:9; 51:14. *Daughter Zion.* A personification of Jerusalem (see note on 2Ki 19:21).
52:3 *sold for nothing.* The enemy paid the Lord nothing for acquiring Jerusalem. See 45:13; 50:1 and notes. *without money… redeemed.* See 41:14 and note; 43:1; 45:13.
52:4 *Assyria…oppressed them.* See 9:4 and note.
52:5 Quoted in part in Ro 2:24. *for nothing.* See v. 3 and note.

my name is…blasphemed. The captivity brought disrespect to the God of helpless Jerusalem (see Eze 36:20–23 and notes). Cf. Assyria's blasphemy in 37:23–24.
52:6 *know my name.* See 49:26 and note. *in that day.* The day of deliverance from Babylon. See 10:20,27 and note. *foretold it.* The return from exile.

52:7 *feet of those who bring good news.* A reference to messengers who ran from the scene of a battle to bring news of the outcome to a waiting king and people (see 2Sa 18:26; Na 1:15 and note). Here the news refers to the return from exile (vv. 11–12; see 40:9 and note; 41:27), a deliverance that prefigures Christ's deliverance from sin. See Ro 10:15; Eph 6:15 and notes. *salvation.* See 49:8 and note. *Your God reigns!* See Ps 93:1 and note. The return of God's people to Jerusalem emphasizes his sovereign rule over the world (see 40:9 and note). God's kingdom will come more fully at the second coming of Christ (see Rev 19:6).

who bring good tidings,
who proclaim salvation,
who say to Zion,
"Your God reigns!" ᵛ

⁸ Listen! Your watchmen ʷ lift up their voices; ˣ
together they shout for joy. ʸ
When the LORD returns ᶻ to Zion, ᵃ
they will see it with their own eyes.

⁹ Burst into songs of joy ᵇ together,
you ruins ᶜ of Jerusalem,
for the LORD has comforted ᵈ his people,
he has redeemed Jerusalem. ᵉ

¹⁰ The LORD will lay bare his holy arm ᶠ
in the sight of all the nations, ᵍ
and all the ends of the earth ʰ will see
the salvation ⁱ of our God.

¹¹ Depart, ʲ depart, go out from there!
Touch no unclean thing! ᵏ
Come out from it and be pure, ˡ
you who carry the articles ᵐ of the LORD's house.

¹² But you will not leave in haste ⁿ
or go in flight;
for the LORD will go before you, ᵒ
the God of Israel will be your rear guard. ᵖ

THE SUFFERING AND GLORY OF THE SERVANT

¹³ See, my servant ᑫ will act wisely ᵃ;
he will be raised and lifted up and highly exalted. ʳ

¹⁴ Just as there were many who were appalled ˢ at him ᵇ—
his appearance was so disfigured ᵗ beyond that of any human being
and his form marred beyond human likeness ᵘ—

¹⁵ so he will sprinkle ᵛ many nations, ᶜ
and kings ʷ will shut their mouths ˣ because of him.
For what they were not told, they will see,
and what they have not heard, they will understand. ʸ

53

Who has believed our message ᶻ
and to whom has the arm ᵃ of the LORD been revealed? ᵇ

² He grew up before him like a tender shoot, ᶜ
and like a root ᵈ out of dry ground.

ᵃ 13 Or *will prosper*   ᵇ 14 Hebrew *you*   ᶜ 15 Or *so will many nations be amazed at him* (see also Septuagint)

52:7 ᵛ S 1Ch 16:31;
S Ps 97:1; 1Co 15:24-25
52:8 ʷ S 1Sa 14:16;
Isa 56:10; 62:6;
Jer 6:17; 31:6;
Eze 3:17; 33:7
ˣ Isa 40:9 ʸ S Isa 12:6
ᶻ S Nu 10:36
ᵃ Isa 59:20; Zec 8:3
52:9 ᵇ S Ps 98:4;
S Isa 35:2 ᶜ S Ps 74:3;
S Isa 51:3 ᵈ S Isa 40:1;
Lk 2:25 ᵉ S Ezr 9:9;
S Isa 48:20
52:10 ᶠ S 2Ch 32:8;
S Ps 44:3; S Isa 30:30
ᵍ Isa 66:18
ʰ S Jos 4:24;
S Isa 11:9 ⁱ S Ps 67:2;
Lk 2:30; 3:6
52:11 ʲ S Isa 48:20
ᵏ S Isa 1:16; 2Co 6:17*
ˡ Nu 8:6; 2Ti 2:19
ᵐ S 2Ch 36:10
52:12 ⁿ S Ex 12:11
ᵒ Mic 2:13; Jn 10:4
ᵖ S Ex 14:19
52:13 ᑫ S Jos 1:8;
S Isa 4:2; S 20:3
ʳ S Isa 6:1; 57:15;
Ac 3:13; S Php 2:9
52:14 ˢ S Lev 26:32;
S Job 18:20
ᵗ S 2Sa 10:4
ᵘ S Job 2:12; S 16:16
52:15 ᵛ S Lev 14:7;
S 16:14-15
ʷ S Isa 49:7
ˣ S Jdg 18:19;
Ps 107:42 ʸ Ro 15:21*;
Eph 3:4-5
53:1 ᶻ S Isa 28:9;
Ro 10:16* ᵃ S Ps 98:1;
S Isa 30:30
ᵇ Jn 12:38*
53:2 ᶜ S 2Ki 19:26;
S Job 14:7; S Isa 4:2
ᵈ S Isa 11:10

52:8 *watchmen*. Stationed on Jerusalem's walls (see 62:6–7; Ps 127:1 and note).
52:9 *Burst into songs*. See 44:23 and note. *comforted*. See 49:13 and note. *redeemed*. See v. 3 and note.
52:10 *holy arm*. See 51:9 and note. God's arm is often associated with redemption and salvation (see Ex 6:6). *all the ends of the earth*. Equivalent to all humankind (see note on 40:5). Cf. 45:22.
52:11 Quoted in part in 2Co 6:17. *Depart, depart ...!* See note on 40:1. *unclean thing*. Perhaps referring to pagan religious objects (cf. Ge 31:19; 35:2). *you who carry the articles*. Cyrus allowed the people to take back the articles of the temple seized by Nebuchadnezzar (Ezr 1:7–11). The priests and Levites were responsible for them (see Nu 3:6–8; 2Ch 5:4–7).
52:12 *not leave in haste*. See 48:20 and note. *go before you ... be your rear guard*. As he did for the Israelites when they were freed from Egypt (see Ex 13:21; 14:19–20 and notes; cf. Isa 42:16; 49:10; 58:8).
52:13—53:12 The fourth and longest of the four servant songs (see note on 42:1–4). It constitutes the central and most important unit in chs. 40–66, as well as in chs. 49–57 (see note on 39:8). The song contains five stanzas of three numbered verses each. It is quoted more frequently in the NT than any other

OT passage and is often referred to as the "gospel in the OT."

52:13 *my servant*. See note on 42:1. *act wisely*. A mark of God's blessing (see 1Sa 18:14) and of obedience to God's word (see Jos 1:8). The Messianic King will "reign wisely" (Jer 23:5). Cf. 53:10. *raised and lifted up*. Words that describe the Lord in Isaiah's vision (see 6:1 and note; 57:15). Christ's exaltation is referred to in Ac 2:33; 3:13; Eph 1:20–23; Php 2:9–11 (see also 1Pe 1:10–11).

52:14 *appalled at him*. When they saw Christ's suffering on the cross. Cf. the reaction to the ruined city of Tyre (Eze 27:35). *disfigured*. A term used of a "blemished animal," which should not be offered to the Lord (Mal 1:14). Cf. the disgraceful treatment of the servant (see 50:6 and note). *beyond that of any human being*. Cf. Ps 22:6. His treatment was inhuman.

52:15 *sprinkle many nations*. With the sprinkling of cleansing (see Lev 14:7; Nu 8:7; 19:18–19) and/or of consecration (see Ex 29:21; Lev 8:11,30). But see TNIV text note. *kings will shut their mouths*. In astonishment at the suffering and exaltation of the servant (see 49:6–7 and notes). *For what ... understand*. Quoted in Ro 15:21. Even though they have not heard the prophetic word, kings will understand the mission of the servant when they see his humiliation and exaltation (contrast 6:9–10).

53:2 *e* Isa 52:14
53:3 *f* Ps 69:29
g ver 4,10; S Ex 1:10;
S Mt 16:21; Lk 18:31-
33; Heb 5:8
h S Dt 31:17; Isa 1:15
i S 1Sa 2:30;
S Ps 22:6; Mt 27:29;
Jn 1:10-11
53:4 *j* Mt 8:17*
k S Dt 5:24; S Job 4:5;
Jer 23:5-6; 25:34;
Eze 34:23-24;
Mic 5:2-4; Zec 13:7;
Jn 19:7 *l* S ver 3;
S Ge 12:17; S Ru 1:21
53:5 *m* S Ps 22:16
n S Ex 28:38;
S Ps 39:8; S Jn 3:17;
Ro 4:25; 1Co 15:3;
Heb 9:28 *o* Ps 34:18
p S Isa 50:6
q S Isa 9:6; Ro 5:1
r Isa 1:6; Mt 27:26;
Jn 19:1 *s* S Dt 32:39;
S 2Ch 7:14; 1Pe 2:24-
25
53:6 *t* S Ps 95:10;
1Pe 2:24-25
u S 1Sa 8:3; Isa 56:11;
57:17; Mic 3:5
v ver 12; S Ex 28:38;
Ro 4:25
53:7 *w* Isa 49:26
x S Mk 14:61; 1Pe 2:23
y Mt 27:31; S Jn 1:29
z S Ps 44:22
53:8 *a* Mk 14:49
b Ps 88:5; Da 9:26;
Ac 8:32-33* *c* ver 12;
S Ps 39:8
53:9 *d* Mt 27:38;
Mk 15:27; Lk 23:32;
Jn 19:18 *e* Mt 27:57-
60; Mk 15:43-46;
Lk 23:50-53;
Jn 19:38-41 *f* Isa 42:1-
3 *g* S Job 16:17;
1Pe 2:22*; 1Jn 3:5;
Rev 14:5

He had no beauty or majesty to attract us to him,
　　nothing in his appearance *e* that we should desire him.
³ He was despised and rejected by others,
　　a man of suffering, *f* and familiar with pain. *g*
Like one from whom people hide *h* their faces
　　he was despised, *i* and we held him in low esteem.

⁴ Surely he took up our pain
　　and bore our suffering, *j*
yet we considered him punished by God, *k*
　　stricken by him, and afflicted. *l*
⁵ But he was pierced *m* for our transgressions, *n*
　　he was crushed *o* for our iniquities;
the punishment *p* that brought us peace *q* was on him,
　　and by his wounds *r* we are healed. *s*
⁶ We all, like sheep, have gone astray, *t*
　　each of us has turned to our own way; *u*
and the LORD has laid on him
　　the iniquity *v* of us all.

⁷ He was oppressed *w* and afflicted,
　　yet he did not open his mouth; *x*
he was led like a lamb *y* to the slaughter, *z*
　　and as a sheep before its shearers is silent,
　　so he did not open his mouth.
⁸ By oppression *a* and judgment *a* he was taken away.
　　Yet who of his generation protested?
For he was cut off from the land of the living; *b*
　　for the transgression *c* of my people he was punished. *b*
⁹ He was assigned a grave with the wicked, *d*
　　and with the rich *e* in his death,
though he had done no violence, *f*
　　nor was any deceit in his mouth. *g*

---

a 8 Or *From arrest*   *b* 8 Or *generation considered / that he was cut off from the land of the living, / that he was punished for the transgression of my people?*

53:1 Quoted in whole in Jn 12:38 and in part in Ro 10:16. *our message.* The good news about salvation, given by the prophets to Israel and the nations (see 52:7,10). *arm of the LORD.* See 51:9 and note.
53:2 *tender shoot.* The Messiah would grow from the "stump of Jesse" (11:1; see note there; cf. 4:2; Zec 3:8 and notes). His beginnings would be humble. *root.* See 11:10 and note. *beauty.* The Hebrew for this word is used of David in 1Sa 16:18, where it is translated "fine-looking." *majesty.* Christ had nothing of the bearing or trappings of royalty.
53:3 *despised.* See 49:7 and note; Ps 22:6. *rejected ... held ... in low esteem.* The Hebrew words used here occur together also in 2:22 (see note there). Cf. Jn 1:10-11. *suffering.* The Hebrew for this word is used of both physical and mental pain (see v. 4; Ex 3:7). *hide their faces.* See 1:15 and note; 8:17.
53:4 Quoted in part in Mt 8:17 with reference to Jesus' healing ministry. *pain.* Diseases often result from sinful living and are ultimately the consequences of original (Adamic) sin. See 1:5-6 and note. *punished by God.* With a terrible disease (see Ge 12:17; 2Ki 15:5). People (Israel in particular) thought the servant was suffering for his own sins. *afflicted.* Or "humbled" or "oppressed" (see v. 7; 58:10).
53:5 *pierced.* See Ps 22:16; Zec 12:10; Jn 19:34 and notes. *crushed.* In spirit (see Ps 34:18; cf. Isa 57:15). The sins of the world weighed heavily upon him. *healed.* Here probably equivalent to "forgiven" (see 6:10; Jer 30:17; see also note on 1Pe 2:24).

53:6 *have gone astray.* Cf. Ps 119:176 and note; Jer 50:6; Eze 34:4-6,16; 1Pe 2:25 and note. *laid on him the iniquity of us all.* Just as the priest laid his hands on the scapegoat and

symbolically put Israel's sins on it (see Lev 16:20-22 and note). See 1Pe 2:24 and note.
53:7-8 Verses read by the Ethiopian eunuch in the presence of Philip (see Ac 8:34 and note).

53:7 *oppressed.* Like Israel. See 49:26 and note. The Hebrew for this word is translated "slave drivers" in Ex 5:6. *lamb to the slaughter.* Cf. Ps 44:22; Rev 5:6 and note. John the Baptist called Jesus "the Lamb of God" (Jn 1:29,36; see note on 1:29). *did not open his mouth.* Jesus remained silent before the chief priests and Pilate (Mt 27:12-14; Mk 14:60-61; 15:4-5; Jn 19:8-9) and before Herod (Lk 23:8-9).
53:8 *By oppression and judgment.* Jesus was given an unfair trial. See TNIV text notes.

53:9 *the wicked.* The manner of his death would indicate that, as far as those who condemned him were concerned, he was to be buried with executed criminals. *the rich.* Not as a burial with honor. The parallelism (with its effective wordplay in Hebrew) makes clear that Isaiah here associates the rich with the wicked, as do many OT writers— because they acquired their wealth by wicked means and/or trusted in their wealth rather than in God (see, e.g., Ps 37:16,35; Pr 18:23; 28:6,20; Jer 5:26-27; Mic 6:10,12). According to the Gospels (Mt 27:57-60 and parallels), the wealthy Joseph of Arimathea gave Jesus an honorable burial by placing his body in his own tomb. But this was undoubtedly an act of love growing out of his awareness that he had been forgiven much (see Lk 7:47). Thus the fulfillment fitted but also transcended the prophecy. *he had done no violence, nor ... deceit in his mouth.* Peter quotes these lines as he encourages believers to endure unjust suffering (1Pe 2:22).

¹⁰ Yet it was the LORD's will ʰ to crush ⁱ him and cause him to suffer, ʲ
   and though the LORD makes ᵃ his life an offering for sin, ᵏ
he will see his offspring ˡ and prolong his days,
   and the will of the LORD will prosper ᵐ in his hand.
¹¹ After he has suffered, ⁿ
   he will see the light ᵒ of life ᵇ and be satisfied ᶜ;
by his knowledge ᵈ my righteous servant ᵖ will justify ᑫ many,
   and he will bear their iniquities. ʳ
¹² Therefore I will give him a portion among the great, ᵉ ˢ
   and he will divide the spoils ᵗ with the strong, ᶠ
because he poured out his life unto death, ᵘ
   and was numbered with the transgressors. ᵛ
For he bore ʷ the sin of many, ˣ
   and made intercession ʸ for the transgressors.

THE FUTURE GLORY OF ZION

54

"Sing, barren woman, ᶻ
   you who never bore a child;
burst into song, shout for joy, ᵃ
   you who were never in labor; ᵇ
because more are the children ᶜ of the desolate ᵈ woman
   than of her who has a husband, ᵉ"
                                         says the LORD.

² "Enlarge the place of your tent, ᶠ
   stretch your tent curtains wide,
   do not hold back;
lengthen your cords,
   strengthen your stakes. ᵍ
³ For you will spread out to the right and to the left;
   your descendants ʰ will dispossess nations ⁱ
   and settle in their desolate ʲ cities.

⁴ "Do not be afraid; ᵏ you will not be put to shame. ˡ
   Do not fear disgrace; ᵐ you will not be humiliated.
You will forget the shame of your youth ⁿ
   and remember no more the reproach ᵒ of your widowhood. ᵖ
⁵ For your Maker ᑫ is your husband ʳ—
   the LORD Almighty is his name—

ᵃ 10 Hebrew *though you make*   ᵇ 11 Dead Sea Scrolls (see also Septuagint); Masoretic Text does not have *the light of life.*   ᶜ 11 Or (with Masoretic Text) ¹¹*He will see the fruit of his suffering / and will be satisfied*   ᵈ 11 Or *by knowledge of him*   ᵉ 12 Or *many*   ᶠ 12 Or *numerous*

53:10 ʰ Isa 46:10; 55:11; Ac 2:23 ʲ ver 5
ʲ S ver 3; S Ge 12:17
ᵏ S Lev 5:15; Jn 3:17
ˡ S Ps 22:30
ᵐ S Jos 1:8; S Isa 49:4
53:11 ⁿ Jn 10:14-18
ᵒ S Job 33:30
ᵖ S Isa 20:3; Ac 7:52
ᑫ S Isa 6:7; Jn 1:29; Ac 10:43; S Ro 4:25
ʳ S Ex 28:38
53:12 ˢ S Isa 6:1; S Php 2:9 ᵗ S Ex 15:9; S Ps 119:162; Lk 11:22
ᵘ Mt 26:28,38,39,42
ᵛ Mt 27:38; Mk 15:27*; Lk 22:37*; 23:32
ʷ S ver 6; 1Pe 2:24
ˣ Heb 9:28
ʸ Isa 59:16; S Ro 8:34
54:1 ᶻ S Ge 30:1
ᵃ S Ge 21:6; S Ps 98:4
ᵇ Isa 66:7 ᶜ Isa 49:20
ᵈ S Isa 49:19
ᵉ S 1Sa 2:5; Gal 4:27*
54:2 ᶠ S Ge 26:22; Isa 26:15; 49:19-20
ᵍ Ex 35:18; 39:40
54:3 ʰ S Ge 13:14; S Isa 48:19
ⁱ S Job 12:23; S Isa 14:2; 60:4-11
ʲ S Isa 49:19
54:4 ᵏ Jer 30:10; Joel 2:21 ˡ S Isa 28:16; S 29:22 ᵐ S Ge 30:23; S Ps 119:39; S Isa 41:11
ⁿ S Ps 25:7; S Jer 2:2; S 22:21 ᵒ S Isa 51:7
ᵖ S Isa 47:8
54:5 ᑫ S Ps 95:6; S 149:2; S Isa 51:13
ʳ S SS 3:11; Jer 3:14; 31:32; Hos 2:7,16

53:10 *crush him.* See v. 5 and note. *an offering for sin.* Or "a guilt offering," an offering where restitution was usually required and the offender sacrificed a ram (but see note on Lev 5:15). *his offspring.* Spiritual progeny. *prolong his days.* Christ would live forever (see 9:7 and note). *prosper.* See 52:13 and TNIV text note there.

▲ **53:11** *light of life.* A reference to the resurrection of Christ; see 1Co 15:4 (but see also the first two TNIV text notes here). For "of life," see Job 33:30 and note; Ps 49:19; 56:13 and note. *be satisfied.* In 1:11, where the same Hebrew word appears, God had "more than enough" of innumerable sacrifices that accomplished nothing. Here the one sacrifice of Christ brings perfect satisfaction. *his knowledge.* His true knowledge of the true God (see 1:3; 6:9; 43:10; 45:4–5; 52:6; 56:10). The Spirit of knowledge (11:2) rested on the Messiah (but see the third TNIV text note here). Cf. 52:13. *my ... servant.* See 41:8–9; 42:1 and notes. *justify.* Cause many to be declared righteous. See 5:23 ("acquit"); Ro 5:19 and note. *many.* See TNIV text notes on v. 12; see also 52:15; Da 12:3.

▲ **53:12** *among the great ... with the strong.* God will reward his servant as if he were a king sharing in the spoils of a great victory (see 52:15). *divide the spoils.* God's gift to his suffering servant (cf. 9:3). *poured out his life.* As a sacrifice (see v. 10). *unto death.* See Php 2:8 and note. *and was numbered with*

the transgressors. Quoted in Lk 22:37 with reference to Jesus (see note there). *bore.* The Hebrew for this verb is translated "took up" in v. 4. *made intercession.* See Jer 7:16 ("pray"); 27:18 ("plead"). Cf. 59:16; Heb 7:25.
54:1 This verse is applied by Paul to Sarah and the covenant of promise, representing "the Jerusalem that is above" (Gal 4:26–27; see notes there). *Sing ... burst into song.* See 12:6; 44:23; 52:9 and notes. *barren woman.* Jerusalem (representing Israel), especially during the exile (see 49:21). In the Near East, barrenness was considered a disgrace (see 49:19–20 and note). *more are the children of the desolate woman.* See 49:19–20 and note. Israel will be restored, both physically and spiritually (cf. 62:4). *husband.* See 50:1 and note.
54:2 See 26:15; 33:20 and notes. *your tent.* Jerusalem is viewed as a woman living in her own tent.
54:3 *spread out.* See 49:19–20 and note; cf. Ge 28:14. *dispossess nations.* See 11:14; 49:7 and notes.
54:4 *not be put to shame ... disgrace.* See 29:22 and note; 45:17. *shame of your youth.* Probably the period of slavery in Egypt. Cf. Jer 31:19; Eze 16:60. *reproach of your widowhood.* Probably referring to the exile, when Israel was alone, like a widow (vv. 6–7).
54:5 *husband.* See 62:4–5. *Holy One of Israel ... Redeemer.* See 1:4; 41:14 and notes.

54:5 *S Isa 1:4;
49:7; 55:5; 60:9
*S Isa 48:17
*S Isa 6:3; S 12:4
54:6 *Isa 49:14-21
*ver 6; Isa 1:4;
50:1-2; 60:15; 62:4,
12; Jer 44:2; Hos 1:10
*S Ex 20:14; Mal 2:15
54:7 *S Job 14:13;
Isa 26:20 *S Ps 71:11;
S Isa 27:8 *S Ps 51:1
*S Isa 49:18
54:8 *Isa 9:12;
26:20; 60:10
*S Isa 1:15 *ver 10;
S Ps 25:6; 92:2;
Isa 55:3; 63:7
*S Ps 102:13;
S Isa 14:1; Hos 2:19
*S Isa 48:17
54:9 *S Ge 8:21
*S Isa 14:24; S 49:18
*Ps 13:1; 103:9;
Isa 12:1; 57:16;
Jer 3:5,12; Eze 39:29;
Mic 7:18 *S Dt 28:20
54:10 *Rev 6:14
*S Ps 46:2 *S Ps 6:4
*S Isa 51:6;
Heb 12:27
*S Ge 9:16; Ex 34:10;
Ps 89:34; S Isa 42:6
*S Nu 25:12 *ver 8;
S Isa 14:1; 55:7
54:11 *S Isa 14:32
*Isa 28:2; 29:6
*S Isa 51:19
*1Ch 29:2; Rev 21:18
*S Isa 28:16;
Rev 21:19-20
*S Ex 24:10;
S Job 28:6
54:12 *Rev 21:21
54:13 *S Isa 28:9;
Mic 4:2; Jn 6:45*;
Heb 8:11 *S Lev 26:6;
S Isa 48:18
54:14 *S Isa 26:2
*Jer 30:20
*2Sa 7:10; S Isa 9:4
*Zep 3:15; Zec 9:8
*S Isa 17:14
54:15 *Isa 41:11-16
54:16 *S Isa 44:12
*S Isa 10:5 / S Isa 13:5
54:17 *S Isa 29:8
*S Isa 41:11

the Holy One *s* of Israel is your Redeemer; *t*
he is called the God of all the earth. *u*

6 The LORD will call you back *v*
as if you were a wife deserted *w* and distressed in spirit—
a wife who married young, *x*
only to be rejected," says your God.

7 "For a brief moment *y* I abandoned *z* you,
but with deep compassion *a* I will bring you back. *b*

8 In a surge of anger *c*
I hid *d* my face from you for a moment,
but with everlasting kindness *e*
I will have compassion *f* on you,"
says the LORD your Redeemer. *g*

9 "To me this is like the days of Noah,
when I swore that the waters of Noah would never again cover the
earth. *h*
So now I have sworn *i* not to be angry *j* with you,
never to rebuke *k* you again.

10 Though the mountains be shaken *lm*
and the hills be removed,
yet my unfailing love *n* for you will not be shaken *o*
nor my covenant *p* of peace *q* be removed,"
says the LORD, who has compassion *r* on you.

11 "Afflicted *s* city, lashed by storms *t* and not comforted, *u*
I will rebuild you with stones of turquoise, *a v*
your foundations *w* with lapis lazuli. *x*

12 I will make your battlements of rubies,
your gates *y* of sparkling jewels,
and all your walls of precious stones.

13 All your children will be taught by the LORD, *z*
and great will be their peace. *a*

14 In righteousness *b* you will be established: *c*
Tyranny *d* will be far from you;
you will have nothing to fear. *e*
Terror *f* will be far removed;
it will not come near you.

15 If anyone does attack you, it will not be my doing;
whoever attacks you will surrender *g* to you.

16 "See, it is I who created the blacksmith *h*
who fans the coals into flame
and forges a weapon *i* fit for its work.
And it is I who have created the destroyer *j* to work havoc;

17 no weapon forged against you will prevail, *k*
and you will refute *l* every tongue that accuses you.

---

a 11 The meaning of the Hebrew for this word is uncertain.

54:6–7 *wife deserted...abandoned.* Israel's experience in exile
(see 49:14; 50:1 and note; 62:4).
54:7–8,10 *compassion.* See 14:1; 49:10,13; 51:3.
54:7 *brief moment.* The Babylonian exile was relatively brief
(see 26:20; 50:1 and notes).
54:8 *surge of anger.* See 9:12,17,21 and note; 60:10. *hid my face.*
See 1:15 and note. *everlasting kindness.* See v. 10; 55:3 and note.
Cf. 45:17. *Redeemer.* See v. 5.
54:9 *never again cover the earth.* See Ge 9:11 and note. *not to
be angry.* Cf. 12:1 and note. *never to rebuke you again.* As I did
when I sent you into exile.
54:10 *mountains...be removed.* Cf. 51:6; Ps 46:2; 102:26–27. *unfailing love...covenant of peace.* A reference to God's covenantal
commitments to Israel, embodied in the Abrahamic, Sinaitic and
Davidic covenants (see chart, p. 20). Cf. Jer 33:20–21; for the language, see Nu 25:11–13.

54:11–12 A figurative description of restored Jerusalem, echoed
in the description of the new Jerusalem in Rev 21:10,18–21.
54:11 *Afflicted city.* Jerusalem. See 51:21. *lashed by storms.* See
28:2 and note. *turquoise.* A bluish-green stone. It was used in
Solomon's temple (1Ch 29:2). *lapis lazuli.* Cf. the "pavement made
of lapis lazuli" (a blue stone) in Ex 24:10 (see also Eze 1:26; 10:1).
54:12 *battlements.* Parapets on the top of walls. Cf. 26:1.
54:13–14 *peace...righteousness.* See 48:18 and note.
54:13 Quoted in part in Jn 6:45. *taught by the LORD.* Like the
servant of the Lord in 50:4. Cf. Jer 31:34 and note.
54:14 *Tyranny...Terror...far removed.* Cf. 14:4; 33:18–19.
54:15 *surrender to you.* See v. 3.
54:16 *created the destroyer.* God raised up nations such as Assyria and Babylonia to punish Israel (see 10:5; 33:1 and notes).
54:17 *refute every tongue.* Just as no legitimate charges
could be brought against the servant of 50:8–9. *servants*

This is the heritage of the servants ^{m} of the Lord,
  and this is their vindication ^{n} from me,"

                                        declares the Lord.

INVITATION TO THE THIRSTY

55 "Come, all you who are thirsty, ^{o}
      come to the waters; ^{p}
    and you who have no money,
      come, buy ^{q} and eat!
    Come, buy wine and milk ^{r}
      without money and without cost. ^{s}
  ^{2} Why spend money on what is not bread,
      and your labor on what does not satisfy? ^{t}
    Listen, listen to me, and eat what is good, ^{u}
      and you will delight in the richest ^{v} of fare.
  ^{3} Give ear and come to me;
      listen, ^{w} that you may live. ^{x}
    I will make an everlasting covenant ^{y} with you,
      my faithful love ^{z} promised to David. ^{a}
  ^{4} See, I have made him a witness ^{b} to the peoples,
      a ruler and commander ^{c} of the peoples.
  ^{5} Surely you will summon nations ^{d} you know not,
      and nations you do not know will come running to you, ^{e}
    because of the Lord your God,
      the Holy One ^{f} of Israel,
    for he has endowed you with splendor." ^{g}

  ^{6} Seek ^{h} the Lord while he may be found; ^{i}
      call ^{j} on him while he is near.
  ^{7} Let the wicked forsake ^{k} their ways
      and the unrighteous their thoughts. ^{l}
    Let them turn ^{m} to the Lord, and he will have mercy ^{n} on them,
      and to our God, for he will freely pardon. ^{o}

  ^{8} "For my thoughts ^{p} are not your thoughts,
      neither are your ways my ways," ^{q}

                                        declares the Lord.

  ^{9} "As the heavens are higher than the earth, ^{r}
      so are my ways higher than your ways
    and my thoughts than your thoughts. ^{s}
  ^{10} As the rain ^{t} and the snow
      come down from heaven,
    and do not return to it
      without watering the earth

54:17 ^{m} Isa 56:6-8;
63:17; 65:8,9,13-15;
66:14 ^{n} S Ps 17:2;
Zec 1:20-21
55:1 ^{o} S Pr 9:5;
S Isa 35:7; Mt 5:6;
Lk 6:21; Jn 4:14; 7:37
^{p} Jer 2:13; Eze 47:1,
12; Zec 14:8 ^{q} La 5:4;
Mt 13:44; Rev 3:18
^{r} SS 5:1; 1Pe 2:2
^{s} Hos 14:4; Mt 10:8;
Rev 21:6; 22:17
55:2 ^{t} Ps 22:26;
Ecc 6:2; Isa 49:4;
Jer 12:13; Hos 4:10;
8:7; Mic 6:14; Hag 1:6
^{u} S Isa 1:19
^{v} S Isa 30:23
55:3 ^{w} S Ps 78:1
^{x} S Lev 18:5;
S Jn 6:27; Ro 10:5
^{y} S Ge 9:16;
S Isa 54:10;
S Heb 13:20
^{z} S Isa 54:8
^{a} Ac 13:34*
55:4 ^{b} Rev 1:5
^{c} S Isa 13:14;
S 2Ch 7:18; S Isa 32:1
55:5 ^{d} S Isa 49:6
^{e} S Isa 2:3 ^{f} S Isa 12:6;
S 54:5 ^{g} S Isa 44:23
55:6 ^{h} S Dt 4:29;
S 2Ch 15:2; S Isa 9:13
^{i} Ps 32:6; Isa 49:8;
Ac 17:27; 2Co 6:1-2
^{j} S Ps 50:15;
Isa 65:24; Jer 29:12;
33:3
55:7 ^{k} S 2Ch 7:14;
S 30:9; Eze 18:27-28
^{l} Isa 32:7; 59:7
^{m} S Isa 44:22;
S Jer 26:3;
S Eze 18:32
^{n} S Isa 54:10
^{o} S 2Ch 6:21; Isa 1:18;
40:2
55:8 ^{p} Php 2:5; 4:8
^{q} Isa 53:6; Mic 4:12
55:9 ^{r} S Job 11:8;
Ps 103:11
^{s} S Nu 23:19;
S Isa 40:13-14
55:10 ^{t} Isa 30:23

---

of the Lord. After ch. 53 the singular "servant" no longer occurs in Isaiah. The "servants" (see 63:17; 65:8–9,13–15; 66:14) are true believers—both Jew and Gentile (see 56:6–8)—who are faithful to the Lord. They are in a sense the "offspring" of the servant (53:10). See 49:19–20 and note.

A **55:1** The exiles are summoned to return and be restored. *thirsty.* Spiritual thirst is primarily in view (see 41:17; 44:3; Ps 42:1–2 and notes; 63:1). *waters.* Figurative for spiritual refreshment. Cf. Wisdom's invitation in Pr 9:5 (see note there). Christ similarly invited people to drink the water of life (see Jn 4:14 and note; 7:37; cf. Rev 22:17). *no money.* In hard times even water had to be purchased (see La 5:4). *wine and milk.* Symbols of abundance, enjoyment and nourishment. *without money.* The death of the servant (53:5–9) paid for the free gift of life (see Ro 6:23 and note).

55:2 *what is not bread.* Perhaps the husks of pagan religious practices. Cf. Dt 8:3 and note. *richest of fare.* Great spiritual blessings are compared to a banquet (see 25:6 and note; Ps 22:26; 34:8; Jer 31:14).

A **55:3** *everlasting covenant.* David had been promised an unending dynasty, one that would culminate in the Mes-

siah (see 9:7; 54:10; 61:8; 2Sa 7:14–16 and notes). *faithful love.* Assuring the continuation of the nation. See 54:8 and note. Christ's resurrection was further proof of God's faithfulness to David (see Ac 13:34, which quotes this verse).

A **55:4** *witness to the peoples.* A reference either to David, who exalted the Lord among the nations (see Ps 18:43, 49–50 and notes), or to David's Son, the Messiah, who was a light to the nations (see 42:6; 49:6 and notes). *ruler . . . of the peoples.* Similar titles are used of David (1Sa 13:14; 25:30) and the Messiah (Da 9:25).

A **55:5** *you will summon nations.* The attraction of nations to Zion and to the God of Israel is a major Biblical theme (see, e.g., 2:2–4; 45:14; Zec 8:22 and notes). *Holy One of Israel.* See 1:4; 41:14 and notes. *endowed . . . with splendor.* See 4:2; 60:9. The nation will be restored physically and spiritually.

55:6 *Seek the Lord.* See Jer 29:13–14; Hos 3:5; Am 5:4,6,14 (contrast the hypocritical seeking of 58:2).

55:7 *wicked forsake.* See 1:16. *turn to the Lord . . . freely pardon.* See 43:25; 44:22 and notes.

55:9 *my ways higher.* See Ps 145:3.

55:10 *u* S Lev 25:19;
S Job 14:9; S Ps 67:6
v S Ge 47:23
w 2Co 9:10
55:11 *x* S Dt 32:2;
Jn 1:1 *y* Isa 40:8;
45:23; S Mt 5:18;
Heb 4:12 *z* S Pr 19:21;
S Isa 44:26;
Eze 12:25
55:12 *a* S Ps 98:4;
S Isa 35:2 *b* Isa 54:10,
13 *c* S Ps 65:12-13;
S 96:12-13
d S 1Ch 16:33
e Ps 98:8
55:13 *f* S Nu 33:55;
S Isa 5:6 *g* Isa 41:19
h S Ps 102:12;
Isa 63:12; Jer 32:20;
33:9
56:1 *i* S Ps 11:7;
S Isa 1:17; S Jer 22:3
j S Isa 26:8
k S Ps 85:9 *l* Jer 23:6;
Da 9:24
56:2 *m* S Ps 119:2
n S Ex 20:8,10
56:3 *o* S Ex 12:43;
S 1Ki 8:41; S Isa 11:10;
Zec 8:20-23 *p* Dt 23:3
q S Lev 21:20;
Jer 38:7 fn; Ac 8:27
56:4 *r* Jer 38:7 fn
s S Ex 31:13
56:5 *t* Isa 26:1; 60:18
u S Nu 32:42;
1Sa 15:12 *v* S Isa 43:7

and making it bud and flourish, *u*
  so that it yields seed *v* for the sower and bread for the eater, *w*
[11] so is my word *x* that goes out from my mouth:
  It will not return to me empty, *y*
but will accomplish what I desire
  and achieve the purpose *z* for which I sent it.
[12] You will go out in joy *a*
  and be led forth in peace; *b*
the mountains and hills
  will burst into song *c* before you,
and all the trees *d* of the field
  will clap their hands. *e*
[13] Instead of the thornbush will grow the juniper,
  and instead of briers *f* the myrtle *g* will grow.
This will be for the LORD's renown, *h*
  for an everlasting sign,
  that will endure forever."

SALVATION FOR OTHERS

56 This is what the LORD says:

"Maintain justice *i*
  and do what is right, *j*
for my salvation *k* is close at hand
  and my righteousness *l* will soon be revealed.
[2] Blessed *m* are those who do this—
  who hold it fast,
those who keep the Sabbath *n* without desecrating it,
  and keep their hands from doing any evil."

[3] Let no foreigners *o* who have bound themselves to the LORD say,
  "The LORD will surely exclude me from his people." *p*
And let no eunuch *q* complain,
  "I am only a dry tree."

[4] For this is what the LORD says:

"To the eunuchs *r* who keep my Sabbaths,
  who choose what pleases me
  and hold fast to my covenant *s*—
[5] to them I will give within my temple and its walls *t*
  a memorial *u* and a name
  better than sons and daughters;
I will give them an everlasting name *v*

55:11 *my word.* Especially the promises of vv. 3,5,12. The word is viewed as a messenger also in 9:8; Ps 107:20 (see note there). Cf. Jn 1:1 and note. *achieve the purpose.* See 46:10–11 and note; cf. 40:8; Heb 4:12 and note.
55:12 *go out in joy.* The departure from Babylon provides the background (see 35:10; 52:9–12 and notes). *mountains ... will burst into song.* See 44:23 and note. *hands.* Branches. The language is figurative (cf. 1Ch 16:33; Ps 98:8 and note; 114:3–6).
55:13 *thornbush ... juniper ... briers ... myrtle.* The reverse of the desolation Isaiah had prophesied about earlier (5:6; 32:13). For the significance of trees, see 35:2; see also 41:19 and note. *LORD's renown.* Similar to God's fame in the exodus (see 63:12, 14). *everlasting sign.* God's deliverance would never be forgotten. Cf. 19:20; 56:5.
56:1 *justice ... what is right.* See note on Ps 119:121. *salvation ... righteousness.* See 45:8; 46:13; 51:5 and notes.
A 56:2 *keep the Sabbath.* See vv. 4,6. Just as the Sabbath had been instituted after the exodus from Egypt (see notes on Ex 20:8–10) as a sign of the Sinaitic covenant (see Ex 31:13–17 and notes), so God's new deliverance (55:12) afforded an opportunity to obey him fully, an obedience summed up in

"keeping the Sabbath" (see 58:13; 66:23; Jer 17:21–27 and notes; Eze 20:20–21).
56:3 *foreigners.* See v. 6. Members of certain nations who came to live among the Israelites had been excluded from worship, at least for several generations (see Ex 12:43; Dt 23:3,7–8). But the work of the servant of the Lord would change this (see 49:19–20; 54:17; 60:10 and notes). Cf. 14:1. *eunuch.* See v. 4; Mt 19:12 and note. Eunuchs were also excluded from the assembly of the Lord (see Dt 23:1 and note), but they could still be part of God's people (see Ac 8:27, 38–40).
56:4,6 *hold fast to my covenant.* Keeping the Sabbath was a sign of the Sinaitic covenant (see note on v. 2; see also Eze 20:12, 20 and note on 20:12; cf. notes on Ge 9:12–13; 17:11).
56:5 *memorial.* Absalom built a "Monument" (same Hebrew word) as a memorial since he had no surviving sons (2Sa 18:18). *name.* The Hebrew for this word is translated "renown" in 55:13. The Hebrew for "a memorial and a name" (*yad vashem*) was chosen from v. 5 as the name of the main Holocaust monument in Jerusalem in modern Israel. *that will endure forever.* An idiom sometimes referring to the preserving of a name through one's descendants.

that will endure forever. *w*

⁶ And foreigners *x* who bind themselves to the LORD
to minister *y* to him,
to love the name *z* of the LORD,
and to be his servants,
all who keep the Sabbath *a* without desecrating it
and who hold fast to my covenant—
⁷ these I will bring to my holy mountain *b*
and give them joy in my house of prayer.
Their burnt offerings and sacrifices *c*
will be accepted on my altar;
for my house will be called
a house of prayer for all nations. *d" e*

⁸ The Sovereign LORD declares—
he who gathers the exiles of Israel:
"I will gather *f* still others to them
besides those already gathered."

GOD'S ACCUSATION AGAINST THE WICKED

⁹ Come, all you beasts of the field, *g*
come and devour, all you beasts of the forest!
¹⁰ Israel's watchmen *h* are blind,
they all lack knowledge; *i*
they are all mute dogs,
they cannot bark;
they lie around and dream,
they love to sleep. *j*
¹¹ They are dogs with mighty appetites;
they never have enough.
They are shepherds *k* who lack understanding; *l*
they all turn to their own way, *m*
they seek their own gain. *n*
¹² "Come," each one cries, "let me get wine! *o*
Let us drink our fill of beer!
And tomorrow will be like today,
or even far better." *p*

57 The righteous perish, *q*
and no one takes it to heart; *r*
the devout are taken away,
and no one understands
that the righteous are taken away
to be spared from evil. *s*
² Those who walk uprightly *t*
enter into peace;
they find rest *u* as they lie in death.

³ "But you—come here, you children of a sorceress, *v*
you offspring of adulterers *w* and prostitutes! *x*
⁴ Whom are you mocking?

56:5 *w* S Isa 48:19; 55:13
56:6 *x* S Ex 12:43; S 1Ki 8:41
y S 1Ch 22:2; Isa 60:7, 10; 61:5 *z* Mal 1:11
a ver 2, 4
56:7 *b* S Isa 2:2; Eze 20:40
c S Isa 19:21; Ro 12:1; Php 4:18; Heb 13:15
d Mt 21:13*;
Lk 19:46* *e* Mk 11:17*
56:8 *f* S Dt 30:4; S Isa 1:9; S 11:12; 60:3-11; Eze 34:12; Jn 10:16
56:9 *g* Isa 18:6; Jer 12:9; Eze 34:5,8; 39:17-20
56:10 *h* S Isa 52:8; 62:6; Jer 6:17; 31:6; Eze 3:17; 33:7
i Jer 2:8; 10:21; 14:13-14 *j* Na 3:18
56:11 *k* Jer 23:1; Eze 34:2 *l* Isa 1:3
m S Isa 53:6;
Hos 4:7-8 *n* Isa 57:17; Jer 6:13; 8:10; 22:17; Eze 13:19; Mic 3:11
56:12 *o* S Lev 10:9; S Pr 23:20;
S Isa 22:13 *p* Ps 10:6; Lk 12:18-19
57:1 *q* S Ps 12:1; Eze 21:3 *r* S Isa 42:25
s 2Ki 22:20
57:2 *t* Isa 26:7
u Da 12:13
57:3 *v* S Ex 22:18; Mal 3:5 *w* ver 7-8; Mt 16:4; Jas 4:4
x Isa 1:21; Jer 2:20

56:6 *minister.* Cf. 60:7,10.

56:7 *my holy mountain.* See 2:2–4 and note. *offerings... accepted on my altar.* Cf. 60:7; contrast 1:11–13. *my house... for all nations.* Quoted by Jesus in Mk 11:17 and parallels. *house of prayer for all nations.* Solomon may have anticipated this in his prayer of dedication for the temple (see 1Ki 8:41–42 and notes).

56:8 *gathers the exiles.* See 11:11–12 and notes. *gather still others.* Including Gentiles (see v. 3 and note; cf. Jn 10:16 and note).

56:9—59:15 Many verses in these sections could apply to conditions before or during the Babylonian exile.

56:9 *beasts.* Foreign invaders (see 18:6 and note).

56:10 *watchmen.* The prophets (see note on Eze 3:17; cf. note on Isa 52:8). *blind... love to sleep.* Cf. 29:9–10. *mute dogs.* Watchdogs who guarded the sheep (cf. Job 30:1).

56:11 *mighty appetites.* They devour the sheep. See Eze 34:3. *shepherds.* Rulers may be included. See Eze 34:2–5 and notes.

56:12 *wine... beer.* Cf. the behavior of priests and prophets in 28:7. *tomorrow will be... far better.* Cf. the words of the rich fool in Lk 12:19.

57:1 *spared from evil.* Huldah explained that righteous King Josiah would die before disaster struck (2Ki 22:19–20).

57:2 *peace.* Contrast v. 21. *find rest.* Cf. Paul's words in Php 1:21,23.

57:3 *sorceress.* A woman who practices magic or consults evil spirits (see 3:2–3 and note; 47:12; Dt 18:10). *adulterers and prostitutes.* Spiritual adultery (idolatry) is in view (see vv. 5–8; see also Ex 34:15 and note).

57:4 *mocking... sneer.* The people mocked Isaiah in 28:9,14. *brood of rebels.* See 1:4; 46:8 and note.

57:4 ʸS Isa 1:2
57:5 ᶻS Isa 1:29
ᵃ S Dt 12:2; 2Ki 16:4
ᵇ S Lev 18:21;
S Dt 18:10; Ps 106:37-
38; Eze 16:20
57:6 ᶜS 2Ki 17:10;
Jer 3:9; Hab 2:19
ᵈ Jer 7:18; 19:13; 44:18
ᵉ Jer 5:9,29; 9:9
57:7 ᶠJer 3:6;
Eze 6:3; 16:16; 20:29
ᵍ Isa 65:7; Jer 13:27;
Eze 6:13; 20:27-28
57:8 ʰ Eze 16:26;
23:7 ʲEze 16:15,36;
23:18
57:9 ʲS Lev 18:21;
S 1Ki 11:5 ᵏS SS 4:10
ˡ Eze 23:16,40
ᵐ S Isa 8:19
57:10 ⁿS Isa 47:13
ᵒ Jer 2:25; 18:12;
Mal 3:14 ᵖ S 1Sa 2:4
57:11 ᵠS 2Ki 1:15;
Pr 29:25; Isa 7:2
ʳ S Isa 17:10; Jer 2:32;
3:21; 13:25; 18:15;
Eze 22:12
ˢ S Isa 42:23
ᵗ S Est 4:14;
S Ps 50:21; S 83:1
57:12 ᵘ Isa 29:15;
58:1; 59:6,12; 65:7;
66:18; Eze 16:2;
Mic 3:2-4,8
57:13 ᵛ Jer 22:20;
30:15 ʷ S Jdg 10:14
ˣ Isa 40:7,24
ʸ S Ps 118:8
ᶻS Ps 37:9 ᵃ Isa 2:2-
3; 56:7; 65:9-11

At whom do you sneer
and stick out your tongue?
Are you not a brood of rebels, ʸ
the offspring of liars?
⁵ You burn with lust among the oaks ᶻ
and under every spreading tree; ᵃ
you sacrifice your children ᵇ in the ravines
and under the overhanging crags.
⁶ The idols ᶜ among the smooth stones of the ravines are your portion;
they, they are your lot.
Yes, to them you have poured out drink offerings ᵈ
and offered grain offerings.
In view of all this, should I relent? ᵉ
⁷ You have made your bed on a high and lofty hill; ᶠ
there you went up to offer your sacrifices. ᵍ
⁸ Behind your doors and your doorposts
you have put your pagan symbols.
Forsaking me, you uncovered your bed,
you climbed into it and opened it wide;
you made a pact with those whose beds you love, ʰ
and you looked on their nakedness. ʲ
⁹ You went to Molek ᵃ ʲ with olive oil
and increased your perfumes. ᵏ
You sent your ambassadors ᵇ ˡ far away;
you descended to the very realm of the dead! ᵐ
¹⁰ You wearied ⁿ yourself by such going about,
but you would not say, 'It is hopeless.' ᵒ
You found renewal of your strength, ᵖ
and so you did not faint.

¹¹ "Whom have you so dreaded and feared ᵠ
that you have not been true to me,
and have neither remembered ʳ me
nor taken this to heart? ˢ
Is it not because I have long been silent ᵗ
that you do not fear me?
¹² I will expose your righteousness and your works, ᵘ
and they will not benefit you.
¹³ When you cry out ᵛ for help,
let your collection of idols save ʷ you!
The wind will carry all of them off,
a mere breath will blow ˣ them away.
But whoever takes refuge ʸ in me
will inherit the land ᶻ
and possess my holy mountain." ᵃ

ᵃ 9 Or *to the king*   ᵇ 9 Or *idols*

57:5 *oaks.* Sacred trees (see 1:29 and note). *spreading tree.* Associated with high places of pagan worship in 1Ki 14:23. Cf. Jer 2:20 and note; 3:13. *sacrifice your children.* Often associated with the worship of Molek (cf. v. 9; see note on 30:33) or Baal (Jer 19:5; see notes on Jer 7:31–32). Ps 106:37–38 says that children were sacrificed to idols and demons.
57:6 *ravines.* Possibly the Hinnom Valley (see Jer 7:31 and note). *drink offerings.* These pagan libations were especially popular.
57:7 *high and lofty hill.* "High places" or "mountain shrines" (see Jer 3:6; Eze 6:3 and note; 16:16; 22:9).
57:8 *those … you love.* Pagan deities or idols.
57:9 *Molek.* The main god of the Ammonites (see v. 5; 1Ki 11:5 and notes). *olive oil.* Used as an ointment for perfume. See SS

4:10, where the Hebrew word for "oil" is translated "perfume." *to the … realm of the dead.* Cf. 8:19.
57:10 *It is hopeless.* Ironically, the people said that turning away from their own plans or from foreign gods was hopeless. *renewal of your strength.* Cf. 40:31 and note.
57:11 *so dreaded and feared.* They feared mere mortals (see 51:12). *neither remembered me.* See 51:13. *long been silent.* God had not acted in judgment (see 42:14 and note).
57:12 *righteousness.* See 58:2–3; 64:6.
57:13 *collection of idols save you.* See 44:17 and note. *wind will carry … breath will blow.* Idols are no stronger than their worshipers. *takes refuge in me.* See 25:4. *inherit the land.* See 49:8 and note. *my holy mountain.* See 2:2–4 and note.

COMFORT FOR THE CONTRITE

[14] And it will be said:

"Build up, build up, prepare the road! [b]
    Remove the obstacles out of the way of my people." [c]
[15] For this is what the high and exalted [d] One says—
    he who lives forever, [e] whose name is holy:
"I live in a high [f] and holy place,
    but also with those who are contrite [g] and lowly in spirit, [h]
to revive the spirit of the lowly
    and to revive the heart of the contrite. [i]
[16] I will not accuse [j] them forever,
    nor will I always be angry, [k]
for then they would faint away because of me—
    the very people [l] I have created.
[17] I was enraged by their sinful greed; [m]
    I punished them, and hid [n] my face in anger,
    yet they kept on in their willful ways. [o]
[18] I have seen their ways, but I will heal [p] them;
    I will guide [q] them and restore comfort [r] to them,
[19]   creating praise on the lips [s] of the mourners in Israel.
Peace, peace, [t] to those far and near," [u]
    says the LORD. "And I will heal them."
[20] But the wicked [v] are like the tossing sea, [w]
    which cannot rest,
    whose waves cast up mire [x] and mud.
[21] "There is no peace," [y] says my God, "for the wicked." [z]

TRUE FASTING

58

"Shout it aloud, [a] do not hold back.
    Raise your voice like a trumpet. [b]
Declare to my people their rebellion [c]
    and to the house of Jacob their sins. [d]
[2] For day after day they seek [e] me out;
    they seem eager to know my ways,
as if they were a nation that does what is right
    and has not forsaken [f] the commands of its God.
They ask me for just decisions
    and seem eager for God to come near [g] them.
[3] 'Why have we fasted,' [h] they say,
    'and you have not seen it?
Why have we humbled [i] ourselves,
    and you have not noticed?' [j]

"Yet on the day of your fasting, you do as you please [k]
    and exploit all your workers.
[4] Your fasting ends in quarreling and strife, [l]
    and in striking each other with wicked fists.

57:14 [b] S Isa 11:16
[c] Isa 62:10; Jer 18:15
57:15 [d] S Isa 52:13
[e] S Dt 33:27;
S Ps 90:2 [f] S Job 16:19
[g] Ps 147:3 [h] Ps 34:18;
51:17; Isa 66:2;
Mic 6:8; Mt 5:3
[i] S 2Ki 22:19;
S Job 5:18; S Mt 23:12
57:16 [j] S Ps 50:21;
Isa 3:13-14
[k] S Ps 103:9;
S Isa 54:9 [l] S Ge 2:7;
Zec 12:1
57:17 [m] S Isa 56:11;
Jer 8:10 [n] S Isa 1:15
[o] Isa 1:4; S 30:15;
S 53:6; 66:3
57:18 [p] S Dt 32:39;
S 2Ch 7:14;
S Isa 30:26
[q] S Ps 48:14;
S Isa 42:16; S 48:17
[r] Isa 49:13; 61:1-3
57:19 [s] Isa 6:7;
51:16; 59:21;
Heb 13:15 [t] S Isa 2:4;
26:3,12; 32:17;
S Lk 2:14 [u] Ac 2:39
57:20 [v] Job 18:5-21
[w] S Ge 49:4;
Eph 4:14; Jude 13
[x] Ps 69:14
57:21 [y] S Isa 26:3;
59:8; Eze 13:16
[z] S Isa 48:22
58:1 [a] Isa 40:6
[b] S Eze 20:18
[c] S Isa 24:20; S 48:8
[d] S Isa 57:12; Eze 3:17
58:2 [e] S Isa 48:1;
Tit 1:16; Jas 4:8
[f] S Dt 32:15;
S Ps 119:87
[g] Isa 29:13
58:3 [h] S Lev 16:29
[i] S Ex 10:3;
S 2Ch 6:37; Jer 44:10
[j] Mal 3:14 [k] Isa 22:13;
Zec 7:5-6
58:4 [l] 1Ki 21:9-13;
Isa 59:6; Jer 6:7;
Eze 7:11; Mal 2:16

57:14 *Build up, build up.* See note on 40:1. *prepare the road.* See 40:3 and note.

57:15 *high and exalted One.* See 6:1; 52:13 and notes; cf. 33:5. *contrite.* Or "crushed" (see 53:5).

57:16 *not accuse them forever.* He had taken Israel to court repeatedly (see 3:13–14). *nor … be angry.* See 54:9 and note; Jer 3:12.

57:17 *hid my face in anger.* See 54:8; see also 1:15 and note.

57:18 *heal them.* See v. 19; 6:10; 30:26; Jer 3:22. God will forgive and restore his people. *guide.* Cf. 40:11; 42:16; 49:10. *restore comfort.* See 49:13 and note.

A **57:19** *mourners.* Those mourning the judgment on Jerusalem (see 66:10). *Peace, peace.* Contrast Jer 6:13–14 (see note on 6:14). *those far.* Either Gentiles or exiled Jews. Paul probably had this verse in mind in Eph 2:17.

57:20 *like the tossing sea.* See Jer 49:23. *cannot rest.* Contrast v. 2.

57:21 Almost identical to 48:22 (see note there; see also 39:8 and note).

58:1 *voice like a trumpet.* God's powerful voice is compared to a trumpet blast at Mount Sinai (see Ex 19:19; 20:18–19). *rebellion.* See 1:2 and note. *sins.* See 1:4; 59:12–13.

58:2 *seek me out.* See 55:6 and note. Cf. the frequent sacrifices of 1:11. *eager for God to come near.* The same hypocrisy is mentioned in 29:13 (see note there).

58:3 *fasted … fasting.* See v. 6; a time of self-denial, self-humbling and repentance for sin. After the fall of Jerusalem, the number of days for fasting increased (see Lev 16:29 and TNIV text note; see also Zec 8:19 and note). *humbled ourselves.* Cf. 2Ch 7:14; 1Ki 21:29. *you have not noticed.* The same attitude is seen in Mal 3:14 (see note there; cf. Lk 18:12). *exploit all your workers.* See 3:14–15; 10:2.

58:4 *m* S 1Sa 8:18;
Isa 59:2; La 3:44;
Eze 8:18; Mic 3:4
58:5 *n* Zec 7:5
o 1Ki 21:27; Mt 6:16
p S Isa 36:6
q S Job 2:8
58:6 *r* Joel 2:12-14
s Ne 5:10-11
t S Dt 14:29; Isa 61:1;
Jer 34:9; Am 4:1;
S Lk 4:19 *u* S Isa 9:4
58:7 *v* S Job 22:7;
Eze 18:16; Lk 3:11
w Isa 16:4; Heb 13:2
x Job 31:19-20;
S Mt 25:36
y S Ge 29:14;
Lk 10:31-32
58:8 *z* S Job 11:17;
S Isa 9:2 *a* S Isa 1:5;
S 30:26 *b* S Isa 26:2
c S Ex 14:19
58:9 *d* S Ps 50:15
e S Job 8:6;
S Isa 30:19; Da 9:20;
S Zec 10:6 *f* S Pr 6:13
g Ps 12:2; Isa 59:13
58:10 *h* Dt 15:7-8
i S Isa 42:16
j S Job 11:17
58:11 *k* S Ps 48:14;
S Isa 42:16; S 48:17
l S Ps 104:28; S 107:9
m S Ps 68:6
n S Ps 72:16
o S SS 4:15
p S Isa 35:7; Jn 4:14
58:12 *q* S Isa 49:8
r S Isa 44:28 *s* Ne 2:17
58:13 *t* S Ex 20:8

You cannot fast as you do today
  and expect your voice to be heard *m* on high.
5 Is this the kind of fast *n* I have chosen,
  only a day for people to humble *o* themselves?
Is it only for bowing one's head like a reed *p*
  and for lying in sackcloth and ashes? *q*
Is that what you call a fast,
  a day acceptable to the LORD?

6 "Is not this the kind of fasting *r* I have chosen:
to loose the chains of injustice *s*
  and untie the cords of the yoke,
to set the oppressed *t* free
  and break every yoke? *u*
7 Is it not to share your food with the hungry *v*
  and to provide the poor wanderer with shelter *w*—
when you see the naked, to clothe *x* them,
  and not to turn away from your own flesh and blood? *y*
8 Then your light will break forth like the dawn, *z*
  and your healing *a* will quickly appear;
then your righteousness *a b* will go before you,
  and the glory of the LORD will be your rear guard. *c*
9 Then you will call, *d* and the LORD will answer; *e*
  you will cry for help, and he will say: Here am I.

"If you do away with the yoke of oppression,
  with the pointing finger *f* and malicious talk, *g*
10 and if you spend yourselves in behalf of the hungry
  and satisfy the needs of the oppressed, *h*
then your light *i* will rise in the darkness,
  and your night will become like the noonday. *j*
11 The LORD will guide *k* you always;
  he will satisfy your needs *l* in a sun-scorched land *m*
  and will strengthen *n* your frame.
You will be like a well-watered garden, *o*
  like a spring *p* whose waters never fail.
12 Your people will rebuild the ancient ruins *q*
  and will raise up the age-old foundations; *r*
you will be called Repairer of Broken Walls, *s*
  Restorer of Streets with Dwellings.

13 "If you keep your feet from breaking the Sabbath *t*
  and from doing as you please on my holy day,

a 8 Or *your righteous One*

58:4 *to be heard on high.* Such hypocritical religious activity is actually a hindrance to prayer (see 1:15; 59:2).
58:5 *fast…humble themselves.* See Mt 6:16–18. *like a reed.* A sign of weakness and humility (see 42:3 and note). *sackcloth and ashes…fast.* See notes on Ge 37:34; Ezr 8:23; 10:6; Joel 1:13–14; Jnh 3:5–6; Rev 11:3. *acceptable.* A term often applied to sacrifices (see 56:7; 60:7; Lev 1:3; cf. Ro 12:1).
58:6 *chains of injustice.* During the siege of Jerusalem, Hebrew slaves were rightly released—only to be reclaimed by their masters (see Jer 34:8–11 and notes). *yoke.* See v. 9; 9:4; 10:27, where the yoke imposed by Assyria is mentioned. *oppressed.* See 1:17.
58:7 *share your food…provide…shelter…clothe.* The outward evidence of genuine righteousness. See Job 31:17–20; Eze 18:7,16 and Jesus' identification with the hungry and naked in Mt 25:34–40 (see notes there). *flesh and blood.* Probably refers to close relatives (Ge 37:27), but see 2Sa 5:1 and note.
58:8 *light.* The joy, prosperity and salvation brought by the Lord (see 9:2; 60:1–3; Ps 27:1 and note). *healing.* See 57:18 and note. *go before you … be your rear guard.* See 52:12 and note. The Lord will protect them and guide them. *glory of the LORD.*

Probably a reference to the pillar of cloud and fire in the desert (see 4:5–6; Ex 13:21; 14:20 and notes).
58:9 *LORD will answer.* See 30:19 and note. *Here am I.* See 65:1. *pointing finger.* A gesture of either contempt or accusation (see note on Pr 6:12–14). *malicious talk.* See Pr 2:12; 6:12,17,19 and notes.
58:10 *hungry…oppressed.* See vv. 6–7 and notes. *light.* See v. 8 and note.
58:11 *guide you.* See 57:18 and note. *needs.* Both material and spiritual (see note on 32:2). *sun-scorched land.* See 35:7; 49:10. *well-watered garden.* In 1:30 Jerusalem was a garden without water. *spring…never fail.* Contrast Jer 15:18 (see note there). Cf. the "living water" Jesus gives in Jn 4:10,14 (see notes there).
58:12 *ancient ruins … age-old foundations.* See 44:26,28 and notes; 61:4; Eze 36:10; Am 9:11,13–15 and notes. *Repairer of Broken Walls.* Cf. the work of Nehemiah in Ne 2:17 (see note there).
58:13 *Sabbath.* See 56:2 and note. *my holy day.* A day set apart to God (see Ex 3:5 and note). *delight.* They were also to delight themselves in the Lord (Ps 37:4) and in his law (see Ps 1:2 and note). *going your own way.* Perhaps to engage in business (see Am 8:5).

if you call the Sabbath a delight ^u
    and the Lord's holy day honorable,
and if you honor it by not going your own way
    and not doing as you please or speaking idle words, ^v
¹⁴ then you will find your joy ^w in the Lord,
    and I will cause you to ride in triumph on the heights ^x of the land
    and to feast on the inheritance ^y of your father Jacob."
        For the mouth of the Lord has spoken. ^z

SIN, CONFESSION AND REDEMPTION

59

Surely the arm ^a of the Lord is not too short ^b to save,
    nor his ear too dull to hear. ^c
² But your iniquities have separated ^d
    you from your God;
your sins have hidden his face from you,
    so that he will not hear. ^e
³ For your hands are stained with blood, ^f
    your fingers with guilt. ^g
Your lips have spoken falsely, ^h
    and your tongue mutters wicked things.
⁴ No one calls for justice; ⁱ
    no one pleads their case with integrity.
They rely ^j on empty arguments, they utter lies; ^k
    they conceive trouble and give birth to evil. ^l
⁵ They hatch the eggs of vipers ^m
    and spin a spider's web. ⁿ
Whoever eats their eggs will die,
    and when one is broken, an adder is hatched.
⁶ Their cobwebs are useless for clothing;
    they cannot cover themselves with what they make. ^o
Their deeds are evil deeds,
    and acts of violence ^p are in their hands.
⁷ Their feet rush into sin;
    they are swift to shed innocent blood. ^q
They pursue evil schemes; ^r
    acts of violence mark their ways. ^s
⁸ The way of peace they do not know; ^t
    there is no justice in their paths.
They have turned them into crooked roads; ^u
    no one who walks along them will know peace. ^v

⁹ So justice is far from us,
    and righteousness does not reach us.
We look for light, but all is darkness; ^w
    for brightness, but we walk in deep shadows.
¹⁰ Like the blind ^x we grope along the wall,
    feeling our way like people without eyes.
At midday we stumble ^y as if it were twilight;

58:13 ^u Ps 37:4; 42:4; 84:2,10
^v Isa 59:3
58:14 ^w S Job 22:26
^x S Dt 32:13
^y Ps 105:10-11
^z S Isa 1:20
59:1 ^a S Isa 41:20
^b S Isa 50:2
^c Isa 30:19; 58:9; 65:24
59:2 ^d Jer 5:25; Eze 39:23
^e S Ps 18:41; S Isa 58:4; S Jer 11:11; S Jn 9:31
59:3 ^f S 2Ki 21:16; S Isa 1:15; S Eze 22:9
^g Ps 7:3 ^h S Isa 3:8
59:4 ⁱ S Isa 5:23
^j S Job 15:31
^k S Isa 44:20
^l S Job 4:8; S Isa 29:20; Jas 1:15
59:5 ^m S Isa 11:8; Mt 3:7 ⁿ S Job 8:14
59:6 ^o Isa 28:20
^p S Ps 55:9; S Pr 4:17; S Isa 58:4
59:7 ^q S 2Ki 21:16; S Pr 6:17; S Mic 3:10
^r S Pr 24:2; S Isa 26:10; Mk 7:21-22 ^s Ro 3:15-17*
59:8 ^t Ro 3:15-17*
^u S Jdg 5:6
^v S Isa 57:21; Lk 1:79
59:9 ^w S Job 19:8; S Ps 107:14; S Isa 5:30; S 8:20; S Lk 1:79
59:10 ^x Dt 28:29; S Isa 6:9-10; 56:10; La 4:14; Zep 1:17
^y S Job 3:23; S Isa 8:15; Jn 11:9-10

58:14 *joy in the Lord.* See 61:10. *ride in triumph on the heights.* Thus controlling the land. See 33:16 and note; see also Hab 3:19. *feast on the inheritance.* Enjoying plentiful food in the promised land (see Dt 32:13–14). *mouth ... has spoken.* See 40:5 and note.
59:1 *arm ... too short.* See 51:9 and note. *too dull to hear.* See 30:19 and note.
59:2 *hidden his face ... he will not hear.* See 1:15 and note.
59:3–4 *spoken falsely ... utter lies.* See v. 13; 28:15; Hos 4:2 and note.
59:3 *stained with blood.* See v. 7; 1:15,21; Eze 7:23; see also notes on Eze 18:4,21.
59:4 *justice ... pleads their case.* The poor and helpless could not receive fair trials (see v. 14; 1:17–23; 5:7,23). *they conceive ... evil.* Identical to Job 15:35 (see note there). Cf. Isa 33:11; Ps 7:14.
59:5 *spider's web.* Verse 6 and Job 8:14–15 stress how fragile it is.
59:6 *acts of violence.* See v. 3; Jer 6:7; Eze 7:11.

A **59:7–8** Quoted in part in Ro 3:15–17 by Paul to show the universality of sin.
59:7 *Their feet rush ... to shed innocent blood.* This sentence appears in Pr 1:16 (see note there). *evil schemes.* God's thoughts are different (see 55:7–9). *acts of violence.* Contrast 60:18.
59:8 *way of peace.* Cf. 26:3,12; 57:20–21; Lk 1:79. *crooked roads.* Unsafe (see Jdg 5:6 and note).
59:9 *justice ... righteousness.* Personified here and in v. 14. See v. 4 and note; 1:21. *us ... We.* The prophet includes himself with the people. *We look for ... but.* See v. 11; cf. note on 5:2. *darkness ... deep shadows.* Similar language describes conditions when Assyria invaded Israel (see 5:30; 8:21–22; 9:1–2). Contrast 58:8.
59:10 *Like the blind we grope ... At midday.* The fulfillment of the curse for disobedience in Dt 28:29. Cf. Job 5:14. *strong.* Perhaps enemies or oppressors.

59:10 ᶻLa 3:6
59:11 ᵃS Ge 8:8;
Ps 74:19; Isa 38:14;
Jer 48:28; Eze 7:16;
Na 2:7
59:12 ᵇS Ezr 9:6;
ᶜS Isa 57:12 ᶜS Ge 4:7;
S Isa 3:9; S Jer 2:19
ᵈPs 51:3
59:13 ᵉIsa 46:8;
48:8 ᶠS Nu 11:20;
S Pr 30:9; Mt 10:33;
Tit 1:16 ᵍS Ps 12:5;
S Isa 5:7 ʰS Isa 3:8;
S 44:20; Mk 7:21-22
59:14 ⁱS Isa 29:21
ʲS Isa 1:21
ᵏS Isa 48:1;
S Jer 33:16
59:15 ˡJer 7:28; 9:5;
Da 8:12 ᵐS Isa 5:7
59:16 ⁿS Isa 41:28
ᵒS Isa 53:12
ᵖS Isa 51:5 �q Isa 45:8,
13; 46:13
59:17 ʳEph 6:14;
1Th 5:8 ˢEph 6:17;
1Th 5:8 ᵗS Job 27:6;
Isa 63:3 ᵘS Isa 1:24
ᵛIsa 9:7; Eze 5:13
59:18 ʷS Lev 26:28
; S Nu 10:35;
S Isa 34:8; S Mt 16:27
ˣIsa 11:11; 41:5
59:19 ʸS Isa 49:12;
S Mt 8:11 ᶻS Ps 113:3
ᵃPs 97:6; S Isa 24:15;
35:2; 40:5; 52:10;
66:18 ᵇS Isa 11:4
59:20 ᶜS Job 19:25;
Isa 60:16; 63:16
ᵈS Isa 52:8;
S Joel 3:21
ᵉS Job 22:23;
S Isa 1:27; S Jer 35:15;
Ac 2:38-39; Ro 11:26-
27*

among the strong, we are like the dead. ᶻ
¹¹ We all growl like bears;
    we moan mournfully like doves. ᵃ
We look for justice, but find none;
    for deliverance, but it is far away.

¹² For our offenses ᵇ are many in your sight,
    and our sins testify ᶜ against us.
Our offenses are ever with us,
    and we acknowledge our iniquities: ᵈ
¹³ rebellion ᵉ and treachery against the LORD,
    turning our backs ᶠ on our God,
inciting revolt and oppression, ᵍ
    uttering lies ʰ our hearts have conceived.
¹⁴ So justice ⁱ is driven back,
    and righteousness ʲ stands at a distance;
truth ᵏ has stumbled in the streets,
    honesty cannot enter.
¹⁵ Truth ˡ is nowhere to be found,
    and whoever shuns evil becomes a prey.

The LORD looked and was displeased
    that there was no justice. ᵐ
¹⁶ He saw that there was no one, ⁿ
    he was appalled that there was no one to intervene; ᵒ
so his own arm achieved salvation ᵖ for him,
    and his own righteousness �q sustained him.
¹⁷ He put on righteousness as his breastplate, ʳ
    and the helmet ˢ of salvation on his head;
he put on the garments ᵗ of vengeance ᵘ
    and wrapped himself in zeal ᵛ as in a cloak.
¹⁸ According to what they have done,
    so will he repay ʷ
wrath to his enemies
    and retribution to his foes;
    he will repay the islands ˣ their due.
¹⁹ From the west, ʸ people will fear the name of the LORD,
    and from the rising of the sun, ᶻ they will revere his glory. ᵃ
For he will come like a pent-up flood
    that the breath ᵇ of the LORD drives along. ᵃ

²⁰ "The Redeemer ᶜ will come to Zion, ᵈ
    to those in Jacob who repent of their sins," ᵉ
                      declares the LORD.

ᵃ 19 Or *When enemies come in like a flood, / the Spirit of the LORD will put them to flight*

59:11 *growl like bears.* Impatient and frustrated.
  59:12 *offenses . . . sins . . . iniquities.* In Hebrew the three most common OT words for evil thoughts and deeds (see Ps 32:5 and note). *offenses are many.* See 58:1. *we acknowledge our iniquities.* Like Ezra (9:6–7), Isaiah confesses the sins of the nation.
59:13 *rebellion and treachery. turning our backs.* See 1:4. *oppression.* See 30:12. *lies.* See vv. 3–4.
59:14 *justice . . . truth.* Cf. the personification of wisdom in Pr 8:1—9:12 (see note on 8:1–36). *righteousness stands at a distance.* Cf. v. 9; contrast 46:13 (see note there).
59:15 *Truth.* Restored Jerusalem is called the "City of Truth" in Zec 8:3 (see 1:21,26 and notes). *becomes a prey.* See 32:7.
59:16 *there was no one.* To help (see 63:5, a parallel to the whole verse). Cf. Eze 22:30 and note. *appalled.* Cf. the reaction to the servant in 52:14. *intervene.* Cf. the intercession of the servant in 53:12 (see note there). *his own arm achieved salvation.* See 51:9; 52:10. For the meaning of salvation, see 43:3; 49:8; 52:7 and notes. *righteousness.* For the relationship between righteousness and salvation, see 45:8; 46:13 and notes.

59:17 *put on . . . wrapped himself in.* See note on Ps 109:29. *righteousness as his breastplate.* The Lord's armor is compared to the believer's armor in the battle against Satan in Eph 6:14 (see note there). *garments of vengeance.* Cf. the blood-spattered garments of 63:1–3. God's vengeance is described also in 34:8 (see note there); 63:4. It is part of the day of the Lord (see 34:2 and note). *zeal.* God's jealous love (see 9:7 and note; 37:32; 42:13).
59:18 *enemies . . . foes.* God will judge the nations, but he must also punish wicked Israelites (see 65:6–7; 66:6; Jer 25:29). Only the remnant will be blessed (see v. 20; see also 1:9 and note). *islands.* See note on 11:11.
59:19 *From the west . . . rising of the sun.* All nations will see God's saving work in behalf of his people (see 40:5; 45:6; 52:10 and notes). *name.* See 30:27 and note. *pent-up flood.* The coming of the Lord will be irresistible, like a "rushing torrent" (30:28) that overwhelms the enemy.
  59:20 *Redeemer.* See 41:14 and note. *come to Zion.* In the return from exile, but more fully in the person of Christ

²¹"As for me, this is my covenant ᶠ with them," says the LORD. "My Spirit, ᵍ who is on you, and my words that I have put in your mouth ʰ will not depart from your mouth, ᶦ or from the mouths of your children, or from the mouths of their descendants from this time on and forever," says the LORD.

THE GLORY OF ZION

60 "Arise, ʲ shine, for your light ᵏ has come,
and the glory ˡ of the LORD rises upon you.
² See, darkness ᵐ covers the earth
and thick darkness ⁿ is over the peoples,
but the LORD rises upon you
and his glory appears over you.
³ Nations ᵒ will come to your light, ᵖ
and kings �q to the brightness of your dawn.

⁴ "Lift up your eyes and look about you:
All assemble ʳ and come to you;
your sons come from afar, ˢ
and your daughters ᵗ are carried on the hip. ᵘ
⁵ Then you will look and be radiant, ᵛ
your heart will throb and swell with joy; ʷ
the wealth ˣ on the seas will be brought to you,
to you the riches of the nations will come.
⁶ Herds of camels ʸ will cover your land,
young camels of Midian ᶻ and Ephah. ᵃ
And all from Sheba ᵇ will come,
bearing gold and incense ᶜ
and proclaiming the praise ᵈ of the LORD.
⁷ All Kedar's ᵉ flocks will be gathered to you,
the rams of Nebaioth will serve you;
they will be accepted as offerings ᶠ on my altar, ᵍ
and I will adorn my glorious temple. ʰ

⁸ "Who are these ᶦ that fly along like clouds, ʲ
like doves to their nests?
⁹ Surely the islands ᵏ look to me;
in the lead are the ships of Tarshish, ᵃ ˡ

ᵃ 9 Or *the trading ships*

59:21 ᶠ S Ge 9:16;
S Dt 29:14; S Isa 42:6
ᵍ S Isa 11:2; S 44:3
ʰ S Ex 4:15 ᶦ S Jos 1:8
60:1 ʲ Isa 52:2
ᵏ S Ps 36:9; S 118:27;
S Isa 9:2; Jn 8:12;
Eph 5:14 ˡ S Ex 16:7;
S Isa 4:5; Rev 21:11
60:2 ᵐ S 1Sa 2:9;
S Ps 82:5; S 107:14;
S Isa 8:20 ⁿ Jer 13:16;
Col 1:13
60:3 ᵒ S Isa 44:5;
S 45:14; Mt 2:1-11;
Rev 21:24 ᵖ S Isa 9:2;
42:6 q S Isa 49:23
60:4 ʳ S Isa 11:12
ˢ S Isa 2:3; Jer 30:10
ᵗ S Isa 43:6
ᵘ Isa 49:20-22
60:5 ᵛ S Ex 34:29
ʷ Isa 35:2; 65:13;
66:14; Zec 10:7
ˣ S Dt 33:19;
S Jdg 3:15; Rev 21:26
60:6 ʸ S Jdg 6:5
ᶻ S Ge 25:2 ᵃ Ge 25:4
ᵇ S Ge 10:7,28
ᶜ Isa 43:23; Jer 6:20;
Mt 2:11 ᵈ S 1Ki 5:7;
S Isa 42:10
60:7 ᵉ S Ge 25:13
ᶠ Isa 18:7; Eze 20:40;
43:27; Zep 3:10
ᵍ S Isa 19:21 ʰ ver 13;
Hag 2:3,7,9
60:8 ᶦ Isa 49:21
ʲ Isa 19:1
60:9 ᵏ S Isa 11:11
ˡ S Ge 10:4;
Isa 2:16 fn

(see Ro 11:26–27 and notes). See 35:4; 40:9; 52:7 and notes. Cf. Zec 8:3. *those . . . who repent.* See 1:27–28 and note; 30:15; 31:6; see also Eze 18:30–32 and notes.

59:21 *covenant.* The description best fits the "new covenant" (see 42:6; Jer 31:31–34 and notes). *My Spirit.* See 11:2; 32:15; Eze 36:27; Jn 16:13 and notes. *you . . . your . . . your . . . your.* In Hebrew the pronouns are singular but are probably intended in a collective sense—the citizens of Zion. *my words . . . in your mouth.* Then Israel will truly be God's people (see 51:16; Jer 31:33 and notes). *not depart from your mouth.* See Jos 1:8.

60:1–2 *glory.* Probably an allusion to the pillar of cloud, but announcing a new manifestation of God's redeeming glory (see 58:8 and note). See also 35:2 and note.

60:1 *light.* See 58:8 and note. Here the Lord himself is viewed as the light (see vv. 19–20).

60:2 *darkness.* A symbol of gloom, oppression and sin (see 8:22; 9:2; 59:9).

60:3 *Nations will come.* See vv. 5,10–12 and notes. This theme was first mentioned in 2:2–4 (see note there). *light.* See 42:6; 49:6 and notes.

60:4 The first two lines are almost identical to the beginning of 49:18, the last two to the end of 49:22 (see note there). The setting there was the return from exile, but here much broader implications are involved. *afar.* See v. 9; 49:12 and note.

60:5 *wealth on the seas.* Jerusalem will be enriched by the nations (see v. 11; 61:6; 66:12; see also 18:7; 23:18; 45:14

and notes). The contribution of King Darius to Zerubbabel's temple may be a partial fulfillment (see Ezr 6:8–9 and notes). Some interpret this verse as referring to conditions during the future phase of the Messianic kingdom, while others apply it to the influx of Gentiles into the church (see note on 2:2–4). See Rev 21:26 (the new Jerusalem); see also Hag 2:7; Zec 14:14 and notes.

60:6 *camels will cover your land.* As caravans bringing goods. Ironically it was on camels that the Midianites once devastated Israel (see 9:4; Jdg 6:1–6 and notes). *Midian.* Abraham's son through Keturah (Ge 25:2). The Midianites roamed the deserts of Transjordan. *Ephah.* A son of Midian (Ge 25:4). *Sheba.* A wealthy land in southern Arabia, perhaps roughly equal to modern Yemen (see Ge 25:3; 1Ki 10:1 and note). *gold and incense.* The queen of Sheba brought gold and spices to Solomon (1Ki 10:2). Jer 6:20 mentions the incense of Sheba. Cf. Ps 72:10; Mt 2:11. *proclaiming the praise.* Cf. the queen's words in 1Ki 10:9 (but see note there).

60:7 *Kedar's flocks.* See note on 21:16. *Nebaioth.* The firstborn son of Ishmael (Ge 25:13). The name is probably preserved in that of the later Nabatean kingdom. *serve.* See v. 10; 56:6. *accepted as offerings.* See 56:7; 58:5 and notes.

60:9 *islands look to me.* See 11:11 and note. *ships of Tarshish.* See note on 2:16. *bringing your children.* See 49:22 and note. *silver and gold.* Ships of Tarshish had brought these to Solomon every three years (1Ki 10:22). *Holy One of Israel.* See v. 14; 1:4 and note. *endowed . . . with splendor.* See 55:5 and note.

60:9 *m* S Isa 14:2;
S 43:6. *n* S 1Ki 10:22
o S Ps 22:23 *p* ver 14;
Isa 1:4; S 54:5
q S Isa 44:23; 55:5;
Jer 30:19
60:10 *r* S Ex 1:11;
S Isa 14:1-2; S 56:6
s S Ezr 1:2; Rev 21:24
t S Isa 49:8
u S Ps 102:13
60:11 *v* ver 18;
S Ps 24:7; Isa 62:10;
Mic 2:13; Rev 21:25
w S ver 5; Isa 61:6;
Rev 21:26 *x* Ps 149:8;
S Isa 2:12
60:12 *y* S Isa 11:14;
S 14:2 *z* S Ge 27:29;
S Ps 110:5; Da 2:34
60:13 *a* S Ezr 3:7
b Isa 41:19 *c* S ver 7
d S 1Ch 28:2
60:14 *e* S Isa 14:2
f S Ge 27:29;
S Isa 2:3; Rev 3:9
g S Ge 32:28;
S Isa 1:26 *h* Heb 12:22
i S ver 9
60:15 *j* Isa 1:7-9;
S 6:12; S 54:6
k S Isa 33:8 *l* S Isa 4:2
m S Ps 126:5;
Isa 65:18
60:16 *n* S Ex 6:2;
Isa 49:23; 66:11,12
o S Ex 6:7
p S Ex 14:30;
S Isa 25:9
q S Job 19:25;
S Isa 59:20
r S Ge 49:24;
S Ps 132:2
60:17 *s* 1Ki 10:21
t S Ps 85:8; Isa 66:12;
Hag 2:9 *u* S Isa 9:7
60:18 *v* S Lev 26:6;
S 2Sa 7:10; S Isa 9:4
w S Isa 49:19; S 51:19
x S Isa 33:6
y Isa 61:11; 62:7;
Jer 33:9; Zep 3:20

bringing *m* your children from afar,
  with their silver and gold, *n*
to the honor *o* of the LORD your God,
  the Holy One *p* of Israel,
  for he has endowed you with splendor. *q*

10 "Foreigners *r* will rebuild your walls,
  and their kings *s* will serve you.
Though in anger I struck you,
  in favor *t* I will show you compassion. *u*
11 Your gates *v* will always stand open,
  they will never be shut, day or night,
so that people may bring you the wealth of the nations *w*—
  their kings *x* led in triumphal procession.
12 For the nation or kingdom that will not serve *y* you will perish;
  it will be utterly ruined. *z*

13 "The glory of Lebanon *a* will come to you,
  the juniper, the fir and the cypress together, *b*
to adorn my sanctuary; *c*
  and I will glorify the place for my feet. *d*
14 The children of your oppressors *e* will come bowing before you;
  all who despise you will bow down *f* at your feet
and will call you the City *g* of the LORD,
  Zion *h* of the Holy One *i* of Israel.

15 "Although you have been forsaken *j* and hated,
  with no one traveling *k* through,
I will make you the everlasting pride *l*
  and the joy *m* of all generations.
16 You will drink the milk of nations
  and be nursed *n* at royal breasts.
Then you will know *o* that I, the LORD, am your Savior, *p*
  your Redeemer, *q* the Mighty One of Jacob. *r*
17 Instead of bronze I will bring you gold, *s*
  and silver in place of iron.
Instead of wood I will bring you bronze,
  and iron in place of stones.
I will make peace *t* your governor
  and well-being your ruler. *u*
18 No longer will violence *v* be heard in your land,
  nor ruin or destruction *w* within your borders,
but you will call your walls Salvation *x*
  and your gates Praise. *y*
19 The sun will no more be your light by day,
  nor will the brightness of the moon shine on you,

60:10 *Foreigners … kings.* See vv. 12,14; 49:7,23; 61:5. *will rebuild your walls.* In 444 B.C. King Artaxerxes issued the decree allowing Nehemiah to rebuild the walls of Jerusalem (Ne 2:8). Some also apply the rebuilt walls to the building up of the church through Gentile believers (Ac 15:14–16). *Though in anger … compassion.* See 54:7–8 and notes.
60:11 *gates … always … open.* As are the gates of the new Jerusalem (Rev 21:25). *wealth.* See v. 5 and note.
60:12 *nation … will perish.* Israel's future political domination is referred to also in 11:14; 14:2; 49:23 (cf. vv. 10,14).
60:13 *glory of Lebanon.* Its magnificent cedar trees, which were used in the construction of Solomon's temple, along with juniper trees (1Ki 5:10,18). See also 35:2. The glory of Solomon's era would return. *juniper … fir … cypress.* See 41:19 and note. Perhaps the trees would be ornamental rather than building material. *adorn … sanctuary.* See v. 7. *place for my feet.* The temple, and especially the ark of the covenant, God's "footstool." **60:14** *oppressors … bow down.* See 49:7,23 and notes. Cf. vv. 10,12. *City of the LORD.* Cf. the names for the future Jerusalem in

1:26; 62:4; Eze 48:35; Zec 8:3; Heb 12:22 (see notes there).
60:15 *forsaken and hated.* See 6:11–12; 62:4; Jer 30:17. *pride … joy.* See 4:2 and note.
60:16 *nursed at royal breasts.* Jerusalem will receive the very best nourishment, the "riches of the nations" (v. 5). *Then … Jacob.* For this sentence, see 49:26 and note.

60:17 *gold … silver.* As in Solomon's day gold and silver were plentiful (1Ki 10:21,27), so the future Jerusalem will have the most valuable metals, as well as the strongest ("iron"). Cf. 9:10. *peace … well-being.* Both are also present in the rule of the Messianic king in 9:7 (where the Hebrew for "well-being" is rendered "righteousness"). See note on 48:18.
60:18 *No longer … violence.* Cf. 54:14. *ruin or destruction.* See 51:19 and note. *walls Salvation.* See 26:1.

60:19 *sun … moon.* According to Rev 21:23; 22:5 their light will no longer be needed in the new Jerusalem, since God and the Lamb will be the "everlasting light." *glory.* See vv. 1–2 and note; Zec 2:5; cf. notes on Ex 40:34; Ps 26:8.

for the LORD will be your everlasting light, [z]
 and your God will be your glory. [a]
 [20] Your sun [b] will never set again,
 and your moon will wane no more;
 the LORD will be your everlasting light,
 and your days of sorrow [c] will end.
 [21] Then will all your people be righteous [d]
 and they will possess [e] the land forever.
 They are the shoot I have planted, [f]
 the work of my hands, [g]
 for the display of my splendor. [h]
 [22] The least of you will become a thousand,
 the smallest a mighty nation. [i]
 I am the LORD;
 in its time I will do this swiftly." [j]

THE YEAR OF THE LORD'S FAVOR

61 The Spirit [k] of the Sovereign LORD [l] is on me,
 because the LORD has anointed [m] me
 to proclaim good news [n] to the poor. [o]
 He has sent me to bind up [p] the brokenhearted,
 to proclaim freedom [q] for the captives [r]
 and release from darkness for the prisoners, [a]
 [2] to proclaim the year of the LORD's favor [s]
 and the day of vengeance [t] of our God,
 to comfort [u] all who mourn, [v]
 [3] and provide for those who grieve in Zion—
 to bestow on them a crown [w] of beauty
 instead of ashes, [x]
 the oil [y] of joy
 instead of mourning, [z]
 and a garment of praise
 instead of a spirit of despair.
 They will be called mighty oaks,
 a planting [a] of the LORD
 for the display of his splendor. [b]

 [4] They will rebuild the ancient ruins [c]
 and restore the places long devastated;
 they will renew the ruined cities
 that have been devastated for generations.
 [5] Strangers [d] will shepherd your flocks;

---

[a] 1 Hebrew; Septuagint *the blind*

60:19 [z] S Ps 36:9;
S 118:27; Rev 22:5
[a] S Ps 85:9;
S Isa 24:16,23;
Rev 21:23
60:20 [b] Isa 30:26
[c] S Isa 30:19; S 35:10;
S Rev 7:17
60:21 [d] S Isa 4:3;
S 26:2; Rev 21:27
[e] Ps 37:11,22;
Isa 49:8; 57:13; 61:7;
65:9; Zec 8:12
[f] S Ex 15:17; Ps 44:2;
80:8-11; Jer 32:41;
Am 9:15; Mt 15:13
[g] S Job 10:3; S Ps 8:6;
S Isa 19:25; Eph 2:10
[h] S Lev 10:3;
S Isa 44:23
60:22 [i] S Ge 12:2;
S Dt 1:10 / Isa 5:19
61:1 [k] S Isa 11:2;
2Co 3:17 [l] S Isa 50:4
[m] S Ps 45:7;
S Da 9:24-26;
S Ac 4:26
[n] S 2Sa 18:26;
S Isa 40:9
[o] S Job 5:16;
S Mt 11:5; Lk 7:22
[p] 2Ki 22:19;
S Job 5:18
[q] S Lev 25:10
[r] S Ps 68:6; S Isa 49:9
61:2 [s] S Isa 49:8;
S Lk 4:18-19*
[t] S Isa 1:24
[u] S Isa 40:1; Mt 5:4
[v] S Job 5:11; Lk 6:21
61:3 [w] S Isa 3:23
[x] S Job 2:8 [y] S Ru 3:3;
S Isa 1:6; Heb 1:9
[z] Jer 31:13; Mt 5:4
[a] Ps 1:3; 92:12-13;
Mt 15:13; 1Co 3:9
[b] S Isa 44:23
61:4 [c] S Isa 44:26;
51:3; 65:21;
Eze 36:33; Am 9:14;
Zec 1:16-17
61:5 [d] S Isa 14:1-2;
S 56:6

60:20 *sun will never set.* There will be no night there (cf. Rev 22:5) but only the light of joy and salvation (see 58:8 and note). *sorrow will end.* See 25:8; 35:10; 51:11; 65:19; Rev 21:4.

60:21 *people be righteous.* Only the redeemed will be there (see 4:3; 35:8; Rev 21:27). *possess the land forever.* Enter into full blessing (see 49:8 and note; see also 57:13; 61:7; Ps 37:11,22). *shoot I have planted.* Cf. the vineyard of 5:2,7 (see also 11:1). *work of my hands.* God made them as a potter forms clay (see 64:8; see also 29:23; 45:11). *display of my splendor.* They are the evidence of God's redemptive work. See 49:3; 61:3; see also notes on 35:2; 40:5.

60:22 *least ... will become a thousand.* See 51:2; 54:3 and notes. The blessing of Lev 26:8 is similar. *do this swiftly.* Cf. 5:19, where the same Hebrew verb is translated "hasten."

61:1–2 Jesus applied these verses to himself in the synagogue at Nazareth (see Lk 4:16–20 and notes; cf. Mt 11:5).

61:1 *Spirit ... is on me.* The statement may refer to Isaiah in a limited sense, but the Messianic servant is the main figure intended (cf. what is said of him in 42:1; see 11:2; 48:16 and notes). *Sovereign LORD.* See 50:4–5,7,9 and note. *anointed me.* See 45:1 and note. *good news.* See 40:9 and note. *poor.* Cf.

11:4; 29:19. *bind up the brokenhearted.* See 30:26 and note. *freedom for the captives.* Freedom is proclaimed in the Year of Jubilee in Lev 25:10 (see 49:8 and note).

61:2 *year of the LORD's favor.* Corresponds to the "day of salvation" in 49:8 (see note there) and the "year for me to redeem" in 63:4. Christ ended his quotation at this point (Lk 4:19–20), probably because the "day of vengeance" will not occur until his second coming. *day of vengeance.* See 34:2,8 and notes. *comfort all who mourn.* See 49:13; 57:19 and notes; 66:10; Jer 31:13; Mt 5:4.

61:3 *bestow on them ... a garment of praise.* See note on Ps 109:29. *crown of beauty.* A "turban" (as the Hebrew for this phrase is translated in Eze 24:17) or headdress. In 3:20 the women of Jerusalem were to lose their beautiful headdresses. *oil of joy.* Anointing with olive oil was common on joyous occasions (see Ps 23:5; 45:7 and notes; 104:15; 133:1–2; cf. 2Sa 14:2). See also 1:6 and note. *garment of praise.* Contrast the "garments of vengeance" in 59:17. *mighty oaks.* Contrast the oaks of 1:30. *planting ... for the display.* See 60:21 and note.

61:4 *rebuild the ancient ruins ... ruined cities.* See 58:12 and note.

61:5 *Strangers ... foreigners.* See 14:1–2; 56:3; 60:10 and notes.

61:6 *e* S Ex 19:6;
1Pe 2:5 *f* Dt 33:19;
S Isa 60:11
61:7 *g* S Isa 29:22;
S 41:11 *h* S Dt 21:17;
S Isa 40:2
i S Isa 60:21
j S Ps 126:5;
S Isa 25:9
61:8 *k* S Ps 11:7;
S Isa 1:17; S 5:16
l S Ge 9:16;
S Isa 42:6;
S Heb 13:20
61:9 *m* S Isa 43:5;
S 48:19 *n* S Ge 12:2;
S Dt 28:3-12
61:10 *o* S Ps 2:11;
S Isa 7:13; S 25:9;
Hab 3:18; S Lk 1:47
p S Job 27:6;
S Ps 132:9; S Isa 52:1;
Rev 19:8 *q* S Ex 39:28
r S Isa 49:18; Rev 21:2
61:11 *s* S Ge 47:23;
Isa 58:11 *t* S Isa 45:8
62:1 *u* S Est 4:14;
S Ps 50:21; S 83:1
v S Isa 1:26; S 45:8
w S Job 11:17
x S Ps 67:2
62:2 *y* S Ps 67:2;
S Isa 40:5; S 45:14;
52:10 *z* S Ge 32:28;
S Isa 1:26; Rev 2:17;
3:12
62:3 *a* S Isa 28:5;
1Th 2:19
62:4 *b* S Lev 26:43;
S Isa 6:12; S 54:6
c S Ge 49:19; S 51:19
d 2Ki 21:1

foreigners will work your fields and vineyards.
⁶ And you will be called priests *e* of the LORD,
you will be named ministers of our God.
You will feed on the wealth *f* of nations,
and in their riches you will boast.

⁷ Instead of your shame *g*
you will receive a double *h* portion,
and instead of disgrace
you will rejoice in your inheritance.
And so you will inherit *i* a double portion in your land,
and everlasting joy *j* will be yours.

⁸ "For I, the LORD, love justice; *k*
I hate robbery and wrongdoing.
In my faithfulness I will reward my people
and make an everlasting covenant *l* with them.
⁹ Their descendants *m* will be known among the nations
and their offspring among the peoples.
All who see them will acknowledge
that they are a people the LORD has blessed." *n*

¹⁰ I delight greatly in the LORD;
my soul rejoices *o* in my God.
For he has clothed me with garments of salvation
and arrayed me in a robe of his righteousness, *p*
as a bridegroom adorns his head *q* like a priest,
and as a bride *r* adorns herself with her jewels.
¹¹ For as the soil makes the sprout come up
and a garden *s* causes seeds to grow,
so the Sovereign LORD will make righteousness *t*
and praise spring up before all nations.

ZION'S NEW NAME

62 For Zion's sake I will not keep silent, *u*
for Jerusalem's sake I will not remain quiet,
till her vindication *v* shines out like the dawn, *w*
her salvation *x* like a blazing torch.
² The nations *y* will see your vindication,
and all kings your glory;
you will be called by a new name *z*
that the mouth of the LORD will bestow.
³ You will be a crown *a* of splendor in the LORD's hand,
a royal diadem in the hand of your God.
⁴ No longer will they call you Deserted, *b*
or name your land Desolate. *c*
But you will be called Hephzibah, *a* *d*

---

a 4 *Hephzibah* means *my delight is in her.*

61:6 *priests of the LORD.* See 66:21. True Israel will be a
"kingdom of priests" among the Gentiles (see Ex 19:6; Zec
3:1–10 and notes). *ministers.* Priests. See 1Ki 8:11, where the Hebrew word for "minister" is translated "perform their service."
wealth of nations. See 60:5 and note.
61:7 *shame ... disgrace.* See 45:17; 54:4. *double portion.* The
firstborn son received a double share of the inheritance (see Dt
21:17; Zec 9:12 and notes). Contrast the "double" punishment Israel received (40:2). *everlasting joy.* See 35:10; 51:11; cf. Ps 16:11.
61:8 *love justice.* Cf. 30:18; 59:15. *robbery and wrongdoing.* Israel had been mistreated by her conquerors. Cf. 42:24; 59:18. *everlasting covenant.* Probably the new covenant (see 55:3; 59:21
and notes; cf. Jer 31:35–37; 32:40 and notes).
61:9 *people the LORD has blessed.* See 44:3; 65:23 and the promises to Abraham in Ge 12:1–3 (see notes there).
61:10 Zion is probably the speaker. *clothed me with ... arrayed
me in.* See note on Ps 109:29. *garments of salvation.* See v. 3; 52:1

and note. *head like a priest.* Putting on a turban or headband
(see note on v. 3). *bride ... with her jewels.* See 49:18 and note.
61:11 *sprout ... grow.* Cf. 55:10. *righteousness and praise spring
up.* See 45:8 and note.
62:1 *not keep silent ... quiet.* See v. 6; 42:14; 57:11 and note;
64:12; 65:6; see also Ps 28:1. *vindication ... salvation.* See 46:13
and note (there the Hebrew for "vindication" is translated "righteousness"). *dawn.* Cf. 58:8.
62:2 *nations will see ... glory.* See 52:10; see also 40:5; 60:3 and
notes. *your.* Jerusalem's (see vv. 1,6). *new name.* To reflect a new
status (see vv. 4,12; see also 1:26; 60:14; Ge 32:28 and notes).
62:3 *crown of splendor.* In 28:5 the Lord is a "glorious crown" for
his people (cf. Zec 9:16).
62:4 *Deserted ... Desolate.* See 54:6–7; 60:15 and note. *Hephzibah.* See TNIV text note; also the name of Hezekiah's wife (2Ki
21:1). *Beulah.* See TNIV text note. *married.* Israel's relationship
with the Lord will be restored. See 50:1 and note.

and your land Beulah[a];
for the LORD will take delight[e] in you,
  and your land will be married.[f]
5 As a young man marries a young woman,
  so will your Builder marry you;
as a bridegroom[g] rejoices over his bride,
  so will your God rejoice[h] over you.

6 I have posted watchmen[i] on your walls, Jerusalem;
  they will never be silent day or night.
You who call on the LORD,
  give yourselves no rest,[j]
7 and give him no rest[k] till he establishes Jerusalem
  and makes her the praise[l] of the earth.

8 The LORD has sworn[m] by his right hand
  and by his mighty arm:
"Never again will I give your grain[n]
  as food for your enemies,
and never again will foreigners drink the new wine
  for which you have toiled;
9 but those who harvest it will eat[o] it
  and praise the LORD,[p]
and those who gather the grapes will drink it
  in the courts of my sanctuary."[q]

10 Pass through, pass through the gates![r]
  Prepare the way for the people.
Build up, build up the highway![s][t]
  Remove the stones.
Raise a banner[u] for the nations.

11 The LORD has made proclamation
  to the ends of the earth:[v]
"Say to Daughter Zion,[w]
  'See, your Savior comes![x]
See, his reward is with him,
  and his recompense accompanies him.' "[y]
12 They will be called[z] the Holy People,[a]
  the Redeemed[b] of the LORD;
and you will be called Sought After,
  the City No Longer Deserted.[c]

GOD'S DAY OF VENGEANCE AND REDEMPTION

63 Who is this coming from Edom,[d]
  from Bozrah,[e] with his garments stained crimson?[f]
Who is this, robed in splendor,
  striding forward in the greatness of his strength?[g]

---

[a] 4 *Beulah* means *married.*

62:4 [e] Isa 65:19;
Jer 32:41; Zep 3:17;
Mal 3:12 [f] Isa 54:5;
Jer 3:14; Hos 2:19
62:5 [g] S SS 3:11
[h] S Dt 28:63;
Isa 65:19; Jer 31:12;
Zep 3:17
62:6 [i] S Isa 52:8;
Heb 13:17 [j] Ps 132:4
62:7 [k] Mt 15:21-28;
Lk 18:1-8 [l] S Dt 26:19;
S Isa 60:18
62:8 [m] S Ge 22:16;
S Isa 14:24; S 49:18
[n] Dt 28:30-33;
S Isa 1:7
62:9 [o] S Isa 1:19;
Am 9:14 [p] S Dt 12:7;
Joel 2:26 [q] Lev 23:39
62:10 [r] S Ps 24:7;
S Isa 60:11 [s] Isa 57:14
[t] S Isa 11:16
[u] S Isa 11:10
62:11 [v] S Dt 30:4
[w] S Ps 9:14; Zec 9:9;
Mt 21:5 [x] S Isa 35:4;
Rev 22:12
[y] S Isa 40:10
62:12 [z] S Ge 32:28
[a] S Ex 19:6; 1Pe 2:9
[b] S Ps 106:10;
S Isa 35:9; S 44:23
[c] S Ps 27:9; Isa 42:16;
S 54:6
63:1 [d] S 2Ch 28:17;
S Isa 11:14
[e] S Ge 36:33; Am 1:12
[f] Rev 19:13 [g] S Job 9:4;
S Isa 45:24

62:5 *Builder marry you.* See note on 49:17.
62:6 *watchmen.* Probably those (the prophets especially; see note on 56:10) waiting for the messenger with good news (see 52:8 and note). *never be silent.* They will be praying that God will not be silent (see v. 1) but will restore Jerusalem. *give yourselves no rest.* Cf. David's intense prayer as he searched for a home for the ark (Ps 132:1-5).
62:7 *praise of the earth.* Cf. Jer 33:9; Zep 3:19-20; see 60:3 and note.
62:8 *has sworn.* Cf. 45:23; 54:9. *mighty arm.* See 51:9 and note. *grain . . . for your enemies . . . foreigners drink the new wine.* Punishment Moses warned about in Lev 26:16; Dt 28:33. See also 52:1 and note; Jer 5:17.
62:9 *eat it . . . drink it.* See 65:13,21-23. *in the courts of my sanctuary.* During a festival, or when they brought the tithe to the Lord (Lev 23:39-40; Dt 14:22-26).

62:10 *Pass through, pass through.* See note on 40:1. *gates.* Probably of Babylon (cf. 48:20; Mic 2:12-13). *Prepare the way . . . build up the highway.* See 40:3; 49:11 and notes. *Remove the stones.* See 57:14. *banner.* See 5:26 and note.
62:11 *ends of the earth.* See 11:12; 49:6 and notes. *Daughter Zion.* A personification of Jerusalem (see note on 2Ki 19:21). *your Savior comes!* See 40:9; 43:3; Zec 9:9 and notes; Mt 21:5. *reward . . . recompense.* See 40:10 and note.
62:12 *Holy People.* See 4:3; Ex 19:6 and notes. *Redeemed.* See 35:9 and note. *Sought After . . . No Longer Deserted.* See v. 4.

63:1 *Edom.* See 21:11; 34:5 and notes. Edom here symbolizes a world that hates God's people. *Bozrah.* See 34:6 and note. *stained crimson.* Cf. Christ's robe "dipped in blood" (Rev 19:13; see note there) as he wages war at his second coming. *righteousness, mighty to save.* See 45:8; 46:13; 59:16 and notes.

63:1 *h* ver 5;
Isa 46:13; S 51:5;
Jer 42:11; Zep 3:17
63:2 *i* S Ge 49:11
63:3 *j* S Jdg 6:11;
S Rev 14:20
k S Job 40:12;
S Ps 108:13; S Isa 5:5
l S Isa 22:5
m Rev 19:13
63:4 *n* S Isa 1:24;
S Jer 50:15
63:5 *o* S 2Ki 14:26;
S Isa 41:28
p S Ps 44:3; S 98:1;
S Isa 33:2 *q* Isa 59:16
63:6 *r* S Job 40:12;
S Ps 108:13
s S Isa 29:9; La 4:21
t S Isa 34:3
63:7 *u* S Isa 54:8
v S Ex 18:9
w S Ps 51:1; Eph 2:4
63:8 *x* S Ps 100:3;
S Isa 51:4
y S Ex 14:30;
S Isa 25:9
63:9 *z* S Ex 14:19
a S Ex 33:14 *b* Dt 7:7-
8; S Ezr 9:9;
S Isa 48:20
c S Dt 1:31; S Ps 28:9
d S Dt 32:7;
S Job 37:23
63:10 *e* S Ps 78:17;
Eze 20:8; Ac 7:39-42
f S Ps 51:11; Ac 7:51;
Eph 4:30 *g* Ps 106:40;
S Isa 10:4
h S Jos 10:14
63:11 *i* S Ex 14:22,
30

"It is I, speaking in righteousness,
    mighty to save." *h*

²Why are your garments red,
    like those of one treading the winepress? *i*

³ "I have trodden the winepress *j* alone;
    from the nations no one was with me.
I trampled *k* them in my anger
    and trod them down in my wrath; *l*
their blood spattered my garments, *m*
    and I stained all my clothing.
⁴ It was for me the day of vengeance; *n*
    the year for me to redeem had come.
⁵ I looked, but there was no one *o* to help,
    I was appalled that no one gave support;
so my own arm *p* achieved salvation for me,
    and my own wrath sustained me. *q*
⁶ I trampled *r* the nations in my anger;
    in my wrath I made them drunk *s*
    and poured their blood *t* on the ground."

PRAISE AND PRAYER

⁷ I will tell of the kindnesses *u* of the LORD,
    the deeds for which he is to be praised,
    according to all the LORD has done for us—
yes, the many good things *v* he has done
    for the house of Israel,
according to his compassion *w* and many kindnesses.
⁸ He said, "Surely they are my people, *x*
    children who will be true to me";
    and so he became their Savior. *y*
⁹ In all their distress he too was distressed,
    and the angel *z* of his presence *a* saved them. *a*
In his love and mercy he redeemed *b* them;
    he lifted them up and carried *c* them
    all the days of old. *d*
¹⁰ Yet they rebelled *e*
    and grieved his Holy Spirit. *f*
So he turned and became their enemy *g*
    and he himself fought *h* against them.

¹¹ Then his people recalled *b* the days of old,
    the days of Moses and his people—
    where is he who brought them through the sea, *i*

a 9 Or *Savior* ⁹*in their distress.* / *It was no envoy or angel* / *but his own presence that saved them*
b 11 Or *But may he recall*

63:2 *Why ...?* Isaiah responds with a question. *treading the winepress.* See 16:10 and note.
63:3 *trodden the winepress.* A figure of judgment (see notes on La 1:15; Joel 3:13; Rev 14:19; 19:15). *in my anger ... wrath.* On the day of the Lord. See v. 6; 13:3; 34:2 and notes.
63:4 *day of vengeance ... year for me to redeem.* See 61:2 and note. The day of judging the enemy meant at the same time redemption for God's people. See 35:9; 41:14 and notes.
63:5 See 59:16 (a parallel to the whole verse) and note. *wrath.* In 59:16 "righteousness" is used. God's righteousness and holiness resulted in his wrath.
63:6 *made them drunk.* They drank the "cup of his wrath" (see 51:17 and note). *poured their blood.* Here the battle is compared to a sacrifice, as in 34:6.
63:7—64:12 A prayer of Isaiah, asking the Lord to bring about the redemption he has promised—as one of the "watchmen" the Lord has posted on the walls of Jerusalem (see 62:6 and note). It is similar to a national lament (see, e.g., Ps 44).

63:7 *kindnesses.* A demonstration of God's unfailing love as he stood true to his covenant with Israel. *many good things.* Cf. Jos 21:45; 1Ki 8:66. *compassion.* See 54:7–8,10 and note.
63:8 *my people, children who will be true to me.* But see 1:2–4. *Savior.* See 43:3 and note.
63:9 *In all their distress ... distressed.* The suffering in Egypt and during the period of the judges is probably in view (see Jdg 10:16). *angel of his presence.* See Ex 23:20–23; 33:14–15. *redeemed.* See 41:14; 43:1 and notes. *lifted ... carried.* Like a father (see Dt 1:31; 32:10–12).
63:10 *rebelled.* In the desert (see 1:2 and note; 30:1; Nu 20:10; Ps 78:40–55 and note). *grieved his Holy Spirit.* See Ps 106:33 and note; cf. Isa 11:1–2; 42:1; Eph 4:30 and note. *became their enemy.* See 43:28 and note.
63:11 *sea.* The Red Sea (see 50:2 and note; 51:10). *shepherd.* Moses. *Holy Spirit.* See note on Ps 51:11. The Spirit rested on Moses and 70 elders (Nu 11:17,25). See also v. 14.

with the shepherd of his flock?[j]
Where is he who set
  his Holy Spirit[k] among them,
[12] who sent his glorious arm[l] of power
  to be at Moses' right hand,
who divided the waters[m] before them,
  to gain for himself everlasting renown,[n]
[13] who led[o] them through the depths?[p]
Like a horse in open country,
  they did not stumble;[q]
[14] like cattle that go down to the plain,
  they were given rest[r] by the Spirit of the LORD.
This is how you guided your people
  to make for yourself a glorious name.

[15] Look down from heaven[s] and see,
  from your lofty throne,[t] holy and glorious.
Where are your zeal[u] and your might?
  Your tenderness and compassion[v] are withheld[w] from us.
[16] But you are our Father,[x]
  though Abraham does not know us
  or Israel acknowledge[y] us;
you, LORD, are our Father,
  our Redeemer[z] from of old is your name.
[17] Why, LORD, do you make us wander[a] from your ways
  and harden our hearts[b] so we do not revere[c] you?
Return[d] for the sake of your servants,
  the tribes that are your inheritance.[e]
[18] For a little while[f] your people possessed your holy place,
  but now our enemies have trampled[g] down your sanctuary.[h]
[19] We are yours from of old;
  but you have not ruled over them,
  they have not been called[a] by your name.[i]

64

*Oh, that you would rend the heavens[j] and come down,[k]
  that the mountains[l] would tremble before you!
*[2] As when fire sets twigs ablaze
  and causes water to boil,
come down to make your name[m] known to your enemies
  and cause the nations to quake[n] before you!
[3] For when you did awesome[o] things that we did not expect,
  you came down, and the mountains trembled[p] before you.
[4] Since ancient times no one has heard,
  no ear has perceived,
  no eye has seen any God besides you,[q]

---

a 19 Or *We are like those you have never ruled, / like those never called*

* 64:1 is numbered 63:19b in Hebrew texts.   * 64:2-12 is numbered 64:1-11 in Hebrew texts.

63:11 /S Ps 77:20
k Nu 11:17
63:12 /S Ge 49:24;
S Ex 3:20 m Ex 14:21-22; Isa 11:15
n S Ps 102:12;
S Isa 55:13; S Jer 13:11
63:13 o S Dt 32:12
p S Ex 14:22
q S Ps 119:11; Jer 31:9
63:14 r S Ex 33:14;
S Dt 12:9
63:15 s S Dt 26:15;
La 3:50 t S 1Ki 22:19;
S Ps 123:1 u S Isa 9:7;
S 26:11 v S 1Ki 3:26;
S Ps 25:6
w S Ge 43:31;
Isa 64:12
63:16 x S Ex 4:22;
S Jer 3:4; Jn 8:41
y S Job 14:21
z Isa 41:14; 44:6;
S 59:20
63:17 a S Ge 20:13;
La 3:9 b S Ex 4:21
c Isa 29:13
d Nu 10:36
e S Ex 34:9
63:18 f Dt 4:26;
11:17 g S Isa 28:18;
Da 8:13; S Lk 21:24
h S Lev 26:31;
S 2Ki 25:9
63:19 i S Isa 43:7;
S Jer 14:9
64:1 j Ps 18:9; 144:5
k ver 3; Mic 1:3
l S Ex 19:18
64:2 m S Isa 30:27
n Ps 99:1; 119:120;
Jer 5:22; 33:9
64:3 o S Ps 65:5
p S Ps 18:7
64:4 q S Isa 43:10-11

63:12 *arm of power.* See 51:9 and note; Ex 15:16. *divided the waters.* See Ex 14:21; cf. Isa 11:15; 51:10. *everlasting renown.* See 55:13 and note.
63:13 *depths.* Of the Red Sea (see Ex 15:5,8; Ps 106:9). But the crossing of the Jordan (Jos 3) may be intended as well (see v. 14 and note).
63:14 *to the plain.* To find pasture and water. *given rest.* They found a home in Canaan, the promised land (see Dt 12:9; Jos 1:13 and note; 21:44).
63:15 *lofty throne.* See 6:1. *zeal.* See 9:7; 42:13 and notes. *tenderness and compassion.* Cf. Hos 11:8. *withheld.* See 42:14 and note.
63:16 *Father.* See 64:8; Dt 32:6. *Abraham does not know.* Even if their human fathers abandon them, God will not (see 49:14–15 and notes). *Redeemer.* See 41:14 and note.
63:17 *make us wander.* When Israel went astray (see 53:6), God

let his people wander. *harden our hearts.* Their hearts were hard (see 6:10; Ps 95:8), and the Lord confirmed that condition (see 6:10; Ex 4:21 and notes). *servants.* True believers (see 54:17 and note).
63:18 *enemies.* The Babylonians. *trampled down your sanctuary.* Graphically described in Ps 74:3–8 (see notes there); cf. Isa 64:11. Since it was God's sanctuary, his honor was at stake (cf. 48:11).
63:19 *called by your name.* See 43:7 and note.
64:1 *rend the heavens.* The sky is compared to a tent curtain. For this and the further description of the cosmic effects of God's coming in judgment and redemption, see Jdg 5:4–5; Ps 18:7–15; 144:5; Na 1:5; Hab 3:3–7 and notes.
64:2 *make your name known.* See 30:27 and note.
64:3 *awesome things.* See Ps 66:3,5–7 and notes.
64:4 *no … God besides you.* See 43:11 and note. *wait for him.* See 30:18; see also 40:31 and note.

64:4 ʳS Isa 30:18;
1Co 2:9*
64:5 ˢS Isa 26:8
ᵗS Isa 10:4
64:6 ᵘS Lev 5:2;
S 12:2 ᵛIsa 46:12;
48:1 ʷS Ps 1:3; 90:5-
6 ˣPs 1:4; Jer 4:12
64:7 ʸS Isa 41:28;
59:4; 63:5; Jer 8:6;
Eze 22:30 ᶻS Ps 14:4
ᵃDt 31:18; Isa 1:15;
54:8 ᵇS Isa 9:18;
Eze 22:18-22
64:8 ᶜS Ex 4:22;
S Jer 3:4
ᵈS Isa 29:16;
Ro 9:20-21
ᵉS Job 10:3;
S Isa 19:25
64:9 ᶠIsa 54:8;
57:17; 60:10; La 5:22
ᵍS Isa 43:25
ʰS Ps 100:3;
S Isa 51:4
64:10 ᶦPs 78:54;
S Isa 1:26 ʲS Dt 29:23
64:11 ᵏS Lev 26:31;
2Ki 25:9; Ps 74:3-7;
La 2:7 ˡver 10-11;
La 1:7,10
64:12 ᵐS Ge 43:31;
Ps 74:10-11
ⁿS Est 4:14;
S Ps 50:21; S 83:1
65:1 ᵒHos 1:10;
Ro 9:24-26; 10:20*
ᵖRo 9:30; Eph 2:12
ᵍS Ps 14:4; S Isa 43:7
65:2 ʳS Ps 78:8;
S Isa 1:2,23;
Ro 10:21* ˢPs 81:11-
12; S Pr 24:2;
Isa 66:18
65:3 ᵗS Job 1:11

who acts on behalf of those who wait for him. ʳ
⁵ You come to the help of those who gladly do right, ˢ
　　who remember your ways.
But when we continued to sin against them,
　　you were angry. ᵗ
　　How then can we be saved?
⁶ All of us have become like one who is unclean, ᵘ
　　and all our righteous ᵛ acts are like filthy rags; ʷ
we all shrivel up like a leaf, ʷ
　　and like the wind our sins sweep us away. ˣ
⁷ No one ʸ calls on your name ᶻ
　　or strives to lay hold of you;
for you have hidden ᵃ your face from us
　　and have given us over ᵇ to ᵃ our sins.

⁸ Yet you, Lᴏʀᴅ, are our Father. ᶜ
　　We are the clay, you are the potter; ᵈ
　　we are all the work of your hand. ᵉ
⁹ Do not be angry ᶠ beyond measure, Lᴏʀᴅ;
　　do not remember our sins ᵍ forever.
Oh, look on us, we pray,
　　for we are all your people. ʰ
¹⁰ Your sacred cities ᶦ have become a wasteland;
　　even Zion is a wasteland, Jerusalem a desolation. ʲ
¹¹ Our holy and glorious temple, ᵏ where our ancestors praised you,
　　has been burned with fire,
　　and all that we treasured ˡ lies in ruins.
¹² After all this, Lᴏʀᴅ, will you hold yourself back? ᵐ
　　Will you keep silent ⁿ and punish us beyond measure?

JUDGMENT AND SALVATION

65 "I revealed myself to those who did not ask for me;
　　I was found by those who did not seek me. ᵒ
To a nation ᵖ that did not call on my name, ᵍ
　　I said, 'Here am I, here am I.'
² All day long I have held out my hands
　　to an obstinate people, ʳ
who walk in ways not good,
　　pursuing their own imaginations ˢ—
³ a people who continually provoke me
　　to my very face, ᵗ

ᵃ 7 Septuagint, Syriac and Targum; Hebrew *have made us melt because of*

64:5 *do right.* See 56:1. *you were angry.* See 9:12,17,21 and note. God's anger culminated in the exile. *saved.* Or "delivered" (see 43:3 and note).
64:6 *unclean.* Ceremonially unclean, like a person with a terrible disease (see 6:5; see also notes on Lev 4:12; 11:2; 13:45–46; cf. Introduction to Leviticus: Theological Themes). *righteous acts.* See 57:12 and note. *filthy rags.* The cloths a woman uses during her period, a time when she is "unclean" (see Lev 15:19–24; Eze 36:17). *shrivel up like a leaf.* A figure used also in 1:30. *like the wind.* Which blows away the chaff (see 17:13; 40:24; Ps 1:4 and notes).
A **64:7** *No one calls on your name.* The Lord urges earnest prayer in times of distress (see, e.g., 2Ch 7:14). *hidden your face.* See 1:15 and note.
64:8 *Father.* See 63:16 and note. *clay … potter.* See 29:16 and note. *work of your hand.* See 60:21 and note.
64:9 *Do not be angry.* Cf. the promise to end that anger in 54:7–8 (see notes there). *do not remember our sins.* See 43:25 and note; Jer 31:34; Mic 7:18. *your people.* See 63:17–19; Ps 79:13.
64:10 *sacred cities.* Sacred because Israel was the "holy land" (Zec 2:12 [see note there]; cf. Ps 78:54). Jerusalem is often called the "holy city" (see 48:2 and note). *Zion is a wasteland … desola-*

tion. See 1:7–9 and note; 6:11; Jer 12:11.
64:11 *holy and glorious temple.* See 60:7; 63:15. *burned with fire.* Isaiah here reaches the climax of his lament. See 63:18 and note.
64:12 *hold yourself back … keep silent.* See 42:14; 57:11; 62:1, 6–7 and notes.
65:1—66:24 The grand conclusion to chs. 58–66, as well as to chs. 40–66 and to the whole book.
65:1–2 *I revealed … people.* Paul makes use of these prophetic words in Ro 10:20–21. *a nation … an obstinate people.* See v. 3; see also note on 6:9–10.
A **65:1** *did not ask … did not seek.* The Lord now proceeds to answer Isaiah's prayer. Israel failed to stay close to the Lord, though the people sought him in a superficial way (see 55:6; 58:2 and notes). *did not call on my name.* See 64:7. *Here am I.* See 58:9.
65:2 *obstinate people.* See 1:2; 30:1,9 and notes. *imaginations.* See 59:7 and note.
65:3 *provoke me.* By worshiping idols (see Jdg 2:12–13 and notes). *to my very face.* Defiantly (cf. 3:8–9). *gardens.* See 1:29 and note. *burning incense.* As when worshiping the Queen of Heaven (as in Jer 44:17–19 and notes).

offering sacrifices in gardens[u]
and burning incense[v] on altars of brick;
[4] who sit among the graves[w]
and spend their nights keeping secret vigil;
who eat the flesh of pigs,[x]
and whose pots hold broth of impure meat;
[5] who say, 'Keep away; don't come near me,
for I am too sacred[y] for you!'
Such people are smoke[z] in my nostrils,
a fire that keeps burning all day.

[6] "See, it stands written before me:
I will not keep silent[a] but will pay back[b] in full;
I will pay it back into their laps[c]—
[7] both your sins[d] and the sins of your ancestors,"[e]
says the LORD.
"Because they burned sacrifices on the mountains
and defied me on the hills,[f]
I will measure into their laps
the full payment[g] for their former deeds."

[8] This is what the LORD says:

"As when juice is still found in a cluster of grapes[h]
and people say, 'Don't destroy it,
there is still a blessing in it,'
so will I do in behalf of my servants;[i]
I will not destroy them all.
[9] I will bring forth descendants[j] from Jacob,
and from Judah those who will possess[k] my mountains;
my chosen[l] people will inherit them,
and there will my servants live.[m]
[10] Sharon[n] will become a pasture for flocks,[o]
and the Valley of Achor[p] a resting place for herds,
for my people who seek[q] me.

[11] "But as for you who forsake[r] the LORD
and forget my holy mountain,[s]
who spread a table for Fortune
and fill bowls of mixed wine[t] for Destiny,
[12] I will destine you for the sword,[u]
and all of you will fall in the slaughter;[v]
for I called but you did not answer,[w]
I spoke but you did not listen.[x]
You did evil in my sight
and chose what displeases me."[y]

65:3 [u] S Isa 1:29
[v] S Lev 2:2; Jer 41:5;
44:17; Eze 23:41
65:4 [w] S Lev 19:31;
S Isa 8:19 [x] S Lev 11:7
65:5 [y] S Ps 40:4;
Mt 9:11; Lk 7:39;
18:9-12 [z] Pr 10:26
65:6 [a] S Ps 50:3
[b] S 2Ch 6:23;
Isa 59:18; Jer 16:18
[c] S Ps 79:12; Eze 9:10;
Lk 6:38
65:7 [d] S Isa 22:14
[e] Ex 20:5; Jer 32:18
[f] S Isa 57:7
[g] S Pr 10:24;
S Isa 10:12
65:8 [h] Isa 5:2
[i] S Isa 54:17
65:9 [j] S Isa 45:19
[k] S Nu 34:13;
S Isa 60:21; Jer 50:19;
Am 9:11-15 [l] S Isa 14:1
[m] Isa 32:18
65:10 [n] S 1Ch 27:29
; S Isa 35:2; Ac 9:35
[o] Jer 31:12; 33:12;
Eze 34:13-14
[p] S Jos 7:26
[q] S Isa 51:1
65:11 [r] Dt 28:20;
29:24-25; S 32:15;
Isa 1:28; Jer 2:13; 19:4
[s] S Dt 33:19;
S Ps 137:5 [t] S Isa 5:22
65:12 [u] S Isa 1:20;
S 27:1 [v] S Isa 30:25
[w] S Pr 1:24-25;
S Isa 41:28; 66:4;
Jer 7:27 [x] 2Ch 36:15-
16; Jer 7:13; 13:11;
25:3; 26:5 [y] Ps 149:7;
Isa 1:24; 66:4;
Mic 5:15

65:4 *sit among the graves.* Perhaps to consult the dead (see 8:19 and note; 57:9; Dt 18:11). *flesh of pigs.* Considered ceremonially unclean (see 66:3,17; Lev 11:7–8).
65:5 *I am too sacred for you.* Those who engage in pagan rituals often believe they are superior to others (cf. the attitude of the Pharisees in Mt 9:11; Lk 7:39; 18:9–12).
65:6 *not keep silent.* The answer to 64:12. *pay back.* See 59:18 and note.
65:7 *burned sacrifices on the mountains.* Offered to Baal on the high places (see 57:7; Hos 2:13 and note). *defied me.* See Eze 20:27–28.
65:8 *cluster of grapes.* Israel was a vineyard that had produced bad grapes (5:2,4,7). *my servants.* See vv. 9,13–14; 54:17 and note. Here the Lord's servants are equivalent to the remnant (see 1:9 and note).
65:9 *descendants.* See Jer 31:36 and note. *Jacob . . . Judah.* The northern and southern kingdoms, respectively. *possess my mountains.* See 49:8; 60:21 and notes. "Mountains" refers to the

whole land, since so much of it was hilly (see Jdg 1:9; Eze 6:2–3). *chosen people.* See 41:8–9 and note. *inherit.* See 57:13 and note.
65:10 *Sharon.* See 33:9 and note. *Valley of Achor.* A valley near Jericho (see Jos 7:24,26; Hos 2:15 and notes). Since Sharon and Achor are on the western and eastern edges of the land, respectively, they probably represent the whole country. *seek me.* See v. 1; 51:1 and notes.
65:11 *forsake the LORD.* See 1:4. *holy mountain.* See 2:2–4 and note. *spread a table . . . mixed wine.* A meal and drink offering presented to deities. See note on 5:22; cf. v. 3; Jer 7:18 and note. *Fortune . . . Destiny.* The pagan gods of good fortune and fate. See Jos 11:17, where "Gad" may mean "Fortune."
65:12 *sword.* Designed for God's enemies, such as Edom (34:5–6), but the wicked of Israel would also suffer (see 1:20; 59:18 and note; 66:16). *called . . . not answer.* See 50:2; 2Ch 24:19 and notes. *chose what displeases me.* Contrast the faithfulness of the eunuchs in 56:4. The last four lines of v. 12 are almost identical to those of 66:4.

65:13 *z* S Isa 1:19
a S Job 18:12; Lk 6:25
b S Isa 33:16
c S Isa 3:1; 41:17
d S Isa 60:5; 61:7
e S Isa 44:9
65:14 *f* S Ps 109:28;
Zep 3:14-20; Jas 5:13
g S Isa 15:2; Mt 8:12;
Lk 13:28
65:15 *h* S Nu 5:27;
S Ps 102:8
i Ge 32:28; Rev 2:17
65:16 *j* S Dt 29:19
k Ps 31:5; Rev 3:14
l S Ps 63:11;
S Isa 19:18
m S Job 11:16
65:17 *n* S Isa 41:22;
66:22; 2Co 5:17;
S 2Pe 3:13 *o* Isa 43:18;
Jer 3:16; S Rev 7:17
65:18 *p* S Dt 32:43;
Ps 98:1-9; S Isa 25:9
q Rev 21:2
65:19 *r* S Isa 35:10;
S 62:5 *s* S Dt 30:9
t S Isa 25:8; Rev 7:17
65:20 *u* Isa 11:8
v Ge 5:1-32; S 15:15;
S Ecc 8:13; Zec 8:4
65:21 *w* S Isa 32:18;
S 61:4 *x* S 2Ki 19:29;
S Isa 37:30;
Eze 28:26; Am 9:14

13 Therefore this is what the Sovereign LORD says:

"My servants will eat, *z*
     but you will go hungry; *a*
my servants will drink, *b*
     but you will go thirsty; *c*
my servants will rejoice, *d*
     but you will be put to shame. *e*
14 My servants will sing *f*
     out of the joy of their hearts,
but you will cry out *g*
     from anguish of heart
     and wail in brokenness of spirit.
15 You will leave your name
     for my chosen ones to use in their curses; *h*
the Sovereign LORD will put you to death,
     but to his servants he will give another name. *i*
16 Whoever invokes a blessing *j* in the land
     will do so by the one true God; *k*
whoever takes an oath in the land
     will swear *l* by the one true God.
For the past troubles *m* will be forgotten
     and hidden from my eyes.

NEW HEAVENS AND A NEW EARTH

17 "See, I will create
     new heavens and a new earth. *n*
The former things will not be remembered, *o*
     nor will they come to mind.
18 But be glad and rejoice *p* forever
     in what I will create,
for I will create Jerusalem *q* to be a delight
     and its people a joy.
19 I will rejoice *r* over Jerusalem
     and take delight *s* in my people;
the sound of weeping and of crying *t*
     will be heard in it no more.

20 "Never again will there be in it
     infants *u* who live but a few days,
     or older people who do not live out their years; *v*
those who die at a hundred
     will be thought mere youths;
those who fail to reach *a* a hundred
     will be considered accursed.
21 They will build houses *w* and dwell in them;
     they will plant vineyards and eat their fruit. *x*

---

a 20 Or youths; / sinners who reach

65:13 *eat . . . drink.* See 41:17–18; 49:10. *go hungry . . . thirsty.* See 5:13; 8:21. *rejoice.* See 61:7 and note; 66:14. *put to shame.* See 42:17; 44:9,11.

65:14 *sing out of . . . joy.* See 35:10; 54:1 and notes. *brokenness of spirit.* They had refused God's healing. See 61:1 and note.

65:15 *chosen ones.* See v. 9 and note. *use in their curses.* The rebellious Israelites will be used as an example when curses are uttered (see Jer 29:22). *another name.* Perhaps the "new name" of 62:2 (see note there).

65:16 *invokes a blessing.* See 48:1; Dt 29:19. *one true God.* God is true to his promises. The Hebrew word for "true" here is *amen* (see Dt 27:15; Ro 1:25; 1Co 14:15–17; 2Co 1:20; Rev 3:14 and notes). *swear by.* See 45:23. Perhaps a contrast is intended with those who took oaths in the name of Baal (see Jer 12:16).

65:17 *new heavens and a new earth.* See 66:22; the climax of the "new things" Isaiah has been promising (see 42:9; 48:6; 2Pe

3:13 and notes). *former things.* The "old order of things" (Rev 21:4), including pain and sorrow.

65:18 *be glad and rejoice.* See 66:10; see also 51:3 and note. *create Jerusalem.* John links the notion of a new heaven and a new earth with the "new Jerusalem" (Rev 21:1–2). A restored Jerusalem after the exile and in the Messianic kingdom points toward this greater Jerusalem. See note on 54:11–12.

65:19 *rejoice . . . take delight.* See 62:4–5 and notes. *weeping . . . crying.* See 25:8 and note; 35:10.

65:20–25 See 11:6–9 and note.

65:20 *hundred . . . mere youths.* Comparable to the longevity of Adam and his early descendants. See the genealogy of Ge 5 (but see note on Ge 5:5).

65:21–22 Contrast Moses' curse for disobedience in Dt 28:30; cf. the same contrast in Am 5:11; 9:14; cf. also Mic 6:15.

65:21 *plant vineyards.* See 62:8–9.

²² No longer will they build houses and others live in them,[y]
  or plant and others eat.
For as the days of a tree,[z]
  so will be the days[a] of my people;
my chosen[b] ones will long enjoy
  the work of their hands.
²³ They will not labor in vain,[c]
  nor will they bear children doomed to misfortune;[d]
for they will be a people blessed[e] by the Lord,
  they and their descendants[f] with them.
²⁴ Before they call[g] I will answer;[h]
  while they are still speaking[i] I will hear.
²⁵ The wolf and the lamb[j] will feed together,
  and the lion will eat straw like the ox,[k]
  but dust will be the serpent's[l] food.
They will neither harm nor destroy
  on all my holy mountain,"[m]

                                    says the Lord.

JUDGMENT AND HOPE

66 This is what the Lord says:

"Heaven is my throne,[n]
  and the earth is my footstool.[o]
Where is the house[p] you will build for me?
  Where will my resting place be?
² Has not my hand made all these things,[q]
  and so they came into being?"

                                    declares the Lord.

"These are the ones I look on with favor:
  those who are humble and contrite in spirit,[r]
  and who tremble at my word.[s]
³ But whoever sacrifices a bull
  is like one who kills a human being,
and whoever offers a lamb
  is like one who breaks a dog's neck;
whoever makes a grain offering
  is like one who presents pig's[u] blood,
and whoever burns memorial incense[v]
  is like one who worships an idol.
They have chosen their own ways,[w]
  and they delight in their abominations;[x]
⁴ so I also will choose harsh treatment for them
  and will bring on them what they dread.[y]
For when I called, no one answered,[z]
  when I spoke, no one listened.
They did evil[a] in my sight
  and chose what displeases me."[b]

⁵ Hear the word of the Lord,
  you who tremble at his word:[c]

65:22 [y] S Dt 28:30
[z] Ps 1:3; 92:12-14
[a] Ps 21:4; 91:16
[b] S Isa 14:1
65:23 [c] S Isa 49:4; 1Co 15:58 [d] Dt 28:32, 41; Jer 16:3-4
[e] S Ge 12:2; S Dt 28:3-12
[f] S Isa 44:3; Ac 2:39
65:24 [g] S Isa 55:6; Mt 6:8 [h] S Job 8:6; S Isa 30:19; S Zec 10:6 [i] Da 9:20-23; 10:12
65:25 [j] Isa 11:6
[k] Job 40:15
[l] Ge 3:14; Mic 7:17
[m] S Job 5:23; S Isa 2:4
66:1 [n] S 2Ch 6:18; S Ps 2:4; S 9:7; Mt 23:22 [o] S 1Ki 8:27; Mt 5:34-35
[p] 2Sa 7:7; Jn 4:20-21; Ac 7:49*; 17:24
66:2 [q] S Isa 40:26; Ac 7:50*; 17:24
[r] S Isa 57:15; Mt 5:3-4; Lk 18:13-14
[s] S Ezr 9:4
66:3 [t] S Isa 1:11
[u] S Lev 11:7
[v] S Lev 2:2
[w] S Isa 57:17 [x] ver 17; S Dt 27:15; Eze 8:9-13
66:4 [y] S Pr 10:24; S Isa 10:12
[z] S 1Sa 8:19; S Isa 41:28 [a] 2Ki 21:2, 4, 6; S Isa 59:12
[b] S Isa 65:12
66:5 [c] S Ezr 9:4

65:22 *days of a tree.* Compared to the righteous also in Ps 1:3 (see note there); 92:12-14. *chosen ones.* See 41:8-9 and note. *long enjoy.* Cf. Ps 91:16.
65:23 *labor in vain.* See 49:4 and note. *misfortune.* Such as death or captivity. *people blessed by the Lord.* See 61:9 and note.
65:24 *Before they call I will answer.* See 30:19; 58:9; Ps 118:5 and note; Mt 6:8.
65:25 *wolf…lamb…lion.* See 11:6-9 and notes. *dust…serpent's food.* See Ge 3:14 and note. The serpent will be harmless (see 11:8). *They…mountain.* Identical to the first two lines of 11:9.
66:1 *throne…footstool.* See 40:22 and note. *Where is the house…?* Solomon realized that God could not be local-

ized in a temple built by humans, magnificent though it may be (see 1Ki 8:27 and note).
66:2 *made all these things.* See 40:26 and note. *humble and contrite.* See 57:15 and note.
66:3 Cf. Isaiah's harsh words in 1:11-14 about ineffective sacrifices. *breaks a dog's neck.* The dog was "unclean" and not used in offerings. Cf. the law in Ex 13:13 about breaking a donkey's neck. *pig's blood.* See 65:4 and note. The dog and pig are mentioned together also in Mt 7:6; 2Pe 2:22 (see note there). *worships an idol.* See 44:19 and note. *abominations.* Probably idols (see Jer 4:1).
66:4 *choose harsh treatment.* Cf. 65:7. *For when…displeases me.* For these last four lines, see 65:12 and note.

66:5 *d* Ps 38:20;
Isa 60:15; Jn 15:21
e S Isa 44:9; Lk 13:17
66:6 *f* S Isa 2:10;
S Ps 68:33
g S Lev 26:28;
Isa 65:6; Joel 3:7
66:7 *h* S Isa 54:1
i Rev 12:5
66:8 *j* Isa 64:4;
Jer 18:13 *k* S Isa 49:20
l S Isa 49:21
66:9 *m* S Isa 37:3
66:10 *n* S Dt 32:43;
S Isa 25:9; Ro 15:10
o S Ps 26:8
p Isa 57:19; 61:2
66:11 *q* S Nu 11:12;
S Isa 60:16 *r* Ge 49:25
s S Nu 25:1; S Isa 25:6
66:12 *t* S Ps 119:165;
S Isa 9:6 *u* S Isa 33:21
v Ps 72:3; Isa 60:5;
61:6 *w* S Nu 11:12;
Isa 60:4
66:13 *x* S Isa 49:15;
1Th 2:7 *y* S Isa 40:1;
S 2Co 1:4
66:14 *z* S Isa 25:9;
S 60:5; S Joel 2:23
a S Ps 72:16
b S Ezr 5:5;
S Isa 41:20
c S Isa 54:17
d S Isa 10:5; S 30:27
66:15 *e* S Isa 1:31;
S 42:25 *f* S 2Ki 2:11;
S Ps 68:17 *g* S 2Ki 2:1
h S Dt 28:20;
S Ps 9:5; S 39:11
66:16 *i* Isa 30:30;
Am 7:4; Mal 4:1
j S Isa 1:20; S 27:1;
S Eze 14:21

"Your own people who hate *d* you,
    and exclude you because of my name, have said,
'Let the LORD be glorified,
    that we may see your joy!'
Yet they will be put to shame. *e*

⁶ Hear that uproar from the city,
    hear that noise from the temple!
It is the sound *f* of the LORD
    repaying *g* his enemies all they deserve.

⁷ "Before she goes into labor, *h*
    she gives birth;
before the pains come upon her,
    she delivers a child. *i*
⁸ Who has ever heard of such things?
    Who has ever seen *j* things like this?
Can a country be born in a day *k*
    or a nation be brought forth in a moment?
Yet no sooner is Zion in labor
    than she gives birth to her children. *l*
⁹ Do I bring to the moment of birth *m*
    and not give delivery?" says the LORD.
"Do I close up the womb
    when I bring to delivery?" says your God.

¹⁰ "Rejoice *n* with Jerusalem and be glad for her,
    all you who love *o* her;
rejoice greatly with her,
    all you who mourn *p* over her.
¹¹ For you will nurse *q* and be satisfied
    at her comforting breasts; *r*
you will drink deeply
    and delight in her overflowing abundance." *s*

¹² For this is what the LORD says:

"I will extend peace *t* to her like a river, *u*
    and the wealth *v* of nations like a flooding stream;
you will nurse and be carried *w* on her arm
    and dandled on her knees.
¹³ As a mother comforts her child, *x*
    so will I comfort *y* you;
    and you will be comforted over Jerusalem."

¹⁴ When you see this, your heart will rejoice *z*
    and you will flourish *a* like grass;
the hand *b* of the LORD will be made known to his servants, *c*
    but his fury *d* will be shown to his foes.
¹⁵ See, the LORD is coming with fire, *e*
    and his chariots *f* are like a whirlwind; *g*
he will bring down his anger with fury,
    and his rebuke *h* with flames of fire.
¹⁶ For with fire *i* and with his sword *j*

66:5 *tremble.* See v. 2. *Your own people.* Lit. "Your brothers," i.e., your fellow Israelites (see Ac 11:1 and note). *Let . . . joy.* Apparently spoken sarcastically, much like 5:19; Ps 22:8.
66:6 *city.* Probably Jerusalem. *repaying his enemies.* See 59:18 and note; 65:6–7.
66:7 *Before . . . labor.* See 54:1 (and note), where Zion was barren.
66:8 *country . . . born in a day.* See 49:19–20 and note.
66:9 *moment of birth.* See 37:3 and note.
66:10 *Rejoice . . . be glad.* See 65:18 and note. *all . . . who love her.* Cf. Ps 137:6. *who mourn.* See 57:19; 61:2 and notes.
66:11 *nurse and be satisfied.* In 60:16 (see note there) Jerusalem was drinking the milk of nations. Here she is the mother (cf. v. 12; 49:23).

66:12 *peace . . . like a river.* See 48:18 and note. *wealth of nations.* See 60:5 and note. *flooding stream.* Contrast the destructive flood of 8:7–8 (see note there). *on her arm.* See 40:11.
66:13 *comforted over Jerusalem.* See 49:13 and note. Cf. 2Co 1:3–4.
66:14 *heart will rejoice.* See 60:5. *grass.* Usually a symbol of weakness. See 37:27 and note; 51:12; but contrast 44:4. *hand of the LORD.* Cf. Ezr 7:9; 8:31. *servants.* See 54:17 and note. *fury.* See v. 15; 13:3 and note.
66:15–16 *fire.* A figure of judgment (see 1:31 and note; 30:27).
66:15 *chariots . . . like a whirlwind.* See 5:28; 2Ki 2:11 and note; 6:17; Ps 68:17 and note. *anger.* See 34:2; 42:25 and notes. *rebuke.* See 51:20 and note.

the LORD will execute judgment[k] on all people,
and many will be those slain[l] by the LORD.

[17]"Those who consecrate and purify themselves to go into the gardens,[m] following one who is among those who eat the flesh of pigs,[n] rats[o] and other unclean things—they will meet their end[p] together with the one they follow," declares the LORD.

[18]"And I, because of what they have planned and done,[q] am about to come[a] and gather the people of all nations[r] and languages, and they will come and see my glory.[s]

[19]"I will set a sign[t] among them, and I will send some of those who survive[u] to the nations—to Tarshish, to the Libyans,[v] to the Libyans[b] and Lydians[w] (famous as archers), to Tubal[x] and Greece,[y] and to the distant islands[z] that have not heard of my fame or seen my glory.[a] They will proclaim my glory among the nations. [20]And they will bring[b] all your people, from all the nations, to my holy mountain[c] in Jerusalem as an offering to the LORD—on horses, in chariots and wagons, and on mules and camels,"[d] says the LORD. "They will bring them, as the Israelites bring their grain offerings, to the temple of the LORD in ceremonially clean vessels.[e] [21]And I will select some of them also to be priests[f] and Levites," says the LORD.

[22]"As the new heavens and the new earth[g] that I make will endure before me," declares the LORD, "so will your name and descendants endure.[h] [23]From one New Moon to another and from one Sabbath[i] to another, all people will come and bow down[j] before me," says the LORD. [24]"And they will go out and look on the dead bodies[k] of those who rebelled[l] against me; their worm[m] will not die, nor will their fire be quenched,[n] and they will be loathsome to the whole human race."

---

[a] *18* The meaning of the Hebrew for this clause is uncertain.   [b] *19* Some Septuagint manuscripts *Put* (Libyans); Hebrew *Pul*

66:24 [l] S Isa 1:2 [m] S Isa 14:11 [n] S Isa 1:31; S Mt 25:41; Mk 9:48*

66:16 [k] S Isa 13:9, 11; S Jer 2:35; S Eze 36:5 [l] S Isa 10:4
66:17 [m] S Isa 1:29
[n] S Lev 11:7
[o] Lev 11:29
[p] Ps 37:20; Isa 1:28
66:18 [q] S Pr 24:2; S Isa 65:2 [r] S Isa 2:3; S Zec 12:3 [s] S Ex 16:7; S Isa 59:19
66:19 [t] Isa 11:10; 49:22; Mt 24:30
[u] S 2Ki 19:31
[v] S Isa 2:16
[w] Jer 46:9; Eze 27:10
[x] S Ge 10:2
[y] Jer 31:10; Da 11:18
[z] Isa 11:11
[a] S 1Ch 16:24; S Isa 24:15
66:20 [b] S Isa 11:12; S Jer 25:22; Eze 34:13
[c] S Dt 33:19; S Isa 2:2; Jer 31:23
[d] S Ezr 2:66
[e] Isa 52:11
66:21 [f] S Ex 19:6; 1Pe 2:5,9
66:22 [g] S Isa 65:17; Heb 12:26-27; S 2Pe 3:13
[h] S Isa 48:19; Jn 10:27-29; 1Pe 1:4-5
66:23 [i] Eze 46:1-3
[j] S Ps 22:29; S Isa 19:21; S 44:5; Rev 15:4
66:24 [k] S Ps 110:6

66:16 *sword.* See 27:1; 31:8; 35:5–6 and note on Ps 7:12–13. *execute judgment.* The day of the Lord (see note on 2:11,17,20; cf. Eze 38:21–22).

66:17 *consecrate and purify themselves.* By special rituals required by their pagan religion. Cf. 2Ch 30:17. *gardens.* See 1:29 and note. *flesh of pigs.* See 65:4 and note.

66:18 *what they have planned and done.* Wicked Israelites may be the antecedent. *gather...all nations.* Cf. Joel 3:2 and note; Zep 3:8; Zec 12:3 and note. *see my glory.* Usually linked with God's deliverance of his people (see 35:2–4; 40:5 and notes).

66:19 *sign.* Possibly the banner of 11:10,12 (see note on 5:26; cf. Ps 74:4). Cf. the "sign of the Son of Man" (Mt 24:30) at the second coming. *those who survive.* After the judgment of v. 16. Cf. Zec 14:16. *Tarshish.* See 23:6 and note. *Libyans.* People who lived west of Egypt. See Na 3:9. *Lydians.* People probably from western Asia Minor (see Ge 10:13 and note). *archers.* See Jer 46:9. *Tubal.* Usually mentioned with Meshek (see Ge 10:2; Eze 27:13; 38:2–3; 39:1 and notes). It was probably a region southeast of the Black Sea. For the location of several of these nations, see map, p. 23. *islands.* See 11:11 and note. *proclaim my glory.* See 42:12; 1Ch 16:24.

66:20 *bring all your people.* Gentiles will bring back the remnant (see 11:11–12; 49:22; 60:4 and notes). *holy mountain.* See 2:2–4 and note. *as an offering...to the temple.* As the Israelites were to bring their tithes and offerings (see Dt 12:5–7).

66:21 *some of them.* A reference either to believing Jews (see 61:6 and note) or to Gentiles as part of the church or Messianic kingdom (see 1Pe 2:5,9 and notes).

66:22 *new heavens...new earth.* See 65:17 and note. *name and descendants endure.* See 48:19 and note.

66:23 *New Moon.* See 1:14 and note. *all people...bow down.* See 19:21; Zec 14:16 and notes.

66:24 Quoted in part in Mk 9:48 (see note there; see also Mk 9:47, where "hell" renders Greek *gehenna*). The Valley of Hinnom (Hebrew *ge' hinnom,* from which the word Gehenna comes) was located southwest of Jerusalem and became a picture of hell (see note on Mt 5:22). See Ne 11:30; Jer 7:31 and note. *dead bodies.* See 5:25; 34:3. *rebelled.* See 1:2 and note; 24:20. *worm will not die.* There will be everlasting torment. See 14:11; 48:22; 50:11; 57:21. *fire...quenched.* See 1:31 and note; Mt 3:12. *loathsome.* The Hebrew for this word is translated "contempt" in Da 12:2.

JEREMIAH

C The book preserves an account of the prophetic ministry of Jeremiah, whose personal life and struggles are shown to us in greater depth and detail than those of any other OT prophet. The meaning of his name is uncertain. Suggestions include "The LORD exalts" and "The LORD establishes," but a more likely proposal is "The LORD throws," either in the sense of "hurling" the prophet into a hostile world or of "throwing down" the nations in divine judgment for their sins. Jeremiah's prophetic ministry began in 626 B.C. and ended sometime after 586 (see notes on 1:2–3). His ministry was immediately preceded by that of Zephaniah. Habakkuk was a contemporary, and Obadiah may have been also. Since Ezekiel began his ministry in Babylon in 593, he too was a late contemporary of the great prophet in Jerusalem. How and when Jeremiah died is not known; Jewish tradition, however, asserts that while living in Egypt he was put to death by being stoned (cf. Heb 11:37).

Jeremiah was a member of the priestly household of Hilkiah. His hometown was Anathoth (1:1), so he may have been a descendant of Abiathar (1Ki 2:26), a priest during the days of King Solomon. The Lord commanded Jeremiah not to marry and raise children because the impending divine judgment on Judah would sweep away the next generation (16:1–4). Primarily a prophet of doom, he attracted only a few friends, among whom were Ahikam (26:24), Gedaliah (Ahikam's son, 39:14) and Ebed-Melek (38:7–13; cf. 39:15–18). Jeremiah's closest companion was his faithful secretary, Baruch, who wrote down Jeremiah's words as the prophet dictated them (36:4–32). He was advised by Jeremiah not to succumb to the temptations of ambition but to be content with his lot (ch. 45). He also received from Jeremiah and deposited for safekeeping a deed of purchase (32:11–16) and accompanied the prophet on the long road to exile in Egypt (43:6–7). It is possible that Baruch was also responsible for the final compilation of the book of Jeremiah itself, since no event recorded in chs. 1–51 occurred after 580 B.C. (ch. 52 is an appendix added by a later hand).

Given to self-analysis and self-criticism (10:24), Jeremiah has revealed a great deal about himself. Although timid by nature (1:6), he received the Lord's assurance that he would become strong and courageous (1:18; 6:27; 15:20). In his "confessions" (see 11:18–23; 12:1–4; 15:10–21; 17:12–18; 18:18–23; 20:7–18 and notes) he laid bare the deep struggles of his inmost being, sometimes making startling statements about his feelings toward God (12:1; 15:18). On occasion, he engaged in calling for redress against his personal enemies (12:1–3; 15:15; 17:18; 18:19–23; see note on Ps 5:10)—a practice that explains the origin of the English word *jeremiad*, referring to a denunciatory tirade or complaint. Jeremiah, so often expressing his anguish of spirit (4:19; 9:1; 10:19–20; 23:9), has justly been called the "weeping prophet." But it is also true that the memory of his divine call (1:17) and the Lord's frequent reaffirmations of his commissioning as a prophet (see, e.g., 3:12; 7:2,27–28; 11:2,6; 13:12–13; 17:19–20) made Jeremiah fearless and faithful in the service of his God (cf. 15:20).

BACKGROUND

Jeremiah began prophesying in Judah halfway through the reign of Josiah (640–609 B.C.) and continued throughout the reigns of Jehoahaz (609), Jehoiakim (609–598), Jehoiachin (598–597) and Zedekiah (597–586). It was a period of storm and stress, when the doom of entire nations—including Judah itself—was being sealed. The smaller states of western Asia were often pawns in the power plays of such imperial giants as Egypt, Assyria and Babylon, and the time of Jeremiah's ministry was no exception. Ashurbanipal, last of the great Assyrian rulers, died in 627. His successors were no match for Nabopolassar, the founder of the Neo-Babylonian empire, who began his rule in 626 (the year of Jeremiah's call to prophesy). Soon after Assyria's capital city, Nineveh, fell under the onslaught of a coalition of Babylonians and Medes in 612, Egypt (no friend of Babylon) marched northward in an attempt to rescue Assyria, which would soon be destroyed. King Josiah of Judah made the mistake of trying to stop the Egyptian advance, and his untimely death near Megiddo in 609 at the hands of Pharaoh Necho II was the sad result (2Ch 35:20–24). Jeremiah, who had found a kindred spirit in the godly Josiah and perhaps had proclaimed the messages recorded in 11:1–8; 17:19–27 during the king's reformation movement, lamented Josiah's death (see 2Ch 35:25 and note).

Josiah's son Jehoahaz (see TNIV text note on 22:11), also known as Shallum, is mentioned only briefly in the book of Jeremiah (22:10b–12), and then in an unfavorable way. Necho put Jehoahaz in chains and made Eliakim, another of Josiah's sons, king in his place, renaming him Jehoiakim. Jehoahaz had ruled for a scant three months (2Ch 36:2), and his reign marks the turning point in the king's attitude toward Jeremiah. Once the friend and confidant of the king, the prophet now entered a dreary round of persecution and imprisonment, alternating with only brief periods of freedom (20:1–2; 26:8–9; 32:2–3; 33:1; 36:26; 37:12–21; 38:6–13,28).

Jehoiakim remained relentlessly hostile toward Jeremiah. On one occasion, when an early draft of the prophet's writings was being read to Jehoiakim (36:21), the king used a scribe's knife to cut the scroll apart, three or four columns at a time, and threw it piece by piece into the firepot in his winter apartment (vv. 22–23). At the Lord's command, however, Jeremiah simply dictated his prophecies to Baruch a second time, adding "many similar words" to them (v. 32).

Just prior to this episode in Jeremiah's life, an event of extraordinary importance took place that changed the course of history: In 605 B.C., the Egyptians were crushed at Carchemish on the Euphrates by Nebuchadnezzar (46:2), the gifted general who succeeded his father, Nabopolassar, as ruler of Babylon that same year. Necho returned to Egypt after heavy losses, and Babylon was given a virtually free hand in western Asia for the next 70 years. Nebuchadnezzar besieged Jerusalem in 605, humiliating Jehoiakim (Da 1:1–2) and carrying off Daniel and his three companions to Babylon (Da 1:3–6). Later, in 598–597, Nebuchadnezzar attacked Jerusalem again, and the rebellious Jehoiakim was heard of no more. His son Jehoiachin ruled Judah for only three months (2Ch 36:9), and Jeremiah foretold the captivity of Jehoiachin and his followers (22:24–30), a prediction that was later fulfilled (24:1; 29:1–2).

Mattaniah, Jehoiachin's uncle and a son of Josiah, was renamed Zedekiah and placed on Judah's throne by Nebuchadnezzar in 597 B.C. (37:1; 2Ch 36:9–14). Zedekiah, a weak and vacillating ruler, sometimes befriended Jeremiah and sought his advice but at other times allowed the prophet's enemies to mistreat and imprison him. Near the end of Zedekiah's reign, Jeremiah entered into an agreement with him to reveal God's will to him in exchange for his own personal safety (38:14–27). Even then the prophet was under virtual house arrest until Jerusalem was captured in 586 (38:28).

While trying to flee the city, Zedekiah was overtaken by the pursuing Babylonians. In his presence his sons were executed, after which he himself was blinded by Nebuchadnezzar (39:1–7). Nebuzaradan, commander of the imperial guard, advised Jeremiah to live with Gedaliah, whom Nebuchadnezzar had made governor over Judah (40:1–6). After a brief term of office, Gedaliah was murdered by his opponents (41:1–9). Others in Judah feared Babylonian reprisal and fled to Egypt, taking Jeremiah and Baruch with them (43:4–7). By that time the prophet was probably over

70 years old. His last recorded words are found in 44:24–30, the last verse of which is the only explicit reference in the Bible to Pharaoh Hophra, who ruled Egypt from 589 to 570 B.C.

THEOLOGICAL THEMES AND MESSAGE

Referred to frequently as "Jeremiah the prophet" (or "the prophet Jeremiah") in the book that bears his name (20:2; 25:2; 28:5,10–12,15; 29:1,29; 32:2; 34:6; 36:8,26; 37:2, 3,6; 38:9–10,14; 42:2,4; 43:6; 45:1; 46:1,13; 47:1; 49:34; 50:1) and elsewhere (2Ch 36:12; Da 9:2; Mt 2:17; 27:9; see Mt 16:14), Jeremiah was ever conscious of his call from the Lord (1:5; 15:19) to be a prophet. As such, he proclaimed words given him by God himself (19:2) and therefore certain of fulfillment (28:9; 32:24). Jeremiah had only contempt for false prophets (14:13–18; 23:13–40; 27:14–18) like Hananiah (ch. 28) and Shemaiah (29:24–32). Many of his own predictions were fulfilled in the short term (e.g., 16:15; 20:4; 25:11–14; 27:19–22; 29:10; 34:4–5; 43:10–11; 44:30; 46:13), and others were—or will yet be—fulfilled in the long term (e.g., 23:5–6; 30:8–9; 31:31–34; 33:15–16).

As hinted earlier, an aura of conflict surrounded Jeremiah almost from the beginning. He lashed out against the sins of his countrymen (44:23), excoriating them severely for their idolatry (16:10–13,20; 22:9; 32:29; 44:2–3,8,17–19,25)—which sometimes even involved sacrificing their children to foreign gods (see 7:30–34 and notes). But Jeremiah loved the people of Judah in spite of their sins, and he prayed for them (14:7,20) even when the Lord told him not to (7:16; 11:14; 14:11).

Judgment is one of the all-pervasive themes in Jeremiah's writings, though he was careful to point out that repentance, if sincere, would postpone the otherwise inevitable. His counsel of submission to Babylon and his message of "life as usual" for the exiles of the early deportations branded him as a traitor in the eyes of many. Actually, of course, his advice not to rebel against Babylon marked him as a true patriot, a man who loved his own people too much to stand by silently and watch them destroy themselves. By warning them to submit and not rebel, Jeremiah was revealing God's will to them—always the most sensible prospect under any circumstances.

For Jeremiah, God was ultimate. The prophet's theology conceived of the Lord as the Creator of all that exists (10:12–16; 51:15–19), as all-powerful (32:27; 48:15; 51:57) and everywhere present (23:24). Jeremiah ascribed the most elevated attributes to the God he served (32:17–25), viewing him as the Lord not only of Judah but also of the nations (5:15; 18:7–10; 25:17–28; chs. 46–51).

At the same time, God is very much concerned about individual people and their accountability to him. Jeremiah's emphasis in this regard (see, e.g., 31:29–30) is similar to that of Ezekiel (see Eze 18:2–4), and the two men have become known as the "prophets of individual responsibility." The undeniable relationship between sin and its consequences, so visible to Jeremiah as he watched his beloved Judah in her death throes, made him—in the pursuit of his divine vocation—a fiery preacher (5:14; 20:9; 23:29) of righteousness, and his oracles have lost none of their power with the passing of the centuries.

Called to the unhappy task of announcing the destruction of the kingdom of Judah (thoroughly corrupted by the long and evil reign of Manasseh and only superficially affected by Josiah's efforts at reform), it was Jeremiah's commission to lodge God's indictment against his people and proclaim the end of an era. At long last, the Lord was about to inflict on the remnant of his people the ultimate covenant curse (see Lev 26:31–33; Dt 28:49–68). He would undo all that he had done for them since the day he brought them out of Egypt. It would then seem that the end had come, that Israel's stubborn and uncircumcised (unconsecrated) heart had sealed her final destiny, that God's chosen people had been cast off, that all the ancient promises and covenants had come to nothing.

But God's judgment of his people (and the nations), though terrible, was not to be the last word, the final work of God in history. Mercy and covenant faithfulness would triumph over wrath. Beyond the judgment would come restoration and renewal. Israel would be restored, the nations that crushed her would be crushed, and the old covenants (with Israel, David and the Levites) would be honored. God would make a new covenant with his people, in which he would write his law on their hearts (see 31:31–34 and notes; see also Heb 8:8–12 and note) and thus consecrate them to his service. The new covenant was cast in the form of ancient Near Eastern royal grant treaties and contained unconditional, gracious and profoundly spiritual, moral, ethical and relational promises (see chart, p. 20). The house of David would rule God's people in righteousness, and faithful priests would serve. God's commitment to Israel's redemption was as unfailing as the secure order of creation (ch. 33).

Jeremiah's message illumined the distant as well as the near horizon. It was false prophets who proclaimed peace to a rebellious nation, as though the God of Israel's peace were indifferent to her unfaithfulness. But the very God who compelled Jeremiah to denounce sin and pronounce judgment was the God who authorized him to announce that the divine wrath had its bounds, its 70 years. Afterward forgiveness and cleansing would come—and a new day, in which all the old expectations, aroused by God's past acts and his promises and covenants, would yet be fulfilled in a manner transcending all God's mercies of old.

LITERARY FEATURES

Jeremiah is the longest book in the Bible, containing more words than any other book. Although a number of chapters were written mainly in prose (chs. 7; 11; 16; 19; 21; 24–29; 32–45), including the appendix (ch. 52), most sections are predominantly poetic in form. Jeremiah's poetry is lofty and lyrical. A creator of beautiful phrases, he has given us an abundance of memorable passages (e.g., 2:13,26–28; 7:4,11,34; 8:20,22; 9:23–24; 10:6–7,10,12–13; 13:23; 15:20; 17:5–9; 20:13; 29:13; 30:7,22; 31:3,15, 29–30,31–34; 33:3; 51:10).

Poetic repetition was used by Jeremiah with particular skill (see, e.g., 4:23–26; 51:20–23). He understood the effectiveness of repeating a striking phrase over and over. An example is "sword, famine and plague," found in 15 separate verses (14:12; 21:7,9; 24:10; 27:8,13; 29:17–18; 32:24,36; 34:17; 38:2; 42:17,22; 44:13). He made use of cryptograms (see TNIV text notes on 25:26; 51:1,41) on appropriate occasions. Alliteration and assonance were also a part of his literary style, examples being *zarim wezeruha* ("foreigners . . . to winnow her," 51:2) and *pahad wapahat wapah* ("Terror and pit and snare," 48:43; see note on Isa 24:17). Like Ezekiel, Jeremiah was often instructed to use symbolism to highlight his message: a ruined and useless belt (13:1–11), a smashed clay jar (19:1–12), a yoke of straps and crossbars (ch. 27), large stones in a brick pavement (43:8–13). Symbolic value is also seen in the Lord's commands to Jeremiah not to marry and raise children (16:1–4), not to enter a house where there was a funeral meal or where there was feasting (16:5–9), and to buy a field in his hometown, Anathoth (32:6–15). Similarly, the Lord used visual aids in conveying his message to Jeremiah: potter's clay (18:1–10) and two baskets of figs (ch. 24).

OUTLINE

Unlike Ezekiel, the oracles in Jeremiah are not arranged in chronological order. Had they been so arranged, the sequence of sections within the book would have been approximately as follows: 1:1—7:15; ch. 26; 7:16—20:18; ch. 25; chs. 46–51; 36:1–8; ch. 45; 36:9–32; ch. 35; chs. 21–24; chs. 27–31; 34:1–7; 37:1–10; 34:8–22; 37:11—38:13; 39:15–18; chs. 32–33; 38:14—39:14; 52:1–30; chs. 40–44; 52:31–34. The outline below represents an analysis of the book of Jeremiah in its present canonical order.

1:1 *a* S Jos 21:18
1:2 *b* Eze 1:3;
Hos 1:1; Joel 1:1
c S 2Ki 22:1
1:3 *d* S 2Ki 23:34
Dan 24:17
f Ezr 5:12; Jer 52:15
1:5 *g* S Ps 139:13
h Ps 139:16
i Isa 49:1 / Jn 10:36
k ver 10; Jer 25:15-26
1:6 *l* S Ex 3:11; S 6:12
m 1Ki 3:7
1:8 *n* S Ge 15:1;
S Jos 8:1 *o* S Ge 26:3;
S Jos 1:5; Jer 15:20
p ver 19; Jer 15:21;
26:24; 36:26; 42:11
q Jer 20:11
1:9 *r* S Isa 6:7
1:10 *t* Jer 25:17; 46:1
s S Ex 4:12
u Jer 12:17 *v* Jer 18:7-
10; 24:6; 31:4,28

The words of Jeremiah son of Hilkiah, one of the priests at Anathoth *a* in the territory of Benjamin. ²The word of the LORD came *b* to him in the thirteenth year of the reign of Josiah *c* son of Amon king of Judah, ³and through the reign of Jehoiakim *d* son of Josiah king of Judah, down to the fifth month of the eleventh year of Zedekiah *e* son of Josiah king of Judah, when the people of Jerusalem went into exile. *f*

THE CALL OF JEREMIAH

⁴The word of the LORD came to me, saying,

⁵ "Before I formed you in the womb *g* I knew *a h* you,
    before you were born *i* I set you apart; *j*
    I appointed you as a prophet to the nations. *k*"

⁶"Ah, Sovereign LORD," I said, "I do not know how to speak; *l* I am too young." *m*
⁷But the LORD said to me, "Do not say, 'I am too young.' You must go to everyone I send you to and say whatever I command you. ⁸Do not be afraid *n* of them, for I am with you *o* and will rescue *p* you," declares the LORD. *q*
⁹Then the LORD reached out his hand and touched *r* my mouth and said to me, "I have put my words in your mouth. *s* ¹⁰See, today I appoint you over nations *t* and kingdoms to uproot *u* and tear down, to destroy and overthrow, to build and to plant." *v*

a 5 Or *chose*

1:1–3 The background and setting of Jeremiah's call are stated concisely but comprehensively.

1:1 *The words of.* See 36:10; see also Ne 1:1; Ecc 1:1; Am 1:1; cf. Dt 1:1. *Jeremiah.* For the meaning of the name, see Introduction: Author and Date. Nine other OT men had the same name (see 1Ch 5:24; 12:4,10,13; Ne 10:2; 12:1,12,34), two of whom were the prophet's contemporaries (Jer 35:3; 52:1). *Hilkiah.* Means "The LORD is my portion." For Hilkiah's possible relationship to a priestly house dating back to King Solomon, see Introduction: Author and Date. Two other men named Hilkiah (a common OT name) were also Jeremiah's contemporaries (see 29:3; Ezr 7:1 and note). *priests.* Like Ezekiel (Eze 1:3) and Zechariah (see Introduction to Zechariah: Author), Jeremiah was both a prophet and a member of a priestly family. *Anathoth.* See 11:21–23; 32:6–9. The Hebrew word is the plural form of the name of the Canaanite deity Anat(h), goddess of war. Anathoth had had priestly connections in Israel as early as the times of Joshua (Jos 21:18) and Solomon (1Ki 2:26), and its pagan origins had presumably been almost forgotten by Jeremiah's time. Present-day Anata, three miles northeast of Jerusalem, preserves the ancient name and may be the ancient site itself. *Benjamin.* Anathoth was one of the four Levitical towns in the tribal territory of Benjamin (Jos 21:17–18), and after the exile Benjamites settled there again (Ne 11:31–32).

1:2 *The word of the LORD came.* The most common way of introducing a divine oracle at the beginning of a prophetic book (see Eze 1:3; Jnh 1:1 and note; Hag 1:1; Zec 1:1 and note; cf. Hos 1:1; Joel 1:1 and note; Mic 1:1; Zep 1:1). *to him.* Beginning in v. 4, Jeremiah speaks in the first person (see, e.g., vv. 11,13; 2:1). *thirteenth year.* 626 B.C. (see 25:3). *Josiah.* See 3:6; 36:2. He was the last good and godly king of Judah. Jeremiah sympathized with and supported his attempts at spiritual reformation and renewal (see 22:15b–16), which began in earnest in 621 (see 2Ki 22:3—23:25; 2Ch 34:8—35:19; cf. 2Ch 34:3–7).

1:3 *Jehoiakim.* His predecessor (Jehoahaz) and successor (Jehoiachin) are not mentioned, since they each reigned only three months. In contrast to his father, Josiah, Jehoiakim was a wicked ruler (see 2Ki 23:36–37; 2Ch 36:5)—as Jeremiah discovered almost immediately (see Introduction: Background; see also 22:13–15a,17–19; 26:20–23). *fifth month of the eleventh year.* Ab (July–August), 586 B.C. (see 52:12). *Zedekiah.* The last king of Judah (see Introduction: Background), as wicked in his own way as Jehoiakim (see 52:1–2; 2Ch 36:11–14; see also Jer 24:8; 37:1–2). *exile.* The main captivity of Judah's people coincided with the destruction of Jerusalem and Solomon's temple by Nebuchadnezzar in 586 (see 2Ki 25:8–11).

1:4–19 The account of Jeremiah's call includes two prophetic visions (vv. 10–16) and some closing words of exhortation and encouragement (vv. 17–19).

1:4 See note on v. 2.

1:5 *I formed you.* See Isa 49:5. God's creative act (see Ge 2:7; Ps 119:73) is the basis of his sovereign right (see 18:4–6; Isa 43:21) to call Jeremiah into his service. *I knew you.* In the sense of making Jeremiah the object of his choice (see TNIV text note). The Hebrew verb used here is translated "chosen" in Ge 18:19; Am 3:2. *I set you apart.* I consecrated you (cf. Jdg 13:5; Isa 49:1; Ro 1:1; Gal 1:15 and note). *I appointed you.* The Hebrew for this verb is not the same as that in v. 10, but both refer to the commissioning of the prophet. *prophet.* Lit. "one who has been called" to be God's spokesman (see Ex 7:1–2; 1Sa 9:9 and notes). *nations.* Although Judah's neighbors are probably the primary focus (see 25:8–38; chs. 46–51), Judah herself is not excluded.

1:6 *Do not know how to speak.* Like Moses (see Ex 4:10 and note), Jeremiah claimed inability to be a prophet; God nevertheless made him his spokesman (15:19). *too young.* See 1Ki 3:7. Jeremiah's objection is denied immediately by the Lord (v. 7).

1:7 Youth and inexperience do not disqualify when God calls (see 1Ti 4:12); he equips and sustains those he commissions.

1:8 *Do not be afraid.* See 10:5; 30:10; 40:9; 42:11; 46:27–28; 51:46; see also Isa 35:4 and note; 41:10,13–14; 43:1; Zep 3:11; Hag 2:5. *I am with you.* See v. 19; 15:20. God's promise of his continuing presence should calm the fears of the most reluctant of prophets (see Ge 26:3; Ex 3:12–15; Jos 1:5 and notes). *rescue.* See v. 19; 15:20; 39:17. The Lord does not promise that Jeremiah will not be persecuted or imprisoned but that no serious physical harm will come to him.

1:9 *touched my mouth.* Either in prophetic vision (see note on v. 11) or figuratively—or both (cf. Isa 6:7). *I have put my words in your mouth.* Continues the figure of speech begun earlier in the verse and provides a classic description of the relationship between the Lord and his prophet (see 5:14; Ex 4:15; Nu 22:38; 23:5,12,16; Dt 18:18; Isa 51:16; cf. 2Pe 1:21).

1:10 *appoint.* See note on v. 5. *uproot and tear down . . . destroy and overthrow . . . build and . . . plant.* See 12:14–15,17; 18:7–10; 24:6; 31:28; 42:10; 45:4. The first two pairs of verbs are negative, stressing the fact that Jeremiah is to be primarily a prophet of doom, while the last pair is positive, indicating that he is also to be a prophet of restoration—even if only secondarily. The first verb ("uproot") is the opposite of the last ("plant"), and fully half of the verbs ("tear down," "destroy," "overthrow") are the opposite of "build."

1:11 ʷ Jer 24:3;
Am 7:8
1:12 ˣ S Job 29:2;
Jer 44:27
1:13 ʸ Jer 24:3;
Zec 4:2; 5:2
1:14 ᶻ S Isa 14:31
1:15 ᵃ Jer 4:16; 9:11;
10:22
1:16 ᵇ Jer 4:12
ᶜ S Ge 6:5; Jer 44:5
ᵈ Jer 2:13; 17:13
ᵉ S Ex 20:3; Jer 7:9;
19:4; 44:3 ᶠ S Nu 25:3
ᵍ Ps 115:4-8; S 135:15
1:17 ʰ ver 7;
Jer 7:27; 26:2,15; 42:4
ⁱ S Dt 31:6; S 2Ki 1:15
1:18 ʲ S Isa 50:7
1:19 ᵏ S Ps 129:2
ˡ S Ge 26:3; Isa 43:2;
Jer 20:11 ᵐ S ver 8;
S Pr 20:22; Ac 26:17
2:1 ⁿ Isa 38:4;
Eze 1:3; Mic 1:1
2:2 ᵒ Ps 71:17;
Isa 54:4; Jer 3:4;
Eze 16:8-14,60;
Hos 2:15; 11:1;
Rev 2:4 ᵖ S Ex 13:21;
S Dt 1:19
2:3 �q S Dt 7:6
ʳ S Ex 19:6; S Dt 7:6

¹¹The word of the Lᴏʀᴅ came to me: "What do you see, Jeremiah?"ʷ

"I see the branch of an almond tree," I replied.

¹²The Lᴏʀᴅ said to me, "You have seen correctly, for I am watchingᵃˣ to see that my word is fulfilled."

¹³The word of the Lᴏʀᴅ came to me again: "What do you see?"ʸ

"I see a pot that is boiling," I answered. "It is tilting toward us from the north."

¹⁴The Lᴏʀᴅ said to me, "From the northᶻ disaster will be poured out on all who live in the land. ¹⁵I am about to summon all the peoples of the northern kingdoms,"ᵃ declares the Lᴏʀᴅ.

> "Their kings will come and set up their thrones
> in the entrance of the gates of Jerusalem;
> they will come against all her surrounding walls
> and against all the towns of Judah.ᵃ
> ¹⁶I will pronounce my judgmentsᵇ on my people
> because of their wickednessᶜ in forsaking me,ᵈ
> in burning incense to other godsᵉ
> and in worshipingᶠ what their hands have made.ᵍ

¹⁷"Get yourself ready! Stand up and sayʰ to them whatever I command you. Do not be terrifiedⁱ by them, or I will terrify you before them. ¹⁸Today I have made youʲ a fortified city, an iron pillar and a bronze wall to stand against the whole land—against the kings of Judah, its officials, its priests and the people of the land. ¹⁹They will fight against you but will not overcomeᵏ you, for I am with youˡ and will rescueᵐ you," declares the Lᴏʀᴅ.

ISRAEL FORSAKES GOD

 The wordⁿ of the Lᴏʀᴅ came to me: ²"Go and proclaim in the hearing of Jerusalem:

"This is what the Lᴏʀᴅ says:

> " 'I remember the devotion of your youth,ᵒ
> how as a bride you loved me
> and followed me through the wilderness,ᵖ
> through a land not sown.
> ³Israel was holy�q to the Lᴏʀᴅ,ʳ

ᵃ 12 The Hebrew for *watching* sounds like the Hebrew for *almond tree*.

1:11 *What do you see . . . ?* Often spoken by the Lord (or his representative) to introduce a prophetic vision (see v. 13; Am 7:8; 8:2; Zec 4:2; 5:2).

1:12 *watching.* See TNIV text note. Just as the almond tree (v. 11) blooms first in the year (and therefore "wakes up" early—the Hebrew word for "watching" means to be wakeful), so the Lord is ever watchful to make sure his word is fulfilled.

1:13 *pot.* The Hebrew for this word is translated "caldron" in Job 41:31 and stresses its large size (see Eze 24:3–5).

1:14 *From the north disaster.* See note on Isa 41:25. *will be poured out* For this word has a sound similar to that for "boiling" in v. 13. *land.* Judah (see v. 15).

1:15 *northern kingdoms.* Since Assyria posed a minimal threat to Judah after the death of Ashurbanipal in 627 B.C., reference is most likely to Babylon and her allies. *set up their thrones in . . . the gates of Jerusalem.* For the fulfillment, see 39:3. Since the gateway of a city was the place where its ruling council sat (see notes on Ge 19:1; Ru 4:1), the Babylonians replaced Judah's royal authority with their own (cf. 43:10; 49:38).

1:16 *my judgments on my people.* God, sovereign over his own, judges them for their sins, using the Babylonians as his agents of judgment. *burning incense to other gods.* A common feature of pagan worship (e.g., 7:9; 11:12–13,17; 18:15; 19:13; 32:29; 44:17). *what their hands have made.* Idols (see 16:19–20; 25:6; 2Ki 22:17; 2Ch 33:22; Isa 46:6).

1:17 *Get yourself ready!* Lit. "Tighten your belt around your waist!" For related expressions, see Ex 12:11; 1Ki 18:46; 2Ki 4:29; 9:1; Job 38:3; 40:7.

1:18 *fortified city.* A symbol of security and impregnability (see 5:17; Pr 18:11,19). *iron pillar.* Unique in the OT, the expression signifies dignity and strength. *bronze wall.* See 15:20. Jeremiah would be able to withstand the abuse and persecution that his divine commission would evoke, even though his enemies themselves would be "bronze and iron" (6:28). *kings . . . officials . . . priests . . . people.* The whole nation would defy the prophet and his God (see, e.g., 2:26; 23:8; 32:32).

1:19 See note on v. 8; see also 15:20.

2:1—6:30 It is generally agreed that these chapters are among Jeremiah's earliest discourses, delivered during the reign of Josiah (3:6). The basic theme is the virtually total apostasy of Judah (chs. 2–5), leading inevitably to divine retribution through foreign invasion (ch. 6).

2:1—3:5 The wickedness and backsliding of God's people are vividly portrayed in numerous colorful figures of speech.

2:1 See note on 1:2.

2:2 *devotion.* The Hebrew for this word refers to the most intimate degree of loyalty, love and faithfulness that can exist between two people or between an individual and the Lord. *youth . . . as a bride.* Early in her history, Israel had enjoyed a close and cordial relationship with the Lord, who is often described figuratively as Israel's husband (3:14; 31:32; Isa 54:5; Hos 2:16). *you loved me.* But later God's people forsook him and loved "foreign gods" (v. 25), tragically abandoning their first love (cf. Rev 2:4). *followed me.* They followed "worthless idols" (vv. 5,8), "the Baals" (v. 23). *wilderness.* Sinai (see v. 6).

2:3 *holy to the Lᴏʀᴅ.* Set apart to him and his service (see notes

the firstfruits ^{s} of his harvest;
all who devoured ^{t} her were held guilty, ^{u}
and disaster overtook them,' "

declares the LORD.

⁴ Hear the word of the LORD, house of Jacob,
all you clans of the house of Israel.

⁵ This is what the LORD says:

"What fault did your ancestors find in me,
that they strayed so far from me?
They followed worthless idols ^{v}
and became worthless ^{w} themselves.
⁶ They did not ask, 'Where is the LORD,
who brought us up out of Egypt ^{x}
and led us through the barren wilderness,
through a land of deserts ^{y} and ravines, ^{z}
a land of drought and utter darkness,
a land where no one travels ^{a} and no one lives?'
⁷ I brought you into a fertile land
to eat its fruit and rich produce. ^{b}
But you came and defiled my land
and made my inheritance detestable. ^{c}
⁸ The priests did not ask,
'Where is the LORD?'
Those who deal with the law did not know me; ^{d}
the leaders ^{e} rebelled against me.
The prophets prophesied by Baal, ^{f}
following worthless idols. ^{g}

⁹ "Therefore I bring charges ^{h} against you again,"

declares the LORD.

"And I will bring charges against your children's children.
¹⁰ Cross over to the coasts of Cyprus ^{i} and look,
send to Kedar $^{a\,j}$ and observe closely;
see if there has ever been anything like this:
¹¹ Has a nation ever changed its gods?

___

^{a} 10 In the Syro-Arabian desert

2:3 ^{s} Lev 23:9-14;
Jas 1:18; Rev 14:4
^{t} Isa 41:11; Jer 10:25;
30:16 ^{u} Jer 50:7
2:5 ^{v} S Dt 32:21;
S 1Sa 12:21; Ps 31:6
^{w} 2Ki 17:15
2:6 ^{x} S Ex 6:6;
Hos 13:4 ^{y} S Dt 1:19
^{z} S Dt 32:10
^{a} Jer 51:43
2:7 ^{b} S Nu 13:27;
Dt 8:7-9; 11:10-12
^{c} Ps 106:34-39;
Jer 3:9; 7:30; 16:18;
Eze 11:21; 36:17
2:8 ^{d} S 1Sa 2:12;
Jer 4:22 ^{e} Jer 3:15;
23:1; 25:34; 50:6
^{f} S 1Ki 18:22 ^{g} ver 25;
S Isa 40:19; S 56:10;
Jer 5:19; 9:14; 16:19;
22:9
2:9 ^{h} Jer 25:31;
Hos 4:1; Mic 6:2
2:10 ^{i} S Ge 10:4
^{j} S Ge 25:13

on Ex 3:5; Lev 11:44; Dt 7:6). *firstfruits.* Just as the "best of the firstfruits" of Israel's crops were to be brought to the Lord (Ex 23:19; see Nu 18:12; 2Ch 31:5; Eze 44:30), so also the people themselves were his first and choicest treasure (cf. Jas 1:18; Rev 14:4 and note). *disaster overtook them.* See, e.g., Ex 17:8–16.
2:4 *Hear.* A common divine imperative in prophetic writings, summoning God's people—as well as the nations—into his courts to remind them of their legal obligations to him and, when necessary, to pass judgment on them (see, e.g., 7:2; 17:20; 19:3; 21:11; 22:2,29; 31:10; 42:15; 44:24,26; Isa 1:10; Eze 13:2; Hos 4:1; Am 7:16).
2:5 *This is what the LORD says.* The so-called messenger formula, introducing God's word through the prophet. Though frequent in overall occurrence, its use is restricted to Jeremiah, Isaiah (e.g., 7:7), Ezekiel (e.g., 2:4), Amos (e.g., 1:3), Obadiah (1), Micah (3:5), Nahum (1:12), Haggai (e.g., 1:2), Zechariah (e.g., 1:3) and Malachi (1:4). *strayed.* See 4:1; 23:13,32; 31:19; 50:6; Isa 53:6; Eze 34:4–6,16; 1Pe 2:25. *followed worthless idols.* See vv. 8,23; see also note on v. 2. "Worthless" is Jeremiah's favorite way of describing idols (8:19; 10:8,15; 14:22; 16:19; 51:18). *became worthless themselves.* See 2Ki 17:15. Idolaters are no better than the idols they worship (see Ps 115:8 and note).
2:6 *LORD ... brought us up out of Egypt.* The Lord, Israel's Redeemer (see notes on Ge 2:4; Ex 3:15), freed his people from Egyptian bondage so that they might serve him alone (Ex 20:2–6). *led us.* As a shepherd leads his sheep (see v. 17; Dt 8:15; Ps 23:2–3). *land of deserts ... land of ... darkness.* The desert of-

ten symbolized darkness with its attendant dangers, including death (see v. 31 and note; 9:10; 12:12; 17:6; 23:10; Ps 44:19).
2:7 *fertile.* The Hebrew for this word is *karmel,* translated "orchards" in 48:33 and also used as the name of a place (see Isa 33:9 and note). Rendered "fruitful land" in 4:26, it is the opposite of a desert. *defiled my land.* Made it ceremonially unclean (see 3:1–2,9; 16:18; see also note on Lev 4:12). *inheritance.* The promised land, given by God to Israel as a legacy and often intimately associated with the people themselves (see especially 12:7–9, 14–15). *detestable.* See note on Lev 7:21.
2:8 No one consulted the Lord (see v. 6). *priests ... leaders ... prophets.* See note on 1:18. *Those who deal with the law.* Priests (see Dt 31:11 and note). *leaders.* Lit. "shepherds," a term used elsewhere to denote rulers (23:1–4; 49:19; 50:44; see especially Eze 34:1–10,23–24). *by Baal.* In the name of Baal (cf. 11:21; 14:15; 23:25; 26:9; see note on Jdg 2:13). *following worthless idols.* See v. 23. *worthless.* Lit. "unprofitable" (see v. 11).
2:9 *bring charges against.* See note on v. 4; see also 25:31; Hos 4:1; 12:2; Mic 6:2.
2:10 *Cyprus.* See Nu 24:24; Eze 27:6 and notes. *Kedar.* Represents the eastern nations and regions (see TNIV text note; see also 49:28; Isa 21:16 and note).
2:11 *Has ... gods?* A rhetorical question, clearly expecting a negative answer and emphasizing how incredible is Judah's practice of substituting idolatry for the worship of the Lord. *their glorious God.* See Ps 106:20; Hos 4:7; see also 1Sa 15:29. *worthless.* See note on v. 8.

2:11 *k* Isa 37:19;
Jer 16:20; Gal 4:8
l 1Sa 4:21; Ro 1:23
2:13 *m* S Dt 31:16;
S Isa 65:11
n S Isa 12:3; Jn 4:14
2:14 *o* Ex 4:22;
Jer 31:9
2:15 *p* Jer 4:7; 50:17
q S Isa 1:7 *r* S 2Ki 25:9
s Lev 26:43
2:16 *t* S Isa 19:13
u Jer 43:7-9
2:17 *v* Jer 4:18
w S Isa 1:28; Jer 17:13;
19:4
2:18 *x* S Isa 30:2
y S Jos 13:3
z 2Ki 16:7; Hos 5:13;
7:11; 8:9 *a* S Isa 7:20
2:19 *b* Jer 3:11,22;
7:24; 11:10; 14:7;
Hos 14:4 *c* Isa 3:9;
59:12; Hos 5:5
d S Job 20:14;
Am 8:10 *e* Jer 19:4
f S Ps 36:1
2:20 *g* S Lev 26:13
h Ps 2:3; Jer 5:5
i S Job 21:14 / Isa 57:7;
Jer 3:23; 17:2
k S Dt 12:2 *l* S Isa 1:21;
Eze 16:15
2:21 *m* S Ex 15:17
n S Ps 80:8

(Yet they are not gods *k* at all.)
But my people have exchanged their glorious *l* God
for worthless idols.
¹² Be appalled at this, you heavens,
and shudder with great horror,"

declares the LORD.

¹³ "My people have committed two sins:
They have forsaken *m* me,
the spring of living water, *n*
and have dug their own cisterns,
broken cisterns that cannot hold water.
¹⁴ Is Israel a servant, a slave *o* by birth?
Why then has he become plunder?
¹⁵ Lions *p* have roared;
they have growled at him.
They have laid waste *q* his land;
his towns are burned *r* and deserted. *s*
¹⁶ Also, the men of Memphis *t* and Tahpanhes *u*
have cracked your skull.
¹⁷ Have you not brought this on yourselves *v*
by forsaking *w* the LORD your God
when he led you in the way?
¹⁸ Now why go to Egypt *x*
to drink water from the Nile*a*? *y*
And why go to Assyria *z*
to drink water from the Euphrates? *a*
¹⁹ Your wickedness will punish you;
your backsliding *b* will rebuke *c* you.
Consider then and realize
how evil and bitter *d* it is for you
when you forsake *e* the LORD your God
and have no awe *f* of me,"

declares the Lord, the LORD Almighty.

²⁰ "Long ago you broke off your yoke *g*
and tore off your bonds; *h*
you said, 'I will not serve you!' *i*
Indeed, on every high hill *j*
and under every spreading tree *k*
you lay down as a prostitute. *l*
²¹ I had planted *m* you like a choice vine *n*

a 18 Hebrew *Shihor*; that is, a branch of the Nile

2:12 *Be appalled...you heavens.* See note on Isa 1:2; see also Mic 6:1–2 and note. The Hebrew for these phrases offers a striking play on words: *shommu shamayim.*
2:13 *forsaken me.* See v. 19. *me, the spring of living water.* See 17:13. God himself provides life-giving power to his people (see Ps 36:9; see also note on Jn 4:10; Isa 55:1 and note; Rev 21:6). *broken cisterns.* Watertight plaster was used to keep cisterns from losing water. Idols, like broken cisterns, will always fail their worshipers; by contrast, God provides life abundant and unfailing (cf. Jn 10:10 and note).
2:14 *Is...birth?* Another rhetorical question (see note on v. 11), again expecting a negative answer in the light of God's redemptive acts during the period of the exodus (see Ex 6:6; 20:2). *plunder.* To Assyria and Egypt (see vv. 15–16).
2:15 *Lions.* Probably symbolizing Assyria (see v. 18; 50:17; see also notes on 4:7; Isa 15:9). *roared...growled.* See Am 3:4. *laid waste his land.* See 4:7; 18:16; 50:3. *towns are burned and deserted.* The Hebrew for this phrase is very similar to that in 4:7, rendered there "towns will lie in ruins without inhabitant" (cf. 22:6).
2:16 *Memphis.* See 44:1; 46:14,19; see also note on Isa 19:13. *Tahpanhes.* Probably the city later called Daphnai by the Greeks, located just south of Lake Menzaleh in the eastern delta region

of Egypt and known today as Tell Defneh (see 43:7–9; 44:1; 46:14; Eze 30:18).
2:17 *he led you.* See note on v. 6. *the way.* See Ex 18:8; 23:20; Dt 1:33.
2:18 See v. 36. The tendency of Israel or Judah to seek help alternately from Egypt and Assyria was not restricted to Jeremiah's time (see, e.g., Hos 7:11; 12:2). *drink water.* Provided by enemies, whether national or spiritual, rather than by God (see v. 13; Isa 8:6–8 and notes).
2:19 *backsliding.* See 3:22; 5:6; 14:7. The word implies repeated apostasy. *LORD Almighty.* A title for God occurring about 75 times in Jeremiah—more than in any other OT book (see note on 1Sa 1:3).
2:20—3:6 The rebellion of Judah against God is vividly portrayed by Jeremiah with the use of numerous figures of speech.
2:20 Like a stubborn draft animal (see Hos 4:16), Judah refuses to obey the Lord's commands. *broke off your yoke and tore off your bonds.* See 5:5; see also 31:18; cf. Ps 2:3. Judah has broken God's law and violated his covenant. *on every high hill and under every spreading tree.* Locales of pagan worship (see 1Ki 14:23; 2Ki 17:10; Eze 6:13). *as a prostitute.* See v. 2; Ex 34:15 and notes.

of sound and reliable stock.
How then did you turn against me
into a corrupt, *o* wild vine?
²² Although you wash*p* yourself with soap*q*
and use an abundance of cleansing powder,
the stain of your guilt is still before me,"

declares the Sovereign LORD.*r*

²³ "How can you say, 'I am not defiled;*s*
I have not run after the Baals'?*t*
See how you behaved in the valley;*u*
consider what you have done.
You are a swift she-camel
running*v* here and there,
²⁴ a wild donkey*w* accustomed to the desert,*x*
sniffing the wind in her craving—
in her heat who can restrain her?
Any males that pursue her need not tire themselves;
at mating time they will find her.
²⁵ Do not run until your feet are bare
and your throat is dry.
But you said, 'It's no use!*y*
I love foreign gods,*z*
and I must go after them.'*a*

²⁶ "As a thief is disgraced*b* when he is caught,
so the house of Israel is disgraced—
they, their kings and their officials,
their priests*c* and their prophets.*d*
²⁷ They say to wood,*e* 'You are my father,'
and to stone,*f* 'You gave me birth.'
They have turned their backs*g* to me
and not their faces;*h*
yet when they are in trouble,*i* they say,
'Come and save*j* us!'
²⁸ Where then are the gods*k* you made for yourselves?
Let them come if they can save you
when you are in trouble!*l*
For you, Judah, have as many gods
as you have towns.*m*

²⁹ "Why do you bring charges against me?
You have all*n* rebelled against me,"

declares the LORD.

³⁰ "In vain I punished your people;
they did not respond to correction.*o*

2:21 *o* S Isa 5:4
2:22 *p* S Ps 51:2;
La 1:8,17 *q* S Job 9:30
r Jer 17:1
2:23 *s* S Pr 30:12
t ver 25; Jer 9:14;
23:27 *u* S 2Ki 23:10;
Jer 7:31; 19:2; 31:40
v ver 33; Jer 31:22
2:24 *w* S Ge 16:12;
Jer 14:6 *x* S Job 39:6
2:25 *y* S Isa 57:10
z Dt 32:16; Jer 3:13;
14:10 *a* S ver 8,S 23
2:26 *b* Jer 48:27;
La 1:7; Eze 16:54;
36:4 *c* Eze 22:26
d Jer 32:32; 44:17,21
2:27 *e* Jer 10:8
f Jer 3:9 *g* S 1Ki 14:9;
S 2Ch 29:6; Ps 14:3;
Eze 8:16 *h* Jer 18:17;
32:33; Eze 7:22
i Jdg 10:10; Isa 26:16
j Isa 37:20; Hos 5:15
2:28 *k* S Isa 45:20
l S Dt 32:37;
S Isa 40:19
m S 2Ki 17:29
2:29 *n* Jer 5:1; 6:13;
Da 9:11; Mic 3:11; 7:2
2:30 *o* S Lev 26:23

2:21 See Isa 5:1–7; see also Ps 80:8–16; Eze 17:1–10; Hos 10:1–2; cf. Jn 15:1–8. *choice vine.* See Isa 5:2. The Hebrew for this word refers to a grape of exceptional quality. *wild.* Lit. "foreign." A vine symbolizing Israel should not be like a vine symbolizing Israel's enemies (see Dt 32:32).

2:22 *soap … cleansing powder.* Vegetable alkali and mineral alkali, respectively. Sins can be removed and forgiven (see Ps 51:2,7; Isa 1:18), but only when the sinner repents and confesses (see Pr 28:13; cf. 1Jn 1:7,9).

2:23 *defiled.* Ceremonially unclean (see 19:13; see also note on Lev 4:12). *run after.* See note on v. 2; see also v. 25. *Baals.* See 9:14; see also notes on Jdg 2:11,13. *the valley.* Probably the Hinnom Valley (see note on Jos 15:5), known also as the Valley of Ben Hinnom (7:31–32; 19:2,6; 32:35). *running here and there.* Instead, the people of Judah should have been obeying the Lord, not turning aside either "to the right or to the left" (Dt 28:14).
2:24 *wild donkey.* Properly the wild ass, an unruly (see Ge 16:12) and intractable (see Job 39:5–8) animal. *accustomed to the desert.* See 14:6; Job 24:5. *sniffing the wind.* The picture is one of active searching, not passive waiting (see Hos 2:7,13).

2:25 *your feet are bare.* You wear out your sandals. *It's no use!* See 18:12 and note. *I love foreign gods.* As opposed to the love Judah was expected to express toward God under the terms of their covenant relationship (see, e.g., Dt 6:5; 7:9; Hos 2:16; see also Ex 39:15 and note). *go after them.* See v. 23; see also note on v. 2.
2:26 *disgraced when he is caught.* See, e.g., Ex 22:3–4. The Hebrew word underlying "disgraced" means lit. "shame," a term often used as a pejorative synonym for the name of Baal, the chief god of Canaan (see 11:13 and note; Hos 9:10; see also note on Jdg 6:32). *kings … officials … priests … prophets.* See note on 1:18.
2:27 See Isa 44:13–17; contrast Dt 32:6,18; Isa 64:8; Mal 2:10. *wood … stone.* Materials used to make idols (see 3:9 and note). *Come … save.* See v. 28.
2:28 *as many gods as … towns.* See 11:13; cf. 1Co 8:5. Every ancient Near Eastern town of any importance had its own patron deity (cf. Ac 19:28, 34–35), and many towns were named after deities (see, e.g., note on 1:1).
2:29 *bring charges against.* Cf. v. 9; see 12:1; Job 33:13.
2:30 *I punished your people.* Cf. Heb 12:6. *did not respond to cor-*

2:30 P S Ne 9:26;
S Jer 11:21; Ac 7:52;
1Th 2:15
2:31 q Isa 45:19
r S Job 21:14
2:32 s S Dt 32:18;
S Isa 57:11
2:33 t S ver 23
2:34 u S 2Ki 21:16;
S Pr 6:17 v S Ex 22:2
2:35 w S Pr 30:12
x Isa 66:16; Jer 25:31;
39:7; 45:5; Eze 17:20;
20:35; Joel 3:2
y S 2Sa 12:13; 1Jn 1:8,
10
2:36 z Jer 31:22
a S Ps 108:12;
S Isa 30:2,3,7;
Jer 37:7
2:37 b 2Sa 13:19
c Jer 37:7
3:1 d Dt 24:1-4
e S Ge 3:17
f S 2Ki 16:7;
S Isa 1:21; Jer 2:20,
25; 4:30; La 1:2;
Eze 16:26,29;
Hos 2:5,12; 3:1
g Hos 2:7
3:2 h ver 21
i Ge 38:14; Eze 16:25
j ver 9 k S Nu 15:39;
S Isa 1:21

Your sword has devoured your prophets P
    like a ravenous lion.

31 "You of this generation, consider the word of the LORD:

"Have I been a desert to Israel
    or a land of great darkness? q
Why do my people say, 'We are free to roam;
    we will come to you no more'? r
32 Does a young woman forget her jewelry,
    a bride her wedding ornaments?
Yet my people have forgotten s me,
    days without number.
33 How skilled you are at pursuing t love!
    Even the worst of women can learn from your ways.
34 On your clothes is found
    the lifeblood u of the innocent poor,
    though you did not catch them breaking in. v
Yet in spite of all this
35   you say, 'I am innocent; w
    he is not angry with me.'
But I will pass judgment x on you
    because you say, 'I have not sinned.' y
36 Why do you go about so much,
    changing z your ways?
You will be disappointed by Egypt a
    as you were by Assyria.
37 You will also leave that place
    with your hands on your head, b
for the LORD has rejected those you trust;
    you will not be helped c by them.

3 "If a man divorces d his wife
    and she leaves him and marries another man,
should he return to her again?
    Would not the land be completely defiled? e
But you have lived as a prostitute with many lovers f—
    would you now return to me?" g

                  declares the LORD.

2 "Look up to the barren heights h and see.
    Is there any place where you have not been ravished?
By the roadside i you sat waiting for lovers,
    sat like a nomad in the desert.
You have defiled the land j
    with your prostitution k and wickedness.

---

rection. See 5:3. *sword has devoured your prophets.* See, e.g.,
26:20–23; 2Ki 21:16; 24:4; see also Ne 9:26.
2:31 *generation.* Often has negative connotations (see, e.g., Dt
1:35; 32:5; Mt 12:39; 16:4; 17:17; Ac 2:40; Php 2:15; Heb 3:10).
Have I been a desert . . . a land of great darkness? On the contrary,
the Lord led his people through the desert and its darkness (v.
6). The phrase "great darkness" translates the Hebrew for "darkness of the LORD" (i.e., darkness sent by the Lord; cf. 1Sa 26:12),
just as "mighty flame" in SS 8:6 translates "flame of the LORD"
(see TNIV text note there).
    2:32 See Isa 49:15,18 and notes. *bride.* Cf. v. 2. *my people
    have forgotten me.* See 18:15; see also 3:21; 13:25; Isa
17:10; Eze 22:12; 23:35; Hos 8:14. Israel was always to "remember" the Lord and all that he had done for her (Dt 7:18; 8:18) and
so trust and worship him alone, but she often "forgot" him—put
him out of mind (see Jdg 2:10; Hos 2:13).
2:33 *love.* See v. 25 and note.
2:34 See Am 2:6–8; 4:1; 5:11–12. *catch them breaking in.* See Ex
22:2 and note.

2:36 *disappointed by Egypt . . . by Assyria.* See vv. 15–18 and
notes. The days of Ahaz (see 2Ch 28:21), and perhaps the days of
Zedekiah (see 37:7), are in view here.
    2:37 *with your hands on your head.* Ancient reliefs depict
    captives with wrists tied together above their heads.
those you trust. Egypt and Assyria.
    3:1 *If . . . defiled?* Cf. Dt 24:1–4. Divorce and remarriage on
    a widespread scale defiles not only the participants but
also the land in which they live (cf. v. 2; Lev 18:25–28). *lived as a
prostitute with many lovers.* A metaphor carried forward from
ch. 2 and used throughout ch. 3 (see 2:20,25,33 and note on
2:25). *many.* See note on 2:28. *return to me.* Repent of your sins
against me (see vv. 12–14,22; 4:1).
3:2 *barren heights.* Places where pagan gods were consulted
and worshiped (see v. 21; 12:12; Nu 23:3). *ravished.* Cf. Dt 28:30.
By the roadside you sat. See Ge 38:14 and note; Pr 7:10,12. *like a
nomad in the desert.* Waiting in ambush to waylay a traveler (cf.
Lk 10:30). *defiled the land.* See v. 9.

³ Therefore the showers have been withheld, ^{l}
  and no spring rains ^{m} have fallen.
Yet you have the brazen ^{n} look of a prostitute;
  you refuse to blush with shame. ^{o}
⁴ Have you not just called to me:
  'My Father, ^{p} my friend from my youth, ^{q}
⁵ will you always be angry? ^{r}
  Will your wrath continue forever?'
This is how you talk,
  but you do all the evil you can."

UNFAITHFUL ISRAEL

⁶ During the reign of King Josiah, ^{s} the LORD said to me, "Have you seen what faithless ^{t} Israel has done? She has gone up on every high hill and under every spreading tree ^{u} and has committed adultery ^{v} there. ⁷ I thought that after she had done all this she would return to me but she did not, and her unfaithful sister ^{w} Judah saw it. ^{x} ⁸ I gave faithless Israel ^{y} her certificate of divorce ^{z} and sent her away because of all her adulteries. Yet I saw that her unfaithful sister Judah had no fear; ^{a} she also went out and committed adultery. ⁹ Because Israel's immorality mattered so little to her, she defiled the land ^{b} and committed adultery ^{c} with stone ^{d} and wood. ^{e} ¹⁰ In spite of all this, her unfaithful sister Judah did not return ^{f} to me with all her heart, but only in pretense, ^{g} " declares the LORD. ^{h}

¹¹ The LORD said to me, "Faithless Israel is more righteous ^{i} than unfaithful ^{j} Judah. ^{k} ¹² Go, proclaim this message toward the north: ^{l}

" 'Return, ^{m} faithless ^{n} Israel,' declares the LORD,
  'I will frown on you no longer,
  for I am faithful,' ^{o} declares the LORD,
  'I will not be angry ^{p} forever.
¹³ Only acknowledge ^{q} your guilt—
  you have rebelled against the LORD your God,
  you have scattered your favors to foreign gods ^{r}
  under every spreading tree, ^{s}
  and have not obeyed ^{t} me,' "

declares the LORD.

¹⁴ "Return, ^{u} faithless people," declares the LORD, "for I am your husband. ^{v} I will choose you—one from a town and two from a clan—and bring you to Zion. ¹⁵ Then I will give you shepherds ^{w} after my own heart, ^{x} who will lead you with knowledge and understanding. ¹⁶ In those days, when your numbers have increased greatly in the land," declares the LORD,

---

3:3 /Lev 26:19;
Jer 5:25; Am 4:7
^{m} S Dt 11:14; Jer 14:4;
Joel 1:10 ^{n} Eze 3:7;
16:30 ^{o} Jer 6:15; 8:12;
Zep 2:1; 3:5
3:4 ^{p} ver 19;
S Dt 32:6; S Ps 89:26;
Isa 63:16; 64:8;
Jer 31:9 ^{q} S Jer 2:2
3:5 ^{r} S Ps 103:9;
S Isa 54:9
3:6 ^{s} S 1Ch 3:14
^{t} ver 12,22;
S Isa 24:16; Jer 31:22;
49:4 ^{u} S Dt 12:2;
Jer 17:2; Eze 20:28;
Hos 4:13 ^{v} S Lev 17:7;
Jer 2:20
3:7 ^{w} Eze 16:46;
23:2,11 ^{x} Am 4:8
3:8 ^{y} Jer 11:10
^{z} S Dt 4:27; S 24:1
^{a} Eze 16:47; 23:11
3:9 ^{b} ver 2
^{c} S Lev 17:7; S Isa 1:21
^{d} S Isa 57:6 ^{e} Jer 2:27
3:10 ^{f} Isa 31:6;
^{g} Jer 12:2; Eze 33:31
^{h} Jer 2:5; 2Ki 17:19
3:11 ^{i} Eze 16:52;
23:11 ^{j} ver 7
^{k} S Jer 2:19
3:12 /2Ki 17:3-6
^{m} ver 14; S Dt 4:30;
Jer 31:21,22; Eze 14:6;
33:11; Hos 14:1
^{n} S ver 6 ^{o} S 1Ki 3:26;
S Ps 6:2 ^{p} S Ps 103:9;
S Isa 54:9
3:13 ^{q} Dt 30:1-3;
Jer 14:20; 1Jn 1:9
^{r} S Jer 2:25 ^{s} S Dt 12:2
^{t} ver 25; Jer 22:21
3:14 ^{u} S ver 12;
S Job 22:23; Jer 4:1
^{v} S Isa 54:5
3:15 ^{w} S Isa 31:4
^{x} Ac 13:22

3:3 *showers have been withheld.* See 14:1–6; Am 4:7–8. This is the reverse of God's gracious response to his people in Hos 2:21; 6:3. *spring rains.* See notes on Dt 11:14; Jas 5:7. *brazen look.* See Pr 7:13.

3:4 *My Father.* See v. 19; contrast 2:27 and see note there. Compared to the NT, the title "Father" for God is relatively rare in the OT. However, it often occurs in personal names—compound names that begin with Abi- (e.g., Abinadab and Abiram) refer to God as "(my) Father." *my friend.* Claiming intimate association (see Ps 55:13; Pr 16:28; 17:9; Mic 7:5); perhaps even claiming to be the Lord's faithful wife (cf. Pr 2:17). *from my youth.* See note on 2:2.

3:5 *Will your wrath continue forever?* Not if God's people repent (vv. 12–13).

3:6—6:30 The unfaithfulness of Judah (3:6—5:31) will ultimately bring the Babylonians as God's instrument of judgment (ch. 6).

3:6 *King Josiah.* See Introduction: Background; see also note on 1:2. *faithless Israel.* The northern kingdom, destroyed in 722–721 B.C. (see vv. 8,11–12).

3:7 *her unfaithful sister Judah.* The southern kingdom (see vv. 8,10–11). Samaria (Israel's capital) and Jerusalem (Judah's capital) are similarly compared as adulterous sisters in Eze 23. *it.* Israel's adultery.

3:8 *certificate of divorce.* See v. 1 and note; see also Dt 24:1–4; Isa 50:1 and notes. *sent her away.* Into exile in 721 B.C. *Judah had no fear.* She refused to learn from Israel's tragic experience.

3:9 *committed adultery with stone and wood.* Worshiped pagan deities (see notes on 2:27; Ex 34:15).

3:10 *in pretense.* Judah's response to Josiah's reform measures (see note on 1:2) was superficial and hypocritical.

3:11 *Israel is more righteous than . . . Judah.* See note on v. 8; see also Eze 16:51–52; 23:11.

3:12 *Go, proclaim.* See 2:2. *north.* Assyria's northern provinces, to which many Israelites had been exiled. *Return.* Repent (see v. 13). *faithful.* The Hebrew for this word is used of God elsewhere only in Ps 145:13,17. *not be angry forever.* See note on v. 5.

3:13 *scattered your favors.* See Eze 16:15,33–34 and note on 16:33. *foreign gods.* See note on 2:25. *under every spreading tree.* See note on 2:20.

3:14 *husband.* See 31:32; Hos 2:16–17. The Hebrew root underlying this word is *ba'al.* Instead of allowing God to be Israel's husband, his people followed "the Baals" (2:23; see note on Jdg 2:11). *one . . . two.* A remnant will return (see note on Isa 10:20–22). *Zion.* Jerusalem.

3:15 See 23:4. *shepherds.* Rulers (see note on 2:8). *after my own heart.* Like David (see 1Sa 13:14; see also Eze 34:23; Hos 3:5).

3:16 *In those days.* The Messianic age (see v. 18; 31:29). *numbers have increased.* See 23:3; Eze 36:11. For the fuller meaning of the Hebrew underlying this phrase, see note on Ge 1:28. *nor will another one be made.* The ark of the covenant, formerly symbolizing God's royal presence (see 1Sa 4:3 and note), will be irrelevant when the Messiah comes.

3:16 ʸS Nu 3:31;
S 1Ch 15:25
ᶻS Isa 65:17
3:17 ᵃS Ps 47:8;
Jer 17:12; 33:16;
Eze 1:26; 43:7; 48:35
ᵇS Isa 2:3; Mic 4:1
ᶜS Ps 22:23; Jer 13:11;
33:9 ᵈPs 81:12;
Jer 7:24; 9:14; 11:8;
13:10; 16:12; 18:12
3:18 ᵉJer 30:3;
Eze 37:19
ᶠS Isa 11:13; Jer 50:4
ᵍJer 16:15; 31:8
ʰDt 31:7; S Isa 14:1;
Eze 11:17; 37:22;
Am 9:15
3:19 ⁱS Dt 8:7
ʲPs 106:24; Eze 20:6
ᵏS ver 4; S Ex 4:22;
S 2Sa 7:14
3:20 ˡS Isa 24:16
3:21 ᵐver 2
ⁿJer 31:18
ᵒS Isa 57:11
3:22 ᵖS ver 12;
S Job 22:23
�q S Isa 30:26; 57:18;
Jer 33:6; Hos 6:1
ʳS Jer 2:19
3:23 ˢS Jer 2:20
ᵗPs 3:8; Jer 17:14
3:24 ᵘJer 11:13;
Hos 9:10
3:25 ᵛS Ezr 9:6;
Jer 31:19; Da 9:7
ʷS Jdg 10:10;
S 1Ki 8:47 ˣJer 14:20
ʸS Ps 25:7;
S Jer 22:21 ᶻS ver 13;
Eze 2:3
4:1 ᵃS Dt 4:30;
S 2Ki 17:13;
S Hos 12:6
ᵇS 2Ki 21:4; Jer 16:18;
35:15; Eze 8:5

"people will no longer say, 'The ark ʸ of the covenant of the Lᴏʀᴅ.' It will never enter their minds or be remembered; ᶻ it will not be missed, nor will another one be made. ¹⁷At that time they will call Jerusalem The Throne ᵃ of the Lᴏʀᴅ, and all nations ᵇ will gather in Jerusalem to honor ᶜ the name of the Lᴏʀᴅ. No longer will they follow the stubbornness of their evil hearts. ᵈ¹⁸In those days the house of Judah will join the house of Israel, ᵉ and together ᶠ they will come from a northern ᵍ land to the land ʰ I gave your ancestors as an inheritance.

¹⁹"I myself said,

" 'How gladly would I treat you like my children
    and give you a pleasant land, ⁱ
    the most beautiful inheritance ʲ of any nation.'
I thought you would call me 'Father' ᵏ
    and not turn away from following me.
²⁰But like a woman unfaithful to her husband,
    so you, house of Israel, have been unfaithful ˡ to me,"
                      declares the Lᴏʀᴅ.

²¹A cry is heard on the barren heights, ᵐ
    the weeping ⁿ and pleading of the people of Israel,
because they have perverted their ways
    and have forgotten ᵒ the Lᴏʀᴅ their God.

²²"Return, ᵖ faithless people;
    I will cure q you of backsliding." ʳ

"Yes, we will come to you,
    for you are the Lᴏʀᴅ our God.
²³Surely the ⌊idolatrous⌋ commotion on the hills ˢ
    and mountains is a deception;
surely in the Lᴏʀᴅ our God
    is the salvation ᵗ of Israel.
²⁴From our youth shameful ᵘ gods have consumed
    the fruits of our ancestors' labor—
their flocks and herds,
    their sons and daughters.
²⁵Let us lie down in our shame, ᵛ
    and let our disgrace cover us.
We have sinned ʷ against the Lᴏʀᴅ our God,
    both we and our ancestors; ˣ
from our youth ʸ till this day
    we have not obeyed ᶻ the Lᴏʀᴅ our God."

4 "If you, Israel, will return, ᵃ
    then return to me,"
                      declares the Lᴏʀᴅ.
"If you put your detestable idols ᵇ out of my sight
    and no longer go astray,

3:17 *Throne.* The Lord sat "enthroned between the cherubim" above the ark (see 1Sa 4:4 and note), but Jerusalem itself would someday be his throne. *all nations will gather.* See Zec 2:11; see also note on Isa 2:2–4. *they.* Israel. *follow the stubbornness of their evil hearts.* A stock phrase referring to Israel's disobedience and often involving the worship of pagan gods (see 9:14; 11:8; 13:10; 16:12; 18:12; 23:17).
3:18 *Judah will join … Israel.* In the Messianic age God's divided people will again be united (see, e.g., 31:31; Isa 11:12; Eze 37:15–23; Hos 1:11). *northern land.* Where they had been exiles (see note on v. 12; see also 31:8). *land I gave … as an inheritance.* See note on 2:7.
3:19 *my children.* Israel was the Lord's firstborn (see Ex 4:22; cf. Hos 11:1). *pleasant land.* See Ps 106:24; Zec 7:14. *beautiful inheritance.* Judah, Jerusalem, the people themselves—ideally, all were beautiful in God's eyes (see 6:2; 11:16). *Father.* See note on v. 4.
3:20 A concise summary of the story told in Hos 1–3 (see note on Ex 34:15).

3:21 *barren heights.* See note on v. 2. *weeping and pleading.* A description of repentance, verbalized in vv. 22b–25. *forgotten.* See note on 2:32.
3:22 See v. 14. *Return, faithless … backsliding.* Each of these three words is derived from the same Hebrew root, producing a striking series of puns. *I will cure you.* See 30:17; 33:6; Hos 6:1; 14:4. *Yes.* The people's repentance begins.
3:23 *commotion.* See, e.g., 1Ki 18:25–29. *in the Lᴏʀᴅ … is … salvation.* See Ge 49:18; Ps 3:8; Jnh 2:9 and note.
3:24 *our youth.* The period of the judges. *shameful gods.* See notes on 2:26; 11:13. *consumed the fruits.* False worship is costly, both financially and spiritually. *sons and daughters.* Often sacrificed to pagan gods (see note on 7:31).
3:25 *shame.* The Hebrew for this word is translated "shameful gods" in v. 24.
4:1 *go astray.* The Hebrew for this word implies wandering, as in Ge 4:12,14 (see TNIV text note on Ge 4:16).

4:2 ^cDt 10:20;
S Isa 19:18; 65:16
^dS Nu 14:21; Jer 5:2;
12:16; 44:26; Hos 4:15
^eS Ge 12:2; Gal 3:8
^fJer 9:24
4:3 ^gHos 10:12
^hMk 4:18
4:4 ⁱS Lev 26:41
^jZep 1:18; 2:2
^kS Job 41:21
^lS Isa 1:31; Am 5:6
^mIsa 1:31; Am 5:6
4:5 ⁿJer 5:20; 11:2,6
^oS ver 21; S Nu 10:2,
7; S Job 39:24
^pS Jos 10:20
4:6 ^qver 21; Ps 74:4;
S Isa 11:10; 31:9;
Jer 50:2 ^rJer 11:11;
18:11 ^sS Isa 14:31;
Jer 50:3
4:7 ^tS 2Ki 24:1;
S Jer 2:15 ^uJer 25:38;
Hos 5:14; 13:7;
Na 2:12 ^vJer 6:26;
15:8; 22:7; 48:8; 51:1,
53; Eze 21:31; 25:7
^wS Isa 1:7; Eze 12:20
^xver 29; S Lev 26:31;
S Isa 6:11
4:8 ^y1Ki 21:27;
S Isa 3:24; Jer 6:26;
Eze 7:18; Joel 1:8
^zJer 7:29; 9:20;
Am 5:1 ^aS Isa 10:4;
S Jer 30:24
4:9 ^bS 1Sa 17:32
^cS Isa 29:9
4:10 ^dS Ex 5:23;
2Th 2:11 ^eIsa 30:10;
Jer 6:14; 8:11; 14:13;
23:17; Eze 13:10;
Mic 3:5; 1Th 5:3

²and if in a truthful, just and righteous way
    you swear, ^c 'As surely as the LORD lives,' ^d
then the nations will invoke blessings ^e by him
    and in him they will boast. ^f"

³This is what the LORD says to the people of Judah and to Jerusalem:

"Break up your unplowed ground ^g
    and do not sow among thorns. ^h
⁴Circumcise yourselves to the LORD,
    circumcise your hearts, ⁱ
you people of Judah and inhabitants of Jerusalem,
or my wrath ^j will flare up and burn like fire ^k
    because of the evil ^l you have done—
    burn with no one to quench ^m it.

DISASTER FROM THE NORTH

⁵"Announce in Judah and proclaim ⁿ in Jerusalem and say:
    'Sound the trumpet ^o throughout the land!'
Cry aloud and say:
    'Gather together!
    Let us flee to the fortified cities!' ^p
⁶Raise the signal ^q to go to Zion!
    Flee for safety without delay!
For I am bringing disaster ^r from the north, ^s
    even terrible destruction."

⁷A lion ^t has come out of his lair; ^u
    a destroyer ^v of nations has set out.
He has left his place
    to lay waste ^w your land.
Your towns will lie in ruins ^x
    without inhabitant.
⁸So put on sackcloth, ^y
    lament ^z and wail,
for the fierce anger ^a of the LORD
    has not turned away from us.

⁹"In that day," declares the LORD,
    "the king and the officials will lose heart, ^b
the priests will be horrified,
    and the prophets will be appalled." ^c

¹⁰Then I said, "Ah, Sovereign LORD, how completely you have deceived ^d this people and Jerusalem by saying, 'You will have peace,' ^e when the sword is at our throats."

4:2 *truthful, just and righteous.* The piling up of qualifying words underscores the need for repentance that is sincere and not perfunctory. *As surely as the LORD lives.* See note on Ge 42:15. *nations will invoke blessings by him.* Reflects the language of the seventh of God's great promises to Abram (see Ge 12:2–3 and note). Israel's repentance is a necessary precondition for the ultimate blessing of the nations.

4:3 *Break up your unplowed ground.* Probably quoted from Hos 10:12. *do not sow among thorns.* See Mt 13:7,22. Openness to the Lord's overtures is necessary, as is total commitment to him (see Eze 18:31).

4:4 *circumcise your hearts.* Consecrate your hearts (see 6:10 and TNIV text note; 9:26; see also Ge 17:10 and note; Dt 10:16; 30:6; cf. Ro 2:29 and note; 1Co 7:19; Col 2:11). *wrath will ... burn with no one to quench.* See 21:12; see also Isa 1:31; Am 5:6 and note. *because of the evil you have done.* Probably quoted from Dt 28:20.

4:5–31 The invaders from the north will bring God's judgment against his unrepentant people (see ch. 6).

4:5 *Sound the trumpet.* To warn of impending doom (see 6:1; see also note on Joel 2:1). *flee to the fortified cities.* See v. 6. To

avoid capture by hostile troops, people living in the countryside would take refuge in the nearest walled town (see 5:17; 8:14; 34:7; 48:18).

4:6 *Raise the signal.* See note on Isa 5:26. *disaster from the north.* See 1:14; 6:22; the Babylonians (see 25:9; Isa 41:25 and notes). *terrible destruction.* See 6:1; cf. 48:3; 50:22; 51:54.

4:7 *lion.* A symbol of Babylon (see note on 2:15). *destroyer.* Usually refers to Babylon (6:26; 15:8; 48:8,32), but in 51:1,56 it refers to Persia and her allies (see 51:48,53). *towns ... without inhabitant.* See note on 2:15; see also v. 25; 46:19.

4:8 *sackcloth.* See notes on Ge 37:34; Rev 11:3. *anger ... has not turned away.* Contrast 2:35.

4:9 *In that day.* See note on Isa 2:11,17,20. *king ... officials ... priests ... prophets.* See note on 1:18.

4:10 *you have deceived.* Not directly, but through false prophets (see, e.g., 1Ki 22:20–23 and note on 22:23). *You will have peace.* Here the words of false prophets, not of God (see 14:13; 23:17; see also 6:13–14; 8:10–11). *throats.* The Hebrew for this word is usually translated "soul" or "life," but originally it had the meaning "throat, neck" (see, e.g., Ps 69:1).

4:11 ^fS Ge 41:6;
S Lev 26:33;
S Job 1:19
4:12 ^gS Isa 64:6
^hJer 1:16
4:13 ⁱS 2Sa 22:10;
Isa 19:1 / Isa 66:15;
Eze 26:10; Na 2:4
^kS 2Ki 2:1 / Hab 3:8
^mS Dt 28:49; Hab 1:8
ⁿver 20, 27; Isa 6:11;
24:3; Jer 7:34; 9:11,
19; 12:11; 25:11; 44:6;
Mic 2:4
4:14 ^oS Ru 3:3;
S Ps 51:2; Jas 4:8
^pIsa 45:22 ^qS Ps 6:3
4:15 ^rS Ge 30:6
^sJer 31:6
4:16 ^tS Dt 28:49
^uver 19; Eze 21:22
^vS Jer 1:15
4:17 ^wS 2Ki 25:1,4
^xS 1Sa 12:15; Jer 5:23
4:18 ^yPs 107:17;
S Isa 1:28; Jer 5:25
^zJer 2:17 ^aJer 2:19
4:19 ^bIsa 22:4;
Jer 6:24; 9:10; La 1:20
^cS Job 6:10; S 14:22;
Jer 10:19 ^dS Job 37:1;
Jer 23:9 ^eS Job 4:2;
Jer 20:9 ^fS ver 21;
S Nu 10:2;
S Job 39:24
^gS ver 16; Nu 10:9;
Jer 49:2; Zep 1:16
4:20 ^hS Dt 31:17
ⁱS ver 13 ^jS Nu 24:5;
Jer 10:20; La 2:4
4:21 ^kS ver 6;
S Nu 2:2; S Isa 18:3
^lver 5,19; S Jos 6:20;
Jer 6:1; Hos 5:8;
Am 3:6; Zep 1:16
4:22 ^mJer 5:21; 10:8
ⁿS Isa 1:3; 27:11;
Jer 2:8; 8:7; Hos 5:4;
6:6 ^oS Ps 14:4; S 53:2

¹¹At that time this people and Jerusalem will be told, "A scorching wind ^f from the barren heights in the desert blows toward my people, but not to winnow or cleanse; ¹²a wind ^g too strong for that comes from me.^a Now I pronounce my judgments ^h against them."

¹³Look! He advances like the clouds, ⁱ
  his chariots ^j come like a whirlwind, ^k
  his horses ^l are swifter than eagles. ^m
  Woe to us! We are ruined! ⁿ
¹⁴Jerusalem, wash ^o the evil from your heart and be saved. ^p
  How long ^q will you harbor wicked thoughts?
¹⁵A voice is announcing from Dan, ^r
  proclaiming disaster from the hills of Ephraim. ^s
¹⁶"Tell this to the nations,
  proclaim concerning Jerusalem:
  'A besieging army is coming from a distant land, ^t
  raising a war cry ^u against the cities of Judah. ^v
¹⁷They surround ^w her like people guarding a field,
  because she has rebelled ^x against me,' "
                                                     declares the LORD.

¹⁸"Your own conduct and actions ^y
  have brought this on you. ^z
  This is your punishment.
  How bitter ^a it is!
  How it pierces to the heart!"

¹⁹Oh, my anguish, my anguish! ^b
  I writhe in pain. ^c
  Oh, the agony of my heart!
  My heart pounds ^d within me,
  I cannot keep silent. ^e
  For I have heard the sound of the trumpet; ^f
  I have heard the battle cry. ^g
²⁰Disaster follows disaster; ^h
  the whole land lies in ruins. ⁱ
  In an instant my tents ^j are destroyed,
  my shelter in a moment.
²¹How long must I see the battle standard ^k
  and hear the sound of the trumpet? ^l

²²"My people are fools; ^m
  they do not know me. ⁿ
  They are senseless children;
  they have no understanding. ^o

^a 12 Or *comes at my command*

4:11 *scorching wind.* The sirocco or khamsin, a hot, dry wind that brings sand and dust (see Ps 11:6; Isa 11:15; Jnh 4:8). *winnow.* See note on Ru 1:22.
4:12 *too strong for that.* Neither winnowing (separating grain from chaff) nor cleansing (blowing dust from the grain), God's judgments will sweep away good and bad alike.
4:13 *advances like the clouds.* Cf. Eze 38:16. *chariots . . . like a whirlwind.* See 2Ki 2:11; 6:17; Ps 68:17; Isa 66:15. *horses are swifter than eagles.* See Hab 1:8, where the Babylonians (Hab 1:6) use horses that are "swifter than leopards" and employ cavalry that "fly like a vulture" (the Hebrew word for "vulture" is translated "eagle" here; see Dt 28:49). *ruined.* See v. 20; 9:19; 48:1.
4:14 *Jerusalem.* As the royal city of Judah and the most important metropolis of the nation, Jerusalem is addressed as representative of the nation. *wash.* See 2:22 and note. *wicked thoughts.* Against other people (see Pr 6:18; Isa 59:7).
4:15 *Dan.* Far away, close to the northern border of Israel (see 8:16). *Ephraim.* A few miles north of Jerusalem. The enemy, in the mind's eye of the prophet, is making fearfully rapid progress toward the holy city.

4:16 *besieging army.* See Isa 1:8. *distant land.* Babylon. *raising a war cry.* The Hebrew underlying this phrase is translated "growled" in 2:15.
4:17 *surround her.* See 1:15.
4:19–26 A brief personal interlude, broken only by the divine complaint in v. 22. Jeremiah voices his agony at the approaching destruction of his beloved land and its people.
4:19 See 10:19–20. *anguish.* Often associated with labor pangs, as here (see 6:24; 49:24; 50:43). *heart pounds.* See Job 37:1; Ps 38:10; Hab 3:16. *sound of the trumpet.* See note on v. 5.
4:20 *lies in ruins.* See v. 13; 9:19; 48:1. *shelter.* Lit. "tent curtains" (as in Isa 54:2), usually made of goat hair (see Ex 26:7) and therefore strong enough to protect from cold and rain (see 10:20).
4:21 *battle standard . . . sound of the trumpet.* See notes on vv. 5–6.
4:22 The Lord speaks. *fools.* See TNIV text note on Pr 1:7. *do not know me.* See 2:8. Leaders and people alike had committed the ultimate sin (see Isa 1:2–3; Hos 4:1). *senseless.* See 5:21; 10:8,14,21; 51:17. *skilled in doing evil.* See Mic 7:3. *know not how to do good.* See Ps 14:1–3 and note on 14:1.

They are skilled in doing evil;[p]
    they know not how to do good."[q]

23 I looked at the earth,
    and it was formless and empty;[r]
and at the heavens,
    and their light[s] was gone.
24 I looked at the mountains,
    and they were quaking;[t]
all the hills were swaying.
25 I looked, and there were no people;
    every bird in the sky had flown away.[u]
26 I looked, and the fruitful land was a desert;[v]
    all its towns lay in ruins[w]
before the LORD, before his fierce anger.[x]

27 This is what the LORD says:

"The whole land will be ruined,[y]
    though I will not destroy[z] it completely.
28 Therefore the earth will mourn[a]
    and the heavens above grow dark,[b]
because I have spoken and will not relent,[c]
    I have decided and will not turn back.[d]"

29 At the sound of horsemen and archers[e]
    every town takes to flight.[f]
Some go into the thickets;
    some climb up among the rocks.[g]
All the towns are deserted;[h]
    no one lives in them.

30 What are you doing,[i] you devastated one?
    Why dress yourself in scarlet
    and put on jewels[j] of gold?
Why color your eyes with paint?[k]
    You adorn yourself in vain.
Your lovers[l] despise you;
    they seek your life.[m]

31 I hear a cry as of a woman in labor,[n]
    a groan as of one bearing her first child—
the cry of Daughter Zion[o] gasping for breath,[p]
    stretching out her hands[q] and saying,
"Alas! I am fainting;
    my life is given over to murderers."[r]

4:22 [p] Jer 13:23;
S 1Co 14:20
[q] S Ps 36:3
4:23 [r] S Ge 1:2
[s] ver 28; S Job 9:7;
30:26; S Isa 5:30;
59:9; La 3:2
4:24 [t] S Ex 19:18;
S Job 9:6
4:25 [u] Jer 7:20; 9:10;
12:4; Hos 4:3; Zep 1:3
4:26 [v] S Ge 13:10;
Jer 12:4; 23:10
[w] S Isa 6:11
[x] Jer 12:13; 25:38
4:27 [y] S ver 13
[z] S Lev 26:44;
Jer 5:10,18; 12:12;
30:11; 46:28;
Eze 20:17; Am 9:8
4:28 [a] Jer 12:4,11;
14:2; Hos 4:3
[b] S ver 23
[c] S Nu 23:19 [d] ver 8;
Jer 23:20; 30:24
4:29 [e] S ver 13;
Jer 6:23; 8:16
[f] 2Ki 25:4
[g] S Ex 33:22;
S 1Sa 26:20 [h] S ver 7;
S Isa 6:12
4:30 [i] Isa 10:3-4
[j] Eze 16:11; 23:40
[k] S 2Ki 9:30
[l] Job 19:14; La 1:2;
Eze 23:9,22
[m] S Ps 35:4
4:31 [n] S Ge 3:16;
Jer 6:24; 13:21; 22:23;
30:6; Mic 4:10
[o] S Ps 9:14 [p] Isa 42:14
[q] Isa 1:15; La 1:17
[r] S Dt 32:25; La 2:21

4:23–26 The striking repetition of "I looked" at the beginning of each verse ties this poem together and underscores its visionary character, as the prophet sees his beloved land in ruins after the Babylonian onslaught. Creation, as it were, has been reversed.
4:23 *formless and empty.* The phrase occurs elsewhere only in Ge 1:2 (see note there). In Jeremiah's vision, the primeval chaos has returned. *light was gone.* Contrast Ge 1:3.
4:24 See Na 1:5.
4:25 *there were no people.* The Hebrew underlying this phrase occurs elsewhere only in Ge 2:5, where it is translated "there was no one." Again, uncreation has replaced creation.
4:26 *fruitful land.* See note on 2:7. *fierce anger.* See v. 8; Isa 13:13; Na 1:6.
4:27 *not destroy it completely.* See 5:10,18; 30:11; 46:28. God's mercy tempers the total judgment envisioned by Jeremiah in vv. 23–26.
4:28 *will not relent.* Unless his people repent (see 18:7–10 and note).

4:29 *archers.* Babylon's evil deeds against Judah will someday recoil on her (see 50:29). *Some go.* See Jdg 6:2; 1Sa 13:6; Isa 2:19,21. Even people living in fortified towns feel unsafe. *deserted.* Contrast Isa 62:4.
4:30 *you ... yourself.* All the second person pronouns in this verse represent feminine pronouns or verbs in Hebrew, indicating that Jerusalem is being addressed (see v. 14 and note). She is here portrayed as an adulterous wife trying to allure her lovers. *paint.* Antimony, a black powder used to enlarge the eyes and make them more attractive (see 2Ki 9:30; Eze 23:40). *lovers.* The Hebrew root underlying this word is found elsewhere only in Eze 23:5,7,9,12,16,20, where it is used of Samaria and Jerusalem, the adulterous sisters (see notes on Jer 2:25; 3:1,7) who "lusted" after foreign nations and their gods. *seek your life.* They are intent only on murdering you (see v. 31).
4:31 *woman in labor.* See 6:24; 13:21; 22:23; 30:6; 31:8; 48:41; 49:22,24; 50:43; see also v. 19; Isa 13:8 and notes. *Daughter Zion.* A personification of Jerusalem (see note on 2Ki 19:21). *stretching out her hands.* In prayer for help (see Job 11:13).

NOT ONE IS UPRIGHT

5 "Go up and down ˢ the streets of Jerusalem,
    look around and consider, ᵗ
    search through her squares.
If you can find but one person ᵘ
    who deals honestly ᵛ and seeks the truth,
    I will forgive ʷ this city.
² Although they say, 'As surely as the LORD lives,' ˣ
    still they are swearing falsely. ʸ

³ LORD, do not your eyes ᶻ look for truth?
    You struck ᵃ them, but they felt no pain;
    you crushed them, but they refused correction. ᵇ
They made their faces harder than stone ᶜ
    and refused to repent. ᵈ
⁴ I thought, "These are only the poor;
    they are foolish, ᵉ
for they do not know ᶠ the way of the LORD,
    the requirements of their God.
⁵ So I will go to the leaders ᵍ
    and speak to them;
surely they know the way of the LORD,
    the requirements of their God."
But with one accord they too had broken off the yoke
    and torn off the bonds. ʰ
⁶ Therefore a lion from the forest ⁱ will attack them,
    a wolf from the desert will ravage ʲ them,
a leopard ᵏ will lie in wait near their towns
    to tear to pieces any who venture out,
for their rebellion is great
    and their backslidings many. ˡ

⁷ "Why should I forgive you?
    Your children have forsaken me
    and sworn ᵐ by gods that are not gods. ⁿ
I supplied all their needs,
    yet they committed adultery ᵒ
    and thronged to the houses of prostitutes. ᵖ
⁸ They are well-fed, lusty stallions,
    each neighing for another man's wife. q
⁹ Should I not punish them for this?" ʳ
    declares the LORD.
"Should I not avenge ˢ myself
    on such a nation as this?

¹⁰ "Go through her vineyards and ravage them,
    but do not destroy them completely. ᵗ

5:1–31 Jeremiah resumes his vivid description of the wickedness of the people of Judah and Jerusalem.

5:1 See Zep 1:12. The Lord challenges anyone to find just one righteous person in Israel—a rhetorical way of charging that corruption pervaded the city (see Ps 14:1–3; Isa 64:6–7; Hos 4:1–2; Mic 7:2). *If you can find . . . I will forgive.* See Ge 18:26–32.
5:2 *As surely as the LORD lives.* See 4:2; see also Ge 42:15 and note. *they are swearing falsely.* In violation of Lev 19:12 (see note on Ex 20:7). The Hebrew underlying this phrase is translated "commit . . . perjury" in 7:9 (see TNIV text note there).
5:3 *refused correction.* See 2:30. *made their faces harder than stone.* A striking portrayal of rebellion (see Eze 3:7–9).
5:4 *poor.* Concerned about basic physical needs (cf. 39:10; 40:7), they are uninformed of God's word and way. *foolish.* See 4:22; see also Nu 12:11 and TNIV text note on Pr 1:7. *do not know . . . requirements of their God.* They are more ignorant than the birds of the heavens (see 8:7).
5:5 *leaders.* Lit. "great ones." Although possessing every advan-

tage, they were no more righteous than the poorest of the common people. *broken . . . bonds.* See note on 2:20.
5:6 *lion . . . wolf . . . leopard.* See Lev 26:22; Eze 14:15; cf. 2Ki 17:25–26. *lie in wait.* The Hebrew for this phrase is translated "watching" in 1:12. *backslidings.* See 2:19; 3:22; 14:7. The word implies repeated apostasy.
5:7 *Why should I forgive you?* See v. 1. *Your children.* Jerusalem is depicted as the "mother" city of the nation. *gods that are not gods.* Idols (see 2:11). *I supplied . . . yet they.* See Dt 32:15–16; Hos 2:8. *committed adultery.* See 2:25 and note.
5:8 *lusty stallions.* See 13:27; 50:11; Eze 23:20.
5:9 *Should I not punish . . . such a nation as this?* Repeated in v. 29; 9:9.
5:10 *Go.* Addressed to Israel's enemies (see v. 15). *vineyards.* Vines and vineyards are often symbolic of Israel (see notes on 2:21; Isa 5:1). *not destroy them completely.* See v. 18; see also note on 4:27. *Strip off her branches.* See Isa 18:5; Jn 15:2,6. *people do not belong to the LORD.* See Hos 1:9.

Strip off her branches,
for these people do not belong to the LORD.
¹¹ The house of Israel and the house of Judah
have been utterly unfaithful ᵘ to me,"

declares the LORD.

¹² They have lied ᵛ about the LORD;
they said, "He will do nothing!
No harm will come to us; ʷ
we will never see sword or famine. ˣ
¹³ The prophets ʸ are but wind ᶻ
and the word is not in them;
so let what they say be done to them."

¹⁴Therefore this is what the LORD God Almighty says:

"Because the people have spoken these words,
I will make my words in your mouth ᵃ a fire ᵇ
and these people the wood it consumes. ᶜ
¹⁵ House of Israel," declares the LORD,
"I am bringing a distant nation ᵈ against you—
an ancient and enduring nation,
a people whose language ᵉ you do not know,
whose speech you do not understand.
¹⁶ Their quivers ᶠ are like an open grave;
all of them are mighty warriors.
¹⁷ They will devour ᵍʰ your harvests and food,
devour ⁱʲ your sons and daughters;
they will devour ᵏ your flocks and herds,
devour your vines and fig trees. ˡ
With the sword ᵐ they will destroy
the fortified cities ⁿ in which you trust. ᵒ

¹⁸"Yet even in those days," declares the LORD, "I will not destroy ᵖ you completely. ¹⁹And when the people ask, �q 'Why has the LORD our God done all this to us?' you will tell them, 'As you have forsaken me and served foreign gods ʳ in your own land, so now you will serve foreigners ˢ in a land not your own.'

²⁰ "Announce this to the house of Jacob
and proclaim ᵗ it in Judah:
²¹ Hear this, you foolish and senseless people, ᵘ
who have eyes ᵛ but do not see,
who have ears but do not hear; ʷ
²² Should you not fear ˣ me?" declares the LORD.
"Should you not tremble ʸ in my presence?
I made the sand a boundary for the sea, ᶻ
an everlasting barrier it cannot cross.
The waves may roll, but they cannot prevail;
they may roar, ᵃ but they cannot cross it.
²³ But these people have stubborn and rebellious ᵇ hearts;
they have turned aside ᶜ and gone away.
²⁴ They do not say to themselves,

5:11 ᵘS 1Ki 19:10; S Ps 73:27; S Isa 24:16
5:12 ᵛIsa 28:15; ʷJer 23:17 ˣJer 14:13; 27:8
5:13 ʸJer 14:15; ᶻS 2Ch 36:16; S Job 6:26
5:14 ᵃHos 6:5; ᵇS Ps 39:3; Jer 23:29; ᶜS Isa 1:31
5:15 ᵈS Dt 28:49; S 2Ki 24:2; ᵉS Ge 11:7; S Isa 28:11
5:16 ᶠS Job 39:23
5:17 ᵍS Isa 1:7; Jer 8:16; 30:16; ʰLev 26:16 ⁱJer 50:7, 17 ʲDt 28:32; ᵏDt 28:31; ˡS Nu 16:14; Jer 8:13; Hos 2:12; ᵐS Lev 26:25; ⁿS Jos 10:20; ᵒDt 28:33
5:18 ᵖS Jer 4:27
5:19 �q S Dt 4:28; S 1Ki 9:9 ʳS Jer 2:8; 15:14; 16:13; 17:4; ˢDt 28:48
5:20 ᵗS Jer 4:5
5:21 ᵘver 4; S Dt 32:6; S Jer 4:22; Hab 2:18 ᵛIsa 6:10; Eze 12:2 ʷS Dt 29:4; S Isa 42:20; S Mt 13:15; Mk 8:18
5:22 ˣS Dt 28:58; ʸS Job 4:14; S Isa 64:2 ᶻS Ge 1:9; ᵃS Ps 46:3
5:23 ᵇS Dt 21:18; ᶜPs 14:3

5:11 See note on 3:7.
5:12 *He will do nothing.* Either good or bad (see Zep 1:12). *sword or famine.* Jeremiah introduces us to the first two elements of his characteristic triad: "sword, famine and plague" (see note on 14:12).
5:13 *prophets are but wind.* Like images of false gods (see Isa 41:29). *let what they say be done to them.* See note on 4:29; see also Ps 7:16; 54:5.
5:14 *my words in your mouth a fire.* In contrast to the total lack of God's word in the mouths of false prophets (v. 13). See 20:9 and note. *consumes.* See note on Isa 1:31.
5:15 *distant nation.* See note on 4:16. *ancient and enduring nation.* Babylon's history reached back 2,000 years and more. *whose language you do not know.* See Dt 28:49 and note.

5:16 *open grave.* Symbolizing insatiability, destruction and death (see Ps 5:9; Pr 30:15–16).
5:17 *devour your sons and daughters.* Either as sacrifices to pagan gods (see note on 3:24) or as casualties of war (see 10:25). *fortified cities in which you trust.* See note on 4:5; see also Dt 28:52.
5:18 See v. 10; see also note on 4:27.
5:21 *Hear this.* See note on 2:4. *foolish and senseless.* See 4:22; see also TNIV text note on Pr 1:7. *who have eyes ... do not hear.* See note on Isa 6:10; see also Dt 29:4; Ps 115:4–8; 135:15–18.
5:22 *fear me.* See note on Ge 20:11. *boundary for the sea.* See Job 38:8–11; Ps 104:6–9.
5:23 Though the sea never crosses its divinely appointed boundaries, God's people have violated the limits he has set for them.

5:24 ^dDt 6:24
^eS Lev 26:4;
S 2Sa 1:21; Jas 5:7
^fS Ge 8:22; Am 14:17
5:25 ^gPs 84:11
5:26 ^hS Mt 7:15
ⁱS Ps 10:8 / Ecc 9:12;
Jer 9:8; Hos 5:1;
Mic 7:2
5:27 ^kJer 8:5; 9:6
^jJer 12:1
5:28 ^mS Dt 32:15
ⁿZec 7:10 ^oEx 22:21-
24; S Ps 82:3;
S Isa 1:23; Jer 7:6;
Eze 16:49; Am 5:12
5:29 ^pS Isa 57:6
5:30 ^qver 30-31;
Jer 18:13; 23:14;
Hos 6:10
5:31 ^rS ver 1;
Mic 2:11 ^sLa 4:13
^tHos 9:5
6:1 ^uS Nu 10:7;
S Jer 4:21 ^v2Ch 11:6;
Am 1:1 ^wNe 3:14
^xS Jer 4:6
6:2 ^yS Ps 9:14
^zLa 4:5
6:3 ^aJer 12:10
^bS 2Ki 25:4; Lk 19:43

'Let us fear ^d the L<small>ORD</small> our God,
who gives autumn and spring rains ^e in season,
who assures us of the regular weeks of harvest.' ^f
²⁵ Your wrongdoings have kept these away;
your sins have deprived you of good. ^g

²⁶ "Among my people are the wicked ^h
who lie in wait ⁱ like those who snare birds
and like those who set traps ^j to catch people.
²⁷ Like cages full of birds,
their houses are full of deceit; ^k
they have become rich ^l and powerful
²⁸   and have grown fat ^m and sleek.
Their evil deeds have no limit;
they do not seek justice.
They do not promote the case of the fatherless; ⁿ
they do not defend the just cause of the poor. ^o
²⁹ Should I not punish them for this?"
declares the L<small>ORD</small>.
"Should I not avenge ^p myself
on such a nation as this?

³⁰ "A horrible ^q and shocking thing
has happened in the land:
³¹ The prophets prophesy lies, ^r
the priests ^s rule by their own authority,
and my people love it this way.
But what will you do in the end? ^t

JERUSALEM UNDER SIEGE

"Flee for safety, people of Benjamin!
Flee from Jerusalem!
Sound the trumpet ^u in Tekoa! ^v
Raise the signal over Beth Hakkerem! ^w
For disaster looms out of the north, ^x
even terrible destruction.
² I will destroy Daughter Zion, ^y
so beautiful and delicate. ^z
³ Shepherds ^a with their flocks will come against her;
they will pitch their tents around ^b her,
each of them tending their own portion."

5:24 *God, who gives.* See v. 7 and note. *autumn and spring rains.* See 3:3; see also note on Dt 11:14. *regular weeks of harvest.* Perhaps the seven weeks between Passover and the Festival of Weeks (see Lev 23:15–16).
5:26 *traps.* Lit. "destroyer" (see, e.g., Ex 12:23) or "destruction" (see, e.g., Eze 21:31). *people.* Innocent (see Isa 29:21), godly, upright people (see Mic 7:2).
5:27 *cages.* Traps woven of wicker; the Hebrew for this word is translated "basket" in Am 8:1–2. *deceit.* Riches gained through extortion and deception (see Hab 2:6).
5:28 *grown fat and sleek.* Symbolic of prosperity (see Dt 32:15; Jas 5:5 and note). *evil deeds have no limit.* See Ps 73:7. *They do not promote the case.* What the wicked will not do, God must do (see Dt 10:18)—and so must those who truly know and serve him (see 22:16; Jas 1:27).
5:29 Repeated from v. 9; see also 9:9.
5:31 See 1:18 and note. *prophesy lies.* See 20:6 (often, and arrogantly, in God's name; see 23:25; 27:15; 29:9). *my people love it this way.* See note on Am 4:5.
6:1–30 The prophet envisions the future Babylonian attack on Jerusalem.
6:1 The Lord speaks in vv. 1–3. Verse 1 is strongly reminiscent of 4:6 (see note there). But whereas in 4:6 the

command was to seek protection in Jerusalem, in 6:1 the people are to flee from Jerusalem, because no place—not even the holy city itself—will be safe from the invader. *Benjamin.* The tribal territory bordering Judah north of Jerusalem. Jeremiah himself was from Benjamite territory (see 1:1). *Sound . . . Tekoa.* In the Hebrew there is a play on these words. Tekoa was the hometown of Amos (see Introduction to Amos: Author). *Raise . . . signal.* In the Hebrew there is a play on words, made possible by using a different Hebrew word (found also in Lachish Letter 4:10) for "signal" (caused by the smoke of a fire; see Jdg 20:38, 40) than the one used in 4:6. *Beth Hakkerem.* Mentioned elsewhere only in Ne 3:14 (see note there). *disaster . . . out of the north.* See 1:14 and note.
6:2 *Daughter Zion.* A personification of Jerusalem (see note on 2Ki 19:21). *delicate.* Used to describe the city of Babylon in Isa 47:1.
6:3 See 1:15. *Shepherds with their flocks.* Rulers (see note on 2:8) with their troops. *pitch.* The Hebrew for this verb continues the pun on "Tekoa" in v. 1 (see note on v. 8). *each . . . their own portion.* The Hebrew for this phrase is used similarly ("each . . . their own place") in Nu 2:17. *tending.* Grazing or depasturing, and thus destroying.

4 "Prepare for battle against her!
  Arise, let us attack at noon![c]
But, alas, the daylight is fading,
  and the shadows of evening grow long.
5 So arise, let us attack at night
  and destroy her fortresses!"

6 This is what the LORD Almighty says:

"Cut down the trees[d]
  and build siege ramps[e] against Jerusalem.
This city must be punished;
  it is filled with oppression.[f]
7 As a well pours out its water,
  so she pours out her wickedness.
Violence[g] and destruction[h] resound in her;
  her sickness and wounds are ever before me.
8 Take warning, Jerusalem,
  or I will turn away[i] from you
and make your land desolate
  so no one can live in it."

9 This is what the LORD Almighty says:

"Let them glean the remnant[j] of Israel
  as thoroughly as a vine;
pass your hand over the branches again,
  like one gathering grapes."

10 To whom can I speak and give warning?
  Who will listen[k] to me?
Their ears are closed[a][l]
  so they cannot hear.[m]
The word[n] of the LORD is offensive to them;
  they find no pleasure in it.
11 But I am full of the wrath[o] of the LORD,
  and I cannot hold it in.[p]

"Pour it out on the children in the street
  and on the youths[q] gathered together;
both husband and wife will be caught in it,
  and the old, those weighed down with years.[r]
12 Their houses will be turned over to others,[s]
  together with their fields and their wives,[t]
when I stretch out my hand[u]
  against those who live in the land,"

declares the LORD.

a 10 Hebrew *uncircumcised*

6:4 c Jer 15:8; 22:7
6:6 d Dt 20:19-20
e S 2Sa 20:15;
Jer 32:24; 52:4;
Eze 26:8 f S Dt 28:33;
Jer 25:38; Zep 3:1
6:7 g Ps 55:9;
S Isa 58:4 h Jer 20:8
6:8 i Eze 23:18
6:9 j S Ge 45:7
6:10 k Jer 7:13,24;
35:15 l Jer 4:4; Ac 7:51
m S Isa 42:20
n Jer 15:10,15; 20:8
6:11 o Jer 7:20;
15:17 p Job 32:20;
Jer 20:9
q S 2Ch 36:17;
S Isa 40:30 r La 2:21
6:12 s S Dt 28:30;
Mic 2:4 t 1Ki 11:4;
Jer 8:10; 29:23; 38:22;
43:6; 44:9,15
u Isa 5:25; Jer 21:5;
32:21; Eze 6:14; 35:3;
Zep 1:4

6:4 The invaders speak in vv. 4–5. *Prepare for.* Lit. "Consecrate" (also in Joel 3:9; Mic 3:5). Since ancient battles had religious connotations, soldiers had to prepare themselves ritually, as well as militarily (see Dt 20:2–4; 1Sa 21:4 and note). *at noon.* To take advantage of the element of surprise, since the usual time of attack was early in the morning (see, e.g., Jos 8:10,14).
6:5 *at night.* Since attacking soldiers normally retired for the night and resumed siege the following morning, the phrase underscores their eagerness and determination (see Jdg 7:19 and note).
6:6 The Lord addresses the Babylonian troops. *siege ramps.* To help them bring up battering rams and scale Jerusalem's walls (see 33:4). *oppression.* Against its own people (see note on Isa 30:12).
6:7 *sickness and wounds.* Jerusalem suffers from spiritual decay and disease (see v. 14) and is not aware of it.
6:8 *Take warning.* The better part of wisdom (see v. 10; Ps 2:10). *turn away.* In sorrow, but also in disgust. The Hebrew for this phrase continues the pun on "Tekoa" in v. 1 (see note on v. 3). *desolate so no one can live in it.* See 22:6.

6:9 *glean.* See notes on Ru 2:2; Isa 17:5. *remnant.* See 11:23; 23:3; 31:7; 40:11,15; 42:2,15,19; 43:5; 44:7,12,14,28; 50:20; see also note on Isa 10:20–22. *thoroughly.* Stopping just short of complete destruction (see 4:27; 5:10,18; 30:11; 46:28). *vine.* Symbolic of Israel (see 2:21 and note; 5:10).
6:10 Jeremiah speaks. *give warning.* See note on v. 8. *ears are closed.* See TNIV text note; see also 4:4 and note. The imagery of uncircumcised ears is found elsewhere only in Ac 7:51 (see note there).
6:11 The prophet speaks, then the Lord resumes his speech (through v. 23). *full of the wrath.* See 25:15 and note. *children . . . youths . . . husband and wife . . . old.* All will be judged, from youngest to oldest (see v. 13). *in the street.* Where children play (see 9:21; Zec 8:5).
6:12–15 Repeated almost verbatim in 8:10–12.
6:12 *houses . . . fields . . . wives.* Cf. Ex 20:17; Dt 5:21. *turned over to others.* As Dt 28:30 warned—one of the covenant curses. *stretch out my hand against.* To destroy (see 15:6).

6:13 ᵛS Jer 2:29
ʷS Isa 56:11 ˣLa 4:13
6:14 ʸS Isa 30:10;
S Jer 4:10
6:15 ᶻJer 3:3; 8:10-
12; Mic 3:7; Zec 13:4
ᵃ2Ch 25:16; Jer 27:15
6:16 ᵇJer 18:15
ᶜS 1Ki 8:36;
S Ps 119:3 ᵈS Jos 1:13;
S Isa 11:10; Mt 11:29
6:17 ᵉS Isa 52:8
ᶠS Ex 20:18 ᵍJer 11:7-
8; Eze 33:4; Zec 1:4
6:19 ʰS Dt 4:26;
Jer 22:29; Mic 1:2
ⁱS Jos 23:15; Jer 11:11;
19:3 / Pr 1:31
ᵏJer 29:19 ˡJer 8:9;
Eze 20:13; Am 2:4
6:20 ᵐS Ge 10:7
ⁿS Ex 30:23
ᵒAm 5:22; Mal 1:9
ᵖPs 50:8-10; Jer 7:21;
Mic 6:7-8 ᑫS Isa 1:11;
Jer 14:12; Hos 8:13;
9:4
6:21 ʳS Lev 26:37;
S Isa 8:14
6:22 ˢS Jer 4:6
ᵗS Dt 28:49
6:23 ᵘS Isa 13:18

13 "From the least to the greatest,
　　all ᵛ are greedy for gain; ʷ
prophets and priests alike,
　　all practice deceit. ˣ
14 They dress the wound of my people
　　as though it were not serious.
'Peace, peace,' they say,
　　when there is no peace. ʸ
15 Are they ashamed of their detestable conduct?
　　No, they have no shame at all;
　　they do not even know how to blush. ᶻ
So they will fall among the fallen;
　　they will be brought down when I punish ᵃ them,"
　　　　　　　　　　　　　　　　　　　　says the LORD.

16 This is what the LORD says:

"Stand at the crossroads and look;
　　ask for the ancient paths, ᵇ
ask where the good way ᶜ is, and walk in it,
　　and you will find rest ᵈ for your souls.
But you said, 'We will not walk in it.'
17 I appointed watchmen ᵉ over you and said,
　　'Listen to the sound of the trumpet!' ᶠ
But you said, 'We will not listen.' ᵍ
18 Therefore hear, you nations;
　　you who are witnesses,
　　observe what will happen to them.
19 Hear, you earth: ʰ
　　I am bringing disaster ⁱ on this people,
　　the fruit of their schemes, ʲ
because they have not listened to my words ᵏ
　　and have rejected my law. ˡ
20 What do I care about incense from Sheba ᵐ
　　or sweet calamus ⁿ from a distant land?
Your burnt offerings are not acceptable; ᵒ
　　your sacrifices ᵖ do not please me." ᑫ

21 Therefore this is what the LORD says:

"I will put obstacles before this people.
　　Parents and children alike will stumble ʳ over them;
　　neighbors and friends will perish."

22 This is what the LORD says:

"Look, an army is coming
　　from the land of the north; ˢ
a great nation is being stirred up
　　from the ends of the earth. ᵗ
23 They are armed with bow and spear;
　　they are cruel and show no mercy. ᵘ

6:13 See 1:18 and note.
6:14 *wound.* See note on v. 7. *Peace … when there is no peace.* A common message of false and greedy prophets (see Eze 13:10; Mic 3:5). The wicked, in any case, cannot expect to enjoy peace (Isa 48:22; 57:21).

6:16 *ancient paths.* The tried and true ways of Judah's godly ancestors (see 18:15; Dt 32:7). *walk in it.* See Isa 30:21. *you will find rest for your souls.* Quoted by Jesus in Mt 11:29 (see Isa 28:12; cf. Ps 119:165).
6:17 *watchmen.* True prophets (see Eze 3:17 and note; Hab 2:1). To warn of approaching danger (see v. 1; see also note on Joel 2:1).
6:18 *hear, you nations.* See Mic 1:2.
6:19 *rejected my law.* Disobeyed the law of Moses (see 8:8–9).

6:20 *Sheba.* Located in southwestern Arabia, it was the center of the spice trade (see Isa 60:6 and note). *calamus.* See Ex 25:6; SS 4:14; Isa 43:24 and notes. It probably came from India and was an ingredient in the sacred anointing oil (Ex 30:25). *burnt offerings are not acceptable.* The attitude of one's heart and the manner of one's life are far more important than the ritual of sacrifice (see note on Isa 1:11–15).
6:21 *obstacles.* The Babylonian invaders (see v. 22).
6:22–24 Repeated almost verbatim in 50:41–43.
6:22 *land of the north.* Babylonia (see 4:6; Isa 41:25 and notes). *from the ends of the earth.* See 25:32; 31:8.
6:23 *spear.* The Hebrew for this word is translated "javelin" in 1Sa 17:6. Another possibility is "sword," as attested in *The War of the Sons of Light against the Sons of Darkness,* one of the

They sound like the roaring sea ^{v}
  as they ride on their horses; ^{w}
they come like men in battle formation
  to attack you, Daughter Zion. ^{x} "

24 We have heard reports about them,
  and our hands hang limp. ^{y}
Anguish ^{z} has gripped us,
  pain like that of a woman in labor. ^{a}
25 Do not go out to the fields
  or walk on the roads,
for the enemy has a sword,
  and there is terror on every side. ^{b}
26 Put on sackcloth, ^{c} my people,
  and roll in ashes; ^{d}
mourn with bitter wailing ^{e}
  as for an only son, ^{f}
for suddenly the destroyer ^{g}
  will come upon us.

27 "I have made you a tester ^{h} of metals
  and my people the ore,
that you may observe
  and test their ways.
28 They are all hardened rebels, ^{i}
  going about to slander. ^{j}
They are bronze and iron; ^{k}
  they all act corruptly.
29 The bellows blow fiercely
  to burn away the lead with fire,
but the refining ^{l} goes on in vain;
  the wicked are not purged out.
30 They are called rejected silver, ^{m}
  because the LORD has rejected them." ^{n}

FALSE RELIGION WORTHLESS

7 This is the word that came to Jeremiah from the LORD: 2 "Stand ^{o} at the gate of the LORD's house and there proclaim this message:
" 'Hear the word of the LORD, all you people of Judah who come through these gates to worship the LORD. 3 This is what the LORD Almighty, the God of Israel, says: Reform your ways ^{p} and your actions, and I will let you live ^{q} in this place. 4 Do not trust ^{r} in

### Cross references (right margin)
6:23 ^{v} S Ps 18:4; S 93:3 ^{w} S Jer 4:29 ^{x} S Isa 10:32
6:24 ^{y} Isa 13:7 ^{z} S Jer 4:19 ^{a} S Jer 4:31; 50:41-43
6:25 ^{b} S Job 15:21; S Ps 31:13; Jer 49:29
6:26 ^{c} S Jer 4:8 ^{d} S Job 2:8; Jer 25:34; Eze 27:30; Jnh 3:6 ^{e} Jer 9:1; 18:22; 20:16; 25:36 ^{f} S Ge 21:16 ^{g} S Ex 12:23; S Jer 4:7
6:27 ^{h} Jer 9:7; Zec 13:9
6:28 ^{i} Jer 5:23 ^{j} S Lev 19:16 ^{k} Eze 22:18
6:29 ^{l} Mal 3:3
6:30 ^{m} Pr 17:3; Eze 22:18 ^{n} Ps 53:5; 119:119; Jer 7:29; La 5:22; Hos 9:17
7:2 ^{o} Jer 17:19
7:3 ^{p} Jer 18:11; 26:13; 35:15 ^{q} ver 7
7:4 ^{r} S Job 15:31

Dead Sea Scrolls (see essay, pp. 1595–1596). *like the roaring sea.* See Isa 5:30; see also Isa 17:12 and note. *horses.* See note on 4:13; see also 8:16. *Daughter Zion.* See v. 2 and note.
6:24–26 The prophet speaks to, and on behalf of, the people of Judah.
6:24 *hands hang limp.* Courage fails (see 47:3; Isa 13:7 and notes). *Anguish.* See note on 4:19. *woman in labor.* See note on 4:31.
6:25 *terror on every side.* A favorite expression of Jeremiah (20:10; 46:5; 49:29; cf. La 2:22); it is used once as a proper name (20:3).
6:26 *Put on sackcloth.* See 4:8; see also note on Ge 37:34. *roll in ashes; mourn.* See Eze 27:30–31; cf. Mic 1:10. *only son.* A father's most precious possession (see Ge 22:12,16; Ex 11:5 and note; Am 8:10; Zec 12:10; Ro 8:32). *destroyer.* Babylon (see note on 4:7).
6:27–30 The Lord speaks to Jeremiah and appoints him to test the people of Judah as a refiner tests metals (see 9:7; Ps 12:6 and note; Isa 1:25; Mal 3:2–3).
6:27 *tester of metals.* See Job 23:10.
6:28 *going about to slander.* Contrary to Lev 19:16. *bronze and iron.* Base metals when compared to gold and silver. *act corruptly.* See Eze 22:18; Isa 1:4.
6:29 In ancient times, lead was added to silver ore in the refining process. The crucible was heated, the lead oxidized and acted as a flux to remove the alloys. Here the process fails

because the ore is not pure enough (cf. Eze 24:11–13).
6:30 *They are ... rejected.* The "hardened rebels" (v. 28), the "wicked" (v. 29), have failed to pass the Lord's test. Nothing worthwhile can be made of them.
A 7:1—10:25 A series of temple messages delivered by Jeremiah, perhaps over a period of several years. Since 26:2–6,12–15 is very similar in content to ch. 7, it is possible that chs. 7–10 (or at least ch. 7) date to the reign of Jehoiakim (see 26:1). On the other hand, Jeremiah may have repeated various themes on several occasions during his lengthy ministry. In any event, nothing in chs. 7–10 is inappropriate to the time of King Josiah.
A 7:1—8:3 The straightforward narrative of this section asserts that Solomon's temple in Jerusalem will not escape the fate of the earlier sanctuary at Shiloh if the people of Judah persist in worshiping false gods.
7:1 *the word that came.* See 1:2 and note; 1:4,11,13; 2:1.
7:2 *gate.* In the wall between the inner and outer courts of the temple, perhaps the so-called New Gate (26:10; 36:10). *Hear.* See note on 2:4. *all you people ... who come ... to worship.* Perhaps during one of the three annual pilgrimage festivals (see Dt 16:16 and note). *gates.* Leading into the outer court.
7:3 *this place.* Used almost 30 times in Jeremiah to designate the land God had given them (see, e.g., v. 7; 14:13,15; 24:5–6).

7:4 ⁵ver 8; Jer 28:15;
Mic 3:11
7:5 ᵗver 3; Jer 18:11;
26:13; 35:15
ᵘS Ex 22:22;
S Lev 25:17; S Isa 1:17
7:6 ᵛS Jer 5:28;
Eze 22:7
ʷS 2Ki 21:16;
Jer 2:34; 19:4; 22:3
ˣS Ex 20:3; S Dt 8:19
7:7 ʸS Dt 4:40
ᶻS Jos 1:6
7:8 ᵃS Job 15:31
ᵇS ver 4
7:9 ᶜEx 20:15
ᵈEx 20:13 ᵉEx 20:14;
S Nu 25:1 ᶠEx 20:16;
S Lev 19:12; Zec 8:17;
Mal 3:5 ᵍS Isa 1:13
ʰJer 11:13,17; 32:29
ⁱS Ex 20:3; Hos 2:13
7:10 ʲS Isa 48:1
ᵏver 30; 2Ki 21:4-5;
Jer 23:11; 32:34;
Eze 23:38-39
ˡEze 33:25
7:11 ᵐIsa 56:7
ⁿMt 21:13*;
Mk 11:17*; Lk 19:46*
ᵒGe 31:50; Jdg 11:10;
Jer 29:23; 42:5
7:12 ᵖS Jos 18:1;
S 1Sa 2:32
ᵍS Ex 40:2;
S Jos 18:10 ʳDa 9:18
ˢS 1Sa 4:10-11,22;
Ps 78:60-64
7:13 ᵗPs 71:17;
Isa 48:17; Jer 32:33
ᵘS 2Ch 36:15
ᵛS ver 26; S Isa 65:12
ʷS Pr 1:24 ˣJer 35:17

deceptive ˢ words and say, "This is the temple of the Lᴏʀᴅ, the temple of the Lᴏʀᴅ, the temple of the Lᴏʀᴅ!" ⁵If you really change ᵗ your ways and your actions and deal with each other justly, ᵘ ⁶if you do not oppress ᵛ the foreigner, the fatherless or the widow and do not shed innocent blood ʷ in this place, and if you do not follow other gods ˣ to your own harm, ⁷then I will let you live in this place, in the land ʸ I gave your ancestors ᶻ for ever and ever. ⁸But look, you are trusting ᵃ in deceptive ᵇ words that are worthless.

⁹ 'Will you steal ᶜ and murder, ᵈ commit adultery ᵉ and perjury, ᵃ ᶠ burn incense to Baal ᵍʰ and follow other gods ⁱ you have not known, ¹⁰and then come and stand ʲ before me in this house, ᵏ which bears my Name, and say, "We are safe"—safe to do all these detestable things? ˡ ¹¹Has this house, ᵐ which bears my Name, become a den of robbers ⁿ to you? But I have been watching! ᵒ declares the Lᴏʀᴅ.

¹²" 'Go now to the place in Shiloh ᵖ where I first made a dwelling ᵍ for my Name, ʳ and see what I did ˢ to it because of the wickedness of my people Israel. ¹³While you were doing all these things, declares the Lᴏʀᴅ, I spoke ᵗ to you again and again, ᵘ but you did not listen; ᵛ I called ʷ you, but you did not answer. ˣ ¹⁴Therefore, what I did to Shiloh ʸ I will now do to the house that bears my Name, ᶻ the temple ᵃ you trust in, the place I gave to you and your ancestors. ¹⁵I will thrust you from my presence, ᵇ just as I did all your fellow Israelites, the people of Ephraim.' ᶜ

¹⁶"So do not pray for this people nor offer any plea ᵈ or petition for them; do not plead with me, for I will not listen ᵉ to you. ¹⁷Do you not see what they are doing in the towns of Judah and in the streets of Jerusalem? ¹⁸The children gather wood, the fathers light the fire, and the women knead the dough and make cakes to offer to the Queen of Heaven. ᶠ They pour out drink offerings ᵍ to other gods to arouse ʰ my anger. ¹⁹But am I the one they are provoking? ⁱ declares the Lᴏʀᴅ. Are they not rather harming themselves, to their own shame? ʲ

ᵃ 9 Or *and swear by false gods*

7:14 ʸS Jdg 18:31; S 1Sa 2:32 ᶻS 1Ki 9:7 ᵃver 4; Eze 24:21 7:15 ᵇS Ge 4:14; S Ex 33:15; S 2Ki 17:20; Jer 23:39 ᶜS Ps 78:67
7:16 ᵈS Ex 32:10; Dt 9:14; Jer 15:1 ᵉS Nu 23:19 7:18 ᶠJer 44:17-19 ᵍS Isa 57:6 ʰS Dt 31:17; S 1Ki 14:9 7:19 ⁱDt 32:21; Jer 44:3
ʲS Job 7:20; Jer 9:19; 20:11; 22:22

7:4 *deceptive words.* Spoken by false prophets. The idea that God would not destroy Jerusalem simply because his dwelling, the temple, was located there was a delusion, fostered in part by the miraculous deliverance of the city during the reign of Hezekiah (see 2Ki 19:32–36; cf. 2Sa 7:11b–13; Ps 132:13–14). In the light of Judah's sinful rebellion against the Lord, such an idea was "worthless" (v. 8; see Mic 3:11). *This is.* Lit. "They are," referring to the buildings that constituted the entire temple complex. *temple … temple … temple.* Vain and repetitious babbling (cf. Mt 6:7). Often such a threefold repeating of a word or phrase is for emphasis (see 22:29; see also note on Isa 6:3).

7:6 Rulers and people alike needed to hear and act on these prophetic words (see 22:2–3). *foreigner … fatherless … widow.* See Dt 16:11,14; 24:19–21; 26:12–13; 27:19; cf. Jas 1:27. *innocent blood.* See 19:4; 22:17; 26:15; see also the frightening example of King Manasseh (2Ki 21:16).

7:7 *land … for ever and ever.* See Ge 17:8 and note.

7:8 *deceptive words.* See note on v. 4.

7:9 This one verse mentions the violation of fully half of the Ten Commandments (cf. Hos 4:2 and note). *burn incense to Baal.* See note on 1:16. *follow other gods you have not known.* See 19:4. Tragically, such sins would be the cause of their exile to lands they had not known (see 9:14,16; 16:11,13).

7:10 *house, which bears my Name.* See vv. 11,14,30; 25:29; 32:34; 34:15; Dt 12:5 and note; 1Ki 8:16 and note; 2Ch 6:33; 20:9; Da 9:18. The "Name" of God is equivalent to his gracious presence in such passages (see vv. 12,15; see also note on Ps 5:11). *We are safe.* See 12:12. *detestable.* See 2:7; see also note on Lev 7:21.

7:11 Together with the last half of Isa 56:7, part of this verse is quoted by Jesus in Mt 21:13; Mk 11:17; Lk 19:46. *den of robbers.* As thieves hide in caves and think they are safe, so the people of Judah falsely trust in the temple to protect them in spite of their sins.

7:12 See note on 7:1—8:3. *place in Shiloh … see what I did to it.* See v. 14; 26:6,9; Ps 78:60–61. The tabernacle had

been set up in Shiloh after the conquest of Canaan (Jos 18:1) and was still there at the end of the period of the judges (see 1Sa 1:9). Modern Seilun, near a main highway about 18 miles north of Jerusalem, preserves the name of the ancient site. Archaeological excavations there indicate that it was destroyed by the Philistines c. 1050 b.c. It was included in that destruction, since it was still in existence at Gibeon during David's reign (see 1Ch 21:29). One or more auxiliary buildings had apparently been erected at Shiloh near the tabernacle in connection with various aspects of public worship there (cf. the reference to the "doors of the house of the Lᴏʀᴅ" in 1Sa 3:15; see note on 1Sa 1:9). Such structures would have been destroyed with the city itself, perhaps sometime after the events of 1Sa 4.

7:13 *again and again.* The Hebrew idiom underlying this phrase is found frequently in Jeremiah (v. 25; 11:7; 25:3–4; 26:5; 29:19; 32:33; 35:14–15; 44:4) but appears nowhere else in the OT.

7:15 *thrust you from my presence.* Into exile (see Dt 29:28). *just as I did all your fellow Israelites.* God sent Israel, the northern kingdom, into captivity in 721 b.c. (see 2Ki 17:20). *Ephraim.* Another name for Israel (see, e.g., 31:9)—and, ironically, the tribal territory in which Shiloh was located.

7:16 Perhaps the events of ch. 26 belong chronologically between vv. 15 and 16 (see Introduction: Outline). *do not pray for this people.* As a true prophet would (see 27:18; Ex 32:31–32; 1Sa 12:23). See 11:14; 14:11. There is virtually no hope for them (cf. Eze 14:14,20). On various occasions, however, Jeremiah prayed for his countrymen (see, e.g., 18:20). *this people.* See note on Ex 17:4.

7:18 *children … fathers … women.* Entire families participate in idolatrous worship. *cakes.* See 44:19. *Queen of Heaven.* A Babylonian title for Ishtar, an important goddess in the Babylonian pantheon (see 44:17–19,25). *drink offerings to other gods.* And sometimes to the Queen of Heaven herself (see 44:19,25). *arouse my anger.* See Dt 31:29.

7:19 *their own shame.* See 3:25.

²⁰" 'Therefore this is what the Sovereign ^k Lord says: My anger ^l and my wrath will be poured ^m out on this place—on people and animals, on the trees of the field and on the crops of your land—and it will burn and not be quenched. ⁿ

²¹" 'This is what the Lord Almighty, the God of Israel, says: Go ahead, add your burnt offerings to your other sacrifices ^o and eat ^p the meat yourselves! ²²For when I brought your ancestors out of Egypt and spoke to them, I did not just give them commands ^q about burnt offerings and sacrifices, ^{r 23}but I gave them this command: ^s Obey ^t me, and I will be your God and you will be my people. ^u Walk in obedience to all ^v I command you, that it may go well ^w with you. ²⁴But they did not listen ^x or pay attention; ^y instead, they followed the stubborn inclinations of their evil hearts. ^z They went backward ^a and not forward. ²⁵From the time your ancestors left Egypt until now, day after day, again and again ^b I sent you my servants ^c the prophets. ^{d 26}But they did not listen to me or pay attention. ^e They were stiff-necked ^f and did more evil than their ancestors.' ^g

²⁷"When you tell ^h them all this, they will not listen ⁱ to you; when you call to them, they will not answer. ^{j 28}Therefore say to them, 'This is the nation that has not obeyed the Lord its God or responded to correction. ^k Truth ^l has perished; it has vanished from their lips.

²⁹" 'Cut off ^m your hair and throw it away; take up a lament ⁿ on the barren heights, for the Lord has rejected and abandoned ^o this generation that is under his wrath.

THE VALLEY OF SLAUGHTER

³⁰" 'The people of Judah have done evil ^p in my eyes, declares the Lord. They have set up their detestable idols ^q in the house that bears my Name and have defiled ^r it. ³¹They have built the high places of Topheth ^s in the Valley of Ben Hinnom ^t to burn their sons and daughters ^u in the fire—something I did not command, nor did it enter my mind. ^{v 32}So beware, the days are coming, declares the Lord, when people will no longer call it Topheth or the Valley of Ben Hinnom, but the Valley of Slaughter, ^w for they will bury ^x the dead in Topheth until there is no more room. ³³Then the carcasses ^y of this people will become food ^z for the birds and the wild animals, and there will be no one to frighten them away. ^{a 34}I will bring an end to the sounds ^b of joy and gladness and to the voices of bride

7:30 ^qS Jer 2:7; S 4:1; Eze 7:20-22 ^rS Lev 20:3; Jer 32:34   **7:31** ^sS 2Ki 23:10 ^tS Jos 15:8; 2Ch 33:6 ^uS Lev 18:21; Eze 16:20 ^vJer 19:5; 32:35; Eze 20:31; Mic 6:7   **7:32** ^wJer 19:6 ^xJer 19:11   **7:33** ^yS Ge 15:11 ^zS Dt 28:26; Eze 29:5 ^aJer 6:11; 14:16   **7:34** ^bS Isa 24:8

Cross-reference column

7:20 ^kS Isa 30:15 ^lJob 40:11; Jer 42:18; La 2:3-5 ^mJer 6:11-12; La 4:11 ⁿS Isa 1:31; Jer 11:16; 13:14; 15:6,14; 17:4, 27; Eze 20:47-48
7:21 ^oS Jer 6:20; Am 5:21-22 ^pS 1Sa 2:12-17; Hos 8:13
7:22 ^qIsa 43:23
7:23 ^r*1Jn 3:23 ^sS Ex 19:5 ^tS Lev 26:12; Jer 11:4 ^uS Lev 26:12; S Isa 51:16 ^vS 1Ki 8:36; S Ps 119:3 ^wS Dt 5:33
7:24 ^xS Jer 6:10 ^yJer 11:8; 17:23; 34:14 ^zS Jer 3:17 ^aS Jer 2:19; Eze 37:23
7:25 ^bS 2Ch 36:15 ^cS Isa 20:3 ^dS Nu 11:29; Jer 25:4; 35:15
7:26 ^ever 13,24; S 2Ch 36:16; Ps 81:11; Jer 13:11; 22:21; 25:3; 35:15; Eze 20:8,21 ^fS Ex 32:9; Ac 7:51 ^gJer 16:12; Mal 3:7; Lk 11:47
7:27 ^hEze 2:7 ⁱver 13; Eze 3:7; Zec 7:13 ^jS Isa 65:12
7:28 ^kS Lev 26:23; Zep 3:7 ^lS Ps 15:2; S Isa 59:15
7:29 ^mS Jer 21:5; S Job 1:20 ⁿS Jer 4:8; S Eze 19:1 ^oS Jer 6:30; 12:7; Hos 11:8; Mic 5:3
7:30 ^pS ver 10; S Lev 18:21

7:20 All nature suffers when God judges sinners (see 5:17; Ro 8:20–22). *burn and not be quenched.* See 4:4; 21:12; see also Isa 1:31; Am 5:6.

🅐 **7:21** Because of your sinful deeds your sacrifices are worthless, so you might as well eat them yourselves.

🅐 **7:22–23** Sacrifices are valid only when accompanied by sincere repentance and joyful obedience (see 6:20; Isa 1:11–15 and notes).

🅐 **7:23** *your God ... my people.* The most basic summary of the relationship between God and Israel implied in the covenant at Sinai (see Ex 6:7; Lev 26:12; Zec 8:8 and notes; Dt 26:17–18).

7:24 *followed ... evil hearts.* See note on 3:17; see also Ge 6:5 and note.

7:25 *again and again.* See note on v. 13. *my servants the prophets.* See 25:4; 26:5; 29:19; 35:15; 44:4; see also Zec 1:6 and note. God had promised that Moses would be the first in a long line of prophets who would speak in the Lord's name and serve him faithfully (see Dt 18:15–22 and notes).

7:26 *stiff-necked.* See 17:23; 19:15; Ex 32:9 and note.

7:28 *not ... responded to correction.* See 2:30; 5:3. *Truth ... has vanished from their lips.* No one seeks the truth (see 5:1 and note).

7:29 Addressed to Jerusalem. *Cut off your hair.* A sign of mourning (see Job 1:20; Mic 1:16). The Hebrew for the word "hair" is related to the word "Nazirite" (see Nu 6:2) and referred originally to the diadem worn by the high priest (see Ex 29:6). The Nazirite's hair was the symbol of his separation or consecration (Nu 6:7). As the Nazirite was commanded to cut off his hair when he became ceremonially unclean (Nu 6:9), so also Jerusalem must cut off her hair because of her sins. *lament on the barren heights.* See 3:21; see also note on 3:2.

🅐 **7:30** *set up their ... idols in the house.* Manasseh had put a carved Asherah pole (see TNIV text note on 2Ki 13:6) in the temple (2Ki 21:7). Jeremiah's contemporary, the good King

Josiah, removed the pole and other accessories to idol worship (2Ki 23:4–7). But less than 20 years after Josiah's death, Ezekiel reported that there were numerous idols in the temple courts (see Eze 8:3,5–6,10,12). *defiled it.* See note on 2:7.

🅐 **7:31** *high places.* Pagan shrines, usually (but not here) located on natural heights (see 1Sa 9:13–14; 10:5; 1Ki 11:7). *Topheth.* See v. 32; 19:6,11–14; see also note on Isa 30:33. The word is of Aramaic origin and means "fireplace," though in cultures outside Israel it was used as a common noun meaning "place of child sacrifice." Its vowel pattern was perhaps intentionally conformed to that of Hebrew *bosheth,* "shameful thing" (see note on Jdg 6:32), often used in connection with idol worship (see notes on 2:26; 3:25). The OT Topheth had a fire pit (see Isa 30:33), into which the hapless children were apparently thrown. *Valley of Ben Hinnom.* See v. 32; 19:2,6; 32:35; see also note on Jos 15:5. It was used as a trash dump and also as a place for sacrificing children to pagan gods. The abbreviated Hebrew name *ge' hinnom* ("Valley of Hinnom"; see Ne 11:30 and note) became "Gehenna" (Greek *geenna*), consistently translated in the NT as "hell," the place of eternal, fiery punishment (see Mt 5:22 and note; 18:9; Mk 9:47–48). *burn their sons and daughters in the fire.* A horrible ritual, prohibited in the law of Moses (see Lev 18:21 and note; Dt 18:10) but practiced by Ahaz (see 2Ki 16:2–3) and Manasseh (2Ki 21:1,6). *nor did it enter my mind.* Stresses how terribly evil such an act is to God (see 19:5; 32:35).

7:32 *So beware ... Valley of Slaughter.* Repeated almost verbatim in 19:6. Their place of sacrifice would become their cemetery when the people of Judah were slaughtered by the Babylonian invaders.

7:33 The punishment announced here is one of the curses for covenant disobedience (see Dt 28:26). *food for the birds ... wild animals.* See 16:4; 19:7; see also 34:20, where the same judgment is the result of violating God's covenant (34:18–19). To remain unburied was an unspeakable abomination in ancient times.

7:34 *c* Rev 18:23
d Isa 24:7-12;
Jer 33:10
e S Lev 26:34;
Zec 7:14; Mt 23:38
8:1 *f* S Ps 53:5
g S Isa 14:19
8:2 *h* S 2Ki 23:5;
Jer 19:13; Zep 1:5;
Ac 7:42 *i* S Job 31:27
j Jer 14:16; Eze 29:5;
37:1 *k* S 2Ki 9:37;
Jer 31:40; 36:30
8:3 *l* Dt 29:28
m S Job 3:22; Rev 9:6
8:4 *n* Pr 24:16;
Mic 7:8 *o* Ps 119:67;
Jer 31:19
8:5 *p* S Jer 5:27
q Zec 7:11
8:6 *r* Mal 3:16
s Rev 9:20 *t* Ps 14:1-3
8:7 *u* S Dt 32:28;
S Jer 4:22
8:8 *v* Ro 2:17
8:9 *w* S Isa 29:14
x S 2Ki 19:26
y S Job 5:13
z S Jer 6:19 *a* Pr 1:7;
1Co 1:20
8:10 *b* S Jer 6:12

and bridegroom *c* in the towns of Judah and the streets of Jerusalem, *d* for the land will become desolate. *e*

8 " 'At that time, declares the LORD, the bones of the kings and officials of Judah, the bones of the priests and prophets, and the bones *f* of the people of Jerusalem will be removed *g* from their graves. ²They will be exposed to the sun and the moon and all the stars of the heavens, which they have loved and served *h* and which they have followed and consulted and worshiped. *i* They will not be gathered up or buried, *j* but will be like dung lying on the ground. *k* ³Wherever I banish them, *l* all the survivors of this evil nation will prefer death to life, *m* declares the LORD Almighty.'

SIN AND PUNISHMENT

⁴"Say to them, 'This is what the LORD says:

" 'When people fall down, do they not get up? *n*
    When people turn away, *o* do they not return?
⁵Why then have these people turned away?
    Why does Jerusalem always turn away?
They cling to deceit; *p*
    they refuse to return. *q*
⁶I have listened *r* attentively,
    but they do not say what is right.
None of them repent *s* of their wickedness,
    saying, "What have I done?"
They each pursue their own course *t*
    like a horse charging into battle.
⁷Even the stork in the sky
    knows her appointed seasons,
and the dove, the swift and the thrush
    observe the time of their migration.
But my people do not know *u*
    the requirements of the LORD.

⁸" 'How can you say, "We are wise,
    for we have the law *v* of the LORD,"
when actually the lying pen of the scribes
    has handled it falsely?
⁹The wise *w* will be put to shame;
    they will be dismayed *x* and trapped. *y*
Since they have rejected the word *z* of the LORD,
    what kind of wisdom *a* do they have?
¹⁰Therefore I will give their wives to other men
    and their fields to new owners. *b*
From the least to the greatest,

7:34 See 16:9; 25:10; contrast 33:10–11. *land will become desolate.* Another covenant curse (Lev 26:31,33).

8:1 *bones ... removed from their graves.* A gross indignity and sacrilege (see 2Ki 23:16,18; Am 2:1 and note). *kings ... officials ... priests ... prophets.* See 2:26; see also note on 1:18.

8:2 *exposed to the sun ... moon ... stars.* To hasten their disintegration, and perhaps also to demonstrate that the heavenly bodies, which had been worshiped by some of Judah's kings, among others, were powerless to help. *loved and served and ... followed and consulted and worshiped.* Acts of homage and adoration that should have been given to God alone. *They.* The bones. *not be gathered up or buried.* Contrast 2Sa 21:13–14. *dung.* See 9:22; 16:4; 25:33.

8:3 *survivors.* See note on 6:9.

8:4—9:26 In contrast to 7:1—8:3, this section is almost completely in poetic form. Jeremiah resumes his extended commentary on the inevitability of divine judgment against sinners.

8:4 *Say to them.* Connects this section with the previous (see 7:28). *turn away ... return.* The Hebrew for these two verbs is identical, forming a play on words.

8:5 The general truths stated in v. 4 are routinely and perversely violated by the people of Jerusalem. *turned away ... turn away ... return.* Continuing the wordplay of v. 4.

8:6 *I. The Lord. pursue.* The Hebrew for this word continues the wordplay of vv. 4–5. *their own course.* And therefore evil (see 23:10).

8:7 See Isa 1:3. Although migratory birds obey their God-given instincts, God's rebellious people refuse to obey his laws. *swift.* Of similar build and habit as the swallow but not related to it (see 38:14, where it is also linked with the thrush). *do not know ... requirements of the LORD.* See note on 5:4.

8:8—9 *law of the LORD ... word of the LORD.* Misinterpreting and manipulating the first (the written law of Moses) leads to rejection of the second (God's truth as found in the law and proclaimed by his servants the prophets).

8:8 *lying pen.* Symbolizes mistreatment of the written law. *scribes.* The earliest mention of them as a recognizable group. They were apparently organized on the basis of families (see 1Ch 2:55; 2Ch 34:13; see also note on Ezr 7:6). *handled it falsely.* Contrast 2Ti 2:15.

8:9 *rejected ... wisdom.* Contrast Dt 4:5–6.

8:10–12 See 6:12–15 and notes.

all are greedy for gain; [c]
prophets [d] and priests alike,
all practice deceit. [e]

[11] They dress the wound of my people
as though it were not serious.
"Peace, peace," they say,
when there is no peace. [f]

[12] Are they ashamed of their detestable conduct?
No, they have no shame [g] at all;
they do not even know how to blush.
So they will fall among the fallen;
they will be brought down when they are punished, [h]

says the LORD. [i]

[13] " 'I will take away their harvest,

declares the LORD.

There will be no grapes on the vine. [j]
There will be no figs [k] on the tree,
and their leaves will wither. [l]
What I have given them
will be taken [m] from them. [a] ' "

[14] Why are we sitting here?
Gather together!
Let us flee to the fortified cities [n]
and perish there!
For the LORD our God has doomed us to perish
and given us poisoned water [o] to drink,
because we have sinned [p] against him.
[15] We hoped for peace [q]
but no good has come,
for a time of healing
but there is only terror. [r]
[16] The snorting of the enemy's horses [s]
is heard from Dan; [t]
at the neighing of their stallions
the whole land trembles. [u]
They have come to devour [v]
the land and everything in it,
the city and all who live there.

[17] "See, I will send venomous snakes [w] among you,
vipers that cannot be charmed, [x]
and they will bite you,"

declares the LORD.

[18] You who are my Comforter [b] in sorrow,
my heart is faint [y] within me.
[19] Listen to the cry of my people

---

[a] 13 The meaning of the Hebrew for this sentence is uncertain.   [b] 18 The meaning of the Hebrew for this word is uncertain.

8:10 [c] S Isa 56:11
[d] Jer 14:14; La 2:14
[e] Jer 23:11,15
8:11 [f] ver 15;
S Jer 4:10; Eze 7:25
8:12 [g] S Jer 3:3
[h] Ps 52:5-7; Isa 3:9
[i] S Jer 6:15
8:13 [j] Hos 2:12;
Joel 1:7 [k] Lk 13:6
[l] Mt 21:19 [m] S Jer 5:17
8:14 [n] S Jos 10:20;
Jer 35:11 [o] S Dt 29:18;
Jer 9:15; 23:15
[p] Jer 14:7,20; Da 9:5
8:15 [q] S ver 11
[r] S Job 19:8; Jer 14:19
8:16 [s] S Jer 4:29
[t] S Ge 30:6 [u] Jer 51:29
[v] S Jer 5:17
8:17 [w] Nu 21:6;
S Dt 32:24
[x] S Ps 58:5; S Isa 3:3
8:18 [y] La 5:17

8:11 *my people.* Lit. "the Daughter of my people" (also in v. 21; see Isa 22:4 and note).
8:13—9:24 This section is read aloud in synagogues every year on the ninth of Ab (see chart, p. 105), the day the temple in Jerusalem was destroyed by the Babylonians in 586 B.C. and by the Romans in A.D. 70.
8:13 *grapes ... figs.* Symbolic of individual people also in Mic 7:1; see ch. 24. *vine.* Israel (see 2:21 and note). *leaves will wither.* Contrast 17:8; Ps 1:3.
8:14—16 On behalf of the people the prophet speaks, envisioning the Babylonian invasion.
8:14 *Gather together!* See 4:5. The Hebrew for this phrase forms a wordplay with the Hebrew for "take away" and "harvest" in v. 13. *flee to the fortified cities.* See note on 4:5. *poisoned water.* The phrase

is unique to the prophet Jeremiah (see 9:15; 23:15; cf. 25:15).
8:15 Repeated almost verbatim in 14:19. *peace.* Under the circumstances, a false hope (see notes on 4:10; 6:14). *healing.* See note on 6:7.
8:16 *the enemy's horses.* See note on 4:13. *Dan.* Close to the northern border of Israel. It would be the first to feel the effects of the Babylonian invasion. *stallions.* Lit. "mighty ones"; the Hebrew word is translated "stallions" again in 50:11, "steeds" in 47:3.
8:17 *vipers that cannot be charmed.* Such are the wicked always (see Ps 58:4-5).
8:18 The prophet speaks. *my heart is faint.* See La 1:22; 5:17.
8:19 The prophet speaks in the first part of the verse, the Lord in the last part. *my people from a land far away.* Judah in Babylonian exile (see Ps 137:1-4) as Jeremiah envisions the future.

8:19 *z* Dt 28:64;
Jer 9:16 *a* Mic 4:9
b Jer 44:3
c S Isa 41:24
d S Dt 32:21
8:21 *e* S Ps 94:5
f Ps 78:40; Isa 43:24;
Jer 4:19; 10:19; 14:17;
30:14; La 2:13;
Eze 6:9
8:22 *g* S Ge 37:25
h Job 13:4 *i* S Isa 1:6;
Jer 30:12
9:1 *j* S Ps 119:136
k Jer 13:17; 14:17;
La 2:11,18; 3:48
l Isa 22:4
9:2 *m* Ps 55:7
n S Nu 25:1; Jer 23:10;
Hos 4:2; 7:4
o 1Ki 19:10;
S Isa 24:16
9:3 *p* ver 8;
S Ex 20:16; Ps 64:3;
S Isa 44:20; Jer 18:18;
Mic 6:12 *q* S Isa 1:3
9:4 *r* S 2Sa 15:12
s Mic 7:5-6
t S Ge 27:35
u S Ex 20:16;
S Lev 19:16
9:5 *v* S Lev 6:2
w S Ps 15:2;
S Isa 59:15
x S Ps 52:3
9:6 *y* S Jer 5:27

from a land far away: *z*
"Is the LORD not in Zion?
Is her King *a* no longer there?"

"Why have they aroused *b* my anger with their images,
with their worthless *c* foreign idols?" *d*

²⁰ "The harvest is past,
the summer has ended,
and we are not saved."

²¹ Since my people are crushed, *e* I am crushed;
I mourn, *f* and horror grips me.
²² Is there no balm in Gilead? *g*
Is there no physician *h* there?
Why then is there no healing *i*
for the wound of my people?

9

^{*1} Oh, that my head were a spring of water
and my eyes a fountain of tears! *j*
I would weep *k* day and night
for the slain of my people. *l*
^{*2} Oh, that I had in the desert *m*
a lodging place for travelers,
so that I might leave my people
and go away from them;
for they are all adulterers, *n*
a crowd of unfaithful *o* people.

³ "They make ready their tongue
like a bow, to shoot lies; *p*
it is not by truth
that they triumph *a* in the land.
They go from one sin to another;
they do not acknowledge *q* me,"

declares the LORD.

⁴ "Beware of your friends; *r*
do not trust any of your people. *s*
For every one of them is a deceiver, *b t*
and every friend a slanderer. *u*
⁵ Friend deceives friend, *v*
and no one speaks the truth. *w*
They have taught their tongues to lie; *x*
they weary themselves with sinning.
⁶ You *c* live in the midst of deception; *y*
in their deceit they refuse to acknowledge me,"

declares the LORD.

---

a 3 Or *lies; / they are not valiant for truth*
is singular)   *b* 4 Or *a deceiving Jacob*   *c* 6 That is, Jeremiah (the Hebrew

* 9:1 is numbered 8:23 in Hebrew texts.   * 9:2-26 is numbered 9:1-25 in Hebrew texts.

Is the LORD not in Zion? Cf. Mic 3:11. The people are perplexed at their fate, still wondering how God could have permitted the destruction of his land and temple (see note on 7:4). *King.* God (see Isa 33:22 and note). *aroused my anger.* See 7:18; Dt 31:29. *worthless...idols.* See note on 2:5.

8:20 The people speak from the hopelessness of their exile. *we are not saved.* We have been captured by the enemy.

8:21 Jeremiah identifies himself with his exiled countrymen. *grips me.* See 6:24.

8:22 *balm in Gilead.* See 46:11; cf. 51:8. The territory of Gilead was an important source of spices and medicinal herbs (see Ge 37:25 and note). *no healing for the wound.* Contrast 30:17.

9:1–2 The prophet's frustration is highlighted as he speaks to his countrymen with tender sympathy in v. 1 and with indignant disgust in v. 2.

A **9:1** Jeremiah is often called the "weeping prophet"—a well-deserved title (see v. 10; the book of Lamentations;

cf. 2Sa 18:33; Lk 19:41; Ro 9:2–4; 10:1).

9:2 The prophet wants to get as far away from his wicked countrymen as possible (cf. Ps 55:6–8). *adulterers...unfaithful people.* See v. 14; see also Ex 34:15 and note. *crowd.* The Hebrew for this word is always used elsewhere in the OT in the sense of a solemn religious assembly (see, e.g., Dt 16:8), sometimes perverted by the worshipers and therefore falling under divine judgment (see Isa 1:13; Am 5:21).

9:3–9 The Lord speaks.

9:3 *tongue like a bow.* See vv. 5,8; see also Ps 64:3–4; cf. Jas 3:5–12. *do not acknowledge me.* See v. 6; Jdg 2:10; 1Sa 2:12; Job 18:21; Hos 4:1 and note; Ro 1:28; contrast Hos 6:3.

9:4 *deceiver.* See TNIV text note; Ge 25:26 and note; TNIV text note on Ge 27:36; Hos 12:2–3 and TNIV text note on 12:2.

A **9:6** *refuse to acknowledge me.* The situation has deteriorated even further (v. 3 says simply "do not acknowledge me").

[7] Therefore this is what the LORD Almighty says:

> "See, I will refine[z] and test[a] them,
>> for what else can I do
>> because of the sin of my people?
> [8] Their tongue[b] is a deadly arrow;
>> it speaks deceitfully.
> With their mouths they all speak cordially to their neighbors,[c]
>> but in their hearts they set traps[d] for them.[e]
> [9] Should I not punish them for this?"
>> declares the LORD.
> "Should I not avenge[f] myself
>> on such a nation as this?"

> [10] I will weep and wail for the mountains
>> and take up a lament concerning the wilderness grasslands.[g]
> They are desolate and untraveled,
>> and the lowing of cattle is not heard.
> The birds[h] have all fled
>> and the animals are gone.

> [11] "I will make Jerusalem a heap[i] of ruins,
>> a haunt of jackals;[j]
> and I will lay waste the towns of Judah[k]
>> so no one can live there."[l]

[12] Who is wise[m] enough to understand this? Who has been instructed by the LORD and can explain it? Why has the land been ruined and laid waste like a desert that no one can cross?

[13] The LORD said, "It is because they have forsaken my law, which I set before them; they have not obeyed me or followed my law.[n] [14] Instead, they have followed[o] the stubbornness of their hearts;[p] they have followed the Baals, as their ancestors taught them." [15] Therefore, this is what the LORD Almighty, the God of Israel, says: "See, I will make this people eat bitter food[q] and drink poisoned water.[r] [16] I will scatter them among nations[s] that neither they nor their ancestors have known,[t] and I will pursue them with the sword[u] until I have made an end of them."[v]

[17] This is what the LORD Almighty says:

> "Consider now! Call for the wailing women[w] to come;
>> send for the most skillful of them.
> [18] Let them come quickly
>> and wail over us
> till our eyes overflow with tears
>> and water streams from our eyelids.[x]
> [19] The sound of wailing is heard from Zion:
>> 'How ruined[y] we are!
> How great is our shame!
> We must leave our land
>> because our houses are in ruins.' "

9:7 [z] S Job 28:1; S Isa 1:25 [a] S Jer 6:27
9:8 [b] S ver 3; S Ps 35:20 [c] S Isa 3:5 [d] S Jer 5:26 [e] ver 4
9:9 [f] S Dt 32:43; S Isa 10:3
9:10 [g] Jer 23:10; Joel 1:19 [h] S Jer 4:25; 12:4; Hos 4:3; Joel 1:18
9:11 [i] Jer 26:18 [j] S Job 30:29; S Isa 34:13 [k] S Jer 1:15 [l] Lev 26:31; Isa 25:2; S Jer 4:13; 26:9; 33:10; 50:3,13; 51:62; La 1:4
9:12 [m] S Ps 107:43
9:13 S 2Ch 7:19; S Ps 89:30-32
9:14 [o] S Jer 2:8,23; Am 2:4 [p] S Jer 3:17; S 7:24
9:15 [q] La 3:15 [r] S Jer 8:14
9:16 [s] S Lev 26:33 [t] S Dt 4:32; S Jer 8:19 [u] Jer 14:12; 24:10; Eze 5:2 [v] Jer 44:27; Eze 5:12
9:17 [w] S Ecc 12:5
9:18 [x] S Ps 119:136; La 3:48
9:19 [y] S Jer 4:13

9:7 *refine and test.* See 6:27–30 and notes. The Lord will test his people "in the furnace of affliction" (Isa 48:10; see note there).
9:8 *tongue…speaks deceitfully.* See v. 3 and note. *With their mouths…but in their hearts.* See Ps 55:21. *cordially.* The Hebrew for this word is translated "peace" in 6:14 (see note there).
9:9 Repeated from 5:9,29.
9:10 The prophet speaks. See 4:23–26 and notes. *weep and wail.* See v. 18; see also note on v. 1. *wilderness grasslands.* Good for poor grazing at best (see 1Sa 17:28; cf. Ex 3:1). *desolate.* Lit. "burned" (as in 2:15); here parched by the blazing sun. *untraveled.* See v. 12; Eze 33:28.
9:11 The Lord speaks. *haunt of jackals.* See 10:22; 49:33; 51:37; Ps 44:19; Isa 13:21–22; La 5:18; Eze 13:4; Mal 1:3; contrast Isa 35:7. *no one can live there.* See 2:15; 4:7 and notes.
9:12 The prophet asks a series of questions. *Who is wise…?* See Hos 14:9.

9:13 The Lord answers the prophet and then continues to speak through v. 19. *law, which I set before them.* In the days of Moses (see Dt 4:8).
9:14 *stubbornness.* See note on 3:17. *Baals.* See 2:23 and note.
9:15 *eat bitter food and drink poisoned water.* Repeated in 23:15; see note on 8:14. Centuries earlier, Moses had warned the Israelites concerning just such a fate (see Dt 29:18).
9:16 *I will scatter them.* See 13:24; 18:17; 30:11; 46:28. This warning was given in Dt 28:64 as one of the curses for persistent covenant unfaithfulness. *pursue them with the sword.* See 42:16. *made an end of them.* But not to the last man (see note on 4:27; see especially 44:27–28).
9:17 *wailing women.* Professionals, paid to mourn at funerals and other sorrowful occasions (see 2Ch 35:25; Ecc 12:5; Am 5:16).
9:18 *wail.* See v. 10. *eyes overflow with tears.* See v. 1.
9:19 *How ruined we are!* See 4:13,20; cf. 48:1.

9:20 ᶻ Jer 23:16
ᵃ Isa 32:9-13
9:21 ᵇ Joel 2:9
ᶜ S 2Ch 36:17;
S Isa 40:30; S Jer 16:6
9:22 ᵈ S 2Ki 9:37
9:23 ᵉ S Job 4:12;
S Ecc 9:11
ᶠ S 1Ki 20:11
ᵍ Ps 62:10; S Pr 11:28;
Jer 48:7; 49:4;
Eze 28:4-5
9:24 ʰ S Ps 34:2;
1Co 1:31*; Gal 6:14
ⁱ S Ps 36:10
ʲ 2Co 10:17*; ᵏ Ps 51:1
ˡ Ps 36:6
9:25 ᵐ S Lev 26:41;
Ro 2:25
9:26 ⁿ Jer 25:23;
49:32; S Isa 14:6;
Eze 31:18 ᵒ Ac 7:51
10:2 �q S Ex 23:24;
S Lev 20:23
ʳ S Ge 1:14

²⁰ Now, you women, hear the word of the LORD;
    open your ears to the words of his mouth. ᶻ
Teach your daughters how to wail;
    teach one another a lament. ᵃ
²¹ Death has climbed in through our windows ᵇ
    and has entered our fortresses;
it has removed the children from the streets
    and the youths ᶜ from the public squares.

²²Say, "This is what the LORD declares:

" 'Dead bodies will lie
    like dung ᵈ on the open field,
like cut grain behind the reaper,
    with no one to gather them.' "

²³This is what the LORD says:

"Let not the wise boast of their wisdom ᵉ
    or the strong boast of their strength ᶠ
    or the rich boast of their riches, ᵍ
²⁴ but let those who boast boast ʰ about this:
    that they understand and know ⁱ me,
that I am the LORD, ʲ who exercises kindness, ᵏ
    justice and righteousness ˡ on earth,
for in these I delight,"

                       declares the LORD.

²⁵"The days are coming," declares the LORD, "when I will punish all who are circumcised only in the flesh ᵐ— ²⁶Egypt, Judah, Edom, Ammon, Moab and all who live in the wilderness in distant places. ᵃ ⁿ For all these nations are really uncircumcised, ᵒ and even the whole house of Israel is uncircumcised in heart. ᵖ"

GOD AND IDOLS
10:12–16pp — Jer 51:15–19

10 Hear what the LORD says to you, house of Israel. ²This is what the LORD says:

"Do not learn the ways of the nations �q
    or be terrified by signs ʳ in the sky,
    though the nations are terrified by them.
³ For the practices of the peoples are worthless;

ᵃ 26 Or *wilderness and who clip the hair by their foreheads*

9:20–21 The prophet speaks.
9:20 The wailing women will have to teach their daughters how to lament, so great will be the need for their services.
9:21 *Death.* Personified here (as in Hab 2:5). Canaanite mythology included a deity named Mot (a word related to the Hebrew word for "death"), the god of infertility and the netherworld. *climbed in through our windows.* Said of an army of "locusts" in Joel 2:9 (see note there). *children . . . youths.* See 6:11.
9:22 *Dead bodies.* See 7:33 and note. *like dung.* See note on 8:2. *reaper.* The concept of death as the "grim reaper" comes largely from this verse.
9:23 *Let not . . . the rich boast of their riches.* An almost exact parallel occurs in the Aramaic *Words of Ahiqar,* written about a century after Jeremiah's time: "Let not the rich say, 'In my riches I am glorious.'"
9:24 1Co 1:31 summarizes: "Let those who boast boast in the Lord." *this . . . these.* Ultimately, only God and our knowledge of and love for him are worthwhile. *understand and know.* See 3:15; see also note on 4:22. *I am the LORD.* Ex 6:2–8, a key passage on the doctrine of redemption, begins and ends with this statement of divine self-disclosure. *kindness.* The Hebrew for this word is translated "devotion" in 2:2 (see note there). *in these I delight.* See Ps 11:7; 33:5; 99:4; 103:6; Mic 6:8; 7:18.
9:25–26 See Ro 2:25–29; see also note on Ge 17:10.

9:26 *who live . . . in distant places.* Arab tribes (see 25:23; 49:32), later to be attacked by the Babylonians under Nebuchadnezzar (see 49:28–33). With the TNIV text note contrast Lev 19:27. *uncircumcised in heart.* See 4:4 and note.
10:1–25 Jeremiah concludes his series of temple messages with a poetic section that focuses primarily on the vast difference between idols and the Lord (vv. 2–16). Idols and their worshipers are condemned in vv. 2–5,8–9,11,14–15, while the one true God is praised in the alternate passages (vv. 6–7,10,12–13,16). See Isa 40:18–20 and note; 41:7; 44:9–20; 46:5–7.
10:1 *Hear.* See note on 2:4.
10:2 *Do not . . . be terrified.* See 1:17. *ways.* The Hebrew for this word is singular and refers to the religious practices of the nations. The early Christians often called their distinctive beliefs and lifestyle the "Way" (see Ac 9:2; 19:9,23; 22:4; 24:14,22). *signs in the sky.* The heavenly bodies were created by the Lord for purposes other than idolatrous worship (see Ge 1:14–18 and notes). *nations are terrified.* Not only by the heavenly bodies themselves but also by unusual phenomena associated with them (such as comets, meteors and eclipses).
10:3 *worthless.* See note on 2:5. *cut a tree.* See Isa 44:14–15. *skilled worker.* The Hebrew for this phrase is often used of idol-makers who work usually—but not always (see Isa 40:19)—with wood (see Isa 41:7). *chisel.* Cf. Isa 44:13.

they cut a tree out of the forest,
    and a skilled worker[s] shapes it with a chisel.[t]
[4] They adorn it with silver[u] and gold;
    they fasten it with hammer and nails
    so it will not totter.[v]
[5] Like a scarecrow in a melon patch,
    their idols cannot speak;[w]
they must be carried
    because they cannot walk.[x]
Do not fear them;
    they can do no harm[y]
    nor can they do any good."[z]

[6] No one is like you,[a] Lord;
    you are great,[b]
    and your name is mighty in power.
[7] Who should not fear[c] you,
    King of the nations?[d]
    This is your due.
Among all the wise rulers of the nations
    and in all their kingdoms,
    there is no one like you.

[8] They are all senseless[e] and foolish;[f]
    they are taught by worthless wooden idols.[g]
[9] Hammered silver is brought from Tarshish[h]
    and gold from Uphaz.
What the goldsmith and engraver have made[i]
    is then dressed in blue and purple—
    all made by skilled workers.
[10] But the Lord is the true God;
    he is the living God,[j] the eternal King.[k]
When he is angry,[l] the earth trembles;[m]
    the nations cannot endure his wrath.[n]

[11]"Tell them this: 'These gods, who did not make the heavens and the earth, will perish[o] from the earth and from under the heavens.' "[a]

[12] But God made[p] the earth[q] by his power;
    he founded the world by his wisdom[r]
    and stretched out the heavens[s] by his understanding.
[13] When he thunders,[t] the waters in the heavens roar;
    he makes clouds rise from the ends of the earth.
He sends lightning[u] with the rain[v]
    and brings out the wind from his storehouses.[w]

---

[a] 11 The text of this verse is in Aramaic.

10:3 ˢ S Isa 40:19
ᵗ Dt 9:21; S 1Ki 8:36;
Jer 44:8; Eze 7:20
10:4 ᵘ Ps 135:15;
Hos 13:2; Hab 2:19
ᵛ S 1Sa 5:3; Isa 41:7
10:5 ʷ S 1Ki 18:26;
1Co 12:2 ˣ S Isa 45:20
ʸ Isa 41:23
ᶻ S Isa 41:24; 44:9-
20; 46:7; Jos 9:26
10:6 ᵃ S Ex 8:10
ᵇ S Ps 48:1
10:7 ᶜ Jer 5:22
ᵈ Ps 22:28; S Isa 12:4;
Rev 15:4
10:8 ᵉ S Isa 44:18
ᶠ S Isa 40:19;
S Jer 4:22
ᵍ S Dt 32:21
10:9 ʰ S Ge 10:4
ⁱ Ps 115:4; S Isa 40:19
10:10 ʲ S Jos 3:10;
S Mt 16:16
ᵏ S Ge 21:33; Da 6:26
ˡ Ps 18:7
ᵐ S Jdg 5:4; S Job 9:6;
Ps 29:8; Ps 76:7;
Jer 21:12; Na 1:6
10:11 ᵒ S Isa 2:18
10:12 ᵖ S 1Sa 2:8
�q S ver 16 ʳ S Ge 1:31
ˢ S Ge 1:1,8
10:13 ᵗ S Job 36:29
ᵘ S Job 36:30
ᵛ S Ps 104:13; S 135:7
ʷ S Dt 28:12

10:4 *silver and gold.* Wooden idols were plated with precious metals to beautify them (see Isa 30:22; 40:19). *fasten it ... so it will not totter.* See Isa 40:20; 41:7; cf. 46:7; contrast 1Sa 5:2–4.

10:5 The impotence of idols is described in classic form in Ps 115:4–7; 135:15–18. *scarecrow.* Verse 70 in the Apocryphal *Letter of Jeremiah* uses the same imagery. *melon patch.* See Isa 1:8 and note. *must be carried.* Usually on the backs of animals. See Isa 46:1. *harm nor ... good.* Idols can do nothing at all (see Isa 41:22–24).

10:6 *No one.* Among the gods (see Ps 86:8). *your name is mighty in power.* See 16:21.

10:7 *King of the nations.* See Ps 47:8–9 and notes; 96:10; Rev 15:3–4. Unlike the gods of the surrounding nations, limited to their own territories, the Lord is King over all. *This.* Reverence ("fear"). *Among all the wise rulers ... no one like you.* See Isa 19:12; 29:14; 1Co 1:20.

10:8 *senseless and foolish.* See vv. 14,21; 51:17; see also TNIV text note on Pr 1:7. *taught by ... idols.* Instead of by the Lord (see Dt 11:2; Job 5:17; Pr 3:11, where the Hebrew word for "taught by" is

translated "discipline"). *worthless.* See note on v. 3.

10:9 *silver ... from Tarshish.* See Eze 27:12; see also note on Isa 23:6. *Uphaz.* Mentioned only here; location unknown. *goldsmith and engraver.* See Isa 40:19 and note. *dressed in blue and purple.* To make it look regal. *all.* The idols.

10:10 Everything that idols are not, the Lord is. *true.* See 1Th 1:9. *living God.* See 23:36; Dt 5:26; 2Ki 19:4 and note. *eternal.* See Ex 15:18; Ps 10:16; 29:10. *When ... wrath.* See Ps 97:5; Na 1:5.

10:11 See TNIV text note. The other major Aramaic passages in the OT are Ezr 4:8—6:18; 7:12–26; Da 2:4—7:28. *them.* Pagan idolaters, who would have been more likely to understand Aramaic (the language of diplomacy during this period) than Hebrew.

10:12–16 Repeated almost verbatim in 51:15–19.

10:12 *But God.* In contrast to the false gods of v. 11. *stretched out the heavens.* Like a tent or canopy (see Ps 104:2; Isa 40:22 and note).

10:13 *he makes clouds ... his storehouses.* Repeated in Ps 135:7, where the one true God is contrasted to false gods (see Ps 135:5,15–17); cf. Job 38:22.

10:14 ˣ S Ps 97:7;
S Isa 1:29
ʸ S Isa 44:20
10:15 ᶻ S Isa 41:24;
S Jer 14:22
10:16 ᵃ S Dt 32:9;
S Ps 119:57 ᵇ ver 12;
Jer 32:17; 33:2
ᶜ S Ex 34:9; Ps 74:2
ᵈ Jer 31:35; 32:18
10:17 ᵉ Eze 12:3-12
10:18 ᶠ S Isa 25:29;
S Isa 22:17
ᵍ S Dt 28:52
10:19 ʰ Job 34:6;
Jer 14:17; 15:18; 30:12,
15; La 2:13; Mic 1:9;
Na 3:19 ⁱ Mic 7:9
10:20 ʲ S Jer 4:20
ᵏ Jer 31:15; La 1:5
10:21 ˡ Jer 22:22;
23:1; 25:34; 50:6
ᵐ ver 8 ⁿ S Isa 56:10
ᵒ Jer 22:30 ᵖ Jer 23:2;
Eze 34:6
10:22 ᑫ Jer 6:22;
27:6; 49:28,30
ʳ Eze 12:19
ˢ S Isa 34:13
10:23 ᵗ S Job 33:29;
S Pr 3:5-6; 20:24
10:24 ᵘ Ps 6:1; 38:1;
S Jer 7:20; 18:23
ᵛ Jer 46:28 ʷ S Jer 30:11
10:25 ˣ S Ps 69:24;
Zep 2:2; 3:8
ʸ S Ps 14:4
ᶻ S Ps 79:7; S Jer 2:3

¹⁴ Everyone is senseless and without knowledge;
　　all goldsmiths are shamed ˣ by their idols.
　Their images are a fraud; ʸ
　　they have no breath in them.
¹⁵ They are worthless, ᶻ the objects of mockery;
　　when their judgment comes, they will perish.
¹⁶ He who is the Portion ᵃ of Jacob is not like these,
　　for he is the Maker of all things, ᵇ
　including Israel, the tribe of his inheritance ᶜ—
　　the LORD Almighty is his name. ᵈ

COMING DESTRUCTION

¹⁷ Gather up your belongings ᵉ to leave the land,
　　you who live under siege.
¹⁸ For this is what the LORD says:
　　"At this time I will hurl ᶠ out
　　　those who live in this land;
　　I will bring distress ᵍ on them
　　　so that they may be captured."

¹⁹ Woe to me because of my injury!
　　My wound ʰ is incurable!
　Yet I said to myself,
　　"This is my sickness, and I must endure ⁱ it."
²⁰ My tent ʲ is destroyed;
　　all its ropes are snapped.
　My children are gone from me and are no more; ᵏ
　　no one is left now to pitch my tent
　　or to set up my shelter.
²¹ The shepherds ˡ are senseless ᵐ
　　and do not inquire of the LORD; ⁿ
　so they do not prosper ᵒ
　　and all their flock is scattered. ᵖ
²² Listen! The report is coming—
　　a great commotion from the land of the north! ᑫ
　It will make the towns of Judah desolate, ʳ
　　a haunt of jackals. ˢ

JEREMIAH'S PRAYER

²³ LORD, I know that people's lives are not their own;
　　it is not for them to direct their steps. ᵗ
²⁴ Discipline me, LORD, but only in due measure—
　　not in your anger, ᵘ
　　or you will reduce me to nothing. ᵛʷ
²⁵ Pour out your wrath on the nations ˣ
　　that do not acknowledge you,
　　on the peoples who do not call on your name. ʸ
　For they have devoured ᶻ Jacob;

10:14 *senseless.* See vv. 8,21; see also note on 4:22. *images.* Cast in metal; the Hebrew for this word is translated "metal god" in Isa 48:5 and "metal images" in Da 11:8. *no breath.* See Ps 135:17.
10:15 *worthless.* See note on v. 3.
10:16 *Portion of Jacob.* A title for God, used again only in 51:19 (see Ps 73:26 and note; 119:57; 142:5; La 3:24). *tribe of his inheritance.* See Isa 63:17. *The LORD Almighty is his name.* See 2:19 and note; Isa 54:5; Am 4:13.
10:17–22 Destruction and exile are imminent.
10:18 *hurl out.* As from a sling.
10:19–20 On behalf of his countrymen, the prophet bemoans their fate and his own (see 4:19–21).
10:20 *My children.* The people of Judah and Jerusalem (Jeremiah never married or had children; see 16:2). *shelter.* See note on 4:20.

10:21 *shepherds…flock.* Rulers and people (see note on 2:8). *senseless.* See vv. 8,14; see also note on 4:22. *do not inquire of the LORD.* Instead, they consult the heavenly bodies (see 8:2). *scattered.* See note on 9:16.
10:22 *great commotion.* The sound of the invaders (see 6:23; 8:16). *land of the north.* Babylonia (see 4:6; 6:22; see also note on Isa 41:25). *haunt of jackals.* See 9:11 and note.
A **10:23–25** On the people's behalf, the prophet prays for divine justice.
A **10:23** Only the Lord can direct people's steps (see Ps 37:23; Pr 16:9 and note).
A **10:25** Repeated almost verbatim in Ps 79:6–7, where the context (see Ps 79:1–5) shows that the prayer is not vengeful but is an appeal for God's justice (see note on Ps 5:10). The verse is recited annually by Jews during their Passover service.

they have devoured him completely
and destroyed his homeland. [a]

THE COVENANT IS BROKEN

11 This is the word that came to Jeremiah from the LORD: [2]"Listen to the terms of this covenant [b] and tell them to the people of Judah and to those who live in Jerusalem. [3]Tell them that this is what the LORD, the God of Israel, says: 'Cursed [c] is everyone who does not obey the terms of this covenant— [4]the terms I commanded your ancestors when I brought them out of Egypt, [d] out of the iron-smelting furnace. [e]' I said, 'Obey [f] me and do everything I command you, and you will be my people, [g] and I will be your God. [5]Then I will fulfill the oath I swore [h] to your ancestors, to give them a land flowing with milk and honey' [i]—the land you possess today."

I answered, "Amen, [j] LORD."

[6]The LORD said to me, "Proclaim [k] all these words in the towns of Judah and in the streets of Jerusalem: 'Listen to the terms of this covenant and follow [l] them. [7]From the time I brought your ancestors up from Egypt until today, I warned them again and again, [m] saying, "Obey me." [8]But they did not listen or pay attention; [n] instead, they followed the stubbornness of their evil hearts. [o] So I brought on them all the curses [p] of the covenant I had commanded them to follow but that they did not keep.' "

[9]Then the LORD said to me, "There is a conspiracy [r] among the people of Judah and those who live in Jerusalem. [10]They have returned to the sins of their ancestors, [s] who refused to listen to my words. [t] They have followed other gods [u] to serve them. [v] Both the house of Israel and the house of Judah have broken the covenant [w] I made with their ancestors. [11]Therefore this is what the LORD says: 'I will bring on them a disaster [x] they cannot escape. [y] Although they cry [z] out to me, I will not listen [a] to them. [12]The towns of Judah and the people of Jerusalem will go and cry out to the gods to whom they burn incense, [b] but they will not help them at all when disaster [c] strikes. [13]You, Judah, have as many gods [d] as you have towns; [e] and the altars you have set up to burn incense [f] to that shameful [g] god Baal are as many as the streets of Jerusalem.'

[14]"Do not pray [h] for this people or offer any plea or petition for them, because I will not listen [i] when they call to me in the time of their distress.

[15] "What is my beloved doing in my temple
as she, with many others, works out her evil schemes?
Can consecrated meat [j] avert your punishment? [k]
When you engage in your wickedness,
then you rejoice. [a]"

[16] The LORD called you a thriving olive tree [l]
with fruit beautiful in form.

[a] 15 Or *Could consecrated meat avert your punishment? / Then you would rejoice*

10:25 [a] Ps 79:6-7
11:2 [b] S Dt 5:2
11:3 [c] Dt 11:26-28; 27:26; 28:15-68; Gal 3:10
11:4 [d] ver 7
[e] S 1Ki 8:51
[f] S Ex 24:8; Jer 7:23
[g] Jer 7:23; 31:33; Eze 11:20
11:5 [h] S Ex 6:8; 13:5; Dt 7:12; Ps 105:8-11 [i] S Ex 3:8
[j] S Dt 27:26
11:6 [k] S Jer 4:5
[l] S Ex 15:26; S Dt 15:5; Jas 1:22
11:7 [m] S 2Ch 36:15
11:8 [n] S Jer 7:26
[o] S Ecc 9:3; S Jer 3:17
[p] Lev 26:14-43; Dt 28:15-68; S Jos 23:15
[q] S 2Ch 7:19; Ps 78:10; Jer 26:4; 32:23; 44:10
11:9 [r] Eze 22:25
11:10 [s] Dt 9:7; S 2Ch 30:7 [t] Zec 7:11
[u] S Jdg 2:12-13; S 10:13 [v] Jer 16:11; Eze 20:8 [w] Isa 24:5; Jer 34:18; Hos 6:7; 8:1
11:11 [x] S 2Ki 22:16; S Jer 4:6
[y] S Job 11:20; La 2:22
[z] S Job 27:9; Jer 14:12; Eze 8:18; Mal 2:13
[a] ver 14; S Ps 66:18; Pr 1:28; S Isa 1:15; 59:2; Eze 8:8; Zec 7:13
11:12 [b] S Dt 32:38; S Jer 44:17
[c] S Dt 32:37; S Jdg 10:14
11:13 [d] S Ex 20:3; Jer 19:4 [e] S 2Ki 17:29
[f] S Jer 7:9; 44:21
[g] S Jer 3:24
11:14 [h] S Ex 32:10
[i] S ver 11
11:15 [j] Hag 2:12
[k] S Jer 7:9-10
11:16 [l] S Ps 1:3; Hos 14:6

11:1—13:27 Because of Judah's violations of its covenant obligations, the people will be exiled to Babylonia. The section is perhaps to be dated to the reign of Josiah (but see note on 13:18).

11:1–17 God's people have broken his covenant with them.

11:2 *Listen.* See note on 2:4. *terms.* Lit. "words," a technical term for covenant stipulations (see vv. 3–4,6; 34:18; see also note on Ex 20:1). *this covenant.* See vv. 3,6,8,10; Dt 29:9. Reference is to the covenant established by God with Israel through Moses at Mount Sinai (see v. 4; Ex 19–24). *tell them.* Periodic public reading of covenants was a common and necessary practice (see Dt 31:10–13; Jos 8:34–35).

11:3 *Cursed is everyone.* "Cursed is anyone" appears at the beginning of every covenant curse in Dt 27:15–26, and the people respond to each of the curses with their "Amen." Blessings resulted from obedience to the covenant (see Dt 28:1–14); curses resulted from disobedience (see Dt 28:15–68; see also Dt 11:26–28; 29:20–21).

11:4 *out of Egypt ... the iron-smelting furnace.* See note on Dt 4:20. *Obey me.* See v. 7; 7:23; Ex 19:5. *my people ... your God.* See note on 7:23.

11:5 *fulfill the oath I swore.* See Ge 15:17–18 and notes; Dt 7:8. *land flowing with milk and honey.* See Ex 32:22; see also note on Ex 3:8. *Amen.* See note on v. 3.

11:6 *Proclaim.* See 2:2; 3:12.

11:7 *again and again.* See note on 7:13.

11:8 *stubbornness of their evil hearts.* See note on 3:17. *So I brought on them.* See 2Ki 17:18–23. *curses of the covenant.* See note on v. 3.

11:9 *conspiracy.* Against the intended reforms of Josiah (see Introduction: Background; see also note on 1:2).

11:10 *refused.* Their sin was deliberate (see note on 9:6). *the covenant.* Lit. "my covenant," emphasizing its origin in God himself.

11:11 *I will bring on them.* Judah will be judged, just as Israel had been judged earlier (see v. 10; see also 2Ki 17:18–23).

11:12 *burn incense.* See vv. 13,17; see also note on 1:16.

11:13 *as many gods as ... towns.* See note on 2:28. *altars ... as many as the streets.* See 2Ch 28:24. *to that shameful god Baal.* See 3:24; see also notes on 2:26; Jdg 6:32.

11:14 *Do not pray for this people.* See note on 7:16; cf. 1Jn 5:16.

11:15 See 7:10–11,21–24. *my beloved.* Judah (see 12:7; cf. Dt 33:12, where Benjamin is called the "beloved of the LORD").

11:16 *called you ... olive tree.* See Ps 52:8; 128:3. *storm.* The Hebrew for this word appears elsewhere only in Eze 1:24, where it is translated "tumult" in reference to the noise made by an army (see Isa 13:4). *branches will be broken.* See Eze 31:12.

11:16 *m* S Jer 7:20;
21:14 *n* S Isa 27:11;
Ro 11:17-24
11:17 *o* S Ex 15:17;
Isa 5:2; Jer 12:2; 45:4
p ver 11 *q* Jer 7:18
r S Jer 7:9
11:19 *s* S Ps 44:22
t ver 21; S Ps 44:16;
54:3; 71:10; Jer 18:18;
20:10 *u* S Job 28:13;
S Ps 116:9; Isa 53:8
v Ps 83:4
11:20 *w* Ps 7:11
x S 1Sa 2:3;
S 1Ch 29:17
y S Ps 26:2
z S Ps 58:10; La 3:60
11:21 *a* S Jos 21:18
b S ver 19; Jer 12:6;
21:7; 34:20
c S Isa 30:10
d Jer 2:30; 18:23; 26:8,
11; 38:4
11:22 *e* S Isa 9:17;
Jer 18:21
11:23 *f* Jer 6:9
g Jer 23:12
12:1 *h* S Ezr 9:15;
Job 8:3; Da 9:14
i S Job 5:8 *j* Eze 18:25
k S Job 21:7,13;
Ps 37:7; Jer 5:27-28
12:2 *l* S Jer 11:17
m S Job 5:3
n S Isa 29:13;
S Jer 3:10;
S Eze 22:27; Mt 15:8;
Mk 7:6; Tit 1:16
12:3 *o* Ps 7:9; 11:5;
139:1-4 *p* S Ps 44:11
q Jer 16:18; 17:18;
20:11

> But with the roar of a mighty storm
> he will set it on fire, *m*
> and its branches will be broken. *n*

¹⁷The LORD Almighty, who planted *o* you, has decreed disaster *p* for you, because the house of Israel and the house of Judah have done evil and aroused *q* my anger by burning incense to Baal. *r*

PLOT AGAINST JEREMIAH

¹⁸Because the LORD revealed their plot to me, I knew it, for at that time he showed me what they were doing. ¹⁹I had been like a gentle lamb led to the slaughter; *s* I did not realize that they had plotted *t* against me, saying,

> "Let us destroy the tree and its fruit;
> let us cut him off from the land of the living, *u*
> that his name be remembered *v* no more."
> ²⁰But you, LORD Almighty, who judge righteously *w*
> and test the heart *x* and mind, *y*
> let me see your vengeance *z* on them,
> for to you I have committed my cause.

²¹"Therefore this is what the LORD says about the people of Anathoth *a* who are seeking your life *b* and saying, 'Do not prophesy *c* in the name of the LORD or you will die *d* by our hands'— ²²therefore this is what the LORD Almighty says: 'I will punish them. Their young men *e* will die by the sword, their sons and daughters by famine. ²³Not even a remnant *f* will be left to them, because I will bring disaster on the people of Anathoth in the year of their punishment. *g*' "

JEREMIAH'S COMPLAINT

12
> You are always righteous, *h* LORD,
> when I bring a case *i* before you.
> Yet I would speak with you about your justice: *j*
> Why does the way of the wicked prosper? *k*
> Why do all the faithless live at ease?
> ²You have planted *l* them, and they have taken root;
> they grow and bear fruit. *m*
> You are always on their lips
> but far from their hearts. *n*
> ³Yet you know me, LORD;
> you see me and test *o* my thoughts about you.
> Drag them off like sheep *p* to be butchered!
> Set them apart for the day of slaughter! *q*

11:17 Fulfilled when Judah was destroyed in 586 B.C. (see 44:2–3). *aroused my anger.* See 8:19; Dt 31:29.

11:18–23 The first of Jeremiah's six "confessions" (see Introduction: Author and Date).

11:18 *their . . . they.* Jeremiah's personal enemies, the "people of Anathoth" (vv. 21,23), his hometown.

11:19 *lamb led to the slaughter.* See 51:40; see also Isa 53:7 and note. *destroy the tree and its fruit.* Contrast 12:2. *cut him off from the land of the living.* See Isa 53:8; contrast Ps 27:13. *name.* Since Jeremiah had no children (see 16:2), his name would die with him. *be remembered no more.* As though he were evil (see Job 24:20; Eze 21:32).

11:20 Repeated almost verbatim in 20:12; see also 17:10. *you . . . who judge righteously.* See note on Ge 18:25.

11:21 *people of Anathoth who are seeking your life.* See 12:6. "Your enemies are the members of your own household" (Mic 7:6, quoted by Jesus in Mt 10:36).

11:22 *sword . . . famine.* See note on 5:12.

11:23 *remnant.* See 6:9; Isa 10:20–22 and notes. *them.* The conspirators in Anathoth, not its entire population, since 128 men of Anathoth returned to their hometown after the exile (see Ezr 2:23).

12:1–4 The second of Jeremiah's "confessions" (see Introduc-

tion: Author and Date), continuing and closely related to the first (11:18–23). Jeremiah speaks in vv. 1–4, and God responds in vv. 5–6.

12:1 *You are . . . righteous.* See note on Ge 18:25; see also 11:20; Ps 51:4; Ro 3:4. Because God is righteous, he is a dependable arbiter and judge. *Yet.* He is nevertheless ready to listen to our questions and complaints. *Why does . . . the wicked prosper?* The question is not unique to Jeremiah (see, e.g., Job 21:7–15; Mal 3:15). The Lord replies that ultimately the wicked in Judah will perish (vv. 7–13) and that the wicked invaders who destroy them will themselves be destroyed (vv. 14–17).

12:2 *You have planted them.* But a sovereign God can always reconsider his intentions if conditions warrant a change (see 18:9–10). *bear fruit.* The wicked flourish, while Jeremiah's fellow citizens plot to destroy his own "fruit" (see 11:19). *on their lips . . . far from their hearts.* Quoted in part by Jesus in Mt 15:8–9.

12:3 *test my thoughts.* See 11:20. *like sheep to be butchered.* Jeremiah asks that his wicked countrymen receive the fate mentioned in 11:19. His request arises not so much out of a desire for revenge as for the vindication of God's righteousness (see note on 10:25). *day of slaughter.* An expression found elsewhere only in Jas 5:5 (see note there).

⁴ How long will the land lie parched^r
    and the grass in every field be withered?^s
Because those who live in it are wicked,
    the animals and birds have perished.^t
Moreover, the people are saying,
    "He will not see what happens to us."

GOD'S ANSWER

⁵ "If you have raced with people on foot
    and they have worn you out,
    how can you compete with horses?
If you stumble^a in safe country,
    how will you manage in the thickets^u by^b the Jordan?
⁶ Your relatives, members of your own family—
    even they have betrayed you;
    they have raised a loud cry against you.^v
Do not trust them,
    though they speak well of you.^w

⁷ "I will forsake^x my house,
    abandon^y my inheritance;
I will give the one I love^z
    into the hands of her enemies.^a
⁸ My inheritance has become to me
    like a lion^b in the forest.
She roars at me;
    therefore I hate her.^c
⁹ Has not my inheritance become to me
    like a speckled bird of prey
    that other birds of prey surround and attack?
Go and gather all the wild beasts;
    bring them to devour.^d
¹⁰ Many shepherds^e will ruin my vineyard
    and trample down my field;
they will turn my pleasant field
    into a desolate wasteland.^f
¹¹ It will be made a wasteland,^g
    parched and desolate before me;^h
the whole land will be laid waste
    because there is no one who cares.
¹² Over all the barren heights in the desert
    destroyers will swarm,
for the swordⁱ of the Lord^j will devour^k
    from one end of the land to the other;^l

---

^a 5 Or *you feel secure only*   ^b 5 Or *the flooding of*

12:4 ^r S Jer 4:28
^s S ver 11; S Jer 4:26;
Joel 1:10-12; Am 1:2
^t Dt 28:15-18;
S Jer 4:25; S 9:10
12:5 ^u Jer 49:19;
50:44
12:6 ^v S Pr 26:24-
25; Jer 9:4 ^w Ps 12:2
12:7 ^x S 2Ki 21:14
^y S Jer 7:29 ^z Isa 5:1
^a Jer 17:4
12:8 ^b S Ps 17:12
^c Ps 5:5; Hos 9:15;
Am 6:8
12:9 ^d S Dt 28:26;
Isa 56:9; Jer 15:3;
Eze 23:25; 39:17-20
12:10 ^e Jer 23:1;
25:34; Eze 34:2-10
^f Isa 5:1-7; Jer 9:10;
25:11
12:11 ^g S Isa 5:6;
S 24:4 ^h ver 4;
Jer 9:12; 14:4; 23:10
12:12 ⁱ Eze 21:3-4
^j S Isa 34:2; Jer 31:8;
Jer 46:10; 47:6;
Eze 14:17; 21:28; 33:2
^k S Dt 32:42 ^l Jer 3:2

12:4 *parched...withered.* See 23:10; see also 3:3; 14:1 note. Apparently there was a series of droughts in Judah during Jeremiah's ministry. *He will not see.* The prophet's enemies do not believe that his predictions will be fulfilled. Or they believe that if they are, Jeremiah will not live to see their fulfillment.
12:5 The Lord warns Jeremiah that in the future his troubles will increase (see, e.g., 38:4–6). *stumble.* The Hebrew for this word usually means "trust" (see TNIV text note). *thickets.* Providing cover for lions (see 49:19; 50:44; Zec 11:3). If the Hebrew for this word means "flooding" (see TNIV text note) here, an ancient example is described in Jos 3:15.
12:6 *family.* Lit. "house," linking this verse verbally with the following context (see v. 7). Apparently, members of Jeremiah's own family were included in the "people of Anathoth" (11:21,23) who wanted to kill him.
12:7–17 The Lord will judge Judah (vv. 7–13) as well as the wicked neighboring nations (vv. 14–17).
12:7 *house.* Judah (see, e.g., 11:17). *inheritance.* God's land and

people (see vv. 8–9,14–15; see also Ex 15:17 and note; Dt 4:20; Isa 19:25; 47:6). *the one I love.* See note on 11:15.
12:8 *I hate her.* I will withdraw my love from her by giving her "into the hands of her enemies" (v. 7; see Mal 1:3 and note).
12:9 *other birds of prey...wild beasts.* Judah's enemies (see Isa 56:9 and note).
12:10 *shepherds.* Rulers (see note on 2:8). *my vineyard.* Judah (see 2:21 and note). *pleasant field.* See 3:19 and note.
12:11 *parched.* See v. 4 and note. A total of seven s-sounds and seven m-sounds in the Hebrew of this brief verse punctuate its theme and provide a striking example of Jeremiah's literary gifts (see Introduction: Literary Features).
12:12 *barren heights.* Places of idolatrous worship (see 3:2; Nu 23:3). *destroyers.* The Babylonians (see note on 4:7). *sword of the Lord.* Symbolizing God's instruments of judgment (see 25:29; 47:6 and note on Ps 7:12–13). *from one end...to the other.* See 25:33. *no one will be safe.* Lit. "there will be no peace/safety for anyone" (see 6:14 and note).

12:12 *m* Jer 7:10
12:13 *n* S Lev 26:20;
S Dt 28:38
o S Ex 15:7; S Jer 4:26
12:14 *p* S Dt 29:28;
S 2Ch 7:20 *q* S Ps 9:6;
Zec 2:7-9
r S Dt 28:63
12:15 *s* Ps 6:2
t S Dt 30:3; Am 9:14-15
12:16 *u* Jer 18:8
v S Jer 4:2
w S Jos 23:7
x S Isa 26:18; 49:6;
Jer 3:17
12:17 *y* S Ge 27:29
13:3 *z* Jer 33:1
13:4 *a* S Ge 2:14
13:5 *b* Ex 40:16
13:9 *c* S Lev 26:19;
S Mt 23:12; S Lk 1:51
13:10 *d* Jer 22:21
e S Ecc 9:3; S Jer 3:17
f S Dt 8:19; Jer 9:14
g S Jdg 10:13
h Eze 15:3
13:11 *i* Isa 63:12;
Jer 32:20 *j* Ex 19:5-6;
Isa 43:21; S Jer 3:17
k S Isa 65:12;
S Jer 7:26

no one will be safe. *m*

13 They will sow wheat but reap thorns;
 they will wear themselves out but gain nothing. *n*
They will bear the shame of their harvest
 because of the LORD's fierce anger." *o*

¹⁴This is what the LORD says: "As for all my wicked neighbors who seize the inheritance *p* I gave my people Israel, I will uproot *q* them from their lands and I will uproot *r* the house of Judah from among them. ¹⁵But after I uproot them, I will again have compassion *s* and will bring *t* each of them back to their own inheritance and their own country. ¹⁶And if they learn *u* well the ways of my people and swear by my name, saying, 'As surely as the LORD lives' *v*—even as they once taught my people to swear by Baal *w*—then they will be established among my people. *x* ¹⁷But if any nation does not listen, I will completely uproot and destroy *y* it," declares the LORD.

A LINEN BELT

13 This is what the LORD said to me: "Go and buy a linen belt and put it around your waist, but do not let it touch water." ²So I bought a belt, as the LORD directed, and put it around my waist.

³Then the word of the LORD came to me a second time: *z* ⁴"Take the belt you bought and are wearing around your waist, and go now to Perath *a* *a* and hide it there in a crevice in the rocks." ⁵So I went and hid it at Perath, as the LORD told me. *b*

⁶Many days later the LORD said to me, "Go now to Perath and get the belt I told you to hide there." ⁷So I went to Perath and dug up the belt and took it from the place where I had hidden it, but now it was ruined and completely useless.

⁸Then the word of the LORD came to me: ⁹"This is what the LORD says: 'In the same way I will ruin the pride of Judah and the great pride *c* of Jerusalem. ¹⁰These wicked people, who refuse to listen *d* to my words, who follow the stubbornness of their hearts *e* and go after other gods *f* to serve and worship them, *g* will be like this belt—completely useless! *h* ¹¹For as a belt is bound around the waist, so I bound the whole house of Israel and the whole house of Judah to me,' declares the LORD, 'to be my people for my renown *i* and praise and honor. *j* But they have not listened.' *k*

WINESKINS

¹²"Say to them: 'This is what the LORD, the God of Israel, says: Every wineskin should be filled with wine.' And if they say to you, 'Don't we know that every wineskin should be filled with wine?' ¹³then tell them, 'This is what the LORD says: I am going to fill with

---

a 4 Or possibly *to the Euphrates*; similarly in verses 5-7

12:13 See 14:2–4.
12:14 *wicked neighbors.* See, e.g., 2Ki 24:2. *seize.* Lit. "touch," used in the context of attack and plunder in Zec 2:8. *uproot.* Carry off into exile (see, e.g., 1Ki 14:15).
12:15 The exiles from Judah, and those from the neighboring nations, will eventually be brought back to their respective lands (v. 16; 32:37,44; 33:26; 48:47; 49:6).
12:16 To be fulfilled in the Messianic age (see Isa 56:6–7 and note on 56:7). *ways.* See note on 10:2. *Baal.* See note on Jdg 2:13. *be established.* The Hebrew for this phrase is translated "prosper" in Mal 3:15.
13:1–27 A series of five warnings, the first two (vv. 1–11,12–14) written in prose and the last three (vv. 15–17,18–19,20–27) in poetry.
13:1–11 The story of the ruined, useless belt is the first major example of the Lord's commanding Jeremiah to perform symbolic acts to illustrate his message (see Introduction: Literary Features).

13:1–2,4–7 *Go and buy … So I bought … Take the belt … and hide it … So I went and hid it … Go now to Perath and get the belt … So I went to Perath and dug up the belt.* Like his spiritual ancestor Abraham (see note on Ge 12:4), Jeremiah was characterized by prompt obedience.
13:1 *linen.* The material of which the priests' garments were made (see Eze 44:17–18), symbolic of Israel's holiness as a "kingdom of priests" (see Ex 19:6 and note). The linen belt is a symbol of the formerly intimate relationship between God and Judah

(see v. 11). *do not let it touch water.* Do not wash it—symbolic of Judah's sinful pride (see v. 9).
13:3 *Then.* Some time later.
13:4 *Perath.* Perhaps the same as Parah (Jos 18:23), near the modern Wadi Farah, three miles northeast of Anathoth. Since in other contexts the Hebrew for Perath refers to the river Euphrates (see TNIV text note), it serves as an appropriate symbol of the corrupting Assyrian and Babylonian influence on Judah that began during the reign of Ahaz (see 2Ki 16). *crevice in the rocks.* See note on 16:16.
13:6 *Many days later.* Perhaps a reference to the lengthy Babylonian exile.
13:7 *dug up.* The belt had either been buried by the prophet or silted over by the water of the wadi. *it was ruined.* As foreseen in Lev 26:39, God's people in exile would waste away because of their sins and the sins of their ancestors.
13:9 *pride … great pride.* Contrast 9:23–24. Judah's vaunted pride would be a cause of her downfall and exile (see vv. 15,17), as foreshadowed in Lev 26:19.
13:10 *refuse to listen.* See note on 9:6. *stubbornness of their hearts.* See note on 3:17. *completely useless.* See 24:8.
13:11 *But they have not listened.* And therefore the promise of Dt 26:19 can no longer be fulfilled in them.
13:12–14 The Lord uses the imagery of filled wineskins to point toward the eventual destruction of Judah's leaders and people.

drunkenness *l* all who live in this land, including the kings who sit on David's throne, the priests, the prophets and all those living in Jerusalem. ¹⁴I will smash them one against the other, parents and children alike, declares the LORD. I will allow no pity *m* or mercy or compassion *n* to keep me from destroying *o* them.' "

THREAT OF CAPTIVITY

¹⁵ Hear and pay attention,
    do not be arrogant,
    for the LORD has spoken. *p*
¹⁶ Give glory *q* to the LORD your God
    before he brings the darkness,
    before your feet stumble *r*
    on the darkening hills.
You hope for light,
    but he will turn it to utter darkness
    and change it to deep gloom. *s*
¹⁷ If you do not listen, *t*
    I will weep in secret
    because of your pride;
my eyes will weep bitterly,
    overflowing with tears, *u*
    because the LORD's flock *v* will be taken captive. *w*

¹⁸ Say to the king *x* and to the queen mother, *y*
    "Come down from your thrones,
    for your glorious crowns *z*
    will fall from your heads."
¹⁹ The cities in the Negev will be shut up,
    and there will be no one to open them.
All Judah *a* will be carried into exile,
    carried completely away.

²⁰ Look up and see
    those who are coming from the north. *b*
Where is the flock *c* that was entrusted to you,
    the sheep of which you boasted?
²¹ What will you say when ˻the LORD˼ sets over you
    those you cultivated as your special allies? *d*
Will not pain grip you
    like that of a woman in labor? *e*
²² And if you ask yourself,
    "Why has this happened to me?" *f*—
    it is because of your many sins *g*
    that your skirts have been torn off *h*
    and your body mistreated. *i*

13:13 *l* Ps 60:3;
75:8; S Isa 29:9;
Jer 25:18; 51:57
13:14 *m* Eze 7:4;
8:18; 9:5,10; 24:14;
Zec 11:6 *n* S Isa 9:17;
Jer 16:5 *o* Dt 29:20;
Isa 9:19-21;
S Jer 7:20; 49:32,36;
La 2:21; Eze 5:10
13:15 *p* S Ex 23:21;
Ps 95:7-8
13:16 *q* S Jos 7:19
r S Lev 26:37;
S Job 3:23; Isa 51:17;
Jer 23:12 *s* S 1Sa 2:9;
S Job 3:5; S Ps 82:5
13:17 *t* Mal 2:2
u S Jer 9:1 *v* Ps 80:1;
Jer 23:1 *w* Jer 14:18;
29:1
13:18 *x* Jer 21:11;
22:1 *y* S 1Ki 2:19;
S 2Ki 24:8;
S Isa 22:17
z S 2Sa 12:30; La 5:16;
Eze 16:12; 21:26
13:19 *a* Jer 20:4;
52:30; La 1:3
13:20 *b* Jer 6:22;
Hab 1:6 *c* Jer 23:2
13:21 *d* S Ps 41:9;
Jer 4:30; 20:10; 38:22;
Ob 1:7 *e* S Jer 4:31
13:22 *f* S 1Ki 9:9
g Jer 9:2-6; 16:10-12
h S Isa 20:4 *i* La 1:8;
Eze 16:37; 23:26;
Na 3:5-6

13:13 *drunkenness.* In a literal sense (see, e.g., Isa 28:7), but also symbolizing the effects of the wine of God's wrath (see 25:15–29; Ps 60:3; Isa 51:17–23; Eze 23:32–34). *kings...priests ...prophets...all those living in Jerusalem.* See 26:16; see also note on 1:18.
13:14 *smash them one against the other.* The various factions in Judah produced only confusion and chaos in the face of determined outside enemies. *no pity or mercy or compassion.* See 21:7; see also Eze 5:11.
13:15–17 Sinful pride carries the seeds of its own destruction, says the prophet.
13:15 *Hear.* See note on 2:4. *do not be arrogant.* See v. 17; see also note on v. 9.
13:16 *Give glory to...God.* Confess your sins (cf. Jos 7:19; Jn 9:24). *You hope for light, but.* Cf. the description of the day of the Lord in Am 5:18–20; 8:9.
13:17 *I will weep.* See note on 9:1. *pride.* See v. 15; see also note on v. 9. *flock.* People (see v. 20; Zec 10:3; see also note on 10:21). *taken captive.* Into exile (see v. 19).

13:18–19 The prophet speaks: Exile is imminent.
13:18 *king and...queen mother.* Probably Jehoiachin and Nehushta (2Ki 24:8). If so, the date is 597 B.C., about 12 years after Josiah's death (see note on 11:1—13:27). *your...crowns will fall.* See 22:24–26; 29:2; 2Ki 24:15; cf. Eze 21:25–27 and notes.
13:19 *Negev.* The dry southland (see note on Ge 12:9). *shut up.* Blocked by debris (see Isa 24:10). *All Judah.* The nation as a whole. *carried completely away.* Cf. Am 1:6,9 ("whole communities").
13:20–27 First the prophet speaks (vv. 20–23), then the Lord (vv. 24–27). Judah's willful rebellion has made exile inevitable.
13:20 *you...you.* Jerusalem, personified as a woman (see vv. 21–22,26–27), is being addressed. *the north.* Babylonia (see 4:6; see also note on Isa 41:25). *flock...sheep.* See note on v. 17.
13:21 *special allies.* Perhaps Egypt and Babylon, who alternated in dominating Judah (see Introduction: Background). *like...a woman in labor.* See note on 4:31.
13:22 *skirts...torn off.* Disgraced publicly, like a common prostitute (see vv. 26–27; Isa 47:2–3; Hos 2:3,10).

13:23 /S 2Ch 6:36
13:24 *k* S Ps 1:4
/S Lev 26:33;
S Job 1:19; S 27:21
13:25 *m* S Job 20:29
; Mt 24:51
n S Isa 17:10
o S Dt 31:20; S Ps 4:2;
106:19-21
13:26 *p* La 1:8;
Eze 16:37; Na 3:5
13:27 *q* Eze 23:29
/r S Isa 57:7; Eze 6:13
s Hos 8:5
14:1 /t S Dt 28:22;
S Isa 5:6
14:2 *u* S Isa 3:26
14:3 *v* S Dt 28:48;
S 2Ki 18:31; Job 6:19-
20 *w* S Est 6:12
14:4 *x* S Jer 3:3;
S 12:11; Am 4:8;
Zec 14:17
14:5 *y* Isa 15:6
14:6 *z* S Job 39:5-6;
S Ps 104:11; S Jer 2:24
a S Ge 47:4
14:7 *b* S Isa 3:9;
Hos 5:5 *c* S 1Sa 12:22;
S Ps 79:9

23 Can an Ethiopian[a] change his skin
    or a leopard its spots?
Neither can you do good
    who are accustomed to doing evil.[j]

24 "I will scatter you like chaff[k]
    driven by the desert wind.[l]
25 This is your lot,
    the portion[m] I have decreed for you,"

                        declares the LORD,

"because you have forgotten[n] me
    and trusted in false gods.[o]
26 I will pull up your skirts over your face
    that your shame may be seen[p]—
27 your adulteries and lustful neighings,
    your shameless prostitution![q]
I have seen your detestable acts
    on the hills and in the fields.[r]
Woe to you, Jerusalem!
    How long will you be unclean?"[s]

DROUGHT, FAMINE, SWORD

14 This is the word of the LORD that came to Jeremiah concerning the drought:[t]

2 "Judah mourns,[u]
    her cities languish;
they wail for the land,
    and a cry goes up from Jerusalem.
3 The nobles send their servants for water;
    they go to the cisterns
    but find no water.[v]
They return with their jars unfilled;
    dismayed and despairing,
    they cover their heads.[w]
4 The ground is cracked
    because there is no rain in the land;[x]
the farmers are dismayed
    and cover their heads.
5 Even the doe in the field
    deserts her newborn fawn
    because there is no grass.[y]
6 Wild donkeys stand on the barren heights[z]
    and pant like jackals;
their eyes fail
    for lack of food."[a]

7 Although our sins testify[b] against us,
    do something, LORD, for the sake of your name.[c]

---

a 23 Hebrew *Cushite* (probably a person from the upper Nile region)

13:23 *Can...spots?* A rhetorical question, expecting a negative answer (see 17:9).
13:24 *like chaff driven.* The fate of the wicked (see, e.g., Ps 1:4). *desert wind.* See note on 4:11.
13:25 *forgotten me.* See 2:32 and note.
13:26 See v. 22 and note.
13:27 *adulteries and lustful neighings.* See note on 5:8. *shameless prostitution.* See Eze 16:26; see also Ex 34:15 and note. *How long....?* There is yet hope, however slender, to postpone the divine wrath (cf., e.g., 12:14–16).
14:1—15:21 Messages delivered by Jeremiah during an especially severe drought, the date of which is unknown.
14:1—15:9 After an initial vivid description of the drought (14:2–6), Jeremiah alternately prays (14:7–9, 13,19–22) and God responds (14:10–12, 14–18; 15:1–9).

14:1 *drought.* See 17:8. Unlike that in 3:3; 12:4, the suffering is increased because an enemy has invaded the land (see v. 18). Drought was one of the curses threatened (see 23:10) for disobedience to the covenant (see Lev 26:19–20; Dt 28:22–24).
14:2 *cities.* Lit. "gates" (see note on Ge 22:17); see 15:7.
14:3 *nobles.* A drought is no respecter of class distinctions. *cover their heads.* In mourning (see v. 4; 2Sa 15:30; cf. 2Sa 19:4).
14:4 *because there is no rain.* See 1Ki 17:7. Unlike Egypt, where the mighty Nile waters the ground, the Holy Land depends on adequate rainfall.
14:6 *pant.* The Hebrew underlying this word is translated "sniffing the wind" in 2:24. There a female wild donkey (Jerusalem) was in the heat of desire, while here the male wild donkeys are panting because of a drought brought on by Judah's sin. *eyes fail.* See Ps 6:7 and note.

For our backsliding[d] is great;
　　we have sinned[e] against you.
[8] You who are the hope[f] of Israel,
　　its Savior[g] in times of distress,[h]
　why are you like a stranger in the land,
　　like a traveler who stays only a night?
[9] Why are you like someone taken by surprise,
　　like a warrior powerless to save?[i]
You are among[j] us, Lord,
　　and we bear your name;[k]
　do not forsake[l] us!

[10] This is what the Lord says about this people:

"They greatly love to wander;
　　they do not restrain their feet.[m]
So the Lord does not accept[n] them;
　he will now remember[o] their wickedness
　　and punish them for their sins."[p]

[11] Then the Lord said to me, "Do not pray[q] for the well-being of this people. [12] Although they fast, I will not listen to their cry;[r] though they offer burnt offerings[s] and grain offerings,[t] I will not accept[u] them. Instead, I will destroy them with the sword,[v] famine[w] and plague."[x]

[13] But I said, "Ah, Sovereign Lord, the prophets[y] keep telling them, 'You will not see the sword or suffer famine.[z] Indeed, I will give you lasting peace[a] in this place.' "

[14] Then the Lord said to me, "The prophets are prophesying lies[b] in my name. I have not sent[c] them or appointed them or spoken to them. They are prophesying to you false visions,[d] divinations,[e] idolatries[a] and the delusions of their own minds. [15] Therefore, this is what the Lord says about the prophets who are prophesying in my name: I did not send them, yet they are saying, 'No sword or famine will touch this land.' Those same prophets will perish[f] by sword and famine.[g] [16] And the people they are prophesying to will be thrown out into the streets of Jerusalem because of the famine and sword. There will be no one to bury[h] them, their wives, their sons and their daughters.[i] I will pour out on them the calamity they deserve.[j]

[17] "Speak this word to them:

" 'Let my eyes overflow with tears[k]
　　night and day without ceasing,
　for the Virgin[l] Daughter, my people,
　　has suffered a grievous wound,
　　a crushing blow.[m]
[18] If I go into the country,
　　I see those slain by the sword;
　if I go into the city,
　　I see the ravages of famine.[n]

---

[a] 14 Or *visions, worthless divinations*

### Cross references (right margin)

14:7 [d] S Jer 2:19; 5:6
[e] S Jer 8:14
14:8 [f] S Ps 9:18; Jer 17:13; 50:7
[g] Ps 18:46; S Isa 25:9
[h] Ps 46:1
14:9 [i] S Isa 50:2
[j] S Ge 17:7; Jer 8:19
[k] Isa 63:19; Jer 15:16
[l] S Ps 27:9
14:10 [m] Ps 119:101; Jer 2:25 [n] Jer 6:20; Am 5:22 [o] Hos 7:2; 9:9; Am 8:7
[p] Jer 44:21-23; Hos 8:13; Am 3:2
14:11 [q] S Ex 32:10; S 1Sa 2:25
14:12 [r] S Dt 1:45; S 1Sa 8:18; S Jer 11:11
[s] Lev 1:1-17; Jer 7:21
[t] S Lev 2:1-16
[u] Am 5:22
[v] S Isa 51:19; S Jer 9:16 [w] Jer 15:2; 16:4 [x] Jer 21:6; 27:8, 13; 32:24; 34:17; Eze 14:21
14:13 [y] Dt 18:22; Jer 27:14; 37:19
[z] S Jer 5:12
[a] S Isa 30:10; S Jer 4:10
14:14 [b] S Jer 5:1; 23:25; 27:14; Eze 13:2 [c] Jer 23:21,32; 29:31; Eze 13:6 [d] Jer 23:16; La 2:9 [e] Eze 12:24
14:15 [f] Jer 20:6; Eze 14:9 [g] Jer 5:12-13; 16:4; La 1:19
14:16 [h] Ps 79:3
[i] S Jer 7:33 / S Pr 1:31; S Jer 17:10
14:17 [k] S Ps 119:136
[l] S 2Ki 19:21; S Isa 23:12
[m] S Jer 8:21
14:18 [n] Eze 7:15

Study notes (bottom)

14:7–9 The prophet prays on behalf of the people (see v. 11).
14:7 *for the sake of your name.* See v. 21; Jos 7:9; Isa 48:9–11. *backsliding.* See 2:19; 3:22; 5:6. The word implies apostasy.
14:8 *hope of Israel.* See v. 22; 17:13; 50:7; Ac 28:20.
14:9 *we bear your name.* We belong to you, our ever-present Savior (see note on 7:10).
14:10–12 The Lord responds.
14:10–11 *this people.* God does not acknowledge them as his own (see Isa 6:9–10; 8:6,11–12; see also note on Ex 17:4).
14:10 *wander.* After false gods. See v. 10. *the Lord does not ...their sins.* The Hebrew for these three lines is quoted verbatim from Hos 8:13 (cf. Hos 9:9).
14:11 *Do not pray.* See note on 7:16; cf. 1Sa 7:8; 12:19.

14:12 *not accept them.* Sacrifice is to no avail when unaccompanied by repentance (see note on 6:20). *sword, famine and plague.* Curses for violating God's covenant (see Lev 26:25–26); the first occurrence of this triad, which oc-

curs 15 times in Jeremiah (see Introduction: Literary Features; see also Eze 5:16–17 and note).
14:13 Jeremiah reminds the Lord of what the false prophets are saying. *not ... sword or ... famine.* See 5:12. *lasting peace.* Jeremiah's elaboration of the false prophets' "Peace, peace" (see 6:14; 8:11).
14:14–18 The Lord responds.
14:14 *lies.* See 5:12. *in my name.* See Dt 18:20,22. *delusions of their own minds.* See 23:26.
14:15 *Those ... prophets will perish.* See 28:15–17; Dt 18:20.
14:16 *no one to bury them.* See note on 7:33. *wives ... sons ... daughters.* All would perish, because all had worshiped false gods (see note on 7:18).
14:17 *my eyes overflow with tears.* See 9:18; 13:17. *Virgin Daughter, my people.* Lit. "the virgin of the daughter of my people" (see 8:11; Isa 22:4 and note on 2Ki 19:21).

14:18 ºS 2Ch 36:10;
S Jer 13:17
14:19 ᵖ Jer 7:29
ᑫ S Isa 1:6; Jer 30:12-
13 ʳ S Job 19:8;
S Jer 8:15
14:20 ˢ S Jer 3:13
ᵗ S Lev 26:40;
S 1Ki 8:47; S Ezr 9:6
ᵘ S Jdg 10:10;
Da 9:7-8
14:21 ᵛver 7;
S Jos 7:9 ʷIsa 62:7;
Jer 3:17 ˣS Ex 2:24
14:22 ʸS Isa 41:24;
S 44:10; Jer 10:15;
16:19; Hab 2:18
ᶻS 1Ki 8:36;
S Ps 135:7
ªS Isa 43:10
15:1 ᵇS Ex 32:11;
Nu 14:13-20
ᶜS 1Sa 1:20; S 7:8
ᵈS 1Sa 2:25;
S Jer 7:16
ᵉS 2Ki 17:20;
Jer 16:13
15:2 ᶠJer 42:22;
43:11; 44:13
ᵍS Dt 28:26;
S Jer 14:12; La 4:9
ʰEze 12:11; Rev 13:10
15:3 ⁱS Nu 33:4
ʲS Lev 26:25
ᵏS 1Ki 21:19;
S 2Ki 9:36
ˡS Dt 28:26
ᵐS Lev 26:22;
Eze 14:21; 33:27
15:4 ⁿJer 24:9;
29:18; 34:17
ºS Dt 28:25;
S Job 17:6
ᵖS 2Ki 21:2; 23:26-27
15:5 ᑫJer 27:11;
51:19; S Jer 13:14;
16:13; 21:7; Na 3:7
15:6 ʳS Dt 32:15;
Jer 6:19

Both prophet and priest
⠀⠀have gone to a land they know not. º ' "

¹⁹ Have you rejected Judah completely? ᵖ
⠀⠀Do you despise Zion?
Why have you afflicted us
⠀⠀so that we cannot be healed? ᑫ
We hoped for peace
⠀⠀but no good has come,
for a time of healing
⠀⠀but there is only terror. ʳ
²⁰ We acknowledge ˢ our wickedness, Lᴏʀᴅ,
⠀⠀and the guilt of our ancestors; ᵗ
⠀⠀we have indeed sinned ᵘ against you.
²¹ For the sake of your name ᵛ do not despise us;
⠀⠀do not dishonor your glorious throne. ʷ
Remember your covenant ˣ with us
⠀⠀and do not break it.
²² Do any of the worthless idols ʸ of the nations bring rain? ᶻ
⠀⠀Do the skies themselves send down showers?
No, it is you, Lᴏʀᴅ our God.
⠀⠀Therefore our hope is in you,
⠀⠀for you are the one who does all this. ª

15 Then the Lᴏʀᴅ said to me: "Even if Moses ᵇ and Samuel ᶜ were to stand before me, my heart would not go out to this people. ᵈ Send them away from my presence! ᵉ Let them go! ²And if they ask you, 'Where shall we go?' tell them, 'This is what the Lᴏʀᴅ says:

" 'Those destined for death, to death;
⠀⠀those for the sword, to the sword; ᶠ
⠀⠀those for starvation, to starvation; ᵍ
⠀⠀those for captivity, to captivity.' ʰ

³"I will send four kinds of destroyers ⁱ against them," declares the Lᴏʀᴅ, "the sword ʲ to kill and the dogs ᵏ to drag away and the birds ˡ and the wild animals to devour and destroy. ᵐ ⁴I will make them abhorrent ⁿ to all the kingdoms of the earth º because of what Manasseh ᵖ son of Hezekiah king of Judah did in Jerusalem.

⁵"Who will have pity ᑫ on you, Jerusalem?
⠀⠀Who will mourn for you?
⠀⠀Who will stop to ask how you are?
⁶ You have rejected ʳ me," declares the Lᴏʀᴅ.
⠀⠀"You keep on backsliding.

14:19–22 The prophet prays on behalf of the people.

14:20 *guilt of our ancestors.* See 2:5–6; 7:25–26. *we have ...sinned.* Repentance brings restoration (see Dt 30:2–3).
14:21 *For the sake of your name.* See Eze 20:9 and note. *your glorious throne.* The Jerusalem temple (see 17:12; 2Ki 19:14–15; Ps 99:1–2). *Remember your covenant...do not break it.* Jeremiah pleads the ancient promise of God found in Lev 26:44–45.
14:22 See Hos 2:8,21–22. *worthless idols.* See note on 2:5. *it is you.* Only the Lord (not Baal) can send the showers to end the drought (see v. 1). *our hope is in you.* See note on v. 8.
15:1–9 The Lord responds, concluding this section (see note on 14:1—15:9).
15:1 *Moses and Samuel.* Famed for their intercession for sinful Israel (see Ex 32:11–14,30–34; Nu 14:13–23; Dt 9:18–20,25–29; 1Sa 7:5–9; 12:19–25; Ps 99:6–8). *stand before me.* The posture of God's servants as they are about to pray to him (see Ge 18:22; Mk 11:25). *Send them away.* The people are so wicked that God refuses to hear prayers offered on their behalf. They are beyond divine help (see 7:16; 14:11–12).
15:2 See Eze 14:21; 33:27. *death.* Probably by plague; see 14:12 (and note), where "sword, famine and plague" are God's three agents of destruction, paralleling the first three here (the He-

brew word for "starvation" here is the same as that for "famine" in 14:12).
15:3–4 Foreseen in Dt 28:25–26.
15:3 *four kinds.* Not the same four as in v. 2, but an elaboration of three of the fates awaiting the corpses of those killed by the sword. The seventh-century B.C. vassal treaties of Esarhaddon present similar curses: "May Ninurta, leader of the gods, fell you with his fierce arrow, fill the plain with your corpses, and give your flesh to the eagles and vultures to feed on ...May dogs and pigs eat your flesh." *dogs.* See 1Ki 21:23. *wild animals.* See Rev 6:8.
15:4 *abhorrent.* The Hebrew for this word is translated "a thing of horror" in the parallel in Dt 28:25. *what Manasseh ...did in Jerusalem.* Manasseh, good King Josiah's grandfather, was the most wicked king in Judah's long history (see 2Ki 21:1–11,16). His sins were a primary cause of Judah's eventual destruction (see 2Ki 21:12–15; 23:26–27; 24:3–4).
15:5–9 A poem concerning the forthcoming destruction of Jerusalem in 586 B.C (see La 1:1,12,21; 2:13,20).
15:5 Cf. Mt 23:37.
15:6 *You keep on backsliding.* Lit. "You go backward" (cf. 7:24; see note on 2:19).

So I will lay hands [s] on you and destroy you;
I am tired of holding back. [t]
[7] I will winnow [u] them with a winnowing fork
at the city gates of the land.
I will bring bereavement [v] and destruction on my people, [w]
for they have not changed their ways. [x]
[8] I will make their widows [y] more numerous
than the sand of the sea.
At midday I will bring a destroyer [z]
against the mothers of their young men;
suddenly I will bring down on them
anguish and terror. [a]
[9] The mother of seven will grow faint [b]
and breathe her last. [c]
Her sun will set while it is still day;
she will be disgraced [d] and humiliated.
I will put the survivors to the sword [e]
before their enemies,"[f]

declares the LORD.

[10] Alas, my mother, that you gave me birth, [g]
a man with whom the whole land strives and contends! [h]
I have neither lent [i] nor borrowed,
yet everyone curses [j] me.

[11] The LORD said,

"Surely I will deliver you [k] for a good purpose;
surely I will make your enemies plead [l] with you
in times of disaster and times of distress.

[12] "Can anyone break iron—
iron from the north [m]—or bronze?

[13] "Your wealth [n] and your treasures
I will give as plunder, [o] without charge, [p]
because of all your sins
throughout your country. [q]
[14] I will enslave you to your enemies
in[a] a land you do not know, [r]
for my anger will kindle a fire [s]
that will burn against you."

[15] LORD, you understand;
remember me and care for me.

---

[a] 14 Some Hebrew manuscripts, Septuagint and Syriac (see also Jer. 17:4); most Hebrew manuscripts
I will cause your enemies to bring you / into

15:6 [s] Isa 31:3;
Zep 1:4 [t] S Jer 7:20;
Am 7:8
15:7 [u] S Isa 41:16
[v] Isa 3:26 [w] Jer 18:21
[x] S 2Ch 28:22
15:8 [y] S Isa 47:9
[z] S Jer 4:7; S 6:4
[a] S Job 18:11
15:9 [b] Isa 2:5
[c] S Job 8:13 [d] Jer 7:19
[e] Jer 21:7; 25:31
[f] 2Ki 25:7; Jer 19:7
15:10 [g] S Job 3:1;
S 10:18-19 [h] Jer 1:19
[i] S Lev 25:36; Ne 5:1-
12 [j] S Jer 6:10
15:11 [k] ver 21;
Jer 40:4 [l] Jer 21:1-2;
37:3; 42:1-3
15:12 [m] S Dt 28:48;
Jer 28:14; La 1:14;
Hos 10:11
15:13 [n] S 2Ki 25:15
[o] S 2Ki 24:13;
Eze 38:12-13
[p] S Ps 44:12 [q] Jer 17:3
15:14 [r] S Dt 28:36;
S Jer 5:19 [s] S Ps 21:9

15:7 *winnow.* See note on Ru 1:22. Winnowing as a figure of judgment is found also in 51:2; Pr 20:8,26; Isa 41:16. *city gates of the land.* Or, more simply, "gates of the land" (as in Na 3:13), i.e., the approaches to the land. *bereavement . . . on my people.* The young men will fall in battle, and Judah and Jerusalem will be childless (see Eze 5:17). *not changed.* Lit. "not repented of," reminiscent of the refrain in Am 4:6,8–11: "yet you have not returned to me," where the same Hebrew verb is used (see note on 3:1).
15:8 *widows more numerous than the sand of the sea.* A tragic reversal of the covenant promise of innumerable offspring (see Ge 22:17 and note). *At midday . . . suddenly.* Military attacks at noon were unexpected (see note on 6:4). *destroyer.* Babylon (see note on 4:7). *anguish.* See note on 4:19.
15:9 *seven.* The complete, ideal number of sons (see Ru 4:15 and note)—soon to be destroyed. *sun will set while it is still day.* See Am 8:9; cf. Mt 27:45 and note. *survivors.* Lit. "remnant" (see note on 6:9). Even they will be put to the sword (see Mic 6:14).
15:10–21 The third of Jeremiah's "confessions" (see Introduction: Author and Date), including in this case two responses by

the Lord (vv. 11–14,19–21).
15:10 See 20:14–15 and notes; Job 3:3–10. *have neither lent nor borrowed.* Have not become involved in matters likely to evoke dispute or difference of opinion.
15:11–14 The Lord speaks, first to Jeremiah (v. 11), then to the people of Judah (vv. 12–14).
15:11 God encourages Jeremiah. *I will make your enemies plead with you.* Fulfilled, e.g., in 21:1–2; 37:3; 38:14–26; 42:1–3.
15:12 A rhetorical question assuming a negative answer. *iron.* Symbolic of great strength (see 28:13). *from the north.* From Babylonia (see note on Isa 41:25).
15:13–14 Repeated in large part in 17:3–4.
15:13 Fulfilled in 52:17–23. *without charge.* Cf. Isa 55:1. People and plunder alike would be free for the taking (see note on Isa 52:3).
15:14 *for my anger will kindle a fire.* Quoted verbatim from Dt 32:22, where the same Hebrew is translated "For a fire will be kindled by my wrath."
15:15 *you understand.* The Lord is aware of what Jeremiah has

15:15 ᵗJdg 16:28;
S Ps 119:84
ᵘS Ex 34:6
ᵛPs 44:22; 69:7-9;
S Jer 6:10
15:16 ʷEze 2:8;
3:3; Rev 10:10
ˣS Job 15:11;
Ps 119:72,103
ʸS Isa 43:7;
S Jer 14:9
15:17 ᶻRu 3:3;
Ps 1:1; 26:4-5; Jer 16:8
ᵃS 2Ki 3:15
15:18 ᵇS Job 6:4;
S Jer 10:19; 30:12;
Mic 1:9 ᶜS Job 6:15;
S Ps 9:10
15:19 ᵈZec 3:7
ᵉS Ex 4:16
15:20 ᶠS Isa 50:7
ᵍS Ps 129:2
ʰS Jer 1:8; 20:11;
42:11; Eze 3:8
15:21 ⁱS Jer 1:8
ʲS Ps 97:10
ᵏJer 50:34
ˡS Ge 48:16
16:2 ᵐMt 19:12;
1Co 7:26-27
16:3 ⁿJer 6:21
16:4 ᵒver 6;
Jer 25:33 ᵖS Jer 9:22
ᵍS Jer 14:15
ʳS Dt 28:26; Ps 79:1-
3; S Jer 14:12; 19:7

Avenge me on my persecutors. ᵗ
You are long-suffering ᵘ—do not take me away;
   think of how I suffer reproach for your sake. ᵛ
¹⁶ When your words came, I ate ʷ them;
   they were my joy and my heart's delight, ˣ
for I bear your name, ʸ
   LORD God Almighty.
¹⁷ I never sat ᶻ in the company of revelers,
   never made merry with them;
I sat alone because your hand ᵃ was on me
   and you had filled me with indignation.
¹⁸ Why is my pain unending
   and my wound grievous and incurable? ᵇ
You are to me like a deceptive brook,
   like a spring that fails. ᶜ

¹⁹ Therefore this is what the LORD says:

"If you repent, I will restore you
   that you may serve ᵈ me;
if you utter worthy, not worthless, words,
   you will be my spokesman. ᵉ
Let this people turn to you,
   but you must not turn to them.
²⁰ I will make you a wall ᶠ to this people,
   a fortified wall of bronze;
they will fight against you
   but will not overcome ᵍ you,
for I am with you
   to rescue and save you," ʰ

declares the LORD.

²¹ "I will save ⁱ you from the hands of the wicked ʲ
   and deliver ᵏ you from the grasp of the cruel." ˡ

DAY OF DISASTER

16 Then the word of the LORD came to me: ²"You must not marry ᵐ and have sons or daughters in this place." ³For this is what the LORD says about the sons and daughters born in this land and about the women who are their mothers and the men who are their fathers: ⁿ ⁴"They will die of deadly diseases. They will not be mourned or buried ᵒ but will be like dung lying on the ground. ᵖ They will perish by sword and famine, ᵍ and their dead bodies will become food for the birds and the wild animals." ʳ

---

suffered (see v. 10). *remember.* Express concern for (see note on Ge 8:1).

A **15:16** *your words . . . I ate them.* I digested them, I assimilated them, I made them a part of me (see Eze 2:8—3:3; Rev 10:9–10). *came.* Lit. "were found"—perhaps referring to the discovery of the Book of the Law in the temple during the reign of Josiah in 621 B.C. (see 2Ki 22:13; 23:2; see also note on 1:2). *they were . . . my heart's delight.* See Mic 1:2. *I bear your name.* See 14:9. I belong to you (see note on 7:10).

15:17 *sat alone.* Jeremiah never married (see 16:2), and he attracted only a few friends (see Introduction: Author and Date). *your hand.* Divine constraint (see 2Ki 3:15; Isa 8:11 and note; Eze 1:3; 3:14,22; 37:1; 40:1). *indignation.* At the sins of Judah (see 6:11).

C **15:18** Two rhetorical questions used by Jeremiah to express his nagging doubts about himself, his mission and God's faithfulness. *pain unending . . . wound grievous and incurable.* Jerusalem is similarly described in 30:12–15, together with God's promise of healing in 30:17. *deceptive brook.* See Mic 1:14, where also "deceptive" probably refers to the kind of intermittent streams described in Job 6:15–20. Jeremiah here accuses God of being undependable, in contrast to the Lord's own earlier description of himself as a "spring of living water" (see 2:13 and note).

A **15:19–21** The Lord commands Jeremiah to repent, then encourages him and renews his call.

15:19 *repent . . . restore . . . turn . . . turn.* The Hebrew root is the same for all four words (see notes on 3:1; Isa 1:25–26). *serve.* Lit. "stand before"—the appropriate posture for the obedient servant (see Nu 16:9; Dt 10:8). *spokesman.* Lit. "mouth" (see 1:9 and note; Ex 4:15–16; see also note on Ex 7:1–2).

15:20 See 1:8,18–19 and notes.

15:21 *save you from . . . the wicked.* See, e.g., 36:26; 38:6–13.

16:1—17:18 Messages of disaster and comfort, with the note of disaster predominating (16:1–13,16–18; 16:21—17:6; 17:9–13,18). The first half of the section is prose (16:1–18), the second half poetry (16:19—17:18).

A **16:2** Jeremiah's ministry was such that he had to face life alone (see note on 15:17), without the comfort and support a family can provide. *You must not.* The Hebrew underlying this phrase is used for the most forceful of negative commands, as, e.g., in the Ten Commandments (see Ex 20:3–4,7, 13–17). *this place.* Judah and Jerusalem, especially the latter (see, e.g., Zep 1:4).

16:4 *diseases.* The Hebrew for this word is translated "ravages" in 14:18. *not be mourned or buried.* See v. 6; 7:33 and note; 8:2; 14:16; 25:33. *dung.* See 8:2; 9:22; 25:33. *perish by sword and famine.* See 14:15–16; see also note on 5:12. *food for the birds and the wild animals.* See note on 7:33.

⁵For this is what the LORD says: "Do not enter a house where there is a funeral meal; do not go to mourn or show sympathy, because I have withdrawn my blessing, my love and my pity ˢ from this people," declares the LORD. ⁶"Both high and low will die in this land. ᵗ They will not be buried or mourned, ᵘ nor will people cut ᵛ themselves or shave ʷ their heads for them. ⁷No one will offer food ˣ to comfort those who mourn ʸ for the dead—not even for a father or a mother—nor will anyone give them a drink to console ᶻ them.

⁸"And do not enter a house where there is feasting and sit down to eat and drink. ᵃ ⁹For this is what the LORD Almighty, the God of Israel, says: Before your eyes and in your days I will bring an end to the sounds ᵇ of joy and gladness and to the voices of bride ᶜ and bridegroom in this place. ᵈ

¹⁰"When you tell these people all this and they ask you, 'Why has the LORD decreed such a great disaster against us? What wrong have we done? What sin have we committed against the LORD our God?' ᵉ ¹¹then say to them, 'It is because your ancestors forsook me,' declares the LORD, 'and followed other gods and served and worshiped ᶠ them. They forsook me and did not keep my law. ᵍ ¹²But you have behaved more wickedly than your ancestors. ʰ See how all of you are following the stubbornness of your evil hearts ⁱ instead of obeying me. ¹³So I will throw you out of this land ʲ into a land neither you nor your ancestors have known, ᵏ and there you will serve other gods ˡ day and night, for I will show you no favor.' ᵐ

¹⁴"However, the days are coming," ⁿ declares the LORD, "when people will no longer say, 'As surely as the LORD lives, who brought the Israelites up out of Egypt,' ᵒ ¹⁵but they will say, 'As surely as the LORD lives, who brought the Israelites up out of the land of the north ᵖ and out of all the countries where he had banished them.' �q For I will restore ʳ them to the land I gave their ancestors. ˢ

¹⁶"But now I will send for many fishermen," declares the LORD, "and they will catch them. ᵗ After that I will send for many hunters, and they will hunt ᵘ them down on every mountain and hill and from the crevices of the rocks. ᵛ ¹⁷My eyes are on all their ways; they are not hidden ʷ from me, nor is their sin concealed from my eyes. ˣ ¹⁸I will repay ʸ them double ᶻ for their wickedness and their sin, because they have defiled my land ᵃ with the lifeless forms of their vile images ᵇ and have filled my inheritance with their detestable idols. ᶜ" ᵈ

> ¹⁹ LORD, my strength and my fortress,
> my refuge ᵉ in time of distress,
> to you the nations will come ᶠ
> from the ends of the earth and say,

16:18 ᵈS Jer 2:7; S 4:1; Eze 5:11; 8:10 16:19 ᵉS 2Sa 22:3; S Ps 46:1 ᶠS Isa 2:2; Jer 3:17

16:5 ˢS Jer 15:5
16:6 ᵗJer 9:21;
Eze 9:5-6 ᵘS ver 4
ᵛS Lev 19:28
ʷS Lev 21:5;
S Job 1:20
16:7 ˣS 2Sa 3:35
ʸJer 22:10; Eze 24:17;
Hos 9:4 ᶻLa 1:9,16
16:8 ᵃS Ex 32:6;
S Ecc 7:2-4;
S Jer 15:17
16:9 ᵇS Isa 24:8;
S 51:3; Eze 26:13;
Am 6:4-7 ᶜS Ps 78:63
ᵈIsa 22:12-14;
Rev 18:23
16:10 ᵉS Dt 29:24;
Jer 5:19
16:11 ᶠS Job 31:27
ᵍDt 29:25-26;
S 1Ki 9:9; Ps 106:35-43
16:12 ʰS Ex 32:8;
S Jer 7:26; Eze 20:30;
Am 2:4 ⁱS Ecc 9:3;
S Jer 3:17
16:13 ʲS 2Ch 7:20
ᵏS Dt 28:36;
S Jer 5:19 ˡS Dt 4:28;
S 1Ki 9:9 ᵐS Jer 15:5
16:14 ⁿJer 29:10;
30:3; 31:27,38
ᵒS Dt 15:15
16:15 ᵖS Jer 3:18
qS Isa 11:11; Jer 23:8
ʳPs 53:6; S Isa 11:12;
Jer 30:3; 32:44;
Eze 38:14; Joel 3:1
ˢS Dt 30:3; S Isa 14:1
16:16 ᵗAm 4:2;
Hab 1:14-15 ᵘAm 9:3;
Mic 7:2 ᵛS 1Sa 26:20
16:17 ʷS Ge 3:8;
S Ecc 12:14;
S Mk 4:22; 1Co 4:5;
S Heb 4:13
ˣS Ps 51:9; Pr 15:3;
Zep 1:12
16:18 ʸS Isa 65:6
ᶻS Isa 40:2;
S Jer 12:3; Rev 18:6
ᵃNu 35:34; Jer 2:7
ᵇS Ps 101:3
ᶜS 1Ki 14:24

16:5 *do not go to mourn.* See the similar command of God in Eze 24:16–17,22–23.

16:6 *cut themselves … shave their heads.* Actions forbidden in the law (see Lev 19:28; 21:5 and note; Dt 14:1 and note), but sometimes practiced by Israelites as a sign of mourning (see 41:5; Eze 7:18; Mic 1:16).

16:7 Food was customarily offered to mourners (see 2Sa 3:35; 12:16–17; Eze 24:17,22; Hos 9:4). *drink to console them.* Lit. "cup of consolation," in later Judaism a special cup of wine for the chief mourner.

16:8 *do not enter a house where there is feasting.* The present crisis is a time for neither feasting nor mourning (see v. 5).

16:9 See 7:34; 25:10; contrast 33:10–11.

16:10–13 The same question but a more elaborate answer than in 5:19 (see 9:12–16; 22:8–9; Dt 29:24–28; 1Ki 9:8–9).

16:10 Cf. the similar questions in Mal 1:6–7; 2:17; 3:7–8,13.

16:11 See 11:10, where committing sins like those mentioned here is called breaking the Lord's covenant.

Ⓐ **16:12** *behaved more wickedly than your ancestors.* See 1Ki 14:9. The coming judgment cannot be blamed on the sins of previous generations (see 31:29–30 and notes; Eze 18:2–4). *following the stubbornness of your evil hearts.* See note on 3:17; see also 7:24.

16:13 See Dt 28:36,64. *I will throw you out.* Into exile (see 7:15; 22:26; Dt 29:28). *land neither you nor your ancestors have known.* Babylonia (see 9:16).

16:14–15 Repeated almost verbatim in 23:7–8, the passage

outlines nearly 1,000 years of Israelite history: exodus (c. 1446 B.C.), exile (586), restoration (537). See Isa 43:16–21; 48:20–21; 51:9–11. *As surely as the LORD lives.* See note on Ge 42:15.

16:15 *land of the north.* Babylonia (see note on Isa 41:25).

16:16 *fishermen … hunters.* Symbolic of conquerors (see Eze 12:13; 29:4; Am 4:2 and note). *mountain and hill.* To which the people would flee in vain (see 4:29 and note). *crevices of the rocks.* The phrase occurs outside Jeremiah only in Isa 7:19. The Lord may be recalling here the episode of the ruined linen belt, hidden in a "crevice in the rocks" (13:4).

16:17 *My eyes are on all their ways.* See 32:19. *they are not hidden from me.* See 23:24 and note.

16:18 *repay them double.* See 17:18; Isa 40:2 and note. *defiled my land.* Made it ceremonially unclean (see 2:7; 3:1–2; see also note on Lev 4:12). *lifeless forms of their vile images.* See Lev 26:30. Idols have no life in them (see Ps 115:4–7; 135:15–17). *my inheritance.* God's land (see 17:4; see also note on 2:7). *detestable.* Abominable in the Lord's eyes (see 2:7; see also note on Lev 7:21).

16:19–20 The prophet interjects a few brief words of hope.

Ⓐ **16:19** *strength … fortress … refuge in time of distress.* Such descriptions of God's dependability and protecting power are common in the Psalms (see, e.g., Ps 18:1–2; 28:7–8; 59:9,16–17). *to you the nations will come.* See 4:2 and note; see also Isa 2:2–4; 42:4; 45:14; 49:6; Zec 8:20–23; 14:16. *worthless idols.* See note on 2:5. *did them no good.* Were unprofitable to them (see note on 2:8).

16:19 g S Ps 4:2
h S Dt 32:21;
S 1Sa 12:21
i S Isa 40:19;
S Jer 14:22
16:20 j Ps 115:4-7;
S Jer 2:11; Ro 1:23
16:21 k S Ex 3:15
17:1 l Job 19:24
m S Dt 6:6; S 2Co 3:3
n S Ex 27:2
17:2 o S 2Ch 24:18
p S Jer 2:20
17:3 q S 2Ki 24:13
r Jer 26:18; Mic 3:12
s Jer 15:13
17:4 t La 5:2
u Dt 28:48; S Jer 12:7
v Jer 16:13; 22:28
w S Jer 7:20
17:5 x S Ps 108:12;
S Isa 2:22 y 2Co 1:9
17:6 z Job 30:3
a Dt 29:23;
S Job 39:6; Ps 107:34;
Jer 48:9
17:7 b S Ps 146:5
c S Ps 26:1; 34:8;
40:4; Pr 16:20;
Jer 39:18

"Our ancestors possessed nothing but false gods, [g]
worthless idols [h] that did them no good. [i]
[20] Do people make their own gods?
Yes, but they are not gods!" [j]

[21] "Therefore I will teach them—
this time I will teach them
my power and might.
Then they will know
that my name [k] is the Lord.

17

"Judah's sin is engraved with an iron tool, [l]
inscribed with a flint point,
on the tablets of their hearts [m]
and on the horns [n] of their altars.
[2] Even their children remember
their altars and Asherah poles [a] [o]
beside the spreading trees
and on the high hills. [p]
[3] My mountain in the land
and your [b] wealth and all your treasures
I will give away as plunder, [q]
together with your high places, [r]
because of sin throughout your country. [s]
[4] Through your own fault you will lose
the inheritance [t] I gave you.
I will enslave you to your enemies [u]
in a land [v] you do not know,
for you have kindled my anger,
and it will burn [w] forever."

[5] This is what the Lord says:

"Cursed are those who trust in mortals, [x]
who depend on flesh for their strength
and whose hearts turn away from the Lord. [y]
[6] They will be like a bush in the wastelands;
they will not see prosperity when it comes.
They will dwell in the parched places [z] of the desert,
in a salt [a] land where no one lives.

[7] "But blessed [b] are those who trust [c] in the Lord,
whose confidence is in him.
[8] They will be like a tree planted by the water

---

[a] 2 That is, wooden symbols of the goddess Asherah   [b] 2,3 Or hills / [3] and the mountains of the land. / Your

---

16:20 not gods. See 5:7.

16:21—17:4 The Lord responds to Jeremiah and continues his solemn warnings that began in v. 1.

16:21 teach … teach … know. The same Hebrew root underlies each of these words. God would "cause them to know," and then they would surely "know." them … they. Probably includes Judah as well as the nations (see Eze 36:23; 37:14). know that my name is the Lord. "Name" often means "person" or "being" in the OT (see note on Ps 5:11). Ezekiel's equivalent of Jeremiah's phrase is "know that I am the Lord," found in his prophecy about 70 times (see Introduction to Ezekiel: Themes; see also notes on Eze 5:13; 6:7).

17:1 engraved with an iron tool. The method used to inscribe the most permanent of records (see Job 19:24). flint. An extremely hard stone from which tools and weapons were made (see notes on Ex 4:25; Jos 5:2; see also Eze 3:9; Zec 7:12). tablets of their hearts. For the same imagery, see Pr 3:3; 7:3. horns of their altars. The people of Judah had backslid so badly that their sins are engraved not only on their hearts but also on their altars—to be remembered by God rather than to be atoned for (see Lev 16:18).

17:2 altars and Asherah poles. See notes on Ex 34:13; Dt 7:5.

spreading trees … high hills. See note on 2:20.

17:3–4 Repeated in large part from 15:13–14 (see notes there).

17:3 My mountain. Mount Zion, the location of the temple in Jerusalem (see Ps 24:3; Isa 2:3; Zec 8:3). high places. Locales of idolatrous worship (see note on 1Ki 3:2).

17:4 inheritance. The land of Canaan (see 16:18; see also note on 2:7).

17:5–8 See Ps 1 and notes.

17:5 Cursed. See note on 11:3. flesh. The opposite of "spirit" (see Isa 31:3; cf. Job 10:4).

17:6 bush. The Hebrew for this word suggests destitution (see Ps 102:17, "destitute"). prosperity. Lit. "good." The Hebrew for this word is translated "bounty" in Dt 28:12, where it refers to rain. salt land. An evidence of God's curse also in Dt 29:23.

17:7 trust … confidence. The same Hebrew root underlies both words.

17:8 planted. Or "transplanted." stream. See Isa 44:4, where the same Hebrew root is used again to illustrate the source of the righteous person's strength. drought. See note on 14:1. bear fruit. The Lord's answer to Jeremiah's complaint in 12:1–2 (see notes there).

that sends out its roots by the stream. *d*
It does not fear when heat comes;
  its leaves are always green.
It has no worries in a year of drought *e*
  and never fails to bear fruit." *f*

⁹ The heart *g* is deceitful above all things
  and beyond cure.
  Who can understand it?

¹⁰ "I the LORD search the heart *h*
  and examine the mind, *i*
to reward *j* everyone according to their conduct,
  according to what their deeds deserve." *k*

¹¹ Like a partridge that hatches eggs it did not lay
  are those who gain riches by unjust means.
When their lives are half gone, their riches will desert them,
  and in the end they will prove to be fools. *l*

¹² A glorious throne, *m* exalted from the beginning,
  is the place of our sanctuary.
¹³ LORD, you are the hope *n* of Israel;
  all who forsake *o* you will be put to shame.
Those who turn away from you will be written in the dust *p*
  because they have forsaken the LORD,
  the spring of living water. *q*

¹⁴ Heal me, LORD, and I will be healed; *r*
  save *s* me and I will be saved,
  for you are the one I praise. *t*
¹⁵ They keep saying to me,
  "Where is the word of the LORD?
  Let it now be fulfilled!" *u*
¹⁶ I have not run away from being your shepherd;
  you know I have not desired the day of despair.
  What passes my lips *v* is open before you.
¹⁷ Do not be a terror *w* to me;
  you are my refuge *x* in the day of disaster. *y*
¹⁸ Let my persecutors be put to shame,
  but keep me from shame;
let them be terrified,
  but keep me from terror.
Bring on them the day of disaster;
  destroy them with double destruction. *z*

17:8 *d* Job 14:9
e Jer 14:1-6 *f* Ps 1:3;
92:12-14; Eze 19:10;
47:12
17:9 *g* S Ecc 9:3;
Mt 13:15; Mk 7:21-22
17:10 *h* S Jos 22:22;
S 2Ch 6:30;
S Rev 2:23 *i* Ps 17:3;
139:23; Jer 11:20;
20:12; Eze 11:5; 38:10
j S Lev 26:28;
Ps 62:12; Jer 32:19;
S Mt 16:27 *k* Jer 12:13;
14:16; 21:14; 32:19
17:11 *l* Lk 12:20
17:12 *m* S Jer 3:17
17:13 *n* Ps 71:5;
Jer 14:8 *o* S Jer 2:17
p S Ps 69:28; 87:6;
Eze 13:9; Da 12:1
q S Isa 12:3; Jn 4:10
17:14 *r* S Isa 30:26;
Jer 15:18 *s* Ps 119:94
t S Ex 15:2; S Ps 109:1
17:15 *u* S Isa 5:19;
2Pe 3:4
17:16 *v* Ps 139:4
17:17 *w* Ps 88:15-16
x S Ps 46:1; Jer 16:19;
Na 1:7 *y* S Ps 18:18
17:18 *z* Ps 35:1-8;
S Isa 40:2; S Jer 12:3

A **17:9** The prophet makes an observation, then asks a rhetorical question. *heart.* Wickedness must not be allowed to take root in one's heart (see Ps 4:7 and note; Pr 4:23). *deceitful.* The Hebrew root for this word is the basis of the name Jacob (see TNIV text note on Ge 27:36).
17:10 The Lord responds to Jeremiah's question. *search ... examine.* See 11:20; 12:3. *mind.* Lit. "kidneys" (see 11:20). The Hebrew for this word is translated "hearts" in 12:2. *what their deeds deserve.* Lit. "the fruit of their deeds" (cf. 6:19).
17:11 The prophet uses a proverb to make his point (as in v. 9). *partridge.* Mentioned elsewhere in the OT only in 1Sa 26:20. *fools.* Morally and spiritually bankrupt (see note on Pr 1:7).
17:12–18 The fourth of Jeremiah's "confessions" (see Introduction: Author and Date).
17:12 *glorious throne.* See note on 14:21; see also Isa 6:1. The Lord is often represented as sitting on a throne between the cherubim on the ark of the covenant in the temple (see, e.g., Ps 80:1; 99:1). *exalted from the beginning.* From time immemorial, Zion had been chosen by God as the place of his sanctuary (see Ex 15:17).

B **17:13** *hope of Israel.* See note on 14:8. *dust.* Lit. "earth," sometimes referring to the netherworld (see note on Ps 61:2; see also note on Job 7:21), as also in Canaanite and Mesopotamian literature. "Written in the dust" would then mean "destined for death," the opposite of "written in the book" of life (see Ex 32:32; Da 12:1; see also Ps 69:28; Lk 10:20; Rev 3:5 and notes). *forsaken ... spring of living water.* Contrast 15:18; see note on 2:13.
17:14 *Heal me.* See 15:18; Ps 6:2. *you are the one I praise.* Lit. "you are my praise" (see Ps 22:3 and note).
17:15 See 20:8. Jeremiah's enemies accuse him of being a false prophet (see Dt 18:21-22). The accusation must have been voiced before the first invasion of Judah by the Babylonians in 605 B.C., after the battle of Carchemish (see 46:2; see also Introduction: Background).
17:16 *shepherd.* Symbolic of leadership and therefore of Jeremiah's role as a prophet (see notes on 2:8; Ps 23:1; Jn 10:1-30).
17:17 *my refuge.* See 16:19 and note. *day of disaster.* See v. 18; 15:11.
17:18 *my persecutors.* See 15:15. *double.* See 16:18; Isa 40:2 and note.

17:19 ^a Jer 7:2; 26:2
17:20 ^b Jer 19:3
^c Jer 22:2
17:21 ^d Nu 15:32-
36; S Dt 5:14;
Ne 13:15-21; Jn 5:10
17:22 ^e S Ge 2:3;
S Ex 20:8; Isa 56:2-6
17:23 ^f Jer 7:26
^g Jer 19:15
^h S 2Ch 28:22;
S Jer 7:28; Zec 7:11
17:24 ⁱ ver 22
17:25 ^j S 2Sa 7:13;
Isa 9:7; Jer 22:2,4;
Lk 1:32 ^k Jer 30:10;
33:16; Eze 28:26
17:26 ^l Jer 32:44;
33:13; Zec 7:7
17:27 ^m S 1Ki 9:6;
Jer 22:5 ⁿ S Ne 10:31
^o S Jer 7:20
^p S 2Ki 25:9;
Hos 8:14; Am 2:5
18:6 ^q S Isa 29:16;
45:9; Ro 9:20-21
^r S Ge 2:7

KEEPING THE SABBATH DAY HOLY

¹⁹This is what the Lord said to me: "Go and stand at the gate of the people, through which the kings of Judah go in and out; stand also at all the other gates of Jerusalem.^a ²⁰Say to them, 'Hear the word of the Lord, you kings of Judah and all people of Judah and everyone living in Jerusalem^b who come through these gates.^c ²¹This is what the Lord says: Be careful not to carry a load on the Sabbath^d day or bring it through the gates of Jerusalem. ²²Do not bring a load out of your houses or do any work on the Sabbath, but keep the Sabbath day holy, as I commanded your ancestors.^e ²³Yet they did not listen or pay attention;^f they were stiff-necked^g and would not listen or respond to discipline.^h ²⁴But if you are careful to obey me, declares the Lord, and bring no load through the gates of this city on the Sabbath, but keep the Sabbath day holyⁱ by not doing any work on it, ²⁵then kings who sit on David's throne^j will come through the gates of this city with their officials. They and their officials will come riding in chariots and on horses, accompanied by the men of Judah and those living in Jerusalem, and this city will be inhabited forever.^k ²⁶People will come from the towns of Judah and the villages around Jerusalem, from the territory of Benjamin and the western foothills, from the hill country and the Negev,^l bringing burnt offerings and sacrifices, grain offerings and incense, and bringing thank offerings to the house of the Lord. ²⁷But if you do not obey^m me to keep the Sabbathⁿ day holy by not carrying any load as you come through the gates of Jerusalem on the Sabbath day, then I will kindle an unquenchable fire^o in the gates of Jerusalem that will consume her fortresses.' "^p

AT THE POTTER'S HOUSE

18 This is the word that came to Jeremiah from the Lord: ²"Go down to the potter's house, and there I will give you my message." ³So I went down to the potter's house, and I saw him working at the wheel. ⁴But the pot he was shaping from the clay was marred in his hands; so the potter formed it into another pot, shaping it as seemed best to him.

⁵Then the word of the Lord came to me. ⁶He said, "Can I not do with you, house of Israel, as this potter does?" declares the Lord. "Like clay^q in the hand of the potter, so are you in my hand,^r house of Israel. ⁷If at any time I announce that a nation or kingdom is to

---

17:19–27 An extended commentary on the Sabbath-day commandment (the covenant sign of God's relationship with Israel; see Ex 31:13–17; Eze 20:12), probably the version recorded in Dt 5:12–15 (see note on v. 22 below).

17:19 *people.* Lit. "sons of the people." The Hebrew for this word is translated "common people" in 26:23; 2Ki 23:6 and "lay people" in 2Ch 35:5,7. The latter meaning seems intended here, and therefore the "gate of the people" is likely the east gate of the temple, where the people assembled in large numbers and which the kings would be expected to use frequently.

17:20 *kings of Judah.* The current king and all subsequent ruling members of David's dynasty (see, e.g., v. 25; 1:18; 2:26; 13:13; 19:3).

17:21 *Be careful.* See Jos 23:11. The Hebrew underlying this phrase is translated "watch yourselves ... carefully" in Dt 4:15, and a similar expression is translated "be on your guard" in Mal 2:15, stressing the urgency and solemnity of God's command.

17:22 *Do not.* See note on 16:2. The Hebrew for this negative expression is stronger than that in v. 21. *not ... do any work ... keep the Sabbath day holy.* Specific references to the Sabbath-day commandment of Ex 20:8,10; Dt 5:12,14. *as I commanded.* The Hebrew underlying this phrase is unique to the Ten Commandments as recorded in Deuteronomy (see Dt 5:12, 15–16; see note on vv. 19–27).

17:23 *did not listen ... were stiff-necked.* Repeated from 7:26 (see note there; see also 11:10). *not ... respond to discipline.* See 2:30; 5:3.

17:25 Repeated in part in 22:4. King David's dynasty will last forever (see 23:5–6; 30:9; 33:15; 2Sa 7:12–17), and Jerusalem will be inhabited for all time (31:38–40; 2:2–12; 8:3; 14:11), if the people of Judah obey the Lord (see v. 27)—and they will, according to 31:33–34.

17:26 *territory of Benjamin.* Jeremiah's hometown was located

there (see 1:1). *western foothills ... hill country.* See note on Dt 1:7. *Negev.* See note on Ge 12:9. *bringing thank offerings.* See 33:11.

17:27 Disobedience will bring disaster and will negate —at least temporarily—the promises of vv. 24–26. *gates of Jerusalem.* The symbols of Sabbath violation would be the first structures destroyed. *kindle ... fire ... consume her fortresses.* Common prophetic language for divine judgment against rebellious cities (see 49:27; 50:32; Am 1:4,7,10,12,14; 2:2,5; cf. Jer 21:14).

18:1—20:18 Three chapters focusing on lessons the Lord taught Jeremiah at the potter's workshop, probably before 605 B.C. (see note on 17:15).

18:1–17 As the potter controls what he does with the clay, so the Lord is sovereign over the people of Judah.

18:2 *Go down.* The potter's workshop was probably located on the slopes of the Valley of Ben Hinnom, near the Potsherd Gate (see 19:2 and note).

18:3 *wheel.* Lit. "two stones." Both wheels were attached to a single upright shaft, one end of which was sunk permanently in the ground. The potter would spin the lower wheel with his foot and would work the clay on the upper wheel; the process is described in the Apocryphal book of Ecclesiasticus (38:29–30).

18:4 *marred.* The Hebrew for this word is translated "ruined" in 13:7 with respect to the linen belt that Jeremiah had hidden (see note there). *as seemed best to him.* The flaw was in the clay itself, not in the potter's skill.

18:6 *Like clay ... so are you.* Biblical imagery often pictures humankind as made of clay by a potter (see Job 4:19 and note). *potter.* The Hebrew for this word is translated "Maker" in 10:16 with reference to God.

18:7–10 *If ... if ... if ... if.* God's promises and threats are conditioned on human actions. God, who himself does be uprooted, ^{s} torn down and destroyed, ^{8}and if that nation I warned repents of its evil, then I will relent ^{t} and not inflict on it the disaster ^{u} I had planned. ^{9}And if at another time I announce that a nation or kingdom is to be built ^{v} up and planted, ^{10}and if it does evil ^{w} in my sight and does not obey me, then I will reconsider ^{x} the good I had intended to do for it. ^{y}

^{11}"Now therefore say to the people of Judah and those living in Jerusalem, 'This is what the LORD says: Look! I am preparing a disaster ^{z} for you and devising a plan ^{a} against you. So turn ^{b} from your evil ways, ^{c} each one of you, and reform your ways and your actions.' ^{d} ^{12}But they will reply, 'It's no use. ^{e} We will continue with our own plans; we will all follow the stubbornness of our evil hearts. ^{f} '"

^{13}Therefore this is what the LORD says:

"Inquire among the nations:
　　Who has ever heard anything like this? ^{g}
A most horrible ^{h} thing has been done
　　by Virgin ^{i} Israel.
^{14} Does the snow of Lebanon
　　ever vanish from its rocky slopes?
Do its cool waters from distant sources
　　ever cease to flow? ^{a}
^{15} Yet my people have forgotten ^{j} me;
　　they burn incense ^{k} to worthless idols, ^{l}
which made them stumble ^{m} in their ways,
　　in the ancient paths. ^{n}
They made them walk in byways,
　　on roads not built up. ^{o}
^{16} Their land will be an object of horror ^{p}
　　and of lasting scorn; ^{q}
all who pass by will be appalled ^{r}
　　and will shake their heads. ^{s}
^{17} Like a wind ^{t} from the east,
　　I will scatter them before their enemies;
I will show them my back and not my face ^{u}
　　in the day of their disaster."

^{18}They said, "Come, let's make plans ^{v} against Jeremiah; for the teaching of the law by the priest ^{w} will not cease, nor will counsel from the wise, ^{x} nor the word from the prophets. ^{y} So come, let's attack him with our tongues ^{z} and pay no attention to anything he says."

^{19} Listen to me, LORD;
　　hear what my accusers ^{a} are saying!

---

^{a} 14 The meaning of the Hebrew for this sentence is uncertain.

18:7 ^{s} Jer 1:10
18:8 ^{t} S Ex 32:14; Ps 25:11; Jer 26:13; 36:3; Jnh 3:8-10 ^{u} Jer 31:28; 42:10; Da 9:14; Hos 11:8-9; Joel 2:13; Jnh 4:2
18:9 ^{v} Jer 1:10; 31:28
18:10 ^{w} Eze 33:18 ^{x} 1Sa 2:29-30; 13:13 ^{y} S Jer 1:10
18:11 ^{z} S 2Ki 22:16; S Jer 4:6 ^{a} ver 18 ^{b} S Dt 4:30; S 2Ki 17:13; Isa 1:16-19 ^{c} S Jer 7:3 ^{d} S Job 16:17
18:12 ^{e} S Isa 57:10 ^{f} S Jer 3:17
18:13 ^{g} S Isa 66:8 ^{h} S Jer 5:30 ^{i} S 2Ki 19:21
18:15 ^{j} S Isa 17:10 ^{k} S Isa 1:13; Jer 44:15, 19 ^{l} Jer 10:15; 51:18; Hos 11:2 ^{m} Eze 44:12; Mal 2:8 ^{n} Jer 6:16 ^{o} S Isa 57:14; 62:10
18:16 ^{p} S Dt 28:37; Jer 25:9; Eze 33:28-29 ^{q} Jer 19:8; 42:18 ^{r} S Lev 26:32 ^{s} S 2Ki 19:21; S Job 16:4; Ps 22:7; La 1:12
18:17 ^{t} S Job 7:10; Jer 13:24 ^{u} S 2Ch 29:6; S Jer 2:27
18:18 ^{v} ver 11; Jer 11:19 ^{w} Jer 2:8; Hag 2:11; Mal 2:7 ^{x} S Job 5:13; Eze 7:26 ^{y} Jer 5:13 ^{z} Ps 52:2; 64:2-8; S Jer 9:3
18:19 ^{a} Ps 71:13

---

not change (see Nu 23:19; Mal 3:6; Jas 1:17), nevertheless does change his preannounced response to people, depending on what they do (see note on 4:28; see also Joel 2:13; Jnh 3:8—4:2 and note on 3:9; 4:11).
18:7 *uprooted, torn down and destroyed.* See 1:10 and note.
18:8 See 26:3. *evil ... disaster.* The Hebrew is the same for both words (also in v. 11).
18:9 *built up and planted.* See 1:10 and note.
18:11 *devising a plan.* See Est 8:3; 9:25; Eze 38:10. *turn from.* The Hebrew underlying this phrase is translated "repents of" in v. 8.
18:12 *It's no use.* See 2:25; see also note on Isa 57:10. *follow the stubbornness of our evil hearts.* See note on 3:17.
18:13–17 See 2:10–13.
18:13 *horrible thing.* See 5:30; 23:14; Hos 6:10. *Virgin Israel.* See note on 2Ki 19:21.

A **18:14–15** Although nature is reliable (v. 14), Judah is fickle and unfaithful (v. 15).

18:14 *Lebanon.* One of the highest of the northern mountains (see 22:6), reaching an altitude of over 10,000 feet.
18:15 *my people have forgotten me.* Repeated from 2:32 (see note there). *burn incense.* See note on 1:16. *worthless idols.* Lit. "nothing" (Ps 31:6; see Jer 2:8 and note). *which made them stum-*

ble. See 2Ch 28:23. *ancient paths.* See note on 6:16. *roads not built up.* See note on Isa 35:8.
18:16 *object of horror ... appalled.* The same Hebrew root underlies both words. *lasting scorn.* See 19:8; 25:9,18; 29:18; 51:37. The phrase implies hissing or whistling to express shock, ridicule and contempt. *all ... appalled.* See 19:8; 1Ki 9:8. *shake their heads.* See 48:27; Job 16:4 and note; see also Ps 44:14; 109:25.

A **18:17** *wind from the east.* See 4:11; Ps 48:7 and notes. *show them my back and not my face.* As the people themselves had done to God (see 2:27). His face symbolizes his gracious blessing and favor (see Nu 6:24–26).

18:18–23 The fifth of Jeremiah's "confessions" (see Introduction: Author and Date).
18:18 *They.* Jeremiah's enemies (see note on 17:15). *plans against Jeremiah.* See v. 12; 11:18–23; 12:6; 15:10–11,15–21. *teaching of the law.* Delegated to the priests (see note on Hos 4:4–9). *priest ... wise ... prophets.* Despite Jeremiah's prophecies to the contrary (see 6:13–15; cf. 23:9–40; Eze 7:26 and note), the people thought that the various sources for receiving guidance from the Lord would continue as usual. *attack him with our tongues.* See note on 9:3.

18:20 *b* S Ge 44:4
c Ps 35:7; 57:6;
S 119:85 *d* Jer 15:1
e S Ge 20:7;
S Dt 9:19; Ps 106:23;
Jer 14:7-9
18:21 *f* Jer 11:22;
14:16 *g* S Ps 63:10
h S 1Sa 15:33;
Ps 109:9; S Isa 47:9;
La 5:3 *i* S Isa 9:17
18:22 *j* S Ge 6:26
k S Ps 119:85
l Ps 35:15; 140:5;
Jer 5:26; 20:10
18:23 *m* S Jer 11:21;
37:15 *n* S Ne 4:5
o Ps 59:5; S Jer 10:24
19:1 *p* Jer 18:2
q S Nu 11:17; 1Ki 8:1
19:2 *r* S Jos 15:8
19:3 *s* Jer 17:20
t S Jer 6:19
u S 1Sa 3:11
19:4 *v* S Dt 31:16;
Dt 28:20; S Isa 65:11
w S Ex 20:3; S Jer 1:16
x S Lev 18:21
y S 2Ki 21:16
19:5 *z* S Lev 18:21;
S 2Ki 3:27;
Ps 106:37-38
a S Jer 7:31; Eze 16:36
19:6 *b* S 2Ki 23:10
c S Jos 15:8 *d* Jer 7:32
19:7 *e* Ps 33:10-11
f S ver 9; S Lev 26:17;
S Dt 28:25
g S Jer 16:4; 34:20
h S Dt 28:26
19:8 *i* S Dt 28:37;
S Jer 18:16; 25:9
j S Lev 26:32;
La 2:15-16

20 Should good be repaid with evil? *b*
  Yet they have dug a pit *c* for me.
  Remember that I stood *d* before you
  and spoke in their behalf *e*
  to turn your wrath away from them.
21 So give their children over to famine; *f*
  hand them over to the power of the sword. *g*
  Let their wives be made childless and widows; *h*
  let their men be put to death,
  their young men *i* slain by the sword in battle.
22 Let a cry *j* be heard from their houses
  when you suddenly bring invaders against them,
  for they have dug a pit *k* to capture me
  and have hidden snares *l* for my feet.
23 But you, LORD, know
  all their plots to kill *m* me.
  Do not forgive *n* their crimes
  or blot out their sins from your sight.
  Let them be overthrown before you;
  deal with them in the time of your anger. *o*

19 This is what the LORD says: "Go and buy a clay jar from a potter. *p* Take along some of the elders *q* of the people and of the priests ²and go out to the Valley of Ben Hinnom, *r* near the entrance of the Potsherd Gate. There proclaim the words I tell you, ³and say, 'Hear the word of the LORD, you kings *s* of Judah and people of Jerusalem. This is what the LORD Almighty, the God of Israel, says: Listen! I am going to bring a disaster *t* on this place that will make the ears of everyone who hears of it tingle. *u* ⁴For they have forsaken *v* me and made this a place of foreign gods *w*; they have burned incense *x* in it to gods that neither they nor their ancestors nor the kings of Judah ever knew, and they have filled this place with the blood of the innocent. *y* ⁵They have built the high places of Baal to burn their children *z* in the fire as offerings to Baal—something I did not command or mention, nor did it enter my mind. *a* ⁶So beware, the days are coming, declares the LORD, when people will no longer call this place Topheth *b* or the Valley of Ben Hinnom, *c* but the Valley of Slaughter. *d*

⁷" 'In this place I will ruin *a* the plans *e* of Judah and Jerusalem. I will make them fall by the sword before their enemies, *f* at the hands of those who seek their lives, and I will give their carcasses *g* as food *h* to the birds and the wild animals. ⁸I will devastate this city and make it an object of horror and scorn; *i* all who pass by will be appalled *j* and will scoff be-

---

a 7 The Hebrew for *ruin* sounds like the Hebrew for *jar* (see verses 1 and 10).

18:20 *good ... repaid with evil.* See Ps 35:12. *dug a pit.* Symbolic of his enemies' plots against him (see v. 22; Ps 57:6 and note; Pr 22:14; 23:27). *stood before you.* See note on 15:1. *spoke in their behalf.* See 14:7–9, 21.
18:21 *hand them over to the power of the sword.* The Hebrew underlying this phrase occurs also in Ps 63:10; Eze 35:5. *be put to death.* Lit. "be slain by death," probably referring to plague, as in 15:2 (see note there).
18:22–23 See Ps 141:8–10.
18:22 *hidden snares.* See Ps 140:5; 142:3.
18:23 *you, LORD, know.* See 12:3; 15:15. *Do not forgive their crimes ... Let them be overthrown before you.* A prayer not for human vengeance but for divine vindication (see note on 10:25). *blot out their sins.* See Ps 51:1–2 and notes.
19:1–15 A jar deliberately broken by Jeremiah (vv. 1–10) symbolizes the forthcoming destruction of Judah and Jerusalem (vv. 11–15). In ch. 18 the potter's clay was still moist and pliable, making it possible to reshape and rework it (see 18:1–11). In ch. 19, however, the clay jar is hard and, if unsuitable for the owner's use, can only be destroyed (see v. 11).
19:1 *jar.* The Hebrew for this word implies a vessel with a narrow neck, perhaps the water decanter frequently found in excavations and ranging from 5 to 12 inches high. *elders.* See note on Ex 3:16. *of the people.* See 1Ki 8:1–3. *of the priests.* See 2Ki 19:2, "leading priests" (lit. "elders of the priests").

Elders in Israel were of two kinds, one performing primarily civil functions and the other primarily religious functions.
19:2 *Valley of Ben Hinnom.* See note on 7:31. *Potsherd Gate.* The Jerusalem Targum (an ancient Aramaic paraphrase) identifies the Potsherd Gate (so called because it overlooked the main dump for broken pottery) with the Dung Gate of Ne 2:13 (see note there); 3:13–14; 12:31.
19:3 *kings.* See note on 17:20. *disaster ... make the ears ... tingle.* Echoed from 2Ki 21:12 (see 1Sa 3:11). The phrase refers to the shock of hearing an announcement of threatened punishment.
19:4 *they.* All who tried to combine the worship of idols with the worship of the one true God. *this ... place.* Jerusalem. *burned incense.* See note on 1:16. *filled this place with the blood of the innocent.* The blood of godly people (see 2:34; 7:6; 22:3,17; 26:15), specifically as shed by wicked King Manasseh (see 15:4 and note; see also 2Ki 21:16).
19:5–6 Repeated in large part from 7:31–32 (see notes there).
19:7 *ruin.* Lit. "pour out"; see TNIV text note (see also note on v. 1). As Jeremiah was saying this, he may have been pouring water from the jar to the ground (cf. 2Sa 14:14). *fall by the sword before their enemies.* The Babylonians are the instruments of the divine threat (see 20:6). *carcasses as food ... wild animals.* See 7:33 and note.
19:8 Echoes the language of 18:16 (see note there; see also Eze 27:35; Zep 2:15). *devastate ... appalled.* The same Hebrew root

cause of all its wounds. *k* 9I will make them eat *l* the flesh of their sons and daughters, and they will eat one another's flesh because their enemies *m* will press the siege so hard against them to destroy them.'

10"Then break the jar *n* while those who go with you are watching, 11and say to them, 'This is what the LORD Almighty says: I will smash *o* this nation and this city just as this potter's jar is smashed and cannot be repaired. They will bury *p* the dead in Topheth until there is no more room. 12This is what I will do to this place and to those who live here, declares the LORD. I will make this city like Topheth. 13The houses *q* in Jerusalem and those of the kings of Judah will be defiled *r* like this place, Topheth—all the houses where they burned incense on the roofs *s* to all the starry hosts *t* and poured out drink offerings *u* to other gods.' "

14Jeremiah then returned from Topheth, where the LORD had sent him to prophesy, and stood in the court *v* of the LORD's temple and said to all the people, 15"This is what the LORD Almighty, the God of Israel, says: 'Listen! I am going to bring on this city and all the villages around it every disaster *w* I pronounced against them, because they were stiff-necked *x* and would not listen *y* to my words.' "

JEREMIAH AND PASHHUR

20 When the priest Pashhur son of Immer, *z* the official *a* in charge of the temple of the LORD, heard Jeremiah prophesying these things, 2he had Jeremiah the prophet beaten *b* and put in the stocks *c* at the Upper Gate of Benjamin *d* at the LORD's temple. 3The next day, when Pashhur released him from the stocks, Jeremiah said to him, "The LORD's name *e* for you is not Pashhur, but Terror on Every Side. *f* 4For this is what the LORD says: 'I will make you a terror to yourself and to all your friends; with your own eyes *g* you will see them fall by the sword of their enemies. I will give *h* all Judah into the hands of the king of Babylon, who will carry *i* them away to Babylon or put them to the sword. 5I will deliver all the wealth *j* of this city into the hands of their enemies—all its products, all its valuables and all the treasures of the kings of Judah. They will take it away *k* as plunder and carry it off to Babylon. 6And you, Pashhur, and all who live in your house will go into exile to Babylon. There you will die and be buried, you and all your friends to whom you have prophesied *l* lies.' "

19:8 *k* S Dt 29:22
19:9 *l* S Lev 26:29;
Dt 28:49-57; La 4:10
m S ver 7; Jer 21:7;
34:20
19:10 *n* ver 1;
S Ps 2:9; Jer 13:14
19:11 *o* Ps 2:9;
Isa 30:14 *p* Jer 7:32
19:13 *q* Jer 32:29;
52:13; Eze 16:41
r Ps 74:7 *s* S 2Ki 23:12
t Dt 4:19; S 2Ki 17:16;
S Job 38:32; Jer 8:2;
Ac 7:42 *u* S Isa 57:6;
Eze 20:28
19:14 *v* 2Ch 20:5;
S Jer 7:2; 26:2
19:15 *w* ver 3;
Jer 11:11 *x* S Ne 9:16;
Ac 7:51 *y* Jer 22:21
20:1 *z* S 1Ch 24:14
a 2Ki 25:18; Lk 22:52
20:2 *b* Dt 25:2-3;
S Jer 1:19; 15:15;
37:15; 2Co 11:24
c S Job 13:27;
Jer 29:26; Ac 16:24;
Heb 11:36
d S Job 29:7;
Jer 37:13; 38:7;
Zec 14:10
20:3 *e* Hos 1:4
f S ver 10; S Ps 31:13
20:4 *g* Jer 29:21
h Jer 21:10; 25:9
i Jer 13:19; 39:9; 52:27
20:5 *j* S 2Ki 25:15;
Jer 17:3 *k* S 2Ki 20:17
20:6 *l* S Jer 14:15;
La 2:14

---

underlies both words—the devastation of the city will have a similar effect on those who see its ruins. *scorn … scoff.* The same Hebrew root underlies both words.

19:9 One of the covenant curses (see Lev 26:29; Dt 28:53–57). *eat the flesh of their sons and daughters … eat one another's flesh.* When Jerusalem's food supply ran out during the Babylonian siege in 586 B.C., cannibalism resulted (see La 2:20; 4:10; Eze 5:10). Such shocking activity was not unprecedented in Israel (see 2Ki 6:28–29), and it would occur again in A.D. 70 during the Roman siege of Jerusalem (see Zec 11:9 and note):"A woman …who … had fled to Jerusalem … killed her son, roasted him, and ate one half, concealing and saving the rest" (Josephus, *Wars*, 6.3.4).

19:11 *smash this nation … as this potter's jar is smashed.* Egyptians of the 12th Dynasty (1991–1786 B.C.) inscribed the names of their enemies on pottery bowls and then smashed them, hoping to break the power of their enemies by so doing. *cannot be repaired.* See note on vv. 1–15.

19:13 *will be defiled like … Topheth.* King Josiah had earlier"desecrated Topheth" (2Ki 23:10). *burned incense.* See note on 1:16. *on the roofs.* See 32:29; see also note on Isa 15:3. The kings of Judah had built pagan altars on the roof of the palace in Jerusalem (see 2Ki 23:12). The Ugaritic Keret epic of the 14th century B.C. (see chart, p. xxiv) describes a similar practice:"Go to the top of a tower, bestride the top of the wall … Honor Baal with your sacrifice … Then descend … from the housetops." *starry hosts.* Worship of the sun, moon and stars was common in Judah throughout much of the later history of the monarchy (see, e.g., 2Ki 17:16; 21:3,5; 23:4–5; Zep 1:5). *drink offerings to other gods.* See note on 7:18.

19:14 *all the people.* A much larger audience than the elders of v. 1.

19:15 *the villages around it.* The towns of Judah that were dependent on Jerusalem (see 1:15; 9:11). *were stiff-necked and would not listen.* Repeated from 7:26 (see note there; see also 11:10).

20:1–6 Pashhur's response to Jeremiah's symbolic act (vv. 1–2), and Jeremiah's rejoinder (vv. 3–6).
20:1 *Pashhur.* One or more different men with the same name appear in 21:1; 38:1. *Immer.* Perhaps a descendant of the head of the 16th division of priests in the Jerusalem temple (see 1Ch 24:14). *official in charge.* The priest in charge of punishing troublemakers, real or imagined, in the temple courts (see v. 2; 29:26). The position was second only to that of the chief priest himself (compare 29:25–26 with 52:24).

20:2 The first of many recorded acts of physical violence against Jeremiah. *the prophet.* The first time Jeremiah is so called in the book (see Introduction: Theological Themes and Message), here to stress the enormity of Pashhur's actions. Probably in accordance with the Mosaic law of Dt 25:2–3 (see note on Dt 25:3). *stocks.* Lit."restraint, confinement." *Upper Gate of Benjamin.* Probably the same as the "north gate of the inner court" (Eze 8:3; see 2Ki 15:35; see also Eze 9:2). *at the LORD's temple.* This qualifying phrase distinguishes the temple's Gate of Benjamin from the "Benjamin Gate" in the city wall (37:13; 38:7). Both gates were in the northern part of the city, facing the territory of Benjamin.
20:3 *Terror on Every Side.* See note on 6:25.
20:4 Pashhur's new name symbolizes terror to all Judah, whose people will be exiled to Babylonia or put to death. *friends.* Associates and allies in the sense of covenant partners (see v. 6). *king of Babylon.* Nebuchadnezzar, who acceded to the Babylonian throne in 605 B.C. (see notes on 17:15; 18:1—20:18).
20:5 Fulfilled in 597 B.C. (see 2Ki 24:13) and in 586 (see 52:17–23; 2Ki 25:13–17).
20:6 *you, Pashhur, … will go into exile.* Probably in 597 B.C., because shortly after that year (see 29:2) two other men in succession had replaced Pashhur as chief officer in the temple (see 29:25–26). *you have prophesied lies.* The priest Pashhur had pretended to be a prophet.

20:7 ᵐS Ex 5:23;
22:16 ⁿIsa 8:11;
Am 3:8; 1Co 9:16
ᵒJob 12:4
ᵖS Job 17:2;
S Ps 119:21
20:8 ᵍJer 6:7; 28:8
ʳS 2Ch 36:16;
S Jer 6:10
20:9 ˢJer 44:16
ᵗS Ps 39:3; S Jer 4:19
ᵘS Job 4:2; S Jer 6:11;
Am 3:8; Ac 4:20
20:10 ᵛJer 6:25
ʷNe 6:6-13; Isa 29:21
ˣS Job 19:14;
S Jer 13:21
ʸS Ps 57:4;
S Jer 18:22; Lk 11:53-
54 ᶻS 1Ki 19:2
ᵃS 1Sa 18:25;
S Jer 11:19
20:11 ᵇJer 1:8;
Ro 8:31 ᶜJer 15:15;
17:18 ᵈS Ps 129:2
ᵉS Jer 7:19; 23:40
20:12 ᶠS Ps 7:9;
S Jer 17:10 ᵍDt 32:35;
S Ro 12:19 ʰPs 62:8;
Jer 11:20
20:13 ⁱS Isa 12:6
ʲPs 34:6; 35:10
ᵏS Ps 97:10
20:14 ˡS Job 3:8,16;
Jer 15:10

JEREMIAH'S COMPLAINT

⁷You deceived ᵃᵐ me, LORD, and I was deceived ᵃ;
　　you overpowered ⁿ me and prevailed.
I am ridiculed ᵒ all day long;
　　everyone mocks ᵖ me.
⁸Whenever I speak, I cry out
　　proclaiming violence and destruction. ᵍ
So the word of the LORD has brought me
　　insult and reproach ʳ all day long.
⁹But if I say, "I will not mention his word
　　or speak anymore in his name," ˢ
his word is in my heart like a fire, ᵗ
　　a fire shut up in my bones.
I am weary of holding it in; ᵘ
　　indeed, I cannot.
¹⁰I hear many whispering,
　　"Terror ᵛ on every side!
Denounce ʷ him! Let's denounce him!"
All my friends ˣ
　　are waiting for me to slip, ʸ saying,
"Perhaps he will be deceived;
　　then we will prevail ᶻ over him
　　and take our revenge ᵃ on him."

¹¹But the LORD ᵇ is with me like a mighty warrior;
　　so my persecutors ᶜ will stumble and not prevail. ᵈ
They will fail and be thoroughly disgraced; ᵉ
　　their dishonor will never be forgotten.
¹²LORD Almighty, you who examine the righteous
　　and probe the heart and mind, ᶠ
let me see your vengeance ᵍ on them,
　　for to you I have committed ʰ my cause.

¹³Sing ⁱ to the LORD!
　　Give praise to the LORD!
He rescues ʲ the life of the needy
　　from the hands of the wicked. ᵏ

¹⁴Cursed be the day I was born! ˡ
　　May the day my mother bore me not be blessed!
¹⁵Cursed be the man who brought my father the news,

ᵃ 7 Or *persuaded*

C **20:7–18** The sixth, last and longest of Jeremiah's "confessions" (see Introduction: Author and Date; see also note on 11:18–23). In some respects, it is the most daring and bitter of them all.
20:7 Cf. 15:18. *deceived.* Lit. "seduced" (Ex 22:16) or "enticed" (1Ki 22:20–22); see v. 10. Jeremiah feels that when the Lord originally called him to be a prophet he had overly persuaded him (see TNIV text note; see also 1:7–8,17–19; cf. Eze 14:9).
20:8 Jeremiah attributes his suffering to the Lord's demands on his life. *violence and destruction.* The prophet's message echoes the Lord's word (see 6:7). *reproach.* See Ps 44:13; 79:4.
A **20:9** A classic description of prophetic reluctance overcome by divine compulsion (see 1:6–8; Am 3:8; Ac 4:20; 1Co 9:16). *his word is ... like a fire.* See 5:14; 23:29. The figure is unique to the prophet Jeremiah (see also La 1:13).
20:10 The Hebrew of the first two lines is identical with that of the first two lines of Ps 31:13. *Terror on every side!* See note on 6:25. The phrase is here used to mock Jeremiah in the light of his doleful message. *friends.* Lit. "men of my peace/welfare" (cf. Ps 41:9 and note). *waiting for me to slip.* See Ps 35:15; 38:16. *deceived.* See v. 7 and note. *we will prevail over him.* Or so they think (see v. 11). *take our revenge on him.* His enemies will not give up, no matter what it takes (see 11:19; 12:6; 26:11; cf. Ps 56:5–6; 71:10).

20:11 *the LORD is with me.* See 1:8 and note. *mighty.* The Hebrew for this word is translated "cruel" in 15:21, where it describes Jeremiah's enemies. Here it has a different nuance and is applied to God, whose "might" overcomes all "cruelty." *warrior.* See notes on Ex 14:14; 15:3.
20:12 Repeated almost verbatim from 11:20.
20:13 *Sing ... Give praise.* See 31:7; see also introduction to Ps 9. *rescues ... from the hands of the wicked.* See 15:21; 21:12. *needy.* See 22:16. By Jeremiah's time, "poor/needy" had become virtually synonymous with "righteous" (see Am 2:6; see also notes on Ps 9:18; 34:6).
A C **20:14–18** See Job 3:3–19. From the heights of exultation (v. 13) Jeremiah now sinks to the depths of despair. The irreversibility of his divine call (v. 9), the betrayal of his friends (v. 10), the relentless pursuit of his enemies (vv. 7,11), the negative and condemnatory nature of his message (v. 8)—all have combined to bring to his lips a startling expression of despondency and hopelessness. The passage serves also as a transition to the next major section of the book. Judah and Jerusalem, Jeremiah will soon say, are now irrevocably doomed (see 21:1–10).
20:14 *Cursed be the day I was born!* See note on Job 3:3. The prophet questions the very basis of his divine commission (see 1:5).

who made him very glad, saying,
"A child is born to you—a son!"
¹⁶ May that man be like the towns ^m
the LORD overthrew without pity.
May he hear wailing ⁿ in the morning,
a battle cry at noon.
¹⁷ For he did not kill me in the womb, ^o
with my mother as my grave,
her womb enlarged forever.
¹⁸ Why did I ever come out of the womb^p
to see trouble ^q and sorrow
and to end my days in shame? ^r

GOD REJECTS ZEDEKIAH'S REQUEST

21 The word came to Jeremiah from the LORD when King Zedekiah ^s sent to him Pashhur ^t son of Malkijah and the priest Zephaniah ^u son of Maaseiah. They said: ²"Inquire ^v now of the LORD for us because Nebuchadnezzar^{a w} king of Babylon ^x is attacking us. Perhaps the LORD will perform wonders ^y for us as in times past so that he will withdraw from us."

³But Jeremiah answered them, "Tell Zedekiah, ⁴'This is what the LORD, the God of Israel, says: I am about to turn ^z against you the weapons of war that are in your hands, which you are using to fight the king of Babylon and the Babylonians^b who are outside the wall besieging ^a you. And I will gather them inside this city. ⁵I myself will fight ^b against you with an outstretched hand^c and a mighty arm ^d in furious anger and in great wrath. ⁶I will strike ^e down those who live in this city—both people and animals—and they will die of a terrible plague. ^{f 7}After that, declares the LORD, I will give Zedekiah ^g king of Judah, his officials and the people in this city who survive the plague, ^h sword and famine, into the hands of Nebuchadnezzar king of Babylon ⁱ and to their enemies ^j who seek their lives. ^k He will put them to the sword; ^l he will show them no mercy or pity or compassion.'^m

⁸"Furthermore, tell the people, 'This is what the LORD says: See, I am setting before you the way of life ⁿ and the way of death. ⁹Whoever stays in this city will die by the sword,

^a 2 Hebrew *Nebuchadrezzar*, of which *Nebuchadnezzar* is a variant; here and often in Jeremiah and Ezekiel   ^b 4 Or *Chaldeans*; also in verse 9

20:16 ^m S Ge 19:25
ⁿ S Jer 6:26
20:17 ^o S Job 3:16;
S 10:18-19
20:18 ^p S Job 3:10-
11; S Ecc 4:2
^q S Ge 3:17; S Job 5:7
^r S 1Ki 19:4; Ps 90:9;
102:3
21:1 ^s 2Ki 24:18;
Jer 52:1 ^t S 1Ch 9:12
^u S 2Ki 25:18
21:2 ^v S Ge 25:22;
S 2Ki 22:18
^w S 2Ki 25:1
^x S Ge 10:10
^y Ps 44:1-4; Jer 32:17
21:4 ^z Jer 32:5
^a Jer 37:8-10
21:5 ^b S Jos 10:14;
Eze 29:19
^c S Jer 6:12 ^d S Ex 3:20
S Jer 7:20
21:6 ^e S Jer 7:20
^f S Jer 14:12
21:7 ^g S 2Ki 25:7;
Jer 52:9; Eze 12:14
^h Jer 14:12; 27:8
ⁱ S 2Ch 36:10;
Jer 27:6; 32:4; 34:3;
37:17; 38:18; 39:5;
^j S Lev 26:17;
S Jer 19:9 ^k S Jer 11:21
^l S Jer 15:9
^m S 2Ch 36:17;
S Jer 15:5; Eze 7:9;
Hab 1:6
21:8 ⁿ S Dt 30:15

20:15 *News of the birth of a son,* normally a blessing in ancient times (see, e.g., Ge 29:31–35), Jeremiah sees as a curse in his own case. *Cursed be the man.* A rhetorical curse, not directed against the man personally.

20:16 *towns the LORD overthrew.* Sodom and Gomorrah (see Ge 19:24–25,29). By Jeremiah's time their wickedness had long been proverbial (see 23:14; Dt 29:23; see also note on Isa 1:9–10). *battle cry.* See 4:19. *at noon.* See note on 6:4.

20:17 *enlarged.* Lit."pregnant." In his anguish, Jeremiah wishes that his mother's womb, which gave him birth, had been instead his eternal tomb.

21:1—24:10 The prophet denounces Judah's rulers (21:1—23:7), false prophets (23:8–40) and sinful people (ch. 24). Although for the most part chs. 1–20 relate events in chronological order, chs. 21–52 are arranged on the basis of subject matter rather than chronology (see 24:1; 25:1; 26:1; 27:1; 29:2; 32:1; 35:1; 36:1; 37:1; 45:1; 49:34; 51:59; 52:4).

A **21:1—23:7** The rulers of Judah, who bear the primary responsibility for the nation's economic, social and spiritual ills, are the first to be denounced by Jeremiah.

21:1 *The word came.* The phrase does not appear again until 25:1, suggesting that chs. 21–24 constitute an integral section in the book. *Zedekiah.* Means "The LORD is my righteousness." See Introduction: Background. *Pashhur son of Malkijah.* Not the same as the Pashhur of 20:1–6 (see 38:1). *the priest Zephaniah son of Maaseiah.* Not the same as the prophet Zephaniah (see 29:25,29; 37:3; 52:24; see also Zep 1:1).

21:2 *Inquire … of the LORD.* A request for knowledge or information (see Ge 25:22; 2Ki 22:13), not necessarily for help. *Nebuchadnezzar.* See TNIV text note; see also chart, p. 482, and note

on 2Ki 24:1. *is attacking.* About 588, because the brash Zedekiah had rebelled against Babylon (see 52:3). *us.* Jerusalem. *perform wonders … as in times past.* For example, in the days of Hezekiah (see Isa 37:36). *he will withdraw.* See Isa 37:37.

21:4 *turn against you the weapons.* Your defense of Jerusalem will fail. *Babylonians.* See TNIV text note; see also note on Job 1:17. *gather them inside this city.* Either (1) the weapons, meaning that Judah's troops would be totally unable to defend the approaches to the city, or (2) the Babylonians, meaning that Jerusalem's defeat is imminent and inevitable.

21:5 *I myself will fight against you.* The Lord, usually his people's defender, will now destroy them and seal their doom. *with an outstretched hand and a mighty arm.* See 27:5; 32:17. A similar phrase is used to describe God's powerful redemption of Israel at the exodus (see 32:21; Dt 4:34; 5:15; 7:19; 26:8), but here God turns his wrath against his own people. *in furious anger and in great wrath.* Probably quoted from Dt 29:28.

21:7 *I will give Zedekiah … his officials and the people … into the hands of Nebuchadnezzar.* Fulfilled in 52:8–11,24–27 (see Eze 12:13–14). *plague, sword and famine.* See v. 9. For this triad see note on 14:12. *no mercy or pity or compassion.* For this triad see 13:14; see also Eze 5:11. The three triads here heighten the literary effect of the passage.

21:8–10 See 27:12–13. Similar advice is offered in 38:2–3,17–18 (see Dt 30:15–20).

21:8 *See, I am setting before you.* See Dt 11:26. The people are offered a choice, but few of them will make the right decision. *the way of life and the way of death.* See Dt 30:15,19; see also Pr 6:23.

C **21:9** Repeated almost verbatim in 38:2. Jeremiah's counsel of surrender branded him as a traitor in the eyes of

21:9 °Jer 14:12;
Eze 5:12 °Jer 27:11;
40:9 °Jer 27:12; 38:2,
17; 39:18; 45:5
21:10 °Jer 44:11,27;
Am 9:4 °S Jer 20:4;
32:28; 38:2-3
°S 2Ki 25:9;
S 2Ch 36:19
21:11 °S Jer 13:18
21:12 °S Ex 22:22;
S Lev 25:17
°S Ps 27:11
°S Isa 42:25;
S Jer 10:10 °Jer 23:2
°S Isa 1:31
21:13 °Jer 23:30;
50:31; 51:25; Eze 5:8;
13:8; 21:3; 29:10;
34:10; Na 2:13; 3:5
°Ps 125:2 °2Sa 5:6-
7; Jer 49:4; La 4:12;
Ob 1:3-4
21:14 °S Pr 1:31;
S Isa 3:10-11;
S Jer 17:10
°S 2Ch 36:19; La 2:3
°S 2Ki 19:23;
Eze 20:47
22:1 °S Jer 13:18;
34:2
22:2 °Am 7:16
°S Jer 17:25; Lk 1:32
°Jer 17:20
22:3 °S Lev 25:17;
Isa 56:1; Jer 5:1;
Eze 33:14; 45:9;
Hos 12:6; Am 5:24;
Mic 6:8; Zec 7:9
°Ps 72:4; Jer 21:12
°Ex 22:22;
S Isa 1:17; Jer 5:28
°S Jer 7:6
22:4 °S Jer 17:25
22:5 °S Jer 17:27
°S Ge 22:16;
Heb 6:13
22:6 °S Ge 31:21;
S SS 4:1 °S 1Ki 7:2;
S Isa 33:9 °Mic 3:12

famine or plague. ° But whoever goes out and surrenders° to the Babylonians who are besieging you will live; they will escape with their lives. ° ¹⁰I have determined to do this city harm ' and not good, declares the LORD. It will be given into the hands ˢ of the king of Babylon, and he will destroy it with fire.' ᵗ

¹¹"Moreover, say to the royal house ° of Judah, 'Hear the word of the LORD. ¹²This is what the LORD says to you, house of David:

" 'Administer justice ° every morning;
  rescue from the hands of their oppressors ʷ
  those who have been robbed,
or my wrath will break out and burn like fire ˣ
  because of the evil ʸ you have done—
  burn with no one to quench ᶻ it.
¹³ I am against ° you, Jerusalem,
  you who live above this valley ᵇ
  on the rocky plateau, declares the LORD—
you who say, "Who can come against us?
  Who can enter our refuge?" ᶜ
¹⁴ I will punish you as your deeds ᵈ deserve,
  declares the LORD.
I will kindle a fire ᵉ in your forests ᶠ
  that will consume everything around you.' "

JUDGMENT AGAINST WICKED KINGS

22 This is what the LORD says: "Go down to the palace of the king ᵍ of Judah and proclaim this message there: ²'Hear ʰ the word of the LORD to you, king of Judah, you who sit on David's throne '—you, your officials and your people who come through these gates. ' ³This is what the LORD says: Do what is just ᵏ and right. Rescue from the hands of their oppressors ' those who have been robbed. Do no wrong or violence to the foreigner, the fatherless or the widow, ᵐ and do not shed innocent blood ⁿ in this place. ⁴For if you are careful to carry out these commands, then kings ° who sit on David's throne will come through the gates of this palace, riding in chariots and on horses, accompanied by their officials and their people. ⁵But if you do not obey ° these commands, declares the LORD, I swear ° by myself that this palace will become a ruin.' "

⁶For this is what the LORD says about the palace of the king of Judah:

"Though you are like Gilead ' to me,
  like the summit of Lebanon, ˢ
I will surely make you like a wasteland, ᵗ
  like towns not inhabited.

---

many (see 37:13), but he was in fact a true patriot who wanted to stay in Judah even after Jerusalem was destroyed (see 37:14; 40:6; 42:7–22). *whoever … surrenders to the Babylonians … will live.* Fulfilled in 39:9; 52:15. *they will escape with their lives.* Lit. "their lives will be their (only) booty." The victorious in battle can expect to share plunder; the defeated are fortunate indeed if their lives are spared.
21:10 *determined.* Lit. "set my face" (see 44:11; Isa 50:7 and note). *harm and not good.* See Am 9:4; contrast 24:6. *It will be given … destroy it with fire.* See 34:2.
21:12 *Administer justice.* See 5:28; 22:16; 1Ki 3:28; La 3:59. The king was obliged and expected to do so, as was the future Messiah (see 23:5; 33:15). *every morning.* When the mind is clear and the day is cool (see Ps 101:8 and note). *rescue … robbed.* Repeated in 22:3. *or my wrath … no one to quench it.* Repeated from 4:4 (see Am 5:6). *wrath will … burn.* See 15:14; 17:4,27.
21:13 *valley.* Jerusalem, surrounded on three sides by valleys (see note on Isa 22:7), is called the "Valley of Vision" in Isa 22:1,5. *rocky plateau.* Mount Zion. The pronouns are plural in the second half of the verse (referring to Jerusalem's inhabitants), singular in the first half (referring to Jerusalem personified). *Who can come against us?* The people think that no one can successfully besiege them (see notes on 7:4; 8:19).
21:14 *as your deeds deserve.* See note on 17:10. *kindle a fire … consume.* See note on 17:27. *forests.* The Hebrew for this word is

singular and perhaps refers figuratively to Jerusalem's royal palace, called the "Palace of the Forest of Lebanon" (1Ki 7:2; 10:17,21; see Isa 22:8) because of the cedar (see 22:7,14,15,23) used in its construction. The palace (see 22:1) is compared to the "summit of Lebanon" in 22:6 (see 22:23 and TNIV text note).
22:1 *Go down.* The palace was at a lower elevation than the temple (see 26:10; 36:10–12). *king of Judah.* Probably Zedekiah (see 21:3,7; compare v. 3 with 21:12), whose predecessors are mentioned in sequence later in the chapter (Josiah, vv. 10a, 15b–16; Jehoahaz/Shallum, vv. 10b–12; Jehoiakim, vv. 13–15a, 17–19; Jehoiachin/Coniah, vv. 24–30).

22:2 *David's throne.* Though all the kings of the Davidic dynasty failed to a greater or lesser degree, the victorious Messiah would someday appear as the culmination of David's royal line (see 23:5 and TNIV text note; 33:15; Eze 34:23–24; Mt 1:1). *who come through these gates.* See 17:25 and note.
22:3 Contrast Isa 11:3–5 with Eze 22:6–7.
22:4 Repeated in part from 17:25.
22:5 See 17:27 and note. *swear by myself.* See notes on Ge 22:16; Isa 45:23; see also 49:13; 51:14; cf. 44:26. *become a ruin.* Fulfilled in 52:13 (see 27:17).
22:6 *Gilead … Lebanon.* Renowned for their forests. Lebanon in particular supplied cedar for the royal palace (see note on 21:14; see also 1Ki 5:6,8–10; 7:2–3; 10:27).

⁷I will send destroyers ᵘ against you,
  each man with his weapons,
  and they will cut ᵛ up your fine cedar beams
  and throw them into the fire. ʷ

⁸"People from many nations will pass by this city and will ask one another, 'Why has the LORD done such a thing to this great city?' ˣ ⁹And the answer will be: 'Because they have forsaken the covenant of the LORD their God and have worshiped and served other gods. ʸ ' "

¹⁰Do not weep for the dead ᶻ ⌊king⌋ or mourn ᵃ his loss;
  rather, weep bitterly for him who is exiled,
  because he will never return ᵇ
  nor see his native land again.

¹¹For this is what the LORD says about Shallum ᵃ ᶜ son of Josiah, who succeeded his father as king of Judah but has gone from this place: "He will never return. ¹²He will die ᵈ in the place where they have led him captive; he will not see this land again."

¹³"Woe ᵉ to him who builds ᶠ his palace by unrighteousness,
  his upper rooms by injustice,
  making his subjects work for nothing,
  not paying ᵍ them for their labor.
¹⁴He says, 'I will build myself a great palace ʰ
  with spacious upper rooms.'
So he makes large windows in it,
  panels it with cedar ⁱ
  and decorates it in red. ʲ

¹⁵"Does it make you a king
  to have more and more cedar?
Did not your father have food and drink?
  He did what was right and just, ᵏ
  so all went well ˡ with him.
¹⁶He defended the cause of the poor and needy, ᵐ
  and so all went well.
Is that not what it means to know ⁿ me?"
  declares the LORD.
¹⁷"But your eyes and your heart
  are set only on dishonest gain, ᵒ
  on shedding innocent blood ᵖ
  and on oppression and extortion." �q

ᵃ *11* Also called *Jehoahaz*

22:7 | ᵘ S Jer 4:7;
S 6:4; ᵛ Ps 74:5;
Isa 10:34
ʷ S 2Ch 36:19;
Zec 11:1
22:8 | ˣ Dt 29:25-26;
1Ki 9:8-9; Jer 16:10-11
22:9 | ʸ S 1Ki 9:9;
Jer 16:11; Eze 39:23
22:10 | ᶻ S Ecc 4:2
ᵃ ver 18; Eze 24:16
ᵇ ver 27; Jer 24:9;
29:18; 42:18
22:11 | ᶜ 2Ki 23:31
22:12 | ᵈ 2Ki 23:34
22:13 | ᵉ S Isa 5:8
ᶠ Mic 3:10; Hab 2:9
ᵍ S Lev 19:13; Jas 5:4
22:14 | ʰ Isa 5:8-9
ⁱ 2Sa 7:2 / Eze 23:14
22:15 | ᵏ 2Ki 23:25
ˡ Ps 128:2; S Isa 3:10
22:16 | ᵐ Ps 72:1-4,
12-13; S 82:3;
S Pr 24:23
ⁿ S Ps 36:10
22:17 | ᵒ S Isa 56:11
ᵖ 2Ki 24:4
q S Dt 28:33;
Eze 18:12; Mic 2:2

22:7 *send.* Lit. "consecrate" (see note on 6:4). *destroyers.* The Babylonians (see note on 4:7; see also 12:12). *each man with his weapons.* See Eze 9:2. *cut up your ... cedar.* Cf. Isa 10:33–34; cf. especially the vivid description of the Babylonian troops smashing the carved paneling of the Jerusalem temple with their axes and hatchets (Ps 74:3–6).
22:8–9 Echoed in 1Ki 9:8–9; see Dt 29:24–26.
22:9 *forsaken the covenant ... and served other gods.* A gross violation of the first and second stipulations of the Sinaitic covenant (see Ex 20:3–5 and notes).
22:10 *weep for the dead* ⌊*king*⌋. Josiah, who was mourned long after his death (see 2Ch 35:24–25). *him who is exiled.* Jehoahaz/Shallum. In 609 B.C. the Egyptian pharaoh Necho "carried him off to Egypt, and there he died" (2Ki 23:34).
22:11 *Shallum.* See 1Ch 3:15. "Shallum" was his personal name, "Jehoahaz" his throne name (the latter means "The LORD seizes").
22:12 *the place where they have led him captive.* Egypt (see note on v. 10).
22:13–19 A scathing denunciation of King Jehoiakim, who is described in the third person (vv. 13–14), then rhetorically addressed in the second person (vv. 15,17) and identified by name (v. 18), meaning "The LORD raises up." Good King Josiah is referred to in vv. 15b–16 by way of contrast.
22:13 *Woe to him who builds.* See Hab 2:9,12. *by unrighteousness*

... by injustice. Contrast v. 3; 21:12. *upper rooms.* See note on Jdg 3:20. *making his subjects work for nothing.* Contrary to the law (see Lev 25:39; Dt 24:14–15). Jehoiakim's refusal to pay them may have been due partly to inability, since Judah was under heavy tribute to Egypt during the early part of his reign (see 2Ki 23:35).
22:14 *large windows.* The windows described here may well be the same as those found in the ruins of Beth Hakkerem (see 6:1; see also note on Ne 3:14) by archaeologists in the early 1960s. *panels.* Haggai similarly deplores the use of paneling as an extravagant and unneeded luxury in certain situations (see Hag 1:4).
22:15 *your father.* Josiah. *have food and drink.* Enjoy life (see Ecc 2:24–25; 3:12–13). *did what was right and just.* Like his ancestor David (see 2Sa 8:15); contrast v. 13 (see note there; see also note on Ps 119:121).
22:16 James defines a proper relationship to God in similar terms (Jas 1:27); contrast 5:28 (see note there). *poor and needy.* See note on 20:13. *to know me.* To love God fully, which results in living a pious life and serving those in need (see Dt 10:12–13; Hos 6:6; Mic 6:8).
22:17 *your.* Jehoiakim's (see v. 18). *dishonest gain.* See 6:13; 8:10. *shedding innocent blood.* See note on 19:4; for an illustration of Jehoiakim's cruelty in this regard, see 26:20–23. *oppression.* See v. 3; 6:6; 21:12.

22:18 ʳS 2Sa 1:26
22:19 ˢ 2Ki 24:6
ᵗ Jer 8:2; 36:30
22:20 ᵘ S Isa 57:13
ᵛ S Ps 68:15
ʷ S Nu 27:12 ˣ ver 22;
Jer 30:14; La 1:19;
Eze 16:33-34;
Hos 8:9
22:21 ʸ Zec 7:7
ᶻ Dt 9:7; Ps 25:7;
Isa 54:4; Jer 3:25;
31:19; 32:30
ᵃ S Jer 3:13; 7:23-28;
Zep 3:2
22:22 ᵇ S Dt 28:64;
S Job 27:21
ᶜ S Jer 10:21
ᵈ S ver 20 ᵉ S Jer 7:19
22:23 ᶠ S 1Ki 7:2;
Eze 17:3 ᵍ S Jer 4:31
22:24 ʰ S 2Ki 24:6,8
ⁱ S Ge 38:18
22:25 ʲ S 2Ki 24:16;
S 2Ch 36:10
22:26 ᵏ S 1Sa 25:29;
S 2Ki 24:8;
2Ch 36:10;
S Isa 22:17; Eze 19:9-
14 ˡ S 1Ki 2:19
22:27 ᵐ S ver 10
22:28 ⁿ S 2Ki 24:6
ᵒ Ps 31:12; S Jer 19:10;
25:34; 48:38 ᵖ Jer 15:1
�q S Jer 17:4
22:29 ʳ S Jer 6:19

¹⁸Therefore this is what the Lord says about Jehoiakim son of Josiah king of Judah:

"They will not mourn ʳ for him:
    'Alas, my brother! Alas, my sister!'
They will not mourn for him:
    'Alas, my master! Alas, his splendor!'
¹⁹ He will have the burial ˢ of a donkey—
    dragged away and thrown ᵗ
    outside the gates of Jerusalem."

²⁰ "Go up to Lebanon and cry out, ᵘ
    let your voice be heard in Bashan, ᵛ
cry out from Abarim, ʷ
    for all your allies ˣ are crushed.
²¹ I warned you when you felt secure, ʸ
    but you said, 'I will not listen!'
This has been your way from your youth; ᶻ
    you have not obeyed ᵃ me.
²² The wind ᵇ will drive all your shepherds ᶜ away,
    and your allies ᵈ will go into exile.
Then you will be ashamed and disgraced ᵉ
    because of all your wickedness.
²³ You who live in 'Lebanon, ᵃ ᶠ'
    who are nestled in cedar buildings,
how you will groan when pangs come upon you,
    pain ᵍ like that of a woman in labor!

²⁴ "As surely as I live," declares the Lord, "even if you, Jehoiachin ᵇ ʰ son of Jehoiakim king of Judah, were a signet ring ⁱ on my right hand, I would still pull you off. ²⁵ I will deliver ʲ you into the hands of those who seek your life, those you fear—Nebuchadnezzar king of Babylon and the Babylonians. ᶜ ²⁶ I will hurl ᵏ you and the mother ˡ who gave you birth into another country, where neither of you was born, and there you both will die. ²⁷ You will never come back to the land you long to return ᵐ to."

²⁸ Is this man Jehoiachin ⁿ a despised, broken pot, ᵒ
    an object no one wants?
Why will he and his children be hurled ᵖ out,
    cast into a land �q they do not know?
²⁹ O land, ʳ land, land,
    hear the word of the Lord!

ᵃ 23 That is, the palace in Jerusalem (see 1 Kings 7:2)   ᵇ 24 Hebrew *Koniah,* a variant of *Jehoiachin;* also in verse 28   ᶜ 25 Or *Chaldeans*

22:18 Contrast 2Ch 35:24–25. *They will not mourn for him: "Alas, my brother!"* Contrast 1Ki 13:30.
22:19 *burial of a donkey.* Tantamount to no burial at all (see 36:30); fulfilled in 2Ki 24:6, where no burial is described and where it says that Jehoiakim "rested with his ancestors," a euphemism for dying (see notes on Ge 25:8; 1Ki 1:21). *dragged away.* See 15:3.
22:20–23 The Lord speaks to Jerusalem, which is personified as a woman (see v. 23).
22:20 *Lebanon . . . Bashan . . . Abarim.* Mountainous regions (see v. 6; Nu 27:12; Dt 32:49; Jdg 3:3; Ps 68:15), the first two in the north and the third in the south, suitable heights from which the whole land of Israel could be rhetorically addressed. *allies.* Lit. "lovers" (see 4:30 and note), here referring to nations joined together by treaty. Judah's onetime allies included Egypt, Assyria (see 2:36), Edom, Moab, Ammon and Phoenicia (see 27:3), all of whom had been—or soon would be—conquered by Babylonia (see 27:6–7; 28:14). *crushed.* See 14:17.
22:21 *not listen . . . not obeyed me.* See 7:22–26; 11:7–8. *your youth.* The days of Israel's early history in Egypt (see 2:2 and note; Hos 2:15).
22:22 *wind will drive . . . away.* See 13:24; Job 27:21; Isa 27:8. *shepherds.* See 2:8 and note; 10:21; 23:1–4. The initial fulfillment of this verse took place in 597 B.C. (see 2Ki 24:12–16).

22:23 *Lebanon . . . cedar.* See TNIV text note; see also 21:14 and note; Eze 17:3–4,12. *pain like that of a woman in labor.* See 4:19, 31 and notes.
22:24–30 A prophecy against King Jehoiachin (fulfilled in 24:1; 29:2), who was also known as Koniah (see TNIV text note on v. 24), a shortened form of Jeconiah (see TNIV text note on 24:1); see Introduction: Background. All three forms of the name mean "The Lord establishes."
22:24 *As surely as I live.* See note on Ge 42:15. *even if you . . . were a signet ring.* The curse on Jehoiachin is apparently reversed in Hag 2:23 (see note there).
22:25 *deliver you into the hands of . . . those you fear.* Contrast 39:17.
22:26 Fulfilled in 597 B.C. (see 29:2; 2Ki 24:15). *hurl . . . into another country.* Send into exile in Babylonia (see 7:15; 16:13; Dt 29:28). *you and the mother who gave you birth.* Jehoiachin and Nehushta (see note on 13:18).
22:28 Two rhetorical questions, answered in v. 30. *broken pot . . . hurled out.* Jehoiachin and his descendants, like Judah itself (see 19:10–11), are under God's judgment. *he and his children.* Though Jehoiachin was only 18 years old at the time of his exile (see 2Ki 24:8), he already had more than one wife (see 2Ki 24:15) and therefore probably one or more children.
22:29 *land, land, land.* The repetition implies the strongest pos-

[30] This is what the LORD says:
"Record this man as if childless, [s]
a man who will not prosper [t] in his lifetime,
for none of his offspring [u] will prosper,
none will sit on the throne [v] of David
or rule anymore in Judah."

THE RIGHTEOUS BRANCH

23 "Woe to the shepherds [w] who are destroying and scattering [x] the sheep of my pasture!" [y] declares the LORD. [2] Therefore this is what the LORD, the God of Israel, says to the shepherds [z] who tend my people: "Because you have scattered my flock [a] and driven them away and have not bestowed care on them, I will bestow punishment on you for the evil [b] you have done," declares the LORD. [3] "I myself will gather the remnant [c] of my flock out of all the countries where I have driven them and will bring them back to their pasture, [d] where they will be fruitful and increase in number. [4] I will place shepherds [e] over them who will tend them, and they will no longer be afraid [f] or terrified, nor will any be missing, [g]" declares the LORD.

[5] "The days are coming," declares the LORD,
"when I will raise up for David [a] a righteous Branch, [h]
a King [i] who will reign [j] wisely
and do what is just and right [k] in the land.
[6] In his days Judah will be saved
and Israel will live in safety. [l]
This is the name [m] by which he will be called:
The LORD Our Righteous Savior. [n]

[7] "So then, the days are coming," [o] declares the LORD, "when people will no longer say, 'As surely as the LORD lives, who brought the Israelites up out of Egypt,' [p] [8] but they will say, 'As surely as the LORD lives, who brought the descendants of Israel up out of the land of the north and out of all the countries where he had banished them.' Then they will live in their own land." [q]

LYING PROPHETS

[9] Concerning the prophets:

My heart [r] is broken within me;
all my bones tremble. [s]

---

[a] 5 Or *up from David's line*

22:30 *Ch 3:18;
Jer 38:23; 52:10;
Mt 1:12 *Jer 10:21
[u] S Job 18:19
[v] S Ps 94:20
23:1 [w] Jer 10:21;
12:10; 25:36;
Eze 34:1-10; Zec 10:2;
Zec 11:15-17
[x] S Isa 56:11
[y] Ps 100:3; S Jer 13:17;
Eze 34:31
23:2 [z] Jn 10:8
[a] S Jer 10:21; 13:20
[b] Jer 21:12; Eze 34:8-
10
23:3 [c] Isa 11:10-12;
Jer 32:37; Eze 34:11-
16 [d] S 1Ki 8:48
23:4 [e] S Ge 48:15;
S Isa 31:4; Jer 31:10
[f] Jer 30:10; 46:27-28
[g] S Jn 6:39
23:5 [h] S 2Ki 19:26;
S Isa 4:2; Eze 17:22
[i] S Mt 2:2 / Isa 9:7;
S Mt 1:1 [k] S Ge 18:19
23:6 [l] S Lev 25:18;
S Dt 32:8; Hos 2:18
[m] Ex 23:21; Jer 33:16;
Mt 1:21-23
[n] S Ezr 9:15;
S Isa 42:6; Ro 3:21-
22; S 1Co 1:30
23:7 [o] Jer 30:3
[p] S Dt 15:15
23:8 [q] S Isa 14:1;
S 43:5-6; Jer 30:10;
Eze 20:42; 34:13;
Am 9:14-15
23:9 [r] S Jer 4:19
[s] S Job 4:14

---

sible emphasis and intensity (see 7:4 and note; 23:30–32; Isa 6:3 and note; Eze 21:27).

22:30 *as if childless.* Not in the sense of Jehoiachin's having no children at all (he had at least seven; see 1Ch 3:17–18), but of having none to sit on the throne of David in Judah. Jehoiachin's grandson Zerubbabel (1Ch 3:17–19; Mt 1:12) became governor of Judah (see Hag 1:1), but not king. Zedekiah was a son of Josiah (see 37:1), not of Jehoiachin, and he and his sons died before the latter (see 52:10–11). Jehoiachin therefore was Judah's last surviving Davidic king—until Christ.

23:1–8 A summary statement (probably dating to Zedekiah's reign; see note on v. 6) that includes God's intention to judge the wicked rulers and leaders of Judah (vv. 1–2), to ultimately bring his people back from exile (vv. 3–4,7–8) and to raise up an ideal Davidic King (vv. 5–6).

23:1 See 10:21 and note. *sheep.* The people of Judah (see v. 2).
23:2 *bestowed care . . . bestow punishment.* The same Hebrew root underlies both phrases (see v. 4 and note). What Judah's rulers had failed to do is summarized in Eze 34:4.

23:3 *remnant.* See note on 6:9. *I have driven.* Although Judah's sins and the sins of her leaders had caused the people to be "driven . . . away" (v. 2) into exile, the Lord himself ultimately carried out the results of their repeated violations of their covenant commitments. *be fruitful and increase.* See note on Ge 1:28.
23:4 *be afraid . . . terrified.* The absence of a concerned shepherd invites attacks by wild animals (see Eze 34:8). *be missing.*

See Nu 31:49. The Hebrew root underlying this phrase is the same as that for "bestowed care" and "bestow punishment" in v. 2 (see note there).

23:5–6 One of the most important Messianic passages in Jeremiah, echoed in 33:15–16.

23:5 *raise up.* See 2Sa 7:12; see also 30:9; Eze 34:23–24; 37:24. The Hebrew for this phrase is translated "place" in v. 4. *for David.* See TNIV text note; see also Mt 1:1 and TNIV text note. The Messiah, unlike any previous descendant of David, would be the ideal King. He would sum up in himself all the finest qualities of the best rulers, and infinitely more. *Branch.* A Messianic title (see note on Isa 4:2; Zec 3:8; 6:12). The Targum (ancient Aramaic paraphrase) reads "Messiah" here. *reign wisely.* See note on Isa 52:13. *do what is just and right.* See 22:3,15 and note on 22:15; said also of King David (see 2Sa 8:15).

23:6 *Judah . . . and Israel.* God's reunited people will be restored (see 31:31 and note; Eze 37:15–22). *be saved . . . live in safety.* The deliverance will be both spiritual and physical (see Dt 33:28–29). *The LORD Our Righteous Savior.* Although Zedekiah did not live up to the meaning of his name, "The LORD is my righteousness," the Messiah would bestow on his people the abundant blessings (see Eze 34:25–31) that come from the hands of a King who does "what is just and right" (v. 5).
23:7–8 Repeated almost verbatim from 16:14–15 (see notes there).
23:9–40 False prophets denounced (see 2:8; 4:9; 5:30–31;

23:9 ᵗ Jer 20:8-9
23:10 ᵘ S Jer 9:2
ᵛ Dt 28:23-24
ʷ Ps 107:34;
S Jer 9:10 ˣ S Jer 4:26;
S 12:11
23:11 ʸ Jer 6:13;
S 8:10; Zep 3:4
ᶻ S 2Ki 21:4; S Jer 7:10
23:12 ᵃ S Dt 32:35;
S Job 3:23; Jer 13:16
ᵇ Jer 11:23
23:13 ᶜ S 1Ki 18:22
ᵈ ver 32; S Isa 3:12;
Eze 13:10
23:14 ᵉ S Jer 5:30;
Hos 6:10 ᶠ Jer 29:23
ᵍ ver 22 ʰ S Isa 5:18
ⁱ S Ge 18:20; Mt 11:24
ʲ Jer 20:16; Am 4:11
23:15 ᵏ S Jer 8:14;
9:15 ˡ S Jer 8:10
23:16 ᵐ Jer 27:9-10,
14; S Mt 7:15
ⁿ S Jer 14:14; Eze 13:3
ᵒ Jer 9:20
23:17 ᵖ ver 31
�q S 1Ki 22:8;
S Jer 4:10 ʳ S Jer 13:10
ˢ Jer 5:12; Am 9:10;
Mic 3:11

I am like a drunken man,
  like one overcome by wine,
because of the LORD
  and his holy words. ᵗ
¹⁰ The land is full of adulterers; ᵘ
  because of the curse ᵃ ᵛ the land lies parched
  and the pastures ʷ in the wilderness are withered. ˣ
The ₗprophets₎ follow an evil course
  and use their power unjustly.

¹¹ "Both prophet and priest are godless; ʸ
  even in my temple ᶻ I find their wickedness,"

> declares the LORD.

¹² "Therefore their path will become slippery; ᵃ
  they will be banished to darkness
  and there they will fall.
I will bring disaster on them
  in the year they are punished, ᵇ"

> declares the LORD.

¹³ "Among the prophets of Samaria
  I saw this repulsive thing:
They prophesied by Baal ᶜ
  and led my people Israel astray. ᵈ
¹⁴ And among the prophets of Jerusalem
  I have seen something horrible: ᵉ
They commit adultery and live a lie. ᶠ
They strengthen the hands of evildoers, ᵍ
  so that none of them turn from their wickedness. ʰ
They are all like Sodom ⁱ to me;
  the people of Jerusalem are like Gomorrah." ʲ

¹⁵ Therefore, this is what the LORD Almighty says concerning the prophets:

"I will make them eat bitter food
  and drink poisoned water, ᵏ
because from the prophets of Jerusalem
  ungodliness ˡ has spread throughout the land."

¹⁶ This is what the LORD Almighty says:

"Do not listen ᵐ to what the prophets are prophesying to you;
  they fill you with false hopes.
They speak visions ⁿ from their own minds,
  not from the mouth ᵒ of the LORD.
¹⁷ They keep saying ᵖ to those who despise me,
  'The LORD says: You will have peace.' q
And to all who follow the stubbornness ʳ of their hearts
  they say, 'No harm ˢ will come to you.'

ᵃ 10 Or *because of these things*

6:13–15; 8:10–12; 14:13–15; 18:18–23; 26:8,11,16; 27–28; Isa 28:7–13; Eze 13; Mic 3:5–12).
23:9 *Concerning.* Introduces headings also in 46:2; 48:1; 49:1, 7,23,28. *his holy words.* Contrast the unholy words of the false prophets (see vv. 16–18).
23:10 See Isa 24:4–6. *adulterers.* See 5:7–8; 9:2 and notes. *curse.* Brought on by violating the Lord's covenant (see 11:3 and note; 11:8). *parched ... withered.* See 12:4 and note. To worship other gods is to deny to the land the fertility that only the Lord can bring (see Hos 2:5–8,21–22; Am 4:4–9). *pastures in the wilderness.* See note on 9:10. *evil course.* Evil because it is their own and not God's (see 8:6).
23:11 *even in my temple ... wickedness.* For examples, see 32:34; 2Ki 16:10–14; 21:5; Eze 8:5,10,14,16.
23:12 *their path will become slippery ... banished to darkness.* See Ps 35:5–6; see also Ps 73:18.

23:13 *prophesied by Baal.* See 2:8 and note; see also 1Ki 18:19–40.
23:14 *They ... live a lie.* See 14:13 and note; cf. 1Jn 1:6. *strengthen the hands of.* The Hebrew underlying this phrase is translated "encouraged" in Eze 13:22. *none of them turn from their wickedness.* See Eze 13:22. *like Sodom ... like Gomorrah.* See note on 20:16.
23:15 *I will make ... poisoned water.* Repeated almost verbatim from 9:15 (see note there). *ungodliness.* See v. 11.
23:16 *visions.* "Revelations" or "prophecies" (see 1Sa 3:1; Pr 29:18; Isa 1:1; Ob 1 and notes). *from their own minds.* See v. 26; 14:14. False prophets are like preachers of a "different gospel" (Gal 1:6–9).
23:17 *You will have peace.* The essential message of the false prophets (see 6:14 and note; 8:11; 14:13 and note; cf. 28:8–9). *stubbornness of their hearts.* See note on 3:17.

¹⁸ But which of them has stood in the council ᵗ of the LORD
  to see or to hear his word?
  Who has listened and heard his word?
¹⁹ See, the storm ᵘ of the LORD
  will burst out in wrath,
  a whirlwind ᵛ swirling down
  on the heads of the wicked.
²⁰ The anger ʷ of the LORD will not turn back ˣ
  until he fully accomplishes
  the purposes of his heart.
  In days to come
  you will understand it clearly.
²¹ I did not send ʸ these prophets,
  yet they have run with their message;
  I did not speak to them,
  yet they have prophesied.
²² But if they had stood in my council, ᶻ
  they would have proclaimed ᵃ my words to my people
  and would have turned ᵇ them from their evil ways
  and from their evil deeds. ᶜ

²³ "Am I only a God nearby, ᵈ"

  declares the LORD,

  "and not a God far away?
²⁴ Who can hide ᵉ in secret places
  so that I cannot see them?"

  declares the LORD.

  "Do not I fill heaven and earth?" ᶠ

  declares the LORD.

²⁵ "I have heard what the prophets say who prophesy lies ᵍ in my name. They say, 'I had a dream! ʰ I had a dream!' ²⁶ How long will this continue in the hearts of these lying prophets, who prophesy the delusions ⁱ of their own minds? ʲ ²⁷ They think the dreams they tell one another will make my people forget ᵏ my name, just as their ancestors forgot ˡ my name through Baal worship. ᵐ ²⁸ Let the prophets who have dreams ⁿ tell their dreams, but let the one who has my word ᵒ speak it faithfully. For what has straw to do with grain?" declares the LORD. ²⁹ "Is not my word like fire," ᵖ declares the LORD, "and like a hammer ᑫ that breaks a rock in pieces?

³⁰ "Therefore," declares the LORD, "I am against ʳ the prophets ˢ who steal from one another words supposedly from me. ³¹ Yes," declares the LORD, "I am against the prophets who wag their own tongues and yet declare, 'The LORD declares.' ᵗ ³² Indeed, I am against those who prophesy false dreams, ᵘ" declares the LORD. "They tell them and lead my peo-

23:18 ᵗ S 1Ki 22:19;
S Ro 11:34
23:19 ᵘ Isa 30:30;
Jer 25:32; 30:23
ᵛ Zec 7:14
23:20 ʷ S 2Ki 23:26
ˣ S Jer 4:28
23:21 ʸ S Jer 14:14;
27:15
23:22 ᶻ S 1Ki 22:19
ᵃ S Dt 33:10
ᵇ S 2Ki 17:13;
Jer 25:5; Zec 1:4
ᶜ ver 14; Am 3:7
23:23 ᵈ Ps 139:1-10
23:24 ᵉ S Ge 3:8;
S Job 11:20; 22:12-14;
S Ecc 12:14;
S Isa 28:15; 1Co 4:5
ᶠ S 1Ki 8:27
23:25 ᵍ ver 16;
Jer 14:14; 27:10
ʰ ver 28,32; S Dt 13:1;
Jer 27:9; 29:8
23:26 ⁱ S Isa 30:10;
1Ti 4:1-2 ʲ Jer 14:14;
Eze 13:2
23:27 ᵏ Dt 13:1-3;
Jer 29:8 ˡ S Jdg 3:7;
S 8:33-34
ᵐ S Jer 2:23
23:28 ⁿ S ver 25
ᵒ S 1Sa 3:17
23:29 ᵖ S Ps 39:3;
Jer 5:14; S 1Co 3:13
ᑫ Heb 4:12
23:30 ʳ S Ps 34:16
ˢ ver 2; Dt 18:20;
Jer 14:15; S 21:13
23:31 ᵗ ver 17
23:32 ᵘ S ver 25

23:18 *council of the LORD.* God's heavenly confidants (see v. 22; Job 15:7–10 and note; see also 1Ki 22:19–22; Job 1:6; 2:1; 29:4 and note; Ps 89:7). In Am 3:7 the Hebrew for "council" is translated "plan," the purposes that God has promised to reveal to his chosen servants (see v. 20).
23:19–20 Repeated almost verbatim in 30:23–24.
23:19 *storm . . . whirlwind.* A vivid image of God's wrath.
23:20 *you will understand it clearly.* Unlike the false prophets, who continued to mislead their hearers even in Babylonia after the exile of 597 B.C. (see 29:20–23).
23:21 *I did not send.* See v. 32; 29:9; contrast 1:7; Isa 6:8; Eze 3:5. *did not speak to them.* See 29:23.
23:22 *my council.* See note on v. 18.
23:23 *God nearby . . . God far away.* God is both immanent and transcendent; he lives "in a high and holy place, but also with those who are . . . lowly in spirit" (Isa 57:15).
23:24 *hide . . . so that I cannot see them.* See Job 26:6; Ps 139:7–12; Am 9:2–4. *I fill heaven and earth.* See Isa 66:1.
23:25 *lies.* See 5:12. *in my name.* See Dt 18:20,22. *dream.* An infrequent mode of divine revelation to a true prophet (see 27:9; Dt 13:1–3; 1Sa 28:6; Zec 10:2; but cf. Nu 12:6; Joel 2:28).
23:26 *hearts . . . minds.* The Hebrew is the same for both words

(see note on Ps 4:7). *their own minds.* See note on v. 16.
23:27 *my name.* To forget the Lord's name is tantamount to forgetting him (see note on Ps 5:11). *forgot . . . through Baal worship.* When Judah's ancestors forgot God, they began to serve Baal (see Jdg 3:7; 1Sa 12:9–10). *forgot.* See Ps 9:17 and note.
23:28–29 The true word of God is symbolized in three figures of speech (grain, fire, hammer).
23:28 *straw . . . grain.* Of the two, only grain can feed and nourish (see note on 15:16).
23:29 *like fire.* See note on 20:9. The fire of the divine word ultimately tests "the quality of each person's work" (1Co 3:13; see note there). *like a hammer.* Similarly, the divine word works relentlessly, like a sword or hammer, to judge "the thoughts and attitudes of the heart" (Heb 4:12; see note there).
23:30–32 *I am against.* The threefold statement is for emphasis (see note on 22:29).
23:31 *prophets who . . . declare.* False prophets are claiming that their own prophecies are the oracles of God. The Hebrew for this verb is used only here with someone other than God as the subject. The phrase "declares the LORD" or its equivalent occurs hundreds of times in the OT, more frequently in Jeremiah (over 175 times) than in any other book.

23:32 ʸS ver 13;
S Jer 50:6
ʷS Job 13:4;
Eze 13:3; 22:28
ˣS Jer 14:14 ʸJer 7:8;
La 2:14
23:33 ᶻMal 1:1
ᵃS 2Ki 21:14
23:34 ᵇLa 2:14
ᶜZec 13:3
23:35 ᵈJer 33:3;
42:4
23:36 ᵉGal 1:7-8;
2Pe 3:16 ᶠS Jos 3:10
23:39 ᵍS Jer 7:15
23:40 ʰS Jer 20:11;
Eze 5:14-15
24:1 ⁱS 2Ki 24:16;
S 2Ch 36:9 ʲEx 23:19;
Dt 26:2; Am 8:1-2
24:2 ᵏS SS 2:13
ˡS Isa 5:4
24:3 ᵐJer 1:11;
Am 8:2
24:5 ⁿJer 29:4,20
24:6 ᵒS Dt 30:3;
Jer 27:22; 29:10; 30:3;
Eze 11:17 ᵖJer 33:7;
42:10 �qS Dt 30:9;
S Jer 1:10; Am 9:14-15
24:7 ʳS Isa 11:9
ˢS Lev 26:12;
S Isa 51:16;
S Zec 2:11; Heb 8:10
ᵗJer 32:40
ᵘS 2Ch 6:37;
Eze 11:19
24:8 ᵛJer 29:17
ʷJer 32:4-5; 38:18,
23; 39:5; 44:30
ˣJer 39:6 ʸJer 39:9

ple astray ᵛ with their reckless lies, ʷ yet I did not send ˣ or appoint them. They do not benefit ʸ these people in the least," declares the LORD.

FALSE PROPHECY

³³"When these people, or a prophet or a priest, ask you, 'What is the message ᶻ from the LORD?' say to them, 'What message? I will forsake ᵃ you, declares the LORD.' ³⁴If a prophet or a priest or anyone else claims, 'This is a message ᵇ from the LORD,' I will punish ᶜ them and their households. ³⁵This is what each of you keeps saying to your friends and other Israelites: 'What is the LORD's answer?' ᵈ or 'What has the LORD spoken?' ³⁶But you must not mention 'a message from the LORD' again, because everyone's own word becomes a message from God. So you distort ᵉ the words of the living God, ᶠ the LORD Almighty, our God. ³⁷This is what you keep saying to a prophet: 'What is the LORD's answer to you?' or 'What has the LORD spoken?' ³⁸Although you claim, 'This is a message from the LORD,' this is what the LORD says: You used the words, 'This is a message from the LORD,' even though I told you that you must not claim, 'This is a message from the LORD.' ³⁹Therefore, I will surely forget you and cast ᵍ you out of my presence along with the city I gave to you and your ancestors. ⁴⁰I will bring on you everlasting disgrace ʰ—everlasting shame that will not be forgotten."

TWO BASKETS OF FIGS

24 After Jehoiachin ᵃ ⁱ son of Jehoiakim king of Judah and the officials, the artisans and the other skilled workers of Judah were carried into exile from Jerusalem to Babylon by Nebuchadnezzar king of Babylon, the LORD showed me two baskets of figs ʲ placed in front of the temple of the LORD. ²One basket had very good figs, like those that ripen early; ᵏ the other basket had very bad ˡ figs, so bad they could not be eaten.

³Then the LORD asked me, "What do you see, ᵐ Jeremiah?"

"Figs," I answered. "The good ones are very good, but the bad ones are so bad they cannot be eaten."

⁴Then the word of the LORD came to me: ⁵"This is what the LORD, the God of Israel, says: 'Like these good figs, I regard as good the exiles from Judah, whom I sent ⁿ away from this place to the land of the Babylonians. ᵇ ⁶My eyes will watch over them for their good, and I will bring them back ᵒ to this land. I will build ᵖ them up and not tear them down; I will plant q them and not uproot them. ⁷I will give them a heart to know ʳ me, that I am the LORD. They will be my people, ˢ and I will be their God, for they will return ᵗ to me with all their heart. ᵘ

⁸"But like the bad ᵛ figs, which are so bad they cannot be eaten,' says the LORD, 'so will I deal with Zedekiah ʷ king of Judah, his officials ˣ and the survivors ʸ from Jerusa-

---

ᵃ *1* Hebrew *Jeconiah,* a variant of *Jehoiachin*   ᵇ *5* Or *Chaldeans*

23:32 *did not send.* See v. 21 and note.
23:33 *message.* The Hebrew for this word can also mean "burden," a term that may refer to a burdensome message from the Lord (see, e.g., Na 1:1).
23:36 The three divine titles at the end of the verse enhance the solemnity of what is being said. *living God.* See 10:10; Dt 5:26.
23:39 *forget.* The Hebrew for this word is a pun on the Hebrew for the word "message" in vv. 33–34,36,38—by which Jeremiah highlights his word of judgment. *the city.* Jerusalem.
23:40 Echoed from 20:11.
24:1–10 See Am 8:1–3. Having denounced Judah's leaders (21:1—23:8) and false prophets (23:9–40), Jeremiah now describes the division of Judah's people into good and bad (24:1–3) and summarizes the Lord's determination to restore the good (vv. 4–7) but destroy the bad (vv. 8–10).
24:1 *Jehoiachin ... and the officials ... were carried into exile.* In 597 B.C. *artisans and the other skilled workers.* See 29:2; 2Ki 24:14, 16. Only the poorest and weakest people were left behind in Judah (see 2Ki 24:14; for the later period [586], cf. Jer 39:10). *the LORD showed me.* A common way of introducing prophetic visions (see Am 7:1,4,7). *figs.* See note on 8:13. *placed.* The Hebrew root underlying this word is translated "meet" in Ex 29:42–43. As the Lord desired to "meet" with the Israelites at the entrance to

the tabernacle, so the figs (symbolizing the people of Judah) would be "met" by him in front of the Jerusalem temple.
24:2 *very good figs ... that ripen early.* The first figs in June are especially juicy and delicious (see Isa 28:4; Hos 9:10; Mic 7:1; Na 3:12).
24:3 *What do you see ...?* See note on 1:11.
24:5–6 Just as good figs should be protected and preserved by their owner, so also the exiles of 597 B.C., who were the best of Judah's leaders and craftsmen (see 2Ki 24:14–16), would be watched over and cared for by the Lord (see 29:4–14).
24:6 *My eyes will watch over them for their good.* Contrast the word of judgment in Am 9:4. *bring them back.* In 538/537 B.C. *build them up ... tear them down ... plant ... uproot.* See 1:10 and note.
24:7 *a heart to know me.* For a more comprehensive prediction including the same promise, see 31:31–34. *my people ... their God.* The classic statement of covenant relationship (see 31:33; 32:38; see also notes on 7:23; Ge 17:7; Zec 8:8). *with all their heart.* See 29:13.
24:8 *live in Egypt.* Perhaps those deported with Jehoahaz in 609 B.C. (see 22:10b–12 and notes; 2Ki 23:31–34) and/or those who fled to Egypt after the Babylonians defeated the Egyptians in the battle of Carchemish in 605 (see 46:2).

lem, whether they remain in this land or live in Egypt. *z* 9I will make them abhorrent *a* and an offense to all the kingdoms of the earth, a reproach and a byword, *b* a curse *a c* and an object of ridicule, wherever I banish *d* them. 10I will send the sword, *e* famine *f* and plague *g* against them until they are destroyed from the land I gave to them and their ancestors. *h*'"

SEVENTY YEARS OF CAPTIVITY

25 The word came to Jeremiah concerning all the people of Judah in the fourth year of Jehoiakim *i* son of Josiah king of Judah, which was the first year of Nebuchadnezzar *j* king of Babylon. 2So Jeremiah the prophet said to all the people of Judah *k* and to all those living in Jerusalem: 3For twenty-three years—from the thirteenth year of Josiah *l* son of Amon king of Judah until this very day—the word of the LORD has come to me and I have spoken to you again and again, *m* but you have not listened. *n*

4And though the LORD has sent all his servants the prophets *o* to you again and again, you have not listened or paid any attention. *p* 5They said, "Turn *q* now, each of you, from your evil ways and your evil practices, and you can stay in the land *r* the LORD gave to you and your ancestors for ever and ever. 6Do not follow other gods *s* to serve and worship them; do not arouse my anger with what your hands have made. Then I will not harm you."

7"But you did not listen to me," declares the LORD, "and you have aroused *t* my anger with what your hands have made, *u* and you have brought harm *v* to yourselves."

8Therefore the LORD Almighty says this: "Because you have not listened to my words, 9I will summon *w* all the peoples of the north *x* and my servant *y* Nebuchadnezzar *z* king of Babylon," declares the LORD, "and I will bring them against this land and its inhabitants and against all the surrounding nations. I will completely destroy *b a* them and make them an object of horror and scorn, *b* and an everlasting ruin. *c* 10I will banish from them the sounds *d* of joy and gladness, the voices of bride and bridegroom, *e* the sound of millstones *f* and the light of the lamp. *g* 11This whole country will become a desolate wasteland, *h* and these nations will serve *i* the king of Babylon seventy years. *j*

12"But when the seventy years *k* are fulfilled, I will punish the king of Babylon *l* and his nation, the land of the Babylonians, *c* for their guilt," declares the LORD, "and will make it desolate *m* forever. 13I will bring on that land all the things I have spoken against it, all that are written *n* in this book and prophesied by Jeremiah against all the nations. 14They themselves will be enslaved *o* by many nations *p* and great kings; I will repay *q* them according to their deeds and the work of their hands."

---

a 9 That is, their names will be used in cursing (see Jer. 29:22); or, others will see that they are cursed.
b 9 The Hebrew term refers to the irrevocable giving over of things or persons to the LORD, often by totally destroying them.   *c* 12 Or *Chaldeans*

25:14 *P* Jer 50:9; 51:27-28 *q* S Dt 32:41; S Job 21:19; S Jer 51:6

24:8 *z* Jer 44:1,26; 46:14
24:9 *a* S Jer 15:4; 25:18 *b* S Dt 28:25; S 1Ki 9:7 *c* S 2Ki 22:19; S Jer 29:18
  d S Dt 28:37; Da 9:7
24:10 *e* S Jer 15:19; S Jer 9:16; Rev 6:8 *f* Jer 15:2 *g* Jer 27:8 *h* S Dt 28:21
25:1 *i* S 2Ki 24:2 *j* S 2Ki 24:1
25:2 *k* Jer 18:11
25:3 *l* S 1Ch 3:14 *m* Jer 11:7; 26:5 *n* S Isa 65:12; S Jer 7:26
25:4 *o* Jer 6:17; S Jer 29:19
  P S Jer 7:26; 34:14; 44:5
25:5 *q* S Jdg 6:8; S 2Ch 7:14; S 30:9; S Jer 23:22
  r S Ge 12:7; S Dt 4:40
25:6 *s* S Ex 20:3; S Dt 8:19
25:7 *t* Jer 30:14; 32:35; 44:5 *u* Dt 32:21
  v 2Ki 17:20; 21:15
25:9 *w* Isa 13:3-5 *x* S Isa 14:31
  y S Isa 41:2; Jer 27:6
  z S 2Ch 36:6
  a S Nu 21:2
  b S 2Ch 29:8
  c S Jer 19:8; S 20:4; Eze 12:20
25:10 *d* S Isa 24:8; Eze 26:13 *e* Jer 7:34; 33:11 *f* Ecc 12:3-4
  g S Job 18:5; La 5:15; Rev 18:22-23
25:11 *h* S Lev 26:31, 32; Jer 4:26-27; 12:11-12 *i* Jer 28:14
  j S 2Ch 36:21
25:12 *k* Jer 27:7; 29:10 *l* S Ge 10:10; S Ps 137:8
  m S Isa 13:19-22; 14:22-23
25:13 *n* S Isa 30:8
25:14 *o* Isa 14:6; Jer 27:7

24:9 *abhorrent...to all the kingdoms.* See 34:17. *reproach...object of ridicule.* See Dt 28:37. *byword.* See notes on 1Ki 9:7; Job 17:6.
24:10 *sword, famine and plague.* See note on 14:12. *destroyed from the land.* In 586 B.C. (see 52:4–27).
25:1—29:32 The dominant theme in chs. 25–29 is the forthcoming destruction of Jerusalem and exile to Babylonia in 586 B.C. (hinted at briefly in 24:10).
25:1–38 Divine judgment will descend not only on Judah but on "all the surrounding nations" (v. 9) as well (cf. note on Mic 1:2).
25:1 *fourth year of Jehoiakim...first year of Nebuchadnezzar.* The synchronism yields the date 605 B.C. (see note on Da 1:1).
25:3 *twenty-three years.* Nineteen under Josiah and four under Jehoiakim (see v. 1). *thirteenth year of Josiah.* 626 B.C. (or possibly as early as 627); see 1:2. *again and again.* See v. 4; see also note on 7:13. *you have not listened.* Jeremiah, now halfway through his prophetic ministry, had been warned at the time of his call that the people of Judah would oppose him (see 1:17–19).
25:4 Echoed from 7:25–26; see also 35:15. *his servants the prophets.* See note on 7:25.
25:5 *stay in the land the LORD gave...your ancestors for ever and ever.* Echoed from 7:7; see Ge 17:8 and note.
25:6 *arouse my anger.* See 7:18; Dt 31:29. *what your hands have made.* Idols (see note on 1:16).
25:7 *brought harm to yourselves.* See 7:6.
A **25:9** *peoples of the north.* Babylonia and her allies (see 1:15 and note). *my servant Nebuchadnezzar.* See 27:6; 43:10. "Servant" is used here not in the sense of "worshiper" but

of "vassal" or "agent of judgment," just as the pagan ruler Cyrus is called the Lord's "shepherd" in Isa 44:28 and his "anointed" in Isa 45:1. *this land.* Judah. *surrounding nations.* Named in vv. 19–26. *completely destroy.* See TNIV text note; 50:21,26; 51:3; see also note on Dt 2:34. *object of horror and scorn.* See note on 18:16. *everlasting ruin.* See 49:13; Ps 74:3; Isa 58:12 and note.
25:11–12 *seventy years.* This round number (as in Ps 90:10; Isa 23:15) represents the period from 605 (see notes on v. 1; Da 1:1) to 538/537 B.C., which marked the beginning of Judah's return from exile (see 2Ch 36:20–23; see also notes on Da 9:1–2). The 70 years of Zec 1:12 are not necessarily the same as those here and in 29:10. They probably represent the period from 586 (when Solomon's temple was destroyed) to 516 (when Zerubbabel's temple was completed). See note on Zec 7:5.
25:11 *This...country...and these nations.* Judah and the nations named in vv. 19–26.
25:12 *punish the king...and his nation.* See 50:18. The city of Babylon was captured by the Medes and Persians in 539 B.C. (near the end of Jeremiah's 70 years; see note on vv. 11–12). *for their guilt.* See 50:11,31–32; 51:6,49,53,56; Isa 13:19. *make it desolate forever.* See 50:12–13; 51:26; see also note on Isa 13:20.
25:13 *book.* After this word, the Septuagint (the pre-Christian Greek translation of the OT) inserts the material found in chs. 46–51, though rearranged.
25:14 *many nations.* Media, Persia and their allies. *great kings.* Cyrus and his associates. *repay them according to their deeds.* See 50:29; 51:24.

25:15 ʳS Isa 51:17;
Jer 49:12; La 4:21;
Eze 23:31; Rev 14:10
ˢ Jer 1:5
25:16 ᵗ ver 26
ᵘ S Ps 60:3 ᵛ Jer 51:7
ʷ ver 27-29
25:17 ˣ Jer 1:10;
27:3
25:18 ʸ S Jer 13:13
ᶻ S Job 12:19
ᵃ S 2Ch 29:8
ᵇ S Jer 24:9
ᶜ S Ge 19:13;
Jer 44:22
25:19 ᵈ S 2Ki 18:21
ᵉ Isa 19:1; 20:3;
Jer 44:30; Eze 29:2
25:20 ᶠ S Ge 10:23
ᵍ S Jos 13:3;
S 2Ch 26:6; S 28:18;
Zep 2:4-7 ʰ S Ge 10:19
25:21 ⁱ S Ge 25:30
ᵏ S Ge 19:37;
S Dt 23:6
ˡ S Ge 19:38; Jer 27:3;
49:1
25:22 ᵐ S Jos 19:29
ⁿ S Ge 10:15 ᵒ Isa 11:11;
48:20; 66:20; Jer 31:10;
Eze 27:15; 39:6;
Da 11:18
25:23 ᵖ S Ge 25:3
�q S Ge 25:15 ʳ S Ge 2
2:21 ˢ Jer 9:26; 49:32
25:24 ᵗ S 2Ch 9:14
ᵘ ver 20
25:25 ᵛ Ge 25:2
ʷ S Ge 10:22
ˣ S Isa 21:2
25:26 ʸ ver 9;
Jer 50:3,9; 51:11,48
ᶻ Isa 23:17 ᵃ Jer 51:41
25:27 ᵇ ver 16,28;
S Isa 29:9; S 49:26;
Jer 51:57; Eze 23:32-
34; Na 3:18; Hab 2:16
ᶜ S Jer 12:12;
Eze 14:17; 21:4

THE CUP OF GOD'S WRATH

¹⁵This is what the Lᴏʀᴅ, the God of Israel, said to me: "Take from my hand this cup ʳ filled with the wine of my wrath and make all the nations to whom I send ˢ you drink it. ¹⁶When they drink ᵗ it, they will stagger ᵘ and go mad ᵛ because of the sword ʷ I will send among them."

¹⁷So I took the cup from the Lᴏʀᴅ's hand and made all the nations to whom he sent ˣ me drink it: ¹⁸Jerusalem ʸ and the towns of Judah, its kings and officials, to make them a ruin ᶻ and an object of horror and scorn, ᵃ a curse ᵇ—as they are today; ᶜ ¹⁹Pharaoh king ᵈ of Egypt, ᵉ his attendants, his officials and all his people, ²⁰and all the foreign people there; all the kings of Uz; ᶠ all the kings of the Philistines ᵍ (those of Ashkelon, ʰ Gaza, ⁱ Ekron, and the people left at Ashdod); ²¹Edom, ʲ Moab ᵏ and Ammon; ˡ ²²all the kings of Tyre ᵐ and Sidon; ⁿ the kings of the coastlands ᵒ across the sea; ²³Dedan, ᵖ Tema, q Buz ʳ and all who are in distant places ᵇ; ˢ ²⁴all the kings of Arabia ᵗ and all the kings of the foreign people ᵘ who live in the wilderness; ²⁵all the kings of Zimri, ᵛ Elam ʷ and Media; ˣ ²⁶and all the kings of the north, ʸ near and far, one after the other—all the kingdoms ᶻ on the face of the earth. And after all of them, the king of Sheshak ᶜ ᵃ will drink it too.

²⁷"Then tell them, 'This is what the Lᴏʀᴅ Almighty, the God of Israel, says: Drink, get drunk ᵇ and vomit, and fall to rise no more because of the sword ᶜ I will send among you.' ²⁸But if they refuse to take the cup from your hand and drink ᵈ, tell them, 'This is what the Lᴏʀᴅ Almighty says: You must drink it! ²⁹See, I am beginning to bring disaster ᵉ on the city that bears my Name, ᶠ and will you indeed go unpunished? ᵍ You will not go unpunished, for I am calling down a sword ʰ on all ⁱ who live on the earth, ʲ declares the Lᴏʀᴅ Almighty.'

³⁰"Now prophesy all these words against them and say to them:

" 'The Lᴏʀᴅ will roar ᵏ from on high;
he will thunder ˡ from his holy dwelling ᵐ
and roar mightily against his land.
He will shout like those who tread ⁿ the grapes,
shout against all who live on the earth.

ᵃ 18 That is, their names to be used in cursing (see Jer. 29:22); or, to be seen by others as cursed
ᵇ 23 Or who clip the hair by their foreheads ᶜ 26 Sheshak is a cryptogram for Babylon.

25:28 ᵈ S Isa 51:23 **25:29** ᵉ S 2Sa 5:7; Isa 10:12; Jer 13:12-14; 39:1 ᶠ S Dt 28:10; S Isa 37:17 ᵍ S Pr 11:31 ʰ ver 27 ⁱ ver 30-31; Isa 34:2 ʲ S Isa 24:1 **25:30** ᵏ Isa 16:10; S 42:13 ˡ S Ps 46:6 ᵐ S Ps 68:5 ⁿ Isa 63:3; Joel 3:13; Rev 14:19-20

25:15 *cup filled with the wine of my wrath.* Symbolic of divine judgment, especially against wicked nations (see Isa 51:17 and note; see also 51:7; Rev 18:6). *nations to whom I send you.* See 1:5 and note.

25:16 *stagger and go mad.* See 13:12-14 and notes; Rev 14:8. *because of the sword.* As the sting of wine causes people to stagger, so the stroke of the sword causes them to fall, never to rise again (see v. 27).

25:17 A symbolic description of Jeremiah's announcement of divine judgment against the nations.

25:18 *Jerusalem and ... Judah.* God's own people are to be judged first (see v. 29; see also Eze 9:6; 1Pe 4:17). *its kings.* See note on 17:20. *ruin ... horror ... scorn ... curse.* See vv. 9,11; 18:16; 19:8.

25:19-26 The roster of nations begins with Egypt and ends with Babylon, as in chs. 46-51; but Damascus (see 49:23-27) is omitted, and a few other regions are added.

25:19 *Egypt.* See 46:2-28.

25:20 *foreign people.* See v.24; Ne 13:3. *Uz.* See note on Job 1:1. *Philistines.* See ch. 47; see also note on Ge 10:14. *Ashkelon, Gaza, Ekron.* See note on Jdg 1:18; see also map, p. 338. *people left at Ashdod.* According to the Greek historian Herodotus (2.157), the Egyptian pharaoh Psammetichus I (664-610 B.C.) destroyed Ashdod after a long siege. By Nehemiah's time it was inhabited again (see note on Ne 4:7). The fifth main Philistine city, Gath (see Jos 13:3), though important earlier (see, e.g., 1Sa 21:10-12), was destroyed and apparently not rebuilt (in later centuries it is not mentioned with the other four cities; see Am 1:6-8; Zep 2:4; Zec 9:5-6).

25:21-22 See 27:3-5.

25:21 *Edom.* See 49:7-22; see also note on Ge 36:1. *Moab and Ammon.* See 48:1—49:6; see also note on Ge 19:36-38.

25:22 *Tyre and Sidon.* See 47:4; see also notes on Isa 23:1-2, 4,12. *coastlands across the sea.* Mediterranean islands and maritime regions, some of them Phoenician colonies (see Eze 27:15; Da 11:18 and notes).

25:23 *Dedan.* See 49:8; see also note on Isa 21:13; Eze 25:13. *Tema.* See note on Isa 21:14. *Buz.* A desert region in the east. *who are in distant places.* See note on 9:26.

25:24 *Arabia.* See 49:28-33. *foreign people.* See v. 20; Ne 13:3. The same Hebrew root underlies "Arabia" and "foreign people."

25:25 *Zimri.* Not to be confused with the Israelite king of that name; Zimri is perhaps the same as Zimran, whom Keturah bore to Abraham (see Ge 25:1-2). The region known as Zimri (location unknown) would then have been named after him. *Elam.* See 49:34-39; see also note on Ge 10:22. *Media.* Later to join the Persians in conquering Babylon (see 51:11,28; see also note on Isa 13:17).

25:26 *Sheshak.* See TNIV text note. The cryptogram is formed by substituting the first consonant of the Hebrew alphabet for the last, the second for the next-to-last, etc. Its purpose is not fully understood, though in some cases the cryptogram itself bears a suitable meaning (see note on 51:1). *will drink it too.* The Lord's agents of judgment are not themselves exempt from his judgment (see 51:48-49).

25:27 *fall ... because of the sword.* See note on v. 16.

25:29 *beginning.* See note on v. 18. *city that bears my Name.* Jerusalem (see note on 7:10). *sword.* See note on 12:12.

25:30 *The Lord will roar ... thunder.* An echo of Joel 3:16; Am 1:2 (see note there; see also Hos 11:10; Am 3:8). *his land.* Judah. *shout like those who tread the grapes.* See Isa 9:3; 16:9-10; 63:3 and note; see also Isa 16:10 and note.

³¹ The tumult ^o will resound to the ends of the earth,
 for the LORD will bring charges ^p against the nations;
he will bring judgment ^q on all ^r humankind
 and put the wicked to the sword, ^s'"

declares the LORD.

³² This is what the LORD Almighty says:

"Look! Disaster ^t is spreading
 from nation to nation; ^u
a mighty storm ^v is rising
 from the ends of the earth." ^w

³³ At that time those slain ^x by the LORD will be everywhere—from one end of the earth to the other. They will not be mourned or gathered ^y up or buried, ^z but will be like dung lying on the ground.

³⁴ Weep and wail, you shepherds; ^a
 roll ^b in the dust, you leaders of the flock.
For your time to be slaughtered ^c has come;
 you will fall like the best of the rams. ^{a d}
³⁵ The shepherds will have nowhere to flee,
 the leaders of the flock no place to escape. ^e
³⁶ Hear the cry ^f of the shepherds, ^g
 the wailing of the leaders of the flock,
for the LORD is destroying their pasture.
³⁷ The peaceful meadows will be laid waste
 because of the fierce anger of the LORD.
³⁸ Like a lion ^h he will leave his lair,
 and their land will become desolate ⁱ
because of the sword ^b of the oppressor ^j
 and because of the LORD's fierce anger. ^k

JEREMIAH THREATENED WITH DEATH

26 Early in the reign of Jehoiakim ^l son of Josiah king of Judah, this word came from the LORD: ²"This is what the LORD says: Stand in the courtyard ^m of the LORD's house and speak to all the people of the towns of Judah who come to worship in the house of the LORD. ⁿ Tell ^o them everything I command you; do not omit ^p a word. ³Perhaps they will listen and each will turn ^q from their evil ways. Then I will relent ^r and not inflict on them the disaster I was planning because of the evil they have done. ⁴Say to them, 'This is what the LORD says: If you do not listen ^s to me and follow my law, ^t which I have set before you, ⁵and if you do not listen to the words of my servants the prophets, whom I have sent to you again and again (though you have not listened ^u), ⁶then I will make this house like Shiloh ^v and this city a curse ^{c w} among all the nations of the earth.' "

⁷The priests, the prophets and all the people heard Jeremiah speak these words in the house of the LORD. ⁸But as soon as Jeremiah finished telling all the people everything the

^a 34 Septuagint; Hebrew *fall and be shattered like fine pottery* ^b 38 Some Hebrew manuscripts and Septuagint (see also Jer. 46:16 and 50:16); most Hebrew manuscripts *anger* ^c 6 That is, their names will be used in cursing (see Jer. 29:22); or, others will see that they are cursed.

25:31 ^o Jer 23:19
^p S Jer 2:9
^q S 1Sa 12:7;
S Jer 2:35; S Eze 36:5
^r S ver 29 ^s S Jer 15:9
25:32 ^t S Isa 30:25
^u Isa 34:2
^v S Jer 23:19
^w S Dt 28:49
25:33 ^x Isa 66:16;
Eze 39:17-20
^y S Jer 8:2 ^z S Ps 79:3
25:34 ^a S Jer 2:8;
Zec 10:3 ^b S Jer 6:26
^c S Ps 44:22;
S Isa 34:6; Jer 50:27;
51:40; Zec 11:4,7
^d S Jer 22:28
25:35 ^e S Job 11:20
25:36 ^f S Jer 6:26
^g S Jer 23:1; Zec 11:3
25:38 ^h S Job 10:16;
S Jer 4:7 ⁱ Jer 44:22
^j Jer 46:16; 50:16
^k S Ex 15:7; S Jer 4:26
26:1 ^l 2Ki 23:36
26:2 ^m Jer 19:14
ⁿ S Jer 17:19
^o S ver 12; S Jer 1:17;
Mt 28:20; Ac 20:27
^p Dt 4:2
26:3 ^q Dt 30:2;
2Ch 33:12-13;
Isa 55:7; Jer 35:15;
36:7 ^r S Jer 18:8
26:4 ^s Lev 26:14;
Jer 25:3 ^t Ex 20:1-
23:33; S 1Ki 9:6;
S Jer 11:8
26:5 ^u S Pr 1:24;
S Isa 65:12; Jer 25:4;
44:5
26:6 ^v S Jos 18:1;
S Jdg 18:31
^w S Dt 28:25;
S 2Ki 22:19

25:31 *tumult.* The sounds of war (see Am 2:2). *bring charges … bring judgment.* See note on 2:9; see also 2:35; 12:1.

25:32 *mighty storm … from the ends of the earth.* The wrath of God (see 23:19), mediated through the coming invasion of the Babylonians (see note on Isa 41:25).

25:33 *not be mourned … like dung lying on the ground.* Repeated from 8:2 (see there); 16:4.

25:34–36 *shepherds … leaders of the flock.* See 2:8 and note; 10:21; 22:22; Eze 34:2 and note.

25:34 *roll in the dust.* Or "roll in ashes" (as in 6:26). *your time … has come.* See La 4:18. *fall like the best of the rams.* See TNIV text note. For the reading given there, cf. the description of Jehoiachin in 22:28.

25:36 *their pasture.* The land of Judah.

26:1–24 A summary (vv. 2–6)—and its results (vv. 7–24)—of

one of Jeremiah's temple messages in ch. 7 (see note on 7:1—10:25).

26:1 *Early in the reign.* See 27:1. The Babylonian equivalent of the Hebrew for this phrase implies that the first year of King Jehoiakim (609–608 B.C.) is probably meant.

26:2 *courtyard of the LORD's house.* Perhaps near the New Gate (see v. 10; see also note on 7:2). *who come to worship.* See 7:2 and note. *do not omit a word.* See Dt 4:2 and note.

26:3 See 7:3,5–7. *relent.* See vv. 13,19; see also notes on 4:28; 18:7–10.

26:4 *If you do not listen.* See v. 5; 7:13. *my law.* See 7:6,9 and notes.

26:5 See 7:13,25–26. *my servants the prophets.* See note on 7:25. *again and again.* See note on 7:13.

26:6 *make this house like Shiloh.* See v. 9; see also note on 7:12. *this city.* Jerusalem. *curse.* See TNIV text note and 24:9; 25:18; see also note on Zec 8:13.

26:8 ˣJer 43:1
ʸAc 6:12; 21:27
ᶻLev 24:15-16;
S Ne 9:26; S Jer 11:21
26:9 ᵃS Lev 26:32;
S Jer 9:11 ᵇAc 21:32
26:10 ᶜver 16;
Jer 34:19; Eze 22:27
ᵈS Ge 23:10
26:11 ᵉDt 18:20;
S Jer 11:21; 18:23;
Mt 26:66; Ac 6:11
ᶠS Ps 44:1
26:12 ᵍJer 1:18
ʰS Isa 6:8; Am 7:15;
Ac 4:18-20; 5:29
ⁱS ver 2,15
26:13 ʲS Jer 7:5;
Joel 2:12-14 ᵏJer 11:4
ˡS Jer 18:8
26:14 ᵐJos 9:25;
Jer 38:5
26:15 ⁿS Dt 19:10
ᵒS ver 12; S Jer 1:17
26:16 ᵖS ver 10;
S Ac 23:9 ᵠAc 23:29
26:18 ʳMic 1:1
ˢIsa 2:3 ᵗS 2Ki 25:9;
S Ne 4:2; Jer 9:11
ᵘMic 4:1; Zec 8:3
ᵛS Jer 17:3
26:19 ʷS 1Ch 3:13;
2Ch 32:24-26;
Isa 37:14-20
ˣS 1Sa 13:12
ʸS Ex 32:14;
S Jer 18:8 ᶻJer 44:7
ᵃHab 2:10
26:20 ᵇS Jos 9:17
26:21 ᶜS 1Ki 19:2
ᵈver 10 ᵉJer 2:30;
Mt 23:37 ᶠS Ge 31:21;
Mt 10:23
26:22 ᵍJer 36:12,25

Lᴏʀᴅ had commandedˣ him to say, the priests, the prophets and all the people seizedʸ him and said, "You must die!ᶻ ⁹Why do you prophesy in the Lᴏʀᴅ's name that this house will be like Shiloh and this city will be desolate and deserted?"ᵃ And all the people crowded ᵇ around Jeremiah in the house of the Lᴏʀᴅ.

¹⁰When the officialsᶜ of Judah heard about these things, they went up from the royal palace to the house of the Lᴏʀᴅ and took their places at the entrance of the New Gateᵈ of the Lᴏʀᴅ's house. ¹¹Then the priests and the prophets said to the officials and all the people, "This man should be sentenced to deathᵉ because he has prophesied against this city. You have heard it with your own ears!"ᶠ

¹²Then Jeremiah said to all the officialsᵍ and all the people: "The Lᴏʀᴅ sent me to prophesyʰ against this house and this city all the things you have heard.ⁱ ¹³Now reformʲ your ways and your actions and obeyᵏ the Lᴏʀᴅ your God. Then the Lᴏʀᴅ will relentˡ and not bring the disaster he has pronounced against you. ¹⁴As for me, I am in your hands;ᵐ do with me whatever you think is good and right. ¹⁵Be assured, however, that if you put me to death, you will bring the guilt of innocent bloodⁿ on yourselves and on this city and on those who live in it, for in truth the Lᴏʀᴅ has sent me to you to speak all these wordsᵒ in your hearing."

¹⁶Then the officialsᵖ and all the people said to the priests and the prophets, "This man should not be sentenced to death!ᵠ He has spoken to us in the name of the Lᴏʀᴅ our God."

¹⁷Some of the elders of the land stepped forward and said to the entire assembly of people, ¹⁸"Micahʳ of Moresheth prophesied in the days of Hezekiah king of Judah. He told all the people of Judah, 'This is what the Lᴏʀᴅ Almighty says:

" 'Zionˢ will be plowed like a field,
　　Jerusalem will become a heap of rubble,ᵗ
　　the temple hillᵘ a mound overgrown with thickets.'ᵃ ᵛ

¹⁹"Did Hezekiah king of Judah or anyone else in Judah put him to death? Did not Hezekiahʷ fear the Lᴏʀᴅ and seekˣ his favor? And did not the Lᴏʀᴅ relent,ʸ so that he did not bring the disasterᶻ he pronounced against them? We are about to bring a terrible disasterᵃ on ourselves!"

²⁰(Now Uriah son of Shemaiah from Kiriath Jearimᵇ was another man who prophesied in the name of the Lᴏʀᴅ; he prophesied the same things against this city and this land as Jeremiah did. ²¹When King Jehoiakimᶜ and all his officers and officialsᵈ heard his words, the king sought to put him to death.ᵉ But Uriah heard of it and fledᶠ in fear to Egypt. ²²King Jehoiakim, however, sent Elnathanᵍ son of Akbor to Egypt, along with some other men.

ᵃ 18 Micah 3:12

26:8 *You must die!* A similar phrase describes the ultimate penalty for gross violations of the law of Moses (see, e.g., Ex 21:15-17; Lev 24:16-17,21; Dt 18:20; cf. 1Ki 21:13).
26:9 *crowded around.* With hostile intent (see Nu 16:3).
26:10 *officials of Judah.* Those responsible for making legal decisions concerning disputes taking place in the temple precincts. The priests and (false) prophets, who had a vested interest in Jerusalem and its temple, felt that Jeremiah should be sentenced to death because he was predicting the destruction of both the city and the Lord's house (see vv. 8-9,11). After hearing Jeremiah's defense (vv. 12-15), the officials decided in his favor (v. 16). The people, fickle and easily swayed, first opposed Jeremiah (vv. 8-9), then supported him (v. 16). *New Gate.* See 36:10; possibly the same as the "Upper Gate of Benjamin" (see 20:2 and note).
26:11 Jeremiah's enemies judge him before he has a chance to defend himself (cf. Dt 19:6; Jos 20:1-9 and note).
26:12 *The Lᴏʀᴅ sent me.* Contrast 23:21.
26:13 *reform your ways and your actions.* Repeated from 7:3 (see also 18:11; 35:15). *relent.* See vv. 3,19; see also notes on 4:28; 18:7-10.
26:15 *innocent blood.* See 7:6 and note; see also Mt 27:24-25; Ac 5:28.
26:16 Contrast v. 11; see note on v. 10.
26:17 *elders.* See 19:1 and note.
△ 26:18-19 The elders cite the precedent of Micah, who lived a century earlier and who (together with Isaiah) convinced King Hezekiah to pray for forgiveness on behalf of his people. The Lord answered the prayers of the king and the

prophets, and in 701 B.C. Jerusalem and the temple were spared (see Isa 37:33-37).
26:18 *Micah of Moresheth.* See Introduction to Micah: Author. *Zion will be plowed . . . overgrown with thickets.* Quoted verbatim from Mic 3:12 (see note there)—the only place in the OT where one prophet quotes another and identifies his source.
26:19 *seek his favor.* Lit. "stroke his face" (cf. Ps 119:58), "pat his cheek." See Ex 32:11; 1Sa 13:12; 2Ki 13:4. *relent.* See vv. 3,13; see also notes on 4:28; 18:7-10.
■ 26:20-23 A parenthesis, cited as an example of the contrast between how a good king, Hezekiah, treated the Lord's prophets and how a wicked king, Jehoiakim, was known to have treated them.
■ 26:20 *Uriah.* Not mentioned elsewhere in the OT, though it has been claimed (but not substantiated) that he appears in one of the Lachish letters (see note on 34:7; see also chart, p. xxiii).
26:21 *officers.* Lit. "strong men" (perhaps the royal bodyguard). *Uriah . . . fled . . . to Egypt.* A fatal mistake, for now he could be accused of treason and sedition.
26:22 *Elnathan son of Akbor.* One of King Jehoiakim's highest officials (see 36:12), he was impressed on another occasion by Jeremiah's prophecies (see 36:16), "urged the king not to burn" Jeremiah's scroll (36:25), and warned the prophet to hide (see 36:19). An Elnathan (perhaps the same man) was Jehoiakim's father-in-law (see 2Ki 24:6,8). An Akbor (perhaps the father of this Elnathan) was one of King Josiah's officials (see 2Ki 22:12,14; see also note on v. 24).

²³They brought Uriah out of Egypt and took him to King Jehoiakim, who had him struck down with a sword ^h and his body thrown into the burial place of the common people.) ⁱ

²⁴Furthermore, Ahikam ^j son of Shaphan supported Jeremiah, and so he was not handed over to the people to be put to death.

JUDAH TO SERVE NEBUCHADNEZZAR

27 Early in the reign of Zedekiah ^{a k} son of Josiah king of Judah, this word came to Jeremiah from the LORD: ²This is what the LORD said to me: "Make a yoke ^l out of straps and crossbars and put it on your neck. ³Then send ^m word to the kings of Edom, Moab, Ammon, ⁿ Tyre and Sidon ^o through the envoys who have come to Jerusalem to Zedekiah king of Judah. ⁴Give them a message for their masters and say, 'This is what the LORD Almighty, the God of Israel, says: "Tell this to your masters: ⁵With my great power and outstretched arm ^p I made ^q the earth and its people and the animals ^r that are on it, and I give ^s it to anyone I please. ⁶Now I will give all your countries into the hands of my servant ^t Nebuchadnezzar ^u king of Babylon; I will make even the wild animals subject to him. ^v ⁷All nations will serve ^w him and his son and his grandson until the time ^x for his land comes; then many nations and great kings will subjugate ^y him.

⁸" ' "If, however, any nation or kingdom will not serve Nebuchadnezzar king of Babylon or bow its neck under his yoke, I will punish ^z that nation with the sword, ^a famine ^b and plague, ^c declares the LORD, until I destroy it by his hand. ⁹So do not listen to your prophets, ^d your diviners, ^e your interpreters of dreams, ^f your mediums ^g or your sorcerers ^h who tell you, 'You will not serve ⁱ the king of Babylon.' ¹⁰They prophesy lies ^j to you that will only serve to remove ^k you far from your lands; I will banish you and you will perish. ¹¹But if any nation will bow its neck under the yoke ^l of the king of Babylon and serve him, I will let that nation remain in its own land to till it and to live ^m there, declares the LORD." ' "

¹²I gave the same message to Zedekiah king of Judah. I said, "Bow your neck under the yoke ⁿ of the king of Babylon; serve him and his people, and you will live. ^o ¹³Why will you and your people die ^p by the sword, famine and plague ^q with which the LORD has threatened any nation that will not serve the king of Babylon? ¹⁴Do not listen ^r to the words of the prophets ^s who say to you, 'You will not serve the king of Babylon,' for they are proph-

26:23 ^h Heb 11:37
ⁱ 2Ki 23:6
26:24 ^j S 2Ki 22:12
27:1 ^k S 2Ch 36:11
27:2 ^l S Lev 26:13;
S 1Ki 22:11
27:3 ^m S Jer 25:17
ⁿ S Jer 25:21
^o S Ge 10:15;
S Jer 25:22
27:5 ^p S Dt 9:29
^q S Ge 1:1 ^r S Ge 1:25
^s Ps 115:16; Da 4:17
27:6 ^t S Jer 25:9
^u S Jer 21:7
^v Jer 28:14; Da 2:37-38
27:7 ^w S 2Ch 36:20;
Da 5:18 ^x S Jer 25:12
^y S Jer 25:14; 51:47;
Da 5:28
27:8 ^z Jer 9:16
^a Jer 21:9 ^b S Jer 5:12
^c S Jer 14:12
27:9 ^d Eze 13:1-23
^e S Ge 30:27;
S Isa 44:25
^f S Dt 13:1; S Jer 23:25
^g S Dt 18:11
^h S Ex 7:11 ⁱ Jer 6:14
27:10 ^j S Jer 23:25;
S Mk 13:5
^k S 2Ki 23:27
27:11 ^l S Jer 21:9
^m Dt 6:2
27:12 ⁿ Jer 17:4
^o S Jer 21:9
27:13 ^p Eze 18:31
^q S Jer 14:12
27:14 ^r S Jer 23:16
^s S Jer 14:13

^a 1 A few Hebrew manuscripts and Syriac (see also Jer. 27:3, 12 and 28:1); most Hebrew manuscripts *Jehoiakim* (Most Septuagint manuscripts do not have this verse.)

26:23 *brought Uriah out of Egypt.* Mutual rights of extradition were a part of the treaty imposed on Judah by Egypt when Jehoiakim became the vassal of the Egyptian pharaoh Necho II (see 2Ki 23:34–35). *Jehoiakim ... had him struck down.* Apart from divine intervention, Jeremiah probably would have fallen victim to the same fate (see 36:26). *burial place of the common people.* See note on 17:19. Commoners were buried in the Kidron Valley east of Jerusalem (see 2Ki 23:6).

26:24 *Ahikam son of Shaphan.* One of King Josiah's officials (see 2Ki 22:12,14), along with an Akbor who may have been the father of the Elnathan in v. 22 (see note there). Ahikam was also the father of Gedaliah, who would become governor of Judah after Jerusalem was destroyed in 586 B.C. (see 40:5) and who also befriended Jeremiah (see 39:14). *supported Jeremiah.* Ahikam's high position in Jehoiakim's court was doubtless instrumental in saving the prophet's life.

27:1—29:32 Further attempts by Jeremiah to counteract the teachings of false prophets, who were claiming that Babylon's doom was near and that rebellion against Nebuchadnezzar was therefore warranted and desirable.

27:1–22 Jeremiah tells the nations (vv. 3–11), King Zedekiah (vv. 12–15) and the priests and people of Judah (vv. 16–22) to submit to the Babylonian yoke.

27:1 *Early in the reign.* See note on 26:1. In this case, however, the phrase has been extended in meaning to include Zedekiah's fourth year (593 B.C.; see 28:1).

27:2 *yoke.* Of the kind worn by oxen, it was a symbol of political submission (see vv. 8,11–12; Lev 26:13). That Jeremiah actually wore such a yoke for a time is clear from 28:10,12.

27:3 *send word.* In his role as a "prophet to the nations" (1:5). *Edom, Moab, Ammon.* Lands east and south of Judah (see 25:21

and note). *Tyre and Sidon.* Prominent cities in Phoenicia, north of Judah (see 25:22 and note). *envoys ... have come ... to Zedekiah.* Perhaps to discuss rebellion against Babylonia. They may have counted on support from Egypt, where Psammetichus II had become pharaoh a year earlier (594 B.C.). Zedekiah went to Babylon in 593 (see 51:59), perhaps to be interrogated by Nebuchadnezzar. In any case, Zedekiah rebelled against him (see 52:3).

27:5 *great power and outstretched arm.* See note on 21:5.

27:6 *my servant Nebuchadnezzar.* See note on 25:9. *make ... wild animals subject to him.* Nothing would be beyond the reach of Nebuchadnezzar's dominion (see 28:14; Da 2:38).

27:7 *him ... his son ... his grandson.* Three generations of rulers, not necessarily in direct father-son relationships (see note on Da 5:1; see also TNIV text notes on Ge 10:2,8). *time for his land comes.* Babylonia will be judged (see note on 25:26). *many nations and great kings.* See note on 25:14.

27:8 *sword, famine and plague.* See note on v. 2. *sword, famine and plague.* See note on 14:12. *until I destroy.* See 9:16; 24:10.

27:9 See 29:8. *your prophets.* False prophets. *diviners ... mediums ... sorcerers.* Forbidden in Israel (see Lev 19:26; Dt 18:10–11). *interpreters of dreams.* Including prophets and diviners (see 23:25–28; 29:8).

27:10 *prophesy lies.* See note on 5:31; cf. 2Ti 4:3–4.

27:11 *yoke.* See note on v. 2. *serve ... till.* The Hebrew underlying both words is the same ("work" is the common denominator in serving and tilling).

27:12 *your neck ... serve ... live.* The Hebrew for all these words is plural, since Jeremiah is speaking to the people of Judah as well as to Zedekiah (see v. 13). *yoke.* See note on v. 2.

27:13 See v. 8. *sword, famine and plague.* See note on 14:12.

27:14 See vv. 9–10.

27:14 ʳS Jer 14:14;
S Mt 7:15
27:15 ᵘS Jer 23:21
ᵛJer 29:9; 44:16
ʷS Jer 6:15; Mt 15:12-
14
27:16 ˣ1Ki 7:48-50;
S 2Ki 24:13
27:17 ʸJer 23:16
ᶻJer 42:11
27:18 ªS Nu 21:7;
S 1Sa 7:8
27:19 ᵇ1Ki 7:23-26
ᶜS 1Ki 7:51; Jer 52:17-
23
27:20 ᵈS Dt 28:36;
S 2Ch 36:10
ᵉJer 24:24; Mt 1:11
27:22 ᶠS 2Ki 20:17;
25:13 ᵍS 2Ch 36:21;
S Jer 24:6 ʰS Ezr 7:19
28:1 ⁱS 2Ch 36:11
ʲS Jos 9:3
28:2 ᵏJer 27:12
28:3 ˡS 2Ki 24:13
28:4 ᵐS 2Ki 25:30;
Jer 22:24-27
ⁿHos 7:3
28:6 ᵒZec 6:10
28:8 ᵖLev 26:14-17;
Isa 5:5-7; Na 1:14
28:9 �q S Dt 18:22;
Eze 33:33
28:10 ʳS Lev 26:13;
S 1Ki 22:11
28:11 ˢJer 14:14;
27:10

esying lies ᵗ to you. ¹⁵'I have not sent ᵘ them,' declares the LORD. 'They are prophesying lies in my name. ᵛ Therefore, I will banish you and you will perish, ʷ both you and the prophets who prophesy to you.' "

¹⁶Then I said to the priests and all these people, "This is what the LORD says: Do not listen to the prophets who say, 'Very soon now the articles ˣ from the LORD's house will be brought back from Babylon.' They are prophesying lies to you. ¹⁷Do not listen ʸ to them. Serve the king of Babylon, and you will live. ᶻ Why should this city become a ruin? ¹⁸If they are prophets and have the word of the LORD, let them plead ª with the LORD Almighty that the articles remaining in the house of the LORD and in the palace of the king of Judah and in Jerusalem not be taken to Babylon. ¹⁹For this is what the LORD Almighty says about the pillars, the Sea, ᵇ the movable stands and the other articles ᶜ that are left in this city, ²⁰which Nebuchadnezzar king of Babylon did not take away when he carried ᵈ Jehoiachin ª ᵉ son of Jehoiakim king of Judah into exile from Jerusalem to Babylon, along with all the nobles of Judah and Jerusalem— ²¹yes, this is what the LORD Almighty, the God of Israel, says about the things that are left in the house of the LORD and in the palace of the king of Judah and in Jerusalem: ²²They will be taken ᶠ to Babylon and there they will remain until the day ᵍ I come for them,' declares the LORD. 'Then I will bring ʰ them back and restore them to this place.' "

THE FALSE PROPHET HANANIAH

28 In the fifth month of that same year, the fourth year, early in the reign of Zedekiah ⁱ king of Judah, the prophet Hananiah son of Azzur, who was from Gibeon,ʲ said to me in the house of the LORD in the presence of the priests and all the people: ²"This is what the LORD Almighty, the God of Israel, says: 'I will break the yoke ᵏ of the king of Babylon. ³Within two years I will bring back to this place all the articles ˡ of the LORD's house that Nebuchadnezzar king of Babylon removed from here and took to Babylon. ⁴I will also bring back to this place Jehoiachin ª ᵐ son of Jehoiakim king of Judah and all the other exiles from Judah who went to Babylon,' declares the LORD, 'for I will break the yoke of the king of Babylon.' " ⁿ

⁵Then the prophet Jeremiah replied to the prophet Hananiah before the priests and all the people who were standing in the house of the LORD. ⁶He said, "Amen! May the LORD do so! May the LORD fulfill the words you have prophesied by bringing the articles of the LORD's house and all the exiles back to this place from Babylon. ᵒ ⁷Nevertheless, listen to what I have to say in your hearing and in the hearing of all the people: ⁸From early times the prophets who preceded me and you have prophesied war, disaster and plague ᵖ against many countries and great kingdoms. ⁹But the prophet who prophesies peace will be recognized as one truly sent by the LORD only if his prediction comes true. q"

¹⁰Then the prophet Hananiah took the yoke ʳ off the neck of the prophet Jeremiah and broke it, ¹¹and he said ˢ before all the people, "This is what the LORD says: 'In the same

---

ª 20,4 Hebrew *Jeconiah*, a variant of *Jehoiachin*

27:15 See 14:14; 23:21 and note.
27:16 *prophets who say, 'Very soon now…'* As the prophet Hananiah was saying (see 28:1–3). *articles from the LORD's house.* Some were carried off to Babylon by Nebuchadnezzar in 605 B.C. (see Da 1:1–2), others in 597 (see 2Ki 24:13). Still others would be carried off in 586 (see vv. 21–22; 52:17–23).

27:18 *If they are prophets…let them plead.* If they are true prophets and in communion with the Lord, let them intercede for Judah, because the Lord has announced his intention to judge the nation.
27:19 *the pillars, the Sea, the movable stands.* See 52:17; see also 1Ki 7:15–37 and notes.
27:22 *They will be taken to Babylon.* In 586 B.C. (see 52:17–23). *I will bring them back.* In 538/537 and shortly afterward (see Ezr 1:7–11).
28:1–17 The true prophet Jeremiah confronts the false prophet Hananiah.
28:1 *fourth year…of Zedekiah.* 593 B.C. *early in the reign.* See notes on 26:1; 27:1. *prophet.* The word is used for all prophets, whether true or false (vv. 5,10–12,15) or false (vv. 1,5,10,12,15,17). *Hananiah.* Means "The LORD is gracious," an appropriate name for a prophet who believed strongly (though mistakenly) that the Lord would soon bring back the exiles of Judah and the temple articles

(see vv. 3–4,11). *Gibeon.* See 41:12,16; see also note on Jos 9:3.
28:2 *This is what the LORD…says.* See v. 11. Though a false prophet, Hananiah claims to have the same authority as Jeremiah (see vv. 13–14,16; see also 23:31). *yoke.* See note on 27:2.
28:3 Hananiah's prediction directly contradicts the words of Jeremiah (see 27:16–22 and notes). *two years.* See v. 11. Contrast Jeremiah's 70 years (25:11–12; 29:10).
28:4 *bring back.* Contradicting Jeremiah's prophecy (see 22:24–27), which was fulfilled (see 52:34). *Jehoiachin…went to Babylon.* In 597 B.C. *yoke.* See note on 27:2.
28:6 See 1Ki 1:36. *Amen.* See 11:5 and note. *May the LORD fulfill.* One of the signs of true prophecy (see v. 9; see also Dt 18:21–22 and note). For another sign (or test), see Dt 13:1–5 and note.
28:7 *Nevertheless.* Though in sympathy with what Hananiah is predicting, Jeremiah reminds him that their true predecessors were basically prophets of doom (see v. 8).
28:8 *war, disaster and plague.* An appropriate modification of Jeremiah's usual triad (see note on 14:12).
28:9 *peace.* Ordinarily the message of false prophets (see 6:14 and note).
28:10 *yoke off the neck of the prophet.* See note on 27:2. *broke it.* Perhaps symbolically to break the power of Jeremiah's earlier prophecies (see 25:11–12; 27:7), which contradicted his own.

way I will break the yoke of Nebuchadnezzar king of Babylon off the neck of all the nations within two years.' " At this, the prophet Jeremiah went on his way.

¹²After the prophet Hananiah had broken the yoke off the neck of the prophet Jeremiah, the word of the LORD came to Jeremiah: ¹³"Go and tell Hananiah, 'This is what the LORD says: You have broken a wooden yoke, but in its place you will get a yoke of iron. ¹⁴This is what the LORD Almighty, the God of Israel, says: I will put an iron yoke ^{t} on the necks of all these nations to make them serve ^{u} Nebuchadnezzar ^{v} king of Babylon, and they will serve him. I will even give him control over the wild animals. ^{w} ' "

¹⁵Then the prophet Jeremiah said to Hananiah the prophet, "Listen, Hananiah! The LORD has not sent ^{x} you, yet you have persuaded this nation to trust in lies. ^{y} ¹⁶Therefore, this is what the LORD says: 'I am about to remove you from the face of the earth. ^{z} This very year you are going to die, ^{a} because you have preached rebellion ^{b} against the LORD.' "

¹⁷In the seventh month of that same year, Hananiah the prophet died. ^{c}

A LETTER TO THE EXILES

29 This is the text of the letter ^{d} that the prophet Jeremiah sent from Jerusalem to the surviving elders among the exiles and to the priests, the prophets and all the other people Nebuchadnezzar had carried into exile from Jerusalem to Babylon. ^{e} ²(This was after King Jehoiachin $^{a\,f}$ and the queen mother, ^{g} the court officials and the leaders of Judah and Jerusalem, the artisans and the other skilled workers had gone into exile from Jerusalem.) ³He entrusted the letter to Elasah son of Shaphan and to Gemariah son of Hilkiah, whom Zedekiah king of Judah sent to King Nebuchadnezzar in Babylon. It said:

⁴This is what the LORD Almighty, the God of Israel, says to all those I carried ^{h} into exile from Jerusalem to Babylon: ⁵"Build ^{i} houses and settle down; plant gardens and eat what they produce. ⁶Marry and have sons and daughters; find wives for your sons and give your daughters in marriage, so that they too may have sons and daughters. Increase in number there; do not decrease. ^{j} ⁷Also, seek ^{k} the peace and prosperity of the city to which I have carried you into exile. Pray ^{l} to the LORD for it, because if it prospers, you too will prosper." ⁸Yes, this is what the LORD Almighty, the God of Israel, says: "Do not let the prophets ^{m} and diviners among you deceive ^{n} you. Do not listen to the dreams ^{o} you encourage them to have. ^{p} ⁹They are prophesying lies ^{q} to you in my name. I have not sent ^{r} them," declares the LORD.

¹⁰This is what the LORD says: "When seventy years ^{s} are completed for Babylon, I

---

^{a} 2 Hebrew *Jeconiah,* a variant of *Jehoiachin*

28:14 ^{r} S Dt 28:48;
S Jer 15:12 ^{u} Jer 25:11
^{v} Jer 39:1; Da 1:1; 5:18
^{w} S Jer 27:6
28:15 ^{x} Jer 29:31
^{y} S Jer 7:4; 20:6;
29:21; La 2:14;
Eze 13:6
28:16 ^{z} S Ge 7:4
^{a} Dt 18:20; Zec 13:3
^{b} Dt 13:5; Jer 29:32
28:17 ^{c} S 2Ki 1:17
29:1 ^{d} ver 28
^{e} S 2Ch 36:10;
S Jer 13:17
29:2 ^{f} S 2Ki 24:12
^{g} S 2Ki 24:8
29:4 ^{h} S Jer 24:5
29:5 ^{i} ver 28
29:6 ^{j} Jer 30:19
29:7 ^{k} S Est 3:8
^{l} 1Ti 2:1-2
29:8 ^{m} 1Jn 4:1
^{n} Jer 37:9 ^{o} S Dt 13:1;
S Jer 23:25
^{p} S Jer 23:27
29:9 ^{q} S Jer 27:15;
La 2:14; Eze 13:6
^{r} Jer 23:21
29:10 ^{s} S 2Ch 36:21;
S Da 9:2

28:11 *two years.* See note on v. 3.

28:13 *yoke of iron.* The wooden yoke of submission (see note on 27:2) would be exchanged for the iron yoke of servitude (see v. 14; 38:17–23).

28:14 *all these nations … will serve him.* See 27:7. *control over the wild animals.* See 27:6 and note.

28:15 *The LORD has not sent you.* A mark of the false prophet (see 23:21 and note).

28:16 *remove.* The Hebrew root behind this word is the same as that underlying "sent" in v. 15. The Lord had not "sent" Hananiah to prophesy; therefore he would soon be "sent away" to his death. *preached rebellion.* Such activity on the part of false prophets was punishable by death (see Dt 13:5; see also Dt 18:20; cf. Eze 11:13; Ac 5:1–11).

28:17 *In the seventh month … Hananiah … died.* He who had falsely prophesied restoration "within two years" (vv. 3, 11) himself died within two months (see v. 1).

29:1–32 Jeremiah's letter to the exiles of 597 B.C. (vv. 4–23) is followed by God's message of judgment against the false prophet Shemaiah (vv. 24–32).

29:2 *queen mother.* Nehushta (see note on 13:18). *artisans and the other skilled workers.* See 24:1 and note.

29:3 *entrusted the letter to.* Placed it in the ancient equivalent of the diplomatic pouch to ensure its safe arrival. *Shaphan.* Perhaps the father also of Ahikam (see 26:24 and note) and/or Gemariah (see 36:10), both of whom were sympathetic to Jeremiah and his mission. *Gemariah.* A common name in Jeremiah's time (see, e.g., 36:10), found on

one of the Lachish ostraca (see note on 34:7), as well as in at least two of the Elephantine papyri (see note on 32:11) a century later. *Hilkiah.* Perhaps the Hilkiah who was high priest under Josiah (see 2Ki 22:12, where Hilkiah and one or more Shaphans are mentioned together). *Zedekiah … sent to King Nebuchadnezzar.* Possibly at or about the same time (593 B.C.) that Zedekiah himself went to Babylon for a brief period (see 51:59). The purpose of the journey(s) is unknown.

29:4 *I.* The Lord (see v. 7). Since it is God who has exiled his people, they are to submit to their captors and not rebel against them.

29:5 *Build … plant.* Reminiscent of Jeremiah's call (see 1:10), but here used in a literal sense. *settle down.* Ezekiel, e.g., lived in his own house in Babylonia (see Eze 8:1 and note).

29:6 *find wives.* But among the exiles themselves, not among the women of Babylonia (cf. Dt 7:3–4; Ezr 9:1–2).

29:7 An unprecedented and unique concept in the ancient world: working toward and praying for the prosperity of one's captors. *peace and prosperity … prospers … prosper.* The Hebrew word is *shalom* in all three cases. *city.* Every place in which the exiles settle down. *Pray … for it.* See Ezr 6:10 and note; Mt 5:44; in the Apocrypha, cf. 1 Maccabees 7:33.

29:8 *prophets and diviners … dreams.* See 27:9 and note. *among you.* The exiles in Babylon had their share of false prophets (see vv. 21,31), who had doubtless accompanied them when they were deported in 597 B.C.

29:9 See v. 31; see also notes on 23:16,21.

29:10 *seventy years.* See note on 25:11–12. *bring you back.* See note on 27:22.

29:10 ʳS Ru 1:6
ᵘ1Ki 8:56; Jer 32:42;
33:14 ᵛS Jer 16:14;
S 24:6
29:11 ʷPs 40:5
ˣIsa 55:12 ʸS Job 8:7;
Zec 8:15
29:12 ᶻHos 2:23;
Zep 3:12; Zec 13:9
ᵃS 1Ki 8:30
ᵇPs 145:19; S Isa 55:6
29:13 ᶜMt 7:7
ᵈS Dt 4:29;
S 2Ch 6:37
29:14 ᵉS Dt 30:3;
Jer 30:3; Eze 39:25;
Am 9:14; Zep 3:20
ᶠJer 23:3-4; 30:10;
46:27; Eze 37:21
29:17 ᵍJer 27:8
ʰS Isa 5:4
29:18 ᶦS Jer 15:4
ʲS Nu 5:27;
S Jer 18:16; S 22:10;
44:12 ᵏS Dt 28:25
ˡS Dt 28:37;
S Isa 28:22; S Mic 2:6
29:19 ᵐJer 6:19
ⁿJer 7:25 ᵒS Jer 25:4
29:20 ᵖS Jer 24:5
29:21 �q ver 9;
Jer 14:14
29:22 ʳDa 3:6
29:23 ˢS Jer 23:14
ᵗS Heb 4:13
ᵘS Ge 31:48;
S Jer 7:11
29:25 ᵛS 2Ki 25:18
29:26 ʷS 1Sa 10:11;
Hos 9:7; S Jn 10:20
ˣJer 20:2
29:28 ʸver 1 ᶻver 10
ᵃver 5

will come to you ᵗ and fulfill my good promise ᵘ to bring you back ᵛ to this place. ¹¹For I know the plans ʷ I have for you," declares the Lᴏʀᴅ, "plans to prosper ˣ you and not to harm you, plans to give you hope and a future. ʸ ¹²Then you will call ᶻ on me and come and pray ᵃ to me, and I will listen ᵇ to you. ¹³You will seek ᶜ me and find me when you seek me with all your heart. ᵈ ¹⁴I will be found by you," declares the Lᴏʀᴅ, "and will bring you back ᵉ from captivity.ᵃ I will gather you from all the nations and places where I have banished you," declares the Lᴏʀᴅ, "and will bring you back to the place from which I carried you into exile." ᶠ

¹⁵You may say, "The Lᴏʀᴅ has raised up prophets for us in Babylon," ¹⁶but this is what the Lᴏʀᴅ says about the king who sits on David's throne and all the people who remain in this city, your fellow citizens who did not go with you into exile— ¹⁷yes, this is what the Lᴏʀᴅ Almighty says: "I will send the sword, famine and plague ᵍ against them and I will make them like figs ʰ that are so bad they cannot be eaten. ¹⁸I will pursue them with the sword, famine and plague and will make them abhorrent ᶦ to all the kingdoms of the earth, a curse ᵇ ʲ and an object of horror, ᵏ of scorn ˡ and reproach, among all the nations where I drive them. ¹⁹For they have not listened to my words," ᵐ declares the Lᴏʀᴅ, "words that I sent to them again and again ⁿ by my servants the prophets. ᵒ And you exiles have not listened either," declares the Lᴏʀᴅ.

²⁰Therefore, hear the word of the Lᴏʀᴅ, all you exiles whom I have sent ᵖ away from Jerusalem to Babylon. ²¹This is what the Lᴏʀᴅ Almighty, the God of Israel, says about Ahab son of Kolaiah and Zedekiah son of Maaseiah, who are prophesying lies �q to you in my name: "I will deliver them into the hands of Nebuchadnezzar king of Babylon, and he will put them to death before your very eyes. ²²Because of them, all the exiles from Judah who are in Babylon will use this curse: 'May the Lᴏʀᴅ treat you like Zedekiah and Ahab, whom the king of Babylon burned ʳ in the fire.' ²³For they have done outrageous things in Israel; they have committed adultery ˢ with their neighbors' wives, and in my name they have uttered lies—which I did not authorize. I know ᵗ it and am a witness ᵘ to it," declares the Lᴏʀᴅ.

MESSAGE TO SHEMAIAH

²⁴Tell Shemaiah the Nehelamite, ²⁵"This is what the Lᴏʀᴅ Almighty, the God of Israel, says: You sent letters in your own name to all the people in Jerusalem, to the priest Zephaniah ᵛ son of Maaseiah, and to all the other priests. You said to Zephaniah, ²⁶'The Lᴏʀᴅ has appointed you priest in place of Jehoiada to be in charge of the house of the Lᴏʀᴅ; you should put any crazy person ʷ who acts like a prophet into the stocks ˣ and neck-irons. ²⁷So why have you not reprimanded Jeremiah from Anathoth, who poses as a prophet among you? ²⁸He has sent this message ʸ to us in Babylon: It will be a long time. ᶻ Therefore build ᵃ houses and settle down; plant gardens and eat what they produce.' "

ᵃ 14 Or *will restore your fortunes*   ᵇ 18 That is, their names will be used in cursing (see Jer. 29:22); or, others will see that they are cursed.

29:11 *I know.* See v. 23. Appearances to the contrary notwithstanding, the Lord has not forgotten his people. *prosper.* See note on v. 7. *and not...harm.* God is the ultimate source of both prosperity and disaster (see Isa 45:7).

29:12–13 Echoed from Dt 4:29–30. The Lord's gracious gift of prosperity is contingent on his people's willingness to repent.

29:14 A summary of Dt 30:3–5. *bring you back from captivity.* See TNIV text note; see also 30:3,18; 31:23; 32:44; 33:7,11,26; 48:47; 49:6,39; and note on Ps 126:4.

29:15 *prophets...in Babylon.* See note on v. 8.

29:16 *the king...on David's throne.* Zedekiah. *sits...remain.* The Hebrew for both words is identical. King and people alike are guilty.

29:17 *sword, famine and plague.* See v. 18; see also note on 14:12. *like figs...so bad they cannot be eaten.* See 24:8.

29:18 See 24:9 and note.

29:19 *again and again.* See note on 7:13. *my servants the prophets.* See note on 7:25. *you exiles have not listened.* See Eze 2:5,7; 3:7,11.

29:21 *Ahab...and Zedekiah.* Not the well-known kings (of Is-

rael and Judah respectively); rather, they were false prophets (see note on v. 8).

29:22 *fire.* Used in Babylonia as a method of execution (see Da 3:6,24; this is also evident in the Code of Hammurapi, sections 25; 110; 157).

29:23 *done outrageous things in Israel.* See Ge 34:7 and note. *committed adultery...and...uttered lies.* See note on 23:10. *I know.* See v. 11.

29:24 *Shemaiah.* A false prophet (see v. 31). *Nehelamite.* The Hebrew root underlying this word is the same as that for "dreams" in v. 8 (see 27:9 and note). Jeremiah is perhaps suggesting that Shemaiah is not a true prophet but a mere dreamer.

29:25 *Zephaniah.* Not the prophet of that name (see note on 21:1).

29:26 *Jehoiada.* Not the same as the priest during the days of King Joash (see 2Ki 12:7). *in charge of the house of the Lᴏʀᴅ.* See note on 20:1. *crazy person.* Prophetic behavior sometimes appeared deranged to the casual observer (see 2Ki 9:11). *stocks.* See 20:2 and note.

29:27 *Anathoth.* See note on 1:1.

29:28 See v. 5 and note. *a long time.* Here 70 years (see 25:11–12 and note; see also 2Sa 3:1).

²⁹Zephaniah ᵇ the priest, however, read the letter to Jeremiah the prophet. ³⁰Then the word of the Lᴏʀᴅ came to Jeremiah: ³¹"Send this message to all the exiles: 'This is what the Lᴏʀᴅ says about Shemaiah ᶜ the Nehelamite: Because Shemaiah has prophesied to you, even though I did not send ᵈ him, and has persuaded you to trust in lies, ³²this is what the Lᴏʀᴅ says: I will surely punish Shemaiah the Nehelamite and his descendants. ᵉ He will have no one left among this people, nor will he see the good ᶠ things I will do for my people, declares the Lᴏʀᴅ, because he has preached rebellion ᵍ against me.' "

RESTORATION OF ISRAEL

30 This is the word that came to Jeremiah from the Lᴏʀᴅ: ²"This is what the Lᴏʀᴅ, the God of Israel, says: 'Write ʰ in a book all the words I have spoken to you. ³The days ⁱ are coming,' declares the Lᴏʀᴅ, 'when I will bring ʲ my people Israel and Judah back from captivity ᵃ and restore ᵏ them to the land I gave their ancestors to possess,' says the Lᴏʀᴅ."

⁴These are the words the Lᴏʀᴅ spoke concerning Israel and Judah. ⁵"This is what the Lᴏʀᴅ says:

" 'Cries of fear ˡ are heard—
   terror, not peace.
⁶ Ask and see:
   Can a man bear children?
Then why do I see every strong man
   with his hands on his stomach like a woman in labor, ᵐ
   every face turned deathly pale? ⁿ
⁷ How awful that day ᵒ will be!
   None will be like it.
It will be a time of trouble ᵖ for Jacob,
   but he will be saved ᵠ out of it.

⁸ " 'In that day,' declares the Lᴏʀᴅ Almighty,
   'I will break the yoke ʳ off their necks
and will tear off their bonds; ˢ
   no longer will foreigners enslave them. ᵗ
⁹ Instead, they will serve the Lᴏʀᴅ their God
   and David ᵘ their king, ᵛ
   whom I will raise up for them.

¹⁰ " 'So do not be afraid, ʷ Jacob my servant; ˣ
   do not be dismayed, Israel,'

declares the Lᴏʀᴅ.

ᵃ 3 Or *will restore the fortunes of my people Israel and Judah*

29:29 *Zephaniah ... however.* He was apparently sympathetic toward Jeremiah (see 21:1–2; 37:3).
29:31–32 The Lord's threat against Shemaiah is similar to that against Hananiah (see 28:15–16).
29:31 *persuaded you to trust in lies.* See 28:15.
29:32 *preached rebellion against.* See 28:16 and note.
30:1—33:26 Often called Jeremiah's "book of consolation," the section depicts the ultimate restoration of both Israel (the northern kingdom) and Judah (the southern kingdom) and is the longest sustained passage in Jeremiah concerned with the future hope of the people of God (for other and briefer passages on restoration, see 3:14–18; 16:14–15; 23:3–8; 24:4–7). The information in 32:1 may be used to date the entire section to 587 ʙ.ᴄ., the year before Jerusalem was destroyed by Nebuchadnezzar and its people exiled to Babylon.
30:1—31:40 Written almost entirely in poetry, these two chapters are filled with optimism as the prophet looks forward to the time when God would redeem his people.
30:1 The heading for chs. 30–31 (and perhaps chs. 32–33 as well).
30:2 *Write.* In order to preserve for future generations the predictions of restoration. *book.* In scroll form (see, e.g., 36:2,4; 45:1; see also Ex 17:14 and note). *all the words I have spoken to you.* Concerning the future redemption of God's people. The phrase is less comprehensive here than in 36:2.

30:3 *bring ... back from captivity.* See note on 29:14. *Israel and Judah.* The northern and southern kingdoms, the first of which was exiled in 721 ʙ.ᴄ. and the second of which would be entering the final stage of its exile in about a year (see note on 30:1—33:26).
30:5 *Cries of fear ... terror.* The sounds of battle and destruction.
30:6 *woman in labor.* A symbol of anguish and distress (see notes on 4:19,31).
30:7 A description of the day of the Lord (see notes on Isa 2:11,17,20; Am 5:18; 8:9). Jeremiah's immediate reference is to the foreseeable future (see vv. 8,18), but a more remote time in the Messianic age is also in view. *awful.* Lit. "great" (as in Joel 2:11; Zep 1:14; cf. Joel 1:15). *None will be like it.* See Da 12:1; Joel 2:2; Mt 24:21. *time of trouble.* The Hebrew for this phrase is translated "time of distress" in Da 12:1 (see Mt 24:21 and note; Rev 16:18). *Jacob.* Israel (see v. 10).
30:8 *In that day.* See note on Isa 2:11,17,20. *yoke.* See note on 27:2. *tear off their bonds.* The Hebrew underlying this phrase is translated "break their chains" in Ps 2:3, where the nations plot to free themselves from the Lord and his anointed ruler. Here the Lord promises to free his people from enslavement to the nations. *foreigners.* Including, but not limited to, Babylonia.
30:9 *David their king.* The Messiah (see note on 23:5). The Targum (ancient Aramaic paraphrase) here reads "Messiah, the son of David, their king." *raise up.* See 23:5 and note.

30:10 ʸS ver 7;
S Jer 29:14 ᶻIsa 35:9;
S Jer 17:25
ᵃS Isa 29:22; S 54:4;
S Jer 23:4; Eze 34:25-
28
30:11 ᵇS Jos 1:5
ᶜS Lev 26:44;
S Jer 5:18; 46:28
ᵈS Jer 10:24
ᵉHos 11:9; Am 9:8
30:12 ᶠS Job 6:4;
S Jer 10:19
ᵍS Jer 8:22
30:13 ʰS Jdg 6:31
ⁱS Jer 8:22; 14:19;
46:11; Na 3:19
30:14 ʲS Jer 22:20;
La 1:2 ᵏS Job 13:24
ˡS Job 30:21
ᵐS Jer 25:7
30:15 ⁿS Jer 10:19
ᵒS Pr 1:31; La 1:5
30:16 ᵖS Isa 29:8;
S 33:1; S Jer 2:3
�q S Isa 14:2; Joel 3:4-
8 ʳJer 49:2; 50:10
30:17 ˢS Isa 1:5;
Hos 6:1 ᵗS Isa 6:12;
Jer 33:24 ᵘPs 142:4
30:18 ᵛver 3;
S Dt 30:3; Jer 31:23;
32:44 ʷS Nu 24:5
ˣPs 102:13; Jer 33:26;
Eze 39:25 ʸJer 31:4,
24,38; 33:7;
Eze 36:10,33;
Am 9:14
30:19 ᶻS Ps 9:2;
Isa 35:10; S 51:11
ᵃS Isa 51:3
ᵇPs 126:1-2; Jer 31:4
ᶜS Ge 15:5; 22:17;
Jer 33:22; Eze 37:26;
Zec 2:4

'I will surely save ʸ you out of a distant place,
  your descendants from the land of their exile.
Jacob will again have peace and security, ᶻ
  and no one will make him afraid. ᵃ
¹¹ I am with you ᵇ and will save you,'
  declares the LORD.
'Though I completely destroy all the nations
  among which I scatter you,
  I will not completely destroy ᶜ you.
I will discipline ᵈ you but only in due measure;
  I will not let you go entirely unpunished.' ᵉ

¹²This is what the LORD says:

" 'Your wound ᶠ is incurable,
  your injury beyond healing. ᵍ
¹³ There is no one to plead your cause, ʰ
  no remedy for your sore,
  no healing ⁱ for you.
¹⁴ All your allies ʲ have forgotten you;
  they care nothing for you.
I have struck you as an enemy ᵏ would
  and punished you as would the cruel, ˡ
because your guilt is so great
  and your sins ᵐ so many.
¹⁵ Why do you cry out over your wound,
  your pain that has no cure? ⁿ
Because of your great guilt and many sins
  I have done these things to you. ᵒ

¹⁶ " 'But all who devour ᵖ you will be devoured;
  all your enemies will go into exile. q
Those who plunder ʳ you will be plundered;
  all who make spoil of you I will despoil.
¹⁷ But I will restore you to health
  and heal ˢ your wounds,'

                                    declares the LORD,

'because you are called an outcast, ᵗ
  Zion for whom no one cares.' ᵘ

¹⁸"This is what the LORD says:

" 'I will restore the fortunes ᵛ of Jacob's tents ʷ
  and have compassion ˣ on his dwellings;
the city will be rebuilt ʸ on her ruins,
  and the palace will stand in its proper place.
¹⁹ From them will come songs ᶻ of thanksgiving ᵃ
  and the sound of rejoicing. ᵇ
I will add to their numbers, ᶜ
  and they will not be decreased;

30:10–11 Repeated almost verbatim in 46:27–28.
30:10 *Jacob my servant.* See Isa 41:8–9 and note; 44:1–2,21; 45:4; 48:20. *no one will make him afraid.* Contrast v. 5; see Lev 26:6; Job 11:19; Isa 17:2; Eze 34:28; 39:26; Mic 4:4 and note; Zep 3:13.
30:11 *I am with you and will save you.* Words spoken originally to Jeremiah alone (see 1:8,19; 15:20) are now spoken to all God's people. *scatter.* See 9:16 and note; 23:1–2. *not completely destroy.* See 4:27 and note. *not…go…unpunished.* See 25:29; 49:12.
30:12–13 See 8:22; Hos 5:13; 6:1; 7:1; 11:3.
30:12 *Your.* Judah's. *wound is incurable.* See 15:18 and note. *injury beyond healing.* See 14:17.
30:13 *plead your cause.* Against your enemies. *no remedy for your sore.* See Hos 5:13.
30:14 *allies.* See note on 22:20. Egypt, e.g., often supported Judah against the Babylonians (see 37:5–7). *because your guilt…*

so many. See 5:6; 13:22. The Hebrew for this clause is repeated verbatim in v. 15.
30:16 *all who devour you.* See 3:24; 5:17; 8:16; 10:25. *will be devoured.* See note on 25:26; see also 51:48–49. *will be plundered.* See Isa 17:14.
30:17 *restore you to health.* Contrast 8:22; see 33:6; Isa 58:8. *Zion.* See note on 2Sa 5:7.
30:18 *restore the fortunes.* See note on 29:14. *the city…the palace.* Lit. "a city…a palace," perhaps referring to Judah's cities and palaces in general (see Am 9:14). It is possible, however, that only Jerusalem and its palace are intended (see 31:38). *ruins.* The Hebrew for this word is *tel(l)*, referring to a mound of ruins resulting from the accumulation of the debris of many years or centuries of occupation and on which successive series of towns were often built (see, e.g., Jos 11:13 and note).
30:19 *songs of thanksgiving.* See 33:11. *rejoicing.* See 31:4 and

I will bring them honor, *d*
    and they will not be disdained.
²⁰ Their children *e* will be as in days of old,
    and their community will be established *f* before me;
    I will punish *g* all who oppress them.
²¹ Their leader *h* will be one of their own;
    their ruler will arise from among them. *i*
I will bring him near *j* and he will come close to me—
    for who is he who will devote himself
        to be close to me?'

²² " 'So you will be my people, *k*
    and I will be your God. *l* ' "

²³ See, the storm *m* of the LORD
    will burst out in wrath,
a driving wind swirling down
    on the heads of the wicked.
²⁴ The fierce anger *n* of the LORD will not turn back *o*
    until he fully accomplishes
        the purposes of his heart.
In days to come
    you will understand *p* this.

31 "At that time," declares the LORD, "I will be the God *q* of all the families of Israel, and they will be my people."
²This is what the LORD says:

"The people who survive the sword
    will find favor *r* in the wilderness;
    I will come to give rest *s* to Israel."

³The LORD appeared to us in the past, *a* saying:

"I have loved *t* you with an everlasting love;
    I have drawn *u* you with unfailing kindness.
⁴ I will build you up again,
    and you, Virgin *v* Israel, will be rebuilt. *w*
Again you will take up your timbrels *x*
    and go out to dance *y* with the joyful. *z*

declares the LORD.

---

a 3 Or LORD has appeared to us from afar

30:19 *d* S Isa 44:23;
S 60:9
30:20 *e* Isa 54:13;
Jer 31:17; Zec 8:5
f Isa 54:14
g S Ex 23:22
30:21 *h* S ver 9;
Jer 23:5-6 *i* Dt 17:15
j Nu 16:5
30:22 *k* Isa 19:25;
Hos 2:23 *l* S Lev 26:12
30:23 *m* S Jer 23:19
30:24 *n* Jer 4:8;
La 1:12 *o* S Jer 4:28
p Jer 23:19-20
31:1 *q* S Lev 26:12
31:2 *r* Nu 14:20
s Ex 33:14;
S Dt 12:9
31:3 *t* S Dt 4:37
u Hos 11:4; Jn 6:44
31:4 *v* S 2Ki 19:21
w S Jer 1:10; S 30:18
x S Ge 31:27
y S Ex 15:20
z S Jer 30:19

---

note; contrast 15:17. *add . . . not be decreased.* See 29:6; Eze
36:37–38. *honor . . . not be disdained.* See Isa 9:1.
30:20 *days of old.* Probably the early days of the united kingdom, especially the reign of David. *community.* In 1Ki 12:20 the
Hebrew for this word is translated "assembly," the political and
religious governing body of the people. *will be established before me.* See Ps 102:28 and note.

30:21 *leader . . . ruler.* Although the Targum renders "Messiah" here, the terms probably refer in the first place to
the rulers of Judah immediately after the exile. But Jesus Christ
ultimately fulfills the promise. *one of their own . . . from among
them.* Not foreigners (cf. Dt 18:15,18). *bring him near . . . come
close.* See Nu 16:5; contrast Ex 24:2. Unauthorized approaches
into God's presence were punishable by death (see Ex 19:21; Nu
8:19).
30:22 See 31:1; see also note on 7:23.
30:23–24 Repeated almost verbatim from 23:19–20 (see
notes there).
31:1–40 Continuing the theme of restoration begun in 30:1,
Jeremiah records the words of the Lord to (1) all the people of
God, v. 1 (prose); (2) the restored northern kingdom of Israel, vv.
2–22 (poetry); (3) the restored southern kingdom of Judah, vv.
23–26 (prose); and (4) Israel and Judah together, vv. 27–40
(prose prologue, vv. 27–30; poetic body, vv. 31–37; prose epi-

logue, vv. 38–40—each section beginning with the words "The
days are coming"; see note on v. 31).
31:1 See 30:22; see also note on 7:23. *God of . . . my people.* See
note on Zec 8:8. *all the families of Israel.* All 12 tribes.
31:2 *people who survive the sword.* The righteous remnant (see
v. 7; see also note on 6:9), who will return from captivity. *wilderness.* The Arabian Desert, the antitype of the Sinai Desert
through which Israel's ancestors marched after the exodus. Return from exile is often pictured as or compared to release from
Egyptian slavery at the time of the exodus (see 16:14–15; Isa
35:1–11 and notes; 40:3–4; 42:14–16; 43:18–21; 48:20–21;
51:9–11; cf. Hos 2:14–15). *rest.* See 6:16; contrast Dt 28:65. See
notes on Dt 3:20; Jos 1:13. *Israel.* The northern kingdom (see
also vv. 4,7,9–10,21). Other names for it are Samaria (v. 5),
Ephraim (vv. 6,9,18,20), Jacob (vv. 7,11) and Rachel (v. 15).

31:3 *drawn . . . with unfailing kindness.* The Hebrew underlying this phrase is translated "Continue . . . love" in Ps
36:10 (see note on Ps 6:4).
31:4 *build.* See 1:10 and note. *Virgin Israel.* See note on 2Ki
19:21. *timbrels.* Used on joyful occasions (see Ps 68:25), especially following a military victory (see Ex 15:20 and note; Jdg 11:34)
—in contrast to Judah's experience during the exile (see Ps
137:1–3). *dance.* See v. 13; often a religious activity in ancient
times (see 2Sa 6:14; Ps 149:3; 150:4).

31:5 ᵃ S Dt 20:6
ᵇ Jer 33:13; 50:19;
Ob 1:19 ᶜ S Isa 37:30;
Am 9:14
31:6 ᵈ S Isa 52:8;
S 56:10 ᵉ ver 12;
S Dt 33:19; Jer 50:4-
5; Mic 4:2
31:7 ᶠ S Isa 12:6
ᵍ Dt 28:13; Isa 61:9
ʰ Ps 14:7; 28:9
ⁱ S Isa 37:31
31:8 ʲ S Jer 3:18
ᵏ S Ge 33:13;
S Dt 30:4;
S Ps 106:47;
Eze 34:12-14
ˡ Isa 42:16
ᵐ Eze 34:14; Mic 4:6
31:9 ⁿ S Ezr 3:12;
Ps 126:5 ᵒ Isa 63:13
ᵖ S Nu 20:8; S Ps 1:3;
S Isa 32:2
�q S Isa 40:4; S 49:11
ʳ S Ex 4:22; S Jer 3:4
31:10 ˢ Isa 49:1;
S 66:19; S Jer 25:22
ᵗ S Lev 26:33
ᵘ S Dt 30:4;
S Isa 11:12; Jer 50:19
ᵛ Isa 40:11; Eze 34:12
31:11 ʷ S Ex 6:6;
Zec 9:16 ˣ Ps 142:6
31:12 ʸ S Ps 126:5
ᶻ Eze 17:23; 20:40;
40:2; Mic 4:1
ᵃ S Ps 36:8; Joel 3:18
ᵇ S Nu 18:12;
Hos 2:21-22; Joel 2:19
ᶜ ver 24; S Isa 65:10
ᵈ S S 4:15
ᵉ S Isa 30:19; S 62:5;
Jn 16:22; S Rev 7:17

⁵Again you will plant ᵃ vineyards
    on the hills of Samaria; ᵇ
the farmers will plant them
    and enjoy their fruit. ᶜ
⁶There will be a day when watchmen ᵈ cry out
    on the hills of Ephraim,
'Come, let us go up to Zion,
    to the Lᴏʀᴅ our God.' " ᵉ

⁷This is what the Lᴏʀᴅ says:

"Sing ᶠ with joy for Jacob;
    shout for the foremost ᵍ of the nations.
Make your praises heard, and say,
    'Lᴏʀᴅ, save ʰ your people,
    the remnant ⁱ of Israel.'
⁸See, I will bring them from the land of the north ʲ
    and gather ᵏ them from the ends of the earth.
Among them will be the blind ˡ and the lame, ᵐ
    expectant mothers and women in labor;
    a great throng will return.
⁹They will come with weeping; ⁿ
    they will pray as I bring them back.
I will lead ᵒ them beside streams of water ᵖ
    on a level q path where they will not stumble,
because I am Israel's father, ʳ
    and Ephraim is my firstborn son.

¹⁰"Hear the word of the Lᴏʀᴅ, you nations;
    proclaim it in distant coastlands: ˢ
'He who scattered ᵗ Israel will gather ᵘ them
    and will watch over his flock like a shepherd.' ᵛ
¹¹For the Lᴏʀᴅ will deliver Jacob
    and redeem ʷ them from the hand of those stronger ˣ than they.
¹²They will come and shout for joy ʸ on the heights ᶻ of Zion;
    they will rejoice in the bounty ᵃ of the Lᴏʀᴅ—
the grain, the new wine and the olive oil, ᵇ
    the young of the flocks ᶜ and herds.
They will be like a well-watered garden, ᵈ
    and they will sorrow ᵉ no more.
¹³Then young women will dance and be glad,
    young men and old as well.

31:5 *plant.* See 1:10 and note. *Samaria.* Conquered in 722–721
B.C. (see 2Ki 17:24), it would someday be resettled by God's people. *plant them and enjoy their fruit.* See Dt 28:30; Isa 62:8–9;
65:21–22. Since the law stipulated that the fruit of a tree could
not be eaten until the fifth year after planting it (see Lev 19:23–
25), a return to normalcy is envisioned here.
31:6 *watchmen . . . on the hills.* Watchmen were stationed in appropriate locations to observe and give notice of the appearance of various phases of the moon to fix the times of the most
important festivals (see Dt 16:16 and note). *Ephraim . . . to Zion.*
In the days of Jeroboam I the people of the northern kingdom
had been required to worship at northern shrines (see 1Ki
12:26–30). In the future, however, they would worship the Lord
only in Jerusalem (cf. Jn 4:20). *go up.* In ancient Israel one always
"went up" to Jerusalem (see, e.g., Ezr 1:3; 7:7; Isa 2:3; Jn 2:13), not
only because its elevation was above the surrounding countryside but also because it was the royal city and the main center
of the nation's religious life.

A **31:7** *foremost of the nations.* See Dt 26:19; Am 6:1. Israel
was the greatest nation, not because of intrinsic merit but
because of divine grace and appointment (see Dt 7:6–8; 2Sa
7:23–24). *save.* The Hebrew for this word is the basis of "Hosanna," the cry of the people of Jerusalem on Palm Sunday (see Mt
21:9 and TNIV text note; see also Ps 20:9; 28:9; 86:2; and espe-

cially 118:25). *remnant.* See note on 6:9.
31:8 *land of the north.* See 3:18; 4:6 and notes; 6:22; 16:15. *ends
of the earth.* See 6:22; 25:32. *blind . . . lame.* See Isa 35:5–6 and
notes; 42:16. *women in labor.* See note on 4:31.
31:9 *with weeping.* Contrast Ps 126:5–6; Isa 55:12. *lead them.*
See Isa 40:11; 48:21; contrast Isa 20:4. *beside streams of water.*
See Isa 49:10; see also 41:18. *level path.* See Isa 40:3–4 and
notes; 43:16,19. *I am Israel's father.* See 3:4 and note; see also Dt
32:6; Isa 63:16; 64:8. *firstborn son.* Cf. v. 20; see Ex 4:22 and note;
Hos 11:1–4.
31:10 *distant coastlands.* Remote areas to the west of Israel
(see 2:10; 25:22 and note; 47:4; Ps 72:10; Isa 41:1,5; 42:10,12;
49:1). *scattered Israel . . . watch over his flock like a shepherd.* See
23:1–3 and notes.
31:11 *redeem.* See note on Ru 2:20. As the Lord had redeemed
his people from Egyptian slavery (see Ex 6:6 and note; 15:13; Dt
7:8; 9:26), so now he would redeem their descendants from Babylonian exile (see Isa 41:14; 43:1 and notes; 52:9). *from . . . those
stronger than they.* See Ps 35:10.
31:12 *heights of Zion.* See note on 17:12. *bounty of the Lᴏʀᴅ.*
Primarily material blessings (see v. 14; Hos 3:5). *grain . . . new
wine . . . olive oil.* See note on Dt 7:13; see also Hos 2:8. *like a well-
watered garden.* See Isa 58:11 and note. *sorrow no more.* See
Isa 25:8.

I will turn their mourning [f] into gladness;
I will give them comfort [g] and joy [h] instead of sorrow.
[14] I will satisfy [i] the priests [j] with abundance,
and my people will be filled with my bounty, [k]"

declares the LORD.

[15] This is what the LORD says:

"A voice is heard in Ramah, [l]
mourning and great weeping,
Rachel weeping for her children
and refusing to be comforted, [m]
because they are no more." [n]

[16] This is what the LORD says:

"Restrain your voice from weeping
and your eyes from tears, [o]
for your work will be rewarded, [p]"

declares the LORD.

"They will return [q] from the land of the enemy.
[17] So there is hope [r] for your descendants,"

declares the LORD.

"Your children [s] will return to their own land.

[18] "I have surely heard Ephraim's moaning:
'You disciplined [t] me like an unruly calf, [u]
and I have been disciplined.
Restore [v] me, and I will return,
because you are the LORD my God.
[19] After I strayed, [w]
I repented;
after I came to understand,
I beat [x] my breast.
I was ashamed [y] and humiliated
because I bore the disgrace of my youth.' [z]
[20] Is not Ephraim my dear son,
the child [a] in whom I delight?
Though I often speak against him,
I still remember [b] him,
Therefore my heart yearns for him;
I have great compassion [c] for him,"

declares the LORD.

[21] "Set up road signs;
put up guideposts. [d]
Take note of the highway, [e]
the road that you take.
Return, [f] Virgin [g] Israel,

31:13 [f] Isa 61:3
[g] S Isa 40:1
[h] Ps 30:11; S Isa 51:11
31:14 [i] ver 25
[j] Lev 7:35-36
[k] S Ps 36:8;
S Isa 30:23
31:15 [l] S Jos 18:25
[m] S Ge 37:35
[n] S Jer 10:20;
Mt 2:17-18*
31:16 [o] S Ps 30:5;
S Isa 25:8; 30:19
[p] S Ru 2:12;
S 2Ch 15:7 [q] Jer 30:3;
Eze 11:17
31:17 [r] S Job 8:7;
La 3:29 [s] Jer 30:20
31:18 [t] S Job 5:17
[u] Jer 50:11; Hos 4:16;
10:11 [v] S Ps 80:3
31:19 [w] S Ps 95:10;
S Jer 8:4; Eze 36:31
[x] Eze 21:12; Lk 18:13
[y] Ezr 9:6 [z] S Ps 25:7;
S Jer 22:21
31:20 [a] La 3:33
[b] S Isa 44:21
[c] S 1Ki 3:26; S Ps 6:2;
Isa 55:7; Mic 7:18
31:21 [d] Eze 21:19
[e] Isa 35:8; Jer 50:5
[f] Isa 52:11; S Jer 3:12
[g] ver 4

31:14 *abundance.* Either (1) a synonym for God's bounty (see Ps 36:8; 63:5; Isa 55:2) or (2) a reference to the special portions of the sacrificial animal reserved for the priests (see Lev 7:31–36).

C **31:15** Quoted in Mt 2:18, where Herod's orders to kill all the male infants "in Bethlehem and its vicinity" (Mt 2:16) are stated to be a fulfillment of this passage. *Ramah.* Located about five miles north of Jerusalem, it was one of the towns through which Jerusalem's people passed on their way to exile in Babylonia (see 40:1; cf. Isa 10:29; Hos 5:8). *Rachel.* Jacob's favorite wife (see Ge 29:30) and the grandmother of Ephraim and Manasseh (see Ge 30:22–24; 48:1–2), the two most powerful tribes in the northern kingdom. The name is used here to personify that kingdom (see note on v. 2).
31:16 *for your work will be rewarded.* Echoed in 2Ch 15:7. Here the work is the bearing and raising of children.
31:17 *hope for your descendants.* See 29:11. *children will return.* Cf. Hos 11:10–11.

31:18–19 *Restore...return...strayed.* The same Hebrew root underlies all three words (see 8:4–5 and notes).
31:18 *like an unruly calf.* See Hos 4:16 and note.

B **31:19** *beat my breast.* A gesture of mourning and grief (see Eze 21:12; Lk 23:48 and note). Similar expressions are found in other ancient literature, such as the Babylonian *Descent of Ishtar*, verse 21; Homer, *Iliad*, 15.397–398; 16.125; *Odyssey*, 13.198–199. *ashamed and humiliated.* See Isa 45:16. *youth.* Early history (see 2:2; 3:24–25; 22:21; 32:30; Isa 54:4; Eze 16:22).
31:20 *child in whom I delight.* Cf. Isa 5:7. *Though...I have great compassion for him.* See Hos 11:1–4,8–9. *my heart yearns.* See Isa 16:11.
31:21 The departing exiles are advised to set up markers along their path to exile so that in due time they will be able to find their way back to Judah (see notes on 30:1—33:26; 32:1). *road signs.* Tombstone-shaped markers (see 2Ki 23:17; Eze 39:15). *Virgin Israel.* See v. 4 and note.

31:22 ʰS Jer 2:23
ⁱS Jer 3:6 / Isa 43:19
ᵏS Dt 32:10
31:23 ʲS Jer 30:18
ᵐS Ge 28:3;
S Nu 6:24 ⁿS Isa 1:26
ᵒS Ps 48:1; S Isa 2:2
31:24 ᵖS Jer 30:18;
Zec 8:4-8 �ۣS Ver 12
31:25 ʳS Isa 40:29
ˢJn 4:14
31:26 ᵗZec 4:1
31:27 ᵘS Jer 16:14
ᵛHos 2:23
31:28 ʷS Job 29:2
ˣS Jer 29:28
ʸS Jer 18:8
ᶻS Dt 28:63; S 30:9;
S Jer 1:10; Eze 36:10-
11; Am 9:14
31:29 ᵃS Ge 9:25;
Dt 24:16; La 5:7
ᵇEze 18:2
31:30 ᶜS 2Ki 14:6;
S Isa 3:11; Gal 6:7
31:31 ᵈS Dt 29:14;
S Isa 42:6; S 54:10;
S Lk 22:20; Heb 8:8-
12*; 10:16-17
31:32 ᵉS Ex 24:8
ᶠDt 5:3 ᵍJer 11:4
ʰS Isa 54:5

return to your towns.
²² How long will you wander, ʰ
unfaithful ⁱ Daughter Israel?
The LORD will create a new thingʲ on earth—
the woman will return toᵃ ᵏ the man.'"

²³This is what the LORD Almighty, the God of Israel, says: "When I bring them back from captivity,ᵇ ⁱ the people in the land of Judah and in its towns will once again use these words: 'The LORD bless ᵐ you, you prosperous city, ⁿ you sacred mountain.' ᵒ ²⁴People will live ᵖ together in Judah and all its towns—farmers and those who move about with their flocks. ᵠ ²⁵I will refresh the wearyʳ and satisfy the faint." ˢ

²⁶At this I awoke ᵗ and looked around. My sleep had been pleasant to me.

²⁷"The days are coming," ᵘ declares the LORD, "when I will plant ᵛ the house of Israel and the house of Judah with the offspring of people and of animals. ²⁸Just as I watchedʷ over them to uprootˣ and tear down, and to overthrow, destroy and bring disaster,ʸ so I will watch over them to build and to plant," ᶻ declares the LORD. ²⁹"In those days people will no longer say,

'The parents ᵃ have eaten sour grapes,
and the children's teeth are set on edge.' ᵇ

³⁰Instead, everyone will die for their own sin; ᶜ whoever eats sour grapes—their own teeth will be set on edge.

³¹"The days are coming," declares the LORD,
"when I will make a new covenant ᵈ
with the house of Israel
and with the house of Judah.
³² It will not be like the covenant ᵉ
I made with their ancestors ᶠ
when I took them by the hand
to lead them out of Egypt, ᵍ
because they broke my covenant,
though I was a husband ʰ toᶜ them, ᵈ"

declares the LORD.

ᵃ 22 Or will protect   ᵇ 23 Or I restore their fortunes   ᶜ 32 Hebrew; Septuagint and Syriac / and I
turned away from   ᵈ 32 Or was their master

A **31:22** *unfaithful Daughter.* A personification of the people of Judah (see note on 2Ki 19:21), who are apostate (see 3:14,22). *create a new thing.* See Isa 42:9 and note. *return to.* Judah would someday return to the Lord and love him as her husband without reservation (see v. 32 and note). The meaning of the TNIV text note ("protect") may be that, instead of God protecting Israel, Israel will at last protect God's interests (cf. Zec 3:7 and note).

31:23 *bring . . . back from captivity.* See note on 29:14. *The LORD bless you.* See Ps 128:5; 134:3. *prosperous city.* Jerusalem (cf. Isa 1:21,26). *sacred mountain.* The temple hill (see Ps 2:6; 48:1–2; Isa 2:2–3; 11:9; 27:13; 66:20).

31:26 *I awoke.* Jeremiah had evidently received the previous divine revelation (beginning in 30:3) in a dream (for similar examples, see Da 10:9; Zec 4:1). *sleep . . . pleasant.* See Pr 3:24 and note.

31:27 *plant . . . offspring.* See Eze 36:8–11. The same Hebrew root underlies both words. *Israel and . . . Judah.* North and south would again be united (see 3:18 and note.)

31:28 *watched . . . watch.* See note on 1:12. *uproot . . . tear down . . . overthrow, destroy . . . build . . . plant.* See note on 1:10.

A **31:29** *The parents . . . set on edge.* Repeated in Eze 18:2. This was apparently a popular proverb that originated in a misunderstanding of such passages as Ex 20:5 and Nu 14:18, which teach that sins can have a negative effect on descendants. In the time of Jeremiah and Ezekiel, many people felt that God's hand of judgment against them was due not to their own sins but to the sins of their ancestors.

A **31:30** *everyone will die for their own sin.* See Dt 24:16; Eze 18:3,20; 33:7–18. Although group or collective responsi-

bility is an important concept, Jeremiah and Ezekiel emphasize individual responsibility as both preparation and explanation for the imminent destruction of Jerusalem, which the people might have been tempted to blame on the sins of their ancestors.

A **31:31–34** The high point of Jeremiah's prophecies, this passage is the longest sequence of OT verses to be quoted in its entirety in the NT (see note on Heb 8:8–12; see also Heb 10:16–17). Verse 31 contains the only OT use of the phrase "new covenant," which (together with its NT echoes) has come down to us (via Latin) as "new testament," the name that would later be applied to the distinctively Christian part of the Biblical canon.

A **31:31** *The days are coming.* See vv. 27,38; a phrase that often refers to the Messianic era. *make.* Lit. "cut" (see notes on 34:18; Ge 15:18). *new covenant.* See note on vv. 31–34. As the old covenant was put into effect with the shedding of the blood of animals (Ex 24:4–8), so the new would be put into effect with the shedding of the blood of Christ (see Mt 26:28 and TNIV text note; Mk 14:24; Lk 22:20 and notes; 1Co 11:25; 2Co 3:6; Heb 9:15; 12:24). *house of Israel . . . house of Judah.* The reunited people of God (see 3:18 and note).

31:32 *covenant I made with their ancestors.* See 7:23; 11:1–8; Ex 19:5; 20:22—23:19 and notes. The covenant at Sinai eventually became known as the "old covenant" (2Co 3:14) or "first covenant" (Heb 8:7; 9:15,18). *took them by the hand.* See Hos 11:3–4. *they broke my covenant.* See 11:10. The people, not God, were responsible for violating his covenant (see note on Isa 24:5). *I was a husband.* See 3:14 and note.

33 "This is the covenant I will make with the house of Israel
    after that time," declares the LORD.
"I will put my law in their minds[i]
    and write it on their hearts.[j]
I will be their God,
    and they will be my people.[k]
34 No longer will they teach[l] their neighbors,
    or say to one another, 'Know the LORD,'
because they will all know[m] me,
    from the least of them to the greatest,"

                                      declares the LORD.

"For I will forgive[n] their wickedness
    and will remember their sins[o] no more."

35 This is what the LORD says,

he who appoints[p] the sun
    to shine by day,
who decrees the moon and stars
    to shine by night,[q]
who stirs up the sea[r]
    so that its waves roar[s]—
    the LORD Almighty is his name:[t]
36 "Only if these decrees[u] vanish from my sight,"
    declares the LORD,
"will the descendants[v] of Israel ever cease
    to be a nation before me."

37 This is what the LORD says:

"Only if the heavens above can be measured[w]
    and the foundations of the earth below be searched out
will I reject[x] all the descendants of Israel
    because of all they have done,"

                                      declares the LORD.

38 "The days are coming," declares the LORD, "when this city will be rebuilt[y] for me from the Tower of Hananel[z] to the Corner Gate.[a] 39 The measuring line[b] will stretch from there straight to the hill of Gareb and then turn to Goah. 40 The whole valley[c] where dead bodies[d] and ashes are thrown, and all the terraces out to the Kidron Valley[e] on the east as far as the corner of the Horse Gate,[f] will be holy[g] to the LORD. The city will never again be uprooted or demolished."

31:33 [i] S Ex 4:15
[j] S Dt 6:6; S 2Co 3:3
[k] S Jer 11:4; Heb 10:16
31:34 [l] Jn 2:27
[m] S Isa 11:9; S Jn 6:45
[n] Ps 85:2; 130:4;
Jer 33:8; 50:20
[o] S Job 7:21;
S Isa 38:17; Mic 7:19;
Heb 10:17*
31:35 [p] Ps 136:7-9
[q] S Ge 1:16
[r] S Ex 14:21
[s] S Ps 93:3
[t] S Jer 10:16
31:36 [u] S Job 38:33;
Jer 33:20-26
[v] Ps 89:36-37
31:37 [w] S Job 38:5;
Jer 33:22 [x] Jer 33:24-26; Ro 11:1-5
31:38 [y] S Jer 30:18
[z] S Ne 3:1
[a] S 2Ki 14:13;
S 2Ch 25:23
31:39 [b] S 1Ki 7:23
31:40 [c] S Jer 2:23;
7:31-32 [d] S Jer 8:2
[e] S 2Sa 15:23; Jn 18:1
[f] S 2Ki 11:16
[g] S Isa 4:3; Joel 3:17;
Zec 14:21

31:33 *house of Israel.* Here includes both Israel and Judah (see v. 31 and note on 3:18). *put my law in their minds.* Internally (see Dt 6:6; 11:18; 30:14; Eze 11:19; 18:31; 36:26–27), in contrast to setting it before them externally (see 9:13; Dt 4:8; 11:32). *write it on their hearts.* So that it effectively governs their lives, in contrast to the ineffectiveness of merely presenting it in writing, though inscribed on durable stone (see Ex 24:4; 31:18; 32:15–16; 34:28–29; Dt 4:13; 5:22; 9:9,11; 10:4). *their God … my people.* See note on 7:23. The "new" covenant fulfills the "old" and achieves its purpose (cf. Mt 5:17 and note).

31:34 *No longer … teach their neighbors.* When the Lord has done his new work, there will no longer be among his people those who are ignorant of him and his will for human lives. True knowledge of the Lord will be shared by all—young and old, the peasant and the powerful (see 5:4–5 and notes; see also 32:38–40; Isa 54:13 and note; Eze 11:19–20; 36:25–27; Eph 3:12; Heb 4:16; 10:19–22). *Know.* In the experiential, not the academic, sense (see Ex 6:3 and note). *I will forgive … their sins.* The glorious basis of the new covenant (see Ro 11:27; Heb 10:14–17).

31:35 *appoints the sun … moon … stars.* See Ge 1:16–18 and

notes. *who stirs up … is his name.* The same line is found in Isa 51:15 (see Ps 46:3; Isa 17:12).

31:36 See 33:20–21,25–26. Just as God's creation order is established and secure, so also Israel will always have descendants.

31:37 *reject all.* Israel will continue to exist as a remnant (cf. Lev 26:44; Ro 11:5 and notes), even though a terrible judgment is about to sweep the kingdom of Judah away.

31:38–40 See Zec 14:10–11.

31:38 *this city.* Jerusalem. *Tower of Hananel … Corner Gate.* The eastern and western ends of the northern wall (see note on Zec 14:10).

31:39 *measuring line.* Mentioned in connection with restored Jerusalem also in Eze 40:3; Zec 1:16; 2:1. *Gareb … Goah.* Probably west of Jerusalem.

31:40 *valley.* Probably the Hinnom Valley (see 2:23 and note). *Horse Gate.* See note on Ne 3:28. *holy to the LORD.* See Zec 14:20 and note. *uprooted … demolished.* See note on 1:10. Jerusalem, the city of God, will endure. For the ultimate fulfillment, cf. Gal 4:26 and note; Rev 21:1–5.

32:1 ʰ 2Ki 25:1
ⁱ Jer 25:1
32:2 ʲ S 2Ki 25:1
ᵏ S Ps 88:8 ˡ S Ne 3:25
32:3 ᵐ Jer 26:8-9
ⁿ ver 28; Jer 21:4;
34:2-3
32:4 ᵒ Jer 34:21;
44:30 ᵖ S Jer 21:7;
38:18,23; 39:5-7;
52:9 ᵠ ver 24
32:5 ʳ Jer 39:7;
Eze 12:13 ˢ S 2Ki 25:7
ᵗ Jer 21:4; La 1:14
32:7 ᵘ S Jos 21:18
ᵛ Lev 25:24-25;
S Ru 4:3-4;
Mt 27:10*
32:8 ʷ ver 25
32:9 ˣ Jer 37:12
ʸ S Ge 23:16
32:10 ᶻ Ge 23:20
ᵃ S Isa 8:2
32:12 ᵇ ver 16;
Jer 36:4; 43:3,6; 45:1
ᶜ Jer 51:59
32:14 ᵈ Jer 36:4
32:15 ᵉ ver 43-44;
Isa 44:26; Jer 30:18;
Eze 28:26; Am 9:14-
15
32:16 ᶠ S ver 12
32:17 ᵍ Jer 1:6
ʰ S Ge 1:1; S Jer 10:16
ⁱ S Dt 9:29; 2Ki 19:15;
Ps 102:25 ʲ S 2Ki 3:18;
Jer 51:15; S Mt 19:26
32:18 ᵏ S Dt 5:10

JEREMIAH BUYS A FIELD

32 This is the word that came to Jeremiah from the LORD in the tenth ʰ year of Zedekiah king of Judah, which was the eighteenth ⁱ year of Nebuchadnezzar. ²The army of the king of Babylon was then besieging ʲ Jerusalem, and Jeremiah the prophet was confined ᵏ in the courtyard of the guard ˡ in the royal palace of Judah.

³Now Zedekiah king of Judah had imprisoned him there, saying, "Why do you prophesy ᵐ as you do? You say, 'This is what the LORD says: I am about to give this city into the hands of the king of Babylon, and he will capture ⁿ it. ⁴Zedekiah ᵒ king of Judah will not escape ᵖ the Babylonians ᵃ ᵠ but will certainly be given into the hands of the king of Babylon, and will speak with him face to face and see him with his own eyes. ⁵He will take ʳ Zedekiah to Babylon, where he will remain until I deal with him, ˢ declares the LORD. If you fight against the Babylonians, you will not succeed.' " ᵗ

⁶Jeremiah said, "The word of the LORD came to me: ⁷Hanamel son of Shallum your uncle is going to come to you and say, 'Buy my field at Anathoth, ᵘ because as nearest relative it is your right and duty ᵛ to buy it.'

⁸"Then, just as the LORD had said, my cousin Hanamel came to me in the courtyard of the guard and said, 'Buy my field ʷ at Anathoth in the territory of Benjamin. Since it is your right to redeem it and possess it, buy it for yourself.'

"I knew that this was the word of the LORD; ⁹so I bought the field ˣ at Anathoth from my cousin Hanamel and weighed out for him seventeen shekels ᵇ of silver. ʸ ¹⁰I signed and sealed the deed, ᶻ had it witnessed, ᵃ and weighed out the silver on the scales. ¹¹I took the deed of purchase—the sealed copy containing the terms and conditions, as well as the unsealed copy— ¹²and I gave this deed to Baruch ᵇ son of Neriah, ᶜ the son of Mahseiah, in the presence of my cousin Hanamel and of the witnesses who had signed the deed and of all the Jews sitting in the courtyard of the guard.

¹³"In their presence I gave Baruch these instructions: ¹⁴'This is what the LORD Almighty, the God of Israel, says: Take these documents, both the sealed ᵈ and unsealed copies of the deed of purchase, and put them in a clay jar so they will last a long time. ¹⁵For this is what the LORD Almighty, the God of Israel, says: Houses, fields and vineyards will again be bought in this land.' ᵉ

¹⁶"After I had given the deed of purchase to Baruch ᶠ son of Neriah, I prayed to the LORD:

¹⁷"Ah, Sovereign LORD, ᵍ you have made the heavens and the earth ʰ by your great power and outstretched arm. ⁱ Nothing is too hard ʲ for you. ¹⁸You show love ᵏ to thou-

---

ᵃ 4 Or *Chaldeans*; also in verses 5, 24, 25, 28, 29 and 43   ᵇ 9 That is, about 7 ounces or about 200 grams

---

32:1–44 Though with some reluctance (see v. 25), Jeremiah obeys the Lord's command to buy a field in Anathoth from his cousin (see vv. 8–9) even as the Babylonians are besieging Jerusalem (see vv. 2, 24).

32:1 *tenth year of Zedekiah … eighteenth year of Nebuchadnezzar.* 587 B.C., the year before Jerusalem was destroyed by the Babylonians (see 52:12–13). The siege began in 588 (see 39:1; 52:4).

32:2 *confined in the courtyard of the guard.* See Ne 3:25 and note. Jeremiah was imprisoned by King Zedekiah (see 37:21) and remained in the courtyard of the guard until Jerusalem fell (see 38:13,28; 39:14).

32:3–5 See 21:3–7; 34:2–5; 37:17. The fulfillment is recorded in 52:7–14.

32:5 *until I deal with him.* After his capture by the Babylonians, Zedekiah was taken to Babylon, where he eventually died (see 52:11). *you will not succeed.* See note on 29:4.

32:7 *Anathoth.* Jeremiah's hometown (see note on 1:1). *as nearest relative … duty to buy it.* In accordance with the ancient law of redemption (see Lev 25:23–25 and notes on 25:24–25; see also notes on Ru 2:20; 4:3).

32:8 *came to me in the courtyard.* Though imprisoned, Jeremiah was allowed to have visitors. *in the territory of Benjamin.* Some time earlier Jeremiah had been on his way home "to get his share of the property" in Benjamin (37:12), but he was arrested, falsely accused of treason and thrown into prison (see 37:13–16).

32:9 *so I bought.* In obedience to the Lord's command (see v. 7). *weighed out.* Coinage had not yet been invented. *seventeen shekels of silver.* See TNIV text note. The size of the field is un-

known, but the price was probably not exorbitant (contrast Ge 23:15; see note here).

32:10 *sealed.* Not to attest his signature (as, e.g., in Est 3:12; see note on Ge 38:18) but to guarantee the contents of the deed and keep it from being tampered with (see Isa 8:16; 29:11; Da 12:4,9; Rev 15:1–5).

32:11 *unsealed copy.* For ready reference, the authenticity of which would then be guaranteed by the sealed copy if the unsealed deed should be lost, damaged or changed (deliberately or otherwise). Examples of tied and sealed papyrus documents of the fifth and subsequent centuries B.C. have been found at Elephantine in southern Egypt, in the desert of Judah west of the Dead Sea, and elsewhere (see chart, p. xxiii).

32:12 *Baruch.* Means "blessed (by the LORD)." He was Jeremiah's faithful secretary and friend (see Introduction: Author and Date).

32:14 *put them in a clay jar so they will last a long time.* Documents found in clay jars at Elephantine (see note on v. 11) and Qumran (west of the Dead Sea) were preserved almost intact for more than 2,000 years (see essay, pp. 1595–1596).

32:15 Jeremiah's deed of purchase would enable him (or his heirs) to reclaim the field as soon as normal economic activity resumed after the exile.

32:17 See 27:5. *great power and outstretched arm.* See v. 21; see also note on 21:5. *Nothing is too hard for you.* See note on Ge 18:14. The Lord's reply to Jeremiah echoes these words (see v. 27).

32:18 *show love to thousands but … punishment for the parents' sins.* See Ex 20:5–6; 34:7; see also note on Ex 20:6. *bring … into the laps.* A symbol of retribution (see Ps 79:12; Isa 65:6–7; cf. Lk 6:38 and note). *Great and mighty God.* See Dt 10:17. *whose name* sands but bring the punishment for the parents' sins into the laps *l* of their children *m* after them. Great and mighty God, *n* whose name is the LORD Almighty, *o* 19great are your purposes and mighty are your deeds. *p* Your eyes are open to the ways of all; *q* you reward everyone according to their conduct and as their deeds deserve. *r* 20You performed signs and wonders *s* in Egypt *t* and have continued them to this day, both in Israel and among all nations, and have gained the renown *u* that is still yours. 21You brought your people Israel out of Egypt with signs and wonders, by a mighty hand *v* and an outstretched arm *w* and with great terror. *x* 22You gave them this land you had sworn to give their ancestors, a land flowing with milk and honey. *y* 23They came in and took possession *z* of it, but they did not obey you or follow your law; *a* they did not do what you commanded them to do. So you brought all this disaster *b* on them.

24"See how the siege ramps *c* are built up to take the city. Because of the sword, famine and plague, *d* the city will be given into the hands of the Babylonians who are attacking it. What you said *e* has happened, *f* as you now see. 25And though the city will be given into the hands of the Babylonians, you, Sovereign LORD, say to me, 'Buy the field *g* with silver and have the transaction witnessed. *h* ' "

26Then the word of the LORD came to Jeremiah: 27"I am the LORD, the God of the whole human race. *i* Is anything too hard for me? *j* 28Therefore, this is what the LORD says: I am about to give this city into the hands of the Babylonians and to Nebuchadnezzar *k* king of Babylon, who will capture it. *l* 29The Babylonians who are attacking this city will come in and set it on fire; they will burn it down, *m* along with the houses *n* where the people aroused my anger by burning incense on the roofs to Baal and by pouring out drink offerings *o* to other gods. *p*

30"The people of Israel and Judah have done nothing but evil in my sight from their youth; *q* indeed, the people of Israel have done nothing but arouse my anger *r* with what their hands have made, *s* declares the LORD. 31From the day it was built until now, this city *t* has so aroused my anger and wrath that I must remove *u* it from my sight. 32The people of Israel and Judah have provoked *v* me by all the evil *w* they have done—they, their kings and officials, *x* their priests and prophets, the people of Judah and those living in Jerusalem. 33They turned their backs *y* to me and not their faces; though I taught *z* them again and again, they would not listen or respond to discipline. *a* 34They set up their vile images *b* in the house that bears my Name *c* and defiled *d* it. 35They built high places for Baal in the Valley of Ben Hinnom *e* to sacrifice their sons and daughters to Molek, *f* though I never commanded—nor did it enter my mind *g*—that they should do such a detestable *h* thing and so make Judah sin. *i*

36"You are saying about this city, 'By the sword, famine and plague *j* it will be given into the hands of the king of Babylon'; but this is what the LORD, the God of Israel, says: 37I will surely gather *k* them from all the lands where I banish them in my furious anger *l* and great wrath; I will bring them back to this place and let them live in safety. *m* 38They will be my

32:36 *j* ver 24   32:37 *k* S Isa 11:12 *l* Jer 21:5 *m* S Lev 25:18; Eze 34:28; 39:26

32:18 *l* S Ps 79:12
m S Ex 20:5;
S Ps 109:14 *n* Jer 10:6
o S Jer 10:16
32:19 *p* S Job 12:13;
Da 2:20 *q* S Job 14:16;
S Pr 5:21; Jer 16:17
r S Job 34:11;
S Mt 16:27
32:20 *s* S Ex 3:20;
S Job 9:10 *t* Ex 9:16
u S Isa 55:13;
S Jer 13:11
32:21 *v* S Ex 6:6;
Da 9:15 *w* S Dt 5:15;
S Jer 6:12 *x* S Dt 26:8
32:22 *y* S Ex 3:8;
Eze 20:6
32:23 *z* S Ps 44:2;
78:54-55
a S Ex 16:28; S Jos 1:7;
S 1Ki 9:6; S Jer 11:8
b S Dt 28:64; 31:29;
Da 9:14
32:24 *c* S 2Sa 20:15;
S Jer 6:6 *d* S Jer 14:12
e Dt 4:25-26;
Jos 23:15-16
f S Dt 28:2
32:25 *g* S ver 8
h S Isa 8:2
32:27 *i* S Nu 16:22
j S Ge 18:14;
S 2Ki 3:18
32:28 *k* S 2Ch 36:17
l S ver 3; S Jer 21:10
32:29 *m* S 2Ch 36:1
n S Jer 19:13
o Jer 44:18 *p* S Jer 7:9
32:30 *q* S Ps 25:7;
S Jer 22:21 *r* Jer 8:19
s Jer 25:7
32:31 *t* 1Ki 11:7-8;
2Ki 21:4-5; Mt 23:37
u S 2Ki 23:27
32:32 *v* S 1Ki 14:9
w Da 9:8 *x* S Jer 2:26;
S 44:9
32:33 *y* S 1Ki 14:9;
S Ps 14:3; Jer 2:27
z S Dt 4:5; S Isa 28:9;
S Jer 7:13 *a* S Jer 7:28
32:34 *b* S 2Ki 21:4;
Eze 8:3-16 *c* Jer 7:10;
34:15 *d* S Jer 7:30
32:35 *e* Jer 19:2
f S Lev 18:21
g S Jer 19:5
h S 1Ki 14:24
i S Jer 25:7

---

is the LORD Almighty. See 31:35; Isa 54:5; Am 4:13; see also note on 1Sa 1:3.

32:19 *great are your purposes and...deeds.* See Ps 66:5; Isa 9:6; 28:29. *you reward everyone...as their deeds deserve.* Repeated verbatim from 17:10 (see note there; see also Ro 2:6 and note; 1Co 3:8; Eph 6:8).

32:20 *signs and wonders.* See v. 21; Ex 7:3; see also notes on Ex 3:12; 4:8.

32:21 Echoes Dt 26:8 (see also Dt 4:34). *mighty hand...outstretched arm.* See v. 17 and note on 21:5. *great terror.* See Ex 15:14–16.

32:22 *land flowing with milk and honey.* See 11:5; see also note on Ex 3:8.

32:24 *siege ramps.* See 6:6; 33:4; see also note on Isa 37:33. *sword, famine and plague.* See note on 14:12.

32:25 Jeremiah expresses his doubts concerning what must seem to him to be an unwise investment. Nevertheless, he remains the obedient servant (see vv. 8–9).

32:27 *the LORD, the God of the whole human race.* Echoes Nu 16:22; 27:16, emphasizing God's universal dominion. *Is anything too hard for me?* Responds to the description in Jeremiah's prayer (see v. 17 and note on Ge 18:14), stressing God's omnipotence. God is worthy of obedience because he is always

faithful in fulfilling his promises.

32:29 *burn it down.* See 21:10; 34:2; 37:8. *aroused my anger.* See 7:18; Dt 31:29. *burning incense...to Baal.* See 1:16 and note. *on the roofs.* See note on 19:13. *drink offerings to other gods.* See 7:18 and note; 19:13.

32:30 Echoes Dt 31:29. *youth.* See note on 31:19. *what their hands have made.* A reference to idols.

32:31 *remove it from my sight.* See 52:3; 2Ki 24:3.

32:32 *kings...officials...priests...prophets.* See 1:18 and note.

32:33 *again and again.* See note on 7:13. *not...respond to discipline.* See 2:30; 5:3; 7:28; 17:23.

32:34–35 Repeated from 7:30–31 (see notes there).

32:34 *house that bears my Name.* See 7:10 and note.

32:35 *Molek.* The god of the Ammonites (see 49:1,3; see also note on Lev 18:21). *nor did it enter my mind.* See 7:31 and note.

32:36 *You.* The people of Judah as a whole. *sword, famine and plague.* See note on 14:12. *but.* After judgment on the wicked comes restoration for the righteous.

32:37 See Dt 30:1–5. *furious anger and great wrath.* See note on 21:5. *bring them back...let them live.* See Eze 36:11,33; Hos 11:11. The Hebrew underlying the first phrase sounds like that underlying the second.

32:38 See 31:33; see also note on 7:23.

32:38 ⁿ Jer 24:7;
2Co 6:16*
32:39 ᵒ S 2Ch 30:12;
S Ps 86:11; Jn 17:21;
Ac 4:32 ᵖ S Dt 6:24;
S 10:16
32:40 ᵍ S Ge 9:16;
S Isa 42:6 ʳ S Dt 4:10
ˢ S Jer 24:7
32:41 ᵗ S Dt 28:63;
S Isa 62:4
ᵘ S Dt 28:3-12
ᵛ Jer 24:6; 31:28
ʷ Mic 7:18
32:42 ˣ La 3:38
ʸ S Jer 29:10
32:43 ᶻ ver 15
ᵃ Jer 33:12
32:44 ᵇ ver 10
ᶜ S Ru 4:9; S Isa 8:2
ᵈ S Jer 17:26
ᵉ S Ezr 9:9; Ps 14:7
33:1 ᶠ S Ps 88:8
ᵍ Jer 37:21; 38:28
ʰ Jer 13:3
33:2 ⁱ S Ps 136:6;
S Jer 10:16 / S Ex 3:15
33:3 ᵏ S Isa 55:6
ˡ S Job 28:11
33:4 ᵐ S 2Ki 25:1;
Eze 4:2 ⁿ Jer 32:24;
Eze 26:8; Hab 1:10
33:5 ᵒ Jer 21:4-7
ᵖ S Dt 31:17;
S Isa 8:17
33:6 ᵍ S Dt 32:39;
S Isa 30:26 ʳ S Isa 9:6
33:7 ˢ Jer 32:44
ᵗ Jer 30:3; Eze 39:25;
Am 9:14 ᵛ S Jer 24:6
ᵛ S Isa 1:26
33:8 ʷ S Lev 16:30;
Heb 9:13-14
ˣ S 2Sa 24:14;
S Jer 31:34
33:9 ʸ S Isa 55:13
ᶻ S Isa 60:18
ᵃ S Jer 3:17
ᵇ S Isa 64:2
33:10 ᶜ Jer 32:43

people, ⁿ and I will be their God. ³⁹ I will give them singleness ᵒ of heart and action, so that they will always fear ᵖ me and that all will then go well for them and for their children after them. ⁴⁰ I will make an everlasting covenant ᵍ with them: I will never stop doing good to them, and I will inspire ʳ them to fear me, so that they will never turn away from me. ˢ ⁴¹ I will rejoice ᵗ in doing them good ᵘ and will assuredly plant ᵛ them in this land with all my heart and soul. ʷ

⁴² "This is what the LORD says: As I have brought all this great calamity ˣ on this people, so I will give them all the prosperity I have promised ʸ them. ⁴³ Once more fields will be bought ᶻ in this land of which you say, 'It is a desolate ᵃ waste, without people or animals, for it has been given into the hands of the Babylonians.' ⁴⁴ Fields will be bought for silver, and deeds ᵇ will be signed, sealed and witnessed ᶜ in the territory of Benjamin, in the villages around Jerusalem, in the towns of Judah and in the towns of the hill country, of the western foothills and of the Negev, ᵈ because I will restore ᵉ their fortunes, ᵃ declares the LORD."

PROMISE OF RESTORATION

33 While Jeremiah was still confined ᶠ in the courtyard ᵍ of the guard, the word of the LORD came to him a second time: ʰ ² "This is what the LORD says, he who made the earth, ⁱ the LORD who formed it and established it—the LORD is his name: ʲ ³ 'Call ᵏ to me and I will answer you and tell you great and unsearchable ˡ things you do not know.' ⁴ For this is what the LORD, the God of Israel, says about the houses in this city and the royal palaces of Judah that have been torn down to be used against the siege ᵐ ramps ⁿ and the sword ⁵ in the fight with the Babylonians ᵇ: 'They will be filled with the dead bodies of the people I will slay in my anger and wrath. ᵒ I will hide my face ᵖ from this city because of all its wickedness.

⁶ 'Nevertheless, I will bring health and healing to it; I will heal ᵍ my people and will let them enjoy abundant peace ʳ and security. ⁷ I will bring Judah ˢ and Israel back from captivity ᶜ ᵗ and will rebuild ᵘ them as they were before. ᵛ ⁸ I will cleanse ʷ them from all the sin they have committed against me and will forgive ˣ all their sins of rebellion against me. ⁹ Then this city will bring me renown, ʸ joy, praise ᶻ and honor ᵃ before all nations on earth that hear of all the good things I do for it; and they will be in awe and will tremble ᵇ at the abundant prosperity and peace I provide for it.'

¹⁰ "This is what the LORD says: 'You say about this place, "It is a desolate waste, without people or animals." ᶜ Yet in the towns of Judah and the streets of Jerusalem that are

---

ᵃ 44 Or *will bring them back from captivity and Israel*   ᵇ 5 Or *Chaldeans*   ᶜ 7 Or *will restore the fortunes of Judah and Israel*

32:39 *singleness of heart.* See 24:7; 31:32 and note; Eze 11:19. *their children after them.* See Dt 4:9–10.
32:40 *everlasting covenant.* See Isa 55:3 and note; Eze 16:60; 37:26. Unlike the old covenant (see 31:32; Isa 24:5), the new covenant would never be broken. *inspire them to fear me.* See Dt 6:24; see also note on Ge 20:11. *never turn away from me.* See 26:3; Isa 53:6.
32:41 *rejoice in doing them good.* See Dt 30:9; Isa 62:5; 65:19.
32:43–44 *fields will be bought.* The field purchased by Jeremiah (see v. 9) is symbolic of the many fields that will be purchased in Judah after the Babylonian exile, when economic conditions return to normal (see note on v. 15).
32:43 *you.* See note on v. 36. *desolate waste, without people or animals.* See 4:23–26 and notes.
32:44 *territory of Benjamin.* See 1:1. Here Benjamin is mentioned first because it was the region in which Jeremiah's hometown was located (see vv. 7–8 and notes). *hill country . . . western foothills.* See note on Dt 1:7. *Negev.* See note on Ge 12:9. *restore their fortunes.* See TNIV text note; see also note on 29:14.
33:1–26 Concluding Jeremiah's "book of consolation" (see note on 30:1—33:26), the section is divided into two roughly equal parts: (1) vv. 1–13, which continue and build on ch. 32, and (2) vv. 14–26, which summarize a wider range of earlier passages in Jeremiah and elsewhere. This section is not found in the Septuagint (the pre-Christian Greek translation of the OT).
33:1 *still confined.* In 587 B.C. (see note on 32:1). *courtyard of the guard.* See 32:2 and note. *a second time.* Ch. 32 comprises the first time.

33:2 See 10:12; 32:17; 51:15; see also 31:35 and note.
33:3 *Call . . . and I will answer.* The prayers of God's people invite—and assure—God's response (see Ps 3:4; 4:3; 18:6; 27:7; 28:1–2; 30:8; 55:17; 118:5 and note; Mt 7:7; contrast 11:14). *great and unsearchable.* The Hebrew for this phrase usually refers to the formidable cities of Canaan and is translated "large, with walls up to the sky" (Dt 1:28; see Nu 13:28; Dt 9:1; Jos 14:12). *unsearchable things you do not know.* The Hebrew (with the change of one letter) for this phrase echoes Isa 48:6: "hidden things unknown to you." As the rest of ch. 33 demonstrates, the Lord will first judge his people (vv. 4–5) and then restore them in ways that will be nothing short of incredible (vv. 6–26).
33:4 *Jerusalem's houses*—including those of the king—were torn down so that their stones could be used to repair the city's battered walls (see Isa 22:10 and note). *siege ramps.* See 6:6 and note.
33:5 *fight with the Babylonians.* See 32:5. *dead bodies.* Of Jerusalem's defenders.
33:6–16 The glorious restoration of Jerusalem (see Isa 35:1–10 and notes).
33:6 *health and healing.* See 30:17; contrast 8:22.
33:7 *bring . . . back from captivity.* See v. 11, 26; see also note on 29:14. *Judah and Israel.* See note on 3:18.
33:8 *forgive all their sins.* The basis of the institution of the new covenant (see 31:34 and note; see also 50:20; Eze 36:25–26).
33:9 *tremble at the abundant prosperity.* See Hos 3:5 and note.
33:10 See 32:43 and note.

deserted, *d* inhabited by neither people nor animals, there will be heard once more ¹¹the sounds of joy and gladness, *e* the voices of bride and bridegroom, and the voices of those who bring thank offerings *f* to the house of the LORD, saying,

> "Give thanks to the LORD Almighty,
>   for the LORD is good; *g*
>   his love endures forever." *h*

For I will restore the fortunes *i* of the land as they were before, *j* ' says the LORD.

¹²"This is what the LORD Almighty says: 'In this place, desolate *k* and without people or animals *l*—in all its towns there will again be pastures for shepherds to rest their flocks. *m* ¹³In the towns of the hill *n* country, of the western foothills and of the Negev, *o* in the territory of Benjamin, in the villages around Jerusalem and in the towns of Judah, flocks will again pass under the hand *p* of the one who counts them,' says the LORD.

¹⁴" 'The days are coming,' declares the LORD, 'when I will fulfill the good promise *q* I made to the house of Israel and to the house of Judah.

¹⁵" 'In those days and at that time
    I will make a righteous *r* Branch *s* sprout from David's line; *t*
    he will do what is just and right in the land.
¹⁶In those days Judah will be saved *u*
    and Jerusalem will live in safety. *v*
This is the name by which it *a* will be called: *w*
    The LORD Our Righteous Savior.' *x*

¹⁷For this is what the LORD says: 'David will never fail *y* to have a man to sit on the throne of the house of Israel, ¹⁸nor will the Levitical *z* priests *a* ever fail to have a man to stand before me continually to offer burnt offerings, to burn grain offerings and to present sacrifices. *b* ' "

¹⁹The word of the LORD came to Jeremiah: ²⁰"This is what the LORD says: 'If you can break my covenant with the day *c* and my covenant with the night, so that day and night no longer come at their appointed time, *d* ²¹then my covenant *e* with David my servant— and my covenant with the Levites *f* who are priests ministering before me—can be broken and David will no longer have a descendant to reign on his throne. *g* ²²I will make the descendants of David my servant and the Levites who minister before me as countless *h* as the stars in the sky and as measureless as the sand on the seashore.' "

²³The word of the LORD came to Jeremiah: ²⁴"Have you not noticed that these people are saying, 'The LORD has rejected the two kingdoms *b i* he chose'? So they despise *j* my

---

a 16 Or He   *b* 24 Or families

33:10 *d* S Lev 26:32; S Jer 9:11
33:11 *e* S Ps 51:8; S Isa 24:8; S 51:3
f S Lev 7:12
g S 2Ch 7:3; Ps 25:8; S 136:1; Na 1:7
h S 1Ch 16:34; 2Ch 5:13; Ps 100:4-5
i Ps 14:7 / S Isa 1:26
33:12 *k* Jer 32:43
l ver 10 *m* Isa 65:10; Eze 34:11-15
33:13 *n* S Jer 31:5
o S Jer 17:26; Ob 1:20
p S Lev 27:32
33:14 *q* Dt 28:1-14; S Jos 23:15; S Jer 29:10
33:15 *r* S Ps 72:2
s S Isa 4:2 *t* S 2Sa 7:12
33:16 *u* S Isa 45:17
v S Jer 17:25; S 32:37
w Isa 59:14; Jer 3:17; Eze 48:35; Zep 3:13; Zec 8:3,16
x S 1Co 1:30
33:17 *y* S 2Sa 7:13; S 2Ch 7:18; Ps 89:29-37; S Lk 1:33
33:18 *z* S Dt 18:1
a S Nu 25:11-13; Heb 7:17-22
b Heb 13:15
33:20 *c* Ps 89:36
d S Ge 1:14
33:21 *e* Ps 89:34
f S Dt 18:1
g S 2Sa 7:13; S 2Ch 7:18
33:22 *h* S Ge 12:2; S Jer 30:19; Hos 1:10
33:24 *i* Eze 37:22
j S Ne 4:4

33:11 *joy and gladness ... bride and bridegroom.* The glorious reversal of the judgment proclaimed in 7:34; 16:9; 25:10. *those who bring thank offerings.* See note on 17:26. *restore the fortunes.* See note on 29:14.

33:13 *hill country ... towns of Judah.* See 17:26 and note; 32:44. *flocks ... pass under the hand ... counts them.* See Eze 20:37 and note.

33:15–16 Repeated from 23:5–6 (see notes there).

33:15 *what is just and right.* See note on Ps 119:121.

33:16 *it will be called.* Because of Jerusalem's intimate relationship to the Messiah, it is given the same name by which he is called in 23:6 (for other examples, see Jdg 6:24; Eze 48:35). But see TNIV text note.

A **33:17–26** In the face of the impending judgment in which the nation will be swept away and the promised land reduced to a desolate wasteland, all God's past covenants with his people appear to be rendered of no effect—his covenants with Israel, with David and with Phinehas (see chart, p. 20). This series of oracles, however, gives reassurance that the ancient covenants are not being repudiated, that they are as secure as God's covenant concerning the creation order and that in the future restoration they will all yet be fulfilled.

A **33:17** See 2Sa 7:12–16; 1Ki 2:4; 8:25; 9:5; 2Ch 6:16; 7:18. This passage is fulfilled ultimately in Jesus (see Lk 1:32–33 and notes).

A **33:18** See Nu 25:13. The priestly covenant with the Levites, like the royal covenant with David, was not a private grant to the priestly family involving only that family and the Lord. It was rather an integral part of the Lord's dealings with his people, in which Israel was assured of the ministry of a priesthood that was acceptable to the Lord and through whose mediation God's people could enjoy communion with him. That ministry was and is being fulfilled by Jesus, who administers a higher and better priesthood (see Ps 110:4; Heb 5:6–10; 6:19–20; 7:11–25). *Levitical priests.* See Dt 17:9,18.

33:20 *covenant with the day and ... the night.* See v. 25; 31:35–36. Although reference may be to God's sovereign establishment of the creation order in the beginning, more likely the covenant of Ge 9:8–17 (see Ge 8:22) is in view.

33:21 *covenant with the Levites.* See Mal 2:4.

A **33:22** In words that echo the covenant promises to the patriarchs (Abraham, Ge 22:17; Isaac, Ge 26:4; Jacob, Ge 32:12), the Lord assures the flourishing of the two mediatorial (royal and priestly) families and thus the continuation of this ministry in the spiritual commonwealth he has established with his people. This promise of a numerous progeny to both the royal and priestly families is no doubt fulfilled in that great throng who (will) reign with Christ (see Ro 5:17; 8:17; 1Co 6:3; 2Ti 2:12; Rev 3:21; 5:10; 20:5–6; 22:5; see also Mt 19:28; Lk 22:30) and who in Christ have been consecrated to be priests (see 1Pe 2:5,9; Rev 1:6; 5:10; 20:6; see also Isa 66:21; Ro 6:13; 12:1; 15:16; Eph 5:2; Php 4:18; Heb 13:15–16).

33:24 *two kingdoms.* Israel and Judah. But since the Hebrew uses a word here that commonly refers to families (see TNIV text

33:24 k S Jer 30:17;
Eze 36:20
33:25 l S Ge 1:18
m S Ps 148:6
n Ps 74:16-17
33:26 o S Lev 26:44
p S Isa 14:1 q ver 7;
Ps 14:7 r S Jer 30:18
34:1 s Jer 27:7
t 2Ki 25:1; Jer 39:1
34:2 u S 2Ch 36:11
v ver 22; Jer 32:29;
37:8
34:3 w S 2Ki 25:7;
S Jer 21:7
34:4 x Jer 52:11
34:5 y S 2Ch 16:14
z Jer 22:18
34:7 a Jos 10:3
b Jos 10:10; 2Ch 11:9
34:8 c S 2Ki 11:17
d S Ex 21:2; Lev 25:10,
39-41; Ne 5:5-8
34:9 e Dt 15:12-18

people and no longer regard them as a nation. k 25This is what the LORD says: 'If I have not made my covenant with day and night l and established the laws m of heaven and earth, n 26then I will reject o the descendants of Jacob p and David my servant and will not choose one of his sons to rule over the descendants of Abraham, Isaac and Jacob. For I will restore their fortunes a q and have compassion r on them.' "

WARNING TO ZEDEKIAH

34 While Nebuchadnezzar king of Babylon and all his army and all the kingdoms and peoples s in the empire he ruled were fighting against Jerusalem t and all its surrounding towns, this word came to Jeremiah from the LORD: 2"This is what the LORD, the God of Israel, says: Go to Zedekiah u king of Judah and tell him, 'This is what the LORD says: I am about to give this city into the hands of the king of Babylon, and he will burn it down. v 3You will not escape from his grasp but will surely be captured and given into his hands. w You will see the king of Babylon with your own eyes, and he will speak with you face to face. And you will go to Babylon.

4" 'Yet hear the LORD's promise to you, Zedekiah king of Judah. This is what the LORD says concerning you: You will not die by the sword; x 5you will die peacefully. As people made a funeral fire y in honor of your ancestors, the former kings who preceded you, so they will make a fire in your honor and lament, "Alas, z master!" I myself make this promise, declares the LORD.' "

6Then Jeremiah the prophet told all this to Zedekiah king of Judah, in Jerusalem, 7while the army of the king of Babylon was fighting against Jerusalem and the other cities of Judah that were still holding out—Lachish a and Azekah. b These were the only fortified cities left in Judah.

FREEDOM FOR SLAVES

8The word came to Jeremiah from the LORD after King Zedekiah had made a covenant with all the people c in Jerusalem to proclaim freedom d for the slaves. 9Everyone was to free their Hebrew slaves, both male and female; no one was to hold another Jew in bondage. e 10So all the officials and people who entered into this covenant agreed that they would free their male and female slaves and no longer hold them in bondage. They agreed,

a 26 Or will bring them back from captivity

---

note), the reference may be to the two mediatorial (royal and priestly) families, or to the families of Jacob and David (see v. 26). he chose. See Am 3:2 and note.
33:25–26 See v. 20 and note.
33:26 restore their fortunes and have compassion. Echoes Dt 30:3; see note on 29:14.
34:1—35:19 The first major division of the book (chs. 2–35) now comes to a close. Jeremiah's warnings and exhortations to Judah are concluded with a historical appendix (chs. 34–35), a technique used to conclude the third major division of the book (chs. 39–45) as well (see note on 45:1–5). Ch. 52, written by someone other than Jeremiah, serves as a fitting historical appendix to the entire book.
34:1–22 The chapter divides naturally into two parts (vv. 1–7 and 8–22), each of which dates to 588 B.C. (see notes on vv. 7, 21–22).
34:1–7 Jeremiah's warning to King Zedekiah parallels the prophet's similar admonition in 21:1–10 (see notes there).
34:1 kingdoms and peoples in the empire he ruled. Nebuchadnezzar's empire was vast (see Eze 26:7; Da 3:2–4; 4:1; cf. the similar description of the Medes in 51:28). fighting against Jerusalem. Subject nations were expected to supply troops to fight alongside those of their overlord (see 2Ki 24:2). In a 14th-century B.C. treaty between the Hittite ruler Mursilis II and Duppi-Tessub, king of the Amorites, Mursilis says, "If you do not send your son or brother with your foot soldiers and charioteers to help the Hittite king, you act in disregard of the gods of the oath." all its surrounding towns. See 19:15 and note.
34:2–3 See 32:3–5 and note; see also 39:4–7; Eze 12:12–13; 17:11–20.
34:4 not die by the sword. See 32:5; 38:17,20; 52:11; Eze 17:16.

34:5 funeral fire in honor of … the former kings. Not cremation (see 2Ch 16:14; 21:19; see also note on Am 6:10). Alas, master! Words of mourning at the death of a king (see 22:18; cf. 1Ki 13:30).
34:7 Lachish and Azekah. Solomon's son Rehoboam had fortified them (see 2Ch 11:5,9), but Lachish was later besieged (701 B.C.) during Hezekiah's reign by the Assyrian king Sennacherib (see 2Ch 32:9). A contemporary relief depicting Sennacherib's conquest states that he "sat on a throne and passed in review the plunder taken from Lachish." In 1935, 18 ostraca (broken pottery fragments used as writing material) were discovered at Lachish (see chart, p. xxiii), nearly all of them in the ruins of the latest occupation level (588 B.C.) of the Israelite gate-tower. Ostracon 4, written to the commander at Lachish shortly before the events described here, ends as follows: "We are watching for the fire-signals of Lachish … for we cannot see Azekah." See note on 6:1.
34:8–22 Contemporary with the events of 37:4–12 (see note on vv. 21–22).
34:8 proclaim freedom. See Lev 25:10 and note. freedom for the slaves. In accordance with the general provisions of the law of Moses (see Ex 21:2–11 and notes; Lev 25:39–55; Dt 15:12–18).
34:9 Hebrew. See Ex 21:2 and note. no one … hold another Jew in bondage. See Lev 25:39,42. Jew. A shortened form of "Judahite" (an inhabitant of the kingdom of Judah, where a remnant of the Israelites was still living). Strictly speaking, the term "Jew" is properly applied only to the OT people of God and their descendants from the time of the Babylonian exile on.
34:10 They … set them free. To gain God's blessing, and/or in the hope that the freed slaves would be more willing to help defend Jerusalem.

and set them free. [11]But afterward they changed their minds[f] and took back the slaves they had freed and enslaved them again.

[12]Then the word of the LORD came to Jeremiah: [13]"This is what the LORD, the God of Israel, says: I made a covenant with your ancestors[g] when I brought them out of Egypt, out of the land of slavery.[h] I said, [14]'Every seventh year each of you must free any other Hebrews who have sold themselves to you. After they have served you six years, you must let them go free.'[a][i] Your ancestors, however, did not listen to me or pay attention[j] to me. [15]Recently you repented and did what is right in my sight: Each of you proclaimed freedom to your own people.[k] You even made a covenant before me in the house that bears my Name.[l] [16]But now you have turned around[m] and profaned[n] my name; each of you has taken back the male and female slaves you had set free to go where they wished. You have forced them to become your slaves again.

[17]"Therefore, this is what the LORD says: You have not obeyed me; you have not proclaimed freedom to your own people. So I now proclaim 'freedom' for you,[o] declares the LORD—'freedom' to fall by the sword, plague[p] and famine.[q] I will make you abhorrent to all the kingdoms of the earth.[r] [18]Those who have violated my covenant[s] and have not fulfilled the terms of the covenant they made before me, I will treat like the calf they cut in two and then walked between its pieces.[t] [19]The leaders of Judah and Jerusalem, the court officials,[u] the priests and all the people of the land who walked between the pieces of the calf, [20]I will deliver[v] into the hands of their enemies who seek their lives.[w] Their dead bodies will become food for the birds and the wild animals.[x]

[21]"I will deliver Zedekiah[y] king of Judah and his officials[z] into the hands of their enemies[a] who seek their lives, to the army of the king of Babylon,[b] which has withdrawn[c] from you. [22]I am going to give the order, declares the LORD, and I will bring them back to this city. They will fight against it, take[d] it and burn[e] it down. And I will lay waste[f] the towns of Judah so no one can live there."

THE REKABITES

35 This is the word that came to Jeremiah from the LORD during the reign of Jehoiakim[g] son of Josiah king of Judah: [2]"Go to the Rekabite[h] family and invite them to come to one of the side rooms[i] of the house of the LORD and give them wine to drink."

[3]So I went to get Jaazaniah son of Jeremiah, the son of Habazziniah, and his brothers

---

a 14 Deut. 15:12

**Cross references (right margin):**

34:11 f Ps 78:37
34:13 g S Ex 24:8
  h S Dt 15:15
34:14 i S Ex 21:2
  j 2Ki 17:14; S Jer 7:26
34:15 k ver 8
  l S Jer 32:34
34:16 m Eze 3:20;
  18:24 n S Lev 19:12
34:17 o S Mt 7:2;
  Gal 6:7 p Jer 21:7
  q S Jer 14:12 r Jer 15:4;
  S 24:9; S 29:18
  S 34:18 s S Jer 11:10
  t S Ge 15:10
34:19 u S Jer 26:10;
  Zep 3:3-4
34:20 v Jer 21:7;
  Eze 16:27; 23:28
  w S Jer 11:21
  x S Dt 28:26
34:21 y S Jer 32:4
  z 2Ki 25:21; Jer 39:6;
  52:24-27 a S Jer 21:7
  b S 2Ch 36:10
  c Jer 37:5
34:22 d Jer 39:1-2
  e S Ne 2:17; Jer 38:18;
  39:8; Eze 23:47
  f S Lev 26:32;
  S Isa 1:7
35:1 g S 2Ch 36:5
35:2 h S 2Ki 10:15
  i S 1Ki 6:5

34:11 *afterward.* When the Babylonian siege was temporarily lifted due to Egyptian intervention (see vv. 21–22; 37:5,11). *took back the slaves they had freed.* In violation of Dt 15:12. *enslaved them.* Cf. 2Ch 28:10.

34:13 *land of slavery.* Lit. "house of slaves" (see Ex 13:3, 14; 20:2; Dt 5:6; 6:12; 8:14; 13:5; Jos 24:17; Jdg 6:8). The Israelites were to free their slaves because God had earlier freed the Israelites (see Dt 15:15).

34:14 *Every seventh year … let them go free.* A loose quotation of Dt 15:12.

34:15–16 *you repented … you have turned around.* The Hebrew for the two phrases is identical, providing an ironic play on words (see note on v. 18).

34:15 *house that bears my Name.* See 7:10 and note.

34:16 *you have … profaned my name.* By breaking the Lord's covenant, Zedekiah was a man whose word could not be trusted (see Eze 17:15,18). *go where they wished.* See Dt 21:14.

34:17 *sword, plague and famine.* See note on 14:12. *abhorrent to all the kingdoms of the earth.* See 15:4 and note.

34:18 *violated … walked.* The Hebrew root underlying both words is the same, again providing an ironic play on words (see note on vv. 15–16). *made … cut.* The Hebrew for the two words is identical. In ancient times, making a covenant involved a self-maledictory oath ("May thus and so be done to me if I do not keep this covenant"), which was often symbolized by cutting an animal in two and walking between the two halves (see Ge 15:18 and note). *between its pieces.* See note on Ge 15:17.

34:20 *food for the birds … wild animals.* See 7:33 and note.

34:21–22 Because of the arrival of the Egyptians on the scene,

the Babylonians in 588 B.C. temporarily lifted the siege of Jerusalem (see notes on v. 11; 37:3).

34:21 *withdrawn from you.* See the hope expressed in 21:2.

34:22 *I will bring them back.* See 37:8.

35:1–19 The family of the Rekabites, who obeyed their forefather's command, are an example and rebuke to the people of Judah, who have disobeyed the Lord (see v. 16). The mention of "Babylonian and Aramean armies" (v. 11) dates the chapter to no earlier than the eighth year of King Jehoiakim, who began his reign in 609 B.C., whose capital city of Jerusalem was besieged in 605 (see Da 1:1 and note) by Nebuchadnezzar and who rebelled against Nebuchadnezzar three or four years later—an unwise act that led to raids on his territory by Babylonians, Arameans and others (see 2Ki 24:1–2). (The raids are perhaps reflected in 12:7–13.)

35:1 *during the reign of Jehoiakim.* Chs. 35–36 (see 36:1) are a flashback to the reign of Jehoiakim (609–598 B.C.; see Introduction: Outline).

35:2 *Rekabite family.* A nomadic tribal group related to the Kenites (see 1Ch 2:55), some of whom lived among or near the Israelites (see Jdg 1:16; 4:11; 1Sa 27:10) and were on friendly terms with them (see 1Sa 15:6; 30:26,29). *side rooms of the house of the LORD.* Used for storage and/or as living quarters (see 1Ki 6:5; 1Ch 28:12; 2Ch 31:11; Ne 13:4–5).

35:3 *Jaazaniah.* Means "The LORD hears." It was a common name in Jeremiah's time (see 40:8; Eze 8:11; 11:1) and appears on a stamp seal (discovered at Tell en-Nasbeh north of Jerusalem and dating c. 600 B.C.), as well as on one of the Lachish ostraca (see note on 34:7). *Jeremiah.* Not the prophet.

35:4 *j* S Dt 33:1
k 1Ch 9:19
l S 2Ki 12:9; S 23:4
35:6 *m* S 2Ki 10:15
n S Lev 10:9; Nu 6:2-4; S Lk 1:15
35:7 *o* Heb 11:9
p S Ex 20:12;
Eph 6:2-3
35:8 *q* Pr 1:8;
Col 3:20
35:9 *r* 1Ti 6:6
35:11 *s* 2Ki 24:1
t S Jos 10:20; Jer 8:14
35:13 *u* Jer 11:6
v Jer 6:10; 32:33
35:14 *w* ver 6-10,16
x S Jer 7:13 *y* Isa 30:9
35:15 *z* S Jer 7:25
a S 2Ki 17:13;
S Jer 26:3 *b* S Isa 1:16-17; S Jer 4:1;
18:11; Eze 14:6; 18:30
c S Ex 20:3
d S Dt 4:40; Jer 25:5
e S Jer 6:10; S 7:26;
44:4-5
35:16 *f* S Lev 20:9;
Mal 1:6
35:17 *g* S Jos 23:15;
S 1Ki 13:34; Jer 21:4-7
h S Pr 1:24; Ro 10:21
i Jer 7:13
35:18 *j* S Ge 31:35
35:19 *k* S Isa 48:19;
Jer 33:17 *l* Jer 15:19
36:1 *m* S 2Ch 36:5
36:2 *n* S ver 4;
S Ex 17:14; S Ps 40:7;
Jer 30:2; Hab 2:2
o Eze 2:7

and all his sons—the whole family of the Rekabites. [4]I brought them into the house of the LORD, into the room of the sons of Hanan son of Igdaliah the man of God.*j* It was next to the room of the officials, which was over that of Maaseiah son of Shallum *k* the doorkeeper.*l* [5]Then I set bowls full of wine and some cups before the members of the Rekabite family and said to them, "Drink some wine."

[6]But they replied, "We do not drink wine, because our ancestor Jehonadab*a m* son of Rekab gave us this command: 'Neither you nor your descendants must ever drink wine.*n* [7]Also you must never build houses, sow seed or plant vineyards; you must never have any of these things, but must always live in tents.*o* Then you will live a long time in the land*p* where you are nomads.' [8]We have obeyed everything our ancestor *q* Jehonadab son of Rekab commanded us. Neither we nor our wives nor our sons and daughters have ever drunk wine [9]or built houses to live in or had vineyards, fields or crops.*r* [10]We have lived in tents and have fully obeyed everything our ancestor Jehonadab commanded us. [11]But when Nebuchadnezzar king of Babylon invaded*s* this land, we said, 'Come, we must go to Jerusalem *t* to escape the Babylonian*b* and Aramean armies.' So we have remained in Jerusalem."

[12]Then the word of the LORD came to Jeremiah, saying: [13]"This is what the LORD Almighty, the God of Israel, says: Go and tell *u* the people of Judah and those living in Jerusalem, 'Will you not learn a lesson *v* and obey my words?' declares the LORD. [14]Jehonadab son of Rekab ordered his descendants not to drink wine and this command has been kept. To this day they do not drink wine, because they obey their ancestor's command. *w* But I have spoken to you again and again, *x* yet you have not obeyed *y* me. [15]Again and again I sent all my servants the prophets *z* to you. They said, "Each of you must turn *a* from your wicked ways and reform *b* your actions; do not follow other gods *c* to serve them. Then you will live in the land *d* I have given to you and your ancestors." But you have not paid attention or listened *e* to me. [16]The descendants of Jehonadab son of Rekab have carried out the command their ancestor *f* gave them, but these people have not obeyed me.'

[17]"Therefore, this is what the LORD God Almighty, the God of Israel, says: 'Listen! I am going to bring on Judah and on everyone living in Jerusalem every disaster *g* I pronounced against them. I spoke to them, but they did not listen; *h* I called to them, but they did not answer.' " *i*

[18]Then Jeremiah said to the family of the Rekabites, "This is what the LORD Almighty, the God of Israel, says: 'You have obeyed the command of your ancestor *j* Jehonadab and have followed all his instructions and have done everything he ordered.' [19]Therefore, this is what the LORD Almighty, the God of Israel, says: 'Jehonadab son of Rekab will never fail *k* to have a descendant to serve *l* me.' "

JEHOIAKIM BURNS JEREMIAH'S SCROLL

36 In the fourth year of Jehoiakim *m* son of Josiah king of Judah, this word came to Jeremiah from the LORD: [2]"Take a scroll *n* and write on it all the words *o* I have spoken to you concerning Israel, Judah and all the other nations from the

---

a 6 Hebrew *Jonadab*, a variant of *Jehonadab*; here and often in this chapter   *b* 11 Or *Chaldean*

35:4 *sons.* Perhaps here in the sense of "disciples" (see Am 7:14 and note). *man of God.* A synonym for "prophet" (see 1Ki 12:22; see also note on 1Sa 9:9), emphasizing his relationship to the One who has called him. *Maaseiah.* Perhaps the man of the same name mentioned in 21:1; 29:25; 37:3. *doorkeeper.* One of three supervisors (see 52:24) over those who guarded the entrances to the temple (see 2Ki 12:9).
35:5 *bowls.* Large vessels, from which smaller cups would be filled.
35:6 *We do not drink wine.* A permanent vow taken by the Rekabites; cf. the Nazirites' temporary vow (see Nu 6:2-3,20; Jdg 13:4-7). Malkijah son of Rekab may have been a later renegade exception to the Rekabite vow, since he was "ruler of the district of Beth Hakkerem" (Ne 3:14), which means "house of the vineyard." *Jehonadab.* See 2Ki 10:15,23. Nearly 250 years before the days of Jeremiah, he helped King Jehu destroy Baal worship (at least temporarily) in the northern kingdom.
35:7 *must always live in tents.* Except during times of national emergency (see v. 11). *Then you will live a long time in the land.* An echo of Ex 20:12, where honoring one's parents is commanded.
35:8 *We have obeyed ... Jehonadab.* Contrast Judah's disobedience toward God (see v. 16).
35:11 See note on vv. 1-19.

35:13 *learn a lesson.* The Hebrew underlying this phrase is translated "respond(ed) to correction" in 2:30; 7:28 (see 5:3; 17:23 and note).
35:14-15 *again and again.* See note on 7:13.
35:15 See 25:4-5 and notes.
35:17 See 11:11.
35:19 *never fail to have a descendant to serve me.* See 33:18. Various traditions in the Jewish Mishnah (see note on Ne 10:34) claim that the Rekabites were later given special duties to perform in connection with the Jerusalem temple built after the return from Babylonian exile.
36:1—38:28 Three chapters united by the common theme of Jeremiah's suffering and persecution.
36:1-32 An account of King Jehoiakim's attempt to destroy Jeremiah's written prophecies.
36:1 *fourth year of Jehoiakim.* 605 B.C.—a critical year in Judah's history (see notes on 25:1; 46:2).
36:2 *scroll.* See notes on 30:2; Ex 17:14. *write on it.* To preserve Jeremiah's messages for future generations. *all the words I have spoken to you.* This "earliest edition" of Jeremiah's prophecies may have included all or most of chs. 1-26; 46-51. *began speaking to you in the reign of Josiah.* See note on 1:2.

36:2 *p* Jer 1:2; 25:3
36:3 *q* ver 7;
Eze 12:3; Am 5:15
r Isa 6:9; Mk 4:12
s 2Ki 17:13;
S Isa 44:22;
S Jer 26:3; Ac 3:19
t Jer 18:8
36:4 *u* S Jer 32:12
v Jer 51:59 *w* ver 18
x ver 2; Eze 2:9;
Da 7:1; Zec 5:1
36:6 *y* ver 9
z S Ex 4:16 *a* 2Ch 20:4
36:7 *b* Jer 37:20;
42:2 *c* S Jer 26:3
d S Dt 31:17
36:9 *e* ver 22
f S 2Ch 20:3
36:10 *g* ver 12,25;
Jer 29:3 *h* Jer 26:24
i Jer 52:25
j S Ge 23:10
36:12 *k* S 2Sa 8:17
l S Jer 26:22
m Jer 38:4
36:14 *n* ver 21
o ver 4
36:16 *p* S Ps 36:1
36:17 *q* Jer 30:2
36:18 *r* ver 4
36:19 *s* Jer 26:16
t S 1Ki 17:3
36:21 *u* ver 14
v 2Ki 22:10
36:22 *w* Am 3:15
36:23 *x* ver 2
y 1Ki 22:8
36:24 *z* S Ps 36:1

time I began speaking to you in the reign of Josiah *p* till now. ³Perhaps *q* when the people of Judah hear *r* about every disaster I plan to inflict on them, they will each turn *s* from their wicked ways; then I will forgive *t* their wickedness and their sin."

⁴So Jeremiah called Baruch *u* son of Neriah, *v* and while Jeremiah dictated *w* all the words the LORD had spoken to him, Baruch wrote them on the scroll. *x* ⁵Then Jeremiah told Baruch, "I am restricted; I am not allowed to go to the LORD's temple. ⁶So you go to the house of the LORD on a day of fasting *y* and read to the people from the scroll the words of the LORD that you wrote as I dictated. *z* Read them to all the people of Judah *a* who come in from their towns. ⁷Perhaps they will bring their petition *b* before the LORD, and will all turn *c* from their wicked ways, for the anger *d* and wrath pronounced against this people by the LORD are great."

⁸Baruch son of Neriah did everything Jeremiah the prophet told him to do; at the LORD's temple he read the words of the LORD from the scroll. ⁹In the ninth month *e* of the fifth year of Jehoiakim son of Josiah king of Judah, a time of fasting *f* before the LORD was proclaimed for all the people in Jerusalem and those who had come from the towns of Judah. ¹⁰From the room of Gemariah *g* son of Shaphan *h* the secretary, *i* which was in the upper courtyard at the entrance of the New Gate *j* of the temple, Baruch read to all the people at the LORD's temple the words of Jeremiah from the scroll.

¹¹When Micaiah son of Gemariah, the son of Shaphan, heard all the words of the LORD from the scroll, ¹²he went down to the secretary's *k* room in the royal palace, where all the officials were sitting: Elishama the secretary, Delaiah son of Shemaiah, Elnathan *l* son of Akbor, Gemariah son of Shaphan, Zedekiah son of Hananiah, and all the other officials. *m* ¹³After Micaiah told them everything he had heard Baruch read to the people from the scroll, ¹⁴all the officials sent Jehudi *n* son of Nethaniah, the son of Shelemiah, the son of Cushi, to say to Baruch, "Bring the scroll *o* from which you have read to the people and come." So Baruch son of Neriah went to them with the scroll in his hand. ¹⁵They said to him, "Sit down, please, and read it to us."

So Baruch read it to them. ¹⁶When they heard all these words, they looked at each other in fear *p* and said to Baruch, "We must report all these words to the king." ¹⁷Then they asked Baruch, "Tell us, how did you come to write *q* all this? Did Jeremiah dictate it?"

¹⁸"Yes," Baruch replied, "he dictated *r* all these words to me, and I wrote them in ink on the scroll."

¹⁹Then the officials *s* said to Baruch, "You and Jeremiah, go and hide. *t* Don't let anyone know where you are."

²⁰After they put the scroll in the room of Elishama the secretary, they went to the king in the courtyard and reported everything to him. ²¹The king sent Jehudi *u* to get the scroll, and Jehudi brought it from the room of Elishama the secretary and read it to the king *v* and all the officials standing beside him. ²²It was the ninth month and the king was sitting in the winter apartment, *w* with a fire burning in the firepot in front of him. ²³Whenever Jehudi had read three or four columns of the scroll, *x* the king cut them off with a scribe's knife and threw them into the firepot, until the entire scroll was burned in the fire. *y* ²⁴The king and all his attendants who heard all these words showed no fear, *z* nor did they tear

---

A **36:3** *Perhaps ... then.* If the people repent, the Lord will relent (see 18:7–10 and note; 26:3).
36:4 *Baruch.* See note on 32:12.
36:5 *I am restricted.* Perhaps because of his unpopular temple message(s) (see 7:2–15; 26:2–6), or perhaps because of the events recorded in 19:1—20:6.
36:6 *day of fasting.* Proclaimed because of a national emergency (cf. Joel 2:15), perhaps in this case the Babylonian attack of 605 B.C. (see Da 1:1 and note).
36:7 See v. 3 and note.
36:8 If the book presented Jeremiah's prophecies in chronological order, ch. 45 would appear after this verse (see Introduction: Outline).
36:9 *ninth month of the fifth year.* December, 604 B.C., during a time of cold weather (see v. 22).
B **36:10** Cf. 2Ki 23:2. *room.* See note on 35:2. *Gemariah son of Shaphan.* This official's name has been found in Jerusalem on a seal impression. *Shaphan.* Secretary of state under King Josiah (see 2Ki 22:3; see also notes on 26:24; 29:3). *entrance of the New Gate.* See 26:10 and note.
36:12 *Elnathan son of Akbor.* See note on 26:22.

B **36:18** *ink.* Mentioned only here in the OT (but see also 2Co 3:3; 2Jn 12; 3Jn 13). In ancient times, ink was made from soot or lampblack mixed with gum arabic, oil, or a metallic substance (as in the case of the Lachish ostraca; see note on 34:7).
36:19 The officials were understandably concerned about the safety of Jeremiah and Baruch (cf. 26:20–23).
36:20 *put.* For safekeeping (the Hebrew root for this word is translated "store" in Isa 10:28).
36:22 *ninth month.* See note on v. 9. *winter apartment.* Lit. "winter house" (as in Am 3:15), here probably a large room in the king's palace. *firepot.* A depression or container in the middle of the floor where coals were kept burning to warm the room.
36:23 Contrast King Josiah's desire to know the word of God and obey it (see 2Ki 22:11—23:3; 23:21–24). *columns.* Lit. "doors," so called because of their rectangular shape. *cut.* Lit. "tore." Instead of tearing his clothes in repentance (see note on v. 24), the king tore the prophet's scroll.
36:24 *attendants ... showed no fear.* See v. 31. Contrast the response of the "officials" (v. 12; see vv. 16,25). *nor did they tear their clothes.* Contrast the response of Jehoiakim's father, Josiah (see 2Ki 22:11; cf. 1Ki 21:27).

36:24 ᵃS Ge 37:29;
S Nu 14:6
36:25 ᵇver 12
ᶜS ver 10
36:26 ᵈMt 23:34
ᵉS 1Ki 17:3; Ps 11:1;
S Jer 1:8; 15:21
36:27 ᶠver 4
36:28 ᵍver 2
36:29 ʰS Isa 30:10
ⁱJer 33:12
36:30 ʲJer 52:2
ᵏS Isa 14:19
ˡS 2Ki 24:6
ᵐS Jer 8:2
36:31 ⁿEx 20:5
ᵒS Pr 29:1 ᵖS Pr 1:24
36:32 ᑫver 4
ʳEx 34:1; Jer 30:2
ˢver 23
37:1 ᵗS 2Ki 24:17
ᵘ1Sa 11:1; Eze 17:13
ᵛS 2Ki 24:8,12;
Jer 22:24
37:2 ʷS 2Ki 24:19
37:3 ˣver 17;
Jer 38:14 ʸJer 38:1
ᶻS 2Ki 25:18;
Jer 29:25; 52:24
ᵃS Ex 8:28;
S Nu 21:7; 1Sa 12:19;
1Ki 13:6; 2Ki 19:4;
Jer 42:2
37:4 ᵇver 15;
Jer 32:2
37:5 ᶜS Ge 15:18;
Isa 31:1; Eze 17:15
ᵈJer 34:21
ᵉS Isa 30:5; Jer 34:11
37:7 ᶠS Ge 25:22;
S 2Ki 22:18 ᵍver 5
ʰS 2Ki 18:21;
S Jer 2:36; La 1:7;
4:17
37:8 ⁱJer 38:3
ʲJer 21:10; 38:18; 39:8
37:9 ᵏJer 29:8;
S Mk 13:5
37:10 ˡJer 21:10
37:11 ᵐver 5

their clothes.ᵃ ²⁵Even though Elnathan, Delaiahᵇ and Gemariahᶜ urged the king not to burn the scroll, he would not listen to them. ²⁶Instead, the king commanded Jerahmeel, a son of the king, Seraiah son of Azriel and Shelemiah son of Abdeel to arrestᵈ Baruch the scribe and Jeremiah the prophet. But the LORD had hiddenᵉ them.

²⁷After the king burned the scroll containing the words that Baruch had written at Jeremiah's dictation,ᶠ the word of the LORD came to Jeremiah: ²⁸"Take another scrollᵍ and write on it all the words that were on the first scroll, which Jehoiakim king of Judah burned up. ²⁹Also tell Jehoiakim king of Judah, 'This is what the LORD says: You burned that scroll and said, "Why did you write on it that the king of Babylon would certainly come and destroy this land and wipe from itʰ both people and animals?"ⁱ ³⁰Therefore, this is what the LORD says about Jehoiakimʲ king of Judah: He will have no one to sit on the throne of David; his body will be thrown outᵏ and exposedˡ to the heat by day and the frost by night.ᵐ ³¹I will punish him and his childrenⁿ and his attendants for their wickedness; I will bring on them and those living in Jerusalem and the people of Judah every disasterᵒ I pronounced against them, because they have not listened.ᵖ' "

³²So Jeremiah took another scroll and gave it to the scribe Baruch son of Neriah, and as Jeremiah dictated,ᑫ Baruch wroteʳ on it all the words of the scroll that Jehoiakim king of Judah had burnedˢ in the fire. And many similar words were added to them.

JEREMIAH IN PRISON

37 Zedekiahᵗ son of Josiah was made kingᵘ of Judah by Nebuchadnezzar king of Babylon; he reigned in place of Jehoiachinᵃ ᵛ son of Jehoiakim. ²Neither he nor his attendants nor the people of the land paid any attentionʷ to the words the LORD had spoken through Jeremiah the prophet.

³King Zedekiah, however, sentˣ Jehukalʸ son of Shelemiah with the priest Zephaniahᶻ son of Maaseiah to Jeremiah the prophet with this message: "Please prayᵃ to the LORD our God for us."

⁴Now Jeremiah was free to come and go among the people, for he had not yet been put in prison.ᵇ ⁵Pharaoh's army had marched out of Egypt,ᶜ and when the Babyloniansᵇ who were besieging Jerusalem heard the report about them, they withdrewᵈ from Jerusalem.ᵉ

⁶Then the word of the LORD came to Jeremiah the prophet: ⁷"This is what the LORD, the God of Israel, says: Tell the king of Judah, who sent you to inquireᶠ of me, 'Pharaoh's army, which has marchedᵍ out to support you, will go back to its own land, to Egypt.ʰ ⁸Then the Babylonians will return and attack this city; they will captureⁱ it and burnʲ it down.'

⁹"This is what the LORD says: Do not deceiveᵏ yourselves, thinking, 'The Babylonians will surely leave us.' They will not! ¹⁰Even if you were to defeat the entire Babylonianᶜ army that is attacking you and only wounded men were left in their tents, they would come out and burnˡ this city down."

¹¹After the Babylonian army had withdrawnᵐ from Jerusalem because of Pharaoh's

---

ᵃ *1* Hebrew *Koniah,* a variant of *Jehoiachin*   ᵇ *5* Or *Chaldeans;* also in verses 8, 9, 13 and 14
ᶜ *10* Or *Chaldean;* also in verse 11

B **36:26** *Jerahmeel, a son of the king.* This official's name, along with his title, has been found on a seal impression discovered in a burnt archive near Jerusalem. *son of the king.* Since Jehoiakim was only about 30 years old (see 2Ki 23:36), the phrase probably is not to be understood literally but means "member of the royal court" (as also in 38:6; 1Ki 22:26; Zep 1:8).
36:30 *Jehoiakim . . . will have no one to sit on the throne.* His son Jehoiachin (see 2Ki 24:6) ruled only 3 months (see 2Ki 24:8) and then was captured and carried off to exile in Babylonia (see 2Ki 24:15), where he eventually died (see 52:33–34). *his body will be thrown out.* As punishment for the fact that he "threw" (v. 23) the prophet's scroll into the fire (see 22:18–19 and notes).
36:31 See 11:11; 19:15; 35:17. *attendants.* See note on v. 24.

B **36:32** *another scroll.* Cf. similarly Ex 34:1. *the scribe Baruch son of Neriah.* This precise identification has been found on two seal impressions (made with the same seal) discovered in the same burnt archive mentioned in the note on v. 26.
37:1—38:28 During the last two years of Zedekiah's reign (588–586 B.C.) Jeremiah is imprisoned by the authorities (see 20:2 and note).

C **37:1** See 2Ki 24:15,17–18. *Zedekiah.* Means "The LORD is my righteousness." See Introduction: Background. *reigned in place of Jehoiachin.* In 597 B.C. This fulfills the prophecy concerning Jehoiakim in 36:30.

C **37:3** *Zedekiah . . . sent . . . to Jeremiah.* See 21:1. *Jehukal son of Shelemiah.* Later became Jeremiah's enemy (see 38:1,4). *the priest Zephaniah son of Maaseiah.* See 21:1 and note. *pray . . . for us.* See 21:2 and note; perhaps to ask the Lord to make the temporary withdrawal of the Babylonians in 588 B.C. (see note on 34:21–22) permanent.

B **37:5** *Pharaoh's army.* The troops of Hophra (see 44:30). *marched out of Egypt.* Probably to help Zedekiah at his request; Lachish ostracon 3 (see note on 34:7) mentions a visit to Egypt made by the commander of Judah's army. All such ploys by Zedekiah would fail, however (see Eze 17:15,17). *Babylonians . . . withdrew.* To deal with the Egyptian threat (see 34:21 and note).
37:7 *Pharaoh's army . . . will go back . . . to Egypt.* Hophra would soon be defeated by Nebuchadnezzar (see note on Eze 30:21).
37:10 *wounded.* Lit. "pierced through," "mortally wounded." Though seriously handicapped, the Babylonians would still destroy Jerusalem.

army, [12]Jeremiah started to leave the city to go to the territory of Benjamin to get his share of the property[n] among the people there. [13]But when he reached the Benjamin Gate,[o] the captain of the guard, whose name was Irijah the son of Shelemiah, the son of Hananiah, arrested him and said, "You are deserting to the Babylonians!"[p]

[14]"That's not true!" Jeremiah said. "I am not deserting to the Babylonians." But Irijah would not listen to him; instead, he arrested[q] Jeremiah and brought him to the officials. [15]They were angry with Jeremiah and had him beaten[r] and imprisoned[s] in the house[t] of Jonathan the secretary, which they had made into a prison.

[16]Jeremiah was put into a vaulted cell in a dungeon, where he remained a long time. [17]Then King Zedekiah sent[u] for him and had him brought to the palace, where he asked[v] him privately,[w] "Is there any word from the LORD?"

"Yes," Jeremiah replied, "you will be delivered[x] into the hands of the king of Babylon."

[18]Then Jeremiah said to King Zedekiah, "What crime[y] have I committed against you or your attendants or this people, that you have put me in prison? [19]Where are your prophets[z] who prophesied to you, 'The king of Babylon will not attack you or this land'? [20]But now, my lord the king, please listen. Let me bring my petition before you: Do not send me back to the house of Jonathan the secretary, or I will die there."[a]

[21]King Zedekiah then gave orders for Jeremiah to be placed in the courtyard of the guard and given a loaf of bread from the street of the bakers each day until all the bread[b] in the city was gone.[c] So Jeremiah remained in the courtyard of the guard.[d]

JEREMIAH THROWN INTO A CISTERN

38

Shephatiah son of Mattan, Gedaliah son of Pashhur,[e] Jehukal[a][f] son of Shelemiah, and Pashhur son of Malkijah heard what Jeremiah was telling all the people when he said, [2]"This is what the LORD says: 'Whoever stays in this city will die by the sword, famine or plague,[g] but whoever goes over to the Babylonians[b] will live. They will escape with their lives; they will live.'[h] [3]And this is what the LORD says: 'This city will certainly be given into the hands of the army of the king of Babylon, who will capture it.'"[i]

[4]Then the officials[j] said to the king, "This man should be put to death.[k] He is discouraging[l] the soldiers who are left in this city, as well as all the people, by the things he is saying to them. This man is not seeking the good of these people but their ruin."

[5]"He is in your hands,"[m] King Zedekiah answered. "The king can do nothing[n] to oppose you."

[6]So they took Jeremiah and put him into the cistern of Malkijah, the king's son, which was in the courtyard of the guard.[o] They lowered Jeremiah by ropes[p] into the cistern; it had no water in it,[q] only mud, and Jeremiah sank down into the mud.[r]

[7]But Ebed-Melek,[s] a Cushite,[c] an official[d][t] in the royal palace, heard that they had put

---

a 1 Hebrew *Jukal*, a variant of *Jehukal*   b 2 Or *Chaldeans*; also in verses 18, 19 and 23   c 7 Probably from the upper Nile region   d 7 Or *a eunuch*

37:12 [n]S Jer 32:9
37:13 [o]S Jer 20:2
[p]Jer 21:9
37:14 [q]Isa 58:6;
Jer 40:4
37:15 [r]S Jer 20:2;
Heb 11:36
[s]S 1Ki 22:27 [t]ver 20;
Jer 38:26
37:17 [u]S ver 3
[v]S Ge 25:22; Jer 15:11
[w]Jer 38:16 [x]S Jer 21:7
37:18 [y]S 1Sa 26:18;
37:19 [z]S Jer 14:13;
Eze 13:2
37:20 [a]S ver 15
37:21 [b]S Lev 26:26;
Isa 33:16; Jer 38:9;
La 1:11 [c]S 2Ki 25:3
[d]Jer 32:2; 38:6,13,28;
39:13-14
38:1 [e]S 1Ch 9:12
[f]Jer 37:3
38:2 [g]Jer 34:17
[h]ver 17; S Jer 21:9;
39:18; 45:5
38:3 [i]S Jer 21:4,10
38:4 [j]S Jer 36:12
[k]S Jer 11:21
[l]S Isa 17:32
38:5 [m]S Jer 26:14
[n]1Sa 15:24
38:6 [o]S Jer 37:21
[p]S Jos 2:15
[q]S Ge 37:24
38:7 [s]Jer 39:16
[t]fn Isa 56:3-5;
Ac 8:27

37:12 *territory of Benjamin.* Where Jeremiah's hometown, Anathoth, was located (see note on 1:1). *get his share of the property.* While there was a brief lull in the Babylonian invasion, Jeremiah wanted to settle matters of estate with the other members of his family.

37:13 *Benjamin Gate.* See 38:7; see also note on Zec 14:10. *You are deserting to the Babylonians.* Irijah's fear was understandable, since Jeremiah recommended surrendering to the Babylonians (see 21:9; 38:2) and since many Judahites in fact defected (see 38:19; 39:9; 52:15).

37:14 *That's not true!* Lit. "A lie" (see 2Ki 9:12).

37:15 *had him beaten.* See 20:2 and note. *house of Jonathan.* Jeremiah would later look back on this prison as a place of great danger for him (see v. 20; 38:26).

37:16 *dungeon.* Lit. "house of the cistern" (see Ex 12:29).

37:17 *Zedekiah ... asked him privately.* Not wanting to do so in the presence of his officials, whom he apparently feared (see note on 38:5). *you will be delivered into the hands of the king of Babylon.* See 32:4; 34:3.

37:19 *your prophets.* False prophets (see Dt 18:22 and note).

37:20 *bring my petition before you.* See 36:7.

37:21 *courtyard of the guard.* A less objectionable prison than the dungeon of v. 16 (see note on 32:2). *street of the bakers.* Perhaps near the Tower of the Ovens (see note on Ne 3:11). *until all*

the bread ... was gone. The Hebrew word for "bread" is translated "food" in 52:6.

38:1 *Pashhur.* See note on 20:1. *Jehukal son of Shelemiah.* See note on 37:3. *Pashhur son of Malkijah.* See note on 21:1. *Jeremiah was telling all the people.* Though he was confined in the courtyard of the guard (see 37:21), he was allowed to have visitors and to speak freely to them (see 32:8,12).

38:2 Echoes 21:9 (see note there).

38:3 Echoes 32:28 (see note 34:2; 37:8).

B **38:4** *officials.* Those named in v. 1. *discouraging.* See Ezr 4:4; lit. "weakening the hands of," as in a similar situation in Lachish ostracon 6 (see note on 34:7): "The words of the officials are not good; they serve only to weaken our hands." Contrast Isa 35:3. *seeking the good.* The Hebrew underlying this phrase is translated "seek the peace and prosperity" in 29:7 (see note there). *good ... ruin.* The Hebrew for these words is translated "prosperity ... disaster" in Isa 45:7.

A **38:5** *The king can do nothing.* Not because of inability or lack of authority but through failure of nerve. He feared his own officials (see vv. 25–26; see also 37:17 and note).

38:6 *cistern.* A pit with a relatively small opening at the top (see 37:16 and note). *king's son.* See note on 36:26. *cistern ... had no water in it.* Zedekiah's officials wanted to kill Jeremiah (see v. 4), but not by taking his life with their own hands (cf. Ge 37:20–24).

38:7 ^u S Job 29:7
38:9 ^v S Ge 37:20
^w S Jer 37:21
38:11 ^x S Jos 2:15
38:13 ^y S Jer 37:21
38:14 ^z S Jer 37:3
^a S 1Sa 3:17
38:16 ^b Jer 37:17
^c Isa 42:5; 57:16
^d ver 4
38:17 ^e Jer 27:8
^f S Jer 21:9
38:18 ^g ver 3
^h S Jer 37:8
ⁱ S Jer 24:8; S 32:4
38:19 ^j Isa 51:12;
Jn 12:42 ^k Jer 39:9;
52:15
38:20 ^l Jer 11:4
^m S Dt 5:33; Jer 40:9
ⁿ Isa 55:3
38:22 ^o S Jer 6:12
^p S Job 19:14;
S Jer 13:21
^q S Job 30:19;
Ps 69:14
38:23 ^r S 2Ki 25:6
^s S Jer 32:4; Eze 17:15
^t S Jer 24:8
^u Jer 21:10; 37:8
38:24 ^v Jer 37:17

Jeremiah into the cistern. While the king was sitting in the Benjamin Gate, ^u ⁸Ebed-Melek went out of the palace and said to him, ⁹"My lord the king, these men have acted wickedly in all they have done to Jeremiah the prophet. They have thrown him into a cistern, ^v where he will starve to death when there is no longer any bread ^w in the city."

¹⁰Then the king commanded Ebed-Melek the Cushite, "Take thirty men from here with you and lift Jeremiah the prophet out of the cistern before he dies."

¹¹So Ebed-Melek took the men with him and went to a room under the treasury in the palace. He took some old rags and worn-out clothes from there and let them down with ropes ^x to Jeremiah in the cistern. ¹²Ebed-Melek the Cushite said to Jeremiah, "Put these old rags and worn-out clothes under your arms to pad the ropes." Jeremiah did so, ¹³and they pulled him up with the ropes and lifted him out of the cistern. And Jeremiah remained in the courtyard of the guard. ^y

ZEDEKIAH QUESTIONS JEREMIAH AGAIN

¹⁴Then King Zedekiah sent ^z for Jeremiah the prophet and had him brought to the third entrance to the temple of the LORD. "I am going to ask you something," the king said to Jeremiah. "Do not hide ^a anything from me."

¹⁵Jeremiah said to Zedekiah, "If I give you an answer, will you not kill me? Even if I did give you counsel, you would not listen to me."

¹⁶But King Zedekiah swore this oath secretly ^b to Jeremiah: "As surely as the LORD lives, who has given us breath, ^c I will neither kill you nor hand you over to those who are seeking your life." ^d

¹⁷Then Jeremiah said to Zedekiah, "This is what the LORD God Almighty, the God of Israel, says: 'If you surrender ^e to the officers of the king of Babylon, your life will be spared and this city will not be burned down; you and your family will live. ^f ¹⁸But if you will not surrender to the officers of the king of Babylon, this city will be given into the hands ^g of the Babylonians and they will burn ^h it down; you yourself will not escape ⁱ from them.' "

¹⁹King Zedekiah said to Jeremiah, "I am afraid ^j of the Jews who have gone over ^k to the Babylonians, for the Babylonians may hand me over to them and they will mistreat me."

²⁰"They will not hand you over," Jeremiah replied. "Obey ^l the LORD by doing what I tell you. Then it will go well ^m with you, and your life ⁿ will be spared. ²¹But if you refuse to surrender, this is what the LORD has revealed to me: ²²All the women ^o left in the palace of the king of Judah will be brought out to the officials of the king of Babylon. Those women will say to you:

> " 'They misled you and overcame you—
> those trusted friends ^p of yours.
> Your feet are sunk in the mud; ^q
> your friends have deserted you.'

²³"All your wives and children ^r will be brought out to the Babylonians. You yourself will not escape ^s from their hands but will be captured ^t by the king of Babylon; and this city will ^a be burned down." ^u

²⁴Then Zedekiah said to Jeremiah, "Do not let anyone know ^v about this conversation,

---

^a 23 Or *and you will cause this city to*

38:7 *Ebed-Melek.* Means "king's servant." *king was sitting in the Benjamin Gate.* See 37:13; see also note on Zec 14:10. Since a city gateway was often used as a courtroom or town hall (see notes on Ge 19:1; Ru 4:1), Zedekiah may have been settling various legal complaints on this occasion (see 2Sa 15:2–4) and would therefore have been in a position to help Ebed-Melek.
38:9 *no longer any bread in the city.* See 37:21 and note.
38:10 *thirty men.* The large number was probably to keep the officials (see v. 4) and their friends from trying to prevent Jeremiah's rescue.
38:11 *room under the treasury.* Perhaps a wardrobe storeroom (see 2Ki 10:22).

[A] **38:12** *Put these old rags . . . to pad the ropes.* Ebed-Melek's kindnesses to Jeremiah were evidence that he trusted in the Lord, and the Lord rewarded him (see 39:15–18).
38:13 *remained in the courtyard of the guard.* See note on 32:2.
38:14–26 Jeremiah's final interview with King Zedekiah.
38:14 *third entrance.* Mentioned only here; perhaps the king's private access to the temple. *something . . . anything.* Lit. "a word

. . . a word," probably referring to a "word" from the Lord (see 37:17).
38:16 *As surely as the LORD lives.* See note on Ge 42:15. *those who are seeking your life.* Zedekiah's officials (see v. 4 and note).
38:17–18 See vv. 2–3; 21:9–10; 32:3–4; 34:2–5. *surrender.* Lit. "come out" (see 2Ki 18:31; 24:12). *officers of the king of Babylon.* Those in charge of the siege of Jerusalem (see 39:3,13).

[A] **38:19** *I am afraid.* See v. 5 and note. If Zedekiah had trusted in the Lord, he would not have had to fear either officials or deserters (see Pr 29:25 and note). *gone over to the Babylonians.* See 37:13 and note. *mistreat me.* Do violence to me (see Jdg 19:25; 1Ch 10:4).
38:22 *women . . . in the palace . . . brought out to the officials.* Women in a conquered king's harem became the property of the conquerors (cf. 2Sa 16:21–22). *misled you and overcame you—those trusted friends of yours.* Repeated almost verbatim in Ob 7 (see 20:10 and note). Zedekiah's so-called friends were his officials (see v. 4) and false prophets (see 37:19). *feet are sunk in the mud.* Symbolic of great distress (see Ps 69:14).

or you may die. ²⁵If the officials hear that I talked with you, and they come to you and say, 'Tell us what you said to the king and what the king said to you; do not hide it from us or we will kill you,' ²⁶then tell ^w them, 'I was pleading with the king not to send me back to Jonathan's house ^x to die there.' "

²⁷All the officials did come to Jeremiah and question him, and he told them everything the king had ordered him to say. So they said no more to him, for no one had heard his conversation with the king.

²⁸And Jeremiah remained in the courtyard of the guard ^y until the day Jerusalem was captured.

THE FALL OF JERUSALEM

39:1–10pp — 2Ki 25:1–12; Jer 52:4–16

39 This is how Jerusalem ^z was taken: ¹In the ninth year of Zedekiah ^a king of Judah, in the tenth month, Nebuchadnezzar ^b king of Babylon marched against Jerusalem with his whole army and laid siege ^c to it. ²And on the ninth day of the fourth ^d month of Zedekiah's eleventh year, the city wall ^e was broken through. ^{f 3}Then all the officials ^g of the king of Babylon came and took seats in the Middle Gate: Nergal-Sharezer of Samgar, Nebo-Sarsekim ^a a chief officer, Nergal-Sharezer a high official and all the other officials of the king of Babylon. ⁴When Zedekiah king of Judah and all the soldiers saw them, they fled; they left the city at night by way of the king's garden, through the gate between the two walls, ^h and headed toward the Arabah. ^{b i}

⁵But the Babylonian ^c army pursued them and overtook Zedekiah ^j in the plains of Jericho. They captured ^k him and took him to Nebuchadnezzar king of Babylon at Riblah ^l in the land of Hamath, where he pronounced sentence on him. ⁶There at Riblah the king of Babylon slaughtered the sons of Zedekiah before his eyes and also killed all the nobles ^m of Judah. ⁷Then he put out Zedekiah's eyes ⁿ and bound him with bronze shackles to take him to Babylon. ^o

⁸The Babylonians ^d set fire ^p to the royal palace and the houses of the people and broke down the walls ^q of Jerusalem. ⁹Nebuzaradan commander of the imperial guard carried into exile to Babylon the people who remained in the city, along with those who had gone over to him, ^r and the rest of the people. ^{s 10}But Nebuzaradan the commander of the guard left behind in the land of Judah some of the poor people, who owned nothing; and at that time he gave them vineyards and fields.

¹¹Now Nebuchadnezzar king of Babylon had given these orders about Jeremiah through Nebuzaradan commander of the imperial guard: ¹²"Take him and look after him; don't harm ^t him but do for him whatever he asks." ¹³So Nebuzaradan the commander of the guard, Nebushazban a chief officer, Nergal-Sharezer a high official and all the other officers ^u of the king of Babylon ¹⁴sent and had Jeremiah taken out of the courtyard of the guard. ^v They turned him over to Gedaliah ^w son of Ahikam, ^x the son of Shaphan, ^y to take him back to his home. So he remained among his own people. ^z

---

^a 3 Or *Nergal-Sharezer, Samgar-Nebo, Sarsekim*   ^b 4 Or *the Jordan Valley*   ^c 5 Or *Chaldean*
^d 8 Or *Chaldeans*

38:26 ^w 1Sa 16:2
^x S Jer 37:15
38:28 ^y S Jer 37:21
^z S Jer 25:29
39:1 ^a S 2Ch 36:11
^b S 2Ki 24:1;
S Jer 28:14
^c S 2Ki 25:1; Jer 52:4;
Eze 4:3; 24:2
39:2 ^d Zec 8:19
^e S 2Ki 14:13
^f Eze 33:21
39:3 ^g ver 13;
Jer 21:4
39:4 ^h S Isa 22:11
ⁱ Eze 12:12
39:5 ^j S Jer 24:8;
S 32:4 ^k S Jer 21:7
^l S Nu 34:11
39:6 ^m S Isa 34:12
39:7 ⁿ S Nu 16:14;
Eze 12:13 ^o S Jer 2:35
39:8 ^p S Jer 34:22
^q S Ne 1:3; S Ps 80:12;
S Isa 22:5; La 2:8
39:9 ^r Jer 21:9
^s Jer 40:1; La 1:5
39:12 ^t S Pr 16:7;
Jer 15:20-21; 1Pe 3:13
39:13 ^u S ver 3
39:14 ^v S Ne 3:25;
Jer 37:21
^w S 2Ki 25:22
^x S 2Ki 22:12
^y S 2Ki 22:3 ^z Jer 40:5

38:26 See 37:20. *Jonathan's house.* See 37:15 and note.

38:27 *told them everything the king had ordered him to say.* Jeremiah was not obliged to give the officials the other information, which had been shared in confidence.

38:28 *remained in the courtyard of the guard.* See v. 13; see also note on 32:2.

39:1—45:5 The most detailed account in the OT of the Babylonian conquest of Jerusalem and its aftermath. The section concludes with a brief appendix (ch. 45).

39:1–10 A vivid summary of the siege and fall of Jerusalem and of the exile of its inhabitants (see 52:4–27).

39:1–2 Summarizes 52:4–7a.

39:1 *ninth year of Zedekiah ... tenth month.* The final Babylonian siege of Jerusalem began on the tenth day of the month (see 52:4; 2Ki 25:1; Eze 24:1–2), i.e., Jan. 15, 588 B.C.

39:2 *ninth day ... fourth month ... eleventh year.* July 18, 586 B.C. (see 52:5–6; 2Ki 25:2–3). The siege lasted just over two and a half years.

39:3 *took seats in the Middle Gate.* In fulfillment of 1:15. The Middle Gate may have been located in the wall separating the citadel of Mount Zion from the lower city, therefore

serving as a strategic vantage point for the invaders. *Nergal-Sharezer.* Means "Nergal [a god; see 2Ki 17:30], protect the king." One of the two men so named here (see v. 13) is probably Neriglissar, who later became a successor of Nebuchadnezzar as ruler of Babylonia (560–556 B.C.). *chief officer.* See v. 13; see also note on 2Ki 18:17. *high official.* See v. 13. The Hebrew for this phrase is cognate to Babylonian *rab mu(n)gi,* a high military official who sometimes served as an envoy to foreign rulers.

39:4–7 See 52:7–11; see also 2Ki 25:4–7 and notes.

39:4 *Arabah.* See note on Dt 1:1.

39:5 *plains.* The Hebrew for this word is the plural of the word for "Arabah" (v. 4).

39:8–10 See 52:12–16; see also 2Ki 25:8–12 and notes.

39:12 *look after him.* See note on 40:4.

39:14 *had Jeremiah taken out.* Either (1) a summary statement of Jeremiah's release from prison, the specific details of which are given in 40:1–6; or (2) a brief description of the first of two releases, the second of which (made necessary because Jeremiah had been arrested again by mistake in the confusion surrounding the capture and transporting of thousands of exiles) is detailed in 40:1–6. *courtyard of the guard.* See

39:16 *a* Jer 38:7
b Ps 33:11; Isa 14:27;
40:8; Jer 44:28;
La 2:17; S Mt 1:22
c S Jos 23:15; Jer 21:10
39:17 *d* Ps 34:22;
41:1-2
39:18 *e* S 1Sa 17:47;
Ac 16:31 *f* S Job 5:20
g S Jer 21:9; S 38:2
h S Jer 17:7; Ro 10:11
40:1 *i* S Jos 18:25;
1Sa 8:4; Mt 2:18
j S Dt 21:10;
S 2Ki 24:1;
S 2Ch 36:10; Na 3:10
40:2 *k* Ro 13:4
l S Isa 10:22
m S 2Ch 34:24;
S Ps 18:18; S Pr 8:36;
Gal 6:7-8
n S Jos 23:15
40:3 *o* S Pr 13:21;
Ro 6:23; Jas 1:15
p S Lev 26:33;
Dt 28:45-52; 29:24-
28; 31:17-18;
S 1Ki 9:9; Jer 22:8-9;
Da 9:14; Ac 7:39;
Ro 2:5-9
40:4 *q* Ps 105:18-20;
S Jer 37:14 *r* La 3:7
s S Ge 13:9
40:5 *t* S 2Ki 25:22
u 2Ki 22:12-14
v Ne 5:14; Jer 41:2
w Jer 44:2; Zec 1:12
x Jer 39:14
y S Ge 32:20;
S 1Sa 9:7
40:6 *z* ver 10;
Jdg 20:1; 1Sa 7:5-17
40:7 *a* S Ge 41:41;
S Ne 5:14
b S 2Ki 24:14;
S Ac 24:17; Jas 2:5
40:8 *c* ver 13
d ver 14; Jer 41:1,2
e ver 15; Jer 41:11
f S 2Sa 23:28
g S Dt 23:34
40:9 *h* Jer 5:19;
27:11; Ro 13:1-2;
Eph 6:5-8 *i* Eze 23:23
j S Jer 38:20; La 1:1
40:10 *k* S ver 6
l S Ge 27:28;
S Ex 23:16 *m* Ex 7:19;
2Co 4:7 *n* Dt 1:39
40:11 *o* S Nu 21:11;
25:1 *p* S Ge 25:30
q Jer 12:14

¹⁵While Jeremiah had been confined in the courtyard of the guard, the word of the LORD came to him: ¹⁶"Go and tell Ebed-Melek *a* the Cushite, 'This is what the LORD Almighty, the God of Israel, says: I am about to fulfill my words *b* against this city—words concerning disaster, *c* not prosperity. At that time they will be fulfilled before your eyes. ¹⁷But I will rescue *d* you on that day, declares the LORD; you will not be given into the hands of those you fear. ¹⁸I will save *e* you; you will not fall by the sword *f* but will escape with your life, *g* because you trust *h* in me, declares the LORD.' "

JEREMIAH FREED

40 The word came to Jeremiah from the LORD after Nebuzaradan commander of the imperial guard had released him at Ramah. *i* He had found Jeremiah bound in chains among all the captives *j* from Jerusalem and Judah who were being carried into exile to Babylon. ²When the commander *k* of the guard found Jeremiah, he said to him, "The LORD your God decreed *l* this disaster *m* for this place. *n* ³And now the LORD has brought it about; he has done just as he said he would. All this happened because you people sinned *o* against the LORD and did not obey *p* him. ⁴But today I am freeing *q* you from the chains *r* on your wrists. Come with me to Babylon, if you like, and I will look after you; but if you do not want to, then don't come. Look, the whole country lies before you; go wherever you please." *s* ⁵However, before Jeremiah turned to go, *a* Nebuzaradan added, "Go back to Gedaliah *t* son of Ahikam, *u* the son of Shaphan, whom the king of Babylon has appointed *v* over the towns *w* of Judah, and live with him among the people, or go anywhere else you please." *x*

Then the commander gave him provisions and a present *y* and let him go. ⁶So Jeremiah went to Gedaliah son of Ahikam at Mizpah *z* and stayed with him among the people who were left behind in the land.

GEDALIAH ASSASSINATED

40:7–9; 41:1–3pp — 2Ki 25:22–26

⁷When all the army officers and their men who were still in the open country heard that the king of Babylon had appointed Gedaliah son of Ahikam as governor *a* over the land and had put him in charge of the men, women and children who were the poorest *b* in the land and who had not been carried into exile to Babylon, ⁸they came to Gedaliah at Mizpah *c*—Ishmael *d* son of Nethaniah, Johanan *e* and Jonathan the sons of Kareah, Seraiah son of Tanhumeth, the sons of Ephai the Netophathite, *f* and Jaazaniah *b* the son of the Maakathite, *g* and their men. ⁹Gedaliah son of Ahikam, the son of Shaphan, took an oath to reassure them and their men. "Do not be afraid to serve *h* the Babylonians, *c i*" he said. "Settle down in the land and serve the king of Babylon, and it will go well with you. *j* ¹⁰I myself will stay at Mizpah *k* to represent you before the Babylonians who come to us, but you are to harvest the wine, *l* summer fruit and olive oil, and put them in your storage jars, *m* and live in the towns you have taken over." *n*

¹¹When all the Jews in Moab, *o* Ammon, Edom *p* and all the other countries *q* heard that

a 5 Or *Jeremiah answered*   *b* 8 Hebrew *Jezaniah*, a variant of *Jaazaniah*   *c* 9 Or *Chaldeans*; also in verse 10

---

note on 32:2. *Gedaliah son of Ahikam, the son of Shaphan.* See note on 26:24. *his home.* The governor's residence. An early sixth-century seal impression found at Lachish reads:"Belonging to Gedaliah [probably the man named in this verse], who is over the house."

39:15–18 See note on 38:12.

39:16 *Go and tell.* Though confined in prison, Jeremiah was permitted to have visitors (see note on 38:1). *I am about to fulfill my words against this city.* See 19:15.

39:17 *those you fear.* The court officials (see 38:1), who, in Ebed-Melek's judgment, had "acted wickedly" (38:9).

39:18 *escape with your life.* See note on 21:9. *you trust in me.* Ebed-Melek had expressed his faith in God by securing Jeremiah's release from the cistern (see 38:7–13; see also note on 38:12).

40:1—44:30 A lively narrative of the aftermath of the fall of Jerusalem. Chronologically, the chapters are the latest in the book (although 52:31–34 is later, it is part of the appendix and not of the book proper).

40:1 *The word came.* A heading introducing the prophecies of

Jeremiah after the exile, just as "The word . . . came" (1:2) introduces his prophecies from the time of his call up to the exile (see 1:3). *Nebuzaradan . . . released him.* See note on 39:14. *Ramah.* See note on 31:15. *chains.* Manacles that were fastened to the wrists (see v. 4; see also Job 36:8; Isa 45:14).

40:2–3 Nebuzaradan doubtless knew the basic content of Jeremiah's prophetic message against Jerusalem, and he here repeats it to the prophet in summary fashion.

40:4 *I will look after you.* Nebuzaradan promises to carry out Nebuchadnezzar's wishes concerning Jeremiah (see 39:12). *the whole country lies before you.* Cf. Abram's offer to Lot in Ge 13:9.

40:5–9 See 2Ki 25:22–24 and notes.

40:5 *Gedaliah son of Ahikam.* See note on 26:24. *provisions.* The Hebrew for this word is translated "allowance" in 52:34.

40:8 *Jaazaniah.* See note on 2Ki 25:23.

40:10 *harvest the wine, summer fruit and olive oil.* Nebuzaradan (see 39:9) had arrived in Jerusalem in August of 586 B.C. (see note on 2Ki 25:8). Grapes, figs and olives were harvested in the Holy Land during August and September.

the king of Babylon had left a remnant in Judah and had appointed Gedaliah son of Ahikam, the son of Shaphan, as governor over them, ¹²they all came back to the land of Judah, to Gedaliah at Mizpah, from all the countries where they had been scattered. ʳ And they harvested an abundance of wine and summer fruit.

¹³Johanan ˢ son of Kareah and all the army officers still in the open country came to Gedaliah at Mizpah ᵗ ¹⁴and said to him, "Don't you know that Baalis king of the Ammonites ᵘ has sent Ishmael ᵛ son of Nethaniah to take your life?" But Gedaliah son of Ahikam did not believe them.

¹⁵Then Johanan ʷ son of Kareah said privately to Gedaliah in Mizpah, "Let me go and kill ˣ Ishmael son of Nethaniah, and no one will know it. Why should he take your life and cause all the Jews who are gathered around you to be scattered ʸ and the remnant ᶻ of Judah to perish?"

¹⁶But Gedaliah son of Ahikam said to Johanan ᵃ son of Kareah, "Don't do such a thing! What you are saying about Ishmael is not true."

41 In the seventh month Ishmael ᵇ son of Nethaniah, the son of Elishama, who was of royal blood and had been one of the king's officers, came with ten men to Gedaliah son of Ahikam at Mizpah. While they were eating together there, ²Ishmael ᶜ son of Nethaniah and the ten men who were with him got up and struck down Gedaliah son of Ahikam, the son of Shaphan, with the sword, ᵈ killing the one whom the king of Babylon had appointed ᵉ as governor over the land. ᶠ ³Ishmael also killed all the men of Judah who were with Gedaliah at Mizpah, as well as the Babylonian ᵃ soldiers who were there.

⁴The day after Gedaliah's assassination, before anyone knew about it, ⁵eighty men who had shaved off their beards, ᵍ torn their clothes ʰ and cut ⁱ themselves came from Shechem, ʲ Shiloh ᵏ and Samaria, ˡ bringing grain offerings and incense ᵐ with them to the house of the Lord. ⁿ ⁶Ishmael son of Nethaniah went out from Mizpah to meet them, weeping ᵒ as he went. When he met them, he said, "Come to Gedaliah son of Ahikam." ᵖ ⁷When they went into the city, Ishmael son of Nethaniah and the men who were with him slaughtered them and threw them into a cistern. ᑫ ⁸But ten of them said to Ishmael, "Don't kill us! We have wheat and barley, olive oil and honey, hidden in a field." ʳ So he let them alone and did not kill them with the others. ⁹Now the cistern where he threw all the bodies of the men he had killed along with Gedaliah was the one King Asa ˢ had made as part of his defense ᵗ against Baasha ᵘ king of Israel. Ishmael son of Nethaniah filled it with the dead.

¹⁰Ishmael made captives of all the rest of the people ᵛ who were in Mizpah—the king's daughters ʷ along with all the others who were left there, over whom Nebuzaradan commander of the imperial guard had appointed Gedaliah son of Ahikam. Ishmael son of Nethaniah took them captive and set out to cross over to the Ammonites. ˣ

ᵃ 3 Or *Chaldean*

Cross references:
40:12 ʳ Jer 43:5
40:13 ˢ Jer 42:1
ᵗ ver 8
40:14 ᵘ S Ge 19:38;
2Sa 10:1-19; Jer 25:21;
41:10; 49:1 ᵛ S ver 8
40:15 ʷ S ver 8
ˣ S Dt 5:17; Mt 5:21-
22 ʸ S Ge 11:4;
S Lev 26:33;
Mt 26:31; Jn 11:52;
Jas 1:1 ᶻ S 2Ki 21:14;
S Isa 1:9; Ro 11:5
40:16 ʸ Jer 43:2
41:1 ᵇ S Jer 40:8
41:2 ᶜ Ps 41:9; 109:5
ᵈ S Jos 11:10;
Jer 40:15; Heb 11:37
ᵉ S Jer 40:5
ᶠ 2Sa 3:27; 20:9-10;
S Jer 40:8
41:5 ᵍ S Lev 19:27;
Jer 47:5; 48:37
ʰ S Ge 37:29;
S Lev 10:6;
S Mk 14:63
ⁱ S Lev 19:28
ʲ Ge 12:6; 33:18;
Jdg 9:1-57; 1Ki 12:1
ᵏ S Jos 18:1 ˡ 1Ki 16:24
ᵐ S Nu 16:40;
S Lk 1:9 ⁿ 1Ki 3:2;
6:38; 2Ki 25:9
41:6 ᵒ 2Sa 3:16
ᵖ Ps 5:9; Hos 7:11;
Rev 20:10
41:7 ᑫ S Ge 37:24;
2Ki 10:14
41:8 ʳ Isa 45:3
41:9 ˢ S 1Ki 15:22;
S 2Ch 16:6 ᵗ S Jdg 6:2
ᵘ S 2Ch 16:1
41:10 ᵛ Jer 40:7,12
ʷ Jer 38:23
ˣ S Jer 40:14

B **40:14** *Baalis.* Three royal inscriptions have been found that may relate to this king: (1) "King Ba'lay," as his name is written on an early sixth-century B.C. bottle discovered in Jordan; (2) "Ba'al-Yasha," an Ammonite king whose name appears on a stamp seal found at Tell el-'Umeiri in Jordan in 1984; (3) "Baalis king of [the Ammonites]," as his name reads on an Ammonite stamp seal that came to light in 1998. *Ammonites.* Ammon was among the nations that earlier had been allies against Babylonia (see 27:3 and note; see also Eze 21:18-32).
40:15 *privately.* See note on 38:16. *remnant.* See note on 6:9.
40:16 *not true.* Lit. "a lie" (see 37:14 and note). Gedaliah's naive faith in Ishmael's integrity would cost him his life (see 41:2).
41:1-3 See 2Ki 25:25 and note.
C **41:1** *one of the king's officers.* Ishmael's loyalty to Zedekiah might explain his assassination of Gedaliah, whom he considered to be a Babylonian puppet ruler. *they were eating together.* Ancient custom with respect to hospitality probably made Gedaliah assume that his guests would not harm him, much less kill him (see note on Jdg 4:21).
41:5 *had shaved off their beards, torn their clothes and cut themselves.* Signs of mourning (see 16:6 and note; see also note on Ezr 9:3), probably over the destruction of Jerusalem. *came.* In the "seventh month" (v. 1) to celebrate the Festival of Tabernacles (see note on Ex 23:16). *Shechem, Shiloh and Samaria.* Formerly

worship centers in the north (see notes on 7:12; Ge 12:6; see also Jos 24:25-26). After the northern kingdom was destroyed in 722-721 B.C., many Israelites made periodic pilgrimages to Jerusalem, especially during the reform movements of Hezekiah (see 2Ch 30:11) and Josiah (see 2Ch 34:9). *grain offerings and incense.* Bloodless offerings, since the altar of the Jerusalem temple had been destroyed. *house of the Lord.* Though the temple itself was in ruins, the site was still considered holy.
41:6 *weeping.* Pretending to share the sorrow of the mourners from the north.
41:7 *the city.* Mizpah. *cistern.* A favorite place to dispose of victims, whether living or dead (see 37:16 and note; 38:6).
41:8 *wheat and barley, olive oil and honey.* Supplies that Ishmael perhaps would have taken with him when he fled to Ammon (see v. 15).
B **41:9** *the cistern … was the one King Asa had made.* Probably as part of the fortifications Asa had built at Mizpah (see 1Ki 15:22), since cisterns were essential for storing water during times of siege. Archaeologists have discovered numerous cisterns in the ruins of ancient Mizpah (modern Tell en-Nasbeh, seven and a half miles north of Jerusalem).
41:10 *king's daughters.* Women who had been members of King Zedekiah's court, not necessarily daughters of the king himself (see note on 36:26). *Ammonites.* See 40:14 and note.

41:11 ʸ S Jer 40:8
41:12 ᶻ S Ex 14:14;
Jn 18:36 ᵃ S Jos 9:3;
Jn 9:7
41:13 ᵇ ver 10
41:14 ᶜ Jer 40:6
41:15 ᵈ Job 21:30;
S Pr 28:17
41:16 ᵉ Jer 42:1;
43:2 ᶠ Isa 1:9;
Jer 43:4; Eze 7:16;
14:22; Zep 2:9
41:17 ᵍ 2Sa 19:37
ʰ Ge 35:19; Mic 5:2
ⁱ Jer 42:14
41:18 ʲ S Nu 14:9;
Isa 51:12; Jer 42:16;
Lk 12:4-5
ᵏ S 2Ki 25:22
42:1 ˡ S Ge 40:13
ᵐ S Jer 41:16
ⁿ Jer 6:13; 44:12
42:2 ᵒ S Ge 20:7;
S Jer 36:7; Ac 8:24;
Jas 5:16 ᵖ S Isa 1:9
�q S Lev 26:22; La 1:1
42:3 ʳ ver 20;
Ps 86:11; S Pr 3:6;
S Jer 15:11
42:4 ˢ Ex 8:29;
1Sa 12:23 ᵗ S Jer 1:17
ᵘ S Nu 22:18;
S 1Sa 3:17
42:5 ᵛ 1Ki 22:16;
Ps 119:160; Ro 3:4
ʷ S Dt 7:9; Jn 8:26;
S 1Co 1:9
ˣ S Ge 31:48;
S Dt 4:26; S Isa 1:2;
S Ro 1:9; Rev 1:5
42:6 ʸ Dt 5:29; 6:3;
Jer 7:23; 22:15
ᶻ S ver 19; S Ex 24:7;
S Jos 24:24
42:8 ᵃ ver 1
ᵇ Jer 41:16;
S Mk 9:35; Lk 7:28;
Heb 8:11
42:9 ᶜ ver 2
ᵈ 2Ki 22:15
42:10 ᵉ Jer 43:4
ᶠ S Jer 24:6 ᵍ S Dt 30:9
ʰ S Dt 29:28; Ecc 3:2;
Jer 45:4; Eze 36:36;
Da 11:4 ⁱ S 2Ch 34:24;
Isa 30:26; S Jer 18:8
42:11 ʲ Jer 27:11
ᵏ S Nu 14:9;
S 1Sa 15:24; Ps 23:4;
Mt 10:28; 2Ti 1:7
ˡ Ps 18:27; 69:35;
S 119:94; S Isa 63:1;
Heb 7:25 ᵐ S Ps 3:7;
S Pr 20:22; S Jer 1:8;
Ro 8:31
42:12 ⁿ S Ex 3:21;
S 2Sa 24:14; 2Co 1:3
ᵒ S Ge 31:3; S Ne 1:9;
Ps 106:46
42:13 ᵖ S Dt 11:28
42:14 q S Nu 11:4-5;
S Dt 17:16; S Isa 30:2

[11]When Johanan[y] son of Kareah and all the army officers who were with him heard about all the crimes Ishmael son of Nethaniah had committed, [12]they took all their men and went to fight[z] Ishmael son of Nethaniah. They caught up with him near the great pool[a] in Gibeon. [13]When all the people[b] Ishmael had with him saw Johanan son of Kareah and the army officers who were with him, they were glad. [14]All the people Ishmael had taken captive at Mizpah[c] turned and went over to Johanan son of Kareah. [15]But Ishmael son of Nethaniah and eight of his men escaped[d] from Johanan and fled to the Ammonites.

FLIGHT TO EGYPT

[16]Then Johanan son of Kareah and all the army officers[e] who were with him led away all the people of Mizpah who had survived,[f] whom Johanan had recovered from Ishmael son of Nethaniah after Ishmael had assassinated Gedaliah son of Ahikam—the soldiers, women, children and court officials he had recovered from Gibeon. [17]And they went on, stopping at Geruth Kimham[g] near Bethlehem[h] on their way to Egypt[i] [18]to escape the Babylonians.[a] They were afraid[j] of them because Ishmael son of Nethaniah had killed Gedaliah[k] son of Ahikam, whom the king of Babylon had appointed as governor over the land.

42 Then all the army officers, including Johanan[l] son of Kareah and Jezaniah[b] son of Hoshaiah,[m] and all the people from the least to the greatest[n] approached [2]Jeremiah the prophet and said to him, "Please hear our petition[p] and pray[o] to the LORD your God for this entire remnant.[p] For as you now see, though we were once many, now only a few[q] are left. [3]Pray that the LORD your God will tell us where we should go and what we should do."[r]

[4]"I have heard you," replied Jeremiah the prophet. "I will certainly pray[s] to the LORD your God as you have requested; I will tell[t] you everything the LORD says and will keep nothing back from you."[u]

[5]Then they said to Jeremiah, "May the LORD be a true[v] and faithful[w] witness[x] against us if we do not act in accordance with everything the LORD your God sends you to tell us. [6]Whether it is favorable or unfavorable, we will obey the LORD our God, to whom we are sending you, so that it will go well[y] with us, for we will obey[z] the LORD our God."

[7]Ten days later the word of the LORD came to Jeremiah. [8]So he called together Johanan son of Kareah and all the army officers[a] who were with him and all the people from the least to the greatest.[b] [9]He said to them, "This is what the LORD, the God of Israel, to whom you sent me to present your petition,[c] says: [10]'If you stay in this land, I will build[f] you up and not tear you down; I will plant[g] you and not uproot you,[h] for I have relented concerning the disaster I have inflicted on you.[i] [11]Do not be afraid of the king of Babylon,[j] whom you now fear.[k] Do not be afraid of him, declares the LORD, for I am with you and will save[l] you and deliver you from his hands.[m] [12]I will show you compassion[n] so that he will have compassion on you and restore you to your land.'[o]

[13]"However, if you say, 'We will not stay in this land,' and so disobey[p] the LORD your God, [14]and if you say, 'No, we will go and live in Egypt,[q] where we will not see war or hear the trumpet[r] or be hungry for bread,'[s] [15]then hear the word of the LORD,[t] you remnant of Judah. This is what the LORD Almighty, the God of Israel, says: 'If you are determined to go to Egypt and you do go to settle there, [16]then the sword[u] you fear[v] will overtake you there, and the famine[w] you dread will follow you into Egypt, and there you will die.[x] [17]In-

---

ᵃ **18** Or *Chaldeans*   ᵇ **1** Hebrew; Septuagint (see also 43:2) *Azariah*

42:14 ʳ S Jos 6:20; S Mt 24:31 ˢ S Dt 8:3; 1Sa 2:5; Pr 10:3; Isa 65:13; Mt 4:2-4   **42:15** ᵗ Jer 44:24   **42:16** ᵘ S Lev 26:33; Eze 11:8; 14:17
ᵛ S Jer 41:18 ʷ S Ge 41:55 ˣ S Ge 2:17; 2Ch 25:4; S Job 21:20; Eze 3:19; 18:4

41:12 *great pool in Gibeon.* Perhaps the same as the one mentioned in 2Sa 2:13.

41:15 *eight of his men escaped.* Ishmael lost only two of his men (see v. 2) in the fight with Johanan.

41:17 *Geruth Kimham.* Perhaps means "lodging place of Kimham," a friend of David who returned with him to Jerusalem after Absalom's death (see 2Sa 19:37-40).

42:1 *Jezaniah son of Hoshaiah.* Possibly the same as "Jaazaniah the son of the Maacathite" (40:8; see TNIV text note there). Apparently Jezaniah was also known as Azariah (see TNIV text note; see also 43:2), as was King Uzziah (see TNIV text notes on 2Ki 14:21; 2Ch 26:1).

42:2 *Jeremiah.* Had probably been among the "people of Mizpah who had survived" (41:16). *hear our petition.* See v.9; 37:20. *remnant.* See vv. 15,19; see also note on 6:9.

42:3 The people may be asking the Lord to confirm what they sincerely believe to be their only option: flight to Egypt (see v. 17; 41:17).

42:6 *we will obey the LORD our God.* Though they twice declare here their desire to do God's will, they soon demonstrate that they have already decided to follow their own inclinations (see 43:2).

42:7 *Ten days later.* Jeremiah does not bring God's word to the people until he is sure of it himself (see 28:10-17).

42:10 *build you up...tear you down...plant...uproot.* See 1:10 and note; see also 31:4,28; 33:7.

42:12 *he will have compassion on you.* For similar examples, see Ge 43:14; 1Ki 8:50.

42:16 *the sword you fear will overtake you there.* See 43:11 and note.

deed, all who are determined to go to Egypt to settle there will die by the sword, famine and plague;^y not one of them will survive or escape the disaster I will bring on them.' ¹⁸This is what the LORD Almighty, the God of Israel, says: 'As my anger and wrath^z have been poured out on those who lived in Jerusalem,^a so will my wrath be poured out on you when you go to Egypt. You will be a curse^{a b} and an object of horror,^c a curse^a and an object of reproach;^d you will never see this place again.'^e

¹⁹"Remnant^f of Judah, the LORD has told you, 'Do not go to Egypt.'^g Be sure of this: I warn you today ²⁰that you made a fatal mistake when you sent me to the LORD your God and said, 'Pray to the LORD our God for us; tell us everything he says and we will do it.'^h ²¹I have told you today, but you still have not obeyed the LORD your God in all he sent me to tell you.ⁱ ²²So now, be sure of this: You will die by the sword, famine^j and plague^k in the place where you want to go to settle."^l

43

When Jeremiah had finished telling the people all the words of the LORD their God—everything the LORD had sent him to tell them^m—²Azariah son of Hoshaiahⁿ and Johanan^o son of Kareah and all the arrogant^p men said to Jeremiah, "You are lying!^q The LORD our God has not sent you to say, 'You must not go to Egypt to settle there.'^r ³But Baruch^s son of Neriah is inciting you against us to hand us over to the Babylonians,^b so they may kill us or carry us into exile to Babylon."^t

⁴So Johanan son of Kareah and all the army officers and all the people^u disobeyed the LORD's command^v to stay in the land of Judah.^w ⁵Instead, Johanan son of Kareah and all the army officers led away all the remnant of Judah who had come back to live in the land of Judah from all the nations where they had been scattered.^x ⁶They also led away all those whom Nebuzaradan commander of the imperial guard had left with Gedaliah son of Ahikam, the son of Shaphan—the men, the women,^y the children and the king's daughters. And they took Jeremiah the prophet and Baruch^z son of Neriah along with them. ⁷So they entered Egypt^a in disobedience to the LORD and went as far as Tahpanhes.^b

⁸In Tahpanhes^c the word of the LORD came to Jeremiah: ⁹"While the Jews are watching, take some large stones^d with you and bury them in clay in the brick^e pavement at the entrance to Pharaoh's palace^f in Tahpanhes. ¹⁰Then say to them, 'This is what the LORD Almighty, the God of Israel, says: I will send for my servant^g Nebuchadnezzar^h king of Babylon, and I will set his throneⁱ over these stones I have buried here; he will spread his royal canopy^j above them. ¹¹He will come and attack Egypt,^k bringing death^l to those destined^m for death, captivity to those destined for captivity,ⁿ and the sword to those destined for the sword.^o ¹²He will set fire^p to the temples^q of the gods^r of Egypt; he will burn their temples and take their gods captive.^s As a shepherd picks^t his garment clean of lice, so he will pick Egypt clean and depart. ¹³There in the temple of the sun^{c u} in Egypt he will demolish the sacred pillars^v and will burn down the temples of the gods of Egypt.' "

---

^a 18 That is, your name will be used in cursing (see Jer. 29:22); or, others will see that you are cursed.
^b 3 Or *Chaldeans* ^c 13 Or *in Heliopolis*

^{43:12} ^rver 13; S Ex 12:12; S Isa 2:18; Jer 46:25; Eze 30:13; Zec 13:2 ^sDa 11:8 ^tS Ps 104:2; 109:18-19 ^{43:13} ^uS Ge 1:16; Isa 19:18 *fn*; S Dt 4:19 ^vJer 52:17; Eze 26:11

42:17 ^yver 22; S Jer 21:7; 44:13
42:18 ^zDt 29:18-20; S 2Ch 12:7
^aS 2Ch 36:19; Jer 39:1-9
^bS Nu 5:27; S Jer 25:18
^cS Dt 28:25,37
^dS Ps 44:13
^eS Jer 22:10
42:19 ^fJer 40:15
Isa 30:7; S Jer 43:2; 44:16
42:20 ^hver 2; Eze 14:7-8
42:21 ⁱS Ex 24:7; 12:2; Zec 7:11-12
42:22 ^jS Isa 1:28
^kS ver 17; Jer 24:10; Eze 6:11 ^lS Jer 15:2; Hos 9:6
43:1 ^mJer 26:8; 42:9-22
43:2 ⁿS Jer 41:16
^oJer 40:16
^pS Ne 9:29; 1Co 4:18-21 ^qS Ge 19:14;
S Dt 13:3; Ro 9:1; 2Co 11:31; 1Ti 2:7
^rS Ex 24:7; 2Ki 25:24; Jer 18:19; S 42:19; Eze 37:14
43:3 ^sS Jer 32:12
^tJer 38:4; 41:18; 52:30
43:4 ^uS Jer 41:16
^v2Ch 25:16; Jer 42:5-6 ^wJer 42:10
43:5 ^xJer 40:12
43:6 ^yS Jer 6:12
^zS Jer 32:12
43:7 ^aS 2Ki 25:26
^bJer 2:16; 44:1; 46:14; Eze 30:18
43:8 ^cPs 139:7; Jer 2:16
43:9 ^dS Ge 31:45-53; Jos 4:1-7; 1Ki 18:31-32 ^eS Ge 11:3
^fS Ge 47:14
43:10 ^gS Isa 44:28; 45:1; Jer 25:9; 27:6 ^hJer 46:13 ⁱJer 49:38 ^jS Ps 18:11
43:11 ^kJer 46:13-26; Eze 29:19-20 ^lS Pr 11:19; Ro 6:23 ^mS Ps 49:14; Heb 9:27
ⁿS Dt 28:64; Rev 13:10 ^oS Jer 15:2; Eze 32:11; Zec 11:9
43:12 ^pS Jos 7:15
^qS 1Ki 16:32

42:17–18 See 44:11–14.
42:17 *sword, famine and plague.* See note on 14:12.
42:18 *my anger and wrath have been poured out.* See 7:20; 44:6. *curse…reproach.* See TNIV text note; see also notes on 24:9; 25:18; cf. 29:18. *this place.* Jerusalem.
42:19 *I warn you.* See 11:7.
43:2 *Azariah.* See note on 42:1. *arrogant men.* They demonstrate themselves to be such by their words.
43:3 *Baruch.* See note on 32:12. Jeremiah's opponents decide to put the blame on someone they consider less spiritually formidable than the prophet himself.
43:5 *remnant of Judah.* Jews who had fled from the Babylonians to neighboring countries (see 40:11–12).
43:6 *king's daughters.* See note on 41:10. *Jeremiah…and Baruch.* No doubt they went to Egypt unwillingly, in the light of 32:6–15; 40:1–6; 42:13–22.
43:7 *Tahpanhes.* See note on 2:16.
43:9 *Pharaoh's palace.* Not necessarily his main residence. One of the Elephantine papyri (see chart, p. xxiii),

e.g., mentions the "king's house," apparently a more modest dwelling for the pharaoh's use when he visited Elephantine in southern Egypt.
43:10 *my servant Nebuchadnezzar.* See note on 25:9. *his throne.* Symbolizing his authority.
43:11 See 15:2 and note. *He will…attack Egypt.* A fragmentary text now owned by the British Museum in London states that Nebuchadnezzar carried out a punitive expedition against Egypt in his 37th year (568–567 B.C.) during the reign of Pharaoh Amasis (see Eze 29:17–20 and notes).
43:12 *As a shepherd picks his garment clean…so he will pick Egypt clean.* Routinely and confidently.
43:13 *temple of the sun in Egypt.* Lit. "Beth Shemesh in Egypt," not to be confused with "Beth Shemesh in Judah" (2Ki 14:11). The Egyptian city is probably to be identified with Heliopolis (Greek for "city of the sun"; see TNIV text note), called *On* in Hebrew (see note on Ge 41:45). *sacred pillars.* Obelisks, for which ancient Heliopolis was famous.

44:1 ʷS Dt 32:42;
S Jer 24:8 ˣS Ex 14:2
ʸS Jer 43:7,8
ᶻS Isa 19:13
ᵃS Isa 11:11
44:2 ᵇS 2Ch 34:24
ᶜS Jer 40:5
ᵈS Lev 26:31;
S Dt 29:23; S Isa 6:11
44:3 ᵉS Ex 32:22
ᶠS Nu 11:33
ᵍS Nu 16:40 ʰver 8;
S Nu 25:3; Dt 13:6-11;
29:26; Isa 19:1
ⁱS Jdg 2:17
44:4 ʲS Jer 7:13
ᵏS Nu 11:29
ˡS Dt 18:9;
S 1Ki 14:24; 1Pe 4:3
44:5 ᵐDa 9:6
ⁿS Jer 25:4
ᵒS Ge 6:5; Ro 1:18;
2Ti 2:19 ᵖver 21;
Jer 1:16; Eze 8:11;
16:18; 23:41 ᵠJer 11:8-
10; S 25:7
44:6 ʳEze 8:18;
20:34 ˢS Lev 26:31,
34; S Dt 29:23;
La 1:13; Zec 7:14
44:7 ᵗJer 26:19
ᵘJer 51:22
ᵛS 2Ki 21:14
44:8 ʷS Isa 40:18-
20; S Jer 10:3; Ro 1:23
ˣver 17-25; Jer 41:5
ʸS ver 3; S Ex 12:12
ᶻS 1Co 10:22
ᵃS Ps 44:13
44:9 ᵇS Jdg 2:19
ᶜS 2Ki 23:11
ᵈ1Ki 21:25
ᵉS Pr 31:10; S Jer 6:12
ᶠver 17,21; Jer 11:2;
32:32
44:10 ᵍS Dt 8:3;
S Mt 23:12; Php 2:8
ʰS Dt 6:13; 10:12
ⁱS Jos 1:7; S Jer 11:8;
Mt 5:17-20; Gal 3:19;
1Jn 3:4 ʲS Lev 18:4
ᵏ1Ki 9:6-9; 2Ki 17:17
44:11 ˡRev 4:8
ᵐS 2Ch 34:24;
Am 9:4
44:12 ⁿver 7;
Jer 40:15 ᵒS Jer 42:1
ᵖS Isa 1:28
ᵠS Dt 28:25;
S Jer 29:18
44:13 ʳS Ex 32:34;
Lev 26:14-17
ˢS Jer 15:2
ᵗS Jer 42:17
44:14 ᵘJer 22:24-
27; 49:5; La 4:15;
Eze 6:8; S Ro 9:27

DISASTER BECAUSE OF IDOLATRY

44 This word came to Jeremiah concerning all the Jews living in Lower Egypt ʷ—in Migdol, ˣ Tahpanhes ʸ and Memphis ᶻ—and in Upper Egypt: ᵃ ²"This is what the LORD Almighty, the God of Israel, says: You saw the great disaster ᵇ I brought on Jerusalem and on all the towns of Judah. ᶜ Today they lie deserted and in ruins ᵈ ³because of the evil ᵉ they have done. They aroused my anger ᶠ by burning incense ᵍ to and worshiping other gods ʰ that neither they nor you nor your ancestors ⁱ ever knew. ⁴Again and again ʲ I sent my servants the prophets, ᵏ who said, 'Do not do this detestable ˡ thing that I hate!' ⁵But they did not listen or pay attention; ᵐⁿ they did not turn from their wickedness ᵒ or stop burning incense ᵖ to other gods. ᵠ ⁶Therefore, my fierce anger was poured out; ʳ it raged against the towns of Judah and the streets of Jerusalem and made them the desolate ruins ˢ they are today.

⁷"Now this is what the LORD God Almighty, the God of Israel, says: Why bring such great disaster ᵗ on yourselves by cutting off from Judah the men and women, ᵘ the children and infants, and so leave yourselves without a remnant? ᵛ ⁸Why arouse my anger with what your hands have made, ʷ burning incense ˣ to other gods in Egypt, ʸ where you have come to live? ᶻ You will destroy yourselves and make yourselves a curse ᵃ and an object of reproach ᵃ among all the nations on earth. ⁹Have you forgotten the wickedness committed by your ancestors ᵇ and by the kings ᶜ and queens ᵈ of Judah and the wickedness committed by you and your wives ᵉ in the land of Judah and the streets of Jerusalem? ᶠ ¹⁰To this day they have not humbled ᵍ themselves or shown reverence, ʰ nor have they followed my law ⁱ and the decrees ʲ I set before you and your ancestors. ᵏ

¹¹"Therefore, this is what the LORD Almighty, ˡ the God of Israel, says: I am determined to bring disaster ᵐ on you and to destroy all Judah. ¹²I will take away the remnant ⁿ of Judah who were determined to go to Egypt to settle there. They will all perish in Egypt; they will fall by the sword or die from famine. From the least to the greatest, ᵒ they will die by sword or famine. ᵖ They will become a curse and an object of horror, a curse and an object of reproach. ᵠ ¹³I will punish ʳ those who live in Egypt with the sword, ˢ famine and plague, ᵗ as I punished Jerusalem. ¹⁴None of the remnant of Judah who have gone to live in Egypt will escape or survive to return to the land of Judah, to which they long to return and live; none will return except a few fugitives." ᵘ

¹⁵Then all the men who knew that their wives ᵛ were burning incense ʷ to other gods, along with all the women ˣ who were present—a large assembly—and all the people living in Lower and Upper Egypt, ʸ said to Jeremiah, ¹⁶"We will not listen ᶻ to the message you have spoken to us in the name of the LORD! ᵃ ¹⁷We will certainly do everything we said we would: ᵇ We will burn incense ᶜ to the Queen of Heaven ᵈ and will pour out drink offerings to her just as we and our ancestors, our kings and our officials ᵉ did in the towns of Judah and in the streets of Jerusalem. ᶠ At that time we had plenty of food ᵍ and were well off and suffered no harm. ʰ ¹⁸But ever since we stopped burning incense to the Queen of

---

ᵃ 8 That is, your name will be used in cursing (see Jer. 29:22); or, others will see that you are cursed; also in verse 12; similarly in verse 22.

44:15 ᵛS Pr 31:10; S Jer 6:12 ʷS Jer 18:15 ˣS Ge 3:6; 1Ti 2:14 ʸS Isa 11:11   **44:16** ᶻS Isa 8:19; Job 15:25-26; Jer 11:8-10 ᵃS Jer 42:19
44:17 ᵇver 28; Dt 23:23; Zec 1:6 ᶜS Isa 65:3 ᵈver 25; Jer 11:12 ᵉNe 9:34 ᶠS ver 9; S Jer 2:26 ᵍS Ex 16:3; Nu 11:4-6 ʰS Job 21:15; Isa 3:9;
Hos 2:5-13; 9:1

44:1–30 The last of Jeremiah's recorded prophecies (see note on 40:1—44:30).

44:1 *Jews living in … Egypt.* As a result of previous deportations (see, e.g., 2Ki 23:34) and/or the Jews mentioned in 43:5–7. In either case, some time must have elapsed between chs. 43 and 44 to bring about the gathering mentioned in v. 15. *Lower Egypt … Upper Egypt.* See note on Isa 11:11. *Migdol.* Probably in northern Egypt (see 46:14). The name means "watchtower." *Tahpanhes and Memphis.* See notes on 2:16; Isa 19:13.

44:3 See note on 1:16; see also 11:17; 19:4; 32:32.

44:4 See 7:25 and note. *Do not do this detestable thing.* See Jdg 19:24.

44:6 *my fierce anger was poured out.* See 7:20; 42:18.

44:7 *bring … disaster on yourselves.* See 26:19. *men and women, the children and infants.* A stock phrase meaning "everyone" (see 1Sa 15:3; 22:19).

44:8 *what your hands have made.* Idols (see 1:16 and note; see also note on Ex 34:15). *curse and … reproach.* See 42:18 and note; see also notes on 24:9; 25:18.

44:9 *wickedness committed by … queens … and your wives.* The women joined their husbands in worshiping the "Queen of Heaven" (v. 19; see v. 15).

44:10 *nor … followed my law.* See 9:13; 26:4; see also 7:9 and note.

44:11–14 See 42:17–18 and notes.

44:11 *am determined.* Lit. "set my face" (see 21:10 and note).

44:15 *wives … women.* See v. 19; see also note on v. 9. *Lower and Upper Egypt.* See v. 1; see also note on Isa 11:11.

44:17 *Queen of Heaven.* See note on 7:18. *At that time we … were well off.* Judah had been relatively prosperous during King Manasseh's lengthy reign.

44:18 *ever since we stopped.* As a result of King Josiah's reform movement, which began in 621 B.C. *we have had nothing.* Beginning with Josiah's death in 609, a series of disasters, including invasion and exile, had struck Judah. The people understandably (though mistakenly) attributed their misfortune to their failure to worship the Queen of Heaven.

Heaven and pouring out drink offerings *i* to her, we have had nothing and have been perishing by sword and famine.*j k*

¹⁹The women added, "When we burned incense *l* to the Queen of Heaven *m* and poured out drink offerings to her, did not our husbands *n* know that we were making cakes *o* impressed with her image *p* and pouring out drink offerings to her?"

²⁰Then Jeremiah said to all the people, both men and women, who were answering him, ²¹"Did not the Lᴏʀᴅ remember *q* and call to mind the incense *r* burned in the towns of Judah and the streets of Jerusalem *s* by you and your ancestors, *t* your kings and your officials and the people of the land? *u* ²²When the Lᴏʀᴅ could no longer endure *v* your wicked actions and the detestable things you did, your land became a curse *w* and a desolate waste *x* without inhabitants, as it is today. *y* ²³Because you have burned incense and have sinned against the Lᴏʀᴅ and have not obeyed him or followed *z* his law or his decrees *a* or his stipulations, this disaster *b* has come upon you, as you now see." *c*

²⁴Then Jeremiah said to all the people, including the women, *d* "Hear the word of the Lᴏʀᴅ, all you people of Judah in Egypt. *e* ²⁵This is what the Lᴏʀᴅ Almighty, the God of Israel, says: You and your wives *f* have done what you said you would do when you promised, 'We will certainly carry out the vows we made to burn incense and pour out drink offerings to the Queen of Heaven.' *g*

"Go ahead then, do what you promised! Keep your vows! *h* ²⁶But hear the word of the Lᴏʀᴅ, all you Jews living in Egypt: *i* 'I swear *j* by my great name,' says the Lᴏʀᴅ, 'that no one from Judah living anywhere in Egypt will ever again invoke my name or swear, "As surely as the Sovereign *k* Lᴏʀᴅ lives." *l* ²⁷For I am watching *m* over them for harm, *n* not for good; the Jews in Egypt will perish *o* by sword and famine *p* until they are all destroyed. *q* ²⁸Those who escape the sword *r* and return to the land of Judah from Egypt will be very few. *s* Then the whole remnant *t* of Judah who came to live in Egypt will know whose word will stand *u*—mine or theirs. *v*

²⁹" 'This will be the sign *w* to you that I will punish *x* you in this place,' declares the Lᴏʀᴅ, 'so that you will know that my threats of harm against you will surely stand.' *y* ³⁰This is what the Lᴏʀᴅ says: 'I am going to deliver Pharaoh *z* Hophra king of Egypt into the hands of his enemies who seek his life, just as I gave Zedekiah *a* king of Judah into the hands of Nebuchadnezzar king of Babylon, the enemy who was seeking his life.' " *b*

A MESSAGE TO BARUCH

45 When Baruch *c* son of Neriah *d* wrote on a scroll *e* the words Jeremiah the prophet dictated in the fourth year of Jehoiakim *f* son of Josiah king of Judah, Jeremiah said this to Baruch: ²"This is what the Lᴏʀᴅ, the God of Israel, says to you, Baruch: ³You said, 'Woe *g* to me! The Lᴏʀᴅ has added sorrow *h* to my pain; *i* I am worn out with groaning *j* and find no rest.' *k* ⁴But the Lᴏʀᴅ has told me to say to you, 'This is what the Lᴏʀᴅ says: I will overthrow what I have built and uproot *l* what I have planted, *m* throughout the earth. *n* ⁵Should you then seek great *o* things for yourself? Do not seek them. *p* For I will bring disaster *q* on all people, *r* declares the Lᴏʀᴅ, but wherever you go I will let you escape *s* with your life.' " *t*

45:3 *i* S Job 6:10 *j* S Job 23:2; Ps 69:3 *k* S Jos 1:13; Mt 11:28; Heb 4:3 **45:4** *l* S Jer 42:10 *m* S Jer 11:17 *n* S Dt 28:63; S 30:9; Isa 5:5-7; Jer 18:7-10 **45:5** *o* Ps 131:1 *p* Mt 6:25-27,33 *q* Jer 11:11; 40:2 *r* S Jer 2:35 *s* S Ps 68:20; S Jer 44:28 *t* S Jer 21:9

44:18 *i* Lev 23:18
j Mal 3:13-15
k Jer 42:16
44:19 *l* S Jer 18:15
m Jer 7:18 *n* S Ge 3:6;
Eph 5:22 *o* Lev 7:12
p S Lev 26:1; Ac 17:29
44:21 *q* Isa 64:9;
S Jer 14:10; Hos 8:13
r S Jer 11:13 *s* ver 9
t S Ps 79:8 *u* S Jer 2:26
44:22 *v* S Isa 1:14
w S Jer 25:18
x S Lev 26:31,32
y S Ge 19:13;
Ps 107:33-34;
Eze 33:28-29
44:23 *z* S 1Ki 9:6
a S Lev 18:4 *b* Jer 40:2
c S Lev 26:33;
S 1Ki 9:9; Jer 7:13-15;
Eze 39:23; Da 9:11-12
44:24 *d* S Ge 3:6
e Jer 43:7
44:25 *f* S Pr 31:10
g S ver 17; S Dt 32:38
h S Pr 20:25;
Eze 20:39; Jas 1:13-15
44:26 *i* S Jer 24:8
j S Ge 22:16;
S Isa 48:1; Ac 19:13;
Heb 6:13-17
k S Ge 15:2 *l* Dt 32:40;
Ps 50:16; S Jer 4:2
44:27 *m* S Jer 1:12
n S Jer 21:10
o S Lev 26:38;
S Job 15:22; 2Pe 3:9
p S Ge 41:55
q S Jer 9:16; Da 9:14;
Am 9:8
44:28 *r* Jer 45:5;
Eze 6:8 *s* ver 13-14;
S Isa 10:19
t S 2Ki 21:14
u S Isa 7:9;
S Jer 39:16; 42:15-18
v S ver 17,25-26
44:29 *w* S Ge 24:14;
S Ex 3:12; S Nu 16:38;
S Mt 12:38; 24:3
x S Ex 32:34
y S Pr 19:21
44:30 *z* S Jer 25:19;
46:26; Eze 30:21;
32:32 *a* 2Ki 25:1-7;
S Jer 24:8 *b* Jer 43:9-13
45:1 *c* S Jer 32:12
d Jer 51:59
e S Ex 17:14;
S Ps 40:7
f S 2Ch 36:5
45:3 *g* S Isa 24:16;
1Co 9:16
h S Ps 119:28;
Mk 14:34; Ro 9:2

B **44:19** *women.* Since Ishtar (the "Queen of Heaven") was a Babylonian goddess of fertility, women played a major role in her worship. *did not our husbands know …?* To have validity, a religious vow made by a married woman (see v. 25) had to be confirmed by her husband (see Nu 30:10–15). *we were making cakes impressed with her image.* See 7:18.

44:22 *curse.* See v. 12. *desolate waste.* See v. 6.

44:23 *stipulations.* Of the Lord's covenant with his people (see Dt 4:45; 6:17,20).

44:25 *Go ahead then.* Spoken in irony (see 7:21 and note).

44:26 *I swear by my great name.* See note on 22:5. *As surely as the Sovereign Lord lives.* See note on 4:2.

44:27 *watching.* See note on 1:12; see also 31:28.

44:28 *very few.* See v. 14.

44:30 *Hophra.* Ruled Egypt 589–570 B.C. (see 37:5 and note). *his enemies who seek his life.* Hophra was killed by his Egyptian rivals during a power struggle. *I gave Zedekiah … into the hands of Nebuchadnezzar.* See 39:5–7.

C **45:1–5** A brief message of encouragement to Baruch, Jeremiah's faithful secretary (see note on 32:12). Though out of chronological order, the section provides a suitable historical appendix to chs. 39–44, as well as a smooth transition to chs. 46–51 (see notes on v. 1; 46:2).

45:1 *wrote on a scroll.* See 36:4; see also 36:2 and note. *fourth year of Jehoiakim.* 605 B.C. Ch. 45 fits chronologically between 36:8 and 36:9 (see note on 36:8).

45:3 To some extent Baruch shared Jeremiah's anguish, the result of Jeremiah's prophetic call and ministry (see, e.g., 8:18—9:2; 20:7–18). *worn out with groaning.* See Ps 6:6. *find no rest.* See La 5:5.

45:4 *overthrow … built … uproot … planted.* See note on 1:10; see also 2:21; 31:4–5,28,40; 32:41; 33:7. *earth.* See "all people" in v. 5; see also 25:15,31; 46–51.

A C **45:5** *great things … Do not seek them.* See Ps 131:1. Baruch's brother Seraiah would occupy an important position under King Zedekiah (see 32:12; 51:59), but Baruch himself was not to be ambitious or self-seeking. *escape with your life.* See note on 21:9.

46:1 *u* S Jer 1:10
46:2 *v* S Ex 1:8
w S 2Ki 23:29
x S 2Ch 35:20
y S Ge 2:14 *z* Jer 1:3;
25:1; 35:1; 36:1; 45:1;
Da 1:1
46:3 *a* S Isa 21:5
46:4 *b* Eze 21:9-11
c Isa 17:5,38;
2Ch 26:14; Ne 4:16
46:5 *d* ver 21;
Jer 48:44 *e* S Ps 31:13;
S 48:5
46:6 *f* Isa 30:16
g Ge 2:14; 15:18
h ver 12,16; S Ps 20:8
46:7 *i* Jer 47:2
46:8 *j* Eze 29:3,9;
30:12; Am 8:8
k Da 11:10
46:9 *l* Jer 47:3;
Eze 26:10; Na 3:2
m S Ge 10:6
n S Isa 66:19
46:10 *o* Eze 32:10;
Joel 1:15; Ob 1:15
p S Nu 31:3;
S Dt 32:41;
2Ki 23:29-30

A MESSAGE ABOUT EGYPT

46 This is the word of the LORD that came to Jeremiah the prophet concerning the nations: *u*

²Concerning Egypt: *v*

This is the message against the army of Pharaoh Necho *w* king of Egypt, which was defeated at Carchemish *x* on the Euphrates *y* River by Nebuchadnezzar king of Babylon in the fourth year of Jehoiakim *z* son of Josiah king of Judah:

³ "Prepare your shields, *a* both large and small,
 and march out for battle!
⁴ Harness the horses,
 mount the steeds!
Take your positions
 with helmets on!
Polish *b* your spears,
 put on your armor! *c*
⁵ What do I see?
 They are terrified,
they are retreating,
 their warriors are defeated.
They flee *d* in haste
 without looking back,
 and there is terror *e* on every side,"

declares the LORD.

⁶ "The swift cannot flee *f*
 nor the strong escape.
In the north by the River Euphrates *g*
 they stumble and fall. *h*

⁷ "Who is this that rises like the Nile,
 like rivers of surging waters? *i*
⁸ Egypt rises like the Nile, *j*
 like rivers of surging waters.
She says, 'I will rise and cover the earth;
 I will destroy cities and their people.' *k*
⁹ Charge, you horses!
 Drive furiously, you charioteers! *l*
March on, you warriors—men of Cush *a m* and Put who carry shields,
 men of Lydia *n* who draw the bow.
¹⁰ But that day *o* belongs to the Lord, the LORD Almighty—
 a day of vengeance *p*, for vengeance on his foes.

a 9 That is, the upper Nile region

46:1—51:64 See notes on 25:1–38; 25:13; 25:19–26. Chs. 46–51 consist of a series of prophecies against the nations (see Isa 13–23; Eze 25–32; Am 1–2; Zep 2:4–15). They begin with Egypt (ch. 46) and end with Babylonia (chs. 50–51), the two powers that vied for control of Judah during Jeremiah's ministry. The arrangement of the prophecies is in a generally west-to-east direction.

46:1 *This is the word of the LORD ... concerning.* See 14:1; 47:1; 49:34; 50:1. *nations.* To whom Jeremiah was called to prophesy (see 1:5 and note).

46:2 *Concerning Egypt.* See Isa 19–20; Eze 29–32. *Necho.* Ruled Egypt 610–595 B.C. *Carchemish.* See 2Ch 35:20; Isa 10:9 and note. The name means "fortress of Chemosh" (chief god of Moab; see 2Ki 23:13), as clarified by the Ebla tablets (see Introduction to Genesis: Background; see also chart, p. xxiii). *Euphrates River.* See note on Ge 15:18. *by Nebuchadnezzar.* Egypt's defeat by Babylonia at Carchemish was one of the most decisive battles in the ancient world, ending Egypt's agelong claims and pretensions to power in Syro-Palestine. *fourth year of Jehoiakim.* 605 B.C., the first year of Nebuchadnezzar's reign (see 25:1).

46:3 *Prepare.* Spoken to the Egyptians in sarcasm (see, e.g., Na 2:1; 3:14 and notes).

46:4 *horses.* Egypt was a prime source for the finest horses (see 1Ki 10:28). *put on your armor.* See 51:3.

46:5 *terror on every side.* The phrase is used in 6:25 (see note there) with reference to the Babylonian army (see 6:22 and note).

46:7–8 *rivers of surging waters.* In the northern Egyptian delta, where the Nile branches out into numerous streams.

46:8 *rise and cover the earth.* The same metaphor is used of Assyria in Isa 8:7–8 (see note there). *cities.* The Hebrew for this word is in the singular but is used as a generic plural ("city" is generic also in 8:16).

46:9 *Charge.* See note on v. 3; see also 8:6; Na 3:3. *Drive furiously, you charioteers!* See Na 2:4. *Put.* See note on Ge 10:6. *Lydia.* See note on Isa 66:19. Men from Cush, Put and Lydia were mercenaries in the Egyptian army.

46:10 *day of vengeance.* See Isa 34:8 and note. The Lord will avenge Egypt's cruelties toward Judah (see, e.g., 2Ki 23:29,33–35). *sword will devour.* See v. 14. *quenched its thirst with blood ... offer sacrifice.* Slaughter in battle is often compared with sacrifices (see Isa 34:5–7 and notes; Zep 1:7–8).

The sword will devour [q] till it is satisfied,
till it has quenched its thirst with blood. [r]
For the Lord, the Lord Almighty, will offer sacrifice [s]
in the land of the north by the River Euphrates. [t]

[11] "Go up to Gilead and get balm, [u]
Virgin [v] Daughter Egypt.
But you multiply remedies in vain;
there is no healing [w] for you.
[12] The nations will hear of your shame;
your cries will fill the earth.
One warrior will stumble over another;
both will fall [x] down together."

[13] This is the message the Lord spoke to Jeremiah the prophet about the coming of Nebuchadnezzar king of Babylon [y] to attack Egypt: [z]

[14] "Announce this in Egypt, and proclaim it in Migdol;
proclaim it also in Memphis [a] and Tahpanhes: [b]
'Take your positions and get ready,
for the sword devours [c] those around you.'
[15] Why will your warriors be laid low?
They cannot stand, for the Lord will push them down. [d]
[16] They will stumble [e] repeatedly;
they will fall [f] over each other.
They will say, 'Get up, let us go back
to our own people [g] and our native lands,
away from the sword of the oppressor.' [h]
[17] There they will exclaim,
'Pharaoh king of Egypt is only a loud noise; [i]
he has missed his opportunity.' [j]

[18] "As surely as I live," declares the King, [k]
whose name is the Lord Almighty,
"one will come who is like Tabor [l] among the mountains,
like Carmel [m] by the sea.
[19] Pack your belongings for exile, [n]
you who live in Egypt,
for Memphis [o] will be laid waste [p]
and lie in ruins without inhabitant.

[20] "Egypt is a beautiful heifer,
but a gadfly is coming
against her from the north. [q]
[21] The mercenaries [r] in her ranks

46:10 [q] S Dt 32:42; S 2Sa 2:26; Zep 2:12
[r] S Dt 32:42
[s] S Lev 3:9; Zep 1:7
[t] Ge 2:14; 15:18
46:11 [u] S Ge 37:25
[v] S 2Ki 19:21
[w] S Jer 30:13; S Mic 1:9
46:12 [x] S ver 6; Isa 19:4; Na 3:8-10
46:13 [y] ver 26; Eze 32:11 [z] Isa 19:1; Jer 27:7
46:14 [a] S Isa 19:13
[b] S Jer 43:8
[c] S Dt 32:42; S 2Sa 2:26; S Jer 24:8
46:15 [d] S Jos 23:5; Isa 66:15-16
46:16 [e] S Lev 26:37 [f] S ver 6 [g] S Isa 13:14 [h] S Jer 25:38
46:17 [i] 1Ki 20:10-11 [j] Isa 19:11-16
46:18 [k] Jer 48:15 [l] S Jos 19:22 [m] 1Ki 18:42
46:19 [n] S Isa 20:4 [o] S Isa 19:13 [p] Eze 29:10,12; 35:7
46:20 [q] ver 24; S Isa 14:31; Jer 47:2
46:21 [r] S 2Ki 7:6

46:11 *Gilead . . . balm.* See 8:22 and note. *Virgin Daughter Egypt.* A personification of Egypt (see note on 2Ki 19:21). *remedies in vain . . . no healing for you.* The statement is ironic in the light of Egypt's reputation for expertise in the healing arts.
46:12 *stumble . . . fall.* See vv. 6,16.
46:13 *Nebuchadnezzar . . . to attack Egypt.* In 568–567 B.C. (see note on 43:11), long after the battle of Carchemish (see note on v. 2).
46:14 *Migdol.* See note on 44:1. *Memphis and Tahpanhes.* See 44:1; see also notes on 2:16; Isa 19:13. *Take your positions.* See v. 4. *sword devours.* See v. 10.
46:15 *warriors.* The Hebrew for this word is not the same as that for "warrior" in vv. 5,9,12. It is lit. "strong ones," often referring to powerful animals ("stallions" in 8:16; 50:11; "steeds" in 47:3; Jdg 5:22). In Ps 22:12; 50:13; 68:30; Isa 34:7 the Hebrew word is translated "bulls" (see note on Ps 68:30). *be laid low.* The Hebrew for this phrase is translated "Apis has fled" in the Septuagint (the pre-Christian Greek translation of the OT). Apis was a bull-god worshiped in Egypt, especially at Memphis (see v. 14). An alternative translation of v. 15 would then read as follows: "Why did Apis flee? Why did your bull [many manuscripts have the singular form] not stand? Because the Lord pushed him down."
46:16 *They will stumble repeatedly.* See vv. 6,12; lit. "He will make many stumble." *They will say, '. . . let us go.'* The mercenaries in the pharaoh's army (see v. 9 and note) will decide to return to their homelands. *sword of the oppressor.* See 25:38; 50:16.
46:17 *only a loud noise.* In Isa 30:7, Egypt is called "the Do-Nothing." *missed his opportunity.* After the battle of Carchemish (see v. 2), Nebuchadnezzar returned to Babylonia on learning of his father's death. Egypt failed to press its advantage at that time.
46:18 *As surely as I live.* See notes on Ge 22:16; 42:15. *King.* God is called "King" also in 8:19; 10:7,10; 48:15; 51:57. *one.* Nebuchadnezzar. *Tabor . . . Carmel.* Two prominent mountains in Israel (see notes on Jdg 4:6; SS 7:5; Isa 33:9).
46:19 *Pack your belongings for exile.* Echoed in Eze 12:3. *Egypt.* Lit. "Daughter (of) Egypt" (see v. 11 and note). *laid waste.* Judah is so described in 2:15; 9:12.
46:20 *heifer.* Perhaps an ironic reference to Egyptian bull-worship (see note on v. 15). *gadfly.* Nebuchadnezzar. Insects are often used to symbolize an attacking enemy (see note on Ex 23:28).
46:21 *mercenaries.* See note on v. 9. *calves.* See note on v. 20.

46:21 ˢLk 15:27
ᵗS ver 5; S Job 20:24
ᵘPs 18:18; 37:13;
Jer 18:17; ᵛS Job 18:20
46:22 ʷPs 74:5
46:23 ˣS Dt 28:42;
S Jdg 7:12
46:24 ʸS 2Ki 24:7
46:25 ᶻEze 30:14;
Na 3:8 ᵃ2Ki 24:7;
Eze 30:22
ᵇS Jer 43:12
ᶜIsa 20:6
46:26 ᵈS Jer 44:30
ᵉS ver 13; S Isa 19:4
ᶠEze 29:11-16
46:27 ᵍIsa 43:5;
Jer 51:46 ʰIsa 41:8;
44:1; Mal 1:2
ⁱS Isa 44:2
ʲS Isa 11:11;
S Jer 29:14; 50:19
46:28 ᵏS Ex 14:22;
S Nu 14:9; Isa 8:9-10
ˡS Jer 4:27
47:1 ᵐS Ge 10:14;
S Jdg 3:31
ⁿS Ge 10:19;
Zec 9:5-7
47:2 ᵒS Isa 14:31
ᵖS Isa 15:3

are like fattened calves. ˢ
They too will turn and flee ᵗ together,
    they will not stand their ground,
for the day ᵘ of disaster is coming upon them,
    the time ᵛ for them to be punished.
²² Egypt will hiss like a fleeing serpent
    as the enemy advances in force;
they will come against her with axes,
    like those who cut down trees. ʷ
²³ They will chop down her forest,"

                                declares the LORD,

"dense though it be.
They are more numerous than locusts, ˣ
    they cannot be counted.
²⁴ Daughter Egypt will be put to shame,
    given into the hands of the people of the north. ʸ"

²⁵ The LORD Almighty, the God of Israel, says: "I am about to bring punishment on Amon god of Thebes, ᶻ on Pharaoh, ᵃ on Egypt and her gods ᵇ and her kings, and on those who rely ᶜ on Pharaoh. ²⁶ I will give them into the hands ᵈ of those who seek their lives—Nebuchadnezzar king ᵉ of Babylon and his officers. Later, however, Egypt will be inhabited ᶠ as in times past," declares the LORD.

²⁷ "Do not be afraid, ᵍ Jacob ʰ my servant; ⁱ
    do not be dismayed, Israel.
I will surely save you out of a distant place,
    your descendants from the land of their exile. ʲ
Jacob will again have peace and security,
    and no one will make him afraid.
²⁸ Do not be afraid, Jacob my servant,
    for I am with you," ᵏ declares the LORD.
"Though I completely destroy ˡ all the nations
    among which I scatter you,
I will not completely destroy you.
I will discipline you but only in due measure;
    I will not let you go entirely unpunished."

A MESSAGE ABOUT THE PHILISTINES

47 This is the word of the LORD that came to Jeremiah the prophet concerning the Philistines ᵐ before Pharaoh attacked Gaza: ⁿ

² This is what the LORD says:

"See how the waters are rising in the north; ᵒ
    they will become an overflowing torrent.
They will overflow the land and everything in it,
    the towns and those who live in them.
The people will cry out;
    all who dwell in the land will wail ᵖ
³ at the sound of the hooves of galloping steeds,

---

day of disaster. See 18:17. *time for them to be punished.* See 11:23; 23:12; 50:27.

46:22 *serpent.* Often used by Egyptian pharaohs as a symbol of their sovereignty (see note on Ex 4:3). *the enemy . . . like those who cut down trees.* See 21:14; see also Isa 10:18–19,33–34 and notes.

46:23 *more numerous than locusts.* Here an invading army is compared to locusts. In Joel 2:11,25 locusts are compared to an invading army (see also 51:14).

46:24 *Daughter Egypt.* See v. 11 and note.

46:25 *Amon.* The chief god of Egypt during much of its history. Wicked King Manasseh may have named his son after the Egyptian deity (see 2Ki 21:18; 2Ch 33:22). *Thebes.* The capital of Upper (southern) Egypt (see Eze 30:14–16).

46:26 *Egypt will be inhabited as in times past.* Cf. 48:47; 49:6,39.

Egypt would be restored in the Messianic age (see Isa 19:23–25 and notes).

46:27–28 Repeated almost verbatim from 30:10–11 (see notes there).

47:1 *concerning the Philistines.* See Isa 14:28–32; Eze 25:15–17; Am 1:6–8; Zep 2:4–7. *Pharaoh.* It is uncertain whether Necho II (see 46:2; see also note on 2Ki 23:29) or Hophra (see notes on 37:5; 44:30) is intended. *Gaza.* See v. 5; 25:20; see also note on Jdg 1:18.

47:2 *waters are rising.* See notes on 46:7–8. *the north.* Babylonia, as in 1:13–14; 46:20. *the land . . . live in them.* The Hebrew for this phrase is repeated verbatim from 8:16. *land.* Phoenicia and Philistia. *towns.* See note on 46:8; includes Tyre and Sidon (see v. 4) as well as Gaza, Ashkelon (see v. 5) and other Philistine cities.

47:3 *steeds.* Lit. "strong ones" (see note on 46:15). *hands will hang limp.* Paralyzed by terror (see 6:24; Isa 13:7 and notes).

at the noise of enemy chariots [q]
and the rumble of their wheels.
Parents will not turn to help their children;
their hands will hang limp. [r]
⁴ For the day has come
to destroy all the Philistines
and to remove all survivors
who could help Tyre [s] and Sidon. [t]
The LORD is about to destroy the Philistines, [u]
the remnant from the coasts of Caphtor. [a v]
⁵ Gaza will shave [w] her head in mourning;
Ashkelon [x] will be silenced.
You remnant on the plain,
how long will you cut [y] yourselves?

⁶ " 'Ah, sword [z] of the LORD,' [you cry,]
'how long till you rest?
Return to your sheath;
cease and be still.' [a]
⁷ But how can it rest
when the LORD has commanded it,
when he has ordered it
to attack Ashkelon and the coast?" [b]

A MESSAGE ABOUT MOAB

48:29–36pp — Isa 16:6–12

48

Concerning Moab: [c]

This is what the LORD Almighty, the God of Israel, says:

"Woe to Nebo, [d] for it will be ruined.
Kiriathaim [e] will be disgraced and captured;
the stronghold [b] will be disgraced and shattered.
² Moab will be praised [f] no more;
in Heshbon [c g] people will plot her downfall:
'Come, let us put an end to that nation.' [h]
You, the people of Madmen, [d] will also be silenced;
the sword will pursue you.
³ Cries of anguish arise from Horonaim, [i]
cries of great havoc and destruction.
⁴ Moab will be broken;
her little ones will cry out. [d]
⁵ They go up the hill to Luhith, [j]

---

[a] 4 That is, Crete   [b] 1 Or *captured;* / *Misgab*   [c] 2 The Hebrew for *Heshbon* sounds like the Hebrew
for *plot.*   [d] 2 The name of the Moabite town Madmen sounds like the Hebrew for *be silenced.*
[e] 4 Hebrew; Septuagint / *proclaim it to Zoar*

47:3 [q] S Jer 46:9;
S Eze 23:24 [r] Isa 13:7;
Jer 50:43; Eze 7:17;
21:7
47:4 [s] S Isa 23:1;
Am 1:9-10; Zec 9:2-4
[t] S Ge 10:15;
S Jer 25:22
[u] S Ge 10:14; Joel 3:4
[v] S Dt 2:23
47:5 [w] S Jer 41:5
[x] S Jer 25:20
[y] S Lev 19:28
47:6 [z] S Isa 34:5;
Jer 12:12; 48:10; 50:35
[a] Eze 21:30
47:7 [b] Eze 25:15-17
48:1 [c] S Ge 19:37;
S Dt 23:6
[d] S Nu 32:38
[e] S Nu 32:37;
S Jos 13:19
48:2 [f] Isa 16:14
[g] S Nu 21:25;
S Jos 13:26 [h] ver 42
48:3 [i] S Isa 15:5
48:5 [j] Isa 15:5

47:4 *Tyre and Sidon.* See notes on v. 2; 25:22; 27:3. *remnant.* See
v. 5; see also 2Ki 19:30–31; Isa 1:9; 10:20–22 and notes. *Caphtor.*
Crete (see TNIV text note; the Kerethites of Zep 2:5 and elsewhere
were probably Cretans), one of many islands in the Mediterranean believed to be the original homeland of the Philistines
(see Ge 10:14 and note; see also Dt 2:23).
47:5 *Gaza.* See v. 1; 25:20; see also note on Jdg 1:18. *shave her
head in mourning.* See note on 16:6; see also 48:37 and notes on
Isa 3:17; 7:20. *Ashkelon.* See v. 7; 25:20; see also note on Jdg 1:18.
be silenced. A sign of mourning (see La 2:10). *plain.* Roughly
equivalent to the modern Gaza Strip, it lay west of the foothills
that separated Philistia from Judah. *cut yourselves.* See note on
16:6; see also 48:37.
47:6 *sword.* See 12:12 and note. *you.* The Philistines.
47:7 *attack Ashkelon.* The immediate fulfillment took place under Nebuchadnezzar in 604 B.C. *coast.* See Eze 25:16; the Philistine plain (see note on v. 5).

B **48:1** *Concerning Moab.* See Isa 15–16; Eze 25:8–11; Am
2:1–3; Zep 2:8–11. Josephus (*Antiquities,* 10.9.7) implies
that Jeremiah's prophecy concerning the future destruction of
Moab was fulfilled in the "twenty-third year of Nebuchadnezzar's
reign" (582 B.C.). *Nebo.* See v. 22; a town originally allotted to the
tribe of Reuben (see Nu 32:3,37–38; see also Isa 15:2 and note).
Kiriathaim. See v. 23. An ancient town (see Ge 14:5), it too was allotted to Reuben (see Jos 13:19 and note). Nebo, Kiriathaim and
several other towns referred to in this chapter are mentioned
also in an important Moabite inscription written by Mesha, king
of Moab (see 2Ki 3:4), and discovered in 1868 (see chart, p. xxiv).
48:2 *Heshbon.* See vv. 34,45; 49:3; Nu 21:25. Originally allotted
to Reuben (see Nu 32:37; Jos 13:17), it was later reassigned to
Gad as a Levitical town (see Jos 21:39). *Madmen.* Perhaps a
longer spelling of "Dimon" (Isa 15:9—but see note there). In Isa
25:10 the feminine form of the Hebrew word *madmen* is translated "manure." *sword will pursue you.* See 9:16; 42:16.
48:4 *broken.* Like a clay jar (see 19:11).

48:5 *k* ver 3
48:6 *l* S Ge 19:17
m Jer 17:6
48:7 *n* S Ps 49:6;
S Pr 11:28
o Nu 21:29
p Isa 46:1-2; Jer 49:3
q Am 2:3
48:8 *r* S Ex 12:23;
S Jer 4:7 *s* S Jos 13:9
48:9 *t* Jdg 9:45
u Jer 51:29
48:10 *v* S Jer 47:6
w S 1Sa 15:11;
1Ki 20:42; 2Ki 13:15-
19
48:11 *x* Zec 1:15
y Zep 1:12
48:13 *z* Hos 10:6
a ver 7 *b* S Jos 7:2
48:14 *c* Ps 33:16
48:15 *d* S Isa 9:17
e Jer 51:40
f S Jer 46:18
g Jer 51:57
48:16 *h* Isa 13:22

weeping bitterly as they go;
on the road down to Horonaim *k*
anguished cries over the destruction are heard.
⁶ Flee! *l* Run for your lives;
become like a bush *a* in the desert. *m*
⁷ Since you trust in your deeds and riches, *n*
you too will be taken captive,
and Chemosh *o* will go into exile, *p*
together with his priests and officials. *q*
⁸ The destroyer *r* will come against every town,
and not a town will escape.
The valley will be ruined
and the plateau *s* destroyed,
because the LORD has spoken.
⁹ Put salt *t* on Moab,
for she will be laid waste *b*; *u*
her towns will become desolate,
with no one to live in them.

¹⁰ "A curse on those who are lax in doing the LORD's work!
A curse on those who keep their swords *v* from bloodshed! *w*

¹¹ "Moab has been at rest *x* from youth,
like wine left on its dregs, *y*
not poured from one jar to another—
she has not gone into exile.
So she tastes as she did,
and her aroma is unchanged.
¹² But days are coming,"
declares the LORD,
"when I will send people who pour from jars,
and they will pour her out;
they will empty her jars
and smash her jugs.
¹³ Then Moab will be ashamed *z* of Chemosh, *a*
as the house of Israel was ashamed
when they trusted in Bethel. *b*

¹⁴ "How can you say, 'We are warriors, *c*
men valiant in battle'?
¹⁵ Moab will be destroyed and her towns invaded;
her finest young men *d* will go down in the slaughter, *e*"
declares the King, *f* whose name is the LORD Almighty. *g*
¹⁶ "The fall of Moab is at hand; *h*
her calamity will come quickly.

a 6 Or like Aroer   *b 9 Or Give wings to Moab, / for she will fly away*

48:6 *Flee! Run for your lives.* See 51:6. *like a bush.* See note on 17:6.
48:7 *Chemosh.* See vv. 13,46; the national god of Moab (see 1Ki 11:7,33; 2Ki 23:13). The Hebrew text here implies the alternate spelling Chemish, as in "Carchemish" (see note on 46:2). *will go into exile ... and officials.* A stock phrase (see 49:3; Am 1:15). Images of pagan deities were often carried about from place to place (see 43:12; Am 5:26).
48:8 *destroyer.* See v. 32; probably Nebuchadnezzar. *valley ... plateau.* Much of western Moab overlooks the Jordan Valley.
48:9 See 17:6. *Put salt on Moab.* To make its farmland unproductive and barren (see note on Jdg 9:45).
48:10 *lax.* Or "lazy" (as in Pr 10:4; 12:24). Those whom the Lord designates to destroy Moab are urged on in their appointed task.
48:11 A copy of the Hebrew text of this verse has been found inscribed on a large clay seal, dating to the early Christian era and apparently used for stamping the bitumen with which the mouths of wine jars were sealed. *from youth.* From her early history. *like wine.* An apt figure, since Moab was

noted for her vineyards (see vv. 32–33; Isa 16:8–10). *left on its dregs.* In order to improve with age (see Isa 25:6). *she has not gone into exile.* Unlike Israel.
48:12 *days are coming.* Moab will be destroyed (see note on v. 1). *pour from jars.* Ordinarily in order to leave the unwanted sediment in the bottom, but these people will be the agents of divine judgment and will "smash" Moab (see v. 4 and note).
48:13 *house of Israel.* The northern kingdom, destroyed and exiled in 722–721 B.C. *Bethel.* Either (1) the well-known town where one of Jeroboam's golden calves was placed (see 1Ki 12:28–30) or, (2) in parallelism with Chemosh, the West Semitic deity known from contemporary Babylonian inscriptions, as well as from the Elephantine papyri a century later (see chart, p. xxiii).
48:14 *How can you say ... ?* See 2:23; 8:8.
48:15 *go down in the slaughter.* See 50:27; for war depicted as the slaughter of sacrificial animals, see Isa 34:6 and note. *King.* See note on 46:18. The true King is the Lord, not Chemosh.
48:16 See Dt 32:35.

[17] Mourn for her, all who live around her,
  all who know her fame; [i]
say, 'How broken is the mighty scepter, [j]
  how broken the glorious staff!'

[18] "Come down from your glory
  and sit on the parched ground, [k]
  you inhabitants of Daughter Dibon, [l]
for Moab's destroyer
  will come up against you
  and ruin your fortified cities. [m]
[19] Stand by the road and watch,
  you who live in Aroer. [n]
Ask the man fleeing and the woman escaping,
  ask them, 'What has happened?'
[20] Moab is disgraced, for she is shattered.
  Wail [o] and cry out!
Announce by the Arnon [p]
  that Moab is destroyed.
[21] Judgment has come to the plateau [q]—
  to Holon, [r] Jahzah [s] and Mephaath, [t]
[22] to Dibon, [u] Nebo [v] and Beth Diblathaim,
[23] to Kiriathaim, [w] Beth Gamul and Beth Meon, [x]
[24] to Kerioth [y] and Bozrah [z]—
  to all the towns [a] of Moab, far and near.
[25] Moab's horn [a] [b] is cut off;
  her arm [c] is broken,"

                                    declares the LORD.

[26] "Make her drunk, [d]
  for she has defied [e] the LORD.
Let Moab wallow in her vomit; [f]
  let her be an object of ridicule. [g]
[27] Was not Israel the object of your ridicule? [h]
  Was she caught among thieves, [i]
  that you shake your head [j] in scorn [k]
  whenever you speak of her?
[28] Abandon your towns and dwell among the rocks,
  you who live in Moab.
Be like a dove [l] that makes its nest
  at the mouth of a cave. [m]

[29] "We have heard of Moab's pride [n]—
  her overweening pride and conceit,
  her pride and arrogance

---

[a] 25 *Horn* here symbolizes strength.

48:17 [i] 2Ki 3:4-5
[j] S Ps 110:2
48:18 [k] Isa 47:1
[l] S Nu 21:30;
S Jos 13:9 [m] ver 8
48:19 [n] S Nu 32:34
48:20 [o] S Isa 16:7
[p] S Nu 21:13
48:21 [q] S Jos 13:9,
21 [r] S Jos 15:51
[s] S Nu 21:23;
S Isa 15:4 [t] S Jos 13:18
48:22 [u] S Nu 21:30;
S Jos 13:9,17
[v] S Nu 32:38
48:23 [w] S Nu 32:37;
S Jos 13:19
[x] S Jos 13:17
48:24 [y] Am 2:2
[z] Jer 49:13 [a] S Isa 15:1
48:25 [b] Ps 75:10
[c] Ps 10:15; 37:17;
Eze 30:21
48:26 [d] Jer 25:16,
27; 51:39 [e] ver 42;
1Sa 17:26 [f] S Isa 28:8
[g] ver 39
48:27 [h] S Jer 2:26
[i] 2Ki 17:3-6
[j] S Job 16:4; Ps 44:14;
Jer 18:16 [k] S Dt 28:37;
Mic 7:8-10; Zep 2:8,
10
48:28 [l] S Ge 8:8;
S SS 1:15 [m] S Jdg 6:2
48:29 [n] S Lev 26:19;
S Job 40:12

48:17 *who live around her ... who know her fame.* Nations near and far, respectively. *mighty.* At one time Moab had been powerful and feared (see 27:3; 2Ki 1:1; 3:5; 24:2). *scepter ... staff.* Symbols of authority and dominion (see Ge 49:10; Nu 24:17 and note; Ps 2:9; Eze 19:11,14; 21:10,13 and notes).

48:18 *Come down ... sit.* See Isa 47:1 and note. *Daughter Dibon.* A personification of the important (apparently at one time royal) Moabite city of Dibon (see note on 2Ki 19:21), where the famous Moabite Stone of King Mesha was discovered (see chart, p. xxiv; see also Introduction to 1Kings: Theme: Kingship and Covenant). *Dibon.* See v. 22; Nu 21:30; see also note on Isa 15:2.

48:19 *Aroer.* See TNIV text note on v. 6; see also Nu 32:34; Dt 2:36.

48:20 *Arnon.* Moab's most important river.

48:21 *plateau.* See note on v. 8. *Holon.* Not the same as the town mentioned in Jos 15:51; 21:15. *Jahzah.* See 1Ch 6:78; elsewhere called Jahaz (see v. 34; see also Isa 15:4 and note).

48:22 *Dibon.* See v. 18. *Nebo.* See note on v. 1. *Beth Diblathaim.*

Perhaps the same as, or near, Almon Diblathaim (see Nu 33:46).

48:23 *Kiriathaim.* See note on v. 1. *Beth Gamul.* Modern Khirbet Jumeil, five miles east of Aroer. *Beth Meon.* The same as Baal Meon (see Nu 32:38) and Beth Baal Meon (see Jos 13:17).

48:24 *Kerioth.* See note on Am 2:2. *Bozrah.* Not the same as Bozrah in Edom (see 49:13,22), but another name for Bezer in Moab (see note on Dt 4:43).

48:26 The Lord speaks to the Babylonian invaders. *Make her drunk.* By drinking down the cup of God's wrath (see 13:13; 25:15–17,28). *wallow in her vomit.* See 25:27; Isa 19:14. *let her be an object of ridicule.* As she had once ridiculed others (see v. 27; Zep 2:8,10).

48:27 *shake your head in scorn.* See 18:16 and note; see also Ps 64:8.

48:28 *like a dove ... mouth of a cave.* See Ps 55:6–8; SS 2:14.

48:29–30 An expanded version of the description of Moab found in Isa 16:6.

48:29 *Moab's pride.* It had long since become proverbial (see Isa 25:10–11; Zep 2:8–10).

48:29 ᵒ S Ps 10:5;
S Pr 16:18
48:30 ᵖ S Ps 10:3
48:31 ᵠ ver 36;
Isa 15:5-8 ʳ S 2Ki 3:25
48:32 ˢ S Jos 13:25
ᵗ S Nu 32:3
48:33 ᵘ S Isa 24:7
ᵛ Joel 1:12; Am 5:17
48:34 ʷ S Nu 21:25;
S Jos 13:26
ˣ S Nu 32:3
ʸ S Nu 21:23;
S Isa 15:4 ᶻ S Ge 13:10
ᵃ S Isa 15:5
ᵇ S Isa 15:6
48:35 ᶜ S Isa 15:2
ᵈ Jer 11:13
48:36 ᵉ S ver 31
ᶠ S 2Ki 3:25
ᵍ S Isa 15:7
48:37 ʰ S Isa 15:2;
S Jer 41:5; Eze 27:31;
29:18 ⁱ S Lev 19:27;
S 2Sa 10:4
ʲ S Ge 37:34;
S Isa 3:24; Jer 16:6;
Am 8:10
48:38 ᵏ S Isa 15:3
ˡ S Jer 22:28
48:39 ᵐ Jer 50:23
ⁿ ver 26
48:40 ᵒ S Dt 28:49;
Hab 1:8 ᵖ S Isa 8:8

and the haughtiness ᵒ of her heart.
³⁰ I know her insolence but it is futile,"

declares the LORD,

"and her boasts ᵖ accomplish nothing.
³¹ Therefore I wail ᵠ over Moab,
for all Moab I cry out,
I moan for the people of Kir Hareseth. ʳ
³² I weep for you, as Jazer ˢ weeps,
you vines of Sibmah. ᵗ
Your branches spread as far as the sea ᵃ;
they reached as far as ᵇ Jazer.
The destroyer has fallen
on your ripened fruit and grapes.
³³ Joy and gladness are gone
from the orchards and fields of Moab.
I have stopped the flow of wine ᵘ from the presses;
no one treads them with shouts of joy. ᵛ
Although there are shouts,
they are not shouts of joy.

³⁴ "The sound of their cry rises
from Heshbon ʷ to Elealeh ˣ and Jahaz, ʸ
from Zoar ᶻ as far as Horonaim ᵃ and Eglath Shelishiyah,
for even the waters of Nimrim are dried up. ᵇ
³⁵ In Moab I will put an end
to those who make offerings on the high places ᶜ
and burn incense ᵈ to their gods,"

declares the LORD.

³⁶ "So my heart laments ᵉ for Moab like the music of a pipe;
it laments like a pipe for the people of Kir Hareseth. ᶠ
The wealth they acquired ᵍ is gone.
³⁷ Every head is shaved ʰ
and every beard ⁱ cut off;
every hand is slashed
and every waist is covered with sackcloth. ʲ
³⁸ On all the roofs in Moab
and in the public squares ᵏ
there is nothing but mourning,
for I have broken Moab
like a jar ˡ that no one wants,"

declares the LORD.

³⁹ "How shattered ᵐ she is! How they wail!
How Moab turns her back in shame!
Moab has become an object of ridicule, ⁿ
an object of horror to all those around her."

⁴⁰ This is what the LORD says:

"Look! An eagle is swooping ᵒ down,
spreading its wings ᵖ over Moab.

ᵃ 32 Probably the Dead Sea   ᵇ 32 Two Hebrew manuscripts and Septuagint; most Hebrew manuscripts *as far as the Sea of*

48:31–33 See Isa 16:7–10.
48:31–32 *l.* The prophet (as in Isa 16:9; cf. Isa 15:5).
48:31 *moan.* Like a mourning dove (see Isa 38:14; 59:11). *Kir Hareseth.* See Isa 16:7,11; see also note on Isa 15:1.
48:32 *as Jazer.* Or "more than Jazer" (so also in Isa 16:9). *Jazer ... Sibmah ... sea.* See note on Isa 16:8. *vines.* See note on v. 11. *destroyer.* See v. 8; probably Nebuchadnezzar.
48:33 *orchards.* See note on 2:7. *treads.* See note on Isa 16:10. *not shouts of joy.* Instead, shouts of judgment (see 25:30; 51:14).
48:34 See Isa 15:4–6 and notes.
48:36 See Isa 16:11. *pipe.* Played by mourners at funerals (see

Mt 9:23–24 and note on 9:23).
48:37 Signs of mourning (see Isa 15:2–3 and notes). *is slashed.* See note on 16:6.
48:38 *broken ... like a jar that no one wants.* See v. 4 and note on v. 12; cf. the description of King Jehoiachin in 22:28 (see note there).
48:39 *object of ridicule.* See v. 26 and note.
48:40–41 Echoed in 49:22 with respect to Edom.
48:40 *eagle.* Nebuchadnezzar (as in Eze 17:3); see Dt 28:49 and note.

⁴¹Kerioth[a][q] will be captured
  and the strongholds taken.
In that day the hearts of Moab's warriors[r]
  will be like the heart of a woman in labor.[s]
⁴²Moab will be destroyed[t] as a nation[u]
  because she defied[v] the LORD.
⁴³Terror[w] and pit and snare[x] await you,
  you people of Moab,"

declares the LORD.

⁴⁴"Whoever flees[y] from the terror
  will fall into a pit,
whoever climbs out of the pit
  will be caught in a snare;
for I will bring on Moab
  the year[z] of her punishment,"

declares the LORD.

⁴⁵"In the shadow of Heshbon
  the fugitives stand helpless,
for a fire has gone out from Heshbon,
  a blaze from the midst of Sihon;[a]
it burns the foreheads of Moab,
  the skulls[b] of the noisy boasters.
⁴⁶Woe to you, Moab![c]
  The people of Chemosh are destroyed;
your sons are taken into exile
  and your daughters into captivity.

⁴⁷"Yet I will restore[d] the fortunes of Moab
  in days to come,"

declares the LORD.

Here ends the judgment on Moab.

A MESSAGE ABOUT AMMON

49

Concerning the Ammonites:[e]

This is what the LORD says:

"Has Israel no children?
  Has she no heirs?
Why then has Molek[b][f] taken possession of Gad?[g]
  Why do his people live in its towns?
²But the days are coming,"
  declares the LORD,
"when I will sound the battle cry[h]
  against Rabbah[i] of the Ammonites;

ᵃ 41 Or The cities   ᵇ 1 Or their king; also in verse 3

48:41 [q] S Isa 15:1
[r] Am 2:16 [s] S Isa 21:3
48:42 [t] S Isa 16:14
[u] ver 2 [v] S ver 26
48:43 [w] Jer 49:5
[x] S Isa 24:17
48:44 [y] 1Ki 19:17;
S Job 20:24;
Isa 24:18; S Jer 46:5
[z] Jer 11:23; 23:12
48:45 [a] S Nu 21:21,
26-28; S Jos 12:2
[b] Nu 24:17
48:46 [c] S Nu 21:29
48:47 [d] Ps 14:7;
Isa 11:11; Jer 12:15;
49:6, 39; Eze 16:53;
Da 11:41
49:1 [e] S Ge 19:38;
S 1Sa 11:1-11;
2Sa 10:1-19
[f] S Lev 18:21
[g] Ge 30:11
49:2 [h] S Jer 4:19
[i] S Dt 3:11

48:41 *woman in labor.* See note on 4:31.
48:43 *Terror and pit and snare.* The Hebrew original illustrates Jeremiah's fondness for the well-turned phrase (see Introduction: Literary Features)—though in this case Jeremiah was not its creator (see Isa 24:17–18 and note on 24:17).

48:44 *Whoever flees ... will fall ... whoever climbs ... will be caught.* Divine judgment, once determined, is unavoidable (see Am 5:19).
48:45–46 Echoed from Nu 21:28–29; 24:17. Balaam's oracles against Moab are about to be fulfilled.
48:45 *Heshbon.* See note on v. 2. Apparently at this time it was controlled by the Ammonites (see 49:3). *Sihon.* Refers to the associates of Sihon, king of the Amorites, whose chief city was Heshbon (see Nu 21:27) during the time of the exodus. *boasters.* See note on v. 29.
48:46 *Chemosh.* See note on v. 7.
48:47 See 46:26. *restore the fortunes.* See note on 29:14. *in days*

to come. During the Messianic era. *Here ends.* A note by the final compiler of the book of Jeremiah (see 51:64).
49:1 *Concerning the Ammonites.* See Eze 25:1–7; Am 1:13–15; Zep 2:8–11. Ammon was east of the Jordan and north of Moab (see note on Ge 19:36–38). *Has Israel no ... heirs?* Rhetorical questions to underscore how the Ammonites have humiliated Israel. *Molek.* The chief god of the Ammonites (see 1Ki 11:5,7, 33), also known as Milkom (see note on 1Ki 11:5). Both titles are related to the West Semitic word for "king" (see TNIV text note here). *taken possession of Gad.* Probably refers to the aftermath of Tiglath-Pileser III's conquest of Transjordan in 734–732 B.C. The Ammonites later apparently recovered from their defeat and overran some of the territory owned by the Israelite tribe of Gad. *his.* Molek's.
49:2 *battle cry.* See Am 1:14. *Rabbah of the Ammonites.* See note on Dt 3:11. *mound of ruins.* See 30:18 and note.

49:2 *i* S Dt 13:16
k S Isa 14:2;
S Jer 30:16;
Eze 21:28-32; 25:2-11
49:3 *l* S Jos 13:26
m S Ge 12:8;
S Jos 8:28
n S Ge 37:34 *o* Zep 1:5
p S Jer 48:7
49:4 *q* S Jer 3:6
r S Jer 9:23; 1Ti 6:17
s S Jer 21:13
49:5 *t* S Jer 44:14
49:6 *u* Jer 12:14-17;
S 48:47
49:7 *v* S Ge 25:30;
S Ps 83:6
w S Ge 36:11,15,34
49:8 *x* S Jdg 6:2
y S Ge 10:7; S 25:3
49:10 *z* S Ge 3:8
a Isa 34:10-12;
S Jer 11:23; Eze 35:4;
Ob 1:18; Mal 1:2-5

it will become a mound of ruins,[i]
and its surrounding villages will be set on fire.
Then Israel will drive out
those who drove her out,[k]"

says the LORD.

[3] "Wail, Heshbon,[l] for Ai[m] is destroyed!
Cry out, you inhabitants of Rabbah!
Put on sackcloth[n] and mourn;
rush here and there inside the walls,
for Molek[o] will go into exile,[p]
together with his priests and officials.
[4] Why do you boast of your valleys,
boast of your valleys so fruitful?
Unfaithful Daughter Ammon,[q]
you trust in your riches[r] and say,
'Who will attack me?'[s]
[5] I will bring terror on you
from all those around you,"

declares the Lord, the LORD Almighty.

"Every one of you will be driven away,
and no one will gather the fugitives.[t]

[6] "Yet afterward, I will restore[u] the fortunes of the Ammonites,"

declares the LORD.

A MESSAGE ABOUT EDOM

49:9–10pp — Ob 5–6
49:14–16pp — Ob 1–4

[7] Concerning Edom:[v]

This is what the LORD Almighty says:

"Is there no longer wisdom in Teman?[w]
Has counsel perished from the prudent?
Has their wisdom decayed?
[8] Turn and flee, hide in deep caves,[x]
you who live in Dedan,[y]
for I will bring disaster on Esau
at the time when I punish him.
[9] If grape pickers came to you,
would they not leave a few grapes?
If thieves came during the night,
would they not steal only as much as they wanted?
[10] But I will strip Esau bare;
I will uncover his hiding places,[z]
so that he cannot conceal himself.
His armed men are destroyed,
also his allies and neighbors,
so there is no one[a] to say,

49:3 *Heshbon.* See note on 48:45; see also Jdg 11:26–27. *Ai.* Not the Ai of Jos 8. *walls.* The Hebrew for this word refers not to city walls but to walls separating vineyards from each other (see Nu 22:24; Isa 5:5). *Molek.* See note on v. 1. *will go into exile . . . and officials.* See note on 48:7.

49:4 *Unfaithful Daughter.* A personification of the Ammonites (see note on 2Ki 19:21); the same language is used of the people of Judah in 31:22. *you trust in your riches.* Spoken to Moab in 48:7. *Who will attack me?* According to Josephus (*Antiquities,* 10.9.7) Nebuchadnezzar destroyed Ammon in the 23rd year of his reign (582 B.C.).

49:7–22 Shares many memorable phrases and concepts with the book of Obadiah (see Introduction to Obadiah: Unity and Theme).

49:7 *Concerning Edom.* See Isa 21:11–12; Eze 25:12–14; Am

1:11–12; Ob 1–16. *wisdom.* For which Edom was justly famed (see notes on Job 1:1; 2:11). *Teman.* An important Edomite town located south of the Dead Sea (see note on Job 2:11). In v. 20 it is used in parallelism with Edom itself.

49:8 *Turn and flee.* See v. 24; 46:21. *Dedan.* See 25:23; see also notes on Isa 21:13; Eze 25:13. *Esau.* The patriarch Jacob's brother, and another name for Edom (see Ge 25:29–30; 36:1), just as Israel was another name for Jacob (see Ge 32:28). The fact that Esau was Jacob's brother made Edom's enmity toward Israel all the more reprehensible (see Am 1:11; Ob 10 and notes).

49:9–10 Paralleled in Ob 5–6 (see notes there).

49:9 *grape pickers.* See note on v. 13. *leave a few grapes.* For the poor to glean (see note on Ru 2:2).

49:10 *strip . . . bare.* See note on 13:22. *destroyed.* See 31:15; Isa 19:7.

¹¹ 'Leave your fatherless children; ᵇ I will keep them alive.
  Your widows ᶜ too can depend on me.' "

¹²This is what the LORD says: "If those who do not deserve to drink the cup ᵈ must drink it, why should you go unpunished? ᵉ You will not go unpunished, but must drink it. ¹³I swear ᶠ by myself," declares the LORD, "that Bozrah ᵍ will become a ruin and a curse, ᵃ an object of horror ʰ and reproach; ⁱ and all its towns will be in ruins forever." ʲ

¹⁴ I have heard a message from the LORD;
    an envoy was sent to the nations to say,
  "Assemble yourselves to attack it!
    Rise up for battle!"

¹⁵ "Now I will make you small among the nations,
    despised among the peoples.
¹⁶ The terror you inspire
    and the pride ᵏ of your heart have deceived you,
  you who live in the clefts of the rocks, ˡ
    who occupy the heights of the hill.
  Though you build your nest ᵐ as high as the eagle's,
    from there I will bring you down,"

                                          declares the LORD.

¹⁷ "Edom will become an object of horror; ⁿ
    all who pass by will be appalled and will scoff
    because of ᵒ all its wounds.
¹⁸ As Sodom ᵖ and Gomorrah ᵠ were overthrown,
    along with their neighboring towns,"

                                          says the LORD,

  "so no one will live there;
    no one will dwell ʳ in it.

¹⁹ "Like a lion ˢ coming up from Jordan's thickets ᵗ
    to a rich pastureland,
  I will chase Edom from its land in an instant.
    Who is the chosen one I will appoint for this?
  Who is like ᵘ me and who can challenge me? ᵛ
    And what shepherd ʷ can stand against me?"

²⁰ Therefore, hear what the LORD has planned against Edom, ˣ
    what he has purposed ʸ against those who live in Teman: ᶻ
  The young of the flock ᵃ will be dragged away;
    their pasture will be appalled at their fate. ᵇ
²¹ At the sound of their fall the earth will tremble; ᶜ
    their cry ᵈ will resound to the Red Sea. ᵇ
²² Look! An eagle will soar and swoop ᵉ down,
    spreading its wings over Bozrah. ᶠ

ᵃ 13 That is, its name will be used in cursing (see Jer. 29:22); or, others will see that it is cursed.
ᵇ 21 Or the Sea of Reeds

49:11 ᵇ Hos 14:3
ᶜ S Dt 10:18; Jas 1:27
49:12 ᵈ S Isa 51:23; S Jer 25:15; Mt 20:22
ᵉ S Pr 11:31
49:13 ᶠ S Ge 22:16
ᵍ S Ge 36:33 ʰ ver 17
ⁱ Jer 42:18 ʲ S Jer 19:8; Eze 35:9
49:16 ᵏ Eze 35:13; Ob 1:12 ˡ S Job 39:28
ᵐ S Job 39:27
49:17 ⁿ ver 13
ᵒ S Dt 29:22; Eze 35:7
49:18 ᵖ Jer 23:14
ᵠ S Ge 19:24 ʳ ver 33; S Isa 34:10
49:19 ˢ S 1Sa 17:34
ᵗ S Jer 12:5
ᵘ S Ex 8:10; S 2Ch 20:6; S Isa 46:5
ᵛ S Job 9:19; Jer 50:44
ʷ 1Sa 17:35
49:20 ˣ Isa 34:5
ʸ Isa 14:27 ᶻ ver 7; S Ge 36:11 ᵃ Jer 50:45
ᵇ Jer 50:45
49:21 ᶜ Ps 114:7; Eze 26:15; 27:28; 31:16 ᵈ Jer 50:46; 51:29; Eze 26:18
49:22 ᵉ S Dt 28:49; Hos 8:1; Hab 1:8
ᶠ S Ge 36:33

49:11 When the men of Edom go off to war and die, the Lord will protect their widows and orphans.

49:12 Echoed from 25:28–29. *those who do not deserve …must drink it.* Though they are God's chosen ones, the people of Judah will be punished because of their sin (see 25:28; Am 3:2 and notes).

49:13 *swear by myself.* See notes on Ge 22:16; Isa 45:23; see also 22:5; 51:14. *Bozrah.* Not the Bozrah of 48:24 (see note there); the Edomite Bozrah was probably the capital of Edom in the days of Jeremiah (see v. 22; Ge 36:33; see also notes on Isa 34:6; Am 1:12). The Hebrew root underlying Bozrah is the same as that for "grape pickers" in v. 9. *ruin …reproach.* See 25:18. *towns.* Surrounding villages. *in ruins forever.* See 25:9; Ps 74:3; Isa 58:12 and note.

49:14–16 Paralleled in Ob 1–4.

49:16 *pride.* Edom's besetting sin (see v. 4; Ob 11–13; cf. 48:29–30). *rocks.* Perhaps a reference to Petra (see note on 2Ki 14:7), the most spectacular of the mountain strongholds for which Edom was noted.

49:17 Echoed from 19:8.

49:18 Repeated almost verbatim in 50:40, and echoed in part in v. 33. *Sodom and Gomorrah were overthrown.* See Ge 19:24–25. Later calamities were often compared with the one that befell Sodom and Gomorrah (see note on Am 4:11). *their neighboring towns.* Primarily Admah and Zeboyim (see Ge 14:2,8; Dt 29:23; Hos 11:8 and note).

49:19–21 Repeated almost verbatim in the oracle against Babylon (see 50:44–46).

49:19 *Jordan's thickets.* See 12:5 and note. *shepherd.* Ruler (see note on 2:8).

49:20 *Teman.* See note on v. 7. *flock.* The people of Edom.

49:22 Echoed from 48:40–41. *eagle.* Represents Nebuchadnezzar in 48:40 (see note there), and probably here also. A more complete subjugation of the Edomites, however, was accomplished by Nabatean Arabs (perhaps the "desert jackals" of Mal 1:3) beginning c. 550 B.C. *Bozrah.* See note on v. 13. *woman in labor.* See note on 4:31.

49:22 *a* Jer 50:36;
Na 3:13 *h* Isa 13:8
49:23 *i* S Ge 14:15;
2Ki 14:28; 2Ch 16:2;
Ac 9:2 *j* 1Ki 8:65;
Isa 10:9; Eze 47:16;
Am 6:2; Zec 9:2
k S 2Ki 18:34; S 19:13
l S Ge 49:4
49:24 *m* Jer 13:21
49:26 *n* S Isa 9:17;
S 13:18 *o* Isa 17:12-14
49:27 *p* Jer 21:14;
43:12; 50:32;
Eze 30:8; 39:6;
Am 1:4 *q* S Ge 14:15
r Isa 17:1 *s* S 1Ki 15:18
49:28 *t* S Ge 25:13
u S Jos 11:1
v S Jer 10:22
w S Jdg 6:3
49:29 *x* ver 32
y S Jer 6:25
49:30 *z* S Jdg 6:2
a Jos 11:1 *b* S Jer 10:22
49:31 *c* Eze 38:11
49:32 *d* S Jdg 6:5
e ver 29 *f* ver 36;
Jer 13:24 *g* S Jer 9:26

> In that day the hearts of Edom's warriors[g]
> will be like the heart of a woman in labor.[h]

A MESSAGE ABOUT DAMASCUS

23Concerning Damascus:[i]

> "Hamath[j] and Arpad[k] are dismayed,
> for they have heard bad news.
> They are disheartened,
> troubled like[a] the restless sea.[l]
> 24Damascus has become feeble,
> she has turned to flee
> and panic has gripped her;
> anguish and pain have seized her,
> pain like that of a woman in labor.[m]
> 25Why has the city of renown not been abandoned,
> the town in which I delight?
> 26Surely, her young men[n] will fall in the streets;
> all her soldiers will be silenced[o] in that day,"

> > declares the LORD Almighty.

> 27"I will set fire[p] to the walls of Damascus;[q]
> it will consume[r] the fortresses of Ben-Hadad.[s]"

A MESSAGE ABOUT KEDAR AND HAZOR

28Concerning Kedar[t] and the kingdoms of Hazor,[u] which Nebuchadnezzar[v] king of Babylon attacked:

This is what the LORD says:

> "Arise, and attack Kedar
> and destroy the people of the East.[w]
> 29Their tents and their flocks[x] will be taken;
> their shelters will be carried off
> with all their goods and camels.
> People will shout to them,
> 'Terror[y] on every side!'

> 30"Flee quickly away!
> Stay in deep caves,[z] you who live in Hazor,[a]"

> > declares the LORD.

> "Nebuchadnezzar[b] king of Babylon has plotted against you;
> he has devised a plan against you.

> 31"Arise and attack a nation at ease,
> which lives in confidence,"

> > declares the LORD,

> "a nation that has neither gates nor bars;[c]
> its people live far from danger.
> 32Their camels[d] will become plunder,
> and their large herds[e] will be booty.
> I will scatter to the winds[f] those who are in distant places[b][g]

---

a 23 Hebrew *on* or *by*   *b 32* Or *who clip the hair by their foreheads*

49:23 *Concerning Damascus.* See Isa 17; Am 1:3–5 (see also note on Isa 17:1). *Hamath.* An important city in the kingdom of Aram (see Isa 10:9; Zec 9:2 and notes). *Arpad.* See note on Isa 10:9. *bad news.* The threat of Babylonian invasion. *troubled like the restless sea.* See Isa 57:20.
49:24 *anguish.* See note on 4:19.
49:26 Repeated almost verbatim in 50:30.
49:27 A conventional word of judgment (see note on Am 1:4).
49:28 *Concerning Kedar.* See Isa 21:13–17; see also 2:10 and note. *kingdoms of Hazor.* See vv. 30,33; not the Hazor north of the Sea of Galilee (see Jos 11:1). These kingdoms may have included Dedan, Tema, Buz and other Arab regions (see 25:23–24 and notes), since the Hebrew root of the proper name Hazor of-

ten serves as a common noun meaning "settlement" (see especially Isa 42:11; see also Ge 25:16). *Nebuchadnezzar . . . attacked.* In 599–598 B.C. *people of the East.* See Jdg 6:3 and note; Job 1:3; Eze 25:4.
49:29 *Terror on every side.* See note on 6:25.
49:30 *Stay in deep caves.* See v. 8.
49:31 *at ease.* Completely secure (see Job 21:23). *in confidence.* In safety, unsuspecting (see Jdg 18:7 and note; Eze 38:11). *has neither gates nor bars.* Lives in unwalled villages (see Dt 3:5; cf. 1Sa 23:7).
49:32 *scatter to the winds.* See Eze 5:12; 12:4. *who are in distant places.* See note on 9:26. *disaster . . . from every side.* Contrast the description of Solomon's realm in 1Ki 5:4.

and will bring disaster on them from every side,"

> declares the LORD.

33 "Hazor[h] will become a haunt of jackals,[i]
a desolate[j] place forever.
No one will live there;
no one will dwell[k] in it."

A MESSAGE ABOUT ELAM

34 This is the word of the LORD that came to Jeremiah the prophet concerning Elam,[l] early in the reign of Zedekiah[m] king of Judah:

35 This is what the LORD Almighty says:

> "See, I will break the bow[n] of Elam,
> the mainstay of their might.
> 36 I will bring against Elam the four winds[o]
> from the four quarters of the heavens;[p]
> I will scatter them to the four winds,
> and there will not be a nation
> where Elam's exiles do not go.
> 37 I will shatter Elam before their foes,
> before those who seek their lives;
> I will bring disaster on them,
> even my fierce anger,"[q]

> declares the LORD.

> "I will pursue them with the sword[r]
> until I have made an end of them.
> 38 I will set my throne in Elam
> and destroy her king and officials,"

> declares the LORD.

> 39 "Yet I will restore[s] the fortunes of Elam
> in days to come,"

> declares the LORD.

A MESSAGE ABOUT BABYLON

51:15–19pp — Jer 10:12–16

50 This is the word the LORD spoke through Jeremiah the prophet concerning Babylon[t] and the land of the Babylonians[a]:

2 "Announce and proclaim[u] among the nations,
lift up a banner[v] and proclaim it;
keep nothing back, but say,
'Babylon will be captured;[w]
Bel[x] will be put to shame,[y]
Marduk[z] filled with terror.
Her images will be put to shame
and her idols[a] filled with terror.'

---

[a] 1 Or *Chaldeans*; also in verses 8, 25, 35 and 45

49:33 [h] S Jos 11:1
[i] S Isa 13:22 [j] Jer 48:9
[k] S ver 18; Jer 51:37
49:34 4:16 [l] S Ge 10:22
[m] 2Ki 24:18
49:35 [n] S Ps 37:15;
S Isa 22:6
49:36 [o] S ver 32
[p] Da 11:4
49:37 [q] Jer 30:24
[r] Jer 9:16; Eze 32:24
49:39 [s] S Jer 48:47
50:1 [t] S Ge 10:10;
S Ps 137:8
50:2 [u] S Dt 30:4;
Jer 4:16 [v] S Ps 20:5;
S Isa 13:2 [w] ver 9;
Jer 51:31 [x] S Isa 21:9;
S 46:1 [y] Ps 97:7;
Jer 51:52 [z] ver 38;
Isa 46:6; Jer 51:47
[a] S Lev 26:30

49:33 *haunt of jackals.* See note on 9:11. *No one … dwell in it.* Echoes v. 18.
49:34 *This is the word of the LORD … concerning.* See note on 46:1. *Elam.* See note on Isa 11:11.
49:35 *bow.* The Elamites were skilled archers (see Isa 22:6).
49:36 Contrast Isa 11:12. *to the four winds.* In every direction (see Eze 37:9; Da 7:2; 8:8).
49:37 *I will pursue … made an end of them.* Echoes 9:16.
49:38 *set my throne in.* See 1:15 and note.
50:1—51:64 See Isa 13:1—14:23; 21:1–9. Jeremiah's prophecy concerning Babylon is by far the longest of his oracles against foreign nations (chs. 46–51) and expands on his earlier and briefer statements (see 25:12–14,26). Its date, in whole or in part, is 593 B.C. (see 51:59 and note). The two chapters divide into three main sections (50:2–28; 50:29—51:26; 51:27–58),

each of which begins with a summons concerning war against Babylon, Judah's mortal enemy (see 50:2–3; 50:29–32; 51:27–32).
50:1 *word.* Or "message" (as in 46:13), comprising chs. 50–51. *through.* See 37:2. The message would eventually be sent by the prophet to Babylon itself (see 51:59–61).
50:2 *Announce and proclaim.* See 4:5; 46:14. *lift up a banner.* See note on Isa 5:26. The Hebrew for this phrase is translated "raise the signal" in 4:6. *Babylon will be captured.* Fulfilled in 539 B.C. *Bel.* See 51:44; Isa 46:1 and note. *put to shame … filled with terror.* The repetition of each of these phrases emphasizes that the chief god of Babylon and his images and idols are alike doomed. *Her … her.* Babylon's. *idols.* See note on Lev 26:30. Derogatory references concerning idols and idolatry are common in the OT (see, e.g., Isa 44:9–20).

50:3 *b* S ver 26;
S Isa 41:25;
S Jer 25:26 *c* S ver 13;
S Isa 14:22-23;
S Jer 9:11 *d* Zep 1:3
50:4 *e* S Jer 3:18;
Eze 37:22 *f* S Ezr 3:12
g S Isa 9:13;
Eze 37:17; Hos 3:5
50:5 *h* S Isa 11:16;
S Jer 31:21
i S Isa 29:1; Jer 33:7
j S Dt 29:14; Isa 55:3;
Jer 32:40; Heb 8:6-10
50:6 *k* S Ps 119:176;
Mt 9:36; 10:6
l S Jer 2:8; S 10:21
m S Ps 95:10;
Jer 23:32; Eze 13:10
n Jer 3:6; Eze 34:6
o ver 19
50:7 *p* S Jer 5:17;
10:25; Eze 35:12
q Jer 2:3 *r* S Jer 14:8
50:8 *s* S Isa 48:20
t ver 28
50:9 *u* S Isa 13:17
v S Jer 25:14
w S Isa 41:25;
S Jer 25:26 *x* S ver 2
y S Isa 13:18
50:10 *z* Isa 47:11;
S Jer 30:16
50:11 *a* S Isa 47:6
b S Jer 31:18
50:12 *c* Jer 51:47
d ver 13; S Isa 21:1;
Jer 25:12; 51:26
50:13 *e* ver 3, S 12;
S Jer 9:11; 48:9; 51:62

³ A nation from the north *b* will attack her
 and lay waste her land.
No one will live *c* in it;
 both people and animals *d* will flee away.

⁴ "In those days, at that time,"
 declares the LORD,
 "the people of Israel and the people of Judah together *e*
 will go in tears *f* to seek *g* the LORD their God.
⁵ They will ask the way *h* to Zion
 and turn their faces toward it.
They will come *i* and bind themselves to the LORD
 in an everlasting covenant *j*
 that will not be forgotten.

⁶ "My people have been lost sheep; *k*
 their shepherds *l* have led them astray *m*
 and caused them to roam on the mountains.
They wandered over mountain and hill *n*
 and forgot their own resting place. *o*
⁷ Whoever found them devoured *p* them;
 their enemies said, 'We are not guilty, *q*
for they sinned against the LORD, their verdant pasture,
 the LORD, the hope *r* of their ancestors.'

⁸ "Flee *s* out of Babylon; *t*
 leave the land of the Babylonians,
 and be like the goats that lead the flock.
⁹ For I will stir *u* up and bring against Babylon
 an alliance of great nations *v* from the land of the north. *w*
They will take up their positions against her,
 and from the north she will be captured. *x*
Their arrows *y* will be like skilled warriors
 who do not return empty-handed.
¹⁰ So Babylonia *a* will be plundered; *z*
 all who plunder her will have their fill,"

declares the LORD.

¹¹ "Because you rejoice and are glad,
 you who pillage my inheritance, *a*
because you frolic like a heifer *b* threshing grain
 and neigh like stallions,
¹² your mother will be greatly ashamed;
 she who gave you birth will be disgraced. *c*
She will be the least of the nations—
 a wilderness, a dry land, a desert. *d*
¹³ Because of the LORD's anger she will not be inhabited
 but will be completely desolate. *e*

---

a 10 Or *Chaldea*

50:3 *nation from the north.* In Jeremiah, the foe from the north is almost always Babylon (see, e.g., 1:14–15). Here, however, the reference is probably to Persia. Babylon's nemesis is expanded to "an alliance of great nations" in v. 9, specified by name in 51:27–28. *people and animals will flee.* Babylon will suffer the same fate as Jerusalem (see 33:12).
50:4 *Israel and . . . Judah together.* See note on 3:18. *tears.* Of repentance (see 3:21–22; 31:9).
50:5 *everlasting covenant.* See 32:40 and note; see also 31:31–34; 33:20–21.
50:6 *lost sheep.* See Jesus' parable in Lk 15:3–7. *shepherds.* Rulers (see note on 2:8). *mountain and hill.* Places where pagan gods were worshiped (see note on 2:20). *their own resting place.* The Lord (see v. 7).
50:7 *hope of their ancestors.* A phrase found only here (see 14:8,22; cf. Ac 28:20).

50:8 *like the goats that lead the flock.* Judah would be among the first of the captive peoples to be released from exile in Babylon.
50:9 *alliance of great nations.* See Isa 13:4. They are named in 51:27–28 (see note on v. 3).
50:11 *you.* Babylon. *my inheritance.* God's land and people (see 2:7; 12:7 and notes). *frolic like a heifer.* See Mal 4:2. *stallions.* See note on 8:16.
50:12 *mother.* Either (1) the city or, more likely, (2) the land (see Isa 50:1; Hos 2:5). *least.* Lit. "last." As Amalek, "first among the nations" (Nu 24:20) to attack Israel, was destroyed, so Babylon, the last to attack Israel (up to Jeremiah's time), would be destroyed.
50:13 *not be inhabited.* See Isa 13:20 and note. *All who pass . . . because of all her wounds.* Said of Jerusalem in 19:8 and of Edom in 49:17.

All who pass Babylon will be appalled;*f*
  they will scoff*g* because of all her wounds. *h*

14 "Take up your positions around Babylon,
  all you who draw the bow. *i*
Shoot at her! Spare no arrows,*j*
  for she has sinned against the LORD.
15 Shout*k* against her on every side!
  She surrenders, her towers fall,
  her walls*l* are torn down.
Since this is the vengeance*m* of the LORD,
  take vengeance on her;
  do to her*n* as she has done to others. *o*
16 Cut off from Babylon the sowers,
  and the reapers with their sickles at harvest.
Because of the sword*p* of the oppressor
  let everyone return to their own people, *q*
  let everyone flee to their own land. *r*

17 "Israel is a scattered flock*s*
  that lions*t* have chased away.
The first to devour*u* them
  was the king*v* of Assyria;
the last to crush their bones*w*
  was Nebuchadnezzar*x* king*y* of Babylon."

18 Therefore this is what the LORD Almighty, the God of Israel, says:

"I will punish the king of Babylon and his land
  as I punished the king*z* of Assyria. *a*
19 But I will bring*b* Israel back to their own pasture,
  and they will graze on Carmel and Bashan;
their appetite will be satisfied*c*
  on the hills*d* of Ephraim and Gilead. *e*
20 In those days, at that time,"
  declares the LORD,
"search will be made for Israel's guilt,
  but there will be none, *f*
and for the sins*g* of Judah,
  but none will be found,
  for I will forgive*h* the remnant*i* I spare.

21 "Attack the land of Merathaim
  and those who live in Pekod.*j*
Pursue, kill and completely destroy*a* them,"

declares the LORD.

a 21 The Hebrew term refers to the irrevocable giving over of things or persons to the LORD, often by totally destroying them; also in verse 26.

50:13 *f* Jer 51:41
g S Jer 18:16; 51:37;
Eze 27:36; Hab 2:6
h S Dt 29:22
50:14 *i* ver 29, 42
j S Isa 13:18
50:15 *k* Jer 51:14
l S 2Ki 25:4;
S Jer 51:44, 58
m ver 28; S Isa 10:3;
63:4; Jer 51:6
n ver 29; Ps 137:8;
Rev 18:6 *o* Jer 51:24;
Hab 2:7-8
50:16 *p* S Jer 25:38
q S Isa 13:14 *r* Jer 51:9
50:17 *s* S Lev 26:33;
S Ps 119:176
t S 2Ki 24:1; S Jer 2:15
u S Jer 5:17
v S Dt 4:27;
S 2Ki 15:29
w S Nu 24:8; La 3:4
x Jer 51:34
y S 2Ki 24:17; S 25:7
50:18 *z* S Isa 10:12
a Eze 31:3; Zep 2:13
50:19 *b* S Jer 31:10;
Eze 34:13 *c* Jer 31:14
d S Jer 31:5
e Mic 7:14; Zec 10:10
50:20 *f* S Ps 17:3
g Ps 103:12;
S Isa 38:17;
Eze 33:16; Mic 7:18,
19; Zec 3:4, 9
h S Isa 33:24
i S Ge 45:7; Isa 1:9;
10:20-22; S Ro 9:27
50:21 *j* Eze 23:23

50:14 *you who draw the bow.* Including the Medes (see Isa 13:17–18).
50:15 *Shout.* Give the battle cry (see Jos 6:16). *vengeance of the LORD.* See v. 28; 51:11. Though originating in his sovereign holiness, it was often carried out by his people (see Nu 31:3). *do to her . . . to others.* See v. 29; Ob 15 and note; cf. Gal 6:7–8.
50:16 *sword of the oppressor.* See 46:16. *let everyone . . . to their own land.* The Hebrew for this passage has a parallel in Isa 13:14. The captive peoples are warned to flee Babylon in order to avoid being cut down by her invaders.
50:17 *scattered flock.* See Joel 3:2. *lions.* Symbolic of Assyria and Babylon (see 4:7; Isa 15:9 and notes). *The first . . . was the king of Assyria.* The Assyrians destroyed Israel (the northern kingdom) in 722–721 B.C. *the last . . . was Nebuchadnezzar.* The Babylonians destroyed Judah (the southern kingdom) in 586 B.C.
50:18 *I punished the king of Assyria.* Nineveh, the proud Assyr-

ian capital, fell in 612 B.C., and Assyria herself was conquered by a coalition of Medes and Babylonians in 609.
50:19 *Carmel.* See Isa 33:9 and note. *Bashan.* See note on Isa 2:13. *hills of Ephraim.* The lush mountains of central Israel (see Eze 34:13–14). *Gilead.* See note on Ge 31:21; see also Nu 32:1; Mic 7:14.
50:20 See 33:8 and note; see also 36:3; Mic 7:18–19.
50:21 *Merathaim.* Means "double rebellion [against the Lord]," perhaps referring to vv. 24,29 (see Jdg 3:8; Isa 40:2 and notes). It is probably a pun on the Babylonian word *marratu,* which sometimes referred to a region in southern Babylonia that was characterized by briny waters. *Pekod.* See Eze 23:23; means "punishment [from the Lord]," a pun on *Puqudu,* the Babylonian name for an Aramean tribe living on the eastern bank of the lower Tigris River. *completely destroy.* See TNIV text note; v. 26; 25:9; 51:3; see also note on Dt 2:34.

50:22 k Jer 4:19-21;
51:54
50:23 l S Isa 10:5
m Jer 51:25
n S Isa 14:16
50:24 o Jer 51:12
p Jer 51:31 q Job 9:4
50:25 r S Isa 13:5
s Jer 51:25,55
50:26 t ver 3, 41;
Jer 51:11 u S Ru 3:7
v S Isa 14:22-23
50:27 w S Ps 68:30;
Jer 48:15
x S Isa 30:25;
S Jer 25:34
y S Job 18:20 z Jer 51:6
50:28 a ver 8
b Isa 48:20; Jer 51:10
c S ver 15 d 2Ki 24:13;
Jer 51:11; 52:13
50:29 e S ver 14
f S Isa 13:18; Jer 51:3
g S Dt 32:41;
S Job 21:19;
S Jer 51:6; Rev 18:6
h Eze 35:11; Ob 1:15
i S Isa 14:13-14;
47:10; Da 5:23
j Ps 78:41; Isa 41:20;
Jer 51:5
50:30 k S Isa 13:18
50:31 l S Jer 21:13
m S Job 18:20;
Rev 18:7-8
50:32 n S Ps 119:21
o S Ps 20:8 p Am 5:2
q S Jer 49:27

"Do everything I have commanded you.
²² The noise ^k of battle is in the land,
    the noise of great destruction!
²³ How broken and shattered
    is the hammer ^l of the whole earth! ^m
How desolate ⁿ is Babylon
    among the nations!
²⁴ I set a trap ^o for you, Babylon,
    and you were caught before you knew it;
you were found and captured ^p
    because you opposed ^q the LORD.
²⁵ The LORD has opened his arsenal
    and brought out the weapons ^r of his wrath,
for the Sovereign LORD Almighty has work to do
    in the land of the Babylonians. ^s
²⁶ Come against her from afar. ^t
    Break open her granaries;
    pile her up like heaps of grain. ^u
Completely destroy ^v her
    and leave her no remnant.
²⁷ Kill all her young bulls; ^w
    let them go down to the slaughter! ^x
Woe to them! For their day ^y has come,
    the time ^z for them to be punished.
²⁸ Listen to the fugitives ^a and refugees from Babylon
    declaring in Zion ^b
how the LORD our God has taken vengeance, ^c
    vengeance for his temple. ^d

²⁹ "Summon archers against Babylon,
    all those who draw the bow. ^e
Encamp all around her;
    let no one escape. ^f
Repay ^g her for her deeds; ^h
    do to her as she has done.
For she has defied ⁱ the LORD,
    the Holy One ^j of Israel.
³⁰ Therefore, her young men ^k will fall in the streets;
    all her soldiers will be silenced in that day,"
                                            declares the LORD.

³¹ "See, I am against ^l you, you arrogant one,"
    declares the Lord, the LORD Almighty,
"for your day ^m has come,
    the time for you to be punished.
³² The arrogant ⁿ one will stumble and fall ^o
    and no one will help her up; ^p
I will kindle a fire ^q in her towns
    that will consume all who are around her."

50:22 *great destruction.* See 4:6; 6:1; cf. 48:3; 51:54.
50:23 *hammer of the whole earth.* See note on Isa 10:5. *How desolate . . . among the nations!* The Hebrew for this sentence is repeated verbatim in 51:41.
50:24 *caught before you knew it.* The Persian attack in 539 B.C. would catch the city of Babylon completely by surprise (see 51:8; Isa 47:11).
50:25 *weapons of his wrath.* The nations (see 51:27-28) that the Lord would use to conquer Babylon (see Isa 13:5 and note). *the . . . LORD . . . has work to do.* See 48:10.
50:26 *heaps of grain.* The Hebrew for this expression is used in Ne 4:2 to describe heaps of rubble that had been burned. *Completely destroy her.* By burning (see note on v. 21; see also Jos 11:11-13).
50:27 *young bulls.* The people of Babylon, including especially

her fighting men (see Isa 34:6-7 and notes). *go down to the slaughter.* See note on 48:15. *time for them to be punished.* See 11:23; 23:12; 46:21.
50:28 *fugitives and refugees.* Jewish exiles who had fled the destruction overtaking Babylon. *vengeance, vengeance for his temple.* See v. 15 and note; 46:10; 51:6. The conquest of Babylon was the Lord's response to Babylon's burning of the Jerusalem temple.
50:29 *Repay her for her deeds.* Echoed from 25:14 (see 51:24). *do to her as she has done.* See v. 15 and note. *Holy One of Israel.* A title of God found frequently in Isaiah (see note on Isa 1:4), it occurs in Jeremiah only here and in 51:5.
50:30 Echoes 49:26.
50:31-32 A distant echo of 21:13-14, spoken there to Jerusalem but here to Babylon.

33 This is what the LORD Almighty says:

"The people of Israel are oppressed,[r]
　　and the people of Judah as well.
All their captors hold them fast,
　　refusing to let them go.[s]
34 Yet their Redeemer[t] is strong;
　　the LORD Almighty[u] is his name.
He will vigorously defend their cause[v]
　　so that he may bring rest[w] to their land,
　　but unrest to those who live in Babylon.

35 "A sword[x] against the Babylonians!"[y]
　　declares the LORD—
"against those who live in Babylon
　　and against her officials and wise[z] counselors!
36 A sword against her false prophets!
　　They will become fools.
A sword against her warriors![a]
　　They will be filled with terror.[b]
37 A sword against her horses and chariots[c]
　　and all the foreigners in her ranks!
　　They will become weaklings.[d]
A sword against her treasures![e]
　　They will be plundered.
38 A drought on[a] her waters![f]
　　They will dry[g] up.
For it is a land of idols,[h]
　　idols that will go mad with terror.

39 "So desert creatures[i] and hyenas will live there,
　　and there the owl will dwell.
It will never again be inhabited
　　or lived in from generation to generation.[j]
40 As I overthrew Sodom and Gomorrah[k]
　　along with their neighboring towns,"

declares the LORD,

"so no one will live there;
　　no one will dwell in it.[l]

41 "Look! An army is coming from the north;[m]
　　a great nation and many kings
　　are being stirred[n] up from the ends of the earth.[o]
42 They are armed with bows[p] and spears;
　　they are cruel[q] and without mercy.[r]
They sound like the roaring sea[s]
　　as they ride on their horses;
they come like men in battle formation
　　to attack you, Daughter Babylon.[t]
43 The king of Babylon has heard reports about them,
　　and his hands hang limp.[u]
Anguish has gripped him,

---

[a] 38 Or *A sword against*

50:33 [r] Isa 58:6;
[s] S Isa 14:17
50:34 [t] S Ex 6:6;
S Job 19:25
[u] Jer 31:35; 51:19
[v] S Ps 119:154;
S Isa 49:25; Jer 15:21;
51:36; La 3:58
[w] S Isa 14:7
50:35 [x] S Jer 47:6
[y] S Isa 45:1 [z] Da 5:7
50:36 [a] S Jer 49:22
[b] Jer 51:30, 32
50:37 [c] S 2Ki 19:23;
Jer 51:21 [d] S Isa 19:16
[e] S Isa 45:3
50:38 [f] Ps 137:1;
Jer 51:13 [g] S Isa 11:15;
Jer 51:36 [h] S ver 2
50:39 [i] S Ps 74:14
[j] Isa 13:19-22; 34:13-
15; Jer 51:37; Rev 18:2
50:40 [k] S Ge 19:24;
S Mt 10:15 [l] Jer 51:62
50:41 [m] S ver 26;
S Isa 41:25
[n] S Isa 13:17
[o] S Isa 13:4;
Jer 51:22-28
50:42 [p] S ver 14
[q] S Job 30:21
[r] S Isa 13:18
[s] S Isa 5:30
[t] S Isa 47:1
50:43 [u] S Jer 47:3

50:33 *their captors.* See Isa 14:2. *refusing to let them go.* Reminiscent of the pharaoh's repeated refusals before the exodus (see, e.g., Ex 7:14; 8:2,32; 9:2,7).
50:34 *Redeemer.* See 31:11 and note. *defend their cause.* See 51:36. *bring rest.* See 31:2 and note; see also Isa 14:3,7 and notes on Dt 3:20; Jos 1:13.
50:35–38 Cf. Eze 21.
50:36 *false prophets . . . will become fools.* See Isa 44:25; see also Nu 12:11 and TNIV text note on Pr 1:7.
50:37 *against her horses and chariots.* See Isa 43:17; see also Ps

20:7. *foreigners.* See 25:20,24; Ne 13:3. *will become weaklings.* See Na 3:13 and note.
50:38 *idols.* See 51:52; see also note on Isa 21:9. *go mad.* See 25:16 and note.
50:39 See Isa 13:20–22 and notes.
50:40 Echoes 49:18 (see note there).
50:41–43 Echoes 6:22–24 (see notes there). The earlier oracle, referring to Jerusalem, is here applied to Babylon.
50:42 *Daughter Babylon.* A personification of the city of Babylon (see note on 2Ki 19:21).
50:43 *woman in labor.* See note on 4:31.

50:43 ᵛ Jer 6:22-24
50:44 ʷ S Jer 12:5
ˣ S Nu 16:5
ʸ S Job 41:10;
Isa 46:9; S Jer 49:19
50:45 ᶻ Ps 33:11;
Jer 51:11 ᵃ S Isa 48:14
50:46 ᵇ S Jdg 5:4;
S Jer 49:21
ᶜ S Job 24:12;
Rev 18:9-10
51:1 ᵈ S Isa 13:17
ᵉ Jer 25:12
51:2 ᶠ Isa 13:5
ᵍ S Isa 41:16; Mt 3:12
ʰ S Isa 13:9
51:3 ⁱ S Jer 50:29
ʲ Jer 46:4
51:4 ᵏ Isa 13:15
ˡ S Isa 13:18
51:5 ᵐ S Lev 26:44;
Isa 54:6-8 ⁿ Hos 4:1
51:6 ᵒ S Isa 48:20
ᵖ Nu 16:26; Rev 18:4
�q Jer 50:27
ʳ S Isa 1:24;
S Jer 50:15 ˢ ver 24,
56; Dt 32:35;
S Job 21:19; Jer 25:14;
50:29; La 3:64
51:7 ᵗ S Isa 51:22;
Jer 25:15-16; 49:12;
Rev 14:8-10
51:8 ᵘ S Isa 14:15;
S 21:9; S Rev 14:8
ᵛ Jer 8:22; 46:11

pain like that of a woman in labor. ᵛ
⁴⁴ Like a lion coming up from Jordan's thickets ʷ
to a rich pastureland,
I will chase Babylon from its land in an instant.
Who is the chosen ˣ one I will appoint for this?
Who is like me and who can challenge me? ʸ
And what shepherd can stand against me?"

⁴⁵ Therefore, hear what the LORD has planned against Babylon,
what he has purposed ᶻ against the land of the Babylonians: ᵃ
The young of the flock will be dragged away;
their pasture will be appalled at their fate.
⁴⁶ At the sound of Babylon's capture the earth will tremble; ᵇ
its cry ᶜ will resound among the nations.

51

This is what the LORD says:

"See, I will stir ᵈ up the spirit of a destroyer
against Babylon ᵉ and the people of Leb Kamai. ᵃ
² I will send foreigners ᶠ to Babylon
to winnow ᵍ her and to devastate her land;
they will oppose her on every side
in the day ʰ of her disaster.
³ Let not the archer string his bow, ⁱ
nor let him put on his armor. ʲ
Do not spare her young men;
completely destroy ᵇ her army.
⁴ They will fall ᵏ down slain in Babylon, ᶜ
fatally wounded in her streets. ˡ
⁵ For Israel and Judah have not been forsaken ᵐ
by their God, the LORD Almighty,
though their land ᵈ is full of guilt ⁿ
before the Holy One of Israel.

⁶ "Flee ᵒ from Babylon!
Run for your lives!
Do not be destroyed because of her sins. ᵖ
It is time q for the LORD's vengeance; ʳ
he will repay ˢ her what she deserves.
⁷ Babylon was a gold cup ᵗ in the LORD's hand;
she made the whole earth drunk.
The nations drank her wine;
therefore they have now gone mad.
⁸ Babylon will suddenly fall ᵘ and be broken.
Wail over her!
Get balm ᵛ for her pain;
perhaps she can be healed.

⁹ " 'We would have healed Babylon,
but she cannot be healed;

ᵃ 1 *Leb Kamai* is a cryptogram for Chaldea, that is, Babylonia.   ᵇ 3 The Hebrew term refers to the irrevocable giving over of things or persons to the LORD, often by totally destroying them.   ᶜ 4 Or *Chaldea*   ᵈ 5 Or *Almighty, / and the land* ˡof the Babylonians ˡ

50:44–46 Echoes 49:19–21 (see notes there). The oracle against Edom is here applied to Babylon.

51:1 *stir up the spirit.* See 1Ch 5:26; Hag 1:14. The Hebrew underlying this phrase is translated "aroused...the hostility of" in 2Ch 21:16. *destroyer.* See note on 4:7; here including the "kings of the Medes" (v. 11). *Leb Kamai.* Lit. "the heart of my attackers" (cf. Rev 17:5, where Babylon is called "the mother of prostitutes and of the abominations of the earth"). See TNIV text note; see also note on 25:26.

51:2 *foreigners...to winnow her.* The Hebrew for this phrase is an excellent example of alliteration and assonance (see Introduction: Literary Features).

51:3 *completely destroy.* See TNIV text note; 25:9; 50:21,26; see also note on Dt 2:34.

51:4 *fall...in her streets.* See Jer 49:26; 50:30.

51:5 *forsaken.* Lit. "widowed"; contrast Isa 54:4,6–7 and notes. *Holy One of Israel.* See note on 50:29.

51:6 *Flee...! Run for your lives!* See v. 45; 48:6. This was spoken to the people of Judah (as in 50:8). *the LORD's vengeance.* See note on 50:15. *repay her what she deserves.* See Isa 59:18; 66:6.

51:7 See 25:15–16 and notes. *Babylon was...gold.* See note on Da 2:32–43.

51:8 *Babylon will...fall.* See Isa 21:9 and note. *balm.* See note on 8:22.

let us leave ^w her and each go to our own land,
for her judgment ^x reaches to the skies,
it rises as high as the heavens.'

¹⁰ " 'The LORD has vindicated ^y us;
come, let us tell in Zion
what the LORD our God has done.' ^z

¹¹ "Sharpen the arrows, ^a
take up the shields! ^b
The LORD has stirred up the kings ^c of the Medes, ^d
because his purpose ^e is to destroy Babylon.
The LORD will take vengeance, ^f
vengeance for his temple. ^g
¹² Lift up a banner ^h against the walls of Babylon!
Reinforce the guard,
station the watchmen, ⁱ
prepare an ambush! ^j
The LORD will carry out his purpose, ^k
his decree against the people of Babylon.
¹³ You who live by many waters ^l
and are rich in treasures, ^m
your end has come,
the time for you to be destroyed. ⁿ
¹⁴ The LORD Almighty has sworn by himself: ^o
I will surely fill you with troops, as with a swarm of locusts, ^p
and they will shout ^q in triumph over you.

¹⁵ "He made the earth by his power;
he founded the world by his wisdom ^r
and stretched ^s out the heavens by his understanding. ^t
¹⁶ When he thunders, ^u the waters in the heavens roar;
he makes clouds rise from the ends of the earth.
He sends lightning with the rain ^v
and brings out the wind from his storehouses. ^w

¹⁷ "Everyone is senseless and without knowledge;
all goldsmiths are shamed by their idols.
Their images are a fraud; ^x
they have no breath in them.
¹⁸ They are worthless, ^y the objects of mockery;
when their judgment comes, they will perish.
¹⁹ He who is the Portion ^z of Jacob is not like these,
for he is the Maker of all things,
including the tribe of his inheritance ^a—
the LORD Almighty is his name.

²⁰ "You are my war club, ^b
my weapon for battle—
with you I shatter ^c nations, ^d
with you I destroy kingdoms,

51:9 ^w S Isa 13:14;
S 31:9; Jer 50:16
^x Rev 18:4-5
51:10 ^y Mic 7:9
^z Ps 64:9; S Jer 50:28
51:11 ^a Jer 50:9
^b S Isa 21:5
^c S Isa 41:2 ^d ver 28;
S Isa 13:3; S 41:25
^e S Jer 50:45
^f S Lev 26:25
^g S Jer 50:28
51:12 ^h ver 27;
S Ps 20:5 ⁱ 2Sa 18:24;
Eze 33:2 ^j Jer 50:24
^k S Ps 33:11
51:13 ^l S Jer 50:38
^m S Isa 45:3;
Eze 22:27; Hab 2:9
ⁿ Jer 50:3
51:14 ^o S Ge 22:16;
Am 6:8 ^p ver 27;
Am 7:1; Na 3:15
^q Jer 50:15
51:15 ^r Ps 104:24
^s S Ge 1:1; S Ps 104:2
^t S Ps 136:5
51:16 ^u Ps 18:11-13
^v S Job 28:26
^w S Dt 28:12;
S Ps 135:7; Jnh 1:4
51:17 ^x S Isa 44:20;
Hab 2:18-19
51:18 ^y S Jer 18:15
51:19 ^z S Ps 119:57
^a S Ex 34:9
51:20 ^b S Isa 10:5;
Zec 9:13
^c S Job 34:24;
Mic 4:13 ^d S Isa 45:1

51:9 The speakers are the nations conquered by Babylon. *each go to our own land.* See 50:16 and note. *her judgment.* Her sin, deserving of judgment. *reaches to the skies . . . high as the heavens.* Poetic exaggeration (see Dt 1:28; Ps 57:10; 108:4).
51:10 Judah speaks (see 50:28). *The LORD has vindicated us.* See Ps 37:6.
51:11 *stirred up.* Lit. "stirred up the spirit of" (see note on v. 1). *Medes.* See v. 28; Isa 13:17 and note; 21:2; Da 5:28,31; 6:8,12,15; 8:20. *vengeance, vengeance for his temple.* See note on 50:28.
51:12 *prepare an ambush.* To keep defenders from retreating to the safety of their fortifications (see Jos 8:14–22; Jdg 20:29–39).
51:13 *many waters.* The "rivers of Babylon" (Ps 137:1), including the mighty Euphrates, along with a magnificent system of irri-

gation canals, were proverbial. *destroyed.* Like a thread from the loom (see Isa 38:12).
51:14 *sworn by himself.* See note on Ge 22:16. *as with . . . locusts.* See 46:23. *shout in triumph.* See note on 48:33.
51:15–19 Echoes 10:12–16 (see notes there).
51:20–23 Illustrates Jeremiah's fondness for the effective use of repetition (see 4:23–26; see also Introduction: Literary Features).
51:20 *You are my war club.* Cf. Pr 25:18; either (1) Cyrus of Persia, soon to conquer Babylon, or, more likely, (2) Babylon, destroyer of nations (see 50:23; see also note on Isa 10:5). *shatter.* See vv. 21–23. The Hebrew root for this verb is the same as that for "war club." See also Ex 15:6. The Hebrew verb is translated "dash (to pieces)" in Ps 2:9; 137:9; Hos 10:14; 13:16.

51:21 *e* S Ex 15:1
f S Isa 43:17;
S Jer 50:37
51:22 *g* S 2Ch 36:17;
Isa 13:17-18
51:23 *h* ver 57
51:24 *i* S ver 6,35;
S Dt 32:41;
S Jer 50:15; La 3:64
j S Isa 45:1
51:25 *k* S Jer 21:13
l Jer 50:23
m S Ex 3:20 *n* Zec 4:7
51:26 *o* ver 29;
S Isa 13:19-22;
S Jer 50:12
51:27 *p* S Ps 20:5;
S Isa 13:2
q S Jer 25:14
r S Ge 8:4 *s* Ge 10:3
t S ver 14
51:28 *u* S ver 11
v ver 48
51:29 *w* S Jdg 5:4;
S Jer 49:21
x S Ps 33:11 *y* Jer 48:9
z ver 43; S Isa 13:20
51:30 *a* S Jer 50:36
b S Isa 19:16
c S Isa 47:14
d S Isa 45:2
51:31 *e* 2Sa 18:19-31
f S Jer 50:2; Da 5:30

21 with you I shatter horse and rider, *e*
  with you I shatter chariot *f* and driver,
22 with you I shatter man and woman,
  with you I shatter old man and youth,
  with you I shatter young man and young woman, *g*
23 with you I shatter shepherd and flock,
  with you I shatter farmer and oxen,
  with you I shatter governors and officials. *h*

24 "Before your eyes I will repay *i* Babylon *j* and all who live in Babylonia *a* for all the wrong they have done in Zion," declares the LORD.

25 "I am against *k* you, you destroying mountain,
  you who destroy the whole earth," *l*
                                          declares the LORD.

  "I will stretch out my hand *m* against you,
  roll you off the cliffs,
  and make you a burned-out mountain. *n*
26 No rock will be taken from you for a cornerstone,
  nor any stone for a foundation,
  for you will be desolate *o* forever,"
                                          declares the LORD.

27 "Lift up a banner *p* in the land!
  Blow the trumpet among the nations!
  Prepare the nations for battle against her;
  summon against her these kingdoms: *q*
  Ararat, *r* Minni and Ashkenaz. *s*
  Appoint a commander against her;
  send up horses like a swarm of locusts. *t*
28 Prepare the nations for battle against her—
  the kings of the Medes, *u*
  their governors and all their officials,
  and all the countries they rule. *v*
29 The land trembles *w* and writhes,
  for the LORD's purposes *x* against Babylon stand—
  to lay waste *y* the land of Babylon
  so that no one will live there. *z*
30 Babylon's warriors *a* have stopped fighting;
  they remain in their strongholds.
  Their strength is exhausted;
  they have become weaklings. *b*
  Her dwellings are set on fire; *c*
  the bars *d* of her gates are broken.
31 One courier *e* follows another
  and messenger follows messenger
  to announce to the king of Babylon
  that his entire city is captured, *f*
32 the river crossings seized,

---

a 24 Or *Chaldea*; also in verse 35

51:24 *your.* Judah's. *repay . . . for all the wrong they have done.*
See v. 6; 50:15,29 and notes.
51:25 *destroying mountain.* Symbolizes a powerful kingdom
(see Da 2:35,44–45), here Babylon. *burned-out mountain.* After
being judged by the Lord, Babylon will be like an extinct volcano.
51:26 *desolate forever.* See 25:12; 50:12–13; see also note on
Isa 13:20.

B **51:27** See 50:29. *Lift up a banner . . . ! Blow the trumpet . . . !*
See 4:5–6; 6:1 and notes. *Prepare . . . for battle.* Lit. "Consecrate" (see note on 6:4). *these kingdoms.* Allies of the Medes (see
v. 11 and note). *Ararat.* See note on Ge 8:4. *Minni.* A region mentioned in Assyrian inscriptions, it was located somewhere in Armenia. *Ashkenaz.* See note on Ge 10:3. *commander.* The Hebrew

for this word appears again in the OT only in Na 3:17 ("officials").
It is a Babylonian loanword meaning lit. "scribe." *like . . . locusts.*
See note on 46:23.
51:28 *Medes.* See note on v. 11. *all the countries they rule.* See
note on 34:1; see also 1Ki 9:19.
51:29 *land trembles and writhes.* At the fearful prospect of war.
51:30 *exhausted . . . weaklings.* In the Hebrew there is a play on
words. *become weaklings.* See 50:37; Na 3:13 and note.
51:31 *One courier follows another.* They run to the palace from
all parts of the city.
51:32 *river crossings.* Fords and ferries (and perhaps bridges).
marshes set on fire. To destroy the reeds and prevent fugitives
from hiding among them.

the marshes set on fire, *g*
and the soldiers terrified. *h*"

³³This is what the LORD Almighty, the God of Israel, says:

"Daughter Babylon *i* is like a threshing floor *j*
at the time it is trampled;
the time to harvest *k* her will soon come. *l*"

³⁴ "Nebuchadnezzar *m* king of Babylon has devoured *n* us, *o*
he has thrown us into confusion,
he has made us an empty jar.
Like a serpent he has swallowed us
and filled his stomach with our delicacies,
and then has spewed *p* us out.
³⁵ May the violence *q* done to our flesh *a* be on Babylon,"
say the inhabitants of Zion.
"May our blood be on those who live in Babylonia,"
says Jerusalem. *r*

³⁶Therefore, this is what the LORD says:

"See, I will defend your cause *s*
and avenge *t* you;
I will dry up *u* her sea
and make her springs dry.
³⁷Babylon will be a heap of ruins,
a haunt *v* of jackals,
an object of horror and scorn, *w*
a place where no one lives. *x*
³⁸ Her people all roar like young lions, *y*
they growl like lion cubs.
³⁹ But while they are aroused,
I will set out a feast for them
and make them drunk, *z*
so that they shout with laughter—
then sleep forever *a* and not awake,"

declares the LORD. *b*

⁴⁰ "I will bring them down
like lambs to the slaughter,
like rams and goats. *c*

⁴¹ "How Sheshak *b d* will be captured, *e*
the boast of the whole earth seized!
How desolate *f* Babylon will be
among the nations!
⁴² The sea will rise over Babylon;
its roaring waves *g* will cover her.
⁴³ Her towns will be desolate,
a dry and desert *h* land,
a land where no one lives,
through which no one travels. *i*

---

a 35 Or *done to us and to our children*   *b* 41 *Sheshak* is a cryptogram for Babylon.

51:32 *a* S Isa 47:14
h S Jer 50:36
51:33 *i* S Isa 47:1
j S Isa 21:10
k S Isa 17:5
l S Isa 13:22
51:34 *m* S Jer 50:17
n Na 2:12 *o* Hos 8:8
p ver 44; S Lev 18:25
51:35 *q* Joel 3:19;
Hab 2:17 *r* S ver 24;
Ps 137:8
51:36 *s* Ps 140:12;
Jer 50:34; La 3:58
t ver 6; Jer 20:12;
S Ro 12:19
u S Isa 11:15; S 19:5;
Hos 13:15
51:37 *v* S Isa 13:22;
Rev 18:2 *w* Na 3:6;
Mal 2:9 *x* S Jer 50:13,
39
51:38 *y* S Isa 5:29
51:39 *z* S Isa 21:5
a S Ps 13:3 *b* ver 57;
S Jer 50:24
51:40 *c* Eze 39:18
51:41 *d* S Jer 25:26
e Isa 13:19 *f* Jer 50:13
51:42 *g* S Ps 18:4;
Isa 8:7
51:43 *h* S Isa 21:1
i ver 29,62;
S Isa 13:20; Jer 2:6

51:33 *Daughter Babylon.* A personification of the city of Babylon (see note on 2Ki 19:21). *threshing floor.* The destruction of a city or nation is often depicted as a harvest (see Isa 27:12; Joel 3:13 and notes; Mic 4:12–13; cf. Rev 14:14–20 and note on 14:15).
51:34 *serpent.* The Hebrew for this word is translated "monster" in Isa 51:9, where it symbolizes Egypt (see Ge 1:21 and note). *delicacies.* See Ge 49:20.
51:35 *flesh.* See Mic 3:2–3.
51:36 *avenge you.* See vv. 6,11; see also note on 50:15. *sea ... springs.* See note on v. 13. Babylonia is called the "Desert by the

Sea" in Isa 21:1 (see note there).
51:37 See 9:11; 18:16 and notes.
51:38 *roar like young lions.* See 2:15 and note.
51:39 *aroused.* Lit. "heated"; for a similar image, see Hos 7:4–7. *drunk.* See v. 57; see also notes on 25:15–16,26.
51:40 *lambs ... rams and goats.* Symbolic of the people (see Isa 34:6; Eze 39:18) of Babylon. *slaughter.* See Isa 53:7 and note.
51:41 *Sheshak.* See TNIV text note; see also note on 25:26.
51:42 *sea ... its roaring waves.* See Isa 17:12 and note; here and in v. 55, Babylon's enemies (see 46:7 and note).
51:43 See 48:9; 49:18,33; 50:12–13.

51:44 *i* S Isa 21:9;
S 46:1 *k* S ver 34
l ver 58; S 2Ki 25:4;
Isa 25:12; Jer 50:15
51:45 *m* ver 50
n S Isa 48:20
o Ps 76:10; 79:6
51:46 *p* Ps 18:45
q S Jer 46:27
r S 2Ki 19:7
51:47 *s* S Isa 46:1-2;
S Jer 50:2 *t* Jer 50:12
u S Jer 27:7
51:48 *v* S Job 3:7;
S Ps 149:2; Rev 18:20
w ver 11; S Isa 41:25;
S Jer 25:26 *x* ver 53,
56
51:49 *y* Ps 137:8;
S Jer 50:29
51:50 *z* ver 45
a S Ps 137:6
b Jer 23:23
51:51 *c* Ps 44:13-16;
79:4 *d* La 1:10
51:52 *e* ver 47
f S Job 51:12
51:53 *g* S Ge 11:4;
S Isa 14:13-14
h S ver 48; S Job 15:21
51:54 *i* S Job 24:12
j S Jer 50:22
51:55 *k* Isa 25:5

44 I will punish Bel *j* in Babylon
    and make him spew out *k* what he has swallowed.
The nations will no longer stream to him.
    And the wall *l* of Babylon will fall.

45 "Come out *m* of her, my people!
    Run *n* for your lives!
    Run from the fierce anger *o* of the LORD.
46 Do not lose heart *p* or be afraid *q*
    when rumors *r* are heard in the land;
one rumor comes this year, another the next,
    rumors of violence in the land
    and of ruler against ruler.
47 For the time will surely come
    when I will punish the idols *s* of Babylon;
her whole land will be disgraced *t*
    and her slain will all lie fallen within her. *u*
48 Then heaven and earth and all that is in them
    will shout *v* for joy over Babylon,
for out of the north *w*
    destroyers *x* will attack her,"

                    declares the LORD.

49 "Babylon must fall because of Israel's slain,
    just as the slain in all the earth
    have fallen because of Babylon. *y*
50 You who have escaped the sword,
    leave *z* and do not linger!
Remember *a* the LORD in a distant land, *b*
    and call to mind Jerusalem."

51 "We are disgraced, *c*
    for we have been insulted
    and shame covers our faces,
because foreigners have entered
    the holy places of the LORD's house." *d*

52 "But days are coming," declares the LORD,
    "when I will punish her idols, *e*
and throughout her land
    the wounded will groan. *f*
53 Even if Babylon reaches the sky *g*
    and fortifies her lofty stronghold,
    I will send destroyers *h* against her,"

                    declares the LORD.

54 "The sound of a cry *i* comes from Babylon,
    the sound of great destruction *j*
    from the land of the Babylonians. *a*
55 The LORD will destroy Babylon;
    he will silence *k* her noisy din.

---

a 54 Or Chaldeans

51:44 *Bel.* See 50:2; Isa 46:1 and note. *what he has swallowed.* Captive peoples (including Judah) and plundered goods (including vessels from the temple in Jerusalem; see Da 5:2–3). *wall of Babylon.* A wall of double construction, the outer wall (12 feet thick) being separated from the inner wall (21 feet thick) by a dry moat 23 feet wide.
51:45 *Run for your lives!* See note on v. 6. *fierce anger.* See 4:8,26; Isa 13:13; Na 1:6.
51:46 *Do not ... be afraid when rumors are heard.* While giving his Olivet discourse, Jesus may have had this passage in mind (see Mt 24:6; Mk 13:7; Lk 21:9).
51:47 *punish the idols of Babylon.* See v. 52; see also note on 50:2.

51:48 *heaven and earth ... will shout for joy.* See Isa 44:23; Rev 18:20; 19:1–3. *out of the north.* See note on 50:3.
51:49 See note on 25:26.
51:50 *leave.* See note on v. 6.
51:51 *foreigners have entered the holy places.* Refers to Nebuchadnezzar's defiling the Jerusalem temple in 586 B.C. The same sacrilege would occur under Antiochus Epiphanes in 168 B.C. and under the Romans in A.D. 70.
51:53 *reaches the sky.* See Ge 11:4 and note; Isa 14:13–15. *destroyers.* See vv. 48,56.
51:54 See 50:46. *great destruction.* See note on 4:6.

Waves *l* of enemies will rage like great waters;
  the roar of their voices will resound.
⁵⁶A destroyer *m* will come against Babylon;
  her warriors will be captured,
  and their bows will be broken. *n*
For the LORD is a God of retribution;
  he will repay *o* in full.
⁵⁷I will make her officials *p* and wise *q* counselors drunk, *r*
  her governors, officers and warriors as well;
they will sleep *s* forever and not awake,"
  declares the King, *t* whose name is the LORD Almighty.

⁵⁸This is what the LORD Almighty says:

"Babylon's thick wall *u* will be leveled
  and her high gates *v* set on fire;
the peoples *w* exhaust *x* themselves for nothing,
  the nations' labor is only fuel for the flames." *y*

⁵⁹This is the message Jeremiah the prophet gave to the staff officer Seraiah son of Ne-riah, *z* the son of Mahseiah, when he went to Babylon with Zedekiah *a* king of Judah in the fourth *b* year of his reign. ⁶⁰Jeremiah had written on a scroll *c* about all the disasters that would come upon Babylon—all that had been recorded concerning Babylon. ⁶¹He said to Seraiah, "When you get to Babylon, see that you read all these words aloud. ⁶²Then say, 'LORD, you have said you will destroy this place, so that neither people nor animals will live in it; it will be desolate *d* forever.' ⁶³When you finish reading this scroll, tie a stone to it and throw it into the Euphrates. *e* ⁶⁴Then say, 'So will Babylon sink to rise no more *f* because of the disaster I will bring on her. And her people *g* will fall.' " *h*

The words of Jeremiah end *i* here.

THE FALL OF JERUSALEM
52:1–3pp — 2Ki 24:18–20; 2Ch 36:11–16
52:4–16pp — Jer 39:1–10
52:4–21pp — 2Ki 25:1–21; 2Ch 36:17–20

52 Zedekiah *j* was twenty-one years old when he became king, and he reigned in Jerusalem eleven years. His mother's name was Hamutal daughter of Jere-miah; she was from Libnah. *k* ²He did evil in the eyes of the LORD, just as Je-hoiakim *l* had done. ³It was because of the LORD's anger that all this happened to Jerusalem and Judah, *m* and in the end he thrust them from his presence. *n*

Now Zedekiah rebelled *o* against the king of Babylon.

⁴So in the ninth year of Zedekiah's reign, on the tenth *p* day of the tenth month, Neb-uchadnezzar king of Babylon marched against Jerusalem *q* with his whole army. They en-camped outside the city and built siege works *r* all around it. *s* ⁵The city was kept under siege until the eleventh year of King Zedekiah.

⁶By the ninth day of the fourth month the famine in the city had become so severe that

51:55 *l* Ps 18:4
51:56 *m* S ver 48;
S Job 15:21
51:56 *n* Ps 46:9
o S ver 6; S Ge 4:24;
S Dt 32:41; Ps 94:1-2;
Hab 2:8
51:57 *p* S ver 23
q S Job 5:13
r S Isa 21:5 *s* S ver 39;
Ps 76:5; S Jer 25:27
t S Isa 6:5
51:58 *u* S ver 44;
S 2Ki 25:4; S Isa 15:1
v S Isa 13:2 *w* ver 64
x S Isa 47:13
y S Isa 47:14
51:59 *z* Jer 36:4
a Jer 52:1 *b* Jer 28:1
51:60 *c* S Ex 17:14;
Jer 30:2; 36:2
51:62 *d* S Isa 13:20;
S Jer 9:11; S 50:13,39
51:63 *e* S Ge 2:14
51:64 *f* Eze 26:21;
28:19 *g* S ver 58
h Rev 18:21
i S Jer 48:33
52:1 *j* S 2Ki 24:17
k S Nu 33:20;
Jos 10:29; 2Ki 8:22
52:2 *l* S Jer 36:30
52:3 *m* Isa 3:1
n S Ge 4:14;
S Ex 33:15
o Eze 17:12-16
52:4 *p* Zec 8:19
q Jer 34:1 *r* S Jer 6:6
s Eze 24:1-2

51:55 *Waves.* See note on v. 42. *like great waters.* See note on Ps 32:6.
51:56 *God of retribution.* See note on v. 24.

A **51:57** *officials and wise counselors.* See 50:35. *drunk.* See v. 39; see also notes on 25:15–16,26. *King.* See note on 46:18. The true King is the Lord, not Bel/Marduk (see 50:2 and note).

B **51:58** *thick wall.* See note on v. 44. *high gates.* The fa-mous Ishtar Gate was almost 40 feet high. *the peoples … fuel for the flames.* Very similar to Hab 2:13.
51:59–64 A prose conclusion to the book in general and to the oracle against Babylon in particular.

B **51:59** *staff officer.* Lit. "resting-place officer" (see Nu 10:33), the official responsible for determining when and where his men on the march should stay overnight. *Seraiah son of Neriah.* An ancient seal has been found that bears the inscrip-tion "Belonging to Seraiah son of Neriah," and it no doubt refers to the man mentioned here. He was a brother of Jeremiah's sec-retary, Baruch (see 32:12). *he.* Seraiah. *Zedekiah … fourth year.*

593 B.C. Zedekiah may have been summoned to Babylon by Nebuchadnezzar to be interrogated by him (see note on 27:3).
51:60 *scroll.* See note on Ex 17:14. *all that had been recorded concerning Babylon.* Probably the oracle of 50:2—51:58 (see note on 50:1).
51:62 *you have said.* See v. 26.
51:64 *The words of Jeremiah end here.* A note by the final com-piler of the book of Jeremiah (see 48:47).
52:1–27,31–34 Paralleled almost verbatim in 2Ki 24:18—25:21,27–30 (see notes there). (52:4–27 is summarized in 39:1–10; see notes there.) The writer(s) of Kings and the writer of the appendix to Jeremiah (perhaps Baruch) doubtless had access to the same sources. It is unlikely that either of the two accounts copied from the other, since each has peculiarities characteristic of the larger work that it concludes. In a few pas-sages, Jeremiah is fuller than Kings (compare especially vv. 10–11 with 2Ki 25:7; v. 15 with 2Ki 25:11; vv. 19–23 with 2Ki 25:15–17; v. 31 with 2Ki 25:27; v. 34 with 2Ki 25:30).
52:1 *Jeremiah.* Not the prophet. *Libnah.* See note on 2Ki 8:22.

52:6 ʳS Lev 26:26;
S Isa 3:1; La 1:11
52:7 ᵘLa 4:19
52:9 ᵛS Jer 21:7;
S 32:4 ᵂS Nu 34:11
ˣS Nu 13:21
52:10 ʸS Jer 22:30
52:11 ᶻJer 34:4;
Eze 12:13; 17:16
52:12 ᵃZec 7:5;
8:19 ᵇver 26
52:13 ᶜS 2Ch 36:19;
S Ps 74:8; La 2:6
ᵈS Dt 29:24; Ps 79:1;
Mic 3:12 ᵉS Dt 13:16;
S Jer 19:13
52:14 ᶠS Ne 1:3;
La 2:8
52:15 ᵍS 2Ki 24:1;
S Jer 1:3 ʰS Jer 38:19
52:16 ⁱJer 40:6
52:17 ʲS 1Ki 7:15
ᵏ1Ki 7:27-37
ˡS 1Ki 7:23
ᵐJer 27:19-22
52:18 ⁿS Nu 4:14
ᵒS Ex 27:3; 1Ki 7:45
52:19 ᵖS Lev 10:1;
S 1Ki 7:50 �qS Nu 3:31
ʳEx 25:29 ˢS Nu 4:7
ᵗS Ezr 1:7; Da 5:2
52:20 ᵘ1Ki 7:25
ᵛS 1Ki 7:47
52:21 ᵂS 1Ki 7:15
52:22 ˣS 1Ki 7:16
ʸS Ex 28:33
52:23 ᶻ1Ki 7:20
ᵃS ver 17; S Jer 27:19
52:24 ᵇS 2Ki 25:18
ᶜS 2Ki 25:18;
S Jer 37:3 ᵈS 2Ki 12:9
52:25 ᵉJer 36:10
52:26 ᶠS ver 12
52:27 ᵍS Nu 34:11
ʰS Jer 20:4
52:28 ⁱS Dt 28:36;
S 2Ch 36:20; S Ne 1:2
52:30 ʲS Jer 43:3
ᵏS Jer 13:19

there was no food for the people to eat. ᶠ7Then the city wall was broken through, and the whole army fled. ᵘ They left the city at night through the gate between the two walls near the king's garden, though the Babyloniansᵃ were surrounding the city. They fled toward the Arabah,ᵇ 8but the Babylonianᶜ army pursued King Zedekiah and overtook him in the plains of Jericho. All his soldiers were separated from him and scattered, 9and he was captured.ᵛ

He was taken to the king of Babylon at Riblahᵂ in the land of Hamath,ˣ where he pronounced sentence on him. 10There at Riblah the king of Babylon killed the sonsʸ of Zedekiah before his eyes; he also killed all the officials of Judah. 11Then he put out Zedekiah's eyes, bound him with bronze shackles and took him to Babylon, where he put him in prison till the day of his death.ᶻ

12On the tenth day of the fifthᵃ month, in the nineteenth year of Nebuchadnezzar king of Babylon, Nebuzaradanᵇ commander of the imperial guard, who served the king of Babylon, came to Jerusalem. 13He set fireᶜ to the templeᵈ of the LORD, the royal palace and all the housesᵉ of Jerusalem. Every important building he burned down. 14The whole Babylonian army, under the commander of the imperial guard, broke down all the wallsᶠ around Jerusalem. 15Nebuzaradan the commander of the guard carried into exileᵍ some of the poorest people and those who remained in the city, along with the rest of the skilled workersᵈ and those who had desertedʰ to the king of Babylon. 16But Nebuzaradan left behindⁱ the rest of the poorest people of the land to work the vineyards and fields.

17The Babylonians broke up the bronze pillars,ʲ the movable standsᵏ and the bronze Seaˡ that were at the temple of the LORD and they carried all the bronze to Babylon.ᵐ 18They also took away the pots, shovels, wick trimmers, sprinkling bowls,ⁿ dishes and all the bronze articles used in the temple service.ᵒ 19The commander of the imperial guard took away the basins, censers,ᵖ sprinkling bowls, pots, lampstands,q dishesʳ and bowls used for drink offeringsˢ—all that were made of pure gold or silver.ᵗ

20The bronze from the two pillars, the Sea and the twelve bronze bullsᵘ under it, and the movable stands, which King Solomon had made for the temple of the LORD, was more than could be weighed.ᵛ 21Each pillar was eighteen cubits high and twelve cubits in circumferenceᵉ; each was four fingers thick, and hollow.ᵂ 22The bronze capitalˣ on top of one pillar was five cubitsᶠ high and was decorated with a network and pomegranatesʸ of bronze all around. The other pillar, with its pomegranates, was similar. 23There were ninety-six pomegranates on the sides; the total number of pomegranatesᶻ above the surrounding network was a hundred.ᵃ

24The commander of the guard took as prisoners Seraiahᵇ the chief priest, Zephaniahᶜ the priest next in rank and the three doorkeepers.ᵈ 25Of those still in the city, he took the officer in charge of the fighting men, and seven royal advisers. He also took the secretaryᵉ who was chief officer in charge of conscripting the people of the land, sixty of whom were found in the city. 26Nebuzaradanᶠ the commander took them all and brought them to the king of Babylon at Riblah. 27There at Riblah,ᵍ in the land of Hamath, the king had them executed.

So Judah went into captivity, awayʰ from her land. 28This is the number of the people Nebuchadnezzar carried into exile:ⁱ

in the seventh year, 3,023 Jews;
29in Nebuchadnezzar's eighteenth year,
    832 people from Jerusalem;
30in his twenty-third year,
    745 Jews taken into exileʲ by Nebuzaradan the commander of the imperial guard. There were 4,600 people in all.ᵏ

ᵃ 7 Or *Chaldeans*; also in verse 17   ᵇ 7 Or *the Jordan Valley*   ᶜ 8 Or *Chaldean*; also in verse 14   ᵈ 15 Or *the populace*   ᵉ 21 That is, about 27 feet high and 18 feet in circumference or about 8.2 meters high and 5.4 meters in circumference   ᶠ 22 That is, about 7 1/2 feet or about 2.3 meters

---

52:12 *tenth day.* The parallel in 2Ki 25:8 reads "seventh day"; one of the numbers is a copyist's error, but we cannot tell which (see vv. 22,25,31 and notes).
52:18–19 See notes on 1Ki 7:40,45,50.
52:20 *twelve bronze bulls.* See note on 2Ch 4:4.
52:21–23 See notes on 1Ki 7:15–23.
52:22 *five.* The parallel in 2Ki 25:17 reads "three" (see TNIV text note there), probably a copyist's error (see also note on 2Ki 25:17).
52:25 *seven.* The parallel in 2Ki 25:19 reads "five"; see note on v. 12.

52:28 *seventh year.* Of Nebuchadnezzar's reign (see vv. 29–30), which was 597 B.C. *3,023.* Probably includes only adult males, since the corresponding figure(s) in 2Ki 24:14,16 are significantly higher.
52:29 *eighteenth year.* 586 B.C. In v. 12 the same year is called the "nineteenth year"; the difference is due to alternate ways of computing regnal years (for a similar case, see note on Da 1:1).
52:30 *twenty-third year.* 581 B.C. *taken into exile by Nebuzaradan.* Either (1) to quell further rebellion (see v. 3) or (2) in belated reprisal for Gedaliah's assassination (see 41:1–3).

JEHOIACHIN RELEASED

52:31–34pp — 2Ki 25:27–30

52:31 *l* S 2Ch 36:9
52:33 *m* 2Sa 9:7
52:34 *n* 2Sa 9:10

³¹In the thirty-seventh year of the exile of Jehoiachin *l* king of Judah, in the year Awel-Marduk became king of Babylon, on the twenty-fifth day of the twelfth month, he released Jehoiachin king of Judah and freed him from prison. ³²He spoke kindly to him and gave him a seat of honor higher than those of the other kings who were with him in Babylon. ³³So Jehoiachin put aside his prison clothes and for the rest of his life ate regularly at the king's table. *m* ³⁴Day by day the king of Babylon gave Jehoiachin a regular allowance *n* as long as he lived, till the day of his death.

52:31–34 Paralleled almost verbatim in 2Ki 25:27–30 (see notes there). Jeremiah and Kings thus conclude with the same happy ending.

52:31 *twenty-fifth.* The parallel in 2Ki 25:27 reads "twenty-seventh"; see note on v. 12.

52:32 See 2Ki 25:28 and note.

52:34 *till the day of his death.* See v. 11. Since the phrase does not appear in the parallel verses in 2 Kings in either case, its intention is probably to highlight the contrast between Zedekiah, who remained in prison till the day he died (see v. 11), and Jehoiachin, who was released from prison and treated well by the Babylonian kings till the day he died.

LAMENTATIONS

The Hebrew title of the book is *'ekah* ("How . . . !"), the first word not only in 1:1 but also in 2:1; 4:1. Because of its subject matter, the book is also referred to in Jewish tradition as *qinot,* "Lamentations," a title taken over by the Septuagint (the pre-Christian Greek translation of the OT) and by the fourth-century Latin Vulgate.

AUTHOR AND DATE

Lamentations is anonymous, although ancient Jewish and early Christian traditions ascribe it to Jeremiah. These traditions are based in part on 2Ch 35:25 (though the "Laments" referred to there are not to be identified with the OT book of Lamentations); in part on such texts as Jer 7:29; 8:21; 9:1,10,20; and in part on the similarity of vocabulary and style between Lamentations and the prophecies of Jeremiah. Moreover, such an ascription gains a measure of plausibility from the fact that Jeremiah was an eyewitness to the divine judgment on Jerusalem in 586 B.C., which is so vividly portrayed here. Nevertheless, we cannot be certain who authored these carefully crafted poems or who is responsible for putting them together into a single scroll. Lamentations poignantly expresses the people's overwhelming sense of loss that accompanied the destruction of Jerusalem and the temple, as well as the exile of Judah's inhabitants from the land Yahweh had covenanted to give Israel as a perpetual national homeland.

The earliest possible date for the book is 586 B.C., and the latest is 516 (when the rebuilt Jerusalem temple was dedicated). The graphic immediacy of Lamentations argues for an earlier date, probably before 575.

LITERARY FEATURES

The entire book is poetic. The first, second, fourth and fifth laments each contains 22 verses, reflecting the number of letters in the Hebrew alphabet. In the first and second laments each verse contains three poetic lines; in the fourth each verse contains two lines; and in the fifth each verse contains but one line. The first four laments are alphabetic acrostics (see TNIV text notes on 1:1; 2:1; 3:1; 4:1). In the first, second and fourth, each numbered verse begins with the letter of the Hebrew alphabet dictated by the traditional order of that alphabet. The third (middle) lament is distinctive in that while it too is made up of 22 three-line units (like laments 1 and 2), in it the three lines of each unit all begin with the sequenced order of the letters of the alphabet (thus three *aleph* lines followed by three *beth* lines, etc.)—after the manner of Ps 119. The fifth lament continues to reflect the alphabetic pattern in its 22-line structure, but the initial letters of these lines do not follow the alphabetic sequence (see note on 5:1–22). Use of the alphabet as a formal structuring element indicates that, however passionate these laments, they were composed with studied care.

THEMES AND THEOLOGY

Lamentations is not the only OT book that contains individual or community laments. (A large number of the Psalms are lament poems, and every prophetic book except Haggai includes one or more examples of the lament genre.) Lamentations is the only book, however, that consists solely of laments.

B C As a series of laments over the destruction of Jerusalem (the royal city of the Lord's kingdom) in 586 B.C., it stands in a tradition with such ancient non-Biblical writings as the Sumerian "Lamentation over the Destruction of Ur," "Lamentation over the Destruction of Sumer and Ur," and "Lamentation over the Destruction of Nippur." Orthodox Jews customarily read it aloud in its entirety on the ninth day of Ab, the traditional date of the destruction of Solomon's temple in 586, as well as the date of the destruction of Herod's temple in A.D. 70. Many also read it each week at the Western Wall (the "Wailing Wall") in the Old City of Jerusalem. In addition, the book is important in traditional Roman Catholic liturgy, where it is customarily read during the last three days of Holy Week.

This Christian practice reminds us that the book of Lamentations not only bemoans Jerusalem's destruction but also contains profound theological insights. The horrors accompanying the Babylonian destruction of Judah are recited in some detail:

1. Wholesale devastation and slaughter engulfed kings (2:6,9; 4:20), princes (1:6; 2:2,9; 4:7–8; 5:12), elders (1:19; 2:10; 4:16; 5:12), priests (1:4,19; 2:6,20; 4:16), prophets (2:9,20) and commoners (2:10–12; 3:48; 4:6) alike.

2. Starving mothers were reduced to cannibalism (2:20; 4:10).

3. The flower of Judah's inhabitants was dragged off into ignominious exile (1:3,18).

4. An elaborate system of ceremony and worship came to an end (1:4,10). But this recital is integrally woven into the fabric of a poetic wrestling with the ways of God who, as the Lord of history, was dealing with his wayward people.

The author of these laments and those who preserved them understood clearly that the Babylonians were merely the human agents of divine judgment. It was God himself who had destroyed the city and temple (1:12–15; 2:1–8,17,22; 4:11). This was not a merely arbitrary act on the Lord's part; blatant, God-defying sin and covenant-breaking rebellion were at the root of his people's woes (1:5,8–9; 4:13; 5:7,16). Although weeping (1:16; 2:11,18; 3:48–51) is to be expected and cries for redress against the enemy (1:22; 3:59–66) are understandable (see note on Ps 5:10), the proper response to judgment is acknowledgment of sin (1:5,8,14,22; 2:14; 3:39; 4:13; 5:7,16) and heartfelt contrition (3:40–42). Trust in God's mercies and faithfulness must not falter. The book that begins with lament (1:1–2) rightly ends with an appeal to the Lord for restoration (5:21–22).

In the middle of the book, the theology of Lamentations reaches its apex as it focuses on the goodness of God. He is the Lord of hope (3:21,24–25), of love (3:22), of faithfulness (3:23), of salvation and restoration (3:26). In spite of all evidence to the contrary, "his compassions never fail. / They are new every morning; / great is your faithfulness" (3:22–23).

Near the end of the book, faith rises from Jerusalem's lamentable condition to acknowlege Yahweh's eternal reign: "You, LORD, reign forever; / your throne endures from generation to generation" (5:19; see introductions to Ps 47; 93; see also note on Ps 102:12).

OUTLINE

I. Jerusalem's Misery and Desolation (ch. 1)
II. The Lord's Anger against His People (ch. 2)
III. Judah's Complaint—and Basis for Consolation (ch. 3)
IV. The Contrast between Zion's Past and Present (ch. 4)
V. Judah's Appeal to the Lord for Forgiveness and Restoration (ch. 5)

1:1 *a* S Lev 26:43
b S Jer 42:2
c S Isa 47:8
d S 1Ki 4:21 *e* Isa 3:26;
S Jer 40:9; Eze 5:5
1:2 *f* Ps 6:6
g S Jer 3:1
h S Jer 4:30; Mic 7:5
i ver 16; S Jer 30:14
1:3 *j* S Jer 13:19
k Dt 28:65 *l* S Ex 15:9
1:4 *m* S Ps 137:1
n S Isa 27:10;
S Jer 9:11 *o* ver 21;
Joel 1:8-13
1:5 *p* S Isa 22:5;
S Jer 30:15 *q* S Ps 5:10
r S Jer 10:20; S 39:9;
52:28-30 *s* S Ps 137:3;
La 2:17
1:6 *t* S Ps 9:14;
Jer 13:18
u S Lev 26:36

1 ^a

How deserted ^a lies the city,
    once so full of people! ^b
How like a widow ^c is she,
    who once was great ^d among the nations!
She who was queen among the provinces
    has now become a slave. ^e

² Bitterly she weeps ^f at night,
    tears are on her cheeks.
Among all her lovers ^g
    there is none to comfort her.
All her friends have betrayed ^h her;
    they have become her enemies. ⁱ

³ After affliction and harsh labor,
    Judah has gone into exile. ^j
She dwells among the nations;
    she finds no resting place. ^k
All who pursue her have overtaken her ^l
    in the midst of her distress.

⁴ The roads to Zion mourn, ^m
    for no one comes to her appointed festivals.
All her gateways are desolate, ⁿ
    her priests groan,
her young women grieve,
    and she is in bitter anguish. ^o

⁵ Her foes have become her masters;
    her enemies are at ease.
The LORD has brought her grief ^p
    because of her many sins. ^q
Her children have gone into exile, ^r
    captive before the foe. ^s

⁶ All the splendor has departed
    from Daughter Zion. ^t
Her princes are like deer
    that find no pasture;
in weakness they have fled ^u
    before the pursuer.

⁷ In the days of her affliction and wandering
    Jerusalem remembers all the treasures

^a This chapter is an acrostic poem, the verses of which begin with the successive letters of the Hebrew alphabet.

1:1–22 As is widely done in OT prophecy and psalmody, Jerusalem is here presented as a woman—and represents the nation of which she is the political head and symbolic heart.
1:1–11 In the first half of this first lament, Jerusalem's condition is described by one who speaks of her in the third person—yet as one who bemoans the city's desperate situation. For the transition to Jerusalem's own voice, see the quoted words at the end of v. 11.
1:1 *How . . . !* Expresses a mixture of shock and deep dismay (see 2:1; 4:1–2; 2Sa 1:25,27; Jer 9:19; 48:17,39; Eze 26:17). *deserted lies.* The Hebrew underlying this phrase is translated "sat alone" in Jer 15:17. There the prophet sat alone; here his beloved city does the same. *city.* Jerusalem. *once so full of people.* Cf. Isa 1:21. *great among the nations.* Cf. Jer 49:15. *slave.* The Hebrew for this word is translated "forced labor" in Ex 1:11; 1Ki 4:6.
1:2 *Bitterly she weeps.* As did Jeremiah, and for much the same reason (Jer 13:17). *at night.* See 2:18–19. *lovers . . . friends.* International allies to whom the people of Jerusalem and Judah looked for security rather than to the Lord (see Jer 2:36–37; 27:3; Eze 16:26,28–29; 23:11–21; see also Ex 34:15 and note). *none to comfort her.* See vv. 9,16–17,21. *All . . . have betrayed her.*

See v. 19; like Edom (4:21–22; Ps 137:7) and Ammon (Jer 40:14; Eze 25:2–3,6). *become her enemies.* See v. 17.
1:3 *gone into exile.* To Babylonia (see Jer 20:4–5 and thereafter in Jeremiah). *among the nations . . . finds no resting place.* As Moses warned in Dt 28:65.
1:4 *mourn.* Are deserted and desolate (see Jdg 5:6; Isa 33:8 and notes). *appointed festivals.* See Ex 23:14–17 and notes; Lev 23:2. *young women grieve.* A sign of utter defeat (see Jer 9:20; contrast Ex 15:20 and note; 1Sa 18:6; Ps 68:25; Jer 31:13).
1:5 *masters.* Lit. "head"—in accordance with Dt 28:44 (contrast Dt 28:13).
1:6 *Daughter Zion.* A personification of Jerusalem (see note on 2Ki 19:21). *Her princes . . . have fled before the pursuer.* See Jer 52:7–8. *like deer that find no pasture.* Hence are weakened and become easy prey for predators.
1:7 *affliction and wandering.* See 3:19. *treasures.* See vv. 10–11. *days of old.* For example, the days of David and Solomon. *fell into enemy hands.* See 2Sa 24:14. *destruction.* Lit. "cessation" (see notes on Ge 2:2–3). The Hebrew root for this word is the same as that for "Sabbath"—and may be intended as an ironic pun (see Lev 26:34–35).

that were hers in days of old.
When her people fell into enemy hands,
   there was no one to help her. ^v
Her enemies looked at her
   and laughed ^w at her destruction.

⁸ Jerusalem has sinned ^x greatly
   and so has become unclean. ^y
All who honored her despise her,
   for they have seen her nakedness; ^z
she herself groans ^a
   and turns away.

⁹ Her filthiness clung to her skirts;
   she did not consider her future. ^b
Her fall ^c was astounding;
   there was none to comfort ^d her.
"Look, LORD, on my affliction, ^e
   for the enemy has triumphed."

¹⁰ The enemy laid hands
   on all her treasures; ^f
she saw pagan nations
   enter her sanctuary ^g—
those you had forbidden ^h
   to enter your assembly.

¹¹ All her people groan ⁱ
   as they search for bread; ^j
they barter their treasures for food
   to keep themselves alive.
"Look, LORD, and consider,
   for I am despised."

¹² "Is it nothing to you, all you who pass by? ^k
   Look around and see.
Is any suffering like my suffering ^l
   that was inflicted on me,
that the LORD brought on me
   in the day of his fierce anger? ^m

¹³ "From on high he sent fire,
   sent it down into my bones. ⁿ
He spread a net ^o for my feet
   and turned me back.
He made me desolate, ^p
   faint ^q all the day long.

¹⁴ "My sins have been bound into a yoke^a; ^r
   by his hands they were woven together.

---

^a 14 Most Hebrew manuscripts; many Hebrew manuscripts and Septuagint *He kept watch over my sins*

1:7 *v* S 2Ki 14:26;
S Jer 37:7; La 4:17
w S Jer 2:26
1:8 *x* ver 20;
Isa 59:2-13
y S Jer 2:22
z S Jer 13:22,26
a ver 21,22; S Ps 6:6;
S 38:8
1:9 *b* Dt 32:28-29;
Eze 24:13 *c* Jer 13:18
d S Ecc 4:1; S Jer 16:7
e Ps 25:18
1:10 *f* S Isa 64:11
g Ps 74:7-8; 79:1;
Jer 51:51 *h* Dt 23:3
1:11 *i* S Ps 6:6;
S 38:8 *j* S Jer 37:21;
S 52:6
1:12 *k* S Jer 18:16
l ver 18 *m* S Isa 10:4;
13:13; S Jer 30:24
1:13 *n* S Job 30:30;
Ps 102:3 *o* S Job 18:8
p S Jer 44:6
q Hab 3:16
1:14 *r* S Dt 28:48;
S Isa 47:6; S Jer 15:12

1:8 *unclean.* See v. 17 and note. It refers to the ceremonial uncleanness of a woman during her monthly period (see Lev 12:2, 5; 15:19). *her nakedness.* See Isa 47:3; Eze 16:37 and notes.
1:9 *filthiness.* Ceremonial uncleanness (see note on Lev 4:12), here caused by willful sin. *did not consider her future.* Just as Babylon did not (Isa 47:7). *Look, LORD.* Jerusalem's desolation is further depicted by quoting the cry that bursts from her lips (see v. 11 and note). *enemy has triumphed.* See v. 16.
1:10 *forbidden to enter your assembly.* See Eze 44:7,9 and notes.
1:11 *search for bread.* Food shortages were an ever-present problem during and after the siege of Jerusalem. *keep themselves alive.* See v. 19; 2Ki 6:24-29. *Look, LORD.* Again, Jerusalem's desperate cry to the Lord is suddenly introduced. From here to the end of this lament, personified Jerusalem speaks.
1:12 *who pass by.* See Jer 18:16 and note. *Look ... like my suffer-*

ing. In his magisterial *The Messiah,* Handel borrowed these lines (as they appeared in the KJV: "Behold, and see if there be any sorrow like unto my sorrow") and placed them on the lips of the Messiah—perhaps associating them with Isa 53:4 ("Surely he hath borne our griefs and carried our sorrows ..."); cf. also Isa 53:3 ("man of sorrows"). *fierce anger.* See 2:3,6; 4:11. The expression is common in Jeremiah (see Jer 4:8,26; 12:13; 25:37-38; 44:6; 49:37; 51:45).
1:13 *From on high he sent fire.* The fire of his judgment (see 2:3-4; Lev 10:2; Nu 11:1-3; 16:35; 2Ki 1:10,12; Isa 29:6; 30:30; 66:15-16; Jer 4:4; 21:14; 49:27; 50:32; Am 7:4). *my bones.* The bones of Jerusalem (personified as a woman; see note on v. 8). In a strikingly similar image, the word of the Lord was like fire in the bones of the prophet (see Jer 20:9 and note). *spread a net for my feet.* See Ps 57:6; Pr 29:5. *desolate.* Like Absalom's sister Tamar (see 2Sa 13:20).

1:14 ˢ S Jer 32:5
1:15 ᵗ Jer 37:10
ᵘ Isa 41:2 ᵛ Isa 28:18;
S Jer 18:21
ʷ S Jdg 6:11
ˣ S Isa 5:5 ʸ Jer 14:17
1:16 ᶻ Job 7:3;
S Ps 119:136;
S Isa 22:4; La 2:11,18;
3:48-49 ᵃ S Ps 69:20;
Ecc 4:1; S Jer 16:7
ᵇ S ver 2; Jer 13:17;
14:17
1:17 ᶜ S Jer 4:31
ᵈ S Ex 23:21 ᵉ Jer 2:22
ᶠ S Lev 18:25-28
1:18 ᵍ S Ex 9:27;
S Ezr 9:15
ʰ S 1Sa 12:14 ⁱ ver 12
ʲ Dt 28:32,41
1:19 ᵏ S Jer 22:20
ˡ S Jer 14:15; La 2:20
1:20 ᵐ S Jer 4:19
ⁿ La 2:11 ᵒ S Job 20:2
ᵖ S ver 8 ᵠ S Dt 32:25;
Eze 7:15
1:21 ʳ S ver 8;
S Ps 6:6; S 38:8
ˢ ver 4 ᵗ La 2:15
ᵘ Isa 47:11; Jer 30:16

They have been hung on my neck,
　and the Lord has sapped my strength.
He has given me into the hands ˢ
　of those I cannot withstand.

¹⁵ "The Lord has rejected
　all the warriors in my midst; ᵗ
he has summoned an army ᵘ against me
　to ᵃ crush my young men. ᵛ
In his winepress ʷ the Lord has trampled ˣ
　Virgin Daughter ʸ Judah.

¹⁶ "This is why I weep
　and my eyes overflow with tears. ᶻ
No one is near to comfort ᵃ me,
　no one to restore my spirit.
My children are destitute
　because the enemy has prevailed." ᵇ

¹⁷ Zion stretches out her hands, ᶜ
　but there is no one to comfort her.
The Lᴏʀᴅ has decreed for Jacob
　that his neighbors become his foes; ᵈ
Jerusalem has become
　an unclean ᵉ thing ᶠ among them.

¹⁸ "The Lᴏʀᴅ is righteous, ᵍ
　yet I rebelled ʰ against his command.
Listen, all you peoples;
　look on my suffering. ⁱ
My young men and young women
　have gone into exile. ʲ

¹⁹ "I called to my allies ᵏ
　but they betrayed me.
My priests and my elders
　perished ˡ in the city
while they searched for food
　to keep themselves alive.

²⁰ "See, Lᴏʀᴅ, how distressed ᵐ I am!
　I am in torment ⁿ within,
and in my heart I am disturbed, ᵒ
　for I have been most rebellious. ᵖ
Outside, the sword bereaves;
　inside, there is only death. ᵠ

²¹ "People have heard my groaning, ʳ
　but there is no one to comfort me. ˢ
All my enemies have heard of my distress;
　they rejoice ᵗ at what you have done.
May you bring the day ᵘ you have announced
　so they may become like me.

²² "Let all their wickedness come before you;
　deal with them

ᵃ 15 Or has set a time for me / when he will

1:15 *In his winepress . . . trampled.* A common metaphor of divine judgment (see Isa 63:2–3; Joel 3:13; Rev 14:19–20; 19:15). *Virgin Daughter Judah.* A personification of Judah (see note on 2Ki 19:21).
1:16 *eyes overflow with tears.* See 2:11; 3:48; Jer 9:1,18 and note on 9:1; 13:17; 14:17. *enemy has prevailed.* See v. 9.
1:17 *become his foes.* See v. 2. *unclean thing.* See note on v. 8; for the same imagery elsewhere, see Ezr 9:11; Isa 30:22; 64:6; Eze 7:19–20; 36:17.
1:18 *is righteous.* Has dealt rightly with me. *yet I rebelled.* Better "for I have rebelled." *Listen . . . look.* The nations are called to take

note of the Lord's righteous acts of judgment, as well as of his righteous acts of deliverance.
1:19 *allies . . . betrayed me.* See v. 2 and note. *keep themselves alive.* See note on v. 11.
1:20 *I am in torment within.* Repeated in 2:11. *Outside . . . inside.* See Jer 14:18. The Sumerian "Lamentation over the Destruction of Ur" contains a striking parallel: "Inside it we die of famine, outside we are killed by weapons" (lines 403–404).
1:21 *day you have announced.* Day of God's judgment on the nations (see 4:21–22; Jer 25:15–38 and notes).

as you have dealt with me
because of all my sins. *v*
My groans *w* are many
and my heart is faint."

2 ᵃ How the Lord has covered Daughter Zion
with the cloud of his anger! *b! x*
He has hurled down the splendor of Israel
from heaven to earth;
he has not remembered his footstool *y*
in the day of his anger. *z*

² Without pity *a* the Lord has swallowed *b* up
all the dwellings of Jacob;
in his wrath he has torn down
the strongholds *c* of Daughter Judah.
He has brought her kingdom and its princes
down to the ground *d* in dishonor.

³ In fierce anger he has cut off
every horn *c e* of Israel.
He has withdrawn his right hand *f*
at the approach of the enemy.
He has burned in Jacob like a flaming fire
that consumes everything around it. *g*

⁴ Like an enemy he has strung his bow; *h*
his right hand is ready.
Like a foe he has slain
all who were pleasing to the eye; *i*
he has poured out his wrath *j* like fire *k*
on the tent *l* of Daughter Zion.

⁵ The Lord is like an enemy; *m*
he has swallowed up Israel.
He has swallowed up all her palaces
and destroyed her strongholds. *n*
He has multiplied mourning and lamentation *o*
for Daughter Judah. *p*

⁶ He has laid waste his dwelling like a garden;
he has destroyed *q* his place of meeting. *r*
The LORD has made Zion forget
her appointed festivals and her Sabbaths; *s*
in his fierce anger he has spurned
both king and priest. *t*

ᵃ This chapter is an acrostic poem, the verses of which begin with the successive letters of the Hebrew alphabet.   ᵇ 1 Or *How the Lord in his anger / has treated Daughter Zion with contempt*   ᶜ 3 Or *off / all the strength*; or *every king*; horn here symbolizes strength.

1:22 ᵛ Ne 4:5
ʷ S ver 8; S Ps 6:6
2:1 ˣ La 3:44
ʸ Ps 99:5; 132:7
ᶻ S Jer 12:7
2:2 ᵃ ver 17; La 3:43
ᵇ Ps 21:9 ᶜ Ps 89:39-40; Mic 5:11
ᵈ S Isa 25:12
2:3 ᵉ Ps 75:5,10
ᶠ Ps 74:11
ᵍ S Isa 42:25;
Jer 21:4-5,14
2:4 ʰ S Job 3:23;
16:13; La 3:12-13
ⁱ S Ps 48:2; Eze 24:16,
25 / S 2Ch 34:21;
Eze 20:34 ᵏ Isa 42:25;
S Jer 7:20 ˡ S Jer 4:20
2:5 ᵐ S Job 13:24
ⁿ ver 2 ᵒ S Isa 29:2
ᵖ S Jer 7:20; 9:17-20
2:6 ᵠ 2Ch 36:19
ʳ S Jer 52:13
ˢ Zep 3:18 ᵗ Isa 43:28;
S Jer 7:14; La 4:16;
5:12

1:22 *wickedness . . . before you.* See Ps 109:14–15. *my heart is faint.* The same expression is found in Jer 8:18; see La 5:17; Isa 1:5.
2:1–22 Jerusalem is again personified as a woman—and represents the nation (see note on 1:1–22). In vv. 1–10 Jerusalem's experience of God's wrath is described by a voice that speaks of her in the third person. In vv. 12–19 Jerusalem is directly addressed (second-person pronouns abound). At the center (vv. 11–12) the author begins to speak in the first person (see note on 1:1–11). The first-person voice of vv. 20–22 is that of Jerusalem.
2:1 *How . . . !* See note on 1:1. *Daughter Zion.* A personification of Jerusalem (see the same or similar idiom in vv. 2,4–5,8,10, 13,15,18; see also note on 2Ki 19:21). *hurled down the splendor of Israel.* The imagery is that of a falling star (as in Isa 14:12). *footstool.* Either (1) the ark of the covenant (see 1Ch 28:2) or, more likely, (2) Mount Zion (see Ps 99:5 and note).

2:2 *swallowed up all the dwellings.* See v. 5. *Daughter Judah.* See note on v. 1.
2:3 *cut off every horn.* See TNIV text note. *flaming fire that consumes.* See 1:13 and note.
2:4 *strung his bow.* See 3:12; Dt 32:42; Ps 7:12–13; Hab 3:9. *poured out.* Widely used imagery in the OT for the display of God's wrath (see Ps 69:24; 79:6; Jer 6:11; 7:20; 10:25; 42:18; 44:6; Hos 5:10; Zep 3:8). *Daughter Zion.* See note on v. 1.
2:5 *palaces . . . strongholds.* See Hos 8:14. *multiplied mourning and lamentation.* The Sumerian "Lamentation over the Destruction of Sumer and Ur" offers this parallel: "In the desolate city there was uttered nothing but laments and dirges" (lines 361–362, 486–487). *Daughter Judah.* See note on v. 1.
2:6 *his dwelling . . . his place of meeting.* The temple in Jerusalem (see 1Ki 8:29; 9:3; 2Ch 6:2; 7:1–3; Ps 27:7–10 and note; 132:8,13–14). *like a garden.* Cf. Isa 5:5–6; Jer 5:10; 12:10.

2:7 ᵘ S Lev 26:31;
S Eze 7:24 ᵛ Ps 74:7-
8; S Isa 64:11;
Jer 33:4-5; Eze 7:21-
22 ʷ Jer 21:4; 52:13
2:8 ˣ ver 18
ʸ S 2Ki 21:13
ᶻ S Ps 48:13
ᵃ Isa 3:26; S Jer 39:8;
S 52:14
2:9 ᵇ S Ne 1:3
ᶜ S Isa 45:2; Hos 11:6
ᵈ Dt 28:36;
S 2Ki 24:15; Jer 16:13;
Hos 3:4 ᵉ S 2Ch 15:3
ᶠ S Isa 3:1
ᵍ S Jer 14:14
2:10 ʰ La 3:28
ⁱ S Jos 7:6 ʲ Job 2:12
ᵏ S Isa 3:24
ˡ S Job 2:13;
S Isa 3:26; Eze 27:30-
31
2:11 ᵐ S Ps 119:82;
S Isa 15:3; S La 1:16;
3:48-51 ⁿ S Job 30:27;
La 1:20 ᵒ S Isa 1:5
ᵖ ver 19; Ps 22:14
�q S Jer 9:1 ʳ La 4:4
2:12 ˢ Isa 24:11
ᵗ S Job 3:24 ᵘ La 4:4
2:13 ᵛ S Isa 1:6
ʷ S Isa 1:6
ˣ Isa 37:22 ʸ Jer 14:17;
30:12-15; La 1:12

⁷ The Lord has rejected his altar
  and abandoned his sanctuary. ᵘ
He has given the walls of her palaces ᵛ
  into the hands of the enemy;
they have raised a shout in the house of the Lord
  as on the day of an appointed festival. ʷ

⁸ The Lord determined to tear down
  the wall around Daughter Zion. ˣ
He stretched out a measuring line ʸ
  and did not withhold his hand from destroying.
He made ramparts ᶻ and walls lament;
  together they wasted away. ᵃ

⁹ Her gates ᵇ have sunk into the ground;
  their bars ᶜ he has broken and destroyed.
Her king and her princes are exiled ᵈ among the nations,
  the law ᵉ is no more,
and her prophets ᶠ no longer find
  visions ᵍ from the Lord.

¹⁰ The elders of Daughter Zion
  sit on the ground in silence; ʰ
they have sprinkled dust ⁱ on their heads ʲ
  and put on sackcloth. ᵏ
The young women of Jerusalem
  have bowed their heads to the ground. ˡ

¹¹ My eyes fail from weeping, ᵐ
  I am in torment within ⁿ;
my heart ᵒ is poured out ᵖ on the ground
  because my people are destroyed, q
because children and infants faint ʳ
  in the streets of the city.

¹² They say to their mothers,
  "Where is bread and wine?" ˢ
as they faint like the wounded
  in the streets of the city,
as their lives ebb away ᵗ
  in their mothers' arms. ᵘ

¹³ What can I say for you? ᵛ
  With what can I compare you,
  Daughter ʷ Jerusalem?
To what can I liken you,
  that I may comfort you,
  Virgin Daughter Zion? ˣ
Your wound is as deep as the sea. ʸ
  Who can heal you?

2:7 *rejected…abandoned.* These two verbs are found in Ps
89:38–39 ("rejected…renounced") in connection with the Lord's
forsaking of the king from the dynasty of David. *raised a shout in
the house of the Lord.* See Ps 74:4. *as on the day of an appointed
festival.* See Ps 42:4; 47:5; 81:1–4. But there is bitter irony in the
fact that the triumphant shouts of the enemy have silenced the
joyful shouts of those who had worshiped at the temple.
2:8 *determined to tear down.* See Jer 1:15; 32:31. *Daughter Zion.*
See note on v. 1. *stretched out a measuring line.* To destroy with
the same standards of precision used in building (see Isa 28:17;
Am 7:7–8 and notes). *ramparts…walls.* Cf. Isa 26:1. The ramparts were the outer fortifications (see 2Sa 20:15).

A **2:9** *the law is no more.* There are no longer any priests
(see v. 20) to teach and interpret the covenant law (see
Jer 18:18; Hos 4:4–9 and notes). *prophets no longer find visions.*
The Lord was no longer communicating to his people through
prophets (see Ps 74:9; Am 8:11 and note; Mic 3:7).

2:10 *elders.* See note on Ex 3:16. *Daughter Zion.* See note on v.
1. *sit on the ground in silence…sprinkled dust on their heads and
put on sackcloth…bowed their heads.* Signs of mourning (see
Job 2:12–13; Ps 35:13–14). *young women of Jerusalem.* See 1:4
and note.
2:11 *My…I…my…my.* See note on vv. 1–22. Presumably the
speaker is the same as that heard in vv. 1–10 and in 1:1–11 (see
note there). He begins at this point with an expression of deep
personal grief over Jerusalem's condition, especially that of her
little ones (vv. 11–12), and then addresses Jerusalem directly
(vv. 13–19). *weeping.* See note on 1:16. *I am in torment within.*
Repeated from 1:20. *my people.* Lit. "the daughter of my people"
(see note on v. 1). This particular phrase occurs also in 3:48;
4:3,6,10; Isa 22:4; Jer 8:11,21; cf. Jer 14:17.
2:13 *What can I say for you?* The author has no words that can
bring comfort to suffering Jerusalem. *Daughter Jerusalem…Vir-
gin Daughter Zion.* See note on v. 1.

14 The visions of your prophets
were false[z] and worthless;
they did not expose your sin
to ward off your captivity. [a]
The prophecies they gave you
were false and misleading. [b]

15 All who pass your way
clap their hands at you; [c]
they scoff[d] and shake their heads[e]
at Daughter Jerusalem: [f]
"Is this the city that was called
the perfection of beauty, [g]
the joy of the whole earth?" [h]

16 All your enemies open their mouths
wide against you; [i]
they scoff and gnash their teeth[j]
and say, "We have swallowed her up. [k]
This is the day we have waited for;
we have lived to see it." [l]

17 The LORD has done what he planned;
he has fulfilled[m] his word,
which he decreed long ago. [n]
He has overthrown you without pity, [o]
he has let the enemy gloat over you, [p]
he has exalted the horn[a] of your foes. [q]

18 The hearts of the people
cry out to the Lord. [r]
You walls of Daughter Zion, [s]
let your tears[t] flow like a river
day and night; [u]
give yourself no relief,
your eyes no rest. [v]

19 Arise, cry out in the night,
as the watches of the night begin;
pour out your heart[w] like water
in the presence of the Lord. [x]
Lift up your hands[y] to him
for the lives of your children,
who faint[z] from hunger
at every street corner.

20 "Look, LORD, and consider:
Whom have you ever treated like this?
Should women eat their offspring, [a]

---

a 17 *Horn* here symbolizes strength.

2:14 [z] S Jer 28:15
[a] Jer 8:11 [b] Jer 2:8;
S 20:6; 23:25-32, 33-
40; S 29:9; Eze 13:3;
22:28
2:15 [c] S Nu 24:10;
Eze 25:6
[d] S Dt 28:37;
S Isa 28:22; Jer 19:8;
S Na 3:19 [e] S Job 16:4
[f] S La 1:21 [g] Ps 45:11;
S 48:2; 50:2;
Eze 16:14 [h] Ps 48:2
2:16 [i] Ps 22:13;
La 3:46 [j] S Job 16:9
[k] S Ps 35:25
[l] Eze 36:3; Mic 4:11
2:17 [m] S Jer 39:16
[n] Dt 28:15-45
[o] S ver 2; Eze 5:11;
7:9; 8:18 [p] S Ps 22:17
[q] Ps 89:42;
S Isa 44:26; S La 1:5;
Zec 1:6
2:18 [r] S Ps 119:145
[s] ver 8 [t] S La 1:16
[u] S Jer 9:1 [v] La 3:49
2:19 [w] Isa 1:15
[x] S ver 11; Isa 26:9
[y] S Ps 28:2
[z] S Isa 51:20
2:20 [a] S Dt 28:53;
Jer 19:9; Eze 5:10

2:14 *prophets . . . false.* Jeremiah often denounced the false prophets (see Jer 5:12–13; 6:13–14; 8:10–11; 14:13–15; 23:9–40; 27:9—28:17; cf. Jer 26:7–11,16; Eze 22:26, 28). *worthless.* Or "mere whitewash"; for an explanation of this image, see Eze 13:10–16; 22:28. *misleading.* The unusual Hebrew word underlying this word comes from the same root as that underlying "banish" in Jer 27:10,15: The lies of false prophets "mislead" the people and thus lead to "banishment" by the Lord—so they are "banishing" in their effect.
2:15 *who pass your way.* See 1:12. *clap their hands.* See Job 27:23; 34:37. *scoff.* See v. 16; see also note on Jer 19:8. *shake their heads.* See Job 16:4 and note; Ps 44:14; 64:8; 109:25; Jer 18:16. *Daughter Jerusalem.* See note on v. 1. *was called the perfection of beauty.* As in Ps 50:2 (see note there). *was called . . . the joy of the whole earth.* As in Ps 48:2 (see note there; cf. Jer 51:41).
2:16 *open their mouths wide.* To taunt or to devour (see Nu

16:30; Ps 22:13; Isa 5:14; 9:12). *swallowed her up.* See vv. 2,5; Jer 51:34.
2:17 *fulfilled his word.* See Isa 55:11 and note. *long ago.* The days of Moses (see, e.g., the threats of Lev 26:23–39; Dt 28:15–68). *exalted the horn.* Increased the strength (see TNIV text note; see also 1Sa 2:1; Ps 75:4).
2:18 See Jer 14:17. *You walls.* A city gate is similarly addressed in Isa 14:31. *Daughter Zion.* See note on v. 1.
2:19 *watches of the night begin.* See note on Jdg 7:19; see also Ps 63:6. *pour out your heart.* In earnest prayer (see Ps 62:8). *like water.* A common simile with "pour out" (see Dt 12:16,24; 15:23; Ps 79:3; Hos 5:10). *Lift up your hands.* In prayer (see Ps 28:2 and note; 1Ti 2:8). *children, who faint from hunger.* See vv. 11–12.
2:20–22 Jerusalem's heartbroken prayer in response to v. 19.
2:20 *women eat their offspring.* See note on Jer 19:9.

2:20 *b* La 4:10
c Ps 78:64;
S Jer 14:15; 23:11-12
d S La 1:19
2:21 *e* S Dt 32:25;
S 2Ch 36:17;
Ps 78:62-63; Jer 6:11
f S Jer 13:14; La 3:43;
Zec 11:6
2:22 *g* S Ps 31:13;
S Jer 20:10
h S Jer 11:11
i Job 27:14; Hos 9:13
3:1 *j* Jer 15:17-18
k S Job 19:21; Ps 88:7
3:2 *l* S Job 19:8;
S Ps 82:5; S Jer 4:23
3:3 *m* Ps 38:2;
Isa 5:25
3:4 *n* S Job 30:30;
La 4:8 *o* Ps 51:8;
S Isa 38:13;
S Jer 50:17
3:5 *p* ver 19
q Jer 23:15
3:6 *r* Ps 88:5-6;
143:3; Isa 59:10
3:7 *s* S Job 3:23
t Jer 40:4
3:8 *u* Ps 5:2 *v* ver 44;
S Dt 1:45;
S Job 30:20; Ps 22:2
3:9 *w* S Job 19:8
x S Job 9:24;
S Isa 63:17; Hos 2:6
3:10 *y* S Job 10:16
z Hos 13:8; Am 5:18-19
3:11 *a* Hos 6:1

the children they have cared for? *b*
Should priest and prophet be killed *c*
in the sanctuary of the Lord? *d*

21 "Young and old lie together
in the dust of the streets;
my young men and young women
have fallen by the sword. *e*
You have slain them in the day of your anger;
you have slaughtered them without pity. *f*

22 "As you summon to a feast day,
so you summoned against me terrors *g* on every side.
In the day of the LORD's anger
no one escaped *h* or survived;
those I cared for and reared *i*
my enemy has destroyed."

3 *a*

I am one who has seen affliction *j*
by the rod of the LORD's wrath. *k*
2 He has driven me away and made me walk
in darkness *l* rather than light;
3 indeed, he has turned his hand against me *m*
again and again, all day long.

4 He has made my skin and my flesh grow old *n*
and has broken my bones. *o*
5 He has besieged me and surrounded me
with bitterness *p* and hardship. *q*
6 He has made me dwell in darkness
like those long dead. *r*

7 He has walled me in so I cannot escape; *s*
he has weighed me down with chains. *t*
8 Even when I call out or cry for help, *u*
he shuts out my prayer. *v*
9 He has barred *w* my way with blocks of stone;
he has made my paths crooked. *x*

10 Like a bear lying in wait,
like a lion *y* in hiding, *z*
11 he dragged me from the path and mangled *a* me

---

a This chapter is an acrostic poem; the verses of each stanza begin with the successive letters of the Hebrew alphabet, and the verses within each stanza begin with the same letter.

2:21 See Jer 6:11 and note.
2:22 *summon to a feast day.* The same Lord who had called Israel to come to him in worship and to celebrate his saving acts in her history (see, e.g., Ps 81; 95; 114) now issues a quite different summons. *summoned against me.* See 1:15. *terrors on every side.* See note on Jer 6:25. *day of the LORD's anger.* The lament ends as it began (see v. 1). *no one escaped or survived.* See Jer 42:17; 44:14. *those I cared for.* Jerusalem's inhabitants.
3:1–66 This lament at the center of the book stands apart in significant ways. As to form: Like chs. 1 and 2, it is an alphabetic acrostic and is made up of 22 three-line units, but here each line of each unit begins with the same letter (see Introduction: Literary Features). That probably accounts for why in this lament each poetic line, rather than each stanza, has traditionally been set off as a grammatical unit and assigned a separate verse number. As to content: It begins (vv. 1–39) like the prayers of individuals found in the Psalter (which it extensively echoes) without any clear reference to the destruction of Jerusalem and the exile of the nation. This extended introduction may have been intended to put the communal lament that follows (vv. 40–66; see note on vv. 48–66) in a context that models how the community should react to its present distress.

3:1 The exact center of the book. The speaker identifies himself as one who exemplifies those who have suffered much under the rod of God's wrath. *affliction.* See v. 19. *rod of the LORD's wrath.* See Job 9:34; 21:9; cf. Isa 10:5 and note.
3:2 *darkness rather than light.* See Job 12:25; Ps 143:3; Isa 50:10; 59:9; cf. Am 5:18 and note.
3:4 *grow old.* See Ps 32:3 ("wasted away"); Ps 49:14 ("decay"). *broken my bones.* See Ps 51:8; Isa 38:13 and note.
3:5 *surrounded me.* See Job 19:6. *bitterness.* Lit. "poison" (see Jer 8:14 and note). *hardship.* See Ex 18:8; Nu 20:14; Ne 9:32.
3:6 See Ps 143:3 and note.
3:7 *walled.* The Hebrew for this word is the same as that for "barred" in v. 9 (see Job 19:8; Hos 2:6). *cannot escape.* See Ps 88:8.
3:8 *shuts out my prayer.* See v. 44; Job 30:20; Ps 18:41; 22:2; Pr 1:28; Jer 7:16 and note.
3:9 *blocks of stone.* Of enormous size, like those used in the foundation of Solomon's temple (see 1Ki 5:17). *made … crooked.* Rather than level (see Isa 26:7; 45:2; Jer 31:9 and note) or straight (see Ps 5:8; Pr 3:6 and notes; 11:5; Isa 45:13).
3:10 *Like a bear … like a lion.* See Jer 4:7; 5:6; 49:19; 50:44; Am 1:2 and note; 5:19; cf. Ps 7:2 and note.
3:11 See 1:2.

and left me without help.
12 He drew his bow [b]
    and made me the target [c] for his arrows. [d]

13 He pierced [e] my heart
    with arrows from his quiver. [f]
14 I became the laughingstock [g] of all my people; [h]
    they mock me in song [i] all day long.
15 He has filled me with bitter herbs
    and sated me with gall. [j]

16 He has broken my teeth with gravel; [k]
    he has trampled me in the dust. [l]
17 I have been deprived of peace;
    I have forgotten what prosperity is.
18 So I say, "My splendor is gone
    and all that I had hoped from the LORD." [m]

19 I remember my affliction and my wandering,
    the bitterness [n] and the gall. [o]
20 I well remember them,
    and my soul is downcast [p] within me. [q]
21 Yet this I call to mind
    and therefore I have hope:

22 Because of the LORD's great love [r] we are not consumed, [s]
    for his compassions never fail. [t]
23 They are new every morning;
    great is your faithfulness. [u]
24 I say to myself, "The LORD is my portion; [v]
    therefore I will wait for him."

25 The LORD is good to those whose hope is in him,
    to the one who seeks him; [w]
26 it is good to wait quietly [x]
    for the salvation of the LORD. [y]
27 It is good for people to bear the yoke
    while they are young.

28 Let them sit alone in silence, [z]
    for the LORD has laid it on them.
29 Let them bury their faces in the dust [a]—
    there may yet be hope. [b]

3:12 [b] S La 2:4
[c] Job 7:20
[d] S Job 16:12; Ps 7:12-13; 38:2
3:13 [e] S Job 16:13
[f] Job 6:4
3:14 [g] S Ge 38:23; Ps 22:6-7; Jer 20:7
[h] S Job 17:2
[i] S Job 30:9
3:15 [j] ver 19; Jer 9:15
3:16 [k] S Pr 20:17
[l] S Ps 7:5
3:18 [m] S ver 54; S Job 17:15
3:19 [n] ver 5
[o] S ver 15
3:20 [p] S Ps 42:5
[q] Ps 42:11; 43:5
3:22 [r] S Ps 103:11
[s] S Job 34:15; S Hos 11:9 [t] Ps 78:38; 130:7
3:23 [u] S Ex 34:6; Zep 3:5
3:24 [v] S Ps 119:57
3:25 [w] S Ps 33:18; Isa 25:9; S 30:18
3:26 [x] S Isa 7:4
[y] Ps 37:7; 40:1
3:28 [z] Jer 15:17; La 2:10
3:29 [a] S Job 2:8
[b] S Jer 31:17

3:12 *drew his bow.* See note on 2:4. *made me the target.* See note on Job 6:4.
3:13 *heart.* Lit. "kidneys" (as in Job 16:13). *with arrows.* See Ps 38:2 and note.
3:14 See Jeremiah's complaint in Jer 20:7. *mock me in song.* See v. 63; Ps 69:12; see also Ps 22:6–7; cf. Isa 28:9–10 and note.
3:15 *filled me with bitter herbs.* The Hebrew underlying this phrase is translated "overwhelm me with misery" in Job 9:18 (see note on Jer 9:15). For the significance of the bitter herbs eaten during the Passover meal, see note on Ex 12:8.
3:16 *broken my teeth with gravel.* Cf. Ps 72:9; Mic 7:17. *trampled me in the dust.* See Ps 7:5.
3:18 *all that I had hoped from the LORD.* See Ps 39:7; the first explicit mention of God in ch. 3.
3:19–20 The author again recalls all his troubles but now in preparation for his words of hope and encouragement in vv. 21–39.
3:19 *affliction and . . . wandering.* See 1:7. *the bitterness and the gall.* See vv. 5, 15; cf. Jer 9:15.

△ 3:21–26 The theological—and spiritual—high point of the book of Lamentations (see Introduction: Themes and Theology).

△ 3:22 *great love.* See v. 32. The Hebrew for this phrase is plural (also in Ps 107:43) and denotes the Lord's loving

faithfulness to his covenant promises (see Ps 89:1). See note on Ps 6:4; see also Isa 63:7 ("kindnesses") and note. *we.* The Lord's people.

△ 3:23 *They.* The "great love" and "compassions" (v. 22) of the Lord. *new every morning.* See Ps 30:5 and note; Isa 33:2. *great is your faithfulness.* It is beyond measure (see note on v. 32; see also Ps 36:5 and note).

△ 3:24 *The LORD is my portion.* See Ps 73:26; 142:5 and notes. He was the inheritance share of the priests and Levites (see Nu 18:20; see also note on Ge 15:1). *therefore I will wait.* See Ps 27:14; 71:14 and notes. The Hebrew for this phrase is the same as that for "therefore I have hope" in v. 21 and serves as a refrain.

3:25 *The LORD is good.* See Ps 34:8 and note on 34:8–14; 86:5. *whose hope is in him.* See Ps 25:3; 33:18; 37:9 and note.
3:26 See Ps 40:1; Isa 26:3; 30:15.
3:27 *It is good.* See Pr 3:11–12 and note. *people to bear the yoke.* Echoes the thought of v. 1: "one who has seen affliction." *while . . . young.* Cf. Ecc 12:1.
3:28 *sit alone.* Patiently suffering the mockery of his enemies (see v. 30). *in silence.* See v. 39; Ps 39:9. *it.* The yoke (see v. 27).
3:29 *bury their faces in the dust.* Showing humble submission to God. *there may yet be hope.* See 2Sa 12:22; Job 2:14; Am 5:15; Jnh 3:9.

3:30 c S Job 16:10;
S Isa 50:6 d Mic 5:1
3:31 e Ps 94:14;
Isa 54:7
3:32 f Ps 78:38;
106:43-45; Hos 11:8;
Na 1:12
3:33 g S Job 37:23;
S Jer 31:20;
Eze 18:23; 33:11
3:35 h Ge 14:18,19,
20,22
3:36 i Ps 140:12;
S Pr 17:15; S Jer 22:3;
Hab 1:13
3:37 j Ps 33:9-11;
S Pr 19:21; S 21:30
3:38 k S Job 2:10;
S Isa 45:7; Jer 32:42
3:39 l S Jer 30:15;
Mic 7:9
3:40 m 2Co 13:5
n Ps 119:59; 139:23-
24
3:41 o S Ps 25:1;
S 28:2
3:42 p Jer 14:20;
Da 9:5 q S 2Ki 24:4;
Jer 5:7-9
3:43 r ver 66;
Ps 35:6 s S La 2:2,17,
21
3:44 t Ps 97:2;
La 2:1 u S ver 8;
Zec 7:13 v S Isa 58:4
3:45 w 1Co 4:13
3:46 x Ps 22:13
y La 2:16
3:47 z Jer 48:43
a S Isa 24:17-18;
S 51:19
3:48 b S Ps 119:136
c S Jer 9:1,18; La 1:16
d La 2:11

30 Let them offer their cheeks to one who would strike them, c
    and let them be filled with disgrace. d

31 For people are not cast off
    by the Lord forever. e
32 Though he brings grief, he will show compassion,
    so great is his unfailing love. f
33 For he does not willingly bring affliction
    or grief to any human being. g

34 To crush underfoot
    all prisoners in the land,
35 to deny people their rights
    before the Most High, h
36 to deprive them of justice—
    would not the Lord see such things? i

37 Who can speak and have it happen
    if the Lord has not decreed it? j
38 Is it not from the mouth of the Most High
    that both calamities and good things come? k
39 Why should the living complain
    when punished for their sins? l

40 Let us examine our ways and test them, m
    and let us return to the LORD. n
41 Let us lift up our hearts and our hands
    to God in heaven, o and say:
42 "We have sinned and rebelled p
    and you have not forgiven. q

43 "You have covered yourself with anger and pursued r us;
    you have slain without pity. s
44 You have covered yourself with a cloud t
    so that no prayer u can get through. v
45 You have made us scum w and refuse
    among the nations.

46 "All our enemies have opened their mouths
    wide x against us. y
47 We have suffered terror and pitfalls, z
    ruin and destruction. a"
48 Streams of tears b flow from my eyes c
    because my people are destroyed. d

3:30 *offer their cheeks.* See Mt 5:39. *filled with disgrace.* See Ps 123:3–4.
3:31 *people are not cast off . . . forever.* See Isa 49:14–16; cf. note on Jer 3:5; cf. also Ro 11:11–32 and notes.
3:32 The same God who judges also restores (see Ps 30:5; Isa 54:7–8). *great is his unfailing love.* See note on v. 22; see also "great is your faithfulness" (v. 23)—faithfulness and unfailing love are often used together to sum up God's covenant mercies toward his people (see Ps 25:10; 26:3 and notes).
3:33 *does not willingly bring affliction.* See Eze 18:23,32; Hos 11:8; 2Pe 3:9.
3:34 *crush underfoot.* As the Babylonians had done in 586 B.C.
3:35 *deny . . . rights.* As the leaders of Judah had done, in direct violation of the law (see Ex 23:6). *before the Most High.* In the presence of those whom the Most High designates to dispense justice (see Ex 22:8–9 and TNIV text notes; see also introduction to Ps 82). *Most High.* See note on Ge 14:19.
3:36 *deprive . . . of justice.* People might, but God never does (see Job 8:3; 34:12). *the Lord see such things.* Contrary to what the wicked think (see Ps 10:11 and note), the Lord does see and will call to account (see Psalm 10:13–15).
3:37 *speak and have it happen.* No one is equal to God (see Ge 1:3 and note; Ps 33:9–11 and note on 33:4–11); so

no one can override the Lord's governing authority (cf. Job 1:12; 2:6 and notes).
3:38 See Job 2:10; Pr 3:11–12; Isa 45:7; Am 3:3–6 and notes; see also Jer 32:42.
3:39 *complain.* See v. 28 and note.
3:40–41 Here the voice of the community breaks in, responding to the model set before them in vv. 1–39 (see note on v. 1). Appropriately, the community begins with a confession of sin (see 1:8 and note; see also Ps 32:3–5; 39:7–10; 40:11–12; 41:4). **3:40** *let us return to the LORD.* See Hos 6:1; cf. Jer 3:1; 4:1; Hos 14:1; Joel 2:12–13; Zec 1:3.
3:41 *lift up . . . hands.* See note on 2:19. *heaven.* Where God is enthroned (see Ps 2:4; Isa 63:15; 66:1).
3:42 *We have sinned and rebelled.* For similar confessions, see Ps 106:6; Da 9:5.
3:43 *covered yourself with anger.* Cf. Isa 59:17–18. *pursued us . . . slain without pity.* See v. 66; 2:21; Jer 29:18.
3:46 See 2:16 and note.
3:48–66 The voice returns to first-person singular. It could be the same voice as that heard in vv. 1–39, but more likely the community now speaks in first-person singular (see, e.g., Ps 44:1,4 and note on 44:4). To its prayer the community adds expressions of assurance of being heard and a call for redress

⁴⁹ My eyes will flow unceasingly,
  without relief, *e*
⁵⁰ until the LORD looks down
  from heaven and sees. *f*
⁵¹ What I see brings grief to my soul
  because of all the women of my city.

⁵² Those who were my enemies without cause
  hunted me like a bird. *g*
⁵³ They tried to end my life in a pit *h*
  and threw stones at me;
⁵⁴ the waters closed over my head, *i*
  and I thought I was about to perish. *j*

⁵⁵ I called on your name, LORD,
  from the depths *k* of the pit. *l*
⁵⁶ You heard my plea: *m* "Do not close your ears
  to my cry for relief."
⁵⁷ You came near *n* when I called you,
  and you said, "Do not fear." *o*

⁵⁸ You, Lord, took up my case; *p*
  you redeemed my life. *q*
⁵⁹ LORD, you have seen the wrong done to me. *r*
  Uphold my cause! *s*
⁶⁰ You have seen the depth of their vengeance,
  all their plots against me. *t*

⁶¹ LORD, you have heard their insults, *u*
  all their plots against me—
⁶² what my enemies whisper and mutter
  against me all day long. *v*
⁶³ Look at them! Sitting or standing,
  they mock me in their songs. *w*

⁶⁴ Pay them back what they deserve, LORD,
  for what their hands have done. *x*
⁶⁵ Put a veil over their hearts, *y*
  and may your curse be on them!
⁶⁶ Pursue *z* them in anger and destroy them
  from under the heavens of the LORD.

4 ᵃ How the gold has lost its luster,
    the fine gold become dull!
  The sacred gems are scattered
    at every street corner. *a*

ᵃ This chapter is an acrostic poem, the verses of which begin with the successive letters of the Hebrew alphabet.

3:49 *e* Jer 14:17;
S La 2:18
3:50 *f* S Ps 14:2;
80:14; S Isa 63:15
3:52 *g* Ps 35:7
3:53 *h* Jer 37:16;
S 38:6
3:54 *i* Ps 69:2;
Jnh 2:3-5 *j* ver 18;
Ps 88:5; Eze 37:11
3:55 *k* S Ps 88:6
l Ps 130:1; Jnh 2:2
3:56 *m* S Ps 55:1;
116:1-2
3:57 *n* S Ps 46:1
o Isa 41:10
3:58 *p* S Jer 51:36
q Ps 34:22;
S Jer 50:34
3:59 *r* Jer 18:19-20
s Ps 35:23; 43:1
3:60 *t* S Jer 11:20;
18:18
3:61 *u* Ps 89:50;
Zep 2:8
3:62 *v* Eze 36:3
3:63 *w* S Job 30:9
3:64 *x* S Ps 28:4;
S Jer 51:6
3:65 *y* Ex 14:8;
Dt 2:30; Isa 6:10
3:66 *z* S ver 43
4:1 *a* Eze 7:19

---

against the enemies who have attacked them "without cause" (v. 52)—both of which are common elements in the prayers of individuals in the Psalter (cf. Ps 5:10; Ps 54 and notes).
3:48 *tears flow from my eyes.* See note on 1:16. *my people.* Lit. "the daughter of my people" (see note on 2:11).
3:50 *looks down . . . sees.* See Ps 5:1; Ps 80:14; Isa 63:15.
3:51 *women of my city.* See 1:4,18; 2:20–21; 5:11.
3:52 *enemies without cause.* See note on Ps 35:19. *like a bird.* See Ps 124:7.
3:53 *end my life in a pit.* See Ps 35:7. *threw stones at.* See 2Sa 16:6; 1Ki 12:18.
3:54 *waters closed over my head.* See Ps 32:6; 42:7; 69:1–2 and notes. *perish.* Cf. Ps 18:4–5; 30:3 and notes; Isa 53:8; Jnh 2:2 and note.
3:55 *from the depths of the pit.* See Ps 30:1 and note.
3:56 *cry for relief.* See Job 32:20; Ps 118:5.
3:57 *near when I called.* See Ps 145:18. *Do not fear.* A frequent

reassuring word from God (see Jer 1:8 and note).
3:58 *redeemed my life.* See Ps 25:22; 103:4 and notes.
3:59 *you have seen.* See Ps 10:14; 35:22. *Uphold my cause!* See Ps 35:23; 43:1; 119:154.
3:61 *you have heard.* The Lord has heard, as well as seen (vv. 59–60), what the enemies are doing.
3:62 *whisper . . . mutter.* See Ps 5:9 and note.
3:63 *Sitting or standing.* Engaging in any kind of activity (see Dt 6:7; 11:19; Ps 139:2; Isa 37:28). *mock me in their songs.* See note on v. 14.
3:64 Paralleled in Ps 28:4; see Ps 5:10 and note.
3:65 *Put a veil over their hearts.* So they cannot see the error of their ways or foresee the consequences. *may your curse be on them!* See Ps 109:16–20 and note.
3:66 *Pursue them.* Just as you have pursued us without pity because of our sins (v. 43), so now pursue them without pity for what they have done to us.

4:2 b Isa 51:18
4:3 c S Job 39:16
4:4 d S Dt 28:48;
S 2Ki 18:31
e S Ps 22:15 f La 2:11,
12
4:5 g Jer 6:2
h S Isa 3:26;
Am 6:3-7
4:6 i S Ge 19:25
4:8 j S Job 30:28
k Ps 102:3-5; S La 3:4
4:9 l S 2Ki 25:3
m S Jer 15:2; S 16:4;
La 5:10
4:10 n S Lev 26:29;
Dt 28:53-57; Jer 19:9;
La 2:20; Eze 5:10
4:11 o S Job 20:23
p S 2Ch 34:21
q Na 1:6; Zep 2:2; 3:8
r Jer 17:27
s S Dt 32:22;
S Jer 7:20; Eze 22:31

2 How the precious children of Zion, b
   once worth their weight in gold,
are now considered as pots of clay,
   the work of a potter's hands!

3 Even jackals offer their breasts
   to nurse their young,
but my people have become heartless
   like ostriches in the desert. c

4 Because of thirst d the infant's tongue
   sticks to the roof of its mouth; e
the children beg for bread,
   but no one gives it to them. f

5 Those who once ate delicacies
   are destitute in the streets.
Those nurtured in purple g
   now lie on ash heaps. h

6 The punishment of my people
   is greater than that of Sodom, i
which was overthrown in a moment
   without a hand turned to help her.

7 Their princes were brighter than snow
   and whiter than milk,
their bodies more ruddy than rubies,
   their appearance like lapis lazuli.

8 But now they are blacker j than soot;
   they are not recognized in the streets.
Their skin has shriveled on their bones; k
   it has become as dry as a stick.

9 Those killed by the sword are better off
   than those who die of famine; l
racked with hunger, they waste away
   for lack of food from the field. m

10 With their own hands compassionate women
   have cooked their own children, n
who became their food
   when my people were destroyed.

11 The Lord has given full vent to his wrath; o
   he has poured out p his fierce anger. q
He kindled a fire r in Zion
   that consumed her foundations. s

12 The kings of the earth did not believe,
   nor did any of the peoples of the world,

4:1–22 Another lamentation over the conquest of Jerusalem by the Babylonians—apparently by someone who had experienced the long siege of the city and the subsequent dispersion of its people. Verses 1–10 describe the terrible conditions of the siege, vv. 11–19 speak of the taking of the city and the fate of the refugees, v. 20 expresses the people's shock and dismay at the crushing of the Davidic king, and vv. 21–22 close the lament with words about the contrasting futures of exultant Edom and desolate Zion.

4:1 *How ...!* See note on 1:1. *gold ... gems.* Metaphors for God's chosen people (see v. 2). For similar imagery, see SS 5:11–12, 14–15; Zec 9:16; see also "The Babylonian Theodicy": "O ... mighty brother, ... jewel of gold" (lines 56–57). *at every street corner.* See 2:19; Isa 51:20.

4:3 *my people.* Lit. "the daughter of my people" (see note on 2:11). *become heartless.* See v. 10 and note. *like ostriches.* See Job 39:14–16.

4:5 *delicacies ... purple.* See Ge 49:20. Purple was the color of royalty (see, e.g., Jdg 8:26; see also note on SS 7:5); cf. the expressions "born to the purple" and "royal blue." *lie on ash heaps.* See Job 2:8 and note; cf. Jer 6:26 and note.

4:6 *my people.* Lit. "the daughter of my people" (see note on 2:11). *Sodom.* See note on Jer 20:16. *overthrown in a moment. And therefore spared the suffering of a lengthy siege (like that of Jerusalem).

4:7 *whiter ... ruddy.* The Hebrew underlying these two words is translated "radiant ... ruddy" in SS 5:10. *than rubies.* See Job 28:18. *lapis lazuli.* See SS 5:14; Isa 54:11 and notes.

4:8 *skin has shriveled on their bones.* See Job 19:20.

4:10 See Jer 19:9 and note. *my people.* Lit. "the daughter of my people" (see note on 2:11).

4:11 *fierce anger.* See 1:12 and note. *kindled a fire ... consumed.* See Jer 17:27 and note.

that enemies and foes could enter
　　the gates of Jerusalem. [t]

[13] But it happened because of the sins of her prophets
　　and the iniquities of her priests, [u]
who shed within her
　　the blood [v] of the righteous.

[14] Now they grope through the streets
　　as if they were blind. [w]
They are so defiled with blood [x]
　　that no one dares to touch their garments.

[15] "Go away! You are unclean!" people cry to them.
　　"Away! Away! Don't touch us!"
When they flee and wander [y] about,
　　people among the nations say,
　　"They can stay here no longer." [z]

[16] The LORD himself has scattered them;
　　he no longer watches over them. [a]
The priests are shown no honor,
　　the elders [b] no favor. [c]

[17] Moreover, our eyes failed,
　　looking in vain [d] for help; [e]
from our towers we watched
　　for a nation [f] that could not save us.

[18] People stalked us at every step,
　　so we could not walk in our streets.
Our end was near, our days were numbered,
　　for our end had come. [g]

[19] Our pursuers were swifter
　　than eagles [h] in the sky;
they chased us [i] over the mountains
　　and lay in wait for us in the desert. [j]

[20] The LORD's anointed, [k] our very life breath,
　　was caught in their traps. [l]
We thought that under his shadow [m]
　　we would live among the nations.

[21] Rejoice and be glad, Daughter Edom,
　　you who live in the land of Uz. [n]
But to you also the cup [o] will be passed;
　　you will be drunk and stripped naked. [p]

[22] Your punishment will end, Daughter Zion; [q]
　　he will not prolong your exile.

4:12 [r] S 1Ki 9:9;
S Jer 21:13
4:13 [u] Jer 5:31; 6:13;
Eze 22:28; Mic 3:11
[v] S 2Ki 21:16
4:14 [w] S Isa 59:10
[x] Jer 19:4
4:15 [y] S Jer 44:14
[z] Lev 13:46; Mic 2:10
4:16 [a] Isa 9:14-16
[b] La 5:12 [c] S La 2:6
4:17 [d] S Ge 15:18;
S Isa 20:5; Eze 29:16
[e] S La 1:7 [f] Jer 37:7
4:18 [g] Eze 7:2-12;
Am 8:2
4:19 [h] S Dt 28:49
[i] S Lev 26:36;
Isa 5:26-28 [j] Jer 52:7
4:20 [k] S Isa 26:9;
2Sa 19:21 [l] Jer 39:5;
Eze 12:12-13; 19:4,8
[m] S Ps 91:1
4:21 [n] S Ge 10:23
[o] S Ps 16:5;
S Jer 25:15 [p] Isa 34:6-
10; S 63:6; Eze 35:15;
Am 1:11-12; Ob 1:16;
Hab 2:16
4:22 [q] Isa 40:2;
Jer 33:8

4:12 *peoples.* Or "rulers" (parallel to "kings"); the Hebrew form underlying this word is translated "king" in Am 1:5,8.
4:13 See 2:14 and note; see also Eze 22:26,28.
4:14 *grope . . . as if they were blind.* See Dt 28:28–29; Isa 29:9 and note; 59:10 and note; Zep 1:17. *defiled with blood.* See Isa 59:3.
4:15 *unclean!* The cry of the person with a much dreaded skin disease (see Lev 13:45). *people . . . no longer.* Threatened in Dt 28:65–66.
4:16 As threatened in Dt 28:49–50.
4:17 *our eyes failed.* See Dt 28:28; Ps 69:3. *nation that could not save us.* For example, Egypt (see Eze 29:16).
4:19 *eagles.* See Jer 4:13; 48:40 and notes.
◩ ◪ **4:20** *The LORD's anointed.* King Zedekiah of the dynasty of David—under which the people of Judah felt secure because of God's covenant with David (see 2Sa 7; Ps 89; 132; Isa 55:3 and note). *our very life breath.* Lit. "the breath of

our nostrils" (a title used also of Pharaoh Rameses II in an inscription found at Abydos in Egypt). *was caught.* See Jer 39:4–7; 52:7–11. *shadow.* Protection (see Jdg 9:15; Ps 17:8 and notes). This verse beautifully expresses the hope that came to be focused in the promised Messiah—the "Anointed One" from the house of David.
4:21 *Rejoice and be glad.* Irony—exult for the little time you have left before God's judgment sweeps over you (see v. 22). *Daughter Edom.* A personification of Edom (see note on 2Ki 19:21). *Edom.* Because of its close relationship with Israel from earliest times and its persistent hostility (see note on Ge 25:26), Edom often served OT writers as representative of all Israel's enemies (see Ps 137:7 and note; Isa 13:1–6 and note on 13:1; 34:5 and note; Jer 49:7–22 and note on 49:8; Am 9:12 and note; Introduction to Obadiah: Unity and Theme; Ob 8 and note). *land of Uz.* See Jer 25:20; see also note on Job 1:1. *cup.* See note on Jer 25:15. *stripped naked.* See 1:8; see also Jer 49:10; Na 3:5.

4:22 *r* S Ps 137:7;
Eze 25:12-14; Mal 1:4
5:1 *s* Ps 44:13-16;
89:50
5:2 *t* Ps 79:1
u S Ps 109:11
v Zep 1:13 *w* Jer 17:4
5:3 *x* S Ex 22:24;
Jer 15:8; S 18:21
5:4 *y* S Isa 55:1;
Eze 4:16-17 *z* Isa 3:1
5:5 *a* S Ne 9:37;
Isa 47:6 *b* S Jos 1:13
5:6 *c* Jer 2:36;
Hos 5:13; 7:11; 9:3
5:7 *d* S Jer 31:29
e Jer 14:20; 16:12
5:8 *f* Ne 5:15
g Zec 11:6
5:10 *h* S Job 30:30;
S La 4:8-9
5:11 *i* S Ge 34:29;
Zec 14:2
5:12 *j* S Lev 19:32
k S La 2:6; 4:16
5:14 *l* S Isa 24:8;
Jer 7:34
5:15 *m* S Jer 25:10;
Am 8:10
5:16 *n* Ps 89:39;
S Jer 13:18
o S Job 19:9
p S Isa 3:11; Jer 14:20
5:17 *q* S Isa 1:5
r S Jer 8:18 *s* Ps 6:7
t S Job 16:8
5:18 *u* S Ps 74:2-3
v S Isa 27:10; Mic 3:12

But he will punish your sin, Daughter Edom,
  and expose your wickedness. *r*

Remember, LORD, what has happened to us;
  look, and see our disgrace. *s*
2 Our inheritance *t* has been turned over to strangers, *u*
  our homes *v* to foreigners. *w*
3 We have become fatherless,
  our mothers are widows. *x*
4 We must buy the water we drink; *y*
  our wood can be had only at a price. *z*
5 Those who pursue us are at our heels;
  we are weary *a* and find no rest. *b*
6 We submitted to Egypt and Assyria *c*
  to get enough bread.
7 Our parents *d* sinned and are no more,
  and we bear their punishment. *e*
8 Slaves *f* rule over us,
  and there is none to free us from their hands. *g*
9 We get our bread at the risk of our lives
  because of the sword in the desert.
10 Our skin is hot as an oven,
  feverish from hunger. *h*
11 Women have been ravished *i* in Zion,
  and virgins in the towns of Judah.
12 Princes have been hung up by their hands;
  elders *j* are shown no respect. *k*
13 Young men toil at the millstones;
  boys stagger under loads of wood.
14 The elders are gone from the city gate;
  the young men have stopped their music. *l*
15 Joy is gone from our hearts;
  our dancing has turned to mourning. *m*
16 The crown *n* has fallen from our head. *o*
  Woe to us, for we have sinned! *p*
17 Because of this our hearts *q* are faint, *r*
  because of these things our eyes *s* grow dim *t*
18 for Mount Zion, *u* which lies desolate, *v*
  with jackals prowling over it.

4:22 *Daughter Zion.* A personification of Jerusalem (see note on 2Ki 19:21). *will not prolong your exile.* See Jer 31–33. *expose your wickedness.* Contrast Ps 32:1; 85:2.

5:1–22 Although not an explicitly alphabetic acrostic like chs. 1–4, this lament is still controlled by the alphabet in that it is composed of just 22 poetic lines (see introduction to Ps 33). The first-person plural language identifies it as the voice of the community (like Ps 44; 60; 74; 80). The circumstances described suggest the time immediately after the fall of Jerusalem, when all was chaotic in the land (see v. 18; see also Jer 40:7—41:45). Some interpreters have suggested that the diminution of formal structure in this final lament may have been chosen to reflect the social disintegration brought on by the Babylonian destruction of the state of Judah.

5:1 *Remember . . . see.* Initial appeal to the Lord to give his full attention to the plight of his people (see Ps 44:13; 79:4).

5:2 *Our inheritance.* The land of Judah (see Jer 2:7 and note; 3:18).

5:3 *have become fatherless . . . widows.* Are as helpless as these (see notes on Ex 22:21–27; Isa 1:17).

5:4 *We must buy the water . . . wood.* Contrast Dt 29:11; Jos 9:21,23,27. *wood.* Firewood.

5:5 *find no rest.* The promised "rest" has been taken from them (see Dt 3:20 and note).

5:6 *submitted.* See 1Ch 29:24; 2Ch 30:8; Jer 50:15; lit. "gave the hand" (as in 2Ki 10:15; Ezr 10:19; Eze 17:18). *Egypt . . . Assyria.* By this

time a conventional way of referring to the great world powers to which the Israelites had often turned for protective alliances (see Isa 7:18; 11:16; 19:23–25; 52:4; Jer 2:18,36; see also Hos 7:11; 9:3; 11:5,11; 12:1 and notes; cf. Mic 7:12; Zec 10:10 and note).

5:7 Fathers and sons alike are responsible for the calamity that has befallen Jerusalem (see v. 16; Jer 3:25; 16:11–12; 31:29–30; Eze 18:2–4; cf. Isa 65:7).

5:8 *Slaves.* An ironic reference to the Babylonian officials who now rule over Jerusalem (formerly "queen among the provinces," 1:1); see Pr 30:21–22.

5:9 *sword in the desert.* Marauding bandits.

5:12 *hung.* An added indignity following execution (see notes on Dt 21:22–23).

5:13 *toil at the millstones.* Humiliating work (see note on Jdg 9:53; see also Isa 47:2).

5:14 *city gate.* The municipal court (see Jos 20:4), but also a gathering place for conversation and entertainment (cf. 1:4).

5:15 See Jer 7:34; 16:9; 25:10; contrast Ps 30:11; Jer 31:13.

5:16 *crown.* Symbolizes the glory and honor embodied in the city of Jerusalem (see 1:1; 2:15; cf. Isa 28:1,3).

5:17 *hearts are faint.* See note on 1:22. *eyes grow dim.* See 2:11; see also note on Ps 6:7.

5:18 *jackals.* The Hebrew for this word, different from that used in 4:3, can also mean "foxes" (see note on Jdg 15:4). For similar imagery of desolation, see Isa 13:21–22; 34:11–15; Zep 2:13–15.

¹⁹ You, Lᴏʀᴅ, reign forever;ʷ
　your throne enduresˣ from generation to generation.
²⁰ Why do you always forget us?ʸ
　Why do you forsakeᶻ us so long?
²¹ Restoreᵃ us to yourself, Lᴏʀᴅ, that we may return;
　renew our days as of old
²² unless you have utterly rejected usᵇ
　and are angry with us beyond measure.ᶜ

5:19 wS 1Ch 16:31
ˣS Ps 45:6; 102:12, 24-27
5:20 ʸS Ps 13:1; 44:24 ᶻS Ps 71:11
5:21 ᵃS Ps 80:3; Isa 60:20-22
5:22 ᵇS Ps 53:5; 60:1-2; S Jer 6:30
ᶜS Isa 64:9

5:19 Paralleled in Ps 102:12 (see note there). Elsewhere also prayer begins with praise (see Ps 44:1–8; 74:12–14; 80:1–2; 89:1–18; cf. Ac 24:23 and note).

5:20 *Why … ? Why … ?* See note on Ps 6:3.

5:21 *Restore us to yourself.* This language suggests a prayer for renewed commitment to the Lord (see 1Ki

8:33,48; Ne 1:9; Jer 3:7,10; Hos 7:10). *we may return.* See Jer 31:18 and note on 31:18–19. *renew.* See Ps 104:30.

5:22 See Jer 14:19. *unless.* Or "but." A similarly somber ending characterizes not only other laments (e.g., Ps 88) but also other OT books (e.g., Isaiah and Malachi).

Ezekiel lived during a time of international upheaval. The Assyrian empire that had once conquered the Syro-Palestinian area and destroyed the northern kingdom of Israel (which fell to the Assyrians in 722–721 B.C.) began to crumble under the blows of a resurgent Babylon. In 612 the great Assyrian city of Nineveh fell to a combined force of Babylonians and Medes. Three years later, Pharaoh Necho II of Egypt marched north to assist the Assyrians and to try to reassert Egypt's age-old influence over Canaan and Aram (Syria). At Megiddo, King Josiah of Judah, who may have been an ally of Babylon as King Hezekiah had been, attempted to intercept the Egyptian forces but was crushed, losing his life in the battle (see 2Ki 23:29–30 and note on 23:29; 2Ch 35:20–24).

Jehoahaz, a son of Josiah, ruled Judah for only three months, after which Necho installed Jehoiakim, another son of Josiah, as his royal vassal in Jerusalem (609 B.C.). In 605 the Babylonians overwhelmed the Egyptian army at Carchemish (see Jer 46:2), then pressed south as far as the Philistine plain. In the same year, Nebuchadnezzar was elevated to the Babylonian throne and Jehoiakim shifted allegiance to him. When a few years later the Egyptian and Babylonian forces met in a standoff battle, Jehoiakim rebelled against his new overlord.

Nebuchadnezzar soon responded by sending a force against Jerusalem, subduing it in 597 B.C. Jehoiakim's son Jehoiachin and about 10,000 Jews (see 2Ki 24:14), including Ezekiel, were exiled to Babylon, where they joined those who had been exiled in Jehoiakim's "third year" (see Da 1:1 and note). Nebuchadnezzar placed Jehoiachin's uncle, Zedekiah, on the throne in Jerusalem, but within five or six years he too rebelled. The Babylonians laid siege to Jerusalem in 588, and in July, 586, the walls were breached and the city plundered. On Aug. 14, 586, the city and temple were burned.

Under Nebuchadnezzar and his successors, Babylon dominated the international scene until it was crushed by Cyrus the Persian in 539 B.C. The reign of the house of David came to an end; the kingdom of Judah ceased to be an independent nation; Jerusalem and the Lord's temple lay in ruins.

AUTHOR

C What is known of Ezekiel is derived solely from the book that bears his name. He was among the Jews exiled to Babylon by Nebuchadnezzar in 597 B.C., and there among the exiles he received his call to become a prophet (see 1:1–3). He was married (see 24:15–18), lived in a house of his own (see 3:24; 8:1) and along with his fellow exiles, though confined to Babylonia, had a relatively free existence there.

He was a member of a priestly family (see note on 1:3) and therefore was eligible to serve as a priest. As a priest-prophet called to minister to the exiles (separated from the temple of the Lord with its symbolism, sacrifices, priestly ministrations and worship rituals), his message had much to do with the temple (see especially chs. 8–11; 40–48) and its ceremonies.

Ezekiel was obviously a man of broad knowledge, not only of his own national traditions but also of international affairs and history. His acquaintance with general matters of culture, from shipbuilding to literature, is equally amazing. He was gifted with a powerful intellect and was capable of grasping large issues and of dealing with them in grand and compelling images. His style is often detached, but in places it is passionate and earthy (see chs. 16; 23).

More than any other prophet (more even than Hosea and Jeremiah) he was directed to involve himself personally in the divine word by acting it out in prophetic symbolism.

OCCASION, PURPOSE AND SUMMARY OF CONTENTS

Though Ezekiel lived with his fellow exiles in Babylon, his divine call forced him to suppress any natural expectations he may have had of an early return to an undamaged Jerusalem. For the first seven years of his ministry (593–586 B.C.) he faithfully relayed to his fellow Jews the stern, heartrending, hope-crushing word of divine judgment: Because of all her sins, Jerusalem would fall (see chs. 1–24). The fact that Israel was God's covenant people and that Jerusalem was the city of his temple would not bring early release from exile or prevent Jerusalem from being destroyed (see Jer 29–30). The only hope the prophet was authorized to extend to his hearers was that of living at peace with themselves and with God during their exile.

After being informed by the Lord that Jerusalem was under siege and would surely fall (24:1–14), Ezekiel was told that his beloved wife would soon die. The delight of his eyes would be taken from him, just as the temple, the delight of Israel's eyes, would be taken from her. He was not to mourn openly for his wife, as a sign to his people not to mourn openly for Jerusalem (24:15–27). He was then directed to pronounce a series of judgments on Ammon, Moab, Edom, Philistia, Tyre, Sidon and Egypt (chs. 25–32). The day of God's wrath was soon to come, but not on Israel alone.

Once news was received that Jerusalem had fallen, Ezekiel's message turned to the Lord's consoling word of hope for his people—they would experience revival, restoration and a glorious future as the redeemed and perfected kingdom of God in the world (chs. 33–48).

DATE

B Since the book of Ezekiel contains more dates (see chart, p. 1364) than any other OT prophetic book, its prophecies can be dated with considerable precision. In addition, modern scholarship, using archaeology (Babylonian annals on cuneiform tablets) and astronomy (accurate dating of eclipses referred to in ancient archives), provides precise modern calendar equivalents.

Twelve of the 13 dates specify times when Ezekiel received a divine message. The other is the date of the arrival of the messenger who reported the fall of Jerusalem (33:21).

Having received his call in July, 593 B.C., Ezekiel was active for 22 years, his last dated oracle being received in April, 571 (see 29:17). If the "thirtieth year" of 1:1 refers to Ezekiel's age at the time of his call, his prophetic career exceeded a normal priestly term of service by two years (see Nu 4:3). His period of activity coincides with Jerusalem's darkest hour, preceding the 586 destruction by 7 years and following it by 15.

THEMES

The OT in general and the prophets in particular presuppose and teach God's sovereignty over all creation, over people and nations and the course of history. And nowhere in the Bible are God's initiative and control expressed more clearly and pervasively than in the book of Ezekiel. From the first chapter, which graphically describes the overwhelming invasion of the divine presence into Ezekiel's world, to the last phrase of Ezekiel's vision ("THE LORD IS THERE"), the book sounds and echoes God's sovereignty.

    This sovereign God resolved that he would be known and acknowledged. Approximately 65 occurrences of the clause (or variations on) "Then they will know that I am the LORD" testify to that divine desire and intention (see note on 6:7). Overall, chs. 1–24 teach that God will be revealed in the fall of Jerusalem and the destruction of the temple; chs. 25–32 teach that the nations likewise will know God through his judgments; and chs. 33–48 promise that God will be known through the restoration and spiritual renewal of Israel.

    God's total sovereignty is also evident in his mobility. He is not limited to the temple in Jerusalem. He can respond to his people's sin by leaving his sanctuary in Israel, and he can graciously condescend to visit his exiled children in Babylon.

    God is free to judge, and he is equally free to be gracious. His stern judgments on Israel ultimately reflect his grace. He allows the total dismemberment of Israel's political and religious life so that her renewed life and his presence with her will be clearly seen as a gift from the Lord of the universe.

    Furthermore, as God's spokesman, Ezekiel's "son of man" status (see note on 2:1) testifies to the sovereign God he was commissioned to serve.

    See also Theological Significance, below.

LITERARY FEATURES

The three major prophets (Isaiah, Jeremiah, Ezekiel) and Zephaniah all have the same basic sequence of messages: (1) oracles against Israel, (2) oracles against the

DATES IN EZEKIEL

REFERENCE	YEAR	MONTH	DAY	MODERN RECKONING	EVENT
1. 1:1	30	4	5	July 31, 593 B.C.	Inaugural vision
1:2	5	—	5		
3:16	"At the end of seven days"				
2. 8:1	6	6	5	Sept. 17, 592	Transport to Jerusalem
3. 20:1–2	7	5	10	Aug. 14, 591	Negative view of Israel's history
4. 24:1	9	10	10	Jan. 15, 588	Beginning of siege (see also 2Ki 25:1)
5. 26:1	11	—	1	Apr. 23, 587 to Apr. 13, 586	Oracle against Tyre (but see note on 26:1)
6. 29:1	10	10	12	Jan. 7, 587	Oracle against Egypt
7. 29:17	27	1	1	Apr. 26, 571	Egypt in exchange for Tyre
8. 30:20	11	1	7	Apr. 29, 587	Oracle against Pharaoh
9. 31:1	11	3	1	June 21, 587	Oracle against Pharaoh
10. 32:1	12	12	1	Mar. 3, 585	Lament over Pharaoh
11. 32:17	12	—	15	Apr. 13, 586 to Apr. 1, 585	Egypt dead
12. 33:21	12	10	5	Jan. 8, 585	Arrival of first fugitive
13. 40:1	25	1	10	Apr. 28, 573	Vision of the future
40:1	"fourteenth year after the fall of the city"				

nations, (3) consolation for Israel. In no other book is this pattern clearer than in Ezekiel (see Outline).

Besides clarity of structure, the book of Ezekiel reveals symmetry. The vision of the desecrated temple fit for destruction (chs. 8–11) is balanced by the vision of the restored and purified temple (chs. 40–48). The God presented in agitated wrath (ch. 1) is also shown to be a God of comfort ("THE LORD IS THERE," 48:35). Ezekiel's call to be a watchman announcing divine judgment (ch. 3) is balanced by his call to be a watchman announcing the new age to follow (ch. 33). In one place (ch. 6) the mountains of Israel receive a prophetic rebuke, but in another (ch. 36) they are consoled.

Prophetic books are usually largely poetic, the prophets apparently having spoken in imaginative and rhythmic styles. Most of Ezekiel, however, is prose, perhaps due to his priestly background. His repetitions have an unforgettable hammering effect, and his priestly orientation is also reflected in a case-law type of sentence (compare 3:19, "If you do warn the wicked . . . ," with Ex 21:2, "If you buy a Hebrew servant . . .").

The book contains four major visions (chs. 1–3; 8–11; 37:1–14; 40–48) and 12 symbolic acts (3:22–26; 4:1–3; 4:4–8; 4:9–11; 4:12–14; 5:1–3; 12:1–16; 12:17–20; 21:6–7; 21:18–24; 24:15–24; 37:15–28). Five messages are in the form of parables (chs. 15–17; 19; 23).

THEOLOGICAL SIGNIFICANCE

Other prophets deal largely with Israel's idolatry, with her moral corruption in public and private affairs and with her international intrigues and alliances, upon which she relied instead of on the Lord. They announce God's impending judgment on his rebellious nation but speak also of a future redemption: a new exodus, a new covenant, a restored Jerusalem, a revived Davidic dynasty, a worldwide recognition of the Lord and his Messiah and a paradise-like peace.

The contours and sweep of Ezekiel's message are similar, but he focuses uniquely on Israel as the holy people of the holy temple, the holy city and the holy land. By defiling her worship, Israel had rendered herself unclean and had defiled temple, city and land. From such defilement God could only withdraw and judge his people with national destruction.

But God's faithfulness to his covenant and his desire to save were so great that he would revive his people once more, shepherd them with compassion, cleanse them of all their defilement, reconstitute them as a perfect expression of his kingdom under the hand of "David" (34:23–24), overwhelm all the forces and powers arrayed against them, display his glory among the nations and restore the glory of his presence to the holy city.

Ezekiel powerfully depicts the grandeur and glory of God's sovereign rule (see Themes) and his holiness, which he jealously safeguards. The book's theological center is the unfolding of God's saving purposes in the history of the world—from the time in which he must withdraw from the defilement of his covenant people to the culmination of his grand design of redemption. The message of Ezekiel, which is ultimately eschatological, anticipates—even demands—God's future works in history proclaimed by the NT.

OUTLINE

III. Oracles of Consolation for Israel (chs. 33–48)
  A. Renewal of Ezekiel's Call as Watchman (33:1–20)
  B. Jerusalem's Fall Reported and Its Remnant Condemned (33:21–33)
  C. The Lord to Be Israel's Shepherd (ch. 34)
  D. A Prophecy against Edom (ch. 35)
  E. Israel's Complete Restoration Announced (ch. 36)
  F. Israel's Dry Bones Revived and Unity Restored (ch. 37)
    1. Israel's dry bones restored to life (37:1–14)
    2. Again one nation under one King (37:15–28)
  G. The Great Battle of the Ages (chs. 38–39)
  H. The New Order for Purified Israel (chs. 40–48)
    1. The temple area restored (40:1–47)
    2. The new temple (40:48—42:20)
    3. God's glory returns to the temple (43:1–12)
    4. Restoration of the great altar (43:13–27)
    5. Restoration of the priesthood (ch. 44)
    6. Restoration of the theocratic order (chs. 45–46)
    7. The river of life from the temple (47:1–12)
    8. The boundaries of the land (47:13–23)
    9. The distribution of the land (48:1–29)
    10. The twelve gates of the new city (48:30–35)

1:1 *a* S Dt 21:10;
Eze 11:24-25
b S Ps 137:1
c S Mt 3:16
d S Ex 24:10
1:2 *e* S 2Ki 24:15
1:3 *f* Eze 24:24
g S 2Ki 3:15; Isa 8:11;
Eze 3:14,22; 8:1;
33:22; 37:1; 40:1
1:4 *h* S Job 38:1
i Jer 1:14 *j* Eze 8:2
1:5 *k* S Isa 6:2;
Rev 4:6 *l* ver 26;
Da 7:13
1:6 *m* Eze 10:14
1:7 *n* Eze 40:3;
Da 10:6; S Rev 1:15
1:8 *o* Eze 10:8
1:9 *p* Eze 10:22
1:10 *q* Eze 10:14;
Rev 4:7
1:11 *r* Isa 6:2
1:12 *s* Eze 10:16-19
1:13 *t* S 2Sa 22:9
u Rev 4:5
1:14 *v* Ps 29:7
1:15 *w* Eze 3:13
x Eze 10:2; Da 7:9
1:16 *y* S Ex 28:20

EZEKIEL'S INAUGURAL VISION

1 In my thirtieth year, in the fourth month on the fifth day, while I was among the exiles *a* by the Kebar River, *b* the heavens were opened *c* and I saw visions *d* of God. ²On the fifth of the month—it was the fifth year of the exile of King Jehoiachin *e*— ³the word of the LORD came to Ezekiel *f* the priest, the son of Buzi, by the Kebar River in the land of the Babylonians. *a* There the hand of the LORD was on him. *g*

⁴I looked, and I saw a windstorm *h* coming out of the north *i*—an immense cloud with flashing lightning and surrounded by brilliant light. The center of the fire looked like glowing metal, *j* ⁵and in the fire was what looked like four living creatures. *k* In appearance their form was human, *l* ⁶but each of them had four faces *m* and four wings. ⁷Their legs were straight; their feet were like those of a calf and gleamed like burnished bronze. *n* ⁸Under their wings on their four sides they had human hands. *o* All four of them had faces and wings, ⁹and the wings of one touched the wings of another. Each one went straight ahead; they did not turn as they moved. *p*

¹⁰Their faces looked like this: Each of the four had the face of a human being, and on the right side each had the face of a lion, and on the left the face of an ox; each also had the face of an eagle. *q* ¹¹Such were their faces. They each had two wings *r* spreading out upward, each wing touching that of the creature on either side; and each had two other wings covering its body. ¹²Each one went straight ahead. Wherever the spirit would go, they would go, without turning as they went. *s* ¹³The appearance of the living creatures was like burning coals *t* of fire or like torches. Fire moved back and forth among the creatures; it was bright, and lightning *u* flashed out of it. ¹⁴The creatures sped back and forth like flashes of lightning. *v*

¹⁵As I looked at the living creatures, *w* I saw a wheel *x* on the ground beside each creature with its four faces. ¹⁶This was the appearance and structure of the wheels: They sparkled like topaz, *y* and all four looked alike. Each appeared to be made like a wheel intersecting a wheel. ¹⁷As they moved, they would go in any one of the four directions the

a 3 Or *Chaldeans*

1:1–28 Forced into Babylonian exile far from the Lord's temple with its symbolic evocations of God's glory (see notes on Ex 26:1; 40:34; Ps 24:2; see also Ps 24:8–10; 26:8; 29:9; 96:6 and notes), Ezekiel is inaugurated into his prophetic mission (see 1:1 and note) with an overwhelming vision of God's glory (see note on 1:28)—much as Isaiah was granted an awesome vision of God enthroned on high and attended by winged "seraphs" (see Isa 6:1–2 and notes) at the inauguration of his prophetic ministry (cf. 1Ki 22:19 and note).
1:1 *thirtieth year.* Ezekiel's age. According to Nu 4:3, a person entered active priestly ministry in his 30th year. Denied the ministry of the priesthood, Ezekiel received another commission—that of prophet. *Kebar River.* A canal of the Euphrates near the city of Nippur, south of Babylon, and possibly a place of prayer for the exiles (see Ps 137:1; cf. Ac 16:13). *visions of God.* A special term, always in the plural and always with the word "God" (not with the more personal "LORD"). The expression precedes this and the two other major visions of the prophet (8:3; 40:2).
1:2 *fifth year of the exile.* Verses 2–3, written in the third person (the only third-person narrative in the book), clarify the date in v. 1. *King Jehoiachin.* Was forced to accompany an early group of exiles to Babylon in 597 B.C. (see Introduction: Background). Ezekiel was among them and received his prophetic call in 593.
1:3 *Ezekiel.* The prophet's name occurs elsewhere in the book only in 24:24 (see note there) and thus frames the first major literary unit in his prophecy. His name means "God is strong" (cf. 3:14), "God strengthens" (cf. 30:25; 34:16) or "God makes hard" (cf. 3:8). *priest.* Member of a priestly family. *hand of the LORD.* A phrase occurring seven times in the book (see also 3:14,22; 8:1; 33:22; 37:1; 40:1), indicating an overpowering experience of divine revelation.
1:4 *I looked.* Introduces the first part of the vision: storm and living creatures (vv. 4–14). The "I looked" of v. 15 introduces the second part: wheels and the glory of the Lord. *a windstorm.* A storm cloud—accompanied by wind, lightning and thunder— often served as symbolic of God's powerful and active presence

(see Ex 19:16–18; Ps 18:7–15; 77:16–19 and notes; cf. Job 38:1).
1:5 *four living creatures.* "Four," which stands for completeness (cf. the four directions in Ge 13:14 and the four quarters of the earth in Isa 11:12), is used often in this chapter—and over 40 times in the book. The living creatures, called "cherubim" in ch. 10, are throne attendants (see Ex 25:18 and note). Here (see v. 10 and note) they contribute to the whole complex scenario that symbolically represents God's creation. These four creatures (cf. the "seraphs" of Isa 6:2–4) appear again in Rev 4:7. They were often depicted in the paintings and sculptures of the Middle Ages, but in this later use they represent the four Gospels. *their form … human.* God's noblest creature on earth (see v. 10 and note).
1:6 *four faces.* See v. 10 and note. *four wings.* Signifying their mobility as throne attendants of the heavenly King, who is ever on the move through history.
1:7 *like those of a calf.* Perhaps indicates agility (cf. Ps 29:6; Mal 4:2).
1:10 *face of a human being.* God's appointed ruler in the earth (see Ge 1:26–28; Ps 8:3–8 and notes). *a lion.* The most ferocious of wild animals known in Israel and Mesopotamia, and reputedly the strongest of such beasts (see Jdg 14:18). *an ox.* The most powerful of domesticated animals. *an eagle.* The mightiest of the birds. Cf. Rev 4:7 and note.
1:12 *straight ahead … without turning.* In their mobility they were multidirectional (see v. 14). *the spirit.* The directing presence in the cherubim (see v. 20).
1:13 *like burning coals.* Cf. Ps 18:8. *like torches.* Cf. Ge 15:17.
1:15 *wheel.* Also symbolic of mobility (see note on v. 12).
1:16 *topaz.* The precise identification of this stone is uncertain. See Ex 28:20 (and TNIV text note), where the stone appears in the priestly breastplate. *a wheel intersecting a wheel.* Probably two wheels intersecting at right angles in order to move in all four directions (see v. 17). The imagery symbolizes the omnipresence of God.

creatures faced; the wheels did not change direction *z* as the creatures went. ¹⁸Their rims were high and awesome, and all four rims were full of eyes *a* all around.

¹⁹When the living creatures moved, the wheels beside them moved; and when the living creatures rose from the ground, the wheels also rose. ²⁰Wherever the spirit would go, they would go, *b* and the wheels would rise along with them, because the spirit of the living creatures was in the wheels. ²¹When the creatures moved, they also moved; when the creatures stood still, they also stood still; and when the creatures rose from the ground, the wheels rose along with them, because the spirit of the living creatures was in the wheels. *c*

²²Spread out above the heads of the living creatures was what looked something like a vault, *d* sparkling like crystal, and awesome. ²³Under the vault their wings were stretched out one toward the other, and each had two wings covering its body. ²⁴When the creatures moved, I heard the sound of their wings, like the roar of rushing *e* waters, like the voice *f* of the Almighty, *a* like the tumult of an army. *g* When they stood still, they lowered their wings.

²⁵Then there came a voice from above the vault over their heads as they stood with lowered wings. ²⁶Above the vault over their heads was what looked like a throne *h* of lapis lazuli, *i* and high above on the throne was a figure like that of a man. *j* ²⁷I saw that from what appeared to be his waist up he looked like glowing metal, as if full of fire, and that from there down he looked like fire; and brilliant light surrounded him. *k* ²⁸Like the appearance of a rainbow *l* in the clouds on a rainy day, so was the radiance around him. *m*

This was the appearance of the likeness of the glory *n* of the LORD. When I saw it, I fell facedown, *o* and I heard the voice of one speaking.

EZEKIEL'S CALL TO BE A PROPHET

2 He said to me, "Son of man, *b p* stand *q* up on your feet and I will speak to you. *r*" ²As he spoke, the Spirit came into me and raised me *s* to my feet, and I heard him speaking to me.

³He said: "Son of man, I am sending you to the Israelites, to a rebellious nation that has rebelled against me; they and their ancestors have been in revolt against me to this very day. *t* ⁴The people to whom I am sending you are obstinate and stubborn. *u* Say to them, 'This is what the Sovereign LORD says.' *v* ⁵And whether they listen or fail to listen *w*—for they are a rebellious house *x*—they will know that a prophet has been among them. *y* ⁶And you, son of man, do not be afraid *z* of them or their words. Do not be afraid, though briers and thorns *a* are all around you and you live among scorpions. Do not be afraid of what they say or be terrified by them, though they are a rebellious house. *b* ⁷You must speak *c* my words to them, whether they listen or fail to listen, for they are rebellious. *d* ⁸But you, son

---

1:17 *z* ver 9
1:18 *a* Rev 4:6
1:20 *b* ver 12
1:21 *c* Eze 10:9-12
1:22 *d* Eze 10:1
1:24 *e* S Ps 46:3;
Eze 3:13 *f* Eze 10:5;
43:2; Da 10:6;
Rev 1:15; 14:2; 19:6
g S 2Ki 7:6
1:26 *h* S 1Ki 22:19;
Isa 6:1; S Jer 3:17
i S Ex 24:10 *j* S ver 5;
S Eze 2:1; S Rev 1:13
1:27 *k* Eze 8:2
1:28 *l* S Ge 9:13;
Rev 10:1 *m* S Rev 4:2
n S Ex 16:7; S 24:16;
Lk 2:9 *o* S Ge 17:3;
S Nu 14:5
2:1 *p* S Job 25:6;
Ps 8:4; S Eze 1:26;
Da 7:13; 8:15
q Da 10:11; Ac 14:10;
26:16 *r* Ac 9:6
2:2 *s* Eze 3:24;
Da 8:18
2:3 *t* S Jer 3:25;
Eze 5:6; 20:8-24;
24:3
2:4 *u* S Ex 32:9;
S Isa 9:9; Eze 3:7
v Am 7:15
2:5 *w* Eze 3:11
x Eze 3:27 *y* S Jer 5:3;
Eze 33:33; Jn 15:22
2:6 *z* S Dt 31:6;
S 2Ki 1:15
a S Nu 33:55;
Isa 9:18; Mic 7:4
b S Isa 1:2; 30:9;
Eze 24:3; 44:6
2:7 *c* Jer 7:27
d Jer 1:7; S 42:21;
Eze 3:10-11

---

a 24 Hebrew *Shaddai*   *b 1* The Hebrew phrase *ben adam* means *human being.* The phrase *son of man* is retained as a form of address here and throughout Ezekiel because of its traditional associations.

1:18 *full of eyes.* Symbolizes God's all-seeing nature.

1:22 *vault.* The same word occurs in Ge 1:6–8, where its function is to separate the waters above from the waters below. Here it separates the creatures from the glory of the Lord. *like crystal . . . awesome.* Cf. Rev 4:6 and note; 15:2.

1:25 *stood with lowered wings.* Awaiting a word from the throne.

1:26 *Above the vault . . . on the throne.* Cf. Ex 24:10. *a figure like that of a man.* Ezekiel is reporting his vision of God, but he carefully avoids saying he saw God directly (see Ge 16:13; Ex 3:6; Jdg 13:22).

1:28 *appearance of the likeness.* See note on v. 26. *glory of the LORD.* See note on 1:1–28. When God's glory was symbolically revealed, it took the form of brilliant light (see Ex 40:34 and note; Isa 6:3). What is remarkable about Ezekiel's experience is that God's glory had for centuries been associated with the temple in Jerusalem (see 1Ki 8:11; Ps 26:8; 63:2; 96:6; 102:16). Now God had left his temple and was appearing to his exiled people in Babylon—a major theme in the first half of Ezekiel's message (see 10:4; 11:23). In his vision of the restored Jerusalem the prophet saw the glory of the Lord returning (43:2). *I fell facedown.* See Ge 17:3; Ex 3:6; cf. Isa 6:5.

2:1—3:15 God does not abandon his covenant people even though he banishes them from the promised land because of their long history of rebellion against him. He commissions Ezekiel to bring his word to those in exile, still calling them by their covenant name, "Israel" (see 2:3; 3:4–5,7; cf. Am 8:11 and note). Ezekiel's mission to the exiles overlapped that of Jeremiah, another member of a priestly family called to the prophetic office, whose mission was to the Israelites still living in and around Jerusalem.

2:1 *Son of man.* See TNIV text note; a term used 93 times in Ezekiel, emphasizing the prophet's humanity as he was addressed by the transcendent God (see note on Ps 8:4). Da 7:13 and 8:17 are the only other places where the phrase is used as a title in the OT. Jesus' frequent use of the phrase in referring to himself showed that he was the eschatological figure spoken of in Da 7:13 (see, e.g., Mk 8:31 and note).

2:2 *the Spirit came into me and raised me to my feet.* The Spirit of God governs and empowers the prophet's entire ministry (see 11:5; 36:27; 37:14; 39:29; see also 3:12 and note).

2:3 *to a rebellious nation.* A theme that became a keynote of Ezekiel's preaching.

2:6 *briers and thorns . . . scorpions.* Vivid images of those who would make life difficult for the prophet.

2:8 *e* Nu 20:10-13
f Isa 8:11 *g* S Isa 50:5
h Ps 81:10; S Jer 15:16;
Rev 10:9
2:9 *i* Eze 8:3
j S Ps 40:7; S Jer 36:4;
Rev 5:1-5; 10:8-10
2:10 *k* Isa 3:11;
Rev 8:13
3:3 *l* S Jer 15:16
m S Ps 19:10;
Rev 10:9-10
3:4 *n* Eze 11:4,25
3:5 *o* S Isa 28:11;
Jnh 1:2
3:6 *p* Jnh 3:5-10;
Mt 11:21-23;
Ac 13:46-48
3:7 *q* S Jer 7:27
r Isa 48:4; Jer 3:3;
S Eze 2:4; Jn 15:20-
23
3:8 *s* Jer 1:18; S 15:20
3:9 *t* S Isa 48:4
u S Jer 5:3 *v* Isa 50:7;
Eze 2:6; 44:6; Mic 3:8
3:10 *w* S Job 22:22
3:11 *x* S Isa 6:9
y ver 27 *z* Eze 2:4-5,7;
11:24-25
3:12 *a* ver 14;
Eze 8:3; 43:5
3:13 *b* Eze 1:15
c Eze 1:24; 10:5,16-17
3:14 *d* S 1Ki 18:12
e S ver 12 *f* ver 22;
S Isa 8:11; Eze 37:1
3:15 *g* S Ps 137:1
h S Ge 50:10
3:16 *i* Jer 42:7
3:17 *j* S Isa 52:8
k S Isa 58:1; Jer 1:17;
Eze 11:4; Hab 2:1
3:18 *l* S Ge 2:17;
Jn 8:21,24

of man, listen to what I say to you. Do not rebel *e f* like that rebellious house; *g* open your mouth and eat *h* what I give you."

⁹Then I looked, and I saw a hand *i* stretched out to me. In it was a scroll, *j* ¹⁰which he unrolled before me. On both sides of it were written words of lament and mourning and woe. *k*

3 And he said to me, "Son of man, eat what is before you, eat this scroll; then go and speak to the house of Israel." ²So I opened my mouth, and he gave me the scroll to eat.

³Then he said to me, "Son of man, eat this scroll I am giving you and fill your stomach with it." So I ate *l* it, and it tasted as sweet as honey *m* in my mouth.

⁴He then said to me: "Son of man, go now to the house of Israel and speak my words to them. *n* ⁵You are not being sent to a people of obscure speech and strange language, *o* but to the house of Israel— ⁶not to many peoples of obscure speech and strange language, whose words you cannot understand. Surely if I had sent you to them, they would have listened to you. *p* ⁷But the house of Israel is not willing to listen *q* to you because they are not willing to listen to me, for the whole house of Israel is hardened and obstinate. *r* ⁸But I will make you as unyielding and hardened as they are. *s* ⁹I will make your forehead *t* like the hardest stone, harder than flint. *u* Do not be afraid of them or terrified by them, though they are a rebellious house. *v*"

¹⁰And he said to me, "Son of man, listen carefully and take to heart *w* all the words I speak to you. ¹¹Go *x* now to your people in exile and speak to them. Say to them, 'This is what the Sovereign LORD says,' *y* whether they listen or fail to listen. *z*"

¹²Then the Spirit lifted me up, *a* and I heard behind me a loud rumbling sound as the glory of the LORD rose from the place where it was standing. *a* ¹³It was the sound of the wings of the living creatures *b* brushing against each other and the sound of the wheels beside them, a loud rumbling sound. *c* ¹⁴The Spirit *d* then lifted me up *e* and took me away, and I went in bitterness and in the anger of my spirit, with the strong hand of the LORD *f* on me. ¹⁵I came to the exiles who lived at Tel Aviv near the Kebar River. *g* And there, where they were living, I sat among them for seven days *h*—deeply distressed.

EZEKIEL'S TASK AS WATCHMAN

¹⁶At the end of seven days the word of the LORD came to me: *i* ¹⁷"Son of man, I have made you a watchman *j* for the house of Israel; so hear the word I speak and give them warning from me. *k* ¹⁸When I say to the wicked, 'You will surely die, *l*' and you do not warn them or speak out to dissuade them from their evil ways in order to save their lives, those

a 12 Probable reading of the original Hebrew text; Masoretic Text *sound—may the glory of the LORD be praised from his place*

2:10 *On both sides.* Normally, ancient scrolls were written on one side only. See Ex 32:15 and note. *lament and mourning and woe.* Although Ezekiel was later commanded to preach hope (see note on 33:1—48:35), his initial commission (until the fall of Jerusalem) was to declare God's displeasure and the certainty of his judgment on Jerusalem and all of Judah.

3:1 *eat this scroll.* Ezekiel must ingest the Lord's message that he is commissioned to bring to the exiles, so that it becomes, as it were, a very part of his being (cf. Jer 15:16 and note).

3:3 *sweet as honey in my mouth.* What Jeremiah experienced emotionally (Jer 15:16) was experienced by Ezekiel in a more sensory way: Words from God are sweet to the taste (see Ps 19:10; 119:103)—even when their content is bitter (see Rev 10:9—10).

3:6 *Surely if I had sent you to them, they would have listened.* For the greater readiness of other peoples to hear and heed the word of God, see Jnh 3:5; Mal 1:10—11; Mt 11:20—24; Ro 10:20—21.

3:9 *I will make your forehead like the hardest stone.* Strength and courage were necessary equipment for a prophet, especially when preaching judgment. Jeremiah was similarly equipped (see Jer 1:18; cf. Isa 50:7).

3:10 *listen carefully and take to heart.* The prophet is to stand in marked contrast to the people, who do not listen.

3:11 *Go now to your people in exile.* Ezekiel's ministry was to the exilic community, most of whom refused to believe that God would abandon Jerusalem and the temple. After the fall of

Jerusalem, therefore, they were strongly inclined to despair.

3:12—15 The dramatic conclusion to Ezekiel's call experience, with echoes of his initial vision.

3:12 *the Spirit lifted me up.* See v. 14; 8:3; 11:1,24; 37:1; 43:5; cf. 2:2 and note.

3:14 *in bitterness and in the anger of my spirit.* The prophet, knowing the righteousness of God's anger, personally identified with the divine emotions. *strong hand of the LORD on me.* See note on 1:3.

3:15 *Tel Aviv.* The only mention of the specific place where the exiles lived. In Babylonian the name meant "mound of the deluge" and was used to refer to ancient (antediluvian) cities that had been reduced to mere mounds (*tells*). When used of the modern Israeli city of Tel Aviv, this name is understood to mean "hill of new growth." *seven days.* The traditional period of mourning (see Ge 50:10; 1Sa 31:13). *deeply distressed.* Because of his horror over Judah's impending doom (cf. Ezr 9:3—4; Job 2:13 and note; Da 8:27).

3:16—21 Ezekiel's appointment to serve as a "watchman" for Israel—a metaphor drawn from urban life. His special task as watchman is spelled out here; its urgency is more fully elaborated in ch. 18.

3:17 *I have made you a watchman.* In ancient Israel, watchmen were stationed on city walls to serve as the eyes of the city (see 2Sa 18:24—27; 2Ki 9:17—20; SS 3:3; 5:7; Isa 52:8; 62:6), especially to warn of approaching danger (see 33:2—3,6; Ps 127:1; Isa 21:6; 56:10; Jer 6:17; Hos 9:8).

wicked people will die for[a] their sins, and I will hold you accountable for their blood. [m]
[19]But if you do warn the wicked and they do not turn[n] from their wickedness[o] or from their evil ways, they will die[p] for their sins; but you will have saved yourself. [q]

[20]"Again, when the righteous turn[r] from their righteousness and do evil, and I put a stumbling block[s] before them, they will die. Since you did not warn them, they will die for their sins. The righteous things they did will not be remembered, and I will hold you accountable for their blood. [t] [21]But if you do warn the righteous not to sin and they do not sin, they will surely live because they took warning, and you will have saved yourself. [u]

[22]The hand of the LORD[v] was on me there, and he said to me, "Get up and go[w] out to the plain,[x] and there I will speak to you." [23]So I got up and went out to the plain. And the glory of the LORD was standing there, like the glory I had seen by the Kebar River,[y] and I fell facedown. [z]

[24]Then the Spirit came into me and raised me[a] to my feet. He spoke to me and said: "Go, shut yourself inside your house. [b] [25]And you, son of man, they will tie with ropes; you will be bound so that you cannot go out among the people. [c] [26]I will make your tongue stick to the roof[d] of your mouth so that you will be silent and unable to rebuke them, for they are a rebellious house. [e] [27]But when I speak to you, I will open your mouth and you shall say to them, 'This is what the Sovereign LORD says.' [f] Whoever will listen let them listen, and whoever will refuse let them refuse; for they are a rebellious house. [g]

SIEGE OF JERUSALEM SYMBOLIZED

4 "Now, son of man, take a block of clay, put it in front of you and draw the city of Jerusalem on it. [2]Then lay siege to it: Erect siege works against it, build a ramp[h] up to it, set up camps against it and put battering rams around it. [i] [3]Then take an iron pan,[j] place it as an iron wall between you and the city and turn your face toward[k] it. It will be under siege, and you shall besiege it. This will be a sign[l] to the house of Israel. [m]

[4]"Then lie on your left side and put the sin of the house of Israel upon yourself. [b] You are to bear their sin for the number of days you lie on your side. [5]I have assigned you the same number of days as the years of their sin. So for 390 days you will bear the sin of the house of Israel.

[6]"After you have finished this, lie down again, this time on your right side, and bear the sin[n] of the house of Judah. I have assigned you 40 days, a day for each year. [o] [7]Turn your face[p] toward the siege of Jerusalem and with bared arm prophesy against her. [8]I will tie

a 18 Or in; also in verses 19 and 20   b 4 Or upon your side

3:20 *I put a stumbling block before them.* Those who have abandoned righteousness and embraced what is evil will be put to the test by the Lord himself (see 14:9; cf. Dt 13:3; 2Sa 24:1 and note; 2Ch 32:31; Ps 66:10 and note; see also Mt 6:13).

3:22–27 God places severe limitations on Ezekiel's freedom to carry out his mission, very likely to signify that the Lord knows that the exiles will not be responsive to his warnings.

3:22 *hand of the LORD.* See note on 1:3.

3:25 *you . . . they will tie with ropes.* Perhaps better: "you . . . will be tied with ropes" (metaphorically)—the Hebrew construction sometimes is equivalent to a passive. Reference is to the restraints that God will place on Ezekiel's movements (cf. 4:8).

3:26 *you will be silent.* Verses 26–27 indicate that the prophet would be unable to speak except when he had a direct word from the Lord. His enforced silence underscored Israel's stubborn refusal to take God's word seriously—and was itself a part of God's judgment on his rebellious people (see 7:26 and note; 20:3,31). This condition was relieved only after the fall of Jerusalem (24:27; 33:22). From that time on Ezekiel was given messages of hope, which he continually shared with his fellow exiles.

4:1—5:17 By means of a series of symbolic acts, Ezekiel is to portray the siege of Jerusalem and its outcome. In 4:1–3 the siege itself is portrayed; in 4:4–8 Ezekiel symbolically bears the punishment of the people of Israel and Judah; in 4:9–17 Ezekiel's assigned food symbolizes both the limitations of food that those under siege will suffer and the fact that they and the exiles will be forced to eat food the law specified to be "unclean" and therefore prohibited; in 5:1–4 Ezekiel is instructed to shave

off his hair and use it to symbolize that only a small remnant of Israel will be left from God's unfolding judgment; in 5:5–17 these symbolic acts are explained.

4:1 *take a block of clay.* The first of several symbolic acts to be performed by the prophet. After inscribing a likeness of the city of Jerusalem on a moist clay block, Ezekiel was to place around it models of siege works to represent the city under attack (v. 2). He was then to place an iron pan (perhaps a baking griddle) between himself and the symbolized city (v. 3) to indicate the unbreakable strength of the siege.

4:3 *you shall besiege it.* Ezekiel's own presence in the scene signified that the siege would actually be laid by the Lord himself. *sign.* For Ezekiel as a "sign," see also 12:6,11; 24:24,27. These references to "sign" mark off significant literary transitions in the book (see notes on 12:1–28; 24:15–27).

4:4 *You are to bear their sin.* A representative rather than a substitutionary bearing of sin. The prophet's action symbolized the punishment Israel would suffer for her sins; it did not remove the sins.

4:5 *for 390 days.* The 390 years (see v. 6) may represent the period from the time of Solomon's unfaithfulness to the fall of Jerusalem. Correspondingly, the 40 years of v. 6 may represent the long reign of wicked Manasseh before his repentance (see 2Ki 21:11–15; 23:26–27; 24:3–4; 2Ch 33:12–13).

4:6 *on your right side.* Lying on his left side (v. 4) while facing Jerusalem (v. 7) probably placed Ezekiel to the north of the symbolic city (v. 1); lying on his right side would then have placed him to the south—signifying the northern and southern kingdoms, respectively.

4:7 *prophesy against her.* By means of his symbolic actions.

3:18 m ver 20
3:19 n S Ps 7:12
o S Ge 6:5
p S Jer 42:16
q S 2Ki 17:13;
Eze 14:14,20; Ac 18:6;
20:26; 1Ti 4:14-16
3:20 r S Jer 34:16
s S Lev 26:37;
t S Isa 8:14; S Eze 7:19
u ver 18; Ps 125:5;
Eze 18:24; 33:12,18
3:21 u Ac 20:31
3:22 v S ver 14;
S Eze 1:3 w S Ac 9:6
x Eze 8:4
3:23 y Eze 1:1
z S Ge 17:3
3:24 a S Eze 2:2
b Jer 15:17
3:25 c Eze 4:8
3:26 d S Ps 22:15
e Eze 2:5; 24:27;
33:22; Hos 4:4
3:27 f ver 11
g Eze 2:5; 12:3; 24:27;
29:21; 33:22;
Rev 22:11
4:2 h S Jer 6:6;
Eze 17:17; Da 11:15
i S Jer 33:4; Eze 21:22
4:3 j S Lev 2:5
k ver 7; Eze 20:46;
21:2 l S Isa 8:18;
S 20:3; Jer 13:1-7;
18:1-4; 19:1-2; Eze
5:1-4; 12:3-6
m S Jer 39:1
4:6 n S Ex 28:38
o Nu 14:34; Da 9:24-
26; 12:11-12
4:7 p S ver 3;
Eze 6:2; S 13:17

4:8 *q* Eze 3:25
4:9 *r* S Isa 28:25
4:10 *s* S Ex 30:13
4:11 *t* ver.16
4:12 *u* S Isa 36:12
4:13 *v* Hos 9:3;
Am 7:17
4:14 *w* Jer 1:6;
Eze 9:8; 20:49
x S Lev 11:39
y S Ex 22:31; Dt 14:3;
32:37-38; Da 1:8;
Hos 9:3-4
4:16 *z* S Ps 105:16
a ver 10-11;
S Lev 26:26; Isa 3:1;
Eze 12:19
4:17 *b* La 5:4;
Eze 5:16; 12:18-19;
Am 4:8 *c* S Lev 26:39;
Eze 24:23; 33:10
5:1 *d* S Nu 6:5
e Eze 44:20
f S Lev 21:5;
S 2Sa 10:4
5:2 *g* Jer 21:10;
Eze 15:7 *h* Zec 13:8
i ver 10; Jer 13:24
j ver 12; S Lev 26:33;
S Jer 9:16; S 39:1-2
5:3 *k* 2Ki 25:12;
S Ps 74:1l; Jer 39:10
5:4 *l* Eze 10:7; 15:7
5:5 *m* S Dt 4:6;
S La 1:1; Eze 16:14
5:6 *n* S 2Ki 17:15;
Ne 9:17; Jer 11:10;
S Eze 2:3; 16:47-51;
Zec 7:11
5:7 *o* S 2Ki 21:9;
S 2Ch 33:9; Jer 2:10-
11; Eze 16:47
5:8 *p* S Jer 21:5,13;
24:9; Eze 11:9; 15:7;
Zec 14:2
5:9 *q* Da 9:12;
S Mt 24:21
5:10 *r* S Lev 26:29;
S La 2:20
s S Lev 26:33;
S Ps 44:11;
S Jer 13:14; Eze 12:14
5:11 *t* S Nu 14:21
u S Ge 15:2

you up with ropes so that you cannot turn from one side to the other until you have fin-ished the days of your siege. *q*

9"Take wheat and barley, beans and lentils, millet and spelt; *r* put them in a storage jar and use them to make bread for yourself. You are to eat it during the 390 days you lie on your side. ¹⁰Weigh out twenty shekels *a s* of food to eat each day and eat it at set times. ¹¹Also measure out a sixth of a hin *b* of water and drink it at set times. *t* ¹²Eat the food as you would a loaf of barley bread; bake it in the sight of the people, using human excre-ment *u* for fuel." ¹³The Lord said, "In this way the people of Israel will eat defiled food among the nations where I will drive them." *v*

¹⁴Then I said, "Not so, Sovereign Lord! *w* I have never defiled myself. From my youth until now I have never eaten anything found dead *x* or torn by wild animals. No impure meat has ever entered my mouth. *y*"

¹⁵"Very well," he said, "I will let you bake your bread over cow dung instead of human excrement."

¹⁶He then said to me: "Son of man, I am about to cut off *z* the food supply in Jerusalem. The people will eat rationed food in anxiety and drink rationed water in despair, *a* ¹⁷for food and water will be scarce. *b* They will be appalled at the sight of each other and will waste away because of *c* their sin. *c*

GOD'S RAZOR OF JUDGMENT

5 "Now, son of man, take a sharp sword and use it as a barber's razor *d* to shave *e* your head and your beard. *f* Then take a set of scales and divide up the hair. ²When the days of your siege come to an end, burn *g* a third *h* of the hair inside the city. Take a third and strike it with the sword all around the city. And scatter a third to the wind. *i* For I will pursue them with drawn sword. *j* ³But take a few hairs and tuck them away in the folds of your garment. *k* ⁴Again, take a few of these and throw them into the fire *l* and burn them up. A fire will spread from there to the whole house of Israel.

⁵"This is what the Sovereign Lord says: This is Jerusalem, which I have set in the cen-ter of the nations, with countries all around her. *m* ⁶Yet in her wickedness she has rebelled against my laws and decrees more than the nations and countries around her. She has re-jected my laws and has not followed my decrees. *n*

⁷"Therefore this is what the Sovereign Lord says: You have been more unruly than the nations around you and have not followed my decrees or kept my laws. You have not even *d* conformed to the standards of the nations around you. *o*

⁸"Therefore this is what the Sovereign Lord says: I myself am against you, Jerusalem, and I will inflict punishment on you in the sight of the nations. *p* ⁹Because of all your de-testable idols, I will do to you what I have never done before and will never do again. *q* ¹⁰Therefore in your midst parents will eat their children, and children will eat their par-ents. *r* I will inflict punishment on you and will scatter all your survivors to the winds. *s* ¹¹Therefore as surely as I live, *t* declares the Sovereign *u* Lord, because you have defiled

---

a 10 That is, about 8 ounces or about 230 grams   *b 11* That is, about 1 1/3 pints or about 0.6 liter   *c 17* Or *away in*   *d 7* Most Hebrew manuscripts; some Hebrew manuscripts and Syriac *You have*

4:9 *Take wheat and barley, beans and lentils, millet and spelt.* A scant, vegetarian diet representing the meager provisions of a besieged city.

4:15 *cow dung.* When thoroughly dried, it was commonly used in the Near East as a fuel for baking and is still sometimes so used even today. Ezekiel again showed his sensitivity to things ceremonially unclean (see note on 1:3), and God graciously re-sponded to the prophet's objection by allowing this substitute for human excrement.

5:1–17 The fate of the people of Jerusalem in the judgment that is about to overtake them—only the merest remnant will be left (cf. notes on 2Ki 19:30–31; Isa 1:9; 10:20–22).

5:1 *take a sharp sword.* What Isaiah had expressed in a meta-phor (Isa 7:20) Ezekiel acted out in prophetic symbolism.

5:2 *with drawn sword.* See 12:14; 21:3–5; 30:25; 32:10; Ps 7:12–13 and note.

5:5 *This is Jerusalem.* After wordlessly acting out the symbols (beginning in 4:1), Ezekiel received and probably related the divine explanations. *center of the nations.* God had chosen for his people Israel and for his earthly temple a place at the crossroads of the continents of Africa, Asia and Europe so that Israel and what he does for them might be a strong witness

to the nations that he is the one and only God with whom all peoples have to do and from whom alone come life and bless-ing. This made Israel's responsibility and judgment all the more severe (see also 38:12 and note).

5:6 *more than the nations … around her.* See v. 7; 16:47–48; 2Ki 21:9; Am 3:9 and note.

5:8 *I myself am against you.* A short and effective phrase of judgment used often by Ezekiel (see 13:8; 21:3; 26:3; 28:22; 29:3,10; 30:22; 34:10; 35:3; 38:3; 39:1; see also Jer 23:30–32; 50:31; 51:25; Na 2:13; 3:5). *inflict punishment on you in the sight of the nations.* Just as he had acted to bring about Israel's free-dom and privileged position as his people (see Lev 26:45; Jos 2:11; 5:1; cf. Isa 52:10).

5:10 *parents will eat their children.* Cannibalism, the most grue-some extremity of life under siege (see 2Ki 6:28), was threat-ened as a consequence of breaking the covenant (Dt 28:53; see Jer 19:9 and note; La 2:20; Zec 11:9 and note).

5:11 *as surely as I live.* A divine oath, revealing God's unalter-able intention. It is used often in Ezekiel (see 14:16,18,20; 16:48; 17:16,19; 18:3; 20:3,31,33; 33:11,27; 34:8; 35:6,11; see also Heb 6:13 and note). *you have defiled my sanctuary.* See ch. 8.

my sanctuary [v] with all your vile images [w] and detestable practices, [x] I myself will shave you; I will not look on you with pity or spare you. [y] 12A third of your people will die of the plague or perish by famine inside you; a third will fall by the sword outside your walls; and a third I will scatter to the winds [z] and pursue with drawn sword. [a]

13"Then my anger will cease and my wrath [b] against them will subside, and I will be avenged. [c] And when I have spent my wrath on them, they will know that I the LORD have spoken in my zeal. [d]

14"I will make you a ruin and a reproach among the nations around you, in the sight of all who pass by. [e] 15You will be a reproach [f] and a taunt, a warning [g] and an object of horror to the nations around you when I inflict punishment on you in anger and in wrath and with stinging rebuke. [h] I the LORD have spoken. [i] 16When I shoot at you with my deadly and destructive arrows of famine, I will shoot to destroy you. I will bring more and more famine upon you and cut off your supply of food. [j] 17I will send famine and wild beasts [k] against you, and they will leave you childless. Plague and bloodshed [l] will sweep through you, and I will bring the sword against you. I the LORD have spoken. [m]"

DOOM FOR THE MOUNTAINS OF ISRAEL

6 The word of the LORD came to me: 2"Son of man, set your face [n] against the mountains [o] of Israel; prophesy against them [p] 3and say: 'You mountains of Israel, hear the word of the Sovereign LORD. This is what the Sovereign LORD says to the mountains and hills, to the ravines and valleys: [q] I am about to bring a sword against you, and I will destroy your high places. [r] 4Your altars will be demolished and your incense altars [s] will be smashed; and I will slay your people in front of your idols. [t] 5I will lay the dead bodies of the Israelites in front of their idols, and I will scatter your bones [u] around your altars. [v] 6Wherever you live, [w] the towns will be laid waste and the high places [x] demolished, so that your altars will be laid waste and devastated, your idols [y] smashed and ruined, your incense altars [z] broken down, and what you have made wiped out. [a] 7Your people will fall slain [b] among you, and you will know that I am the LORD. [c]

8" 'But I will spare some, for some of you will escape [d] the sword when you are scattered among the lands and nations. [e] 9Then in the nations where they have been carried captive, those who escape will remember [f] me—how I have been grieved [g] by their adulterous hearts, which have turned away from me, and by their eyes, which have lusted after their idols. [h] They will loathe themselves for the evil [i] they have done and for all their detestable practices. [j] 10And they will know that I am the LORD; [k] I did not threaten in vain to bring this calamity on them. [l]

11" 'This is what the Sovereign LORD says: Strike your hands together and stamp your feet and cry out "Alas!" because of all the wicked and detestable practices of the house of Israel, for they will fall by the sword, famine and plague. [m] 12Those who are far away will die of the plague, and those who are near will fall by the sword, and those who survive and are spared will die of famine. So will I spend my wrath [n] on them. [o] 13And they will know

---

6:9 [f] S Ps 137:6; Zec 10:9 [g] S Isa 7:13; S Jer 8:21 [h] S Ex 22:20; Eze 20:7,24; Mic 5:13 [i] S Ex 32:22 [j] S Job 42:6; Eze 20:43; 23:14-16; 36:31
6:10 [k] S ver 7 [l] S Dt 28:52; Jer 40:2 **6:11** [m] S Jer 42:22; Eze 21:14,17; 22:13; 25:6 **6:12** [n] S Job 20:23 [o] S Eze 5:12; 7:15

5:11 [v] S Lev 15:31
[w] Eze 7:20; 11:18
[x] 2Ch 36:14; Eze 8:6
[y] S Job 27:22;
S Jer 16:18; S La 2:17;
Eze 7:4,9; 8:18; 9:5
5:12 [z] ver 10;
Jer 13:24 [a] S ver 2,17;
S Ps 107:39;
S Jer 15:2; S 21:9;
Eze 6:11-12; 7:15;
12:14; Am 9:4;
Zec 13:8; Rev 6:8
5:13 [b] S 2Ch 12:7;
S Job 20:23;
Eze 21:17; 24:13
[c] S Isa 1:24
[d] S Isa 59:17;
Eze 16:42; 38:19;
Hos 10:10; Zec 6:8
5:14 [e] S Lev 26:32;
Ne 2:17; Ps 74:3-10;
79:1-4; Isa 64:11;
Eze 6:6; 22:4;
Da 9:16; Mic 3:12
5:15 [f] S Isa 43:28
[g] S Dt 28:46
[h] S Dt 28:20;
S 1Ki 9:7; S Jer 22:8-
9; 24:9; Eze 14:8
[i] S Jer 23:40
5:16 [j] S Lev 26:26;
S Dt 32:24
5:17 [k] Eze 14:15
[l] Eze 38:22 [m] S ver 12;
S Lev 26:25;
Eze 14:21; 28:23
6:2 [n] S Eze 4:7
[o] Eze 18:6; Mic 6:1
[p] ver 13
6:3 [q] Eze 36:4
[r] S Lev 26:30
6:4 [s] S 2Ch 14:5
[t] Eze 9:6; 14:3; 20:16
6:5 [u] S Nu 19:16;
S Ps 53:5; Jer 8:1-2
[v] ver 13; S Lev 26:30
6:6 [w] S Ex 12:20
[x] Hos 10:8
[y] Eze 30:13; Mic 1:7;
Zec 13:2 [z] S Lev 26:30
[a] S 1Sa 5:4; Isa 6:11;
S Eze 5:14
6:7 [b] Eze 9:7
[c] ver 10,13,14;
Eze 11:10-12
6:8 [d] S Ps 68:20;
S Jer 44:28
[e] S Ge 11:4;
S Ps 44:11; Isa 6:13;
S Jer 44:14; Eze 7:16;
12:16; 14:22

5:13 *spent my wrath on.* An expression frequently used by the Lord in this book (see 6:12; 7:8; 13:15; 20:8,21). *they will know that I the LORD have spoken.* See 17:21; 36:36; 37:14; see also 6:7 and note.
5:15 *a reproach and a taunt, a warning and an object of horror.* A fourfold list (see note on 1:5).
5:16–17 These verses contain echoes of the threatened forces of judgment for covenant unfaithfulness found in Dt 32:22–25. Note especially that God's "arrows" of judgment are the four main causes of death among the peoples of the ancient Near East: famine, disease, sword (violent death at human hands) and wild beasts (see 14:12–21; see also 6:11–12; 7:15; 12:16; cf. 34:25–31; see also Jer 14:12 and note; cf. Rev 6:8).
5:16 *my...arrows.* A widely used metaphor for God's judgments (see note on Ge 9:13).
6:1–14 After announcing judgment on Jerusalem (chs. 4–5), Ezekiel is instructed to pronounce judgment on the whole land; the "mountains of Israel" were the heavily cultivated central highlands (see Ps 104:13–15 and note), which also provided the principal sites for the pagan sanctuaries set up to worship the Baals. The judgment Ezekiel is to pronounce echoes Lev 26:27–39.
6:3 *high places.* Open-air sanctuaries of Canaanite origin, condemned throughout the OT. The high places, together with the

"altars," "incense altars" and "idols" (v. 4), make up a list of four objects (see note on 1:5).
6:4 *incense altars.* Made of burnt clay, about two feet high, usually inscribed with animal figures and idols of Canaanite gods. *idols.* The Hebrew word is a derisive term (see note on Lev 26:30) used especially by Ezekiel (38 times, as opposed to only 9 times elsewhere in the OT).

6:7 *you will know that I am the LORD.* See 36:11 and note. This assertion that God's mighty acts in history (his dealings with Israel in judgment and redemption and his dealings with the nations in judgment) will result in his being known and acknowledged by Israel and the nations echoes throughout chs. 6–39 (see Introduction: Themes; see also 5:13 and note).
6:9 *those who escape will remember me.* The corrective outcome God intends from the severe judgment to come (see v. 10). *their adulterous hearts...lusted after their idols.* See Ex 34:15 and note.
6:11 *Strike your hands together and stamp your feet.* A command to Ezekiel to punctuate his words of judgment with symbolic acts (see 21:14,17)—acts of quite different intent from those of Israel's enemies in 25:6. *sword, famine and plague.* See 5:16–17 and note.

6:13 *P* S Lev 26:30
q Isa 1:29
r S 1Ki 14:23;
S Jer 2:20; Eze 18:6;
20:28; Hos 4:13
6:14 *s* S Ex 7:5;
S Job 30:21;
S Jer 6:12; 51:25;
Eze 20:34 *t* Eze 12:19;
14:13
7:2 *u* Am 8:2,10
v Rev 7:1; 20:8
7:3 *w* Eze 18:30
x S Ge 6:13
7:4 *y* S Jer 13:14;
S Eze 5:11
z S Eze 5:11; 23:49
7:5 *a* S 2Ki 21:12
7:6 *b* Eze 39:8
7:7 *c* S Job 18:20;
S Isa 2:12; Am 5:18-
20 *d* Eze 12:23; 30:3;
Zep 1:14; Mal 3:2
7:8 *e* Isa 42:25;
Eze 9:8; 14:19; 22:22;
Hos 5:10; Na 1:6
f Eze 20:8,21; 36:19
7:9 *g* S Jer 21:7;
S Eze 5:11 *h* Eze 22:31
i Dt 32:35; S Ps 39:10;
S Isa 9:13
7:10 *i* Ps 89:32;
Isa 10:5
7:11 *k* S Ps 55:9;
S Isa 58:4

that I am the LORD, when their people lie slain among their idols[P] around their altars, on every high hill and on all the mountaintops, under every spreading tree and every leafy oak[q]—places where they offered fragrant incense to all their idols.[r] [14]And I will stretch out my hand[s] against them and make the land a desolate waste from the desert to Diblah[a]—wherever they live. Then they will know that I am the LORD.[t] ' "

THE END HAS COME

7 The word of the LORD came to me: [2]"Son of man, this is what the Sovereign LORD says to the land of Israel:

" 'The end![u] The end has come
upon the four corners[v] of the land!
[3] The end is now upon you,
and I will unleash my anger against you.
I will judge you according to your conduct[w]
and repay you for all your detestable practices.[x]
[4] I will not look on you with pity;[y]
I will not spare you.
I will surely repay you for your conduct
and for the detestable practices among you.

" 'Then you will know that I am the LORD.'[z]

[5]"This is what the Sovereign LORD says:

" 'Disaster![a] Unheard-of[b] disaster!
See, it comes!
[6] The end[b] has come!
The end has come!
It has roused itself against you.
See, it comes!
[7] Doom has come upon you,
upon you who dwell in the land.
The time has come! The day[c] is near![d]
There is panic, not joy, on the mountains.
[8] I am about to pour out my wrath[e] on you
and spend my anger against you.
I will judge you according to your conduct
and repay you for all your detestable practices.[f]
[9] I will not look on you with pity;
I will not spare you.[g]
I will repay you for your conduct
and for the detestable practices among you.[h]

" 'Then you will know that it is I the LORD who strikes you.[i]

[10] " 'See, the day!
See, it comes!
Doom has burst forth,
the rod[j] has budded,
arrogance has blossomed!
[11] Violence[k] has arisen,[c]
a rod to punish the wicked.
None of the people will be left,

---

[a] 14 Most Hebrew manuscripts; a few Hebrew manuscripts *Riblah*   [b] 5 Most Hebrew manuscripts; some Hebrew manuscripts and Syriac *Disaster after*   [c] 11 Or *The violent one has become*

6:14 *I will stretch out my hand against.* A common expression in Ezekiel (see 14:9,13; 16:27; 25:7; 35:3). *Diblah.* Perhaps the Beth Diblathaim of Jer 48:22, a city in Moab; or Riblah, a city north of Damascus on the Orontes River (see TNIV text note).
7:1–27 God's word of judgment on the "mountains of Israel" (6:2; see ch. 6 and note on 6:1–14) is elaborated under the fateful declaration that God's patience with Israel's stubborn rebelliousness has run out: "The end! The end has come" (v. 2; see vv. 3,6,24; see also Jer 51:13; La 4:18; cf. Am 7:8; 8:2).

7:7 *The day.* The "day of the LORD's wrath" (v. 19), i.e., the day of reckoning when God brings down his righteous judgments on the wickedness of his people (see also vv. 10,12). Ezekiel's language may be a deliberate echo of the "day of the LORD" of which many of the prophets spoke (see Am 5:18 and note). *panic, not joy.* Cf. Am 5:20 ("darkness, not light").
7:8 *pour out my wrath.* A common expression in Ezekiel (see 9:8; 14:19; 20:8,13,21; 22:31; 30:15; 36:18).

none of that crowd—
none of their wealth,
nothing of value. [l]
[12] The time has come!
The day has arrived!
Let not the buyer [m] rejoice
nor the seller grieve,
for my wrath is on the whole crowd. [n]
[13] The sellers will not recover
the property they have sold—
as long as both buyers and sellers live.
For the vision concerning the whole crowd
will not be reversed.
Because of their sins, not one of them
will preserve their life. [o]

[14] " 'They have blown the trumpet, [p]
they have made all things ready,
but no one will go into battle,
for my wrath [q] is on the whole crowd.
[15] Outside is the sword;
inside are plague and famine.
Those in the country
will die by the sword;
those in the city
will be devoured by famine and plague. [r]
[16] The fugitives [s] who escape
will flee to the mountains.
Like doves [t] of the valleys,
they will all moan,
each for their own sins. [u]
[17] Every hand will go limp; [v]
every knee will be wet with urine. [w]
[18] They will put on sackcloth [x]
and be clothed with terror. [y]
Every face will be covered with shame,
and every head will be shaved. [z]

[19] " 'They will throw their silver into the streets, [a]
and their gold will be treated as a thing unclean.
Their silver and gold
will not be able to deliver them
in the day of the Lord's wrath. [b]
It will not satisfy [c] their hunger
or fill their stomachs,
for it has caused them to stumble [d] into sin. [e]
[20] They took pride in their beautiful jewelry
and used it to make [f] their detestable idols.
They made it into vile images; [g]
therefore I will make it a thing unclean for them. [h]
[21] I will give their wealth as plunder [i] to foreigners
and as loot to the wicked of the earth,
who will defile it. [j]
[22] I will turn my face [k] away from the people,
and robbers will desecrate the place I treasure.
They will enter it
and will defile it. [l]

7:11 [l] Jer 16:6;
Zep 1:18
7:12 [m] S Isa 24:2
[n] ver 7; Isa 5:13-14;
Eze 30:3
7:13 [o] Lev 25:24-28
7:14 [p] S Job 39:24
[q] Jer 25:38
7:15 [r] S Dt 32:25;
Jer 14:18; S La 1:20;
S Eze 5:12; 33:27
7:16 [s] S Isa 10:20;
S Jer 41:16; 42:17
[t] S Ge 8:8; S Isa 59:11
[u] S Ezr 9:15; Jer 9:19;
S Eze 6:8
7:17 [v] S 2Ki 19:26;
S Jer 47:3; Eze 21:7;
22:14 [w] Da 5:6
7:18 [x] S Jer 4:8;
48:37; 49:3
[y] S Ps 55:5
[z] S Isa 15:2-3;
Eze 27:31; Am 8:10
7:19 [a] S La 4:1
[b] Isa 42:25; Eze 13:5;
30:3; Joel 1:15; 2:1;
Zep 1:7,18; 2:2
[c] Isa 55:2 [d] Eze 3:20;
14:3; Hos 4:5
[e] S Pr 11:4
7:20 [f] S Jer 10:3
[g] S Eze 5:11
[h] S Isa 2:20; 30:22;
Eze 16:17
7:21 [i] S Nu 14:3
[j] S 2Ki 24:13
7:22 [k] S Jer 2:27;
Eze 39:23-24
[l] Ps 74:7-8; Jer 19:13;
S La 2:7

7:12 *Let not the buyer rejoice.* Advice similar to that of Jesus
(see Mt 24:17–18).
7:15 *sword…plague and famine.* See 5:16–17 and note.
7:17 *Every hand will go limp.* See 21:7; 30:25; Isa 13:7 and note;
Jer 6:24; 47:3 and note; 50:43; Zep 3:16 and note.
7:18 *They will put on sackcloth…every head will be shaved.* As

signs of intense mourning (see Ge 37:34; Job 1:20; Isa 15:2; Rev
11:3 and notes).
7:19 *They will throw their silver.* See Isa 2:20.
7:20 *beautiful jewelry.* See Ex 32:2–4.
7:22 *the place I treasure.* The Jerusalem temple.

7:23 *m* S 2Ki 21:16;
S Isa 1:15; S Eze 22:9
n S Ge 6:11; Eze 11:6
7:24 *o* La 2:7;
Eze 24:21 *p* 2Ch 7:20;
Eze 28:7
7:25 *q* Jer 6:14;
S 8:11; Eze 13:10,16
7:26 *r* S Dt 29:21;
S 31:17 *s* S 1Sa 3:1
t Isa 47:11; S Jer 18:18;
Eze 20:1-3; Am 8:11;
Mic 3:6
7:27 *u* S Ps 109:19;
Eze 26:16 *v* S Isa 3:11;
Eze 18:20 *w* S ver 4
8:1 *x* S 2Ki 6:32;
Eze 14:1 *y* Eze 33:31
z Eze 1:1-3; 24:1; 40:1
8:2 *a* Eze 1:4,26-27
8:3 *b* S Eze 2:9
c S Eze 3:12; 11:1
d S Ex 24:10 *e* ver 16
f ver 5; Ex 20:5;
Dt 32:16
8:4 *g* S Ex 24:16
h Eze 3:22
8:5 *i* Ps 78:58;
S Jer 4:1; 32:34
8:6 *j* Ps 78:60;
S Eze 5:11 *k* Hos 5:6

23 " 'Prepare chains!
  For the land is full of bloodshed, *m*
  and the city is full of violence. *n*
24 I will bring the most wicked of nations
  to take possession of their houses.
  I will put an end to the pride of the mighty,
  and their sanctuaries *o* will be desecrated. *p*
25 When terror comes,
  they will seek peace in vain. *q*
26 Calamity upon calamity *r* will come,
  and rumor upon rumor.
  They will go searching for a vision from the prophet, *s*
  priestly instruction in the law will cease,
  the counsel of the elders will come to an end. *t*
27 The king will mourn,
  the prince will be clothed with despair, *u*
  and the hands of the people of the land will tremble.
  I will deal with them according to their conduct, *v*
  and by their own standards I will judge them.

" 'Then they will know that I am the Lord.' " *w*

IDOLATRY IN THE TEMPLE

8 In the sixth year, in the sixth month on the fifth day, while I was sitting in my house and the elders *x* of Judah were sitting before *y* me, the hand of the Sovereign Lord came on me there. *z* 2 I looked, and I saw a figure like that of a man. *a* From what appeared to be his waist down he was like fire, and from there up his appearance was as bright as glowing metal. *a* 3 He stretched out what looked like a hand *b* and took me by the hair of my head. The Spirit lifted me up *c* between earth and heaven and in visions *d* of God he took me to Jerusalem, to the entrance of the north gate of the inner court, *e* where the idol that provokes to jealousy *f* stood. 4 And there before me was the glory *g* of the God of Israel, as in the vision I had seen in the plain. *h*

5 Then he said to me, "Son of man, look toward the north." So I looked, and in the entrance north of the gate of the altar I saw this idol *i* of jealousy.

6 And he said to me, "Son of man, do you see what they are doing—the utterly detestable *j* things the house of Israel is doing here, things that will drive me far from my sanctuary? *k* But you will see things that are even more detestable."

a 2 Or *saw a fiery figure*

7:23 *full of bloodshed . . . violence.* See 9:9; 11:6; 12:19; see also 2Ki 21:16; 24:4; Jer 19:4; 22:17; La 4:13; Mic 3:10; Hab 1:2–4; cf. Hab 2:8,12,17.
7:24 *pride of the mighty.* The Jerusalem temple, described by the word "pride" (as in 24:21; 33:28).
7:26 *prophet . . . priestly . . . elders.* There would be no guidance from God and no direction from the elders (see 1Sa 28:6; Am 8:11–12 and note on 8:11; Mic 3:6–7; see also Jer 18:18 and note).
7:27 *king . . . prince.* Here both nouns probably refer to the same person, namely, King Jehoiachin. *clothed with.* See note on Ps 109:29. *people of the land.* The full citizens of Judah (those holding inherited family property and subject to military service; see 12:19; 45:16,22; 46:3).
8:1—11:25 The vision has six movements: (1) God shows Ezekiel the idolatry practiced in the temple in Jerusalem (ch. 8); (2) God pronounces his judgment on the idolaters there (ch. 9); (3) Ezekiel is shown God's glory departing from the temple (ch. 10); (4) God declares that the complacent Jerusalemites will not escape his judgment (11:1–13); (5) God promises that the exiles, whom those still in Jerusalem have written off, will be restored (11:14–21); and (6) the conclusion of the vision (11:22–25).
8:1–8 Ezekiel is shown four examples of idolatrous worship being carried on in the very temple of the Lord: (1) "idol of jealousy" (v. 5), (2) "crawling things and unclean animals" (v. 10),

(3) "mourning the god Tammuz" (v. 14), and (4) "bowing down to the sun" (v. 16).
8:1 *In the sixth year, in the sixth month on the fifth day.* Sept. 17, 592 B.C.—the second of 13 dates in Ezekiel (see chart, p. 1364). This one, like those in 1:2 and 40:1, introduces a vision. *sitting in my house.* The exiles were free to build houses (see Jer 29:5). *elders of Judah were sitting before me.* They also had freedom of movement, assembly and worship (see 14:1; 20:1). A year and two months after his inaugural vision and preaching, the prophet commanded a hearing. Some have seen in such meetings the beginnings of the synagogue form of worship. *hand of the Sovereign Lord.* See note on 1:3.
8:2 *figure like that of a man.* An angel, similar in appearance to the vision of God in 1:26–27. *like fire . . . as bright as glowing metal.* A way of describing the blinding brightness of the divine messenger (see Mt 28:3; cf. Ac 9:3).
8:3 *The Spirit lifted me up.* See 3:12 and note. *took me to Jerusalem.* Ezekiel had been directed to prophesy stern judgments on Jerusalem (chs. 1–7). Now he was transported to Jerusalem in visions of God (see 11:24) and shown the reason for the judgments. *idol that provokes to jealousy.* Any idol in the temple provoked the Lord to jealousy (see Ex 20:5 and note), but this one seems to be a statue of Asherah, the Canaanite goddess of fertility, which Josiah had removed some 30 years previously (see 2Ki 23:6).
8:5 *idol of jealousy.* See note on v. 3.

⁷Then he brought me to the entrance to the court. I looked, and I saw a hole in the wall. ⁸He said to me, "Son of man, now dig into the wall." So I dug into the wall and saw a doorway there.

⁹And he said to me, "Go in and see the wicked and detestable things they are doing here." ¹⁰So I went in and looked, and I saw portrayed all over the walls *l* all kinds of crawling things and unclean *m* animals and all the idols of the house of Israel. *n* ¹¹In front of them stood seventy elders *o* of the house of Israel, and Jaazaniah son of Shaphan was standing among them. Each had a censer *p* in his hand, and a fragrant cloud of incense *q* was rising. *r*

¹²He said to me, "Son of man, have you seen what the elders of the house of Israel are doing in the darkness, *s* each at the shrine of his own idol? They say, 'The Lord does not see *t* us; the Lord has forsaken the land.' " ¹³Again, he said, "You will see them doing things that are even more detestable."

¹⁴Then he brought me to the entrance of the north gate of the house of the Lord, and I saw women sitting there, mourning the god Tammuz. *u* ¹⁵He said to me, "Do you see this, son of man? You will see things that are even more detestable than this."

¹⁶He then brought me into the inner court *v* of the house of the Lord, and there at the entrance to the temple, between the portico and the altar, *w* were about twenty-five men. With their backs toward the temple of the Lord and their faces toward the east, they were bowing down to the sun *x* in the east. *y*

¹⁷He said to me, "Have you seen this, son of man? Is it a trivial matter for the house of Judah to do the detestable things *z* they are doing here? Must they also fill the land with violence *a* and continually arouse my anger? *b* Look at them putting the branch to their nose! ¹⁸Therefore I will deal with them in anger; *c* I will not look on them with pity *d* or spare them. Although they shout in my ears, I will not listen *e* to them."

JUDGMENT ON THE IDOLATERS

9 Then I heard him call out in a loud voice, "Bring near those who are appointed to execute judgment on the city, each with weapon in hand." ²And I saw six men coming from the direction of the upper gate, which faces north, each with a deadly weapon in his hand. With them was a man clothed in linen *f* who had a writing kit at his side. They came in and stood beside the bronze altar.

³Now the glory *g* of the God of Israel went up from above the cherubim, *h* where it had been, and moved to the threshold of the temple. Then the Lord called to the man clothed in linen who had the writing kit at his side ⁴and said to him, "Go throughout the city of Jerusalem *i* and put a mark *j* on the foreheads of those who grieve and lament *k* over all the detestable things that are done in it. *l*"

⁵As I listened, he said to the others, "Follow him through the city and kill, without showing pity *m* or compassion. *n* ⁶Slaughter *o* the old men, the young men and women, the mothers and children, *p* but do not touch anyone who has the mark. *q* Begin at my sanctuary." So they began with the old men *r* who were in front of the temple. *s*

⁷Then he said to them, "Defile the temple and fill the courts with the slain. *t* Go!" So they went out and began killing throughout the city. ⁸While they were killing and I was

---

Right margin cross-references:

8:10 *l* S Jdg 17:4-5; Eze 23:14 *m* Jer 44:4 *n* Ex 20:4; Dt 4:15-18; S Jer 16:18; Eze 11:12
8:11 *o* S Ex 3:16 *p* S Lev 10:1; Nu 16:17 *q* Nu 16:35; S Jer 44:5 *r* Eze 11:1-2
8:12 *s* S Job 22:13 *t* S 2Ki 21:16; Ps 10:11; S Isa 29:15; Eze 9:9; Zep 1:12
8:14 *u* Eze 11:12
8:16 *v* ver 3 *w* Joel 2:17 *x* S Ge 1:16 *y* Dt 4:19; S 17:3; S Job 31:28; S Jer 2:27; Eze 9:6; 11:1,12; 40:6; 43:1
8:17 *z* Eze 16:2 *a* S Ge 6:11 *b* S Nu 11:33; S 1Ki 14:9; Eze 16:26
8:18 *c* S Jer 44:6 *d* S Jer 13:14; S Eze 5:11; 9:10; 24:14 *e* S Isa 8:18; S Isa 58:4; S Jer 11:11
9:2 *f* S Lev 16:4; Eze 10:2; Da 10:5; 12:6; Rev 15:6
9:3 *g* S 1Sa 4:21; Eze 10:4 *h* Eze 11:22
9:4 *i* Jer 25:29 *j* S Ge 4:15; Ex 12:7; 2Co 1:22; S Rev 7:3 *k* Ps 119:136; Jer 7:29; 13:17; Eze 21:6; Am 6:6 *l* Ps 119:53
9:5 *m* S Jer 13:14; S Eze 5:11 *n* S Ex 32:27; Isa 13:18
9:6 *o* Jer 7:32 *p* S Jer 16:6 *q* S Ge 4:15; S Ex 12:7 *r* Eze 8:11-13,16 *s* S 2Ch 36:17; Jer 25:29; S Eze 6:4; 1Pe 4:17
9:7 *t* Eze 6:7

8:10 *all kinds of crawling things and unclean animals.* Probably reflecting Egyptian influence (cf. 2Ki 23:31–35).

8:11 *Jaazaniah.* Not the same person as in 11:1. Ironically, the name means "The Lord hears," and the irony is sharpened by the quotation in v. 12.

■ **8:14** *Tammuz.* The only Biblical reference to this Babylonian fertility god. The women of Jerusalem were bewailing his dying (which supposedly happened seasonally at the height of the summer heat), which they thought caused the annual summer die-off of the vegetation. According to some interpreters, he is alluded to in Da 11:37 ("the one desired by women"; see note there).

8:16 *twenty-five men.* A representative number (see 11:1). *With their backs toward the temple.* Almost all ancient temples were oriented toward the east. Worshiping the sun as it rose required people to turn their backs to the temple. *bowing down to the sun.* For other references to sun worship, see Dt 4:19; 17:3; 2Ki 23:5,11; cf. 2Ki 17:16; 21:3,5; Jer 43:13.

8:17 *fill the land with violence.* See 7:23 and note. *putting the*

branch to their nose. A ceremonial gesture in pagan worship, not documented elsewhere in the Bible.

9:1–11 See note on 8:1—11:25.

9:1 *loud voice.* The thunderous voice of God (see Ex 19:19 and TNIV text note; see also Ps 29).

9:2 *six men coming from the direction of the upper gate.* These six guardian angels of the city, plus the seventh clothed in linen, came from the place where the idol that provoked to jealousy stood (see 8:3 and note).

9:3 *the glory … went up.* God began to vacate the temple, his glory moving to the door (see note on 8:1—11:25).

9:4 *mark.* A *taw,* the last letter of the Hebrew alphabet, which originally looked like an "x" (see Rev 7:2–4 and note on 7:2; cf. Rev 13:16 and note). *those who grieve and lament.* The remnant (see 1Ki 19:18).

9:5 *kill, without showing pity.* See La 2:21.

■ **9:6** *Begin at my sanctuary.* Because that was a primary source of the evil that pervaded Jerusalem (see ch. 8). Cf. an echo in 1Pe 4:17.

9:8 *u* S Jos 7:6
v S Eze 4:14
w S Eze 7:8
x Eze 11:13; Am 7:1-6
9:9 *y* S Ps 58:2;
Jer 12:1; Eze 22:29;
Hab 1:4 *z* S Job 22:13;
S Eze 8:12; 14:23
9:10 *a* S Jer 13:14;
S Eze 8:18
b S Isa 22:5; S 65:6;
Eze 11:21; 23:49
10:1 *c* S Rev 4:2
d S Ex 24:10
e Eze 1:22 *f* S Ge 3:24
10:2 *g* S Eze 9:2
h S Eze 1:15 *i* Rev 8:5
j S 2Sa 22:9
10:4 *k* S Ex 24:16;
Eze 9:3; 44:4
10:5 *l* S Job 40:9
m S Eze 3:13
10:6 *n* Da 7:9
10:7 *o* S Eze 5:4
10:8 *p* Eze 1:8
10:9 *q* S Ex 28:20;
Rev 21:20
10:12 *r* Rev 4:6-8
s Eze 1:15-21
10:14 *t* 1Ki 7:36
u Eze 1:6 *v* 1Ki 7:29
w Eze 1:10; 41:19;
Rev 4:7
10:15 *x* S Isa 6:2
y S Ps 137:1
10:17 *z* S Eze 3:13
10:18 *a* S 1Sa 4:21
b S Ps 18:10
10:19 *c* Eze 11:1,22

left alone, I fell facedown, *u* crying out, "Ah, Sovereign Lᴏʀᴅ! *v* Are you going to destroy the entire remnant of Israel in this outpouring of your wrath *w* on Jerusalem? *x* "

⁹He answered me, "The sin of the house of Israel and Judah is exceedingly great; the land is full of bloodshed and the city is full of injustice. *y* They say, 'The Lᴏʀᴅ has forsaken the land; the Lᴏʀᴅ does not see.' *z* ¹⁰So I will not look on them with pity *a* or spare them, but I will bring down on their own heads what they have done. *b* "

¹¹Then the man in linen with the writing kit at his side brought back word, saying, "I have done as you commanded."

GOD'S GLORY DEPARTS FROM THE TEMPLE

10 I looked, and I saw the likeness of a throne *c* of lapis lazuli *d* above the vault *e* that was over the heads of the cherubim. *f* ²The Lᴏʀᴅ said to the man clothed in linen, *g* "Go in among the wheels *h* beneath the cherubim. Fill *i* your hands with burning coals *j* from among the cherubim and scatter them over the city." And as I watched, he went in.

³Now the cherubim were standing on the south side of the temple when the man went in, and a cloud filled the inner court. ⁴Then the glory of the Lᴏʀᴅ *k* rose from above the cherubim and moved to the threshold of the temple. The cloud filled the temple, and the court was full of the radiance of the glory of the Lᴏʀᴅ. ⁵The sound of the wings of the cherubim could be heard as far away as the outer court, like the voice *l* of God Almighty *a* when he speaks. *m*

⁶When the Lᴏʀᴅ commanded the man in linen, "Take fire from among the wheels, *n* from among the cherubim," the man went in and stood beside a wheel. ⁷Then one of the cherubim reached out his hand to the fire *o* that was among them. He took up some of it and put it into the hands of the man in linen, who took it and went out. ⁸(Under the wings of the cherubim could be seen what looked like human hands.) *p*

⁹I looked, and I saw beside the cherubim four wheels, one beside each of the cherubim; the wheels sparkled like topaz. *q* ¹⁰As for their appearance, the four of them looked alike; each was like a wheel intersecting a wheel. ¹¹As they moved, they would go in any one of the four directions the cherubim faced; the wheels did not turn about *b* as the cherubim went. The cherubim went in whatever direction the head faced, without turning as they went. ¹²Their entire bodies, including their hands and their wings, were completely full of eyes, *r* as were their four wheels. *s* ¹³I heard the wheels being called "the whirling wheels." ¹⁴Each of the cherubim *t* had four faces: *u* One face was that of a cherub, the second the face of a human being, the third the face of a lion, *v* and the fourth the face of an eagle. *w*

¹⁵Then the cherubim rose upward. These were the living creatures *x* I had seen by the Kebar River. *y* ¹⁶When the cherubim moved, the wheels beside them moved; and when the cherubim spread their wings to rise from the ground, the wheels did not leave their side. ¹⁷When the cherubim stood still, they also stood still; and when the cherubim rose, they rose with them, because the spirit of the living creatures was in them. *z*

¹⁸Then the glory *a* of the Lᴏʀᴅ departed from over the threshold of the temple and stopped above the cherubim. *b* ¹⁹While I watched, the cherubim spread their wings and rose from the ground, and as they went, the wheels went with them. *c* They stopped at

---

a 5 Hebrew *El-Shaddai*   *b* 11 Or *aside*

9:8 *Ah, Sovereign Lᴏʀᴅ!* See 11:13. As those who served as intermediaries between God and his people, the prophets frequently interceded on behalf of the people when God's judgments threatened (see Ex 32:31; Nu 14:13–19; 1Sa 12:23; Jer 14:19–21; 15:1; Am 7:2,5).
9:9 *land is full of bloodshed.* See 7:23 and note.
10:1–22 See note on 8:1—11:25.
10:1 *I looked.* Ch. 10 echoes ch. 1, underscoring the identity of what Ezekiel saw at the Kebar River with what he now sees in his vision (see 8:4). The creatures in ch. 1 are here called cherubim (see note on 1:5).
10:2 *burning coals.* While in 1:13 the living creatures looked like burning coals, here there are real coals. *scatter them over the city.* A judgment by fire (see Ge 19:24; Am 7:4).
10:3 *cloud.* The cloud that enclosed the "glory of the Lᴏʀᴅ" (v. 4), which otherwise would have blinded those who saw it (see 1:4; Ex 16:10; 24:15–17; 40:34–35,38; Nu 9:15–16; 16:42; Dt 5:23;

1Ki 8:10–12; Hag 2:7 and note; cf. Mt 13:5; 24:30; 26:64; Mk 9:7; 13:26; 14:62; Lk 9:34–35; 21:27; Ac 1:9; Rev 1:7; 14:14–16).
10:7 *one of the cherubim reached out his hand.* Though the "man clothed in linen" was initially commanded to get the coals himself (v. 2), he received them from the hand of one of the creatures (see 1:8). *who took it and went out.* No further report is given, but the destructive spreading of the coals over Jerusalem is assumed.
10:14 *One face was that of a cherub.* While the faces of the human being, lion and eagle are identical with those in 1:10 (see note on 1:5), the ox is here called a cherub (see note on Ge 3:24).
10:15 *Kebar River.* See 1:1 and note.
10:19 *east gate … and the glory of the God of Israel was above them.* A second movement of the glory, again in an easterly direction (see 9:3; 10:4; see also note on 8:1—11:25). See ch. 43 for the return of the glory of the Lord to the temple by way of the east gate (see note on 43:1–12).

the entrance of the east gate of the Lord's house, and the glory ^d of the God of Israel was above them.

²⁰These were the living creatures I had seen beneath the God of Israel by the Kebar River, ^e and I realized that they were cherubim. ²¹Each had four faces ^f and four wings, ^g and under their wings was what looked like human hands. ²²Their faces had the same appearance as those I had seen by the Kebar River. ^h Each one went straight ahead.

GOD'S SURE JUDGMENT ON JERUSALEM

11 Then the Spirit lifted me up and brought me to the gate of the house of the Lord that faces east. There at the entrance of the gate were twenty-five men, and I saw among them Jaazaniah son of Azzur and Pelatiah ⁱ son of Benaiah, leaders ^j of the people. ^k ²The Lord said to me, "Son of man, these are the men who are plotting evil ^l and giving wicked advice in this city. ^m ³They say, 'Haven't our houses been recently rebuilt? This city is a pot, ⁿ and we are the meat in it.' ^o ⁴Therefore prophesy ^p against them; prophesy, son of man."

⁵Then the Spirit of the Lord came on me, and he told me to say: "This is what the Lord says: That is what you are saying, house of Israel, but I know what is going through your mind. ^q ⁶You have killed many people in this city and filled its streets with the dead. ^r

⁷"Therefore this is what the Sovereign Lord says: The bodies you have thrown there are the meat and this city is the pot, ^s but I will drive you out of it. ^t ⁸You fear the sword, ^u and the sword is what I will bring against you, declares the Sovereign Lord. ^v ⁹I will drive you out of the city and deliver you into the hands ^w of foreigners and inflict punishment on you. ^x ¹⁰You will fall by the sword, and I will execute judgment on you at the borders of Israel. ^y Then you will know that I am the Lord. ¹¹This city will not be a pot ^z for you, nor will you be the meat in it; I will execute judgment on you at the borders of Israel. ¹²And you will know that I am the Lord, ^a for you have not followed my decrees ^b or kept my laws but have conformed to the standards of the nations around you. ^c"

¹³Now as I was prophesying, Pelatiah ^d son of Benaiah died. Then I fell facedown and cried out in a loud voice, "Ah, Sovereign Lord! Will you completely destroy the remnant of Israel? ^e"

THE PROMISE OF ISRAEL'S RETURN

¹⁴The word of the Lord came to me: ¹⁵"Son of man, the people of Jerusalem have said of your fellow exiles and the whole house of Israel, ^a 'They are far away from the Lord; this land was given to us as our possession.' ^f

¹⁶"Therefore say: 'This is what the Sovereign Lord says: Although I sent them far away among the nations and scattered them among the countries, yet for a little while I have been a sanctuary ^g for them in the countries where they have gone.'

¹⁷"Therefore say: 'This is what the Sovereign Lord says: I will gather you from the nations and bring you back from the countries where you have been scattered, and I will give you back the land of Israel again.' ^h

¹⁸"They will return to it and remove all its vile images ⁱ and detestable idols. ^j ¹⁹I will give them an undivided heart ^k and put a new spirit in them; I will remove from them their heart of stone ^l and give them a heart of flesh. ^m ²⁰Then they will follow my decrees and be careful to keep my laws. ⁿ They will be my people, ^o and I will be their God. ^p ²¹But as

^a 15 Or said of your brothers—your brothers who are your blood relatives and the whole house of Israel—

11:1–13 See note on 8:1—11:25.
11:1 *the Spirit lifted me up.* See 3:12 and note. *twenty-five men.* See 8:16 and note. *Jaazaniah.* See note on 8:11. *Pelatiah.* Means "The Lord delivers."
11:3 *Haven't our houses been recently rebuilt?* The residents of Jerusalem who were not exiled by the Babylonians in 597 B.C. felt smugly secure, thinking they had no further Babylonian threat to fear. *pot.* As in ch. 24, Jerusalem is compared to a cooking pot. Those left behind boasted that they were the "meat," the choice portions—the inference being that the exiles in Babylon were the discarded bones (see v. 15).
11:5 *the Spirit of the Lord came on me.* See 2:2 and note.
11:6 *killed many … filled its streets with the dead.* See 7:23 and note.
11:7 *The bodies you have thrown there are the meat.* The meat, redefined by the prophet, is not those in power in Jerusalem

(who will be driven out) but the innocent people they killed.
11:11 *at the borders of Israel.* At Riblah (see 2Ki 25:20–21).
11:13 *Ah, Sovereign Lord!* See note on 9:8.
11:14–21 See note on 8:1—11:25.

11:16 *I have been a sanctuary for them.* A key verse in Ezekiel. Although the exiles had been driven from Jerusalem and its sanctuary (the symbol of God's presence among his people), God himself became their sanctuary, i.e., he was present among them to preserve and bless them.

11:19 *undivided heart … new spirit.* Inner spiritual and moral transformation that results in single-minded commitment to the Lord and to his will (see 36:26). *remove … heart of stone … give … heart of flesh.* Give Israel a new heart, responsive to God's will (see 2Co 3:3 and note).

11:20 *my people … their God.* The heart of God's covenant promise (see Ex 6:7; Jer 7:23; Zec 8:8 and notes).

10:19 ^d Eze 43:4
10:20 ^e Eze 1:1
10:21 ^f Eze 41:18
^g Eze 1:6
10:22 ^h Eze 1:1
11:1 ⁱ ver 13 / Jer 5:5
^k S Eze 8:16; S 10:19; 43:4-5
11:2 ^l S Isa 29:20; Na 1:11 ^m Eze 8:11
11:3 ⁿ Jer 1:13; Eze 24:3 ^o ver 7,11; Eze 12:22,27; Mic 3:3
11:4 ^p S Eze 3:4,17
11:5 ^q S Ps 26:2; S Jer 17:10
11:6 ^r S Eze 7:23; 22:6
11:7 ^s Jer 1:13
^t ver 3; Eze 24:3-13; Mic 3:2-3
11:8 ^u S Lev 26:25; S Jer 42:16
^v S Pr 10:24; Isa 66:4
11:9 ^w Ps 106:41
^x Dt 28:36; S Eze 5:8
11:10 ^y 2Ki 14:25
11:11 ^z ver 3; Eze 24:6
11:12 ^a S Eze 6:7
^b S Lev 18:4; Eze 18:9
^c Eze 8:10
11:13 ^d ver 1
^e S Eze 9:8; Am 7:2
11:15 ^f Eze 33:24
11:16 ^g Ps 31:20; 90:1; 91:9; S Isa 4:6
11:17 ^h S Ne 1:9; S Jer 3:18; 24:5-6; S 31:16; Eze 20:41; 28:25; 34:13; 36:28
11:18 ⁱ S Eze 5:11
^j Eze 37:23
11:19 ^k S 2Ch 30:12; S Ps 86:11 ^l Zec 7:12; Ro 2:5 ^m Eze 18:31; S 2Co 3:3
11:20 ⁿ S Ps 1:2
^o S Jer 11:4; 32:38
^p S Eze 14:11; 34:30; 36:26-28; Hos 1:9; Zec 8:8; Heb 8:10

11:21 *q* Jer 16:18
r Jer 16:11; S Eze 9:10; 16:43
11:22 *s* S Ex 24:16
t Eze 9:3; S 10:19
11:23 *u* Eze 1:28; S 10:4 *v* Zec 14:4
11:24 *w* Eze 37:1; 43:5 *x* 2Co 12:2-4
11:25 *y* S Eze 3:4,11
12:2 *z* Ps 78:40; S Jer 42:21
a S Isa 6:10; S Mt 13:15; Mk 4:12; 8:18
12:3 *b* S Jer 36:3
c Jer 26:3 *d* ver 11; S Eze 3:27; 2Ti 2:25-26
12:4 *e* ver 12; 2Ki 25:4; S Jer 39:4
12:5 *f* Jer 52:7; Am 4:3
12:6 *g* ver 12; S Isa 8:18; S 20:3
12:7 *h* Eze 24:18; 37:10
12:9 *i* Eze 17:12; 20:49; 24:19
12:11 *i* Isa 8:18; Zec 3:8 *k* S 2Ki 25:7; S Jer 15:2; 52:15
12:12 *l* S Jer 39:4
m Jer 52:7
12:13 *n* Eze 17:20; 19:8; 32:3; Hos 7:12
o S Isa 24:17-18
p Eze 1:3 *q* S Jer 39:7
r S Jer 24:8; S 52:11; S La 4:20; Eze 17:16
12:14 *s* S 2Ki 25:5; S Jer 21:7; S Eze 5:10, 12; 17:21
12:15 *t* S Lev 26:33
12:16 *u* S Eze 22:8-9; Eze 6:8-10; 14:22; 36:20
12:18 *v* La 5:9

for those whose hearts are devoted to their vile images and detestable idols, *q* I will bring down on their own heads what they have done, declares the Sovereign Lord. *r* ”

²²Then the cherubim, with the wheels beside them, spread their wings, and the glory *s* of the God of Israel was above them. *t* ²³The glory *u* of the Lord went up from within the city and stopped above the mountain *v* east of it. ²⁴The Spirit *w* lifted me up and brought me to the exiles in Babylonia *a* in the vision *x* given by the Spirit of God.

Then the vision I had seen went up from me, ²⁵and I told the exiles everything the Lord had shown me. *y*

THE EXILE SYMBOLIZED

12 The word of the Lord came to me: ²“Son of man, you are living among a rebellious people. *z* They have eyes to see but do not see and ears to hear but do not hear, for they are a rebellious people. *a*

³“Therefore, son of man, pack your belongings for exile and in the daytime, as they watch, set out and go from where you are to another place. Perhaps *b* they will understand, *c* though they are a rebellious house. *d* ⁴During the daytime, while they watch, bring out your belongings packed for exile. Then in the evening, while they are watching, go out like those who go into exile. *e* ⁵While they watch, dig through the wall *f* and take your belongings out through it. *f* ⁶Put them on your shoulder as they are watching and carry them out at dusk. Cover your face so that you cannot see the land, for I have made you a sign *g* to the house of Israel.”

⁷So I did as I was commanded. *h* During the day I brought out my things packed for exile. Then in the evening I dug through the wall with my hands. I took my belongings out at dusk, carrying them on my shoulders while they watched.

⁸In the morning the word of the Lord came to me: ⁹“Son of man, did not that rebellious house of Israel ask you, ‘What are you doing?’ *i*

¹⁰“Say to them, ‘This is what the Sovereign Lord says: This prophecy concerns the prince in Jerusalem and the whole house of Israel who are there.’ ¹¹Say to them, ‘I am a sign *i* to you.’

“As I have done, so it will be done to them. They will go into exile as captives. *k*

¹²“The prince among them will put his things on his shoulder *l* and leave, and a hole will be dug in the wall for him to go through. He will cover his face so that he cannot see the land. *m* ¹³I will spread my net *n* for him, and he will be caught in my snare; *o* I will bring him to Babylonia, the land of the Chaldeans, *p* but he will not see *q* it, and there he will die. *r* ¹⁴I will scatter to the winds all those around him—his staff and all his troops—and I will pursue them with drawn sword. *s*

¹⁵“They will know that I am the Lord, when I disperse them among the nations *t* and scatter them through the countries. ¹⁶But I will spare a few of them from the sword, famine and plague, so that in the nations where they go they may acknowledge all their detestable practices. Then they will know that I am the Lord. *u* ”

¹⁷The word of the Lord came to me: ¹⁸“Son of man, tremble as you eat your food, *v* and

---

a 24 Or *Chaldea*

11:22—25 See note on 8:1—11:25.
11:23 *The glory of the Lord went up.* The final eastward movement of the glory (as the Lord left his temple), which stopped above the Mount of Olives (see 9:3; 10:4,19; see also note on 8:1—11:25).
11:24 See note on 8:3.
12:1—28 The first series of oracles concludes with Ezekiel being called upon to symbolize by personal actions the coming exile of Jerusalem—just as the second series of oracles culminates (24:15–27) in Ezekiel suffering the death of his wife as a symbolic representation of the fall of Jerusalem. Verses 1–2 and v. 28 frame the chapter; two symbolic acts (vv. 3–16,17–20) are followed by the refutation of two sayings with which the Jerusalemites vainly try to reassure themselves (vv. 21–25,26–27).

12:2 *eyes to see but do not see.* The hardening about which the Lord had spoken to Isaiah (see Isa 6:8–10 and notes). The Israelites in Jerusalem refuse to recognize that the end has come for them (see v. 28; 7:2–6).
12:3 *pack your belongings.* Another symbolic act, which, like those in chs. 4–5, follows a vision. *Perhaps they will understand.* Some hope remained that they would change.
12:5 *dig through the wall.* Not the city wall, which was made of

stone and was many feet thick, but the sun-dried brick wall of his house.
12:6 *sign.* Prophets were often instructed to perform symbolic acts (see, e.g., v. 11; 24:24,27; cf. 1Ki 11:29–31; 13:23–32; 20:35–43; Isa 8:18; Jer 13:1–11; 16:1–9; 19:1–15; 27:2—28:14; 32:6–15).
12:8 *In the morning.* After Ezekiel “did as … commanded” (v. 7). Again the divine explanation follows the prophet's unquestioning obedience (see note on 8:3).
12:9 *What are you doing?* The book's first indication of the people's response to the prophet's symbolic acts.
12:10 *prince in Jerusalem.* Zedekiah.
12:13 *Chaldeans.* See notes on 23:23; Ezr 5:12; Job 1:17. *he will not see it.* Nebuchadnezzar's men would put out Zedekiah's eyes (see 2Ki 25:7).
12:14 *with drawn sword.* See 5:2 and note.
12:15 *know that I am the Lord.* See vv. 16,20; see also note on 6:7.
12:16 *sword, famine and plague.* See 5:16–17 and note.
12:18 *tremble as you eat.* Another prophetic symbol. Ezekiel's trembling must have been particularly violent, because the Hebrew word for “tremble” is used elsewhere to describe an earthquake (see 1Ki 19:11; Am 1:1).

shudder in fear as you drink your water. ¹⁹Say to the people of the land: 'This is what the Sovereign LORD says about those living in Jerusalem and in the land of Israel: They will eat their food in anxiety and drink their water in despair, for their land will be stripped of everything ᵂ in it because of the violence of all who live there. ˣ ²⁰The inhabited towns will be laid waste and the land will be desolate. Then you will know that I am the LORD. ʸ ' "

THERE WILL BE NO DELAY

²¹The word of the LORD came to me: ²²"Son of man, what is this proverb ᶻ you have in the land of Israel: 'The days go by and every vision comes to nothing'? ᵃ ²³Say to them, 'This is what the Sovereign LORD says: I am going to put an end to this proverb, and they will no longer quote it in Israel.' Say to them, 'The days are near ᵇ when every vision will be fulfilled. ᶜ ²⁴For there will be no more false visions or flattering divinations ᵈ among the people of Israel. ²⁵But I the LORD will speak what I will, and it shall be fulfilled without delay. ᵉ For in your days, you rebellious house, I will fulfill ᶠ whatever I say, declares the Sovereign LORD. ᵍ ' "

²⁶The word of the LORD came to me: ²⁷"Son of man, the house of Israel is saying, 'The vision he sees is for many years from now, and he prophesies about the distant future.' ʰ ²⁸"Therefore say to them, 'This is what the Sovereign LORD says: None of my words will be delayed any longer; whatever I say will be fulfilled, declares the Sovereign LORD.' "

FALSE PROPHETS CONDEMNED

13 The word of the LORD came to me: ²"Son of man, prophesy against the prophets ⁱ of Israel who are now prophesying. Say to those who prophesy out of their own imagination: ʲ 'Hear the word of the LORD! ᵏ ³This is what the Sovereign LORD says: Woe to the foolish ᵃ prophets ˡ who follow their own spirit and have seen nothing! ᵐ ⁴Your prophets, Israel, are like jackals among ruins. ⁵You have not gone up to the breaches in the wall to repair ⁿ it for the house of Israel so that it will stand firm in the battle on the day of the LORD. ᵒ ⁶Their visions are false ᵖ and their divinations a lie. Even though the LORD has not sent ᑫ them, they say, "The LORD declares," and expect him to fulfill their words. ʳ ⁷Have you not seen false visions ˢ and uttered lying divinations when you say, "The LORD declares," though I have not spoken?

⁸" 'Therefore this is what the Sovereign LORD says: Because of your false words and lying visions, I am against you, ᵗ declares the Sovereign LORD. ⁹My hand will be against the prophets who see false visions and utter lying ᵘ divinations. They will not belong to the council of my people or be listed in the records ᵛ of the house of Israel, nor will they enter the land of Israel. Then you will know that I am the Sovereign LORD. ᵂ

¹⁰" 'Because they lead my people astray, ˣ saying, "Peace," ʸ when there is no peace,

---

ᵃ 3 Or *wicked*

12:19 ʷ Jer 10:22;
S Eze 6:6-14;
Mic 7:13; Zec 7:14
ˣ S Eze 4:16; 23:33
12:20 ʸ Isa 7:23-24;
S Jer 4:7; S 25:9
12:22 ᶻ S Ps 49:4
ᵃ S Isa 5:19; Eze 11:3;
Am 6:3; 2Pe 3:4
12:23 ᵇ S Eze 7:7
ᶜ S Ps 37:13; Eze 18:3;
Joel 2:1; Zep 1:14
12:24 ᵈ Jer 14:14;
Eze 13:23; Mic 3:6;
Zec 13:2-4
12:25 ᵉ Hab 2:3
ᶠ S Nu 11:23; Eze 13:6
ᵍ Nu 14:28-34;
S Isa 14:24; S 55:11;
Jer 16:9; Hab 1:5
12:27 ʰ S Eze 11:3;
Da 10:14; Mt 24:48-
50; 2Pe 3:4
13:2 ⁱ S Isa 9:15
ʲ Jer 28:15 ᵏ ver 17;
S Jer 23:16; S 37:19;
Eze 22:28
13:3 ˡ S La 2:14;
Hos 9:7
ᵐ S Jer 23:25-32
13:5 ⁿ Isa 58:12;
Eze 22:30
ᵒ S Eze 7:19; 30:3
13:6 ᵖ S Jer 5:1;
23:16 ᑫ S Jer 14:14
ʳ S Jer 28:15; S 29:9;
Eze 12:24-25; 22:28
13:7 ˢ S Isa 30:10
13:8 ᵗ S Jer 21:13
13:9 ᵘ S Dt 13:3
ᵛ S Ex 32:32;
S Jer 17:13 ᵂ S Ex 6:2;
Jer 20:3-6; Eze 20:38
13:10 ˣ S Jer 23:13;
S 50:6 ʸ S Jer 4:10

12:19 *people of the land.* See note on 7:27. *because of the violence.* See 7:23 and note.
12:22 For more than 30 years Jeremiah had been prophesying Jerusalem's fall, but the city still stood. So among its inhabitants, whose ears were deaf to Jeremiah's warnings (v. 2), a mocking proverb was making the rounds, reinforced by the false prophets (see ch. 13; Jer 23:9–40; 28), which said in effect: "The days go by" and none of the visions of coming disaster have come true, so forget them.
12:23 The Lord refutes the first saying (v. 22) of the Israelites that dismisses his prophet's announcements of impending judgment.
12:24 *no more false visions ... divinations.* Events will silence the false prophets, whose "visions are false and their divinations a lie" (13:6).
12:27 Another saying (see note on v. 23) is being passed around among the Israelites, this one apparently among those in exile. It pertains to Ezekiel's "visions" and dismisses them as having to do only with far-off events that need not concern the present generation.
12:28 *None of my words will be delayed any longer.* The Lord also refutes this saying (v. 27) circulating among his "rebellious people" (v. 2; see note on 12:1–28).
13:1–23 The Lord's condemnation of the false prophets, both men and women—as through Jeremiah in Jerusalem (Jer 23:9–40; 28), so through Ezekiel in Babylonia. This begins a series of oracles concerning God's judgment on Judah that con-

cludes with a parable in which Jerusalem is likened to a pot cooking on a fire (24:1–14).
13:2 *out of their own imagination.* Cf. Jer 23:16, 26–32.
13:3 *have seen nothing.* No revelation from God was received (cf. Jer 23:18,22 and note on 23:18).
13:4 *jackals.* Animals that travel in packs and feed on dead flesh—a powerfully negative image (see Ps 63:10; La 5:18).
13:5 *to repair it for the house of Israel.* The function of true prophets is described (cf. 22:30; Ps 106:23). *day of the LORD.* See note on 7:7.
13:6 *Their visions are false.* Whether the false prophets had actual visions is unknown, but they claimed to have received revelations from God when in reality their messages only proclaimed what their hearers wanted to hear (see Isa 30:10; Jer 23:9–17; 2Ti 4:3).
13:8 *I am against you.* See 5:8 and note.
13:9 *They will not belong ... land of Israel.* A threefold punishment, resulting in total exclusion from the community. *council of my people.* See Ps 111:1 and note. *records of the house of Israel.* See Ezr 2:62; cf. Da 12:1; see also Ps 69:28 and note.
13:10 *saying, "Peace."* Very likely in echo of the priestly benediction (see Nu 6:24–26 and note on 6:26), ignoring the fact that God's promise of "peace" to his people was conditional on their faithfulness to him. *when there is no peace.* See v. 16; Jer 6:14 and 8:11. *whitewash.* See vv. 11,14–15; 22:28; an uncommon word used only by Ezekiel, perhaps chosen by

13:10 *z* S Eze 7:25; 22:28
13:11 *a* S Jos 10:11
b S Job 38:23
c Ps 11:6; Eze 38:22
13:13 *d* S Jos 10:11; Rev 11:19; 16:21
e Job 14:19
f S Ex 9:25; S Job 38:23; Isa 30:30
13:14 *g* S Isa 22:5
h Mic 1:6 *i* Jer 6:15
13:16 *j* S Isa 57:21; Jer 6:14; S Eze 7:25
13:17 *k* S Eze 4:7; 25:2; 28:21
l S Ex 15:20; Rev 2:20
m ver 2
13:19 *n* Jer 44:26; Eze 20:39; 22:26; 36:20; 39:7
o S Isa 56:11
p Pr 28:21; Mic 3:11
13:20 *q* Ps 124:7
13:21 *r* Ps 91:3
13:22 *s* S Isa 9:15
t Jer 23:14; Eze 18:21; 33:14-16
13:23 *u* Ne 6:12
v S Eze 12:24
w S Ps 72:14 *x* Mic 3:6
14:1 *y* S Eze 8:1; 20:1
14:3 *z* S Eze 6:4
a S ver 7; S Eze 7:19
b Isa 1:15; Eze 20:31
14:5 *c* S Dt 32:15; Eze 16:45; Hos 5:7; Zec 11:8 *d* Jer 2:11
14:6 *e* Ne 1:9; S Jer 3:12; S 35:15
f S Isa 2:20; S 30:22
14:7 *g* Ex 12:48; 20:10 *h* ver 3; S Isa 8:14; Hos 4:5; 5:5 *i* S Ge 25:22

and because, when a flimsy wall is built, they cover it with whitewash, *z* [11]therefore tell those who cover it with whitewash that it is going to fall. Rain will come in torrents, and I will send hailstones *a* hurtling down, *b* and violent winds will burst forth. *c* [12]When the wall collapses, will people not ask you, "Where is the whitewash you covered it with?"

[13]" 'Therefore this is what the Sovereign LORD says: In my wrath I will unleash a violent wind, and in my anger hailstones *d* and torrents of rain *e* will fall with destructive fury. *f* [14]I will tear down the wall *g* you have covered with whitewash and will level it to the ground so that its foundation *h* will be laid bare. When it *a* falls, *i* you will be destroyed in it; and you will know that I am the LORD. [15]So I will spend my wrath against the wall and against those who covered it with whitewash. I will say to you, "The wall is gone and so are those who whitewashed it, [16]those prophets of Israel who prophesied to Jerusalem and saw visions of peace for her when there was no peace, declares the Sovereign LORD." *j* '

[17]"Now, son of man, set your face *k* against the daughters *l* of your people who prophesy out of their own imagination. Prophesy against them *m* [18]and say, 'This is what the Sovereign LORD says: Woe to the women who sew magic charms on all their wrists and make veils of various lengths for their heads in order to ensnare people. Will you ensnare the lives of my people but preserve your own? [19]You have profaned *n* me among my people for a few handfuls of barley and scraps of bread. *o* By lying to my people, who listen to lies, you have killed those who should not have died and have spared those who should not live. *p*

[20]" 'Therefore this is what the Sovereign LORD says: I am against your magic charms with which you ensnare people like birds and I will tear them from your arms; I will set free the people that you ensnare like birds. *q* [21]I will tear off your veils and save my people from your hands, and they will no longer fall prey to your power. Then you will know that I am the LORD. *r* [22]Because you disheartened the righteous with your lies, *s* when I had brought them no grief, and because you encouraged the wicked not to turn from their evil ways and so save their lives, *t* [23]therefore you will no longer see false visions *u* or practice divination. *v* I will save *w* my people from your hands. And then you will know that I am the LORD. *x* ' "

IDOLATERS CONDEMNED

14 Some of the elders of Israel came to me and sat down in front of me. *y* [2]Then the word of the LORD came to me: [3]"Son of man, these men have set up idols in their hearts *z* and put wicked stumbling blocks *a* before their faces. Should I let them inquire of me at all? *b* [4]Therefore speak to them and tell them, 'This is what the Sovereign LORD says: When any of the Israelites set up idols in their hearts and put a wicked stumbling block before their faces and then go to a prophet, I the LORD will answer them myself in keeping with their great idolatry. [5]I will do this to recapture the hearts of the people of Israel, who have all deserted *c* me for their idols.' *d*

[6]"Therefore say to the house of Israel, 'This is what the Sovereign LORD says: Repent! *e* Turn from your idols and renounce all your detestable practices! *f*

[7]" 'When any of the Israelites or any foreigner *g* residing in Israel separate themselves from me and set up idols in their hearts and put a wicked stumbling block *h* before their faces and then go to a prophet to inquire *i* of me, I the LORD will answer them myself. [8]I

a 14 Or *the city*

---

him to evoke the like-sounding word rendered "repulsive thing" in Jer 23:13 and "worthless" in La 2:14, both pertaining to the proclamations of the false prophets.

13:11 *Rain will come in torrents.* The violent thunderstorm of God's judgment (imagery frequently used in the OT) was about to sweep them away (see, e.g., Ps 18:7–15; 77:17–18; 83:15; Isa 28:17; 30:30; Jer 23:19; 30:23).

13:18 *magic charms.* Exactly what the women were doing is not known, but that it was some kind of black magic or voodoo is clear. The Bible consistently avoids explicit description of occult practices.

A **13:19** *profaned me.* See note on Lev 18:21. *for a few handfuls of barley.* Involvement in religious matters of any kind for mere gain is consistently condemned in the Bible (see, e.g., Jer 6:13; 8:10; Mic 3:5,11; Ac 8:9–24; 2Co 2:17; Tit 1:11). For the proper attitude and motivation, see 2Co 11:7; 2Th 3:8; 1Ti 3:3. *you have killed.* The women had used their evil powers for unjust ends, involving even matters of life and death.

14:1–11 The idolatry among the Israelites that God here con-

demns took the form of worshiping the gods of neighboring peoples (see notes on Ge 20:9; Ex 34:15) along with the worship of Yahweh—the people thought they should take all the gods seriously—an apostasy that struck at the very heart of Israel's covenant relationship with Yahweh (see Ex 20:3–5 and notes). And this idolatry was not limited to those still living in Jerusalem; Ezekiel had to confront it also among the exiles.

14:1 *elders of Israel.* Apparently interchangeable with "elders of Judah" (see note on 8:1).

14:3 *idols.* See note on 6:4. *wicked stumbling blocks.* The physical representations of the idols. *inquire.* A technical term for seeking an oracle from a prophet (see 2Ki 1:16; 3:11; 8:8).

14:4 *I the LORD will answer them myself.* Not through a prophet but by direct action. The punishment for idolatry was death (Dt 13:6–18).

14:6 *Repent!* First of three calls for repentance from Ezekiel, who elsewhere proclaims inescapable judgment (see 18:30; 33:11).

will set my face against[j] them and make them an example[k] and a byword. [l] I will remove them from my people. Then you will know that I am the LORD. [m]

⁹ 'And if the prophet[n] is enticed[o] to utter a prophecy, I the LORD have enticed that prophet, and I will stretch out my hand against him and destroy him from among my people Israel. [p] ¹⁰They will bear their guilt—the prophet will be as guilty as the one who consults him. ¹¹Then the people of Israel will no longer stray[q] from me, nor will they defile themselves anymore with all their sins. They will be my people,[r] and I will be their God, declares the Sovereign LORD. [s] '"

JERUSALEM'S JUDGMENT INESCAPABLE

¹²The word of the LORD came to me: ¹³"Son of man, if a country sins[t] against me by being unfaithful and I stretch out my hand against it to cut off its food supply[u] and send famine upon it and kill its people and their animals, [v] ¹⁴even if these three men—Noah, [w] Daniel[a x] and Job[y]—were in it, they could save only themselves by their righteousness, [z] declares the Sovereign LORD.

¹⁵"Or if I send wild beasts[a] through that country and they leave it childless and it becomes desolate so that no one can pass through it because of the beasts, [b] ¹⁶as surely as I live, declares the Sovereign LORD, even if these three men were in it, they could not save their own sons or daughters. They alone would be saved, but the land would be desolate. [c]

¹⁷"Or if I bring a sword[d] against that country and say, 'Let the sword pass throughout the land,' and I kill its people and their animals, [e] ¹⁸as surely as I live, declares the Sovereign LORD, even if these three men were in it, they could not save their own sons or daughters. They alone would be saved.

¹⁹"Or if I send a plague into that land and pour out my wrath[f] on it through bloodshed, [g] killing its people and their animals, [h] ²⁰as surely as I live, declares the Sovereign LORD, even if Noah, Daniel and Job were in it, they could save neither son nor daughter. They would save only themselves by their righteousness. [i]

²¹"For this is what the Sovereign LORD says: How much worse will it be when I send against Jerusalem my four dreadful judgments[j]—sword[k] and famine[l] and wild beasts and plague[m]—to kill its men and their animals! [n] ²²Yet there will be some survivors[o]—sons and daughters who will be brought out of it. [p] They will come to you, and when you see their conduct[q] and their actions, you will be consoled[r] regarding the disaster I have brought on Jerusalem—every disaster I have brought on it. ²³You will be consoled when you see their conduct and their actions, for you will know that I have done nothing in it without cause, declares the Sovereign LORD. [s]"

JERUSALEM AS A USELESS VINE

15 The word of the LORD came to me: ²"Son of man, how is the wood of a vine[t] different from that of a branch from any of the trees in the forest? ³Is wood ever taken from it to make anything useful?[u] Do they make pegs[v] from it to hang things on? ⁴And after it is thrown on the fire as fuel and the fire burns both ends and chars the middle, is it then useful for anything? [w] ⁵If it was not useful for anything when it was whole, how much less can it be made into something useful when the fire has burned it and it is charred?

---

a 14 Or *Daniel*, a man of renown in ancient literature; also in verse 20

14:8 *i* Eze 15:7
k S Nu 16:38
l S Ps 102:8;
S Eze 5:15
m S Jer 42:20
14:9 *n* S Jer 14:15
o Isa 63:17; Jer 4:10
p 1Ki 22:23;
S 2Ch 18:22; Zec 13:3
14:11 *q* Eze 48:11
r S Isa 51:16
s S Eze 11:19-20;
37:23
14:13 *t* S Pr 13:21
u S Lev 26:26
v S Eze 5:16; 6:14;
15:8
14:14 *w* Ge 6:8
x ver 20; Eze 28:3;
Da 1:6; 6:13 *y* S Job 1:1
z S Ge 6:9;
S Job 42:9; Jer 15:1;
Eze 3:19; 18:20
S Ge 6:22
14:15 *a* Eze 5:17
b S Lev 26:22
14:16 *c* S Ge 19:29;
Eze 18:20
14:17 *d* S Lev 26:25;
S Jer 25:27; S 42:16
e Eze 25:13; Zep 1:3
14:19 *f* S Eze 7:8
g S Isa 34:3
h Jer 14:12; Eze 38:22
14:20 *i* S ver 14
14:21 *j* S Nu 33:4
k Isa 31:8; 34:6; 66:16;
Eze 21:3,19
l S 2Sa 24:13
m S Jer 14:12; 27:8
n S Jer 15:3;
S Eze 5:17; 33:27;
Am 4:6-10; Rev 6:8
14:22 *o* S Jer 41:16
p S Eze 12:16
q Eze 20:43
r Eze 31:16; 32:31
14:23 *s* S Jer 22:8-9;
Eze 8:6-18; S 9:9
15:2 *t* Ps 80:8-16;
Isa 5:1-7; 27:2-6;
Jer 2:21; Hos 10:1;
S Jn 15:2
15:3 *u* Jer 13:10
v S Isa 22:23
15:4 *w* Eze 17:3-10;
19:14; Jn 15:6

14:9 *enticed.* Related to God's testing of his people's loyalty (see 3:20 and note; cf. 1Ki 22:19–23).

A 14:11 The harsh judgment about to fall on idolatrous Israel has a redemptive purpose: to restore Israel to covenant faithfulness (see 20:32–44; cf. 33:11). *my people . . . their God.* Covenant terminology (see note on 11:20).

14:12–23 Israel must know that once God's judgments have been sent upon an unfaithful nation no one can persuade him to call them back—and that will be even more true of Jerusalem (cf. Jer 15:1 and note). The judgments in view here include the four often mentioned in Ezekiel: famine (v. 13), wild beasts (v. 15), sword (v. 17) and plague (v. 19; see also v. 21 and note on 5:16–17).

B 14:14,20 *Noah, Daniel and Job.* Three ancient men of renown, selected because of their proverbial righteousness. As the TNIV text note indicates, another Daniel may be referred to (Ugaritic literature speaks of an honored "Danel"; see chart, p. xxiv), since the Biblical Daniel's righteousness probably

had not become proverbial so soon (Daniel and Ezekiel were contemporaries; see Da 1:1).

A 14:20 *neither son nor daughter.* When God comes in judgment against a nation or people, they cannot count on another's righteousness—not even that of their parents—to deliver them.

14:23 *You.* Plural; i.e., the exiles in Babylon. *will be consoled.* When the exiles see the wickedness of those brought to Babylon from Jerusalem, they will know that God's judgment on the city was just.

15:1–8 God compares Jerusalem to a vine (cf. Ps 80:8–16 and note) that yields no grapes and is therefore good for nothing but to be used as fuel.

15:3 *Do they make pegs from it to hang things on?* See Isa 22:23–25.

15:4 *is it then useful for anything?* Whereas Isaiah (5:1–7) and Jeremiah (2:21) express divine disappointment over Israel's failure to produce good fruit, Ezekiel typically laments her total uselessness.

15:7 ˣS Lev 26:17;
Ps 34:16; Eze 14:8
ʸS Eze 5:2
ᶻS Eze 5:4
ᵃIsa 24:18; Am 9:1-4
15:8 ᵇS Eze 14:13
ᶜEze 17:20; 18:24
16:2 ᵈS Isa 57:12;
Eze 23:36 ᵉEze 8:17;
20:4; 22:2
16:3 ᶠGe 11:25-29;
Eze 21:30
ᵍS Ge 12:18
ʰS Ge 15:16 ⁱver 45;
S Ge 10:15; S Dt 7:1;
Jos 24:14-15
16:4 ʲHos 2:3
16:6 ᵏver 22;
S Eze 19:4; Eze 18:23,
32
16:7 ˡS Dt 1:10
ᵐS Ex 1:7
16:8 ⁿRu 3:9
ᵒver 59; S Jer 11:10;
Mal 2:14 ᵖJer 2:2;
Hos 2:7,19-20
16:9 �qS Ru 3:3
16:10 ʳS Ex 26:36;
S Isa 19:9 ˢEze 27:16
ᵗver 18; S Isa 3:23
16:11 ᵘS Jer 4:30;
Eze 23:40 ᵛIsa 3:19;
Eze 23:42
ʷS Ge 41:42;
S Ps 73:6
16:12 ˣIsa 3:21
ʸS Ge 35:4
ᶻS Isa 28:5;
S Jer 13:18 ᵃPr 1:9;
S Isa 3:19
16:13 ᵇEst 5:1
ᶜ1Sa 10:1 ᵈDt 32:13-
14; S 1Ki 4:21;
S Est 2:9,17
16:14 ᵉ1Ki 10:24

⁶"Therefore this is what the Sovereign LORD says: As I have given the wood of the vine among the trees of the forest as fuel for the fire, so will I treat the people living in Jerusalem. ⁷I will set my face against ˣ them. Although they have come out of the fire ʸᶻ, the fire will yet consume them. And when I set my face against them, you will know that I am the LORD. ᵃ ⁸I will make the land desolate ᵇ because they have been unfaithful, ᶜ declares the Sovereign LORD."

JERUSALEM AS AN ADULTEROUS WIFE

16 The word of the LORD came to me: ²"Son of man, confront ᵈ Jerusalem with her detestable practices ᵉ ³and say, 'This is what the Sovereign LORD says to Jerusalem: Your ancestry ᶠ and birth were in the land of the Canaanites; your father ᵍ was an Amorite ʰ and your mother a Hittite. ⁱ ⁴On the day you were born ʲ your cord was not cut, nor were you washed with water to make you clean, nor were you rubbed with salt or wrapped in cloths. ⁵No one looked on you with pity or had compassion enough to do any of these things for you. Rather, you were thrown out into the open field, for on the day you were born you were despised.

⁶" 'Then I passed by and saw you kicking about in your blood, and as you lay there in your blood I said to you, "Live!" ᵃᵏ ⁷I made you grow ˡ like a plant of the field. You grew and developed and entered puberty. Your breasts had formed and your hair had grown, yet you were stark naked. ᵐ

⁸" 'Later I passed by, and when I looked at you and saw that you were old enough for love, I spread the corner of my garment ⁿ over you and covered your nakedness. I gave you my solemn oath and entered into a covenant ᵒ with you, declares the Sovereign LORD, and you became mine. ᵖ

⁹" 'I bathed you with water and washed q the blood from you and put ointments on you. ¹⁰I clothed you with an embroidered ʳ dress and put sandals of fine leather on you. I dressed you in fine linen ˢ and covered you with costly garments. ᵗ ¹¹I adorned you with jewelry: ᵘ I put bracelets ᵛ on your arms and a necklace ʷ around your neck, ¹²and I put a ring on your nose, ˣ earrings ʸ on your ears and a beautiful crown ᶻ on your head. ᵃ ¹³So you were adorned with gold and silver; your clothes ᵇ were of fine linen and costly fabric and embroidered cloth. Your food was honey, olive oil ᶜ and the finest flour. You became very beautiful and rose to be a queen. ᵈ ¹⁴And your fame ᵉ spread among the nations on ac-

---

ᵃ 6 A few Hebrew manuscripts, Septuagint and Syriac; most Hebrew manuscripts repeat the last clause.

15:7 *Although they have come out of the fire.* A reference to the siege of Jerusalem in 597 B.C., which resulted in the exile of which Ezekiel was a part (see 1:2; 2Ki 24:10–16). *fire will yet consume them.* Prophecy threatening another and more devastating siege—Ezekiel's main message before 586 (see 5:2,4; 10:2,7).

16:1–63 The whole history of God's dealings with Jerusalem is graphically portrayed in an allegory that highlights the Lord's great goodness to the city on the one hand and the depth of the city's unfaithfulness to him on the other. Here Jerusalem as a royal city among the other cities of the world is in focus and serves as an analogue and representative of Israel. She is the city God had chosen to be the site of his temple (see 1Ki 9:3; 2Ch 7:1–3; Ps 68:16; 78:68–69; 132:13–16), and he had elevated her as "the city of the Great King" (Ps 48:2), to be the earthly center of his kingly rule in human affairs. He had married her (see v. 8 and note) and provided for her richly. But she turned to the false gods to supply her needs and allied herself with the great empires around her (Egypt [v. 26], Assyria [v. 28] and Babylon [v. 29]) to provide her security. So God accuses her of unfaithfulness to him, like that of an adulterous wife (see Ex 34:15 and note).

16:3 *Your ancestry and birth.* Jerusalem had a centuries-old, pre-Israelite history (see notes on Ge 14:18; Ecc 1:16), and the city had long resisted Israelite conquest (Jos 15:63). It became fully Israelite only after David's conquest (2Sa 5:6–9). *father ... mother.* A reference to Jerusalem's non-Israelite origin generally, not to any specific individuals. *Amorite.* Cf. v. 45. Like the Canaanites, the Amorites were pre-Israelite, Semitic inhabitants of Canaan (see Ge 10:16 and note; 48:22; Jos 5:1 and note; 10:5; Jdg 1:34–36). *Hittite.* The Hittites were non-Semitic residents of Canaan, who had flourished in Asia Minor during the second millennium B.C. (see Ge 10:15 and note; 23:10–20; 26:34; 1Sa 26:6; 2Sa 11:2–27; 1Ki 11:1).

16:4 *rubbed with salt.* This practice has been observed among Arab peasants as late as A.D. 1918. *wrapped in cloths.* Cf. Lk 2:7.
16:5 *thrown out into the open field.* Abandoned to die. Exposure of infants, common in ancient pagan societies, was abhorrent to Israel.

16:6 *blood.* Of childbirth. *Live!* God's basic desire for all people, summed up in one word (see 18:23,32; 1Ti 2:4; 2Pe 3:9).
16:7 *hair.* Pubic hair.
16:8 *spread the corner of my garment.* Symbolic of entering a marriage relationship (see notes on Dt 22:30; Ru 3:9). *covenant.* Since the young woman symbolizes Jerusalem, this does not refer to the Sinai covenant but to marriage as a covenant (see Mal 2:14).
16:9 *blood.* Menstrual blood, indicating sexual maturity.
16:10 *embroidered dress ... sandals of fine leather ... fine linen.* Representative of the very best garments. *embroidered dress.* See 27:16,24; colored, variegated material fit for a queen (see Ps 45:14). *sandals of fine leather.* The same kind of leather was used to cover the tabernacle (see Ex 25:5; 26:14).
16:11 *bracelets on your arms.* See Ge 24:22.
16:12 *ring.* Not piercing the nose but worn on the outer part of the nose (see Ge 24:47). *earrings.* Circular ear ornaments, worn by men (Nu 31:50). The Hebrew for this word is not the same as that used in Ge 35:4; Ex 32:2–3. *crown.* The wedding crown (see SS 3:11, where the groom wears it).
16:13 *gold and silver.* Cf. Hos 2:8. *olive oil.* Cf. Hos 2:8. For the combination of honey and oil, see Dt 32:13. *finest flour.* Used in offerings and therefore of high quality (see v. 19; 46:14). *You became very beautiful.* Cf. Eph 5:27.
16:14 *your fame spread.* Especially in the time of David and Solomon.

count of your beauty, *f* because the splendor I had given you made your beauty perfect, declares the Sovereign LORD. *g*

¹⁵" 'But you trusted in your beauty and used your fame to become a prostitute. You lavished your favors on anyone who passed by *h* and your beauty became his. *i* ¹⁶You took some of your garments to make gaudy high places, *j* where you carried on your prostitution. *k* You went to him, and he possessed your beauty. *a* ¹⁷You also took the fine jewelry I gave you, the jewelry made of my gold and silver, and you made for yourself male idols and engaged in prostitution with them. *l* ¹⁸And you took your embroidered clothes to put on them, and you offered my oil and incense *m* before them. ¹⁹Also the food I provided for you—the flour, olive oil and honey I gave you to eat—you offered as fragrant incense before them. That is what happened, declares the Sovereign LORD. *n*

²⁰" 'And you took your sons and daughters *o* whom you bore to me *p* and sacrificed them as food to the idols. Was your prostitution not enough? *q* ²¹You slaughtered my children and sacrificed them to the idols. *r* ²²In all your detestable practices and your prostitution you did not remember the days of your youth, *s* when you were naked and bare, *t* kicking about in your blood. *u*

²³" 'Woe! *v* Woe to you, declares the Sovereign LORD. In addition to all your other wickedness, ²⁴you built a mound for yourself and made a lofty shrine *w* in every public square. *x* ²⁵At every street corner *y* you built your lofty shrines and degraded your beauty, spreading your legs with increasing promiscuity to anyone who passed by. *z* ²⁶You engaged in prostitution *a* with the Egyptians, *b* your neighbors with large genitals, and aroused my anger *c* with your increasing promiscuity. *d* ²⁷So I stretched out my hand *e* against you and reduced your territory; I gave you over *f* to the greed of your enemies, the daughters of the Philistines, *g* who were shocked by your lewd conduct. ²⁸You engaged in prostitution with the Assyrians *h* too, because you were insatiable; and even after that, you still were not satisfied. *i* ²⁹Then you increased your promiscuity to include Babylonia, *b j* a land of merchants, but even with this you were not satisfied. *k*

³⁰" 'I am filled with fury against you, *c* declares the Sovereign LORD, when you do all these things, acting like a brazen prostitute! *l* ³¹When you built your mounds at every street corner and made your lofty shrines *m* in every public square, you were unlike a prostitute, because you scorned payment.

³²" 'You adulterous wife! You prefer strangers to your own husband! ³³All prostitutes receive gifts, *n* but you give gifts *o* to all your lovers, bribing them to come to you from everywhere for your illicit favors. *p* ³⁴So in your prostitution you are the opposite of others; no one runs after you for your favors. You are the very opposite, for you give payment and none is given to you.

³⁵" 'Therefore, you prostitute, hear the word of the LORD! ³⁶This is what the Sovereign LORD says: Because you poured out your lust and exposed your nakedness in your promiscuity with your lovers, and because of all your detestable idols, and because you gave them your children's blood, *q* ³⁷therefore I am going to gather all your lovers, with whom you found pleasure, those you loved as well as those you hated. I will gather them against you from all around and will strip *r* you in front of them, and they will see all your nakedness. *s* ³⁸I will sentence you to the punishment of women who commit adultery and who shed

---

a 16 The meaning of the Hebrew for this sentence is uncertain.   *b 29* Or *Chaldea*   *c 30* Or *How feverish is your heart,*

16:14 *r* S Est 1:11;
S Ps 48:2; S La 2:15
g S Eze 5:5
16:15 *h* ver 25
i S Isa 57:8;
S Jer 2:20; Eze 23:3;
27:3
16:16 *j* S Isa 57:7
k S 2Ki 23:7
16:17 *l* S Eze 7:20;
Hos 2:13
16:18 *m* S Jer 44:5
16:19 *n* Hos 2:8
16:20 *o* S Jer 7:31
p Ex 13:2 *q* Ps 106:37-
38; S Isa 57:5
Eze 23:37
16:21 *r* S 2Ki 17:17;
S Jer 19:5
16:22 *s* S Ps 25:7;
S 88:15; Jer 2:2;
Hos 2:15; 11:1
t Hos 2:3 *u* ver 6
16:23 *v* Eze 24:6
16:24 *w* ver 31;
Isa 57:7 *x* Ps 78:58;
S Jer 2:20; 3:2;
S 44:21; Eze 20:28
16:25 *y* S Jer 3:2
z ver 15; S Pr 9:14
16:26 *a* S Isa 23:17
b S Jer 3:1
c S 1Ki 14:9;
S Eze 8:17
d S Isa 57:8; Jer 11:15;
Eze 20:8; 23:19-21
16:27 *e* Eze 20:33;
25:13 *f* S Jer 34:20
g S 2Ch 28:18
16:28 *h* S 2Ki 16:7
i Isa 57:8
16:29 *j* S Jer 3:1;
Eze 23:14-17 *k* Na 3:4
16:30 *l* S Jer 3:3
16:31 *m* S ver 24
16:33 *n* S Ge 30:15
o Isa 30:6; 57:9
p Hos 8:9-10
16:36 *q* S Jer 19:5;
Eze 23:10
16:37 *r* Hos 2:3
s S Isa 47:3;
S Jer 13:22;
Eze 23:22; Hos 2:10;
8:10; Rev 17:16

16:15 *favors.* Sexual favors. Verb and noun forms of the Hebrew for this word occur 23 times in this chapter. *anyone who passed by.* Cf. Ge 38:14-16.

16:16 *garments.* All of the Lord's previous gifts were used by Jerusalem in prostituting herself. Cloths of some kind were needed in the Asherah worship practices (see 2Ki 23:7). They may have been used as curtains or as bedding (see Am 2:7-8).

16:20 *sons and daughters . . . sacrificed.* See 20:26,31 and note; 23:37; 2Ki 21:6; 23:10; Jer 7:31 and note; 19:5; 32:35. For laws against child sacrifice, see Lev 18:21; Dt 18:10; cf. Lev 20:2-5; Dt 12:31.

16:24 *mound . . . lofty shrine.* Centers of idol worship were built not only in the countryside but also in Jerusalem itself.

16:26-29 *Egyptians . . . Philistines . . . Assyrians . . . Babylonia.* The historical sequence of Jerusalem's political alliances with these four powers.

16:26 *neighbors.* Nowhere else in the OT are the Egyptians called "neighbors." *large genitals.* See 23:20. The language re-

flects both God's and Ezekiel's disgust with Jerusalem's apostasy.

16:27 *reduced your territory.* After the 701 B.C. siege of Jerusalem, the Assyrian king, Sennacherib, gave some of Jerusalem's territory to the Philistines. *shocked by your lewd conduct.* Cf. Am 3:9,13 and notes.

16:29 *Babylonia, a land of merchants.* See note on Rev 14:8; see also Rev 18:11-19,23.

16:32 *your own husband.* The Lord himself (see v. 8 and note). Elsewhere the prophets speak about the Lord as the husband of his people (see Jer 3:14; 31:32; Hos 2:16-17 and notes; cf. Ex 34:15 and note).

16:33 *you give gifts to all your lovers.* Jerusalem's perversity is here pictured as worse than adultery and ordinary prostitution (see also v. 34).

16:37 *strip you.* A reversal of the marriage covering (v. 8) and a return to the state described in v. 7.

16:38 *sentence you.* The punishment prescribed in the law was death (see Lev 20:10; Dt 22:22) by stoning (Dt 22:21-24; Jn

16:38 ᵗ S Ge 38:24
ᵘ S Lev 20:10;
Ps 79:3,5; Eze 23:25;
Zep 1:17
16:39 ᵛ S 2Ki 18:11
ʷ Eze 21:31; Hos 2:3
16:40 ˣ Jn 8:5,7
16:41 ʸ S Dt 13:16;
S Jer 19:13 ᶻ Eze 23:10
ᵃ Eze 22:15; 23:27,48
16:42 ᵇ 2Sa 24:25;
Isa 40:1-2; 54:9;
S Eze 5:13; 39:29
16:43 ᶜ S Ex 15:24;
Ps 78:42 ᵈ Eze 22:31
ᵉ Eze 11:21
16:44 ᶠ S Ps 49:4
16:45 ᵍ S Eze 14:5
ʰ Jer 44:19 / ver 3;
Eze 23:2
16:46 ⁱ S Jer 3:7
ᵏ Ge 13:10-13;
S 18:20; Jer 3:8-11;
Eze 23:4; Rev 11:8
16:47 ˡ S Eze 5:7
16:48 ᵐ S Ge 15:2
ⁿ S Ge 19:25
ᵒ Mt 10:15; 11:23-24
16:49 ᵖ S Isa 1:10
�q Ps 138:6; Eze 28:2
ʳ Isa 22:13
ˢ S Ge 13:13; 19:9;
S Jer 5:28; Eze 18:7,
12,16; Am 6:4-6;
Lk 12:16-20; 16:19;
Jas 5:5
16:50 ᵗ Ps 18:27
ᵘ Ge 18:20-21; S 19:5
16:51 ᵛ Jer 3:8-11;
Eze 5:6-7; 23:11
16:52 ʷ S Jer 3:11
ˣ Eze 23:35
16:53 ʸ S Dt 30:3;
Isa 19:24-25;
S Jer 48:47
ᶻ Eze 39:25
16:54 ᵃ S Jer 2:26
16:55 ᵇ Eze 36:11;
Mal 3:4
16:57 ᶜ S Ps 137:3
ᵈ 2Ki 16:6
16:58 ᵉ Eze 23:49
16:59 ᶠ S ver 8;
Eze 17:19
16:60 ᵍ S Ge 6:18;
S 9:15 ʰ S Ps 25:7;
S Jer 2:2 ⁱ S Ge 9:16;
Eze 37:26
16:61 ʲ ver 63;
Eze 20:43; 43:10;
44:13

blood; ᶠ I will bring on you the blood vengeance of my wrath and jealous anger. ᵘ ³⁹Then I will deliver you into the hands ᵛ of your lovers, and they will tear down your mounds and destroy your lofty shrines. They will strip you of your clothes and take your fine jewelry and leave you naked and bare. ʷ ⁴⁰They will bring a mob against you, who will stone ˣ you and hack you to pieces with their swords. ⁴¹They will burn down ʸ your houses and inflict punishment on you in the sight of many women. ᶻ I will put a stop ᵃ to your prostitution, and you will no longer pay your lovers. ⁴²Then my wrath against you will subside and my jealous anger will turn away from you; I will be calm and no longer angry. ᵇ

⁴³" 'Because you did not remember ᶜ the days of your youth but enraged me with all these things, I will surely bring down ᵈ on your head what you have done, declares the Sovereign Lᴏʀᴅ. Did you not add lewdness to all your other detestable practices? ᵉ

⁴⁴" 'Everyone who quotes proverbs ᶠ will quote this proverb about you: "Like mother, like daughter." ⁴⁵You are a true daughter of your mother, who despised ᵍ her husband ʰ and her children; and you are a true sister of your sisters, who despised their husbands and their children. Your mother was a Hittite and your father an Amorite. ⁱ ⁴⁶Your older sister ʲ was Samaria, who lived to the north of you with her daughters; and your younger sister, who lived to the south of you with her daughters, was Sodom. ᵏ ⁴⁷You not only followed their ways and copied their detestable practices, but in all your ways you soon became more depraved than they. ˡ ⁴⁸As surely as I live, declares the Sovereign ᵐ Lᴏʀᴅ, your sister Sodom ⁿ and her daughters never did what you and your daughters have done. ᵒ

⁴⁹" 'Now this was the sin of your sister Sodom: ᵖ She and her daughters were arrogant, q overfed and unconcerned; ʳ they did not help the poor and needy. ˢ ⁵⁰They were haughty ᵗ and did detestable things before me. Therefore I did away with them as you have seen. ᵘ ⁵¹Samaria did not commit half the sins you did. You have done more detestable things than they, and have made your sisters seem righteous by all these things you have done. ᵛ ⁵²Bear your disgrace, for you have furnished some justification for your sisters. Because your sins were more vile than theirs, they appear more righteous ʷ than you. So then, be ashamed and bear ˣ your disgrace, for you have made your sisters appear righteous.

⁵³" 'However, I will restore ʸ the fortunes of Sodom and her daughters and of Samaria and her daughters, and your fortunes along with them, ᶻ ⁵⁴so that you may bear your disgrace ᵃ and be ashamed of all you have done in giving them comfort. ⁵⁵And your sisters, Sodom with her daughters and Samaria with her daughters, will return to what they were before; and you and your daughters will return to what you were before. ᵇ ⁵⁶You would not even mention your sister Sodom in the day of your pride, ⁵⁷before your wickedness was uncovered. Even so, you are now scorned ᶜ by the daughters of Edom ᵃ ᵈ and all her neighbors and the daughters of the Philistines—all those around you who despise you. ⁵⁸You will bear the consequences of your lewdness and your detestable practices, declares the Lᴏʀᴅ. ᵉ

⁵⁹" 'This is what the Sovereign Lᴏʀᴅ says: I will deal with you as you deserve, because you have despised my oath by breaking the covenant. ᶠ ⁶⁰Yet I will remember the covenant ᵍ I made with you in the days of your youth, ʰ and I will establish an everlasting covenant ⁱ with you. ⁶¹Then you will remember your ways and be ashamed ʲ when you receive

ᵃ 57 Many Hebrew manuscripts and Syriac; most Hebrew manuscripts, Septuagint and Vulgate *Aram*

8:5–7).*jealous anger.* See v. 42; see also notes on Ex 20:5; Zec 1:14.
16:39 *your mounds … your lofty shrines.* See vv. 24–25.
16:40 See 23:46–47.
16:43 *bring down on your head what you have done.* See note on Ob 15.

▲ **16:44** *Like mother, like daughter.* Referring to Jerusalem's continual and seemingly hereditary tendency toward evil (cf. vv. 3,45).
16:45 *Hittite … Amorite.* See note on v. 3.
16:46 *Your older sister was Samaria.* Historically, Samaria was not founded as a royal city until after 880 B.C. (see note on 1Ki 16:24), so "older" in this allegory apparently alludes to the fact that Samaria ruled over a significantly larger kingdom than Jerusalem did. *daughters.* Suburbs or satellite cities.

▲ **16:47** *more depraved than they.* The Bible frequently compares a city or people to Sodom (see v. 46) as the epitome of evil and degradation (see Ge 13:10 and note; Dt 29:23; 32:32; Isa 1:9–10 and note; 3:9; Jer 23:14; La 4:6; Mt 10:15; 11:23–24; Jude 7).

▲ **16:49** *sin of your sister Sodom.* Here social injustice rather than sexual perversion (Ge 19) is highlighted.
16:51–52 *righteous.* Relatively innocent.
16:56 *day of your pride.* Referring to a time long before Ezekiel, when Jerusalem (as an Israelite city) was still relatively uncorrupted—as in the days of David and the early years of Solomon.
16:57 *scorned by the daughters of Edom.* The OT frequently condemns Edom for this (see 25:12–14; 35:5 and note; Isa 63:1; Introduction to Obadiah: Unity and Theme; Ob 10–14 and notes).
16:59–63 In God's concluding word concerning Jerusalem's future reformation and restoration, the city's role as representative of Israel in the allegory is foregrounded (see note on vv. 1–63), so that his words about remembering the covenant and establishing an everlasting covenant (see v. 60; cf. v. 62) parallel what is elsewhere said of Israel itself (see 37:26; Isa 55:3; Jer 32:40 and notes).
16:59 *covenant.* See v. 8 and note.
16:60 *I will remember the covenant.* Though Jerusalem did not (v. 43).
16:61 *will remember … be ashamed.* See v. 63. Jerusalem (Israel) will remember—to her everlasting shame.

your sisters, both those who are older than you and those who are younger. I will give them to you as daughters, *k* but not on the basis of my covenant with you. ⁶²So I will establish my covenant *l* with you, and you will know that I am the LORD. *m* ⁶³Then, when I make atonement *n* for you for all you have done, you will remember and be ashamed *o* and never again open your mouth *p* because of your humiliation, declares the Sovereign LORD. *q* ' "

TWO EAGLES AND A VINE

17 The word of the LORD came to me: ²"Son of man, set forth an allegory and tell it to the house of Israel as a parable. *r* ³Say to them, 'This is what the Sovereign LORD says: A great eagle *s* with powerful wings, long feathers and full plumage of varied colors came to Lebanon. *t* Taking hold of the top of a cedar, ⁴he broke off *u* its topmost shoot and carried it away to a land of merchants, where he planted it in a city of traders.

⁵ 'He took one of the seedlings of the land and put it in fertile soil. He planted it like a willow by abundant water, *v* ⁶and it sprouted and became a low, spreading vine. Its branches *w* turned toward him, but its roots remained under it. So it became a vine and produced branches and put out leafy boughs. *x*

⁷ 'But there was another great eagle with powerful wings and full plumage. The vine now sent out its roots toward him from the plot where it was planted and stretched out its branches to him for water. *y* ⁸It had been planted in good soil by abundant water so that it would produce branches, *z* bear fruit and become a splendid vine.'

⁹"Say to them, 'This is what the Sovereign LORD says: Will it thrive? Will it not be uprooted and stripped of its fruit so that it withers? All its new growth will wither. It will not take a strong arm or many people to pull it up by the roots. *a* ¹⁰It has been planted, *b* but will it thrive? Will it not wither completely when the east wind strikes it—wither away in the plot where it grew? *c* ' "

¹¹Then the word of the LORD came to me: ¹²"Say to this rebellious house, 'Do you not know what these things mean? *d* ' Say to them: 'The king of Babylon went to Jerusalem and carried off her king and her nobles, *e* bringing them back with him to Babylon. *f* ¹³Then he took a member of the royal family and made a treaty *g* with him, putting him under oath. *h* He also carried away the leading men *i* of the land, ¹⁴so that the kingdom would be brought low, *j* unable to rise again, surviving only by keeping his treaty. ¹⁵But the king rebelled *k* against him by sending his envoys to Egypt *l* to get horses and a large army. *m* Will he succeed? Will he who does such things escape? Will he break the treaty and yet escape? *n*

¹⁶" 'As surely as I live, declares the Sovereign LORD, he shall die *o* in Babylon, in the land of the king who put him on the throne, whose oath he despised and whose treaty he broke. *p* ¹⁷Pharaoh *q* with his mighty army and great horde will be of no help to him in war, when ramps *r* are built and siege works erected to destroy many lives. *s* ¹⁸He despised the oath by breaking the covenant. Because he had given his hand in pledge *t* and yet did all these things, he shall not escape.

¹⁹" 'Therefore this is what the Sovereign LORD says: As surely as I live, I will bring down on his head my oath that he despised and my covenant that he broke. *u* ²⁰I will spread my net *v* for him, and he will be caught in my snare. I will bring him to Babylon and execute

---

16:61 *k* S Isa 43:6
16:62 *l* S Dt 29:14
m S Jer 24:7;
Eze 20:37, 43-44;
34:25; 37:26;
Hos 2:19-20
16:63 *n* Ps 65:3;
78:38; 79:9
o Eze 36:31-32
p Ro 3:19 *q* Ps 39:9;
Da 9:7-8
17:2 *r* S Jdg 14:12;
S Eze 20:49
17:3 *s* S Dt 28:49;
Jer 49:22; Da 7:4;
Hos 8:1 *t* S Jer 22:23
17:4 *u* S Isa 10:33
17:5 *v* Dt 8:7-9;
Ps 1:3; Isa 44:4;
Eze 31:5
17:6 *w* S Isa 18:5
x S Job 5:3
17:7 *y* Eze 31:4
17:8 *z* Job 18:19;
Mal 4:1
17:9 *a* Jer 42:10;
Am 2:9
17:10 *b* S Job 1:19;
Hos 12:1; 13:15
c S Eze 15:4
17:12 *d* S Eze 12:9
e 2Ki 24:15
f S Dt 21:10;
S 2Ch 36:10;
Eze 24:19
17:13 *g* S Ex 23:32;
S Jer 37:1 *h* 2Ch 36:13
i Isa 3:2
17:14 *j* Eze 29:14
17:15 *k* Jer 52:3
l S Isa 30:2; S Jer 37:5
m S Dt 17:16
n S Ps 56:7;
S Isa 30:5; Jer 34:3;
38:18; Eze 29:16
17:16 *o* S Jer 52:11;
Eze 12:13
p S 2Ki 24:17
17:17 *q* Jer 37:7
S Eze 4:2
s S Isa 36:6; Jer 37:5;
Eze 29:6-7
17:18 *t* S 2Ki 10:15;
1Ch 29:24
17:19 *u* Jer 7:9;
S Eze 16:59; 21:23;
Hos 10:4
17:20 *v* S Eze 12:13;
32:3

A **16:63** *when I make atonement for you.* God himself will do for faithless Jerusalem what she cannot do for herself (cf. Ro 3:23; 1Jn 2:2 and notes).

C **17:1-24** An allegory/parable symbolizing King Zedekiah's vacillating royal policy that led to his downfall. The allegory is presented in vv. 1-10; its explanation follows in vv. 11-21; and vv. 22-24 append a promise of better times to come, utilizing the imagery of the allegory.

17:3 *great eagle.* Nebuchadnezzar (see v. 12). *Lebanon.* Jerusalem (see v. 12). *cedar.* David's dynasty; his royal family.

17:4 *topmost shoot.* Jehoiachin. *land of merchants.* The country of Babylonia (see v. 12; 16:29 and note). *city of traders.* Babylon.

17:5 *one of the seedlings.* Zedekiah, son of Josiah; he was the brother of Jehoahaz and Jehoiakim and uncle of Jehoiachin (see 2Ki 23-24). *planted it.* Made him king (2Ki 24:17).

17:6 *low, spreading vine.* No longer a tall cedar, because thousands of Judah's leading citizens had been deported (see 2Ki 24:15-16; see also Jer 52:28). But see note on 15:1-8.

C **17:7** *another great eagle.* An Egyptian pharaoh, either Psammetichus II (595-589 B.C.) or Hophra (589-570).

Hophra, mentioned in Jer 44:30, is probably the pharaoh who offered help to Jerusalem in 586 (see Jer 37:5). If the fact that ch. 17 is located between ch. 8 (dated 592) and ch. 20 (dated 591) is chronologically meaningful, Psammetichus is meant. *sent out its roots toward him.* Zedekiah appealed to Egypt for military aid (v. 15), an act of rebellion against Nebuchadnezzar (see 2Ki 24:20).

17:10 *east wind.* The hot, dry wind known today as the khamsin, which withers vegetation (see 19:12). Here it stands for Nebuchadnezzar and his Babylonian forces.

17:12 *this rebellious house.* See 2:3 and note.

17:15 *Will he break the treaty and yet escape?* The point of the chapter (see vv. 16,18).

17:16 *he shall die in Babylon.* See 2Ki 25:7.

A **17:19** *my oath ... my covenant.* The king of Judah would have sworn faithfulness to the treaty in the name of the Lord. His oath would have taken some such form as "May the Lord slay me if I do not remain true to this treaty" (a self-maledictory oath; see notes on Ge 9:13; 15:17; 17:10). To swear such an oath and then violate it was to treat the Lord as if he were powerless.

17:20 ʷS Jer 2:35
ˣS Eze 15:8
17:21 ʸS Eze 12:14
ᶻ2Ki 25:11
ᵃS Lev 26:33;
S 2Ki 25:5; Zec 2:6
ᵇS Jer 27:8
17:22 ᶜS 2Ki 19:30;
S Isa 4:2 ᵈver 23;
Isa 2:2; S Jer 23:5;
Eze 20:40; 36:1,36;
37:22; 40:2; 43:12
17:23 ᵉS ver 22;
S Jer 31:12 ᶠS Isa 27:6
ᵍPs 92:12; S Isa 2:2;
Eze 31:6; Da 4:12;
Hos 14:5-7;
S Mt 13:32
17:24 ʰS Ps 96:12;
Isa 2:13 ⁱS Ps 52:5
ʲS Nu 17:8; Da 5:21
ᵏS 1Sa 2:7-8;
Eze 19:12; 21:26;
22:14; 37:13; Am 9:11
18:2 ˡS Job 21:19;
Isa 3:15; Jer 31:29
18:3 ᵐS Ps 49:4
18:4 ⁿS 2Ki 14:6;
S Pr 13:21 ᵒver 20;
S Ge 18:23;
S Ex 17:14;
S Job 21:20; Isa 42:5;
Eze 33:8; S Ro 6:23
18:6 ᵖS Eze 6:2
ᵠDt 4:19; S Eze 6:13;
20:24; Am 5:26
ʳS Lev 12:2; S 15:24
18:7 ˢS Ex 22:21;
Mal 3:5; Jas 5:4
ᵗS Ex 22:26
ᵘS Ex 20:15
ᵛS Job 22:7
ʷDt 15:11;
S Eze 16:49;
S Mt 25:36; Lk 3:11

judgment ʷ on him there because he was unfaithful ˣ to me. ²¹All his choice troops will fall by the sword, ʸ and the survivors ᶻ will be scattered to the winds. ᵃ Then you will know that I the LORD have spoken. ᵇ

²²" 'This is what the Sovereign LORD says: I myself will take a shoot ᶜ from the very top of a cedar and plant it; I will break off a tender sprig from its topmost shoots and plant it on a high and lofty mountain. ᵈ ²³On the mountain heights ᵉ of Israel I will plant it; it will produce branches and bear fruit ᶠ and become a splendid cedar. Birds of every kind will nest in it; they will find shelter in the shade of its branches. ᵍ ²⁴All the trees of the forest ʰ will know that I the LORD bring down ⁱ the tall tree and make the low tree grow tall. I dry up the green tree and make the dry tree flourish. ʲ

" 'I the LORD have spoken, and I will do it. ᵏ ' "

THE ONE WHO SINS WILL DIE

18 The word of the LORD came to me: ²"What do you people mean by quoting this proverb about the land of Israel:

" 'The parents eat sour grapes,
　and the children's teeth are set on edge'? ˡ

³"As surely as I live, declares the Sovereign LORD, you will no longer quote this proverb ᵐ in Israel. ⁴For everyone belongs to me, the parent as well as the child—both alike belong to me. The one who sins ⁿ is the one who will die. ᵒ

⁵ "Suppose there is a righteous man
　who does what is just and right.
⁶ He does not eat at the mountain ᵖ shrines
　or look to the idols ᵠ of the house of Israel.
He does not defile his neighbor's wife
　or have sexual relations with a woman during her period. ʳ
⁷ He does not oppress ˢ anyone,
　but returns what he took in pledge ᵗ for a loan.
He does not commit robbery ᵘ
　but gives his food to the hungry ᵛ
　and provides clothing for the naked. ʷ
⁸ He does not lend to them at interest

A **17:22** *I myself.* A beautiful Messianic promise follows, using the previous imagery in a totally new and unexpected way. *shoot.* A member of David's family (cf. Isa 11:1; Zec 3:8; 6:12 and notes). *cedar.* See note on v. 3. *plant it.* Make him king (see v. 5). *high and lofty mountain.* Jerusalem (see Isa 2:2–4 and note).
17:23 *Birds ... will nest in it.* For similar imagery applied to a mighty king, see Da 4:10–12,20–22; cf. Mk 4:32.
17:24 *trees of the forest.* Kings and rulers of the world. *bring down the tall tree ... make the dry tree flourish.* See 1Sa 2:4–8 and notes; cf. Isa 2:12–18.

A **C** **18:1–32** A word to silence those who complained that they were being made to suffer for the sins of their ancestors rather than for their own sins. That sin and guilt are not always purely individual but often have a communal and thus also a cumulative dimension is the pervasive testimony of the OT (see, e.g., Ex 20:5; Jdg 7:24; 1Ki 14:14–16 and notes; see also Ex 34:7; 1Ki 22:16–20; 23:26–27; 24:1–4; 2Ki 21:10–15; Isa 5:1–7; Jer 1:15–16; 5:1–17; 17:1–4; Am 2:4–16; 5:12). But when the Jerusalemites charged God with injustice, as if they themselves were not guilty, that called for a sharp corrective word—they had not turned away from the sinful ways of their ancestors after the manner specified in vv. 14–17, 27–28. This justification of God's way with Israel stands at the center of the series of oracles found in 13:1—24:14 (see note on 13:1–23).
A **18:2** *this proverb.* Jer 31:29 indicates that the proverb arose first in Jerusalem. Jeremiah predicted the cessation of the proverb, and Ezekiel said that its end had come. *about the land of Israel.* And about the fate of those who have suffered loss. *The parents ... on edge.* The proverb expresses self-pity and mocks the justice of God. *set on edge.* The Hebrew for this phrase per-

haps means "blunted" or "worn" (cf. Ecc 10:10), but it may refer to the sensation in the mouth when eating something bitter or sour.
18:3 *As surely as I live.* See note on 5:11.
A **18:4** *The one who sins is the one who will die.* Or "Only the one ..." Ezekiel spoke out against a false use the people were making of a doctrine of inherited guilt (perhaps based on a false understanding of Ex 20:5; 34:7). What follows is his description of three men, standing for three generations, who break the three/four-generation pattern.
18:5 *righteous man.* The first generation that keeps the law. The following 15 commandments are partly ceremonial but are mostly moral injunctions. See the Ten Commandments in Ex 20 and Dt 5; cf. Ps 15:2–5; 24:3–6; Isa 33:15; cf. also notes on Ps 1:5; 119:121. *just and right.* Emphasized by Ezekiel in chs. 18 (see vv. 19,21,27) and 33 (see vv. 14,16,19; see also note on Ps 119:121).
18:6 *eat at the mountain shrines.* Eating meat sacrificed to idols on the high places (see 6:3; Hos 4:13). *look to.* Seek help from (see 23:27; 33:25; Ps 121:1). *idols.* See note on 6:4. *defile.* Adultery (condemned in Ex 20:14; Dt 22:22; Lev 18:20; 20:10) is here associated with a menstrual prohibition (see Lev 15:19–24; 18:19; 20:18) which is absent from the two listings that follow (cf. vv. 11,15).
18:7 *oppress.* The rich taking advantage of the poor. *returns what he took in pledge.* See Ex 22:26; Dt 24:12–13; Am 2:8. *robbery.* See the commandment against stealing in Ex 20:15; Dt 5:19. This is violent (armed) robbery rather than secret theft or burglary (see Lev 19:13). *food to the hungry.* See Dt 15:7–11; Mt 25:31–46.
18:8 *lend ... at interest.* See 22:12; see also Ex 22:25–27 and note.

or take a profit from them. *x*
He withholds his hand from doing wrong
     and judges fairly *y* between two parties.
    [9] He follows my decrees *z*
     and faithfully keeps my laws.
    That man is righteous; *a*
     he will surely live, *b*

declares the Sovereign LORD.

[10] "Suppose he has a violent son, who sheds blood *c* or does any of these other things *a*
[11] (though the father has done none of them):

    "He eats at the mountain shrines. *d*
    He defiles his neighbor's wife.
    [12] He oppresses the poor *e* and needy.
    He commits robbery.
    He does not return what he took in pledge. *f*
    He looks to the idols.
    He does detestable things. *g*
    [13] He lends at interest and takes a profit. *h*

Will such a man live? He will not! Because he has done all these detestable things, he is
to be put to death; his blood will be on his own head. *i*
    [14] "But suppose this son has a son who sees all the sins his father commits, and though
he sees them, he does not do such things: *j*

    [15] "He does not eat at the mountain shrines *k*
     or look to the idols *l* of the house of Israel.
    He does not defile his neighbor's wife.
    [16] He does not oppress anyone
     or require a pledge for a loan.
    He does not commit robbery
     but gives his food to the hungry *m*
     and provides clothing for the naked. *n*
    [17] He withholds his hand from mistreating the poor
     and takes no interest or profit from them.
    He keeps my laws *o* and follows my decrees.

He will not die for his father's sin; he will surely live. [18] But his father will die for his own
sin, because he practiced extortion, robbed his brother and did what was wrong among
his people.
    [19] "Yet you ask, 'Why does the son not share the guilt of his father?' Since the son has
done what is just and right and has been careful to keep all my decrees, he will surely
live. *p* [20] The one who sins is the one who will die. *q* The child will not share the guilt of the
parent, nor will the parent share the guilt of the child. The righteousness of the righteous
will be credited to them, and the wickedness of the wicked will be charged against them. *r*
    [21] "But if *s* the wicked turn away from all the sins they have committed and keep all my
decrees *t* and do what is just and right, they will surely live; they will not die. *u* [22] None of
the offenses they have committed will be remembered against them. Because of the righteous things they have done, they will live. *v* [23] Do I take any pleasure in the death of the
wicked? declares the Sovereign LORD. Rather, am I not pleased *w* when they turn from
their ways and live? *x*
    [24] "But if the righteous turn *y* from their righteousness and commit sin and do the same

---

a 10 Or things to a brother

18:8 *x* S Ex 18:21;
22:25; S Lev 25:35-
37; Dt 23:19-20
y S Jer 22:3; Zec 8:16
18:9 *z* S Lev 19:37
a Hab 2:4
b S Lev 18:5;
S Eze 11:12; 20:11;
Am 5:4
18:10 *c* Ex 21:12;
Eze 22:6
18:11 *d* Eze 22:9
18:12 *e* S Ex 22:22;
S Job 24:9; Am 4:1
f S Ex 22:27
g 2Ki 21:11; Isa 59:6-
7; S Jer 22:17;
S Eze 16:49; Hab 2:6
18:13 *h* Ex 22:25
i S Lev 20:9;
Eze 33:4-5; Hos 12:14
18:14 *j* S Pr 23:24
18:15 *k* Eze 22:9
l S Ps 24:4
18:16 *m* Isa 58:7
n S Ex 22:27; Ps 41:1;
Isa 58:10; S Eze 16:49
18:17 *o* S Ps 1:2
18:19 *p* Ex 20:5;
Dt 5:9; Jer 15:4;
Zec 1:3-6
18:20 *q* S Nu 15:31
r Dt 24:16; S 1Ki 8:32;
2Ki 14:6; Isa 3:11;
S Eze 7:27; S 14:14;
S Mt 16:27; Jn 9:2
18:21 *s* Jer 18:8
t S Ge 26:5
u S Eze 13:22; 36:27
18:22 *v* Ps 18:20-24;
S Isa 43:25; Da 4:27;
Mic 7:19
18:23 *w* Ps 147:11
x S Job 37:23;
S La 3:33; S Eze 16:6;
Mic 7:18; S 1Ti 2:4
18:24 *y* S Jer 34:16

18:9 *That man is righteous; he will surely live.* After the
checklist of commandments has been gone over, the verdict is rendered (cf. Ps 15:5; 24:5). *live.* See note on 16:6. This is
life as more than mere existence; it includes communion with
God (see Ps 63:3; 73:27-28).
18:10 *violent son.* Evil, second generation. About half (eight) of
the previous commandments follow, but in a different order.
18:13 *his blood will be on his own head.* He is held responsible for his own sin (see Lev 20:9,11-12,16,27).
18:14 *a son.* Righteous, third generation. Twelve commandments follow.

18:20 *righteousness … credited to them.* See Ps 106:31 and note.
18:21 *But if the wicked turn … and keep … they will surely
live.* Verses 1-20 indicate that the chain of inherited guilt
can be broken, and vv. 21-29 teach that the power of guilt accumulated within a person's life can be overcome.
18:23 *Do I take any pleasure in the death of the wicked?* In addition to the answer in this verse and in v. 32, see 33:11; Jnh 4:11
and notes.
18:24 *But if the righteous turn.* See Heb 2:3; 2Pe 2:20-22
for warnings against those who knowingly and willfully
turn from righteousness.

18:24 ᶻS Eze 15:8
ᵃS 1Sa 15:11;
2Ch 24:17-20;
S Job 35:8; Pr 21:16;
S Eze 3:20; 20:27;
2Pe 2:20-22
18:25 ᵇJer 2:29
ᶜS Ge 18:25; Jer 12:1;
Eze 33:17; Zep 3:5;
Mal 2:17; 3:13-15
18:27 ᵈS Isa 1:18;
S Eze 13:22
18:28 ᵉS Isa 55:7
18:30 ᶠS Isa 1:27;
S Jer 35:15; Mt 3:2
ᵍEze 7:3; 24:14;
33:20; Hos 12:6;
1Pe 1:17
18:31 ʰS Jdg 6:8
ⁱPs 51:10 / Jer 27:13
ᵏS Isa 1:16-17;
S Eze 11:19; 36:26
18:32 ʲS Job 22:23;
Isa 55:7; Mal 3:7
ᵐS 2Ch 7:14;
S Job 37:23;
S Eze 16:6; 33:11
19:1 ⁿver 14;
Jer 7:29; 9:10,20;
Eze 26:17; 27:2,32;
28:12; 32:2,16; Am 5:1
ᵒS 2Ki 24:6
19:2 ᵖS Nu 23:24
�q S Ge 49:9
19:4 ʳS Job 41:2
ˢ2Ki 23:33-34;
2Ch 36:4; S La 4:20
19:5 ᵗS Ge 49:9
ᵘ2Ki 23:34
19:6 ᵛ2Ki 24:9;
2Ch 36:9
19:7 ʷEze 29:10;
30:12

detestable things the wicked do, will they live? None of the righteous things they have done will be remembered. Because of the unfaithfulness ᶻ they are guilty of and because of the sins they have committed, they will die. ᵃ

²⁵"Yet you say, 'The way of the Lord is not just.' ᵇ Hear, house of Israel: Is my way unjust? ᶜ Is it not your ways that are unjust? ²⁶If the righteous turn from their righteousness and commit sin, they will die for it; because of the sin they have committed they will die. ²⁷But if the wicked turn away from the wickedness they have committed and do what is just and right, they will save their lives. ᵈ ²⁸Because they consider all the offenses they have committed and turn away from them, they will surely live; they will not die. ᵉ ²⁹Yet the house of Israel says, 'The way of the Lord is not just.' Are my ways unjust, house of Israel? Is it not your ways that are unjust?

³⁰"Therefore, house of Israel, I will judge each of you according to your own ways, declares the Sovereign Lᴏʀᴅ. Repent! ᶠ Turn away from all your offenses; then sin will not be your downfall. ᵍ ³¹Rid ʰ yourselves of all the offenses you have committed, and get a new heart ⁱ and a new spirit. Why ʲ will you die, house of Israel? ᵏ ³²For I take no pleasure in the death of anyone, declares the Sovereign Lᴏʀᴅ. Repent ˡ and live! ᵐ

A LAMENT OVER ISRAEL'S PRINCES

19 "Take up a lament ⁿ concerning the princes ᵒ of Israel ²and say:

" 'What a lioness ᵖ was your mother
   among the lions!
She lay down among them
   and reared her cubs. q

³ She brought up one of her cubs,
   and he became a strong lion.
He learned to tear the prey
   and he devoured people.
⁴ The nations heard about him,
   and he was trapped in their pit.
They led him with hooks ʳ
   to the land of Egypt. ˢ

⁵ " 'When she saw her hope unfulfilled,
   her expectation gone,
she took another of her cubs ᵗ
   and made him a strong lion. ᵘ
⁶ He prowled among the lions,
   for he was now a strong lion.
He learned to tear the prey
   and he devoured people. ᵛ
⁷ He broke downᵃ their strongholds
   and devastated ʷ their towns.
The land and all who were in it
   were terrified by his roaring.

ᵃ 7 Targum (see Septuagint); Hebrew *He knew*

18:25 *Is my way unjust?* See 33:17; cf. Ge 18:25 and note; Dt 32:4; Jer 12:1 and note.

18:26 *If the righteous.* Verses 26–29 repeat the argument developed in vv. 21–25.

A **18:30** *Therefore.* Concluding summary oracle. Compare the language of this conclusion with the closing words of the last (the 14th) oracle in this series (24:14). *each of you.* While the house of Israel as a whole was guilty, God's judgment would be just and individual. *Repent!* Second call to repentance (see 14:6 and note).

18:31 *get a new heart.* What had been promised unconditionally (11:19; 36:26) is here portrayed as attainable but not inevitable (cf. the same tension between Php 2:12 and 2:13).

A **18:32** *I take no pleasure.* Verse 23 is echoed in this final, grand summary, called by some the most important message in the whole book of Ezekiel (see note on 16:6).

19:1–14 A twofold dirge lamenting the fall of the royal family of Judah, one part employing the imagery of a lioness and her

brood of whelps (vv. 1–9), the other utilizing the imagery of a once flourishing vine (vv. 10–14).

19:1 *lament.* A chant usually composed for funerals of fallen leaders (as in 2Sa 1:17–27), but often used sarcastically by the OT prophets to lament or to ironically predict the death of a nation (see Isa 14:4–21; Am 5:1–3 and note on 5:1). See also 2:10. *princes.* Kings.

19:2 An allegorical reference to the people of Israel or the nation of Judah.

19:3 *one of her cubs.* Jehoahaz (see 2Ki 23:31–34; Jer 22:10–12), who reigned only three months. *devoured people.* A reference to his oppressive policies.

C **19:5** *another of her cubs.* Perhaps Jehoiachin (who reigned only three months, 2Ki 24:8), but probably Zedekiah (of whom v. 7 appears a more likely description). Both were taken to Babylon (v. 9). If the reference is to Jehoiachin (2Ki 24:15), this was a true lament; if to Zedekiah, it was a prediction (2Ki 25:7).

⁸ Then the nations^x came against him,
    those from regions round about.
They spread their net^y for him,
    and he was trapped in their pit.^z
⁹ With hooks^a they pulled him into a cage
    and brought him to the king of Babylon.^b
They put him in prison,
    so his roar^c was heard no longer
    on the mountains of Israel.^d

¹⁰ " 'Your mother was like a vine in your vineyard^{a e}
    planted by the water;^f
it was fruitful and full of branches
    because of abundant water.^g
¹¹ Its branches were strong,
    fit for a ruler's scepter.
It towered high
    above the thick foliage,
conspicuous for its height
    and for its many branches.^h
¹² But it was uprootedⁱ in fury
    and thrown to the ground.
The east wind^j made it shrivel,
    it was stripped of its fruit;
its strong branches withered
    and fire consumed them.^k
¹³ Now it is planted in the desert,^l
    in a dry and thirsty land.^m
¹⁴ Fire spread from one of its main^b branches
    and consumedⁿ its fruit.
No strong branch is left on it
    fit for a ruler's scepter.'^o

"This is a lament^p and is to be used as a lament."

REBELLIOUS ISRAEL PURGED

20 In the seventh year, in the fifth month on the tenth day, some of the elders of Israel came to inquire^q of the LORD, and they sat down in front of me.^r ²Then the word of the LORD came to me: ³"Son of man, speak to the elders^s of Israel and say to them, 'This is what the Sovereign LORD says: Have you come to inquire^t of me? As surely as I live, I will not let you inquire of me, declares the Sovereign LORD.^u'

⁴"Will you judge them? Will you judge them, son of man? Then confront them with the detestable practices of their ancestors^v ⁵and say to them: 'This is what the Sovereign LORD says: On the day I chose^w Israel, I swore with uplifted hand^x to the descendants of the house of Jacob and revealed myself to them in Egypt. With uplifted hand I said to them, "I am the LORD your God.^y" ⁶On that day I swore^z to them that I would bring them out of

---

^a 10 Two Hebrew manuscripts; most Hebrew manuscripts *your blood*   ^b 14 Or *from under its*

19:10 *Your mother was like a vine.* The one previously pictured as a lioness (v. 2) is here a vine (for other uses of the vine imagery, see 15:1–8; 17:7 and notes).

19:12 *east wind.* Nebuchadnezzar and his army (see note on 17:10).

19:13 *desert.* Babylonia—which to Israel seemed like a desert (see 20:35).

19:14 *Fire.* Rebellion (see 2Ki 24:20). *one of its main branches.* Zedekiah. *to be used as a lament.* Indicates repeated use (see Ps 137:1).

A C **20:1–44** This word to be addressed to the elders of Israel came to Ezekiel on Aug. 14, 591 B.C., some 11 months after the preceding dated vision (see 8:1 and note on 8:1—11:25; see also chart, p. 1364). It begins with an overview of Israel's long history of apostasy (vv. 1–29), which leads into an announcement of the Lord's purpose to purge and renew his apostate people through the judgment now overtaking them (vv. 30–44).

20:1 *seventh year … fifth month … tenth day.* The third date (see previous note) supplied in the book of Ezekiel (see 1:2; 8:1). *elders of Israel.* See notes on 8:1; 14:1. *inquire.* See v. 3 and note on 14:3.

20:3 *As surely as I live.* See note on 5:11. *I will not let you inquire of me.* See v. 31; see also 3:26; 7:26 and notes.

20:4 *Will you judge them? … Then confront them.* As the one sent to pronounce God's judgment on Israel, Ezekiel is instructed to spell out the "detestable practices" for which that judgment comes on them (see also 22:2; 23:36).

20:5–26 These verses present Israel's history of apostasy in three acts (Act 1: vv. 5–9, Egypt; Act 2: vv. 10–17, Desert, Part 1; Act 3: vv. 18–26, Desert, Part 2). Each act has four scenes: (1) revelation, (2) rebellion, (3) wrath, (4) reconsideration. But see also note on v. 28.

20:5 *With uplifted hand.* A symbolic act accompanying the swearing of an oath (see vv. 15,23,42; Ge 14:22 and note; Ex 6:8). *I am the LORD your God.* See Ex 3:6,14–15 and notes.

19:8 ^x 2Ki 24:2
^y S Eze 12:13
^z 2Ki 24:11; S La 4:20
19:9 ^a S 2Ki 19:28
^b S 2Ki 25:7;
S 2Ch 36:6 ^c Zec 11:3
^d S 2Ki 24:15
19:10 ^e S Ge 49:22
^f S Jer 17:8 ^g S Ps 80:8-11
19:11 ^h Eze 31:3;
Da 4:11
19:12 ⁱ S Dt 29:28
^j S Ge 41:6
^k S Isa 27:11;
S Eze 17:24; 28:17;
Hos 13:15
19:13 ^l Eze 20:35;
Hos 2:14 ^m Hos 2:3
19:14 ⁿ Eze 20:47
^o S Eze 15:4 ^p S ver 1
20:1 ^q S Ge 25:22
^r Eze 1:1-2; S 8:1; 21:1
20:3 ^s S Eze 7:26
^t S Ge 25:22; Eze 14:3
^u S 1Sa 28:6; Isa 1:15;
Am 8:12; Mic 3:7
20:4 ^v S Eze 16:2;
22:2; Mt 23:32
20:5 ^w S Dt 7:6
^x S Ge 14:22;
S Nu 14:30
^y S Lev 11:44
20:6 ^z S Ex 6:8

20:6 *ª* S Ex 3:8
b S Dt 8:7; Da 8:9;
11:41; Mal 3:12
20:7 *ᶜ* Ex 20:4
d S Eze 6:9
e S Ex 20:2; Lev 18:3;
Dt 29:18
20:8 *f* S Jer 7:26
g S Jer 11:10;
S Eze 7:8; S 16:26
h S Ex 32:7; Dt 9:7;
S Isa 63:10
20:9 *i* Eze 36:22;
39:7 / S Isa 48:11
20:10 *k* S Ex 13:18;
19:1
20:11 *l* Lev 20:1-23;
Lev 18:5; Dt 4:7-8;
S Eze 18:9; S Ro 10:5
20:12 *m* S Ex 20:10
n S Ex 31:13 *º* Jer 17:22
p S Lev 20:8
20:13 *q* Ps 78:40
r S Jer 6:19; 11:8
s ver 24 *t* S Dt 9:8
u S Ex 32:10
v Lev 26:15,43;
S Nu 14:29; Ps 95:8-
10; Isa 56:6
20:14 *w* S Isa 48:11
x Eze 36:23
20:15 *y* S Dt 1:34
z Nu 14:22-23;
Ps 95:11; 106:26;
Heb 3:11
20:16 *a* Jer 11:8;
Am 2:4 *b* S Nu 15:39
ᶜ ver 24; S Eze 6:4;
Am 5:26
20:17 *d* S Jer 4:27
20:18 *e* S 2Ch 30:7;
Zec 1:4 *f* S Ps 106:39
20:19 *g* S Ex 20:2
h Dt 5:32-33; 6:1-2;
S 8:1; 11:1; S 12:1
20:20 *i* S Ex 20:10
j S Ex 31:13 *k* Jer 17:22
20:21 *l* S Jer 7:26
m Nu 25:3 *n* S Eze 7:8
20:22 *º* Ps 78:38
p S Isa 48:11
20:23 *q* S Lev 26:33;
S Ps 9:11
20:24 *r* Am 2:4
s ver 13 *t* S Eze 6:9
u S ver 16; S Eze 2:3;
S 18:6
20:25 *v* S Ps 81:12;
Ro 1:28 *w* Isa 66:4;
2Th 2:11

Egypt into a land I had searched out for them, a land flowing with milk and honey, *ª* the most beautiful of all lands. *b* 7And I said to them, "Each of you, get rid of the vile images *ᶜ* you have set your eyes on, and do not defile yourselves with the idols *d* of Egypt. I am the LORD your God. *e*"

8 " 'But they rebelled against me and would not listen to me; *f* they did not get rid of the vile images they had set their eyes on, nor did they forsake the idols of Egypt. *g* So I said I would pour out my wrath on them and spend my anger against them in Egypt. *h* 9But for the sake of my name, I brought them out of Egypt. *i* I did it to keep my name from being profaned *j* in the eyes of the nations among whom they lived and in whose sight I had revealed myself to the Israelites. 10Therefore I led them out of Egypt and brought them into the wilderness. *k* 11I gave them my decrees and made known to them my laws, through which people will live if they obey them. *l* 12Also I gave them my Sabbaths *m* as a sign *n* between us, *º* so they would know that I the LORD made them holy. *p*

13 " 'Yet the people of Israel rebelled *q* against me in the wilderness. They did not follow my decrees but rejected my laws *r*—through which people will live if they obey them—and they utterly desecrated my Sabbaths. *s* So I said I would pour out my wrath *t* on them and destroy *u* them in the wilderness. *v* 14But for the sake of my name I did what would keep it from being profaned *w* in the eyes of the nations in whose sight I had brought them out. *x* 15Also with uplifted hand I swore *y* to them in the wilderness that I would not bring them into the land I had given them—a land flowing with milk and honey, the most beautiful of all lands *z*— 16because they rejected my laws *ª* and did not follow my decrees and desecrated my Sabbaths. For their hearts *b* were devoted to their idols. *ᶜ* 17Yet I looked on them with pity and did not destroy *d* them or put an end to them in the wilderness. 18I said to their children in the wilderness, "Do not follow the statutes of your parents *e* or keep their laws or defile yourselves *f* with their idols. 19I am the LORD your God; *g* follow my decrees and be careful to keep my laws. *h* 20Keep my Sabbaths *i* holy, that they may be a sign *j* between us. Then you will know that I am the LORD your God. *k*"

21 " 'But the children rebelled against me: They did not follow my decrees, they were not careful to keep my laws, *l* of which I said, "Whoever obeys them will live by them," and they desecrated my Sabbaths. So I said I would pour out my wrath on them and spend my anger *m* against them in the wilderness. *n* 22But I withheld *º* my hand, and for the sake of my name *p* I did what would keep it from being profaned in the eyes of the nations in whose sight I had brought them out. 23Also with uplifted hand I swore to them in the wilderness that I would disperse them among the nations and scatter *q* them through the countries, 24because they had not obeyed my laws but had rejected my decrees and desecrated my Sabbaths, *s* and their eyes lusted after *t* their parents' idols. *u* 25So I gave *v* them other statutes that were not good and laws through which they could not live; *w* 26I defiled them through their gifts—the sacrifice *x* of every firstborn—that I might fill them with horror so they would know that I am the LORD. *y* '

20:26 *x* S Lev 18:21 *y* Lev 20:2-5; 2Ki 17:17

20:6 *land flowing with milk and honey.* See note on Ex 3:8. *most beautiful of all lands.* Cf. Dt 8:7–10; Jer 3:19 for the land's natural beauty. Its real beauty lay in being selected as God's dwelling place (Dt 12:5,11).
20:7 *idols.* See note on 6:4.
20:8 *But they rebelled.* See vv. 13,21; see also Jos 24:14. *So I said I would pour out my wrath on them.* An internal refrain (see vv. 13,21); see also note on 7:8. *spend my anger against.* See note on 5:13.
20:9 *for the sake of my name.* See vv. 14,22,44. Name and person are closely connected in the Bible. God's name is his identity and reputation—that by which he is known (see note on Ps 5:11). The phrase used here is equivalent to "for my own sake" (cf. Isa 37:35; 43:25). God's acts of deliverance—past and future—identify him, revealing his true nature (see 36:22; Ps 23:3 and notes; Isa 48:9). *profaned.* Made light of—as through ridicule (see Nu 14:15–16).
20:10 *wilderness.* Act 2 (see note on vv. 5–26).
20:11 *will live.* See vv. 13,21; contrast v. 25. See notes on 16:6; 18:9; see also Lev 18:5 and note.
20:12 *Sabbaths as a sign.* Israel's observance of the Sabbath was to serve as a sign that she was the Lord's holy people (see Ex 31:16–17 and note). Ezekiel highlights the Sabbath (see 22:8,26; 23:38; 44:24; 45:17; 46:3), as did Jeremiah (Jer 17:19–27;

cf. Ne 13:17–18). Jewish legalism later corrupted the Sabbath law (see Mt 12:1–14).
20:13 *desecrated.* By not observing the Sabbath-rest (see Jer 17:21–23) or by not observing it in the manner and spirit God intended (see Am 8:5).
20:15 *land flowing with milk and honey.* See note on Ex 3:8.
20:18 *I said to their children.* Act 3 (see note on vv. 5–26). God began anew with the second generation in the desert (see Nu 14:26–35).
20:25 *So I gave them … laws through which they could not live.* Just as God's judgments undo the creation order (see note on Ge 6:9—9:29) and undo human history (see note on Ge 11:1–9), so as an act of judgment he turns the laws he gave as the way to life (see vv. 12–13,21 and note on v. 11) into laws that produced death. This is a hard saying, but it most likely refers to God's requirement that Israel dedicate to him every firstborn male (Ex 13:2; 22:29)—which kings Ahaz and Manasseh, under the influence of the pagan religions of Israel's neighbors, radicalized into a law calling for actual sacrifice of the firstborn (v. 26; cf. Ro 1:24–32 and notes).
20:26 *sacrifice of every firstborn.* See v. 31 and note on 16:20. *so they would know that I am the LORD.* God will go to any lengths to get his people to acknowledge him (see note on 6:7).

²⁷"Therefore, son of man, speak to the people of Israel and say to them, 'This is what the Sovereign Lord says: In this also your ancestors ^z blasphemed ^a me by being unfaithful to me: ^{b 28}When I brought them into the land ^c I had sworn to give them and they saw any high hill or any leafy tree, there they offered their sacrifices, made offerings that aroused my anger, presented their fragrant incense and poured out their drink offerings. ^d ²⁹Then I said to them: What is this high place ^e you go to?' " (It is called Bamah ^a to this day.)

REBELLIOUS ISRAEL RENEWED

³⁰"Therefore say to the house of Israel: 'This is what the Sovereign Lord says: Will you defile yourselves ^f the way your ancestors did and lust after their vile images? ^g ³¹When you offer your gifts—the sacrifice of your children ^h in the fire—you continue to defile yourselves with all your idols to this day. Am I to let you inquire of me, house of Israel? As surely as I live, declares the Sovereign Lord, I will not let you inquire of me. ⁱ

³² 'You say, "We want to be like the nations, like the peoples of the world, who serve wood and stone." But what you have in mind will never happen. ³³As surely as I live, declares the Sovereign Lord, I will reign over you with a mighty hand and an outstretched arm ^j and with outpoured wrath. ^{k 34}I will bring you from the nations ^l and gather ^m you from the countries where you have been scattered—with a mighty hand ⁿ and an outstretched arm and with outpoured wrath. ^{o 35}I will bring you into the wilderness ^p of the nations and there, face to face, I will execute judgment ^q upon you. ³⁶As I judged your ancestors in the wilderness of the land of Egypt, so I will judge you, declares the Sovereign Lord. ^{r 37}I will take note of you as you pass under my rod, ^s and I will bring you into the bond of the covenant. ^{t 38}I will purge ^u you of those who revolt and rebel against me. Although I will bring them out of the land where they are living, yet they will not enter the land of Israel. Then you will know that I am the Lord. ^v

³⁹" 'As for you, house of Israel, this is what the Sovereign Lord says: Go and serve your idols, ^w every one of you! But afterward you will surely listen to me and no longer profane my holy name ^x with your gifts and idols. ^{y 40}For on my holy mountain, the high mountain of Israel, ^z declares the Sovereign Lord, there in the land the entire house of Israel will serve me, and there I will accept them. There I will require your offerings ^a and your choice gifts, ^b along with all your holy sacrifices. ^{b 41}I will accept you as fragrant incense ^c when I bring you out from the nations and gather ^d you from the countries where you have been scattered, and I will be proved holy ^e through you in the sight of the nations. ^{f 42}Then you will know that I am the Lord, ^g when I bring you into the land of Israel, ^h the land I had sworn with uplifted hand to give to your ancestors. ^{i 43}There you will remember your conduct ^j and all the actions by which you have defiled yourselves, and you will loathe yourselves ^k for all the evil you have done. ^{l 44}You will know that I am the Lord, when I deal with you for my name's sake ^m and not according to your evil ways and your corrupt practices, house of Israel, declares the Sovereign Lord. ⁿ' "

---

^a 29 *Bamah* means *high place.*   ^b 40 Or *and the gifts of your firstfruits*

20:28 *When I brought them into the land.* Apparently Act 4 in Ezekiel's history (see note on vv. 5–26), but it is not carried through with the same schematic consistency.
20:30–44 See note on vv. 1–44.
20:30 *Will you defile yourselves the way your ancestors did. . .?* See note on vv. 5–26.
20:31 *inquire.* See v. 3 and note.

C **20:32** *like the nations.* The temptation to lose its uniqueness was always present for Israel (see 1Sa 8:5 and note). *will never happen.* As happened to those who were exiled to Egypt (see Jer 44:15–19). God will not abandon them to their idolatrous ways but will firmly turn them back to the way of covenant faithfulness to him.
20:33 *mighty hand . . . outstretched arm.* Terminology of the exodus (cf. Dt 4:34; 5:15; 7:19; 11:2; 26:8).
20:35 *wilderness of the nations.* Exile among the nations would be for Israel like a return to the wilderness through which she journeyed on the way to the promised land (see Hos 2:14 and note).
20:37 *pass under my rod.* The way a shepherd counts or separates his flock (see Lev 27:32; Jer 33:13; cf. Mt 25:32–33). *I will bring you into the bond of the covenant.* As he had in the Sinai

Desert (see note on 16:59–63).
20:38 *purge.* As in the first desert experience, many were not allowed to enter the land (see Nu 14:26–35 and notes).
20:39 *Go and serve your idols.* Irony, as in Am 4:4. *profane my holy name.* See Lev 18:21 and note.
20:40 *my holy mountain.* Mentioned only here in Ezekiel, it refers to Jerusalem or Zion (see Ps 2:6; Isa 2:2–4 and notes; 65; Ob 16; Zep 3:11). *entire house of Israel.* Includes a remnant of the northern kingdom, which fell in 722–721 b.c. (see 11:15; 36:10 and note). *offerings.* Possibly refers to a prescribed contribution. The other 19 occurrences in Ezekiel of the Hebrew for this word are confined to chs. 44–48, where the reference is to the land set aside for the temple and priests (see 45:1; 48:8–10, "portion") or to the special gifts for the priests (see 44:30). *choice gifts.* Voluntary contributions (but see TNIV text note).
20:41 *as fragrant incense.* In a metaphorical sense (as in Eph 5:2). *bring you out.* Cf. v. 34. *I will be proved holy.* See Lev 10:3 and note.
20:43 *you will remember . . . and . . . loathe yourselves.* A thorough repentance (see 6:9 and note; 16:63; 36:31; Lk 15:17–19).
20:44 *for my name's sake.* Summarizes and concludes the oracle (see note on v. 9).

20:27 ^z S Ps 78:57
^a S Nu 15:30; Ro 2:24
^b S Eze 18:24
20:28 ^c Ne 9:23;
Ps 78:55,58
^d S Jer 2:7; S 3:6;
S 19:13; S Eze 6:13
20:29 ^e Eze 16:16;
43:7
20:30 ^f ver 43
^g S Jdg 2:16-19;
S Jer 16:12
20:31 ^h S Eze 16:20
ⁱ Ps 106:37-39;
S Jer 7:31; S Eze 14:3;
Am 8:12; Zec 7:13
20:33 ^j S Eze 16:27
^k Jer 21:5; Eze 25:16
20:34 ^l 2Co 6:17*
^m S Dt 30:4;
S Ps 106:47
ⁿ S Isa 31:3
20:35 ^o Isa 27:12-13;
S Jer 44:6; S La 2:4;
S Eze 6:14
^p S Eze 19:13
20:36 ^q S 1Sa 12:7;
S Job 22:4; S Jer 2:35
^r Nu 11:1-35;
14:28-30; 1Co 10:5-10
20:37 ^s S Lev 27:32
^t S Eze 16:62
20:38 ^u Eze 34:17-22; Am 9:9-10
^v Ps 95:11; Jer 44:14;
S Eze 13:9; 23:49;
Hos 2:14; Zec 13:8-9;
Mal 3:3; 4:1-3;
Heb 4:3
20:39 ^w S Jer 44:25
^x S Ex 20:7;
S Eze 13:19
^y Eze 43:7; Am 4:4
20:40 ^z S Eze 17:22;
34:14 ^a S Isa 60:7
^b S Isa 56:7; Mal 3:4
20:41 ^c S 2Co 2:14
^d S Dt 30:4
Eze 28:25; 36:23
^e S Isa 5:16;
S Eze 11:17; 2Co 6:17
20:42 ^g Eze 38:23
^h S Jer 23:8; Eze 34:13;
36:24 ⁱ Jer 30:3;
Eze 34:27; 37:21
20:43 ^j Eze 14:22
^k S Lev 26:41
^l S Eze 6:9; S 16:61;
Hos 5:15
20:44 ^m Ps 109:21;
Isa 43:25; Eze 36:22
ⁿ S Eze 16:62; 36:32

20:46 °S Eze 4:3;
S 13:17 °Eze 21:2;
Am 7:16 °Isa 30:6;
Jer 13:19
20:47 °S 2Ki 19:23
° Eze 19:14 °Eze 21:4
°Isa 9:18-19; S 13:8
20:48 °S Jer 7:20;
Eze 21:5,32; 23:25
20:49 °S Eze 4:14
× S Jdg 14:12;
S Ps 78:2; S Eze 12:9;
Mt 13:13; S Jn 16:25
21:1 °S Eze 20:1
21:2 °S Eze 13:17
°Eze 9:6 °Jer 26:11-
12; S Eze 20:46
21:3 °S Jer 21:13
°S Isa 27:1;
S Eze 14:21 °ver 9-11;
S Job 9:22; S Isa 57:1;
Jer 47:6-7
21:4 °S Lev 26:25;
S Jer 25:27
°Eze 20:47
21:5 °S Isa 34:5
°ver 30 °S Eze 20:47-
48; Na 1:9
21:6 °ver 12;
S Isa 22:4; Jer 30:6;
S Eze 9:4
21:7 °S Job 23:2
°S Jos 7:5
°S Jer 47:3;
Eze 22:14 °S Ps 6:2
°S Lev 26:36;
S Job 11:16
21:10 °Ps 110:5-6;
Isa 34:5-6 °Dt 32:41
21:11 °Jer 46:4

PROPHECY AGAINST THE SOUTH

*⁴⁵The word of the Lᴏʀᴅ came to me: ⁴⁶"Son of man, set your face toward° the south; preach against the south and prophesy against ° the forest of the southland. ° ⁴⁷Say to the southern forest: ° 'Hear the word of the Lᴏʀᴅ. This is what the Sovereign Lᴏʀᴅ says: I am about to set fire to you, and it will consume ° all your trees, both green and dry. The blazing flame will not be quenched, and every face from south to north ° will be scorched by it. ° ⁴⁸Everyone will see that I the Lᴏʀᴅ have kindled it; it will not be quenched. ° ' "

⁴⁹Then I said, "Ah, Sovereign Lᴏʀᴅ! ° They are saying of me, 'Isn't he just telling parables?ˣ' "

BABYLON AS GOD'S SWORD OF JUDGMENT

21 *The word of the Lᴏʀᴅ came to me: ʸ ²"Son of man, set your face against ᶻ Jerusalem and preach against the sanctuary. ° Prophesy against ° the land of Israel ³and say to her: 'This is what the Lᴏʀᴅ says: I am against you. ° I will draw my sword ° from its sheath and cut off from you both the righteous and the wicked. ° ⁴Because I am going to cut off the righteous and the wicked, my sword ° will be unsheathed against everyone from south to north. ° ⁵Then all people will know that I the Lᴏʀᴅ have drawn my sword ° from its sheath; it will not return ° again.' ʲ

⁶"Therefore groan, son of man! Groan before them with broken heart and bitter grief. ° ⁷And when they ask you, 'Why are you groaning?' you shall say, 'Because of the news that is coming. Every heart will melt ° and every hand go limp; ° every spirit will become faint ° and every knee be wet with urine.' ° It is coming! It will surely take place, declares the Sovereign Lᴏʀᴅ."

⁸The word of the Lᴏʀᴅ came to me: ⁹"Son of man, prophesy and say, 'This is what the Lord says:

" 'A sword, a sword,
    sharpened and polished—
¹⁰sharpened for the slaughter, °
    polished to flash like lightning!

" 'Shall we rejoice in the scepter of my royal son? The sword despises every such stick. ʳ

¹¹" 'The sword is appointed to be polished, °
    to be grasped with the hand;
it is sharpened and polished,
    made ready for the hand of the slayer.
¹²Cry out and wail, son of man,
    for it is against my people;
it is against all the princes of Israel.

*20:45-49 is numbered 21:1-5 in Hebrew texts.   *21:1-32 is numbered 21:6-37 in Hebrew texts.

20:45—21:32 Babylon will be God's sword to bring a ruinous destruction as total as that of a forest fire—primarily on Judah and Jerusalem (20:45—21:27), but also on the Ammonites (21:28–29)—and then Babylon, too, will feel God's wrath (21:30–32).

20:46 *set your face.* A posture required eight times of Ezekiel (here; 13:17; 21:2; 25:2; 28:21; 29:2; 35:2; 38:2). *toward the south.* Toward Judah and Jerusalem. Any Babylonian invasion would traverse Israel from north to south (see 26:7 and note).

20:47 *set fire.* Common figurative language for God's devastating judgments (see Isa 10:16–19), which often took the form of invasion by some world power (see Am 1:4 and note). *both green and dry.* All trees (cf. 17:24; Lk 23:31). *from south to north.* Expresses totality, not direction; equivalent to saying, "from the border on the right to that on the left."

20:49 *parables.* See note on 17:1–24; for other ridiculing of the prophet, see 12:21–28; 33:32.

21:2 *set your face.* See note on 20:46. *against the sanctuary.* See 9:6 and note.

21:3–5 *my sword . . . my sword . . . my sword.* See 5:2 and note. The threefold repetition is for emphasis (see note on Jer 7:4).

21:3 *I am against you.* See note on 5:8. *my sword.* This is the first of five sword oracles (see vv. 8–17, 18–24, 25–27, 28–32). Here the sword refers to Babylon and Nebuchadnezzar (v. 19).

both the righteous and the wicked. Indicates the completeness of the judgment that is about to come on Israel. No one will escape its devastating effects, not even the righteous in the land. Contrast God's deliverance of Noah (Ge 6:7–8) and Lot (Ge 18:23; 19:12–13).

21:4 *from south to north.* See note on 20:47.

21:6 *groan . . . with broken heart and bitter grief.* Ezekiel's display of intense grief is to serve as another prophetic sign and as an occasion for a new message of impending judgment. This is Ezekiel's seventh symbolic act (see Introduction: Literary Features).

21:7 *every knee be wet with urine.* See 7:17.

21:9 *A sword, a sword.* A sword song (see vv. 3–5 and note), possibly accompanied by dancing or symbolic actions. Such songs may have been sung by warriors about to go into battle (see note on 2Sa 1:18).

21:10 *Shall we rejoice . . . every such stick.* To think that the Babylonians would conquer every other country except Judah was a false hope. *scepter.* Represents rule, government or kingdom. *my royal son.* Referring to the reigning king of the house of David (see vv. 25–27; Ps 2:7 and notes). *sword.* Babylon and Nebuchadnezzar (v. 19).

21:11 *slayer.* Nebuchadnezzar (v. 19).

21:12 *Cry out and wail . . . beat your breast.* Eighth symbolic act (see Introduction: Literary Features).

They are thrown to the sword
     along with my people.
Therefore beat your breast. *t*

¹³" 'Testing will surely come. And what if even the scepter, which the sword despises, does not continue? declares the Sovereign Lᴏʀᴅ.'

¹⁴"So then, son of man, prophesy
     and strike your hands *u* together.
Let the sword strike twice,
     even three times.
It is a sword for slaughter—
     a sword for great slaughter,
     closing in on them from every side. *v*
¹⁵ So that hearts may melt *w*
     and the fallen be many,
I have stationed the sword for slaughter *a*
     at all their gates.
Oh! It is made to flash like lightning,
     it is grasped for slaughter. *x*
¹⁶ Slash to the right, you sword,
     then to the left,
     wherever your blade is turned.
¹⁷ I too will strike my hands *y* together,
     and my wrath *z* will subside.
I the Lᴏʀᴅ have spoken. *a*"

¹⁸The word of the Lᴏʀᴅ came to me: ¹⁹"Son of man, mark out two roads for the sword *b* of the king of Babylon to take, both starting from the same country. Make a signpost *c* where the road branches off to the city. ²⁰Mark out one road for the sword to come against Rabbah of the Ammonites *d* and another against Judah and fortified Jerusalem. ²¹For the king of Babylon will stop at the fork in the road, at the junction of the two roads, to seek an omen: He will cast lots *e* with arrows, he will consult his idols, *f* he will examine the liver. *g* ²²Into his right hand will come the lot for Jerusalem, where he is to set up battering rams, to give the command to slaughter, to sound the battle cry, *h* to set battering rams against the gates, to build a ramp *i* and to erect siege works. *j* ²³It will seem like a false omen to those who have sworn allegiance to him, but he will remind *k* them of their guilt *l* and take them captive.

²⁴"Therefore this is what the Sovereign Lᴏʀᴅ says: 'Because you people have brought to mind your guilt by your open rebellion, revealing your sins in all that you do—because you have done this, you will be taken captive.

²⁵" 'You profane and wicked prince of Israel, whose day has come, *m* whose time of punishment has reached its climax, *n* ²⁶this is what the Sovereign Lᴏʀᴅ says: Take off the turban, remove the crown. *o* It will not be as it was: The lowly will be exalted and the ex-

---

a 15 Septuagint; the meaning of the Hebrew for this word is uncertain.

21:13 *come.* On Judah. *what if even the scepter … does not continue?* See note on v. 10. The question anticipates the final interruption of Davidic kingship, which came in 586 B.C. (see vv. 25–27).
21:14 *strike your hands.* See 6:11 and note. *Let the sword strike twice.* Cf. 2Ki 13:18–19.
21:17 *strike my hands.* As Ezekiel was commanded to do in v. 14.
21:19 *king of Babylon.* Nebuchadnezzar. *same country.* Babylon, or possibly Aram (Syria)—Nebuchadnezzar headquartered at Riblah in northern Aram (see 2Ki 25:6).
21:20 *Rabbah.* Capital of Ammon (Jer 49:2); modern Amman (capital of Jordan).
21:21 *cast lots with arrows.* Divination with arrows, for the purpose of seeking good omens for the coming campaign—a practice not elsewhere mentioned in the Bible. Apparently arrows were labeled (e.g., "Rabbah," "Jerusalem"), placed into a quiver and drawn out, one with each hand. Right-hand selection was seen as a good omen (see v. 22). *idols.* The Hebrew for this word is translated "household gods" in Ge 31:19 (see note there). Consulting them is referred to in Hos 3:4; Zec 10:2. The

household gods of Ge 31:19–35 were small enough to hide in a saddle, but others were life-size (1Sa 19:13–16). *examine the liver.* Looking at the color and configurations of sheep livers to foretell the future was common in ancient Babylonia and Rome, but the practice is not mentioned elsewhere in the Bible.
21:23 *false omen.* The leaders of Jerusalem, once submissive to Nebuchadnezzar but now in rebellion (2Ki 24:20), hoped that the result of the omen-seeking (vv. 21–22) was misleading.
21:25,29 *whose day … has reached its climax.* The same fate that awaits the Ammonites also awaits Judah's king.
21:25 *prince of Israel.* Zedekiah (see note on 7:27).
21:26 *turban.* Only here is it mentioned as royal headwear. Elsewhere it is worn by priests (Ex 28:4,37,39; 29:6; 39:28,31; Lev 8:9; 16:4) as a setting for the crown (Ex 28:36–37; 29:6; 39:31; Lev 8:9). It was made of fine linen (Ex 28:39; 39:28). *lowly … exalted … exalted … brought low.* A common Biblical expression for the reversal of human conditions because of the intervention of the Lord (see 17:24 and note; 1Sa 2:7–8; Ob 15 and note; Lk 1:52–53).

21:12 *t* Jer 31:19
21:14 *u* ver 17;
S Nu 24:10
v S Eze 6:11; 30:24
21:15 *w* S 2Sa 17:10
x Ps 22:14
21:17 *y* ver 14;
Eze 22:13 *z* S Eze 5:13
a S Eze 6:11; S 16:42
21:19 *b* S Eze 14:21;
32:11 *c* Jer 31:21
21:20 *d* S Dt 3:11
21:21 *e* S Pr 16:33
f Zec 10:2 *g* Nu 22:7;
S 23:23
21:22 *h* S Jer 4:16
i Jer 32:24
j S Eze 4:2; 26:9
21:23 *k* S Nu 5:15
l S Eze 17:19
21:25 *m* Eze 22:4
n Eze 35:5
21:26 *o* S Isa 28:5;
S Jer 13:18

21:26 ᵖ Ps 75:7;
Isa 40:4; S Eze 17:24;
S Mt 23:12
21:27 ᵍ Ge 49:10
ʳ Ps 2:6; Jer 23:5-6;
Eze 37:24; Hag 2:21-
22
21:28 ˢ S Ge 19:38;
Zep 2:8 ᵗ S Jer 12:12
21:29 ᵘ Jer 27:9
ᵛ ver 25; Eze 22:28;
35:5
21:30 ʷ ver 5;
Jer 47:6 ˣ S Eze 16:3
21:31 ʸ Ps 18:15;
S Isa 11:4 ᶻ Ps 79:6;
Eze 22:20-21
ᵃ S Jer 4:7; 51:20-23;
S Eze 16:39
21:32 ᵇ S Eze 20:47-
48; Mal 4:1 ᶜ Eze 25:10
22:2 ᵈ Eze 24:6,9;
Hos 4:2; Na 3:1;
Hab 2:12 ᵉ S Eze 16:2;
23:36
22:3 ᶠ ver 6,13,27;
Eze 23:37,45; 24:6
22:4 ᵍ S 2Ki 21:16
ʰ Eze 21:25
ⁱ S Ps 137:3
ʲ Ps 44:13-14;
S Eze 5:14
22:5 ᵏ S Isa 22:2
22:6 ˡ S Eze 11:6;
18:10; 33:25
22:7 ᵐ S Dt 5:16;
Mic 7:6 ⁿ S Ex 23:9
ᵒ S Ex 22:21-22
22:8 ᵖ S Ex 20:8;
Eze 23:38-39
22:9 ᵍ S Lev 19:16

alted will be brought low. ᵖ ²⁷A ruin! A ruin! I will make it a ruin! The crown will not be restored until he to whom it rightfully belongs shall come; ᵍ to him I will give it.' ʳ

²⁸"And you, son of man, prophesy and say, 'This is what the Sovereign LORD says about the Ammonites ˢ and their insults:

" 'A sword, ᵗ a sword,
　drawn for the slaughter,
polished to consume
　and to flash like lightning!
²⁹ Despite false visions concerning you
　and lying divinations ᵘ about you,
it will be laid on the necks
　of the wicked who are to be slain,
whose day has come,
　whose time of punishment has reached its climax. ᵛ

³⁰ " 'Let the sword return to its sheath. ʷ
In the place where you were created,
in the land of your ancestry, ˣ
　I will judge you.
³¹ I will pour out my wrath on you
　and breathe ʸ out my fiery anger ᶻ against you;
I will deliver you into the hands of brutal men,
　men skilled in destruction. ᵃ
³² You will be fuel for the fire, ᵇ
　your blood will be shed in your land,
you will be remembered ᶜ no more;
　for I the LORD have spoken.' "

JUDGMENT ON JERUSALEM'S SINS

22 The word of the LORD came to me:

²"Son of man, will you judge her? Will you judge this city of bloodshed? ᵈ Then confront her with all her detestable practices ᵉ ³and say: 'This is what the Sovereign LORD says: You city that brings on herself doom by shedding blood ᶠ in her midst and defiles herself by making idols, ⁴you have become guilty because of the blood you have shed ᵍ and have become defiled by the idols you have made. You have brought your days to a close, and the end of your years has come. ʰ Therefore I will make you an object of scorn ⁱ to the nations and a laughingstock to all the countries. ʲ ⁵Those who are near and those who are far away will mock you, you infamous city, full of turmoil. ᵏ

⁶ " 'See how each of the princes of Israel who are in you uses his power to shed blood. ˡ ⁷In you they have treated father and mother with contempt; ᵐ in you they have oppressed the foreigner ⁿ and mistreated the fatherless and the widow. ᵒ ⁸You have despised my holy things and desecrated my Sabbaths. ᵖ ⁹In you are slanderers ᵍ who are bent on shedding

---

A **21:27** *A ruin! A ruin!... a ruin!* Threefold repetition for emphasis (see Isa 6:3; Jer 7:4 and notes). *The crown.* Representing dominion (the kingdom of Judah). *until he to whom it rightfully belongs shall come.* The Messiah; probably an allusion to Ge 49:10 (see note there).

21:28 *Ammonites.* See v. 20. After judgment on Jerusalem, they too will be dealt with (see 25:1-7; see also Jer 9:26; 49:1-6; Am 1:13-15; Zep 2:8-11). *their insults.* See 25:3,6; also cf. 36:15. *A sword, a sword.* Nebuchadnezzar's (see vv. 9,19 and notes).

21:29 *false visions... lying divinations.* Apparently Ammon also had false prophets of peace (see v. 10 and note; 13:10; Jer 6:14; 8:11-12). *it.* The sword.

C **21:30-32** When the Lord has accomplished his purpose through the Babylonians, they too will come under his judgment for all their evil ways (see Jer 50:15,27,29,31; 51:6,49; Hab 2:4-20; cf. Isa 10:5-19 and note on 10:12).

21:30 *Let the sword return.* Addressing Nebuchadnezzar.

21:31 *brutal men.* The people of the East, as in 25:4.

21:32 *fuel for the fire.* See 20:47 and note.

C **22:1-31** Ezekiel is instructed to confront Jerusalem (vv. 1-12) and the land of Judah (vv. 23-29) with all the sins of which they are guilty and for which they were about to feel the fiery wrath of Yahweh (vv. 13-22,30-31). Under Manasseh, Amon and Jehoiakim, Jerusalem had become a city of idolatry and pervasive moral corruption (see 2Ki 21:2-26; Jer 22:13-17). In the land of Judah all who held power cruelly exploited the weak.

22:2 *will you judge her?* Cf. 20:4 and note. *this city.* Jerusalem, the usual focal point of Ezekiel's prophecy (see 5:5 and note).

A **22:3** *shedding blood... making idols.* Two categories of sins are developed: social injustices and idol worship. *idols.* See note on 6:4.

22:6 *princes of Israel.* Leaders generally, not kings; contrast 21:12 with 19:1.

A **22:7** *treated father and mother with contempt.* See Mic 7:6 and note. Both passages are the opposite of what God commands in Ex 20:12 (see note there). *foreigner... fatherless... widow.* See Ex 22:21-27 and notes; Dt 10:18; 16:11,14; 24:17; 27:19; Ps 68:5-6 and note; 82:3; Isa 1:17 and note; 23; Jer 7:6; 22:3; Jas 1:27.

22:8 *Sabbaths.* A major concern in Ezekiel (see note on 20:12).

blood; ^r in you are those who eat at the mountain shrines ^s and commit lewd acts. ^t ¹⁰In you are those who dishonor their father's bed; ^u in you are those who violate women during their period, ^v when they are ceremonially unclean. ^w ¹¹In you one man commits a detestable offense with his neighbor's wife, ^x another shamefully defiles his daughter-in-law, ^y and another violates his sister, ^z his own father's daughter. ^a ¹²In you are people who accept bribes ^b to shed blood; you take interest ^c and make a profit from the poor. You extort unjust gain from your neighbors. ^d And you have forgotten ^e me, declares the Sovereign Lord. ^f

¹³ " 'I will surely strike my hands ^g together at the unjust gain ^h you have made and at the blood ⁱ you have shed in your midst. ^j ¹⁴Will your courage endure ^k or your hands ^l be strong in the day I deal with you? I the Lord have spoken, ^m and I will do it. ⁿ ¹⁵I will disperse you among the nations and scatter ^o you through the countries; and I will put an end to ^p your uncleanness. ^q ¹⁶When you have been defiled ^a in the eyes of the nations, you will know that I am the Lord.' "

¹⁷Then the word of the Lord came to me: ¹⁸"Son of man, the house of Israel has become dross ^r to me; all of them are the copper, tin, iron and lead left inside a furnace. ^t ¹⁹Therefore this is what the Sovereign Lord says: 'Because you have all become dross, ^u I will gather you into Jerusalem. ²⁰As silver, copper, iron, lead and tin are gathered into a furnace to be melted with a fiery blast, so will I gather you in my anger and my wrath and put you inside the city and melt you. ^v ²¹I will gather you and I will blow ^w on you with my fiery wrath, and you will be melted inside her. ^x ²²As silver is melted ^y in a furnace, so you will be melted inside her, and you will know that I the Lord have poured out my wrath ^z on you.' " ^a

²³Again the word of the Lord came to me: ²⁴"Son of man, say to the land, 'You are a land that has not been cleansed or rained on in the day of wrath.' ^b ²⁵There is a conspiracy ^c of her princes ^b within her like a roaring lion ^d tearing its prey; they devour people, ^e take treasures and precious things and make many widows ^f within her. ²⁶Her priests do violence to my law ^g and profane my holy things; they do not distinguish between the holy and the common; ^h they teach that there is no difference between the unclean and the clean; ⁱ and they shut their eyes to the keeping of my Sabbaths, so that I am profaned ^j among them. ^k ²⁷Her officials ^l within her are like wolves ^m tearing their prey; they shed blood and kill people ⁿ to make unjust gain. ^o ²⁸Her prophets whitewash ^p these deeds for them by false visions and lying divinations. ^q They say, 'This is what the Sovereign Lord says'—when the Lord has not spoken. ^r ²⁹The people of the land practice extortion and commit robbery; ^s they oppress the poor and needy and mistreat the foreigner, ^t denying them justice. ^u

³⁰"I looked for someone among them who would build up the wall ^v and stand before me in the gap on behalf of the land so I would not have to destroy it, but I found no one. ^w ³¹So I will pour out my wrath on them and consume them with my fiery anger, ^x bringing down ^y on their own heads all they have done, declares the Sovereign Lord. ^z"

TWO ADULTEROUS SISTERS

23 The word of the Lord came to me: ²"Son of man, there were two women, daughters of the same mother. ^a ³They became prostitutes in Egypt, ^b engaging in prostitution ^c from their youth. ^d In that land their breasts were fondled

^a 16 Or *When I have allotted you your inheritance*   ^b 25 Septuagint; Hebrew *prophets*

22:29 ^uS Isa 5:7   **22:30** ^vS Eze 13:5; ^wS Ps 106:23; S Isa 64:7; Jer 5:1   **22:31** ^xS Ex 32:10; S Isa 30:27; S La 4:11; ^yEze 16:43; ^zEze 7:8-9; Ro 2:8   **23:2** ^aS Jer 3:7; S Eze 16:45   **23:3** ^bJos 24:14; ^cS Lev 17:7; S Isa 1:21; ^dS Ps 25:7

22:9 ^rIsa 59:3; S Eze 11:6; Hos 4:2; 6:9; ^sEze 18:11; ^tEze 23:29; Hos 4:10, 14
22:10 ^uLev 18:7; ^vS Lev 12:2; ^wS Lev 18:8,19
22:11 ^xS Jer 5:8; ^yS Ge 11:31; Lev 18:15; ^zS Lev 18:9; S 2Sa 13:14; ^aEze 18:6
22:12 ^bS Ex 18:21; Dt 27:25; Ps 26:10; Isa 5:23; Am 5:12; Mic 7:3; ^cS Eze 18:8; ^dLev 19:13; ^ePs 106:21; S Isa 17:10; S 57:11; ^fS Eze 11:6
22:13 ^gS Nu 24:10; S Eze 21:17; ^hS ver 27; S Isa 33:15; ⁱS ver 3 / S Eze 6:11
22:14 ^kPs 76:7; Joel 2:11; Na 1:6; Mal 3:2 / ^lS Eze 7:17; ^mEze 24:14; ⁿS Eze 17:24
22:15 ^oS Lev 26:33; Dt 4:27; Zec 7:14; ^pS Eze 16:41; ^qEze 24:11
22:18 ^rS Ps 119:119; ^sIsa 48:10 / Jer 6:28-30
22:19 ^uS Ps 119:119
22:20 ^vHos 8:10; Mal 3:2
22:21 ^wIsa 40:7; Hag 1:9; ^xPs 68:2; Eze 21:31
22:22 ^yS Isa 1:25; ^zS Eze 7:8; ^aS Isa 64:7
22:24 ^bEze 24:13
22:25 ^cJer 11:9; ^dS Ps 22:13; ^eHos 6:9; ^fJer 15:8; 18:21
22:26 ^gHos 9:7-8; Zep 3:4; Mal 2:7-8; ^hEze 42:20; 44:23; ⁱS Lev 20:25; S Eze 18:21; S Eze 13:19; ^kver 8; S 1Sa 2:12-17; Jer 2:8, 26; Hag 2:11-14
22:27 ^lS Jer 26:10; Zep 3:3; ^mMt 7:15; ⁿS ver 3; S Eze 11:6; 33:25; 34:2-3; Mic 3:2,10; ^over 13
22:28 ^pS Eze 13:10; ^qS La 2:14; S 4:13; S Eze 21:29; ^rS Eze 13:2,6-7
22:29 ^sS Ps 62:10; ^tS Ex 22:21

22:9 *eat at the mountain shrines.* See 18:6 and note. *commit lewd acts.* In their pagan worship practices (see Hos 4:14 and note).
22:10 *violate women.* Cf. 18:6 and note.
22:11 *detestable offense.* All the sins mentioned in this verse were specifically forbidden in the law (Lev 18:7-20; 20:10-21; Dt 22:22-23,30; 27:22).
22:12 *you take interest and make a profit from the poor.* See 18:8 and note.
22:13 *strike my hands.* In anger (21:14,17).
22:17-22 Jerusalem will become God's "furnace" in which he melts down all those remaining in and around the city in order to cleanse away the "dross" (see Ps 12:6 and note).
22:25 *princes.* Ezekiel begins to speak plainly concerning the "dross" of vv. 18-22. All of Jerusalem's leaders and people were included: princes (here), priests (v. 26), officials (v. 27), prophets (v. 28), people (v. 29). *like a roaring lion.* Cf. v. 27; 19:3; 13:4; Zep 3:3.

22:26 *distinguish between the holy and the common.* One of the main duties of the priests (see 44:23 and note; see also Lev 10:10 and note). *Sabbaths.* See note on v. 8. *I am profaned.* See Lev 18:21 and note.
22:28 *whitewash.* See 13:10 and note.
22:29 *people of the land.* See 7:27 and note.
22:30 *I looked for someone.* Cf. Isa 59:16; 63:5 and notes. *stand before me in the gap.* See 13:5 and note. Some interpret the task here as prophetic intercession with God in behalf of the people (see Ge 20:7; 1Sa 12:23; Jer 37:3; 42:2). Others interpret it as teaching, particularly calling the people to repentance. Cf. the task of the prophetic "watchman" (3:17-21; 33:1-6).
22:31 *bringing down on their own heads all they have done.* See note on 16:43.
23:1-49 This extended allegory depicting in lurid colors the sins of Israel (similar to that found in ch. 16) climaxes the series

23:3 *e* S Eze 16:15
23:4 *f* S Eze 16:46
23:5 *g* S 2Ki 16:7;
Hos 5:13 *h* Hos 8:9
23:7 *i* Isa 57:8;
Hos 5:3; 6:10
23:8 *j* Ex 32:4
k S Eze 16:15
23:9 *l* S 2Ki 18:11
m S Jer 4:30
n Hos 11:5
23:10 *o* Hos 2:10
p Eze 16:41 *q* Jer 42:10
r Eze 16:36
23:11 *s* S Jer 3:7
t Jer 3:8-11;
S Eze 16:51
23:12 *v* 2Ki 16:7-15;
S 2Ch 28:16;
S Eze 16:15,28
23:13 *v* S 2Ki 17:19;
Hos 12:2
23:14 *w* S Eze 8:10
x Jer 22:14; Na 2:3
23:15 *y* S Isa 5:27
23:16 *z* S Isa 57:9
a S Eze 6:9
23:17 *b* Jer 40:9
c S Eze 16:29
23:18 *d* S Isa 57:8
e Ps 78:59; 106:40;
Jer 6:8 *f* Jer 12:8;
Am 5:21
23:21 *g* S Eze 16:26
23:22 *h* S Jer 4:30
i S Eze 16:37
23:23 *j* 2Ki 20:14-
18; S Jer 40:9
k S Ge 11:28 *l* Jer 50:21
m S 2Ki 24:2
23:24 *n* Jer 47:3;
Eze 26:7,10; Na 2:4
o Jer 39:5-6
23:25 *p* S Dt 29:20
q ver 47; Eze 24:21
r S Jer 12:9;
S Eze 16:38; S 20:47-
48
23:26 *s* S Jer 13:22
t S Isa 3:18-23;
S Eze 16:39
23:27 *u* S Eze 16:41
23:28 *v* S Jer 34:20

and their virgin bosoms caressed. *e* ⁴The older was named Oholah, and her sister was Oholibah. They were mine and gave birth to sons and daughters. Oholah is Samaria, and Oholibah is Jerusalem. *f*

⁵"Oholah engaged in prostitution while she was still mine; and she lusted after her lovers, the Assyrians *g*—warriors *h* ⁶clothed in blue, governors and commanders, all of them handsome young men, and mounted horsemen. ⁷She gave herself as a prostitute to all the elite of the Assyrians and defiled herself with all the idols of everyone she lusted after. *i* ⁸She did not give up the prostitution she began in Egypt, *j* when during her youth men slept with her, caressed her virgin bosom and poured out their lust on her. *k*

⁹"Therefore I delivered her into the hands *l* of her lovers, *m* the Assyrians, for whom she lusted. *n* ¹⁰They stripped *o* her naked, took away her sons and daughters and killed her with the sword. She became a byword among women, *p* and punishment was inflicted *q* on her. *r*

¹¹"Her sister Oholibah saw this, *s* yet in her lust and prostitution she was more depraved than her sister. *t* ¹²She too lusted after the Assyrians—governors and commanders, warriors in full dress, mounted horsemen, all handsome young men. *u* ¹³I saw that she too defiled herself; both of them went the same way. *v*

¹⁴"But she carried her prostitution still further. She saw men portrayed on a wall, *w* figures of Chaldeans *a* portrayed in red, *x* ¹⁵with belts *y* around their waists and flowing turbans on their heads; all of them looked like Babylonian chariot officers, natives of Chaldea. *b* ¹⁶As soon as she saw them, she lusted after them and sent messengers *z* to them in Chaldea. *a* ¹⁷Then the Babylonians *b* came to her, to the bed of love, and in their lust they defiled her. After she had been defiled by them, she turned away from them in disgust. *c* ¹⁸When she carried on her prostitution openly and exposed her nakedness, *d* I turned away *e* from her in disgust, just as I had turned away from her sister. *f* ¹⁹Yet she became more and more promiscuous as she recalled the days of her youth, when she was a prostitute in Egypt. ²⁰There she lusted after her lovers, whose genitals were like those of donkeys and whose emission was like that of horses. ²¹So you longed for the lewdness of your youth, when in Egypt your bosom was caressed and your young breasts fondled. *c g*

²²"Therefore, Oholibah, this is what the Sovereign Lᴏʀᴅ says: I will stir up your lovers *h* against you, those you turned away from in disgust, and I will bring them against you from every side *i*— ²³the Babylonians *j* and all the Chaldeans, *k* the men of Pekod *l* and Shoa and Koa, and all the Assyrians with them, handsome young men, all of them governors and commanders, chariot officers and men of high rank, all mounted on horses. *m* ²⁴They will come against you with weapons, *d* chariots and wagons *n* and with a throng of people; they will take up positions against you on every side with large and small shields and with helmets. I will turn you over to them for punishment, *o* and they will punish you according to their standards. ²⁵I will direct my jealous anger *p* against you, and they will deal with you in fury. They will cut off your noses and your ears, and those of you who are left will fall by the sword. They will take away your sons and daughters, *q* and those of you who are left will be consumed by fire. *r* ²⁶They will also strip *s* you of your clothes and take your fine jewelry. *t* ²⁷So I will put a stop *u* to the lewdness and prostitution you began in Egypt. You will not look on these things with longing or remember Egypt anymore.

²⁸"For this is what the Sovereign Lᴏʀᴅ says: I am about to deliver you into the hands *v* of those you hate, to those you turned away from in disgust. ²⁹They will deal with you in

---

a 14 Or *Babylonians*   *b* 15 Or *Babylonia*; also in verse 16   *c* 21 Syriac (see also verse 3); Hebrew *caressed because of your young breasts*   *d* 24 The meaning of the Hebrew for this word is uncertain.

---

of oracles of judgment on Jerusalem and Judah begun in ch. 13 (see notes on 13:1–23; 18:1–32).

23:4 *The older.* See 16:46 and note. *Oholah.* Means "her tent," probably referring to the fact that Samaria had its own unauthorized sanctuary. *Oholibah.* Means "My tent is in her," probably referring to the Lord's sanctuary in Jerusalem. Cf. the two sisters of Jer 3:6–12 and note on 3:7.

A **23:5** *prostitution.* Here represents political alliances with pagan powers—not idolatry as in ch. 16 (see Eze 34:15 and note). The graphic language of the chapter underscores God's and Ezekiel's disgust with Israel for playing the worldly game of international politics rather than relying on the Lord for her security—as clear a case of religious prostitution as idolatry. *Assyrians.* See 2Ki 15:19 and note.

C **23:8** *in Egypt.* Cf. 20:5–8. Israel's entire history was marked by unfaithfulness. For her attachment to Egypt, see Ex 17:3; Nu 11:5,18,20; 14:2–4; 21:5.

23:10 *stripped her naked.* A reference to the fall of Samaria to the Assyrians in 722–721 B.C.

23:14 *portrayed in red.* Jeremiah, too, noted red interior decorations with disfavor (Jer 22:14).

23:15 *belts.* Cf. Isa 5:27 for similar Assyrian military equipment.

23:20 *genitals.* See note on 16:26.

23:23 *Babylonians . . . Chaldeans.* Often identified with one another (see 1:3 and TNIV text note there; 12:13), here distinguished (as in v. 15), probably because the Chaldeans were relative newcomers. *Pekod.* Aramaic people located east of Babylon. *Shoa and Koa.* Babylonian allies of uncertain origin and location.

23:24 *their standards.* Which were cruel and gruesome (see v. 25).

23:25 *jealous anger.* See 16:38 and note. *fire.* See notes on 15:7; 20:47.

23:27 *in Egypt.* See note on v. 8.

hatred and take away everything you have worked for. They will leave you stark naked, [w] and the shame of your prostitution will be exposed. [x] Your lewdness [y] and promiscuity [z] [30]have brought this on you, because you lusted after the nations and defiled yourself with their idols. [a] [31]You have gone the way of your sister; so I will put her cup [b] into your hand. [c]

[32]"This is what the Sovereign LORD says:

"You will drink your sister's cup,
    a cup large and deep;
it will bring scorn and derision, [d]
    for it holds so much. [e]
[33]You will be filled with drunkenness and sorrow,
    the cup of ruin and desolation,
    the cup of your sister Samaria. [f]
[34]You will drink it [g] and drain it dry
    and chew on its pieces—
    and you will tear your breasts.

I have spoken, declares the Sovereign LORD. [h]

[35]"Therefore this is what the Sovereign LORD says: Since you have forgotten [i] me and thrust me behind your back, [j] you must bear [k] the consequences of your lewdness and prostitution."

[36]The LORD said to me: "Son of man, will you judge Oholah and Oholibah? Then confront [l] them with their detestable practices, [m] [37]for they have committed adultery and blood is on their hands. They committed adultery with their idols; they even sacrificed their children, whom they bore to me, as food for them. [n] [38]They have also done this to me: At that same time they defiled my sanctuary [o] and desecrated my Sabbaths. [p] [39]On the very day they sacrificed their children to their idols, they entered my sanctuary and desecrated [q] it. That is what they did in my house. [r]

[40]"They even sent messengers for men who came from far away, [s] and when they arrived you bathed yourself for them, painted your eyes [t] and put on your jewelry. [u] [41]You sat on an elegant couch, [v] with a table [w] spread before it on which you had placed the incense [x] and olive oil that belonged to me. [y]

[42]"The noise of a carefree [z] crowd was around her; drunkards [a] were brought from the desert along with men from the rabble, and they put bracelets [b] on the arms of the woman and her sister and beautiful crowns on their heads. [c] [43]Then I said about the one worn out by adultery, 'Now let them use her as a prostitute, [d] for that is all she is.' [44]And they slept with her. As men sleep with a prostitute, so they slept with those lewd women, Oholah and Oholibah. [45]But righteous judges will sentence them to the punishment of women who commit adultery and shed blood, [e] because they are adulterous and blood is on their hands. [f]

[46]"This is what the Sovereign LORD says: Bring a mob [g] against them and give them over to terror and plunder. [h] [47]The mob will stone them and cut them down with their swords; they will kill their sons and daughters [i] and burn [j] down their houses. [k]

[48]"So I will put an end [l] to lewdness in the land, that all women may take warning and not imitate you. [m] [49]You will suffer the penalty for your lewdness and bear the consequences of your sins of idolatry. [n] Then you will know that I am the Sovereign LORD. [o]"

JERUSALEM AS A COOKING POT

24 In the ninth year, in the tenth month on the tenth day, the word of the LORD came to me: [p] [2]"Son of man, record [q] this date, this very date, because the king of Babylon has laid siege to Jerusalem this very day. [r] [3]Tell this rebellious house [s] a parable [t] and say to them: 'This is what the Sovereign LORD says:

23:29 [w] Mic 1:11
[x] S Jer 13:27
[y] S Eze 22:9
[z] Dt 28:48;
S Eze 16:36
23:30 [a] Ps 106:37-38; Zep 3:1
23:31 [b] S Jer 25:15
[c] 2Ki 21:13
23:32 [d] Ps 44:13;
Hos 7:16 [e] Ps 60:3;
Isa 51:17; Jer 25:15
23:33 [f] Jer 25:15-16;
S Eze 12:19
23:34 [g] S Ps 16:5
[h] S Jer 25:27
23:35 [i] S Dt 32:18;
S Isa 17:10
[j] S 1Ki 14:9;
S 2Ch 29:6
[k] Eze 16:52
23:36 [l] S Eze 16:2
[m] Isa 58:1;
S Eze 22:2; Mic 3:8
23:37 [n] S Eze 16:36
23:38 [o] S Lev 15:31
[p] S Ne 10:31
23:39 [q] S 2Ki 21:4
[r] S Jer 7:10; Eze 22:8
23:40 [s] S Isa 57:9
[t] 2Ki 9:30
23:41 [v] S Est 1:6;
S Pr 7:17 [w] Isa 65:11;
Eze 41:22; 44:16;
Mal 1:7,12 [x] Isa 57:9;
S 65:3; S Jer 44:5
[y] S Nu 18:12
23:42 [z] S Ps 73:5
[a] S 2Ch 9:1
[b] S Ge 24:30
[c] S Eze 16:11-12
23:43 [d] ver 3
23:45 [e] S Eze 22:3
[f] S Lev 20:10;
S Eze 16:38; Hos 2:2;
6:5
23:46 [g] Eze 16:40
[h] S Dt 28:25;
S Jer 25:9
23:47 [i] S ver 25
[j] 2Ch 36:19;
S Jer 34:22
[k] S 2Ch 36:17
23:48 [l] Eze 16:41
[m] 2Pe 2:6
23:49 [n] Eze 24:13
[o] S Eze 7:4; S 9:10;
16:58; S 20:38
24:1 [p] S Eze 8:1;
26:1; 29:17
24:2 [q] Isa 30:8;
Hab 2:2 [r] 2Ki 25:1;
S Jer 39:1
24:3 [s] S Isa 1:2;
S Eze 2:3,6
[t] S Eze 20:49

23:31 *cup.* Filled with the anger of the Lord. To drink it was to die. For a development of the imagery, see Ps 16:5 and note; 75:8; Isa 51:17,22; Jer 25:15 and note; 49:12; La 4:21; Ob 16 and note; Hab 2:16; Mt 20:22; 26:39; Rev 14:10 and note.
23:34 *tear your breasts.* Beating the breasts—a sign of mourning (see 21:12; see also Jer 31:19; Lk 23:48 and notes)—is here poetically intensified to the point of tearing them in a frantic attempt to find relief from intolerable suffering.
23:35 *you have forgotten me.* See 22:12; Jer 2:32 and note.
23:37 *sacrificed their children.* See note on 16:20.
23:38 *defiled my sanctuary.* See ch. 8. *Sabbaths.* See note on 22:8.
23:40 *They even sent messengers for men.* Possibly a reference

to the Jerusalem summit meeting in Zedekiah's time (Jer 27). *you. Jerusalem. painted your eyes.* By daubing them with kohl, a soot-like compound, to draw attention to the eyes.
23:41 *couch, with a table spread before it.* Ready for a banquet (see Isa 21:5; also Pr 9:2).
23:42 *drunkards.* Drunkenness is consistently condemned in Scripture (see notes on Pr 20:1; Isa 5:11–13).
24:1–14 The series of oracles beginning with ch. 13 (see note on 13:1–23) ends with a depiction of Jerusalem as a pot cooking over an open fire, concluding with words that echo the final words of the seventh oracle in this series (see 18:30; 24:14 and notes).
24:1 *ninth year . . . tenth month . . . tenth day.* Of King Zedekiah's

24:3 *u* S Eze 11:3
24:4 *v* S Eze 11:7
24:5 *w* S Isa 34:12;
Jer 52:10 *x* Jer 52:24-
27; Mic 3:2-3
24:6 *y* S Eze 16:23
z S Eze 22:2
a S Job 6:27; Joel 3:3;
Ob 1:11; Na 3:10
b S Eze 11:11
24:7 *c* S Lev 17:13
24:11 *d* Jer 21:10
24:13 *e* S Isa 22:14
f Jer 6:28-30; La 1:9;
S Eze 16:42; 22:24;
23:36-49; Hos 7:1;
Zec 6:8
24:14 *g* Eze 22:14
h S Nu 11:23
i S Eze 8:18
j S Job 27:22
k Eze 36:19; Zec 8:14
l S Isa 3:11;
S Eze 18:30

" 'Put on the cooking pot; *u* put it on
    and pour water into it.
⁴ Put into it the pieces of meat,
    all the choice pieces—the leg and the shoulder.
Fill it with the best of these bones; *v*
⁵   take the pick of the flock. *w*
Pile wood beneath it for the bones;
    bring it to a boil
    and cook the bones in it. *x*

⁶ " 'For this is what the Sovereign Lᴏʀᴅ says:

" 'Woe *y* to the city of bloodshed, *z*
    to the pot now encrusted,
    whose deposit will not go away!
Take the meat out piece by piece
    in whatever order *a* it comes. *b*

⁷ " 'For the blood she shed is in her midst:
    She poured it on the bare rock;
she did not pour it on the ground,
    where the dust would cover it. *c*
⁸ To stir up wrath and take revenge
    I put her blood on the bare rock,
    so that it would not be covered.

⁹ " 'Therefore this is what the Sovereign Lᴏʀᴅ says:

" 'Woe to the city of bloodshed!
    I, too, will pile the wood high.
¹⁰ So heap on the wood
    and kindle the fire.
Cook the meat well,
    mixing in the spices;
    and let the bones be charred.
¹¹ Then set the empty pot on the coals
    till it becomes hot and its copper glows,
so that its impurities may be melted
    and its deposit burned away. *d*
¹² It has frustrated all efforts;
    its heavy deposit has not been removed,
    not even by fire.

¹³ " 'Now your impurity is lewdness. Because I tried to cleanse you but you would not be cleansed *e* from your impurity, you will not be clean again until my wrath against you has subsided. *f*

¹⁴ " 'I the Lᴏʀᴅ have spoken. *g* The time has come for me to act. *h* I will not hold back; I will not have pity, *i* nor will I relent. *j* You will be judged according to your conduct and your actions, *k* declares the Sovereign Lᴏʀᴅ. *l* ' "

---

reign (2Ki 25:1); Jan. 15, 588 ʙ.ᴄ., some two and a half years after the preceding dated oracle (see 20:1 and chart, p. 1364); Ezekiel's fourth date (see 1:2; 8:1; 20:1).
24:2 *record this date . . . because.* God revealed to Ezekiel what was happening in Jerusalem.
24:3 *rebellious house.* The last occurrence of this condemning phrase in Ezekiel (see 2:5,6,8; 3:9, 26–27; 12:2–3,9,25; 17:12). Jerusalem's rebellion would soon be crushed. *parable.* Cf. 17:2. *cooking pot.* A reuse of the imagery found in 11:3–12. The cooking pot is Jerusalem (cf. 11:3 and note). In what follows, the imagery shifts from cooking the meat and bones in the pot (vv. 4–5) to burning away the impurities that adhere to the pot (vv. 6–8) and then repeats the cycle (vv. 9–10, cooking the meat and bones; vv. 11–12, burning off the encrusted impurities).
24:4 *choice pieces.* The people of Jerusalem who thought they were spared the exile in 597 ʙ.ᴄ. because of their goodness (see 11:3 and note).

24:5 *wood.* Nebuchadnezzar's siege equipment.
24:6 *city of bloodshed.* Cf. v. 9; 22:2–3. *encrusted.* Representing Jerusalem's irredeemable situation. *in whatever order it comes.* After the siege of Jerusalem in 597, perhaps the Babylonians had cast lots to see whom they would take away into exile. Now everyone would go.
24:7 *blood . . . on the bare rock.* Jerusalem had brazenly left on display the blood she unjustly shed (cf. Isa 3:9). For uncovered blood, see Ge 4:10; Job 16:18 and notes; cf. Lev 17:13–14.

A   **24:8** *wrath.* God's wrath. What Jerusalem had done would be done to her (see 16:43 and note; see also 1Ki 8:32; Isa 3:1; cf. Ex 4:21; 21:23–25; Lev 24:17–22; Dt 19:21 and notes).
24:11 *empty pot.* Jerusalem, emptied of inhabitants, would be set to the torch in a vain, final effort at purification.
24:13 *lewdness.* See 16:1–63; 23:1–49 and notes.
24:14 *The time has come.* See 7:2–3 and note on 7:1–27.

EZEKIEL'S WIFE DIES

¹⁵The word of the LORD came to me: ¹⁶"Son of man, with one blow ᵐ I am about to take away from you the delight of your eyes. ⁿ Yet do not lament or weep or shed any tears. ᵒ ¹⁷Groan quietly; ᵖ do not mourn for the dead. Keep your turban �ۊ fastened and your sandals ʳ on your feet; do not cover your mustache and beard ˢ or eat the customary food ⌞of mourners⌟. ᵗ"

¹⁸So I spoke to the people in the morning, and in the evening my wife died. The next morning I did as I had been commanded. ᵘ

¹⁹Then the people asked me, "Won't you tell us what these things have to do with us? ᵛ Why are you acting like this?"

²⁰So I said to them, "The word of the LORD came to me: ²¹Say to the house of Israel, 'This is what the Sovereign LORD says: I am about to desecrate my sanctuary ᵂ—the stronghold in which you take pride, ˣ the delight of your eyes, ʸ the object of your affection. The sons and daughters ᶻ you left behind will fall by the sword. ᵃ ²²And you will do as I have done. You will not cover your mustache and beard ᵇ or eat the customary food ⌞of mourners⌟. ᶜ ²³You will keep your turbans ᵈ on your heads and your sandals ᵉ on your feet. You will not mourn ᶠ or weep but will waste away ᵍ because ofᵃ your sins and groan among yourselves. ʰ ²⁴Ezekiel ⁱ will be a sign ʲ to you; you will do just as he has done. When this happens, you will know that I am the Sovereign LORD.'

²⁵"And you, son of man, on the day I take away their stronghold, their joy and glory, the delight of their eyes, ᵏ their heart's desire, ˡ and their sons and daughters ᵐ as well— ²⁶on that day a fugitive will come to tell you ⁿ the news. ²⁷At that time your mouth will be opened; you will speak with him and will no longer be silent. ᵒ So you will be a sign to them, and they will know that I am the LORD. ᵖ"

A PROPHECY AGAINST AMMON

25 The word of the LORD came to me: ²"Son of man, set your face against ᵠ the Ammonites ʳ and prophesy against them. ˢ ³Say to them, 'Hear the word of the Sovereign LORD. This is what the Sovereign LORD says: Because you said "Aha! ᵗ" over my sanctuary when it was desecrated ᵘ and over the land of Israel when it was laid waste and over the people of Judah when they went into exile, ᵛ ⁴therefore I am going to give you to the people of the East ᵂ as a possession. They will set up their camps ˣ and pitch their tents among you; they will eat your fruit and drink your milk. ʸ ⁵I will turn

---

ᵃ 23 Or *away in*

24:16 ᵐ S Ps 39:10	
ⁿ ver 21; Ps 84:1;	
S La 2:4 ᵒ Jer 13:17;	
16:5; S 22:10	
24:17 ᵖ Ps 39:9	
ᵠ S Ex 28:39;	
S Isa 3:20 ʳ S Isa 20:2	
ˢ S Lev 13:45 ᵗ ver 22;	
S Jer 16:7	
24:18 ᵘ S Eze 12:7	
24:19 ᵛ Eze 12:9;	
37:18	
24:21 ᵂ S Lev 26:31;	
S Eze 7:24	
ˣ S Lev 26:19	
ʸ S ver 16; Ps 27:4	
ᶻ S Eze 23:25	
ᵃ Jer 7:14,15;	
Hos 9:12,16; Mal 2:12	
24:22 ᵇ S Lev 13:45	
ᶜ Jer 16:7	
24:23 ᵈ S Ex 28:39;	
S Isa 3:20 ᵉ S Isa 20:2	
ᶠ Ex 33:4	
ᵍ S Lev 26:16	
ʰ Ps 78:64	
24:24 ⁱ Eze 1:3	
ʲ S Isa 20:3; Eze 12:11	
24:25 ᵏ S La 2:4	
ˡ S Ps 20:4	
ᵐ Dt 28:32; Jer 11:22	
24:26 ⁿ S 1Sa 4:12;	
Job 1:15-19	
24:27 ᵒ Da 10:15	
ᵖ S Eze 3:26; 33:22	
25:2 ᵠ S Eze 13:17;	
29:2 ʳ S Eze 21:28	
ˢ Jer 49:1-6	
25:3 ᵗ S Ps 35:21;	
Eze 26:2; 36:2	
ᵘ Zep 2:8 ᵛ S Pr 17:5	
25:4 ᵂ S Ge 25:6;	
S Jdg 6:3 ˣ S Nu 31:10	
ʸ Dt 28:33,51;	
S Jdg 6:33	

---

judged according to your conduct and your actions. See notes on Ro 2:1–16; 2:6–8; Rev 20:12.

24:15–27 Following the series of oracles concerning God's judgment on Judah (13:1—24:14), Ezekiel's action upon the death of his wife serves to symbolize how the exiles would react to the fall of Jerusalem, just as his earlier symbolic actions symbolized the exile of the people of Jerusalem (see 12:1–28 and note). These two symbolic acts thus serve as a literary frame around this second series of oracles in Ezekiel.

24:16 *blow.* Some swiftly fatal disease, one that often reached plague proportions (see Ex 9:14; Nu 14:37). *delight of your eyes.* The object of loving attention (see vv. 21,25)—apparently a conventional way of referring to a man's wife (cf. Jdg 14:3, "She's the right one for me" [lit. "She is right in my eyes"]; see also SS 8:10).

24:17 *Keep your turban fastened.* Mourners normally removed turbans and put dust on their heads (see Jos 7:6; 1Sa 4:12 and notes). *sandals on your feet.* Another time showed grief (see 2Sa 15:30 and note). *cover . . . mustache and beard.* A gesture of shame (Mic 3:7). *food ⌞of mourners⌟.* The funeral meal (see Jer 16:7 and note).

24:18 *in the evening my wife died.* She died the same day the temple was burned (Aug. 14, 586 B.C.; see vv. 25–27; 2Ki 25:8 and note; see also Introduction: Occasion, Purpose and Summary of Contents).

24:19 *Then the people asked me.* The third time the people responded to Ezekiel's behavior (see 12:9; 21:7 and notes).

24:21 *desecrate.* By letting Nebuchadnezzar burn it down.

24:24 *Ezekiel.* The Lord speaks of Ezekiel in the third person. Elsewhere the prophet's name occurs only in 1:3 (see note there). *sign.* See v. 27 and note on 12:6.

24:26 *fugitive.* The first of the exiles of 586 B.C. *news.* About the siege—its beginning (verifying the accuracy of vv. 1–2) and its ending (see note on 33:21).

24:27 *At that time.* When the fugitive arrived from Jerusalem (see 33:21 and note). *no longer be silent.* The muteness that had been imposed on him at the beginning of his ministry was now lifted (see 3:26 and note).

25:1—32:32 Oracles against the nations. Frequently in the prophets, God's word of judgment on Israel is accompanied by oracles of judgment on the nations (see note on Jer 46:1—51:64). These make clear that, while judgment begins "with God's household" (1Pe 4:17), the pagan nations would not escape God's wrath. Often these judgments are implicit messages of salvation for Israel (see 28:25–26 and notes) since the Lord's victories over hostile powers remove an enemy of his people or punish them for their cruel attacks on his people. In the case of Ezekiel, there are seven oracles (the seventh of which has seven parts, each introduced by the phrase "The word of the LORD came to me"; see Introduction: Outline). The structure of these oracles follows the pattern "Because [introducing the evil committed] . . . , therefore [introducing the judgment] . . . know that I am the LORD" (e.g., 25:3–7).

25:2 *set your face.* See note on 20:46. *Ammonites.* Ammon (part of modern Jordan) was immediately east of Israel (see 21:20 and note; see also Jer 9:26; 49:1–6; Am 1:13–15; Zep 2:8–11). For hostile Ammonite action during this time and later, see 2Ki 24:2; Ne 4:7.

25:3 *Aha!* A cry of malicious joy (cf. 26:2; 36:2; Ps 35:21–25).

25:4 *people of the East.* Probably nomadic tribes of the desert east of Ammon, though this could be a reference to Nebuchadnezzar and his army (see 21:31).

25:5 ʲS Dt 3:11
ᵃS S Isa 17:2
25:6 ᵇS Nu 24:10
ᶜS Eze 6:11; Ob 1:12;
Zep 2:8
25:7 ᵈZep 1:4
ᵉS Nu 14:3
ᶠEze 21:31;ᵛver 13-
14,17; Am 1:14-15
25:8 ʰS Ge 19:37;
S Dt 23:6; S Isa 16:6
ⁱS Ge 14:6
25:9 ʲS Nu 33:49
ᵏS Nu 32:3;
S Jos 13:17
ˡS Nu 32:37;
S Jos 13:19
25:10 ᵐEze 21:32
25:11 ⁿIsa 15:9;
16:1-14; Jer 48:1;
Am 2:1-3
25:12 ᵒS 2Sa 8:13-
14; S 2Ch 28:17;
S Isa 11:14
25:13 ᵖS Ex 7:5;
S Eze 16:27
�q Eze 29:8
ʳS Ge 36:11,15,34
ˢJer 25:23
ᵗS Jer 49:10;
S Eze 14:17
25:14 ᵘEze 35:11
ᵛS Ps 137:7;
Eze 32:29; 35:2-3;
36:5; Am 1:11; Ob 1:1,
10-16; Mal 1:4
25:15 ʷS Jos 13:3;
S 2Ch 28:18
ˣS Ps 73:8
25:16 ʸS 2Ch 26:6;
Am 1:8;ᶻS 1Sa 30:14
ᵃS Eze 20:33
25:17 ᵇS Nu 31:3
ᶜJer 44:13 ᵈS Ex 6:2;
S 8:22 ᵉS Isa 11:14
ᶠS Isa 14:30; Jer 47:7;
Joel 3:4
26:1 ᵍS Eze 24:1;
29:1; 30:20
26:2 ʰS Jos 19:29;
2Sa 5:11 ⁱS Eze 25:3

Rabbah ᶻ into a pasture for camels and Ammon into a resting place for sheep. ᵃ Then you will know that I am the Lᴏʀᴅ. ⁶For this is what the Sovereign Lᴏʀᴅ says: Because you have clapped your hands ᵇ and stamped your feet, rejoicing with all the malice of your heart against the land of Israel, ᶜ ⁷therefore I will stretch out my hand ᵈ against you and give you as plunder ᵉ to the nations. I will wipe you out from among the nations and exterminate you from the countries. I will destroy ᶠ you, and you will know that I am the Lᴏʀᴅ. ᵍ' "

A PROPHECY AGAINST MOAB

⁸"This is what the Sovereign Lᴏʀᴅ says: 'Because Moab ʰ and Seir ⁱ said, "Look, the house of Judah has become like all the other nations," ⁹therefore I will expose the flank of Moab, beginning at its frontier towns—Beth Jeshimoth ʲ, Baal Meon ᵏ and Kiriathaim ˡ— the glory of that land. ¹⁰I will give Moab along with the Ammonites to the people of the East as a possession, so that the Ammonites will not be remembered ᵐ among the nations; ¹¹and I will inflict punishment on Moab. Then they will know that I am the Lᴏʀᴅ.' " ⁿ

A PROPHECY AGAINST EDOM

¹²"This is what the Sovereign Lᴏʀᴅ says: 'Because Edom ᵒ took revenge on the house of Judah and became very guilty by doing so, ¹³therefore this is what the Sovereign Lᴏʀᴅ says: I will stretch out my hand ᵖ against Edom and kill its people and their animals. q I will lay it waste, and from Teman ʳ to Dedan ˢ they will fall by the sword. ᵗ ¹⁴I will take vengeance on Edom by the hand of my people Israel, and they will deal with Edom in accordance with my anger ᵘ and my wrath; they will know my vengeance, declares the Sovereign Lᴏʀᴅ.' " ᵛ

A PROPHECY AGAINST PHILISTIA

¹⁵"This is what the Sovereign Lᴏʀᴅ says: 'Because the Philistines ʷ acted in vengeance and took revenge with malice ˣ in their hearts, and with ancient hostility sought to destroy Judah, ¹⁶therefore this is what the Sovereign Lᴏʀᴅ says: I am about to stretch out my hand against the Philistines, ʸ and I will wipe out the Kerethites ᶻ and destroy those remaining along the coast. ᵃ ¹⁷I will carry out great vengeance ᵇ on them and punish ᶜ them in my wrath. Then they will know that I am the Lᴏʀᴅ, ᵈ when I take vengeance on them. ᵉᶠ' "

A PROPHECY AGAINST TYRE

26 In the eleventh month of the twelfth ᵃ year, on the first day of the month, the word of the Lᴏʀᴅ came to me: ᵍ ²"Son of man, because Tyre ʰ has said of Jerusalem, 'Aha! ⁱ The gate to the nations is broken, and its doors have swung

---

ᵃ 1 Probable reading of the original Hebrew text; Masoretic Text does not have *month of the twelfth*.

25:5 *Rabbah.* See note on 21:20. *pasture...resting place.* A common OT description for destroyed cities (see Isa 34:13–15; Zep 2:13–15). The sites were returned to the conditions they were in before the cities were built, representing the undoing of human efforts.

25:6 *clapped your hands.* See 6:11 and note.

25:7 *I will stretch out my hand against.* See note on 6:14. *plunder to the nations.* Cf. 26:5; 34:28. *wipe you out.* Cf. v. 16.

25:8 *Moab.* Immediately to the south of Ammon, east of the Dead Sea (see Ge 19:36–38 and note; Isa 15–16; Jer 48; Am 2:1–3; Zep 2:8–11). *Seir.* Edom, a country south of Moab and southeast of the Dead Sea (see ch. 35, especially v. 15; 36:5; Isa 34:5–17; 63:1–6; Jer 49:7–11; Am 1:11–12). *like all the other nations.* Israel wanted to be like the nations (see 20:32 and note), but when the nations saw Judah in her apparent vulnerability and lost their awe of her, they failed to take her God seriously (cf. La 4:12).

B **25:9** *flank of Moab.* Lower hills rising from the Dead Sea, visible from Jerusalem. *Beth Jeshimoth.* A town in the plains of Moab. *Baal Meon.* A major Moabite town mentioned in an inscribed monument of Mesha, king of Moab (see chart, p. xxiv). *Kiriathaim.* A city also mentioned in the Mesha inscription (cf. 2Ki 3:4–5 and note on 2Ki 1:1).

25:12 *Edom.* See note on v. 8 ("Seir"). *took revenge.* By not harboring Judah's refugees after 586 B.C. (see Ob 11–14 and notes).

25:13 *Teman.* A district near Petra in central Edom (see Jer 49:7,20; Am 1:12; Ob 9; Hab 3:3 and notes). *Dedan.* A tribe and territory in southern Edom (see 27:20; 38:13; Isa 21:13 and note; Jer 49:8).

25:15 *Philistines.* Inhabitants of the coastal plain along the Mediterranean west of Judah (1Sa 6:17; see note on Ge 10:14), who strove for control of Canaan until subdued by David. Their hostility to Israel continued, however (see Isa 14:29–31; Jer 47; Am 1:6–8; Zep 2:4–7), until Nebuchadnezzar deported them.

25:16 *Kerethites.* Related to, if not identical with, the Philistines (see 1Sa 30:14 and note; 2Sa 8:18; 15:18; 20:7). *coast.* Of the Mediterranean.

26:1—28:19 A series of prophecies against Tyre, the chief seaport of Phoenicia (present-day Lebanon). Tyre was an island fortress that had an additional harbor on the mainland. After Nebuchadnezzar's victory at Carchemish in 605 B.C., it acknowledged the hegemony of the Babylonian king, but in 594 B.C. it joined a coalition of states to throw off the Babylonian yoke (Jer 27:3). Ancient historians relate that Nebuchadnezzar laid siege to Tyre for 15 years (cf. 29:18 and note) and may have succeeded in once more establishing some kind of authority over it, but he did not succeed in destroying the city. The island fortress was not overrun until Alexander the Great conquered it after a seven-month siege in 332 B.C. (see notes on Isa 23:1; Zec 9:3).

26:1 *eleventh month of the twelfth year...first day of the month.* The fifth date in the book (see 1:2; 8:1; 20:1; 24:1). As the TNIV text note indicates, the Masoretic Text (the traditional Hebrew text) does not have "month of the twelfth." Thus it reads "eleventh year," which dates from Apr. 23, 587, to Apr. 13, 586 B.C. If this is the correct text, the prophecy must date from the end of that year, in the 11th (Feb. 13, 586) or the 12th month (Mar. 15, 586). But there is a problem with these dates: This prophecy open to me; now that she lies in ruins I will prosper,' ³therefore this is what the Sovereign Lord says: I am against you, Tyre, and I will bring many nations against you, like the sea*ʲ* casting up its waves. ⁴They will destroy*ᵏ* the walls of Tyre*ˡ* and pull down her towers; I will scrape away her rubble and make her a bare rock. ⁵Out in the sea*ᵐ* she will become a place to spread fishnets,*ⁿ* for I have spoken, declares the Sovereign Lord. She will become plunder*ᵒ* for the nations,*ᵖ* ⁶and her settlements on the mainland will be ravaged by the sword. Then they will know that I am the Lord.

⁷"For this is what the Sovereign Lord says: From the north I am going to bring against Tyre Nebuchadnezzar*ᵃ �q* king of Babylon, king of kings,*ʳ* with horses and chariots,*ˢ* with horsemen and a great army. ⁸He will ravage your settlements on the mainland with the sword; he will set up siege works*ᵗ* against you, build a ramp*ᵘ* up to your walls and raise his shields against you. ⁹He will direct the blows of his battering rams against your walls and demolish your towers with his weapons. ¹⁰His horses will be so many that they will cover you with dust. Your walls will tremble at the noise of the warhorses, wagons and chariots*ʷ* when he enters your gates as men enter a city whose walls have been broken through. ¹¹The hooves*ˣ* of his horses will trample all your streets; he will kill your people with the sword, and your strong pillars*ʸ* will fall to the ground.*ᶻ* ¹²They will plunder your wealth and loot your merchandise; they will break down your walls and demolish your fine houses and throw your stones, timber and rubble into the sea.*ᵃ* ¹³I will put an end*ᵇ* to your noisy songs,*ᶜ* and the music of your harps*ᵈ* will be heard no more.*ᵉ* ¹⁴I will make you a bare rock, and you will become a place to spread fishnets. You will never be rebuilt,*ᶠ* for I the Lord have spoken, declares the Sovereign Lord.

¹⁵"This is what the Sovereign Lord says to Tyre: Will not the coastlands*ᵍ* tremble*ʰ* at the sound of your fall, when the wounded groan*ⁱ* and the slaughter takes place in you? ¹⁶Then all the princes of the coast will step down from their thrones and lay aside their robes and take off their embroidered*ʲ* garments. Clothed*ᵏ* with terror, they will sit on the ground,*ˡ* trembling*ᵐ* every moment, appalled*ⁿ* at you. ¹⁷Then they will take up a lament*ᵒ* concerning you and say to you:

" 'How you are destroyed, city of renown,
　　peopled by men of the sea!
You were a power on the seas,
　　you and your citizens;
you put your terror
　　on all who lived there.*ᵖ*
¹⁸Now the coastlands tremble*�q*
　　on the day of your fall;
the islands in the sea
　　are terrified at your collapse.'*ʳ*

26:3 ʲ ver 19; Isa 5:30; Jer 50:42; 51:42
26:4 ᵏ S Isa 23:1,11 ˡ Am 1:10
26:5 ᵐ Eze 27:32 ⁿ Eze 47:10 ᵒ S Nu 14:3; Eze 29:19 ᵖ Zec 9:2-4
26:7 ᵍ Jer 27:6; 39:1 ʳ Ezr 7:12 ˢ S Eze 23:24; Na 2:3-4
26:8 ᵗ S Jer 6:6 ᵘ S Jer 33:4
26:9 ᵛ S Eze 21:22
26:10 ʷ S Jer 4:13; S 46:9; S Eze 23:24
26:11 ˣ Isa 5:28 ʸ S Jer 43:13
26:12 ᵃ Isa 23:8; S Jer 4:7; Eze 27:3-27; 28:8; Hab 1:8
26:13 ᵇ S Jer 7:34 ᶜ Isa 23:7 ᵈ S Ps 137:2; S Isa 14:11 ᵉ S Job 30:31; S Jer 16:9; S 25:10; Rev 18:22
26:14 ᶠ S Job 12:14; Mal 1:4
26:15 ᵍ Isa 41:5; Eze 27:35 ʰ S Jer 49:21 ⁱ S Job 24:12
26:16 ʲ S Ex 26:36 ᵏ S Job 8:22 ˡ S Job 2:8,13 ᵐ Hos 11:10 ⁿ S Lev 26:32; Eze 32:10
26:17 ᵒ S Eze 19:1 ᵖ Isa 14:12
26:18 ᵍ S Ps 46:6; S Jer 49:21 ʳ Isa 23:5; S 41:5; Eze 27:35

ᵃ 7 Hebrew *Nebuchadrezzar*, of which *Nebuchadnezzar* is a variant; here and often in Ezekiel and Jeremiah

describes Tyre's gloating over the destruction of Jerusalem (v. 2), yet Jerusalem did not fall until July 18, 586 (see note on 2Ki 25:2–3), and was not burned until Aug. 14, 586 (see note on 2Ki 25:8)—several months after the date given here for Tyre's celebration of the fact that Jerusalem "now ...lies in ruins" (v. 2). To solve the problem, many interpreters believe that the probable reading of the original Hebrew text was "In the eleventh month of the twelfth year, on the first day of the month" and that the words "month of the twelfth" must have been inadvertently omitted by a copyist (hence the TNIV reading). The restored reading would yield the date Feb. 3, 585, which would nicely fit the chronology in 33:21 (see note there). If, on the other hand, the Hebrew text that has come down to us is correct, then the Lord (through Ezekiel) is prophesying what Tyre's response to Jerusalem's fall will be and how the Lord, in turn, will judge Tyre.
26:2 *Tyre.* For other prophecies against Tyre, see Isa 23; Jer 25:22; 47:4; Joel 3:4–5; Am 1:9–10; Zec 9:2–4). *Aha!* See note on 25:3. *gate to the nations.* Because of its geographical location, its political importance and the central role it played in international trade. The anti-Babylonian summit meeting was held there (see Jer 27).
26:3 *I am against you.* See note on 5:8. *like the sea casting up its waves.* For invading armies likened to waves of the sea, cf. Isa 17:12–13. Since Tyre was mainly a fortified island, the metaphor

is especially appropriate here.
26:5 *plunder for the nations.* Cf. 25:7; 34:28.
26:6 *know that I am the Lord.* See Introduction: Themes.
26:7 *north.* The direction from which Nebuchadnezzar would descend on Tyre after first marching his army up the Euphrates River valley rather than across the Arabian Desert (cf. Jer 1:13). *I am going to bring.* A clear indication of God's sovereignty over the nations (cf. 28:7; 29:8). *Nebuchadnezzar.* The first of four references to him in Ezekiel (see 29:18–19; 30:10). He ruled from 605 to 562 B.C., and his name means "O (god) Nabu, protect my son" or "O (god) Nabu, protect my boundary." Jeremiah and Ezekiel both proclaimed that this pagan king would be used by God to do his work (see Jer 25:9 and note; 27:6).
26:8 *siege.* See note on 26:1—28:19.
26:14 *never be rebuilt.* Eventually fulfilled by Alexander's devastating siege in 332 B.C. (see note on Isa 23:1).
26:16 *princes of the coast.* In 27:35, they were probably trading partners with Tyre. *lay aside their robes.* Usually mourners tore their clothes (Job 2:12) and put on sackcloth, but cf. the king of Nineveh (Jnh 3:6). *Clothed with terror.* Because of political shock waves from the fall of such a powerful city (cf. 7:27; Ps 35:26; 109:29 and note).
26:17 *lament.* See note on 19:1.

26:19 ᵍS Ge 7:11
ᵗS ver 3; Isa 8:7-8
26:20 ᵘNu 16:30;
Ps 28:1; 88:6;
Eze 31:14; 32:18;
Am 9:2; Jnh 2:2, 6
ᵛS Job 28:13;
S Isa 14:9-10;
Eze 32:24, 30
26:21 ʷS Jer 51:64;
Da 11:19 ˣJer 20:4;
Eze 27:36; 28:19;
Rev 18:21
27:2 ʸS Eze 19:1
27:3 ᶻS Ps 83:7
ᵃver 33; Hos 9:13
ᵇS Isa 23:9;
S Eze 16:15
27:4 ᶜEze 28:12
27:5 ᵈS Dt 3:9
ᵉS Isa 2:13
27:6 ᶠNu 21:33;
S Ps 29:9; Jer 22:20;
Zec 11:2 ᵍS Ge 10:4;
Isa 23:12
27:7 ʰS Ex 26:36;
S Isa 19:9 ⁱEx 25:4;
Jer 10:9 ʲGe 10:4
27:8 ᵏGe 10:18
ˡ1Ki 9:27
27:9 ᵐS Jos 13:5
ⁿS Ps 104:26
27:10 ᵒ2Ch 36:20;
Ezr 1:1; Eze 38:5;
Da 8:20 ᵖS Isa 66:19
�q S Ge 10:6; Eze 30:5;
Na 3:9 ʳSS 4:4

[19]"This is what the Sovereign LORD says: When I make you a desolate city, like cities no longer inhabited, and when I bring the ocean depths ᵍ over you and its vast waters cover you,ᵗ [20]then I will bring you down with those who go down to the pit,ᵘ to the people of long ago. I will make you dwell in the earth below, as in ancient ruins, with those who go down to the pit, and you will not return or take your placeᵃ in the land of the living.ᵛ [21]I will bring you to a horrible end and you will be no more.ʷ You will be sought, but you will never again be found, declares the Sovereign LORD."ˣ

A LAMENT OVER TYRE

27 The word of the LORD came to me: [2]"Son of man, take up a lamentʸ concerning Tyre. [3]Say to Tyre,ᶻ situated at the gateway to the sea,ᵃ merchant of peoples on many coasts, 'This is what the Sovereign LORD says:

  " 'You say, Tyre,
    "I am perfect in beauty.ᵇ"
[4]Your domain was on the high seas;
  your builders brought your beauty to perfection.ᶜ
[5]They made all your timbers
  of juniper from Senir;ᵇ·ᵈ
  they took a cedar from Lebanon ᵉ
  to make a mast for you.
[6]Of oaks ᶠ from Bashan
  they made your oars;
  of cypress woodᶜ from the coasts of Cyprus ᵍ
  they made your deck, inlaid with ivory.
[7]Fine embroidered linen ʰ from Egypt was your sail
  and served as your banner;
  your awnings were of blue and purpleⁱ
  from the coasts of Elishah.ʲ
[8]Men of Sidon and Arvad ᵏ were your oarsmen;
  your skilled men, Tyre, were aboard as your sailors.ˡ
[9]Veteran craftsmen of Byblos ᵐ were on board
  as shipwrights to caulk your seams.
  All the ships of the sea ⁿ and their sailors
  came alongside to trade for your wares.

[10]" 'Men of Persia,ᵒ Lydiaᵖ and Putq
  served as soldiers in your army.
  They hung their shieldsʳ and helmets on your walls,
  bringing you splendor.
[11]Men of Arvad and Helek
  guarded your walls on every side;
  men of Gammad

ᵃ 20 Septuagint; Hebrew *return, and I will give glory*   ᵇ 5 That is, Mount Hermon   ᶜ 6 Targum; the Masoretic Text has a different division of the consonants.

26:19 *ocean depths.* The primeval, chaotic mass—the "deep" of Ge 1:2. Tyre's collapse into the sea is described in almost cosmic terms.

26:20 *pit.* The grave, "the earth below" (see note on Ps 30:1). *people of long ago.* Those long dead (Ps 143:3; La 3:6). *not return or take your place in the land of the living.* As Israel would (see 37:1–14).

26:21 See 27:36; 28:19.

27:2 *lament.* See note on 19:1.

27:3 *I am perfect in beauty.* See 28:12 and note; cf. 28:2 for a similar prideful statement. Since Tyre is described as a stately ship in the following verses, some translate, "You are a ship, perfect in beauty."

27:4 *brought your beauty to perfection.* See v. 11.

27:5 *Senir.* Amorite name for Hermon, the Anti-Lebanon mountain (or range) famed for cedar.

27:6 *Bashan.* See note on 39:18. *Cyprus.* Translates Hebrew *Kittim,* originally the name of a town in southern Cyprus colonized by Phoenicia.

27:7 *Elishah.* A city on the east side of Cyprus; also the oldest name for Cyprus (but see note on Ge 10:4).

27:8 *Sidon.* A harbor city 25 miles north of Tyre, which sometimes rivaled her in political and commercial importance (see note on 28:21). *Arvad.* Another Phoenician island-city, off the Mediterranean coast and north of Sidon.

27:9 *Byblos.* An important ancient city on the coast between Sidon and Arvad (see 1Ki 5:18; see also map No. 5 at the end of this study Bible).

27:10 *Persia.* Or "Paras" (identification uncertain). *Lydia.* In Asia Minor; the Lydians are known to have served as mercenaries for the Egyptians. *Put.* Libya, in North Africa, west of Egypt. *soldiers.* The ship image is abandoned, and Tyre is now described literally—as a city (note references to walls and towers here and in v. 11), complete with a mercenary army gathered from many peoples.

27:11 *Arvad.* See note on v. 8. *Helek.* Cilicia, the mountainous region in southeast Asia Minor. *Gammad.* Either (1) northern Asia Minor or (2) a coastal town near Arvad.

were in your towers.
They hung their shields around your walls;
    they brought your beauty to perfection. [s]

[12]" 'Tarshish[t] did business with you because of your great wealth of goods; [u] they exchanged silver, iron, tin and lead for your merchandise.

[13]" 'Greece,[v] Tubal and Meshek[w] did business with you; they traded human beings[x] and articles of bronze for your wares.

[14]" 'Men of Beth Togarmah[y] exchanged chariot horses, cavalry horses and mules for your merchandise.

[15]" 'The men of Rhodes[a][z] traded with you, and many coastlands[a] were your customers; they paid you with ivory[b] tusks and ebony.

[16]" 'Aram[b][c] did business with you because of your many products; they exchanged turquoise,[d] purple fabric, embroidered work, fine linen,[e] coral[f] and rubies for your merchandise.

[17]" 'Judah and Israel traded with you; they exchanged wheat[g] from Minnith[h] and confections,[c] honey, olive oil and balm[i] for your wares.[j]

[18]" 'Damascus[k] did business with you because of your many products and great wealth of goods.[l] They offered wine from Helbon, wool from Zahar [19]and casks of wine from Izal[m] in exchange for your wares: wrought iron, cassia[n] and calamus.

[20]" 'Dedan[o] traded in saddle blankets with you.

[21]" 'Arabia[p] and all the princes of Kedar[q] were your customers; they did business with you in lambs, rams and goats.

[22]" 'The merchants of Sheba[r] and Raamah traded with you; for your merchandise they exchanged the finest of all kinds of spices[s] and precious stones, and gold.[t]

[23]" 'Harran,[u] Kanneh and Eden[v] and merchants of Sheba, Ashur[w] and Kilmad traded with you. [24]In your marketplace they traded with you beautiful garments, blue fabric, embroidered work and multicolored rugs with cords twisted and tightly knotted.

[25]" 'The ships of Tarshish[x] serve
        as carriers for your wares.
    You are filled with heavy cargo
        as you sail the sea.[y]
[26] Your oarsmen take you
        out to the high seas.
    But the east wind[z] will break you to pieces
        far out at sea.

---

[a] 15 Septuagint; Hebrew *Dedan*   [b] 16 Most Hebrew manuscripts; some Hebrew manuscripts and Syriac *Edom*   [c] 17 The meaning of the Hebrew for this word is uncertain.

27:11 ˢ ver 27
27:12 ᵗ S Ge 10:4; ᵘ ver 18,33
27:13 ᵛ Joel 3:6; ʷ Ge 10:2; Isa 66:19; Eze 32:26; 38:2; 39:1; ˣ Rev 18:13
27:14 ʸ S Ge 10:3
27:15 ᶻ S Ge 10:7; ᵃ S Jer 25:22; ᵇ 1Ki 10:22; Rev 18:12
27:16 ᶜ Jdg 10:6; Isa 7:1-8 ᵈ Ex 28:18; 39:11; Eze 28:13; ᵉ S Eze 16:10; ᶠ Job 28:18
27:17 ᵍ S 1Ki 5:9; ʰ Jdg 11:33; ⁱ S Ge 43:11 / Ac 12:20
27:18 ᵏ S Ge 14:15; ˡ S ver 12
27:19 ᵐ Ge 10:27; ⁿ S Ex 30:24
27:20 ᵒ S Ge 10:7
27:21 ᵖ S 2Ch 9:14; �q S Ge 25:13; Isa 21:17
27:22 ʳ S Ge 10:7,28; ˢ S Ge 43:11; ᵗ Rev 18:12
27:23 ᵘ S Ge 11:26; ᵛ Isa 37:12; ʷ S Ge 10:22; S Nu 24:24
27:25 ˣ S Ge 10:4; Isa 2:16 ᶠⁿ ʸ Rev 18:3
27:26 ᶻ S Ge 41:6; Jer 18:17

27:12 *Tarshish.* Traditionally located on the coast of southern Spain, but the island of Sardinia has also been suggested. Passages such as 1Ki 10:22; Jnh 1:3 imply that it was a long distance from the Canaanite coast. The list of places in vv. 12–23 generally follows a west-to-east direction.

27:13 *Tubal and Meshek.* Both in Asia Minor.

27:14 *Beth Togarmah.* In eastern Asia Minor, present-day Armenia (see 38:6). *chariot horses.* Asia Minor was known for its horses (see 1Ki 10:28 and TNIV text note there on "Kue").

27:15 *Rhodes.* A large island off the southwest coast of Asia Minor that served as gateway to the Aegean islands. It was an early major trading center (see Ac 21:1).

27:16 *Aram.* Since Damascus, the capital of Aram, is mentioned in v. 18, perhaps Edom is meant here (see TNIV text note; see also 25:12 and note).

27:17 *Israel traded with you.* In the past. Since 722–721 B.C. Israel had ceased to exist as a political state. *Minnith.* An Ammonite town, apparently famous for its wheat; "wheat from Minnith" possibly denoted a superior quality of wheat. *balm.* Gum or oil from one of several plants; a product of Gilead (see Ge 37:25 and note; Jer 8:22; 46:11).

27:18 *Damascus.* Capital of Aram (see note on v. 16; see also Isa 7:8). *Helbon.* A town north of Damascus, still in existence and still a wine-making center. The name occurs only here in the Bible. *Zahar.* Modern Sahra, an area northwest of Damascus, where grazing is still common today.

27:19 *Izal.* Perhaps the area between Harran and the Tigris. *cassia.* Similar to the cinnamon tree. The only other Biblical mention of it is in Ex 30:24, where it appears in a list of aromatic plants. *calamus.* An aromatic reed.

27:20 *Dedan.* See note on 25:13.

27:21 *Arabia and … Kedar.* A general expression for the nomadic tribes from Aram to the Arabian Desert. For Kedar, see Isa 21:16 and note; 42:11; 60:7; Jer 49:28.

27:22 *Sheba.* See note on 23:42. *Raamah.* A city in southern Arabia.

27:23 *Harran.* A city east of Carchemish, in present-day eastern Turkey. It was well-known in ancient times as a center both for trade and for the worship of the moon-god, Sin. From here Abraham moved to Canaan (see Ge 11:31 and note; 12:4). *Kanneh.* Of uncertain location, presumably in Mesopotamia. It is often identified with Kalno or Kalneh (Isa 10:9; Am 6:2). *Eden.* A district south of Harran, mentioned in connection with Harran in 2Ki 19:12 (see note there). Cf. Beth Eden in Am 1:5 (but see note there). *Sheba.* See note on 23:42. *Ashur.* Can mean the city, the country (Assyria) or the people (Assyrians). Here it is probably the city south of Nineveh that gave its name to the country. *Kilmad.* If a town, it is yet unidentified; presumably in Mesopotamia. Some read "all Media."

27:25 *Tarshish.* See note on v. 12. The ship image is resumed (see notes on vv. 3,10).

27:26 *east wind.* Disastrous at sea (Ps 48:7) as well as on land (Jer 18:17). It possibly symbolizes Nebuchadnezzar (as in 17:10; 19:12).

27:27 *a* Pr 11:4
b Eze 28:8
27:28 *c* S Jer 49:21
27:30 *d* S Jos 7:6;
S 2Sa 1:2 *e* S Jer 6:26
f Rev 18:18-19
27:31 *g* S Lev 13:40;
S Job 1:20; S Isa 3:17;
S Jer 48:37
h S Isa 16:9; Rev 18:15
i S Est 4:1; Job 3:20;
Isa 22:12; Jer 6:26;
S La 2:10; S Eze 7:18
27:32 *j* S Eze 19:1
k Isa 23:1-6; Eze 26:5
27:33 *l* S ver 3
m S ver 12;
Eze 28:4-5
27:34 *n* Zec 9:4
27:35 *o* S Eze 26:15
p S Lev 26:32;
S Job 18:20
q S Eze 26:17-18;
32:10
27:36 *r* Jer 19:8;
S 49:17; S 50:13;
Zep 2:15 *s* S Ps 37:10,
36; S Eze 26:21
28:2 *t* S Isa 13:11
u S Isa 14:13
v Zep 2:15 *w* S Ge 3:5;
S Ps 9:20; 82:6-7;
S Eze 16:49; 2Th 2:4
28:3 *x* S Eze 14:14;
Da 1:20; 2:20-23,28;
5:11-12

²⁷ Your wealth, *a* merchandise and wares,
    your mariners, sailors and shipwrights,
your merchants and all your soldiers,
    and everyone else on board
will sink into the heart of the sea *b*
    on the day of your shipwreck.
²⁸ The shorelands will quake *c*
    when your sailors cry out.
²⁹ All who handle the oars
    will abandon their ships;
the mariners and all the sailors
    will stand on the shore.
³⁰ They will raise their voice
    and cry bitterly over you;
they will sprinkle dust *d* on their heads
    and roll *e* in ashes. *f*
³¹ They will shave their heads *g* because of you
    and will put on sackcloth.
They will weep *h* over you with anguish of soul
    and with bitter mourning. *i*
³² As they wail and mourn over you,
    they will take up a lament *j* concerning you:
"Who was ever silenced like Tyre,
    surrounded by the sea? *k*"
³³ When your merchandise went out on the seas, *l*
    you satisfied many nations;
with your great wealth *m* and your wares
    you enriched the kings of the earth.
³⁴ Now you are shattered by the sea
    in the depths of the waters;
your wares and all your company
    have gone down with you. *n*
³⁵ All who live in the coastlands *o*
    are appalled *p* at you;
their kings shudder with horror
    and their faces are distorted with fear. *q*
³⁶ The merchants among the nations scoff at you; *r*
    you have come to a horrible end
    and will be no more. *s* "

A PROPHECY AGAINST THE KING OF TYRE

28 The word of the LORD came to me: ²"Son of man *t*, say to the ruler of Tyre, 'This is what the Sovereign LORD says:

" 'In the pride of your heart
    you say, "I am a god;
I sit on the throne *u* of a god
    in the heart of the seas." *v*
But you are a mortal and not a god,
    though you think you are as wise as a god. *w*
³ Are you wiser than Daniel *a*? *x*
    Is no secret hidden from you?
⁴ By your wisdom and understanding
    you have gained wealth for yourself

a 3 Or *Danel,* a man of renown in ancient literature

27:30 *dust on their heads.* See 26:16 for a similar scene. *roll in ashes.* Cf. Mic 1:10 and note.
27:31 *shave their heads.* Cf. 7:18; Isa 15:2 and note; 22:12. *sackcloth.* See notes on Ge 37:34; Rev 11:3.
27:36 *horrible end … be no more.* See 26:21; 28:19; see also note on Isa 23:1.
28:2,8 *in the heart of the seas.* Emphasizes Tyre's location as an

island fortress and as a dominant force in maritime commerce.
28:2 *ruler of Tyre.* May refer to the city of Tyre as ruler, or to Ethbaal II, Tyre's king (see v. 12), not to be confused with Ethbaal I (see 1Ki 16:31). *pride.* Cf. 27:3; Pr 11:2 and note; 16:18; Ac 12:21–23. *I am a god.* Cf. the proud boasts of the king of Babylon in Isa 14:12–15 (see note there).
28:3 *Daniel.* See note on 14:14.

and amassed gold and silver
   in your treasuries. [y]
[5] By your great skill in trading [z]
   you have increased your wealth, [a]
and because of your wealth
   your heart has grown proud. [b]

[6] " 'Therefore this is what the Sovereign LORD says:

" 'Because you think you are wise,
   as wise as a god,
[7] I am going to bring foreigners against you,
   the most ruthless of nations; [c]
they will draw their swords against your beauty and wisdom [d]
   and pierce your shining splendor. [e]
[8] They will bring you down to the pit, [f]
   and you will die a violent death [g]
   in the heart of the seas. [h]
[9] Will you then say, "I am a god,"
   in the presence of those who kill you?
You will be but a mortal, not a god, [i]
   in the hands of those who slay you. [j]
[10] You will die the death of the uncircumcised [k]
   at the hands of foreigners.

I have spoken, declares the Sovereign LORD.' "

[11] The word of the LORD came to me: [12] "Son of man, take up a lament [l] concerning the king of Tyre and say to him: 'This is what the Sovereign LORD says:

" 'You were the seal of perfection,
   full of wisdom and perfect in beauty. [m]
[13] You were in Eden, [n]
   the garden of God; [o]
every precious stone [p] adorned you:
   carnelian, chrysolite and emerald,
   topaz, onyx and jasper,
   lapis lazuli, turquoise [q] and beryl. [a]
Your settings and mountings [b] were made of gold;
   on the day you were created they were prepared. [r]
[14] You were anointed [s] as a guardian cherub, [t]
   for so I ordained you.
You were on the holy mount of God;
   you walked among the fiery stones.
[15] You were blameless in your ways
   from the day you were created
   till wickedness was found in you.
[16] Through your widespread trade

---

[a] 13 The precise identification of some of these precious stones is uncertain.   [b] 13 The meaning of the Hebrew for this phrase is uncertain.

28:7 *foreigners.* The Babylonians; see next phrase.
28:8 *pit.* Cf. Job 33:22,24; see note on 26:20.
28:10 *uncircumcised.* Used here in the sense of barbarian or uncouth. The Phoenicians, like the Israelites and the Egyptians, practiced circumcision (see 31:18; 32:19).
28:12 *lament.* See note on 19:1. *king of Tyre.* Cf. v. 2, but see note on Isa 14:12–15. *seal of perfection.* For "seal," see Hag 2:23, where Zerubbabel is called God's "signet ring" (see note there). With cutting irony Ezekiel depicts the proud king of Tyre as the first man created, radiant with wisdom and beauty. *perfect in beauty.* See 27:3 and note.
28:13 *You were in Eden.* Like Adam (Ge 2:15). Ezekiel continues to use imagery of the creation and the fall to picture the career of the king of Tyre (see 31:9,16,18). *every precious stone.* Unlike Adam, who was naked (Ge 2:25), the king is pictured as a fully

clothed priest, ordained (v. 14) to guard God's holy place. The 9 stones are among the 12 worn by the priest (Ex 28:17–20). (The Septuagint, the pre-Christian Greek translation of the OT, lists all 12.) *settings and mountings.* For the precious stones. *on the day you were created.* Cf. v. 15; Ge 5:2.
28:14 *as a guardian cherub.* Cf. v. 16. The Genesis account has cherubim (plural) stationed at the border of the garden after the expulsion of Adam and Eve (see Ge 3:24 and note). Some read "with" instead of "as." *holy mount of God.* Cf. v. 16. This does not reflect the Genesis story. See Isa 14:13 for the figure of God dwelling on a mountain. *fiery stones.* The precious stones (v. 13; cf. Rev 4:1–6; 21:15–21).
28:15 *You were blameless … till.* The parallel to Ge 2–3 is clear (see Ge 6:9 and note; 17:1).
28:16 *widespread trade … filled with violence.* Tyre's major crime.

28:4 [y] Isa 10:13;
Zec 9:3
28:5 [z] Isa 23:8
[a] S Jer 9:23;
S Eze 27:33
[b] S Job 31:25; Ps 52:7;
62:10; Hos 12:8; 13:6
28:7 [c] Eze 30:11;
31:12; 32:12; Hab 1:6
[d] Jer 9:23
[e] S Eze 7:24
28:8 [f] S Ps 55:23;
Eze 32:30 [g] Rev 18:7
[h] S Eze 26:12; 27:27
28:9 [i] S Isa 31:3
[j] S Eze 16:49
28:10 [k] S 1Sa 14:6;
S Jer 9:26; Eze 32:19,
24
28:12 [l] S Eze 19:1
[m] Eze 27:2-4
28:13 [n] S Ge 2:8
[o] Eze 31:8-9
[p] Rev 17:4
[q] S Eze 27:16
[r] Isa 14:11; Rev 21:20
28:14 [s] Ex 30:26;
40:9 [t] Ex 25:17-20

28:16 ᵘ S Ge 6:11;
Hab 2:17 ᵛ S Ge 3:24
28:17 ʷ Isa 10:12;
Eze 16:49; 31:10
ˣ S Eze 19:12
28:18 ʸ Ob 1:18
ᶻ Mal 4:3 ᵃ Zec 9:2-4
28:19 ᵇ S Lev 26:32
ᶜ S Jer 51:64;
S Eze 26:21
28:21 ᵈ S Eze 13:17
ᵉ S Ge 10:15;
S Jer 25:22
28:22 ᶠ Eze 39:13
ᵍ Eze 30:19
ʰ S Lev 10:3
28:23 ᶦ S Eze 5:17;
38:22
28:24 ʲ S Isa 5:6;
S Eze 2:6
28:25 ᵏ S Ps 106:47;
Jer 32:37 ˡ S Isa 11:12
ᵐ S Eze 20:41
ⁿ Jer 12:15; 23:8;
S Eze 11:17; 34:27;
37:25
28:26 ᵒ S Lev 25:18;
S 1Ki 4:25; S Jer 17:25
ᵖ Dt 20:6
�q S Ps 149:9
ʳ S Isa 65:21;
S Jer 32:15; Eze 38:8;
39:26-27; Hos 2:15;
11:11; Am 9:14-15
29:1 ˢ ver 17;
S Eze 26:1
29:2 ᵗ S Eze 25:2
ᵘ S Jer 25:19
ᵛ Isa 19:1-17; Jer 46:2;
Eze 30:1-26; 31:1-18;
32:1-32

you were filled with violence, ᵘ
   and you sinned.
So I drove you in disgrace from the mount of God,
   and I expelled you, guardian cherub, ᵛ
   from among the fiery stones.
¹⁷ Your heart became proud ʷ
   on account of your beauty,
and you corrupted your wisdom
   because of your splendor.
So I threw you to the earth;
   I made a spectacle of you before kings. ˣ
¹⁸ By your many sins and dishonest trade
   you have desecrated your sanctuaries.
So I made a fire ʸ come out from you,
   and it consumed you,
and I reduced you to ashes ᶻ on the ground
   in the sight of all who were watching. ᵃ
¹⁹ All the nations who knew you
   are appalled ᵇ at you;
you have come to a horrible end
   and will be no more. ᶜ ' "

A PROPHECY AGAINST SIDON

²⁰ The word of the LORD came to me: ²¹ "Son of man, set your face against ᵈ Sidon; ᵉ prophesy against her ²² and say: 'This is what the Sovereign LORD says:

" 'I am against you, Sidon,
   and among you I will display my glory. ᶠ
You will know that I am the LORD,
   when I inflict punishment ᵍ on you
   and within you am proved to be holy. ʰ
²³ I will send a plague upon you
   and make blood flow in your streets.
The slain will fall within you,
   with the sword against you on every side.
Then you will know that I am the LORD. ᶦ

²⁴ " 'No longer will the people of Israel have malicious neighbors who are painful briers and sharp thorns. ʲ Then they will know that I am the Sovereign LORD.

²⁵ " 'This is what the Sovereign LORD says: When I gather ᵏ the people of Israel from the nations where they have been scattered, ˡ I will be proved holy ᵐ through them in the sight of the nations. Then they will live in their own land, which I gave to my servant Jacob. ⁿ ²⁶ They will live there in safety ᵒ and will build houses and plant ᵖ vineyards; they will live in safety when I inflict punishment q on all their neighbors who maligned them. Then they will know that I am the LORD their God. ʳ ' "

A PROPHECY AGAINST EGYPT

JUDGMENT ON PHARAOH

29 In the tenth year, in the tenth month on the twelfth day, the word of the LORD came to me: ˢ ² "Son of man, set your face against ᵗ Pharaoh king of Egypt ᵘ and prophesy against him and against all Egypt. ᵛ ³ Speak to him and say: 'This is what the Sovereign LORD says:

28:17 *threw you to the earth.* Expulsion from the heavenly garden.
28:19 *horrible end . . . be no more.* See note on 27:36.
28:21 *set your face.* See note on 20:46. *Sidon.* See 27:8 and note. This is the only time in the OT that Sidon is mentioned apart from Tyre (cf. Isa 23:1–4; Jer 47:4; Joel 3:4; Zec 9:2).
28:22 *I am against you.* Possibly because of Sidon's involvement in the Jerusalem summit conference (Jer 27:3; see note on 5:8). *among you I will display my glory.* The Lord's glory would be recognized in Sidon's punishment. *am proved to be holy.* See v. 25; Lev 10:3 and note.

28:24 *painful briers.* For references to Israel's enemies as briers, see Nu 33:55; Jos 23:13.
28:25 *When I gather . . . Israel.* A frequent promise in Ezekiel and later (see 11:17; 20:34,41–42; 29:13; 34:13; 36:24; 37:21; 38:8; 39:27; Ne 1:9; Zec 10:8,10). *my servant Jacob.* Cf. 37:25. For the promise, see Ge 28:13; 35:12; Ps 105:10–11.
28:26 *live there in safety.* A perennial ideal that had become an especially meaningful promise (cf. 34:28; 38:8,11,14; 39:26; Lev 25:18–19; Jer 23:6; 32:37; 33:16)—closely related to God's promised "rest" (see Dt 3:20 and note). *houses . . . vineyards.* Basic necessities of the good life (cf. Isa 65:21; Jer 29:5,28; Am 9:14).

" 'I am against you, Pharaoh ^{w} king of Egypt,
　　you great monster ^{x} lying among your streams.
You say, "The Nile ^{y} belongs to me;
　　I made it for myself."
^{4}But I will put hooks ^{z} in your jaws
　　and make the fish of your streams stick to your scales.
I will pull you out from among your streams,
　　with all the fish sticking to your scales. ^{a}
^{5}I will leave you in the desert,
　　you and all the fish of your streams.
You will fall on the open field
　　and not be gathered ^{b} or picked up.
I will give you as food
　　to the beasts of the earth and the birds of the sky. ^{c}

^{6}Then all who live in Egypt will know that I am the LORD.

" 'You have been a staff of reed ^{d} for the house of Israel. ^{7}When they grasped you with their hands, you splintered ^{e} and you tore open their shoulders; when they leaned on you, you broke and their backs were wrenched. $^{a\,f}$

^{8}" 'Therefore this is what the Sovereign LORD says: I will bring a sword against you and kill your people and their animals. ^{g} ^{9}Egypt will become a desolate wasteland. Then they will know that I am the LORD.

" 'Because you said, "The Nile ^{h} is mine; I made it, $^{i\,}$" ^{10}therefore I am against you ^{j} and against your streams, and I will make the land of Egypt ^{k} a ruin and a desolate waste ^{l} from Migdol ^{m} to Aswan, ^{n} as far as the border of Cush. $^{b\,o}$ ^{11}No foot will pass through it, neither people nor animals; no one will live there for forty years. ^{p} ^{12}I will make the land of Egypt desolate ^{q} among devastated lands, and her cities will lie desolate forty years among ruined cities. And I will disperse the Egyptians among the nations and scatter them through the countries. ^{r}

^{13}" 'Yet this is what the Sovereign LORD says: At the end of forty years I will gather the Egyptians from the nations where they were scattered. ^{14}I will bring them back from captivity and return them to Upper Egypt, ^{s} the land of their ancestry. There they will be a lowly ^{t} kingdom. ^{u} ^{15}It will be the lowliest of kingdoms and will never again exalt itself above the other nations. ^{v} I will make it so weak that it will never again rule over the nations. ^{16}Egypt will no longer be a source of confidence ^{w} for the people of Israel but will be a reminder ^{x} of their sin in turning to her for help. ^{y} Then they will know that I am the Sovereign LORD. $^{z\,}$' "

NEBUCHADNEZZAR'S REWARD

^{17}In the twenty-seventh year, in the first month on the first day, the word of the LORD came to me: ^{a} ^{18}Son of man, Nebuchadnezzar ^{b} king of Babylon drove his army in a hard

---

^{a} 7 Syriac (see also Septuagint and Vulgate); Hebrew *and you caused their backs to stand*　　^{b} 10 That is, the upper Nile region

---

29:3 ^{w} Jer 44:30
^{x} S Ps 68:30; S 74:13;
Eze 32:2 ^{y} S Jer 46:8
29:4 ^{z} S 2Ki 19:28;
S Job 41:2 ^{a} Eze 38:4
29:5 ^{b} S Jer 8:2
^{c} S Jer 7:33; 34:20;
Eze 31:13; 32:4-6;
39:4
29:6 ^{d} S 2Ki 18:21
29:7 ^{e} 2Ki 18:21;
Isa 36:6 ^{f} Jer 17:5;
Eze 17:15-17
29:8 ^{g} Eze 25:13;
32:11-13
29:9 ^{h} S Jer 46:8
^{i} Eze 30:7-8,13-19
29:10 ^{j} S Jer 21:13
^{k} Ex 3:22
^{l} S Jer 46:19
^{m} S Ex 14:2
^{n} Eze 30:6 ^{o} Isa 18:1;
Eze 30:4
29:11 ^{p} Eze 32:13
29:12 ^{q} S Isa 34:10
^{r} S Jer 46:19;
29:14 ^{s} S Isa 11:11;
Eze 30:7,23,26
29:14 ^{t} Eze 17:14
^{u} S Isa 19:22;
Jer 46:26
29:15 ^{v} Zec 10:11
29:16 ^{w} 2Ch 32:10
^{x} Nu 5:15
^{y} S La 4:17 ^{z} Isa 20:5;
S 30:2; Hos 8:13
29:17 ^{a} S ver 1;
S Eze 24:1; 30:20;
40:1
29:18 ^{b} Jer 27:6;
39:1

29:1—32:32 A series of seven prophecies against Egypt (for their dates, see notes below), most of which came during Jerusalem's last years when the Egyptian pharaoh was offering encouragement to King Zedekiah to rebel against Nebuchadnezzar (see 17:15; Jer 37:5–8).
29:1 *tenth year ... tenth month ... twelfth day.* Jan. 7, 587 B.C.; the sixth date in Ezekiel (see 1:2; 8:1; 20:1; 24:1; 26:1). All the prophecies against Egypt are dated except one (30:1).
29:2 *set your face.* See note on 20:46. *Pharaoh.* Hophra, 589–570 B.C. (see Jer 44:30).
29:3 *I am against you.* See note on 5:8. *great monster.* Or "crocodile"; pictured as being in the Nile. See notes on Job 41:1; Ps 74:13–14; Isa 27:1. *your streams.* Nile delta and canals (cf. Isa 7:18; 19:6; 37:25). *You say.* Boasts inscribed on Egyptian monuments had become proverbial.
29:4 *hooks.* Cf. 19:4. *fish of your streams.* Egypt's conquered territories or mercenaries.
29:5 *food to the beasts.* Particularly frustrating to the pharaoh's great hopes for an afterlife, as symbolized by the pyramids and expressed in the Egyptian "Book of the Dead."

29:6 *You have been a staff of reed.* A comparison made earlier (see Isa 36:6 and note). Hophra briefly but unsuccessfully diverted the Babylonians' pharaoh from laying siege to Jerusalem (see Jer 37:1–10).
29:8 *sword.* Nebuchadnezzar's (see 5:2 and note).
29:10 *Migdol.* Probably in northern Egypt (see Jer 44:1 and note). *Aswan.* A town in southern Egypt. "From Migdol to Aswan" (30:6) probably indicated all Egypt, just as "from Dan to Beersheba" meant all Israel (see, e.g., Jdg 20:1; 1Sa 3:20 and notes).
29:11 *forty years.* Sometimes used to signify a long and difficult period (cf. 4:6).
29:14 *Upper Egypt.* Southern Egypt (see 30:14; Isa 11:11 and note; Jer 44:1,15).
29:17 The second prophecy against Egypt (see note on v. 1). *twenty-seventh year ... first month ... first day.* Apr. 26, 571 B.C.; the seventh date in Ezekiel (see v. 1; 1:2; 8:1; 20:1; 24:1; 26:1). This is the latest date in Ezekiel; accordingly, this oracle intrudes in the series of dated oracles against Egypt, all the rest of which come within the years 587–585.
29:18 *hard campaign.* Nebuchadnezzar besieged Tyre for 15

29:18 ʿS Lev 13:40;
S Job 1:20;
S Jer 48:37 ᵈ Ge 49:15
29:19 ᵉ S Isa 19:4
ᶠ S Eze 26:5
ᵍ Jer 43:10-13;
Eze 30:4,10,24-25;
32:11
29:20 ʰ S Isa 43:3
ⁱ Isa 10:6-7; 45:1;
S Jer 25:9
29:21 ʲ S Ps 132:17;
S Lk 1:69 ᵏ Eze 33:22
ˡ S Eze 3:27
30:2 ᵐ S Isa 13:6;
Jas 5:1
30:3 ⁿ S Eze 7:7;
Joel 1:15; 2:1,11;
Ob 1:15 ᵒ ver 18;
S Eze 7:12,19; 32:7;
34:12
30:4 ᵖ Jer 25:19;
Da 11:43 ᵠ S Ge 10:6;
S Eze 29:10
ʳ S Eze 29:19
30:5 ˢ S Eze 27:10
ᵗ S 2Ch 9:14
ᵘ Jer 25:20 ᵛ Na 3:9
30:6 ʷ Eze 29:10
30:7 ˣ S Eze 29:12
30:8 ʸ S Jer 49:27;
Eze 39:6; Am 1:4,7,
10; Na 1:6
ᶻ S Eze 29:9
30:9 ᵃ S Ge 10:6
ᵇ Isa 23:5 ᶜ Eze 32:9-
10; Zep 2:12
30:10 ᵈ Jer 39:1
ᵉ S Eze 29:19
30:11 ᶠ S Eze 28:7

campaign against Tyre; every head was rubbed bare ᶜ and every shoulder made raw. ᵈ Yet he and his army got no reward from the campaign he led against Tyre. ¹⁹ Therefore this is what the Sovereign Lord says: I am going to give Egypt to Nebuchadnezzar king ᵉ of Babylon, and he will carry off its wealth. He will loot and plunder ᶠ the land as pay for his army. ᵍ ²⁰ I have given him Egypt ʰ as a reward for his efforts because he and his army did it for me, declares the Sovereign Lord. ⁱ

²¹ On that day I will make a horn ᵃ ʲ grow for the house of Israel, and I will open your mouth ᵏ among them. Then they will know that I am the Lord. ˡ"

A LAMENT OVER EGYPT

30 The word of the Lord came to me: ²"Son of man, prophesy and say: 'This is what the Sovereign Lord says:

" 'Wail ᵐ and say,
  "Alas for that day!"
³ For the day is near, ⁿ
  the day of the Lord ᵒ is near—
a day of clouds,
  a time of doom for the nations.
⁴ A sword will come against Egypt, ᵖ
  and anguish will come upon Cush. ᵇ ᵠ
When the slain fall in Egypt,
  her wealth will be carried away
  and her foundations torn down. ʳ

⁵ Cush and Libya, ˢ Lydia and all Arabia, ᵗ Kub and the people ᵘ of the covenant land will fall by the sword along with Egypt. ᵛ

⁶ " 'This is what the Lord says:

" 'The allies of Egypt will fall
  and her proud strength will fail.
From Migdol to Aswan ʷ
  they will fall by the sword within her,

                              declares the Sovereign Lord.

⁷ " 'They will be desolate
    among desolate lands,
  and their cities will lie
    among ruined cities. ˣ
⁸ Then they will know that I am the Lord,
  when I set fire ʸ to Egypt
  and all her helpers are crushed. ᶻ

⁹ " 'On that day messengers will go out from me in ships to frighten Cush ᵃ out of her complacency. Anguish ᵇ will take hold of them on the day of Egypt's doom, for it is sure to come. ᶜ

¹⁰ " 'This is what the Sovereign Lord says:

" 'I will put an end to the hordes of Egypt
  by the hand of Nebuchadnezzar ᵈ king of Babylon. ᵉ
¹¹ He and his army—the most ruthless of nations ᶠ—

ᵃ 21 *Horn* here symbolizes strength.   ᵇ 4 That is, the upper Nile region; also in verses 5 and 9

---

years, from 586 to 571 B.C. (see 26:7–14). *every head was rubbed bare.* Probably from the leather helmets.

A **29:19** *I am going to give.* God's sovereignty over the nations is again proclaimed.

29:21 *make a horn grow for.* Revive the strength of (see TNIV text note). The passage is not a Messianic prophecy. *open your mouth.* Ezekiel's muteness (3:26; 24:27) would be removed, which anticipates 33:22.

30:1 The third prophecy against Egypt (see note on 29:1). No date is given, but it was probably between January and April of 587 B.C. Compare 29:1 with 30:20. Jerusalem was under siege at this time.

30:2–3 *that day . . . the day of the Lord.* The day of God's coming in judgment (see 7:7 and note). Egypt's judgment is announced.
30:3 *the day is near.* See 7:2–3,6 and note on 7:1–27; cf. Isa 13:6. *day of clouds.* Cf. Joel 2:2; Zep 1:15.
30:4 *sword.* Nebuchadnezzar's (see 29:8 and note).
30:5 *Libya.* In North Africa (see note on 27:10). *Lydia.* See 27:10 and note. *Kub.* Probably best understood as an unidentified place. *people of the covenant land.* Apparently Jews living in Egypt (see Jer 44 and note on 44:1).
30:6 *From Migdol to Aswan.* See note on 29:10.
30:8 *set fire to.* See note on 20:47.
30:9 *messengers . . . in ships.* See Isa 18 for a similar oracle on Cush, involving ships on the Nile.

will be brought in to destroy the land.
They will draw their swords against Egypt
and fill the land with the slain. *g*

¹²I will dry up *h* the waters of the Nile *i*
and sell the land to an evil nation;
by the hand of foreigners
I will lay waste *j* the land and everything in it.

I the LORD have spoken.

¹³" 'This is what the Sovereign LORD says:

" 'I will destroy the idols *k*
and put an end to the images in Memphis. *l*
No longer will there be a prince in Egypt, *m*
and I will spread fear throughout the land.
¹⁴I will lay *n* waste Upper Egypt,
set fire to Zoan *o*
and inflict punishment on Thebes. *p*
¹⁵I will pour out my wrath on Pelusium,
the stronghold of Egypt,
and wipe out the hordes of Thebes.
¹⁶I will set fire *q* to Egypt;
Pelusium will writhe in agony.
Thebes will be taken by storm;
Memphis *r* will be in constant distress.
¹⁷The young men of Heliopolis *s* and Bubastis
will fall by the sword,
and the cities themselves will go into captivity.
¹⁸Dark will be the day at Tahpanhes *t*
when I break the yoke of Egypt; *u*
there her proud strength will come to an end.
She will be covered with clouds,
and her villages will go into captivity. *v*
¹⁹So I will inflict punishment *w* on Egypt,
and they will know that I am the LORD.' "

PHARAOH'S ARMS ARE BROKEN

²⁰In the eleventh year, in the first month on the seventh day, the word of the LORD came to me: *x* ²¹"Son of man, I have broken the arm *y* of Pharaoh *z* king of Egypt. It has not been bound up to be healed *a* or put in a splint so that it may become strong enough to hold a sword. ²²Therefore this is what the Sovereign LORD says: I am against Pharaoh king of Egypt. *b* I will break both his arms, the good arm as well as the broken one, and make the sword fall from his hand. *c* ²³I will disperse the Egyptians among the nations and scatter them through the countries. *d* ²⁴I will strengthen *e* the arms of the king of Babylon and put my sword *f* in his hand, but I will break the arms of Pharaoh, and he will groan *g* before him like someone mortally wounded. ²⁵I will strengthen the arms of the king of Babylon, but the arms of Pharaoh will fall limp. Then they will know that I am the LORD, when I put my sword *h* into the hand of the king of Babylon and he brandishes it against Egypt. *i*

30:11 *g* ver 24-25
30:12 *h* S Isa 19:6
i S Jer 46:8; Eze 29:9
j S Eze 19:7
30:13 *k* S Jer 43:12;
S Eze 6:6 *l* S Isa 19:13
m Zec 10:11
30:14 *n* S Eze 29:14
o S Nu 13:22
p S Jer 46:25
30:16 *q* S Jos 7:15
r S Isa 19:13
30:17 *s* Ge 41:45
30:18 *t* S Jer 43:7
u S Lev 26:13;
S Isa 9:4 *v* S ver 3
30:19 *w* Eze 28:22
30:20 *x* S Eze 26:1;
S 29:17; 31:1; 32:1
30:21 *y* S Jer 48:25
z Jer 44:30
a Jer 30:13; 46:11
30:22 *b* S Ge 15:18;
S Jer 46:25 *c* Ps 37:17;
Zec 11:17
30:23 *d* S Eze 29:12
30:24 *e* Zec 10:6,12;
12:5 *f* S Eze 21:14;
Zep 2:12 *g* Jer 51:52
30:25 *h* 1Ch 21:12
i S Isa 10:5; 45:1,5;
S Eze 29:19

30:11 *most ruthless of nations.* A common phrase for the Babylonians, who were known for their cruelty (see 2Ki 25:7).

30:13 *idols.* See note on 6:4. *Memphis.* Located 15 miles south of Cairo, Memphis was a former capital of Egypt and one of her largest cities. The list of towns shows no discernible geographical pattern but is a literary device used to underscore the scope of the destruction (cf. Isa 10:9–11,27–32; Mic 1:10–15; Zep 2:4). *prince.* King.

30:14 *Upper Egypt.* See 29:14 and note. *Zoan.* A city in northeast Egypt in the delta region; also called Rameses (see Ge 47:11 and note; Ex 1:11), Avaris and Tanis (see Isa 19:11,13; 30:4 and notes). *Thebes.* Capital of Upper Egypt; present-day Luxor and Karnak.

30:15 *Pelusium.* A fortress in the eastern delta region of the Nile.

30:17 *Heliopolis.* Greek name (meaning "city of the sun") for

Hebrew *On,* located six miles northeast of Cairo. *Bubastis.* At one time the capital of Lower (northern) Egypt; located 40 miles northeast of Cairo.

30:18 *Dark.* A common Biblical metaphor describing ruin, destruction or death. *Tahpanhes.* In extreme northeast Egypt. Johanan, son of Kareah, and his men fled there after the murder of Gedaliah (see Jer 43:4–7). *covered with clouds.* See v. 3 and note; 32:7.

30:20 The fourth oracle against Egypt (see note on 29:1). *eleventh year . . . first month . . . seventh day.* Apr. 29, 587 B.C.; the eighth date in Ezekiel (see 1:2; 8:1; 20:1; 24:1; 26:1; 29:1,17).

30:21 *broken the arm.* Refers to Pharaoh Hophra's defeat by Nebuchadnezzar the previous year (see notes on 29:6; Jer 37:10).

30:24 *put my sword in his hand.* See note on 21:3.

30:25 *my sword.* See 5:2 and note.

30:26 / S Eze 29:12
31:1 *k* Jer 52:5
l S Eze 30:20; 32:17
31:3 *m* S Jer 50:18
n S 2Ki 19:23;
Hab 2:17; Zec 11:1
o Isa 10:34;
S Eze 19:11
31:4 *p* Eze 17:7
q Da 4:10
31:5 *r* ver 10
s S Nu 24:6;
S Eze 17:5
31:6 *t* S Ge 31:7-9
u S Eze 17:23;
S Mt 13:32
31:7 *v* S Job 14:9
31:8 *w* Ps 80:10
x S Ge 30:37
y Ge 2:8-9
31:9 *z* S Ge 2:8
a S Ge 13:10;
Eze 28:13
31:10 *b* S Isa 2:11;
S 14:13-14;
S Eze 28:17
31:11 *c* Da 5:20
31:12 *d* S Eze 28:7
e Eze 32:5; 35:8
f Eze 32:11-12;
Da 4:14
31:13 *g* S Isa 18:6;
S Eze 29:5; 32:4

[26]I will disperse the Egyptians among the nations and scatter them through the countries. Then they will know that I am the LORD.*j*"

PHARAOH AS A FELLED CEDAR OF LEBANON

31 In the eleventh year,*k* in the third month on the first day, the word of the LORD came to me:[2]"Son of man, say to Pharaoh king of Egypt and to his hordes:

" 'Who can be compared with you in majesty?
[3]Consider Assyria,*m* once a cedar in Lebanon,*n*
   with beautiful branches overshadowing the forest;
it towered on high,
   its top above the thick foliage.*o*
[4]The waters*p* nourished it,
   deep springs made it grow tall;
their streams flowed
   all around its base
and sent their channels
   to all the trees of the field.*q*
[5]So it towered higher*r*
   than all the trees of the field;
its boughs increased
   and its branches grew long,
   spreading because of abundant waters.*s*
[6]All the birds of the sky
   nested in its boughs,
all the animals of the wild
   gave birth*t* under its branches;
all the great nations
   lived in its shade.*u*
[7]It was majestic in beauty,
   with its spreading boughs,
for its roots went down
   to abundant waters.*v*
[8]The cedars*w* in the garden of God
   could not rival it,
nor could the junipers
   equal its boughs,
nor could the plane trees*x*
   compare with its branches—
no tree in the garden of God
   could match its beauty.*y*
[9]I made it beautiful
   with abundant branches,
the envy of all the trees of Eden*z*
   in the garden of God.*a*

[10]" 'Therefore this is what the Sovereign LORD says: Because the great cedar towered over the thick foliage, and because it was proud*b* of its height, [11]I gave it into the hands of the ruler of the nations, for him to deal with according to its wickedness. I cast it aside,*c* [12]and the most ruthless of foreign nations*d* cut it down and left it. Its boughs fell on the mountains and in all the valleys;*e* its branches lay broken in all the ravines of the land. All the nations of the earth came out from under its shade and left it.*f* [13]All the birds settled on the fallen tree, and all the wild animals lived among its branches.*g* [14]Therefore no other trees by the waters are ever to tower proudly on high, lifting their tops above the thick

---

31:1 The fifth prophecy against Egypt (see note on 29:1). *eleventh year ... third month ... first day.* June 21, 587 B.C.; the ninth date in Ezekiel (see 1:2; 8:1; 20:1; 24:1; 26:1; 29:1,17; 30:20).
31:3 *Consider Assyria.* A great nation that had fallen. In 609 B.C. Pharaoh Necho and his army marched north to help the Assyrians who were reeling from Babylonian attacks. The effort ultimately failed, and Assyria passed from history. *once a cedar.* The beginning of another allegory (see Ezekiel's allegorical use of the cedar in ch. 17). *Lebanon.* Known for its cedars (see vv.

15–18; Jdg 9:15; 1Ki 4:33; 5:6; 2Ki 14:9; Ezr 3:7; Ps 29:5; 92:12; 104:16).
31:4 *waters.* The Tigris and Euphrates. *deep springs.* Or "the deep" (see note on 26:19).
31:6 *birds of the sky.* See 17:23 and note.
31:8 *garden of God.* Cf. 28:13.
31:11 *ruler of the nations.* Probably Nabopolassar, or possibly Nebuchadnezzar. *its wickedness.* Pride (see v. 10; Ge 11:1–8).
31:12 *most ruthless.* Babylon (see note on 30:11).

foliage. No other trees so well-watered are ever to reach such a height; they are all destined *h* for death, *i* for the earth below, among mortals who go down to the realm of the dead. *j*

15 " 'This is what the Sovereign Lord says: On the day it was brought down to the realm of the dead I covered the deep springs with mourning for it; I held back its streams, and its abundant waters were restrained. Because of it I clothed Lebanon with gloom, and all the trees of the field withered away. *k* 16 I made the nations tremble *l* at the sound of its fall when I brought it down to the realm of the dead to be with those who go down to the pit. Then all the trees *m* of Eden, *n* the choicest and best of Lebanon, the well-watered trees, were consoled *o* in the earth below. *p* 17 They too, like the great cedar, had gone down to the realm of the dead, to those killed by the sword, *q* along with the armed men who lived in its shade among the nations.

18 " 'Which of the trees of Eden can be compared with you in splendor and majesty? Yet you, too, will be brought down with the trees of Eden to the earth below; you will lie among the uncircumcised, *r* with those killed by the sword.

" 'This is Pharaoh and all his hordes, declares the Sovereign Lord.' "

A LAMENT OVER PHARAOH

32 In the twelfth year, in the twelfth month on the first day, the word of the Lord came to me: *s* 2 "Son of man, take up a lament *t* concerning Pharaoh king of Egypt and say to him:

" 'You are like a lion *u* among the nations;
  you are like a monster *v* in the seas *w*
thrashing about in your streams,
  churning the water with your feet
  and muddying the streams. *x*

3 " 'This is what the Sovereign Lord says:

" 'With a great throng of people
  I will cast my net over you,
  and they will haul you up in my net. *y*
4 I will throw you on the land
  and hurl you on the open field.
I will let all the birds of the sky settle on you
  and all the animals of the wild gorge themselves on you. *z*
5 I will spread your flesh on the mountains
  and fill the valleys *a* with your remains.
6 I will drench the land with your flowing blood *b*
  all the way to the mountains,
  and the ravines will be filled with your flesh. *c*
7 When I snuff you out, I will cover the heavens
  and darken their stars;
I will cover the sun with a cloud,
  and the moon will not give its light. *d*
8 All the shining lights in the heavens
  I will darken *e* over you;
  I will bring darkness over your land, *f*

declares the Sovereign Lord.

31:14 *h* S Ps 49:14
i S Ps 82:7
j S Nu 14:11; Ps 63:9;
S Eze 26:20; 32:24
31:15 *k* S 2Sa 1:21
31:16 *l* S Jer 49:21
m S Isa 14:8
n S Ge 2:8
o S Eze 14:22
p S Isa 14:15;
Eze 32:18
31:17 *q* Ps 9:17
31:18 *r* S Jer 9:26
32:1 *s* S Eze 31:1;
33:21
32:2 *t* 2Sa 1:17; 3:33;
2Ch 35:25; S Eze 19:1
u S Eze 19:1-
13 *v* S Job 3:8;
S Ps 74:13 *w* S Ge 1:21
x ver 13; Job 41:31;
S Eze 29:3; 34:18
32:3 *y* S Eze 12:13;
Hab 1:15
32:4 *z* S Isa 18:6;
Eze 31:12-13; 39:4-5,
17
32:5 *a* S Eze 31:12
32:6 *b* S Isa 34:3
c S Eze 29:5
32:7 *d* S Isa 13:10;
34:4; S Eze 30:3;
Joel 2:2, 31; 3:15;
S Mt 24:29; Rev 8:12
32:8 *e* S Ps 102:26
f S Job 9:7; S Jer 4:23;
Joel 2:10

31:14 *the earth below … the realm of the dead.* See note on Ps 30:1.
31:15 *deep springs.* See v. 4 and note on 26:19. *clothed … with gloom.* See note on Ps 109:29.
31:16 *nations tremble.* As at Tyre's fall (see 27:35; 28:19). *were consoled.* Because the mightiest of trees had joined them in the "realm of the dead" (Sheol). See note on Ps 30:1.
31:17 *those killed by the sword.* Those who met a premature death.
31:18 *you.* The Egyptian pharaoh. *you, too.* What had happened to Assyria would also happen to the pharaoh. *uncircumcised.* See note on 28:10.
32:1 The sixth prophecy against Egypt (see note on 29:1). *twelfth year … twelfth month … first day.* Mar. 3, 585 B.C.; the tenth date in Ezekiel (see 1:2; 8:1; 20:1; 24:1; 26:1; 29:1, 17; 30:20; 31:1). If the

Septuagint (the pre-Christian Greek translation of the OT) is followed ("eleventh year"), then the chronological order of the Egypt oracles is preserved (and the date would be Mar. 13, 586). Cf. 29:1; 30:20; 31:1; see v. 17 and note.
32:2 *lament.* See note on 19:1. *lion among the nations.* A figure for royalty and grandeur (see 19:1-9). *monster.* See 29:3 and note. *seas … streams.* Canals of the Nile (see note on 29:3).
32:3 *cast my net.* Earlier it was Zedekiah over whom God's net was thrown (see 12:13; 17:20; 19:8).
32:4 *I will throw.* God's actions here are very similar to those described in 29:3-5.
32:7-8 A piling up of language that evokes the darkness associated with the day of the Lord (see Joel 2:2, 10, 31 and note on 2:2; 3:15; Am 5:18 and note; Zep 1:15).

32:10 *g* S Isa 30:32
h S Jer 46:10
i S Eze 26:16; S 27:35;
30:9; Rev 18:9-10
32:11 *j* S Eze 21:19
k S Isa 19:4;
S Jer 46:13
l S Eze 29:19
32:12 *m* S Eze 28:7
n Eze 31:11-12
32:13 *o* S ver 2;
S Eze 29:8,11
32:15 *p* Ex 7:5;
S 14:4,18; Ps 107:33-
34
32:16 *q* S Ge 50:10;
S Eze 19:1
32:17 *r* S ver 1
32:18 *s* Jer 1:10
t Eze 26:20; S 31:14,
16; Mic 1:8
32:19 *u* ver 29-30;
S Eze 28:10
32:20 *v* Ps 28:3
w Eze 31:17-18
32:21 *x* S Isa 14:9
y Eze 28:10
32:23 *z* S Isa 14:15
a Na 1:14
32:24 *b* S Ge 10:22
c S Jer 49:37
d S Job 28:13
e S Eze 26:20

⁹ I will trouble the hearts of many peoples
> when I bring about your destruction among the nations,
> among[a] lands you have not known.
¹⁰ I will cause many peoples to be appalled at you,
> and their kings will shudder with horror because of you
> when I brandish my sword *g* before them.
> On the day *h* of your downfall
> each of them will tremble
> every moment for his life. *i*

¹¹" 'For this is what the Sovereign LORD says:

> " 'The sword *j* of the king of Babylon *k*
> will come against you. *l*
¹² I will cause your hordes to fall
> by the swords of mighty men—
> the most ruthless of all nations. *m*
> They will shatter the pride of Egypt,
> and all her hordes will be overthrown. *n*
¹³ I will destroy all her cattle
> from beside abundant waters
> no longer to be stirred by human feet
> or muddied by the hooves of cattle. *o*

¹⁴ Then I will let her waters settle
> and make her streams flow like oil,
> > > > declares the Sovereign LORD.

¹⁵ When I make Egypt desolate
> and strip the land of everything in it,
> when I strike down all who live there,
> then they will know that I am the LORD. *p*'

¹⁶"This is the lament *q* they will chant for her. The daughters of the nations will chant it; for Egypt and all her hordes they will chant it, declares the Sovereign LORD."

EGYPT'S DESCENT INTO THE REALM OF THE DEAD

¹⁷In the twelfth year, on the fifteenth day of the month, the word of the LORD came to me: *r* ¹⁸"Son of man, wail for the hordes of Egypt and consign *s* to the earth below both her and the daughters of mighty nations, along with those who go down to the pit. *t* ¹⁹Say to them, 'Are you more favored than others? Go down and be laid among the uncircumcised.' *u* ²⁰They will fall among those killed by the sword. The sword is drawn; let her be dragged *v* off with all her hordes. *w* ²¹From within the realm of the dead *x* the mighty leaders will say of Egypt and her allies, 'They have come down and they lie with the uncircumcised, *y* with those killed by the sword.'

²²"Assyria is there with her whole army; she is surrounded by the graves of all her slain, all who have fallen by the sword. ²³Their graves are in the depths of the pit *z* and her army lies around her grave. *a* All who had spread terror in the land of the living are slain, fallen by the sword.

²⁴"Elam *b* is there, with all her hordes around her grave. All of them are slain, fallen by the sword. *c* All who had spread terror in the land of the living *d* went down uncircumcised to the earth below. They bear their shame with those who go down to the pit. *e* ²⁵A bed is made for her among the slain, with all her hordes around her grave. All of them are un-

---

a 9 Hebrew; Septuagint *bring you into captivity among the nations, / to*

32:9 *trouble the hearts.* This and the next verse reflect the fear brought about whenever great world powers fall, reminding lesser nations that they are even more vulnerable. Cf. similar feelings aroused by Tyre's fall (26:16–18; 27:35; 28:19).
32:10 *my sword.* See 5:2 and note.
32:11 *king of Babylon.* Nebuchadnezzar (cf. 21:19).
32:12 *most ruthless of all nations.* Babylon (see note on 30:11). *pride of Egypt.* The army in which she took pride ("her hordes"; cf. Am 6:8).
32:14 *streams flow like oil.* Their surface undisturbed by any form of life.

32:16 *daughters of the nations.* A world chorus of professional wailers (see Jer 9:17–18 and notes).
32:17 The seventh and last prophecy against Egypt (see note on 29:1). *twelfth year ... fifteenth day.* No month is given (as in 26:1; 40:1). The whole year dates from Apr. 13, 586, to Apr. 1, 585 B.C. The Septuagint suggests the first month, the 15th day of which would be Apr. 27, 586.
32:18 *earth below.* Same as "realm of the dead" (Sheol) in 31:15. *daughters of mighty nations.* See note on v. 16.
32:19 *uncircumcised.* See note on 28:10.
32:24 *Elam.* A country east of Assyria, in present-day Iran (see note on Isa 11:11).

circumcised,[f] killed by the sword. Because their terror had spread in the land of the living, they bear their shame with those who go down to the pit; they are laid among the slain.

26"Meshek and Tubal[g] are there, with all their hordes around their graves. All of them are uncircumcised, killed by the sword because they spread their terror in the land of the living. 27But they do not lie with the fallen warriors of old,[a] [h] who went down to the realm of the dead with their weapons of war—their swords placed under their heads and their shields[b] resting on their bones—though these warriors also had terrorized the land of the living.

28"You too, Pharaoh, will be broken and will lie among the uncircumcised, with those killed by the sword.

29"Edom[i] is there, her kings and all her princes; despite their power, they are laid with those killed by the sword. They lie with the uncircumcised, with those who go down to the pit.[j]

30"All the princes of the north[k] and all the Sidonians[l] are there; they went down with the slain in disgrace despite the terror caused by their power. They lie uncircumcised[m] with those killed by the sword and bear their shame with those who go down to the pit.[n]

31"Pharaoh—he and all his army—will see them and he will be consoled[o] for all his hordes that were killed by the sword, declares the Sovereign Lord. 32Although I had him spread terror in the land of the living, Pharaoh[p] and all his hordes will be laid among the uncircumcised, with those killed by the sword, declares the Sovereign Lord."[q]

RENEWAL OF EZEKIEL'S CALL AS WATCHMAN

33

The word of the Lord came to me: 2"Son of man, speak to your people and say to them: 'When I bring the sword[r] against a land, and the people of the land choose one of their men and make him their watchman,[s] 3and he sees the sword coming against the land and blows the trumpet[t] to warn the people, 4then if anyone hears the trumpet but does not heed the warning[u] and the sword comes and takes their life, their blood will be on their own head. [v] 5Since they heard the sound of the trumpet but did not heed the warning, their blood will be on their own head. [w] If they had heeded the warning, they would have saved themselves. [x] 6But if the watchman sees the sword coming and does not blow the trumpet to warn the people and the sword comes and takes someone's life, that person's life will be taken because of their sin, but I will hold the watchman accountable for their blood.' [y]

7"Son of man, I have made you a watchman[z] for the house of Israel; so hear the word I speak and give them warning from me. [a] 8When I say to the wicked, 'You wicked people, you will surely die,[b]' and you do not speak out to dissuade them from their ways, those wicked people will die for[c] their sins, and I will hold you accountable for their blood. [c] 9But if you do warn the wicked to turn from their ways and they do not do so,[d] they will die for their sins, though you yourself will be saved. [e]

10"Son of man, say to the house of Israel, 'This is what you are saying: "Our offenses and sins weigh us down, and we are wasting away[f] because of[d] them. How then can we live?[g]' ' 11Say to them, 'As surely as I live, declares the Sovereign Lord, I take no pleasure in the death of the wicked, but rather that they turn from their ways and live. [h] Turn![i] Turn from your evil ways! Why will you die, house of Israel?'[j]

---

[a] 27 Septuagint; Hebrew *warriors who were uncircumcised*   [b] 27 Probable reading of the original Hebrew text; Masoretic Text *punishment*   [c] 8 Or *in*; also in verse 9   [d] 10 Or *away in*

32:26 *Meshek and Tubal.* Peoples and territories in Asia Minor (see 38:2 and note).

32:29 *Edom.* See note on Ge 36:1,8; see also Isa 34:5; Am 1:11–12; Introduction to Obadiah: Unity and Theme; map, p. 508.

32:30 *Sidonians.* See note on 28:21.

33:1—37:28 A section depicting consolation for Israel (see Introduction: Outline).

🅰 **33:1—48:35** Sermons and messages of comfort following the fall of Jerusalem. Interspersed are words of warning and judgment (e.g., 33:23–33; 34:1–19; 35).

33:1–20 At this juncture, when his message takes on a radically different theme, Ezekiel's call to be a "watchman" for Israel is renewed (see 3:16–19 and note on 3:17).

33:2 *your people.* Fellow Israelites in exile with Ezekiel. *sword.* The invading army (cf. 5:2 and note). *people of the land.* See note on 7:27.

33:3 *trumpet.* An instrument made from a ram's horn (see notes on Jos 6:4–5), used to warn of approaching danger (Ne 4:18–20; Jer 4:19; Am 3:6).

33:4 *their blood will be on their own head.* See note on 18:13.

33:6 *their blood.* Their life, blood being the life principle (see Ge 9:5; 42:22; Lev 17:11 and note).

33:7–9 Cf. 3:17–19.

🅰 **33:10** *Our offenses and sins.* The first time the exiles expressed consciousness of sin. Previously they had blamed their fathers (18:2) and even God (18:19,25).

🅰 **33:11** *As surely as I live.* See note on 5:11. *I take no pleasure.* The question of 18:23 (see note there) is now a statement. God's basic intention for his creation is life, not death (see note on 16:6). *Turn!* The third call for repentance (see 14:6; 18:30).

32:25 *r* Eze 28:10
32:26 *g* S Eze 27:13
32:27 *h* Eze 28:10
32:29 *i* S Ps 137:7;
Isa 34:5-15; Jer 49:7;
Eze 35:15; Ob 1:1
j Eze 25:12-14
32:30 *k* S Isa 14:31;
Jer 25:26; Eze 38:6;
39:2 *l* S Ge 10:15;
S Jer 25:22
m Eze 28:10
n S Eze 26:20; S 28:8
32:31 *o* S Eze 14:22
32:32 *p* S Jer 44:30
q S Job 3:14
33:2 *r* S Lev 26:25;
S Jer 12:12
s S 1Sa 14:16;
Isa 21:6-9; S Jer 51:12
33:3 *t* S Ex 20:18;
S Nu 10:7; Hos 5:8;
8:1
33:4 *u* 2Ch 25:16
v S Lev 20:9;
S Jer 6:17; Zec 1:4;
Ac 18:6
33:5 *w* S Lev 20:9
x S Ex 9:21
33:6 *y* Isa 56:10-11;
S Eze 3:18
33:7 *z* S Isa 52:8
a Jer 1:17; 26:2
33:8 *b* ver 14
c S Isa 3:11;
S Eze 18:4
33:9 *d* S Ps 7:12
e Eze 3:17-19
33:10 *f* S Lev 26:16
S Eze 4:17
33:11 *h* S La 3:33
i S 2Ch 30:9;
S Isa 19:22; S Jer 3:12
j Jer 14:7-8;
S Eze 18:23; Hos 11:8;
Joel 2:12; S 1Ti 2:4

33:12 *k* ver 2
l 2Ch 7:14;
S Eze 3:20; S 18:21
33:13 *m* Heb 10:38;
2Pe 2:20-21
33:14 *n* S Jer 22:3
33:15 *o* S Ex 22:26
p Ex 22:1-4;
S Lev 6:2-5
q Isa 55:7; Jer 18:7-8;
S Lk 19:8
33:16 *r* S Jer 50:20
s S Isa 43:25
33:18 *t* Jer 18:10
u S Eze 3:20
33:19 *v* Ver 14-15
33:20 *w* S Job 34:11
33:21 *x* Eze 24:26
y S 2Ki 25:4,10;
Jer 39:1-2; 52:4-7;
S Eze 32:1
33:22 *z* S Eze 1:3
a Eze 29:21; Lk 1:64
b Eze 3:26-27;
S 24:27
33:24 *c* Eze 36:4
d S Dt 1:10 *e* Isa 51:2;
Jer 40:7; Eze 11:15;
Lk 3:8; Ac 7:5
33:25 *f* Jer 7:21
g S Ge 9:4 *h* Jer 7:9-
10; S Eze 22:6,27
33:26 *i* Jer 41:7
j Eze 22:11
33:27 *k* Isa 13:6;
Isa 2:19; S Jer 42:22;
S Eze 7:15; S 14:21;
39:4
33:28 *l* S Isa 41:15
m S Ge 6:7; Jer 9:10
33:29 *n* S Lev 26:34
o S Jer 18:16; S 44:22;
Eze 36:4; Mic 7:13
33:31 *p* S Eze 8:1
q Ps 119:36
r Ps 78:36-37;
S Isa 29:13; S 33:15;
S Jer 3:10; S 6:17;
S Eze 22:27;
Mt 13:22; 1Jn 3:18

[12]"Therefore, son of man, say to your people, *k* 'If someone who is righteous disobeys, that person's former righteousness will count for nothing. And if someone who is wicked repents, that person's former wickedness will not bring condemnation. The righteous, if they sin, will not be allowed to live because of their former righteousness.' *l* [13]If I tell the righteous that they will surely live, but then they trust in their righteousness and do evil, none of the righteous things they have done will be remembered; they will die for the evil they have done. *m* [14]And if I say to the wicked, 'You will surely die,' but they then turn away from their sins and do what is just *n* and right— [15]if they give back what they took in pledge *o* for a loan, return what they have stolen, *p* follow the decrees that give life, and do no evil, they will surely live; they will not die. *q* [16]None of the sins *r* they have committed will be remembered against them. They have done what is just and right; they will surely live. *s*

[17]"Yet your people say, 'The way of the Lord is not just.' But it is their way that is not just. [18]If the righteous turn from their righteousness and do evil, *t* they will die for it. *u* [19]And if the wicked turn away from their wickedness and do what is just and right, they will live by doing so. *v* [20]Yet you say, house of Israel, 'The way of the Lord is not just.' But I will judge each of you according to your own ways." *w*

JERUSALEM'S FALL EXPLAINED

[21]In the twelfth year of our exile, in the tenth month on the fifth day, a man who had escaped *x* from Jerusalem came to me and said, "The city has fallen!" *y* [22]Now the evening before the man arrived, the hand of the Lord was on me, *z* and he opened my mouth *a* before the man came to me in the morning. So my mouth was opened and I was no longer silent. *b*

[23]Then the word of the Lord came to me: [24]"Son of man, the people living in those ruins *c* in the land of Israel are saying, 'Abraham was only one man, yet he possessed the land. But we are many; *d* surely the land has been given to us as our possession.' *e* [25]Therefore say to them, 'This is what the Sovereign Lord says: Since you eat *f* meat with the blood *g* still in it and look to your idols and shed blood, should you then possess the land? *h* [26]You rely on your sword, you do detestable things, *i* and each of you defiles his neighbor's wife. *j* Should you then possess the land?'

[27]"Say this to them: 'This is what the Sovereign Lord says: As surely as I live, those who are left in the ruins will fall by the sword, those out in the country I will give to the wild animals to be devoured, and those in strongholds and caves will die of a plague. *k* [28]I will make the land a desolate waste, and her proud strength will come to an end, and the mountains *l* of Israel will become desolate so that no one will cross them. *m* [29]Then they will know that I am the Lord, when I have made the land a desolate *n* waste because of all the detestable things they have done.' *o*

[30]"As for you, son of man, your people are talking together about you by the walls and at the doors of the houses, saying to each other, 'Come and hear the message that has come from the Lord.' [31]My people come to you, as they usually do, and sit before *p* you to hear your words, but they do not put them into practice. Their mouths speak of love, but their hearts are greedy *q* for unjust gain. *r* [32]Indeed, to them you are nothing more than

---

33:12–20 Cf. 18:21–29 (see notes there).
33:14 *what is just and right.* See notes on 18:5; Ps 119:121.

🅰 **33:15** *give back what they took in pledge ... return what they have stolen.* See note on 18:7. *decrees that give life.* The purpose of God's law was to foster and protect life (see note on 20:11). *they will surely live.* The entire section is Ezekiel's answer to the despairing question of v. 10.

33:17 *The way of the Lord is not just.* See note on 18:25.
33:21–33 When news of Jerusalem's fall reaches Ezekiel, he must still reinforce his earlier word that "the end" (7:2) had truly come on the city (see note on 7:1–27); even the remnant eking out an existence in the ruins of the city will be destroyed.

🅰 **33:21** *twelfth year ... tenth month ... fifth day.* Jan. 8, 585 B.C., five months after the Jerusalem temple was burned. See date in 2Ki 25:8, which in modern reckoning is Aug. 14, 586. The journey between Jerusalem and Babylon could be made in four months (Ezr 7:9). *man who had escaped.* The first of the exiles of 586 (see 24:26, "fugitive"; see also note there). He had "escaped" alive from the disaster at Jerusalem. *The city has fallen!* With this statement all of Ezekiel's previous prophecies were

fulfilled and vindicated. He was then sent with a new mission: pastoral comfort.

33:22 *no longer silent.* See 24:27 and note.
33:24 *people living in those ruins.* The residents of Jerusalem not exiled in 586 B.C. *Abraham was only one man ... But we are many.* A boast by the unrepentant, similar to that of 11:15 (cf. Lk 3:8).
33:25 *eat meat with the blood.* Forbidden in Ge 9:4 (see note there; see also note on Lev 17:11). *look to your idols.* See note on 18:6.
33:27 *As surely as I live.* See note on 5:11. *sword ... wild animals ... plague.* Cf. the threefold threat in 5:12; 7:15; 12:16 and the fourfold threat in 14:12–21 (see note on 5:16–17).
33:29 *know that I am the Lord.* See Introduction: Themes.
33:30–33 Words addressed to Ezekiel, but included here as a rebuke and admonition to the remnant from Jerusalem living in exile.

🅰 **33:31** *sit before you.* As the elders had (8:1; 14:1). *greedy.* The people were waiting for Ezekiel to tell them how they could personally profit from the situation. They were not interested in God's designs for them (cf. Mt 20:20–28).

one who sings love songs *s* with a beautiful voice and plays an instrument well, for they hear your words but do not put them into practice. *t*

³³"When all this comes true—and it surely will—then they will know that a prophet has been among them. *u*"

THE LORD WILL BE ISRAEL'S SHEPHERD

34 The word of the LORD came to me: ²"Son of man, prophesy against the shepherds of Israel; prophesy and say to them: 'This is what the Sovereign LORD says: Woe to you shepherds of Israel who only take care of yourselves! Should not shepherds take care of the flock? *v* ³You eat the curds, clothe yourselves with the wool and slaughter the choice animals, but you do not take care of the flock. *w* ⁴You have not strengthened the weak or healed *x* the sick or bound up *y* the injured. You have not brought back the strays or searched for the lost. You have ruled them harshly and brutally. *z* ⁵So they were scattered because there was no shepherd, *a* and when they were scattered they became food for all the wild animals. *b* ⁶My sheep wandered over all the mountains and on every high hill. *c* They were scattered *d* over the whole earth, and no one searched or looked for them. *e*

⁷'Therefore, you shepherds, hear the word of the LORD: ⁸As surely as I live, declares the Sovereign LORD, because my flock lacks a shepherd and so has been plundered *f* and has become food for all the wild animals, *g* and because my shepherds did not search for my flock but cared for themselves rather than for my flock, *h* ⁹therefore, you shepherds, hear the word of the LORD: ¹⁰This is what the Sovereign LORD says: I am against *i* the shepherds and will hold them accountable for my flock. I will remove them from tending the flock so that the shepherds can no longer feed themselves. I will rescue *j* my flock from their mouths, and it will no longer be food for them. *k*

¹¹'For this is what the Sovereign LORD says: I myself will search for my sheep *l* and look after them. ¹²As shepherds *m* look after their scattered flocks when they are with them, so will I look after my sheep. I will rescue them from all the places where they were scattered on a day of clouds and darkness. *n* ¹³I will bring them out from the nations and gather *o* them from the countries, and I will bring them into their own land. *p q r s* I will pasture them on the mountains of Israel, in the ravines and in all the settlements in the land. *t u v* ¹⁴I will tend them in a good pasture, and the mountain heights of Israel *w* will be their grazing land. There they will lie down in good grazing land, and there they will feed in a rich pasture *x* on the mountains of Israel. *y* ¹⁵I myself will tend my sheep and have them lie down, *z* declares the Sovereign LORD. *a* ¹⁶I will search for the lost and bring back the strays. I will bind up *b* the injured and strengthen the weak, *c* but the sleek and the strong I will destroy. *d* I will shepherd the flock with justice. *e*

¹⁷'As for you, my flock, this is what the Sovereign LORD says: I will judge between one sheep and another, and between rams and goats. *f* ¹⁸Is it not enough *g* for you to feed on

---

33:32 *one who sings.* May indicate that Ezekiel chanted his oracles (see 2Ki 3:15; Isa 5:1), but more likely the prophet was using a metaphor. *they hear … but do not … practice.* See Isa 29:13 and note; Mt 21:28–32; cf. Jas 1:22–25.

34:1–31 The Lord gives the Israelites in exile the reassuring word that in the future he will himself be their Shepherd. In vv. 1–10 he denounces Israel's worthless "shepherds"; in vv. 11–16 he promises to seek out his scattered flock; in vv. 17–22 he declares that he will judge the strong sheep who have oppressed the weak; in vv. 23–24 he promises to set over his flock his servant "David"; in vv. 25–31 he speaks climactically of his "covenant of peace" that will secure Israel's blessed state.

34:2 *shepherds of Israel.* Those responsible for providing leadership, especially the kings and their officials (see 2Sa 7:7 and note; Jer 25:18–19), but also the prophets and priests (see Isa 56:11; Jer 23:9–11). Ezekiel had earlier singled out the princes, priests and prophets for special rebuke (ch. 22). To call a king a shepherd was common throughout the ancient Near East (see note on Ps 23:1). For David's rise from shepherd to shepherd-king, see Ps 78:70–71. For condemnation of the shepherds, cf. Jer 23:1–4.

34:3 *eat … clothe … slaughter.* Legitimate rewards for shepherds. Their crime was that they did not care for the flock.
34:4 *searched for the lost.* Cf. Jer 50:6; Zec 11:15–17; Mt 18:12–14; Lk 15:4; 19:10.

34:5 *scattered.* Often used by Ezekiel to describe Israel's exile and dispersion (11:16–17; 12:15; 20:23,34,41; 22:15; 28:25). *no shepherd.* That is, no true shepherd (cf. Mk 6:34).

34:8 *wild animals.* Hostile foreign nations; but see v. 28, where they are contrasted.

34:10 *I am against the shepherds.* See note on 5:8.

34:11 *I myself will search for my sheep.* Having dealt with the faithless shepherds (vv. 1–10), the Lord committed himself to shepherd his flock (see Jer 23:3–4).

34:12 *from all the places.* Babylon was not the only place where the Israelites had gone (see Jer 43:1–7). *day of clouds and darkness.* The day of the Lord that had come upon Israel when Jerusalem fell in the summer of 586 B.C. (see 7:7; 32:7 and notes).

34:13 *I will bring them out.* The promises of restoration—begun in 11:17 and repeated in 20:34,41–42; 28:25—find special emphasis in this part (chs. 33–39) of Ezekiel (see 36:24–32 and notes; 37:21; 38:8 and note; 39:27). *mountains of Israel.* Compare the tone of 6:3–7 with judgment now past (see v. 12). The mountains perhaps represented the scene of salvation.

34:14 *I will tend them.* See Isa 40:11; Jn 10:11.

34:16 *the sleek and the strong.* Those with power who had fattened themselves by oppressing the other "sheep" (see vv. 17–22).

34:17 *rams and goats.* People of power and influence who were oppressing poorer Israelites. This prophetic word shows the same concern for social justice found else-

34:18 ʰ S Eze 32:2
34:20 ⁱ Mt 25:32
34:21 ʲ S Dt 33:17
34:22 ᵏ Ps 72:12-14;
Jer 23:2-3;
Eze 20:37-38
34:23 ˡ Isa 40:11
ᵐ S Isa 31:4; Mic 5:4
34:24 ⁿ Eze 36:28
ᵒ Ps 89:49
ᵖ S Isa 53:4; Zec 13:7
ᵠ Jer 23:4-5; S 30:9;
S 33:14; Jn 10:16;
Rev 7:17
34:25 ʳ S Eze 16:62
ˢ S Nu 25:12
ᵗ Lev 26:6
ᵘ S Lev 25:18;
Isa 11:6-9; Hos 2:18
34:26 ᵛ S Ge 12:2
ʷ Ps 68:9; Joel 2:23
ˣ Dt 11:13-15; S 28:12;
Isa 44:3
34:27 ʸ S Ps 72:16
ᶻ S Job 14:9; S Ps 67:6
ᵃ S Nu 24:21
ᵇ S Lev 26:13
ᶜ S Jer 30:8;
S Eze 20:42; S 28:25
34:28 ᵈ S Jer 32:37
ᵉ S Jer 30:10;
S Eze 28:26; 39:26;
Hos 11:11; Am 9:15;
Zep 3:13; Zec 14:11
34:29 ᶠ S Isa 4:2
ᵍ Eze 36:29
ʰ S Ps 137:3;
Eze 36:6; Joel 2:19
ⁱ Eze 36:15
34:30 ʲ S Eze 14:11;
37:27
34:31 ᵏ S Ps 28:9
ˡ S Jer 23:1
35:2 ᵐ S Ge 14:6
35:3 ⁿ S Jer 6:12
ᵒ S Isa 34:10;
Eze 25:12-14
35:4 ᵖ Jer 44:2
ᵠ ver 9; S Jer 49:10
35:5 ʳ S Ps 63:10
ˢ Ob 1:13 ; Ps 137:7;
S Eze 21:29
35:6 ᵘ S Isa 34:3
ᵛ Isa 63:2-6

the good pasture? Must you also trample the rest of your pasture with your feet?ʰ Is it not enough for you to drink clear water? Must you also muddy the rest with your feet? ¹⁹Must my flock feed on what you have trampled and drink what you have muddied with your feet?

²⁰ 'Therefore this is what the Sovereign LORD says to them: See, I myself will judge between the fat sheep and the lean sheep.ⁱ ²¹Because you shove with flank and shoulder, butting all the weak sheep with your hornsʲ until you have driven them away, ²²I will save my flock, and they will no longer be plundered. I will judge between one sheep and another.ᵏ ²³I will place over them one shepherd, my servant David, and he will tendˡ them; he will tend them and be their shepherd.ᵐ ²⁴I the LORD will be their God,ⁿ and my servant Davidᵒ will be prince among them.ᵖ I the LORD have spoken.ᵠ

²⁵ 'I will make a covenantʳ of peaceˢ with them and rid the land of savage beastsᵗ so that they may live in the wilderness and sleep in the forests in safety.ᵘ ²⁶I will make them and the places surrounding my hill a blessing.ᵃ ᵛ I will send down showers in season;ʷ there will be showers of blessing.ˣ ²⁷The trees will yield their fruitʸ and the ground will yield its crops;ᶻ the people will be secureᵃ in their land. They will know that I am the LORD, when I break the bars of their yokeᵇ and rescue them from the hands of those who enslaved them.ᶜ ²⁸They will no longer be plundered by the nations, nor will wild animals devour them. They will live in safety,ᵈ and no one will make them afraid.ᵉ ²⁹I will provide for them a land renownedᶠ for its crops, and they will no longer be victims of famineᵍ in the land or bear the scornʰ of the nations.ⁱ ³⁰Then they will know that I, the LORD their God, am with them and that they, the house of Israel, are my people, declares the Sovereign LORD.ʲ ³¹You are my sheep,ᵏ the sheep of my pasture,ˡ and I am your God, declares the Sovereign LORD.' "

A PROPHECY AGAINST EDOM

35 The word of the LORD came to me: ²"Son of man, set your face against Mount Seir;ᵐ prophesy against it ³and say: 'This is what the Sovereign LORD says: I am against you, Mount Seir, and I will stretch out my handⁿ against you and make you a desolate waste.ᵒ ⁴I will turn your towns into ruinsᵖ and you will be desolate. Then you will know that I am the LORD.ᵠ

⁵ 'Because you harbored an ancient hostility and delivered the Israelites over to the swordʳ at the time of their calamity,ˢ the time their punishment reached its climax,ᵗ ⁶therefore as surely as I live, declares the Sovereign LORD, I will give you over to bloodshedᵘ and it will pursue you.ᵛ Since you did not hate bloodshed, bloodshed will pursue you. ⁷I

ᵃ 26 Or I will cause them and the places surrounding my hill to be named in blessings (see Gen. 48:20); or I will cause them and the places surrounding my hill to be seen as blessed

---

where in the prophets (see Isa 3:13–15; 5:8; Am 5:12; 6:1–7; see also Mic 2:1–5 and notes). Cf. the treatment of slaves Jeremiah observed (Jer 34:8–11).

A **34:23–24** *my servant David.* A ruler like David and from his line (see Ps 89:4,20,29; see also Jer 23:5–6 and notes).

A **34:24** *prince.* The Lord announced a kingdom where he would be King and the earthly king a "prince" (cf. 37:25; 44:3; 45:7,16–17,22; 46:2–18; 48:21–22).

A **34:25** *covenant of peace.* Cf. 37:26. All of God's covenants aim at peace (see Ge 15:1; Nu 25:12; Isa 54:10; Mal 2:5). This covenant (the "new covenant" spoken of by Jeremiah, 31:31–34) looks to the final peace, initiated by Christ (Php 4:7) and still awaiting final fulfillment. The "peace" (Hebrew *shalom*) envisioned here is that of a restored relationship with God and the secure enjoyment of a life made full and rich through his blessings. None of the threats to life experienced under God's judgments will mar this "peace" (compare vv. 25–29 with 5:16–17 and note). *sleep in the forests.* Often dangerous (see Ps 104:20–21; Jer 5:6).

A **34:26** *showers in season.* Autumn rains, which signal the beginning of the rainy season, and spring rains, which come at the end (cf. Jer 5:24). *showers of blessing.* Blessing, the power of life promised to God's people through Abraham (Ge 12:1–3), is beautifully symbolized in the life-giving effects of rain.

34:27 *bars of their yoke.* The bars were wooden pegs inserted down through holes in the yoke and tied below the animal's neck with cords (Isa 58:6) to form a collar (cf. 30:18; Lev 26:13;

Jer 27:2; 28:10–13). The entire picture represents foreign domination.

34:29 *scorn of the nations.* See 22:4.

A **34:30** *their God … my people.* Covenant language (see 11:20; Ex 6:7; Hos 1:9; Zec 8:8 and notes).

C **35:1–15** The counterpart of Israel's restoration as the Lord's people is the desolation of her enemies—of which Edom serves here as representative (see 36:5). Given the historic relationship between Israel and Edom (see notes on vv. 2,5), the spiteful treatment of Judah by the Edomites at the time of Jerusalem's fall was especially reprehensible (see Isa 63:1–6 and notes; Introduction to Obadiah: Unity and Theme; see also notes on Am 9:12; Ob 8).

35:2 *set your face against.* See note on 20:46. *Mount Seir.* Edom (v. 15), Israel's relative (Jacob and Esau being twins, Ge 25:21–30) and constant enemy, from whom brotherhood was sought but seldom found (cf. Am 1:11). Edom had to be dealt with before Israel could find peace (cf. Ge 32–33). See 25:12 and note.

35:3 *I am against you.* See note on 5:8.

35:5 *ancient hostility.* Beginning with Jacob's deception of Isaac for Esau's blessing (Ge 27; see especially v. 41) and continuing later (Nu 20:14–21; 2Sa 8:13–14; 1Ki 9:26–28). *time of their calamity.* Edom looted Jerusalem in 586 B.C. (see Ob 11–14 and notes).

35:6 *as surely as I live.* See note on 5:11. *bloodshed will pursue you.* Retributive justice, in accordance with Ge 9:6 (see note there).

will make Mount Seir a desolate waste *w* and cut off from it all who come and go. *x* 8I will fill your mountains with the slain; those killed by the sword will fall on your hills and in your valleys and in all your ravines. *y* 9I will make you desolate forever; *z* your towns will not be inhabited. Then you will know that I am the LORD. *a*

10" 'Because you have said, "These two nations and countries will be ours and we will take possession *b* of them," even though I the LORD was there, 11therefore as surely as I live, declares the Sovereign LORD, I will treat you in accordance with the anger *c* and jealousy you showed in your hatred of them and I will make myself known among them when I judge you. *d* 12Then you will know that I the LORD have heard all the contemptible things you have said against the mountains of Israel. You said, "They have been laid waste and have been given over to us to devour. *e*" 13You boasted *f* against me and spoke against me without restraint, and I heard it. *g* 14This is what the Sovereign LORD says: While the whole earth rejoices, I will make you desolate. *h* 15Because you rejoiced *i* when the inheritance of the house of Israel became desolate, that is how I will treat you. You will be desolate, Mount Seir, *j* you and all of Edom. *k* Then they will know that I am the LORD.' "

HOPE FOR THE MOUNTAINS OF ISRAEL

36 "Son of man, prophesy to the mountains of Israel *l* and say, 'Mountains of Israel, hear the word of the LORD. 2This is what the Sovereign LORD says: *m* The enemy said of you, "Aha! *n* The ancient heights *o* have become our possession. *p*" ' 3Therefore prophesy and say, 'This is what the Sovereign LORD says: Because they ravaged *q* and crushed you from every side so that you became the possession of the rest of the nations and the object of people's malicious talk and slander, *r* 4therefore, mountains of Israel, hear the word of the Sovereign LORD: This is what the Sovereign LORD says to the mountains and hills, to the ravines and valleys, *s* to the desolate ruins *t* and the deserted *u* towns that have been plundered and ridiculed *v* by the rest of the nations around you— 5this is what the Sovereign LORD says: In my burning *x* zeal I have spoken against the rest of the nations, and against all Edom, for with glee and with malice in their hearts they made my land their own possession so that they might plunder its pastureland.' *y* 6Therefore prophesy concerning the land of Israel and say to the mountains and hills, to the ravines and valleys: 'This is what the Sovereign LORD says: I speak in my jealous wrath because you have suffered the scorn of the nations. *z* 7Therefore this is what the Sovereign LORD says: I swear with uplifted hand *a* that the nations around you will also suffer scorn. *b*

8" 'But you, mountains of Israel, will produce branches and fruit *c* for my people Israel, for they will soon come home. 9I am concerned for you and will look on you with favor; you will be plowed and sown, *d* 10and I will multiply the number of people living on you, even the whole house of Israel. The towns will be inhabited and the ruins *e* rebuilt. *f* 11I will increase the number of people and animals living on you, and they will be fruitful *g* and become numerous. I will settle people *h* on you as in the past *i* and will make you

35:7 *w* S Jer 46:19
x S Jer 49:17
35:8 *y* S Eze 31:12
35:9 *z* Ob 1:10
a S Isa 34:5-6;
S Jer 49:13
35:10 *b* S Ps 83:12;
Eze 36:2,5
35:11 *c* Eze 25:14
d S Ps 9:16; Ob 1:15;
S Mt 7:2
35:12 *e* S Jer 50:7
35:13 *f* S Jer 49:16
g Da 11:36
35:14 *h* Jer 51:48
35:15 *i* Eze 36:5;
Ob 1:12 / ver 3
k S Isa 34:5-6,11;
Jer 50:11-13;
S La 4:21;
S Eze 32:29
36:1 *l* S Eze 17:22
36:2 *m* Eze 6:2-3
n S Eze 25:3
o S Dt 32:13
p S Eze 35:10
36:3 *q* Ob 1:13
r Ps 44:13-14;
S La 2:16; 3:62
36:4 *s* Eze 6:3
t Eze 33:24
u S Lev 26:43
v S Jer 2:26 *w* Dt 11:11;
S Ps 79:4;
S Eze 33:28-29
36:5 *x* S Dt 29:20
y Isa 66:16; Jer 25:31;
50:11; Eze 25:12-14;
S 35:10,15; 38:22;
Joel 3:2,14
36:6 *z* Ps 123:3-4;
Eze 34:29
36:7 *a* S Nu 14:30
b S Jer 25:9
36:8 *c* S Isa 4:2;
S 27:6; Eze 47:12
36:9 *d* ver 34-36;
Jer 31:27
36:10 *e* S Isa 49:8
f Isa 49:17-23;
S Jer 30:18
36:11 *g* S Ge 1:22
h S Isa 49:19
i Mic 7:14

35:9 *desolate forever.* To experience no restoration like Egypt's (see 29:13–16). *know that I am the LORD.* See Introduction: Themes.
35:10 *These two nations.* Israel and Judah. *I the LORD was there.* See 48:35 and note.
35:13 *You boasted against me.* Cf. Ob 12; Zep 2:8,10; also Ps 35:26; Jer 48:26,42.
36:1–38 How God, whose name has been profaned among the nations, will display his holiness in the restoration of his people: Verses 1–15 set forth God's promise to cause the now desolate land ("mountains") of Israel to prosper once more so that it is a place of blessing for Israel, thereby removing its disgrace; vv. 16–38 spell out God's promise to cleanse and restore his now defiled and scattered people, thereby removing the disgrace that Israel has brought on his name and once again showing to all nations his holiness.
36:1–15 The comforting counterpart to ch. 6. Verses 1–7 announce God's coming judgment on the nations for the scorn they heaped on the land of Israel; vv. 8–15 announce God's future renewal of the prosperity of the land.
36:2 *The enemy said of you.* See 25:3; 26:2. *Aha!* See note on 25:3. *ancient heights.* The promised land, of which the elevated region between the Jordan Valley and the Mediterranean coast was the central core.
36:3 *rest of the nations.* All nations that in the past had con-

quered parts of Israel—until finally they took full possession.
36:4 *mountains…hills…ravines…valleys.* See 6:3 and note on 1:5.
36:5 *my burning zeal.* The Lord was personally offended by the ridicule of the nations because it was his special land they were mocking and plundering (see "my land" later in the verse). *Edom.* Singled out because of its long-standing hostility to Israel (see ch. 35, especially vv. 2,5 and notes).
36:6 *jealous wrath.* See 16:38 and note.
36:7 *with uplifted hand.* See 20:5 and note.
36:8 *branches and fruit.* Signs of productivity (see 17:8,23) and the Lord's restored favor (see Eze 26:3–5); to be contrasted with Edom's desolation in 35:3,7,15. *soon.* Even as judgment fell, a speedy return of the exiles was announced.
36:9 *I…will look on you with favor.* Cf. Lev 26:9 for the identical clause in a similar context.
36:10 *even the whole house of Israel.* In this chapter (as in 37:15–23) Ezekiel is speaking of the restoration of all Israel.
36:11 *be fruitful and become numerous.* Identical terminology to the divine blessing at creation (Ge 1:22,28; see Ge 8:17; 9:1,7) and the subsequent covenant blessing (see Ge 17:6; 35:11; 48:3–4; Ex 1:7). *know that I am the LORD.* See note on 6:7. These words of recognition, used throughout the book to express God's revelation through judgment, here point to God's self-disclosure in salvation (see 35:9 and note).

36:11 *j* Lev 26:9;
Job 42:13; S Jer 31:28;
S Eze 16:55; Zec 10:8
36:12 *k* Eze 47:14,
22
36:13 *l* S Nu 13:32
36:15 *m* Ps 89:50-
51; Isa 54:4;
S Eze 34:29
36:17 *n* S Lev 5:2;
S 12:2 *o* Ps 106:37-38;
S Jer 2:7
36:18 *q* 2Ch 34:21
36:19 *q* Dt 28:64
r Lev 18:24-28;
S Eze 7:8; S 24:14;
39:24
36:20 *s* S Lev 18:21;
S Eze 13:19; Ro 2:24
t Isa 52:5; S Jer 33:24;
S Eze 12:16
36:21 *u* Ps 74:18;
Isa 48:9
36:22 *v* S Isa 37:35;
S Eze 20:44
w Ro 2:24* *x* Dt 9:5-
6; Ps 106:8;
S Eze 20:9
36:23 *y* S Nu 6:27
z S Isa 37:23
a S Ps 46:10
b S Eze 20:41
c Ps 126:2; S Isa 5:16;
Eze 20:14; 38:23;
39:7,27-28
36:24 *d* S Isa 43:5-
6; S Eze 34:13; 37:21
36:25 *e* S Lev 14:7;
S 16:14-15; Heb 9:13
f S Ps 51:2,7
g S Ezr 6:21 *h* Isa 2:18;
Joel 3:21; Zec 3:4;
13:2; S Ac 22:16
36:26 *i* Jer 24:7
j S Jer 5:3 *k* S Ps 51:10;
S Eze 18:31;
S 2Co 3:3
36:27 *l* S Isa 44:3;
Joel 2:29; Jn 3:5
m S Eze 18:21
n Jer 50:20; 1Th 4:8

prosper more than before. *j* Then you will know that I am the Lord. ¹²I will cause people, my people Israel, to live on you. They will possess you, and you will be their inheritance; *k* you will never again deprive them of their children.

¹³" 'This is what the Sovereign Lord says: Because some say to you, "You devour your people *l* and deprive your nation of its children," ¹⁴therefore you will no longer devour people or make your nation childless, declares the Sovereign Lord. ¹⁵No longer will I make you hear the taunts of the nations, and no longer will you suffer the scorn of the peoples or cause your nation to fall, declares the Sovereign Lord. *m* '"

ISRAEL'S RESTORATION ASSURED

¹⁶Again the word of the Lord came to me: ¹⁷"Son of man, when the people of Israel were living in their own land, they defiled it by their conduct and their actions. Their conduct was like a woman's monthly uncleanness *n* in my sight. *o* ¹⁸So I poured out *p* my wrath on them because they had shed blood in the land and because they had defiled it with their idols. ¹⁹I dispersed them among the nations, and they were scattered *q* through the countries; I judged them according to their conduct and their actions. *r* ²⁰And wherever they went among the nations they profaned *s* my holy name, for it was said of them, 'These are the Lord's people, and yet they had to leave his land.' *t* ²¹I had concern for my holy name, which the house of Israel profaned among the nations where they had gone. *u*

²²"Therefore say to the house of Israel, 'This is what the Sovereign Lord says: It is not for your sake, house of Israel, that I am going to do these things, but for the sake of my holy name, *v* which you have profaned *w* among the nations where you have gone. *x* ²³I will show the holiness of my great name, *y* which has been profaned *z* among the nations, the name you have profaned among them. Then the nations will know that I am the Lord, *a* declares the Sovereign Lord, when I am proved holy *b* through you before their eyes. *c*

²⁴" 'For I will take you out of the nations; I will gather you from all the countries and bring you back into your own land. *d* ²⁵I will sprinkle *e* clean water on you, and you will be clean; I will cleanse *f* you from all your impurities *g* and from all your idols. *h* ²⁶I will give you a new heart *i* and put a new spirit in you; I will remove from you your heart of stone *j* and give you a heart of flesh. *k* ²⁷And I will put my Spirit *l* in you and move you to follow my decrees *m* and be careful to keep my laws. *n* ²⁸Then you will live in the land I gave your ancestors; you will be my people, *o* and I will be your God. *p* ²⁹I will save you from all your uncleanness. I will call for the grain and make it plentiful and will not bring famine *q* upon

36:28 *o* Jer 30:22; 31:33 *p* S Eze 11:17; S 14:11; 34:24; 37:14,27; Zec 8:8   **36:29** *q* Eze 34:29

36:12 *live on you.* The mountains of Israel are still being addressed. *deprive them of their children.* The mountains are poetically pictured as having contributed to the depopulation brought by the exile. This may refer to the fact that the promised land had contained the Canaanites and their religious centers ("high places"), which had led Israel astray and so brought God's wrath down on his people (see 6:3 and note).

36:16–38 God's restoration of his defiled and scattered people. Verses 16–23 remind Israel that the nation was exiled from her land because of her uncleanness and that her restoration is for the sake of God's holy name; vv. 24–27 announce God's renewal of defiled Israel and its effects on Israel (vv. 28–32) and on the nations (vv. 33–36); vv. 37–38 provide a concluding summary.

36:18 *shed blood . . . defiled it with their idols.* A summary reference to Israel's social injustices and idolatrous religious practices (see 22:3 and note). *idols.* See note on 6:4.

36:20 *they profaned my holy name.* Because Israel had been removed from her land, it seemed to the nations that her God was unable to protect and preserve his people (see 20:9 and note; cf. Nu 14:15–16; 2Ki 18:32–35; 19:10–12).

36:22 *It is not for your sake.* Not because God did not care for Israel, but because his people did not deserve what he was about to do (cf. Dt 9:4–6). Statements like these make Ezekiel a preacher of pure grace. *for the sake of my holy name.* The reason given in ch. 20 for the withholding of divine punishment (see 20:9,14,22) is here given as a reason for divine restoration.

36:23 *Then the nations will know that I am the Lord.* The ultimate purpose of God's plans with Israel is that the whole world may know the true God (see v. 11 and note). *I am*

proved holy. See Lev 10:3 and note.

36:24–27 The four elements in the promised restoration: (1) return of the exiles (v. 24), (2) cleansing from sin (v. 25), (3) renewal of heart (v. 26) and (4) enablement by God's Spirit to live God's way (v. 27).

36:25 *I will sprinkle clean water.* For sprinkling with water as a ritual act of cleansing, see Ex 30:19–20; Lev 14:51; Nu 19:18; cf. Zec 13:1; Heb 10:22. *I will cleanse.* See v. 33; 37:23; Jer 33:8. *idols.* See note on 6:4.

36:26–27 Contains "new covenant" terminology (see Jer 31:33–34 and notes).

36:26 *new heart.* See notes on 11:19; 18:31. *put a new spirit in you.* Transform your mind and heart. Here and in 11:19 God declared that he would bring about the change. In 18:31 (see note there) he called on his people to effect the change. What he requires of his people he always provides. *heart of flesh.* "Flesh" in the OT is often a symbol for weakness and frailty (Isa 31:3); in the NT it often stands for the sinful nature as a God-opposing force (as in Ro 8:5–8). Here it stands (in opposition to stone) for a pliable, teachable heart.

36:27 *my Spirit.* God bestows his Spirit to enable the human spirit to do his will (see 37:14 and note on 2:2). Verses 25–27 are closely paralleled in Ps 51:7–11 (see notes there).

36:28–32 The results of Israel's renewal: restoration to prosperity (vv. 28–30) and a deep sense of shame for all her sins (vv. 31–32).

36:28 *my people . . . your God.* Covenant language (see 11:20 and note).

36:29 *from all your uncleanness.* From idol worship and moral defilement (see v. 25; 37:23).

you. ³⁰I will increase the fruit of the trees and the crops of the field, so that you will no longer suffer disgrace among the nations because of famine.ʳ ³¹Then you will remember your evil ways and wicked deeds, and you will loathe yourselves for your sins and detestable practices.ˢ ³²I want you to know that I am not doing this for your sake, declares the Sovereign Lᴏʀᴅ. Be ashamedᵗ and disgraced for your conduct, house of Israel!ᵘ

³³" 'This is what the Sovereign Lᴏʀᴅ says: On the day I cleanseᵛ you from all your sins, I will resettle your towns, and the ruinsʷ will be rebuilt.ˣ ³⁴The desolate land will be cultivated instead of lying desolate in the sight of all who pass through it. ³⁵They will say, "This land that was laid waste has become like the garden of Eden;ʸ the cities that were lying in ruins, desolate and destroyed, are now fortified and inhabited.ᶻ" ³⁶Then the nations around you that remain will know that I the Lᴏʀᴅ have rebuilt what was destroyed and have replanted what was desolate. I the Lᴏʀᴅ have spoken, and I will do it.'ᵃ

³⁷"This is what the Sovereign Lᴏʀᴅ says: Once again I will yield to the pleaᵇ of the house of Israel and do this for them: I will make their people as numerous as sheep,ᶜ ³⁸as numerous as the flocks for offeringsᵈ at Jerusalem during her appointed festivals. So will the ruined cities be filled with flocks of people. Then they will know that I am the Lᴏʀᴅ.ᵉ"

THE VALLEY OF DRY BONES

37 The hand of the Lᴏʀᴅ was on me,ᶠ and he brought me out by the Spiritᵍ of the Lᴏʀᴅ and set me in the middle of a valley;ʰ it was full of bones.ⁱ ²He led me back and forth among them, and I saw a great many bones on the floor of the valley, bones that were very dry. ³He asked me, "Son of man, can these bones live?"

I said, "Sovereign Lᴏʀᴅ, you alone know.ʲ"

⁴Then he said to me, "Prophesy to these bones and say to them, 'Dry bones, hear the word of the Lᴏʀᴅ!ᵏ ⁵This is what the Sovereign Lᴏʀᴅ says to these bones: I will make breathᵃ enter you, and you will come to life.ˡ ⁶I will attach tendons to you and make flesh come upon you and cover you with skin; I will put breath in you, and you will come to life. Then you will know that I am the Lᴏʀᴅ.ᵐ' "

⁷So I prophesied as I was commanded. And as I was prophesying, there was a noise, a rattling sound, and the bones came together, bone to bone. ⁸I looked, and tendons and flesh appeared on them and skin covered them, but there was no breath in them.

⁹Then he said to me, "Prophesy to the breath;ⁿ prophesy, son of man, and say to it, 'This is what the Sovereign Lᴏʀᴅ says: Come, breath, from the four windsᵒ and breathe into these slain, that they may live.' " ¹⁰So I prophesied as he commandedᵖ me, and breath entered them; they came to life and stood up on their feet—a vast army. q

¹¹Then he said to me: "Son of man, these bones are the whole house of Israel. They say, 'Our bones are dried up and our hope is gone; we are cut off.'ʳ ¹²Therefore prophesy and say to them: 'This is what the Sovereign Lᴏʀᴅ says: My people, I am going to open your graves and bring you up from them; I will bring you back to the land of Israel.ˢ ¹³Then

---

ᵃ 5 The Hebrew for this word can also mean *wind* or *spirit* (see verses 6-14).

36:30 ʳLev 26:4-5; S Eze 34:13-14; Hos 2:21-22
36:31 ˢIsa 6:5; S Jer 31:19; S Eze 6:9
36:32 ᵗEze 16:63 ᵘDt 9:5
36:33 ᵛS Lev 16:30 ʷS Lev 26:31 ˣS Isa 49:8
36:35 ʸS Ge 2:8 ᶻAm 9:14
36:36 ᵃS Jer 42:10; S Eze 17:22; 37:14; 39:27-28
36:37 ᵇZec 10:6; 13:9 ᶜPs 102:17; Jer 29:12-14
36:38 ᵈ1Ki 8:63; 2Ch 35:7-9 ᵉS Ex 6:2
37:1 ᶠS Eze 1:3
37:2 ᵍS Eze 11:24; Lk 4:1; Ac 8:39 ʰJer 7:32
37:3 ⁱS Jer 8:2; Eze 40:1
37:3 ʲDt 32:39; 1Co 15:35
37:4 ᵏJer 22:29
37:5 ˡS Ge 2:7; Ps 104:29-30; Rev 11:11
37:6 ᵐS Ex 6:2; Eze 38:23
37:9 ⁿver 14; Ps 104:30; Isa 32:15; Eze 39:29; Zec 12:10 ᵒJer 49:36; Da 7:2; 8:8; 11:4; Zec 2:6; 6:5; Rev 7:1
37:10 ᵖS Eze 12:7 ᵠRev 11:11
37:11 ʳS Job 17:15; S La 3:54
37:12 ˢver 21; Dt 32:39; 1Sa 2:6; Isa 26:19; Jer 29:14; Hos 13:14; Am 9:14-15; Zep 3:20; Zec 8:8

36:30 *disgrace.* As in v. 15.

36:31 *Then you will remember.* God's undeserved grace leads to recollection and repentance (cf. 6:9; 16:63; 20:43; Ps 130:4).

36:32 *not . . . for your sake.* See note on v. 22.

36:33–36 The impact of Israel's restoration on the nations.

36:33 *On the day.* Connects the promise of cleansing (vv. 24–32) and the promise of repopulation (vv. 33–36).

36:35 *garden of Eden.* Cf. 28:13; 31:9. *fortified.* In contrast to 38:11.

36:36 *nations . . . will know.* See note on v. 23.

36:37–38 In summary, Israel's full standing with God will be restored.

36:37 *yield to the plea.* Allowing petitions to come to him again, God reversed his earlier refusals to hear (cf. 14:3; 20:3,31).

36:38 *as numerous as the flocks for offerings.* See 1Ki 8:63; 1Ch 29:21; 2Ch 35:7 for the appropriateness of the comparison.

37:1–28 Although one of Ezekiel's major visions, it surprisingly bears no date (see chart, p. 1364). However, it must have come to Ezekiel sometime after 586 B.C. The symbolic vision given to Ezekiel (vv. 1–15) is immediately followed by a symbolic act that Ezekiel is instructed to perform (vv. 16–28). Both speak of the restoration of Israel, the central theme of chs. 34–36.

37:1 *hand of the Lᴏʀᴅ.* See note on 1:3. *brought me out by the*

Spirit. See 3:12 and note. *valley.* The Hebrew for this word is the same as that translated "plain" in 3:22–23; 8:4. Ezekiel now received a message of hope, whereas previously he had heard God's word of judgment. *bones.* Verse 11 interprets them as symbolizing Israel's apparently hopeless condition in exile.

37:2 *a great many bones.* Symbolizing the whole community of exiles. *very dry.* Long dead, far beyond the reach of resuscitation (1Ki 17:17–24; 2Ki 4:18–37; but see 2Ki 13:21).

37:4 *Prophesy to these bones.* Ezekiel had previously prophesied to inanimate objects (mountains, 6:2; 36:1; forests, 20:47); now he prophesies to lifeless bones and "the breath" (v. 9). Cf. Jn 5:25 and note.

37:6 *tendons . . . flesh . . . skin . . . breath.* Lists of four items are common in Ezekiel (see note on 1:5).

37:8 *but there was no breath.* This visionary re-creation of God's people recalls the two-step creation of Adam in Ge 2:7.

37:9 *breath.* See TNIV text note on v. 5. *four.* See note on 1:5. *slain.* What Ezekiel saw was a battlefield strewn with the bones of the fallen (see v. 10).

37:11 *Our bones . . . cut off.* A sense of utter despair, to which the vision offers hope.

37:12 *graves.* The imagery shifts from a scattering of bones on a battlefield (see note on v. 9) to a cemetery with sealed graves.

37:13 ʳS Ex 6:2
ᵘS Eze 17:24;
Hos 13:14
37:14 �ᵛS ver 9;
S Isa 11:2; Joel 2:28-
29 ʷS Jer 43:2
ˣEze 36:27-28,36;
Rev 11:11
37:16 ʸS 1Ki 12:20;
2Ch 10:17-19
ᶻNu 17:2-3; 2Ch 15:9
37:17 ᵃver 24;
Isa 11:13; S Jer 50:4;
Hos 1:11
37:18 ᵇS Eze 24:19
37:19 ᶜZec 10:6
37:21 ᵈS ver 12;
S Isa 43:5-6;
S Eze 20:42; 39:27;
Mic 4:6
37:22 ᵉS Eze 17:22;
S 34:13-14 ᶠIsa 11:13;
Jer 33:24; S 50:4;
Hos 1:11
37:23 ᵍEze 43:7
ʰS Jer 7:24
ⁱEze 11:18; S 36:28;
Na 2:2
37:24 ʲIsa 55:4;
Hos 3:5 ᵏS 1Sa 13:14;
S Isa 32:1 ˡZec 13:7
ᵐPs 78:70-71;
S Jer 30:21;
S Eze 21:27
37:25 ⁿS Eze 28:25
ᵒS Ezr 9:12; Am 9:15
ᵖS Ps 89:3-4;
Isa 11:1; S Eze 34:23-
24
37:26 ᵠS Nu 25:12
ʳS Ge 9:16;
S Dt 29:14;
S Heb 13:20
ˢS Jer 30:19
ᵗLev 26:11
ᵘS Eze 16:62
37:27 ᵛS Lev 26:11
ʷS Eze 34:30;
S 36:28; S 2Co 6:16*
37:28 ˣS Ex 31:13
ʸHos 1:10-11
ᶻEze 43:9; Zep 3:15
38:2 ᵃver 14;
Eze 39:11 ᵇS Ge 10:2
ᶜS Eze 27:13

you, my people, will know that I am the LORD, ᵗ when I open your graves and bring you up from them. ᵘ ¹⁴I will put my Spirit ᵛ in you and you will live, and I will settle ʷ you in your own land. Then you will know that I the LORD have spoken, and I have done it, declares the LORD. ˣ ' "

ONE NATION UNDER ONE KING

¹⁵The word of the LORD came to me: ¹⁶"Son of man, take a stick of wood and write on it, 'Belonging to Judah and the Israelites ʸ associated with him. ᶻ ' Then take another stick of wood, and write on it, 'Belonging to Joseph (that is, to Ephraim) and all the house of Israel associated with him.' ¹⁷Join them together into one stick so that they will become one in your hand. ᵃ

¹⁸"When your people ask you, 'Won't you tell us what you mean by this?' ᵇ ¹⁹say to them, 'This is what the Sovereign LORD says: I am going to take the stick of Joseph—which is in Ephraim's hand—and of the Israelite tribes associated with him, and join it to Judah's stick. I will make them into a single stick of wood, and they will become one in my hand.' ᶜ ²⁰Hold before their eyes the sticks you have written on ²¹and say to them, 'This is what the Sovereign LORD says: I will take the Israelites out of the nations where they have gone. I will gather them from all around and bring them back into their own land. ᵈ ²²I will make them one nation in the land, on the mountains of Israel. ᵉ There will be one king over all of them and they will never again be two nations or be divided into two kingdoms. ᶠ ²³They will no longer defile ᵍ themselves with their idols and vile images or with any of their offenses, for I will save them from all their sinful backsliding, ᵃ ʰ and I will cleanse them. They will be my people, and I will be their God. ⁱ

²⁴" 'My servant David ʲ will be king ᵏ over them, and they will all have one shepherd. ˡ They will follow my laws and be careful to keep my decrees. ᵐ ²⁵They will live in the land I gave to my servant Jacob, the land where your ancestors lived. ⁿ They and their children and their children's children will live there forever, ᵒ and David my servant will be their prince forever. ᵖ ²⁶I will make a covenant of peace ᵠ with them; it will be an everlasting covenant. ʳ I will establish them and increase their numbers, ˢ and I will put my sanctuary among them ᵗ forever. ᵘ ²⁷My dwelling place ᵛ will be with them; I will be their God, and they will be my people. ʷ ²⁸Then the nations will know that I the LORD make Israel holy, ˣ when my sanctuary is among them forever. ʸᶻ ' "

THE LORD'S GREAT VICTORY OVER THE NATIONS

38 The word of the LORD came to me: ²"Son of man, set your face against Gog, ᵃ of the land of Magog, ᵇ the chief prince of ᵇ Meshek and Tubal; ᶜ prophesy against him ³and say: 'This is what the Sovereign LORD says: I am against you,

---

ᵃ 23 Many Hebrew manuscripts (see also Septuagint); most Hebrew manuscripts *all their dwelling places where they sinned*   ᵇ 2 Or *the prince of Rosh,*

37:14 *I will put my Spirit in you.* See 36:27 and note. *I will settle you in your own land.* These words make it clear that the Lord is not speaking of a resurrection from the dead but of the national restoration of Israel.

37:16 *take a stick.* Ezekiel's last symbolic act involving a material object (cf. 4:1,3,9; 5:1). *write on it.* Zec 11:7 seems to be based on this passage in Ezekiel.

37:18 *Won't you tell us … ?* The symbolic act successfully aroused the people's curiosity (see 12:9; 21:7; 24:19).

37:19 *they will become one in my hand.* God would duplicate Ezekiel's symbolic act by uniting the two kingdoms separated since Solomon's death (see 1Ki 12). For similar prophecies of the reunion of Israel, see 33:23,29; Jer 3:18; 23:5–6; Hos 1:11; Am 9:11.

37:22 *mountains of Israel.* See 6:2–3; 34:13; 36:1. *one king.* Only here and in v. 24 is the word "king" used of the future ruler. Usually "prince" is used (see note on 34:24), as in v. 25. See 7:27 and note; see also 44:3; 45:7–9 and frequently in chs. 45–48, where the ruler in the ideal age is always referred to as "prince."

37:23 *idols.* The old and basic offense (see note on 6:4). *backsliding.* Cf. Jer 2:19; 3:22. *cleanse.* Cf. 36:25 for the same notion. *my people … their God.* See 11:20 and note.

37:24–25 These verses appear to recall the Davidic covenant (v. 24a), the Sinaitic covenant (v. 24b) and the Abrahamic covenant (v. 25)—all of which will be fulfilled in the "covenant of peace" (v. 26).

37:24 *My servant David.* As in 34:23 (see note there) the coming Messianic ruler is called David because he would be a descendant of David and would achieve for Israel what David had—except more fully. *king.* See note on v. 22. *shepherd.* As in 34:23 the coming ruler is likened to a shepherd who cares for his flock (cf. Jn 10, especially v. 16).

37:25 *my servant Jacob.* See 28:25 and note.

37:26 *covenant of peace.* See vv. 24–26; 34:25 and notes. *everlasting covenant.* See note on 16:59–63. The phrase occurs 16 times in the OT, referring at times to the Noahic covenant (Ge 9:16), the Abrahamic (Ge 17:7,13,19), the Davidic (2Sa 23:5) and the "new" (Jer 32:40). Cf. the covenant with Phinehas (Nu 25:12–13). *put my sanctuary among them.* As he had done before. This word is further developed in Ezekiel's vision of the future age, in which the rebuilt sanctuary would have central position (chs. 40–48). See vv. 27–28 and map, p. 1439.

37:27 *their God … my people.* See note on Zec 8:8.

38:1—39:29 The great battle of the ages, when the future restoration of Israel under the reign of the house of David (ch. 37) evokes a massive coalition of world powers to destroy God's kingdom. The vast host that comes against Jerusalem will end up as dead bodies strewn over the fields of the promised land, which will become the cemetery of all the enemy hordes that invade it (cf. ch. 39). Three oracles against Gog (38:1–13,14–23; 39:1–16) are followed by the depiction of a great feast in which

Gog, chief prince of[a] Meshek and Tubal.[d] [4]I will turn you around, put hooks[e] in your jaws and bring you out with your whole army—your horses, your horsemen fully armed, and a great horde with large and small shields, all of them brandishing their swords.[f] [5]Persia, Cush[b][g] and Put[h] will be with them, all with shields and helmets, [6]also Gomer[i] with all its troops, and Beth Togarmah[j] from the far north[k] with all its troops—the many nations with you.

[7]" 'Get ready; be prepared,[l] you and all the hordes gathered about you, and take command of them. [8]After many days[m] you will be called to arms. In future years you will invade a land that has recovered from war, whose people were gathered from many nations[n] to the mountains of Israel, which had long been desolate. They had been brought out from the nations, and now all of them live in safety.[o] [9]You and all your troops and the many nations with you will go up, advancing like a storm;[p] you will be like a cloud[q] covering the land.[r]

[10]" 'This is what the Sovereign LORD says: On that day thoughts will come into your mind[s] and you will devise an evil scheme.[t] [11]You will say, "I will invade a land of unwalled villages; I will attack a peaceful and unsuspecting people[u]—all of them living without walls and without gates and bars.[v] [12]I will plunder and loot and turn my hand against the resettled ruins and the people gathered from the nations, rich in livestock and goods, living at the center of the land.[c]" [13]Sheba[w] and Dedan[x] and the merchants of Tarshish[y] and all her villages[d] will say to you, "Have you come to plunder? Have you gathered your hordes to loot, to carry off silver and gold, to take away livestock and goods and to seize much plunder?[z]" '

[14]"Therefore, son of man, prophesy and say to Gog: 'This is what the Sovereign LORD says: In that day, when my people Israel are living in safety,[a] will you not take notice of it? [15]You will come from your place in the far north,[b] you and many nations with you, all of them riding on horses, a great horde, a mighty army.[c] [16]You will advance against my people Israel like a cloud[d] that covers the land.[e] In days to come, Gog, I will bring you against my land, so that the nations may know me when I am proved holy[f] through you before their eyes.[g]

---

[a] 3 Or Gog, prince of Rosh,   [b] 5 That is, the upper Nile region   [c] 12 The Hebrew for this phrase means the navel of the earth.   [d] 13 Or her strong lions

---

38:3 [d] Eze 39:1
38:4 [e] S 2Ki 19:28
[f] S Isa 43:17;
Eze 29:4; 39:2;
Da 11:40
38:5 [g] S Ge 10:6
[h] S Ge 10:6;
S Eze 27:10
38:6 [i] S Ge 10:2
[j] S Ge 10:3
[k] S Eze 32:30
38:7 [l] S Isa 8:9
38:8 [m] Isa 24:22
[n] S Isa 11:11 [o] ver 14;
Jer 23:6; S Eze 28:26;
Joel 3:1
38:9 [p] Isa 25:4; 28:2
[q] ver 16; Jer 4:13;
Joel 2:2 [r] Rev 20:8
38:10 [s] S Jer 17:10
[t] Ps 36:4; Mic 2:1
38:11 [u] S Ge 34:25
[v] Jer 49:31; Zec 2:4
38:13 [w] S Ge 10:7
[x] S Ge 25:3
[y] S Ge 10:4 [z] Isa 10:6;
33;23; S Jer 15:13
38:14 [a] S ver 8;
S Lev 25:18;
S Jer 16:15; Zec 2:5
38:15 [b] Eze 32:30
[c] Eze 39:2; Rev 20:8
38:16 [d] S ver 9
[e] Joel 3:11 [f] S Lev 10:3
[g] Isa 29:23; Eze 39:21

---

the enemy warriors are described in terms of sacrificial animals (39:17–20). Two final words put this great battle in the context of God's ways with Israel in exile and restoration: (1) The nations will then know that Israel was carried into exile not because her God was incapable of protecting his own but because he had punished them for being unfaithful to him (39:21–24), and (2) Israel's restoration following her punishment will show the nations that Israel's God is truly the Holy One (39:25–29).

38:1 This statement, repeated often for receiving God's word, stands as an introduction to chs. 38–39, which are a unit.
38:2 Son of man. See note on 2:1. set your face. See note on 20:46. Gog. Apparently a leader or king whose name appears only in chs. 38–39; Rev 20:8. Several identifications have been attempted, notably Gyges, king of Lydia (c. 660 B.C.). Possibly the name is purposely vague, standing for a mysterious, as yet undisclosed, enemy of God's people. of the land of Magog. In Ge 10:2; 1Ch 1:5 Magog is one of the sons of Japheth, thus the name of a people. In Eze 39:6 it appears to refer to a people. But since the prefix ma- can mean "place of," Magog may here simply mean "land of Gog." Israel had long experienced the hostility of the Hamites and other Semitic peoples; the future coalition here envisioned will include—and in fact be led by—peoples descended from Japheth (cf. Ge 10). chief prince. Military commander-in-chief. The TNIV text note gives the possible translation "prince of Rosh," and if it is correct, Rosh is probably the name of an unknown people or place. Identification with Russia is unlikely and in any case cannot be proven. Meshek and Tubal. These sons of Japheth (see Ge 10:2 and note; 1Ch 1:5) are probably located in eastern Asia Minor (cf. 27:13; 32:26). They are peoples and territories to the north of Israel (cf. vv. 6, 15; 39:2). As in the days of the Assyrians and Babylonians, the major attack will come from the north.
38:3 I am against you. See note on 5:8.

A **38:4** I will turn you around. Emphasis is on the fact that God is in complete control of all that is to follow. put

hooks in your jaws. As with the pharaoh in 29:4, Gog is likened to a beast led around by God.
38:5 Cush. See TNIV text note. The invading forces from the north (see v. 2 and note) are joined by armies from the south. Put. Libya.
38:6 Gomer. Another of Gog's northern allies (see note on v. 2), mentioned in Ge 10:3 and 1Ch 1:6 as one of the sons of Japheth. According to non-Biblical sources, these peoples originated north of the Black Sea. Beth Togarmah. See note on 27:14. According to Ge 10:3 and 1Ch 1:6, Togarmah is one of the children of Gomer.
38:8 After many days … In future years. After all the events of Israel's restoration described in chs. 34–37 are completed.
38:9 like a cloud. In Jer 4:13 Jeremiah similarly describes an invasion from the north.
38:10 On that day. A phrase also common to other prophetic writings; here it refers to the day of Gog's invasion of Israel. thoughts will come into your mind. The divine initiative (v. 4) is paralleled, as it often is in Scripture, by human action (cf. Dt 31:3; Isa 10:6–7). evil scheme. A raiding expedition (see v. 12).

A **38:11** land of unwalled villages. Speaks of a blissfully peaceful, ideal future time when walls will no longer be needed. See Zec 2:4–5 (and notes), which assumes, as does this passage, that the Lord alone is sufficient protection (cf. 36:35–36).

A **38:12** center of the land. The Hebrew for "center" also means "navel," a graphic image for the belief that Israel was the vital link between God and the world (the idea occurs also in 5:5). Since the Hebrew for "land" can also mean "earth," theologically Jerusalem is both the center of the land of Israel and the center of the world.
38:13 Sheba. Southwest corner of the Arabian peninsula (modern Yemen), known for trading (Job 6:19; see 23:42; 27:22; Ge 10:28 and note). Dedan. See note on 25:13. Tarshish. See note on 27:12.
38:16 I am proved holy. See Lev 10:3 and note.

38:19 *h* Isa 24:18;
Joel 2:10; 3:16;
S Rev 6:12 *i* Ps 18:7;
S Eze 5:13; Hag 2:6,
21
38:20 *j* S Ex 15:14
k Isa 42:15 *l* Job 14:18
m Ps 76:8; Hos 4:3;
Na 1:5
38:21 *n* Isa 66:16;
Jer 25:29
o S 1Sa 14:20;
S 2Ch 20:23;
Hag 2:22
38:22 *p* Isa 66:16;
Jer 25:31; S Eze 36:5
q S Eze 14:19; S 28:23
r S Eze 9:18; Ps 18:12;
Rev 16:21
s S Ge 19:24;
S Rev 9:17
t S Eze 13:11
38:23 *u* Eze 20:42;
S 36:23; S 37:6
39:1 *v* Rev 20:8
w S Ge 10:2
x S Eze 27:13;
S 38:2,3
39:2 *y* S Eze 32:30
z S Eze 38:4,15
39:3 *a* Hos 1:5;
Am 2:15 *b* Ps 76:3
39:4 *c* S Ge 40:19
d ver 17-20;
S Jer 25:33;
S Eze 29:5; S 33:27
39:5 *e* S Eze 32:4
39:6 *f* S Eze 30:8;
Rev 20:9 *g* S Ge 10:2
h S Jer 25:22
i S Ex 6:7
39:7 *j* S Ex 20:7;
S Eze 13:19
k S Isa 49:26
l S Isa 12:6; S 54:5;
S Eze 20:9; S 36:16,
23
39:8 *m* Eze 7:6
39:9 *n* Ps 76:3
o S Ps 46:9
39:10 *p* S Ex 3:22
q S Isa 14:2; S 33:1;
Hab 2:8
39:11 *r* S Isa 34:3
s S Eze 38:2
39:12 *t* Dt 21:23
39:13 *u* Eze 28:22

¹⁷ " 'This is what the Sovereign LORD says: You are the one I spoke of in former days by my servants the prophets of Israel. At that time they prophesied for years that I would bring you against them. ¹⁸This is what will happen in that day: When Gog attacks the land of Israel, my hot anger will be aroused, declares the Sovereign LORD. ¹⁹In my zeal and fiery wrath I declare that at that time there shall be a great earthquake *h* in the land of Israel. *i* ²⁰The fish in the sea, the birds in the sky, the beasts of the field, every creature that moves along the ground, and all the people on the face of the earth will tremble *j* at my presence. The mountains will be overturned, *k* the cliffs will crumble *l* and every wall will fall to the ground. *m* ²¹I will summon a sword *n* against Gog on all my mountains, declares the Sovereign LORD. Every man's sword will be against his fellow. *o* ²²I will execute judgment *p* on him with plague and bloodshed; *q* I will pour down torrents of rain, hailstones *r* and burning sulfur *s* on him and on his troops and on the many nations with him. *t* ²³And so I will show my greatness and my holiness, and I will make myself known in the sight of many nations. Then they will know that I am the LORD. *u* '

39 "Son of man, prophesy against Gog *v* and say: 'This is what the Sovereign LORD says: I am against you, Gog, chief prince of *a* Meshek *w* and Tubal. *x* ²I will turn you around and drag you along. I will bring you from the far north *y* and send you against the mountains of Israel. *z* ³Then I will strike your bow *a* from your left hand and make your arrows *b* drop from your right hand. ⁴On the mountains of Israel you will fall, you and all your troops and the nations with you. I will give you as food to all kinds of carrion birds *c* and to the wild animals. *d* ⁵You will fall in the open field, for I have spoken, declares the Sovereign LORD. *e* ⁶I will send fire *f* on Magog *g* and on those who live in safety in the coastlands, *h* and they will know *i* that I am the LORD.

⁷ " 'I will make known my holy name among my people Israel. I will no longer let my holy name be profaned, *j* and the nations will know *k* that I the LORD am the Holy One in Israel. *l* ⁸It is coming! It will surely take place, declares the Sovereign LORD. This is the day *m* I have spoken of.

⁹ " 'Then those who live in the towns of Israel will go out and use the weapons for fuel and burn them up—the small and large shields, the bows and arrows, *n* the war clubs and spears. For seven years they will use them for fuel. *o* ¹⁰They will not need to gather wood from the fields or cut it from the forests, because they will use the weapons for fuel. And they will plunder *p* those who plundered them and loot those who looted them, declares the Sovereign LORD. *q*

¹¹ " 'On that day I will give Gog a burial place in Israel, in the valley of those who travel east of the Sea. It will block the way of travelers, because Gog and all his hordes will be buried *r* there. So it will be called the Valley of Hamon Gog. *b s*

¹² " 'For seven months the house of Israel will be burying them in order to cleanse the land. *t* ¹³All the people of the land will bury them, and the day I display my glory *u* will be a memorable day for them, declares the Sovereign LORD. ¹⁴People will be continually employed in cleansing the land. They will spread out across the land and, along with others, they will bury any bodies that are lying on the ground.

" 'After the seven months they will carry out a more detailed search. ¹⁵As they go

---

a 1 Or *Gog, prince of Rosh,*   *b* 11 *Hamon Gog* means *hordes of Gog.*

38:17 *You are the one I spoke of.* Probably a general reference to earlier prophecies of divine judgment on the nations arrayed against God and his people (see note on v.2, "Gog").
38:19 *earthquake.* Signaling the mighty presence of God, who comes to overwhelm the great army invading his land.
38:20 The fourfold listing of the animal world indicates the totality of nature (see note on 1:5; cf. Ge 9:2; 1Ki 4:33; Job 12:7–8 for similar listings).
38:21 *I will summon a sword.* God's sword of judgment (see 5:2 and note). *Every man's sword will be against his fellow.* The coalition of Israel's enemies will turn on itself, as did the armies that attacked Judah in the time of Jehoshaphat (2Ch 20:22–23).
38:22 The list of divine weapons suggests that God will intervene directly, without the benefit of an earthly army.
39:1–16 The same basic events as those of ch. 38 are described, though some new details are added.
39:1 *Gog, chief prince of Meshek.* See note on 38:2.
39:2 *from the far north.* As in 38:6,15.
39:3 *bow.* Cf. Jer 6:23. The Lord will disarm Israel's enemies before they can shoot an arrow.

39:4 *food to all kinds of carrion birds.* A theme expanded in vv. 17–20.
39:6 *I will send fire.* See 20:47 and note.
39:7 *let my holy name be profaned.* See Lev 18:21 and note. *the Holy One.* See Lev 11:44 and note.
39:9 *seven.* A symbolic number stressing the size of the invading armies and the finality of this great battle against God's people, though some understand "seven years" literally.
39:11 *the Sea.* The Mediterranean Sea according to some, the Dead Sea according to others. *Hamon Gog.* See TNIV text note.
39:12 *seven.* Cf. v. 9 and note. *cleanse the land.* Ritual purity is a basic element in Ezekiel's theology (see 22:26; 24:13; 36:25,33; 37:23). Corpses were especially unclean (see Lev 5:2; 21:1,11; 22:4; Nu 5:2; 6:6–12; 19:16; 31:19).
39:13 *people of the land.* See 7:27 and note, though here a special class may not be implied.
39:14 *People will be continually employed.* After the seven-month burial period observed by all the people, special squads will be hired full time to ensure total cleansing of the land— by marking for burial any human bones that may have been missed. Total ritual purity is the aim.

through the land, anyone who sees a human bone will leave a marker beside it until the gravediggers bury it in the Valley of Hamon Gog, ¹⁶near a town called Hamonah. ᵃ And so they will cleanse the land.'

¹⁷"Son of man, this is what the Sovereign Lᴏʀᴅ says: Call out to every kind of bird ᵛ and all the wild animals: 'Assemble and come together from all around to the sacrifice I am preparing for you, the great sacrifice on the mountains of Israel. There you will eat flesh and drink blood. ʷ ¹⁸You will eat the flesh of mighty men and drink the blood of the princes of the earth as if they were rams and lambs, goats and bulls—all of them fattened animals from Bashan. ˣ ¹⁹At the sacrifice ʸ I am preparing for you, you will eat fat till you are glutted and drink blood till you are drunk. ²⁰At my table you will eat your fill of horses and riders, mighty men and soldiers of every kind,' declares the Sovereign Lᴏʀᴅ. ᶻ

²¹"I will display my glory among the nations, and all the nations will see the punishment I inflict and the hand I lay on them. ᵃ ²²From that day forward the house of Israel will know that I am the Lᴏʀᴅ their God. ²³And the nations will know that the people of Israel went into exile for their sin, because they were unfaithful to me. So I hid my face from them and handed them over to their enemies, and they all fell by the sword. ᵇ ²⁴I dealt with them according to their uncleanness and their offenses, and I hid my face from them. ᶜ

²⁵"Therefore this is what the Sovereign Lᴏʀᴅ says: I will now restore the fortunes of Jacobᵇ ᵈ and will have compassion ᵉ on all the people of Israel, and I will be zealous for my holy name. ᶠ ²⁶They will forget their shame and all the unfaithfulness they showed toward me when they lived in safety ᵍ in their land with no one to make them afraid. ʰ ²⁷When I have brought them back from the nations and have gathered them from the countries of their enemies, I will be proved holy through them in the sight of many nations. ⁱ ²⁸Then they will know that I am the Lᴏʀᴅ their God, for though I sent them into exile among the nations, I will gather themʲ to their own land, not leaving any behind. ᵏ ²⁹I will no longer hide my face ˡ from them, for I will pour out my Spirit ᵐ on the house of Israel, declares the Sovereign Lᴏʀᴅ. ⁿ"

THE TEMPLE AREA RESTORED

40 In the twenty-fifth year of our exile, at the beginning of the year, on the tenth of the month, in the fourteenth year after the fall of the city ᵒ—on that very day the hand of the Lᴏʀᴅ was on meᵖ and he took me there. ²In visions ᑫ of

---

ᵃ 16 *Hamonah* means *horde.*   ᵇ 25 Or *now bring Jacob back from captivity*

39:17–20 These verses involve a restating of vv. 9–16, employing a different figure (see Isa 34:6 and note; Jer 46:10; Zep 1:7). The metaphor of sacrifice suggests a consecration to the Lord in judgment, as with Jericho (see Jos 6:17 and TNIV text note there).
39:18 *You will eat the flesh of mighty men.* A gory description of what birds of prey commonly do (see previous note and Rev 19:17–21). *as if they were.* The bodies of the victims are compared to animals commonly used for sacrifices. *Bashan.* Rich pastureland east of the Sea of Galilee, known for its sleek cattle (Dt 32:14; Ps 22:12; Am 4:1) and its oak trees (27:6; Isa 2:13).
39:19 *eat fat … drink blood.* Further indication that this is the Lord's sacrificial feast, in that fat and blood were normally reserved for God (see 44:15; see also Lev 3:16; 1Sa 2:15; Isa 34:6 and notes).
39:20 *my table.* Sacrificial altar. See 40:38–43 and 41:22 for description of the tables in the new temple.

⚫ **39:21** *my glory.* God's visible presence in the world (see note on 1:28). Here that visibility is due to divine intervention in history.

⚫ **39:22–23** *the house of Israel will know … And the nations will know.* As God had made himself known to Israel and the nations through his saving acts in Israel's behalf (see Ex 6:7; 7:5,17; 10:2; 14:18; 16:6–7,12; Jos 3:10; 4:24; cf. Jos 2:9–11; 5:1), so now Israel and the nations see him at work as he judges his people for their sin (see v. 27; 6:7 and note).
39:23 *I hid my face.* Expression of divine displeasure (see Ps 13:1 and note; 30:7; Isa 54:8; 57:17).
39:24 *their uncleanness and their offenses.* Spelled out especially in ch. 22, but also throughout chs. 6–24.
39:25 *Jacob.* The nation of Israel, as in 20:5. *my holy name.* See 20:9 and note.
39:26 *They will forget their shame.* The remembrance of shame

previously called for (6:9; 20:43; 36:31) is here erased.

⚫ **39:27** *I will be proved holy through them.* God will reveal himself anew in a restored, holy people (see Lev 10:3 and note).

39:28 *know that I am the Lᴏʀᴅ.* See note on vv. 22–23.

⚫ **39:29** *I will pour out my Spirit.* The gift of God's enabling Spirit (see 36:27; 37:14; see also notes on 2:2; Joel 2:28).

⚫ **40:1—48:35** The restoration of Israel as a purified people calls for a purified land and a new order in the commonwealth of the people of God. This is the subject of Ezekiel's last vision, which presents an idealized picture of the new order to be put in place. For the basic outline of the vision's various topics, see Introduction: Outline under "The New Order for Purified Israel," as well as the summary (overview) notes below.
40:1–47 Restoration of the temple area.
40:1 *twenty-fifth year … beginning … tenth.* Apr. 28, 573 B.C. *of our exile.* All the dates in the book of Ezekiel (see chart, p. 1364) are reckoned from the 597 exile, but only here and in 33:21 is the exile specifically mentioned (see 1:2). *the beginning of the year.* Hebrew *Rosh Hashanah,* the well-known Jewish New Year festival. It had long occurred in the fall (in either September or October), but since throughout the book Ezekiel uses a different and older religious calendar, the spring date as given above is correct (see note on Lev 23:24). *hand of the Lᴏʀᴅ was on me.* See note on 1:3.

⚫ **40:2** *visions of God.* Introduces all three of Ezekiel's major visions (see 1:1; 8:3). *very high mountain.* Mount Zion, also seen as extraordinarily high in other prophetic visions (17:22; Isa 2:2; Mic 4:1; Zec 14:10). Height here signifies importance, as the earthly seat of God's reign. *on whose south side.* With the city located on its southern slopes, the mountain is to the north (cf. Ps 48; see Ps 48:2 and note).

39:17 ᵛ S Job 15:23
ʷ S Eze 32:4
39:18 ˣ S Ps 22:12; Jer 51:40
39:19 ʸ S Lev 3:9
39:20 ᶻ S Isa 56:9; S Jer 12:9; Rev 19:17-18
39:21 ᵃ Eze 9:16; Isa 37:20; S Eze 38:16
39:23 ᵇ Isa 1:15; 59:2; S Jer 22:8-9; S 44:23
39:24 ᶜ 2Ki 17:23; Jer 2:17,19; 4:18; S Eze 7:22; Da 9:7
39:25 ᵈ S Jer 33:7
ᵉ Isa 27:12-13; S Eze 16:53
39:26 ᵍ S 1Ki 4:25; S Jer 32:37; S Eze 38:8 ʰ Isa 17:2; Eze 34:28; Mic 4:4
39:27 ⁱ S Eze 37:21
39:28 ʲ Ps 147:2
ᵏ S Eze 36:23,36
39:29 ˡ S Dt 31:17
ᵐ S Isa 11:2; S Eze 37:9; S Ac 2:17
ⁿ S Eze 16:42
40:1 ᵒ S 2Ki 25:7; Jer 39:1-10; 52:4-11
ᵖ S Eze 1:3; S 29:17
40:2 ᑫ S Eze 24:10; Da 7:1,7

40:2 ʳS Jer 31:12;
S Eze 17:22;
Rev 21:10
40:3 ˢS Eze 1:7;
Rev 1:15 ᵗEze 47:3;
Zec 2:1-2; Rev 11:1;
21:15
40:4 ᵘS Dt 6:6
ᵛJer 26:2 ʷEze 44:5
40:5 ˣEze 42:20
40:6 ʸS Eze 8:16
40:7 ᶻver 36
40:14 ᵃS Ex 27:9
40:16 ᵇver 21-22;
2Ch 3:5; Eze 41:26
40:17 ᶜRev 11:2
ᵈEze 41:6 ᵉEze 42:1
40:19 ᶠEze 46:1
ᵍver 23,27

God he took me to the land of Israel and set me on a very high mountain, ʳ on whose south side were some buildings that looked like a city. ³He took me there, and I saw a man whose appearance was like bronze; ˢ he was standing in the gateway with a linen cord and a measuring rod ᵗ in his hand. ⁴The man said to me, "Son of man, look carefully and listen closely and pay attention to everything I am going to show you, ᵘ for that is why you have been brought here. Tell ᵛ the house of Israel everything you see. ʷ"

THE EAST GATE TO THE OUTER COURT

⁵I saw a wall completely surrounding the temple area. The length of the measuring rod in the man's hand was six long cubits,ᵃ each of which was a cubit and a handbreadth. He measuredˣ the wall; it was one measuring rod thick and one rod high.

⁶Then he went to the east gate.ʸ He climbed its steps and measured the threshold of the gate; it was one rod deep. ⁷The alcovesᶻ for the guards were one rod long and one rod wide, and the projecting walls between the alcoves were five cubitsᵇ thick. And the threshold of the gate next to the portico facing the temple was one rod deep.

⁸Then he measured the portico of the gateway; ⁹itᶜ was eight cubitsᵈ deep and its jambs were two cubitsᵉ thick. The portico of the gateway faced the temple.

¹⁰Inside the east gate were three alcoves on each side; the three had the same measurements, and the faces of the projecting walls on each side had the same measurements. ¹¹Then he measured the width of the entrance of the gateway; it was ten cubits and its length was thirteen cubits.ᶠ ¹²In front of each alcove was a wall one cubit high, and the alcoves were six cubits square. ¹³Then he measured the gateway from the top of the rear wall of one alcove to the top of the opposite one; the distance was twenty-five cubitsᵍ from one parapet opening to the opposite one. ¹⁴He measured along the faces of the projecting walls all around the inside of the gateway—sixty cubits.ʰ The measurement was up to the porticoⁱ facing the courtyard.ⁱ ᵃ¹⁵The distance from the entrance of the gateway to the far end of its portico was fifty cubits.ᵏ ¹⁶The alcoves and the projecting walls inside the gateway were surmounted by narrow parapet openings all around, as was the portico; the openings all around faced inward. The faces of the projecting walls were decorated with palm trees.ᵇ

THE OUTER COURT

¹⁷Then he brought me into the outer court.ᶜ There I saw some rooms and a pavement that had been constructed all around the court; there were thirty roomsᵈ along the pavement.ᵉ ¹⁸It abutted the sides of the gateways and was as wide as they were long; this was the lower pavement. ¹⁹Then he measured the distance from the inside of the lower gateway to the outside of the inner court;ᶠ it was a hundred cubitsⁱᵍ on the east side as well as on the north.

ᵃ 5 That is, about 10 feet or about 3.1 meters; also in verse 12. The long cubit of about 21 inches or about 52 centimeters is the basic unit of measurement of length throughout Ezekiel 40–48. ᵇ 7 That is, about 8 1/2 feet or about 2.6 meters; also in verse 48 ᶜ 8,9 Many Hebrew manuscripts, Septuagint, Vulgate and Syriac; most Hebrew manuscripts *gateway facing the temple; it was one rod deep. ⁹Then he measured the portico of the gateway; it* ᵈ 9 That is, about 14 feet or about 4.2 meters ᵉ 9 That is, about 3 1/2 feet or about 1 meter ᶠ 11 That is, about 17 feet wide and 22 feet long or about 5.2 meters wide and 6.8 meters long ᵍ 13 That is, about 43 feet or about 13 meters; also in verses 21, 25, 29, 30, 33 and 36 ʰ 14 That is, about 103 feet or about 31 meters ⁱ 14 Septuagint; Hebrew *projecting wall* ᶦ 14 The meaning of the Hebrew for this verse is uncertain. ᵏ 15 That is, about 85 feet or about 26 meters; also in verses 21, 25, 29, 33 and 36 ᶦ 19 That is, about 170 feet or about 52 meters; also in verses 23, 27 and 47

40:3 *like bronze.* Indicates that the man was other than human. *in the gateway.* Presumably of the outer court (see vv. 17–19). *linen cord.* Used for longer measurements, such as those in 47:3. *measuring rod.* Used for shorter measurements—about ten feet and four inches long.

40:5 *wall completely surrounding the temple area.* Separating the sacred from the secular. *six long cubits.* In using the long cubit (seven handbreadths, or about 21 inches), which was older than the shorter cubit (six handbreadths, or about 18 inches), Ezekiel was returning to more ancient standards for the new community (see 2Ch 3:3).

40:6 *east gate.* The gate of the outer court. The three gates (east, north, south) of the outer court were similar to the three in the inner court (v. 32), having six alcoves for the guards (three on each side) and a portico (vv. 8–9). Comparable gate plans have been discovered at Megiddo, Gezer and Hazor, all dating from the time of Solomon (see 1Ki 9:15 and note). The guards kept out anyone who might profane the temple area

(see Ezr 2:62). *climbed its steps.* The first of three sets of stairs leading to the temple. This one had seven steps (v. 22); the next one (inner court), eight (v. 31); the last (temple), ten (v. 49; see TNIV text note there)—possibly indicating increasing degrees of "holiness" (sacredness).

40:9 *portico of the gateway faced the temple.* The reverse position of the porticoes of the inner court gates, which faced away from the temple (v. 34).

40:10 *three alcoves.* The alcoves for the guards, mentioned in v. 7.

40:16 *palm trees.* As in Solomon's temple (see 1Ki 6:29,32,35 and note on 6:29).

40:17 *thirty rooms.* The exact location of these rooms is not given. They were probably intended for the people's use (see Jer 35:2,4 and note on 35:2).

40:19 *hundred cubits.* Over 170 feet (see note on v. 5) separated the outer wall from the inner wall and was the width of the outer court.

EZEKIEL'S TEMPLE

A. Wall (40:5,16-20)
B. East gate (40:6-14,16)
C. Portico (40:8)
D. Outer court (40:17)
E. Pavement (40:17)
F. Inner court (40:19)
G. North gate (40:20-22)
H. Inner court (40:23)
I. South gate (40:24-26)
J. South inner court (40:27)
K. Gateway (40:28-31)
L. Gateway (40:32-34)
M. Gateway (40:35-38)
N. Priests' rooms (40:44-45)

O. Court (40:47)
P. Temple portico (40:48-49)
Q. Outer sanctuary (41:1-2)
R. Most Holy Place (41:3-4)
S. Temple walls (41:5-7,9,11)
T. Base (41:8)
U. Open area (41:10)
V. West building (41:12)
W. Priests' rooms (42:1-10)
X. Altar (43:13-17)
AA. Rooms for preparing
sacrifices (40:39-43)
BB. Ovens (46:19-20)
CC. Kitchens (46:21-24)

Ezekiel uses a long or "royal" cubit,
c. 21 inches or 52 cm ("cubit and a handbreadth," Eze 40:5) as opposed
to the standard Hebrew cubit of c. 18
inches or 45 cm.

Scripture describes a floor plan but provides few height dimensions. This art-
work shows an upward projection of the
temple over the floor plan. This temple
existed only in a vision of Ezekiel (Eze
40:2) and has never actually been built,
as were the temples of Solomon, Zerubbabel and Herod.

Floor plan of sanctuary

Side rooms

NORTH

NORTH

SOUTH

EAST

Height of this wall has
been exaggerated slightly
to avoid optical illusion

Kitchens were in
all four corners

40:21 ^h ver 7
ⁱ ver 30
40:22 ^j ver 49
^k S ver 16,26
40:23 ^l S ver 19
40:24 ^m ver 32,35
40:25 ⁿ ver 33
40:26 ^o S ver 22
40:27 ^p ver 32
^q S ver 19
40:28 ^r ver 35
40:29 ^s ver 7
^t ver 25
40:30 ^u ver 21
40:31 ^v ver 22
^w ver 34,37
40:32 ^x S ver 24
40:33 ^y ver 7
40:34 ^z ver 22
40:35 ^a Eze 44:4;
47:2 ^b S ver 24
40:36 ^c ver 7
40:37 ^d ver 22
^e ver 34
40:38 ^f S 2Ch 4:6;
Eze 42:13
40:39 ^g Eze 46:2
^h Lev 4:3,28
ⁱ S Lev 7:1 ^j ver 42
40:42 ^k Ex 20:25
^l ver 39

THE NORTH GATE

²⁰Then he measured the length and width of the north gate, leading into the outer court. ²¹Its alcoves ^h—three on each side—its projecting walls and its portico ⁱ had the same measurements as those of the first gateway. It was fifty cubits long and twenty-five cubits wide. ²²Its openings, its portico ^j and its palm tree decorations had the same measurements as those of the gate facing east. Seven steps led up to it, with its portico opposite them. ^k ²³There was a gate to the inner court facing the north gate, just as there was on the east. He measured from one gate to the opposite one; it was a hundred cubits. ^l

THE SOUTH GATE

²⁴Then he led me to the south side and I saw the south gate. He measured its jambs and its portico, and they had the same measurements ^m as the others. ²⁵The gateway and its portico had narrow openings all around, like the openings of the others. It was fifty cubits long and twenty-five cubits wide. ⁿ ²⁶Seven steps led up to it, with its portico opposite them; it had palm tree decorations on the faces of the projecting walls on each side. ^o ²⁷The inner court ^p also had a gate facing south, and he measured from this gate to the outer gate on the south side; it was a hundred cubits. ^q

THE GATES TO THE INNER COURT

²⁸Then he brought me into the inner court through the south gate, and he measured the south gate; it had the same measurements ^r as the others. ²⁹Its alcoves, ^s its projecting walls and its portico had the same measurements as the others. The gateway and its portico had openings all around. It was fifty cubits long and twenty-five cubits wide. ^t ³⁰(The porticoes ^u of the gateways around the inner court were twenty-five cubits wide and five cubits deep.) ³¹Its portico ^v faced the outer court; palm trees decorated its jambs, and eight steps led up to it. ^w

³²Then he brought me to the inner court on the east side, and he measured the gateway; it had the same measurements ^x as the others. ³³Its alcoves, ^y its projecting walls and its portico had the same measurements as the others. The gateway and its portico had openings all around. It was fifty cubits long and twenty-five cubits wide. ³⁴Its portico ^z faced the outer court; palm trees decorated the jambs on either side, and eight steps led up to it.

³⁵Then he brought me to the north gate ^a and measured it. It had the same measurements ^b as the others, ³⁶as did its alcoves, ^c its projecting walls and its portico, and it had openings all around. It was fifty cubits long and twenty-five cubits wide. ³⁷Its portico ^a ^d faced the outer court; palm trees decorated the jambs on either side, and eight steps led up to it. ^e

THE ROOMS FOR PREPARING SACRIFICES

³⁸A room with a doorway was by the portico in each of the inner gateways, where the burnt offerings ^f were washed. ³⁹In the portico of the gateway were two tables on each side, on which the burnt offerings, ^g sin offerings ^b ^h and guilt offerings ⁱ were slaughtered. ^j ⁴⁰By the outside wall of the portico of the gateway, near the steps at the entrance of the north gateway were two tables, and on the other side of the steps were two tables. ⁴¹So there were four tables on one side of the gateway and four on the other—eight tables in all—on which the sacrifices were slaughtered. ⁴²There were also four tables of dressed stone ^k for the burnt offerings, each a cubit and a half long, a cubit and a half wide and a cubit high. ^c On them were placed the utensils for slaughtering the burnt offerings and the other sacrifices. ^l ⁴³And double-pronged hooks, each a handbreadth ^d long, were attached to the wall all around. The tables were for the flesh of the offerings.

---

^a 37 Septuagint (see also verses 31 and 34); Hebrew *jambs*   ^b 39 Or *purification offerings*   ^c 42 That is, about 2 1/2 feet long and wide and 21 inches high or about 78 centimeters long and wide and 52 centimeters high   ^d 43 That is, about 3 1/2 inches or about 9 centimeters

---

40:20 *north gate.* Both it and the south gate (v. 24) were identical to the east gate (see note on v. 6).

40:22 *Seven steps.* See note on v. 6.

40:28 *south gate.* Of the inner wall, which is not described but must be assumed. *it had the same measurements as the others.* In both the outer walls (see note on v. 6).

40:34 *eight steps.* See note on v. 6.

40:38 *portico in each of the inner gateways.* The porticoes of the inner gateways were on the side of the outer court, facing away from the temple. *washed.* The inner parts and the legs were washed (Lev 1:9).

40:39 *burnt offerings.* Probably one of the oldest kinds of sacrifice. The entire animal was burned in consecration to God (see note on Lev 1:3). *sin offerings and guilt offerings.* Discussed in Lev 4—7 (see notes there). The fellowship offerings, which were more festive, are notable by their absence from this listing (see 43:27; 45:17; 46:2,12; see also chart, p. 155).

THE ROOMS FOR THE PRIESTS

⁴⁴Outside the inner gate, within the inner court, were two rooms, one ᵃ at the side of the north gate and facing south, and another at the side of the south ᵇ gate and facing north. ⁴⁵He said to me, "The room facing south is for the priests who guard the temple, ᵐ ⁴⁶and the room facing north ⁿ is for the priests who guard the altar. ᵒ These are the sons of Zadok, ᵖ who are the only Levites who may draw near to the LORD to minister before him. �q"

⁴⁷Then he measured the court: It was square—a hundred cubits long and a hundred cubits wide. And the altar was in front of the temple. ʳ

THE NEW TEMPLE

⁴⁸He brought me to the portico of the temple ˢ and measured the jambs of the portico; they were five cubits wide on either side. The width of the entrance was fourteen cubits ᶜ and its projecting walls were ᵈ three cubits ᵉ wide on either side. ⁴⁹The portico ᵗ was twenty cubits ᶠ wide, and twelve ᵍ cubits ʰ from front to back. It was reached by a flight of stairs, ⁱ and there were pillars ᵘ on each side of the jambs.

41 Then the man brought me to the main hall ᵛ and measured the jambs; the width of the jambs was six cubits ʲ on each side. ᵏ ²The entrance was ten cubits ˡ wide, and the projecting walls on each side of it were five cubits ᵐ wide. He also measured the main hall; it was forty cubits long and twenty cubits wide. ⁿ ʷ

³Then he went into the inner sanctuary and measured the jambs of the entrance; each was two cubits ᵒ wide. The entrance was six cubits wide, and the projecting walls on each side of it were seven cubits ᵖ wide. ⁴And he measured the length of the inner sanctuary; it was twenty cubits, and its width was twenty cubits across the end of the main hall. ˣ He said to me, "This is the Most Holy Place. ʸ"

⁵Then he measured the wall of the temple; it was six cubits thick, and each side room around the temple was four cubits q wide. ⁶The side rooms were on three levels, one above another, thirty ᶻ on each level. There were ledges all around the wall of the temple to serve as supports for the side rooms, so that the supports were not inserted into the wall of the temple. ᵃ ⁷The side rooms all around the temple were wider at each successive level. The structure surrounding the temple was built in ascending stages, so that the rooms widened as one went upward. A stairway ᵇ went up from the lowest floor to the top floor through the middle floor.

⁸I saw that the temple had a raised base all around it, forming the foundation of the side rooms. It was the length of the rod, six long cubits. ⁹The outer wall of the side rooms was five cubits thick. The open area between the side rooms of the temple ¹⁰and the ⌊priests'⌋ rooms was twenty cubits wide all around the temple. ¹¹There were entrances to the side rooms from the open area, one on the north and another on the south; and the base adjoining the open area was five cubits wide all around.

¹²The building facing the temple courtyard on the west side was seventy cubits ʳ wide. The wall of the building was five cubits thick all around, and its length was ninety cubits. ˢ

ᵃ 44 Septuagint; Hebrew *were rooms for singers, which were*   ᵇ 44 Septuagint; Hebrew *east*   ᶜ 48 That is, about 24 feet or about 7.3 meters   ᵈ 48 Septuagint; Hebrew *entrance was*   ᵉ 48 That is, about 5 1/4 feet or about 1.5 meters   ᶠ 49 That is, about 34 feet or about 10.4 meters   ᵍ 49 Septuagint; Hebrew *eleven*   ʰ 49 That is, about 21 feet or about 6.2 meters   ⁱ 49 Hebrew; Septuagint *Ten steps led up to it*   ʲ 1 That is, about 10 feet or about 3 meters; also in verses 3, 5 and 8   ᵏ 1 One Hebrew manuscript and Septuagint; most Hebrew manuscripts *side, the width of the tent*   ˡ 2 That is, about 17 feet or about 5.2 meters   ᵐ 2 That is, about 8 1/2 feet or about 2.6 meters; also in verses 9, 11 and 12   ⁿ 2 That is, about 68 feet long and 34 feet wide or about 21 meters long and 10.4 meters wide   ᵒ 3 That is, about 3 1/2 feet or about 1 meter; also in verse 22   ᵖ 3 That is, about 12 feet or about 3.6 meters   q 5 That is, about 7 feet or about 2.1 meters   ʳ 12 That is, about 120 feet or about 36 meters   ˢ 12 That is, about 154 feet or about 47 meters

---

40:46 *sons of Zadok.* For the distinction between the sons of Zadok and the Levites, see the fuller discussion in the notes on 44:15–31.

40:47 *altar.* Described in 43:13–17 (see notes there).

40:48—42:20 Description of the new temple (see diagram, p. 1427).

40:48 *portico.* Similar to the portico in Solomon's temple but slightly larger (see 1Ki 6:3).

40:49 *pillars.* Called Jakin and Boaz in Solomon's temple (see 1Ki 7:21 and TNIV text notes).

41:1 *main hall.* Or nave, the largest of the three rooms comprising the temple (see 1Ki 6:3–5). This main hall was identical in size to Solomon's (see 1Ki 6:17).

41:3 *he went into the inner sanctuary.* Only the angel, not Ezekiel, entered the Most Holy Place. Lev 16 forbids any but the high priest to enter it, and then only once a year (see Heb 9:7 and note). *six cubits wide.* Note the progressive narrowing of the door openings as one approaches the inner sanctuary (40:48, 14 cubits; 41:2, 10 cubits; here, 6 cubits).

41:4 *Most Holy Place.* See notes on Ex 26:31–35; 27:12–13; 1Ki 6:2,23; 2Ch 3:8; Ezr 6:15; Ps 28:2; Mt 27:51; Heb 8:2; 10:19–20.

41:6 *thirty on each level.* These 90 side rooms were probably storerooms for the priests, possibly for the tithes (see Mal 3:10 and note).

41:13 *hundred.* The 100-cubit symmetry stood for perfection.

40:45 ᵐ 1Ch 9:23
40:46 ⁿ Eze 42:13
ᵒ Nu 18:5
ᵖ S 2Sa 8:17;
S Ezr 7:2 q Nu 16:5;
Eze 43:19; 44:15;
45:4; 48:11
40:47 ʳ Eze 41:13-14
40:48 ˢ 1Ki 6:2
40:49 ᵗ ver 22;
1Ki 6:3 ᵘ S 1Ki 7:15
41:1 ᵛ ver 23
41:2 ʷ 2Ch 3:3
41:4 ˣ 1Ki 6:20
ʸ S Ex 26:33;
Heb 9:3-8
41:6 ᶻ Eze 40:17
ᵃ S 1Ki 6:5
41:7 ᵇ 1Ki 6:8

41:14 *c* Eze 40:47
41:15 *d* Eze 42:3
41:16 *e* 1Ki 6:4
f ver 25-26; 1Ki 6:15;
Eze 42:3
41:18 *g* S 1Ki 6:18
h Ex 37:7; S 2Ch 3:7
i S 1Ki 6:29; 7:36
j Eze 10:21
41:19 *k* S Eze 10:14
41:21 *l* ver 1
41:22 *m* S Ex 30:1
n S Ex 25:23;
S Eze 23:41
41:23 *o* ver 1
p 1Ki 6:32
41:24 *q* 1Ki 6:34
41:26 *r* ver 15-16;
Eze 40:16
42:1 *s* ver 13
t S Ex 27:9;
Eze 41:12-14
u Eze 40:17
42:3 *v* Eze 41:15
w Eze 41:16
42:4 *x* Eze 46:19
42:9 *y* Eze 44:5;
46:19
42:10 *z* Eze 41:12-14
a ver 1
42:13 *b* Eze 40:46
c ver 1 *d* Eze 41:12-14

[13] Then he measured the temple; it was a hundred cubits [a] long, and the temple courtyard and the building with its walls were also a hundred cubits long. [14] The width of the temple courtyard on the east, including the front of the temple, was a hundred cubits. [c]

[15] Then he measured the length of the building facing the courtyard at the rear of the temple, including its galleries [d] on each side; it was a hundred cubits.

The main hall, the inner sanctuary and the portico facing the court, [16] as well as the thresholds and the narrow windows [e] and galleries around the three of them—everything beyond and including the threshold was covered with wood. The floor, the wall up to the windows, and the windows were covered. [f] [17] In the space above the outside of the entrance to the inner sanctuary and on the walls at regular intervals all around the inner and outer sanctuary [18] were carved [g] cherubim [h] and palm trees. [i] Palm trees alternated with cherubim. Each cherub had two faces: [j] [19] the face of a human being toward the palm tree on one side and the face of a lion toward the palm tree on the other. They were carved all around the whole temple. [k] [20] From the floor to the area above the entrance, cherubim and palm trees were carved on the wall of the main hall.

[21] The main hall [l] had a rectangular doorframe, and the one at the front of the Most Holy Place was similar. [22] There was a wooden altar [m] three cubits [b] high and two cubits square [c]; its corners, its base [d] and its sides were of wood. The man said to me, "This is the table [n] that is before the Lord." [23] Both the main hall [o] and the Most Holy Place had double doors. [p] [24] Each door had two leaves—two hinged leaves [q] for each door. [25] And on the doors of the main hall were carved cherubim and palm trees like those carved on the walls, and there was a wooden overhang on the front of the portico. [26] On the sidewalls of the portico were narrow windows with palm trees carved on each side. The side rooms of the temple also had overhangs. [r]

THE ROOMS FOR THE PRIESTS

42 Then the man led me northward into the outer court and brought me to the rooms [s] opposite the temple courtyard [t] and opposite the outer wall on the north side. [u] [2] The building whose door faced north was a hundred cubits long and fifty cubits wide. [e] [3] Both in the section twenty cubits [f] from the inner court and in the section opposite the pavement of the outer court, gallery [v] faced gallery at the three levels. [w] [4] In front of the rooms was an inner passageway ten cubits wide and a hundred cubits [g] long. [h] Their doors were on the north. [x] [5] Now the upper rooms were narrower, for the galleries took more space from them than from the rooms on the lower and middle floors of the building. [6] The rooms on the top floor had no pillars, as the courts had; so they were smaller in floor space than those on the lower and middle floors. [7] There was an outer wall parallel to the rooms and the outer court; it extended in front of the rooms for fifty cubits. [8] While the row of rooms on the side next to the outer court was fifty cubits long, the row on the side nearest the sanctuary was a hundred cubits long. [9] The lower rooms had an entrance [y] on the east side as one enters them from the outer court.

[10] On the south side [i] along the length of the wall of the outer court, adjoining the temple courtyard [z] and opposite the outer wall, were rooms [a] [11] with a passageway in front of them. These were like the rooms on the north; they had the same length and width, with similar exits and dimensions. Similar to the doorways on the north [12] were the doorways of the rooms on the south. There was a doorway at the beginning of the passageway that was parallel to the corresponding wall extending eastward, by which one enters the rooms.

[13] Then he said to me, "The north [b] and south rooms [c] facing the temple courtyard [d] are the priests' rooms, where the priests who approach the Lord will eat the most holy offer-

a 13 That is, about 170 feet or about 52 meters; also in verses 14 and 15   *b 22* That is, about 5 1/4 feet or about 1.5 meters   *c 22* Septuagint; Hebrew *long*   *d 22* Septuagint; Hebrew *length*   *e 2* That is, about 170 feet long and 85 feet wide or about 52 meters long and 26 meters wide   *f 3* That is, about 34 feet or about 10.4 meters   *g 4* Septuagint and Syriac; Hebrew *and one cubit*   *h 4* That is, about 17 feet wide and 170 feet long or about 5.2 meters wide and 52 meters long   *i 10* Septuagint; Hebrew *Eastward*

41:16 *everything … was covered with wood.* As in Solomon's temple (1Ki 6:15).

41:18 *cherubim.* Who served as guards (cf. Ge 3:24 and note). These, as opposed to those mentioned in ch. 10 (see note on 1:5), have only two faces—a man's and a lion's (see 1Ki 6:29,32,35).

41:22 *wooden altar.* As the great altar stood outside the temple proper (43:13–17), so a smaller altar (3'5" square by 5' high) stood outside the Most Holy Place. It served as a table, no doubt to hold the bread of the Presence (see Ex 25:30; Lev 24:5–9; 1Ki 7:48 and notes). Ezekiel makes no mention of an altar of incense

or of lampstands, such as were found in Solomon's temple and in the tabernacle before it. Also not included are the "Sea" (1Ki 7:23) and the ark of the covenant (see notes on Ezr 6:15; Jer 3:16).

41:23 *double doors.* Folding doors, so that the entry could be made still narrower.

42:1 *rooms opposite the temple courtyard.* Their function is described in vv. 13–14. They have no parallel in Solomon's temple as described in 1Ki 6.

42:13 *priests who approach the Lord.* The sons of Zadok (see 40:6 and note on 44:15). *eat the most holy offerings.* The priests ings. There they will put the most holy offerings—the grain offerings, *e* the sin offerings *a f* and the guilt offerings *g*—for the place is holy. *h* ¹⁴Once the priests enter the holy precincts, they are not to go into the outer court until they leave behind the garments *i* in which they minister, for these are holy. They are to put on other clothes before they go near the places that are for the people. *j*"

¹⁵When he had finished measuring what was inside the temple area, he led me out by the east gate *k* and measured the area all around: ¹⁶He measured the east side with the measuring rod; it was five hundred cubits. *b, c* ¹⁷He measured the north side; it was five hundred cubits *d* by the measuring rod. ¹⁸He measured the south side; it was five hundred cubits by the measuring rod. ¹⁹Then he turned to the west side and measured; it was five hundred cubits by the measuring rod. ²⁰So he measured *l* the area *m* on all four sides. It had a wall around it, *n* five hundred cubits long and five hundred cubits wide, *o* to separate the holy from the common. *p*

GOD'S GLORY RETURNS TO THE TEMPLE

43 Then the man brought me to the gate facing east, *q* ²and I saw the glory of the God of Israel coming from the east. His voice was like the roar of rushing waters, *r* and the land was radiant with his glory. *s* ³The vision I saw was like the vision I had seen when he *e* came to destroy the city and like the visions I had seen by the Kebar River, and I fell facedown. ⁴The glory *t* of the LORD entered the temple through the gate facing east. *u* ⁵Then the Spirit *v* lifted me up *w* and brought me into the inner court, and the glory *x* of the LORD filled the temple. *y*

⁶While the man was standing beside me, I heard someone speaking to me from inside the temple. ⁷He said: "Son of man, this is the place of my throne *z* and the place for the soles of my feet. This is where I will live among the Israelites forever. The house of Israel will never again defile *a* my holy name—neither they nor their kings—by their prostitution and the funeral offerings *f* for their kings at their death. *g b* ⁸When they placed their threshold next to my threshold and their doorposts beside my doorposts, with only a wall between me and them, they defiled my holy name by their detestable practices. So I destroyed them in my anger. ⁹Now let them put away from me their prostitution and the funeral offerings for their kings, and I will live among them forever. *c*

¹⁰"Son of man, describe the temple to the people of Israel, that they may be ashamed *d* of their sins. Let them consider its perfection, ¹¹and if they are ashamed of all they have done, make known to them the design of the temple—its arrangement, its exits and entrances—its whole design and all its regulations *h* and laws. Write these down before them so that they may be faithful to its design and follow all its regulations. *e*

---

a 13 Or *purification offerings*   *b* 16 See Septuagint of verse 17; Hebrew *rods*; also in verses 18 and 19.
c 16 Five hundred cubits equal about 850 feet or about 260 meters; also in verses 17, 18 and 19.
d 17 Septuagint; Hebrew *rods*   *e* 3 Some Hebrew manuscripts and Vulgate; most Hebrew manuscripts *l*
f 7 Or the *memorial monuments*; also in verse 9   *g* 7 Or *their high places*   *h* 11 Some Hebrew manuscripts and Septuagint; most Hebrew manuscripts *regulations and its whole design*

42:13 *e* Jer 41:5
f S Lev 10:17
g Lev 14:13
h S Ex 29:31;
S Lev 6:29; 7:6;
10:12-13; Nu 18:9-10
42:14 *i* Lev 16:23;
Eze 44:19 / Ex 29:9;
S Lev 8:7-9
42:15 *k* Eze 43:1
42:20 *l* Eze 40:5
m Eze 43:12 *n* Zec 2:5
o Eze 45:2; Rev 21:16
p S Eze 22:26
43:1 *q* S 1Ch 9:18;
S Eze 8:16; 42:15;
44:1
43:2 *r* S Ps 18:4;
S Rev 1:15 *s* Isa 6:3;
Rev 18:1; 21:11
43:4 *t* Eze 1:28
u Eze 10:19; 44:2
43:5 *v* S Eze 11:24
w S Eze 3:12
x S Ex 16:7 *y* S Isa 6:4
43:7 *z* S Jer 3:17
a S Eze 37:23
b S Lev 26:30;
Eze 20:29,39
43:9 *c* Eze 37:26-28
43:10 *d* S Eze 16:61
43:11 *e* Eze 44:5

---

normally received partial maintenance by being allowed to eat certain sacrifices (see Lev 2:3; 5:13; 6:16,26,29; 7:6,10). *the place is holy.* See note on Lev 11:44; see also Introduction to Leviticus: Theological Themes.

42:20 *five hundred cubits long and five hundred cubits wide.* Perfect symmetry in the ideal temple's total area.

43:1-5 God's glory returns to the new temple.

43:2 *I saw the glory.* The high point of chs. 40-48. The temple had been prepared for this moment, and all that follows flows from this appearance. *coming from the east.* The direction from which God's glory had seen God leave (see 11:23 and note). In the book of Ezekiel God's glory is always active (see vv. 4-5; 3:23; 9:3; 10:4,18; 44:4). *like the roar of rushing waters.* Ezekiel experienced an audition as well as a vision. For the comparison, see 1:24; Rev 1:15; 14:2; 19:6. *the land was radiant with his glory.* God's visible glory is always described as being very bright (see 10:4; Lk 2:9; Rev 21:11,23).

43:3 *like the vision I had seen.* But somewhat different, for no creatures or wheels are mentioned here. *when he came to destroy the city.* See ch. 9. *Kebar River.* See 1:1 and note. *I fell facedown.* See 1:28; 3:23; 9:8; 11:13; 44:4.

43:4 *through the gate facing east.* See note on v. 2.

43:5 *Then the Spirit lifted me up.* With God being nearer, the function of the guiding angel was taken over by the

Spirit of God. Ezekiel was transported into the inner court but not into the temple (cf. 3:12 and note). *filled the temple.* As at the consecration of Solomon's temple (1Ki 8:10-11; see notes on Ex 40:34; 1Ki 8:10; cf. Isa 6:4).

43:6 *someone.* God, but out of reverence not named here, preserving an air of awe and mystery.

43:7 *place of my throne.* See 1Sa 4:4; Ps 47:8 and notes. *place for the soles of my feet.* See 1Ch 28:2; Ps 99:5 and note; 132:7; Isa 60:13 and note; La 2:1. *I will live among the Israelites forever.* Renewing the promise of 37:26-28 (see v. 9; 1Ki 6:13; Zec 2:11). *defile my holy name.* See note 18:21 and note. *prostitution.* See note on Ex 34:15. *funeral offerings.* As the TNIV text note indicates, the reference is either to funeral offerings or to memorial monuments for past kings. Fourteen kings of Judah were buried in Jerusalem, possibly near (too near for Ezekiel) the temple area (see 2Ki 21:18,26; 23:30).

43:8 *their threshold next to my threshold.* Solomon's temple was surrounded by many of his own private structures (see 1Ki 7:1-12). The distinction between God's holy temple and the rest of the world is a central idea in the book of Ezekiel (see v. 12; 44:23). *So I destroyed them.* As elsewhere in Ezekiel, the unstable practices of the people and their kings brought about their destruction (see 5:11; 18:10-12; and especially 22:1-15).

43:12 ᶠEze 42:20
ᵍS Eze 17:22
43:13 ʰS Ex 20:24;
2Ch 4:1
43:15 ⁱIsa 29:2
ʲS Ex 27:2
43:16 ᵏRev 21:16
43:17 ˡver 20;
Eze 45:19 ᵐEx 20:26
ⁿS Ex 27:1
43:18 ᵒEx 40:29
ᵖLev 1:5,11;
Heb 9:21-22
43:19 �q S Lev 4:3
ʳS 2Sa 8:17; S Ezr 7:2
ˢNu 16:40;
S Eze 40:46
43:20 ᵗS Lev 4:7
ᵘS ver 17 ᵛLev 16:19
43:21 ʷEx 29:14;
Heb 13:11
43:23 ˣEx 29:1;
S Lev 22:20
43:24 ʸS Lev 2:13;
Mk 9:49-50
43:25 ᶻS Lev 8:33
ᵃS Ex 29:37
43:27 ᵇLev 9:1
ᶜS Isa 60:7
ᵈS Ex 32:6;
S Lev 17:5
44:1 ᵉS Eze 43:1
44:2 ᶠEze 43:4-5

¹²"This is the law of the temple: All the surrounding area ᶠ on top of the mountain will be most holy. ᵍ Such is the law of the temple.

THE GREAT ALTAR RESTORED

¹³"These are the measurements of the altar ʰ in long cubits, ᵃ that cubit being a cubit and a handbreadth: Its gutter is a cubit deep and a cubit wide, with a rim of one span ᵇ around the edge. And this is the height of the altar: ¹⁴From the gutter on the ground up to the lower ledge that goes around the altar it is two cubits high, and the ledge is a cubit wide. ᶜ From this lower ledge to the upper ledge that goes around the altar it is four cubits high, and that ledge is also a cubit wide. ᵈ ¹⁵Above that, the altar hearth ⁱ is four cubits high, and four horns ʲ project upward from the hearth. ¹⁶The altar hearth is square, twelve cubits ᵉ long and twelve cubits wide. ᵏ ¹⁷The upper ledge ˡ also is square, fourteen cubits ᶠ long and fourteen cubits wide. All around the altar is a gutter of one cubit with a rim of half a cubit. ᵍ The steps ᵐ of the altar face east. ⁿ"

¹⁸Then he said to me, "Son of man, this is what the Sovereign Lᴏʀᴅ says: These will be the regulations for sacrificing burnt offerings ᵒ and splashing blood ᵖ against the altar when it is built: ¹⁹You are to give a young bull �q as a sin offering ʰ to the Levitical priests of the family of Zadok, ʳ who come near ˢ to minister before me, declares the Sovereign Lᴏʀᴅ. ²⁰You are to take some of its blood and put it on the four horns of the altar ᵗ and on the four corners of the upper ledge ᵘ and all around the rim, and so purify the altar ᵛ and make atonement for it. ²¹You are to take the bull for the sin offering and burn it in the designated part of the temple area outside the sanctuary. ʷ

²²"On the second day you are to offer a male goat without defect for a sin offering, and the altar is to be purified as it was purified with the bull. ²³When you have finished purifying it, you are to offer a young bull and a ram from the flock, both without defect. ˣ ²⁴You are to offer them before the Lᴏʀᴅ, and the priests are to sprinkle salt ʸ on them and sacrifice them as a burnt offering to the Lᴏʀᴅ.

²⁵"For seven days ᶻ you are to provide a male goat daily for a sin offering; you are also to provide a young bull and a ram from the flock, both without defect. ᵃ ²⁶For seven days they are to make atonement for the altar and cleanse it; thus they will dedicate it. ²⁷At the end of these days, from the eighth day ᵇ on, the priests are to present your burnt offerings ᶜ and fellowship offerings ᵈ on the altar. Then I will accept you, declares the Sovereign Lᴏʀᴅ."

THE PRIESTHOOD RESTORED

44 Then the man brought me back to the outer gate of the sanctuary, the one facing east, ᵉ and it was shut. ²The Lᴏʀᴅ said to me, "This gate is to remain shut. It must not be opened; no one may enter through it. ᶠ It is to remain shut

---

ᵃ 13 That is, about 21 inches or about 52 centimeters; also in verses 14 and 17. The long cubit is the basic unit for linear measurement throughout Ezekiel 40–48.   ᵇ 13 That is, about 10 inches or about 26 centimeters   ᶜ 14 That is, about 3 1/2 feet high and 1 3/4 feet wide or about 104 centimeters high and 52 centimeters wide   ᵈ 14 That is, about 7 feet high and 1 3/4 feet wide or about 2.1 meters high and 52 centimeters wide   ᵉ 16 That is, about 21 feet or about 6.2 meters   ᶠ 17 That is, about 24 feet or about 7.3 meters   ᵍ 17 That is, about 10 inches or about 26 centimeters   ʰ 19 Or purification offering; also in verses 21, 22 and 25

43:12 This is the law. Refers to the contents of chs. 40–42.
43:13–27 Restoration of the great altar.

B **43:13** altar. Alluded to in 40:47 and here described in detail. Although the material is not mentioned, dressed stones were probably to be used. Ex 20:24–26 allowed an altar to be made of earth, but use of dressed stones for those altars was strictly forbidden (see notes on Ex 20:24–25). Solomon's altar was bronze (1Ki 8:64). Ezekiel's altar, much larger than Solomon's, was over 20 feet tall (including the horns, v. 15), made up of three slabs of decreasing size, like an Egyptian pyramid or Babylonian ziggurat: the "lower ledge" (v. 14) two cubits high; the "upper ledge" (v. 14) four cubits high; and the "altar hearth" (v. 15) four cubits high.
43:15 altar hearth. The Hebrew for this term appears only here in the OT and may also mean "mountain of God" or "lion of God"; it is a variant of a form that appears in Isa 29:1–2,7 (see note there). four horns. Stone projections from each of the four corners of the altar hearth. On earlier altars they afforded a refuge of last resort for an accused person (see Ex 21:12–14; 1Ki 1:50–51; 2:28–29).

43:17 steps of the altar. Forbidden in Ex 20:26 but here required because of the size (see note on v. 13).
43:18 burnt offerings. See note on 40:39. splashing blood. See Ex 29:16; Lev 4:6; 5:9.
43:19 sin offering. To cleanse the altar from the pollution of human sin (see note on 40:39). of the family of Zadok. See note on 44:15.
43:21 outside the sanctuary. As prescribed in Ex 29:14; Lev 4:12,21; 8:17; 9:11; 16:27. This action foreshadows one aspect of Christ's sacrifice (see Heb 13:11–13 and notes).
43:22 purified. By the sprinkling of the blood (see v. 20).
43:27 fellowship offerings. After the seven-day consecration by burnt offerings and sin offerings, the altar was ready for the celebration of the more festive fellowship offerings, where the people partook of some of the meat (see note on Lev 3:1).
44:1–31 Restoration of the priesthood.
44:2 It is to remain shut because. The reason given here is that God entered through the east gate (43:1–2), thus making it holy. Related reasons may be that God would never again leave

because the LORD, the God of Israel, has entered through it. [3]The prince himself is the only one who may sit inside the gateway to eat in the presence[g] of the LORD. He is to enter by way of the portico of the gateway and go out the same way.[h]"

[4]Then the man brought me by way of the north gate[i] to the front of the temple. I looked and saw the glory of the LORD filling the temple[j] of the LORD, and I fell facedown.[k]

[5]The LORD said to me, "Son of man, look carefully, listen closely and give attention to everything I tell you concerning all the regulations and instructions regarding the temple of the LORD. Give attention to the entrance[l] to the temple and all the exits of the sanctuary.[m] [6]Say to the rebellious house[n] of Israel, 'This is what the Sovereign LORD says: Enough of your detestable practices, house of Israel! [7]In addition to all your other detestable practices, you brought foreigners uncircumcised in heart[o] and flesh into my sanctuary, desecrating my temple while you offered me food, fat and blood, and you broke my covenant.[p] [8]Instead of carrying out your duty in regard to my holy things, you put others in charge of my sanctuary.[q] [9]This is what the Sovereign LORD says: No foreigner uncircumcised in heart and flesh is to enter my sanctuary, not even the foreigners who live among the Israelites.[r]

[10]"'The Levites who went far from me when Israel went astray[s] and who wandered from me after their idols must bear the consequences of their sin.[t] [11]They may serve in my sanctuary, having charge of the gates of the temple and serving in it; they may slaughter the burnt offerings[u] and sacrifices for the people and stand before the people and serve them.[v] [12]But because they served them in the presence of their idols and made the house of Israel fall[w] into sin, therefore I have sworn with uplifted hand[x] that they must bear the consequences of their sin, declares the Sovereign LORD.[y] [13]They are not to come near to serve me as priests or come near any of my holy things or my most holy offerings; they must bear the shame[z] of their detestable practices.[a] [14]And I will appoint them to guard the temple for all the work that is to be done in it.[b]

[15]"'But the Levitical priests, who are descendants of Zadok[c] and who guarded my sanctuary when the Israelites went astray from me, are to come near to minister before me; they are to stand before me to offer sacrifices of fat[d] and blood, declares the Sovereign LORD.[e] [16]They alone are to enter my sanctuary; they alone are to come near my table[f] to minister before me and serve me as guards.[g]

[17]"'When they enter the gates of the inner court, they are to wear linen clothes;[h] they must not wear any woolen garment while ministering at the gates of the inner court or inside the temple. [18]They are to wear linen turbans[i] on their heads and linen undergarments[j] around their waists. They must not wear anything that makes them perspire.[k] [19]When they go out into the outer court where the people are, they are to take off the clothes they have been ministering in and are to leave them in the sacred rooms, and put on other clothes, so that the people are not consecrated[l] through contact with their garments.[m]

[20]"'They must not shave[n] their heads or let their hair grow long, but they are to keep

---

44:3 [g]S Eze 24:9-11
[h]Eze 46:2,8
44:4 [i]S Eze 40:35
44:5 [j]S Isa 6:4; S Eze 10:4; Rev 15:8 [k]Da 8:17
44:6 [n]S Eze 3:9
44:7 [o]S Lev 26:41
[p]Ge 17:14; Ex 12:48; Lev 22:25
44:8 [q]Lev 22:2; Nu 18:7
44:9 [r]Joel 3:17; Zec 14:21
44:10 [s]Ps 95:10
[t]Nu 18:23
44:11 [u]2Ch 29:34
[v]Nu 3:5-37; S 16:9; S 1Ch 26:12-19
44:12 [w]S Jer 18:15
[x]Ps 106:26
[y]2Ki 16:10-16; Jer 14:10
44:13 [z]S Eze 16:61
[a]Nu 18:3; Hos 5:1
44:14 [b]1Sa 2:36; 2Ki 23:9; S 1Ch 23:28-32
44:15 [c]S 2Sa 8:17; S Ezr 7:2 [d]S Eze 29:13
[e]S Jer 33:18; S Eze 40:46; Zec 3:7
44:16 [f]S Eze 41:22
[g]Lev 3:16-17; 17:5-6; Nu 18:5; S 1Sa 2:35; Zec 3:7
44:17 [h]Rev 19:8
44:18 [i]S Eze 28:39; S Isa 3:20 [j]S Ex 28:42 [k]S Lev 16:4
44:19 [l]S Lev 6:27 [m]Ex 39:27-29; Lev 6:10-11; S Eze 42:14
44:20 [n]Eze 5:1

---

as before (10:19; 11:23) and that sun worship would be made impossible (see 8:16). Today the east gate (called the Golden Gate) of the sacred Moslem area (*Haram esh-Sharif*) in Jerusalem is likewise sealed shut as a result of a later but possibly related tradition.

44:3 *prince.* The first mention of the prince in chs. 40–48 (see 34:24 and note). *to eat.* Probably his part of the fellowship offering (see Lev 7:15; Dt 12:7; see also Eze 43:27 and note). While this honor is accorded the prince, it is significant that he is given no other part in the ceremonial functions, reserved now solely for the priests (see 2Ch 26:16–20). *by way of the portico.* From the inside of the outer court.

44:7 *uncircumcised in heart.* Spiritually unfit.

44:9 *No foreigner uncircumcised ... is to enter my sanctuary.* Nehemiah enforced this restriction when he dismissed Tobiah (Ne 13:8), an Ammonite (Ne 2:10; see Dt 23:3). Foreigners could, however, be a part of Israel (see 47:22).

44:10 *Levites.* Some members of the tribe of Levi served as priests (see Dt 33:8–11; Jdg 17:13). *when Israel went astray.* The reference is mainly to the period of the monarchy, especially to the last years, during which Ezekiel so often criticized the people's idolatry (see 6:3–6; 14:3–11; 16:18–21; 23:36–49; 36:17–18; 37:23).

44:11 *stand before the people.* Cf. standing before the Lord (see v. 15); the Levites still had an honorable position.

44:12 *with uplifted hand.* See 20:5 and note.

■ B ■ C 44:15 *Zadok.* Traced his Levitical lineage to Aaron through Aaron's son Eleazar (1Ch 6:50–53). He served as priest under David, along with Abiathar (see 2Sa 8:17 and note; 15:24–29; 20:25). He supported Solomon (as opposed to Abiathar, who pledged himself to Adonijah) and thus secured for himself and his descendants the privilege of serving in the Jerusalem temple (see 1Ki 1). Later the Zadokites were removed from office, but the Qumran (Dead Sea Scrolls) community remained loyal to them. *who guarded my sanctuary.* Contrast 22:26 and the thrust of all of ch. 8. In chs. 40–48 the Zadokites received special consideration because of their faithfulness (cf. Zec 3:7 and note). *fat and blood.* See 39:19 and note.

44:16 *They alone are to enter.* This elevation of the Zadokite priests and demotion of the Levites were part of the concern for ritual purity, a major theme of chs. 40–48. Only the fittest were to serve. *my table.* Either the table that held the bread (see 41:22 and note) or the large altar on which the Lord's food was presented (v. 7).

44:17 *linen.* Cooler than wool (see v. 18).

44:18 *turbans.* Ezekiel wore one (24:17).

44:19 *take off the clothes.* In the interest of ritual purity.

44:20 *must not shave their heads.* Because it was a mourning ritual (7:18) that rendered the mourner unclean (see Lev 21:1–5). *or let their hair grow long.* Because it implied the taking of a vow that might prevent the priest from serving (see Nu 6:5; Ac 21:23–26).

44:20 °S Lev 21:5;
Nu 6:5
44:21 °S Lev 10:9
44:22 °Lev 21:7
44:23 °S Eze 22:26
°S Ge 7:2; Lev 13:50;
15:31; Jer 15:19;
Hag 2:11-13
44:24 °Dt 17:8-9;
19:17; 21:5;
S 1Ch 23:4
°S Lev 23:2
°2Ch 19:8
44:25 °Lev 21:1- 4
44:26 °Nu 19:14
44:27 °S Nu 3:28
°S Lev 4:28; Nu 6:11
44:28 °S Nu 18:20;
Dt 18:1-2; S Jos 13:33
44:29 °Lev 6:16
°S Lev 27:21
°Nu 18:9,14;
S Jos 13:14
44:30 °Nu 18:12-13;
S 2Ch 31:5
°S Nu 15:18-21
°S Lev 25:21
°S 2Ch 31:10;
Ne 10:35-37
44:31 °S Lev 11:39
°S Ex 22:31;
S Lev 11:40
45:1 °S Nu 34:13
°Eze 48:8-9,29
45:2 °Eze 42:20
45:4 °S Eze 40:46
°Eze 48:10-11
45:5 °Eze 48:13
45:6 °Eze 48:15-18

the hair of their heads trimmed. ° ²¹No priest is to drink wine when he enters the inner court. ᵖ ²²They must not marry widows or divorced women; they may marry only virgins of Israelite descent or widows of priests. �q ²³They are to teach my people the difference between the holy and the common ʳ and show them how to distinguish between the unclean and the clean. ˢ

²⁴" 'In any dispute, the priests are to serve as judges ᵗ and decide it according to my ordinances. They are to keep my laws and my decrees for all my appointed festivals, ᵘ and they are to keep my Sabbaths holy. ᵛ

²⁵" 'A priest must not defile himself by going near a dead person; however, if the dead person was his father or mother, son or daughter, brother or unmarried sister, then he may defile himself. ʷ ²⁶After he is cleansed, he must wait seven days. ˣ ²⁷On the day he goes into the inner court of the sanctuary ʸ to minister in the sanctuary, he is to offer a sin offeringᵃᶻ for himself, declares the Sovereign LORD.

²⁸" 'I am to be the only inheritance ᵃ the priests have. You are to give them no possession in Israel; I will be their possession. ²⁹They will eat ᵇ the grain offerings, the sin offerings and the guilt offerings; and everything in Israel devotedᵇ to the LORD ᶜ will belong to them. ᵈ ³⁰The best of all the firstfruits ᵉ and of all your special gifts will belong to the priests. You are to give them the first portion of your ground meal ᶠ so that a blessingᵍ may rest on your household. ʰ ³¹The priests must not eat anything, whether bird or animal, found dead ⁱ or torn by wild animals.ʲ

ISRAEL FULLY RESTORED

45 " 'When you allot the land as an inheritance, ᵏ you are to present to the LORD a portion of the land as a sacred district, 25,000 cubitsᶜ long and 20,000ᵈ cubitsᵉ wide; the entire area will be holy. ¹ ²Of this, a section 500 cubitsᶠ square ᵐ is to be for the sanctuary, with 50 cubitsᵍ around it for open land. ³In the sacred district, measure off a section 25,000 cubits long and 10,000 cubitsʰ wide. In it will be the sanctuary, the Most Holy Place. ⁴It will be the sacred portion of the land for the priests, ⁿ who minister in the sanctuary and who draw near to minister before the LORD. It will be a place for their houses as well as a holy place for the sanctuary. ° ⁵An area 25,000 cubits long and 10,000 cubits wide will belong to the Levites, who serve in the temple, as their possession for towns to live in.ⁱᵖ

⁶" 'You are to give the city as its property an area 5,000 cubitsʲ wide and 25,000 cubits long, adjoining the sacred portion; it will belong to the whole house of Israel. �q

⁷" 'The prince will have the land bordering each side of the area formed by the sacred district and the property of the city. It will extend westward from the west side and east-

---

ᵃ 27 Or *purification offering*; also in verse 29   ᵇ 29 The Hebrew term refers to the irrevocable giving over of things or persons to the LORD.   ᶜ 1 That is, about 8 miles or about 13 kilometers; also in verses 3, 5 and 6   ᵈ 1 Septuagint (see also verses 3 and 5 and 48:9); Hebrew *10,000*   ᵉ 1 That is, about 6 1/2 miles or about 10 kilometers   ᶠ 2 That is, about 850 feet or about 260 meters   ᵍ 2 That is, about 85 feet or about 26 meters   ʰ 3 That is, about 3 miles or about 5.2 kilometers; also in verse 5   ⁱ 5 Septuagint; Hebrew *temple; they will have as their possession 20 rooms*   ʲ 6 That is, about 1 2/3 miles or about 2.6 kilometers

---

44:23 *difference between the holy and the common.* One of Ezekiel's central concerns. The important task of declaring God's will on matters of clean and unclean food, the fitness of sacrificial animals and ritual purity either had been done for pay (see Mic 3:11) or had been neglected altogether (see Jer 2:8; Eze 22:26 and note). See Hag 2:10–13 for a positive example. *distinguish between the unclean and the clean.* See Lev 11; Dt 14:3–21 and notes.

44:24 *priests are to serve as judges.* One of their functions from earliest days (see TNIV text note on 1Sa 4:18; see also 2Ch 19:8–11).

44:25 *dead person.* Contact with the dead made a person ceremonially unclean (Lev 21:1–3; Hag 2:13).

44:28 *no possession.* The statement that priests were not to own land agrees with Nu 18:20,23–24; Dt 10:9; Jos 13:14,33; 18:7.

44:31 *found dead.* This restriction applied to all Israel according to Lev 7:24.

45:1—46:24 An idealized depiction of the restoration of Israel's theocratic order.

45:1 *When you allot the land.* Envisioned a new acquisition and redistribution of the land. *present to the LORD.* The entire square area in the center of the land was to be set aside for the Lord. *20,000 cubits.* With the 5,000-cubit city area (v. 6) it was a per-

fect square. *entire area will be holy.* Set apart for the Lord and owned by no tribe.

45:2 *section 500 cubits square.* The temple area discussed in 42:16–20. *open land.* An unoccupied strip of land that served as a buffer between the more holy and the less holy, though the whole area was holy (see 42:20).

45:3 *measure off a section.* The middle strip of the holy square was specifically for the temple (see map, p. 1439).

45:4 *land for the priests.* Not to own (see 44:28) but to live on.

45:5 *area . . . to the Levites.* A section of equal size just to the north was for the Levites to dwell on, even though it was in the holy area. The Levites, as opposed to the Zadokite priests, could hold land as a possession.

45:6 *city.* The former Jerusalem contained the temple area. The new holy city would not, but would be adjacent to the temple. *5,000 cubits wide.* The southernmost section of the city completed the perfectly square area. *it will belong to the whole house of Israel.* Not to any one tribe or person, as in former days.

45:7 *The prince will have the land.* A considerable portion of territory. In view of the next verse (cf. 46:18), the generous allotment should have kept the prince from greed like that of Ahab (see 1Ki 21). The prince was also responsible for sizable offerings (v. 17).

ward from the east side, running lengthwise from the western to the eastern border parallel to one of the tribal portions. [r] 8 This land will be his possession in Israel. And my princes will no longer oppress my people but will allow the house of Israel to possess the land according to their tribes. [s]

9 " 'This is what the Sovereign LORD says: You have gone far enough, princes of Israel! Give up your violence and oppression [t] and do what is just and right. [u] Stop dispossessing my people, declares the Sovereign LORD. 10 You are to use accurate scales, [v] an accurate ephah [a][w] and an accurate bath. [b] 11 The ephah [x] and the bath are to be the same size, the bath containing a tenth of a homer and the ephah a tenth of a homer; the homer is to be the standard measure for both. 12 The shekel [c] is to consist of twenty gerahs. [y] Twenty shekels plus twenty-five shekels plus fifteen shekels equal one mina. [d]

13 " 'This is the special gift you are to offer: a sixth of an ephah [e] from each homer of wheat and a sixth of an ephah [f] from each homer of barley. 14 The prescribed portion of olive oil, measured by the bath, [g] is a tenth of a bath from each cor (which consists of ten baths or one homer, for ten baths are equivalent to a homer). 15 Also one sheep is to be taken from every flock of two hundred from the well-watered pastures of Israel. These will be used for the grain offerings, burnt offerings [z] and fellowship offerings to make atonement [a] for the people, declares the Sovereign LORD. 16 All the people of the land will be required to give this special offering to the prince in Israel. 17 It will be the duty of the prince to provide the burnt offerings, grain offerings and drink offerings at the festivals, the New Moons [b] and the Sabbaths [c]—at all the appointed festivals of the house of Israel. He will provide the sin offerings, [h] grain offerings, burnt offerings and fellowship offerings to make atonement for the house of Israel. [d]

18 " 'This is what the Sovereign LORD says: In the first month [e] on the first day you are to take a young bull without defect [f] and purify the sanctuary. [g] 19 The priest is to take some of the blood of the sin offering and put it on the doorposts of the temple, on the four corners of the upper ledge [h] of the altar [i] and on the gateposts of the inner court. 20 You are to do the same on the seventh day of the month for anyone who sins unintentionally [j] or through ignorance; so you are to make atonement for the temple.

21 " 'In the first month on the fourteenth day you are to observe the Passover, [k] a festival lasting seven days, during which you shall eat bread made without yeast. 22 On that day the prince is to provide a bull as a sin offering for himself and for all the people of the land. [l] 23 Every day during the seven days of the festival he is to provide seven bulls and seven rams [m] without defect as a burnt offering to the LORD, and a male goat for a sin offering. [n] 24 He is to provide as a grain offering [o] an ephah for each bull and an ephah for each ram, along with a hin [i] of olive oil for each ephah. [p]

25 " 'During the seven days of the festival, [q] which begins in the seventh month on the fifteenth day, he is to make the same provision for sin offerings, burnt offerings, grain offerings and oil. [r]

46 " 'This is what the Sovereign LORD says: The gate of the inner court [s] facing east [t] is to be shut on the six working days, but on the Sabbath day and on the day of the New Moon [u] it is to be opened. 2 The prince is to enter from the out-

---

[a] 10 An ephah was a dry measure equaling about 3/5 bushel or about 22 liters.   [b] 10 A bath was a liquid measure equaling about 6 gallons or about 22 liters.   [c] 12 A shekel weighed about 2/5 ounce or about 11.5 grams.   [d] 12 That is, 60 shekels; the common mina was 50 shekels. Sixty shekels were about 1 1/2 pounds or about 680 grams.   [e] 13 That is, probably about 6 pounds or about 2.8 kilograms [f] 13 That is, probably about 5 pounds or about 2.3 kilograms   [g] 14 That is, about 5 pints or about 2.2 liters   [h] 17 Or *purification offerings*; also in verses 19, 22, 23 and 25   [i] 24 That is, about 1 gallon or about 3.6 liters

---

45:9 *princes of Israel!* The language of this verse is reminiscent of the preaching Ezekiel did before 586 B.C. (see 22:6). *what is just and right.* See note on 33:14.

45:10 *You are to use accurate scales.* Israel was not to repeat the economic injustices of the past. The OT often warns against cheating in weights and measures (see Lev 19:35 and note; Dt 25:13–16; Mic 6:10–12).

45:11 *same size.* A little more than half a bushel. *homer.* About six bushels.

45:13 *special gift.* Given to the prince, as distinct from the gifts given to the priests (44:30). The prince is to use these gifts in part for the offerings he is to provide (see v. 16).

45:15 *make atonement.* See notes on Ex 25:17; Lev 16:20–22; 17:11; Ro 3:25.

45:16 *people of the land.* See v. 22; 7:27 and note.

45:17 *drink offerings.* Usually wine is meant (see Nu 15:5; Hos 9:4), though olive oil, not wine, is mentioned here (vv. 14,24).

45:18—46:24 This entire section involves so many variations from Pentateuchal law that the rabbis spent a great deal of effort trying to reconcile them. For example, the provision in 45:18 for an annual purification of the temple does not seem to take into consideration the Day of Atonement ritual of Lev 16.

45:19 *priest.* High priest.

45:20 *sins unintentionally or through ignorance.* See Nu 15:22–30 and notes.

45:22 *sin offering.* See note on 40:39.

45:25 *the festival, which begins in the seventh month.* In some respects the most important of the festivals—called the Festival of Ingathering (Ex 23:16; 34:22) and the Festival of Tabernacles (Dt 16:16; see note on Zec 14:16).

45:7 [r] Eze 48:21
45:8 [s] Nu 26:53; Eze 46:18
45:9 [t] Ps 12:5
10; 8:16
[u] S Jer 22:3; Zec 7:9-
45:10 [v] Dt 25:15; S Pr 11:1; Am 8:4-6; Mic 6:10-11
[w] S Lev 19:36
45:11 [x] Isa 5:10
45:12 [y] Ex 30:13; Lev 27:25; Nu 3:47
45:15 [z] S Lev 1:4
[a] Lev 6:30
45:17 [b] S Nu 10:10
[c] S Lev 23:38;
Isa 66:23 [d] S 1Ki 8:62; S 2Ch 31:3; Eze 46:4-12
45:18 [e] Ex 12:2
[f] S Lev 22:20; Heb 9:14
[g] S Lev 16:16,33
45:19 [h] S Eze 43:17
[i] Lev 16:18-19
45:20 [j] Lev 4:27
45:21 [k] S Ex 12:11
45:22 [l] Lev 4:14
45:23 [m] S Nu 22:40; S Job 42:8
[n] Nu 28:16-25
45:24 [o] Nu 28:12-13
[p] Eze 46:5-7
45:25 [q] Dt 16:13
[r] Lev 23:34-43; Nu 29:12-38
46:1 [s] S Eze 40:19
[t] S 1Ch 9:18 [u] ver 6; Isa 66:23

46:2 ᵛver 8
ᵂEze 40:39 ˣver 12;
S Eze 44:3
46:3 ʸS Isa 66:23
ᶻLk 1:10
46:5 ᵃver 11
46:6 ᵇver 1;
S Nu 10:10
ᶜS Lev 22:20
46:7 ᵈEze 45:24
46:8 ᵉver 2
ᶠEze 44:3
46:9 ᵍS Ex 23:14;
S 34:20
46:10 ʰ2Sa 6:14-15;
Ps 42:4
46:11 ᶦver 5
46:12 ʲS Eze 45:17
ᵏS Lev 7:16 ᶦver 2
46:13 ᵐS Ps 5:3
ⁿEx 29:38; S Nu 28:3
46:14 ᵒNu 15:6
ᵖDa 8:11
46:15 ᵍS Ex 29:42
ʳS Ex 29:38;
Nu 28:5-6
46:16 ᵍ2Ch 21:3
46:17 ᵗS Lev 25:10
46:18 ᵘ1Sa 8:14
ᵛS Lev 25:23;
Eze 45:8; Mic 2:1-2
46:19 ᵂS Eze 42:9
ˣEze 44:3
46:20 ʸS Lev 6:27
ᶻver 24; Zec 14:20

side through the portico ᵛ of the gateway and stand by the gatepost. The priests are to sacrifice his burnt offering ᵂ and his fellowship offerings. He is to bow down in worship at the threshold of the gateway and then go out, but the gate will not be shut until evening. ˣ ³On the Sabbaths ʸ and New Moons the people of the land are to worship in the presence of the LORD at the entrance of that gateway. ᶻ ⁴The burnt offering the prince brings to the LORD on the Sabbath day is to be six male lambs and a ram, all without defect. ⁵The grain offering given with the ram is to be an ephah, ᵃ and the grain offering with the lambs is to be as much as he pleases, along with a hin ᵇ of olive oil for each ephah. ᵃ ⁶On the day of the New Moon ᵇ he is to offer a young bull, six lambs and a ram, all without defect. ᶜ ⁷He is to provide as a grain offering one ephah with the bull, one ephah with the ram, and with the lambs as much as he wants to give, along with a hin of oil for each ephah. ᵈ ⁸When the prince enters, he is to go in through the portico ᵉ of the gateway, and he is to come out the same way. ᶠ

⁹" 'When the people of the land come before the LORD at the appointed festivals, ᵍ whoever enters by the north gate to worship is to go out the south gate; and whoever enters by the south gate is to go out the north gate. No one is to return through the gate by which he entered, but each is to go out the opposite gate. ¹⁰The prince is to be among them, going in when they go in and going out when they go out. ʰ ¹¹At the feasts and the appointed festivals, the grain offering is to be an ephah with a bull, an ephah with a ram, and with the lambs as much as he pleases, along with a hin of oil for each ephah. ᶦ

¹²" 'When the prince provides ʲ a freewill offering ᵏ to the LORD—whether a burnt offering or fellowship offerings—the gate facing east is to be opened for him. He shall offer his burnt offering or his fellowship offerings as he does on the Sabbath day. Then he shall go out, and after he has gone out, the gate will be shut. ᶦ

¹³" 'Every day you are to provide a year-old lamb without defect for a burnt offering to the LORD; morning by morning ᵐ you shall provide it. ⁿ ¹⁴You are also to provide with it morning by morning a grain offering, consisting of a sixth of an ephah ᶜ with a third of a hin ᵈ of oil ᵒ to moisten the flour. The presenting of this grain offering to the LORD is a lasting ordinance. ᵖ ¹⁵So the lamb and the grain offering and the oil shall be provided morning by morning for a regular ᵍ burnt offering. ʳ

¹⁶" 'This is what the Sovereign LORD says: If the prince makes a gift from his inheritance to one of his sons, it will also belong to his descendants; it is to be their property by inheritance. ˢ ¹⁷If, however, he makes a gift from his inheritance to one of his servants, the servant may keep it until the year of freedom; ᵗ then it will revert to the prince. His inheritance belongs to his sons only; it is theirs. ¹⁸The prince must not take ᵘ any of the inheritance ᵛ of the people, driving them off their property. He is to give his sons their inheritance out of his own property, so that not one of my people will be separated from their property.' "

¹⁹Then the man brought me through the entrance ᵂ at the side of the gate to the sacred rooms facing north, ˣ which belonged to the priests, and showed me a place at the western end. ²⁰He said to me, "This is the place where the priests are to cook the guilt offering and the sin offering ᵉ and bake the grain offering, to avoid bringing them into the outer court and consecrating ʸ the people." ᶻ

ᵃ 5 That is, probably about 36 pounds or about 16 kilograms; also in verses 7 and 11   ᵇ 5 That is, about 1 gallon or about 3.6 liters; also in verses 7 and 11   ᶜ 14 That is, probably about 6 pounds or about 2.8 kilograms   ᵈ 14 That is, about 2 2/3 pints or about 1.2 liters   ᵉ 20 Or purification offering

---

46:1 *gate of the inner court.* While the east gate of the outer court was permanently closed (44:2), the east gate of the inner court could be opened on festival days.

46:2 *through the portico of the gateway.* The portico of the gate of the inner court faced the outer court. *stand by the gatepost.* Which had been ritually cleansed (45:19). From there the prince could observe the sacrifices being performed on the great altar in the inner court, but he was not allowed into the inner court itself.

46:3 *people of the land.* See note on 7:27. *at the entrance of that gateway.* But in the outer court.

46:4 *six male lambs and a ram.* Another example of a difference from Pentateuchal laws (see note on 45:18—46:24). Nu 28:9 calls for two lambs and no ram on the Sabbath.

46:5 *ephah.* Contrast Nu 28:9.

46:6 *day of the New Moon.* The first day of the month. Contrast the requirement of Nu 28:11.

46:7 *as a grain offering one ephah.* Contrast Nu 28:12.

46:9 *whoever enters by the north gate.* These appear to be

crowd control measures. If so, the new era would see masses of people thronging the sanctuary on the festival day.

46:12 *freewill offering.* Above and beyond what was required of the prince.

46:13 *morning by morning.* Contrast Nu 28:3–8, where the daily sacrifice consists of one lamb in the morning and one in the evening (see 1Ch 16:40; 2Ch 13:11; 31:3). A different custom appears in 2Ki 16:15, where a burnt offering was offered in the mornings, a grain offering in the evenings.

46:14 *sixth of an ephah … third of a hin.* Contrast Nu 28:5.

46:16 *his descendants.* Ezekiel pictured a hereditary rulership.

46:17 *until the year of freedom.* The Year of Jubilee—held, theoretically, every 50th year (see Lev 25:8–15, especially v. 13).

46:18 *The prince must not take.* See note on 45:7.

46:19–24 Fits well after 42:13–14, where other rooms for priests are described. The provisions here are a fitting conclusion to the sacrifice laws. The priests' area (vv. 19–20) was to be kept separate from the cooking areas of the Levites (vv. 21–24).

²¹He then brought me to the outer court and led me around to its four corners, and I saw in each corner another court. ²²In the four corners of the outer court were enclosed[a] courts, forty cubits long and thirty cubits wide;[b] each of the courts in the four corners was the same size. ²³Around the inside of each of the four courts was a ledge of stone, with places for fire built all around under the ledge. ²⁴He said to me, "These are the kitchens where those who minister at the temple are to cook the sacrifices of the people."

THE RIVER FROM THE TEMPLE

47 The man brought me back to the entrance to the temple, and I saw water[a] coming out from under the threshold of the temple toward the east (for the temple faced east). The water was coming down from under the south side of the temple, south of the altar.[b] ²He then brought me out through the north gate[c] and led me around the outside to the outer gate facing east, and the water was trickling from the south side.

³As the man went eastward with a measuring line[d] in his hand, he measured off a thousand cubits[c] and then led me through water that was ankle-deep. ⁴He measured off another thousand cubits and led me through water that was knee-deep. He measured off another thousand and led me through water that was up to the waist. ⁵He measured off another thousand, but now it was a river[e] that I could not cross, because the water had risen and was deep enough to swim in—a river that no one could cross.[f] ⁶He asked me, "Son of man, do you see this?"

Then he led me back to the bank of the river. ⁷When I arrived there, I saw a great number of trees on each side of the river.[g] ⁸He said to me, "This water flows toward the eastern region and goes down into the Arabah,[d][h] where it enters the Dead Sea. When it empties into the sea, the salty water there becomes fresh.[i] ⁹Swarms of living creatures will live wherever the river flows. There will be large numbers of fish, because this water flows there and makes the salt water fresh; so where the river flows everything will live.[j] ¹⁰People will fish[k] along the shore; from En Gedi[l] to En Eglaim there will be places for spreading nets.[m] The fish will be of many kinds[n]—like the fish of the Mediterranean Sea.[o] ¹¹But the swamps and marshes will not become fresh; they will be left for salt.[p] ¹²Fruit trees of all kinds will grow on both banks of the river.[q] Their leaves will not wither, nor will their fruit[r] fail. Every month they will bear fruit, because the water from the sanctuary[s] flows to them. Their fruit will serve for food and their leaves for healing.[t]"

THE BOUNDARIES OF THE LAND

¹³This is what the Sovereign LORD says: "These are the boundaries[u] of the land that you will divide among the twelve tribes of Israel as their inheritance, with two portions for Joseph.[v] ¹⁴You are to divide it equally among them. Because I swore with uplifted hand to give it to your ancestors, this land will become your inheritance.[w]

[a] 22 The meaning of the Hebrew for this word is uncertain.   [b] 22 That is, about 68 feet long and 51 feet wide or about 21 meters long and 16 meters wide   [c] 3 That is, about 1,700 feet or about 520 meters   [d] 8 Or the Jordan Valley

47:1 #S Isa 55:1
bPs 46:4; Joel 3:18;
Rev 22:1
47:2 cS Eze 40:35
47:3 dS Eze 40:3
47:5 eS Ge 2:10
fIsa 11:9; Hab 2:14
47:7 gver 12;
Rev 22:2
47:8 hS Dt 1:1;
S 3:17 iIsa 41:18
47:9 jIsa 12:3; 55:1;
Jn 4:14; 7:37-38
47:10 kS Isa 19:8;
Mt 4:19 iS Jos 15:62
mEze 26:5
nS Ps 104:25;
Mt 13:47 oS Nu 34:6
47:11 pS Dt 29:23
47:12 qver 7;
Rev 22:2 rS Ps 1:3
sS Isa 55:1 tS Ge 2:9;
S Jer 17:8; Eze 36:8
47:13 uNu 34:2-12
vS Ge 48:16; S 49:26
47:14 wS Ge 12:7;
S Dt 1:8; S Eze 36:12

47:1–12 The river of life flowing from the temple.

47:1 *man.* The angelic guide (40:3), who here appears for the last time, concluded Ezekiel's visionary tour of the new temple. *entrance to the temple.* Ezekiel was standing in the inner court. *water.* The rest of this section (vv. 1–12) makes it clear that healing, life-nurturing water is meant (see Ps 36:8; 46:4 and notes; see also Joel 3:18; Zec 13:1; 14:8; Rev 22:1–2). In the larger background was the river flowing from the Garden of Eden (Ge 2:10).
47:2 *brought me out through the north gate.* Because the east gate was closed (44:2).
47:5 *measured off another thousand.* For a total of four measurings (see note on 1:5). *river that no one could cross.* Amazing, in that a stream fed by no tributaries does not increase as it flows.
47:7 *great number of trees.* Reminiscent of Eden (Ge 2:9).

47:7 *toward the eastern region.* Contrast Zec 14:8. *Arabah.* Here the waterless region between Jerusalem and the Dead Sea (see TNIV text note). *becomes fresh.* The Hebrew says, figuratively, "becomes healed." That lowest (1,300 feet below sea level) and saltiest (25 percent) body of water in the world should sustain such an abundance of life indicates the wonderful renewing power of this "river of the water of life" (Rev 22:1).

47:9 *Swarms of living creatures.* Overtones of Ge 1:20–21 point to a new creation.
47:10 *En Gedi.* Means "spring of the goat"; a strong spring midway along the western side of the Dead Sea. *En Eglaim.* Means "spring of the two calves." It is possibly Ain Feshkha, at the northwestern corner of the Dead Sea, though some suggest a location on the east bank.
47:11 *they will be left for salt.* Perhaps to provide the salt needed in the sacrifices (43:24).
47:12 *Every month they will bear.* A marvelous extension of the promises in 34:27; 36:30 (see Am 9:13; cf. Rev 22:2).
47:13–23 The boundaries of the land in the new order (see map, p. 1439).
47:13 *two portions for Joseph.* Since the tribe of Levi received none (44:28), Ephraim and Manasseh, Joseph's two sons adopted by Jacob (Ge 48:5, 17–20), each received an allotment (see 48:4–5).
47:14 *Because I swore.* A reference to the covenant made with Abram (see Ge 15:9–21 and notes; Eze 20:5; 36:28). *with uplifted hand.* See 20:5 and note.

47:15 ˣ Nu 34:2
ʸ ver 19; S Nu 34:6
ᶻ Eze 48:1
47:16 ᵃ 2Sa 8:8
ᵇ Nu 13:21;
S Jer 49:23; Eze 48:1
47:17 ᶜ Eze 48:1
47:18 ᵈ S Eze 27:18
47:19 ᵉ Dt 32:51
ᶠ S Ge 15:18; Isa 27:12
ᵍ S ver 15; Eze 48:28
47:20 ʰ S Nu 13:21;
Eze 48:1 ⁱ Nu 34:6
47:22 ʲ S Eze 36:12
ᵏ S Dt 24:19;
S Isa 14:1; Mal 3:5
ˡ S Lev 24:22;
Nu 15:29; 26:55-56;
Isa 56:6-7; Ro 10:12;
Eph 2:12-16; 3:6;
Col 3:11
47:23 ᵐ S Dt 10:19
48:1 ⁿ S Ge 30:6
ᵒ Eze 47:15-17
ᵖ S Eze 47:20
48:2 �q Jos 19:24-31
48:3 ʳ Jos 19:32-39
48:4 ˢ Jos 17:1-11
48:5 ᵗ Jos 16:5-9
ᵘ Jos 17:7-10
ᵛ Jos 17:17
48:6 ʷ Jos 13:15-21

¹⁵"This is to be the boundary of the land:ˣ

"On the north side it will run from the Mediterranean Seaʸ by the Hethlon roadᶻ past Lebo Hamath to Zedad, ¹⁶Berothahᵃ ᵃ and Sibraim (which lies on the border between Damascus and Hamath), ᵇ as far as Hazer Hattikon, which is on the border of Hauran. ¹⁷The boundary will extend from the sea to Hazer Enan,ᵇ along the northern border of Damascus, with the border of Hamath to the north. This will be the northern boundary. ᶜ

¹⁸ "On the east side the boundary will run between Hauran and Damascus, along the Jordan between Gilead and the land of Israel, to the Dead Sea and as far as Tamar.ᶜ This will be the eastern boundary. ᵈ

¹⁹ "On the south side it will run from Tamar as far as the waters of Meribah Kadesh,ᵉ then along the Wadi of Egyptᶠ to the Mediterranean Sea. ᵍ This will be the southern boundary.

²⁰ "On the west side, the Mediterranean Sea will be the boundary to a point opposite Lebo Hamath. ʰ This will be the western boundary. ⁱ

²¹"You are to distribute this land among yourselves according to the tribes of Israel. ²²You are to allot it as an inheritanceʲ for yourselves and for the foreigners ᵏ residing among you and who have children. You are to consider them as native-born Israelites; along with you they are to be allotted an inheritance among the tribes of Israel. ˡ ²³In whatever tribe foreigners reside, there you are to give them their inheritance," declares the Sovereign Lord. ᵐ

THE DIVISION OF THE LAND

48 "These are the tribes, listed by name: At the northern frontier, Dan ⁿ will have one portion; it will follow the Hethlon roadᵒ to Lebo Hamath; ᵖ Hazar Enan and the northern border of Damascus next to Hamath will be part of its border from the east side to the west side.

²"Asher q will have one portion; it will border the territory of Dan from east to west.

³"Naphtali ʳ will have one portion; it will border the territory of Asher from east to west.

⁴"Manasseh ˢ will have one portion; it will border the territory of Naphtali from east to west.

⁵"Ephraim ᵗ will have one portion; it will border the territory of Manasseh ᵘ from east to west. ᵛ

⁶"Reuben ʷ will have one portion; it will border the territory of Ephraim from east to west.

ᵃ *15,16* See Septuagint and Ezekiel 48:1; Hebrew *road to go into Zedad,* ¹⁶*Hamath, Berothah.*
ᵇ *17* Hebrew *Enon,* a variant of *Enan*   ᶜ *18* See Syriac; Hebrew *Israel. You will measure to the Dead Sea.*

47:15 *This is to be the boundary.* Approximates Israel's borders at the time of David and Solomon, except that Transjordan is not included (see v. 18)—which, in any event, was never within the boundaries of the promised land proper. The following specified boundaries closely resemble those in Nu 34:1–12. *Hethlon road.* Probably situated on the Mediterranean coast, somewhere in present-day Lebanon. *Lebo Hamath.* Lebo is now identified with modern Lebweh, about 15 miles northeast of Baalbek and 20 miles southwest of Kadesh on the Orontes River, near Riblah. At one time Lebo must have served as a fortress guarding the southern route to Hamath. Perhaps the phrase should be translated "Lebo of Hamath." It is often referred to in Scripture as the northern limit of Israel (see v. 20; 48:1; Nu 13:21; 34:8; Jos 13:5; 1Ki 8:65; 2Ki 14:25; Am 6:14). *Zedad.* Mentioned in Nu 34:8 but otherwise unknown.
47:16 *Berothah.* Probably to be identified with the Berothai of 2Sa 8:8, but otherwise unknown. *Sibraim.* Location unknown; probably the Sepharvaim of 2Ki 17:24; 18:34. *Damascus.* Capital of Aram (Syria); according to v. 17 it was included in Israel. *Hamath.* A city about 120 miles north of Damascus on the Orontes River. *Hazer Hattikon.* Means "the middle enclosure." Its location is unknown, but it is possibly the same as Hazar Enan in v. 17.
47:18 *Dead Sea.* See Joel 2:20; Zec 14:8. *Tamar.* Means "(place of) palms" (see v. 19; 48:28); mentioned in Ge 14:7 (Hazazon Tamar) and 1Ki 9:18 (see TNIV text note) and identified with En Gedi (see note on v. 10) in 2Ch 20:2.

47:19 *Meribah Kadesh.* A district about 50 miles south of Beersheba, identified with Kadesh Barnea in Nu 34:4. *Wadi of Egypt.* The Wadi el-Arish, a deeply cut riverbed with seasonal flow that runs from the Sinai north-northwest until it enters the Mediterranean, 50 miles southwest of Gaza. It marked the southernmost extremity of Solomon's kingdom (1Ki 8:65).
47:22 *You are to consider them as native-born Israelites.* A gracious inclusiveness that went beyond the provision of 14:7. It reflects the same universalism that is found in such prophecies as Isa 56:3–8 (see notes there).
48:1–29 The distribution of the land in the new order (see map, p. 1439).
48:1 *Dan.* Occupies its historical location as the northernmost tribe (see the phrase "from Dan to Beersheba," giving northern and southern boundaries—e.g., in Jdg 20:1; 1Sa 3:20). Dan was born to Rachel's maidservant Bilhah (Ge 35:25). *Hethlon ... Lebo Hamath.* See note on 47:15. *Hazar Enan.* See note on 47:16.
48:2 *Asher.* Born to Leah's maidservant Zilpah (Ge 35:26). The tribes descended from maidservants were placed farthest from the sanctuary (see Dan, v. 1; Naphtali, v. 3; Gad, v. 27).
48:3 *Naphtali.* Born to Rachel's maidservant Bilhah (see note on v. 2).
48:4 *Manasseh.* See note on 47:13.
48:5 *Ephraim.* See note on 47:13.
48:6 *Reuben.* Leah's firstborn (Ge 29:31).

BOUNDARIES OF THE LAND IN EZEKIEL'S VISION

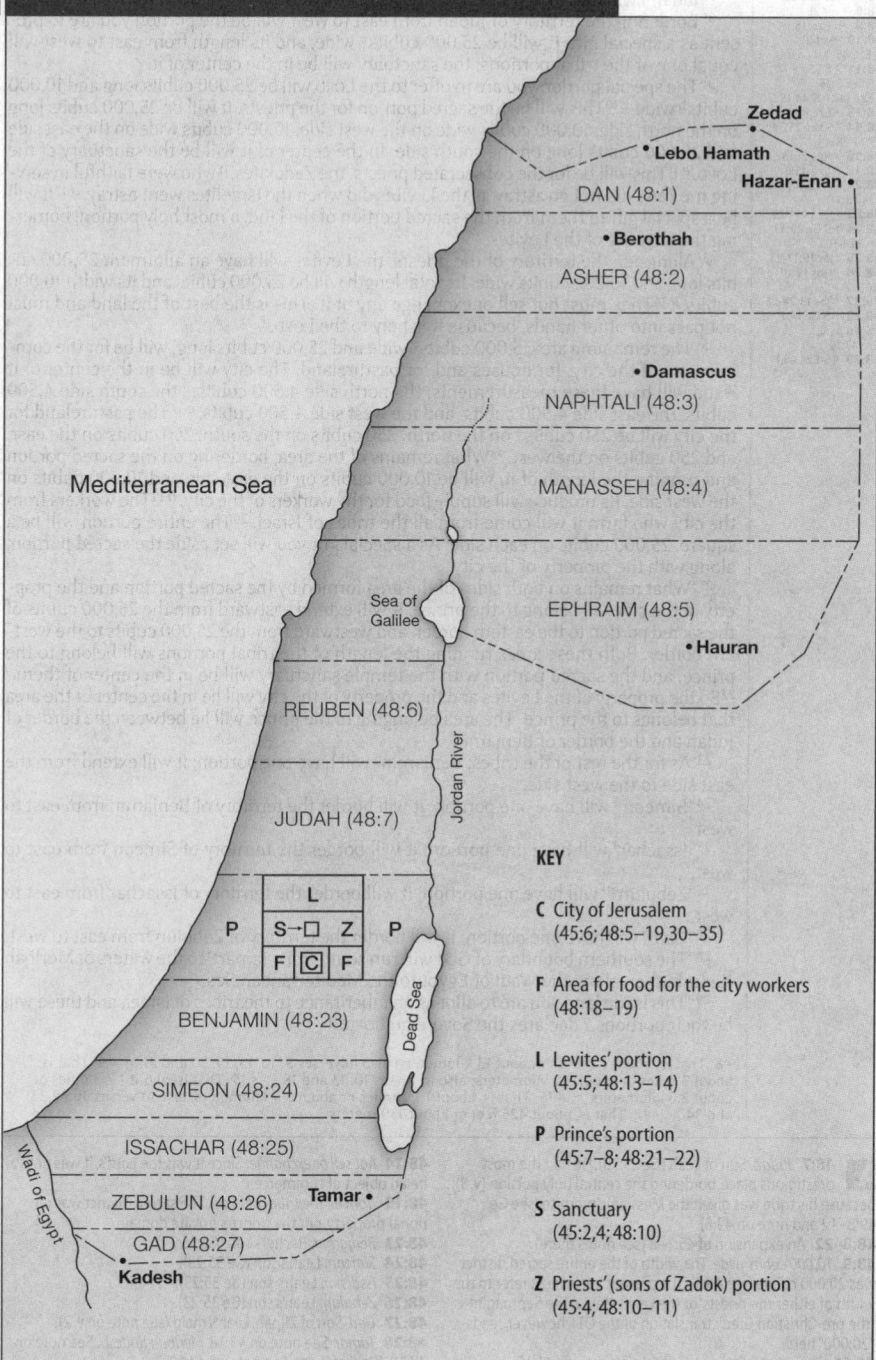

Mediterranean Sea

Zedad

Lebo Hamath

Hazar-Enan

DAN (48:1)

Berothah

ASHER (48:2)

Damascus

NAPHTALI (48:3)

MANASSEH (48:4)

Sea of Galilee

EPHRAIM (48:5)

Hauran

REUBEN (48:6)

Jordan River

JUDAH (48:7)

Dead Sea

L

P S→□ Z P

F □C F

BENJAMIN (48:23)

SIMEON (48:24)

ISSACHAR (48:25)

Wadi of Egypt

ZEBULUN (48:26) Tamar

GAD (48:27)

Kadesh

KEY

C City of Jerusalem
(45:6; 48:5–19,30–35)

F Area for food for the city workers
(48:18–19)

L Levites' portion
(45:5; 48:13–14)

P Prince's portion
(45:7–8; 48:21–22)

S Sanctuary
(45:2,4; 48:10)

Z Priests' (sons of Zadok) portion
(45:4; 48:10–11)

48:7 ˣ Jos 15:1-63
48:8 ʸ ver 21
48:9 ᶻ S Eze 45:1
48:10 ᵃ ver 21;
S Eze 45:3-4
48:11 ᵇ S 2Sa 8:17
ᶜ S Lev 8:35
ᵈ Eze 14:11; S 44:15
48:13 ᵉ Eze 45:5
48:14 ᶠ S Lev 25:34;
27:10,28
48:16 ᵍ Rev 21:16
48:18 ʰ Eze 45:6
48:21 ⁱ ver 8,10;
Eze 45:7
48:23 ʲ Jos 18:11-28
48:24 ᵏ S Ge 29:33;
Jos 19:1-9
48:25 ˡ Jos 19:17-23
48:26 ᵐ Jos 19:10-
16
48:27 ⁿ Jos 13:24-28
48:28 ᵒ S Ge 14:7
ᵖ S Nu 34:6;
Eze 47:19
48:29 �q S Eze 45:1

⁷"Judah ˣ will have one portion; it will border the territory of Reuben from east to west.

⁸"Bordering the territory of Judah from east to west will be the portion you are to present as a special gift. It will be 25,000 cubits ᵃ wide, and its length from east to west will equal one of the tribal portions; the sanctuary will be in the center of it. ʸ

⁹"The special portion you are to offer to the LORD will be 25,000 cubits long and 10,000 cubits ᵇ wide. ᶻ ¹⁰This will be the sacred portion for the priests. It will be 25,000 cubits long on the north side, 10,000 cubits wide on the west side, 10,000 cubits wide on the east side and 25,000 cubits long on the south side. In the center of it will be the sanctuary of the LORD. ᵃ ¹¹This will be for the consecrated priests, the Zadokites, ᵇ who were faithful in serving me ᶜ and did not go astray as the Levites did when the Israelites went astray. ᵈ ¹²It will be a special gift to them from the sacred portion of the land, a most holy portion, bordering the territory of the Levites.

¹³"Alongside the territory of the priests, the Levites will have an allotment 25,000 cubits long and 10,000 cubits wide. Its total length will be 25,000 cubits and its width 10,000 cubits. ᵉ ¹⁴They must not sell or exchange any of it. This is the best of the land and must not pass into other hands, because it is holy to the LORD. ᶠ

¹⁵"The remaining area, 5,000 cubits ᶜ wide and 25,000 cubits long, will be for the common use of the city, for houses and for pastureland. The city will be in the center of it ¹⁶and will have these measurements: the north side 4,500 cubits, ᵈ the south side 4,500 cubits, the east side 4,500 cubits, and the west side 4,500 cubits. ᵍ ¹⁷The pastureland for the city will be 250 cubits ᵉ on the north, 250 cubits on the south, 250 cubits on the east, and 250 cubits on the west. ¹⁸What remains of the area, bordering on the sacred portion and running the length of it, will be 10,000 cubits on the east side and 10,000 cubits on the west side. Its produce will supply food for the workers of the city. ʰ ¹⁹The workers from the city who farm it will come from all the tribes of Israel. ²⁰The entire portion will be a square, 25,000 cubits on each side. As a special gift you will set aside the sacred portion, along with the property of the city.

²¹"What remains on both sides of the area formed by the sacred portion and the property of the city will belong to the prince. It will extend eastward from the 25,000 cubits of the sacred portion to the eastern border, and westward from the 25,000 cubits to the western border. Both these areas running the length of the tribal portions will belong to the prince, and the sacred portion with the temple sanctuary will be in the center of them. ⁱ ²²So the property of the Levites and the property of the city will lie in the center of the area that belongs to the prince. The area belonging to the prince will lie between the border of Judah and the border of Benjamin.

²³"As for the rest of the tribes: Benjamin ʲ will have one portion; it will extend from the east side to the west side.

²⁴"Simeon ᵏ will have one portion; it will border the territory of Benjamin from east to west.

²⁵"Issachar ˡ will have one portion; it will border the territory of Simeon from east to west.

²⁶"Zebulun ᵐ will have one portion; it will border the territory of Issachar from east to west.

²⁷"Gad ⁿ will have one portion; it will border the territory of Zebulun from east to west.

²⁸"The southern boundary of Gad will run south from Tamar ᵒ to the waters of Meribah Kadesh, then along the Wadi of Egypt to the Mediterranean Sea. ᵖ

²⁹"This is the land you are to allot as an inheritance to the tribes of Israel, and these will be their portions," declares the Sovereign LORD. q

---

ᵃ 8 That is, about 8 miles or about 13 kilometers; also in verses 9, 10, 13, 15, 20 and 21   ᵇ 9 That is, about 3 miles or about 5.2 kilometers; also in verses 10, 13 and 18   ᶜ 15 That is, about 1 2/3 miles or about 2.6 kilometers   ᵈ 16 That is, about 1 1/2 miles or about 2.4 kilometers; also in verses 30,32,33 and 34   ᵉ 17 That is, about 425 feet or about 130 meters

---

48:7 *Judah.* Son of Leah (Ge 35:23). He had the most prestigious place, bordering the central holy portion (v. 8), because his tribe was given the Messianic promise (see Ge 49:8–12 and note on 49:8).

48:8–22 An expansion of 45:1–8 (see notes there).

48:9 *10,000 cubits wide.* The width of the entire sacred district was 20,000 cubits (see 45:1). The present verse must refer to the width of either the priests' or the Levites' area. The Septuagint (the pre-Christian Greek translation of the OT), however, reads "20,000" here.

48:11 *Zadokites, who were faithful.* See note on 44:15.

48:14 *not sell or exchange.* Since it was the Lord's, it was not to be an object of commerce.

48:19 *from all the tribes of Israel.* The sacred district was national property, not the prince's private domain.

48:23 *Benjamin.* Rachel's son (Ge 35:24).

48:24 *Simeon.* Leah's son (Ge 35:23).

48:25 *Issachar.* Leah's son (Ge 35:23).

48:26 *Zebulun.* Leah's son (Ge 35:23).

48:27 *Gad.* Son of Zilpah, Leah's maid (see note on v. 2).

48:28 *Tamar.* See note on 47:18. *Meribah Kadesh.* See note on 47:19. *Wadi of Egypt.* See note on 47:19.

THE GATES OF THE NEW CITY

48:34 ʳS 2Ch 4:4;
Rev 21:12-13
48:35 ˢS Isa 12:6;
S 24:23; S Jer 3:17;
14:9; Joel 3:21;
Rev 3:12; S 21:3

³⁰"These will be the exits of the city: Beginning on the north side, which is 4,500 cubits long, ³¹the gates of the city will be named after the tribes of Israel. The three gates on the north side will be the gate of Reuben, the gate of Judah and the gate of Levi.

³²"On the east side, which is 4,500 cubits long, will be three gates: the gate of Joseph, the gate of Benjamin and the gate of Dan.

³³"On the south side, which measures 4,500 cubits, will be three gates: the gate of Simeon, the gate of Issachar and the gate of Zebulun.

³⁴"On the west side, which is 4,500 cubits long, will be three gates: the gate of Gad, the gate of Asher and the gate of Naphtali. ʳ

³⁵"The distance all around will be 18,000 cubits. ᵃ

"And the name of the city from that time on will be:

THE LORD IS THERE. ˢ"

ᵃ 35 That is, about 6 miles or about 9.4 kilometers

48:30–35 The 12 gates of the new city of Jerusalem.
48:31 *Reuben ... Judah ... Levi.* Reuben (representing the firstborn), Judah (the Messianic tribe) and Levi (the tribe of the priesthood) had gates together on the north side. Since Levi was included in this list, Joseph (v. 32) represented Ephraim and Manasseh (see note on 47:13) in order to keep the number at 12. For the gates, cf. Rev 21:12–14.

48:35 *THE LORD IS THERE.* The great decisive word concerning the holy city. The Hebrew for this clause is *Yahweh Shammah*, which may be a wordplay on *Yerushalayim*, the Hebrew pronunciation of Jerusalem. For other names of Jerusalem, see 23:4; Isa 1:26; 60:14; 62:2–4,12; Jer 3:17; 33:16; Zec 8:3. The book of Joel has a similar ending (see note on Joel 3:21).

The book implies in several passages, such as 9:2; 10:2, that Daniel was its author. That Jesus concurred is clear from his reference to "'the abomination that causes desolation,' spoken of through the prophet Daniel" (Mt 24:15; see note there), quoting 9:27 (see note there); 11:31 (see note there); 12:11. The book was probably completed c. 530 B.C., shortly after Cyrus the Great, king of Persia, captured the city of Babylon in 539.

The widely held view that the book of Daniel is largely fictional rests mainly on the modern philosophical assumption that long-range predictive prophecy is impossible. Therefore all fulfilled predictions in Daniel, it is claimed, had to have been composed no earlier than the Maccabean period (second century B.C.), after the fulfillments had taken place. But objective evidence excludes this hypothesis on several counts:

1. To avoid fulfillment of long-range predictive prophecy in the book, the adherents of the late-date view usually maintain that the four empires of chs. 2 and 7 are Babylon, Media, Persia and Greece. But in the mind of the author, "the Medes and Persians" (5:28; see note there) together constituted the second in the series of four kingdoms (2:32–43; see note there). Thus it becomes clear that the four empires are the Babylonian, Medo-Persian, Greek and Roman. See chart, p. 1455.

B 2. The language itself argues for a date earlier than the second century. Linguistic evidence from the Dead Sea Scrolls (which furnish authentic samples of Hebrew and Aramaic writing from the third and second centuries B.C.; see essay, pp. 1595–1596) demonstrates that the Hebrew and Aramaic chapters of Daniel must have been composed centuries earlier. Furthermore, as recently demonstrated, the Persian and Greek words in Daniel do not require a late date. Some of the technical terms appearing in ch. 3 were already so obsolete by the second century B.C. that translators of the Septuagint (the pre-Christian Greek translation of the OT) translated them incorrectly.

3. Several of the fulfillments of prophecies in Daniel could not have taken place by the second century anyway, so the prophetic element cannot be dismissed. The symbolism connected with the fourth kingdom makes it unmistakably predictive of the Roman empire (see 2:33; 7:7,19), which did not take control of Syro-Palestine until 63 B.C. Also, a plausible interpretation of the prophecy concerning the coming of "the Anointed One, the ruler," approximately 483 years after the word went out "to restore and rebuild Jerusalem" (9:25; see note on 9:25–27), works out to the time of Jesus' ministry.

Objective evidence, therefore, appears to exclude the late-date hypothesis and indicates that there is insufficient reason to deny Daniel's authorship.

THEOLOGICAL THEME

The theological theme of the book is summarized in 4:17; 5:21: "The Most High (God) is sovereign over the kingdoms on earth." Daniel's visions always show God as triumphant (7:11,26–27; 8:25; 9:27). The climax of his sovereign rule is described in Revelation: "The kingdom of the world has become the kingdom of our Lord and of his Messiah ['Anointed One'], and he will reign for ever and ever" (Rev 11:15; see Da 2:44; 7:27 and notes).

KEY   **A** APPLICATION FOR LIVING   **B** BACKGROUND NOTES   **C** CHARACTER INFORMATION

LITERARY FORM

The book is made up primarily of historical narrative (found mainly in chs. 1–6) and apocalyptic ("revelatory") material (found mainly in chs. 7–12). The latter may be defined as symbolic, visionary, prophetic literature, usually composed during oppressive conditions and being chiefly eschatological in theological content. Apocalyptic literature is primarily a literature of encouragement to the people of God (see Introduction to Zechariah: Literary Form and Themes; see also Introduction to Revelation: Literary Form). For the symbolic use of numbers in apocalyptic literature, see Introduction to Revelation: Distinctive Feature.

OUTLINE

1:1 *a* S Jer 46:2
b S 2Ki 24:1;
S Jer 28:14 *c* Jer 50:1
d 2Ki 24:1;
S 2Ch 36:6; Jer 35:11
1:2 *e* S 2Ki 24:13
f S 2Ch 36:7;
Jer 27:19-20; Zec 5:5-11
1:3 *g* S 2Ki 20:18;
S 24:15; Isa 39:7
1:4 *h* S Ge 39:6
i ver 17 *i* S Ezr 4:7
1:5 *k* ver 8,10
l S Est 2:9 *m* ver 18
n ver 19; S Est 2:5-6
1:6 *o* S Eze 14:14
p Da 2:17,25
1:7 *q* Da 2:26; 4:8;
5:12; 10:1 *r* S Isa 39:7;
Da 2:49; 3:12
1:8 *s* S Eze 4:13-14
1:9 *t* S Ge 39:21;
S Pr 16:7 *u* S 1Ki 8:50
1:10 *v* ver 5
1:12 *w* Rev 2:10
1:13 *x* ver 16
1:14 *y* Rev 2:10
1:15 *z* Ex 23:25
1:16 *a* ver 12-13
1:17 *b* S Job 12:13
c Da 2:23; Col 1:9;
Jas 1:5 *d* Da 2:19,30;
5:11; 7:1; 8:1
1:18 *e* ver 5
1:19 *f* S Ge 41:46

DANIEL'S TRAINING IN BABYLON

1 In the third year of the reign of Jehoiakim *a* king of Judah, Nebuchadnezzar *b* king of Babylon *c* came to Jerusalem and besieged it. *d* 2And the Lord delivered Jehoiakim king of Judah into his hand, along with some of the articles from the temple of God. These he carried *e* off to the temple of his god in Babylonia *a* and put in the treasure house of his god. *f*

3Then the king ordered Ashpenaz, chief of his court officials, to bring into the king's service some of the Israelites from the royal family and the nobility *g*— 4young men without any physical defect, handsome, *h* showing aptitude for every kind of learning, *i* well informed, quick to understand, and qualified to serve in the king's palace. He was to teach them the language *j* and literature of the Babylonians. *b* 5The king assigned them a daily amount of food and wine *k* from the king's table. *l* They were to be trained for three years, *m* and after that they were to enter the king's service. *n*

6Among those who were chosen were some from Judah: Daniel, *o* Hananiah, Mishael and Azariah. *p* 7The chief official gave them new names: to Daniel, the name Belteshazzar; *q* to Hananiah, Shadrach; to Mishael, Meshach; and to Azariah, Abednego. *r*

8But Daniel resolved not to defile *s* himself with the royal food and wine, and he asked the chief official for permission not to defile himself this way. 9Now God had caused the official to show favor *t* and compassion *u* to Daniel, 10but the official told Daniel, "I am afraid of my lord the king, who has assigned your *c* food and drink. *v* Why should he see you looking worse than the other young men your age? The king would then have my head because of you."

11Daniel then said to the guard whom the chief official had appointed over Daniel, Hananiah, Mishael and Azariah, 12"Please test *w* your servants for ten days: Give us nothing but vegetables to eat and water to drink. 13Then compare our appearance with that of the young men who eat the royal food, and treat your servants in accordance with what you see." *x* 14So he agreed to this and tested *y* them for ten days.

15At the end of the ten days they looked healthier and better nourished than any of the young men who ate the royal food. *z* 16So the guard took away their choice food and the wine they were to drink and gave them vegetables instead. *a*

17To these four young men God gave knowledge and understanding *b* of all kinds of literature and learning. *c* And Daniel could understand visions and dreams of all kinds. *d*

18At the end of the time *e* set by the king to bring them into his service, the chief official presented them to Nebuchadnezzar. 19The king talked with them, and he found none equal to Daniel, Hananiah, Mishael and Azariah; so they entered the king's service. *f* 20In every matter of wisdom and understanding about which the king questioned them, he

---

a 2 Hebrew *Shinar*　　*b* 4 Or *Chaldeans*　　*c* 10 The Hebrew for *your* and *you* in this verse is plural.

B **1:1** *third year.* According to the Babylonian system of computing the years of a king's reign, the third year of Jehoiakim would have been 605 B.C., since his first full year of kingship began on New Year's Day after his accession in 608. But according to the system in Judah, which counted the year of accession as the first year of reign, this was "the fourth year of Jehoiakim" (Jer 25:1; 46:2; see notes there). *Jehoiakim king of Judah.* See 2Ki 23:34; 2Ch 36:5–8 and notes. *Nebuchadnezzar king of Babylon.* 605 B.C. was also the first year of his reign (see Jer 25:1; 2Ki 24:1 and note; see also chart, p. 482).

A **1:2** *carried off.* Judah was exiled to Babylonia because she disobeyed God's word regarding covenant-keeping, the sabbath years and idolatry (see Lev 25:4 and note; 26:27–35; Dt 28:15–68; 2Ki 25:1 and note; 2Ch 36:20–21 and note). The first deportation (605 B.C.) included Daniel, and the second (597) included Ezekiel. A third deportation took place in 586, when the Babylonians destroyed the city of Jerusalem and Solomon's temple. *his god.* Marduk (see note on Isa 45:4).

B **1:4** *language and literature of the Babylonians.* Including the classical literature in Sumerian and Akkadian cuneiform, a complicated syllabic writing system. But the language of normal communication in multiracial Babylon was Aramaic, written in an easily learned alphabetic script (see 2:4 and note).

1:6 *Daniel.* Means "God is (my) Judge." *Hananiah.* Means "The LORD shows grace." *Mishael.* Means "Who is what God is?" *Azariah.* Means "The LORD helps."

1:7 *gave them new names.* Indicating that they were now subject to Nebuchadnezzar's authority (see Ge 17:5; 41:45; 2Ki 23:34; 24:17 and notes). *Belteshazzar.* Probably means, in Babylonian, "Bel (i.e., Marduk), protect his life!" *Shadrach.* Probably means "command of Aku (Sumerian moon-god)." *Meshach.* Probably means "Who is what Aku is?" *Abednego.* Means "servant of Nego/Nebo (i.e., Nabu)."

A **1:8** *royal food and wine.* Israelites considered food from Nebuchadnezzar's table to be contaminated because the first portion of it was offered to idols. Likewise, a portion of the wine was poured out on a pagan altar. Ceremonially unclean animals were used and were neither slaughtered nor prepared according to the regulations of the law. *he asked ... not to defile himself.* He demonstrated the courage of his convictions.

C **1:9** *God had caused the official to show favor ... to Daniel.* The careers of Joseph and Daniel were similar in many respects (see Ge 39–41).

A **1:12** *test your servants.* Daniel used good judgment by offering an alternative instead of rebelling. *ten.* Often symbolized completeness.

A **1:17** With God's help, Daniel and his friends mastered the essential Babylonian literature on astrology and divination by dreams. But in the crucial tests of interpretation and prediction (see 2:2–11; 4:6–7), all the pagan literature proved worthless. Only by God's special revelation (2:17–28) was Daniel able to interpret correctly.

found them ten times better than all the magicians[g] and enchanters in his whole kingdom.[h]

21And Daniel remained there until the first year of King Cyrus.[i]

NEBUCHADNEZZAR'S DREAM

2 In the second year of his reign, Nebuchadnezzar had dreams;[j] his mind was troubled[k] and he could not sleep.[l] 2So the king summoned the magicians,[m] enchanters, sorcerers[n] and astrologers[a][o] to tell him what he had dreamed.[p] When they came in and stood before the king, 3he said to them, "I have had a dream that troubles[q] me and I want to know what it means.[b]"

4Then the astrologers answered the king,[c][r] "May the king live forever![s] Tell your servants the dream, and we will interpret it."

5The king replied to the astrologers, "This is what I have firmly decided:[t] If you do not tell me what my dream was and interpret it, I will have you cut into pieces[u] and your houses turned into piles of rubble.[v] 6But if you tell me the dream and explain it, you will receive from me gifts and rewards and great honor.[w] So tell me the dream and interpret it for me."

7Once more they replied, "Let the king tell his servants the dream, and we will interpret it."

8Then the king answered, "I am certain that you are trying to gain time, because you realize that this is what I have firmly decided: 9If you do not tell me the dream, there is only one penalty[x] for you. You have conspired to tell me misleading and wicked things, hoping the situation will change. So then, tell me the dream, and I will know that you can interpret it for me."[y]

10The astrologers[z] answered the king, "There is not a person on earth who can do what the king asks! No king, however great and mighty, has ever asked such a thing of any magician or enchanter or astrologer.[a] 11What the king asks is too difficult. No one can reveal it to the king except the gods,[b] and they do not live among human beings."

12This made the king so angry and furious[c] that he ordered the execution[d] of all the wise men of Babylon. 13So the decree was issued to put the wise men to death, and men were sent to look for Daniel and his friends to put them to death.[e]

14When Arioch, the commander of the king's guard, had gone out to put to death the wise men of Babylon, Daniel spoke to him with wisdom and tact. 15He asked the king's officer, "Why did the king issue such a harsh decree?" Arioch then explained the matter to Daniel. 16At this, Daniel went in to the king and asked for time, so that he might interpret the dream for him.

17Then Daniel returned to his house and explained the matter to his friends Hananiah, Mishael and Azariah.[f] 18He urged them to plead for mercy[g] from the God of heaven[h] concerning this mystery,[i] so that he and his friends might not be executed with the rest of the wise men of Babylon. 19During the night the mystery[j] was revealed to Daniel in a vision.[k] Then Daniel praised the God of heaven[l] 20and said:

"Praise be to the name of God for ever and ever;[m]
    wisdom and power[n] are his.
21He changes times and seasons;[o]

---

[a] 2 Or *Chaldeans;* also in verses 4, 5 and 10   [b] 3 Or *was*   [c] 4 At this point the Hebrew text has *in Aramaic,* indicating that the text from here through the end of chapter 7 is in Aramaic.

1:20 [g] S Ge 41:8
[h] S 1Ki 4:30; Est 2:15;
S Eze 28:3; Da 2:13,
28; 4:18; 6:3
1:21 [i] S 2Ch 36:22;
Da 6:28; 10:1
2:1 [j] ver 3;
S Ge 20:3;
S Job 33:15,18; Da 4:5
[k] Ge 41:8 [l] S Est 6:1
2:2 [m] S Ge 41:8
[n] Ex 7:11; Jer 27:9
[o] S ver 10; S Isa 19:3;
S 44:25 [p] Da 4:6
2:3 [q] Da 4:5
2:4 [r] S Ezr 4:7
[s] S Ne 2:3
2:5 [t] Ge 41:32
[u] ver 12 [v] Ezr 6:11;
Da 3:29
2:6 [w] ver 48; Da 5:7,
16
2:9 [x] Est 4:11
[y] Isa 41:22-24
2:10 [z] ver 2; Da 3:8;
4:7 [a] ver 27; Da 5:8
2:11 [b] S Ge 41:38
2:12 [c] Da 3:13,19
[d] ver 5
2:13 [e] S Da 1:20;
5:19
2:17 [f] S Da 1:6
2:18 [g] S Isa 37:4
[h] Ezr 1:2; Ne 1:4;
Jnh 1:9; Rev 11:13
[i] ver 23; Jer 33:3
2:19 [j] ver 28
[k] S Job 33:15;
S Da 1:17 [l] S Jos 22:33
2:20 [m] S Ps 113:2;
145:1-2 [n] S Job 9:4;
S Jer 32:19
2:21 [o] Da 7:25

1:20 *ten.* See note on v. 12. *magicians.* See note on Ge 41:8.
1:21 *there.* In Babylonia. *first year of King Cyrus.* Over Babylon (539 B.C.; see chart, p. 482). Daniel spent about 70 years in Babylonia and was still living in the year 537 (10:1), so he saw the exiles return to Judah from Babylonian captivity.
2:1 *second year of . . . Nebuchadnezzar.* 604 B.C. (see 1:1 and note). *he could not sleep.* See 6:18; Est 6:1 and note.
2:2 *magicians, enchanters, sorcerers.* See Dt 18:9–14 and note on 18:9.

2:4 See TNIV text note. Since the astrologers were of various ethnic and cultural backgrounds, they communicated in Aramaic, the language everyone understood. From here to the end of ch. 7 the entire narrative is in Aramaic. These six chapters deal with matters of importance to the Gentile nations of the Near East and were written in a language understandable to all. But the last five chapters (8–12) revert to Hebrew, since they deal

with special concerns of the chosen people. *your servants.* Us.
2:5 See 3:29.

2:10 *not a person on earth who can do what the king asks.* But "God in heaven" can (through Daniel; see vv. 27–28).
2:11 *do not live among human beings.* Are not readily accessible.
2:14 *Arioch.* Also the name of a Mesopotamian king who lived centuries earlier (Ge 14:1,9).

2:18 *God of heaven.* In this chapter this Persian title for a high god (see note on Ezr 1:2) is used to refer to Yahweh, the God of Israel. *mystery.* A key word in Daniel (vv. 19,27–30,47; 4:9). It also appears often in the writings (Dead Sea Scrolls) of the Qumran sect (see essay, pp. 1595–1597). The Greek equivalent is used in the NT to refer to the secret purposes of God that he reveals only to his chosen prophets and apostles (see notes on Ro 11:25; Rev 10:7).

2:21 ᵖS Job 12:19;
Ps 75:6-7; Ro 13:1
ᵍDa 4:17
ʳS Ps 119:34; Jas 1:5
ˢS 2Sa 14:17
2:22 ᵗS Ge 40:8;
S Job 12:22; Da 5:11;
1Co 2:10 ᵘJob 12:22;
Ps 139:11-12;
Jer 23:24; S Heb 4:13
ᵛIsa 45:7; Jas 1:17
2:23 ʷS Ge 31:5;
S Ex 3:15 ˣS Da 1:17
ʸS Eze 28:3
2:24 ᶻver 14
2:25 ᵃS Dt 21:10
ᵇS Da 1:6; 5:13; 6:13
2:26 ᶜS Da 1:7
2:27 ᵈS ver 10;
S Ge 41:8
2:28 ᵉS Ge 40:8;
Jer 10:7; Am 4:13
ᶠS Ge 49:1; Da 10:14;
Mt 24:6; Rev 1:1; 22:6
ᵍDa 4:5 ʰS Ps 4:4
ⁱS Eze 28:3;
S Da 1:20
2:29 ʲS Ge 41:25
2:30 ᵏIsa 45:3;
S Da 1:17; Am 4:13
2:31 ˡHab 1:7
ᵐIsa 25:3-5
2:34 ⁿS Job 12:19;
Zec 4:6 ᵒS Job 34:24
ᵖver 44-45; Ps 2:9;
S Isa 60:12; Da 8:25
2:35 ᵍPs 1:4; 37:10;
S Isa 17:13; 41:15-16
ʳIsa 2:3; Mic 4:1
ˢZec 12:3
2:36 ᵗS Ge 40:12
2:37 ᵘS Ezr 7:12
ᵛS Jer 27:7; Da 4:26
2:38 ʷS Jer 27:6;
Da 4:21-22; 5:18
2:39 ˣDa 7:5
2:40 ʸDa 7:7,23

he deposes ᵖ kings and raises up others. ᵍ
He gives wisdom ʳ to the wise
and knowledge to the discerning. ˢ
²²He reveals deep and hidden things; ᵗ
he knows what lies in darkness, ᵘ
and light ᵛ dwells with him.
²³I thank and praise you, God of my ancestors: ʷ
You have given me wisdom ˣ and power,
you have made known to me what we asked of you,
you have made known to us the dream of the king. ʸ"

DANIEL INTERPRETS THE DREAM

²⁴Then Daniel went to Arioch, ᶻ whom the king had appointed to execute the wise men of Babylon, and said to him, "Do not execute the wise men of Babylon. Take me to the king, and I will interpret his dream for him."

²⁵Arioch took Daniel to the king at once and said, "I have found a man among the exiles ᵃ from Judah ᵇ who can tell the king what his dream means."

²⁶The king asked Daniel (also called Belteshazzar), ᶜ "Are you able to tell me what I saw in my dream and interpret it?"

²⁷Daniel replied, "No wise man, enchanter, magician or diviner can explain to the king the mystery he has asked about, ᵈ ²⁸but there is a God in heaven who reveals mysteries. ᵉ He has shown King Nebuchadnezzar what will happen in days to come. ᶠ Your dream and the visions that passed through your mind ᵍ as you were lying in bed ʰ are these: ⁱ

²⁹"As Your Majesty was lying there, your mind turned to things to come, and the revealer of mysteries showed you what is going to happen. ʲ ³⁰As for me, this mystery has been revealed ᵏ to me, not because I have greater wisdom than anyone else alive, but so that Your Majesty may know the interpretation and that you may understand what went through your mind.

³¹"Your Majesty looked, and there before you stood a large statue—an enormous, dazzling statue, ˡ awesome ᵐ in appearance. ³²The head of the statue was made of pure gold, its chest and arms of silver, its belly and thighs of bronze, ³³its legs of iron, its feet partly of iron and partly of baked clay. ³⁴While you were watching, a rock was cut out, but not by human hands. ⁿ It struck the statue on its feet of iron and clay and smashed ᵒ them. ᵖ ³⁵Then the iron, the clay, the bronze, the silver and the gold were all broken to pieces and became like chaff on a threshing floor in the summer. The wind swept them away ᵍ without leaving a trace. But the rock that struck the statue became a huge mountain ʳ and filled the whole earth. ˢ

³⁶"This was the dream, and now we will interpret it to the king. ᵗ ³⁷Your Majesty, you are the king of kings. ᵘ The God of heaven has given you dominion ᵛ and power and might and glory; ³⁸in your hands he has placed all people everywhere and the beasts of the field and the birds in the sky. Wherever they live, he has made you ruler over them all. ʷ You are that head of gold.

³⁹"After you, another kingdom will arise, inferior to yours. Next, a third kingdom, one of bronze, will rule over the whole earth. ˣ ⁴⁰Finally, there will be a fourth kingdom, strong as iron—for iron breaks and smashes everything—and as iron breaks things to pieces, so it will crush and break all the others. ʸ ⁴¹Just as you saw that the feet and toes were partly of baked clay and partly of iron, so this will be a divided kingdom; yet it will have some of the strength of iron in it, even as you saw iron mixed with clay. ⁴²As the toes were partly iron and partly clay, so this kingdom will be partly strong and partly brittle. ⁴³And just

2:21 He gives wisdom ... to the discerning. See Pr 1:2–5 and note on 1:2.

2:22 light dwells with him. See Ps 36:9 and note.

2:29 the revealer of mysteries. God (see v. 47).

2:32–43 See map No. 8b and map No. 14 at the end of this study Bible; see also chart, p. 1455. The gold head represents the Neo-Babylonian empire (v. 38; see Jer 51:7 and note; see also map, p. 1449); the silver chest and arms the Medo-Persian empire established by Cyrus in 539 B.C. (the date of the fall of Babylon); the bronze belly and thighs the Greek empire established by Alexander the Great c. 330; the iron legs and feet the Roman empire. The toes (v. 41) are understood by some to represent a later confederation of states occupying the territory formerly

controlled by the Roman empire. The diminishing value of the metals from gold to silver to bronze to iron represents the decreasing power and grandeur (v. 39) of the rulers of the successive empires, from the absolute despotism of Nebuchadnezzar to the democratic system of checks and balances that characterized the Roman senates and assemblies. The metals also symbolize a growing degree of toughness and endurance, with each successive empire lasting longer than the preceding one.

2:33 partly of iron and partly of baked clay. "Partly strong and partly brittle" (v. 42).

2:35 broken to pieces. See Lk 20:18 and note.

2:37 king of kings. That is, the greatest king (cf. v. 47; Ezr 7:12 and note; 1Ti 6:15; Rev 17:14 and note; 19:16).

as you saw the iron mixed with baked clay, so the people will be a mixture and will not remain united, any more than iron mixes with clay.

⁴⁴"In the time of those kings, the God of heaven will set up a kingdom that will never be destroyed, nor will it be left to another people. It will crush ᶻ all those kingdoms ᵃ and bring them to an end, but it will itself endure forever. ᵇ ⁴⁵This is the meaning of the vision of the rock ᶜ cut out of a mountain, but not by human hands ᵈ—a rock that broke the iron, the bronze, the clay, the silver and the gold to pieces.

"The great God has shown the king what will take place in the future. ᵉ The dream is true ᶠ and its interpretation is trustworthy."

⁴⁶Then King Nebuchadnezzar fell prostrate ᵍ before Daniel and paid him honor and ordered that an offering ʰ and incense be presented to him. ⁴⁷The king said to Daniel, "Surely your God is the God of gods ⁱ and the Lord of kings ʲ and a revealer of mysteries, ᵏ for you were able to reveal this mystery. ˡ"

⁴⁸Then the king placed Daniel in a high ᵐ position and lavished many gifts on him. He made him ruler over the entire province of Babylon and placed him in charge of all its wise men. ⁿ ⁴⁹Moreover, at Daniel's request the king appointed Shadrach, Meshach and Abednego administrators over the province of Babylon, ᵒ while Daniel himself remained at the royal court. ᵖ

THE IMAGE OF GOLD AND THE BLAZING FURNACE

3 King Nebuchadnezzar made an image �q of gold, sixty cubits high and six cubits wide, ᵃ and set it up on the plain of Dura in the province of Babylon. ²He then summoned the satraps, ʳ prefects, governors, advisers, treasurers, judges, magistrates and all the other provincial officials ˢ to come to the dedication of the image he had set up. ³So the satraps, prefects, governors, advisers, treasurers, judges, magistrates and all the other provincial officials assembled for the dedication of the image that King Nebuchadnezzar had set up, and they stood before it.

⁴Then the herald loudly proclaimed, "Nations and peoples of every language, ᵗ this is what you are commanded to do: ⁵As soon as you hear the sound of the horn, flute, zither, lyre, harp, ᵘ pipe and all kinds of music, you must fall down and worship the image ᵛ of gold that King Nebuchadnezzar has set up. ʷ ⁶Whoever does not fall down and worship will immediately be thrown into a blazing furnace." ˣ

⁷Therefore, as soon as they heard the sound of the horn, flute, zither, lyre, harp and all kinds of music, all the nations and peoples of every language fell down and worshiped the image of gold that King Nebuchadnezzar had set up. ʸ

⁸At this time some astrologers ᵇ ᶻ came forward and denounced the Jews. ⁹They said to King Nebuchadnezzar, "May the king live forever! ᵃ ¹⁰Your Majesty has issued a decree ᵇ that everyone who hears the sound of the horn, flute, zither, lyre, harp, pipe and all kinds of music must fall down and worship the image of gold, ᶜ ¹¹and that whoever does not fall down and worship will be thrown into a blazing furnace. ¹²But there are some Jews whom you have set over the affairs of the province of Babylon—Shadrach, Meshach and Abednego ᵈ—who pay no attention ᵉ to you, Your Majesty. They neither serve your gods nor worship the image of gold you have set up." ᶠ

¹³Furious ᵍ with rage, Nebuchadnezzar summoned Shadrach, Meshach and Abednego.

ᵃ *1* That is, about 90 feet high and 9 feet wide or about 27 meters high and 2.7 meters wide
ᵇ *8* Or *Chaldeans*

2:44 The fifth kingdom is the eternal kingdom of God (see Rev 11:15), built on the ruins of the sinful empires of the world. Its authority will extend over "the whole earth" (v. 35) and ultimately over "a new heaven and a new earth" (Rev 21:1).
2:46 *offering . . . be presented to him.* As to a god (cf. Ac 14:12 and note).
2:48 Cf. the story of Joseph (Ge 41:41–43).
2:49 Daniel requests that his administrative authority be shared with his three Jewish friends.

3:1 *image of gold.* Large statues of this kind were not made of solid gold but were plated with gold. *sixty cubits high.* Including the lofty pedestal on which it no doubt stood (see TNIV text note; cf. Est 5:14 and note). *Dura.* Either the name of a place now marked by a series of mounds (located a few miles south of Babylon) or a common noun meaning "walled enclosure."
3:2 The seven classifications of government officials were to

pledge full allegiance to the newly established empire as they stood before the image. The image probably represented the god Nabu, whose name formed the first element in Nebuchadnezzar's name (see note on 2Ki 24:1).
3:4 *every language.* Nebuchadnezzar's Babylon had become a cosmopolitan city whose population included people of many national and ethnic origins (see v. 7).

3:5 The words for "zither," "harp" and "pipe" (or perhaps "small drum") are Greek loanwords in Daniel. Greek musicians and instruments are mentioned in Assyrian inscriptions written before the time of Nebuchadnezzar. *fall down and worship the image.* See Ex 20:4–5 and note on 20:4.
3:8 *Jews.* A shortened form of "Judahites" (see Jer 34:9 and note).

3:12 *They neither serve your gods nor worship the image.* They obeyed the word of God (Ex 20:3–5) above the word of the king.

2:44 ᶻ S Ge 27:29; Ps 2:9; S 110:5; Mt 21:43-44; 1Co 15:24
ᵃ S 1Sa 9:20; Hag 2:22 ᵇ Ps 145:13; S Isa 9:7; Da 4:34; 6:26; 7:14,27; Ob 1:21; Mic 4:7,13; S Lk 1:33; Rev 11:15
2:45 ᶜ S Isa 28:16 ᵈ Da 8:25 ᵉ S Ge 41:25 ᶠ Rev 22:6
2:46 ᵍ Da 8:17; Ac 10:25 ʰ Ac 14:13
2:47 ⁱ S Dt 10:17; Da 11:36 ʲ Da 4:25; 1Ti 6:15 ᵏ S ver 22,28 ˡ Da 1:17; 1Co 14:25
2:48 ᵐ S 2Ki 25:28 ⁿ S ver 6; S Est 8:2; S Da 1:20; 4:9; 5:11; 8:27
2:49 ᵒ S Da 1:7; 3:30 ᵖ Da 6:2
3:1 �q ver 14; S Isa 46:6; Jer 16:20; Hab 2:19
3:2 ʳ S Est 1:1 ˢ ver 27; Da 6:7
3:4 ᵗ Da 4:1; 6:25; Rev 10:11
3:5 ᵘ S Ge 4:21 ᵛ Rev 13:12 ʷ ver 10, 15
3:6 ˣ ver 11,15,21; Jer 29:22; Da 5:19; 6:7; Mt 13:42,50; Rev 13:15
3:7 ʸ S ver 5
3:8 ᶻ S Isa 19:3; S Da 2:10
3:9 ᵃ S Ne 2:3; Da 5:10; 6:6
3:10 ᵇ Da 6:12 ᶜ ver 4-6
3:12 ᵈ S Da 2:49 ᵉ Da 6:13 ᶠ S Est 3:3
3:13 ᵍ S Da 2:12

3:14 *h* Isa 46:1;
Jer 50:2 *i* S ver 1
3:15 *j* S Isa 36:18-20
k S 2Ch 32:15
3:16 *l* S Da 1:7
3:17 *m* S Ge 48:16;
S Ps 18:48; 27:1-2
n S Job 5:19; Jer 1:8;
Da 6:20
3:18 *o* ver 28;
S Ex 1:17; S Jos 24:15
3:19 *p* Lev 26:18-28
3:20 *q* S Da 1:7
3:22 *r* S Da 1:7
3:26 *s* Da 4:2,34
3:27 *t* ver 2; Da 6:7
u Ps 91:3-11;
S Isa 43:2; Heb 11:32-
34 *v* Da 6:23
3:28 *w* S Ps 34:7;
Da 6:22; Ac 5:19
x S Ps 97:10; Ac 12:11
y S Dt 31:20;
S Job 13:15; S Ps 26:1;
84:12 *z* S ver 18
3:29 *a* Da 6:26
b S Ezr 6:11 *c* Da 6:27
3:30 *d* S Da 2:49
4:1 *e* S Da 3:4
f Da 6:25

So these men were brought before the king, [14]and Nebuchadnezzar said to them, "Is it true, Shadrach, Meshach and Abednego, that you do not serve my gods *h* or worship the image *i* of gold I have set up? [15]Now when you hear the sound of the horn, flute, zither, lyre, harp, pipe and all kinds of music, if you are ready to fall down and worship the image I made, very good. But if you do not worship it, you will be thrown immediately into a blazing furnace. Then what god *j* will be able to rescue *k* you from my hand?"

[16]Shadrach, Meshach and Abednego *l* replied to him, "King Nebuchadnezzar, we do not need to defend ourselves before you in this matter. [17]If the God we serve is able to deliver *m* us, then he will deliver *n* us from the blazing furnace and from Your Majesty's hand. [18]But even if he does not, we want you to know, Your Majesty, that we will not serve your gods or worship the image of gold you have set up. *o*"

[19]Then Nebuchadnezzar was furious with Shadrach, Meshach and Abednego, and his attitude toward them changed. He ordered the furnace heated seven *p* times hotter than usual [20]and commanded some of the strongest soldiers in his army to tie up Shadrach, Meshach and Abednego *q* and throw them into the blazing furnace. [21]So these men, wearing their robes, trousers, turbans and other clothes, were bound and thrown into the blazing furnace. [22]The king's command was so urgent and the furnace so hot that the flames of the fire killed the soldiers who took up Shadrach, Meshach and Abednego, *r* [23]and these three men, firmly tied, fell into the blazing furnace.

[24]Then King Nebuchadnezzar leaped to his feet in amazement and asked his advisers, "Weren't there three men that we tied up and threw into the fire?"

They replied, "Certainly, Your Majesty."

[25]He said, "Look! I see four men walking around in the fire, unbound and unharmed, and the fourth looks like a son of the gods."

[26]Nebuchadnezzar then approached the opening of the blazing furnace and shouted, "Shadrach, Meshach and Abednego, servants of the Most High God, *s* come out! Come here!"

So Shadrach, Meshach and Abednego came out of the fire, [27]and the satraps, prefects, governors and royal advisers *t* crowded around them. *u* They saw that the fire *v* had not harmed their bodies, nor was a hair of their heads singed; their robes were not scorched, and there was no smell of fire on them.

[28]Then Nebuchadnezzar said, "Praise be to the God of Shadrach, Meshach and Abednego, who has sent his angel *w* and rescued *x* his servants! They trusted *y* in him and defied the king's command and were willing to give up their lives rather than serve or worship any god except their own God. *z* [29]Therefore I decree *a* that the people of any nation or language who say anything against the God of Shadrach, Meshach and Abednego be cut into pieces and their houses be turned into piles of rubble, *b* for no other god can save *c* in this way."

[30]Then the king promoted Shadrach, Meshach and Abednego in the province of Babylon. *d*

NEBUCHADNEZZAR'S DREAM OF A TREE

4 *King Nebuchadnezzar,

To the nations and peoples of every language, *e* who live in all the earth:

May you prosper greatly! *f*

* 4:1-3 is numbered 3:31-33 in Aramaic texts.

3:15 *what god will be able to rescue you from my hand?* Such boastful taunts were characteristic of proud Mesopotamian rulers (see Isa 36:18–20 and note).

3:17 See vv. 26–27; Heb 11:34 and note. *If the God we serve is able to deliver us.* For what God is "able" to do, see, e.g., 4:37; 6:19–22 (cf. Ro 11:23; 2Co 9:8; Heb 7:25; Jude 24–25 and notes).

3:18 *if he does not.* Whether God decides to rescue them (v. 17) or not, their faith is fully resigned to his will.

3:19 *seven times hotter than usual.* Probably figurative for "as hot as possible" (seven signifies completeness).

3:25 See Ps 91:9–12. *son of the gods.* Nebuchadnezzar was speaking as a pagan polytheist and was content to

conceive of the fourth figure as a lesser heavenly being ("angel," v. 28) sent by the all-powerful God of the Jews (see also 6:22).

3:26 *Most High God.* Nebuchadnezzar had earlier acknowledged that Daniel's God is "the God of gods and the Lord of kings" (2:47).

3:28 *They trusted in him.* See 6:23 and note; Ps 11; 16; 23; 31; 52; Pr 3:5 and note.

3:29 See 2:5. *no other god can save.* See Isa 40:18–20; 41:24; 44:17 and notes (cf. Jn 14:6 and note).

4:1–3 Nebuchadnezzar reached this conclusion after the experiences of vv. 4–33. The language of his confession may reflect Daniel's influence.

²It is my pleasure to tell you about the miraculous signs *g* and wonders that the Most High God *h* has performed for me.

³ How great are his signs,
  how mighty his wonders! *i*
His kingdom is an eternal kingdom;
  his dominion endures *j* from generation to generation.

*⁴I, Nebuchadnezzar, was at home in my palace, contented *k* and prosperous. ⁵I had a dream *l* that made me afraid. As I was lying in bed, *m* the images and visions that passed through my mind *n* terrified me. *o* ⁶So I commanded that all the wise men of Babylon be brought before me to interpret *p* the dream for me. ⁷When the magicians, *q* enchanters, astrologers *a* and diviners *r* came, I told them the dream, but they could not interpret it for me. *s* ⁸Finally, Daniel came into my presence and I told him the dream. (He is called Belteshazzar, *t* after the name of my god, and the spirit of the holy gods *u* is in him.)

⁹I said, "Belteshazzar, chief *v* of the magicians, I know that the spirit of the holy gods *w* is in you, and no mystery is too difficult for you. Here is my dream; interpret it for me. ¹⁰These are the visions I saw while lying in bed: *x* I looked, and there before me stood a tree in the middle of the land. Its height was enormous. *y* ¹¹The tree grew

a 7 Or *Chaldeans*
* 4:4-37 is numbered 4:1-34 in Aramaic texts.

4:2 *g* Ps 74:9
h S Da 3:26
4:3 *i* S Ps 105:27;
Da 6:27 / Da 2:44
4:4 *k* Ps 30:6;
S Isa 32:9
4:5 *l* S Da 2:1
m Ps 4:4 *n* Da 2:28
o ver 19; S Ge 41:8;
S Job 3:26; Da 2:3;
5:6
4:6 *p* Da 2:2
4:7 *q* S Ge 41:8
r S Isa 44:25;
S Da 2:2 *s* S Da 2:10
4:8 *t* S Da 1:7
u S Ge 41:38
4:9 *v* Da 2:48
w Da 5:11-12
4:10 *x* S ver 5;
Ps 4:4 *y* Eze 31:3-4

4:3 *His kingdom ... from generation to generation.* See v. 34 and note.
4:8 *after the name of my god.* See note on 1:7. Bel ("lord") was a title for the Babylonian god Marduk.

4:9 *chief of the magicians.* See 2:48.
4:10 *tree.* Interpreted in v. 22.

B **4:11** *grew large and strong.* In one of Nebuchadnezzar's building inscriptions, Babylon is compared to a spreading

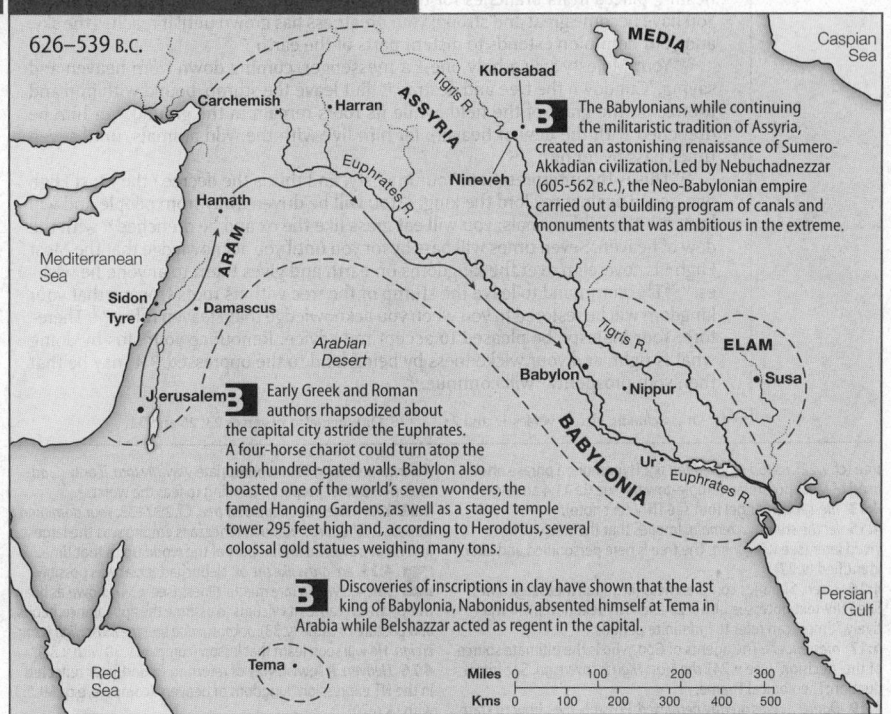

THE NEO-BABYLONIAN EMPIRE

626–539 B.C.

MEDIA

Caspian Sea

Khorsabad

Carchemish • Harran

ASSYRIA

Nineveh

Hamath

Tigris R.

Euphrates R.

Mediterranean Sea

ARAM

Sidon
Tyre •
• Damascus

Arabian Desert

Jerusalem

Tigris R.

ELAM

Babylon •
• Nippur

• Susa

BABYLONIA

Ur •

Euphrates R.

Persian Gulf

Red Sea

Tema •

B The Babylonians, while continuing the militaristic tradition of Assyria, created an astonishing renaissance of Sumero-Akkadian civilization. Led by Nebuchadnezzar (605-562 B.C.), the Neo-Babylonian empire carried out a building program of canals and monuments that was ambitious in the extreme.

B Early Greek and Roman authors rhapsodized about the capital city astride the Euphrates. A four-horse chariot could turn atop the high, hundred-gated walls. Babylon also boasted one of the world's seven wonders, the famed Hanging Gardens, as well as a staged temple tower 295 feet high and, according to Herodotus, several colossal gold statues weighing many tons.

B Discoveries of inscriptions in clay have shown that the last king of Babylonia, Nabonidus, absented himself at Tema in Arabia while Belshazzar acted as regent in the capital.

Miles	0	100	200	300
Kms	0	100 200	300 400	500

4:11 z S Eze 19:11;
31:5
4:12 a S Eze 17:23;
S Mt 13:32
4:13 b ver 10; Da 7:1
c S ver 23; S Dt 33:2
4:14 d S Job 24:20
e S Eze 31:12;
S Mt 3:10
4:16 f ver 23,32
4:17 g ver 2,25;
Ps 83:18
h S Ps 103:19;
Jer 27:5-7; Da 2:21;
5:18-21; Ro 13:1
i Da 11:21; Mt 23:12
4:18 j S Ge 41:8;
Da 5:8,15 k S Ge 41:15
l S Ge 41:38 m ver 7-
9; S Da 1:20
4:19 n S ver 5;
S Ge 41:8; Da 7:15,
28; 8:27; 10:16-17
o S Ge 40:12
4:21 p S Eze 31:6
4:22 q S 2Sa 12:7
r Jer 27:7; Da 5:18-19
4:23 s ver 13;
Da 8:13 t Da 5:21
u S Eze 31:3-4
4:24 v Job 40:12;
Ps 107:40; Jer 40:2
4:25 w S Job 24:8
x S ver 17 y Jer 27:5;
S Da 2:47; 5:21
4:26 z ver 15
a S Da 2:37
4:27 b Isa 55:6-7
c Jer 29:7
d S Dt 24:13;
1Ki 21:29; S Ps 41:3;
S Pr 28:13;
S Eze 18:22

large and strong and its top touched the sky; it was visible to the ends of the earth. z [12]Its leaves were beautiful, its fruit abundant, and on it was food for all. Under it the wild animals found shelter, and the birds lived in its branches; a from it every creature was fed.

[13]"In the visions I saw while lying in bed, b I looked, and there before me was a holy one, c a messenger, a coming down from heaven. [14]He called in a loud voice: 'Cut down the tree d and trim off its branches; strip off its leaves and scatter its fruit. Let the animals flee from under it and the birds from its branches. e [15]But let the stump and its roots, bound with iron and bronze, remain in the ground, in the grass of the field.

" 'Let him be drenched with the dew of heaven, and let him live with the animals among the plants of the earth. [16]Let his mind be changed from that of a human being and let him be given the mind of an animal, till seven times b pass by for him. f

[17]'The decision is announced by messengers, the holy ones declare the verdict, so that the living may know that the Most High g is sovereign h over the kingdoms on earth and gives them to anyone he wishes and sets over them the lowliest i of people.'

[18]"This is the dream that I, King Nebuchadnezzar, had. Now, Belteshazzar, tell me what it means, for none of the wise men in my kingdom can interpret it for me. j But you can, k because the spirit of the holy gods l is in you." m

DANIEL INTERPRETS THE DREAM

[19]Then Daniel (also called Belteshazzar) was greatly perplexed for a time, and his thoughts terrified n him. So the king said, "Belteshazzar, do not let the dream or its meaning alarm you." o

Belteshazzar answered, "My lord, if only the dream applied to your enemies and its meaning to your adversaries! [20]The tree you saw, which grew large and strong, with its top touching the sky, visible to the whole earth, [21]with beautiful leaves and abundant fruit, providing food for all, giving shelter to the wild animals, and having nesting places in its branches for the birds p— [22]Your Majesty, you are that tree! q You have become great and strong; your greatness has grown until it reaches the sky, and your dominion extends to distant parts of the earth. r

[23]"Your Majesty saw a holy one, s a messenger, coming down from heaven and saying, 'Cut down the tree and destroy it, but leave the stump, bound with iron and bronze, in the grass of the field, while its roots remain in the ground. Let him be drenched with the dew of heaven; let him live with the wild animals, until seven times pass by for him.' t u

[24]"This is the interpretation, Your Majesty, and this is the decree v the Most High has issued against my lord the king: [25]You will be driven away from people and will live with the wild animals; you will eat grass like the ox and be drenched w with the dew of heaven. Seven times will pass by for you until you acknowledge that the Most High x is sovereign over the kingdoms on earth and gives them to anyone he wishes. y [26]The command to leave the stump of the tree with its roots z means that your kingdom will be restored to you when you acknowledge that Heaven rules. a [27]Therefore, Your Majesty, be pleased to accept my advice: Renounce your sins by doing what is right, and your wickedness by being kind to the oppressed. b It may be that then your prosperity c will continue. d"

---

a 13 Or *watchman*; also in verses 17 and 23   b 16 Or *years*; also in verses 23, 25 and 32

---

tree (cf. v. 22). *its top touched the sky.* Hyperbole; a phrase often used of Mesopotamian temple-towers (see Ge 11:4 and note).
4:13 *messenger.* Angel (but see TNIV text note).
4:15 *let the stump . . . remain.* Implies that the tree will be revived later (see v. 26). *him.* The tree is here personified and later identified (v. 22).
4:16 *seven.* Signifies completeness (i.e., a full measure). *times.* See TNIV text note; see also 7:25 and TNIV text note). Alternatively, "times" can refer to indefinite periods.
4:17 *messengers.* The agents of God, who is the ultimate source of the "decision" (see v. 24). *the Most High is sovereign.* See Introduction: Theological Theme.
4:19 *Daniel . . . was greatly perplexed.* Possibly over how to state

the interpretation in an appropriate way. *My lord, if only . . . adversaries!* Daniel prepared the king to fear the worst.
4:22 *Your Majesty, you are that tree.* Cf. 2:37–38. *your dominion extends . . . the earth.* Nebuchadnezzar's empire was the largest and most powerful in that part of the world up to that time.

4:25 *eat grass like the ox.* Nebuchadnezzar was possibly stricken with a rare mental illness (see v. 34) known as boanthropy, which causes its victims to assume the appearance, habits and posture of cattle (v. 33). *acknowledge that the Most High is sovereign.* He will soon learn that lesson (compare v. 30 with v. 37).
4:26 *Heaven.* A Jewish way of referring to God, later reflected in the NT expression "kingdom of heaven" (compare, e.g., Mt 5:3 with Lk 6:20).

THE DREAM IS FULFILLED

²⁸All this happened ᵉ to King Nebuchadnezzar. ²⁹Twelve months later, as the king was walking on the roof of the royal palace of Babylon, ³⁰he said, "Is not this the great Babylon I have built as the royal residence, by my mighty power and for the glory ᶠ of my majesty?" ᵍ

³¹Even as the words were on his lips, a voice came from heaven, "This is what is decreed for you, King Nebuchadnezzar: Your royal authority has been taken from you. ʰ ³²You will be driven away from people and will live with the wild animals; you will eat grass like the ox. Seven times will pass by for you until you acknowledge that the Most High is sovereign over the kingdoms on earth and gives them to anyone he wishes." ⁱ

³³Immediately what had been said about Nebuchadnezzar was fulfilled. He was driven away from people and ate grass like the ox. His body was drenched ʲ with the dew of heaven until his hair grew like the feathers of an eagle and his nails like the claws of a bird. ᵏ

³⁴At the end of that time, I, Nebuchadnezzar, raised my eyes toward heaven, and my sanity ˡ was restored. Then I praised the Most High; I honored and glorified him who lives forever. ᵐ

His dominion is an eternal dominion;
    his kingdom ⁿ endures from generation to generation. ᵒ
³⁵All the peoples of the earth
    are regarded as nothing. ᵖ
He does as he pleases �q
    with the powers of heaven
    and the peoples of the earth.
No one can hold back ʳ his hand ˢ
    or say to him: "What have you done?" ᵗ

³⁶At the same time that my sanity was restored, my honor and splendor were returned to me for the glory of my kingdom. ᵘ My advisers and nobles sought me out, and I was restored to my throne and became even greater than before. ³⁷Now I, Nebuchadnezzar, praise and exalt ᵛ and glorify ʷ the King of heaven, because everything he does is right and all his ways are just. ˣ And those who walk in pride ʸ he is able to humble. ᶻ

THE WRITING ON THE WALL

5 King Belshazzar ᵃ gave a great banquet ᵇ for a thousand of his nobles ᶜ and drank wine with them. ²While Belshazzar was drinking ᵈ his wine, he gave orders to bring in the gold and silver goblets ᵉ that Nebuchadnezzar his father ᵃ had taken from the temple in Jerusalem, so that the king and his nobles, his wives and his concubines ᶠ might drink from them. ᵍ ³So they brought in the gold goblets that had been taken from the temple of God in Jerusalem, and the king and his nobles, his wives and his concubines drank from them. ⁴As they drank the wine, they praised the gods ʰ of gold and silver, of bronze, iron, wood and stone. ⁱ

⁵Suddenly the fingers of a human hand appeared and wrote on the plaster of the wall, near the lampstand in the royal palace. The king watched the hand as it wrote. ⁶His face

---

ᵃ 2 Or *ancestor*; or *predecessor*; also in verses 11, 13 and 18

4:28 ᵉ Nu 23:19
4:30 ᶠ Isa 13:19
ᵍ S Isa 10:13; S 37:24-25; Da 5:20; Hab 1:11; 2:4
4:31 ʰ S 2Sa 22:28; Da 5:20
4:32 ⁱ S Job 9:12
4:33 ʲ S Job 24:8
ᵏ Da 5:20-21
4:34 ˡ S Job 12:20
ᵐ Da 12:7 ⁿ Isa 37:16
ᵒ Ps 145:13;
S Da 2:44; 5:21; 6:26; Lk 1:33
4:35 ᵖ S Isa 40:17
q Dt 21:8; Ps 115:3; S 135:6; Jnh 1:14
ʳ S Isa 14:27
ˢ S Dt 32:39
ᵗ S Job 9:4;
S Isa 14:24; S 45:9; Da 5:21; Ro 9:20
4:36 ᵘ S Pr 22:4; Da 5:18
4:37 ᵛ S Ex 15:2
ʷ S Ps 34:3 ˣ Dt 32:4; Ps 33:4-5 ʸ Ps 18:27; S 119:21 ᶻ S Job 31:4; 40:11-12; S Isa 13:11; Da 5:20,23; Mt 23:12
5:1 ᵃ ver 30; Da 7:1; 8:1 ᵇ S 1Ki 3:15
ᶜ Jer 50:35
5:2 ᵈ S Isa 21:5
ᵉ S 2Ki 24:13;
S 2Ch 36:10;
S Jer 52:19
ᶠ S Est 2:14
ᵍ S Est 1:7; Da 1:2
5:4 ʰ Jdg 16:24
ⁱ S Est 1:10; Ps 135:15-18; Hab 2:19; Rev 9:20

4:28 *All this happened.* But only because Nebuchadnezzar did not follow Daniel's "advice" (v. 27).
4:30 *great Babylon.* Illustrated, e.g., in the city's ramparts, temples and hanging gardens (see note on Isa 13:19; see also map, p. 1449).
4:31 *as the words were on his lips.* See Lk 12:19–20.
4:33 *what had been said ... was fulfilled.* See Pr 11:2 and note; 16:18. *driven away.* Possibly into the palace gardens. His counselors, perhaps led by Daniel (see 2:48–49), could have administered the kingdom efficiently.
4:34 *At the end of that time.* Perhaps as much as seven years (see v. 16 and note). *His dominion ... from generation to generation.* Nebuchadnezzar returns to the grand theme with which he began (see v. 3; see also 6:26; 7:14).
4:35 See Ps 115:3 and note.
4:36 Cf. Job 42:10,12.

4:37 *everything he does is right and ... just.* See notes on Ps 119:121; Eze 18:25. *those who walk in pride he is able to humble.* See Pr 3:34; Jas 4:6,10; 1Pe 5:5–6.
5:1–4 The orgy of revelry and blasphemy on such occasions is mentioned also by the ancient Greek historians Herodotus and Xenophon.
5:1 *King.* Belshazzar (meaning "Bel, protect the king!") was the son and viceroy of Nabonidus (see chart, p. 482). He is called the "son" of Nebuchadnezzar (v. 22), but the Aramaic term could also mean "grandson" or "descendant" or even "successor" (see TNIV text note on v. 22). See also note on v. 10 and TNIV text note on v. 2.
5:2 *gold ... that Nebuchadnezzar ... had taken from the temple.* In the eighth year of his reign (597 B.C.; see 2Ki 24:12–13 and note on 24:12).
5:5 *Suddenly.* See 4:31; see also Pr 29:1; 1Th 5:3 and notes.

5:6 /S Job 4:15
k S Da 4:5
/ S Ps 22:14; Eze 7:17
m S Isa 7:2
5:7 *n* S Ge 41:8
o S Isa 19:3
p Isa 44:25
q Jer 50:35; Da 4:6-7
r S Ge 41:42 *s* Est 10:3
t Da 2:5-6,48
5:8 *u* S Ex 8:18
v S Da 2:10,27; S 4:18
5:9 *w* S Ps 48:5;
S Isa 21:4
5:10 *x* S Ne 2:3;
S Da 3:9
5:11 *y* S Ge 41:38
z ver 14; S Da 1:17
a S Da 2:22
b Da 2:47-48
5:12 *c* S Da 1:7
d S Nu 12:8 *e* ver 14-
16; Da 6:3
f S Eze 28:3
5:13 *g* S Est 2:5-6;
Da 6:13
5:14 *h* S Ge 41:38
/ S Da 2:22
5:15 / Da 4:18
5:16 *k* S Ge 41:15
/ S Ge 41:42
m S Est 5:3; S Da 2:6
5:17 *n* S 2Ki 5:16
5:18 *o* S Jer 28:14
p S Jer 27:7;
S Da 2:37-38; S 4:36
5:19 *q* Da 2:12-13;
S 3:6 *r* S Da 4:22
5:20 *s* Da 4:30
t Jer 43:10 *u* Jer 13:18;
S Da 4:31
v S Job 40:12;
Isa 14:13-15;
Eze 31:10-11; Da 8:8
5:21 *w* S Ge 17:24
x Da 4:16-17,35
5:22 *y* S Ex 10:3
5:23 *z* S Isa 14:13;
S Jer 50:29 *a* Jer 44:9
b Ps 115:4-8;
Hab 2:19; Rev 9:20
c Job 12:10; Ac 17:28
d S Job 31:4;
S Isa 13:11; Jer 10:23;
S 48:26

turned pale[j] and he was so frightened[k] that his legs became weak[l] and his knees were knocking.[m]

[7]The king summoned the enchanters,[n] astrologers[a][o] and diviners.[p] Then he said to these wise[q] men of Babylon, "Whoever reads this writing and tells me what it means will be clothed in purple and have a gold chain placed around his neck,[r] and he will be made the third[s] highest ruler in the kingdom."[t]

[8]Then all the king's wise men[u] came in, but they could not read the writing or tell the king what it meant.[v] [9]So King Belshazzar became even more terrified[w] and his face grew more pale. His nobles were baffled.

[10]The queen,[b] hearing the voices of the king and his nobles, came into the banquet hall. "May the king live forever!"[x] she said. "Don't be alarmed! Don't look so pale! [11]There is a man in your kingdom who has the spirit of the holy gods[y] in him. In the time of your father he was found to have insight and intelligence and wisdom[z] like that of the gods.[a] Your father, King Nebuchadnezzar, appointed him chief of the magicians, enchanters, astrologers and diviners.[b] [12]He did this because Daniel, whom the king called Belteshazzar,[c] was found to have a keen mind and knowledge and understanding, and also the ability to interpret dreams, explain riddles[d] and solve difficult problems.[e] Call for Daniel, and he will tell you what the writing means."[f]

[13]So Daniel was brought before the king, and the king said to him, "Are you Daniel, one of the exiles my father the king brought from Judah?[g] [14]I have heard that the spirit of the gods[h] is in you and that you have insight, intelligence and outstanding wisdom.[i] [15]The wise men and enchanters were brought before me to read this writing and tell me what it means, but they could not explain it.[j] [16]Now I have heard that you are able to give interpretations and to solve difficult problems.[k] If you can read this writing and tell me what it means, you will be clothed in purple and have a gold chain placed around your neck,[l] and you will be made the third highest ruler in the kingdom."[m]

[17]Then Daniel answered the king, "You may keep your gifts for yourself and give your rewards to someone else.[n] Nevertheless, I will read the writing for the king and tell him what it means.

[18]"Your Majesty, the Most High God gave your father Nebuchadnezzar[o] sovereignty and greatness and glory and splendor.[p] [19]Because of the high position he gave him, all the nations and peoples of every language dreaded and feared him. Those the king wanted to put to death, he put to death; those he wanted to spare, he spared; those he wanted to promote, he promoted; and those he wanted to humble, he humbled.[r] [20]But when his heart became arrogant and hardened with pride,[s] he was deposed from his royal throne[t] and stripped[u] of his glory.[v] [21]He was driven away from people and given the mind of an animal; he lived with the wild donkeys and ate grass like the ox; and his body was drenched with the dew of heaven, until he acknowledged that the Most High God is sovereign[w] over the kingdoms on earth and sets over them anyone he wishes.[x]

[22]"But you, Belshazzar, his son,[c] have not humbled[y] yourself, though you knew all this. [23]Instead, you have set yourself up against[z] the Lord of heaven. You had the goblets from his temple brought to you, and you and your nobles, your wives[a] and your concubines drank wine from them. You praised the gods of silver and gold, of bronze, iron, wood and stone, which cannot see or hear or understand.[b] But you did not honor the God who holds in his hand your life[c] and all your ways.[d] [24]Therefore he sent the hand that wrote the inscription.

[25]"This is the inscription that was written:

MENE, MENE, TEKEL, PARSIN

---

a 7 Or *Chaldeans;* also in verse 11   *b* 10 Or *queen mother*   *c* 22 Or *descendant;* or *successor*

5:7 *third highest ruler in the kingdom.* Nabonidus was first, Belshazzar second (see last notation on map, p. 1449).

5:10 *queen.* See TNIV text note. She could have been (1) the wife of Nebuchadnezzar, (2) the daughter of Nebuchadnezzar and wife of Nabonidus or (3) the wife of Nabonidus but not the daughter of Nebuchadnezzar.

5:11 *the time of your father.* Nebuchadnezzar had died in 562 B.C.; the year is now 539.

5:16 *third highest ruler.* See v. 7 and note.

5:17 *keep your gifts for yourself.* See Ge 14:23; 2Ki 5:16 and notes.

5:21 *He was ... given the mind of an animal.* See 4:25 and note. *until he acknowledged.* See note on 4:25. *the Most High God is*

sovereign over the kingdoms on earth. See Introduction: Theological Theme.

5:22–23 Three charges were brought against Belshazzar: (1) He sinned through disobedience and pride, not through ignorance (v. 22); (2) he defied God by desecrating the sacred vessels (v. 23a); and (3) he praised idols and so did not honor God (v. 23b).

5:23 The stark contrast between the false gods of the nations and the one true God is a pervasive theme in the prophets (see, e.g., 3:29 and note; Isa 41:5–10; 44:6–23; Jer 10:1–16; Eze 8–9; Hos 13:1–8; Hab 2:18–20; see also Ps 115:2–8; 135:15–18).

5:24 *he sent the hand.* Daniel waits until the last moment before informing the king that God himself is the source of the inscription.

²⁶"This is what these words mean:

> *Mene*^a: God has numbered the days^e of your reign and brought it to an end.^f
> ²⁷*Tekel*^b: You have been weighed on the scales^g and found wanting.^h
> ²⁸*Peres*^c: Your kingdom is divided and given to the Medesⁱ and Persians."^j

²⁹Then at Belshazzar's command, Daniel was clothed in purple, a gold chain was placed around his neck,^k and he was proclaimed the third highest ruler in the kingdom.^l
³⁰That very night Belshazzar,^m kingⁿ of the Babylonians,^d was slain,^o ^{*31}and Darius^p the Mede^q took over the kingdom, at the age of sixty-two.

DANIEL IN THE DEN OF LIONS

6 [*]It pleased Darius^r to appoint 120 satraps^s to rule throughout the kingdom, ²with three administrators over them, one of whom was Daniel.^t The satraps were made accountable^u to them so that the king might not suffer loss. ³Now Daniel so distinguished himself among the administrators and the satraps by his exceptional qualities that the king planned to set him over the whole kingdom.^v ⁴At this, the administrators and the satraps tried to find grounds for charges^w against Daniel in his conduct of government affairs, but they were unable to do so. They could find no corruption in him, because he was trustworthy and neither corrupt nor negligent. ⁵Finally these men said, "We will never find any basis for charges against this man Daniel unless it has something to do with the law of his God."^x

⁶So these administrators and satraps went as a group to the king and said: "May King Darius live forever!^y ⁷The royal administrators, prefects, satraps, advisers and governors^z have all agreed that the king should issue an edict and enforce the decree that anyone who prays to any god or human being during the next thirty days, except to you, Your Majesty, shall be thrown into the lions' den.^a ⁸Now, Your Majesty, issue the decree and put it in writing so that it cannot be altered—in accordance with the law of the Medes and Persians, which cannot be repealed."^b ⁹So King Darius put the decree in writing.

¹⁰Now when Daniel learned that the decree had been published, he went home to his upstairs room where the windows opened toward^c Jerusalem. Three times a day he got down on his knees^d and prayed, giving thanks to his God, just as he had done before.^e ¹¹Then these men went as a group and found Daniel praying and asking God for help.^f ¹²So they went to the king and spoke to him about his royal decree: "Did you not publish a decree that during the next thirty days anyone who prays to any god or human being except to you, Your Majesty, would be thrown into the lions' den?"

The king answered, "The decree stands—in accordance with the law of the Medes and Persians, which cannot be repealed."^g

¹³Then they said to the king, "Daniel, who is one of the exiles from Judah,^h pays no attentionⁱ to you, Your Majesty, or to the decree you put in writing. He still prays three times a day." ¹⁴When the king heard this, he was greatly distressed;^j he was determined to rescue Daniel and made every effort until sundown to save him.

¹⁵Then the men went as a group to King Darius and said to him, "Remember, Your Maj-

---

^a 26 *Mene* can mean *numbered* or *mina* (a unit of money).   ^b 27 *Tekel* can mean *weighed* or *shekel*.
^c 28 *Peres* (the singular of *Parsin*) can mean *divided* or *Persia* or *a half mina* or *a half shekel*.
^d 30 Or *Chaldeans*
[*] 5:31 is numbered 6:1 in Aramaic texts.   [*] 6:1-28 is numbered 6:2-29 in Aramaic texts.

5:26–28 See TNIV text notes. Three weights (mina, shekel and half mina/shekel) may be intended, symbolizing three rulers, (respectively): (1) Nebuchadnezzar, (2) either Evil-Merodach (see 2Ki 25:27 and note) or Nabonidus, and (3) Belshazzar.

A **5:27** *weighed on the scales.* Measured in the light of God's standards (see Job 31:6 and note; Ps 62:9).
5:28 *divided…Persians.* Daniel employs a telling wordplay (see TNIV text note). *Medes and Persians.* The second kingdom of the series of four predicted in ch. 2 (see Introduction: Author, Date and Authenticity; see also chart, p. 1455).
5:29 *gold chain was placed around his neck.* As a symbol of authority (see Ge 41:42 and note).
5:30 *That very night.* See Pr 6:15 and note; Lk 12:20.
B **5:31** *Darius the Mede.* Perhaps another name for Gubaru, referred to in Babylonian inscriptions as the governor that Cyrus put in charge of the newly conquered Babylonian territo-

ries. Or "Darius the Mede" may have been Cyrus's throne name in Babylon (see TNIV text note on 6:28; see also 1Ch 5:26 and note). *took over the kingdom.* In 539 B.C. The "head of gold" (2:38) is now no more, as predicted in 2:39.
6:7 The conspirators lied in stating that "all" the royal administrators supported the proposed decree since they knew that Daniel (totally unaware of the proposal) was the foremost of the three administrators. *lions' den.* A pit with a relatively small opening at the top (see v. 17), making it impossible for a prisoner to escape.
6:8,12 *law of the Medes and Persians, which cannot be repealed.* See v. 15; see also notes on Est 1:19; 8:8.
A **6:10** *toward Jerusalem.* See 2Ch 6:38–39. *Three times a day.* Cf. Ps 55:17. *prayed…just as he had done before.* Not even the threat of death could keep Daniel from honoring his customary times of prayer to "his God."
6:13 *pays no attention to you.* But see vv. 22,24.

*Cross references (right margin):*

5:26 *e* Jer 27:7
f Isa 13:6
5:27 *g* S Job 6:2
h Ps 62:9
5:28 *i* Isa 13:17
j S Jer 27:7; 50:41-43; Da 6:28
5:29 *k* S Ge 41:42
l S Da 2:6
5:30 *m* S ver 1
n Jer 50:35
o S Isa 21:9; S Jer 51:31
5:31 *p* Jer 50:41; Da 6:1; 9:1; 11:1
q S Isa 13:3
6:1 *r* S Da 5:31
s S Est 1:1
6:2 *t* Da 2:48-49
6:3 *v* S Ge 41:41; S Est 10:3; S Da 1:20; 5:12-14
6:4 *w* Jer 20:10
6:5 *x* Ac 24:13-16
6:6 *y* S Ne 2:3
6:7 *z* S Da 3:2
a Ps 59:3; 64:2-6; S Da 3:6
6:8 *b* S Est 1:19
6:10 *c* S 1Ki 8:29
d Ps 95:6 *e* Mt 6:6; Ac 5:29
6:11 *f* 1Ki 8:48-50; Ps 55:17; 1Th 5:17-18
6:12 *g* S Est 1:19;
6:13 *h* S Eze 14:14; Da 2:25 *i* S Est 3:8
6:14 *j* Mk 6:26

6:15 *k* S Est 8:8
6:16 *l* S ver 7
m S Job 5:19;
Ps 37:39-40; S 97:10
6:17 *n* Mt 27:66
6:18 *o* S 2Sa 12:17;
Da 10:3 *p* S Est 6:1
6:20 *q* S Da 3:17
6:21 *r* S Ne 2:3;
Da 3:9
6:22 *s* S Ge 32:1;
S Da 3:28 *t* ver 27;
Ps 91:11-13; Heb 11:33
u Ac 12:11; 2Ti 4:17
6:23 *v* Da 3:27
w S 1Ch 5:20;
S Isa 12:2
6:24 *x* Dt 19:18-19;
Est 7:9-10; Ps 54:5
y Dt 24:16; 2Ki 14:6
z S Isa 38:13
6:25 *a* S Da 3:4
b Da 4:1
6:26 *c* S Ps 5:7
d S Est 8:17; Ps 99:1-3; Da 3:29
e S Jos 2:11; S 3:10
f S Jer 10:10; Da 12:7;
Rev 1:18 *g* S Da 2:44
6:27 *h* Da 3:29
i S Da 4:3 *j* S ver 22
6:28 *k* S 2Ch 36:22;
S Da 1:21 *l* S Da 5:28
7:1 *m* S Da 5:1
n S Eze 40:2
o S Da 1:17 *p* Ps 4:4;
S Da 4:13 *q* S Jer 36:4
7:2 *r* S Eze 37:9;
Da 8:8; 11:4; Rev 7:1
7:3 *s* Rev 13:1
7:4 *t* S 2Ki 24:1;
Ps 7:2; Jer 4:7;
Rev 13:2 *u* S Eze 17:3

esty, that according to the law of the Medes and Persians no decree or edict that the king issues can be changed." *k*

¹⁶So the king gave the order, and they brought Daniel and threw him into the lions' den. *l* The king said to Daniel, "May your God, whom you serve continually, rescue *m* you!"

¹⁷A stone was brought and placed over the mouth of the den, and the king sealed *n* it with his own signet ring and with the rings of his nobles, so that Daniel's situation might not be changed. ¹⁸Then the king returned to his palace and spent the night without eating *o* and without any entertainment being brought to him. And he could not sleep. *p*

¹⁹At the first light of dawn, the king got up and hurried to the lions' den. ²⁰When he came near the den, he called to Daniel in an anguished voice, "Daniel, servant of the living God, has your God, whom you serve continually, been able to rescue you from the lions?" *q*

²¹Daniel answered, "May the king live forever! *r* ²²My God sent his angel, *s* and he shut the mouths of the lions. *t* They have not hurt me, because I was found innocent in his sight. *u* Nor have I ever done any wrong before you, Your Majesty."

²³The king was overjoyed and gave orders to lift Daniel out of the den. And when Daniel was lifted from the den, no wound *v* was found on him, because he had trusted *w* in his God.

²⁴At the king's command, the men who had falsely accused Daniel were brought in and thrown into the lions' den, *x* along with their wives and children. *y* And before they reached the floor of the den, the lions overpowered them and crushed all their bones. *z*

²⁵Then King Darius wrote to all the nations and peoples of every language *a* in all the earth:

"May you prosper greatly! *b*

²⁶I issue a decree that in every part of my kingdom people must fear and reverence *c* the God of Daniel. *d*

"For he is the living God *e*
and he endures forever; *f*
his kingdom will not be destroyed,
his dominion will never end. *g*
²⁷He rescues and he saves; *h*
he performs signs and wonders *i*
in the heavens and on the earth.
He has rescued Daniel
from the power of the lions." *j*

²⁸So Daniel prospered during the reign of Darius and the reign of Cyrus *a* *k* the Persian. *l*

DANIEL'S DREAM OF FOUR BEASTS

7 In the first year of Belshazzar *m* king of Babylon, Daniel had a dream, and visions *n* passed through his mind *o* as he was lying in bed. *p* He wrote *q* down the substance of his dream.

²Daniel said: "In my vision at night I looked, and there before me were the four winds of heaven *r* churning up the great sea. ³Four great beasts, *s* each different from the others, came up out of the sea.

⁴"The first was like a lion, *t* and it had the wings of an eagle. *u* I watched until its wings

a 28 Or *Darius, that is, the reign of Cyrus*

6:16 *serve continually.* See 1Co 15:58 and note.
6:18 *he could not sleep.* See 2:1; Est 6:1 and note.
6:20 *has your God . . . been able to rescue you . . . ?* See 3:17 and note.

6:23 *no wound was found on him.* See 3:27. *he . . . trusted in his God.* That the lions were ravenously hungry (v. 24) was no obstacle to the Lord's rewarding Daniel's faith by saving his life (see 3:28 and note).
6:24 *along with their wives and children.* In accordance with Persian custom (cf. Jos 7:24 and note).
6:28 See TNIV text note.
7:1 *first year of Belshazzar.* Probably 553 B.C. The events of ch. 7 preceded those of ch. 5.
7:2 *the great sea.* The world of nations and peoples (see also vv. 3,17).
7:4–7 The lion with an eagle's wings is a cherub symbolizing

the Neo-Babylonian empire (see Ge 3:24 and note). The rest of v. 4 perhaps reflects the humbling of Nebuchadnezzar, as recorded in ch. 4. The bear (v. 5), "raised up on one of its sides," refers to the superior status of the Persians in the Medo-Persian alliance. The three ribs may represent its three principal conquests: Lydia (546 B.C.), Babylon (539) and Egypt (525). The leopard with four wings (v. 6) represents the speedy conquests of Alexander the Great (334–330), and the four heads correspond to the four main divisions into which his empire fell after his untimely death in 323 (see 8:22): Macedon and Greece (under Antipater and Cassander), Thrace and Asia Minor (under Lysimachus), Syria (under Seleucus I), the Holy Land and Egypt (under Ptolemy I). The fourth beast (v. 7), with its irresistible power surpassing all its predecessors, points to the Roman empire (cf. 11:30 and note; in the Apocrypha, see 2 Esdras 12:11). Its ten horns correspond to the ten toes of 2:41–42 (see note on 2:32–43).

were torn off and it was lifted from the ground so that it stood on two feet like a human being, and a human mind was given to it.

⁵"And there before me was a second beast, which looked like a bear. It was raised up on one of its sides, and it had three ribs in its mouth between its teeth. It was told, 'Get up and eat your fill of flesh!' ᵛ

⁶"After that, I looked, and there before me was another beast, one that looked like a leopard. ʷ And on its back it had four wings like those of a bird. This beast had four heads, and it was given authority to rule.

⁷"After that, in my vision ˣ at night I looked, and there before me was a fourth beast— terrifying and frightening and very powerful. It had large iron ʸ teeth; it crushed and de-voured its victims and trampled ᶻ underfoot whatever was left. ᵃ It was different from all the former beasts, and it had ten horns. ᵇ

⁸"While I was thinking about the horns, there before me was another horn, a little ᶜ one, which came up among them; and three of the first horns were uprooted before it. This horn had eyes like the eyes of a human being ᵈ and a mouth that spoke boastfully. ᵉ

⁹"As I looked,

"thrones were set in place,
  and the Ancient of Days ᶠ took his seat. ᵍ
His clothing was as white as snow; ʰ
  the hair of his head was white like wool. ⁱ
His throne was flaming with fire,
  and its wheels ʲ were all ablaze.

7:5 ᵛDa 2:39
7:6 ʷRev 13:2
7:7 ˣS Eze 40:2
ʸS Da 2:40 ᶻDa 8:10
ᵃDa 8:7 ᵇS Rev 12:3
7:8 ᶜDa 8:9
ᵈRev 9:7 ᵉS Ps 12:3;
Rev 13:5-6
7:9 ᶠver 22
ᵍS 1Ki 22:19;
2Ch 18:18; Mt 19:28;
Rev 4:2; 20:4
ʰS Mt 28:3 ⁱRev 1:14
ʲS Eze 1:15; 10:6

7:7 *iron.* See 2:40–43 and note on 2:32–43. *ten horns.* Indicative of the comprehensiveness of the beast's sphere of authority (see note on 1:12).

7:8 *another horn, a little one.* The antichrist, or a world power

sharing in the characteristics of the antichrist. *mouth that spoke boastfully.* See 11:36; 2Th 2:4 and notes; Rev 13:5–6.

7:9 *Ancient of Days.* God. *hair of his head was white like wool.* See Rev 1:14 and note. *throne…wheels.* See Eze 1:15–21,26–27.

VISIONS IN DANIEL

IDENTIFICATION OF THE FOUR KINGDOMS					CHRONOLOGY OF MAJOR EMPIRES IN DANIEL
Vision in Ch. 2	Vision in Ch. 7	Vision in Ch. 8	IDENTIFICATION	600	626 B.C.
HEAD OF GOLD	LION		BABYLON 2:37–38		**BABYLONIA**
				500	539 B.C.
CHEST AND ARMS OF SILVER	BEAR	RAM	MEDO-PERSIA 8:20	400	**MEDO-PERSIA**
				300	330 B.C.
BELLY AND THIGHS OF BRONZE	LEOPARD	GOAT	GREECE 8:21	200	**GREECE** (Including Ptolemies and Seleucids) (167 B.C. Maccabees and Hasmoneans)
				100	
LEGS OF IRON	TERRIFYING AND FRIGHTENING BEAST		ROME	63 B.C.	63 B.C. **ROME**
FEET OF CLAY AND IRON MIXED				A.D. 70 100	A.D. 70 Fall of Jerusalem

7:10 *k* Ps 50:3; 97:3;
Isa 30:27 *l* S Dt 33:2;
Ps 68:17; Jude 1:14;
Rev 5:11 *m* S Ex 32:32;
S Ps 56:8; Rev 20:11-
15
7:11 *n* Rev 13:5-6
o Rev 19:20
7:13 *p* S Eze 1:5;
S 2:1; Mt 8:20*;
Rev 1:13*; 14:14*
q Isa 13:6; Zep 1:14;
Mal 3:2; 4:1
r S Dt 33:26;
S Rev 1:7
7:14 *s* S Mt 28:18
t Ps 72:11; 102:22
u S Isa 16:5
v S Da 2:44;
Heb 12:28; Rev 11:15
7:15 *w* S Job 4:15;
S Da 4:19
7:16 *x* Da 8:16; 9:22;
Zec 1:9
7:18 *y* S Ps 16:3
z S Ps 49:14
a Isa 60:12-14;
Lk 12:32; Heb 12:28;
Rev 2:26; 20:4
7:20 *b* Rev 17:12
c Rev 13:5-6
7:21 *d* Rev 13:7
7:22 *e* Mk 8:35
7:23 *f* S Da 2:40
7:24 *g* Rev 17:12
7:25 *h* S Isa 37:23;
Da 11:36 *i* Rev 16:6
j Da 2:21; Mk 1:15;
Lk 21:8; Ac 1:6-7
k Da 8:24; 12:7;
S Rev 11:2
7:26 *l* Rev 19:20
7:27 *m* S Isa 14:2
n 1Co 6:2 *o* Ge 14:18
p S 2Sa 7:13;
Ps 145:13; S Da 2:44;
S 4:34; S Lk 1:33;
Rev 11:15; 22:5
q S Ps 22:27; 72:11;
86:9
7:28 *r* S Isa 21:3;
S Da 4:19 *s* S Ps 13:2
t S Job 4:15

^{10}A river of fire ^{k} was flowing,
    coming out from before him. ^{l}
Thousands upon thousands attended him;
    ten thousand times ten thousand stood before him.
The court was seated,
    and the books ^{m} were opened.

^{11}"Then I continued to watch because of the boastful words the horn was speaking. ^{n} I kept looking until the beast was slain and its body destroyed and thrown into the blazing fire. ^{o} ^{12}(The other beasts had been stripped of their authority, but were allowed to live for a period of time.)

^{13}"In my vision at night I looked, and there before me was one like a son of man, $^{a\,p}$ coming ^{q} with the clouds of heaven. ^{r} He approached the Ancient of Days and was led into his presence. ^{14}He was given authority, ^{s} glory and sovereign power; all nations and peoples of every language worshiped him. ^{t} His dominion is an everlasting dominion that will not pass away, and his kingdom ^{u} is one that will never be destroyed. ^{v}

THE INTERPRETATION OF THE DREAM

^{15}"I, Daniel, was troubled in spirit, and the visions that passed through my mind disturbed me. ^{w} ^{16}I approached one of those standing there and asked him the meaning of all this.

"So he told me and gave me the interpretation ^{x} of these things: ^{17}'The four great beasts are four kings that will rise from the earth. ^{18}But the holy people ^{y} of the Most High will receive the kingdom ^{z} and will possess it forever—yes, for ever and ever.' ^{a}

^{19}"Then I wanted to know the meaning of the fourth beast, which was different from all the others and most terrifying, with its iron teeth and bronze claws—the beast that crushed and devoured its victims and trampled underfoot whatever was left. ^{20}I also wanted to know about the ten horns ^{b} on its head and about the other horn that came up, before which three of them fell—the horn that looked more imposing than the others and that had eyes and a mouth that spoke boastfully. ^{c} ^{21}As I watched, this horn was waging war against the holy people and defeating them, ^{d} ^{22}until the Ancient of Days came and pronounced judgment in favor of the holy people of the Most High, and the time came when they possessed the kingdom. ^{e}

^{23}"He gave me this explanation: 'The fourth beast is a fourth kingdom that will appear on earth. It will be different from all the other kingdoms and will devour the whole earth, trampling it down and crushing it. ^{f} ^{24}The ten horns ^{g} are ten kings who will come from this kingdom. After them another king will arise, different from the earlier ones; he will subdue three kings. ^{25}He will speak against the Most High ^{h} and oppress his holy people ^{i} and try to change the set times ^{j} and the laws. The holy people will be delivered into his hands for a time, times and half a time. $^{b\,k}$

^{26}"'But the court will sit, and his power will be taken away and completely destroyed ^{l} forever. ^{27}Then the sovereignty, power and greatness of all the kingdoms ^{m} under heaven will be handed over to the holy people ^{n} of the Most High. ^{o} His kingdom will be an everlasting ^{p} kingdom, and all rulers will worship ^{q} and obey him.'

^{28}"This is the end of the matter. I, Daniel, was deeply troubled ^{r} by my thoughts, ^{s} and my face turned pale, ^{t} but I kept the matter to myself."

---

^{a} 13 The Aramaic phrase *bar enash* means *human being*. The phrase *son of man* is retained as a form of address here because of its traditional associations. ^{b} 25 Or *for a year, two years and half a year*

7:10 *Thousands...ten thousand.* See 1Sa 18:7 and note. *court was seated...books were opened.* John echoes the language of this judgment scene in Rev 20:12.

🅰 **7:13** *like a son of man.* See Mk 8:31 and note; Rev 1:13. This is the first reference to the Messiah as the Son of Man, a title that Jesus applied to himself. He will be enthroned as ruler over the whole earth (previously misruled by the four kingdoms that oppose God's kingdom), and his kingdom "will never be destroyed" (v. 14), whether on earth or in heaven. *coming with the clouds of heaven.* See Mk 14:62 and note; Rev 1:7.

7:16 *one of those standing there.* An angel.

7:17 *four kings.* See 2:38–40 and note on 2:32–43. *the earth.* The world of nations and peoples—referred to as "the (great) sea" in vv. 2–3.

🅰 **7:18** *holy people.* Exalted privileges will be enjoyed by Christ's followers in the Messianic kingdom (see Mt 19:28–29; see also Lk 22:29–30; Rev 1:6; 20:2–6 and notes). *will receive the kingdom.* See vv. 22,27 and note.

7:24 *ten kings.* All the political powers (see note on 1:12; see also Rev 17:12–14) that will arise out of the fourth kingdom—not necessarily simultaneously (but see 2:44 and note). *three kings.* Some of the ten. Three often signified a small, indefinite number (see Ex 3:18 and note).

7:25 *He.* See v. 8 and note. *a time, times and half a time.* See TNIV text note.

🅰 **7:27** *handed over to the holy people.* For their benefit. God and the Messiah will rule, as the last sentence in the verse makes clear (see v. 14 and note on v. 13; see also Rev 19–22).

DANIEL'S VISION OF A RAM AND A GOAT

8 In the third year of King Belshazzar's[u] reign, I, Daniel, had a vision,[v] after the one that had already appeared to me. [2]In my vision I saw myself in the citadel of Susa[w] in the province of Elam;[x] in the vision I was beside the Ulai Canal. [3]I looked up,[y] and there before me was a ram[z] with two horns, standing beside the canal, and the horns were long. One of the horns was longer than the other but grew up later. [4]I watched the ram as it charged toward the west and the north and the south. No animal could stand against it, and none could rescue from its power.[a] It did as it pleased[b] and became great.

[5]As I was thinking about this, suddenly a goat with a prominent horn between its eyes came from the west, crossing the whole earth without touching the ground. [6]It came toward the two-horned ram I had seen standing beside the canal and charged at it in great rage. [7]I saw it attack the ram furiously, striking the ram and shattering its two horns. The ram was powerless to stand against it; the goat knocked it to the ground and trampled on it,[c] and none could rescue the ram from its power.[d] [8]The goat became very great, but at the height of its power the large horn was broken off,[e] and in its place four prominent horns grew up toward the four winds of heaven.[f]

[9]Out of one of them came another horn, which started small[g] but grew in power to the south and to the east and toward the Beautiful Land.[h] [10]It grew until it reached[i] the host of the heavens, and it threw some of the starry host down to the earth[j] and trampled[k] on them. [11]It set itself up to be as great as the commander[l] of the army of the Lord;[m] it took away the daily sacrifice[n] from the Lord, and his sanctuary was thrown down.[o] [12]Because of rebellion, the Lord's people[a] and the daily sacrifice were given over to it. It prospered in everything it did, and truth was thrown to the ground.[p]

[13]Then I heard a holy one[q] speaking, and another holy one said to him, "How long will it take for the vision to be fulfilled[r]—the vision concerning the daily sacrifice, the rebellion that causes desolation, the surrender of the sanctuary and the trampling underfoot[s] of the Lord's people?"

[14]He said to me, "It will take 2,300 evenings and mornings; then the sanctuary will be reconsecrated."[t]

THE INTERPRETATION OF THE VISION

[15]While I, Daniel, was watching the vision[u] and trying to understand it, there before me stood one who looked like a man.[v] [16]And I heard a man's voice from the Ulai[w] calling, "Gabriel,[x] tell this man the meaning of the vision."[y]

[17]As he came near the place where I was standing, I was terrified and fell prostrate.[z] "Son of man,"[b] he said to me, "understand that the vision concerns the time of the end."[a]

[18]While he was speaking to me, I was in a deep sleep, with my face to the ground.[b] Then he touched me and raised me to my feet.[c]

---

[a] 12 Or *rebellion, the armies*   [b] 17 The Hebrew phrase *ben adam* means *human being*. The phrase *son of man* is retained as a form of address here because of its traditional associations.

8:1 [u] S Da 5:1
[v] S Da 1:17
8:2 [w] S Ezr 4:9;
S Est 2:8 • S Ge 10:22
8:3 [y] Da 10:5
[z] Rev 13:11
8:4 [a] Isa 41:3
[b] Da 11:3,16
8:7 [c] S Da 7:7
[d] Da 11:11,16
8:8 [e] 2Ch 26:16-21;
S Da 5:20 • S Da 7:2;
Rev 7:1
8:9 [f] Da 7:8
[h] S Eze 20:6; Da 11:16
8:10 [i] S Isa 14:13
[j] Rev 8:10; 12:4
[k] S Da 7:7
8:11 [l] ver 25
[m] Da 11:36-37
[n] Eze 46:13-14
[o] Da 11:31; 12:11
8:12 [p] S Isa 48:1
8:13 [q] S Dt 33:2;
S Da 4:23 • [r] Da 12:6
[s] S Isa 28:18;
S Lk 21:24; Rev 11:2
8:14 [t] Da 12:11-12
8:15 [u] ver 1
[v] S Eze 2:1; Da 10:16-18
8:16 [w] ver 2
[x] Da 9:21; S Lk 1:19
[y] S Da 7:16
8:17 [z] Eze 1:28;
44:4; S Da 2:46;
Rev 1:17 • [a] ver 19;
Hab 2:3
8:18 [b] Da 10:9
[c] S Eze 2:2; Da 10:16-18; Zec 4:1

8:1—12:13 These chapters are written in Hebrew (see note on 2:4).

8:1 *third year.* About 551 B.C. The events of ch. 8 preceded those of ch. 5. *after the one that had already appeared to me.* Two years earlier (see 7:1 and note).

8:2 *citadel of Susa...Elam.* See notes on Ezr 4:9; Est 1:2.

8:3 The ram represents the Medo-Persian empire (v. 20). The longer of his two horns reflects the predominant position of Persia (see 7:5 and note on 7:4–7).

8:5 The rapidly charging goat is Greece, and the "prominent horn" is Alexander the Great, "the first king" (v. 21; see chart, p. 1455).

8:7 *shattering its two horns.* Greece crushes Medo-Persia.

8:8 *large horn was broken off.* The death of Alexander the Great at the height of his power (323 B.C.). *four prominent horns.* Equivalent to the "four heads" of 7:6 (see note on 7:4–7).

8:9–12 "Another horn" (v. 9) emerges not from the ten horns belonging to the fourth kingdom (as in 7:8) but rather from one of the four horns belonging to the third kingdom. The horn that "started small" is Antiochus IV Epiphanes, who during the last few years of his reign (168–164 B.C.) made a determined effort to destroy the Jewish faith. He in turn served as a type of the even more ruthless beast of the last days (the

antichrist), who is also referred to in 7:8 as a "little" horn. Antiochus was to extend his power over Israel, "the Beautiful Land" (v. 9; see Jer 3:19 and note), and defeat the godly believers there (referred to as "the host of the heavens," v. 10; see also v. 12), many of whom died for their faith. Then he set himself up to be the equal of "the commander of the army of the Lord" (v. 11) and ordered the daily sacrifices to end. Eventually the army of Judas Maccabeus recaptured Jerusalem and rededicated the temple (v. 14) to the Lord (December, 165)—the origin of the Festival of Hanukkah (see Jn 10:22 and note), still celebrated by Jews today (in the Apocrypha see 1 Maccabees 1–4; see also bottom of chart, pp. 180–181).

8:13 *a holy one.* An angel.

8:14 There were two daily sacrifices for the continual burnt offering (see 9:21; Ex 29:38–39 and note), representing the atonement required for Israel as a whole. The "2,300 evenings and mornings" probably refer to the number of sacrifices consecutively offered on 1,150 days, the interval between the desecration of the Lord's altar by Antiochus Epiphanes and its reconsecration on Kislev 25, 165 B.C.

8:16 *Gabriel.* An angel (see Lk 1:19 and note).

8:17 *Son of man.* Not to be confused with the "one like a son of man" in 7:13 (see note there; see also note on Eze 2:1).

8:19 *d* S Isa 10:25
e S Ps 102:13
f Hab 2:3
8:20 *g* S Eze 27:10
8:21 *h* Da 10:20
i Da 11:3
8:24 *j* S Da 7:25;
11:36
8:25 *k* Da 11:23
l Da 11:36
m S Da 2:34; 11:21
8:26 *n* Da 10:1
o S Isa 8:16; S 29:11;
Rev 10:4; 22:10
p Da 10:14
8:27 *q* Da 10:8
r S Da 2:48
s S Isa 21:3; S Da 4:19
9:1 *t* S Da 5:31
u S Ezr 4:6
9:2 *v* S 2Ch 36:21;
Jer 29:10; Zec 1:12;
7:5
9:3 *w* S 2Ch 20:3
x S 2Sa 13:19;
S Ne 1:4; Jer 29:12;
Da 10:12; Jnh 3:6
9:4 *y* S 1Ki 8:30
z S Dt 7:21 *a* Dt 7:9;
S 1Ki 8:23
9:5 *b* S Jer 8:14
c Ps 106:6 *d* Isa 53:6
e ver 11; La 1:20;
S 3:42
9:6 *f* S 2Ki 18:12
g S 2Ch 36:16;
S Jer 44:5; Jas 5:10;
Rev 10:7 *h* S 2Ch 29:6
9:7 *i* S Ezr 9:15;
S Isa 42:6 *j* Ezr 9:7;
Ps 44:15 *k* Dt 4:27;
Am 9:9 *l* S Dt 7:3
m S Jer 3:25; S 24:9;
S Eze 39:23-24
9:8 *n* S Ne 9:33;
S Jer 14:20;
S Eze 16:63
9:9 *o* S Ex 34:7;
S 2Sa 24:14; Jer 42:12
p S Ne 9:17; La 1:47
9:10 *q* 2Ki 17:13-15;
S 18:12; Rev 10:7
9:11 *r* S Jer 2:29
s 2Ki 22:16
t S Dt 11:26; S 13:15;
S 28:15 *u* 2Ki 17:23
v Isa 1:4-6; Jer 8:5-10
9:12 *w* S Isa 44:26;
Zec 1:6 *x* S Jer 44:23
y Jer 30:7 *z* Jer 44:2-6;
Eze 5:9; Da 12:1;
Joel 2:2; Zec 7:12
9:13 *a* S Dt 4:29;
S Isa 31:1 *b* S Isa 9:13;
Jer 2:30

[19]He said: "I am going to tell you what will happen later in the time of wrath, *d* because the vision concerns the appointed time *e* of the end. *f* [20]The two-horned ram that you saw represents the kings of Media and Persia. *g* [21]The shaggy goat is the king of Greece, *h* and the large horn between its eyes is the first king. *i* [22]The four horns that replaced the one that was broken off represent four kingdoms that will emerge from his nation but will not have the same power.

[23]"In the latter part of their reign, when rebels have become completely wicked, a fierce-looking king, a master of intrigue, will arise. [24]He will become very strong, but not by his own power. He will cause astounding devastation and will succeed in whatever he does. He will destroy the mighty warriors, the holy people. *j* [25]He will cause deceit *k* to prosper, and he will consider himself superior. When they feel secure, he will destroy many and take his stand against the Prince of princes. *l* Yet he will be destroyed, but not by human power. *m*

[26]"The vision of the evenings and mornings that has been given you is true, *n* but seal *o* up the vision, for it concerns the distant future." *p*

[27]I, Daniel, was worn out. I lay exhausted *q* for several days. Then I got up and went about the king's business. *r* I was appalled *s* by the vision; it was beyond understanding.

DANIEL'S PRAYER

9 In the first year of Darius *t* son of Xerxes *b u* (a Mede by descent), who was made ruler over the Babylonian *c* kingdom— [2]in the first year of his reign, I, Daniel, understood from the Scriptures, according to the word of the LORD given to Jeremiah the prophet, that the desolation of Jerusalem would last seventy *v* years. [3]So I turned to the Lord God and pleaded with him in prayer and petition, in fasting, *w* and in sackcloth and ashes. *x*

[4]I prayed to the LORD my God and confessed: *y*

"Lord, the great and awesome God, *z* who keeps his covenant of love *a* with those who love him and keep his commandments, [5]we have sinned *b* and done wrong. *c* We have been wicked and have rebelled; we have turned away *d* from your commands and laws. *e* [6]We have not listened *f* to your servants the prophets, *g* who spoke in your name to our kings, our princes and our ancestors, *h* and to all the people of the land.

[7]"Lord, you are righteous, *i* but this day we are covered with shame*j*—the people of Judah and Jerusalem and all Israel, both near and far, in all the countries where you have scattered *k* us because of our unfaithfulness *l* to you. *m* [8]We and our kings, our princes and our ancestors are covered with shame, LORD, because we have sinned against you. *n* [9]The Lord our God is merciful and forgiving, *o* even though we have rebelled against him; *p* [10]we have not obeyed the LORD our God or kept the laws he gave us through his servants the prophets. *q* [11]All Israel has transgressed *r* your law *s* and turned away, refusing to obey you.

"Therefore the curses *t* and sworn judgments *u* written in the Law of Moses, the servant of God, have been poured out on us, because we have sinned *v* against you. [12]You have fulfilled *w* the words spoken against us and against our rulers by bringing on us great disaster. *x* Under the whole heaven nothing has ever been done like *y* what has been done to Jerusalem. *z* [13]Just as it is written in the Law of Moses, all this disaster has come on us, yet we have not sought the favor of the LORD *a* our God by turning from our sins and giving attention to your truth. *b* [14]The LORD did not hesi-

---

a 19 Or *because the end will be at the appointed time*   *b* 1 Hebrew *Ahasuerus*   *c* 1 Or *Chaldean*

8:21 See v. 5 and note.
8:22 See v. 8 and note.
C 8:23–25 A description of Antiochus IV and his rise to power by intrigue and deceit (he was not the rightful successor to the Seleucid throne).
C 8:25 *consider himself superior.* Antiochus IV called himself Epiphanes ("God manifest"). *Prince of princes.* God. *destroyed, but not by human power.* Antiochus died in 164 B.C. at Tabae in Persia through illness or accident; God "destroyed" him.
8:26 *vision of the evenings and mornings.* See v. 14 and note.
9:1 *first year.* 539–538 B.C. *Darius . . . a Mede.* See 5:31 and note. *Xerxes.* See TNIV text note; not the later Xerxes of the book of Esther.
9:2 *Jeremiah . . . seventy years.* See note on Jer 25:11–12.

A 9:3–19 Daniel's prayer contains expressions of humility (v. 3), worship (v. 4), confession (vv. 5–15) and petition (vv. 16–19). See similar prayers in Ezr 9:5–15; Ne 9:5–37 (see note there).
9:3 *sackcloth and ashes.* See notes on Ge 37:34; Rev 11:3.
9:4 *who keeps his covenant of love.* See Dt 7:9,12 and note. *who love him and keep his commandments.* See Ne 1:5; cf. Ex 20:6 and note.
9:6 *your servants the prophets.* See v. 10; see also Jer 7:25; Zec 1:6 and notes.
9:7 *scattered us because of our unfaithfulness.* See 2Ki 17:7–23 and note; 2Ch 36:15–20.
9:11 *curses . . . written in the Law.* See Lev 26:33; Dt 28:64 and note.

tate to bring the disaster [c] on us, for the LORD our God is righteous in everything he does; [d] yet we have not obeyed him. [e]

[15] "Now, Lord our God, who brought your people out of Egypt with a mighty hand [f] and who made for yourself a name [g] that endures to this day, we have sinned, we have done wrong. [16] Lord, in keeping with all your righteous acts, [h] turn away [i] your anger and your wrath [j] from Jerusalem, [k] your city, your holy hill. [l] Our sins and the iniquities of our ancestors have made Jerusalem and your people an object of scorn [m] to all those around us.

[17] "Now, our God, hear the prayers and petitions of your servant. For your sake, Lord, look with favor [n] on your desolate sanctuary. [18] Give ear, [o] our God, and hear; [p] open your eyes and see [q] the desolation of the city that bears your Name. [r] We do not make requests of you because we are righteous, but because of your great mercy. [s] [19] Lord, listen! Lord, forgive! [t] Lord, hear and act! For your sake, [u] my God, do not delay, because your city and your people bear your Name."

THE SEVENTY "SEVENS"

[20] While I was speaking and praying, confessing [v] my sin and the sin of my people Israel and making my request to the LORD my God for his holy hill [w]— [21] while I was still in prayer, Gabriel, [x] the man I had seen in the earlier vision, came to me in swift flight about the time of the evening sacrifice. [y] [22] He instructed me and said to me, "Daniel, I have now come to give you insight and understanding. [z] [23] As soon as you began to pray, [a] a word went out, which I have come to tell you, for you are highly esteemed. [b] Therefore, consider the word and understand the vision: [c]

[24] "Seventy 'sevens' [a] are decreed for your people and your holy city [d] to finish [b] transgression, to put an end to sin, to atone [e] for wickedness, to bring in everlasting righteousness, [f] to seal up vision and prophecy and to anoint the Most Holy Place. [c]

[25] "Know and understand this: From the time the word goes out to restore and rebuild [g] Jerusalem until the Anointed One, [d] [h] the ruler, [i] comes, there will be seven 'sevens,' and sixty-two 'sevens.' It will be rebuilt with streets and a trench, but in times of trouble. [j] [26] After the sixty-two 'sevens,' the Anointed One will be put to death [k] and will have nothing. [e] The people of the ruler who will come will destroy the city and the sanctuary. The end will come like a flood: [l] War will continue until the end, and desolations [m] have been decreed. [n] [27] He will confirm a covenant with many for one 'seven.' [f] In the middle of the 'seven' [f] he will put an end to sacrifice and offering. And at the temple [g] he will set up an abomination that causes desolation, until the end that is decreed [o] is poured out on him." [h] [i]

[a] 24 Or 'weeks'; also in verses 25 and 26   [b] 24 Or restrain   [c] 24 Or the most holy One   [d] 25 Or an anointed one; also in verse 26   [e] 26 Or death and will have no one; or death, but not for himself   [f] 27 Or 'week'   [g] 27 Septuagint and Theodotion; Hebrew wing   [h] 27 Or it   [i] 27 Or And one who causes desolation will come upon the wing of the abominable ⌊temple⌋, until the end that is decreed is poured out on the desolated ⌊city⌋

9:14 [c] S Jer 18:8;
S 44:27 [d] S Ge 18:25;
S 2Ch 12:6; S Jer 12:1
[e] S Ne 9:33;
S Jer 32:23; S 40:3
9:15 [f] S Ex 3:20;
S Jer 32:21
[g] S Ne 9:10
9:16 [h] S Jdg 5:11;
Ps 31:1 [i] S Isa 5:25
[j] S Ps 85:3 [k] Jer 32:32
[l] S Ex 15:17; S Ps 48:1
[m] S Ps 39:8;
S Eze 5:14
9:17 [n] Nu 6:24-26;
Ps 80:19
9:18 [o] S Ps 5:1
[p] Ps 116:1 [q] Ps 80:14
[r] S Dt 28:10;
S Isa 37:17; Jer 7:10-
12; 25:29 [s] Lk 18:13
9:19 [t] Ps 44:23
[u] S 1Sa 12:22
9:20 [v] S Ezr 10:1
[w] S ver 3; Ps 145:18;
S Isa 58:9
9:21 [x] S Da 8:16;
S Lk 1:19 [y] S Ex 29:39
9:22 [z] S Da 7:16;
10:14; Am 3:7
9:23 [a] S Isa 65:24
[b] Da 10:19; Lk 1:28
[c] Da 10:11-12;
Mt 24:15
9:24 [d] S Isa 1:26
[e] S Isa 53:10
[f] S Isa 56:1; Heb 9:12
9:25 [g] S Ezr 4:24;
S Isa 1:17;
Jn 4:25 [i] S 1Sa 13:14
[j] S Ezr 3:3
9:26 [k] S Isa 53:8;
Mt 16:21 [l] Isa 28:2;
Da 11:10; Na 1:8
[m] S Ps 46:8 [n] Isa 61:1;
S Eze 4:5-6;
Hag 2:23; Zec 4:14
9:27 [o] S Isa 10:22

9:14 the LORD our God is righteous. See Ps 4:1; Jer 12:1 and notes.

⚑ **9:18** city that bears your Name. Jerusalem (1Ki 11:36; cf. Ps 132:13 and note; see Jer 25:29 and note). Name. See Dt 12:5 and note. because of your great mercy. God answers prayer because of his grace, not because of our works.

9:20 While I was speaking. See Isa 65:24. holy hill. Zion (see Ps 2:6 and note).

9:21 Gabriel. See 8:16 and note. evening sacrifice. See note on Ps 141:2.

9:24 sevens. Probably seven-year periods of time, making a total of 490 years, but some take the numbers as symbolic. Of the six purposes mentioned (all to be fulfilled through the Messiah), some believe that the last three were not achieved by the crucifixion and resurrection of Christ but await his further action: the establishment of everlasting righteousness (on earth), the complete fulfillment of vision and prophecy and the anointing of the "Most Holy Place" (see TNIV text note).

⚑ **9:25–27** The time between the decree authorizing the rebuilding of Jerusalem (v. 25) and the coming of the Messiah ("the Anointed One") was to be 69 (7 plus 62) "sevens," or 483 years (see note on Ezr 7:11). The "seven 'sevens'" may refer to the period of the complete restoration of Jerusalem (partially narrated in Ezra and Nehemiah) and the "sixty-two 'sevens'" to the period between that restoration and the Messiah's coming

to Israel. The final (70th) "seven" is not mentioned specifically until v. 27, following the prophecy of the destruction of Jerusalem by "the people of the ruler who will come" (Titus in A.D. 70). Therefore, while many hold that the 70th "seven" was fulfilled during Christ's earthly ministry and the years immediately following, others conclude that there is an indeterminate interval between the 69th and the 70th "seven"—a period of "war" and "desolations" (v. 26). According to this latter opinion, in the 70th "seven" the little horn or beast (the antichrist) of the last days (referred to here as the one who sets up an "abomination that causes desolation" and who is the antitype of the Roman Titus; see Rev 13:1–8 and notes) will establish a covenant for seven years with the Jews (the "many") but will violate the covenant halfway through that period (but see also note on v. 27). The cutting off of the Anointed One (v. 26) refers to the crucifixion of Christ.

⚑ **9:27** He will confirm a covenant ... will put an end to sacrifice. According to some, a reference to the Messiah's ("the Anointed One," v. 26) instituting the new covenant and putting "an end" to the OT sacrificial system; according to others, a reference to the antichrist's ("the [ultimate] ruler who will come," v. 26) making a treaty with the Jews in the future and then disrupting their system of worship. abomination that causes desolation. See note on 11:31.

10:1 *P* S Da 1:21
q S Da 1:7 / Da 8:26
10:2 *s* S Ezr 9:4
10:3 *t* S Da 6:18
10:4 *u* Da 12:5
v S Ge 2:14
10:5 *w* Da 8:3
x S Eze 9:2; Rev 15:6
y Jer 10:9
10:6 *z* S Da 8:20
a Mt 17:2; S 28:3
b Job 41:19; Rev 19:12
c S Eze 1:7; S Rev 1:15
d S Eze 1:24
10:7 *e* 2Ki 6:17-20;
Ac 9:7
10:8 *f* Ge 32:24
g S Job 4:14; Da 8:27
h S Job 4:15 / Hab 3:16
10:9 *i* Da 8:18;
Mt 17:6
10:10 *k* Jer 1:9
l Rev 1:17
10:11 *m* S Ge 6:9;
Da 9:23 *n* S Eze 2:1
10:12 *o* S Mt 14:27
p S Lev 16:31;
S Da 9:3 *q* S Isa 65:24
r Da 9:20
10:13 *s* Isa 24:21
t ver 21; Da 12:1;
S Jude 1:9
10:14 *u* S Da 9:22

DANIEL'S VISION OF A MAN

10 In the third year of Cyrus[p] king of Persia, a revelation was given to Daniel (who was called Belteshazzar).[q] Its message was true[r] and it concerned a great war.[a] The understanding of the message came to him in a vision.

²At that time I, Daniel, mourned[s] for three weeks. ³I ate no choice food; no meat or wine touched my lips;[t] and I used no lotions at all until the three weeks were over.

⁴On the twenty-fourth day of the first month, as I was standing on the bank[u] of the great river, the Tigris,[v] ⁵I looked up[w] and there before me was a man dressed in linen,[x] with a belt of fine gold[y] from Uphaz around his waist. ⁶His body was like topaz,[z] his face like lightning,[a] his eyes like flaming torches,[b] his arms and legs like the gleam of burnished bronze,[c] and his voice[d] like the sound of a multitude.

⁷I, Daniel, was the only one who saw the vision; those who were with me did not see it,[e] but such terror overwhelmed them that they fled and hid themselves. ⁸So I was left alone,[f] gazing at this great vision; I had no strength left,[g] my face turned deathly pale[h] and I was helpless.[i] ⁹Then I heard him speaking, and as I listened to him, I fell into a deep sleep, my face to the ground.[j]

¹⁰A hand touched me[k] and set me trembling on my hands and knees.[l] ¹¹He said, "Daniel, you who are highly esteemed,[m] consider carefully the words I am about to speak to you, and stand up,[n] for I have now been sent to you." And when he said this to me, I stood up trembling.

¹²Then he continued, "Do not be afraid,[o] Daniel. Since the first day that you set your mind to gain understanding and to humble[p] yourself before your God, your words[q] were heard, and I have come in response to them.[r] ¹³But the prince[s] of the Persian kingdom resisted me twenty-one days. Then Michael,[t] one of the chief princes, came to help me, because I was detained there with the king of Persia. ¹⁴Now I have come to explain[u] to you

---

a 1 Or true and burdensome

10:1 *third year of Cyrus.* 537 B.C. This is the third year after his conquest of Babylonia in 539 (see note on 1:1).
10:3 See 1:8–16 and note on 1:8.
10:5–6 See 7:9; Rev 1:12–16 and notes.
10:7 Cf. Ac 9:7.

10:13 *prince of the Persian kingdom.* Apparently a demon exercising influence over the Persian realm in the interests of Satan (see also v. 20). His resistance was finally overcome by the archangel Michael, "the great prince who protects" the people of God (12:1).

PTOLEMIES AND SELEUCIDS

Ptolemy I Lagi Soter
(323–285 B.C.)

Seleucus I Nicator
(311–280 B.C.)

Ptolemy II Philadelphus
(285–246)

Antiochus I Soter
(280–261)

Ptolemy III Euergetes I
(246–221)

Berenice [m.] ····▶ Antiochus II Theos ◀····· [m.] Laodice
(261–246)

Ptolemy IV Philopator
(221–203)

Seleucus II Callinicus
(246–226)

Antiochus III (the Great)
(223–187)

Seleucus III Ceraunus
(226–223)

Ptolemy V Epiphanes ◀······· [m.] Cleopatra I
(203–181)

Antiochus IV Epiphanes
(175–164)

Seleucus IV Philopator
(187–175)

Ptolemy VI Philometor
(181–146)

Antiochus V Eupator
(163–162)

Demetrius I
(162–150)

what will happen to your people in the future,[v] for the vision concerns a time yet to come.[w]"

[15]While he was saying this to me, I bowed with my face toward the ground and was speechless.[x] [16]Then one who looked like a man[a] touched my lips, and I opened my mouth and began to speak.[y] I said to the one standing before me, "I am overcome with anguish[z] because of the vision, my lord, and I feel very weak. [17]How can I, your servant, talk with you, my lord? My strength is gone and I can hardly breathe."[a]

[18]Again the one who looked like a man touched[b] me and gave me strength.[c] [19]"Do not be afraid, you who are highly esteemed,"[d] he said. "Peace![e] Be strong now; be strong."[f]

When he spoke to me, I was strengthened and said, "Speak, my lord, since you have given me strength."[g]

[20]So he said, "Do you know why I have come to you? Soon I will return to fight against the prince of Persia, and when I go, the prince of Greece[h] will come; [21]but first I will tell you what is written in the Book of Truth.[i] (No one supports me against them except Michael,[j] your prince. [1]And in the first year of Darius[k] the Mede, I took my stand to support and protect him.)

THE KINGS OF THE SOUTH AND THE NORTH

[2]"Now then, I tell you the truth:[l] Three more kings will arise in Persia, and then a fourth, who will be far richer than all the others. When he has gained power by his wealth, he will stir up everyone against the kingdom of Greece.[m] [3]Then a mighty king will arise, who

---

[a] 16 Most manuscripts of the Masoretic Text; one manuscript of the Masoretic Text, Dead Sea Scrolls and Septuagint *Then something that looked like a human hand*

10:14 [v]S Eze 12:27
[w]S Da 2:28; 8:26;
Hab 2:3
10:15 [x]Eze 24:27;
Lk 1:20
10:16 [y]S Isa 6:7;
Jer 1:9; Da 8:15-18
[z]S Isa 21:3
10:17 [a]S Da 4:19
10:18 [b]ver 16
[c]S Da 8:18
10:19 [d]S Da 9:23
[e]Jdg 6:23; S Isa 35:4
[f]Jos 1:9; Isa 6:1-8
10:20 [h]Da 8:21; 11:2
10:21 [i]Da 11:2
[j]S ver 13; S Jude 1:9
11:1 [k]S Da 5:31
11:2 [l]Da 10:21
[m]S Da 10:20

10:14 *what will happen to your people in the future.* See chs. 11–12.

10:16 *touched my lips, and I ... began to speak.* See Isa 6:7; Jer 1:9 and notes.

10:20 *prince of Greece.* See note on v. 13. This spiritual power will also have to be opposed.

10:21 *Book of Truth.* See 12:1; perhaps a reference to God's

book of the destinies of all human beings (see Ex 32:32; Ps 69:28 and notes).

11:1 *Darius the Mede.* See note on 5:31.

11:2 *Three more kings.* Cambyses (530–522 B.C.), Pseudo-Smerdis or Gaumata (522) and Darius I (522–486). *fourth.* Xerxes I (486–465; see note on Est 1:1), who attempted to conquer Greece in 480.

11:3 *mighty king.* Alexander the Great (336–323).

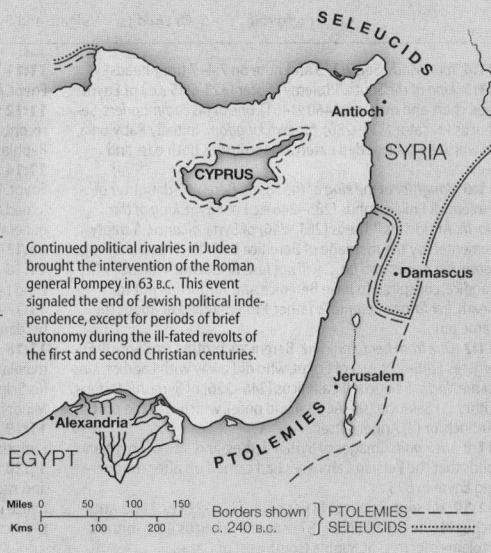

Soon after the death of Alexander the Great in 323 B.C., his generals divided his empire into four parts, two of which—Egypt and Syria—were under the rule of the Ptolemies and Seleucids, respectively. The Holy Land was controlled from Egypt by the Ptolemaic dynasty from 323 to 198 and was subsequently governed by the Seleucids of Syria from 198 to 142.

The Diadochi, as the successors of Alexander were called, struggled bitterly for power over his domain. At first Ptolemy I seized his own satrapy, Egypt and North Africa, which had splendid resources and natural defense capabilities. Seleucus gained Syria and Mesopotamia, and by 301 Lysimachus held Thrace and Asia Minor, while Cassander ruled Macedon. The situation changed again by 277, when only three major Hellenistic kingdoms stabilized in Egypt, in Syria and in Macedonia under the Antigonids (277–168). Each continued until the eventual triumph of Rome.

Da 11 treats the "king of the South" and the "king of the North," describing their conflicts, wars and alliances. Their hostility toward the people of God culminated in the "abomination that causes desolation" (11:31), identified historically with the reign of Antiochus IV Epiphanes (175–164). The Maccabean revolt followed, leading eventually to the founding of the Hasmonean dynasty.

Continued political rivalries in Judea brought the intervention of the Roman general Pompey in 63 B.C. This event signaled the end of Jewish political independence, except for periods of brief autonomy during the ill-fated revolts of the first and second Christian centuries.

SELEUCIDS

Antioch

SYRIA

CYPRUS

Damascus

Jerusalem

Alexandria

PTOLEMIES

EGYPT

| Miles | 0 | 50 | 100 | 150 |
| Kms | 0 | 100 | 200 | |

Borders shown
c. 240 B.C.

PTOLEMIES - - - -
SELEUCIDS ·········

11:3 *n* S Da 8:4,21
11:4 *o* S Da 7:2;
8:22 *p* S Jer 42:10
11:7 *q* ver 6
11:8 *r* Isa 37:19;
S 46:1-2 *s* Jer 43:12
11:10 *t* Isa 8:8;
Jer 46:8; S Da 9:26
11:11 *u* Da 8:7-8
11:15 *v* S Eze 4:2
11:16 *w* S Da 8:4
x S Jos 1:5; S Da 8:7
y S Da 8:9
11:17 *z* S Ps 20:4
11:18 *a* S Isa 66:19;
S Jer 25:22
b Hos 12:14
11:19 *c* S Ps 27:2;
S 46:2 *d* S Ps 37:36;
S Eze 26:21
11:20 *e* Isa 60:17

will rule with great power and do as he pleases. *n* 4After he has arisen, his empire will be broken up and parceled out toward the four winds of heaven. *o* It will not go to his descendants, nor will it have the power he exercised, because his empire will be uprooted *p* and given to others.

5"The king of the South will become strong, but one of his commanders will become even stronger than he and will rule his own kingdom with great power. 6After some years, they will become allies. The daughter of the king of the South will go to the king of the North to make an alliance, but she will not retain her power, and he and his power*a* will not last. In those days she will be betrayed, together with her royal escort and her father*b* and the one who supported her.

7"One from her family line will arise to take her place. He will attack the forces of the king of the North *q* and enter his fortress; he will fight against them and be victorious. 8He will also seize their gods, *r* their metal images and their valuable articles of silver and gold and carry them off to Egypt. *s* For some years he will leave the king of the North alone. 9Then the king of the North will invade the realm of the king of the South but will retreat to his own country. 10His sons will prepare for war and assemble a great army, which will sweep on like an irresistible flood *t* and carry the battle as far as his fortress.

11"Then the king of the South will march out in a rage and fight against the king of the North, who will raise a large army, but it will be defeated. *u* 12When the army is carried off, the king of the South will be filled with pride and will slaughter many thousands, yet he will not remain triumphant. 13For the king of the North will muster another army, larger than the first; and after several years, he will advance with a huge army fully equipped.

14"In those times many will rise against the king of the South. Those who are violent among your own people will rebel in fulfillment of the vision, but without success. 15Then the king of the North will come and build up siege ramps *v* and will capture a fortified city. The forces of the South will be powerless to resist; even their best troops will not have the strength to stand. 16The invader will do as he pleases; *w* no one will be able to stand against him. *x* He will establish himself in the Beautiful Land and will have the power to destroy it. *y* 17He will determine to come with the might of his entire kingdom and will make an alliance with the king of the South. And he will give him a daughter in marriage in order to overthrow the kingdom, but his plans*c* will not succeed*z* or help him. 18Then he will turn his attention to the coastlands*a* and will take many of them, but a commander will put an end to his insolence and will turn his insolence back on him. *b* 19After this, he will turn back toward the fortresses of his own country but will stumble and fall, *c* to be seen no more. *d*

20"His successor will send out a tax collector to maintain the royal splendor. *e* In a few years, however, he will be destroyed, yet not in anger or in battle.

a 6 Or *offspring*   *b* 6 Or *child* (see Vulgate and Syriac)   *c* 17 Or *but she*

11:4 *four winds.* See 7:2–3 and note on 7:4–7 (four heads).
11:5 *king of the South.* Ptolemy I Soter (323–285 B.C.) of Egypt (see chart and map, pp. 1460–1461). *one of his commanders.* Seleucus I Nicator (311–280). *his own kingdom.* Initially Babylonia, to which he then added extensive territories both east and west.
11:6 *daughter of the king of the South.* Berenice, daughter of Ptolemy II Philadelphus (285–246 B.C.) of Egypt. *king of the North.* Antiochus II Theos (261–246) of Syria. *alliance.* A treaty cemented by the marriage of Berenice to Antiochus. *she will not retain her power, and he … will not last.* Antiochus's former wife, Laodice, conspired to have Berenice and Antiochus put to death. *her father.* Berenice's father, Ptolemy, died at about the same time.
11:7 *One from her family line.* Berenice's brother, Ptolemy III Euergetes (246–221 B.C.) of Egypt, who did away with Laodice. *king of the North.* Seleucus II Callinicus (246–226) of Syria. *his fortress.* Either (1) Seleucia (see Ac 13:4 and note), which was the port of Antioch, or (2) Antioch itself.
11:8 *their gods.* Images of Syrian deities, and also of Egyptian gods that the Persian Cambyses had carried off after conquering Egypt in 525 B.C.
11:10 *His sons.* Seleucus III Ceraunus (226–223 B.C.) and Antiochus III (the Great) (223–187), sons of Seleucus II. *his fortress.* Ptolemy's fortress at Raphia (southwest of Gaza).

11:11 *king of the South.* Ptolemy IV Philopator (221–203 B.C.) of Egypt. *king of the North.* Antiochus III. *defeated.* At Raphia in 217.
11:12 *slaughter many thousands.* The Greek historian Polybius records that Antiochus lost nearly 10,000 infantrymen at Raphia.
11:14 *king of the South.* Ptolemy V Epiphanes (203–181 B.C.) of Egypt. *Those who are violent among your own people.* Jews who joined the forces of Antiochus. *without success.* The Ptolemaic general Scopas crushed the rebellion in 200.
11:15 *fortified city.* The Mediterranean port of Sidon.
11:16 *The invader.* Antiochus, who was in control of the Holy Land by 197 B.C. *Beautiful Land.* See note on 8:9–12.
11:17 *he will give him a daughter in marriage.* Antiochus gave his daughter Cleopatra I in marriage to Ptolemy V in 194 B.C.
11:18 *he.* Antiochus. *coastlands.* Asia Minor and perhaps also mainland Greece. *commander.* The Roman consul Lucius Cornelius Scipio Asiaticus, who defeated Antiochus at Magnesia in Asia Minor in 190 B.C.
11:19 *stumble and fall.* Antiochus died in 187 B.C. while attempting to plunder a temple in the province of Elymais.
11:20 *His successor.* Seleucus IV Philopator (187–175 B.C.), son and successor of Antiochus the Great. *tax collector.* Seleucus's finance minister, Heliodorus. *he will be destroyed.* Seleucus was the victim of a conspiracy engineered by Heliodorus.

21"He will be succeeded by a contemptible [f] person who has not been given the honor of royalty. [g] He will invade the kingdom when its people feel secure, and he will seize it through intrigue. 22Then an overwhelming army will be swept away [h] before him; both it and a prince of the covenant will be destroyed. [i] 23After coming to an agreement with him, he will act deceitfully, [j] and with only a few people he will rise to power. 24When the richest provinces feel secure, he will invade them and will achieve what neither his fathers nor his forefathers did. He will distribute plunder, loot and wealth among his followers. [k] He will plot the overthrow of fortresses—but only for a time.

25"With a large army he will stir up his strength and courage against the king of the South. The king of the South will wage war with a large and very powerful army, but he will not be able to stand because of the plots devised against him. 26Those who eat from the king's provisions will try to destroy him; his army will be swept away, and many will fall in battle. 27The two kings, with their hearts bent on evil, [l] will sit at the same table and lie [m] to each other, but to no avail, because an end will still come at the appointed time. [n] 28The king of the North will return to his own country with great wealth, but his heart will be set against the holy covenant. He will take action against it and then return to his own country.

29"At the appointed time he will invade the South again, but this time the outcome will be different from what it was before. 30Ships of the western coastlands [o] will oppose him, and he will lose heart. [p] Then he will turn back and vent his fury [q] against the holy covenant. He will return and show favor to those who forsake the holy covenant.

31"His armed forces will rise up to desecrate the temple fortress and will abolish the daily sacrifice. [r] Then they will set up the abomination that causes desolation. [s] 32With flattery he will corrupt those who have violated the covenant, but the people who know their God will firmly resist [t] him.

33"Those who are wise will instruct [u] many, though for a time they will fall by the sword or be burned or captured or plundered. [v] 34When they fall, they will receive a little help, and many who are not sincere [w] will join them. 35Some of the wise will stumble, so that they may be refined, [x] purified and made spotless until the time of the end, for it will still come at the appointed time.

THE KING WHO EXALTS HIMSELF

36"The king will do as he pleases. He will exalt and magnify himself [y] above every god and will say unheard-of things [z] against the God of gods. [a] He will be successful until the time of wrath [b] is completed, for what has been determined must take place. [c] 37He will show no regard for the gods of his ancestors or for the one desired by women, nor will he regard any god, but will exalt himself above them all. 38Instead of them, he will honor a god of fortresses; a god unknown to his ancestors he will honor with gold and silver, with precious stones and costly gifts. 39He will attack the mightiest fortresses with the help of a foreign god and will greatly honor those who acknowledge him. He will make them rulers over many people and will distribute the land at a price. [a]

[a] 39 Or land for a reward

11:21 *contemptible person.* Seleucus's younger brother, Antiochus IV Epiphanes (175–164 B.C.). *not been given the honor of royalty.* Antiochus seized power while the rightful heir to the throne, the son of Seleucus (later to become Demetrius I), was still very young. *kingdom.* Syro-Palestine.
11:22 *prince of the covenant.* Either the high priest Onias III, who was murdered in 170 B.C., or, if the Hebrew for this phrase is translated "confederate prince," Ptolemy VI Philometor (181–146) of Egypt.
11:23 *he.* Antiochus.
11:24 *richest provinces.* Either of the Holy Land or of Egypt. *fortresses.* In Egypt.
11:25 *king of the South.* Ptolemy VI.
11:26 *his army.* Ptolemy's.
11:27 *two kings.* Antiochus and Ptolemy, who was living in Antiochus's custody.
11:28 *against the holy covenant.* In 169 B.C. Antiochus plundered the temple in Jerusalem, set up a garrison there and massacred many Jews in the city.
11:30 *Ships of the western coastlands.* Roman vessels under the command of Popilius Laenas. *those who forsake the holy covenant.* Apostate Jews (see also v. 32).

11:31 *abomination that causes desolation.* See 9:27; 12:11; the altar to the pagan god Zeus Olympius, set up in 168 B.C. by Antiochus Epiphanes and prefiguring a similar abomination that Jesus predicted would be erected (see Mt 24:15; Lk 21:20 and notes).
11:33 *Those who are wise.* The godly leaders of the Jewish resistance movement, also called the Hasidim. *fall by the sword or be burned or captured or plundered.* See Heb 11:36–38.
11:34 *a little help.* The early successes of the guerrilla uprising (168 B.C.) that originated in Modein, 17 miles northwest of Jerusalem, under the leadership of Mattathias and his son Judas Maccabeus. In December, 165, the altar of the temple was rededicated.
11:35 *time of the end.* See v. 40; 12:4,9. Daniel concludes his predictions about Antiochus Epiphanes and begins to prophesy concerning the more distant future.
11:36 From here to the end of ch. 11 the antichrist (see notes on 7:8; 9:27) is in view. The details of this section do not fit what is known of Antiochus Epiphanes. See 2Th 2:3–4 and notes; cf. Rev 13:5–8.
11:37 *the one desired by women.* Usually interpreted as either Tammuz (see Eze 8:14 and note) or the Messiah (see Hag 2:7 and note).

Cross reference column:

11:21 [f] Da 4:17
[g] S Da 8:25
11:22 [h] S Isa 28:15
[i] Da 8:10-11
11:23 [j] Da 8:25
11:24 [k] Ne 9:25
11:27 [l] Ps 64:6
[m] Ps 12:2; Jer 9:5
[n] Hab 2:3
11:30 [o] S Ge 10:4
[p] S 1Sa 17:32
[q] S Job 15:13
11:31 [r] Hos 3:4
[s] S Jer 19:4; Da 8:11-13; S 9:27; Mt 24:15*; Mk 13:14*
11:32 [t] Mic 5:7-9
11:33 [u] Da 12:3; Mal 2:7 v Mt 24:9; Jn 16:2; Heb 11:32-38
11:34 [w] Mt 7:15; Ro 16:18
11:35 [x] S Job 28:1; S Ps 78:38; S Isa 48:10; Da 12:10; Zec 13:9; Jn 15:2
11:36 [y] Jude 1:6
[z] Rev 13:5-6
[a] S Dt 10:17; S Isa 14:13-14; S Da 7:25; 8:11-12,25; 2Th 2:4 [b] S Isa 10:25; 26:20 [c] Eze 35:13; S Da 8:24

11:40 *d* S Isa 21:1
e Isa 5:28 *f* S Isa 8:7;
S Eze 38:4
11:41 *g* S Eze 20:6;
Mal 3:12 *h* S Isa 11:14
i S Jer 48:47
11:43 *j* S Eze 30:4
k 2Ch 12:3; Na 3:9
11:45 *l* S Isa 2:2,4;
Da 8:9
12:1 *m* S Da 10:13;
Jude 1:9 *n* S Da 9:12;
S Mt 24:21; Mk 13:19;
Rev 16:18
o S Ex 32:32;
S Ps 56:8; S Jer 17:13;
S Lk 10:20 *p* Jer 30:7
12:2 *q* Jn 11:24
r S Isa 26:19;
Mt 25:46
12:3 *s* S Da 11:33
t Mt 13:43; Jn 5:35;
Php 2:15 *u* S Isa 6:7
v S Pr 4:18; 1Co 15:42
12:4 *w* S Isa 8:16
x ver 9,13; Rev 22:10
y Jer 5:1
12:5 *z* Da 10:4
12:6 *a* S Eze 9:2
b Da 8:13
12:7 *c* S Ge 14:22
d S Da 6:26; Rev 10:5-
6 *e* S Da 7:25;
S Rev 11:2 *f* S Da 8:24
g Lk 21:24; Rev 10:7
12:9 *h* S Isa 29:11
i S ver 4
12:10 *j* S Da 1:25;
S Da 11:35
k S Isa 32:7; Rev 22:11
l Hos 14:9
12:11 *m* S Ex 29:38
n S Da 8:11; S 9:27;
Mt 24:15*; Mk 13:14*
o Rev 11:2
12:12 *p* S Isa 30:18
q S Eze 4:5-6;
Da 8:14
12:13 *r* S ver 4
s Isa 57:2 *t* Ps 16:5;
Rev 14:13 *u* Mt 10:22;
Jas 1:12

40"At the time of the end the king of the South *d* will engage him in battle, and the king of the North will storm *e* out against him with chariots and cavalry and a great fleet of ships. He will invade many countries and sweep through them like a flood. *f* 41He will also invade the Beautiful Land. *g* Many countries will fall, but Edom, *h* Moab *i* and the leaders of Ammon will be delivered from his hand. 42He will extend his power over many countries; Egypt will not escape. 43He will gain control of the treasures of gold and silver and all the riches of Egypt, *j* with the Libyans *k* and Cushites *a* in submission. 44But reports from the east and the north will alarm him, and he will set out in a great rage to destroy and annihilate many. 45He will pitch his royal tents between the seas at *b* the beautiful holy mountain. *l* Yet he will come to his end, and no one will help him.

THE END TIMES

12 "At that time Michael, *m* the great prince who protects your people, will arise. There will be a time of distress *n* such as has not happened from the beginning of nations until then. But at that time your people—everyone whose name is found written in the book *o*—will be delivered. *p* 2Multitudes who sleep in the dust of the earth will awake: *q* some to everlasting life, others to shame and everlasting contempt. *r* 3Those who are wise *c* *s* will shine *t* like the brightness of the heavens, and those who lead many to righteousness, *u* like the stars for ever and ever. *v* 4But you, Daniel, close up and seal *w* the words of the scroll until the time of the end. *x* Many will go here and there *y* to increase knowledge."

5Then I, Daniel, looked, and there before me stood two others, one on this bank of the river and one on the opposite bank. *z* 6One of them said to the man clothed in linen, *a* who was above the waters of the river, "How long will it be before these astonishing things are fulfilled?" *b*

7The man clothed in linen, who was above the waters of the river, lifted his right hand *c* and his left hand toward heaven, and I heard him swear by him who lives forever, *d* saying, "It will be for a time, times and half a time. *d* *e* When the power of the holy people *f* has been finally broken, all these things will be completed. *g*"

8I heard, but I did not understand. So I asked, "My lord, what will the outcome of all this be?"

9He replied, "Go your way, Daniel, because the words are closed up and sealed *h* until the time of the end. *i* 10Many will be purified, made spotless and refined, *j* but the wicked will continue to be wicked. *k* None of the wicked will understand, but those who are wise will understand. *l*

11"From the time that the daily sacrifice *m* is abolished and the abomination that causes desolation *n* is set up, there will be 1,290 days. *o* 12Blessed is the one who waits *p* for and reaches the end of the 1,335 days. *q*

13"As for you, go your way till the end. *r* You will rest, *s* and then at the end of the days you will rise to receive your allotted inheritance. *t* *u*"

---

a 43 That is, people from the upper Nile region   *b* 45 Or *the sea and*   *c* 3 Or *who impart wisdom*   *d* 7 Or *a year, two years and half a year*

11:40–45 Conflicts to be waged between the antichrist and his political enemies. He will meet his end "at the beautiful holy mountain" (v. 45), Jerusalem's temple mount, perhaps in connection with the battle of Armageddon (Rev 16:13–16).

11:41 *Beautiful Land.* See note on 8:9–12.

12:1 *Michael.* See note on 10:13. *time of distress.* See Jer 30:7; Mt 24:21 and notes; cf. Rev 16:18. *book.* See 10:21; Ps 9:5; 51:1; 69:28 and notes.

12:2 *Multitudes who sleep in the dust of the earth will awake.* They will rise from the dead (see Isa 26:19 and note). *some to everlasting life, others to shame.* The first clear reference to a resurrection of both the righteous and the wicked. See Jn 5:24–29 and notes. *everlasting life.* The phrase occurs only here in the OT.

12:5 *two others.* Two was the minimum number of witnesses to an oath (see v. 7; Dt 17:6 and note; 19:15).

12:7 *time, times and half a time.* See TNIV text note; cf. 7:25.

12:11–12 Apparently representing either (1) further calculations relating to the persecutions of Antiochus Epiphanes (see 8:14; 11:28 and notes) or (2) further end-time calculations.

12:11 *daily sacrifice is abolished ... abomination that causes desolation is set up.* See 11:31 and note.

12:13 *rest.* Die (see Job 3:17).

In Ecclesiasticus (an Apocryphal book written c. 190 B.C.), Jesus ben Sira spoke of "the twelve prophets" (Ecclesiasticus 49:10) as a unit parallel to Isaiah, Jeremiah and Ezekiel. He thus indicated that these 12 prophecies were at that time thought of as a unit and were probably already written together on one scroll, as is the case in later times. Josephus (*Against Apion,* 1.8.3) also was aware of this grouping. Augustine (*The City of God,* 18.25) called them the "Minor Prophets," referring to the small size of these books by comparison with the major prophetic books and not at all suggesting that they are of minor importance.

In the traditional Jewish canon these works are arranged in what was thought to be their chronological order: (1) the books that came from the period of Assyrian power (Hosea, Joel, Amos, Obadiah, Jonah, Micah), (2) those written about the time of the decline of Assyria (Nahum, Habakkuk, Zephaniah) and (3) those dating from the postexilic era (Haggai, Zechariah, Malachi). On the other hand, their order in the Septuagint (the pre-Christian Greek translation of the OT) is: Hosea, Amos, Micah, Joel, Obadiah, Jonah, Nahum, Habakkuk, Zephaniah, Haggai, Zechariah, Malachi (the order of the first six was probably determined by length, except for Jonah, which is placed last among them because of its different character).

In any event, it appears that within a century after the composition of Malachi the Jews had brought together the 12 shorter prophecies to form a book (scroll) of prophetic writing, which was received as canonical and paralleled the three major prophetic books of Isaiah, Jeremiah and Ezekiel. The great Greek manuscripts Alexandrinus and Vaticanus place the Twelve before the major prophets, but in the traditional Jewish canon and in all modern versions they appear after them.

JERUSALEM DURING THE TIME OF THE PROPHETS

c. 750–586 B.C.

Refugees arrived in Jerusalem about the time of the fall of the northern kingdom (722 B.C.). Settlement spread to the western hill, and a new wall was added for protection. King Hezekiah's engineers carved an underground aqueduct out of solid rock to bring an ample water supply inside the city walls, enabling Jerusalem to survive the siege of Sennacherib in 701.

©1982 Hugh Claycombe

Jerusalem is shown from above and at an angle; therefore wall shapes appear different from those on flat maps. Wall locations have been determined from limited archaeological evidence; houses are artist's concept.

In Ecclesiasticus (an Apocryphal book written c. 190 B.C.), Jesus Ben Sira spoke of "the twelve prophets." (Ecclesiasticus 49:10) as did Ezekiel. He thus indicated that [text faded/obscured]

HOSEA

AUTHOR AND DATE | INTRODUCTION

C Hosea, son of Beeri, prophesied about the middle of the eighth century B.C., his ministry beginning during or shortly after that of Amos. Amos threatened God's judgment on Israel at the hands of an unnamed enemy; Hosea identifies that enemy as Assyria (7:11; 8:9; 10:6; 11:11). Judging from the kings mentioned in 1:1, Hosea must have prophesied for at least 38 years, though almost nothing is known about him from sources outside his book. He was the only one of the writing prophets to come from the northern kingdom (Israel), and his prophecy is primarily directed to that kingdom. But since his prophetic activity is dated by reference to kings of Judah, the book was probably written in Judah after the fall of the northern capital, Samaria (722–721 B.C.)—an idea suggested by references to Judah throughout the book (1:7,11; 4:15; 5:5,10,12–13; 6:4,11; 10:11; 11:12; 12:2). Whether Hosea himself authored the book that preserves his prophecies is not known. The book of Hosea stands first in the division of the Bible called the Book of the Twelve (in the Apocrypha cf. Ecclesiasticus 49:10; see essay, p. 1465) or the Minor Prophets (a name referring to the brevity of these books as compared to Isaiah, Jeremiah and Ezekiel).

BACKGROUND

Hosea lived in the tragic final days of the northern kingdom, during which six kings (following Jeroboam II) reigned within 25 years (2Ki 15:8—17:6). Four (Zechariah, Shallum, Pekahiah, Pekah) were murdered by their successors while in office, and one (Hoshea) was captured in battle; only one (Menahem) was succeeded on the throne by his son. These kings, given to Israel by God "in my anger" and taken away "in my wrath" (13:11), floated away "like a twig on the surface of the waters" (10:7). "Bloodshed" followed "bloodshed" (4:2). Assyria was expanding westward, and Menahem accepted that world power as overlord and paid tribute (2Ki 15:19–20). But shortly afterward, in 733 B.C., Israel was dismembered by Assyria because of the intrigue of Pekah (who had gained Israel's throne by killing Pekahiah, Menahem's son and successor). Only the territories of Ephraim and western Manasseh were left to the king of Israel. Then, because of the disloyalty of Hoshea (Pekah's successor), Samaria was captured and its people exiled in 722–721, bringing the northern kingdom to an end.

THEOLOGICAL THEME AND MESSAGE

C The first part of the book (chs. 1–3) narrates the family life of Hosea as a symbol (similar to the symbolism in the lives of Isaiah, Jeremiah and Ezekiel) to convey the message the prophet had from the Lord for his people. God ordered Hosea to marry a promiscuous woman, Gomer, and their three children were each given a symbolic name representing part of the ominous message. Ch. 2 alternates between Hosea's relation to Gomer and its symbolic representation of God's relation to Israel. The children are told to drive the unfaithful mother out of the house, but it was her reform, not her riddance, that was sought. The prophet was ordered to continue loving her, and he took her back and kept her in isolation for a while (ch. 3). The affair graphically represents the Lord's relation to the Israelites (cf. 2:4,9,18), who had been disloyal to him by worshiping Canaanite deities as the source of their abun-

KEY   **A** APPLICATION FOR LIVING   **B** BACKGROUND NOTES   **C** CHARACTER INFORMATION

dance. Israel was to go through a period of exile (cf. 7:16; 9:3,6,17; 11:5). But the Lord still loved his covenant people and longed to take them back, just as Hosea took back Gomer. This return is described with imagery recalling the exodus from Egypt and settlement in Canaan (cf. 1:11; 2:14–23; 3:5; 11:10–11; 14:4–7). Hosea saw Israel's past experiences with the Lord as the fundamental pattern, or type, of God's future dealings with his people.

B The second part of the book (chs. 4–14) gives the details of Israel's involvement in Canaanite religion, but a systematic outline of the material is difficult. Like other prophetic books, Hosea issued a call to repentance. Israel's alternative to destruction was to forsake her idols and return to the Lord (chs. 6; 14). Information gleaned from materials discovered at Ugarit (dating from the 15th century B.C.; see chart, p. xxiv) enables us to know more clearly the religious practices against which Hosea protested.

Hosea saw the failure to acknowledge God (4:1,6; 8:2–3; 13:4) as Israel's basic problem. God's relation to Israel was that of love (2:19; 4:1; 6:6; 10:12; 12:6). The intimacy of the covenant relationship between God and Israel, illustrated in the first part of the book by the husband-wife relationship, is later amplified by the father-child relationship (11:1–4). Disloyalty to God was spiritual adultery (4:13–14; 5:4; 9:1; cf. Jer 3; see note on Ex 34:15). Israel had turned to Baal worship and had sacrificed at the pagan high places, which included associating with the sacred prostitutes at the sanctuaries (4:14) and worshiping the calf images at Samaria (8:5; 10:5–6; 13:2). There was also international intrigue (5:13; 7:8–11) and materialism. Yet despite God's condemnation and the harshness of language with which the unavoidable judgment was announced, the major purpose of the book is to proclaim God's compassion and covenant love that cannot—finally—let Israel go.

SPECIAL PROBLEMS

The book of Hosea has at least two perplexing problems. The first concerns the nature of the story told in chs. 1–3 and the character of Gomer. While some interpreters have thought the story to be merely an allegory of the relation between God and Israel, others claim, more plausibly, that it is to be taken literally. Among the latter, some insist that Gomer was faithful at first and later became unfaithful, others that she was unfaithful even before the marriage.

The second problem of the book is the relation of ch. 3 to ch. 1. Despite the fact that no children are mentioned in ch. 3, some interpreters claim that the two chapters are different accounts of the same episode. The traditional interpretation, however, is more likely, namely, that ch. 3 is a sequel to ch. 1—i.e., after Gomer proved unfaithful, Hosea was instructed to take her back.

OUTLINE

1

The word of the LORD that came[a] to Hosea son of Beeri during the reigns of Uzziah,[b] Jotham,[c] Ahaz[d] and Hezekiah,[e] kings of Judah,[f] and during the reign of Jeroboam[g] son of Jehoash[a] king of Israel:[h]

HOSEA'S WIFE AND CHILDREN

²When the LORD began to speak through Hosea, the LORD said to him, "Go, marry a promiscuous[i] woman and have children with her, for like an adulterous wife this land is guilty of unfaithfulness[j] to the LORD." ³So he married Gomer[k] daughter of Diblaim, and she conceived and bore him a son.

⁴Then the LORD said to Hosea, "Call him Jezreel,[l] because I will soon punish the house of Jehu for the massacre at Jezreel, and I will put an end to the kingdom of Israel. ⁵In that day I will break Israel's bow in the Valley of Jezreel.[m]"

⁶Gomer conceived again and gave birth to a daughter. Then the LORD said to Hosea, "Call her Lo-Ruhamah (which means "not loved"),[o] for I will no longer show love to the house of Israel,[p] that I should at all forgive them. ⁷Yet I will show love to the house of Judah; and I will save them—not by bow,[q] sword or battle, or by horses and horsemen, but by the LORD their God.[r]"

⁸After she had weaned Lo-Ruhamah,[s] Gomer had another son. ⁹Then the LORD said, "Call him Lo-Ammi (which means "not my people"), for you are not my people, and I am not your God.[b][t]

*¹⁰"Yet the Israelites will be like the sand on the seashore, which cannot be measured or counted.[u] In the place where it was said to them, 'You are not my people,' they will be called 'children of the living God.'[v][w] ¹¹The people of Judah and the people of Israel will come together;[x] they will appoint one leader[y] and will come up out of the land,[z] for great will be the day of Jezreel.[a]

2

*"Say of your brothers, 'My people,' and of your sisters, 'My loved one.'[b]

ISRAEL PUNISHED AND RESTORED

² "Rebuke your mother,[c] rebuke her,
for she is not my wife,

---

[a] *1* Hebrew *Joash*, a variant of *Jehoash*   [b] *9* Or *your I* AM
* 1:10-11 is numbered 2:1-2 in Hebrew texts.   * 2:1-23 is numbered 2:3-25 in Hebrew texts.

1:1 *word of the LORD.* A claim of authority paralleling that of Jeremiah (1:2,4), Ezekiel (1:3), Joel (1:1), Jonah (1:1; 3:1), Micah (1:1), Zephaniah (1:1), Haggai (1:1,3; 2:1,10,20), Zechariah (1:1,7; 9:1; 12:1) and Malachi (1:1). *Hosea.* Means "salvation." *Uzziah.* Reigned 792–740 B.C.; also known as Azariah (see 2Ki 14:21 and TNIV text note). *Jotham.* 750–732. *Ahaz.* 735–715. *Hezekiah.* 729–686. Some of the reigns overlapped, the coregency of Ahaz and Hezekiah being the longest (see note on Isa 36:1). *Jeroboam.* Jeroboam II, 793–753. Hosea was a contemporary of Isaiah, Amos and Micah (see the similar first verse in their prophecies).

1:2 *marry a promiscuous woman.* See Introduction: Special Problems. *unfaithfulness.* The one great sin of which the Lord (through Hosea) accuses Israel.

1:3 *Gomer.* Not mentioned outside this book. *him.* The omission of this word in vv. 6,9 may indicate that Hosea was not the father of Gomer's next two children.

1:4 *Jezreel.* Means "God scatters," here used to reinforce the announcement of judgment on the reigning dynasty (see notes on v. 11; 2:22). Jeroboam II was of the dynasty of Jehu (841–814 B.C.), which was established at Jezreel by the overthrow of Ahab's son Joram (see 2Ki 9:14–29; see also 1Ki 19:16–17 and notes). Jehu's dynasty ended with the murder of Zechariah in 753 (2Ki 15:8–10).

1:5 *Israel's bow.* Israel's military power, broken in 725 B.C., though Samaria held out under siege for three years longer (see 2Ki 17:5–6 and notes). *Valley of Jezreel.* Located east of Megiddo, it provides the only major pass through the mountain range that traverses Israel from north to south and was therefore a major battleground in ancient times.

1:6 *Lo-Ruhamah.* The naming represents a reversal of the love (compassion) that God had earlier shown to Israel (see Ex 33:19;

Dt 7:6–8 and note on 7:8) but that later was promised again (see 2:23 and TNIV text note).

1:7 *Yet.* See v. 10 and note. *Judah . . . I will save.* God's people were saved from Assyria by the Lord in 722–721 B.C. and again in 701 (see 2Ki 19:32–36).

1:9 *Lo-Ammi.* The naming represents a break in the covenant relationship between the Lord and Israel (see Ex 6:7; Jer 7:23 and note), which later, however, would be restored (v. 10; 2:1,23; see notes there). The warnings became more severe in moving from the first to the third child.

1:10 Cited in Ro 9:26; 1Pe 2:10 (see note there) and applied to the mission to the Gentiles. *Yet.* The threatened punishment (vv. 4–6,9) would be for only a limited time, and a period of blessing would follow. *sand on the seashore.* See the promise to Abraham and Jacob (Ge 22:17; 32:12; cf. Jer 33:22 and note; Heb 11:12). *children of the living God.* Contrasts with "children of adultery" (2:4; cf. 1:2). *living God.* Contrasts with idols—"which are not God" (Dt 32:17).

1:11 *come together.* Israel and Judah would become one nation again. *out of the land.* Possibly the land of exile (cf. Ex 1:10). Another interpretation is that they would spring up from the ground as plants do. *Jezreel.* Here "God scatters" (see note on v. 4) refers to sowing or planting, indicating a reversal of the meaning of the first child's name (see 2:21–23 and notes).

2:1 *My people . . . My loved one.* The negatives associated with the names of Hosea's children (see notes [*Lo = "not"*] on 1:6,9) are dropped.

2:2 The Lord speaks to Hosea's children, continuing the analogy between Gomer and Israel. *not my wife.* The marriage was broken by unfaithfulness, but reconciliation, not divorce, was sought (cf. vv. 7–15).

**Marginal references:**

1:1 [a]S Jer 1:2
[b]S 2Ki 14:21
[c]S 1Ch 3:12
[d]S 1Ch 3:13
[e]S 1Ch 3:13 [f]Isa 1:1;
Mic 1:1 [g]S 2Ki 13:13
[h]Am 1:1
1:2 [i]S Jer 3:1;
Hos 2:2,5; 3:1
[j]Dt 31:16; Jer 3:14;
Eze 23:3-21; Hos 5:3
1:3 [k]ver 6
1:4 [l]ver 11;
S 1Sa 29:1; 1Ki 18:45;
2Ki 10:1-14; Hos 2:22
1:5 [m]S Jos 15:56;
S 1Sa 29:1; 2Ki 15:29
1:6 [n]ver 3 [o]ver 8;
Hos 2:23 [p]Hos 2:4
1:7 [q]S Ps 44:6
[r]Zec 4:6
1:8 [s]S ver 6
1:9 [t]ver 10;
S Eze 11:19-20;
1Pe 2:10
1:10 [u]S Ge 22:17;
S Jer 33:22 [v]S ver 9;
Hos 2:23; Ro 9:26[w]
[w]S Jos 3:10
1:11 [x]S Isa 11:12,13
[y]Jer 23:5-8; 30:9
[z]S Eze 37:15-28
[a]S ver 4
2:1 [b]ver 23;
1Pe 2:10
2:2 [c]ver 5;
S Isa 50:1; S Hos 1:2;
4:5

2:2 *d* S Isa 1:21;
S Eze 23:45
2:3 *e* S Eze 16:37
f Eze 16:4,22
g Isa 32:13-14
2:4 *h* S Eze 8:18;
Hos 1:6 *i* Hos 5:7
2:5 *j* S Jer 3:6;
S Hos 1:2 *k* Jer 44:17-
18
2:6 *l* S Job 3:23;
S 19:8; S La 3:9
2:7 *m* Hos 5:13
n S Isa 54:5 *o* Jer 2:2;
S 3:1 *p* S Eze 16:8
2:8 *q* S Isa 1:3
r S Nu 18:12
s S Dt 8:18 *t* ver 13;
Eze 16:15-19; Hos 8:4
2:9 *u* Hos 8:7
v Hos 9:2
2:10 *w* Eze 23:10
x Jer 13:26
y S Eze 16:37
2:11 *z* Jer 7:34
a S Isa 24:8
b S Isa 1:14; Jer 16:9;
Hos 3:4; 9:5;
Am 5:21; 8:10
2:12 *c* S Isa 7:23;
S Jer 8:13 *d* S Jer 5:17
e S Jer 3:1 *f* S Isa 5:6
g Hos 5:7; 13:8

and I am not her husband.
Let her remove the adulterous *d* look from her face
and the unfaithfulness from between her breasts.
³ Otherwise I will strip *e* her naked
and make her as bare as on the day she was born; *f*
I will make her like a desert, *g*
turn her into a parched land,
and slay her with thirst.
⁴ I will not show my love to her children, *h*
because they are the children of adultery. *i*
⁵ Their mother has been unfaithful
and has conceived them in disgrace.
She said, 'I will go after my lovers, *j*
who give me my food and my water,
my wool and my linen, my olive oil and my drink.' *k*
⁶ Therefore I will block her path with thornbushes;
I will wall her in so that she cannot find her way. *l*
⁷ She will chase after her lovers but not catch them;
she will look for them but not find them. *m*
Then she will say,
'I will go back to my husband *n* as at first, *o*
for then I was better off *p* than now.'
⁸ She has not acknowledged *q* that I was the one
who gave her the grain, the new wine and oil, *r*
who lavished on her the silver and gold *s*—
which they used for Baal. *t*

⁹ "Therefore I will take away my grain *u* when it ripens,
and my new wine *v* when it is ready.
I will take back my wool and my linen,
intended to cover her nakedness.
¹⁰ So now I will expose *w* her lewdness
before the eyes of her lovers; *x*
no one will take her out of my hands. *y*
¹¹ I will stop *z* all her celebrations: *a*
her yearly festivals, her New Moons,
her Sabbath days—all her appointed festivals. *b*
¹² I will ruin her vines *c* and her fig trees, *d*
which she said were her pay from her lovers; *e*
I will make them a thicket, *f*
and wild animals will devour them. *g*
¹³ I will punish her for the days

2:3 *strip her.* The husband supplied the wife's clothing (see Ex 21:10; Eze 16:10), and here her unfaithfulness was exposed (see Jer 13:26; Eze 16:39). *bare.* As Israel was when the Lord found her in Egypt—in slavery and with nothing (cf. Eze 16:4–8; Na 3:5).
2:4 *children of adultery.* See 1:2 and note. This contrasts with being "children of the living God" (1:10; cf. 11:1).
2:5 *go after.* The wife was chasing other men (see v. 13; Jer 3:2; Eze 16:33–34). *lovers.* See vv. 7,10. The reference is to Canaanite deities (such as Baal), whose worshipers hoped to gain agricultural fertility (see note on Ex 34:15). *who give me my food . . . my drink.* Ugaritic texts attribute crops to rain given by Baal. *wool . . . linen . . . olive oil . . . drink.* The agricultural staples of the Holy Land. Israel does not know the true source of her blessings.
2:6 *block her path . . . wall her in.* Rather than punish Israel with death (cf. Dt 22:21; Eze 16:39–40; 23:47; Na 3:5–7), the Lord would isolate her.
2:7 *look for.* See 5:6,15 ("seek"). *not find.* See 5:6 and note. *go back.* The Hebrew for this expression often means "repent." *my husband.* The Lord.
2:8 *She has not acknowledged.* The Canaanites attributed to Baal the "grain, the new wine and oil" (Dt 7:13; Joel 1:10; Hag 1:11 and notes). *silver and gold.* Used for making idols

(see 8:4; 13:2). *Baal.* The Canaanite god who was believed to control the weather and the fertility of crops, animals and people (see note on Jdg 2:13).
2:9 *take away.* By withholding the fruits of field and flock, the Lord made known the true source of those blessings.
2:10 *expose her lewdness.* The unfaithful wife was exposed to public shame (see La 1:8; Eze 16:37; 23:29). *no one will take her.* Baal had no power.
2:11 *stop . . . celebrations.* In exile these joyous seasons would be only a memory. *yearly festivals.* See Ex 23:14–17; Dt 16:16 and notes. See also chart, pp. 180–181. *New Moons.* See 2Ki 4:23; Isa 1:14; Am 8:5 and notes. *Sabbath.* See Ex 20:8–11.
2:12 *pay from her lovers.* The prostitute's pay (see v. 5; 9:1; Dt 23:18; Eze 16:33; Mic 1:7). Israel attributed her agricultural products to the false gods she worshiped rather than to the Lord (see Dt 11:13–14).
2:13 *days.* Festival days. *Baals.* See v. 17; 11:2. Hosea used the plural here, suggesting the idols at the many local shrines (see Jdg 2:11–13 and notes; Jer 2:23,28 and note; 9:14). *went after.* See note on v. 5. *forgot.* The opposite of "acknowledge" (see note on v. 20) in Hosea (see 13:4–6 and note on 13:6; see also note on 1Sa 12:9).

she burned incense [h] to the Baals; [i]
she decked herself with rings and jewelry, [j]
and went after her lovers, [k]
but me she forgot, [l] "

declares the LORD. [m]

14 "Therefore I am now going to allure her;
I will lead her into the wilderness [n]
and speak tenderly to her.

15 There I will give her back her vineyards,
and will make the Valley of Achor [a] [o] a door of hope.
There she will respond [b] [p] as in the days of her youth, [q]
as in the day she came up out of Egypt. [r]

16 "In that day," declares the LORD,
"you will call me 'my husband'; [s]
you will no longer call me 'my master.' [c]'

17 I will remove the names of the Baals from her lips; [t]
no longer will their names be invoked. [u]

18 In that day I will make a covenant for them
with the beasts of the field, the birds in the sky
and the creatures that move along the ground. [v]
Bow and sword and battle
I will abolish [w] from the land,
so that all may lie down in safety. [x]

19 I will betroth [y] you to me forever;
I will betroth you in [d] righteousness and justice, [z]
in [e] love and compassion. [a]

20 I will betroth you in faithfulness,
and you will acknowledge [b] the LORD. [c]

21 "In that day I will respond,"
declares the LORD—
"I will respond [d] to the skies,
and they will respond to the earth;

22 and the earth will respond to the grain,
the new wine and the olive oil, [e]
and they will respond to Jezreel. [f] [f]

23 I will plant [g] her for myself in the land;
I will show my love to the one I called 'Not my loved one. [g] [h]'

---

[a] 15 *Achor* means *trouble.*   [b] 15 Or *sing*   [c] 16 Hebrew *baal*   [d] 19 Or *with*; also in verse 20
[e] 19 Or *with*   [f] 22 *Jezreel* means *God plants.*   [g] 23 Hebrew *Lo-Ruhamah* (see 1:6)

2:13 [h] Isa 65:7
[i] ver 8; S Jer 7:9;
Hos 11:2 [j] S Eze 16:17;
S 23:40 [k] Hos 4:13
[l] Hos 4:6; 8:14; 13:6
[m] S Jer 44:17;
Hos 13:1
2:14 [n] S Eze 19:13
2:15 [o] S Jos 7:24,26
[p] Ex 15:1-18
[q] S Jer 2:2;
S Eze 16:22
[r] S Eze 28:26;
Hos 12:9
2:16 [s] S Isa 54:5
2:17 [t] Ex 23:13;
Ps 16:4 [u] S Jos 23:7;
Zec 13:2
2:18 [v] S Job 5:22
[w] S Ps 46:9; S Isa 2:4;
Zec 9:10 [x] S Job 5:23;
S Jer 23:6; Eze 34:25
2:19 [y] S Isa 62:4;
2Co 11:2 [z] S Isa 1:27
[a] S Isa 54:8
2:20 [b] Jer 31:34;
Hos 4:1; 6:6; 13:4
[c] S Eze 16:8
2:21 [d] Isa 55:10;
Zec 8:12; Mal 3:10-11
2:22 [e] S Jer 31:12;
Hos 14:7; Joel 2:19
[f] S Eze 36:29-30;
S Hos 1:4
2:23 [g] S Jer 31:27
[h] S Hos 1:6

2:14 *into the wilderness.* For a second betrothal (see vv. 19–20). It refers back to the days of Israel's wilderness wandering, before she was tempted by the Baals in Canaan. *speak tenderly to.* Reassure, encourage, comfort (cf. Ge 34:3; Ru 2:13; Isa 40:2). God continually shows love in the midst of judgment.

2:15 *Valley of Achor.* Near Jericho (see Jos 7:24,26; Isa 65:10). As the prophet reversed the meaning of the names of his children, so also the meaning of Achor (see TNIV text note)—where God first judged his people in the promised land—became a symbol of new opportunity.

2:16–17 *husband…master…Baals.* A play on words. Of the two Hebrew words for husband, one (master) is identical with the name of the god Baal (see TNIV text note on v. 16). There will be such a vigorous reaction against Baal worship that this Hebrew word for "master" will no longer be used of the Lord.

2:18 *make a covenant.* See 6:7; 8:1. Animals, the instruments of destruction in v. 12, as well as birds and insects, would no longer threaten life. Nature and history combine in a picture of peace (see Isa 11:6–9 and note; 65:25). *War* is terminated. *land.* Israel (see 1:2; 4:1,3; 9:3 and note; 10:1). *lie down in safety.* See Jer 33:16; Eze 34:24–28.

2:19–20 Rather than money, these five traits necessary to the covenant relationship make up the bride-price (see Ex 22:16; 1Sa 18:25 and notes).

2:19 *righteousness.* See 10:12; Ps 4:1; Jer 23:6 and notes. *justice.* See Am 5:24 and note. *love.* See 4:1; 6:4; 10:12 and note; 12:6. *compassion.* A reversal of God's threatened withdrawal of compassion (see 1:6 and note). "Lo-Ruhamah" means lit. "not shown compassion" (cf. Ps 51:1; 103:3–14).

2:20 *faithfulness.* Dependability (see Dt 32:4; Ps 88:11). *acknowledge.* The Hebrew for this word can refer to intimate sexual relations (Ge 19:8; Nu 31:17–18, 35 ["slept with"]), but it also refers to active acknowledgment of a covenant partner (see 6:3 and note; 8:2; 13:4).

2:21 *respond.* The woman (Israel) responded to the Lord's overtures (see TNIV text note on v. 15); now God responded to her new behavior. The land also responded by becoming productive (vv. 21–22).

2:22 *Jezreel.* Here used in the sense "God plants" (see TNIV text note and v. 23; see also 1:4,11 and notes). The threats represented by the names of the children are turned into blessings (see 1:10 and note). The basic statement describing the covenant relationship was "I will be your God and you will be my people" (Jer 7:23; see notes on Ex 6:7; Zec 8:8).

2:23 *i* S ver 1;
S Isa 19:25;
S Hos 1:10
j S Jer 29:12;
Ro 9:25*; 1Pe 2:10
3:1 *k* S Hos 1:2
l S 2Sa 6:19
3:4 *m* Hos 13:11
n Da 11:31; S Hos 2:11
o Hos 10:1 *p* S Ex 25:7
q Jdg 17:5-6; 18:14-17;
S La 2:9; Zec 10:2
3:5 *r* S Dt 4:29;
S Isa 9:13; S 10:20;
Hos 5:15; Mic 4:1-2
s S 1Sa 13:14
t S Ps 18:45
u S Dt 4:30;
S Jer 50:4-5;
Hos 11:10
4:1 *v* S Job 10:2;
S Jer 2:9 *w* Joel 1:2,14
x S Pr 24:2
y S Pr 10:21; S Isa 1:3;
Jer 7:28; S Hos 2:20
z S Jer 51:5
4:2 *a* Isa 59:3;
Hos 7:3; 10:4; 11:12
b Hos 5:2; 6:9
c Hos 7:1 *d* S Jer 9:2
e S 2Ki 21:16;
S Isa 1:15; S Eze 22:2,
9; Hos 5:2; 10:13
4:3 *f* S Jer 4:28
g S Isa 15:6; S 33:9
h S Jer 4:25; S 9:10;
S Eze 38:20; Zep 1:3

I will say to those called 'Not my people,'*a* 'You are my people';*i*
and they will say, 'You are my God.'*j* "

HOSEA'S RECONCILIATION WITH HIS WIFE

3 The LORD said to me, "Go, show your love to your wife again, though she is loved
by another and is an adulteress. *k* Love her as the LORD loves the Israelites, though
they turn to other gods and love the sacred raisin cakes.*l*"

²So I bought her for fifteen shekels*b* of silver and about a homer and a lethek*c* of barley. ³Then I told her, "You are to live with me many days; you must not be a prostitute or
be intimate with any man, and I will behave the same way toward you."

⁴For the Israelites will live many days without king or prince,*m* without sacrifice*n* or sacred stones,*o* without ephod*p* or household gods.*q* ⁵Afterward the Israelites will return
and seek*r* the LORD their God and David their king.*s* They will come trembling*t* to the
LORD and to his blessings in the last days.*u*

THE CHARGE AGAINST ISRAEL

4 Hear the word of the LORD, you Israelites,
because the LORD has a charge*v* to bring
against you who live in the land:*w*
"There is no faithfulness,*x* no love,
no acknowledgment*y* of God in the land.*z*
²There is only cursing,*d* lying*a* and murder,*b*
stealing*c* and adultery;*d*
they break all bounds,
and bloodshed follows bloodshed.*e*
³Because of this the land dries up,*f*
and all who live in it waste away;*g*
the beasts of the field, the birds in the sky
and the fish in the sea are swept away.*h*

⁴"But let no one bring a charge,
let no one accuse another,

---

a 23 Hebrew *Lo-Ammi* (see 1:9)   *b 2* That is, about 6 ounces or about 170 grams   *c 2* A homer and a
lethek possibly weighed about 430 pounds or about 195 kilograms.   *d 2* That is, to pronounce a curse on

---

2:23 *my people … my God.* See note on v. 22. *You are my God.* The people respond to God's graciousness. This verse is quoted in part in Ro 9:25; 1Pe 2:10 and applied to Gentiles coming into the church.

3:1 *said to me.* Ch. 3 is narrated in the first person, ch. 1 in the third person. *Go … love … your wife.* Hosea's love for unfaithful Gomer illustrated God's love for unfaithful Israel. God's love for Israel (see 11:1 and note; 14:4) is the basic theme of the book. *other gods.* See Ex 20:3; Dt 31:20. *raisin cakes.* Offered to Baal in thanksgiving for harvest.

3:2 Gomer had evidently become a slave, and Hosea bought her back. *fifteen shekels.* Half the usual price of a slave (see Ex 21:32 and note) or of the redemption value of a woman's vow (Lev 27:4). *lethek.* See TNIV text note. It appears that half her price was paid in money (silver) and half in produce (barley)—for a total value of 30 shekels.

3:3–5 A picture of exile and return.

3:3 *live with.* Suggests a period of isolation (see 2:6 and note), comparable to Israel's exile. *many days.* Not forever. There would be an "afterward" (v. 5), a future (see Jer 29:11).

3:4 *king.* See 1:4; 5:1; 8:4,10; 10:15; 13:10–11. *prince.* See 7:3,5; 8:4; 13:10. *without sacrifice.* See 6:6; 8:11,13. *sacred stones.* See 10:1–2; 1Ki 14:23 and note; 2Ki 17:10; Mic 5:13. *ephod.* Here an image associated with idols (see Jdg 8:27; 17:5 and notes). *household gods.* See Ge 31:19,30,34 and note on 31:19.

3:5 *return.* A basic word in Hosea's vocabulary (see 2:7 ["go back"]; 5:4; 6:1; 7:10; 11:5; 12:6; 14:1–2). *seek.* Israel's repentance is envisioned (see 5:15 and note)—the reverse of her present stubborn rebellion (7:10). *LORD their God.* See 12:9; 13:4; Jer 50:4. *David their king.* The Messianic king from the dynasty of David (see Jer 30:9; Eze 34:24 and note). After the death

of Solomon, Israel (the northern kingdom) had abandoned the Davidic kings. *his blessings.* The vineyards and olive groves that had been taken away (see 2:12) and all of God's gifts (cf. Jer 31:12–14). *last days.* The Hebrew for this phrase occurs 13 times in the OT, sometimes simply meaning the future ("days to come," Ge 49:1), but most of the time, as no doubt here, referring to the Messianic age ("afterward," Joel 2:28; cf. Ac 2:17; Heb 1:2).

4:1—14:9 Deals with Israel's involvement in Canaanite religion, her moral sins and her international intrigues.

4:1 *Hear the word.* See Jer 2:4 and note. *charge.* As the Lord's spokesman, Hosea brought charges against unfaithful, covenant-breaking Israel (cf. v. 4; 12:2; Isa 3:13; Jer 2:9; Mic 6:2). *faithfulness.* Loyalty (see 2:20 and note) to the covenant Lord (Jos 24:14) and right dealing with others (cf. Pr 3:3). *love.* See 2:19; 10:12. *acknowledgment of God.* See 2:20; 6:3 and notes.

4:2 *cursing … adultery.* The sins detailed (paralleled in Jer 7:9) transgress several of the Ten Commandments (see Ex 20:13–16 and notes on 20:1–2). *bloodshed.* Includes (1) murder (see 6:8–9); (2) the assassinations following the death of Jeroboam II, when three kings reigned in one year (2Ki 15:10–14); and (3) human sacrifice (Ps 106:38; Eze 16:20–21; 23:37). Where God is not acknowledged (v. 1), moral uprightness disappears.

4:3 *land dries up.* God's judgment on human sin affects all living things in the world (see, e.g., Isa 24:3–6; Jer 4:23–28). *waste away.* See Isa 19:8; Jer 14:2; 15:9; Joel 1:10.

4:4–9 An indictment against the priests, whose duty it was to be guardians of God's law and to furnish religious instruction (see Lev 10:11; Dt 31:9–13; 33:10; 2Ch 17:8–9; Ezr 7:6,10; Jer 18:18; Eze 7:26 and note; Zep 3:4; Hag 2:11; Mal 2:7–9). Hosea warned the priests not to lodge charges against

for your people are like those
  who bring charges against a priest. *i*
[5] You stumble *j* day and night,
  and the prophets stumble with you.
So I will destroy your mother *k*—
[6]   my people are destroyed from lack of knowledge. *l*

"Because you have rejected knowledge,
  I also reject you as my priests;
because you have ignored the law *m* of your God,
  I also will ignore your children.
[7] The more the priests increased,
  the more they sinned against me;
they exchanged their glorious God *a n* for something disgraceful. *o*
[8] They feed on the sins of my people
  and relish their wickedness. *p*
[9] And it will be: Like people, like priests. *q*
  I will punish both of them for their ways
  and repay them for their deeds. *r*

[10] "They will eat but not have enough; *s*
  they will engage in prostitution *t* but not increase,
because they have deserted *u* the LORD
  [11]to give themselves to prostitution; *v*
old wine *w* and new wine
  take away their understanding. *x*
[12] My people consult a wooden idol *y*
  and are answered by a stick of wood. *z*
A spirit of prostitution *a* leads them astray; *b*
  they are unfaithful *c* to their God.
[13] They sacrifice on the mountaintops
  and burn offerings on the hills,
under oak, *d* poplar and terebinth,
  where the shade is pleasant. *e*
Therefore your daughters turn to prostitution *f*
  and your daughters-in-law to adultery. *g*

[14] "I will not punish your daughters
  when they turn to prostitution,
nor your daughters-in-law
  when they commit adultery,
because the men themselves consort with harlots *h*

---

a 7 Syriac (see also an ancient Hebrew scribal tradition); Masoretic Text *I will exchange their glory*

4:4 *i* Dt 17:12;
S Eze 3:26
4:5 *j* S Eze 7:19;
S 14:7 *k* S Hos 2:2
4:6 *l* S Pr 10:21;
S Isa 1:3; S Hos 2:13;
Mal 2:7-8 *m* Hos 8:1,
12
4:7 *n* Hab 2:16
o Hos 9:11; 10:1,6;
13:6
4:8 *p* S Isa 56:11;
Hos 14:1; Mic 3:11
4:9 *q* S Isa 24:2
r Jer 5:31; Hos 8:13;
9:9,15; 10:10; 12:2
4:10 *s* S Lev 26:26;
S Isa 55:2; Mic 6:14
t S Eze 22:9
u Hos 7:14; 9:17
4:11 *v* ver 14;
Hos 5:4 *w* S Lev 10:9;
S 1Sa 25:36
x S Pr 20:1
4:12 *y* Jer 2:27
z Hab 2:19
a S Nu 15:39
b S Isa 44:20
c S Ps 73:27
4:13 *d* S Isa 1:29
e S Jer 3:6; Hos 10:8;
11:2 *f* Jer 2:20;
Am 7:17 *g* Hos 2:13
4:14 *h* S ver 11

---

the people for bringing God's judgment down on the nation, for they themselves were guilty, and the people could also bring charges against them—as Hosea proceeded to do (see v. 9; cf. Isa 28:7; Jer 2:26; 4:9; 23:11).
4:5 *stumble.* Experience calamity (see 5:5). *prophets.* See Mic 2:6,11; 3:5–7. *your mother.* The nation (see 2:2,5; Isa 50:1).

4:6 *my people.* Israel (see vv. 8,12; 2:1,23; 6:11; 11:7; Mic 6:3,5). *destroyed from lack of knowledge.* Partly because the priests had failed to teach God's word to the people. *rejected knowledge ... reject you.* Punishment in kind. *law of your God.* Israel's source of life (see Dt 30:20 and note), which the priests should have been faithfully promoting.
4:7 *their glorious God.* See Ps 106:20 and note.

4:8 *feed on the sins.* Priests devoured the sacrifices (see 1Sa 2:13–17 and notes), profiting from the continuation of the sin rather than helping to cure it (see 8:13 and note).

4:9 *Like people, like priests.* Without exception, all would be punished for their sins.

4:10 *eat but not have enough.* The punishment (a "futility curse"; see note on Hag 1:6) fit the sin. *prostitution.* See vv. 12,18; 2:4; 6:10; 9:1; Jdg 2:17 and note; Ps 106:39. Instead of giv-

ing themselves to the Lord, they gave themselves to prostitution (vv. 11–15; see notes on Ge 20:9; Ex 34:15; Ps 73:27).
4:11 *old wine.* See 7:5. *new.* See 2:8–9,22; 7:14; 9:2.
4:12 *wooden idol.* An image of a god (see Jer 2:27; 10:8; Hab 2:19). *stick of wood.* Either the wooden idol or a diviner's rod. *spirit of prostitution.* See 5:4. Hebrew idioms often speak of inner tendencies in terms of "spirit."

4:13 *mountaintops.* Places commonly chosen for pagan altars (see 10:8; Dt 12:2; 1Ki 3:2 and note; Jer 2:20; 3:6). Clay tablets from Ugarit (see chart, p. xxiv) tell of fertility rites carried out by the Canaanites at the high places. *oak ... terebinth.* Trees noted for their shade. *turn to prostitution.* Canaanite fertility rites involved sexual activity (v. 14) that led to general erosion of morals (see, e.g., Nu 25:1–18 and notes).

4:14 *not punish.* The men would punish their women for immorality, but God would have no part in their hypocrisy. *harlots.* Common prostitutes (see Ge 34:31; Lev 21:14; Eze 16:31). *shrine prostitutes.* Women of the sanctuaries who served as partners for men in sexual activity that was part of their religious ritual (cf. Ge 38:21 and note; Dt 23:18). *without understanding.* Contrast 14:9.

4:14 *i* S Ge 38:21;
Hos 9:10 / S Pr 10:21
k ver 19
4:15 *l* Hos 9:15;
12:11; Am 4:4; 5:5
m S Jos 7:2; S Hos 5:8
n S Jer 4:2
4:16 *o* S Ex 32:9
p S Jer 31:18
q Isa 5:17; 7:25
4:19 *r* Hos 12:1;
13:15 *s* ver 13-14;
Isa 1:29
5:1 *t* S Job 10:2
u Hos 6:9; 9:8
v S Jer 5:26
5:2 *w* S Hos 4:2
x Hos 9:15
5:3 *y* Am 5:12
z S Eze 23:7;
S Hos 1:2; 6:10
5:4 *a* Hos 7:10
b S Hos 4:11
c S Jer 4:22; S
Hos 4:6

and sacrifice with shrine prostitutes *i*—
a people without understanding *j* will come to ruin! *k*

15 "Though you, Israel, commit adultery,
do not let Judah become guilty.

"Do not go to Gilgal; *l*
do not go up to Beth Aven. *a m*
And do not swear, 'As surely as the LORD lives!' *n*
16 The Israelites are stubborn, *o*
like a stubborn heifer. *p*
How then can the LORD pasture them
like lambs *q* in a meadow?
17 Ephraim is joined to idols;
leave him alone!
18 Even when their drinks are gone,
they continue their prostitution;
their rulers dearly love shameful ways.
19 A whirlwind *r* will sweep them away,
and their sacrifices will bring them shame. *s*

JUDGMENT AGAINST ISRAEL

5 "Hear this, you priests!
Pay attention, you Israelites!
Listen, royal house!
This judgment *t* is against you:
You have been a snare *u* at Mizpah,
a net *v* spread out on Tabor.
2 The rebels are deep in slaughter. *w*
I will discipline all of them. *x*
3 I know all about Ephraim;
Israel is not hidden *y* from me.
Ephraim, you have now turned to prostitution;
Israel is corrupt. *z*

4 "Their deeds do not permit them
to return *a* to their God.
A spirit of prostitution *b* is in their heart;
they do not acknowledge *c* the LORD.

a 15 *Beth Aven* means *house of wickedness* (a derogatory name for Bethel, which means *house of God*).

4:15 *commit adultery.* See notes on Ge 20:9; Ex 34:15. *Judah.* An aside warning (see Introduction: Author and Date). *guilty.* See 10:2; 13:1. *Do not go.* The nation as a whole was addressed. *Gilgal.* A site near Jericho (see 9:15; 12:11; Jos 4:19; 1Sa 11:14 and notes) where the Israelites had established a religious shrine. *Beth Aven.* A sarcastic substitute name for Bethel (see TNIV text note; see also 5:8), site of one of the two major worship centers established by Jeroboam I (see 1Ki 12:29 and note). *As surely as the LORD lives.* A form of solemn oath (see Ge 42:15 and note; Jdg 8:19; Ru 3:13; 1Sa 14:39; 26:10,16; Jer 4:2; 38:16). Though proper in itself—since it invoked the true God (Dt 6:13; 10:20; cf. Jos 23:7)—it was here forbidden because it was being used deceitfully, as though the Israelites were truly honoring the Lord (see Jer 5:2 and note).

4:16 *stubborn.* See Ne 9:29; Zec 7:11. *stubborn heifer.* See Jer 2:20; 31:18 and notes; an apt figure for unruly Israel (Hos 10:11; cf. 11:4).

4:17 *Ephraim.* Israel's largest tribe (see notes on 9:11; 13:1), whose name came to be used of the northern kingdom as a whole. *idols.* The golden calf (see 8:5 and note) and the Baals (see 2:8,13 and notes). *leave him alone.* Nothing could be done to help (see 2Sa 16:11; 2Ki 23:18).

4:19 *A whirlwind will sweep them away.* Lit. "The wind will catch them up with its wings," probably a metaphor from the threshing floor (see 13:3; Ru 1:22; Ps 1:4 and notes) for

the sudden violence that would bring the exile. Since the Hebrew for the words "wind" and "spirit" is the same, there is a possible wordplay with the "spirit of prostitution" (see v. 12 and note). *shame.* By means of their sacrifices they hoped to flourish, but God's punishment for their idolatry would bring them into disgrace among the nations (see 10:6).

5:1 *priests ... Israelites ... royal house.* The three groups addressed were all responsible for maintaining justice, but it miscarried at their hands. *snare ... net.* Devices for catching animals and birds, here used as metaphors for those who by economic and legal schemes took cruel advantage of innocent people (see Job 18:8–10; Ps 140:5; Pr 29:5–6; La 1:13). *Mizpah.* Either (1) Mizpah in Gilead east of the Jordan (Ge 31:43–49) or (2) Mizpah in Benjamin (see 1Sa 7:5 and note). *Tabor.* A mountain at the southeastern edge of the Jezreel Valley. Reference must have been to well-known events that illustrated Israel's corruption.

5:2 *discipline.* A significant word in the prophets for God's corrective action against his people (see Isa 26:16; Jer 2:30; 5:3; 7:28).

5:3 *Ephraim.* See note on 4:17. *prostitution.* See note on 4:10.

5:4 *Their deeds.* See 4:9; 7:2; 9:15; 12:2. Persistent sin can make repentance impossible (see Jer 13:23; Jn 8:34; Ro 6:6,16). *spirit of prostitution.* See 4:12 and note. *not acknowledge the LORD.* See 4:6; Isa 1:3 and note.

⁵Israel's arrogance testifies *d* against them;
  the Israelites, even Ephraim, stumble *e* in their sin;
  Judah also stumbles with them. *f*
⁶When they go with their flocks and herds
    to seek the LORD, *g*
  they will not find him;
  he has withdrawn *h* himself from them.
⁷They are unfaithful *i* to the LORD;
  they give birth to illegitimate *j* children.
  When they celebrate their New Moon feasts, *k*
    he will devour *a l* their fields.

⁸"Sound the trumpet *m* in Gibeah, *n*
    the horn in Ramah. *o*
  Raise the battle cry in Beth Aven *b; p*
    lead on, Benjamin.
⁹Ephraim will be laid waste *q*
    on the day of reckoning. *r*
  Among the tribes of Israel
    I proclaim what is certain. *s*
¹⁰Judah's leaders are like those
    who move boundary stones. *t*
  I will pour out my wrath *u* on them
    like a flood of water.
¹¹Ephraim is oppressed,
    trampled in judgment,
  intent on pursuing idols. *c v*
¹²I am like a moth *w* to Ephraim,
  like rot *x* to the people of Judah.

¹³"When Ephraim *y* saw his sickness,
    and Judah his sores,
  then Ephraim turned to Assyria, *z*
    and sent to the great king for help. *a*
  But he is not able to cure *b* you,
    not able to heal your sores. *c*
¹⁴For I will be like a lion *d* to Ephraim,
    like a great lion to Judah.
  I will tear them to pieces *e* and go away;
    I will carry them off, with no one to rescue them. *f*
¹⁵Then I will return to my lair *g*

---

a 7 Or *Now their New Moon feasts / will devour them and* derogatory name for Bethel, which means *house of God*). *c* 11 The meaning of the Hebrew for this word is uncertain.

b 8 *Beth Aven* means *house of wickedness* (a

5:5 *d* S Isa 3:9;
S Jer 2:19; Hos 7:10
e Eze 14:7 *f* Hos 14:1
5:6 *g* Mic 6:6-7
h S Pr 1:28; Isa 1:15;
Eze 8:6; Mal 1:10
5:7 *i* S Isa 24:16;
Hos 6:7 *j* Hos 2:4
k Isa 1:14 *l* S Hos 2:11-12
5:8 *m* S Nu 10:2;
S Jer 4:21; S Eze 33:3
n Jdg 19:12; Hos 9:9;
10:9 *o* S Hos 10:29
p S Jos 7:2; Hos 4:15;
10:5
5:9 *q* S Isa 7:16
r Isa 37:3; Hos 9:11-17
s Isa 46:10; Zec 1:6
5:10 *t* S Dt 19:14
u S Eze 7:8
5:11 *v* Hos 9:16;
Mic 6:16
5:12 *w* S Job 13:28;
S Isa 51:8
x S Job 18:16
5:13 *y* S Isa 7:16
z Eze 23:5;
Hos 7:11; 8:9; 12:1
a La 5:6; Hos 7:8;
10:6 *b* S Hos 3:7;
Hos 14:3 *c* Hos 2:7
5:14 *d* S Job 10:16;
S Jer 4:7; Am 3:4
e Hos 6:1 *f* S Dt 32:39;
Mic 5:8
5:15 *g* S Isa 18:4

5:5 *arrogance.* Stubborn rebellion against the Lord (see Dt 1:43; 1Sa 15:23; Ne 9:16; Job 35:12; Ps 10:2; Eze 16:56–57). *testifies.* In the case God presented against his people (see 4:1 and note). *stumble.* See 4:5 and note. *Judah.* See Introduction: Author and Date.

5:6 *seek the LORD.* Go to him with prayer and sacrifices (see 3:5 and note; Am 5:4–5). *not find him.* Offering sacrifices in their situation was useless (see 2:7; cf. Isa 1:10–15; Am 5:21–24; Mic 6:6–8). The Lord would be "found" by Israel only when she turned to him with integrity of heart (see v. 15; 3:5; Dt 4:29–31; Jer 29:13).

5:7 *unfaithful.* See 1:2 and note. *New Moon.* Usually a festive occasion (see, e.g., 2:11; 1Sa 20:5 and note; Am 8:5; Col 2:16), but now a time of judgment. Or the meaning may be that one month would be sufficient to accomplish their punishment.

5:8 Some interpreters suggest that the Aramean (Syrian)-Ephraimite (Israelite) war (see 2Ki 16:5–9; Isa 7:1–9 and notes) forms the background of the oracle in chs. 4–5. *trumpet.* Made of a ram's horn, which here sounds the alarm that an army is approaching (see 8:1; Joel 2:1 and note; Am 3:6). *Gibeah.* Two miles

north of Jerusalem. *Ramah.* North of Gibeah. *Beth Aven.* See note on 4:15. *lead on, Benjamin.* Perhaps a Benjamite war cry.

5:9 *laid waste.* See Jer 25:11,38.

5:10 *move boundary stones.* Judah had seized Israelite territory (1Ki 15:16–22; see Dt 19:14 and note; 27:17; Pr 15:25 and note; 23:10; Isa 5:8; Mic 2:2). *my wrath.* See 13:11.

5:12 *moth . . . rot.* Both consume (see Job 13:28).

5:13 *sickness . . . sores.* Metaphors for the national wounds that Israel and Judah had suffered at the hands of their enemies (see Isa 1:5–6; 17:11; Jer 15:18; 30:12–15). *turned to Assyria.* Assyrian records tell of the tribute paid to Tiglath-Pileser III by the Israelite kings Menahem and Hoshea (cf. 2Ki 15:19–20; 17:3). *not able to cure.* The alliances were worthless.

5:14 *lion.* See 13:7; Am 1:2 and note; 3:8. The Lord might use human agents (see Isa 10:5 and note), but he would be responsible for Israel's punishment, from which there was no escape (see Isa 5:29; 42:22; Am 9:1–4).

5:15 *return to my lair.* God threatened to withdraw from Israel until, out of desperation, she truly repented. This idea sets the stage for the prophet's next theme. *lair.* See v. 14.

5:15 *h* S Lev 26:40
i S Nu 21:7; S Ps 24:6;
S Hos 3:5 *j* S Ps 50:15;
S Jer 2:27 *k* Isa 64:9;
S Eze 20:43
6:1 *l* S Isa 10:20;
S 19:22 *m* S Job 16:9;
La 3:11; Hos 5:14
n S Nu 12:13;
S Jer 3:22
o S Dt 32:39;
S Job 5:18;
S Jer 30:17; Hos 14:4
6:2 *p* Ps 30:5;
S 80:18 *q* S Mt 16:21
r S Ps 71:20
6:3 *s* S Job 4:3;
Joel 2:23 *t* Ps 72:6;
Hos 11:10; 12:6
6:4 *u* Hos 11:8
v Hos 7:1; 13:3
6:5 *w* Jer 1:9-10;
5:14; 23:29
x Heb 4:12
6:6 *y* S 1Sa 15:22;
S Isa 1:11; Mt 9:13*;
12:7*; Mk 12:33
z S Jer 4:22;
S Hos 2:20
a S Ps 40:6; Mic 6:8
6:7 *b* S Ge 9:11;
S Jer 11:10; Hos 8:1
c S Hos 5:7
6:8 *d* Hos 12:11
6:9 *e* Ps 10:8
f S Hos 4:2 *g* Jer 5:30-
31; 7:9-10;
S Eze 22:9; S Hos 5:1;
7:1
6:10 *h* S Jer 5:30
i S Jer 23:14;
S Eze 23:7; S Hos 5:3

until they have borne their guilt *h*
   and seek my face *i*—
in their misery *j*
   they will earnestly seek me. *k*"

ISRAEL UNREPENTANT

6 "Come, let us return *l* to the LORD.
He has torn us to pieces *m*
   but he will heal us; *n*
he has injured us
   but he will bind up our wounds. *o*
2 After two days he will revive us; *p*
   on the third day *q* he will restore *r* us,
   that we may live in his presence.
3 Let us acknowledge the LORD;
   let us press on to acknowledge him.
As surely as the sun rises,
   he will appear;
he will come to us like the winter rains, *s*
   like the spring rains that water the earth. *t*"

4 "What can I do with you, Ephraim? *u*
   What can I do with you, Judah?
Your love is like the morning mist,
   like the early dew that disappears. *v*
5 Therefore I cut you in pieces with my prophets,
   I killed you with the words of my mouth *w*—
   then my judgments go forth like the sun. *a x*
6 For I desire mercy, not sacrifice, *y*
   and acknowledgment *z* of God rather than burnt offerings. *a*
7 As at Adam, *b* they have broken the covenant; *b*
   they were unfaithful *c* to me there.
8 Gilead is a city of wicked people, *d*
   stained with footprints of blood.
9 As marauders lie in ambush for a victim, *e*
   so do bands of priests;
they murder *f* on the road to Shechem,
   carrying out their wicked schemes. *g*
10 I have seen a horrible *h* thing
   in the house of Israel.
There Ephraim is given to prostitution
   and Israel is defiled. *i*

---

a 5 The meaning of the Hebrew for this line is uncertain.   *b* 7 Or *Like Adam;* or *Like human beings*

6:1 *let us return.* A shallow (see v. 4) proposal of repentance (using phrases from 5:13–15), in which Israel acknowledged that God, not Assyria (cf. 5:13), was the true physician (cf. 7:1).

6:2 *two days … third day.* A brief time. Israel supposed that God's wrath would only be temporary.

6:3 *acknowledge the LORD.* A key concept in Hosea (see v. 6; 2:20 and note; 4:1,6; 5:4). *like the winter rains … spring rains.* Israel believed that, as surely as seasonal rains fell, reviving the earth, God's favor would return and restore her.

6:4 *What can I do … ?* See Isa 5:4. God saw through Israel's superficial repentance. *Ephraim.* See note on 4:17. *Judah.* See Introduction: Author and Date. *love.* See 2:19; see also note on v. 6. *morning mist … dew.* Figurative for that which is temporary.

6:5 *my prophets.* God's spokesmen had denounced the people's sin. *words of my mouth.* The judgments spoken by the Lord's faithful prophets (see Jer 1:9; 15:19 and notes).

6:6 *mercy.* Hebrew *hesed,* a word that can refer to right conduct toward one's neighbor or loyalty to the Lord or

both—the sum of what God requires of his servants. Here it perhaps refers to both. The same Hebrew word is translated "love" in v. 4 (see note on Ps 6:4). *not sacrifice.* Sacrifice apart from faithfulness to the Lord's will is wholly unacceptable to him (see 1Sa 15:22–23; Isa 1:11–15; Jer 7:21–23; Am 5:21–24; Mic 6:6–8; Mt 9:13; 12:7). *acknowledgment of God.* See v. 3; 2:20 and notes.

6:7 *As at Adam.* Adam is probably Tell ed-Damiyeh at the Jordan (see Jos 3:16 and notes on 3:13,15), as suggested by the reference to "there" at the end of the sentence. The allusion in "Like Adam" (see TNIV text note) is uncertain since Scripture records no covenant with Adam. A third interpretation ("Like human beings"; see TNIV text note) takes Hebrew *'adam* to mean "humankind." *broken the covenant.* See 8:1; Jos 7:11.

6:8 *Gilead.* See 12:11; Jdg 10:17; 12:7. *footprints of blood.* The allusion is unclear, but Hosea may have been referring to a more recent event than the bloodbath of Jdg 12:1–6—such as Pekah's rebellion against Pekahiah (see 2Ki 15:25).

6:9 *they murder.* The specific event is unknown. *Shechem.* See Ge 33:18 and note.

6:10 *prostitution.* See note on 4:10.

11 "Also for you, Judah,
    a harvest[j] is appointed.

"Whenever I would restore the fortunes[k] of my people,
1   whenever I would heal Israel,
    the sins of Ephraim are exposed
    and the crimes of Samaria revealed.[l]
They practice deceit,[m]
    thieves break into houses,[n]
    bandits rob in the streets;[o]
2 but they do not realize
    that I remember[p] all their evil deeds.[q]
Their sins engulf them;[r]
    they are always before me.

3 "They delight the king with their wickedness,
    the princes with their lies.[s]
4 They are all adulterers,[t]
    burning like an oven
whose fire the baker need not stir
    from the kneading of the dough till it rises.
5 On the day of the festival of our king
    the princes become inflamed with wine,[u]
    and he joins hands with the mockers.[v]
6 Their hearts are like an oven;[w]
    they approach him with intrigue.
Their passion smolders all night;
    in the morning it blazes like a flaming fire.
7 All of them are hot as an oven;
    they devour their rulers.
All their kings fall,[x]
    and none of them calls[y] on me.

8 "Ephraim mixes[z] with the nations;
    Ephraim is a flat loaf not turned over.
9 Foreigners sap his strength,[a]
    but he does not realize it.
His hair is sprinkled with gray,
    but he does not notice.
10 Israel's arrogance testifies against him,[b]
    but despite all this
he does not return[c] to the LORD his God
    or search[d] for him.

11 "Ephraim is like a dove,[e]
    easily deceived and senseless—

6:11 *j* Jer 51:33;
Joel 3:13 *k* S Ps 126:1;
Zep 2:7
7:1 *l* S Eze 24:13;
S Hos 6:4 *m* ver 13
n S Ex 22:2; Hos 4:2
o S Hos 6:9; 12:1
7:2 *p* S Ps 14:10;
S 44:21; S Hos 8:13
q S Job 35:15;
Hos 9:15 *r* Jer 2:19;
4:18
7:3 *s* Jer 28:1-4;
S Hos 4:2; 10:13;
Mic 7:3
7:4 *t* S Jer 9:2
7:5 *u* S Isa 28:1,7
v S Ps 1:1
7:6 *w* Ps 21:9
7:7 *x* Hos 13:10
y ver 16; S Ps 14:4;
S Isa 9:13; Zep 1:6
7:8 *z* ver 11;
Ps 106:35; S Hos 5:13
7:9 *a* Isa 1:7; Hos 8:7
7:10 *b* Hos 5:5
c Hos 5:4 *d* ver 14;
S Isa 9:13
7:11 *e* S Ge 8:8

6:11 *harvest.* Figurative for God's judgments (see 8:7; 10:12–13; Jer 51:33; Mt 13:30,39–42; Rev 14:15). *restore the fortunes.* Paralleling "heal" (7:1), the phrase refers to the restoration of the wounded national body (see Joel 3:1; Zep 3:20).

🅰 **7:1** *heal.* See 5:13; 6:1; 11:3; 14:4; Jer 51:8–9. *sins.* See 4:8; 5:5; 8:13. *Ephraim.* See note on 4:17. *exposed … revealed.* God sees them. *crimes.* See v. 3. *Samaria.* Another name for the northern kingdom, of which Samaria was the royal city, selected by Omri to be capital of Israel (see 1Ki 16:24 and note). *deceit.* See Jer 6:13; 8:10; probably refers to both feigned repentance and treacherous foreign alliances. *thieves.* See 4:2. *bandits.* See 6:9; Ge 49:19; Jer 18:22.

🅰 **7:2** See Ps 90:8 and note. *I remember.* Everything is open before the Lord, but the wicked believe that God does not see (see Ps 10:6,11 and notes).

7:3 *delight the king.* Perhaps in conjunction with one of the palace revolts (see 2Ki 15:8–30). They were entertaining and flattering the king and princes while engaging in the "wickedness" of preparing to stab them in the back (vv. 6–7; see note on v. 7). *lies.* See 11:12; Ps 10:7 and note; Na 3:1.

7:4 *adulterers.* See note on 4:15. *fire.* A metaphor for political intrigue (see vv. 6–7). The fire was banked until ready to use; then it broke out. *baker.* Perhaps the leader of the conspiracy.
7:5 *festival of our king.* Probably a coronation or birthday that became a drunken orgy. King Elah died in drunkenness (see 1Ki 16:9 and note). *mockers.* See Pr 1:22 and note. Isaiah (28:1–8,14) condemned Israel's drunkenness and her scoffers.
7:6 The intrigue was kept secret until a suitable time.

🅰 **7:7** *rulers … kings.* Four kings were assassinated in 20 years, Zechariah and Shallum in a seven-month period (2Ki 15:10–14). *none of them calls on me.* The reason for the shameful situation.

7:8 *mixes with the nations.* See v. 11 and note. *flat loaf.* A metaphor describing unwise policies. Baked on hot stones (cf. 1Ki 19:6), the loaf was burned on the bottom and undone on the top.
7:9 *Foreigners sap his strength.* Tribute to Assyria (2Ki 15:19–20) and to Egypt (v. 11) had weakened the country economically. *hair … gray.* He was old before his time but ignored the danger signals.
7:10 *return.* See 3:5; 5:4; Am 4:6–11. *search.* See 3:5; 5:6,15 and notes.

7:11 *f* ver 16;
Hos 9:6 *g* S ver 8;
S Jer 2:18; S La 5:6;
Hos 9:3; 12:1
7:12 *h* S Eze 12:13;
S 32:3
7:13 *i* Hos 9:12
j Jer 14:10;
S Eze 34:4-6;
Hos 9:17 *k* ver 1;
Jer 51:9; Mt 23:37
l S Ps 116:11
7:14 *m* Jer 3:10
n Am 2:8 *o* S ver 10;
S Hos 4:10; 9:1; 13:16
7:15 *p* Hos 11:3
q Ps 2:1; S 140:2;
Na 1:9,11
7:16 *r* S ver 7
s S Ps 78:9,57
t Mal 1:14
u S Eze 23:32
v S ver 11; Hos 9:3;
11:5
8:1 *w* S Nu 10:2;
S Eze 33:3
x S Dt 28:49; Jer 4:13
y S Jer 11:10
z S Hos 4:6; S 6:7
8:3 *a* S Mt 7:23;
Tit 1:16
8:4 *b* Hos 13:10
c S Hos 2:8; 13:1-2
8:5 *d* ver 6; Hos 10:5
e Jer 13:27

now calling to Egypt, *f*
  now turning to Assyria. *g*
[12] When they go, I will throw my net *h* over them;
  I will pull them down like the birds in the sky.
When I hear them flocking together,
  I will catch them.
[13] Woe *i* to them,
  because they have strayed *j* from me!
Destruction to them,
  because they have rebelled against me!
I long to redeem them
  but they speak about me *k* falsely. *l*
[14] They do not cry out to me from their hearts *m*
  but wail on their beds.
They slash themselves, *a* appealing to their gods
  for grain and new wine, *n*
  but they turn away from me. *o*
[15] I trained *p* them and strengthened their arms,
  but they plot evil *q* against me.
[16] They do not turn to the Most High; *r*
  they are like a faulty bow. *s*
Their leaders will fall by the sword
  because of their insolent *t* words.
For this they will be ridiculed *u*
  in the land of Egypt. *v*

ISRAEL TO REAP THE WHIRLWIND

8

"Put the trumpet *w* to your lips!
  An eagle *x* is over the house of the LORD
because the people have broken my covenant *y*
  and rebelled against my law. *z*
[2] Israel cries out to me,
  'Our God, we acknowledge you!'
[3] But Israel has rejected what is good;
  an enemy will pursue him. *a*
[4] They set up kings without my consent;
  they choose princes without my approval. *b*
With their silver and gold
  they make idols *c* for themselves
  to their own destruction.
[5] Samaria, throw out your calf-idol! *d*
  My anger burns against them.
How long will they be incapable of purity? *e*

a 14 Some Hebrew manuscripts and Septuagint; most Hebrew manuscripts *They gather together*

7:11 *dove.* See 11:11 and note, where a different image is intended. See also note on Ps 68:13. *senseless.* See Jer 5:21. Menahem turned to Assyria (2Ki 15:19–20); Hoshea alternated in allegiance to Assyria and Egypt (2Ki 17:3–4).

7:12 *my net.* The Lord himself was the hunter—not the nations—and Israel was certain to be caught.

7:13 *Woe.* Often used in conjunction with threats of judgment (see 9:12). *Destruction.* See 9:6; Isa 13:6. *redeem.* See 13:14; also used for deliverance from Egypt (see, e.g., Ex 6:6; Mic 6:4). *speak about me falsely.* Possibly by ascribing prosperity and destiny to gods other than the Lord.

7:14 *wail.* See Joel 1:13. *They slash themselves.* See Lev 19:28; 21:5 and notes. *grain and new wine.* See 2:8,22; 9:1–2.

7:15 *I trained them.* As children (see 11:3 and note) or, perhaps, as troops. *strengthened their arms.* See Eze 30:24–25.

7:16 *Most High.* See 11:7; Dt 32:8 and note. *faulty bow.* See Ps 78:57. The arrow missed the mark; Israel missed her purpose for being. *ridiculed.* Egypt would fail to assist Israel and then would belittle God's power (see Dt 9:28). *Egypt.* See 8:13; 11:5 and

notes. There is no record of a forced exile of large numbers to Egypt. Some captives were taken there (2Ki 23:34; Jer 22:11–14), and some fugitives voluntarily went there (2Ki 25:26; Jer 42–44). A return from Egypt is envisioned in 11:11; Isa 11:11; 27:13; Zec 10:10.

8:1 *trumpet.* See 5:8 and note. *your.* Hosea's. *eagle.* Or "vulture," referring to Assyria. *house of the LORD.* The land of Israel, not just the temple (see 9:15 and note; cf. Ex 15:17).

8:2 *we acknowledge you.* See 2:20; 6:3 and notes; but their worship of the Lord was thoroughly corrupted by pagan notions and practices, as vv. 3–6 indicate (see Am 2:4,7–8; 3:14; 5:26).

8:3 *an enemy.* The Assyrians.

8:4 *set up kings.* After Jeroboam II, five kings ruled over Israel in 13 years (2Ki 15:8–30), three of whom seized the throne by violence (see 7:7 and note).

8:5 *Samaria.* See note on 7:1. *calf-idol.* See 10:5; 13:2. Jeroboam I (930–909 B.C.) had set up golden calves in Bethel and Dan, saying, "Here are your gods" (see 1Ki 12:28–33 and note on 12:28).

⁶ They are from Israel!
This calf—a metalworker has made it;
    it is not God. *f*
It will be broken in pieces,
    that calf *g* of Samaria. *h*

⁷ "They sow the wind
    and reap the whirlwind. *i*
The stalk has no head;
    it will produce no flour. *j*
Were it to yield grain,
    foreigners would swallow it up. *k*
⁸ Israel is swallowed up; *l*
    now she is among the nations
    like something no one wants. *m*
⁹ For they have gone up to Assyria *n*
    like a wild donkey *o* wandering alone.
Ephraim has sold herself to lovers. *p*
¹⁰ Although they have sold themselves among the nations,
    I will now gather them together. *q*
They will begin to waste away *r*
    under the oppression of the mighty king.

¹¹ "Though Ephraim built many altars for sin offerings,
    these have become altars for sinning. *s*
¹² I wrote for them the many things of my law,
    but they regarded them as something foreign. *t*
¹³ Though they offer sacrifices as gifts to me,
    and though they eat *u* the meat,
    the LORD is not pleased with them. *v*
Now he will remember *w* their wickedness
    and punish their sins: *x*
They will return to Egypt. *y*
¹⁴ Israel has forgotten *z* their Maker *a*
    and built palaces;
Judah has fortified many towns.
But I will send fire on their cities
    that will consume their fortresses." *b*

PUNISHMENT FOR ISRAEL

9 Do not rejoice, Israel;
    do not be jubilant *c* like the other nations.
For you have been unfaithful *d* to your God;
    you love the wages of a prostitute *e*

8:6 *a metalworker has made it.* For prophetic satire on idolatry, see Isa 40:20; 41:22–24; 44:9–20; see also Ps 115:4–8 and notes. Israel's leaders (Ex 32:4) and Jeroboam I had said "These are your gods," but Hosea said "It is not God."

8:7 *They sow … whirlwind.* A familiar proverb about the results of doing evil (see 10:13; Job 4:8; Ps 126:5–6; Pr 11:18; 22:8; 2Co 9:6; Gal 6:7). Israel sowed the wind of idolatry and reaped the whirlwind of Assyria. *stalk … flour.* The prophet played on the similar sound of the Hebrew words. *foreigners.* Assyria.

8:8 Israel was chosen to be God's own people (see Ex 19:5; Am 3:2 and notes), but since she had conformed to the other nations she lost her special identity and so became to God "like something no one wants."

8:9 *wild donkey wandering alone.* See Jer 2:24 and note. *Ephraim.* See note on 4:17. *sold herself to lovers.* For the prostitute's fees (see 9:1 and note) of Assyrian protection. Menahem (2Ki 15:19) and Hoshea (2Ki 17:3), kings of Israel, paid tribute to Assyria.

8:10 Even though Israel paid tribute to Assyria, that would not buy her security, for God would send judgment by the king of Assyria. Israel's real enemy was the Lord himself (see 2:8–13; 7:12 and note).

8:13 *offer sacrifices.* See v. 2 and note. *eat the meat.* Some of the sacrifices were partly eaten by the offerer and priests (see Lev 7:11–18,28–36; Dt 12:7; Jer 7:21). *not pleased with them.* See 6:6 and note. *Egypt.* Israel, who had trusted in Egypt and Assyria, was to go back to "Egypt," i.e., into bondage in a foreign land, primarily Assyria (see 9:3). But see note on 7:16.

8:14 *Israel has forgotten.* The cause of all her problems (see 2:13 and note; cf. Jdg 2:10). *built palaces … fortified many towns.* Israel's trust was not in her Maker but in what she herself had accomplished. *Judah.* See Introduction: Author and Date. *fire … that will consume.* See Am 1:4 and note.

9:1 This verse begins a section that was probably spoken at a harvest festival, such as the Festival of Tabernacles (Lev 23:33–43; Dt 16:13–15). *unfaithful.* See 1:2; 2:2–5 and notes. *wages of a prostitute.* See 2:12 and note; not to be taken literally, but in the sense of spiritual adultery (see 2:12; Ex 34:15 and notes). *at every threshing floor.* Since the threshing floor at threshing time was a man's world—the threshers feasted there at the end of the day's labors and stayed all night to protect the grain (see Ru 3:2–3 and notes)—prostitutes were not uncommon visitors.

8:6 *f* S Jer 16:20; Hos 14:3 *g* S Ex 32:4 *h* S ver 5
8:7 *i* S Job 4:8; Pr 22:8; Isa 66:15; Hos 10:12-13; Na 1:3; Gal 6:8 *j* S Dt 28:38; S Isa 17:11; Hos 9:16 *k* Hos 2:9; S 7:9
8:8 *l* Jer 51:34
m Jer 22:28
8:9 *n* S Jer 2:18 *o* S Ge 16:12 *p* S Jer 22:20; Eze 23:5; S Hos 5:13
8:10 *q* S Eze 16:37; S 22:20 *r* Jer 42:2
8:11 *s* Hos 10:1; 12:11
8:12 *t* S ver 1
8:13 *u* S Jer 7:21 *v* S Jer 6:20; Hos 9:4 *w* Hos 7:2; 9:9; Am 8:7 *x* S Hos 4:9 *y* Hos 9:3,6
8:14 *z* S Dt 32:18; S Isa 17:10; S Hos 2:13 *a* S Ps 95:6 *b* Jer 5:17; S 17:27; Am 2:5
9:1 *c* Isa 22:12-13 *d* S Ps 73:27; S Isa 24:16; S Hos 7:14; 10:5 *e* S Ge 30:15

9:2 *f* Isa 24:7;
Hos 2:9; Joel 1:10
9:3 *g* Lev 25:23
h S Hos 7:16; S 8:13
i Eze 4:13; S Hos 7:11;
10:5; Am 7:17
9:4 *j* Joel 1:9,13; 2:14
k S Hos 8:13
l S Jer 16:7
m S Dt 26:14;
Hag 2:13-14
n S Eze 4:13-14
9:5 *o* Isa 10:3;
Jer 5:31 *p* S Hos 2:11
9:6 *q* S Hos 7:11;
S 8:13 *r* S Isa 19:13
s S Jer 42:22 *t* Zep 1:11
u Isa 5:6; Hos 10:8
9:7 *v* Isa 34:8;
Jer 10:15; Mic 7:4;
Lk 21:22 *w* S Job 31:14
x Jer 16:18
y S 1Sa 10:11;
Isa 44:25; S La 2:14;
Eze 14:9-10
z S Jer 29:26; Hos 14:1
9:8 *a* S Hos 5:1
b S Eze 22:26
9:9 *c* Zep 3:7
d Jdg 19:16-30;
S Hos 5:8
e S Hos 8:13
f S Hos 4:9
9:10 *g* S SS 2:13
h S Isa 28:4 *i* Nu 25:1-
5; Ps 106:28-29

at every threshing floor.
² Threshing floors and winepresses will not feed the people;
the new wine *f* will fail them.
³ They will not remain *g* in the LORD's land;
Ephraim will return to Egypt *h*
and eat unclean food in Assyria. *i*
⁴ They will not pour out wine offerings *j* to the LORD,
nor will their sacrifices please *k* him.
Such sacrifices will be to them like the bread of mourners; *l*
all who eat them will be unclean. *m*
This food will be for themselves;
it will not come into the temple of the LORD. *n*

⁵ What will you do *o* on the day of your appointed festivals, *p*
on the festal days of the LORD?
⁶ Even if they escape from destruction,
Egypt will gather them, *q*
and Memphis *r* will bury them. *s*
Their treasures of silver *t* will be taken over by briers,
and thorns *u* will overrun their tents.
⁷ The days of punishment *v* are coming,
the days of reckoning *w* are at hand.
Let Israel know this.
Because your sins *x* are so many
and your hostility so great,
the prophet is considered a fool, *y*
anyone who is inspired a maniac. *z*
⁸ The prophet, along with my God,
is the watchman over Ephraim, *a*
yet snares *a* await him on all his paths,
and hostility in the house of his God. *b*
⁹ They have sunk deep into corruption, *c*
as in the days of Gibeah. *d*
God will remember *e* their wickedness
and punish them for their sins. *f*

¹⁰ "When I found Israel,
it was like finding grapes in the desert;
when I saw your ancestors,
it was like seeing the early fruit *g* on the fig *h* tree.
But when they came to Baal Peor, *i*

a 8 Or *The prophet is the watchman over Ephraim, / the people of my God*

9:3 *LORD's land.* The promised land, which the Lord claimed as his own (see Lev 25:23; Jos 22:19 and note; Jer 2:7; Eze 38:16; Joel 1:6). *Ephraim.* See note on 4:17. *Egypt . . . Assyria.* Israel was threatened with exile to the lands it depended on—where the temple sacrifice could not be offered (see 7:16; 8:13 and notes). *unclean.* A foreign country was ceremonially unclean (see Am 7:17 and note). What grew there was likewise unclean, because it was the product of fertility credited to pagan gods (see 2:5 and note; Eze 4:13).
9:4 *bread of mourners.* Unclean, like bread in a house where there had been a death (see Nu 19:14 and note; Dt 26:14; Jer 16:7). All who touched it became ceremonially unclean. *not come into the temple of the LORD.* In exile Israel would have no place (not even those places established by Jeroboam I; 1Ki 12:28–33) where she could bring sacrifices to the Lord or celebrate her religious festivals (v. 5).
9:5 *appointed festivals . . . festal days.* See 2:11 and note.
9:6 *Egypt.* See 7:16; 8:13; 11:5 and notes. *Memphis.* The capital of Lower (northern) Egypt. *briers, and thorns.* Cf. a similar threat against Edom (Isa 34:13).
9:7 *inspired.* See Mic 3:8 and note. *maniac.* See 2Ki 9:11; Jer 29:26 and notes; cf. 1Sa 21:15.

9:8 *watchman.* See Eze 3:17; Hab 2:1 and notes. *snares . . . hostility.* Israel showed only hostility toward the watchmen (the true prophets) whom God sent to warn his people of the great dangers that threatened (see Jer 1:19; 11:19; 15:10; Am 7:10–13).
9:9 *corruption.* The word used of the Israelites who worshiped the golden calf (see Ex 32:7 and note; Dt 9:12). *days of Gibeah.* A reference to the corrupt behavior of the Benjamites so graphically described in Jdg 19–21. *God will remember.* Sins unrepented of are remembered, as well as the accumulated sins of generations (see 13:12).
9:10 *I found Israel . . . I saw your ancestors.* The covenant relation is traced back to "the wilderness" (see 2:14–15 and note on 2:14; 13:5; Dt 32:10). *grapes . . . fig.* Refreshing delicacies (see SS 2:13; Isa 28:4; Mic 7:1). The images used here (grapes in the wilderness, early fruit of the fig tree) beautifully convey God's delight in Israel when she, out of all the nations, committed herself to him in covenant at Sinai. *Baal Peor.* Peor was a mountain (Nu 23:28). "Baal Peor" refers to the god of Peor (Nu 25:1–3) and is here used to refer to Beth Peor, "the sanctuary of Peor" (see Dt 3:29 and note; 4:3,46; Jos 13:20). Hosea refers here to the incident in Nu 25. *that shameful idol.* See Jdg 6:32; Jer 2:26 and notes. *became . . . vile.* See Isa 5:2,4,7.

they consecrated themselves to that shameful idol[j]
and became as vile as the thing they loved.
[11] Ephraim's glory[k] will fly away like a bird[l]—
no birth, no pregnancy, no conception.[m]
[12] Even if they rear children,
I will bereave[n] them of every one.
Woe[o] to them
when I turn away from them![p]
[13] I have seen Ephraim, like Tyre,
planted in a pleasant place.[r]
But Ephraim will bring out
their children to the slayer."[s]

[14] Give them, LORD—
what will you give them?
Give them wombs that miscarry
and breasts that are dry.[t]

[15] "Because of all their wickedness in Gilgal,[u]
I hated them there.
Because of their sinful deeds,[v]
I will drive them out of my house.
I will no longer love them;[w]
all their leaders are rebellious.[x]
[16] Ephraim[y] is blighted,
their root is withered,
they yield no fruit.[z]
Even if they bear children,
I will slay[a] their cherished offspring."

[17] My God will reject[b] them
because they have not obeyed[c] him;
they will be wanderers among the nations.[d]

10

Israel was a spreading vine;[e]
he brought forth fruit for himself.
As his fruit increased,
he built more altars;[f]
as his land prospered,[g]
he adorned his sacred stones.[h]
[2] Their heart is deceitful,[i]
and now they must bear their guilt.[j]
The LORD will demolish their altars[k]
and destroy their sacred stones.[l]

[3] Then they will say, "We have no king
because we did not revere the LORD.
But even if we had a king,
what could he do for us?"
[4] They make many promises,
take false oaths[m]

9:10 [j] Jer 11:13; S Hos 4:14
9:11 [k] S Isa 17:3 [l] S Hos 4:7; 10:5 [m] ver 14
9:12 [n] ver 16; S Eze 24:21 [o] Hos 7:13 [p] S Dt 31:17
9:13 [q] S Ps 78:67 [r] S Eze 27:3 [s] S Job 15:22; S La 2:22
9:14 [t] ver 11; Lk 23:29
9:15 [u] S Hos 4:15 [v] S Hos 7:2 [w] S Jer 12:8 [x] S Isa 1:23; S Hos 4:9; 5:2
9:16 [y] S Hos 5:11 [z] Job 15:32; S Hos 8:7 [a] S ver 12
9:17 [b] S Jer 6:30 [c] S Hos 4:10 [d] S Dt 28:65; S Hos 7:13
10:1 [e] S Eze 15:2 [f] S 1Ki 14:23 [g] Hos 13:15 [h] Hos 3:4; S 4:7; S 8:11; 12:11
10:2 [i] 1Ki 18:21 [j] Hos 13:16 [k] ver 8 [l] Mic 5:13
10:4 [m] S Hos 4:2

9:11 *Ephraim's glory.* Her large population and prosperity. The punishment fit the sin. Prostitution produces no increase (see 4:10; Jdg 2:17 and notes). *fly away like a bird.* Never to return (see Pr 23:5).
9:12 *Woe.* See 7:13 and note.
9:13 *Tyre.* Noted for its wealth, pleasant environment and security (see Eze 27:3–25).
9:14 Hosea did not pray out of hateful vengeance against Israel but because he shared God's holy wrath against her sins.
9:15 *Gilgal.* See note on 4:15. *drive them out of my house.* As the unfaithful wife was driven from her husband's house, so Israel was driven from God's "house"—i.e., his land (see 8:1 and note). *no longer love them.* Because of their sins. But when they repent and ask the Lord to forgive them (see 14:1–2

and notes), he will "love them freely" (14:4).
9:17 *My God.* Hosea's words alone, for God was no longer Israel's God. *reject.* See 4:6; 2Ki 17:20. *wanderers.* Like Cain (Ge 4:12–16).
10:1 *Israel.* The nation personified and called by the name of its ancestor. *vine.* A frequent metaphor for Israel (see Ps 80:8–16 and note). *prospered.* The prosperity during the period of Jeroboam II (793–753 B.C.) is probably in view. *sacred stones.* See 3:4 and note.
10:2 *Their heart is deceitful.* See ver 16 and note. Israel formally cried out to God, but the people dishonored him by pagan worship (see 8:2 and note).
10:3 *We have no king.* Such would soon be their condition when Assyria destroyed the nation.
10:4 *They make many promises.* The last kings of Israel were notoriously corrupt and deceitful.

10:4 *n* S Eze 17:19;
Am 5:7 *o* Am 6:12
10:5 *p* S Ex 32:4;
S Isa 44:17-20
q ver 8; S Hos 5:8
r S 2Ki 23:5; Zep 1:4
s S Jdg 18:17-18;
S Hos 8:5; S 9:1,3,11
10:6 *t* S 2Ki 16:7;
Hos 11:5 *u* S Jdg 3:15
v S Hos 5:13
w Isa 30:3; S Hos 4:7
x Jer 48:13
10:7 *y* ver 15;
Hos 13:11
10:8 *z* S Eze 6:6
a S ver 5; 1Ki 12:28-
30; S Hos 4:13
b S Hos 9:6 *c* ver 2;
S Isa 32:13
d S Job 30:6;
Am 3:14-15 *e* Am 7:9;
Lk 23:30*; Rev 6:16
10:9 *f* S Hos 5:8
g S Jos 7:11
10:10 *h* S Eze 5:13;
S Hos 4:9
10:11 *i* S Jer 15:12;
S 31:18
10:12 *j* S Ecc 11:1
k S Pr 11:18; Jas 3:18
l Jer 4:3 *m* S Isa 19:22;
Hos 12:6 *n* S Isa 45:8
10:13 *o* S Job 4:8;
S Hos 7:3; 11:12;
Gal 6:7-8 *p* S Pr 11:18;
S Hos 8:7 *q* Ps 33:16

and make agreements; *n*
therefore lawsuits spring up
  like poisonous weeds *o* in a plowed field.
[5] The people who live in Samaria fear
  for the calf-idol *p* of Beth Aven. *a q*
Its people will mourn over it,
  and so will its idolatrous priests, *r*
those who had rejoiced over its splendor,
  because it is taken from them into exile. *s*
[6] It will be carried to Assyria *t*
  as tribute *u* for the great king. *v*
Ephraim will be disgraced; *w*
Israel will be ashamed *x* of its foreign alliances.
[7] Samaria's king will be destroyed, *y*
  swept away like a twig on the surface of the waters.
[8] The high places *z* of wickedness *b a* will be destroyed—
  it is the sin of Israel.
Thorns *b* and thistles will grow up
  and cover their altars. *c*
Then they will say to the mountains, "Cover us!" *d*
  and to the hills, "Fall on us!" *e*

[9] "Since the days of Gibeah, *f* you have sinned, *g* Israel,
  and there you have remained. *c*
Will not war again overtake
  the evildoers in Gibeah?
[10] When I please, I will punish *h* them;
  nations will be gathered against them
  to put them in bonds for their double sin.
[11] Ephraim is a trained heifer
  that loves to thresh;
so I will put a yoke *i*
  on her fair neck.
I will drive Ephraim,
  Judah must plow,
  and Jacob must break up the ground.
[12] Sow *j* for yourselves righteousness, *k*
  reap the fruit of unfailing love,
and break up your unplowed ground; *l*
  for it is time to seek *m* the LORD,
until he comes
  and showers his righteousness *n* on you.
[13] But you have planted wickedness,
  you have reaped evil, *o*
  you have eaten the fruit of deception. *p*
Because you have depended on your own strength
  and on your many warriors, *q*

---

a 5 Beth Aven means *house of wickedness* (a derogatory name for Bethel, which means *house of God*).
b 8 Hebrew *aven*, a reference to Beth Aven (a derogatory name for Bethel); see verse 5. *c 9* Or *there a stand was taken*

10:5 *Samaria.* The royal city of Israel (see note on 7:1). *calf-idol of Beth Aven.* The idol that Jeroboam I had set up at Bethel (see TNIV text note; see also 8:5 and note).
10:6 *tribute for the great king.* See 5:13 and note. *Ephraim.* See note on 4:17.
10:8 *high places.* See 4:13–14 and note on 4:13. *wickedness.* See TNIV text note. *Cover us! ... Fall on us!* Cries of utter despair; quoted by Jesus (see Lk 23:30 and note) and alluded to in Rev 6:16.
10:9 *Gibeah.* See 9:9 and note. As war came on Gibeah, so war and captivity would come on Israel.
10:11 *trained heifer.* Up to now Ephraim (Israel) had been as contented as a young cow that ate while threshing grain. But now God would cause Israel (here called both Ephraim and Ja-

cob) and Judah to do the heavy work of plowing and harrowing under a yoke—a picture of going into the Assyrian and Babylonian captivities. *Judah.* See Introduction: Author and Date.

10:12 *reap the fruit of unfailing love.* If Israel would only do what was right ("unfailing love" translates the Hebrew word *hesed;* see note on 6:6), God would bless her. *break up your unplowed ground.* Be no longer unproductive, but repentant, making a radical new beginning and becoming productive and fruitful. *righteousness.* God's covenant blessings that in righteousness he would shower on his people if they in righteousness were loyal to him, their covenant Lord.

10:13 *deception.* Israel had been living a lie—and by lies (see v. 4; 7:3; 11:12; 12:1; cf. 1Jn 1:6).

14the roar of battle will rise against your people,
    so that all your fortresses will be devastated *r*—
as Shalman *s* devastated Beth Arbel on the day of battle,
    when mothers were dashed to the ground with their children. *t*
15So will it happen to you, Bethel,
    because your wickedness is great.
When that day dawns,
    the king of Israel will be completely destroyed. *u*

GOD'S LOVE FOR ISRAEL

11 "When Israel was a child, *v* I loved *w* him,
    and out of Egypt I called my son. *x*
2But the more they were called,
    the more they went away from me. *a y*
They sacrificed to the Baals *z*
    and they burned incense to images. *a*
3It was I who taught Ephraim to walk,
    taking them by the arms; *b*
but they did not realize
    it was I who healed *c* them.
4I led them with cords of human kindness,
    with ties of love. *d*
To them I was like one who lifts
    a little child to the cheek,
and I bent down to feed *e* them. *f*

5"Will they not return to Egypt *g*
    and will not Assyria *h* rule over them
because they refuse to repent? *i*
6Swords *j* will flash in their cities,
    will destroy the bars *k* of their gates
    and put an end to their plans.
7My people are determined to turn *l* from me. *m*
    Even though they call me God Most High,
    I will by no means exalt them.

8"How can I give you up, *n* Ephraim? *o*
    How can I hand you over, Israel?
How can I treat you like Admah?
    How can I make you like Zeboyim? *p*
My heart is changed within me;
    all my compassion *q* is aroused. *r*
9I will not carry out my fierce anger, *s*

---

a 2 Septuagint; Hebrew *them*

10:14 *r* S Isa 17:3;
Mic 5:11 *s* S 2Ki 17:3
t S Isa 13:16;
Hos 13:16
10:15 *u* S ver 7
11:1 *v* S Jer 2:2;
S Eze 16:22
w S Dt 4:37
x S Ex 4:22; Hos 12:9,
13; 13:4; Mt 2:15*
11:2 *y* ver 7
z S Hos 2:13
a S 2Ki 17:15;
Isa 65:7; S Jer 18:15;
S Hos 4:13; 13:1
11:3 *b* S Dt 1:31;
S 32:11; Hos 7:15
c S Ex 15:26; Jer 30:17
11:4 *d* Jer 31:2-3
e Ex 16:32; Ps 78:25
f Jer 31:20
11:5 *g* S Hos 7:16
h S Hos 10:6
i S Ex 13:17
11:6 *j* Hos 13:16
k S La 2:9
11:7 *l* S Isa 26:10
m ver 2; Jer 3:6-7; 8:5
11:8 *n* S Jer 7:29
o Hos 6:4 *p* S Ge 14:8;
S La 3:32
q S 1Ki 3:26; S Ps 25:6
r S Eze 33:11; Am 7:3
11:9 *s* S Jer 18:8; S 30:11

10:14 *Shalman devastated Beth Arbel.* The event is otherwise unknown, as are the names mentioned—though Shalman may be an abbreviated form of Shalmaneser V, the Assyrian king who laid siege to Samaria in 725 B.C. (see 2Ki 17:3–5). In any event, atrocities against civilians were common in ancient warfare (see 9:13; 13:16; see also Ps 137:9 and note).
10:15 *Bethel.* See v. 8 and TNIV text note; 12:4 and note.
11:1 A third appeal to history (see 9:10; 10:9) traces God's choice of Israel back to Egypt, the exodus from that country (cf. 12:9; 13:4) having given birth to the nation. Israel's response to the Lord is now illustrated by the wayward son rather than by the unfaithful wife (chs. 1–3). Israel is also referred to as God's "son/child" elsewhere (see Ex 4:22–23 and notes; Isa 1:2,4). For God as Israel's "Father," see Dt 32:6; Isa 63:16; 64:8. Hosea saw God's love as the basis (see 3:1 and note) for the election of Israel. Matthew saw in Jesus' return from Egypt a typological fulfillment of Israel's deliverance from Egypt (see Mt 2:15 and note).
11:2 *Baals.* See 2:13 and note. *images.* See Dt 7:25.
11:3 *Ephraim.* See note on 4:17. *walk.* This picture of a father

teaching his child to walk is one of the most tender in the OT. *did not realize.* See 2:5–8 and note on 2:8. *healed.* See 5:13; 6:1 and note; 7:1.
11:4 The imagery is unclear, but the figure seems to change to a farmer tending his work animals. Another interpretation sees a continuation of the son image, with the father lifting the son to his cheek. *feed them.* God supplied miraculous food in the wilderness (see Ex 16; Dt 8:16).
11:5 *Egypt . . . Assyria.* See 8:13; 9:3 and notes. The tender tone (vv. 1–4) changes to threat of exile to the two countries between which Israel had vacillated. It is ironic that the people rescued from Egypt should be returned there because of their disloyalty to the one who had rescued them.
11:7 *Most High.* See 7:16 and note.
11:8 The stubborn son was subject to stoning (Dt 21:18–21), but the Lord's compassion overcame his wrath and he refused to destroy Ephraim (Israel). *Admah . . . Zeboyim.* Cities of the plain (see Ge 10:19 and note; 14:2,8), overthrown when Sodom was destroyed (Ge 19:24–25; Dt 29:23; Jer 49:18) and symbolizing total destruction (see Am 4:11 and note).

11:9 ʳLa 3:22;
Mal 3:6 ᵘS Nu 23:19
ᵛS 2Ki 19:22;
S Isa 31:1
11:10 ʷS Isa 42:13
ˣS Isa 31:4
ʸS Ps 18:45
ᶻS Hos 3:5; S 6:1-3
11:11 ᵃS Ge 8:8
ᵇS Isa 11:11
ᶜS Eze 28:26;
S 34:25-28
11:12 ᵈS Hos 4:2
ᵉS Dt 7:9
ᶠS Hos 10:13
12:1 ᵍS Ps 78:67
ʰS Ge 41:6;
S Eze 17:10
ⁱS Hos 4:19; S 7:1
ʲHos 5:13; S 7:11
ᵏS 2Ki 17:4
12:2 ˡS Job 10:2;
Mic 6:2 ᵐAm 2:4
ⁿEx 32:34
ᵒS Hos 4:9; S 9:15
12:3 ᵖGe 25:26
ᑫGe 32:24-29
12:4 ʳS Ge 12:8;
S 35:15
12:5 ˢS Ex 3:15
12:6 ᵗS Isa 19:22;
Jer 4:1; Joel 2:12
ᵘS Ps 106:3;
S Jer 22:3
ᵛS Eze 18:30;
Hos 6:1-3; 10:12;
Mic 7:7
12:7 ʷS Lev 19:36;
Am 8:5

nor will I devastate ᵗEphraim again.
For I am God, and not a human being ᵘ—
the Holy One ᵛ among you.
I will not come against their cities.
¹⁰ They will follow the Lᴏʀᴅ;
he will roar ʷ like a lion. ˣ
When he roars,
his children will come trembling ʸ from the west. ᶻ
¹¹ They will come trembling
like birds from Egypt,
like doves ᵃ from Assyria. ᵇ
I will settle them in their homes," ᶜ
declares the Lᴏʀᴅ.

ISRAEL'S SIN

*¹² Ephraim has surrounded me with lies, ᵈ
the house of Israel with deceit.
And Judah is unruly against God,
even against the faithful ᵉ Holy One. ᶠ

12

*¹Ephraim ᵍ feeds on the wind; ʰ
he pursues the east wind all day
and multiplies lies and violence. ⁱ
He makes a treaty with Assyria ʲ
and sends olive oil to Egypt. ᵏ
² The Lᴏʀᴅ has a charge ˡ to bring against Judah; ᵐ
he will punish ⁿ Jacob ᵃ according to his ways
and repay him according to his deeds. ᵒ
³ In the womb he grasped his brother's heel; ᵖ
as a man he struggled ᑫ with God.
⁴ He struggled with the angel and overcame him;
he wept and begged for his favor.
He found him at Bethel ʳ
and talked with him there—
⁵ the Lᴏʀᴅ God Almighty,
the Lᴏʀᴅ is his name! ˢ
⁶ But you must return ᵗ to your God;
maintain love and justice, ᵘ
and wait for your God always. ᵛ
⁷ The merchants use dishonest scales; ʷ
they love to defraud.

ᵃ *2 Jacob* means *he grasps the heel*, a Hebrew idiom for *he takes advantage of* or *he deceives.*
* 11:12 is numbered 12:1 in Hebrew texts.   * 12:1-14 is numbered 12:2-15 in Hebrew texts.

11:9 *God, and not a human being.* God will not be untrue to the love he has shown toward Israel (see vv. 1–4; 1Sa 15:29; Mal 3:6). Israel was to be punished, but not destroyed. *the Holy One among you.* God's holiness is alluded to in Hosea both here and in v. 12 (see notes on Ex 3:5; Lev 11:44).
11:10 The return from exile. *roar like a lion.* Rather than threatening destruction (cf. 5:14; 13:7), God's roar was now a clear signal to return from exile. *the west.* The islands and coastlands of the Mediterranean Sea.
11:11 *like birds ... like doves.* Suggests swiftness of return (cf. Isa 60:8) and is not derogatory, as was the earlier comparison to a silly dove (7:11). *from Egypt ... Assyria.* See 7:16 and note; 9:3.
11:12 *lies ... deceit.* See 10:13 and note. *Judah.* See Introduction: Author and Date. *unruly against God.* See Jer 2:31. *Holy One.* See v. 9 and note.
12:1 *Ephraim.* See note on 4:17. *wind.* See 8:7; Ecc 1:14. *east wind.* See 13:15; Job 15:2; Jer 18:17. Pursuing the wind symbolized Israel's futile foreign policy, which vacillated between Egypt (2Ki 17:4; Isa 30:6–7) and Assyria (see 5:13; 7:11; 8:9 and notes; 2Ki 17:3).

12:2 *charge.* See 4:1 and note. *Judah.* See Introduction: Author and Date. *Jacob.* Israel (see 10:11). The Lord indicted both kingdoms—all the descendants of Father Jacob. In their deceitfulness Israel and Judah were living up to the name of their forefather (see TNIV text note).
12:3 *In the womb.* See Ge 25:26; 27:36 and notes. *grasped his brother's heel.* See TNIV text note on v. 2. God's covenant people here relived the experiences of Father Jacob and now had to return to God, just as Jacob was called back to Bethel (Ge 35:1–15).
12:4 *struggled with the angel.* See Ge 32:22–28 and TNIV text note on 32:28. *Bethel.* See Ge 28:12–19 and TNIV text note on 28:19; 35:1–15. In Hosea's time, Bethel was the most important royal sanctuary in the northern kingdom (cf. Am 7:13).
12:6 *love.* Hebrew *hesed;* see 6:6 ("mercy") and note. *justice.* See Am 5:24; Mic 6:8 and notes.
12:7 *merchants.* As Hosea had played on the meaning of Jacob in v. 2, he here uses a wordplay on Canaan (the Hebrew for "merchant" sounds like Canaan) to charge that Israel was no better than a Canaanite (see note on Zec 14:21). *dishonest scales.* See Lev 19:35; Pr 11:1 and notes.

12:8 ˣ S Eze 28:5
ʸ Ps 62:10; Rev 3:17
12:9 ᶻ Lev 23:43;
S Hos 2:15; S 11:1
ᵃ S Ne 8:17
12:10 ᵇ S Jdg 14:12;
S Eze 20:49
ᶜ 2Ki 17:13; Jer 7:25
12:11 ᵈ S Hos 6:8
ᵉ S Hos 4:15
ᶠ S Hos 8:11
12:12 ᵍ Ge 28:5
ʰ S Ge 29:18
12:13 ⁱ S Hos 11:1
ʲ Ex 13:3; 14:19-22;
Isa 63:11-14
12:14 ᵏ S Eze 18:13
ˡ Da 11:18
13:1 ᵐ Jdg 12:1
ⁿ S Jdg 8:1
ᵒ S Hos 11:2
13:2 ᵖ Jer 44:8
�q S Isa 46:6;
S Jer 10:4 ʳ Hos 14:3
ˢ 1Ki 19:18
ᵗ S Isa 44:17-20;
S Hos 8:4
13:3 ᵘ S Hos 6:4

⁸Ephraim boasts,ˣ
  "I am very rich; I have become wealthy.ʸ
With all my wealth they will not find in me
    any iniquity or sin."

⁹"I have been the Lᴏʀᴅ your God
    ever since you came out of Egypt;ᶻ
I will make you live in tentsᵃ again,
    as in the days of your appointed festivals.
¹⁰I spoke to the prophets,
    gave them many visions
    and told parablesᵇ through them."ᶜ

¹¹Is Gilead wicked?ᵈ
    Its people are worthless!
Do they sacrifice bulls in Gilgal?ᵉ
    Their altars will be like piles of stones
    on a plowed field.ᶠ
¹²Jacob fled to the country of Aramᵃ;ᵍ
    Israel served to get a wife,
    and to pay for her he tended sheep.ʰ
¹³The Lᴏʀᴅ used a prophet to bring Israel up from Egypt,ⁱ
    by a prophet he cared for him.ʲ
¹⁴But Ephraim has aroused his bitter anger;
    his Lord will leave on him the guilt of his bloodshedᵏ
    and will repay him for his contempt.ˡ

THE LORD'S ANGER AGAINST ISRAEL

13 When Ephraim spoke, people trembled;ᵐ
    he was exaltedⁿ in Israel.
But he became guilty of Baal worshipᵒ and died.
²Now they sin more and more;
    they makeᵖ idols for themselves from their silver,�q
cleverly fashioned images,
    all of them the work of skilled hands.ʳ
It is said of them,
    "They offer human sacrifices!
    They kissᵇ ˢ calf-idols!ᵗ"
³Therefore they will be like the morning mist,
    like the early dew that disappears,ᵘ

ᵃ 12 That is, Northwest Mesopotamia   ᵇ 2 Or "Men who sacrifice / kiss

---

12:8 *I am very rich.* Riches brought a sense of self-sufficiency (cf. 10:13; Dt 32:15–18; Lk 12:19; Rev 3:17). *not find in me any iniquity.* Like a dishonest merchant, Ephraim (Israel) was confident that her deceitfulness (see 10:13 and note) would not come to light.
12:9 *I have been the Lᴏʀᴅ your God ever since.* See 13:4; Ex 20:2 and note. *tents.* Recalling the wilderness journey of long ago (cf. 2:14–15). *appointed festivals.* Probably the Festival of Tabernacles (see Lev 23:33–43 and note on 23:42), which commemorated the wilderness journey.
12:10 *spoke to the prophets.* See 6:5; Am 2:11 and notes; Heb 1:1. There have been ample warning. *visions.* Revelations (see Nu 12:6–8 and note; Am 1:1). *parables.* Containing messages of warning from God (see 2Sa 12:1–4; Ps 78:2; Isa 5:1–7; Eze 17:2; 24:3).
12:11 *Gilead wicked.* See 6:8–9 and notes. Gilead was overrun by Assyria in 734–732 ʙ.ᴄ. (2Ki 15:29). *Gilgal.* See 4:15 and note. The Hebrew contains a wordplay between "Gilgal" and "piles" (Hebrew *gallim*). Rather than assuring safety, the altars themselves would be destroyed. Israelite farmers gathered into piles the stones turned up by their plows.
12:12 Jacob fled from Esau to Paddan Aram (Ge 28:2,5), serving Laban seven years for each wife (Ge 29:20–28), and then continued six more years as Laban's herdsman (Ge 30:31; 31:41).
12:13 *prophet.* Moses (cf. Nu 12:6–8; Dt 18:15; 34:10). *cared for him.* As Jacob had cared for Laban's flocks, so the Lord cared for

Israel during her wilderness wandering. Earlier leadership by the prophet Moses stands in contrast with Israel's present disregard for prophets (cf. 4:5; 6:5; 9:7).
12:14 *Ephraim ... aroused his bitter anger.* Despite warnings. *bloodshed.* Cf. 1:4; 4:2; 5:2; 6:8. This refers to violence committed against others, including human sacrifice (see 13:2 and note). In legal passages such as Lev 20:11–27, "their blood will be on their own heads" describes guilt. The prophet drew a contrast between past divine preservation and present divine anger that would bring punishment. *repay.* See Isa 65:7.
13:1 *When Ephraim spoke.* In accordance with Jacob's blessing (Ge 48:10–20), Ephraim became a powerful tribe (Jdg 8:1–3; 12:1–6; 1Sa 1:1–4), from which came such prominent leaders as Joshua (Nu 13:8,16; Jos 24:29–30) and Jeroboam I (1Ki 11:26; 12:20). *Ephraim.* See note on 4:17. *Israel.* The 12 tribes. *died.* The wages of sin was death (cf. Ro 6:23), and the end of the nation was at hand.
13:2 *idols.* See 4:12; 8:5–6 and notes; 11:2. *human sacrifices.* See Lev 18:21; 2Ki 16:13; 17:17; 23:10; Jer 7:31 and notes; Eze 20:26; Mic 6:7. For the sense of the TNIV text note, see 1Ki 12:26–33. *kiss.* Show homage to (see Ps 2:12 and note). *calf-idols.* See 8:5 and note; 10:5.
13:3 "Mist" and "dew" (see 6:4), "chaff" (see Ps 1:4 and note; 35:5; Isa 17:13; 29:5; Zep 2:2) and "smoke" (see Ps 37:20; 68:2; Isa

13:3 ʸS Job 13:25;
Ps 1:4; S Isa 17:13
ʷDa 2:35 ˣPs 68:2
13:4 ʸS Jer 2:6;
S Hos 12:9
ᶻS Hos 2:20
ᵃS Ex 20:3
ᵇS Dt 28:29;
Ps 18:46; Isa 43:11;
45:21-22
13:5 ᶜS Dt 1:19
13:6 ᵈS Eze 28:5
ᵉS Dt 32:18;
S Isa 17:10 ᶠDt 32:12-
15; S Pr 30:7-9;
S Jer 5:7; S Hos 2:13;
S 4:7
13:7 ᵍS Job 10:16;
S Jer 4:7
13:8 ʰ2Sa 17:8
ⁱS 1Sa 17:34; Ps 17:12
ʲPs 50:22; S La 3:10;
S Hos 2:12
13:9 ᵏJer 2:17-19
ˡS Dt 33:29
13:10 ᵐ2Ki 17:4;
Hos 7:7 ⁿ1Sa 8:6;
Hos 8:4
13:11 ᵒS Nu 11:20
ᵖS Jos 24:20;
S 1Sa 13:14;
S 1Ki 14:10; Hos 3:4;
S 10:7
13:12 ᵍS Dt 32:34
13:13 ʳIsa 13:8;
Mic 4:9-10 ˢ2Ki 19:3
ᵗIsa 66:9
13:14 ᵘS Ps 16:10;
49:15; S Eze 37:12-13
ᵛS Isa 25:8
ʷ1Co 15:55ˣ
13:15 ˣS Hos 10:1
ʸS Job 1:19;
S Eze 19:12;
S Hos 4:19
ᶻS Jer 51:36 ᵃJer 20:5

like chaff ᵛ swirling from a threshing floor, ʷ
like smoke ˣ escaping through a window.

⁴ "But I have been the LORD your God
    ever since you came out of Egypt. ʸ
You shall acknowledge ᶻ no God but me, ᵃ
    no Savior ᵇ except me.
⁵ I cared for you in the wilderness, ᶜ
    in the land of burning heat.
⁶ When I fed them, they were satisfied;
    when they were satisfied, they became proud; ᵈ
    then they forgot ᵉ me. ᶠ
⁷ So I will come upon them like a lion, ᵍ
    like a leopard I will lurk by the path.
⁸ Like a bear robbed of her cubs, ʰ
    I will attack them and rip them open;
like a lion ⁱ I will devour them—
    a wild animal will tear them apart. ʲ

⁹ "You are destroyed, Israel,
    because you are against me, ᵏ against your helper. ˡ
¹⁰ Where is your king, ᵐ that he may save you?
    Where are your rulers in all your towns,
of whom you said,
    'Give me a king and princes'? ⁿ
¹¹ So in my anger I gave you a king, ᵒ
    and in my wrath I took him away. ᵖ
¹² The guilt of Ephraim is stored up,
    his sins are kept on record. ᵍ
¹³ Pains as of a woman in childbirth ʳ come to him,
    but he is a child without wisdom;
when the time ˢ arrives,
    he does not come to the opening of the womb. ᵗ

¹⁴ "I will deliver them from the power of the grave; ᵘ
    I will redeem them from death. ᵛ
Where, O death, are your plagues?
    Where, O grave, is your destruction? ʷ

"I will have no compassion,
¹⁵ even though he thrives ˣ among his brothers.
An east wind ʸ from the LORD will come,
    blowing in from the desert;
his spring will fail
    and his well dry up. ᶻ
His storehouse will be plundered ᵃ
    of all its treasures.

51:6) are all figurative for Ephraim, which was soon to vanish as
a nation.
13:4 *I have been the LORD your God ever since.* See 12:9; Ex 20:2 and
note. The contrast is with Jeroboam's declaration, "Here are your
gods" (1Ki 12:28). *acknowledge . . . God.* See 2:20; 6:3 and notes.
13:5 *wilderness.* See 2:14; 9:10 and notes.
13:6 *satisfied.* See Dt 6:11–12; 8:10–14; 11:15. *forgot me.* See
2:13; Dt 6:10–12 and notes; 8:11,14,19; 32:18.
13:7–8 The Lord, previously pictured as a shepherd (4:16),
would attack like the wild beasts that often ravaged the flocks.
13:7 *lion.* See 5:14 and note. *leopard.* See Jer 5:6; Rev 13:2.
13:8 *bear robbed of her cubs.* See 2Sa 17:8; Pr 17:12 and note.
13:9 *helper.* See Ps 10:14; 30:10; 54:4.

13:10 *Where is your king . . . ?* Help comes only from the
Lord (Ps 121:2), not from kings. The prophet likely alludes
to the royal assassinations of his day (see 7:7; 8:4 and notes).
Give me a king. Though all Israel asked for a king in the days of
Samuel (see 1Sa 8:5 and note), the reference here is only to the
northern monarchy. Israel selected Jeroboam I (1Ki 12:20) in

preference to the Davidic kings.
13:11 Reference is to the kings of the northern kingdom of Israel.
13:12 See 9:9 and note; Job 14:17. *sins . . . on record.* See 7:2
and note; Dt 32:34.
13:13 *Pains as of . . . childbirth.* Their helpless situation was
comparable to that of a woman in childbirth (see Isa 13:8 and
note; 21:3; Jer 13:21; Mic 4:9–10; Mt 24:8) who cannot deliver
the child (see 2Ki 19:3) and consequently dies.
13:14 *I will deliver.* A promise of rescue from death. *Where, O
death . . . ?* The personified reference is to the death of the nation
(see note on v. 1). Paul applies this passage to resurrection (1Co
15:55). *grave.* For a description of "the grave" (Hebrew *Sheol*),
see Job 3:13–19; Isa 14:9–10; see also note on Ge 37:35.
13:15 *thrives.* In Hebrew a wordplay on Ephraim (meaning "fruitful"). *east wind.* The drought-bringing east wind (see 12:1; Ge 41:7
and note; Job 1:19; Isa 27:8; Jer 4:11; 13:24; 18:17) is here a figure
for Assyria, an instrument of the Lord (see Isa 10:5 and note). Assyria invaded the northern kingdom in 734 B.C., then crushed it
and exiled its people in 722–721. *all its treasures.* See Na 2:9.

*[16] The people of Samaria [b] must bear their guilt, [c]
    because they have rebelled [d] against their God.
They will fall by the sword; [e]
    their little ones will be dashed [f] to the ground,
    their pregnant women [g] ripped open."

REPENTANCE TO BRING BLESSING

14

*[1] "Return, [h] Israel, to the LORD your God.
    Your sins [i] have been your downfall! [j]
[2] Take words with you
    and return to the LORD.
Say to him:
    "Forgive [k] all our sins
and receive us graciously, [l]
    that we may offer the fruit of our lips. [a] [m]
[3] Assyria cannot save us; [n]
    we will not mount warhorses. [o]
We will never again say 'Our gods' [p]
    to what our own hands have made, [q]
    for in you the fatherless [r] find compassion."

[4] "I will heal [s] their waywardness [t]
    and love them freely, [u]
    for my anger has turned away [v] from them.
[5] I will be like the dew [w] to Israel;
    he will blossom like a lily. [x]
Like a cedar of Lebanon [y]
    he will send down his roots; [z]
[6]   his young shoots will grow.
His splendor will be like an olive tree, [a]
    his fragrance like a cedar of Lebanon. [b]
[7] People will dwell again in his shade; [c]
    they will flourish like the grain,
they will blossom [d] like the vine—
    Israel's fame will be like the wine [e] of Lebanon. [f]
[8] Ephraim, what more have I [b] to do with idols? [g]
    I will answer him and care for him.
I am like a flourishing juniper; [h]
    your fruitfulness comes from me."

[9] Who is wise? [i] Let them realize these things.
    Who is discerning? Let them understand. [j]
The ways of the LORD are right; [k]
    the righteous walk [l] in them,
    but the rebellious stumble in them.

---

[a] 2 Or *offer our lips as sacrifices of bulls*   [b] 8 Or Hebrew; Septuagint *What more has Ephraim*
* 13:16 is numbered 14:1 in Hebrew texts.   * 14:1-9 is numbered 14:2-10 in Hebrew texts.

13:16 *Samaria.* See 7:1 and note; 8:5–6; 10:5,7; here, the northern kingdom. *rebelled against.* See Ps 5:10; Isa 1:2 and note; Eze 20:8,13,21. *little ones … women.* For atrocities against women and children, see 10:14; Ps 137:9 and notes.

🅰 **14:1** *Return.* Another appeal for repentance (see 10:12; 12:6). Unlike that of ch. 6, this repentance would have to be sincere in order for the people to receive the gracious response from the Lord promised in vv. 4–8 (cf. Ps 130:7–8; Isa 55:6–7).

🅰 **14:2** *Take words.* None could appear before the Lord empty-handed (Ex 23:15; 34:20), but animal sacrifices would not be enough. Only words of true repentance would be sufficient. *fruit of our lips.* As thank offerings to the Lord (see Heb 13:15).

14:3 *what our own hands have made.* Idols (see v. 8; 13:2 and note). *fatherless.* Penitent Israel (see Ps 10:14; 68:5; La 5:3). *find compassion.* Cf. the name of the child Lo-Ruhamah (see 1:6 and note; see also 2:1,23).

14:4 *heal.* See 11:3 and note. *waywardness.* See 11:7. *love them*

freely. That is, love them out of my own free choice (cf. 9:15 and note). *love.* See 3:1; 11:1 and notes. *anger … turned away.* Contrasts with the burning anger that brought destruction (see 8:5).

14:5 *dew.* Here not a symbol of transitoriness (cf. 6:4; 13:3) but of God's blessing (see Dt 33:13; Mic 5:7 and note). *cedar of Lebanon.* See notes on Jdg 9:15; 1Ki 5:6; Isa 9:10. *cedar.* See Ps 80:8–11. *Lebanon.* See Ps 104:16–18 and note.

14:7 *shade.* See Jdg 9:15 and note; SS 2:3; Eze 31:6). *vine.* See 10:1; Ps 80:8–16 and note.

14:8 *Ephraim.* See note on 4:17. *flourishing juniper.* Only here in the OT is God compared to a tree. For the point of the imagery, see Eze 31:3–7; Da 4:12. *fruitfulness.* Ephraim ("fruitful"; see Ge 41:52 and note) received his fruitfulness from the Lord (cf. 2:8).

🅰 **14:9** *ways of the LORD.* See Ps 18:21; 25:4 and note. The prophet concludes by offering each reader the alternatives of walking or stumbling (cf. 4:5; 5:5)—of obedience or rebellion. *right.* See note on Ps 119:121.

13:16 [b] 2Ki 17:5
[c] Hos 10:2
[d] S Hos 7:14
[e] Hos 11:6
[f] S 2Ki 8:12;
  S Hos 10:14
[g] 2Ki 15:16; Isa 13:16;
  Am 1:13
14:1 [h] S Isa 19:22;
  S Jer 3:12 [i] S Hos 4:8
[j] S Hos 5:5; S 9:7
14:2 [k] S Ex 34:9
[l] Ps 51:16-17;
  Mic 7:18-19
[m] Heb 13:15
14:3 [n] S Hos 5:13
[o] Ps 33:17; S Isa 31:1;
  Mic 5:10 [p] Hos 8:6
[q] ver 28; Hos 13:2
[r] Ps 10:14; 68:5;
  Jer 49:11
14:4 [s] S Isa 30:26;
  S Hos 6:1 [t] S Jer 2:19
[u] S Isa 55:1; Jer 31:20;
  Zep 3:17 [v] S Job 13:16
14:5 [w] S Ge 27:28;
  S Isa 18:4 [x] S SS 2:1
[y] Isa 35:2 [z] Job 29:19
14:6 [a] Ps 52:8;
  S Jer 11:16
[b] S Ps 92:12;
  S SS 4:11
14:7 [c] Ps 91:1-4
[d] S Ge 40:10
[e] S Hos 2:22
[f] S Eze 17:23
14:8 [g] S ver 3
[h] S Isa 37:24
14:9 [i] S Ps 107:43
[j] S Pr 10:29;
  S Isa 1:28; Da 12:10
[k] Ps 111:7-8; Zep 3:5;
  Ac 13:10 [l] Isa 26:7

AUTHOR — JOEL — INTRODUCTION

C The prophet Joel cannot be identified with any of the 12 other figures in the OT who have the same name. He is not mentioned outside the books of Joel and Acts (Ac 2:16). The non-Biblical legends about him are unconvincing. His father, Pethuel (1:1), is also unknown. Judging from his concern with Judah and Jerusalem (see 2:32; 3:1,6,8,16–20), it seems likely that Joel lived in that area. See note on 1:1.

DATE

The book contains no references to datable historical events. Many interpreters date it somewhere between the late seventh and early fifth centuries B.C. In any case, its message is not significantly affected by its dating.

The book of Joel has striking linguistic parallels to the language of Amos, Micah, Zephaniah, Jeremiah and Ezekiel. Some scholars maintain that the prophets borrowed phrases from one another; others hold that they drew more or less from the religious literary traditions that they and their readers shared in common—liturgical and otherwise.

THEOLOGICAL MESSAGE

Joel sees the massive locust plague and severe drought devastating Judah as a harbinger of the "great and dreadful day of the LORD" (2:31). (The locusts he mentions in 1:4; 2:25 are best understood as real insects, not as allegorical representations of the Babylonians, Medo-Persians, Greeks and Romans, as held by some interpreters.) Confronted with this crisis, he calls on everyone to repent: old and young (1:2–3), drunkards (1:5), farmers (1:11) and priests (1:13). He describes the locusts as the Lord's army and sees in their coming a reminder that the day of the Lord is near. He does not voice the popular notion that the day will be one of judgment on the nations but deliverance and blessing for Israel. Instead—with Isaiah (2:10–21), Jeremiah (4:5–9), Amos (5:18–20) and Zephaniah (1:7–18)—he describes the day as one of punishment of unfaithful Israel as well. Restoration and blessing will come only after judgment and repentance.

OUTLINE

 KEY   **A** APPLICATION FOR LIVING   **B** BACKGROUND NOTES   **C** CHARACTER INFORMATION

The word of the LORD that came *a* to Joel *b* son of Pethuel.

AN INVASION OF LOCUSTS

² Hear this, *c* you elders; *d*
    listen, all who live in the land. *e*
Has anything like this ever happened in your days
    or in the days of your ancestors? *f*
³ Tell it to your children, *g*
    and let your children tell it to their children,
    and their children to the next generation. *h*
⁴ What the locust *i* swarm has left
    the great locusts have eaten;
what the great locusts have left
    the young locusts have eaten;
what the young locusts have left *j*
    other locusts *a* have eaten. *k*

⁵ Wake up, you drunkards, and weep!
    Wail, all you drinkers of wine; *l*
wail because of the new wine,
    for it has been snatched *m* from your lips.
⁶ A nation has invaded my land,
    a mighty army without number; *n*
it has the teeth *o* of a lion,
    the fangs of a lioness.
⁷ It has laid waste *p* my vines
    and ruined my fig trees. *q*
It has stripped off their bark
    and thrown it away,
    leaving their branches white.

⁸ Mourn like a virgin in sackcloth *r*
    grieving for the betrothed of her youth.
⁹ Grain offerings and drink offerings *s*
    are cut off from the house of the LORD.
The priests are in mourning, *t*
    those who minister before the LORD.
¹⁰ The fields are ruined,
    the ground is dried up; *u*

ᵃ 4 The precise meaning of the four Hebrew words used here for locusts is uncertain.

1:1 *aS* Jer 1:2
b Ac 2:16
1:2 *c* Hos 5:1
d Joel 2:16 *e* S Hos 4:1
f Joel 2:2
1:3 *g* S Ex 10:2
h S Ps 71:18
1:4 *i* S Ex 10:14
j S Ex 10:5
k S Ex 10:15;
S Dt 28:39; Am 7:1;
Na 3:15
1:5 *l* Joel 3:3
m S Isa 24:7
1:6 *n* Ps 105:34;
Joel 2:2,11,25
o Rev 9:8
1:7 *p* Isa 5:6
q Am 4:9
1:8 *r* ver 13;
Isa 22:12; Am 8:10
1:9 *s* S Hos 9:4
t S Isa 22:12
1:10 *u* S Isa 5:6;
S 24:4; S Jer 3:3

1:1 *word of the LORD.* See Hos 1:1 and note. *Joel.* Means "The LORD is God"; cf. Elijah's name, which means "(My) God is the LORD."
1:2 *elders.* Either the older men of the community or the recognized officials (see v. 14; 2:16,28; see also note on Ex 3:16).
1:4 *locust swarm … great locusts … young locusts … other locusts.* Either (1) various species of locusts or (2) locusts in various stages of their life cycle. See 2:25; Ex 10:4 and note.

A **1:5** *drunkards.* Although Joel calls for repentance, drunkenness is the only specific sin mentioned in the book (see notes on Pr 20:1; Eze 23:42). It suggests a self-indulgent lifestyle (cf. Isa 28:7–8; Am 4:1) pursued by those who value material things more than spiritual. *weep.* Various segments of the community (drunkards, here; farmers, v. 11; priests, v. 13) are called upon to mourn. The destruction of the vines by the locusts leaves the drunkards without a source of wine.

B **1:6** The locusts are compared here to a nation; cf. the ants and hyraxes in Pr 30:25–26, where the Hebrew word for "creatures" means lit. "(a) people." Elsewhere the locusts are called the Lord's "army" (2:11,25). The reverse comparison—that of armies to locusts in regard to numbers—is as old as Ugaritic literature (15th century B.C.; see chart, p. xxiv) and is common in

the OT (see Jdg 6:5 and note; Jer 46:23; 51:14,27; Na 3:15). *without number.* A phrase used to describe the locusts in the plague in Egypt (see Ps 105:34; see also Ex 10:4–6,12–15). *teeth.* Joel's comparison of the locusts' teeth to lions' teeth is reflected in Rev 9:8.

1:7 *my.* The personal pronouns here and elsewhere in Joel (vv. 6,13–14; 2:1,13–14,17–18,23,26–27; 3:2–5,17) offer a hint of hope, since they indicate that the people belong to the Lord (cf. Jos 22:19).
1:8 *virgin.* The community is addressed. In Israel, when a woman was pledged to be married to a man, he was called her husband and she his wife, though she was still a virgin (see Dt 22:23–24). This verse refers to such a husband who died before the marriage was consummated. *sackcloth.* See v. 13; Ge 37:34; Rev 11:3 and notes.
1:9 *offerings.* See v. 13; 2:14. The locusts have left nothing that can be offered as sacrifice. The grain offering (Lev 2:1–2) and the drink offering, which was a libation of wine (Lev 23:13), were part of the daily offering (Ex 29:40; Nu 28:5–8).
1:10 *dried up.* The destruction caused by the locusts was intensified by drought. *grain … new wine … olive oil.* An important OT triad, related to the agriculture of that day (see 2:19).

1:10 ᵛ S Hos 9:2
ʷ S Nu 18:12
1:11 ˣ S Job 6:20;
Am 5:16 ʸ S Ex 9:31
ᶻ S Isa 17:11
1:12 ᵃ S Isa 15:6
ᵇ S Ex 28:33
ᶜ S Isa 16:8; Hag 2:19
1:13 ᵈ S Ge 37:34;
S Jer 4:8 ᵉ Joel 2:17
ᶠ ver 9; S Hos 9:4;
Joel 2:14
1:14 ᵍ S 2Ch 20:3
ʰ S Hos 4:1 ⁱ Jnh 3:8
ʲ 2Ch 20:4
1:15 ᵏ S Isa 2:12;
Jer 30:7; S 46:10;
S Eze 30:3; Mal 4:5
ˡ Joel 2:1,11,31; 3:14;
Am 5:18; Zep 1:14;
Zec 14:1 ᵐ S Ge 17:1
1:16 ⁿ Isa 3:7
ᵒ S Ps 51:8 ᵖ Dt 12:7
1:17 ᵠ S Isa 17:10-11
1:18 ʳ S Ge 47:4
ˢ S Jer 9:10

the grain is destroyed,
    the new wine ᵛ is dried up,
    the olive oil fails. ʷ

¹¹ Despair, you farmers, ˣ
    wail, you vine growers;
grieve for the wheat and the barley, ʸ
    because the harvest of the field is destroyed. ᶻ
¹² The vine is dried up
    and the fig tree is withered; ᵃ
the pomegranate, ᵇ the palm and the apple ᵃ tree—
    all the trees of the field—are dried up. ᶜ
Surely the people's joy
    is withered away.

A CALL TO LAMENTATION

¹³ Put on sackcloth, ᵈ you priests, and mourn;
    wail, you who minister ᵉ before the altar.
Come, spend the night in sackcloth,
    you who minister before my God;
for the grain offerings and drink offerings ᶠ
    are withheld from the house of your God.
¹⁴ Declare a holy fast; ᵍ
    call a sacred assembly.
Summon the elders
    and all who live in the land ʰ
to the house of the Lᴏʀᴅ your God,
    and cry out ⁱ to the Lᴏʀᴅ. ʲ

¹⁵ Alas for that ᵏ day!
    For the day of the Lᴏʀᴅ ˡ is near;
    it will come like destruction from the Almighty. ᵇ ᵐ

¹⁶ Has not the food been cut off ⁿ
    before our very eyes—
joy and gladness ᵒ
    from the house of our God? ᵖ
¹⁷ The seeds are shriveled
    beneath the clods. ᶜ ᵠ
The storehouses are in ruins,
    the granaries have been broken down,
    for the grain has dried up.
¹⁸ How the cattle moan!
    The herds mill about
because they have no pasture; ʳ
    even the flocks of sheep are suffering. ˢ

ᵃ 12 Or possibly *apricot*   ᵇ 15 Hebrew *Shaddai*   ᶜ 17 The meaning of the Hebrew for this word is uncertain.

1:13 *my God … your God.* See note on v. 7. *grain offerings and drink offerings.* See note on v. 9.

![A] **1:14** *fast … assembly.* See 2:15. Fasting, required on the Day of Atonement (see note and TNIV text note on Lev 16:29) and also practiced in times of calamity (see Jdg 20:26; 2Sa 12:16; Est 4:3,16; Jer 14:12; Jnh 3:4–5; Zec 7:3), was a sign of penitence and humility. The Bible speaks against outward signs that do not reflect a corresponding inward belief or attitude (see Mt 6:1–8,16–18; 23:1–36). *elders.* See notes on v. 2; Ex 3:16; 2Sa 3:17.

![A] **1:15** *day of the LORD.* See notes on Isa 2:11,17,20; 10:20,27; Am 5:18. This phrase occurs five times in Joel and is its dominant theme (here; 2:1,11,31; 3:14). Six other prophets also use it: Isaiah (13:6,9), Ezekiel (13:5; 30:3), Amos (5:18,20), Obadiah (15), Zephaniah (1:7,14) and Malachi (4:5); and an equivalent expression occurs in Zec 14:1. Sometimes abbreviated as "that day," the term often refers to the decisive in-

tervention of God in history, such as through the invasion of locusts in Joel or at the battle of Carchemish, 605 B.C. (see Jer 46:2,10). It can also refer to Christ's coming to consummate history (see Mal 4:5; 1Co 5:5; 2Co 1:14; 1Th 5:2 and note; 2Pe 3:10). When the term is not used for divine judgments in the midst of history, it refers to the final day of the Lord, which generally has two aspects: (1) God's triumph over and punishment of his enemies and (2) his granting of rest (security) and blessing to his people. *destruction … Almighty.* See Isa 13:6 and note.

1:18 Cf. the description of a drought in Jer 14:5–6. *moan.* The Hebrew for this word is used for the groaning of Israel in Egypt (Ex 2:23) and of others in distress (Pr 29:2; Isa 24:7; La 1:4,8,11, 21; Eze 9:4; 21:12). *mill about.* The Hebrew for this verb is used to describe Israel's confused movements in the wilderness (Ex 14:3). *even … sheep.* Sheep are the last to suffer, because they can even grub the grass roots out of the soil.

¹⁹ To you, LORD, I call,^t
for fire^u has devoured the pastures^v in the wilderness
and flames have burned up all the trees of the field.
²⁰ Even the wild animals pant for you;^w
the streams of water have dried up^x
and fire has devoured the pastures^y in the wilderness.

AN ARMY OF LOCUSTS

2
Blow the trumpet^z in Zion;^a
sound the alarm on my holy hill.^b

Let all who live in the land tremble,
for the day of the LORD^c is coming.
It is close at hand^d—
² a day of darkness^e and gloom,^{fg}
a day of clouds^h and blackness.ⁱ
Like dawn spreading across the mountains
a large and mighty army^j comes,
such as never was of old^k
nor ever will be in ages to come.

³ Before them fire^l devours,
behind them a flame blazes.
Before them the land is like the garden of Eden,^m
behind them, a desert wasteⁿ—
nothing escapes them.
⁴ They have the appearance of horses;^o
they gallop along like cavalry.
⁵ With a noise like that of chariots^p
they leap over the mountaintops,
like a crackling fire^q consuming stubble,
like a mighty army drawn up for battle.

⁶ At the sight of them, nations are in anguish;^r
every face turns pale.^s
⁷ They charge like warriors;^t
they scale walls like soldiers.
They all march in line,^u
not swerving^v from their course.
⁸ They do not jostle each other;
each marches straight ahead.
They plunge through defenses
without breaking ranks.
⁹ They rush upon the city;
they run along the wall.

1:19 ^t Ps 50:15
^u S Ps 97:3; Am 7:4
^v S Jer 9:10
1:20 ^w S Ps 42:1;
S 104:21 ^x 1Ki 17:7
^y Joel 2:22
2:1 ^z S Nu 10:2,7
^a ver 15 ^b S Ex 15:17
^c S Joel 1:15; Zep 1:14-
16 ^d S Eze 12:23;
S 30:3; Ob 1:15
2:2 ^e ver 10,31;
S Job 9:7; S Isa 8:22;
S 13:10; Am 5:18
^f S Da 9:12;
S Mt 24:21
^g S Eze 34:12
^h S Eze 38:9
ⁱ Zep 1:15; Rev 9:2
^j S Joel 1:6 ^k Joel 1:2
2:3 ^l S Ps 97:3;
S Isa 1:31 ^m S Ge 2:8
ⁿ Ex 10:12-15;
Ps 105:34-35;
S Isa 14:17
2:4 ^o Rev 9:7
2:5 ^p Rev 9:9
^q Isa 5:24; 30:30
2:6 ^r S Isa 13:8
^s S Isa 29:22
2:7 ^t S Job 16:14
^u Pr 30:27 ^v Isa 5:27

1:19–20 *fire.* Although the destruction caused by the locusts is elsewhere compared to that of a fire (see 2:3), here the prophet may be describing the effects of a drought. In both cases he evokes the fire of God's judgment (see, e.g., Jer 4:4; 15:14; 17:27 and note; Eze 5:4; 15:6–7 and note on 15:7; 20:47; 21:32; Hos 8:14; Am 1:4 and note).
2:1 *trumpet.* See v. 15. Made of a ram's or bull's horn, it was used to signal approaching danger (see Jer 4:5; Eze 33:3 and notes). Its sound brought trembling (from fear) to the people (see Am 3:6). *Zion.* See v. 15; 3:17,21. Here it refers to Jerusalem as the capital of the nation. *day of the LORD.* See 1:15; Isa 2:11,17,20 and notes.
2:2 *day of darkness.* Darkness is a common prophetic figure used of the day of the Lord (see Am 5:18 and note; Zep 1:15) and is generally a metaphor for distress and suffering (see Isa 50:3; 59:9; Jer 2:6; 13:16; La 3:6; Eze 34:12 and notes). *dawn.* Usually suggests relief from sorrow or gloom, the end of darkness (cf. Isa 8:20; 58:8). Here, however, it is used as bitter irony, describing the locust infestation that fans out across the land like the light of dawn, which first lights up the eastern horizon and

then spreads across the whole countryside.
2:3–11 The staccato character of the poetry is appropriate for the imagery of war (see Na 3:1–3).
2:3 *Before them.* Joel creates a special impact by using this phrase three times (twice in v. 3 and once in v. 10), "behind them" twice (v. 3) and "At the sight of them" once (v. 6). *fire.* See note on 1:19–20. *Eden.* See Ge 2:8,15 (the garden before the fall); Ge 13:10 (the Jordan Valley before the destruction of Sodom); and Isa 51:3; Eze 31:8–9,16,18; 36:35 (all of which describe a desert that has become like Eden).
2:4 *horses.* Whereas the book of Job compares the horse to a locust (Job 39:19–20), Joel does the opposite.
2:5 *leap over the mountaintops.* Mountains, though barriers to ordinary horses and chariots, are no deterrent to locusts.
2:6 *At the sight of them.* Parallels "Before them" (vv. 3,10). *in anguish.* Because of the famine that the locusts will cause.
2:9 *climb into the houses.* As in the Egyptian plague of locusts (Ex 10:6). Latticed windows with no glass would not stop them.

2:9 ʷ Ex 10:6
ˣ Jer 9:21
2:10 ʸ Ps 18:7;
Na 1:5 ᶻ S Eze 38:19
ᵃ S ver 2; S Isa 5:30;
S Mt 24:29;
Mk 13:24; Rev 9:2
ᵇ S Job 9:7;
S Ps 102:26; Isa 13:10;
S Eze 32:8
2:11 ᶜ S Isa 2:12;
S Eze 30:3;
S Joel 1:15; Ob 1:15
ᵈ S Ps 29:3 ᵉ S ver 2,
25 ᶠ Zep 1:14
ᵍ S Eze 22:14;
Zep 2:11; Rev 6:17
2:12 ʰ S Dt 4:30;
S Eze 33:11; S Hos
12:6 ⁱ S Isa 7:3
2:13 ʲ Ps 51:17;
Isa 57:15
ᵏ S Ge 37:29;
S Nu 14:6; Job 1:20
ˡ S Isa 19:22
ᵐ S Dt 4:31 ⁿ Ex 34:6;
S Ps 86:5,15
ᵒ S Jer 18:8; Jnh 4:2
2:14 ᵖ Jer 26:3;
Jnh 3:9 �q Am 5:15;
Jnh 1:6 ʳ Jer 31:14;
Hag 2:19; Zec 8:13;
Mal 3:10 ˢ S Joel 1:13
2:15 ᵗ S Nu 10:2
ᵘ ver 1 ᵛ S 2Ch 20:3;
Jer 36:9 ʷ S Ex 32:5;
Nu 10:3
2:16 ˣ S Ex 19:10,22
ʸ Joel 1:2 ᶻ Ps 19:5
2:17 ᵃ Joel 1:13
ᵇ S Isa 22:12
ᶜ Eze 8:16; Mt 23:35
ᵈ Dt 9:26-29;
Ps 44:13

They climb into the houses; ʷ
  like thieves they enter through the windows. ˣ

¹⁰ Before them the earth shakes, ʸ
  the heavens tremble, ᶻ
the sun and moon are darkened, ᵃ
  and the stars no longer shine. ᵇ
¹¹ The Lᴏʀᴅ ᶜ thunders ᵈ
  at the head of his army; ᵉ
his forces are beyond number,
  and mighty is the army that obeys his command.
The day of the Lᴏʀᴅ is great; ᶠ
  it is dreadful.
Who can endure it? ᵍ

REND YOUR HEART

¹² "Even now," declares the Lᴏʀᴅ,
  "return ʰ to me with all your heart, ⁱ
  with fasting and weeping and mourning."

¹³ Rend your heart ʲ
  and not your garments. ᵏ
Return ˡ to the Lᴏʀᴅ your God,
  for he is gracious and compassionate, ᵐ
slow to anger and abounding in love, ⁿ
  and he relents from sending calamity. ᵒ
¹⁴ Who knows? He may turn ᵖ and relent �q
  and leave behind a blessing ʳ—
grain offerings and drink offerings ˢ
  for the Lᴏʀᴅ your God.

¹⁵ Blow the trumpet ᵗ in Zion, ᵘ
  declare a holy fast, ᵛ
  call a sacred assembly. ʷ
¹⁶ Gather the people,
  consecrate ˣ the assembly;
bring together the elders, ʸ
  gather the children,
  those nursing at the breast.
Let the bridegroom ᶻ leave his room
  and the bride her chamber.
¹⁷ Let the priests, who minister ᵃ before the Lᴏʀᴅ,
  weep ᵇ between the portico and the altar. ᶜ
Let them say, "Spare your people, Lᴏʀᴅ.
  Do not make your inheritance an object of scorn, ᵈ

2:10 *earth shakes.* See Ps 68:8; 77:18; Isa 24:18–20; Jer 4:24; Am 8:8; Na 1:5. *heavens tremble.* See 2Sa 22:8; Isa 13:13; Hag 2:6,21; Heb 12:26–28. *darkened.* Joel links God's judgment through the locusts to the cosmic phenomena of the day of the Lord.
2:11 Just as Isaiah saw the Assyrians (see Isa 10:5 and note) and Jeremiah the Babylonians (Jer 25:9; 43:10) as the Lord's weapons, so Joel sees the locusts as the Lord's army (cf. Jos 5:14; Ps 68:17; Hab 3:8–9)—the army of the Lord with which he will come against his enemies in the day of the Lord (see 3:9–11 and note). This passage parallels Zep 1:14 (cf. v. 31; 3:14; Mal 4:1,5). *thunders.* See 3:16 and note. *great ... dreadful.* Two ideas often associated in the OT, though sometimes the Hebrew word underlying "dreadful" means "awesome" (see Dt 7:21; 10:21; Ps 106:21–22). The terms are frequently used to describe the day of the Lord (see v. 31; Mal 4:5). *Who can endure it?* See Na 1:6 and note; Mal 3:2; Rev 6:17. There is no escape except in turning to God.
2:12–17 The first half of the book ends with a call to repentance ("return," vv. 12–13; see Hos 14:1 and note) and prayer (v. 17), balancing the call to mourning and prayer with which the section begins (1:2–14).

2:13 *Rend your heart.* See Ps 51:17 and note. *gracious ... abounding in love.* Recalls the great self-characterization of God in Ex 34:6–7, which runs like a golden thread through the OT (see note on Ex 34:6–7; see also Dt 4:31; Mic 7:18).
2:14 *grain offerings and drink offerings.* See note on 1:9.
2:15 *trumpet.* Not an alarm as in v. 1, but a call to religious assembly (see Lev 23:24; 25:9; Nu 10:10; Jos 6:4–5; 2Ch 15:14; Ps 98:6 and note). *fast ... assembly.* See note on 1:14.
2:16 As with the call to mourning in ch. 1, no segment of the community was exempt. *assembly.* The Hebrew for this word refers to the religious community (see Nu 16:3; 2Ch 30:2,4,23–25; Mic 2:5). *elders.* See note on 1:2. *chamber.* The place where the marriage was consummated.
2:17 *your inheritance.* Israel is God's special possession (see Ex 34:9; Jer 3:19 and note). Judah is to plead, not her innocence, but that God's honor is at stake before the world (see Ex 32:12; see also Nu 14:13; Jos 7:9 and notes). *byword.* See note on 1Ki 9:7. *Where is their God?* A rhetorical question with sarcastic intent (see Ps 3:2; 10:11; 115:2 and notes).

a byword^e among the nations.
Why should they say among the peoples,
'Where is their God?^f'"

THE LORD'S ANSWER

¹⁸ Then the Lord was jealous^g for his land
and took pity^h on his people.

¹⁹The Lord replied^a to them:

"I am sending you grain, new wineⁱ and olive oil,^j
enough to satisfy you fully;^k
never again will I make you
an object of scorn^l to the nations.

²⁰ "I will drive the northern horde^m far from you,
pushing it into a parched and barren land;
its eastern ranks will drown in the Dead Sea
and its western ranks in the Mediterranean Sea.
And its stenchⁿ will go up;
its smell will rise."

Surely he has done great things!
²¹ Do not be afraid, ^o land of Judah;
be glad and rejoice.^p
Surely the Lord has done great things!^q
²² Do not be afraid, you wild animals,
for the pastures in the wilderness are becoming green.^r
The trees are bearing their fruit;
the fig tree^s and the vine^t yield their riches.^u
²³ Be glad, people of Zion,
rejoice^v in the Lord your God,
for he has given you
the autumn rains in righteousness.^w
He sends you abundant showers,^x
both autumn^y and spring rains,^z as before.
²⁴ The threshing floors will be filled with grain;
the vats will overflow^a with new wine^b and oil.

²⁵ "I will repay you for the years the locusts^c have eaten^d—
the great locust and the young locust,
the other locusts and the locust swarm^b—
my great army^e that I sent among you.
²⁶ You will have plenty to eat, until you are full,^f
and you will praise^g the name of the Lord your God,
who has worked wonders^h for you;
never again will my people be shamed.ⁱ
²⁷ Then you will know^j that I am in Israel,

---

^a 18,19 Or Lord will be jealous . . . / and take pity . . . / ¹⁹The Lord will reply   ^b 25 The precise meaning of
the four Hebrew words used here for locusts is uncertain.

2:17 ^e S 1Ki 9:7;
S Job 17:6 ^f S Ps 42:3
2:18 ^g S Isa 26:11;
Zec 1:14; 8:2
^h S Ps 72:13
2:19 ⁱ Ps 4:7
^j S Jer 31:12
^k S Lev 26:5
^l S Eze 34:29
2:20 ^m Jer 1:14-15
ⁿ S Isa 34:3
2:21 ^o S Isa 29:22;
S 54:4; Zep 3:16-17
^p S Ps 9:2
^q S Ps 126:3;
S Isa 25:1
2:22 ^r S Ps 65:12
^s S 1Ki 4:25
^t S Nu 16:14
^u Joel 1:18-20;
Zec 8:12
2:23 ^v Ps 33:21;
97:12; 149:2; Isa 12:6;
41:16; 66:14;
Hab 3:18; Zec 10:7
^w S Isa 45:8
^x S Job 36:28;
S Eze 34:26 ^y Ps 84:6
^z S Lev 26:4;
S Ps 135:7; Jas 5:7
2:24 ^a Lev 26:10;
Mal 3:10 ^b S Pr 3:10;
Joel 3:18; Am 9:13
2:25 ^c S Ex 10:14;
Am 4:9 ^d S Dt 28:39
^e S Joel 1:6
2:26 ^f S Lev 26:5
^g S Lev 23:40;
S Isa 62:9
^h S Ps 126:3;
S Isa 25:1
ⁱ S Isa 29:22
2:27 ^j S Ex 6:7

2:18 Joel begins a new section by turning from the destruction caused by the locusts to the blessings God gave (or will give; see TNIV text note on vv. 18,19) to a repentant people. *jealous.* See note on Ex 20:5. The Lord responded (or will respond) to the prayer of v. 17 and aroused (or will arouse) himself to defend his honor and have pity on his people.
2:19 *grain, new wine and olive oil.* See note on 1:10.
2:20 *northern horde.* Since enemies in ancient times did not invade from the sea or across the desert, Canaan's geographical location made her vulnerable only from the south (Egypt) and from the north (Assyria and Babylon). The hordes of locusts are pictured here as a vast army of Israel's most feared enemies. *stench.* Because the locusts are now dead.
2:21–23 As there was a multiple call to grief (1:5,8, 11,13), so there is a multiple call to joy: The land (v. 21), the wild animals (v. 22) and the people (v. 23) are called on to

rejoice in the Lord's bounty.
2:22 The wild animals now find green open pastures (cf. 1:19–20). The same land, with its trees that the locusts and drought had devastated (see 1:7,12,19), is now productive.
2:23 *autumn and spring rains.* See notes on Dt 11:14; Jas 5:7.
2:24 *threshing floors.* See note on Ru 1:22. *vats.* See note on Hag 2:16.
2:25 See 1:4 and note.
2:26 *wonders.* God performed wonders for the people when they were in Egypt (see Ex 3:20 and note; 7:3), and now he will work wonders in restoring the devastated land.
2:27 *Israel.* Probably refers to all God's people, with no distinction between the northern and southern kingdoms, as also in 3:2,16. *I am the Lord your God.* This clause recalls the covenant at Sinai (see Ex 20:2 and note). *there is no other.* See note on Dt 4:35.

2:27 *k* S Ex 6:2;
S Isa 44:8; Joel 3:17
l Isa 45:17; 54:4;
Zep 3:11
2:28 *m* S Isa 11:2;
S 44:3 *n* S Nu 11:17;
S Mk 1:8; Gal 3:14
o S 1Sa 19:20
p Jer 23:25
2:29 *q* 1Co 12:13;
Gal 3:28 *r* S Eze 36:27
2:30 *s* Lk 21:11
t Mk 13:24-25
2:31 *u* S ver 2;
S Isa 22:5; S Jer 4:23;
S Mt 24:29
v S Joel 1:15; Ob 1:15;
Mal 3:2; 4:1,5
2:32 *w* S Ge 4:26;
S Ps 105:1
x S Ps 106:8; Ac 2:17-
21*; Ro 10:13*
y S Isa 46:13 *z* Ob 1:17
a S Isa 1:9; 11:11;
Mic 4:7; 7:18;
S Ro 9:27 *b* Ac 2:39
3:1 *c* S Dt 30:3;
S Jer 16:15;
S Eze 38:8; Zep 3:20
d Jer 40:5
3:2 *e* Zep 3:8
f ver 12; S Isa 22:1
g S Isa 13:9;
S Jer 2:35; S Eze 36:5
h S Ge 11:4;
S Lev 26:33
3:3 *i* S Job 6:27;
S Eze 24:6 *j* Joel 1:5;
Am 2:6

that I am the Lord *k* your God,
  and that there is no other;
never again will my people be shamed. *l*

THE DAY OF THE LORD

*28 "And afterward,
  I will pour out my Spirit *m* on all people. *n*
  Your sons and daughters will prophesy, *o*
  your old men will dream dreams, *p*
  your young men will see visions.
29 Even on my servants, *q* both men and women,
  I will pour out my Spirit in those days. *r*
30 I will show wonders in the heavens *s*
  and on the earth, *t*
  blood and fire and billows of smoke.
31 The sun will be turned to darkness *u*
  and the moon to blood
  before the coming of the great and dreadful day of the Lord. *v*
32 And everyone who calls
  on the name of the Lord *w* will be saved; *x*
for on Mount Zion *y* and in Jerusalem
  there will be deliverance, *z*
  as the Lord has said,
even among the survivors *a*
  whom the Lord calls. *b*

THE NATIONS JUDGED

3 * "In those days and at that time,
  when I restore the fortunes *c* of Judah *d* and Jerusalem,
2 I will gather *e* all nations
  and bring them down to the Valley of Jehoshaphat. *a f*
There I will enter into judgment *g* against them
  concerning my inheritance, my people Israel,
for they scattered *h* my people among the nations
  and divided up my land.
3 They cast lots *i* for my people
  and traded boys for prostitutes;
  they sold girls for wine *j*
    that they might drink.

a 2 *Jehoshaphat* means *the Lord judges*; also in verse 12.
* 2:28-32 is numbered 3:1-5 in Hebrew texts.   * 3:1-21 is numbered 4:1-21 in Hebrew texts.

2:28–32 Quoted by Peter on the day of Pentecost (Ac 2:16–21), but with a few variations from both the Hebrew text and the Septuagint (the pre-Christian Greek translation of the OT).

2:28 *afterward*. In the Messianic period, beyond the restoration just spoken of. *pour out my Spirit*. See v. 29; Isa 32:15; 44:3; Eze 39:29 and note; Zec 12:10—13:1. *all people*. All will participate without regard to gender, age or rank; and then Moses' wish (see Nu 11:29 and note) will be realized (cf. Gal 3:28). Peter extends the "all" of this verse and the "everyone" of v. 32 to the Gentiles ("all who are far off," Ac 2:39; see also note on Ac 2:17), who will not be excluded from the Spirit's outpouring or deliverance (cf. Ro 11:11–24). *prophesy … dream dreams … see visions*. See Nu 12:6.

2:30–31 These cosmic events are often associated with the day of the Lord (see Isa 13:9–10,13; 34:4; Mt 24:29; Rev 6:12–13; 8:8–9; 9:1–19; 14:14–20; 16:4, 8–9).

2:30 *blood … fire … smoke*. From war; fire and smoke can also be signs of God's presence (see Ge 15:17 and note).

2:31 *darkness*. See v. 2 and note. *blood*. The moon will become blood-red. *great and dreadful day of the Lord*. See v. 11; 1:15 and notes.

2:32 *calls on the name of the Lord*. Worships God and prays to him (see Ge 4:26; 12:8; Ps 116:4). *saved*. Delivered from the wrath of God's judgment (see Mt 24:13). *as the Lord has said*. Perhaps Joel is recalling the Lord's covenant with David (see 2Sa 7; Ps 132:11–18). *survivors*. See Zec 13:8–9 and notes; 14:2.

3:1 *In those days*. At the time of Israel's final redemption (see v. 18 and note). *restore the fortunes of*. Or "bring back from captivity" (see vv. 6–7; see also note on Jer 29:14 and TNIV text note there).

3:2 *Valley of Jehoshaphat*. See v. 12. Called the "valley of decision" in v. 14, it seems to be a symbolic name for a valley near Jerusalem that is here depicted as the place of God's ultimate judgment on the nations gathered against Jerusalem (see TNIV text note; cf. Zec 6:1 and note). There King Jehoshaphat had witnessed one of the Lord's historic victories over the nations (see 2Ch 20:1–30). *my inheritance*. See note on 2:17. Eight times in three verses (vv. 2–3,5) God uses "my," emphasizing his covenant relationship with Israel. *Israel*. See note on 2:27.

3:3 *cast lots for my people*. This happened to Judah at the time of the captivity (586 B.C.) and is mentioned in Ob 11. The Israelites were treated by their enemies as mere chattel, to be traded off for the pleasures of prostitution and wine.

4"Now what have you against me, Tyre and Sidon ^{k} and all you regions of Philistia? ^{l} Are you repaying me for something I have done? If you are paying me back, I will swiftly and speedily return on your own heads what you have done. ^{m} ^{5}For you took my silver and my gold and carried off my finest treasures to your temples. ^{a} ^{n} ^{6}You sold the people of Judah and Jerusalem to the Greeks, ^{o} that you might send them far from their homeland.

7"See, I am going to rouse them out of the places to which you sold them, ^{p} and I will return ^{q} on your own heads what you have done. ^{8}I will sell your sons ^{r} and daughters to the people of Judah, ^{s} and they will sell them to the Sabeans, ^{t} a nation far away." The LORD has spoken. ^{u}

9 Proclaim this among the nations:
　　Prepare for war! ^{v}
　Rouse the warriors! ^{w}
　　Let all the fighting men draw near and attack.
10 Beat your plowshares into swords
　　and your pruning hooks ^{x} into spears. ^{y}
　Let the weakling ^{z} say,
　　"I am strong!" ^{a}
11 Come quickly, all you nations from every side,
　　and assemble ^{b} there.

　Bring down your warriors, ^{c} LORD!

12 "Let the nations be roused;
　　let them advance into the Valley of Jehoshaphat, ^{d}
　for there I will sit
　　to judge ^{e} all the nations on every side.
13 Swing the sickle, ^{f}
　　for the harvest ^{g} is ripe.
　Come, trample the grapes, ^{h}
　　for the winepress ^{i} is full
　　and the vats overflow—
　　so great is their wickedness!"

14 Multitudes, ^{j} multitudes
　　in the valley ^{k} of decision!
　For the day of the LORD ^{l} is near
　　in the valley of decision. ^{m}
15 The sun and moon will be darkened,
　　and the stars no longer shine. ^{n}
16 The LORD will roar ^{o} from Zion

---

^{a} 5 Or *palaces*

**Cross references (right margin):**

3:4 ^{k} S Ge 10:15;
S Mt 11:21 ^{l} S Ps 87:4;
Isa 14:29-31;
Jer 47:1-7
^{m} S Lev 26:28;
S Isa 34:8;
S Eze 25:15-17;
Zec 9:5-7
3:5 ^{n} S 1Ki 15:18;
S 2Ch 21:16-17
3:6 ^{o} Eze 27:13;
Zec 9:13
3:7 ^{p} S Isa 43:5-6;
Jer 23:8 ^{q} S Isa 66:6
3:8 ^{r} Isa 60:14
^{s} Isa 14:2 ^{t} S Ge 10:7;
S 2Ch 9:1 ^{u} S Isa 23:1;
S Jer 30:16
3:9 ^{v} S Isa 8:9
^{w} Jer 46:4
3:10 ^{x} Isa 2:4
^{y} S Nu 25:7 ^{z} Zec 12:8
^{a} S Jos 1:6
3:11 ^{b} Eze 38:15-16;
Zep 3:8 ^{c} S Isa 13:3
3:12 ^{d} S ver 2
^{e} S Ps 82:1; S Isa 2:4
3:13 ^{f} Mk 4:29
^{g} S Isa 17:5;
S Hos 6:11; Mt 13:39;
Rev 14:15-19
^{h} S Jer 25:30
^{i} S Jdg 6:11;
S Rev 14:20
3:14 ^{j} Isa 13:4
^{k} S Isa 22:1 ^{l} Isa 34:2-
8; S Joel 1:15;
S Zep 1:7 ^{m} S Isa 2:4;
S Eze 36:5
3:15 ^{n} S Job 9:7;
S Eze 32:7
3:16 ^{o} S Isa 42:13

3:4–8 A parenthetical interlude. In vv. 1–3,9–16 God announces judgment against the nations hostile to Israel, but here he addresses the nations directly.

3:4 *me*. The Lord. *Tyre … Sidon … Philistia*. Tyre and Philistia had sold Israelites as slaves (see Am 1:6,9 and notes), and Philistia had often plundered Israel (see Jdg 13:1; 1Sa 5:1; 2Ch 21:16–17; Eze 25:15–17 and note on 25:15). God punished these nations by allowing Sidon to be destroyed and many of its people enslaved by Artaxerxes III c. 345 B.C. and by allowing Tyre to be captured by the Greeks (under Alexander the Great) in 332. *return on your own heads what you have done*. See v. 7; Ob 15 and note.

B **3:6** The Greeks were trading with the Phoenicians as early as 800 B.C.

3:8 *Sabeans*. See Job 1:15 and note; from Sheba, whose queen visited Solomon (see 1Ki 10:1–13 and note on 10:1). *far away*. It was located in the southern part of the Arabian peninsula (present-day Yemen).

3:9–21 In vv. 9–11 Joel is the speaker; in vv. 12–13 God speaks; in vv. 14–16, Joel; and in vv. 17–21, God. When Joel speaks, he does so as the spokesman of the Lord, who has commissioned him to be his prophet.

3:9–11 Joel commands that the nations be told to prepare for battle, for the Lord would come against them with his invincible

heavenly army and bring them into judgment (cf. Eze 38–39; Rev 19).

3:10 The first part of this verse is the reverse of Isa 2:4 (see note there) and Mic 4:3, where the peaceful effect of God's reign is portrayed. Here God's enemies are summoned to their last great confrontation with him. *plowshares*. See note on Isa 2:4.

3:11 *assemble there*. In the Valley of Jehoshaphat for judgment (vv. 2,12).

3:13 As a result of the Lord's great army of locusts that had marched against Judah (see 2:3–11 and note on 2:11), there had been no harvest (2:3). But that harvest was to be restored (2:19,22,24,26). In the final great day of the Lord, there will also be a harvest—the harvest of God's judgment on the nations. Rev 14:14–20 draws heavily on this picture of judgment (see notes on Rev 14:15,18–20). *vats*. See 2:24 and note.

3:14 *valley of decision*. The Valley of Jehoshaphat (judgment) of vv. 2,12. "Jehoshaphat" speaks of God's role as Judge (see note on v. 2). Here "decision" (from a different Hebrew word) refers to the heavenly Judge's decision or judicial decree. The valley is now viewed as the place where that decree will be executed. *day of the LORD*. See 1:15 and note.

3:15 See 2:10 and note.

3:16 *roar*. Like a lion, God will destroy the nations. The first two

3:16 ᵖ Am 1:2
�q S Jdg 5:4;
S Isa 14:16;
S Eze 38:19
ʳ S Ps 46:1; S Isa 25:4;
Zec 12:8 ˢ S 2Sa 22:3;
Jer 16:19; Zec 9:12
3:17 ᵗ S Ex 6:7
ᵘ S Joel 2:27
ᵛ S Ps 74:2; S Isa 4:3
ʷ Ps 2:6; S Isa 2:2;
S Eze 17:22
ˣ S Jer 31:40
ʸ S Isa 52:1;
S Eze 44:9; Zec 9:8
3:18 ᶻ S Joel 2:24
ᵃ Ex 3:8; S SS 5:1
ᵇ S Isa 30:25; 35:6;
S 44:3 ᶜ Rev 22:1-2
ᵈ S Nu 25:1;
S Isa 25:6; S Jer 31:12;
S Eze 47:1; Am 9:13
3:19 ᵉ S Isa 19:1
ᶠ S Isa 11:14; S 34:11
ᵍ S Jer 51:35; Ob 1:10
3:20 ʰ S Ezr 9:12;
Am 9:15
3:21 ⁱ S Isa 1:15
ʲ S Eze 36:25
ᵏ S Ps 74:2; Isa 59:20;
S Eze 48:35; Zec 8:3

and thunder from Jerusalem; ᵖ
 the earth and the heavens will tremble. �q
But the LORD will be a refuge ʳ for his people,
 a stronghold ˢ for the people of Israel.

BLESSINGS FOR GOD'S PEOPLE

¹⁷ "Then you will know ᵗ that I, the LORD your God, ᵘ
 dwell in Zion, ᵛ my holy hill. ʷ
Jerusalem will be holy; ˣ
 never again will foreigners invade her. ʸ

¹⁸ "In that day the mountains will drip new wine, ᶻ
 and the hills will flow with milk; ᵃ
all the ravines of Judah will run with water. ᵇ
A fountain will flow out of the LORD's house ᶜ
 and will water the valley of acacias. ᵃ ᵈ
¹⁹ But Egypt ᵉ will be desolate,
 Edom ᶠ a desert waste,
because of violence ᵍ done to the people of Judah,
 in whose land they shed innocent blood.
²⁰ Judah will be inhabited forever ʰ
 and Jerusalem through all generations.
²¹ Shall I leave their innocent blood unpunished? ⁱ
 No, I will not. ʲ "

The LORD dwells in Zion! ᵏ

ᵃ 18 Or *Valley of Shittim*

---

lines occur also in Am 1:2 (see note there; see also Jer 25:30). *from Zion.* See note on Am 1:2. *thunder.* As God at the head of his army had thundered against Jerusalem (2:11), so he will then thunder against Jerusalem's enemies, and he will do so from his royal city, from which he rules his "inheritance" (see v. 17; Am 1:2). *the earth and the heavens will tremble.* See 2:10 and note. *Israel.* See note on 2:27.

A **3:17–21** God blesses his people in a dual way: negatively, by destroying their enemies; and positively, by giving them good things.

A **3:17** *dwell in Zion.* The Lord himself will dwell with them (see v. 21). The same picture is found in 2:27; Ps 46:4 (cf. Rev 21:3). The final, blessed state of the now unholy and vulnerable city will be God's abiding presence in her (see v. 21 and note; Rev 21). Then she will be holy and impregnable (see Zec 14:21 and note). *Zion.* See 2:1 and note.

A **3:18** *In that day.* The same as "In those days" of v. 1. The Edenic lushness pictured in this verse is in great contrast to the drought in 1:10 (see Am 9:13). *mountains . . . hills.* See Ps 104:13–15; Hag 1:11 and notes. *A fountain will flow out of the*

LORD's house. Flowing from God's presence, streams of blessing will refresh his people and make their place endlessly fruitful (see Ps 36:8; 46:4 and notes; 87:7; Eze 47:1–12; Rev 22:1–2). *acacias.* See Ex 25:5 and note. Since acacias flourish in dry soil, the picture is that of a well-watered desert.

A **3:19** *Egypt . . . Edom.* As old enemies of Israel, they here represent all the nations hostile to God's people (see notes on Eze 35:1–15; Zec 10:10). *desolate . . . desert waste.* Figures for the removal of all life-sustaining blessings, thus setting in sharp focus the contrasting destinies of God's people and the enemies of God's kingdom. This picture of desolation also recalls the earlier description of Judah's condition (2:3).

A **3:20** *will be inhabited forever.* When God's judgment and redemption are consummated, his kingdom will endure and flourish eternally.

A **3:21** This book of judgment ends on a promising and encouraging note: "The LORD dwells in Zion," and therefore all is right with those who trust in God and live with him. The book of Ezekiel has a similar ending (see note on Eze 48:35).

AUTHOR · AMOS · INTRODUCTION

C Amos was from Tekoa (1:1), a small town in Judah about 6 miles south of Bethlehem and 11 miles from Jerusalem. He was not a man of the court like Isaiah, or a member of a priestly family like Jeremiah and Ezekiel. He earned his living from the flock and the sycamore-fig grove (1:1; 7:14–15). Whether he owned the flocks and groves or only worked as a hired hand is not known. His skill with words and the strikingly broad range of his general knowledge of history and the world preclude his being an ignorant peasant. Though his home was in Judah, he was sent to announce God's judgment on the northern kingdom (Israel). He probably ministered for the most part at Bethel (7:10–13; see 1Ki 12:28–30 and notes), Israel's main religious sanctuary, where the upper echelons of the northern kingdom worshiped.

The book brings his prophecies together in a carefully organized form intended to be read as a unit. It offers few, if any, clues as to the chronological order of his spoken messages—he may have repeated them on many occasions to reach everyone who came to worship. The book is ultimately addressed to all Israel (hence the references to Judah and Jerusalem).

DATE AND HISTORICAL SITUATION

According to the first verse, Amos prophesied during the reigns of Uzziah over Judah (792–740 B.C.) and Jeroboam II over Israel (793–753). The main part of his ministry was probably carried out c. 760–750. Both kingdoms were enjoying great prosperity and had reached new political and military heights (cf. 2Ki 14:23—15:7; 2Ch 26). It was also a time of idolatry, extravagant indulgence in luxurious living, immorality, corruption of judicial procedures and oppression of the poor. As a consequence, God would soon bring about the Assyrian captivity of the northern kingdom (722–721).

Israel at the time was politically secure and spiritually smug. About 40 years earlier, at the end of his ministry, Elisha had prophesied the resurgence of Israel's power (2Ki 13:17–19), and more recently Jonah had prophesied her restoration to a glory not known since the days of Solomon (2Ki 14:25). The nation felt sure, therefore, that she was in God's good graces. But prosperity increased Israel's religious and moral corruption. God's past punishments for unfaithfulness were forgotten, and his patience was at an end—which he sent Amos to announce.

With Amos, the messages of the prophets began to be preserved in permanent form, being brought together in books that would accompany Israel through the coming debacle and beyond. (Since Amos was a contemporary of Hosea and Jonah, see Introductions to those books.)

THEOLOGICAL THEME AND MESSAGE

The dominant theme is clearly stated in 5:24, which calls for social justice as the indispensable expression of true piety. Amos was a vigorous spokesman for God's justice and righteousness, whereas Hosea emphasized God's love, grace, mercy and forgiveness. Amos declared that God was going to judge his unfaithful, disobedient, covenant-breaking people. Despite the Lord's special choice of Israel and his kindnesses to her during the exodus and conquest and in the days of David and Solomon,

KEY · **A** APPLICATION FOR LIVING · **B** BACKGROUND NOTES · **C** CHARACTER INFORMATION his people continually failed to honor and obey him. The shrines at Bethel and other places of worship were often paganized, and Israel had a worldly view of even the ritual that the Lord himself had prescribed. The people thought performance of the rites was all God required, and, with that done, they could do whatever they pleased—an essentially pagan notion. Without commitment to God's law, they had no basis for standards of conduct. Amos condemns all who make themselves powerful or rich at the expense of others. Those who had acquired two splendid houses (3:15), expensive furniture and richly laden tables by cheating, perverting justice and crushing the poor, would lose everything they had.

God's imminent judgment on Israel would not be a mere punitive blow to warn (as often before; see 4:6–11 and note), but an almost total destruction. The unthinkable was about to happen: Because they had not faithfully consecrated themselves to his lordship, God would uproot his chosen people by the hands of a pagan nation. Even so, if they would repent, there was hope that "the LORD God Almighty (would) have mercy on the remnant" (5:15; see 5:4–6,14). In fact, the Lord had a glorious future for his people, beyond the impending judgment. The house of David would again rule over Israel—even extend its rule over many nations—and Israel would once more be secure in the promised land, feasting on wine and fruit (9:11–15). The God of Israel, the Lord of history, would not abandon his chosen people or his chosen program of redemption.

The God for whom Amos speaks is God of more than merely Israel. He also uses one nation against another to carry out his purposes (6:14). He is the Great King who rules the whole universe (4:13; 5:8; 9:5–6). Because he is all-sovereign, the God of Israel holds the history and destiny of all peoples and of the world in his hands. Israel must know not only that he is the Lord of her future, but also that he is Lord over all, and that he has purposes and concerns that reach far beyond her borders. Israel had a unique, but not an exclusive, claim on God. She needed to remember not only his covenant commitments to her but also her covenant obligations to him. (See further the prophecy of Jonah.)

OUTLINE

1:1 ᵃ S 2Sa 14:2
ᵇ Zec 14:5
ᶜ S 2Ki 14:21;
S 2Ch 26:23
ᵈ S 2Ki 14:23
ᵉ S Hos 1:1
1:2 ᶠ S Isa 42:13
ᵍ S Ps 29:3 ʰ Joel 3:16
ⁱ Am 9:3 / S Jer 12:4
1:3 ᵏ Isa 7:8; 8:4;
17:1-3 ˡ ver 6,9,11,13;
Am 2:6
1:4 ᵐ S Jer 49:27;
S Eze 30:8
ⁿ S 1Ki 19:17; 2Ki 8:7-
15 ᵒ Jer 17:27
ᵖ 1Ki 20:1; Jer 6:24;
Jer 49:23-27
1:5 ᵍ Jer 51:30
ʳ S Isa 37:12
ˢ S 2Ki 16:9;
S Isa 22:6; Zec 9:1
ᵗ S Isa 7:16; Jer 49:27
1:6 ᵘ S Ge 10:19;
1Sa 6:17; Zep 2:4
ᵛ S ver 3

1 The words of Amos, one of the shepherds of Tekoa ᵃ—the vision he saw concerning Israel two years before the earthquake, ᵇ when Uzziah ᶜ was king of Judah and Jeroboam ᵈ son of Jehoash ᵃ was king of Israel. ᵉ

²He said:

> "The LORD roars ᶠ from Zion
>   and thunders ᵍ from Jerusalem; ʰ
> the pastures of the shepherds dry up,
>   and the top of Carmel ⁱ withers." ʲ

JUDGMENT ON ISRAEL'S NEIGHBORS

³This is what the LORD says:

> "For three sins of Damascus, ᵏ
>   even for four, I will not turn back ⌐my wrath⌐. ˡ
> Because she threshed Gilead
>   with sledges having iron teeth,
> ⁴I will send fire ᵐ on the house of Hazael ⁿ
>   that will consume the fortresses ᵒ of Ben-Hadad. ᵖ
> ⁵I will break down the gate ᵍ of Damascus;
>   I will destroy the king who is in ᵇ the Valley of Aven ᶜ
> and the one who holds the scepter in Beth Eden. ʳ
>   The people of Aram will go into exile to Kir, ˢ"

says the LORD. ᵗ

⁶This is what the LORD says:

> "For three sins of Gaza, ᵘ
>   even for four, I will not turn back ⌐my wrath⌐. ᵛ
> Because she took captive whole communities

ᵃ 1 Hebrew *Joash*, a variant of *Jehoash*   ᵇ 5 Or *the inhabitants of*   ᶜ 5 *Aven* means *wickedness.*

1:1 *Amos.* Apparently a shortened form of a name like Amasiah (2Ch 17:16), meaning "The LORD carries" or "The LORD upholds." *shepherds.* The Hebrew for this word occurs elsewhere in the OT only in reference to the king of Moab (2Ki 3:4, where it is translated "raised sheep"). Cf. 7:14, where a different Hebrew word is used. Amos was not a professional prophet who earned his living from his ministry; he stood outside religious institutions. *Tekoa.* See Introduction: Author. *saw.* Received by divine revelation. *earthquake.* Evidently a major shock, long remembered, and probably the one mentioned in Zec 14:5. Recent geological studies have detected a mammoth seismic event in this area dating to c. 750 B.C. Reference to the earthquake suggests that the author viewed it as a kind of divine reinforcement of the words of judgment. *Uzziah.* See Introduction: Date and Historical Situation; see also note on Isa 6:1. *Jeroboam.* See Introduction: Date and Historical Situation.
1:2 A thematic verse, ominously announcing the main thrust of Amos's message. *roars.* Amos, a shepherd, was sent to Israel to warn her that he had heard a lion roar and that the lion is none other than the Lord himself, who has only wanted to be Israel's shepherd. For the use of this imagery in other contexts, see Jer 25:30; Joel 3:16. *from Zion.* The Lord established his earthly throne in Jerusalem, among his special people, and from there he announces his judgments on them, as well as on the other nations. *pastures ... top of Carmel.* See 9:3. From the lowest and driest portions of the land to the highest and greenest, the Lord's judgment will be felt like a severe drought that devastates the whole land.
1:3—2:16 A series of oracles against the nations; for parallel sections in other prophets, see Isa 13:1—23:18 and note. After pronouncing judgment on Israel's neighbors for various atrocities—judgment that Israel would naturally applaud—Amos announces God's condemnation of his own two kingdoms for despising God's laws. His listing of Israel's sins under the same form of indictment used against the other nations shockingly pictures Israel's sins alongside those of her pagan neighbors.

1:3 *This is what the LORD says.* See vv. 6,9,11,13; 2:1,4,6. Amos, the Lord's spokesman, uses the messenger formula that identifies the true source of his oracles. *For three sins ... four.* For their many sins, especially the one named; see also vv. 6,9,11,13; 2:1,4,6. For similar numerical expressions, see Job 5:19; Pr 6:16; Mic 5:5 and notes. *Damascus.* Capital of the Aramean state directly north of Israel (see note on Isa 17:1) and a constant enemy in that day. Her crime was brutality to the conquered people of Gilead, Israel's territory east of Galilee. *not turn back ⌐my wrath⌐.* See Isa 9:12,17,21 and note; Jer 23:20. *threshed ... sledges.* Heads of grain were threshed by driving a wooden sledge fitted with sharp teeth over the cut grain (cf. Job 41:30; Isa 28:27; 41:15; Hab 3:12; see 2Ki 13:7 and note on Ru 1:22).
1:4 *fire ... that will consume.* See vv. 7,10,12,14; 2:2,5; a common description of the threat of divine judgment, usually carried out by a devastating war that resulted in the burning of major cities and fortresses (see Jer 17:27 and note; Hos 8:14). *Hazael.* King of Damascus and founder of a new line of kings (see 2Ki 8:7–15 and note on 8:15). *fortresses.* See vv. 7,10,12,14; 2:2,5; perhaps referring not only to citadels but also to the fortress-like palatial dwellings of the rich and powerful. *Ben-Hadad.* Son of Hazael (see 2Ki 13:3 and note) and the second (or possibly third) king with this name (cf. 2Ki 8:14–15).
1:5 *king.* See v. 8; lit. "one who sits [enthroned]." *Valley of Aven.* Possibly the Beqaa Valley between the Lebanon and Anti-Lebanon mountains, but may refer to the river valley in which Damascus is located (see note on 2Ki 5:12), calling it the "valley of wickedness" (see TNIV text note). *Beth Eden.* Probably Damascus, the garden spot of that region. *Aram.* See note on Dt 26:5. *Kir.* An unidentified place, possibly in the vicinity of Elam (see 9:7 and note), from which the Arameans are said to have come (9:7).
1:6 *Gaza.* One of the five major Philistine cities (see map, p. 338); it guarded the entry to Canaan from Egypt. *whole communities.* See v. 9; not just warriors captured in battle. The reference may be to villages in south Judah on the trade route from Edom to Gaza. *to Edom.* See v. 9; trading the people like cattle to another country.

and sold them to Edom,[w]
⁷I will send fire on the walls of Gaza
  that will consume her fortresses.
⁸I will destroy the king[a] of Ashdod[x]
  and the one who holds the scepter in Ashkelon.
I will turn my hand[y] against Ekron,
  till the last of the Philistines[z] are dead,"[a]

says the Sovereign LORD.[b]

⁹This is what the LORD says:

"For three sins of Tyre,[c]
  even for four, I will not turn back ⌊my wrath⌋.[d]
Because she sold whole communities of captives to Edom,
  disregarding a treaty of brotherhood,[e]
¹⁰I will send fire on the walls of Tyre
  that will consume her fortresses.[f]"

¹¹This is what the LORD says:

"For three sins of Edom,[g]
  even for four, I will not turn back ⌊my wrath⌋.
Because he pursued his brother with a sword[h]
  and slaughtered the women of the land,
because his anger raged continually
  and his fury flamed unchecked,[i]
¹²I will send fire on Teman[j]
  that will consume the fortresses of Bozrah.[k]"

¹³This is what the LORD says:

"For three sins of Ammon,[l]
  even for four, I will not turn back ⌊my wrath⌋.
Because he ripped open the pregnant women[m] of Gilead
  in order to extend his borders,
¹⁴I will set fire to the walls of Rabbah[n]
  that will consume[o] her fortresses
amid war cries[p] on the day of battle,
  amid violent winds[q] on a stormy day.
¹⁵Their king[b] will go into exile,
  he and his officials together,[r]"

says the LORD.[s]

2

This is what the LORD says:

"For three sins of Moab,[t]
  even for four, I will not turn back ⌊my wrath⌋.
Because he burned to lime[u]
  the bones of Edom's king,
²I will send fire on Moab

---

[a] 8 Or *inhabitants*   [b] 15 Or */Molek*

1:6 [w] S Ge 14:6;
Ob 1:11
1:8 [x] S 2Ch 26:6
[y] Ps 81:14
[z] S Eze 25:16
[a] S Isa 34:8
[b] Isa 14:28-32;
Zep 2:4-7
1:9 [c] 1Ki 5:1; 9:11-14;
Jer 25:22; Joel 3:4; S
Mt 11:21 [d] ver 3
[e] S 1Ki 5:12
1:10 [f] Isa 23:1-18;
S 34:8; S Jer 47:4;
Eze 26:2-4; Zec 9:1-4
1:11 [g] Nu 20:14-21;
S 2Ch 28:17;
S Ps 83:6 [h] S Ps 63:10
[i] Eze 25:12-14;
Zec 1:15
1:12 [j] S Eze 36:11,15
[k] S Isa 34:5; 63:1-6;
Jer 25:21; Eze 25:12-
14; 35:1-15; Ob 1:1;
Mal 1:2-5
1:13 [l] S Ge 19:38;
S Eze 21:28
[m] S Ge 34:29;
S 2Ki 8:12;
S Hos 13:16
1:14 [n] S Dt 3:11
[o] Isa 30:30
[p] S Job 39:25
[q] Jer 23:19
1:15 [r] S Jer 25:21
[s] 1Ch 20:1; S Jer 49:1;
Eze 21:28-32; 25:2-7
2:1 [t] S Isa 16:6
[u] Isa 33:12

1:8 *Ashdod...Ashkelon...Ekron.* Three more cities of the Philistine group (see note on v. 6). Gath, the fifth (cf. 6:2), may already have been subdued by Uzziah (see 2Ch 26:6). *the last.* There would be no remnant. Philistia was finally destroyed by Nebuchadnezzar.
1:9 *Tyre.* The dominant Phoenician merchant city, allied to Israel by a "treaty of brotherhood" in the days of David (1Ki 5:1), later in the time of Solomon (1Ki 5:12) and later still during the reign of Ahab, whose father-in-law ruled Tyre and Sidon (1Ki 16:30–31). *she sold.* Her crime was like Philistia's (v. 6).
1:10 *walls.* Tyre was an almost impregnable island, boastful of her security (cf. Eze 26:1—28:19).
1:11 *Edom.* The nation descended from Esau (Ge 36; see Ge 25:23–30; 27:39–40 and TNIV text note on 25:25). *brother.* Israel (see Ob 8–10 and note on Ob 10). Reference may be to a treaty "brother" (see note on v. 9). Edom's crime was in violating this relationship by persistent hostility.

1:12 *Teman...Bozrah.* Major cities of Edom, the former thought to be near Petra (see note on Ob 9), the latter now identified with Buseirah, 37 miles to the north. With their destruction, Edom would lose its capacity for continual warfare.
1:13 *Ammon.* Judgment centered on Rabbah (v. 14; see note on Dt 3:11), modern Amman. Greed for land bred a brutal genocide that would be punished by a tumult of men and nature, leaving the state without leaders to continue such practices (see 1Ki 8:12 and note).
1:14 Fulfilled through the Assyrians.
1:15 *Their king.* See TNIV text note; see also Jer 49:3 and note on 49:1.
2:1 *Moab.* Located east of the Dead Sea (see note on Isa 15:1). *burned...the bones of Edom's king.* Thus depriving the king's spirit of the rest that was widely believed to result from decent burial.

2:2 ᵛ Jer 48:24
ʷ S Job 39:25
ˣ S Jos 6:20
2:3 ʸ S Ps 2:10
ᶻ S Isa 40:23
2:4 ᵃ Isa 15:1-9; 16:1-14;
S 25:10; Jer 48:1;
S Eze 25:8-11;
Zep 2:8-9
2:4 ᵇ 2Ki 17:19;
Hos 12:2 ᶜ S Jer 6:19
ᵈ S Eze 20:24
ᵉ Isa 9:16 ᶠ S Ex 34:15;
S Dt 31:20; S Ps 4:2
ᵍ S 2Ki 22:13;
S Jer 9:14; S 16:12
2:5 ʰ S 2Ki 25:9;
S 2Ch 36:19 ᶦ Am 3:11
ʲ S Jer 17:27;
S Hos 8:14
2:6 ᵏ S Am 1:3
ˡ S Joel 3:3; Am 8:6
2:7 ᵐ S Lev 18:21;
Am 5:11-12; 8:4
2:8 ⁿ S Ex 22:26;
Dt 24:12-13
ᵒ Hos 7:14; Am 4:1;
6:6 ᵖ Hab 2:6
2:9 �q Nu 21:23-26;
Jos 10:12 ʳ S Isa 10:33
ˢ S Ps 29:9
ᵗ S 2Ki 19:30;
S Job 18:16;
S Eze 17:9

that will consume the fortresses of Kerioth.ᵃ ᵛ
Moab will go down in great tumult
    amid war criesʷ and the blast of the trumpet.ˣ
³ I will destroy her rulerʸ
    and kill all her officials with him,"ᶻ

               says the LORD.ᵃ

⁴This is what the LORD says:

"For three sins of Judah, ᵇ
    even for four, I will not turn back ⌞my wrath⌟.
Because they have rejected the lawᶜ of the LORD
    and have not kept his decrees, ᵈ
because they have been led astrayᵉ by false gods,ᵇ ᶠ
    the godsᶜ their ancestors followed,ᵍ
⁵ I will send fireʰ on Judah
    that will consume the fortressesᶦ of Jerusalem.ʲ"

JUDGMENT ON ISRAEL

⁶This is what the LORD says:

"For three sins of Israel,
    even for four, I will not turn back ⌞my wrath⌟. ᵏ
They sell the innocent for silver,
    and the needy for a pair of sandals. ˡ
⁷ They trample on the heads of the poor
    as on the dust of the ground
    and deny justice to the oppressed.
Father and son use the same girl
    and so profane my holy name. ᵐ
⁸ They lie down beside every altar
    on garments taken in pledge. ⁿ
In the house of their god
    they drink wineᵒ taken as fines. ᵖ

⁹ "Yet I destroyed the Amorites q before them,
    though they were tallʳ as the cedars
    and strong as the oaks. ˢ
I destroyed their fruit above
    and their rootsᵗ below.

ᵃ 2 Or of her cities   ᵇ 4 Or by lies   ᶜ 4 Or lies

2:2 *Kerioth.* Perhaps a plural noun meaning "cities" (see TNIV text note) or the name of a major town (see Jer 48:24) and shrine of Chemosh, the national god of Moab (see 1Ki 11:7,33).

2:4 *rejected the law of the LORD.* Judah's sins differed in kind from those of the other nations. Those nations violated the generally recognized laws of humanity, but Judah disobeyed the revealed law of God. These sins may be included in the indictment against Israel that follows.

2:5 *fire … consume the fortresses.* See 1:4 and note. Judah's punishment is the same as Aram's (1:4), Philistia's (1:7), Phoenicia's (1:10), Edom's (1:12), Ammon's (1:14) and Moab's (2:2)—loss of the defenses and wealth in which they trusted.

2:6 Israel's sins revealed the general moral deterioration of the nation. *the innocent.* Probably those who were not in debt and whom there was no lawful reason to sell (cf. Lev 25:39–43). Alternatively, the "innocent" here may refer to "the poor" (v. 7; cf. 5:12; 8:6), in contrast to the sinfully wicked behavior of the wealthy and powerful (see 4:1–5; 6:1–7). *the needy.* God had commanded that they be helped (see Dt 15:7–11 and note on 15:11), but they were instead sold for failure to repay a (perhaps paltry) debt, for which a "pair of sandals" had been given in pledge (see 8:6).

2:7 *trample.* See 5:11; 8:4. *poor … oppressed.* To care for them and to protect them from injustice were clearly commanded by Israel's law (Ex 23:6–8); also, throughout the ancient Near East,

kings were supposed to defend such people. *Father and son use the same girl.* Whether the girl in question was a household servant (in which case father and son used her as a family prostitute) is not clear. In any case, the law required that if there were sexual relations with a girl, marriage was obligatory (Ex 22:16; Dt 22:28–29). For a father and son to have sexual relations with the same girl or woman was strictly forbidden (Lev 18:7–8,15; 20:11–12). *profane my holy name.* Cf. Lev 18:21 and note; 19:12; 20:3; 21:6; 22:2,32; see Jer 34:16; Eze 20:9 and notes; 36:20–23; 39:7.

2:8 *beside every altar … In the house of their god.* Israelites who broke the laws protecting the powerless brazenly used their wrongly gotten gains even in places supposed to be holy. *garments taken in pledge.* The law prohibited keeping a man's cloak overnight as security for a debt (see Ex 22:26–27 and note; Dt 24:12–13), or taking a widow's cloak at all (Dt 24:17). *fines.* Claimed as restitution for damages suffered. Exorbitant claims or even false charges of damage seem to be suggested.

2:9 *I destroyed.* Israel not only had known God's law but had been specially favored by his powerful help. *Amorites.* Here used for all the inhabitants of Canaan (see notes on Ge 10:16; 15:16; Jdg 6:10). *tall … strong.* Neither the size of Canaan's people nor their military power (see Nu 13:27–33) was able to prevent God's victory over them (see Jos 10:5,12–13). *their fruit above and their roots below.* That is, totally.

¹⁰ I brought you up out of Egypt ^u
 and led ^v you forty years in the wilderness ^w
 to give you the land of the Amorites. ^x

¹¹ "I also raised up prophets ^y from among your children
 and Nazirites ^z from among your youths.
 Is this not true, people of Israel?"

 declares the LORD.

¹² "But you made the Nazirites drink wine
 and commanded the prophets not to prophesy. ^a

¹³ "Now then, I will crush you
 as a cart crushes when loaded with grain. ^b
¹⁴ The swift will not escape, ^c
 the strong ^d will not muster their strength,
 and the warrior will not save his life. ^e
¹⁵ The archer ^f will not stand his ground,
 the fleet-footed soldier will not get away,
 and the horseman ^g will not save his life. ^h
¹⁶ Even the bravest warriors ⁱ
 will flee naked on that day,"

 declares the LORD.

WITNESSES SUMMONED AGAINST ISRAEL

3 Hear this word, people of Israel, the word the LORD has spoken against you ^j—against the whole family I brought up out of Egypt: ^k

² "You only have I chosen ^l
 of all the families of the earth;
 therefore I will punish ^m you
 for all your sins. ⁿ"

³ Do two walk together
 unless they have agreed to do so?
⁴ Does a lion roar ^o in the thicket
 when it has no prey? ^p
Does it growl in its den
 when it has caught nothing?
⁵ Does a bird swoop down to a trap on the ground
 when no bait ^q is there?
Does a trap spring up from the ground
 if it has not caught anything?
⁶ When a trumpet ^r sounds in a city,
 do not the people tremble?
When disaster ^s comes to a city,
 has not the LORD caused it? ^t

2:10 ^u S Ex 6:6;
20:2; Am 3:1
^v S Dt 8:2 ^w S Dt 2:7
^x S Ex 3:8;
S Nu 21:25;
S Jos 13:4; Am 9:7
2:11 ^y Dt 18:18;
Jer 7:25 ^z S Jdg 13:5
2:12 ^a Isa 30:10;
Jer 11:21; Am 7:12-13;
Mic 2:6
2:13 ^b Am 7:16-17
2:14 ^c S Job 11:20
^d S 1Ki 20:11
^e Ps 33:16; Isa 30:16-17
2:15 ^f S Eze 39:3
^g S Ex 15:21; Zec 10:5
^h Ecc 9:11
2:16 ⁱ Jer 48:41
3:1 ^j Zep 2:5
^k S Am 2:10
3:2 ^l S Ex 19:6;
Dt 7:6; Lk 12:47
^m ver 14 ⁿ S Jer 14:10;
Mic 2:3; 1Pe 4:17
3:4 ^o S Isa 42:13
^p Ps 104:21;
S Hos 5:14
3:5 ^q S Ps 119:110
3:6 ^r S Nu 10:2;
S Job 39:24;
S Jer 4:21 ^s S Isa 31:2
^t Isa 14:24-27

2:10 *I brought you up.* See 3:1; see also Ex 20:2 and note. God's great blessings to Israel in the past added to her guilt, and now they are recalled as a part of the Lord's indictment against his people.

2:11 *I also raised up prophets…and Nazirites.* Prophets, as God's faithful spokesmen (see Dt 18:15–20 and note on 18:15), and Nazirites, as those uniquely dedicated to him (see Nu 6:1–21 and note on 6:2; Jdg 13:5 and note), are singled out as special gifts to his people. These persons who were outside the priesthood were used by God through word and example to call his people to faithfulness.

2:12 *But you.* Israel showed utter disdain for God's faithful servants and thus demonstrated her callous insensitivity to God's working among them (cf. 7:16).

2:13 A loaded cart crushes anything that falls beneath its wheels.

2:14–16 None who might be expected to stand their ground

or escape would be able to save themselves.

2:16 *that day.* The day God comes in judgment (see 5:18; Joel 1:15 and notes)—as he did through the Assyrian invasion that swept the northern kingdom away.

3:1—5:17 Oracles that underscore the certainty of God's judgment on Israel.

3:1 *Hear this word.* See 4:1; 5:1. The Lord calls his people to account because of their sins.

3:2 *You only.* Israel's present strength and prosperity gave rise to complacency about her privileged status as the Lord's chosen people. She is shockingly reminded of the long-forgotten responsibilities her privileges entailed.

3:3–6 With these rhetorical questions (involving comparisons) Amos builds up to the statements of vv. 7–8, to explain why he is speaking such terrifying words. Each picture is of cause and effect, using figures drawn from daily life—and culminating in divine action (v. 6).

3:7 u Ge 18:17;
S 1Sa 3:7; S Da 9:22;
Jn 15:15; Rev 10:7
v S Jer 23:22
3:8 w S Isa 31:4
x S Isa 42:13
y S Jer 20:9; Jnh 1:1-3;
3:1-3; Ac 4:20
3:9 z S Jos 13:3;
S 2Ch 26:6 a Am 4:1;
6:1
3:10 b Am 5:7; 6:12
c S Ps 36:3; Mic 6:10;
Zep 1:9 d Hab 2:8
3:11 e Am 2:5; 6:14
3:12 f S 1Sa 17:34
g S Est 1:6; Am 6:4
3:13 h Eze 2:7
3:14 i S ver 2;
S Lev 26:18
j S Ge 12:8; Am 5:5-6
k S Ex 27:2
3:15 l Jer 36:22
m Jdg 3:20
n S 1Ki 22:39
o Am 5:11; 6:11
p S Isa 34:5
q Hos 10:5-8,14-15

[7] Surely the Sovereign Lord does nothing
    without revealing his plan [u]
    to his servants the prophets. [v]

[8] The lion [w] has roared [x]—
    who will not fear?
    The Sovereign Lord has spoken—
    who can but prophesy? [y]

[9] Proclaim to the fortresses of Ashdod [z]
    and to the fortresses of Egypt:
"Assemble yourselves on the mountains of Samaria; [a]
    see the great unrest within her
    and the oppression among her people."

[10] "They do not know how to do right, [b]" declares the Lord,
    "who store up in their fortresses [c]
    what they have plundered [d] and looted."

[11] Therefore this is what the Sovereign Lord says:

"An enemy will overrun your land,
    pull down your strongholds
    and plunder your fortresses. [e]"

[12] This is what the Lord says:

"As a shepherd saves from the lion's [f] mouth
    only two leg bones or a piece of an ear,
so will the Israelites be saved,
those who sit in Samaria
    on the edge of their beds
    and in Damascus on their couches. [a] [g]"

[13] "Hear this and testify [h] against the house of Jacob," declares the Lord, the Lord God Almighty.

[14] "On the day I punish [i] Israel for her sins,
    I will destroy the altars of Bethel; [j]
the horns [k] of the altar will be cut off
    and fall to the ground.
[15] I will tear down the winter house [l]
    along with the summer house; [m]
the houses adorned with ivory [n] will be destroyed
    and the mansions [o] will be demolished, [p]"

declares the Lord. [q]

a 12 Or Israelites living in Samaria be saved, / with only the head of a bed / and a piece of fabric from a couch

---

3:7 his servants the prophets. See Jer 7:25; Zec 1:6 and notes.
3:8 lion has roared. Echoes 1:2 (see note there). who can but prophesy? Amos must speak because God has spoken.

▲ **3:9** The rich and powerful of Philistia and Egypt are summoned to witness the Lord's indictment against those who store up ill-gotten riches in the fortresses of Samaria (see v. 15). fortresses. See note on 1:4. great unrest. The result of a violent, selfish power structure that was heedless of the justice called for in God's law.

▲ **3:10** who store up. Cf. 2:6–8. The prosperity of Israel's wealthy depended on oppression and robbery. The following verses announce God's judgment on such greed (cf. Hab 2:6–11).
3:11 enemy. Assyria. plunder your fortresses. Those that Samaria's wealthy had greedily filled with plunder.
3:12 As a shepherd saves … only two leg bones. To prove to the owner that the sheep had been eaten by a wild animal, not stolen by the shepherd. be saved. Only a mutilated remnant would survive. The nation as such would be more than wounded—it would be destroyed. those who sit. In idle luxury (see

6:4). in Damascus on their couches. See TNIV text note. Since at this time Israel had extended its influence over Damascus, the rich merchants of Samaria may have maintained luxurious houses also in Damascus, along with market privileges in that city (see 1Ki 20:34 and note).
3:13 Hear … testify. Addressed to those summoned in v. 9. The rich and powerful of Philistia and Egypt are called upon to hear the Lord's indictment of the rich and powerful in Samaria and to testify that his indictment is true and that his judgment is warranted. Even these pagans will agree with God's judgment.
3:14 altars of Bethel. Israel's sins were rooted in the false shrine built by Jeroboam I at Bethel (1Ki 12:26–33). horns of the altar. Even the last refuge for a condemned person (cf. 1Ki 1:50–53) will afford Israel no protection.

■ **3:15** winter house … summer house. Cf. 6:11; further signs of opulence that would not benefit their owners on the day of God's judgment—nor would expensive imported decorations, carvings and inlays of ivory (cf. 6:4). Many examples of such carvings have been found in ruined palaces in Samaria and other cities (see 1Ki 22:39 and note).

ISRAEL HAS NOT RETURNED TO GOD

4 Hear this word, you cows of Bashan[r] on Mount Samaria,[s]
   you women who oppress the poor[t] and crush the needy[u]
   and say to your husbands,[v] "Bring us some drinks!"[w]
² The Sovereign LORD has sworn by his holiness:
   "The time[x] will surely come
when you will be taken away[y] with hooks,[z]
   the last of you with fishhooks.[a]
³ You will each go straight out
   through breaches in the wall,[a]
   and you will be cast out toward Harmon,[b]"

declares the LORD.

⁴ "Go to Bethel[b] and sin;
   go to Gilgal[c] and sin yet more.
Bring your sacrifices every morning,[d]
   your tithes[e] every three years.[c][f]
⁵ Burn leavened bread[g] as a thank offering
   and brag about your freewill offerings[h]—
boast about them, you Israelites,
   for this is what you love to do,"

declares the Sovereign LORD.

⁶ "I gave you empty stomachs in every city
   and lack of bread in every town,
   yet you have not returned to me,"

declares the LORD.[i]

⁷ "I also withheld[j] rain from you
   when the harvest was still three months away.
I sent rain on one town,
   but withheld it from another.[k]
One field had rain;
   another had none and dried up.
⁸ People staggered from town to town for water[l]
   but did not get enough[m] to drink,
   yet you have not returned[n] to me,"

declares the LORD.[o]

⁹ "Many times I struck your gardens and vineyards,
   destroying them with blight and mildew.[p]

---

[a] 2 Or *away in baskets, / the last of you in fish baskets*   [b] 3 Masoretic Text; with a different word division of the Hebrew (see Septuagint) *out, you mountain of oppression*   [c] 4 Or *days*

4:1 [r] S Ps 22:12
[s] S Am 3:9
[t] S Isa 58:6;
S Eze 18:12
[u] S Dt 24:14
[v] Jer 44:19
[w] S Am 2:8; 5:11; 8:6
4:2 [x] Jer 31:31
[y] Am 6:8
[z] S 2Ki 19:28;
S 2Ch 33:11;
S Isa 19:8
4:3 [a] S Eze 12:5
4:4 [b] S Jos 7:2
[c] S Hos 4:15
[d] S Nu 28:3
[e] Dt 14:28
[f] S Eze 20:39;
Am 5:21-22
4:5 [g] S Lev 7:13
[h] S Lev 22:18-21
4:6 [i] S Isa 3:1;
S 9:13; S Jer 5:3;
Hag 2:17
4:7 [j] S Jer 3:3;
Zec 14:17 [k] Eze 9:4,26;
Dt 11:17; S 2Ch 7:13;
S Isa 5:6
4:8 [l] S Eze 4:16-17
[m] Hag 1:6 [n] S Jer 3:7
[o] S Job 36:31;
S Jer 14:4
4:9 [p] S Dt 28:22

4:1 *Hear this word.* See note on 3:1. *cows of Bashan.* Upper-class women, directly addressed, are compared with the best breed of cattle in ancient Canaan, which were raised (and pampered) in the pastures of northern Transjordan (see Ps 22:12; Eze 39:18 and notes). Whether the metaphor was intended as an insult or as ironic flattery is uncertain. *Mount Samaria.* See 6:1 and note.

4:2 *The Sovereign LORD has sworn.* Stresses the solemnity of the situation and the certainty of the events. *by his holiness.* Contrasts with Israel's sin, reminding God's people of what they could have been (see Ex 19:6 and note) if they had faithfully kept their side of the covenant—as God had his. *hooks.* According to Assyrian reliefs (pictures engraved on stone), prisoners of war were led away with a rope fastened to a hook that pierced the nose or lower lip (see 2Ki 19:28 and note; 2Ch 33:11; Eze 19:4,9; Hab 1:15). The Hebrew word here may, in fact, refer to ropes.

4:3 *breaches in the wall.* Cf. 2Ki 17:5; Eze 13:5. *Harmon.* Appears to be a place-name, though it is not otherwise known (see TNIV text note).

4:4–5 Spoken in irony.

4:4 *Bethel … Gilgal.* These towns had historical importance as places where God's help was commemorated (Ge 35:1–15; Jos 4:20–24), and both were popular places of worship in Amos's day (5:5; Hos 4:15; 12:4 and notes). *sacrifices every morning.* See Ex

29:38–41. *tithes.* Apparently the special tithe that was to be brought "every three years" (Dt 14:28; 26:12). *years.* See TNIV text note. The Hebrew word for "days" sometimes stands for years.

4:5 *leavened bread.* The burning of leavened bread in the sacrifices was strictly forbidden (see Lev 2:11; 6:17). Either Amos rebukes the Israelites for willful transgression of the law, or he speaks of burning in a general way for offering inappropriate gifts to the Lord. Leavened bread could accompany a fellowship offering (see Lev 7:13). *what you love to do.* They loved the forms and rituals of religion but did not love what God loves—goodness, mercy, justice (see 5:15; Isa 5:7; 61:8; Hos 6:6 and note; Mic 6:8).

4:6–11 In the past, God had used natural disasters to discipline and warn his people, but those lessons were soon forgotten (cf. the covenant curses in Dt 28:22–24,39–40, 42,48,56–57).

4:6 *I.* These were not simply natural disasters; they were direct acts of God (3:6). *yet you have not returned to me.* A recurring accusation that runs like a refrain through vv. 8–11.

4:7–8 Lack of rain three months before harvest would prevent full development of the grain.

4:9 *blight and mildew.* See Hag 2:17 and note. *Locusts.* See Ex 10:14 and note.

4:9 q S Ex 10:13;
S Joel 2:25 r Joel 1:7
s S Isa 9:13; S Jer 3:10
4:10 t S Isa 9:3
u Ex 11:5 v S Isa 9:17
w S Isa 34:3
x S Dt 28:21
y S Isa 9:13
4:11 z S Ge 19:24;
S Jer 23:14
a S Isa 7:4; Jude 1:23
b S Job 36:13
4:13 c Ps 65:6
d Ps 135:7 e S Da 2:28
f Mic 1:3 g S Isa 47:4;
Am 5:8,27; 9:6
5:1 h S Jer 4:8;
S Eze 19:1
5:2 i S 2Ki 19:21;
Jer 14:17 j Jer 50:32;
Am 8:14
5:3 k Isa 6:13;
Am 6:9
5:4 l S Dt 4:29
m Dt 32:46-47;
Isa 55:3; Jer 29:13;
S Eze 18:9
5:5 n 1Sa 11:14;
S Hos 4:15 o Ge 21:31;
Am 8:14 p S 1Sa 7:16;
S 8:2
5:6 q Ps 22:26;
105:4; S Isa 31:1;
55:6; Zep 2:3 r ver 14;
S Lev 18:5

Locusts q devoured your fig and olive trees, r
    yet you have not returned s to me,"

             declares the LORD.

10 "I sent plagues t among you
    as I did to Egypt. u
I killed your young men v with the sword,
    along with your captured horses.
I filled your nostrils with the stench w of your camps,
    yet you have not returned to me," x

             declares the LORD. y

11 "I overthrew some of you
    as I overthrew Sodom and Gomorrah. z
You were like a burning stick a snatched from the fire,
    yet you have not returned to me,"

             declares the LORD. b

12 "Therefore this is what I will do to you, Israel,
    and because I will do this to you, Israel,
    prepare to meet your God."

13 He who forms the mountains, c
    who creates the wind, d
and who reveals his thoughts e to mortals,
    who turns dawn to darkness,
    and treads on the heights of the earth f—
    the LORD God Almighty is his name. g

A LAMENT AND CALL TO REPENTANCE

5 Hear this word, house of Israel, this lament h I take up concerning you:

2 "Fallen is Virgin i Israel,
    never to rise again,
deserted in her own land,
    with no one to lift her up. j"

3 This is what the Sovereign LORD says to the house of Israel:

    "Your city that marches out a thousand strong
        will have only a hundred left;
    your town that marches out a hundred strong
        will have only ten left. k"

4 This is what the LORD says to the house of Israel:

    "Seek l me and live; m
5   do not seek Bethel,
do not go to Gilgal, n
    do not journey to Beersheba. o
For Gilgal will surely go into exile,
    and Bethel will be reduced to nothing. a p"
6 Seek q the LORD and live, r

a 5 Hebrew aven, a reference to Beth Aven (a derogatory name for Bethel); see Hosea 4:15.

4:10 plagues...as...Egypt. See Ex 7:14—12:30.
4:11 Sodom and Gomorrah. Exemplified total destruction,
God's judgment on those cities (see Ge 19:24–25) eventually
becoming proverbial (see Dt 29:23; Isa 1:9; 13:19; see also Jer
49:18; Zep 2:9 and notes). burning stick snatched from the fire.
Saved only by God's grace (see Zec 3:2 and note).
4:12 prepare to meet your God. Devastated Israel, brought to
her knees by the Assyrians, would meet the God she had covenanted with at Sinai and had now so grievously offended.
4:13 See note on 5:8–9. The God of such power and majesty is
easily able to execute the judgment announced in v. 12.
5:1 Hear this word. See note on 3:1. this lament. Amos sorrow-
fully fashioned a lament as if Israel were already dead.

5:2 Virgin Israel. A personification of Israel (see note on 2Ki 19:21).
deserted. Left like a dead body on the open field (see Jer 8:2; 9:22).
5:3 city...town. The Hebrew expression denotes communities
of varying size, all of which would suffer.
A **5:4** Seek me and live. This gracious invitation is expanded
in v. 6, and yet again in v. 14, to heighten the rhetorical effect. If the people of Israel would seek the Lord, they (or at least
a "remnant," v. 15) could yet escape the violent death anticipated in Amos's lament (see Zep 2:3 and note).
5:5 Bethel...Gilgal. Located in the south of Judah, it also had evidently become a place of pilgrimage and idolatry (see 8:14). All shrines where the worship of
God was abused would be destroyed.

or he will sweep through the house of Joseph like a fire; [s]
it will devour them,
    and Bethel [t] will have no one to quench it. [u]

[7] There are those who turn justice into bitterness [v]
    and cast righteousness [w] to the ground. [x]

[8] He who made the Pleiades and Orion, [y]
    who turns midnight into dawn [z]
    and darkens day into night, [a]
who calls for the waters of the sea
    and pours them out over the face of the land—
    the LORD is his name. [b]
[9] He flashes destruction on the stronghold
    and brings the fortified city to ruin. [c]

[10] There are those who hate the one who reproves in court [d]
    and detest the one who tells the truth. [e]

[11] You levy a straw tax on the poor [f]
    and impose a tax on their grain.
Therefore, though you have built stone mansions, [g]
    you will not live in them; [h]
though you have planted lush vineyards,
    you will not drink their wine. [i]
[12] For I know how many are your offenses
    and how great your sins. [j]

There are those who oppress the innocent and take bribes [k]
    and deprive the poor [l] of justice in the courts. [m]
[13] Therefore the prudent keep quiet [n] in such times,
    for the times are evil. [o]

[14] Seek good, not evil,
    that you may live. [p]
Then the LORD God Almighty will be with you,
    just as you say he is.
[15] Hate evil, [q] love good; [r]
    maintain justice in the courts. [s]
Perhaps [t] the LORD God Almighty will have mercy [u]
    on the remnant [v] of Joseph.

5:6 [s] Dt 4:24
[t] S Am 3:14 [u] S Jer 4:4
5:7 [v] Isa 5:20;
Am 6:12 [w] S Am 3:10
[x] S Hos 10:4
5:8 [y] S Ge 1:16;
S Job 38:31
[z] S Job 38:12;
Isa 42:16
[a] S Ps 104:20; Am 8:9
[b] Ps 104:6-9;
Jer 16:21; S Am 4:13
5:9 [c] Mic 5:11
5:10 [d] S Isa 29:21
[e] 1Ki 22:8; Gal 4:16
5:11 [f] Am 8:6
[g] S Am 3:15
[h] S Dt 28:30; Mic 1:6
[i] S Jdg 9:27; S Am 4:1;
9:14; Mic 6:15;
Zep 1:13
5:12 [j] Hos 5:3
[k] S Job 36:18;
S Isa 1:23;
S Eze 22:12
[l] S Jer 5:28
[m] S Job 5:4;
S Isa 5:23;
S Am 2:6-7
5:13 [n] S Est 4:14
[o] Mic 2:3
5:14 [p] S ver 6
5:15 [q] S Ps 52:3;
S 97:10; Ro 12:9
[r] S Ge 18:25
[s] S Isa 1:17; S 29:21;
Zec 8:16 [t] S Jer 36:3
[u] S Joel 2:14
[v] Mic 5:7,8; 7:18

5:6 The places of idolatry were doomed; yet if Israel turned to God, there was hope for her as a nation. Otherwise her people, too, would be destroyed. *Seek … live.* See v. 4 and note. *house of Joseph.* The northern kingdom of Israel, dominated by the tribe of Ephraim, descendants of Joseph (see v. 15; 6:6; Hos 4:7 and note). *Bethel.* The main religious center of the northern kingdom (see 3:14; 4:4; 7:13; Hos 12:4 and notes). The god the Israelites worshiped there would be powerless to save the place when the true God brought his judgment.

5:7 *those who turn justice into bitterness.* They corrupted the procedures and institutions of justice (the courts), making them instruments of injustice ("bitterness"). Turning God's order upside down is inevitable in a society that ignores his law and despises true religion (see 6:12 and note).

5:8–9 As in 4:13, a brief hymn is inserted (see 9:5–6 and notes). Here Amos highlights the contrast between "those who turn" good into bad (v. 7) and the One "who turns" night into day and governs the order of the universe—and whose power can smash the walls his people hide behind.

5:8 *Pleiades.* A group of seven stars (part of the constellation Taurus); always mentioned in connection with Orion (see note on Job 9:9). *midnight into dawn … day into night.* The orderly sequence of day and night (see Ge 8:22; Jer 31:35). *waters of the sea.* The waters above the expanse (see 9:6; Ge 1:7; see also notes on Ps 36:8; 42:7; 104:3); alternatively, waters evaporated from the sea and condensed as rain. *the LORD is his name.* The

middle of three occurrences of this refrain (see 4:13, where the refrain is expanded; 9:6).

5:10 Continues the sentence begun in v. 7. This poetic paragraph is continued and completed in vv. 12b–13, which (in the Hebrew) use the third person, while the preceding passage (vv. 11–12a) uses the second person. The indictment of vv. 7, 10, 12b–13 is therefore more objective and descriptive, while that of vv. 11–12a is more direct and pointed. *reproves … tells the truth.* Those who are concerned that the courts uphold justice.

5:11 *levy a straw tax on the poor.* Echoes the initial indictment against Israel (2:7). *though you have built.* God would take away their prized possessions acquired through wrongful gain. Their prosperity would be turned to grief (see the covenant curses in Dt 28:30, 38–40).

5:13 *the prudent.* They know they cannot change the state of affairs, and therefore only await judgment.

5:14 *Seek good.* Cf. "Seek me" (v. 4; see note there; see also Isa 1:16–17 and note on 1:17). *that you may live.* The purpose is more definitely expressed than in vv. 4, 6, and the way to change is explicit. *with you.* As your security and source of blessing.

5:15 *Perhaps.* Emphasizes the danger of presuming on God's grace. Even a widespread change of attitude would need the test of time to prove its genuineness. *remnant.* Implies that a change now would benefit the individual survivors of the disaster, though the nation as a whole would perish. *Joseph.* See note on v. 6.

5:16 _w_ Jer 9:17;
Am 8:3; Zep 1:10
_x_ Jer 7:34 _y_ S Joel 1:11
5:17 _z_ S Ex 11:6
_a_ Ex 12:12 _b_ Isa 16:10;
S Jer 48:33
5:18 _c_ S Isa 2:12;
S Joel 1:15 _d_ S Jer 30:5
_e_ S 1Sa 2:9; S Joel 2:2
_f_ S Job 20:28;
Isa 5:19,30; Jer 30:7
5:19 _g_ S La 3:10
_h_ S Dt 32:24;
Job 20:24; S Ecc 10:8;
Isa 24:17-18; Jer 15:2-
3; 48:44
5:20 _i_ S 1Sa 2:9
_j_ S Isa 13:10;
S Eze 7:7; Ob 1:15;
Zep 1:15
5:21 _k_ Jer 44:4
_l_ S Lev 26:31;
S Hos 2:11
_m_ S Eze 23:18
5:22 _n_ Lev 26:31
_o_ S Jer 7:21
_p_ S Ps 40:6
_q_ Jer 14:12; S Am 4:4;
Mic 6:6-7 _r_ Isa 1:11-
16; S 66:3
5:23 _s_ Am 6:5
5:24 _t_ S Jer 22:3
_u_ S Isa 45:8 _v_ Mic 6:8
5:25 _w_ S Isa 43:23
_x_ S Ex 16:35
5:26 _y_ S Eze 18:6;
S 20:16

16Therefore this is what the Lord, the LORD God Almighty, says:

"There will be wailing _w_ in all the streets _x_
and cries of anguish in every public square.
The farmers _y_ will be summoned to weep
and the mourners to wail.
17 There will be wailing _z_ in all the vineyards,
for I will pass through _a_ your midst,"

says the LORD. _b_

THE DAY OF THE LORD

18 Woe to you who long
for the day of the LORD! _c_
Why do you long for the day of the LORD? _d_
That day will be darkness, _e_ not light. _f_
19 It will be as though a man fled from a lion
only to meet a bear, _g_
as though he entered his house
and rested his hand on the wall
only to have a snake bite him. _h_
20 Will not the day of the LORD be darkness, _i_ not light—
pitch-dark, without a ray of brightness? _j_

21 "I hate, _k_ I despise your religious festivals; _l_
I cannot stand your assemblies. _m_
22 Even though you bring me burnt offerings _n_ and grain offerings,
I will not accept them. _o p_
Though you bring choice fellowship offerings,
I will have no regard for them. _q r_
23 Away with the noise of your songs!
I will not listen to the music of your harps. _s_
24 But let justice _t_ roll on like a river,
righteousness _u_ like a never-failing stream! _v_

25 "Did you bring me sacrifices _w_ and offerings
forty years _x_ in the wilderness, house of Israel?
26 You have lifted up the shrine of your king,
the pedestal of your idols, _y_
the star of your god _a_—
which you made for yourselves.

_a_ 26 Or _lifted up Sakkuth your king / and Kaiwan your idols, / your star-gods;_ Septuagint _lifted up the shrine of Molek / and the star of your god Rephan, / their idols_

5:16–17 A return to the theme of lament with which this section began (vv. 1–2). _streets ... square ... farmers ... vineyards._ All will be affected by God's punishment. Even farmers, usually too busy for such things, would join the professional mourners in lament, and mourning would overflow from the cities to the vineyards (see Joel 1:5 and note). When the holy God "will pass through" (as he did in Egypt, Ex 12:12), punishment for the unholy and unjust will be inescapable (cf. Isa 6:5).
5:18 _day of the LORD._ The time when God will show himself the victor over the world, vindicating his claims to be the Lord over all the earth (see notes on 8:9; Isa 2:11,17,20; Joel 1:15). Israel expected to be exalted as his people and longed for that day to come. Amos warned that the day would come, but not as Israel expected (8:9 and note) for her, because she had not been faithful to God. (Cf. "the day of our Lord Jesus Christ" and variations in 1Co 1:8; 3:12–15; 5:5; 2Co 1:14; Php 1:6,10; 2:16.) Amos speaks primarily of an imminent and decisive judgment on Israel, not exclusively of the last day.
5:19–20 The two pictures (v. 19) emphasize vividly the inescapability of God's coming judgment.
5:21–27 Again God directly addresses Israel with the charge of unfaithfulness.

5:21–23 These three verses summarize and reject the current practice of religion in Israel. The institutions were not wrong in themselves; it was the worshipers and the ways they worshiped that were wrong. The people had no basis on which to come to God, because their conduct reflected disobedience to his law (see Isa 1:11–15 and note).
5:21 _I cannot stand._ Lit. "I do not inhale with delight."
5:24 _justice ... righteousness._ Prerequisites for acceptance by God (see Mic 6:8 and note); but these are what Israel had rejected and scorned (cf. vv. 7,10,12b). _river ... never-failing stream._ In contrast to stream beds that are dry much of the year (see Jer 15:18 and note). The simile is especially apt: As plant and animal life flourishes where there is water, so human life flourishes where there is justice and righteousness.
5:25 Israel's right relationship with the Lord was never established primarily by sacrifices. It was above all based on obedience (see 1Sa 15:22 and note; cf. Ro 1:5). _forty years in the wilderness._ See Nu 14:32–35 and note on 14:34.
5:26 The obscure language of this verse speaks of Israelite idolatry, but whether it was in the wilderness long ago or more recently in the promised land, or both, is not clear. The TNIV text note takes two nouns as proper names derived from Akkadian. The Septuagint (the pre-Christian Greek translation of the OT) represents a somewhat different text, which is followed by Ac 7:43.

²⁷Therefore I will send you into exile^z beyond Damascus,"
says the LORD, whose name is God Almighty.^a

WOE TO THE COMPLACENT

6 Woe to you^b who are complacent^c in Zion,
and to you who feel secure^d on Mount Samaria,^e
you notable men of the foremost nation,
to whom the people of Israel come!^f
²Go to Kalneh^g and look at it;
go from there to great Hamath,^h
and then go down to Gathⁱ in Philistia.
Are they better off than^j your two kingdoms?
Is their land larger than yours?
³You put off the evil day
and bring near a reign of terror.^k
⁴You lie on beds inlaid with ivory
and lounge on your couches.^l
You dine on choice lambs
and fattened calves.^m
⁵You strum away on your harpsⁿ like David
and improvise on musical instruments.^o
⁶You drink wine^p by the bowlful
and use the finest lotions,
but you do not grieve^q over the ruin of Joseph.^r
⁷Therefore you will be among the first to go into exile;^s
your feasting and lounging will end.^t

THE LORD ABHORS THE PRIDE OF ISRAEL

⁸The Sovereign LORD has sworn by himself^u—the LORD God Almighty declares:

"I abhor^v the pride of Jacob^w
and detest his fortresses;^x
I will deliver up^y the city
and everything in it.^z"

⁹If ten^a people are left in one house, they too will die. ¹⁰And if the relative who comes to carry the bodies out of the house to burn them^{a b} asks anyone who might be hiding there, "Is anyone else with you?" and he says, "No," then he will go on to say, "Hush!^c We must not mention the name of the LORD."

¹¹For the LORD has given the command,
and he will smash^d the great house^e into pieces
and the small house into bits.^f

¹²Do horses run on the rocky crags?
Does one plow the sea^b with oxen?

^a 10 Or to make a funeral fire in honor of the dead   ^b 12 With a different word division of the Hebrew; Masoretic Text plow there

---

5:27 ^z Am 6:7; 7:11, 17; Mic 1:16
^a Dt 32:17-19; Jer 38:17; S Am 4:13; Ac 7:42-43*
6:1 ^b Lk 6:24
^c Zep 1:12
^d S Job 24:23
^e S Am 3:9 ^f Isa 32:9-11
6:2 ^g S Ge 10:10
^h S 2Ki 17:24;
S Jer 49:23
ⁱ S Jos 11:22; 2Ch 26:6
^j Na 3:8
6:3 ^k S Isa 56:12;
S Eze 12:22; Am 9:10
6:4 ^l S Est 1:6;
S Pr 7:17 ^m S Isa 1:11;
S Eze 34:2-3;
S Am 3:12
6:5 ⁿ S Ps 137:2;
S Isa 14:11; Am 5:23
^o S 1Ch 15:16
6:6 ^p S Isa 28:1;
S Am 2:8 ^q S Eze 9:4
^r S Eze 16:49
6:7 ^s S Am 5:27
^t S Jer 16:9; S La 4:5
6:8 ^u S Ge 22:16;
Heb 6:13
^v S Lev 26:30
^w S Ps 47:4
^x S Jer 12:8 ^y Am 4:2
^z S Lev 26:19;
Dt 32:19
6:9 ^a S Am 5:3
6:10 ^b S 1Sa 31:12
^c Am 8:3
6:11 ^d S Isa 34:5
^e S Am 3:15 ^f Isa 55:11

5:27 This punishment is the final one—exile from the God-given land to remote foreign places.
6:1 in Zion . . . on Mount Samaria. Although Amos spoke primarily to Israel, Judah and Jerusalem (Zion) also deserved his rebuke (cf. 2:4–5), for Israel properly comprised all 12 tribes. Mount Samaria. See 4:1; Israel's capital city, founded by King Omri. It was located on an easily defended, lofty hill (see 1Ki 16:24 and note). foremost nation. In Amos's self-complacent eyes in this time of her newly recovered power and prosperity (see Introduction: Date and Historical Situation).
6:2 Perhaps Kalneh and Hamath had fallen in Jeroboam II's campaign (see 2Ki 14:25,28 and notes), and the wall of Gath had been broken down by Uzziah (2Ch 26:6). These words may have been spoken by the "people of Israel" (v. 1) who, when they came before their notables, flattered their vanity and thus reinforced their arrogant complacency.
6:3 evil day. See note on 5:18.
6:4 lie . . . lounge on your couches. See 3:12 and note. ivory. See

3:15 and note.
6:5 like David. See 1Sa 16:15–23; 2Sa 23:1.
6:6 by the bowlful. To extravagant and intemperate excess. Joseph. See note on 5:6.
6:8 sworn by himself. See notes on Ge 22:16; Heb 6:13. By this oath God declares that the verdict is final. the pride of Jacob. The strongholds in which the people took pride ("his fortresses"; cf. Eze 32:12 and note). fortresses. See note on 1:4.
6:10–11 A fearful scene: Apparently a survivor is cowering inside the house, the relative forbidding him even to pray because God's wrath had fallen on the city.
6:10 carry the bodies out . . . to burn them. Reference may be to burning a memorial fire in honor of the dead (see Jer 34:5 and note). Cremation was not generally practiced, being reserved primarily for serious offenders (see Ge 38:24; Lev 20:14; 21:9; Jos 7:15,25; 1Sa 31:12 and note).
6:11 great house . . . small house. Cf. perhaps the "summer house" and "winter house" of 3:15.

6:12 *g* Hos 10:4
h S Am 3:10
i S Isa 1:21; S Am 5:7
6:13 *j* S Job 8:15;
Isa 28:14-15
6:14 *k* Jer 5:15
l S Nu 13:21
m S Am 3:11
7:1 *n* ver 7; Am 8:1
o Ps 78:46;
S Jer 51:14; S Joel 1:4
7:2 *p* S Ex 10:15
q S Isa 37:4
r S Eze 11:13;
S Am 4:9
7:3 *s* S Ex 32:14;
Dt 32:36; S Jer 18:8;
26:19 *t* S Hos 11:8
7:4 *u* S Isa 66:16;
S Joel 1:19 *v* Dt 32:22
7:5 *w* S ver 1-2;
Joel 2:17
7:6 *x* S Ex 32:14;
S Jer 18:8; Jnh 3:10
y Jer 42:10; S Eze 9:8
7:8 *z* Jer 1:11,13
a Am 8:2 *b* S 2Ki 21:13
c S Jer 15:6; Eze 7:2-9
7:9 *d* S Lev 26:30
e S Lev 26:31
f S 1Ki 13:34;
2Ki 15:9; Isa 63:18;
S Hos 10:8
7:10 *g* S Jos 7:2
h S 2Ki 14:23

But you have turned justice into poison *g*
    and the fruit of righteousness *h* into bitterness *i*—
¹³ you who rejoice in the conquest of Lo Debar *a*
    and say, "Did we not take Karnaim *b* by our own strength? *j*"

¹⁴ For the LORD God Almighty declares,
    "I will stir up a nation *k* against you, house of Israel,
that will oppress you all the way
    from Lebo Hamath *l* to the valley of the Arabah. *m*"

LOCUSTS, FIRE AND A PLUMB LINE

7 This is what the Sovereign LORD showed me: *n* He was preparing swarms of locusts *o* after the king's share had been harvested and just as the late crops were coming up. ²When they had stripped the land clean, *p* I cried out, "Sovereign LORD, forgive! How can Jacob survive? *q* He is so small! *r*"

³So the LORD relented. *s*

"This will not happen," the LORD said. *t*

⁴This is what the Sovereign LORD showed me: The Sovereign LORD was calling for judgment by fire; *u* it dried up the great deep and devoured *v* the land. ⁵Then I cried out, "Sovereign LORD, I beg you, stop! How can Jacob survive? He is so small! *w*"

⁶So the LORD relented. *x*

"This will not happen either," the Sovereign LORD said. *y*

⁷This is what he showed me: The Lord was standing by a wall that had been built true to plumb, *c* with a plumb line *d* in his hand. ⁸And the LORD asked me, "What do you see, *z* Amos? *a*"

"A plumb line, *b*" I replied.

Then the Lord said, "Look, I am setting a plumb line among my people Israel; I will spare them no longer. *c*

⁹ "The high places *d* of Isaac will be destroyed
    and the sanctuaries *e* of Israel will be ruined;
with my sword I will rise against the house of Jeroboam. *f*"

AMOS AND AMAZIAH

¹⁰Then Amaziah the priest of Bethel *g* sent a message to Jeroboam *h* king of Israel:

---

a 13 *Lo Debar* means *nothing.*   *b 13* *Karnaim* means *horns; horn* here symbolizes strength.   *c 7* The meaning of the Hebrew for this phrase is uncertain.   *d 7* The meaning of the Hebrew for this phrase is uncertain; also in verse 8.

6:12 *plow the sea with oxen.* See TNIV text note. Israel's perversion of justice flies in the face of even common human wisdom about the right order of things. See 5:7 and note.
6:13 *Lo Debar ... Karnaim.* See TNIV text notes for Amos's ironic play on the meanings of these place names. The towns may have been regained from Hazael by Jehoash (2Ki 10:32–33; 13:25) or by Jeroboam II (see 2Ki 14:25 and note), then taken by the Assyrians soon after Amos's day (2Ki 15:29)—beginning the sequence of events that would lead to the loss of all territory conquered by Jeroboam II.
6:14 *nation.* Assyria. *from Lebo Hamath to the valley of the Arabah.* From the Orontes River in north Lebanon to the Dead Sea—thus the whole land (see 2Ki 14:25).
7:1 *showed me.* Introduces reports of visions that convey God's message through things seen, as well as heard (see vv. 4,7; 8:1; Jer 1:11 and note; cf. Am 9:1). *locusts.* See 4:9; Ex 10:4 and note. *king's share.* Apparently the earlier crop, from which the royal taxes were taken. *late crops.* The growth that came up in the fields after the grains and early hay were harvested. On these the flocks and herds pastured until the summer dry season stopped all growth.
7:2 See v. 5. *How ... survive?* Mass starvation would afflict all the people. *Jacob.* Israel. *so small.* Powerless to withstand the calamity. Amos makes no appeal to the Lord's covenant with Israel—perhaps because Israel's unfaithfulness had removed all right to such an appeal.

7:3 See v. 6. *the LORD relented.* In response to the prophetic intercession (see Ge 20:7)—but forgiveness is not offered.
7:4 *great deep.* Probably the Mediterranean Sea. *land.* Lit. "portion," probably referring to the promised land or, more precisely, to everything growing on the land (cf. Joel 1:19).
7:5 See note on v. 2.
7:6 See note on v. 3.
7:7 Israel is compared to a wall built "true to plumb"—what she should have been, after all the Lord had done for her.
7:8–9 In vv. 1–6 God proposed wholesale punishments amounting to total destruction, but relented at Amos's prayer—though without promise of forgiveness. Now the Lord is no longer open to such intercession (see Jer 7:16; 15:1 and notes).
7:8 *What do you see ... ?* See note on Jer 1:11. *plumb line.* God's people had been "built" (v. 7) according to God's standards. They were expected to be true to those standards, but were completely out of plumb when tested (see 2Ki 21:13 and note). *my people.* Here, for the first time in the book of Amos, the Lord calls Israel "my people" (see v. 15; 8:2; 9:10,14; see also note on Ex 17:4). *spare them no longer.* See 8:2; cf. 9:1–4.
7:9 *high places ... sanctuaries ... house.* The centers of religious and political pretension and of self-righteous pride would be wiped out. *Isaac.* Israel's (Jacob's) father, a way of referring to Israel found only in Amos (see v. 16). *Jeroboam.* The oracles of chs. 1–6 were spoken to the leading people of Israel and Samaria as a whole; here Amos names one man, King Jeroboam II.

"Amos is raising a conspiracy[i] against you in the very heart of Israel. The land cannot bear all his words.[j] [11]For this is what Amos is saying:

" 'Jeroboam will die by the sword,
 and Israel will surely go into exile,[k]
 away from their native land.' "[l]

[12]Then Amaziah said to Amos, "Get out, you seer![m] Go back to the land of Judah. Earn your bread there and do your prophesying there.[n] [13]Don't prophesy anymore at Bethel,[o] because this is the king's sanctuary and the temple[p] of the kingdom.[q]"

[14]Amos answered Amaziah, "I was neither a prophet[r] nor the disciple of a prophet, but I was a shepherd, and I also took care of sycamore-fig trees.[s] [15]But the LORD took me from tending the flock[t] and said to me, 'Go,[u] prophesy[v] to my people Israel.'[w] [16]Now then, hear[x] the word of the LORD. You say,

" 'Do not prophesy against[y] Israel,
 and stop preaching against the house of Isaac.'

[17]"Therefore this is what the LORD says:

" 'Your wife will become a prostitute[z] in the city,
 and your sons and daughters will fall by the sword.
Your land will be measured and divided up,
 and you yourself will die in a pagan[a] country.
And Israel will surely go into exile,[a]
 away from their native land.[b]' "

A BASKET OF RIPE FRUIT

8 This is what the Sovereign LORD showed me:[c] a basket of ripe fruit. [2]"What do you see,[d] Amos?[e]" he asked.

"A basket[f] of ripe fruit," I answered.

Then the LORD said to me, "The time is ripe for my people Israel; I will spare them no longer.[g]

[3]"In that day," declares the Sovereign LORD, "the songs in the temple will turn to wailing.[b][h] Many, many bodies—flung everywhere! Silence![i]"

[4]Hear this, you who trample the needy
 and do away with the poor[j] of the land,[k]

[5]saying,

"When will the New Moon[l] be over

---

[a] 17 Hebrew *an unclean*   [b] 3 Or *"the temple singers will wail*

7:10 [i]Jer 38:4
[j]2Ki 14:24; Jer 26:8-11
7:11 [k]S Am 5:27
[l]Jer 36:16
7:12 [m]S 1Sa 9:9
[n]Mt 8:34
7:13 [o]S Jos 7:2;
S 1Ki 12:29 [p]Jer 36:5
[q]S Jer 20:2;
S Am 2:12; Ac 4:18
7:14 [r]S 1Sa 10:5;
2Ki 2:5; 4:38;
Zec 13:5 [s]S 1Ki 10:27;
S Isa 9:10
7:15 [t]S Ge 37:2;
S 2Sa 7:8 [u]S Isa 6:9
[v]S Jer 26:12 [w]Jer 7:1-2; S Eze 2:3-4
7:16 [x]Jer 22:2
[y]S Eze 20:46;
Mic 2:6
7:17 [z]S Hos 4:13
[a]S Am 5:27
[b]2Ki 17:6;
S Eze 4:13; S Hos 9:3;
Am 2:12-13
8:1 [c]S Am 7:1
8:2 [d]Jer 1:13; 24:3
[e]Am 7:8 [f]S Ge 40:16
[g]S La 4:18; Eze 7:2-9
8:3 [h]S Am 5:16
[i]Am 6:10
8:4 [j]S Pr 30:14
[k]S Job 20:19;
S Ps 14:4; S Am 2:7
8:5 [l]S Nu 10:10

7:11 Amaziah's words summarize Amos's message (see note on v. 17). *Jeroboam.* That is, his "house" (v. 9), the king's name also representing his dynasty. *will die.* Jeroboam died naturally (2Ki 14:29), but his son and successor Zechariah (2Ki 15:8) was assassinated (2Ki 15:10).

7:12 *seer.* Amaziah dismissed Amos as a prophet for hire whom he need not take seriously. *Go back to…Judah…and do your prophesying there.* Return to your homeland (see Introduction: Author). You have no business or standing among us.

7:13 *king's sanctuary.* Amaziah served the king in Samaria, not Israel's heavenly King; hence he would not allow a prophetic word to be spoken against Jeroboam or his realm at the royal chapel.

7:14 *neither a prophet nor the disciple of a prophet.* Amos denied any previous connection with the prophets or their disciples (see note on 1Ki 20:35). No one had hired him to come and announce judgment on Jeroboam and Israel. *shepherd.* See note on 1:1, but the Hebrew uses a different word here—one not found elsewhere in the OT. The Hebrew for this word is, however, related to a word for "cattle," suggesting that Amos may also have tended cattle. *sycamore-fig trees.* They yield fig-like fruit, though smaller than figs and of inferior quality. To ensure good fruit, the gardener had to slit the top of each fig—which may be the procedure referred to by the obscure Hebrew

word here rendered "took care of."

7:15 *tending.* Or "following" (as in 2Sa 7:8), the Hebrew for which stresses the location of the shepherd rather than his activity. *Go.* Amos was in Bethel because God had sent him to prophesy there.

7:16 *Do not prophesy.* Cf. 2:12.

7:17 Amos turned to condemn the priest personally. *prostitute.* With the exile of Amaziah, the death of his children and the loss of the family estate, Amaziah's wife would be reduced to prostitution to survive. *Your land.* Amaziah's private estate would be "divided up" and given to others. *pagan country.* Where his ceremonial purity as a priest would be defiled (see TNIV text note). *And Israel…native land.* Amos repeats—verbatim in the Hebrew—the last two lines of Amaziah's earlier summary of Amos's message (v. 11).

8:1 *showed me.* See note on 7:1.

8:2 *What do you see…?* See 7:8 and note. *ripe fruit…time is ripe.* A wordplay in Hebrew; Israel was ready to be plucked. *my people.* See 7:8 and note. *spare them no longer.* See 7:8.

8:3 *that day.* See 5:18 and note. *wailing…Silence!* There would be no thanksgiving songs for this harvest (contrast Lev 23:39–41)—only silence in the face of divine judgment (see note on Hab 2:20).

8:4 *Hear this.* See 3:1 and note. *trample.* See 5:11 and note.

8:5 _m_ Isa 58:13
_n_ S Ne 10:31
_o_ S Ge 31:7
_p_ Dt 25:15; 2Ki 4:23;
Ne 13:15-16;
Eze 45:10-12;
S Hos 12:7; Mic 6:10-
11; Zec 5:6
8:6 _q_ Am 5:11
_r_ S Am 2:6; S 4:1
8:7 _s_ Ps 47:4
_t_ S Hos 8:13
_u_ S Job 35:15
8:8 _v_ S Job 9:6;
Jer 51:29 _w_ Ps 18:7;
S Jer 46:8; Am 9:5
8:9 _x_ S Job 5:14;
Isa 59:9-10; Jer 13:16;
15:9; S Eze 32:7;
S Am 5:8; Mic 3:6;
Mt 27:45; Mk 15:33;
Lk 23:44-45
8:10 _y_ S Lev 26:31
_z_ S La 5:15; S Hos 2:11
_a_ S Joel 1:8
_b_ S Lev 13:40;
S Isa 3:17 _c_ S Ge 21:16
_d_ S Jer 2:19;
S Eze 7:18
8:11 _e_ Jer 30:3;
31:27 _f_ S Isa 30:20
_g_ S 1Sa 3:1; S 28:6;
S 2Ch 15:3
8:12 _h_ S Eze 20:3,31
8:13 _i_ S Isa 9:17
_j_ Isa 41:17; Hos 2:3
8:14 _k_ Mic 1:5
_l_ S 1Ki 12:29
_m_ S Am 5:5
_n_ S Ps 46:2
_o_ S Am 5:2

that we may sell grain,
 and the Sabbath be ended
  that we may market _m_ wheat?" _n_—
 skimping on the measure,
  boosting the price
  and cheating _o_ with dishonest scales, _p_
  ⁶ buying the poor _q_ with silver
  and the needy for a pair of sandals,
  selling even the sweepings with the wheat. _r_

⁷ The LORD has sworn by himself, the Pride of Jacob: _s_ "I will never forget _t_ anything they
have done. _u_

⁸ "Will not the land tremble _v_ for this,
 and all who live in it mourn?
The whole land will rise like the Nile;
 it will be stirred up and then sink
 like the river of Egypt. _w_

⁹ "In that day," declares the Sovereign LORD,

 "I will make the sun go down at noon
 and darken the earth in broad daylight. _x_
 ¹⁰ I will turn your religious festivals _y_ into mourning
 and all your singing into weeping. _z_
I will make all of you wear sackcloth _a_
 and shave _b_ your heads.
I will make that time like mourning for an only son _c_
 and the end of it like a bitter day. _d_

¹¹ "The days are coming," _e_ declares the Sovereign LORD,
 "when I will send a famine through the land—
not a famine of food or a thirst for water,
 but a famine _f_ of hearing the words of the LORD. _g_
¹² People will stagger from sea to sea
 and wander from north to east,
searching for the word of the LORD,
 but they will not find it. _h_

¹³ "In that day

 "the lovely young women and strong young men _i_
 will faint because of thirst. _j_
 ¹⁴ Those who swear by the sin of Samaria _k_—
 who say, 'As surely as your god lives, Dan,' _l_
 or, 'As surely as the god _a_ of Beersheba _m_ lives'—
 they will fall, _n_ never to rise again. _o_ "

_a_ 14 Hebrew _the way_

8:5 _New Moon ... Sabbath._ The official religious festivals, when commerce ceased (see Nu 28:9–15; 2Ki 4:23 and note). _skimping on the measure, boosting the price ... dishonest scales._ See Lev 19:35; Pr 11:1 and notes; Hos 12:7.

8:6 See note on 2:6.

8:7 _The LORD has sworn by himself, the Pride of Jacob._ In ironic fashion, Amos echoes the phrase "pride of Jacob" in 6:8, where it refers not to God (as here) but to the fortresses of Israel.

8:8 See 9:5. _rise like the Nile._ Because of the heavy seasonal rains in Ethiopia, the Nile in Egypt annually rose by as much as 25 feet, flooding the whole valley except for the towns and villages standing above it. Its waters carried a large amount of rich soil, which was deposited on the land—perhaps referred to by the words "stirred up."

8:9 _that day._ See 5:18 and note. _darken the earth._ As elsewhere, the "day of the LORD" is described as one in which the cosmic (world) order is disrupted and light is turned to darkness (see 5:18,20; Isa 13:10; 24:23; 34:4; 50:3; Eze 32:7–8; Joel 2:2,10,31 and note on 2:2; Mic 3:6; Zep 1:15; Rev 6:12), as if creation is being undone (see Jer 4:23 and note).

8:10 _mourning._ Illustrated by King David (2Sa 18:33). _wear sackcloth ... shave your heads._ Signs of mourning (see Ge 37:34; Isa 15:2–3 and notes). _only son._ On whose life the future of the family depended (cf. 2Sa 18:18). _bitter day._ The opposite of the "day of celebration" (Est 9:22).

8:11 _days._ When God's judgment begins to take effect. _famine of hearing the words of the LORD._ In times of great distress Israel turned to the Lord for a prophetic word of hope or guidance (see, e.g., 2Ki 19:1–4,14–15; 22:13–14; Jer 21:1–2; Eze 14:7), but in the coming judgment the Lord will answer all such appeals with silence—the awful silence of God (see Eze 7:26 and note; 20:1–3; Mic 3:4,7).

8:12 _sea to sea ... north to east._ Throughout the land of Israel, from the Mediterranean to the Dead Sea, even to the Transjordan.

8:13 _thirst._ Both physical and spiritual. Their strength sapped, even the "lovely young women and strong young men" of the nation would faint and fall useless.

8:14 _Those who swear._ By the gods of their various religious centers—the false gods in which they trusted rather than in the Lord. _Samaria._ See note on 6:1. _Dan ... Beersheba._ Cities that not

ISRAEL TO BE DESTROYED

9 I saw the Lord standing by the altar, and he said:

"Strike the tops of the pillars
so that the thresholds shake.
Bring them down on the heads[p] of all the people;
those who are left I will kill with the sword.
Not one will get away,
none will escape.[q]

[2] Though they dig down to the depths below,[r]
from there my hand will take them.
Though they climb up to the heavens above,[s]
from there I will bring them down.[t]

[3] Though they hide themselves on the top of Carmel,[u]
there I will hunt them down and seize them.[v]
Though they hide from my eyes at the bottom of the sea,[w]
there I will command the serpent[x] to bite them.[yz]

[4] Though they are driven into exile by their enemies,[a]
there I will command the sword[a] to slay them.

"I will fix my eyes on them
for evil[b] and not for good.[c″ d]

[5] The Lord, the LORD Almighty—
he touches the earth and it melts,[e]
and all who live in it mourn;
the whole land rises like the Nile,
then sinks like the river of Egypt;[f]

[6] he builds his lofty palace[a g] in the heavens
and sets its foundation[b] on the earth;
he calls for the waters of the sea
and pours them out over the face of the land—
the LORD is his name.[h]

[7] "Are not you Israelites
the same to me as the Cushites[c]?"[i]

declares the LORD.

"Did I not bring Israel up from Egypt,
the Philistines[j] from Caphtor[d k]
and the Arameans from Kir?[l]

[8] "Surely the eyes of the Sovereign LORD
are on the sinful kingdom.

---

[a] 6 The meaning of the Hebrew for this phrase is uncertain.   [b] 6 The meaning of the Hebrew for this word is uncertain.   [c] 7 That is, people from the upper Nile region   [d] 7 That is, Crete

9:1 [p] Ps 68:21
[q] Jer 11:11
9:2 [r] S Job 7:9;
S Eze 26:20
[s] Jer 51:53 [t] Ob 1:4
9:3 [u] Am 1:2
[v] Ps 139:8-10
[w] Ps 68:22 × Isa 27:1
[y] Jer 16:16-17
[z] S Ge 49:17;
S Job 11:20
9:4 [a] S Lev 26:33;
S Eze 5:12
[b] S Jer 21:10
[c] Jer 39:16; S Eze 15:7
[d] S Jer 44:11
9:5 [e] S Ps 46:2
[f] S Am 8:8
9:6 [g] Jer 43:9
[h] Ps 104:1-3,5-6,13;
S Am 5:8
9:7 [i] S 2Ch 12:3;
Isa 20:4; 43:3
[j] S Ge 10:14
[k] S Dt 2:23
[l] 2Ki 16:9;
S Isa 22:6; S Am 2:10

---

only marked the northern and southern limits of Israel (see note on Jdg 20:1) but also were noted as sites where pagan shrines had been built (see 5:5; 1Ki 12:29 and notes).
9:1 *I saw the Lord.* See note on 7:1. God is now poised on earth. *by the altar.* God is about to initiate the destruction from the very place from which the people expect to hear a word of peace and blessing. *tops of the pillars.* God will shatter the temple completely, from the decorated capitals down to the heavy stone "thresholds." The next lines depict the destruction. *Not one ... will escape.* See note on 7:8.
9:2–4 See note on 7:8. These verses emphasize the impossibility of escape from God's impending judgment. The imaginary extremes to which a person might go may be compared with those in Ps 139:7–12 (see note there). God's domain includes every place, even the realm of the grave (v. 2).
9:3 *top of Carmel.* See note on 1:2. *serpent.* In pagan mythology, the fierce monster of the sea (see Ps 74:13–14 and note). If some of "the people" (v.1) should seek to escape by hiding in the depths, they could still not evade God, for even there all are subject to him.

9:4 *driven ... by their enemies ... I will command.* Even those dispersed among the nations will not escape God's judgment. *I will fix my eyes ... for evil.* Contrast Ps 33:18–19; 34:15.
9:5 *The Lord ... he touches.* Introduces a hymnic reminder that Israel's God is the Creator and Sustainer of the universe, thus underlining the pronouncements of the previous verses (see 4:13; 5:8–9 and notes). *earth ... melts.* See note on Ps 46:6. *rises like the Nile.* See 8:8 and note.
9:6 *his lofty palace.* Contrasts the scale of God with the scale of human beings, whose structures fall at the movement of the earth (v. 5). See Ps 104:3 and note. *waters of the sea.* See 5:8 and note.
9:7 *Cushites.* A dark-skinned people who lived south of Egypt (see Jer 13:23 and TNIV text note there). *Did I not bring Israel up ... ?* See note on Ex 20:2. Israel could not rely on God's past blessings as an assurance of his future benevolence. Her stubborn rebelliousness robbed the exodus of all special meaning for her; her journey from Egypt is reduced to no more significance than the movements of other peoples. *Philistines from Caphtor.* See note on Jer 47:4. *Kir.* See note on 1:5.
9:8 *sinful kingdom.* Israel, the chosen, whose disobedience was

9:8 _m_ S Jer 4:27
_n_ S Jer 44:27
9:9 _o_ Lk 22:31
_p_ Isa 30:28
_q_ S Jer 31:36; S Da 9:7
9:10 _r_ Jer 49:37
_s_ Jer 5:12; S 23:17;
S Eze 20:38;
S Am 6:3
9:11 _t_ S Isa 7:2
_u_ S Ge 26:22
_v_ Ps 53:6; S Isa 49:8
_w_ Ps 80:12;
S Eze 17:24; Mic 7:8,
11; Zec 12:7; 14:10
9:12 _x_ S Nu 24:18
_y_ Isa 43:7; Jer 25:29
_z_ Ac 15:16-17*
9:13 _a_ Jer 31:38;
33:14 _b_ S Ru 2:3
_c_ Lev 26:5
_d_ S Jdg 9:27
_e_ S Joel 2:24
_f_ S Joel 3:18
9:14 _g_ S Jer 29:14
_h_ S Jer 33:7
_i_ S Isa 32:18; S 49:8;
S 61:4 _j_ S 2Ki 19:29
_k_ S Isa 62:9;
S Jer 30:18; S 31:28;
Eze 28:25-26;
S 34:13-14; S Am 5:11
9:15 _l_ S Ex 15:17;
S Isa 60:21
_m_ S Jer 23:8
_n_ S Joel 3:20
_o_ S Isa 65:9;
S Jer 3:18; Ob 1:17
_p_ S Jer 18:9; S 24:6;
S 32:15; S Eze 28:26;
S 34:25-28; S 37:12,
25

I will destroy _m_ it
  from the face of the earth.
Yet I will not totally destroy
  the house of Jacob,"

declares the LORD. _n_

⁹"For I will give the command,
  and I will shake the house of Israel
  among all the nations
as grain _o_ is shaken in a sieve, _p_
  and not a pebble will reach the ground. _q_
¹⁰All the sinners among my people
  will die by the sword, _r_
all those who say,
  'Disaster will not overtake or meet us.' _s_

ISRAEL'S RESTORATION

¹¹"In that day

I will restore David's _t_ fallen shelter _u_—
  I will repair its broken walls
  and restore its ruins _v_—
  and will rebuild it as it used to be, _w_
¹²so that they may possess the remnant of Edom _x_
  and all the nations that bear my name, _a y_"
declares the LORD, who will do these things. _z_

¹³"The days are coming," _a_ declares the LORD,

"when the reaper _b_ will be overtaken by the one who plows _c_
  and the planter by the one treading _d_ grapes.
New wine _e_ will drip from the mountains
  and flow from all the hills, _f_
¹⁴ and I will bring _g_ my people Israel back from exile. _b h_

"They will rebuild the ruined cities _i_ and live in them.
  They will plant vineyards _j_ and drink their wine;
  they will make gardens and eat their fruit. _k_
¹⁵I will plant _l_ Israel in their own land, _m_
  never again to be uprooted _n_
  from the land I have given them," _o_
says the LORD your God. _p_

_a 12_ Hebrew; Septuagint _so that the remnant of people / and all the nations that bear my name may seek the Lord,_   _b 14_ Or _will restore the fortunes of my people Israel_

---

far worse than the sins of other nations (see 1:3—2:16; 3:1–2 and note on 3:2). _Yet I will not totally destroy._ See note on v. 11.
9:9 _sieve._ Separates the wheat from small stones and other refuse gathered with it when scooped up from the ground. _not a pebble will reach._ Only the grain drops through, the refuse being screened out to be discarded.
9:10 _All the sinners . . . will die._ For their persistent rebellion. _my people._ See 7:8 and note.
9:11–12 Quoted in Ac 15:16–17 (see note on Ac 15:16).
9:11 The verse is also regarded as Messianic in the Jewish Talmud. _I will restore._ Raises a hope underlying Amos's words—one that runs through the whole OT from Ge 3:15 on: God will bring blessing after judgment and will not ultimately reject Israel. _shelter._ Lit. "hut" (or rough booth)—either the dynasty ("house") of David or the united kingdom of the 12 tribes (David's kingdom). The word "hut" may have been chosen to recall David's humble beginnings. _as it used to be._ In the days of David and Solomon.
9:12 _remnant of Edom._ Whatever is left of Israel's bitter enemy (see note on 1:11) after her punishment. _all the nations that bear my name._ Refers to the extent of the rule of the

Lord's anointed future King, recalling that David had reigned over many nations surrounding Israel. It represents the fulfillment of the Abrahamic and Davidic covenants. The Messiah will reign even over former enemies, of whom Edom is symbolic (see notes on Isa 34:5; Joel 3:19; Ob 8). _will do these things._ God does what he says.
9:13–15 After all the forecasts of destruction, dearth and death (see, e.g., 5:9,11,27), Amos's final words picture a glorious Edenic prosperity, when the seasons will run together so that sowing and reaping are without interval, and there will be a continuous supply of fresh produce—a reversal of the conditions portrayed in 4:6–11 (see notes there).
9:13 See Joel 3:18 and note.
9:14–15 _I will bring . . . They will rebuild . . . They will plant . . . I will plant._ In the promised land God will make his people productive, fruitful and secure.
9:14 _my people._ See note on 7:8; contrast Hos 1:9, but see Hos 2:23. _rebuild the ruined cities._ See Isa 58:12 and note.
9:15 _never again._ When Israel is finally and fully restored, she will never again be destroyed. _your God._ Contrast Hos 1:9, but see Hos 2:23.

AUTHOR

OBADIAH

INTRODUCTION

The author's name is Obadiah, which means "servant (or worshiper) of the LORD." His was a common name (see 1Ki 18:3–16; 1Ch 3:21; 7:3; 8:38; 9:16; 12:9; 27:19; 2Ch 17:7; 34:12; Ezr 8:9; Ne 10:5; 12:25). Neither his father's name nor the place of his birth is given.

DATE AND PLACE OF WRITING

The date and place of composition are disputed. Dating the prophecy is mainly a matter of relating vv. 11–14 to one of two specific events in Israel's history:

1. The rebellion of Edom against Judah during the reign of Jehoram (853–841 B.C.); see 2Ki 8:20–22; 2Ch 21:8–15. In this case, Obadiah would be a contemporary of Elisha.

2. The Babylonian attacks on Jerusalem (605–586). Obadiah would then be a contemporary of Jeremiah. This alternative seems more likely.

The striking parallels between Ob 1–6 and Jer 49:9–10,14–16 have caused many to suggest some kind of interdependence between Obadiah and Jeremiah, but it may be that both prophets were drawing on a common source not otherwise known to us.

UNITY AND THEME

There is no compelling reason to doubt the unity of this brief prophecy, the shortest book in the OT. Its theme is that Edom, proud over her own security, has gloated over Israel's devastation by foreign powers. However, Edom's participation in that disaster will bring on God's wrath. She herself will be destroyed, but Mount Zion and Israel will be delivered and God's kingdom will triumph.

Edom's hostile activities have spanned the centuries of Israel's existence. The following Biblical references are helpful in understanding the relation of Israel and Edom: Ge 27:41–45; 32:1–21; 33; 36; Ex 15:15; Nu 20:14–21; Dt 2:1–6; 23:7–8; 1Sa 22 with Ps 52; 2Sa 8:13–14; 2Ki 8:20–22; 14:7; Ps 83; Eze 35; Joel 3:18–19; Am 1:11–12; 9:11–12.

Since the Edomites are related to the Israelites (v. 10), their hostility is all the more reprehensible. Edom is fully responsible for her failure to assist Israel and for her open aggression. The fact that God rejected Esau (Ge 25:23; Mal 1:3; Ro 9:13) in no way exonerates the Edomites. Edom, smug in its mountain strongholds, will be dislodged and sacked. But Israel will prosper because God is with her.

OUTLINE

   I. Title and Introduction (1)
  II. Judgment on Edom (2–14)
     A. Edom's Destruction Announced (2–7)
       1. The humbling of her pride (2–4)
       2. The completeness of her destruction (5–7)
     B. Edom's Destruction Reaffirmed (8–14)
       1. Her shame and destruction (8–10)
       2. Her crimes against Israel (11–14)
  III. The Day of the Lord (15–21)
     A. Judgment on the Nations but Deliverance for Zion (15–18)
     B. The Lord's Kingdom Established (19–21)

KEY   **APPLICATION FOR LIVING**   **BACKGROUND NOTES**   **C** CHARACTER INFORMATION

1 *a* S Isa 1:1
b S Ge 25:14;
S Isa 11:14; S 34:11;
63:1-6; Jer 49:7-22;
S Eze 25:12-14;
S 32:29; S Am 1:11-12
c Isa 18:2 *d* Jer 6:4-5
2 *e* Nu 24:18
3 *f* S Isa 16:6
g fn Isa 16:1
h S 2Ch 25:11-12
4 *i* S Isa 10:14
j S Isa 14:13
k S Job 20:6
5 *l* S Dt 4:27; 24:21;
S Isa 24:13
7 *m* Jer 30:14
n S Ps 41:9
8 *o* Job 5:12;
Isa 29:14
9 *p* S Ge 36:11,34
10 *q* S Joel 3:19
r Ps 137:7; Am 1:11-12

¹The vision *a* of Obadiah.

1–4pp — *Jer 49:14–16*
5–6pp — *Jer 49:9–10*

This is what the Sovereign Lᴏʀᴅ says about Edom *b*—

> We have heard a message from the Lᴏʀᴅ:
> An envoy *c* was sent to the nations to say,
> "Rise, let us go against her for battle" *d*—

² "See, I will make you small *e* among the nations;
> you will be utterly despised.
³ The pride *f* of your heart has deceived you,
> you who live in the clefts of the rocks *a g*
> and make your home on the heights,
you who say to yourself,
> 'Who can bring me down to the ground?' *h*
⁴ Though you soar like the eagle
> and make your nest *i* among the stars,
> from there I will bring you down," *j*

declares the Lᴏʀᴅ. *k*

⁵ "If thieves came to you,
> if robbers in the night—
oh, what a disaster awaits you!—
> would they not steal only as much as they wanted?
If grape pickers came to you,
> would they not leave a few grapes? *l*
⁶ But how Esau will be ransacked,
> his hidden treasures pillaged!

⁷ All your allies *m* will force you to the border;
> your friends will deceive and overpower you;
those who eat your bread *n* will set a trap for you, *b*
> but you will not detect it.

⁸ "In that day," declares the Lᴏʀᴅ,
> "will I not destroy *o* the wise in Edom,
> people of understanding in the mountains of Esau?
⁹ Your warriors, Teman, *p* will be terrified,
> and everyone in Esau's mountains
> will be cut down in the slaughter.
¹⁰ Because of the violence *q* against your brother Jacob, *r*

a 3 Or *of Sela*   *b 7* The meaning of the Hebrew for this clause is uncertain.

1–4 Paralleled in Jer 49:14–16.
1 *vision.* Commonly used in the OT to designate a revelation from God (see Pr 29:18; Isa 1:1 and notes). *Obadiah.* See Introduction: Author. *We.* Either (1) the editorial "we," (2) the prophet's association of Israel with himself or (3) other prophets' pronouncements against Edom. In any case, the rest of the verse sets the stage for Obadiah's prophetic message, which begins with v. 2. *message.* Or "report." An envoy had been sent to the nations, calling them to battle against Edom. Perhaps a conspiracy was under way among some of Edom's allies (v. 7). Although Edom feels secure (trusting in her mountain fortresses and her wise men, vv. 2–4,8–9), Obadiah announces God's judgment on her for her hostility to Israel.
2 *I will make you small.* Cf. the colloquial expression, "cut one down to size."
3 *pride.* See v. 12; Jer 49:16 and note. *rocks.* See TNIV text note. Sela was the capital of Edom. Perhaps the later Petra (both Sela and Petra mean "rock" or "cliff"), this rugged site is located some 50 miles south of the southern end of the Dead Sea (see notes on 2Ki 14:7; Isa 16:1).
4 *eagle.* A proud and regal bird, noted for strength, keenness of vision and power of flight (see Dt 28:49; Isa 40:31; Jer 4:13; 49:22; Eze 17:3). *stars.* Hyperbole for high, inaccessible places in the mountains.

5–6 Paralleled in Jer 49:9–10.
5 *leave a few grapes.* See Jer 49:9 and note.
6 *hidden treasures.* The ancient Greek historian Diodorus Siculus indicates that the Edomites put their wealth—accumulated from trade—in vaults in the rocks.
7 *eat your bread.* See Ps 41:9 and note. *set a trap for you.* However the Hebrew for this expression is understood (see TNIV text note), it must indicate some act of treachery on the part of previously trusted close friends.
8 *In that day.* The day of Edom's destruction; but the words also have an eschatological ring (see v. 15 and note). Since in OT prophecy Edom was often emblematic of all the world powers hostile to God and his kingdom, her judgment anticipates God's complete removal of all such opposition in that day (see note on Am 9:12). *the wise.* In whom Edom put so much confidence for her security (see Jer 49:7 and note). Eliphaz, one of Job's three friends, was a Temanite (see note on v. 9). *Esau.* Another name for Edom (see Ge 36:1 and note).
9 *Teman.* A reference to all Edom, as in Jer 49:7,20 (see notes on Jer 49:7; Am 1:12). Teman means "south," and the name probably refers to Edom as the southland. Some, however, identify Teman with Tawilan, a site about three miles east of Petra.
10 *your brother Jacob.* Edom's violent crimes are all the more

you will be covered with shame;
you will be destroyed forever. ^s
¹¹ On the day you stood aloof
while strangers carried off his wealth
and foreigners entered his gates
and cast lots ^t for Jerusalem,
you were like one of them. ^u
¹² You should not gloat ^v over your brother
in the day of his misfortune, ^w
nor rejoice ^x over the people of Judah
in the day of their destruction, ^y
nor boast ^z so much
in the day of their trouble. ^a
¹³ You should not march through the gates of my people
in the day of their disaster,
nor gloat over them in their calamity ^b
in the day of their disaster,
nor seize their wealth
in the day of their disaster.
¹⁴ You should not wait at the crossroads
to cut down their fugitives, ^c
nor hand over their survivors
in the day of their trouble.

¹⁵ "The day of the LORD is near ^d
for all nations.
As you have done, it will be done to you;
your deeds ^e will return upon your own head.
¹⁶ Just as you drank ^f on my holy hill, ^g
so all the nations will drink ^h continually;
they will drink and drink
and be as if they had never been. ⁱ
¹⁷ But on Mount Zion will be deliverance; ^j
it will be holy, ^k
and the house of Jacob
will possess its inheritance. ^l
¹⁸ The house of Jacob will be a fire
and the house of Joseph a flame;
the house of Esau will be stubble,
and they will set it on fire ^m and consume ⁿ it.
There will be no survivors ^o
from the house of Esau."

The LORD has spoken.

¹⁹ People from the Negev will occupy
the mountains of Esau,

10 ^s S Ps 137:7;
S Eze 25:12-14; 35:9
11 ^t S Job 6:27;
S Eze 24:6 ^u S Am 1:6
12 ^v Pr 24:17
^w S Job 31:29
^x S Eze 35:15
^y S Pr 17:5 ^z Ps 137:7
^a S Eze 25:6;
Mic 4:11; 7:8
13 ^b S Eze 35:5
14 ^c S 1Ki 18:4
15 ^d S Jer 46:10;
S Eze 30:3;
S Joel 2:31; S Am 5:18
^e S Jer 50:29; Hab 2:8
16 ^f Isa 51:17
^g S Ex 15:17
^h Jer 25:15; 49:12;
S La 4:21-22
ⁱ S La 4:21;
S Eze 25:12-14
17 ^j S Ps 69:35;
S Isa 14:1-2;
Joel 2:32; S Am 9:11-
15 ^k S Ps 74:2;
S Isa 4:3 ^l Zec 8:12
18 ^m S Isa 1:31
ⁿ Zec 12:6
^o S Jer 49:10

reprehensible because they were committed against the brother nation. *covered with shame.* A striking expression, since
shame is usually associated with nakedness.
11 See Introduction: Date and Place of Writing. *strangers ... foreigners.* These terms put in relief the sin of Edom: He did not act
like a brother (v. 12) but was like one of the strangers. *cast lots
for Jerusalem.* See Eze 24:6 and note.
12–14 A rebuke of Edom's hostile actions. The eight rebukes in
this section proceed from the general to the particular. See Ps
137:7; Eze 35:13 for examples of Edom's reactions to Judah's
misfortunes (see also note on Ps 137:7).
12 *boast.* See v. 3; Jer 49:16 and note.
15 *The day of the LORD is near for all nations.* If there was
an eschatological glimmering in "In that day" (v. 8), it here
becomes a strong ray. The day of the Lord brings judgment for
the nations (including, but not limited to, Edom) and salvation
for the house of Jacob (see v. 17; Am 5:18; Joel 1:15 and notes).
upon your own head. The situation will be reversed in retribution
for Edom's hostility against God's people, detailed in vv. 11–14.

Ezekiel's denunciation of Edom (ch. 35) reflects a similar punish-
ment-fits-the-crime principle (see also Eze 16:43).
16 *Just as you drank.* As the Edomites profaned the holy
mountain by carousing, so the nations "will drink and
drink." Their drinking, however, is that of the bitter potion of God's
judgment—which they will be compelled to keep on drinking.
For drinking as punishment, see Jer 25:15–16; 49:12 and notes.
17 *But on Mount Zion will be deliverance.* Beginning with
this verse the blessings on the house of Jacob are mentioned. Eschatological references are twofold: judgment on God's
enemies, blessing on God's people. *inheritance.* The land that God
had promised them (see Jer 3:19; 12:7 and notes).
18 *Jacob ... Joseph.* Previously it was stated that the Lord
would destroy Edom, using other nations (v. 7); now it is to be
done by God's people. *no survivors.* The final word to Esau is that
his house (or nation) will be totally destroyed; there will be no
Edomite survivors. Yet compare Am 9:12 with Ac 15:17, and see
note and TNIV text note on Am 9:12.
19 *People ... will occupy.* With Edom annihilated, others will oc-

19 P Isa 11:14
9 S Jer 31:5
r S Nu 1:36
20 s 1Ki 17:9-10;
Lk 4:26 t S Jer 33:13
21 u S Dt 28:29;
S Jdg 3:9
v S Ps 22:28; 47:9;
66:4; S Da 2:44;
Zec 14:9,16; Mal 1:14;
Rev 11:15

and people from the foothills will possess
    the land of the Philistines. P
They will occupy the fields of Ephraim and Samaria, 9
    and Benjamin r will possess Gilead.
20 This company of Israelite exiles who are in Canaan
    will possess ⌊the land⌋ as far as Zarephath; s
the exiles from Jerusalem who are in Sepharad
    will possess the towns of the Negev. t
21 Deliverers u will go up on a Mount Zion
    to govern the mountains of Esau.
And the kingdom will be the LORD's. v

---

a 21 Or *from*

---

cupy Edomite territory. Although not expressly identified, these are most likely the remnant of Israel referred to in the lines immediately following. *Negev.* See note on Ge 12:9. *foothills.* See note on Mic 1:10–15. *Philistines.* See note on Ge 10:14. *Gilead.* See notes on Ge 31:21; SS 4:1.

20 *Zarephath.* See note on 1Ki 17:9. *Sepharad.* Usually taken to refer to Sardis in Asia Minor (present-day Turkey), though some think that Sparta (the city in Greece) might be meant.

A **21** *Deliverers.* Having developed the theme of possessing lands around Zion, the prophet now turns to the center. The "deliverers" come from Mount Zion and rule over the mountains of Esau. Mount Zion is exalted over the mountains of Esau. The Messiah, the Deliverer par excellence, may ultimately be in view. *the kingdom will be the LORD's.* The conclusion of the prophecy—and the final outcome of history. The last book of the Bible echoes this theme (Rev 11:15).

DATE OF WRITING

TITLE JONAH | INTRODUCTION

The book is named after its principal character, whose name means "dove"; see the simile used of Ephraim in Hos 7:11 to portray the northern kingdom as "easily deceived and senseless." See also Ps 68:13; 74:19 and notes.

AUTHOR

C Though the book does not identify its author, tradition has ascribed it to the prophet himself, Jonah, son of Amittai (1:1), from Gath Hepher (2Ki 14:25; see note there) in Zebulun (Jos 19:10,13). In view of its many similarities with the narratives about Elijah and Elisha, however, it may come from the same prophetic circles that originally composed the accounts about those prophets, perhaps in the eighth century B.C. (see Introduction to 1 Kings: Author, Sources and Date).

BACKGROUND

In the half-century during which the prophet Jonah ministered (800–750 B.C.), a significant event affected the northern kingdom of Israel: King Jeroboam II (793–753) restored her traditional borders, ending almost a century of sporadic, seesaw conflict between Israel and Damascus.

Jeroboam, in God's good providence (2Ki 14:26–27), capitalized on Assyria's defeat of Damascus (in the latter half of the ninth century), which temporarily crushed that center of Aramean power. Prior to that time, not only had Israel been considerably reduced in size but the king of Damascus had even been able to control internal affairs in the northern kingdom (2Ki 13:7). However, after the Assyrian campaign against Damascus in 797, Jehoash, king of Israel, had been able to recover the territory lost to the king of Damascus (2Ki 13:25). Internal troubles in Assyria subsequently allowed Jeroboam to complete the restoration of Israel's northern borders. Nevertheless, Assyria remained the real threat from the north at this time.

The prophets of the Lord were speaking to Israel regarding these events. About 797 B.C. Elisha spoke to the king of Israel concerning future victories over Damascus (2Ki 13:14–19). A few years later Jonah prophesied the restoration that Jeroboam accomplished (2Ki 14:25). But soon after Israel had triumphed, she began to gloat over her newfound power. Because she was relieved of foreign pressures—relief that had come in accordance with encouraging words from Elisha and Jonah—she felt jealously complacent about her favored status with God (Am 6:1). She focused her religion on expectations of the "day of the LORD" (Am 5:18–20), when God's darkness would engulf the other nations, leaving Israel to bask in his light.

It was in such a time that the Lord sent Amos and Hosea to announce to his people Israel that he would "spare them no longer" (Am 7:8; 8:2) but would send them into exile "beyond Damascus" (Am 5:27), i.e., to Assyria (Hos 9:3; 10:6; 11:5). During this time the Lord also sent Jonah to Nineveh to warn it of the imminent danger of divine judgment.

Since Jonah was a contemporary of Amos, see Introduction to Amos: Date and Historical Situation, for additional details.

DATE OF WRITING

For a number of reasons, including the preaching to Gentiles, the book is often assigned a postexilic date. At least, it is said, the book must have been written after the destruction of Nineveh in 612 B.C. But these considerations are not decisive. The similarity of this narrative to the Elijah-Elisha accounts has already been noted. One may also question whether mention of the repentance of Nineveh and the consequent averted destruction of the city would have had so much significance to the author after Nineveh's overthrow. And to suppose that proclaiming God's word to Gentiles had no relevance in the eighth century is to overlook the fact that already in the previous century Elijah and Elisha had extended their ministries to foreign lands (1Ki 17:7–24; 2Ki 8:7–15). Moreover, the prophet Amos (c. 760–750) set God's redemptive work in behalf of Israel in the context of his dealings with the nations (Am 1:3—2:16; 9:7,12). Perhaps the third quarter of the eighth century is the most likely date for the book, after the public ministries of Amos and Hosea and before the fall of Samaria to Assyria in 722–721.

INTERPRETATION

Many have questioned whether the book of Jonah is historical. The supposed legendary character of some of the events (e.g., the episode involving the great fish) has caused them to suggest alternatives to the traditional view that the book is historical, biographical narrative. Although their specific suggestions range from fictional short story to allegory to parable, they share the common assumption that the account sprang essentially from the author's imagination, despite its serious and gracious message.

Such interpretations, often based in part on doubt about the miraculous as such, too quickly dismiss (1) the similarities between the narrative of Jonah and other parts of the OT and (2) the pervasive concern of the OT writers, especially the prophets, for history. They also fail to realize that OT narrators had a keen ear for recognizing how certain past events in Israel's pilgrimage with God illumine (by way of analogy) later events. (For example, the events surrounding the birth of Moses illumine the exodus, those surrounding Samuel's birth illumine the series of events narrated in the books of Samuel, and the ministries of Moses and Joshua illumine those of Elijah and Elisha.) Similarly, the prophets recognized that the future events they announced could be illumined by reference to analogous events of the past. Overlooking these features in OT narrative and prophecy, many have supposed that a story that too neatly fits the author's purpose must therefore be fictional.

On the other hand, it must be acknowledged that Biblical narrators were more than historians. They interpretatively recounted the past with the unswerving purpose of bringing it to bear on the present and the future. In the portrayal of past events, they used their materials to achieve this purpose effectively. Nonetheless, the integrity with which they treated the past ought not to be questioned. The book of Jonah recounts real events in the life and ministry of the prophet himself.

LITERARY CHARACTERISTICS

Unlike most other prophetic parts of the OT, this book is a narrative account of a single prophetic mission. Its treatment of that mission is thus similar to the accounts of the ministries of Elijah and Elisha found in 1,2 Kings and to certain narrative sections of Isaiah, Jeremiah and Ezekiel.

As is often the case in Biblical narratives, the author has compressed much into a small space; 40 verses tell the entire story (eight additional verses of poetry are devoted to Jonah's prayer of thanksgiving). In its scope (a single extended episode), compactness, vividness and character delineation, it is much like the book of Ruth.

Also as in Ruth, the author uses structural symmetry effectively. The story is developed in two parallel cycles that call attention to a series of comparisons and contrasts (see Outline). The story's climax is Jonah's grand prayer of confession, "Salvation comes from the LORD"—the middle confession of three from his lips (1:9; 2:9; 4:2). The last sentence emphasizes that the Lord's word is final and decisive, while Jonah is left sitting in the hot, open country outside Nineveh.

The author uses the art of representative roles in a straightforward manner. In this story of God's loving concern for all people, Nineveh, the great menace to Israel, is representative of the Gentiles. Correspondingly, stubbornly reluctant Jonah represents Israel's jealousy of her favored relationship with God and her unwillingness to share the Lord's compassion with the nations.

The book depicts the larger scope of God's purpose for Israel: that she might rediscover the truth of his concern for the whole creation and better understand her own role in carrying out that concern.

OUTLINE

1:1 ^aMt 12:39-41;
16:4; Lk 11:29-32
^b2Ki 14:25
1:2 ^cS Ge 10:11;
S Na 1:1
1:3 ^dPs 139:7
^eS Ge 10:4
^fS Jos 19:46; Ac 9:36,
43 ^gEx 4:13;
S Jer 20:9; S Am 3:8
1:4 ^hPs 107:23-26
1:5 ⁱAc 27:18-19
1:6 ^jJnh 3:8
^kS Ps 107:28
1:7 ^lNu 32:23;
Jos 7:10-18;
S 1Sa 14:42
^mS Pr 16:33
1:9 ⁿS Ps 96:9
^oS Da 2:18; Ac 17:24
^pS Ne 9:6 ^qS Ge 1:9
1:12 ^r2Sa 24:17;
1Ch 21:17

JONAH FLEES FROM THE LORD

1 The word of the LORD came to Jonah ^a son of Amittai: ^{b 2}"Go to the great city Nineveh ^c and preach against it, because its wickedness has come up before me."
³But Jonah ran ^d away from the LORD and headed for Tarshish ^e. He went down to Joppa, ^f where he found a ship bound for that port. After paying the fare, he went aboard and sailed for Tarshish to flee from the LORD. ^g

⁴Then the LORD sent a great wind on the sea, and such a violent storm arose that the ship threatened to break up. ^{h 5}All the sailors were afraid and each cried out to his own god. And they threw the cargo into the sea to lighten the ship. ⁱ

But Jonah had gone below deck, where he lay down and fell into a deep sleep. ⁶The captain went to him and said, "How can you sleep? Get up and call ^j on your god! Maybe he will take notice of us so that we will not perish." ^k

⁷Then the sailors said to each other, "Come, let us cast lots to find out who is responsible for this calamity." ^l They cast lots and the lot fell on Jonah. ^{m 8}So they asked him, "Tell us, who is responsible for making all this trouble for us? What kind of work do you do? Where do you come from? What is your country? From what people are you?"

⁹He answered, "I am a Hebrew and I worship the LORD, ⁿ the God of heaven, ^o who made the sea ^p and the dry land. ^q"

¹⁰This terrified them and they asked, "What have you done?" (They knew he was running away from the LORD, because he had already told them so.)

¹¹The sea was getting rougher and rougher. So they asked him, "What should we do to you to make the sea calm down for us?"

¹²"Pick me up and throw me into the sea," he replied, "and it will become calm. I know that it is my fault that this great storm has come upon you." ^r

---

A C **1:1** *word of the LORD.* See 3:1; Hos 1:1 and note. *Jonah.* See Introduction: Title; Author. In his account of Jonah's mission to Nineveh written for Israel's instruction, the author probably presents Jonah as a cameo representation of Israel, the people called out from the nations by God to be the channel of his redemptive purposes for the peoples of the world. In this narrative, the people of Israel are to see themselves as in a mirror: their unique position of privilege as the people to whom God had revealed himself in a special way, their particular vocation as God's chosen kingdom people, their stubborn resistance to fulfilling that vocation and the reason Israel must die as a nation (the judgment the prophets were announcing) and be raised up again, refined and renewed the more distant future the prophets were envisioning). Cf. note on Jdg 13:1—16:31.

A **1:2** *great city.* See 3:2; 4:11; see also note on 3:3. According to Ge 10:11, Nineveh was first built by Nimrod and was traditionally known as the "great city" (see Ge 10:12 and note). About 700 B.C. Sennacherib made it the capital of Assyria, which it remained until its fall in 612 (see Introduction to Nahum: Background). Nineveh is over 500 miles from Gath Hepher, Jonah's hometown. *its wickedness has come up.* Cf. Sodom and Gomorrah (see Ge 18:20–21 and note on 18:20). Except for the "violence" (3:8) of Nineveh, her "evil ways" (3:8,10) are not described in Jonah. Nahum later states that Nineveh's sins included plotting evil against the Lord, cruelty and plundering in war, prostitution, witchcraft and commercial exploitation (Na 1:11; 2:12–13; 3:1,4,16,19).

A **1:3** *ran away.* Jonah gives his reason in 4:2. The futility of trying to run away from the Lord is acknowledged in Ps 139:7–12 (see note there). *Tarshish.* Perhaps the city of Tartessus in southern Spain, a Phoenician mining colony near Gibraltar. By heading in the opposite direction from Nineveh (see map, p. 1523), to what seemed like the end of the world, Jonah intended to escape his divinely appointed task. *Joppa.* See note on Ac 9:36.

A C **1:4–16** Probably this account of the storm at sea is intended to be a graphic depiction, in exquisite miniature, of the pagan world of many nations (represented by the sailors) threatened by the judgments of God (represented by the storm), with Israel in their midst (represented by Jonah).

If Jonah (Israel) does not fulfill his mission, the sailors (nations) will die calling on their gods. And because he is rebelling against his mission, he must "die" to save them. See note on 1:1; cf. note on Ac 27:13–44.
1:4–5 Although Jonah's mission was to bring God's warning of impending judgment to the pagan world, his refusal to go to Nineveh brings these pagan sailors into peril.

A **1:4** *the LORD sent a great wind.* God's sovereign working in Jonah's mission is evident at several other points also: the fish (v. 17), the release of Jonah (2:10), the vine (4:6), the worm (4:7) and the "scorching east wind" (4:8).
1:5 *his own god.* Apparently the sailors, who may have come from various ports, worshiped several different pagan gods (see note on Ge 28:15).
1:6 *The captain went to him.* The pagan captain's concern for everyone on board contrasts with the believing prophet's refusal to carry God's warning to Nineveh.
1:7 *let us cast lots.* The casting of lots was a custom widely practiced in the ancient Near East. The precise method is unclear, though it appears that, for the most part, sticks or marked pebbles were drawn from a receptacle into which they had been "cast" (see notes on Ex 28:30; Ne 11:1; Pr 16:33; Eze 21:21; Ac 1:26). *lot fell on Jonah.* By the lot of judgment the Lord exposed the guilty one (see Jos 7:14–26 and note on 7:14; 1Sa 14:37–44 and note on 14:37).

A **1:9** *Hebrew.* See note on Ge 14:13. *God of heaven, who made the sea and the dry land.* See note on Ezr 1:2. The sailors would have understood Jonah's words as being descriptive of the highest deity. Their present experiences confirmed this truth, since, in the religions of the ancient Near East generally, the supreme god was master of the seas (see note on Jos 3:10). This is Jonah's first confessional statement, and, like those that follow (2:9d; 4:2), it is thoroughly orthodox. Though orthodox in his beliefs, Jonah refuses to fulfill his divine mission to Nineveh.
1:10 *What have you done?* This rhetorical question is really an accusation.
1:12 *throw me into the sea.* Jonah's readiness to die to save the terrified sailors contrasts with his later callous departure from Nineveh to watch from a safe distance while the city perishes— at least he still hoped it would perish (see 4:5 and note).

N of the LORD

¹³Instead, the men did their best to row back to land. But they could not, for the sea grew even wilder than before. ⁱ ¹⁴Then they cried out to the LORD, "Please, LORD, do not let us die for taking this man's life. Do not hold us accountable for killing an innocent man, ᵗ for you, LORD, have done as you pleased." ᵘ ¹⁵Then they took Jonah and threw him overboard, and the raging sea grew calm. ᵛ ¹⁶At this the men greatly feared ʷ the LORD, and they offered a sacrifice to the LORD and made vows ˣ to him.

*¹⁷Now the LORD provided ʸ a huge fish to swallow Jonah, ᶻ and Jonah was in the belly of the fish three days and three nights.

JONAH'S PRAYER

2 *From inside the fish Jonah prayed to the LORD his God. ²He said:

"In my distress I called ᵃ to the LORD, ᵇ
    and he answered me.
From deep in the realm of the dead ᶜ I called for help,

---

* 1:17 is numbered 2:1 in Hebrew texts.   * 2:1-10 is numbered 2:2-11 in Hebrew texts.

1:13 ˢ S Pr 21:30
1:14 ᵗ Dt 21:8
ᵘ S Da 4:35
1:15 ᵛ S Ps 107:29;
Lk 8:24
1:16 ʷ Mk 4:41
ˣ S Nu 30:2; Ps 66:13-
14
1:17 ʸ Jnh 4:6,7
ᶻ Mt 12:40; 16:4;
Lk 11:30
2:2 ᵃ La 3:55
ᵇ Ps 18:6; 120:1
ᶜ Ps 86:13

C **1:13** *did their best to row.* The Hebrew uses the picturesque word meaning "to dig" (with oars) to indicate strenuous effort. The ship could be driven by sails oars or both. The reluctance of the sailors to throw Jonah into the sea stands in sharp contrast to Jonah's reluctance to warn Nineveh of impending judgment.
1:14 *cried out to the LORD.* Earlier the sailors had cried out to their own gods (see v. 5 and note), but now in their desperation they plead for help from Jonah's God.
1:16 *greatly feared the LORD.* There is no evidence that the sailors renounced all other gods (contrast Naaman; see 2Ki 5:15 and note). Ancient pagans were ready to recognize the existence and power of many gods. At the least, however, the sailors acknowledged that the God of Israel was in control of the present events, that he was the one who both stirred up and calmed the storm and that at this moment he was the one to be recognized and worshiped.

A **1:17** *the LORD provided.* This characteristic phrase occurs also in 4:6-8. *huge fish.* The Hebrew here and the Greek of Mt 12:40 are both general terms for a large fish, not necessarily

a whale. This great fish is carefully distinguished from the sinister "serpent" of the sea (Am 9:3)—otherwise called "Leviathan" (Isa 27:1), the "monster of the deep" (Job 7:12; see Ps 74:13; Eze 32:2). *three days and three nights.* The phrase used here may, as in Mt 12:40, refer to a period of time including one full day and parts of two others (see notes on Mt 12:40; 1Co 15:4). In any case, the NT clearly uses Jonah's experience as a type (foreshadowing) of the burial and resurrection of Jesus, who was entombed for "three days and three nights" (Mt 12:40; see Mt 16:4; Lk 11:29-30 and note on 11:30).

A **2:2–9** A psalm of thanksgiving for deliverance from death in the Mediterranean Sea. Jonah recalls his prayer for help as he was sinking into the depths. His gratitude is heightened by his knowledge that he deserved death but that God had shown him extraordinary mercy. The language of this song indicates that Jonah was familiar with the praise literature of the Psalms.
2:2 *I called . . . he answered.* See note on Ps 118:5. *realm of the dead.* Figurative for Jonah's near-death experience in the sea (see Ps 30:3 and note). See also note on Ge 37:35.

THE BOOK OF JONAH

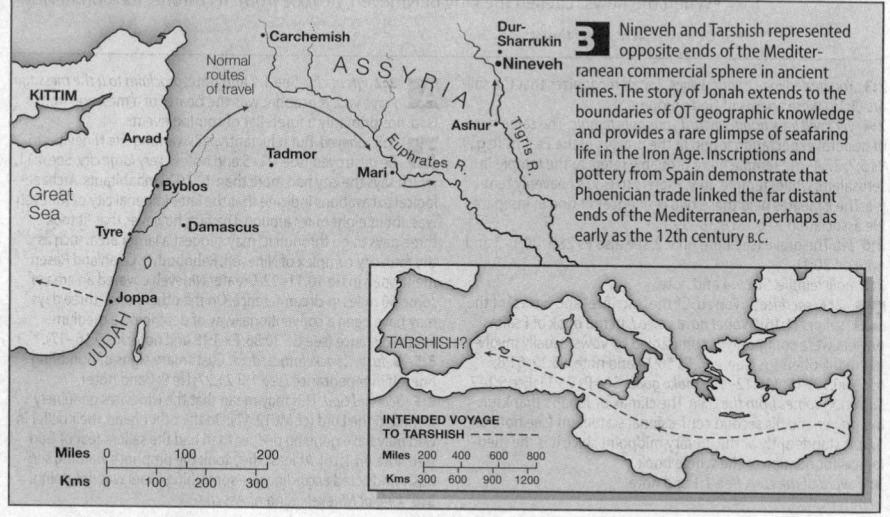

B Nineveh and Tarshish represented opposite ends of the Mediterranean commercial sphere in ancient times. The story of Jonah extends to the boundaries of OT geographic knowledge and provides a rare glimpse of seafaring life in the Iron Age. Inscriptions and pottery from Spain demonstrate that Phoenician trade linked the far distant ends of the Mediterranean, perhaps as early as the 12th century B.C.

2:3 ^d S Ps 88:6
^e S 2Sa 22:5
^f S Ps 42:7
2:4 ^g Ps 31:22;
Jer 7:15 ^h S 1Ki 8:48
2:5 ⁱ Ps 69:1-2
2:6 ^j Job 28:9
^k S Job 17:16; S 33:18;
S Ps 30:3
2:7 ^l Ps 77:11-12
^m 2Ch 30:27
ⁿ S Ps 11:4; 18:6
2:8 ^o S Dt 32:21;
S 1Sa 12:21
2:9 ^p S Ps 42:4
^q Ps 50:14,23;
Heb 13:15
^r S Nu 30:2; Ps 116:14;
S Ecc 5:4-5
^s S Ex 15:2; S Ps 3:8
3:1 ^t Jnh 1:1
3:4 ^u S Jer 18:7-10
3:5 ^v Da 9:3;
Mt 11:21; 12:41;
Lk 11:32

and you listened to my cry.
³ You hurled me into the deep, ^d
into the very heart of the seas,
and the currents swirled about me;
all your waves ^e and breakers
swept over me. ^f
⁴ I said, 'I have been banished
from your sight; ^g
yet I will look again
toward your holy temple.' ^h
⁵ The engulfing waters threatened me, ^a
the deep surrounded me;
seaweed was wrapped around my head. ⁱ
⁶ To the roots of the mountains ^j I sank down;
the earth beneath barred me in forever.
But you, LORD my God,
brought my life up from the pit. ^k

⁷ "When my life was ebbing away,
I remembered ^l you, LORD,
and my prayer ^m rose to you,
to your holy temple. ⁿ

⁸ "Those who cling to worthless idols ^o
forfeit God's love for them.
⁹ But I, with shouts of grateful praise, ^p
will sacrifice ^q to you.
What I have vowed ^r I will make good.
I will say, 'Salvation ^s comes from the LORD.' "

¹⁰ And the LORD commanded the fish, and it vomited Jonah onto dry land.

JONAH GOES TO NINEVEH

3 Then the word of the LORD came to Jonah ^t a second time: ² "Go to the great city of Nineveh and proclaim to it the message I give you."
³ Jonah obeyed the word of the LORD and went to Nineveh. Now Nineveh was a very large city; it took three days to go through it. ⁴ Jonah began by going a day's journey into the city, proclaiming, ^u "Forty more days and Nineveh will be overthrown." ⁵ The Ninevites believed God. They declared a fast, and all of them, from the greatest to the least, put on sackcloth. ^v
⁶ When the news reached the king of Nineveh, he rose from his throne, took off his roy-

^a 5 Or *waters were at my throat*

2:3 *You hurled me ... your waves.* Jonah recognizes that the sailors (1:15) were agents of God's judgment.

2:4 *yet I will look again toward your holy temple.* The same note of hopeful expectation found in the prayers of the Psalms (e.g., Ps 5:7; 27:4–6). "Temple" here probably refers to the temple in Jerusalem, while "temple" in v. 7 refers to God's heavenly temple. The Israelites held these two residences of God in inseparable association (see 1Ki 8:38–39).

2:6 *pit.* The grave (see note on v. 2; see also Ps 28:1; 30:1–3 and note on 30:1).

2:7 *holy temple.* See v. 4 and note.

2:9 *sacrifice ... vowed.* Cf. the "sacrifice" and "vows" of the sailors (1:16). *What I have vowed.* In the book of Psalms prayers were commonly accompanied by vows, usually involving thank offerings (see, e.g., Ps 50:14 and note; 56:12; 61:8; 65:1; 66:13–15; 116:12–19). *make good.* See Ps 76:11; Ecc 5:1–7. *Salvation comes from the LORD.* The climax of Jonah's thanksgiving prayer and his second confessional statement (see note on 1:9). It stands aptly at the literary midpoint since it is the theological foundation of the whole book.

3:1 *word of the LORD.* See 1:1 and note.

3:2 *great city.* See 1:2 and note. *proclaim to it the message I give you.* A prophet was the bearer of a message from God, not primarily a foreteller of coming events.

3:3 *obeyed.* But reluctantly, still wanting the Ninevites to be destroyed (see 4:1–5 and notes). *very large city.* See 4:11, which says the city had more than 120,000 inhabitants. Archaeological excavations indicate that the later imperial city of Nineveh was about eight miles around. The fact, however, that "it took three days to go through it" may suggest a larger area, such as the four-city complex of Nineveh, Rehoboth Ir, Calah and Resen mentioned in Ge 10:11–12. Greater Nineveh covered an area of some 60 miles in circumference. On the other hand, "three days" may have been a conventional way of describing a medium-length distance (see Ge 30:36; Ex 3:18 and note; Jos 9:16–17).

3:5–6 *fast ... sackcloth ... dust.* Customary signs of humbling oneself in repentance (see 1Ki 21:27; Ne 9:1 and note).

3:5 *believed God.* This may mean that the Ninevites genuinely turned to the Lord (cf. Mt 12:41). On the other hand, their belief in God may have gone no deeper than had the sailors' fear of God (see note on 1:16). At least they took the prophet's warning seriously and acted accordingly—something Israel was not doing!

3:6 *king of Nineveh.* King of Assyria.

al robes, covered himself with sackcloth and sat down in the dust. *w* 7Then he issued a proclamation in Nineveh:

"By the decree of the king and his nobles:

Do not let people or animals, herds or flocks, taste anything; do not let them eat or drink. *x* 8But let people and animals be covered with sackcloth. Let everyone call *y* urgently on God. Let them give up *z* their evil ways *a* and their violence. *b* 9Who knows? *c* God may yet relent *d* and with compassion turn *e* from his fierce anger *f* so that we will not perish."

10When God saw what they did and how they turned from their evil ways, he relented *g* and did not bring on them the destruction *h* he had threatened. *i*

JONAH'S ANGER AT THE LORD'S COMPASSION

4 But to Jonah this seemed very wrong, and he became angry. *j* 2He prayed to the LORD, "Isn't this what I said, LORD, when I was still at home? That is what I tried to forestall by fleeing to Tarshish. I knew *k* that you are a gracious *l* and compassionate God, slow to anger and abounding in love, *m* a God who relents *n* from sending calamity. *o* 3Now, LORD, take away my life, *p* for it is better for me to die *q* than to live." *r*

4But the LORD replied, "Is it right for you to be angry?" *s*

5Jonah went out and sat down at a place east of the city. There he made himself a shelter, sat in its shade and waited to see what would happen to the city. 6Then the LORD God provided *t* a gourd *a* and made it grow up over Jonah to give shade for his head to ease his discomfort, and Jonah was very happy about the gourd. 7But at dawn the next day God provided a worm, which chewed the gourd so that it withered. *u* 8When the sun rose, God provided a scorching east wind, and the sun blazed on Jonah's head so that he grew faint. He wanted to die, *v* and said, "It would be better for me to die than to live."

9But God said to Jonah, "Is it right for you to be angry about the gourd?" *w*

"It is," he said. "And I'm so angry I wish I were dead."

10But the LORD said, "You have been concerned about this gourd, though you did not tend it or make it grow. It sprang up overnight and died overnight. 11And should I not have concern *x* for the great city Nineveh, *y* in which there are more than a hundred and twenty thousand people who cannot tell their right hand from their left—and also many animals?"

a 6 The precise identification of this plant is uncertain; also in verses 7, 9 and 10.

Cross references (right column):

3:6 *w* Est 4:1-3; S Job 2:8,13; S Eze 27:30-31
3:7 *x* S 2Ch 20:3; S Ezr 10:6
3:8 *y* Ps 130:1; Jnh 1:6 *z* Jer 25:5 *a* Jer 7:3 *b* S Job 16:17
3:9 *c* 2Sa 12:22 *d* S Jer 18:8 *e* S Joel 2:14 *f* S Ps 85:3
3:10 *g* S Am 7:6 *h* S Jer 18:8 *i* S Ex 32:14
4:1 *j* ver 4; Mt 20:11; Lk 15:28
4:2 *k* Jer 20:7-8 *l* S Dt 4:31; Ps 103:8 *m* S Ex 22:27; Ps 86:5, 15 *n* S Nu 14:18 *o* S Joel 2:13
4:3 *p* S Nu 11:15 *q* S Job 7:15 *r* Jer 8:3
4:4 *s* Ge 4:6; Mt 20:11-15
4:6 *t* S Jnh 1:17
4:7 *u* Joel 1:12
4:8 *v* S 1Ki 19:4
4:9 *w* ver 4
4:11 *x* Jnh 3:10 *y* Jnh 1:2; 3:2

3:8 *animals.* Inclusion of the domestic animals (see 4:11) was unusual and expressed the urgency with which the Ninevites sought mercy.

[A] **3:9** God often responds in mercy to human repentance by canceling threatened punishment (v. 10). See note on Jer 18:7-10.

3:10 *did not bring on them the destruction . . . threatened.* See 1Ki 21:28–29 and note on 21:29; see also Introduction to Nahum: Background; Na 3:19 and note.

[A] **4:1** *angry.* Jonah was angry that God would have compassion on an enemy of Israel. He wanted God's goodness to be shown only to Israelites, not to Gentiles.

[A] **4:2** *prayed to the LORD.* Now in anger, not in distress (see 2:1–2 and note on 2:2). *That is what I tried to forestall by fleeing to Tarshish.* See 1:3 and note. *gracious . . . love.* See Ex 34:6–7 and note. This is the third and last of Jonah's confessional statements (see notes on 1:9; 2:9). *slow to anger.* In contrast, Jonah became angry quickly (vv. 1,9).

[C] **4:3** *take away my life.* See 1Ki 19:4 and note (Elijah). To Jonah, God's mercy to the Ninevites meant an end to Israel's favored standing with him. Jonah shortly before had rejoiced in his deliverance from death (2:2–9), but now that Nineveh lives, he prefers to die.

4:5 *shelter.* Apparently this shelter did not provide enough shade since the next verse indicates that God provided a gourd to give more shade. *waited to see.* Jonah still hoped that Nineveh would be destroyed.

4:6 *the LORD God provided.* This characteristic phrase occurs also in vv. 7–8; 1:17. *gourd.* See TNIV text note. It may have been a castor oil plant, a shrub growing over 12 feet high with large, shady leaves. God graciously increased the comfort of his stubbornly defiant prophet.

4:8 *better for me to die.* See note on v. 3.

4:10 *sprang up overnight and died overnight.* Indicative of fleeting value.

[A] **4:11** *should I not have concern . . . ?* God had the first word (1:1–2), and he also has the last. The commission he gave Jonah displayed his mercy and compassion to the Ninevites, and his last word to Jonah emphatically proclaimed that concern for every creature, both people and animals. Not only does the Lord "preserve both people and animals" (Ps 36:6; see Ne 9:6; Ps 145:16), but he takes "no pleasure in the death of the wicked, but [desires] rather that they turn from their ways and live" (Eze 33:11; see Eze 16:6; 18:23; 33:11 and notes; cf. 2Pe 3:9 and note). Jonah and his fellow Israelites traditionally rejoiced in God's special mercies to Israel but wished only his wrath on their enemies. God here rebukes such hardness and proclaims his own gracious benevolence. *great city.* See 1:2 and note. The book begins and ends by referring to Nineveh, the unlikely and unexpected scene of a remarkable display of divine compassion. *cannot tell their right hand from their left.* Like small children (see Dt 1:39 and note), the Ninevites needed God's fatherly compassion. *also many animals.* God's concern extended even to domestic animals (cf. 3:8 and chart, p. 275 [item 16]).

AUTHOR — MICAH — INTRODUCTION

C Little is known about the prophet Micah beyond what can be learned from the book itself and from Jer 26:18. Micah was from the town of Moresheth (1:1), probably Moresheth Gath (1:14) in southern Judah. The prophecy attests to Micah's deep sensitivity to the social ills of his day, especially as they affected the small towns and villages of his homeland.

DATE

Micah prophesied sometime between 750 and 686 B.C. during the reigns of Jotham, Ahaz and Hezekiah, kings of Judah (1:1; Jer 26:18). He was therefore a contemporary of Isaiah (see Isa 1:1) and Hosea (see Hos 1:1). Micah predicted the fall of Samaria (1:6), which took place in 722–721. This would place his early ministry in the overlapping reigns of Jotham (750–732) and Ahaz (735–715). Micah's message reflects social conditions prior to the religious reforms under Hezekiah (715–686), and his ministry most likely fell within the period 735–700.

If Micah himself wrote out his messages, the date for the earliest written form of his work would be c. 700. If one of his disciples arranged his messages in their present form, the date would be the early seventh century B.C. If a later editor collected and arranged his messages, the date would still need to be early enough in the seventh century to allow time for his prophecy of Jerusalem's fall (3:12) to become familiar enough to be quoted in Jer 26:18 c. 608.

HISTORICAL BACKGROUND

The background of the book is the same as that found in the earlier portions of Isaiah, though Micah does not exhibit the same knowledge of Jerusalem's political life as Isaiah does. Perhaps this is because he, like Amos, was from a village in Judah. The relevant Biblical texts covering this period (see Date, above) are 2Ki 15:32—20:21; 2Ch 27–32; Isa 7; 20; 36–39.

Israel was in an apostate condition. Micah predicted the fall of her capital, Samaria (1:5–7), and also foretold the inevitable desolation of Judah (1:9–16).

Several significant historical events occurred during this period:

1. In 734–732 B.C. Tiglath-Pileser III of Assyria led a military campaign against Aram (Syria), Philistia and parts of Israel and Judah. Ashkelon and Gaza were defeated. Judah, Ammon, Edom and Moab paid tribute to the Assyrian king, but Israel did not fare as well. According to 2Ki 15:29 the northern kingdom lost most of its territory, including all of Gilead and much of Galilee. Damascus fell in 732 and was annexed to the Assyrian empire.

2. In 722–721 Samaria fell, and the northern kingdom of Israel was conquered by Assyria.

3. In 712 King Sargon II of Assyria captured Ashdod (see Isa 20:1 and note).

4. In 701 Judah joined a revolt against Assyria and was overrun by King Sennacherib and his army, though Jerusalem was spared.

LITERARY ANALYSIS

1. *Structure.* The book's collection of short prophetic messages is organized in a pattern of three cycles of judgment and salvation/deliverance oracles (see Outline to follow).

2. *Forms.* The book contains at least seven different literary forms. These are identified in the notes on the individual units.

3. *Style.* Micah's style is similar to that of Isaiah. Both prophets use vigorous language and many figures of speech (see, e.g., Mic 1:4–5,7; 2:4,6,11; 3:2–3; 4:3–4,12–13; 5:1); both show great tenderness in threatening punishment and in promising justice. Micah makes frequent use of plays on words, 1:10–15 (see TNIV text notes there) being the classic example.

THEME AND MESSAGE

As the Outline shows, Micah's message alternates between oracles of doom and oracles of hope—in terms of Ro 11:22, between God's "sternness" and his "kindness." The theme is divine judgment and deliverance. Micah also stresses that God hates idolatry, injustice, rebellion and empty ritualism (see 3:8 and note) but delights in pardoning the penitent (see 7:18–19 and notes). Finally, the prophet declares that Zion will have greater glory in the future than ever before (see, e.g., 4:1–2 and note on 4:1–5). The Davidic kingdom, though it will seem to come to an end, will reach greater heights through the coming Messianic deliverer (see note on 5:1–4). Key passages include 1:2; 3:8–12; 5:1–4; 6:2,6–8; 7:18–20.

OUTLINE

1:1 *a* ver 14;
Jer 26:18 *b* S 1Ch 3:12
c S 1Ch 3:13
d S 1Ch 3:13 *e* Hos 1:1
f Isa 1:1
1:2 *g* S Dt 32:1
h Ps 50:7 *i* S Ge 6:19
j S Ge 31:50;
S Dt 4:26; S Isa 1:2
k S Ps 11:4
1:3 *l* S Isa 18:4
m S Isa 64:1
n S Am 4:13
1:4 *o* S Ps 46:2,6
p S Job 9:5
q S Nu 16:31; Na 1:5
1:5 *r* Am 8:14
1:6 *s* S Dt 20:6
t S Am 5:11
u Eze 13:14
1:7 *v* S Eze 6:6
w S Ex 32:20
x S Dt 9:21
y Dt 23:17-18
1:8 *z* S Isa 15:3
a S Isa 20:2

The word of the LORD that came to Micah of Moresheth *a* during the reigns of Jotham, *b* Ahaz *c* and Hezekiah, *d* kings of Judah *e*—the vision *f* he saw concerning Samaria and Jerusalem.

² Hear, *g* you peoples, all of you, *h*
listen, earth *i* and all who live in it,
that the Sovereign LORD may witness *j* against you,
the Lord from his holy temple. *k*

JUDGMENT AGAINST SAMARIA AND JERUSALEM

³ Look! The LORD is coming from his dwelling *l* place;
he comes down *m* and treads on the heights of the earth. *n*
⁴ The mountains melt *o* beneath him *p*
and the valleys split apart, *q*
like wax before the fire,
like water rushing down a slope.
⁵ All this is because of Jacob's transgression,
because of the sins of the house of Israel.
What is Jacob's transgression?
Is it not Samaria? *r*
What is Judah's high place?
Is it not Jerusalem?

⁶ "Therefore I will make Samaria a heap of rubble,
a place for planting vineyards. *s*
I will pour her stones *t* into the valley
and lay bare her foundations. *u*
⁷ All her idols *v* will be broken to pieces; *w*
all her temple gifts will be burned with fire;
I will destroy all her images. *x*
Since she gathered her gifts from the wages of prostitutes, *y*
as the wages of prostitutes they will again be used."

WEEPING AND MOURNING

⁸ Because of this I will weep *z* and wail;
I will go about barefoot *a* and naked.
I will howl like a jackal
and moan like an owl.

1:1 *word of the LORD.* See Hos 1:1 and note. *Micah.* Means "Who is like the LORD?" (cf. 7:18 and note). *Moresheth.* See Introduction: Author. *Jotham, Ahaz and Hezekiah.* See Introduction: Date. For background on these kings and the book of Micah, see Introduction: Historical Background. Isaiah, Hosea and Micah prophesied at roughly the same time (see Isa 1:1; Hos 1:1). *vision.* See Pr 29:18; Isa 1:1 and notes. *Samaria and Jerusalem.* The capitals of Israel and Judah, respectively. The judgment predicted by Micah involved these nations and not just their capital cities.

1:2—2:13 The first cycle of judgment (1:2—2:11) and salvation/restoration (2:12–13; see Introduction: Outline).

1:2–7 A divine covenant lawsuit, including a theophany (appearance of God, vv. 3–4). The Divine Warrior comes to judge Samaria and Israel (through Assyria).

1:2 *Hear.* The Hebrew for this word introduces prophetic addresses also in 3:1 and 6:1, where it is translated "Listen" (see also 3:9; 6:2). *peoples ... earth.* All nations—an announcement that the day of the Lord is at hand (see Am 5:18 and note), when God will call the nations to account. In view of that day Micah speaks in his prophecy of the impending judgments on Israel and Judah. *holy temple.* Heaven (see v. 3), as in Ps 11:4; Jnh 2:7; Hab 2:20.

1:3 *The LORD is coming.* An OT expression describing the Lord's intervention in history (see Ps 18:9; 96:13 and note; 144:5; Isa 26:21; 31:4; 64:1–3). *heights of the earth.* May refer to mountains as well as to pagan shrines, since both are cited here (vv. 4–5). Cf. Am 4:13; see Dt 33:29.

1:4 *mountains melt ... like wax.* See Ps 18:6–7; 97:5; Na 1:5; Hab 3:3 and note.

1:5 *All this.* The Lord's coming in judgment (vv. 3–4). *Jacob's.* Jacob was an alternate name for Israel (see Ge 32:28 and note; 35:10). *Israel.* Here (and in v. 13) specifically the northern kingdom, but Micah uses the name also for the southern kingdom (see 3:1,8–9; 5:1,3; 6:2) or for the whole covenant people (see vv. 14–15; 2:12; 5:2). *high place.* Pagan center of idolatry (see note on 1Ki 3:2).

1:6–7 God is the speaker. This prophecy was fulfilled during Micah's lifetime when Assyria destroyed Samaria in 722–721 B.C. (see 2Ki 17:6 and note).

1:6 *into the valley.* Samaria was built on a hill (see 1Ki 16:24 and note).

1:7 *prostitutes.* Prostitution is often an OT symbol for idolatry or spiritual unfaithfulness (see Ex 34:15 and note; Jdg 2:17; Eze 23:29–30). *wages.* The wealth that Samaria had gained from her idolatry will be taken by the Assyrians and placed in their own temples, to be used again in the worship of idols.

1:8–16 Micah laments not only the imminent destruction of Samaria but also the coming invasion of Judah, fulfilled by Sennacherib of Assyria in 701 B.C.

1:8 *this.* The coming destruction of Samaria. *barefoot.* A sign of mourning (see 2Sa 15:30 and note). It is possible that Micah actually walked stripped and barefoot through Jerusalem (cf. Isa 20:2). The concept of mourning frames this section (see v. 16). *naked.* Perhaps clothed only in a loincloth.

9 For Samaria's wound [b] is incurable; [c]
  it has come to Judah. [d]
  It has reached the very gate [e] of my people,
    even to Jerusalem itself.
10 Tell it not in Gath [a];
  weep not at all.
  In Beth Ophrah [b]
    roll in the dust.
11 Pass on in nakedness [f] and shame,
    you who live in Shaphir. [c]
  Those who live in Zaanan [d]
    will not come out.
  Beth Ezel is in mourning;
    its protection is taken from you.
12 Those who live in Maroth [e] writhe in pain,
    waiting for relief, [g]
  because disaster [h] has come from the LORD,
    even to the gate of Jerusalem.
13 You who live in Lachish, [f] [i]
    harness the team to the chariot.
  You were the beginning of sin
    to Daughter Zion, [j]
  for the transgressions of Israel
    were found in you.
14 Therefore you will give parting gifts [k]
    to Moresheth [l] Gath.
  The town of Akzib [g] [m] will prove deceptive [n]
    to the kings of Israel.
15 I will bring a conqueror against you
    who live in Mareshah. [h] [o]
  The nobles of Israel
    will flee to Adullam. [p]
16 Shave [q] your head in mourning
    for the children in whom you delight;
  make yourself as bald as the vulture,
    for they will go from you into exile. [r]

---

a 10 *Gath* sounds like the Hebrew for *tell*.   b 10 *Beth Ophrah* means *house of dust*.   c 11 *Shaphir*
means *pleasant*.   d 11 *Zaanan* sounds like the Hebrew for *come out*.   e 12 *Maroth* sounds like the
Hebrew for *bitter*.   f 13 *Lachish* sounds like the Hebrew for *team*.   g 14 *Akzib* means *deception*.
h 15 *Mareshah* sounds like the Hebrew for *conqueror*.

1:9 *wound.* The judgment about to overtake Samaria. *incurable.* See Isa 1:6; see also Isa 17:11; Jer 30:12 and notes. *gate.* The Assyrian destruction of the northern kingdom will spread like a malignant disease to the gate of Jerusalem (v. 12). The gate was where the process of town government was carried on (see Ge 19:1 and note; Ru 4:1–4 and note on 4:1).

1:10–15 Several plays on words are explained in the TNIV text notes. The towns mentioned lie in the Shephelah, i.e., the foothills (500–1,500 feet high) between the Mediterranean coastal plain and the mountains of Judah.

1:10 *Tell it not in Gath.* These words introduce a funeral lament over Judah. Micah did not want the pagan people in Gath to gloat over the downfall of God's people (see 2Sa 1:20 and note). *roll in the dust.* As a sign of grief over the coming catastrophe. See Isa 47:1 and note.

1:11 *nakedness and shame.* A reference to their future humiliation as prisoners (see Isa 20:4). *will not come out.* Because of the invasion, the people will not dare to go outside their houses.

1:12 *has come.* Micah foresees the future so clearly that to him it seems as though it has already come (see v. 3 and note).

1:13 *Lachish.* One of the largest towns in Judah (see Isa 36:2 and note). Later, Sennacherib was so proud of capturing it that he decorated his palace at Nineveh with a relief picturing his exploits. *harness the team.* In order to escape. *Daughter Zion.* A personification of Jerusalem (see note on 2Ki 19:21). *Israel.* See note on v. 5.

1:14 *parting gifts.* The Hebrew for these words is translated "wedding gift" in 1Ki 9:16. Jerusalem must give up Moresheth Gath to Assyria, as a father gives a "wedding gift" to his daughter when she marries. *Akzib.* See TNIV text note. The word "deceptive" is used in Jer 15:18 (see note there) to describe a brook that has dried up in summer. Like such a brook, the city of Akzib will cease to exist. *Israel.* See note on v. 5.

1:15 Micah again represents God as speaking, as in vv. 6–7. *nobles of Israel.* "Nobles" is lit. "glory," referring to Israel's leaders (see Isa 5:13, "those of high rank," lit. "glory").

1:16 *Shave your head in mourning.* See note in Jer 16:6. *exile.* Israel was taken into exile by the Assyrians in 722–721 B.C. and Judah by the Babylonians in 586.

1:9 b Jer 46:11
c S Jer 10:19
d S 2Ki 18:13
e Isa 3:26
1:11 f Eze 23:29
1:12 g Jer 14:19
h Jer 40:2
1:13 i S Jos 10:3
j S Ps 9:14
1:14 k 2Ki 16:8
l S ver 1 m S Jos 15:44
n Jer 15:18
1:15 o Jos 15:44
p S Jos 12:15
1:16 q S Lev 13:40;
S Job 1:20 r S Dt 4:27;
S Am 5:27

2:1 *a* S Isa 29:20
t Ps 36:4
2:2 *u* Isa 5:8
v S Pr 30:14
w S Jer 22:17
x S 1Sa 8:14;
S Isa 1:23;
S Eze 46:18
2:3 *y* Jer 18:11;
S Am 3:1-2 *z* Isa 2:12
2:4 *a* S Lev 26:31;
S Jer 4:13 *b* S Jer 6:12
2:5 *c* Dt 32:13;
Jos 18:4 *d* S Nu 34:13
2:6 *e* Ps 44:13;
Jer 18:16; 19:8; 25:18;
29:18; Mic 6:16
f S Am 2:12
2:7 *g* S Ps 119:65
h Is 15:2; 84:11
2:9 *i* Jer 10:20
2:10 *j* S Dt 12:9
k Lev 18:25-29;
Ps 106:38-39;
S La 4:15

| HUMAN PLANS AND GOD'S PLANS

2 Woe to those who plan iniquity,
  to those who plot evil *s* on their beds! *t*
At morning's light they carry it out
  because it is in their power to do it.
² They covet fields *u* and seize them, *v*
  and houses, and take them.
They defraud *w* people of their homes,
  they rob them of their inheritance. *x*

³ Therefore, the LORD says:

"I am planning disaster *y* against this people,
  from which you cannot save yourselves.
You will no longer walk proudly, *z*
  for it will be a time of calamity.
⁴ In that day people will ridicule you;
  they will taunt you with this mournful song:
'We are utterly ruined; *a*
  my people's possession is divided up. *b*
He takes it from me!
  He assigns our fields to traitors.' "

⁵ Therefore you will have no one in the assembly of the LORD
  to divide the land *c* by lot. *d*

FALSE PROPHETS

⁶ "Do not prophesy," their prophets say.
  "Do not prophesy about these things;
  disgrace *e* will not overtake us. *f*"
⁷ House of Jacob, should it be said,
  "Does the LORD become *a* impatient?
  Does he do such things?"

"Do not my words do good *g*
  to those whose ways are upright? *h*
⁸ Lately my people have risen up
  like an enemy.
You strip off the rich robe
  from those who pass by without a care,
  like men returning from battle.
⁹ You drive the women of my people
  from their pleasant homes. *i*
You take away my blessing
  from their children forever.
¹⁰ Get up, go away!
  For this is not your resting place, *j*
because it is defiled, *k*
  it is ruined, beyond all remedy.

a 7 Or *Is the Spirit of the LORD*

2:1–5 A judgment woe is pronounced on wealthy and oppressive land-grabbers. Their slogan is "Might makes right."

2:1 *plot evil.* Cf. Pr 6:14,18; Zec 7:10. *power to do it.* The rich, oppressing classes continued to get rich at the expense of the poor because they controlled the power structures of their society.

2:2 *They covet.* In violation of the tenth commandment (see Ex 20:17 and note; Dt 5:21). *inheritance.* Land that was to be the permanent possession of a particular family. See notes on Lev 25:13 (Year of Jubilee); Nu 27:1–11; 36:1–12 (Zelophehad's daughters); 1Ki 21:3 (Naboth's vineyard).

2:3 *Therefore.* Because of the sins of Israel's influential classes, calamity will strike. *disaster.* The impending exile.

2:4 *We . . . me.* The rich landowners, on whom God's judgment

will fall. *He.* God. *traitors.* The treacherous Assyrians (see Isa 33:1 and note), who will capture the land.

2:5 *you.* The oppressing classes—the rich landowners. *no one . . . to divide the land.* They will be cut off from all the promises of the covenant people.

2:6–11 A disputation: Micah and his God versus the wealthy wicked and their false prophets. The unit is framed by "prophesy" (vv. 6,11).

2:6 *their prophets.* The false prophets whose words were addressed to Micah.

2:7 Verses 6–7a are spoken by Micah; vv. 7b–13 are spoken by God.

2:10 *resting place.* A place that could be regarded as one's own possession, where a people could settle in security (see Dt 3:20 and note; Jos 21:43–44; 22:4).

¹¹ If liars and deceivers ⁱ come and say,
　'We will prophesy for you plenty of wine and beer,' ᵐ
　they would be just the prophets for this people! ⁿ

DELIVERANCE PROMISED

¹² "I will surely gather all of you, Jacob;
　I will surely bring together the remnant ᵒ of Israel.
I will bring them together like sheep in a pen,
　like a flock in its pasture;
　the place will throng with people. ᵖ
¹³ One who breaks open the way will go up before �q them;
　they will break through the gate ʳ and go out.
Their King will pass through before them,
　the LORD at their head."

LEADERS AND PROPHETS REBUKED

3 Then I said,

"Listen, you leaders ˢ of Jacob,
　you rulers of the house of Israel.
Should you not know justice,
² 　you who hate good and love evil;
who tear the skin from my people
　and the flesh from their bones; ᵗ
³ who eat my people's flesh, ᵘ
　strip off their skin
　and break their bones in pieces; ᵛ
who chop ʷ them up like meat for the pan,
　like flesh for the pot? ˣ"

⁴ Then they will cry out to the LORD,
　but he will not answer them. ʸ
At that time he will hide his face ᶻ from them
　because of the evil they have done. ᵃ

⁵ This is what the LORD says:

"As for the prophets
　who lead my people astray, ᵇ
if you feed them,
　they proclaim 'peace'; ᶜ
if you do not,
　they prepare to wage war against you.
⁶ Therefore night will come over you, without visions,
　and darkness, without divination. ᵈ
The sun will set for the prophets, ᵉ
　and the day will go dark for them. ᶠ
⁷ The seers will be ashamed ᵍ
　and the diviners disgraced. ʰ

2:11 ⁱ S 2Ch 36:16;
Jer 5:31 ᵐ S Lev 10:9
ⁿ Isa 30:10
2:12 ᵒ Mic 4:7; 5:7;
7:18 ᵖ S Ne 1:9
2:13 q S Isa 52:12
ʳ S Isa 60:11
3:1 ˢ S Jer 5:5
3:2 ᵗ Ps 53:4;
S Eze 22:27
3:3 ᵘ S Ps 14:4
ᵛ S Eze 34:4; Zep 3:3
ʷ S Job 24:14
ˣ S Eze 11:7; S 24:4-5
3:4 ʸ S Dt 1:45;
S 1Sa 8:18; S Isa 58:4;
S Jer 11:11 ᶻ S Dt 31:17
ᵃ S Job 15:31;
S Eze 8:18
3:5 ᵇ S Isa 3:12;
S 9:16; S 53:6
ᶜ S Jer 4:10
3:6 ᵈ Isa 8:19-22;
S Eze 12:24
ᵉ Isa 29:10
ᶠ S Eze 7:26;
S Am 8:11
3:7 ᵍ S Jer 6:15;
Mic 7:16 ʰ S Isa 44:25

2:11 Anyone who promised greater affluence would gain a hearing.

2:12–13 A salvation oracle of deliverance. Although Israel will be carried into exile, a remnant will return (see note on Isa 1:9).

2:12 *Jacob ... Israel.* Here perhaps the entire nation, north and south. Contrast 1:5 (see note there).

2:13 *One who breaks open ... Their King ... the LORD.* Rabbinic interpretation refers all three to the Messiah.

3:1—5:15 The second cycle of judgment (ch. 3) and salvation/restoration (chs. 4–5; see Introduction: Outline).

3:1–12 Verses 1–4 deal with the sins of the leaders of Israel, vv. 5–7 with the false prophets and vv. 9–12 with the leaders, priests and prophets.

3:1–4 Probably another divine covenant lawsuit (see 1:2–7), in which God charges the civil leaders with acting like cannibals.

3:1 *Listen.* See note on 1:2; see also 6:1. *Jacob ... Israel.* Both

names refer here to Judah (see vv. 9–10; 1:5 and note).

3:2–3 *tear the skin ... like flesh for the pot.* A series of figures of speech describing the cruel way the leaders treat the people.

3:2 *hate good and love evil.* Contrast Am 5:15; Ro 12:9.

3:4 *they.* The leaders. *he will not answer.* See v. 7. *hide his face.* See Dt 31:17; Isa 1:15 and note. Disobedience leads to separation from God.

3:5–8 Another disputation (see note on 2:6–11): Micah and the false prophets of peace.

3:5 *proclaim 'peace.'* The false prophets predicted peace for Judah, while Micah predicted destruction and captivity (see v. 12; 4:10). See also Jer 6:13–14 and note on 6:14; 8:10–11.

3:6–7 *without visions ... no answer from God.* See Jer 18:18 and note; Am 8:11–12 and note on 8:11.

3:7 *seers.* An older term for "prophets" (see note on 1Sa 9:9). *cover their faces.* In shame and humiliation.

3:7 *i* S Est 6:12
j S Lev 13:45
k S Eze 20:3
3:8 *l* S Isa 57:12; 61:2
3:9 *m* Ps 58:1-2;
S Isa 1:23
3:10 *n* S Jer 22:13
o Isa 59:7; Mic 7:2;
Na 3:1; Hab 2:12
p Jer 22:17;
S Eze 22:27
3:11 *q* S Ex 23:8;
S Lev 19:15; Mal 2:9
r S Eze 13:19
s Isa 1:23; S 56:11;
Jer 6:13; S La 4:13;
S Hos 4:8,18
t S Isa 10:20 *u* Jer 7:4;
S Eze 34:2
3:12 *v* 2Ki 25:9;
S Isa 6:11
w S Jer 52:13
x S Lev 26:31;
S Jer 17:3; S 22:6;
S La 5:18; S Eze 5:14
4:1 *y* S Ps 48:1;
Zec 8:3 *z* S Eze 17:22
a S Ps 22:27; 86:9;
S Jer 3:17; S 31:12;
S Da 2:35
4:2 *b* S Jer 31:6;
S Eze 20:40
c Zec 2:11; 14:16
d S Ps 119:171
e Ps 25:8-9;
S Isa 54:13
f Dt 18:18
4:3 *g* S Isa 11:4
h Joel 3:10; Zec 9:10
i S Ps 46:9 *j* Zec 8:20-
22
4:4 *k* S 1Ki 4:25
l S Lev 26:6;
S Eze 39:26

They will all cover[i] their faces[j]
    because there is no answer from God.[k]"
[8] But as for me, I am filled with power,
    with the Spirit of the LORD,
    and with justice and might,
to declare to Jacob his transgression,
    to Israel his sin.[l]

[9] Hear this, you leaders of the house of Jacob,
    you rulers of the house of Israel,
who despise justice
    and distort all that is right;[m]
[10] who build[n] Zion with bloodshed,[o]
    and Jerusalem with wickedness.[p]
[11] Her leaders judge for a bribe,[q]
    her priests teach for a price,[r]
    and her prophets tell fortunes for money.[s]
Yet they lean[t] upon the LORD and say,
    "Is not the LORD among us?
    No disaster will come upon us."[u]
[12] Therefore because of you,
    Zion will be plowed like a field,
Jerusalem will become a heap of rubble,[v]
    the temple[w] hill a mound overgrown with thickets.[x]

THE MOUNTAIN OF THE LORD
4:1–3pp — Isa 2:1–4

4 In the last days

the mountain[y] of the LORD's temple will be established
    as chief among the mountains;
it will be raised above the hills,[z]
    and peoples will stream to it.[a]

[2] Many nations will come and say,

"Come, let us go up to the mountain of the LORD,[b]
    to the house of the God of Jacob.[c]
He will teach us[d] his ways,[e]
    so that we may walk in his paths."
The law[f] will go out from Zion,
    the word of the LORD from Jerusalem.
[3] He will judge between many peoples
    and will settle disputes for strong nations far and wide.[g]
They will beat their swords into plowshares
    and their spears into pruning hooks.[h]
Nation will not take up sword against nation,
    nor will they train for war[i] anymore.[j]
[4] Everyone will sit under their own vine
    and under their own fig tree,[k]
    and no one will make them afraid,[l]

3:8 *filled … with the Spirit.* The prophets were Spirit-filled messengers (see Isa 48:16; 61:1 and note). *to declare … his sin.* One of the chief purposes of Micah was to declare to Israel its sin.
3:9–12 An oracle of indictment and of judgment on corrupt leaders, resulting in Zion's fall.
3:9 *Hear.* See note on 1:2. *Jacob … Israel.* See v. 1 and note.
3:10 *who build Zion with bloodshed.* See Eze 7:23 and note.
3:11 *for a bribe.* See 1Sa 8:3 and note; Isa 1:23; 5:23.
3:12 The destruction of Jerusalem occurred in 586 B.C. This verse was quoted a century later in Jer 26:18 (see note there). Jer 26:19 indicates that Micah's preaching may have been instrumental in the reformation under King Hezekiah (see 2Ki

18:1–6; 2Ch 29–31). *Jerusalem … heap of rubble.* Just like Samaria (see 1:6).
4:1–5 An eschatological ("In the last days," v. 1) salvation oracle: Zion's future exaltation. Although the temple will be destroyed (3:12), in the Zion of the future it will be restored in even grander style to become the worship and learning center for all nations.
4:1–3 See notes on Isa 2:2–4, a passage that is almost the same as these verses.
4:3 *plowshares.* See note on Isa 2:4.
4:4 *vine and … fig tree.* A reference to the peaceful security of the kingdom of God. See 1Ki 4:25; 2Ki 18:31; Zec 3:10. *no one will make them afraid.* Quoted in Zep 3:13. Fear will be a thing of the past.

for the Lord Almighty has spoken. *m*
⁵All the nations may walk
in the name of their gods; *n*
we will walk in the name of the Lord
our God for ever and ever. *o*

THE LORD'S PLAN

⁶"In that day," declares the Lord,

"I will gather the lame; *p*
I will assemble the exiles *q*
and those I have brought to grief. *r*
⁷I will make the lame a remnant, *s*
those driven away a strong nation. *t*
The Lord will rule over them in Mount Zion *u*
from that day and forever. *v*
⁸As for you, watchtower of the flock,
stronghold *a* of Daughter Zion,
the former dominion will be restored *w* to you;
kingship will come to Daughter Jerusalem. *x*"

⁹Why do you now cry aloud—
have you no king *b y*?
Has your ruler *c* perished,
that pain seizes you like that of a woman in labor? *z*
¹⁰Writhe in agony, Daughter Zion,
like a woman in labor,
for now you must leave the city
to camp in the open field.
You will go to Babylon; *a*
there you will be rescued.
There the Lord will redeem *b* you
out of the hand of your enemies.

¹¹But now many nations
are gathered against you.
They say, "Let her be defiled,
let our eyes gloat *c* over Zion!"
¹²But they do not know
the thoughts of the Lord;
they do not understand his plan, *d*
he who gathers them like sheaves to the threshing floor.
¹³"Rise and thresh, *e* Daughter Zion,
for I will give you horns of iron;
I will give you hooves of bronze,
and you will break to pieces many nations." *f*
You will devote their ill-gotten gains to the Lord, *g*
their wealth to the Lord of all the earth.

a 8 Or *hill*   *b 9* Or *King*   *c 9* Or *Ruler*

4:4 *m* S Isa 1:20
4:5 *n* 2Ki 17:29;
Ac 14:16 *o* Jos 24:14-
15; Isa 26:8; Zec 10:12
4:6 *p* S Jer 31:8
q S Ps 106:47
r S Eze 34:13,16;
S 37:21; Zep 3:19
4:7 *s* S Joel 2:32;
S Mic 2:12 *t* S Ge 12:2
u S Isa 2:2
v S Da 2:44; S 7:14;
S Lk 1:33; Rev 11:15
4:8 *w* S Isa 1:26
x Zec 9:9
4:9 *y* Jer 8:19
z S Ge 3:16; Jer 30:6;
48:41
4:10 *a* S Dt 21:10;
2Ki 20:18; Isa 43:14
b S Isa 48:20
4:11 *c* S La 2:16;
S Ob 1:12; Mic 7:8
4:12 *d* S Ge 50:20;
S Isa 55:8; Ro 11:33-
34
4:13 *e* S Isa 21:10
f S Isa 45:1; S Da 2:44
g S Isa 23:18

4:5 *walk in the name of the Lord.* Confess, love, obey and rely on the Lord. Cf. Zec 10:12.

4:6–8 Another eschatological ("In that day," v. 6) salvation oracle: restoration of a remnant and Zion.

4:6 *In that day.* The Messianic period (see v. 1; see also notes on Isa 2:11,17,20; Joel 1:15).

4:7 *remnant.* The people of God (see 2:12; see also note on Isa 1:9).

4:8 *watchtower of the flock.* Jerusalem, the capital city of David, the shepherd-king. *Daughter Zion ... Daughter Jerusalem.* See vv. 10,13; a personification of Jerusalem (see note on 2Ki 19:21). *former dominion.* The kingdom of David will be restored

under the Messiah.

4:9–13 In vv. 9–10 Micah foresees the collapse of the monarchy and the impending exile in 586 b.c., as well as the restoration beginning in 538. Verses 11–13 are a prophecy of judgment against the gloating enemies of Jerusalem.

4:9–10 An oracle of both judgment and salvation. The next three units (vv. 9–10,11–13; 5:1–4) all begin with the Hebrew word for "now" and end with an assertion that the present or anticipated bad situation will be changed for the better (here: from distress to deliverance).

4:11–13 An oracle of judgment and salvation: from siege to victory (see note on vv. 9–10).

5:1 *h* La 3:30
5:2 *i* S Jn 7:42
j S Ge 35:16; S 48:7
k S Nu 24:19;
S 1Sa 13:14;
S 2Sa 6:21;
S 2Ch 7:18 *l* Ps 102:25
m Mt 2:6*
5:3 *n* S Jer 7:29
5:4 *o* Isa 40:11; 49:9;
S Eze 34:11-15,23;
Mic 7:14 *p* Isa 52:13;
Lk 1:32
5:5 *q* S Isa 9:6;
S Lk 2:14; Col 1:19-20
r Isa 8:7 *s* Isa 10:24-27
5:6 *t* Ge 10:8
u Zep 2:13 *v* Na 2:11-13
5:7 *w* S Am 5:15;
S Mic 2:12
x Ps 133:3 *y* Isa 44:4
5:8 *z* S Ge 49:9

A PROMISED RULER FROM BETHLEHEM

5

** Marshal your troops now, city of troops,
    for a siege is laid against us.
They will strike Israel's ruler
    on the cheek *h* with a rod.

**2 "But you, Bethlehem *i* Ephrathah, *j*
    though you are small among the clans *a* of Judah,
out of you will come for me
    one who will be ruler *k* over Israel,
whose origins are from of old, *l*
    from ancient times." *m*

3 Therefore Israel will be abandoned *n*
    until the time when she who is in labor gives birth
and the rest of his brothers return
    to join the Israelites.

4 He will stand and shepherd his flock *o*
    in the strength of the LORD,
    in the majesty of the name of the LORD his God.
And they will live securely, for then his greatness *p*
    will reach to the ends of the earth.

5 And he will be our peace *q*
    when the Assyrians invade *r* our land
    and march through our fortresses.
We will raise against them seven shepherds,
    even eight commanders, *s*
6 who will rule *b* the land of Assyria with the sword,
    the land of Nimrod *t* with drawn sword. *c u*
He will deliver us from the Assyrians
    when they invade our land
    and march into our borders. *v*

7 The remnant *w* of Jacob will be
    in the midst of many peoples
like dew *x* from the LORD,
    like showers on the grass, *y*
which do not wait for mortals
    or depend on any human being.
8 The remnant of Jacob will be among the nations,
    in the midst of many peoples,
like a lion among the beasts of the forest, *z*

a 2 Or *rulers*   *b* 6 Or *crush*   *c* 6 Or *Nimrod in its gates*

** 5:1 is numbered 4:14 in Hebrew texts.   ** 5:2-15 is numbered 5:1-14 in Hebrew texts.

5:1–4 An oracle of judgment and salvation: from helpless ruler to ideal King (see note on 4:9–10), who will be born in Bethlehem and whose "greatness will reach to the ends of the earth" (v. 4).
5:1 Jerusalem will be besieged, and her kings will be seized and taken to Babylon (the last king, Zedekiah, was blinded; see 2Ki 25:7 and note).
5:2 Quoted in part in Mt 2:6. In contrast to the dire prediction of v. 1, Micah shifts to a positive note. *Ephrathah.* The region in which Bethlehem was located (see Ru 1:2 and note). *ruler.* Ultimately Christ, who will rule (see note on 4:8) for God the Father. *origins … from of old.* His beginnings were much earlier than his human birth (see Jn 8:58). *from ancient times.* Within history (see 2Sa 7:12–16; Isa 9:6–7 and notes; Am 9:11) —and even from eternity (see Jn 1:1,14,18; 8:58; 17:5; Phil 2:5–11; Col 1:15–20; Heb 1:1–3 and notes).
5:3 *Israel will be abandoned.* Until the Messiah is born and begins his rule. *Israel.* See note on 1:5.

5:4 The Messiah will shepherd and rule in the "strength" and "majesty" of God the Father.
5:5–6 A salvation oracle of deliverance: The ideal King will "deliver" (v. 6) his people. Note the *a–b–b/a–b-b* scansion pattern at the beginning and end of this unit. Or one could analyze the structure of the entire unit as consisting of an *a–b–c–d/d–a–b–c* pattern (a "chiasmus"), with *d* representing two lines.
5:5 *our peace.* Jesus is "our peace" (Eph 2:14). In addition to freedom from war, the Hebrew word for "peace" also connotes prosperity in the OT. See notes on Isa 9:6 ("Prince of Peace"); Lk 2:14. *Assyrians.* Symbolic of all the enemies of God's people in every age. See Isa 11:11; Zec 10:10 and notes. *We.* The people of God. *seven … eight.* A figurative way of saying "many" (see note on Job 5:19).
5:6 *land of Nimrod.* Assyria. See Ge 10:8–12. *He.* The ruler of v. 2.
5:7–9 A salvation oracle of deliverance: the remnant among the nations.
5:7–8 *remnant.* See note on 4:7.
5:7 *like dew from the LORD.* See Hos 14:5 and note.

like a young lion among flocks of sheep,
which mauls and mangles *a* as it goes,
and no one can rescue. *b*
⁹ Your hand will be lifted up *c* in triumph over your enemies,
and all your foes will be destroyed.

¹⁰ "In that day," declares the LORD,

"I will destroy your horses from among you
and demolish your chariots. *d*
¹¹ I will destroy the cities *e* of your land
and tear down all your strongholds. *f*
¹² I will destroy your witchcraft
and you will no longer cast spells. *g*
¹³ I will destroy your idols *h*
and your sacred stones from among you; *i*
you will no longer bow down
to the work of your hands. *j*
¹⁴ I will uproot from among you your Asherah poles *a k*
when I demolish your cities.
¹⁵ I will take vengeance *l* in anger and wrath
on the nations that have not obeyed me."

THE LORD'S CASE AGAINST ISRAEL

6 Listen to what the LORD says:

"Stand up, plead my case before the mountains; *m*
let the hills hear what you have to say.

² "Hear, *n* you mountains, the LORD's accusation; *o*
listen, you everlasting foundations of the earth.
For the LORD has a case *p* against his people;
he is lodging a charge *q* against Israel.

³ "My people, what have I done to you?
How have I burdened *r* you? *s* Answer me.
⁴ I brought you up out of Egypt *t*
and redeemed you from the land of slavery. *u*
I sent Moses *v* to lead you,
also Aaron *w* and Miriam. *x*
⁵ My people, remember
what Balak *y* king of Moab plotted
and what Balaam son of Beor answered.
Remember your journey from Shittim *z* to Gilgal, *a*
that you may know the righteous acts *b* of the LORD."

---

a 14 That is, wooden symbols of the goddess Asherah

5:8 *a* Mic 4:13;
Zec 10:5 *b* S Ps 50:22;
S Isa 5:29; S Hos 5:14
5:9 *c* S Ps 10:12
5:10 *d* Ex 15:4,19;
S Hos 14:3; Hag 2:22;
Zec 9:10
5:11 *e* S Dt 29:23;
Isa 6:11 *f* S La 2:2;
S Hos 10:14; Am 5:9
5:12 *d* Dt 18:10-12;
Isa 2:6; 8:19
5:13 *h* Na 1:14
i Hos 10:2 *j* S Isa 2:18;
S Eze 6:9; Zec 13:2
5:14 *k* S Ex 34:13;
S Jdg 3:7; S 2Ki 17:10
5:15 *l* S Isa 65:12
6:1 *m* S Ps 50:1;
S Eze 6:2
6:2 *n* Dt 32:1
o S Hos 12:2
p S Isa 3:13 *q* Ps 50:7;
S Jer 2:9
6:3 *r* Jer 2:5 *s* Jer 2:5
6:4 *t* S Ex 3:10; S 6:6
u Dt 7:8 *v* S Ex 4:16
w S Nu 33:1; Ps 77:20
x S Ex 15:20
6:5 *y* S Nu 22:2
z S Nu 25:1
a S Dt 11:30; Jos 5:9-
10 *b* Jdg 5:11; 1Sa 12:7

5:8 *lion.* Like the previous simile (v. 7), this pictures the inevitable progress of the people of God toward triumph over their enemies (v. 9). God's kingdom will be victorious.
5:9 *Your.* The remnant (vv. 7–8).
5:10–15 An eschatological ("In that day," v. 10) salvation oracle: obliteration of military power and pagan worship. In the Messianic era the people of God will not depend on weapons of war or pagan idols. The successes of his people are always achieved by dependence on him (cf. Isa 2:6–8).
5:10 *In that day.* See note on 4:6.
5:14 *Asherah poles.* See Ex 34:13 and note.
6:1—7:20 The third cycle of judgment (6:1—7:7) and salvation/restoration (7:8–20; see Introduction: Literary Analysis; Outline).
6:1–16 This chapter depicts a courtroom scene in which the Lord lodges a legal complaint against Israel.
6:1–8 A divine covenant lawsuit. In v. 1 the Lord instructs his prophet to present his (i.e., the Lord's; see v. 2) case; in v. 2 he

summons the mountains to listen as witnesses to his accusation. Then the Lord speaks to his people in vv. 3–5, poignantly reminding them of his gracious acts in their behalf. In vv. 6–7 Israel speaks, and in v. 8 Micah responds directly to the nation, answering the questions of vv. 6–7.
6:1–2 *mountains ... foundations of the earth.* Inanimate objects were called on as third-party witnesses because of their enduring nature and because they were witnesses to his covenant (see Dt 32:1; Jos 24:27; Isa 1:2 and note).
6:1 *Listen.* See note on 1:2; see also 3:1.
6:2 *Israel.* Primarily Judah here (see note on 1:5).
6:3,5 *My people.* Covenant language (see note on v. 8).
6:4 *brought you up out of Egypt.* See Ex 20:2 and note. *Moses ... Aaron and Miriam.* See Nu 12:1–2 and note on 12:2.
6:5 *Balak ... Balaam.* See Nu 22–24 and note on 22:8. *Shittim to Gilgal.* See Nu 25:1; Jos 2:1; 3:1—4:25; 4:19 and notes. *righteous acts of the LORD.* See 1Sa 12:7 and note.

6:6 ᶜS Ps 95:2
ᵈPs 40:6-8; 51:16-17
6:7 ᵉS Isa 1:11;
S 40:16 ᶠPs 50:8-10
ᵍS Lev 18:21;
S 2Ki 3:27 ʰHos 5:6;
S Am 5:22
6:8 ⁱS Isa 1:17;
S Jer 22:3
ʲS 2Ki 22:19;
S Isa 57:15
ᵏS Ge 5:22; Dt 10:12-
13; 1Sa 15:22;
Hos 6:6; Zec 7:9-10;
Mt 9:13; 23:23;
Mk 12:33; Lk 11:42
6:9 ˡS Ge 17:1;
Isa 11:4
6:10 ᵐEze 45:9-10;
S Am 3:10; 8:4-6
6:11 ⁿS Lev 19:36
ᵒS Dt 25:13
6:12 ᵖS Isa 1:23
ᵠS Ps 116:11; Isa 3:8
ʳS Ps 35:20; S Jer 9:3
6:13 ˢIsa 1:7; 6:11
6:14 ᵗS Isa 9:20;
S Hos 4:10 ᵘIsa 30:6
6:15 ᵛS Dt 28:38;
Jer 12:13 ʷJob 24:11;
S Am 5:11; Zep 1:13
6:16 ˣS 1Ki 16:25
ʸ1Ki 16:29-33
ᶻJer 7:24 ᵃS Jer 25:9
ᵇS Dt 28:37;
S Jer 51:51; S Mic 2:6

⁶ With what shall I come before ᶜ the LORD
  and bow down before the exalted God?
Shall I come before him with burnt offerings,
  with calves a year old? ᵈ
⁷ Will the LORD be pleased with thousands of rams, ᵉ
  with ten thousand rivers of olive oil? ᶠ
Shall I offer my firstborn ᵍ for my transgression,
  the fruit of my body for the sin of my soul? ʰ
⁸ He has shown all you people what is good.
  And what does the LORD require of you?
To act justly ⁱ and to love mercy
  and to walk humbly ᵃʲ with your God. ᵏ

ISRAEL'S GUILT AND PUNISHMENT

⁹ Listen! The LORD is calling to the city—
  and to fear your name is wisdom—
  "Heed the rod ˡ and the One who appointed it. ᵇ
¹⁰ Am I still to forget your ill-gotten treasures, you wicked house,
  and the short ephah, ᶜ which is accursed? ᵐ
¹¹ Shall I acquit a person with dishonest scales, ⁿ
  with a bag of false weights? ᵒ
¹² Her rich people are violent; ᵖ
  her inhabitants are liars ᵠ
  and their tongues speak deceitfully. ʳ
¹³ Therefore, I have begun to destroy ˢ you,
  to ruin ᵈ you because of your sins.
¹⁴ You will eat but not be satisfied; ᵗ
  your stomach will still be empty. ᵉ
You will store up but save nothing, ᵘ
  because what you save ᶠ I will give to the sword.
¹⁵ You will plant but not harvest; ᵛ
  you will press olives but not use the oil on yourselves,
  you will crush grapes but not drink the wine. ʷ
¹⁶ You have observed the statutes of Omri ˣ
  and all the practices of Ahab's ʸ house;
  you have followed their traditions. ᶻ
Therefore I will give you over to ruin ᵃ
  and your people to derision;
  you will bear the scorn ᵇ of the nations. ᵍ"

ᵃ 8 Or *prudently*   ᵇ 9 The meaning of the Hebrew for this line is uncertain.   ᶜ 10 An ephah was a dry measure.   ᵈ 13 Or *Therefore, I will make you ill and destroy you; / I will ruin*   ᵉ 14 The meaning of the Hebrew for this word is uncertain.   ᶠ 14 Or *You will press toward birth but not give birth, / and what you bring to birth*   ᵍ 16 Septuagint; Hebrew *scorn due my people*

6:6 The same thought is expressed in 1Sa 15:22; Ps 51:17; Isa 1:11–15; Hos 6:6 (see notes on these verses). Micah does not deny the desirability of sacrifices but shows that it does no good to offer them without obedience.
6:7 These rhetorical questions, charged with hyperbole, demand a resoundingly negative answer.

6:8 The most memorable statement in the OT defining a proper relationship to God (see Jer 22:16; Hos 6:6 and notes; cf. Jas 1:27). Micah here summarizes major themes found in the prophecies of his near contemporaries: Amos ("act justly"; cf. Am 5:24), Hosea ("love mercy"; cf. Hos 6:6) and Isaiah ("walk humbly with your God"; cf. Isa 29:19). Cf. also Mt 23:23. *all you people.* Micah is speaking to all Israel (see also Dt 10:12–13). *act justly . . . love mercy.* The kind of obedience God expects from his covenant people. *act justly.* See note on Zec 8:16. *humbly.* Or "prudently" (see TNIV text note), "carefully" or "wisely." *your God.*

Covenant language in accordance with "My people" in vv. 3,5 (see note on Zec 8:8).
6:9–16 A divine covenant lawsuit containing further charges and the sentence (a life of futility, frustration, scorn and destruction, vv. 13–15). Its outline: (1) opening statement (v. 9), (2) a list of commercial and social sins (vv. 10–12), (3) announcement of divine punishment (vv. 13–15) and (4) summary statement (v. 16).
6:9 *city.* Jerusalem.
6:10 *ephah.* About half a bushel.
6:11 See Lev 19:35; Pr 11:1 and notes; Hos 12:7; Am 8:5.
6:12 *Her.* Jerusalem's.
6:13 *Therefore.* See note on 2:3.
6:14–15 See Hag 1:6 and note.

6:16 *Omri . . . Ahab's.* 1Ki 16:25,30 says that they did more evil than all the kings who preceded them. *ruin.* Disobedience brings disaster.

ISRAEL'S MISERY

7 What misery is mine!
I am like one who gathers summer fruit
at the gleaning of the vineyard;
there is no cluster of grapes to eat,
none of the early figs[c] that I crave.
[2] The faithful have been swept from the land;[d]
not one[e] upright person remains.
Everyone lies in wait[f] to shed blood;[g]
they hunt each other[h] with nets.[i]
[3] Both hands are skilled in doing evil;[j]
the ruler demands gifts,
the judge accepts bribes,[k]
the powerful dictate what they desire—
they all conspire together.
[4] The best of them is like a brier,[l]
the most upright worse than a thorn[m] hedge.
The day of your watchmen has come,
the day God visits you.
Now is the time of their confusion.[n]
[5] Do not trust a neighbor;
put no confidence in a friend.[o]
Even with the woman who lies in your embrace
be careful of your words.
[6] For a son dishonors his father,
a daughter rises up against her mother,[p]
a daughter-in-law against her mother-in-law—
your enemies are the members of your own household.[q]

[7] But as for me, I watch[r] in hope[s] for the LORD,
I wait for God my Savior;
my God will hear[t] me.

ISRAEL WILL RISE

[8] Do not gloat over me,[u] my enemy!
Though I have fallen, I will rise.[v]
Though I sit in darkness,
the LORD will be my light.[w]
[9] Because I have sinned against him,
I will bear the LORD's wrath,[x]
until he pleads my case[y]
and establishes my right.
He will bring me out into the light;[z]
I will see his righteousness.[a]
[10] Then my enemy will see it
and will be covered with shame,[b]
she who said to me,
"Where is the LORD your God?"[c]
My eyes will see her downfall;[d]
even now she will be trampled[e] underfoot
like mire in the streets.

Cross references (right column)

7:1 [c] S SS 2:13
7:2 [d] S Ps 12:1
[e] S Jer 2:29; 8:6
[f] Ps 10:8 [g] S Pr 6:17;
S Mic 3:10 [h] S Isa 3:5
[i] S Jer 5:26
7:3 [j] S Pr 4:16
[k] S Ex 23:8;
S Eze 22:12
7:4 [l] S Nu 33:55;
S Eze 2:6
[m] S 2Sa 23:6
[n] S Job 31:14;
Isa 22:5; S Hos 9:7
7:5 [o] Jer 9:4
7:6 [p] S Eze 22:7
[q] Mt 10:35-36*;
S Mk 13:12
7:7 [r] S Isa 21:8
[s] Ps 130:5; Isa 25:9
[t] S Ps 4:3
7:8 [u] S Ps 22:17;
S Pr 24:17; S Mic 4:11
[v] Ps 20:8; 37:24;
S Am 9:11
[w] S 2Sa 22:29; Isa 9:2
7:9 [x] La 3:39-40
[y] S Ps 119:154
[z] S Ps 107:10
[a] Isa 46:13
7:10 [b] S Ps 35:26
[c] S Ps 42:3
[d] S Isa 51:23
[e] S 2Sa 22:43;
S Job 40:12; S Isa 5:5;
Zec 10:5

Footnotes / study notes (bottom)

7:1–20 The speakers in this chapter are Micah (vv. 1–7), Zion (vv. 8–10), Micah (vv. 11–13), either Micah or Zion (v. 14), God (v. 15) and Micah (vv. 16–20). The chapter begins on a note of gloom but ends with a statement of hope.
7:1–7 Micah's lament over a decadent society.
7:1–2 Looking for the godly is like looking for summer fruit when the harvest has ended (see also Jer 5:1; 8:20 and notes).
7:3 Power often corrupts. *accepts bribes.* See 1Sa 8:3 and note; 12:3.
7:4 *day of your watchmen.* The day of judgment that the prophets warned about (see Eze 3:17–21 and note on 3:17). *visits you.* For punishment.
7:6 The family unit was disintegrating (cf. Mt 10:21,34–36).

7:7 Micah's complaint (vv. 1–6) is followed by his expression of confidence. Such a hopeful element is actually quite common in laments (see, e.g., Ps 55:16–17).
7:8–20 This completes the final salvation section in the three cycles of judgment and salvation. The unit is a prophetic liturgy made up of four subunits: (1) an expression of trust (vv. 8–10); (2) a promise of restoration (vv. 11–13); (3) a prayer, the Lord's answer and the response (vv. 14–17); and (4) a hymn of praise (vv. 18–20).
7:8 *me.* Zion. *my enemy.* Other nations (see v. 10). *Though I have fallen.* Micah foresees the destruction of Jerusalem in 586 B.C.
7:10 *Where is the LORD …?* See notes on Ps 3:2; 10:11; 115:2; Joel 2:17; see also Ps 42:3,10; 79:10.

7:11 *f* Isa 54:11;
S Am 9:11
7:12 *g* S Isa 11:11
h Isa 19:23-25; 60:4
7:13 *i* Isa 3:10-11;
S Eze 12:19; S 33:28-29
7:14 *j* S Ps 28:9;
S Mic 5:4 *k* Ps 23:4
l Ps 95:7 *m* S Isa 33:9
n S SS 4:1; S Jer 50:19
o Eze 36:11
7:15 *p* S Ex 3:20;
Ps 78:12
7:16 *q* Isa 26:11
r S Jdg 18:19
7:17 *s* Ge 3:14
t 2Sa 22:46 *u* Isa 25:3;
59:19
7:18 *v* S Ex 8:10;
S 1Sa 2:2
w S Isa 43:25;
S Jer 50:20; Zec 3:4
x S 2Ch 6:21;
Ps 103:8-13
y S Joel 2:32;
S Am 5:15; S Mic 2:12
z S Ex 34:9
a S Ps 103:9;
S Isa 54:9
b S 2Ch 30:9;
S Jer 31:20; 32:41;
S Eze 18:23
7:19 *c* S Isa 43:25
d S Jer 31:34
7:20 *e* Gal 3:16
f Dt 7:8; Lk 1:72
g Ps 108:4

11 The day for building your walls *f* will come,
    the day for extending your boundaries.
12 In that day people will come to you
    from Assyria *g* and the cities of Egypt,
even from Egypt to the Euphrates
    and from sea to sea
    and from mountain to mountain. *h*
13 The earth will become desolate because of its inhabitants,
    as the result of their deeds. *i*

PRAYER AND PRAISE

14 Shepherd *j* your people with your staff, *k*
    the flock of your inheritance,
which lives by itself in a forest,
    in fertile pasturelands. *a l*
Let them feed in Bashan *m* and Gilead *n*
    as in days long ago. *o*

15 "As in the days when you came out of Egypt,
    I will show them my wonders. *p*"

16 Nations will see and be ashamed, *q*
    deprived of all their power.
They will put their hands over their mouths *r*
    and their ears will become deaf.
17 They will lick dust *s* like a snake,
    like creatures that crawl on the ground.
They will come trembling *t* out of their dens;
    they will turn in fear *u* to the LORD our God
    and will be afraid of you.
18 Who is a God *v* like you,
    who pardons sin *w* and forgives *x* the transgression
    of the remnant *y* of his inheritance? *z*
You do not stay angry *a* forever
    but delight to show mercy. *b*
19 You will again have compassion on us;
    you will tread our sins underfoot
    and hurl all our iniquities *c* into the depths of the sea. *d*
20 You will be faithful to Jacob,
    and show love to Abraham, *e*
as you pledged on oath to our ancestors *f*
    in days long ago. *g*

---

a 14 Or *in the middle of Carmel*

7:12 *In that day.* See Isa 2:11,17,20; 10:20,27; Joel 1:15 and notes. *people will come.* See 4:2.
7:14–17 It is possible that these verses constitute a prayer that God will show his wonders again as in the exodus, that the nations will see and be ashamed and that they will turn to the Lord in fear.
7:14 *Shepherd.* Rule over (see 5:4; Ps 23:1; Jer 2:8; Eze 34:2 and notes). *inheritance.* The land and people of Israel (see v. 18; Ps 94:14; see also Ps 127:3; Jer 2:7 and notes). *Bashan and Gilead.* Fertile areas with rich pasturelands (see Ge 31:21; Ps 22:12; Eze 39:18; Am 4:1 and notes).
7:16 When the nations see the awesome display of God's power (v. 15), they will be amazed.
7:17 *lick dust like a snake.* A picture of defeat and death (see Ge 3:14 and note).
7:18–20 The conclusion to the whole book, not just to ch. 7.

7:18–19a See Ex 34:6–7a.
7:18 *Who is a God like you …?* Perhaps a pun on Micah's name (see note on 1:1). See Ex 15:11 and note.
7:19 *tread … underfoot.* Or "subdue." When God takes away sin's guilt so that it does not condemn us (v. 18), he also takes away its power so that it does not rule over us (see Ps 19:13; cf. Ro 6:14). *iniquities into the depths of the sea.* See note on Isa 38:17; see also Jer 50:2.
7:20 *Jacob … Abraham.* God had sworn to Abraham (see Ge 13:16; 15:5; 22:17 and notes) and Jacob (Ge 28:14) that their descendants would be as numerous as the stars in the sky, the dust of the earth and the sand on the seashore, and he had promised Abraham that he would be the father of many nations (Ge 17:5; cf. Lk 1:54–55). All believers are ultimately included in this promise (Ro 4; Gal 3:6–29; Heb 11:12).

AUTHOR NAHUM | INTRODUCTION

C The book contains the "vision of Nahum" (1:1), whose name means "comfort" and is related to the name Nehemiah, meaning "The LORD comforts" or "comfort of the LORD." (Nineveh's fall, which is Nahum's theme, would bring comfort to Judah.) Nothing is known about him except his hometown (Elkosh), and even its general location is uncertain.

DATE

In 3:8–10 the author speaks of the fall of Thebes, which happened in 663 B.C., as already past. In all three chapters Nahum prophesied Nineveh's fall, which was fulfilled in 612. Nahum therefore uttered this oracle between 663 and 612, perhaps near the end of this period since he represents the fall of Nineveh as imminent (2:1; 3:14, 19). This would place him during the reign of Josiah and make him a contemporary of Zephaniah and the young Jeremiah.

BACKGROUND

C Assyria (represented by Nineveh, 1:1) had already destroyed Samaria (722–721 B.C.), resulting in the captivity of the northern kingdom of Israel, and posed a present threat to Judah. The Assyrians were brutally cruel, their kings often being depicted as gloating over the gruesome punishments inflicted on conquered peoples. They conducted their wars with shocking ferocity, uprooted whole populations as state policy and deported them to other parts of their empire. The leaders of conquered cities were tortured and horribly mutilated before being executed (see note on 3:3). No wonder the dread of Assyria fell on all her neighbors!

About 700 B.C. King Sennacherib made Nineveh the capital of the Assyrian empire, and it remained the capital until it was destroyed in 612. Jonah had announced its destruction earlier (Jnh 3:4), but the people put on at least a show of repentance, and the destruction was temporarily averted (see Jnh 3:10 and note). Not long after that, however, Nineveh reverted to its extreme wickedness, cruelty and pride. The brutality reached its peak under Ashurbanipal (669–627), the last great ruler of the Assyrian empire. After his death Assyria's influence and power waned rapidly until 612, when Nineveh was overthrown (see notes on 1:14; 2:1). (Further historical information is given in notes throughout the book.)

RECIPIENTS

Some words are addressed to Judah (see 1:12–13,15), but most are addressed to Nineveh (see 1:11,14; 2:1,13; 3:5–17,19) or its king (3:18). The book, however, was meant for Israelite readers living in Judah.

LITERARY STYLE

The contents are primarily made up of judgment oracles, with appropriate descriptions and vocabulary, expressing intense moods, sights and sounds. The language is

| KEY | **A** APPLICATION FOR LIVING | **B** BACKGROUND NOTES | **C** CHARACTER INFORMATION |

poetic, with frequent use of metaphors and similes, vivid word pictures, repetition and many short—often staccato—phrases (see, e.g., 3:1–3). Rhetorical questions punctuate the flow of thought, which has a marked stress on moral indignation toward injustice (cf. note on Zec 8:16).

THEOLOGICAL THEMES

The focal point of the entire book is the Lord's judgment on Nineveh for her oppression, cruelty, idolatry and wickedness. The book ends with the destruction of the city.

According to Ro 11:22, God is not only kind but also stern. In Nahum, God is not only "slow to anger" (1:3) and "a refuge . . . for those who trust in him" (1:7) but also one who "will not leave the guilty unpunished" (1:3). God's righteous and just kingdom will ultimately triumph, for kingdoms built on wickedness and tyranny must eventually fall, as Assyria did.

In addition, Nahum declares the universal sovereignty of God. God is Lord of history and of all nations; as such, he controls their destinies.

OUTLINE

I. Title (1:1)
II. Nineveh's Judge (1:2–15)
   A. The Lord's Kindness and Sternness (1:2–8)
   B. Nineveh's Overthrow and Judah's Joy (1:9–15)
III. Nineveh's Judgment (ch. 2)
   A. Nineveh Besieged (2:1–10)
   B. Nineveh's Desolation Contrasted with Her Former Glory (2:11–13)
IV. Nineveh's Total Destruction (ch. 3)
   A. Nineveh's Sins (3:1–4)
   B. Nineveh's Doom (3:5–19)

A prophecy [a] concerning Nineveh. [b] The book of the vision [c] of Nahum the Elkoshite.

THE LORD'S ANGER AGAINST NINEVEH

[2] The Lord is a jealous [d] and avenging God;
  the Lord takes vengeance [e] and is filled with wrath.
The Lord takes vengeance on his foes
  and vents his wrath against his enemies. [f]
[3] The Lord is slow to anger [g] but great in power;
  the Lord will not leave the guilty unpunished. [h]
His way is in the whirlwind [i] and the storm, [j]
  and clouds [k] are the dust of his feet.
[4] He rebukes [l] the sea and dries it up; [m]
  he makes all the rivers run dry.
Bashan and Carmel [n] wither
  and the blossoms of Lebanon fade.
[5] The mountains quake [o] before him
  and the hills melt away. [p]
The earth trembles [q] at his presence,
  the world and all who live in it. [r]
[6] Who can withstand [s] his indignation?
  Who can endure [t] his fierce anger? [u]
His wrath is poured out like fire; [v]
  the rocks are shattered [w] before him.

[7] The Lord is good, [x]
  a refuge in times of trouble. [y]
He cares for [z] those who trust in him, [a]
[8]   but with an overwhelming flood [b]
he will make an end of Nineveh;
  he will pursue his foes into darkness.

[9] Whatever they plot [c] against the Lord
  he [a] will bring to an end;
  trouble will not come a second time.
[10] They will be entangled among thorns [d]
  and drunk [e] from their wine;
  they will be consumed like dry stubble. [b] [f]
[11] From you, Nineveh, has one come forth
  who plots evil against the Lord
  and devises wicked plans.

---

[a] 9 Or *What do you foes plot against the Lord? / He*   [b] 10 The meaning of the Hebrew for this verse is uncertain.

### Cross references (right margin)

1:1 [a] S Isa 13:1; 19:1; Jer 23:33-34
  [b] S Ge 10:11; S Jer 50:18; Na 2:8; 3:7 [c] S Isa 1:1
1:2 [d] S Ex 20:5
  [e] S Ge 4:24; S Dt 32:41; Ps 94:1
  [f] S Dt 7:10
1:3 [g] S Ne 9:17
  [h] S Ex 34:7
  [i] S Ex 14:21; S 2Ki 2:1
  [j] S Ps 50:3
  [k] S 2Sa 22:10; S Ps 104:3
1:4 [l] S 2Sa 22:16
  [m] S Ex 14:22
  [n] S Isa 33:9
1:5 [o] S Ex 19:18; S Job 9:6 [p] S Mic 1:4
  [q] S Joel 2:10
  [r] S Eze 38:20
1:6 [s] S Ps 130:3
  [t] S Eze 22:14
  [u] S Ps 76:7
  [v] S Isa 5:24-25; S 42:25; S Jer 10:10
  [w] 1Ki 19:11
1:7 [x] S Jer 33:11
  [y] S Jer 17:17 [z] S Ps 1:6
  [a] S Ps 22:9
1:8 [b] S Isa 8:7; S Da 9:26
1:9 [c] S Hos 7:15
1:10 [d] S 2Sa 23:6
  [e] S Isa 49:26
  [f] S Isa 5:24; Mal 4:1

Study notes (bottom)

1:1 The title of the book. *prophecy.* See Isa 13:1; Hab 1:1 and notes. *Nineveh.* See Introduction: Background; see also notes on Jnh 1:2; 3:3. Here the capital city stands for the entire Assyrian empire. *vision.* See Pr 29:18; Isa 1:1; Ob 1 and notes. *Nahum the Elkoshite.* See Introduction: Author.

1:2–3 The covenant name Yahweh ("the Lord") is emphasized (see notes on Ge 2:4; Ex 3:14–15; 6:6; Dt 28:58).

1:2 *jealous.* See note on Ex 20:5. *avenging ... vengeance ... vengeance.* God acts justly in judgment against all who oppose him and his kingdom. The repetition is for emphasis (see note on Jer 7:4)."It is mine to avenge; I will repay" (Dt 32:35; see note there), says the Lord. *wrath.* See notes on Ps 2:5; Ro 1:18.

1:3 *slow to anger ... not leave the guilty unpunished.* See Ex 34:6–7 and note. *the guilty.* Such as Nineveh. *whirlwind ... storm ... clouds.* Awesome natural phenomena that display God's majesty and power. See notes on Job 38:1; Ps 18:7–15; 68:4; 77:16–19; 104:3–4.

1:4 *rebukes the sea and dries it up.* As at the crossing of the Red Sea (see Ex 14:1—15:12; see also Ps 18:15 and note). *makes all the rivers run dry.* As at the crossing of the Jordan (see Jos 3:1—4:24 and note). *Bashan ... Carmel ... Lebanon.* See notes on Ps

22:12; SS 7:5; Isa 2:13; 33:9; 35:2; Eze 39:18; Am 4:1. These three places were noted for their fertility, vineyards and trees, but at the Lord's word they wither.

1:5 *mountains ... hills ... earth ... world.* Emblems of stability and permanence.

1:6 *Who can withstand ...? Who can endure ...?* Rhetorical questions. If mountains quake before the Lord (v. 5), what human beings can think that they are not vulnerable? Cf. Ro 2:3–5; Rev 6:17.

1:7 *those who trust in him.* Such as Judah.

1:8 *overwhelming flood.* Symbolic of an invading army (see Isa 8:7–8; 28:17–19). *end ... darkness.* In 612 B.C. that end came for Nineveh, and the darkness enveloped her.

1:9 *they plot.* See note on v. 11. *trouble will not come a second time.* God never permitted the Assyrians a second victory over Judah; the first was the fall of Samaria (722–721 B.C.) and of the northern kingdom (Sennacherib's invasion in 701 was not a complete victory; see 2Ki 18:13—19:36).

1:10 *drunk from their wine.* See 3:11 and note; but perhaps the line here should read: "and drenched as with their wine,/yet they ..." (see TNIV text note).

1:12 *g* S Isa 10:34
h Isa 54:6-8;
S La 3:31-32
1:13 *i* S Isa 9:4
j S Job 12:18;
S Ps 107:14
1:14 *k* S Isa 14:22
l Mic 5:13
m S Jer 28:8;
Eze 32:22-23
1:15 *n* Isa 40:9;
Ro 10:15 *o* S Isa 52:7;
Ac 10:36 *p* Lev 23:2-4
q S Isa 52:1
2:1 *r* Jer 51:20
2:2 *s* Eze 37:23
t Isa 60:15
2:3 *u* Eze 23:14-15
2:4 *v* S Jer 4:13;
S Eze 23:24

¹²This is what the LORD says:

"Although they have allies and are numerous,
　　they will be destroyed *g* and pass away.
Although I have afflicted you, Judah,
　　I will afflict you no more. *h*
¹³ Now I will break their yoke *i* from your neck
　　and tear your shackles away." *j*

¹⁴ The LORD has given a command concerning you, Nineveh:
　　"You will have no descendants to bear your name. *k*
I will destroy the images *l* and idols
　　that are in the temple of your gods.
I will prepare your grave, *m*
　　for you are vile."

*¹⁵ Look, there on the mountains,
　　the feet of one who brings good news, *n*
　　who proclaims peace! *o*
Celebrate your festivals, *p* Judah,
　　and fulfill your vows.
No more will the wicked invade you; *q*
　　they will be completely destroyed.

NINEVEH TO FALL

2 *An attacker *r* advances against you, Nineveh.
　　Guard the fortress,
　　watch the road,
　　brace yourselves,
　　marshal all your strength!

² The LORD will restore *s* the splendor *t* of Jacob
　　like the splendor of Israel,
though destroyers have laid them waste
　　and have ruined their vines.

³ The shields of the soldiers are red;
　　the warriors are clad in scarlet. *u*
The metal on the chariots flashes
　　on the day they are made ready;
　　the spears of juniper are brandished. *a*
⁴ The chariots *v* storm through the streets,
　　rushing back and forth through the squares.
They look like flaming torches;
　　they dart about like lightning.

---

a 3 Hebrew; Septuagint and Syriac *ready; / the horsemen rush to and fro.*

* 1:15 is numbered 2:1 in Hebrew texts.　　* 2:1-13 is numbered 2:2-14 in Hebrew texts.

1:11 *one … who plots evil.* Possibly the Assyrian king Ashurbanipal (669–627 B.C.), the last great Assyrian emperor, whose western expeditions succeeded in subduing Egypt and to whom King Manasseh had to submit as a vassal (see 2Ch 33:11–13 and notes on 33:11; Ezr 4:9–10). *plots evil against the LORD.* All such schemes end in futility and destruction (Ps 2:1–4). **1:12** *they.* The Assyrians. *I have afflicted you.* God had used Assyria as the rod of his anger against his covenant-breaking people in the days of Ahaz (Isa 10:5) and again in the time of Manasseh. **1:13** See Jer 27:2 and note. *I will break their yoke.* Judah was Assyria's vassal; that yoke would be broken. **1:14** *I will prepare your grave.* God used the Babylonians and Medes to dig Nineveh's grave in 612 B.C. For the fulfillment of this prophecy, see Eze 32:22–23. **1:15** *mountains.* Of Judah. *feet of one who brings good news.* This verse sets forth a principle that is applicable in several contexts of deliverance. Here the reference is to the good news of deliverance from the Assyrian threat; in Isa 52:7,

deliverance from Babylonian exile; in Ro 10:15, deliverance from sin through the gospel ("good news") of Christ. *Celebrate your festivals.* In the joy of your deliverance. *fulfill your vows.* Those you uttered in the time of distress (see notes on Ps 7:17; 50:14; Jnh 2:9). *No more will the wicked invade you.* The Assyrian invasion in the days of Manasseh was the last (see v. 12 and note). *wicked.* See note on Dt 13:13. *completely destroyed.* Fulfilled in 612 when Nineveh fell (see note on v. 14). **2:1** *attacker.* Refers to the alliance of the Medes under Cyaxares and the Babylonians under Nabopolassar. *Guard the fortress … marshal all your strength!* Probably irony, touched with sarcasm. *road.* By which the enemies will come. **2:2** *restore the splendor of Jacob … Israel.* The nation will be restored to its previous greatness. **2:3** *the soldiers.* Those of the attacker (v. 1), or perhaps those of Nineveh itself. *red.* Either (1) the color of the shields, (2) a reference to blood on them or (3) the result of the reflection of the sun shining on them. *brandished.* Ready to use.

2:5 w Jer 46:12
2:6 x Isa 45:1;
Na 3:13
2:7 y S Ge 8:8;
S Isa 59:11 z Isa 32:12
2:10 a S Jos 2:11;
S 7:5 b S Isa 29:22
2:11 c Isa 5:29
2:12 d S Jer 51:34
e S Jer 4:7
f S Isa 37:18
2:13 g Isa 10:5-13;
S Jer 21:13; Na 3:5
h Ps 46:9 i S 2Sa 2:26
j S Mic 5:6

⁵ Nineveh summons her picked troops,
    yet they stumble ʷ on their way.
They dash to the city wall;
    the protective shield is put in place.
⁶ The river gates ˣ are thrown open
    and the palace collapses.
⁷ It is decreed ᵃ that Nineveh
    be exiled and carried away.
Her female slaves moan ʸ like doves
    and beat on their breasts. ᶻ
⁸ Nineveh is like a pool
    whose water is draining away.
"Stop! Stop!" they cry,
    but no one turns back.
⁹ Plunder the silver!
    Plunder the gold!
The supply is endless,
    the wealth from all its treasures!
¹⁰ She is pillaged, plundered, stripped!
    Hearts melt, ᵃ knees give way,
    bodies tremble, every face grows pale. ᵇ

¹¹ Where now is the lions' den, ᶜ
    the place where they fed their young,
where the lion and lioness went,
    and the cubs, with nothing to fear?
¹² The lion killed ᵈ enough for his cubs
    and strangled the prey for his mate,
filling his lairs ᵉ with the kill
    and his dens with the prey. ᶠ

¹³ "I am against ᵍ you,"
    declares the LORD Almighty.
"I will burn up your chariots in smoke, ʰ
    and the sword ⁱ will devour your young lions.
I will leave you no prey on the earth.
The voices of your messengers
    will no longer be heard." ʲ

ᵃ 7 The meaning of the Hebrew for this word is uncertain.

2:4 *chariots…rushing.* Refers to either (1) the Assyrian war chariots, as the Assyrians take frantic but vain steps to defend themselves, or (2) the chariots of Nineveh's invaders.

2:5 *Nineveh.* That is, the king of Assyria. *city wall.* A moat 150 feet wide had to be filled in before reaching Nineveh's wall, which was almost 8 miles long with 15 gates. Then battering rams were moved up. *protective shield.* A large defensive framework covered with hides to deflect stones and arrows.

2:6 *river gates.* Perhaps the dams on the Khoser River, which ran through the city to the Tigris River. They were either already in place or quickly built to back up the river water, then suddenly released so the flood would damage the walls. *palace collapses.* One ancient historian (the author of the *Babylonian Chronicles*) speaks of a flood that washed away some of the wall, making it easier for the invaders to enter the city.

2:7 *female slaves.* Even the lowest in the social order will not escape the judgment.

2:8 *like a pool…water is draining away.* Some think that this refers to the Tigris and the smaller rivers encircling and running through parts of the city, as well as to a system of dams to make the city more impenetrable. Others take the language less literally as a reference to Nineveh's people fleeing, like water draining from a pool.

2:9 The cry of the invaders.

2:10 *pillaged, plundered, stripped!* The *Babylonian Chronicles* confirms the fact that a great quantity of plunder was carried off by the invaders. *Hearts melt.* The powerful, insolent Ninevites become helpless with fear.

2:11–13 Nahum ironically contrasts the devastated and desolate city of Nineveh with its former glory and power, expressed in figurative terms.

2:11 *lion and lioness.* See Isa 5:29; Jer 4:7. The lion is an appropriate image to apply to Assyria because of the rapacious ways of the Assyrian monarchs and because Nineveh contained numerous lion sculptures.

2:12 *filling his lairs…with the prey.* Nineveh was filled with the spoils of war from many conquered nations.

2:13 *I will burn up.* Nineveh's fall will be an act of divine judgment. Nineveh had been put on trial, found guilty and sentenced to destruction. *voices…no longer be heard.* History has confirmed this prediction.

3:1 kS Eze 22:2;
S Mic 3:10 lPs 12:2
3:3 m2Ki 19:35;
Isa 34:3; Jer 47:3
3:4 nS Isa 47:9
oS Isa 23:17;
Eze 16:25-29
3:5 pS Na 2:13
qS Isa 20:4; Jer 13:22
rS Isa 47:3
3:6 sS Ex 29:14;
S Job 9:31
tS 1Sa 2:30;
S Jer 51:37 uIsa 14:16
3:7 vS Isa 13:14;
S 31:9 wS Na 1:1
xS Job 3:14
yS Jer 15:5
zS Isa 51:19
3:8 aAm 6:2
bS Jer 46:25
cIsa 19:6-9
3:9 dS Ge 10:6;
S 2Ch 12:3
eS Eze 27:10
fEze 30:5
3:10 gS Isa 20:4
hS 2Ki 8:12;
S Isa 13:16; Hos 13:16
iS Job 6:27;
S Eze 24:6 jS Jer 40:1
3:11 kS Isa 49:26

WOE TO NINEVEH

3 Woe to the city of blood, [k]
full of lies, [l]
full of plunder,
never without victims!
[2] The crack of whips,
the clatter of wheels,
galloping horses
and jolting chariots!
[3] Charging cavalry,
flashing swords
and glittering spears!
Many casualties,
piles of dead,
bodies without number,
people stumbling over the corpses [m]—
[4] all because of the wanton lust of a prostitute,
alluring, the mistress of sorceries, [n]
who enslaved nations by her prostitution [o]
and peoples by her witchcraft.

[5] "I am against [p] you," declares the LORD Almighty.
"I will lift your skirts [q] over your face.
I will show the nations your nakedness [r]
and the kingdoms your shame.
[6] I will pelt you with filth, [s]
I will treat you with contempt [t]
and make you a spectacle. [u]
[7] All who see you will flee [v] from you and say,
'Nineveh [w] is in ruins [x]—who will mourn for her?' [y]
Where can I find anyone to comfort [z] you?"

[8] Are you better than [a] Thebes, [b]
situated on the Nile, [c]
with water around her?
The river was her defense,
the waters her wall.
[9] Cush [a] [d] and Egypt were her boundless strength;
Put [e] and Libya [f] were among her allies.
[10] Yet she was taken captive [g]
and went into exile.
Her infants were dashed [h] to pieces
at every street corner.
Lots [i] were cast for her nobles,
and all her great men were put in chains. [j]
[11] You too will become drunk; [k]

---

a 9 That is, the upper Nile region

3:1–3 See note on Joel 2:3–11.
3:1 *city of blood.* Nineveh's bloody massacres of her conquered rivals were well known. *never without victims.* The Assyrians were noted for their ruthlessness, brutality and terrible atrocities. Many of their victims were beheaded, impaled or burned.

3:3 *piles of dead.* The Assyrian king Shalmaneser III boasted of erecting a pyramid of chopped-off heads in front of an enemy's city. Other Assyrian kings stacked corpses like cordwood by the gates of defeated cities. Nahum's description of the cruel Assyrians is apropos.

3:4 *prostitute…prostitution.* The lure of luxury and wealth brought multitudes to Nineveh, but like the allurements of a prostitute it did not yield life's true pleasures. *sorceries…witchcraft.* Pagan practices (see Dt 18:10 and note on 18:9).

3:5 *lift your skirts over your face.* A common punishment of prostitutes and adulteresses (see notes on Isa 47:3; Jer 13:22; Hos 2:3,10).

3:7 *who…? Where…?* Rhetorical questions. Nineveh will receive no sympathy.

3:8 *Thebes.* Hebrew *No Amon,* which means "city of (the god) Amun." Thebes was the great capital of Upper (southern) Egypt. Its site is occupied today by the towns of Luxor and Karnak. It was destroyed by the Assyrians in 663 B.C.

3:9 *Put and Libya.* Perhaps better "Put (i.e., Libya)"; see notes on Ge 10:6; Eze 27:10; 30:5.

3:10 *Her infants were dashed to pieces.* See Ps 137:9; Isa 13:16; Hos 13:16 and notes. *her great men were put in chains.* Assyrian kings often did this; e.g., King Ashurbanipal gave this description of his treatment of a captured leader: "I … put a dog chain on him and made him occupy a kennel at the eastern gate of Nineveh."

3:11 *will become drunk.* Probably from the cup of God's wrath (see Isa 51:17; Jer 25:15; Eze 23:31 and notes).

you will go into hiding[l]
and seek refuge from the enemy.

[12] All your fortresses are like fig trees
with their first ripe fruit;[m]
when they are shaken,
the figs[n] fall into the mouth of the eater.

[13] Look at your troops—
they are all weaklings.[o]
The gates[p] of your land
are wide open to your enemies;
fire has consumed the bars of your gates.[q]

[14] Draw water for the siege,[r]
strengthen your defenses![s]
Work the clay,
tread the mortar,
repair the brickwork!

[15] There the fire[t] will consume you;
the sword[u] will cut you down—
they will devour you like a swarm of locusts.
Multiply like grasshoppers,
multiply like locusts![v]

[16] You have increased the number of your merchants
till they are more than the stars in the sky,
but like locusts[w] they strip the land
and then fly away.

[17] Your guards are like locusts,[x]
your officials like swarms of locusts
that settle in the walls on a cold day—
but when the sun appears they fly away,
and no one knows where.

[18] King of Assyria, your shepherds[a] slumber;[y]
your nobles lie down to rest.
Your people are scattered[a] on the mountains
with no one to gather them.

[19] Nothing can heal you;[b]
your wound is fatal.
All who hear the news about you
clap their hands[c] at your fall,
for who has not felt
your endless cruelty?[d]

---

[a] 18 That is, rulers

3:11 [l] S Isa 2:10
3:12 [m] S SS 2:13
[n] S Isa 28:4
3:13 [o] S Isa 19:16
[p] S Na 2:6
[q] S Isa 45:2
3:14 [r] S 2Ch 32:4
[s] Na 2:1
3:15 [t] S Isa 27:1
[u] S 2Sa 2:26
[v] S Jer 51:14;
S Joel 1:4
3:16 [w] S Ex 10:13
3:17 [x] Jer 51:27
3:18 [y] Ps 76:5-6;
S Jer 25:27 [z] Isa 56:10
[a] S 1Ki 22:17
3:19 [b] S Jer 30:13;
S Mic 1:9
[c] S Job 27:23;
S La 2:15; Zep 2:15
[d] Isa 37:18

3:12 *like fig trees with their first ripe fruit.* A simile for the eagerness with which the victors gather the rich loot of Nineveh. *figs fall into the mouth of the eater.* Nineveh's fortresses will finally fall just as easily.

3:13 *your troops … are all weaklings.* They are unable to stand against the invading armies.

3:14 *Draw water.* A normal preparation for siege. *strengthen your defenses!* Irony, the point being that it will do no good (see 2:1 and note).

3:15 *There.* Inside your strong fortifications. *fire will consume you.* Confirmed by history and archaeology. Assyria's king died in the flames of his palace.

3:16 *your merchants … are more than the stars.* Speaks of Assyria's vast trading and commercial enterprises.

3:17 *locusts.* Feared by the farmers of the ancient Near East, because they came in huge swarms and devoured everything in their path. Their activity provided an apt simile for

the exploitative actions of Nineveh's officials during their destruction. *no one knows where.* Thus will Nineveh's officials disappear, without a trace. Interestingly, for centuries no one knew where Nineveh itself lay buried; in 1845 it was finally uncovered by archaeologists (see note on Zep 2:13).

3:18 *King.* The reigning king at the time of Nineveh's fall was Sin-Shar-Ishkun, so these words are prophetically addressed to him. *shepherds.* Leaders (see Jer 2:8 and note). *lie down to rest.* Die. *people are scattered.* The age-old scene of refugees fleeing a place of destruction is repeated at Nineveh.

3:19 *your wound is fatal.* Nineveh was so totally destroyed that it was never rebuilt, and within a few centuries it was covered with windblown sand. So that "great city" (Jnh 1:2; 3:2; 4:11; see note on Jnh 3:3) fell in 612 B.C., never to rise again—all in fulfillment of God's word through his prophet Nahum. *your endless cruelty.* But now you lie in endless ruin.

AUTHOR — HABAKKUK | INTRODUCTION

C Little is known about Habakkuk except that he was a contemporary of Jeremiah and a man of vigorous faith rooted deeply in the religious traditions of Israel. The account of his ministering to the needs of Daniel in the lions' den in the Apocryphal book *Bel and the Dragon* is legendary rather than historical.

DATE

The prediction of the coming Babylonian invasion (1:6) indicates that Habakkuk lived in Judah toward the end of Josiah's reign (640–609 B.C.) or at the beginning of Jehoiakim's (609–598). The prophecy is generally dated a little before or after the battle of Carchemish (605), when Egyptian forces, which had earlier gone to the aid of the last Assyrian king, were routed by the Babylonians under Nabopolassar and Nebuchadnezzar and were pursued as far as the Egyptian border (Jer 46). Habakkuk, like Jeremiah, probably lived to see the initial fulfillment of his prophecy when Jerusalem was attacked by the Babylonians in 597.

THEOLOGICAL MESSAGE

Among the prophetic writings, Habakkuk is somewhat unique in that it includes no oracle addressed to Israel. It contains, rather, a dialogue between the prophet and God (see Outline). (The book of Jonah, while narrative, presents an account of conflict between the Lord and one of his prophets.) In the first two chapters, Habakkuk argues with God over his ways that appear to him unfathomable, if not unjust. Having received replies, he responds with a beautiful confession of faith (ch. 3).

This account of wrestling with God is, however, not just a fragment from a private journal that has somehow entered the public domain. It was composed for Israel. No doubt it represented the voice of the godly in Judah, struggling to comprehend the ways of God. God's answers therefore spoke to all who shared Habakkuk's troubled doubts. And Habakkuk's confession became a public expression—as indicated by its liturgical notations (see note on 3:1).

Habakkuk was perplexed that wickedness, strife and oppression were rampant in Judah but that God seemingly did nothing. When told that the Lord was preparing to do something about it through the "ruthless" Babylonians (1:6), his perplexity only intensified: How could God, who is "too pure to look on evil" (1:13), appoint such a nation "to execute judgment" (1:12) on a people "more righteous than themselves" (1:13)?

God makes it clear, however, that eventually the corrupt destroyer will itself be destroyed. In the end, Habakkuk learns to rest in God's sovereign appointments and await his working in a spirit of worship. He learns to wait patiently in faith (2:3–4) for God's kingdom to be expressed universally (2:14). See note on 3:18–19.

LITERARY FEATURES

B The author wrote clearly and with great feeling, and he penned many memorable phrases (2:2,4,14,20; 3:2,17–19). The book was popular during the intertestamental period; a complete commentary on its first two chapters has been found among the Dead Sea Scrolls (see essay, pp. 1595–1596).

OUTLINE

I. Title (1:1)
II. Habakkuk's First Complaint: Why Does the Evil in Judah Go Unpunished? (1:2–4)
III. God's Answer: The Babylonians Will Punish Judah (1:5–11)
IV. Habakkuk's Second Complaint: How Can a Just God Use the Wicked Babylonians to Punish a People More Righteous Than Themselves? (1:12—2:1)
V. God's Answer: Babylonia Will Be Punished, and Faith Will Be Rewarded (2:2–20)
VI. Habakkuk's Prayer: After Asking for Manifestations of God's Wrath and Mercy (As He Has Seen in the Past), He Closes with a Confession of Trust and Joy in God (ch. 3)

1:1 ᵃS Na 1:1
1:2 ᵇS Ps 6:3
ᶜPs 13:1-2; 22:1-2
ᵈJer 14:9; Zec 1:12
1:3 ᵉver 13
ᶠS Job 9:23 ᵍJer 20:8
ʰS Ps 55:9
1:4 ⁱPs 119:126
ʲS Isa 29:21
ᵏS Job 19:7;
S Isa 1:23; 5:20;
S Eze 9:9
1:5 ˡS Isa 29:9
ᵐAc 13:41*
1:6 ⁿS Dt 28:49;
S 2Ki 24:2 ᵒRev 20:9
ᵖS Jer 13:20; S 21:7
1:7 ᵠIsa 18:7;
Jer 39:5-9
1:8 ʳS Jer 4:13
ˢS Ge 49:27
1:9 ᵗHab 2:5

1   The prophecy ᵃ that Habakkuk the prophet received.

HABAKKUK'S COMPLAINT

² How long, ᵇ Lᴏʀᴅ, must I call for help,
     but you do not listen? ᶜ
Or cry out to you, "Violence!"
     but you do not save? ᵈ
³ Why do you make me look at injustice?
     Why do you tolerate ᵉ wrongdoing? ᶠ
Destruction and violence ᵍ are before me;
     there is strife, ʰ and conflict abounds.
⁴ Therefore the law ⁱ is paralyzed,
     and justice never prevails.
The wicked hem in the righteous,
     so that justice ʲ is perverted. ᵏ

THE LORD'S ANSWER

⁵ "Look at the nations and watch—
     and be utterly amazed. ˡ
For I am going to do something in your days
     that you would not believe,
     even if you were told. ᵐ
⁶ I am raising up the Babylonians, ᵃ ⁿ
     that ruthless and impetuous people,
who sweep across the whole earth ᵒ
     to seize dwellings not their own. ᵖ
⁷ They are a feared and dreaded people; ᵠ
     they are a law to themselves
     and promote their own honor.
⁸ Their horses are swifter ʳ than leopards,
     fiercer than wolves ˢ at dusk.
Their cavalry gallops headlong;
     their horsemen come from afar.
They fly like a vulture swooping to devour;
⁹   they all come bent on violence.
Their hordes ᵇ advance like a desert wind
     and gather prisoners ᵗ like sand.

ᵃ 6 Or *Chaldeans*   ᵇ 9 The meaning of the Hebrew for this word is uncertain.

1:1 *prophecy.* Such as the two found here (vv. 5–11; 2:2–20). Prophecies were frequently received in visions. The Hebrew word for "prophecy" (possibly meaning "burden," but perhaps only "pronouncement") often refers to revelations containing warnings of impending doom (see Isa 13:1 and note; 15:1; 19:1; 22:1), but in Zec 9:1; 12:1; Mal 1:1 it refers to messages (see notes on those passages). *Habakkuk.* The name is probably Babylonian and refers to a kind of garden plant. *prophet.* Habakkuk is called a prophet also in 3:1, tying ch. 3 closely to chs. 1–2. See notes on Ex 3:4; 7:1–2; 1Ki 22:19; Jnh 3:2; Zec 1:1.

1:2—2:20 A dialogue between the prophet and God. The basic themes are age-old: Why does evil seem to go unpunished? Why does God not respond to prayer?

1:2 *How long . . . ?* See Ps 6:3 and note; 13:1–2; 22:1–2. *Violence!* At this time Judah was probably under King Jehoiakim, who was ambitious, cruel and corrupt. Habakkuk describes the social corruption and spiritual apostasy of Judah in the late seventh century B.C.

1:3 *you tolerate.* See v. 13. The prophet was amazed that God seemed to condone cruelty and violence. *Destruction and violence are before me.* Jeremiah complains to the Lord in a similar vein (Jer 20:8).

1:4 *law is paralyzed . . . justice is perverted.* Because wealthy

landowners controlled the courts through bribery (see Mic 3:11; 7:3).

1:5 Paul concludes his sermon in Pisidian Antioch by quoting these words (Ac 13:41). *your . . . you . . . you.* Judah as a whole is addressed (the pronouns are plural). *would not believe.* To the people of Judah it was incredible that God would give them over to the arrogant Babylonians.

1:6 *I am raising up the Babylonians.* See Isa 10:5–6 and note on 10:5. The apostate nation of Judah is to be punished by an invasion of the Babylonians, a powerful people who regained their independence from Assyria in 626 B.C., destroyed Assyrian power completely in 612–605 and flourished until 539. In this context, the Chaldeans (see TNIV text note) are synonymous with the newly resurgent Babylonians. *seize dwellings.* See 2:6–8.

1:7 *promote their own honor.* A mark of arrogance.

1:8 The speed with which Babylonia conquered her enemies had become proverbial. *vulture.* The Hebrew for "vulture" may also refer to an eagle (see Dt 28:49–50 and note on 28:49).

1:9 *violence.* The rapacious cruelty of the Babylonians was more than a match for that of the people of Judah (see v. 2 and note; see also v. 3). *gather prisoners like sand.* Like their Assyrian predecessors, the Babylonians deported conquered peoples as a matter of deliberate national policy (see 2:5).

¹⁰ They mock kings
  and scoff at rulers. ^u
They laugh at all fortified cities;
  by building earthen ramps ^v they capture them.
¹¹ Then they sweep past like the wind ^w and go on—
  guilty people, whose own strength is their god." ^x

HABAKKUK'S SECOND COMPLAINT

¹² LORD, are you not from everlasting? ^y
  My God, my Holy One, ^z you^a will never die. ^a
You, LORD, have appointed ^b them to execute judgment;
  you, my Rock, ^c have ordained them to punish.
¹³ Your eyes are too pure ^d to look on evil;
  you cannot tolerate wrongdoing. ^e
Why then do you tolerate ^f the treacherous? ^g
  Why are you silent while the wicked
  swallow up those more righteous than themselves? ^h
¹⁴ You have made people like the fish in the sea,
  like the sea creatures that have no ruler.
¹⁵ The wicked ⁱ foe pulls all of them up with hooks, ^j
  he catches them in his net, ^k
he gathers them up in his dragnet;
  and so he rejoices and is glad.
¹⁶ Therefore he sacrifices to his net
  and burns incense ^l to his dragnet,
for by his net he lives in luxury
  and enjoys the choicest food.
¹⁷ Is he to keep on emptying his net,
  destroying nations without mercy? ^m

2
I will stand at my watch ⁿ
  and station myself on the ramparts; ^o
I will look to see what he will say ^p to me,
  and what answer I am to give to this complaint. ^{b q}

THE LORD'S ANSWER

² Then the LORD replied:

  "Write ^r down the revelation
  and make it plain on tablets
  so that a herald ^c may run with it.
³ For the revelation awaits an appointed time; ^s
  it speaks of the end ^t

---

^a 12 An ancient Hebrew scribal tradition; Masoretic Text *we rebuked*   ^b 1 Or *and what to answer when I am*   ^c 2 Or *so that whoever reads it*

1:10 *building earthen ramps.* A siege method.
1:11 *whose own strength is their god.* The Babylonians were so proud and confident of their military might that it had virtually become their god (see v. 16).
1:12 Habakkuk cannot see the justice in Judah's being punished by an even more wicked nation, and he thinks that the Babylonians surely would not be allowed to conquer Judah completely. *from everlasting.* See Ps 90:2. *You, LORD, have appointed them.* The prophet recognizes Babylonia as God's agent of judgment (cf. Isa 7:18–20; 44:28—45:1). *Rock.* See 1Sa 2:2 and note.

A **1:13** A classic statement of the problem of evil within the context of Israel's faith: Why does evil appear to flourish unchecked by a just and holy God? See Ps 37; 73 and notes. *you tolerate.* See v. 3 and note. *treacherous ... wicked.* The Babylonians. *those more righteous.* Judah.

B **1:15** *hooks.* See note on Am 4:2. *catches them in his net.* Babylonia's victims are as powerless as fish swimming into a net. Mesopotamian reliefs symbolically portray conquerors capturing their enemies in fishnets.

1:16 See note on v. 11.
2:1 See Eze 3:17 and note. *I will stand at my watch.* The figure of a guard looking out from a tower and expecting a response to his challenge. Any rebuke (see TNIV text note) would be for questioning God's justice. *ramparts.* The walls of Jerusalem. *he.* God.
2:2–3 *revelation.* See 1Ch 17:15; Pr 29:18 and note. The Hebrew for this word refers specifically to a prophet's vision (see, e.g., Isa 1:1 and note).
2:2 *Write down.* See Isa 30:8; Jer 36:2 and note. *so that a herald may run with it.* Lit. "so that he who reads it may run," i.e., so that a messenger may run to deliver the message and read it to those to whom he has been sent.
2:3 *the end.* Of the Babylonians, though some refer it to the end times, when God's redemptive purposes would be completed. *wait for it.* The following message deals with the fall of Babylon in 539 B.C., about 66 years after Habakkuk's prophecy. The Lord tells Habakkuk (and Judah) that fulfillment of the prophecy may "linger" but that he and the people are to expect it (see 3:16).

1:10 ^u S 2Ch 36:6
  ^v S Jer 33:4
1:11 ^w Jer 4:11-12
  ^x S Da 4:30
1:12 ^y S Ge 21:33
  ^z Isa 31:1; 37:23
  ^a Ps 118:17 ^b Isa 10:6
  ^c S Ge 49:24;
  S Ex 33:22
1:13 ^d Ps 18:26
  ^e S La 3:34-36 ^f ver 3
  ^g S Ps 25:3
  ^h S Job 21:7
1:15 ⁱ Jer 5:26
  ^j Isa 19:8
  ^k S Job 18:8; Jer 16:16
1:16 ^l Jer 44:8
1:17 ^m S Isa 14:6;
  19:8
2:1 ⁿ S Isa 21:8
  ^o S Ps 48:13 ^p Ps 85:8
  ^q S Ps 5:3; S Eze 3:17
2:2 ^r S Isa 30:8;
  S Jer 36:2;
  S Eze 24:2;
  S Ro 4:24; Rev 1:19
2:3 ^s Da 11:27
  ^t Da 8:17

2:3 *u* S Ps 27:14
v S Eze 12:25
2:4 *w* S Eze 18:9
x Ro 1:17*; Gal 3:11*;
Heb 10:37-38*
2:5 *y* S Pr 20:1
z S Isa 2:11
a S Pr 27:20; S 30:15-
16 *b* Hab 1:9
2:6 *c* S Isa 14:4
d Am 2:8
2:7 *e* S Pr 29:1
2:8 *f* Isa 33:1;
Jer 50:17-18;
S Ob 1:15; Zec 2:8-9
g ver 17 *h* S Eze 39:10
2:9 *i* S Jer 22:13
j S Jer 51:13
k S Job 39:27;
S Isa 10:14
2:10 *l* Jer 26:19
m ver 16; S Na 3:6
2:11 *n* S Jos 24:27;
Zec 5:4; Lk 19:40
2:12 *o* S Eze 22:2;
S Mic 3:10
2:13 *p* Isa 50:11
q S Isa 47:13
2:14 *r* S Ex 16:7;
S Nu 14:21 *s* S Isa 11:9

and will not prove false.
Though it linger, wait *u* for it;
  it *a* will certainly come
and will not delay. *v*

4 "See, he is puffed up;
  his desires are not upright—
but the righteous *w* will live by their faithfulness *b x*—
5 indeed, wine *y* betrays him;
  he is arrogant *z* and never at rest.
Because he is as greedy as the grave
  and like death is never satisfied, *a*
he gathers to himself all the nations
  and takes captive *b* all the peoples.

6 "Will not all of them taunt *c* him with ridicule and scorn, saying,

  " 'Woe to him who piles up stolen goods
  and makes himself wealthy by extortion! *d*
  How long must this go on?'
7 Will not your creditors suddenly arise?
  Will they not wake up and make you tremble?
  Then you will become their prey. *e*
8 Because you have plundered many nations,
  the peoples who are left will plunder you. *f*
For you have shed human blood; *g*
  you have destroyed lands and cities and everyone in them. *h*

9 "Woe to him who builds *i* his house by unjust gain, *j*
  setting his nest *k* on high
to escape the clutches of ruin!
10 You have plotted the ruin *l* of many peoples,
  shaming *m* your own house and forfeiting your life.
11 The stones *n* of the wall will cry out,
  and the beams of the woodwork will echo it.

12 "Woe to him who builds a city with bloodshed *o*
  and establishes a town by injustice!
13 Has not the LORD Almighty determined
  that the people's labor is only fuel for the fire, *p*
  that the nations exhaust themselves for nothing? *q*
14 For the earth will be filled with the knowledge of the glory *r* of the LORD
  as the waters cover the sea. *s*

---

a 3 Or *Though he linger, wait for him; / he*   *b* 4 Or *faith*

2:4 *he.* Collective for the Babylonians, but with special reference to their king. *but.* In contrast to the Babylonians, whose "desires are not upright." *the righteous will live by their faithfulness.* See TNIV text note; Eze 18:9; see also Isa 26, especially vv. 1–6. In light of God's revelation about how (and when) he is working, his people are to wait patiently and live by faith—trusting in their sovereign God. The clause is quoted frequently in the NT to support the teaching that people are saved by grace through faith (Ro 1:17; Gal 3:11; cf. Eph 2:8 and note) and should live by faith (Heb 10:38–39; 11:7). Together with Ge 15:6 (see note there; see also Ro 4:3,9, 22–23; Gal 3:6; Jas 2:23 and note on 2:21), it became the rallying cry of the Protestant Reformation in the 16th century. The same principle that was applicable in the realm of national deliverance is applicable in the area of spiritual deliverance (salvation).
2:5 *greedy as the grave.* The grave never says, "Enough" (see Isa 5:14 and note; see also Pr 30:15–16 and notes on Ps 49:14; Pr 30:16).
2:6–20 This taunt, an extended commentary on v. 4a (see note on 3:1), falls into two halves of ten (Hebrew) lines each (vv. 6–14 and vv. 15–20), each half concluding with a significant theological statement (vv. 14,20). Together these two statements set the

five "woes" pronounced against Babylon (vv. 6,9, 12,15,19; cf. Isa 5:8–23; Mt 23:13–32; Lk 6:24–26; Rev 9:12; 11:14) in a larger frame of reference. In addition, the first and fourth "woes" echo each other (see vv. 8,17).
2:6 *all of them taunt him.* The threatened victims of the Babylonian onslaught, especially Judah, will taunt ruthless Babylon (see Isa 14:4). *Woe.* The Babylonians' greed for conquest is condemned.
2:8 *you have shed human blood.* See v. 17. Therefore Babylon's blood would be shed (see Ge 9:6 and note).
2:9 *Woe.* The Babylonians' pride in building is condemned (see v. 12; cf. Jer 22:13). *nest on high.* Like the eagle building an inaccessible nest, the Babylonians thought their empire to be unconquerable (see Isa 14:4,13–15; cf. Ob 3–4).
2:11 *The stones . . . will cry out, and the beams.* The stones and beams in Babylonian houses were purchased with plunder and thus testified against the occupants. Cf. Lk 19:40.
2:12 *Woe.* Babylonian injustice is condemned. Cf. Mic 3:10; Zec 8:16 and note.
2:13 *fuel for the fire.* The cities built by the labor of the Babylonians (v. 12) will be burned (see Jer 51:58 and note).

¹⁵"Woe to him who gives drink^t to his neighbors,
    pouring it from the wineskin till they are drunk,
    so that he can gaze on their naked bodies!
¹⁶You will be filled with shame^u instead of glory.^v
    Now it is your turn! Drink^w and let your nakedness be exposed^a!^x
    The cup^y from the LORD's right hand is coming around to you,
    and disgrace will cover your glory.
¹⁷The violence^z you have done to Lebanon will overwhelm you,
    and your destruction of animals will terrify you.^a
    For you have shed human blood;^b
    you have destroyed lands and cities and everyone in them.

¹⁸"Of what value^c is an idol^d that someone has carved?
    Or an image^e that teaches lies?
    For those who make them trust in their own creations;
    they make idols that cannot speak.^f
¹⁹Woe to him who says to wood, 'Come to life!'
    Or to lifeless stone, 'Wake up!'^g
    Can it give guidance?
    It is covered with gold and silver;^h
    there is no breath in it."ⁱ

²⁰The LORD is in his holy temple;^j
    let all the earth be silent^k before him.

HABAKKUK'S PRAYER

3 A prayer of Habakkuk the prophet. On *shigionoth*.^b*^l*

²LORD, I have heard^m of your fame;
    I stand in aweⁿ of your deeds, LORD.^o
    Renew^p them in our day,
    in our time make them known;
    in wrath remember mercy.^q

³God came from Teman,^r
    the Holy One^s from Mount Paran.^c^t

^a 16 Masoretic Text; Dead Sea Scrolls, Aquila, Vulgate and Syriac (see also Septuagint) *and stagger*
^b 1 Probably a literary or musical term   ^c 3 The Hebrew has *Selah* (a word of uncertain meaning) here and at the middle of verse 9 and at the end of verse 13.

2:14 Habakkuk quotes Isa 11:9 and expands its language. The Lord's future destruction of proud Babylonia and all her worldly glory will cause his greater glory to be known throughout the world (cf. Ex 14:4,17–18; Rev 17:1—19:4).

2:15 Cf. Ge 9:20–22. *Woe.* Babylonian violence is condemned. Her rapacious treatment of her neighbors, which stripped them of all their wealth (cf. what she later did to Jerusalem, 2Ki 25:8–21), is compared to one who makes her neighbors drunk so he can take lewd pleasure from their nakedness.

2:16 *be filled with shame … be exposed.* The Lord will do to Babylonia what she has done to others (see note on Ob 15). *cup from the LORD's right hand.* A symbol of divine retribution (see Ps 16:5 and note; Isa 51:17,21–22; Jer 25:15–17; La 4:21; Rev 14:10 and note; 16:19; see also note on Na 3:11).

2:17 *violence you have done to Lebanon.* The Babylonians apparently had ravaged the cedar forests of Lebanon to adorn their temples and palaces (see Isa 14:8 and note). *destruction of animals.* Assyrian inscriptions record hunting expeditions in the Lebanon range, and such sport may have been indulged in by the invading Babylonians as well. Babylonian violence was destructive of all forms of life, not only of lands and cities. *you have shed human blood.* See v. 8 and note.

2:18 *idols.* The Hebrew for this word means "godlets" or "nonentities" (cf. Isa 41:29; 44:9; Jer 10:15 and the condemnation of idolatry in Ex 20:4–5; see Ps 115:4–7 and note).

2:19 *Woe.* Babylonian idolatry is condemned. *Wake up!* Cf. Elijah's taunt of Baal's prophets on Mount Carmel (1Ki 18:27).

2:20 *The LORD is in his holy temple.* From his heavenly temple (cf. Jnh 2:7) he judges all people in accordance with his righteousness (see Ps 11:4–7 and note; Mic 1:2). *be silent before him.* The stone and wooden idols of the nations (v. 19) are to be silent in unprotecting submission to the awesome divine judgment (see Zep 1:7; Zec 2:13; cf. Am 6:10; 8:3 and note).

3:1 *prayer.* In the strict sense, petition is found in this prayer only in v. 2 but, as with many of the psalms, it is set in a larger context of recollection (vv. 3–15) and expression of confidence and trust (vv. 16–19). In fact, Habakkuk's prayer, an extended commentary on 2:4b (see note on 2:6–20), appears to have been used as a psalm; note the psalm-like heading (v. 1) and the musical and/or literary notations (vv. 1,3 [see TNIV text note on this verse],9,13,19). *prophet.* See 1:1 and note. *shigionoth.* See Ps 7 title and note.

3:2 *heard of your fame.* See Ps 44:1; 78:3. In vv. 3–15 Habakkuk recites a poetic celebration of God's mighty, saving acts of old—perhaps one he had heard at the temple (see v. 16).

3:3 *God came.* When celebrating the exodus, the OT poets (and poet-prophets) combined recollections of the mighty acts of God with conventional images of a fearsome manifestation of the Lord. He came down with his heavenly host and rode on the mighty thunderstorm as his chariot, with his arrows (lightning

---

(Right margin cross-references:)

2:15 ^tS Pr 23:20
2:16 ^uS ver 10
    ^vS Eze 23:32-34;
    Hos 4:7 ^wS Lev 10:9
    ^xS La 4:21
    ^yS Ps 16:5;
    S Isa 51:22
2:17 ^zS Jer 51:35
    ^aS Jer 50:15 ^bver 8
2:18 ^cS 1Sa 12:21
    ^dS Jdg 10:14;
    S Isa 40:19;
    S Jer 5:21; S 14:22
    ^eS Lev 26:1
    ^fPs 115:4-5; Jer 10:14;
    1Co 12:2
2:19 ^g1Ki 18:27
    ^hS Jer 10:4 ⁱS Da 5:4,
    23; S Hos 4:12
2:20 ^jS Ps 11:4
    ^kS Isa 41:1
3:1 ^lPs 7 Title
3:2 ^mS Job 26:14;
    Ps 44:1 ⁿS Ps 119:120
    ^oS Ps 90:16 ^pPs 85:6
    ^qIsa 54:8
3:3 ^rS Ge 36:11,15
    ^sIsa 31:1 ^tS Nu 10:12

3:3 ᵘ S Ps 8:1
ᵛ Ps 48:10
3:4 ʷ S Isa 18:4
ˣ S Job 9:6
3:5 ʸ S Lev 26:25
3:6 ᶻ S Ps 46:2
ᵃ Ge 49:26
ᵇ S Ex 19:18; Ps 18:7;
114:1-6 ᶜ S Ge 21:33
3:7 ᵈ S Ge 25:2;
S Nu 25:15; Jdg 7:24-
25 ᵉ Ex 15:14
3:8 ᶠ S Ex 7:20
ᵍ S Ps 77:16
ʰ S 2Ki 2:11;
S Ps 68:17
3:9 ⁱ S Dt 32:23;
Ps 7:12-13
3:10 ʲ S Ps 77:16
ᵏ Ps 98:7 ⁱ Ps 93:3
3:11 ᵐ Jos 10:13
ⁿ Ps 18:14
ᵒ S Ps 144:6; Zec 9:14
3:12 ᵖ S Isa 41:15
3:13 �q S Ex 13:21
ʳ S Ps 20:6; S 28:8
ˢ S 2Sa 23:1
ᵗ Ps 68:21; 110:6
3:14 ᵘ Jdg 7:22
ᵛ Ps 64:2-5
3:15 ʷ S Job 9:8
ˣ Ex 15:8

His glory covered the heavens ᵘ
    and his praise filled the earth. ᵛ
⁴ His splendor was like the sunrise; ʷ
    rays flashed from his hand,
    where his power ˣ was hidden.
⁵ Plague ʸ went before him;
    pestilence followed his steps.
⁶ He stood, and shook the earth;
    he looked, and made the nations tremble.
The ancient mountains crumbled ᶻ
    and the age-old hills ᵃ collapsed ᵇ—
    but he marches on forever. ᶜ
⁷ I saw the tents of Cushan in distress,
    the dwellings of Midian ᵈ in anguish. ᵉ

⁸ Were you angry with the rivers, ᶠ LORD?
    Was your wrath against the streams?
Did you rage against the sea ᵍ
    when you rode your horses
    and your chariots to victory? ʰ
⁹ You uncovered your bow,
    you called for many arrows. ⁱ
You split the earth with rivers;
¹⁰   the mountains saw you and writhed. ʲ
Torrents of water swept by;
    the deep roared ᵏ
    and lifted its waves ⁱ on high.

¹¹ Sun and moon stood still ᵐ in the heavens
    at the glint of your flying arrows, ⁿ
    at the lightning ᵒ of your flashing spear.
¹² In wrath you strode through the earth
    and in anger you threshed ᵖ the nations.
¹³ You came out q to deliver ʳ your people,
    to save your anointed ˢ one.
You crushed ᵗ the leader of the land of wickedness,
    you stripped him from head to foot.
¹⁴ With his own spear you pierced his head
    when his warriors stormed out to scatter us, ᵘ
    gloating as though about to devour
    the wretched ᵛ who were in hiding.
¹⁵ You trampled the sea ʷ with your horses,
    churning the great waters. ˣ

---

bolts; see note on Ps 18:14) flying in all directions, a cloudburst of rain descending on the earth and the mountains quaking before him (see Jdg 5:4–5; Ps 18:7–15; 68:7–10; 77:16–19; Mic 1:3 and notes). Such figures characterize many of the references in the following verses. *Teman.* Means "southland." God is pictured during the exodus as coming from the area south of Judah. *Mount Paran.* See Dt 33:2 and note; probably northwest of the Gulf of Aqaba and south of Kadesh Barnea, between Edom and Sinai. For *Selah* see TNIV text note and Introduction to Psalms: Authorship and Titles (or Superscriptions), last paragraph. *filled the earth.* See note on 2:14.

3:5 *Plague . . . pestilence.* Means of divine punishment (cf. Ex 7:14—12:30; Lev 26:25; Ps 91:3,6).

3:6 God's presence was frequently marked by earthquakes (see Ex 19:18; Ps 18:7; Jer 4:24; 10:10; Na 1:5). Landslides may also be alluded to here.

3:7 *Cushan . . . Midian.* Arab tribes living near Edom. *distress . . . anguish.* When Israel was delivered from Egypt under Moses, neighboring peoples were filled with fear (see Ex 15:14–16; Jos 2:9–10).

3:8 Poetic allusions to the plague on the Nile (Ex 7:20–24)

and/or the stopping of the Jordan (Jos 3:15–17), as well as to the parting of the Red Sea (Ex 14:15–31).

3:9 *arrows.* Probably lightning bolts unleashed by the heavenly archer (see Ps 18:14 and note; 144:6). *rivers.* Caused by the accompanying thunderstorms.

3:11 *Sun and moon stood still.* Probably an allusion to the victory at Gibeon (see Jos 10:12–13 and note on 10:13), indicating that God's triumph over his enemies would be just as complete as on that occasion.

3:12 *threshed.* See note on Am 1:3.

3:13 *deliver your people.* God fought against the nations of Canaan (v. 12) but delivered his people. *save.* By giving victory to. *anointed one.* The covenant nation ("your people"; see Ps 28:9), the "kingdom of priests" (Ex 19:6; see note there), which God came to deliver. He destroyed the enemy and in this great act of wrath (v. 12) remembered mercy (v. 2). *leader of the land of wickedness.* The pharaoh (see Ex 14:5–9).

3:14–15 Another reference to the destruction of the Egyptians in the Red Sea. God will likewise vanquish present foes.

3:15 *horses.* See v. 8 and note.

¹⁶I heard and my heart pounded,
    my lips quivered at the sound;
decay crept into my bones,
    and my legs trembled. ^y
Yet I will wait patiently ^z for the day of calamity
    to come on the nation invading us.
¹⁷Though the fig tree does not bud
    and there are no grapes on the vines,
though the olive crop fails
    and the fields produce no food, ^a
though there are no sheep in the pen
    and no cattle in the stalls, ^b
¹⁸yet I will rejoice in the LORD, ^c
    I will be joyful in God my Savior. ^d

¹⁹The Sovereign LORD is my strength; ^e
    he makes my feet like the feet of a deer,
    he enables me to tread on the heights. ^f

For the director of music. On my stringed instruments.

3:16 ^y S Job 4:14
^z S Ps 37:7
3:17 ^a Joel 1:10-12,
18 ^b Jer 5:17
3:18 ^c Ps 97:12;
S Isa 61:10; Php 4:4
^d S Ex 15:2; S Lk 1:47
3:19 ^e S Dt 33:29;
Ps 46:1-5 ^f S Dt 32:13;
Ps 18:33

3:16 The hymnic recollection of God's mighty deeds of old in Israel's behalf (vv. 3–15) fills the prophet with an awe so profound that he feels physically weak. Alternatively, it is possible that the message from the Lord that Babylon would be sent against Judah (1:5–11) had so devastated him that he felt ill—until he heard the Lord's further word. *wait patiently.* See 2:3 and note; Ps 37:7. *nation invading us.* Babylonia.
3:17 Probably anticipates the awful results of the imminent Babylonian invasion and devastation.

3:18–19 Habakkuk has learned the lesson of faith (2:4)—to trust in God's providence regardless of circum-

stances. He declares that even if God should send suffering and loss, he would still rejoice in God his Savior—one of the strongest affirmations of faith in all Scripture.
3:18 *rejoice in the LORD.* See Ps 32:11; Php 3:1; 4:4. *be joyful in God my Savior.* See Lk 1:47.

3:19 *makes my feet like the feet of a deer.* Gives me surefooted confidence (see Ps 18:33). *director.* Probably the conductor of the temple musicians. This chapter may have formed part of the temple prayers that were chanted with the accompaniment of instruments (see 1Ch 16:4–7). *stringed instruments.* Including harp and lyre (Ps 33:2; 92:3; 144:9).

ZEPHANIAH

AUTHOR

INTRODUCTION

ZEPHANIAH

C The prophet Zephaniah was evidently a person of considerable social standing in Judah and was probably related to the royal line. The prophecy opens with a statement of the author's ancestry (1:1), which in itself is an unusual feature of the Hebrew prophetic tradition. Zephaniah was a fourth-generation descendant of Hezekiah, a notable king of Judah from 715 to 686 B.C. Apart from this statement, nothing more is said about his background. Whereas the prophet Micah dealt carefully and sympathetically with the problems of the common people of Judah, Zephaniah's utterances show a much greater familiarity with court circles and current political issues. Zephaniah was probably familiar with the writings of such prominent eighth-century prophets as Isaiah and Amos, whose utterances he reflects, and he may also have been aware of the ministry of the young Jeremiah.

DATE

According to 1:1, Zephaniah prophesied during the reign of King Josiah (640–609 B.C.), making him a contemporary of Jeremiah, Nahum and perhaps Habakkuk. His prophecy is probably to be dated relatively early in Josiah's reign, before that king's attempt at reform (and while conditions brought about by the reigns of Manasseh and Amon still prevailed) and before the Assyrian king Ashurbanipal's death in 627 (while Assyria was still powerful, though threatened).

BACKGROUND

See Introductions to Jeremiah and Nahum: Background; see also 2Ki 22:1—23:30; 2Ch 34:1—36:1 and notes.

PURPOSE AND THEOLOGICAL THEME

The intent of the author was to announce to Judah God's approaching judgment. A Scythian incursion into Canaan may have provided the immediate occasion. This fierce, horse-mounted people originated in what is now southern Russia, but by the seventh century B.C. they had migrated across the Caucasus and settled in and along the northern territories of the Assyrian empire. Alternately the enemies and allies of Assyria, they seem to have thrust south along the Mediterranean sometime in the 620s, destroying Ashkelon and Ashdod and halting at the Egyptian border only because of a payoff by Pharaoh Psamtik (Psammetichus). Ultimately, however, the destruction prophesied by Zephaniah came at the hands of the Babylonians after they had overpowered Assyria and brought that ancient power to its end.

Zephaniah's main theme is the coming of the day of the Lord (see notes on Isa 2:11,17,20; Joel 1:15; 2:2; Am 5:18; 8:9), when God will severely punish the nations, including apostate Judah. Zephaniah portrays the stark horror of that ordeal with the same graphic imagery found elsewhere in the prophets. But he also makes it clear that God will yet be merciful toward his people; like many other prophets, he ends his pronouncements of doom on the positive note of Judah's restoration by Yahweh, "King of Israel" (3:15; see note there).

OUTLINE

I. Introduction (1:1–3)
    A. Title: The Prophet Identified (1:1)
    B. Prologue: Double Announcement of Total Judgment (1:2–3)
II. The Day of the Lord Coming on Judah and the Nations (1:4–18)
    A. Judgment on the Idolaters in Judah (1:4–9)
    B. Wailing throughout Jerusalem (1:10–13)
    C. The Inescapable Day of the Lord's Wrath (1:14–18)
III. God's Judgment on the Nations (2:1—3:8)
    A. Call to Judah to Repent (2:1–3)
    B. Judgment on Philistia (2:4–7)
    C. Judgment on Moab and Ammon (2:8–11)
    D. Judgment on Cush (2:12)
    E. Judgment on Assyria (2:13–15)
    F. Judgment on Jerusalem (3:1–5)
    G. Jerusalem's Refusal to Repent (3:6–8)
IV. Redemption of the Remnant (3:9–20)
    A. The Nations Purified, the Remnant Restored, Jerusalem Purged (3:9–13)
    B. Rejoicing in the City (3:14–17)
    C. The Nation Restored (3:18–20)

1:1 *a* 2Ki 22:1;
2Ch 34:1–35:25
b S 1Ch 3:14
1:2 *c* S Ge 6:7
1:3 *d* Jer 50:3
e S Jer 4:25 *f* ver 18;
S Hos 4:3
g S Eze 14:17
1:4 *h* S Jer 6:12
i Mic 5:13; Zep 2:11
j S Jer 15:6;
S Hos 10:5
1:5 *k* S Jer 8:2
l S Lev 18:21; Jer 5:7
1:6 *m* Isa 1:4;
Jer 2:13 *n* S Isa 9:13
o S Hos 7:7
1:7 *p* S Isa 41:1
q ver 14; Isa 13:6;
S Eze 7:19;
S Joel 3:14;
S Am 5:18-20
r S Lev 3:9;
S Jer 46:10
1:8 *s* Isa 24:21
t Jer 39:6
1:9 *u* 1Sa 5:5
v S Am 3:10

1

The word of the LORD that came to Zephaniah son of Cushi, the son of Gedaliah, the son of Amariah, the son of Hezekiah, during the reign of Josiah *a* son of Amon *b* king of Judah:

JUDGMENT ON THE WHOLE EARTH IN THE DAY OF THE LORD

² "I will sweep away everything
  from the face of the earth," *c*
                                    declares the LORD.
³ "I will sweep away both people and animals; *d*
  I will sweep away the birds in the sky *e*
  and the fish in the sea—
  and the idols that cause the wicked to stumble." *a*

  "When I destroy all people
  on the face of the earth," *f*
                                    declares the LORD, *g*
⁴ "I will stretch out my hand *h* against Judah
  and against all who live in Jerusalem.
 I will destroy every remnant of Baal worship in this place, *i*
  every remembrance of the idolatrous priests *j*—
⁵ those who bow down on the roofs
  to worship the starry host, *k*
 those who bow down and swear by the LORD
  and who also swear by Molek, *b l*
⁶ those who turn back from following *m* the LORD
  and neither seek *n* the LORD nor inquire *o* of him."

⁷ Be silent *p* before the Sovereign LORD,
  for the day of the LORD *q* is near.
 The LORD has prepared a sacrifice; *r*
  he has consecrated those he has invited.

⁸ "On the day of the LORD's sacrifice
  I will punish *s* the officials
  and the king's sons *t*
 and all those clad
  in foreign clothes.
⁹ On that day I will punish
  all who avoid stepping on the threshold, *c u*
 who fill the temple of their gods
  with violence and deceit. *v*

a 3 The meaning of the Hebrew for this line is uncertain.   *b* 5 Hebrew *Malkam*   *c* 9 See 1 Samuel 5:5.

1:1 *word of the LORD.* A common introductory phrase in the prophets (see Jer 1:2; Hos 1:1 and notes). *Zephaniah.* Means "The LORD hides" or "The LORD protects," perhaps implying a prayer for God's protection of the child Zephaniah during the infamous reign of Manasseh. *son of ... Hezekiah.* Judging from the author's pedigree, it is likely that he was in his early 20s when he began to prophesy. He is more closely identified with the ruling class than was Isaiah, although Isaiah also moved regularly in court circles and was perhaps of noble birth.
1:2–3 *sweep away.* Zephaniah speaks of the coming catastrophe in language reminiscent of God's utterances prior to the flood (Ge 6:7). But this time it will be by God's fire (v. 18; 3:8).
1:3 *idols that cause the wicked to stumble.* See TNIV text note; see also Ps 115:4–8; Isa 44:9–20; Hos 8:4–8; 9:10 and notes.
1:4–6 Seems to indicate that Zephaniah's main ministry took place before 621 B.C., since the practices condemned here were abolished in Josiah's reforms (see 2Ki 23:4–16 and notes). Perhaps Zephaniah's message was partly instrumental in motivating King Josiah to undertake his reforms (cf. 2Ch 34:1–7).
1:4 Judah is censured for its unrepentant participation in the gross idolatry of Baal worship. *Baal.* See note on Jdg 2:13. *this place.* Jerusalem, where Zephaniah probably lived.
1:5 *on the roofs.* See 2Ki 23:12; Jer 19:13 and notes. *worship the*

starry host. See Dt 4:19; 2Ki 17:16 and note; 21:3; Isa 47:13. *swear by the LORD ... also swear by Molek.* Syncretism (worship of one's own god along with other gods). *Molek.* Worshiped by the Ammonites, his rituals sometimes involved child sacrifice. Molek worship was forbidden to the Israelites (see Lev 18:21 and note; 20:1–5). Despite this, Solomon set up an altar to Molek on the Mount of Olives (1Ki 11:7). Manasseh established the rituals in the Valley of Ben Hinnom (see 2Ch 33:6; Jer 7:31 and note; 32:35).
1:7 *Be silent before the Sovereign LORD.* See Hab 2:20 and note. *day of the LORD.* Zephaniah's main theme (see Introduction: Purpose and Theological Theme); not of deliverance for Judah but of divine vengeance on the idolatrous covenant nation. See notes on Isa 2:11,17,20; 10:20,27; Joel 1:15; Am 5:18. *sacrifice.* The victim is Judah. *consecrated.* Since the coming slaughter of judgment is called a sacrifice, God's preparation of his guests is called his consecration of them—in preparation for their feasting on the plunder. *those ... invited.* The pagan conquerors (mainly Babylonia).
1:8 *foreign clothes.* Dress that indicated conformity to Babylonian, Egyptian or Assyrian ways.
1:9 *avoid stepping on the threshold.* Perhaps referring to a pagan custom that began in the time of Samuel (see 1Sa 5:5 and note).

[10] "On that day,[w]
  declares the LORD,
"a cry will go up from the Fish Gate,[x]
  wailing[y] from the New Quarter,
  and a loud crash from the hills.
[11] Wail,[z] you who live in the market district[a];
  all your merchants will be wiped out,
  all who trade with[b] silver will be destroyed. [a]
[12] At that time I will search Jerusalem with lamps
  and punish those who are complacent,[b]
  who are like wine left on its dregs,[c]
  who think, 'The LORD will do nothing,[d]
  either good or bad.'[e]
[13] Their wealth will be plundered,[f]
  their houses demolished.
Though they build houses,
  they will not live in them;
though they plant vineyards,
  they will not drink the wine."[g]

[14] The great day of the LORD[h] is near[i]—
  near and coming quickly.
The cry on the day of the LORD is bitter;
  the Mighty Warrior shouts his battle cry.
[15] That day will be a day of wrath—
  a day of distress and anguish,
    a day of trouble and ruin,
    a day of darkness[j] and gloom,
      a day of clouds and blackness[k]—
[16]   a day of trumpet and battle cry[l]
against the fortified cities
  and against the corner towers.[m]

[17] "I will bring such distress[n] on all people
  that they will grope about like those who are blind,[o]
  because they have sinned against the LORD.
Their blood will be poured out[p] like dust
  and their entrails like dung. [q]
[18] Neither their silver nor their gold
  will be able to save them
  on the day of the LORD's wrath."[r]

In the fire of his jealousy[s]
  the whole earth will be consumed,[t]
for he will make a sudden end
  of all who live on the earth. [u]

---

[a] 11 Or *the Mortar*   [b] 11 Or *in*

1:10 [w] Isa 22:5
[x] S 2Ch 33:14
[y] S Am 5:16
1:11 [z] Jas 5:1
[a] Hos 9:6
1:12 [b] Am 6:1
[c] Jer 48:11
[d] S 2Ki 21:16;
S Eze 8:12
[e] S Job 22:13
1:13 [f] S 2Ki 24:13;
Jer 15:13 [g] Dt 28:30,
39; La 5:2; S Am 5:11
1:14 [h] S ver 7;
S Joel 1:15 [i] S Eze 7:7;
S Da 7:13
1:15 [j] S Isa 2:9
[k] S Am 22:5; Joel 2:2;
Mk 13:24-25
1:16 [l] S Jer 4:19
[m] S Dt 28:52;
S Isa 2:15; S Joel 2:1
1:17 [n] S Dt 28:52
[o] S Isa 59:10
[p] Ps 79:3 [q] S Ps 83:10
1:18 [r] S Job 20:20;
S 40:11; S Jer 4:4;
S Eze 7:19
[s] S Dt 29:20 [t] S ver 2-
3; Zep 3:8 [u] S Ge 6:7;
S Eze 7:11

1:10–13 Wailing throughout the city (contrast 3:14–17).
  1:10 Merchants who had grown rich through corrupt
  business practices would be destroyed. *Fish Gate.* In the
north wall of the city (see note on Ne 3:3). Jerusalem was most
vulnerable to attacks from the north. *New Quarter.* See note on
2Ki 22:14.
1:11 *market district.* May have been an area in the Tyropoeon
Valley (see note on Ne 2:13).
1:12 *search Jerusalem with lamps.* The Babylonians later dragged
people from houses, streets, sewers and tombs, where they had
hidden. *like wine left on its dregs.* See Isa 25:6 and note. *The LORD will
do nothing.* A typical depiction of the arrogance of the wicked (see
note on Ps 10:11).

1:13 The assets of those who have become wealthy
  through dishonesty will be exposed and plundered (see
Dt 28:30).
1:14–18 In a dramatic passage of great lyrical power, the Lord
describes the destruction that will sweep the earth in the day of
God's wrath.
1:15 *That day will be a day of wrath.* The inspiration for Thomas
of Celano's great medieval hymn, *Dies Irae Dies Illa* (c. A.D. 1250).
darkness . . . blackness. See Am 5:18–20.
1:17 *like those who are blind.* See Dt 28:28–29.
  1:18 *Neither . . . silver nor . . . gold will . . . save them.* In the
  day of God's judgment, material wealth cannot buy deliverance from punishment. *fire of his jealousy.* See vv. 2–3 and
note; 3:8.

2:1 ᵛ2Ch 20:4;
Joel 1:14 ʷS Jer 3:3;
6:15
2:2 ˣIsa 17:13;
Hos 13:3
ʸS Jer 10:25;
S La 4:11 ᶻS Jer 4:4;
S Eze 7:19
2:3 ᵃS Am 5:6
ᵇS Isa 1:17 ᶜPs 45:4
ᵈPs 57:1
2:4 ᵉS Ge 10:19;
S Am 1:6-8; Zec 9:5-7
ᶠJer 47:5
2:5 ᵍS 1Sa 30:14
ʰS Lev 26:31; Am 3:1
ⁱS Isa 14:30
2:6 ʲS Isa 5:17
2:7 ᵏS Ge 45:7
ˡS Dt 30:3; Ps 126:4;
Jer 32:44; S Hos 6:11;
S Joel 3:1; Am 1:6-8
2:8 ᵐS Jer 48:27
ⁿS Ge 19:37;
S Isa 16:6
ᵒS Eze 21:28
ᵖEze 25:3 ᵠS La 3:61
ʳS Dt 23:6; Isa 15:1-
16:14; Jer 48:1-47;
Eze 25:8-11
ˢDt 29:23; Isa 13:19;
Jer 49:18

JUDAH AND JERUSALEM JUDGED ALONG WITH THE NATIONS

JUDAH SUMMONED TO REPENT

2 Gather together, ᵛ gather yourselves together,
you shameful ʷ nation,
² before the decree takes effect
and that day passes like windblown chaff, ˣ
before the LORD's fierce anger ʸ
comes upon you,
before the day of the LORD's wrath ᶻ
comes upon you.
³ Seek ᵃ the LORD, all you humble of the land,
you who do what he commands.
Seek righteousness, ᵇ seek humility; ᶜ
perhaps you will be sheltered ᵈ
on the day of the LORD's anger.

PHILISTIA

⁴ Gaza ᵉ will be abandoned
and Ashkelon ᶠ left in ruins.
At midday Ashdod will be emptied
and Ekron uprooted.
⁵ Woe to you who live by the sea,
you Kerethite ᵍ people;
the word of the LORD is against you, ʰ
Canaan, land of the Philistines.
He says, "I will destroy you,
and none will be left." ⁱ
⁶ The land by the sea will become pastures
having wells for shepherds
and pens for flocks. ʲ
⁷ That land will belong
to the remnant ᵏ of the house of Judah;
there they will find pasture.
In the evening they will lie down
in the houses of Ashkelon.
The LORD their God will care for them;
he will restore their fortunes. ᵃ ˡ

MOAB AND AMMON

⁸ "I have heard the insults ᵐ of Moab ⁿ
and the taunts of the Ammonites, ᵒ
who insulted ᵖ my people
and made threats against their land. ᵠ
⁹ Therefore, as surely as I live,"
declares the LORD Almighty,
the God of Israel,
"surely Moab ʳ will become like Sodom, ˢ

ᵃ 7 Or will bring back their captives

2:1–3 The prophet's exhortation to Judah to repent. This call to repentance and the later indictment of Jerusalem for refusal to repent (see 3:6–8 and note) frame the series of judgments that illustratively detail God's acts in the coming day of the Lord (2:4—3:5).
2:2 like windblown chaff. See Ps 1:4 and note; 35:5; Isa 17:13; 29:5; Hos 13:3.
2:3 Seek the LORD. Even though destruction is imminent, there is still time to be sheltered from the calamity if only the nation will repent (see Am 5:4 and note). humble. Those who abandon the arrogance of their idolatry and wickedness and "seek humility."
2:4—3:8 God's coming judgment on the nations—including Jerusalem (see Am 1:3—2:16 and note).

2:4 Gaza … Ashkelon … Ashdod … Ekron. Philistine cities located west of Judah "by the sea" (vv. 5–6; see notes on Am 1:6,8; see also map, p. 338).
2:5 Kerethite. See note on 1Sa 30:14. Canaan. See note on Ge 10:6. I … left. The Lord's announced purpose.
2:6 The once-populous Philistine cities will revert to pastureland.
2:7 The faithful remnant of Judah will occupy this land and graze their flocks on it. restore their fortunes. See TNIV text note. Here and in vv. 9,11 the prophet anticipates the ultimate outcome of the day of the Lord, which he spells out more fully in 3:9–20.
2:8 Moab … Ammonites. Peoples living east of Judah (see notes on Ge 19:36–38; Am 1:13; 2:3). For the hostility of Ammon and Moab toward Israel, see Am 1:13; 2:3. They had often threatened to occupy Israelite territory (see Jdg 11:13 and note; Eze 25:2–7).

the Ammonites[t] like Gomorrah—
a place of weeds and salt pits,
a wasteland forever.
The remnant of my people will plunder[u] them;
the survivors[v] of my nation will inherit their land.[w]"

[10] This is what they will get in return for their pride,[x]
for insulting[y] and mocking
the people of the LORD Almighty.[z]
[11] The LORD will be awesome[a] to them
when he destroys all the gods[b] of the earth.[c]
Distant nations will bow down to him,[d]
all of them in their own lands.

CUSH

[12] "You Cushites,[a][e] too,
will be slain by my sword.[f]"

ASSYRIA

[13] He will stretch out his hand against the north
and destroy Assyria,[g]
leaving Nineveh[h] utterly desolate
and dry as the desert.[i]
[14] Flocks and herds[j] will lie down there,
creatures of every kind.
The desert owl[k] and the screech owl[l][m]
will roost on her columns.
Their hooting will echo through the windows,
rubble will fill the doorways,
the beams of cedar will be exposed.
[15] This is the city of revelry[n]
that lived in safety.[o]
She said to herself,
"I am the one! And there is none besides me."[p]
What a ruin she has become,
a lair for wild beasts![q]
All who pass by her scoff[r]
and shake their fists.[s]

JERUSALEM

3

Woe to the city of oppressors,[t]
rebellious[u] and defiled![v]
[2] She obeys[w] no one,
she accepts no correction.[x]
She does not trust[y] in the LORD,
she does not draw near[z] to her God.
[3] Her officials within her
are roaring lions;[a]
her rulers are evening wolves,[b]

---

[a] 12 That is, people from the upper Nile region

2:8 [t] Jer 49:1-6;
Eze 25:1-7
[u] S Isa 11:14
[v] S 2Ki 19:31
[w] S Am 2:1-3
2:10 [x] S Job 40:12;
S Isa 16:6
[y] S Jer 48:27
[z] S Ps 9:6
2:11 [a] S Joel 2:11
[b] S Zep 1:4
[c] S 1Ch 19:1;
Eze 25:6-7 [d] Ps 86:9;
S Isa 12:4; Zep 3:9
2:12 [e] S Ge 10:6;
S Isa 20:4
[f] S Jer 46:10
2:13 [g] S Isa 10:5
[h] S Ge 10:11; S Na 1:1
[i] S Mic 5:6; Zec 10:11
2:14 [j] S Isa 5:17
[k] S Isa 14:23
[l] Rev 18:2
[m] S Ps 102:6
2:15 [n] S Isa 32:9
[o] Isa 47:8 [p] Eze 28:2
[q] Jer 49:33
[r] S Isa 28:22;
S Na 3:19
[s] S Eze 27:36
3:1 [t] S Jer 6:6
[u] S Dt 21:18
[v] S Eze 23:30
3:2 [w] S Jer 22:21
[x] S Lev 26:23;
S Jer 7:28 [y] S Dt 1:32
[z] S Ps 73:28
3:3 [a] S Ps 22:13
[b] S Ge 49:27

2:9 *Sodom . . . Gomorrah.* See Ge 19. They were used in the OT to typify complete destruction at the hands of God (see Am 4:11 and note), and their mention added ominous overtones to the prophet's description of the day of the Lord. *weeds.* A symbol of depopulation (cf. Isa 7:23–25). *remnant . . . will inherit their land.* See note on v. 7.
2:10 *in return for their pride, for insulting and mocking.* In reprisal, the faithful remnant will occupy Ammonite and Moabite territory.
2:11 *nations will bow down to him.* See 3:9 and note.
2:12 *You . . . too.* Without elaboration, the prophet simply announces God's purpose against Egypt, located southwest of Judah (see vv. 5,8 and notes). *Cushites.* See TNIV text note. Egypt was ruled from 715 to 663 B.C. by a Cushite dynasty. *my sword.* Probably Babylonia (see Eze 21:9–13,19; see also notes on Ps 7:12–13; Isa 10:5).

2:13 *north.* Although Nineveh was east of Judah, Assyrian armies normally invaded Canaan from the north (see notes on v. 12; 1:10), having first marched west along the Euphrates instead of through the Arabian Desert. *Nineveh.* See the books of Jonah and Nahum. Since Nineveh was destroyed in 612 B.C., Zephaniah's ministry had to be before that date. *utterly desolate.* Even the site of Nineveh was later forgotten—until discovered through modern excavations (see Na 3:17 and note).
2:15 *I am . . . none besides me.* See Isa 47:10. Assyria's boast belongs properly to God alone (see Isa 47:8,10 and note). *has become.* Anticipating Nineveh's impending destruction.
3:1 *city.* Apostate Jerusalem is condemned for its sins. *oppressors.* See Jer 22:3.

3:3 ^cS Mic 3:3
3:4 ^dS Ps 25:3;
S Isa 48:8; Jer 3:20;
9:4; Mal 2:10
^eS Jer 23:11;
S Eze 22:26
3:5 ^fS Ezr 9:15
^gDt 32:4 ^hS Ps 5:3
ⁱS La 3:23 ^jS Jer 3:3;
S Eze 18:25
3:6 ^kS Lev 26:31
3:7 ^lS Jer 7:28
^mS Hos 9:9
3:8 ⁿS Ps 27:14
^oS Joel 3:11
^pS Isa 2:3 ^qPs 79:6;
Rev 16:1 ^rS Jer 10:25;
S La 4:11 ^sS Zep 1:18
3:9 ^tS Zep 2:11
^uS Ge 4:26
^vS Isa 19:18
3:10 ^wS Ge 10:6;
S Ps 68:31
^xS 2Ch 32:23;
S Isa 60:7
3:11 ^yS Isa 29:22;
S Joel 2:26-27
^zS Ge 50:15

who leave nothing for the morning. ^c
⁴ Her prophets are unprincipled;
    they cannot be trusted. ^d
Her priests profane the sanctuary
    and do violence to the law. ^e
⁵ The LORD within her is righteous; ^f
    he does no wrong. ^g
Morning by morning ^h he dispenses his justice,
    and every new day he does not fail, ⁱ
    yet the unrighteous know no shame. ^j

JERUSALEM REMAINS UNREPENTANT

⁶ "I have destroyed nations;
    their strongholds are demolished.
I have left their streets deserted,
    with no one passing through.
Their cities are laid waste; ^k
    they are deserted and empty.
⁷ Of Jerusalem I thought,
    'Surely you will fear me
    and accept correction!' ^l
Then her place of refuge ^a would not be destroyed,
    nor all my punishments come upon ^b her.
But they were still eager
    to act corruptly ^m in all they did.
⁸ Therefore wait ⁿ for me,"
    declares the LORD,
    "for the day I will stand up to testify. ^c
I have decided to assemble ^o the nations, ^p
    to gather the kingdoms
and to pour out my wrath ^q on them—
    all my fierce anger. ^r
The whole world will be consumed ^s
    by the fire of my jealous anger.

RESTORATION OF ISRAEL'S REMNANT

⁹ "Then I will purify the lips of the peoples,
    that all of them may call ^t on the name of the LORD ^u
    and serve ^v him shoulder to shoulder.
¹⁰ From beyond the rivers of Cush ^{d w}
    my worshipers, my scattered people,
    will bring me offerings. ^x
¹¹ On that day you, Jerusalem, will not be put to shame ^y
    for all the wrongs you have done to me, ^z

^a 7 Or *her sanctuary*   ^b 7 Or *all those I appointed over*   ^c 8 Septuagint and Syriac; Hebrew *will rise up to plunder*   ^d 10 That is, the upper Nile region

---

3:3–4 *officials…rulers…prophets…priests.* All classes of Judah's leaders are castigated for indulging in conduct completely opposed to their vocations and responsibilities (see Jer 1:18 and note).
3:3 *roaring lions…evening wolves.* Those in power are rapacious.
3:4 *unprincipled…cannot be trusted.* Claiming to be prophets of the Lord, they proclaimed only lies (see Jer 5:31 and note; 14:14; 23:16,32). *priests…do violence to the law.* When they should have been teachers of the law (see Dt 31:9–13; 2Ch 17:8–9; 19:8; Ezr 7:6; Jer 2:8; 18:18; Mal 2:7).
3:5 *Morning by morning…he does not fail.* Cf. La 3:22–23 and notes.
3:6–8 Jerusalem's refusal to repent (see 2:1–3 and note).
3:6 *I have destroyed nations.* The destruction of other nations was meant to serve as a warning to wanton Judah, but to no avail (see v. 7).
3:7 *eager to act corruptly.* See, e.g., Jer 7:13,25–26.
3:8 *wait.* A sarcastic statement to Judah to wait for the threat-

ened catastrophe. *to testify.* To lodge accusations (see Ps 50:7)—and then proceed to execute judgments. *I have decided.* Or "For I have decided." The Lord concludes his announcement of judgment with a general declaration of his intent. *consumed by the fire of my jealous anger.* See 1:2–3 and note; 1:18; La 1:13 and note.
3:9–20 A three-stanza oracle (vv. 9–13, 14–17, 18–20) announcing redemption that will follow God's judgment.
3:9–13 The Lord gives assurance that the nations will be purified, the scattered remnant restored and Jerusalem purged.
3:9 God's fearful judgment of the nations will effect (or be followed by) their purification, so that they will call on his name and serve him. Israel's God will be acknowledged by the nations, and God's people will be held in honor by them (cf. vv. 19–20).
3:10 *Cush.* See TNIV text note; the most distant area imaginable (see 2:12; Isa 18:1 and notes). The most widely dispersed will be restored. *bring me offerings.* Rather than to Baal and Molek (cf. 1:4–5).

because I will remove from you
   those who revel in your glory. *a*
Never again will you be haughty
   on my holy hill. *b*
¹² But I will leave within you
   the meek *c* and humble.
The remnant of Israel
   will trust *d* in the name of the LORD.
¹³ They *e* will do no wrong; *f*
   they will tell no lies. *g*
A deceitful tongue
   will not be found in their mouths. *h*
They will eat and lie down *i*
   and no one will make them afraid. *j*"

¹⁴ Sing, Daughter Zion; *k*
   shout aloud, *l* Israel!
Be glad and rejoice *m* with all your heart,
   Daughter Jerusalem!
¹⁵ The LORD has taken away your punishment,
   he has turned back your enemy.
The LORD, the King of Israel, is with you; *n*
   never again will you fear *o* any harm. *p*
¹⁶ On that day
   they will say to Jerusalem,
"Do not fear, Zion;
   do not let your hands hang limp. *q*
¹⁷ The LORD your God is with you,
   the Mighty Warrior who saves. *r*
He will take great delight *s* in you;
   in his love he will no longer rebuke you, *t*
   but will rejoice over you with singing." *u*

¹⁸ "I will remove from you
   all who mourn over the loss of your appointed festivals,
   which is a burden and reproach for you.
¹⁹ At that time I will deal
   with all who oppressed *v* you.
I will rescue the lame;
   I will gather the exiles. *w*
I will give them praise *x* and honor
   in every land where they have suffered shame.
²⁰ At that time I will gather you;
   at that time I will bring *y* you home.
I will give you honor *z* and praise *a*
   among all the peoples of the earth
when I restore your fortunes *a* *b*
   before your very eyes,"

says the LORD.

a 20 Or *I bring back your captives*

3:11 *a* S Ps 59:12
b S Ex 15:17;
S Lev 26:19
3:12 *c* Isa 14:32
d Jer 29:12; Na 1:7
3:13 *e* S Isa 10:21
f Ps 119:3; S Isa 4:3
g Jer 33:16; Rev 14:5
h S Job 16:17
i Eze 34:15; Zep 2:7
j S Lev 26:6;
S Eze 34:25-28
3:14 *k* S Ps 9:14;
Zec 2:10 *l* S Ps 95:1;
Isa 12:6; Zec 2:10
m S Ps 9:2; S Isa 51:11
3:15 *n* Eze 37:26-28
o S Isa 54:14
p Zec 9:9
3:16 *q* S 2Ki 19:26;
S Job 4:3; Isa 35:3-4;
Heb 12:12
3:17 *r* S Isa 63:1;
S Joel 2:21
s S Dt 28:63;
S Isa 62:4
t S Hos 14:4
u S Isa 40:1
3:19 *v* S Isa 14:2
w S Eze 34:16;
S Mic 4:6 *x* Isa 60:18
3:20 *y* S Jer 29:14;
S Eze 37:12 *z* Isa 56:5;
66:22 *a* S Dt 26:19;
S Isa 60:18
b S Joel 3:1

3:11 *me./because.* In the Hebrew, this new line begins the same as the first line of v. 9. Hence it may be better to read: "me./Then." Thus vv. 9–11a constitute a three-line unit (in Hebrew) and vv. 11b,c–12 a three-line unit. The latter speaks of a purified Jerusalem. Verse 13 is a summary conclusion. *my holy hill.* Mount Zion (see Ps 2:6 and note).
3:12 *remnant.* See 2:7; Isa 1:9 and notes.
3:13 *no one will make them afraid.* Quoted verbatim from Mic 4:4.
3:14–17 Joy in the restored city (in two parts: vv. 14–15 and vv. 16–17)—the prophet's reassurance (contrast 1:10–13).
3:14 *Daughter Zion … Daughter Jerusalem.* A personification of Jerusalem (see note on 2Ki 19:21).
3:15 *your enemy.* All those arrayed against Israel. *The LORD, the*

King of Israel. See Isa 44:6; see also Introduction to Psalms: Theology: Major Themes.
3:16 *do not let your hands hang limp.* Do not be discouraged (see Jer 47:3 and note).
3:18–20 Summary announcement of restoration—the Lord's final assurance.
3:18 *mourn.* Israel's sorrow at not being able to celebrate its great religious festivals. *appointed festivals.* See Lev 23 and chart, pp. 180–181.
3:19–20 *gather the exiles … give them … gather you … give you.* The level of intimacy increases as the Lord concludes his words of assurance.
3:20 *give you honor and praise.* See v. 19; see also Ge 12:2–3 and note.

AUTHOR HAGGAI | INTRODUCTION

C Haggai (1:1) was a prophet who, along with Zechariah, encouraged the re-turned exiles to rebuild the temple (see Ezr 5:1–2; 6:14). Haggai means "festal," which may indicate that the prophet was born during one of the three pilgrimage festivals (Unleavened Bread, Pentecost or Weeks, and Tabernacles; cf. Dt 16:16). Based on 2:3 (see note there) Haggai may have witnessed the destruction of Solomon's temple. If so, he must have been in his 70s during his ministry.

BACKGROUND

In 538 B.C. the conqueror of Babylon, Cyrus, king of Persia, issued a decree allowing the Jews to return to Jerusalem and rebuild the temple (see Ezr 1:2–4; 6:3–5). Led by Zerubbabel (but see note on Ezr 1:8, "Sheshbazzar"), about 50,000 Jews journeyed home and began work on the temple. About two years later (536) they completed the foundation amid great rejoicing (Ezr 3:8–11). Their success aroused the Samaritans and other neighbors who feared the political and religious implications of a rebuilt temple in a thriving Jewish state. They therefore opposed the project vigorously and managed to halt work until 520, after Darius the Great became king of Persia in 522 (Ezr 4:1–5,24).

    Darius was interested in the religions of his empire, and Haggai and Zechari-ah began to preach in his second year, 520 B.C. (see 1:1; Zec 1:1). The Jews were more to blame for their inactivity than their opponents, and Haggai tried to arouse them from their lethargy. When the governor of Trans-Euphrates and other officials tried to interfere with the rebuilding efforts, Darius fully supported the Jews (Ezr 5:3–6; 6:6–12). In 516 the temple was finished and dedicated (Ezr 6:15–18).

DATE

Haggai's messages are among the most carefully and precisely dated in the entire OT. They were given during a four-month period in 520 B.C., the second year of King Darius. The first message was delivered on the first day of the sixth month (Aug. 29), the last on the 24th day of the ninth month (Dec. 18). See notes on 1:1; 2:1,10; see also Introduction to Zechariah: Dates.

THEMES AND THEOLOGICAL TEACHING

Apart from Obadiah, Haggai is the shortest book in the OT, but its teachings are none the less significant. Haggai clearly shows the consequences of disobedience (1:6,11; 2:16–17) and obedience (2:7–9,19). When the people give priority to God and his house, they are blessed rather than cursed (cf. Lk 12:31 and note). Obedience brings the encouragement and strength of the Spirit of God (2:4–5).

    In ch. 2 God gives great encouragement to those laboring under difficult conditions to rebuild his temple by assuring them that the future glory of the modest temple they are able to build will be greater than that of the temple Solomon had built in the time of Israel's greatest wealth and power. The Jews in Judah may now be a much reduced community and under the hegemony of a powerful world em-

KEY   **A** APPLICATION FOR LIVING   **B** BACKGROUND NOTES   **C** CHARACTER INFORMATION

pire, but the Lord will shake up the present world order and assert his claim to all the world's wealth, so that the glory of his future temple will be without rival. "What is desired by all nations will come, and I will fill this house with glory" (see 2:6–7; Eze 1:28; 43:2 and notes).

LITERARY FEATURES

Like Malachi, Haggai uses a number of questions to highlight key issues (see 1:4,9; 2:3,19). He also makes effective use of repetition: "Give careful thought" occurs in 1:5,7; 2:15,18, and "I am with you" in 1:13; 2:4. "Shake the heavens and the earth" is found in 2:6,21. The major sections of the book are marked off by the date on which the word of the Lord came "through" (or "to") Haggai (1:1; 2:1,10,20).

    Several times the prophet appears to reflect other passages of Scripture (compare 1:6 with Dt 28:38–39 and 2:17 with Dt 28:22). The threefold use of "Be strong" in 2:4 (see note there) echoes the encouragement given in Jos 1:6–7,9,18. (For chiasm, see Outline below.)

OUTLINE

    I. First Message: The Call to Rebuild the Temple (1:1–11)
       A. The People's Lame Excuse (1:1–4)
       B. The Poverty of the People (1:5–6)
       C. The Reason God Has Cursed Them (1:7–11)
    II. The Response of Zerubbabel and the People (1:12–15)
       A. The Leaders and Remnant Obey (1:12)
       B. The Lord Strengthens the Workers (1:13–15)
    III. Second Message: The Temple to Be Filled with Glory (2:1–9)
       A. The People Encouraged (2:1–5)
       B. The Promise of Glory and Peace (2:6–9)
    IV. Third Message: A Defiled People Purified and Blessed (2:10–19)
       A. The Rapid Spread of Sin (2:10–14)
       B. Poor Harvests because of Disobedience (2:15–17)
       C. Blessing to Come as the Temple Is Rebuilt (2:18–19)
    V. Fourth Message: The Promise to Zerubbabel (2:20–23)
       A. The Judgment of the Nations (2:20–22)
       B. The Significance of Zerubbabel (2:23)

It is also possible to outline the book in a chiastic *a-b / b-a* pattern:
    a Negative effects of the unbuilt house (1:1–11)
       b The Lord's presence energizes the present work (1:12–15)
       b¹ The Lord's presence guarantees future glory (2:1–9)
    a¹ Positive effects of the rebuilt house (2:10–23)
Similar chiastic patterns exist in the subunits within these larger units.

1:1 ᵃS Ezr 4:24
ᵇS Ezr 5:1
ᶜS 1Ch 3:19; Mt 1:12-13 ᵈEzr 5:3;
S Ne 5:14 ᵉS Ezr 2:2
ᶠS 1Ch 6:15; S Ezr 3:2
ᵍZec 3:8
1:2 ʰIsa 13:4
ⁱS Isa 29:13 / Ezr 1:2
1:3 ᵏS Ezr 5:1
1:4 ˡS 2Sa 7:2
ᵐver 9; Jer 33:12
1:5 ⁿver 7; La 3:40;
Hag 2:15,18
1:6 ᵒS Lev 26:20;
S Isa 5:10
ᵖS Isa 9:20; S 55:2
�q Am 4:8 ʳHag 2:16;
Zec 8:10
1:7 ˢS ver 5
1:8 ᵗS 1Ch 14:1
ᵘS Job 22:3;
Ps 132:13-14
ᵛS Ex 29:43; Jer 13:11
1:9 ʷS Dt 28:38;
S Isa 5:10
ˣS Ps 103:16;
S Eze 22:21 ʸS ver 4;
S Ne 13:11
1:10 ᶻS Dt 28:24
ᵃS Ge 27:28; 1Ki 17:1
ᵇLev 26:19; Dt 28:23
1:11 ᶜS Dt 11:26;
S 28:22; S Ru 1:1;
S 1Ki 17:1; S Isa 5:6
ᵈIsa 7:25
ᵉS Dt 28:51; Ps 4:7
ᶠS Nu 18:12
ᵍHag 2:17
1:12 ʰver 1 ⁱver 14;
Isa 1:9; Hag 2:2
ʲS Job 36:11
ᵏS Isa 50:10; Mt 28:20
ᵏS Dt 31:12; S Isa 1:2
1:13 ˡver 1
ᵐS Nu 27:21;
S 2Ch 36:15
ⁿS Ge 26:3;
S Nu 14:9;
S Mt 28:20; Ro 8:31
1:14 ᵒS Ezr 1:5
ᵖS Ezr 5:2
ᵠS 1Ch 6:15 ʳS ver 12

A CALL TO BUILD THE HOUSE OF THE LORD

¹In the second year of King Darius,ᵃ on the first day of the sixth month, the word of the LORD came through the prophet Haggaiᵇ to Zerubbabelᶜ son of Shealtiel, governorᵈ of Judah, and to Joshuaᵃ ᵉ son of Jozadak,ᵇ ᶠ the high priest:ᵍ

²This is what the LORD Almightyʰ says: "These peopleⁱ say, 'The time has not yet come to rebuild the LORD's house.ʲ'"

³Then the word of the LORD came through the prophet Haggai:ᵏ ⁴"Is it a time for you yourselves to be living in your paneled houses,ˡ while this house remains a ruin?ᵐ"

⁵Now this is what the LORD Almighty says: "Give careful thoughtⁿ to your ways. ⁶You have planted much, but have harvested little.ᵒ You eat, but never have enough. ᵖYou drink, but never have your fill.ᵠ You put on clothes, but are not warm. You earn wages,ʳ only to put them in a purse with holes in it."

⁷This is what the LORD Almighty says: "Give careful thoughtˢ to your ways. ⁸Go up into the mountains and bring down timberᵗ and build the house, so that I may take pleasureᵘ in it and be honored,ᵛ" says the LORD. ⁹"You expected much, but see, it turned out to be little.ʷ What you brought home, I blewˣ away. Why?" declares the LORD Almighty. "Because of my house, which remains a ruin,ʸ while each of you is busy with his own house. ¹⁰Therefore, because of you the heavens have withheldᶻ their dewᵃ and the earth its crops.ᵇ ¹¹I called for a droughtᶜ on the fields and the mountains,ᵈ on the grain, the new wine,ᵉ the olive oilᶠ and everything else the ground produces, on people and livestock, and on all the labor of your hands.ᵍ"

¹²Then Zerubbabelʰ son of Shealtiel, Joshua son of Jozadak, the high priest, and the whole remnantⁱ of the people obeyedʲ the voice of the LORD their God and the message of the prophet Haggai, because the LORD their God had sent him. And the people fearedᵏ the LORD.

¹³Then Haggai,ˡ the LORD's messenger,ᵐ gave this message of the LORD to the people: "I am withⁿ you," declares the LORD. ¹⁴So the LORD stirred upᵒ the spirit of Zerubbabelᵖ son of Shealtiel, governor of Judah, and the spirit of Joshua son of Jozadak,ᵠ the high priest, and the spirit of the whole remnantʳ of the people. They came and began to work on the house of the LORD Almighty, their God, ¹⁵on the twenty-fourth day of the sixth month.ˢ

ᵃ 1 A variant of *Jeshua*; here and elsewhere in Haggai in verses 12 and 14   ᵇ 1 Hebrew *Jehozadak*, a variant of *Jozadak*; also

1:15 ˢver 1; Hag 2:10,20

1:1 *second year … first day … sixth month.* Aug. 29, 520 B.C. *King Darius.* Darius Hystaspes ruled Persia from 522 to 486 B.C. (see chart, p. 482). It was he who prepared the trilingual inscription on the Behistun cliff wall (located in modern Iran), through which cuneiform inscriptions were deciphered and the culture and history of ancient Mesopotamia were brought to light. *first day.* The New Moon was the day on which prophets were sometimes consulted (see 2Ki 4:22–23 and note on 4:23; see also note on Isa 1:14). *word of the LORD.* See v. 3; 2:2; Hos 1:1 and note. *Zerubbabel.* See note on Ezr 1:8, "Sheshbazzar." *son of Shealtiel.* See 1Ch 3:17–19 and note on 3:19. *governor … high priest.* The civil and religious leaders of the restored Jewish community. *Joshua.* See note on Ezr 2:2; mentioned with Zerubbabel also in vv. 12,14; 2:2,4. *Jozadak.* Had been taken captive by Nebuchadnezzar (1Ch 6:15).

1:2 *LORD Almighty.* Used more than 90 times in Haggai, Zechariah and Malachi. See notes on 1Sa 1:3; Isa 13:4. *These people.* See 2:14. Because of their sin, the nation is not called "my people" (see Isa 6:9–10; 8:6,11–12; Jer 14:10–11; see also notes on Ex 17:4; Hos 1:9). *time has not yet come.* After the foundation of the temple had been laid in 536 B.C., the people became discouraged and halted the work until 520 (see Ezr 4:1–5,24).

1:4 *paneled houses.* Usually connected with royal dwellings, which had cedar paneling (see 1Ki 7:3,7; Jer 22:14–15 and note on 22:14).

1:5 *Give careful thought.* Repeated in v. 7; 2:15,18.

1:6 *planted much … harvested little.* A curse for disobedience (see Dt 28:38–39). Lev 26:20 also describes the unfruitfulness of a land judged by God. *drink … fill.* Cf. Isa 55:1–2.

The people experience futility in all their activities, legitimate or illegitimate (cf. Hos 4:10–11; Mic 6:13–15). *purse with holes.* Famine causes prices to rise sharply.

1:8 *mountains … timber.* Perhaps wood from nearby hills was to supplement the cedar wood already purchased from Lebanon (see Ezr 3:7). *take pleasure in it.* And in the sacrifices offered there (contrast Isa 1:11). *be honored.* An obedient nation would bring praise and honor to God (see Jer 13:11).

1:9 *busy with.* Lit. "running to."

1:10 *dew.* Normally abundant in the growing season, and often as valuable as rain (see 2Sa 1:21; 1Ki 17:1).

1:11 *mountains.* The hills were cultivated, especially through terracing (see Ps 104:13–15; Isa 7:25; Joel 3:18). *the grain, the new wine, the olive oil.* The three basic crops of the land, often mentioned in a context of blessing or cursing (see Dt 7:13; Joel 1:10 and notes). Olive oil was used as food, ointment and medicine. *people and livestock.* The drought affected people and cattle and so could be said to be "on" them too.

1:12 *remnant.* See note on Isa 1:9. *feared the LORD.* Showing reverence, respect and obedience (see Ge 20:11 and note; Dt 31:12–13; Mal 1:6; 3:5,16).

1:13 *messenger.* A title for prophets (see 2Ch 36:15–16; Isa 42:19 and note) or priests (see Mal 2:7 and note). *I am with you.* A sure indication of success (see 2:4; Ge 26:3; Nu 14:9 and notes).

1:14 *stirred up the spirit.* The Hebrew for this expression is translated "(whose) heart (God) had moved" in Ezr 1:5, where God stirred up many of these same people to return home and rebuild the temple.

1:15 *twenty-fourth day of the sixth month.* Sept. 21, 520 B.C.

THE PROMISED GLORY OF THE NEW HOUSE

2 In the second year of King Darius, [t] on the twenty-first day of the seventh month, [u] the word of the LORD came through the prophet Haggai: [v] ²"Speak to Zerubbabel [w] son of Shealtiel, governor of Judah, to Joshua son of Jozadak, [a][x] the high priest, and to the remnant [y] of the people. Ask them, ³'Who of you is left who saw this house [z] in its former glory? How does it look to you now? Does it not seem to you like nothing? [a] ⁴But now be strong, Zerubbabel,' declares the LORD. 'Be strong, [b] Joshua son of Jozadak, [c] the high priest. Be strong, all you people of the land,' declares the LORD, 'and work. For I am with [d] you,' declares the LORD Almighty. ⁵'This is what I covenanted [e] with you when you came out of Egypt. [f] And my Spirit [g] remains among you. Do not fear.' [h]

⁶"This is what the LORD Almighty says: 'In a little while [i] I will once more shake the heavens and the earth, [j] the sea and the dry land. ⁷I will shake all nations, and what is desired [k] by all nations will come, and I will fill this house [l] with glory, [m] says the LORD Almighty. ⁸'The silver is mine and the gold [n] is mine,' declares the LORD Almighty. ⁹'The glory [o] of this present house [p] will be greater than the glory of the former house,' says the LORD Almighty. 'And in this place I will grant peace, [q]' declares the LORD Almighty."

BLESSINGS FOR A DEFILED PEOPLE

¹⁰On the twenty-fourth day of the ninth month, [r] in the second year of Darius, the word of the LORD came to the prophet Haggai: ¹¹"This is what the LORD Almighty says: 'Ask the priests [s] what the law says: ¹²If a person carries consecrated meat [t] in the fold of his garment, and that fold touches some bread or stew, some wine, olive oil or other food, does it become consecrated? [u]' "

The priests answered, "No."

¹³Then Haggai said, "If a person defiled by contact with a dead body touches one of these things, does it become defiled?"

"Yes," the priests replied, "it becomes defiled. [v]"

¹⁴Then Haggai said, " 'So it is with this people [w] and this nation in my sight,' declares the LORD. 'Whatever they do and whatever they offer [x] there is defiled.

---

[a] 2 Hebrew *Jehozadak*, a variant of *Jozadak*; also in verse 4

### Cross references (right margin)

1:15 ʳS Ezr 4:24
2:1 ᵘver 10, 20;
S Lev 23:34; Jn 7:37
ᵛS Ezr 5:1
2:2 ʷHag 1:1
ˣS 1Ch 6:15
ʸS Hag 1:12
2:3 ᶻS Ezr 3:12;
S Isa 60:7 ᵃZec 4:10
2:4 ᵇS 1Ch 28:20;
Zec 8:9; S Eph 6:10
ᶜS 1Ch 6:15
ᵈS Ex 33:14;
S Nu 14:9; S 2Sa 5:10;
Ac 7:9
2:5 ᵉS Ge 6:18
ᶠS Ex 29:46
ᵍS Ne 9:20
ʰS Ge 15:1; 1Ch 28:20;
S Ezr 5:2; Zec 8:13
2:6 ⁱS Isa 10:25
ʲS Ex 19:18; S Job 9:6;
S Isa 14:16;
S Eze 38:19;
Heb 12:26*
2:7 ᵏS 1Sa 9:20
ˡS Isa 60:7
ᵐS Ex 16:7; S 29:43;
Lk 2:32
2:8 ⁿS 1Ch 29:2
2:9 ᵒS Ps 85:9;
S Isa 11:10 ᵖS Ezr 3:12;
S Isa 60:7 ᵠS Lev 26:6;
S Isa 60:17
2:10 ʳS ver 1;
S Hag 1:15
2:11 ˢS Lev 10:10-
11; Dt 17:8-11; 33:8;
S Jer 18:18
2:12 ᵗJer 11:15
ᵘS Ge 7:2;
S Lev 6:27; Mt 23:19
2:13 ᵛLev 22:4-6;
Nu 19:13
2:14 ʷS Isa 29:13
ˣS Ps 51:17; S Isa 1:13

Study notes

2:1 *twenty-first day of the seventh month.* Oct. 17, 520 B.C., the last day of the Festival of Tabernacles. It was a time to celebrate the summer harvest (see Lev 23:34–43), though the crops were meager (see 1:11; cf. Jn 7:37). Solomon had dedicated his temple during this festival (see 1Ki 8:2 and note).

2:3 *is left.* Some of the older exiles (perhaps including Haggai himself) had seen Solomon's magnificent temple, destroyed by the Babylonians 66 years earlier. *this house in its former glory.* See vv. 7,9. Zerubbabel's temple was considered a continuation of Solomon's. *seem ... like nothing.* Cf. the reaction when the foundation of the temple was finished (Ezr 3:12).

2:4 *be strong ... work.* David used these words in 1Ch 28:20 when he encouraged Solomon to build the temple. The Lord had exhorted Joshua, son of Nun, with similar words (Jos 1:6–7,9,18). *be strong ... Be strong.... Be strong.* See note on Jer 7:4. *I am with you.* See 1:13 and note; 1Ch 28:20. The same God who helped Solomon will empower Zerubbabel.

2:5 *my Spirit.* The Holy Spirit had rested on Moses and the 70 elders as they had led the people out of Egypt and through the desert (see Nu 11:16–17,25; Isa 63:11). See also Ps 51:11; Zec 4:6 and notes. *Do not fear.* See notes on v. 4; Jos 1:18; Isa 41:10.

2:6 An announcement of the coming day of God's judgment on the nations—which the fall of Persia to Alexander the Great (333–330 B.C.) would foreshadow. Heb 12:26–27 relates this verse to the judgment of the nations at the second coming of Christ. The background for the shaking of the nations here and in vv. 21–22 is the judgment on Egypt at the Red Sea. Cf. also Isa 14:16–17.

2:7 *desired ... will come.* "Desired" can refer to individuals, as in Da 9:23 (where the same Hebrew verb is translated "highly esteemed"); cf. 1Sa 9:20. Thus it may have Messianic significance (see Da 11:37 and note; Mal 3:1). The same Hebrew word can also refer to articles of value, however (see 2Ch 20:25; 32:27)—such as the contribution of King Darius to the temple

(Ezr 6:8). If that is the intent here, the bringing of the "riches of the nations" to Zion in Isa 60:5 is a close parallel (see note there). *fill ... with glory.* "Glory" can refer to material splendor (see Isa 60:7,13 and notes) or to the presence of God (Ex 40:34–35; 1Ki 8:10–11; Eze 10:4). The latter references connect the glory of the Lord with the cloud that filled the sanctuary. When Christ came to the earthly temple, God's presence was evident as never before (see Lk 2:27,32). Cf. notes on Eze 1:28; 43:2.

2:8 *silver ... gold.* Provided for Solomon's temple (1Ch 29:2,7) and for Zerubbabel's (Ezr 6:5).

2:9 *glory ... greater.* Ultimately because the Messiah would be present there (see v. 7 and note). *former house.* Solomon's temple. *this place.* Perhaps Jerusalem (see Zep 1:4 and note). *I will grant peace.* Perhaps an allusion to the priestly benediction (see Nu 6:26 and note).

2:10 *twenty-fourth day ... ninth month.* Dec. 18, 520 B.C.—when winter crops were planted.

2:11 *priests.* They were consulted about the precise meaning of the law (see Dt 31:11; Jer 18:18; Mal 2:7–9 and notes).

2:12 *consecrated meat.* Meat from an animal set apart for a sacrifice. *does it become consecrated?* A question about transmitting holiness. Consecrated meat made the garment "holy" because it was in direct contact with that garment (see Lev 6:27), but the garment could not pass on that holiness to a third object.

2:13 *does it become defiled?* Ceremonial uncleanness is transmitted much more easily than holiness. Anything touched by an unclean person becomes unclean (see Nu 19:11–13,22).

2:14 *this people.* See 1:2 and note. *Whatever they do ... is defiled.* Even though the people were back in the holy land, that holiness did not make them pure. They needed to obey the Lord, particularly with regard to rebuilding the temple. See notes on vv. 12–13.

2:15 ʸ S Hag 1:5
ᶻ S Ezr 3:10 ᵃ Ezr 4:24
2:16 ᵇ S Ru 3:7
ᶜ S Job 24:11;
S Isa 5:2
ᵈ S Dt 28:38;
S Isa 5:10; S Hag 1:6
2:17 ᵉ Hag 1:11
ᶠ S Dt 28:22
ᵍ S Ex 9:18; Ps 78:48
ʰ S Isa 9:13; S Jer 3:10
ⁱ S Am 4:6
2:18 ʲ S Hag 1:5
ᵏ S Ezr 3:11
2:19 ˡ S Ex 28:33
ᵐ S Joel 1:12
ⁿ S Ge 12:2;
S Lev 25:21; Ps 128:1-
6; S Joel 2:14
2:20 ᵒ S Ezr 5:1
ᵖ S ver 1; S Hag 1:15
2:21 �q S Ezr 5:2
ʳ S Isa 14:16;
Eze 38:19-20
2:22 ˢ S Ge 19:25;
S Job 2:13 ᵗ S Da 2:44
ᵘ S Mic 5:10
ᵛ S Ex 15:21
ʷ S Jdg 7:22;
S Eze 38:21
2:23 ˣ S Isa 2:11;
10:20; Zec 4:10
ʸ S Isa 20:3;
S Da 9:24-26

¹⁵" 'Now give careful thought ʸ to this from this day on ᵃ—consider how things were before one stone was laid ᶻ on another in the Lᴏʀᴅ's temple. ᵃ ¹⁶When anyone came to a heap ᵇ of twenty measures, there were only ten. When anyone went to a wine vat ᶜ to draw fifty measures, there were only twenty. ᵈ ¹⁷I struck all the work of your hands ᵉ with blight, ᶠ mildew and hail, ᵍ yet you did not return ʰ to me,' declares the Lᴏʀᴅ. ⁱ ¹⁸'From this day on, from this twenty-fourth day of the ninth month, give careful thought ʲ to the day when the foundation ᵏ of the Lᴏʀᴅ's temple was laid. Give careful thought: ¹⁹Is there yet any seed left in the barn? Until now, the vine and the fig tree, the pomegranate ˡ and the olive tree have not borne fruit. ᵐ

" 'From this day on I will bless ⁿ you.' "

ZERUBBABEL THE LORD'S SIGNET RING

²⁰The word of the Lᴏʀᴅ came to Haggai ᵒ a second time on the twenty-fourth day of the month: ᵖ ²¹"Tell Zerubbabel q governor of Judah that I am going to shake ʳ the heavens and the earth. ²²I will overturn ˢ royal thrones and shatter the power of the foreign kingdoms. ᵗ I will overthrow chariots ᵘ and their drivers; horses and their riders ᵛ will fall, each by the sword of his comrade. ʷ

²³" 'On that day, ˣ' declares the Lᴏʀᴅ Almighty, 'I will take you, my servant ʸ Zerubbabel ᶻ son of Shealtiel,' declares the Lᴏʀᴅ, 'and I will make you like my signet ring, ᵃ for I have chosen you,' declares the Lᴏʀᴅ Almighty."

ᵃ 15 Or *to the days past*

2:23 ᶻ Mt 1:12 ᵃ S Ge 38:18; S Ex 28:9; 2Co 1:22

2:15 *before one stone was laid.* Before the 24th day of the sixth month (1:14–15).
2:16 *heap.* Probably of grain (see Jer 50:26). *only ten ... only twenty.* The poor harvests were related to the sin of the people (see 1:11; Isa 5:10 and note). *wine vat.* Usually a shallow pit cut into solid rock, into which grape juice flowed when the grapes were trodden and where it was retained until fermentation had begun. The juice was later transferred to jars or skins for further fermentation and storage.
2:17 *blight, mildew.* Mentioned as a curse for disobedience in Dt 28:22 (see also 1Ki 8:37; Am 4:9). The blight was probably caused by a scorching east wind (see Ge 41:6 and note). *hail.* Sent to destroy the fields and livestock of Egypt (see Ex 9:25; Ps 78:47–48). *you did not return.* See Am 4:6,8–11.
2:18 *when the foundation ... was laid.* The same potential for blessing had existed at the time when the foundation of the temple was laid in 536 B.C. (Ezr 3:11). This is a warning not to fail again.
2:19 *vine ... fig tree ... pomegranate ... olive tree.* Grapes, figs and pomegranates ripened in August and September, and olives from September to November. These harvests, like the earlier grain crops, had produced little (see 1:11 and note). *I will bless you.* Because of their response to Haggai's message, future

abundance is assured. Cf. Mal 3:10.
2:20 See note on v. 10.
2:21 *shake ... the earth.* See v. 6 and note.
2:22 *overturn ... overthrow.* The Hebrew for these words is used with reference to Sodom and Gomorrah (see Ge 19:25; Am 4:11). *chariots ... horses ... riders.* Cf. the destruction of the pharaoh's army at the Red Sea (Ex 15:1,4,19,21). *each by ... his comrade.* The plight of the armies of Midian (see Jdg 7:22 and note), Gog (see Eze 38:21 and note) and the nations fighting against Jerusalem in the last days (Zec 14:13).

▲ **2:23** *On that day.* The day of the Lord (see Isa 2:11,17,20; 10:20,27; Joel 1:15; Zec 2:11). *my servant.* A term applied to prophets (see Isa 20:3 and note), political leaders (Isa 22:20) and the Messiah (see Isa 41:8–9; 42:1 and notes). *signet ring.* A kind of seal that functioned as a signature (see Est 8:8) and was worn on one's finger (Est 3:10). Like other seals (see Ge 38:18 and note), it could be used as a pledge or guarantee of full payment. Its mention here apparently reverses the curse placed on King Jehoiachin in Jer 22:24 (see also Jdg 17:2 and note). Zerubbabel would then be a guarantee that indeed the future glory of the temple will be realized (see vv. 6–7,9; Zec 4:6–7 and notes). *chosen you.* See Isa 41:8–9; 42:1 and notes.

BACKGROUND ZECHARIAH | INTRODUCTION

Zechariah's prophetic ministry took place in the postexilic period, the time of the Jewish restoration from Babylonian captivity. For historical details, see Introduction to Haggai: Background.

AUTHOR AND UNITY

C Like Jeremiah (1:1) and Ezekiel (1:3), Zechariah was not only a prophet (1:1) but also a member of a priestly family. He was born in Babylonia and was among those who returned to Judah in 538/537 B.C. under the leadership of Zerubbabel and Joshua (his grandfather Iddo is named among the returnees in Ne 12:4). At a later time, when Joiakim was high priest (see note on Ne 12:12–21), Zechariah apparently succeeded Iddo (1:1,7) as head of that priestly family (Ne 12:10–16). Since the grandson succeeded the grandfather, it has been suggested that the father (Berekiah, 1:1,7) died at an early age.

Zechariah was a contemporary of Haggai (Ezr 5:1; 6:14) but continued his ministry long after him (compare 1:1 and 7:1 with Hag 1:1; see also Ne 12:1–16). His young age (see 2:4 and note) in the early period of his ministry makes it possible that he ministered even into the reign of Artaxerxes I (465–424 B.C.).

Most likely Zechariah wrote the entire book that bears his name. Some have questioned his authorship of chs. 9–14, citing differences in style and other compositional features and giving historical and chronological references that allegedly require a different date and author from those of chs. 1–8. All these objections, however, can be explained in other satisfactory ways, so there is no compelling reason to question the unity of the book.

DATES

The dates of Zechariah's recorded messages are best correlated with those of Haggai and with other historical events as follows:

1. Haggai's first message (Hag 1:1–11; Ezr 5:1)	Aug. 29, 520 B.C.
2. Resumption of the building of the temple (Hag 1:12–15; Ezr 5:2) (The rebuilding seems to have been hindered from 536 to c. 530 [Ezr 4:1–5], and the work ceased altogether from c. 530 to 520 [Ezr 4:24].)	Sept. 21, 520
3. Haggai's second message (Hag 2:1–9)	Oct. 17, 520
4. Beginning of Zechariah's preaching (1:1–6)	Oct./Nov., 520
5. Haggai's third message (Hag 2:10–19)	Dec. 18, 520
6. Haggai's fourth message (Hag 2:20–23)	Dec. 18, 520
7. Tattenai's letter to Darius concerning the rebuilding of the temple (Ezr 5:3—6:14) (There must have been a lapse of time between the resumption of the building and Tattenai's appearance.)	519–518
8. Zechariah's eight night visions (1:7—6:8)	Feb. 15, 519
9. Joshua crowned (6:9–15)	Feb. 16 (?), 519
10. Repentance urged, blessings promised (chs. 7–8)	Dec. 7, 518
11. Dedication of the temple (Ezr 6:15–18)	Mar. 12, 516
12. Zechariah's final prophecies (chs. 9–14)	After 480 (?)

OCCASION AND PURPOSE

The occasion is the same as that of the book of Haggai (see Background; Dates). The chief purpose of Zechariah (and Haggai) was to rebuke the people of Judah and to encourage and motivate them to complete the rebuilding of the temple (Zec 4:8–10; Hag 1–2), though both prophets were clearly interested in spiritual renewal as well. In addition, the purpose of the eight night visions (1:7—6:8) is explained in 1:3,5–6: The Lord said that if the people of Judah would return to him, he would return to them. Furthermore, his word would continue to be fulfilled.

THEOLOGICAL TEACHING

The theology of Zechariah's prophecy matches his name, which means "The Lord (Yahweh) remembers." "The Lord" is the personal, covenant name of God and is a perpetual testimony to his faithfulness to his promises (see notes on Ge 2:4; Ex 3:14–15; 6:6; Dt 28:58). He "remembers" his covenant promises and takes action to fulfill them. In the book of Zechariah God's promised deliverance from Babylonian exile, including a restored kingdom community and a functioning temple (the earthly throne of the divine King; see Introduction to Psalms: Theology: Major Themes), leads into even grander pictures of the salvation and restoration to come through the Messiah (see notes on 3:8–9; 4:3,14; 6:9–15; 9:9–10; 10:2,4; 11:4–14; 12:10—13:1; 13:7; 14:4–9).

     The book as a whole also teaches the sovereignty of God in history, over people and nations—past, present and future (see, e.g., 1:10–11; 2:13; 4:10,14 and note; 6:5,7; 8:20–23; 9:10,13–14; 10:11; 12:1–5; 14:9,16–19). See also Literary Forms and Themes, below.

LITERARY FORMS AND THEMES

The book is primarily a mixture of exhortation (call to repentance, 1:2–6); prophetic visions (1:7—6:8); a prophetic oracle of instruction or exhortation involving a symbolic coronation scene (6:9–15); hortatory messages (mainly of rebuke and hope), prompted by a question about fasting (chs. 7–8); and judgment and salvation oracles (chs. 9–14). The prophetic visions of 1:7—6:8 are called apocalyptic (revelatory) literature, which is essentially a literature of encouragement to God's people. When the apocalyptic section is read along with the salvation (or deliverance) oracles in chs. 9–14, it becomes obvious that the dominant emphasis of the book is encouragement because of the glorious future that awaits the people of God.

     In fact, encouragement is the book's central theme—primarily encouragement to complete the rebuilding of the temple. Various means are used to accomplish this end, and these function as subthemes. For example, great stress is laid on the coming of the Messiah and the overthrow of all anti-kingdom forces by him so that God's rule can be finally and fully established on earth. The then-current local scene thus becomes the basis for contemplating the universal, eschatological picture.

     Several interpreters have arranged the eight visions of 1:7—6:8 in a chiastic (or concentric) pattern of *a - b - b - c / c¹ - b¹ - b¹ - a¹*:

  a   The Lord controls the events of history (1:7–17)
     b   Nations that devastated Israel will in turn be devastated (1:18–21)
     b   Israel will be fully restored (ch. 2)
        c   Israel will be restored as a priestly nation (ch. 3)
        c¹   Israel will be restored under royal and priestly leadership (ch. 4)
     b¹   Lawbreakers will be purged from Israel (5:1–4)
     b¹   The whole sinful system will be removed from the land (5:5–11)
  a¹   The Lord controls the events of history (6:1–8)

1:1 ᵃS Ezr 4:24;
S 6:15 ᵇS Ezr 5:1
ᶜMt 23:35; Lk 11:51
ᵈver 7; S Ne 12:4
1:2 ᵉS 2Ch 36:16
1:3 ᶠS Job 22:23
ᵍMal 3:7; Jas 4:8
1:4 ʰS 2Ch 36:15
ⁱZec 7:7 ʲS 2Ki 17:13;
S 2Ch 7:14; Ps 106:6;
S Jer 23:22
ᵏS 2Ch 24:19;
Ps 78:8; S Jer 6:17;
17:23 ˡS Eze 20:18;
S 33:4
1:6 ᵐS Isa 44:26
ⁿS Dt 28:2;
S Da 9:12; S Hos 5:9
ᵒJer 12:14-17; La 2:17
ᵖJer 23:20; 39:16;
S 44:17
1:7 ᑫS ver 1
1:8 ʳRev 6:4
ᶻZec 6:2-7
1:9 ᵗZec 4:1,4-5; 5:5
ᵘS Da 7:16
1:10 ᵛZec 6:5-8
1:11 ʷZec 16:7
ˣS Isa 14:7
1:12 ʸS Ps 6:3
ᶻPs 40:11 ᵃS Jer 40:5
ᵇS 2Ch 36:21;
S Da 9:2
1:13 ᶜS Isa 35:4
ᵈS Job 15:11 ᵉZec 4:1
1:14 ᶠS Isa 26:11;
S Joel 2:18
1:15 ᵍJer 48:11
ʰS 2Ch 28:9
ⁱS Ps 69:26; 123:3-4;
S Am 1:11

A CALL TO RETURN TO THE LORD

1 In the eighth month of the second year of Darius, ᵃ the word of the LORD came to the prophet Zechariah ᵇ son of Berekiah, ᶜ the son of Iddo: ᵈ

²"The LORD was very angry ᵉ with your ancestors. ³Therefore tell the people: This is what the LORD Almighty says: 'Return ᶠ to me,' declares the LORD Almighty, 'and I will return to you,' ᵍ says the LORD Almighty. ⁴Do not be like your ancestors, ʰ to whom the earlier prophets ⁱ proclaimed: This is what the LORD Almighty says: 'Turn from your evil ways ʲ and your evil practices.' But they would not listen or pay attention to me, ᵏ declares the LORD. ˡ ⁵Where are your ancestors now? And the prophets, do they live forever? ⁶But did not my words ᵐ and my decrees, which I commanded my servants the prophets, overtake your ancestors? ⁿ

"Then they repented and said, 'The LORD Almighty has done to us what our ways and practices deserve, ᵒ just as he determined to do.' " ᵖ

THE MAN AMONG THE MYRTLE TREES

⁷On the twenty-fourth day of the eleventh month, the month of Shebat, in the second year of Darius, the word of the LORD came to the prophet Zechariah son of Berekiah, the son of Iddo. ᑫ

⁸During the night I had a vision, and there before me was a man mounted on a red ʳ horse. He was standing among the myrtle trees in a ravine. Behind him were red, brown and white horses. ˢ

⁹I asked, "What are these, my lord?"

The angel ᵗ who was talking with me answered, "I will show you what they are." ᵘ

¹⁰Then the man standing among the myrtle trees explained, "They are the ones the LORD has sent to go throughout the earth." ᵛ

¹¹And they reported to the angel of the LORD ʷ who was standing among the myrtle trees, "We have gone throughout the earth and found the whole world at rest and in peace." ˣ

¹²Then the angel of the LORD said, "LORD Almighty, how long ʸ will you withhold mercy ᶻ from Jerusalem and from the towns of Judah, ᵃ which you have been angry with these seventy ᵇ years?" ¹³So the LORD spoke ᶜ kind and comforting words ᵈ to the angel who talked with me. ᵉ

¹⁴Then the angel who was speaking to me said, "Proclaim this word: This is what the LORD Almighty says: 'I am very jealous ᶠ for Jerusalem and Zion, ¹⁵and I am very angry with the nations that feel secure. ᵍ I was only a little angry, ʰ but they added to the calamity.' ⁱ

1:1 *eighth month of the second year.* October-November, 520 B.C. Haggai also began his prophetic ministry in Darius's second year (see chart, p. 482), on the first day of the sixth month, i.e., on Aug. 29, 520 (Hag 1:1). *word of the LORD.* A technical phrase for the prophetic word of revelation (see v. 7; 9:1; 12:1; see also 4:8; Hos 1:1 and notes). *prophet.* One called by God to speak his word on his behalf (see note on Ex 7:1–2). *Iddo.* See v. 7; Ezr 5:1; 6:14; Ne 12:4,16; see also Introduction: Author and Unity.
1:2 *very angry with your ancestors.* The Lord was angry because of the covenant-breaking sins of the Jews' preexilic ancestors, resulting in the destruction of Jerusalem and the temple in 586 B.C., followed by exile to Babylonia (2Ch 36:15–21).
■ 1:3 *the LORD Almighty.* See note on 1Sa 1:3. *Return to me ... and I will return to you.* Cf. 7:13; 8:3; Mal 3:7. If the people of Zechariah's day would change their course and go in the opposite direction from that of their ancestors (v. 4), the Lord would return to them with blessing instead of with a curse (see v. 16; see also Jer 18:7–10 and note).
1:4 *earlier prophets.* Such as Isaiah (see Isa 45:22 and note), Jeremiah (see Jer 18:11 and note) and Ezekiel (see Eze 33:11 and note). See also 7:7,12; Jer 25:4–5; 35:15.
1:5 *do they live forever?* No, but God's words live on to be fulfilled (see v. 6).
1:6 *did not my words ... overtake your ancestors?* Cf. Isa 40:6–8; 55:10–11. For the imagery of "overtake," see Dt 28:2 ("accompany" is lit. "overtake"),15,45. *my servants the prophets.* See 2Ki 9:7; 17:13,23; 21:10; 24:2; Ezr 9:11; Jer 7:25 and note; 25:4; Eze 38:17; Da 9:6,10; Am 3:7. *they repented.* Apparently a reference to what happened to some of the preexilic ancestors and/or their off-

spring during the exile and immediately afterward (cf. Ezr 9:1—10:17; Da 9:3–19).
1:7–6:8 See Introduction: Literary Forms and Themes.
■ 1:7–17 The first vision. Although God's covenant people are troubled while the oppressing nations are at ease, God is jealous (see note on Ex 20:5) for his people and will restore them and their towns and the temple. The imagery of the first vision is reflected in that of the eighth and final vision (6:1–8).
1:7 *twenty-fourth day of ... Shebat.* Feb. 15, 519 B.C., about three months after the date of v. 1.
1:8 *During the night.* Zechariah had all eight visions (1:7—6:8) in one night. *vision.* Not a dream (see 4:1; see also Pr 29:18; Isa 1:1; Ob 1 and notes). The visions were given to Zechariah while he was fully awake. *man mounted on.* Later identified as the angel of the Lord (v. 11). He must not be confused with the interpreting angel, who is mentioned in vv. 9,13–14,19; 2:3; 4:1, 4–5; 5:5,10; 6:4–5.
1:9 *angel.* See note on v. 8.
1:11 *angel of the LORD.* See 3:1; see also note on Ge 16:7. *at rest.* Cf. 6:8. While the Persian empire as a whole was secure and at ease by this time (v. 15), the Jews in Judah were oppressed and still under foreign domination (v. 12).
1:12 *mercy.* Tender compassion (also in v. 16). *seventy years.* See 7:5; Ezr 1:1; Jer 25:11–12 and notes.
1:13 *comforting words.* Those of vv. 14–17.
■ 1:14 *jealous.* See 8:2. Through the use of such language the Lord's love for Judah is shown (see note on Ex 20:5; cf. Jas 4:4). The key idea is that of God avenging Judah for the violations against her (v. 15; see Dt 32:35,41; Jer 50:15; 51:6,11).

[16]"Therefore, this is what the LORD says: 'I will return[j] to Jerusalem with mercy, and there my house will be rebuilt. And the measuring line[k] will be stretched out over Jerusalem,' declares the LORD Almighty.[l]

[17]"Proclaim further: This is what the LORD Almighty says: 'My towns will again overflow with prosperity, and the LORD will again comfort[m] Zion and choose[n] Jerusalem.' "[o]

FOUR HORNS AND FOUR CRAFTSMEN

*[18]Then I looked up, and there before me were four horns. [19]I asked the angel who was speaking to me, "What are these?"

He answered me, "These are the horns[p] that scattered Judah, Israel and Jerusalem."

[20]Then the LORD showed me four craftsmen. [21]I asked, "What are these coming to do?"

He answered, "These are the horns that scattered Judah so its people could not raise their heads, but the craftsmen have come to terrify them and throw down these horns of the nations who lifted up their horns[q] against the land of Judah to scatter its people."[r]

A MAN WITH A MEASURING LINE

2 *[1]Then I looked up, and there before me was a man with a measuring line in his hand. [2]I asked, "Where are you going?"

He answered me, "To measure Jerusalem, to find out how wide and how long it is."[s]

[3]While the angel who was speaking to me was leaving, another angel came to meet him [4]and said to him: "Run, tell that young man, 'Jerusalem will be a city without walls[t] because of the great number[u] of people and animals in it. [v] [5]And I myself will be a wall[w] of fire[x] around it,' declares the LORD, 'and I will be its glory[y] within.'[za]

[6]"Come! Come! Flee from the land of the north," declares the LORD, "for I have scattered[b] you to the four winds of heaven,"[c] declares the LORD. [d]

[7]"Come, Zion! Escape,[e] you who live in Daughter Babylon!"[f] [8]For this is what the LORD Almighty says: "After the Glorious One has sent me against the nations that have plundered you—for whoever touches you touches the apple of his eye[g]— [9]I will surely raise my hand against them so that their slaves will plunder them.[a] [h] Then you will know that the LORD Almighty has sent me.[i]

[10]"Shout[j] and be glad, Daughter Zion. [k]For I am coming,[l] and I will live among you,"[m] declares the LORD. [n] [11]"Many nations will be joined with the LORD in that day and will become my people. [o] I will live among you and you will know that the LORD Almighty has sent me to you.[p] [12]The LORD will inherit[q] Judah[r] as his portion in the holy land and will again

---

[a] 8,9 Or says after . . . eye: [9]"I . . . plunder them."

* [1]:18-21 is numbered 2:1-4 in Hebrew texts.   * 2:1-13 is numbered 2:5-17 in Hebrew texts.

Cross references (right column)

1:16 [j] Zec 8:3
[k] Job 38:5; Zec 2:1-2 [l] S Ezr 1:1
1:17 [m] S Isa 40:1
[n] S Isa 14:1
[o] S Ezr 9:9;
S Ps 51:18; Isa 54:8-10; S 61:4
1:19 [p] Am 6:13
1:21 [q] S 1Ki 22:11;
Ps 75:4 [r] S Ps 75:10;
S Isa 54:16-17;
Zec 12:9
2:2 [s] S Eze 40:3;
S Zec 1:16; Rev 21:15
2:4 [t] S Eze 38:11
[u] S Isa 49:20;
S Jer 30:19; S 33:22
[v] Zec 14:11
2:5 [w] S Isa 26:1;
Eze 42:20
[x] S Isa 10:17
[y] S Ps 85:9;
S Isa 11:10; S 24:23;
Rev 21:23 [z] S Ps 125:2
[a] S Ps 46:5;
S Eze 38:14
2:6 [b] S Ps 44:11
[c] S Eze 17:21; S 37:9
[d] Mt 24:31; Mk 13:27
2:7 [e] S Isa 42:7
[f] S Isa 48:20; Jer 3:18
2:8 [g] S Dt 32:10
2:9 [h] S Isa 14:2;
S Jer 12:14; S Hab 2:8
[i] S Isa 48:16; Zec 4:9;
6:15
2:10 [j] S Zep 3:14
[k] S Isa 23:12;
S Zep 3:14 [l] Zec 9:9
[m] S Ex 25:8;
Lev 26:12;
S Nu 23:21; Zec 8:3
[n] S Rev 21:3
2:11 [o] S Jer 24:7;
S Mic 4:2; Zec 8:8,
20-22 [p] Zec 4:9; 6:15
2:12 [q] S Ex 34:9;
Ps 33:12; Jer 10:16
[r] Jer 40:5

Study notes (bottom)

1:15 *nations that feel secure.* A security that will be completely undone (see Isa 32:9–13; Hag 2:6–7 and notes).*added to the calamity.* God was angry with Israel and used the Assyrians (see Isa 10:5 and note) and Babylonians (see Isa 47:6; Jer 25:9 and notes) to punish her, but they went too far by trying to destroy Israel as a people.

1:16 *I will return.* See note on v. 3. *mercy.* See v. 12 and note. *my house will be rebuilt.* See Ezr 6:14–16; Hag 1:8; see also Introduction to Haggai: Background. *measuring line.* A symbol of restoration (see Jer 31:38–40 and note on 31:39).

1:17 *Zion.* See v. 14 and note. *choose Jerusalem.* See 2:12; 3:2.

1:18–21 The second vision. The nations that devastated Israel (v. 19) will in turn be destroyed by other nations.

1:18 *four.* If the number is to be taken literally, the reference is probably to Assyria, Egypt, Babylonia and Persia. *horns.* Probably metallic, either bronze or iron; symbolic of strength in general (Ps 18:2) or of the strength of a country, i.e., its king (Ps 89:17; Da 7:7–8; 8:20–21; Rev 17:12) or, as here (see v. 21), the power of a nation in general.

1:20 *four.* If the number is to be understood literally, perhaps the reference is to Egypt, Babylonia, Persia and Greece. What is clear is that all Israel's enemies will ultimately be defeated (v. 21). *craftsmen.* Probably metalsmiths (see 1Ki 22:11).

1:21 *terrify them.* Contrast vv. 11 ("at rest and in peace") and 15 ("feel secure"; see note there).

2:1–13 The third vision. There will be full restoration and blessing for the covenant people, temple and city.

2:1 *measuring line.* See note on 1:16.

2:4 *young man.* Evidently Zechariah. *without walls.* The city's population will overflow to the point that it will be as though it had no walls (see 10:8,10; see also note on Isa 49:19–20).

2:5 *wall of fire.* Here symbolic of divine protection (see 9:8; see also Ex 13:21; Isa 4:5–6 and notes).*glory.* See Ex 40:34; Eze 1:28; 43:2; Hag 2:9 and notes.

2:6 *land of the north.* Babylonia (v. 7) invaded Judah from the north (see Isa 41:25 and note; Jer 1:14; 4:6; 6:1,22; 10:22). *to the four winds.* In all directions. The exiles would return from north, south, east and west (Isa 43:5–6; 49:12).

2:7 *Zion.* Jerusalem's exiles in Babylon. *Escape . . . Babylon.* Cf. Rev 18:2–4. *Daughter Babylon.* A personification of Babylon (see note on 2Ki 19:21).

2:8 *me.* See also v. 9; probably the angel of the Lord (see 1:8 and note). *apple of his eye.* See note on Dt 32:10.

2:10 See 9:9 and note. *Daughter Zion.* A personification of Jerusalem (see v. 7 and note). *I will live among you.* See v. 11; 8:3; Lev 26:11–12; Eze 37:27; Jn 1:14; 2 Co 6:16; Rev 21:3.

2:11 *Many nations.* In fulfillment of the promise to Abraham (Ge 12:3; cf. Zec 8:20–23; 14:16; Ge 18:18; 22:18; Isa 2:2–4 and note; 19:24–25). *that day.* The day of the Lord (see 3:10; see also 12:3; Isa 2:11,17,20; Joel 1:15; Am 5:18 and notes).

2:12 *S* Dt 12:5;
S Isa 14:1
2:13 *t* S Ex 14:14;
S Isa 41:1 *u* S Dt 26:15
3:1 *v* S Ezr 2:2;
Zec 6:11 *w* S 2Sa 24:1;
S 2Ch 18:21;
S Ps 109:6; S Mt 4:10
3:2 *x* Jude 1:9
y S Isa 14:1 *z* S Isa 7:4
a Jude 1:23
3:4 *b* S 2Sa 12:13;
S Eze 36:25;
S Mic 7:18
c S Ge 41:42;
S Ps 132:9; S Isa 52:1;
Rev 19:8
3:5 *d* S Ex 29:6
3:7 *e* S Lev 8:35
f Dt 17:8-11;
S Eze 44:15-16
g 2Ch 23:6 *h* Jer 15:19;
Zec 6:15
3:8 *i* Hag 1:1
j S Dt 28:46;
S Eze 12:11
k S Isa 4:2; S 49:3;
S Eze 17:22
3:9 *l* S Ezr 2:2
m S 2Ch 16:9
n Isa 28:16
o S 2Sa 12:13;
S Jer 50:20
3:10 *p* S Job 11:18
q S Nu 16:14;
S 1Ki 4:25; Mic 4:4
4:1 *r* S Da 8:18
s Jer 31:26
4:2 *t* S Jer 1:13
u S Ex 25:31; Rev 1:12
v Rev 4:5

choose *s* Jerusalem. [13]Be still *t* before the LORD, all people, because he has roused himself from his holy dwelling. *u*"

CLEAN GARMENTS FOR THE HIGH PRIEST

3 Then he showed me Joshua *a v* the high priest standing before the angel of the LORD, and Satan *b w* standing at his right side to accuse him. [2]The LORD said to Satan, "The LORD rebuke you, *x* Satan! The LORD, who has chosen *y* Jerusalem, rebuke you! Is not this man a burning stick *z* snatched from the fire?" *a*

[3]Now Joshua was dressed in filthy clothes as he stood before the angel. [4]The angel said to those who were standing before him, "Take off his filthy clothes."

Then he said to Joshua, "See, I have taken away your sin, *b* and I will put fine garments *c* on you."

[5]Then I said, "Put a clean turban *d* on his head." So they put a clean turban on his head and clothed him, while the angel of the LORD stood by.

[6]The angel of the LORD gave this charge to Joshua: [7]"This is what the LORD Almighty says: 'If you will walk in obedience to me and keep my requirements, *e* then you will govern my house *f* and have charge *g* of my courts, and I will give you a place among these standing here. *h*

[8]"'Listen, High Priest *i* Joshua, you and your associates seated before you, you who are symbolic *j* of things to come: I am going to bring my servant, the Branch. *k* [9]See, the stone I have set in front of Joshua! *l* There are seven eyes *c m* on that one stone, *n* and I will engrave an inscription on it,' says the LORD Almighty, 'and I will remove the sin *o* of this land in a single day.

[10]"'In that day each of you will invite your neighbor to sit *p* under your vine and fig tree, *q*' declares the LORD Almighty."

THE GOLD LAMPSTAND AND THE TWO OLIVE TREES

4 Then the angel who talked with me returned and wakened *r* me, as one is wakened from sleep. *s* [2]He asked me, "What do you see?" *t*

I answered, "I see a solid gold lampstand *u* with a bowl at the top and seven lamps *v*

---

a 1 A variant of *Jeshua*; here and elsewhere in Zechariah   *b 1* Hebrew *satan* means *adversary*.
c 9 Or *facets*

2:12 *holy land.* See Ps 78:54. The land was rendered holy chiefly because it was the site of the earthly throne and sanctuary of the holy King, who dwelt there among his covenant people (see note on Ex 3:5). *choose Jerusalem.* See 1:17; 3:2.
2:13 *Be still before the LORD.* See Hab 2:20 and note. *roused himself.* To judge (cf. v. 9).

3:1–10 The fourth vision. Israel will be cleansed and restored as a priestly nation (see Ex 19:6 and note).
3:1 *Joshua.* For its Aramaic equivalent (Jeshua), see TNIV text note; see also TNIV text note on Hag 1:1. Here he represents the sinful nation of Israel (see vv. 8–9). The names Joshua and Jeshua were common in ancient times. The Greek equivalent is spelled "Jesus" in English, and all three forms of the name mean "The LORD saves" (see TNIV text note on Mt 1:21). *standing before.* Ministering before—as priest (see Dt 10:8; 2Ch 29:11; Eze 44:15). *angel of the LORD.* See 1:11; see also note on Ge 16:7. *Satan.* See TNIV text note; Job 1:6–12 and note on 1:6; 2:1–7; Rev 12:10 and note. *right side.* See Ps 109:6. *accuse.* The Hebrew for this word has the same root as the Hebrew for "Satan."
3:2 *rebuke … rebuke.* Repeated for emphasis (see 4:7; see also note on Isa 40:1). *chosen Jerusalem.* See 1:17; 2:12. *burning stick snatched from the fire.* The Jews were retrieved from the fire of Babylonian exile to carry out God's future purpose for them (see Am 4:11 and note; see also Zec 13:8–9; Dt 4:20 and note; 7:7–8; Jer 30:7; Rev 12:13–16; cf. 1Co 3:15; Jude 23 and notes).
3:4 *those who were standing before him.* Probably angels (see also v. 7). *Take off his filthy clothes.* Thus depriving him of his priestly office. The act is here symbolic also of the removal of sin (see note on v. 9; cf. Isa 64:6).
3:5 *Put a clean turban on his head.* Thus reinstating him into his high-priestly function so that Israel once again has a divinely authorized priestly mediator. On the front of the turban were

the words "HOLY TO THE LORD" (Ex 28:36–37; 39:30–31; see Zec 14:20 and note).
3:7 If Joshua and his priestly associates are faithful, they will be co-workers with the angels in carrying out God's purposes for Zion and Israel (cf. Jer 31:22 and note). *these standing here.* See note on v. 4.
3:8 *associates.* Fellow priests. *my servant.* See notes on Ex 14:31; Ps 18 title; Isa 41:8–9; 42:1–4; 42:1; Ro 1:1. *Branch.* A Messianic title (see 6:12; Isa 4:2 and notes; 11:1; Jer 23:5 and note; 33:15).
3:9 *stone.* Probably another figure of the Messiah (see Ps 118:22; Isa 8:14; 28:16 and notes; Da 2:35,45). *seven eyes.* Perhaps symbolic of infinite intelligence (omniscience). See note on 4:10. *I will remove the sin of this land.* The symbolic act of v. 4 is now explained. "Land" stands for the people of Israel. For the cleansing spoken of here, see also 12:10—13:1; cf. Ro 11:26–27 and notes. *in a single day.* Ultimately Good Friday, though some believe that the reference also includes Christ's second coming.
3:10 *that day.* See 2:11 and note. *sit under your vine and fig tree.* A proverbial picture of peace, security and contentment (see Mic 4:4 and note; cf. 2Ki 18:31).

4:1–14 The fifth vision. The Jews are encouraged to rebuild the temple by being reminded of their divine resources. The light from the lampstand in the tabernacle/temple represents the reflection of God's glory in the consecration and holy service of God's people (see note on Ex 25:37)—made possible only by the power of God's Spirit (see v. 6; symbolized by the oil, v. 12). This enabling power will equip and sustain Zerubbabel in the rebuilding of the temple (vv. 6–10). And in the performance of their offices, Zerubbabel and Joshua (as representatives of the royal and priestly mediatorial offices) will channel the Spirit's enablement to God's people (vv. 11–14).
4:1 *wakened me.* On the same night (see note on 1:8).

on it, with seven channels to the lamps. ³Also there are two olive trees ʷ by it, one on the right of the bowl and the other on its left."

⁴I asked the angel who talked with me, "What are these, my lord?"

⁵He answered, "Do you not know what these are?"

"No, my lord," I replied. ˣ

⁶So he said to me, "This is the word of the LORD to Zerubbabel: ʸ 'Not ᶻ by might nor by power, ᵃ but by my Spirit,' ᵇ says the LORD Almighty.

⁷"What are you, mighty mountain? Before Zerubbabel you will become level ground. ᶜ Then he will bring out the capstone ᵈ to shouts ᵉ of 'God bless it! God bless it!' "

⁸Then the word of the LORD came to me: ⁹"The hands of Zerubbabel have laid the foundation ᶠ of this temple; his hands will also complete it. ᵍ Then you will know that the LORD Almighty has sent me ʰ to you.

¹⁰"Who dares despise the day ⁱ of small things, ʲ since the seven eyes ᵏ of the LORD that range throughout the earth will rejoice when they see the chosen capstoneᵃ in the hand of Zerubbabel?"ˡ

¹¹Then I asked the angel, "What are these two olive trees ᵐ on the right and the left of the lampstand?"

¹²Again I asked him, "What are these two olive branches beside the two gold pipes that pour out golden oil?"

¹³He replied, "Do you not know what these are?"

"No, my lord," I said.

¹⁴So he said, "These are the two who are anointed ⁿ toᵇ serve the Lord of all the earth."

THE FLYING SCROLL

5 I looked again, and there before me was a flying scroll. ᵒ
²He asked me, "What do you see?" ᵖ
I answered, "I see a flying scroll, twenty cubits long and ten cubits wide. ᶜ"

ᵃ 10 Or *the plumb line*   ᵇ 14 Or *two who bring oil and*   ᶜ 2 That is, about 30 feet long and 15 feet wide or about 9 meters long and 4.5 meters wide

4:3 ʷ ver 11;
S Ps 1:3; S Rev 11:4
4:5 ˣ S Zec 1:9
4:6 ʸ S 1Ch 3:19;
S Ezr 5:2
ᶻ S 1Sa 13:22;
S 1Ki 19:12 ᵃ S 1Sa 2:9
ᵇ S Ne 9:20; Isa 11:2-
4; S Da 2:34; Hos 1:7
4:7 ᶜ S Ps 26:12;
Jer 51:25 ᵈ S Ps 118:22
ᵉ S 1Ch 15:28
4:9 ᶠ S Ezr 3:11
ᵍ Ezr 3:8; S 6:15;
Zec 6:12 ʰ S Zec 2:9
4:10 ⁱ S Hag 2:23
ʲ Ezr 3:12
ᵏ 2Ch 16:9; Rev 5:6
ˡ S Ezr 5:1; S Ne 12:1;
S Job 38:5
4:11 ᵐ S ver 3;
S Rev 11:4
4:14 ⁿ Ex 29:7;
40:15; S Ps 45:7;
S Isa 20:3;
S Da 9:24-26
5:1 ᵒ S Ps 40:7;
S Jer 36:4; Rev 5:1
5:2 ᵖ S Jer 1:13

4:2 *What do you see?* See 5:2; see also Jer 1:11 and note. The vision here was probably of seven lamps arranged around a large bowl that served as a bountiful reservoir of oil. The "seven channels to the lamps" conveyed the oil from the bowl to the lamps. But the text is also open to a different interpretation, namely, that the "channels" are "lips" or "spouts" that held the wicks of these oil lamps and that each of these lamps had seven of them (thus a total of 49 flames; see note on Ex 25:37). In any event, the bowl represents an abundant supply of oil, symbolizing the fullness of God's power through his Spirit, and the "seven ... seven" represents the abundant light shining from the lamps (seven being the number of fullness).

4:3 *two olive trees.* Cf. Rev 11:4. The two olive trees stand for the priestly and royal offices and symbolize a continuing supply of oil. The two olive branches (v. 12) stand for Joshua, the priest (ch. 3), and Zerubbabel, from the royal house of David (ch. 4; cf. v. 14). These two leaders were to do God's work (e.g., on the temple and in the lives of the people) in the power of his Spirit (v. 6). The combination of the priestly and royal lines and their functions points ultimately to the Messianic King-Priest and his offices and functions (cf. 6:13).

4:4 *these.* The two olive trees of v. 3, as v. 11 makes clear. The answer to the question is postponed until v. 14.

4:6 *Not by might nor by power.* Zerubbabel does not possess the royal might and power that David and Solomon had enjoyed, and in any event such worldly power is inadequate for the purpose of rebuilding the Lord's temple. *by my Spirit.* Interprets the symbolism of the oil (v. 12). The angel encouraged Zerubbabel to complete the rebuilding of the temple (vv. 7–10) and assured him of the Spirit's enablement (see Hag 2:5 and note).

4:7 *mountain ... level ground.* Faith in the power of God's Spirit (v. 6) can overcome mountainous obstacles. The figurative mountain probably included opposition (Ezr 4:1–5:24) and the people's unwillingness to persevere (cf. Hag 1:14;

2:1–5). Cf. the same or similar imagery in Isa 40:4; 41:15; 49:11; Mt 17:20; 21:21; 1Co 13:2; 2Co 10:4. *capstone.* The final stone to be put in place (see Ps 118:22 and note), marking the completion of the restoration temple by Zerubbabel (see v. 9). *God bless it! God bless it!* Repeated for emphasis (see 3:2; see also note on Isa 40:1).

4:8 Introduces a prophetic oracle (see 6:9; 7:4,8; 8:1,18; see also note on Hos 1:1).

4:9 *laid the foundation.* In 536 B.C. (Ezr 3:8–11; 5:16). *complete it.* In 516 (see Ezr 6:15 and note).

4:10 *day of small things.* Some thought the work on the temple was insignificant (see Ezr 3:12; Hag 2:3 and note), but God was in the rebuilding program and, by his Spirit (v. 6), would enable Zerubbabel to finish it. *seven eyes.* See note on 3:9. God oversees the whole earth and is therefore in control of the situation in Judah (cf. 2Ch 16:9). *chosen capstone.* See TNIV text note ("plumb line"), but the main TNIV text is preferable contextually (v.7).

4:14 The meaning of the vision is now explained. *two ... anointed.* Zerubbabel, from the royal line of David, and Joshua, the priest. The oil (v. 12) used in anointing symbolizes the Holy Spirit (v. 6). The combination of ruler and priest points ultimately to the Messianic King-Priest (cf. 6:13; see Ps 110; Heb 7). *Lord of all the earth.* See 6:5; the master of the circumstances in which Zerubbabel and the people found themselves.

5:1–4 The sixth vision. Lawbreakers are condemned by the law they have broken; sinners will be purged from the land.

5:1 *flying.* Unrolled and waving like a banner, for all to read. *scroll.* See note on Ex 17:14.

5:2 *He.* The interpreting angel (v.5; 4:11). *What do you see?* See 4:2 and note. *twenty ... ten.* Unusually large (especially in its width), for all to see (see TNIV text note). Such a bold, clear message of judgment against sin should spur the people on to repentance and righteousness.

5:3 *q* Isa 24:6; 34:2;
43:28; Mal 3:9; 4:6
r Ex 20:15; Mal 3:8
s Ex 20:7; Isa 48:1
5:4 *t* Zec 8:17
u Lev 14:34-45;
S Pr 3:33; S Hab 2:9-
11; Mal 3:5
5:6 *v* Mic 6:10
5:8 *w* Mic 6:11
5:9 *x* Lev 11:19
5:11 *y* S Ge 10:10
z Jer 29:5,28
a S Da 1:2
6:1 *b* ver 5;
S 2Ki 2:11
6:2 *c* Rev 6:5
6:3 *d* Rev 6:2
6:5 *e* S Eze 37:9;
Mt 24:31; Rev 7:1
f S Jos 3:11
6:7 *g* Isa 43:6;
Zec 1:8

[3]And he said to me, "This is the curse [q] that is going out over the whole land; for according to what it says on one side, every thief [r] will be banished, and according to what it says on the other, everyone who swears falsely [s] will be banished. [4]The LORD Almighty declares, 'I will send it out, and it will enter the house of the thief and the house of anyone who swears falsely [t] by my name. It will remain in that house and destroy it completely, both its timbers and its stones. [u]' "

THE WOMAN IN A BASKET

[5]Then the angel who was speaking to me came forward and said to me, "Look up and see what this is that is appearing."

[6]I asked, "What is it?"

He replied, "It is a basket. [v]" And he added, "This is the iniquity [a] of the people throughout the land."

[7]Then the cover of lead was raised, and there in the basket sat a woman! [8]He said, "This is wickedness," and he pushed her back into the basket and pushed the lead cover down over its mouth. [w]

[9]Then I looked up—and there before me were two women, with the wind in their wings! They had wings like those of a stork, [x] and they lifted up the basket between heaven and earth.

[10]"Where are they taking the basket?" I asked the angel who was speaking to me.

[11]He replied, "To the country of Babylonia [b] [y] to build a house [z] for it. When it is ready, the basket will be set there in its place." [a]

FOUR CHARIOTS

6 I looked up again, and there before me were four chariots [b] coming out from between two mountains—mountains of bronze. [2]The first chariot had red horses, the second black, [c] [3]the third white, [d] and the fourth dappled—all of them powerful. [4]I asked the angel who was speaking to me, "What are these, my lord?"

[5]The angel answered me, "These are the four spirits [c] [e] of heaven, going out from standing in the presence of the Lord of the whole world. [f] [6]The one with the black horses is going toward the north country, the one with the white horses toward the west, [d] and the one with the dappled horses toward the south."

[7]When the powerful horses went out, they were straining to go throughout the earth. [g] And he said, "Go throughout the earth!" So they went throughout the earth.

---

a 6 Or *appearance*   *b* 11 Hebrew *Shinar*   *c* 5 Or *winds*   *d* 6 Or *horses after them*

5:3 *curse.* See Dt 27:26 and note. *on one side ... on the other.* Like the two tablets of the law (Ex 32:15), the scroll is inscribed on both sides (see Eze 2:10 and note). *thief.* One who breaks the eighth commandment (Ex 20:15). *everyone who swears falsely.* See 8:17. Such a person violates the third commandment (compare v. 4 with Ex 20:7). Although theft and perjury may have been the most common forms of lawbreaking at the time, they are probably intended as representative sins. The people of Judah had been guilty of infractions against the whole law (see Jas 2:10 and note).

5:4 *The LORD Almighty.* See note on 1Sa 1:3. *it will enter ... and destroy.* "It" refers to the curse (v. 3). God's word, whether promise (ch. 4) or warning (as here), always accomplishes its purpose (cf. Ps 147:15; Isa 55:10-11; see Heb 4:12-13 and notes).

5:5-11 The seventh vision. Not only must flagrant, persistent sinners be removed from the land (vv. 1-4), but the whole sinful system will be removed—apparently to a more fitting place (Babylonia).

5:6 *basket.* Hebrew "ephah." A normal ephah-sized container would not be large enough to hold a person. This one was undoubtedly enlarged (like the flying scroll of vv. 1-2) for the purpose of the vision. *iniquity.* See v. 8 ("wickedness").

5:7 *woman.* Perhaps the reason the people's wickedness was personified as a woman (cf. Rev 17:1-6) is that the Hebrew word for "wickedness" (v. 8) is feminine in gender.

5:8 *wickedness.* A general word denoting moral, religious and civil evil—frequently used as an antonym of righteousness (e.g., Pr 13:6; Eze 33:12). The whole evil system was to

be destroyed (cf. 2Th 2:6-8).

5:9 *two women.* Divinely chosen agents. *wind.* Also an instrument of God (see Ps 104:3-4 and note). The removal of wickedness would be the work of God alone.

5:11 *Babylonia.* See Ge 10:10 and TNIV text note; 11:2 and TNIV text note; Rev 17-18. Babylonia, a land of idolatry, was an appropriate locale for wickedness—but not Israel, where God chose to dwell with his people. Only after being purged of its evil would the promised land truly be the "holy land" (2:12).

6:1-8 The eighth and last vision. It corresponds to the first (1:7-17), though there are differences in details, such as in the order and colors of the horses. As in the first vision, the Lord is depicted as the one who controls the events of history (see Introduction: Literary Forms and Themes). He will conquer the nations that oppress Israel.

6:1 *four chariots.* Angelic spirits as agents of divine judgment (v. 5). *two mountains.* Possibly Mount Zion and the Mount of Olives, with the Kidron Valley between them (cf. Joel 3:2 and note), or perhaps reference is to the creation of two mountains through the splitting of the Mount of Olives in 14:4. *bronze.* Perhaps symbolic of judgment (cf. Nu 21:9).

6:2-3 *red ... black ... white ... dappled.* The horses may signify various divine judgments on the earth (see note on v. 8; see also Rev 6:1-8 and note on 6:2).

6:4 *these.* The chariots, with the horses harnessed to them.

6:5 *four spirits.* See note on v. 1. *Lord of the whole world.* See note on 4:14.

⁸Then he called to me, "Look, those going toward the north country have given my Spirit[a] rest[h] in the land of the north."[i]

A CROWN FOR JOSHUA

⁹The word of the LORD came to me: ¹⁰"Take ⌐silver and gold⌐ from the exiles Heldai, Tobijah and Jedaiah, who have arrived from Babylon.[j] Go the same day to the house of Josiah son of Zephaniah. ¹¹Take the silver and gold and make a crown,[k] and set it on the head of the high priest, Joshua[l] son of Jozadak.[b m] ¹²Tell him this is what the LORD Almighty says: 'Here is the man whose name is the Branch,[n] and he will branch out from his place and build the temple of the LORD.[o] ¹³It is he who will build the temple of the LORD, and he will be clothed with majesty and will sit and rule on his throne. And he[c] will be a priest[p] on his throne. And there will be harmony between the two.' ¹⁴The crown will be given to Heldai,[d] Tobijah, Jedaiah and Hen[e] son of Zephaniah as a memorial[q] in the temple of the LORD. ¹⁵Those who are far away will come and help to build the temple of the LORD,[r] and you will know that the LORD Almighty has sent me to you.[s] This will happen if you diligently obey[t] the LORD your God."

JUSTICE AND MERCY, NOT FASTING

7 In the fourth year of King Darius, the word of the LORD came to Zechariah[u] on the fourth day of the ninth month, the month of Kislev.[v] ²The people of Bethel had sent Sharezer and Regem-Melek, together with their men, to entreat[w] the LORD[x] ³by asking the priests of the house of the LORD Almighty and the prophets, "Should I mourn[y] and fast in the fifth[z] month, as I have done for so many years?"

⁴Then the word of the LORD Almighty came to me: ⁵"Ask all the people of the land and the priests, 'When you fasted[a] and mourned in the fifth and seventh[b] months for the past seventy years,[c] was it really for me that you fasted? ⁶And when you were eating and drinking, were you not just feasting for yourselves?[d] ⁷Are these not the words the LORD proclaimed through the earlier prophets[e] when Jerusalem and its surrounding towns were at rest[f] and prosperous, and the Negev and the western foothills[g] were settled?' "[h]

⁸And the word of the LORD came again to Zechariah: ⁹"This is what the LORD Almighty said: 'Administer true justice;[i] show mercy and compassion to one another.[j] ¹⁰Do not op-

---

[a] 8 Or spirit   [b] 11 Hebrew Jehozadak, a variant of Jozadak   [c] 13 Or there   [d] 14 Syriac; Hebrew Helem   [e] 14 Or and the gracious one, the

---

Right margin cross-references:

6:8 ʰS Eze 5:13; S 24:13 ¹S Zec 1:10
6:10 ʲEzr 7:14-16; Jer 28:6
6:11 ᵏPs 21:3 ˡS Ezr 2:2; S Zec 3:1 ᵐS 1Ch 6:15; S Ezr 3:2
6:12 ⁿS Isa 4:2; S Eze 17:22 ᵒEzr 3:8-10; Zec 4:6-9
6:13 ᵖS Ps 110:4
6:14 ᑫS Ex 28:12
6:15 ʳIsa 60:10 ˢZec 2:9-11 ᵗIsa 58:12; Jer 7:23; S Zec 3:7
7:1 ᵘS Ezr 5:1
7:2 ʷJer 26:19; Zec 8:21 ˣHag 2:10-14
7:3 ʸZec 12:12-14 ᶻ2Ki 25:9; Jer 52:12-14
7:5 ᵃIsa 58:5 ᵇ2Ki 25:25 ᶜS Da 9:2
7:6 ᵈS Isa 43:23
7:7 ᵉIsa 1:11-20; Zec 1:4 ᶠJer 22:21 ᵍS Jer 17:26 ʰJer 44:4-5
7:9 ⁱS Jer 22:3; 42:5; Zec 8:16 ʲS Dt 22:1

6:8 *north country.* Primarily Babylonia, but also the direction from which most of Israel's foes invaded them (see note on 2:6). *my Spirit.* If the alternative translation in the TNIV text note ("spirit") is taken, the meaning is that the angelic beings dispatched to the north have triumphed and thus have pacified or appeased God's spirit (i.e., his anger; cf. Ecc 10:4, where the same Hebrew word is translated "anger"). See 1:15, where God's displeasure was aroused against oppressive nations. In either case, since conquest was announced in the north, victory was assured over all enemies.

6:9-15 The two central visions (the fourth and fifth) were concerned with the high priest and the civil governor (in the Davidic line); see Introduction: Literary Forms and Themes. Zechariah now relates the message of those two visions to the Messianic King-Priest.

6:9 See note on 4:8.

6:10 ⌐silver and gold⌐. Gifts for the temple (cf. Ezr 6:5; Hag 2:8).

6:11 *crown.* The Hebrew for this word is not the same as that used for the high priest's turban but refers to an ornate crown (cf. Rev 19:12). The royal crowning of the high priest foreshadows the goal and consummation of prophecy—the crowning and reign of the Messianic King-Priest (see vv. 12-13; cf. Ps 110:4; Heb 7:1-3).

6:12 *Here is the man.* Cf. Pilate's introduction of Jesus in Jn 19:5. *Branch.* See note on 3:8. According to the Aramaic Targum (a paraphrase), the Jerusalem Talmud (a collection of religious instruction) and the Midrash (practical exposition), Jews early regarded this verse as Messianic. *branch out.* The TNIV here reflects the wordplay in the Hebrew text. *temple.* Cf. Isa 2:2-3; Eze 40-43; Hag 2:6-9.

6:13 *clothed with.* See note on Ps 109:29. *his throne.* See 2Sa 7:11,16; Isa 9:7; Lk 1:32 and notes. *priest on his throne.* The coming Davidic King will also be a priest. *two.* Probably the royal and priestly offices. Such a combination was not normally possible in Israel. For this reason, the sect of Qumran (see essay, pp. 1596-1597) expected two Messianic figures—a high-priestly Messiah and a Davidic one. But the two offices and functions would in fact be united in the one person of the Messiah (cf. Ps 110; Heb 7).

6:14 *Hen.* Means "gracious one" (see TNIV text note), perhaps another name for Josiah—to honor him for his hospitality (v. 10).

6:15 *Those who are far away will ... help.* Cf. Isa 60:4-7.

7:1 *fourth year ... fourth day ... ninth month.* Dec. 7, 518 B.C.—not quite two years after the eight night visions (see note on 1:7).

7:3 *prophets.* Including Zechariah. *I.* The people of Bethel collectively. *fast in the fifth month.* See note on 8:19. *so many years.* "The past seventy years" (v. 5).

7:4-7 A rebuke for selfish and insincere fasting on the part of the people and the priests.

7:4,8 See note on 4:8.

7:5 *fasted ... fifth and seventh.* See note on 8:19. *seventy years.* See 1:12 and note. Since these fasts commemorated events related to the destruction of Jerusalem and the temple (see note on 8:19), the 70 years here are to be reckoned from 586 B.C. Strictly speaking, 68 years had transpired; 70 is thus a round number.

7:6 *for yourselves.* Cf. Isa 1:11-17; 58:1-7,13-14.

7:7,12 *earlier prophets.* See note on 1:4.

7:7 *Negev.* See note on Ge 12:9. *western foothills.* Sloping toward the Mediterranean.

7:9-10 Four tests of faithful covenant living, consisting of a series of social, moral and ethical commands.

7:9 *justice.* The proper ordering of all society (see 8:16-17 and

7:10 ᵏJer 49:11
ˡS Ex 22:21
ᵐS Lev 25:17;
Isa 1:23 ⁿS Ex 22:22;
S Job 35:8; S Isa 1:17;
S Eze 45:9; S Mic 6:8
7:11 ᵒS Isa 6:9
ᵖS Jer 32:33
qS Jer 5:3; 8:5; 11:10;
S 17:23; S Eze 5:6
7:12 ʳS Jer 5:3; 17:1;
S Eze 11:19
ˢS Ne 9:29
ᵗS Jer 42:21;
S Da 9:12
7:13 ᵘS Jer 7:27
ᵛIsa 1:15; S Jer 11:11;
14:12; S Mic 3:4
ᵂS Pr 1:28;
S La 3:44;
S Eze 20:31
7:14 ˣS Lev 26:33;
Dt 4:27; 28:64-67;
S Ps 44:11 ʸJer 23:19
ᶻS Isa 33:8
ᵃS Jer 7:34; S 44:6;
S Eze 12:19
8:2 ᵇS Joel 2:18
8:3 ᶜZec 1:16
ᵈS Isa 52:8;
S Joel 3:21
ᵉS Zec 2:10
ᶠS Ps 15:2; S Isa 1:26;
S 48:1; S Jer 33:16
ᵍS Jer 26:18
ʰS Isa 1:26; S Mic 4:1
8:4 ⁱS Isa 65:20
8:5 ʲS Jer 30:20;
31:13
8:6 ᵏPs 118:23;
126:1-3 ˡJer 32:17,27
8:7 ᵐPs 107:3;
S Isa 11:11; S 43:5
8:8 ⁿS Eze 37:12;
Zec 10:10
ᵒS Jer 31:24
ᵖS Isa 51:16;
S Eze 11:19-20;
S 36:28; S Zec 2:11;
Heb 8:10 qJer 11:4;
Zec 10:6
8:9 ʳS Hag 2:4
ˢS Ezr 5:1 ᵗS Ezr 3:11

press the widowᵏ or the fatherless, the foreignerˡ or the poor.ᵐ Do not plot evil against each other.'ⁿ

¹¹"But they refused to pay attention; stubbornlyᵒ they turned their backsᵖ and covered their ears.q ¹²They made their hearts as hard as flintʳ and would not listen to the law or to the words that the LORD Almighty had sent by his Spirit through the earlier prophets.ˢ So the LORD Almighty was very angry.ᵗ

¹³" 'When I called, they did not listen;ᵘ so when they called, I would not listen,'ᵛ says the LORD Almighty.ᵂ ¹⁴I scatteredˣ them with a whirlwindʸ among all the nations, where they were strangers. The land they left behind them was so desolate that no one traveled through it.ᶻ This is how they made the pleasant land desolate.ᵃ' "

THE LORD PROMISES TO BLESS JERUSALEM

8 The word of the LORD Almighty came to me. ²This is what the LORD Almighty says: "I am very jealousᵇ for Zion; I am burning with jealousy for her."

³This is what the LORD says: "I will returnᶜ to Zionᵈ and dwell in Jerusalem.ᵉ Then Jerusalem will be called the City of Truth,ᶠ and the mountainᵍ of the LORD Almighty will be called the Holy Mountain.ʰ"

⁴This is what the LORD Almighty says: "Once again men and women of ripe old age will sit in the streets of Jerusalem,ⁱ each of them with cane in hand because of their age. ⁵The city streets will be filled with boys and girls playing there.ʲ"

⁶This is what the LORD Almighty says: "It may seem marvelous to the remnant of this people at that time,ᵏ but will it seem marvelous to me?ˡ" declares the LORD Almighty.

⁷This is what the LORD Almighty says: "I will save my people from the countries of the east and the west.ᵐ ⁸I will bring them backⁿ to liveᵒ in Jerusalem; they will be my people,ᵖ and I will be faithful and righteous to them as their God.q"

⁹This is what the LORD Almighty says: "Now hear these words, 'Let your hands be strongʳ so that the temple may be built.' This is also what the prophetsˢ said who were present when the foundationᵗ was laid for the house of the LORD Almighty. ¹⁰Before that time there were no wagesᵘ for people or animals. People could not go about their business safelyᵛ because of conflicts, since I had turned them all against each other. ¹¹But now I will not deal with the remnant of this people as I did in the past,"ᵂ declares the LORD Almighty.

¹²"The seed will grow well, the vine will yield its fruit,ˣ the ground will produce its

8:10 ᵘS Isa 5:10; S Hag 1:6 ᵛS 2Ch 15:5   8:11 ᵂIsa 12:1   8:12 ˣS Ps 85:12; S Joel 2:22

---

note on 8:16; Isa 42:1,4; Mic 6:8 and notes). *mercy.* Or "faithful love" (see Hos 10:12; 12:6 and notes). *compassion.* See note on 1:12.

A **7:10** *oppress.* Oppression is denounced frequently in the OT (see, e.g., Am 2:6–8 and notes; 4:1; 5:11–12,21–24; 8:4–6). *widow ... fatherless ... foreigner ... poor.* For the Biblical concern for such people, see, e.g., Dt 10:18; Isa 1:17 and note; Jer 5:28; Jas 1:27; 1Jn 3:16–18. In the ancient Near East, the ideal king was expected to protect the oppressed and needy members of society. *plot evil against each other.* See 8:17; cf. Mic 2:1–2 and note on 2:1.
7:11 *they.* The preexilic ancestors, as the reference to the "earlier prophets" in v. 12 shows. *stubbornly they turned their backs.* See Dt 9:6,13,27. *covered their ears.* See Ps 58:4; Isa 6:10 and notes; cf. Isa 33:15.
A **7:12** *hard as flint.* See Eze 3:8–9. *words ... sent by his Spirit.* The words of the prophets were inspired by God's Spirit (see Ne 9:30; Mic 3:8; 2Pe 1:21 and note). *very angry.* See 1:2,15.
7:13 See note on 1:3.
7:14 *scattered them.* One of the curses for covenant disobedience (see Dt 28:36–37,64–68 and note on 28:64). *whirlwind.* See Pr 1:27 and note; Isa 40:24; Hos 4:19. *land ... desolate.* See Dt 28:41–42,45–52. *This is how.* By their sins. *pleasant land.* See Ps 106:24 and note.
A **8:1–23** Ten promises of blessing, each beginning with "This is what the LORD (Almighty) says" (vv. 2,3,4,6,7,9,14, 19,20,23).
8:1,18 See note on 4:8.
8:2 *jealous.* See 1:14 and note.
8:3 *I will return.* See 1:3 and note; 1:16. *dwell.* See note on 2:10.

the City of Truth. Cf. v. 16; see Isa 1:26 and note. *the Holy Mountain.* Cf. 14:20–21.
8:4–5 See Isa 11:6–9 and note; 65:20–25.
8:6,11–12 *remnant.* See notes on Isa 1:9; 10:20–22.
8:6 *will it seem marvelous to me?* See Jer 32:27 and note.
8:7 *save my people.* Deliver them from exile, bondage and dispersion (cf. Isa 11:11–12; 43:5–7; Jer 30:7–11; 31:7–8). *from the countries of the east and the west.* Lit. "from the land of the sunrise and from the land of the going in of the sun," i.e., from everywhere—wherever the people are (cf. Ps 50:1; 113:3; Mal 1:11).
A **8:8** *they will be my people, and I will be ... their God.* Covenant terminology, pertaining to intimate fellowship in the covenant relationship between God and his people (see 13:9; Ge 17:7 and note; Ex 6:7; 29:45–46; Lev 11:45; 22:33; 25:38; 26:12,45; Nu 15:41; Dt 29:13; Jer 24:7 and note; Eze 34:30–31; 36:28; 37:27; Hos 1:9–10; 11:20; 2Co 6:16; Heb 8:10; Rev 21:3). *faithful and righteous.* Judah's restoration to covenant favor and blessing rests on the faithfulness (dependability) and righteousness of God.
8:9 *hands be strong.* See v. 13. The Hebrew for this expression is translated "be encouraged" in Jdg 7:11. *prophets.* Including Haggai (1:1) and Zechariah (1:1; see Ezr 5:1–2).
8:10 *Before that time.* Before the temple foundation was laid (see v. 9). *no wages.* See Hag 1:6–11; 2:15–19. *conflicts.* For example, with the Samaritans (Ezr 4:1–5).
8:11 *But now.* The reasons for discouragement have passed; God will now provide the grounds for encouragement.
A **8:12** Contrast with Hag 1:10–11. In Hag 2:19 God had predicted just such a reversal as is depicted here. Fertility

crops, *y* and the heavens will drop their dew. *z* I will give all these things as an inheritance *a* to the remnant of this people. *b* 13Just as you, Judah and Israel, have been a curse *a c* among the nations, so I will save *d* you, and you will be a blessing. *b e* Do not be afraid, *f* but let your hands be strong. *g*"

14This is what the LORD Almighty says: "Just as I had determined to bring disaster *h* on you and showed no pity when your ancestors angered me," says the LORD Almighty, 15"so now I have determined to do good *i* again to Jerusalem and Judah. *j* Do not be afraid. 16These are the things you are to do: Speak the truth *k* to each other, and render true and sound judgment *l* in your courts; *m* 17do not plot evil *n* against each other, and do not love to swear falsely. *o* I hate all this," declares the LORD.

18The word of the LORD Almighty came to me.

19This is what the LORD Almighty says: "The fasts of the fourth, *p* fifth, *q* seventh *r* and tenth *s* months will become joyful *t* and glad occasions and happy festivals for Judah. Therefore love truth *u* and peace."

20This is what the LORD Almighty says: "Many peoples and the inhabitants of many cities will yet come, 21and the inhabitants of one city will go to another and say, 'Let us go at once to entreat *v* the LORD and seek *w* the LORD Almighty. I myself am going.' 22And many peoples and powerful nations will come to Jerusalem to seek the LORD Almighty and to entreat him." *x*

23This is what the LORD Almighty says: "In those days ten people from all languages and nations will take firm hold of one Jew by the hem of his robe and say, 'Let us go with you, because we have heard that God is with you.' " *y*

JUDGMENT ON ISRAEL'S ENEMIES

9 A prophecy: *z*

> The word of the LORD is against the land of Hadrak
> and will come to rest on Damascus *a*—
> for the eyes of all people and all the tribes of Israel
> are on the LORD— *c*

---

a 13 That is, your name has been used in cursing (see Jer. 29:23); or, you have been regarded as under a curse.   *b* 13 Or and your name will be used in blessings (see Gen. 48:20); or and you will be seen as blessed   *c* 1 Or Damascus. / For the eye of the LORD is on all people, / as well as on the tribes of Israel,

8:12 *y* S Ps 67:6
z S Ge 27:28
a S Ps 65:13;
S Isa 60:21; Ob 1:17
b S Hos 2:21
8:13 *c* S Nu 5:27;
S Dt 13:15;
S Ps 102:8; Jer 42:18
d S Ps 48:8
e S Ge 12:2;
S Joel 2:14 *f* S Hag 2:5
g ver 9
8:14 *h* S Eze 24:14
8:15 *i* ver 13;
S Jer 29:11; Mic 7:18-
20 / Jer 31:28; 32:42
8:16 *k* S Ps 15:2;
S Jer 33:16;
S Eph 4:25
l S Eze 18:8
m S Eze 45:9;
S Am 5:15; S Zec 7:9
8:17 *n* Pr 3:29
o S Pr 6:16-19;
S Jer 7:9; Zec 5:4
8:19 *p* S 2Ki 25:7;
Jer 39:2 *q* S Jer 52:12
r 2Ki 25:25 *s* Jer 52:4
t Ps 30:11 *u* ver 16
8:21 *v* S Zec 7:2
w Jer 26:19
8:22 *x* S Ps 86:9;
117:1; Isa 2:2-3;
S 44:5; S 45:14; 49:6;
S Zec 2:11
8:23 *y* S Ps 102:22;
S Isa 14:1; S 45:14;
S 56:3; 1Co 14:25
9:1 *z* S Isa 13:1;
Jer 23:33 *a* Isa 17:1;
S Am 1:5

---

and bounty are part of the covenant blessings for obedience promised in Lev 26:3–10; Dt 28:11–12; cf. Eze 34:25–27; Hos 1:21–24.
8:13 *curse among the nations.* Part of the covenant curses for disobedience threatened in Dt 28:15–68 (see Dt 28:37; Jer 24:9; 25:18). *Judah and Israel.* The whole nation will experience this deliverance and blessing (cf. Jer 31:1–31; Eze 37:15–28). *blessing.* See vv. 20–23; cf. Ge 12:2. *hands be strong.* See note on v. 9.
8:14–17 Verses 14–15 specify God's part in the people's restoration to favor and blessing; vv. 16–18 delineate their part.
8:14 *your ancestors angered me.* See note on 1:2.
8:15 *do good.* See vv. 12–13.
8:16–17 See 7:9–10. Such moral and ethical behavior sums up the character of those who are in covenant relationship with the Lord.
8:16 *Speak the truth to each other.* See Eph 4:25 and note. *render true and sound judgment.* God requires justice (see 7:9; Dt 24:17–18; Ps 33:5; 89:14; 99:4; Am 2:7; 5:24 and notes; see also Introduction to Amos: Theological Theme and Message) and hates injustice (see v. 17; 5:3; 2Ch 19:7; Pr 6:16–19; Hab 1:4 and notes). *courts.* Lit. "gates" (see Ge 19:1 and note; 2Sa 18:24).
8:17 *swear falsely.* Perjure oneself (see note on 5:3). *I hate all this.* Pr 6:16–19 lists seven things the Lord hates, three of which relate directly to vv. 16–17 here: "a lying tongue," "a heart that devises wicked schemes" and "a false witness who pours out lies."
8:19 See 7:2–6. *fourth.* The fast that lamented the breaching of the walls of Jerusalem by Nebuchadnezzar (2Ki 25:3–4; Jer 39:2). *fifth.* Commemorated the burning of the temple and the other important buildings (2Ki 25:8–10). *seventh.* Marked the

anniversary of Gedaliah's assassination (2Ki 25:22–25; Jer 41:1–3). *tenth.* Mourned the beginning of Nebuchadnezzar's siege of Jerusalem (2Ki 25:1; Jer 39:1; Eze 24:1–2). *happy festivals.* Cf. Isa 65:18–19; Jer 31:10–14.
8:20–23 For similar predictions about Gentiles seeking the Lord, see 2:11 and note; Mic 4:1–5.
8:22 *powerful.* Or "numerous" (as in Ex 1:9; see also TNIV text note on Isa 53:12); anticipates a fulfillment of the promise of Gentile blessing in the Abrahamic covenant (Ge 12:3; Gal 3:8,26–29; see also Isa 55:5; 56:6–7; Mk 11:17 and note).
8:23 *ten.* One way of indicating a large or complete number in Hebrew (see Ge 31:7 and note; Lev 26:26; Nu 14:22 and note; 1Sa 1:8; Ne 4:12). *Jew.* The word is ordinarily used in the OT only of the people of Judah after the exile (see note on Jer 34:9). *we have heard that God is with you.* True godliness attracts others to the Lord (see Ge 21:22; 26:28; 30:27; see also notes on Ge 39:2–6; 1Co 14:24).
9:1–8 Probably a prophetic description of the Lord's march south to Jerusalem, destroying—as Divine Warrior—the traditional enemies of Israel. As history shows, the agent of his judgment was Alexander the Great (333–332 B.C.; see essay, p. 1594).
9:1 *A prophecy: The word of the LORD.* The Hebrew for this phrase occurs only two other times in the OT (12:1; Mal 1:1), making it likely that Zec 9–14 and Malachi were written during the same general period. *word of the LORD.* See 1:1; 12:1; Hos 1:1 and note. *Hadrak.* Hatarikka, north of Hamath on the Orontes River (see v. 2). *Damascus.* The leading city-state of the Arameans (see notes on Dt 26:5; Isa 17:1). *eyes . . . on the LORD.* The thought may be that the eyes of people, especially all the tribes of Israel, are turned toward the Lord (for deliverance). But see TNIV text note.

9:2 *b* S Jer 49:23
c Eze 28:1-19
d S Ge 10:15
9:3 *e* Job 27:16;
S Eze 28:4
9:4 *f* S Isa 23:11
g S Isa 23:1; Jer 25:22;
Eze 26:3-5; 27:32-36;
28:18
9:5 *h* Jer 47:5
9:6 *i* S Isa 14:30
9:7 *j* S Job 25:2
k S Jer 47:1;
S Joel 3:4; S Zep 2:4
9:8 *l* S Isa 26:1
m Zec 14:21
n S Isa 52:1; S 54:14;
S Joel 3:17
9:9 *o* S Isa 62:11
p S 1Ki 1:39
q S Ps 24:7; S 149:2;
Mic 4:8 *r* Isa 9:6-7;
43:3-11; Jer 23:5-6;
Zep 3:14-15; Zec 2:10
s S Ge 49:11;
S 1Ki 1:33 *t* Mt 21:5*;
Jn 12:15*

² and on Hamath *b* too, which borders on it,
   and on Tyre *c* and Sidon, *d* though they are very skillful.
³ Tyre has built herself a stronghold;
   she has heaped up silver like dust,
   and gold like the dirt of the streets. *e*
⁴ But the Lord will take away her possessions
   and destroy *f* her power on the sea,
   and she will be consumed by fire. *g*
⁵ Ashkelon *h* will see it and fear;
   Gaza will writhe in agony,
   and Ekron too, for her hope will wither.
Gaza will lose her king
   and Ashkelon will be deserted.
⁶ A mongrel people will occupy Ashdod,
   and I will put an end *i* to the pride of the Philistines.
⁷ I will take the blood from their mouths,
   the forbidden food from between their teeth.
Those who are left will belong to our God *j*
   and become a clan in Judah,
   and Ekron will be like the Jebusites. *k*
⁸ But I will encamp *l* at my temple
   to guard it against marauding forces. *m*
Never again will an oppressor overrun my people,
   for now I am keeping watch. *n*

THE COMING OF ZION'S KING

⁹ Rejoice greatly, Daughter Zion! *o*
   Shout, *p* Daughter Jerusalem!
See, your king comes to you, *q*
   righteous and having salvation, *r*
lowly and riding on a donkey, *s*
   on a colt, the foal of a donkey. *t*
¹⁰ I will take away the chariots from Ephraim
   and the warhorses from Jerusalem,

9:2 *on Hamath too.* Judgment will rest upon Hamath, just as upon Hadrak and Damascus. Hamath is modern Hama (see Isa 10:9 and note). *it. Damascus. Tyre and Sidon.* Phoenician (modern Lebanese) coastal cities (see notes on Isa 23:1; 23:2,4,12). Their judgment (vv. 3–4) is also foretold in Isa 23; Eze 26:3–14; 28:20–24; Am 1:9–10.
9:3 *stronghold.* The Hebrew for this word is a pun on the Hebrew for "Tyre" (meaning "rock"). The stronghold was Tyre's island fortress (Isa 23:4; Eze 26:5). It fell (v. 4) to Alexander in July, 332 B.C., after a siege of seven months (see note on Eze 26:1—28:19). *silver like dust ... gold like the dirt.* Cf. 1Ki 10:21,27. Tyre was a center of trade and commerce, and her wealth was proverbial (see Isa 23:2–3,8,18; Eze 26:12; 27:3–27,33; 28:4–5,7, 12–14,16–18).
9:4 *her power on the sea.* Tyre's exploitation of commercial sea lanes in the Mediterranean was the source of much of her wealth.
9:5–7 The Philistine cities were greatly alarmed at Alexander's steady advance.
9:5 *Ashkelon ... Gaza ... Ekron.* Three of the five major Philistine cities (see map, p. 338). *her hope will wither.* As the northernmost city of Philistia, Ekron would be the first to suffer. Her hope that Tyre would stem the tide would meet with disappointment.
9:6 *mongrel people.* People of mixed nationality; they characterized the postexilic period (Ne 13:23–24). *Ashdod.* The fourth remaining city in the Philistine group (see notes on v. 5; Am 1:8). *l.* God. *Philistines.* See note on Ge 10:14. At one time their control of Canaan was so extensive that the land was eventually named after them ("Palestine").
9:7 *blood.* Of idolatrous sacrifices. *forbidden food.* Ceremonially

unclean food. *Jebusites.* These ancient inhabitants of Jerusalem (see notes on Ge 10:16; 2Sa 5:6) were absorbed into Judah (e.g., Araunah in 2Sa 24:16–24). So would it be with a remnant of the Philistines.
9:8 *encamp at my temple to guard it against marauding forces.* See 2:5. Alexander spared the temple and the city of Jerusalem. *oppressor.* The Hebrew for this word is translated "slave driver" in Ex 3:7; 5:6,10 and elsewhere; thus it echoes the Egyptian bondage motif. *keeping watch.* See Ex 3:7; Ps 32:8; 121.
🔺 9:9 Quoted in the NT as Messianic and as referring ultimately to Jesus' entry into Jerusalem as King (Mt 21:5; Jn 12:15). *Daughter Zion ... Daughter Jerusalem.* A personification of Jerusalem (see note on 2Ki 19:21). *your king.* The Davidic ("your") Messianic King. *righteous.* Conforming to the divine standard of morality and ethics, particularly as revealed in the Mosaic legislation; a characteristic of the ideal king (see 2Sa 23:3–4 and note on 23:3; Ps 4:1 and note; 72:1–3; Isa 9:7 and note; 53:11; Jer 23:6 and note). *lowly.* Or "humble" (cf. Isa 53:2–3,7; Mt 11:29). *riding on a donkey.* A suitable choice, since the donkey was a lowly animal of peace (contrast the warhorse of v. 10), as well as a princely mount (Jdg 10:4; 12:14; 2Sa 16:2) before the horse came into common use. The royal mount used by David and his sons was the mule (see 2Sa 13:29 and note).
🔺 9:10 *take away the chariots ... warhorses ... battle bow.* A similar era of disarmament is foreseen in Isa 2:4; 9:5–7; 11:1–10; Mic 5:10–11. *Ephraim.* See note on v. 13. *peace to the nations.* In sharp contrast to Alexander's empire, which was founded on bloodshed, the Messianic King will establish a universal kingdom of peace as the ultimate fulfillment of the Abrahamic covenant (cf. 14:16; see Ge 12:2–3 and note, but cf. Rev

and the battle bow will be broken. [u]
He will proclaim peace [v] to the nations.
His rule will extend from sea to sea
and from the River[a] to the ends of the earth. [w]
[11] As for you, because of the blood of my covenant [x] with you,
I will free your prisoners [y] from the waterless pit. [z]
[12] Return to your fortress, [a] you prisoners of hope;
even now I announce that I will restore twice [b] as much to you.
[13] I will bend Judah as I bend my bow [c]
and fill it with Ephraim. [d]
I will rouse your sons, Zion,
against your sons, Greece, [e]
and make you like a warrior's sword. [f]

THE LORD WILL APPEAR

[14] Then the LORD will appear over them; [g]
his arrow will flash like lightning. [h]
The Sovereign LORD will sound the trumpet; [i]
he will march in the storms [j] of the south,
[15]   and the LORD Almighty will shield [k] them.
They will destroy
and overcome with slingstones. [l]
They will drink and roar as with wine; [m]
they will be full like a bowl [n]
used for sprinkling [b] the corners [o] of the altar.
[16] The LORD their God will save his people on that day [p]
as a shepherd saves his flock.
They will sparkle in his land
like jewels in a crown. [q]
[17] How attractive and beautiful they will be!
Grain will make the young men thrive,
and new wine the young women.

THE LORD WILL CARE FOR JUDAH

10 Ask the LORD for rain in the springtime;
it is the LORD who sends the thunderstorms.
He gives showers of rain [r] to all people,
and plants of the field [s] to everyone.
[2] The idols [t] speak deceitfully,

---

[a] 10 That is, the Euphrates   [b] 15 Or bowl, / like

9:10 [u] Hos 1:7; 2:18;
Mic 4:3; 5:10;
Zec 10:4 [v] S Isa 2:4
[w] Ps 72:8
9:11 [x] S Ex 24:8;
S Mt 26:28;
S Lk 22:20
[y] S Isa 10:4; S 42:7
[z] Jer 38:6
9:12 [a] S Joel 3:16
[b] S Dt 21:17;
S Isa 40:2
9:13 [c] S 2Sa 22:35
[d] S Isa 49:2
[e] S Joel 3:6
[f] S Jer 51:20
9:14 [g] Isa 31:5
[h] Ps 18:14; S Hab 3:11
[i] S Lev 25:9;
S Mt 24:31 [j] Isa 21:1;
66:15
9:15 [k] Isa 31:5;
37:35; Zec 12:8
[l] Zec 14:3 [m] Zec 10:7
[n] Zec 14:20
[o] S Ex 27:2
9:16 [p] S Isa 10:20
[q] S Jer 31:11
10:1 [r] S Lev 26:4;
S 1Ki 8:36;
S Ps 104:13; S 135:7
[s] S Job 14:9
10:2 [t] Eze 21:21

19:11 and note). *from sea to sea.* Variously explained as "from the Nile to the Euphrates," "from the Mediterranean to the Red Sea" and "from the Mediterranean to the Dead Sea." The question is not important because the phrase is used to indicate totality or universality, as is true also of "from the River to the ends of the earth." The point is that the Davidic Messiah's rule will be universal (see Ps 22:27–28 and notes; 72:8–11 and note on 72:8; Isa 45:22; 52:10; 66:18).

9:11 *blood of my covenant with you.* Probably the Sinaitic covenant (Ex 24:3–8). *prisoners.* Perhaps those still in Babylonia, the land of exile. *waterless pit.* Cf. Ge 37:24; Jer 38:6.

9:12 *fortress.* Either (1) Jerusalem (Zion) and environs or (2) God himself (cf. 2:5). *hope.* In the future delivering King (vv. 9–10). *twice as much.* Full or complete restoration (Isa 61:7).

9:13 See note on 10:4. The Lord compares himself to a warrior who uses Judah as his bow and Ephraim (the northern kingdom) as his arrow. *your sons, Zion.* The Maccabees (see note on Da 11:34; see also essay, p. 1594). *your sons, Greece.* The Seleucids of Syria (after the breakup of Alexander's empire).

9:14 See Hab 3:3–15 and note on 3:3. *trumpet.* Probably a reference to thunder (see Ex 19:16–19 and note on 19:16). *south.* In the region of Mount Sinai, where the Sinaitic covenant was given (see v. 11 and note) and where the Lord's dwelling was

(see Jdg 5:4–5; Ps 68:8; Hab 3:3 and note).

9:15 The Apocryphal book 1 Maccabees (3:16–24; 4:6–16; 7:40–50) records a partial fulfillment of this verse. *slingstones.* Hurled at defenders on the city wall and onto the inhabitants inside. *bowl used for sprinkling.* See Ex 27:1–3 and note on 27:3; Lev 4:6–7.

9:16 *that day.* See note on 2:11.

[A] 10:1 *it is the LORD who…gives showers…plants.* The Lord, not the Canaanite god Baal, is the one who controls the weather and the rain, giving life and fertility to the land (see Jer 14:22; Hos 2:8 and note; 6:3; Joel 2:21–27; Am 5:8; Mt 5:45). Therefore God's people are to pray to and trust in him.

[A] 10:2 *idols.* Household gods (see Ge 31:19 and note). They were used for divination during the period of the judges (see Jdg 17:5 and note; 18:14–20). *diviners.* Included among false prophets, they were the occult counterpart to true prophets. See Jer 27:9–10 and note on 27:9. Resorting to such sources for information and guidance is expressly forbidden in Dt 18:9–14 because God provided true prophets (and ultimately the Messianic Prophet) for that purpose (see Dt 13:1–5 and notes; 18:15–22 and note on 18:15; Isa 8:19–20 and notes; Jn 4:25; 6:14 and note; Ac 3:22–26 and note; see also note on Ge 30:27). *they give comfort in vain.* For example, when they wrong-

10:2 ᵘ S Isa 44:25
ᵛ Jer 23:16
ʷ S Isa 40:19
ˣ S Nu 27:17;
S Jer 23:1; S Hos 3:4;
S Mt 9:36
10:3 ʸ Isa 14:9;
S Jer 25:34
ᶻ S Eze 34:8-10
10:4 ᵃ S Ps 118:22;
S Ac 4:11
ᵇ S Isa 22:23
ᶜ S Zec 9:10
10:5 ᵈ S 2Sa 22:43;
S Mic 7:10
ᵉ S Am 2:15;
S Mic 5:8; Hag 2:22;
Zec 12:4
10:6 ᶠ S Eze 30:24
ᵍ S Ps 102:13;
S Isa 14:1
ʰ S Eze 36:37; 37:19;
S Zec 8:7-8
ⁱ Ps 34:17; Isa 58:9;
65:24; Zec 13:9
10:7 ʲ Zec 9:15
ᵏ S 1Sa 2:1; S Isa 60:5;
S Joel 2:23
10:8 ˡ Isa 5:26
ᵐ S Jer 33:22;
S Eze 36:11
10:9 ⁿ S Isa 44:21;
S Eze 6:9
10:10 ᵒ S Isa 11:11;
S Zec 8:8
ᵖ S Jer 50:19

diviners ᵘ see visions that lie;
they tell dreams ᵛ that are false,
  they give comfort in vain. ʷ
Therefore the people wander like sheep
  oppressed for lack of a shepherd. ˣ

³ "My anger burns against the shepherds,
  and I will punish the leaders; ʸ
for the Lᴏʀᴅ Almighty will care
  for his flock, the house of Judah,
  and make them like a proud horse in battle. ᶻ
⁴ From Judah will come the cornerstone, ᵃ
  from him the tent peg, ᵇ
from him the battle bow, ᶜ
  from him every ruler.
⁵ Together theyᵃ will be like mighty warriors in battle
  trampling their enemy into the mud of the streets. ᵈ
They will fight because the Lᴏʀᴅ is with them,
  and they will put the enemy horsemen to shame. ᵉ

⁶ "I will strengthen ᶠ the house of Judah
  and save the house of Joseph.
I will restore them
  because I have compassion ᵍ on them. ʰ
They will be as though
  I had not rejected them,
for I am the Lᴏʀᴅ their God
  and I will answer ⁱ them.
⁷ The Ephraimites will become like mighty warriors,
  and their hearts will be glad as with wine.ʲ
Their children will see it and be joyful;
  their hearts will rejoice ᵏ in the Lᴏʀᴅ.
⁸ I will signal ˡ for them
  and gather them in.
Surely I will redeem them;
  they will be as numerous ᵐ as before.
⁹ Though I scatter them among the peoples,
  yet in distant lands they will remember me. ⁿ
They and their children will survive,
  and they will return.
¹⁰ I will bring them back from Egypt
  and gather them from Assyria. ᵒ
I will bring them to Gileadᵖ and Lebanon,

ᵃ 4,5 Or *ruler, all of them together.* / ⁵*They*

---

ly promise rain, fruitful seasons, fertility, prosperity, peace and
blessing. *people wander like sheep.* See Isa 53:6 and note.*lack of
a shepherd.* Spiritual leadership is missing (cf. Mk 6:34)."Shepherd" is primarily a royal motif, whether referring to human
kings (see Isa 44:28; Jer 2:8 and notes), to God as King (see Ps
23:1 and note) or to the Messianic, Davidic King (Eze 34:23–24;
Jn 10:11–16; Heb 13:20; 1Pe 5:4; Rev 7:17).
10:3 *I will punish the leaders.* Cf. Eze 34:1–10. *like a proud horse.*
Triumphant.
10:4 Probably Messianic (indicated by the Aramaic Targum).
From Judah. See Ge 49:10; Jer 30:21 and note; Mic 5:2. *cornerstone.* See 3:9; Eph 2:20 and notes. *tent peg.* The ruler as the support of the state (see note on Isa 22:23; see also Isa 22:24). *battle
bow.* Part of the Divine Warrior terminology (cf. 9:13; Ps 7:12;
45:5; La 2:4; 3:12; Hab 3:9).
10:5 *they.* Judah (v. 4), i.e., its people. *the Lᴏʀᴅ is with them.* See
Jos 1:5; Jer 1:8 and note. *put the enemy horsemen to shame.* Partly fulfilled in the Maccabean victories (during the period between the OT and the NT; see essay, p. 1594).

10:6 *Judah … Joseph.* The people of the southern and northern
kingdoms will be reunited (see note on 8:13).
10:7 *Ephraimites.* See note on 9:13. *glad as with wine.* See Ps
104:15.
10:8 *signal.* Lit."whistle," a continuation of the shepherd metaphor (vv. 2–3; see Jdg 5:16). *redeem.* The Hebrew for this word is
often used of ransoming from slavery or captivity (see Isa 35:10;
Mic 6:4; cf. 1Pe 1:18–19). *as numerous as before.* See Ex 1:6–20
and note on 1:7.
10:9 *they will remember me.* According to the meaning
of Zechariah's name,"the Lᴏʀᴅ remembers" (his covenant
people and promises). Now they will remember him.
10:10 *Egypt … Assyria.* See v. 11; Hos 7:16 and note. Probably
representing all the countries where the Israelites are dispersed,
these two evoke memories of slavery and exile. *gather them.*
See Isa 11:11–16; Eze 39:27–29. *Gilead.* See Ge 31:21 and note;
SS 6:5; Jer 50:19; Mic 7:14 and note. *Lebanon.* See 2Ki 19:23; see
also Isa 33:9; 35:2; Jer 22:6 and notes. *not be room enough.* See
v. 8; 2:4 and note; see also note on Isa 49:19–20.

and there will not be room �q enough for them.
¹¹ They will pass through the sea of trouble;
the surging sea will be subdued
and all the depths of the Nile will dry up. ʳ
Assyria's pride ˢ will be brought down
and Egypt's scepter ᵗ will pass away. ᵘ
¹² I will strengthen ᵛ them in the LORD
and in his name they will live securely, ʷ"

declares the LORD.

11 Open your doors, Lebanon, ˣ
so that fire ʸ may devour your cedars!
² Wail, you juniper, for the cedar has fallen;
the stately trees are ruined!
Wail, oaks ᶻ of Bashan;
the dense forest ᵃ has been cut down! ᵇ
³ Listen to the wail of the shepherds;
their rich pastures are destroyed!
Listen to the roar of the lions; ᶜ
the lush thicket of the Jordan is ruined! ᵈ

TWO SHEPHERDS

⁴ This is what the LORD my God says: "Shepherd the flock marked for slaughter. ᵉ ⁵ Their buyers slaughter them and go unpunished. Those who sell them say, 'Praise the LORD, I am rich!' Their own shepherds do not spare them. ᶠ ⁶ For I will no longer have pity on the people of the land," declares the LORD. "I will give everyone into the hands of their neighbors ᵍ and their king. They will devastate the land, and I will not rescue them from their hands." ʰ

⁷ So I shepherded the flock marked for slaughter, ⁱ particularly the oppressed of the flock. Then I took two staffs and called one Favor and the other Union, and I shepherded the flock. ⁸ In one month I got rid of the three shepherds.

The flock detested ʲ me, and I grew weary of them ⁹ and said, "I will not be your shepherd. Let the dying die, and the perishing perish. ᵏ Let those who are left eat ˡ one another's flesh."

¹⁰ Then I took my staff called Favor ᵐ and broke it, revoking ⁿ the covenant I had made

10:10 �q S Isa 49:19
10:11 ʳ Isa 19:5-7;
S 51:10 ˢ Zep 2:13
ᵗ Eze 30:13
ᵘ Eze 29:15
10:12 ᵛ S Jer 30:24
ʷ S Mic 4:5
11:1 ˣ S Eze 31:3
ʸ S 2Ch 36:19;
Zec 12:6
11:2 ᶻ S Isa 2:13
ᵃ Isa 32:19
ᵇ S Isa 10:34
11:3 ᶜ S Isa 5:29
ᵈ Jer 2:15; 50:44;
Eze 19:9
11:4 ᵉ S Jer 25:34
11:5 ᶠ Jer 50:7;
S Eze 34:2-3
11:6 ᵍ Zec 14:13
ʰ Isa 9:19-21;
S Jer 13:14; S La 2:21;
5:8; S Mic 5:8; 7:2-6
11:7 ⁱ S Jer 25:34
11:8 ʲ S Eze 14:5
11:9 ᵏ S Jer 43:11
ˡ S Isa 9:20
11:10 ᵐ ver 7
ⁿ S Ps 89:39; Jer 14:21

10:11 *pass through the sea of trouble.* As at the Red Sea (see Ex 14:22 and note).

11:1–3 Some interpret this brief poem as a taunt song related to the lament that will be sung over the destruction of the nations' power and arrogance (ch. 10), represented by the cedar, the pine and the oak (vv. 1–2). Their kings are represented by the shepherds and the lions (v. 3). Understood in this way, vv. 1–3 would provide the conclusion to the preceding section. Other interpreters, however, without denying the presence of figurative language, see the piece more literally as a description of the devastation of Syro-Palestine due to the rejection of the Messianic Good Shepherd (vv. 4–14). Verses 1–3 would then furnish the introduction to the next section. The geography of the text—Lebanon, Bashan and Jordan— would seem to favor this interpretation. Part of the fulfillment would be the destruction and further subjugation of the area by the Romans, including the fall of Jerusalem in A.D. 70 and of Masada in 73. Understood in this way, the passage is in sharp contrast with ch. 10 and its prediction of Israel's full deliverance and restoration to the covenant land. Now the scene is one of desolation for the land (vv. 1–3), followed by the threat of judgment and disaster for both land and people (vv. 4–6).

11:1 *Lebanon.* See 10:10 and note.

11:2 *Bashan.* See note on Isa 2:13. The Israelites took this region from the Amorite king, Og, at the time of the conquest of Canaan (Nu 21:33–35). It was allotted to the half-tribe of Manasseh (Jos 13:29–30; 17:5). *dense forest.* Of Lebanon.

11:3 If the language is figurative, the shepherds and lions represent the rulers or leaders of the Jews (see v. 5; 10:3; cf. Jer 25:34–36). *lush thicket of the Jordan.* Where the lions had their lairs.

A **11:4–14** The reason for the judgment on Israel in vv. 1–3 is now given, namely, the people's rejection of the Messianic Shepherd-King. Just as the Servant in the "servant songs" (see note on Isa 42:1–4) is rejected, so here the Good Shepherd (a royal figure) is rejected. The same Messianic King is in view in both instances.

11:4 *says.* To Zechariah. *flock.* Israel.

11:5 *buyers.* The sheep (the Jews) are bought as slaves by outsiders. Part of the fulfillment came in A.D. 70 and the following years. *Those who sell them.* "Their own shepherds (rulers or leaders)."

11:6 *land.* Israel. *king.* Perhaps the Roman emperor (cf. Jn 19:15). *They.* Includes the Romans prophetically.

11:7 *I.* Zechariah, as a type (foreshadowing) of the Messianic Shepherd-King. *called one Favor.* To ensure divine favor on the flock. *Union.* See Eze 37:15–28 and note on 37:16. Such unity would be the result of the gracious leadership of the Good Shepherd. (For the significance of the subsequent breaking of the two staffs, see vv. 10,14 and notes.)

11:8 *got rid of the three shepherds.* Although the three cannot be specifically identified, the Good Shepherd will dispose of all such unfit leaders. *I grew weary of them.* Cf. Isa 1:13–14.

11:9 *Let the dying die.* The Good Shepherd terminates his providential care of the sheep. *eat one another's flesh.* According to Josephus, this actually happened during the Roman siege of Jerusalem in A.D. 70 (see Jer 19:9 and note).

11:10 *covenant.* Apparently a covenant of security and restraint, by which the Shepherd had been keeping the nations from attacking his people (cf. Eze 34:25; Hos 2:18). Now, however, the nations (e.g., the Romans) will be permitted to overrun them.

with all the nations. ¹¹It was revoked on that day, and so the oppressed of the flock who were watching me knew it was the word of the LORD.

¹²I told them, "If you think it best, give me my pay; but if not, keep it." So they paid me thirty pieces of silver. °

¹³And the LORD said to me, "Throw it to the potter"—the handsome price at which they valued me! So I took the thirty pieces of silver ᵖ and threw them to the potter at the house of the LORD. ᵠ

¹⁴Then I broke my second staff called Union, breaking the family bond between Judah and Israel.

¹⁵Then the LORD said to me, "Take again the equipment of a foolish shepherd. ¹⁶For I am going to raise up a shepherd over the land who will not care for the lost, or seek the young, or heal the injured, or feed the healthy, but will eat the meat of the choice sheep, tearing off their hooves.

¹⁷"Woe to the worthless shepherd, ʳ
who deserts the flock!
May the sword strike his arm ˢ and his right eye!
May his arm be completely withered,
his right eye totally blinded!" ᵗ

JERUSALEM'S ENEMIES TO BE DESTROYED

12 A prophecy: ᵘ The word of the LORD concerning Israel.

The LORD, who stretches out the heavens, ᵛ who lays the foundation of the earth, ʷ and who forms the spirit in human beings, ˣ declares: ²"I am going to make Jerusalem a cup ʸ that sends all the surrounding peoples reeling. ᶻ Judah ᵃ will be besieged as well as Jerusalem. ³On that day, when all the nations ᵇ of the earth are gathered against her, I will make Jerusalem an immovable rock ᶜ for all the nations. All who try to move it will injure ᵈ themselves. ⁴On that day I will strike every horse with panic and its rider with madness," declares the LORD. "I will keep a watchful eye over the house of Judah, but I will blind all the horses of the nations. ᵉ ⁵Then the clans of Judah will say in their hearts, 'The people of Jerusalem are strong, ᶠ because the LORD Almighty is their God.'

⁶"On that day I will make the clans of Judah like a firepot ᵍ in a woodpile, like a flam-

---

11:11 *the oppressed of the flock.* Probably the faithful few, who recognize the authoritative word of the Lord (see also v. 7). *it was the word of the LORD.* The faithful discern that what happens (e.g., the judgment on Jerusalem and the temple in A.D. 70) is a fulfillment of God's prophetic word—as a result of such actions as those denounced in Mt 23, which led to the rejection of the Good Shepherd.

11:12 *give me my pay.* Refers to the severance of the relationship. *keep it.* A more emphatic way of ending the relationship. *thirty pieces of silver.* The price of a slave among the Israelites in ancient times (see notes on Ex 21:32; Mt 26:15).

11:13 *handsome price.* Irony and sarcasm. *threw them to the potter at the house of the LORD.* For the NT use of vv. 12–13, see Mt 26:14–15; 27:3–10 and note on 27:9.

11:14 *broke my second staff called Union.* Signifying the dissolution of the covenant nation, particularly of the unity between the south and the north. The breaking up of the nation into parties hostile to each other was characteristic of later Jewish history; it greatly hindered the popular cause in the war against Rome (cf. Jn 11:48).

11:15 *again.* See v. 7. *foolish shepherd.* With the Shepherd of the Lord's choice removed from the scene, a foolish and worthless (v. 17) shepherd replaces him. A selfish, greedy, corrupt leader will arise and afflict the flock (the people of Israel).

11:16 *seek the young.* Cf. Ge 33:13; Isa 40:11. *tearing off their hooves.* Apparently in a greedy search for the last edible piece.

11:17 *worthless shepherd.* See note on v. 15. This counterfeit shepherd may have found a partial historical fulfillment in such leaders as Simeon bar Kosiba or Kokhba (who led the Jewish revolt against the Romans in A.D. 132–135 and who was hailed as the Messiah by Rabbi Akiba). But it would seem that the final

stage of the progressive fulfillment of this prophecy awaits the rise of the final antichrist (cf. Eze 34:2–4; Da 11:36–39; Jn 5:43; 2Th 2:3–10; Rev 13:1–8). *deserts the flock.* Contrast the Good Shepherd of Jn 10:11–16. *May his arm be completely withered.* May his power be paralyzed. *his right eye totally blinded.* May his intelligence be nullified. Thus this leader will be powerless to fight.

12:1—14:21 This second oracle in Part II of the book revolves around two scenes: the final siege of Jerusalem and the Messiah's return to defeat Israel's enemies and establish his kingdom.

12:1 *A prophecy: The word of the LORD.* See note on 9:1. *Israel.* The whole nation, not just the northern kingdom. Judah and Jerusalem, however, are the main focus of attention (see v. 2). *The LORD, who stretches . . . lays . . . forms.* This description of the Lord's creative power shows that he is able to perform what he predicts; it also strengthens the royal and sovereign authority of the message.

12:2 *cup that sends all . . . reeling.* See notes on Ps 16:5; Isa 51:17; Jer 25:15; Ob 16; Hab 2:16.

12:3 *that day.* See note on 2:11. The phrase is used often in chs. 12–14 (12:4,6,8–9,11; 13:1–2,4; 14:4,6,8–9,13,20–21). *all the nations . . . gathered against her.* See 14:2,12; Joel 3:9–16; cf. Rev 16:16–21.

12:4 *panic . . . madness . . . blind.* Listed in Dt 28:28 among Israel's curses for disobeying the stipulations of the covenant. Now these curses are turned against Israel's enemies. *watchful eye.* See Ps 32:8; 33:18; 121.

12:5 *the LORD Almighty.* See note on 1Sa 1:3.

12:6 Like a fire destroying wood and sheaves of grain, Judah's discerning leaders (see v. 5) will consume their enemies (cf. Jdg 15:3–5; Mic 5:5–6; see note on Isa 1:31).

ing torch among sheaves. They will consume [h] right and left all the surrounding peoples, but Jerusalem will remain intact [i] in her place.

[7]"The LORD will save the dwellings of Judah first, so that the honor of the house of David and of Jerusalem's inhabitants may not be greater than that of Judah. [j] [8]On that day the LORD will shield [k] those who live in Jerusalem, so that the feeblest [l] among them will be like David, and the house of David will be like God, [m] like the angel of the LORD going before [n] them. [9]On that day I will set out to destroy all the nations [o] that attack Jerusalem. [p]

MOURNING FOR THE ONE THEY PIERCED

[10]"And I will pour out on the house of David and the inhabitants of Jerusalem a spirit [a] [q] of grace and supplication. [r] They will look on [b] me, the one they have pierced, [s] and they will mourn for him as one mourns for an only child, [t] and grieve bitterly for him as one grieves for a firstborn son. [u] [11]On that day the weeping [v] in Jerusalem will be great, like the weeping of Hadad Rimmon in the plain of Megiddo. [w] [12]The land will mourn, [x] each clan by itself, with their wives by themselves: the clan of the house of David and their wives, the clan of the house of Nathan and their wives, [13]the clan of the house of Levi and their wives, the clan of Shimei and their wives, [14]and all the rest of the clans and their wives. [y]

CLEANSING FROM SIN

13 "On that day a fountain [z] will be opened to the house of David and the inhabitants of Jerusalem, to cleanse [a] them from sin and impurity.

[2]"On that day, I will banish the names of the idols [b] from the land, and they will be remembered no more," [c] declares the LORD Almighty. "I will remove both the prophets [d] and the spirit of impurity from the land. [3]And if some still prophesy, their fathers and mothers, to whom they were born, will say to them, 'You must die, because you have told lies [e] in the LORD's name.' When they prophesy, their own parents will stab them. [f]

[4]"On that day the prophets will all be ashamed [g] of their prophetic visions. They will not put on a prophet's garment [h] of hair [i] in order to deceive. [j] [5]Every one of them will say, 'I am not a prophet. I am a farmer; the land has been my livelihood since my youth. [c] [k] [6]If someone asks, 'What are these wounds on your body [d]?' they will answer, 'The wounds I was given at the house of my friends.'

---

[a] 10 Or *the Spirit*   [b] 10 Or *to*   [c] 5 Or *farmer; a man sold me in my youth*   [d] 6 Or *wounds between your hands*

12:6 [h] Ob 1:18
[i] Zec 14:10
12:7 [j] Jer 30:18;
S Am 9:11
12:8 [k] S Ps 91:4;
S Joel 3:16; S Zec 9:15
[l] Joel 3:10 [m] Ps 82:6
[n] Mic 7:8
12:9 [o] S Isa 29:7
[p] S Zec 1:21; 14:2-3
12:10 [q] S Eze 37:9
[r] Isa 44:3;
S Eze 39:29;
Joel 2:28-29
[s] S Ps 22:16; Jn 19:34,
37* [t] Jdg 11:34
[u] S Ge 21:16; Jer 31:19
12:11 [v] Jer 50:4
[w] 2Ki 23:29
12:12 [x] Mt 24:30;
Rev 1:7
12:14 [y] Zec 7:3
13:1 [z] Jer 17:13
[a] S Lev 16:30;
S Ps 51:2; Heb 9:14
13:2 [b] S Jer 43:12;
S Eze 6:6; S 36:25; S
Hos 2:17 [c] S Mic 5:13
[d] 1Ki 22:22; Jer 23:14-
15
13:3 [e] S Jer 28:16
[f] Dt 13:6-11; 18:20;
S Ne 6:14; Jer 23:34;
S Eze 14:9
13:4 [g] S Jer 6:15
[h] Mt 3:4 [i] S 1Ki 18:7;
S Isa 20:2
[j] S Eze 12:24
13:5 [k] S Am 7:14

12:8 *like David.* Like a great warrior. *like God.* Cf. Ex 4:16; 7:1. *like the Angel of the LORD.* See Ge 48:16 and note; Ex 14:19; 23:20; 32:34; 33:2; Hos 12:3–4; see also Ge 16:7 and note.

12:10 *a spirit.* See TNIV text note; Isa 32:15; Eze 36:26–27 and notes; see also Isa 44:3; 59:20–21; Eze 39:29; Joel 2:28–29. *look on.* See TNIV text note. The emphasis seems to be on looking "to" the Messiah in faith (cf. Nu 21:9; Isa 45:22; Jn 3:14–15). *me . . . him . . . him.* Same person. *pierced.* See Ps 22:16 and note; Jn 19:37. *mourns for an only child.* See Jer 6:26 and note. *grieves for a firstborn son.* Cf. Ex 11:5; Jer 6:26 and notes.

12:11 *Hadad Rimmon.* The name of either (1) a place near Megiddo, where the people mourned the death of King Josiah (2Ch 35:20–27; see v. 22 there for the plain of Megiddo and vv. 24–25 for the mourning); or (2) a Semitic storm god (see 2Ki 5:18 and note), whose name means "Hadad the thunderer" in Babylonian (as in the *Epic of Gilgamesh,* 11:98; see chart, p. xxiii; see also Eze 8:14 for an example of the practice of weeping for a Babylonian deity).

12:12 *Nathan.* David's son (2Sa 5:14; Lk 3:31).

12:13 *Shimei.* Son of Gershon, the son of Levi (Nu 3:17–18,21). The repentance and mourning are led, then, by the civil (royal) and religious leaders.

13:1 *cleanse them from sin.* See 3:4–9 and note on 3:9; one of the provisions of the new covenant (Jer 31:34; Eze 36:25).

13:2 *names of the idols.* The influence and fame, and even the very existence, of the idols. *prophets.* False prophecy was still a

problem in the postexilic period (see Ne 6:12–14) and would again be a problem in the future (see Mt 24:4–5,11,23–24; 2Th 2:2–4).

13:3 *lies.* False prophecies. *parents will stab them.* See Dt 13:3,6–10. The Hebrew for "stab" is the same as the verb for "pierced" in 12:10, perhaps indicating that the feelings and actions exhibited in piercing the Messiah will now be directed toward the false prophets.

13:4–6 Because of the stern measures just mentioned, a false prophet will be reluctant to identify himself as such and will be evasive in his responses to interrogation. To help conceal his true identity, he will not wear a "prophet's garment of hair" (v. 4), such as Elijah wore (see 2Ki 1:8 and note). Instead, to avoid the death penalty (v. 3), he will deny being a prophet and will claim to have been a farmer since his youth (v. 5). And if a suspicious person notices marks on his body and inquires about them (v. 6), he will claim to have received them in a scuffle with friends (or perhaps as discipline from his parents during childhood). Apparently the accuser suspects that the false prophet's wounds were self-inflicted to arouse his prophetic ecstasy in idolatrous rites (as in 1Ki 18:28; see Jer 16:6 and note; 48:37).

13:5 *the land . . . my youth.* If the alternative translation in the TNIV text note is taken, the meaning is that someone sold him as a slave while he was still young.

13:6 Some take this verse as Messianic, but the interpretation given above seems preferable in this context (e.g., v. 5).

13:7 [l] S Isa 34:5;
Jer 47:6 [m] Isa 40:11;
S 53:4; Eze 37:24
[n] S 2Sa 17:2;
Mt 26:31*; Mk 14:27*
13:8 [o] S Eze 5:2-4,
12; Zec 14:2
13:9 [p] S Isa 4:4;
33:14; Mal 3:2
[q] S Ps 12:6;
S Da 11:35; 1Pe 1:6-7
[r] S Job 6:29;
S Jer 6:27 [s] S Ps 50:15
[t] Ps 105:1 [u] S Ps 86:7;
S Isa 30:19;
S Zec 10:6
[v] S Lev 26:12;
S Jer 30:22
[w] S Isa 44:5;
S Jer 29:12;
S Eze 20:38
14:1 [x] Isa 13:6;
S Joel 1:15; Mal 4:1
[y] S Isa 13:16
14:2 [z] S Isa 2:3;
S Zec 12:3 [a] S Eze 5:8
[b] S Ge 34:29;
S La 5:11 [c] Isa 13:6;
S Zec 13:8
14:3 [d] Zec 9:14-15
[e] S Isa 8:9; S Zec 12:9
14:4 [f] Eze 11:23
[g] S Nu 16:31
14:5 [h] Am 1:1
[i] Isa 29:6; 66:15-16
[j] S Dt 33:2; Mt 16:27;
25:31; Jude 14
14:6 [k] S Isa 13:10;
S Jer 4:23
14:7 [l] Jer 30:7
[m] Rev 21:23-25; 22:5
[n] S Isa 13:10; S 30:26
14:8 [o] Eze 47:1-12;
Jn 7:38; Rev 22:1-2
[p] S Isa 30:25
[q] Joel 2:20 [r] S Ge 8:22
14:9 [s] S Ps 22:28;
S Ob 1:21 [t] S Dt 6:4;
Ps 47:7; Isa 45:24;
Rev 11:15 [u] Hab 2:14;
Eph 4:5-6
14:10 [v] 1Ki 15:22
[w] S Jos 15:32

THE SHEPHERD STRUCK, THE SHEEP SCATTERED

⁷ "Awake, sword, [l] against my shepherd, [m]
    against the man who is close to me!"
    declares the LORD Almighty.
"Strike the shepherd,
    and the sheep will be scattered, [n]
    and I will turn my hand against the little ones.
⁸ In the whole land," declares the LORD,
    "two-thirds will be struck down and perish;
    yet one-third will be left in it. [o]
⁹ This third I will bring into the fire; [p]
    I will refine them like silver [q]
    and test them like gold. [r]
They will call [s] on my name [t]
    and I will answer [u] them;
I will say, 'They are my people,' [v]
    and they will say, 'The LORD is our God.' [w]"

THE LORD COMES AND REIGNS

14 A day of the LORD [x] is coming, Jerusalem, when your possessions [y] will be plundered and divided up within your walls. ²I will gather all the nations [z] to Jerusalem to fight against it; [a] the city will be captured, the houses ransacked, and the women ravished. [b] Half of the city will go into exile, but the rest of the people will not be taken from the city. [c] ³Then the LORD will go out and fight [d] against those nations, as he fights on a day of battle. [e] ⁴On that day his feet will stand on the Mount of Olives, [f] east of Jerusalem, and the Mount of Olives will be split [g] in two from east to west, forming a great valley, with half of the mountain moving north and half moving south. ⁵You will flee by my mountain valley, for it will extend to Azel. You will flee as you fled from the earthquake[a] [h] in the days of Uzziah king of Judah. Then the LORD my God will come, [i] and all the holy ones with him. [j]

⁶On that day there will be no sunlight, [k] no cold, frosty darkness. ⁷It will be a unique [l] day—a day known only to the LORD—with no distinction between day and night. [m] When evening comes, there will be light. [n]

⁸On that day living water [o] will flow [p] out from Jerusalem, half of it east [q] to the Dead Sea and half of it west to the Mediterranean Sea, in summer and in winter. [r]

⁹The LORD will be king [s] over the whole earth. [t] On that day there will be one LORD, and his name the only name. [u]

¹⁰The whole land, from Geba [v] to Rimmon, [w] south of Jerusalem, will become like the

---

[a] 5 Or ⁵My mountain valley will be blocked and will extend to Azel. It will be blocked as it was blocked
because of the earthquake

13:7 *my shepherd.* The royal (Messianic) Good Shepherd (cf. the true Shepherd of 11:4–14; contrast the foolish and worthless shepherd of 11:15–17). *Strike the shepherd.* In 11:17 it was the worthless shepherd who was to be struck; now it is the Good Shepherd (cf. also 12:10). *sheep will be scattered.* In partial fulfillment of the curses for covenant disobedience (see Dt 28:64 and note; 29:24–25). These two clauses are quoted by Jesus not long before his arrest (Mt 26:31; Mk 14:27) and applied to the scattering of the apostles (Mt 26:56; Mk 14:49–50), who in turn are probably typological of the dispersion of the Jews in A.D. 70 and subsequent years.
13:8–9 These verses depict a refining process for Israel (see note on Isa 48:10).
13:8 *one-third.* A remnant, thus revealing God's mercy in the midst of judgment.
13:9 *I will refine them.* See Ps 12:6 and note. *my people ... our God.* See note on 8:8. They will be restored to proper covenant relationship with the Lord (see also Eze 20:30–44).
14:1 *A day of the LORD.* Cf. Isa 2:12; Eze 30:3; Joel 1:15 and note. *your ... your.* Jerusalem (v. 2) is the object of the plunder.
14:2 *all the nations ... fight against it.* See v. 12; see also note on 12:3.
14:3 *day of battle.* Any occasion when the Lord supernaturally

intervenes to deliver his people, such as at the Red Sea (see Ex 14:14 and note).
14:4 *Mount of Olives.* Called by this name elsewhere in the OT only in 2Sa 15:30. It faced the temple mount and, being about 2,700 feet high, rose about 200 feet above it. Cf. Eze 11:23. This prophecy is probably referred to in Ac 1:11–12.
14:5 *Azel.* The name of a place east of Jerusalem, marking the eastern end of the newly formed valley. *earthquake in the days of Uzziah.* Amos dates his prophecy by referring to it (see Am 1:1 and note). *holy ones.* May include both believers and angels. They will accompany our Lord when he comes (cf. Mt 25:31; 1Th 3:13; Jude 14; Rev 19:14).
14:7 *unique day.* Due to the topographical, cosmic and cataclysmic changes. See also Isa 60:19–20 and notes.
14:8 *living water will flow.* Perhaps both literal and symbolic (see Isa 8:6; Joel 3:18 and note; Jn 7:38).
14:9 *The LORD will be king over the whole earth.* A pervasive theological theme in Scripture (see Introduction to Psalms: Theology: Major Themes). *one LORD.* See Dt 6:4; Isa 43:11 and notes.
14:10 *Geba.* About six miles north-northeast of Jerusalem at the northern boundary of Judah (see 2Ki 23:8 and note). *Rimmon.* Also called En Rimmon (see Ne 11:29 and note), it was

Arabah. But Jerusalem will be raised up˟ high from the Benjamin Gateʸ to the site of the First Gate, to the Corner Gate,ᶻ and from the Tower of Hananelᵃ to the royal winepresses, and will remain in its place.ᵇ ¹¹It will be inhabited;ᶜ never again will it be destroyed. Jerusalem will be secure.ᵈ

¹²This is the plague with which the Lord will strikeᵉ all the nations that fought against Jerusalem: Their flesh will rot while they are still standing on their feet, their eyes will rot in their sockets, and their tongues will rot in their mouths.ᶠ ¹³On that day people will be stricken by the Lord with great panic.ᵍ They will seize each other by the hand and attack one another.ʰ ¹⁴Judahⁱ too will fight at Jerusalem. The wealth of all the surrounding nations will be collectedʲ—great quantities of gold and silver and clothing. ¹⁵A similar plagueᵏ will strike the horses and mules, the camels and donkeys, and all the animals in those camps.

¹⁶Then the survivorsˡ from all the nations that have attacked Jerusalem will go up year after year to worshipᵐ the King,ⁿ the Lord Almighty, and to celebrate the Festival of Tabernacles.ᵒ ¹⁷If any of the peoples of the earth do not go up to Jerusalem to worshipᵖ the King, the Lord Almighty, they will have no rain.�q ¹⁸If the Egyptian people do not go up and take part, they will have no rain. The Lordᵃ will bring on them the plagueʳ he inflicts on the nations that do not go up to celebrate the Festival of Tabernacles.ˢ ¹⁹This will be the punishment of Egypt and the punishment of all the nations that do not go up to celebrate the Festival of Tabernacles.ᵗ

²⁰On that day Holy to the Lordᵘ will be inscribed on the bells of the horses, and the cooking potsᵛ in the Lord's house will be like the sacred bowlsʷ in front of the altar. ²¹Every pot in Jerusalem and Judah will be holy˟ to the Lord Almighty, and all who come to sacrifice will take some of the pots and cook in them. And on that dayʸ there will no longer be a Canaaniteᵇᶻ in the houseᵃ of the Lord Almighty.ᵇ

ᵃ 18 Or part, then the Lord   ᵇ 21 Or merchant

---

about 35 miles south-southwest of Jerusalem, where the hill country of Judah slopes away into the Negev. *Arabah.* See note on Dt 1:1. All the land around Jerusalem is to be leveled. *Jerusalem will be raised up.* See Isa 2:2–4 and note. The elevation may be both physical and in prominence. *Benjamin Gate . . . First Gate . . . Tower of Hananel.* All were probably at the northeastern part of the city wall (cf. Jer 31:38; 37:12–13; 38:7). *Corner Gate.* At the northwest corner (cf. Jer 31:38). *royal winepresses.* Just south of the city. Thus the whole city is included.

14:11 *inhabited.* See 2:4 and note. *never again . . . destroyed.* As at the time of the exile to Babylonia (see Isa 43:28 and note). *Jerusalem will be secure.* See Jer 31:40.

14:12 *plague.* See Isa 37:36 and note. *nations that fought against Jerusalem.* See v. 2; see also note on 12:3.

14:13 *great panic . . . attack one another.* See Jdg 7:22 and note.

14:14 *gold and silver and clothing.* The plunder of battle, thus reversing the situation in v. 1.

14:15 A similar plague will strike the beasts of burden, preventing the people from using them to escape.

A **14:16** See Isa 2:2–4 and note. *Festival of Tabernacles.* See notes on Ex 23:16; Ps 81:3. Of the three great pilgrimage festivals (see Ex 23:14–17), perhaps Tabernacles was selected as the one for representatives of the various Gentile nations because it was the last and greatest festival of the Hebrew calendar, gathering up into itself the year's worship (see note on Eze

45:25). It was to be a time of grateful rejoicing (see Lev 23:40; Dt 16:13–15; Ne 8:17 and note). Beginning with the period of Ezra and Nehemiah, the reading and teaching of "the Book of the Law of God" became an integral part of the festivities (Ne 8:18; cf. Isa 2:3). The festival seems to speak of the final, joyful regathering and restoration of Israel, as well as of the ingathering of the nations. See chart, pp. 180–181.

14:17 *no rain.* One of the curses for covenant disobedience (Dt 28:22–24; cf. Zec 9:11—10:1).

14:18 *Egyptian people . . . will have no rain.* See TNIV text note. With either reading, the withholding of rain may still be included, for drought (v. 17) in the upper reaches of the Nile would cause the annual flooding of the Nile to fail.

A **14:20** *Holy to the Lord.* Engraved on the gold plate worn on the high priest's turban (Ex 28:36–38) as a reminder of his consecration to the Lord's service (see note on 3:5). God's original purpose for Israel (see Ex 19:6 and note) will be realized.

A **14:21** *Every pot in Jerusalem . . . holy.* See Joel 3:17 and note. Even common things become holy when they are used for God's service. *cook.* Portions from the sacrifices. *Canaanite.* Represents anyone who is morally or spiritually unclean—anyone who is not included among the chosen people of God (cf. Isa 35:8; Eze 43:7; 44:9; Rev 21:27).

14:10 ˟ Isa 2:2; Jer 30:18; S Am 9:11
ʸ S Jer 20:2
ᶻ S 2Ki 14:13
ᵃ S Ne 3:1 ᵇ Zec 12:6
14:11 ᶜ Zec 2:4
ᵈ S Ps 48:8; S Eze 34:25-28
14:12 ᵉ S Isa 11:4
ᶠ ver 18; S Lev 26:16;
S Dt 28:22; Job 18:13
14:13 ᵍ S Ge 35:5
ʰ S Jdg 7:22; S Zec 11:6
14:14 ⁱ Zec 12:2
ʲ S Isa 23:18
14:15 ᵏ ver 12
14:16 ˡ S 2Ki 19:31
ᵐ S Zec 22:29; S 86:9;
S Isa 19:21 ⁿ S Ob 1:21
ᵒ S Ex 23:16;
Isa 60:6-9; S Mic 4:2
14:17 ᵖ S 2Ch 32:23
q S Jer 14:4; S Am 4:7
14:18 ʳ S Ge 27:29
ˢ S ver 12
14:19 ᵗ S Zec 14:16
14:20 ᵘ S Ex 39:30
ᵛ S Eze 46:20
ʷ Zec 9:15
14:21 ˟ S Jer 31:40;
Ro 14:6-7; 1Co 10:31
ʸ Ne 8:10 ᶻ Zec 9:8
ᵃ S Ne 11:1
ᵇ S Eze 44:9

MALACHI — INTRODUCTION

AUTHOR

C The book is ascribed to Malachi, whose name means "my messenger." Since the term occurs in 3:1, and since both prophets and priests were called messengers of the Lord (see 2:7; Hag 1:13), some have thought "Malachi" to be only a title that tradition has given the author. The view has been supported by appeal to the pre-Christian Greek translation of the OT (the Septuagint), which translates the term in 1:1 "his messenger" rather than as a proper noun. The matter, however, remains uncertain, and it is still very likely that Malachi was in fact the author's name.

BACKGROUND

Spurred on by the prophetic activity of Haggai and Zechariah, the returned exiles under the leadership of their governor, Zerubbabel, finished the temple in 516 B.C. In 458 the community was strengthened by the coming of the priest Ezra and several thousand more Jews. Artaxerxes, king of Persia, encouraged Ezra to reconstitute the temple worship (Ezr 7:17) and to make sure the law of Moses was being obeyed (Ezr 7:25–26).

Fourteen years later (444) the same Persian king permitted his cupbearer Nehemiah to return to Jerusalem and rebuild its walls (Ne 6:15). As newly appointed governor, Nehemiah also spearheaded reforms to help the poor (Ne 5:2–13) and convinced the people to shun mixed marriages (Ne 10:30), to keep the Sabbath (Ne 10:31) and to bring their tithes and offerings faithfully (Ne 10:37–39).

In 433 B.C. Nehemiah returned to the service of the Persian king, and during his absence the Jews fell into sin once more. Later, however, Nehemiah came back to Jerusalem to discover that the tithes were ignored, the Sabbath was broken, the people had intermarried with foreigners and the priests had become corrupt (Ne 13:7–31). Several of these same sins are condemned by Malachi (see 1:6–14; 2:14–16; 3:8–11).

DATE

The similarity between the sins denounced in Nehemiah and those denounced in Malachi suggests that the two leaders were contemporaries. Malachi may have been written after Nehemiah returned to Persia in 433 B.C. or during his second period as governor. Since the governor mentioned in 1:8 (see note there) was probably not Nehemiah, the first alternative may be more likely. Malachi was most likely the last prophet of the OT era (though some place Joel later).

THEMES AND THEOLOGY

The theological message of the book can be summed up in one sentence: The Great King (1:14) will come not only to judge his people (3:1–5; 4:1) but also to bless and restore them (3:6–12; 4:2).

Although the Jews had been allowed to return from exile and rebuild the temple, several discouraging factors brought about a general religious malaise: (1) Their land remained but a small province in the backwaters of the Persian empire, (2) the glorious future announced by the prophets (including the other postexilic prophets, Haggai and Zechariah) had not (yet) been realized and (3) their God had not (yet) come to his temple (3:1) with majesty and power (as celebrated in Ps 68) to exalt his

KEY **A** APPLICATION FOR LIVING **B** BACKGROUND NOTES **C** CHARACTER INFORMATION

kingdom in the sight of the nations. Doubting God's covenant love (1:2) and no longer trusting his justice (2:17; 3:14–15), the Jews of the restored community began to lose hope. So their worship degenerated into a listless perpetuation of mere forms, and they no longer took the law seriously.

Malachi rebukes their doubt of God's love (1:2–5) and the faithlessness of both priests (1:6—2:9) and people (2:10–16). To their charge that God is unjust (2:17) because he has failed to come in judgment to exalt his people, Malachi answers with an announcement and a warning. The Lord they seek will come—but he will come "like a refiner's fire" (3:1–4). He will come to judge—but he will judge his people first (3:5).

Because the Lord does not change in his commitments and purpose, Israel has not been completely destroyed for her persistent unfaithfulness (3:6). But only through repentance and reformation will she again experience God's blessing (3:6–12). Those who honor the Lord will be spared when he comes to judge (3:16–18).

In conclusion, Malachi once more reassures and warns his readers that "the day ['that great and dreadful day of the Lord,' 4:5] is coming" and that "it will burn like a furnace" (4:1). In that day the righteous will rejoice, and "you will trample on the wicked" (4:2–3). So "remember the law of my servant Moses" (4:4). To prepare his people for that day the Lord will send "the prophet Elijah" to call them back to the godly ways of their forefathers (4:5–6).

LITERARY FEATURES

Malachi is called a "prophecy" (1:1) and is written in what might be called lofty prose. The text features a series of questions asked by both God and the people. Frequently the Lord's statements are followed by sarcastic questions introduced by "(But) you ask" (1:2,6–7; 2:14,17; 3:7–8,13; cf. 1:13). In each case the Lord's response is given.

Repetition is a key element in the book. The name "Lord Almighty" occurs 20 times (see note on 1Sa 1:3). The book begins with a description of the wasteland of Edom (1:3–4) and ends with a warning of Israel's destruction (4:6).

Several vivid figures are employed within the book of Malachi. The priests sniff contemptuously at the altar of the Lord (1:13), and the Lord spreads on their faces the dung from their sacrifices (see 2:3 and note). As Judge, "he will be like a refiner's fire or a launderer's soap" (3:2), but for the righteous "the sun of righteousness will rise with healing in its rays. And you will go out and frolic like well-fed calves " (4:2).

OUTLINE

I. Title (1:1)
II. Introduction: God's Faithful Covenant Love for Israel Affirmed (1:2–5)
III. Israel's Unfaithfulness Rebuked (1:6—2:16)
    A. The Unfaithfulness of the Priests (1:6—2:9)
        1. They dishonor God in their sacrifices (1:6–14)
        2. They do not faithfully teach the law (2:1–9)
    B. The Unfaithfulness of the People (2:10–16)
IV. The Lord's Coming Announced (2:17—4:6)
    A. The Lord Will Come to Purify the Priests and Judge the People (2:17—3:5)
    B. A Call to Repentance in View of the Lord's Coming (3:6–18)
        1. An exhortation to faithful giving (3:6–12)
        2. An exhortation to faithful service (3:13–18)
    C. The Day of the Lord Announced (ch. 4)

1:1 ^a S Na 1:1
^b Ac 7:38; Ro 3:1-2;
1Pe 4:11
1:2 ^c S Dt 4:37
^d ver 6,7; Mal 2:14,
17; 3:7,13
^e S Jer 46:27;
Ro 9:13*
1:3 ^f Lk 14:26
^g S Isa 34:10
^h S Isa 13:22
1:4 ⁱ S Isa 11:14;
S 34:11 i Isa 9:10
^k S Isa 34:5
^l S La 4:22;
S Eze 25:12-14;
S 26:14
1:5 ^m Ps 35:27; 48:1;
Mic 5:4 ⁿ Isa 45:22;
52:10; S Am 1:11-12
1:6 ^o S Lev 20:9;
Mt 15:4; 23:9
^p Lk 6:46 ^q S Dt 32:6;
S Isa 1:2 ^r Job 5:17
^s S ver 2
1:7 ^t ver 12; Lev 21:6
^u S ver 2
^v S Eze 23:41
1:8 ^w S Lev 1:3;
S Dt 15:21
^x S Ge 32:20
^y S Isa 43:23
1:9 ^z Lev 23:33-44;
Ps 51:17; Mic 6:6-8;
Ro 12:1; Heb 13:16
^a S Jer 6:20
1:10 ^b 2Ch 28:24
^c S Hos 5:6
^d Lev 22:20 ^e ver 13;
Isa 1:11-14; Jer 14:12;
Mal 2:12
1:11 ^f S Isa 24:15;
56:6 ^g S Isa 6:3;
S 12:4 ^h S Ps 113:3;
S Mt 8:11 ⁱ Isa 60:6-7;
Rev 5:8; 8:3
^j S Isa 19:21;
Heb 13:15
1:12 ^k S Eze 41:22
^l S ver 7

1 A prophecy:^a The word^b of the Lord to Israel through Malachi.^a

ISRAEL DOUBTS GOD'S LOVE

²"I have loved^c you," says the Lord.

"But you ask,^d 'How have you loved us?'

"Was not Esau Jacob's brother?" declares the Lord. "Yet I have loved Jacob,^e ³but Esau I have hated,^f and I have turned his hill country into a wasteland^g and left his inheritance to the desert jackals.^h"

⁴Edomⁱ may say, "Though we have been crushed, we will rebuild^j the ruins."

But this is what the Lord Almighty says: "They may build, but I will demolish.^k They will be called the Wicked Land, a people always under the wrath of the Lord.^l ⁵You will see it with your own eyes and say, 'Great^m is the Lord—even beyond the borders of Israel!'ⁿ

BREAKING COVENANT THROUGH BLEMISHED SACRIFICES

⁶"A son honors his father,^o and slaves honor their master.^p If I am a father, where is the honor due me? If I am a master, where is the respect^q due me?" says the Lord Almighty.^r

"It is you priests who show contempt for my name.

"But you ask,^s 'How have we shown contempt for your name?'

⁷"By offering defiled food^t on my altar.

"But you ask,^u 'How have we defiled you?'

"By saying that the Lord's table^v is contemptible. ⁸When you offer blind animals for sacrifice, is that not wrong? When you sacrifice lame or diseased animals,^w is that not wrong? Try offering them to your governor! Would he be pleased^x with you? Would he accept you?" says the Lord Almighty.^y

⁹"Now implore God to be gracious to us. With such offerings^z from your hands, will he accept^a you?"—says the Lord Almighty.

¹⁰"Oh, that one of you would shut the temple doors,^b so that you would not light useless fires on my altar! I am not pleased^c with you," says the Lord Almighty, "and I will accept^d no offering^e from your hands. ¹¹My name will be great^f among the nations,^g from where the sun rises to where it sets.^h In every place incenseⁱ and pure offerings^j will be brought to me, because my name will be great among the nations," says the Lord Almighty.

¹²"But you profane it by saying, 'The Lord's table^k is defiled,' and, 'Its food^l is con-

---

^a 1 Malachi means my messenger.

1:1 A prophecy: The word of the Lord. See Zec 9:1 and note; 12:1; see also Hab 1:1 and note. word of the Lord. See Hos 1:1 and note.

1:2 loved you. The Lord's reassuring word to his disheartened people.

🅰 1:3 Esau I have hated. If God's people doubt his covenant love, they should consider the contrast between God's ways with them and his ways with Jacob's (Israel's) brother, Esau (Edom). Paul explains God's love for Jacob and hatred for Esau on the basis of election (see Ro 9:10–13 and note on 9:13). God chose Jacob but not Esau. For the intended sense of "love" and "hate" here, see Ge 29:31–33; Lk 14:26 and note. wasteland. Malachi's words about Edom echo those of the earlier prophets (see Am 1:11–12; Isa 34:5–15; Jer 49:7–22; Eze 25:12–14; 35:1–15; Obadiah). Between c. 550 and 400 b.c. the Nabatean Arabs gradually forced the Edomites from their homeland.

1:4 Edom may say. Her proud self-reliance has not assured her security and will not secure her future (cf. Jer 49:16).

🅰 1:5 Great … Israel. When she sees the ultimate fate of Edom, doubting Israel will acknowledge that the Lord is the great Ruler over all the nations (see Ps 47:2; 96:10; 97:1,9; see also 99:1–3 and notes).

1:6—2:9 The Lord rebukes the priests for unacceptable worship.

1:6 son honors his father. Cf. Isa 1:2–3. priests who show con-

tempt for my name. Contrast 2:5; cf. Isa 1:4.

🅰 1:7 food. The animal offerings (see v. 12; Lev 21:8,21). defiled you. By offering defiled sacrifices they defile the Lord himself. the Lord's table. The altar (see v. 12; see also v. 8; Eze 44:16 and notes). Since the priests ate from the sacrifices, the altar was also the table from which they got their food. contemptible. As the priests considered the Lord's altar and its sacrifices (v. 12) contemptible, so the Lord would cause the priests to be considered contemptible by the people (see 2:9 and note).

🅰 1:8 blind … lame. Animals with defects or serious flaws were unacceptable as sacrifices (see Lev 1:3 and note; Dt 15:21). God desires the best. governor. Probably the Persian governor.

🅰 1:10 shut the temple doors. Better no sacrifices at all than sacrifices offered with contempt (see Isa 1:11–15 and note).

1:11 great among the nations. Cf. v. 14. God's judgment on Edom (v. 5) and other nations demonstrates his superiority over their gods, and it ultimately will evoke their recognition of him (see Zep 2:11; 3:9 and note). incense and pure offerings. Cf. the acceptable offerings presented by foreigners in Isa 56:6–7; 60:7. Some interpreters understand "incense" to mean "prayer" (cf. Rev 5:8) and "offerings" to mean "praise" (cf. Heb 13:15 and note).

1:12 defiled … contemptible. See v. 7 and note.

temptible.' [13]And you say, 'What a burden!' [m] and you sniff at it contemptuously, [n]" says the LORD Almighty.

"When you bring injured, lame or diseased animals and offer them as sacrifices, [o] should I accept them from your hands?" [p] says the LORD. [14]"Cursed is the cheat who has an acceptable male in his flock and vows to give it, but then sacrifices a blemished animal [q] to the Lord. For I am a great king, [r]" says the LORD Almighty, [s] "and my name is to be feared [t] among the nations. [u]

ADDITIONAL WARNING TO THE PRIESTS

2 "And now, you priests, this warning is for you. [v] [2]If you do not listen, [w] and if you do not resolve to honor [x] my name," says the LORD Almighty, "I will send a curse [y] on you, and I will curse your blessings. [z] Yes, I have already cursed them, because you have not resolved to honor me.

[3]"Because of you I will rebuke your descendants [a]; I will smear on your faces the dung [a] from your festival sacrifices, and you will be carried off with it. [b] [4]And you will know that I have sent you this warning so that my covenant with Levi [c] may continue," says the LORD Almighty. [5]"My covenant was with him, a covenant [d] of life and peace, [e] and I gave them to him; this called for reverence [f] and he revered me and stood in awe of my name. [6]True instruction [g] was in his mouth and nothing false was found on his lips. He walked [h] with me in peace [i] and uprightness, [j] and turned many from sin. [k]

[7]"For the lips of a priest [l] ought to preserve knowledge, because he is the messenger [m] of the LORD Almighty and people seek instruction from his mouth. [n] [8]But you have turned from the way [o] and by your teaching have caused many to stumble; [p] you have violated the covenant [q] with Levi," [r] says the LORD Almighty. [9]"So I have caused you to be despised [s] and humiliated [t] before all the people, because you have not followed my ways but have shown partiality [u] in matters of the law." [v]

BREAKING COVENANT THROUGH DIVORCE

[10]Do we not all have one Father [b]? [w] Did not one God create us? [x] Why do we profane the covenant [y] of our ancestors by being unfaithful [z] to one another?

[11]Judah has been unfaithful. A detestable [a] thing has been committed in Israel and in Jerusalem: Judah has desecrated the sanctuary the LORD loves [b] by marrying [c] women who worship a foreign god. [d] [12]If anyone does this, whoever he may be, may the LORD remove [e] him from the tents of Jacob [c] [f]—even though he brings an offering [g] to the LORD Almighty.

---

[a] 3 Or *will blight your grain*   [b] 10 Or *father*   [c] 12 Or [12]*May the* LORD *remove from the tents of Jacob anyone who gives testimony in behalf of the man who does this*

2:11 [b] S Dt 4:37 [c] S Ne 13:23 [d] S Ex 34:16; Jer 3:7-9   **2:12** [e] S 1Sa 2:30-33; S Eze 24:21 [f] S Nu 24:5; 2Sa 20:1 [g] S Mal 1:10

1:13 [m] Isa 43:22-24
[n] S Nu 14:11 [o] S ver 10
[p] S Dt 15:21
1:14 [q] Lev 12:5;
S Lev 22:18-21
[r] Ps 95:3; S Ob 1:21;
1Ti 6:15 [s] Jer 46:18
[t] S Dt 28:58
[u] Ps 72:8-11
2:1 [v] ver 7
2:2 [w] Jer 13:17
[x] Mt 15:7-9; Jn 5:23;
1Ti 6:16; Rev 5:12-13
[y] S Dt 11:26; S 28:20
[z] Nu 6:23-27
2:3 [a] S Ex 29:14;
S Lev 4:11; S Job 9:31
[b] 1Ki 14:10
2:4 [c] S Nu 3:12
2:5 [d] Dt 33:9;
Ps 25:10; 103:18;
S Mt 26:28;
S Lk 22:20; Heb 7:22
[e] S Nu 25:12
[f] S Dt 14:23; S 28:58;
Ps 119:161; Heb 12:28
2:6 [g] S Dt 33:10
[h] S Ge 5:22 [i] Lk 2:14;
S Jn 14:27; Gal 5:22
[j] S Ps 25:21
[k] S Ro 11:14; Jas 5:19-
20
2:7 [l] S Jer 18:18
[m] S Nu 27:21;
S 2Ch 36:15; Mt 11:10;
Mk 1:2 [n] S Lev 10:11;
S 2Ch 17:7
2:8 [o] S Ex 32:8;
Jer 2:8 [p] S Jer 18:15
[q] Jer 33:21;
S Eze 22:26
[r] S Hos 4:6
2:9 [s] 1Sa 2:30;
S Ps 22:6; S Jer 51:37
[t] S Ps 31:25; Jer 3:25;
Ac 8:32-33
[u] S Ex 18:16;
S Lev 19:15; Ac 10:34;
Ro 2:11 [v] S 1Sa 2:17
2:10 [w] S Ex 4:22;
Mt 5:16; 6:4,18;
Lk 11:2; 1Co 8:6
[x] S Job 4:17; Isa 43:1
[y] Ex 19:5; S 2Ki 17:15;
Jer 31:32 [z] S Zep 3:3-4
2:11 [a] S Isa 1:13;
S 48:8

1:13 *sniff at it contemptuously.* Cf. the behavior of Eli's sons in 1Sa 2:15–17. *injured...diseased.* See v. 8 and note.
1:14 *vows...a blemished animal.* An animal sacrificed in fulfillment of a vow had to be male without defect or blemish (see Lev 22:18–23). *great king.* See Zec 14:9 and note. *my name... feared.* More than the governor of v. 8 (see v. 11 and note).
2:2 *curse your blessings.* It was the function of the priests to pronounce God's blessing (see Nu 6:23–27), but their blessings will become curses so that their uniquely priestly function will be worse than useless.
2:3 *Because of you.* Because of what you have done. *smear on your faces.* To disgrace you (see Na 3:6).
2:4 *Levi.* The priests were chosen from the tribe of Levi (see Dt 21:5 and note).
2:5 *covenant of life and peace.* An allusion to the covenant with Phinehas, Aaron's grandson, in Nu 25:10–13 (see note on Nu 25:11). *he revered me.* Phinehas showed this by his zeal for God (see Nu 25:13).
2:6–7 *instruction.* Priests were responsible to teach the law of Moses (see Lev 10:11; see also notes on Zep 3:4; Hag 2:11).
2:6 *peace and uprightness.* Linked together also in Ps 37:37, but here "walked with me in peace and uprightness" probably refers to covenant loyalty.
2:7 *messenger.* As teacher of the law and as one through whom

people could inquire of God (see notes on 3:1; Hag 1:13).
2:8 *violated the covenant.* By unfaithful teaching, but also, it seems, by intermarriage with pagan foreigners (see Ezr 9:1 and note; 10:18–22; Ne 13:27–29). *with Levi.* See v. 4 and note on v. 5.
2:9 *despised.* In Hebrew the same word that is translated "contemptible" in 1:7,12 (see note on 1:7). *shown partiality.* Forbidden in Lev 19:15. The priests were to be like God in this respect (see Dt 10:17).

2:10–16 Malachi rebukes the people—in a passage framed by references to being "unfaithful." Two examples of their sin are specifically mentioned: marrying pagan women and divorce.
2:10 *one Father.* See Isa 63:16. *create us.* As his special people (see Isa 43:1 and note). *covenant of our ancestors.* The covenant God had made with their ancestors at Mount Sinai. *being unfaithful.* The people could not even trust their own fellow Israelites or the national leaders—like the priests (see v. 16).

2:11 *women who worship a foreign god.* Pagan women. Such marriages were strictly forbidden in the covenant law, not for ethnic or cultural reasons but because they would lead to apostasy (see Ex 34:15–16; Dt 7:2–5 and notes; Jos 23:12–13 and note on 23:12). Ezra and Nehemiah both wrestled with this problem (see note on v. 8).
2:12 The alternative given in the TNIV text note (particularly "gives testimony") is supported, e.g., by the use of the same Hebrew verb in Ge 30:33; Dt 5:20; 1Sa 12:3; 2Sa 1:16; Isa 3:9; Jer

2:13 *h* S Jer 11:11
i Ps 39:12 / Ps 66:18;
Jer 14:12 *k* Isa 58:2
2:14 *l* S Mal 1:2
m S Ge 21:30;
S Jos 24:22
n S Pr 5:18
o S Eze 16:8;
Heb 13:4
2:15 *p* S Ge 2:24;
Mt 19:4-6 *q* S Dt 14:2;
1Co 7:14 *r* S Dt 4:15
s S Isa 54:6; 1Co 7:10;
Heb 13:4
2:16 *t* S Dt 24:1;
Mt 5:31-32; 19:4-9;
Mk 10:4-5
u S Ge 6:11; 34:25;
S Pr 4:17; S Isa 58:4
v Ps 51:10
2:17 *w* S Isa 1:14
x S Mal 1:2 *y* Ps 5:4
z S Ge 18:25;
S Job 8:3; S Eze 18:25
3:1 *a* S Nu 27:21;
S 2Ch 36:15
b S Isa 40:3; S Mt 3:3;
11:10*a*; Mk 1:2*a*;
Lk 7:27*a* *c* Mic 5:2
d S Isa 42:6
e S 1Sa 9:20
3:2 *f* S Eze 22:14;
Rev 6:17 *g* S Eze 7:7;
S Da 7:13; S Joel 2:31;
S Mt 16:27; Jas 5:8;
2Pe 3:4; S Rev 1:7
h S 1Sa 6:20
i S Isa 1:31; S 30:30;
S Zec 13:9; Mt 3:10-
12 / S Job 9:30
3:3 *k* S Da 12:10;
S 1Co 3:13
l S 1Ch 23:28;
S Isa 1:25 *m* S Job 28:1;
S Ps 12:6; 1Pe 1:7;
Rev 3:18 *n* S Ps 132:9
3:4 *o* 2Ch 7:12;
Ps 51:19; Mal 1:11
p S 2Ch 7:3;
S Eze 20:40
3:5 *q* S Ex 7:11;
S Isa 47:9 *r* Ex 20:14;
Jas 2:11; 2Pe 2:12-14
s Lev 19:11-12;
S Jer 7:9

¹³Another thing you do: You flood the Lᴏʀᴅ's altar with tears. *h* You weep and wail *i* because he no longer looks with favor *j* on your offerings or accepts them with pleasure from your hands. *k* ¹⁴You ask, *l* "Why?" It is because the Lᴏʀᴅ is the witness *m* between you and the wife of your youth. *n* You have been unfaithful to her, though she is your partner, the wife of your marriage covenant. *o*

¹⁵Has not the Lᴏʀᴅ made the two of you one? *p* You belong to him in body and spirit. And why has he made you one? Because he was seeking godly offspring. *a* *q* So be on your guard, *r* and do not be unfaithful *s* to the wife of your youth.

¹⁶"I hate divorce, *t* " says the Lᴏʀᴅ God of Israel, "and I hate it when people clothe themselves with injustice," *u* says the Lᴏʀᴅ Almighty.

So be on your guard, *v* and do not be unfaithful.

BREAKING COVENANT THROUGH INJUSTICE

¹⁷You have wearied *w* the Lᴏʀᴅ with your words.

"How have we wearied him?" you ask. *x*

By saying, "All who do evil are good in the eyes of the Lᴏʀᴅ, and he is pleased *y* with them" or "Where is the God of justice? *z* "

3 "I will send my messenger, *a* who will prepare the way before me. *b* Then suddenly the Lord *c* you are seeking will come to his temple; the messenger of the covenant, *d* whom you desire, *e* will come," says the Lᴏʀᴅ Almighty.

²But who can endure *f* the day of his coming? *g* Who can stand *h* when he appears? For he will be like a refiner's fire *i* or a launderer's soap. *j* ³He will sit as a refiner and purifier of silver; *k* he will purify *l* the Levites and refine them like gold and silver. *m* Then the Lᴏʀᴅ will have men who will bring offerings in righteousness, *n* ⁴and the offerings *o* of Judah and Jerusalem will be acceptable to the Lᴏʀᴅ, as in days gone by, as in former years. *p*

⁵"So I will come to put you on trial. I will be quick to testify against sorcerers, *q* adulterers *r* and perjurers, *s* against those who defraud laborers of their wages, *t* who oppress the widows *u* and the fatherless, and deprive the foreigners *v* among you of justice, but do not fear *w* me," says the Lᴏʀᴅ Almighty.

BREAKING COVENANT BY WITHHOLDING TITHES

⁶"I the Lᴏʀᴅ do not change. *x* So you, the descendants of Jacob, are not destroyed. *y* ⁷Ever since the time of your ancestors you have turned away *z* from my decrees and have not kept them. Return *a* to me, and I will return to you," *b* says the Lᴏʀᴅ Almighty.

a 15 The meaning of the Hebrew for the first part of this verse is uncertain.

3:5 *t* S Lev 19:13; Jas 5:4 *u* S Ex 22:22 *v* S Ex 22:21; S Dt 24:19; S Eze 22:7 *w* S Dt 31:12; S Isa 1:2   **3:6** *x* S Nu 23:19; S Heb 7:21; Jas 1:17
y S Job 34:15; S Hos 11:9   **3:7** *z* S Ex 32:8; S Jer 7:26; Ac 7:51 *a* S Isa 44:22; S Eze 18:32 *b* S Zec 1:3; Jas 4:8

14:7. On this reading, the one who is to be cut off is the one who speaks in defense of the wrongdoer. *tents of Jacob.* A figurative expression for the community (see Jer 30:18).

2:13 *weep and wail.* Because the Lord does not respond to their sacrifices with blessing, they add wailing to their prayers. **2:14** *witness ... marriage covenant.* Marriage was a covenant (see Pr 2:17; Eze 16:8 and notes), and covenants were affirmed before witnesses (see notes on Dt 30:19; 1Sa 20:23; Isa 8:1–2). **2:15** *one.* See Ge 2:24 and note. *godly offspring.* Marriage "sanctifies" the children (see 1Co 7:14 and note). But see TNIV text note.

2:16 *I hate divorce.* See Isa 50:1 and note. *injustice.* See 3:5. *do not be unfaithful.* See note on vv. 10–16; see also v. 10 and note.

2:17—4:6 The second half of Malachi's prophecy speaks of God's coming to his people. They had given up on God (2:17) and had grown religiously cynical and morally corrupt. So God's coming will mean judgment and purification, as well as redemption.

2:17 *wearied the Lᴏʀᴅ with your words.* In Isa 43:24 Israel's sins had wearied God. *All who do evil are good.* Such was the depth of their cynicism. *Where is ... justice?* Cf. the sarcastic taunts of Isa 5:19.

3:1 *my messenger.* The Hebrew for these words is *mal'aki* (see TNIV text note on 1:1); it is normally used of a priest or prophet (see Hag 1:13 and note). These words are fulfilled in John the Baptist (see Mt 11:7–10; Mk 1:2–4; Lk 1:76). *who will prepare the way.* When the Lord comes, it will be to purify (v. 3) and judge (v. 5), but he will mercifully send one before him to prepare his

people (see 4:5–6; Isa 40:3 and notes). *the Lord you are seeking ... whom you desire, will come.* See Hag 2:7 and note. *messenger of the covenant.* The Messiah, who as the Lord's representative will confirm and establish the covenant (see note on Isa 42:6).

3:2 *day of his coming.* The day of the Lord (see 4:1; see also Isa 2:11,17,20; Joel 1:15 and notes). Malachi announces the Lord's coming to complete God's work in history, especially the work he outlines in the rest of his book. His word is fulfilled in the accomplishments of the Messiah. *Who can stand ... ?* Those who desire the Lord's coming must know that clean hands and a pure heart are required (see Ps 24:3–4 and note on 24:4; Isa 33:14–15). *refiner's fire.* See Isa 1:25; Zec 13:8–9 and notes. *launderer's soap.* White clothes signified purity (cf. Mk 9:3; Rev 3:5).

3:3 *sit as a refiner and purifier.* See Ps 12:6 and note. *purify the Levites.* Those who are supposed to be "messengers" of the Lord and who serve at the altar will be purged of their sins and unfaithfulness—such as those the Lord has rebuked in 1:6—2:9.

3:4 *be acceptable.* See 1:8 and note. *days gone by.* Probably the time of Moses and Phinehas (see note on 2:5).

3:5 When he comes, the Lord will both purify the Levites (vv. 3–4) and judge the people. *sorcerers.* Common in the ancient Near East (see Ex 7:11; Dt 18:10 and note on 18:9).

3:6 *do not change.* See Jas 1:17. Contrary to what many in Malachi's day were thinking, God remains faithful to his covenant. *not destroyed.* In contrast to Edom (1:3–5) and in spite of Israel's history of unfaithfulness.

"But you ask, *c* 'How are we to return?'

8"Will a mere mortal rob *d* God? Yet you rob me.

"But you ask, 'How are we robbing you?'

"In tithes *e* and offerings. 9You are under a curse *f*—your whole nation—because you are robbing me. 10Bring the whole tithe *g* into the storehouse, *h* that there may be food in my house. Test me in this," says the LORD Almighty, "and see if I will not throw open the floodgates *i* of heaven and pour out *j* so much blessing *k* that there will not be room enough to store it. *l* 11I will prevent pests from devouring *m* your crops, and the vines in your fields will not drop their fruit before it is ripe, *n*" says the LORD Almighty. 12"Then all the nations will call you blessed, *o* for yours will be a delightful land," *p* says the LORD Almighty. *q*

ISRAEL SPEAKS ARROGANTLY AGAINST GOD

13"You have spoken arrogantly *r* against me," says the LORD.

"Yet you ask, *s* 'What have we said against you?'

14"You have said, 'It is futile *t* to serve *u* God. What do we gain by carrying out his requirements *v* and going about like mourners *w* before the LORD Almighty? 15But now we call the arrogant *x* blessed. Certainly evildoers *y* prosper, *z* and even when they put God to the test, they get away with it.' "

THE FAITHFUL REMNANT

16Then those who feared the LORD talked with each other, and the LORD listened and heard. *a* A scroll *b* of remembrance was written in his presence concerning those who feared *c* the LORD and honored his name.

17"On the day when I act," says the LORD Almighty, "they will be my *d* treasured possession. *e* I will spare *f* them, just as a father has compassion and spares his son *g* who serves him. 18And you will again see the distinction between the righteous *h* and the wicked, between those who serve God and those who do not. *i*

JUDGMENT AND COVENANT RENEWAL

4 **"Surely the day is coming; *j* it will burn like a furnace. *k* All the arrogant *l* and every evildoer will be stubble, *m* and the day that is coming will set them on fire, *n*" says the LORD Almighty. "Not a root or a branch *o* will be left to them. 2But for you who revere my name, *p* the sun of righteousness *q* will rise with healing *r* in its rays. And you will go out and frolic *s* like well-fed calves. 3Then you will trample *t* on the wicked; they will be ashes *u* under the soles of your feet on the day when I act," says the LORD Almighty.

* 4:1-6 is numbered 3:19-24 in Hebrew texts.

4:2 *r* S 2Ch 7:14; S Isa 30:26; S Mt 4:23; Rev 22:2 *s* S Isa 35:6   **4:3** *t* S Job 40:12; Ps 18:40-42 *u* Eze 28:18

3:7 *c* S Mal 1:2
3:8 *d* S Zec 5:3
e S Lev 27:30;
Nu 18:21; S Ne 13:10-12; Lk 18:12
3:9 *f* S Dt 11:26;
28:15-68; S Zec 5:3
3:10 *g* S Ex 22:29
h S Ne 13:12 *i* S 2Ki 7:2
j Isa 44:3 *k* S Lev 25:21;
S Joel 2:14; 2Co 9:8-11
l S Joel 2:24
3:11 *m* S Ex 10:15;
S Dt 28:39
n S Ex 23:26
3:12 *o* S Dt 28:3-12;
Isa 61:9 *p* S Isa 62:4;
S Eze 20:6
q S 2Ch 31:10
3:13 *r* Mal 2:17
s S Mal 1:2
3:14 *t* Ps 73:13;
S Isa 57:10
u Ps 100:2; Jn 12:26;
Ro 12:11 *v* S Jos 22:5;
S Isa 1:14 *w* Isa 58:3
3:15 *x* S Ps 119:21
y Ps 14:1; 36:1-2;
Jer 7:10 *z* S Job 21:7
3:16 *a* S Ps 34:15
S 87:6; S Lk 10:20
c S Dt 28:58; S 31:12;
Ps 33:18; S Pr 1:7;
Rev 11:18
3:17 *d* Isa 43:21
e S Ex 8:22; S Dt 7:6;
S Ro 8:14; S Tit 2:14
f Ne 13:22; Ps 103:13;
Isa 26:20; Lk 15:1-32
g Ro 8:32
3:18 *h* S Ge 18:25
i Dt 32:4; Mt 25:32-33, 41
4:1 *j* S Da 7:13;
S Joel 2:31; Mt 11:14;
Ac 2:20 *k* S Isa 31:9
l S Isa 2:12
m S Isa 5:24;
S Na 1:10 *n* S Isa 1:31
o S 2Ki 10:11;
S Eze 17:8; S Mt 3:10
4:2 *p* S Dt 28:58;
Ps 61:5; 111:9;
Rev 14:1
q S Ps 118:27;
S Isa 9:2; S 45:8;
Lk 1:78; Eph 5:14

3:7 *Return ... and I will return.* If the Lord is to come for Israel's redemption, she must repent (see Zec 1:3 and note).
3:9–10 *curse ... blessing.* See Dt 11:26–28.
3:10 *storehouse.* The treasury rooms of the sanctuary (see 1Ki 7:51; 2Ch 31:11–12; Ne 13:12). *floodgates of heaven.* Elsewhere the idiom refers to abundant provision of food (see 2Ki 7:2,19; Ps 78:23–24 and note on 78:23). *pour out ... blessing.* The promised covenant blessing (see Dt 28:12; cf. Isa 44:3).
3:11 *pests ... drop their fruit.* Examples of the threatened covenant curses (see Dt 28:39–40).
3:12 *call you blessed.* In fulfillment of the promise to Abraham (see Ge 12:2–3; Isa 61:9 and notes).
3:14 *It is futile to serve God.* Because the redemption they longed for had not yet been realized. *like mourners.* In sackcloth and ashes.
3:15 *arrogant.* Evildoers—those who challenge God (see note on Ps 10:11). *blessed.* In their unbelief, the Jews call blessed those whom the godly know to be cursed (see Ps 119:21 and note)—but it is they who will be called blessed if they repent (v. 12). *evildoers prosper ... get away with it.* The psalmist struggled with the prosperity of the wicked in Ps 73:3,9–12 (see also Hab 1:2–4 and notes).
3:16 *those who feared the LORD.* Those who had not given way to doubts and cynicism. *talked with each other.* In the face of the widespread complaining against God (vv. 14–15),

they sought mutual encouragement in fellowship. *scroll of remembrance.* Analogous to the records of notable deeds kept by earthly rulers (see Est 6:1–3; Isa 4:3; Da 7:10; 12:1). *honored his name.* Contrast the priests (1:12) and many among the people (vv. 14–15; 2:17).
3:17 *my treasured possession.* See note on Ex 19:5. *spare them.* In the day of judgment (see 4:1–2). *who serves him.* Cf. 1:6.
3:18 *you will again see.* As they apparently do not now see—hence their cynicism. *the righteous and the wicked.* See 2:17 and note.
4:1 *the day.* The day of the Lord (see v. 5; 3:2 and note). *burn like a furnace.* See 3:2–3; Isa 1:31; 66:15–16 and notes. *arrogant.* See 3:15 and note. *stubble ... fire.* See Isa 47:14 and note; see also John the Baptist's prophecy about the work of Christ in Mt 3:12. *Not a root or a branch.* Nothing of them will be left (see Eze 17:8–9).
4:2 *sun of righteousness.* God and his glory are compared with the sun in Isa 60:19 (see note there). Christ is the "rising sun" from heaven (see Lk 1:78–79 and note on 1:78; see also Isa 9:2 and note). *righteousness ... healing.* Salvation and renewal are intended (see Isa 45:8; 46:13; 53:5; Jer 30:17 and notes). *its rays.* Cf. Ps 139:9. *like well-fed calves.* Frisky young calves often frolic about when released from confinement.
4:3 *trample ... the wicked.* As one treads the winepress (see Isa 63:2–3 and notes).

4:4 ᵛS Dt 28:61;
S Ps 147:19; Mt 5:17;
7:12; Ro 2:13; 4:15;
Gal 3:24 ʷS Ex 3:1
ˣS Ex 20:1
4:5 ʸS 1Ki 17:1;
S Mt 11:14; 16:14
ᶻS Joel 2:31
4:6 ᵃLk 1:17
ᵇS Isa 11:4; Rev 19:15
4:6 ᶜS Dt 11:26; S 13:15; S Jos 6:17; S 23:15; S Zec 5:3

⁴"Remember the law ᵛ of my servant Moses, the decrees and laws I gave him at Horeb ʷ for all Israel. ˣ

⁵"See, I will send the prophet Elijah ʸ to you before that great and dreadful day of the LORD comes. ᶻ ⁶He will turn the hearts of the parents to their children, ᵃ and the hearts of the children to their parents; or else I will come and strike ᵇ the land with total destruction." ᶜ

4:4 *Remember the law.* A final exhortation to those who impatiently wait for the Lord's coming. *my servant Moses.* See Ex 14:31; Dt 34:5 and notes. *Horeb.* Mount Sinai (see Ex 3:1 and note).

4:5 See 3:1 and note. *Elijah.* As Elijah came before Elisha (whose ministry was one of judgment and redemption), so "Elijah" will be sent to prepare God's people for the Lord's coming. John the Baptist ministered "in the spirit and power of

Elijah" (see Lk 1:17 and note; see also Mt 11:13–14; 17:12–13; Mk 9:11–13 and note on 9:13). And some feel that Elijah may also be one of the two witnesses in Rev 11:3 (see note there). *great and dreadful day.* See v. 1; see also 3:2; Joel 2:11 and note.

4:6 *turn the hearts.* Cf. Ge 18:19. According to Lk 1:17 John the Baptist sought to accomplish this. *total destruction.* If Israel does not repent, she will be dealt with as God had dealt with Edom (see 1:3–4; Isa 34:5).

FROM MALACHI TO CHRIST

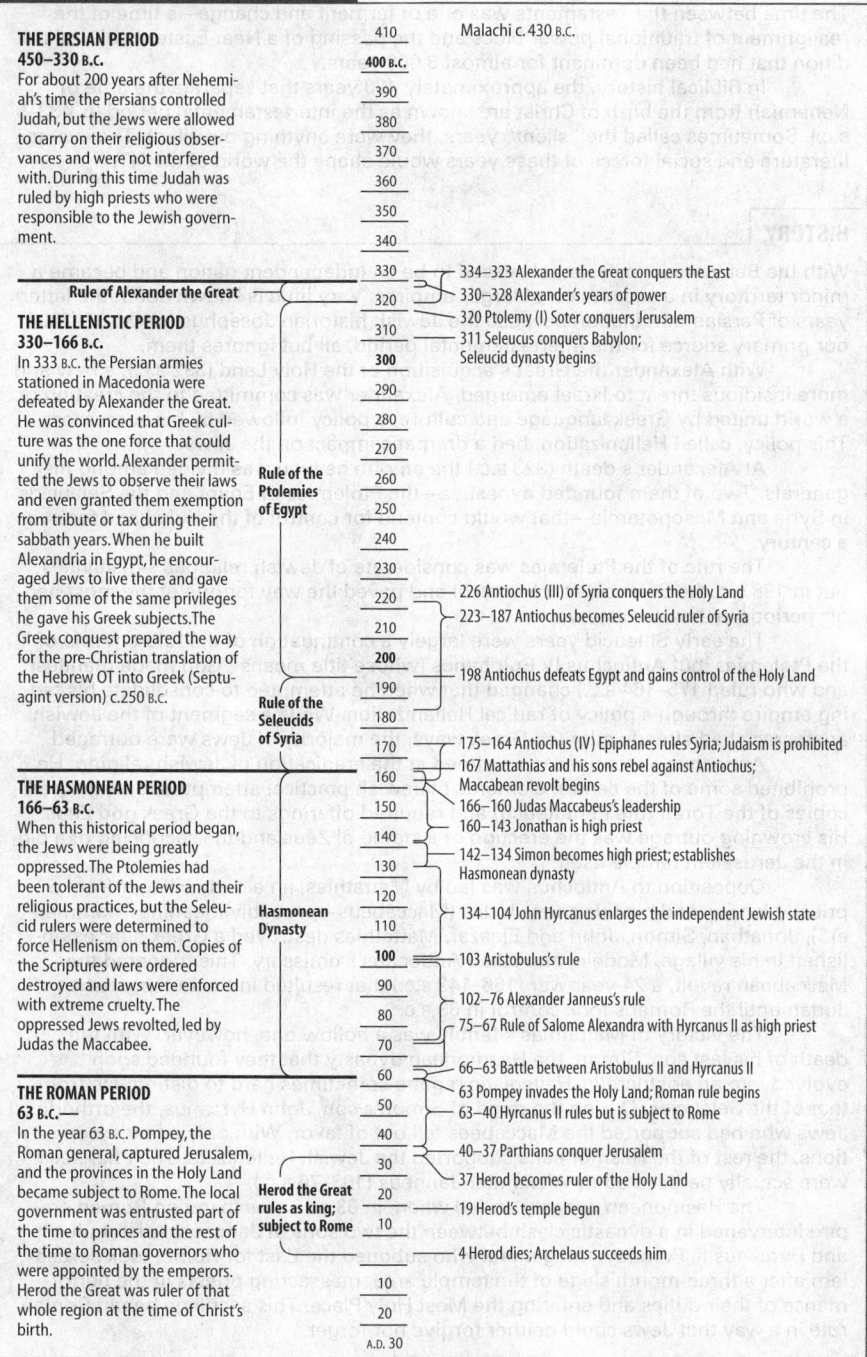

THE PERSIAN PERIOD
450–330 B.C.
For about 200 years after Nehemiah's time the Persians controlled Judah, but the Jews were allowed to carry on their religious observances and were not interfered with. During this time Judah was ruled by high priests who were responsible to the Jewish government.

Rule of Alexander the Great

THE HELLENISTIC PERIOD
330–166 B.C.
In 333 B.C. the Persian armies stationed in Macedonia were defeated by Alexander the Great. He was convinced that Greek culture was the one force that could unify the world. Alexander permitted the Jews to observe their laws and even granted them exemption from tribute or tax during their sabbath years. When he built Alexandria in Egypt, he encouraged Jews to live there and gave them some of the same privileges he gave his Greek subjects. The Greek conquest prepared the way for the pre-Christian translation of the Hebrew OT into Greek (Septuagint version) c.250 B.C.

Rule of the Ptolemies of Egypt

Rule of the Seleucids of Syria

THE HASMONEAN PERIOD
166–63 B.C.
When this historical period began, the Jews were being greatly oppressed. The Ptolemies had been tolerant of the Jews and their religious practices, but the Seleucid rulers were determined to force Hellenism on them. Copies of the Scriptures were ordered destroyed and laws were enforced with extreme cruelty. The oppressed Jews revolted, led by Judas the Maccabee.

Hasmonean Dynasty

THE ROMAN PERIOD
63 B.C.—
In the year 63 B.C. Pompey, the Roman general, captured Jerusalem, and the provinces in the Holy Land became subject to Rome. The local government was entrusted part of the time to princes and the rest of the time to Roman governors who were appointed by the emperors. Herod the Great was ruler of that whole region at the time of Christ's birth.

Herod the Great rules as king; subject to Rome

Timeline (years):
410
400 B.C.
390
380
370
360
350
340
330
320
310
300
290
280
270
260
250
240
230
220
210
200
190
180
170
160
150
140
130
120
110
100
90
80
70
60
50
40
30
20
10
A.D. 10
20
A.D. 30

Malachi c. 430 B.C.

334–323 Alexander the Great conquers the East
330–328 Alexander's years of power
320 Ptolemy (I) Soter conquers Jerusalem
311 Seleucus conquers Babylon; Seleucid dynasty begins

226 Antiochus (III) of Syria conquers the Holy Land
223–187 Antiochus becomes Seleucid ruler of Syria

198 Antiochus defeats Egypt and gains control of the Holy Land

175–164 Antiochus (IV) Epiphanes rules Syria; Judaism is prohibited
167 Mattathias and his sons rebel against Antiochus; Maccabean revolt begins
166–160 Judas Maccabeus's leadership
160–143 Jonathan is high priest
142–134 Simon becomes high priest; establishes Hasmonean dynasty

134–104 John Hyrcanus enlarges the independent Jewish state

103 Aristobulus's rule

102–76 Alexander Janneus's rule
75–67 Rule of Salome Alexandra with Hyrcanus II as high priest
66–63 Battle between Aristobulus II and Hyrcanus II
63 Pompey invades the Holy Land; Roman rule begins
63–40 Hyrcanus II rules but is subject to Rome
40–37 Parthians conquer Jerusalem
37 Herod becomes ruler of the Holy Land
19 Herod's temple begun

4 Herod dies; Archelaus succeeds him

The time between the Testaments was one of ferment and change—a time of the realignment of traditional power blocs and the passing of a Near Eastern cultural tradition that had been dominant for almost 3,000 years.

In Biblical history, the approximately 400 years that separate the time of Nehemiah from the birth of Christ are known as the intertestamental period (c. 433–5 B.C.). Sometimes called the "silent" years, they were anything but silent. The events, literature and social forces of these years would shape the world of the NT.

HISTORY

With the Babylonian exile, Israel ceased to be an independent nation and became a minor territory in a succession of larger empires. Very little is known about the latter years of Persian domination because the Jewish historian Josephus (c. A.D. 37–100), our primary source for the intertestamental period, all but ignores them.

With Alexander the Great's acquisition of the Holy Land (332 B.C.), a new and more insidious threat to Israel emerged. Alexander was committed to the creation of a world united by Greek language and culture, a policy followed by his successors. This policy, called Hellenization, had a dramatic impact on the Jews.

At Alexander's death (323 B.C.) the empire he won was divided among his generals. Two of them founded dynasties—the Ptolemies of Egypt and the Seleucids in Syria and Mesopotamia—that would contend for control of the Holy Land for over a century.

The rule of the Ptolemies was considerate of Jewish religious sensitivities, but in 198 B.C. the Seleucids took control and paved the way for one of the most heroic periods in Jewish history.

The early Seleucid years were largely a continuation of the tolerant rule of the Ptolemies, but Antiochus IV Epiphanes (whose title means "God made manifest" and who ruled 175–164 B.C.) changed that when he attempted to consolidate his fading empire through a policy of radical Hellenization. While a segment of the Jewish aristocracy had already adopted Greek ways, the majority of Jews were outraged.

Antiochus's atrocities were aimed at the eradication of Jewish religion. He prohibited some of the central elements of Jewish practice, attempted to destroy all copies of the Torah (the Pentateuch) and required offerings to the Greek god Zeus. His crowning outrage was the erection of a statue of Zeus and the sacrificing of a pig in the Jerusalem temple itself.

Opposition to Antiochus was led by Mattathias, an elderly villager from a priestly family, and his five sons: Judas (Maccabeus—probably meaning "hammerer"), Jonathan, Simon, John and Eleazar. Mattathias destroyed a Greek altar established in his village, Modein, and killed Antiochus's emissary. This triggered the Maccabean revolt, a 24-year war (166–142 B.C.) that resulted in the independence of Judah until the Romans took control in 63 B.C.

The victory of Mattathias's family was a hollow one, however. With the death of his last son, Simon, the Hasmonean dynasty that they founded soon evolved into an aristocratic, Hellenistic regime sometimes hard to distinguish from that of the Seleucids. During the reign of Simon's son, John Hyrcanus, the orthodox Jews who had supported the Maccabees fell out of favor. With only a few exceptions, the rest of the Hasmoneans supported the Jewish Hellenizers. The Pharisees were actually persecuted by Alexander Janneus (103–76 B.C.).

The Hasmonean dynasty ended when, in 63 B.C., an expanding Roman empire intervened in a dynastic clash between the two sons of Janneus, Aristobulus II and Hyrcanus II. Pompey, the general who subdued the East for Rome, took Jerusalem after a three-month siege of the temple area, massacring priests in the performance of their duties and entering the Most Holy Place. This sacrilege began Roman rule in a way that Jews could neither forgive nor forget.

LITERATURE

During these unhappy years of oppression and internal strife, the Jewish people produced a sizable body of literature that both recorded and addressed their era. Three of the more significant works are the Septuagint, the Apocrypha and the Dead Sea Scrolls.

Septuagint. Jewish legend says that 72 scholars, under the sponsorship of Ptolemy Philadelphus (c. 250 B.C.), were brought together on the island of Pharos, near Alexandria, where they produced a Greek translation of the OT in 72 days. From this tradition the Latin word for 70, "Septuagint," became the name attached to the translation. The Roman numeral for 70, LXX, is used as an abbreviation for it.

Behind the legend lies the probability that at least the Torah (the five books of Moses) was translated into Greek c. 250 B.C. for the use of the Greek-speaking Jews of Alexandria. The rest of the OT and some noncanonical books were also included in the LXX before the dawning of the Christian era, though it is difficult to be certain when.

The Septuagint quickly became the Bible of the Jews outside the Holy Land who, like the Alexandrians, no longer spoke Hebrew. It would be difficult to overestimate its influence. It made the Scriptures available both to the Jews who no longer spoke their ancestral language and to the entire Greek-speaking world. It later became the Bible of the early church. Also, its widespread popularity and use contributed to the retention of the Apocrypha by some branches of Christendom.

Apocrypha. Derived from a Greek word that means "hidden," Apocrypha has acquired the meaning "false," but in a technical sense it describes a specific body of writings. This collection consists of a variety of books and additions to canonical books that, with the exception of 2 Esdras (c. A.D. 90), were written during the intertestamental period. Their recognition as authoritative in Roman and Eastern Christianity is the result of a complex historical process.

The limits of the Hebrew canon of the OT, also accepted by most Protestants today, were very likely established by the dawn of the second century A.D. In spite of disagreements among some of the church fathers as to which books were canonical and which were not, the Apocryphal books (which were included in the Septuagint) continued in common use by most Christians until the Reformation. During this period most Protestants decided to follow the original Hebrew canon, while Rome, at the Council of Trent (1546), and more recently at the First Vatican Council (1869–70), affirmed the larger "Alexandrian" canon that includes the Apocrypha.

The Apocryphal books have retained their place primarily through the weight of ecclesiastical authority, without which they would not commend themselves as canonical literature. There is no clear evidence that Jesus or the apostles ever quoted any Apocryphal works as inspired Scripture. The Jewish community that produced them repudiated them, and the historical surveys in the apostolic sermons recorded in Acts completely ignore the period they cover. Even the sober, historical account of 1 Maccabees is tarnished by numerous errors and anachronisms.

There is nothing of theological value in the Apocryphal books that cannot be duplicated in canonical Scripture, and they contain much that runs counter to its teachings. Nonetheless, this body of literature does provide a valuable source of information for the study of the intertestamental period.

B *Dead Sea Scrolls.* In the spring of 1947 an Arab shepherd chanced upon a cave in the hills overlooking the southwestern shore of the Dead Sea that contained what has been called "the greatest manuscript discovery of modern times." The documents and fragments of documents found in a group of such caves, dubbed the "Dead Sea Scrolls," included OT books, a few books of the Apocrypha, apocalyptic works, pseudepigrapha (books that purport to be the work of ancient heroes of the faith) and a number of books peculiar to the sect that produced them.

Approximately a third of the documents are Biblical, with Psalms, Deuteronomy and Isaiah—the books quoted most often in the NT—occurring most frequently. One of the most remarkable finds was a complete, 24-foot-long scroll of Isaiah.

The Scrolls have made a significant contribution to the quest for a form of the OT texts most accurately reflecting the original manuscripts; they provide copies 1,000 years closer to the originals than were previously known. The understanding of Biblical Hebrew and Aramaic and knowledge of the development of Judaism between the Testaments have been increased significantly. Of great importance to readers of the Bible is the demonstration of the care with which OT texts were copied, thus providing objective evidence for the general reliability of those texts.

SOCIAL DEVELOPMENTS

The Judaism of Jesus' day is, to a large extent, the result of changes that came about in response to the pressures of the intertestamental period.

Diaspora. The Diaspora (dispersion) of Israel begun in the exile accelerated during these years until a writer of the day could say that Jews filled "every land and sea."

Jews outside the Holy Land, cut off from the temple, concentrated their religious life in the study of the Torah and the life of the synagogue (see below). The missionaries of the early church began their Gentile ministries among the Diaspora, using their Greek translation of the OT (the Septuagint).

Sadducees. In the Holy Land, the Greek world made its greatest impact through the party of the Sadducees. Made up of aristocrats, it became the temple party. Because of their position, the Sadducees had a vested interest in the status quo.

Relatively few in number, they wielded disproportionate political power and controlled the high priesthood. They rejected all religious writings except the Torah, as well as any doctrine (such as resurrection from the dead) not found in those five books.

Synagogue. During the Babylonian exile, Israel was cut off from the temple, divested of nationhood and surrounded by pagan religious practices. The nation's faith was threatened with extinction. Under these circumstances, the exiles turned their religious focus from what they had lost to what they retained—the Torah and the belief that they were God's people. They concentrated on the law rather than nationhood, on personal piety rather than sacramental rectitude and on prayer as an acceptable replacement for the sacrifices denied to them.

When they returned from the exile, they brought with them this new form of religious expression, as well as the synagogue (its center), and Judaism became a faith that could be practiced wherever the Torah could be carried. The emphases on personal piety and a relationship with God, which characterized synagogue worship, not only helped preserve Judaism but also prepared the way for the Christian gospel.

Pharisees. As the party of the synagogue, the Pharisees strove to reinterpret the law. They built a "hedge" around it to enable Jews to live righteously before God in a world that had changed drastically since the days of Moses. Although they were comparatively few in number, the Pharisees enjoyed the support of the people and influenced popular opinion, if not national policy. They were the only party to survive the destruction of the temple in A.D. 70 and were the spiritual progenitors of modern Judaism.

B   *Essenes.* An almost forgotten Jewish sect (but referred to by Josephus) until the discovery of the Dead Sea Scrolls, the Essenes were a small, separatist group that grew out of the conflicts of the Maccabean age. Like the Pharisees, they stressed strict legal observance, but they considered the temple priesthood corrupt and rejected much of the temple ritual and sacrificial system. Though they are mentioned by several ancient writers, the precise nature of the Essenes is still not certain, though it is generally agreed that the Qumran community that produced the Dead Sea Scrolls was an Essene group.

Because they were convinced that they were the true remnant, these Qumran Essenes had separated themselves from Judaism at large and devoted themselves to personal purity and preparation for the final war between the "Sons of Light and the Sons of Darkness." They practiced an apocalyptic faith, looking back to the contributions of their "Teacher of Righteousness" and forward to the coming of two, and possibly three, Messiahs. The destruction of the temple in A.D. 70, however, seems to have delivered a death blow to their apocalyptic expectations.

Attempts have been made to equate aspects of the beliefs of the Qumran community with the origins of Christianity. Some have seen a prototype of Jesus in their "Teacher of Righteousness," and both John the Baptist and Jesus have been assigned membership in the sect. There is, however, only a superficial, speculative base for these conjectures.

A careful comparison of the four Gospels reveals that Matthew, Mark and Luke are noticeably similar, while John is quite different. The first three Gospels agree extensively in language, in the material they include, and in the order in which events and sayings from the life of Christ are recorded. (Chronological order does not appear to have been rigidly followed in any of the Gospels, however.) Because of this agreement, these three books are called the Synoptic Gospels (*syn*, "together with"; *optic*, "seeing"; thus "seeing together"). For an example of agreement in content, see Mt 9:2–8; Mk 2:3–12; Lk 5:18–26. An instance of verbatim agreement is found in Mt 10:22a; Mk 13:13a; Lk 12:17. A mathematical comparison shows that 91 percent of Mark's Gospel is contained in Matthew, while 53 percent of Mark is found in Luke. Such agreement raises questions as to the origin of the Synoptic Gospels. Did the authors rely on a common source? Were they interdependent? Questions such as these constitute what is known as the Synoptic Problem. Several suggested solutions have been advanced:

1. *The use of oral tradition.* Some have thought that oral tradition had become so stereotyped that it provided a common source from which all the Synoptic writers drew.

2. *The use of an early Gospel.* Some have postulated that the Synoptic authors all had access to an earlier Gospel, now lost.

3. *The use of written fragments.* Some have assumed that written fragments had been composed concerning various events from the life of Christ and that these were used by the Synoptic authors.

4. *Mutual dependence.* Some have suggested that the Synoptic writers drew from each other, with the result that what they wrote was often very similar.

5. *The use of two major sources.* The most common view currently is that the Gospel of Mark and a hypothetical document, called *Quelle* (German for "source") or *Q*, were used by Matthew and Luke as sources for most of the materials included in their Gospels.

6. *The priority and use of Matthew.* Another view suggests that the other two Synoptics drew from Matthew as their main source.

7. *The priority and use of Luke.* A similar view suggests that the other two Synoptics drew from Luke as their main source.

8. *A combination of the above.* This theory assumes that the authors of the Synoptic Gospels made use of oral tradition, written fragments, mutual dependence on other Synoptic writers or on their Gospels, and the testimony of eyewitnesses.

9. *Complete independence.* Some hold that the Synoptic writers worked independently of each other. According to this view, the similar—sometimes even verbatim—choice and order of words and events are best explained by the infallible guidance of the Holy Spirit on the authors.

DATING THE SYNOPTIC GOSPELS

MARK
MATTHEW   LUKE

ASSUMPTION A
Matthew and Luke used Mark as a major source

View No. 1 Mark written in the 50s or early 60s A.D.
(1) Matthew written in late 50s or the 60s
(2) Luke written 59–63

View No. 2 Mark written 65–70
(1) Matthew written in the 70s or later
(2) Luke written in the 70s or later

MATTHEW | MARK | LUKE

ASSUMPTION B
Matthew and Luke did not use Mark as a source

View No. 1 Mark could have been written anytime between 50 and 70
View No. 2 Mark written 65–70
(1) Matthew written in the 50s (see Introduction to Matthew: Date and Place of Writing)
(2) Luke written 59–63 (see Introduction to Luke: Date and Place of Writing)

MATTHEW | INTRODUCTION

C Although the first Gospel is anonymous, the early church fathers were unanimous in holding that Matthew, one of the 12 apostles, was its author. However, the results of modern critical studies—in particular those that stress Matthew's alleged dependence on Mark for a substantial part of his Gospel—have caused some Biblical scholars to abandon Matthean authorship. Why, they ask, would Matthew, an eyewitness to the events of our Lord's life, depend so heavily on Mark's account? The best answer seems to be that he agreed with it and wanted to show that the apostolic testimony to Christ was not divided.

Matthew, whose name means "gift of the LORD," was a tax collector who left his work to follow Jesus (9:9–13). In Mark and Luke he is called by his other name, Levi.

DATE AND PLACE OF WRITING

Some have argued on the basis of its Jewish characteristics that Matthew's Gospel was written in the early church period, possibly the early part of A.D. 50, when the church was largely Jewish and the gospel was preached to Jews only (Ac 11:19). However, those who have concluded that both Matthew and Luke drew extensively from Mark's Gospel date it later—after the Gospel of Mark had been in circulation for a period of time. See essay and chart, p. 1601. Accordingly, some feel that Matthew would have been written in the late 50s or in the 60s. Others, who assume that Mark was written between 65 and 70, place Matthew in the 70s or even later. However, there is insufficient evidence to be dogmatic about either view.

The Jewish nature of Matthew's Gospel may suggest that it was written in the Holy Land, though many think it may have originated in Syrian Antioch.

RECIPIENTS

Since his Gospel was written in Greek, Matthew's readers were obviously Greek-speaking. They also seem to have been Jews. Many elements point to Jewish readership: Matthew's concern with fulfillment of the OT (he has more quotations from and allusions to the OT than any other NT author); his tracing of Jesus' descent from Abraham (1:1–17); his lack of explanation of Jewish customs (especially in contrast to Mark); his use of Jewish terminology (e.g., "kingdom of heaven," where "heaven" reveals the Jewish reverential reluctance to use the name of God; see note on 3:2); his emphasis on Jesus' role as "Son of David" (1:1; 9:27; 12:23; 15:22; 20:30–31; 21:9, 15; 22:41–45). This does not mean, however, that Matthew restricts his Gospel to Jews. He records the coming of the Magi (non-Jews) to worship the infant Jesus (2:1–12), as well as Jesus' statement that the "field is the world" (13:38). He also gives a full statement of the Great Commission (28:18–20). These passages show that, although Matthew's Gospel is Jewish, it has a universal outlook.

PURPOSE

Matthew's main purpose is to prove to his Jewish readers that Jesus is their Messiah. He does this primarily by showing how Jesus in his life and ministry fulfilled the

OT Scriptures. Although all the Gospel writers quote the OT, Matthew includes nine proof texts unique to his Gospel (1:22–23; 2:15; 2:17–18; 2:23; 4:14–16; 8:17; 12:17–21; 13:35; 27:9–10) to drive home his basic theme: Jesus is the fulfillment of the OT predictions of the Messiah. Matthew even finds the history of God's people in the OT recapitulated in some aspects of Jesus' life (see, e.g., his quotation of Hos 11:1 in 2:15). To accomplish his purpose Matthew also emphasizes Jesus' Davidic lineage (see Recipients, p. 1603).

STRUCTURE

The way the material is arranged reveals an artistic touch. The whole Gospel is woven around five great discourses: (1) chs. 5–7; (2) ch. 10; (3) ch. 13; (4) ch. 18; (5) chs. 24–25. That this is deliberate is clear from the refrain that concludes each discourse: "When Jesus had finished saying these things," or similar words (7:28; 11:1; 13:53; 19:1; 26:1). The narrative sections, in each case, appropriately lead up to the discourses. The Gospel has a fitting prologue (chs. 1–2) and a challenging epilogue (28:16–20).

      The fivefold division may suggest that Matthew has modeled his book on the structure of the Pentateuch (the first five books of the OT). He may also be presenting the gospel as a new Torah and Jesus as a new and greater Moses.

OUTLINE

1:1 *a* 2Sa 7:12-16;
Isa 9:6,7; 11:1; Jer
23:5,6; S Mt 9:27;
Lk 1:32,69; Rev 22:16
b Ge 22:18; S Gal 3:16
1:2 *c* Ge 21:3,12
d Ge 25:26
e Ge 29:35; 49:10
1:3 *f* Ge 38:27-30
1:5 *g* S Heb 11:31
1:6 *h* Isa 16:1; 17:12
i 2Sa 12:24
1:10 *j* 2Ki 20:21
1:11 *k* 2Ki 24:14-16;
Jer 27:20; 40:1;
Da 1:1,2
1:12 *l* 1Ch 3:17
m 1Ch 3:19; Ezr 3:2

THE GENEALOGY OF JESUS THE MESSIAH

1:1–17pp — Lk 3:23–38
1:3–6pp — Ru 4:18–22
1:7–11pp — 1Ch 3:10–17

1 This is the genealogy[a] of Jesus the Messiah[b] the son of David,[a] the son of Abraham:[b]

2 Abraham was the father of Isaac,[c]
  Isaac the father of Jacob,[d]
  Jacob the father of Judah and his brothers,[e]
3 Judah the father of Perez and Zerah, whose mother was Tamar,[f]
  Perez the father of Hezron,
  Hezron the father of Ram,
4 Ram the father of Amminadab,
  Amminadab the father of Nahshon,
  Nahshon the father of Salmon,
5 Salmon the father of Boaz, whose mother was Rahab,[g]
  Boaz the father of Obed, whose mother was Ruth,
  Obed the father of Jesse,
6 and Jesse the father of King David.[h]

David was the father of Solomon, whose mother had been Uriah's wife,[i]
7 Solomon the father of Rehoboam,
  Rehoboam the father of Abijah,
  Abijah the father of Asa,
8 Asa the father of Jehoshaphat,
  Jehoshaphat the father of Jehoram,
  Jehoram the father of Uzziah,
9 Uzziah the father of Jotham,
  Jotham the father of Ahaz,
  Ahaz the father of Hezekiah,
10 Hezekiah the father of Manasseh,[j]
  Manasseh the father of Amon,
  Amon the father of Josiah,
11 and Josiah the father of Jeconiah[c] and his brothers at the time of the exile to Babylon.[k]

12 After the exile to Babylon:
  Jeconiah was the father of Shealtiel,[l]
  Shealtiel the father of Zerubbabel,[m]
13 Zerubbabel the father of Abiud,
  Abiud the father of Eliakim,
  Eliakim the father of Azor,

---

a 1 Or *is an account of the origin*   *b 1* Or *Jesus Christ. Messiah* (Hebrew) and *Christ* (Greek) both mean
Anointed One; also in verse 18.   *c 11* That is, Jehoiachin; also in verse 12

1:1–16 For a comparison of Matthew's genealogy with Luke's see note on Lk 3:23–38. The types of people mentioned in this genealogy reveal the broad scope of those who make up the people of God as well as the genealogy of Jesus.
1:1 *son of David.* A Messianic title (see Introduction: Recipients and Purpose; see also note on 9:27) found several times in this Gospel (in 1:20 it is not a Messianic title). Jesus fulfills the Davidic covenant (see 2Sa 7:5–16 and note on 7:11). *son of Abraham.* Because Matthew was writing to Jews, it was important to identify Jesus in this way. Jesus fulfills the Abrahamic covenant (see Ge 12:2–3; 15:9–21; 17; Zec 9:10 and note).
1:3 *Tamar.* In Matthew's genealogy five women are named: Tamar (here), Rahab (v. 5), Ruth (v. 5), Bathsheba (not by name but by description—"Solomon, whose mother had been Uriah's wife," v. 6), and, of course, Mary (v. 16). At least three of these women were Gentiles (Tamar, Rahab and Ruth). Bathsheba was probably an Israelite (1Ch 3:5) but was closely associated with the Hittites because of Uriah, her Hittite husband. By including these women (contrary to custom) in his genealogy, Matthew may be indicating at the very outset of his Gospel

that God's activity is not limited to men or to the people of Israel.
1:4 *Amminadab.* Father-in-law of Aaron (Ex 6:23).
1:5 *Rahab.* See note on v. 3; see also Jos 2. Since quite a long time had elapsed between Rahab and David and because of Matthew's desire for systematic organization (see note on v. 17), many of the generations between these two ancestors were assumed, but not listed, by Matthew. *Ruth.* See note on v. 3.
1:6 *Solomon, whose mother.* His mother was Bathsheba (see note on v. 3).
1:8 *Jehoram the father.* Matthew calls Jehoram the father of Uzziah, but from 2Ch 21:4—26:23 it is clear that, again, several generations were assumed (Ahaziah, Joash and Amaziah) and that "father" is used in the sense of "forefather" or "ancestor" (see TNIV text notes on 1Ch 1:5,10).
1:11 *Josiah the father.* Similarly (see note on v. 8), Josiah is called the father of Jeconiah (i.e., Jehoiachin; see TNIV text note), whereas he was actually the father of Jehoiakim and the grandfather of Jehoiachin (2Ch 36:1–9).
1:12 *Shealtiel the father.* See note on 1Ch 3:19.

1:16 ⁿLk 1:27
ᵒMt 27:17
1:18 ᵖLk 1:35
1:19 ᑫLk 24:1
1:20 ʳs Ac 5:19
ˢMt 27:19
1:21 ᵗs Lk 1:31
ᵘPs 130:8; S Lk 2:11;
S Jn 3:17; Ac 5:31;
S Ro 11:14; Tit 2:14
1:22 ᵛMt 2:15,17,
21:4; 26:54,56; 27:9;
Lk 4:21; 21:22; 24:44;
Jn 13:18; 19:24,28,36
1:23 ʷIsa 7:14;
8:8,10
1:24 ˣS Ac 5:19
1:25 ʸver 21;
S Lk 1:31
2:1 ᶻLk 2:4-7
ᵃLk 1:5
2:2 ᵇJer 23:5;
Mt 27:11; Mk 15:2;
Lk 23:38; Jn 1:49;
18:33-37 ᶜNu 24:17

¹⁴Azor the father of Zadok,
   Zadok the father of Akim,
   Akim the father of Eliud,
¹⁵Eliud the father of Eleazar,
   Eleazar the father of Matthan,
   Matthan the father of Jacob,
¹⁶and Jacob the father of Joseph, the husband of Mary,ⁿ and Mary was the mother
   of Jesus who is called the Messiah.ᵒ

¹⁷Thus there were fourteen generations in all from Abraham to David, fourteen from
David to the exile to Babylon, and fourteen from the exile to the Messiah.

JOSEPH ACCEPTS JESUS AS HIS SON

¹⁸This is how the birth of Jesus the Messiah came aboutᵃ: His mother Mary was pledged
to be married to Joseph, but before they came together, she was found to be pregnant
through the Holy Spirit.ᵖ ¹⁹Because Joseph her husband was a righteous man and did not
want to expose her to public disgrace, he had in mind to divorceᑫ her quietly.

²⁰But after he had considered this, an angelʳ of the Lord appeared to him in a dreamˢ
and said, "Joseph son of David, do not be afraid to take Mary home as your wife, because
what is conceived in her is from the Holy Spirit. ²¹She will give birth to a son, and you are
to give him the name Jesus,ᵇᵗ because he will save his people from their sins."ᵘ

²²All this took place to fulfillᵛ what the Lord had said through the prophet: ²³"The virgin will conceive and give birth to a son, and they will call him Immanuel"ᶜʷ (which
means "God with us").

²⁴When Joseph woke up, he did what the angelˣ of the Lord had commanded him and
took Mary home as his wife. ²⁵But he had no union with her until she gave birth to a son.
And he gave him the name Jesus.ʸ

THE MAGI VISIT THE MESSIAH

2 After Jesus was born in Bethlehem in Judea,ᶻ during the time of King Herod,ᵃ Magiᵈ
from the east came to Jerusalem ²and asked, "Where is the one who has been born
king of the Jews?ᵇ We saw his starᶜ when it rose and have come to worship him."

ᵃ 18 Or *The origin of Jesus the Messiah was like this*   ᵇ 21 *Jesus* is the Greek form of *Joshua*, which means
the Lᴏʀᴅ saves.   ᶜ 23 Isaiah 7:14   ᵈ 1 Traditionally *wise men*

1:16 *husband of Mary.* Matthew does not say that Joseph was
the father of Jesus but only that he was the husband of Mary
and that Jesus was born of her. In this genealogy Matthew
shows that, although Jesus is not the physical son of Joseph, he
is the legal son and therefore a descendant of David (see Lk 2:33;
Jn 1:45 and notes). *Mary ... mother of Jesus.* See note on v. 3.
1:17 *fourteen generations ... fourteen ... fourteen.* These divisions reflect two characteristics of Matthew's Gospel: (1) an apparent fondness for numbers and (2) concern for systematic
arrangement. The number 14 may have been chosen because it
is twice seven (the number of completeness) and/or because it
is the numerical value of the name David (see notes on Pr 10:1;
Rev 13:17). For the practice of telescoping genealogies to
achieve the desired number of names see Introduction to
1 Chronicles: Genealogies.
1:18 *pledged to be married.* There were no sexual relations during a Jewish betrothal period, but it was a much more binding
relationship than a modern engagement and could be broken
only by divorce (see v. 19). In Dt 22:24 a betrothed woman is
called a "wife," though the preceding verse speaks of her as being "pledged to be married." Matthew uses the terms "husband"
(v. 19) and "wife" (v. 24) of Joseph and Mary before their marriage was consummated (see note on Joel 1:8). *the Holy Spirit.*
The common NT way of referring to the divine Spirit, who in the
OT was almost always called "the Spirit of God" or "the Spirit of
the Lᴏʀᴅ." See Ps 51:11 and note. Christian reflection on the Biblical word about him (see 3:16–17; 28:19; 2Co 13:14 and notes)
led to the understanding that he is one of the three persons of
the Trinity.
1:19 *righteous.* To Jews this meant being zealous in keeping the
law. *divorce her quietly.* He would sign the necessary legal papers

but not have her judged publicly and stoned (see Dt 22:23–24).
1:20 *in a dream.* The phrase occurs five times in the first two
chapters of Matthew (here; 2:12–13,19,22) and indicates the
means the Lord used for speaking to Joseph. *Joseph son of David.* See notes on 1:1,16; perhaps a hint that the message of the
angel related to the expected Messiah. *take Mary home as your
wife.* They were legally pledged to each other, but not yet living
together as husband and wife. *what is conceived in her is from
the Holy Spirit.* This agrees perfectly with the announcement to
Mary (Lk 1:35), except that the latter is more specific (see note
on Lk 1:26–35).
1:21 *the name Jesus.* See TNIV text note; the meaning is more
specifically explained in the rest of the verse. *save.* See Lk 2:11
and note.
1:22 *fulfill.* Twelve times (here; 2:15,23; 3:15; 4:14; 5:17; 8:17;
12:17; 13:14,35; 21:4; 27:9) Matthew speaks of the OT being fulfilled, i.e., of events in NT times that were prophesied in the OT
—a powerful testimony to the divine origin of Scripture and its
accuracy even in small details. In the fulfillments we also see the
writer's concern for linking the gospel with the OT.
1:23 See note on Isa 7:14. This is the first of at least 47 quotations, most of them Messianic, that Matthew takes from the OT
(see TNIV text notes throughout Matthew).
1:24 *angel of the Lord.* See Lk 2:9 and note.
1:25 *he had no union with her until she gave birth.* Both Matthew and Luke (1:26–35) make it clear that Jesus was born of a
virgin. Although this doctrine is often ridiculed, it is an important part of the evangelical faith.

2:1 *Bethlehem in Judea.* A village about five miles
south of Jerusalem. Matthew says nothing of
the events in Nazareth (cf. Lk 1:26–56). Possibly wanting to

³When King Herod heard this he was disturbed, and all Jerusalem with him. ⁴When he had called together all the people's chief priests and teachers of the law, he asked them where the Messiah was to be born. ⁵"In Bethlehem*d* in Judea," they replied, "for this is what the prophet has written:

> ⁶ " 'But you, Bethlehem, in the land of Judah,
>   are by no means least among the rulers of Judah;
> for out of you will come a ruler
>   who will shepherd my people Israel.'*a*"*e*

⁷Then Herod called the Magi secretly and found out from them the exact time the star had appeared. ⁸He sent them to Bethlehem and said, "Go and make a careful search for the child. As soon as you find him, report to me, so that I too may go and worship him."

⁹After they had heard the king, they went on their way, and the star they had seen when it rose went ahead of them until it stopped over the place where the child was. ¹⁰When they saw the star, they were overjoyed. ¹¹On coming to the house, they saw the child with his mother Mary, and they bowed down and worshiped him.*f* Then they opened their treasures and presented him with gifts*g* of gold, frankincense and myrrh. ¹²And having been warned*h* in a dream*i* not to go back to Herod, they returned to their country by another route.

THE ESCAPE TO EGYPT

¹³When they had gone, an angel*j* of the Lord appeared to Joseph in a dream.*k* "Get up," he said, "take the child and his mother and escape to Egypt. Stay there until I tell you, for Herod is going to search for the child to kill him."*l*

¹⁴So he got up, took the child and his mother during the night and left for Egypt, ¹⁵where he stayed until the death of Herod. And so was fulfilled*m* what the Lord had said through the prophet: "Out of Egypt I called my son."*b**n*

¹⁶When Herod realized that he had been outwitted by the Magi, he was furious, and he gave orders to kill all the boys in Bethlehem and its vicinity who were two years old and under, in accordance with the time he had learned from the Magi. ¹⁷Then what was said through the prophet Jeremiah was fulfilled:*o*

a 6 Micah 5:2,4   *b* 15 Hosea 11:1

emphasize Jesus' Davidic background, he begins with the events that happened in David's city. It is called "Bethlehem in Judea," not only to distinguish it from the town of the same name about seven miles northwest of Nazareth, but also to emphasize that Jesus came from the tribe (Judah) and territory that produced the line of Davidic kings. That Jews expected the Messiah to be born in Bethlehem and to be from David's family is clear from Jn 7:42. *King Herod.* Herod the Great (37–4 B.C.), to be distinguished from the other Herods in the Bible (see chart, p. 1608). Herod a non-Jew, an Idumean, who was appointed king of Judea by the Roman Senate in 40 B.C. and gained control in 37. Like most rulers of the day, he was ruthless, murdering his wife, his three sons, mother-in-law, brother-in-law, uncle and many others— not to mention the babies in Bethlehem (v. 16). His reign was also noted for splendor, as seen in the many theaters, amphitheaters, monuments, pagan altars, fortresses and other buildings he erected or refurbished—including the greatest work of all, the rebuilding of the temple in Jerusalem, begun in 20 B.C. and finished 68 years after his death. *Magi.* Probably astrologers, perhaps from Persia or southern Arabia, both of which are east of the Holy Land. *Jerusalem.* Since they were looking for the "king of the Jews" (v. 2), they naturally came to the Jewish capital city (see map No. 10 at the end of this study Bible).

A **2:2** *born king.* The Magi realized that Jesus was born a king, not that he would become one later on. *king of the Jews.* Indicates the Magi were Gentiles. Matthew wants to show that people of all nations acknowledged Jesus as "king of the Jews" and came to worship him as Lord. *star.* Probably not an ordinary star, planet or comet, though some interpreters have identified it with the conjunction of Jupiter and Saturn or with other astronomical phenomena (cf. Nu 24:17 and note).

2:4 *chief priests.* See note on Mk 8:31; Sadducees (see note on

3:7) who were in charge of worship at the temple in Jerusalem. *teachers of the law.* The Jewish scholars of the day, professionally trained in the development, teaching and application of OT law. Their authority was strictly human and traditional (see notes on Mk 2:16; Lk 5:17).

2:6 See Mic 5:2 and note.

2:11 *house.* Contrary to tradition, the Magi did not visit Jesus at the manger on the night of his birth as did the shepherds. They came some months later and visited him as a "child" in his "house." *the child with his mother Mary.* Every time the child Jesus and his mother are mentioned together, he is mentioned first (vv. 11,13–14,20–21). *gold...frankincense...myrrh.* The three gifts perhaps gave rise to the legend that there were three "wise men." But the Bible does not indicate the number of the magi, and they were almost certainly not kings. *myrrh.* See note on Ge 37:25.

2:13 *angel of the Lord.* See note on Lk 2:9.

A **2:15** *the death of Herod.* In 4 B.C. *Out of Egypt I called my son.* This quotation from Hos 11:1 originally referred to God's calling the nation of Israel out of Egypt in the time of Moses. But Matthew, under the inspiration of the Spirit, applies it also to Jesus. He sees the history of Israel (God's "son") recapitulated in the life of Jesus (God's unique Son). Just as Israel as an infant nation went down into Egypt, so the child Jesus went there. And as Israel was led by God out of Egypt, so also was Jesus. How long Jesus and his parents were in Egypt is not known.

2:16 *kill all the boys...two years old and under.* The number killed has often been exaggerated as being in the thousands. In so small a village as Bethlehem, however (even with the surrounding area included), the number was probably not large— though the act, of course, was no less brutal.

HOUSE OF HEROD

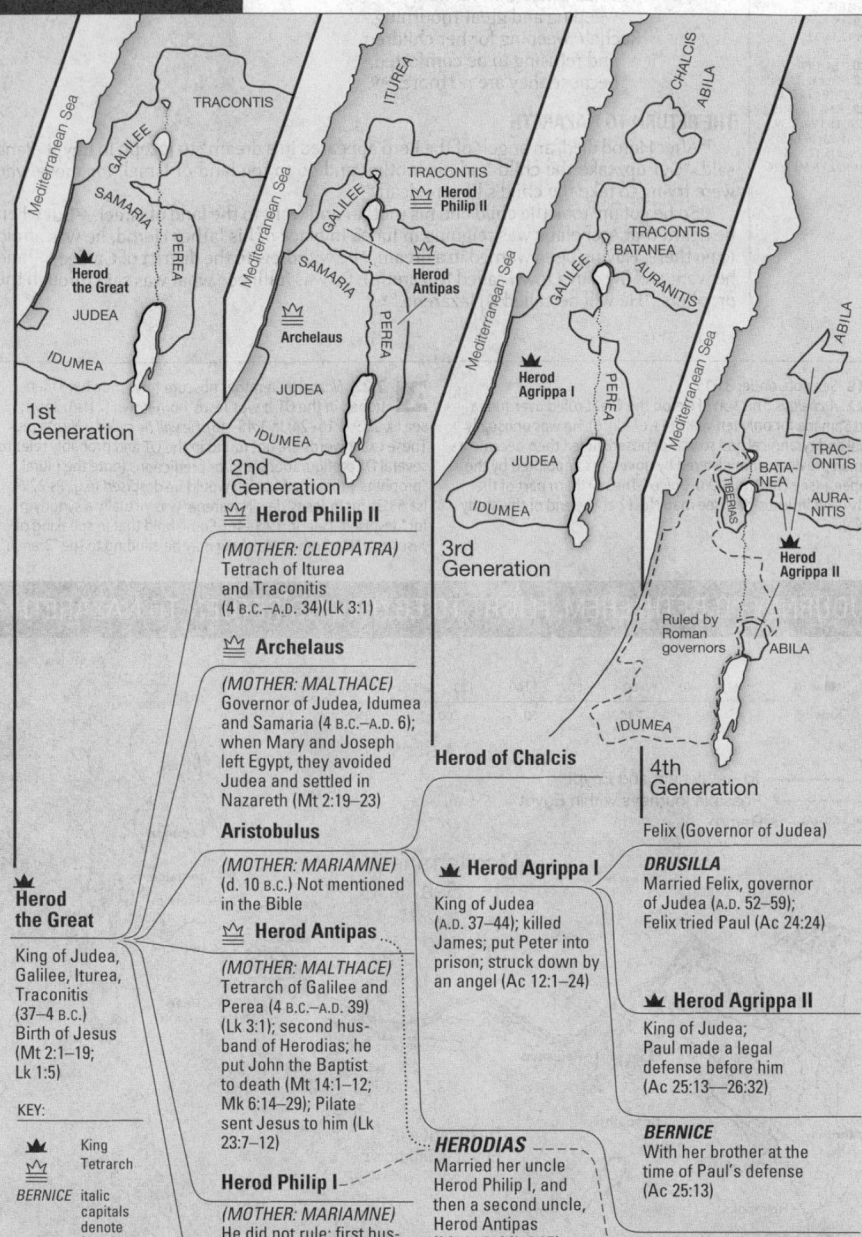

1st Generation

Mediterranean Sea · GALILEE · SAMARIA · PEREA · TRACONTIS
👑 Herod the Great
JUDEA · IDUMEA

2nd Generation

Mediterranean Sea · GALILEE · SAMARIA · PEREA · ITUREA
👑 Herod Philip II
👑 Herod Antipas
👑 Archelaus
JUDEA · IDUMEA

3rd Generation

Mediterranean Sea · GALILEE · PEREA · TRACONTIS · BATANEA · AURANITIS · CHALCIS · ABILA
👑 Herod Agrippa I
JUDEA · IDUMEA

4th Generation

Mediterranean Sea · GALILEE · PEREA · TIBERIAS · BATANEA · TRACONITIS · AURANITIS · ABILA
👑 Herod Agrippa II
Ruled by Roman governors · ABILA · IDUMEA

👑 Herod the Great

King of Judea, Galilee, Iturea, Traconitis (37–4 B.C.) Birth of Jesus (Mt 2:1–19; Lk 1:5)

KEY:

👑 King

♔ Tetrarch

BERNICE italic capitals denote females

Antipater bold type: bloodline of Herod the Great

Felix light type: non-bloodline

♔ Herod Philip II

(MOTHER: CLEOPATRA) Tetrarch of Iturea and Traconitis (4 B.C.–A.D. 34)(Lk 3:1)

♔ Archelaus

(MOTHER: MALTHACE) Governor of Judea, Idumea and Samaria (4 B.C.–A.D. 6); when Mary and Joseph left Egypt, they avoided Judea and settled in Nazareth (Mt 2:19–23)

Aristobulus

(MOTHER: MARIAMNE) (d. 10 B.C.) Not mentioned in the Bible

♔ Herod Antipas

(MOTHER: MALTHACE) Tetrarch of Galilee and Perea (4 B.C.–A.D. 39) (Lk 3:1); second husband of Herodias; he put John the Baptist to death (Mt 14:1–12; Mk 6:14–29); Pilate sent Jesus to him (Lk 23:7–12)

Herod Philip I

(MOTHER: MARIAMNE) He did not rule; first husband of Herodias (Mt 14:3; Mk 6:17) (d.c. A.D. 34)

Antipater

(MOTHER: DORIS)

Herod of Chalcis

👑 Herod Agrippa I

King of Judea (A.D. 37–44); killed James; put Peter into prison; struck down by an angel (Ac 12:1–24)

HERODIAS

Married her uncle Herod Philip I, and then a second uncle, Herod Antipas (Mt 14:3; Mk 6:17)

·········· Denotes Herodias's marriage to Herod Antipas

– – – – Denotes Herodias's marriage to Herod Philip I and daughter of that marriage

---

Felix (Governor of Judea)

DRUSILLA

Married Felix, governor of Judea (A.D. 52–59); Felix tried Paul (Ac 24:24)

👑 Herod Agrippa II

King of Judea; Paul made a legal defense before him (Ac 25:13—26:32)

BERNICE

With her brother at the time of Paul's defense (Ac 25:13)

SALOME

Daughter of Herodias and Herod Philip I; danced for the head of John the Baptist (Mt 14:1–12; Mk 6:14–29)

[18] "A voice is heard in Ramah,
  weeping and great mourning,
Rachelᵖ weeping for her children
  and refusing to be comforted,
  because they are no more."ᵃᵠ

THE RETURN TO NAZARETH

[19]After Herod died, an angelʳ of the Lord appeared in a dreamˢ to Joseph in Egypt [20]and said, "Get up, take the child and his mother and go to the land of Israel, for those who were trying to take the child's life are dead."ᵗ

[21]So he got up, took the child and his mother and went to the land of Israel. [22]But when he heard that Archelaus was reigning in Judea in place of his father Herod, he was afraid to go there. Having been warned in a dream,ᵘ he withdrew to the district of Galilee,ᵛ [23]and he went and lived in a town called Nazareth.ʷ So was fulfilledˣ what was said through the prophets: "He will be called a Nazarene."ʸ

ᵃ 18 Jer. 31:15

2:18 See note on Jer 31:15.
2:22 *Archelaus.* This son of Herod the Great ruled over Judea and Samaria for only ten years (4 B.C.–A.D. 6). He was unusually cruel and tyrannical and so was deposed. Judea then became a Roman province, administered by governors appointed by the emperor (see chart, p. 1608). *Galilee.* The northern part of the Holy Land in Jesus' day (see map No. 12 at the end of this study Bible).

A 2:23 *Nazareth.* A rather obscure town, nowhere mentioned in the OT. It was Jesus' hometown (21:11; 26:71; see Lk 2:39; 4:16–24; Jn 1:45–46). *He will be called a Nazarene.* These exact words are not found in the OT and probably refer to several OT prefigurations and/or predictions (note the plural, "prophets") that the Messiah would be despised (e.g., Ps 22:6; Isa 53:3), for in Jesus' day "Nazarene" was virtually a synonym for "despised" (see Jn 1:45–46). Some hold that in speaking of Jesus as a "Nazarene," Matthew may be alluding to the "Branch"

JOURNEY TO BETHLEHEM, FLIGHT TO EGYPT AND RETURN TO NAZARETH

Miles 0 20 40 60 80 100 120 140 160
Kms 0   50   100   150   200   250

⟵——— To Bethlehem and Egypt
⟵- - - - Possible journeys within Egypt
··········▸ Return

Mediterranean Sea

GALILEE
Nazareth

Lebonah

Jerusalem
Ashkelon Bethlehem JUDEA
Gaza   Hebron

PHILISTIA

Beer-sheba

Jordan R.

Dead Sea

Pelusium

Athribis
Succoth
Pithom

Destination in Egypt is unknown

River of Egypt (dry Canyon)

(Wadi El Arabah)
(Great Rift Valley)

Heliopolis

EGYPT

Memphis

Nile R.

Red Sea (western arm)

SINAI

Ezion Geber

JOHN THE BAPTIST PREPARES THE WAY

3:1–12pp — Mk 1:3–8; Lk 3:2–17

3 In those days John the Baptist[z] came, preaching in the wilderness of Judea [2]and saying, "Repent, for the kingdom of heaven[a] has come near." [3]This is he who was spoken of through the prophet Isaiah:

"A voice of one calling in the wilderness,
'Prepare the way for the Lord,
  make straight paths for him.' "[a][b]

[4]John's[c] clothes were made of camel's hair, and he had a leather belt around his waist.[d] His food was locusts[e] and wild honey. [5]People went out to him from Jerusalem and all Judea and the whole region of the Jordan. [6]Confessing their sins, they were baptized[f] by him in the Jordan River.

[7]But when he saw many of the Pharisees and Sadducees coming to where he was baptizing, he said to them: "You brood of vipers![g] Who warned you to flee from the coming wrath?[h] [8]Produce fruit in keeping with repentance.[i] [9]And do not think you can say to yourselves, 'We have Abraham as our father.'[i] I tell you that out of these stones God can raise up children for Abraham. [10]The ax is already at the root of the trees, and every tree that does not produce good fruit will be cut down and thrown into the fire.[k]

[11]"I baptize you with[b] water for repentance.[l] But after me comes one who is more powerful than I, whose sandals I am not worthy to carry. He will baptize you with[b] the Holy Spirit[m] and fire.[n] [12]His winnowing fork is in his hand, and he will clear his threshing floor, gathering his wheat into the barn and burning up the chaff with unquenchable fire."[o]

---

[a] 3 Isaiah 40:3   [b] 11 Or *in*

3:1 [z] ver 13,14;
Mt 9:14; 11:2-14; 14:1-
12; Lk 1:13,57-66;
3:2-19; Ac 19:3,4
3:2 [a] Da 7:14;
Mt 4:17; 6:10; 7:21;
S 25:34; Lk 11:20;
17:20,21; 19:11; 21:31;
Jn 3:3,5; Ac 1:3,6
3:3 [b] Isa 40:3;
Mal 3:1; Lk 1:76;
Jn 1:23
3:4 [c] S Mt 3:1
[d] 2Ki 1:8 [e] Lev 11:22
3:6 [f] ver 11; S Mk 1:4
3:7 [g] Mt 12:34;
23:33 [h] S Ro 1:18
3:8 [i] Ac 26:20
3:9 [i] S Lk 3:8
3:10 [k] Mt 7:19;
Lk 3:9; 13:6-9;
Jn 15:2,6
3:11 [l] ver 6;
S Mk 1:4 [m] S Mk 1:8
[n] Isa 4:4; Ac 2:3,4
3:12 [o] Mt 13:30;
S 25:41

(Hebrew *neser*) of Isa 11:1, since the word also appears in the Targums (see note on Ne 8:8), Rabbinic literature, and the Dead Sea Scrolls (see essay, pp. 1595–1596) as a Messianic title.

3:1 *John the Baptist.* The forerunner of Jesus, born c. 7 B.C. to Zechariah, a priest, and his wife Elizabeth (see Lk 1:5–80). *wilderness of Judea.* An area that stretched some 20 miles from the Jerusalem-Bethlehem plateau down to the Jordan River and the Dead Sea, perhaps the same region where John lived (cf. Lk 1:80). The people of Qumran (often associated with the Dead Sea Scrolls) lived in this area too (see essay, pp. 1596–1597).

3:2 *Repent.* Repentance is not merely a change of mind but a radical change in one's life as a whole that especially involves forsaking sin and turning or returning to God. *kingdom of heaven.* A phrase found only in Matthew, where it occurs 33 times. See Introduction: Recipients. Mark and Luke refer to "the kingdom of God," a term Matthew uses only four times (see note on Mk 11:30). The "kingdom of heaven/God" in the preaching of Jesus as recounted in the Gospels is the reign of God that he brings about through Jesus Christ—i.e., the establishment of God's rule in the hearts and lives of his people, the overcoming of all the forces of evil, the removal from the world of all the consequences of sin—including death and all that diminishes life—and the creation of a new order of righteousness and peace. The idea of God's kingdom is central to Jesus' teaching and is mentioned 50 times in Matthew alone. *has come near.* See note on Mk 1:15.

3:3 All three Synoptic Gospels quote Isa 40:3 (Luke quotes two additional verses) and apply it to John the Baptist. *make straight paths for him.* Equivalent to "Prepare the way for the Lord" (see note on Lk 3:4). The preparation was to be moral and spiritual.

3:4 *leather belt.* Used to bind up the loose outer garments. Camel's hair and a leather belt were worn by Elijah and other prophets (see 2Ki 1:8 and note; Zec 13:4). *locusts and wild honey.* No one living in the wilderness hesitated to eat insects, and locusts were among the clean foods (Lev 11:21–22). John's simple food, clothing and lifestyle were a visual protest against self-indulgence.

3:6 *Jordan River.* See note on Mk 1:5.

3:7 *Pharisees and Sadducees.* See essay, p. 1596, and chart, p. 1650. The Pharisees (see notes on Mk 2:16; Lk 5:17) were a legalistic and separatistic group who strictly, but often hypocritically, kept the law of Moses and the unwritten "tradition of the elders" (15:2). The Sadducees (see notes on Mk 12:18; Lk 20:27; Ac 4:1) were more worldly and politically minded, and were theologically unorthodox—among other things denying the resurrection, angels and spirits (Ac 23:8). *baptizing.* See note on Mk 1:4. *the coming wrath.* The arrival of the Messiah will bring repentance (v. 8) or judgment.

3:9 *We have Abraham as our father.* See Jn 8:39. Salvation does not come as a birthright (even for the Jews) but through faith in Christ (Ro 2:28–29; Gal 3:7,9,29). *these stones.* John may have pointed to the stones in the Jordan River. *children for Abraham.* The true people of God are not limited to the physical descendants of Abraham (cf. Ro 9:6–8 and notes).

3:10 *The ax is already at the root of the trees.* Judgment is near. *every tree that does not produce good fruit.* Cf. Jn 15:2 and note.

3:11 *with water for repentance.* John's baptism presupposed repentance; he would not baptize the Pharisees and Sadducees because they failed to give any evidence of repentance (vv. 7–8). *whose sandals I am not worthy to carry.* See note on Jn 1:27. *carry.* Mark (1:7) and Luke (3:16) have "untie," but the Greek for "carry" can also mean "remove." *baptize you with the Holy Spirit.* See Jn 1:33 and note. *with the Holy Spirit and fire.* Demonstrated in a dramatic way at Pentecost (Ac 1:5,8; 2:1–13; 11:16), though here "fire" may refer to judgment to come (see v. 12). The outpouring of the Holy Spirit on all God's people was promised in Joel 2:28–29 and at least partially fulfilled in Ac 2:16–21.

3:12 *His winnowing fork.* For the process of winnowing see note on Ru 1:22. Here it is figurative for the separation of the righteous ("wheat") from the wicked ("chaff"). *unquenchable fire.* Eschatological judgment (see 25:41 and note; cf. La 1:13 and note). The OT prophets and NT writers sometimes compress the first and second comings of Christ so that they seem to be one event (see, e.g., Isa 61:2 and note).

3:13 *p* S Mt 3:1;
S Mk 1:4
3:16 *q* Eze 1:1;
Jn 1:51; Ac 7:56; 10:11;
Rev 4:1; 19:11
r Isa 11:2; 42:1
3:17 *s* Dt 4:12;
Mt 17:5; Jn 12:28
t Ps 2:7; Ac 13:33;
Heb 1:1-5; 5:5;
2Pe 1:17,18 *u* Isa 42:1;
Mt 12:18; 17:5;
Mk 1:11; 9:7; Lk 3:22;
9:35; 2Pe 1:17
4:1 *v* Heb 4:15
w Ge 3:1-7
4:2 *x* Ex 34:28;
1Ki 19:8
4:3 *y* 1Th 3:5
z S Mt 3:17; 14:33;
16:16; 27:54; Mk 3:11;
Lk 1:35; 22:70;
Jn 1:34,49; 5:25;
11:27; 20:31; Ac 9:20;
Ro 1:4; 1Jn 5:10-13,
20; Rev 2:18

THE BAPTISM OF JESUS

3:13–17pp — Mk 1:9–11; Lk 3:21,22; Jn 1:31–34

¹³Then Jesus came from Galilee to the Jordan to be baptized by John.*p* ¹⁴But John tried to deter him, saying, "I need to be baptized by you, and do you come to me?"

¹⁵Jesus replied, "Let it be so now; it is proper for us to do this to fulfill all righteousness." Then John consented.

¹⁶As soon as Jesus was baptized, he went up out of the water. At that moment heaven was opened,*q* and he saw the Spirit of God*r* descending like a dove and alighting on him. ¹⁷And a voice from heaven*s* said, "This is my Son,*t* whom I love; with him I am well pleased."*u*

JESUS IS TESTED IN THE WILDERNESS

4:1–11pp — Mk 1:12,13; Lk 4:1–13

4 Then Jesus was led by the Spirit into the wilderness to be tempted*a v* by the devil.*w* ²After fasting forty days and forty nights,*x* he was hungry. ³The tempter*y* came to him and said, "If you are the Son of God,*z* tell these stones to become bread."

a 1 The Greek for *tempted* can also mean *tested.*

3:13 *Jesus … baptized by John.* See map and accompanying text, below.

3:15 Jesus' baptism marked the beginning of his Messianic ministry. There were several reasons for his baptism: 1. The first, mentioned here, was "to fulfill all righteousness." His baptism indicated that he was consecrated to God and officially approved by him, as especially shown in the descent of the Holy Spirit (v. 16) and the words of the Father (v. 17; cf. Ps 2:7; Isa 42:1). All God's righteous requirements for the Messiah were fully met in Jesus. 2. At Jesus' baptism John publicly announced the arrival of the Messiah and the inception of his ministry (Jn 1:31–34). 3. By his baptism Jesus completely identified himself with humanity's sin and failure (though he himself needed no repentance or cleansing from sin), becoming our substitute (2Co 5:21). 4. His baptism was an example to his followers.

3:16–17 All three persons of the Trinity are clearly seen here (see 28:19 and note).

3:16 *Spirit of God.* The Holy Spirit came upon Jesus not to overcome sin (for he was sinless), but to equip him (see

note on Jdg 3:10) for his work as the divine-human Messiah. *like a dove.* Either in the form of a dove or in a descent like a dove. See also note on Mk 1:10.

3:17 *voice from heaven.* The voice (1) authenticated Jesus' unique sonship and echoes Ps 2:7 ("This is my Son"), (2) identified Jesus with the suffering servant of Isa 42:1 ("whom I love"), and (3) offered the Father's support of Jesus in his mission ("with him I am well pleased"). This word from the Father must have greatly encouraged Jesus at the very outset of his earthly ministry. *my Son.* See notes on 14:33; Jn 3:16. *I am well pleased.* The tense of the Greek verb used here is timeless. God has always been and always will be "well pleased" with his Son.

4:1–11 The significance of Jesus' temptations, especially because they occurred at the outset of his public ministry, seems best understood in terms of the kind of Messiah he was to be. He would not accomplish his mission by using his supernatural power for his own needs (first temptation), by using his power to win a large following by miracles or magic (second

---

JESUS' BAPTISM AND TEMPTATION

Events surrounding Jesus' baptism reveal the intense religious excitement and social ferment of the early days of John the Baptist's ministry. Herod had been rapacious and extravagant; Roman military occupation was harsh. Some agitation centered around the change of governors from Gratus to Pilate in A.D. 26. Most of the people hoped for a religious solution to their intolerable political situation, and when they heard of a new prophet, they flocked out into the desert to hear him. The religious sect (Essenes) from Qumran professed similar doctrines of repentance and baptism. Jesus was baptized at Bethany on the other side of the Jordan (see Jn 1:28). John also baptized at "Aenon near Salim" (Jn 3:23).

The temptations took place (1) in the desert region of the lower Jordan Valley, (2) on a high mountain (possibly one of the abrupt cliffs near Jericho that present an unsurpassed panorama) and (3) on the highest point of the temple, from which the priests sounded the trumpet to call the city's attention to important events.

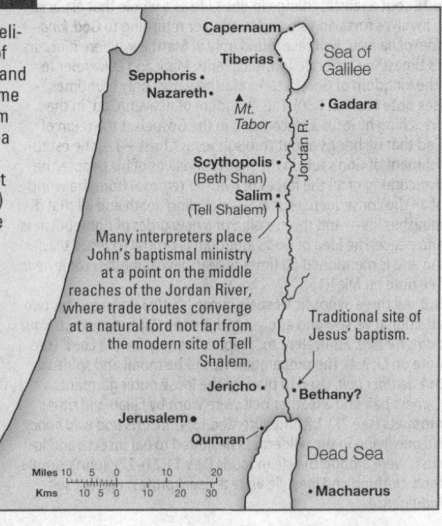

⁴Jesus answered, "It is written: 'People do not live on bread alone, but on every word that comes from the mouth of God.'ᵃ"ᵃ

⁵Then the devil took him to the holy cityᵇ and had him stand on the highest point of the temple. ⁶"If you are the Son of God,"ᶜ he said, "throw yourself down. For it is written:

" 'He will command his angels concerning you,
    and they will lift you up in their hands,
    so that you will not strike your foot against a stone.'ᵇ"ᵈ

⁷Jesus answered him, "It is also written: 'Do not put the Lord your God to the test.'ᶜ"ᵉ

⁸Again, the devil took him to a very high mountain and showed him all the kingdoms of the world and their splendor. ⁹"All this I will give you," he said, "if you will bow down and worship me."

¹⁰Jesus said to him, "Away from me, Satan!ᶠ For it is written: 'Worship the Lord your God, and serve him only.'ᵈ"ᵍ

¹¹Then the devil left him,ʰ and angels came and attended him.ⁱ

JESUS BEGINS TO PREACH

¹²When Jesus heard that John had been put in prison,ʲ he withdrew to Galilee.ᵏ ¹³Leaving Nazareth, he went and lived in Capernaum,ˡ which was by the lake in the area of Zebulun and Naphtali— ¹⁴to fulfillᵐ what was said through the prophet Isaiah:

¹⁵ "Land of Zebulun and land of Naphtali,
       the Way of the Sea, beyond the Jordan,
       Galilee of the Gentiles—

ᵃ 4 Deut. 8:3   ᵇ 6 Psalm 91:11,12   ᶜ 7 Deut. 6:16   ᵈ 10 Deut. 6:13

4:4 ᵃ Dt 8:3; Jn 4:34
4:5 ᵇ Ne 11:1;
Da 9:24; Mt 27:53
4:6 ᶜ S ver 3
ᵈ Ps 91:11,12
4:7 ᵉ Dt 6:16
4:10 ᶠ 1Ch 21:1;
Job 1:6-9; Mt 16:23;
Mk 4:15; Lk 10:18;
13:16; 22:3, 31;
Ro 16:20; 2Co 2:11;
11:14; 2Th 2:9;
Rev 12:9 ᵍ Dt 6:13
4:11 ʰ Jas 4:7
ⁱ Mt 26:53; Lk 22:43;
Heb 1:14
4:12 ʲ Mt 14:3
ᵏ Mk 1:14
4:13 ˡ Mk 1:21; 9:33;
Lk 4:23, 31; Jn 2:12;
4:46, 47
4:14 ᵐ S Mt 1:22

temptation) or by compromising with Satan (third temptation). Jesus had no inward desire or inclination to sin, for these in themselves are sin (Mt 5:28). Because he was God he did not sin in any way, whether by actions or word or inner desire (see 2Co 5:21; Heb 7:26; 1Pe 2:22 and note; 1Jn 3:5). Yet Jesus' temptation was real, not merely symbolic. He was "tempted in every way, just as we are—yet he did not sin" (see Heb 4:15 and note). He was confronted by the tempter with a real opportunity to sin. Although Jesus was the Son of God, he defeated Satan by using a weapon that everyone has at their disposal: "the sword of the Spirit, which is the word of God" (Eph 6:17). He met all three temptations with Scriptural truth (vv. 4,7,10) from Deuteronomy.

4:1 *Jesus ... tempted by the devil.* See map and accompanying text, p. 1612. *led by the Spirit ... to be tempted.* This testing of Jesus (the Greek verb translated "tempted" can also be rendered "tested"), which was divinely intended, has as its primary background Dt 8:1–5, from which Jesus also quotes in his first reply to the devil (see v. 4 and TNIV text note). There Moses recalls how the Lord led the Israelites in the desert 40 years "to humble and test you in order to know what was in your heart, whether or not you would keep his commands" (Dt 8:2). Here at the beginning of his ministry Jesus is subjected to a similar test and shows himself to be the true Israelite who lives "on every word that comes from the mouth of the Lᴏʀᴅ" (Dt 8:3). And whereas Adam failed the great test and plunged the whole race into sin (Ge 3), Jesus was faithful and thus demonstrated his qualification to become the Savior of all who receive him. It was, moreover, important that Jesus be tested/tempted as Israel and we are, so that he could become our "merciful and faithful high priest" (Heb 2:17; see note there) and thus be "able to help those who are being tempted" (Heb 2:18; see Heb 4:15–16). Finally, as the one who remained faithful in temptation he became the model for all believers when they are tempted. *by the devil.* God surely tests his people, but it is the devil who tempts to evil (see notes on Ge 22:1; Jas 1:13; see also 1Jn 3:8; Rev 2:9–10 and notes; Rev 12:9–10). Like the Hebrew for "Satan," the Greek for "devil" means "accuser" or "slanderer." The devil is a personal being, not a mere force or influence. He is the great archenemy of God and the leader of the hosts of darkness.
4:2 *forty days and forty nights.* The number recalls the experiences of Moses (Ex 24:18; 34:28) and Elijah (1Ki 19:8), as well as

the 40 years of Israel's temptation (testing) in the wilderness (see note on v. 1).
4:3 *If you are the Son of God.* Meaning "Since you are." The devil is not casting doubt on Jesus' divine sonship but is tempting him to use his supernatural powers as the Son of God for his own ends. *Son of God.* See notes on Ps 2:7; 45:6; Jn 3:16. *tell these stones to become bread.* See note on Lk 4:3.
4:4 Just as God gave the Israelites manna in a supernatural way (see Dt 8:3 and note), so also people today must rely on God for spiritual nourishment. Jesus relied on his Father, not his own miracle power, for provision of food (cf. Jn 4:34 and note; 6:27).
4:5 See note on Lk 4:2. *highest point of the temple.* See note on Lk 4:9. *temple.* The temple, including the entire temple area, had been rebuilt by Herod the Great (see notes on 2:1; Jn 2:20). The courtyard had been greatly enlarged, to about 330 by 500 yards. To accomplish this a huge platform had been erected to compensate for the sharp falling off of the land to the southeast. An enormous retaining wall made of massive stones was built to support the platform. On the platform stood the temple building, porches and courtyards flanked by beautiful colonnades (see diagram, p. 1614).
4:6 *throw yourself down.* See note on Lk 4:9. *it is written.* See note on Lk 4:10.
4:9 *worship me.* See note on Lk 4:7.
4:10 *Satan.* See note on v. 1.
4:11 *the devil left him.* See note on Lk 4:13.
4:12 See map No. 11 at the end of this study Bible. *John had been put in prison.* See Mk 1:14 and note on Lk 3:20. The reason for John's imprisonment is given in 14:3–4.
4:13 *Capernaum.* Although not mentioned in the OT, it was evidently a sizable town in Jesus' day. Peter's house there became Jesus' base of operations during his extended ministry in Galilee (see Mk 2:1; 9:33). A fifth-century basilica now stands over the supposed site of Peter's house, and a fourth-century synagogue is located a short distance from it (see diagram, p. 1725).
4:15–16 Another Messianic prophecy from Isaiah. Jesus spent most of his public ministry "in the area of Zebulun and Naphtali" (v. 13), which is north and west of the Sea of Galilee.
4:15 *Galilee of the Gentiles.* A region that, from the Jewish per-

4:16 *n* Isa 9:1,2;
Lk 2:32; Jn 1:4,5,9
4:17 *o* S Mt 3:2
4:18 *p* Mt 15:29;
Mk 7:31; Jn 6:1
q Mt 16:17,18
4:19 *r* ver 20,22;
Mt 8:22; Mk 10:21,28,
52; Lk 5:28; 28:19; Jn 1:43;
21:19,22
4:20 *s* S ver 19

> [16] the people living in darkness
> have seen a great light;
> on those living in the land of the shadow of death
> a light has dawned."[a][n]

[17] From that time on Jesus began to preach, "Repent, for the kingdom of heaven[o] has come near."

JESUS CALLS HIS FIRST DISCIPLES

4:18–22pp — Mk 1:16–20; Lk 5:2–11; Jn 1:35–42

[18] As Jesus was walking beside the Sea of Galilee,[p] he saw two brothers, Simon called Peter[q] and his brother Andrew. They were casting a net into the lake, for they were fishermen. [19] "Come, follow me,"[r] Jesus said, "and I will send you out to fish for people." [20] At once they left their nets and followed him.[s]

---

[a] 16 Isaiah 9:1,2

---

spective in Jesus' day, was "in darkness" and "the land of the shadow of death" (v. 16), probably because it was far removed from the religious influences of Jerusalem and because large numbers of Gentiles lived there. Matthew may have chosen this text (Isa 9:1–2) because of his interest in the universal appeal of the gospel (see 2:1–12; 13:38; 28:19; see also Introduction: Recipients).

4:17 *From that time on.* These words indicate an important turning point in the life of Jesus and occur three times in Mat-

thew's Gospel (see also 16:21; 26:16, TNIV "From then on"). Some think these words mark the three main sections of the book. *Repent.* See note on Mk 1:4. Jesus began his public ministry with the same message as that of John the Baptist (see 3:2 and note). The people must repent because God's reign was drawing near in the person and ministry of Jesus Christ. *kingdom of heaven.* See note on 3:2. *has come near.* See note on Mk 1:15.

4:18 *Sea of Galilee.* See note on Mk 1:16. *net.* A circular casting net used either from a boat or while standing in shallow water.

HEROD'S TEMPLE

20 B.C.–A.D. 70

Begun in 20 B.C., Herod's new structure towered 15 stories high, following the floor dimensions of the former temples in the Holy Place and the Most Holy Place. The high sanctuary shown here in a cutaway view was built on the site of the former temples of Solomon and Zerubbabel.

Holy Place
Golden vine
Holy Place

CUBITS
FEET
Drawn to scale the height of a 6 ft. man equals 4 cubits.

100 cubits high and 100 cubits wide

Most Holy Place

60 cubits

Side rooms within walls

20
40 cubits

The outer courts surrounding the temple mount were not completed until A.D. 64. The entire structure was demolished by the Romans in A.D. 70.

Dimensions of rooms, steps, doorways, cornices and exterior measurements are mentioned in history (Josephus and the Mishnah) but are subject to interpretation, and all drawings vary.

Basin

Altar

N

©1981 Hugh Claycombe

²¹Going on from there, he saw two other brothers, James son of Zebedee and his brother John.ᶠ They were in a boat with their father Zebedee, preparing their nets. Jesus called them, ²²and immediately they left the boat and their father and followed him.ᵘ

JESUS HEALS THE SICK

²³Jesus went throughout Galilee,ᵛ teaching in their synagogues,ʷ proclaiming the good newsˣ of the kingdom,ʸ and healing every disease and sickness among the people.ᶻ ²⁴News about him spread all over Syria,ᵃ and people brought to him all who were ill with various diseases, those suffering severe pain, the demon-possessed,ᵇ those having seizures,ᶜ and the paralyzed;ᵈ and he healed them. ²⁵Large crowds from Galilee, the Decapolis,ᵃ Jerusalem, Judea and the region across the Jordan followed him.ᵉ

INTRODUCTION TO THE SERMON ON THE MOUNT

5 Now when Jesus saw the crowds, he went up on a mountainside and sat down. His disciples came to him, ²and he began to teach them.

THE BEATITUDES

5:3–12pp — Lk 6:20–23

He said:

> ³ "Blessed are the poor in spirit,
>   for theirs is the kingdom of heaven.ᶠ
> ⁴ Blessed are those who mourn,
>   for they will be comforted.ᵍ
> ⁵ Blessed are the meek,

ᵃ 25 That is, the Ten Cities

4:21 ᶠMt 17:1;
20:20; 26:37;
Mk 3:17; 13:3;
Lk 8:51; Jn 21:2
4:22 ᵘS ver 19
4:23 ᵛMk 1:39;
Lk 4:15, 44 ʷMt 9:35;
13:54; Mk 1:21;
Lk 4:15; Jn 6:59;
18:20 ˣMk 1:14
ʸS Mt 3:2; Ac 20:25;
28:23, 31 ᶻMt 8:16;
14:14; 15:30; Mk 3:10;
Lk 7:22; Ac 10:38
4:24 ᵃS Lk 2:2
ᵇMt 8:16, 28; 9:32;
12:22; 15:22; Mk 1:32;
5:15, 16, 18 ᶜMt 17:15
ᵈMt 8:6; 9:2; Mk 2:3
4:25 ᵉMk 3:7, 8;
Lk 6:17
5:3 ᶠver 10, 19;
S Mt 25:34
5:4 ᵍIsa 61:2, 3;
Rev 7:17

4:19 *send you out to fish for people.* Evangelism was at the heart of Jesus' call to his disciples.
4:20 See note on Mk 1:17.

4:21 *boat.* In 1986 the remains of a 2,000-year-old typical fisherman's boat were found off the northwest shore of the Sea of Galilee. Its discoverers named it the Jesus Boat. *preparing their nets.* Washing, mending and hanging the nets up to dry in preparation for the next day's work.

4:23 *teaching . . . proclaiming . . . healing.* Jesus' threefold ministry. The synagogues (see note on Mk 1:21) provided a place for him to teach on the Sabbath. During the week he preached to larger crowds in the open air. *good news.* See note on Mk 1:1.
4:24 *Syria.* The area north of Galilee and between Damascus and the Mediterranean Sea. *those having seizures.* The Greek word for this expression originally meant "moonstruck" and reflects the ancient superstition that seizures were caused by changes of the moon.
4:25 *Large crowds.* Jesus' influence spread quickly over a large geographical area. *the Decapolis.* A league of free cities (see TNIV text note and map, p. 1679) characterized by high Greek culture. All but one, Scythopolis (Beth Shan), were east of the Sea of Galilee and the Jordan River. The league stretched from a point northeast of the Sea of Galilee southward to Philadelphia (modern Amman). *followed him.* Not all who followed were true disciples; many were curious onlookers, as subsequent events revealed only too clearly.

5:1—7:29 The Sermon on the Mount is in effect King Jesus' inaugural address, explaining what he expects of members of his kingdom. It is the first of five great discourses in Matthew (chs. 5–7; 10; 13; 18; 24–25; see Introduction: Structure). It contains three types of material: (1) beatitudes, i.e., declarations of blessedness (5:1–12), (2) ethical admonitions (5:13–20; 6:1—7:23) and (3) contrasts between Jesus' ethical teaching and Jewish legalistic traditions (5:21–48). The Sermon ends with a short parable stressing the importance of practicing what has just been taught (7:24–27) and an expression of amazement by the crowds at the authority with which Jesus spoke (7:28–29).

Opinion differs as to whether the Sermon is a summary of what Jesus taught on one occasion or a compilation of teachings presented on numerous occasions. Matthew possibly took a single sermon and expanded it with other relevant teachings of Jesus. Thirty-four of the verses in Matthew's Sermon occur in different contexts in Luke than the apparently parallel Sermon on the Plain (Lk 6:17–49).

The moral and ethical standard called for in the Sermon on the Mount is so high that some have dismissed the Sermon as being completely unrealistic or have projected its fulfillment to the future kingdom. There is no doubt, however, that Jesus (and Matthew) gave the Sermon as a standard for all Christians, realizing that its demands cannot be met in our own power. It is also true that Jesus occasionally used hyperbole to make his point (see, e.g., note on 5:29–30).
5:1 *mountainside.* The exact location is uncertain. It may have been the gently sloping hillside at the northwest corner of the Sea of Galilee, not far from Capernaum (see note on Lk 6:20–49). The new law, like the old (Ex 19:3), was given from a mountain. *sat down.* It was the custom for Jewish rabbis to be seated while teaching (see Mk 4:1 and note; 9:35; Lk 4:20 and note; 5:3; Jn 8:2). *disciples.* Lit. "learners." Since at the end of the Sermon the "crowds" expressed amazement at Jesus' teaching (7:28), "disciples" may here be used in a broader sense than the Twelve. Or perhaps the Sermon is addressed to the Twelve with the crowds also listening.

5:3 *Blessed.* The word means more than "happy," because happiness is an emotion often dependent on outward circumstances. "Blessed" here refers to the ultimate well-being and distinctive spiritual joy of those who share in the salvation of the kingdom of God. See notes on Ps 1:1; Rev 1:3. *poor in spirit.* In contrast to the spiritually proud and self-sufficient. *theirs is the kingdom of heaven.* The kingdom is not something earned. It is more a gift than a reward.
5:4 *those who mourn.* Over both personal and corporate sins (see Ezr 9:4; Ps 119:36).
5:5 *meek.* This beatitude is taken from Ps 37:11 (see note there) and refers not so much to an attitude toward people as

5:5 h Ps 37:11;
Ro 4:13
5:6 i Isa 55:1,2
5:7 j S Jas 2:13
5:8 k Ps 24:3,4; 73:1
l Ps 17:15; 42:2;
Heb 12:14; Rev 22:4
5:9 m Jas 3:18;
S Ro 14:19 n ver 44,
45; S Ro 8:14
5:10 o S 1Pe 3:14
p ver 3,19; S Mt 25:34
5:11 q Isa 51:7
r S Jn 15:21
5:12 s Ps 9:2;
Ac 5:41; S 2Co 6:10;
12:10; Col 1:24;
Jas 1:2; 1Pe 1:6; 4:13,
16 t 2Ch 36:16;
Mt 23:31,37; Ac 7:52;
1Th 2:15; Heb 11:32-
38
5:13 u Mk 9:50;
Lk 14:34,35
5:14 v Jn 8:12
5:15 w Mk 4:21;
Lk 8:16; 11:33
5:16 x 1Co 10:31;
Php 1:11 y S Tit 2:14
z S Mt 9:8
5:17 a Jn 10:34,35;
Ro 3:31
5:18 b Ps 119:89;
Isa 40:8; 55:11;
Mt 24:35; Mk 13:31;
Lk 16:17; 21:33
5:19 c Jas 2:10

for they will inherit the earth.[h]
[6] Blessed are those who hunger and thirst for righteousness,
　　for they will be filled.[i]
[7] Blessed are the merciful,
　　for they will be shown mercy.[j]
[8] Blessed are the pure in heart,[k]
　　for they will see God.[l]
[9] Blessed are the peacemakers,[m]
　　for they will be called children of God.[n]
[10] Blessed are those who are persecuted because of righteousness,[o]
　　for theirs is the kingdom of heaven.[p]

[11]"Blessed are you when people insult you,[q] persecute you and falsely say all kinds of evil against you because of me.[r] [12]Rejoice and be glad,[s] because great is your reward in heaven, for in the same way they persecuted the prophets who were before you.[t]

SALT AND LIGHT

[13]"You are the salt of the earth. But if the salt loses its saltiness, how can it be made salty again? It is no longer good for anything, except to be thrown out and trampled underfoot.[u]

[14]"You are the light of the world.[v] A city on a hill cannot be hidden. [15]Neither do people light a lamp and put it under a bowl. Instead they put it on its stand, and it gives light to everyone in the house.[w] [16]In the same way, let your light shine before others,[x] that they may see your good deeds[y] and glorify[z] your Father in heaven.

THE FULFILLMENT OF THE LAW

[17]"Do not think that I have come to abolish the Law or the Prophets; I have not come to abolish them but to fulfill them.[a] [18]Truly I tell you, until heaven and earth disappear, not the smallest letter, not the least stroke of a pen, will by any means disappear from the Law until everything is accomplished.[b] [19]Anyone who sets aside one of the least of these commands[c] and teaches others accordingly will be called least in the kingdom of heaven, but whoever practices and teaches these commands will be called great in the kingdom of

---

to a disposition before God, namely, humility. *the earth.* The new promised land (see Rev 21:1; cf. note on Ps 37:9).

A **5:6** *hunger and thirst for righteousness.* Have a deep longing for both personal righteousness and justice for the oppressed.
5:8 *heart.* The center of one's being, including mind, will and emotions (see note on Ps 4:7).
5:9 *peacemakers.* Those who promote peace, as far as it depends on them (Ro 12:18). In so doing, they reflect the character of their heavenly Father and so are called "children of God" (see Jas 3:17–18).
A **5:10** *Blessed.* Because persecution provides an opportunity for believers to prove their fitness for the kingdom (see Heb 12:4–11 and notes). *persecuted.* Righteous living is often offensive to unbelievers (cf. v. 11). *theirs is the kingdom of heaven.* For the blessings of God's kingdom see 3:2 and note.
5:13 *salt.* Used for flavoring and preserving (cf. Mk 9:50 and note). *loses its saltiness.* Most of the salt used in Israel came from the Dead Sea and was full of impurities. This caused it to lose some of its flavor.
A **5:14** *light of the world.* Although Jesus himself fulfilled the mission of the Lord's servant to be "a light for the Gentiles" (Isa 42:6; see also Lk 2:32 and notes on Isa 49:6; Lk 2:31), he expected his followers to carry on the work (see vv. 15–16; cf. Jn 8:12; Php 2:15 and notes).
5:15 *lamp.* In Jesus' day people used small clay lamps that burned olive oil drawn up by a wick (see note on Ex 25:37). *bowl.* A bowl that held about eight quarts of ground meal or flour.
5:16 *glorify your Father.* Good deeds are not to be done in a public way for one's own honor ("in front of others, to be seen by them," 6:1) but for the glory of God (see 1Co 10:31; Php 1:11 and notes; 2:11). *Father in heaven.* Matthew uses the phrase "Fa-

ther in heaven" or "heavenly Father" 17 times, Mark and Luke only once each, and John not at all.
5:17 *the Law.* The first five books of the OT. *the Prophets.* Not only the Latter Prophets—Isaiah, Jeremiah and Ezekiel, which we call Major Prophets, and the 12 Minor Prophets (lumped together by the Jews as "the Book of the Twelve")—but also the Former Prophets (Joshua, Judges, Samuel and Kings). Taken together, "the Law" and "the Prophets" designated the entire OT, including the Writings, the third section of the Hebrew Bible. See 13:35, where Matthew introduces a quotation from the Writings (Ps 78:2) with "what was spoken through the prophet." *fulfill.* Jesus fulfilled the Law in the sense that he gave it its full meaning. He emphasized its deep, underlying principles and total commitment to it rather than mere external acknowledgment and obedience.
A **5:18–20** Jesus is not speaking against observing all the requirements of the Law but against hypocritical, Pharisaical legalism. Such legalism was not the keeping of all details of the Law but the hollow sham of keeping laws externally to gain merit before God while breaking them inwardly. It was following the letter of the Law while ignoring its spirit. Jesus repudiates the Pharisees' interpretation of the Law and their view of righteousness by works. He preaches a righteousness that comes only through faith in him and his work. In the rest of the chapter, he gives six examples of Pharisaical externalism.
5:18 *smallest letter.* One word in Greek (*iota*), which we use when we say, "It doesn't make one iota of difference." It is the nearest Greek equivalent to the Hebrew *yodh,* the smallest letter of the Hebrew alphabet (see Ps 119:73 title). *least stroke of a pen.* The Greek word for this phrase means "horn" and was used to designate the slight embellishment or extension of certain letters of the Hebrew alphabet (somewhat like the bottom of a "j").

heaven. ²⁰For I tell you that unless your righteousness surpasses that of the Pharisees and the teachers of the law, you will certainly not enter the kingdom of heaven.ᵈ

MURDER

5:25,26pp — Lk 12:58,59

²¹"You have heard that it was said to the people long ago, 'You shall not murder,ᵃᵉ and anyone who murders will be subject to judgment.' ²²But I tell you that anyone who is angryᶠ with a brother or sisterᵇ will be subject to judgment.ᵍ Again, anyone who says to a brother or sister, 'Raca,'ᶜ is answerable to the Sanhedrin.ʰ And anyone who says, 'You fool!' will be in danger of the fire of hell.ⁱ

²³"Therefore, if you are offering your gift at the altar and there remember that your brother or sister has something against you, ²⁴leave your gift there in front of the altar. First go and be reconciled to that person; then come and offer your gift.

²⁵"Settle matters quickly with your adversary who is taking you to court. Do it while you are still together on the way, or your adversary may hand you over to the judge, and the judge may hand you over to the officer, and you may be thrown into prison. ²⁶Truly I tell you, you will not get out until you have paid the last penny.

ADULTERY

²⁷"You have heard that it was said, 'You shall not commit adultery.'ᵈʲ ²⁸But I tell you that anyone who looks at a woman lustfully has already committed adultery with her in his heart.ᵏ ²⁹If your right eye causes you to stumble,ˡ gouge it out and throw it away. It is better for you to lose one part of your body than for your whole body to be thrown into hell. ³⁰And if your right hand causes you to stumble,ᵐ cut it off and throw it away. It is better for you to lose one part of your body than for your whole body to go into hell.

DIVORCE

³¹"It has been said, 'Anyone who divorces his wife must give her a certificate of divorce.'ᵉⁿ ³²But I tell you that anyone who divorces his wife, except for sexual immorality, causes her to become an adulteress, and anyone who marries the divorced woman commits adultery.ᵒ

OATHS

³³"Again, you have heard that it was said to the people long ago, 'Do not break your oath,ᵖ but fulfill to the Lord the vows you have made.'�q ³⁴But I tell you, do not swear an oath at all:ʳ either by heaven, for it is God's throne;ˢ ³⁵or by the earth, for it is his footstool; or by Jerusalem, for it is the city of the Great King.ᵗ ³⁶And do not swear by your head, for you cannot make even one hair white or black. ³⁷All you need to say is simply 'Yes' or 'No';ᵘ anything beyond this comes from the evil one.ᶠᵛ

ᵃ 21 Exodus 20:13   ᵇ 22 Some manuscripts *brother or sister without cause*   ᶜ 22 An Aramaic term of contempt   ᵈ 27 Exodus 20:14   ᵉ 31 Deut. 24:1   ᶠ 37 Or *from evil*

5:20 ᵈ Isa 26:2; Mt 18:3; Jn 3:5
5:21 ᵉ Ex 20:13; 21:12; Dt 5:17
5:22 ᶠ Ecc 7:9; 1Co 13:5; Eph 4:26; Jas 1:19,20 ᵍ 1Jn 3:15 ʰ Mt 26:59; Jn 11:47; Ac 5:21,27,34,41; 6:12 ⁱ Mt 18:9; Mk 9:43,48; Lk 16:24; Jas 3:6
5:27 ʲ Ex 20:14; Dt 5:18
5:28 ᵏ Pr 6:25; 2Pe 2:14
5:29 ˡ ver 30; Mt 18:6,8,9; Mk 9:42-47; Lk 17:2; Ro 14:21; 1Co 8:13; S 2Co 6:3; 11:29
5:30 ᵐ S ver 29
5:31 ⁿ Dt 24:1-4
5:32 ᵒ S Lk 16:18
5:33 ᵖ Lev 19:12 q Nu 30:2; Dt 23:21; Mt 23:16-22
5:34 ʳ Jas 5:12 ˢ Isa 66:1; Mt 23:22
5:35 ᵗ Ps 48:2
5:37 ᵘ Jas 5:12 ᵛ Mt 6:13; 13:19,38; Jn 17:15; Eph 6:16; 2Th 3:3; 1Jn 2:13,14; 3:12; 5:18,19

5:20 *Pharisees.* See note on 3:7. *teachers of the law.* See note on 2:4. *kingdom of heaven.* See note on 3:2.

5:21–22 *it was said … But I tell you.* The contrast that Jesus sets up (see also vv. 27–28,31–32,33–34,38–39, 43–44) is not between the OT and his teaching (he has just established the validity of the OT Law). Rather, it is between externalistic interpretation of the Rabbinic tradition on the one hand and Jesus' correct interpretation of the Law on the other. *murder.* Several Hebrew and Greek verbs mean "kill." The ones used here and in Ex 20:13 specifically mean "murder."

5:22 *Raca.* May be related to the Aramaic word for "empty" and mean "Empty-head!" *Sanhedrin.* See note on Mk 14:55. *hell.* The Greek word is *ge(h)enna,* which derives its name from a deep ravine south of Jerusalem, the "Valley of (the Sons of) Hinnom" (Hebrew *ge' hinnom*). During the reigns of the wicked Ahaz and Manasseh, human sacrifices to the Ammonite god Molek were offered there. Josiah desecrated the valley because of the pagan worship there (2Ki 23:10; see Jer 7:31–32; 19:6). It became a sort of perpetually burning city dump and later a figure for the place

of final punishment (see notes on Isa 66:24; Jer 7:31).

5:23–26 Two illustrations of dealing with anger by means of reconciliation.

5:25 Cf. Lk 12:57–59.

5:26 *penny.* The smallest Roman copper coin (see note on Lk 12:59).

5:28 *looks at a woman lustfully.* Not a passing glance but a willful, calculated stare that arouses sexual desire. According to Jesus this is a form of adultery even if it is only "in his heart."

5:29–30 Jesus is not teaching self-mutilation, for even a blind man can lust. What he is saying is that we should deal as drastically as necessary with sin, a point Jesus repeated on at least one other occasion (see 18:8–9; Mk 9:43–48).

5:30 *hell.* See note on v. 22.

5:32 *except for sexual immorality.* See note on 19:3. Neither Mk 10:11–12 nor Lk 16:18 mentions this exception.

5:33–37 The OT allowed oaths except those that profaned the name of God. Jesus would do away with all oaths, in favor of always speaking the truth.

5:38 ʷEx 21:24;
Lev 24:20; Dt 19:21
5:39 ˣLk 6:29;
Ro 12:17,19; 1Pe 3:9
5:42 ʸDt 15:8;
Lk 6:30
5:43 ᶻLev 19:18;
Mt 19:19; 22:39;
Mk 12:31; Lk 10:27;
Ro 13:9; Gal 5:14;
Jas 2:8 ᵃDt 23:6;
Ps 139:21,22
5:44 ᵇLk 6:27,28;
23:34; Jn 15:20;
Ac 7:60; Ro 8:35;
12:14; 1Co 4:12;
1Pe 2:23
5:45 ᶜver 9;
Lk 6:35; S Ro 5:8;
ᵈJob 25:3
5:46 ᵉLk 6:32
5:48 ᶠLev 19:2;
1Pe 1:16
6:1 ᵍMt 5:16; 23:5
6:4 ʰver 6,18;
Col 3:23,24
6:5 ⁱMk 11:25;
Lk 18:10-14
6:6 ʲ2Ki 4:33
6:7 ᵏEcc 5:2

EYE FOR EYE

³⁸"You have heard that it was said, 'Eye for eye, and tooth for tooth.'ᵃʷ ³⁹But I tell you, do not resist an evil person. If anyone slaps you on the right cheek, turn to them the other cheek also.ˣ ⁴⁰And if anyone wants to sue you and take your shirt, hand over your coat as well. ⁴¹If anyone forces you to go one mile, go with them two miles. ⁴²Give to the one who asks you, and do not turn away from the one who wants to borrow from you.ʸ

LOVE FOR ENEMIES

⁴³"You have heard that it was said, 'Love your neighborᵇᶻ and hate your enemy.'ᵃ ⁴⁴But I tell you, love your enemies and pray for those who persecute you,ᵇ ⁴⁵that you may be childrenᶜ of your Father in heaven. He causes his sun to rise on the evil and the good, and sends rain on the righteous and the unrighteous.ᵈ ⁴⁶If you love those who love you, what reward will you get?ᵉ Are not even the tax collectors doing that? ⁴⁷And if you greet only your own people, what are you doing more than others? Do not even pagans do that? ⁴⁸Be perfect, therefore, as your heavenly Father is perfect.ᶠ

GIVING TO THE NEEDY

6 "Be careful not to do your 'acts of righteousness' in front of others, to be seen by them.ᵍ If you do, you will have no reward from your Father in heaven.

²"So when you give to the needy, do not announce it with trumpets, as the hypocrites do in the synagogues and on the streets, to be honored by others. Truly I tell you, they have received their reward in full. ³But when you give to the needy, do not let your left hand know what your right hand is doing, ⁴so that your giving may be in secret. Then your Father, who sees what is done in secret, will reward you.ʰ

PRAYER

6:9–13pp — Lk 11:2–4

⁵"And when you pray, do not be like the hypocrites, for they love to pray standingⁱ in the synagogues and on the street corners to be seen by others. Truly I tell you, they have received their reward in full. ⁶But when you pray, go into your room, close the door and pray to your Father,ʲ who is unseen. Then your Father, who sees what is done in secret, will reward you. ⁷And when you pray, do not keep on babblingᵏ like pagans, for they think

---

ᵃ 38 Exodus 21:24; Lev. 24:20; Deut. 19:21   ᵇ 43 Lev. 19:18

5:38 See notes on Ex 21:23–25; Lev 24:20.

5:39 *resist.* Here it probably means in a court of law. *slaps.* The Greek verb used here means "slaps you with the back of the hand." It was more an insult (cf. 26:67) than an act of violence. The point is that it is better to be insulted even twice than to take the matter to court. Ancient Near Eastern society had become very litigious.

5:40 *shirt … coat.* The first was an undergarment, the second a loose outer one. Since the outer garment was used to sleep in, OT law prohibited anyone from taking it even as a pledge overnight (see Ex 22:26–27; Dt 24:12–13).

5:42 Probably not a general requirement to give to everyone who asks but a reference to the poor (cf. Dt 15:7–11; Ps 112:5,9).

5:43 *hate your enemy.* Words not found anywhere in the OT. However, hatred for one's enemies was an accepted part of the Jewish ethic at that time in some circles (cf., e.g., the Dead Sea Scrolls work, *The Rule of the Community* 1.4,10). See note on Lev 19:18.

5:44 *love your enemies.* See note on Ex 23:4–5. *pray.* Prayer is one of the practical ways love expresses itself (cf. Job 42:8–10 and note on Ps 35:13–14).

5:45 *that you may be children of your Father in heaven.* Loving one's enemy does not make one a child of the heavenly Father. But it does make one known as his child. *the evil and the good.* God shows his love to people without distinction.

5:46 *tax collectors.* Traditionally known as "publicans," these were local men employed by Roman tax contractors to collect taxes for Rome. Because they worked for Rome and often demanded unreasonable payments, the tax collectors gained a bad reputation and were generally hated and considered traitors (see notes on Mk 2:14–15; Lk 3:12).

5:48 *Be perfect.* Christ sets up the high ideal of perfect love (see vv. 43–47)—not that we can fully attain it in this life. That, however, is God's high standard for us.

6:1 *acts of righteousness.* This verse introduces the discussion of three acts of righteousness: (1) giving (vv. 2–4), (2) praying (vv. 5–15) and (3) fasting (vv. 16–18). Jesus' concern here is with the motives behind such acts. *reward from your Father.* Spiritual growth and maturity or perhaps a heavenly reward of some kind—or both.

6:2 *when you give.* Not "if you give." Jesus presupposes the disciples' giving to the poor. *announce it with trumpets.* Perhaps a reference to the noise made by coins as they were thrown into the temple treasury. Or the phrase may be used figuratively to mean "make a big show of it." *hypocrites.* The Greek word means "play-actor." Matthew uses the word 13 times (Mark, twice; Luke, three times). Here it refers to those who fake being pious. *their reward in full.* The honor they receive from people is all the reward they get.

6:3 *do not let your left hand know what your right hand is doing.* Not to be taken literally but as a way of emphasizing that one should not call attention to one's giving. Self-glorification is always a present danger.

6:6 Jesus' followers are not to make a show of their praying, in contrast to "the hypocrites" (v. 5). It does not mean that all prayer should be private, as the plurals "our" and "us" in vv. 9–13 indicate. *room.* The Greek word here probably means "storeroom," because unlike most of the rooms in the house, it had a door that could be shut.

6:7 *babbling like pagans.* They used long lists of the names of their gods in their prayers, hoping that by constantly repeating them they would call on the name of the god that could help they will be heard because of their many words.[*l*] [8]Do not be like them, for your Father knows what you need[*m*] before you ask him.

[9]"This, then, is how you should pray:

" 'Our Father[*n*] in heaven,
hallowed be your name,
[10]your kingdom[*o*] come,
your will be done,[*p*]
on earth as it is in heaven.
[11]Give us today our daily bread.[*q*]
[12]And forgive us our debts,
as we also have forgiven our debtors.[*r*]
[13]And lead us not into temptation,[*a*][*s*]
but deliver us from the evil one.[*b*][*t*]

[14]For if you forgive others when they sin against you, your heavenly Father will also forgive you.[*u*] [15]But if you do not forgive others their sins, your Father will not forgive your sins.[*v*]

FASTING

[16]"When you fast,[*w*] do not look somber[*x*] as the hypocrites do, for they disfigure their faces to show others they are fasting. Truly I tell you, they have received their reward in full. [17]But when you fast, put oil on your head and wash your face, [18]so that it will not be obvious to others that you are fasting, but only to your Father, who is unseen; and your Father, who sees what is done in secret, will reward you.[*y*]

TREASURES IN HEAVEN

6:22,23pp — Lk 11:34–36

[19]"Do not store up for yourselves treasures on earth,[*z*] where moth and rust destroy,[*a*] and where thieves break in and steal. [20]But store up for yourselves treasures in heaven,[*b*] where moth and rust do not destroy, and where thieves do not break in and steal.[*c*] [21]For where your treasure is, there your heart will be also.[*d*]

[22]"The eye is the lamp of the body. If your eyes are healthy,[*c*] your whole body will be

---

[*a*] 13 The Greek for *temptation* can also mean *testing*. [*b*] 13 Or *from evil*; some late manuscripts *one, / for yours is the kingdom and the power and the glory forever. Amen.* [*c*] 22 The Greek for *healthy* here implies *generous*.

6:7 [*l*]1Ki 18:26-29
6:8 [*m*]ver 32
6:9 [*n*]Jer 3:19;
Mal 2:10; 1Pe 1:17
6:10 [*o*]S Mt 3:2
[*p*]S Mt 26:39
6:11 [*q*]Pr 30:8
6:12 [*r*]Mt 18:21-35
6:13 [*s*]Jas 1:13
[*t*]S Mt 5:37
6:14 [*u*]Mt 18:21-35;
Mk 11:25, 26;
Eph 4:32; Col 3:13
6:15 [*v*]Mt 18:35
6:16 [*w*]Lev 16:29, 31;
23:27-32; Nu 29:7
[*x*]Isa 58:5; Zec 7:5;
8:19
6:18 [*y*]ver 4, 6
6:19 [*z*]Pr 23:4;
Lk 12:16-21; Heb 13:5
[*a*]S Jas 5:2, 3
6:20 [*b*]Mt 19:21;
Lk 12:33; 16:9; 18:22;
1Ti 6:19 [*c*]Lk 12:33
6:21 [*d*]Lk 12:34

---

them. Jesus is not necessarily condemning all long prayers, but meaningless verbiage in praying.

6:9–13 Commonly known as "The Lord's Prayer," it is really "The Disciples' Prayer," since it was meant as a model for them. The prayer contains six petitions, three relating more directly to God (vv. 9–10) and three to us (vv. 11–13). When praying this prayer, one should not reverse the order of its petitions. A similar prayer in Lk 11:2–4 occurs in a different historical setting.

6:9 *hallowed.* God is already holy (see Lev 11:44 and note; 1Pe 1:15), so the prayer is not that God be made holy but that he be regarded as holy. By his saving and judging acts in history he proves himself holy (see Lev 10:3; Eze 36:23 and notes). This petition is that he so achieve his saving purposes in the world that his holiness is displayed before the eyes of the world's people and acknowledged by them—which will happen only as his kingdom comes. *name.* See notes on Ps 5:11; Eze 20:9.

6:10 *your kingdom come.* Not in the sense of to "come" into existence—after all, it is already here (see 3:2; Lk 17:21 and notes)—but to "come" more and more completely until its full and final consummation. *your will be done.* Logically follows "your kingdom come." The TNIV scansion and punctuation suggest that "on earth as it is in heaven" be read with each of the three preceding petitions.

6:11 That is, meet our needs "each day" (Lk 11:3; see Ex 16:4 and note).

6:12 *debts.* Moral debts, i.e., sins (see note on Lk 11:4).

6:13 *lead us not into temptation.* That is, do not lead us through trials so deep that they would tempt us to be unfaithful to you. God does not tempt (in the sense of enticing to

sin; see Jas 1:13 and note). *the evil one.* Satan (see 13:19 and note). Others think the reference is to "evil," i.e., evil circumstances (see TNIV text note). Cf. 1Ch 29:10–11 with the longer ending in the TNIV text note.

6:15 *forgive . . . forgive.* See Eph 4:32 and note.

6:16 *fast.* See notes on Mk 2:18; Lk 18:12. Jesus does not condemn fasting as such but ostentation in fasting. *hypocrites.* See note on v. 2. *their reward in full.* See note on v. 2.

6:17 *put oil on your head and wash your face.* That is, maintain your regular appearance. Jews put ashes on their heads when fasting.

6:19–21 The dangers of riches are often mentioned in the NT (e.g., v. 24; 13:22; 19:22; Mk 10:17–30; Lk 12:16–21; 1Ti 6:9–10, 17–19; Heb 13:5; Jas 5:2–3), but nowhere are riches condemned in and of themselves. What Jesus condemns here is greed and the hoarding of money.

6:19 *Do not store up.* Or "Stop storing up." They may have already started to do it. *moth and rust.* Representative of all agents and processes that destroy worldly possessions. *break in and steal.* Houses in the Holy Land had walls made of mud bricks and could be broken into easily.

6:20 *treasures in heaven.* Anything done in this life that has eternal value will be rewarded. Cf. "rich toward God" (Lk 12:21).

6:21 See Lk 12:34. *heart.* See note on 5:8.

6:22 *The eye is the lamp of the body.* It lets light in to illumine the body. *your eyes are healthy.* You recognize the folly of storing up wealth (v. 19)—but see TNIV text note. *whole body.* Entire person.

6:24 *e* Lk 16:13
6:25 *f* ver 27,28,31,
34; Lk 10:41; 12:11,22
6:26 *g* Job 38:41;
Ps 104:21; 136:25;
145:15; 147:9
h Mt 10:29-31
6:27 *i* Ps 39:5
6:29 *i* 1Ki 10:4-7
6:30 *k* Mt 8:26;
14:31; 16:8; Lk 12:28
6:32 *l* ver 8
6:33 *m* S Mt 3:2
n Ps 37:4; Mt 19:29
7:1 *o* Lk 6:37;
Ro 14:4,10,13;
1Co 4:5; 5:12; Jas 4:11,
12
7:2 *p* Eze 35:11;
Mk 4:24; Lk 6:38;
Ro 2:1
7:7 *q* 1Ki 3:5;
Mt 18:19; 21:22;
Jn 14:13,14; 15:7,16;
16:23,24; Jas 1:5-8;
4:2,3; 5:16; 1Jn 3:22;
5:14,15
7:8 *r* Pr 8:17;
Jer 29:12,13
7:11 *s* Jas 1:17

full of light. ²³But if your eyes are unhealthy,ª your whole body will be full of darkness. If then the light within you is darkness, how great is that darkness!

²⁴"No one can serve two masters. Either you will hate the one and love the other, or you will be devoted to the one and despise the other. You cannot serve both God and money.ᵉ

DO NOT WORRY

6:25–33pp — Lk 12:22–31

²⁵"Therefore I tell you, do not worryᶠ about your life, what you will eat or drink; or about your body, what you will wear. Is not life more important than food, and the body more important than clothes? ²⁶Look at the birds of the air; they do not sow or reap or store away in barns, and yet your heavenly Father feeds them.ᵍ Are you not much more valuable than they?ʰ ²⁷Can any one of you by worrying add a single hour to your lifeᵇ?ⁱ

²⁸"And why do you worry about clothes? See how the flowers of the field grow. They do not labor or spin. ²⁹Yet I tell you that not even Solomon in all his splendorʲ was dressed like one of these. ³⁰If that is how God clothes the grass of the field, which is here today and tomorrow is thrown into the fire, will he not much more clothe you—you of little faith?ᵏ ³¹So do not worry, saying, 'What shall we eat?' or 'What shall we drink?' or 'What shall we wear?' ³²For the pagans run after all these things, and your heavenly Father knows that you need them.ˡ ³³But seek first his kingdomᵐ and his righteousness, and all these things will be given to you as well.ⁿ ³⁴Therefore do not worry about tomorrow, for tomorrow will worry about itself. Each day has enough trouble of its own.

JUDGING OTHERS

7:3–5pp — Lk 6:41,42

7 "Do not judge, or you too will be judged.ᵒ ²For in the same way you judge others, you will be judged, and with the measure you use, it will be measured to you.ᵖ ³"Why do you look at the speck of sawdust in someone else's eye and pay no attention to the plank in your own eye? ⁴How can you say, 'Let me take the speck out of your eye,' when all the time there is a plank in your own eye? ⁵You hypocrite, first take the plank out of your own eye, and then you will see clearly to remove the speck from the other person's eye.

⁶"Do not give dogs what is sacred; do not throw your pearls to pigs. If you do, they may trample them under their feet, and then turn and tear you to pieces.

ASK, SEEK, KNOCK

7:7–11pp — Lk 11:9–13

⁷"Ask and it will be given to you;�q seek and you will find; knock and the door will be opened to you. ⁸For everyone who asks receives; those who seek find;ʳ and to those who knock, the door will be opened.

⁹"Which of you, if your son asks for bread, will give him a stone? ¹⁰Or if he asks for a fish, will give him a snake? ¹¹If you, then, though you are evil, know how to give good gifts to your children, how much more will your Father in heaven give good giftsˢ to those who

---

ª 23 The Greek for *unhealthy* here implies stingy.   ᵇ 27 Or *single cubit to your height*

6:23 *your eyes are unhealthy.* They are blind to the deceitfulness of wealth––but see TNIV text note.

6:24 See Lk 16:13; Jas 4:4.

6:25 *do not worry.* See Php 4:6 and note. *worry.* Undue anxiety, not a legitimate concern to provide for one's daily needs (cf. Lk 10:41–42; 2Th 3:6–12).

A **6:27** *add a single hour.* But anxiety may very well shorten one's life span, as modern medicine has shown.

6:30 *thrown into the fire.* Grass was commonly used to heat clay ovens in the Holy Land. *you of little faith.* See 8:26; 14:31; 16:8; 17:20; Lk 12:28.

A **6:33** The heart of the matter. *kingdom.* See note on 3:2. *his righteousness.* The righteous life that God requires, as the content of the Sermon emphasizes (see, e.g., 5:6,10,20; 6:1).

A **7:1** The Christian is not to judge hypocritically or self-righteously, as can be seen from the context (v. 5). The same thought is expressed in 23:13–39 (cf. Ro 2:1). To obey Christ's commands in this chapter, we must first evaluate a person's character—whether one is a "dog" (v. 6) or a false prophet

(v. 15), or whether one's life shows fruit (v. 16). Scripture repeatedly exhorts believers to evaluate carefully (see Jn 7:24) and choose between good and bad people and things (sexually immoral, 1Co 5:9; those who masquerade as angels of light, 2Co 11:14; dogs, Php 3:2; false prophets, 1Jn 4:1). The Christian is to "test them all" (1Th 5:21).

7:3–5 Jesus rebukes hypocritical judging.

7:3 *speck of sawdust…plank.* An example of hyperbole in the teachings of Jesus (cf. 19:24). Its purpose is to drive home a point (see Lk 6:41 and note).

7:5 *hypocrite.* See note on 6:2.

7:6 Teaching about the kingdom should be given in accordance with the spiritual capacity of the learners. *dogs.* The unclean dogs of the street were held in low esteem.

7:7–11 See note on Lk 11:5–13.

A **7:7** *Ask…seek…knock.* Greek present imperatives are used here, indicating constant asking, seeking and knocking. Persistent prayer is being emphasized (cf. Jas 4:2–3).

7:11 *good gifts.* See Lk 11:13 and note.

ask him! [12]So in everything, do to others what you would have them do to you,[t] for this sums up the Law and the Prophets.[u]

THE NARROW AND WIDE GATES

[13]"Enter through the narrow gate.[v] For wide is the gate and broad is the road that leads to destruction, and many enter through it. [14]But small is the gate and narrow the road that leads to life, and only a few find it.

TRUE AND FALSE PROPHETS

[15]"Watch out for false prophets.[w] They come to you in sheep's clothing, but inwardly they are ferocious wolves.[x] [16]By their fruit you will recognize them.[y] Do people pick grapes from thornbushes, or figs from thistles?[z] [17]Likewise, every good tree bears good fruit, but a bad tree bears bad fruit. [18]A good tree cannot bear bad fruit, and a bad tree cannot bear good fruit.[a] [19]Every tree that does not bear good fruit is cut down and thrown into the fire.[b] [20]Thus, by their fruit you will recognize them.

TRUE AND FALSE DISCIPLES

[21]"Not everyone who says to me, 'Lord, Lord,'[c] will enter the kingdom of heaven,[d] but only those who do the will of my Father who is in heaven.[e] [22]Many will say to me on that day,[f] 'Lord, Lord, did we not prophesy in your name and in your name drive out demons and in your name perform many miracles?'[g] [23]Then I will tell them plainly, 'I never knew you. Away from me, you evildoers!'[h]

THE WISE AND FOOLISH BUILDERS
7:24–27pp — Lk 6:47–49

[24]"Therefore everyone who hears these words of mine and puts them into practice[i] is like a wise man who built his house on the rock. [25]The rain came down, the streams rose, and the winds blew and beat against that house; yet it did not fall, because it had its foundation on the rock. [26]But everyone who hears these words of mine and does not put them into practice is like a foolish man who built his house on sand. [27]The rain came down, the streams rose, and the winds blew and beat against that house, and it fell with a great crash."

[28]When Jesus had finished saying these things,[j] the crowds were amazed at his teaching,[k] [29]because he taught as one who had authority, and not as their teachers of the law.

JESUS HEALS A MAN WITH LEPROSY
8:2–4pp — Mk 1:40–44; Lk 5:12–14

8 When Jesus came down from the mountainside, large crowds followed him. [2]A man with leprosy[a][l] came and knelt before him[m] and said, "Lord, if you are willing, you can make me clean."

[3]Jesus reached out his hand and touched the man. "I am willing," he said. "Be clean!"

---

[a] 2 The Greek word traditionally translated *leprosy* was used for various diseases affecting the skin.

7:12 [t] Lk 6:31
[u] Ro 13:8-10; Gal 5:14
7:13 [v] Lk 13:24;
Jn 10:7, 9
7:15 [w] Jer 23:16;
Mt 24:24; Lk 6:26;
2Pe 2:1; 1Jn 4:1;
Rev 16:13 [x] Eze 22:27;
Ac 20:29
7:16 [y] Mt 12:33;
Lk 6:44 [z] Jas 3:12
7:18 [a] Lk 6:43
7:19 [b] S Mt 3:10
7:21 [c] Hos 8:2;
Mt 25:11; S Jn 13:13;
1Co 12:3 [d] S Mt 3:2
[e] Mt 12:50; Ro 2:13;
Jas 1:22; 1Jn 3:18
7:22 [f] S Mt 10:15
[g] Lk 10:20; Ac 19:13;
1Co 13:1-3
7:23 [h] Ps 6:8;
Mt 25:12, 41;
Lk 13:25-27
7:24 [i] ver 21;
Jas 1:22-25
7:28 [j] Mt 11:1; 13:53;
19:1; 26:1 [k] Mt 13:54;
22:33; Mk 1:22; 6:2;
11:18; Lk 4:32; Jn 7:46
8:2 [l] Lev 13:45;
Mt 10:8; 11:5; 26:6;
Lk 5:12; 17:12
[m] Mt 9:18; 15:25;
18:26; 20:20

7:12 The so-called Golden Rule is found in negative form in Rabbinic Judaism and also in Hinduism, Buddhism and Confucianism. It occurred in various forms in Greek and Roman ethical teaching. Jesus stated it in positive form. *in everything.* Probably refers to the teaching of the entire Sermon up to this point. *sums up.* Cf. 22:36–40; Ro 13:8–10 and relevant notes. *the Law and the Prophets.* See note on 5:17.

7:13 *narrow gate.* The gate that leads into the kingdom of heaven is synonymous with "life" (v. 14). *destruction.* Separation from God in hell.

7:15 *false prophets.* People who have not been sent by God but who claim that they have (see 24:24; Jer 23:16 and note).

7:19 See Jn 15:6 and note; cf. Mt 3:10.

7:20 Cf. Jn 15:7 and note.

7:21 *Lord.* Here seems to mean more than merely "sir" or "master" in view of the fact that Jesus is the one who makes the final decision about a person's eternal destiny. *kingdom of heaven.* See note on 3:2. *do the will of my Father.* The deciding factor as to who enters the kingdom (see Mk 3:35 and note).

7:22 *that day.* The day of judgment (cf. Mal 3:17–18). *prophesy.*

In the Bible this verb primarily means to give a message from God, not necessarily to predict. *demons.* See note on Mk 1:23.

7:24–27 This parable ends the Sermon on the Mount and also the Sermon on the Plain (Lk 6:47–49).

7:24 *rock.* The Bible often speaks metaphorically of God or Christ as a "rock" (see Ge 49:24; Ps 18:2; 1Co 10:4 and notes).

7:25 *rain came down.* The Holy Land is known for its torrential rains that often cause disastrous floods.

7:28 *were amazed.* A common reaction by Jesus' listeners to his teaching—both its presentation and its authority (see note on Mk 1:22).

7:29 *authority.* The teachers of the law quoted other rabbis to support their own teaching (see note on 2:4), but Jesus spoke with divine authority (see 9:6,8; cf. Jn 7:46).

8:1 *mountainside.* See 5:1 and note.

8:2 *leprosy.* See TNIV text note; see also note on Lev 13:2. *Lord.* See note on 7:21. *make me clean.* Leprosy made a person ceremonially unclean as well as physically afflicted (see note on Lk 5:12–16).

8:3 *touched the man.* See note on Mk 1:41.

8:4 *n* Mt 9:30; 12:16;
Mk 5:43; 7:36; S 8:30;
Lk 4:41 *o* Lk 17:14
p Lev 14:2-32
8:6 *q* S Mt 4:24
8:8 *r* Ps 107:20
8:10 *s* Mt 15:28
8:11 *t* Ps 107:3;
Isa 49:12; 59:19;
Mal 1:11 *u* Lk 13:29
8:12 *v* Mt 13:38
w Mt 13:42,50; 22:13;
24:51; 25:30; Lk 13:28
8:13 *x* S Mt 9:22
8:16 *y* S Mt 4:23,24
8:17 *z* S Mt 1:22
a Isa 53:4
8:18 *b* Mk 4:35

Immediately he was cleansed of his leprosy. ⁴Then Jesus said to him, "See that you don't tell anyone. *n* But go, show yourself to the priest *o* and offer the gift Moses commanded, *p* as a testimony to them."

THE FAITH OF THE CENTURION

8:5–13pp — Lk 7:1–10

⁵When Jesus had entered Capernaum, a centurion came to him, asking for help. ⁶"Lord," he said, "my servant lies at home paralyzed, *q* suffering terribly."

⁷Jesus said to him, "Shall I come and heal him?"

⁸The centurion replied, "Lord, I do not deserve to have you come under my roof. But just say the word, and my servant will be healed. *r* ⁹For I myself am a man under authority, with soldiers under me. I tell this one, 'Go,' and he goes; and that one, 'Come,' and he comes. I say to my servant, 'Do this,' and he does it."

¹⁰When Jesus heard this, he was amazed and said to those following him, "Truly I tell you, I have not found anyone in Israel with such great faith. *s* ¹¹I say to you that many will come from the east and the west, *t* and will take their places at the feast with Abraham, Isaac and Jacob in the kingdom of heaven. *u* ¹²But the subjects of the kingdom *v* will be thrown outside, into the darkness, where there will be weeping and gnashing of teeth." *w*

¹³Then Jesus said to the centurion, "Go! Let it be done just as you believed it would." *x* And his servant was healed at that very hour.

JESUS HEALS MANY

8:14–16pp — Mk 1:29–34; Lk 4:38–41

¹⁴When Jesus came into Peter's house, he saw Peter's mother-in-law lying in bed with a fever. ¹⁵He touched her hand and the fever left her, and she got up and began to wait on him.

¹⁶When evening came, many who were demon-possessed were brought to him, and he drove out the spirits with a word and healed all the sick. *y* ¹⁷This was to fulfill *z* what was spoken through the prophet Isaiah:

"He took up our infirmities
    and bore our diseases." *a a*

THE COST OF FOLLOWING JESUS

8:19–22pp — Lk 9:57–60

¹⁸When Jesus saw the crowd around him, he gave orders to cross to the other side of the lake. *b* ¹⁹Then a teacher of the law came to him and said, "Teacher, I will follow you wherever you go."

a 17 Isaiah 53:4 (see Septuagint)

8:4 *don't tell anyone.* Perhaps for several reasons: (1) Jesus did not want to be considered just a miracle worker, (2) he did not want his teaching ministry hindered by too much publicity being given to his healing miracles, and (3) he did not want his death to come prematurely, i.e., before he had finished his ministry. See 9:30; 12:16; Mk 1:44; 5:43; 7:36; Lk 8:56. *show yourself to the priest.* See note on Lk 5:14. *a testimony to them.* See note on Mk 1:44. *them.* The priests and the people.

8:5–13 Although the incident in Jn 4:46–54 is similar, it probably is a separate episode in the life of Jesus.

8:5 *Capernaum.* See note on 4:13. *centurion.* A Roman military officer in charge of 100 soldiers. In Luke's account (Lk 7:1–5) Jewish elders and friends of the centurion came to Jesus on his behalf, but Matthew does not mention these intermediaries. A parallel situation was the flogging of Jesus by Pilate, in which the act was obviously not carried out by Pilate himself but by the Roman soldiers at Pilate's command (27:26, lit. "he flogged Jesus").

8:8 *I do not deserve to have you come under my roof.* In Greek the words "I do not deserve" are the same as those used by John the Baptist in 3:11 ("I am not worthy"). The entire statement reveals how highly the centurion regarded Jesus. Or perhaps his response reflects his own sense of moral guilt in the presence of Jesus.

8:10 *he was amazed.* See note on Lk 7:9. In his incarnate state

Jesus experienced every human emotion. *such great faith.* See note on Lk 7:9.

8:11 The universality of the gospel is one of Matthew's themes (see Introduction: Recipients). *feast . . . in the kingdom of heaven.* The eschatological Messianic banquet that symbolizes the blessings of an intimate relationship with God (see Isa 25:6; Lk 14:15; Rev 19:9 and notes).

8:12 *subjects of the kingdom.* Jews who thought their Judaism was an inherited passport for entrance into the kingdom (see 3:9–10 and note on 3:9). *outside, into the darkness.* Hell. *weeping and gnashing of teeth.* A phrase used only in Matthew's Gospel (here; 13:42,50; 22:13; 24:51; 25:30)—though an almost identical phrase occurs in Lk 13:28—to describe the horrible suffering experienced in hell.

8:14 *Peter's mother-in-law.* See notes on Mk 1:30; Lk 4:38.

8:15 *him.* Jesus. Mk 1:31 and Lk 4:39 have "them." She began to serve not only Jesus but also her guests, probably by preparing a meal for them.

8:16 *evening.* See Lk 4:40 and note. *demon-possessed.* See notes on Mk 1:23; Lk 4:33.

8:17 *bore.* Bore the burden of. The diseases were not transferred to Jesus in the sense of making him ill.

8:18 *the other side.* The east side.

8:19 *teacher of the law.* See note on 2:4.

²⁰Jesus replied, "Foxes have holes and birds have nests, but the Son of Man*c* has no place to lay his head."

²¹Another disciple said to him, "Lord, first let me go and bury my father."

²²But Jesus told him, "Follow me,*d* and let the dead bury their own dead."

JESUS CALMS THE STORM
8:23–27pp — Mk 4:36–41; Lk 8:22–25
8:23–27Ref — Mt 14:22–33

²³Then he got into the boat and his disciples followed him. ²⁴Suddenly a furious storm came up on the lake, so that the waves swept over the boat. But Jesus was sleeping. ²⁵The disciples went and woke him, saying, "Lord, save us! We're going to drown!"

²⁶He replied, "You of little faith,*e* why are you so afraid?" Then he got up and rebuked the winds and the waves, and it was completely calm.*f*

²⁷The men were amazed and asked, "What kind of man is this? Even the winds and the waves obey him!"

JESUS RESTORES TWO DEMON-POSSESSED MEN
8:28–34pp — Mk 5:1–17; Lk 8:26–37

²⁸When he arrived at the other side in the region of the Gadarenes,*a* two demon-possessed*g* men coming from the tombs met him. They were so violent that no one could pass that way. ²⁹"What do you want with us,*h* Son of God?" they shouted. "Have you come here to torture us before the appointed time?"*i*

³⁰Some distance from them a large herd of pigs was feeding. ³¹The demons begged Jesus, "If you drive us out, send us into the herd of pigs."

³²He said to them, "Go!" So they came out and went into the pigs, and the whole herd rushed down the steep bank into the lake and died in the water. ³³Those tending the pigs ran off, went into the town and reported all this, including what had happened to the demon-possessed men. ³⁴Then the whole town went out to meet Jesus. And when they saw him, they pleaded with him to leave their region.*j*

JESUS FORGIVES AND HEALS A PARALYZED MAN
9:2–8pp — Mk 2:3–12; Lk 5:18–26

9 Jesus stepped into a boat, crossed over and came to his own town.*k* ²Some men brought to him a paralyzed man,*l* lying on a mat. When Jesus saw their faith,*m* he said to the man, "Take heart,*n* son; your sins are forgiven."*o*

³At this, some of the teachers of the law said to themselves, "This fellow is blaspheming!"*p*

⁴Knowing their thoughts,*q* Jesus said, "Why do you entertain evil thoughts in your hearts? ⁵Which is easier: to say, 'Your sins are forgiven,' or to say, 'Get up and walk'? ⁶But I want you to know that the Son of Man*r* has authority on earth to forgive sins." So he said to the paralyzed man, "Get up, take your mat and go home." ⁷Then the man got up

---

ᵃ 28 Some manuscripts *Gergesenes*; other manuscripts *Gerasenes*

8:20 *c* Da 7:13;
Mt 12:8,32,40; 16:13,
27,28; 17:9; 19:28;
Mk 2:10; 8:31
8:22 *d* S Mt 4:19
8:26 *e* S Mt 6:30
f Ps 65:7; 89:9; 107:29
8:28 *g* S Mt 4:24
8:29 *h* Jdg 11:12;
2Sa 16:10; 1Ki 17:18;
Mk 1:24; Lk 4:34;
Jn 2:4 *i* 2Pe 2:4
8:34 *j* Lk 5:8;
Ac 16:39
9:1 *k* Mt 4:13
9:2 *l* S Mt 4:24
m S ver 22 *n* Jn 16:33
o Lk 7:48
9:3 *p* Mt 26:65;
Jn 10:33
9:4 *q* Ps 94:11;
Mt 12:25; Lk 6:8;
9:47; 11:17; Jn 2:25
9:6 *r* S Mt 8:20

8:20 *Son of Man.* See note on Mk 8:31.
8:21 *bury my father.* See note on Lk 9:59.
8:22 *let the dead bury their own dead.* Let the spiritually dead bury the physically dead. The time of Jesus' ministry was short and demanded full attention and commitment. This statement stresses the radical demands of Jesus' discipleship, since Jews placed great importance on the duty of children to bury their parents.
8:23–27 See note on Mk 4:35–41.
8:24 *furious storm.* See note on Mk 4:37. *But Jesus was sleeping.* See note on Mk 4:38.
8:26 *little faith.* See 6:30 and note.
8:27 *What kind of man is this?* See note on Mk 4:41.
8:28 *region of the Gadarenes.* The region around the city of Gadara, six miles southeast of the Sea of Galilee. Mark and Luke identify the region by the capital city Gerasa, located about 35 miles southeast of the Sea (see note on Mk 5:2 and Lk 8:27 (see note there) mention only one Gadarene demoniac. *demon-possessed.* See note on v. 16.
8:29 *Son of God.* See note on Lk 8:28. *appointed time.* The time of their judgment (see notes on Mk 5:10; Lk 8:31).

8:30 *herd of pigs.* Large numbers of Gentiles lived in Galilee. Normally Jews did not raise pigs, since they were considered the most ceremonially unclean of all animals.
8:32 Though Jesus seemingly consented to the demons' request, the pigs carried the demons into the depths of the sea—perhaps symbolic of the Abyss (see Lk 8:31 and note).
8:34 *pleaded with him to leave.* They were probably more concerned about their financial loss than about the deliverance of the miserable demon-possessed man (see note on Mk 5:17).
9:1 *crossed over.* The northern end of the Sea of Galilee. *his own town.* Capernaum (see note on 4:13).
9:2 *their faith.* The faith of the men who carried him as well as the faith of the paralyzed man. *your sins are forgiven.* See note on Mk 2:5. In this case, perhaps there was a relationship between the man's sin and his paralysis (cf. Jn 9:1–3).
9:3 *blaspheming.* Here the term includes usurping God's prerogative to forgive sins (see notes on Mk 2:7; Lk 5:21).
9:5–6 See notes on Mk 2:9–10; 14:64.
9:6 *Son of Man.* See note on Mk 8:31.

9:8 ᵍ Mt 5:16; 15:31;
Lk 7:16; 13:13; 17:15;
23:47; Jn 15:8;
Ac 4:21; 11:18; 21:20
9:9 ᵗ S Mt 4:19
9:11 ᵘ Mt 11:19;
Lk 5:30; 15:2; 19:7;
Gal 2:15
9:13 ᵛ Hos 6:6;
Mic 6:6-8; Mt 12:7
ʷ Lk 19:10; 1Ti 1:15
9:14 ˣ S Mt 3:1
ʸ Mt 11:18,19; Lk 18:12
9:15 ᶻ Jn 3:29
ᵃ Ac 13:2,3; 14:23
9:18 ᵇ S Mt 8:2
ᶜ S Mk 5:23
9:20 ᵈ Mt 14:36;
Mk 3:10; 6:56; Lk 6:19
9:22 ᵉ ver 2;
Jn 16:33 ᶠ ver 29;
Mt 8:13; Mk 10:52;
Lk 7:50; 17:19; 18:42
ᵍ Mt 15:28
9:23 ʰ 2Ch 35:25;
Jer 9:17,18
9:24 ⁱ Ac 20:10
ʲ Da 12:2; Ps 76:5;
Jn 11:11-14; Ac 7:60;
13:36; 1Co 11:30; 15:6,
18, 20; 1Th 4:13-16
9:25 ᵏ S Lk 7:14
9:26 ˡ ver 31;
Mt 4:24; 14:1;
Mk 1:28,45; Lk 4:14,
37; 5:15; 7:17

and went home. ⁸When the crowd saw this, they were filled with awe; and they praised God,ᵍ who had given such authority to human beings.

THE CALLING OF MATTHEW

9:9–13pp — Mk 2:14–17; Lk 5:27–32

⁹As Jesus went on from there, he saw a man named Matthew sitting at the tax collector's booth. "Follow me,"ᵗ he told him, and Matthew got up and followed him.

¹⁰While Jesus was having dinner at Matthew's house, many tax collectors and sinners came and ate with him and his disciples. ¹¹When the Pharisees saw this, they asked his disciples, "Why does your teacher eat with tax collectors and sinners?"ᵘ

¹²On hearing this, Jesus said, "It is not the healthy who need a doctor, but the sick. ¹³But go and learn what this means: 'I desire mercy, not sacrifice.'ᵃ ᵛ For I have not come to call the righteous, but sinners."ʷ

JESUS QUESTIONED ABOUT FASTING

9:14–17pp — Mk 2:18–22; Lk 5:33–39

¹⁴Then John'sˣ disciples came and asked him, "How is it that we and the Pharisees fast often,ʸ but your disciples do not fast?"

¹⁵Jesus answered, "How can the guests of the bridegroom mourn while he is with them?ᶻ The time will come when the bridegroom will be taken from them; then they will fast.ᵃ

¹⁶"No one sews a patch of unshrunk cloth on an old garment, for the patch will pull away from the garment, making the tear worse. ¹⁷Neither do people pour new wine into old wineskins. If they do, the skins will burst; the wine will run out and the wineskins will be ruined. No, they pour new wine into new wineskins, and both are preserved."

JESUS RAISES A DEAD GIRL AND HEALS A SICK WOMAN

9:18–26pp — Mk 5:22–43; Lk 8:41–56

¹⁸While he was saying this, a synagogue leader came and knelt before himᵇ and said, "My daughter has just died. But come and put your hand on her,ᶜ and she will live." ¹⁹Jesus got up and went with him, and so did his disciples.

²⁰Just then a woman who had been subject to bleeding for twelve years came up behind him and touched the edge of his cloak.ᵈ ²¹She said to herself, "If I only touch his cloak, I will be healed."

²²Jesus turned and saw her. "Take heart,ᵉ daughter," he said, "your faith has healed you."ᶠ And the woman was healed from that moment.ᵍ

²³When Jesus entered the synagogue leader's house and saw the noisy crowd and people playing pipes,ʰ ²⁴he said, "Go away. The girl is not deadⁱ but asleep."ʲ But they laughed at him. ²⁵After the crowd had been put outside, he went in and took the girl by the hand, and she got up.ᵏ ²⁶News of this spread through all that region.ˡ

ᵃ 13 Hosea 6:6

9:9 *Matthew.* Mark and Luke call this disciple Levi in the parallel accounts (but see also Mk 3:18; Lk 6:15; Ac 1:13). *tax collector's booth.* See note on Mk 2:14. *got up and followed him.* See note on Lk 5:28.

9:10 *tax collectors.* See notes on 5:46; Mk 2:16. *sinners.* See note on Mk 2:15.

9:11 *Pharisees.* See note on Mk 2:16.

9:12 *not the healthy who need a doctor, but the sick.* See note on Lk 5:31.

9:13 *I have not come to call the righteous, but sinners.* See note on Mk 2:17.

9:14 See notes on Mk 2:18; Lk 5:33.

9:15 See notes on Mk 2:19–20.

9:17 *new wineskins.* In ancient times goatskins were used to hold wine. As the fresh grape juice fermented, the wine would expand, and the new wineskin would stretch. But a used skin, already stretched, would break (see note on Job 32:19). Jesus brings a newness that cannot be confined within the old forms.

9:18 *synagogue leader.* His name was Jairus (see notes on Mk 5:22; Lk 8:41). *has just died.* Mk 5:23 has "is dying," but Matthew omits reference to the later messengers (Mk 5:35) and condenses (see notes on 21:12–17; 21:18–22) by presenting at the outset what was actually true before Jesus reached the house.

9:20 *subject to bleeding for twelve years.* See notes on Mk 5:25; Lk 8:43.

9:21 See notes on Mk 5:28; Lk 8:45.

9:22 *daughter.* See note on Lk 8:48. *healed.* See note on Mk 5:34.

9:23 *noisy crowd.* Mourners hired to wail and lament (see note on Mk 5:38). *people playing pipes.* Musicians hired to play in mourning ceremonies.

9:24 *not dead but asleep.* See note on Lk 8:52.

9:25 *took the girl by the hand.* Touching a dead body ordinarily resulted in ceremonial uncleanness (see Lev 11:31; 21:1,11 and note on 21:1; 22:4; Nu 19:14 and note), but Jesus' action brought life, not defilement.

JESUS HEALS THE BLIND AND THE MUTE

²⁷As Jesus went on from there, two blind men followed him, calling out, "Have mercy on us, Son of David!"ᵐ

²⁸When he had gone indoors, the blind men came to him, and he asked them, "Do you believe that I am able to do this?"

"Yes, Lord," they replied.ⁿ

²⁹Then he touched their eyes and said, "According to your faith let it be done to you";ᵒ ³⁰and their sight was restored. Jesus warned them sternly, "See that no one knows about this."ᵖ ³¹But they went out and spread the news about him all over that region.ᵠ

³²While they were going out, a man who was demon-possessedʳ and could not talkˢ was brought to Jesus. ³³And when the demon was driven out, the man who had been mute spoke. The crowd was amazed and said, "Nothing like this has ever been seen in Israel."ᵗ

³⁴But the Pharisees said, "It is by the prince of demons that he drives out demons."ᵘ

THE WORKERS ARE FEW

³⁵Jesus went through all the towns and villages, teaching in their synagogues, proclaiming the good news of the kingdom and healing every disease and sickness.ᵛ ³⁶When he saw the crowds, he had compassion on them,ʷ because they were harassed and helpless, like sheep without a shepherd.ˣ ³⁷Then he said to his disciples, "The harvestʸ is plentiful but the workers are few.ᶻ ³⁸Ask the Lord of the harvest, therefore, to send out workers into his harvest field."

JESUS SENDS OUT THE TWELVE

10:2–4pp — Mk 3:16–19; Lk 6:14–16; Ac 1:13
10:9–15pp — Mk 6:8–11; Lk 9:3–5; 10:4–12
10:19–22pp — Mk 13:11–13; Lk 21:12–17
10:26–33pp — Lk 12:2–9
10:34,35pp — Lk 12:51–53

10 Jesus called his twelve disciples to him and gave them authority to drive out evilᵃ spiritsᵃ and to heal every disease and sickness.ᵇ ²These are the names of the twelve apostles: first, Simon (who is called Peter) and his brother Andrew; James son of Zebedee, and his brother John; ³Philip and Bartholomew; Thomas and Matthew the tax collector; James son of Alphaeus, and Thaddaeus; ⁴Simon the Zealot and Judas Iscariot, who betrayed him.ᶜ

⁵These twelve Jesus sent out with the following instructions: "Do not go among the Gentiles or enter any town of the Samaritans.ᵈ ⁶Go rather to the lost sheep of Israel.ᵉ ⁷As you go, proclaim this message: 'The kingdom of heavenᶠ has come near.' ⁸Heal the sick, raise the dead, cleanse those who have leprosy,ᵇ drive out demons. Freely you have received, freely give.

⁹"Do not get any gold or silver or copper to take with you in your beltsᵍ— ¹⁰no bag for

---

ᵃ 1 Greek *unclean*   ᵇ 8 The Greek word traditionally translated *leprosy* was used for various diseases affecting the skin.

9:27 *blind men.* Isaiah predicted the healing of the blind in the Messianic age (Isa 35:5). *Son of David.* A popular Jewish title for the coming Messiah (e.g., 12:23; 20:30; 21:9; 22:41–45; see note on 1:1).
9:29 *According to your faith.* That is, "Because you have faith," not "In proportion to your faith." Jesus did not provide healing according to the amount of faith the blind men had (see 17:20 and note). Cf. 8:13; Mk 9:23 and note; 11:23; Jn 11:40.
9:30 See notes on 8:4; 16:20.
9:32 *could not talk.* Isaiah also (see note on v. 27) predicted that the mute would talk in the Messianic age (Isa 35:6).
9:33 *amazed.* See 8:27; 13:54; 15:31; 21:20; 22:22; cf. Mk 1:22 and note.
9:34 *prince of demons.* See note on 10:25.
9:35 *synagogues.* See note on Mk 1:21. *good news.* See note on Mk 1:1.
9:36 *compassion.* Jesus' compassion for people is often noted in the Gospels (see 14:14; 15:22; 20:34; Mk 1:41; 6:34; 8:2). *like sheep without a shepherd.* See Eze 34:5; Zec 10:2; 13:7 and notes; Mk 6:34.

10:2–4 See notes on Lk 6:14–16.
10:2 *apostles.* The only occurrence of this word in Matthew's Gospel. See note on Mk 6:30.
10:3 *Thaddaeus.* Also called Judas (not Iscariot [Jn 14:22]); see Mk 3:18; Lk 6:16; Ac 1:13 and note.
10:4 *the Zealot.* Either a description of Simon's religious zeal or a reference to his membership in the party of the Zealots, a Jewish revolutionary group violently opposed to Roman rule over the Holy Land (see chart, p. 1650).
10:5 *Do not go.* The good news about the kingdom was to be proclaimed first to Jews only. After his death and resurrection, Jesus commanded the message to be taken to all nations (28:19; cf. 21:43). *Samaritans.* A mixed-blood race resulting from the intermarriage of Israelites left behind when the people of the northern kingdom were exiled and Gentiles who were brought into the land by the Assyrians (2Ki 17:24). Bitter hostility existed between Jews and Samaritans in Jesus' day (see Jn 4:9 and note).
10:7 *kingdom of heaven.* See note on 3:2.
10:8 *leprosy.* See TNIV text note and note on Lev 13:2.
10:9–10 See notes on Mk 6:8–9.

**Cross references (right margin):**

9:27 ᵐ S Mt 1:1; 12:23; 15:22; 20:30, 31; 21:9,15; 22:42; Mk 10:47
9:28 ⁿ Ac 14:9
9:29 ᵒ S ver 22
9:30 ᵖ S Mt 8:4
9:31 ᵠ S ver 26; Mk 7:36
9:32 ʳ S Mt 4:24 ˢ Mt 12:22-24
9:33 ᵗ Mk 2:12
9:34 ᵘ Mt 12:24
9:35 ᵛ S Mt 4:23
9:36 ʷ Mt 14:14; 15:32; Mk 8:2 ˣ Nu 27:17; 1Ki 22:17; Eze 34:5,6; Zec 10:2
9:37 ʸ Jn 4:35
ᶻ Lk 10:2
10:1 ᵃ Mk 3:13-15; 6:7; Lk 4:36; 9:1 ᵇ S Mt 4:23
10:4 ᶜ Mt 26:14-16, 25,47; 27:3; Mk 14:10; Jn 6:71; 12:4; 13:2,26,27; Ac 1:16
10:5 ᵈ 1Ki 16:24; 2Ki 17:24; Lk 9:52; 10:33; 17:16; Jn 4:4-26,39,40; 8:48; Ac 8:5,25
10:6 ᵉ Jer 50:6; Mt 15:24
10:7 ᶠ S Mt 3:2
10:9 ᵍ Lk 22:35

10:10 *h* S 1Ti 5:18
10:12 *i* Isa 25:6
10:14 *j* Ne 5:13;
Mk 6:11; Lk 9:5; 10:11;
Ac 13:51; 18:6
10:15 *k* Ge 18:20;
19:24; 2Pe 2:6; Jude 7
l Mt 12:36; Ac 17:31;
2Pe 2:9; 3:7; 1Jn 4:17;
Jude 6 *m* Mt 11:22,24
10:16 *n* Lk 10:3;
Ac 20:29
o S 1Co 14:20
10:17 *p* S Mt 5:22
q Mt 23:34; Mk 13:9;
Ac 5:40; 22:19; 26:11
10:18 *r* Ac 25:24-26
10:19 *s* Ex 4:12
10:20 *t* Lk 12:11,12;
Ac 4:8
10:21 *u* ver 35,36;
Mic 7:6 *v* Mk 13:12
10:22 *w* S Jn 15:21
x Mt 24:13; Mk 13:13;
Lk 21:19; Rev 2:10
10:23 *y* S Lk 17:30
10:24 *z* S Jn 13:16
10:25 *a* S Mk 3:22
10:26 *b* Mk 4:22;
Lk 8:17
10:28 *c* Isa 8:12,13;
Heb 10:31
10:30 *d* Isa 45:9;
2Sa 14:11; 1Ki 1:52;
Lk 21:18; Ac 27:34
10:31 *e* Mt 6:26;
12:12
10:32 *f* Ro 10:9
10:33 *g* Mk 8:38;
2Ti 2:12

the journey or extra shirt or sandals or a staff, for workers are worth their keep.*h* ¹¹Whatever town or village you enter, search for some worthy person there and stay at that person's house until you leave. ¹²As you enter the home, give it your greeting.*i* ¹³If the home is deserving, let your peace rest on it; if it is not, let your peace return to you. ¹⁴If anyone will not welcome you or listen to your words, shake the dust off your feet*j* when you leave that home or town. ¹⁵Truly I tell you, it will be more bearable for Sodom and Gomorrah*k* on the day of judgment*l* than for that town.*m*

¹⁶"I am sending you out like sheep among wolves.*n* Therefore be as shrewd as snakes and as innocent as doves.*o* ¹⁷Be on your guard; you will be handed over to the local councils*p* and be flogged in the synagogues.*q* ¹⁸On my account you will be brought before governors and kings*r* as witnesses to them and to the Gentiles. ¹⁹But when they arrest you, do not worry about what to say or how to say it.*s* At that time you will be given what to say, ²⁰for it will not be you speaking, but the Spirit of your Father*t* speaking through you.

²¹"Brother will betray brother to death, and a father his child; children will rebel against their parents*u* and have them put to death.*v* ²²Everyone will hate you because of me,*w* but those who stand firm to the end will be saved.*x* ²³When you are persecuted in one place, flee to another. Truly I tell you, you will not finish going through the towns of Israel before the Son of Man comes.*y*

²⁴"Students are not above their teacher, nor servants above their master.*z* ²⁵It is enough for students to be like their teacher, and servants like their master. If the head of the house has been called Beelzebul,*a* how much more the members of his household!

²⁶"So do not be afraid of them. There is nothing concealed that will not be disclosed, or hidden that will not be made known.*b* ²⁷What I tell you in the dark, speak in the daylight; what is whispered in your ear, proclaim from the roofs. ²⁸Do not be afraid of those who kill the body but cannot kill the soul. Rather, be afraid of the One*c* who can destroy both soul and body in hell. ²⁹Are not two sparrows sold for a penny? Yet not one of them will fall to the ground outside your Father's care.*a* ³⁰And even the very hairs of your head are all numbered.*d* ³¹So don't be afraid; you are worth more than many sparrows.*e*

³²"Whoever publicly acknowledges me*f* I will also acknowledge before my Father in heaven. ³³But whoever publicly disowns me I will disown before my Father in heaven.*g*

³⁴"Do not suppose that I have come to bring peace to the earth. I did not come to bring peace, but a sword. ³⁵For I have come to turn

---

a 29 Or *will;* or *knowledge*

10:10 *workers are worth their keep.* Cf. 1Co 9:4–14; 1Ti 5:17–18 and note on 5:18.

10:11 *stay at that person's house.* See note on Lk 9:4.

10:12 *your greeting.* The Jews' greeting was *shalom,* "peace" (see Lk 10:5).

10:13 *If the home is deserving.* That is, "If the head of the house loves peace" (Lk 10:6). *let your peace return to you.* Either (1) retract your blessing, or (2) leave the house.

10:14 *shake the dust off your feet.* A symbolic act practiced by the Pharisees when they left a ceremonially unclean Gentile area. Here it represented an act of solemn warning to those who rejected God's message (see notes on Lk 9:5; Ac 13:51; cf. Ac 18:6).

10:15 *Truly I tell you.* See note on Mk 3:28. *Sodom and Gomorrah.* See Ge 19:23–29; Lk 10:12 and note.

10:16 Cf. 7:15; cf. also Paul's statement in Ro 16:19: "I want you to be wise about what is good, and innocent about what is evil."

10:17 *local councils.* The lower courts, connected with local synagogues, that tried less serious cases and flogged those found guilty. *synagogues.* See notes on Mk 1:21; Lk 21:12.

10:18 Anticipates the mission to the Gentiles. Matthew's Gospel emphasizes the universality of the gospel (see note on 8:11; see also Introduction: Recipients).

10:19 *do not worry about what to say.* Namely, to defend yourselves (Lk 21:14–15). *you will be given what to say.* "Words and wisdom" that cannot be resisted (Lk 21:15; see note there).

10:20 *the Spirit of your Father speaking.* See Mk 13:11; Lk 12:11–12; cf. Lk 21:14–15.

10:21 The allusion is to Mic 7:6, which is quoted in vv. 35–36.

10:22 *Everyone.* Hyperbole. *those who stand firm to the end will be saved.* See note on Mk 13:13.

10:23 Some take Jesus' saying here as a reference to his sec-

ond coming at the end of the age (see 24:30), but it is hard to reconcile this with the failure of the disciples to "finish going through" (evangelize) the cities of Israel before this happens. It is therefore probably best understood as referring to his coming in judgment on the Jews when Jerusalem and the temple were destroyed in A.D. 70.

10:25 *Beelzebul.* The prince of demons (12:24); the Greek form of the Hebrew name Baal-Zebul ("Exalted Baal" or "Baal the Prince"). Baal-Zebub ("lord of flies") is a parody on and mockery of the actual epithet, Baal-Zebul (see note on Jdg 10:6). The name came to be used of Satan.

10:26–33 See Lk 12:2–9 and notes.

10:26 *them.* The persecutors (vv. 21–25).

10:28 *cannot kill the soul.* See Lk 12:4 and note. *soul.* The true self (see note on Ps 6:3). Body and soul are closely related in this life but are separated at death and then reunited at the resurrection (cf. 2Co 5:1–10 and notes; Php 1:23–24). *the One.* God. He alone determines the final destiny of us all. *destroy both soul and body in hell.* See Lk 12:5 and note. *hell.* See note on 5:22.

10:29 *two sparrows sold for a penny.* Cf. Lk 12:6 and note.

10:31 *worth more than many sparrows.* See 6:26.

10:32–33 See Lk 12:8–9 and notes.

10:34 At first glance this saying sounds like a contradiction of Isa 9:6 ("Prince of Peace"), Lk 2:14 ("on earth peace to those on whom his favor rests") and Jn 14:27 ("Peace I leave with you"). It is true that Christ came to bring peace—peace between the believer and God, and peace among humans. Yet the inevitable result of Christ's coming is conflict—between Christ and the antichrist, between light and darkness, between Christ's children and the devil's children. This conflict can occur even between members of the same family (vv. 35–36; Mk 10:29–30).

" 'a man against his father,
    a daughter against her mother,
a daughter-in-law against her mother-in-law[h]—
    [36] your enemies will be the members of your own household.'[a][i]

[37]"Anyone who loves their father or mother more than me is not worthy of me; anyone who loves a son or daughter more than me is not worthy of me.[j] [38]Whoever does not take up their cross and follow me is not worthy of me.[k] [39]Whoever finds their life will lose it, and whoever loses their life for my sake will find it.[l]

[40]"Anyone who welcomes you welcomes me,[m] and anyone who welcomes me welcomes the one who sent me.[n] [41]Whoever welcomes someone known to be a prophet will receive a prophet's reward, and whoever welcomes someone known to be righteous will receive a righteous person's reward. [42]And if anyone gives even a cup of cold water to one of these little ones who is known to be my disciple, truly I tell you, that person will certainly be rewarded."[o]

JESUS AND JOHN THE BAPTIST

11:2–19pp — Lk 7:18–35

11 After Jesus had finished instructing his twelve disciples,[p] he went on from there to teach and preach in the towns of Galilee.[b] [2]When John[q] heard in prison[r] what the Messiah was doing, he sent his disciples [3]to ask him, "Are you the one who was to come,[s] or should we expect someone else?"

[4]Jesus replied, "Go back and report to John what you hear and see: [5]The blind receive sight, the lame walk, those who have leprosy[c] are cleansed, the deaf hear, the dead are raised, and the good news is proclaimed to the poor.[t] [6]Blessed is anyone who does not stumble on account of me."[u]

[7]As John's[v] disciples were leaving, Jesus began to speak to the crowd about John: "What did you go out into the wilderness[w] to see? A reed swayed by the wind? [8]If not, what did you go out to see? A man dressed in fine clothes? No, those who wear fine clothes are in kings' palaces. [9]Then what did you go out to see? A prophet?[x] Yes, I tell you, and more than a prophet. [10]This is the one about whom it is written:

" 'I will send my messenger ahead of you,[y]
    who will prepare your way before you.'[d][z]

[11]Truly I tell you, among those born of women there has not risen anyone greater than John the Baptist; yet whoever is least in the kingdom of heaven is greater than he. [12]From the days of John the Baptist until now, the kingdom of heaven has been subjected to violence,[e] and violent people have been raiding it. [13]For all the Prophets and the Law prophesied until John.[a] [14]And if you are willing to accept it, he is the Elijah who was to come.[b] [15]Whoever has ears, let them hear.[c]

---

[a] 36 Micah 7:6   [b] 1 Greek *in their towns* used for various diseases affecting the skin.   [c] 5 The Greek word traditionally translated *leprosy* was   [d] 10 Mal. 3:1   [e] 12 Or *been forcefully advancing*

10:35 [h] ver 21
10:36 [i] Mic 7:6
10:37 [j] Lk 14:26
10:38 [k] Mt 16:24; Lk 14:27
10:39 [l] S Jn 12:25
10:40 [m] Ex 16:8; Mt 18:5; Gal 4:14
[n] Lk 9:48; 10:16; Jn 12:44; 13:20
10:42 [o] Pr 14:31; 19:17; Mt 25:40; Mk 9:41; Ac 10:4; Heb 6:10
11:1 [p] S Mt 7:28
11:2 [q] S Mt 3:1
[r] Mt 14:3
11:3 [s] Ps 118:26; Jn 11:27; Heb 10:37
11:5 [t] Isa 35:4-6; 61:1; Mt 15:31; Lk 4:18,19
11:6 [u] Mt 13:21; 26:31
11:7 [v] S Mt 3:1
[w] Mt 3:1
11:9 [x] Mt 14:5; 21:26; Lk 1:76; 7:26
11:10 [y] Jn 3:28
[z] Mal 3:1; Mk 1:2; Lk 7:27
11:13 [a] Lk 16:16
11:14 [b] Mal 4:5; Mt 17:10-13; Mk 9:11-13; Lk 1:17; Jn 1:21
11:15 [c] Mt 13:9,43; Mk 4:23; Lk 14:35; S Rev 2:7

10:37 See Lk 14:26 and note.

10:38 *take up their cross.* The first mention of the cross in Matthew's Gospel. The cross was an instrument of death and here symbolizes the necessity of total commitment— even unto death—on the part of Jesus' disciples (see note on Mk 8:34).

10:39 See note on Lk 9:24.

10:40–42 During times of persecution, hospitality was especially important and could be dangerous. So Jesus indicates that those who provide it and show kindness to God's people will receive a reward.

10:42 *cup of cold water.* See note on Mk 9:41.

11:1 While the 12 apostles were carrying out their first mission, Jesus continued his ministry in Galilee. *Galilee.* See note on 2:2.

11:2 *John.* The Baptist (see note on 3:1). *in prison.* See note on Lk 7:19.

11:3 *the one who was to come.* The Messiah. *expect someone else.* See note on Lk 7:19.

11:4 *report to John what you hear and see.* See note on Lk 7:22.

11:5 *leprosy.* See TNIV text note; see also note on Lev 13:2. *the good news is proclaimed to the poor.* See note on Lk 7:22.

11:6 *anyone who does not stumble.* See note on Lk 7:23.

11:7–10 See Lk 7:24–28 and notes.

11:10 See Mal 3:1 and note.

11:11 *greater than he.* John belonged to the age of the old covenant, which was preparatory to Christ. The least NT saint has a higher privilege in Christ as a part of his bride (the church, Eph 5:25–27,32) than John the Baptist, who was only a friend of the bridegroom (Jn 3:29). Another view, however, stresses the expression "whoever is least," holding that the key to its meaning is found in 18:4—"whoever takes a humble place—becoming like this child." Such a person, though "least," is regarded by God as even greater than John the Baptist.

11:12 *From the days of John the Baptist.* From the beginning of Jesus' ministry. *kingdom of heaven.* See note on 3:2. *subjected to violence.* The ongoing persecution of the people of the kingdom. (But see TNIV text note. The main TNIV text, however, is probably to be preferred.)

11:13 *Prophets and the Law.* The entire OT prophesied the coming of the kingdom. John represented the end of the old covenant era.

11:14 *he is the Elijah who was to come.* A reference to Mal 4:5, which prophesied the reappearance of Elijah before the day of the Lord. Some of the people remembered the prophecy and

11:18 *d* Mt 3:4
e S Lk 1:15
11:19 *f* S Mt 9:11
11:21 *g* Mk 6:45;
8:22; Lk 9:10; Jn 1:44;
12:21 *h* Joel 3:4;
Am 1:9; Mt 15:21;
Mk 3:8; Lk 6:17;
Ac 12:20 *i* Jnh 3:5-9
11:22 *i* ver 24;
Mt 10:15
11:23 *k* S Mt 4:13
l Isa 14:13-15
11:24 *m* S Mt 10:15
11:25 *n* Mt 16:17;
Lk 22:42; 23:34;
Jn 11:41; 12:27,28
o S Mt 13:11;
1Co 1:26-29
11:27 *p* S Mt 28:18
q S Jn 3:35 *r* Jn 10:15;
17:25,26
11:28 *s* Jn 7:37
t Ex 33:14
11:29 *u* Jn 13:15;
Php 2:5; 1Pe 2:21;
1Jn 2:6 *v* Ps 116:7;
Jer 6:16
11:30 *w* 1Jn 5:3

16"To what can I compare this generation? They are like children sitting in the market-places and calling out to others:

17 " 'We played the pipe for you,
    and you did not dance;
  we sang a dirge,
    and you did not mourn.'

18For John came neither eating*d* nor drinking,*e* and they say, 'He has a demon.' 19The Son of Man came eating and drinking, and they say, 'Here is a glutton and a drunkard, a friend of tax collectors and sinners.'*f* But wisdom is proved right by her actions."

WOE ON UNREPENTANT TOWNS

11:21–23pp — Lk 10:13–15

20Then Jesus began to denounce the towns in which most of his miracles had been performed, because they did not repent. 21"Woe to you, Chorazin! Woe to you, Bethsaida!*g* If the miracles that were performed in you had been performed in Tyre and Sidon,*h* they would have repented long ago in sackcloth and ashes.*i* 22But I tell you, it will be more bearable for Tyre and Sidon on the day of judgment than for you.*i* 23And you, Capernaum,*k* will you be lifted up to the skies? No, you will go down to the depths.*e l* If the miracles that were performed in you had been performed in Sodom, it would have remained to this day. 24But I tell you that it will be more bearable for Sodom on the day of judgment than for you."*m*

THE FATHER REVEALED IN THE SON

11:25–27pp — Lk 10:21,22

25At that time Jesus said, "I praise you, Father,*n* Lord of heaven and earth, because you have hidden these things from the wise and learned, and revealed them to little children.*o* 26Yes, Father, for this was your good pleasure.

27"All things have been committed to me*p* by my Father.*q* No one knows the Son except the Father, and no one knows the Father except the Son and those to whom the Son chooses to reveal him.*r*

28"Come to me,*s* all you who are weary and burdened, and I will give you rest.*t* 29Take my yoke upon you and learn from me,*u* for I am gentle and humble in heart, and you will find rest for your souls.*v* 30For my yoke is easy and my burden is light."*w*

e 23 Greek *to Hades*

---

asked John the Baptist,"Are you Elijah?"He answered,"I am not" (Jn 1:21). John was not literally the reincarnation of Elijah, but he did fulfill the function and role of the prophet (see Mt 17:10–13 and note on Lk 1:17).
11:16 *like children sitting in the marketplaces.* See note on Lk 7:32.
11:17 *played the pipe.* As at a wedding. *sang a dirge.* As at a funeral. The latter symbolized the ministry of John, the former that of Jesus. The people of Jesus' "generation" (v. 16) were like children who refused to respond on either occasion.
11:19 *Son of Man.* See note on Mk 8:31. *friend of tax collectors and sinners.* See note on Lk 7:34. *wisdom is proved right by her actions.* Apparently means that God (wisdom) had sent both John and Jesus in specific roles, and that this would be vindicated by the lasting works of both Jesus and John (see note on Lk 7:35).
11:20 *repent.* See note on 3:2.
11:21 *Chorazin.* Mentioned in the Bible only twice (here and in Lk 10:13), it was near the Sea of Galilee, probably about two miles north of Capernaum. *Bethsaida.* On the northeast shore of the Sea of Galilee. Philip the tetrarch rebuilt Bethsaida and named it "Julias," after Julia, daughter of Caesar Augustus. *Tyre and Sidon.* Cities on the Phoenician coast north of the Holy Land (see note on Mk 7:31). *sackcloth.* Here a sign of repentance (see note on Ge 37:34). Cf. Rev 6:12. *ashes.* Also a sign of repentance.

11:23 *Capernaum.* See note on Lk 10:15. *Sodom.* See notes on 10:15; Ge 13:10; Lk 10:12.
11:25 *Lord of heaven and earth.* A title for God emphasizing his sovereignty and found only three times in the Bible (here; Lk 10:21; Ac 17:24). *these things.* Either the significance of Jesus' miracles (see vv. 20–24) or of his entire mission. *wise.* According to the standards of this age (see 1Co 1:26–29; cf. 1Co 3:18 and note). *little children.* The disciples or, more generally, the humble followers of Jesus.
11:26 *your good pleasure.* Since God is "Lord of heaven and earth" (v. 25), he sovereignly reveals and conceals.
11:27 *All things.* The full revelation of God (see v. 25). *No one knows the Son.* Total knowledge of the Son belongs only to the Father. Believers can "know" the Son for salvation (1Jn 5:20) and in a deep and satisfying way, but not completely (see Jn 10:14 and note; cf. Php 3:7–11 and notes). *except . . . those to whom the Son chooses to reveal him.* Christ sovereignly chooses those to whom he reveals a saving knowledge of God (see Jn 14:6 and note).
11:28 *weary and burdened.* Probably a reference to the "heavy loads" the Pharisees placed "on other people's shoulders" by insisting on a legalistic interpretation of the law (23:4).
11:29 *yoke.* Cf. v. 30 and note; see note on Eze 34:27. *find rest for your souls.* See Jer 6:16 and note.
11:30 *my burden is light.* Cf. Ps 55:22; 1Jn 5:3 and notes.

JESUS IS LORD OF THE SABBATH

12:1–8pp — Mk 2:23–28; Lk 6:1–5
12:9–14pp — Mk 3:1–6; Lk 6:6–11

12 At that time Jesus went through the grainfields on the Sabbath. His disciples were hungry and began to pick some heads of grain[x] and eat them. [2]When the Pharisees saw this, they said to him, "Look! Your disciples are doing what is unlawful on the Sabbath."[y]

[3]He answered, "Haven't you read what David did when he and his companions were hungry?[z] [4]He entered the house of God, and he and his companions ate the consecrated bread—which was not lawful for them to do, but only for the priests.[a] [5]Or haven't you read in the Law that the priests on Sabbath duty in the temple desecrate the Sabbath[b] and yet are innocent? [6]I tell you that one[a] greater than the temple is here.[c] [7]If you had known what these words mean, 'I desire mercy, not sacrifice,'[b][d] you would not have condemned the innocent. [8]For the Son of Man[e] is Lord of the Sabbath."

[9]Going on from that place, he went into their synagogue, [10]and a man with a shriveled hand was there. Looking for a reason to accuse Jesus,[f] they asked him, "Is it lawful to heal on the Sabbath?"[g]

[11]He said to them, "If any of you has a sheep and it falls into a pit on the Sabbath, will you not take hold of it and lift it out?[h] [12]How much more valuable is a human being than a sheep![i] Therefore it is lawful to do good on the Sabbath."

[13]Then he said to the man, "Stretch out your hand." So he stretched it out and it was completely restored, just as sound as the other. [14]But the Pharisees went out and plotted how they might kill Jesus.[j]

GOD'S CHOSEN SERVANT

[15]Aware of this, Jesus withdrew from that place. A large crowd followed him, and he healed all who were ill.[k] [16]He warned them not to tell others about him.[l] [17]This was to fulfill[m] what was spoken through the prophet Isaiah:

[18] "Here is my servant whom I have chosen,
    the one I love, in whom I delight;[n]
I will put my Spirit on him,[o]
    and he will proclaim justice to the nations.
[19] He will not quarrel or cry out;
    no one will hear his voice in the streets.
[20] A bruised reed he will not break,
    and a smoldering wick he will not snuff out,
    till he leads justice to victory.
[21]   In his name the nations will put their hope."[c][p]

JESUS AND BEELZEBUL

12:25–29pp — Mk 3:23–27; Lk 11:17–22

[22]Then they brought him a demon-possessed man who was blind and mute, and Jesus

---

[a] 6 Or *something*   [b] 7 Hosea 6:6   [c] 21 Isaiah 42:1-4

12:1 *grainfields.* Of wheat or barley, the latter eaten by poorer people. *pick some heads of grain.* See note on Mk 2:23.
12:2 *Pharisees.* See note on 3:7. *what is unlawful on the Sabbath.* See note on Mk 2:24.
12:3 *what David did.* See note on Mk 2:25.
12:4 *consecrated bread.* Each Sabbath, 12 fresh loaves of bread were to be set on a table in the Holy Place (Ex 25:30; Lev 24:5–9). The old loaves were eaten by the priests.
12:5 *desecrate the Sabbath.* By doing required work associated with the sacrifices (see Nu 28:9; cf. Jn 7:22–23 and note on 7:22).
12:8 *the Son of Man is Lord of the Sabbath.* See note on Lk 6:5.
12:9 *synagogue.* See note on Mk 1:21.
12:10 *heal on the Sabbath.* The rabbis prohibited healing on the Sabbath, unless it was feared the victim would die before the next day. Obviously the man with the shriveled hand was in no danger of this.
12:11–12 Jesus contrasts the worth of an animal with that of a human being (cf. Lk 13:15–16; 14:5 and notes).

12:12 *lawful to do good on the Sabbath.* See Mk 3:4; Lk 6:9 and notes.
12:13 *"Stretch out your hand." So he stretched it out.* The fact that the man stretched out his shriveled hand shows there is a connection between faith and Jesus' healing power.
12:14 See notes on Mk 3:6; Lk 6:11.
12:16 *not to tell others about him.* See note on 8:4.
A 12:18–21 Another fulfillment passage (see note on 1:22). This one is from Isaiah's first servant song (see Isa 42:1–4 and note) and is the longest OT quotation in Matthew's Gospel. It summarizes the quiet ministry of the Lord's servant, who will bring justice and hope to the nations.
12:18 *my servant.* Jesus is called God's servant only here and in Ac 3:13,26 (see note on 3:13); 4:27,30. *chosen.* See Lk 9:35 and note. *the one I love, in whom I delight.* See note on 3:17. *put my Spirit on him.* See Isa 11:2; 61:1 and notes.
A 12:20 Jesus mends broken lives (see v. 15; Jn 4:4–42; 8:3–11).
12:22 *demon-possessed.* See notes on Mk 1:23; Lk 4:33.

12:1 [x] Dt 23:25
12:2 [y] ver 10; Ex 20:10; 23:12; Dt 5:14; Lk 13:14; 14:3; Jn 5:10; 7:23; 9:16
12:3 [z] 1Sa 21:6
12:4 [a] Lev 24:5, 9
12:5 [b] Nu 28:9,10; Jn 7:22,23
12:6 [c] ver 41,42
12:7 [d] Hos 6:6; Mic 6:6-8; Mt 9:13
12:8 [e] S Mt 8:20
12:10 [f] Mk 3:2; 12:13; Lk 11:54; 14:1; 20:20 [g] S ver 2
12:11 [h] Lk 14:5
12:12 [i] Mt 6:26; 10:31
12:14 [j] Ge 37:18; Ps 71:10; Mt 26:4; 27:1; Mk 3:6; Lk 6:11; Jn 5:18; 7:1,19; 11:53
12:15 [k] S Mt 4:23
12:16 [l] S Mt 8:4
12:17 [m] S Mt 1:22
12:18 [n] S Mt 3:17
[o] S Jn 3:34
12:21 [p] Isa 42:1-4

12:22 *q* S Mt 4:24
12:23 *r* S Mt 9:27
12:24 *s* Mk 3:22
t Mt 9:34
12:25 *u* S Mt 9:4
12:26 *v* S Mt 4:10
12:27 *w* ver 24
x Ac 19:13
12:28 *y* S Mt 3:2
12:30 *z* Mk 9:40;
Lk 11:23
12:31 *a* Mk 3:28,29;
Lk 12:10
12:32 *b* Tit 2:12
c Mk 10:30; Lk 20:34,
35; Eph 1:21; Heb 6:5
12:33 *d* Mt 7:16,17;
Lk 6:43,44
12:34 *e* Mt 3:7;
23:33 *f* Mt 15:18;
Lk 6:45
12:37 *g* Job 15:6;
Pr 10:14; 18:21; Jas 3:2
12:38 *h* S Jn 2:11;
S 4:48 *i* Mt 16:1;
Mk 8:11,12; Lk 11:16;
Jn 2:18; 6:30; 1Co 1:22
12:39 *j* Mt 16:4;
Lk 11:29
12:40 *k* Jnh 1:17
l S Mt 8:20
m S Mt 16:21
12:41 *n* Jnh 1:2
o Jnh 3:5
12:42 *p* 1Ki 10:1;
2Ch 9:1

healed him, so that he could both talk and see.*q* 23All the people were astonished and said, "Could this be the Son of David?"*r*

24But when the Pharisees heard this, they said, "It is only by Beelzebul,*s* the prince of demons, that this fellow drives out demons."*t*

25Jesus knew their thoughts*u* and said to them, "Every kingdom divided against itself will be ruined, and every city or household divided against itself will not stand. 26If Satan*v* drives out Satan, he is divided against himself. How then can his kingdom stand? 27And if I drive out demons by Beelzebul,*w* by whom do your people*x* drive them out? So then, they will be your judges. 28But if it is by the Spirit of God that I drive out demons, then the kingdom of God*y* has come upon you.

29"Or again, how can anyone enter a strong man's house and carry off his possessions without first tying up the strong man? Then his house can be plundered.

30"Whoever is not with me is against me, and whoever does not gather with me scatters.*z* 31And so I tell you, people will be forgiven every sin and blasphemy. But blasphemy against the Spirit will not be forgiven.*a* 32Anyone who speaks a word against the Son of Man will be forgiven, but anyone who speaks against the Holy Spirit will not be forgiven, either in this age*b* or in the age to come.*c*

33"Make a tree good and its fruit will be good, or make a tree bad and its fruit will be bad, for a tree is recognized by its fruit.*d* 34You brood of vipers,*e* how can you who are evil say anything good? For out of the overflow of the heart the mouth speaks.*f* 35Good people bring good things out of the good stored up in them, and evil people bring evil things out of the evil stored up in them. 36But I tell you that people will have to give account on the day of judgment for every empty word they have spoken. 37For by your words you will be acquitted, and by your words you will be condemned."*g*

THE SIGN OF JONAH

12:39–42pp — Lk 11:29–32
12:43–45pp — Lk 11:24–26

38Then some of the Pharisees and teachers of the law said to him, "Teacher, we want to see a sign*h* from you."*i*

39He answered, "A wicked and adulterous generation asks for a sign! But none will be given it except the sign of the prophet Jonah.*j* 40For as Jonah was three days and three nights in the belly of a huge fish,*k* so the Son of Man*l* will be three days and three nights in the heart of the earth.*m* 41The people of Nineveh*n* will stand up at the judgment with this generation and condemn it; for they repented at the preaching of Jonah,*o* and now one*a* greater than Jonah is here. 42The Queen of the South will rise at the judgment with this generation and condemn it; for she came*p* from the ends of the earth to listen to Solomon's wisdom, and now one greater than Solomon is here.

43"When an evil*b* spirit comes out of anyone, it goes through arid places seeking rest and does not find it. 44Then it says, 'I will return to the house I left.' When it arrives, it finds the house unoccupied, swept clean and put in order. 45Then it goes and takes with

---

a 41 Or *something*; also in verse 42   *b 43* Greek *unclean*

12:23 *Son of David.* See note on 9:27.
12:24 See 10:25; Lk 11:19 and notes.
12:25 *kingdom divided against itself.* See note on Lk 11:17.
12:28 *kingdom of God.* See note on 3:2. *has come upon you.* See note on Mk 1:15.

A **12:30** There can be no double-mindedness in our relationship to Jesus (see note on Lk 11:23; cf. Ps 119:113; Mk 9:40; Lk 9:50 and note; Jas 1:8; 4:8).
12:31 *blasphemy against the Spirit will not be forgiven.* The context (vv. 24,28,32) suggests that the unpardonable sin was attributing to Satan Christ's authenticating miracles done in the power of the Holy Spirit (see note on Mk 3:29).
12:32 *Son of Man.* See note on Mk 8:31. *this age...the age to come.* See Eph 1:21 and note.
12:33 See 3:16; cf. Jas 3:11–12.
12:34 *brood of vipers.* In the NT an expression used only by John the Baptist (3:7; Lk 3:7) and Jesus (here; 23:33). In this context it refers to the Pharisees (v. 24). *out of the overflow of the heart the mouth speaks.* See 15:18–19; Pr 4:23 and note. *heart.* See note on Ps 4:7.

12:36 *day of judgment.* At Christ's second coming; sometimes referred to as "that day" (7:22; 2Ti 1:12,18), "the day of slaughter" (Jas 5:5; see note there).
12:38 *sign.* The Pharisees wanted to see a spectacular miracle, preferably in the sky (see Lk 11:16), as the sign that Jesus was the Messiah. Instead, he cites them a "sign" from history. See note on Mk 1:15.

A **12:39** *adulterous.* Referring to spiritual, not physical, adultery, in the sense that their generation had become unfaithful to its spiritual husband (God; see note on Ex 34:15). *sign of the prophet Jonah.* See note on Lk 11:30.
12:40 *three days and three nights.* Including at least part of the first day and part of the third day, a common Jewish reckoning of time. See note on Lk 24:46. *huge fish.* The Greek word does not mean "whale" but rather "sea creature," i.e., a huge fish (see note on Jnh 1:17). *Son of Man.* See note on Mk 8:31.
12:41–42 *one greater than Jonah...one greater than Solomon.* See note on Lk 11:31–32.
12:42 *Queen of the South.* In 1Ki 10:1 she is called the queen of Sheba, a country in southwest Arabia now called Yemen.
12:43–45 See notes on Lk 11:24–25.

it seven other spirits more wicked than itself, and they go in and live there. And the final condition of that person is worse than the first.q That is how it will be with this wicked generation."

JESUS' MOTHER AND BROTHERS

12:46–50pp — Mk 3:31–35; Lk 8:19–21

⁴⁶While Jesus was still talking to the crowd, his motherr and brotherss stood outside, wanting to speak to him. ⁴⁷Someone told him, "Your mother and brothers are standing outside, wanting to speak to you."

⁴⁸He replied to him, "Who is my mother, and who are my brothers?" ⁴⁹Pointing to his disciples, he said, "Here are my mother and my brothers. ⁵⁰For whoever does the will of my Father in heavent is my brother and sister and mother."

THE PARABLE OF THE SOWER

13:1–15pp — Mk 4:1–12; Lk 8:4–10
13:16,17pp — Lk 10:23,24
13:18–23pp — Mk 4:13–20; Lk 8:11–15

13 That same day Jesus went out of the houseu and sat by the lake. ²Such large crowds gathered around him that he got into a boatv and sat in it, while all the people stood on the shore. ³Then he told them many things in parables, saying: "A farmer went out to sow his seed. ⁴As he was scattering the seed, some fell along the path, and the birds came and ate it up. ⁵Some fell on rocky places, where it did not have much soil. It sprang up quickly, because the soil was shallow. ⁶But when the sun came up, the plants were scorched, and they withered because they had no root. ⁷Other seed fell among thorns, which grew up and choked the plants. ⁸Still other seed fell on good soil, where it produced a crop—a hundred,w sixty or thirty times what was sown. ⁹Whoever has ears, let them hear."x

¹⁰The disciples came to him and asked, "Why do you speak to the people in parables?"

¹¹He replied, "The knowledge of the secrets of the kingdom of heaveny has been given to you,z but not to them. ¹²Those who have will be given more, and they will have an abundance. As for those who do not have, even what they have will be taken from them.a ¹³This is why I speak to them in parables:

"Though seeing, they do not see;
    though hearing, they do not hear or understand.b

¹⁴In them is fulfilledc the prophecy of Isaiah:

" 'You will be ever hearing but never understanding;
    you will be ever seeing but never perceiving.
¹⁵For this people's heart has become calloused;
    they hardly hear with their ears,
    and they have closed their eyes.
Otherwise they might see with their eyes,
    hear with their ears,
    understand with their hearts
and turn, and I would heal them.'ad

a 15 Isaiah 6:9,10 (see Septuagint)

12:45 qⁱ 2Pe 2:20
12:46 rⁱ Mt 1:18; 2:11, 13,14,20; Lk 1:43; 2:33,34,48,51; Jn 2:1, 5; 19:25,26
sⁱ Mt 13:55; Jn 2:12; 7:3,5; Ac 1:14; 1Co 9:5; Gal 1:19
12:50 tⁱ Mt 6:10; Jn 15:14
13:1 uⁱ ver 36; Mt 9:28
13:2 vⁱ Lk 5:3
13:8 wⁱ Ge 26:12
13:9 xⁱ S Mt 11:15
13:11 yⁱ S Mt 3:2
zⁱ Mt 11:25; 16:17; 19:11; Jn 6:65; 1Co 2:10,14; Col 1:27; 1Jn 2:20,27
13:12 aⁱ S Mt 25:29
13:13 bⁱ Dt 29:4; Jer 5:21; Eze 12:2
13:14 cⁱ ver 35; S Mt 1:22
13:15 dⁱ Isa 6:9,10; Jn 12:40; Ac 28:26,27; Ro 11:8

12:46 *mother and brothers.* See note on Lk 8:19.

12:50 *whoever does the will of my Father.* See notes on Mk 3:35; Lk 8:21.

13:1 *went out of the house.* See "went into the house" (v. 36). These two phrases determine the setting of Jesus' teaching in vv. 1–35.

13:2 *sat in it.* See note on Mk 4:1.

13:3–9 See vv. 18–23 for the interpretation of this first parable.

13:3 *parables.* Our word "parable" comes from the Greek *parabolē,* which means "a placing beside"—and thus a comparison or an illustration. Its most common use in the NT is for the illustrative stories that Jesus drew from nature and human life. The Synoptic Gospels contain about 30 of these stories. John's Gospel contains no parables but uses other figures of speech (see notes on Mk 4:2; Lk 8:4; see also chart, p. 1752). *to sow his*

seed. See note on Lk 8:5. According to Mk 4:14; Lk 8:11 (see notes there), the seed is the word of God.

13:4–6 See note on Mk 4:3–8.

13:4 *birds.* Satan, "the evil one" (v. 19).

13:5 *rocky places.* Not ground covered with small stones, but shallow soil on top of solid rock. See note on Lk 8:6.

13:8 *a hundred.* See note on Mk 4:8; Lk 8:8.

13:9 *let them hear.* See note on Lk 8:8.

13:10 See note on Lk 8:9.

13:11 *secrets of the kingdom of heaven.* See notes on Mk 4:11; Lk 8:10.

13:13–14 Jesus speaks in parables because of the spiritual dullness of the people (see note on Lk 8:4).

13:13 *Though seeing, they do not see.* See notes on Mk 4:12; Lk 8:10.

13:14–15 See Isa 6:9–10 and notes.

¹⁶But blessed are your eyes because they see, and your ears because they hear.*e* ¹⁷Truly I tell you, many prophets and righteous people longed to see what you see*f* but did not see it, and to hear what you hear but did not hear it.

¹⁸"Listen then to what the parable of the sower means: ¹⁹When people hear the message about the kingdom*g* and do not understand it, the evil one*h* comes and snatches away what was sown in their hearts. This is the seed sown along the path. ²⁰The seed falling on rocky ground refers to people who hear the word and at once receive it with joy. ²¹But since they have no root, they last only a short time. When trouble or persecution comes because of the word, they quickly fall away.*i* ²²The seed falling among the thorns refers to people who hear the word, but the worries of this life and the deceitfulness of wealth*j* choke the word, making it unfruitful. ²³But the seed falling on good soil refers to people who hear the word and understand it. They produce a crop, yielding a hundred, sixty or thirty times what was sown."*k*

THE PARABLE OF THE WEEDS

²⁴Jesus told them another parable: "The kingdom of heaven is like*l* a man who sowed good seed in his field. ²⁵But while everyone was sleeping, his enemy came and sowed weeds among the wheat, and went away. ²⁶When the wheat sprouted and formed heads, then the weeds also appeared.

²⁷"The owner's servants came to him and said, 'Sir, didn't you sow good seed in your field? Where then did the weeds come from?'

²⁸" 'An enemy did this,' he replied.

"The servants asked him, 'Do you want us to go and pull them up?'

²⁹" 'No,' he answered, 'because while you are pulling the weeds, you may uproot the wheat with them. ³⁰Let both grow together until the harvest. At that time I will tell the harvesters: First collect the weeds and tie them in bundles to be burned; then gather the wheat and bring it into my barn.' "*m*

THE PARABLES OF THE MUSTARD SEED AND THE YEAST

13:31,32pp — Mk 4:30–32
13:31–33pp — Lk 13:18–21

³¹He told them another parable: "The kingdom of heaven is like*n* a mustard seed,*o* which a man took and planted in his field. ³²Though it is the smallest of all seeds, yet when it grows, it is the largest of garden plants and becomes a tree, so that the birds come and perch in its branches."*p*

³³He told them still another parable: "The kingdom of heaven is like*q* yeast that a woman took and mixed into about sixty pounds*a* of flour*r* until it worked all through the dough."*s*

³⁴Jesus spoke all these things to the crowd in parables; he did not say anything to them without using a parable.*t* ³⁵So was fulfilled*u* what was spoken through the prophet:

"I will open my mouth in parables,
I will utter things hidden since the creation of the world."*b* *v*

---

a 33 Or about 27 kilograms   *b 35* Psalm 78:2

13:18 *what the parable of the sower means.* Jesus seldom interpreted his parables, but here he does.
13:19 *message.* Cf. Luke's "word of God" (8:11). *evil one.* Satan (the devil; see Mk 4:15; Lk 8:12 and note).
13:21 Cf. 24:10–12; see note on Lk 8:13.
13:22 *the worries of this life and the deceitfulness of wealth.* Lk 8:14 adds life's "pleasures" to these two phrases. *deceitfulness of wealth.* See note on Mk 4:19.
13:23 *understand.* Cf. the Isaiah quotation in vv. 14–15. Matthew uses this word six times in this chapter (here and in vv. 13–15,19,51). *hundred . . . times.* See note on Lk 8:8.
13:24–30 See vv. 36–43 for the interpretation.
13:24 *The kingdom of heaven is like.* This phrase introduces six of the seven parables in this chapter (all but the parable of the sower).
13:25 *weeds.* Probably darnel, which looks very much like wheat while it is young, but can later be distinguished. This parable does not refer to unbelievers in the professing church. The field is the world (v. 38). Thus in this world the people of the kingdom live side by side with the people of the evil one.

13:30 *harvest.* The final judgment (see notes on Joel 3:13; Mk 4:29; Rev 14:15).
13:31–32 Although the kingdom will seem to have an insignificant beginning, it will eventually spread throughout the world (see note on Mk 4:30–34).
13:32 *the smallest . . . the largest.* The mustard seed is not the smallest seed known today, but it was the smallest seed used by farmers and gardeners there and at that time, and under favorable conditions the plant could reach about ten feet in height. *a tree . . . its branches.* Likely an allusion to Da 4:21, suggesting that the kingdom of heaven will expand to world dominion and that people from all nations will find rest in it (cf. Da 2:35,44–45; 7:27; Rev 11:15).
13:33 In the Bible, yeast usually symbolizes that which is evil or unclean (see note on Mk 8:15). Here, however, it is a symbol of growth. As yeast permeates a batch of dough, so the kingdom of heaven spreads through a person's life. Or it may signify the growth of the kingdom by the inner working of the Holy Spirit (using God's word). See note on Lk 13:21.
13:35 *spoken through the prophet.* The quotation is from Ps 78

THE PARABLE OF THE WEEDS EXPLAINED

³⁶Then he left the crowd and went into the house. His disciples came to him and said, "Explain to us the parable[w] of the weeds in the field."

³⁷He answered, "The one who sowed the good seed is the Son of Man.[x] ³⁸The field is the world, and the good seed stands for the people of the kingdom. The weeds are the people of the evil one,[y] ³⁹and the enemy who sows them is the devil. The harvest[z] is the end of the age,[a] and the harvesters are angels.[b]

⁴⁰"As the weeds are pulled up and burned in the fire, so it will be at the end of the age. ⁴¹The Son of Man[c] will send out his angels,[d] and they will weed out of his kingdom everything that causes sin and all who do evil. ⁴²They will throw them into the blazing furnace, where there will be weeping and gnashing of teeth.[e] ⁴³Then the righteous will shine like the sun[f] in the kingdom of their Father. Whoever has ears, let them hear.[g]

THE PARABLES OF THE HIDDEN TREASURE AND THE PEARL

⁴⁴"The kingdom of heaven is like[h] treasure hidden in a field. When a man found it, he hid it again, and then in his joy went and sold all he had and bought that field.[i]

⁴⁵"Again, the kingdom of heaven is like[j] a merchant looking for fine pearls. ⁴⁶When he found one of great value, he went away and sold everything he had and bought it.

THE PARABLE OF THE NET

⁴⁷"Once again, the kingdom of heaven is like[k] a net that was let down into the lake and caught all kinds[l] of fish. ⁴⁸When it was full, the fishermen pulled it up on the shore. Then they sat down and collected the good fish in baskets, but threw the bad away. ⁴⁹This is how it will be at the end of the age. The angels will come and separate the wicked from the righteous[m] ⁵⁰and throw them into the blazing furnace, where there will be weeping and gnashing of teeth.[n]

⁵¹"Have you understood all these things?" Jesus asked.

"Yes," they replied.

⁵²He said to them, "Therefore every teacher of the law who has been instructed about the kingdom of heaven is like the owner of a house who brings out of his storeroom new treasures as well as old."

A PROPHET WITHOUT HONOR

13:54–58pp — Mk 6:1–6

⁵³When Jesus had finished these parables,[o] he moved on from there. ⁵⁴Coming to his hometown, he began teaching the people in their synagogue,[p] and they were amazed.[q] "Where did this man get this wisdom and these miraculous powers?" they asked. ⁵⁵"Isn't this the carpenter's son?[r] Isn't his mother's[s] name Mary, and aren't his brothers[t] James, Joseph, Simon and Judas? ⁵⁶Aren't all his sisters with us? Where then did this man get all these things?" ⁵⁷And they took offense[u] at him.

But Jesus said to them, "Only in their own towns and in their own homes are prophets without honor."[v]

⁵⁸And he did not do many miracles there because of their lack of faith.

13:36 *w* Mt 15:15
13:37 *x* S Mt 8:20
13:38 *y* Jn 8:44, 45; 1Jn 3:10
13:39 *z* Joel 3:13
a Mt 24:3; 28:20
b Rev 14:15
13:41 *c* S Mt 8:20
d Mt 24:31
13:42 *e* S Mt 8:12
13:43 *f* Da 12:3
g S Mt 11:15
13:44 *h* S ver 24
i Isa 55:1; Mt 19:21; Php 3:7,8
13:45 *j* S ver 24
13:47 *k* S ver 24
l Mt 22:10
13:49 *m* Mt 25:32
13:50 *n* S Mt 8:12
13:53 *o* S Mt 7:28
13:54 *p* S Mt 4:23
q S Mt 7:28
13:55 *r* Lk 3:23; Jn 6:42 *s* S Mt 12:46
t S Mt 12:46
13:57 *u* Jn 6:61
v Lk 4:24; Jn 4:44

(see note on 78:2), a psalm ascribed to Asaph, who according to 2Ch 29:30 was a "seer" (prophet).

13:37,41 *Son of Man.* See note on Mk 8:31.

13:42 *blazing furnace.* Often mentioned in connection with the final judgment in apocalyptic literature (see Rev 19:20; 20:14). *weeping and gnashing of teeth.* Occurs six times in Matthew's Gospel (here; v. 50; 8:12; 22:13; 24:51; 25:30) and nowhere else in the NT (but see note on 8:12).

13:43 *the righteous will shine like the sun.* See Da 12:3. *let them hear.* See note on Lk 8:8.

13:44–46 These two parables teach the same truth: The kingdom is of such great value that one should be willing to give up all one has in order to gain it. Jesus did not imply that one can purchase the kingdom with money or good deeds.

13:44 *treasure hidden in a field.* In ancient times it was common to hide treasure in the ground since there were no banks—though there were "bankers" (25:27; see note there).

13:47–51 The parable of the net teaches the same general lesson as the parable of the weeds: There will be a final separation of the righteous and the wicked. The parable of the weeds also emphasizes that we are not to try to make such a separation now. That is entirely the Lord's business (vv. 28–30,41–42).

13:50 See note on v. 42.

13:51 *Yes.* Probably an overstatement by the disciples, especially in view of Jesus' words in 15:16.

13:53 Concludes a teaching section and introduces a narrative section (cf. 7:28–29).

13:54 *his hometown.* Nazareth (see note on 2:23). *teaching the people in their synagogue.* See note on Mk 1:21. *synagogue.* See note on Mk 1:21. *amazed.* See note on 7:28.

13:55 *carpenter's son.* See note on Mk 6:3. Apparently Joseph was not living at the time of this incident. *brothers.* Sons born to Joseph and Mary after the virgin birth of Jesus (see note on Lk 8:19).

13:58 *lack of faith.* The close relationship between faith and miracles is stressed in Matthew's Gospel (cf. 8:10,13; 9:2,22, 28–29).

14:1 *w* Mk 8:15;
Lk 3:1,19; 13:31; 23:7,
8; Ac 4:27; 12:1
x Lk 9:7-9
14:2 *y* S Mt 3:1
14:3 *z* Mt 4:12; 11:2
a Lk 3:19,20
14:4 *b* Lev 18:16;
20:21
14:5 *c* S Mt 11:9
14:10 *d* Mt 17:12
14:12 *e* Ac 8:2
14:14 *f* S Mt 9:36
g S Mt 4:23
14:17 *h* Mt 16:9
14:19 *i* 1Sa 9:13;
Mt 26:26; Mk 8:6;
Lk 9:16; 24:30;
Ac 2:42; 20:7,11;
27:35; 1Co 10:16;
1Ti 4:4

JOHN THE BAPTIST BEHEADED

14:1–12pp — Mk 6:14–29

14 At that time Herod *w* the tetrarch heard the reports about Jesus, *x* 2and he said to his attendants, "This is John the Baptist; *y* he has risen from the dead! That is why miraculous powers are at work in him."

3Now Herod had arrested John and bound him and put him in prison *z* because of Herodias, his brother Philip's wife, *a* 4for John had been saying to him: "It is not lawful for you to have her." *b* 5Herod wanted to kill John, but he was afraid of the people, because they considered him a prophet. *c*

6On Herod's birthday the daughter of Herodias danced for them and pleased Herod so much 7that he promised with an oath to give her whatever she asked. 8Prompted by her mother, she said, "Give me here on a platter the head of John the Baptist." 9The king was distressed, but because of his oaths and his dinner guests, he ordered that her request be granted 10and had John beheaded *d* in the prison. 11His head was brought in on a platter and given to the girl, who carried it to her mother. 12John's disciples came and took his body and buried it. *e* Then they went and told Jesus.

JESUS FEEDS THE FIVE THOUSAND

14:13–21pp — Mk 6:32–44; Lk 9:10–17; Jn 6:1–13
14:13–21Ref — Mt 15:32–38

13When Jesus heard what had happened, he withdrew by boat privately to a solitary place. Hearing of this, the crowds followed him on foot from the towns. 14When Jesus landed and saw a large crowd, he had compassion on them *f* and healed their sick. *g*

15As evening approached, the disciples came to him and said, "This is a remote place, and it's already getting late. Send the crowds away, so they can go to the villages and buy themselves some food."

16Jesus replied, "They do not need to go away. You give them something to eat."

17"We have here only five loaves *h* of bread and two fish," they answered.

18"Bring them here to me," he said. 19And he directed the people to sit down on the grass. Taking the five loaves and the two fish and looking up to heaven, he gave thanks and broke the loaves. *i* Then he gave them to the disciples, and the disciples gave them to the people. 20They all ate and were satisfied, and the disciples picked up twelve basketfuls of broken pieces that were left over. 21The number of those who ate was about five thousand men, besides women and children.

JESUS WALKS ON THE WATER

14:22–33pp — Mk 6:45–51; Jn 6:16–21
14:34–36pp — Mk 6:53–56

22Immediately Jesus made the disciples get into the boat and go on ahead of him to the other side, while he dismissed the crowd. 23After he had dismissed them, he went up on

---

14:1 *tetrarch.* The ruler of a fourth part of a region. "Herod the tetrarch" (Herod Antipas) was one of several sons of Herod the Great. When Herod the Great died, his kingdom was divided among three of his sons (see chart, p. 1608; see also map, p. 1721). Herod Antipas ruled over Galilee and Perea (4 B.C.–A.D. 39). Matthew correctly refers to him as tetrarch here, as Luke regularly does (Lk 3:19; 9:7; Ac 13:1). But in v. 9 Matthew calls him "king"—as Mk 6:14 also does—because that was his popular title among the Galileans, as well as in Rome.
14:2 *John . . . risen from the dead.* See note on Mk 6:16.
14:3 *Herod had arrested John.* See note on Mk 6:17. *Herodias.* A granddaughter of Herod the Great (see chart, p. 1608). First she married her uncle, Herod Philip (Herod the Great also had another son named Philip), who lived in Rome. While a guest in their home, Herod Antipas persuaded Herodias to leave her husband for him. Marriage to one's brother's wife, while the brother was still living, was forbidden by the Mosaic law (Lev 18:16). *Philip's.* The son of Herod the Great and Mariamne, the daughter of Simon the high priest, and thus a half-brother of Herod Antipas, born to Malthace (see chart, p. 1608).
14:6 *daughter of Herodias.* Salome, according to Josephus. She later married her granduncle, the other Philip (son of Herod the Great), who ruled the northern territories (Lk 3:1). At this time

Salome was a young woman of marriageable age. Her dance was doubtless lascivious, and the performance pleased both Herod and his guests.
14:7 *whatever she asked.* See Mk 6:22 and note.
14:8 *platter.* A flat wooden dish on which meat was served.
14:13–21 See 15:37; Mk 6:32–44; Lk 9:10–17; Jn 6:1–13 and notes.
14:13 *what had happened.* Probably refers to vv. 1–2, namely, Herod's response to reports about Jesus. *withdrew . . . to a solitary place.* To avoid the threat of Herod and the pressing of the crowds. Jesus' time had not yet come (see Jn 2:4 and note; cf. Jn 6:15).
14:14 *compassion.* See note on 9:36.
14:20 *twelve basketfuls.* See note on Jn 6:13.
14:21 *besides women and children.* Matthew alone notes this. He was writing to the Jews, who did not permit women and children to eat with men in public. So they were in a place by themselves.
14:22 *made.* The Greek word used here means "to compel" and suggests a crisis. John records that after the miracle of the loaves and fish the crowds "intended to . . . make him [Jesus] king by force" (6:15). This involved a complete misunderstanding of the mission of Jesus. The disciples may have been caught up in the enthusiasm and needed to be removed from the area quickly.

a mountainside by himself to pray.*j* When evening came, he was there alone, ²⁴but the boat was already a considerable distance from land, buffeted by the waves because the wind was against it.

²⁵Shortly before dawn Jesus went out to them, walking on the lake. ²⁶When the disciples saw him walking on the lake, they were terrified. "It's a ghost,"*k* they said, and cried out in fear.

²⁷But Jesus immediately said to them: "Take courage!*l* It is I. Don't be afraid."*m*

²⁸"Lord, if it's you," Peter replied, "tell me to come to you on the water."

²⁹"Come," he said.

Then Peter got down out of the boat, walked on the water and came toward Jesus. ³⁰But when he saw the wind, he was afraid and, beginning to sink, cried out, "Lord, save me!" ³¹Immediately Jesus reached out his hand and caught him. "You of little faith,"*n* he said, "why did you doubt?"

³²And when they climbed into the boat, the wind died down. ³³Then those who were in the boat worshiped him, saying, "Truly you are the Son of God."*o*

³⁴When they had crossed over, they landed at Gennesaret. ³⁵And when the men of that place recognized Jesus, they sent word to all the surrounding country. People brought all their sick to him ³⁶and begged him to let the sick just touch the edge of his cloak,*p* and all who touched him were healed.

THAT WHICH DEFILES
15:1–20pp — Mk 7:1–23

15 Then some Pharisees and teachers of the law came to Jesus from Jerusalem and asked, ²"Why do your disciples break the tradition of the elders? They don't wash their hands before they eat!"*q*

³Jesus replied, "And why do you break the command of God for the sake of your tradition? ⁴For God said, 'Honor your father and mother'*a r* and 'Anyone who curses their father or mother is to be put to death.'*b s* ⁵But you say that if anyone declares that what might have been used to help their father or mother is 'devoted to God,' ⁶they are not to 'honor their father or mother' with it. Thus you nullify the word of God for the sake of your tradition. ⁷You hypocrites! Isaiah was right when he prophesied about you:

⁸ " 'These people honor me with their lips,
but their hearts are far from me.
⁹ They worship me in vain;
their teachings are merely human rules.'*t c u*

¹⁰Jesus called the crowd to him and said, "Listen and understand. ¹¹What goes into your mouth does not defile you,*v* but what comes out of your mouth, that is what defiles you."*w*

¹²Then the disciples came to him and asked, "Do you know that the Pharisees were offended when they heard this?"

¹³He replied, "Every plant that my heavenly Father has not planted*x* will be pulled up

---

a 4 Exodus 20:12; Deut. 5:16   *b* 4 Exodus 21:17; Lev. 20:9   *c* 9 Isaiah 29:13

### Cross references (margin)

14:23 *j* S Lk 3:21
14:26 *k* Lk 24:37
14:27 *l* Mt 9:2;
Ac 23:11 *m* Da 10:12;
Mt 17:7; 28:10;
Lk 1:13,30; 2:10;
Ac 18:9; 23:11;
Rev 1:17
14:31 *n* S Mt 6:30
14:33 *o* Ps 2:7;
S Mt 4:3
14:36 *p* S Mt 9:20
15:2 *q* Lk 11:38
15:4 *r* Ex 20:12;
Dt 5:16; Eph 6:2
s Ex 21:17; Lev 20:9
15:9 *t* Col 2:20-22
u Isa 29:13; Mal 2:2
15:11 *v* S Ac 10:14,
15 *w* ver 18
15:13 *x* Isa 60:21;
61:3

14:23 *pray.* Matthew speaks of Jesus praying only here and in Gethsemane (cf. 26:36–46).
14:24 *considerable distance from land.* See Jn 6:19 and note.
14:25 *Shortly before dawn.* Lit."During the fourth watch of the night," 3:00–6:00 A.M. According to Roman reckoning the night was divided into four watches: (1) 6:00–9:00 P.M., (2) 9:00–midnight, (3) midnight–3:00 A.M. and (4) 3:00–6:00 A.M. (see note on Mk 13:35).The Jews had only three watches during the night: (1) sunset–10:00 P.M., (2) 10:00 P.M.–2:00 A.M. and (3) 2:00 A.M.–sunrise (see Jdg 7:19 and note; 1Sa 11:11). *walking on the lake.* See note on Mk 6:48. *lake.* The Sea of Galilee (see note on Mk 1:16).
14:26 *ghost.* See note on Mk 6:49.
14:27 *It is I.* Lit."I am" (cf. Ex 3:14; Isa 43:10; 51:12; Jn 8:58 and note).
14:28 *if it's you.* A condition assumed to be true. Peter knew it was Jesus, and that is why he stepped out of the boat onto the water in the first place.
14:31 *You of little faith.* See note on 6:30. *why did you doubt?* See Jas 1:5–8.
14:33 *Son of God.* This is the first time the disciples use the full title in addressing Jesus (cf. 3:17, where God called him "my

Son"; see also Jn 3:16 and note).
14:34 *Gennesaret.* Either the narrow plain (about four miles long and less than two miles wide) on the west side of the Sea of Galilee near the north end (north of Magdala), or a town in the plain.The plain was considered a garden spot, fertile and well watered.
14:36 *just touch the edge of his cloak.* See note on Mk 5:28.
15:2 *tradition of the elders.* After the Babylonian exile, the Jewish rabbis began to make meticulous rules and regulations governing the daily life of the people.These were interpretations and applications of the law of Moses, handed down from generation to generation. In Jesus' day this "tradition of the elders" was in oral form. It was not until c. A.D. 200 that it was put into writing in the Mishnah. *wash.* See note on Mk 7:3.
15:5–6 See notes on Mk 7:11,13.
15:7–20 See Mk 7:6–23 and notes.
15:7 *hypocrites.* See note on 6:2.
15:8–9 See Isa 29:13 and note.
15:13 *Every plant that my heavenly Father has not planted.* Probably refers to the Pharisees and teachers of the law who were in Jesus' audience (vv. 1,12).

15:14 ʸ Mt 23:16, 24; Ro 2:19 ᶻ Lk 6:39
15:15 ᵃ Mt 13:36
15:16 ᵇ Mt 16:9
15:18 ᶜ Mt 12:34; Lk 6:45; Jas 3:6
15:19 ᵈ Gal 5:19-21
15:20 ᵉ Ro 14:14
15:21 ᶠ S Mt 11:21
15:22 ᵍ S Mt 9:27 ʰ S Mt 4:24
15:24 ⁱ Mt 10:6,23; Ro 15:8
15:25 ʲ S Mt 8:2
15:28 ᵏ S Mt 9:22
15:30 ˡ S Mt 4:23
15:31 ᵐ S Mt 9:8
15:32 ⁿ S Mt 9:36
15:36 ᵒ S Mt 14:19
15:37 ᵖ Mt 16:10

by the roots. ¹⁴Leave them; they are blind guides.ᵃʸ If the blind lead the blind, both will fall into a pit."ᶻ

¹⁵Peter said, "Explain the parable to us."ᵃ

¹⁶"Are you still so dull?"ᵇ Jesus asked them. ¹⁷"Don't you see that whatever enters the mouth goes into the stomach and then out of the body? ¹⁸But the things that come out of the mouth come from the heart,ᶜ and these defile you. ¹⁹For out of the heart come evil thoughts, murder, adultery, sexual immorality, theft, false testimony, slander.ᵈ ²⁰These are what defile you;ᵉ but eating with unwashed hands does not defile you."

THE FAITH OF A CANAANITE WOMAN
15:21–28pp — Mk 7:24–30

²¹Leaving that place, Jesus withdrew to the region of Tyre and Sidon.ᶠ ²²A Canaanite woman from that vicinity came to him, crying out, "Lord, Son of David,ᵍ have mercy on me! My daughter is demon-possessed and suffering terribly."ʰ

²³Jesus did not answer a word. So his disciples came to him and urged him, "Send her away, for she keeps crying out after us."

²⁴He answered, "I was sent only to the lost sheep of Israel."ⁱ

²⁵The woman came and knelt before him.ʲ "Lord, help me!" she said.

²⁶He replied, "It is not right to take the children's bread and toss it to the dogs."

²⁷"Yes it is, Lord," she said. "Even the dogs eat the crumbs that fall from their master's table."

²⁸Then Jesus said to her, "Woman,ᵇ you have great faith!ᵏ Your request is granted." And her daughter was healed from that very hour.

JESUS FEEDS THE FOUR THOUSAND
15:29–31pp — Mk 7:31–37
15:32–39pp — Mk 8:1–10
15:32–39Ref — Mt 14:13–21

²⁹Jesus left there and went along the Sea of Galilee. Then he went up on a mountainside and sat down. ³⁰Great crowds came to him, bringing the lame, the blind, the crippled, the mute and many others, and laid them at his feet; and he healed them.ˡ ³¹The people were amazed when they saw the mute speaking, the crippled made well, the lame walking and the blind seeing. And they praised the God of Israel.ᵐ

³²Jesus called his disciples to him and said, "I have compassion for these people;ⁿ they have already been with me three days and have nothing to eat. I do not want to send them away hungry, or they may collapse on the way."

³³His disciples answered, "Where could we get enough bread in this remote place to feed such a crowd?"

³⁴"How many loaves do you have?" Jesus asked.

"Seven," they replied, "and a few small fish."

³⁵He told the crowd to sit down on the ground. ³⁶Then he took the seven loaves and the fish, and when he had given thanks, he broke themᵒ and gave them to the disciples, and they in turn to the people. ³⁷They all ate and were satisfied. Afterward the disciples picked up seven basketfuls of broken pieces that were left over.ᵖ ³⁸The number of those who ate

---

ᵃ 14 Some manuscripts *blind guides of the blind*   ᵇ 28 The Greek for *Woman* does not denote any disrespect.

15:15 *parable.* See note on 13:3. The parable Peter refers to is found in v. 11.

15:21 *Tyre.* See note on Mk 7:24. *Sidon.* About 25 miles north of Tyre.

15:22 *Canaanite.* A term found many times in the OT but only here in the NT. In NT times there was no country known as Canaan. Some think this was the Semitic manner of referring to the people of Phoenicia at this time. Mark says the woman was "a Greek, born in Syrian Phoenicia" (7:26; see note there). *Son of David.* See note on 9:27; shows that this pagan woman had some recognition of Jesus' Messianic claims. *demon-possessed.* See Mk 1:23; Lk 4:33 and notes.

15:26 *children's.* "The lost sheep of Israel" (v. 24). *bread.* God's covenanted blessings. *dogs.* Gentiles. Jesus' point was that the gospel was to be given first to Jews. The woman understood Jesus' implication and was willing to settle for "crumbs" (v. 27). Jesus rewarded her "great faith" (v. 28).

15:28 Jesus was pleased with the woman's reply (v. 27). It revealed not only her wit but also her faith and humility. *Woman.* See TNIV text note; see also note on Jn 2:4.

15:29 *there.* The "region of Tyre and Sidon" (v. 21; see note on Mk 7:31).

15:31 *amazed.* Cf. Mk 1:22 and note.

15:32–39 See notes on Mk 8:1–10.

15:32 *compassion.* See note on 9:36.

15:36 *when he had given thanks.* The Jewish practice at meals (see 1Ti 4:3–5).

15:37 The feeding of the 5,000 is recorded in all four Gospels, but the feeding of the 4,000 is only in Matthew and Mark. The 12 baskets mentioned in the accounts of the feeding of the 5,000 were possibly the lunch baskets of the 12 apostles. The 12 baskets of leftovers may also suggest a sufficient abundance to feed all 12 tribes of Israel (cf. note on Ex 25:30). The seven baskets mentioned here were probably larger.

was four thousand men, besides women and children. ³⁹After Jesus had sent the crowd away, he got into the boat and went to the vicinity of Magadan.

THE DEMAND FOR A SIGN
16:1–12pp — Mk 8:11–21

16 The Pharisees and Sadducees*q* came to Jesus and tested him by asking him to show them a sign from heaven.*r* ²He replied,*a* "When evening comes, you say, 'It will be fair weather, for the sky is red,' ³and in the morning, 'Today it will be stormy, for the sky is red and overcast.' You know how to interpret the appearance of the sky, but you cannot interpret the signs of the times.*s* ⁴A wicked and adulterous generation looks for a sign, but none will be given it except the sign of Jonah."*t* Jesus then left them and went away.

THE YEAST OF THE PHARISEES AND SADDUCEES

⁵When they went across the lake, the disciples forgot to take bread. ⁶"Be careful," Jesus said to them. "Be on your guard against the yeast of the Pharisees and Sadducees."*u*

⁷They discussed this among themselves and said, "It is because we didn't bring any bread."

⁸Aware of their discussion, Jesus asked, "You of little faith,*v* why are you talking among yourselves about having no bread? ⁹Do you still not understand? Don't you remember the five loaves for the five thousand, and how many basketfuls you gathered?*w* ¹⁰Or the seven loaves for the four thousand, and how many basketfuls you gathered?*x* ¹¹How is it you don't understand that I was not talking to you about bread? But be on your guard against the yeast of the Pharisees and Sadducees." ¹²Then they understood that he was not telling them to guard against the yeast used in bread, but against the teaching of the Pharisees and Sadducees.*y*

PETER DECLARES THAT JESUS IS THE MESSIAH
16:13–16pp — Mk 8:27–29; Lk 9:18–20

¹³When Jesus came to the region of Caesarea Philippi, he asked his disciples, "Who do people say the Son of Man is?"

¹⁴They replied, "Some say John the Baptist;*z* others say Elijah; and still others, Jeremiah or one of the prophets."*a*

¹⁵"But what about you?" he asked. "Who do you say I am?"

¹⁶Simon Peter answered, "You are the Messiah, the Son of the living God."*b*

¹⁷Jesus replied, "Blessed are you, Simon son of Jonah, for this was not revealed to you by flesh and blood,*c* but by my Father in heaven.*d* ¹⁸And I tell you that you are Peter,*b*,*e* and

---

a 2 Some early manuscripts do not have the rest of verse 2 and all of verse 3. *b* 18 The Greek for *Peter* means *rock.*

16:1 *q* S Ac 4:1
r S Mt 12:38
16:3 *s* Lk 12:54-56
16:4 *t* Mt 12:39
16:6 *u* Lk 12:1
16:8 *v* S Mt 6:30
16:9 *w* Mt 14:17-21
16:10 *x* Mt 15:34-38
16:12 *y* S Ac 4:1
16:14 *z* S Mt 3:1
a Mk 6:15; Jn 1:21
16:16 *b* S Mt 4:3;
Ps 42:2; Jer 10:10;
Ac 14:15; 2Co 6:16;
1Th 1:9; 1Ti 3:15;
Heb 10:31; 12:22
16:17 *c* 1Co 15:50;
Eph 6:12; Heb 2:14
d S Mt 13:11
16:18 *e* Jn 1:42

15:39 *Magadan.* Also called Magdala, the home of Mary Magdalene. Mk 8:10 has "Dalmanutha."
16:1 *Pharisees and Sadducees.* See note on 3:7. Normally these two groups were opponents, but they had a common enemy in Jesus. *sign from heaven.* See note on Mk 8:11.
16:4 *sign of Jonah.* See 12:39–40 and note on Lk 11:30.
16:6 *yeast of the Pharisees and Sadducees.* See v. 12; see also note on Mk 8:15.
16:7 *because we didn't bring any bread.* Apparently the disciples took Jesus' statement about "yeast" (v. 6) to somehow relate to their being short of bread. Perhaps they thought they would be required to bake bread when they arrived at the other side of the lake and were being warned by Jesus not to use any yeast provided by the spiritually contaminated religious leaders.
16:8 *little faith.* See 14:31 and note on 6:30.
16:12 Matthew often explains the meaning of Jesus' words (cf. 17:13).
16:13 *Caesarea Philippi.* To be distinguished from the magnificent city of Caesarea, which Herod the Great had built on the Mediterranean coast. Caesarea Philippi, rebuilt by Herod's son Philip (who named it after Tiberius Caesar and himself), was north of the Sea of Galilee near the slopes of Mount Hermon on what is today the Golan Heights. Originally it was called Paneas (the ancient name survives today as Banias) in honor of the Greek god Pan, whose shrine was located there. The region was

especially pagan. *Who do people say the Son of Man is?* See note on Lk 9:18. *Son of Man.* See note on Mk 8:31.
16:14 *John the Baptist.* See Mk 6:16 and note. *Elijah.* See Mk 6:15 and note.
16:16 *Peter answered.* See note on Lk 9:20. *Messiah.* See TNIV text note on 1:1; see also note on Jn 1:25. In the OT *Messiah* is used of anyone who was anointed with the holy oil, such as the priests and kings of Israel (e.g., Ex 29:7,21; 1Sa 10;1,6; 16:13; 2Sa 1:14,16). The word carries the idea of being chosen by God, consecrated to his service, and endowed with his power to accomplish the assigned task. Toward the end of the OT period the word assumed a special meaning. It denoted the ideal king anointed and empowered by God to rescue his people from their enemies and establish his righteous kingdom (Da 9:25–26). The ideas that clustered around the title *Messiah* tended to be political and national in nature. Probably for that reason Jesus seldom used the term. When he did accept it as applied to himself, he did so with reservations (cf. Mk 8:27–30; 14:61–63).
16:17 *Simon son of Jonah.* In Jn 1:42 Jesus identifies Peter as "Simon son of John." Probably Simon Peter was the son of Johanan (the Hebrew form of the name), and Jonah is an Aramaic abbreviation of Johanan, while John is from the Greek form of the name. *flesh and blood.* See notes on 1Co 15:50; Gal 1:16.
16:18 *Peter . . . rock . . . church.* In the Greek "Peter" is *petros* ("detached stone"), and "rock" is *petra* ("bedrock"). Several interpre-

16:18 f S Eph 2:20
16:19 g Isa 22:22;
Rev 3:7 h Mt 18:18;
Jn 20:23
16:20 i S Mk 8:30
16:21 j S Lk 9:51
k Ps 22:6; Isa 53:3;
Mt 26:67,68;
Mk 10:34; Lk 17:25;
Jn 18:22,23; 19:3
l Mt 27:1,2 m Ac 2:23;
3:13 n Hos 6:2;
Mt 12:40; Lk 24:21,
46; Jn 2:19; 1Co 15:3,
4 o Mt 17:22,23;
27:63; Mk 9:31;
Lk 9:22; 18:31-33;
24:6,7
16:23 p S Mt 4:10
16:24 q Mt 10:38;
Lk 14:27
16:25 r S Jn 12:25
16:27 s S Mt 8:20
t S Lk 17:30; Jn 14:3;
Ac 1:11; S 1Co 1:7;
S 1Th 2:19; 4:16;
S Rev 1:7; 22:7,12,20
u 2Ch 6:23; Job 34:11;
Ps 62:12; Jer 17:10;
Eze 18:20; 1Co 3:12-
15; 2Co 5:10;
Rev 22:12
17:1 v S Mt 4:21

on this rock I will build my church,f and the gates of deatha will not overcome it. 19I will give you the keysg of the kingdom of heaven; whatever you bind on earth will beb bound in heaven, and whatever you loose on earth will beb loosed in heaven."h 20Then he ordered his disciples not to tell anyonei that he was the Messiah.

JESUS PREDICTS HIS DEATH

16:21–28pp — Mk 8:31—9:1; Lk 9:22–27

21From that time on Jesus began to explain to his disciples that he must go to Jerusalemj and suffer many thingsk at the hands of the elders, the chief priests and the teachers of the law,l and that he must be killedm and on the third dayn be raised to life.o

22Peter took him aside and began to rebuke him. "Never, Lord!" he said. "This shall never happen to you!"

23Jesus turned and said to Peter, "Get behind me, Satan!p You are a stumbling block to me; you do not have in mind the concerns of God, but merely human concerns."

24Then Jesus said to his disciples, "Whoever wants to be my disciple must deny themselves and take up their cross and follow me.q 25For whoever wants to save their lifec will lose it, but whoever loses their life for me will find it.r 26What good will it be for you to gain the whole world, yet forfeit your soul? Or what can you give in exchange for your soul? 27For the Son of Mans is going to comet in his Father's glory with his angels, and then he will reward everyone according to what they have done.u

28"Truly I tell you, some who are standing here will not taste death before they see the Son of Man coming in his kingdom."

THE TRANSFIGURATION

17:1–8pp — Lk 9:28–36
17:1–13pp — Mk 9:2–13

17 After six days Jesus took with him Peter, James and Johnv the brother of James, and led them up a high mountain by themselves. 2There he was transfigured before them. His face shone like the sun, and his clothes became as white as the light. 3Just then there appeared before them Moses and Elijah, talking with Jesus.

---

a 18 Greek *Hades*   b 19 Or *will have been*   c 25 The Greek word means either *life* or *soul*; also in verse 26.

---

tations have been given to these words: The bedrock on which the church is built is (1) Christ; (2) Peter's confession of faith in Jesus as the Messiah (v. 16); (3) Christ's teachings— one of the great emphases of Matthew's Gospel; (4) Peter himself, understood in terms of his role on the day of Pentecost (Ac 2), the Cornelius incident (Ac 10) and his leadership among the apostles. Eph 2:20 indicates that the church is "built on the foundation of the apostles and prophets" (see note on Jn 1:42). *church.* In the Gospels this word is used only by Matthew (here and twice in 18:17). In the Septuagint (the pre-Christian Greek translation of the OT) it is used for the congregation of Israel. In Greek circles of Jesus' day it indicated the assembly of free, voting citizens in a city (cf. Ac 19:32,39,41). *death.* Greek *Hades,* the place of departed spirits, generally equivalent to the Hebrew *Sheol* (see note on Ge 37:35). The "gates of Hades" may mean the "powers of death," i.e., all forces opposed to Christ and his kingdom (but see note on Job 17:16).

16:19 *keys.* Perhaps Peter used these keys on the day of Pentecost (Ac 2) when he announced that the door of the kingdom was unlocked to Jews and proselytes and later when he acknowledged that it was also opened to Gentiles (Ac 10; cf. Isa 22:22; Rev 3:7 and notes). *bind ... loose.* Not authority to determine, but to announce, guilt or innocence (see 18:18 and context; cf. Jn 20:23 and note; Ac 5:3,9).

16:20 *not to tell.* Because of the false concepts of the Jews, who looked for an exclusively national and political Messiah, Jesus didn't want to precipitate a revolution against Rome (see notes on 8:4; Lk 9:21).

16:21 *began.* The beginning of a new emphasis in Jesus' ministry. Instead of teaching the crowds in parables, he concentrated on preparing the disciples for his coming suffering and death.

16:22 *Peter ... began to rebuke him.* See note on Mk 8:32.

16:23 *Satan.* A loanword from Hebrew, meaning "adversary" or

"accuser" (see TNIV text note on Job 1:6; see also notes on Mk 8:33; Rev 2:9).

16:24 See note on Mk 8:34. *take up your cross.* See note on 10:38 (Lk 9:23 adds "daily"; see also note there).

16:25 *save their life.* See note on Mk 8:35. *whoever loses their life.* See note on Lk 9:24.

16:26 *whole world.* See note on Mk 8:36. *soul.* See note on 10:28.

16:27 *Son of Man.* See note on Mk 8:31. *is going to come.* The second coming of Christ. *in his Father's glory.* See note on Mk 8:38; cf. Jn 17:1–5. *according to what they have done.* See Ps 62:12 and note; see also notes on Ro 2:1–16; 2:6–8.

16:28 There are two main interpretations of this verse: 1. It is a prediction of the transfiguration, which happened a week later (17:1) and which demonstrated that Jesus will return "in his Father's glory" (16:27). 2. It refers to the Son of Man's authority and kingly reign in his post-resurrection church. Some of his disciples will witness—even participate in—this as described in the book of Acts. The context seems to favor the first view. See note on 2Pe 1:16.

17:1–9 The transfiguration was: (1) a revelation of the glory of the Son of God, a glory hidden now but to be fully revealed when he returns (see 2Th 1:10); (2) a confirmation of the difficult teaching given to the disciples at Caesarea Philippi (16:13–20); and (3) a beneficial experience for the disciples, who were discouraged after having been reminded so recently of Jesus' impending suffering and death (16:21). See notes on Mk 9:2–7; Lk 9:28–35.

17:1 *six days.* Mark also says "six days" (Mk 9:2), counting just the days between Peter's confession and the transfiguration, whereas Luke, counting all the days involved, says, "About eight days" (Lk 9:28). *Peter, James and John.* See 26:37; Mk 5:37 and note. *high mountain.* See note on Lk 9:28. *by themselves.* Luke adds "to pray" (Lk 9:28).

⁴Peter said to Jesus, "Lord, it is good for us to be here. If you wish, I will put up three shelters—one for you, one for Moses and one for Elijah."

⁵While he was still speaking, a bright cloud covered them, and a voice from the cloud said, "This is my Son, whom I love; with him I am well pleased.ʷ Listen to him!"ˣ

⁶When the disciples heard this, they fell facedown to the ground, terrified. ⁷But Jesus came and touched them. "Get up," he said. "Don't be afraid."ʸ ⁸When they looked up, they saw no one except Jesus.

⁹As they were coming down the mountain, Jesus instructed them, "Don't tell anyoneᶻ what you have seen, until the Son of Manᵃ has been raised from the dead."ᵇ

¹⁰The disciples asked him, "Why then do the teachers of the law say that Elijah must come first?"

¹¹Jesus replied, "To be sure, Elijah comes and will restore all things.ᶜ ¹²But I tell you, Elijah has already come,ᵈ and they did not recognize him, but have done to him everything they wished.ᵉ In the same way the Son of Man is going to sufferᶠ at their hands." ¹³Then the disciples understood that he was talking to them about John the Baptist.ᵍ

JESUS HEALS A DEMON-POSSESSED BOY

17:14–19pp — Mk 9:14–28; Lk 9:37–42

¹⁴When they came to the crowd, a man approached Jesus and knelt before him. ¹⁵"Lord, have mercy on my son," he said. "He has seizuresʰ and is suffering greatly. He often falls into the fire or into the water. ¹⁶I brought him to your disciples, but they could not heal him."

¹⁷"You unbelieving and perverse generation," Jesus replied, "how long shall I stay with you? How long shall I put up with you? Bring the boy here to me." ¹⁸Jesus rebuked the demon, and it came out of the boy, and he was healed from that moment.

¹⁹Then the disciples came to Jesus in private and asked, "Why couldn't we drive it out?"

²⁰[21]He replied, "Because you have so little faith. Truly I tell you, if you have faithⁱ as small as a mustard seed,ʲ you can say to this mountain, 'Move from here to there,' and it will move.ᵏ Nothing will be impossible for you."

JESUS PREDICTS HIS DEATH A SECOND TIME

²²When they came together in Galilee, he said to them, "The Son of Manˡ is going to be delivered over to human hands. ²³He will be killed,ᵐ and on the third dayⁿ he will be raised to life."ᵒ And the disciples were filled with grief.

THE TEMPLE TAX

²⁴After Jesus and his disciples arrived in Capernaum, the collectors of the two-drachma temple taxᵖ came to Peter and asked, "Doesn't your teacher pay the temple tax?"

²⁵"Yes, he does," he replied.

**Cross references (right margin):**

17:5 ʷS Mt 3:17
ˣAc 3:22,23
17:7 ʸS Mt 14:27
17:9 ᶻS Mk 8:30
ᵃS Mt 8:20
ᵇS Mt 16:21
17:11 ᶜMal 4:6; Lk 1:16,17
17:12 ᵈS Mt 11:14
ᵉMt 14:3,10
ᶠS Mt 16:21
17:13 ᵍS Mt 3:1
17:15 ʰMt 4:24
17:20[21] ⁱS Mt 21:21 / Mt 13:31; Lk 17:6
ᵏ1Co 13:2
17:22 ˡS Mt 8:20
17:23 ᵐAc 2:23; 3:13 ⁿS Mt 16:21
ᵒS Mt 16:21
17:24 ᵖEx 30:13

17:2 *he was transfigured.* His appearance changed. The three disciples saw Jesus in his glorified state (see Jn 17:5; 2Pe 1:17).
17:3 *Moses and Elijah.* Moses appears as the representative of the old covenant and the promise of salvation, which was soon to be fulfilled in the death of Jesus. Elijah appears as the appointed restorer of all things (Mal 4:5–6; Mk 9:11–13). Lk 9:31 says that they talked about Christ's death. See note on Lk 9:30.
17:4 *three shelters.* See notes on Mk 9:5; Lk 9:33.
17:5 *bright cloud.* Signifying the presence of God (see Ex 13:21; 19:16 and notes; 24:15–16; 34:5; 40:34–38; see also note on Mk 9:7). *them.* Jesus, Moses and Elijah. *This is my Son, whom I love; with him I am well pleased.* The same words spoken from heaven at Jesus' baptism (see 3:17 and note). No mere man, but the very Son of God, was transfigured. *Listen to him.* See note on Mk 9:7.
17:6 *terrified.* Primarily with a sense of awe at the presence and majesty of God.
17:9 *Don't tell anyone.* See note on Mk 9:9; cf. Lk 9:36.
17:10 Traditional Jewish eschatology, based on Mal 4:5–6, held that Elijah must appear before the coming of the Messiah. The disciples reasoned that if Jesus really was the Messiah, as the transfiguration proved him to be, why had not Elijah appeared?
17:12 *In the same way.* As John the Baptist was not recognized and was killed, so Jesus would be rejected and killed (see 14:1–12).

17:13 See note on 16:12.
17:15 *seizures.* See note on 4:24.
17:17 *unbelieving.* See v. 20 and note.
17:18 Not all seizures were the result of demon possession, but these were.
17:20[21] *little faith.* Not so much the quantity of their faith as its quality—a faith that is bathed in prayer (see Mk 9:29). *mustard seed.* See 13:31–32 and notes. *say to this mountain, 'Move from here to there.'* A proverbial statement meaning to remove great difficulties (cf. Isa 54:10; Zec 4:7 and note; 1Co 13:2). In this context it probably refers to removing the problems associated with the work of the kingdom. Verse 21 ("But this kind does not go out except by prayer and fasting") was probably added here by a later copyist, who thus harmonized this passage with the parallel in Mk 9:29 (see TNIV text note there). It is omitted here by an impressive combination of early manuscripts and other ancient witnesses.
17:22 The second prediction of Christ's death, the first being in 16:21. *Galilee.* See note on Mk 9:30. *Son of Man.* See note on Mk 8:31.
17:24 *Capernaum.* See note on Mk 4:13. *two-drachma temple tax.* The annual temple tax required of every male 20 years of age and older (Ex 30:13; 2Ch 24:9; Ne 10:32). It was worth half a shekel (approximately two days' wages) and was used for the upkeep of the temple.

17:25 *a* Mt 22:17-
21; Ro 13:7
17:27 *r* Jn 6:61
18:3 *s* Mt 19:14;
1Pe 2:2 *t* S Mt 3:2
18:4 *u* S Mk 9:35
18:5 *v* Mt 10:40
18:6 *w* Mk 9:42;
Lk 17:2
18:7 *x* Lk 17:1
18:8 *y* S Mt 5:29
18:9 *z* S Mt 5:29
a S Mt 5:22
18:10[11] *b* Ge 48:1
6; Ps 34:7; Ac 12:11,
15; Heb 1:14
18:15 *c* Lev 19:17;
Lk 17:3; Gal 6:1;
Jas 5:19,20

When Peter came into the house, Jesus was the first to speak. "What do you think, Simon?" he asked. "From whom do the kings of the earth collect duty and taxes *q*—from their own children or from others?"

26 "From others," Peter answered.

"Then the children are exempt," Jesus said to him. 27 "But so that we may not cause offense, *r* go to the lake and throw out your line. Take the first fish you catch; open its mouth and you will find a four-drachma coin. Take it and give it to them for my tax and yours."

THE GREATEST IN THE KINGDOM OF HEAVEN

18:1–5pp — Mk 9:33–37; Lk 9:46–48

18 At that time the disciples came to Jesus and asked, "Who, then, is the greatest in the kingdom of heaven?"

2 He called a little child, whom he placed among them. 3 And he said: "Truly I tell you, unless you change and become like little children, *s* you will never enter the kingdom of heaven. *t* 4 Therefore, whoever takes a humble place—becoming like this child— is the greatest in the kingdom of heaven. *u* 5 And whoever welcomes one such child in my name welcomes me. *v*

CAUSING TO STUMBLE

6 "If anyone causes one of these little ones—those who believe in me—to stumble, it would be better for them if a large millstone were hung around their neck and they were drowned in the depths of the sea. *w* 7 Woe to the world because of the things that cause people to stumble! Such things must come, but woe to the person through whom they come! *x* 8 If your hand or your foot causes you to stumble, *y* cut it off and throw it away. It is better for you to enter life maimed or crippled than to have two hands or two feet and be thrown into eternal fire. 9 And if your eye causes you to stumble, *z* gouge it out and throw it away. It is better for you to enter life with one eye than to have two eyes and be thrown into the fire of hell. *a*

THE PARABLE OF THE WANDERING SHEEP

18:12–14pp — Lk 15:4–7

10[11] "See that you do not despise one of these little ones. For I tell you that their angels *b* in heaven always see the face of my Father in heaven.

12 "What do you think? If a man owns a hundred sheep, and one of them wanders away, will he not leave the ninety-nine on the hills and go to look for the one that wandered off? 13 And if he finds it, truly I tell you, he is happier about that one sheep than about the ninety-nine that did not wander off. 14 In the same way your Father in heaven is not willing that any of these little ones should perish.

DEALING WITH SIN IN THE CHURCH

15 "If a brother or sister sins, *a* go and point out the fault, *c* just between the two of you. If they listen to you, you have won them over. 16 But if they will not listen, take one or two

a 15 Some manuscripts *sins against you*

17:25 *What do you think ...?* Jesus frequently asks this question in Matthew's Gospel (18:12; 21:28; 22:17,42).

17:26 *the children are exempt.* The implication is that Peter and the rest of the disciples belonged to God's royal household, but unbelieving Jews did not (see 21:43).

A **17:27** *not cause offense.* The Son of God, who controls the entire universe (see Heb 1:2–3 and note), is careful not to offend (cf. 11:28–30; 12:20).

18:1 *Who ... is the greatest ...?* See v. 4 and note on Lk 9:46.

18:3 *like little children.* Trusting and unpretentious.

18:4 *greatest.* See note on Lk 9:48.

18:6,10,14 *little ones.* All believers, regardless of age (see Mk 9:42 and note; Lk 17:2).

18:6 *large millstone.* Lit. "millstone of a donkey," i.e., a millstone turned by a donkey—far larger and heavier than the small millstones (24:41) used by women each morning.

A **18:8–9** Hyperbole: Deal as drastically as necessary with sin in order to remove it from your life. This calls for self-discipline. See note on 5:29–30.

18:8 *thrown into eternal fire.* See Rev 19:20 and note; 20:15.

18:9 *hell.* See note on 5:22.

18:10[11] *their angels.* Guardian angels not exclusively for children, but for God's people in general (Ps 34:7; 91:11; Heb 1:14). *always see the face of.* Have constant access to. Some late manuscripts add v. 11: "The Son of Man came to save what was lost." But it is not in any of the earliest manuscripts. A later scribe doubtless copied it here from Lk 19:10, which would explain why it appears only in some late manuscripts.

18:12–14 The parable of the lost/wandering (see vv. 12–13) sheep is also found in Lk 15:3–7. There it applies to unbelievers, here to believers. Jesus used the same parable to teach different truths in different situations.

18:12 *sheep.* See note on Lk 15:4.

18:13 Cf. the "father" in the parable of the lost son (Lk 15:31–32).

18:14 *not willing that any ... should perish.* See 1Ti 2:4; 2Pe 3:9 and notes.

18:15 *brother or sister.* Fellow believer. *just between the two of you.* To protect the brother from the harm caused by gossip.

others along, so that 'every matter may be established by the testimony of two or three witnesses.'ª ᵈ ¹⁷If they still refuse to listen, tell it to the church;ᵉ and if they refuse to listen even to the church, treat them as you would a pagan or a tax collector.ᶠ

¹⁸"Truly I tell you, whatever you bind on earth will beᵇ bound in heaven, and whatever you loose on earth will beᵇ loosed in heaven.ᵍ

¹⁹"Again, truly I tell you that if two of you on earth agree about anything you ask for, it will be done for youʰ by my Father in heaven. ²⁰For where two or three come together in my name, there am I with them."ⁱ

THE PARABLE OF THE UNMERCIFUL SERVANT

²¹Then Peter came to Jesus and asked, "Lord, how many times shall I forgive someone who sins against me?ʲ Up to seven times?"ᵏ

²²Jesus answered, "I tell you, not seven times, but seventy-seven times.ᶜˡ

²³"Therefore, the kingdom of heaven is likeᵐ a king who wanted to settle accountsⁿ with his servants. ²⁴As he began the settlement, a man who owed him ten thousand bags of goldᵈ was brought to him. ²⁵Since he was not able to pay,ᵒ the master ordered that he and his wife and his children and all that he had be soldᵖ to repay the debt.

²⁶"The servant fell on his knees before him.�q 'Be patient with me,' he begged, 'and I will pay back everything.' ²⁷The servant's master took pity on him, canceled the debt and let him go.

²⁸"But when that servant went out, he found one of his fellow servants who owed him a hundred silver coins.ᵉ He grabbed him and began to choke him. 'Pay back what you owe me!' he demanded.

²⁹"His fellow servant fell to his knees and begged him, 'Be patient with me, and I will pay you back.'

³⁰"But he refused. Instead, he went off and had the man thrown into prison until he could pay the debt. ³¹When the other servants saw what had happened, they were greatly distressed and went and told their master everything that had happened.

³²"Then the master called the servant in. 'You wicked servant,' he said, 'I canceled all that debt of yours because you begged me to. ³³Shouldn't you have had mercy on your fellow servant just as I had on you?' ³⁴In anger his master handed him over to the jailers to be tortured, until he should pay back all he owed.

³⁵"This is how my heavenly Father will treat each of you unless you forgive a brother or sister from your heart."ʳ

DIVORCE

19:1–9pp — Mk 10:1–12

19

When Jesus had finished saying these things,ˢ he left Galilee and went into the region of Judea to the other side of the Jordan. ²Large crowds followed him,ᵗ and he healed them there.

³Some Pharisees came to him to test him. They asked, "Is it lawful for a man to divorce his wifeᵘ for any and every reason?"

ᵃ 16 Deut. 19:15   ᵇ 18 Or *will have been*   ᶜ 22 Or *seventy times seven*   ᵈ 24 Greek *ten thousand talents*; a talent was worth about 20 years of a day laborer's wages.   ᵉ 28 Greek *a hundred denarii*; a denarius was the daily wage of a day laborer (see Matt. 20:2).

18:16 ᵈNu 35:30; Dt 17:6; 19:15; Jn 8:17; 2Co 13:1; 1Ti 5:19; Heb 10:28
18:17 ᵉ1Co 6:1-6 ᶠS Ro 16:17
18:18 ᵍMt 16:19; Jn 20:23
18:19 ʰS Mt 7:7
18:20 ⁱS Mt 28:20
18:21 ʲS Mt 6:14 ᵏLk 17:4
18:22 ˡGe 4:24
18:23 ᵐS Mt 13:24 ⁿMt 25:19
18:25 ᵒLk 7:42 ᵖLev 25:39; 2Ki 4:1; Ne 5:5,8
18:26 qS Mt 8:2
18:35 ʳS Mt 6:14; S Jas 2:13
19:1 ˢS Mt 7:28
19:2 ᵗS Mt 4:23
19:3 ᵘMt 5:31

18:17 *church.* Local congregation. Here and 16:18 are the only two places where the Gospels use the word "church." *pagan.* For the Jews this meant any Gentile. *tax collector.* See note on 5:46. This verse establishes one basis for excommunication (when people refuse to respond to church discipline; see 2Th 3:14 and note; cf. Ro 16:17).

18:18 See note on 16:19.

18:19 *anything.* Probably not a reference to prayer generally but to disciplinary decisions, especially in the context of vv. 15–18.

18:20 Christ promises his presence with those involved in the proper disciplinary function of the church.

18:22 *seventy-seven times.* Times without number (see TNIV text note).

18:23 *kingdom of heaven.* See note on 3:2.

18:24 *ten thousand bags of gold.* See TNIV text note.

18:25 For this practice of selling into slavery see Ex 21:2; Lev 25:39; 2Ki 4:1; Ne 5:5; Isa 50:1.

18:28 *hundred silver coins.* See TNIV text note.

18:35 God is very forgiving, but he also judges those who refuse to forgive (v. 34; cf. 6:12, 14–15).

19:1 *Judea.* See note on Mk 10:1. *other side of the Jordan.* The east side, known later as Transjordan or Perea and today simply as Jordan. Jesus now began ministering there (see note on Lk 13:22). *Jordan.* See note on Mk 1:5.

19:3 *Pharisees.* See note on Mk 2:16. *for any and every reason.* This last part of the question is not in the parallel passage in Mark (10:2). Matthew possibly included it because he was writing to Jews, who were aware of the dispute between the schools of Shammai and Hillel over the interpretation of Dt 24:1–4. Shammai held that "something indecent" (Dt 24:1) meant "sexual immorality" (Mt 19:9)—the only allowable cause for divorce. Hillel emphasized the preceding clause, "who becomes displeasing to him" (Dt 24:1). He would allow a man to divorce his wife if she did anything he disliked—even if she burned his food while cooking it. Jesus clearly took the side of Shammai (see v. 9), but only after first pointing back to God's original ideal for marriage in Ge 1:27; 2:24.

19:4 ᵛGe 1:27; 5:2
19:5 ʷGe 2:24;
1Co 6:16; Eph 5:31
19:7 ˣDt 24:1-4;
Mt 5:31
19:9 ʸS Lk 16:18
19:11 ᶻS Mt 13:11;
1Co 7:7-9,17
19:13 ᵃS Mk 5:23
19:14 ᵇS Mt 25:34
ᶜMt 18:3; 1Pe 2:2
19:16 ᵈS Mt 25:46
ᵉLk 10:25
19:17 ᶠLev 18:5
19:18 ᵍJas 2:11
19:19 ʰEx 20:12-16;
Dt 5:16-20
ⁱLev 19:18; S Mt 5:43
19:21 ʲMt 5:48
ᵏS Ac 2:45
ˡS Mt 6:20

⁴"Haven't you read," he replied, "that at the beginning the Creator 'made them male and female,'ᵃ ᵛ ⁵and said, 'For this reason a man will leave his father and mother and be united to his wife, and the two will become one flesh'ᵇ? ʷ ⁶So they are no longer two, but one. Therefore what God has joined together, let no one separate."

⁷"Why then," they asked, "did Moses command that a man give his wife a certificate of divorce and send her away?"ˣ

⁸Jesus replied, "Moses permitted you to divorce your wives because your hearts were hard. But it was not this way from the beginning. ⁹I tell you that anyone who divorces his wife, except for sexual immorality, and marries another woman commits adultery."ʸ

¹⁰The disciples said to him, "If this is the situation between a husband and wife, it is better not to marry."

¹¹Jesus replied, "Not everyone can accept this word, but only those to whom it has been given.ᶻ ¹²For some are eunuchs because they were born that way; others have been made eunuchs; and others have renounced marriageᶜ because of the kingdom of heaven. The one who can accept this should accept it."

THE LITTLE CHILDREN AND JESUS
19:13–15pp — Mk 10:13–16; Lk 18:15–17

¹³Then people brought little children to Jesus for him to place his hands on themᵃ and pray for them. But the disciples rebuked them.

¹⁴Jesus said, "Let the little children come to me, and do not hinder them, for the kingdom of heaven belongsᵇ to such as these."ᶜ ¹⁵When he had placed his hands on them, he went on from there.

THE RICH AND THE KINGDOM OF GOD
19:16–29pp — Mk 10:17–30; Lk 18:18–30

¹⁶Just then a man came up to Jesus and asked, "Teacher, what good thing must I do to get eternal lifeᵈ?"ᵉ

¹⁷"Why do you ask me about what is good?" Jesus replied. "There is only One who is good. If you want to enter life, keep the commandments."ᶠ

¹⁸"Which ones?" he inquired.

Jesus replied, " 'You shall not murder, you shall not commit adultery,ᵍ you shall not steal, you shall not give false testimony, ¹⁹honor your father and mother,'ᵈ ʰ and 'love your neighbor as yourself.'ᵉ ⁱ

²⁰"All these I have kept," the young man said. "What do I still lack?"

²¹Jesus answered, "If you want to be perfect,ʲ go, sell your possessions and give to the poor,ᵏ and you will have treasure in heaven.ˡ Then come, follow me."

²²When the young man heard this, he went away sad, because he had great wealth.

ᵃ 4 Gen. 1:27   ᵇ 5 Gen. 2:24   ᶜ 12 Or *have made themselves eunuchs*   ᵈ 19 Exodus 20:12-16; Deut. 5:16-20   ᵉ 19 Lev. 19:18

19:10–12 See 1Co 7:7–8,26,32–35.

19:11 *this word.* The disciples' conclusion in v. 10: "it is better not to marry." This teaching is not meant for everyone. Jesus then gives three examples of persons for whom it is meant in v. 12.

19:12 *born that way.* Impotent. *made eunuchs.* By castration. *have renounced marriage because of the kingdom of heaven.* Those who have voluntarily adopted a celibate lifestyle in order to give themselves more completely to God's work. Under certain circumstances celibacy is recommended in Scripture (cf. 1Co 7:25–38), but it is never presented as superior to marriage.

19:14 *kingdom of heaven.* See note on 3:2. *belongs to such as these.* See note on Mk 10:14.

19:15 *placed his hands on them.* Mk 10:16 adds "and blessed them."

19:16 *a man.* See note on Mk 10:17. *what good thing must I do ...?* The rich man was thinking in terms of righteousness by works. Jesus had to correct this misunderstanding first before answering the question more fully. *eternal life.* The first use of this term in Matthew's Gospel (see v. 29; 25:46). In John it occurs much more frequently, often taking the place of the term "kingdom of God (or heaven)" used in the Synoptics, which treat the following three expressions as synonymous: (1) eternal life (v. 16; Mk 10:17; Lk 18:18), (2) entering the kingdom of heaven (v.

23; cf. Mk 10:24; Lk 18:24) and (3) being saved (vv. 25–26; Mk 10:26–27; Lk 18:26–27).

19:17 *Why do you ask me about what is good?* Jesus wanted the man to think seriously about what is good, especially since Jesus' concept of it differed widely from that of the religious leaders (cf. Mk 10:18). *There is only One who is good.* The good is not something to be done as meritorious in itself. God alone is good, and all other goodness derives from him—even the keeping of the commandments, which Jesus proceeded to enumerate (vv. 18–20). *If you want to enter life, keep the commandments.* "To enter life" is the same as "to get eternal life" (v. 16). The requirement to "keep the commandments" is not to establish one's merit before God but is to be an expression of true faith. The Bible always teaches that salvation is a gift of God's grace received through faith (see Eph 2:8–9 and notes).

19:19 *love your neighbor as yourself.* See Lev 19:18 and note.

19:20 *All these I have kept.* See note on Mk 10:20.

▲ **19:21** *perfect.* The Greek word means "goal, end" (cf. note on Ro 10:4). His goal was eternal life, but wealth and lack of commitment stood in his way. *go, sell your possessions.* In his listing of the commandments (vv. 18–19), Jesus omitted "you shall not covet." This was the rich man's main problem and was preventing him from entering life (see note on Mk 10:21).

19:22 *went away sad.* See note on Mk 10:22.

19:23 *m* Mt 13:22;
1Ti 6:9,10
19:26 *n* Ge 18:14;
Job 42:2; Jer 32:17;
Lk 1:37; 18:27;
Ro 4:21
19:27 *o* S Mt 4:19
19:28 *p* Mt 20:21;
25:31 *q* Lk 22:28-30;
Rev 3:21; 4:4; 20:4
19:29 *r* Mt 6:33;
S 25:46
19:30 *s* Mt 20:16;
Mk 10:31; Lk 13:30
20:1 *t* S Mt 13:24
u Mt 21:28,33
20:8 *v* Lev 19:13;
Dt 24:15
20:11 *w* Jnh 4:1
20:12 *x* Jnh 4:8;
Lk 12:55; Jas 1:11
20:13 *y* Mt 22:12;
26:50
20:15 *z* Dt 15:9;
Mk 7:22
20:16 *a* S Mt 19:30

²³Then Jesus said to his disciples, "Truly I tell you, it is hard for the rich*m* to enter the kingdom of heaven. ²⁴Again I tell you, it is easier for a camel to go through the eye of a needle than for the rich to enter the kingdom of God."

²⁵When the disciples heard this, they were greatly astonished and asked, "Who then can be saved?"

²⁶Jesus looked at them and said, "With human beings this is impossible, but with God all things are possible."*n*

²⁷Peter answered him, "We have left everything to follow you!*o* What then will there be for us?"

²⁸Jesus said to them, "Truly I tell you, at the renewal of all things, when the Son of Man sits on his glorious throne,*p* you who have followed me will also sit on twelve thrones, judging the twelve tribes of Israel.*q* ²⁹And everyone who has left houses or brothers or sisters or father or mother or wife*a* or children or fields for my sake will receive a hundred times as much and will inherit eternal life.*r* ³⁰But many who are first will be last, and many who are last will be first.*s*

THE PARABLE OF THE WORKERS IN THE VINEYARD

20 "For the kingdom of heaven is like*t* a landowner who went out early in the morning to hire workers for his vineyard.*u* ²He agreed to pay them a denarius for the day and sent them into his vineyard.

³"About nine in the morning he went out and saw others standing in the marketplace doing nothing. ⁴He told them, 'You also go and work in my vineyard, and I will pay you whatever is right.' ⁵So they went.

"He went out again about noon and about three in the afternoon and did the same thing. ⁶About five in the afternoon he went out and found still others standing around. He asked them, 'Why have you been standing here all day long doing nothing?'

⁷"'Because no one has hired us,' they answered.

"He said to them, 'You also go and work in my vineyard.'

⁸"When evening came,*v* the owner of the vineyard said to his supervisor, 'Call the workers and pay them their wages, beginning with the last ones hired and going on to the first.'

⁹"The workers who were hired about five in the afternoon came and each received a denarius. ¹⁰So when those came who were hired first, they expected to receive more. But each one of them also received a denarius. ¹¹When they received it, they began to grumble*w* against the landowner. ¹²'These men who were hired last worked only one hour,' they said, 'and you have made them equal to us who have borne the burden of the work and the heat*x* of the day.'

¹³"But he answered one of them, 'Friend,*y* I am not being unfair to you. Didn't you agree to work for a denarius? ¹⁴Take your pay and go. I want to give the one who was hired last the same as I gave you. ¹⁵Don't I have the right to do what I want with my own money? Or are you envious because I am generous?'*z*

¹⁶"So the last will be first, and the first will be last."*a*

---

a 29 Some manuscripts do not have *or wife.*

19:23 *kingdom of heaven.* See note on 3:2.
19:24 *camel to go through the eye of a needle.* See note on Mk 10:25.
19:26 See note on Mk 10:27.
19:28 *Truly I tell you.* See note on Mk 3:28. *Son of Man.* See note on Mk 8:31. *judging.* Governing or ruling (cf. OT "judge"; see Introduction to Judges: Title).
19:29 *receive a hundred times as much.* Mark adds, "along with persecutions" (see note on Mk 10:30). *inherit eternal life.* Eternal life is not earned; it is a gift. The word "inherit" often occurs in eschatological contexts in the NT (see 5:5; Mk 10:17; 1Co 6:9–10; 15:50; Gal 5:21; Heb 1:14; 6:12; Rev 21:7).
19:30 This saying of Jesus also appears in other contexts (see 20:16; Mk 10:31 and note; Lk 13:30). In the kingdom of heaven there are many reversals, and the day of judgment will bring many surprises.
20:1–16 This parable occurs only in Matthew's Gospel. In its

original setting, its main point seems to be the sovereign graciousness and generosity of God extended to latecomers (the poor and the outcasts of society) into God's kingdom. It is addressed to the grumblers (v. 11) who just cannot handle this amazing expression of God's grace. They almost certainly represent the religious leaders who opposed Jesus.
20:2 *denarius.* The usual daily wage. A Roman soldier also received one denarius a day.
20:8 *When evening came.* Because farm workers were poor, the law of Moses required that they be paid at the end of each day (cf. Lev 19:13; Dt 24:14–15).
20:13 *Friend.* A term of mild rebuke (see 22:12; 26:50).
20:15 *are you envious…?* Lit. "is your eye evil…?" Apparently the evil eye was associated with jealousy and envy (cf. 1Sa 18:9). *because I am generous.* It was not a matter of justice but of generosity.
20:16 See note on 19:30.

20:18 *b* S Lk 9:51
c S Mt 8:20
d Mt 27:1,2
20:19 *e* S Mt 16:21
f S Ac 2:23
g S Mt 16:21
h S Mt 16:21
20:20 *i* S Mt 4:21
j S Mt 8:2
20:21 *k* Mt 19:28
20:22 *l* Isa 51:17,22;
Jer 49:12; Mt 26:39,
42; Mk 14:36;
Lk 22:42; Jn 18:11
20:23 *m* Ac 12:2;
Rev 1:9
20:24 *n* Lk 22:24,25
20:26 *o* S Mk 9:35
20:28 *p* S Mt 8:20
q Isa 42:1; Lk 12:37;
22:27; Jn 13:13-16;
2Co 8:9; Php 2:7
r Ex 30:12; Isa 44:22;
53:10; Mt 26:28;
1Ti 2:6; Tit 2:14;
Heb 9:28; 1Pe 1:18,19
20:30 *s* S Mt 9:27
21:1 *t* Mt 24:3;
26:30; Mk 14:26;
Lk 19:37; 21:37;
22:39; Jn 8:1; Ac 1:12

JESUS PREDICTS HIS DEATH A THIRD TIME
20:17–19pp — Mk 10:32–34; Lk 18:31–33

¹⁷Now Jesus was going up to Jerusalem. On the way, he took the Twelve aside and said to them, ¹⁸"We are going up to Jerusalem,ᵇ and the Son of Manᶜ will be delivered over to the chief priests and the teachers of the law.ᵈ They will condemn him to death ¹⁹and will hand him over to the Gentiles to be mocked and floggedᵉ and crucified.ᶠ On the third dayᵍ he will be raised to life!"ʰ

A MOTHER'S REQUEST
20:20–28pp — Mk 10:35–45

²⁰Then the mother of Zebedee's sonsⁱ came to Jesus with her sons and, kneeling down,ʲ asked a favor of him.

²¹"What is it you want?" he asked.

She said, "Grant that one of these two sons of mine may sit at your right and the other at your left in your kingdom."ᵏ

²²"You don't know what you are asking," Jesus said to them. "Can you drink the cupˡ I am going to drink?"

"We can," they answered.

²³Jesus said to them, "You will indeed drink from my cup,ᵐ but to sit at my right or left is not for me to grant. These places belong to those for whom they have been prepared by my Father."

²⁴When the ten heard about this, they were indignantⁿ with the two brothers. ²⁵Jesus called them together and said, "You know that the rulers of the Gentiles lord it over them, and their high officials exercise authority over them. ²⁶Not so with you. Instead, whoever wants to become great among you must be your servant,ᵒ ²⁷and whoever wants to be first must be your slave— ²⁸just as the Son of Manᵖ did not come to be served, but to serve,�q and to give his life as a ransomʳ for many."

TWO BLIND MEN RECEIVE SIGHT
20:29–34pp — Mk 10:46–52; Lk 18:35–43

²⁹As Jesus and his disciples were leaving Jericho, a large crowd followed him. ³⁰Two blind men were sitting by the roadside, and when they heard that Jesus was going by, they shouted, "Lord, Son of David,ˢ have mercy on us!"

³¹The crowd rebuked them and told them to be quiet, but they shouted all the louder, "Lord, Son of David, have mercy on us!"

³²Jesus stopped and called them. "What do you want me to do for you?" he asked.

³³"Lord," they answered, "we want our sight."

³⁴Jesus had compassion on them and touched their eyes. Immediately they received their sight and followed him.

JESUS COMES TO JERUSALEM AS KING
21:1–9pp — Mk 11:1–10; Lk 19:29–38
21:4–9pp — Jn 12:12–15

21 As they approached Jerusalem and came to Bethphage on the Mount of Olives,ᵗ Jesus sent two disciples, ²saying to them, "Go to the village ahead of you, and at once you will find a donkey tied there, with her colt by her. Untie

---

20:17–19 See Mk 10:32–34; Lk 18:31–33 and notes.
20:19 *will hand him over to the Gentiles to be mocked and flogged and crucified.* An additional statement in this third prediction of the passion. Jesus would not be killed by the Jews, which would have been by stoning, but would be crucified by the Romans. All three predictions include his resurrection on the third day (16:21; 17:23).
20:20 *mother of Zebedee's sons.* Mark has "James and John, the sons of Zebedee," asking the question (Mk 10:35–37), yet there is no contradiction. The three joined in making the petition.
20:21 *want.* See note on Mk 10:35–36. *sit at your right and the other at your left.* See note on Mk 10:37.
20:22 *drink the cup.* A figure of speech meaning to "undergo" or "experience." Here the reference is to suffering (cf. 26:39). The same figure of speech is used in Jer 25:15; Eze 23:31–32; Hab 2:16; Rev 14:10; 16:19; 18:6 for divine wrath or judgment. See note on Mk 10:38.

20:23 *drink from my cup.* James was martyred (see Ac 12:2 and note); John was exiled (see Rev 1:9 and note). *is not for me to grant.* See note on Mk 10:40; see also Mt 11:27; 24:36; Jn 14:28.
20:24 See note on Mk 10:41.
20:26 *Not so with you.* See note on Mk 10:43.
 20:28 *Son of Man.* See note on Mk 8:31. *ransom.* The Greek word was used most commonly for the price paid to redeem a slave. Similarly, Christ paid the ransom price of his own life to free us from the slavery of sin. *for.* Emphasizes the substitutionary nature of Christ's death. *many.* Christ "gave himself as a ransom for all people" (1Ti 2:6). Salvation is offered to "all," but only the "many" (i.e., the elect) receive it. See note on Mk 10:45.
20:29 *Jericho.* See note on Mk 10:46.
20:30 *Two blind men.* The other Synoptics mention only one (see note on Lk 18:35). *Son of David.* A Messianic title (see note on 9:27).
20:34 *compassion.* See note on 9:36.

them and bring them to me. ³If anyone says anything to you, say that the Lord needs them, and he will send them right away.

⁴This took place to fulfill[u] what was spoken through the prophet:

> ⁵ "Say to Daughter Zion,
>   'See, your king comes to you,
>   gentle and riding on a donkey,
>   and on a colt, the foal of a donkey.' "[a][v]

⁶The disciples went and did as Jesus had instructed them. ⁷They brought the donkey and the colt and placed their cloaks[w] on them for Jesus to sit on. ⁸A very large crowd spread their cloaks[w] on the road, while others cut branches from the trees and spread them on the road. ⁹The crowds that went ahead of him and those that followed shouted,

> "Hosanna[b] to the Son of David!"[x]
>
> "Blessed is he who comes in the name of the Lord!"[c][y]
>
> "Hosanna[b] in the highest heaven!"[z]

¹⁰When Jesus entered Jerusalem, the whole city was stirred and asked, "Who is this?" ¹¹The crowds answered, "This is Jesus, the prophet[a] from Nazareth in Galilee."

JESUS AT THE TEMPLE
21:12–16pp — Mk 11:15–18; Lk 19:45–47

¹²Jesus entered the temple courts and drove out all who were buying[b] and selling there. He overturned the tables of the money changers[c] and the benches of those selling doves. [d] ¹³"It is written," he said to them, " 'My house will be called a house of prayer,'[d][e] but you are making it 'a den of robbers.'[e]"[f]

¹⁴The blind and the lame came to him at the temple, and he healed them. [g] ¹⁵But when the chief priests and the teachers of the law saw the wonderful things he did and the children shouting in the temple courts, "Hosanna to the Son of David," [h] they were indignant. [i]

¹⁶"Do you hear what these children are saying?" they asked him.

"Yes," replied Jesus, "have you never read,

> " 'From the lips of children and infants
>   you have ordained praise'[f]?"[j]

¹⁷And he left them and went out of the city to Bethany, [k] where he spent the night.

ª 5 Zech. 9:9   ᵇ 9 A Hebrew expression meaning "Save!" which became an exclamation of praise; also in verse 15   ᶜ 9 Psalm 118:25,26   ᵈ 13 Isaiah 56:7   ᵉ 13 Jer. 7:11   ᶠ 16 Psalm 8:2 (see Septuagint)

21:1 *Jerusalem.* See map No. 10 at the end of this study Bible. *Bethphage.* Means "house of figs." It is mentioned in the Bible only in connection with the Triumphal Entry. See map, p. 1703. *Mount of Olives.* See note on Mk 11:1.
21:2 *donkey.* An animal symbolic of humility, peace and Davidic royalty (see notes on Zec 9:9; Lk 19:30). See also note on Mk 11:2. *colt.* See notes on Mk 11:2; Lk 19:30.
21:3 *Lord.* See note on Lk 19:31.
21:5 See note on Zec 9:9.
21:7 *cloaks ... for Jesus to sit on.* We know from Mark (11:2) and Luke (19:30) that he rode the colt. Typically, a mother donkey followed her offspring closely. Matthew mentions two animals, while the other Gospels have only one (see note on Lk 19:30).
21:8 *spread their cloaks on the road.* An act of royal homage (see 2Ki 9:13). *branches.* See note on Mk 11:8.
21:9 These are three separate quotations, not necessarily spoken at the same time. *Hosanna.* See note on Jer 31:7; expresses both prayer and praise (see TNIV text note). *Son of David.* See note on 9:27. *in the highest heaven.* That is, may those in heaven sing "Hosanna" (see Ps 148:1–2; Lk 2:14). See Ps 118:25–26 and notes.
21:10 *Who is this?* Because of Jesus' dramatic entry into the city, the people were wondering who he really was.
21:11 *the prophet.* Refers either to a prophet in general (see 13:57) or to the prophet predicted in Dt 18:15–18 (see note on 18:15; see also Dt 34:10–12 and note on 34:12).

21:12–17 In the Synoptics the cleansing of the temple occurs during the last week of Jesus' ministry; in John it takes place during the first few months (Jn 2:12–16). Two explanations are possible: 1. There were two cleansings, one at the beginning and the other at the end of Jesus' public ministry. 2. There was only one cleansing, which took place during Passion Week but which John placed at the beginning of his account for theological reasons—to show that God's judgment was operative through the Messiah from the outset of Jesus' ministry. However, different details are present in the two accounts (the selling of cattle and sheep in Jn 2:14, the whip in Jn 2:15, and the statements of Jesus in Mt 21:13; Jn 2:16). From Matthew's and Luke's accounts we might assume that the cleansing of the temple took place on Sunday, following the so-called Triumphal Entry (21:1–11). But Mark (11:15–19) clearly indicates that it was on Monday. Matthew often compressed narratives.
21:12 *temple courts.* The "buying and selling" took place in the large outer court of the Gentiles, which covered several acres (see notes on Mk 11:15; Lk 19:45; Jn 2:14).
21:13 *house of prayer.* Mark adds "for all nations" (11:17; see note there). *den of robbers.* See Jer 7:11 and note.
21:16 See Ps 8:1b–2 and note.
21:17 *Bethany.* See note on Mk 11:1; a village on the eastern slope of the Mount of Olives, about two miles from Jerusalem and the final station on the road from Jericho to Jerusalem. It was the home of Mary, Martha and Lazarus (Jn 12:1–3).

21:4 ᵘ S Mt 1:22
21:5 ᵛ Isa 62:11; Zec 9:9
21:8 ʷ 2Ki 9:13
21:9 ˣ ver 15; S Mt 9:27 ʸ Ps 118:26; Mt 23:39 ᶻ Lk 2:14
21:11 ª Dt 18:15; Lk 7:16,39; 24:19; Jn 1:21,25; 6:14; 7:40
21:12 ᵇ Dt 14:26 ᶜ Ex 30:13 ᵈ Lev 1:14
21:13 ᵉ Isa 56:7 ᶠ Jer 7:11
21:14 ᵍ S Mt 4:23
21:15 ʰ ver 9; S Mt 9:27 ⁱ Lk 19:39
21:16 ʲ Ps 8:2
21:17 ᵏ Mt 26:6; Mk 11:1; Lk 24:50; Jn 11:1,18; 12:1

21:19 *l* Isa 34:4;
Jer 8:13
21:21 *m* Mt 17:20;
Lk 17:6; 1Co 13:2;
Jas 1:6
21:22 *n* S Mt 7:7
21:23 *o* Ac 4:7; 7:27
21:26 *p* S Mt 11:9
21:28 *q* ver 33;
Mt 20:1
21:31 *r* Lk 7:29
s Lk 7:50
21:32 *t* Mt 3:1-12
u Lk 3:12,13; 7:29
v Lk 7:36-50
w Lk 7:30
21:33 *x* Ps 80:8
y Isa 5:1-7 *z* Mt 25:14,
15
21:34 *a* Mt 22:3
21:35 *b* 2Ch 24:21;
Mt 23:34,37;
Heb 11:36,37
21:36 *c* Mt 22:4

JESUS CURSES A FIG TREE

21:18–22pp — Mk 11:12–14,20–24

¹⁸Early in the morning, as he was on his way back to the city, he was hungry. ¹⁹Seeing a fig tree by the road, he went up to it but found nothing on it except leaves. Then he said to it, "May you never bear fruit again!" Immediately the tree withered.*ˡ*

²⁰When the disciples saw this, they were amazed. "How did the fig tree wither so quickly?" they asked.

²¹Jesus replied, "Truly I tell you, if you have faith and do not doubt,*ᵐ* not only can you do what was done to the fig tree, but also you can say to this mountain, 'Go, throw yourself into the sea,' and it will be done. ²²If you believe, you will receive whatever you ask for*ⁿ* in prayer."

THE AUTHORITY OF JESUS QUESTIONED

21:23–27pp — Mk 11:27–33; Lk 20:1–8

²³Jesus entered the temple courts, and, while he was teaching, the chief priests and the elders of the people came to him. "By what authority*ᵒ* are you doing these things?" they asked. "And who gave you this authority?"

²⁴Jesus replied, "I will also ask you one question. If you answer me, I will tell you by what authority I am doing these things. ²⁵John's baptism—where did it come from? Was it from heaven, or of human origin?"

They discussed it among themselves and said, "If we say, 'From heaven,' he will ask, 'Then why didn't you believe him?' ²⁶But if we say, 'Of human origin'—we are afraid of the people, for they all hold that John was a prophet."*ᵖ*

²⁷So they answered Jesus, "We don't know."

Then he said, "Neither will I tell you by what authority I am doing these things.

THE PARABLE OF THE TWO SONS

²⁸"What do you think? There was a man who had two sons. He went to the first and said, 'Son, go and work today in the vineyard.'*q*

²⁹" 'I will not,' he answered, but later he changed his mind and went.

³⁰"Then the father went to the other son and said the same thing. He answered, 'I will, sir,' but he did not go.

³¹"Which of the two did what his father wanted?"

"The first," they answered.

Jesus said to them, "Truly I tell you, the tax collectors*ʳ* and the prostitutes*ˢ* are entering the kingdom of God ahead of you. ³²For John came to you to show you the way of righteousness,*ᵗ* and you did not believe him, but the tax collectors*ᵘ* and the prostitutes*ᵛ* did. And even after you saw this, you did not repent*ʷ* and believe him.

THE PARABLE OF THE TENANTS

21:33–46pp — Mk 12:1–12; Lk 20:9–19

³³"Listen to another parable: There was a landowner who planted*ˣ* a vineyard. He put a wall around it, dug a winepress in it and built a watchtower.*ʸ* Then he rented the vineyard to some farmers and moved to another place.*ᶻ* ³⁴When the harvest time approached, he sent his servants*ᵃ* to the tenants to collect his fruit.

³⁵"The tenants seized his servants; they beat one, killed another, and stoned a third.*ᵇ* ³⁶Then he sent other servants*ᶜ* to them, more than the first time, and the tenants treat-

---

21:18–22 See note on vv. 12–17; another example of compressing narratives. Mark (11:12–14,20–25) places the cursing of the fig tree on Monday morning and the disciples' finding it withered on Tuesday morning. In Matthew's account the tree withered as soon as Jesus cursed it, emphasizing the immediacy of judgment. For the theological meaning of this event, see note on Mk 11:14.
21:18 *city.* Jerusalem.
21:21 *have faith and do not doubt.* See 17:20 and note; Jas 1:5–8. *Go, throw yourself into the sea.* A proverbial hyperbolic statement (cf. 17:20 and note).
21:22 See Lk 5:14–15 and note on 5:14.
21:23 *temple courts.* See note on Mk 11:27. *chief priests and the elders.* See notes on 2:4; Mk 8:31; Lk 19:47. *By what authority … ?* See notes on Mk 11:28; Lk 20:2.

21:25 *from heaven, or of human origin?* See notes on Mk 11:30; Lk 20:4.
21:31 *tax collectors.* See note on 5:46. *kingdom of God.* See notes on 3:2; Lk 4:43; 1Co 4:20.
🅰 21:32 *way of righteousness.* Doing what is right and obeying God's will, which included believing what Jesus was teaching about how one is to enter the kingdom of God.
21:33–46 See notes on Mk 12:1–12; Lk 20:9–19.
21:33 *winepress.* See notes on Isa 5:2; Rev 14:19. *watchtower.* For guarding the vineyard, especially when the grapes ripened, and for shelter (see Isa 5:2 and note).
21:35–37 The tenants are the Jews, or their leaders. The servants represent the OT prophets, many of whom were killed. The son represents Christ, who was condemned to death by the religious leaders.

ed them the same way. [37]Last of all, he sent his son to them. 'They will respect my son,' he said.

[38]"But when the tenants saw the son, they said to each other, 'This is the heir.[d] Come, let's kill him[e] and take his inheritance.'[f] [39]So they took him and threw him out of the vineyard and killed him.

[40]"Therefore, when the owner of the vineyard comes, what will he do to those tenants?"

[41]"He will bring those wretches to a wretched end,"[g] they replied, "and he will rent the vineyard to other tenants,[h] who will give him his share of the crop at harvest time."

[42]Jesus said to them, "Have you never read in the Scriptures:

" 'The stone the builders rejected
    has become the cornerstone;
the Lord has done this,
    and it is marvelous in our eyes'[a]?[i]

[43]"Therefore I tell you that the kingdom of God will be taken away from you[j] and given to a people who will produce its fruit. [44]Anyone who falls on this stone will be broken to pieces, but anyone on whom it falls will be crushed."[b][k]

[45]When the chief priests and the Pharisees heard Jesus' parables, they knew he was talking about them. [46]They looked for a way to arrest him, but they were afraid of the crowd because the people held that he was a prophet.[l]

THE PARABLE OF THE WEDDING BANQUET
22:2–14Ref — Lk 14:16–24

22 Jesus spoke to them again in parables, saying: [2]"The kingdom of heaven is like[m] a king who prepared a wedding banquet for his son. [3]He sent his servants[n] to those who had been invited to the banquet to tell them to come, but they refused to come.

[4]"Then he sent some more servants[o] and said, 'Tell those who have been invited that I have prepared my dinner: My oxen and fattened cattle have been butchered, and everything is ready. Come to the wedding banquet.'

[5]"But they paid no attention and went off—one to his field, another to his business. [6]The rest seized his servants, mistreated them and killed them. [7]The king was enraged. He sent his army and destroyed those murderers[p] and burned their city.

[8]"Then he said to his servants, 'The wedding banquet is ready, but those I invited did not deserve to come. [9]Go to the street corners[q] and invite to the banquet anyone you find.' [10]So the servants went out into the streets and gathered all the people they could find, the bad as well as the good,[r] and the wedding hall was filled with guests.

[11]"But when the king came in to see the guests, he noticed a man there who was not wearing wedding clothes. [12]'Friend,'[s] he asked, 'how did you get in here without wedding clothes?' The man was speechless.

[13]"Then the king told the attendants, 'Tie him hand and foot, and throw him outside, into the darkness, where there will be weeping and gnashing of teeth.'[t]

[14]"For many are invited, but few are chosen."[u]

---

[a] 42 Psalm 118:22,23   [b] 44 Some manuscripts do not have verse 44.

21:41 *other tenants.* Gentiles, to whom Paul turned when Jews, for the most part, rejected the gospel (Ac 13:46; 18:6). By the second century the church was composed almost entirely of Gentiles.

21:42 See note on Ps 118:22. *Have you never read ...?* See v. 16; 12:3; 19:4; Mk 12:10.

21:44 *will be broken to pieces.* See note on Lk 20:18.

21:45 *chief priests.* See notes on 2:4; Mk 8:31; Lk 19:47. *Pharisees.* See notes on 3:7; Mk 2:16; Lk 5:17. *parables.* See notes on 13:3; Mk 4:2; Lk 8:4.

22:1–14 In Luke's Gospel this parable is spoken by Jesus at a banquet in response to a remark made by one of the guests about "the feast in the kingdom of God" (Lk 14:15; see note there).

22:7 *burned their city.* A common military practice; here possibly an allusion to the coming destruction of Jerusalem in A.D. 70.

22:11 *not wearing wedding clothes.* It may have been the custom for a host to provide guests with wedding garments. This would have been necessary for the guests at this banquet in particular, for they were brought in directly from the streets (vv. 9–10). The failure of the man in question to avail himself of a wedding garment was therefore an insult to the host, who had made the garments available.

22:12 *Friend.* See note on 20:13.

22:13 *gnashing of teeth.* See note on 13:42.

22:14 A proverbial summary of the meaning of the parable. God invites "many" (perhaps "all" in view of the Semitic usage of "many") to be part of his kingdom, but only a "few" are chosen by him. This does not mean that God chooses arbitrarily. The invitation must be accepted, followed by appropriate conduct. Proper behavior is evidence of being chosen.

21:38 [d] Heb 1:2
[e] S Mt 12:14 [f] Ps 2:8
21:41 [g] Mt 8:11,12
[h] S Ac 13:46
21:42 [i] Ps 118:22,23;
S Ac 4:11
21:43 [j] Mt 8:12
21:44 [k] S Lk 2:34
21:46 [l] S ver 11,26
22:2 [m] S Mt 13:24
22:3 [n] Mt 21:34
22:4 [o] Mt 21:36
22:7 [p] Lk 19:27
22:9 [q] Eze 21:21
22:10 [r] Mt 13:47,48
22:12 [s] Mt 20:13;
26:50
22:13 [t] S Mt 8:12
22:14 [u] Rev 17:14

22:16 ᵛ Mk 3:6
22:17 ʷ Mt 17:25
22:21 ˣ Ro 13:7
22:22 ʸ Mk 12:12
22:23 ᶻ S Ac 4:1
ᵃ Ac 23:8; 1Co 15:12
22:24 ᵇ Dt 25:5,6
22:29 ᶜ Jn 20:9
22:30 ᵈ Mt 24:38
22:32 ᵉ Ex 3:6;
Ac 7:32
22:33 ᶠ S Mt 7:28
22:34 ᵍ S Ac 4:1
22:35 ʰ Lk 7:30;
10:25; 11:45; 14:3
22:37 ⁱ Dt 6:5
22:39 ʲ Lev 19:18;
S Mt; 5:43
22:40 ᵏ Mt 7:12;
Lk 10:25-28

PAYING THE IMPERIAL TAX TO CAESAR

22:15–22pp — Mk 12:13–17; Lk 20:20–26

¹⁵Then the Pharisees went out and laid plans to trap him in his words. ¹⁶They sent their disciples to him along with the Herodians.ᵛ "Teacher," they said, "we know that you are a man of integrity and that you teach the way of God in accordance with the truth. You aren't swayed by others, because you pay no attention to who they are. ¹⁷Tell us then, what is your opinion? Is it right to pay the imperial taxᵃʷ to Caesar or not?"

¹⁸But Jesus, knowing their evil intent, said, "You hypocrites, why are you trying to trap me? ¹⁹Show me the coin used for paying the tax." They brought him a denarius, ²⁰and he asked them, "Whose image is this? And whose inscription?"

²¹"Caesar's," they replied.

Then he said to them, "Give back to Caesar what is Caesar's,ˣ and to God what is God's."

²²When they heard this, they were amazed. So they left him and went away.ʸ

MARRIAGE AT THE RESURRECTION

22:23–33pp — Mk 12:18–27; Lk 20:27–40

²³That same day the Sadducees,ᶻ who say there is no resurrection,ᵃ came to him with a question. ²⁴"Teacher," they said, "Moses told us that if a man dies without having children, his brother must marry the widow and raise up offspring for him.ᵇ ²⁵Now there were seven brothers among us. The first one married and died, and since he had no children, he left his wife to his brother. ²⁶The same thing happened to the second and third brother, right on down to the seventh. ²⁷Finally, the woman died. ²⁸Now then, at the resurrection, whose wife will she be of the seven, since all of them were married to her?"

²⁹Jesus replied, "You are in error because you do not know the Scripturesᶜ or the power of God. ³⁰At the resurrection people will neither marry nor be given in marriage;ᵈ they will be like the angels in heaven. ³¹But about the resurrection of the dead—have you not read what God said to you, ³²'I am the God of Abraham, the God of Isaac, and the God of Jacob'ᵇ?ᵉ He is not the God of the dead but of the living."

³³When the crowds heard this, they were astonished at his teaching.ᶠ

THE GREATEST COMMANDMENT

22:34–40pp — Mk 12:28–31

³⁴Hearing that Jesus had silenced the Sadducees,ᵍ the Pharisees got together. ³⁵One of them, an expert in the law,ʰ tested him with this question: ³⁶"Teacher, which is the greatest commandment in the Law?"

³⁷Jesus replied: " 'Love the Lord your God with all your heart and with all your soul and with all your mind.'ᶜⁱ ³⁸This is the first and greatest commandment. ³⁹And the second is like it: 'Love your neighbor as yourself.'ᵈʲ ⁴⁰All the Law and the Prophets hang on these two commandments."ᵏ

ᵃ **17** A special tax levied on subject peoples, not on Roman citizens   ᵇ **32** Exodus 3:6   ᶜ **37** Deut. 6:5   ᵈ **39** Lev. 19:18

22:15–17 The Pharisees were ardent nationalists, opposed to Roman rule, while the hated Herodians, as their name indicates, supported the Roman rule of the Herods. Now, however, the Pharisees enlisted the help of the Herodians to trap Jesus in his words (cf. note on Mk 3:6). After trying to put him off guard with flattery, they sprang their question: "Is it right to pay the imperial tax to Caesar or not?" (v. 17). If he said "No," the Herodians would report him to the Roman governor and he would be executed for treason. If he said "Yes," the Pharisees would denounce him to the people as disloyal to his nation.

22:17 *imperial tax to Caesar.* See note on Mk 12:14.

22:18 *hypocrites.* See note on 6:2.

22:19 *denarius.* The common Roman coin of that day (see note on 20:2). On one side was the portrait of Emperor Tiberius and on the other the inscription in Latin: "Tiberius Caesar Augustus, son of the divine Augustus." The coin was issued by Tiberius and was used for paying tax to him.

22:21 *to God what is God's.* In distinguishing clearly between Caesar and God, Jesus also protested against the false and idol-atrous claims made on the coins (see previous note; see also note on Mk 12:17).

22:22 *amazed.* See Mk 1:22 and note.

22:23 *Sadducees.* See notes on 3:7; Ezr 7:2; Mk 12:18; Lk 20:27; Ac 4:1; see also chart, p. 1650, and essay, p. 1596.

22:23–40 See Mk 12:18–31; Lk 20:27–40 and notes.

22:24 *Moses told us.* Jesus quoted from the Pentateuch when arguing with the Sadducees, since those books had special authority for them (see note on Mk 12:18). The reference (Dt 25:5–10) is to the levirate law (from Latin *levir,* "brother-in-law"), which was given to protect the widow and guarantee continuance of the family line.

22:37 *with all your heart . . . soul . . . mind.* With your whole being. The Hebrew of Dt 6:5 (see note there) has "heart . . . soul . . . strength," but some manuscripts of the Septuagint (the pre-Christian Greek translation of the OT) add "mind." Jesus combined all four terms in Mk 12:30. *soul.* See note on 10:28.

22:39 See note on Lev 19:18.

22:40 *the Law and the Prophets.* The entire OT (see note on 5:17).

WHOSE SON IS THE MESSIAH?

22:41–46pp — Mk 12:35–37; Lk 20:41–44

⁴¹While the Pharisees were gathered together, Jesus asked them, ⁴²"What do you think about the Messiah? Whose son is he?"

"The son of David,"*ᴵ* they replied.

⁴³He said to them, "How is it then that David, speaking by the Spirit, calls him 'Lord'? For he says,

⁴⁴ " 'The Lord said to my Lord:
    "Sit at my right hand
    until I put your enemies
    under your feet." ' ᵃᵐ

⁴⁵If then David calls him 'Lord,' how can he be his son?" ⁴⁶No one could say a word in reply, and from that day on no one dared to ask him any more questions.ⁿ

A WARNING AGAINST HYPOCRISY

23:1–7pp — Mk 12:38,39; Lk 20:45,46
23:37–39pp — Lk 13:34,35

23 Then Jesus said to the crowds and to his disciples: ²"The teachers of the lawᵒ and the Pharisees sit in Moses' seat. ³So you must be careful to do everything they tell you. But do not do what they do, for they do not practice what they preach. ⁴They tie up heavy, cumbersome loads and put them on other people's shoulders, but they themselves are not willing to lift a finger to move them.ᵖ

⁵"Everything they do is done for people to see:�q They make their phylacteriesᵇʳ wide and the tassels on their garmentsˢ long; ⁶they love the place of honor at banquets and the most important seats in the synagogues;ᵗ ⁷they love to be greeted with respect in the marketplaces and to have people call them 'Rabbi.'ᵘ

⁸"But you are not to be called 'Rabbi,' for you have only one Master and you are all brothers. ⁹And do not call anyone on earth 'father,' for you have one Father,ᵛ and he is in heaven. ¹⁰Nor are you to be called 'teacher,' for you have one Teacher, the Messiah. ¹¹The greatest among you will be your servant.ʷ ¹²For those who exalt themselves will be humbled, and those who humble themselves will be exalted.ˣ

SEVEN WOES ON THE TEACHERS OF THE LAW AND THE PHARISEES

¹³[14]"Woe to you, teachers of the law and Pharisees, you hypocrites!ʸ You shut the door of the kingdom of heaven in people's faces. You yourselves do not enter, nor will you let those enter who are trying to.ᶻ

¹⁵"Woe to you, teachers of the law and Pharisees, you hypocrites! You travel over land and sea to win a single convert,ᵃ and then you make that convert twice as much a child of hellᵇ as you are.

¹⁶"Woe to you, blind guides!ᶜ You say, 'If anyone swears by the temple, it means nothing; but whoever swears by the gold of the temple is bound by the oath.'ᵈ ¹⁷You blind fools!

ᵃ 44 Psalm 110:1   ᵇ 5 That is, boxes containing Scripture verses, worn on forehead and arm

---

22:42 *ᴵ* S Mt 9:27
22:44 *ᵐ* Ps 110:1;
1Ki 5:3; Ac 2:34,35;
1Co 15:25; Heb 1:13;
10:13
22:46 *ⁿ* Mk 12:34;
Lk 20:40
23:2 *ᵒ* Ezr 7:6,25
23:4 *ᵖ* Lk 11:46;
Ac 15:10; Gal 6:13
23:5 *q* Mt 6:1,2,5,16
ʳ Ex 13:9; Dt 6:8
ˢ Nu 15:38; Dt 22:12
23:6 *ᵗ* Lk 11:43; 14:7;
20:46
23:7 *ᵘ* ver 8;
Mt 26:25,49; Mk 9:5;
10:51; Jn 1:38,49; 3:2,
26; 20:16
23:9 *ᵛ* Mal 1:6;
23:11 *ʷ* S Mk 9:35
23:12 *ˣ* Isa 2:8;
Ps 18:27; Pr 3:34;
Isa 57:15; Eze 21:26;
Lk 1:52; 14:11
23:13[14] *ʸ* ver 15,
23,25,27,29
ᶻ Lk 11:52
23:15 *ᵃ* Ac 2:11; 6:5;
13:43 *ᵇ* Mt 5:22
23:16 *ᶜ* ver 24;
Isa 9:16; Mt 15:14
ᵈ Mt 5:33-35

22:41–46 See notes on Mk 12:35–40; Lk 20:44–47.
22:44 See note on Ps 110:1. Jesus bases his argument on Ps 110, the most frequently quoted OT chapter in the NT (see introduction to Ps 110). He assumes the Davidic authorship of the psalm, which is essential to his argument.
23:2 *teachers of the law.* See note on 2:4. *Pharisees.* See notes on 3:7; Lk 5:17. *sit in Moses' seat.* A position of authority. They considered themselves to be the authorized successors of Moses as teachers of the law.
23:3 *not practice what they preach.* See Jas 1:22–25.
23:4 *tie up heavy, cumbersome loads and put them on other people's shoulders.* Cf. Jesus' words in 11:28–30 and see note on 11:28.
23:5 *phylacteries.* These boxes (see TNIV text note) contained four passages (Ex 13:1–10; 13:11–16; Dt 6:4–9; 11:13–21). *tassels.* See note on Nu 15:38.
23:6 *most important seats in the synagogues.* See note on Mk 12:39.
23:7 *Rabbi.* A Hebrew word meaning "(my) teacher."
23:8–10 The warning is against seeking titles of honor to fos-

ter pride. We should avoid unreasonable literalism in applying such commands.
23:13–32 Seven woes pronounced by Jesus on the religious leaders (cf. the six woes in Lk 11:42–44,46–52; the six in Isa 5:8–25; and the five in Hab 2:6–20).
23:13[14] *hypocrites.* See vv. 15,23,25,27,29; see also note on 6:2. *shut the door of the kingdom ... in people's faces.* See Lk 11:52 and note. Some late manuscripts add v. 14 from Mk 12:40 or Lk 20:47, but it is not in the earliest manuscripts here.
23:15 Jesus does not criticize the Pharisees for their evangelistic zeal. He objects to its results. The converts became even more sons of hell (i.e., bound for hell) than their teachers. *convert.* The Greek for this word is found in the NT only here and in Ac 2:11 (see note there); 6:5 (see note there); 13:43. *hell.* See note on 5:22; Lk 12:5.
23:16–22 When the teachers of the law and the Pharisees took an oath, they differentiated between what was binding and what was not. This allowed for evasive oath-taking. Jesus rejected all such subtleties by showing how foolish they were and by insisting that people simply tell the truth (see 5:33–37, where Jesus abolished all oaths).

23:17 *e* Ex 30:29
23:19 *f* Ex 29:37
23:21 *g* 1Ki 8:13;
Ps 26:8
23:22 *h* Ps 11:4;
Mt 5:34
23:23 *i* Lev 27:30
j Mic 6:8; Lk 11:42
23:24 *k* ver 16
23:25 *l* Mk 7:4
m Lk 11:39
23:27 *n* Lk 11:44;
Ac 23:3

Which is greater: the gold, or the temple that makes the gold sacred?*e* ¹⁸You also say, 'If anyone swears by the altar, it means nothing; but whoever swears by the gift on the altar is bound by the oath.' ¹⁹You blind men! Which is greater: the gift, or the altar that makes the gift sacred?*f* ²⁰Therefore, anyone who swears by the altar swears by it and by everything on it. ²¹And anyone who swears by the temple swears by it and by the one who dwells*g* in it. ²²And anyone who swears by heaven swears by God's throne and by the one who sits on it.*h*

²³"Woe to you, teachers of the law and Pharisees, you hypocrites! You give a tenth*i* of your spices—mint, dill and cumin. But you have neglected the more important matters of the law—justice, mercy and faithfulness.*j* You should have practiced the latter, without neglecting the former. ²⁴You blind guides!*k* You strain out a gnat but swallow a camel.

²⁵"Woe to you, teachers of the law and Pharisees, you hypocrites! You clean the outside of the cup and dish,*l* but inside they are full of greed and self-indulgence.*m* ²⁶Blind Pharisee! First clean the inside of the cup and dish, and then the outside also will be clean.

²⁷"Woe to you, teachers of the law and Pharisees, you hypocrites! You are like whitewashed tombs,*n* which look beautiful on the outside but on the inside are full of the bones

---

23:23 Jesus does not criticize the observance of the minutiae of the law (he says, "without neglecting" them—including the tithe), but he does criticize the hypocrisy often involved (see notes on 5:18–20; Lk 11:42). *cumin.* A spice indigenous to western Asia and resembling caraway in taste and appearance. *justice, mercy and faithfulness.* See Mic 6:6,8 and notes.
23:24 *strain out.* The strict Pharisee would carefully strain his drinking water through a cloth to be sure he did not swallow a gnat, the smallest of ceremonially unclean animals. But, figura-

tively, he would swallow a camel—one of the largest. *swallow a camel.* Hyperbole (see 7:3 and note; 19:24; Mk 10:25 and note).

▲ **23:26** *clean the inside.* A total moral renewal that will manifest itself in righteous living (see v. 23).
23:27 *whitewashed tombs.* A person who stepped on a grave became ceremonially unclean (see Nu 19:16), so graves were whitewashed to make them easily visible, especially at night. They appeared clean and beautiful on the outside, but they were dirty and rotten on the inside.

JEWISH SECTS

PHARISEES Their roots can be traced to the Hasidim of the second century B.C. (see note on Mk 2:16).	1. Along with the Torah, they accepted as equally inspired and authoritative all material contained within the oral tradition. 2. On free will and determination, they held to a mediating view that made it impossible for either free will or the sovereignty of God to cancel out the other. 3. They accepted a rather developed hierarchy of angels and demons. 4. They believed in the resurrection of the dead. 5. They believed in the immortality of the soul and in reward and retribution after death. 6. They were champions of human equality. 7. The emphasis of their teaching was ethical rather than theological.
SADDUCEES They probably had their beginning during the Hasmonean period (166–63 B.C.). Their demise occurred c. A.D. 70 with the fall of Jerusalem and the destruction of the temple.	1. They denied that the oral law was authoritative and binding. 2. They interpreted the Mosaic law more literally than did the Pharisees. 3. They were very exacting in Levitical purity. 4. They attributed everything to free will. 5. They argued that there is neither resurrection of the dead nor a future life. 6. They rejected belief in angels and demons. 7. They rejected the idea of a spiritual world. 8. They considered only the books of Moses to be canonical Scripture.
ESSENES They probably originated among the Hasidim, along with the Pharisees, from whom they later separated (1 Maccabees 2:42; 7:13). They were a group of very strict and zealous Jews who took part with the Maccabeans in a revolt against the Syrians c. 165–155 B.C.	1. They strictly observed the purity laws of the Torah. 2. They practiced communal ownership of property. 3. They had a strong sense of mutual responsibility. 4. Daily worship was an important feature along with daily study of their sacred scriptures. 5. Solemn oaths of piety and obedience had to be taken. 6. Sacrifices were offered on holy days and during sacred seasons. 7. Marriage was not condemned in principle but was avoided. 8. They attributed everything that happened to fate.
ZEALOTS They originated during the reign of Herod the Great c. 6 B.C. and were exterminated at Masada in A.D. 73.	1. They opposed payment of tribute for taxes to a pagan emperor because they believed that allegiance was due to God alone. 2. They were fiercely loyal to Jewish tradition. 3. They believed in violence as long as it accomplished a good end. 4. They were opposed to the use of the Greek language in the Holy Land.

of the dead and everything unclean. ²⁸In the same way, on the outside you appear to people as righteous but on the inside you are full of hypocrisy and wickedness.

²⁹"Woe to you, teachers of the law and Pharisees, you hypocrites! You build tombs for the prophets⁰ and decorate the graves of the righteous. ³⁰And you say, 'If we had lived in the days of our ancestors, we would not have taken part with them in shedding the blood of the prophets.' ³¹So you testify against yourselves that you are the descendants of those who murdered the prophets.ᵖ ³²Fill up, then, the measureᑫ of the sin of your ancestors!ʳ

³³"You snakes! You brood of vipers!ˢ How will you escape being condemned to hell?ᵗ ³⁴Therefore I am sending you prophets and sages and teachers. Some of them you will kill and crucify;ᵘ others you will flog in your synagoguesᵛ and pursue from town to town.ʷ ³⁵And so upon you will come all the righteous blood that has been shed on earth, from the blood of righteous Abelˣ to the blood of Zechariah son of Berekiah,ʸ whom you murdered between the temple and the altar.ᶻ ³⁶Truly I tell you, all this will come on this generation.ᵃ

³⁷"Jerusalem, Jerusalem, you who kill the prophets and stone those sent to you,ᵇ how often I have longed to gather your children together, as a hen gathers her chicks under her wings,ᶜ and you were not willing. ³⁸Look, your house is left to you desolate.ᵈ ³⁹For I tell you, you will not see me again until you say, 'Blessed is he who comes in the name of the Lord.'ᵃ"ᵉ

THE DESTRUCTION OF THE TEMPLE AND SIGNS OF THE END TIMES
24:1–51pp — Mk 13:1–37; Lk 21:5–36

24 Jesus left the temple and was walking away when his disciples came up to him to call his attention to its buildings. ²"Do you see all these things?" he asked. "Truly I tell you, not one stone here will be left on another;ᶠ every one will be thrown down."

³As Jesus was sitting on the Mount of Olives,ᵍ the disciples came to him privately. "Tell us," they said, "when will this happen, and what will be the sign of your comingʰ and of the end of the age?"ⁱ

⁴Jesus answered: "Watch out that no one deceives you.ʲ ⁵For many will come in my name, claiming, 'I am the Messiah,' and will deceive many.ᵏ ⁶You will hear of wars and rumors of wars, but see to it that you are not alarmed. Such things must happen, but the end is still to come. ⁷Nation will rise against nation, and kingdom against kingdom.ˡ There will be faminesᵐ and earthquakes in various places. ⁸All these are the beginning of birth pains.

ᵃ 39 Psalm 118:26

23:29 ⁰ Lk 11:47,48
23:31 ᵖ S Mt 5:12
23:32 ᑫ 1Ti 2:16
ʳ Eze 20:4
23:33 ˢ Mt 3:7; 12:34 ᵗ S Mt 5:22
23:34 ᵘ 2Ch 36:15, 16; Lk 11:49
ᵛ S Mt 10:17
ʷ Mt 10:23
23:35 ˣ Ge 4:8; Heb 11:4 ʸ Zec 1:1
ᶻ 2Ch 24:21
23:36 ᵃ Mt 10:23; 24:34; Lk 11:50, 51
23:37 ᵇ 2Ch 24:21; S Mt 5:12 ᶜ Ps 57:1; 61:4; Isa 31:5
23:38 ᵈ 1Ki 9:7,8; Jer 22:5
23:39 ᵉ Ps 118:26; Mt 21:9
24:2 ᶠ Lk 19:44
24:3 ᵍ S Mt 21:1
ʰ S Lk 17:30
ⁱ Mt 13:39; 28:20
24:4 ʲ S Mk 13:5
24:5 ᵏ ver 11,23,24; 1Jn 2:18
24:7 ˡ Isa 19:2
ᵐ Ac 11:28

23:29 *tombs for the prophets.* See note on Lk 11:47.

23:31 *descendants.* In the sense that they imitate the actions of their murderous ancestors.

23:32 Cf. Ge 15:16; 1Th 2:14–16; spoken ironically. They would bring the sin of their ancestors to completion with the crucifixion of the Son of God (cf. 21:38–39 and note on 21:35–37).

23:33 *hell.* See notes on 5:22; Lk 12:5.

23:34 *prophets and sages and teachers.* Cf. Jer 18:18; Eze 7:26 and notes. *synagogues.* See note on Mk 1:21.

23:35 *Abel to ... Zechariah.* The murder of Abel is recorded in Ge 4:8 and that of Zechariah son (perhaps grandson, since he is here called "son of Berekiah"; see TNIV text note on 1Ch 1:5; see also note on Da 5:1) of Jehoiada in 2Ch 24:20–22 (Chronicles comes at the close of the OT according to the Hebrew arrangement). The expression was somewhat like our "from Genesis to Revelation." Jesus was summing up the history of martyrdom in the OT.

23:36 *all this.* All the righteous blood of the martyrs (see v. 30). *will come on this generation.* Jesus' contemporaries; a prophecy fulfilled, at least in part, in the destruction of Jerusalem and the temple in A.D. 70 (see vv. 37–38).

23:37–39 See notes on Lk 13:34–35.

24:1—25:46 The Olivet discourse, the fifth and last of the great discourses in Matthew's Gospel (see notes on 5:1—7:29; Mk 13:1–37; Lk 21:5–37; see also Introduction: Structure).

24:2 *not one stone ... left.* Fulfilled literally in A.D. 70, when the Romans under Titus completely destroyed

Jerusalem and the temple buildings. Stones were even pried apart to collect the gold leaf that melted from the roof when the temple was set on fire. *stone.* See note on Mk 13:1. *thrown down.* Excavations in 1968 uncovered large numbers of these stones, toppled from the walls by the invaders.

24:3 *Mount of Olives.* A ridge a little more than a mile long, beyond the Kidron Valley east of Jerusalem and rising about 200 feet above the city (see map, pp. 1702–1703). *when will this happen, and what will be the sign of your coming and of the end of the age?* Jesus deals with these questions but does not distinguish them sharply. However, it appears that the description of the last days (which begin with Jesus' incarnation and end with his second coming) is presented in vv. 4–14, the destruction of Jerusalem in vv. 15–22 (see Lk 21:20) and Christ's coming in vv. 23–31. The rest of the discourse is largely taken up with warnings and exhortations to live responsibly and courageously despite trials, persecutions and uncertainty about the exact time of his coming (24:32—25:46). This last section contains several eschatological parables (25:1–13,14–30,31–46).

24:4 *Watch out.* See note on Mk 13:5.

24:5–14 See Lk 21:8–18 and note on 21:9.

24:5 *in my name.* Claiming to be the Messiah (see Mk 13:6 and note). *Messiah.* See TNIV text note on 1:1. *will deceive many.* See 1Jn 2:18 and note.

24:8 *birth pains.* The rabbis spoke of "birth pains," i.e., sufferings, that would precede the coming of the Messiah (see Isa 13:8 and note).

24:9 ⁿMt 10:17
ᵒJn 16:2 ᵖS Jn 15:21
24:11 ᵠS Mt 7:15
ʳS Mk 13:5
24:13 ˢS Mt 10:22
24:14 ᵗS Mt 4:23
ᵘLk 2:1; 4:5; Ac 11:28;
17:6;; S Ro 10:18
24:15 ᵛS Ac 6:13
ʷDa 9:27; 11:31; 12:11
24:17 ˣIsa 9:25;
Mt 10:27; Lk 12:3;
Ac 10:9
24:19 ʸLk 23:29
24:21 ᶻEze 5:9;
Da 12:1; Joel 2:2
24:22 ᵃver 24,31
24:23 ᵇLk 17:23;
21:8
24:24 ᶜEx 7:11,22;
2Th 2:9-11; Rev 13:13;
16:14; 19:20
24:27 ᵈLk 17:24
ᵉS Lk 17:30
ᶠS Mt 8:20
24:28 ᵍLk 17:37
24:29 ʰIsa 13:10;
34:4; Eze 32:7;
Joel 2:10,31; Zep 1:15;
Rev 6:12,13; 8:12
24:30 ⁱRev 1:7
ʲS Rev 1:7
24:31 ᵏMt 13:41
ˡIsa 27:13; Zec 9:14;
1Co 15:52; 1Th 4:16;
Rev 8:2; 10:7; 11:15

⁹"Then you will be handed over to be persecuted ⁿ and put to death,ᵒ and you will be hated by all nations because of me.ᵖ ¹⁰At that time many will turn away from the faith and will betray and hate each other, ¹¹and many false prophets ᵠ will appear and deceive many people.ʳ ¹²Because of the increase of wickedness, the love of most will grow cold, ¹³but whoever stands firm to the end will be saved.ˢ ¹⁴And this gospel of the kingdom ᵗ will be preached in the whole world ᵘ as a testimony to all nations, and then the end will come.

¹⁵"So when you see standing in the holy place ᵛ 'the abomination that causes desolation,'ᵃʷ spoken of through the prophet Daniel—let the reader understand— ¹⁶then let those who are in Judea flee to the mountains. ¹⁷Let no one on the housetop ˣ go down to take anything out of the house. ¹⁸Let no one in the field go back to get their cloak. ¹⁹How dreadful it will be in those days for pregnant women and nursing mothers!ʸ ²⁰Pray that your flight will not take place in winter or on the Sabbath. ²¹For then there will be great distress, unequaled from the beginning of the world until now—and never to be equaled again.ᶻ

²²"If those days had not been cut short, no one would survive, but for the sake of the elect ᵃ those days will be shortened. ²³At that time if anyone says to you, 'Look, here is the Messiah!' or, 'There he is!' do not believe it.ᵇ ²⁴For false messiahs and false prophets will appear and perform great signs and wonders ᶜ to deceive, if possible, even the elect. ²⁵See, I have told you ahead of time.

²⁶"So if anyone tells you, 'There he is, out in the wilderness,' do not go out; or, 'Here he is, in the inner rooms,' do not believe it. ²⁷For as lightning ᵈ that comes from the east is visible even in the west, so will be the coming ᵉ of the Son of Man.ᶠ ²⁸Wherever there is a carcass, there the vultures will gather.ᵍ

²⁹"Immediately after the distress of those days

" 'the sun will be darkened,
    and the moon will not give its light;
the stars will fall from the sky,
    and the heavenly bodies will be shaken.'ᵇʰ

³⁰"At that time the sign of the Son of Man will appear in the sky, and all the peoples of the earthᶜ will mourn.ⁱ They will see the Son of Man coming on the clouds of heaven,ʲ with power and great glory. ³¹And he will send his angels ᵏ with a loud trumpet call,ˡ and they will gather his elect from the four winds, from one end of the heavens to the other.

ᵃ 15 Daniel 9:27; 11:31; 12:11   ᵇ 29 Isaiah 13:10; 34:4   ᶜ 30 Or *the tribes of the land*

24:13 See note on Mk 13:13; cf. 2Ti 2:10–13; Heb 10:36; 11:27; Jas 1:12; 5:11.
24:14 *preached in the whole world.* Despite his Jewish interests, Matthew has a universal outlook (see Introduction: Recipients). *testimony to all nations.* This missionary mandate (see 28:18–20 and notes) must be fulfilled before the end comes.
24:15 *the abomination that causes desolation.* The detestable thing causing the desolation of the holy place. The primary reference in Daniel (see TNIV text note for references) was to 168 B.C., when Antiochus Epiphanes erected a pagan altar to Zeus on the sacred altar in the temple of Jerusalem. According to some, there were still two more stages in the progressive fulfillment of the predictions in Daniel and Matthew: (1) the Roman destruction of the temple in A.D. 70, and (2) the setting up of an image of the antichrist in Jerusalem (see 2Th 2:4; Rev 13:14–15; see also notes on Da 9:25–27; 11:31). *let the reader understand.* These are Jesus' words, not Matthew's. He exhorts the readers of Daniel's prophecy to understand what they read.
24:16 *mountains.* The Transjordan mountains, where Pella was located. Christians in Jerusalem fled to that area during the Roman siege shortly before A.D. 70. Some believe a similar fleeing will occur in a future tribulation period (identified with the 70th "seven" in Da 9:27).
24:17 *housetop.* See notes on Mk 2:4; Lk 17:31.
24:19 See note on Mk 13:17.
24:20 *in winter.* See note on Mk 13:18. *or on the Sabbath.* Matthew alone includes this phrase because he was writing to Jews, who were forbidden to travel more than about three quarters of a mile on the Sabbath ("a Sabbath day's walk," Ac 1:12; see note there).

24:21 *great distress, unequaled.* Josephus, the Jewish historian who was there, describes the destruction of Jerusalem in almost identical language. Some believe the reference is also to a future period of great distress (see note on v. 16; see also Da 12:1 and note; cf. Rev 6–18).
24:22 *days … cut short.* Some hold that this statement means that the distress will be of such intensity that, if allowed to continue, it would destroy everyone. Others believe that Christ is referring to the cutting short of a previously determined time period (such as the 70th "seven" of Da 9:27 or the 42 months of Rev 11:2; 13:5). *the elect.* The people of God.
24:24 *false messiahs.* See 1Jn 2:18 and note.
24:26 *inner rooms.* See Lk 12:3 and note.
24:27 Christ's second coming will not be in secret, witnessed by only a favored few; it will be visible to all (see v. 30). *as lightning.* See note on Lk 17:24.
24:28 *there the vultures will gather.* The gathering of vultures obviously indicates the presence of carrion; the coming of Christ will likewise be obvious. See note on Lk 17:37, where the saying is used in a slightly different sense.
24:29 See note on Mk 13:25.
24:30 *sign.* Here probably means "banner" or "standard" (see Isa 11:12; 18:3; 49:22; Jer 4:21; 51:27). *all the peoples … will mourn.* Because they now face judgment (see Rev 1:7; cf. Zec 12:10–12). *the Son of Man coming on the clouds.* Alludes to Da 7:13 and refers to Christ's second coming (see 2Th 1:7–10; Rev 19:11–16). *Son of Man.* See note on Mk 8:31. *on the clouds.* After the manner in which God came down on Mount Sinai (see 17:5 and note). *with power and great glory.* Cf. 1Ch 29:11; Ps 63:2; 66:2–3; Hab 3:3–4.
24:31 *gather his elect.* See note on Mk 13:27.

³²"Now learn this lesson from the fig tree: As soon as its twigs get tender and its leaves come out, you know that summer is near. ³³Even so, when you see all these things, you know that it^a is near, right at the door. ^m ³⁴Truly I tell you, this generation will certainly not pass away until all these things have happened. ⁿ ³⁵Heaven and earth will pass away, but my words will never pass away. ^o

THE DAY AND HOUR UNKNOWN
24:37–39pp — Lk 17:26,27
24:45–51pp — Lk 12:42–46

³⁶"But about that day or hour no one knows, not even the angels in heaven, nor the Son, ^b but only the Father. ^p ³⁷As it was in the days of Noah, ^q so it will be at the coming of the Son of Man. ³⁸For in the days before the flood, people were eating and drinking, marrying and giving in marriage, ^r up to the day Noah entered the ark; ³⁹and they knew nothing about what would happen until the flood came and took them all away. That is how it will be at the coming of the Son of Man. ^s ⁴⁰Two men will be in the field; one will be taken and the other left. ⁴¹Two women will be grinding with a hand mill; one will be taken and the other left. ^u

⁴²"Therefore keep watch, because you do not know on what day your Lord will come. ^v ⁴³But understand this: If the owner of the house had known at what time of night the thief was coming, ^w he would have kept watch and would not have let his house be broken into. ⁴⁴So you also must be ready, ^x because the Son of Man will come at an hour when you do not expect him.

⁴⁵"Who then is the faithful and wise servant, ^y whom the master has put in charge of the servants in his household to give them their food at the proper time? ⁴⁶It will be good for that servant whose master finds him doing so when he returns. ^z ⁴⁷Truly I tell you, he will put him in charge of all his possessions. ^a ⁴⁸But suppose that servant is wicked and says to himself, 'My master is staying away a long time,' ⁴⁹and he then begins to beat his fellow servants and to eat and drink with drunkards. ^b ⁵⁰The master of that servant will come on a day when he does not expect him and at an hour he is not aware of. ⁵¹He will cut him to pieces and assign him a place with the hypocrites, where there will be weeping and gnashing of teeth. ^c

THE PARABLE OF THE TEN VIRGINS

25 "At that time the kingdom of heaven will be like^d ten virgins who took their lamps^e and went out to meet the bridegroom. ^f ²Five of them were foolish and five were wise. ^g ³The foolish ones took their lamps but did not take any oil with them. ⁴The wise, however, took oil in jars along with their lamps. ⁵The bridegroom was a long time in coming, and they all became drowsy and fell asleep. ^h

⁶"At midnight the cry rang out: 'Here's the bridegroom! Come out to meet him!'

⁷"Then all the virgins woke up and trimmed their lamps. ⁸The foolish ones said to the wise, 'Give us some of your oil; our lamps are going out.' ⁱ

⁹" 'No,' they replied, 'there may not be enough for both us and you. Instead, go to those who sell oil and buy some for yourselves.'

¹⁰"But while they were on their way to buy the oil, the bridegroom arrived. The virgins who were ready went in with him to the wedding banquet. ^j And the door was shut.

¹¹"Later the others also came. 'Sir! Sir!' they said. 'Open the door for us!'

¹²"But he replied, 'Truly I tell you, I don't know you.' ^k

¹³"Therefore keep watch, because you do not know the day or the hour. ^l

^a 33 Or he   ^b 36 Some manuscripts do not have nor the Son.

24:33 ^m Jas 5:9
24:34 ⁿ Mt 16:28; S 23:36
24:35 ^o S Mt 5:18
24:36 ^p Ac 1:7
24:37 ^q Ge 6:5; 7:6-23
24:38 ^r Mt 22:30
24:39 ^s S Lk 17:30
24:40 ^t Lk 17:34
24:41 ^u Lk 17:35
24:42 ^v Mt 25:13; Lk 12:40
24:43 ^w S Lk 12:39
24:44 ^x 1Th 5:6
24:45 ^y Mt 25:21,23
24:46 ^z Rev 16:15
24:47 ^a Mt 25:21,23
24:49 ^b Lk 21:34
24:51 ^c S Mt 8:12
25:1 ^d S Mt 13:24
^e Lk 12:35-38;
Ac 20:8; Rev 4:5
^f Rev 19:7; 21:2
25:2 ^g Mt 24:45
25:5 ^h 1Th 5:6
25:8 ⁱ Lk 12:35
25:10 ^j Rev 19:9
25:12 ^k ver 41;
S Mt 7:23
25:13 ^l Mt 24:42,
44; Mk 13:35;
Lk 12:40

24:33 it. The kingdom of God (see Lk 21:31 and note on 21:29).
24:34 Truly I tell you. See note on Mk 3:28. this generation. See note on Lk 21:32.
24:35 Jesus' words are more certain than the existence of the universe.
24:36 that day. See note on Lk 21:34. nor the Son. See note on Mk 13:32.
24:40–41 taken. See note on Lk 17:35.

A **24:42** keep watch. Vigilance is the order of the day, because the time of Christ's coming is unknown (see notes on Mk 13:32,37).

24:44 be ready. See 25:10,29; 1Th 5:6 and notes; cf. 1Jn 2:28.
24:51 weeping and gnashing of teeth. See note on 13:42.
25:1–12 The parable emphasizes the need for watchfulness in the event of an unexpectedly long delay in Christ's coming (see v. 13 and note).

25:1 At that time. The time of Christ's coming. kingdom of heaven. See note on 3:2. ten virgins. Perhaps the bridesmaids, who were responsible for preparing the bride to meet the bridegroom. lamps. Probably torches that consisted of a long pole with oil-drenched rags at the top.
25:3 oil. Olive oil.
25:7 trimmed. The charred ends of the rags were cut off and oil was added.

A **25:9** No. When Christ returns, preparedness cannot be shared or transferred. Personal responsibility is emphasized (see v. 12). there may not be enough. Torches required large amounts of oil in order to keep burning, and the oil had to be replenished about every 15 minutes.

25:13 keep watch. The main point of the parable. the day or the hour. Of the coming of Christ.

25:14 *m* Mt 21:33;
Lk 19:12
25:15 *n* Mt 18:24,25
25:19 *o* Mt 18:23
25:21 *p* ver 23;
Mt 24:45,47; Lk 16:10
25:23 *q* ver 21
25:29 *r* Mt 13:12;
Mk 4:25; Lk 8:18;
19:26
25:30 *s* S Mt 8:12
25:31 *t* S Lk 17:30
u Mt 19:28
25:32 *v* Mal 3:18
w Eze 34:17,20
25:34 *x* S Mt 3:2;
5:3,10,19; 19:14;
S Ac 20:32;
1Co 15:50; Gal 5:21;
Jas 2:5 *y* Heb 4:3;
9:26; Rev 13:8; 17:8

THE PARABLE OF THE BAGS OF GOLD

25:14–30Ref — Lk 19:12–27

¹⁴"Again, it will be like a man going on a journey,*m* who called his servants and entrusted his wealth to them. ¹⁵To one he gave five bags of gold, to another two bags, and to another one bag,*a* each according to his ability.*n* Then he went on his journey. ¹⁶The man who had received five bags of gold went at once and put his money to work and gained five bags more. ¹⁷So also, the one with two bags of gold gained two more. ¹⁸But the man who had received one bag went off, dug a hole in the ground and hid his master's money.

¹⁹"After a long time the master of those servants returned and settled accounts with them.*o* ²⁰The man who had received five bags of gold brought the other five. 'Master,' he said, 'you entrusted me with five bags of gold. See, I have gained five more.'

²¹"His master replied, 'Well done, good and faithful servant! You have been faithful with a few things; I will put you in charge of many things.*p* Come and share your master's happiness!'

²²"The man with two bags of gold also came. 'Master,' he said, 'you entrusted me with two bags of gold; see, I have gained two more.'

²³"His master replied, 'Well done, good and faithful servant! You have been faithful with a few things; I will put you in charge of many things.*q* Come and share your master's happiness!'

²⁴"Then the man who had received one bag of gold came. 'Master,' he said, 'I knew that you are a hard man, harvesting where you have not sown and gathering where you have not scattered seed. ²⁵So I was afraid and went out and hid your gold in the ground. See, here is what belongs to you.'

²⁶"His master replied, 'You wicked, lazy servant! So you knew that I harvest where I have not sown and gather where I have not scattered seed? ²⁷Well then, you should have put my money on deposit with the bankers, so that when I returned I would have received it back with interest.

²⁸" 'Take the bag of gold from him and give it to the one who has ten bags. ²⁹For those who have will be given more, and they will have an abundance. As for those who do not have, even what they have will be taken from them.*r* ³⁰And throw that worthless servant outside, into the darkness, where there will be weeping and gnashing of teeth.'*s*

THE SHEEP AND THE GOATS

³¹"When the Son of Man comes*t* in his glory, and all the angels with him, he will sit on his glorious throne.*u* ³²All the nations will be gathered before him, and he will separate*v* the people one from another as a shepherd separates the sheep from the goats.*w* ³³He will put the sheep on his right and the goats on his left.

³⁴"Then the King will say to those on his right, 'Come, you who are blessed by my Father; take your inheritance, the kingdom*x* prepared for you since the creation of the world.*y* ³⁵For I was hungry and you gave me something to eat, I was thirsty and you gave

---

a 15 Greek *five talents . . . two talents . . . one talent*; also throughout this parable; a talent was worth about 20 years of a day laborer's wage.

25:14–30 For a similar parable see Lk 19:12–27.
25:15 *bag.* See TNIV text note. The term *talent* was first used for a unit of weight (about 75 pounds), then for a unit of coinage. The present-day use of "talent" to indicate an ability or gift is derived from this parable (see note on Lk 19:13).
25:21 *faithful with a few . . . in charge of many.* Cf. 13:12; see notes on v. 29; Mk 4:25; Lk 19:26.
25:26 See note on Lk 19:22.
25:27 *bankers.* Sat at small tables and changed money (cf. 21:12).
25:29 The main point of the parable. Being ready for Christ's coming involves more than playing it safe and doing little or nothing. It demands the kind of service that produces results (see note on Lk 19:26).
25:30 *weeping and gnashing of teeth.* See note on 13:42.
25:31–46 The two most widely accepted interpretations of this judgment are: 1. It will occur at the beginning of an earthly millennial kingdom (vv. 31,34; see Rev 20:4 and note on 20:2). Its purpose will be to determine who will be allowed to enter the kingdom (v. 34). The basis for judgment will be the kind of treatment shown to the Jewish people ("these brothers and sis-

ters of mine," v. 40) during the preceding great tribulation period (vv. 35–40,42–45). Ultimately, how one treats them will reveal whether or not one is saved (vv. 41,46). 2. The judgment referred to occurs at the great white throne at the end of the age (Rev 20:11–15). Its purpose will be to determine who will be allowed to enter the eternal kingdom of the saved and who will be consigned to eternal punishment in hell (vv. 34,46). The basis for judgment will be whether love is shown to God's people (see 1Jn 3:14–15). See note on v. 40.
25:31 *Son of Man.* See note on Mk 8:31. *in his glory.* See 16:27; 24:30. *angels.* See 13:41–42; 2Th 1:7; Rev 14:17–20. *sit on his glorious throne.* Not only as judge but also as king (vv. 34,40).
25:32 *All the nations.* Both Jews and Gentiles (see 28:19 and note). *separates the sheep from the goats.* Cf. 7:21–23; 13:40–43.
25:33 *on his right.* See Mk 10:37 and note.
25:34–40 Rewards in the kingdom of heaven are given to those who serve without thought of reward. There is no hint of merit here, for God gives out of grace, not debt.
25:34 *inheritance.* See Ac 20:32; Eph 1:14,18; 5:5; Col 1:12; 3:24; Heb 9:15; 1Pe 1:4. *kingdom.* See note on 3:2. *since the creation of the world.* Cf. Eph 1:4 and note.

me something to drink, I was a stranger and you invited me in,[z] [36]I needed clothes and you clothed me,[a] I was sick and you looked after me,[b] I was in prison and you came to visit me.'[c]

[37]"Then the righteous will answer him, 'Lord, when did we see you hungry and feed you, or thirsty and give you something to drink? [38]When did we see you a stranger and invite you in, or needing clothes and clothe you? [39]When did we see you sick or in prison and go to visit you?'

[40]"The King will reply, 'Truly I tell you, whatever you did for one of the least of these brothers and sisters of mine, you did for me.'[d]

[41]"Then he will say to those on his left, 'Depart from me,[e] you who are cursed, into the eternal fire[f] prepared for the devil and his angels.[g] [42]For I was hungry and you gave me nothing to eat, I was thirsty and you gave me nothing to drink, [43]I was a stranger and you did not invite me in, I needed clothes and you did not clothe me, I was sick and in prison and you did not look after me.'

[44]"They also will answer, 'Lord, when did we see you hungry or thirsty or a stranger or needing clothes or sick or in prison, and did not help you?'

[45]"He will reply, 'Truly I tell you, whatever you did not do for one of the least of these, you did not do for me.'[h]

[46]"Then they will go away to eternal punishment, but the righteous to eternal life.[i][j]

THE PLOT AGAINST JESUS

26:2–5pp — Mk 14:1,2; Lk 22:1,2

26 When Jesus had finished saying all these things,[k] he said to his disciples, [2]"As you know, the Passover[l] is two days away—and the Son of Man will be handed over to be crucified."

[3]Then the chief priests and the elders of the people assembled[m] in the palace of the high priest, whose name was Caiaphas,[n] [4]and they plotted to arrest Jesus in some sly way and kill him.[o] [5]"But not during the festival," they said, "or there may be a riot[p] among the people."

JESUS ANOINTED AT BETHANY

26:6–13pp — Mk 14:3–9

26:6–13Ref — Lk 7:37,38; Jn 12:1–8

[6]While Jesus was in Bethany[q] in the home of Simon the Leper, [7]a woman came to him with an alabaster jar of very expensive perfume, which she poured on his head as he was reclining at the table.

[8]When the disciples saw this, they were indignant. "Why this waste?" they asked. [9]"This perfume could have been sold at a high price and the money given to the poor."

[10]Aware of this, Jesus said to them, "Why are you bothering this woman? She has done a beautiful thing to me. [11]The poor you will always have with you,[a][r] but you will not always have me. [12]When she poured this perfume on my body, she did it to prepare me for

[a] 11 See Deut. 15:11.

### Cross-references (right margin)

25:35 [z] Job 31:32; Heb 13:2
25:36 [a] Isa 58:7; Eze 18:7; Jas 2:15,16 [b] Jas 1:27 [c] 2Ti 1:16
25:40 [d] S Mt 10:40, 42; Heb 13:2
25:41 [e] S Mt 7:23 [f] Isa 66:24; Mt 3:12;; S 5:22; Mk 9:43,48; Lk 3:17; Jude 7 [g] 2Pe 2:4
25:45 [h] Pr 14:31; 17:5
25:46 [i] Mt 19:29; Jn 3:15,16,36; 17:2,3; Ro 2:7; Gal 6:8; 1Jn 1:2; 5:11,13,20 [j] Da 12:2; Jn 5:29; Ac 24:15; Ro 2:7,8; Gal 6:8
26:1 [k] S Mt 7:28
26:2 [l] S Jn 11:55
26:3 [m] Ps 2:2 [n] ver 57; Lk 3:2; Jn 11:47-53; 18:13,14, 24,28; Ac 4:6
26:4 [o] S Mt 12:14
26:5 [p] Mt 27:24
26:6 [q] S Mt 21:17
26:11 [r] Dt 15:11

25:40 *least of these brothers and sisters of mine.* To whom does Jesus refer? The principal views are: (1) all who are hungry, thirsty, poor, needy or otherwise distressed—but this seems too comprehensive; (2) apostles and other Christian missionaries—but this seems too restrictive; (3) the Jews mentioned in the first interpretation in the note on vv. 31–46; (4) Jesus' disciples (12:46–50; 28:8–10); (5) "God's people" mentioned in the second interpretation in the note on vv. 31–46.

25:41 *eternal fire prepared for the devil.* See Rev 20:10. *fire.* See Jude 7; Rev 19:20 and notes; 20:15.

25:46 *eternal punishment … eternal life.* See Da 12:2; Jn 5:28–29; see also Jn 5:29; Ro 2:6–8; Gal 6:8 and notes. The parallelism between these two phrases prevents any weakening of the former.

26:2 *Passover.* See notes on Mk 14:1; Jn 2:13. *Son of Man.* See note on Mk 8:31.

B **26:3** *chief priests and the elders of the people.* The priestly and lay leadership of the Sanhedrin (see note on 2:4). *Caiaphas.* High priest A.D. 18–36 and the son-in-law of Annas (see Jn 18:13 and note), a former high priest, who served A.D. 6–15. In 1991 an ossuary (a limestone chest containing the bones of

the dead) was found in Jerusalem inscribed with the name Caiaphas (see chart, p. 1830).

26:5 *there may be a riot.* Hundreds of thousands of Jewish pilgrims came to Jerusalem for Passover (see note on Mk 14:2), and riots were not unknown. The religious leaders (v. 3) knew that many people admired Jesus.

26:6–13 See note on Jn 12:1–11.

26:6 *Bethany.* See note on 21:17. *Simon the Leper.* Mentioned elsewhere only in Mk 14:3, though Simon was a common Jewish name in the first century. He was probably a well-known victim of leprosy who had been healed by Jesus.

26:7 *a woman.* Mary, sister of Martha and Lazarus (see Jn 12:3 and note). *alabaster jar.* Most alabaster of ancient times was actually marble (see note on Mk 14:3).

26:9 *given to the poor.* See note on Mk 14:5.

26:10 *beautiful.* The Greek word has an aesthetic as well as an ethical meaning.

26:11 *The poor you will always have with you.* See note on Mk 14:7.

26:12 *prepare me for burial.* See note on Mk 14:8.

THE LIFE OF CHRIST

CHILDHOOD

Birth of Jesus, BETHLEHEM, 6/5 B.C., Mt 1:18–25; Lk 2:1–7

Visit by shepherds, BETHLEHEM, Lk 2:8–20

Presentation in the temple, JERUSALEM, Lk 2:21–40

Visit by the Magi, BETHLEHEM, Mt 2:1–12

Escape to Egypt, NILE DELTA, Mt 2:13–18

Return to Nazareth, LOWER GALILEE, Mt 2:19–23

Visit to temple as a boy,
JERUSALEM, A.D. 7/8, Lk 2:41–52

YEAR OF INAUGURATION

YEAR OF POPULARITY

YEAR OF OPPOSITION

Begin less than full year of ministry

```
10        5              5    10   15   20   25      30       35
|||||||||||||||||||||||||||||||||||||||||||||||||||||||||
          B.C. | A.D.
```

Jesus baptized
JORDAN RIVER
A.D. 26
Mt 3:13–17; Mk 1:9–11;
Lk 3:21–23; Jn 1:29–39

Jesus tempted by Satan
DESERT OF JUDEA
Mt 4:1–11; Mk 1:12–13; Lk 4:1–13

Jesus' first miracle
CANA
Jn 2:1–11

4 fishermen become Jesus' followers
SEA OF GALILEE
AT CAPERNAUM
A.D. 27
Mt 4:18–22; Mk 1:16–20;
Lk 5:1–11

Jesus heals Peter's mother-in-law
CAPERNAUM
Mt 8:14–17; Mk 1:29–34;
Lk 4:38–41

──── **YEAR OF INAUGURATION** ────⟍ ⟋──── **YEAR OF POPULARITY** ────

A.D.	**27**				**28**	
FALL	**WINTER**	**SPRING**	**SUMMER**	**FALL**	**WINTER**	

Jesus cleanses the temple
A.D. 27
Jn 2:14–22

Jesus and Nicodemus
JERUSALEM
A.D. 27
Jn 3:1–21

Jesus talks to the Samaritan woman
SAMARIA
Jn 4:5–42

Jesus heals a nobleman's son
CANA
Jn 4:46–54

The people of Jesus' hometown try to kill him
NAZARETH
Lk 4:16–31

Jesus begins his first preaching trip through Galilee
Mt 4:23–25; Mk 1:35–39;
Lk 4:42–44

Matthew decides to follow Jesus
CAPERNAUM
Mt 9:9–13; Mk 2:13–17; Lk 5:27–32

Jesus chooses the 12 disciples
A.D. 28
Mk 3:13–19; Lk 6:12–15

Jesus preaches the Sermon on the Mount
Mt 5:1—7:29; Lk 6:20–49

[Dotted lines leading to the timeline are meant to define sequence of events only. All dates are approximate.]

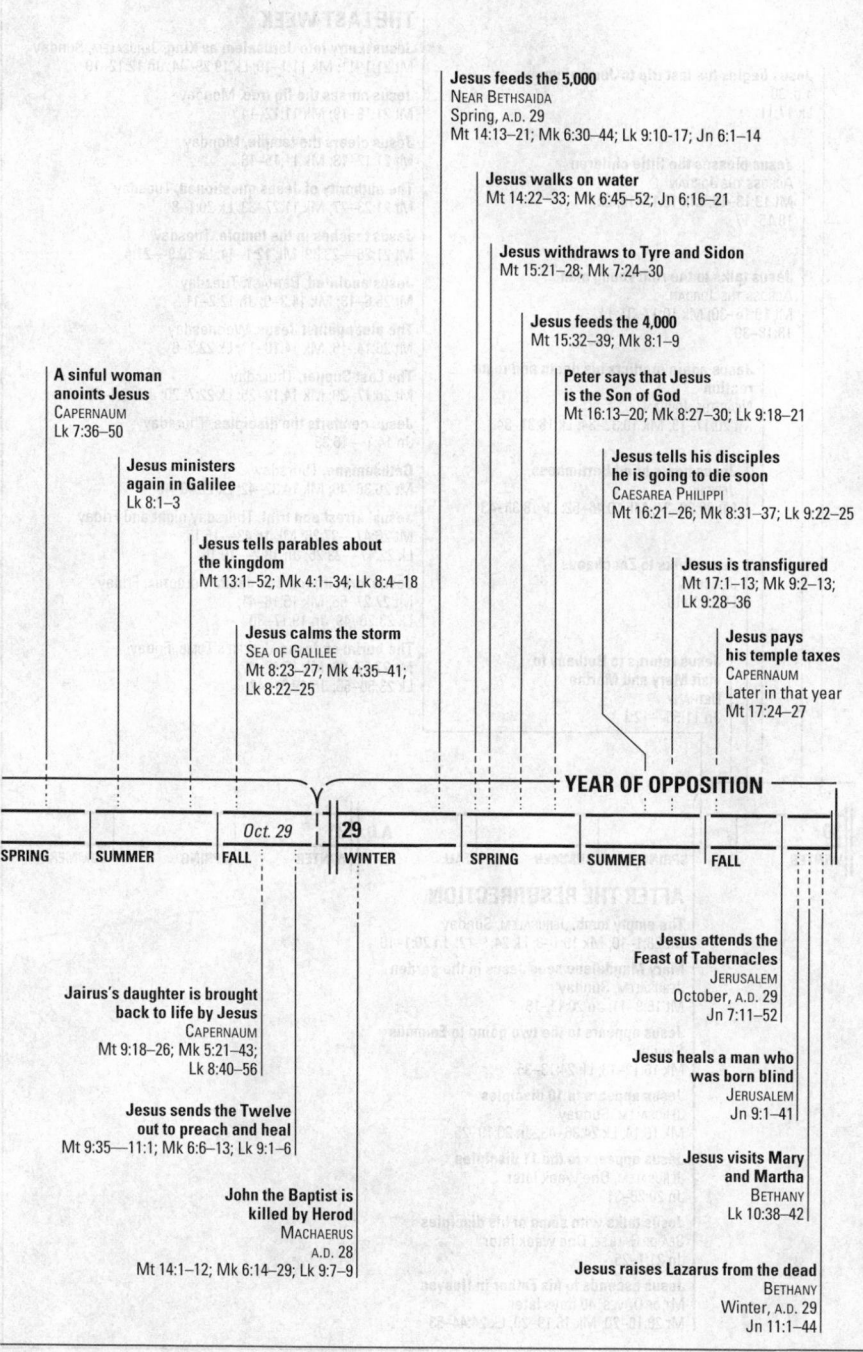

Jesus feeds the 5,000
NEAR BETHSAIDA
Spring, A.D. 29
Mt 14:13–21; Mk 6:30–44; Lk 9:10-17; Jn 6:1–14

Jesus walks on water
Mt 14:22–33; Mk 6:45–52; Jn 6:16–21

Jesus withdraws to Tyre and Sidon
Mt 15:21–28; Mk 7:24–30

Jesus feeds the 4,000
Mt 15:32–39; Mk 8:1–9

Peter says that Jesus is the Son of God
Mt 16:13–20; Mk 8:27–30; Lk 9:18–21

Jesus tells his disciples he is going to die soon
CAESAREA PHILIPPI
Mt 16:21–26; Mk 8:31–37; Lk 9:22–25

Jesus is transfigured
Mt 17:1–13; Mk 9:2–13; Lk 9:28–36

Jesus pays his temple taxes
CAPERNAUM
Later in that year
Mt 17:24–27

A sinful woman anoints Jesus
CAPERNAUM
Lk 7:36–50

Jesus ministers again in Galilee
Lk 8:1–3

Jesus tells parables about the kingdom
Mt 13:1–52; Mk 4:1–34; Lk 8:4–18

Jesus calms the storm
SEA OF GALILEE
Mt 8:23–27; Mk 4:35–41; Lk 8:22–25

YEAR OF OPPOSITION

		Oct. 29	29			
SPRING	SUMMER	FALL	WINTER	SPRING	SUMMER	FALL

Jesus attends the Feast of Tabernacles
JERUSALEM
October, A.D. 29
Jn 7:11–52

Jairus's daughter is brought back to life by Jesus
CAPERNAUM
Mt 9:18–26; Mk 5:21–43; Lk 8:40–56

Jesus heals a man who was born blind
JERUSALEM
Jn 9:1–41

Jesus sends the Twelve out to preach and heal
Mt 9:35—11:1; Mk 6:6–13; Lk 9:1–6

Jesus visits Mary and Martha
BETHANY
Lk 10:38–42

John the Baptist is killed by Herod
MACHAERUS
A.D. 28
Mt 14:1–12; Mk 6:14–29; Lk 9:7–9

Jesus raises Lazarus from the dead
BETHANY
Winter, A.D. 29
Jn 11:1–44

THE LAST WEEK

Jesus' Entry into Jerusalem as King, JERUSALEM, Sunday
Mt 21:1–11; Mk 11:1–10; Lk 19:29–44; Jn 12:12–19

Jesus curses the fig tree, Monday
Mt 21:18–19; Mk 11:12–14

Jesus clears the temple, Monday
Mt 21:12–13; Mk 11:15–18

The authority of Jesus questioned, Tuesday
Mt 21:23–27; Mk 11:27–33; Lk 20:1–8

Jesus teaches in the temple, Tuesday
Mt 21:28—23:39; Mk 12:1–44; Lk 20:9—21:4

Jesus anointed, BETHANY, Tuesday
Mt 26:6–13; Mk 14:3–9; Jn 12:2–11

The plot against Jesus, Wednesday
Mt 26:14–16; Mk 14:10–11; Lk 22:3–6

The Last Supper, Thursday
Mt 26:17–29; Mk 14:12–25; Lk 22:7–20; Jn 13:1–38

Jesus comforts the disciples, Thursday
Jn 14:1—16:33

Gethsemane, Thursday
Mt 26:36–46; Mk 14:32–42; Lk 22:40–46

Jesus' arrest and trial, Thursday night and Friday
Mt 26:47—27:26; Mk 14:43—15:15;
Lk 22:47—23:25; Jn 18:2—19:16

Jesus' crucifixion and death, GOLGOTHA, Friday
Mt 27:27–56; Mk 15:16–41;
Lk 23:26–49; Jn 19:17–30

The burial of Jesus, JOSEPH'S TOMB, Friday
Mt 27:57–66; Mk 15:42–47;
Lk 23:50–56; Jn 19:31–42

Jesus begins his last trip to Jerusalem
A.D. 30
Lk 17:11

Jesus blesses the little children
ACROSS THE JORDAN
Mt 19:13–15; Mk 10:13–16; Lk
18:15–17

Jesus talks to the rich young man
ACROSS THE JORDAN
Mt 19:16–30; Mk 10:17–31; Lk
18:18–30

Jesus again predicts his death and resurrection
NEAR THE JORDAN
Mt 20:17–19; Mk 10:32–34; Lk 18:31–34

Jesus heals blind Bartimaeus
JERICHO
Mt 20:29–34; Mk 10:46–52; Lk 18:35–43

Jesus talks to Zacchaeus
JERICHO
Lk 19:1–10

Jesus returns to Bethany to visit Mary and Martha
BETHANY
Jn 11:55—12:1

30				A.D.	31		
WINTER	SPRING	SUMMER	FALL		WINTER	SPRING	SUMMER

AFTER THE RESURRECTION

The empty tomb, JERUSALEM, Sunday
Mt 28:1–10; Mk 16:1–8; Lk 24:1–12; Jn 20:1–10

Mary Magdalene sees Jesus in the garden
JERUSALEM, Sunday
Mt 16:9–11; Jn 20:11–18

Jesus appears to the two going to Emmaus
Sunday
Mk 16:12–13; Lk 24:13–35

Jesus appears to 10 disciples
JERUSALEM, Sunday
Mk 16:14; Lk 24:36–43; Jn 20:19–25

Jesus appears to the 11 disciples
JERUSALEM, One week later
Jn 20:26–31

Jesus talks with some of his disciples
SEA OF GALILEE, One week later
Jn 21:1–25

Jesus ascends to his Father in Heaven
MT OF OLIVES, 40 days later
Mt 28:16–20; Mk 16:19–20; Lk 24:44–53

burial.*s* 13 Truly I tell you, wherever this gospel is preached throughout the world, what she has done will also be told, in memory of her."

JUDAS AGREES TO BETRAY JESUS

26:14–16pp — Mk 14:10,11; Lk 22:3–6

14 Then one of the Twelve—the one called Judas Iscariot*t*—went to the chief priests 15 and asked, "What are you willing to give me if I deliver him over to you?" So they counted out for him thirty pieces of silver.*u* 16 From then on Judas watched for an opportunity to hand him over.

THE LAST SUPPER

26:17–19pp — Mk 14:12–16; Lk 22:7–13
26:20–24pp — Mk 14:17–21
26:26–29pp — Mk 14:22–25; Lk 22:17–20; 1Co 11:23–25

17 On the first day of the Festival of Unleavened Bread,*v* the disciples came to Jesus and asked, "Where do you want us to make preparations for you to eat the Passover?"*w* 18 He replied, "Go into the city to a certain man and tell him, 'The Teacher says: My appointed time*x* is near. I am going to celebrate the Passover with my disciples at your house.' " 19 So the disciples did as Jesus had directed them and prepared the Passover.

20 When evening came, Jesus was reclining at the table with the Twelve. 21 And while they were eating, he said, "Truly I tell you, one of you will betray me."*y*

22 They were very sad and began to say to him one after the other, "Surely not I, Lord?" 23 Jesus replied, "The one who has dipped his hand into the bowl with me will betray me.*z* 24 The Son of Man will go just as it is written about him.*a* But woe to that man who betrays the Son of Man! It would be better for him if he had not been born."

25 Then Judas, the one who would betray him,*b* said, "Surely not I, Rabbi?"*c* Jesus answered, "You have said so."

26 While they were eating, Jesus took bread, and when he had given thanks, he broke it*d* and gave it to his disciples, saying, "Take and eat; this is my body."

27 Then he took the cup,*e* and when he had given thanks, he gave it to them, saying, "Drink from it, all of you. 28 This is my blood of the*a* covenant,*f* which is poured out for many for the forgiveness of sins.*g* 29 I tell you, I will not drink of this fruit of the vine from now on until that day when I drink it new with you*h* in my Father's kingdom."

30 When they had sung a hymn, they went out to the Mount of Olives.*i*

JESUS PREDICTS PETER'S DENIAL

26:31–35pp — Mk 14:27–31; Lk 22:31–34

31 Then Jesus told them, "This very night you will all fall away on account of me,*j* for it is written:

---

a 28 Some manuscripts *the new*

26:12 *s* Jn 19:40
26:14 *t* ver 25,47;
S Mt 10:4
26:15 *u* Ex 21:32;
Zec 11:12
26:17 *v* Ex 12:18-20
w Dt 16:5-8
26:18 *x* Mk 14:35,
41; Jn 7:6,8,30; 8:20;
12:23; 13:1; 17:1
26:21 *y* Lk 22:21-23;
Jn 13:21
26:23 *z* Ps 41:9;
Jn 13:18
26:24 *a* ver 31,54,
56; Isa 53; Da 9:26;
Mk 9:12; Lk 24:25-27,
46; Ac 17:2,3; 26:22,
23; 1Pe 1:10,11
26:25 *b* S Mt 10:4
c S Mt 23:7
26:26 *d* Mt 14:19
26:27 *e* 1Co 10:16
26:28 *f* Ex 24:6-8;
Zec 9:11; Mal 2:5;
Heb 9:20; 10:29;
S 13:20 *g* S Mt 20:28;
Mk 1:4
26:29 *h* Ac 10:41
26:30 *i* S Mt 21:1
26:31 *j* Mt 11:6;
13:21

26:14 *Iscariot.* See note on Mk 3:19. *chief priests.* See note on 2:4.
26:15 *thirty pieces of silver.* Equivalent to 120 denarii. Laborers customarily received one denarius for a day's work (20:1–16). See notes on 20:2; Zec 11:12.
26:17 *first day of the Festival of Unleavened Bread.* The 14th of Nisan (March-April), it was also called the preparation of the Passover. The Passover meal was eaten the evening of the 14th after sunset—and therefore technically on the 15th, since the Jewish day ended at sunset. The Festival of Unleavened Bread lasted seven days, from the 15th to the 21st of Nisan (see Lev 23:5–6), but in the time of Christ the entire period, Nisan 14–21, was referred to under that name (see note on Mk 14:12).
26:18–30 These verses indicate that Jesus ate the Passover meal with his disciples the night before his crucifixion. For more information on the Lord's Supper see notes on Mk 14:22,24.
26:18 *The Teacher says.* See note on Lk 22:11. *My appointed time.* Jesus' crucifixion.
26:19 *as Jesus had directed them.* See note on Lk 22:13. *prepared the Passover.* See note on Mk 14:15.
26:20 *When evening came.* See note on Mk 14:17. *reclining at the table.* See note on Mk 14:18.
26:21 *Truly I tell you.* See note on Mk 3:28.
26:23 *dipped his hand into the bowl with me.* It was the custom—

still practiced by some in the Middle East—to take a piece of bread, or a piece of meat wrapped in bread, and dip it into a bowl of sauce (made of stewed fruit) on the table. *will betray me.* In that culture, as among Arabs today, to eat with a person was tantamount to saying, "I am your friend and will not hurt you." This fact made Judas's deed all the more despicable (cf. Ps 41:9 and note).
26:24 *as it is written about him.* See note on Mk 14:21. *Son of Man.* See note on Mk 8:31.
26:26–28 See notes on Mk 14:22–24.
26:27 *took the cup.* See note on Lk 22:17.
26:28 *blood of the covenant … poured out for many.* See note on Mk 14:24.
26:29 *drink it new … in my Father's kingdom.* At the Messianic banquet (see Lk 22:16 and note).
26:30 *hymn.* The Passover fellowship was concluded with the second half of the Egyptian Hallel Psalms (Ps 115–118). Ps 113–114 were sung before the meal. *Mount of Olives.* See note on Mk 11:1.
26:31 *all fall away.* Not Peter only, but all the eleven (Judas had previously withdrawn, Jn 13:30). The meaning of the words "fall away" is seen in Peter's denial (vv. 69–75) and in the terrified flight of the other disciples (v. 56). *I will strike the shepherd.* See note on Zec 13:7.

26:31 *k* Zec 13:7;
Jn 16:32
26:32 *l* Mt 28:7,10,
16
26:34 *m* ver 75;
Jn 13:38
26:35 *n* Jn 13:37
26:37 *o* S Mt 4:21
26:38 *p* S Jn 12:27
q ver 40,41
26:39 *r* S Mt 20:22
s ver 42; Ps 40:6-8;
Isa 50:5; Mt 6:10;
Jn 4:34; 5:30; 6:38
26:40 *t* ver 38
26:41 *u* Mt 6:13
26:42 *v* S ver 39
26:45 *w* S ver 18
26:47 *x* S Mt 10:4
26:49 *y* ver 25;
S Mt 23:7
26:50 *z* Mt 20:13;
22:12
26:51 *a* Lk 22:36,38
b Jn 18:10
26:52 *c* Ge 9:6;
Ex 21:12; Rev 13:10

" 'I will strike the shepherd,
and the sheep of the flock will be scattered.'ᵃᵏ

³²But after I have risen, I will go ahead of you into Galilee."ˡ

³³Peter replied, "Even if all fall away on account of you, I never will."

³⁴"Truly I tell you," Jesus answered, "this very night, before the rooster crows, you will disown me three times."ᵐ

³⁵But Peter declared, "Even if I have to die with you,ⁿ I will never disown you." And all the other disciples said the same.

GETHSEMANE
26:36–46pp — Mk 14:32–42; Lk 22:40–46

³⁶Then Jesus went with his disciples to a place called Gethsemane, and he said to them, "Sit here while I go over there and pray." ³⁷He took Peter and the two sons of Zebedeeᵒ along with him, and he began to be sorrowful and troubled. ³⁸Then he said to them, "My soul is overwhelmed with sorrowᵖ to the point of death. Stay here and keep watch with me."ᑫ

³⁹Going a little farther, he fell with his face to the ground and prayed, "My Father, if it is possible, may this cupʳ be taken from me. Yet not as I will, but as you will."ˢ

⁴⁰Then he returned to his disciples and found them sleeping. "Couldn't you men keep watch with meᵗ for one hour?" he asked Peter. ⁴¹"Watch and pray so that you will not fall into temptation.ᵘ The spirit is willing, but the flesh is weak."

⁴²He went away a second time and prayed, "My Father, if it is not possible for this cup to be taken away unless I drink it, may your will be done."ᵛ

⁴³When he came back, he again found them sleeping, because their eyes were heavy. ⁴⁴So he left them and went away once more and prayed the third time, saying the same thing.

⁴⁵Then he returned to the disciples and said to them, "Are you still sleeping and resting? Look, the hourʷ is near, and the Son of Man is delivered into the hands of sinners. ⁴⁶Rise! Let us go! Here comes my betrayer!"

JESUS ARRESTED
26:47–56pp — Mk 14:43–50; Lk 22:47–53

⁴⁷While he was still speaking, Judas,ˣ one of the Twelve, arrived. With him was a large crowd armed with swords and clubs, sent from the chief priests and the elders of the people. ⁴⁸Now the betrayer had arranged a signal with them: "The one I kiss is the man; arrest him." ⁴⁹Going at once to Jesus, Judas said, "Greetings, Rabbi!"ʸ and kissed him.

⁵⁰Jesus replied, "Friend,ᶻ do what you came for."ᵇ

Then the men stepped forward, seized Jesus and arrested him. ⁵¹With that, one of Jesus' companions reached for his sword,ᵃ drew it out and struck the servant of the high priest, cutting off his ear.ᵇ

⁵²"Put your sword back in its place," Jesus said to him, "for all who draw the sword will die by the sword.ᶜ ⁵³Do you think I cannot call on my Father, and he will at once put at

---

ᵃ **31** Zech. 13:7   ᵇ **50** Or *"Friend, why have you come?"*

26:32 *into Galilee.* Cf. 28:10,16–20; Mk 16:7; Jn 21:1–23.

26:34 *before the rooster crows.* The reference may be to the third of the Roman watches into which the night was divided (see note on 14:25; see also Mk 13:35 and note). Or it may simply refer to early morning when the rooster crows.

26:36 *Gethsemane.* The name means "oil press," a place for squeezing the oil from olives (see note on Mk 14:32).

26:37 *Peter and the two sons of Zebedee.* The latter were James and John. These three disciples seem to have been especially close to Jesus (see note on Mk 5:37).

26:38–39 Jesus did not die serenely as many martyrs have. He was no mere martyr; he was the Lamb of God bearing the penalty of the sins of the entire human race. The wrath of God was turned loose on him. Only this can adequately explain what took place at Gethsemane.

26:38 *soul.* See 10:28 and note. *overwhelmed with sorrow.* See Isa 53:3 and note.

26:39 *cup.* A symbol of deep sorrow and suffering. Here it

refers to his Father's face being turned away from him when he who had no sin was made sin (perhaps a sin offering) for us (see 27:46; 2Co 5:21 and note).

26:41 See note on Mk 14:38.

26:45 *the hour.* See note on Lk 22:53. *Son of Man.* see note on Mk 8:31.

26:47 *Judas.* See notes on Jn 6:70; 17:12. *large crowd armed with swords and clubs.* See note on Mk 14:43. *chief priests and the elders.* See notes on v. 3; 2:4.

26:48 *The one I kiss.* See note on Lk 22:47.

26:49 *Rabbi.* Hebrew word for "(my) teacher." *kissed him.* See notes on Mk 14:45; Lk 22:47.

26:50 *Friend.* See note on 20:13.

26:51 *one of Jesus' companions.* Peter (see Jn 18:10 and note). *servant of the high priest.* Malchus (see Jn 18:10 and note). *cutting off his ear.* Perhaps Peter aimed at Malchus's head but missed and only succeeded in "cutting off his ear."

my disposal more than twelve legions of angels?[d] [54]But how then would the Scriptures be fulfilled[e] that say it must happen in this way?"

[55]In that hour Jesus said to the crowd, "Am I leading a rebellion, that you have come out with swords and clubs to capture me? Every day I sat in the temple courts teaching,[f] and you did not arrest me. [56]But this has all taken place that the writings of the prophets might be fulfilled."[g] Then all the disciples deserted him and fled.

JESUS BEFORE THE SANHEDRIN

26:57–68pp — Mk 14:53–65; Jn 18:12,13,19–24

[57]Those who had arrested Jesus took him to Caiaphas[h] the high priest, where the teachers of the law and the elders had assembled. [58]But Peter followed him at a distance, right up to the courtyard of the high priest.[i] He entered and sat down with the guards[j] to see the outcome.

[59]The chief priests and the whole Sanhedrin[k] were looking for false evidence against Jesus so that they could put him to death. [60]But they did not find any, though many false witnesses[l] came forward.

Finally two[m] came forward [61]and declared, "This fellow said, 'I am able to destroy the temple of God and rebuild it in three days.' "[n]

[62]Then the high priest stood up and said to Jesus, "Are you not going to answer? What is this testimony that these men are bringing against you?" [63]But Jesus remained silent.[o]

The high priest said to him, "I charge you under oath[p] by the living God:[q] Tell us if you are the Messiah,[r] the Son of God."[s]

[64]"You have said so,"[t] Jesus replied. "But I say to all of you: From now on you will see the Son of Man sitting at the right hand of the Mighty One[u] and coming on the clouds of heaven."[a][v]

[65]Then the high priest tore his clothes[w] and said, "He has spoken blasphemy! Why do we need any more witnesses? Look, now you have heard the blasphemy. [66]What do you think?"

"He is worthy of death,"[x] they answered.

[67]Then they spit in his face and struck him with their fists.[y] Others slapped him [68]and said, "Prophesy to us, Messiah. Who hit you?"[z]

PETER DISOWNS JESUS

26:69–75pp — Mk 14:66–72; Lk 22:55–62; Jn 18:16–18,25–27

[69]Now Peter was sitting out in the courtyard, and a servant girl came to him. "You also were with Jesus of Galilee," she said.

[70]But he denied it before them all. "I don't know what you're talking about," he said.

[71]Then he went out to the gateway, where another servant girl saw him and said to the people there, "This fellow was with Jesus of Nazareth."

[72]He denied it again, with an oath: "I don't know the man!"

[73]After a little while, those standing there went up to Peter and said, "Surely you are one of them; your accent gives you away."

[74]Then he began to call down curses, and he swore to them, "I don't know the man!"

Immediately a rooster crowed. [75]Then Peter remembered the word Jesus had spoken: "Before the rooster crows, you will disown me three times."[a] And he went outside and wept bitterly.

a 64 See Psalm 110:1; Daniel 7:13.

26:53 d 2Ki 6:17; Da 7:10; Mt 4:11
26:54 e S ver 24; S Mt 1:22
26:55 f Mk 12:35; Lk 22:67; Jn 7:14,28; 18:20
26:56 g S ver 24; S Mt 1:22
26:57 h S ver 3
26:58 i ver 69; Mk 14:66; Lk 22:55; Jn 18:15 J Mk 15:16; Lk 11:21; Jn 7:32,45, 46
26:59 k S Mt 5:22
26:60 l Ps 27:12; 35:11; Ac 6:13
m Dt 19:15
26:61 n S Jn 2:19
26:63 o S Mk 14:61 P Lev 5:1 q S Mt 16:16 r Lk 22:67 s S Mt 4:3
26:64 t Mt 27:11; u S Mk 16:19 v S Rev 1:7
26:65 w S Mk 14:63
26:66 x Lev 24:16; Jn 19:7
26:67 y S Mt 16:21
26:68 z Lk 22:63-65
26:75 a ver 34; Jn 13:58

26:53 *legions.* A Roman legion had 6,000 soldiers.
26:54 *Scriptures be fulfilled.* In view of v. 56 probably a reference to Zec 13:7 (see note on Mk 14:49).
26:55 Jesus protested the manner of his arrest. The crowd sent by the Sanhedrin (see note on Mk 14:55) had come after him as if he were a dangerous criminal or insurrectionist.
26:56 *disciples deserted him.* Contrast v. 35.
26:57—27:26 For a summary of the two stages (religious and civil) of the trial of Jesus see note on Mk 14:53—15:15.
26:57 *Caiaphas.* See v. 3; Jn 11:49 and notes. *teachers of the law.* See note on 2:4. *elders.* See notes on Ex 3:16; 2Sa 3:17.
26:59 *Sanhedrin.* See note on Mk 14:55.
26:61 *I am able to destroy the temple of God.* Possibly an intentional distortion of Jesus' words (see Mk 14:58; Jn 2:19 and notes).
26:63 *I charge you under oath.* Jesus refused to answer the

question of v. 62 (see v. 63a). But when the high priest used this form, Jesus was legally obliged to reply. *Messiah.* See note on 16:16.
26:64 This Son of Man saying brings together Ps 110:1 and Da 7:13. See Mt 17:5; 24:30 and notes.
26:65 *tore his clothes.* Ordinarily the high priest was forbidden by law to do this (Lev 10:6; 21:10), but this was considered a highly unusual circumstance. The high priest interpreted Jesus' answer in v. 64 as blasphemy (see note on Mk 14:64).
26:67–68 Mark (14:65) and Luke (22:64) report that they blindfolded Jesus, which explains the mocking command: "Prophesy . . . Who hit you?"
26:73 *After a little while.* Lk 22:59 says "About an hour later." *your accent gives you away.* Peter had a Galilean accent that was conspicuous in Jerusalem.

27:1 *b* S Mt 12:14;
Mk 15:1; Lk 22:66
27:2 *c* Mt 20:19
d Mk 15:1; Lk 13:1;
Ac 3:13; 1Ti 6:13
27:3 *e* S Mt 10:4
f Mt 26:14,15
27:4 *g* ver 24
27:5 *h* Lk 1:9,21
i Ac 1:18
27:8 *j* Ac 1:19
27:9 *k* S Mt 1:22
27:10 *l* Zec 11:12,13;
Jer 32:6-9
27:11 *m* S Mt 2:2
27:12 *n* S Mk 14:61
27:13 *o* Mt 26:62
27:14 *p* S Mk 14:61
27:15 *q* Jn 18:39
27:17 *r* ver 22;
Mt 1:16
27:19 *s* Jn 19:13
t ver 24 *u* Ge 20:6;
Nu 12:6; 1Ki 3:5;
Job 33:14-16; Mt 1:20;
2:12,13,19,22
27:20 *v* Ac 3:14
27:22 *w* Mt 1:16

JUDAS HANGS HIMSELF

27 Early in the morning, all the chief priests and the elders of the people came to the decision to put Jesus to death.*b* 2They bound him, led him away and handed him over*c* to Pilate the governor.*d*

3When Judas, who had betrayed him,*e* saw that Jesus was condemned, he was seized with remorse and returned the thirty pieces of silver*f* to the chief priests and the elders. 4"I have sinned," he said, "for I have betrayed innocent blood."

"What is that to us?" they replied. "That's your responsibility."*g*

5So Judas threw the money into the temple*h* and left. Then he went away and hanged himself.*i*

6The chief priests picked up the coins and said, "It is against the law to put this into the treasury, since it is blood money." 7So they decided to use the money to buy the potter's field as a burial place for foreigners. 8That is why it has been called the Field of Blood*j* to this day. 9Then what was spoken by Jeremiah the prophet was fulfilled:*k* "They took the thirty pieces of silver, the price set on him by the people of Israel, 10and they used them to buy the potter's field, as the Lord commanded me."*a l*

JESUS BEFORE PILATE

27:11–26pp — Mk 15:2–15; Lk 23:2,3,18–25; Jn 18:29—19:16

11Meanwhile Jesus stood before the governor, and the governor asked him, "Are you the king of the Jews?"*m*

"You have said so," Jesus replied.

12When he was accused by the chief priests and the elders, he gave no answer.*n* 13Then Pilate asked him, "Don't you hear the testimony they are bringing against you?"*o* 14But Jesus made no reply,*p* not even to a single charge—to the great amazement of the governor.

15Now it was the governor's custom at the festival to release a prisoner*q* chosen by the crowd. 16At that time they had a well-known prisoner whose name was Jesus*b* Barabbas. 17So when the crowd had gathered, Pilate asked them, "Which one do you want me to release to you: Jesus Barabbas, or Jesus who is called the Messiah?"*r* 18For he knew it was out of envy that they had handed Jesus over to him.

19While Pilate was sitting on the judge's seat,*s* his wife sent him this message: "Don't have anything to do with that innocent*t* man, for I have suffered a great deal today in a dream*u* because of him."

20But the chief priests and the elders persuaded the crowd to ask for Barabbas and to have Jesus executed.*v*

21"Which of the two do you want me to release to you?" asked the governor.

"Barabbas," they answered.

22"What shall I do, then, with Jesus who is called the Messiah?"*w* Pilate asked.

They all answered, "Crucify him!"

23"Why? What crime has he committed?" asked Pilate.

But they shouted all the louder, "Crucify him!"

---

a 10 See Zech. 11:12,13; Jer. 19:1-13; 32:6-9.   *b* 16 Many manuscripts do not have *Jesus*; also in verse 17.

27:1 *Early in the morning.* Continues the narrative from 26:68. The Sanhedrin could not have a legal session at night, so at daybreak they held a special meeting to make the death sentence (see 26:66) official. See notes on Mk 14:53—15:15; 15:1; Lk 22:66; Jn 18:28.

27:2 *handed him over to Pilate.* The Sanhedrin had been deprived by the Roman government of the right to carry out capital punishment, except in the case of a foreigner who entered the sacred precincts of the temple. So Jesus had to be handed over to Pilate for execution. For additional information about Pilate see note on Mk 15:1.

27:3–10 See Ac 1:16–19.

27:3 *thirty pieces of silver.* See 26:15 and note.

27:5 *temple.* Probably the treasury room of the temple (see v. 6). *hanged himself.* See note on Ac 1:18.

27:8 *Field of Blood.* Cf. "Valley of Slaughter" in Jer 19:6.

27:9 *Jeremiah.* The quotation that follows seems to combine Zec 11:12–13 and Jer 19:1–13 (or perhaps Jer 18:2–12 or 32:6–9). But Matthew attributes it to the better-known prophet Jeremiah, just as Mark (1:2–3) quotes Mal 3:1 and Isa 40:3 but attributes them both to the better-known prophet Isaiah (see note on Mk 1:2).

27:11 *governor.* Pontius Pilate (see note on v. 2). *king of the Jews.* See note on Jn 18:33.

27:14 *Jesus made no reply.* See 26:63; Mk 15:4; Isa 53:7 and notes. *amazement of the governor.* Probably because he had never seen such behavior before. He had no idea that Jesus was carrying out his Father's plan for the redemption of the world (see note on Mk 15:4).

27:15 *governor's custom.* Of which nothing is known outside the Gospels.

27:16 *well-known.* The Greek word here probably means "outstanding" or "notable" (cf. Ro 16:7). Barabbas had taken part in a rebellion (Lk 23:19; Jn 18:40), presumably against the Romans. So he would have been a folk hero among the Jews. See notes on Mk 15:7; Lk 23:18; Jn 18:40. Some manuscripts use Barabbas's full name, Jesus Barabbas, in vv. 16–17 (as in the TNIV; see TNIV text note on v. 16). If that is the correct reading, it sharpens the point of Pilate's question in v. 17.

27:19 Matthew is the only writer who records this incident. *dream.* Dreams play an important role in the life of Jesus in Matthew's Gospel (see 1:20; 2:12,13, 19,22).

²⁴When Pilate saw that he was getting nowhere, but that instead an uproar^x was starting, he took water and washed his hands^y in front of the crowd. "I am innocent of this man's blood,"^z he said. "It is your responsibility!"^a

²⁵All the people answered, "His blood is on us and on our children!"^b

²⁶Then he released Barabbas to them. But he had Jesus flogged,^c and handed him over to be crucified.

THE SOLDIERS MOCK JESUS
27:27–31pp — Mk 15:16–20

²⁷Then the governor's soldiers took Jesus into the Praetorium^d and gathered the whole company of soldiers around him. ²⁸They stripped him and put a scarlet robe on him,^e ²⁹and then twisted together a crown of thorns and set it on his head. They put a staff in his right hand as a scepter. Then they knelt in front of him and mocked him. "Hail, king of the Jews!" they said.^f ³⁰They spit on him, and took the staff and struck him on the head again and again.^g ³¹After they had mocked him, they took off the robe and put his own clothes on him. Then they led him away to crucify him.^h

THE CRUCIFIXION OF JESUS
27:33–44pp — Mk 15:22–32; Lk 23:33–43; Jn 19:17–24

³²As they were going out,ⁱ they met a man from Cyrene,^j named Simon, and they forced him to carry the cross.^k ³³They came to a place called Golgotha (which means "the place of the skull").^l ³⁴There they offered Jesus wine to drink, mixed with gall;^m but after tasting it, he refused to drink it. ³⁵When they had crucified him, they divided up his clothes by casting lots.ⁿ ³⁶And sitting down, they kept watch^o over him there. ³⁷Above his head they placed the written charge against him: THIS IS JESUS, THE KING OF THE JEWS.

³⁸Two rebels were crucified with him,^p one on his right and one on his left. ³⁹Those who passed by hurled insults at him, shaking their heads^q ⁴⁰and saying, "You who are going to destroy the temple and build it in three days,^r save yourself!^s Come down from the cross, if you are the Son of God!"^t

⁴¹In the same way the chief priests, the teachers of the law and the elders mocked him. ⁴²"He saved others," they said, "but he can't save himself! He's the king of Israel!^u Let him come down now from the cross, and we will believe^v in him. ⁴³He trusts in God. Let God rescue him^w now if he wants him, for he said, 'I am the Son of God.' " ⁴⁴In the same way the rebels who were crucified with him also heaped insults on him.

THE DEATH OF JESUS
27:45–56pp — Mk 15:33–41; Lk 23:44–49; Jn 19:29–30

⁴⁵From noon until three in the afternoon darkness^x came over all the land. ⁴⁶About three in the afternoon Jesus cried out in a loud voice, *"Eli, Eli,*^a *lema sabachthani?"* (which means "My God, my God, why have you forsaken me?").^{b y}

⁴⁷When some of those standing there heard this, they said, "He's calling Elijah."

^a 46 Some manuscripts *Eloi, Eloi*   ^b 46 Psalm 22:1

27:24 ^x Mt 26:5
^y Ps 26:6 ^z Dt 21:6-8
^a ver 4
27:25 ^b Jos 2:19;
S Ac 5:28
27:26 ^c Isa 53:5;
Jn 19:1
27:27 ^d Jn 18:28,33;
19:9
27:28 ^e Jn 19:2
27:29 ^f Isa 53:3;
Jn 19:2,3
27:30 ^g S Mt 16:21
27:31 ^h Isa 53:7
27:32 ⁱ Heb 13:12
^j Ac 2:10; 6:9; 11:20;
13:1 ^k Mk 15:21;
Lk 23:26
27:33 ^l Jn 19:17
27:34 ^m ver 48;
Ps 69:21
27:35 ⁿ Ps 22:18
27:36 ^o ver 54
27:38 ^p Isa 53:12
27:39 ^q Ps 22:7;
109:25; La 2:15
27:40 ^r S Jn 2:19
^s ver 42 ^t Mt 4:3,6
27:42 ^u Jn 1:49;
12:13 ^v S Jn 3:15
27:43 ^w Ps 22:8
27:45 ^x Am 8:9
27:46 ^y Ps 22:1

27:24 *washed his hands.* See Dt 21:6; Ps 26:6 and notes; 73:13.

27:25 A chilling response by a bloodthirsty crowd. It has often been used to justify the persecution of the Jewish people. It should be noted, however, that it was not God but the people themselves who uttered these words. If there was a fulfillment of their declaration, it was most likely in the destruction of Jerusalem in A.D. 70. All the following passages should be studied regarding responsibility for Christ's death on the cross: Isa 53:10; Ac 2:23; Jn 10:17–18; Heb 9:14; Mt 26:47,50,57,59,63–66; 27:1–2,20,22,26–27,31,41; Ro 5:8. Because of these and other similar Scriptures, a truly Biblical Christian should never be guilty of anti-Semitism.

27:26 *flogged.* Roman floggings were so brutal that sometimes the victim died before crucifixion (see note on Mk 15:15).

27:27 *Praetorium.* The governor's official residence in Jerusalem (see notes on Mk 15:16; Ac 23:25).

27:28 *scarlet robe.* The outer cloak of a Roman soldier. Mk 15:17, 20; Jn 19:2,5 describe it as purple.

27:29 *crown of thorns.* See note on Mk 15:17. *staff.* A mock scepter. *Hail, king of the Jews!* See note on Mk 15:18.

27:30–31 See Isa 50:6 and note.

27:30 *spit on him.* See note on Mk 15:19.

27:32 *they.* See v. 27. *Cyrene.* See note on Mk 15:21. *Simon . . . to carry the cross.* See note on Mk 15:21.

27:33 *Golgotha.* See note on Mk 15:22.

27:34 *mixed with gall.* Tradition says that the women of Jerusalem customarily furnished this pain-killing narcotic to prisoners who were crucified. Jesus refused to drink it because he wanted to be fully conscious until his death (v. 50).

27:35 *crucified.* See note on Mk 15:24. *casting lots.* Explained more precisely in Jn 19:23–24 (see notes there; see also TNIV text note on Jn 19:24).

27:37 See notes on Mk 15:26; Lk 23:38; Jn 19:19.

27:38 *Two rebels.* See note on Mk 15:27.

27:39 *shaking their heads.* See Ps 22:7 and note.

27:41 *chief priests, the teachers of the law and the elders.* The Sanhedrin (see note on v. 1).

27:43 See Ps 22:8 and note.

27:46 *Eli, Eli, lema sabachthani?* A mixture of Aramaic and Hebrew, translated by Matthew for his readers (see note on Mk 15:34).

27:47 *Elijah.* See note on Mk 15:35.

27:48 *z* ver 34;
Ps 69:21
27:50 *a* Jn 19:30
27:51 *b* Ex 26:31-33;
Heb 9:3,8; 10:19,20
c ver 54
27:53 *d* S Mt 4:5
27:54 *e* ver 36
f S Mt 4:3; 17:5
27:55 *g* Lk 8:2,3
27:56 *h* Mk 15:47;
Lk 24:10; Jn 19:25
27:60 *i* Mt 27:66;
28:2; Mk 16:4;
Ac 13:29
27:63 *j* S Mt 16:21
27:64 *k* Mt 28:13
27:65 *l* ver 66;
Mt 28:11
27:66 *m* Da 6:17
n ver 60; Mt 28:2
o Mt 28:11
28:1 *p* Lk 8:2
q Mt 27:56
28:2 *r* Mt 27:51
s Jn 20:12; S Ac 5:19
t Mt 27:60

⁴⁸Immediately one of them ran and got a sponge. He filled it with wine vinegar,*z* put it on a staff, and offered it to Jesus to drink. ⁴⁹The rest said, "Now leave him alone. Let's see if Elijah comes to save him."

⁵⁰And when Jesus had cried out again in a loud voice, he gave up his spirit.*a*

⁵¹At that moment the curtain of the temple*b* was torn in two from top to bottom. The earth shook, the rocks split*c* ⁵²and the tombs broke open. The bodies of many holy people who had died were raised to life. ⁵³They came out of the tombs after Jesus' resurrection and*a* went into the holy city*d* and appeared to many people.

⁵⁴When the centurion and those with him who were guarding*e* Jesus saw the earthquake and all that had happened, they were terrified, and exclaimed, "Surely he was the Son of God!"*f*

⁵⁵Many women were there, watching from a distance. They had followed Jesus from Galilee to care for his needs.*g* ⁵⁶Among them were Mary Magdalene, Mary the mother of James and Joseph,*b* and the mother of Zebedee's sons.*h*

THE BURIAL OF JESUS
27:57–61pp — Mk 15:42–47; Lk 23:50–56; Jn 19:38–42

⁵⁷As evening approached, there came a rich man from Arimathea, named Joseph, who had himself become a disciple of Jesus. ⁵⁸Going to Pilate, he asked for Jesus' body, and Pilate ordered that it be given to him. ⁵⁹Joseph took the body, wrapped it in a clean linen cloth, ⁶⁰and placed it in his own new tomb*i* that he had cut out of the rock. He rolled a big stone in front of the entrance to the tomb and went away. ⁶¹Mary Magdalene and the other Mary were sitting there opposite the tomb.

THE GUARD AT THE TOMB

⁶²The next day, the one after Preparation Day, the chief priests and the Pharisees went to Pilate. ⁶³"Sir," they said, "we remember that while he was still alive that deceiver said, 'After three days I will rise again.'*j* ⁶⁴So give the order for the tomb to be made secure until the third day. Otherwise, his disciples may come and steal the body*k* and tell the people that he has been raised from the dead. This last deception will be worse than the first."

⁶⁵"Take a guard,"*l* Pilate answered. "Go, make the tomb as secure as you know how." ⁶⁶So they went and made the tomb secure by putting a seal*m* on the stone*n* and posting the guard.*o*

JESUS HAS RISEN
28:1–8pp — Mk 16:1–8; Lk 24:1–10; Jn 20:1–8

28 After the Sabbath, at dawn on the first day of the week, Mary Magdalene*p* and the other Mary*q* went to look at the tomb.

²There was a violent earthquake,*r* for an angel*s* of the Lord came down from heaven and, going to the tomb, rolled back the stone*t* and sat on it. ³His appearance was

---

a 53 Or tombs, and after Jesus' resurrection they   *b 56 Greek Joses, a variant of Joseph*

27:48 *sponge.* See note on Jn 19:29. *wine vinegar.* See notes on Mk 15:36; Lk 23:36; Jn 19:29.

27:49 See note on Mk 15:35.

27:50 *loud voice.* See note on Jn 19:30.

27:51 *curtain.* The curtain that separated the Holy Place from the Most Holy Place. The tearing of the curtain signified Christ's making it possible for believers to go directly into God's presence (see Mk 15:38; Lk 23:45; Heb 9:1–14; 10:14–22 and notes).

27:54 *centurion.* See note on 8:5. *Son of God.* See note on Lk 23:47.

27:55 *women . . . to care for his needs.* Women played a significant role in the ministry of Jesus (see Mk 15:41; Lk 23:49) and his disciples (see Lk 8:3 and note).

27:56 See notes on Mk 15:40; Lk 24:10.

27:57 *Arimathea.* A village in the hill country of Ephraim, about 20 miles northwest of Jerusalem; perhaps to be identified with Ramathaim, the birthplace of the prophet Samuel (see 1Sa 1:1 and note). *Joseph.* See notes on Lk 23:50; Jn 19:38.

27:58 *asked for Jesus' body.* See note on Lk 23:52.

27:60 *new tomb.* See note on Mk 15:46.

27:61 *the other Mary.* Presumably the mother of James and Joseph (v. 56).

27:62 *The next day, the one after Preparation Day.* Saturday, the Sabbath. Friday was the preparation day for the Sabbath (sunset Friday to sunset Saturday).

27:64 *This last deception will be worse than the first.* The first would be that Jesus was the Messiah, the second that he had risen as the Son of God.

27:65 *Take a guard.* Either of Roman soldiers or of their own temple police; 28:14 implies that they were answerable to Pilate ("the governor"), which may favor Roman soldiers. On the other hand, the fact that in 28:11 they "reported to the chief priests" (instead of to Pilate) may favor temple police, who would have been under the authority of the religious leaders. ("Take a guard" may also be rendered "You have a guard.")

28:1 *first day of the week.* See note on Lk 24:1. *the other Mary.* See note on 27:61. Mk 16:1 adds Salome, and Lk 24:10 adds Joanna.

28:2 *There was.* The sense is "Now there had been." The parallel accounts (Mk 16:2–6; Lk 24:1–7; Jn 20:1) make it clear that the events of vv. 2–4 occurred before the women actually arrived at the tomb. *violent earthquake.* Only Matthew mentions this earthquake and the one at Jesus' death (27:51,54).

like lightning, and his clothes were white as snow.*u* 4The guards were so afraid of him that they shook and became like dead men.

5The angel said to the women, "Do not be afraid,*v* for I know that you are looking for Jesus, who was crucified. 6He is not here; he has risen, just as he said.*w* Come and see the place where he lay. 7Then go quickly and tell his disciples: 'He has risen from the dead and is going ahead of you into Galilee.*x* There you will see him.' Now I have told you."

8So the women hurried away from the tomb, afraid yet filled with joy, and ran to tell his disciples. 9Suddenly Jesus met them.*y* "Greetings," he said. They came to him, clasped his feet and worshiped him. 10Then Jesus said to them, "Do not be afraid. Go and tell my brothers*z* to go to Galilee; there they will see me."

THE GUARDS' REPORT

11While the women were on their way, some of the guards*a* went into the city and reported to the chief priests everything that had happened. 12When the chief priests had met with the elders and devised a plan, they gave the soldiers a large sum of money, 13telling them, "You are to say, 'His disciples came during the night and stole him away*b* while we were asleep.' 14If this report gets to the governor,*c* we will satisfy him and keep you out of trouble." 15So the soldiers took the money and did as they were instructed. And this story has been widely circulated among the Jews to this very day.

THE GREAT COMMISSION

16Then the eleven disciples went to Galilee, to the mountain where Jesus had told them to go.*d* 17When they saw him, they worshiped him; but some doubted. 18Then Jesus came to them and said, "All authority in heaven and on earth has been given to me.*e* 19Therefore go and make disciples of all nations,*f* baptizing them in*a* the name of the Father and of the Son and of the Holy Spirit,*g* 20and teaching*h* them to obey everything I have commanded you. And surely I am with you*i* always, to the very end of the age."*j*

a 19 Or *into*; see Acts 8:16; 19:5; Romans 6:3; 1 Cor. 1:13; 10:2; Gal. 3:27.

28:3 *u* Da 7:9; 10:6;
Mk 9:3; S Jn 20:12
28:5 *v* ver 10;
S Mt 14:27
28:6 *w* S Mt 16:21
28:7 *x* ver 10, 16;
Mt 26:32
28:9 *y* Jn 20:14-18
28:10 *z* Mt 12:50;
25:40; Mk 3:34;
Jn 20:17; Ro 8:29;
Heb 2:11-13, 17
28:11 *a* Mt 27:65,66
28:13 *b* Mt 27:64
28:14 *c* S Mt 27:2
28:16 *d* ver 7, 10;
Mt 26:32
28:18 *e* Da 7:13,14;
Lk 10:22; Jn 3:35;
S 13:13; 17:2;
1Co 15:27; Eph 1:20-
22; Php 2:9,10
28:19 *f* Isa 49:6;
Mk 16:15,16;
Lk 24:47; Ac 1:8;
14:21 *g* Ac 1:8; 2:38;
8:16; Ro 6:3,4;
Gal 3:27; Col 2:12
28:20 *h* Jn 14:26;
Ac 2:42 *i* Dt 31:6;
1Ki 8:57; Hag 1:13;
Mt 18:20; Ac 18:10
j Mt 13:39; 24:3

28:6 *just as he said.* See 16:21 and note.
28:7 *going ahead of you into Galilee.* See 26:32 and note.
28:10 *my brothers.* His "disciples" (v. 16).
28:11–15 Only Matthew tells of the posting of the guard (27:62–66), and he follows up by telling about their report.
28:11 *reported to the chief priests.* See note on 27:65.
28:13 *His disciples…stole him away.* One of many human attempts to explain away Christ's resurrection. *while we were asleep.* It is more likely that Jewish temple police would be willing to admit to such dereliction of duty than Roman soldiers would.
28:14 See note on 27:65.
28:16–20 Christ's Great Commission for his church (cf. also Mk 16:15–18; Lk 24:46–48; Jn 17:18; 20:21; Ac 1:8 and relevant notes).
28:16 *eleven.* Judas had committed suicide (see 27:5 and note). *mountain.* Cf. note on 5:1. *had told them.* See v. 10.
28:17 *some.* Probably of the 11 disciples, though it may include others as well. *doubted.* Belief in the resurrection was not instantaneous for them. After the traumatic experience of the

crucifixion, it took time for the disciples to come to full faith (see Lk 24:10–11, 25–26, 36–47).
28:18 *authority.* See 10:1; see also 7:29; 16:28; Jn 17:2 and notes. *in heaven and on earth.* The scope of Christ's authority is the entire universe.

A **28:19–20** Christ's program of missions: "make disciples of all nations." It involves three steps: (1) "go," (2) "baptizing them" and (3) "teaching them to obey everything" Christ has commanded.

A **28:19** *disciples.* See 5:1 and note. *all nations.* Contrast 10:5–6 and note. *baptizing them.* As a sign of their union with and commitment to Christ (see notes on Ac 2:38; Ro 6:3–4). *Father…Son…Holy Spirit.* The Trinitarian formula (see 3:16–17 and note; 1Co 12:4–6; 2Co 13:14 and note; Eph 1:2–13; 4:4–6; 2Th 2:13 and note; Tit 3:4–6; 1Pe 1:2 and note; 1Jn 4:13–14; Rev 1:4–6 and TNIV text note on 14).

A **28:20** *with you.* Matthew ends with the reassuring and empowering words of him who came to earth to be "God with us" (1:23). See note on 2Co 13:14.

Although there is no direct internal evidence of authorship, it was the unanimous testimony of the early church that this Gospel was written by John Mark ("John, also called Mark," Ac 12:12,25; 15:37). The most important evidence comes from Papias (c. A.D. 140), who quotes an even earlier source as saying: (1) Mark was a close associate of Peter, from whom he received the tradition of the things said and done by the Lord (see 1Pe 5:13 and note); (2) this tradition did not come to Mark as a finished, sequential account of the life of our Lord, but as the preaching of Peter—preaching directed to the needs of the early Christian communities; (3) Mark accurately preserved this material. The conclusion drawn from this tradition is that the Gospel of Mark largely consists of the preaching of Peter arranged and shaped by Mark (see note on Ac 10:37).

JOHN MARK IN THE NT

C It is generally agreed that the Mark who is associated with Peter in the early non-Biblical tradition is also the John Mark of the NT. The first mention of him is in connection with his mother, Mary, who had a house in Jerusalem that served as a meeting place for believers (Ac 12:12). When Paul and Barnabas returned to Antioch from Jerusalem after the famine visit, Mark accompanied them (Ac 12:25). Mark next appears as a "helper" to Paul and Barnabas on their first missionary journey (Ac 13:5), but he deserted them at Perga in Pamphylia (see map, p. 1863) to return to Jerusalem (Ac 13:13). Paul must have been deeply disappointed with Mark's actions on this occasion, because when Barnabas proposed taking Mark on the second journey Paul flatly refused, a refusal that broke up their working relationship (Ac 15:36–39). Barnabas took Mark, who was his cousin (Col 4:10), and departed for Cyprus. No further mention is made of either of them in the book of Acts. Mark reappears in Paul's letter to the Colossians, written from Rome. Paul sends a greeting from Mark and adds: "You have received instructions about him; if he comes to you, welcome him" (Col 4:10; see Phm 24, written at about the same time). At this point Mark was apparently beginning to win his way back into Paul's confidence. By the end of Paul's life, Mark had fully regained Paul's favor (see 2Ti 4:11 and note).

DATE OF COMPOSITION

Some, who hold that Matthew and Luke used Mark as a major source, have suggested that Mark may have been composed in the 50s or early 60s. Others have felt that the content of the Gospel and statements made about Mark by the early church fathers indicate that the book was written shortly before the destruction of Jerusalem in A.D. 70. See essay and chart, p. 1601.

PLACE OF ORIGIN

According to early church tradition, Mark was written "in the regions of Italy" (Anti-Marcionite Prologue) or, more specifically, in Rome (Irenaeus; Clement of Alexandria). These same authors closely associate Mark's writing of the Gospel with the apostle Peter. The above evidence is consistent with (1) the historical probability that Peter was in Rome during the last days of his life and was martyred there and (2) the Biblical evidence that Mark also was in Rome about the same time and was closely associated with Peter (see 2Ti 4:11; 1Pe 5:13, where the word "Babylon" may be a cryptogram for Rome; see also Introduction to 1 Peter: Place of Writing).

RECIPIENTS

The evidence points to the church at Rome, or at least to Gentile readers. Mark explains Jewish customs (7:2–4; 15:42), translates Aramaic words (3:17; 5:41; 7:11,34; 15:22,34) and seems to have a special interest in persecution and martyrdom (8:34–38; 13:9–13)—subjects of special concern to Roman believers (and to Peter as well; cf. 1 Peter). A Roman destination would explain the almost immediate acceptance of this Gospel and its rapid dissemination.

OCCASION AND PURPOSE

Since Mark's Gospel is traditionally associated with Rome, it may have been occasioned by the persecutions of the Roman church in the period c. A.D. 64–67. The famous fire of Rome in 64—probably set by Nero himself but blamed on Christians—resulted in widespread persecution. Even martyrdom was not unknown among Roman believers. Mark may be writing to prepare his readers for such suffering by placing before them the life of our Lord. There are many references, both explicit and veiled, to suffering and discipleship throughout his Gospel (see 1:12–13; 3:22,30; 8:34–38; 10:30,33–34,45; 13:8–13).

EMPHASES

1. *The cross.* Both the human cause (12:12; 14:1–2; 15:10) and the divine necessity (8:31; 9:31; 10:33–34) of the cross are emphasized by Mark.

2. *Discipleship.* Special attention should be paid to the passages on discipleship that arise from Jesus' predictions of his passion (8:34—9:1; 9:35—10:31; 10:42–45).

3. *The teachings of Jesus.* Although Mark records far fewer actual teachings of Jesus than the other Gospel writers, there is a remarkable emphasis on Jesus as teacher. The words "teacher," "teach" or "teaching" and "Rabbi" are applied to Jesus in Mark 39 times.

4. *The Messianic secret.* On several occasions Jesus warns his disciples or others to keep silent about who he is or what he has done (see 1:34,44 and notes; 3:12; 5:43; 7:36; 8:30; 9:9).

5. *Son of God.* Although Mark emphasizes the humanity of Jesus (see 3:5; 6:6,31,34; 7:34; 8:12; 10:14; 11:12), he does not neglect his deity (see 1:1,11; 3:11; 5:7; 9:7; 12:1–11; 13:32; 15:39).

SPECIAL CHARACTERISTICS

Mark's Gospel is a simple, succinct, unadorned, yet vivid account of Jesus' ministry, emphasizing more what Jesus did than what he said. Mark moves quickly from one episode in Jesus' life and ministry to another, often using the adverb "immediately" (see note on 1:12). The book as a whole is characterized as "The beginning of the good news" (1:1). The life, death and resurrection of Christ comprise the "beginning," of which the apostolic preaching in Acts is the continuation.

JOHN THE BAPTIST PREPARES THE WAY
1:2–8pp — Mt 3:1–11; Lk 3:2–16

The beginning of the good news about Jesus the Messiah,[a,b] [a] 2as it is written in Isaiah the prophet:

> "I will send my messenger ahead of you,
>   who will prepare your way"[c] [b]—
> 3"a voice of one calling in the wilderness,
>   'Prepare the way for the Lord,
>   make straight paths for him.' "[d] [c]

4And so John the Baptist[d] appeared in the wilderness, preaching a baptism of repentance[e] for the forgiveness of sins.[f] 5The whole Judean countryside and all the people of Jerusalem went out to him. Confessing their sins, they were baptized by him in the Jordan River. 6John wore clothing made of camel's hair, with a leather belt around his waist,[g] and he ate locusts[h] and wild honey. 7And this was his message: "After me comes the one more powerful than I, the thongs of whose sandals I am not worthy to stoop down and untie.[i] 8I baptize you with[e] water, but he will baptize you with[e] the Holy Spirit."[j]

THE BAPTISM AND TESTING OF JESUS
1:9–11pp — Mt 3:13–17; Lk 3:21,22
1:12,13pp — Mt 4:1–11; Lk 4:1–13

9At that time Jesus came from Nazareth[k] in Galilee and was baptized by John[l] in the Jordan. 10Just as Jesus was coming up out of the water, he saw heaven being torn open and the Spirit descending on him like a dove.[m] 11And a voice came from heaven: "You are my Son,[n] whom I love; with you I am well pleased."[o]

---

[a] 1 Or *Jesus Christ. Messiah* (Hebrew) and *Christ* (Greek) both mean *Anointed One.*   [b] 1 Many manuscripts *Messiah, the Son of God*   [c] 2 Mal. 3:1   [d] 3 Isaiah 40:3   [e] 8 Or *in*

**Cross references (right margin):**
1:1 [a] S Mt 4:3
1:2 [b] Mal 3:1;
Mt 11:10; Lk 7:27
1:3 [c] Isa 40:3;
Jn 1:23
1:4 [d] S Mt 3:1
[e] ver 8; Jn 1:26,33;
Ac 1:5, 22; 11:36;
13:24; 18:25; 19:3,4
[f] Lk 1:77
1:6 [g] 2Ki 1:8
[h] Lev 11:22
1:7 [i] Ac 13:25
1:8 [j] Isa 44:3;
Joel 2:28; Jn 1:33;
Ac 1:5; 2:4; 11:16;
19:4-6
1:9 [k] S Mt 2:23
[l] S Mt 3:1
1:10 [m] Jn 1:32
1:11 [n] S Mt 3:17
[o] S Mt 3:17

A **1:1** A summary of the main subject matter of Mark's Gospel (see Introduction: Special Characteristics). *The beginning.* Suggests the opening verse of Genesis (see Jn 1:1). *good news.* The meaning of "gospel," from the Old English *godspel,* "good story" or "good news," which accurately translates the Greek. The good news is that God has provided salvation through the life, death and resurrection of Jesus Christ. *Jesus.* See TNIV text note on Mt 1:21. *Messiah.* See TNIV text note; see also 8:29 and note. For the possibility of reading "the Son of God" at the end of v. 1, see TNIV text note.
1:2 *in Isaiah the prophet.* The quotation that immediately follows (see first two poetry lines) comes from Mal 3:1 (see note there) but is followed (v. 3) by one from Isa 40:3 (see note there). Isaiah here receives pride of place because he stands at the head of the prophetic canon, the division of the Hebrew Bible known as the Latter Prophets (see Introduction to Isaiah: Position in the Canon; cf. Introduction to Joshua: Title and Theme). See also note on Mt 27:9. Understanding the ministry of Jesus must begin with the OT. What Isaiah says about God applies to Jesus, his Son (v. 1). The passages cited speak of the messenger, the wilderness and the Lord, each of which is stressed in vv. 4–8.

A C **1:4** *John ... appeared.* Mark, like John, has no nativity narrative, but begins with the ministry of John the Baptist. This is also where Peter begins in his proclamation of the gospel in Ac 10:37 (see note there; see also Introduction: Place of Origin). The name John means "The LORD is gracious." *wilderness.* The arid region west of the Dead Sea. *baptism.* John's practice of baptizing those who came to him in repentance was so characteristic of his ministry that he became known as "the Baptist" or "the Baptizer." He was preaching repentance-baptism, i.e., baptism that was preceded or accompanied by repentance. Baptism was not new to John's audience. They knew of baptism for Gentile converts but had not heard that the descendants of Abraham (Jews) needed to repent and be baptized. *repentance.* Involves deliberate turning from sin to righteousness, and John's emphasis on repentance recalls the preaching of the

prophets (e.g., Hos 3:4–5). God always grants forgiveness when there is repentance.
1:5 *whole ... all.* Hyperbole, indicating the high interest created by John's preaching. For centuries Israel had had no prophet. *people of Jerusalem.* See note on Jn 7:25. *Jordan River.* The principal river in the Holy Land, beginning in the snows of Mount Hermon and ending in the Dead Sea. Its closest point to Jerusalem is about 20 miles.
1:6 *camel's hair ... leather belt.* Worn by Elijah and other prophets (see 2Ki 1:8 and note; cf. Zec 13:4). *locusts and wild honey.* See note on Mt 3:4.
1:7 *message.* Mark's account of John's message is brief (cf. Mt 3:7–12; Lk 3:7–17) and focuses on the coming of the powerful One. *sandals I am not worthy to ... untie.* See note on Jn 1:27.
1:8 *baptize you with the Holy Spirit.* See note on Mt 3:11.
1:9 *At that time.* Jesus began his public ministry c. A.D. 27 (see chart, p. 1656), when he was approximately 30 years old (Lk 3:23). As far as we know, he had spent most of his previous life in Nazareth. *Nazareth.* See notes on Mt 2:23; Lk 4:23. *baptized by John.* For the significance of Jesus' baptism see Mt 3:15 and note.

A **1:10–11** All three persons of the Trinity are involved in Jesus' baptism: (1) the Father speaks, (2) the Son is baptized and (3) the Holy Spirit descends on the Son (see note on Mt 28:19).

A **1:10** *Spirit descending on him.* Jesus' anointing for ministry—an anointing he claimed in the synagogue at Nazareth (see Lk 4:18 and note). *like a dove.* Symbolizing the gentleness, purity and guilelessness of the Holy Spirit (see Mt 10:16; Lk 3:22 and note).
1:11 An allusion to Ps 2:7; Isa 42:1. *voice.* God sometimes spoke directly from heaven (see 9:7; Lk 3:22 and note; Jn 12:28–29; cf. Ex 19:3). *You are my Son.* In v. 1 Mark proclaims Jesus as the Son of God (if the TNIV text note there is the correct reading); here God the Father himself proclaims Jesus as his Son.

1:13 *p* Ex 24:18;
1Ki 19:8 *q* S Mt 4:10;
Heb 4:15
1:14 *r* S Mt 3:1
s Mt 4:12 *t* Mt 4:23
1:15 *v* Ro 5:6;
Gal 4:4; Eph 1:10
v S Jn 3:15 *w* Ac 20:21
1:18 *x* S Mt 4:19
1:21 *y* ver 39;
S Mt 4:23; S Mk 10:1
1:22 *z* S Mt 7:28,29
1:24 *a* S Mt 8:29
b Mt 2:23; Lk 24:19;
Jn 1:45,46; Ac 4:10;
24:5 *c* Ps 16:10;
Isa 41:14,16,20;
Lk 1:35; Jn 6:69;
Ac 3:14; 1Jn 2:20
1:25 *d* ver 34
1:26 *e* Mk 9:20
1:27 *f* Mk 10:24,32

¹²At once the Spirit sent him out into the wilderness, ¹³and he was in the wilderness forty days, *p* being tempted ᵃ by Satan. *q* He was with the wild animals, and angels attended him.

JESUS ANNOUNCES THE GOOD NEWS

1:16–20pp — Mt 4:18–22; Lk 5:2–11; Jn 1:35–42

¹⁴After John *r* was put in prison, Jesus went into Galilee, *s* proclaiming the good news of God. *t* ¹⁵"The time has come," *u* he said. "The kingdom of God has come near. Repent and believe *v* the good news!" *w*

JESUS CALLS HIS FIRST DISCIPLES

¹⁶As Jesus walked beside the Sea of Galilee, he saw Simon and his brother Andrew casting a net into the lake, because they were fishermen. ¹⁷"Come, follow me," Jesus said, "and I will send you out to fish for people." ¹⁸At once they left their nets and followed him. *x*

¹⁹When he had gone a little farther, he saw James son of Zebedee and his brother John in a boat, preparing their nets. ²⁰Without delay he called them, and they left their father Zebedee in the boat with the hired men and followed him.

JESUS DRIVES OUT AN EVIL SPIRIT

1:21–28pp — Lk 4:31–37

²¹They went to Capernaum, and when the Sabbath came, Jesus went into the synagogue and began to teach. *y* ²²The people were amazed at his teaching, because he taught them as one who had authority, not as the teachers of the law. *z* ²³Just then a man in their synagogue who was possessed by an evil ᵇ spirit cried out, ²⁴"What do you want with us, *a* Jesus of Nazareth? *b* Have you come to destroy us? I know who you are—the Holy One of God!" *c*

²⁵"Be quiet!" said Jesus sternly. "Come out of him!" *d* ²⁶The evil spirit shook the man violently and came out of him with a shriek. *e*

²⁷The people were all so amazed *f* that they asked each other, "What is this? A new

---

ᵃ 13 The Greek for *tempted* can also mean *tested*.   ᵇ 23 Greek *unclean*; also in verses 26 and 27

1:12 *At once.* A distinctive characteristic of Mark's style is his use (some 47 times) of a Greek word that has been variously translated "at once," "without delay," "immediately," "quickly," "just then" (see, e.g., vv. 18,20,23,28,42–43).

1:13 *forty.* See Mt 4:2 and note. *tempted.* See notes on Mt 4:1–11. *Satan.* See Ge 3:1; Job 1:6,9; Zec 3:1; Rev 2:9–10; 12:9–10 and notes. *wild animals.* In Jesus' day there were many more wild animals—including lions—in Israel than today. Only Mark reports their presence in this connection; he emphasizes that God kept Jesus safe in the wilderness. *angels attended him.* As they had attended Israel in the wilderness (see Ex 23:20,23; 32:34).

1:14 *After John was put in prison.* See Mt 4:12; Lk 3:20 and notes. *good news of God.* The good news from, as well as about, God (see 1:1 and note).

1:15 *The time has come.* Not simply chronological time, but the decisive time for God's action. With the coming of the kingdom, God was doing something special. *kingdom of God.* See note on Mt 3:2. *has come near.* The coming of Christ (the King) brings the kingdom near to the people (see Lk 17:21 and note).

1:16 *Sea of Galilee.* A beautiful lake, almost 700 feet below sea level, 14 miles long and 6 miles wide, fed by the waters of the upper Jordan River. It was also called the Lake of Gennesaret (Lk 5:1) and the Sea of Tiberias (Jn 6:1; 21:1). In OT times it was known as the Sea of Kinnereth (e.g., Nu 34:11) because it is shaped like a harp (see note on Dt 3:17). *Simon.* Probably a contraction of the OT name Simeon (see TNIV text note on Ac 15:14). Jesus gave Simon the name Peter (see 3:16; see also Mt 16:18; Jn 1:42 and notes). *net.* See note on Mt 4:18.

🄰 1:17 *Come, follow me.* The call to discipleship is definite and demands a response of total commitment. This was not Jesus' first encounter with Simon and Andrew (see Jn 1:35–42). *send you out to fish for people.* As evangelists (see Lk 5:10).

1:21 *Capernaum.* See Mt 4:13; Lk 10:15 and notes. *Sabbath.* The

seventh day of the week, the day of rest and worship (see 2:27; Ge 2:3; Ex 16:23; Isa 58:13 and notes). *synagogue.* A very important religious institution among the Jews of that day. Originating during the exile, it provided a place where Jews could study the Scriptures and worship God. A synagogue could be established in any town where there were at least ten married Jewish men. See note on Ac 13:14; see also essay, p. 1595, and diagram, p. 1725. *began to teach.* Jesus, like Paul (see Ac 13:14–15 and notes; 14:1; 17:2; 18:4), took advantage of the custom that allowed visiting teachers to participate in the worship service by invitation of the synagogue leaders (see Lk 4:16–17 and notes).

🄰 1:22 *amazed.* Mark frequently reported the amazement that Jesus' teaching and actions produced (see 2:12; 5:20; 42; 6:2,51; 7:37; 10:26,32; 11:18; 12:17; 15:5). In these instances it was Christ's inherent authority that amazed. He did not quote human authorities, as did the teachers of the law, because his authority was directly from God (cf. Lk 2:46–48). *teachers of the law.* See note on Mt 2:4.

1:23 *man in their synagogue ... cried out.* It was actually the demon who cried out (see 5:7 and note). *possessed by an evil spirit.* Demonic possession intended to torment and destroy those who are created in God's image, but the demon recognized that Jesus was a powerful adversary, capable of destroying the forces of Satan.

1:24 *us.* The man was possessed by more than one demon (cf. 5:9), but only one spoke. *Holy One of God.* Apart from the parallel in Lk 4:34, the title is used elsewhere only in Jn 6:69 and points to Christ's divine origin rather than his Messiahship (see Lk 1:35). The name was perhaps used by the demons in accordance with the occult belief that the precise use of a person's name gave certain control over him (see 5:7).

1:25 *Be quiet!* Lit. "Be muzzled!" Jesus' superior power silences the shrieks of the demon-possessed man.

teaching—and with authority! He even gives orders to evil spirits and they obey him." [28]News about him spread quickly over the whole region [g] of Galilee.

JESUS HEALS MANY

1:29–31pp — Mt 8:14,15; Lk 4:38,39
1:32–34pp — Mt 8:16,17; Lk 4:40,41

[29]As soon as they left the synagogue, [h] they went with James and John to the home of Simon and Andrew. [30]Simon's mother-in-law was in bed with a fever, and they immediately told Jesus about her. [31]So he went to her, took her hand and helped her up. [i] The fever left her and she began to wait on them.

[32]That evening after sunset the people brought to Jesus all the sick and demon-possessed. [j] [33]The whole town gathered at the door, [34]and Jesus healed many who had various diseases. [k] He also drove out many demons, but he would not let the demons speak because they knew who he was. [l]

JESUS PRAYS IN A SOLITARY PLACE

1:35–38pp — Lk 4:42,43

[35]Very early in the morning, while it was still dark, Jesus got up, left the house and went off to a solitary place, where he prayed. [m] [36]Simon and his companions went to look for him, [37]and when they found him, they exclaimed: "Everyone is looking for you!"

[38]Jesus replied, "Let us go somewhere else—to the nearby villages—so I can preach there also. That is why I have come." [n] [39]So he traveled throughout Galilee, preaching in their synagogues [o] and driving out demons. [p]

JESUS HEALS A MAN WITH LEPROSY

1:40–44pp — Mt 8:2–4; Lk 5:12–14

[40]A man with leprosy[a] came to him and begged him on his knees, [q] "If you are willing, you can make me clean."

[41]Jesus was indignant. [b] He reached out his hand and touched the man. "I am willing," he said. "Be clean!" [42]Immediately the leprosy left him and he was cleansed.

[43]Jesus sent him away at once with a strong warning: [44]"See that you don't tell this to anyone. [r] But go, show yourself to the priest [s] and offer the sacrifices that Moses commanded for your cleansing, [t] as a testimony to them." [45]Instead he went out and began to talk freely, spreading the news. As a result, Jesus could no longer enter a town openly but stayed outside in lonely places. [u] Yet the people still came to him from everywhere. [v]

---

[a] 40 The Greek word traditionally translated *leprosy* was used for various diseases affecting the skin.
[b] 41 Many manuscripts *Jesus was filled with compassion*

1:28 [g] S Mt 9:26
1:29 [h] ver 21,23
1:31 [i] S Lk 7:14
1:32 [j] S Mt 4:24
1:34 [k] S Mt 4:23
[l] Mk 3:12; Ac 16:17,18
1:35 [m] S Lk 3:21
1:38 [n] Isa 61:1
1:39 [o] S Mt 4:23
[p] S Mt 4:24
1:40 [q] Mk 10:17
1:44 [r] S Mt 8:4
[s] Lev 13:49 [t] Lev 14:1-32
1:45 [u] Lk 5:15,16
[v] Mk 2:13; Lk 5:17; Jn 6:2

1:27 *with authority.* Jesus' authority in how he taught (v. 22) and in what he did (here) impressed the people.

1:29 *home of Simon and Andrew.* Jesus and the disciples probably went there for a meal, since the main Sabbath meal was served immediately following the synagogue service.

1:30 *Simon's mother-in-law.* 1Co 9:5 speaks of Peter's being married.

1:32 *evening.* See Lk 4:40 and note. *people brought.* They waited until the Sabbath was over ("after sunset") before carrying anything (see Jer 17:21–22).

1:34 *not let the demons speak.* See Introduction: Emphases. *because they knew who he was.* Luke says, "because they knew he was the Messiah" (Lk 4:41). Jesus probably wanted first to show by word and deed the kind of Messiah he was (in contrast to popular notions) before he clearly declared himself, and he would not let the demons frustrate this intent.

1:36 *companions.* Andrew, James and John (vv. 16,19,29), and perhaps also Philip and Nathanael (cf. Jn 1:43–45).

1:39 *throughout Galilee.* The first of what seem to be three preaching and healing tours of Galilee (second tour, Lk 8:1; third tour, Mk 6:6 and Mt 11:1).

1:40 *leprosy.* See TNIV text note and Lev 13–14; see also note on Lev 13:2. *make me clean.* See notes on Lev 4:12; Mt 8:2.

1:41 *touched the man.* An act that, according to Mosaic law, brought defilement (see Lev 13, especially vv. 45–46; see also Lev 5:2). Jesus' compassion for the man superseded ceremonial considerations.

1:44 *don't tell this to anyone.* See Introduction: Emphases; see also notes on Mt 8:4; 16:20. *go, show yourself to the priest.* Who would then pronounce him ceremonially clean (see, e.g., Lev 13:6,13,17,23; see also note on Lk 5:14). *testimony to them.* The sacrifices were to be evidence to the priests and the people that the cure was real and that Jesus respected the law. The healing was also a testimony to Jesus' divine power, since Jews believed that only God could cure leprosy (see 2Ki 5:1–14 and notes).

1:45 *no longer enter a town openly.* Jesus' growing popularity with the people (see v. 28; 3:7–8; Lk 7:17) and the increasing opposition from Jewish leaders (see 2:6–7,16,24; 3:2,6,22) sometimes made it necessary for him to withdraw from Galilee into surrounding territories.

2:2 w ver 13;
Mk 1:45
2:3 x S Mt 4:24
2:5 y Lk 7:48
2:7 z Isa 43:25
2:10 a S Mt 8:20
2:12 b S Mt 9:8
c Mt 9:33
2:13 d Mk 1:45;
Lk 5:15; Jn 6:2
2:14 e S Mt 4:19
2:16 f Ac 23:9
g S Mt 9:11
2:17 h Lk 19:10;
1Ti 1:15

JESUS FORGIVES AND HEALS A PARALYZED MAN

2:3–12pp — Mt 9:2–8; Lk 5:18–26

2 A few days later, when Jesus again entered Capernaum, the people heard that he had come home. ²They gathered in such large numbers w that there was no room left, not even outside the door, and he preached the word to them. ³Some men came, bringing to him a paralyzed man, x carried by four of them. ⁴Since they could not get him to Jesus because of the crowd, they made an opening in the roof above Jesus by digging through it and then lowered the mat the man was lying on. ⁵When Jesus saw their faith, he said to the paralyzed man, "Son, your sins are forgiven." y

⁶Now some teachers of the law were sitting there, thinking to themselves, ⁷"Why does this fellow talk like that? He's blaspheming! Who can forgive sins but God alone?" z

⁸Immediately Jesus knew in his spirit that this was what they were thinking in their hearts, and he said to them, "Why are you thinking these things? ⁹Which is easier: to say to this paralyzed man, 'Your sins are forgiven,' or to say, 'Get up, take your mat and walk'? ¹⁰But I want you to know that the Son of Man a has authority on earth to forgive sins." So he said to the man, ¹¹"I tell you, get up, take your mat and go home." ¹²He got up, took his mat and walked out in full view of them all. This amazed everyone and they praised God, b saying, "We have never seen anything like this!" c

JESUS CALLS LEVI AND EATS WITH SINNERS

2:14–17pp — Mt 9:9–13; Lk 5:27–32

¹³Once again Jesus went out beside the lake. A large crowd came to him, d and he began to teach them. ¹⁴As he walked along, he saw Levi son of Alphaeus sitting at the tax collector's booth. "Follow me," e Jesus told him, and Levi got up and followed him.

¹⁵While Jesus was having dinner at Levi's house, many tax collectors and sinners were eating with him and his disciples, for there were many who followed him. ¹⁶When the teachers of the law who were Pharisees f saw him eating with the sinners and tax collectors, they asked his disciples: "Why does he eat with tax collectors and sinners?" g

¹⁷On hearing this, Jesus said to them, "It is not the healthy who need a doctor, but the sick. I have not come to call the righteous, but sinners." h

---

2:1 *home.* When in Capernaum Jesus probably made his home at Peter's house (see 1:21,29).

2:2 *They gathered in … large numbers.* The same enthusiasm that greeted Jesus earlier (1:32–33,37) was evident at his return.

2:3 *paralyzed man.* Nothing definite can be said about the nature of the man's affliction beyond the fact that he could not walk. The determination of the four men to reach Jesus suggests that his condition was desperate.

B **2:4** *made an opening in the roof.* A typical house in the Middle East had a flat roof accessible by means of an outside staircase. The roof was often made of a thick layer of clay (packed with a stone roller), supported by mats of branches across wood beams.

A **2:5** *Jesus saw their faith.* Jesus recognized that the bold action of the paralyzed man and his friends gave evidence of faith. *Son, your sins are forgiven.* Jesus first met the man's deepest need: forgiveness.

A **2:7** *He's blaspheming! Who can forgive sins but God alone?* In Jewish theology even the Messiah could not forgive sins, and Jesus' forgiveness of sin was a claim to deity—which they considered to be blasphemous (see note on 14:64).

A **2:9** *Which is easier … ?* Jesus' point probably was that neither forgiving sins nor healing was easier. Both are equally impossible for people and equally easy for God.

A **2:10** *But I want you to know.* See note on Lk 5:24; spoken to the teachers of the law. The words "So he said to the man" explain a change in the persons addressed. It is clear that one purpose of miracles was to give evidence of Jesus' deity. For the use of miraculous signs in John's Gospel, see Jn 2:11; 20:30–31 and notes. *Son of Man.* See note on 8:31.

2:12 *This amazed everyone.* See note on 1:22.

2:14 *Levi son of Alphaeus.* Matthew (see Mt 9:9; 10:3). His given name was probably Levi (for the possible meaning of the name Levi, see TNIV text note on Ge 29:34), and Matthew ("gift of the LORD") his apostolic name. *tax collector's booth.* Levi was a tax collector (see note on Lk 3:12) under Herod Antipas, tetrarch of Galilee. The tax collector's booth where Jesus found Levi was probably a toll booth on the major international road that went west from Damascus through Capernaum to the Mediterranean coast and then south to Egypt (see Isa 9:1 and note). *Levi got up and followed.* See note on Lk 5:28.

2:15 *tax collectors.* Jewish tax collectors were regarded as outcasts. They could not serve as witnesses or as judges and were expelled from the synagogue. In the eyes of the Jewish community their disgrace extended to their families. See note on Mt 5:46. *sinners.* Notoriously evil people, as well as those who refused to follow the Mosaic law as interpreted by the teachers of the law. The term was commonly used of tax collectors, adulterers, robbers and the like. *were eating.* To eat with a person was a sign of friendship.

2:16 *teachers of the law who were Pharisees.* Not all teachers of the law were Pharisees—successors of the Hasidim, pious Jews who joined forces with the Maccabees during the struggle for freedom from Syrian oppression (166–142 B.C.). They were first called Pharisees during the reign of John Hyrcanus (135–105). Although some, no doubt, were godly, most of those who came into conflict with Jesus were hypocritical, envious, rigid and formalistic. According to Pharisaism, God's grace extended only to those who kept his law. See notes on Mt 2:4; 3:7.

A **2:17** *I have not come to call the righteous, but sinners.* Those who are self-righteous do not realize their need for salvation, but admitted sinners do.

JESUS QUESTIONED ABOUT FASTING

2:18–22pp — Mt 9:14–17; Lk 5:33–38

¹⁸Now John's disciples and the Pharisees were fasting. *ⁱ* Some people came and asked Jesus, "How is it that John's disciples and the disciples of the Pharisees are fasting, but yours are not?"

¹⁹Jesus answered, "How can the guests of the bridegroom fast while he is with them? They cannot, so long as they have him with them. ²⁰But the time will come when the bridegroom will be taken from them,*ʲ* and on that day they will fast.

²¹"No one sews a patch of unshrunk cloth on an old garment. If they do, the new piece will pull away from the old, making the tear worse. ²²And people do not pour new wine into old wineskins. If they do, the wine will burst the skins, and both the wine and the wineskins will be ruined. No, they pour new wine into new wineskins."

JESUS IS LORD OF THE SABBATH

2:23–28pp — Mt 12:1–8; Lk 6:1–5
3:1–6pp — Mt 12:9–14; Lk 6:6–11

²³One Sabbath Jesus was going through the grainfields, and as his disciples walked along, they began to pick some heads of grain. *ᵏ* ²⁴The Pharisees said to him, "Look, why are they doing what is unlawful on the Sabbath?"*ˡ*

²⁵He answered, "Have you never read what David did when he and his companions were hungry and in need? ²⁶In the days of Abiathar the high priest, *ᵐ* he entered the house of God and ate the consecrated bread, which is lawful only for priests to eat. *ⁿ* And he also gave some to his companions." *ᵒ*

²⁷Then he said to them, "The Sabbath was made for people, *ᵖ* not people for the Sabbath. *�q* ²⁸So the Son of Man *ʳ* is Lord even of the Sabbath."

JESUS HEALS ON THE SABBATH

3 Another time Jesus went into the synagogue, *ˢ* and a man with a shriveled hand was there. ²Some of them were looking for a reason to accuse Jesus, so they watched him closely *ᵗ* to see if he would heal him on the Sabbath. *ᵘ* ³Jesus said to the man with the shriveled hand, "Stand up in front of everyone."

⁴Then Jesus asked them, "Which is lawful on the Sabbath: to do good or to do evil, to save life or to kill?" But they remained silent.

2:18 *John's disciples.* John the Baptist's disciples may have been fasting because he was in prison (see 1:14), or this may have been a practice among them as an expression of repentance, intended to hasten the coming of redemption announced by John. *disciples of the Pharisees.* Pharisees as such were not teachers, but some were also "scribes" (teachers of the law), who often had disciples. Or perhaps the phrase is used in a nontechnical way to refer to people influenced by the Pharisees. *fasting.* In the Mosaic law only the fast of the Day of Atonement was required (see Lev 16:29,31 and note; 23:27–32; Nu 29:7). After the Babylonian exile four other yearly fasts were observed by the Jews (see Zec 7:5; 8:19 and notes). In Jesus' time the Pharisees fasted twice a week (see Lk 18:12 and note).
2:19 *How can the guests of the bridegroom fast while he is with them?* Jesus compared his disciples with the guests of a bridegroom. A Jewish wedding was a particularly joyous occasion, and the celebration associated with it often lasted a week. It was unthinkable to fast during such festivities, because fasting was associated with sorrow.
2:20 *bridegroom will be taken from them.* Jesus is the bridegroom who would be taken from them by death, and then fasting would be in order.
2:22 *new wineskins.* See note on Mt 9:17.
2:23 *pick some heads of grain.* There was nothing inherently wrong in the action itself, which comes under the provision of Dt 23:25.
2:24 *what is unlawful on the Sabbath.* According to Jewish tradition (in the Mishnah), harvesting (which is what Jesus' disciples technically were doing) was forbidden on the Sabbath. See Ex 34:21.
2:25 *what David did.* See 1Sa 21:1–6. The relationship between the OT incident and the apparent infringement

of the Sabbath by the disciples lies in the fact that on both occasions godly men did something forbidden. Since, however, it is always "lawful" to do good and to save life (even on the Sabbath), both David and the disciples were within the spirit of the law (see 1Sa 21:4 and note; Isa 58:6–7; Lk 13:10–17; 14:1–6).
2:26 *In the days of Abiathar the high priest.* According to 1Sa 21:1, Ahimelech, Abiathar's father (1Sa 22:20), was then high priest (see note on 2Sa 8:17). *house of God.* The tabernacle (see 1Sa 1:9 and note; 21:1). *consecrated bread.* See note on Mt 12:4.
2:27 *The Sabbath was made for people, not people for the Sabbath.* Jewish tradition had so multiplied the requirements and restrictions for keeping the Sabbath that the burden had become intolerable. Jesus cut across these traditions and emphasized the God-given purpose of the Sabbath—a day intended for the benefit of people (for spiritual, mental and physical restoration; see Ex 20:8–11).
2:28 See note on Lk 6:5.
3:1–6 A demonstration that Jesus is Lord of the Sabbath (see 2:28).
3:2 *Some of them.* The Pharisees (v. 6; cf. Lk 6:7). *to accuse Jesus.* Jesus' presence demanded a decision about his preaching, his acts and his person. The hostility, first seen in 2:6–7, continues to spread. See note on v. 6. *to see if he would heal him on the Sabbath.* An indication that the Pharisees believed in Jesus' power to perform miracles. The question was not "Could he?" but "Would he?" Jewish tradition prescribed that aid could be given the sick on the Sabbath only when the person's life was threatened, which obviously was not the case here. See notes on 2:25; Lk 13:14.
3:4 *to do good or to do evil, to save life or to kill?* Jesus asks: Which is better, to preserve life by healing or to destroy life by refusing to heal? The question is ironic since, whereas Jesus was ready to heal, the Pharisees were plotting to put

---

2:18 *ⁱ* S Mt 6:16-18;
Ac 13:2
2:20 *ʲ* Lk 17:22
2:23 *ᵏ* Dt 23:25
2:24 *ˡ* S Mt 12:2
2:26 *ᵐ* 1Ch 24:6;
2Sa 8:17 *ⁿ* Lev 24:5-9
ᵒ 1Sa 21:1-6
2:27 *ᵖ* Ex 23:12;
Dt 5:14 *q* Col 2:16
2:28 *ʳ* S Mt 8:20
3:1 *ˢ* S Mt 4:23;
Mk 1:21
3:2 *ᵗ* S Mt 12:10
ᵘ Lk 14:1

3:6 ᵛMt 22:16;
Mk 12:13 ʷS Mt 12:14
3:7 ˣMt 4:25
3:8 ʸS Mt 11:21
3:10 ᶻS Mt 4:23
ᵃS Mt 9:20
3:11 ᵇS Mt 4:3;
Mk 1:23,24
3:12 ᶜS Mt 8:4;
Mk 1:24,25,34;
Ac 16:17,18
3:13 ᵈMt 5:1
3:14 ᵉS Mk 6:30
3:15 ᶠS Mt 10:1
3:16 ᵍJn 1:42
3:20 ʰver 7
ⁱMk 6:31
3:21 ʲJn 10:20;
Ac 26:24
3:22 ᵏMt 15:1
ˡMt 10:25; 11:18;
12:24; Jn 7:20; 8:48,
52; 10:20 ᵐMt 9:34

⁵He looked around at them in anger and, deeply distressed at their stubborn hearts, said to the man, "Stretch out your hand." He stretched it out, and his hand was completely restored. ⁶Then the Pharisees went out and began to plot with the Herodians ᵛ how they might kill Jesus. ʷ

CROWDS FOLLOW JESUS

3:7–12pp — Mt 12:15,16; Lk 6:17–19

⁷Jesus withdrew with his disciples to the lake, and a large crowd from Galilee followed. ˣ ⁸When they heard about all he was doing, many people came to him from Judea, Jerusalem, Idumea, and the regions across the Jordan and around Tyre and Sidon. ʸ ⁹Because of the crowd he told his disciples to have a small boat ready for him, to keep the people from crowding him. ¹⁰For he had healed many, ᶻ so that those with diseases were pushing forward to touch him. ᵃ ¹¹Whenever the evilᵃ spirits saw him, they fell down before him and cried out, "You are the Son of God." ᵇ ¹²But he gave them strict orders not to tell others about him. ᶜ

JESUS APPOINTS THE TWELVE

3:16–19pp — Mt 10:2–4; Lk 6:14–16; Ac 1:13

¹³Jesus went up on a mountainside and called to him those he wanted, and they came to him. ᵈ ¹⁴He appointed twelveᵇ ᵉ that they might be with him and that he might send them out to preach ¹⁵and to have authority to drive out demons. ᶠ ¹⁶These are the twelve he appointed: Simon (to whom he gave the name Peter), ᵍ ¹⁷James son of Zebedee and his brother John (to them he gave the name Boanerges, which means "sons of thunder"), ¹⁸Andrew, Philip, Bartholomew, Matthew, Thomas, James son of Alphaeus, Thaddaeus, Simon the Zealot ¹⁹and Judas Iscariot, who betrayed him.

JESUS ACCUSED BY HIS FAMILY AND BY TEACHERS OF THE LAW

3:23–27pp — Mt 12:25–29; Lk 11:17–22
3:31–35pp — Mt 12:46–50; Lk 8:19–21

²⁰Then Jesus entered a house, and again a crowd gathered, ʰ so that he and his disciples were not even able to eat. ⁱ ²¹When his familyᶜ heard about this, they went to take charge of him, for they said, "He is out of his mind." ʲ

²²And the teachers of the law who came down from Jerusalem ᵏ said, "He is possessed by Beelzebul! ˡ By the prince of demons he is driving out demons." ᵐ

ᵃ 11 Greek *unclean*; also in verse 30   ᵇ 14 Some manuscripts *twelve—designating them apostles—*
ᶜ 21 Or *his associates*

---

him to death. It is obvious who was guilty of breaking the Sabbath. *they remained silent.* See 12:34.

3:5 *He looked around at them.* See note on Lk 6:10.

3:6 *the Pharisees ... began to plot.* The decision to seek Jesus' death was not the result of this incident alone but was the response to a series of incidents (see 2:6–7,16–17,24). The plotting of the Pharisees and the Herodians is seen again on Tuesday of Passion Week (see 12:13 and note). *Herodians.* Evidently influential Jews who favored the Herodian dynasty, meaning they were supporters of Rome, from which the Herods received their authority. They joined the Pharisees in opposing Jesus because they feared he might have an unsettling political influence on the people. See Mt 22:15–17 and note.

3:8 Impressive evidence of Jesus' rapidly growing popularity among the people. This geographical list indicates that the crowds came not only from the areas in the vicinity of Capernaum but also from considerable distances. The regions mentioned included virtually all of Israel and its surrounding neighbors. Mark tells of Jesus' work in all these regions except Idumea (see 1:14, Galilee; 5:1 and 10:1, the region across the Jordan; 7:24,31, Tyre and Sidon; 10:1, Judea; 11:11, Jerusalem). *Idumea.* The Greek form of Hebrew Edom, but here referring to an area south of Judea, not to earlier Edomite territory. (See map, p. 1721.)

3:11 *evil spirits.* See note on 1:23. *You are the Son of God.* The evil spirits recognized who Jesus was, but they did not believe in him (see 1:24 and note).

3:12 *not to tell others about him.* See Introduction: Emphases.

The time for revealing Jesus' identity had not yet come (see 1:34 and note; see also notes on Mt 8:4; 16:20), and demons were hardly the proper channel for such disclosure.

3:13 *mountainside.* Probably the hill country of Galilee around the lake.

A **3:14** *that they might be with him.* The training of the Twelve included not only instruction and practice in various forms of ministry but also—first and foremost—continuous association and intimate fellowship with Jesus himself.

3:16–19 See notes on Lk 6:14–16.

3:16 *Simon (to whom he gave the name Peter).* See note on 1:16.

3:17 *Boanerges.* One of many Aramaic words translated by Mark (see Introduction: Recipients). *sons of thunder.* Probably descriptive of their dispositions (see notes on 10:37; Lk 9:54).

3:18 *Thaddaeus.* Apparently the same as "Judas son of James" (see Lk 6:16; Ac 1:13). *the Zealot.* See note on Mt 10:4.

C **3:19** *Iscariot.* Probably means "the man from Kerioth," perhaps the town of Kerioth Hezron (Jos 15:25), 12 miles south of Hebron. For Judas' betrayal of Jesus, see 14:10–11, 43–46.

3:20 *house.* Perhaps the home of Peter and Andrew (see 1:29; 2:1 and notes; see also diagram, p. 1725).

3:21 *his family ... went to take charge of him.* They may have come to Capernaum from Nazareth, about 30 miles away (see v. 31).

3:22 *who came down from Jerusalem.* See 7:1 and note. *Beelzebul.* See note on Mt 10:25.

3:23 *n* Mk 4:2
o S Mt 4:10
3:27 *p* Isa 49:24,25
3:29 *q* Mt 12:31,32;
Lk 12:10
3:31 *r* ver 21
4:1 *s* Mk 2:13; 3:7
4:2 *t* ver 11; Mk 3:23
4:3 *u* ver 26
4:8 *v* Jn 15:5; Col 1:6
4:9 *w* ver 23;
S Mt 11:15
4:11 *x* S Mt 3:2
y 1Co 5:12,13; Col 4:5;
1Th 4:12; 1Ti 3:7
4:12 *z* Isa 6:9,10;
S Mt 13:13-15

²³So Jesus called them over to him and began to speak to them in parables: *ⁿ* "How can Satan *ᵒ* drive out Satan? ²⁴If a kingdom is divided against itself, that kingdom cannot stand. ²⁵If a house is divided against itself, that house cannot stand. ²⁶And if Satan opposes himself and is divided, he cannot stand; his end has come. ²⁷In fact, no one can enter a strong man's house without first tying him up. Then he can plunder the strong man's house. *ᵖ* ²⁸Truly I tell you, people will be forgiven all their sins and all the blasphemies they utter. ²⁹But whoever blasphemes against the Holy Spirit will never be forgiven, but is guilty of an eternal sin." *ᑫ*

³⁰He said this because they were saying, "He has an evil spirit."

³¹Then Jesus' mother and brothers arrived. *ʳ* Standing outside, they sent someone in to call him. ³²A crowd was sitting around him, and they told him, "Your mother and brothers are outside looking for you."

³³"Who are my mother and my brothers?" he asked.

³⁴Then he looked at those seated in a circle around him and said, "Here are my mother and my brothers! ³⁵Whoever does God's will is my brother and sister and mother."

THE PARABLE OF THE SOWER

4:1–12pp — Mt 13:1–15; Lk 8:4–10
4:13–20pp — Mt 13:18–23; Lk 8:11–15

4 Again Jesus began to teach by the lake. *ˢ* The crowd that gathered around him was so large that he got into a boat and sat in it out on the lake, while all the people were along the shore at the water's edge. ²He taught them many things by parables, *ᵗ* and in his teaching said: ³"Listen! A farmer went out to sow his seed. *ᵘ* ⁴As he was scattering the seed, some fell along the path, and the birds came and ate it up. ⁵Some fell on rocky places, where it did not have much soil. It sprang up quickly, because the soil was shallow. ⁶But when the sun came up, the plants were scorched, and they withered because they had no root. ⁷Other seed fell among thorns, which grew up and choked the plants, so that they did not bear grain. ⁸Still other seed fell on good soil. It came up, grew and produced a crop, some multiplying thirty, some sixty, some a hundred times." *ᵛ*

⁹Then Jesus said, "Whoever has ears to hear, let them hear." *ʷ*

¹⁰When he was alone, the Twelve and the others around him asked him about the parables. ¹¹He told them, "The secret of the kingdom of God *ˣ* has been given to you. But to those on the outside *ʸ* everything is said in parables ¹²so that,

" 'they may be ever seeing but never perceiving,
    and ever hearing but never understanding;
    otherwise they might turn and be forgiven!'ᵃ" *ᶻ*

¹³Then Jesus said to them, "Don't you understand this parable? How then will you un-

a 12 Isaiah 6:9,10

3:23 *parables.* In this context the word is used in the general sense of comparisons (see note on 4:2).
3:24 *kingdom is divided against itself.* See note on Lk 11:17.
3:27 *enter a strong man's house . . . plunder.* Jesus was doing this very thing when he freed people from Satan's control.
3:28 *Truly I tell you.* A solemn affirmation used by Jesus to strengthen his assertions (see 8:12; 9:1,41; 10:15,29; 11:23; 12:43; 13:30; 14:9,18,25,30; see also note on Jn 1:51).
3:29 *whoever blasphemes against the Holy Spirit will never be forgiven.* Jesus identifies this sin in v. 30 (cf. v. 22)—the teachers of the law attributed Jesus' healing to Satan's power rather than to the Holy Spirit (see note on Mt 12:31).
3:31 *Jesus' mother and brothers.* See note on Lk 8:19.
3:35 *Whoever does God's will.* Membership in God's spiritual family, evidenced by obedience to him, is more important than membership in our human families (see 10:30 and note).
4:1 *sat in it.* Sitting was the usual position for Jewish teachers (see 9:35; see also Mt 5:1; Lk 4:20 and notes).
4:2 *parables.* Usually stories out of ordinary life used to illustrate spiritual or moral truth, sometimes in the form of brief similes, comparisons (see note on 3:23), analogies or proverbial sayings. They tended to have a single main point, and not every detail

was meant to have significance. See notes on Mt 13:3; Lk 8:4.
4:3–8 In that day seed was broadcast by hand—which, by its nature, scattered some seed on unproductive ground (see note on Lk 8:5).
4:3 *Listen!* This parable begins and ends (v. 9) with a call for careful attention, which suggests that its meaning is not self-evident. *sow his seed.* See note on Lk 8:5.
4:8 *multiplying . . . a hundred times.* A hundredfold yield was an unusually productive harvest (see Ge 26:12–13). Harvest was a common figure for the consummation of God's kingdom (see Joel 3:13; Rev 14:15 and notes).
4:9 See note on Lk 8:8.
4:11 *secret of the kingdom of God.* In the NT "secret" refers to something God has revealed to his people. The secret (that which was previously unknown) is proclaimed to all, but only those who have faith understand. In this context the secret seems to be that the kingdom of God had drawn near (see v. 26; see also notes on 1:15; Mt 3:2) in the coming of Jesus Christ, the King.
4:12 *so that.* Jesus likens his preaching in parables to the ministry of Isaiah, which, while it gained some disciples (Isa 8:16), was also to expose the hardhearted resistance of many to God's warning and appeal.

4:14 *a* Mk 16:20;
Lk 1:2; Ac 4:31; 8:4;
16:6; 17:11; Php 1:14
4:15 *b* S Mt 4:10
4:19 *c* Mt 19:23;
1Ti 6:9,10,17;
1Jn 2:15-17
4:21 *d* S Mt 5:15
4:22 *e* Jer 16:17;
Mt 10:26; Lk 8:17;
12:2
4:23 *f* ver 9;
S Mt 11:15
4:24 *g* S Mt 7:2
4:25 *h* S Mt 25:29
4:26 *i* S Mt 13:24
4:29 *j* Rev 14:15
4:30 *k* S Mt 13:24
4:33 *l* Jn 16:12
4:34 *m* S Jn 16:25
4:36 *n* ver 1; Mk 3:9;
5:2, 21; 6:32, 45

derstand any parable? [14]The farmer sows the word. *a* [15]Some people are like seed along the path, where the word is sown. As soon as they hear it, Satan *b* comes and takes away the word that was sown in them. [16]Others, like seed sown on rocky places, hear the word and at once receive it with joy. [17]But since they have no root, they last only a short time. When trouble or persecution comes because of the word, they quickly fall away. [18]Still others, like seed sown among thorns, hear the word; [19]but the worries of this life, the deceitfulness of wealth *c* and the desires for other things come in and choke the word, making it unfruitful. [20]Others, like seed sown on good soil, hear the word, accept it, and produce a crop—some thirty, some sixty, some a hundred times what was sown."

A LAMP ON A STAND

[21]He said to them, "Do you bring in a lamp to put it under a bowl or a bed? Instead, don't you put it on its stand? *d* [22]For whatever is hidden is meant to be disclosed, and whatever is concealed is meant to be brought out into the open. *e* [23]If anyone has ears to hear, let them hear." *f*

[24]"Consider carefully what you hear," he continued. "With the measure you use, it will be measured to you—and even more. *g* [25]Those who have will be given more; as for those who do not have, even what they have will be taken from them." *h*

THE PARABLE OF THE GROWING SEED

[26]He also said, "This is what the kingdom of God is like. *i* A man scatters seed on the ground. [27]Night and day, whether he sleeps or gets up, the seed sprouts and grows, though he does not know how. [28]All by itself the soil produces grain—first the stalk, then the head, then the full kernel in the head. [29]As soon as the grain is ripe, he puts the sickle to it, because the harvest has come." *j*

THE PARABLE OF THE MUSTARD SEED

4:30–32pp — Mt 13:31,32; Lk 13:18,19

[30]Again he said, "What shall we say the kingdom of God is like, *k* or what parable shall we use to describe it? [31]It is like a mustard seed, which is the smallest of all seeds on earth. [32]Yet when planted, it grows and becomes the largest of all garden plants, with such big branches that the birds can perch in its shade."

[33]With many similar parables Jesus spoke the word to them, as much as they could understand. *l* [34]He did not say anything to them without using a parable. *m* But when he was alone with his own disciples, he explained everything.

JESUS CALMS THE STORM

4:35–41pp — Mt 8:18,23–27; Lk 8:22–25

[35]That day when evening came, he said to his disciples, "Let us go over to the other side." [36]Leaving the crowd behind, they took him along, just as he was, in the boat. *n* There

---

4:14 *the word.* The interpretation calls attention to the response to the word of God that Jesus has been preaching. In spite of many obstacles, God's word will accomplish his purpose (cf. Isa 55:11 and note).

4:17 *trouble or persecution.* See Introduction: Occasion and Purpose; see also 8:34–38; 10:30 and notes; 13:9–13.

4:19 *deceitfulness of wealth.* Prosperity tends to give a false sense of self-sufficiency, security and well-being (see 10:17–25 and notes; Dt 8:17–18; 32:15; Ecc 2:4–11; see also Jas 5:1–6 and notes).

4:20 *hundred times.* See v. 8 and note.

4:21 *Do you bring in a lamp ... ?* As a lamp is placed to give, not hide, light, so Jesus, the light of the world (see Jn 8:12 and note), is destined to be revealed. *lamp.* See Mt 5:15 and note.

4:22 See note on Lk 8:17.

4:23 See note on Lk 8:8.

4:24 See note on Lk 8:18.

4:25 The more we appropriate truth now, the more we will receive in the future; and if we do not respond to what little truth we may know already we will not profit even from that.

4:26–29 Only Mark records this parable. Whereas the parable of the sower stresses the importance of proper soil for the growth of seed and the success of the harvest, here the mysteri-

ous power of the seed itself is emphasized. The gospel message contains its own power.

4:26 *kingdom of God.* See note on v. 11.

4:29 *he puts the sickle to it, because the harvest has come.* A possible allusion to Joel 3:13 (see note there), where harvest is a figure for the consummation of God's kingdom.

4:30–34 The main point of this parable is that the kingdom of God seemingly had insignificant beginnings. It was introduced by the despised and rejected Jesus and his 12 unimpressive disciples. But a day will come when its true greatness and power will be seen by the whole world.

4:31 See notes on Mt 13:31–32.

4:34 *He did not say anything to them without using a parable.* Jesus used parables to illustrate truths, stimulate thinking and awaken spiritual perception. The people in general were not ready for the full truth of the gospel. When alone with his disciples Jesus taught more specifically, but even they usually needed to have things explained.

4:35–41 Although miracles are hard for people to accept today, the NT makes it clear that Jesus is Lord not only over his church but also over all creation.

4:35 *other side.* Jesus left the territory of Galilee to go to the "region of the Gerasenes" (5:1).

JERUSALEM DURING THE MINISTRY OF JESUS

Herod the Great (reigned 37–4 B.C.) rebuilt the temple and its surrounding walls, built a palace, a fortress, a theater and a hippodrome (stadium) for horse and chariot races. He brought the city to the zenith of its architectural beauty and Roman cultural expression. This became Jerusalem in the time of Jesus.

The "THIRD WALL"
(shown with dotted line)
was begun by Herod Agrippa I between A.D. 41 and 44 to enclose the growing northern suburbs, but the work was apparently stopped. Its construction was resumed, in haste, only after the First Jewish Revolt broke out in A.D. 66.

The "SECOND WALL"
was built by Herod I or by earlier Hasmonean kings. Precise location is difficult to determine. This wall was put up around a market area in a valley, protecting it from raiding and looting, but was of questionable military value. At its eastern end, however, Herod built a military barracks (Antonia Fortress).

The "FIRST WALL,"
so named by Josephus, encircled the city during the Hasmonean period, which began in 167 B.C. After the revolt led by Judas Maccabeus in 167, Jerusalem expanded steadily in a period of independence under its own Jewish kings.

Herod's Towers

Herod's Royal Palace*

MT. ZION ("Upper City")

Essene Gate

Traditional Upper Room?

House of Caiaphas the high priest,* identified here with today's Church of St. Peter in Gallicantu.

Theater**

HINNOM VALLEY
FIRST WALL
HINNOM VALLEY
FIRST WALL
SOUTH

Hippodrome**

NORTH

Psephinus Tower*

Tyropoeon Street***
Present Damascus Gate***
Bridge over valley ("Wilson's Arch")***
Xystus (Greek exercise hall)
Hasmonean Palace*
Traditional Crucifixion Site †††

"Garden Tomb" (alternate crucifixion site) †††

Maximum city growth within walls by A.D. 70

Antonia Fortress*** (later Praetorium?)

BEZETHA ("New City")
Pool of Bethesda***

TEMPLE

Gentiles Court

Huldah Gates and Stairways***

Gihon Spring***

Ashpot Gate/ Tekoa Gate

Pool of Siloam***

CITY OF DAVID "Lower City"

KIDRON VALLEY

MOUNT OF OLIVES

Meters / Feet
300 / 1,000
200 / 500
100 / 100

B Archaeological excavations have revealed a monumental stairway and the continuation of Tyropoeon Street,*** which lies along the valley called "Way of the Cheesemongers" by Josephus.

The Siloam aqueduct-tunnel,*** 1,749 ft. long, was cut through solid bedrock, was 5'11" high (average) and followed an "S" shaped course made necessary by engineering difficulties. It was dug by King Hezekiah and provided water during King Sennacherib's threat to lay siege to the city in 701 B.C. (2Ch 32:30). Water flows through it to this very day.

Buildings, streets and roads shown here are artist's concept only unless otherwise named and located. Wall heights remain generally unknown, except for those surrounding the Temple Mount.

Deep valleys on the east, south and west permitted urban expansion only to the north.

* Location generally known, but style of architecture is unknown; artist's concept only, and Roman architecture is assumed.

** Location and architecture unknown, but referred to in written history; shown here for illustrative purposes.

*** Ancient feature has remained, or appearance has been determined from evidence.

4:40 *o* Mt 14:31;
Mk 16:14
5:2 *p* Mk 4:1
q Mk 1:23
5:7 *r* S Mt 8:29
s Mt 4:3; Lk 1:32;
6:35; Ac 16:17;
Heb 7:1
5:9 *t* ver 15

were also other boats with him. ³⁷A furious squall came up, and the waves broke over the boat, so that it was nearly swamped. ³⁸Jesus was in the stern, sleeping on a cushion. The disciples woke him and said to him, "Teacher, don't you care if we drown?"

³⁹He got up, rebuked the wind and said to the waves, "Quiet! Be still!" Then the wind died down and it was completely calm.

⁴⁰He said to his disciples, "Why are you so afraid? Do you still have no faith?" *o*

⁴¹They were terrified and asked each other, "Who is this? Even the wind and the waves obey him!"

JESUS RESTORES A DEMON-POSSESSED MAN

5:1–17pp — Mt 8:28–34; Lk 8:26–37
5:18–20pp — Lk 8:38,39

5They went across the lake to the region of the Gerasenes. *a* ²When Jesus got out of the boat, *p* a man with an evil *b* spirit *q* came from the tombs to meet him. ³This man lived in the tombs, and no one could bind him anymore, not even with a chain. ⁴For he had often been chained hand and foot, but he tore the chains apart and broke the irons on his feet. No one was strong enough to subdue him. ⁵Night and day among the tombs and in the hills he would cry out and cut himself with stones.

⁶When he saw Jesus from a distance, he ran and fell on his knees in front of him. ⁷He shouted at the top of his voice, "What do you want with me, *r* Jesus, Son of the Most High God? *s* In God's name don't torture me!" ⁸For Jesus had said to him, "Come out of this man, you evil spirit!"

⁹Then Jesus asked him, "What is your name?"

"My name is Legion," *t* he replied, "for we are many." ¹⁰And he begged Jesus again and again not to send them out of the area.

¹¹A large herd of pigs was feeding on the nearby hillside. ¹²The demons begged Jesus, "Send us among the pigs; allow us to go into them." ¹³He gave them permission, and the evil spirits came out and went into the pigs. The herd, about two thousand in number, rushed down the steep bank into the lake and were drowned.

¹⁴Those tending the pigs ran off and reported this in the town and countryside, and the people went out to see what had happened. ¹⁵When they came to Jesus, they saw the man

a 1 Some manuscripts *Gadarenes*; other manuscripts *Gergesenes*   *b* 2 Greek *unclean*; also in verses 8 and 13

4:37 *furious squall came up.* Situated in a basin surrounded by mountains, the Sea of Galilee is particularly susceptible to sudden, violent storms. Cool air from the Mediterranean is drawn down through the narrow mountain passes and clashes with the hot, humid air lying over the lake.
4:38 *sleeping on a cushion.* The picture of Jesus, exhausted and asleep, is characteristic of Mark's human touch.
4:41 *Who is this?* In view of what Jesus had just done, the only answer to this rhetorical question was: He is the very Son of God! God's presence, as well as his power, was demonstrated (see Ps 65:6–7; 107:25–30 and notes; Pr 30:4). Mark indicates his answer to this question in the opening line of his Gospel (1:1). By such miracles Jesus sought to establish and increase the disciples' faith in his deity.
5:1–43 The stories of the healing of the demon-possessed man, Jairus's daughter and the woman with the hemorrhage all have to do with ceremonial uncleanness.
5:1 *across the lake.* The east side of the lake, a territory largely inhabited by Gentiles, as indicated by the presence of the large herd of pigs—animals Jews considered ceremonially unclean and therefore unfit to eat (see Isa 65:4 and note). *region of the Gerasenes.* Gerasa, located about 35 miles southeast of the Sea of Galilee, may have had holdings on the eastern shore of the Sea, giving its name to a small village there now known as Khersa. About one mile south is a fairly steep slope within 40 yards of the shore, and about two miles from there are cavern tombs that appear to have been used as dwellings. See note on Lk 8:26.
5:2 *a man.* Mt 8:28 says there were two demon-possessed men (see note on Lk 8:27).
5:3 *lived in the tombs.* It was not unusual for the same cave to

provide burial for the dead and shelter for the living. Very poor people often lived in such caves.
5:4 *often been chained.* Though the villagers no doubt chained him partly for their own protection, this harsh treatment added to his humiliation.
5:5 *cry out and cut himself with stones.* Every word in the story emphasizes the man's pathetic condition, as well as the purpose of demonic possession—to torment and destroy the divine likeness in which human beings are created (see Ge 1:26 and note).
5:6 *fell on his knees.* An act of homage rather than worship. The demon showed respect because he recognized that he was confronted by one greatly superior to him.
5:7 *What do you want with me . . . ?* A way of saying, "What do we have in common?" Similar expressions are found in the OT (e.g., 2Sa 16:10; 19:22), where they mean, "Mind your own business!" The demon was speaking, using the voice of the possessed man (see 1:23 and note). *Son of the Most High God.* See note on 1:24. *In God's name don't torture me!* The demon sensed that he was to be punished and used the strongest basis for an oath that he knew, though his appeal to God was strangely ironic.
5:9 *My name is Legion . . . for we are many.* A Roman legion was made up of 6,000 men. Here the term suggests that the man was possessed by numerous demons and perhaps also represents the many powers opposed to Jesus, who embodies the power of God (see 1:23–24 and notes).
5:10 *not to send them out of the area.* The demons were fearful of being sent into eternal punishment, i.e., "into the Abyss" (Lk 8:31; see note there).
5:11 *pigs.* See note on Lk 8:32.
5:13 *gave them permission.* See note on Mt 8:32.

who had been possessed by the legion ^u of demons, ^v sitting there, dressed and in his right mind; and they were afraid. ¹⁶Those who had seen it told the people what had happened to the demon-possessed man—and told about the pigs as well. ¹⁷Then the people began to plead with Jesus to leave their region.

¹⁸As Jesus was getting into the boat, the man who had been demon-possessed begged to go with him. ¹⁹Jesus did not let him, but said, "Go home to your own people and tell them ^w how much the Lord has done for you, and how he has had mercy on you." ²⁰So the man went away and began to tell in the Decapolis ^a ^x how much Jesus had done for him. And all the people were amazed.

JESUS RAISES A DEAD GIRL AND HEALS A SICK WOMAN
5:22–43pp — Mt 9:18–26; Lk 8:41–56

²¹When Jesus had again crossed over by boat to the other side of the lake, ^y a large crowd gathered around him while he was by the lake. ^z ²²Then one of the synagogue leaders, ^a

^a 20 That is, the Ten Cities

5:15 ^u ver 9 ^v ver 16, 18; S Mt 4:24
5:19 ^w S Mt 8:4
5:20 ^x Mt 4:25; Mk 7:31
5:21 ^y Mt 9:1 ^z Mk 4:1
5:22 ^a ver 35, 36, 38; Lk 13:14; Ac 13:15; 18:8,17

5:16 *told about the pigs as well.* In addition to the remarkable change in the demon-possessed man, the drowning of the pigs seemed to be a major concern, no doubt because it was so dramatic and brought considerable financial loss to the owners.
5:17 *plead with Jesus to leave their region.* Fear of further loss may have motivated this response, but also the fact that a powerful force was at work in their midst, one that they could not comprehend.
5:19 *tell them how much the Lord has done for you.* This is in marked contrast to Jesus' exhortation to silence in the case of the

man cleansed of leprosy (1:44; see 1:34; 3:12; Mt 8:4 and notes), perhaps because the healing of the demoniac was in Gentile territory, where there was little danger that Messianic ideas about Jesus might be circulated (see Introduction: Emphases).
5:20 *Decapolis.* See note on Mt 4:25; see also map, below.
amazed. See 1:22 and note.
5:21 *other side of the lake.* Jesus returned to the west side of the lake, perhaps to Capernaum.
5:22 *synagogue leaders.* A leader of the synagogue was a layman whose responsibilities were administrative and included

THE DECAPOLIS AND THE LANDS BEYOND THE JORDAN

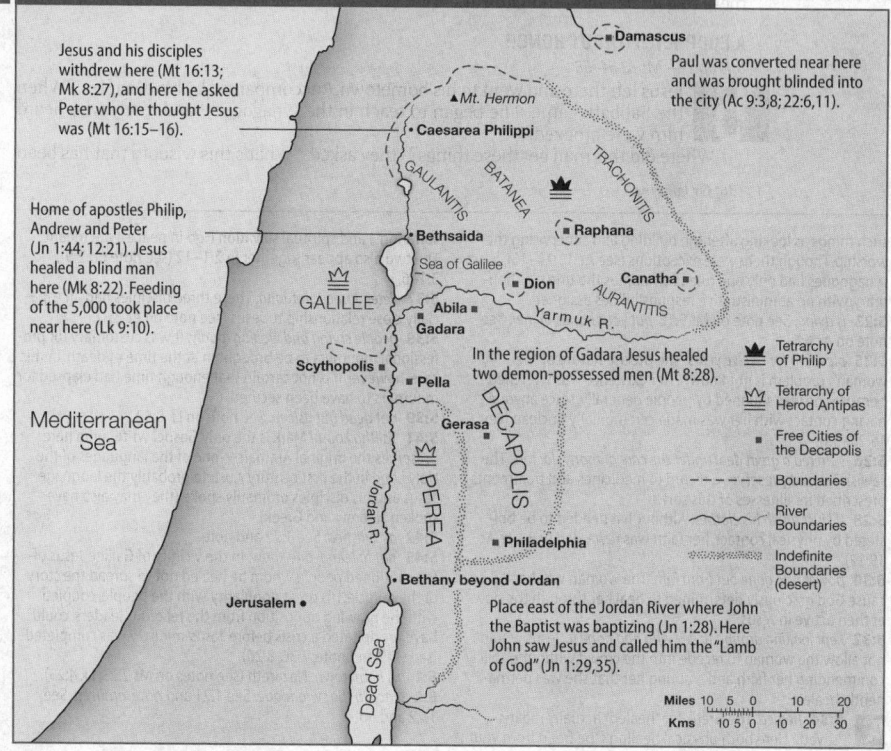

Jesus and his disciples withdrew here (Mt 16:13; Mk 8:27), and here he asked Peter who he thought Jesus was (Mt 16:15–16).

Home of apostles Philip, Andrew and Peter (Jn 1:44; 12:21). Jesus healed a blind man here (Mk 8:22). Feeding of the 5,000 took place near here (Lk 9:10).

Mediterranean Sea

Paul was converted near here and was brought blinded into the city (Ac 9:3,8; 22:6,11).

▪ Damascus
▲ Mt. Hermon
• Caesarea Philippi
GAULANITIS BATANEA TRACHONITIS
• Bethsaida
♔ Raphana
Sea of Galilee
GALILEE
▪ Dion Canatha ▪
AURANTITIS
• Abila Yarmuk R.
• Gadara
Scythopolis ▪ • Pella
DECAPOLIS
Gerasa ▪
PEREA Jordan R.
• Philadelphia
• Bethany beyond Jordan
Jerusalem •
Dead Sea

In the region of Gadara Jesus healed two demon-possessed men (Mt 8:28).

Place east of the Jordan River where John the Baptist was baptizing (Jn 1:28). Here John saw Jesus and called him the "Lamb of God" (Jn 1:29,35).

♔ Tetrarchy of Philip
♔ Tetrarchy of Herod Antipas
▪ Free Cities of the Decapolis
--- Boundaries
～ River Boundaries
Indefinite Boundaries (desert)

Miles 10 5 0   10   20
Kms   10 5 0 10 20 30

5:23 *b* Mt 19:13;
Mk 6:5; 7:32; 8:23;
16:18; Lk 4:40; 13:13;
S Ac 6:6
5:25 *c* Lev 15:25-30
5:28 *d* S Mt 9:20
5:29 *e* ver 34
5:30 *f* Lk 5:17; 6:19
5:34 *g* S Mt 9:22
h S Ac 15:33
5:35 *i* S ver 22
5:37 *j* S Mt 4:21
5:38 *k* S ver 22
5:39 *l* S Mt 9:24
5:41 *m* Mk 1:31
n S Lk 7:14
5:43 *o* S Mt 8:4
6:1 *p* S Mt 2:23
6:2 *q* Mk 1:21
r S Mt 4:23
s S Mt 7:28

named Jairus, came, and when he saw Jesus, he fell at his feet. ²³He pleaded earnestly with him, "My little daughter is dying. Please come and put your hands on *b* her so that she will be healed and live." ²⁴So Jesus went with him.

A large crowd followed and pressed around him. ²⁵And a woman was there who had been subject to bleeding *c* for twelve years. ²⁶She had suffered a great deal under the care of many doctors and had spent all she had, yet instead of getting better she grew worse. ²⁷When she heard about Jesus, she came up behind him in the crowd and touched his cloak, ²⁸because she thought, "If I just touch his clothes, *d* I will be healed." ²⁹Immediately her bleeding stopped and she felt in her body that she was freed from her suffering. *e*

³⁰At once Jesus realized that power *f* had gone out from him. He turned around in the crowd and asked, "Who touched my clothes?"

³¹"You see the people crowding against you," his disciples answered, "and yet you can ask, 'Who touched me?'"

³²But Jesus kept looking around to see who had done it. ³³Then the woman, knowing what had happened to her, came and fell at his feet and, trembling with fear, told him the whole truth. ³⁴He said to her, "Daughter, your faith has healed you. *g* Go in peace *h* and be freed from your suffering."

³⁵While Jesus was still speaking, some people came from the house of Jairus, the synagogue leader. *i* "Your daughter is dead," they said. "Why bother the teacher anymore?"

³⁶Overhearing ª what they said, Jesus told him, "Don't be afraid; just believe."

³⁷He did not let anyone follow him except Peter, James and John the brother of James. *j* ³⁸When they came to the home of the synagogue leader, *k* Jesus saw a commotion, with people crying and wailing loudly. ³⁹He went in and said to them, "Why all this commotion and wailing? The child is not dead but asleep." *l* ⁴⁰But they laughed at him.

After he put them all out, he took the child's father and mother and the disciples who were with him, and went in where the child was. ⁴¹He took her by the hand *m* and said to her, *"Talitha koum!"* (which means "Little girl, I say to you, get up!"). *n* ⁴²Immediately the girl stood up and began to walk around (she was twelve years old). At this they were completely astonished. ⁴³He gave strict orders not to let anyone know about this, *o* and told them to give her something to eat.

A PROPHET WITHOUT HONOR
6:1–6pp — Mt 13:54–58

6 Jesus left there and went to his hometown, *p* accompanied by his disciples. ²When the Sabbath came, *q* he began to teach in the synagogue, *r* and many who heard him were amazed. *s*

"Where did this man get these things?" they asked. "What's this wisdom that has been

---

ª 36 Or *Ignoring*

---

such things as looking after the building and supervising the worship. Though there were exceptions (see Ac 13:14–15), most synagogues had only one ruler. Sometimes the title was honorary, with no administrative responsibilities assigned.

5:23 *is dying.* See note on Mt 9:18. *put your hands on her.* See note on Ac 6:6.

5:25 *bleeding for twelve years.* The precise nature of the woman's problem is not known. Her existence was wretched because she was shunned by people generally, since anyone having contact with her was made ceremonially unclean (Lev 15:25–33).

5:26 *suffered a great deal under the care of many doctors.* The Jewish Talmud preserves a record of medicines and treatments prescribed for illnesses of this sort.

5:28 *If I just touch his clothes.* Although it needed to be bolstered by physical contact, her faith was rewarded (v. 34; cf. Ac 19:12).

5:30 *power had gone out from him.* The woman was healed because God graciously determined to heal her through the power then active in Jesus.

5:32 *kept looking around to see who had done it.* Jesus would not allow the woman to recede into the crowd without publicly commending her faith and assuring her that she was permanently healed.

5:34 *healed.* The Greek for "healed" actually means "saved." Here both physical healing ("be freed from your suffering") and spiritual salvation ("go in peace") are meant. The two also appear together in 2:1–12 (see note on 2:9); 3:1–6.

5:37 *Peter, James and John.* These three disciples had an especially close relationship to Jesus (see note on Ac 3:1).

5:38 *people crying and wailing loudly.* It was customary for professional mourners to be brought in at the time of death. In this case, however, it is not certain that enough time had elapsed for mourners to have been secured.

5:39 *not dead but asleep.* See note on Lk 8:52.

5:41 *Talitha koum!* Mark is the only Gospel writer who here preserves the original Aramaic—one of the languages of the Holy Land in the first century A.D. and probably the language Jesus and his disciples ordinarily spoke (they may also have spoken Hebrew and Greek).

5:42 *astonished.* See 1:22 and note.

5:43 *not to let anyone know.* In the vicinity of Galilee Jesus often cautioned people whom he healed not to spread the story of the miracle. His great popularity with the people, coupled with the growing opposition from the religious leaders, could have precipitated a crisis before Jesus' ministry was completed (see v. 19 and note; 7:36; 8:26).

6:1 *his hometown.* Nazareth (see notes on Mt 2:23; Lk 4:23).

6:2 *teach in the synagogue.* See 1:21 and note. *amazed.* See 1:22 and note.

given him? What are these remarkable miracles he is performing? ³Isn't this the carpenter? Isn't this Mary's son and the brother of James, Joseph,ᵃ Judas and Simon?ᵗ Aren't his sisters here with us?" And they took offense at him.ᵘ

⁴Jesus said to them, "Only in their own towns, among their relatives and in their own homes are prophets without honor."ᵛ ⁵He could not do any miracles there, except lay his hands onʷ a few sick people and heal them. ⁶He was amazed at their lack of faith.

JESUS SENDS OUT THE TWELVE
6:7–11pp — Mt 10:1,9–14; Lk 9:1,3–5

Then Jesus went around teaching from village to village.ˣ ⁷Calling the Twelve to him,ʸ he began to send them out two by twoᶻ and gave them authority over evilᵇ spirits.ᵃ

⁸These were his instructions: "Take nothing for the journey except a staff—no bread, no bag, no money in your belts. ⁹Wear sandals but not an extra shirt. ¹⁰Whenever you enter a house, stay there until you leave that town. ¹¹And if any place will not welcome you or listen to you, shake the dust off your feetᵇ when you leave, as a testimony against them."

¹²They went out and preached that people should repent.ᶜ ¹³They drove out many demons and anointed many sick people with oilᵈ and healed them.

JOHN THE BAPTIST BEHEADED
6:14–29pp — Mt 14:1–12
6:14–16pp — Lk 9:7–9

¹⁴King Herod heard about this, for Jesus' name had become well known. Some were saying,ᶜ "John the Baptistᵉ has been raised from the dead, and that is why miraculous powers are at work in him."

¹⁵Others said, "He is Elijah."ᶠ

And still others claimed, "He is a prophet,ᵍ like one of the prophets of long ago."ʰ

¹⁶But when Herod heard this, he said, "John, whom I beheaded, has been raised from the dead!"

¹⁷For Herod himself had given orders to have John arrested, and he had him bound and put in prison.ⁱ He did this because of Herodias, his brother Philip's wife, whom he had married. ¹⁸For John had been saying to Herod, "It is not lawful for you to have your brother's wife."ʲ ¹⁹So Herodias nursed a grudge against John and wanted to kill him. But she was not able to, ²⁰because Herod feared John and protected him, knowing him to be a righteous and holy man.ᵏ When Herod heard John, he was greatly puzzledᵈ; yet he liked to listen to him.

²¹Finally the opportune time came. On his birthday Herod gave a banquetˡ for his high

---

ᵃ *3* Greek *Joses,* a variant of *Joseph*   ᵇ *7* Greek *unclean*   ᶜ *14* Some early manuscripts *He was saying*
ᵈ *20* Some early manuscripts *he did many things*

6:3 ᵗ S Mt 12:46
ᵘ Mt 11:6; Jn 6:61
6:4 ᵛ Lk 4:24;
Jn 4:44
6:5 ʷ S Mk 5:23
6:6 ˣ Mt 9:35;
Mk 1:39; Lk 13:22
6:7 ʸ Mk 3:13
ᶻ Dt 17:6; Lk 10:1
ᵃ S Mt 10:1
6:11 ᵇ S Mt 10:14
6:12 ᶜ Lk 9:6
6:13 ᵈ S Jas 5:14
6:14 ᵉ S Mt 3:1
6:15 ᶠ Mal 4:5
ᵍ S Mt 21:11
ʰ Mt 16:14; Mk 8:28
6:17 ⁱ Mt 4:12; 11:2;
Lk 3:19,20
6:18 ʲ Lev 18:16;
20:21
6:20 ᵏ S Mt 11:9
6:21 ˡ Est 1:3; 2:18

6:3 *carpenter.* Matthew reports that Jesus was called "the carpenter's son" (Mt 13:55); only in Mark is Jesus himself referred to as a carpenter. The Greek word can also apply to a mason, smith or builder in general. The question is derogatory, meaning, "Isn't he a common worker with his hands like the rest of us?" *brother of James, Joseph, Judas and Simon.* See note on Lk 8:19. *they took offense at him.* They saw no reason to believe that he was different from them, much less that he was specially anointed by God.

6:5 He could not do any miracles there. It was not that Jesus did not have power to perform miracles at Nazareth but that he chose not to in such a climate of unbelief (v. 6).

6:6 *He was amazed.* See note on Lk 7:9.

6:7–13 See note on Lk 9:1–6.

6:7 *the Twelve.* See notes on Ac 1:11; 1Co 15:5. *two by two.* The purpose of going in pairs may have been to bolster credibility by having the testimony of more than one witness (cf. Dt 17:6), as well as to provide mutual support during their training period.

6:8 *no bread, no bag, no money in your belts.* They were to depend entirely on the hospitality of those to whom they testified (see vv. 10–11; see also notes on Lk 9:3; 10:4).

6:9 *not an extra shirt.* At night an extra shirt was helpful as a covering to protect from the cold night air, and the implication

here is that the disciples were to trust in God to provide lodging each night.

6:10 *stay there.* See note on Lk 9:4.

6:11 *shake the dust off your feet.* See note on Mt 10:14.

6:12–13 *preached . . . drove out many demons.* This mission marks the beginning of the disciples' own ministry in Jesus' name (see 3:14–15), and their message was precisely the same as his (1:15).

6:12 *repent.* See 1:4 and note.

6:13 *anointed many sick people with oil.* In the ancient world olive oil was widely used as a medicine (see Jas 5:14 and note).

6:14 *King Herod.* See note on Mt 14:1. Mark may here have used the title "king" sarcastically (since this Herod was actually a tetrarch; see chart, p. 1608), or perhaps he simply used Herod's popular title.

6:15 *He is Elijah.* See Mal 4:5 and note.

6:16 *John . . . has been raised from the dead!* Herod, disturbed by an uneasy conscience and disposed to superstition, feared that John had come back to haunt him.

6:17 *John arrested . . . and put in prison.* See 1:14 and note. Josephus says that John was imprisoned at Machaerus, a fortress in Perea on the eastern side of the Dead Sea (see map, p. 1721). *Herodias.* See note on Mt 14:3. *Philip.* See note on Mt 14:3.

officials and military commanders and the leading men of Galilee. *m* 22When the daughter of*a* Herodias came in and danced, she pleased Herod and his dinner guests.

The king said to the girl, "Ask me for anything you want, and I'll give it to you." 23And he promised her with an oath, "Whatever you ask I will give you, up to half my kingdom." *n*

24She went out and said to her mother, "What shall I ask for?"

"The head of John the Baptist," she answered.

25At once the girl hurried in to the king with the request: "I want you to give me right now the head of John the Baptist on a platter."

26The king was greatly distressed, but because of his oaths and his dinner guests, he did not want to refuse her. 27So he immediately sent an executioner with orders to bring John's head. The man went, beheaded John in the prison, 28and brought back his head on a platter. He presented it to the girl, and she gave it to her mother. 29On hearing of this, John's disciples came and took his body and laid it in a tomb.

JESUS FEEDS THE FIVE THOUSAND

6:32–44pp — Mt 14:13–21; Lk 9:10–17; Jn 6:5–13
6:32–44Ref — Mk 8:2–9

30The apostles *o* gathered around Jesus and reported to him all they had done and taught. *P* 31Then, because so many people were coming and going that they did not even have a chance to eat, *q* he said to them, "Come with me by yourselves to a quiet place and get some rest."

32So they went away by themselves in a boat *r* to a solitary place. 33But many who saw them leaving recognized them and ran on foot from all the towns and got there ahead of them. 34When Jesus landed and saw a large crowd, he had compassion on them, because they were like sheep without a shepherd. *s* So he began teaching them many things.

35By this time it was late in the day, so his disciples came to him. "This is a remote place," they said, "and it's already very late. 36Send the people away so that they can go to the surrounding countryside and villages and buy themselves something to eat."

37But he answered, "You give them something to eat." *t*

They said to him, "That would take almost a year's wages *b*! Are we to go and spend that much on bread and give it to them to eat?"

38"How many loaves do you have?" he asked. "Go and see."

When they found out, they said, "Five—and two fish." *u*

39Then Jesus directed them to have all the people sit down in groups on the green grass. 40So they sat down in groups of hundreds and fifties. 41Taking the five loaves and the two fish and looking up to heaven, he gave thanks and broke the loaves. *v* Then he gave them to his disciples to set before the people. He also divided the two fish among them all. 42They all ate and were satisfied, 43and the disciples picked up twelve basket-

---

a 22 Some early manuscripts *When his daughter*   *b* 37 Greek *take two hundred denarii*

6:22 *daughter of Herodias.* See note on Mt 14:6.
6:23 *up to half my kingdom.* A proverbial reference to generosity, not to be taken literally (see Est 5:3,6). Generosity suited the occasion and would win the approval of the guests.
6:25 *platter.* See note on Mt 14:8.
6:26 *greatly distressed.* The Greek for this phrase is also used to describe Jesus' agony in Gethsemane (14:34, "overwhelmed with sorrow").
6:30–44 The feeding of the 5,000 in Mark's Gospel begins with an elaborate introduction (vv. 30–38), is looked back to on two different occasions (v. 52; 8:17–19) and has a sequel in the feeding of the 4,000 (8:1–10).
6:30 *apostles.* In Mark's Gospel the word occurs only here and in 3:14 (in some manuscripts). The apostles were Jesus' authorized agents or representatives (see Heb 3:1 and note). In the NT the word is sometimes used quite generally (see Jn 13:16, where the Greek *apostolos* is translated "messenger"). In the technical sense it is used (1) of the Twelve (3:14)—in which sense it is also applied to Paul (Ro 1:1)—and (2) of a larger group, including Barnabas (Ac 14:14), James the Lord's brother (Gal 1:19) and possibly Andronicus and Junia (Ro 16:7). *reported to him all they had done and taught.* Because he had commissioned them as his representatives. They were returning from what may have been a third preaching tour in Galilee (see vv. 12–13; 1:39 and notes).

6:32 *went away by themselves in a boat.* John reports that they went to the other side of the Sea of Galilee (Jn 6:1). Luke, more specifically, says they went to Bethsaida (Lk 9:10), which locates the feeding of the 5,000 on the northeast shore (see note on 7:24).
6:33 *ran on foot ... and got there ahead of them.* Perhaps a strong headwind slowed the boat down so that the people had time to go on foot around the lake and arrive before the boat.
6:37 *almost a year's wages.* See TNIV text note. The usual pay for a day's work was one denarius (see Mt 20:2 and note).
6:38 *loaves.* Barley loaves. Unlike our modern loaves, these were small and flat. One could easily eat several at a single meal (see note on Jn 6:9).
6:39 *green grass.* Grass is green around the Sea of Galilee after the late winter or early spring rains.
6:40 *groups of hundreds and fifties.* Recalls the order of the Mosaic camp in the wilderness (e.g., Ex 18:21).
6:42 *all ate and were satisfied.* Attempts to explain away this miracle (e.g., by suggesting that Jesus and his disciples shared their lunch and the crowd followed their good example) are inadequate. If Jesus was, as he claimed to be, God incarnate, the miracle presents no difficulties. God had promised that when the true Shepherd came, the wilderness would become rich pasture where the sheep would be gathered and

fuls of broken pieces of bread and fish. [44]The number of the men who had eaten was five thousand.

JESUS WALKS ON THE WATER

6:45–51pp — Mt 14:22–32; Jn 6:15–21
6:53–56pp — Mt 14:34–36

[45]Immediately Jesus made his disciples get into the boat [w] and go on ahead of him to Bethsaida, [x] while he dismissed the crowd. [46]After leaving them, he went up on a mountainside to pray. [y]

[47]When evening came, the boat was in the middle of the lake, and he was alone on land. [48]He saw the disciples straining at the oars, because the wind was against them. Shortly before dawn he went out to them, walking on the lake. He was about to pass by them, [49]but when they saw him walking on the lake, they thought he was a ghost. [z] They cried out, [50]because they all saw him and were terrified.

Immediately he spoke to them and said, "Take courage! It is I. Don't be afraid." [a] [51]Then he climbed into the boat [b] with them, and the wind died down. [c] They were completely amazed, [52]for they had not understood about the loaves; their hearts were hardened. [d]

[53]When they had crossed over, they landed at Gennesaret and anchored there. [e] [54]As soon as they got out of the boat, people recognized Jesus. [55]They ran throughout that whole region and carried the sick on mats to wherever they heard he was. [56]And wherever he went—into villages, towns or countryside—they placed the sick in the marketplaces. They begged him to let them touch even the edge of his cloak, [f] and all who touched him were healed.

THAT WHICH DEFILES

7:1–23pp — Mt 15:1–20

7 The Pharisees and some of the teachers of the law who had come from Jerusalem gathered around Jesus [2]and saw some of his disciples eating food with hands that were defiled, [g] that is, unwashed. [3](The Pharisees and all the Jews do not eat unless they give their hands a ceremonial washing, holding to the tradition of the elders. [h] [4]When they come from the marketplace they do not eat unless they wash. And they observe many other traditions, such as the washing of cups, pitchers and kettles. [a]) [i]

[5]So the Pharisees and teachers of the law asked Jesus, "Why don't your disciples live according to the tradition of the elders [j] instead of eating their food with defiled hands?"

---

[a] 4 Some early manuscripts *pitchers, kettles and dining couches*

6:45 *w* ver 32
x S Mt 11:21
6:46 *y* S Lk 3:21
6:49 *z* Lk 24:37
6:50 *a* S Mt 14:27
6:51 *b* ver 32
c Mk 4:39
6:52 *d* Mk 8:17-21
6:53 *e* Jn 6:24,25
6:56 *f* S Mt 9:20
7:2 *g* Ac 10:14,28;
11:8; Ro 14:14
7:3 *h* ver 5,8,9,13;
Lk 11:38
7:4 *i* Mt 23:25;
Lk 11:39
7:5 *j* S ver 3;
Gal 1:14; Col 2:8

---

fed (Eze 34:23–31). Jesus is the Shepherd who provides for all our needs, so that we lack nothing (cf. Ps 23:1).

6:43 *twelve basketfuls of broken pieces of bread and fish.* Bread was regarded by Jews as a gift of God, and it was required that scraps that fell on the ground during a meal be picked up. The fragments were collected in small wicker baskets that were carried as a part of daily attire. Each of the disciples returned with his basket full (see note on Mt 15:37).

6:44 *men.* Lit. "males," as in all four Gospels. Matthew further emphasizes the point by adding "besides women and children" (Mt 14:21; see note there). *five thousand.* A number that could easily be calculated because of the division of the crowd into "groups of hundreds and fifties" (v. 40). The size of the crowd is amazing in light of the fact that the neighboring towns of Capernaum and Bethsaida probably had a population of only 2,000–3,000 each.

6:45 *go on ahead of him.* John indicates that the people were ready to take Jesus by force and make him king (see Jn 6:14–15 and note on 6:15), and Jesus therefore sent his disciples across the lake while he slipped away into the hills to pray (v. 46).

6:46 *pray.* Mark's mention of Jesus' praying is further evidence of a crisis situation. On only three occasions in this Gospel (here; 1:35; 14:32–36) does Jesus withdraw to pray; each time a crisis is involved.

6:48 *Shortly before dawn.* Lit. "About the fourth watch of the night," 3:00–6:00 A.M. (see 13:35; Mt 14:25 and notes).

walking on the lake. A special display of the majestic presence and power of the transcendent Lord, who rules over the sea (see Ps 89:9; Isa 51:10,15; Jer 31:35).

6:49 *a ghost.* Popular Jewish superstition held that the appearance of spirits during the night brought disaster. The disciples' terror was prompted by what they may have thought was a water spirit.

6:51 *amazed.* See 1:22 and note.

6:52 *they had not understood about the loaves.* If they had understood the feeding of the 5,000, they would not have been amazed at Jesus' walking on the water or his calming the waves. *hearts were hardened.* They were showing themselves to be similar to Jesus' opponents, who also exhibited hardness of heart (see 3:5; 8:17–21 and note on 8:16; Ex 4:21 and note).

6:53 *Gennesaret.* See note on Mt 14:34.

6:55 *carried the sick on mats.* See 2:3–4.

6:56 *touch even the edge of his cloak.* See note on 5:28.

7:1 *Pharisees . . . had come from Jerusalem.* Another delegation of fact-finding religious leaders from Jerusalem (see 3:22) sent to investigate the Galilean activities of Jesus (see 2:16; Mt 2:4 and notes).

7:3 *ceremonial washing.* See note on Jn 2:6. *tradition of the elders.* Considered to be binding (see v. 5 and note on Mt 15:2).

7:4 *marketplace.* Where Jews would come into contact with Gentiles, or with Jews who did not observe the ceremonial law, and thus become ceremonially unclean.

7:7 *k* Isa 29:13
7:8 *l* S ver 3
7:9 *m* S ver 3
7:10 *n* Ex 20:12;
Dt 5:16 *o* Ex 21:17;
Lev 20:9
7:11 *p* Mt 23:16,18
7:13 *q* S Heb 4:12
r S ver 3
7:17 *s* Mk 9:28
7:19 *t* Ro 14:1-12;
Col 2:16; 1Ti 4:3-5
u S Ac 10:15
7:22 *v* Mt 20:15
7:24 *w* S Mt 11:21
7:25 *x* S Mt 4:24

⁶He replied, "Isaiah was right when he prophesied about you hypocrites; as it is written:

" 'These people honor me with their lips,
    but their hearts are far from me.
⁷They worship me in vain;
    their teachings are merely human rules.'ᵃ ᵏ

⁸You have let go of the commands of God and are holding on to human traditions." ˡ

⁹And he continued, "You have a fine way of setting aside the commands of God in order to observeᵇ your own traditions! ᵐ ¹⁰For Moses said, 'Honor your father and mother,'ᶜ ⁿ and, 'Anyone who curses their father or mother is to be put to death.'ᵈ ᵒ ¹¹But you sayᵖ that if anyone declares that what might have been used to help their father or mother is Corban (that is, devoted to God)— ¹²then you no longer let them do anything for their father or mother. ¹³Thus you nullify the word of God�q by your tradition ʳ that you have handed down. And you do many things like that."

¹⁴Again Jesus called the crowd to him and said, "Listen to me, everyone, and understand this. ¹⁵[¹⁶]Nothing outside you can defile you by going into you. Rather, it is what comes out of you that defiles you."

¹⁷After he had left the crowd and entered the house, his disciples asked himˢ about this parable. ¹⁸"Are you so dull?" he asked. "Don't you see that nothing that enters you from the outside can defile you? ¹⁹For it doesn't go into your heart but into your stomach, and then out of your body." (In saying this, Jesus declared all foodsᵗ clean.) ᵘ

²⁰He went on: "What comes out of you is what defiles you. ²¹For from within, out of your hearts, come evil thoughts, sexual immorality, theft, murder, ²²adultery, greed, ᵛ malice, deceit, lewdness, envy, slander, arrogance and folly. ²³All these evils come from inside and defile you."

JESUS HONORS A SYROPHOENICIAN WOMAN'S FAITH
7:24–30pp — Mt 15:21–28

²⁴Jesus left that place and went to the vicinity of Tyre.ᵉ ʷ He entered a house and did not want anyone to know it; yet he could not keep his presence secret. ²⁵In fact, as soon as she heard about him, a woman whose little daughter was possessed by an evilᶠ spiritˣ came and fell at his feet. ²⁶The woman was a Greek, born in Syrian Phoenicia. She begged Jesus to drive the demon out of her daughter.

ᵃ 6,7 Isaiah 29:13   ᵇ 9 Some manuscripts *set up*   ᶜ 10 Exodus 20:12; Deut. 5:16   ᵈ 10 Exodus 21:17; Lev. 20:9   ᵉ 24 Many early manuscripts *Tyre and Sidon*   ᶠ 25 Greek *unclean*

7:6 *Isaiah … prophesied.* Isaiah roundly denounced the religious leaders of his day (Isa 29:13), and Jesus quotes him to describe the tradition of the elders as "merely human rules" (v. 7). *hypocrites.* See Mt 6:2 and note.

7:8 *commands of God … human traditions.* Jesus clearly contrasts the two. God's commands are found in Scripture and are binding; the "tradition of the elders" (v. 3) is not Biblical and therefore not authoritative or binding.

7:10 The fifth commandment is cited in both its positive and negative forms.

7:11 *Corban.* A Hebrew/Aramaic word meaning "offering" (see note on Lev 1:2). By using this word in a religious vow an irresponsible Jewish son could formally dedicate to God (i.e., to the temple) his earnings that otherwise would have gone for the support of his parents. The money, however, did not necessarily have to go for religious purposes. The Corban formula was simply a means of circumventing the clear responsibility of children toward their parents as prescribed in the law. The teachers of the law held that the Corban oath was binding, even when uttered rashly. The practice was one of many traditions that adhered to the letter of the law while ignoring its spirit. *(that is, devoted to God).* By explaining this word, Mark reveals that he is addressing Gentile readers, probably Romans primarily (see Introduction: Recipients).

7:13 *you nullify the word of God by your tradition.* The teachers of the law appealed to Nu 30:1–2 in support of the Corban vow, but Jesus categorically rejects the practice of using one Biblical teaching to nullify another. The scribal interpretation of Nu 30:1–2 satisfied the letter of the passage but

missed the meaning of the law as a whole. *nullify.* Cf. 2Co 4:2 and note.

7:15[16] Verse 16 ("If anyone has ears to hear, let them hear") appears in some manuscripts, but it is apparently a scribal addition derived from 4:23.

7:19 *(In saying this, Jesus declared all foods clean.)* Mark adds this parenthetical comment to help his readers see the significance of Jesus' pronouncement for them (see Ac 10:9–16 and note on 10:14).

7:20 Jesus replaced the normal Jewish understandings of defilement with the truth that defilement comes from an impure heart, not the violation of external rules. Fellowship with God is not interrupted by unclean hands or food but by sin (see vv. 21–23 and note on Pr 4:23).

7:24 *Tyre.* A Gentile city located in Phoenicia (modern Lebanon), which bordered Galilee to the northwest (see map, p. 1686). A journey of about 30 miles from Capernaum would have brought Jesus "to the vicinity of Tyre." *did not want anyone to know.* Ever since the feeding of the 5,000 (6:30–44) Jesus and his disciples had been, for the most part, skirting the region of Galilee. His purpose was to avoid the opposition in Galilee and to secure opportunity to teach his disciples privately (9:30–31). The regions to which he withdrew were: (1) the northeast shore of the Sea of Galilee (6:30–53), (2) Phoenicia (7:24–30), (3) the Decapolis (7:31—8:10) and (4) Caesarea Philippi (8:27—9:32).

7:26 *Greek.* Here probably equivalent to "Gentile." *Syrian Phoenicia.* At that time Phoenicia belonged administratively to Syria. Mark possibly used the term to distinguish this woman from the Libyan Phoenicians of North Africa.

²⁷"First let the children eat all they want," he told her, "for it is not right to take the children's bread and toss it to the dogs."

²⁸"Lord," she replied, "even the dogs under the table eat the children's crumbs."

²⁹Then he told her, "For such a reply, you may go; the demon has left your daughter."

³⁰She went home and found her child lying on the bed, and the demon gone.

JESUS HEALS A DEAF AND MUTE MAN

7:31–37pp — Mt 15:29–31

³¹Then Jesus left the vicinity of Tyre ʸ and went through Sidon, down to the Sea of Galilee ᶻ and into the region of the Decapolis. ᵃ ᵃ ³²There some people brought to him a man who was deaf and could hardly talk, ᵇ and they begged Jesus to place his hand on ᶜ him.

³³After he took him aside, away from the crowd, Jesus put his fingers into the man's ears. Then he spit ᵈ and touched the man's tongue. ³⁴He looked up to heaven ᵉ and with a deep sigh ᶠ said to him, *"Ephphatha!"* (which means "Be opened!"). ³⁵At this, the man's ears were opened, his tongue was loosened and he began to speak plainly. ᵍ

³⁶Jesus commanded them not to tell anyone. ʰ But the more he did so, the more they kept talking about it. ³⁷People were overwhelmed with amazement. "He has done everything well," they said. "He even makes the deaf hear and the mute speak."

JESUS FEEDS THE FOUR THOUSAND

8:1–9pp — Mt 15:32–39
8:1–9Ref — Mk 6:32–44
8:11–21pp — Mt 16:1–12

8 During those days another large crowd gathered. Since they had nothing to eat, Jesus called his disciples to him and said, ²"I have compassion for these people; ⁱ they have already been with me three days and have nothing to eat. ³If I send them home hungry, they will collapse on the way, because some of them have come a long distance."

⁴His disciples answered, "But where in this remote place can anyone get enough bread to feed them?"

⁵"How many loaves do you have?" Jesus asked.

"Seven," they replied.

⁶He told the crowd to sit down on the ground. When he had taken the seven loaves and given thanks, he broke them and gave them to his disciples to set before the people, and they did so. ⁷They had a few small fish as well; he gave thanks for them also and told the disciples to distribute them. ʲ ⁸The people ate and were satisfied. Afterward the disciples picked up seven basketfuls of broken pieces that were left over. ᵏ ⁹About four thousand were present. And having sent them away, ¹⁰he got into the boat with his disciples and went to the region of Dalmanutha.

ᵃ *31* That is, the Ten Cities

7:31 ʸ ver 24;
S Mt 11:21 ᶻ S Mt 4:18
ᵃ Mt 4:25; Mk 5:20
7:32 ᵇ Mt 9:32;
Lk 11:14 ᶜ S Mk 5:23
7:33 ᵈ Mk 8:23
7:34 ᵉ Mk 6:41;
Jn 11:41 ᶠ Mk 8:12
7:35 ᵍ Isa 35:5,6
7:36 ʰ S Mt 8:4
8:2 ⁱ S Mk 9:36
8:7 ʲ Mt 14:19
8:8 ᵏ ver 20

7:27 *take the children's bread and toss it to the dogs.* See note on Mt 15:26.

7:28 *Lord.* The only time in Mark's Gospel that Jesus is addressed as "Lord"—and this by a Syrian Phoenician woman.

7:31 *left the vicinity of Tyre and went through Sidon, down to the Sea of Galilee.* Apparently Jesus went north from Tyre to Sidon (about 25 miles) and then southeast through the territory of Herod Philip to the east side of the Sea of Galilee (see map, p. 1686). The route was circuitous—possibly to avoid entering Galilee, where Herod Antipas was in power (see 6:14–29) and where many people wanted to take Jesus by force and make him king (see Jn 6:14–15 and note on 6:15). Herod had intimated a hostile interest in Jesus (6:14–16). *Decapolis.* See notes on v. 24; Mt 4:25; see also map, p. 1679.

7:32 *place his hand on him.* In order to heal him (see 1:41; 5:23; Ac 6:6 and note).

7:33 *spit.* See 8:23; Jn 9:6 and note.

7:34 *Ephphatha!* An Aramaic word that Mark translates for his Gentile readers (see Introduction: Recipients).

7:35 *man's ears were opened . . . he began to speak plainly.* Jesus was doing what God had promised to do when he came to redeem his people (see Isa 35:5–6 and notes).

7:36 *not to tell anyone.* See 5:19,43; Mt 8:4; 16:20 and notes.

7:37 *overwhelmed with amazement.* See 1:22 and note.

8:1–10 Although there are striking similarities between this account and 6:34–44, they are two distinct incidents, as indicated by the fact that Jesus himself refers to two feedings (see vv. 18–20).

8:1 *another large crowd gathered.* Since this incident took place in the region of the Decapolis (see 7:31), the crowd may have been made up of both Jews and Gentiles.

8:2 *compassion for these people.* As Jesus had compassion because the people were "like sheep without a shepherd" (6:34), he now has compassion because they have been so long without food.

8:4 *where . . . can anyone get enough bread to feed them?* The disciples' question reflects their inadequacy and acknowledges that Jesus alone could feed the people. They had not forgotten his feeding of the 5,000 (6:34–44) and were probably simply giving back to him the task of procuring bread. Alternatively, their question may reveal their spiritual dullness—they were slow learners (see note on v. 16).

8:8 *seven basketfuls.* See note on Mt 15:37.

8:9 *four thousand.* See note on 6:44.

8:10 *Dalmanutha.* South of the Plain of Gennesaret (see note on Mt 14:34) a cave has been found bearing the

8:11 *ˡ* S Mt 12:38
8:12 *ᵐ* Mk 7:34
8:15 *ⁿ* 1Co 5:6-8
ᵒ Lk 12:1 *ᵖ* S Mt 14:1;
Mk 12:13
8:17 *�q* Isa 6:9,10;
Mk 6:52
8:19 *ʳ* Mt 14:20;
Mk 6:41-44; Lk 9:17;
Jn 6:13
8:20 *ˢ* ver 6-9;
Mt 15:37
8:21 *ᵗ* Mk 6:52

¹¹The Pharisees came and began to question Jesus. To test him, they asked him for a sign from heaven. *ˡ* ¹²He sighed deeply *ᵐ* and said, "Why does this generation ask for a sign? Truly I tell you, no sign will be given to it." ¹³Then he left them, got back into the boat and crossed to the other side.

THE YEAST OF THE PHARISEES AND HEROD

¹⁴The disciples had forgotten to bring bread, except for one loaf they had with them in the boat. ¹⁵"Be careful," Jesus warned them. "Watch out for the yeast *ⁿ* of the Pharisees *ᵒ* and that of Herod." *ᵖ*

¹⁶They discussed this with one another and said, "It is because we have no bread."

¹⁷Aware of their discussion, Jesus asked them: "Why are you talking about having no bread? Do you still not see or understand? Are your hearts hardened? *q* ¹⁸Do you have eyes but fail to see, and ears but fail to hear? And don't you remember? ¹⁹When I broke the five loaves for the five thousand, how many basketfuls of pieces did you pick up?"

"Twelve," *ʳ* they replied.

²⁰"And when I broke the seven loaves for the four thousand, how many basketfuls of pieces did you pick up?"

They answered, "Seven." *ˢ*

²¹He said to them, "Do you still not understand?" *ᵗ*

---

name "Talmanutha," perhaps the spot where Jesus landed. Matthew says Jesus "went to the vicinity of Magadan" (Mt 15:39; see note there). Dalmanutha and Magadan (or Magdala), located on the western shore of the Sea of Galilee, may be names for the same place or for two places located close to each other.

8:11 *Pharisees.* See note on Mt 3:7. *sign from heaven.* The Pharisees wanted more compelling proof of Jesus' divine authority than his miracles, but he refused to perform such a sign because the request came from unbelief.

8:12 *Truly I tell you.* See note on 3:28.

8:13 *other side.* The eastern shore of the Sea of Galilee.

8:15 *yeast.* Here, as generally in the NT (Mt 16:6,11; Lk 12:1; see 1Co 5:6-8; Gal 5:9 and notes, but Mt 13:33 seems to be an exception—see note there), yeast is a symbol of evil or corruption. The metaphor includes the idea of a tiny amount of yeast being able to ferment a large amount of dough. In this

context it refers to the evil disposition of both the Pharisees and Herod Antipas (see Lk 23:8 and note). The Pharisees asked Jesus to produce a sign, i.e., a proof of his divine authority (see note on v. 11).

8:16 Another possible reading of the Greek text could be translated: "They discussed with one another why they had no bread." According to this rendering the disciples were so concerned to find out who was to blame for not bringing more bread that they completely ignored Jesus' warning about the yeast of the Pharisees and of Herod. Such an understanding heightens Mark's depiction of the disciples as slow learners (see 4:13; 5:51-52; 7:18; 8:4,17-21 and note on 8:4; 9:32; 10:13-14, 35-40).

8:17 *hearts hardened.* See v. 4; 6:52 and notes.

8:18-20 These verses indicate two feeding narratives (see note on vv. 1-10).

THE TERRITORIES OF TYRE AND SIDON

In a unique excursion into pagan and semipagan areas, Jesus visited the districts of Tyre and Sidon and the confederation of free cities called the Decapolis (see map, p. 1679). He was called to minister to "the lost sheep of Israel" (Mt 15:24), but the phenomenal public attention in Galilee was intense. Even here his fame had spread, and he could not keep his presence secret. The commercially magnificent cities of Tyre and Sidon had been a source of cultural seductiveness and religious heterodoxy since the time of Jezebel. The cities had been heavily influenced by Hellenism; the sophistication of Greek culture was apparent in their coinage and architecture. Each was also a proud, historic center of Canaanite paganism, with tombs of ancient kings and temples to Melqart/Heracles, Astarte and various other deities.

JESUS HEALS A BLIND MAN AT BETHSAIDA

²²They came to Bethsaida, *u* and some people brought a blind man *v* and begged Jesus to touch him. ²³He took the blind man by the hand and led him outside the village. When he had spit *w* on the man's eyes and put his hands on *x* him, Jesus asked, "Do you see anything?"

²⁴He looked up and said, "I see people; they look like trees walking around."

²⁵Once more Jesus put his hands on the man's eyes. Then his eyes were opened, his sight was restored, and he saw everything clearly. ²⁶Jesus sent him home, saying, "Don't even go into *a* the village."

PETER DECLARES THAT JESUS IS THE MESSIAH

8:27–29pp — Mt 16:13–16; Lk 9:18–20

²⁷Jesus and his disciples went on to the villages around Caesarea Philippi. On the way he asked them, "Who do people say I am?"

²⁸They replied, "Some say John the Baptist; *y* others say Elijah; *z* and still others, one of the prophets."

²⁹"But what about you?" he asked. "Who do you say I am?"

Peter answered, "You are the Messiah." *a*

³⁰Jesus warned them not to tell anyone about him. *b*

JESUS PREDICTS HIS DEATH

8:31 — 9:1pp — Mt 16:21–28; Lk 9:22–27

³¹He then began to teach them that the Son of Man *c* must suffer many things *d* and be rejected by the elders, the chief priests and the teachers of the law, *e* and that he must be killed *f* and after three days *g* rise again. *h* ³²He spoke plainly *i* about this, and Peter took him aside and began to rebuke him.

³³But when Jesus turned and looked at his disciples, he rebuked Peter. "Get behind me, Satan!" *j* he said. "You do not have in mind the concerns of God, but merely human concerns."

THE WAY OF THE CROSS

³⁴Then he called the crowd to him along with his disciples and said: "Whoever wants to be my disciple must deny themselves and take up their cross and follow me. *k* ³⁵For

---

a 26 Some manuscripts *go and tell anyone in*

8:22 *u* S Mt 11:21
v Mk 10:46; Jn 9:1
8:23 *w* Mk 7:33
x S Mk 5:23
8:28 *y* S Mt 3:1
z Mal 4:5
8:29 *a* Jn 6:69; 11:27
8:30 *b* S Mk 8:4;
16:20; 17:9; Mk 9:9;
Lk 9:21
8:31 *c* S Mt 8:20
d S Mt 16:21
e Mt 27:1,2 *f* Ac 2:23;
3:13 *g* S Mt 16:21
h S Mt 16:21
8:32 *i* Jn 18:20
8:33 *j* S Mt 4:10
8:34 *k* Mt 10:38;
Lk 14:27

8:22 *Bethsaida.* See note on Mt 11:21.

8:23 *spit.* See 7:33 and note. *put his hands on him.* See 1:41; Ac 6:6 and note.

8:24 *like trees walking around.* The man had no doubt bumped into trees in his blindness; now he dimly sees something like tree trunks moving about.

8:25 *Once more Jesus put his hands on the man's eyes.* This second laying on of hands is unique in Jesus' healing ministry. *saw everything clearly.* Giving sight to the blind was another indication that Jesus was doing what God had promised to do when he came to bring salvation (see 7:35 and note).

8:26 *Don't even go into the village.* So as not to broadcast what Jesus had done for him and precipitate a crisis before Jesus had completed his ministry (see 5:19,43; Mt 8:4; 16:20 and notes).

8:27 *Caesarea Philippi.* See notes on 7:24; Mt 16:13.

8:29 *Messiah.* See note on Mt 16:16. Because popular Jewish ideas associated with the term "Messiah" were largely political and national, Jesus seldom used it. Of its seven occurrences in Mark, only three appear in the sayings of Jesus (9:41; 12:35; 13:21), and in none of these does he use the title of himself (with the possible exception of 9:41). Mark identifies Jesus as the Messiah in 1:1 (see TNIV text note there).

8:30 *not to tell anyone about him.* See v. 26 and note.

8:31—10:52 A new section begins in 8:31 and centers on three predictions of Jesus' death (8:31; 9:31; 10:33–34). It indicates a geographical shift from Galilee, where most of Jesus' public ministry reported by Mark took place, to Jerusalem and the closing days of Jesus' life on earth. In this section Jesus defines the true meaning of "Messiah" as the title applies to him (see note on v. 29).

8:31 *Son of Man.* Jesus' most common title for himself, used 81 times in the Gospels and never used by anyone but Jesus there. Elsewhere it is used by Stephen (Ac 7:56; see note there) and in John's vision (Rev 1:13). In Da 7:13–14 the Son of Man is pictured as a heavenly figure who in the end times is entrusted by God with authority, glory and sovereign power (see note on Da 7:13). That Jesus considered "Son of Man" to be a Messianic title is evident by his use of it here in juxtaposition to Peter's use of "Messiah" (v. 29; see note there). *must suffer.* As predicted in the Suffering Servant passage in Isa 52:13—53:12 (see note there; see also Mk 9:9,12,31; 10:33–34; 14:21,41 and relevant notes). *elders.* The lay members of the Sanhedrin, the high court of the Jews. *chief priests.* See note on Mt 2:4. These included the ruling high priest, Caiaphas; the former high priest, Annas; and the high priestly families. *teachers of the law.* See note on Mt 2:4. Representatives of the three groups mentioned here constituted the Sanhedrin.

8:32 *Peter…began to rebuke him.* Suffering and rejection had no place in Peter's conception of the Messiah, and he rebuked Jesus for teaching what to him seemed not only inconceivable but also terribly wrong.

8:33 *Satan.* Peter's attempt to dissuade Jesus from going to the cross contained the same temptation Satan gave at the outset of Jesus' ministry (see Mt 4:8–10), so Jesus severely rebuked him.

8:34 *deny themselves.* Cease to make self the object of one's life and actions. *take up their cross.* The picture is of someone, already condemned, required to carry the beam of their own cross to the place of execution (see Jn 19:17 and note). Cross-bearing includes a willingness to suffer and die for

8:35 *l* S Jn 12:25
8:38 *m* S Mt 8:20
n Mt 10:33; Lk 12:9
o S 1Th 2:19
9:1 *p* Mk 13:30;
Lk 22:18 *q* Mt 24:30;
25:31
9:2 *r* S Mt 4:21
9:3 *s* S Mt 28:3
9:5 *t* S Mt 23:7
9:7 *u* Ex 24:16
v S Mt 3:17
9:9 *w* S Mk 8:30
x S Mt 8:20
9:12 *y* S Mt 8:20
z S Mt 16:21 *a* Lk 23:11
9:13 *b* S Mt 11:14

whoever wants to save their life[a] will lose it, but whoever loses their life for me and for the gospel will save it. [l] 36What good is it for you to gain the whole world, yet forfeit your soul? 37Or what can you give in exchange for your soul? 38If any of you are ashamed of me and my words in this adulterous and sinful generation, the Son of Man[m] will be ashamed of you[n] when he comes[o] in his Father's glory with the holy angels."

9

And he said to them, "Truly I tell you, some who are standing here will not taste death before they see that the kingdom of God has come[p] with power."[q]

THE TRANSFIGURATION

9:2–8pp — Lk 9:28–36
9:2–13pp — Mt 17:1–13

2After six days Jesus took Peter, James and John[r] with him and led them up a high mountain, where they were all alone. There he was transfigured before them. 3His clothes became dazzling white,[s] whiter than anyone in the world could bleach them. 4And there appeared before them Elijah and Moses, who were talking with Jesus.

5Peter said to Jesus, "Rabbi,[t] it is good for us to be here. Let us put up three shelters—one for you, one for Moses and one for Elijah." 6(He did not know what to say, they were so frightened.)

7Then a cloud appeared and covered them, and a voice came from the cloud:[u] "This is my Son, whom I love. Listen to him!"[v]

8Suddenly, when they looked around, they no longer saw anyone with them except Jesus.

9As they were coming down the mountain, Jesus gave them orders not to tell anyone[w] what they had seen until the Son of Man[x] had risen from the dead. 10They kept the matter to themselves, discussing what "rising from the dead" meant.

11And they asked him, "Why do the teachers of the law say that Elijah must come first?" 12Jesus replied, "To be sure, Elijah does come first, and restores all things. Why then is it written that the Son of Man[y] must suffer much[z] and be rejected?[a] 13But I tell you, Elijah has come,[b] and they have done to him everything they wished, just as it is written about him."

---

a 35 The Greek word means either *life* or *soul*; also in verses 36 and 37.

---

the Lord's sake. *follow me.* Implying that his own death would be by crucifixion.

8:35 *save their life.* Physical life may be saved by denying Jesus, but eternal life will be lost. *loses their life.* Conversely, discipleship may result in the loss of physical life, but that loss is insignificant when compared with gaining eternal life (see note on Lk 9:24).

8:36 *whole world.* All the things that could possibly be achieved or acquired in this life. *your soul.* Eternal life (also in v. 37).

8:38 *ashamed of me and my words.* Contrast Ro 1:16. Those who are more concerned about fitting into and pleasing their own "adulterous and sinful generation" than about following and pleasing Christ will have no part in God's kingdom. *Son of Man.* See note on v. 31. *when he comes in his Father's glory.* The situation in which Jesus is rejected, humiliated and put to death will be reversed when he returns in glory as the Judge of all people (see 1Th 2:12 and note).

9:1 *Truly I tell you.* See note on 3:28. *not taste death before they see that the kingdom of God has come with power.* See note on Mt 16:28. *kingdom of God.* See note on Mt 3:2.

9:2 *After six days.* See note on Mt 17:1. *Peter, James and John.* See note on 5:37. *high mountain.* See note on Lk 9:28. *transfigured.* See note on Mt 17:2.

9:4 *Elijah and Moses.* See notes on Mt 17:3; Lk 9:30.

9:5 *Rabbi.* Hebrew for "(my) teacher." *three shelters.* Peter may have desired to erect new tents of meeting where God could again communicate with his people (see Ex 29:42). Or he may have been thinking of the booths used at the Festival of Tabernacles (see Lev 23:42 and note). In any case, he seemed eager to find fulfillment of the promised glory at that moment, prior to the sufferings that Jesus had announced as necessary.

9:7 *voice came from the cloud.* A cloud is frequently a symbol of God's presence to protect and guide (see note on Mt 17:5). *This is my Son, whom I love.* An allusion to Ps 2:7; Isa 42:1. *Listen to him!* The full sense includes obeying him. When God is involved, the only true hearing is obedient hearing (see Jas 1:22–25 and note on 1:25).

9:9 *not to tell anyone…until.* See 5:19,43; Mt 8:4; 16:20 and notes. After Jesus' resurrection the disciples were to tell everyone what they had experienced, for Jesus' finished work would have demonstrated his true and full character as the Messiah. *Son of Man.* See note on 8:31.

9:10 *what "rising from the dead" meant.* As Jews they were familiar with the doctrine of the resurrection; it was the resurrection of the Son of Man that baffled them, because their theology had no place for a suffering and dying Messiah.

9:11 *Elijah must come first.* See note on Mt 17:10.

9:12 *Elijah does come first, and restores all things.* A reference to the coming of Elijah, or one like him, in preparation for the coming of the Messiah (see note on Mt 17:10). *Son of Man.* See note on 8:31. *must suffer much and be rejected.* Just as "Elijah" (John the Baptist; see note on v. 13) has been rejected (see note on Mt 17:12).

9:13 *Elijah has come.* A reference to John the Baptist (see Mt 17:13). *they.* Herod and Herodias (see 6:17–29; Mt 14:3 and note). As Elijah was opposed by Ahab and Jezebel, so also John was opposed by a weak ruler and his wicked consort. *as it is written about him.* What Scripture says about Elijah in his relationship to Ahab and Jezebel (see 1Ki 19:1–10 and note on 19:3). There is no prediction of suffering associated with Elijah's ministry in the end times. However, what happened to Elijah under the threats of Jezebel foreshadowed what would happen to John the Baptist. The order of events suggested in vv. 11–13

JESUS HEALS A BOY POSSESSED BY AN EVIL SPIRIT
9:14–28,30–32pp — Mt 17:14–19,22,23; Lk 9:37–45

¹⁴When they came to the other disciples, they saw a large crowd around them and the teachers of the law arguing with them. ¹⁵As soon as all the people saw Jesus, they were overwhelmed with wonder and ran to greet him.

¹⁶"What are you arguing with them about?" he asked.

¹⁷A man in the crowd answered, "Teacher, I brought you my son, who is possessed by a spirit that has robbed him of speech. ¹⁸Whenever it seizes him, it throws him to the ground. He foams at the mouth, gnashes his teeth and becomes rigid. I asked your disciples to drive out the spirit, but they could not."

¹⁹"You unbelieving generation," Jesus replied, "how long shall I stay with you? How long shall I put up with you? Bring the boy to me."

²⁰So they brought him. When the spirit saw Jesus, it immediately threw the boy into a convulsion. He fell to the ground and rolled around, foaming at the mouth. ^c

²¹Jesus asked the boy's father, "How long has he been like this?"

"From childhood," he answered. ²²"It has often thrown him into fire or water to kill him. But if you can do anything, take pity on us and help us."

²³"'If you can'?" said Jesus. "Everything is possible for one who believes." ^d

²⁴Immediately the boy's father exclaimed, "I do believe; help me overcome my unbelief!"

²⁵When Jesus saw that a crowd was running to the scene, ^e he rebuked the evil ^a spirit. "You deaf and mute spirit," he said, "I command you, come out of him and never enter him again."

²⁶The spirit shrieked, convulsed him violently and came out. The boy looked so much like a corpse that many said, "He's dead." ²⁷But Jesus took him by the hand and lifted him to his feet, and he stood up.

²⁸After Jesus had gone indoors, his disciples asked him privately, ^f "Why couldn't we drive it out?"

²⁹He replied, "This kind can come out only by prayer. ^b"

JESUS PREDICTS HIS DEATH A SECOND TIME
9:33–37pp — Mt 18:1–5; Lk 9:46–48

³⁰They left that place and passed through Galilee. Jesus did not want anyone to know where they were, ³¹because he was teaching his disciples. He said to them, "The Son of Man ^g is going to be delivered over to human hands. He will be killed, ^h and after three days ⁱ he will rise." ^j ³²But they did not understand what he meant ^k and were afraid to ask him about it.

³³They came to Capernaum. ^l When he was in the house, ^m he asked them, "What were you arguing about on the road?" ³⁴But they kept quiet because on the way they had argued about who was the greatest. ⁿ

---

^a 25 Greek *unclean*   ^b 29 Some manuscripts *prayer and fasting*

9:20 ^c Mk 1:26
9:23 ^d S Mt 21:21;
Mk 11:23; Jn 11:40
9:25 ^e ver 15
9:28 ^f Mk 7:17
9:31 ^g S Mt 8:20
^h ver 12; Ac 2:23; 3:13
ⁱ S Mt 16:21
^j S Mt 16:21
9:32 ^k Lk 2:50; 9:45;
18:34; Jn 12:16
9:33 ^l S Mt 4:13
^m Mk 1:29
9:34 ⁿ Lk 22:24

---

is as follows: (1) Elijah ministered and suffered in the days of wicked Jezebel; (2) Elijah was a type of John the Baptist, who in turn suffered at the hands of Herodias; (3) the Son of Man suffered and was rejected a short time after John was beheaded.
9:14 *other disciples.* The nine besides Peter, James and John (see v. 2). *teachers of the law.* See note on Mt 2:4. If the transfiguration took place on Mount Hermon (see v. 2 and note), the presence of the teachers of the law so far north in the Holy Land would indicate their concern in monitoring the activities of Jesus.
9:17–18 See Mt 17:15,18 and notes.
9:18 Demonic possession was responsible for the boy's condition (see vv. 20,25–26).
9:19 *unbelieving generation.* Probably the referent should be restricted to the disciples. This cry of Jesus reveals his great disappointment with them (see note on 8:16).
9:22 *to kill him.* See note on 5:5.

▲ **9:23** *If you can? . . . Everything is possible for one who believes.* The question was not whether Jesus had the power to heal the boy but whether the father had faith to believe it. A person who truly believes will set no limits on what God can do.

▲ **9:24** *I do believe; help me overcome my unbelief!* Since human faith is never perfect, belief and unbelief are often mixed.

9:25 *When Jesus saw that a crowd was running to the scene, he rebuked the evil spirit.* As much as possible, Jesus wanted to avoid further publicity.

▲ **9:29** *This kind.* Seems to suggest that there are different kinds of demons. *only by prayer.* The disciples apparently had taken for granted the power given to them or had come to believe that it was inherent in them. Lack of prayer indicated they had forgotten that their power over the demonic spirits came from Jesus (see 3:15; 6:7,13; see also note on 6:12–13).
9:30 *passed through Galilee.* Jesus' public ministry in and around Galilee was now completed (see note on 7:24), and he was on his way to Jerusalem to suffer and die (see 10:32–34). As he had been doing for several months, Jesus continued to focus his teaching ministry on the Twelve (v. 31).
9:31 The second prediction of Jesus' death (see note on 8:31—10:52). *Son of Man.* See note on 8:31.
9:32 *they did not understand.* See v. 10; 8:32–33 and notes.
9:33–37 Parallel to 10:35–45 (see note there).
9:33 *Capernaum.* See Mt 4:13; Lk 10:15 and notes. *house.* Probably the one belonging to Peter and Andrew (see 1:29).

▲ **9:34** *they kept quiet.* No doubt due to embarrassment. *who was the greatest.* Questions of rank and status are normal and played an important role in the life of Jewish

9:35 *o* Mt 18:4;
Mk 10:43; Lk 22:26
9:36 *p* Mk 10:16
9:37 *q* S Mt 10:40
9:38 *r* Nu 11:27-29
9:40 *s* Mt 12:30;
Lk 11:23
9:41 *t* S Mt 10:42
9:42 *u* S Mt 5:29
v Mt 18:6; Lk 17:2
9:43[44] *w* S Mt 5:29
x Mt 5:30; 18:8
y S Mt 25:41
9:45[46] *z* S Mt 5:29
a Mt 18:8
9:47 *b* S Mt 5:29
c Mt 5:29; 18:9
9:48 *d* Isa 66:24;
S Mt 25:41
9:49 *e* Lev 2:13
9:50 *f* Mt 5:13;
Lk 14:34,35 *g* Col 4:6
h Ro 12:18; 2Co 13:11;
1Th 5:13
10:1 *i* Mk 1:5;
Jn 10:40; 11:7
j S Mt 4:23; Mk 2:13;
4:2; 6:6,34

³⁵Sitting down, Jesus called the Twelve and said, "Anyone who wants to be first must be the very last, and the servant of all." *o*

³⁶He took a little child whom he placed among them. Taking the child in his arms, *p* he said to them, ³⁷"Whoever welcomes one of these little children in my name welcomes me; and whoever welcomes me does not welcome me but the one who sent me." *q*

WHOEVER IS NOT AGAINST US IS FOR US

9:38–40pp — Lk 9:49,50

³⁸"Teacher," said John, "we saw someone driving out demons in your name and we told him to stop, because he was not one of us." *r*

³⁹"Do not stop him," Jesus said. "No one who does a miracle in my name can in the next moment say anything bad about me, ⁴⁰for whoever is not against us is for us. *s* ⁴¹Truly I tell you, anyone who gives you a cup of water in my name because you belong to the Messiah will certainly be rewarded. *t*

CAUSING TO STUMBLE

⁴²"If anyone causes one of these little ones—those who believe in me—to stumble, *u* it would be better for them if a large millstone were hung around their neck and they were thrown into the sea. *v* ⁴³[44]If your hand causes you to stumble, *w* cut it off. It is better for you to enter life maimed than with two hands to go into hell, *x* where the fire never goes out. *y* ⁴⁵[46]And if your foot causes you to stumble, *z* cut it off. It is better for you to enter life crippled than to have two feet and be thrown into hell. *a* ⁴⁷And if your eye causes you to stumble, *b* pluck it out. It is better for you to enter the kingdom of God with one eye than to have two eyes and be thrown into hell, *c* ⁴⁸where

" 'their worm does not die,
    and the fire is not quenched.'ᵃ *d*

⁴⁹Everyone will be salted *e* with fire.

⁵⁰"Salt is good, but if it loses its saltiness, how can you make it salty again? *f* Have salt in yourselves, *g* and be at peace with each other." *h*

DIVORCE

10:1–12pp — Mt 19:1–9

10 Jesus then left that place and went into the region of Judea and across the Jordan. *i* Again crowds of people came to him, and as was his custom, he taught them. *j*

ᵃ 48 Isaiah 66:24

---

groups at this time, but they had no place in Jesus' value system (see v. 35; 10:42–44 and note on 10:43).

9:35 See note on Lk 9:48. *Sitting down.* See 4:1 and note.

9:38 *not one of us.* The man apparently was a believer, but he was not a member of the exclusive company of the Twelve. Nevertheless he acted in Jesus' name and had done what the disciples, on at least one occasion, had not been able to do (see vv. 14,28).

A **9:39** *Do not stop him.* Jesus' view of discipleship was far more inclusive than the narrow view held by the Twelve.

9:40 At first glance, this saying appears to contradict the one in Mt 12:30. There, however, reference is to those who vehemently opposed Jesus, whereas here it is to one who was in sympathy with Jesus and his ministry.

A **9:41** *Truly I tell you.* See note on 3:28. *gives you a cup of water.* God remembers even small acts of kindness extended to believers because they are believers (see note on Lk 9:50). *Messiah.* See 8:29 and note. *be rewarded.* Have God's approval.

9:42 *little ones.* See Mt 18:6,10,14 and note; Lk 17:2. To cause believers to sin will bring serious judgment. *millstone.* A heavy stone slab used in grinding grain.

A **9:43[44]** *cut it off.* Hyperbole, a figure of speech that exaggerates to make its point, is used here to emphasize the need for drastic action. Often sin can be conquered only by radical "spiritual surgery." *life.* Eternal life in the presence of God.

hell. See Mt 5:22 and note. Verses 44,46 are inserted from v. 48 in some manuscripts. They are identical with v. 48.

9:47 *kingdom of God.* See note on Mt 3:2.

9:48 Isa 66:24 (see note there) speaks of the punishment for rebellion against God. As the final word of Isaiah's message, the passage became familiar as a picture of endless destruction. *worm does not die.* Worms were always present in the rubbish dump (see Mt 5:22 and note).

9:49 The saying may mean that everyone who enters hell will suffer its fire, or (if only loosely connected with the preceding) it may mean that every Christian in this life can expect to undergo the fire of suffering and purification.

A **9:50** *Salt is good.* The distinctive mark of discipleship typified by salt is allegiance to Jesus and the gospel (see 8:35, 38; Mt 5:13 and notes). *be at peace with each other.* Strife is resolved and peace restored when we recognize in one another a common commitment to Jesus and the gospel.

10:1 *region of Judea.* The Greek and Roman equivalent to the OT land of Judah, essentially the southern part of the Holy Land (now exclusive of Idumea), which formerly had been the southern kingdom. For Jesus' ministry in Judea, see note on Lk 9:51. *Jordan.* See note on 1:5. Jesus' journey took him south from Capernaum, over the mountains of Samaria into Judea and then east across the Jordan into Perea, where Herod Antipas ruled (see note on Mt 14:1). For Jesus' ministry in Perea, see note on Lk 13:22.

10:2 *k* Mk 2:16
10:4 *l* Dt 24:1-4;
Mt 5:31
10:5 *m* Ps 95:8;
Heb 3:15
10:6 *n* Ge 1:27; 5:2
10:8 *o* Ge 2:24;
1Co 6:16
10:11 *p* S Lk 16:18
10:12 *q* Ro 7:3;
1Co 7:10,11
10:14 *r* S Mt 25:34
10:15 *s* Mt 18:3
10:16 *t* Mk 9:36
10:17 *u* Mk 1:40
v Lk 10:25; S Ac 20:32

²Some Pharisees *k* came and tested him by asking, "Is it lawful for a man to divorce his wife?"

³"What did Moses command you?" he replied.

⁴They said, "Moses permitted a man to write a certificate of divorce and send her away." *l*

⁵"It was because your hearts were hard *m* that Moses wrote you this law," Jesus replied. ⁶"But at the beginning of creation God 'made them male and female.' *a n* ⁷'For this reason a man will leave his father and mother and be united to his wife, *b* ⁸and the two will become one flesh.' *c o* So they are no longer two, but one. ⁹Therefore what God has joined together, let no one separate."

¹⁰When they were in the house again, the disciples asked Jesus about this. ¹¹He answered, "Anyone who divorces his wife and marries another woman commits adultery against her. *p* ¹²And if she divorces her husband and marries another man, she commits adultery." *q*

THE LITTLE CHILDREN AND JESUS

10:13–16pp — Mt 19:13–15; Lk 18:15–17

¹³People were bringing little children to Jesus for him to place his hands on them, but the disciples rebuked them. ¹⁴When Jesus saw this, he was indignant. He said to them, "Let the little children come to me, and do not hinder them, for the kingdom of God belongs to such as these. *r* ¹⁵Truly I tell you, anyone who will not receive the kingdom of God like a little child will never enter it." *s* ¹⁶And he took the children in his arms, *t* placed his hands on them and blessed them.

THE RICH AND THE KINGDOM OF GOD

10:17–31pp — Mt 19:16–30; Lk 18:18–30

¹⁷As Jesus started on his way, a man ran up to him and fell on his knees *u* before him. "Good teacher," he asked, "what must I do to inherit eternal life?" *v*

¹⁸"Why do you call me good?" Jesus answered. "No one is good—except God alone. ¹⁹You know the commandments: 'You shall not murder, you shall not commit adultery, you

---

a 6 Gen. 1:27   *b* 7 Some early manuscripts do not have *and be united to his wife*.   *c* 8 Gen. 2:24

10:2 *Pharisees.* See note on 2:16. *came and tested him.* The question of the Pharisees was hostile. It was for unlawful divorce and remarriage that John the Baptist denounced Herod Antipas and Herodias (see 6:17–18), and this rebuke cost him imprisonment and then his life. Jesus was now within Herod's jurisdiction, and the Pharisees may have hoped that Jesus' reply would cause the tetrarch to seize him as he had John. *Is it lawful … to divorce his wife?* Jews of that day generally agreed that divorce was lawful, the only debated issue being the proper grounds for it (see note on Mt 19:3).

10:5 *because your hearts were hard.* See 6:52 and note. Divorce was an accommodation to human weakness and was used to bring order in a society that had disregarded God's will, but it was not the standard God had originally intended, as vv. 6–9 clearly indicate. The purpose of Dt 24:1–4 (see note there) was not to make divorce acceptable but to reduce the hardship of its consequences.

10:6 *at the beginning of creation.* Jesus goes back to the time before human sin to show God's original intention. God instituted marriage as a great unifying blessing, bonding the male and female in his creation.

10:8 *no longer two, but one.* The deduction drawn by Jesus affirms the ideal of the permanence of marriage.

10:9 *Therefore what God has joined together.* Jesus grounds the sanctity of marriage in the authority of God himself, and his "No" to divorce safeguards against human selfishness, which always threatens to destroy marriage.

10:11 *Anyone who divorces his wife.* In Jewish practice divorce was effected by the husband himself, not by a judicial authority or court. *commits adultery against her.* A simple declaration of divorce on the part of a husband could not release him from the divine law of marriage and its moral obligations. This enduring force of the marriage bond was unrecognized in Rabbinic

courts. But see Mt 19:3 and note; see also Mt 19:9, where an exception is mentioned. 1Co 7:15 may contain another exception (see notes on 1Co 7:12,15).

10:12 *she commits adultery.* In this historical and geographical context, Jesus' pronouncements confirm the bold denunciation by John the Baptist and equally condemn Herod Antipas and Herodias.

10:14 *kingdom of God.* See note on Mt 3:2. *belongs to such as these.* The kingdom of God belongs to those who, like children, are prepared to receive the kingdom as a gift of God (see note on v. 15).

10:15 *Truly I tell you.* See note on 3:28. *like a little child.* The point of comparison is the usual openness and receptivity of children. The kingdom of God must be received as a gift; it cannot be achieved by human effort. It can be entered only by those who know they are helpless, without claim or merit (see Mt 18:3; Lk 18:17 and notes).

10:16 *placed his hands on them and blessed them.* See note on Ac 6:6. Jesus visually demonstrated that the blessings of the kingdom are freely given.

10:17 *man.* Lk 18:18 calls him a "ruler," meaning he was probably a member of an official council or court, and Mt 19:20 says he was "young." *what must I do … ?* Cf. Ac 16:30–31 and notes. The rich man was thinking in terms of earning righteousness to merit eternal life, but Jesus taught that it was a gift to be received (see v. 15 and note). *eternal life.* See note on Mt 19:16.

10:18 *Why do you call me good?* Jesus was not denying his own goodness but was forcing the man to recognize that his only hope was in total reliance on God, who alone can give eternal life. He may also have been encouraging the young man to consider the full identity and nature of the One he was addressing.

10:19 ʷEx 20:12-16; Dt 5:16-20
10:21 ˣS Ac 2:45 ʸMt 6:20; Lk 12:33 ᶻS Mt 4:19
10:23 ᵃPs 52:7; 62:10; Mk 4:19; 1Ti 6:9,10,17
10:24 ᵇMt 7:13,14; Jn 3:5
10:25 ᶜLk 12:16-20; 16:19-31
10:27 ᵈS Mt 19:26
10:28 ᵉS Mt 4:19
10:30 ᶠMt 6:33 ᵍS Mt 12:32 ʰS Mt 25:46
10:31 ⁱS Mt 19:30
10:32 ʲMk 3:16-19
10:33 ᵏS Lk 9:51

shall not steal, you shall not give false testimony, you shall not defraud, honor your father and mother.'ᵃ"ʷ

²⁰"Teacher," he declared, "all these I have kept since I was a boy."

²¹Jesus looked at him and loved him. "One thing you lack," he said. "Go, sell everything you have and give to the poor,ˣ and you will have treasure in heaven.ʸ Then come, follow me."ᶻ

²²At this the man's face fell. He went away sad, because he had great wealth.

²³Jesus looked around and said to his disciples, "How hard it is for the richᵃ to enter the kingdom of God!"

²⁴The disciples were amazed at his words. But Jesus said again, "Children, how hard it isᵇ to enter the kingdom of God!ᵇ ²⁵It is easier for a camel to go through the eye of a needle than for the rich to enter the kingdom of God."ᶜ

²⁶The disciples were even more amazed, and said to each other, "Who then can be saved?"

²⁷Jesus looked at them and said, "With human beings this is impossible, but not with God; all things are possible with God."ᵈ

²⁸Then Peter spoke up, "We have left everything to follow you!"ᵉ

²⁹"Truly I tell you," Jesus replied, "no one who has left home or brothers or sisters or mother or father or children or fields for me and the gospel ³⁰will fail to receive a hundred times as muchᶠ in this present age: homes, brothers, sisters, mothers, children and fields—along with persecutions—and in the age to comeᵍ eternal life.ʰ ³¹But many who are first will be last, and the last first."ⁱ

JESUS PREDICTS HIS DEATH A THIRD TIME
10:32–34pp — Mt 20:17–19; Lk 18:31–33

³²They were on their way up to Jerusalem, with Jesus leading the way, and the disciples were astonished, while those who followed were afraid. Again he took the Twelveʲ aside and told them what was going to happen to him. ³³"We are going up to Jerusalem,"ᵏ

ᵃ 19 Exodus 20:12-16; Deut. 5:16-20   ᵇ 24 Some manuscripts *is for those who trust in riches*

10:19 *you shall not defraud.* The prohibition of fraud may have represented the tenth commandment (against covetousness). If so, Jesus here mentions all six commandments that prohibit wrong actions and attitudes against others (see Ex 20:12–17; Dt 5:16–21).

10:20 *all these I have kept.* The man spoke sincerely, because for him keeping the law was a matter of external conformity. That the law also required inner obedience, which no one can fully satisfy, apparently escaped him completely. Paul speaks of having had a similar outlook before his conversion (see Php 3:6 and note). *since I was a boy.* Probably a reference to the age of 13, when a Jewish boy assumed personal responsibility for obeying the commandments and thus became a "son of the commandment(s)" (Aramaic *bar mitzvah*).

10:21 *Jesus . . . loved him.* Jesus recognized the man's earnestness. Jesus' response was not intended to shame the man by exposing failure to understand the spiritual depth of the commandments but was an expression of genuine love. *One thing you lack . . . Go, sell everything.* The young man's primary problem was his wealth (see v. 22 and note), and therefore Jesus' prescription was to rid him of it. There is no indication that Jesus' command to him was meant for all Christians. It applies only to those who have the same spiritual problem. *treasure in heaven.* The gift of eternal life, or salvation. This treasure is not to be earned by self-denial or giving of one's material goods but is to be received by following Jesus. In giving away his wealth, the young man would have removed the obstacle that kept him from trusting in Jesus. *come, follow me.* See note on 1:17.

10:22 *He went away sad, because he had great wealth.* The tragic decision to turn away reflected a greater love for his possessions than for eternal life (see 4:19 and note).

10:25 *eye of a needle.* The camel was the largest animal found in the Holy Land. The vivid contrast between the largest animal and the smallest opening represents what, humanly speaking, is impossible. The oft-repeated suggestion that one of Jerusalem's gates was called the Needle's Eye is unsubstantiated.

10:26 *amazed.* See 1:22 and note.

10:27 *With human beings this is impossible, but not with God.* Salvation is totally the work of God. Every attempt to enter the kingdom on the basis of human achievement or merit is futile. Apart from the grace of God, no one can be saved (cf. Eph 2:8–9; Tit 3:5 and notes).

10:28 See 1:18.

10:29 *Truly I tell you.* See note on 3:28. *gospel.* See 1:1 and note.

10:30 *hundred times as much.* See 4:8 and note. *present age . . . age to come.* These two terms take in all of time from the fall of Adam and Eve to the eternal state. The present age is evil (see Gal 1:4 and note), but the coming righteous age will begin with the second advent of Christ and continue forever. *along with persecutions.* The life of discipleship is a combination of promise and persecution, blessing and suffering. God takes nothing from a Christian without making multiplied restoration in a new and glorious form. Paradoxically, fellowship with other believers develops most deeply in persecution. *eternal life.* Beyond the conflicts of history is the triumph assured to those who belong to God (see Mt 19:16 and note).

10:31 *first will be last.* A warning against pride in sacrificial accomplishments such as Peter had manifested (v. 28; see vv. 42–44 and note on v. 43).

10:32 *on their way up to Jerusalem.* This last journey to Jerusalem began in a city called Ephraim (see Jn 11:54 and note) and took Jesus into Galilee (Lk 17:11), south through Perea to Jericho (Lk 18:35), then to Bethany (Lk 19:29) and finally to Jerusalem (Lk 19:41). See notes on Lk 9:51; 13:22. *astonished.* See 1:22 and note. Perhaps the disciples' astonishment was due to the determination with which Jesus proceeded to his goal (see Isa 50:7 and note). *those who followed.* Perhaps pilgrims on their way to the Passover in Jerusalem.

he said, "and the Son of Man *l* will be delivered over to the chief priests and the teachers of the law. *m* They will condemn him to death and will hand him over to the Gentiles, [34]who will mock him and spit on him, flog him *n* and kill him. *o* Three days later *p* he will rise." *q*

THE REQUEST OF JAMES AND JOHN
10:35–45pp — Mt 20:20–28

[35]Then James and John, the sons of Zebedee, came to him. "Teacher," they said, "we want you to do for us whatever we ask."

[36]"What do you want me to do for you?" he asked.

[37]They replied, "Let one of us sit at your right and the other at your left in your glory." *r*

[38]"You don't know what you are asking," *s* Jesus said. "Can you drink the cup *t* I drink or be baptized with the baptism I am baptized with?" *u*

[39]"We can," they answered.

Jesus said to them, "You will drink the cup I drink and be baptized with the baptism I am baptized with, *v* [40]but to sit at my right or left is not for me to grant. These places belong to those for whom they have been prepared."

[41]When the ten heard about this, they became indignant with James and John. [42]Jesus called them together and said, "You know that those who are regarded as rulers of the Gentiles lord it over them, and their high officials exercise authority over them. [43]Not so with you. Instead, whoever wants to become great among you must be your servant, *w* [44]and whoever wants to be first must be slave of all. [45]For even the Son of Man did not come to be served, but to serve, *x* and to give his life as a ransom for many." *y*

BLIND BARTIMAEUS RECEIVES HIS SIGHT
10:46–52pp — Mt 20:29–34; Lk 18:35–43

[46]Then they came to Jericho. As Jesus and his disciples, together with a large crowd, were leaving the city, a blind man, Bartimaeus (which means "son of Timaeus"), was sitting by the roadside begging. [47]When he heard that it was Jesus of Nazareth, *z* he began to shout, "Jesus, Son of David, *a* have mercy on me!"

[48]Many rebuked him and told him to be quiet, but he shouted all the more, "Son of David, have mercy on me!"

[49]Jesus stopped and said, "Call him."

10:33 *l* S Mt 8:20
m Mt 27:1,2
10:34 *n* S Mt 16:21
o Ac 2:23; 3:13
p S Mt 16:21
q S Mt 16:21
10:37 *r* Mt 19:28
10:38 *s* Job 38:2
t S Mt 20:22
u Lk 12:50
10:39 *v* Ac 12:2;
Rev 1:9
10:43 *w* S Mk 9:35
10:45 *x* S Mt 20:28
y S Mt 20:28
10:47 *z* S Mk 1:24
a S Mt 9:27

10:33–34 The third prediction of Jesus' death (see note on 8:31—10:52). *Gentiles, who will … kill him.* The word "crucify" does not occur in any of the passion predictions in Mark's Gospel, but the statement that Jesus would be handed over to Gentiles to be killed by them suggests crucifixion, since this was the usual means of Roman execution of non-Romans.

10:33 *Son of Man … chief priests … teachers of the law.* See notes on 8:31; Mt 2:4.

10:35–45 Parallel to 9:33–37. Both passages deal with true greatness, and both follow a prediction of Jesus' suffering and death. Both also show how spiritually undiscerning the disciples were (see note on 8:16).

10:35–36 *want … want.* James's and John's desire for position and power would be realized only if they willingly submitted to servanthood (see "wants … wants" in vv. 43–44).

10:35 *James and John, the sons of Zebedee.* See 1:19; 3:17.

10:37 *at your right and … at your left.* Positions of prestige and power.

10:38 *drink the cup I drink.* A Jewish expression that meant to share someone's fate. In the OT the cup of wine was a common metaphor for God's wrath against human sin and rebellion (see Jer 25:15–16 and notes; 49:12). Accordingly, the cup Jesus had to drink refers to divine punishment for sin that he bore for the redemption of the human race (see v. 45; 14:36 and notes). *be baptized with the baptism I am baptized with.* The image of baptism is parallel to that of the cup, referring to his suffering and death as a baptism (see Lk 12:50 and note; cf. Ro 6:3–4 for the figure).

10:40 *is not for me to grant.* Jesus would not usurp his Father's authority.

10:41 *the ten.* The other disciples. *indignant.* Possibly because they desired the positions of prestige and power for themselves.

10:43 *Not so with you.* Jesus overturns the value structure of the world. The life of discipleship is to be characterized by humble and loving service.

10:45 A key verse in Mark's Gospel. Jesus came to this world as a servant—indeed, the Servant—who would suffer and die for our redemption, as Isaiah clearly predicted (Isa 52:13—53:12). *Son of Man.* See note on 8:31. *did not come to be served, but to serve, and to give his life.* See note on Jn 13:5. *ransom.* Means "the price paid for release (from bondage)." Jesus gave his life to release us from bondage to sin and death. *for.* That is, "in place of," pointing to Christ's substitutionary death. *many.* In contrast to the one life given for our ransom. See note on Mt 20:28.

10:46 *Jericho.* A very ancient city located five miles west of the Jordan and about 15 miles northeast of Jerusalem. In Jesus' time OT Jericho was largely abandoned, but a new city, south of the old one, had been built by Herod the Great. *leaving the city.* Luke says Jesus "approached Jericho" (Lk 18:35). He may have been referring to the new Jericho, while Matthew (20:29) and Mark may have meant the old city. *blind man.* See Lk 18:35 and note. *begging.* The presence of a blind beggar just outside the city gates, on a road pilgrims followed on the way to Jerusalem, was a common sight in that day.

10:47 *Nazareth.* See note on Mt 2:23. *Son of David.* A Messianic title (see Isa 11:1–2; Jer 23:5–6; Eze 34:23–24; Mt 1:1; 9:27 and notes). Verses 47–48 are the only places in Mark where it is used to address Jesus. Its only other occurrence in Mark is in 12:35.

10:51 b S Mt 23:7
10:52 c S Mt 9:22
d S Mt 4:19
11:1 e S Mt 21:17
f S Mt 21:1
11:2 g Nu 19:2;
Dt 21:3; 1Sa 6:7
11:4 h Mk 14:16
11:9 i Ps 118:25,26;
Mt 23:39
11:10 j Lk 2:14
11:11 k Mt 21:12,17
11:13 l Lk 13:6-9

So they called to the blind man, "Cheer up! On your feet! He's calling you." [50]Throwing his cloak aside, he jumped to his feet and came to Jesus.

[51]"What do you want me to do for you?" Jesus asked him.

The blind man said, "Rabbi, [b] I want to see."

[52]"Go," said Jesus, "your faith has healed you." [c] Immediately he received his sight and followed [d] Jesus along the road.

JESUS COMES TO JERUSALEM AS KING

11:1–10pp — Mt 21:1–9; Lk 19:29–38
11:7–10pp — Jn 12:12–15

11 As they approached Jerusalem and came to Bethphage and Bethany [e] at the Mount of Olives, [f] Jesus sent two of his disciples, [2]saying to them, "Go to the village ahead of you, and just as you enter it, you will find a colt tied there, which no one has ever ridden. [g] Untie it and bring it here. [3]If anyone asks you, 'Why are you doing this?' say, 'The Lord needs it and will send it back here shortly.' "

[4]They went and found a colt outside in the street, tied at a doorway. [h] As they untied it, [5]some people standing there asked, "What are you doing, untying that colt?" [6]They answered as Jesus had told them to, and the people let them go. [7]When they brought the colt to Jesus and threw their cloaks over it, he sat on it. [8]Many people spread their cloaks on the road, while others spread branches they had cut in the fields. [9]Those who went ahead and those who followed shouted,

"Hosanna! [a]"

"Blessed is he who comes in the name of the Lord!" [b] [i]

[10]"Blessed is the coming kingdom of our father David!"

"Hosanna in the highest heaven!" [j]

[11]Jesus entered Jerusalem and went into the temple courts. He looked around at everything, but since it was already late, he went out to Bethany with the Twelve. [k]

JESUS CURSES A FIG TREE AND CLEARS THE TEMPLE COURTS

11:12–14pp — Mt 21:18–22
11:15–18pp — Mt 21:12–16; Lk 19:45–47; Jn 2:13–16
11:20–24pp — Mt 21:19–22

[12]The next day as they were leaving Bethany, Jesus was hungry. [13]Seeing in the distance a fig tree in leaf, he went to find out if it had any fruit. When he reached it, he found nothing but leaves, because it was not the season for figs. [l] [14]Then he said to the tree, "May no one ever eat fruit from you again." And his disciples heard him say it.

---

a 9 A Hebrew expression meaning "Save!" which became an exclamation of praise; also in verse 10
b 9 Psalm 118:25,26

10:51 Rabbi. See notes on 11:21; Jn 20:16.
10:52 your faith has healed you. See 5:28 and note.

C **11:1–11** At this point a new section in the Gospel of Mark begins. Jesus arrives in Jerusalem, and the rest of his ministry takes place within the confines of the Holy City. Jesus' entry into Jerusalem as King, which inaugurates Passion Week, is a deliberate Messianic action, and the clue to its understanding is found in Zec 9:9 (quoted in Mt 21:5; Jn 12:15). Jesus purposefully offers himself as the Messiah, knowing that this will provoke Jewish leaders to take action against him.
11:1 Bethphage. See note on Mt 21:1. Bethany. See note on Mt 21:17. Mount of Olives. Directly east of Jerusalem, it rises to a height of about 2,700 feet, some 200 feet higher than Mount Zion. Its summit commands a magnificent view of the city, and especially of the temple.
11:2 the village ahead. Probably Bethphage. colt. The Greek word can mean the young of any animal, but here it means the colt of a donkey (see Mt 21:2 and note; Jn 12:15). which no one has ever ridden. Unused animals were regarded as especially suitable for religious purposes (see Nu 19:2; Dt 21:3; 1Sa 6:7).
11:3 If anyone asks you. The message concerning the colt is not directed specifically to the owner but to anyone who might question the disciples' action. Lord. See note on Lk 19:31.

11:8 branches. The word means "leaves" or "leafy branches," which were readily available in nearby fields. Only John mentions palm branches (see Jn 12:13 and note), which may have come from Jericho, since they are not native to Jerusalem.
11:9 Hosanna. See TNIV text note; see also note on Mt 21:9. Blessed is he who comes. A quotation of Ps 118:26 (see note there), one of the Hallel ("Praise") Psalms sung at Passover and especially fitting for this occasion.
11:10 the coming kingdom of our father David. The Messianic kingdom promised to David's son (see 2Sa 7:11–14 and notes).
11:11 temple courts. See note on Mt 4:5. went out to Bethany. Apparently Jesus spent each night through Thursday of Passion Week in Bethany (see note on Mt 21:17) at the home of his friends Mary, Martha and Lazarus (see v. 19; Jn 12:1–3).
11:12 next day. Monday of Passion Week.
11:13 not the season for figs. Fig trees around Jerusalem normally begin to get leaves in March or April but do not produce figs until their leaves are all out in June. This tree was an exception in that it was already, at Passover time, full of leaves.
11:14 May no one ever eat fruit from you again. Perhaps the incident was a parable of judgment, with the fig tree representing Israel (see Jer 24:1; Hos 9:10 and notes; Na 3:12). A tree full of

¹⁵On reaching Jerusalem, Jesus entered the temple courts and began driving out those who were buying and selling there. He overturned the tables of the money changers and the benches of those selling doves, ¹⁶and would not allow anyone to carry merchandise through the temple courts. ¹⁷And as he taught them, he said, "Is it not written: 'My house will be called a house of prayer for all nations'^a? ^m But you have made it 'a den of robbers.'^b" ⁿ

¹⁸The chief priests and the teachers of the law heard this and began looking for a way to kill him, for they feared him, ^o because the whole crowd was amazed at his teaching. ^p

¹⁹When evening came, Jesus and his disciples^c went out of the city. ^q

²⁰In the morning, as they went along, they saw the fig tree withered from the roots. ²¹Peter remembered and said to Jesus, "Rabbi, ^r look! The fig tree you cursed has withered!"

²²"Have faith in God," Jesus answered. ²³"Truly^d I tell you, if you say to this mountain, 'Go, throw yourself into the sea,' and do not doubt in your heart but believe that what you say will happen, it will be done for you. ^s ²⁴Therefore I tell you, whatever you ask for in prayer, believe that you have received it, and it will be yours. ^t ^{25[26]}And when you stand praying, if you hold anything against anyone, forgive them, so that your Father in heaven may forgive you your sins." ^u

THE AUTHORITY OF JESUS QUESTIONED

11:27–33pp — Mt 21:23–27; Lk 20:1–8

²⁷They arrived again in Jerusalem, and while Jesus was walking in the temple courts, the chief priests, the teachers of the law and the elders came to him. ²⁸"By what authority are you doing these things?" they asked. "And who gave you authority to do this?"

²⁹Jesus replied, "I will ask you one question. Answer me, and I will tell you by what authority I am doing these things. ³⁰John's baptism—was it from heaven, or of human origin? Tell me!"

^a *17* Isaiah 56:7   ^b *17* Jer. 7:11   ^c *19* Some early manuscripts *came, Jesus*   ^d *22,23* Some early manuscripts *"If you have faith in God," Jesus answered,* ²³*"truly*

11:17 ^m Isa 56:7
ⁿ Jer 7:11
11:18 ^o Mt 21:46;
Mk 12:12; Lk 20:19
^p S Mt 7:28
11:19 ^q Lk 21:37
11:21 ^r S Mt 23:7
11:23 ^s S Mt 21:21
11:24 ^t S Mt 7:7
11:25[26] ^u S Mt 6:14

leaves normally should have fruit, but this one was cursed because it had none. The fact that the cleansing of the temple (vv. 15–19) is sandwiched between the two parts of the account of the fig tree (vv. 12–14,20–25) may underscore the theme of judgment (see v. 21 and note). The only application Jesus makes, however, is as an illustration of believing prayer (vv. 21–25).

11:15–19 All three Synoptic writers mention a cleansing of the temple at the end of Jesus' ministry. Only John has one at the beginning. See notes on Mt 21:12–17; Jn 2:14–17.

11:15 *temple courts.* The court of the Gentiles, the only part of the temple in which Gentiles could worship God and gather for prayer (see v. 17 and note). *buying and selling.* Pilgrims coming to the Passover Festival needed animals that met the ritual requirements for sacrifice, and the vendors set up their animal pens and money tables in the court of the Gentiles. *tables of the money changers.* Pilgrims needed their money changed into the local currency because the annual temple tax had to be paid in that currency. Also, the Mishnah (see note on Mt 15:2) required currency from Tyre for some offerings. *those selling doves.* Doves were required for the purification of women (Lev 12:6; Lk 2:22–24), the cleansing of those with certain skin diseases (Lev 14:22–23), and other purposes (Lev 15:13–14,28–29). They were also the usual offering of the poor (Lev 5:7).

11:16 *to carry merchandise through the temple courts.* A detail found only in Mark. Apparently the temple area was being used as a shortcut between the city and the Mount of Olives. See note on v. 27.

11:17 *house of prayer for all nations.* Isa 56:7 assured godly Gentiles that they would be allowed to worship God in the temple. By allowing the court of the Gentiles to become a noisy, smelly marketplace, the Jewish religious leaders were interfering with God's provision. *den of robbers.* Not only because they took financial advantage of the people but also because they robbed the temple of its sanctity.

11:18 *chief priests ... teachers of the law.* See note on Mt 2:4. *began looking for a way to kill him.* See note on 3:6. They regarded Jesus as a dangerous threat to their whole way of life. *amazed.* See 1:22 and note.

11:19 *went out of the city.* To Bethany (see note on v. 11).

11:20 *In the morning.* Tuesday morning of Passion Week. *withered from the roots.* This detail indicates that the destruction was total (cf. Job 18:16) and that no one in the future would eat fruit from the tree. It served as a vivid warning of the judgment to come in A.D. 70 (see 13:2; Mt 24:2 and note).

11:21 *Rabbi.* Hebrew for "(my) teacher." *fig tree you cursed.* See note on v. 14. *has withered.* Perhaps prophetic of the fate of the Jewish authorities who were now about to reject their Messiah.

11:23 *Truly I tell you.* See note on 3:28. *this mountain ... into the sea.* The Mount of Olives, from which the Dead Sea is visible. Cf. Mt 17:20 and note.

11:25[26] See Mt 18:35 and note; cf. Eph 4:32 and note. Verse 26 ("But if you do not forgive, neither will your Father who is in heaven forgive your sins") occurs in some manuscripts but is not found at this point in the earliest and best manuscripts of the NT, probably having been inserted from Mt 6:15 by a copyist.

11:27 *temple courts.* Several courts surrounded the main temple buildings, including the court of the women, the court of the men (Israelite) and the court of the Gentiles (see vv. 16–17 and notes). *chief priests ... teachers of the law ... elders.* See notes on 8:31; Mt 2:4.

11:28 *authority.* The Sanhedrin was asking why Jesus performed what appeared to be an official act if he possessed no official status (see note on Lk 20:2).

11:30 *from heaven, or of human origin?* "Heaven" was a common Jewish substitute for the divine name to avoid a possible misuse of God's name (see Ex 20:7 and note; see also Introduction to Matthew: Recipients). Jesus' question implied that his authority, like that of John's baptism, came from God.

11:32 ʸS Mt 11:9
12:1 ʷ Isa 5:1-7
12:6 ˣ Heb 1:1-3
12:10 ʸS Ac 4:11
12:11 ᶻ Ps 118:22,23
12:12 ᵃS Mk 11:18
ᵇ Mt 22:22
12:13 ᶜ Mt 22:16;
Mk 3:6 ᵈS Mt 12:10

³¹They discussed it among themselves and said, "If we say, 'From heaven,' he will ask, 'Then why didn't you believe him?' ³²But if we say, 'Of human origin' . . . ." (They feared the people, for everyone held that John really was a prophet.) ᵛ

³³So they answered Jesus, "We don't know."

Jesus said, "Neither will I tell you by what authority I am doing these things."

THE PARABLE OF THE TENANTS
12:1–12pp — Mt 21:33–46; Lk 20:9–19

12 Jesus then began to speak to them in parables: "A man planted a vineyard. ʷ He put a wall around it, dug a pit for the winepress and built a watchtower. Then he rented the vineyard to some farmers and moved to another place. ²At harvest time he sent a servant to the tenants to collect from them some of the fruit of the vineyard. ³But they seized him, beat him and sent him away empty-handed. ⁴Then he sent another servant to them; they struck this man on the head and treated him shamefully. ⁵He sent still another, and that one they killed. He sent many others; some of them they beat, others they killed.

⁶"He had one left to send, a son, whom he loved. He sent him last of all, ˣ saying, 'They will respect my son.'

⁷"But the tenants said to one another, 'This is the heir. Come, let's kill him, and the inheritance will be ours.' ⁸So they took him and killed him, and threw him out of the vineyard.

⁹"What then will the owner of the vineyard do? He will come and kill those tenants and give the vineyard to others. ¹⁰Haven't you read this passage of Scripture:

" 'The stone the builders rejected
　　has become the cornerstone; ʸ
¹¹the Lord has done this,
　　and it is marvelous in our eyes'ᵃ?" ᶻ

¹²Then the chief priests, the teachers of the law and the elders looked for a way to arrest him because they knew he had spoken the parable against them. But they were afraid of the crowd; ᵃ so they left him and went away. ᵇ

PAYING THE IMPERIAL TAX TO CAESAR
12:13–17pp — Mt 22:15–22; Lk 20:20–26

¹³Later they sent some of the Pharisees and Herodians ᶜ to Jesus to catch him ᵈ in his words. ¹⁴They came to him and said, "Teacher, we know that you are a man of integrity. You aren't swayed by others, because you pay no attention to who they are; but you teach the way of God in accordance with the truth. Is it right to pay the imperial taxᵇ to Caesar or not? ¹⁵Should we pay or shouldn't we?"

But Jesus knew their hypocrisy. "Why are you trying to trap me?" he asked. "Bring me a denarius and let me look at it." ¹⁶They brought the coin, and he asked them, "Whose image is this? And whose inscription?"

"Caesar's," they replied.

ᵃ 11 Psalm 118:22,23　　ᵇ 14 A special tax levied on subject peoples, not on Roman citizens

---

12:1–12 Many of Jesus' parables make one main point. This parable is rather complex, and the details fit the social situation in Jewish Galilee in the first century. Large estates, owned by absentee landlords, were put in the hands of local peasants who cultivated the land as tenant farmers. The parable exposed the planned attempt on Jesus' life, as well as God's judgment on the planners. See notes on Mt 21:35–37,41.

12:1 *them.* The representatives of the Sanhedrin mentioned in 11:27 (see note there). *parables.* See note on 4:2. *A man planted a vineyard.* The description reflects the language of Isa 5:1–2, where the vineyard clearly symbolizes Israel (see Isa 5:7). *watchtower.* See notes on Mt 21:33; Isa 5:2.

12:2 See note on Lk 20:10.

12:6 *son, whom he loved.* See 9:7 and note.

12:7 *inheritance will be ours.* Jewish law provided that a piece of property unclaimed by an heir would be declared ownerless and could then be claimed by others. The tenants assumed that

the son came as heir to claim his property and that if he were slain they could claim the land.

12:10 *cornerstone.* See note on Ps 118:22.

12:13–17 This incident probably took place on Tuesday of Passion Week in one of the temple courts (see map, p. 1702).

12:13 *they.* See note on v. 1. *Pharisees.* See note on Mt 3:7. *Herodians.* See notes on 3:6; Mt 22:15–17. The plan to destroy Jesus, which had originated early in his Galilean ministry, had now matured and was gaining momentum in Jerusalem.

12:14 *pay the imperial tax to Caesar.* Subject peoples were required to pay a poll tax to the Roman emperor (see TNIV text note). The tax was highly unpopular, and some Jews flatly refused to pay it, believing that payment was an admission of Roman right to rule. See note on Mt 22:15–17.

12:15 *hypocrisy.* See 7:6; Mt 5:18–20 and note; 6:2 and note; 23:13–36. *denarius.* See notes on 6:37; Mt 22:19.

¹⁷Then Jesus said to them, "Give back to Caesar what is Caesar's and to God what is God's." ^e

And they were amazed at him.

MARRIAGE AT THE RESURRECTION

12:18–27pp — Mt 22:23–33; Lk 20:27–38

¹⁸Then the Sadducees, ^f who say there is no resurrection, ^g came to him with a question. ¹⁹"Teacher," they said, "Moses wrote for us that if a man's brother dies and leaves a wife but no children, the man must marry the widow and raise up offspring for his brother. ^h ²⁰Now there were seven brothers. The first one married and died without leaving any children. ²¹The second one married the widow, but he also died, leaving no child. It was the same with the third. ²²In fact, none of the seven left any children. Last of all, the woman died too. ²³At the resurrection^a whose wife will she be, since the seven were married to her?"

²⁴Jesus replied, "Are you not in error because you do not know the Scripturesⁱ or the power of God? ²⁵When the dead rise, they will neither marry nor be given in marriage; they will be like the angels in heaven.^j ²⁶Now about the dead rising—have you not read in the Book of Moses, in the account of the burning bush, how God said to him, 'I am the God of Abraham, the God of Isaac, and the God of Jacob'^b? ^k ²⁷He is not the God of the dead, but of the living. You are badly mistaken!"

THE GREATEST COMMANDMENT

12:28–34pp — Mt 22:34–40

²⁸One of the teachers of the law^l came and heard them debating. Noticing that Jesus had given them a good answer, he asked him, "Of all the commandments, which is the most important?"

²⁹"The most important one," answered Jesus, "is this: 'Hear, O Israel: The Lord our God, the Lord is one.^c ³⁰Love the Lord your God with all your heart and with all your soul and with all your mind and with all your strength.'^d ^m ³¹The second is this: 'Love your neighbor as yourself.'^e ⁿ There is no commandment greater than these."

³²"Well said, teacher," the man replied. "You are right in saying that God is one and there is no other but him. ^o ³³To love him with all your heart, with all your understanding and with all your strength, and to love your neighbor as yourself is more important than all burnt offerings and sacrifices." ^p

³⁴When Jesus saw that he had answered wisely, he said to him, "You are not far from the kingdom of God." ^q And from then on no one dared ask him any more questions. ^r

---

^a 23 Some manuscripts *resurrection, when people rise from the dead,*   ^b 26 Exodus 3:6   ^c 29 Or *The Lord our God is one Lord*   ^d 30 Deut. 6:4,5   ^e 31 Lev. 19:18

12:17 ^e Ro 13:7
12:18 ^f S Ac 4:1
^g Ac 23:8; 1Co 15:12
12:19 ^h Dt 25:5
12:24 ⁱ 2Ti 3:15-17
12:25 ^j 1Co 15:42, 49,52
12:26 ^k Ex 3:6
12:28 ^l Lk 10:25-28; 20:39
12:30 ^m Dt 6:4,5
12:31 ⁿ Lev 19:18; S Mt 5:43
12:32 ^o Dt 4:35,39; Isa 45:6,14; 46:9
12:33 ^p 1Sa 15:22; Hos 6:6; Mic 6:6-8; Heb 10:8
12:34 ^q S Mt 3:2
^r Mt 22:46; Lk 20:40

12:17 *Give back to Caesar what is Caesar's.* See Mt 22:21 and note. There are obligations to the state that do not conflict with our obligations to God (see Ro 13:1–7; 1Ti 2:1–3; Tit 3:1–2; 1Pe 2:13–17 and notes). *amazed.* See 1:22 and note.

12:18 *Sadducees.* A Jewish party that represented the wealthy and sophisticated classes. Its members resided largely in Jerusalem and made the temple and its administration their primary interest. Though they were small in number, in Jesus' time they exerted powerful political and religious influence. See notes on Mt 3:7; Lk 20:27; Ac 4:1. *say there is no resurrection.* They denied the resurrection and accepted only the five books of Moses as authoritative. These beliefs set them against the Pharisees and common Jewish piety.

12:19 See note on Mt 22:24.

12:24 *you do not know the Scriptures.* Cf. v. 10; 2:25.

12:25 See note on Lk 20:36. In the resurrection there will be a new order of existence brought about by "the power of God" (v. 24; see 1Co 15:42–44 and note). *like the angels.* The basic characteristics of resurrection life will be fellowship with and service for God (see note on Heb 1:14).

12:26 *Book of Moses.* The Pentateuch, the first five books of the OT. *account of the burning bush.* A common way of referring to Ex 3:1–6 (cf. Ro 11:2, where "the passage about Elijah" refers to 1Ki 19:1–18).

12:28 *which is the most important?* Jewish rabbis counted 613 individual statutes in the law and attempted to differentiate between "heavy" (or "great") and "light" (or "little") commands.

12:29 The OT citation came to be known as the Shema, named after the first word of Dt 6:4 (Hebrew for "Hear"). The Shema became the Jewish confession of faith, which was recited by pious Jews every morning and evening. To this day its recitation begins every synagogue service.

12:30 See notes on Dt 6:5; Mt 22:37; Lk 10:27.

12:31 According to Jesus, the second most important commandment (Lev 19:18) states that love for neighbor is an essential component of love for God (see Jn 13:34; 1Jn 4:19–21 and notes). *neighbor.* See Lk 10:25–37.

12:32 *Well said, teacher.* Cf. Lk 20:39 and note.

12:33 *more important than.* The comparison may have been suggested by the fact that the discussion took place in the temple courtyard (see 11:27 and note). *all burnt offerings and sacrifices.* See 1Sa 15:22; Isa 1:11–15; Hos 6:6; Mic 6:8 and notes.

12:34 *kingdom of God.* See note on Mt 3:2.

12:35 ˢ S Mt 26:55
ᵗ S Mt 9:27
12:36 ᵘ 2Sa 23:2
ᵛ Ps 110:1; S Mt 22:44
12:37 ʷ Jn 12:9
12:39 ˣ Lk 11:43
12:41 ʸ 2Ki 12:9;
Jn 8:20
12:44 ᶻ 2Co 8:12
13:2 ᵃ Lk 19:44
13:3 ᵇ S Mt 21:1
ᶜ S Mt 4:21

WHOSE SON IS THE MESSIAH?

12:35–37pp — Mt 22:41–46; Lk 20:41–44
12:38–40pp — Mt 23:1–7; Lk 20:45–47

³⁵While Jesus was teaching in the temple courts, ˢ he asked, "Why do the teachers of the law say that the Messiah is the son of David? ᵗ ³⁶David himself, speaking by the Holy Spirit, ᵘ declared:

" 'The Lord said to my Lord:
  "Sit at my right hand
  until I put your enemies
  under your feet." 'ᵃ ᵛ

³⁷David himself calls him 'Lord.' How then can he be his son?"
The large crowd ʷ listened to him with delight.

WARNING AGAINST THE TEACHERS OF THE LAW

³⁸As he taught, Jesus said, "Watch out for the teachers of the law. They like to walk around in flowing robes and be greeted with respect in the marketplaces, ³⁹and have the most important seats in the synagogues and the places of honor at banquets. ˣ ⁴⁰They devour widows' houses and for a show make lengthy prayers. These men will be punished most severely."

THE WIDOW'S OFFERING

12:41–44pp — Lk 21:1–4

⁴¹Jesus sat down opposite the place where the offerings were put ʸ and watched the crowd putting their money into the temple treasury. Many rich people threw in large amounts. ⁴²But a poor widow came and put in two very small copper coins, worth only a fraction of a penny.

⁴³Calling his disciples to him, Jesus said, "Truly I tell you, this poor widow has put more into the treasury than all the others. ⁴⁴They all gave out of their wealth; but she, out of her poverty, put in everything—all she had to live on." ᶻ

THE DESTRUCTION OF THE TEMPLE AND SIGNS OF THE END TIMES

13:1–37pp — Mt 24:1–51; Lk 21:5–36

13 As Jesus was leaving the temple, one of his disciples said to him, "Look, Teacher! What massive stones! What magnificent buildings!"
²"Do you see all these great buildings?" replied Jesus. "Not one stone here will be left on another; every one will be thrown down." ᵃ
³As Jesus was sitting on the Mount of Olives ᵇ opposite the temple, Peter, James, John ᶜ

a 36 Psalm 110:1

12:35 *Messiah.* See 8:29 and note. *son of David.* See note on 10:47. Most of the people knew that the Messiah was to be from the family of David.

12:36 *The Lord said to my Lord.* God said to David's Lord, i.e., David's superior—ultimately the Messiah (see note on Ps 110:1). The purpose of the quotation was to show that the Messiah was more than a descendant of David—he was David's Lord (see note on Lk 20:44).

12:37 See note on Lk 20:44.

12:38 *flowing robes.* The teachers of the law wore long robes that were fringed and almost reached to the ground.

12:39 *most important seats in the synagogues.* A reference to the bench that was in front of the "ark" containing the sacred scrolls. Those who sat there could be seen by all the worshipers in the synagogue.

12:40 *devour widows' houses.* Since the teachers of the law were not paid a regular wage, they were dependent on the generosity of patrons for their livelihood. Such a system was open to abuses, and widows were especially vulnerable to exploitation. *for a show make lengthy prayers.* See Mt 6:5–7. *punished most severely.* See note on Lk 20:47.

12:41 *temple treasury.* Located in the court of the women. Both men and women were allowed in this court, but women could go no farther into the temple buildings. It contained 13 trumpet-shaped receptacles for contributions brought by worshipers (see note on Lk 21:1).

12:42 *very small copper coins.* The smallest coins then in circulation in the Holy Land. Though her offering was meager, the widow brought "all she had" (v. 44; see 2Co 8:12 and note).

12:43 *Truly I tell you.* See note on 3:28.

13:1–37 Mark's version of the Olivet discourse (see note on Mt 24:1—25:46). It is the longest connected discourse in Mark's Gospel. The chapter falls into five sections: (1) Jesus' prophecy of the destruction of the temple, which gives rise to the disciples' questions (vv. 1–4); (2) warnings against deceivers, as well as false signs of the end (vv. 5–23); (3) the coming of the Son of Man (vv. 24–27); (4) the lesson of the fig tree (vv. 28–31); and (5) exhortation to watchfulness (vv. 32–37).

13:1 *massive stones.* According to Josephus (*Antiquities,* 15.11.3), they were white, and some of them were 37 feet long, 12 feet high and 18 feet wide. *magnificent buildings.* See note on Lk 21:5.

13:2 See note on Mt 24:2.

13:3 *Mount of Olives.* See note on 11:1; see also map, p. 1703. *Peter, James, John and Andrew.* See 1:16–20; 5:37 and note.

and Andrew asked him privately, [4]"Tell us, when will these things happen? And what will be the sign that they are all about to be fulfilled?"

[5]Jesus said to them: "Watch out that no one deceives you. [d] [6]Many will come in my name, claiming, 'I am he,' and will deceive many. [7]When you hear of wars and rumors of wars, do not be alarmed. Such things must happen, but the end is still to come. [8]Nation will rise against nation, and kingdom against kingdom. There will be earthquakes in various places, and famines. These are the beginning of birth pains.

[9]"You must be on your guard. You will be handed over to the local councils and flogged in the synagogues. [e] On account of me you will stand before governors and kings as witnesses to them. [10]And the gospel must first be preached to all nations. [11]Whenever you are arrested and brought to trial, do not worry beforehand about what to say. Just say whatever is given you at the time, for it is not you speaking, but the Holy Spirit. [f]

[12]"Brother will betray brother to death, and a father his child. Children will rebel against their parents and have them put to death. [g] [13]Everyone will hate you because of me, [h] but those who stand firm to the end will be saved. [i]

[14]"When you see 'the abomination that causes desolation'[a] [j] standing where it [b] does not belong—let the reader understand—then let those who are in Judea flee to the mountains. [15]Let no one on the housetop go down or enter the house to take anything out. [16]Let no one in the field go back to get their cloak. [17]How dreadful it will be in those days for pregnant women and nursing mothers! [k] [18]Pray that this will not take place in winter, [19]because those will be days of distress unequaled from the beginning, when God created the world, [l] until now—and never to be equaled again. [m]

[20]"If the Lord had not cut short those days, no one would survive. But for the sake of the elect, whom he has chosen, he has shortened them. [21]At that time if anyone says to you, 'Look, here is the Messiah!' or, 'Look, there he is!' do not believe it. [n] [22]For false messiahs and false prophets [o] will appear and perform signs and wonders [p] to deceive, if possible, even the elect. [23]So be on your guard; [q] I have told you everything ahead of time.

[24]"But in those days, following that distress,

"'the sun will be darkened,
    and the moon will not give its light;
[25]the stars will fall from the sky,
    and the heavenly bodies will be shaken.'[c] [r]

[26]"At that time people will see the Son of Man coming in clouds [s] with great power and glory. [27]And he will send his angels and gather his elect from the four winds, from the ends of the earth to the ends of the heavens. [t]

---

a [14] Daniel 9:27; 11:31; 12:11   b [14] Or he   c [25] Isaiah 13:10; 34:4

13:5 [d] ver 22; Jer 29:8; Eph 5:6; 2Th 2:3,10-12; 1Ti 4:1; 2Ti 3:13; 1Jn 4:6
13:9 [e] S Mt 10:17
13:11 [f] Mt 10:19,20; Lk 12:11,12
13:12 [g] Mic 7:6; Mt 10:21; Lk 12:51-53
13:13 [h] S Jn 15:21 [i] S Mt 10:22
13:14 [j] Da 9:27; 11:31; 12:11
13:17 [k] Lk 23:29
13:19 [l] Mk 10:6 [m] Da 9:26; 12:1; Joel 2:2
13:21 [n] Lk 17:23; 21:8
13:22 [o] S Mt 7:15 [p] S Jn 4:48; 2Th 2:9, 10
13:23 [q] 2Pe 3:17
13:25 [r] Isa 13:10; 34:4; S Mt 24:29
13:26 [s] S Rev 1:7
13:27 [t] Zec 2:6

13:4 The disciples thought that the destruction of the temple would be one of the events that ushered in the end times (see Mt 24:3 and note). *sign.* The way by which the disciples might know that the destruction of the temple was about to take place and that the end of the age was approaching.
13:5–13 See Lk 21:8–19 and note on 21:9.

A **13:5** *Watch out.* It is clear from such commands as "Watch out" (see also vv. 35,37) and "You must be on your guard" (v. 9; see also vv. 23,33) that one of the main purposes of the Olivet discourse was to alert the disciples to the danger of deception.
13:6 *he.* That is, the Messiah.
13:7 *the end.* Not the destruction of Jerusalem but the end of the age (see Mt 24:3).
13:8 *birth pains.* See note on Mt 24:8.
13:9 *local councils.* See Mt 10:17 and note. *flogged.* Infraction of Jewish regulations was punishable by flogging, the maximum penalty being 39 strokes with a whip (see 2Co 11:23–24). *synagogues.* See note on 1:21.
13:10 *gospel.* See 1:1 and note. *first.* Before the end of the age (see Mt 24:14).

A **13:13** *stand firm to the end.* Such perseverance is a sure indication of salvation (cf. Heb 3:6,14 and notes; 6:11–12; 10:36).
13:14 *abomination that causes desolation.* See note on Mt 24:15. *standing where it does not belong.* Cf. 2Th 2:4 and note. *flee to the mountains.* See note on Mt 24:16.

13:15 *housetop.* See notes on 2:4; Lk 17:31.
13:16 *cloak.* See note on Mt 5:40.
13:17 *pregnant women and nursing mothers.* Representative of anyone forced to flee under especially difficult circumstances.
13:18 *winter.* The time when heavy rains caused streams to become swollen and impossible to cross, preventing many from reaching a place of refuge.
13:19 *days of distress unequaled.* See note on Mt 24:21.
13:20 *cut short those days.* See note on Mt 24:22. *elect.* People of God.
13:21 *Messiah.* See 8:29 and note.

A **13:24–25** Imagery depicting the undoing of creation was commonly used by the OT prophets to describe God's awful judgment on a fallen world (see Isa 13:10; 24:21–23; 34:4; Eze 32:7; Joel 2:10,30–31; Am 8:9 and notes).
13:24 *in those days.* A common OT expression having to do with the Messianic age, the time of Israel's final redemption (see Jer 3:16,18; 31:29; 33:15–16; Joel 3:1; Zec 8:23; Heb 9:26 and note). *distress.* See v. 19 and note on Mt 24:21.
13:26 See Mt 24:30 and note. *Son of Man.* See note on 8:31. *coming in clouds with great power and glory.* A reference to Christ's second coming (see 8:38; Da 7:13; 2Th 1:6–10; Rev 19:11–16 and notes).
13:27 *angels.* Cf. Rev 14:14–16. *gather his elect.* In the OT God is spoken of as gathering his scattered people (Dt 30:3–4; Isa 43:6; Jer 32:37; Eze 34:13; 36:24).

13:30 *u* Lk 17:25
v Mk 9:1
13:31 *w* S Mt 5:18
13:32 *x* Ac 1:7;
1Th 5:1,2
13:33 *y* 1Th 5:6
13:34 *z* Mt 25:14
13:37 *a* Lk 12:35-40
14:1 *b* S Jn 11:55
c S Mt 12:14
14:3 *d* S Mt 21:17
e Lk 7:37-39

²⁸"Now learn this lesson from the fig tree: As soon as its twigs get tender and its leaves come out, you know that summer is near. ²⁹Even so, when you see these things happening, you know that it *a* is near, right at the door. ³⁰Truly I tell you, this generation *u* will certainly not pass away until all these things have happened. *v* ³¹Heaven and earth will pass away, but my words will never pass away. *w*

THE DAY AND HOUR UNKNOWN

³²"But about that day or hour no one knows, not even the angels in heaven, nor the Son, but only the Father. *x* ³³Be on guard! Be alert *b*! *y* You do not know when that time will come. ³⁴It's like a man going away: He leaves his house and puts his servants *z* in charge, each with an assigned task, and tells the one at the door to keep watch.

³⁵"Therefore keep watch because you do not know when the owner of the house will come back—whether in the evening, or at midnight, or when the rooster crows, or at dawn. ³⁶If he comes suddenly, do not let him find you sleeping. ³⁷What I say to you, I say to everyone: 'Watch!' " *a*

JESUS ANOINTED AT BETHANY

14:1–11pp — Mt 26:2–16
14:1,2,10,11pp — Lk 22:1–6
14:3–8Ref — Jn 12:1–8

14 Now the Passover *b* and the Festival of Unleavened Bread were only two days away, and the chief priests and the teachers of the law were looking for some sly way to arrest Jesus and kill him. *c* ²"But not during the festival," they said, "or the people may riot."

³While he was in Bethany, *d* reclining at the table in the home of Simon the Leper, a woman came with an alabaster jar of very expensive perfume, made of pure nard. She broke the jar and poured the perfume on his head. *e*

⁴Some of those present were saying indignantly to one another, "Why this waste of perfume? ⁵It could have been sold for more than a year's wages *c* and the money given to the poor." And they rebuked her harshly.

⁶"Leave her alone," said Jesus. "Why are you bothering her? She has done a beautiful thing to me. ⁷The poor you will always have with you, *d* and you can help them any time

a 29 Or he   *b 33 Some manuscripts alert and pray*   *c 5 Greek than three hundred denarii*   *d 7 See Deut. 15:11.*

13:28 *fig tree.* See notes on 11:13; Lk 21:29.

13:29 *these things.* The signs listed in vv. 5–23 precede the destruction of Jerusalem and/or the end of the age. *it.* Probably a reference to the kingdom of God (see Lk 21:31) coming in the person of King Jesus (see TNIV text note on Mt 24:33).

13:30 *Truly I tell you.* See note on 3:28. *generation.* See note on Lk 21:32.

13:32 *that day.* An OT expression (Am 9:11; Mic 4:6; 5:10). *no one knows.* A specific outline of the future would be a hindrance, not a help, to faith. Certain signs have been given, but not for the purpose of making detailed, sequential predictions (see Ac 1:7; 1Th 5:1 and notes). *nor the Son.* While on earth, even Jesus lived by faith—as his servants must—and obedience was the hallmark of his ministry (see Heb 10:5–7 and note on 10:5).

13:35 *in the evening, or at midnight, or when the rooster crows, or at dawn.* The four watches of the night used by the Romans (see note on Mt 14:25).

13:37 *Watch!* See note on v. 5.

14:1–9 See note on Jn 12:1–11.

14:1 *Passover.* The festival commemorating the time when the angel of the Lord passed over the homes of the Hebrews rather than killing their firstborn sons as he did in the Egyptian homes (see Ex 12:11 and note). The lambs or kids used in the festival were killed on the 14th of Nisan (March-April), and the meal was eaten the same evening between sundown and midnight. Since the Jewish day began at sundown, the Passover Festival took place on the 15th of Nisan (see note on Jn 2:13). *Festival of Unleavened Bread.* This festival followed Passover and lasted seven days (see Ex 12:17; 23:15 and notes).

chief priests. See note on 8:31. *teachers of the law.* See note on Mt 2:4.

14:2 *not during the festival.* During Passover and the weeklong Festival of Unleavened Bread, the population of Jerusalem increased from about 50,000 to several hundred thousand. It would have been too risky to apprehend Jesus with so large and excitable a crowd present.

14:3–9 In John's Gospel this incident is placed before the beginning of Passion Week (see Jn 12:1–11 and note). Matthew and Mark may have placed it here to contrast the hatred of the religious leaders and the betrayal by Judas with the love and devotion of the woman who anointed Jesus.

14:3 *Bethany.* See note on Mt 21:17. *reclining at the table.* The usual posture for eating at a banquet. *Simon the Leper.* See note on Mt 26:6. *woman.* We know from Jn 12:3 that she was Mary, the sister of Martha and Lazarus. *alabaster jar.* A sealed flask with a long neck that was broken off when the contents were used and that contained enough ointment for one application. *nard.* See notes on SS 1:12; Jn 12:3. *poured the perfume on his head.* Anointing was a common custom at feasts (see Ps 23:5 and note). The woman's action expressed her deep devotion to Jesus.

14:4 *Some of those present.* Mt 26:8 identifies them as the disciples, while Jn 12:4–5 singles out Judas Iscariot.

14:5 *given to the poor.* It was a Jewish custom to give gifts to the poor on the evening of Passover (see Jn 13:29).

14:7 *The poor you will always have with you.* See Dt 15:11 and note. Jesus' statement did not express lack of concern for the poor, for their needs lay close to his heart (see Mt 6:2–4; Lk 4:18; 6:20; 14:13,21; 18:22; Jn 13:29). He was simply stating the truth.

you want. *f* But you will not always have me. [8]She did what she could. She poured perfume on my body beforehand to prepare for my burial. *g* [9]Truly I tell you, wherever the gospel is preached throughout the world, *h* what she has done will also be told, in memory of her."

[10]Then Judas Iscariot, one of the Twelve, *i* went to the chief priests to betray Jesus to them. *j* [11]They were delighted to hear this and promised to give him money. So he watched for an opportunity to hand him over.

THE LAST SUPPER

14:12–26pp — Mt 26:17–30; Lk 22:7–23
14:22–25pp — 1Co 11:23–25

[12]On the first day of the Festival of Unleavened Bread, when it was customary to sacrifice the Passover lamb, *k* Jesus' disciples asked him, "Where do you want us to go and make preparations for you to eat the Passover?"

[13]So he sent two of his disciples, telling them, "Go into the city, and a man carrying a jar of water will meet you. Follow him. [14]Say to the owner of the house he enters, 'The Teacher asks: Where is my guest room, where I may eat the Passover with my disciples?' [15]He will show you a large room upstairs, *l* furnished and ready. Make preparations for us there."

[16]The disciples left, went into the city and found things just as Jesus had told them. So they prepared the Passover.

[17]When evening came, Jesus arrived with the Twelve. [18]While they were reclining at the table eating, he said, "Truly I tell you, one of you will betray me—one who is eating with me."

[19]They were saddened, and one by one they said to him, "Surely not I?"

[20]"It is one of the Twelve," he replied, "one who dips bread into the bowl with me. *m* [21]The Son of Man *n* will go just as it is written about him. But woe to that man who betrays the Son of Man! It would be better for him if he had not been born."

[22]While they were eating, Jesus took bread, and when he had given thanks, he broke it *o* and gave it to his disciples, saying, "Take it; this is my body."

[23]Then he took the cup, and when he had given thanks, he gave it to them, and they all drank from it. *p*

[24]"This is my blood of the *a* covenant, *q* which is poured out for many," he said to them. [25]"Truly I tell you, I will not drink again of the fruit of the vine until that day when I drink it new in the kingdom of God." *r*

[26]When they had sung a hymn, they went out to the Mount of Olives. *s*

---

a 24 Some manuscripts *the new*

14:7 *f* Dt 15:11
14:8 *g* Jn 19:40
14:9 *h* S Mt 24:14; Mk 16:15
14:10 *i* Mk 3:16-19 *j* S Mt 10:4
14:12 *k* Ex 12:1-11; Dt 16:1-4; 1Co 5:7
14:15 *l* Ac 1:13
14:20 *m* Jn 13:18-27
14:21 *n* S Mt 8:20
14:22 *o* S Mt 14:19
14:23 *p* 1Co 10:16
14:24 *q* S Mt 26:28
14:25 *r* S Mt 3:2
14:26 *s* S Mt 21:1

14:8 *prepare for my burial.* It was a normal Jewish custom to anoint a dead body with aromatic oils in preparing it for burial (see 16:1 and note). Jesus seems to anticipate suffering a criminal's death, for only in that circumstance was there no anointing of the body.

14:9 *Truly I tell you.* See note on 3:28. *gospel.* See note on 1:1.

14:10 *Judas Iscariot.* See note on 3:19. *chief priests.* See note on 8:31. This was an unexpected opportunity that they seized, even though they had intended not to apprehend Jesus during the festival (see v. 2 and note).

14:11 *money.* Thirty silver coins (see Mt 26:15 and note).

14:12 *first day of the Festival of Unleavened Bread.* Here the 14th of Nisan is meant because Passover lambs were killed on that day (Ex 12:6). The entire eight-day celebration was sometimes referred to as the Festival of Unleavened Bread. *make preparations.* These preparations would have included obtaining food for the meal, such as unleavened bread, wine, bitter herbs and a lamb.

14:13 *two of his disciples.* Peter and John (Lk 22:8). *man carrying a jar.* See note on Lk 22:10.

14:14 *The Teacher asks.* See note on Lk 22:11. *Where is my guest room…?* It was a Jewish custom that anyone in Jerusalem who had a room available would give it upon request to a pilgrim to celebrate the Passover. Apparently Jesus had made previous arrangements with the owner of the house (cf. note on Ac 12:12).

14:16 *as Jesus had told them.* See note on Lk 22:13.

14:17 *evening.* Thursday of Passion Week.

14:18 *reclining at the table eating.* Originally the Passover meal was eaten standing (see Ex 12:11), but in Jesus' time it was cus-

tomary to eat it while reclining (cf. v. 3 and note). *Truly I tell you.* See note on 3:28.

14:20 *dips bread into the bowl with me.* See note on Mt 26:23.

14:21 *Son of Man.* See note on 8:31. *as it is written about him.* Jesus may have had the "suffering servant" passage of Isa 53 in mind.

14:22 The NT gives four accounts of the Lord's Supper (here; Mt 26:26–28; Lk 22:19–20; 1Co 11:23–25). Matthew's account is very much like Mark's, and Luke's and Paul's have similarities. All the accounts include the taking of the bread; the thanksgiving or blessing; the breaking of the bread; the saying, "This is my body"; the taking of the cup; and the explanation of the relation of blood to the covenant. Only Paul and Luke record Jesus' command to continue to celebrate the Supper. *this is my body.* The bread represented his body, given for them (see 1Co 11:24 and note).

14:23 *had given thanks.* The word "Eucharist," often used to refer to the Lord's Supper, is derived from the Greek term used here.

14:24 *my blood of the covenant.* The cup represents the blood of Jesus, which, in turn, represents his poured-out life (i.e., his death). God's commitments to his people in the new covenant are possible only through Christ's atoning death (see Ex 24:6,8; Jer 31:31–34; Lk 22:20; Heb 8:8–12 and notes). *for many.* See Ro 5:15 and note.

14:25 *Truly I tell you.* See note on 3:28. *kingdom of God.* See note on Mt 3:2.

14:26 *hymn.* See note on Mt 26:30. *Mount of Olives.* See note on 11:1.

Bethany, the Mount of Olives and Jerusalem

4. Clearing of the temple
MONDAY
Mt 21:12–17;
Mk 11:15–18;
Lk 19:45–48

Jesus returned to the temple and found the court of the Gentiles full of traders and money changers making a large profit. Jesus drove them out and overturned their benches and tables.

Alternate "Gordon's Calvary"

Present Damascus Gate

Traditional crucifixion and tomb site

NORTH

Jerusalem

Meters Feet
0 100 200 300 500 1,000

KIDRON VALLEY

SOUTH

7. Passover, Last Supper
THURSDAY
Mt 26:17–30;
Mk 14:12–26; Lk 22:7–23

In an upper room Jesus prepared both himself and his disciples for his death. He gave the Passover meal a new meaning. The loaf of bread and cup of wine represented his body, soon to be sacrificed, and his blood, soon to be shed. And so he instituted the "Lord's Supper." After singing a hymn they went to the Garden of Gethsemane, where Jesus prayed in agony, knowing what lay ahead for him.

8. Crucifixion
FRIDAY
Mt 27; Mk 15; Lk 22:66—23:56; Jn 18:28—19:37

Following betrayal, arrest, desertion, false trials, denial, condemnation, beatings and mockery, Jesus was required to carry his cross to The Place of the Skull, where he was crucified with two other prisoners.

9. In the tomb
Jesus' body was placed in the tomb before 6:00 P.M. Friday, when the Sabbath began and all work stopped, and it lay in the tomb throughout the Sabbath.

10. Resurrection
SUNDAY
Mt 28:1–10; Mk 16:1–8; Lk 24:1–49; Jn 20

Early in the morning women went to the tomb and found that the stone closing the tomb's entrance had been rolled back. An angel told them Jesus was alive and gave them a message. Jesus appeared to Mary Magdalene in the garden, to Peter, to two disciples on the road to Emmaus and later that day to all the disciples but Thomas.

5. Day of controversy and parables
TUESDAY
Mt 21:23—24:51; Mk 11:27—13:37; Lk 20:1—21:36

IN JERUSALEM

Jesus evaded the traps set by the priests.

ON THE MOUNT OF OLIVES OVERLOOKING
JERUSALEM

(Tuesday afternoon, exact location unknown)

He taught in parables and warned the people
against the Pharisees. He predicted the
destruction of Herod's great temple and told
his disciples about future events, including his
own return.

6. Day of rest
WEDNESDAY

Although the Gospels do not mention this
day, the counting of the days (Mk 14:1; Jn
12:1) seems to indicate that there was
another day about which the Gospels
record nothing.

KIDRON VALLEY

MOUNT OF OLIVES

To the
Desert
of Judea

Bethphage

The Roman road climbed steeply to the
crest of the Mount of Olives, affording a
spectacular view of the Desert of Judea to
the east and Jerusalem across the Kidron
Valley to the west.

1. Arrival in Bethany
FRIDAY
Jn 12:1

Jesus arrived in Bethany six days before
the Passover to spend some time with his
friends, Mary, Martha and Lazarus. On the following Tuesday evening, while Jesus was still
in Bethany, Mary anointed his feet with costly perfume as an act of humility. This tender
expression of Mary's devotion to
Jesus and her willingness to serve him.

3. Jesus' Entry into Jerusalem
as King
SUNDAY
Mt 21:1–11; Mk 11:1–11;
Lk 19:28–44; Jn 12:12–19

On the first day of the week
Jesus rode into Jerusalem on
a donkey, fulfilling an ancient
prophecy (Zec 9:9). The crowd
welcomed him with the words
of Ps 118:25–26, thus ascribing
to him a Messianic title as the
agent of the Lord, the coming
King of Israel.

2. Sabbath—day of rest
SATURDAY

Not mentioned in the Gospels

The Lord spent the Sabbath day in traditional fashion with his friends.

Bethany

To Jericho and the Dead Sea

14:27 ᶠ Zec 13:7
14:28 ᵘ Mk 16:7
14:30 ᵛ ver 66-72;
Lk 22:34; Jn 13:38
14:31 ʷ Lk 22:33;
Jn 13:37
14:33 ˣ S Mt 4:21
14:34 ʸ Jn 12:27
14:35 ᶻ ver 41;
S Mt 26:18
14:36 ᵃ Ro 8:15;
Gal 4:6 ᵇ S Mt 20:22
ᶜ S Mt 26:39
14:38 ᵈ Mt 6:13
ᵉ Ro 7:22,23
14:41 ᶠ ver 35;
S Mt 26:18
14:43 ᵍ S Mt 10:4
14:45 ʰ S Mt 23:7

JESUS PREDICTS PETER'S DENIAL

14:27–31pp — Mt 26:31–35

²⁷"You will all fall away," Jesus told them, "for it is written;

" 'I will strike the shepherd,
    and the sheep will be scattered.'ᵃ ᵗ

²⁸But after I have risen, I will go ahead of you into Galilee." ᵘ

²⁹Peter declared, "Even if all fall away, I will not."

³⁰"Truly I tell you," Jesus answered, "today—yes, tonight—before the rooster crows twiceᵇ you yourself will disown me three times." ᵛ

³¹But Peter insisted emphatically, "Even if I have to die with you, ʷ I will never disown you." And all the others said the same.

GETHSEMANE

14:32–42pp — Mt 26:36–46; Lk 22:40–46

³²They went to a place called Gethsemane, and Jesus said to his disciples, "Sit here while I pray." ³³He took Peter, James and John ˣ along with him, and he began to be deeply distressed and troubled. ³⁴"My soul is overwhelmed with sorrow to the point of death," ʸ he said to them. "Stay here and keep watch."

³⁵Going a little farther, he fell to the ground and prayed that if possible the hour ᶻ might pass from him. ³⁶"Abba,ᶜ Father," ᵃ he said, "everything is possible for you. Take this cup ᵇ from me. Yet not what I will, but what you will." ᶜ

³⁷Then he returned to his disciples and found them sleeping. "Simon," he said to Peter, "are you asleep? Could you not keep watch for one hour? ³⁸Watch and pray so that you will not fall into temptation. ᵈ The spirit is willing, but the flesh is weak." ᵉ

³⁹Once more he went away and prayed the same thing. ⁴⁰When he came back, he again found them sleeping, because their eyes were heavy. They did not know what to say to him.

⁴¹Returning the third time, he said to them, "Are you still sleeping and resting? Enough! The hour ᶠ has come. Look, the Son of Man is delivered into the hands of sinners. ⁴²Rise! Let us go! Here comes my betrayer!"

JESUS ARRESTED

14:43–50pp — Mt 26:47–56; Lk 22:47–50; Jn 18:3–11

⁴³Just as he was speaking, Judas, ᵍ one of the Twelve, appeared. With him was a crowd armed with swords and clubs, sent from the chief priests, the teachers of the law, and the elders.

⁴⁴Now the betrayer had arranged a signal with them: "The one I kiss is the man; arrest him and lead him away under guard." ⁴⁵Going at once to Jesus, Judas said, "Rabbi!" ʰ and kissed him. ⁴⁶The men seized Jesus and arrested him. ⁴⁷Then one of those

---

ᵃ **27** Zech. 13:7   ᵇ **30** Some early manuscripts do not have *twice.*   ᶜ **36** Aramaic for *Father*

14:27 *You will all fall away.* Not that the disciples will lose their faith in Jesus but that their courage will fail and they will forsake him (see note on Mt 26:31).

14:28 *I will go ahead of you into Galilee.* See 16:7.

14:30 *Truly I tell you.* See note on 3:28. *crows twice.* See TNIV text note here and on v. 72.

14:32 *Gethsemane.* A "garden" (Jn 18:1) on the lower slopes of the Mount of Olives, one of Jesus' favorite places (see Lk 22:39 and note; Jn 18:2). The name is Hebrew and means "oil press," i.e., a place for squeezing the oil from olives.

14:33 *Peter, James and John.* See note on 5:37.

14:36 *Abba, Father.* Expressive of an especially close relationship to God (see also TNIV text note). *this cup.* The chalice of death and of God's wrath that Jesus took from the Father's hand in fulfillment of his mission. What Jesus dreaded was not death as such but the manner of his death as the one who was taking "the sin of the world" (Jn 1:29) upon himself. See 10:38; Mt 26:39 and notes.

14:37 *Simon.* See note on 1:16. Perhaps he is singled out because of his bold assertion that he would not fail Jesus (see vv. 29–31).

14:38 *fall into temptation.* Be attacked by temptation. Here the temptation is to be unfaithful in face of the threatening circumstances confronting them. *The spirit is willing.* The expression is taken from Ps 51:12 (see note on 51:10–12). When one's spirit is under God's control, it strives against human weakness.

14:41 *Son of Man.* See note on 8:31.

14:43 *Judas.* See note on 3:19. *crowd armed with swords and clubs.* Auxiliary police or servants of the court assigned to the task of maintaining public order beyond the precincts of the temple. Jn 18:3 indicates that at least some of the Roman cohort of soldiers were in the arresting group, along with officers of the temple guard. The fact that some carried clubs suggests that they were conscripted at the last moment. *chief priests... teachers of the law... elders.* See notes on 8:31; Mt 2:4. The warrant for Jesus' arrest had been issued by the Sanhedrin.

14:45 *Rabbi.* Hebrew for "(my) teacher." *kissed him.* A token of respect with which disciples customarily greeted their rabbi. See note on Lk 22:47.

standing near drew his sword and struck the servant of the high priest, cutting off his ear.

48"Am I leading a rebellion," said Jesus, "that you have come out with swords and clubs to capture me? 49Every day I was with you, teaching in the temple courts, *i* and you did not arrest me. But the Scriptures must be fulfilled." *j* 50Then everyone deserted him and fled. *k*

51A young man, wearing nothing but a linen garment, was following Jesus. When they seized him, 52he fled naked, leaving his garment behind.

JESUS BEFORE THE SANHEDRIN

14:53–65pp — Mt 26:57–68; Jn 18:12,13,19–24
14:61–63pp — Lk 22:67–71

53They took Jesus to the high priest, and all the chief priests, the elders and the teachers of the law came together. 54Peter followed him at a distance, right into the courtyard of the high priest. *l* There he sat with the guards and warmed himself at the fire. *m*

55The chief priests and the whole Sanhedrin *n* were looking for evidence against Jesus so that they could put him to death, but they did not find any. 56Many testified falsely against him, but their statements did not agree.

57Then some stood up and gave this false testimony against him: 58"We heard him say, 'I will destroy this temple made with human hands and in three days will build another, *o* not made with hands.' " 59Yet even then their testimony did not agree.

60Then the high priest stood up before them and asked Jesus, "Are you not going to answer? What is this testimony that these men are bringing against you?" 61But Jesus remained silent and gave no answer. *p*

Again the high priest asked him, "Are you the Messiah, the Son of the Blessed One?" *q*

62"I am," said Jesus. "And you will see the Son of Man sitting at the right hand of the Mighty One and coming on the clouds of heaven." *r*

63The high priest tore his clothes. *s* "Why do we need any more witnesses?" he asked. 64"You have heard the blasphemy. What do you think?"

14:47 *one of those standing near.* Peter (Jn 18:10). *servant of the high priest.* Malchus (Jn 18:10).

14:48 See note on Mt 26:55.

14:49 *temple courts.* See note on 11:27. *Scriptures must be fulfilled.* Perhaps a reference to Isa 53, or more particularly to Zec 13:7 (see note there), quoted by Jesus in v. 27 and fulfilled (at least in part) at this time (v. 50).

14:50 *deserted him.* In fulfillment of vv. 27–31.

14:51 *young man.* Referred to only in Mark's Gospel. He is not specifically identified, but his anonymity may suggest that he was John Mark, writer of this Gospel (see Introduction: Author; John Mark in the NT). *linen garment.* Ordinarily the outer garment was made of wool. The fine linen garment left behind in the hand of a guard indicates that the youth was from a wealthy family.

14:52 *fled naked.* The absence of an undergarment suggests that he had dressed hastily to follow Jesus.

14:53—15:15 Jesus' trial took place in two stages: a Jewish trial and a Roman trial, each of which had three episodes. For the Jewish trial these were: (1) the preliminary hearing before Annas, the former high priest (reported only in Jn 18:12–14,19–23); (2) the trial before Caiaphas, the ruling high priest, and the Sanhedrin (14:53–65; see Mt 26:57–68; Lk 22:54–65; Jn 18:24); and (3) the final action of the council, which terminated its all-night session (15:1; see Mt 27:1; Lk 22:66–71). The three episodes of the Roman trial were: (1) the trial before Pilate (15:2–5; see Mt 27:11–26; Lk 23:1–5; Jn 18:28—19:16); (2) the trial before Herod Antipas (only in Lk 23:6–12); and (3) the trial before Pilate continued and concluded (15:6–15). Since Matthew, Mark and John give no account of Jesus before Herod Antipas, the trial before Pilate forms a continuous and uninterrupted narrative in these Gospels.

14:53 *high priest.* Caiaphas, son-in-law of Annas, the former high priest (see note on Jn 18:12). *all the chief priests, the elders and the teachers of the law.* The entire Sanhedrin (see note on v. 43).

14:54 *courtyard of the high priest.* The Sanhedrin may have met at Caiaphas's house to ensure secrecy. *warmed himself at the fire.* See note on Jn 18:18.

14:55 *Sanhedrin.* The high court of the Jews. In NT times it was made up of three kinds of members: chief priests, elders and teachers of the law. Its total membership numbered 71, including the high priest, who was presiding officer (see note on Ac 5:21). Under Roman jurisdiction the Sanhedrin was given a great deal of authority, but it could not impose capital punishment (see Mt 27:2; Jn 18:31 and notes).

14:56 *Many testified falsely against him.* In Jewish judicial procedure, witnesses functioned as the prosecution. *did not agree.* According to Dt 17:6 (see note there) a person could not be put to death except on the testimony of two or more witnesses.

14:58 This statement of Jesus is probably an allusion to what is reported in Jn 2:19 (see note there).

14:61 *remained silent.* See Isa 53:7 and note. *Messiah.* See TNIV text note on 1:1. *Son of the Blessed One.* "The Blessed One" was a way of referring to God without pronouncing his name (cf. note on 11:30). The title was therefore equivalent to "Son of God," though in this context it would seem not to refer to deity but to royal Messiahship, since in popular Jewish belief the Messiah was to be a man, not God.

14:62 See Mt 26:64 and note. *I am.* See Ex 3:14 and note; Jn 8:58–59 and note on 8:58. *Son of Man.* See note on 8:31. This Son of Man saying brings together Da 7:13 (see note there) and Ps 110:1 (see note there).

14:63 *tore his clothes.* A sign of great grief or shock (see Ge 37:29; 2Ki 18:37 and note; 19:1). In the case of the high priest it was a form of judicial act expressing the fact that he regarded Jesus' answer as blasphemous (see note on Mt 26:65).

14:64 *blasphemy.* Not only involved reviling the name of God (see Lev 24:10–16) but also included any affront to his majesty or authority (see Mk 2:7 and note; 3:28–29; Jn 5:18 and note; 10:33). Jesus' claim to be the Messiah and, in fact, to have majesty and authority belonging only to God was there-

---

14:49 *i* S Mt 26:55
j Isa 53:7-12;
S Mt 1:22
14:50 *k* ver 27
14:54 *l* S Mt 26:3
m Jn 18:18
14:55 *n* S Mt 5:22
14:58 *o* S Jn 2:19
14:61 *p* Isa 53:7;
Mt 27:12,14; Mk 15:5;
Lk 23:9; Jn 19:9
q Mt 16:16; Jn 4:25,26
14:62 *r* S Rev 1:7
14:63 *s* Lev 10:6;
21:10; Nu 14:6;
Ac 14:14

14:64 *t* Lev 24:16
14:65 *u* S Mt 16:21
14:66 *v* ver 54
14:67 *w* ver 54
x S Mk 1:24
14:68 *y* ver 30,72
14:70 *z* ver 30,68,
72 *a* Ac 2:7
14:71 *b* ver 30,72
14:72 *c* ver 30,68
15:1 *d* Mt 27:1;
Lk 22:66 *e* S Mt 5:22
f S Mt 27:2
15:2 *g* ver 9,12,18,
26; S Mt 2:2
15:5 *h* S Mk 14:61
15:9 *i* S ver 2
15:11 *j* Ac 3:14

They all condemned him as worthy of death. *t* 65 Then some began to spit at him; they blindfolded him, struck him with their fists, and said, "Prophesy!" And the guards took him and beat him. *u*

PETER DISOWNS JESUS

14:66–72pp — Mt 26:69–75; Lk 22:56–62; Jn 18:16–18,25–27

66 While Peter was below in the courtyard, *v* one of the servant girls of the high priest came by. 67 When she saw Peter warming himself, *w* she looked closely at him.

"You also were with that Nazarene, Jesus," *x* she said.

68 But he denied it. "I don't know or understand what you're talking about," *y* he said, and went out into the entryway. *a*

69 When the servant girl saw him there, she said again to those standing around, "This fellow is one of them." 70 Again he denied it. *z*

After a little while, those standing near said to Peter, "Surely you are one of them, for you are a Galilean." *a*

71 He began to call down curses, and he swore to them, "I don't know this man you're talking about." *b*

72 Immediately the rooster crowed the second time. *b* Then Peter remembered the word Jesus had spoken to him: "Before the rooster crows twice *c* you will disown me three times." *c* And he broke down and wept.

JESUS BEFORE PILATE

15:2–15pp — Mt 27:11–26; Lk 23:2,3,18–25; Jn 18:29—19:16

15 Very early in the morning, the chief priests, with the elders, the teachers of the law *d* and the whole Sanhedrin, *e* reached a decision. They bound Jesus, led him away and handed him over to Pilate. *f*

2 "Are you the king of the Jews?" *g* asked Pilate.

"You have said so," Jesus replied.

3 The chief priests accused him of many things. 4 So again Pilate asked him, "Aren't you going to answer? See how many things they are accusing you of."

5 But Jesus still made no reply, *h* and Pilate was amazed.

6 Now it was the custom at the festival to release a prisoner whom the people requested. 7 A man called Barabbas was in prison with the insurrectionists who had committed murder in the uprising. 8 The crowd came up and asked Pilate to do for them what he usually did.

9 "Do you want me to release to you the king of the Jews?" *i* asked Pilate, 10 knowing it was out of envy that the chief priests had handed Jesus over to him. 11 But the chief priests stirred up the crowd to have Pilate release Barabbas *j* instead.

12 "What shall I do, then, with the one you call the king of the Jews?" Pilate asked them.

13 "Crucify him!" they shouted.

---

a 68 Some early manuscripts *entryway and the rooster crowed*   *b* 72 Some early manuscripts do not have *the second time.*   *c* 72 Some early manuscripts do not have *twice.*

---

fore regarded by Caiaphas as blasphemy, for which the Mosaic law prescribed death by stoning (Lev 24:16).

14:65 *began to spit at him ... struck him with their fists.* Conventional gestures of rejection and condemnation (see Nu 12:14; Dt 25:9; Job 30:10; Isa 50:6 and note). *blindfolded him.* A Rabbinic interpretation of Isa 11:2–4 held that the Messiah could judge by smell without the aid of sight. *Prophesy!* Say who it was who struck you!

14:66 *below.* While Jesus was being beaten in an upstairs room of Caiaphas's house, Peter was below in the courtyard. *one of the servant girls.* The doorkeeper (see Jn 18:16; cf. Ac 12:3).

14:67 *Nazarene.* See note on Mt 2:23.

14:68 *I don't know or understand what you're talking about.* An expression used in Jewish law courts for a formal, legal denial.

14:70 *Galilean.* Peter's Galilean dialect showed him to be from Galilee, and his presence among the Judeans in the courtyard suggested he was a follower of Jesus.

14:72 *Before ... times.* See v. 30.

15:1 *Very early in the morning.* The working day of a Roman official began at daylight. *morning.* Friday of Passion Week. *Sanhedrin.* See note on 14:55. *reached a decision.* Apparently to

accuse Jesus before the civil authority for treason rather than blasphemy (see Lk 23:1–14 and note on 23:2). *Pilate.* See note on Lk 3:1.

15:2 *king of the Jews.* See Jn 18:33–37 and notes on 18:33,36. *asked Pilate.* Judgment in a Roman court was the sole responsibility of the imperial magistrate.

15:3 *many things.* See Lk 23:2 and note. Multiple charges were common in criminal cases.

15:4 *Aren't you going to answer?* If Jesus made no defense, according to Roman law Pilate would have to pronounce against him.

15:5 *made no reply.* See 14:61; Isa 53:7 and note.

15:6 *custom.* See note on Jn 18:39. *festival.* Passover (see 14:1–2 and notes).

15:7 *Barabbas.* See Mt 27:16–17 and note on 27:16; probably a member of the Zealots, a Jewish revolutionary group (see Mt 10:4; Jn 18:40; Ac 5:37 and note; see also chart, p. 1650). *uprising.* Nothing from other sources is known about this insurrection, though Mark speaks of it as if it were well known. Under the Roman governors such revolts were common (see Lk 13:1).

15:13–14 *Crucify.* See note on v. 24.

15:15 *k* Isa 53:6
15:16 *l* Jn 18:28, 33;
19:9
15:18 *m* S ver 2
15:20 *n* Heb 13:12
15:21 *o* S Mt 27:32
p Ro 16:13 *q* Mt 27:32;
Lk 23:26
15:23 *r* ver 36;
Ps 69:21; Pr 31:6
15:24 *s* Ps 22:18
15:26 *t* S ver 2
15:29 *u* Ps 22:7;
109:25 *v* S Jn 2:19
15:31 *w* Ps 22:7
15:32 *x* S Mk 14:61

¹⁴"Why? What crime has he committed?" asked Pilate.

But they shouted all the louder, "Crucify him!"

¹⁵Wanting to satisfy the crowd, Pilate released Barabbas to them. He had Jesus flogged, *k* and handed him over to be crucified.

THE SOLDIERS MOCK JESUS

15:16–20pp — Mt 27:27–31

¹⁶The soldiers led Jesus away into the palace *l* (that is, the Praetorium) and called together the whole company of soldiers. ¹⁷They put a purple robe on him, then twisted together a crown of thorns and set it on him. ¹⁸And they began to call out to him, "Hail, king of the Jews!" *m* ¹⁹Again and again they struck him on the head with a staff and spit on him. Falling on their knees, they paid homage to him. ²⁰And when they had mocked him, they took off the purple robe and put his own clothes on him. Then they led him out *n* to crucify him.

THE CRUCIFIXION OF JESUS

15:22–32pp — Mt 27:33–44; Lk 23:33–43; Jn 19:17–24

²¹A certain man from Cyrene, *o* Simon, the father of Alexander and Rufus, *p* was passing by on his way in from the country, and they forced him to carry the cross. *q* ²²They brought Jesus to the place called Golgotha (which means "the place of the skull"). ²³Then they offered him wine mixed with myrrh, *r* but he did not take it. ²⁴And they crucified him. Dividing up his clothes, they cast lots *s* to see what each would get.

²⁵It was nine in the morning when they crucified him. ²⁶The written notice of the charge against him read: THE KING OF THE JEWS. *t* ²⁷[28]They crucified two rebels with him, one on his right and one on his left. ²⁹Those who passed by hurled insults at him, shaking their heads *u* and saying, "So! You who are going to destroy the temple and build it in three days, *v* ³⁰come down from the cross and save yourself!"

³¹In the same way the chief priests and the teachers of the law mocked him *w* among themselves. "He saved others," they said, "but he can't save himself! ³²Let this Messiah, *x*

15:15 *flogged.* The Romans used a whip made of several strips of leather, into which were embedded (near the ends) pieces of bone and lead. The Jews limited the number of stripes to a maximum of 40 (in practice to 39 in case of a miscount; see Dt 25:3 and note), but no such limitation was recognized by the Romans, and victims of Roman floggings often did not survive (cf. Ac 22:24 and note).

15:16 *Praetorium.* The word was used originally of a general's tent or of the headquarters in a military camp (see note on v. 1). *whole company.* The soldiers quartered in the Praetorium were recruited from non-Jewish inhabitants of the Holy Land and assigned to the military governor.

15:17 *purple robe.* Probably an old military cloak, whose color suggested royalty (see Ex 25:4; Mt 27:28; Ac 16:14 and notes). *crown of thorns.* Made from the branches of a thorny tree, of which there were many in the Holy Land. Both robe and crown were parts of the mock royal attire placed on Jesus.

15:18 *Hail, king of the Jews!* A mocking salutation that corresponded to "Hail, Caesar!"

15:19 *spit on him.* Probably a parody on the kiss of homage that was customary when greeting royalty (see note on 14:65).

15:20 *mocked him.* Cf. Ps 22:6–7; Isa 50:6 and note.

15:21 *Cyrene.* See Ac 6:9 and note. *Simon.* Probably a Jew who was in Jerusalem to celebrate the Passover. *Alexander and Rufus.* Mentioned only by Mark, but referred to in such a way as to suggest that they were known by those to whom he wrote (cf. Ro 16:13). *carry the cross.* Men condemned to death were usually forced to carry a beam of the cross, often weighing 30 or 40 pounds, to the place of crucifixion. Jesus started out by carrying his (see Jn 19:17 and note), but he had been so weakened by flogging that Simon was pressed into service.

15:22 *the place of the skull.* It may have been a small hill that looked like a skull, or it may have been so named because of the many executions that took place there.

15:23 *wine mixed with myrrh.* The Talmud gives evidence that incense was mixed with wine to deaden pain (cf. Pr 31:6). Myrrh

is a spice derived from plants native to the Arabian deserts and parts of Africa (see note on Ge 37:25).

15:24 *crucified.* A Roman means of execution in which the prisoner was nailed to a cross (see note on Jn 19:17). Heavy, wrought-iron nails were driven through the wrists and the heel bones. If the victims lingered too long, death was hastened by breaking their legs (see Jn 19:33 and note). Archaeologists have discovered the bones of a crucified man, near Jerusalem, dating between A.D. 7 and 66, which shed light on the position of a person when nailed to a cross. Only slaves, the basest of criminals, and offenders who were not Roman citizens were executed in this manner. First-century authors vividly describe the agony and disgrace of being crucified (see Php 2:8 and note). *Dividing up his clothes.* It was the accepted right of the executioner's squad to claim the minor possessions of the victim. Jesus' clothing probably consisted of an under and an outer garment, a belt, sandals and possibly a head covering (see note on Jn 19:18). *cast lots.* See Ps 22:18 and introduction to that psalm; see also Jn 19:23–24 and notes.

15:25 *nine in the morning.* See Lk 23:44; Jn 19:14 and notes.

15:26 *charge against him.* It was customary to write the charge on a wooden board that was carried before the victim as he walked to the place of execution, and then the board was affixed to the cross above his head. THE KING OF THE JEWS. The wording of the charge differs slightly in the Gospels, but all agree that Jesus was crucified for claiming to be the king of the Jews. One possible reconstruction of the original is THIS IS JESUS OF NAZARETH, THE KING OF THE JEWS (cf. Mt 27:37; Lk 23:38; Jn 19:19).

15:27[28] *two rebels.* Signifies men guilty of insurrection, who were crucified for high treason. The earlier and more reliable Greek manuscripts do not have verse 28. It was probably added from Lk 22:37 (quoting Isa 53:12). Mark does not include many OT quotations (see Introduction: Recipients).

15:29 See 14:58 and note.

15:32 *Messiah.* See TNIV text note on 1:1. *Those crucified with*

15:32 *y* S ver 2
15:33 *z* Am 8:9
15:34 *a* Ps 22:1
15:36 *b* ver 23;
Ps 69:21
15:37 *c* Jn 19:30
15:38 *d* Heb 10:19,
20
15:39 *e* ver 45
f Mk 1:1,11; 9:7;
S Mt 4:3
15:40 *g* Ps 38:11
h Mk 16:1; Lk 24:10;
Jn 19:25
15:41 *i* Mt 27:55,56;
Lk 8:2,3
15:42 *j* Mt 27:62;
Jn 19:31
15:43 *k* S Mt 5:22
l S Mt 3:2; Lk 2:25,38
15:45 *m* ver 9
15:46 *n* Mk 16:3
15:47 *o* ver 40

this king of Israel, *y* come down now from the cross, that we may see and believe." Those crucified with him also heaped insults on him.

THE DEATH OF JESUS

15:33–41pp — Mt 27:45–56; Lk 23:44–49; Jn 19:29–30

³³At noon, darkness came over the whole land until three in the afternoon. *z* ³⁴And at three in the afternoon Jesus cried out in a loud voice, *"Eloi, Eloi, lema sabachthani?"* (which means "My God, my God, why have you forsaken me?"). *a a*

³⁵When some of those standing near heard this, they said, "Listen, he's calling Elijah."

³⁶Someone ran, filled a sponge with wine vinegar, *b* put it on a staff, and offered it to Jesus to drink. "Now leave him alone. Let's see if Elijah comes to take him down," he said.

³⁷With a loud cry, Jesus breathed his last. *c*

³⁸The curtain of the temple was torn in two from top to bottom. *d* ³⁹And when the centurion, *e* who stood there in front of Jesus, saw how he died, *b* he said, "Surely this man was the Son of God!" *f*

⁴⁰Some women were watching from a distance. *g* Among them were Mary Magdalene, Mary the mother of James the younger and of Joseph, *c* and Salome. *h* ⁴¹In Galilee these women had followed him and cared for his needs. Many other women who had come up with him to Jerusalem were also there. *i*

THE BURIAL OF JESUS

15:42–47pp — Mt 27:57–61; Lk 23:50–56; Jn 19:38–42

⁴²It was Preparation Day (that is, the day before the Sabbath). *j* So as evening approached, ⁴³Joseph of Arimathea, a prominent member of the Council, *k* who was himself waiting for the kingdom of God, *l* went boldly to Pilate and asked for Jesus' body. ⁴⁴Pilate was surprised to hear that he was already dead. Summoning the centurion, he asked him if Jesus had already died. ⁴⁵When he learned from the centurion *m* that it was so, he gave the body to Joseph. ⁴⁶So Joseph bought some linen cloth, took down the body, wrapped it in the linen, and placed it in a tomb cut out of rock. Then he rolled a stone against the entrance of the tomb. *n* ⁴⁷Mary Magdalene and Mary the mother of Joseph *o* saw where he was laid.

a 34 Psalm 22:1   *b* 39 Some manuscripts *saw that he died with such a cry*   *c* 40 Greek *Joses,* a variant of *Joseph;* also in verse 47

him. One of the criminals later repented and asked to be included in Jesus' kingdom (Lk 23:39–43).

15:34 The words were spoken in a dialect of Aramaic, one of the languages commonly spoken in the Holy Land in Jesus' day. They reveal how deeply Jesus felt his abandonment by God as he bore "the sin of the world" (Jn 1:29; but see introduction to Ps 22 and note on Ps 22:1).

15:35 *Elijah.* The bystanders mistook the first words of Jesus' cry (*"Eloi, Eloi"*) to be a cry for Elijah. It was commonly believed that Elijah would come in times of critical need to protect the innocent and rescue the righteous (v. 36).

15:36 *wine vinegar.* A sour wine, the drink of laborers and common soldiers (see note on Lk 23:36).

15:37 *With a loud cry.* See note on Jn 19:30. The strength of the cry indicates that Jesus did not die the ordinary death of those crucified, who normally suffered long periods of complete agony, exhaustion and then unconsciousness before dying (see note on v. 24).

A **15:38** *curtain of the temple.* The curtain that separated the Holy Place from the Most Holy Place (see Ex 26:31–35; 26:31 and notes). The tearing of the curtain indicated that Christ had entered heaven itself for us so that we too may now enter God's presence (see Heb 9:8–10,12; 10:19–20 and notes).

15:39 *centurion.* A commander of 100 men in the Roman army (see note on Ac 10:1). *saw how he died.* See note on v. 37. *Son of God.* See note on Mt 27:54.

C **15:40** *Mary Magdalene.* From Lk 8:2 we learn that Jesus had driven seven demons out of her. *Mary the mother of James the younger and of Joseph.* See v. 47; 16:1. *Salome.* Probably the wife of Zebedee and the mother of James and John (see Mt 27:56).

15:41 *women had . . . cared for his needs.* See notes on Mt 27:55; Lk 8:3.

15:42 *Preparation Day.* Friday. Since it was now late in the afternoon, there was an urgency to get Jesus' body down from the cross before sundown, when the Sabbath began.

15:43 *Joseph.* See note on Lk 23:50. *Arimathea.* See note on Mt 27:57. *Council.* The Sanhedrin (see note on 14:55). *kingdom of God.* See note on Mt 3:2. *Pilate.* See note on v. 1. *asked for Jesus' body.* See note on Lk 23:52.

15:44 *surprised.* Crucified men often lived two or three days before dying, and the early death of Jesus was therefore extraordinary.

15:45 *gave the body to Joseph.* The release of the body of one condemned for high treason, and especially to someone who was not an immediate relative, was quite unusual.

B **15:46** *tomb cut out of rock.* Mt 27:60 states that the tomb belonged to Joseph and that it was new, i.e., it had not been used before. Its location was in a garden very near the site of the crucifixion (see Jn 19:41). There is archaeological evidence that the traditional site of the burial of Jesus (the Church of the Holy Sepulchre in Jerusalem) was a cemetery during the

JESUS HAS RISEN

16:1–8pp — Mt 28:1–8; Lk 24:1–10

16 When the Sabbath was over, Mary Magdalene, Mary the mother of James, and Salome bought spices *p* so that they might go to anoint Jesus' body. [2]Very early on the first day of the week, just after sunrise, they were on their way to the tomb [3]and they asked each other, "Who will roll the stone away from the entrance of the tomb?" *q*

[4]But when they looked up, they saw that the stone, which was very large, had been rolled away. [5]As they entered the tomb, they saw a young man dressed in a white robe *r* sitting on the right side, and they were alarmed.

[6]"Don't be alarmed," he said. "You are looking for Jesus the Nazarene, *s* who was crucified. He has risen! He is not here. See the place where they laid him. [7]But go, tell his disciples and Peter, 'He is going ahead of you into Galilee. There you will see him, *t* just as he told you.' " *u*

[8]Trembling and bewildered, the women went out and fled from the tomb. They said nothing to anyone, because they were afraid.

[The earliest manuscripts and some other ancient witnesses do not have Mark 16:9-20.]

[9]*When Jesus rose early on the first day of the week, he appeared first to Mary Magdalene, v out of whom he had driven seven demons. [10]She went and told those who had been with him and who were mourning and weeping. [11]When they heard that Jesus was alive and that she had seen him, they did not believe it. w*

[12]*Afterward Jesus appeared in a different form to two of them while they were walking in the country. x [13]These returned and reported it to the rest; but they did not believe them either.*

[14]*Later Jesus appeared to the Eleven as they were eating; he rebuked them for their lack of faith and their stubborn refusal to believe those who had seen him after he had risen. y*

[15]*He said to them, "Go into all the world and preach the gospel to all creation. z [16]Whoever believes and is baptized will be saved, but whoever does not believe will be condemned. a [17]And these signs b will accompany those who believe: In my name they will drive out demons; c they will speak in new tongues; d [18]they will pick up snakes e with their hands; and when they drink deadly poison, it will not hurt them at all; they will place their hands on f sick people, and they will get well. "*

[19]*After the Lord Jesus had spoken to them, he was taken up into heaven g and he sat at the right hand of God. h [20]Then the disciples went out and preached everywhere, and the Lord worked with them and confirmed his word by the signs i that accompanied it.*

16:1 *p* Lk 23:56;
Jn 19:39,40
16:3 *q* Mk 15:46
16:5 *r* Jn 20:12
16:6 *s* Mk 1:24
16:7 *t* Jn 21:1-23
u Mk 14:28
16:9 *v* Mk 15:47;
Jn 20:11-18
16:11 *w* ver 13,14;
Lk 24:11
16:12 *x* Lk 24:13-32
16:14 *y* Lk 24:36-43
16:15 *z* Mt 28:18-
20; Lk 24:47,48;
Ac 1:8
16:16 *a* Jn 3:16,18,
36; Ac 16:31
16:17 *b* S Jn 4:48
c Mk 9:38; Lk 10:17;
Ac 5:16; 8:7; 16:18;
19:13-16 *d* Ac 2:4;
10:46; 19:6; 1Co 12:10,
28, 30; 13:1; 14:2-39
16:18 *e* Lk 10:19;
Ac 28:3-5 *f* S Ac 6:6
16:19 *g* Lk 24:50, 51;
Jn 6:62; Ac 1:9-11;
1Ti 3:16 *h* Ps 110:1;
Mt 26:64; Ac 2:33;
5:31; Ro 8:34; Col 3:1;
Heb 1:3; 12:2
16:20 *i* S Jn 4:48

first century A.D. *stone*. A large (see 16:4), disc-shaped stone that rolled in a sloped channel.

16:1 *Sabbath was over.* About 6:00 P.M. Saturday evening. No purchases were possible on the Sabbath. *Mary Magdalene, Mary the mother of James, and Salome.* See note on 15:40. *spices.* Embalming was not practiced by the Jews. These spices were brought as an act of devotion and love (see note on Lk 23:56). *anoint Jesus' body.* The women had no expectation of Jesus' resurrection.

16:3 *Who will roll the stone away . . . ?* Setting the large stone in place was a relatively easy task, but once it had slipped into the groove cut in bedrock in front of the entrance it was very difficult to remove.

16:5 *As they entered the tomb.* Inside the large opening of the facade of the tomb was a forechamber, at the back of which a low, rectangular opening led to the burial chamber. *young man dressed in a white robe.* Mt 28:2 identifies him as an angel. See Lk 24:4 and note.

16:6 *Nazarene.* See note on Mt 2:23. *crucified.* See note on 15:24. *He has risen!* The climax of Mark's Gospel is the resurrection, without which Jesus' death, though noble, would be indescribably tragic (see 1Co 15:12–20 and notes). But in the resurrection he "was appointed the Son of God in power by his resurrection from the dead" (Ro 1:4; see TNIV text note there).

16:7 *and Peter.* Jesus showed special concern for Peter, in view

of his confident boasting and subsequent denials (14:29–31, 66–72). *just as he told you.* See 14:28.

16:9–20 Serious doubt exists as to whether these verses belong to the Gospel of Mark. They are absent from important early manuscripts and display certain peculiarities of vocabulary, style and theological content that are unlike the rest of Mark. His Gospel probably ended at 16:8, or its original ending has been lost.

16:9 *Mary Magdalene.* See note on 15:40.

16:11,13 *did not believe.* See vv. 14,16; cf. Jn 20:24–29 and notes on 20:25,29.

16:12–13 A shortened account of the two men going to Emmaus (see Lk 24:13–35).

16:14 *the Eleven.* Judas Iscariot had committed suicide (see Mt 27:5 and note).

16:15–16 See the Great Commission in Mt 28:18–20 (see also note on Mt 28:19–20; cf. Lk 24:46–49; Jn 20:21–23; Ac 1:8.

16:16 *believes and is baptized.* See notes on 1:4; Ro 6:3–4.

16:18 *pick up snakes.* Cf. Paul in Ac 28:1–6. *drink deadly poison.* No occurrence of drinking deadly poison without harm is found in the NT.

16:19 *taken up into heaven.* The ascension was witnessed by the apostles (see Lk 24:51; Ac 1:9; cf. 1Ti 3:16 and note). *right hand of God.* See 14:62; Ps 110:1 and note.

AUTHOR

The author's name does not appear in the book, but much unmistakable evidence points to Luke. This Gospel is a companion volume to the book of Acts, and the language and structure of these two books indicate that both were written by the same person. They are addressed to the same individual, Theophilus, and the second volume refers to the first (Ac 1:1). Certain sections in Acts use the pronoun "we" (Ac 16:10–17; 20:5–15; 21:1–18; 27:1—28:16), indicating that the author was with Paul when the events described in these passages took place. By process of elimination, Paul's "dear friend Luke, the doctor" (Col 4:14) and "fellow worker" (Phm 24) becomes the most likely candidate. His authorship is supported by the uniform testimony of early Christian writings (e.g., the Muratorian Canon, A.D. 170, and the works of Irenaeus, c. 180).

Luke was probably a Gentile by birth, well educated in Greek culture, a physician by profession, a companion of Paul at various times from his second missionary journey to his final imprisonment in Rome and a loyal friend who remained with the apostle after others had deserted him (2Ti 4:11).

Antioch (of Syria) and Philippi are among the places suggested as his hometown.

RECIPIENT AND PURPOSE

The Gospel is specifically directed to Theophilus (1:3), whose name means "one who loves God" and almost certainly refers to a particular person rather than to lovers of God in general. The use of "most excellent" with the name further indicates an individual and supports the idea that he was a Roman official or at least of high position and wealth. He was possibly Luke's patron, responsible for seeing that the writings were copied and distributed. Such a dedication to the publisher was common at that time.

Theophilus, however, was more than a publisher. The message of this Gospel was intended for his own instruction (1:4), as well as for the instruction of those among whom the book would be circulated. The fact that the Gospel was initially directed to Theophilus does not narrow or limit its purpose. It was written to strengthen the faith of all believers and to answer the attacks of unbelievers. It was presented to displace some disconnected and ill-founded reports about Jesus (see 1:1–4 and note). Luke wanted to show that the place of the Gentile Christian in God's kingdom is based on the teaching of Jesus. He wanted to commend the preaching of the gospel to the whole world.

DATE AND PLACE OF WRITING

The two most commonly suggested periods for dating the Gospel of Luke are: (1) A.D. 59–63, and (2) the 70s or the 80s (see essay and chart, p. 1601).

The place of writing was probably Rome, though Achaia, Ephesus and Caesarea have also been suggested. The place to which it was sent would, of course, depend on the residence of Theophilus. By its detailed designations of places in the Holy Land, the Gospel seems to be intended for readers who were unfamiliar with that land. Antioch, Achaia and Ephesus are possible destinations.

STYLE

Luke had outstanding command of the Greek language. His vocabulary is extensive and rich, and his style at times approaches that of classical Greek (as in the preface, 1:1–4), while at other times it is quite Semitic (1:5—2:52)—often like the Septuagint (the pre-Christian Greek translation of the OT).

CHARACTERISTICS

The third Gospel presents the works and teachings of Jesus that are especially important for understanding the way of salvation. Its scope is complete from the birth of Christ to his ascension, its arrangement is orderly and it appeals to both Jews and Gentiles. The writing is characterized by literary excellence, historical detail and warm, sensitive understanding of Jesus and those around him.

Since the Synoptic Gospels (Matthew, Mark and Luke) report many of the same episodes in Jesus' life, one would expect much similarity in their accounts. The dissimilarities reveal the distinctive emphases of the separate writers. Luke's characteristic themes include: (1) universality, recognition of Gentiles as well as Jews in God's plan (see, e.g., 2:30–32 and notes on 2:31; 3:6); (2) emphasis on prayer, especially Jesus' praying before important occasions (see note on 3:21); (3) joy at the announcement of the gospel or "good news" (see note on 1:14); (4) special concern for the role of women (see, e.g., 8:1–3 and notes); (5) special interest in the poor (some of the rich were included among Jesus' followers, but he seemed closest to the poor; see note on 12:33); (6) concern for sinners (Jesus was a friend to those deep in sin); (7) stress on the family circle (Jesus' activity included men, women and children, with the setting frequently in the home); (8) repeated use of the Messianic title "Son of Man" (used 25 times; see 19:10; Da 7:13 and notes); (9) emphasis on the Holy Spirit (see note on 4:1); (10) inclusion of more parables than any other Gospel (see chart, p. 1752); and (11) emphasis on praising God (see 1:64; 24:53 and notes).

SOURCES

Although Luke acknowledges that many others had written of Jesus' life (1:1), he does not indicate that he relied solely on these reports for his own writing. He used personal investigation and arrangement, based on testimony from "eyewitnesses and servants of the word" (1:2)—including the preaching and oral accounts of the apostles. His language differences from the other Synoptics and his blocks of distinctive material (e.g., 10:1—18:14; 19:1–28) indicate independent work, though he obviously used some of the same sources (see essay, p. 1601).

PLAN

Luke's account of Jesus' ministry can be divided into three major parts: (1) the events that occurred in and around Galilee (4:14—9:50), (2) those that took place in Judea and Perea (9:51—19:27) and (3) those of the final week in Jerusalem (19:28—24:53). Luke's uniqueness is especially seen in the amount of material devoted to Jesus' closing ministry in Judea and Perea. This material is predominantly made up of accounts of Jesus' discourses. Twenty-one of the 28 parables that occur in Luke are found in 10:30—19:27. Of the 20 miracles recorded in Luke, only 5 appear in 9:51—19:27. Already in the ninth chapter (see note on 9:51) Jesus is seen anticipating his final appearance in Jerusalem and his crucifixion (see note on 13:22).

The main theme of the Gospel is the nature of Jesus' Messiahship and mission, and a key verse is 19:10.

1:2 *ª*Mk 1:1;
Jn 15:27; Ac 1:21,22
*ᵇ*Heb 2:3; 1Pe 5:1;
2Pe 1:16; 1Jn 1:1
*ᶜ*S Mk 4:14
1:3 *ᵈ*Ac 11:4
*ᵉ*Ac 24:3; 26:25
*ᶠ*Ac 1:1
1:4 *ᵍ*Jn 20:31;
Ac 2:42
1:5 *ʰ*Mt 2:1
*ⁱ*1Ch 24:10
1:6 *ʲ*Ge 6:9; Dt 5:33;
1Ki 9:4; Lk 2:25
1:8 *ᵏ*1Ch 24:19;
2Ch 8:14
1:9 *ˡ*Ac 1:26
*ᵐ*Ex 30:7,8;
1Ch 23:13; 2Ch 29:11;
Ps 141:2
1:10 *ⁿ*Lev 16:17
1:11 *ᵒ*S Ac 5:19
*ᵖ*Ex 30:1-10
1:12 *q*Jdg 6:22,23;
13:22
1:13 *ʳ*ver 30;
S Mt 14:27 *ˢ*ver 60,
63; S Mt 3:1
1:14 *ᵗ*ver 58
1:15 *ᵘ*Nu 6:3;
Lev 10:9; Jdg 13:4;
Lk 7:33 *ᵛ*ver 41,67;
Ac 2:4; 4:8,31; 6:3,5;
9:17; 11:24; Eph 5:18;
S Ac 10:44 *ʷ*Jer 1:5;
Gal 1:15
1:17 *ˣ*ver 76
*ʸ*S Mt 11:14 *ᶻ*Mal 4:5,
6 *ª*S Mt 3:3

INTRODUCTION

1:1–4Ref — Ac 1:1

1 Many have undertaken to draw up an account of the things that have been fulfilled *ª* among us, ²just as they were handed down to us by those who from the first *ª* were eyewitnesses *ᵇ* and servants of the word. *ᶜ* ³With this in mind, since I myself have carefully investigated everything from the beginning, I too decided to write an orderly account *ᵈ* for you, most excellent *ᵉ* Theophilus, *ᶠ* ⁴so that you may know the certainty of the things you have been taught. *ᵍ*

THE BIRTH OF JOHN THE BAPTIST FORETOLD

⁵In the time of Herod king of Judea *ʰ* there was a priest named Zechariah, who belonged to the priestly division of Abijah; *ⁱ* his wife Elizabeth was also a descendant of Aaron. ⁶Both of them were righteous in the sight of God, observing all the Lord's commands and decrees blamelessly. *ʲ* ⁷But they were childless because Elizabeth was not able to conceive, and they were both well advanced in years.

⁸Once when Zechariah's division was on duty and he was serving as priest before God, *ᵏ* ⁹he was chosen by lot, *ˡ* according to the custom of the priesthood, to go into the temple of the Lord and burn incense. *ᵐ* ¹⁰And when the time for the burning of incense came, all the assembled worshipers were praying outside. *ⁿ*

¹¹Then an angel *ᵒ* of the Lord appeared to him, standing at the right side of the altar of incense. *ᵖ* ¹²When Zechariah saw him, he was startled and was gripped with fear. *q* ¹³But the angel said to him: "Do not be afraid, *ʳ* Zechariah; your prayer has been heard. Your wife Elizabeth will bear you a son, and you are to call him John. *ˢ* ¹⁴He will be a joy and delight to you, and many will rejoice because of his birth, *ᵗ* ¹⁵for he will be great in the sight of the Lord. He is never to take wine or other fermented drink, *ᵘ* and he will be filled with the Holy Spirit *ᵛ* even before he is born. *ʷ* ¹⁶Many of the people of Israel will he bring back to the Lord their God. ¹⁷And he will go on before the Lord, *ˣ* in the spirit and power of Elijah, *ʸ* to turn the hearts of the parents to their children *ᶻ* and the disobedient to the wisdom of the righteous—to make ready a people prepared for the Lord." *ª*

ª 1 Or *been surely believed*

1:1–4 Using language similar to classical Greek, Luke begins with a formal preface, common to historical works of that time, in which he states his purpose for writing and identifies the recipient. He acknowledges other reports on the subject, shows the need for this new work and states his method of approach and sources of information.

1:1 *things … fulfilled among us.* Things prophesied in the OT and now fully accomplished.

1:2 *handed down.* A technical term for passing on information as authoritative tradition (see 1Co 15:3 and note). *eyewitnesses and servants of the word.* Luke, though not an eyewitness himself, received testimony from those who were eyewitnesses and were dedicated to spreading the gospel. Apostolic preaching and interviews with other individuals associated with Jesus' ministry were available to him.

1:3 *carefully investigated.* Luke's account was exact in historical detail, having been checked in every way. Inspiration by the Holy Spirit did not rule out human effort. The account is complete, extending back to the very beginning of Jesus' earthly life. It has an orderly, meaningful arrangement that is generally chronological. *most excellent.* Paul used this respectful term for governors Felix (Ac 24:3) and Festus (Ac 26:25). *Theophilus.* See Introduction: Recipient and Purpose.

1:4 *so that you may know.* Cf. John's purpose for writing (Jn 20:31; see note there).

C 1:5 *Herod king of Judea.* Herod the Great reigned 37–4 B.C., and his kingdom also included Samaria, Galilee, Perea and Traconitis (see chart, p. 1608; see also note on Mt 2:1). The time referred to here is probably c. 7–6 B.C. *Zechariah … Elizabeth.* Both were of priestly descent from the line of Aaron. *priestly division of Abijah.* From the time of David the priests were organized into 24 divisions, and Abijah was one of the "heads of the priestly families" (Ne 12:12,17; see 1Ch 24:10 and note).

C 1:6 *righteous … blamelessly.* They were not sinless but were faithful and sincere in keeping God's commandments. Simeon (2:25) and Joseph (Mt 1:19) are given similar praise.

1:7 *childless.* See note on v. 25.

1:9 It was one of the priest's duties to keep the incense burning on the altar in front of the Most Holy Place. He supplied it with fresh incense before the morning sacrifice and again after the evening sacrifice (Ex 30:6–8). Ordinarily a priest would have this privilege very infrequently, and sometimes never, since duty assignments were determined by lot. *chosen by lot.* See notes on Ne 11:1; Pr 16:33; Jnh 1:7; Ac 1:26.

1:11 *angel of the Lord.* See v. 19; see also Ge 16:7 and note.

1:12 *fear.* A common reaction, as with Gideon (Jdg 6:22–23) and Manoah (Jdg 13:22).

A 1:13 *Do not be afraid.* This word of reassurance is given many times in both OT and NT (see, e.g., v. 30; 2:10 and note; 5:10; 8:50; 12:7,32; Ge 15:1; 21:17; 26:24; Dt 1:21 and note; Jos 1:9; 8:1 and note). *John.* The name (derived from Hebrew) means "The LORD is gracious" or "The LORD shows grace."

1:14 *joy.* A keynote of these opening chapters (vv. 44,47,58; 2:10); this Gospel also closes with an expression of "great joy" (24:52).

C 1:15 *wine or other fermented drink.* It appears likely that John was to be subject to the Nazirite vow of abstinence from alcoholic drinks (see Nu 6:2–12 and notes). If so, he was a lifelong Nazirite, as were Samson (Jdg 13:4–7) and Samuel (1Sa 1:11). *filled with the Holy Spirit.* Consistent with his emphasis in his Gospel and in Acts (see note on 4:1), Luke's birth narratives stress the activity of the Holy Spirit (see vv. 35,41,67; 2:25–27). *even before he is born.* In the OT the Holy Spirit came upon individuals temporarily for some special task (see, e.g., Jdg 3:10 and note), but John was to be filled with the Spirit his entire life.

1:17 *Elijah.* John was not Elijah returning in the flesh (see Jn 1:21 and note), but he functioned like that OT preacher of re-

1:18 b Ge 15:8
c ver 34; Ge 17:17
1:19 d ver 26;
Da 8:16; 9:21
1:20 e Ex 4:11;
Eze 3:26
1:22 f ver 62
1:25 g Ge 30:23;
Isa 4:1
1:26 h S ver 19
i S Mt 2:23
1:27 j Mt 1:16,18,20;
Lk 2:4
1:30 k ver 13;
S Mt 14:27 l Ge 6:8
1:31 m Isa 7:14;
Mt 1:21,25; Lk 2:21
1:32 n ver 35,76;
S Mk 5:7 o S Mt 1:1
1:33 p Mt 28:18
q 2Sa 7:16; Ps 89:3,4;
Isa 9:7; Jer 33:17;
Da 2:44; 7:14,27;
Mic 4:7; Heb 1:8
1:35 r Mt 1:18
s ver 32,76; S Mk 5:7
t S Mk 1:24 u S Mt 4:3
1:36 v ver 24
1:37 w S Mt 19:26

[18]Zechariah asked the angel, "How can I be sure of this? [b] I am an old man and my wife is well along in years." [c]

[19]The angel said to him, "I am Gabriel. [d] I stand in the presence of God, and I have been sent to speak to you and to tell you this good news. [20]And now you will be silent and not able to speak [e] until the day this happens, because you did not believe my words, which will come true at their appointed time."

[21]Meanwhile, the people were waiting for Zechariah and wondering why he stayed so long in the temple. [22]When he came out, he could not speak to them. They realized he had seen a vision in the temple, for he kept making signs [f] to them but remained unable to speak.

[23]When his time of service was completed, he returned home. [24]After this his wife Elizabeth became pregnant and for five months remained in seclusion. [25]"The Lord has done this for me," she said. "In these days he has shown his favor and taken away my disgrace [g] among the people."

THE BIRTH OF JESUS FORETOLD

[26]In the sixth month of Elizabeth's pregnancy, God sent the angel Gabriel [h] to Nazareth, [i] a town in Galilee, [27]to a virgin pledged to be married to a man named Joseph, [j] a descendant of David. The virgin's name was Mary. [28]The angel went to her and said, "Greetings, you who are highly favored! The Lord is with you."

[29]Mary was greatly troubled at his words and wondered what kind of greeting this might be. [30]But the angel said to her, "Do not be afraid, [k] Mary; you have found favor with God. [l] [31]You will conceive and give birth to a son, and you are to call him Jesus. [m] [32]He will be great and will be called the Son of the Most High. [n] The Lord God will give him the throne of his father David, [o] [33]and he will reign over the house of Jacob forever; his kingdom [p] will never end." [q]

[34]"How will this be," Mary asked the angel, "since I am a virgin?"

[35]The angel answered, "The Holy Spirit will come on you, [r] and the power of the Most High [s] will overshadow you. So the holy one [t] to be born will be called[a] the Son of God. [u] [36]Even Elizabeth your relative is going to have a child [v] in her old age, and she who was said to be unable to conceive is in her sixth month. [37]For no word from God will ever fail." [w]

[38]"I am the Lord's servant," Mary answered. "May it be to me according to your word." Then the angel left her.

---

a 35 Or So the child to be born will be called holy,

---

pentance and was therefore a fulfillment of Mal 4:5–6 (see notes on Mal 4:5; Mt 11:14; 17:10). *to turn the hearts of the parents to their children.* See Mal 4:6 and note. *people prepared for the Lord.* John helped fulfill Isaiah's prophecy (see Isa 40:3–5 and notes), as Luke shows in 3:4–6.

1:18 *How can I be sure…?* Like Abraham (see Ge 15:8 and note), Gideon (see Jdg 6:17 and note) and Hezekiah (2Ki 20:8), Zechariah asked for a sign (cf. 1Co 1:22).

1:19 *Gabriel.* The name can mean "God is my hero" or "mighty man of God." Only two angels are identified by name in Scripture: Gabriel (Da 8:16; 9:21) and Michael (see Da 10:13,21 and note on 10:13; Jude 9; Rev 12:7 and note).

1:21 *the people were waiting for Zechariah.* They were waiting for him to come out of the Holy Place and pronounce the Aaronic blessing (see Nu 6:24–26 and notes).

1:23 *his time of service.* Each priest was responsible for a week's service at the temple once every six months. *home.* See v. 39.

1:24 *remained in seclusion.* In joy, devotion and gratitude that the Lord had taken away her childlessness.

1:25 *The Lord…has shown his favor and taken away my disgrace.* Not only did lack of children deprive the parents of personal happiness, but it was generally considered to indicate divine disfavor and often brought social reproach (see Ge 16:2, Sarai; 25:21, Rebekah; 30:23, Rachel; 1Sa 1:1–18, Hannah; see also Lev 20:20–21; Ps 128:3; Jer 22:30).

1:26–35 This section speaks clearly of the virginal conception of Jesus (vv. 27,34–35; see Mt 1:18–25 and notes). The conception was the work of the Holy Spirit; the eternal Second Person of the Trinity, while remaining God, also "became

flesh" (Jn 1:14; see note there). From conception he was fully God and fully man.

1:26 *In the sixth month.* That is, from the time of John's conception. *Nazareth.* See note on Mt 2:23.

1:27 *pledged to be married.* See note on Mt 1:18.

1:28 *Greetings. Ave* in the Latin Vulgate (from which comes "Ave Maria").

1:31 *Jesus.* See Mt 1:21 and TNIV text note for the meaning of this name.

1:32 *the Son of the Most High.* This title has two senses: (1) the divine Son of God and (2) the Messiah born in time. His Messiahship is clearly referred to in the following context (vv. 32b–33). *Most High.* A title frequently used of God in both the OT and NT (see vv. 35,76; 6:35; 8:28; Ge 14:19 and note; 2Sa 22:14; Ps 7:10,17). *throne.* Promised in the OT to the Messiah descended from David (see 2Sa 7:13,16; Ps 2:6–7; 89:25–27; Isa 9:6–7 and notes). *his father David.* Mary was a descendant of David, as was Joseph (see Mt 1:16 and note); so Jesus could rightly be called a "son" of David.

1:33 *forever.* See 2Sa 7:16; Ps 45:6 and notes; Rev 11:15. *his kingdom will never end.* Although Christ's role as mediator will one day be finished (see 1Co 15:24–28 and notes), the kingdom of the Father and Son, as one, will never end.

1:34 *How will this be…?* Mary did not ask in disbelief, as Zechariah did (v. 20). See v. 45.

1:35 *holy one.* Jesus never sinned (see 2Co 5:21; Heb 4:15; 7:26 and notes; see also 1Pe 2:22; 1Jn 3:5).

1:36 *Elizabeth your relative.* It is not known whether she was a cousin, aunt or other relation.

1:39 *ver 65
1:41 *s ver 15
1:42 *Jdg 5:24
1:43 *S Jn 13:13
1:46 *Ps 34:2,3
1:47 *Ps 18:46;
Isa 17:10; 61:10;
Hab 3:18; 1Ti 1:1; 2:3;
4:10
1:48 *ver 38;
Ps 138:6 *Lk 11:27
1:49 *Ps 71:19
*Ps 111:9
1:50 *Ex 20:6;
Ps 103:17
1:51 *Ps 98:1;
Isa 40:10 *Ge 11:8;
Ex 18:11; 2Sa 22:28;
Jer 13:9; 49:16
1:52 *S Mt 23:12
1:53 *Ps 107:9
1:54 *Ps 98:3
1:55 *S Gal 3:16
1:59 *Ge 17:12;
Lev 12:3; Lk 2:21;
Php 3:5
1:60 *ver 13,63;
S Mt 3:1
1:62 *ver 22
1:63 *ver 13,60;
S Mt 3:1
1:64 *ver 20;
Eze 24:27
1:65 *ver 39

MARY VISITS ELIZABETH

³⁹At that time Mary got ready and hurried to a town in the hill country of Judea, *
⁴⁰where she entered Zechariah's home and greeted Elizabeth. ⁴¹When Elizabeth heard
Mary's greeting, the baby leaped in her womb, and Elizabeth was filled with the Holy Spirit. * ⁴²In a loud voice she exclaimed: "Blessed are you among women, * and blessed is the
child you will bear! ⁴³But why am I so favored, that the mother of my Lord * should come
to me? ⁴⁴As soon as the sound of your greeting reached my ears, the baby in my womb
leaped for joy. ⁴⁵Blessed is she who has believed that the Lord would fulfill his promises
to her!"

MARY'S SONG

1:46–53pp — 1Sa 2:1–10

⁴⁶And Mary said:

> "My soul glorifies the Lord *
⁴⁷   and my spirit rejoices in God my Savior, *
⁴⁸ for he has been mindful
>   of the humble state of his servant. *
> From now on all generations will call me blessed, *
⁴⁹   for the Mighty One has done great things * for me—
>   holy is his name. *
⁵⁰ His mercy extends to those who fear him,
>   from generation to generation. *
⁵¹ He has performed mighty deeds with his arm; *
>   he has scattered those who are proud in their inmost thoughts. *
⁵² He has brought down rulers from their thrones
>   but has lifted up the humble. *
⁵³ He has filled the hungry with good things *
>   but has sent the rich away empty.
⁵⁴ He has helped his servant Israel,
>   remembering to be merciful *
⁵⁵ to Abraham and his descendants * forever,
>   just as he promised our ancestors."

⁵⁶Mary stayed with Elizabeth for about three months and then returned home.

THE BIRTH OF JOHN THE BAPTIST

⁵⁷When it was time for Elizabeth to have her baby, she gave birth to a son. ⁵⁸Her neighbors and relatives heard that the Lord had shown her great mercy, and they shared her joy.

⁵⁹On the eighth day they came to circumcise * the child, and they were going to name
him after his father Zechariah, ⁶⁰but his mother spoke up and said, "No! He is to be called
John." *

⁶¹They said to her, "There is no one among your relatives who has that name."

⁶²Then they made signs * to his father, to find out what he would like to name the child.
⁶³He asked for a writing tablet, and to everyone's astonishment he wrote, "His name is
John." * ⁶⁴Immediately his mouth was opened and his tongue was loosed, and he began
to speak, * praising God. ⁶⁵The neighbors were all filled with awe, and throughout the hill
country of Judea * people were talking about all these things. ⁶⁶Everyone who heard this

---

1:44 *for joy.* In some mysterious way the Holy Spirit produced
this remarkable response in the unborn baby.
1:46–55 One of four hymns preserved in Lk 1–2 (see vv. 68–
79; 2:14; 2:29–32 and notes). This hymn of praise is known as
the Magnificat because in the Latin Vulgate translation the
opening word is *Magnificat,* which means "glorifies." This song is
like a psalm and should also be compared with the song of
Hannah (1Sa 2:1–10; see note on 1Sa 2:1).

1:50 *those who fear him.* Those who revere God and live
in harmony with his will (see notes on Ge 20:11; Pr 1:7).
1:51 *his arm.* A figurative description of God's powerful acts.
God does not have a body; he is spirit (see Jn 4:24 and note).
1:53 *hungry.* Both physically and spiritually (Mt 5:6; Jn 6:35).
The coming of God's kingdom will bring changes affecting
every area of life.

1:54 *remembering to be merciful.* The song ends with an
assurance that God will be true to his promises to his people (see Ge 22:16–18 and notes).
1:56 *three months.* Mary evidently remained with Elizabeth
until John's birth and then returned to her home in Nazareth
(see v. 36).
1:57–66 The birth of John the Baptist marks the fulfillment of
the prophecy in vv. 5–25.
1:59 *name him after his father.* An accepted practice in that
day, as seen in Josephus (*Life,* 1).
1:62 *they made signs to his father.* Apparently assuming that
since he was mute he was also deaf.
1:63 *a writing tablet.* Probably a small wooden board covered
with wax.
1:64 *praising God.* A common theme in Luke (2:13,20,28; 5:25–
26; 7:16; 13:13; 17:15,18; 18:43; 19:37; 23:47; 24:53).

wondered about it, asking, "What then is this child going to be?" For the Lord's hand was with him. [u]

ZECHARIAH'S SONG

[67] His father Zechariah was filled with the Holy Spirit [v] and prophesied: [w]

[68] "Praise be to the Lord, the God of Israel, [x]
    because he has come to his people and redeemed them. [y]
[69] He has raised up a horn[a] [z] of salvation for us
    in the house of his servant David[a]
[70] (as he said through his holy prophets of long ago), [b]
[71] salvation from our enemies
    and from the hand of all who hate us—
[72] to show mercy to our ancestors [c]
    and to remember his holy covenant, [d]
[73]   the oath he swore to our father Abraham: [e]
[74] to rescue us from the hand of our enemies,
    and to enable us to serve him [f] without fear [g]
[75]   in holiness and righteousness [h] before him all our days.

[76] And you, my child, will be called a prophet [i] of the Most High; [j]
    for you will go on before the Lord to prepare the way for him, [k]
[77] to give his people the knowledge of salvation
    through the forgiveness of their sins, [l]
[78] because of the tender mercy of our God,
    by which the rising sun [m] will come to us from heaven
[79] to shine on those living in darkness
    and in the shadow of death, [n]
    to guide our feet into the path of peace." [o]

[80] And the child grew and became strong in spirit [b; p] and he lived in the wilderness until he appeared publicly to Israel.

THE BIRTH OF JESUS

2 In those days Caesar Augustus [q] issued a decree that a census should be taken of the entire Roman world. [r] [2] (This was the first census that took place while Quirinius was governor of Syria.) [s] [3] And everyone went to their own town to register.

---

[a] 69 *Horn* here symbolizes a strong king.   [b] 80 Or *in the Spirit*

### Cross-references (margin)

1:66 [u] Ge 39:2; Ac 11:21
1:67 [v] ver 15 [w] Joel 2:28
1:68 [x] Ge 24:27; 1Ki 8:15; Ps 72:18 [y] Ps 111:9; Lk 7:16
1:69 [z] 1Sa 2:1,10; 2Sa 22:3; Ps 18:2; 89:17; 132:17; Eze 29:21 [a] S Mt 1:1
1:70 [b] Jer 23:5; Ac 3:21; Ro 1:2
1:72 [c] Mic 7:20 [d] Ps 105:8,9; 106:45; Eze 16:60
1:73 [e] Ge 22:16-18
1:74 [f] Heb 9:14 [g] 1Jn 4:18
1:75 [h] Eph 4:24
1:76 [i] S Mt 11:9 [j] ver 32,35; S Mk 5:7 [k] ver 17; S Mt 3:3
1:77 [l] Jer 31:34; Mt 1:21; Mk 1:4
1:78 [m] Mal 4:2
1:79 [n] Ps 107:14; Isa 9:2; 59:9; Mt 4:16; S Ac 26:18 [o] S Lk 2:14
1:80 [p] Lk 2:40, 52
2:1 [q] Mt 22:17; Lk 3:1 [r] S Mt 24:14
2:2 [s] Mt 4:24; Ac 15:23,41; 21:3; Gal 1:21

1:67 *filled with the Holy Spirit...prophesied.* Prophecy not only predicts but also proclaims God's word. Both Zechariah and Elizabeth (vv. 41–45) were enabled by the Holy Spirit to express what otherwise they could not have formulated.
1:68–79 This hymn is called Benedictus ("Praise be") because the opening word in the Latin Vulgate translation is *Benedictus*. Whereas the Magnificat (see note on 1:46–55) is similar to a psalm, the Benedictus is more like a prophecy.
1:68 *redeemed them.* Not limited to national security (v. 71) but including moral and spiritual salvation (vv. 75,77).
1:69 *horn.* Indicates strength (see TNIV text note), as in the horn of an animal (Dt 33:17; Ps 22:21; Mic 4:13). Jesus, the Messiah from the house of David, has the power to save.
1:74 *to rescue us.* No doubt including liberation from all kinds of oppression and bondage as well as deliverance from sin.
1:76 *called a prophet of the Most High.* But Jesus will be called "the Son of the Most High" (see v. 32 and note). *prepare the way.* See note on 3:4.
1:78 *the rising sun.* A reference to the coming of the Messiah (see also similar figures in Nu 24:17; Isa 9:2; 60:1; Mal 4:2 and notes). Zechariah not only praised his own son, the "prophet of the Most High" (vv. 76–77), but also gave honor to the coming Messiah (vv. 78–79).
1:79 *those living in darkness.* The lost, separated from God (see Isa 9:1–2; Mt 4:15–16 and notes). *peace.* See note on 2:14.

1:80 *lived in the wilderness.* John's parents, old at his birth, probably died while he was young, and he apparently grew up in the Desert of Judea, which lies between Jerusalem and the Dead Sea. *until he appeared publicly.* John's preaching and announcing the coming of the Messiah marked his public appearance. He was about 30 years old when he began his ministry (see note on 3:23).
2:1–7 Jesus' birth marks the fulfillment of the prophecy in 1:26–38.
2:1 Luke is the only Gospel writer who relates his narrative to dates of world history. *Caesar Augustus.* The first and (according to many) greatest Roman emperor (31 B.C.–A.D. 14). Having replaced the republic with an imperial form of government, he expanded the empire to include the entire Mediterranean world, established the famed *Pax Romana* ("Roman Peace") and ushered in the golden age of Roman literature and architecture. Augustus (which means "exalted") was a title conferred on him by the Roman senate in 27 B.C. *census.* Used for military service and taxation. Jews, however, were exempt from Roman military service. God used the decree of a pagan emperor to fulfill the prophecy of Mic 5:2 (see note there; see also Mt 2:3–6). *Roman world.* See map No. 14 at the end of this study Bible.
2:2 *Quirinius.* This official appears to have been in office for two terms, first 6–4 B.C. and then A.D. 6–9. A census is associated with each term. This is the first; Ac 5:37 refers to the second.
2:3 *own town.* Probably the town of their ancestral origin.

2:4 ʳ S Jn 7:42
2:5 ᵘ Lk 1:27
2:9 ᵛ S Ac 5:19
2:10 ʷ S Mt 14:27
2:11 ˣ S Mt 1:21;
S Jn 3:17; 4:42;
Ac 5:31; 13:23;
S Ro 11:14; 1Ti 4:10;
1Jn 4:14 ʸ Mt 1:16;
16:16,20; Jn 11:27;
Ac 2:36; 3:20; S 9:22
ᶻ S Jn 13:13
2:12 ᵃ 1Sa 2:34;
10:7; 2Ki 19:29;
Ps 86:17; Isa 7:14
2:14 ᵇ Isa 9:6; 52:7;
53:5; Mic 5:5;
Lk 1:79; S Jn 14:27;
Ro 5:1; Eph 2:14,17
2:16 ᶜ ver 7
2:19 ᵈ ver 51
2:20 ᵉ S Mt 9:8
2:21 ᶠ S Lk 1:59
ᵍ S Lk 1:31
2:22 ʰ Lev 12:2-8

⁴So Joseph also went up from the town of Nazareth in Galilee to Judea, to Bethlehem ᵗ the town of David, because he belonged to the house and line of David. ⁵He went there to register with Mary, who was pledged to be married to him ᵘ and was expecting a child. ⁶While they were there, the time came for the baby to be born, ⁷and she gave birth to her firstborn, a son. She wrapped him in cloths and placed him in a manger, because there was no guest room available for them.

⁸And there were shepherds living out in the fields nearby, keeping watch over their flocks at night. ⁹An angel ᵛ of the Lord appeared to them, and the glory of the Lord shone around them, and they were terrified. ¹⁰But the angel said to them, "Do not be afraid. ʷ I bring you good news of great joy that will be for all the people. ¹¹Today in the town of David a Savior ˣ has been born to you; he is the Messiah, ʸ the Lord. ᶻ ¹²This will be a sign ᵃ to you: You will find a baby wrapped in cloths and lying in a manger."

¹³Suddenly a great company of the heavenly host appeared with the angel, praising God and saying,

¹⁴"Glory to God in the highest heaven,
    and on earth peace ᵇ to those on whom his favor rests."

¹⁵When the angels had left them and gone into heaven, the shepherds said to one another, "Let's go to Bethlehem and see this thing that has happened, which the Lord has told us about."

¹⁶So they hurried off and found Mary and Joseph, and the baby, who was lying in the manger. ᶜ ¹⁷When they had seen him, they spread the word concerning what had been told them about this child, ¹⁸and all who heard it were amazed at what the shepherds said to them. ¹⁹But Mary treasured up all these things and pondered them in her heart. ᵈ ²⁰The shepherds returned, glorifying and praising God ᵉ for all the things they had heard and seen, which were just as they had been told.

²¹On the eighth day, when it was time to circumcise the child, ᶠ he was named Jesus, the name the angel had given him before he was conceived. ᵍ

JESUS PRESENTED IN THE TEMPLE

²²When the time came for the purification rites required by the Law of Moses, ʰ Joseph and Mary took him to Jerusalem to present him to the Lord ²³(as it is written in the Law

---

2:4 *Nazareth … Bethlehem.* Bethlehem, the town where David was born (1Sa 17:12; 20:6), was at least a three-day trip from Nazareth. *Judea.* The Roman designation for the southern part of the Holy Land, earlier included in the kingdom of Judah.

2:5 *with Mary.* Mary too was of the house of David and probably was required to enroll. In Syria, the Roman province in which the Holy Land was located, women 12 years of age and older were required to pay a poll tax and therefore to register. *pledged to be married.* See Mt 1:18 and note.

2:7 *cloths.* Strips of cloth were regularly used to wrap a newborn infant. *manger.* The feeding trough of the animals. This is the only indication that Christ was born in a stable. Very early tradition suggests that it was a cave, perhaps used as a stable.

2:8 *living out in the fields.* Does not necessarily mean it was summer, the dry season. The flocks reserved for temple sacrifice were kept in the fields near Bethlehem throughout the year. *keeping watch.* Against thieves and predatory animals.

2:9 *An angel of the Lord.* A designation used throughout the birth narratives (see 1:11 and note; Mt 1:20,24; 2:13,19). The angel in 1:11 is identified as Gabriel (1:19; see 1:26). Cf. Ge 16:7 and note.

2:10 *Do not be afraid.* Fear was the common reaction to angelic appearances (see note on 1:13), and encouragement was needed. *great joy.* See note on 1:14.

2:11 *town of David.* Bethlehem (v. 4). *Savior.* Many Jews were looking for a political leader to deliver them from Roman rule, while others were hoping for a savior to deliver them from sickness and physical hardship. But this announcement concerns the Savior who would deliver from sin and death (see Mt 1:21; Jn 4:42 and note). *the Messiah.* See TNIV text note on Mt 1:1. *the Lord.* A designation originally reserved for God but later applied to the Messiah as well (see Ac 2:36; Php 2:11).

2:13,20 *praising God.* See 1:64 and note.

2:14 See note on 1:46–55. This brief hymn is called the Gloria in Excelsis Deo, from the first words of the Latin Vulgate translation (meaning "Glory to God in the Highest"). The angels recognized the glory and majesty of God by giving praise to him. *in the highest heaven.* Where God dwells (cf. Mt 6:9). *peace to those on whom his favor rests.* Peace is not assured to all, but only to those pleasing to God—the objects of his good pleasure (see Luke's use of the words "pleased" and "pleasure" elsewhere: 3:22; 10:21; 12:32). The Roman world was experiencing the *Pax Romana* ("Roman Peace"), marked by external tranquillity. But the angels proclaimed a deeper, more lasting peace than that—a peace of mind and soul made possible by the Savior (v. 11). Peace with God is received by faith in Christ (see Ro 5:1 and note), and it is on believers that "his favor rests." The Davidic Messiah was called "Prince of Peace" (Isa 9:6; see note there), and Christ promised peace to his disciples (see Jn 14:27; Php 4:7 and notes). But Christ also brought conflict (the "sword"; see Mt 10:34 and note; cf. Lk 12:49), for peace with God involves opposition to Satan and his work (see Jas 4:7 and note).

2:19 *treasured up all these things … in her heart.* Cf. v. 51.

2:21 *circumcise.* See Ge 17:10; Jn 7:22 and notes.

2:22 *purification.* Following the birth of a son, the mother had to wait 40 days before going to the temple to offer a sacrifice for her purification. If she could not afford a lamb and a pigeon (or dove), then two pigeons (or doves) would be acceptable (see Lev 12:2–8 and notes; cf. Lev 5:11). *to Jerusalem.* The distance from Bethlehem to Jerusalem was only about five miles. *present him to the Lord.* The firstborn of both people and animals were to be dedicated to the Lord (see v. 23; Ex 13:2–13 and notes). The animals were sacrificed, but the human beings were to serve God throughout their lives. The Levites actually served in the place of all the firstborn males in Israel (see Nu 3:11–13; 8:17–18).

of the Lord, "Every firstborn male is to be consecrated to the Lord"ª), *i* 24and to offer a sacrifice in keeping with what is said in the Law of the Lord: "a pair of doves or two young pigeons."ᵇ*j*

25Now there was a man in Jerusalem called Simeon, who was righteous and devout.ᵏ He was waiting for the consolation of Israel, *l* and the Holy Spirit was on him. 26It had been revealed to him by the Holy Spirit that he would not die before he had seen the Lord's Messiah. 27Moved by the Spirit, he went into the temple courts. When the parents brought in the child Jesus to do for him what the custom of the Law required, *m* 28Simeon took him in his arms and praised God, saying:

> 29"Sovereign Lord, as you have promised, *n*
>   you may now dismissᶜ your servant in peace. *o*
> 30For my eyes have seen your salvation, *p*
> 31   which you have prepared in the sight of all nations:
> 32a light for revelation to the Gentiles,
>   and the glory of your people Israel."*q*

33The child's father and mother marveled at what was said about him. 34Then Simeon blessed them and said to Mary, his mother: *r* "This child is destined to cause the fallingˢ and rising of many in Israel, and to be a sign that will be spoken against, 35so that the thoughts of many hearts will be revealed. And a sword will pierce your own soul too."

36There was also a prophet, *t* Anna, the daughter of Phanuel, of the tribe of Asher. She was very old; she had lived with her husband seven years after her marriage, 37and then had been a widow for eighty-four years. ᵈ*u* She never left the temple but worshiped night and day, fasting and praying. *v* 38Coming up to them at that very moment, she gave thanks to God and spoke about the child to all who were looking forward to the redemption of Jerusalem. *w*

39When Joseph and Mary had done everything required by the Law of the Lord, they returned to Galilee to their own town of Nazareth. *x* 40And the child grew and became strong; he was filled with wisdom, and the grace of God was on him. *y*

THE BOY JESUS AT THE TEMPLE

41Every year Jesus' parents went to Jerusalem for the Festival of the Passover. *z* 42When he was twelve years old, they went up to the festival, according to the custom. 43After the festival was over, while his parents were returning home, the boy Jesus stayed behind in Jerusalem, but they were unaware of it. 44Thinking he was in their company, they traveled on for a day. Then they began looking for him among their relatives and friends. 45When they did not find him, they went back to Jerusalem to look for him. 46After three

ª 23 Exodus 13:2,12   ᵇ 24 Lev. 12:8   ᶜ 29 Or promised, / now dismiss   ᵈ 37 Or then was a widow until she was eighty-four

2:23 *i* Ex 13:2,12,15; Nu 3:13
2:24 *j* Lev 12:8
2:25 *k* Lev 1:6
l ver 38; Isa 52:9; Lk 23:51
2:27 *m* ver 22
2:29 *n* ver 26
ᵒ Ac 2:24
2:30 *p* Isa 40:5; 52:10; Lk 3:6
2:32 *q* Isa 42:6; 49:6; Ac 13:47; 26:23
2:34 *r* S Mt 12:46
ˢ Isa 8:14; Mt 21:44; 1Co 1:23; 2Co 2:16; Gal 5:11; 1Pe 2:7,8
2:36 *t* S Ac 21:9
2:37 *u* 1Ti 5:9
v Ac 13:3; 14:23; 1Ti 5:5
2:38 *w* ver 25; Isa 40:2; 52:9; Lk 1:68; 24:21
2:39 *x* ver 51; S Mt 2:23
2:40 *y* ver 52; Lk 1:80
2:41 *z* Ex 23:15; Dt 16:1-8; Lk 22:8

2:25 *the consolation of Israel.* The comfort the Messiah would bring to his people at his coming (see vv. 26,38; 23:51; 24:21; Isa 40:1–2 and notes; Mt 5:4). *the Holy Spirit was on him.* Not in the way common to all believers after Pentecost. Simeon was given a special insight by the Spirit so that he would recognize the "Messiah" (v. 26; cf. 1:15 and note).
2:28 *praised God.* See 1:64 and note.
2:29–32 See note on 1:46–55. This hymn of Simeon has been called the *Nunc Dimittis,* from the first words of the Latin Vulgate translation, meaning "[You] now dismiss."
2:31 *all nations.* As a Gentile himself, Luke was careful to emphasize the truth that salvation was offered to Gentiles (v. 32) as well as to Jews.
2:33 *child's father.* Luke, aware of the virgin birth of Jesus (1:26–35), is referring to Joseph as Jesus' legal father (see v. 41; Jn 1:45 and note).
2:34 *falling and rising of many in Israel.* Christ raises up those who believe in him but is a stumbling block for those who disbelieve (see 20:17–18 and note on 20:18; 1Co 1:23; 1Pe 2:6–8 and notes). *sign ... spoken against.* This somewhat enigmatic statement may mean that Jesus, a sign from God (v. 12; 11:30), would precipitate division, opposition and rejection.
2:35 *sword will pierce your own soul too.* The word "too" indicates that Mary, as well as Jesus, would suffer deep anguish—the first reference in this Gospel to Christ's suffering and death.

2:36 *prophet.* Other female prophets were Miriam (Ex 15:20), Deborah (Jdg 4:4), Huldah (2Ki 22:14) and the daughters of Philip (Ac 21:9). *Anna.* Same name as OT Hannah (1Sa 1:2), which means "gracious." Anna praised God for the child Jesus, as Hannah had praised God for the child Samuel (1Sa 2:1–10).
2:37 *never left the temple.* Herod's temple was quite large and included rooms for various uses, and Anna may have been allowed to live in one of them. This statement, however, probably means that she spent her waking hours attending and worshiping in the temple.
2:38 *Jerusalem.* The holy city of God's chosen people; here it stands for Israel as a whole. See Introduction to Psalms: Theology: Major Themes, 7 (p. 815).
2:39 *they returned to Galilee.* Luke does not mention the coming of the Magi, the danger from Herod or the flight to and return from Egypt (cf. Mt 2:1–23).
2:41 *Festival of the Passover.* Annual attendance at three festivals by all adult males (normally accompanied by their families) was commanded in the law: Passover, Pentecost and Tabernacles (see notes on Ex 23:14–17; Dt 16:16). Distance prevented many from attending all three, but most Jews tried to be at Passover.
2:42 *twelve years old.* At age 12 boys began preparing to take their places in the religious community the following year.

2:47 *a* S Mt 7:28
2:48 *b* S Mt 12:46
c Lk 3:23; 4:22
2:49 *d* Jn 2:16
2:50 *e* S Mk 9:32
2:51 *f* ver 39;
S Mt 2:23 *g* ver 19
2:52 *h* ver 40;
1Sa 2:26; Pr 3:4;
Lk 1:80
3:1 *i* S Mt 27:2
j S Mt 14:1
3:2 *k* S Mt 26:3
l S Mt 3:1 *m* Lk 1:13
3:3 *n* ver 16;
S Mk 1:4
3:6 *o* Ps 98:2;
Isa 40:3-5; 42:16;
52:10; Lk 2:30
3:7 *p* Mt 12:34;
23:33 *q* S Ro 1:18

days they found him in the temple courts, sitting among the teachers, listening to them and asking them questions. [47]Everyone who heard him was amazed *a* at his understanding and his answers. [48]When his parents saw him, they were astonished. His mother *b* said to him, "Son, why have you treated us like this? Your father *c* and I have been anxiously searching for you."

[49]"Why were you searching for me?" he asked. "Didn't you know I had to be in my Father's house?" *a* [50]But they did not understand what he was saying to them. *e*

[51]Then he went down to Nazareth with them *f* and was obedient to them. But his mother treasured all these things in her heart. *g* [52]And as Jesus grew up, he increased in wisdom and in favor with God and people. *h*

JOHN THE BAPTIST PREPARES THE WAY

3:2–10pp — Mt 3:1–10; Mk 1:3–5
3:16,17pp — Mt 3:11,12; Mk 1:7,8

3 In the fifteenth year of the reign of Tiberius Caesar—when Pontius Pilate *i* was governor of Judea, Herod *j* tetrarch of Galilee, his brother Philip tetrarch of Iturea and Traconitis, and Lysanias tetrarch of Abilene— [2]during the high-priesthood of Annas and Caiaphas, *k* the word of God came to John *l* son of Zechariah *m* in the wilderness. [3]He went into all the country around the Jordan, preaching a baptism of repentance for the forgiveness of sins. *n* [4]As it is written in the book of the words of Isaiah the prophet:

"A voice of one calling in the wilderness,
'Prepare the way for the Lord,
    make straight paths for him.
[5]Every valley shall be filled in,
    every mountain and hill made low.
The crooked roads shall become straight,
    the rough ways smooth.
[6]And all people will see God's salvation.' " *b o*

[7]John said to the crowds coming out to be baptized by him, "You brood of vipers! *p* Who warned you to flee from the coming wrath? *q* [8]Produce fruit in keeping with repentance.

a 49 Or *be about my Father's business*   *b* 6 Isaiah 40:3-5

2:46 *the teachers.* The rabbis, experts in Judaism.

2:49 *in my Father's house.* See TNIV text note. Jesus pointed to his personal duty to his Father in heaven. He contrasted his "my Father" with Mary's "Your father" (v. 48). At 12 years of age he was aware of his unique relationship to God, but he was also obedient to his earthly parents (v. 51).

2:52 Luke says of Jesus what is said of Samuel in 1Sa 2:26 (see note there). *Jesus grew.* Although Jesus was God, there is no indication that he had all knowledge and wisdom from birth. He seems to have matured like any other boy.

3:1–2 Ancient historians frequently dated an event by citing the year in the reign of the ruler at the time the event happened.

3:1 *fifteenth year.* Several possible dates could be indicated by this description, but the date A.D. 25–26 (Tiberius had authority in the provinces beginning in A.D. 11) best fits the chronology of the life of Christ. The other rulers named do not help pinpoint the beginning of John's ministry but only serve to indicate the general historical period. *Pontius Pilate.* The Roman governor of Judea from A.D. 26 to 36, whose official residence was in Caesarea on the Mediterranean coast. (In 1961 archaeologists unearthed a stone step in the Roman amphitheater in Caesarea contemporary with Pilate and bearing a Latin inscription that included these words: "Pontius Pilate, Prefect [Governor] of Judea"; see chart, p. 1830.) When he came to Jerusalem, he stayed in the magnificent palace built by Herod the Great, located southwest of the temple area. Mark calls this palace "the Praetorium" (Mk 15:16; see note there), and it was here that the Roman trial of Jesus took place (see note on Mk 14:53—15:15). *Herod tetrarch of Galilee.* At the death of Herod the Great (4 B.C.), his sons—Archelaus, Herod Antipas and Herod Philip—were given jurisdiction over his divided kingdom. Herod Antipas became the tetrarch of Galilee and Perea (see note on Mt 14:1). *Ly-*

sanias tetrarch of Abilene. Nothing is known of this Lysanias beyond that his name has been found in certain inscriptions (see map, p. 1721).

3:2 *the high-priesthood of Annas and Caiaphas.* Annas was high priest from A.D. 6 until he was deposed by the Roman official Gratus in 15. He was followed by his son Eleazar, his son-in-law Caiaphas and then four more sons. Even though Rome had replaced Annas, the Jews continued to recognize his authority (see Jn 18:13; Ac 4:6 and notes), so Luke included his name as well as that of the Roman appointee, Caiaphas. *word of God.* The source of John's preaching and authority for his baptizing. God's message came to John as it came to the OT prophets (see Jer 1:2; Hos 1:1; Joel 1:1 and notes; see also Eze 1:3). *wilderness.* Refers to a desolate, uninhabited area, not necessarily a sandy, waterless place.

3:3 *baptism of repentance.* See note on Mt 3:11. John's baptism represented a change of heart, which includes sorrow for sin and a determination to lead a holy life. *forgiveness of sins.* Christ would deliver the repentant person from sin's penalty by dying on the cross.

3:4 *Prepare the way.* Before a king made a journey to a distant country, the roads he would travel were improved (see Isa 40:3 and note). Similarly, preparation for the Messiah was made in a moral and spiritual way by the ministry of John, which focused on repentance and forgiveness of sin and the need for a Savior.

3:6 *all people.* God's salvation was to be made known to both Jews and Gentiles—a major theme of Luke's Gospel (see note on 2:31).

3:7 *the coming wrath.* A reference to both the destruction of Jerusalem (21:20–23), which occurred in A.D. 70, and the final judgment (Jn 3:36). But see notes on 1Th 1:10; 5:9.

THE HOLY LAND UNDER HEROD THE GREAT

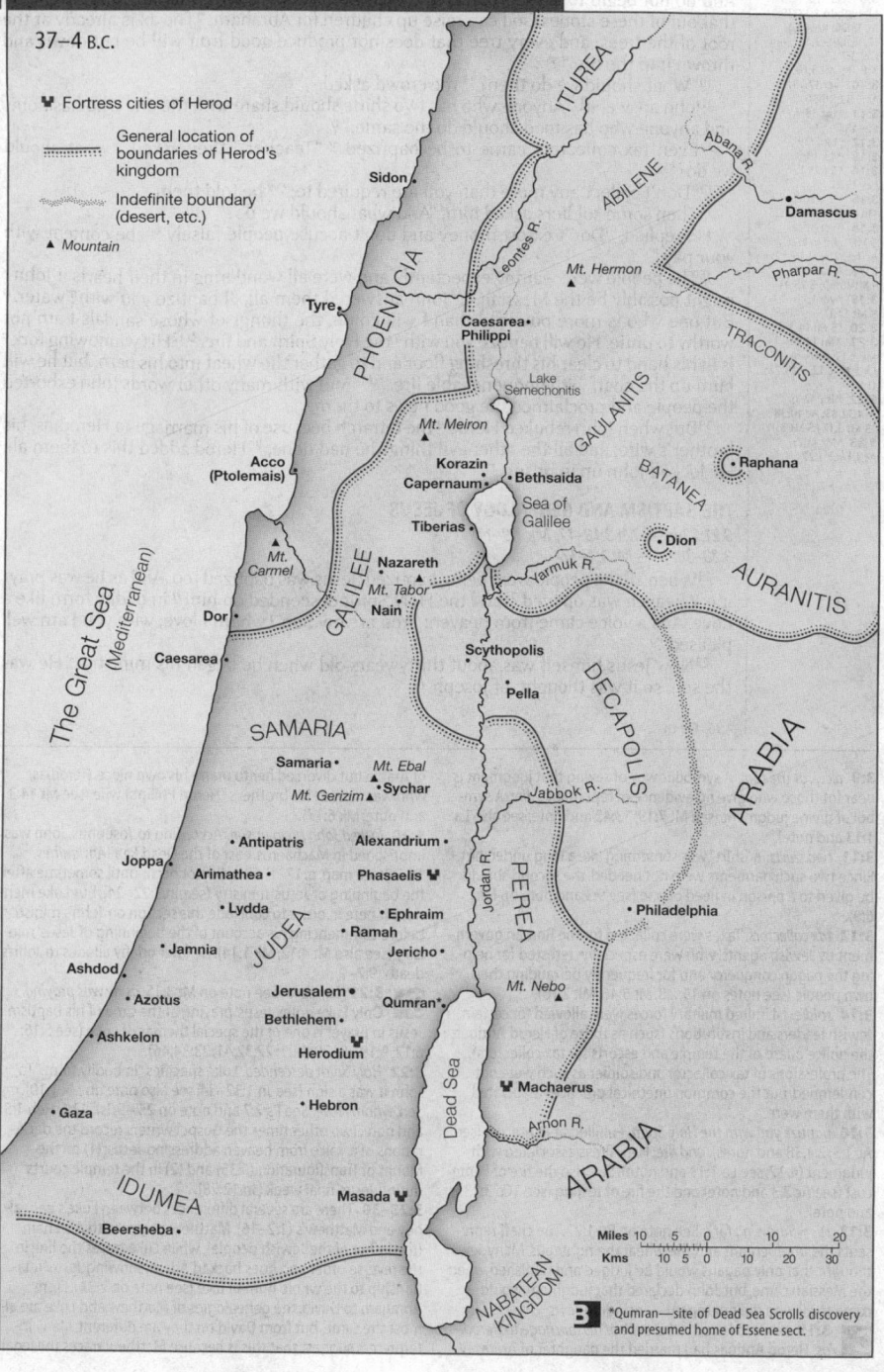

37–4 B.C.

Legend:
- ⚐ Fortress cities of Herod
- ┈┈┈ General location of boundaries of Herod's kingdom
- ∼∼∼ Indefinite boundary (desert, etc.)
- ▲ Mountain

**Labels on map:**

ITUREA

ABILENE

Abana R.

Sidon

Damascus

PHOENICIA

Leontes R.

Mt. Hermon ▲

Pharpar R.

Tyre

Caesarea Philippi

TRACONITIS

Lake Semechonitis

GAULANITIS

BATANEA

Acco (Ptolemais)

Korazin

Bethsaida

Raphana

Capernaum

Sea of Galilee

Mt. Meiron ▲

Tiberias

Dion

GALILEE

Nazareth

AURANITIS

Mt. Carmel ▲

Mt. Tabor ▲

Nain

Yarmuk R.

Dor

Caesarea

Scythopolis

The Great Sea (Mediterranean)

Pella

DECAPOLIS

SAMARIA

ARABIA

Samaria

Mt. Ebal ▲

Sychar

Mt. Gerizim ▲

Jabbok R.

Antipatris

Alexandrium

Joppa

Arimathea

Phasaelis ⚐

Jordan R.

PEREA

Lydda

Ephraim

Ramah

Philadelphia

JUDEA

Jamnia

Jericho

Ashdod

Azotus

Jerusalem

Qumran*

Mt. Nebo ▲

Ashkelon

Bethlehem

Herodium

Dead Sea

Machaerus ⚐

Gaza

Hebron

Arnon R.

IDUMEA

Masada ⚐

ARABIA

Beersheba

NABATEAN KINGDOM

Miles 10 5 0 10 20
Kms 10 5 0 10 20 30

B *Qumran—site of Dead Sea Scrolls discovery and presumed home of Essene sect.

3:8 *i* Isa 51:2;
Lk 19:9; Jn 8:33,39;
Ac 13:26; Ro 4:1,11,
12,16,17; 9:7,8;
Gal 3:7
3:9 *s* S Mt 3:10
3:10 *t* ver 12,14;
Ac 2:37; 16:30
3:11 *u* Isa 58:7;
Eze 18:7
3:12 *v* Lk 7:29
3:13 *w* Lk 19:8
3:14 *x* Ex 23:1;
Lev 19:11
3:15 *y* S Mt 3:1
z Jn 1:19,20; Ac 13:25
3:16 *a* ver 3;
S Mk 1:4 *b* Jn 1:26,33;
Ac 1:5; 2:3; 11:16; 19:4
3:17 *c* Isa 30:24
d Mt 13:30; S 25:41
3:19 *e* ver 1;
S Mt 14:1
3:20 *f* S Mt 14:3,4
3:21 *g* Mt 14:23;
Mk 1:35; 6:46;
Lk 5:16; 6:12; 9:18,28;
11:1
3:22 *h* Isa 42:1;
Jn 1:32,33; Ac 10:38
i S Mt 3:17 *j* S Mt 3:17
3:23 *k* Mt 4:17;
Ac 1:1 *l* Lk 1:27

And do not begin to say to yourselves, 'We have Abraham as our father.' *r* For I tell you that out of these stones God can raise up children for Abraham. [9]The ax is already at the root of the trees, and every tree that does not produce good fruit will be cut down and thrown into the fire." *s*

[10]"What should we do then?" *t* the crowd asked.

[11]John answered, "Anyone who has two shirts should share with the one who has none, and anyone who has food should do the same." *u*

[12]Even tax collectors came to be baptized. *v* "Teacher," they asked, "what should we do?"

[13]"Don't collect any more than you are required to," *w* he told them.

[14]Then some soldiers asked him, "And what should we do?"

He replied, "Don't extort money and don't accuse people falsely *x*—be content with your pay."

[15]The people were waiting expectantly and were all wondering in their hearts if John *y* might possibly be the Messiah. *z* [16]John answered them all, "I baptize you with *a* water. *a* But one who is more powerful than I will come, the thongs of whose sandals I am not worthy to untie. He will baptize you with *a* the Holy Spirit and fire. *b* [17]His winnowing fork *c* is in his hand to clear his threshing floor and to gather the wheat into his barn, but he will burn up the chaff with unquenchable fire." *d* [18]And with many other words John exhorted the people and proclaimed the good news to them.

[19]But when John rebuked Herod *e* the tetrarch because of his marriage to Herodias, his brother's wife, and all the other evil things he had done, [20]Herod added this to them all: He locked John up in prison. *f*

THE BAPTISM AND GENEALOGY OF JESUS
3:21,22pp — Mt 3:13–17; Mk 1:9–11
3:23–38pp — Mt 1:1–17

[21]When all the people were being baptized, Jesus was baptized too. And as he was praying, *g* heaven was opened [22]and the Holy Spirit descended on him *h* in bodily form like a dove. And a voice came from heaven: "You are my Son, *i* whom I love; with you I am well pleased." *j*

[23]Now Jesus himself was about thirty years old when he began his ministry. *k* He was the son, so it was thought, of Joseph, *l*

a 16 Or *in*

3:9 *ax... at the root.* A symbolic way of saying that judgment is near for those who give no evidence of repentance. *fire.* A symbol of divine judgment (see Mt 7:19; 13:42 and note; see also La 1:13 and note).

3:11 *two shirts.* A "shirt" was something like a long undershirt. Since two such garments were not needed, the second should be given to a person in need of one (see 9:3 and note on Mk 6:9).

3:12 *tax collectors.* Taxes were collected for the Roman government by Jewish agents, who were especially detested for helping the pagan conqueror and for frequently defrauding their own people (see notes on 19:2,8; Mt 5:46; Mk 2:16).

3:14 *soldiers.* Limited military forces were allowed for certain Jewish leaders and institutions (such as those of Herod Antipas, the police guard of the temple and escorts for tax collectors). The professions of tax collector and soldier as such were not condemned, but the common unethical practices associated with them were.

3:16 *baptize you with the Holy Spirit.* Fulfilled at Pentecost (see Ac 1:5; 2:4,38 and notes). *and fire.* Here fire is associated with judgment (v. 17; see La 1:13 and note). See also the fire of Pentecost (see Ac 2:3 and note) and the fire of testing (see 1Co 3:13 and note).

3:17 *His winnowing fork.* See note on Ru 1:22. The chaff represents the unrepentant and the wheat the righteous. Many Jews thought that only pagans would be judged and punished when the Messiah came, but John declared that judgment would come to all who did not repent—including Jews.

3:19 *rebuked Herod ... because of his marriage to Herodias.* Herod Antipas had married the daughter of Aretas IV

of Arabia but divorced her to marry his own niece, Herodias, who was already his brother's (Herod Philip's) wife (see Mt 14:3 and note; Mk 6:17).

3:20 *locked John up in prison.* According to Josephus, John was imprisoned in Machaerus, east of the Dead Sea (*Antiquities,* 18.5.2; see map, p. 1721). This did not occur until sometime after the beginning of Jesus' ministry (see Jn 3:22–24), but Luke mentions it here in order to conclude this section on John's ministry before commencing his account of the beginning of Jesus' ministry (see also Mt 4:12; Mk 1:14). He later briefly alludes to John's death (9:7–9).

3:21 *baptized.* See note on Mt 3:15. *as he was praying.* Only Luke notes Jesus' praying at the time of his baptism. Jesus in prayer is one of the special themes of Luke (see 5:16; 6:12; 9:18,28–29; 11:1; 22:32,41; 23:34,46).

3:22 *Holy Spirit descended.* Luke specifies "in bodily form." To John it was a sign (see Jn 1:32–34; see also note on Mk 1:10). *my Son, whom I love.* See Ps 2:7 and note on 2:7–9; Isa 42:1; Heb 1:5 and note. Two other times the Gospel writers record the declarations of a voice from heaven addressing Jesus: (1) on the Mount of Transfiguration (9:35) and (2) in the temple courts during Jesus' final week (Jn 12:28).

3:23–38 There are several differences between Luke's genealogy and Matthew's (1:2–16). Matthew begins with Abraham (the father of the Jewish people), while Luke traces the line in the reverse order and goes back to Adam, showing Jesus' relationship to the whole human race (see note on 2:31). From Abraham to David, the genealogies of Matthew and Luke are almost the same, but from David on they are different. Many interpreters suggest that this is because Matthew traces the legal

the son of Heli, [24]the son of Matthat,
the son of Levi, the son of Melki,
the son of Jannai, the son of Joseph,
[25]the son of Mattathias, the son of Amos,
the son of Nahum, the son of Esli,
the son of Naggai, [26]the son of Maath,
the son of Mattathias, the son of Semein,
the son of Josek, the son of Joda,
[27]the son of Joanan, the son of Rhesa,
the son of Zerubbabel, [m] the son of Shealtiel,
the son of Neri, [28]the son of Melki,
the son of Addi, the son of Cosam,
the son of Elmadam, the son of Er,
[29]the son of Joshua, the son of Eliezer,
the son of Jorim, the son of Matthat,
the son of Levi, [30]the son of Simeon,
the son of Judah, the son of Joseph,
the son of Jonam, the son of Eliakim,
[31]the son of Melea, the son of Menna,
the son of Mattatha, the son of Nathan, [n]
the son of David, [32]the son of Jesse,
the son of Obed, the son of Boaz,
the son of Salmon, [a] the son of Nahshon,
[33]the son of Amminadab, the son of Ram, [b]
the son of Hezron, the son of Perez, [o]
the son of Judah, [34]the son of Jacob,
the son of Isaac, the son of Abraham,
the son of Terah, the son of Nahor, [p]
[35]the son of Serug, the son of Reu,
the son of Peleg, the son of Eber,
the son of Shelah, [36]the son of Cainan,
the son of Arphaxad, [q] the son of Shem,
the son of Noah, the son of Lamech, [r]
[37]the son of Methuselah, the son of Enoch,
the son of Jared, the son of Mahalalel,
the son of Kenan, [s] [38]the son of Enosh,
the son of Seth, the son of Adam,
the son of God. [t]

JESUS IS TESTED IN THE WILDERNESS
4:1–13pp — Mt 4:1–11; Mk 1:12,13

4 Jesus, full of the Holy Spirit, [u] left the Jordan [v] and was led by the Spirit [w] into the wilderness, [2]where for forty days [x] he was tempted[c] by the devil. [y] He ate nothing during those days, and at the end of them he was hungry.

[a] *32* Some early manuscripts *Sala*   [b] *33* Some manuscripts *Amminadab, the son of Admin, the son of Arni*; other manuscripts vary widely.   [c] *2* The Greek for *tempted* can also mean *tested*.

3:27 [m] Mt 1:12
3:31 [n] 2Sa 5:14;
1Ch 3:5
3:33 [o] Ru 4:18-22;
1Ch 2:10-12
3:34 [p] Ge 11:24,26
3:36 [q] Ge 11:12
[r] Ge 5:28-32
3:37 [s] Ge 5:12-25
3:38 [t] Ge 5:1,2,6-9
4:1 [u] ver 14,18;
S Lk 1:15,35; 3:16,22;
10:21 [v] Lk 3:3,21
[w] Eze 37:1; Lk 2:27
4:2 [x] Ex 34:28;
1Ki 19:8 [y] Heb 4:15

descent of the house of David, using only heirs to the throne, while Luke traces the direct bloodline of Joseph to David (see Introduction to 1 Chronicles: Genealogies)—perhaps the preferred view. Another common explanation is that Matthew follows the line of Joseph (Jesus' legal father through Solomon; see Mt 1:6–7, 16), while Luke emphasizes that of Mary (Jesus' blood relative through Nathan, v. 31). Although tracing a genealogy through the mother's side was unusual, so was the virgin birth. Luke's explanation here that Jesus was the son of Joseph, "so it was thought" (v. 23), brings to mind his explicit virgin birth statement (1:34–35) and suggests the importance of the role of Mary in Jesus' genealogy. However, this view is less likely since Luke here so explicitly names Joseph (v. 23), without any reference at all to Mary.
3:23 *about thirty years old.* Luke, a historian, relates the beginning of Jesus' public ministry both to world history (see vv. 1–2) and to the rest of Jesus' life. Thirty was the age when a Levite

undertook his service (Nu 4:47) and when a man was considered mature. *so it was thought.* Luke had already affirmed the virgin birth (1:34–35) and here makes clear again that Joseph was not Jesus' physical father.
4:1 *full of the Holy Spirit.* Luke emphasizes the Holy Spirit not only in his Gospel (1:35,41,67; 2:25–27; 3:16,22; 4:14,18; 10:21; 11:13; 12:10,12) but also in Acts, where the Spirit is mentioned 57 times. *into the wilderness.* The Desert of Judea (see notes on 1:80; Mt 3:1).
4:2 *he was tempted.* See notes on Mt 4:1–11; 4:1; Heb 2:18; 4:15. Luke states that Jesus was tempted for the 40 days he was fasting, and the three specific temptations recounted in Matthew and Luke seem to have occurred at the close of this period—when Jesus' hunger was greatest and his resistance lowest. The sequence of the second and third temptations differs in Matthew and Luke. Matthew probably followed the chronological order, since at the end of the mountain temptation (Mat-

4:3 *z* S Mt 4:3
4:4 *a* Dt 8:3
4:5 *b* S Mt 24:14
4:6 *c* Jn 12:31; 14:30;
1Jn 5:19
4:8 *d* Dt 6:13
4:11 *e* Ps 91:11,12
4:12 *f* Dt 6:16
4:13 *g* Heb 4:15
h Jn 14:30
4:14 *i* Mt 4:12
j S Mt 9:26
4:15 *k* S Mt 4:23
4:16 *l* S Mt 2:23
m Mt 13:54
n S 1Ti 4:13
4:18 *o* S Jn 3:34
p Mk 16:15
4:19 *q* Lev 25:10;
Isa 61:1,2; Ps 102:20;
103:6; Isa 42:7; 49:8,
9; 58:6
4:20 *r* ver 17;
S Mt 26:55

³The devil said to him, "If you are the Son of God, *z* tell this stone to become bread."

⁴Jesus answered, "It is written: 'People do not live on bread alone.'ᵃ" *a*

⁵The devil led him up to a high place and showed him in an instant all the kingdoms of the world. *b* ⁶And he said to him, "I will give you all their authority and splendor; it has been given to me, *c* and I can give it to anyone I want to. ⁷If you worship me, it will all be yours."

⁸Jesus answered, "It is written: 'Worship the Lord your God and serve him only.'ᵇ" *d*

⁹The devil led him to Jerusalem and had him stand on the highest point of the temple. "If you are the Son of God," he said, "throw yourself down from here. ¹⁰For it is written:

" 'He will command his angels concerning you
    to guard you carefully;
¹¹they will lift you up in their hands,
    so that you will not strike your foot against a stone.'ᶜ" *e*

¹²Jesus answered, "It is said: 'Do not put the Lord your God to the test.'ᵈ" *f*

¹³When the devil had finished all this tempting, *g* he left him *h* until an opportune time.

JESUS REJECTED AT NAZARETH

¹⁴Jesus returned to Galilee *i* in the power of the Spirit, and news about him spread through the whole countryside. *j* ¹⁵He was teaching in their synagogues, *k* and everyone praised him.

¹⁶He went to Nazareth, *l* where he had been brought up, and on the Sabbath day he went into the synagogue, *m* as was his custom. He stood up to read, *n* ¹⁷and the scroll of the prophet Isaiah was handed to him. Unrolling it, he found the place where it is written:

¹⁸"The Spirit of the Lord is on me, *o*
    because he has anointed me
    to proclaim good news *p* to the poor.
He has sent me to proclaim freedom for the prisoners
    and recovery of sight for the blind,
to set the oppressed free,
¹⁹ to proclaim the year of the Lord's favor."ᵉ *q*

²⁰Then he rolled up the scroll, gave it back to the attendant and sat down. *r* The eyes

ᵃ *4* Deut. 8:3   ᵇ *8* Deut. 6:13   ᶜ *11* Psalm 91:11,12   ᵈ *12* Deut. 6:16   ᵉ *19* Isaiah 61:1,2 (see Septuagint); Isaiah 58:6

---

thew's third) Jesus told Satan to leave (Mt 4:10). To emphasize a certain point the Gospel writers often bring various events together, not intending to imply chronological sequence. Perhaps Luke's focus here is geographical, as he concludes with Jesus in Jerusalem.

🅰 4:3 *If you are.* See note on Mt 4:3. *tell this stone to become bread.* The devil always makes his temptations seem attractive.

🅲 4:6 *their authority . . . has been given to me.* Satan is elsewhere called "the prince of this world" (Jn 12:31), "the god of this age" (2Co 4:4) and "the ruler of the kingdom of the air" (Eph 2:2)—but remains under God's sovereign power and control (cf. notes on 2Sa 24:1; Job 1:12; 2Co 4:4).

🅰 4:7 *worship me.* The devil was tempting Jesus to avoid the sufferings of the cross, which he came specifically to endure (see Mk 10:45 and note). The temptation offered an easy shortcut to world dominion.

4:9 *the highest point of the temple.* Either the southeast corner of the temple colonnade, from which there was a drop of some 100 feet to the Kidron Valley below, or the pinnacle of the temple proper. *temple.* See note on Mt 4:5. *If you are.* See note on Mt 4:3. *throw yourself down.* Satan was tempting Jesus to test God's faithfulness and to attract public attention dramatically.

4:10 *For it is written.* This time Satan also quoted Scripture, though he misused Ps 91:11–12.

4:12 Jesus answered with Scripture, as he had on each of the other two occasions, quoting from Deuteronomy (see TNIV text notes here).

4:13 *he left him until an opportune time.* Satan continued his testing throughout Jesus' ministry (see Mk 8:33 and note), cul-

minating in the supreme test at Gethsemane.

4:14 *in the power of the Spirit.* See note on v. 1.

4:15 *was teaching in their synagogues.* See note on Mk 1:21.

🅰 4:16 *He went to Nazareth.* Not at the start of his ministry but perhaps almost a year later (v. 23 presupposes that Jesus had already been ministering). Probably all the events of Jn 1:19—4:42 occurred between Lk 4:13 and 4:14. *as was his custom.* Jesus' custom of regular worship sets an example for all his followers. *to read.* Jesus probably read from Isaiah in Hebrew, and then he or someone else paraphrased it in Aramaic, one of the other common languages of the day.

4:17 *the scroll of the prophet Isaiah.* The books of the OT were written on scrolls, kept in a special place in the synagogue and handed to the reader by a special attendant. The passage Jesus read about the Messiah (Isa 61:1–2; see notes there) may have been one he chose to read, or it may have been the assigned passage for the day.

🅰 4:18 This verse tells of the Messiah's ministry of preaching and healing—to meet every human need. *he has anointed me.* Not with literal oil (see Ex 30:22–31), but with the Holy Spirit.

🅰 4:19 *the year of the Lord's favor.* Not a calendar year, but the period when salvation would be proclaimed—the Messianic age. This quotation from Isa 61:1–2 alludes to the Year of Jubilee (Lev 25:8–55), when once every 50 years slaves were freed, debts were canceled and ancestral property was returned to the original family. Isaiah predicted primarily the liberation of Israel from the future Babylonian exile, but Jesus proclaimed liberation from sin and all its consequences.

4:20 *sat down.* It was customary to stand while reading Scripof everyone in the synagogue were fastened on him. ²¹He began by saying to them, "Today this scripture is fulfilled ˢ in your hearing."

²²All spoke well of him and were amazed at the gracious words that came from his lips. "Isn't this Joseph's son?" they asked. ᵗ

²³Jesus said to them, "Surely you will quote this proverb to me: 'Physician, heal yourself!' And you will tell me, 'Do here in your hometown ᵘ what we have heard that you did in Capernaum.' " ᵛ

²⁴"Truly I tell you," he continued, "prophets are not accepted in their hometowns. ʷ ²⁵I assure you that there were many widows in Israel in Elijah's time, when the sky was shut for three and a half years and there was a severe famine throughout the land. ˣ ²⁶Yet Elijah was not sent to any of them, but to a widow in Zarephath in the region of Sidon. ʸ ²⁷And there were many in Israel with leprosyᵃ in the time of Elisha the prophet, yet not one of them was cleansed—only Naaman the Syrian." ᶻ

4:21 ˢ S Mt 1:22
4:22 ᵗ Mt 13:54,55; Jn 6:42; 7:15
4:23 ᵘ ver 16; S Mt 2:23 ᵛ Mk 1:21-28; 2:1-12
4:24 ʷ Mt 13:57; Jn 4:44
4:25 ˣ 1Ki 17:1; 18:1; Jas 5:17,18; Rev 11:6
4:26 ʸ 1Ki 17:8-16; S Mt 11:21
4:27 ᶻ 2Ki 5:1-14

ᵃ 27 The Greek word traditionally translated *leprosy* was used for various diseases affecting the skin.

---

ture (v. 16) but to sit while teaching (see 5:3; Mt 5:1 and note; 26:55; Mk 4:1; 9:35; Jn 8:2; Ac 16:13).

4:23 *hometown.* Nazareth. Although Jesus was born in Bethlehem, he was brought up in Nazareth, in Galilee (see 1:26; 2:39,51; Mt 2:23 and note). *Capernaum.* See note on Mt 4:13.

4:26–27 Mention of Jesus' reference to God's helping two non-Israelites (1Ki 17:1–15; 2Ki 5:1–14) reflects Luke's

special concern for the Gentiles. Jesus' point was that when Israel rejected God's messenger of redemption God sent him to the Gentiles—and so it will be again if they refuse to accept Jesus (see 10:13–15 and notes; Ro 9–11).

4:26 *Sidon.* One of the oldest Phoenician cities, 20 miles north of Tyre. Jesus later healed a Gentile woman's daughter in this region (Mt 15:21–28).

CAPERNAUM SYNAGOGUE

Houses - based on excavations

Side streets (dotted lines) for illustration only— artist's concept

Ancient village was without walls

Extent of ruins

Excavated houses

First-century pavement

Proposed structure

Plan of 4th-century synagogue

Meters 0 10 20 30

Sea wall

Basalt stylobates (low walls to support columns)

Foundations of octagonal Christian church

Excavated houses

Traditional site of Peter's house

Sea wall

N

Sea of Galilee

Capernaum was more than a seaside fishing village in the days of Jesus. It was the place that Christ chose to be the center of his ministry to the entire region of Galilee, and it possessed ideal characteristics as a point of dissemination for the gospel.

There were good reasons for this. The town itself was named *Kephar Nahum,* "village of (perhaps the prophet) Nahum," and was the centerpiece of a densely populated region having a bicultural flavor. On the one hand, there were numerous syna-

gogues in Galilee (in addition to the one in Capernaum), where the ferment of Jewish religious life was profound. On the other hand, there was Hellenism, a pervasive culture already centuries old and potent in its paganism—a lifestyle that influenced manners, dress, architecture and political institutions as well.

B Recent archaeological work at Capernaum (during the latter half of the 20th century) has revealed a section of the pavement of a first-century synagogue below the still-existing ruins of the fourth-century synagogue on the site. A private house later made into a church and a place of pilgrimage has yielded some evidence that may link it to the site of Simon Peter's house (Lk 4:38).

4:29 *a* Nu 15:35;
Ac 7:58; Heb 13:12
4:30 *b* Jn 8:59; 10:39
4:31 *c* ver 23;
S Mt 4:13
4:32 *d* S Mt 7:28
e ver 36; Mt 7:29
4:34 *f* S Mt 8:29
g S Mk 1:24 *h* Jas 2:19
i ver 41; S Mk 1:24
4:35 *j* ver 39, 41;
Mt 8:26; Lk 8:24
4:36 *k* S Mt 7:28
l ver 32; Mt 7:29;
S Mt 10:1
4:37 *m* ver 14;
S Mt 9:26
4:39 *n* ver 35, 41
4:40 *o* S Mk 5:23
p S Mt 4:23
4:41 *q* S Mt 4:3
r S ver 35 *s* Mt 8:4
4:43 *t* S Mt 3:2
4:44 *u* S Mt 4:23
5:1 *v* S Mk 4:14;
S Heb 4:12

28All the people in the synagogue were furious when they heard this. 29They got up, drove him out of the town, *a* and took him to the brow of the hill on which the town was built, in order to throw him off the cliff. 30But he walked right through the crowd and went on his way. *b*

JESUS DRIVES OUT AN EVIL SPIRIT
4:31–37pp — Mk 1:21–28

31Then he went down to Capernaum, *c* a town in Galilee, and on the Sabbath he taught the people. 32They were amazed at his teaching, *d* because his words had authority. *e*

33In the synagogue there was a man possessed by a demon, an evil*a* spirit. He cried out at the top of his voice, 34"Go away! What do you want with us, *f* Jesus of Nazareth? *g* Have you come to destroy us? I know who you are *h*—the Holy One of God!" *i*

35"Be quiet!" Jesus said sternly. *j* "Come out of him!" Then the demon threw the man down before them all and came out without injuring him.

36All the people were amazed *k* and said to each other, "What words these are! With authority *l* and power he gives orders to evil spirits and they come out!" 37And the news about him spread throughout the surrounding area. *m*

JESUS HEALS MANY
4:38–41pp — Mt 8:14–17
4:38–43pp — Mk 1:29–38

38Jesus left the synagogue and went to the home of Simon. Now Simon's mother-in-law was suffering from a high fever, and they asked Jesus to help her. 39So he bent over her and rebuked *n* the fever, and it left her. She got up at once and began to wait on them.

40At sunset, the people brought to Jesus all who had various kinds of sickness, and laying his hands on each one, *o* he healed them. *p* 41Moreover, demons came out of many people, shouting, "You are the Son of God!" *q* But he rebuked *r* them and would not allow them to speak, *s* because they knew he was the Messiah.

42At daybreak, Jesus went out to a solitary place. The people were looking for him and when they came to where he was, they tried to keep him from leaving them. 43But he said, "I must proclaim the good news of the kingdom of God *t* to the other towns also, because that is why I was sent." 44And he kept on preaching in the synagogues of Judea. *u*

JESUS CALLS HIS FIRST DISCIPLES
5:1–11pp — Mt 4:18–22; Mk 1:16–20; Jn 1:40–42

5 One day as Jesus was standing by the Lake of Gennesaret, *b* the people were crowding around him and listening to the word of God. *v* 2He saw at the water's edge two boats, left there by the fishermen, who were washing their nets. 3He got into

a 33 Greek *unclean*; also in verse 36   *b 1* That is, the Sea of Galilee

---

4:28 *furious.* Because of Jesus' inclusion of Gentiles as recipients of God's blessings.

4:30 *walked right through the crowd.* Luke does not explain whether the escape was miraculous or simply the result of Jesus' commanding presence. In any case, his time (to die) had not yet come (see Jn 7:30 and note).

4:32 See note on Mk 1:22.

4:33 *possessed by a demon.* To pagans, "demon" meant a supernatural being, whether good or bad, but Luke makes it clear that this was an evil spirit. Such a demon could cause mental disorder (Jn 10:20), violent action (Lk 8:26–29), bodily disease (13:11,16) and rebellion against God (Rev 16:14).

4:34 *Holy One of God.* See note on Mk 1:24.

4:36 *amazed.* See v. 32 and note on Mk 1:22.

4:38 *synagogue.* See notes on Mt 4:13; Mk 1:21. *home of Simon.* See diagram, p. 1725. *Simon's mother-in-law.* Peter was married (see 1Co 9:5 and note). *high fever.* All three Synoptics tell of this miracle (Mt 8:14–15; Mk 1:29–31), but only Luke, the doctor, uses the more specific phrase "high fever."

4:40 *At sunset.* The Sabbath (v. 31) was over at sundown (about 6:00 P.M.). According to the tradition of the elders, Jews could not carry a burden or travel more than about two-thirds of a mile on the Sabbath. Only after sundown could they carry the sick to Jesus, and their eagerness is seen in the fact that they set out while the sun was still setting.

4:41 *because they knew he was the Messiah.* See note on Mk 1:34.

4:42 *solitary place.* Mark includes the words "where he prayed" (Mk 1:35).

4:43 *kingdom of God.* Luke's first use of this phrase; it occurs over 30 times in his Gospel. Some of its different meanings in the Bible are: the eternal kingship of God; the presence of the kingdom in the person of Jesus, the King; the approaching spiritual form of the kingdom; the future kingdom. See note on Mt 3:2.

4:44 This summary statement includes not only what has just been described (from v. 14 on) but also what lay ahead in Jesus' ministry. No express mention is made in the Synoptics of the early Judean ministry recorded in John (2:13—4:3), though it may be reflected in 13:34 (see note there) and Mt 23:37. *Judea.* Some manuscripts, as well as the parallel accounts (Mt 4:23; Mk 1:39), mention Galilee instead of Judea. In writing to a Gentile (see Introduction: Recipient and Purpose), Luke possibly used "Judea" to refer to the whole land of the Jews (see 23:5 and note; Ac 10:37; 11:1,29; 26:20).

5:1 *Lake of Gennesaret.* Luke is the only one who calls it this. The other Gospel writers call it the Sea of Galilee (see Mk 1:16 and note), and John twice calls it the Sea of Tiberias (see Jn 6:1 and note; 21:1).

5:2 *washing their nets.* After each period of fishing the nets were washed, stretched and prepared for reuse.

one of the boats, the one belonging to Simon, and asked him to put out a little from shore. Then he sat down and taught the people from the boat. *w*

⁴When he had finished speaking, he said to Simon, "Put out into deep water, and let down the nets for a catch." *x*

⁵Simon answered, "Master, *y* we've worked hard all night and haven't caught anything. *z* But because you say so, I will let down the nets."

⁶When they had done so, they caught such a large number of fish that their nets began to break. *a* ⁷So they signaled their partners in the other boat to come and help them, and they came and filled both boats so full that they began to sink.

⁸When Simon Peter saw this, he fell at Jesus' knees and said, "Go away from me, Lord; I am a sinful man!" *b* ⁹For he and all his companions were astonished at the catch of fish they had taken, ¹⁰and so were James and John, the sons of Zebedee, Simon's partners.

Then Jesus said to Simon, "Don't be afraid; *c* from now on you will fish for people." ¹¹So they pulled their boats up on shore, left everything and followed him. *d*

JESUS HEALS A MAN WITH LEPROSY
5:12–14pp — Mt 8:2–4; Mk 1:40–44

¹²While Jesus was in one of the towns, a man came along who was covered with leprosy. *a e* When he saw Jesus, he fell with his face to the ground and begged him, "Lord, if you are willing, you can make me clean."

¹³Jesus reached out his hand and touched the man. "I am willing," he said. "Be clean!" And immediately the leprosy left him.

¹⁴Then Jesus ordered him, "Don't tell anyone, *f* but go, show yourself to the priest and offer the sacrifices that Moses commanded *g* for your cleansing, as a testimony to them."

¹⁵Yet the news about him spread all the more, *h* so that crowds of people came to hear him and to be healed of their sicknesses. ¹⁶But Jesus often withdrew to lonely places and prayed. *i*

JESUS FORGIVES AND HEALS A PARALYZED MAN
5:18–26pp — Mt 9:2–8; Mk 2:3–12

¹⁷One day Jesus was teaching, and Pharisees and teachers of the law *j* were sitting there. They had come from every village of Galilee and from Judea and Jerusalem. And the power of the Lord was with Jesus to heal the sick. *k* ¹⁸Some men came carrying a paralyzed man on a mat and tried to take him into the house to lay him before Jesus. ¹⁹When they could not find a way to do this because of the crowd, they went up on the roof and lowered him on his mat through the tiles into the middle of the crowd, right in front of Jesus.

²⁰When Jesus saw their faith, he said, "Friend, your sins are forgiven." *l*

²¹The Pharisees and the teachers of the law began thinking to themselves, "Who is this fellow who speaks blasphemy? Who can forgive sins but God alone?" *m*

---

a 12 The Greek word traditionally translated *leprosy* was used for various diseases affecting the skin.

5:3 *w* Mt 13:2
5:4 *x* Jn 21:6
5:5 *y* Lk 8:24,45;
9:33,49; 17:13
z Jn 21:3
5:6 *a* Jn 21:11
5:8 *b* Ge 18:27;
Job 42:6; Isa 6:5
5:10 *c* S Mt 14:27
5:11 *d* ver 28;
S Mt 4:19
5:12 *e* S Mt 8:2
5:14 *f* S Mt 8:4
g Lev 14:2-32
5:15 *h* S Mt 9:26
5:16 *i* S Lk 3:21
5:17 *j* Mt 15:1;
Lk 2:46 *k* Mk 5:30;
Lk 6:19
5:20 *l* Lk 7:48,49
5:21 *m* Isa 43:25

5:3 *sat down.* The usual position for teaching (see note on 4:20). The boat provided an ideal arrangement, removed from the press of the crowd but near enough for Jesus to be seen and heard.
5:7 *their partners.* See v. 10.

■ **5:8** *Go away from me, Lord.* The nearer people come to God, the more they feel their own sinfulness and unworthiness—as did Abraham (see Ge 18:27 and note), Job (see 42:6 and note) and Isaiah (6:5).
5:11 *left everything and followed him.* This was not the first time these men had been with Jesus (see Mk 1:17 and note; Jn 1:40–42; 2:1–2). Their periodic and loose association now became a closely knit fellowship as they followed the Master. The scene is the same as Mt 4:18–22 and Mk 1:16–20, but the accounts relate events from different hours of the morning.
5:12–16 The healing of the man with leprosy is described in all three of the Synoptic Gospels, but the setting is different in each.
5:12 *covered with leprosy.* See TNIV text note; see also note on Lev 13:2. Luke alone notes the extent of his disease.
5:14 *Don't tell anyone.* See notes on Mt 8:4; 16:20. *but go, show yourself to the priest.* By this command Jesus urged the man to keep the law, to provide further proof for the actual healing, to testify to the authorities concerning his ministry and to supply

ritual certification of cleansing so the man could be reinstated into society. *a testimony to them.* See note on Mk 1:44.
5:17 *Pharisees and teachers of the law.* See notes on Mt 2:4; 3:7; Mk 2:16. Opposition was rising in Galilee from these religious leaders. *Pharisees.* Mentioned here for the first time in Luke (see essay, p. 1596, and chart, p. 1650). Their name means "separated ones"; they numbered about 6,000 and were spread over the whole of the Holy Land. They were teachers in the synagogues, religious examples in the eyes of the people and self-appointed guardians of the law and its proper observance. They considered the interpretations and regulations handed down by tradition to be virtually as authoritative as Scripture (Mk 7:8–13). Already Jesus had run counter to the Jewish leaders in Jerusalem (Jn 5:16–18). Now they came to a home in Capernaum (Mk 2:1–6) to hear and watch him. *teachers of the law.* "Scribes," who studied, interpreted and taught the law (both written and oral); see note on Ezr 7:6. The majority of these teachers belonged to the party of the Pharisees.
5:19 *roof.* See note on Mk 2:4. *tiles.* Probably ceiling tiles.
5:21 *this fellow . . . speaks blasphemy.* See note on Mk 2:7. The Pharisees considered blasphemy to be the most serious sin anyone could commit (see note on Mk 14:64).

5:24 *n* S Mt 8:20
5:26 *o* S Mt 9:8
5:27 *p* S Mt 4:19
5:28 *q* ver 11;
S Mt 4:19
5:29 *r* Lk 15:1
5:30 *s* Ac 23:9
t S Mt 9:11
5:32 *u* S Jn 3:17
5:33 *v* Lk 7:18;
Jn 1:35; 3:25,26
5:34 *w* Jn 3:29
5:35 *x* Lk 9:22;
17:22; Jn 16:5-7
6:1 *y* Dt 23:25
6:2 *z* S Mt 12:2
6:3 *a* 1Sa 21:6

[22]Jesus knew what they were thinking and asked, "Why are you thinking these things in your hearts? [23]Which is easier: to say, 'Your sins are forgiven,' or to say, 'Get up and walk'? [24]But I want you to know that the Son of Man *n* has authority on earth to forgive sins." So he said to the paralyzed man, "I tell you, get up, take your mat and go home." [25]Immediately he stood up in front of them, took what he had been lying on and went home praising God. [26]Everyone was amazed and gave praise to God. *o* They were filled with awe and said, "We have seen remarkable things today."

JESUS CALLS LEVI AND EATS WITH SINNERS
5:27–32pp — Mt 9:9–13; Mk 2:14–17

[27]After this, Jesus went out and saw a tax collector by the name of Levi sitting at his tax booth. "Follow me," *p* Jesus said to him, [28]and Levi got up, left everything and followed him. *q*

[29]Then Levi held a great banquet for Jesus at his house, and a large crowd of tax collectors *r* and others were eating with them. [30]But the Pharisees and the teachers of the law who belonged to their sect *s* complained to his disciples, "Why do you eat and drink with tax collectors and sinners?" *t*

[31]Jesus answered them, "It is not the healthy who need a doctor, but the sick. [32]I have not come to call the righteous, but sinners to repentance." *u*

JESUS QUESTIONED ABOUT FASTING
5:33–39pp — Mt 9:14–17; Mk 2:18–22

[33]They said to him, "John's disciples *v* often fast and pray, and so do the disciples of the Pharisees, but yours go on eating and drinking."

[34]Jesus answered, "Can you make the friends of the bridegroom *w* fast while he is with them? [35]But the time will come when the bridegroom will be taken from them; *x* in those days they will fast."

[36]He told them this parable: "No one tears a piece out of a new garment to patch an old one. If they do, they will have torn the new garment, and the patch from the new will not match the old. [37]And people do not pour new wine into old wineskins. If they do, the new wine will burst the skins; the wine will run out and the wineskins will be ruined. [38]No, new wine must be poured into new wineskins. [39]And none of you, after drinking old wine, wants the new, for you say, 'The old is better.' "

JESUS IS LORD OF THE SABBATH
6:1–11pp — Mt 12:1–14; Mk 2:23–3:6

6 One Sabbath Jesus was going through the grainfields, and his disciples began to pick some heads of grain, rub them in their hands and eat the kernels. *y* [2]Some of the Pharisees asked, "Why are you doing what is unlawful on the Sabbath?" *z*

[3]Jesus answered them, "Have you never read what David did when he and his companions were hungry? *a* [4]He entered the house of God, and taking the consecrated bread, he

---

5:23 *Which is easier: to say . . . ?* See notes on Mk 2:9–10.

5:24 *I want you to know.* Jesus' power to heal was a visible affirmation of his power to forgive sins. *Son of Man.* See note on Mk 8:31.

5:25 *praising God.* See v. 26; see also 1:64 and note.

5:27 *tax collector.* See note on 3:12. *Levi.* Another name for Matthew (6:15). *tax booth.* The place where customs were collected (see note on Mk 2:14).

5:28 *left everything and followed him.* Since Jesus had been ministering in Capernaum for some time, Levi probably had known him previously (see note on v. 11).

5:29 *great banquet.* When Levi began to follow Jesus, he did not do it secretly (cf. Jn 19:38 and note).

5:30 *Pharisees . . . complained.* They probably stood outside and registered their complaints from a distance. *eat . . . with tax collectors and sinners.* See note on Mk 2:15.

A **5:31** *not the healthy who need a doctor, but the sick.* Not to imply that the Pharisees were "the healthy" but that people must recognize themselves as sinners before they can be spiritually healed (see note on Mk 2:17).

C **5:33** *John's disciples . . . fast and pray.* John the Baptist had grown up in the wilderness and learned to subsist on an austere diet of locusts and wild honey. His ministry was characterized by a sober message and a strenuous schedule. For a contrast between Jesus' ministry and John the Baptist's, see 7:24–28; Mt 11:1–19. The Pharisees also had rigorous lifestyles (see note on 18:12). But Jesus went to banquets, and his disciples enjoyed a freedom not known by the Pharisees. *fast.* See notes on 18:12; Mk 2:18. While Jesus rejected fasting legalistically for display (cf. Isa 58:3–11), he himself fasted privately and permitted voluntary use of fasting for spiritual benefit (Mt 4:2; 6:16–18).

5:35 See notes on Mk 2:19–20.

5:36 *parable.* See notes on Mt 13:3; Mk 4:2.

5:38 *new wineskins.* See note on Mt 9:17.

5:39 *The old is better.* Jesus was indicating the reluctance of some people to change from their traditional religious ways and try the gospel.

6:1 *going through the grainfields.* See note on Mk 2:23.

6:3 *what David did.* See note on Mk 2:25.

6:4 *consecrated bread.* See note on Mt 12:4.

ate what is lawful only for priests to eat.[b] And he also gave some to his companions." [5]Then Jesus said to them, "The Son of Man[c] is Lord of the Sabbath."

[6]On another Sabbath[d] he went into the synagogue and was teaching, and a man was there whose right hand was shriveled. [7]The Pharisees and the teachers of the law were looking for a reason to accuse Jesus, so they watched him closely[e] to see if he would heal on the Sabbath.[f] [8]But Jesus knew what they were thinking[g] and said to the man with the shriveled hand, "Get up and stand in front of everyone." So he got up and stood there.

[9]Then Jesus said to them, "I ask you, which is lawful on the Sabbath: to do good or to do evil, to save life or to destroy it?"

[10]He looked around at them all, and then said to the man, "Stretch out your hand." He did so, and his hand was completely restored. [11]But the Pharisees and the teachers of the law were furious[h] and began to discuss with one another what they might do to Jesus.

THE TWELVE APOSTLES

6:13–16pp — Mt 10:2–4; Mk 3:16–19; Ac 1:13

[12]One of those days Jesus went out to a mountainside to pray, and spent the night praying to God.[i] [13]When morning came, he called his disciples to him and chose twelve of them, whom he also designated apostles:[j] [14]Simon (whom he named Peter), his brother Andrew, James, John, Philip, Bartholomew, [15]Matthew,[k] Thomas, James son of Alphaeus, Simon who was called the Zealot, [16]Judas son of James, and Judas Iscariot, who became a traitor.

BLESSINGS AND WOES

6:20–23pp — Mt 5:3–12

[17]He went down with them and stood on a level place. A large crowd of his disciples was there and a great number of people from all over Judea, from Jerusalem, and from the coastal region around Tyre and Sidon,[l] [18]who had come to hear him and to be healed of their diseases. Those troubled by evil[a] spirits were cured, [19]and the people all tried to touch him,[m] because power was coming from him and healing them all.[n]

[20]Looking at his disciples, he said:

"Blessed are you who are poor,
   for yours is the kingdom of God.[o]
[21]Blessed are you who hunger now,
   for you will be satisfied.[p]

---

a 18 Greek *unclean*

6:4 b Lev 24:5,9
6:5 c Mt 8:20
6:6 d ver 1
6:7 e S Mt 12:10
   f S Mt 12:2
6:8 g S Mt 9:4
6:11 h Jn 5:18
6:12 i S Lk 3:21
6:13 j S Mk 6:30
6:15 k Mt 9:9
6:17 l Mt 4:25;
   S Mt 11:21; Mk 3:7,8
6:19 m S Mt 9:20
   n Mk 5:30; Lk 5:17
6:20 o S Mt 25:34
6:21 p Isa 55:1,2;
   Mt 5:6

6:5 *Son of Man.* See note on Mk 8:31. *Lord of the Sabbath.* Jesus has the authority to overrule human regulations concerning the Sabbath, such as those reflecting the interpretations of the Pharisees (see Mt 12:8; Mk 2:27 and note).

6:7 *to see if he would heal on the Sabbath.* See note on Mk 3:2.

6:8 *stand in front of everyone.* So there would be no question about the healing.

6:9 *which is lawful on the Sabbath . . . ?* Jesus had been enduring questions and attacks from the Pharisees and now took the initiative by putting the questions to everyone in the synagogue (see note on Mk 3:4).

6:10 *He looked around at them.* Jesus wanted to see whether anyone objected to his question or the implied answer, but no one was bold enough to do so.

6:11 *were furious.* Because they could not withstand Jesus' reasoning. Already they were plotting to take his life (see Jn 5:18). See note on Mk 3:6.

6:12 Characteristically, Jesus spent the night in prayer before the important work of selecting his 12 apostles.

6:13 *he called his disciples.* Among those who came to hear Jesus was a group who regularly followed him and were committed to his teachings. At least 72 men were included, since this many disciples were sent out on an evangelistic campaign (10:1,17). Later, 120 believers waited and worshiped in Jerusalem following the ascension (Ac 1:15). From such disciples Jesus at this time chose 12 to be his apostles, a title meaning "ones sent with a special commission" (see notes on Mk 6:30; 1Co 1:1; Heb 3:1).

6:14–16 Lists of the apostles appear also in Mt 10:2–4; Mk

3:16–19; Ac 1:13. Although the order of the names varies, Peter is always first and Judas Iscariot last.

6:14 *Bartholomew.* Seems to be (in the Synoptics) the same as Nathanael (in John). Nathanael is associated with Philip in Jn 1:45.

6:15 *Matthew.* Another name for Levi (5:27). *James son of Alphaeus.* Probably the same as James the younger (Mk 15:40). *the Zealot.* See note on Mt 10:4.

6:16 *Judas son of James.* Another name for Thaddaeus (see Mt 10:3; Mk 3:18 and note). *Judas Iscariot.* Probably the only one from Judea, the rest coming from Galilee (see note on Mk 3:19).

6:17 *stood on a level place.* Perhaps a plateau, which would satisfy both this context and that in Mt 5:1 (see note on Mt 5:1—7:29). *Tyre and Sidon.* In Phoenicia (modern Lebanon); see notes on 4:26; 10:14; Mk 7:24,31; see also map, p. 1721.

6:20–49 Luke's Sermon on the Plain, apparently parallel to Matthew's Sermon on the Mount (Mt 5–7). Although this sermon is much shorter than the one in Matthew, they both begin with the Beatitudes and end with the lesson of the builders. Some of Matthew's Sermon is found in other portions of Luke (e.g., 11:2–4; 12:22–31,33–34), suggesting that the material may have been given on various occasions in Jesus' preaching.

6:20–23 See Mt 5:3–12 and notes. The Beatitudes go deeper than material poverty (v. 20) and physical hunger (v. 21). Matthew's account indicates that Jesus spoke of poverty "in spirit" (Mt 5:3) and hunger "for righteousness" (Mt 5:6).

6:20 *poor.* Those who are aware of their need of God's grace and provisions (cf. Mt 5:3 and note).

6:21 q Isa 61:2,3;
Mt 5:4; Rev 7:17
6:22 r Jn 9:22; 16:2
s Isa 51:7 r S Jn 15:21
6:23 u S Mt 5:12
v S Mt 5:12
6:24 w Jas 5:1
x Lk 16:25
6:25 y Isa 65:13
z Pr 14:13
6:26 a S Mt 7:15
6:27 b ver 35;
Mt 5:44; Ro 12:20
6:28 c S Mt 5:44
6:30 d Dt 15:7,8,10;
Pr 21:26
6:31 e Mt 7:12
6:32 f Mt 5:46
6:34 g Mt 5:42
6:35 h ver 27
i S Ro 8:14 i S Mk 5:7
6:36 k Jas 2:13
l Mt 5:48; 6:1; Lk 11:2;
12:32; Ro 8:15;
Eph 4:6; 1Pe 1:17;
1Jn 1:3; 3:1
6:37 m S Mt 7:1
n Mt 6:14
6:38 o Ps 79:12;
Isa 65:6,7 p S Mt 7:2
6:39 q Mt 15:14
6:40 r S Jn 13:16

> Blessed are you who weep now,
>> for you will laugh. q

22 Blessed are you when people hate you,
> when they exclude you r and insult you s
> and reject your name as evil,
>> because of the Son of Man. t

23 "Rejoice in that day and leap for joy, u because great is your reward in heaven. For that is how their ancestors treated the prophets. v

24 "But woe to you who are rich, w
>> for you have already received your comfort. x

25 Woe to you who are well fed now,
>> for you will go hungry. y

> Woe to you who laugh now,
>> for you will mourn and weep. z

26 Woe to you when everyone speaks well of you,
>> for that is how their ancestors treated the false prophets. a

LOVE FOR ENEMIES

6:29,30pp — Mt 5:39–42

27 "But to you who are listening I say: Love your enemies, do good to those who hate you, b 28 bless those who curse you, pray for those who mistreat you. c 29 If someone slaps you on one cheek, turn the other also. If someone takes your coat, do not withhold your shirt. 30 Give to everyone who asks you, and if anyone takes what belongs to you, do not demand it back. d 31 Do to others as you would have them do to you. e

32 "If you love those who love you, what credit is that to you? f Even sinners love those who love them. 33 And if you do good to those who are good to you, what credit is that to you? Even sinners do that. 34 And if you lend to those from whom you expect repayment, what credit is that to you? g Even sinners lend to sinners, expecting to be repaid in full. 35 But love your enemies, do good to them, h and lend to them without expecting to get anything back. Then your reward will be great, and you will be children i of the Most High, j because he is kind to the ungrateful and wicked. 36 Be merciful, k just as your Father l is merciful.

JUDGING OTHERS

6:37–42pp — Mt 7:1–5

37 "Do not judge, and you will not be judged. m Do not condemn, and you will not be condemned. Forgive, and you will be forgiven. n 38 Give, and it will be given to you. A good measure, pressed down, shaken together and running over, will be poured into your lap. o For with the measure you use, it will be measured to you." p

39 He also told them this parable: "Can the blind lead the blind? Will they not both fall into a pit? q 40 Students are not above their teacher, but all who are fully trained will be like their teacher. r

41 "Why do you look at the speck of sawdust in someone else's eye and pay no attention to the plank in your own eye? 42 How can you say, 'Friend, let me take the speck out of your eye,' when you yourself fail to see the plank in your own eye? You hypocrite, first take the plank out of your eye, and then you will see clearly to remove the speck from the other person's eye.

6:24–26 This section is a point-by-point negative counterpart of vv. 20–22.

6:27 *Love your enemies, do good.* The heart of Jesus' teaching is love. While the Golden Rule (v. 31) is sometimes expressed in negative form outside the Bible (see note on Mt 7:12), Jesus not only forbids treating others spitefully but also commands that we love everyone—even our enemies (see Mt 5:44 and note).

6:29 *turn the other also.* We are not to have a retaliatory attitude.

6:35 *Most High.* God (see Dt 32:8 and note).

6:36 *just as your Father is merciful.* God's perfection should be our example and goal (see Mt 5:48 and note).

6:37 *Do not judge.* Jesus did not relieve his followers of the need for discerning right and wrong (cf. vv. 43–45), but he condemned unjust and hypocritical judging of others (see note on Mt 7:1). *Forgive, and you will be forgiven.* See 11:4 and note.

6:38 *poured into your lap.* Probably refers to the way the outer garment was worn, leaving a fold over the belt that could be used as a large pocket to hold a measure of wheat.

6:41 *speck…plank.* Jesus used hyperbole (a figure of speech that overstates for emphasis) to sharpen the contrast and to emphasize how foolish and hypocritical it is for us to criticize someone for a fault while remaining blind to our own considerable faults (see Mt 7:3–4 and note on 7:3).

6:42 *hypocrite.* See notes on 13:15; Mt 23:23; Ac 5:9.

6:44 ˢ Mt 12:33
6:45 ᵗ Pr 4:23;
Mt 12:34,35; Mk 7:20
6:46 ᵘ S Jn 13:13
6:47 ᵛ Mal 1:6; Mt 7:21
11:28; Jas 1:22-25
7:1 ˣ Mt 7:28
7:7 ʸ Ps 107:20
7:13 ᶻ ver 19;
Lk 10:1; 13:15; 17:5;
22:61; 24:34; Jn 11:2
7:14 ᵃ Mt 9:25;
Mk 1:31; Lk 8:54;
Jn 11:43; Ac 9:40

A TREE AND ITS FRUIT

6:43,44pp — Mt 7:16,18,20

⁴³"No good tree bears bad fruit, nor does a bad tree bear good fruit. ⁴⁴Each tree is recognized by its own fruit. ˢ People do not pick figs from thornbushes, or grapes from briers. ⁴⁵Good people bring good things out of the good stored up in their heart, and evil people bring evil things out of the evil stored up in their heart. For out of the overflow of the heart the mouth speaks. ᵗ

THE WISE AND FOOLISH BUILDERS

6:47–49pp — Mt 7:24–27

⁴⁶"Why do you call me, 'Lord, Lord,'ᵘ and do not do what I say? ᵛ ⁴⁷As for those who come to me and hear my words and put them into practice, ʷ I will show you what they are like. ⁴⁸They are like a man building a house, who dug down deep and laid the foundation on rock. When a flood came, the torrent struck that house but could not shake it, because it was well built. ⁴⁹But those who hear my words and do not put them into practice are like a man who built a house on the ground without a foundation. The moment the torrent struck that house, it collapsed and its destruction was complete."

THE FAITH OF THE CENTURION

7:1–10pp — Mt 8:5–13

7 When Jesus had finished saying all thisˣ to the people who were listening, he entered Capernaum. ²There a centurion's servant, whom his master valued highly, was sick and about to die. ³The centurion heard of Jesus and sent some elders of the Jews to him, asking him to come and heal his servant. ⁴When they came to Jesus, they pleaded earnestly with him, "This man deserves to have you do this, ⁵because he loves our nation and has built our synagogue." ⁶So Jesus went with them.

He was not far from the house when the centurion sent friends to say to him: "Lord, don't trouble yourself, for I do not deserve to have you come under my roof. ⁷That is why I did not even consider myself worthy to come to you. But say the word, and my servant will be healed. ʸ ⁸For I myself am a man under authority, with soldiers under me. I tell this one, 'Go,' and he goes; and that one, 'Come,' and he comes. I say to my servant, 'Do this,' and he does it."

⁹When Jesus heard this, he was amazed at him, and turning to the crowd following him, he said, "I tell you, I have not found such great faith even in Israel." ¹⁰Then the men who had been sent returned to the house and found the servant well.

JESUS RAISES A WIDOW'S SON

7:11–16Ref — 1Ki 17:17–24; 2Ki 4:32–37; Mk 5:21–24,35–43; Jn 11:1–44

¹¹Soon afterward, Jesus went to a town called Nain, and his disciples and a large crowd went along with him. ¹²As he approached the town gate, a dead person was being carried out—the only son of his mother, and she was a widow. And a large crowd from the town was with her. ¹³When the Lordᶻ saw her, his heart went out to her and he said, "Don't cry."

¹⁴Then he went up and touched the bier they were carrying him on, and the bearers stood still. He said, "Young man, I say to you, get up!" ᵃ ¹⁵The dead man sat up and began to talk, and Jesus gave him back to his mother.

6:43–45 Cf. Jas 3:11–12 and note.

6:46–49 See Mt 7:24–27 and notes.

6:47,49 *hear my words and put them into practice ... do not put them into practice.* See Jas 1:22–25 and note on 1:25.

7:1 *Capernaum.* See note on Mt 4:13.

C **7:2** *centurion's servant.* The centurion was probably a member of Herod Antipas's forces, which were organized in Roman fashion, ordinarily in companies of 100 men (see note on Mt 8:5). Roman centurions referred to in the NT showed characteristics to be admired (see e.g., Ac 10:2 and note; 23:17–18; 27:43). This centurion showed genuine concern for his slave, and he was admired by the Jews, who spoke favorably of him even though he was a Gentile (see vv. 5,9).

7:3 *elders of the Jews.* Highly respected Jews of the community, though not necessarily rulers of the synagogue. They were willing to come and plead for the centurion. In Matthew's account (Mt 8:5–13) the centurion speaks with Jesus himself, while in

Luke's account he speaks with Jesus through his friends (see note on Mt 8:5).

7:6 *I do not deserve to have you come under my roof.* See note on Mt 8:8.

A **7:9** Cf. note on Mt 8:11. *he was amazed.* The amazement of Jesus is only mentioned twice, here because of belief and at Nazareth because of unbelief (Mk 6:6; see note on Mk 6:5).

7:11 *Nain.* Mentioned only here. A small village located a few miles south of Nazareth still bears this name. It is generally accepted as the site where this incident took place.

7:14 *touched the bier.* By so doing Jesus risked ritual uncleanness (cf. Nu 19:16). *bier.* The man was probably carried on a bier in an open coffin, suggested by Jewish custom and the fact that he sat up in response to Jesus' command. This is the first of three instances of Jesus' raising someone from the dead, the others being Jairus's daughter (8:40–56) and Lazarus (Jn 11:38–44).

7:15 *gave him back to his mother.* Cf. 1Ki 17:23; 2Ki 4:36–37.

7:16 *b* Lk 1:65
c S Mt 9:8 *d* ver 39;
S Mt 21:11 *e* Lk 1:68
7:17 *f* S Mt 9:26
7:18 *g* S Mt 3:1
h S Lk 5:33
7:21 *i* S Mt 4:23
7:22 *j* Isa 29:18,19;
35:5,6; 61:1,2; Lk 4:18
7:26 *k* S Mt 11:9
7:27 *l* Mal 3:1;
Mt 11:10; Mk 1:2
7:28 *m* S Mt 3:2
7:29 *n* Mt 21:32;
Mk 1:5; Lk 3:12
7:30 *o* S Mt 22:35
7:33 *p* Lk 1:15

¹⁶They were all filled with awe *b* and praised God. *c* "A great prophet *d* has appeared among us," they said. "God has come to help his people." *e* ¹⁷This news about Jesus spread throughout Judea and the surrounding country. *f*

JESUS AND JOHN THE BAPTIST
7:18–35pp — Mt 11:2–19

¹⁸John's *g* disciples *h* told him about all these things. Calling two of them, ¹⁹he sent them to the Lord to ask, "Are you the one who was to come, or should we expect someone else?"

²⁰When the men came to Jesus, they said, "John the Baptist sent us to you to ask, 'Are you the one who was to come, or should we expect someone else?' "

²¹At that very time Jesus cured many who had diseases, sicknesses *i* and evil spirits, and gave sight to many who were blind. ²²So he replied to the messengers, "Go back and report to John what you have seen and heard: The blind receive sight, the lame walk, those who have leprosy *a* are cleansed, the deaf hear, the dead are raised, and the good news is proclaimed to the poor. *j* ²³Blessed is anyone who does not stumble on account of me."

²⁴After John's messengers left, Jesus began to speak to the crowd about John: "What did you go out into the wilderness to see? A reed swayed by the wind? ²⁵If not, what did you go out to see? A man dressed in fine clothes? No, those who wear expensive clothes and indulge in luxury are in palaces. ²⁶But what did you go out to see? A prophet? *k* Yes, I tell you, and more than a prophet. ²⁷This is the one about whom it is written:

" 'I will send my messenger ahead of you,
    who will prepare your way before you.' *b l*

²⁸I tell you, among those born of women there is no one greater than John; yet the one who is least in the kingdom of God *m* is greater than he."

²⁹(All the people, even the tax collectors, when they heard Jesus' words, acknowledged that God's way was right, because they had been baptized by John. *n* ³⁰But the Pharisees and the experts in the law *o* rejected God's purpose for themselves, because they had not been baptized by John.)

³¹Jesus went on to say, "To what, then, can I compare the people of this generation? What are they like? ³²They are like children sitting in the marketplace and calling out to each other:

" 'We played the pipe for you,
    and you did not dance;
  we sang a dirge,
    and you did not cry.'

³³For John the Baptist came neither eating bread nor drinking wine, *p* and you say, 'He has a demon.' ³⁴The Son of Man came eating and drinking, and you say, 'Here is a glut-

a 22 The Greek word traditionally translated *leprosy* was used for various diseases affecting the skin.
b 27 Mal. 3:1

7:16 *praised God.* See 1:64 and note.
7:18 *John's disciples.* See note on 5:33; see also Mk 2:18. Despite John the Baptist's imprisonment, his disciples kept in contact with him and continued his ministry.
7:19 *should we expect someone else?* John had announced the coming of the Messiah, but now he himself had been languishing in prison for months, and the work of Jesus had not brought the results John apparently expected. His disappointment was natural. He wanted reassurance—and perhaps also wanted to urge Jesus to further action.
7:22 *report to John what you have seen and heard.* In answer, Jesus pointed to his healing and life-restoring miracles. He did not give promises but clearly observable evidence —evidence that reflected the predicted ministry of the Messiah. *the good news is proclaimed to the poor.* In Jesus' review of his works he used an ascending scale of impressive deeds, ending with the dead raised and the good news preached to the poor. In this way Jesus reminded John that these were the things predicted of the Messiah in the Scriptures (see Isa 29:18–21; 35:5–6 and notes; 61:1; Lk 4:18 and note).
7:23 *anyone who does not stumble.* Jesus did not want discouragement and doubt to ensnare John.

7:24 *What did you go…to see?* John was not a weak messenger, swayed by the pressures of human opinion. On the contrary, he was a true prophet.
7:26 *more than a prophet.* John was the unique prophet sent to prepare the way for the Messiah (v. 27).
7:28 *one who is least in the kingdom of God.* See note on Mt 11:11.
7:29 *tax collectors.* See note on Mt 5:46.
7:30 *experts in the law.* A designation used by Luke (see 10:25, 37; 11:45–46,52; 14:3; see also Mt 22:35) for the "scribes" (the teachers of the law), most of whom were Pharisees (see note on 5:17). *rejected God's purpose.* Tax collectors had shown their willingness to repent by accepting John's baptism, whereas the Pharisees showed their rejection of God's message by refusing to be baptized.
7:32 *like children sitting in the marketplace.* People had rejected both John and Jesus, but for different reasons—like children who refuse to play either a joyful game or a mournful one. They would not associate with John when he followed the strictest of rules or with Jesus when he freely associated with all kinds of people. *We played the pipe.* See note on Mt 11:17.
7:34 *Son of Man.* See note on Mk 8:31. *friend of tax collectors and sinners.* Jesus ate and talked with people who

ton and a drunkard, a friend of tax collectors and sinners.' *q* 35But wisdom is proved right by all her children."

JESUS ANOINTED BY A SINFUL WOMAN
7:37–39Ref — Mt 26:6–13; Mk 14:3–9; Jn 12:1–8
7:41,42Ref — Mt 18:23–34

36When one of the Pharisees invited Jesus to have dinner with him, he went to the Pharisee's house and reclined at the table. 37A woman in that town who lived a sinful life learned that Jesus was eating at the Pharisee's house, so she came there with an alabaster jar of perfume. 38As she stood behind him at his feet weeping, she began to wet his feet with her tears. Then she wiped them with her hair, kissed them and poured perfume on them.

39When the Pharisee who had invited Jesus saw this, he said to himself, "If this man were a prophet, *r* he would know who is touching him and what kind of woman she is— that she is a sinner."

40Jesus answered him, "Simon, I have something to tell you."

"Tell me, teacher," he said.

41"Two people owed money to a certain moneylender. One owed him five hundred denarii, *a* and the other fifty. 42Neither of them had the money to pay him back, so he forgave the debts of both. Now which of them will love him more?"

43Simon replied, "I suppose the one who had the bigger debt forgiven."

"You have judged correctly," Jesus said.

44Then he turned toward the woman and said to Simon, "Do you see this woman? I came into your house. You did not give me any water for my feet, *s* but she wet my feet with her tears and wiped them with her hair. 45You did not give me a kiss, *t* but this woman, from the time I entered, has not stopped kissing my feet. 46You did not put oil on my head, *u* but she has poured perfume on my feet. 47Therefore, I tell you, her many sins have been forgiven—as her great love has shown. But whoever has been forgiven little loves little."

48Then Jesus said to her, "Your sins are forgiven." *v*

49The other guests began to say among themselves, "Who is this who even forgives sins?"

50Jesus said to the woman, "Your faith has saved you; *w* go in peace." *x*

THE PARABLE OF THE SOWER
8:4–15pp — Mt 13:2–23; Mk 4:1–20

8 After this, Jesus traveled about from one town and village to another, proclaiming the good news of the kingdom of God. *y* The Twelve were with him, 2and also some women who had been cured of evil spirits and diseases: Mary (called Magdalene) *z* from whom seven demons had come out; 3Joanna the wife of Chuza, the manager of Herod's *a* household; Susanna; and many others. These women were helping to support them out of their own means.

a 41 A denarius was the daily wage of a day laborer (see Matt. 20:2).

7:34 *q* Lk 5:29,30; 15:1,2
7:39 *r* ver 16; S Mt 21:11
7:44 *s* Ge 18:4; 19:2; 43:24; Jdg 19:21; Jn 13:4-14; 1Ti 5:10
7:45 *t* Lk 22:47,48; S Ro 16:16
7:46 *u* Ps 23:5; Ecc 9:8
7:48 *v* Mt 9:2
7:50 *w* S Mt 9:22 *x* S Ac 15:33
8:1 *y* S Mt 4:23
8:2 *z* Mt 27:55,56
8:3 *a* S Mt 14:1

were religious and social outcasts. He even called a tax collector to be an apostle (5:27–32).

7:35 *wisdom is proved right by all her children.* In contrast to the rejection by foolish critics, spiritually wise persons could see that the ministries of both John and Jesus were godly, despite their differences. See note on Mt 11:19.

7:36–50 See note on Jn 12:1–11.

7:36 *one of the Pharisees.* See note on 5:17. His motive may have been to entrap Jesus rather than to learn from him.

7:37 *A woman ... who lived a sinful life.* She must have heard Jesus preach, and in repentance she determined to lead a new life. She came out of love and gratitude, in the understanding that she could be forgiven. *alabaster jar.* A long-necked, globular bottle. *perfume.* A perfumed ointment.

7:38 *stood behind him at his feet.* Jesus reclined on a couch with his feet extended away from the table, which made it possible for the woman to wipe his feet with her hair and still not disturb him. *poured perfume on them.* The anointing, perhaps originally intended for Jesus' head, was instead applied to his feet. A similar act was performed by Mary of Bethany just over a week before the crucifixion (see Jn 12:3 and note).

7:41 *five hundred denarii.* See TNIV text note.

7:44 *water for my feet.* The minimal gesture of hospitality.

7:47 *as her great love has shown.* Her love was evidence of her forgiveness, but not the basis for it. Verse 50 clearly states that she was saved by faith. See Eph 2:8 and note.

7:50 *Your faith has saved you.* Her sins were forgiven and she could experience God's peace (see 1:79 and note on 2:14).

8:1 *Jesus traveled about.* Jesus' ministry had been centered in Capernaum, and much of his preaching was in synagogues, but now he traveled again from town to town on a second tour of the Galilean countryside. For the first tour, see 4:43–44; Mt 4:23–25; Mk 1:38–39. For the third tour see note on 9:1–6. *kingdom of God.* See note on 4:43.

8:2 *Mary (called Magdalene).* Her hometown was Magdala. She is not to be confused with the sinful woman of ch. 7 or Mary of Bethany (Jn 11:1).

8:3 *Susanna.* Nothing more is known of her. *helping to support them.* Jesus and his disciples did not provide for themselves by miracles but were supported by the service and means of such grateful people as these women.

8:8 *b* S Mt 11:15
8:10 *c* S Mt 13:11
d Isa 6:9; S Mt 13:13,
14
8:11 *e* S Heb 4:12
8:13 *f* Mt 11:6
8:14 *g* Mt 19:23;
1Ti 6:9,10,17
8:16 *h* S Mt 5:15
8:17 *i* Mt 10:26;
Mk 4:22; Lk 12:2
8:18 *j* S Mt 25:29

⁴While a large crowd was gathering and people were coming to Jesus from town after town, he told this parable: ⁵"A farmer went out to sow his seed. As he was scattering the seed, some fell along the path; it was trampled on, and the birds ate it up. ⁶Some fell on rock, and when it came up, the plants withered because they had no moisture. ⁷Other seed fell among thorns, which grew up with it and choked the plants. ⁸Still other seed fell on good soil. It came up and yielded a crop, a hundred times more than was sown."

When he said this, he called out, "Whoever has ears to hear, let them hear." *b*

⁹His disciples asked him what this parable meant. ¹⁰He said, "The knowledge of the secrets of the kingdom of God has been given to you, *c* but to others I speak in parables, so that,

" 'though seeing, they may not see;
    though hearing, they may not understand.'*a d*

¹¹"This is the meaning of the parable: The seed is the word of God. *e* ¹²Those along the path are the ones who hear, and then the devil comes and takes away the word from their hearts, so that they may not believe and be saved. ¹³Those on the rock are the ones who receive the word with joy when they hear it, but they have no root. They believe for a while, but in the time of testing they fall away. *f* ¹⁴The seed that fell among thorns stands for those who hear, but as they go on their way they are choked by life's worries, riches*g* and pleasures, and they do not mature. ¹⁵But the seed on good soil stands for those with a noble and good heart, who hear the word, retain it, and by persevering produce a crop.

A LAMP ON A STAND

¹⁶"No one lights a lamp and hides it in a clay jar or puts it under a bed. Instead, they put it on a stand, so that those who come in can see the light. *h* ¹⁷For there is nothing hidden that will not be disclosed, and nothing concealed that will not be known or brought out into the open. *i* ¹⁸Therefore consider carefully how you listen. Those who have will be given more; as for those who do not have, even what they think they have will be taken from them." *j*

JESUS' MOTHER AND BROTHERS

8:19-21pp — Mt 12:46-50; Mk 3:31-35

¹⁹Now Jesus' mother and brothers came to see him, but they were not able to get near

a 10 Isaiah 6:9

8:4 *parable.* From this point on in Luke's Gospel Jesus used parables (see notes on Mt 13:3; Mk 4:2; see also Introduction: Characteristics) more extensively as a means of teaching. They were particularly effective and easy to remember because he used familiar scenes. Although parables clarified Jesus' teaching, they also included hidden meanings needing further explanation. These hidden meanings challenged the sincerely interested to further inquiry and taught truths that Jesus wanted to conceal from unbelievers (see v. 10 and note). From parables Jesus' enemies could find no direct statements to use against him. The parable of the sower is one of three parables recorded in each of the Synoptic Gospels (Mt 13:1-23; Mk 4:1-20). The others are those of the mustard seed (13:19; Mt 13:31-32; Mk 4:30-32) and of the vineyard (20:9-19; Mt 21:33- 46; Mk 12:1-12).

8:5 *sow his seed.* In Eastern practice the seed was sometimes sown first and the field plowed afterward. Roads and pathways went directly through many fields, and the traffic made much of the surface too hard for seed to take root.

8:6 *on rock.* On a thin layer of soil that covered solid rock. Any moisture that fell there soon evaporated, and the germinating seed withered and died (see Mt 13:5-6).

8:8 *a hundred times more.* Luke's version is more abbreviated than Matthew's (13:8) and Mark's (4:8), but the point is the same: The quantity of increase depends on the quality of soil. *let them hear.* A challenge for listeners to understand the message and appropriate it for themselves.

8:9 *His disciples.* They included "the Twelve and the others" (Mk 4:10).

8:10 *secrets of the kingdom of God.* Truths that can be known only by revelation from God (cf. Eph 3:3 and note;

1Pe 1:10-12). See note on Mk 4:11. *though seeing, they may not see.* This quotation from Isaiah (6:9) does not express a desire that some would not understand but simply states the sad truth that those who are not willing to receive Jesus' message will find the truth hidden from them. Their ultimate fate is implied in the fuller quotation in Mt 13:14-15 (see note on Mk 4:12).

8:11 *the word of God.* The message that comes from God.

8:12 *may not believe.* The devil's purpose is that people will not hear with understanding and therefore not appropriate the message and be saved.

8:13 *They believe for a while.* This kind of belief is superficial and does not save. It is similar to what James calls "dead" (Jas 2:17,26) or "useless" faith (Jas 2:20; see notes on Jas 2:14-26).

8:16 *lights a lamp.* Although Jesus couched much of his message in parables, he intended that the disciples make the truths known as widely as possible (see note on 11:33). *put it on a stand.* See note on Mt 5:15.

8:17 This verse explains v. 16. It is the destiny of the truth to be made known (cf. 12:2 and note). The disciples were to begin a proclamation that would become universal.

8:18 *consider carefully how you listen.* The disciples heard not only for themselves but also for those to whom they would minister (see Mk 4:24; cf. Jas 1:19-22). Truth that is not understood and appropriated will be lost (see 19:26; Php 3:16 and notes), but truth that is used will be multiplied.

8:19 *Jesus' mother and brothers came.* See note on Mk 3:21. More is known about their motive from Mk 3:21, 31-32. The family, thinking he was "out of his mind" (Mk 3:21), probably wanted to get him away from his heavy schedule.

8:20 *k* Jn 7:5
8:21 *l* Lk 6:47; 11:28; Jn 14:21
8:24 *m* S Lk 5:5
n Lk 4:35,39,41
o Ps 107:29; Jnh 1:15
8:28 *p* S Mt 8:29
q S Mk 5:7
8:31 *r* Rev 9:1,2,11; 11:7; 17:8; 20:1,3
8:33 *s* ver 22,23
8:35 *t* Lk 10:39
8:36 *u* S Mt 4:24
8:37 *v* Ac 16:39

him because of the crowd. [20]Someone told him, "Your mother and brothers[k] are standing outside, wanting to see you."

[21]He replied, "My mother and brothers are those who hear God's word and put it into practice."[l]

JESUS CALMS THE STORM

8:22–25pp — Mt 8:23–27; Mk 4:36–41
8:22–25Ref — Mk 6:47–52; Jn 6:16–21

[22]One day Jesus said to his disciples, "Let us go over to the other side of the lake." So they got into a boat and set out. [23]As they sailed, he fell asleep. A squall came down on the lake, so that the boat was being swamped, and they were in great danger.

[24]The disciples went and woke him, saying, "Master, Master,[m] we're going to drown!"

He got up and rebuked[n] the wind and the raging waters; the storm subsided, and all was calm.[o] [25]"Where is your faith?" he asked his disciples.

In fear and amazement they asked one another, "Who is this? He commands even the winds and the water, and they obey him."

JESUS RESTORES A DEMON-POSSESSED MAN

8:26–37pp — Mt 8:28–34
8:26–39pp — Mk 5:1–20

[26]They sailed to the region of the Gerasenes,[a] which is across the lake from Galilee. [27]When Jesus stepped ashore, he was met by a demon-possessed man from the town. For a long time this man had not worn clothes or lived in a house, but had lived in the tombs. [28]When he saw Jesus, he cried out and fell at his feet, shouting at the top of his voice, "What do you want with me,[p] Jesus, Son of the Most High God?[q] I beg you, don't torture me!" [29]For Jesus had commanded the evil[b] spirit to come out of the man. Many times it had seized him, and though he was chained hand and foot and kept under guard, he had broken his chains and had been driven by the demon into solitary places.

[30]Jesus asked him, "What is your name?"

"Legion," he replied, because many demons had gone into him. [31]And they begged Jesus repeatedly not to order them to go into the Abyss.[r]

[32]A large herd of pigs was feeding there on the hillside. The demons begged Jesus to let them go into the pigs, and he gave them permission. [33]When the demons came out of the man, they went into the pigs, and the herd rushed down the steep bank into the lake[s] and was drowned.

[34]When those tending the pigs saw what had happened, they ran off and reported this in the town and countryside, [35]and the people went out to see what had happened. When they came to Jesus, they found the man from whom the demons had gone out, sitting at Jesus' feet,[t] dressed and in his right mind; and they were afraid. [36]Those who had seen it told the people how the demon-possessed[u] man had been cured. [37]Then all the people of the region of the Gerasenes asked Jesus to leave them,[v] because they were overcome with fear. So he got into the boat and left.

[38]The man from whom the demons had gone out begged to go with him, but Jesus sent

---

[a] 26 Some manuscripts *Gadarenes*; other manuscripts *Gergesenes*; also in verse 37 [b] 29 Greek *unclean*

---

brothers. Did not believe in Jesus at this time (Jn 7:5; see note on Jn 7:4). Various interpretations concerning their relationship to Jesus arose in the early church: They were sons of Joseph by a previous marriage (according to Epiphanius) or were cousins (said Jerome). The most natural conclusion (suggested by Helvidius) is that they were the sons of Joseph and Mary, younger half brothers of Jesus. Four of these brothers are named in Mk 6:3, where sisters are also mentioned. Since Joseph is not mentioned here, it is likely that he had died.

8:21 Jesus' reply was not meant to reject his natural family but to emphasize the higher priority of his spiritual relationship to those who believed in him (see 11:28 and note).
8:22 *lake.* See 5:1 and note.
8:23 *squall.* See note on Mk 4:37.
8:26 *region of the Gerasenes.* The Gospels describe the location of this event in two ways: (1) the region of the Gerasenes (see note on Mk 5:1); (2) the region of the Gadarenes (see note on Mt 8:28). Some manuscripts of Matthew, Mark and Luke read "Gergesenes" (see TNIV text note here), but this spelling may

have been introduced in an attempt to resolve the differences.
8:27 *demon-possessed man.* See note on 4:33. Matthew (8:28) refers to two demon-possessed men, but Mark (5:2) and Luke probably mention only the one who was prominent and did the talking. *tombs.* An isolated burial ground avoided by most people (but see note on Mk 5:3).
8:28 *Son of the Most High God.* Cf. 1:32 and note; 4:34. The title "Most High God" was commonly used by Gentiles (see Ge 14:19 and note; Ac 16:17); its use here perhaps indicates that this man was not a Jew (but see note on Mk 1:24). *don't torture me!* See Mk 1:24 and note.
8:30 *What is your name?* Jesus asked the man his name, but it was the demons who replied, thus showing they were in control. *Legion.* See note on Mk 5:9.
8:31 *Abyss.* A place of confinement for evil spirits and for Satan (see note on Rev 9:1).
8:32 *pigs.* Pigs were unclean to Jews, and eating them was forbidden (Lev 11:7–8), but this was the Decapolis, a predominantly Gentile territory. *he gave them permission.* See note on Mt 8:32.

8:41 ʷ ver 49;
S Mk 5:22
8:43 ˣ Lev 15:25-30
8:44 ʸ S Mt 9:20
8:45 ᶻ S Lk 5:5
8:46 ᵃ Mt 14:36;
Mk 3:10 ᵇ Lk 5:17;
6:19
8:48 ᶜ S Mt 9:22
ᵈ S Ac 15:33
8:49 ᵉ ver 41
8:51 ᶠ S Mt 4:21
8:52 ᵍ Lk 23:27
ʰ S Mt 9:24
8:54 ⁱ S Lk 7:14
8:56 ʲ S Mt 8:4
9:1 ᵏ S Mt 10:1
ˡ S Mt 4:23; Lk 5:17
9:2 ᵐ S Mt 3:2
9:3 ⁿ Lk 10:4; 22:35

him away, saying, ³⁹"Return home and tell how much God has done for you." So the man went away and told all over town how much Jesus had done for him.

JESUS RAISES A DEAD GIRL AND HEALS A SICK WOMAN
8:40–56pp — Mt 9:18–26; Mk 5:22–43

⁴⁰Now when Jesus returned, a crowd welcomed him, for they were all expecting him. ⁴¹Then a man named Jairus, a synagogue leader, ʷ came and fell at Jesus' feet, pleading with him to come to his house ⁴²because his only daughter, a girl of about twelve, was dying.

As Jesus was on his way, the crowds almost crushed him. ⁴³And a woman was there who had been subject to bleeding ˣ for twelve years, ᵃ but no one could heal her. ⁴⁴She came up behind him and touched the edge of his cloak, ʸ and immediately her bleeding stopped.

⁴⁵"Who touched me?" Jesus asked.

When they all denied it, Peter said, "Master, ᶻ the people are crowding and pressing against you."

⁴⁶But Jesus said, "Someone touched me; ᵃ I know that power has gone out from me." ᵇ

⁴⁷Then the woman, seeing that she could not go unnoticed, came trembling and fell at his feet. In the presence of all the people, she told why she had touched him and how she had been instantly healed. ⁴⁸Then he said to her, "Daughter, your faith has healed you. ᶜ Go in peace." ᵈ

⁴⁹While Jesus was still speaking, someone came from the house of Jairus, the synagogue leader. ᵉ "Your daughter is dead," he said. "Don't bother the teacher anymore."

⁵⁰Hearing this, Jesus said to Jairus, "Don't be afraid; just believe, and she will be healed."

⁵¹When he arrived at the house of Jairus, he did not let anyone go in with him except Peter, John and James, ᶠ and the child's father and mother. ⁵²Meanwhile, all the people were wailing and mourning ᵍ for her. "Stop wailing," Jesus said. "She is not dead but asleep." ʰ

⁵³They laughed at him, knowing that she was dead. ⁵⁴But he took her by the hand and said, "My child, get up!" ⁱ ⁵⁵Her spirit returned, and at once she stood up. Then Jesus told them to give her something to eat. ⁵⁶Her parents were astonished, but he ordered them not to tell anyone what had happened. ʲ

JESUS SENDS OUT THE TWELVE
9:3–5pp — Mt 10:9–15; Mk 6:8–11
9:7–9pp — Mt 14:1,2; Mk 6:14–16

9 When Jesus had called the Twelve together, he gave them power and authority to drive out all demons ᵏ and to cure diseases, ˡ ²and he sent them out to proclaim the kingdom of God ᵐ and to heal the sick. ³He told them: "Take nothing for the journey—no staff, no bag, no bread, no money, no extra shirt. ⁿ ⁴Whatever house you enter, stay there until you leave that town. ⁵If people do not welcome you,

---

ᵃ 43 Many manuscripts *years, and she had spent all she had on doctors*

8:39 *Return home and tell how much God has done for you.* Although the man wanted to follow Jesus, he was directed to make the miracle known in his own native territory. There was no danger here of interference with Jesus' ministry (see note on Mk 5:19).

8:41 *synagogue leader.* The leader was responsible for conducting services, selecting participants and maintaining order (see note on Mk 5:22).

8:43 *bleeding.* The hemorrhage had made her ceremonially unclean for 12 years (see Lev 15:19–30 and note on 15:25).

8:45 *Who touched me?* For the woman's good and for a testimony to the crowd, Jesus insisted that the miracle be made known.

8:46 *power has gone out.* See note on Mk 5:30.

8:48 *Daughter.* In the Gospel accounts this woman is the only individual Jesus addressed with this tender term (cf. 23:28). *Go in peace.* Cf. 7:50 and note.

8:50 *will be healed.* See note on Mk 5:34.

8:52 *wailing and mourning.* See note on Mk 5:38. *not dead but asleep.* Jesus meant that she was not permanently dead (see Jn 11:11–14 for a similar statement about Lazarus).

8:56 *ordered them not to tell.* See notes on Mt 8:4; Mk 5:43. Further publicity at this time concerning a raising from the dead would have been counterproductive to Jesus' ministry.

9:1–6 A new phase of Jesus' ministry began when he sent out the apostles to do the type of preaching, teaching and healing they had observed him doing (Mt 9:35). This was the third tour of Galilee by Jesus and his disciples (see note on 8:1). On the first tour Jesus traveled with the four fishermen; on the second all 12 were with him; on the third Jesus traveled alone after sending out the Twelve two by two.

9:1 *the Twelve.* The apostles (see 6:13 and note on Mk 6:30). *power and authority.* Special power to heal (see 5:17; 8:46; Mk 5:30 and note), authority in teaching and control over evil spirits. *demons.* Evil spirits (see note on 4:33).

9:3 *Take nothing.* No excess baggage that would encumber travel, not even the usual provisions. They were to be entirely dependent on the people with whom they were staying (see note on Mk 6:8).

9:4 *stay there.* They were not to move from house to house, seeking better lodging, but use only one home as headquarters while preaching in a community.

shake the dust off your feet when you leave their town, as a testimony against them." [o] [6]So they set out and went from village to village, proclaiming the good news and healing people everywhere.

[7]Now Herod[p] the tetrarch heard about all that was going on. And he was perplexed because some were saying that John[q] had been raised from the dead,[r] [8]others that Elijah had appeared,[s] and still others that one of the prophets of long ago had come back to life.[t] [9]But Herod said, "I beheaded John. Who, then, is this I hear such things about?" And he tried to see him.[u]

JESUS FEEDS THE FIVE THOUSAND
9:10–17pp — Mt 14:13–21; Mk 6:32–44; Jn 6:5–13
9:13–17Ref — 2Ki 4:42–44

[10]When the apostles[v] returned, they reported to Jesus what they had done. Then he took them with him and they withdrew by themselves to a town called Bethsaida,[w] [11]but the crowds learned about it and followed him. He welcomed them and spoke to them about the kingdom of God,[x] and healed those who needed healing.

[12]Late in the afternoon the Twelve came to him and said, "Send the crowd away so they can go to the surrounding villages and countryside and find food and lodging, because we are in a remote place here."

[13]He replied, "You give them something to eat."

They answered, "We have only five loaves of bread and two fish—unless we go and buy food for all this crowd." [14](About five thousand men were there.)

But he said to his disciples, "Have them sit down in groups of about fifty each." [15]The disciples did so, and everyone sat down. [16]Taking the five loaves and the two fish and looking up to heaven, he gave thanks and broke them.[y] Then he gave them to the disciples to set before the people. [17]They all ate and were satisfied, and the disciples picked up twelve basketfuls of broken pieces that were left over.

PETER DECLARES THAT JESUS IS THE MESSIAH
9:18–20pp — Mt 16:13–16; Mk 8:27–29
9:22–27pp — Mt 16:21–28; Mk 8:31—9:1

[18]Once when Jesus was praying[z] in private and his disciples were with him, he asked them, "Who do the crowds say I am?"

[19]They replied, "Some say John the Baptist;[a] others say Elijah; and still others, that one of the prophets of long ago has come back to life."[b]

[20]"But what about you?" he asked. "Who do you say I am?"

Peter answered, "God's Messiah."[c]

JESUS PREDICTS HIS DEATH
[21]Jesus strictly warned them not to tell this to anyone.[d] [22]And he said, "The Son of Man[e] must suffer many things[f] and be rejected by the elders, the chief priests and

9:5 ᵒS Mt 10:14
9:7 ᵖS Mt 14:1
�vS Mt 3:1 ʳver 19
9:8 ˢS Mt 11:14
ᵗver 19; Jn 1:21
9:9 ᵘLk 23:8
9:10 ᵛS Mk 6:30
ʷS Mt 11:21
9:11 ˣver 2;
S Mt 3:2
9:16 ʸS Mt 14:19
9:18 ᶻS Lk 3:21
9:19 ᵃS Mt 3:1
ᵇver 7,8
9:20 ᶜJn 1:49; 6:66-
69; 11:27
9:21 ᵈS Mk 8:30
9:22 ᵉS Mt 8:20
ᶠS Mt 16:21

9:5 *shake the dust off your feet.* A sign of repudiation for their rejection of God's message and a gesture showing separation from everything associated with the place (see 10:11; see also notes on Mt 10:14; Ac 13:51).

9:7 *Herod the tetrarch.* See note on Mt 14:1. *John had been raised from the dead.* See note on Mk 6:16. Luke does not give details about John's death (see Mt 14:1–12; Mk 6:17–29), which occurred about this time, but simply notes that it had taken place (v. 9).

9:8 *Elijah had appeared.* See notes on 1:17; Mk 9:12.

9:9 *he tried to see him.* Herod's desire to see Jesus was not fulfilled until Jesus' trial (23:8–12).

9:10–17 The feeding of the 5,000 is the only miracle besides Jesus' resurrection that is reported in all four Gospels (see notes on Mk 6:30–44; Jn 6:1–14).

9:10 *Bethsaida.* See note on Mt 11:21. Jesus must have retired to a remote area near the town (v. 12).

9:12 *Late in the afternoon.* The question was raised about food and lodging because they were in an isolated place. Jesus may have introduced the question (see Jn 6:5), but the Synoptics indicate that the disciples were also concerned.

9:14 *sit down in groups of about fifty.* See note on Mk 6:40.

9:17 *picked up twelve basketfuls of broken pieces.* This act served as an example of avoiding wastefulness and as a demonstration that everyone had been adequately fed (see note on Mk 6:43).

9:18 *Who do the crowds say I am?* The report brought by the disciples was the same as the one that reached Herod (see vv. 7–8). This event occurred to the north, outside Herod's territory, in the vicinity of Caesarea Philippi (see Mt 16:13 and note; see also note on Mk 7:24).

9:20 *Peter answered.* He was the spokesman for the disciples. *God's Messiah.* See TNIV text note on Mt 1:1. This predicted Deliverer (the Messiah) had been desired for centuries (see notes on Mt 16:18; Mk 8:29; Jn 4:5).

9:21 *warned them not to tell.* The people had false notions about the Messiah and needed to be taught further before Jesus identified himself explicitly to the public. He had a crucial schedule to keep and could not be interrupted by premature reactions (see notes on Mt 8:4; 16:20; Mk 1:34).

9:22 *Son of Man.* See note on Mk 8:31. *must suffer.* Jesus' first explicit prediction of his death (for later references, see v. 44; 12:50; 17:25; 18:31–33; cf. 24:7,25–27).

9:22 ᵍ Mt 27:1,2
ʰ Ac 2:23; 3:13
ⁱ S Mt 16:21
ʲ S Mt 16:21
9:23 ᵏ Mt 10:38;
Lk 14:27
9:24 ˡ S Jn 12:25
9:26 ᵐ Mt 10:33;
Lk 12:9; 2Ti 2:12
ⁿ S Mt 16:27
9:28 ᵒ S Mt 4:21
ᵖ S Lk 3:21
9:31 �q 2Pe 1:15
9:32 ʳ Mt 26:43
9:33 ˢ S Lk 5:5
9:35 ᵗ Isa 42:1
ᵘ S Mt 3:17
9:36 ᵛ Mt 17:9

the teachers of the law,ᵍ and he must be killedʰ and on the third dayⁱ be raised to life."ʲ

²³Then he said to them all: "Whoever wants to be my disciple must deny themselves and take up their cross daily and follow me.ᵏ ²⁴For whoever wants to save their life will lose it, but whoever loses their life for me will save it.ˡ ²⁵What good is it for you to gain the whole world, and yet lose or forfeit your very self? ²⁶If any of you are ashamed of me and my words, the Son of Man will be ashamed of youᵐ when he comes in his glory and in the glory of the Father and of the holy angels.ⁿ

²⁷"Truly I tell you, some who are standing here will not taste death before they see the kingdom of God."

THE TRANSFIGURATION
9:28–36pp — Mt 17:1–8; Mk 9:2–8

²⁸About eight days after Jesus said this, he took Peter, John and Jamesᵒ with him and went up onto a mountain to pray.ᵖ ²⁹As he was praying, the appearance of his face changed, and his clothes became as bright as a flash of lightning. ³⁰Two men, Moses and Elijah, ³¹appeared in glorious splendor, talking with Jesus. They spoke about his departure,ᵃ q which he was about to bring to fulfillment at Jerusalem. ³²Peter and his companions were very sleepy,ʳ but when they became fully awake, they saw his glory and the two men standing with him. ³³As the men were leaving Jesus, Peter said to him, "Master,ˢ it is good for us to be here. Let us put up three shelters—one for you, one for Moses and one for Elijah." (He did not know what he was saying.)

³⁴While he was speaking, a cloud appeared and covered them, and they were afraid as they entered the cloud. ³⁵A voice came from the cloud, saying, "This is my Son, whom I have chosen;ᵗ listen to him."ᵘ ³⁶When the voice had spoken, they found that Jesus was alone. The disciples kept this to themselves and did not tell anyone at that time what they had seen.ᵛ

JESUS HEALS A DEMON-POSSESSED BOY
9:37–42,43–45pp — Mt 17:14–18,22,23; Mk 9:14–27,30–32

³⁷The next day, when they came down from the mountain, a large crowd met him. ³⁸A man in the crowd called out, "Teacher, I beg you to look at my son, for he is my only child. ³⁹A spirit seizes him and he suddenly screams; it throws him into convulsions so that he foams at the mouth. It scarcely ever leaves him and is destroying him. ⁴⁰I begged your disciples to drive it out, but they could not."

ᵃ 31 Greek *exodus*

9:23 *take up their cross daily.* To follow Jesus requires self-denial, complete dedication and willing obedience. Luke emphasizes continued action; "daily" is not mentioned explicitly in the parallel accounts (Mt 16:24–26; Mk 8:34). Disciples from Galilee knew what the cross meant, for hundreds of men had been executed by this means in their region.
9:24 *whoever loses their life for me.* A saying of Jesus found in all four Gospels and in two Gospels more than once (14:26–27; 17:33; Mt 10:38–39; 16:24–25; Mk 8:34–35; Jn 12:25 [see note there]). No other saying of Jesus is given such emphasis.
9:26 *If any of you are ashamed.* See 12:9; see also note on Mk 8:38.
9:27 See note on Mt 16:28. *kingdom of God.* See note on Mt 3:2.
9:28 *About eight days.* Frequently used to indicate a week (e.g., Jn 20:26 in the Greek; see note on Mt 17:1). *Peter, John and James.* These three were also with Jesus at the healing of Jairus's daughter (8:51) and in his last visit to Gethsemane (Mk 14:33). *onto a mountain.* Although Mount Tabor is the traditional site of the Mount of Transfiguration, its distance from Caesarea Philippi (the vicinity of the last scene), its height (about 1,800 feet) and its occupation by a fortress make it unlikely. Mount Hermon fits the context much better by being both closer and higher (over 9,000 feet; see Mk 9:2). *pray.* Again Luke points out the place of prayer in an important event.
9:30 *Moses and Elijah.* Moses, the great OT deliverer and lawgiver, and Elijah, the representative of the prophets.

Moses' work had been finished by Joshua, Elijah's by Elisha (another form of the name Joshua). They now spoke with Jesus (whose Hebrew name was Joshua) concerning the "exodus" he was about to accomplish, by which he would deliver his people from the bondage of sin and bring to fulfillment the work of both Moses and Elijah (see notes on 1Ki 19:16; Mt 17:3).
9:31 *departure.* Greek *exodos,* a euphemism for Jesus' approaching death. It may also link Jesus' saving death and resurrection with God's saving of his people out of Egypt.
9:32 *sleepy.* Perhaps the event was at night. *saw his glory.* See note on Ex 33:18.
9:33 *three shelters.* Temporary structures to prolong the visit of the three important persons: lawgiver, prophet and Messiah. The idea was not appropriate, however, because Jesus had a work to finish in his few remaining days on earth (see note on Mk 9:5).
9:34–35 *cloud.* See Mt 17:5 and note.
9:35 *whom I have chosen.* Or "the Chosen One," related to a Jewish title found in Dead Sea Scrolls literature and possibly echoing Isa 42:1. See also 23:35. *have chosen.* Parallel to "love" (Mt 17:5; see Mt 3:17 and note; 2Pe 1:17).
9:39 *A spirit seizes him.* This evil spirit was causing seizures (Mt 17:15; see note on Mt 4:24) and a speechless condition (Mk 9:17). Evil spirits were responsible for many kinds of affliction (see note on 4:33).

9:41 *w* Dt 32:5
9:44 *x* S ver 22
9:45 *y* S Mk 9:32
9:46 *z* Lk 22:24
9:47 *a* S Mt 9:4
9:48 *b* S Mt 10:40
c S Mk 9:35
9:49 *d* S Lk 5:5
9:50 *e* Mt 12:30;
Lk 11:23
9:51 *f* S Mk 16:19
g Lk 13:22; 17:11;
18:31; 19:28
9:52 *h* S Mt 10:5
9:54 *i* S Mt 4:21
j 2Ki 1:10,12
9:57 *k* ver 51
9:58 *l* S Mt 8:20
9:59 *m* S Mt 4:19
9:60 *n* S Mt 3:2

[41]"You unbelieving and perverse generation,"[w] Jesus replied, "how long shall I stay with you and put up with you? Bring your son here."

[42]Even while the boy was coming, the demon threw him to the ground in a convulsion. But Jesus rebuked the evil[a] spirit, healed the boy and gave him back to his father. [43]And they were all amazed at the greatness of God.

JESUS PREDICTS HIS DEATH A SECOND TIME

While everyone was marveling at all that Jesus did, he said to his disciples, [44]"Listen carefully to what I am about to tell you: The Son of Man is going to be delivered over to human hands."[x] [45]But they did not understand what this meant. It was hidden from them, so that they did not grasp it,[y] and they were afraid to ask him about it.

[46]An argument started among the disciples as to which of them would be the greatest.[z] [47]Jesus, knowing their thoughts,[a] took a little child and had him stand beside him. [48]Then he said to them, "Whoever welcomes this little child in my name welcomes me; and whoever welcomes me welcomes the one who sent me.[b] For whoever is least among you all is the greatest."[c]

[49]"Master,"[d] said John, "we saw someone driving out demons in your name and we tried to stop him, because he is not one of us."

[50]"Do not stop him," Jesus said, "for whoever is not against you is for you."[e]

SAMARITAN OPPOSITION

[51]As the time approached for him to be taken up to heaven,[f] Jesus resolutely set out for Jerusalem.[g] [52]And he sent messengers on ahead, who went into a Samaritan[h] village to get things ready for him; [53]but the people there did not welcome him, because he was heading for Jerusalem. [54]When the disciples James and John[i] saw this, they asked, "Lord, do you want us to call fire down from heaven to destroy them[b]?"[j] [55]But Jesus turned and rebuked them. [56]Then he and his disciples went to another village.

THE COST OF FOLLOWING JESUS
9:57–60pp — Mt 8:19–22

[57]As they were walking along the road,[k] a man said to him, "I will follow you wherever you go."

[58]Jesus replied, "Foxes have holes and birds have nests, but the Son of Man[l] has no place to lay his head."

[59]He said to another man, "Follow me."[m]

But he replied, "Lord, first let me go and bury my father."

[60]Jesus said to him, "Let the dead bury their own dead, but you go and proclaim the kingdom of God."[n]

---

[a] 42 Greek *unclean*   [b] 54 Some manuscripts *them, just as Elijah did*

9:44 Another prediction of Jesus' coming death (see note on v. 22), an indication of how it will be brought about (see 22:21).
9:46 *which ... would be the greatest.* A subject that arose on a number of occasions (see 22:24; see also Mk 10:35–45 and note on Mk 9:34).

9:48 *whoever is least ... is the greatest.* People become great in God's sight as they sincerely and unpretentiously look away from self to revere him (see Mk 10:43 and note).
9:49 *not one of us.* Jesus shifts the pronoun to "you" in v. 50, which may mean that the man had a relationship to Jesus of which the disciples were unaware (see note on Mk 9:38).
9:50 *whoever is not against you is for you.* Spoken in the context of opposition to the disciples' work (cf. 11:23, set in a different context; see note there).
9:51 *taken up to heaven.* See 24:51; Ac 1:9. *set out for Jerusalem.* Lit. "set his face to go to Jerusalem" (cf. Isa 50:7). Luke emphasizes Jesus' determination to complete his mission (see note on 13:22). This journey to Jerusalem, however, is not the one that led to his crucifixion but marks the beginning of a period of ministry in Judea, of which Jerusalem was the central city. Mk 10:1 notes this departure for Judea, which John more specifically describes as a journey to Jerusalem during the Festival of Tabernacles (Jn 7:1–10). The Judean ministry (see Introduction: Outline) is recounted in 9:51—13:21 and Jn 7:10—10:39. Cf.

note on Mk 10:32.
9:52 *a Samaritan village.* Samaritans were particularly hostile to Jews who were on their way to observe religious festivals in Jerusalem. It was at least a three-day journey from Galilee to Jerusalem through Samaria, and Samaritans refused overnight shelter for the pilgrims. Because of this antipathy, Jews traveling between Galilee and Jerusalem frequently went on the east side of the Jordan River.
9:54 *call fire down.* As Elijah had (2Ki 1:9–16). James and John were known as "Sons of Thunder" (Mk 3:17; see note there).
9:55 *rebuked them.* See note on 2Ki 1:10.

9:57–62 The cost of being a true follower of Jesus. Neither hardships (vv. 57–58) nor bereavement (vv. 59–60) nor family ties (v. 61) should keep anyone from following him (v. 62).
9:57 *As they were walking.* Continuing their journey through Samaria to Jerusalem.

9:59 *bury my father.* If his father had already died, the man would have been occupied with the burial. But evidently he wanted to wait until after his father's death, which might have been years away. Jesus told him that the spiritually dead could bury the physically dead and that the spiritually alive should be busy proclaiming the kingdom of God (see Mt 8:21–22 and note on 8:22).

9:61 °1Ki 19:20
10:1 ᵖS Lk 7:13
ᑫLk 9:1,2,51,52
ʳMk 6:7 ˢMt 10:1
10:2 ᵗMt 9:37,38;
Jn 4:35
10:3 ᵘMt 10:16
10:7 ᵛS 1Ti 5:18
10:8 ʷ1Co 10:27
10:9 ˣS Mt 3:2
10:11 ʸS Mt 10:14
ᶻver 9
10:12 ᵃS Mt 10:15
ᵇMt 11:24
10:13 ᶜLk 6:24-26
ᵈS Rev 11:3
10:15 ᵉS Mt 4:13
10:16 ᶠS Mt 10:40
10:17 ᵍver 1
ʰS Mk 16:17
10:18 ⁱS Mt 4:10
ʲIsa 14:12; Rev 9:1;
12:8,9
10:19 ᵏMk 16:18;
Ac 28:3-5
10:20 ˡS Rev 20:12

⁶¹Still another said, "I will follow you, Lord; but first let me go back and say good-by to my family." ᵒ

⁶²Jesus replied, "No one who puts a hand to the plow and looks back is fit for service in the kingdom of God."

JESUS SENDS OUT THE SEVENTY-TWO

10:4–12pp — Lk 9:3–5
10:13–15,21,22pp — Mt 11:21–23,25–27
10:23,24pp — Mt 13:16,17

10 After this the Lordᵖ appointed seventy-twoᵃ othersᑫ and sent them two by two ʳ ahead of him to every town and place where he was about to go.ˢ ²He told them, "The harvest is plentiful, but the workers are few. Ask the Lord of the harvest, therefore, to send out workers into his harvest field.ᵗ ³Go! I am sending you out like lambs among wolves.ᵘ ⁴Do not take a purse or bag or sandals; and do not greet anyone on the road.

⁵"When you enter a house, first say, 'Peace to this house.' ⁶If the head of the house loves peace, your peace will rest on that house; if not, it will return to you. ⁷Stay there, eating and drinking whatever they give you, for workers deserve their wages.ᵛ Do not move around from house to house.

⁸"When you enter a town and are welcomed, eat what is set before you.ʷ ⁹Heal the sick who are there and tell them, 'The kingdom of Godˣ has come near to you.' ¹⁰But when you enter a town and are not welcomed, go into its streets and say, ¹¹'Even the dust of your town we wipe from our feet as a warning to you.ʸ Yet be sure of this: The kingdom of God has come near.'ᶻ ¹²I tell you, it will be more bearable on that day for Sodomᵃ than for that town.ᵇ

¹³"Woe to you,ᶜ Chorazin! Woe to you, Bethsaida! For if the miracles that were performed in you had been performed in Tyre and Sidon, they would have repented long ago, sitting in sacklothᵈ and ashes. ¹⁴But it will be more bearable for Tyre and Sidon at the judgment than for you. ¹⁵And you, Capernaum,ᵉ will you be lifted up to the skies? No, you will go down to the depths.ᵇ

¹⁶"Whoever listens to you listens to me; whoever rejects you rejects me; but whoever rejects me rejects him who sent me."ᶠ

¹⁷The seventy-twoᵍ returned with joy and said, "Lord, even the demons submit to us in your name."ʰ

¹⁸He replied, "I saw Satanⁱ fall like lightning from heaven.ʲ ¹⁹I have given you authority to trample on snakesᵏ and scorpions and to overcome all the power of the enemy; nothing will harm you. ²⁰However, do not rejoice that the spirits submit to you, but rejoice that your names are written in heaven."ˡ

²¹At that time Jesus, full of joy through the Holy Spirit, said, "I praise you, Father, Lord

---

ᵃ 1 Some manuscripts *seventy*; also in verse 17   ᵇ 15 Greek *to Hades*

9:62 *looks back.* Cf. Jn 6:66; Php 3:13 and notes.
10:1 *appointed seventy-two.* Recorded only in Luke, though similar instructions were given to the Twelve (Mt 9:37–38; 10:7–16; Mk 6:7–11; cf. Lk 9:3–5). Certain differences in early manuscripts make it unclear as to whether the number was 72 or 70 (see TNIV text note). Jesus covered Judea with his message (see note on 9:51) as thoroughly as he had Galilee. *two by two.* During his ministry in Galilee, Jesus had also sent out the Twelve two by two (see 9:1–6; Mk 6:7 and notes), a practice continued in the early church (Ac 13:2; 15:27,39–40; 17:14; 19:22).
10:3 *lambs among wolves.* Cf. Mt 7:15; 10:16; Ac 20:29.
10:4 *Do not take a purse or bag or sandals.* They were to travel light, without moneybag, luggage or extra sandals (see note on 9:3). *do not greet anyone.* They were not to stop along the way to visit and exchange customary lengthy greetings. The mission was urgent.
10:7 *workers deserve … wages.* Cf. 1Co 9:3–12; 1Ti 5:18 and note. *Do not move around.* See note on 9:4.
10:9 *The kingdom of God has come near.* The heart of Jesus' message (see notes on 4:43; Mt 3:2).
10:11 *dust … we wipe from.* See note on 9:5.
10:12 *more bearable … for Sodom.* Although Sodom was so sinful that God destroyed it (see Ge 18:20 and note; 19:24–28; Jude 7 and note), the people who heard the message

of Jesus and his disciples were even more accountable, because they had the gospel of the kingdom preached to them. *that day.* Judgment day.
10:13 *Chorazin … Bethsaida.* See note on Mt 11:21. *sackloth and ashes.* See Mt 11:21; Rev 11:3 and notes.
10:14 *Tyre and Sidon.* Gentile cities in Phoenicia (see note on 6:17), north of Galilee, which had not had opportunity to witness Jesus' miracles and hear his preaching as had the people in most of Galilee (see note on v. 12).
10:15 *Capernaum.* Jesus' headquarters on the north shore of Galilee (see Mt 4:13 and note), whose inhabitants had many opportunities to see and hear him. Therefore the condemnation for their rejection was the greater.
10:18 *Satan fall.* Even the demons were driven out by the disciples (v. 17), which meant that Satan was suffering defeat (may echo the language of Isa 14:12; see note on Isa 14:12–15). *Satan.* See notes on Mk 1:13; 1Th 3:5.
10:19 *snakes and scorpions … power of the enemy.* The snakes and scorpions may represent evil spirits; the enemy is Satan himself.
10:20 One's salvation is more important than power to overcome the evil one or escape his harm. *your names are written.* Salvation is recorded in heaven (see Ps 69:28 and note; Da 12:1).
10:21–22 See Mt 11:25–27 and notes.

of heaven and earth, because you have hidden these things from the wise and learned, and revealed them to little children. *m* Yes, Father, for this was your good pleasure.

²²"All things have been committed to me by my Father. *n* No one knows who the Son is except the Father, and no one knows who the Father is except the Son and those to whom the Son chooses to reveal him." *o*

²³Then he turned to his disciples and said privately, "Blessed are the eyes that see what you see. ²⁴For I tell you that many prophets and kings wanted to see what you see but did not see it, and to hear what you hear but did not hear it." *p*

THE PARABLE OF THE GOOD SAMARITAN

10:25–28pp — Mt 22:34–40; Mk 12:28–31

²⁵On one occasion an expert in the law stood up to test Jesus. "Teacher," he asked, "what must I do to inherit eternal life?" *q*

²⁶"What is written in the Law?" he replied. "How do you read it?"

²⁷He answered, " 'Love the Lord your God with all your heart and with all your soul and with all your strength and with all your mind'*a; r* and, 'Love your neighbor as yourself.'*b" s*

²⁸"You have answered correctly," Jesus replied. "Do this and you will live." *t*

²⁹But he wanted to justify himself, *u* so he asked Jesus, "And who is my neighbor?"

³⁰In reply Jesus said: "A man was going down from Jerusalem to Jericho, when he fell into the hands of robbers. They stripped him of his clothes, beat him and went away, leaving him half dead. ³¹A priest happened to be going down the same road, and when he saw the man, he passed by on the other side. *v* ³²So too, a Levite, when he came to the place and saw him, passed by on the other side. ³³But a Samaritan, *w* as he traveled, came where the man was; and when he saw him, he took pity on him. ³⁴He went to him and bandaged his wounds, pouring on oil and wine. Then he put the man on his own donkey, brought him to an inn and took care of him. ³⁵The next day he took out two denarii*c* and gave them to the innkeeper. 'Look after him,' he said, 'and when I return, I will reimburse you for any extra expense you may have.'

³⁶"Which of these three do you think was a neighbor to the man who fell into the hands of robbers?"

³⁷The expert in the law replied, "The one who had mercy on him."

Jesus told him, "Go and do likewise."

AT THE HOME OF MARTHA AND MARY

³⁸As Jesus and his disciples were on their way, he came to a village where a woman named Martha *x* opened her home to him. ³⁹She had a sister called Mary, *y* who sat at the Lord's feet *z* listening to what he said. ⁴⁰But Martha was distracted by all the preparations that had to be made. She came to him and asked, "Lord, don't you care *a* that my sister has left me to do the work by myself? Tell her to help me!"

⁴¹"Martha, Martha," the Lord answered, "you are worried *b* and upset about many things, ⁴²but few things are needed—or indeed only one. *d c* Mary has chosen what is better, and it will not be taken away from her."

a 27 Deut. 6:5 *b 27* Lev. 19:18 *c 35* A denarius was the daily wage of a day laborer (see Matt. 20:2).
d 42 Some manuscripts *but only one thing is needed*

10:23 *see what you see.* The Messiah and his saving work, for which they longed so much.

10:25 *expert in the law.* A scholar well versed in Scripture asked a common question (18:18; cf. Mt 22:35), either to take issue with Jesus or simply to see what kind of teacher he was. See note on 7:30.

A **10:27** *Love … God … Love your neighbor.* Elsewhere Jesus uses these words in reply to another question (see Mt 22:35–40; Mk 12:28–31 and notes), putting the same two Scriptures together (Dt 6:5; Lev 19:18). Whether a fourfold love (heart, soul, strength and mind, as here and in Mk 12:30) or threefold (Dt 6:5; Mt 22:37; Mk 12:33), the significance is that total devotion is demanded.

10:28 *will live.* Will have eternal life (v. 25).

10:29 *to justify himself.* The answer to his first question was obviously one he knew, so to gain credibility he asked for an interpretation. In effect he said, "But the real question is: Who is my neighbor?"

10:30 *Jerusalem to Jericho.* A distance of 17 miles and a descent

from about 2,500 feet above sea level to about 800 feet below sea level. The road ran through rocky, desert country, which provided places for robbers to waylay defenseless travelers.

A **10:31–33** *priest … Levite … Samaritan.* It is significant that the person Jesus commended was neither the religious leader nor the lay associate but a hated foreigner. Jews viewed Samaritans as half-breeds, both physically (see note on Mt 10:5) and spiritually (see notes on Jn 4:20,22). Samaritans and Jews practiced open hostility (see note on 9:52), but Jesus asserted that love knows no national boundaries.

10:34 A demonstration of "Love your neighbor" (v. 27). *oil and wine.* For their healing effects (cf. Isa 1:6 and note; Mk 6:13; Jas 5:14 and note).

10:35 *two denarii.* Two days' wages, which would keep the man for up to two months in an inn.

10:36 *Which … was a neighbor to the man … ?* The question now became: Which one proves he is the good neighbor by his actions?

10:38 *village.* Bethany, about two miles from Jerusalem, was the home of Mary and Martha (Jn 12:1–3; see note on Mt 21:17).

10:21 *m* 1Co 1:26-29
10:22 *n* S Mt 28:18
o Jn 1:18
10:24 *p* 1Pe 1:10-12
10:25 *q* Mt 19:16; Lk 18:18
10:27 *r* Dt 6:5
s Lev 19:18; S Mt 5:43
10:28 *t* S Ro 7:10
10:29 *u* Lk 16:15
10:31 *v* Lev 21:1-3
10:33 *w* S Mt 10:5
10:38 *x* Jn 11:1; 12:2
10:39 *y* Jn 11:1; 12:3
z Lk 8:35
10:40 *a* Mk 4:38
10:41 *b* Mt 6:25-34; Lk 12:11,22
10:42 *c* Ps 27:4

11:1 *d* S Lk 3:21
e S Jn 13:13
11:2 *f* S Mt 3:2
11:4 *g* Mt 18:35;
Mk 11:25 *h* Mt 26:41;
Jas 1:13
11:8 *i* Lk 18:1-6
11:9 *j* S Mt 7:7
11:14 *k* Mt 9:32,33
11:15 *l* S Mk 3:22
m Mt 9:34
11:16 *n* S Mt 12:38
11:17 *o* S Mt 9:4
11:18 *p* S Mt 4:10

JESUS' TEACHING ON PRAYER

11:2–4pp — Mt 6:9–13
11:9–13pp — Mt 7:7–11

11 One day Jesus was praying *d* in a certain place. When he finished, one of his disciples said to him, "Lord, *e* teach us to pray, just as John taught his disciples."

²He said to them, "When you pray, say:

" 'Father, *a*
hallowed be your name,
your kingdom *f* come. *b*
³ Give us each day our daily bread.
⁴ Forgive us our sins,
for we also forgive everyone who sins against us. *c g*
And lead us not into temptation.' *d' " h*

⁵Then Jesus said to them, "Suppose you have a friend, and you go to him at midnight and say, 'Friend, lend me three loaves of bread; ⁶a friend of mine on a journey has come to me, and I have nothing to set before him.' ⁷And suppose the one inside answers, 'Don't bother me. The door is already locked, and my children and I are in bed. I can't get up and give you anything.' ⁸I tell you, even though he will not get up and give you the bread because of friendship, yet because of your shameless audacity *e* he will surely get up and give you as much as you need. *i*

⁹"So I say to you: Ask and it will be given to you; *j* seek and you will find; knock and the door will be opened to you. ¹⁰For everyone who asks receives; those who seek find; and to those who knock, the door will be opened.

¹¹"Which of you fathers, if your son asks for *f* a fish, will give him a snake instead? ¹²Or if he asks for an egg, will give him a scorpion? ¹³If you then, though you are evil, know how to give good gifts to your children, how much more will your Father in heaven give the Holy Spirit to those who ask him!"

JESUS AND BEELZEBUL

11:14,15,17–22,24–26pp — Mt 12:22,24–29,43–45
11:17–22pp — Mk 3:23–27

¹⁴Jesus was driving out a demon that was mute. When the demon left, the man who had been mute spoke, and the crowd was amazed. *k* ¹⁵But some of them said, "By Beelzebul, *l* the prince of demons, he is driving out demons." *m* ¹⁶Others tested him by asking for a sign from heaven. *n*

¹⁷Jesus knew their thoughts *o* and said to them: "Any kingdom divided against itself will be ruined, and a house divided against itself will fall. ¹⁸If Satan *p* is divided against himself, how can his kingdom stand? I say this because you claim that I drive out demons by Beelzebul. ¹⁹Now if I drive out demons by Beelzebul, by whom do your followers drive

---

a 2 Some manuscripts *Our Father in heaven*   *b 2* Some manuscripts *come. May your will be done on earth as it is in heaven.*   *c 4* Greek *everyone who is indebted to us*   *d 4* Some manuscripts *temptation, but deliver us from the evil one*   *e 8* Or *yet to preserve his good name*   *f 11* Some manuscripts *for bread, will give him a stone? Or if he asks for*

11:1 *Jesus was praying.* Not only on special occasions (e.g., baptism, 3:21 [see note there]; choosing the Twelve, 6:12; Gethsemane, 22:41) but also as a regular practice (5:16; Mt 14:23; Mk 1:35; see Introduction: Characteristics). *teach us to pray.* The Lord's model prayer, given here in answer to a request, is similar to Mt 6:9–13, where it is part of the Sermon on the Mount. Six petitions are included in the prayer as given in the Sermon on the Mount by Matthew, whereas five appear in the prayer in Luke.

11:4 *Forgive us our sins.* Mt 6:12 has "debts," but the meaning is the same as "sins." Jesus taught this truth on other occasions as well (see Mt 18:35 and note; Mk 11:25; cf. Eph 4:32 and note).

11:5–13 Jesus now urged boldness in prayer (vv. 5–8) and gave assurance that God answers prayer (vv. 9–13). The argument is from the lesser to the greater (see v. 13).

11:13 *give the Holy Spirit.* Mt 7:11 has "give good gifts," meaning spiritual gifts. Luke emphasizes the work of the Spirit, who is one of the greatest of God's gifts.

11:14 *demon that was mute.* See note on 4:33. This evil spirit caused muteness. The probable parallel passage in Matthew (12:22–30; see also Mk 3:20–27) indicates that the man was also blind.

11:15 *Beelzebul, the prince of demons.* Satan (v. 18). See note on Mt 12:24.

11:16 *sign from heaven.* Jesus had just healed a mute. Here was their sign, and they would not recognize it (see Mk 8:11 and note).

11:17 *kingdom divided against itself.* If Satan gave power to Jesus, who opposed him in every way, he would be supporting an attack upon himself.

11:19 *by whom do your followers...?* Jesus did not say whether the followers of the Pharisees (see Mt 12:24) actually drove out demons (see note on v. 24); but they claimed to drive them out by the power of God, and Jesus claimed the same. So to accuse Jesus of using Satanic power was implicitly to condemn their own followers as well. *your judges.* They will condemn you for your accusation against them.

them out? So then, they will be your judges. ²⁰But if I drive out demons by the finger of God, �q then the kingdom of God ʳ has come upon you.

²¹"When a strong man, fully armed, guards his own house, his possessions are safe. ²²But when someone stronger attacks and overpowers him, he takes away the armor in which the man trusted and divides up his plunder.

²³"Whoever is not with me is against me, and whoever does not gather with me scatters. ˢ

²⁴"When an evilᵃ spirit comes out of anyone, it goes through arid places seeking rest and does not find it. Then it says, 'I will return to the house I left.' ²⁵When it arrives, it finds the house swept clean and put in order. ²⁶Then it goes and takes seven other spirits more wicked than itself, and they go in and live there. And the final condition of that person is worse than the first."ᵗ

²⁷As Jesus was saying these things, a woman in the crowd called out, "Blessed is the mother who gave you birth and nursed you."ᵘ

²⁸He replied, "Blessed rather are those who hear the word of Godᵛ and obey it."ʷ

THE SIGN OF JONAH

11:29–32pp — Mt 12:39–42

²⁹As the crowds increased, Jesus said, "This is a wicked generation. It asks for a sign,ˣ but none will be given it except the sign of Jonah. ʸ ³⁰For as Jonah was a sign to the Ninevites, so also will the Son of Man be to this generation. ³¹The Queen of the South will rise at the judgment with the people of this generation and condemn them, for she came from the ends of the earth to listen to Solomon's wisdom;ᶻ and now oneᵇ greater than Solomon is here. ³²The people of Nineveh will stand up at the judgment with this generation and condemn it, for they repented at the preaching of Jonah; ᵃ and now one greater than Jonah is here.

THE LAMP OF THE BODY

11:34,35pp — Mt 6:22,23

³³"None of you lights a lamp and puts it in a place where it will be hidden, or under a bowl. Instead you put it on its stand, so that those who come in may see the light. ᵇ ³⁴Your eye is the lamp of your body. When your eyes are healthy,ᶜ your whole body also is full of light. But when they are unhealthy,ᵈ your body also is full of darkness. ³⁵See to it, then, that the light within you is not darkness. ³⁶Therefore, if your whole body is full of light, and no part of it dark, it will be just as full of light as when a lamp shines its light on you."

ᵃ *24* Greek *unclean*   ᵇ *31* Or *something*; also in verse 32   ᶜ *34* The Greek for *healthy* here implies *generous.*   ᵈ *34* The Greek for *unhealthy* here implies *stingy.*

11:20 �q Ex 8:19
ʳ S Mt 3:2
11:23 ˢ Mt 12:30;
Mk 9:40; Lk 9:50
11:26 ᵗ 2Pe 2:20
11:27 ᵘ Lk 23:29
11:28 ᵛ S Heb 4:12
ʷ Pr 8:32; Lk 6:47;
8:21; Jn 14:21
11:29 ˣ ver 16;
S Mt 12:38 ʸ Jnh 1:17;
Mt 16:4
11:31 ᶻ 1Ki 10:1;
2Ch 9:1
11:32 ᵃ Jnh 3:5
11:33 ᵇ S Mt 5:15

11:20 *the kingdom of God has come.* In the sense that the King was present in the person of Jesus (see notes on 4:43; 17:21) and that the powers of evil were being overthrown. **11:22** *someone stronger attacks.* Jesus was stronger than Beelzebul, and by his exorcism of demons he demonstrated that he had overpowered Satan and disarmed him. It was therefore foolish to suggest that Jesus had cast out demons by Satan's power.

11:23 The one who does not support Jesus opposes him, making neutrality impossible (see note on Mt 12:30). Even the worker in 9:50, whom the disciples described as "not one of us" (9:49), was apparently a believer, acting in Jesus' name (see note on Mk 9:38), and Jesus did not condemn him. **11:24** *evil spirit comes out.* Jesus is perhaps referring to the work of Jewish exorcists, who claimed to cast out demons (cf. v. 19 and note) but who rejected the kingdom of God and whose exorcisms were therefore ineffective. See Mt 12:43–45, where Jesus makes a similar comment about the Jewish nation of that day.

11:25 *finds the house swept clean.* The place had been cleaned up but left unoccupied. A life reformed but lacking God's presence and power is open to reoccupancy by evil. **11:28** *Blessed rather.* Jesus is not denying the blessedness of Mary. He is stressing that it is even more blessed to be his obedient follower.

11:29 *asks for a sign.* On several occasions Jews asked for miraculous signs (see v. 16; Mt 12:38; Mk 8:11 and notes), but Jesus rejected their requests because they had wrong motives.

11:30 *as Jonah was a sign.* Jonah spent three days (see note on Mt 12:40) "buried" in the huge fish, just as Jesus would be buried for three days before his resurrection.

11:31–32 *one greater than Solomon … one greater than Jonah.* Jesus argued from the lesser to the greater. If the queen of Sheba responded positively to the wisdom of Solomon, and the people of Nineveh to the preaching of Jonah, how much more should the people of Jesus' day have responded to the ministry of Jesus, who is infinitely greater than Solomon or Jonah!

11:31 *The Queen of the South.* The queen of Sheba (see 1Ki 10:1–10 and notes).

11:33 *a bowl.* A container holding about one peck. *may see the light.* A lamp is meant to give light to those who are near it (see v. 36). Jesus had publicly exhibited the light of the gospel for all to see, but "a wicked generation" (v. 29) requested more spectacular signs. The problem was not with any failure on Jesus' part in giving light; it was with the faulty vision of his audience.

11:34 *lamp of your body.* See note on Mt 6:22. *your eyes are healthy.* Those asking for a sign do not need more light; they need good eyes to allow the light to enter. Cf. Mt 6:22–23 and notes.

11:37 c Lk 7:36; 14:1
11:38 d Mk 7:3,4
11:39 e S Lk 7:13
f Mt 23:25,26;
Mk 7:20-23
11:40 g Lk 12:20;
1Co 15:36
11:41 h Lk 12:33
i S Ac 10:15
11:42 j Lk 18:12
k Dt 6:5; Mic 6:8
l Mt 23:23
11:43 m Mt 23:6,7;
Lk 14:7; 20:46
11:44 n Mt 23:27
11:45 o S Mt 23:35
11:46 p S Mt 23:4
11:48 q Mt 23:29-
32; Ac 7:51-53
11:49 r 1Co 1:24,30;
Col 2:3 s Mt 23:34
11:51 t Ge 4:8
u 2Ch 24:20,21
v Mt 23:35,36
11:52 w Mt 23:13
11:54 x S Mt 12:10

WOES ON THE PHARISEES AND THE EXPERTS IN THE LAW

37When Jesus had finished speaking, a Pharisee invited him to eat with him; so he went in and reclined at the table. c 38But the Pharisee was surprised when he noticed that Jesus did not first wash before the meal. d

39Then the Lord e said to him, "Now then, you Pharisees clean the outside of the cup and dish, but inside you are full of greed and wickedness. f 40You foolish people! g Did not the one who made the outside make the inside also? 41But now as for what is inside you— be generous to the poor, h and everything will be clean for you. i

42"Woe to you Pharisees, because you give God a tenth j of your mint, rue and all other kinds of garden herbs, but you neglect justice and the love of God. k You should have practiced the latter without leaving the former undone. l

43"Woe to you Pharisees, because you love the most important seats in the synagogues and respectful greetings in the marketplaces. m

44"Woe to you, because you are like unmarked graves, n which people walk over without knowing it."

45One of the experts in the law o answered him, "Teacher, when you say these things, you insult us also."

46Jesus replied, "And you experts in the law, woe to you, because you load people down with burdens they can hardly carry, and you yourselves will not lift one finger to help them. p

47"Woe to you, because you build tombs for the prophets, and it was your ancestors who killed them. 48So you testify that you approve of what your ancestors did; they killed the prophets, and you build their tombs. q 49Because of this, God in his wisdom r said, 'I will send them prophets and apostles, some of whom they will kill and others they will persecute.' s 50Therefore this generation will be held responsible for the blood of all the prophets that has been shed since the beginning of the world, 51from the blood of Abel t to the blood of Zechariah, u who was killed between the altar and the sanctuary. Yes, I tell you, this generation will be held responsible for it all. v

52"Woe to you experts in the law, because you have taken away the key to knowledge. You yourselves have not entered, and you have hindered those who were entering." w

53When Jesus went outside, the Pharisees and the teachers of the law began to oppose him fiercely and to besiege him with questions, 54waiting to catch him in something he might say. x

---

11:38 *did not first wash.* Especially for ceremonial cleansing, not commanded in the law but added in the tradition of the Pharisees (cf. Mt 15:9 and note on Jn 2:6).
11:39 *clean the outside.* Engage in ceremonial washings of the body. *greed and wickedness.* These Pharisees were more concerned about keeping ceremonies than about being moral (cf. Mk 7:20 and note).
11:40 *make the inside also.* The inside of a person (the heart and inner righteousness) is more important than the outside (ceremonial cleansing).
11:41 *everything will be clean.* Giving from the heart makes everything else right. If one gives to the poor, one's heart is no longer in the grip of "greed and wickedness" (v. 39).
11:42–52 Six woes pronounced by Jesus on the religious leaders (see note on Mt 23:13–32).
11:42 *tenth.* A tithe of all agricultural produce was required by OT law (see Dt 14:22–29 and note). *rue.* Strongly scented herbs with bitter leaves.
11:43 *most important seats in the synagogues.* See Mk 12:39 and note.
11:44 *unmarked graves.* The Jews whitewashed their tombs so that no one would accidentally touch them and be defiled (cf. Nu 19:16; Mt 23:27 and note). Just as touching a grave resulted in ceremonial uncleanness, so also being influenced by these misguided religious leaders could lead to moral uncleanness.
11:45 *experts in the law.* See note on 7:30.

11:46 *load people down.* By adding rules and regulations to the authentic law of Moses (see note on Mt 15:2) and doing nothing to help others keep them (Mt 23:4), while inventing ways for themselves to circumvent them (cf. Mt 11:28 and note).
11:47 *tombs for the prophets.* Outwardly these "experts in the law" (v. 46) appeared to honor the prophets in building or rebuilding memorials, but inwardly they rejected the Messiah the prophets announced. They lived in opposition to the teachings of the prophets, just as their ancestors had done.
11:49 *God in his wisdom said.* Not a quotation from the OT or any other known book. It may refer to God speaking through Jesus, or it may be referring in quotation form to God's decision to send prophets and apostles even though he knew they would be rejected.
11:51 *blood of Abel ... Zechariah.* See note on Mt 23:35.
11:52 *key to knowledge.* The very persons who should have opened the people's minds concerning the law obscured their understanding by faulty interpretation and an erroneous system of theology. They kept themselves and the people in ignorance of the way of salvation, or, as Matthew's account puts it, they "shut the door of the kingdom of heaven in people's faces" (Mt 23:13).
11:54 *waiting to catch him.* The determination of the religious leaders to trap Jesus is evident throughout Luke (see 6:11 and note; 19:47–48; 20:19–20; 22:2).

WARNINGS AND ENCOURAGEMENTS

12:2–9pp — Mt 10:26–33

12 Meanwhile, when a crowd of many thousands had gathered, so that they were trampling on one another, Jesus began to speak first to his disciples, saying: "Be[a] on your guard against the yeast of the Pharisees, which is hypocrisy.[y] ²There is nothing concealed that will not be disclosed, or hidden that will not be made known.[z] ³What you have said in the dark will be heard in the daylight, and what you have whispered in the ear in the inner rooms will be proclaimed from the roofs.

⁴"I tell you, my friends,[a] do not be afraid of those who kill the body and after that can do no more. ⁵But I will show you whom you should fear: Fear him who, after your body has been killed, has authority to throw you into hell. Yes, I tell you, fear him.[b] ⁶Are not five sparrows sold for two pennies? Yet not one of them is forgotten by God. ⁷Indeed, the very hairs of your head are all numbered.[c] Don't be afraid; you are worth more than many sparrows.[d]

⁸"I tell you, whoever publicly acknowledges me, the Son of Man will also acknowledge before the angels of God.[e] ⁹But whoever publicly disowns me will be disowned[f] before the angels of God. ¹⁰And everyone who speaks a word against the Son of Man[g] will be forgiven, but anyone who blasphemes against the Holy Spirit will not be forgiven.[h]

¹¹"When you are brought before synagogues, rulers and authorities, do not worry about how you will defend yourselves or what you will say,[i] ¹²for the Holy Spirit will teach you at that time what you should say."[j]

THE PARABLE OF THE RICH FOOL

¹³Someone in the crowd said to him, "Teacher, tell my brother to divide the inheritance with me."

¹⁴Jesus replied, "Man, who appointed me a judge or an arbiter between you?" ¹⁵Then he said to them, "Watch out! Be on your guard against all kinds of greed; life does not consist in an abundance of possessions."[k]

¹⁶And he told them this parable: "The ground of a certain rich man yielded an abundant harvest. ¹⁷He thought to himself, 'What shall I do? I have no place to store my crops.'

¹⁸"Then he said, 'This is what I'll do. I will tear down my barns and build bigger ones, and there I will store my surplus grain. ¹⁹And I'll say to myself, "You have plenty of grain laid up for many years. Take life easy; eat, drink and be merry."'

²⁰"But God said to him, 'You fool![l] This very night your life will be demanded from you.[m] Then who will get what you have prepared for yourself?'[n]

²¹"This is how it will be with those who store up things for themselves but are not rich toward God."[o]

DO NOT WORRY

12:22–31pp — Mt 6:25–33

²²Then Jesus said to his disciples: "Therefore I tell you, do not worry about your life, what you will eat; or about your body, what you will wear. ²³Life is more than food, and

---

[a] 1 Or *speak to his disciples, saying: "First of all, be*

12:1 *yeast of the Pharisees.* See note on Mk 8:15.

12:2 *nothing concealed that will not be disclosed.* In this context the meaning is that nothing hidden through hypocrisy will fail to be made known (cf. note on 8:17).

12:3 *inner rooms.* Storerooms were surrounded by other rooms so that no one could dig in from outside.

12:4 *after that can do no more.* Encouragement in the face of persecution (see Mt 10:28 and note).

12:5 *authority to throw you into hell.* God alone has this authority. The Greek word for "hell" is *ge(h)enna* (see note on Mt 5:22), not to be confused with Hades, the general name for the place of the dead. *fear him.* Respect his authority, stand in awe of his majesty and trust in him. Verses 6–7 give the basis for trust.

12:6 *five sparrows sold for two pennies.* God even cares for little birds, sold cheaply for food.

12:8 *acknowledges me.* When a person acknowledges that Jesus is the Messiah, the Son of God (see Mt 16:16; 1Jn 2:22 and notes), Jesus acknowledges that the individual is his loyal follower (cf. Mt 7:21).

12:9 *will be disowned.* See Mk 8:38; 2Ti 2:12 and notes; cf. Mt 7:21; 25:41–46. The same Greek word is used in Peter's denial (22:34, "deny"; 22:61, "disown").

12:10 *blasphemes against the Holy Spirit.* See notes on Mt 12:31; Mk 3:29.

12:12 *Holy Spirit will teach you ... what you should say.* See Mt 10:19 and note.

12:13 *divide the inheritance.* Dt 21:17 (see note there) gave the general rule that an elder son received double a younger one's portion. Disputes over such matters were normally settled by rabbis. This man's request of Jesus was selfish and materialistic. There is no indication that the man had been listening seriously to what Jesus had been saying (cf. vv. 1–11). Jesus replied with a parable about the consequences of greed.

12:16 *parable.* See note on 8:4.

12:19 *eat ... be merry.* See Isa 22:13 and note.

12:21 *rich toward God.* Cf. "treasures in heaven" (Mt 6:20; see note there; cf. Lk 12:34).

12:22 *do not worry.* See v. 29; see also Php 4:6–7 and notes.

12:1 ʸMt 16:6,11,12
12:2 ᶻMk 4:22
12:4 ᵃJn 15:14,15
12:5 ᵇHeb 10:31
12:7 ᶜMt 10:30
ᵈMt 12:12
12:8 ᵉLk 15:10
12:9 ᶠMk 8:38;
2Ti 2:12
12:10 ᵍS Mt 8:20
ʰMt 12:31,32;
S 1Jn 5:16
12:11 ᶦMt 10:17,19;
Lk 21:12,14
12:12 ʲEx 4:12;
Mt 10:20; Mk 13:11;
Lk 21:15
12:15 ᵏJob 20:20;
31:24; Ps 62:10
12:20 ᶫJer 17:11;
Lk 11:40 ᵐJob 27:8
ⁿPs 39:6; 49:10
12:21 °ver 33

12:24 P Job 38:41;
Ps 147:9
12:27 9 1Ki 10:4-7
12:28 r S Mt 6:30
12:30 s S Lk 6:36
t Mt 6:8
12:31 u S Mt 3:2
v Mt 19:29
12:32 w S Mt 14:27
x S Mt 25:34
12:33 y S Ac 2:45
z S Mt 6:20 a S Jas 5:2
12:34 b Mt 6:21
12:37 c Mt 24:42,
46; 25:13
d S Mt 20:28
12:39 e Mt 6:19;
1Th 5:2; 2Pe 3:10;
Rev 3:3; 16:15
12:40 f Mk 13:33;
Lk 21:36
12:42 9 S Lk 7:13
12:46 h ver 40
12:47 i Dt 25:2
12:48 j Lev 5:17;
Nu 15:27-30

the body more than clothes. ²⁴Consider the ravens: They do not sow or reap, they have no storeroom or barn; yet God feeds them. P And how much more valuable you are than birds! ²⁵Who of you by worrying can add a single hour to your life a? ²⁶Since you cannot do this very little thing, why do you worry about the rest?

²⁷"Consider how the wild flowers grow. They do not labor or spin. Yet I tell you, not even Solomon in all his splendor q was dressed like one of these. ²⁸If that is how God clothes the grass of the field, which is here today, and tomorrow is thrown into the fire, how much more will he clothe you—you of little faith! r ²⁹And do not set your heart on what you will eat or drink; do not worry about it. ³⁰For the pagan world runs after all such things, and your Father s knows that you need them. t ³¹But seek his kingdom, u and these things will be given to you as well. v

³²"Do not be afraid, w little flock, for your Father has been pleased to give you the kingdom. x ³³Sell your possessions and give to the poor. y Provide purses for yourselves that will not wear out, a treasure in heaven z that will never fail, where no thief comes near and no moth destroys. a ³⁴For where your treasure is, there your heart will be also. b

WATCHFULNESS

12:35,36pp — Mt 25:1–13; Mk 13:33–37
12:39,40; 42–46pp — Mt 24:43–51

³⁵"Be dressed ready for service and keep your lamps burning, ³⁶like servants waiting for their master to return from a wedding banquet, so that when he comes and knocks they can immediately open the door for him. ³⁷It will be good for those servants whose master finds them watching when he comes. c Truly I tell you, he will dress himself to serve, will have them recline at the table and will come and wait on them. d ³⁸It will be good for those servants whose master finds them ready, even if he comes in the middle of the night or toward daybreak. ³⁹But understand this: If the owner of the house had known at what hour the thief e was coming, he would not have let his house be broken into. ⁴⁰You also must be ready, f because the Son of Man will come at an hour when you do not expect him."

⁴¹Peter asked, "Lord, are you telling this parable to us, or to everyone?"

⁴²The Lord g answered, "Who then is the faithful and wise manager, whom the master puts in charge of his servants to give them their food allowance at the proper time? ⁴³It will be good for that servant whom the master finds doing so when he returns. ⁴⁴Truly I tell you, he will put him in charge of all his possessions. ⁴⁵But suppose the servant says to himself, 'My master is taking a long time in coming,' and he then begins to beat the other servants, both men and women, and to eat and drink and get drunk. ⁴⁶The master of that servant will come on a day when he does not expect him and at an hour he is not aware of. h He will cut him to pieces and assign him a place with the unbelievers.

⁴⁷"The servant who knows the master's will and does not get ready or does not do what the master wants will be beaten with many blows. i ⁴⁸But the one who does not know and does things deserving punishment will be beaten with few blows. j From everyone who

---

a 25 Or *single cubit to your height*

12:27 *wild flowers.* See note on Mt 6:28.

12:28 See Mt 6:30 and note.

12:31 *seek his kingdom.* Since v. 32 suggests that Jesus is speaking to believers, who already possess the kingdom, this command probably means that Christians should seek the spiritual benefits of the kingdom rather than the material goods of the world (see Mt 6:33, which says, "seek *first* his kingdom").

12:33 *Sell your possessions.* Jesus does not instruct his disciples to sell all their possessions (see note on Mk 10:21). What is emphasized throughout this Gospel is that wealth is to be generously shared with the poor (see vv. 21–26). *give to the poor.* The danger of riches and the need for giving are characteristic themes in Luke (see 3:11; 6:30; 11:41 and note; 14:13–14; 16:9 and note; 18:22; 19:8). *treasure in heaven.* See v. 21 and note.

12:37 *dress himself to serve.* The master reverses the normal roles and serves the servants (cf. 22:27 and note on 22:26; Mk 10:45; Jn 13:5–14 and notes).

12:38 *middle of the night or toward daybreak.* Lit. "second or

third watch." The second watch was 10:00 P.M.–2:00 A.M., and the third watch was 2:00 A.M.–sunrise. Night was divided into four watches by the Romans (Mk 13:35) and three by the Jews (see Jdg 7:19 and note); see note on Mt 14:25. These were probably the last two of the Jewish watches. The banquet would have begun in the first watch (sunset–10:00 P.M.).

12:40 Christ's return is certain, but the time is not known (see Mt 24:36; Mk 13:32 and note).

12:41 Jesus taught the people in parables but used a more direct approach with the disciples. However, he did not intend these warnings of watchfulness just for the disciples (see Mk 13:37). In the following verses he emphasizes the duty to fulfill responsibilities.

12:42 *wise manager.* An outstanding slave (v. 43) was sometimes left in charge of an estate (see 16:1 and note).

12:46–48 *cut him to pieces…beaten with many blows…beaten with few blows.* Three grades of punishment that the judge will mete out in proportion to both the privileges each person has enjoyed and one's response to those privileges (see Ro 2:12–16 and notes).

has been given much, much will be demanded; and from the one who has been entrusted with much, much more will be asked.

NOT PEACE BUT DIVISION

12:51–53pp — Mt 10:34–36

⁴⁹"I have come to bring fire on the earth, and how I wish it were already kindled! ⁵⁰But I have a baptism ᵏ to undergo, and what constraint I am under until it is completed! ˡ ⁵¹Do you think I came to bring peace on earth? No, I tell you, but division. ⁵²From now on there will be five in one family divided against each other, three against two and two against three. ⁵³They will be divided, father against son and son against father, mother against daughter and daughter against mother, mother-in-law against daughter-in-law and daughter-in-law against mother-in-law." ᵐ

INTERPRETING THE TIMES

⁵⁴He said to the crowd: "When you see a cloud rising in the west, immediately you say, 'It's going to rain,' and it does. ⁿ ⁵⁵And when the south wind blows, you say, 'It's going to be hot,' and it is. ⁵⁶Hypocrites! You know how to interpret the appearance of the earth and the sky. How is it that you don't know how to interpret this present time? ᵒ

⁵⁷"Why don't you judge for yourselves what is right? ⁵⁸As you are going with your adversary to the magistrate, try hard to be reconciled on the way, or your adversary may drag you off to the judge, and the judge turn you over to the officer, and the officer throw you into prison. ᵖ ⁵⁹I tell you, you will not get out until you have paid the last penny." ᑫ

REPENT OR PERISH

13 Now there were some present at that time who told Jesus about the Galileans whose blood Pilate ʳ had mixed with their sacrifices. ²Jesus answered, "Do you think that these Galileans were worse sinners than all the other Galileans because they suffered this way? ˢ ³I tell you, no! But unless you repent, you too will all perish. ⁴Or those eighteen who died when the tower in Siloam ᵗ fell on them—do you think they were more guilty than all the others living in Jerusalem? ⁵I tell you, no! But unless you repent, ᵘ you too will all perish."

⁶Then he told this parable: "A man had a fig tree growing in his vineyard, and he went to look for fruit on it but did not find any. ᵛ ⁷So he said to the man who took care of the vineyard, 'For three years now I've been coming to look for fruit on this fig tree and haven't found any. Cut it down! ʷ Why should it use up the soil?'

⁸ 'Sir,' the man replied, 'leave it alone for one more year, and I'll dig around it and fertilize it. ⁹If it bears fruit next year, fine! If not, then cut it down.' "

JESUS HEALS A CRIPPLED WOMAN ON THE SABBATH

¹⁰On a Sabbath Jesus was teaching in one of the synagogues, ˣ ¹¹and a woman was there who had been crippled by a spirit for eighteen years. ʸ She was bent over and could not straighten up at all. ¹²When Jesus saw her, he called her forward and said to her,

12:50 ᵏ Mk 10:38
ˡ S Jn 19:30
12:53 ᵐ Mic 7:6;
Mt 10:21
12:54 ⁿ Mt 16:2
12:56 ᵒ Mt 16:3
12:58 ᵖ Mt 5:25
12:59 ᑫ Mt 5:26;
Mk 12:42
13:1 ʳ S Mt 27:2
13:2 ˢ Jn 9:2,3
13:4 ᵗ Jn 9:7,11
13:5 ᵘ Mt 3:2;
Ac 2:38
13:6 ᵛ Isa 5:2;
Jer 8:13; Mt 21:19
13:7 ʷ S Mt 3:10
13:10 ˣ S Mt 4:23
13:11 ʸ ver 16

12:49 *fire.* Applied figuratively in different ways in the NT (see note on 3:16). Here it is associated with judgment (v. 49) and division (v. 51). Judgment falls on the wicked, who are separated from the righteous.

12:50 *baptism.* The suffering that Jesus was to endure on the cross (see note on Mk 10:38). *until it is completed.* The words from the cross would pronounce the completion (see Jn 19:28, 30 and note). Jesus wished that the hour of suffering were already past.

12:54–56 Wind from the west was from the Mediterranean Sea; from the south it was from the desert. Although people could use such indicators to forecast the weather, they could not recognize the signs of spiritual crisis, the coming of the Messiah, the threat of his death, the coming confrontation with Rome and the eternal consequences these events would have for their own lives.

12:57 *judge for yourselves.* Despite the insistence of the Pharisees, despite the Roman system and even despite the pressure of family, a person must accept God on his terms. The signs of the times called for immediate decision—before judgment came on the Jewish nation.

12:58 *be reconciled … or.* Settle accounts before it is too late.

13:1 *Galileans whose blood Pilate had mixed with their sacrifices.* Having people killed while offering sacrifices in the temple fits Pilate's reputation.

13:2,4 *worse sinners … more guilty.* In ancient times it was often assumed that a calamity would befall only those who were extremely sinful (see Jn 9:2 and note; see also Job 4:7; 22:5, where Eliphaz falsely accused Job; see note on Job 22:5–11). But Jesus pointed out that all are sinners who must repent or face a fearful end.

13:4 *tower in Siloam.* Built into the southeast section of Jerusalem's wall (cf. note on Jn 9:7).

13:6 *fig tree.* Probably refers to the Jewish nation (see note on Mk 11:14), but it may also apply to an individual.

13:7 *For three years.* A period of ample opportunity.

13:11 *crippled by a spirit.* Various disorders were caused by evil spirits (see note on 4:33). The description of this woman's infirmity suggests that the bones of her spine were rigidly fused together.

13:13 *S Mk 5:23
13:14 *S Mt 12:2
*b S Mk 5:22 *c Ex 20:9
13:15 *d Lk 14:5
13:16 *e S Lk 3:8
*f S Mt 4:10
13:17 *g Isa 66:5
13:18 *h S Mt 3:2
*i S Mt 13:24
13:19 *j Lk 17:6
*k S Mt 13:32
13:21 *l 1Co 5:6
13:22 *m S Lk 9:51
13:24 *n Mt 7:13
13:25 *o Mt 7:23;
25:10-12
13:27 *p S Mt 7:23
13:28 *q S Mt 8:12
13:29 *r S Mt 8:11
13:30 *s S Mt 19:30

"Woman,[a] you are set free from your infirmity." [13]Then he put his hands on her,[z] and immediately she straightened up and praised God.

[14]Indignant because Jesus had healed on the Sabbath,[a] the synagogue leader[b] said to the people, "There are six days for work.[c] So come and be healed on those days, not on the Sabbath."

[15]The Lord answered him, "You hypocrites! Doesn't each of you on the Sabbath untie your ox or donkey from the stall and lead it out to give it water?[d] [16]Then should not this woman, a daughter of Abraham,[e] whom Satan[f] has kept bound for eighteen long years, be set free on the Sabbath day from what bound her?"

[17]When he said this, all his opponents were humiliated,[g] but the people were delighted with all the wonderful things he was doing.

THE PARABLES OF THE MUSTARD SEED AND THE YEAST

13:18,19pp — Mk 4:30–32
13:18–21pp — Mt 13:31–33

[18]Then Jesus asked, "What is the kingdom of God[h] like?[i] What shall I compare it to? [19]It is like a mustard seed, which a man took and planted in his garden. It grew and became a tree,[j] and the birds perched in its branches."[k]

[20]Again he asked, "What shall I compare the kingdom of God to? [21]It is like yeast that a woman took and mixed into about sixty pounds[b] of flour until it worked all through the dough."[l]

THE NARROW DOOR

[22]Then Jesus went through the towns and villages, teaching as he made his way to Jerusalem.[m] [23]Someone asked him, "Lord, are only a few people going to be saved?"

He said to them, [24]"Make every effort to enter through the narrow door,[n] because many, I tell you, will try to enter and will not be able to. [25]Once the owner of the house gets up and closes the door, you will stand outside knocking and pleading, 'Sir, open the door for us.'

"But he will answer, 'I don't know you or where you come from.'[o]

[26]"Then you will say, 'We ate and drank with you, and you taught in our streets.'

[27]"But he will reply, 'I don't know you or where you come from. Away from me, all you evildoers!'[p]

[28]"There will be weeping there, and gnashing of teeth,[q] when you see Abraham, Isaac and Jacob and all the prophets in the kingdom of God, but you yourselves thrown out. [29]People will come from east and west[r] and north and south, and will take their places at the feast in the kingdom of God. [30]Indeed there are those who are last who will be first, and first who will be last."[s]

---

a 12 The Greek for *Woman* does not denote any disrespect.   b 21 Or about 27 kilograms

---

13:12 *Woman.* See TNIV text note; cf. note on Jn 2:4. *set free.* The spirit had been cast out, and the woman was freed from her physical handicap.

13:13 *praised God.* See 1:64 and note.

13:14 *healed on the Sabbath.* A focal point of attack against Jesus was his conduct on the Sabbath (see 6:5; 14:5 and notes; Mt 12:1–8,11–12; Jn 5:10 and note; see also Ex 20:9–10). *synagogue leader.* See note on 8:41.

13:15 *hypocrites.* See note on Mt 6:2. *untie your ox.* They had more regard for the needs of an animal than for the far greater need of a human being. Jesus called his critics "hypocrites" because they pretended zeal for the law, but their motive was to attack him and his healing.

13:19 *mustard seed.* See notes on Mt 13:31–32; Mk 4:31. Trees in Scripture are sometimes symbols of nations (see Eze 17:23; 31:6; Da 4:11 and note).

13:21 *yeast.* See note on Mt 13:33. Its permeating quality is emphasized here as it works from the inside to affect all the dough. This parable speaks of the powerful influence of God's kingdom.

13:22 *through the towns and villages.* See chart, pp. 1656–1658. Somewhere between the events of 11:1 and 13:21 Jesus

left Judea and began his work in and around Perea, which is recorded in 13:22—19:27; Mt 19:1—20:28; Mk 10 (see note on 10:32); Jn 10:40–42. It appears that Jesus went north to Galilee during the last part of the Perean ministry and then traveled south again through Perea to Jericho and to Jerusalem. Some of Jesus' sayings that Luke attributes to the period of ministry in Perea are found in different settings in Matthew (7:13–14,22–23). Perhaps he repeated various sayings on different occasions. *Jerusalem.* Where he would die. Although Jesus was ministering throughout Perea, his eyes were constantly set on the Holy City and his ultimate destiny.

13:23 *only a few … saved?* Perhaps the questioner had observed that in spite of the very large crowds that came to hear Jesus' preaching and be healed, there were only a few followers who were loyal. Jesus did not answer directly but warned that many would try to enter after it was too late.

13:27 *I don't know you.* See Mt 7:23; 25:12.

13:29 *People … from east and west and north and south.* From the four corners of the world (Ps 107:3) and from among all people, including Gentiles. *feast in the kingdom of God.* See 14:15; Mt 8:11 and notes.

13:30 See Mt 19:30 and note.

JESUS' SORROW FOR JERUSALEM
13:34,35pp — Mt 23:37–39
13:34,35Ref — Lk 19:41

13:31 *t* S Mt 14:1
13:32 *u* S Heb 2:10
13:33 *v* S Mt 21:11
13:34 *w* S Mt 23:37
13:35 *x* Jer 12:17; 22:5 *y* Ps 118:26; Lk 19:38
14:1 *z* Lk 7:36; 11:37 *a* S Mt 12:10
14:3 *b* S Mt 22:35 *c* S Mt 12:2
14:5 *d* Lk 13:15
14:7 *e* S Lk 11:43
14:11 *f* S Mt 23:12
14:13 *g* ver 21
14:14 *h* Ac 24:15

³¹At that time some Pharisees came to Jesus and said to him, "Leave this place and go somewhere else. Herod *t* wants to kill you."

³²He replied, "Go tell that fox, 'I will keep on driving out demons and healing people today and tomorrow, and on the third day I will reach my goal.' *u* ³³In any case, I must press on today and tomorrow and the next day—for surely no prophet *v* can die outside Jerusalem!

³⁴"Jerusalem, Jerusalem, you who kill the prophets and stone those sent to you, how often I have longed to gather your children together, as a hen gathers her chicks under her wings, *w* and you were not willing. ³⁵Look, your house is left to you desolate. *x* I tell you, you will not see me again until you say, 'Blessed is he who comes in the name of the Lord.' *a* *y*

JESUS AT A PHARISEE'S HOUSE
14:8–10Ref — Pr 25:6,7

14 One Sabbath, when Jesus went to eat in the house of a prominent Pharisee, *z* he was being carefully watched. *a* ²There in front of him was a man suffering from abnormal swelling of his body. ³Jesus asked the Pharisees and experts in the law, *b* "Is it lawful to heal on the Sabbath or not?" *c* ⁴But they remained silent. So taking hold of the man, he healed him and sent him on his way.

⁵Then he asked them, "If one of you has a child *b* or an ox that falls into a well on the Sabbath day, will you not immediately pull it out?" *d* ⁶And they had nothing to say.

⁷When he noticed how the guests picked the places of honor at the table, *e* he told them this parable: ⁸"When someone invites you to a wedding feast, do not take the place of honor, for a person more distinguished than you may have been invited. ⁹If so, the host who invited both of you will come and say to you, 'Give this person your seat.' Then, humiliated, you will have to take the least important place. ¹⁰But when you are invited, take the lowest place, so that when your host comes, he will say to you, 'Friend, move up to a better place.' Then you will be honored in the presence of all the other guests. ¹¹For all those who exalt themselves will be humbled, and those who humble themselves will be exalted." *f*

¹²Then Jesus said to his host, "When you give a luncheon or dinner, do not invite your friends, your brothers or sisters, your relatives, or your rich neighbors; if you do, they may invite you back and so you will be repaid. ¹³But when you give a banquet, invite the poor, the crippled, the lame, the blind, *g* ¹⁴and you will be blessed. Although they cannot repay you, you will be repaid at the resurrection of the righteous." *h*

a 35 Psalm 118:26   *b* 5 Some manuscripts *donkey*

13:31 *Herod wants to kill you.* See note on Mt 14:1. Jesus was probably in Perea, which was under Herod's jurisdiction (see note on 3:1). The Pharisees wanted to frighten Jesus into leaving this area and going to Judea.
13:32 *fox.* A crafty animal. *today and tomorrow.* In Semitic usage this phrase could refer to an indefinite but limited period of time. *reach my goal.* Jesus' life had a predetermined plan that would be carried out, and no harm could come to him until his purpose was accomplished (cf. 4:43; 9:22).
13:33 *outside Jerusalem.* Jesus' hour had not yet come (see 2:38; Jn 2:4 and note; cf. Jn 8:59; 10:39; 11:54). He would die in Jerusalem as had numerous prophets before him.
13:34 *how often I have longed to gather.* This lament over Jerusalem may suggest that Jesus was in Jerusalem more often than the Synoptics indicate (cf. Jn 2:13; 4:45; 5:1; 7:10; 10:22). However, the statement in vv. 34–35 may have been uttered some distance from Jerusalem, i.e., in Perea. According to Mt 23:37–38, the same utterance was spoken on Tuesday of Passion Week. Jesus repeated many of his teachings and sayings.
13:35 *house is left . . . desolate.* God will abandon his temple and his city (see 21:20,24; Jer 12:7; 22:5 and notes). *not see me again until.* See Zec 12:10 and note; Rev 1:7; cf. Isa 45:23; Ro 14:11; Php 2:10–11.
14:1 Of seven recorded miracles on the Sabbath, Luke includes

five (4:31,38; 6:6; 13:14; here); the other two are Jn 5:10 (see note there); 9:14. Concerning the vigil of the Pharisees, see note on 13:14. Sabbath meals were prepared the day before.
14:2 *abnormal swelling of his body.* Perhaps edema, an excessive accumulation of fluid in the tissues and cavities of the body that indicates illness. The Greek for this word is a medical term found only here in the NT (see Introduction: Author).
14:3 *experts in the law.* See notes on 5:17; 7:30. By questioning them before the miracle, Jesus made it difficult for them to protest afterward.
14:5 *child.* See TNIV text note. The reading "donkey" matches well with the "ox that falls into a well." But in Dt 5:14 the law is specified for both humans and animals; one category opens with "son" and another with "ox." Jesus' action was "unlawful" only according to Rabbinic interpretations, not according to the Mosaic law itself.
14:7 *places of honor.* Maneuvering for better seats may also have caused trouble at the Last Supper (22:24; see also 20:46; Mk 12:39 and note).
14:11 *humble themselves will be exalted.* A basic principle repeated often in the Bible (see 11:43; 18:14; 20:46; 2Ch 7:14–15; Pr 3:34; 25:6–7; Mt 18:4; 23:12; Jas 4:10; 1Pe 5:6).
14:14 *resurrection of the righteous.* All will be resurrected (see Da 12:2; Jn 5:28–29 and notes; Ac 24:15). Some hold

14:15 *i* Isa 25:6;
Mt 26:29; Lk 13:29;
Rev 19:9 *j* S Mt 3:2
14:21 *k* ver 13
14:24 *l* Mt 21:43;
Ac 13:46
14:26 *m* Mt 10:37;
S Jn 12:25
14:27 *n* Mt 10:38;
Lk 9:23
14:33 *o* Php 3:7,8
14:34 *p* Mk 9:50
14:35 *q* Mk 5:13
r S Mt 11:15
15:1 *s* Lk 5:29
15:2 *t* S Mt 9:11

THE PARABLE OF THE GREAT BANQUET

14:16–24Ref — Mt 22:2–14

¹⁵When one of those at the table with him heard this, he said to Jesus, "Blessed are those who will eat at the feast *i* in the kingdom of God." *j*

¹⁶Jesus replied: "A certain man was preparing a great banquet and invited many guests. ¹⁷At the time of the banquet he sent his servant to tell those who had been invited, 'Come, for everything is now ready.'

¹⁸"But they all alike began to make excuses. The first said, 'I have just bought a field, and I must go and see it. Please excuse me.'

¹⁹"Another said, 'I have just bought five yoke of oxen, and I'm on my way to try them out. Please excuse me.'

²⁰"Still another said, 'I just got married, so I can't come.'

²¹"The servant came back and reported this to his master. Then the owner of the house became angry and ordered his servant, 'Go out quickly into the streets and alleys of the town and bring in the poor, the crippled, the blind and the lame.' *k*

²²" 'Sir,' the servant said, 'what you ordered has been done, but there is still room.'

²³"Then the master told his servant, 'Go out to the roads and country lanes and compel them to come in, so that my house will be full. ²⁴I tell you, not one of those who were invited will get a taste of my banquet.' " *l*

THE COST OF BEING A DISCIPLE

²⁵Large crowds were traveling with Jesus, and turning to them he said: ²⁶"If anyone comes to me and does not hate father and mother, wife and children, brothers and sisters—yes, even life itself—such a person cannot be my disciple. *m* ²⁷And whoever does not carry their cross and follow me cannot be my disciple. *n*

²⁸"Suppose one of you wants to build a tower. Won't you first sit down and estimate the cost to see if you have enough money to complete it? ²⁹For if you lay the foundation and are not able to finish it, everyone who sees it will ridicule you, ³⁰saying, 'This person began to build and wasn't able to finish.'

³¹"Or suppose a king is about to go to war against another king. Won't he first sit down and consider whether he is able with ten thousand men to oppose the one coming against him with twenty thousand? ³²If he is not able, he will send a delegation while the other is still a long way off and will ask for terms of peace. ³³In the same way, those of you who do not give up everything you have cannot be my disciples. *o*

³⁴"Salt is good, but if it loses its saltiness, how can it be made salty again? *p* ³⁵It is fit neither for the soil nor for the manure pile; it is thrown out. *q*

"Whoever has ears to hear, let them hear." *r*

THE PARABLE OF THE LOST SHEEP

15:4–7pp — Mt 18:12–14

15 Now the tax collectors *s* and sinners were all gathering around to hear Jesus. ²But the Pharisees and the teachers of the law muttered, "This man welcomes sinners and eats with them." *t*

---

that the resurrection of the righteous (1Co 15:23; 1Th 4:16; Rev 20:4–6) is distinct from the "general" resurrection (1Co 15:12,21; Heb 6:2; Rev 20:11–15). *the righteous.* Those who have been pronounced so by God on the basis of Christ's atonement (see Ro 1:17 and note) and who have evidenced their faith by their actions (cf. Mt 25:34–40).

14:15 *feast in the kingdom.* The great Messianic banquet to come. Association of the future kingdom with a feast was common (see 13:29; Isa 25:6 and note; Mt 8:11 and note; 25:1–10; 26:29 and note; Rev 19:9).

14:16 *Jesus replied.* Jesus used the man's remark as the occasion for a parable warning that not everyone would enter the kingdom.

14:18 *bought a field.* The initial invitation must have been accepted, but when the final invitation came (by Jewish custom the announcement that came when the feast was ready), other interests took priority. None of the excuses given was valid. For example, one did not buy a field without first seeing it, nor oxen without first trying them out (v. 19).

14:24 *those who were invited.* Without explicitly mentioning

them, Jesus warned the Jewish religious leaders that those who refuse the invitation to his Messianic banquet would not get one taste of it, but others would (see 20:9–19; see also note on Mt 21:41).

14:26 *hate father and mother.* A vivid hyperbole, meaning that one must love Jesus even more than one's immediate family (see Mal 1:2–3 for another use of the figure). See Mt 10:37 and note on Mal 1:3.

14:27 *carry their cross.* See 9:23; Mt 10:38 and notes.

14:28 *estimate the cost.* Jesus did not want a blind, naive commitment that expected only blessings. As a builder estimates costs or a king evaluates military strength (v. 31), so people must consider what Jesus expects of his followers before they commit their lives to him.

14:33 *give up everything you have.* The cost, Jesus warned, is complete surrender to him (see Php 3:7–11).

14:34 *Salt is good.* See note on Mk 9:50.

15:1 *tax collectors and sinners.* See notes on 3:12; Mk 2:15.

15:2 *muttered.* Complained among themselves, but not openly. *eats with them.* More than simple association, eating with a

³Then Jesus told them this parable: *u* ⁴"Suppose one of you has a hundred sheep and loses one of them. Doesn't he leave the ninety-nine in the open country and go after the lost sheep until he finds it? *v* ⁵And when he finds it, he joyfully puts it on his shoulders ⁶and goes home. Then he calls his friends and neighbors together and says, 'Rejoice with me; I have found my lost sheep.' *w* ⁷I tell you that in the same way there will be more rejoicing in heaven over one sinner who repents than over ninety-nine righteous persons who do not need to repent. *x*

THE PARABLE OF THE LOST COIN

⁸"Or suppose a woman has ten silver coins *a* and loses one. Doesn't she light a lamp, sweep the house and search carefully until she finds it? ⁹And when she finds it, she calls her friends and neighbors together and says, 'Rejoice with me; I have found my lost coin.' *y* ¹⁰In the same way, I tell you, there is rejoicing in the presence of the angels of God over one sinner who repents." *z*

THE PARABLE OF THE LOST SON

¹¹Jesus continued: "There was a man who had two sons. *a* ¹²The younger one said to his father, 'Father, give me my share of the estate.' *b* So he divided his property *c* between them.

¹³"Not long after that, the younger son got together all he had, set off for a distant country and there squandered his wealth *d* in wild living. ¹⁴After he had spent everything, there was a severe famine in that whole country, and he began to be in need. ¹⁵So he went and hired himself out to a citizen of that country, who sent him to his fields to feed pigs. *e* ¹⁶He longed to fill his stomach with the pods that the pigs were eating, but no one gave him anything.

¹⁷"When he came to his senses, he said, 'How many of my father's hired servants have food to spare, and here I am starving to death! ¹⁸I will set out and go back to my father and say to him: Father, I have sinned *f* against heaven and against you. ¹⁹I am no longer worthy to be called your son; make me like one of your hired servants.' ²⁰So he got up and went to his father.

"But while he was still a long way off, his father saw him and was filled with compassion for him; he ran to his son, threw his arms around him and kissed him. *g*

²¹"The son said to him, 'Father, I have sinned against heaven and against you. *h* I am no longer worthy to be called your son.'

²²"But the father said to his servants, 'Quick! Bring the best robe *i* and put it on him. Put a ring on his finger *j* and sandals on his feet. ²³Bring the fattened calf and kill it. Let's have a feast and celebrate. ²⁴For this son of mine was dead and is alive again; *k* he was lost and is found.' So they began to celebrate. *l*

²⁵"Meanwhile, the older son was in the field. When he came near the house, he heard music and dancing. ²⁶So he called one of the servants and asked him what was going on. ²⁷'Your brother has come,' he replied, 'and your father has killed the fattened calf because he has him back safe and sound.'

²⁸"The older brother became angry *m* and refused to go in. So his father went out and

---

a 8 Greek *ten drachmas*, each worth about a day's wages

15:3 *u* Mt 13:3
15:4 *v* Ps 23;
119:176; Jer 31:10;
Eze 34:11-16; Lk 5:32;
19:10
15:6 *w* ver 9
15:7 *x* ver 10
15:9 *y* ver 6
15:10 *z* ver 7
15:11 *a* Mt 21:28
15:12 *b* Dt 21:17
c ver 30
15:13 *d* ver 30;
Lk 16:1
15:15 *e* Lev 11:7
15:18 *f* Lev 26:40;
Mt 3:2
15:20 *g* Ge 45:14,15;
46:29; Ac 20:37
15:21 *h* Ps 51:4
15:22 *i* Zec 3:4;
Rev 6:11 *j* Ge 41:42
15:24 *k* Eph 2:1,5;
5:14; 1Ti 1:5 *l* ver 32
15:28 *m* Jnh 4:1

---

person indicated acceptance and recognition (cf. Ps 41:9; Jn 13:18 and notes; Ac 11:3; 1Co 5:11 and note; Gal 2:12).

15:3 *this parable.* Jesus responded with a story that contrasted the love of God with the exclusiveness of the Pharisees.

15:4 *lost sheep.* The shepherd theme was familiar (see Ps 23; Isa 40:11; Eze 34:11–16 and notes).

15:7 *rejoicing in heaven.* God's joy over the sinner's repentance is set in stark contrast to the attitude of the Pharisees and the teachers of the law (v. 2). *righteous…do not need to repent.* Probably irony: those who think they are righteous (such as the Pharisees and the teachers of the law) and feel no need to repent.

15:8 *ten silver coins.* See TNIV text note. A *drachma* was a Greek coin approximately equivalent to the Roman *denarius*, worth about an average day's wages (Mt 20:2). *search carefully.* Near Eastern houses frequently had no windows and only earthen floors, making the search for a single coin difficult.

15:12 *share of the estate.* The father might divide the inheritance (double to the older son; see 12:13; Dt 21:17 and notes) but retain the income from it until his death. But to give a

younger son his portion of the inheritance upon request was highly unusual. Cf. Pr 20:21 and note.

15:13 *got together all he had.* The son's motive becomes apparent when he departs, taking with him all his possessions and leaving nothing behind to come back to. He wants to be free of parental restraint and to spend his share of the family wealth as he pleases. *wild living.* More specific in v. 30, though the older brother may have exaggerated because of his bitter attitude.

15:15 *feed pigs.* The ultimate indignity for Jews; the work was distasteful to them because pigs were "unclean" animals (Lev 11:7).

15:16 *pods.* Seeds of the carob tree.

15:22–23 *best robe…ring…sandals…feast.* Each was a sign of position and acceptance (cf. Ge 41:42 and note; Zec 3:4): a long robe of distinction, a signet ring of authority, sandals like a son (slaves went barefoot) and the fattened calf for a special occasion.

A **15:28** *older brother.* The forgiving love of the father symbolizes the divine mercy of God, and the older brother's resentment is like the attitude of the Pharisees and teachers of the law who opposed Jesus (v. 2).

PARABLES OF JESUS

PARABLE	MATTHEW	MARK	LUKE
Lamp under a bowl	5:14–15	4:21–22	8:16; 11:33
Wise and foolish builders	7:24–27		6:47–49
New cloth on an old coat	9:16	2:21	5:36
New wine in old wineskins	9:17	2:22	5:37–38
Sower and the soils	13:3–8,18–23	4:3–8,14–20	8:5–8,11–15
Weeds	13:24–30,36–43		
Mustard seed	13:31–32	4:30–32	13:18–19
Yeast	13:33		13:20–21
Hidden treasure	13:44		
Valuable pearl	13:45–46		
Net	13:47–50		
Owner of a house	13:52		
Lost sheep	18:12–14		15:4–7
Unmerciful servant	18:23–34		
Workers in the vineyard	20:1–16		
Two sons	21:28–32		
Bags of gold	21:33–44	12:1–11	20:9–18
Wedding banquet	22:2–14		
Fig tree	24:32–35	13:28–29	21:29–31
Faithful and wise servant	24:45–51		12:42–48
Ten virgins	25:1–13		
Bags of gold (minas)	25:14–30		19:12–27
Sheep and goats	25:31–46		
Growing seed		4:26–29	
Watchful servants		13:35–37	12:35–40
Moneylender			7:41–43
Good Samaritan			10:30–37
Friend in need			11:5–8
Rich fool			12:16–21
Unfruitful fig tree			13:6–9
Lowest seat at the feast			14:7–14
Great banquet			14:16–24
Cost of discipleship			14:28–33
Lost coin			15:8–10
Lost (prodigal) son			15:11–32
Shrewd manager			16:1–8
Rich man and Lazarus			16:19–31
Master and his servant			17:7–10
Persistent widow			18:2–8
Pharisee and tax collector			18:10–14

pleaded with him. [29]But he answered his father, 'Look! All these years I've been slaving for you and never disobeyed your orders. Yet you never gave me even a young goat so I could celebrate with my friends. [30]But when this son of yours who has squandered your property [n] with prostitutes [o] comes home, you kill the fattened calf for him!'

[31]" 'My son,' the father said, 'you are always with me, and everything I have is yours. [32]But we had to celebrate and be glad, because this brother of yours was dead and is alive again; he was lost and is found.' " [p]

THE PARABLE OF THE SHREWD MANAGER

16 Jesus told his disciples: "There was a rich man whose manager was accused of wasting his possessions. [q] [2]So he called him in and asked him, 'What is this I hear about you? Give an account of your management, because you cannot be manager any longer.'

[3]"The manager said to himself, 'What shall I do now? My master is taking away my job. I'm not strong enough to dig, and I'm ashamed to beg— [4]I know what I'll do so that, when I lose my job here, people will welcome me into their houses.'

[5]"So he called in each one of his master's debtors. He asked the first, 'How much do you owe my master?'

[6]" 'Nine hundred gallons [a] of olive oil,' he replied.

"The manager told him, 'Take your bill, sit down quickly, and make it four hundred and fifty.'

[7]"Then he asked the second, 'And how much do you owe?'

" 'A thousand bushels [b] of wheat,' he replied.

"He told him, 'Take your bill and make it eight hundred.'

[8]"The master commended the dishonest manager because he had acted shrewdly. For the people of this world [r] are more shrewd [s] in dealing with their own kind than are the people of the light. [t] [9]I tell you, use worldly wealth [u] to gain friends for yourselves, so that when it is gone, you will be welcomed into eternal dwellings. [v]

[10]"Whoever can be trusted with very little can also be trusted with much, [w] and whoever is dishonest with very little will also be dishonest with much. [11]So if you have not been trustworthy in handling worldly wealth, [x] who will trust you with true riches? [12]And if you have not been trustworthy with someone else's property, who will give you property of your own?

[13]"No one can serve two masters. Either you will hate the one and love the other, or you will be devoted to the one and despise the other. You cannot serve both God and money." [y]

[14]The Pharisees, who loved money, [z] heard all this and were sneering at Jesus. [a] [15]He said to them, "You are the ones who justify yourselves [b] in the eyes of others, but God knows your hearts. [c] What people value highly is detestable in God's sight.

---

[a] 6 Or about 3,000 liters   [b] 7 Or about 30 tons

15:30 [n] ver 12,13
[o] Pr 29:3
15:32 [p] ver 24;
Mal 3:17
16:1 [q] Lk 15:13,30
16:8 [r] Ps 17:14
[s] Ps 18:26 [t] Jn 12:36;
Eph 5:8; 1Th 5:5
16:9 [u] ver 11,13
[v] Mt 19:21; Lk 12:33
16:10 [w] Mt 25:21,
23; Lk 19:17
16:11 [x] ver 9,13
16:13 [y] ver 9,11;
Mt 6:24
16:14 [z] S 1Ti 3:3
[a] Lk 23:35
16:15 [b] Lk 10:29
[c] S Rev 2:23

15:29 *young goat.* Cheaper food than a fattened calf.

15:30 *this son of yours.* The older brother would not even recognize him as his brother, so bitter was his hatred.

A 15:31 *everything I have is yours.* The father loved both brothers. The parable shows a contrast between the self-centered exclusiveness of the Pharisees, who failed to understand God's love, and his joy over the repentance of sinners.

A 15:32 *dead and is alive.* A beautiful picture of the return of the younger son, which also pictures Christian conversion (see Ro 6:12–13 and note; Eph 2:1,5). The phrase "lost and is found" is often used to mean "perished and is saved" (see 19:10 and note; Mt 10:6; 18:12–14 and note).

16:1 *disciples.* Perhaps more than just the Twelve (see 6:13 and note; 10:1). *manager.* A steward who handled all the business affairs of the owner (cf. 1Co 4:1–2 and note on 4:1). *wasting.* He had squandered his master's possessions, just as the prodigal (wasteful) son had done (15:13).

16:3 *What shall I do now?* The dishonest manager (v. 8) had no scruples against using his position for his own benefit, even if it meant cheating his master. Knowing he would lose his job, the manager planned for his future by discounting the debts owed to his master in order to obligate the debtors to himself. Interpreters disagree as to whether his procedure of discounting was in itself dishonest. Was he giving away what really belonged to

his master, or was he forgoing interest payments his master did not have a right to charge? Originally the manager may have overcharged the debtors, a common way of circumventing the Mosaic law that prohibited taking interest from fellow Jews (see Ex 22:25–27; Lev 25:36 and notes; Dt 23:19–20). So, to reduce the debts, he may have returned the figures to their initial amounts, which would both satisfy his master and gain the good favor of the debtors. In any event, the point remains the same: He was shrewd enough to use the means at his disposal to plan for his future well-being.

16:8 *people of the light.* God's people (see Jn 12:35–36; Eph 5:8; 1Th 5:5 and notes).

A 16:9 *use worldly wealth.* God's people should be alert to make use of what God has given them. *to gain friends.* By helping those in need, who in the future will show their gratitude when they welcome their benefactors into heaven ("eternal dwellings"). In this way worldly wealth may be wisely used to gain eternal benefit.

A 16:10 *trusted with much.* Cf. 19:17; Mt 25:21. Faithfulness is not determined by the amount entrusted but by the character of the person who uses it.

16:11 *true riches.* The things that belong to God's kingdom, in contrast to "worldly wealth."

16:13 *two masters.* See Mt 6:24; cf. Jas 4:4 and note.

16:16 *d* Mt 5:17;
11:12,13 *e* S Mt 4:23
16:17 *f* S Mt 5:18
16:18 *g* Mt 5:31,32;
19:9; Mk 10:11;
Ro 7:2,3; 1Co 7:10,11
16:19 *h* Eze 16:49
16:20 *i* Ac 3:2
16:21 *j* Mt 15:27;
Lk 15:16
16:24 *k* ver 30;
S Lk 3:8 *l* S Mt 5:22
16:25 *m* Ps 17:14
n Lk 6:21,24,25
16:28 *o* Ac 2:40;
20:23; 1Th 4:6
16:29 *p* S Lk 24:27,
44; Jn 1:45; 5:45-47;
Ac 15:21 *q* Lk 4:17;
24:27,44; Jn 1:45
16:30 *r* ver 24;
S Lk 3:8
17:1 *s* S Mt 5:29
t Mt 18:7
17:2 *u* Mk 10:24;
Lk 10:21 *v* S Mt 5:29
17:3 *w* S Mt 18:15
x Eph 4:32; Col 3:13
17:4 *y* Mt 18:21,22

ADDITIONAL TEACHINGS

16 "The Law and the Prophets were proclaimed until John. *d* Since that time, the good news of the kingdom of God is being preached, *e* and people are forcing their way into it. 17 It is easier for heaven and earth to disappear than for the least stroke of a pen to drop out of the Law. *f*

18 "Anyone who divorces his wife and marries another woman commits adultery, and the man who marries a divorced woman commits adultery. *g*

THE RICH MAN AND LAZARUS

19 "There was a rich man who was dressed in purple and fine linen and lived in luxury every day. *h* 20 At his gate was laid a beggar *i* named Lazarus, covered with sores 21 and longing to eat what fell from the rich man's table. *j* Even the dogs came and licked his sores. 22 "The time came when the beggar died and the angels carried him to Abraham's side. The rich man also died and was buried. 23 In Hades, where he was in torment, he looked up and saw Abraham far away, with Lazarus by his side. 24 So he called to him, 'Father Abraham, *k* have pity on me and send Lazarus to dip the tip of his finger in water and cool my tongue, because I am in agony in this fire.' *l*

25 "But Abraham replied, 'Son, remember that in your lifetime you received your good things, while Lazarus received bad things, *m* but now he is comforted here and you are in agony. *n* 26 And besides all this, between us and you a great chasm has been set in place, so that those who want to go from here to you cannot, nor can anyone cross over from there to us.'

27 "He answered, 'Then I beg you, father, send Lazarus to my family, 28 for I have five brothers. Let them warn them, *o* so that they will not also come to this place of torment.'

29 "Abraham replied, 'They have Moses *p* and the Prophets; *q* let them listen to them.'

30 " 'No, father Abraham,' *r* he said, 'but if someone from the dead goes to them, they will repent.'

31 "He said to him, 'If they do not listen to Moses and the Prophets, they will not be convinced even if someone rises from the dead.' "

SIN, FAITH, DUTY

17 Jesus said to his disciples: "Things that cause people to stumble *s* are bound to come, but woe to anyone through whom they come. *t* 2 It would be better for you to be thrown into the sea with a millstone tied around your neck than for you to cause one of these little ones *u* to stumble. *v* 3 So watch yourselves.

"If a brother or sister sins against you, rebuke them; *w* and if they repent, forgive them. *x* 4 Even if they sin against you seven times in a day and seven times come back to you saying 'I repent,' you must forgive them." *y*

16:16 *until John.* The ministry of John the Baptist, which prepared the way for Jesus the Messiah, was the dividing line between the OT (the "Law and the Prophets") and the NT (see notes on Jer 31:31–34; Heb 8:6–12). *forcing their way.* The meaning is disputed, but it probably speaks of the fierce earnestness with which people were responding to the gospel of the kingdom. Multitudes were coming to hear Jesus and to receive his message.

16:17 The ministry of Jesus (introducing the new covenant era) was a fulfillment of the law (defining the old covenant era) in the most minute detail (cf. 21:33). *heaven and earth to disappear.* See Mk 13:24–25; 2Pe 3:7 and notes. *least stroke of a pen.* See Mt 5:17–18 and notes.

16:18 *divorces his wife.* See Mt 5:32; 19:3; Mk 10:11–12; 1Co 7:10–11 and notes. Jesus affirms the continuing authority of the law: For example, adultery was still adultery, still unlawful and still sinful. Matthew's treatment is fuller in that (1) it shows that this law was given because of hardened hearts in regard to divorce, and (2) it includes one exception as permissible grounds for divorce—sexual immorality (Mt 19:9).

16:19 *rich man.* Sometimes given the name Dives (from the Latin for "rich man"). *purple and fine linen.* Characteristic of costly garments.

16:20 *Lazarus.* Not the Lazarus Jesus raised from the dead (Jn 11:43–44). If this is a parable, it is the only one in which Jesus gave a name to one of the characters. *covered with sores.* The

Greek for this phrase is a common medical term found only here in the NT (see Introduction: Author).

16:22 The Talmud mentions both paradise (see 23:43 and note) and Abraham's side as the final home of the righteous. "Abraham's side" refers to the place of blessedness to which the righteous dead go. Its bliss is the quality of blessedness reserved for people like Abraham.

16:23 *Hades.* Here depicted as the place to which the wicked dead go and suffer torment.

16:28 *I have five brothers.* For the first time the rich man showed concern for others.

16:29 *Moses and the Prophets.* A way of designating the whole OT. The rich man had failed to pay attention to Scripture and its teaching and feared his brothers would do the same. *listen to.* Hear and obey.

16:30 *someone from the dead.* The story may suggest that Lazarus was intended, but Luke's account seems to imply that Jesus was speaking also of his own resurrection (cf. v. 31; 9:22). If people's minds are closed and Scripture is rejected, no evidence—not even a resurrection—will change them.

17:2 *millstone.* A heavy stone for grinding grain. *little ones.* See Mt 18:6,10,14; Mk 9:42 and notes.

17:3 *a brother or sister.* See Mt 18:15,17; Mk 3:35 and notes.

17:4 *seven times.* That is, forgiveness is to be unlimited (see notes on Ps 119:164; Mt 18:22).

⁵The apostles^z said to the Lord,^a "Increase our faith!"

⁶He replied, "If you have faith as small as a mustard seed,^b you can say to this mulberry tree, 'Be uprooted and planted in the sea,' and it will obey you.^c

⁷"Suppose one of you has a servant plowing or looking after the sheep. Will he say to the servant when he comes in from the field, 'Come along now and sit down to eat'? ⁸Won't he rather say, 'Prepare my supper, get yourself ready and wait on me^d while I eat and drink; after that you may eat and drink'? ⁹Will he thank the servant because he did what he was told to do? ¹⁰So you also, when you have done everything you were told to do, should say, 'We are unworthy servants; we have only done our duty.' "^e

JESUS HEALS TEN MEN WITH LEPROSY

¹¹Now on his way to Jerusalem,^f Jesus traveled along the border between Samaria and Galilee.^g ¹²As he was going into a village, ten men who had leprosy^a^h met him. They stood at a distanceⁱ ¹³and called out in a loud voice, "Jesus, Master,^j have pity on us!"

¹⁴When he saw them, he said, "Go, show yourselves to the priests."^k And as they went, they were cleansed.

¹⁵One of them, when he saw he was healed, came back, praising God^l in a loud voice. ¹⁶He threw himself at Jesus' feet and thanked him—and he was a Samaritan.^m

¹⁷Jesus asked, "Were not all ten cleansed? Where are the other nine? ¹⁸Was no one found to return and give praise to God except this foreigner?" ¹⁹Then he said to him, "Rise and go; your faith has made you well."ⁿ

THE COMING OF THE KINGDOM OF GOD

17:26,27pp — Mt 24:37–39

²⁰Once, having been asked by the Pharisees when the kingdom of God would come,^o Jesus replied, "The coming of the kingdom of God is not something that can be observed, ²¹nor will people say, 'Here it is,' or 'There it is,'^p because the kingdom of God is in your midst."^b

²²Then he said to his disciples, "The time is coming when you will long to see one of the days of the Son of Man,^q but you will not see it.^r ²³People will tell you, 'There he is!' or 'Here he is!' Do not go running off after them.^s ²⁴For the Son of Man in his day^c will be like the lightning,^t which flashes and lights up the sky from one end to the other. ²⁵But first he must suffer many things^u and be rejected^v by this generation.^w

²⁶"Just as it was in the days of Noah,^x so also will it be in the days of the Son of Man. ²⁷People were eating, drinking, marrying and being given in marriage up to the day Noah entered the ark. Then the flood came and destroyed them all.

²⁸"It was the same in the days of Lot.^y People were eating and drinking, buying and selling, planting and building. ²⁹But the day Lot left Sodom, fire and sulfur rained down from heaven and destroyed them all.

³⁰"It will be just like this on the day the Son of Man is revealed.^z ³¹On that day no one

---

^a 12 The Greek word traditionally translated *leprosy* was used for various diseases affecting the skin.
^b 21 Or is within you   ^c 24 Some manuscripts do not have *in his day*.

17:5 ^z S Mk 6:30
^a S Lk 7:13
17:6 ^b Mt 13:31; 17:20; Lk 13:19
^c S Mt 21:21; Mk 9:23
17:8 ^d Lk 12:37
17:10 ^e 1Co 9:16
17:11 ^f S Lk 9:51
^g Lk 9:51,52; Jn 4:3,4
17:12 ^h S Mt 8:2
ⁱ Lev 13:45,46
17:13 ^j S Lk 5:5
17:14 ^k Lev 14:2; Mt 8:4
17:15 ^l S Mt 9:8
17:16 ^m S Mt 10:5
17:19 ⁿ S Mk 9:22
17:20 ^o S Mt 3:2
17:21 ^p ver 23
17:22 ^q S Mt 8:20
^r S Lk 5:35
17:23 ^s Mt 24:23; Lk 21:8
17:24 ^t Mt 24:27
17:25 ^u S Mt 16:21
^v Lk 9:22; 18:32
^w Mk 13:30; Lk 21:32
17:26 ^x Ge 6:5-8; 7:6-24
17:28 ^y Ge 19:1-28
17:30 ^z Mt 10:23; S 16:27; 24:3,27,37, 39; 25:31; S 1Co 1:7; S 1Th 2:19; 2Th 1:7; 2:8; 2Pe 3:4; S Rev 1:7

17:5 *Increase our faith!* They felt incapable of measuring up to the standards set forth in vv. 1–4. They wanted greater faith to lay hold of the power to live up to Jesus' standards.

17:6 See Mt 17:20 and note; Mk 11:23; see also notes on Mt 13:31–32; Mk 4:31.

17:7 *a servant.* A slave, used to illustrate performance of duty (cf. 12:37 and note).

17:11 *border between Samaria and Galilee.* From this point Jesus seems to have journeyed to Perea, where he ministered on his way south to Jerusalem (see notes on 9:51; 13:22).

17:14 *show yourselves to the priests.* Normal procedure after a cure (see Lev 13:2–3; 14:2–32).

17:15 *praising God.* See v. 18; see also 1:64 and note.

17:16 *Samaritan.* See note on 10:31–33. Normally Jews did not associate with Samaritans (see Jn 4:9 and note), but leprosy broke down some social barriers while erecting others (see notes on Lev 13:2,4, 45–46).

17:19 *your faith has made you well.* See Mt 9:22. The phrase may also be rendered "your faith has saved you" (7:50; see note on Mk 5:34). The fact that the Samaritan returned to thank Jesus may indicate that he had received salva-tion in addition to the physical healing all ten had received (cf. 7:50; 8:48,50 and notes).

17:20 *Pharisees.* See note on 5:17.

17:21 *the kingdom of God is in your midst.* The kingdom is present in the person of King Jesus (see note on 4:43).

17:22 *long to see.* In time of trouble, believers will desire to experience the day when Jesus returns in his glory and delivers his people from distress.

17:23 *Do not go running off after them.* Do not leave your work in order to pursue predictions of Christ's second advent (see note on 1Th 4:11).

17:24 *like the lightning.* His coming will be sudden, unexpected and public (cf. 12:40 and note).

17:25 *he must suffer.* Jesus repeatedly foretold his coming death (see 5:35; 9:22 and note, 43–45; 12:50; 13:32–33; 18:32; 24:7; Mt 16:21; Mk 2:20 and note), which had to occur before his glorious return.

17:28 *in the days of Lot.* See Ge 18:16—19:28.

17:30 *Son of Man is revealed.* At Jesus' second coming he will be plainly visible to all (see 1Co 1:7; 2Th 1:7 and note; 1Pe 1:7, 13; 4:13; Rev 1:7).

17:31 *a* Mt 24:17,18
17:32 *b* Ge 19:26
17:33 *c* S Jn 12:25
17:35[36] *d* Mt 24:
41
17:37 *e* Mt 24:28
18:1 *f* Isa 40:31;
Lk 11:5-8; S Ac 1:14;
S Ro 1:10; 12:12;
Eph 6:18; Col 4:2;
1Th 5:17
18:3 *g* Isa 1:17
18:5 *h* Lk 11:8
18:6 *i* S Lk 7:13
18:7 *j* Rev 22:23;
Ps 88:1; Rev 6:10
18:8 *k* S Mt 8:20
l S Mt 16:27
18:9 *m* Lk 16:15
n Isa 65:5
18:10 *o* Ac 3:1
18:11 *p* Mt 6:5;
Mk 11:25
18:12 *q* Isa 58:3;
Mt 9:14 *r* Mal 3:8;
Lk 11:42
18:13 *s* Isa 66:2;
Jer 31:19; Lk 23:48
t Lk 5:32; 1Ti 1:15
18:14 *u* S Mt 23:12

who is on the housetop, with possessions inside, should go down to get them. Likewise, no one in the field should go back for anything. *a* 32Remember Lot's wife! *b* 33Whoever tries to keep their life will lose it, and whoever loses their life will preserve it. *c* 34I tell you, on that night two people will be in one bed; one will be taken and the other left. 35[36] Two women will be grinding grain together; one will be taken and the other left." *d*

37"Where, Lord?" they asked.

He replied, "Where there is a dead body, there the vultures will gather." *e*

THE PARABLE OF THE PERSISTENT WIDOW

18 Then Jesus told his disciples a parable to show them that they should always pray and not give up. *f* 2He said: "In a certain town there was a judge who neither feared God nor cared what people thought. 3And there was a widow in that town who kept coming to him with the plea, 'Grant me justice *g* against my adversary.'

4"For some time he refused. But finally he said to himself, 'Even though I don't fear God or care what people think, 5yet because this widow keeps bothering me, I will see that she gets justice, so that she won't eventually come and attack me!' " *h*

6And the Lord *i* said, "Listen to what the unjust judge says. 7And will not God bring about justice for his chosen ones, who cry out *j* to him day and night? Will he keep putting them off? 8I tell you, he will see that they get justice, and quickly. However, when the Son of Man *k* comes, *l* will he find faith on the earth?"

THE PARABLE OF THE PHARISEE AND THE TAX COLLECTOR

9To some who were confident of their own righteousness *m* and looked down on everyone else, *n* Jesus told this parable: 10"Two men went up to the temple to pray, *o* one a Pharisee and the other a tax collector. 11The Pharisee stood by himself *p* and prayed: 'God, I thank you that I am not like other people—robbers, evildoers, adulterers—or even like this tax collector. 12I fast *q* twice a week and give a tenth *r* of all I get.'

13"But the tax collector stood at a distance. He would not even look up to heaven, but beat his breast *s* and said, 'God, have mercy on me, a sinner.' *t*

14"I tell you that this man, rather than the other, went home justified before God. For all those who exalt themselves will be humbled, and those who humble themselves will be exalted." *u*

17:31 *on the housetop.* It was customary to relax on the flat rooftop. When the final hour comes, however, the individual there should not be thinking of going into the house to retrieve some material objects. Matthew and Mark refer similarly to flight at the fall of Jerusalem, and indirectly to the end time (Mt 24:17–18; Mk 13:15), but here the reference is explicitly to Jesus' return (see v. 30; cf. 21:21).

17:33 *whoever loses their life will preserve it.* See note on 9:24 (cf. Mt 10:39).

17:35[36] *taken.* Could refer to being "taken to/from destruction" or "taken into the kingdom." What is clear is that no matter how close two people may be in life, they have no guarantee of the same eternal destiny. One may go to judgment and condemnation, the other to salvation, reward and blessing. Verse 36 ("Two men will be in the field; one will be taken and the other left") was probably inserted here from Mt 24:40 by a later copyist. It is not found at this point in Luke in any of the earliest manuscripts.

17:37 *Where . . . there the vultures will gather.* A proverb. See note on Mt 24:28. In response to the disciples' question, Jesus explains that these things will take place wherever there are people to whom the event pertains.

18:2 *nor cared what people thought.* The judge was unconcerned about the needs of others or about their opinion of him.

18:3 *widow.* Particularly helpless and vulnerable because she had no family to uphold her cause. Only justice and her own persistence were in her favor (cf. 1Ti 5:3 and note).

18:7 *will not God bring about justice . . . ?* If an unworthy judge who feels no constraint of right or wrong is com-

pelled by persistence to deal justly with a helpless individual, how much more will God answer prayer! *keep putting them off.* God will not delay his support of the chosen ones when they are right. He is not like the unjust judge, who had to be badgered until he wearied and gave in.

18:8 *will he find faith . . . ?* Particularly faith that perseveres in prayer and loyalty (see Mt 24:12–13). Christ makes a second application that looks forward to the time of his second coming. A period of spiritual decline and persecution is assumed—a time that will require perseverance such as the widow demonstrated.

18:10 *to pray.* Periods for prayer were scheduled daily in connection with the morning and evening sacrifices. People could also go to the temple at any time for private prayer. *tax collector.* See note on Mt 5:46.

18:12 *fast twice a week.* Fasting was not commanded in the Mosaic law except for the fast on the annual Day of Atonement (see Mk 2:18 and note). However, the Pharisees also fasted on Mondays and Thursdays (see 5:33 and note; Mt 6:16; 9:14; Ac 27:9 and note). *a tenth of all I get.* As a typical first-century Pharisee, he tithed all that he acquired, not merely what he earned.

18:13 *beat his breast.* Cf. 23:48 and note. *have mercy on me.* The verb used here means "to be appeased/reconciled" (see note on 1Jn 2:2). The tax collector does not plead his good works but the mercy of God in forgiving his sin.

18:14 *justified before God.* God reckoned him to be righteous, i.e., his sins were forgiven and he was credited with righteousness—not his own (v. 9) but that which comes from God (see Ro 1:17 and note).

THE LITTLE CHILDREN AND JESUS

18:15–17pp — Mt 19:13–15; Mk 10:13–16

¹⁵People were also bringing babies to Jesus for him to place his hands on them. When the disciples saw this, they rebuked them. ¹⁶But Jesus called the children to him and said, "Let the little children come to me, and do not hinder them, for the kingdom of God belongs to such as these. ¹⁷Truly I tell you, anyone who will not receive the kingdom of God like a little child ᵛ will never enter it."

THE RICH AND THE KINGDOM OF GOD

18:18–30pp — Mt 19:16–29; Mk 10:17–30

¹⁸A certain ruler asked him, "Good teacher, what must I do to inherit eternal life?" ʷ

¹⁹"Why do you call me good?" Jesus answered. "No one is good—except God alone. ²⁰You know the commandments: 'You shall not commit adultery, you shall not murder, you shall not steal, you shall not give false testimony, honor your father and mother.'ᵃ"ˣ

²¹"All these I have kept since I was a boy," he said.

²²When Jesus heard this, he said to him, "You still lack one thing. Sell everything you have and give to the poor, ʸ and you will have treasure in heaven. ᶻ Then come, follow me."

²³When he heard this, he became very sad, because he was very wealthy. ²⁴Jesus looked at him and said, "How hard it is for the rich to enter the kingdom of God! ᵃ ²⁵Indeed, it is easier for a camel to go through the eye of a needle than for the rich to enter the kingdom of God."

²⁶Those who heard this asked, "Who then can be saved?"

²⁷Jesus replied, "What is impossible with human beings is possible with God." ᵇ

²⁸Peter said to him, "We have left all we had to follow you!" ᶜ

²⁹"Truly I tell you," Jesus said to them, "no one who has left home or wife or brothers or sisters or parents or children for the sake of the kingdom of God ³⁰will fail to receive many times as much in this age, and in the age to come ᵈ eternal life." ᵉ

JESUS PREDICTS HIS DEATH A THIRD TIME

18:31–33pp — Mt 20:17–19; Mk 10:32–34

³¹Jesus took the Twelve aside and told them, "We are going up to Jerusalem, ᶠ and everything that is written by the prophets ᵍ about the Son of Man ʰ will be fulfilled. ³²He will be delivered over to the Gentiles. ⁱ They will mock him, insult him and spit on him; ³³they will flog him ʲ and kill him. ᵏ On the third day ˡ he will rise again." ᵐ

³⁴The disciples did not understand any of this. Its meaning was hidden from them, and they did not know what he was talking about. ⁿ

A BLIND BEGGAR RECEIVES HIS SIGHT

18:35–43pp — Mt 20:29–34; Mk 10:46–52

³⁵As Jesus approached Jericho, ᵒ a blind man was sitting by the roadside begging. ³⁶When he heard the crowd going by, he asked what was happening. ³⁷They told him, "Jesus of Nazareth is passing by." ᵖ

³⁸He called out, "Jesus, Son of David, ᑫ have mercy ʳ on me!"

³⁹Those who led the way rebuked him and told him to be quiet, but he shouted all the more, "Son of David, have mercy on me!" ˢ

⁴⁰Jesus stopped and ordered the man to be brought to him. When he came near, Jesus asked him, ⁴¹"What do you want me to do for you?"

ᵃ 20 Exodus 20:12-16; Deut. 5:16-20

18:17 ᵛ Mt 11:25; 18:3
18:18 ʷ Lk 10:25
18:20 ˣ Ex 20:12-16; Dt 5:16-20; Ro 13:9
18:22 ʸ S Ac 2:45
ᶻ S Mt 6:20
18:24 ᵃ Pr 11:28
18:27 ᵇ S Mt 19:26
18:28 ᶜ S Mt 4:19
18:30 ᵈ S Mt 12:32
ᵉ S Mt 25:46
18:31 ᶠ S Lk 9:51
ᵍ Ps 22; Isa 53
ʰ S Mt 8:20
18:32 ⁱ Lk 23:1
18:33 ʲ S Mt 16:21
ᵏ S Ac 2:23
ˡ S Mt 16:21
ᵐ S Mt 16:21
18:34 ⁿ S Mk 9:32
18:35 ᵒ S Lk 19:1
18:37 ᵖ Lk 19:4
18:38 ᑫ ver 39; S Mt 9:27 ʳ Mt 17:15; Lk 18:13
18:39 ˢ ver 38

18:17 *like a little child.* With total dependence, full trust, frank openness and complete sincerity (see Mt 18:3; 19:14; Mk 10:14–15 and notes; cf. 1Pe 2:2).

18:18–27 For this event, see notes on Mk 10:17–27.

18:18 *eternal life.* See note on Mt 19:16.

18:20 *You know the commandments.* See Ex 20:1–17; 20:2 and notes.

18:24 *kingdom of God.* See note on Mt 3:2.

18:30 *this age . . . the age to come.* The present age of sin and misery and the future age to be inaugurated by the return of the Messiah (see Mk 10:30 and note).

18:31 *everything that is written by the prophets.* Sometimes referred to as the third prediction of Jesus' death, though the total number is more than three (see note on 17:25). The first distinct

prediction is in 9:22 (see note there) and the second in 9:44 (see note there). The Messiah's death had been predicted and/or prefigured centuries before (see, e.g., 24:25–27; introduction to Ps 22; see also note on Isa 52:13—53:12; Zec 13:7 and note; Mt 26:24,31,54). *Son of Man.* See note on Mk 8:31.

18:35 *approached Jericho.* See note on Mk 10:46. *blind man.* Bartimaeus (Mk 10:46). Matthew reports that two blind men were healed (see note on Mt 20:30). Mark and Luke did not record the presence of the other—possibly because one was the spokesman and therefore more outstanding.

18:38–39 *Son of David.* A Messianic title (see Mt 1:1 and note; 22:41–45; Mk 10:47 and note; 12:35; Jn 7:42; see also 2Sa 7:12–13; Ps 89:3–4; Am 9:11; Mt 12:23 and notes).

18:42 ᵗ S Mt 9:22
18:43 ᵘ S Mt 9:8;
Lk 13:17
19:1 ᵛ Lk 18:35
19:4 ʷ 1Ki 10:27;
1Ch 27:28; Isa 9:10
ˣ Lk 18:37
19:7 ʸ S Mt 9:11
19:8 ᶻ S Lk 7:13
ᵃ Lk 3:12,13 ᵇ Ex 22:1;
Lev 6:4,5; Nu 5:7;
2Sa 12:6; Eze 33:14,
15
19:9 ᶜ S Lk 3:8
19:10 ᵈ Eze 34:12,
16; S Jn 3:17
19:11 ᵉ S Mt 3:2
ᶠ Lk 17:20; Ac 1:6
19:13 ᵍ Mk 13:34
19:17 ʰ Pr 27:18
ⁱ Lk 16:10
19:21 ʲ Mt 25:24
19:22 ᵏ 2Sa 1:16;
Job 15:6

"Lord, I want to see," he replied.

⁴²Jesus said to him, "Receive your sight; your faith has healed you." ᵗ ⁴³Immediately he received his sight and followed Jesus, praising God. When all the people saw it, they also praised God. ᵘ

ZACCHAEUS THE TAX COLLECTOR

19 Jesus entered Jericho ᵛ and was passing through. ²A man was there by the name of Zacchaeus; he was a chief tax collector and was wealthy. ³He wanted to see who Jesus was, but because he was short he could not see over the crowd. ⁴So he ran ahead and climbed a sycamore-fig ʷ tree to see him, since Jesus was coming that way. ˣ

⁵When Jesus reached the spot, he looked up and said to him, "Zacchaeus, come down immediately. I must stay at your house today." ⁶So he came down at once and welcomed him gladly.

⁷All the people saw this and began to mutter, "He has gone to be the guest of a sinner." ʸ

⁸But Zacchaeus stood up and said to the Lord, ᶻ "Look, Lord! Here and now I give half of my possessions to the poor, and if I have cheated anybody out of anything, ᵃ I will pay back four times the amount." ᵇ

⁹Jesus said to him, "Today salvation has come to this house, because this man, too, is a son of Abraham. ᶜ ¹⁰For the Son of Man came to seek and to save what was lost." ᵈ

THE PARABLE OF THE TEN MINAS

19:12-27Ref — Mt 25:14-30

¹¹While they were listening to this, he went on to tell them a parable, because he was near Jerusalem and the people thought that the kingdom of God ᵉ was going to appear at once. ᶠ ¹²He said: "A man of noble birth went to a distant country to have himself appointed king and then to return. ¹³So he called ten of his servants ᵍ and gave them ten minas. ᵃ 'Put this money to work,' he said, 'until I come back.'

¹⁴"But his subjects hated him and sent a delegation after him to say, 'We don't want this man to be our king.'

¹⁵"He was made king, however, and returned home. Then he sent for the servants to whom he had given the money, in order to find out what they had gained with it.

¹⁶"The first one came and said, 'Sir, your mina has earned ten more.'

¹⁷"'Well done, my good servant!' ʰ his master replied. 'Because you have been trustworthy in a very small matter, take charge of ten cities.' ⁱ

¹⁸"The second came and said, 'Sir, your mina has earned five more.'

¹⁹"His master answered, 'You take charge of five cities.'

²⁰"Then another servant came and said, 'Sir, here is your mina; I have kept it laid away in a piece of cloth. ²¹I was afraid of you, because you are a hard man. You take out what you did not put in and reap what you did not sow.' ʲ

²²"His master replied, 'I will judge you by your own words, ᵏ you wicked servant! You

---

ᵃ **13** A mina was about three months' wages.

18:42 *your faith.* See note on 17:19.

18:43 *praising God...praised God.* See 1:64 and note.

19:1 *entered Jericho.* See note on Mk 10:46.

19:2 *chief tax collector.* A position referred to only here in the Bible, probably designating one in charge of a district, with other tax collectors under him. The region was prosperous at this time, so it is no wonder that Zacchaeus had grown rich. See notes on 3:12; Mt 5:46; Mk 2:14-16.

19:4 *sycamore-fig tree.* A sturdy tree from 30 to 40 feet high, with a short trunk and spreading branches, capable of holding a grown man. See note on Am 7:14.

19:5 *I must stay at your house.* Implies a divine necessity.

19:8 *four times.* The full repayment required under the law in case of theft (see Ex 22:1; 2Sa 12:6 and note).

A **19:9** *son of Abraham.* A true Jew—not only of the lineage of Abraham but one who also walks "in the footsteps" of Abraham's faith (Ro 4:12). Jesus recognized the tax collector as such, though Jewish society excluded him.

A **19:10** A key verse in Luke's Gospel. *Son of Man.* A Messianic title (see Introduction: Plan; see also note on Mk 8:31). *to seek and to save.* An important summary of Jesus' pur-

pose—to bring salvation, meaning eternal life (18:18), and the kingdom of God (18:25). See note on 15:32.

19:11 *kingdom...was going to appear.* They expected the Messiah to appear in power and glory and to set up his earthly kingdom, defeating all their political and military enemies.

19:12 *have himself appointed king.* A rather unusual procedure, but the Herods (see chart, p. 1608) did just that when they went to Rome to be appointed rulers over the Jews. Similarly, Jesus was soon to depart and in the future is to return as King. During his absence his servants are entrusted with their master's affairs (for a similar parable, see Mt 25:14-30).

19:13 *ten minas.* See TNIV text note.

19:14 *sent a delegation.* Such an incident had occurred over 30 years earlier in the case of Archelaus (Josephus, *Wars,* 2.6.1; *Antiquities,* 17.9.3), as well as in a number of other instances. This aspect of the story may have been included to warn the Jews against rejecting Jesus as King.

19:22 *You knew...that I am a hard man...?* The master did not admit to the statement of the servant but repeated it in a question. If this was the opinion of the servant, he should have acted accordingly.

knew, did you, that I am a hard man, taking out what I did not put in, and reaping what I did not sow? *l* 23Why then didn't you put my money on deposit, so that when I came back, I could have collected it with interest?'

24"Then he said to those standing by, 'Take his mina away from him and give it to the one who has ten minas.'

25" 'Sir,' they said, 'he already has ten!'

26"He replied, 'I tell you that to everyone who has, more will be given, but as for those who have nothing, even what they have will be taken away. *m* 27But those enemies of mine who did not want me to be king over them—bring them here and kill them in front of me.' "

JESUS COMES TO JERUSALEM AS KING
19:29–38pp — Mt 21:1–9; Mk 11:1–10
19:35–38pp — Jn 12:12–15

28After Jesus had said this, he went on ahead, going up to Jerusalem. *n* 29As he approached Bethphage and Bethany *o* at the hill called the Mount of Olives, *p* he sent two of his disciples, saying to them, 30"Go to the village ahead of you, and as you enter it, you will find a colt tied there, which no one has ever ridden. Untie it and bring it here. 31If anyone asks you, 'Why are you untying it?' say, 'The Lord needs it.' "

32Those who were sent ahead went and found it just as he had told them. *q* 33As they were untying the colt, its owners asked them, "Why are you untying the colt?"

34They replied, "The Lord needs it."

35They brought it to Jesus, threw their cloaks on the colt and put Jesus on it. 36As he went along, people spread their cloaks *r* on the road.

37When he came near the place where the road goes down the Mount of Olives, *s* the whole crowd of disciples began joyfully to praise God in loud voices for all the miracles they had seen:

38"Blessed is the king who comes in the name of the Lord!" *a t*

"Peace in heaven and glory in the highest!" *u*

39Some of the Pharisees in the crowd said to Jesus, "Teacher, rebuke your disciples!" *v*

40"I tell you," he replied, "if they keep quiet, the stones will cry out." *w*

41As he approached Jerusalem and saw the city, he wept over it *x* 42and said, "If you, even you, had only known on this day what would bring you peace—but now it is hidden from your eyes. 43The days will come on you when your enemies will build an embankment against you and encircle you and hem you in on every side. *y* 44They will dash you to the ground, you and the children within your walls. *z* They will not leave one stone on another, *a* because you did not recognize the time of God's coming *b* to you."

a 38 Psalm 118:26

19:22 *l* Mt 25:26
19:26 *m* S Mt 25:29
19:28 *n* Mk 10:32;
S Lk 9:51
19:29 *o* S Mt 21:17
p S Mt 21:1
19:32 *q* Lk 22:13
19:36 *r* 2Ki 9:13
19:37 *s* S Mt 21:1
19:38 *t* Ps 118:26;
Lk 13:35 *u* S Lk 2:14
19:39 *v* Mt 21:15,16
19:40 *w* Hab 2:11
19:41 *x* Isa 22:4;
Lk 13:34,35
19:43 *y* Isa 29:3;
Jer 6:6; Eze 4:2; 26:8;
Lk 21:20
19:44 *z* Ps 137:9
a Lk 21:6 *b* 1Pe 2:12

19:26 *more will be given ... what they have will be taken away.* See 8:18; 17:33 and notes; Mt 13:12. Those who seek spiritual gain in the gospel, for themselves and others, will become richer, and those who neglect or squander what is given them will become impoverished, losing even what they have.

19:27 *those enemies of mine ... kill them.* Perhaps a reference to Jerusalem's destruction in A.D. 70. The punishment of those who rebelled and actively opposed the king (see v. 14 and note) was much more severe than that of the negligent servant.

19:28–44 Jesus' entry into Jerusalem as King occurred on Sunday of Passion Week (see chart, p. 1658, and map, p. 1703; see also notes on Mt 21:1–9; Mk 11:1–10; Jn 12:12–15).

19:29 *Bethphage.* A village near the road going from Jericho to Jerusalem. *Bethany.* Another village about two miles southeast of Jerusalem (Jn 11:18) and the home of Mary, Martha and Lazarus. *Mount of Olives.* A ridge a little more than a mile long (see note on Mk 11:1). For the Mount of Olives, Bethany and Bethphage in relationship to Jerusalem see map, pp. 1702–1703. *two of his disciples.* Not named here or in the parallel passages (Mt 21:1; Mk 11:1; cf. Jn 12:14).

19:30 *village.* Probably Bethphage. *colt.* In other accounts a donkey colt (Jn 12:15) is specified and the mother of the colt (Mt 21:7; see note there) with him. Luke uses a Greek word that the Septuagint (the pre-Christian Greek translation of the OT) frequently employed to translate the Hebrew for "donkey." Jesus chooses to

enter Jerusalem this time mounted on a donkey to claim publicly that he was the chosen Son of David to sit on David's throne (see note on 1Ki 1:33), the one about whom the prophets had spoken (Zec 9:9; see note there). *which no one has ever ridden.* And thus available for sacred use (see note on Mk 11:2).

19:31 *The Lord.* Either God or, more likely, Jesus himself, here claiming his own unique status as Israel's Lord.

19:37 *praise God.* See 1:64 and note. *all the miracles.* The raising of Lazarus and the healing of blind Bartimaeus were recent examples, but included also would be the works recorded in John on various occasions in Jerusalem, as well as the whole of his ministry in Galilee (cf. Mt 21:14; Jn 12:17).

19:40 Perhaps an echo of Hab 2:11.

19:41 *he wept.* One of only two occasions when Jesus is said to have wept (see also Jn 11:35).

19:42 *peace.* That the Messiah would bring. *hidden.* Cf. 18:34.

19:43 *your enemies will build an embankment.* See 21:20 and note; fulfilled when the Romans took Jerusalem in A.D. 70, using an embankment to besiege the city. The description is reminiscent of OT predictions of an earlier destruction of Jerusalem (Isa 29:3; 37:33; Eze 4:1–3).

19:44 *the time of God's coming to you.* God came to the Jews in the person of Jesus the Messiah, but they failed to recognize him and rejected him (see Jn 1:10–11; cf. Lk 20:13–16).

19:46 *c* Isa 56:7
d Jer 7:11
19:47 *e* S Mt 26:55
f S Mt 12:14; Mk 11:18
20:1 *g* S Mt 26:55
h Lk 8:1
20:2 *i* Jn 2:18;
Ac 4:7; 7:27
20:4 *j* S Mk 1:4
20:6 *k* Lk 7:29
l S Mt 11:9
20:9 *m* Isa 5:1-7
n Mt 25:14
20:13 *o* S Mt 3:17
20:16 *p* Lk 19:27

JESUS AT THE TEMPLE

19:45,46pp — Mt 21:12–16; Mk 11:15–18; Jn 2:13–16

45When Jesus entered the temple courts, he began to drive out those who were selling. 46"It is written," he said to them, " 'My house will be a house of prayer'ᵃ; *c* but you have made it 'a den of robbers.' "ᵇˮ *d*

47Every day he was teaching at the temple. *e* But the chief priests, the teachers of the law and the leaders among the people were trying to kill him. *f* 48Yet they could not find any way to do it, because all the people hung on his words.

THE AUTHORITY OF JESUS QUESTIONED

20:1–8pp — Mt 21:23–27; Mk 11:27–33

20 One day as Jesus was teaching the people in the temple courts *g* and proclaiming the good news, *h* the chief priests and the teachers of the law, together with the elders, came up to him. 2"Tell us by what authority you are doing these things," they said. "Who gave you this authority?" *i*

3He replied, "I will also ask you a question. Tell me, 4John's baptism *j* —was it from heaven, or of human origin?"

5They discussed it among themselves and said, "If we say, 'From heaven,' he will ask, 'Why didn't you believe him?' 6But if we say, 'Of human origin,' all the people *k* will stone us, because they are persuaded that John was a prophet." *l*

7So they answered, "We don't know where it was from."

8Jesus said, "Neither will I tell you by what authority I am doing these things."

THE PARABLE OF THE TENANTS

20:9–19pp — Mt 21:33–46; Mk 12:1–12

9He went on to tell the people this parable: "A man planted a vineyard, *m* rented it to some farmers and went away for a long time. *n* 10At harvest time he sent a servant to the tenants so they would give him some of the fruit of the vineyard. But the tenants beat him and sent him away empty-handed. 11He sent another servant, but that one also they beat and treated shamefully and sent away empty-handed. 12He sent still a third, and they wounded him and threw him out.

13"Then the owner of the vineyard said, 'What shall I do? I will send my son, whom I love; *o* perhaps they will respect him.'

14"But when the tenants saw him, they talked the matter over. 'This is the heir,' they said. 'Let's kill him, and the inheritance will be ours.' 15So they threw him out of the vineyard and killed him.

"What then will the owner of the vineyard do to them? 16He will come and kill those tenants *p* and give the vineyard to others."

a 46 Isaiah 56:7   b 46 Jer. 7:11

19:45 Mark (11:11–17) makes clear that this cleansing occurred the day after Jesus' entry into Jerusalem as King, i.e., on Monday of Passion Week. *temple courts.* The outer court (of the Gentiles), where animals for sacrifice were sold at unfair prices (see note on Mk 11:15). John records a cleansing of the temple at the beginning of Jesus' ministry (Jn 2:13–25), but the Synoptics (see Mt 21:12–13; Mk 11:15–17) speak only of a cleansing at the close of Jesus' ministry (see notes on Mt 21:12–17; Jn 2:14–17).

19:47 *chief priests.* See 3:2; 22:52; 23:4; 24:20; see also note on Mt 2:4. They were part of the Sanhedrin, the ruling Jewish council (see note on Mk 14:55). *were trying to kill him.* See 20:19–20 (cf. Jn 7:1; 11:53–57).

20:1 The events of 20:1—21:36 all occurred on Tuesday of Passion Week—a long day of controversy. *One day.* Not specified, but Mark's parallel accounts (Mk 11:19–20,27–33) indicate that this day (Tuesday) followed the cleansing of the temple (Monday), which followed the Triumphal Entry (Sunday). See map, pp. 1702–1703. *chief priests.* See 19:47 and note. *teachers of the law.* See 5:30 and note on 5:17. *elders.* See note on Mt 15:2. Each of these groups was represented in the Jewish council, the Sanhedrin (see 22:66).

20:2 *Who gave you this authority?* They had asked this of John the Baptist (Jn 1:19–25) and of Jesus early in his ministry (Jn 2:18–22). Here the reference is to the cleansing of the temple,

which not only defied the authority of the Jewish leaders but also hurt their monetary profits. The leaders may also have been looking for a way to discredit Jesus in the eyes of the people or raise suspicion of him as a threat to the authority of Rome.

20:4 *John's baptism ... from heaven, or of human origin?* By replying with a question, Jesus put the burden on his opponents—indicating only two alternatives: The work of John was either divinely-inspired or humanly-devised. By refusing to answer, they placed themselves in an awkward position. *from heaven.* See note on Mk 11:30.

20:10 *he sent a servant.* This parable (v. 9) is reminiscent of Isa 5:1–7 (see note on Isa 5:1). The servants who were sent to the tenants represent the prophets God sent in former times who were rejected (see Ne 9:26; Jer 7:25 and note; 25:4–7; Mt 23:34; Ac 7:52; Heb 11:36–38). *give him some of the fruit.* In accordance with a kind of sharecropping agreement, a fixed amount was due the landowner. At the proper time he would expect to receive his share.

20:13 *my son, whom I love.* The specific reference to the beloved son makes clearer the intended application of the son in the parable to the Son, Jesus Christ (see 3:22; Mt 17:5 and notes).

20:14 *inheritance will be ours.* See note on Mk 12:7.

20:16 *give the vineyard to others.* See note on Mt 21:41.

20:17 q Ps 118:22;
S Ac 4:11
20:18 r Isa 8:14,15
20:19 s Lk 19:47
t S Mk 11:18
20:20 u S Mt 12:10
v Mt 27:2
20:21 w Jn 3:2
20:25 x Lk 23:2;
Ro 13:7
20:27 y S Ac 4:1
z Ac 23:8; 1Co 15:12
20:28 a Dt 25:5
20:35 b S Mt 12:32
20:36 c S Jn 1:12

When the people heard this, they said, "God forbid!"

¹⁷Jesus looked directly at them and asked, "Then what is the meaning of that which is written:

" 'The stone the builders rejected
has become the cornerstone'ᵃ? q

¹⁸Everyone who falls on that stone will be broken to pieces, but anyone on whom it falls will be crushed." r

¹⁹The teachers of the law and the chief priests looked for a way to arrest him s immediately, because they knew he had spoken this parable against them. But they were afraid of the people. t

PAYING TAXES TO CAESAR
20:20–26pp — Mt 22:15–22; Mk 12:13–17

²⁰Keeping a close watch on him, they sent spies, who pretended to be sincere. They hoped to catch Jesus in something he said, u so that they might hand him over to the power and authority of the governor. v ²¹So the spies questioned him: "Teacher, we know that you speak and teach what is right, and that you do not show partiality but teach the way of God in accordance with the truth. w ²²Is it right for us to pay taxes to Caesar or not?"

²³He saw through their duplicity and said to them, ²⁴"Show me a denarius. Whose image and inscription are on it?"

"Caesar's," they replied.

²⁵He said to them, "Then give back to Caesar what is Caesar's, x and to God what is God's."

²⁶They were unable to trap him in what he had said there in public. And astonished by his answer, they became silent.

THE RESURRECTION AND MARRIAGE
20:27–40pp — Mt 22:23–33; Mk 12:18–27

²⁷Some of the Sadducees, y who say there is no resurrection, z came to Jesus with a question. ²⁸"Teacher," they said, "Moses wrote for us that if a man's brother dies and leaves a wife but no children, the man must marry the widow and raise up offspring for his brother. a ²⁹Now there were seven brothers. The first one married a woman and died childless. ³⁰The second ³¹and then the third married her, and in the same way the seven died, leaving no children. ³²Finally, the woman died too. ³³Now then, at the resurrection whose wife will she be, since the seven were married to her?"

³⁴Jesus replied, "The people of this age marry and are given in marriage. ³⁵But those who are considered worthy of taking part in the age to come b and in the resurrection from the dead will neither marry nor be given in marriage, ³⁶and they can no longer die; for they are like the angels. They are God's children, c since they are children of the resurrection. ³⁷But in the account of the burning bush, even Moses showed that the dead rise, for

a 17 Psalm 118:22

20:17 *cornerstone.* See Ac 4:11; Ro 9:33; 1Pe 2:7; see also note on Ps 118:22.

20:18 *will be broken to pieces.* As a pot dashed against a stone is broken, and as one lying beneath a falling stone is crushed, so those who reject Jesus the Messiah will be doomed (see Isa 8:14 and note; cf. Da 2:34–35,44; Lk 2:34).

20:19 *teachers of the law.* See note on Mt 2:4. For their opposition to Jesus, see 5:17,30 and note on 5:17; 9:22; 19:47; 22:2; 23:10.

20:20 *authority of the governor.* Fearing to take action themselves, the Jewish religious leaders hoped to draw from Jesus some statement that would bring action from the Roman officials and remove him from his contact with the people.

20:22 *pay taxes to Caesar.* See note on Mk 12:14. To agree to the taxes demanded by Caesar would disappoint the people, but to advise no payment would disturb the Roman officials. The questioners hoped to trap Jesus with this dilemma (see note on Mt 22:15–17).

20:24 *denarius.* A Roman coin worth about a day's wages (see note on Mt 22:19).

20:25 *to God what is God's.* See notes on Mt 22:21; Mk 12:17.

20:27 *Sadducees.* An aristocratic, politically minded group, willing to compromise with secular and pagan leaders. They controlled the high priesthood at this time and held the majority of the seats in the Sanhedrin. They did not believe in the resurrection or an afterlife, and they rejected the oral tradition taught by the Pharisees (Josephus, *Antiquities,* 13.10.6). See notes on Ezr 7:2; Mt 2:4; 3:7; 22:23; Mk 12:18; Ac 4:1; see also essay, p. 1596, and chart, p. 1650.

20:28 *the man must marry the widow.* The levirate law (see note on Mt 22:24; cf. Ge 38:8 and note).

20:34–35 *this age . . . the age to come.* See note on 18:30.

20:36 *like the angels.* The resurrection order cannot be assumed to follow present earthly lines. In the new age there will be no marriage, no procreation and no death (see note on Mk 12:25). *children of the resurrection.* Those who are to take part in the resurrection of the righteous (cf. Mk 12:18; Ac 4:1; 23:6 and notes).

20:37 *account of the burning bush.* Since Scripture chapters and verses were not used at the time of Christ, the passage was identified in this way, referring to Moses' experience with the burning bush (see Ex 3:2–6 and notes).

20:37 ᵈ Ex 3:6
20:40 ᵉ Mt 22:46;
Mk 12:34
20:41 ᶠ S Mt 1:1
20:43 ᵍ Ps 110:1;
S Mt 22:44
20:46 ʰ S Lk 11:43
21:1 ⁱ Mt 27:6;
Jn 8:20
21:4 ʲ 2Co 8:12
21:6 ᵏ Lk 19:44

he calls the Lord 'the God of Abraham, and the God of Isaac, and the God of Jacob.'ᵃ ᵈ ³⁸He is not the God of the dead, but of the living, for to him all are alive."

³⁹Some of the teachers of the law responded, "Well said, teacher!" ⁴⁰And no one dared to ask him any more questions. ᵉ

WHOSE SON IS THE MESSIAH?
20:41–47pp — Mt 22:41–23:7; Mk 12:35–40

⁴¹Then Jesus said to them, "Why is it said that the Messiah is the son of David? ᶠ ⁴²David himself declares in the Book of Psalms:

" 'The Lord said to my Lord:
      "Sit at my right hand
⁴³ until I make your enemies
      a footstool for your feet." 'ᵇ ᵍ

⁴⁴David calls him 'Lord.' How then can he be his son?"

WARNING AGAINST THE TEACHERS OF THE LAW

⁴⁵While all the people were listening, Jesus said to his disciples, ⁴⁶"Beware of the teachers of the law. They like to walk around in flowing robes and love to be greeted with respect in the marketplaces and have the most important seats in the synagogues and the places of honor at banquets. ʰ ⁴⁷They devour widows' houses and for a show make lengthy prayers. These men will be punished most severely."

THE WIDOW'S OFFERING
21:1–4pp — Mk 12:41–44

21 As Jesus looked up, he saw the rich putting their gifts into the temple treasury. ⁱ ²He also saw a poor widow put in two very small copper coins. ³"Truly I tell you," he said, "this poor widow has put in more than all the others. ⁴All these people gave their gifts out of their wealth; but she out of her poverty put in all she had to live on." ʲ

THE DESTRUCTION OF THE TEMPLE AND SIGNS OF THE END TIMES
21:5–36pp — Mt 24; Mk 13
21:12–17pp — Mt 10:17–22

⁵Some of his disciples were remarking about how the temple was adorned with beautiful stones and with gifts dedicated to God. But Jesus said, ⁶"As for what you see here, the time will come when not one stone will be left on another; ᵏ every one of them will be thrown down."

⁷"Teacher," they asked, "when will these things happen? And what will be the sign that they are about to take place?"

⁸He replied: "Watch out that you are not deceived. For many will come in my name,

ᵃ 37 Exodus 3:6   ᵇ 43 Psalm 110:1

20:39 *Well said, teacher!* Even though there was great animosity against Jesus, the teachers of the law (who were Pharisees) sided with Jesus against the Sadducees on the matter of resurrection.

20:44 *David calls him 'Lord.'* Jesus' argument with the Jewish religious leaders is that since the Messiah is a descendant of David, how can this honored king refer to his offspring as Lord? Unless Jesus' opponents were ready to admit that the Messiah was also the divine Son of God, they could not answer his question. See notes on Ps 110:1; Mt 22:44; Mk 12:36.

20:46 *flowing robes . . . important seats.* See notes on Mk 12:38–39.

20:47 *devour widows' houses.* They take advantage of this defenseless group by fraud and schemes for selfish gain. *punished most severely.* Cf. 12:46–48 and note. The higher the esteem received from others, the more severe the demands of true justice, and the more hypocrisy (Mt 23:1–36) the greater the condemnation.

21:1 *temple treasury.* In the court of women, east of Herod's temple, there were 13 boxes shaped like inverted megaphones and positioned to receive the donations of the worshipers (see note on Mk 12:41).

21:2 *very small copper coins.* See note on Mk 12:42.

21:3–4 See note on 2Co 8:12.

21:3 *Truly I tell you.* See note on Mk 3:28.

21:5–36 See note on Mk 13:1–37.

21:5 *how the temple was adorned.* "Whatever was not overlaid with gold was purest white" (Josephus, *Wars*, 5.5.6). Herod gave a golden vine for one of its decorations. Its grape clusters were as tall as a man. The full magnificence of the temple as elaborated and adorned by Herod has only recently come to light through archaeological investigations on the temple hill.

21:6 *not one stone . . . left.* Fulfilled in A.D. 70 when the Romans took Jerusalem and burned the temple (Mt 24:2; see note there).

21:7 *when . . . ?* Mark reports that this question was asked by four disciples: Peter, James, John and Andrew (Mk 13:3). Matthew gives the question in a fuller form, including an inquiry for the sign of Jesus' coming and the end of the age (Mt 24:3; see note there). *what will be the sign . . . ?* What would be the indication that these things are about to happen?

claiming, 'I am he,' and, 'The time is near.' Do not follow them. [l] [9]When you hear of wars and uprisings, do not be frightened. These things must happen first, but the end will not come right away."

[10]Then he said to them: "Nation will rise against nation, and kingdom against kingdom. [m] [11]There will be great earthquakes, famines and pestilences in various places, and fearful events and great signs from heaven. [n]

[12]"But before all this, they will lay hands on you and persecute you. They will deliver you to synagogues and prisons, and you will be brought before kings and governors, and all on account of my name. [13]And so you will bear testimony to me. [o] [14]But make up your mind not to worry beforehand how you will defend yourselves. [p] [15]For I will give you [q] words and wisdom that none of your adversaries will be able to resist or contradict. [16]You will be betrayed even by parents, brothers, sisters, relatives and friends, [r] and they will put some of you to death. [17]Everyone will hate you because of me. [s] [18]But not a hair of your head will perish. [t] [19]Stand firm, and you will win life. [u]

[20]"When you see Jerusalem being surrounded by armies, [v] you will know that its desolation is near. [21]Then let those who are in Judea flee to the mountains, let those in the city get out, and let those in the country not enter the city. [w] [22]For this is the time of punishment [x] in fulfillment [y] of all that has been written. [23]How dreadful it will be in those days for pregnant women and nursing mothers! There will be great distress in the land and wrath against this people. [24]They will fall by the sword and will be taken as prisoners to all the nations. Jerusalem will be trampled [z] on by the Gentiles until the times of the Gentiles are fulfilled.

[25]"There will be signs in the sun, moon and stars. On the earth, nations will be in anguish and perplexity at the roaring and tossing of the sea. [a] [26]People will faint from terror, apprehensive of what is coming on the world, for the heavenly bodies will be shaken. [b] [27]At that time they will see the Son of Man [c] coming in a cloud [d] with power and great glory. [28]When these things begin to take place, stand up and lift up your heads, because your redemption is drawing near." [e]

[29]He told them this parable: "Look at the fig tree and all the trees. [30]When they sprout leaves, you can see for yourselves and know that summer is near. [31]Even so, when you see these things happening, you know that the kingdom of God [f] is near.

[32]"Truly I tell you, this generation [g] will certainly not pass away until all these things have happened. [33]Heaven and earth will pass away, but my words will never pass away. [h]

[34]"Be careful, or your hearts will be weighed down with dissipation, drunkenness and the anxieties of life, [i] and that day will close on you suddenly [j] like a trap. [35]For it will come

21:8 [l] Lk 17:23
21:10 [m] 2Ch 15:6; Isa 19:2
21:11 [n] Isa 29:6; Joel 2:30
21:13 [o] Php 1:12
21:14 [p] Lk 12:11
21:15 [q] S Lk 12:12
21:16 [r] Lk 12:52,53
21:17 [s] S Jn 15:21
21:18 [t] S Mt 10:30
21:19 [u] S Mt 10:22
21:20 [v] S Lk 19:43
21:21 [w] Lk 17:31
21:22 [x] Isa 63:4; Da 9:24-27; Hos 9:7
[y] S Mt 1:22
21:24 [z] Isa 5:5; 63:18; Da 8:13; Rev 11:2
21:25 [a] 2Pe 3:10,12
21:26 [b] S Mt 24:29
21:27 [c] S Mt 8:20
[d] S Rev 1:7
21:28 [e] Lk 18:7
21:31 [f] S Mt 3:2
21:32 [g] Lk 11:50; 17:25
21:33 [h] S Mt 5:18
21:34 [i] Mk 4:19
[j] Lk 12:40,46; 1Th 5:2-7

21:8 *I am he.* I am Jesus, the Messiah (having come a second time). *The time.* The end time.
21:9 *the end will not come right away.* Refers to the end of the age (see Mt 24:3,6). All the events listed in vv. 8–18 are characteristic of the entire present age, not just signs of the end of the age.
21:11 *signs from heaven.* See v. 25. For prophetic descriptions of celestial signs accompanying the day of the Lord, see note on Mk 13:24–25.
21:12 *deliver you to synagogues.* Synagogues were used not only for worship and school but also for community administration and for confinement of accused persons while awaiting trial (see note on Mk 13:9; cf. Mt 23:34).
21:15 *none ... will be able to resist.* See Ac 6:9–10.
21:18 Although persecution and death may come, God is in control, and the ultimate outcome will be eternal victory. *not a hair of your head will perish.* In view of v. 16, this cannot refer to physical safety. The figure indicates that there will be no real— i.e., spiritual and eternal—loss.
21:19 See note on Mk 13:13.
21:20 *surrounded by armies.* See 19:43 and note. The sign that the end was near (cf. v. 7 and note) would be the surrounding of Jerusalem with armies. Associated with this event would be the "abomination that causes desolation" (Mt 24:15; see note there).
21:21 *flee to the mountains.* When an army surrounds a city, it is natural to seek protection inside the walls, but Jesus directs his followers to seek the safety of the mountains because the city was doomed to destruction (see note on Mt 24:16).
21:22 *time of punishment.* God's retributive justice as the consequence of faithlessness (cf. Isa 63:4; Jer 5:29; Hos 9:7).

21:24 *times of the Gentiles.* The Gentiles would have both spiritual opportunities (see Mt 24:14 and note; Mk 13:10; cf. Lk 20:16; Ro 11:25 and note) and domination of Jerusalem, but these times will end when God's purpose for the Gentiles has been fulfilled.
21:27 See Mt 24:30 and note.

A 21:28 *lift up your heads.* Do not be downcast at the appearance of these signs, but look up in joy, hope and trust (cf. Ps 24:7). *redemption.* Final, completed redemption (see Heb 9:28 and note).
21:29 *Look at the fig tree.* The coming of spring is announced by the greening of the trees (cf. Mt 24:32–35; Mk 11:13 and note; 13:28–31). In a similar way, one can anticipate the coming of the kingdom when its signs are seen. But "kingdom" is used in different ways (see note on 4:43). The reference in v. 31 is to the future kingdom.

A 21:32 *this generation.* If reference here is to the destruction of Jerusalem that occurred about 40 years after Jesus spoke these words, "generation" is used in its ordinary sense of a normal life span. "All these things" would then have been fulfilled in the A.D. 70 destruction of Jerusalem. On the other hand, if reference here is to the second coming of Christ, "generation" might refer to a future generation alive at the beginning of "these things." It does not mean that Jesus had a mistaken notion that he was going to return immediately.
21:34 *that day.* When Christ returns and the future aspect of God's kingdom is inaugurated (cf. v. 31). *close on you suddenly.* Does not mean that Christ's second coming will be completely unannounced, since there will be introductory signs (vv. 28,31; cf. 1Th 5:1–3).

21:36   *k* Mt 26:41
21:37   *l* S Mt 26:55
  m Mk 11:19 *n* S Mt 21:1
21:38   *o* Jn 8:2
22:1   *p* S Jn 11:55
22:2   *q* S Mt 12:14
22:3   *r* S Mt 4:10
  s S Mt 10:4
22:4   *t* ver 52; Ac 4:1;
5:24
22:5   *u* Zec 11:12
22:7   *v* Ex 12:18-20;
Dt 16:5-8; S Mk 14:12
22:8   *w* Ac 3:1,11;
4:13,19; 8:14
22:13   *x* Lk 19:32
22:14   *y* S Mk 6:30
  z Mt 26:20; Mt 14:17,
18
22:15   *a* S Mt 16:21
22:16   *b* S Lk 14:15

on all those who live on the face of the whole earth. [36]Be always on the watch, and pray [k] that you may be able to escape all that is about to happen, and that you may be able to stand before the Son of Man."

[37]Each day Jesus was teaching at the temple, [l] and each evening he went out [m] to spend the night on the hill called the Mount of Olives, [n] [38]and all the people came early in the morning to hear him at the temple. [o]

JUDAS AGREES TO BETRAY JESUS
22:1,2pp — Mt 26:2–5; Mk 14:1,2,10,11

22 Now the Festival of Unleavened Bread, called the Passover, was approaching, [p] [2]and the chief priests and the teachers of the law were looking for some way to get rid of Jesus, [q] for they were afraid of the people. [3]Then Satan [r] entered Judas, called Iscariot, [s] one of the Twelve. [4]And Judas went to the chief priests and the officers of the temple guard [t] and discussed with them how he might betray Jesus. [5]They were delighted and agreed to give him money. [u] [6]He consented, and watched for an opportunity to hand Jesus over to them when no crowd was present.

THE LAST SUPPER
22:7–13pp — Mt 26:17–19; Mk 14:12–16
22:17–20pp — Mt 26:26–29; Mk 14:22–25; 1Co 11:23–25
22:21–23pp — Mt 26:21–24; Mk 14:18–21; Jn 13:21–30
22:25–27pp — Mt 20:25–28; Mk 10:42–45
22:33,34pp — Mt 26:33–35; Mk 14:29–31; Jn 13:37,38

[7]Then came the day of Unleavened Bread on which the Passover lamb had to be sacrificed. [v] [8]Jesus sent Peter and John, [w] saying, "Go and make preparations for us to eat the Passover."

[9]"Where do you want us to prepare for it?" they asked.

[10]He replied, "As you enter the city, a man carrying a jar of water will meet you. Follow him to the house that he enters, [11]and say to the owner of the house, 'The Teacher asks: Where is the guest room, where I may eat the Passover with my disciples?' [12]He will show you a large room upstairs, all furnished. Make preparations there."

[13]They left and found things just as Jesus had told them. [x] So they prepared the Passover.

[14]When the hour came, Jesus and his apostles [y] reclined at the table. [z] [15]And he said to them, "I have eagerly desired to eat this Passover with you before I suffer. [a] [16]For I tell you, I will not eat it again until it finds fulfillment in the kingdom of God." [b]

21:35 *whole earth.* The second coming of Christ will involve the whole of humankind, whereas the fall of Jerusalem did not.
21:37 *Each day.* Each day during the final week of his life, from his Triumphal Entry to the time of the Passover (Sunday-Thursday). *Mount of Olives.* See notes on 19:29; Mt 21:17.
22:1 *Festival of Unleavened Bread … Passover.* "Passover" was used in two different ways: (1) a specific meal begun at twilight on the 14th of Nisan (Lev 23:4–5) and (2) the week following the Passover meal (Eze 45:21), otherwise known as the Festival of Unleavened Bread, a week in which no leaven was allowed (see Ex 12:15 and note; 13:3–7; see also notes on Mk 14:1; Jn 2:13). By NT times the two names for the week-long festival were virtually interchangeable.
22:2 *the chief priests and the teachers of the law.* See 20:1 and note.
22:3 *Satan entered Judas.* In the Gospels this expression is used on two separate occasions: (1) before Judas went to the chief priests and offered to betray Jesus (here) and (2) during the Last Supper (Jn 13:27; see note there). Thus the Gospel writers depict Satan's control over Judas, who had never displayed strong commitment to Jesus (see Jn 13:2; see also notes on Jn 17:12; 1Co 15:2). *called Iscariot.* See Jn 6:71 and note.
22:4 *officers of the temple guard.* Jews, selected mostly from the Levites.
22:7 *Passover lamb had to be sacrificed.* On the 14th of Nisan between 2:30 and 5:30 P.M. in the court of the priests—Thursday of Passion Week.
22:10 *man carrying a jar.* It was extraordinary to see a man carrying a jar of water, since this was normally women's work.

22:11 *The Teacher asks.* This form of address may have been chosen because the owner was a follower already known to Jesus.
22:13 *as Jesus had told them.* It may be that Jesus had made previous arrangements with the man in order to make sure that the Passover meal would not be interrupted. Since Jesus did not identify ahead of time just where he would observe Passover, Judas was unable to inform the enemy, who might have interrupted this important occasion.
22:14–30 It appears that Luke does not attempt to be strictly chronological in his account of the Last Supper. He records the most important part of the occasion first—the sharing of the bread and the cup. Then he tells of Jesus' comments about his betrayer and about the argument over who would be greatest, though both of these subjects seem to have been introduced earlier. John's Gospel (13:26–30), e.g., indicates that Judas had already left the room before the bread and cup of the Lord's Supper were shared, but Luke does not tell when he left.
22:14 *reclined at the table.* See note on Mk 14:18.
22:16 *until it finds fulfillment.* Jesus yearned to keep this Passover with his disciples because it was the last occasion before he himself was to be slain as the perfect "Passover lamb" (1Co 5:7; see note there) and thus fulfill this sacrifice for all time. Jesus would eat no more Passover meals until the coming of the future kingdom. After this he will renew fellowship with those who through the ages have commemorated the Lord's Supper. Finally, the fellowship will be consummated in the great Messianic "wedding supper" to come (Rev 19:9).

¹⁷After taking the cup, he gave thanks and said, "Take this and divide it among you. ¹⁸For I tell you I will not drink again of the fruit of the vine until the kingdom of God comes."

¹⁹And he took bread, gave thanks and broke it, *c* and gave it to them, saying, "This is my body given for you; do this in remembrance of me."

²⁰In the same way, after the supper he took the cup, saying, "This cup is the new covenant *d* in my blood, which is poured out for you. ²¹But the hand of him who is going to betray me is with mine on the table. *e* ²²The Son of Man *f* will go as it has been decreed. *g* But woe to that man who betrays him!" ²³They began to question among themselves which of them it might be who would do this.

²⁴A dispute also arose among them as to which of them was considered to be greatest. *h* ²⁵Jesus said to them, "The kings of the Gentiles lord it over them; and those who exercise authority over them call themselves Benefactors. ²⁶But you are not to be like that. Instead, the greatest among you should be like the youngest, *i* and the one who rules like the one who serves. *j* ²⁷For who is greater, the one who is at the table or the one who serves? Is it not the one who is at the table? But I am among you as one who serves. *k* ²⁸You are those who have stood by me in my trials. ²⁹And I confer on you a kingdom, *l* just as my Father conferred one on me, ³⁰so that you may eat and drink at my table in my kingdom *m* and sit on thrones, judging the twelve tribes of Israel. *n*

³¹"Simon, Simon, Satan has asked *o* to sift all of you as wheat. *p* ³²But I have prayed for you, *q* Simon, that your faith may not fail. And when you have turned back, strengthen your brothers." *r*

³³But he replied, "Lord, I am ready to go with you to prison and to death." *s*

³⁴Jesus answered, "I tell you, Peter, before the rooster crows today, you will deny three times that you know me."

³⁵Then Jesus asked them, "When I sent you without purse, bag or sandals, *t* did you lack anything?"

"Nothing," they answered.

³⁶He said to them, "But now if you have a purse, take it, and also a bag; and if you don't have a sword, sell your cloak and buy one. ³⁷It is written: 'And he was numbered with the transgressors'*a; u* and I tell you that this must be fulfilled in me. Yes, what is written about me is reaching its fulfillment."

³⁸The disciples said, "See, Lord, here are two swords."

"That is enough," he replied.

a 37 Isaiah 53:12

22:19 *c* S Mt 14:19
22:20 *d* Ex 24:8;
Isa 42:6; Jer 31:31-34;
Zec 9:11; 2Co 3:6;
Heb 8:6; 9:15
22:21 *e* Ps 41:9
22:22 *f* S Mt 8:20
g Ac 2:23; 4:28
22:24 *h* Mk 9:34;
Lk 9:46
22:26 *i* 1Pe 5:5
j S Mk 9:35
22:27 *k* S Mt 20:28
22:29 *l* S Mt 25:34;
2Ti 2:12
22:30 *m* S Lk 14:15
n S Mt 19:28
22:31 *o* Job 1:6-12
p Am 9:9
22:32 *q* Jn 17:9,15;
S Ro 8:34 *r* Jn 21:15-17
22:33 *s* Jn 11:16
22:35 *t* Mt 10:9,10;
Lk 9:3; 10:4
22:37 *u* Isa 53:12

22:17 *After taking the cup.* Either the first of the four cups shared during regular observance of the Passover meal or the third cup.

22:18 *until the kingdom of God comes.* See notes on v. 16; 4:43.

22:19 *is.* Represents or signifies. *given for you.* Anticipating his substitutionary sacrifice on the cross. *in remembrance of me.* Just as the Passover was a constant reminder and proclamation of God's redemption of Israel from bondage in Egypt, so the keeping of Christ's command would be a remembering and proclaiming of the deliverance of believers from the bondage of sin through Christ's atoning work on the cross.

22:20 *after the supper.* Mentioned only here and in 1Co 11:25; see note on 1Co 11:23–26. *took the cup.* See note on Mk 14:24. *new covenant.* Promised through the prophet Jeremiah (see 31:31–34 and notes)—the fuller administration of God's saving grace, founded on and sealed by the death of Jesus ("in my blood"). See note on 1Co 11:25.

22:22 *as it has been decreed.* See Mk 14:21 and note.

22:25 *Benefactors.* A title assumed by or conferred on rulers in Egypt, Syria and Rome as a display of honor, but frequently not representing actual service rendered.

22:26 *like the one who serves.* Jesus urges and exemplifies servant leadership—a trait that was as uncommon then as it is now (see Mk 10:45; Php 2:5,7 and notes).

22:27 *I am among you as one who serves.* See Jn 13:5 and note.

22:28 *in my trials.* Including temptations (cf. 4:13), hardships (9:58) and rejection (Jn 1:11).

22:29 *confer on you a kingdom.* The following context (v. 30) indicates that this kingdom is the future form of the kingdom (see notes on 4:43; Mt 3:2).

22:30 *sit on thrones.* As they shared in Jesus' trials, so they will share in his rule (see 2Ti 2:12 and note). *judging.* Leading or ruling (see TNIV text note on Jdg 2:16). *twelve tribes of Israel.* See Mt 19:28.

22:31 *sift all of you.* Satan wanted to test the disciples, hoping to bring them to spiritual ruin.

22:34 See Mt 26:34; Jn 13:38 and notes.

22:36 *a purse . . . a bag.* Cf. previous instructions (9:3; 10:4). Until now they had been dependent on generous hospitality, but future opposition would require them to be prepared to pay their own way. *buy one.* An extreme figure of speech used to warn them of the perilous times about to come. They would need defense and protection, as Paul did when he appealed to Caesar (Ac 25:11; see note there) as the one who "bears the sword" (Ro 13:4).

22:37 *numbered with the transgressors.* Jesus was soon to be arrested as a criminal, in fulfillment of prophetic Scripture (see TNIV text note), and his disciples would also be in danger for being his followers.

22:38 *". . . two swords." "That is enough."* Sensing that the disciples had taken him too literally, Jesus ironically closes the discussion with a curt "That's plenty!" Not long after this, Peter was rebuked for using a sword (v. 50).

22:39 ᵛ Lk 21:37
ʷ S Mt 21:1
22:40 ˣ Mt 6:13
22:41 ʸ Lk 18:11
22:42 ᶻ S Mt 20:22
ᵃ S Mt 26:39
22:43 ᵇ Mt 4:11;
Mk 1:13
22:46 ᶜ ver 40
22:49 ᵈ ver 38
22:52 ᵉ ver 4
22:53 ᶠ S Mt 26:55
ᵍ Jn 12:27 ʰ Mt 8:12;
Jn 1:5; 3:20
22:54 ⁱ Mt 26:57;
Mk 14:53 / Mt 26:58;
Mk 14:54; Jn 18:15
22:59 ᵏ Lk 23:6
22:61 ˡ S Lk 7:13

JESUS PRAYS ON THE MOUNT OF OLIVES

22:40–46pp — Mt 26:36–46; Mk 14:32–42

³⁹Jesus went out as usual ᵛ to the Mount of Olives, ʷ and his disciples followed him. ⁴⁰On reaching the place, he said to them, "Pray that you will not fall into temptation." ˣ ⁴¹He withdrew about a stone's throw beyond them, knelt down ʸ and prayed, ⁴²"Father, if you are willing, take this cup ᶻ from me; yet not my will, but yours be done." ᵃ ⁴³An angel from heaven appeared to him and strengthened him. ᵇ ⁴⁴And being in anguish, he prayed more earnestly, and his sweat was like drops of blood falling to the ground. ᵃ

⁴⁵When he rose from prayer and went back to the disciples, he found them asleep, exhausted from sorrow. ⁴⁶"Why are you sleeping?" he asked them. "Get up and pray so that you will not fall into temptation." ᶜ

JESUS ARRESTED

22:47–53pp — Mt 26:47–56; Mk 14:43–50; Jn 18:3–11

⁴⁷While he was still speaking a crowd came up, and the man who was called Judas, one of the Twelve, was leading them. He approached Jesus to kiss him, ⁴⁸but Jesus asked him, "Judas, are you betraying the Son of Man with a kiss?"

⁴⁹When Jesus' followers saw what was going to happen, they said, "Lord, should we strike with our swords?" ᵈ ⁵⁰And one of them struck the servant of the high priest, cutting off his right ear.

⁵¹But Jesus answered, "No more of this!" And he touched the man's ear and healed him.

⁵²Then Jesus said to the chief priests, the officers of the temple guard, ᵉ and the elders, who had come for him, "Am I leading a rebellion, that you have come with swords and clubs? ⁵³Every day I was with you in the temple courts, ᶠ and you did not lay a hand on me. But this is your hour ᵍ—when darkness reigns." ʰ

PETER DISOWNS JESUS

22:55–62pp — Mt 26:69–75; Mk 14:66–72; Jn 18:16–18,25–27

⁵⁴Then seizing him, they led him away and took him into the house of the high priest. ⁱ Peter followed at a distance. ʲ ⁵⁵And when some there had kindled a fire in the middle of the courtyard and had sat down together, Peter sat down with them. ⁵⁶A servant girl saw him seated there in the firelight. She looked closely at him and said, "This man was with him."

⁵⁷But he denied it. "Woman, ᵇ I don't know him," he said.

⁵⁸A little later someone else saw him and said, "You also are one of them."

"Man, I am not!" Peter replied.

⁵⁹About an hour later another asserted, "Certainly this fellow was with him, for he is a Galilean." ᵏ

⁶⁰Peter replied, "Man, I don't know what you're talking about!" Just as he was speaking, the rooster crowed. ⁶¹The Lord ˡ turned and looked straight at Peter. Then Peter re-

---

ᵃ 43,44 Some early manuscripts do not have verses 43 and 44.   ᵇ 57 The Greek for *Woman* does not denote any disrespect.

22:39 *Mount of Olives.* See 19:29 and note. Matthew specifies Gethsemane (Mt 26:36; see note there), and John, a garden (Jn 18:1). The place apparently was located on the lower slopes of the Mount of Olives.
22:40 *temptation.* Here refers to severe trial of the kind referred to in vv. 28–38, which might lead to a faltering of their faith.
22:42 *this cup.* The cup of suffering (see Mt 20:22; Mk 14:36 and notes; cf. Isa 51:17; Eze 23:31 and notes).
22:43 *angel.* Matthew and Mark tell of angels ministering to Jesus at the close of his fasting and temptations (Mt 4:11; Mk 1:13).
22:44 *drops of blood.* Probably perspiration in large drops like blood, or possibly hematidrosis, the actual mingling of blood and sweat as in cases of extreme anguish, strain or sensitivity. Only Luke, the doctor, records this.
22:47 *crowd came up.* They were sent by the chief priests, elders (Mt 26:47) and teachers of the law (Mk 14:43; see note there), and they carried swords and clubs. Included was a detachment of soldiers with officials of the Jews (v. 52; Jn 18:3). *to kiss him.* This signal had been prearranged to identify Jesus to the authorities (Mt 26:48). It was unnecessary because Jesus identified him-

self (Jn 18:5), but Judas acted out his plan anyway.
22:50 *servant of the high priest.* Malchus by name; Simon Peter struck the blow (see Jn 18:10 and note).
22:51 *healed him.* Found only in Luke. Jesus rectified the wrong done by his follower. No faith on the part of Malchus was involved, but to allow such action would have been contrary to Jesus' own teaching.
22:52 See note on Mt 26:55.
22:53 *your hour.* The time appointed for Jesus' enemies to apprehend him, the time when the forces of darkness (the powers of evil) would do their worst to defeat God's plan.
22:54 *house of the high priest.* See notes on 3:2; Mk 14:53.
22:57 *Woman.* See TNIV text note; cf. note on Jn 2:4.
22:59 *he is a Galilean.* Recognized by his speech (see Mt 26:73 and note) and identified by a relative of Malchus, the high priest's slave (see Jn 18:26 and note).
22:61 *The Lord . . . looked straight at Peter.* Peter was outside in the enclosed courtyard, and perhaps Jesus was being taken from the trial by Caiaphas to the Sanhedrin when Jesus caught Peter's eye. *the word the Lord had spoken to him.* See v. 34.

membered the word the Lord had spoken to him: "Before the rooster crows today, you will disown me three times." *m* 62And he went outside and wept bitterly.

THE GUARDS MOCK JESUS

22:63–65pp — Mt 26:67,68; Mk 14:65; Jn 18:22,23

63The men who were guarding Jesus began mocking and beating him. 64They blindfolded him and demanded, "Prophesy! Who hit you?" 65And they said many other insulting things to him. *n*

JESUS BEFORE PILATE AND HEROD

22:67–71pp — Mt 26:63–66; Mk 14:61–63; Jn 18:19–21
23:2,3pp — Mt 27:11–14; Mk 15:2–5; Jn 18:29–37
23:18–25pp — Mt 27:15–26; Mk 15:6–15; Jn 18:39—19:16

66At daybreak the council *o* of the elders of the people, both the chief priests and the teachers of the law, met together, *p* and Jesus was led before them. 67"If you are the Messiah," they said, "tell us."

Jesus answered, "If I tell you, you will not believe me, 68and if I asked you, you would not answer. *q* 69But from now on, the Son of Man will be seated at the right hand of the mighty God." *r*

70They all asked, "Are you then the Son of God?" *s*

He replied, "You say that I am." *t*

71Then they said, "Why do we need any more testimony? We have heard it from his own lips."

23 Then the whole assembly rose and led him off to Pilate. *u* 2And they began to accuse him, saying, "We have found this man subverting our nation. *v* He opposes payment of taxes to Caesar *w* and claims to be Messiah, a king." *x*

3So Pilate asked Jesus, "Are you the king of the Jews?"

"You have said so," Jesus replied.

4Then Pilate announced to the chief priests and the crowd, "I find no basis for a charge against this man." *y*

5But they insisted, "He stirs up the people all over Judea by his teaching. He started in Galilee *z* and has come all the way here."

6On hearing this, Pilate asked if the man was a Galilean. *a* 7When he learned that Jesus was under Herod's jurisdiction, he sent him to Herod, *b* who was also in Jerusalem at that time.

8When Herod saw Jesus, he was greatly pleased, because for a long time he had been wanting to see him. *c* From what he had heard about him, he hoped to see him perform a sign of some sort. 9He plied him with many questions, but Jesus gave him no answer. *d* 10The chief priests and the teachers of the law were standing there, vehemently accusing him. 11Then Herod and his soldiers ridiculed and mocked him. Dressing him in an elegant robe, *e* they sent him back to Pilate. 12That day Herod and Pilate became friends *f*— before this they had been enemies.

13Pilate called together the chief priests, the rulers and the people, 14and said to them,

22:61 *m* ver 34
22:65 *n* S Mt 16:21
22:66 *o* S Mt 5:22
p Mt 27:1; Mk 15:1
22:68 *q* Lk 20:3-8
22:69 *r* S Mk 16:19
22:70 *s* S Mt 4:3
t Mt 27:11; Lk 23:3
23:1 *u* S Mt 27:2
23:2 *v* ver 14
w Lk 20:22 *x* Jn 19:12
23:4 *y* ver 14, 22, 41;
Mt 27:23; Jn 18:38;
1Ti 6:13; S 2Co 5:21
23:5 *z* Mk 1:14
23:6 *a* Lk 22:59
23:7 *b* S Mt 14:1
23:8 *c* Lk 9:9
23:9 *d* S Mk 14:61
23:11 *e* Mk 15:17-19; Jn 19:2,3
23:12 *f* Ac 4:27

22:64 *blindfolded him.* See note on Mk 14:65.

22:66 *At daybreak.* Only after daylight could a legal trial take place for the whole council (Sanhedrin) to pass the death sentence (see note on Mk 14:53—15:15).

22:67 *If you are the Messiah.* This demand is related to a question asked later: "Are you then the Son of God?" (v. 70).

22:69 *Son of Man.* See note on Mk 8:31.

22:71 *We have heard it.* The reaction to Jesus' reply makes clear that his answer was a strong affirmative. Mark has simply, "I am" (Mk 14:62). It was blasphemy to claim to be the Messiah and Son of God—unless, of course, the claim was true (see note on Mk 14:64).

23:1 *whole assembly.* The body of the Sanhedrin (see Mt 26:59; 27:1 and note; Mk 14:55 and note), which had met at the earliest hint of dawn (see 22:66 and note). *led him off to Pilate.* See note on Lk 3:1. *Pilate.* See note on Mk 15:1. The Roman governor had his main headquarters in Caesarea, but he was in Jerusalem during Passover to prevent trouble from the large number of Jews assembled for the occasion.

23:2 *subverting our nation.* Large crowds followed Jesus, but he was not misleading them or turning them against Rome. *op-*

poses payment of taxes. Another untrue charge (see 20:25 and note on Mt 22:21). *claims to be Messiah, a king.* Jesus claimed to be the Messiah, but not a political or military king, the kind Rome would be anxious to eliminate.

23:3 *You have said so.* Jesus somewhat indirectly affirms that he is a king, but then explains that his kingdom is not the kind that characterizes this world (see Jn 18:33–38 and notes).

23:5 *Judea.* May here refer to the whole of the land of the Jews (including Galilee) or to the southern section only, where the region of Judea proper was governed by Pilate (see note on 4:44).

23:7 *Herod's jurisdiction.* See note on 3:1. Although Pilate and Herod were rivals, Pilate did not want to handle this case; so he sent Jesus to Herod (cf. v. 12). *in Jerusalem.* Herod's main headquarters was in Tiberias on the Sea of Galilee; but, like Pilate, he had come to Jerusalem because of the crowds at Passover.

23:8 *wanting to see him.* Herod was worried about Jesus' identity (see 9:9 and note) and had desired to kill him (see 13:31 and note), though the two had never met. There is no record that Jesus ever preached in Tiberias, where Herod's residence was located.

23:11 *elegant robe.* See note on Mk 15:17.

23:14 g S ver 4
23:16[17] h ver 22;
Mt 27:26; Jn 19:1;
Ac 16:37; 2Co 11:23,
24
23:18 i Ac 3:13,14
23:22 j ver 16
23:26 k S Mt 27:32
l Mk 15:21; Jn 19:17
23:27 m Lk 8:52
23:28 n Lk 19:41-
44; 21:23,24
23:29 o Mt 24:19
23:30 p Isa 2:19;
Hos 10:8; Rev 6:16
23:31 q Eze 20:47
23:32 r Isa 53:12;
Mt 27:38; Mk 15:27;
Jn 19:18
23:34 s Mt 11:25
t S Mt 5:44 u Ps 22:18
23:35 v Ps 22:17
w Isa 42:1
23:36 x Ps 22:7
y Ps 69:21; Mt 27:48
23:37 z Lk 4:3,9

"You brought me this man as one who was inciting the people to rebellion. I have examined him in your presence and have found no basis for your charges against him. g 15Neither has Herod, for he sent him back to us; as you can see, he has done nothing to deserve death. 16[17]Therefore, I will punish him h and then release him."

18With one voice they cried out, "Away with this man! Release Barabbas to us!" i 19 (Barabbas had been thrown into prison for an insurrection in the city, and for murder.)

20Wanting to release Jesus, Pilate appealed to them again. 21But they kept shouting, "Crucify him! Crucify him!"

22For the third time he spoke to them: "Why? What crime has this man committed? I have found in him no grounds for the death penalty. Therefore I will have him punished and then release him." j

23But with loud shouts they insistently demanded that he be crucified, and their shouts prevailed. 24So Pilate decided to grant their demand. 25He released the man who had been thrown into prison for insurrection and murder, the one they asked for, and surrendered Jesus to their will.

THE CRUCIFIXION OF JESUS
23:33–43pp — Mt 27:33–44; Mk 15:22–32; Jn 19:17–24

26As the soldiers led him away, they seized Simon from Cyrene, k who was on his way in from the country, and put the cross on him and made him carry it behind Jesus. l 27A large number of people followed him, including women who mourned and wailed m for him. 28Jesus turned and said to them, "Daughters of Jerusalem, do not weep for me; weep for yourselves and for your children. n 29For the time will come when you will say, 'Blessed are the childless women, the wombs that never bore and the breasts that never nursed!' o 30Then

" 'they will say to the mountains, "Fall on us!"
and to the hills, "Cover us!" ' a p

31For if people do these things when the tree is green, what will happen when it is dry?" q

32Two other men, both criminals, were also led out with him to be executed. r 33When they came to the place called the Skull, they crucified him there, along with the criminals—one on his right, the other on his left. 34Jesus said, "Father, s forgive them, for they do not know what they are doing." b t And they divided up his clothes by casting lots. u

35The people stood watching, and the rulers even sneered at him. v They said, "He saved others; let him save himself if he is God's Messiah, the Chosen One." w

36The soldiers also came up and mocked him. x They offered him wine vinegar y 37and said, "If you are the king of the Jews, z save yourself."

a 30 Hosea 10:8   b 34 Some early manuscripts do not have this sentence.

23:16[17] *I will punish him.* Although Pilate found Jesus "not guilty" as charged, he was willing to have him illegally beaten in order to satisfy the chief priests and the people and to warn against any possible trouble in the future. Scourging, though not intended to kill, was sometimes fatal (see note on Mk 15:15). Apparently v. 17 ("Now he was obliged to release one man to them at the festival") was added here in some manuscripts from Mt 27:15 or Mk 15:6 (see note there).
23:18 *Barabbas.* Means "son of Abba" (see Mt 27:16 and note). Pilate offered a choice between Jesus and an obviously evil, dangerous criminal.
23:19 *insurrection ... murder.* This particular uprising is otherwise unknown, but, coupled with murder, it shows the gravity of his deeds (see Jn 18:40 and note).
23:22 *third time.* See vv. 4, 14.
23:25 *surrendered Jesus.* Pilate had already handed Jesus over to the soldiers for scourging before he was convicted (Jn 19:1–5). He now handed him over for crucifixion.
23:26 *Simon.* His sons, Rufus and Alexander (see Mk 15:21 and note), must have been known in Christian circles at a later time, and perhaps were associated with the church at Rome (Ro 16:13). *Cyrene.* A leading city of Libya, west of Egypt (see note on Ac 6:9). *put the cross on him.* See note on Mk 15:21.
23:27–28 Found only in this Gospel. Luke emphasizes the role of women in the gospel story (see Introduction: Characteristics).
23:28 *weep for yourselves and for your children.* Because of the

terrible suffering to befall Jerusalem about 40 years later, when the Romans would besiege the city and utterly destroy the temple.
23:29 *Blessed are the childless women.* It would be better not to have children than to have them experience such suffering. Cf. Jer 16:1–4; 1Co 7:25–35.
23:30 *Fall on us!* People would seek escape through destruction in death rather than endure continuing suffering and judgment (cf. Hos 10:8; Rev 6:16 and notes).
23:31 *tree is green ... dry.* If they treat the Messiah this way when the "tree" is well-watered and green, what will their plight be when he is withdrawn from them and they suffer for their rejection in the dry period?
23:33 *the Skull.* Latin *Calvaria,* hence the name "Calvary" (see note on Mk 15:22). *crucified.* See note on Mk 15:24.
23:34 *they do not know what they are doing.* Cf. Ac 3:17 and note. *divided up his clothes.* Any possessions an executed person had with him were taken by the executioners. Unwittingly the soldiers (cf. Jn 19:23–24) were fulfilling the words of Ps 22:18 (but see introduction to Ps 22 and notes on Ps 22:17,20–21).
23:35 *the Chosen One.* See note on 9:35.
23:36 *wine vinegar.* A sour wine, the drink of laborers and common soldiers. Jesus refused a sedative drink (see Mt 27:34; Mk 15:23 and notes) but later was given the vinegar drink when he cried out in thirst (see Jn 19:28–30 and notes). Luke shows that it was offered in mockery.

23:38 ᵃS Mt 2:2
23:39 ᵇver 35,37
23:41 ᶜS ver 4
23:42 ᵈS Mt 16:27
23:43 ᵉ2Co 12:3,4;
Rev 2:7
23:44 ᶠAm 8:9
23:45 ᵍEx 26:31-33;
Heb 9:3,8
ʰHeb 10:19,20
23:46 ⁱMt 27:50
ʲPs 31:5; 1Pe 2:23
ᵏJn 19:30
23:47 ˡS Mt 9:8
23:48 ᵐLk 18:13
23:49 ⁿLk 8:2
ᵒPs 38:11
23:51 ᵖLk 2:25,38
23:54 ᵠMt 27:62
23:55 ʳver 49

³⁸There was a written notice above him, which read: THIS IS THE KING OF THE JEWS. ᵃ

³⁹One of the criminals who hung there hurled insults at him: "Aren't you the Messiah? Save yourself and us!" ᵇ

⁴⁰But the other criminal rebuked him. "Don't you fear God," he said, "since you are under the same sentence? ⁴¹We are punished justly, for we are getting what our deeds deserve. But this man has done nothing wrong." ᶜ

⁴²Then he said, "Jesus, remember me when you come into your kingdom. ᵃ" ᵈ

⁴³Jesus answered him, "Truly I tell you, today you will be with me in paradise." ᵉ

THE DEATH OF JESUS

23:44–49pp — Mt 27:45–56; Mk 15:33–41; Jn 19:29–30

⁴⁴It was now about noon, and darkness came over the whole land until three in the afternoon, ᶠ ⁴⁵for the sun stopped shining. And the curtain of the temple ᵍ was torn in two. ʰ ⁴⁶Jesus called out with a loud voice, ⁱ "Father, into your hands I commit my spirit." ᵇʲ When he had said this, he breathed his last. ᵏ

⁴⁷The centurion, seeing what had happened, praised God ˡ and said, "Surely this was a righteous man." ⁴⁸When all the people who had gathered to witness this sight saw what took place, they beat their breasts ᵐ and went away. ⁴⁹But all those who knew him, including the women who had followed him from Galilee, ⁿ stood at a distance, ᵒ watching these things.

THE BURIAL OF JESUS

23:50–56pp — Mt 27:57–61; Mk 15:42–47; Jn 19:38–42

⁵⁰Now there was a man named Joseph, a member of the Council, a good and upright man, ⁵¹who had not consented to their decision and action. He came from the Judean town of Arimathea, and he himself was waiting for the kingdom of God. ᵖ ⁵²Going to Pilate, he asked for Jesus' body. ⁵³Then he took it down, wrapped it in linen cloth and placed it in a tomb cut in the rock, one in which no one had yet been laid. ⁵⁴It was Preparation Day, ᵠ and the Sabbath was about to begin.

⁵⁵The women who had come with Jesus from Galilee ʳ followed Joseph and saw the

---

ᵃ 42 Some manuscripts *come with your kingly power*   ᵇ 46 Psalm 31:5

23:38 *written notice.* Indicated the crime for which a person was dying. This was Pilate's way of mocking the Jewish leaders, as well as announcing what Jesus had been accused of. *KING OF THE JEWS.* See note on Mk 15:26.

23:39 *One of the criminals.* See note on Mk 15:32.

23:43 *paradise.* In the Septuagint (the pre-Christian Greek translation of the OT) the word designated a garden (Ge 2:8–10; cf. note on 2:8) or forest (see Ne 2:8 and note), but in the NT (used only here and in 2Co 12:4; Rev 2:7 [see note there]) it refers to the place of bliss and rest between death and resurrection (cf. Lk 16:22; 2Co 12:2).

23:44 *about noon . . . three in the afternoon.* Lit. "about the sixth hour . . . the ninth hour." Jesus had been put on the cross at the "third hour" (9:00 A.M., Mk 15:25). The "sixth hour" of John (Jn 19:14) may be Roman time (6:00 A.M.), when Pilate gave his decision (but see note on Jn 19:14), whereas here it is Jewish time (noon, when darkness began).

23:45 *curtain of the temple.* The curtain between the Holy Place and the Most Holy Place. *was torn.* Its tearing symbolized Christ's opening the way directly to God (see Heb 9:3,8; 10:19–22 and notes on 10:19–20).

23:47 *praised God.* See 1:64 and note; either for having seen God publicly vindicate Jesus by mighty signs from heaven, or out of fear (see Mt 27:54) to appease the heavenly Judge and thus ward off a divine penalty for having carried out an unjust judgment. *this was a righteous man.* Or "this man was the Righteous One." Matthew and Mark report the centurion's words as "this man was the Son (or son) of God." "The Righteous One" and "the Son of God" would have been essentially equivalent terms. Similarly, "the son of God" and "a righteous man" would have been virtual equivalents. Which one the centurion intended is difficult to determine (see note on Mt 27:54). It seems clear, however, that the Gospel writers saw in his declaration a

vindication of Jesus, and since the centurion was the Roman official in charge of the crucifixion his testimony was viewed as significant (see also the declarations of Pilate: vv. 4,14–15,22; Mt 27:23–24).

23:48 *beat their breasts.* A sign of anguish, grief or contrition (cf. 18:13).

23:49 *women . . . from Galilee.* See Mk 15:40; Jn 19:25 and notes; cf. Lk 24:10 and note.

23:50 *Joseph, a member of the Council.* Either Joseph was not present at the meeting of the Sanhedrin (22:66); or he did not support the vote to have Jesus killed (see v. 51). Mk 14:64 suggests that he was not present, for the decision was supported by "all."

23:51 *Arimathea.* See note on Mt 27:57. *waiting for the kingdom of God.* See 2:25 and note.

23:52 The remains of an executed criminal often were left unburied or at best put in a dishonored place in a pauper's field. A near relative, such as a mother, might ask for the body, but it was a courageous gesture for Joseph, a member of the Sanhedrin, to ask for Jesus' body.

23:53 *in which no one had yet been laid.* Rock-hewn tombs were usually made to accommodate several bodies. This one, though finished, had not yet been used. See notes on 19:30; Mk 15:46.

23:54 *Preparation Day.* Friday, the day before the Sabbath, when preparation was made for keeping the Sabbath. It could be used for Passover preparation, but since in this instance it is followed by the Sabbath, it indicates Friday (see note on Mt 27:62).

23:55 *women.* See v. 49 and note; cf. 8:2–3 and notes. They saw where Jesus was buried and would not mistake the location when they returned.

23:56 s Mk 16:1;
Lk 24:1 t Ex 12:16;
20:10
24:1 u Lk 23:56
24:3 v ver 23,24
24:4 w S Jn 20:12
24:6 x Mt 17:22,23;
Lk 9:22; 24:44
24:7 y S Mt 8:20
z S Mt 16:21
24:8 a Jn 2:22
24:10 b Lk 8:1-3
c S Mk 6:30
24:11 d Mk 16:11
24:12 e Jn 20:3-7
f Jn 20:10
24:13 g Mk 16:12
24:15 h ver 36
24:16 i Jn 20:14;
21:4
24:18 j Jn 19:25
24:19 k S Mk 1:24
l S Mt 21:11
24:20 m Lk 23:13
24:21 n Lk 1:68;
2:38; 21:28
o S Mt 16:21

tomb and how his body was laid in it. ⁵⁶Then they went home and prepared spices and perfumes. ˢ But they rested on the Sabbath in obedience to the commandment. ᵗ

JESUS HAS RISEN

24:1–10pp — Mt 28:1–8; Mk 16:1–8; Jn 20:1–8

24 On the first day of the week, very early in the morning, the women took the spices they had prepared ᵘ and went to the tomb. ²They found the stone rolled away from the tomb, ³but when they entered, they did not find the body of the Lord Jesus. ᵛ ⁴While they were wondering about this, suddenly two men in clothes that gleamed like lightning ʷ stood beside them. ⁵In their fright the women bowed down with their faces to the ground, but the men said to them, "Why do you look for the living among the dead? ⁶He is not here; he has risen! Remember how he told you, while he was still with you in Galilee: ˣ ⁷'The Son of Man ʸ must be delivered over to the hands of sinners, be crucified and on the third day be raised again.' " ᶻ ⁸Then they remembered his words. ᵃ

⁹When they came back from the tomb, they told all these things to the Eleven and to all the others. ¹⁰It was Mary Magdalene, Joanna, Mary the mother of James, and the others with them ᵇ who told this to the apostles. ᶜ ¹¹But they did not believe ᵈ the women, because their words seemed to them like nonsense. ¹²Peter, however, got up and ran to the tomb. Bending over, he saw the strips of linen lying by themselves, ᵉ and he went away, ᶠ wondering to himself what had happened.

ON THE ROAD TO EMMAUS

¹³Now that same day two of them were going to a village called Emmaus, about seven miles ᵃ from Jerusalem. ᵍ ¹⁴They were talking with each other about everything that had happened. ¹⁵As they talked and discussed these things with each other, Jesus himself came up and walked along with them; ʰ ¹⁶but they were kept from recognizing him. ⁱ

¹⁷He asked them, "What are you discussing together as you walk along?"

They stood still, their faces downcast. ¹⁸One of them, named Cleopas, ʲ asked him, "Are you only a visitor to Jerusalem and do not know the things that have happened there in these days?"

¹⁹"What things?" he asked.

"About Jesus of Nazareth," ᵏ they replied. "He was a prophet, ˡ powerful in word and deed before God and all the people. ²⁰The chief priests and our rulers ᵐ handed him over to be sentenced to death, and they crucified him; ²¹but we had hoped that he was the one who was going to redeem Israel. ⁿ And what is more, it is the third day ᵒ since all this took

---

ᵃ 13 Or about 11 kilometers

23:56 *spices and perfumes.* Yards of cloth and large quantities of spices were used in preparing a body for burial. Seventy-five pounds of myrrh and aloes were already used on that first evening (see Jn 19:39 and note). More was purchased for the return of the women after the Sabbath (see note on Mk 16:1).
24:1 *first day of the week.* By Jewish time, Sunday began at sundown on Saturday. The women bought spices after sunset on Saturday (see note) and were ready to set out early the next day. When they started out, it was dark (see Jn 20:1 and note), and by the time they arrived at the tomb it was still early dawn (see Mt 28:1; Mk 16:2).
24:2 *the stone rolled away.* A tomb's entrance was ordinarily closed to keep vandals and animals from disturbing the bodies. This stone, however, had been sealed by Roman authority for a different reason (see Mt 27:62–66).
24:4 *two men.* They looked like men, but their clothes were remarkable (see 9:29; Ac 1:10 and note; 10:30 and note). Other reports referring to them call them angels (v. 23; see also Jn 20:12 and note). Although Matthew speaks of one angel, not two (Mt 28:2) and Mark of a young man in white (see Mk 16:5 and note), this is not strange because frequently only the spokesman is noted and an accompanying figure is not mentioned. Words and posture (seated, Jn 20:12; standing, Lk 24:4) often change in the course of events, so these variations are not necessarily contradictory. They are merely evidence of independent accounts.
24:6 *while . . . in Galilee.* Jesus had predicted his death and resurrection on a number of occasions (see 9:22 and note), but the disciples failed to comprehend or accept what he was saying.

24:7 See 9:22; 17:25 and notes.
24:9 *to the Eleven and to all the others.* "Eleven" is sometimes used to refer to the group of apostles (Ac 1:26; 2:14) after the betrayal of Judas. Judas was dead at the time the apostles first met the risen Christ, but the group was still called the Twelve (Jn 20:24). The "others" included disciples who, for the most part, came from Galilee.
24:10 *Mary Magdalene.* See note on 8:2. She is named first in most of the lists of women (see Mt 27:56; Mk 15:40 and note; but cf. Jn 19:25) and was the first to see the risen Christ (Jn 20:13–18). *Joanna.* See 8:3. She is named only by Luke at this point (Mark is the only one who adds Salome at this time, Mk 16:1; see note on Mk 15:40). *Mary the mother of James.* See Mk 16:1. She is the "other Mary" of Mt 28:1 (see note there). The absence of the mother of Jesus is significant. She was probably with John (cf. Jn 19:27 and note).
24:12 *Peter . . . ran.* John's Gospel (20:3–9) includes another disciple, John himself.
24:13 *two of them.* One was named Cleopas (v. 18). *Emmaus.* See map, p. 1784.
24:15 *Jesus . . . came up and walked . . . with them.* See chart, p. 1771.
24:16 *kept from recognizing him.* By special, divine intervention.
24:19 *prophet.* They had respect for Jesus as a man of God, but after his death they apparently were reluctant to call him the Messiah.
24:21 *to redeem Israel.* What they probably meant by this was

place. ²²In addition, some of our women amazed us.^p They went to the tomb early this morning ²³but didn't find his body. They came and told us that they had seen a vision of angels, who said he was alive. ²⁴Then some of our companions went to the tomb and found it just as the women had said, but him they did not see."^q

²⁵He said to them, "How foolish you are, and how slow to believe all that the prophets have spoken! ²⁶Did not the Messiah have to suffer these things and then enter his glory?"^r ²⁷And beginning with Moses^s and all the Prophets,^t he explained to them what was said in all the Scriptures concerning himself.^u

²⁸As they approached the village to which they were going, Jesus continued on as if he were going farther. ²⁹But they urged him strongly, "Stay with us, for it is nearly evening; the day is almost over." So he went in to stay with them.

³⁰When he was at the table with them, he took bread, gave thanks, broke it^v and began to give it to them. ³¹Then their eyes were opened and they recognized him,^w and he disappeared from their sight. ³²They asked each other, "Were not our hearts burning within us^x while he talked with us on the road and opened the Scriptures^y to us?"

³³They got up and returned at once to Jerusalem. There they found the Eleven and those with them, assembled together ³⁴and saying, "It is true! The Lord^z has risen and has appeared to Simon."^a ³⁵Then the two told what had happened on the way, and how Jesus was recognized by them when he broke the bread.^b

24:22 ^p ver 1-10
24:24 ^q ver 12
24:26 ^r Heb 2:10; 1Pe 1:11
24:27 ^s Ge 3:15; Nu 21:9; Dt 18:15
^t Isa 7:14; 9:6; 40:10, 11; 53; Eze 34:23; Da 9:24; Mic 7:20; Mal 3:1 ^u Jn 1:45
24:30 ^v S Mt 14:19
24:31 ^w ver 16
24:32 ^x Ps 39:3 ^y ver 27,45
24:34 ^z S Lk 7:13 ^a 1Co 15:5
24:35 ^b ver 30,31

"to set the Jewish nation free from bondage to Rome and so usher in the kingdom of God" (see 1:68; 2:38; 21:28,31 and note on 21:28; cf. Tit 2:14; 1Pe 1:18 and notes). *the third day.* A reference either to the Jewish belief that after the third day the soul left the body or to Jesus' remark that he would be resurrected on the third day (9:22).
24:23 *vision of angels.* See note on v. 4.
24:24 *some of our companions.* See v. 12 and note.

24:26 *suffer ... enter his glory.* See 1Pe 1:11 and note.
24:27 *Moses and all the Prophets.* A way of designating the whole of the OT Scriptures (see v. 44 and note; 16:16,29).
24:28 *as if he were going farther.* If they had not invited him in, he apparently would have continued on by himself.
24:31 *their eyes were opened.* Cf. v. 16; more than a matter of simple recognition.
24:33 *the Eleven and those with them.* See note on v. 9.

RESURRECTION APPEARANCES

APPEARANCE	PLACE	TIME	MATTHEW	MARK	LUKE	JOHN	ACTS	1 CO
The empty tomb	Jerusalem	Resurrection Sunday	28:1–10	16:1–8	24:1–12	20:1–9		
To Mary Magdalene in the garden	Jerusalem	Resurrection Sunday		16:9–11		20:11–18		
To other women	Jerusalem	Resurrection Sunday	28:9–10					
To two people going to Emmaus	Road to Emmaus	Resurrection Sunday		16:12–13	24:13–32			
To Peter	Jerusalem	Resurrection Sunday			24:34			15:5
To the ten disciples in the upper room	Jerusalem	Resurrection Sunday			24:36–43	20:19–25		
To the 11 disciples in the upper room	Jerusalem	Following Sunday		16:14		20:26–31		15:5
To seven disciples fishing	Sea of Galilee	Some time later				21:1–23		
To the 11 disciples on a mountain	Galilee	Some time later	28:16–20	16:15–18				
To more than 500	Unknown	Some time later						15:6
To James	Unknown	Some time later						15:7
To his disciples at his ascension	Mount of Olives	40 days after Jesus' resurrection			24:44–49		1:3–8	
To Paul	Damascus	Several years later					9:1–19 22:3–16 26:9–18	9:1

JESUS APPEARS TO THE DISCIPLES

³⁶While they were still talking about this, Jesus himself stood among them and said to them, "Peace be with you." c

³⁷They were startled and frightened, thinking they saw a ghost. d ³⁸He said to them, "Why are you troubled, and why do doubts rise in your minds? ³⁹Look at my hands and my feet. It is I myself! Touch me and see; e a ghost does not have flesh and bones, as you see I have."

⁴⁰When he had said this, he showed them his hands and feet. ⁴¹And while they still did not believe it because of joy and amazement, he asked them, "Do you have anything here to eat?" ⁴²They gave him a piece of broiled fish, ⁴³and he took it and ate it in their presence. f

⁴⁴He said to them, "This is what I told you while I was still with you: g Everything must be fulfilled h that is written about me in the Law of Moses, i the Prophets j and the Psalms." k

⁴⁵Then he opened their minds so they could understand the Scriptures. ⁴⁶He told them, "This is what is written: The Messiah will suffer l and rise from the dead on the third day, m ⁴⁷and repentance for the forgiveness of sins will be preached in his name n to all nations, o beginning at Jerusalem. p ⁴⁸You are witnesses q of these things. ⁴⁹I am going to send you what my Father has promised; r but stay in the city until you have been clothed with power from on high."

THE ASCENSION OF JESUS

⁵⁰When he had led them out to the vicinity of Bethany, s he lifted up his hands and blessed them. ⁵¹While he was blessing them, he left them and was taken up into heaven. t ⁵²Then they worshiped him and returned to Jerusalem with great joy. ⁵³And they stayed continually at the temple, u praising God.

24:36 *Jesus himself stood among them.* Behind locked doors (Jn 20:19; see chart, p. 1771), indicating that his body was of a different order. It was his glorified resurrection body. *Peace be with you.* The traditional greeting, now given new significance by the resurrection.

24:39 *my hands and my feet.* Indicating that Jesus' feet as well as his hands were nailed to the cross (see note on Mk 15:24; cf. Jn 20:20,27 and note on 20:20).

24:42 *a piece of broiled fish.* Demonstrating that he had a physical body that could consume food.

24:44 *Law of Moses, the Prophets and the Psalms.* The three parts of the Hebrew OT (Psalms was the most prominent book of the third section, called the Writings), indicating that Christ (the Messiah) was foretold in the whole OT.

24:45 *opened their minds.* By explaining the OT Scriptures (cf. v. 27).

24:46 *suffer . . . rise from the dead . . . third day.* See 1Co 15:3-4. The OT depicts the Messiah as one who would suffer (see introduction to Ps 22; see also Isa 53) and rise from the dead on the third day (compare Ps 16:8-11 with Ac 2:23-33 and notes; see Isa 53:10-11 and notes; compare Jnh 1:17 with Mt 12:40 and note).

24:47 *repentance for the forgiveness of sins.* See Ac 5:31; 10:43; 13:38; 26:18. The prediction of Christ's death and resurrection (v. 46) is joined with the necessary human response (repentance) and the resulting benefit (forgiveness; cf. Isa 49:6; Ac 13:47; 26:22-23). *to all nations.* Prophesied also in Mk 13:10; cf. Mt 28:19-20 and note; Ac 10:34-35; 15:16-17; Ro 1:13-14; 4:16-17; 15:7-12. *beginning at Jerusalem.* See Ac 1:8 and note.

24:49 *what my Father has promised.* See Joel 2:28-32 and notes. The reference is to the coming power of the Spirit, fulfilled in Ac 2:4 (see note there and Ac 2:17-22 and notes).

24:50 *Bethany.* A village on the Mount of Olives (see notes on 19:29; Mt 21:17; see also map, p. 1703).

24:51 *taken up into heaven.* Different from his previous disappearances (4:30; 24:3; Jn 8:59). They saw him ascend into a cloud (see Ac 1:9; see also Ac 1:11-12 and notes).

24:53 *at the temple.* During the period of time immediately following Christ's ascension, the believers met continually at the temple (Ac 2:46; 3:1; 5:21,42), where many rooms were available for meetings (see note on 2:37). *praising God.* The Gospel of Luke begins (1:64; see note there) and ends (here) with praise to God in his temple. This Gospel also begins with the aged Zechariah's doubt (1:18) and unbelief (1:20) and ends with the disciples' worship of the risen and ascended Lord "with great joy" (v. 52; see 1:14 and note). Luke has fittingly prepared the way for what follows in his second volume (see Ac 1:1 and note).

AUTHOR | JOHN | INTRODUCTION

C The author is the apostle John, "the disciple whom Jesus loved" (13:23 [see note there]; 19:26; 20:2; 21:7,20,24). He was prominent in the early church but is not mentioned by name in this Gospel—which would be natural if he wrote it, but hard to explain otherwise. The author knew Jewish life well, as seen from references to popular Messianic speculations (see, e.g., 1:21 and note; 7:40–42); to the hostility between Jews and Samaritans (see 4:9 and note); and to Jewish customs, such as the duty of circumcision on the eighth day taking precedence over the prohibition of working on the Sabbath (see note on 7:22). He knew the geography of the Holy Land, locating Bethany about 15 stadia (about two miles) from Jerusalem (11:18) and mentioning Cana, a village not referred to in any earlier writing known to us (2:1 [see note there]; 21:2). The Gospel of John has many touches that appear to reflect the recollections of an eyewitness—such as the house at Bethany being filled with the fragrance of the broken perfume jar (see 12:3 and note). Early writers such as Irenaeus and Tertullian say that John wrote this Gospel, and all other evidence agrees (see Introduction to 1 John: Author).

DATE

In general, two views of the dating of this Gospel have been advocated:

1. The traditional view places it toward the end of the first century, c. A.D. 85 or later (see Introduction to 1 John: Date).

2. More recently, some interpreters have suggested an earlier date, perhaps as early as the 50s and no later than 70.

The first view may be supported by reference to the statement of Clement of Alexandria (died between 211 and 216) that John wrote to supplement the accounts found in the other Gospels (Eusebius, *Ecclesiastical History,* 6.14.7), and thus his Gospel is later than the first three. It has also been argued that the seemingly more developed theology of the fourth Gospel indicates that it originated later.

The second view has found favor because it has been felt more recently that John wrote independently of the other Gospels (see essay and chart, p. 1601). This does not contradict the statement of Clement, referred to above. Also, those who hold this view point out that developed theology does not necessarily argue for a late origin. The theology of Romans (written c. 57) is every bit as developed as that in John. Further, the statement in 5:2 that there "is" (rather than "was") a pool "near the Sheep Gate" may suggest a time before 70, when Jerusalem was destroyed. Others, however, observe that John elsewhere sometimes used the present tense when speaking of the past.

PURPOSE AND EMPHASES

John's Gospel is rather different from the other three. Whether or not he knew them (or any one of them) continues to be debated. In any event, his witness to Jesus goes its own way, highlighting matters that in the other Gospels remain implicit and underdeveloped. The literary style of this witness of Jesus is also unique among the Gospels; here focus is on the "signs" of Jesus' identity and mission (see note on 2:11) and on lengthy, theologically rich discourses.

KEY   **A** APPLICATION FOR LIVING   **B** BACKGROUND NOTES   **C** CHARACTER INFORMATION

John begins with the profound announcement that Jesus is the "in the beginning" creative Word of God who had become embodied (incarnated) as a human being to be the light of life for the world. After this comes the proclamation that this Jesus is the Son of God sent from the Father to finish the Father's work in the world (see 4:34 and note). God's own glory is made visible in him ("Anyone who has seen me has seen the Father," 14:9), and what he does glorifies the Father. In him the full grace and truth of God has shown itself. Strikingly, a series of "I am" claims on Jesus' lips echoes God's naming of himself in Ex 3:14, further strengthening the link between the Father and the Son (see 6:35 [see also note there]; 8:12; 9:5; 10:7,9, 14; 11:25; 14:6; 15:1,5).

Jesus' words to Nicodemus nicely summarize this Gospel's central theme: "For God so loved the world that he gave his one and only Son, that whoever believes in him shall not perish but have eternal life" (3:16). Although a variety of motivations for the composition of John's Gospel have been posited by interpreters (such as to supplement the other Gospels, to combat some form of heresy or to oppose the continuing followers of John the Baptist), the author himself states his main purpose clearly in 20:31: "that you may believe that Jesus is the Messiah, the Son of God, and that by believing you may have life in his name."

For the main emphases of the book, see notes on 1:4,7,9,14,19,49; 2:4,11; 3:27; 4:34; 6:35; 13:1—17:26; 13:31; 17:1–2,5; 20:31.

OUTLINE

1:1 *a* Isa 55:11;
Rev 19:13 *b* Jn 17:5;
1Jn 1:2 *c* Php 2:6
1:2 *d* Ge 1:1; Jn 8:58;
17:5,24; 1Jn 1:1;
Rev 1:8
1:3 *e* ver 10; 1Co 8:6;
Col 1:16; Heb 1:2
1:4 *f* S Jn 5:26; 6:57;
11:25; 14:6; Ac 3:15;
Heb 7:16; 1Jn 1:1,2;
5:20; Rev 1:18
g Ps 36:9; Jn 3:19;
8:12; 9:5; 12:46
1:5 *h* Ps 18:28
i Jn 3:19
1:6 *j* S Mt 3:1
1:7 *k* ver 15,19,32;
Jn 3:26; 5:33 *l* ver 12;
S Jn 3:15
1:9 *m* 1Jn 2:8
n Isa 49:6
1:10 *o* S ver 3
1:11 *p* Isa 53:3
1:12 *q* ver 7;
S Jn 3:15 *r* S 1Jn 3:23
s Dt 14:1; S Ro 8:14;
8:16,21; Eph 5:1;
1Jn 3:1,2
1:13 *t* Jn 3:6; Tit 3:5;
Jas 1:18; 1Pe 1:23;
1Jn 3:9; 4:7; 5:1,4

THE WORD BECAME FLESH

1 In the beginning was the Word,*a* and the Word was with God,*b* and the Word was God. *c* 2He was with God in the beginning. *d* 3Through him all things were made; without him nothing was made that has been made. *e* 4In him was life,*f* and that life was the light *g* of all people. 5The light shines in the darkness,*h* and the darkness has not overcome*a* it. *i*

6There was a man sent from God whose name was John.*j* 7He came as a witness to testify *k* concerning that light, so that through him all might believe. *l* 8He himself was not the light; he came only as a witness to the light.

9The true light *m* that gives light to everyone *n* was coming into the world. 10He was in the world, and though the world was made through him,*o* the world did not recognize him. 11He came to that which was his own, but his own did not receive him. *p* 12Yet to all who did receive him, to those who believed *q* in his name,*r* he gave the right to become children of God *s*— 13children born not of natural descent, nor of human decision or a husband's will, but born of God. *t*

14The Word became flesh *u* and made his dwelling among us. We have seen his glory,*v* the glory of the one and only ₍Son₎, who came from the Father, full of grace *w* and truth. *x*

15(John testified *y* concerning him. He cried out, saying, "This is he of whom I said, 'He who comes after me has surpassed me because he was before me.' ")*z* 16Out of his full-

a 5 Or *understood*

1:14 *u* Gal 4:4; Php 2:7,8; 1Ti 3:16; Heb 2:14; 1Jn 1:1,2; 4:2 *v* Ex 33:18; 40:34 *w* S Ro 3:24 *x* Jn 14:6   **1:15** *y* ver 7 *z* ver 30; Mt 3:11

A C **1:1** *In the beginning.* A deliberate echo of Ge 1:1 (see note there) to link God's action in behalf of the world through Jesus Christ (cf. 3:16) with his first work, the creation of the world. *Word.* Greek *logos,* a term Greeks used not only of the spoken word but also of the unspoken word, the word still in the mind—the reason. When they applied it to the universe, they meant the rational principle that governs all things. The Jews, however, used it to refer to the "word" of God by which he created the world and governs it (see the Septuagint [the pre-Christian Greek translation of the OT] rendering of Ps 33:6; 119:89; 147:15,18) and to refer to the law of God that he gave the Israelites to be their life (see Dt 32:47 and note on 30:20). Of the law the rabbis said that it was "created before the world," that it "lay on God's bosom while God sat on the throne of glory," that it was divine, that it was God's "firstborn" through whom he "created the heaven and the earth," that it is "light" and "life" for the world and that it "is truth." This Jewish use of *logos* as that which comes from God to fulfill his purpose in and for the world appears to lie behind the heavily freighted affirmation with which John begins his Gospel. *with God.* The Word was distinct from the Father. *was God.* Jesus was God in the fullest sense (see note on Ro 9:5). The prologue (vv. 1–18) begins and ends with a ringing affirmation of his deity (see note on v. 18).

A **1:4** *life.* One of the great concepts of this Gospel. The Greek word for "life" is found 36 times in John, while no other NT book uses it more than 17 times. Life is Christ's gift (10:28), and he, in fact, is "the life" (14:6). *light of all people.* This Gospel also links light with Christ, from whom comes all spiritual illumination. He is the "light of the world," who holds out wonderful hope for humanity (cf. 8:12 and note) and for the creation (see 3:16 and note). For an OT link between life and light, see Ps 36:9 and note.

1:5 *darkness.* The stark contrast between light and darkness is a striking theme in this Gospel (see, e.g., 12:35).

1:6 *John.* In this Gospel the name John always refers to John the Baptist.

A **1:7** *as a witness to testify.* John the Baptist's singular ministry was to testify to Jesus (10:41). "Witness" is another important concept in this Gospel. The Greek noun for "witness" or "testimony" is used 14 times (in Matthew not at all, in Mark three times, in Luke once) and the verb ("testify") 33 times (found once each in Matthew and Luke and not at all in Mark)—in both cases more often than anywhere else in the NT. John (the

author) thereby emphasizes that the facts about Jesus are amply attested. *that through him all might believe.* People were not to believe "in" John the Baptist but "through" him. Similarly, the writer's purpose was to draw them to belief in Christ (20:31 [see note there]); he uses the Greek verb for "believe" 98 times.

1:8 *He himself was not the light.* The greatness of John the Baptist caused some of his followers to have exaggerated ideas about him (see v. 21), but while Jesus affirms John's greatness (see Mt 11:11 and note), he also makes clear his limitations: John is "a lamp" (5:35) but not "the light."

1:9 John is referring to the incarnation of Christ. *world.* Another common word in John's writings, the Greek noun for "world" is found 78 times in this Gospel and 24 times in his letters (only 47 times in all of Paul's writings). It can mean the universe, the earth, the people on earth, most people, people opposed to God or the human system opposed to God's purposes. John emphasizes the word by repetition and moves without explanation from one meaning to another (see, e.g., 17:5,14–15 and notes).

A **1:12** *believed.* See v. 7; 20:31 and notes. *he gave the right.* Membership in God's family is by grace alone—the gift of God (see Eph 2:8–9 and notes). It is never a human achievement, as v. 13 emphasizes; yet the imparting of the gift is dependent on human reception of it, as the words "did receive" and "believed" make clear.

1:13 *born of God.* The "children of God" (v. 12) have been given a new openness to and relationship with God that was not theirs as a result of their natural birth (see 3:3,5; 2Co 5:17; Gal 6:15; Tit 3:5 and notes).

1:14 *flesh.* A strong, almost crude, word that stresses the reality of Christ's humanity. *made his dwelling among us. We have seen his glory.* The Greek for "made his dwelling" is connected with the word for "tent/tabernacle"; the verse would have reminded John's Jewish readers of the Tent of Meeting, which was filled with the glory of God (Ex 40:34–35). Christ revealed his glory to his disciples by the miracles he performed (see 2:11 and note) and by his death and resurrection. *grace and truth.* The corresponding Hebrew terms are often translated "(unfailing) love and faithfulness" (see notes on Ps 26:3; Pr 16:6). *grace.* A significant Christian concept (see notes on Jnh 4:2; Ro 1:7; Gal 1:3; Eph 1:2), though John never uses the word after the prologue (vv. 1–18). *truth.* John uses the Greek word for "truth" 25 times and links it closely with Jesus, who is the truth (see 14:6 and note).

A **1:15** *he was before me.* In ancient times the older person was given respect and regarded as greater than the ness *a* we have all received grace *b* in place of grace already given. ¹⁷For the law was given through Moses; *c* grace and truth came through Jesus Christ. *d* ¹⁸No one has ever seen God, *e* but the one and only ⌞Son⌟, who is himself God and *a f* is in closest relationship with the Father, has made him known.

JOHN THE BAPTIST DENIES BEING THE MESSIAH

¹⁹Now this was John's *g* testimony when the Jewish leaders *h* in Jerusalem sent priests and Levites to ask him who he was. ²⁰He did not fail to confess, but confessed freely, "I am not the Messiah." *i*

²¹They asked him, "Then who are you? Are you Elijah?" *j*

He said, "I am not."

"Are you the Prophet?" *k*

He answered, "No."

²²Finally they said, "Who are you? Give us an answer to take back to those who sent us. What do you say about yourself?"

²³John replied in the words of Isaiah the prophet, "I am the voice of one calling in the wilderness, *l* 'Make straight the way for the Lord.'" *b m*

²⁴Now the Pharisees who had been sent ²⁵questioned him, "Why then do you baptize if you are not the Messiah, nor Elijah, nor the Prophet?"

²⁶"I baptize with *c* water," *n* John replied, "but among you stands one you do not know. ²⁷He is the one who comes after me, *o* the thongs of whose sandals I am not worthy to untie." *p*

²⁸This all happened at Bethany on the other side of the Jordan, *q* where John was baptizing.

JOHN'S TESTIMONY ABOUT JESUS

²⁹The next day John saw Jesus coming toward him and said, "Look, the Lamb of God, *r*

---

a 18 Some manuscripts *but the only Son, who*   *b 23* Isaiah 40:3   *c 26* Or *in*; also in verses 31 and 33 (twice)

1:16 *a* Eph 1:23;
Col 1:19; 2:9
b S Ro 3:24
1:17 *c* Dt 32:46;
Jn 7:19 *d* ver 14
1:18 *e* Ex 33:20;
Jn 6:46; Col 1:15;
1Ti 6:16; 1Jn 4:12
f Jn 3:16,18; 1Jn 4:9
1:19 *g* S Mt 3:1
h Jn 2:18; 5:10,16;
6:41,52; 7:1; 10:24
1:20 *i* Jn 3:28;
Lk 3:15,16
1:21 *j* S Mt 11:14
k Dt 18:15
1:23 *l* Mt 3:1
m Isa 40:3
1:26 *n* S Mk 1:4
1:27 *o* ver 15,30
p Mk 1:7
1:28 *q* Jn 3:26; 10:40
1:29 *r* ver 36;
Ge 22:8; Isa 53:7;
1Pe 1:19; Rev 5:6; 13:8

---

younger. People would normally have ranked Jesus lower in respect than John, who was older. John the Baptist explains that this is only apparent, since Jesus, as the Word, existed before he was born on earth.

1:16 *grace in place of grace already given.* To the blessing that came through Moses has been added the greater blessing that has come through Jesus (see v. 17; see also Heb 1:1–4 and notes).

A **1:18** *the one and only ⌞Son⌟, who is himself God.* An explicit declaration of Christ's deity (see vv. 1,14 and notes; 3:16; see also note on Ro 9:5). *has made him known.* Sometimes in the OT people are said to have seen God (see, e.g., Ex 24:10 and note). But we are also told that no one can see God and live (Ex 33:20). Therefore, since no human being can see God as he really is, those who saw God saw him in a form he took upon himself temporarily for the occasion. Now, however, Christ "has made him known" (see 2Co 4:4; Col 1:15,19; 2:9 and notes).

1:19 *Jewish leaders.* Lit. "Jews," which occurs about 70 times in this Gospel. It is used in a favorable sense (e.g., 4:22) and in a neutral sense (e.g., 2:6). But generally John used it of the Jewish leaders who were hostile to Jesus (e.g., here; 5:10,16; 7:1, etc.). Here it refers to the delegation sent by the Sanhedrin to look into the activities of an unauthorized teacher. *Levites.* Descendants of the tribe of Levi, who were assigned to specific duties in connection with the tabernacle (Nu 3:17–37) and temple. They also had teaching responsibilities (2Ch 35:3; Ne 8:7–9), and it was probably in this role that they were sent with the priests to John the Baptist.

1:20 *I.* Emphatic, contrasting John the Baptist with someone else. Throughout the following verses this emphatic "I" occurs frequently, and almost invariably there is an implied contrast with Jesus, who is always given the higher place.

C **1:21** *Are you Elijah? . . . I am not.* The Jews remembered that Elijah had not died (2Ki 2:11) and believed that he would come back to earth to announce the end time. In this sense, John properly denied that he was Elijah. When Jesus later said the Baptist was Elijah (see Mt 11:14; 17:10 and notes), he

meant it in the sense that John was a fulfillment of the prophecy of Mal 4:5 (see note there). *the Prophet.* The prophet of Dt 18:15 (see note there). The Jewish people expected a variety of persons to be associated with the coming of the Messiah. John the Baptist emphatically denies being "the Prophet." He had come to testify about Jesus, yet the people kept asking him about himself. His answers became progressively more terse.

B **1:23** The Baptist applied the prophecy of Isa 40:3 (see note there) to his own ministry of calling people to repent in preparation for the coming of the Messiah. The men of Qumran (the community that produced the Dead Sea Scrolls; see essay, pp. 1596–1597) applied the same words to themselves, but they prepared for the Lord's coming by isolating themselves from the world to secure their own salvation. John concentrated on helping people come to the Messiah (the Christ).

1:24 *Pharisees.* Members of the conservative religious party, who probed deeper than the rest of the delegation (v. 19). See notes on Mt 3:7; Mk 2:16; Lk 5:17; see also essay, p. 1596, and chart, p. 1650.

A **1:25** *the Messiah.* Means "the Anointed One." In OT times anointing signified being set apart for service, particularly as king (cf. 1Sa 16:1,13) or priest (Ex 28:41; 29:7; 30:30; 40:13,15). But people were looking for not just *an* anointed one but *the* Anointed One, the Messiah (cf. Mt 16:16 and note).

1:27 *whose sandals I am not worthy to untie.* A menial task, fit for a slave. Disciples would perform all sorts of service for their rabbis (teachers), but loosing sandal thongs was expressly excluded.

1:28 *Bethany.* The Bethany mentioned elsewhere in the Gospels was only about two miles from Jerusalem (see note on Mt 21:17). The site of this other Bethany is not known, except that it was located on the east side of the Jordan (see maps, pp. 1612, 1679).

A **1:29** *Lamb of God.* An expression found in the Bible only here and in v. 36. Many suggestions have been made as to which "lamb" John had in mind (e.g., the lamb offered at Passover or the lamb of Isa 53:7, of Jer 11:19, of Ge 22:8 or of Rev 5:6 [see note there]). It may be that John chose this unique way of

1:29 *s* S Jn 3:17
1:30 *t* ver 15,27
1:32 *u* Mt 3:16
1:33 *v* S Mk 1:4
w S Mk 1:8
1:34 *x* ver 49;
S Mt 4:3
1:35 *y* S Mt 3:1
1:36 *z* S ver 29
1:38 *a* ver 49;
S Mt 23:7
1:41 *b* Jn 4:25
1:42 *c* Ge 17:5,15;
32:28; 35:10
d Mt 16:18
1:43 *e* Mt 10:3;
Jn 6:5-7; 12:21,22;
14:8,9 *f* S Mt 4:19
1:44 *g* S Mt 11:21
1:45 *h* Jn 21:2
i S Lk 24:27
j S Lk 24:27
k S Mk 1:24 *l* Lk 3:23
1:46 *m* Jn 7:41,42,
52
1:47 *n* Ro 9:4,6
o Ps 32:2

who takes away the sin of the world! *s* ³⁰This is the one I meant when I said, 'A man who comes after me has surpassed me because he was before me.' *t* ³¹I myself did not know him, but the reason I came baptizing with water was that he might be revealed to Israel."

³²Then John gave this testimony: "I saw the Spirit come down from heaven as a dove and remain on him. *u* ³³And I myself did not know him, but the one who sent me to baptize with water *v* told me, 'The man on whom you see the Spirit come down and remain is the one who will baptize with the Holy Spirit.' *w* ³⁴I have seen and I testify that this is God's Chosen One." *a x*

JOHN'S DISCIPLES FOLLOW JESUS

1:40–42pp — Mt 4:18–22; Mk 1:16–20; Lk 5:2–11

³⁵The next day John *y* was there again with two of his disciples. ³⁶When he saw Jesus passing by, he said, "Look, the Lamb of God!" *z*

³⁷When the two disciples heard him say this, they followed Jesus. ³⁸Turning around, Jesus saw them following and asked, "What do you want?"

They said, "Rabbi" *a* (which means "Teacher"), "where are you staying?"

³⁹"Come," he replied, "and you will see."

So they went and saw where he was staying, and they spent that day with him. It was about four in the afternoon.

⁴⁰Andrew, Simon Peter's brother, was one of the two who heard what John had said and who had followed Jesus. ⁴¹The first thing Andrew did was to find his brother Simon and tell him, "We have found the Messiah" (that is, the Christ). *b* ⁴²And he brought him to Jesus.

Jesus looked at him and said, "You are Simon son of John. You will be called *c* Cephas" (which, when translated, is Peter *b*). *d*

JESUS CALLS PHILIP AND NATHANAEL

⁴³The next day Jesus decided to leave for Galilee. Finding Philip, *e* he said to him, "Follow me." *f*

⁴⁴Philip, like Andrew and Peter, was from the town of Bethsaida. *g* ⁴⁵Philip found Nathanael *h* and told him, "We have found the one Moses wrote about in the Law, *i* and about whom the prophets also wrote *j*—Jesus of Nazareth, *k* the son of Joseph." *l*

⁴⁶"Nazareth! Can anything good come from there?" *m* Nathanael asked.

"Come and see," said Philip.

⁴⁷When Jesus saw Nathanael approaching, he said of him, "Here truly is an Israelite *n* in whom there is no deceit." *o*

⁴⁸"How do you know me?" Nathanael asked.

Jesus answered, "I saw you while you were still under the fig tree before Philip called you."

a 34 See Isaiah 42:1; many manuscripts *is the Son of God.* *b 42* Cephas (Aramaic) and Peter (Greek) both mean *rock.*

---

referring to Jesus' mission to point both to the sacrificial offering that Jesus would become and to his subsequent conquest of all evil powers—the two ways by which he "takes away the sin of the world" (see 1Jn 2:2 and note).

1:31 *I … did not know him.* John the Baptist, who "lived in the wilderness until he appeared publicly to Israel" (Lk 1:80), may not have known Jesus at all. But the words probably mean only that he did not know that Jesus was the Messiah until he saw the sign mentioned in vv. 32–33.

1:32 See note on Mt 3:15 for Jesus' baptism.

1:33 *baptize with the Holy Spirit.* John baptized with water, but Jesus would baptize with the Spirit—by which he would cause those who believe in him to participate in the powers and graces of the new life he came to give (see 20:22; Ac 1:5; 2:4; 11:15–16; 19:4–6; 1Co 12–14; Gal 3:5,14; 4:6; 5:16–25; Eph 1:13; 3:16; 5:18; Php 3:3; 1Th 4:8). *Holy Spirit.* His normal title in the NT, though it appears only here and in 14:26; 20:22 in this Gospel—emphasizing his holiness rather than his power or greatness.

1:34 *God's Chosen One.* See TNIV text note.

1:35 *two.* One was Andrew (v. 40). The other is not named, but from early times it has been thought that he was the author of

this Gospel. *his disciples.* In the sense that they had been baptized by John and looked to him as their religious teacher.

1:36 *Lamb of God.* See note on v. 29.

1:40 *Andrew.* One of the 12 apostles (Mt 10:2). He was from Bethsaida (v. 44) but later lived with Peter at Capernaum (Mk 1:29), where they fished for a living (Mt 4:18).

1:41 *the Messiah.* See note on v. 25.

1:42 *Simon son of John.* See note on Mt 16:17. *Cephas … Peter.* See TNIV text note. In the Gospels, Peter was anything but a rock; he was impulsive and unstable. In Acts, however, he was a pillar of the early church. Jesus named him not for what he was but for what, by God's grace, he would become (see Mt 16:18 and note).

1:44 *Bethsaida.* See note on Mt 11:21.

1:45 *son of Joseph.* Not a denial of the virgin birth of Christ (see Mt 1:18,20,23,25 and note; Lk 1:26–35 and note). Joseph was Jesus' legal, though not his natural, father.

1:46 *Nazareth.* See 7:52; see also note on Mt 2:23.

1:47 *Here truly is an Israelite.* See 2:24–25.

1:48 *fig tree.* Its shade was a favorite place for study and prayer in hot weather.

1:49 ᵖ ver 38;
S Mt 23:7 ᵍ ver 34;
S Mt 4:3 ʳ S Mt 2:2;
27:42; Jn 12:13
1:51 ˢ S Mt 3:16
ᵗ Ge 28:12 ᵘ S Mt 8:20
2:1 ᵛ Jn 4:46; 21:2
ʷ S Mt 12:46
2:4 ˣ Jn 19:26
ʸ Mt 8:29
ᶻ S Mt 26:18
2:5 ᵃ Ge 41:55
2:6 ᵇ Mk 7:3,4;
Jn 3:25
2:9 ᶜ Jn 4:46
2:11 ᵈ ver 23;
Mt 12:38; Jn 3:2;
S 4:48; 6:2,14,26,30;
12:37; 20:30 ᵉ Jn 1:14
ᶠ Ex 14:31
2:12 ᵍ S Mt 4:13
ʰ S Mt 12:46
ⁱ S Mt 12:46

⁴⁹Then Nathanael declared, "Rabbi,ᵖ you are the Son of God;ᵍ you are the king of Israel."ʳ

⁵⁰Jesus said, "You believeᵃ because I told you I saw you under the fig tree. You will see greater things than that." ⁵¹He then added, "Very truly I tell you,ᵇ youᵇ will see 'heaven open,ˢ and the angels of God ascending and descendingᵗ on'ᶜ the Son of Man."ᵘ

JESUS CHANGES WATER INTO WINE

2 On the third day a wedding took place at Cana in Galilee.ᵛ Jesus' motherʷ was there, ²and Jesus and his disciples had also been invited to the wedding. ³When the wine was gone, Jesus' mother said to him, "They have no more wine."

⁴"Woman,ᵈˣ why do you involve me?"ʸ Jesus replied. "My hourᶻ has not yet come."

⁵His mother said to the servants, "Do whatever he tells you."ᵃ

⁶Nearby stood six stone water jars, the kind used by the Jews for ceremonial washing,ᵇ each holding from twenty to thirty gallons.ᵉ

⁷Jesus said to the servants, "Fill the jars with water"; so they filled them to the brim.

⁸Then he told them, "Now draw some out and take it to the master of the banquet."

They did so, ⁹and the master of the banquet tasted the water that had been turned into wine.ᶜ He did not realize where it had come from, though the servants who had drawn the water knew. Then he called the bridegroom aside ¹⁰and said, "Everyone brings out the choice wine first and then the cheaper wine after the guests have had too much to drink; but you have saved the best till now."

¹¹What Jesus did here in Cana of Galilee was the first of the signsᵈ through which he revealed his glory;ᵉ and his disciples put their faith in him.ᶠ

¹²After this he went down to Capernaumᵍ with his motherʰ and brothersⁱ and his disciples. There they stayed for a few days.

ᵃ 50 Or Do you believe . . . ?   ᵇ 51 The Greek is plural.   ᶜ 51 Gen. 28:12   ᵈ 4 The Greek for Woman does not denote any disrespect.   ᵉ 6 Or from about 75 to about 115 liters

---

1:49 *Rabbi.* Hebrew word for "(my) teacher." *the Son of God.* See vv. 14,18,34; 3:16 and note; 20:31. At the beginning of Jesus' ministry Nathanael acknowledged him with this meaningful title; later it was used in mockery (Mt 27:40; cf. Jn 19:7). Andrew's "the Messiah" (v. 41) and Nathanael's "the Son of God" together match Peter's "You are the Messiah, the Son of the living God" (Mt 16:16). *king of Israel.* See 12:13 and note. In Mk 15:32 "Messiah" and "king of Israel" are equated.

1:51 *Very truly I tell you.* See note on Mk 3:28; "truly I tell you" occurs more in this Gospel than in any other Gospel—and nowhere else in the NT. And John alone prefaces the phrase with "Very" a total of 25 times. *heaven open.* In Jesus' ministry the disciples will see heaven's (God's) testimony to Jesus as plainly as if they heard an announcement from heaven concerning him. *the angels of God ascending and descending.* As in Jacob's dream (see Ge 28:12 and note), thus marking Jesus as God's elect one, through whom redemption comes to the world—perhaps identifying Jesus as "truly" the "Israelite" (v. 47). *Son of Man.* Jesus' favorite self-designation (see note on Mk 8:31).

2:1 *third day.* Cf. Ge 22:4 and note. *wedding.* Little is known of how a wedding was performed in the Holy Land in the first century, but clearly the feast was very important and might go on for a week. To fail in proper hospitality was a serious offense. *Cana.* Mentioned only in John's Gospel (v. 11; 4:46; 21:2). It was west of the Sea of Galilee, but the exact location is unknown (see map, p. 1791).

2:3 *When the wine was gone.* More than a minor social embarrassment, since the family had an obligation to provide a feast of the socially required standard. There was no great variety in beverages, and people normally drank water or wine.

2:4 *Woman.* See TNIV text note. *My hour has not yet come.* Several similar expressions scattered through this Gospel (see 7:6, 8,30; 8:20 and notes) picture Jesus moving inevitably toward the destiny for which he had come: the time of his sacrificial

death on the cross. At the crucifixion and resurrection Jesus' "hour" had truly come (see 12:23,27 and notes; 13:1; 16:32; 17:1).

2:6 *ceremonial washing.* Jews became ceremonially defiled during the normal circumstances of daily life and were cleansed by pouring water over their hands. For a lengthy feast with many guests a large amount of water was required for this purpose. *holding.* Refers to capacity, not to actual content.

2:8–9 *master of the banquet.* A function mentioned only here in the NT. Apparently he was one of the guests, charged with serving as master of ceremonies.

2:10 *too much to drink . . . you have saved the best.* Ordinarily, after the guests' taste buds were dulled, the "cheaper wine" was served.

2:11 *signs.* See chart, p. 1780. John always refers to Jesus' miracles as "signs," a word emphasizing the significance of the action rather than the marvel (see, e.g., 4:54; 6:14; 9:16; 11:47 and notes). There are seven (the number of completeness and perfection) such "signs" in the main body of this Gospel; the large catch of fish in 21:1–11 is in the epilogue (see Introduction: Outline; cf. note on 6:35). They revealed Jesus' glory (see 1:14 and note) and likely also pointed to the fullness of the salvation he came to effect. In his account of Jesus' first display of "his glory" by providing an abundance of wine so that a wedding feast of common folk could be fully celebrated, John probably was testifying that Christ's saving mission would culminate in the redemption of the creation from all its distresses, so that the wine of joy would flow fully, as the prophets had announced (see Isa 35:1–2; Joel 3:18; Am 9:13 and notes; cf. Ge 49:11 and note). *his disciples put their faith in him.* See 1:7; 20:31 and notes.

2:12 *went down.* Situated on the shore of the lake, Capernaum was at a lower level than Cana. *Capernaum.* See notes on Mt 4:13; Lk 10:15; see also diagram, p. 1725. *brothers.* See note on Lk 8:19.

MIRACLES OF JESUS

HEALING MIRACLES	MATTHEW	MARK	LUKE	JOHN
Man with leprosy	8:2–4	1:40–42	5:12–13	
Roman centurion's servant	8:5–13		7:1–10	
Peter's mother-in-law	8:14–15	1:30–31	4:38–39	
Two men from Gadara	8:28–34	5:1–15	8:27–35	
Paralyzed man	9:2–7	2:3–12	5:18–25	
Woman with bleeding	9:20–22	5:25–29	8:43–48	
Two blind men	9:27–31			
Mute, demon-possessed man	9:32–33			
Man with a shriveled hand	12:10–13	3:1–5	6:6–10	
Blind, mute, demon-possessed man	12:22		11:14	
Canaanite woman's daughter	15:21–28	7:24–30		
Boy with a demon	17:14–18	9:17–29	9:38–43	
Two blind men (including Bartimaeus)	20:29–34	10:46–52	18:35–43	
Deaf mute		7:31–37		
Possessed man in synagogue		1:23–26	4:33–35	
Blind man at Bethsaida		8:22–26		
Crippled woman			13:11–13	
Man with edema			14:1–4	
Ten men with leprosy			17:11–19	
The high priest's servant			22:50–51	
Official's son at Capernaum				4:46–54
Sick man at pool of Bethesda				5:1–9
Man born blind				9:1–7

MIRACLES SHOWING POWER OVER NATURE				
Calming the storm	8:23–27	4:37–41	8:22–25	
Walking on water	14:25	6:48–51		6:19–21
Feeding of the 5,000	14:15–21	6:35–44	9:12–17	6:6–13
Feeding of the 4,000	15:32–38	8:1–9		
Coin in fish	17:24–27			
Fig tree withered	21:18–22	11:12–14,20–25		
Large catch of fish			5:4–11	
Water turned into wine				2:1–11
Another large catch of fish				21:1–11

MIRACLES OF RAISING THE DEAD				
Jairus's daughter	9:18–19,23–25	5:22–24,38–42	8:41–42,49–56	
Widow's son at Nain			7:11–15	
Lazarus				11:1–44

2:13 *j* Jn 11:55
k Dt 16:1-6; Lk 2:41
2:14 *l* Lev 1:14;
Dt 14:26 *m* Dt 14:25
2:16 *n* Lk 2:49
2:17 *o* Ps 69:9
2:18 *p* S Jn 1:19
q S ver 11 *r* S Mt 12:38
2:19 *s* S Mt 16:21;
26:61; 27:40;
Mk 14:58; 15:29;
Ac 6:14
2:21 *t* 1Co 6:19
2:22 *u* Lk 24:5-8;
Jn 12:16; 14:26
v Ps 16:10; S Lk 24:27
2:23 *w* ver 13
x S ver 11 *y* S Jn 3:15
2:25 *z* Isa 11:3
a Dt 31:21; 1Ki 8:39;
S Mt 9:4; Jn 6:61,64;
13:11
3:1 *b* Jn 7:50; 19:39
c Lk 23:13
3:2 *d* S Mt 23:7
e ver 11 *f* S Jn 2:11
g Jn 10:38; 14:10,11;
Ac 2:22; 10:38
3:3 *h* S Jn 1:13
i S Mt 3:2
3:5 *j* S Ac 22:16
k Tit 3:5
3:6 *l* S Jn 1:13;
1Co 15:50

JESUS CLEARS THE TEMPLE COURTS

2:14–16pp — Mt 21:12,13; Mk 11:15–17; Lk 19:45,46

¹³When it was almost time for the Jewish Passover,*j* Jesus went up to Jerusalem. *k* ¹⁴In the temple courts he found people selling cattle, sheep and doves,*l* and others sitting at tables exchanging money. *m* ¹⁵So he made a whip out of cords, and drove all from the temple courts, both sheep and cattle; he scattered the coins of the money changers and overturned their tables. ¹⁶To those who sold doves he said, "Get these out of here! Stop turning my Father's house *n* into a market!" ¹⁷His disciples remembered that it is written: "Zeal for your house will consume me."*a o*

¹⁸The Jews*p* then responded to him, "What sign*q* can you show us to prove your authority to do all this?"*r*

¹⁹Jesus answered them, "Destroy this temple, and I will raise it again in three days."*s*

²⁰They replied, "It has taken forty-six years to build this temple, and you are going to raise it in three days?" ²¹But the temple he had spoken of was his body. *t* ²²After he was raised from the dead, his disciples recalled what he had said. *u* Then they believed the scripture *v* and the words that Jesus had spoken.

²³Now while he was in Jerusalem at the Passover Festival, *w* many people saw the signs*x* he was performing and believed*y* in his name. *b* ²⁴But Jesus would not entrust himself to them, for he knew all people. ²⁵He did not need human testimony about them, *z* for he knew what was in them. *a*

JESUS TEACHES NICODEMUS

3 Now there was a Pharisee, a man named Nicodemus *b* who was a member of the Jewish ruling council. *c* ²He came to Jesus at night and said, "Rabbi, *d* we know*e* that you are a teacher who has come from God. For no one could perform the signs*f* you are doing if God were not with him."*g*

³Jesus replied, "Very truly I tell you, no one can see the kingdom of God without being born again.*c" h i*

⁴"How can anyone be born when they are old?" Nicodemus asked. "Surely they cannot enter a second time into their mother's womb to be born!"

⁵Jesus answered, "Very truly I tell you, no one can enter the kingdom of God without being born of water and the Spirit.*j k* ⁶Flesh gives birth to flesh, but the Spirit*d* gives birth to spirit. *l* ⁷You should not be surprised at my saying, 'You*e* must be born again.' ⁸The wind

a 17 Psalm 69:9   *b 23* Or *in him*   *c 3* The Greek for *again* also means *from above*; also in verse 7.
d 6 Or *but spirit*   *e 7* The Greek is plural.

2:13 *Passover.* See Ex 12 and notes on Ex 12:11–23; see also notes on Mt 26:17,18–30; Mk 14:1,12; Lk 22:1; and chart, pp. 180–181. Passover was one of the annual festivals that all Jewish men were required to celebrate in Jerusalem. See notes on 5:1; Dt 16:16.
2:14–17 Matthew, Mark and Luke record a cleansing of the temple toward the end of Jesus' ministry (see note on Mt 21:12–17).
2:14 *cattle, sheep and doves.* Required for sacrifices. Jews who came great distances had to be able to buy sacrificial animals near the temple. The merchants, however, were selling them in the outer court of the temple itself, the one place where Gentiles could come to pray. *exchanging money.* Many coins had to be changed into currency acceptable to the temple authorities, which made money changers necessary (see note on Mk 11:15). They should not, however, have been working in the temple itself.
2:17 *His disciples remembered.* Probably after Jesus' crucifixion (see v. 22)—when Ps 69 struck them as a prophecy of his suffering at the hands of those his "zeal" for the true worship of God had deeply antagonized (see introduction to Ps 69).
2:19 *temple.* The Jews thought Jesus was referring to the literal temple, but John tells us that he was not (v. 21). Just a few years later Jesus was accused of saying that he would destroy the temple and raise it again (see Mt 26:61; Mk 14:58 and notes), and mockers repeated the charge as he hung on the cross (Mt 27:40; Mk 15:29). The same misunderstanding may have been behind the charge against Stephen (see Ac 6:13 and note).

2:20 *forty-six years.* The temple was not finally completed until A.D. 64. The meaning is that work had been going on for 46 years. Since it had begun c. 19 or 20 B.C., the year of the event recorded here is c. A.D. 27 (see chart, p. 1656).
2:22 *recalled what he had said.* See 14:26 and note. *Then they believed the scripture.* See 20:9 and note. It is not clear whether reference here is to a particular word from the OT (see, e.g., Ps 16:10; 17:15 and notes) or to the OT in general (cf. 1Co 15:4).
2:23 *Passover Festival.* See note on v. 13. *name.* See notes on Ps 5:11; Eze 20:9.
3:1 *Pharisee.* See note on Mt 3:7; Mk 2:16; Lk 5:17.
3:2 *at night.* Perhaps Nicodemus was afraid to come by day. Or he may have wanted a long talk, which would have been difficult in the daytime with the crowds around Jesus.
3:3,7 *born again.* The Greek may also mean "born from above" (see TNIV text note). Both meanings are consistent with Jesus' redeeming work (see 1:13 and note).
3:5 *kingdom of God.* See note on Mt 3:2. *born of water and the Spirit.* A phrase understood in various ways: 1. It means much the same as "born of the Spirit" (v. 8; cf. Tit 3:5 and note). 2. Water here refers to purification. 3. Water refers to baptism—that of John (1:31) or that of Jesus and his disciples (see v. 22; 4:2 and notes). 4. Water refers to physical birth, specifically to the water of the amniotic sac (cf. v. 6).
3:7 *You.* See TNIV text note. This assertion applies to everyone, not just to Nicodemus. *must.* There are no exceptions. *born again.* See note on v. 3.

3:8 *m* 1Co 2:14-16
3:9 *n* Jn 6:52,60
3:10 *o* Lk 2:46
3:11 *p* Jn 1:18; 7:16,
17 *q* ver 32
3:13 *r* Pr 30:4;
Ac 2:34; Eph 4:8-10
s ver 31; Jn 6:38,42;
Heb 4:14; 9:24
t S Mt 8:20
3:14 *u* Nu 21:8,9
v S Jn 12:32
3:15 *w* ver 16,36;
Ge 15:6; Nu 14:11;
Mt 27:42; Mk 1:15;
Jn 1:7,12; 2:23; 5:24;
7:38; 20:31 Ac 13:39;
16:31; Ro 3:22; 10:9,
10; 1Jn 5:1,5,10
x ver 16,36;
S Mt 25:46; Jn 20:31
3:16 *y* Ro 5:8;
Eph 2:4; 1Jn 4:9,10
z Isa 9:6; Ro 8:32
a Ge 22:12; Jn 1:18
b S ver 15 *c* ver 36;
Jn 6:29, 40; 11:25,26
3:17 *d* Jn 6:29,57;
10:36; 11:42; 17:8,21;
20:21 *e* Isa 53:11;
S Mt 1:21; S Lk 2:11;
19:10; Jn 1:29; 12:47;
S Ro 11:14; 1Ti 1:15;
2:5,6; 1Jn 2:2; 3:5
3:18 *f* Jn 5:24
g Jn 1:18; 1Jn 4:9
3:19 *h* S Jn 1:4
i Ps 52:3; Jn 7:7
3:20 *j* Eph 5:11,13
3:22 *k* Jn 4:2
3:23 *l* S Mt 3:1
3:24 *m* Mt 4:12; 14:3
3:25 *n* Jn 2:6
3:26 *o* Jn 3:7
p Jn 1:7
3:28 *q* Jn 1:20,23
3:29 *r* Mt 9:15
s Jn 16:24; 17:13;
Php 2:2; 1Jn 1:4;
2Jn 12
3:31 *t* ver 13
u Jn 8:23; 1Jn 4:5

blows wherever it pleases. You hear its sound, but you cannot tell where it comes from or where it is going. So it is with everyone born of the Spirit." *a m*

9 "How can this be?" *n* Nicodemus asked.

10 "You are Israel's teacher," *o* said Jesus, "and do you not understand these things? 11 Very truly I tell you, we speak of what we know, *p* and we testify to what we have seen, but still you people do not accept our testimony. *q* 12 I have spoken to you of earthly things and you do not believe; how then will you believe if I speak of heavenly things? 13 No one has ever gone into heaven *r* except the one who came from heaven *s* —the Son of Man. *b t* 14 Just as Moses lifted up the snake in the wilderness, *u* so the Son of Man must be lifted up, *c v* 15 that everyone who believes *w* may have eternal life in him." *d x*

16 For God so loved *y* the world that he gave *z* his one and only Son, *a* that whoever believes *b* in him shall not perish but have eternal life. *c* 17 For God did not send his Son into the world *d* to condemn the world, but to save the world through him. *e* 18 Whoever believes in him is not condemned, *f* but whoever does not believe stands condemned already because they have not believed in the name of God's one and only Son. *g* 19 This is the verdict: Light *h* has come into the world, but people loved darkness instead of light because their deeds were evil. *i* 20 All those who do evil hate the light, and will not come into the light for fear that their deeds will be exposed. *j* 21 But those who live by the truth come into the light, so that it may be seen plainly that what they have done has been done in the sight of God.

JOHN TESTIFIES AGAIN ABOUT JESUS

22 After this, Jesus and his disciples went out into the Judean countryside, where he spent some time with them, and baptized. *k* 23 Now John *l* also was baptizing at Aenon near Salim, because there was plenty of water, and people were coming and being baptized. 24 (This was before John was put in prison.) *m* 25 An argument developed between some of John's disciples and a certain Jew over the matter of ceremonial washing. *n* 26 They came to John and said to him, "Rabbi, *o* that man who was with you on the other side of the Jordan—the one you testified *p* about—look, he is baptizing, and everyone is going to him."

27 To this John replied, "A person can receive only what is given from heaven. 28 You yourselves can testify that I said, 'I am not the Messiah but am sent ahead of him.' *q* 29 The bride belongs to the bridegroom. *r* The friend who attends the bridegroom waits and listens for him, and is full of joy when he hears the bridegroom's voice. That joy is mine, and it is now complete. *s* 30 He must become greater; I must become less." *e*

31 The one who comes from above *t* is above all; the one who is from the earth belongs to the earth, and speaks as one from the earth. *u* The one who comes from heaven is above

---

a 8 The Greek for *Spirit* is the same as that for *wind.*   *b* 13 Some manuscripts *Man, who is in heaven*
c 14 The Greek for *lifted up* also means *exalted.*   *d* 15 Some interpreters end the quotation with verse 21.   *e* 30 Some interpreters end the quotation with verse 36.

3:8 The Holy Spirit is sovereign. He works as he pleases in his renewal of human hearts.

3:11 *testimony.* See note on 1:7.

3:13 *Son of Man.* Jesus' favorite self-designation (see notes on Mk 8:31; Lk 19:10).

3:14 *Moses lifted up the snake.* See notes on Nu 21:8–9; 2Ki 18:4. *the Son of Man must be lifted up.* See 8:28; 12:32 and note; see also TNIV text note.

3:15–16 *believes.* See note on 1:7. *eternal life.* Life in living fellowship with God—both now and forever.

3:16 *God so loved the world.* The great truth that motivated God's plan of salvation (cf. 1Jn 4:9–10). *world.* All people on earth—or perhaps all creation (see notes on 1:4,9). *gave his one and only Son.* Cf. Isa 9:6 ("a son is given," referring to the Messianic Son of David—who is also God's Son [see 2Sa 7:14 and note]). See also 1:14,18 and notes; cf. Ge 22:2,16; Ro 8:32 and notes. Although believers are also called "sons" of God (2Co 6:18; Gal 4:4–6), Jesus is God's Son in a unique sense (see 20:31 and note).

3:18 *believes…does not believe.* John is not speaking of momentary beliefs and doubts but of continuing, settled convictions. *name.* See 2:23 and note.

3:22 *baptized.* According to 4:2 only the disciples actually baptized.

3:23 *Aenon.* Possibly about eight miles south of Scythopolis (Beth Shan), west of the Jordan (see map, p. 1784).

3:24 See note on Lk 3:20.

3:25 *argument…over…ceremonial washing.* See 2:6 and note. The Dead Sea (Qumran) Scrolls (see essay, pp. 1595–1596) show that some Jews were deeply interested in the right way to achieve ceremonial purification.

3:26 *testified.* See note on 1:7. John's disciples knew that he had testified about Jesus, but they loved their master and were apparently envious of Jesus' success.

3:27 The words are true of both Jesus and John (and of everyone). Both had what God had given them, so there was no place for envy. *given.* The Greek verb is used 76 times in this Gospel, especially of the things the Father gives the Son.

3:29 *bridegroom.* The most important man at a wedding, referring here to Jesus. "The friend who attends the bridegroom" is there only to help him, which describes the role of John the Baptist. *full of joy.* Not because he was on center stage but because the bridegroom was there. John's joy was to hear of Jesus' success.

3:30 John the Baptist's pointed way of reaffirming his subordinate position.

3:31 *The one who comes from above.* Jesus, whose heavenly origin (see v. 13; 1Co 15:47) meant much to John. *the one who is from the earth.* A general expression that could apply to anyone, but here it particularly refers to John the Baptist.

all. ³²He testifies to what he has seen and heard, ᵛ but no one accepts his testimony. ʷ ³³The person who has accepted it has certified that God is truthful. ³⁴For the one whom God has sent ˣ speaks the words of God, for God ᵃ gives the Spirit ʸ without limit. ³⁵The Father loves the Son and has placed everything in his hands. ᶻ ³⁶Whoever believes in the Son has eternal life, ᵃ but whoever rejects the Son will not see life, for God's wrath remains on them.

JESUS TALKS WITH A SAMARITAN WOMAN

4 Now Jesus learned that the Pharisees had heard that he was gaining and baptizing more disciples than John ᵇ— ²although in fact it was not Jesus who baptized, but his disciples. ³So he left Judea ᶜ and went back once more to Galilee.

⁴Now he had to go through Samaria. ᵈ ⁵So he came to a town in Samaria called Sychar, near the plot of ground Jacob had given to his son Joseph. ᵉ ⁶Jacob's well was there, and Jesus, tired as he was from the journey, sat down by the well. It was about noon.

⁷When a Samaritan woman came to draw water, Jesus said to her, "Will you give me a drink?" ᶠ ⁸(His disciples had gone into the town ᵍ to buy food.)

⁹The Samaritan woman said to him, "You are a Jew and I am a Samaritan ʰ woman. How can you ask me for a drink?" (For Jews do not associate with Samaritans. ᵇ)

¹⁰Jesus answered her, "If you knew the gift of God and who it is that asks you for a drink, you would have asked him and he would have given you living water." ⁱ

¹¹"Sir," the woman said, "you have nothing to draw with and the well is deep. Where can you get this living water? ¹²Are you greater than our father Jacob, who gave us the well ʲ and drank from it himself, as did also his sons and his flocks and herds?"

¹³Jesus answered, "Everyone who drinks this water will be thirsty again, ¹⁴but those who drink the water I give them will never thirst. ᵏ Indeed, the water I give them will become in them a spring of water ˡ welling up to eternal life." ᵐ

¹⁵The woman said to him, "Sir, give me this water so that I won't get thirsty ⁿ and have to keep coming here to draw water."

¹⁶He told her, "Go, call your husband and come back."

¹⁷"I have no husband," she replied.

Jesus said to her, "You are right when you say you have no husband. ¹⁸The fact is, you

---

ᵃ 34 Greek *he*   ᵇ 9 Or *do not use dishes Samaritans have used*

3:32 *what he has seen and heard.* Jesus taught from divine experience. *no one.* Does not mean that no person accepted what he said (see v. 33) but that people in general refused his teaching.

3:33 *certified.* When people accept Christ's testimony, they accept the truth that Jesus came from heaven and that God was acting in him for the world's salvation. They thereby testify that God is truthful.

3:34 *the one whom God has sent.* Jesus. *without limit.* Some hold that it is only to Jesus that the Spirit is given without limit. Others take the "he" (see TNIV text note) as a reference to Christ's giving the Spirit without limit to believers.

3:36 *has.* Eternal life is a present possession, not something the believer will only obtain later (see note on v. 15). *God's wrath.* A strong expression, since God is actively opposed to everything evil. The word "wrath" occurs only here in John's Gospel (see note on Ro 1:18). *remains.* No one who persists in rejecting the Son of God as Savior and Lord can expect God's wrath eventually to fade away. God's opposition to evil is both total and permanent.

4:1 *Pharisees.* These religious leaders took a close interest in John the Baptist (see 1:24 and note) and then also in Jesus.

4:2 The disciples did not baptize without Jesus' approval (see 3:2 and note).

4:3 *left Judea.* Success (which aroused opposition; see note on 7:1—8:59), not failure, led Jesus to leave Judea.

4:4 *had to go.* Perhaps the necessity lay in Jesus' mission rather than in geography. *Samaria.* Here the whole region, not simply the city. Jews often avoided Samaria by crossing the Jordan and traveling on the east side (see notes on Mt 10:5; Lk 9:52).

4:5 *Sychar.* A small village near Shechem. Jacob bought some land in the vicinity of Shechem (Ge 33:18–19), and it was appar-

ently this land that he gave to Joseph (Ge 48:21–22). See map, p. 1784.

4:6 *Jacob's well.* Mentioned nowhere else in Scripture.

4:7 *to draw water.* People normally drew water at the end of the day rather than in the heat of midday (see Ge 24:11 and note). But the practice is attested by Josephus, who says that the young ladies whom Moses helped (Ex 2:15–17) came to draw water at noon.

4:9 *do not associate with.* The point of the TNIV text note (and probably of the text) is that Jews would become ceremonially unclean if they used a drinking vessel handled by a Samaritan, since they held that all Samaritans were "unclean."

4:10 *gift.* The Greek for this word is used only here in this Gospel and emphasizes God's grace through Christ. Jesus gave life and gave it freely. *living water.* Not stagnant cistern water but fresh, flowing water, as of a spring or mountain stream, that revives and refreshes life. In 7:38–39 the term is explained as referring to the Holy Spirit, but here it refers to that which produces eternal life (see v. 14).

4:11 *deep.* Christian pilgrim sources as early as the fourth century mention a well in this area that was about 100 feet deep. When the present well was cleaned out in 1935, it was found to be 138 feet deep.

4:12 *our father Jacob.* Deep regard for the past prevented her from seeing the great opportunity of the present.

4:14 *welling up.* The expression is a vigorous one, with a meaning like "leaping up." Jesus was speaking of vigorous, abundant life (cf. 10:10).

4:15 Cf. the misunderstanding of Nicodemus (3:4). In both cases the way was opened for further instruction.

3:32 ᵛ Jn 8:26; 15:15
ʷ ver 11
3:34 ˣ S ver 17
ʸ Isa 42:1; Mt 12:18;
Lk 4:18; Ac 10:38
3:35 ᶻ S Mt 28:18
3:36 ᵃ S ver 15;
Jn 5:24; 6:47
4:1 ᵇ Jn 3:22,26
4:3 ᶜ Jn 3:22
4:4 ᵈ S Mt 10:5
4:5 ᵉ Ge 33:19;
Jos 24:32
4:7 ᶠ Ge 24:17;
1Ki 17:10
4:8 ᵍ ver 5,39
4:9 ʰ S Mt 10:5
4:10 ⁱ Isa 44:3; 55:1;
Jer 2:13; 17:13;
Zec 14:8; Jn 7:37,38;
Rev 7:17; 21:6; 22:1,17
4:12 ʲ ver 6
4:14 ᵏ Jn 6:35
ˡ Isa 12:3; 58:11;
Jn 7:38 ᵐ Mt 25:46
4:15 ⁿ Jn 6:34

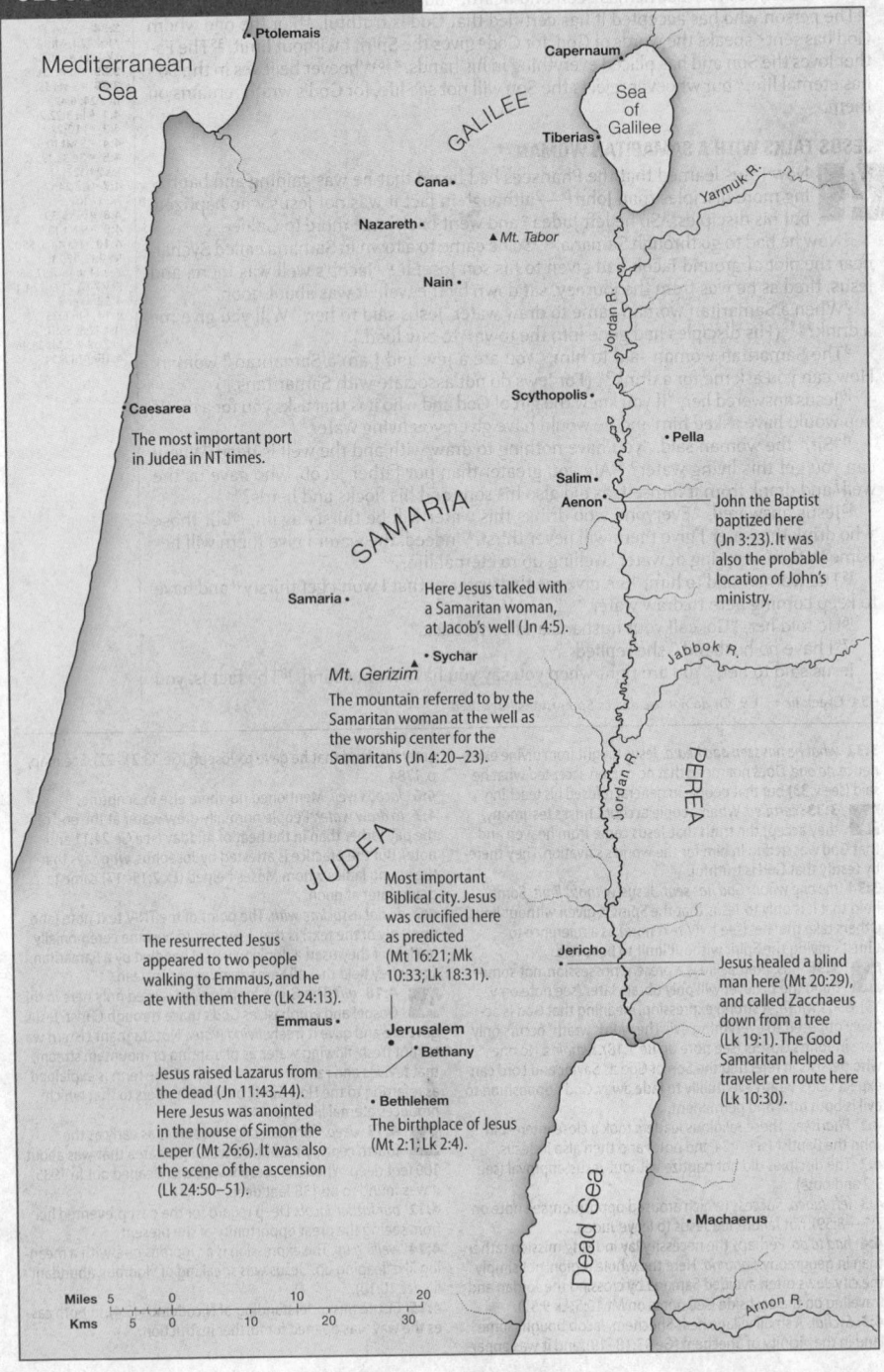

JESUS IN JUDEA AND SAMARIA

Mediterranean
Sea

Ptolemais

GALILEE

Capernaum

Sea
of
Galilee

Tiberias

Cana

Yarmuk R.

Nazareth

▲ Mt. Tabor

Nain

Jordan R.

Caesarea

**The most important port
in Judea in NT times.**

Scythopolis

Pella

SAMARIA

Salim

Aenon

John the Baptist
baptized here
(Jn 3:23). It was
also the probable
location of John's
ministry.

Samaria

**Here Jesus talked with
a Samaritan woman,
at Jacob's well (Jn 4:5).**

Sychar

Jabbok R.

Mt. Gerizim

**The mountain referred to by the
Samaritan woman at the well as
the worship center for the
Samaritans (Jn 4:20–23).**

PEREA

Jordan R.

JUDEA

**Most important
Biblical city. Jesus
was crucified here
as predicted
(Mt 16:21; Mk
10:33; Lk 18:31).**

Jericho

Jesus healed a blind
man here (Mt 20:29),
and called Zacchaeus
down from a tree
(Lk 19:1). The Good
Samaritan helped a
traveler en route here
(Lk 10:30).

**The resurrected Jesus
appeared to two people
walking to Emmaus, and he
ate with them there (Lk 24:13).**

Emmaus

Jerusalem

Bethany

**Jesus raised Lazarus from
the dead (Jn 11:43-44).
Here Jesus was anointed
in the house of Simon the
Leper (Mt 26:6). It was also
the scene of the ascension
(Lk 24:50–51).**

Bethlehem

**The birthplace of Jesus
(Mt 2:1; Lk 2:4).**

Dead Sea

Machaerus

Arnon R.

Miles 5 0 10 20

Kms 5 0 10 20 30

have had five husbands, and the man you now have is not your husband. What you have just said is quite true."

¹⁹"Sir," the woman said, "I can see that you are a prophet. ᵒ ²⁰Our ancestors worshiped on this mountain, ᵖ but you Jews claim that the place where we must worship is in Jerusalem." �q

²¹"Woman," ᵃ Jesus replied, "believe me, a time is coming ʳ when you will worship the Father neither on this mountain nor in Jerusalem. ˢ ²²You Samaritans worship what you do not know; ᵗ we worship what we do know, for salvation is from the Jews. ᵘ ²³Yet a time is coming and has now come ᵛ when the true worshipers will worship the Father in the Spirit ʷ and in truth, for they are the kind of worshipers the Father seeks. ²⁴God is spirit, ˣ and his worshipers must worship in the Spirit and in truth."

²⁵The woman said, "I know that Messiah" (called Christ) ʸ "is coming. When he comes, he will explain everything to us."

²⁶Then Jesus declared, "I, the one speaking to you—I am he." ᶻ

THE DISCIPLES REJOIN JESUS

²⁷Just then his disciples returned ᵃ and were surprised to find him talking with a woman. But no one asked, "What do you want?" or "Why are you talking with her?"

²⁸Then, leaving her water jar, the woman went back to the town and said to the people, ²⁹"Come, see a man who told me everything I ever did. ᵇ Could this be the Messiah?" ᶜ ³⁰They came out of the town and made their way toward him.

³¹Meanwhile his disciples urged him, "Rabbi, ᵈ eat something."

³²But he said to them, "I have food to eat ᵉ that you know nothing about."

³³Then his disciples said to each other, "Could someone have brought him food?"

³⁴"My food," said Jesus, "is to do the will ᶠ of him who sent me and to finish his work. ᵍ ³⁵Don't you have a saying, 'It's still four months until harvest'? I tell you, open your eyes and look at the fields! They are ripe for harvest. ʰ ³⁶Even now those who reap draw their wages, even now they harvest ⁱ the crop for eternal life, ʲ so that the sower and the reaper

ᵃ 21 The Greek for *Woman* does not denote any disrespect.

4:19 ᵒ S Mt 21:11
4:20 ᵖ Dt 11:29;
Jos 8:33 q Lk 9:53
4:21 ʳ Jn 5:28; 16:2
ˢ Mal 1:11; 1Ti 2:8
4:22 ᵗ 2Ki 17:28-41
ᵘ Isa 2:3; Ro 3:1,2;
9:4,5; 15:8,9
4:23 ᵛ Jn 5:25; 16:32
ʷ Php 3:3
4:24 ˣ Php 3:3
4:25 ʸ Mt 1:16;
Jn 1:41
4:26 ᶻ Jn 8:24; 9:35-37
4:27 ᵃ ver 8
4:29 ᵇ ver 17,18
ᶜ Mt 12:23; Jn 7:26,31
4:31 ᵈ S Mt 23:7
4:32 ᵉ Job 23:12;
Mt 4:4; Jn 6:27
4:34 ᶠ S Mt 26:39
ᵍ S Jn 19:30
4:35 ʰ Mt 9:37;
Lk 10:2
4:36 ⁱ Ro 1:13
ʲ S Mt 25:46

4:18 *five husbands.* The Jews held that a woman might be divorced twice or at the most three times. If the Samaritans had the same standard, the woman's life had been exceedingly immoral. Apparently she had not married her present partner.

4:19 *you are a prophet.* Because of his special insight.

4:20 *this mountain.* Perhaps the woman did not like the way the conversation was going and so began to argue. The proper place of worship had long been a source of debate between Jews and Samaritans. Samaritans held that "this mountain" (Mount Gerizim) was especially sacred. Abraham and Jacob had built altars in the general vicinity (Ge 12:6–7; 33:18–20), and the people had been blessed from this mountain (Dt 11:29; 27:12). In the Samaritan Scriptures, Mount Gerizim (rather than Mount Ebal) was the mountain on which Moses had commanded an altar to be built (Dt 27:4–6). The Samaritans had built a temple on Mount Gerizim c. 400 B.C., which the Jews destroyed c. 128. Both actions, of course, increased hostility between the two groups. See map, p. 1784.

4:22 *worship what you do not know.* The Samaritan Bible contained only the Pentateuch. Samaritans worshiped the true God, but their failure to accept much of his revelation meant that they knew little about him. *salvation is from the Jews.* The Messiah would come from God's historic people (see notes on Ro 1:16; 11:18).

A **4:24** *God is spirit ... worship in the Spirit and in truth.* The place of worship is irrelevant, because true worship must be in keeping with God's nature, which is spirit. "True worshipers" (v. 23) must worship God in the power (enablement) of his Spirit and in accordance with truth. In John's Gospel truth is associated with Christ (see notes on 1:14; 14:6), a fact that has great importance for the proper understanding of Christian worship.

4:25 *Messiah ... will explain everything.* The woman's last attempt to evade the issue. The matter was too important, she reasoned, for people like Jesus and herself to work out. Understanding would have to await the coming of the Messiah (see note on 1:25). The Samaritans expected a Messiah, but their rejection of all the inspired writings after the Pentateuch meant that they knew little about him. They thought of him mainly as a teacher.

4:26 *I am he.* The only occasion before his trial on which Jesus specifically said that he was the Messiah (but see Mk 9:41, "Messiah"). The term did not have the political overtones in Samaria that it had in Judea, which may be part of the reason Jesus used the designation here.

4:27 *were surprised.* Jewish religious teachers rarely spoke with women in public.

4:29 *everything I ever did.* An exaggeration, but it shows the impression Jesus made on her. *Could this be the Messiah?* Her question seems full of longing, as though she did not expect them to say "Yes," but she could not say "No."

4:32 Cf. Mt 4:4 and note.

4:33 A misunderstanding similar to that of the woman (see v. 15 and note).

A **4:34** *My food ... is to do the will of him who sent me.* John often mentions that Jesus depended on the Father and did the work the Father sent him to do (see, e.g., 5:30 and note; 6:38; 8:26; 9:4; 10:37–38; 12:50 and note; 14:31 and note; 15:10; 17:4).

4:35 *four months until harvest.* Apparently a proverb that meant something like "Harvest cannot be rushed." But, while the crops must take their time ripening, in the fields that Jesus referred to the harvest is already ripe (cf. Mt 9:36–38).

A **4:36** *draw their wages.* The work, or at least part of it, had been done, and others were working hard. The disciples were not to think that the harvest was far off. Jesus was not speaking of grain but of "the crop for eternal life." There was urgency, for the crop would not wait. *glad together.* There is no competition among Christ's faithful servants, and sower and reaper share in the joy of the crop.

4:37 *k* Job 31:8;
Mic 6:15
4:39 *l* ver 5 *m* ver 29
4:42 *n* S Lk 2:11
4:43 *o* ver 40
4:44 *p* Mt 13:57;
Lk 4:24
4:45 *q* Jn 2:23
4:46 *r* Jn 2:1-11
4:47 *s* ver 3,54
4:48 *t* Da 4:2,3;
S Jn 2:11; Ac 2:43;
14:3; Ro 15:19;
2Co 12:12; Heb 2:4
4:53 *u* S Ac 11:14
4:54 *v* S ver 48;
S Jn 2:11
5:2 *w* Ne 3:1; 12:39
x Jn 19:13,17,20;
20:16; Ac 21:40; 22:2;
26:14

may be glad together. ³⁷Thus the saying 'One sows and another reaps'*k* is true. ³⁸I sent you to reap what you have not worked for. Others have done the hard work, and you have reaped the benefits of their labor."

MANY SAMARITANS BELIEVE

³⁹Many of the Samaritans from that town*l* believed in him because of the woman's testimony, "He told me everything I ever did."*m* ⁴⁰So when the Samaritans came to him, they urged him to stay with them, and he stayed two days. ⁴¹And because of his words many more became believers.

⁴²They said to the woman, "We no longer believe just because of what you said; now we have heard for ourselves, and we know that this man really is the Savior of the world."*n*

JESUS HEALS THE OFFICIAL'S SON

⁴³After the two days*o* he left for Galilee. ⁴⁴(Now Jesus himself had pointed out that prophets have no honor in their own country.)*p* ⁴⁵When he arrived in Galilee, the Galileans welcomed him. They had seen all that he had done in Jerusalem at the Passover Festival,*q* for they also had been there.

⁴⁶Once more he visited Cana in Galilee, where he had turned the water into wine.*r* And there was a certain royal official whose son lay sick at Capernaum. ⁴⁷When this man heard that Jesus had arrived in Galilee from Judea,*s* he went to him and begged him to come and heal his son, who was close to death.

⁴⁸"Unless you people see signs and wonders,"*t* Jesus told him, "you will never believe."
⁴⁹The royal official said, "Sir, come down before my child dies."
⁵⁰"Go," Jesus replied, "your son will live."

The man took Jesus at his word and departed. ⁵¹While he was still on the way, his servants met him with the news that his boy was living. ⁵²When he inquired as to the time when his son got better, they said to him, "Yesterday, at one in the afternoon, the fever left him."

⁵³Then the father realized that this was the exact time at which Jesus had said to him, "Your son will live." So he and his whole household*u* believed.

⁵⁴This was the second sign*v* Jesus performed after coming from Judea to Galilee.

THE HEALING AT THE POOL

5 Some time later, Jesus went up to Jerusalem for one of the Jewish festivals. ²Now there is in Jerusalem near the Sheep Gate*w* a pool, which in Aramaic*x* is called Bethesda*a* and which is surrounded by five covered colonnades. ³[⁴]Here a great number of disabled people used to lie—the blind, the lame, the paralyzed.*b* ⁵One who

---

a 2 Some manuscripts *Bethzatha;* other manuscripts *Bethsaida*   *b 3* Some later manuscripts and some ancient witnesses, wholly or in part, *paralyzed—and they waited for the moving of the waters. ⁴From time to time an angel of the Lord would come down and stir up the waters. The first person into the pool after each such disturbance would be cured of whatever disease they had.*

4:37 See 1Co 3:6–9.
4:38 *Others.* May refer to John the Baptist and his supporters, on whose work the apostles would build. Or perhaps Jesus was looking further back, to the prophets and other godly people of old. Either way, he expected the apostles to be reapers as well as sowers.
4:39 *that town.* Sychar (v. 5).

4:42 *the Savior of the world.* In the NT the expression occurs only here and in 1Jn 4:14. It points to the facts (1) that Jesus not only teaches but also saves and (2) that his salvation extends to the world (see note on 3:16).
4:44 *prophets have no honor in their own country.* Nonetheless, Jesus went to Galilee, because he came to die for our salvation (cf. 1:29 and note).

4:45 *welcomed him.* The welcome of the Galileans actually was a kind of rejection, for they were interested only in Jesus' miracles. They were not welcoming the Messiah who could save them, but only a miracle worker who could amaze them. *all that he had done.* See 20:30 and note. *Passover Festival.* The one narrated in 2:13–25.
4:46 *royal official.* Evidently an officer in Herod's service.
4:48 *Unless you . . . see signs and wonders . . . you will never believe.* The general attitude of Galileans, not that of the official.
4:50 *your son will live.* Not simply a prophecy, but words of

power. Jesus was healing, not forecasting a happy ending (see vv. 51,53).
4:53 *believed.* Cf. the aim of this Gospel (see 20:31 and note; see also Introduction: Purpose and Emphases).
4:54 *second sign.* This was the second time Jesus performed a sign after coming from Judea to Galilee (see 2:11 and note; see also chart, p. 1780).
5:1 *one of the Jewish festivals.* Probably Passover, Pentecost or Tabernacles. The identity of this festival is significant for the attempt to ascertain the number of Passovers included in Jesus' ministry, and thus the number of years his ministry lasted. John explicitly mentions at least three different Passovers: the first in 2:13,23 (see note on 2:13), the second in 6:4 and the third several times (e.g., in 11:55; 12:1), suggesting a public ministry lasting between two and three years. However, if the festival of 5:1 was a fourth Passover or assumes that a fourth Passover had come and gone, Jesus' ministry would have lasted between three and four years.

5:2 *there is.* Use of the present tense may mean that the pool was still in existence and that John wrote his Gospel before the destruction of Jerusalem. However, see Introduction: Date. *Bethesda.* The manuscripts have a variety of names (see TNIV text note), but one of the Dead Sea Scrolls seems to show was there had been an invalid for thirty-eight years. ⁶When Jesus saw him lying there and learned that he had been in this condition for a long time, he asked him, "Do you want to get well?"

⁷"Sir," the invalid replied, "I have no one to help me into the pool when the water is stirred. While I am trying to get in, someone else goes down ahead of me."

⁸Then Jesus said to him, "Get up! Pick up your mat and walk." ^y ⁹At once the man was cured; he picked up his mat and walked.

The day on which this took place was a Sabbath, ^z ¹⁰and so the Jewish leaders ^a said to the man who had been healed, "It is the Sabbath; the law forbids you to carry your mat." ^b

¹¹But he replied, "The man who made me well said to me, 'Pick up your mat and walk.' "

¹²So they asked him, "Who is this fellow who told you to pick it up and walk?"

¹³The man who was healed had no idea who it was, for Jesus had slipped away into the crowd that was there.

¹⁴Later Jesus found him at the temple and said to him, "See, you are well again. Stop sinning ^c or something worse may happen to you." ¹⁵The man went away and told the Jewish leaders ^d that it was Jesus who had made him well.

THE AUTHORITY OF THE SON

¹⁶So, because Jesus was doing these things on the Sabbath, the Jewish leaders began to persecute him. ¹⁷In his defense Jesus said to them, "My Father ^e is always at his work ^f to this very day, and I too am working." ¹⁸For this reason they tried all the more to kill him; ^g not only was he breaking the Sabbath, but he was even calling God his own Father, making himself equal with God. ^h

¹⁹Jesus gave them this answer: "Very truly I tell you, the Son can do nothing by himself; ⁱ he can do only what he sees his Father doing, because whatever the Father does the Son also does. ²⁰For the Father loves the Son ^j and shows him all he does. Yes, and he will show him even greater works than these, ^k so that you will be amazed. ²¹For just as the Father raises the dead and gives them life, ^l even so the Son gives life ^m to whom he is pleased to give it. ²²Moreover, the Father judges no one, but has entrusted all judgment to the Son, ⁿ ²³that all may honor the Son just as they honor the Father. Whoever does not honor the Son does not honor the Father, who sent him. ^o

5:8 *y* Mt 9:5,6
5:9 *z* Mt 12:1-14; Jn 9:14
5:10 *a* ver 16
b Ne 13:15-22; Jer 17:21; S Mt 12:2
5:14 *c* Mk 2:5; Jn 8:11
5:15 *d* S Jn 1:19
5:17 *e* Lk 2:49
f Jn 9:4; 14:10
5:18 *g* S Mt 12:14
h Jn 10:30,33; 19:7
5:19 *i* ver 30; S Jn 14:24
5:20 *j* Jn 3:35
k Jn 14:12
5:21 *l* Ro 4:17; 8:11; 2Co 1:9; Heb 11:19
m Jn 11:25
5:22 *n* ver 27; Ge 18:25; Jdg 11:27; Jn 9:39; S Ac 10:42
5:23 *o* Lk 10:16; S 1Jn 2:23

that Bethesda is the right name. The site is generally identified with the twin pools near the present-day Saint Anne's Church. There would have been a colonnade on each of the four sides and another between the two pools.

5:4 See TNIV text note on v. 3.

5:6 *Do you want to get well?* The man had not asked Jesus for help.

5:7 *when the water is stirred.* The man did not see Jesus as a potential healer, and his mind was set on the supposed curative powers of the water.

5:9 *the man was cured.* Ordinarily, faith in Jesus was essential to the cure (e.g., Mk 5:34), but here the man did not even know who Jesus was (v. 13). So while Jesus usually healed in response to faith, he was not limited by a person's lack of it.

5:10 *the law forbids you to carry your mat.* It was not the law of Moses itself but their traditional interpretation of it that prohibited carrying loads of any kind on the Sabbath. The Jews had very strict regulations on keeping the Sabbath but also had many curious loopholes that their lawyers made full use of (cf. Mt 23:4). It is always lawful to do good and to save life—including on the Sabbath (see v. 17; 7:23; Lk 6:9; 13:15; 14:5 and notes).

5:12 *this fellow.* The Jews were contrasting the authority of the law of God, which in their view prohibited the action, and that of a mere man (as they considered Jesus to be) who permitted it.

5:14 *Stop sinning.* Implies that the man's sins had caused his disability. In 9:1 Jesus repudiates the idea that disabilities (such as blindness there) are always caused by sin, but he does not say they are never caused by sin. *something worse.* The eternal consequences of sin are more serious than any physical ailment.

5:16 *was doing.* The continuous action points to more than one incident, and the Jews (see note on 1:19) apparently dis-

cerned a pattern. *began to persecute him.* John does not tell us what form the persecution took.

5:17 *My Father is always at his work.* Jesus' justification for his action was his close relation to his Father. The Jews did not refer to God as "My Father," regarding the term as too intimate—though they might have used "Our Father" or, in prayer, "My Father in heaven." Jesus also exemplified the way the Sabbath should be observed. God does not stop his deeds of compassion on that day, and neither did Jesus.

5:18 *his own Father.* Referring to a special relationship. The Jews did not object to the idea that God is the Father of all, but they strongly objected to Jesus' claim that he stood in a special relationship to the Father—a relationship so close as to make himself equal with God.

5:19 *can do nothing by himself.* Because of who and what he was, it was not possible for Jesus to act except in dependence on the Father (see 4:34 and note).

5:20 *the Father loves the Son.* Therefore the Father revealed to the Son his plans and purposes, and the Son obediently carried them out (see 17:4). *greater works.* The Son's activities in raising the dead and judging (see following verses).

5:21 *the Father raises the dead.* A firm belief among the Jews (except the Sadducees; see p. 1596). They also held that he did not give this privilege to anyone else. Jesus claimed a prerogative that, according to his opponents, belonged only to God. *the Son gives life.* Probably refers to Christ's gift of abundant life here and now (10:10), though possibly also to the future resurrection (see 11:25 and note).

5:22 *entrusted all judgment to the Son.* The Jews believed that the Father is Judge of the world, so this teaching seemed heretical to them. For other NT assertions that Jesus will be the eschatological Judge, see Mt 25:31–33; Ac 10:42; 17:31; 2Co 5:10; 2Ti 4:1; 1Pe 4:5 and note.

5:24 *P* S Mt 10:40;
S Jn 3:15; S 3:17
q S Mt 25:46 *r* Jn 3:18
s 1Jn 3:14
5:25 *t* Jn 4:23; 16:32
u Jn 8:43, 47
5:26 *v* Dt 30:20;
Job 10:12; 33:4;
Ps 36:9; S Jn 1:4
5:27 *w* S ver 22
5:28 *x* Jn 4:21; 16:2
5:29 *y* S Mt 25:46
5:30 *z* ver 19
a Isa 28:6; Jn 8:16
b S Mt 26:39
5:31 *c* Jn 8:14
5:32 *d* ver 37;
Jn 8:18
5:33 *e* S Jn 1:7
5:34 *f* 1Jn 5:9
g Ac 16:30, 31;
Eph 2:8; Tit 3:5
5:35 *h* Da 12:3;
2Pe 1:19
5:36 *i* 1Jn 5:9
j Jn 14:11; 15:24
k S Jn 3:17
5:37 *l* Jn 8:18
m Dt 4:12; 1Ti 1:17;
S Jn 1:18
5:38 *n* 1Jn 1:10; 2:14
o Isa 26:10 *p* S Jn 3:17
5:39 *q* Ro 2:17, 18
r S Mt 25:46
s S Lk 24:27, 44;
Ac 13:27
5:40 *t* Jn 6:44
5:41 *u* ver 44

²⁴"Very truly I tell you, whoever hears my word and believes him who sent me *p* has eternal life *q* and will not be judged *r* but has crossed over from death to life. *s* ²⁵Very truly I tell you, a time is coming and has now come *t* when the dead will hear *u* the voice of the Son of God and those who hear will live. ²⁶For as the Father has life in himself, so he has granted the Son also to have life *v* in himself. ²⁷And he has given him authority to judge *w* because he is the Son of Man.

²⁸"Do not be amazed at this, for a time is coming *x* when all who are in their graves will hear his voice ²⁹and come out—those who have done what is good will rise to live, and those who have done what is evil will rise to be condemned. *y* ³⁰By myself I can do nothing; *z* I judge only as I hear, and my judgment is just, *a* for I seek not to please myself but him who sent me. *b*

TESTIMONIES ABOUT JESUS

³¹"If I testify about myself, my testimony is not true. *c* ³²There is another who testifies in my favor, *d* and I know that his testimony about me is true.

³³"You have sent to John and he has testified *e* to the truth. ³⁴Not that I accept human testimony; *f* but I mention it that you may be saved. *g* ³⁵John was a lamp that burned and gave light, *h* and you chose for a time to enjoy his light.

³⁶"I have testimony weightier than that of John. *i* For the works that the Father has given me to finish—the very works that I am doing *j*—testify that the Father has sent me. *k* ³⁷And the Father who sent me has himself testified concerning me. *l* You have never heard his voice nor seen his form, *m* ³⁸nor does his word dwell in you, *n* for you do not believe *o* the one he sent. *p* ³⁹You study *a* the Scriptures *q* diligently because you think that in them you possess eternal life. *r* These are the very Scriptures that testify about me, *s* ⁴⁰yet you refuse to come to me *t* to have life.

⁴¹"I do not accept glory from human beings, *u* ⁴²but I know you. I know that you do not have the love of God in your hearts. ⁴³I have come in my Father's name, and you do not

---

a 39 Or ³⁹Study

5:24 *believes him … has eternal life.* Faith and life are connected (see 20:31 and note). *has eternal life.* A present possession (see notes on 3:15,36). *has crossed.* The decisive action has taken place, and the believer no longer belongs to the realm where death reigns supreme but to the realm of life.

5:25 *is coming and has now come.* A reference not only to the future resurrection but also to the fact that Christ gives life now. The spiritually dead who hear him receive life from him.

5:26 *has life in himself.* Must be understood against the background of the OT, where life is spoken of as belonging to God and as being his gift (see Dt 30:20 and note; Job 10:12; 33:4; Ps 16:11; 27:1; 36:9 and note). The Son has been given the same kind of life the Father possesses.

5:27 *authority to judge.* Granted to the Son by the Father (see v. 22 and note). *Son of Man.* See note on 1:51.

5:28–29 See Da 12:2 and note.

5:29 *done what is good … live … done what is evil … condemned.* As always in Scripture, judgment is based on what people have done in their lives (see Ro 2:6–8; Rev 20:12 and notes). Salvation, of course, is a gift from God in response to faith (see v. 24 and note), but true faith in Christ results in changed lives, lived in obedience to Christ as Lord (see Jas 2:14–26 and note).

5:30 *By myself I can do nothing.* Jesus stresses his dependence on the Father (see note on v. 19). He judges only as he hears from the Father, which makes his judgment fair.

5:31–47 This section stresses the testimonies (see note on 1:7) of John the Baptist (v. 33), of the works of Jesus (v. 36), of God the Father (v. 37), of the Scriptures (v. 39) and of Moses (v. 46).

5:31 Jesus' testimony about himself required the support of all God's revelation. Otherwise, it would have been unacceptable.

5:32 *another.* The Father testifies concerning the Son. The Jews might not accept this testimony, but it was the testimony that mattered most.

5:33 *You have sent to John.* A reference to the delegation from the Jewish leaders to John the Baptist (see 1:19 and note). *he*

has testified. The testimony of John was important, though not, of course, equal to the testimony of the Father. But if the Jews had believed John, they would have believed Christ and would have been saved.

5:34 *Not that I accept human testimony.* Probably meaning that he does not rely on human testimony—which is always fallible and often fickle (1Jn 5:9).

5:35 *John was.* The past tense may indicate that John was dead or at least imprisoned. In any case, his work was done. *burned and gave light.* John's giving light was costly to him. *for a time.* The Jewish leaders never came to grips with John's message, and their responses to him were always at best tentative and superficial.

5:36 *works.* The miracles of Jesus, which testified to what he is and to his divine mission (see 10:25 and note).

5:37 *the Father … himself testified … his voice.* Probably a reference to God's voice in the Scriptures (see vv. 38–39). God had also given his voice of approval at Jesus' baptism (see Mt 3:17 and note). *nor seen his form.* Probably refers to their lack of spiritual perception of who Jesus really is.

5:38 *you do not believe.* The Jews did not recognize what God was saying, as their failure to believe Jesus shows.

5:39 *You study the Scriptures diligently.* The Jewish leaders studied Scripture in minute detail. Despite their reverence for the very letter of Scripture (see notes on Mt 5:18–21), they did not recognize the one to whom Scripture bears supreme testimony.

5:41 Jesus did not accept the kind of human praise that his opponents prized (v. 44).

5:42 *love of God.* May mean God's love for them or theirs for God. Probably it is the latter.

5:43–44 The Jews whom Jesus was addressing had their attention firmly fixed on people. Their emphasis on self-seeking and on human praise showed that they did not accept the one who came from God, and therefore they missed the praise that comes from God.

accept me; but if someone else comes in his own name, you will accept him. ⁴⁴How can you believe since you accept glory from one another but do not seek the glory that comes from the only God? ᵃ ˅

⁴⁵"But do not think I will accuse you before the Father. Your accuser is Moses, ʷ on whom your hopes are set. ˣ ⁴⁶If you believed Moses, you would believe me, for he wrote about me. ʸ ⁴⁷But since you do not believe what he wrote, how are you going to believe what I say?" ᶻ

JESUS FEEDS THE FIVE THOUSAND
6:1–13pp — Mt 14:13–21; Mk 6:32–44; Lk 9:10–17

6 Some time after this, Jesus crossed to the far shore of the Sea of Galilee (that is, the Sea of Tiberias), ²and a great crowd of people followed him because they saw the signs ᵃ he had performed by healing the sick. ³Then Jesus went up on a mountainside ᵇ and sat down with his disciples. ⁴The Jewish Passover Festival ᶜ was near.

⁵When Jesus looked up and saw a great crowd coming toward him, he said to Philip, ᵈ "Where shall we buy bread for these people to eat?" ⁶He asked this only to test him, for he already had in mind what he was going to do.

⁷Philip answered him, "It would take almost a year's wages ᵇ to buy enough bread for each one to have a bite!"

⁸Another of his disciples, Andrew, Simon Peter's brother, ᵉ spoke up, ⁹"Here is a boy with five small barley loaves and two small fish, but how far will they go among so many?" ᶠ

¹⁰Jesus said, "Have the people sit down." There was plenty of grass in that place, and they sat down (about five thousand men were there). ¹¹Jesus then took the loaves, gave thanks, ᵍ and distributed to those who were seated as much as they wanted. He did the same with the fish.

¹²When they had all had enough to eat, he said to his disciples, "Gather the pieces that are left over. Let nothing be wasted." ¹³So they gathered them and filled twelve baskets with the pieces of the five barley loaves left over by those who had eaten.

¹⁴After the people saw the sign ʰ Jesus performed, they began to say, "Surely this is the Prophet who is to come into the world." ⁱ ¹⁵Jesus, knowing that they intended to come and make him king ʲ by force, withdrew again to a mountain by himself. ᵏ

JESUS WALKS ON THE WATER
6:16–21pp — Mt 14:22–33; Mk 6:47–51

¹⁶When evening came, his disciples went down to the lake, ¹⁷where they got into a boat and set off across the lake for Capernaum. By now it was dark, and Jesus had not yet joined them. ¹⁸A strong wind was blowing and the waters grew rough. ¹⁹When they had rowed

---

ᵃ 44 Some early manuscripts *the Only One* ᵇ 7 Greek *take two hundred denarii*

**Cross references (right margin):**

5:44 ˅ S Ro 2:29
5:45 ʷ Jn 9:28
ˣ Ro 2:17
5:46 ʸ Ge 3:15;
S Lk 24:27,44;
Ac 26:22
5:47 ᶻ Lk 16:29,31
6:2 ᵃ S Jn 2:11
6:3 ᵇ ver 15
6:4 ᶜ S Jn 11:55
6:5 ᵈ S Jn 1:43
6:8 ᵉ Jn 1:40
6:9 ᶠ 2Ki 4:43
6:11 ᵍ ver 23;
S Mt 14:19
6:14 ʰ S Jn 2:11
ⁱ Dt 18:15,18; Mt 11:3;
S 21:11
6:15 ʲ Jn 18:36
ᵏ Mt 14:23; Mk 6:46

5:43 *if someone else ... you will accept him.* See note on Zec 11:17.

5:45–47 The revelation God gave Moses is inseparable from the revelation God was giving through Jesus (see Lk 16:31; Ro 10:4 and note). Those who refused to believe the witness to Jesus in the earlier revelation would also reject the later revelation coming through him. To their surprise, he declared that his listeners had refused to believe both and should therefore be accused before God by Moses.

5:46 *he wrote about me.* The authors of the NT books sometimes expressly stressed and everywhere assumed that the OT, rightly read, pervasively points to Christ (see Lk 24:25–27,44 and note). Here Jesus applies this truth specifically to the writings traditionally ascribed to Moses. He may have had Dt 18:15,18 especially in mind but probably was thinking more broadly of the whole scope of what the Pentateuch disclosed concerning God's saving program in history, which Jesus the Messiah came to complete.

6:1–15 The feeding of the 5,000 is the one miracle, apart from the resurrection, found in all four Gospels. It shows Jesus as the supplier of human need and also sets the stage for his testimony that he is the bread of life (v. 35).

6:1 *far shore.* The northeast shore, probably near Bethsaida (see Lk 9:10 and map, p. 1791). *Sea of Tiberias.* Probably the offi-

cial Roman name of the Sea of Galilee (see note on Mk 1:16). The name came from the town of Tiberias (named after the emperor Tiberius), founded c. A.D. 20.

6:2 *signs.* See note on 2:11.

6:4 *Passover.* See notes on 2:13; 5:1.

6:5 *Philip.* Since he came from nearby Bethsaida (see 1:44 and note), it was appropriate to ask him.

6:9 *barley loaves.* Cheap bread, the food of the poor.

6:10 *about five thousand men.* Women and children were not included in this number (see Mt 14:21 and note).

6:12 *Gather the pieces.* See note on Mk 6:43.

6:13 *twelve baskets ... left over.* There was abundant supply (see note on Mk 6:43).

6:14 *sign ... Prophet.* It pointed people to the Son of Man and the food for eternal life that he gives (see v. 27 and note), but they thought only of the Prophet, i.e., the prophet of Dt 18:15,18 who would be like Moses (see 1:21 and note). Through Moses God had provided food and water for the people in the wilderness, and they expected the Prophet to do more than this.

6:15 *make him king by force.* Jesus rejected the widely held Jewish view of the Messiah's kingship (cf. notes on 18:36; Lk 24:21).

6:19 *l* Job 9:8
6:20 *m* S Mt 14:27
6:22 *n* ver 2
o ver 15-21
6:23 *p* ver 1 *q* ver 11
6:25 *r* S Mt 23:7
6:26 *s* ver 24
t ver 30; S Jn 2:11
6:27 *u* Isa 55:2
v ver 54; S Mt 25:46
w S Mt 8:20 *x* Ro 4:11;
1Co 9:2; 2Co 1:22;
Eph 1:13; 4:30;
2Ti 2:19; Rev 7:3
6:29 *y* 1Jn 3:23
z S Jn 3:17
6:30 *a* S Jn 2:11
b S Mt 12:38
6:31 *c* Nu 11:7-9
d Ex 16:4,15; Ne 9:15;
Ps 78:24; 105:40
6:33 *e* ver 50;
Jn 3:13,31
6:34 *f* Jn 4:15
6:35 *g* Ex 3:14;
Jn 8:12; 10:7,11; 11:25;
14:6; 15:1 *h* ver 48,51
i S Jn 3:15 *j* Jn 4:14
6:37 *k* ver 39;
Jn 17:2,6,9,24
6:38 *l* Jn 3:13,31
m S Mt 26:39
n S Jn 3:17
6:39 *o* Isa 27:3;
Jer 23:4; Jn 10:28;
17:12; 18:9

about three or three and a half miles, [a] they saw Jesus approaching the boat, walking on the water; [l] and they were frightened. 20But he said to them, "It is I; don't be afraid." [m] 21Then they were willing to take him into the boat, and immediately the boat reached the shore where they were heading.

22The next day the crowd that had stayed on the opposite shore of the lake [n] realized that only one boat had been there, and that Jesus had not entered it with his disciples, but that they had gone away alone. [o] 23Then some boats from Tiberias [p] landed near the place where the people had eaten the bread after the Lord had given thanks. [q] 24Once the crowd realized that neither Jesus nor his disciples were there, they got into the boats and went to Capernaum in search of Jesus.

JESUS THE BREAD OF LIFE

25When they found him on the other side of the lake, they asked him, "Rabbi, [r] when did you get here?"

26Jesus answered, "Very truly I tell you, you are looking for me, [s] not because you saw the signs [t] I performed but because you ate the loaves and had your fill. 27Do not work for food that spoils, but for food that endures [u] to eternal life, [v] which the Son of Man [w] will give you. On him God the Father has placed his seal [x] of approval."

28Then they asked him, "What must we do to do the works God requires?"

29Jesus answered, "The work of God is this: to believe [y] in the one he has sent." [z]

30So they asked him, "What sign [a] then will you give that we may see it and believe you? [b] What will you do? 31Our ancestors ate the manna [c] in the wilderness; as it is written: 'He gave them bread from heaven to eat.' [b] [d]

32Jesus said to them, "Very truly I tell you, it is not Moses who has given you the bread from heaven, but it is my Father who gives you the true bread from heaven. 33For the bread of God is the bread that comes down from heaven [e] and gives life to the world."

34"Sir," they said, "always give us this bread." [f]

35Then Jesus declared, "I am [g] the bread of life. [h] Whoever comes to me will never go hungry, and whoever believes [i] in me will never be thirsty. [j] 36But as I told you, you have seen me and still you do not believe. 37All whom the Father gives me [k] will come to me, and whoever comes to me I will never drive away. 38For I have come down from heaven [l] not to do my will but to do the will [m] of him who sent me. [n] 39And this is the will of him who sent me, that I shall lose none of all those he has given me, [o] but raise them up at the

---

a 19 Or about 5 or 6 kilometers   b 31 Exodus 16:4; Neh. 9:15; Psalm 78:24,25

6:19 *three or three and a half miles.* Mark says they were "in the middle of the lake" (Mk 6:47). *frightened.* They thought they were seeing a ghost (Mt 14:26).

6:21 *immediately the boat reached the shore.* Some think that this was another miracle. In any event, the boat's safe arrival is implicitly credited to Jesus.

6:22–24 The crowd could not figure out what had happened to Jesus. But they wanted to see him again, so they looked for him in the most likely place, Capernaum (see note on 2:12).

6:27 *eternal life.* Not something to be achieved but to be received by faith in Christ (see vv. 28–29; 3:15 and notes). *Son of Man.* See note on Mk 8:31. Submission of the Son to the Father is one of John's major themes (see note on 4:34).

6:28 *What must we do . . . ?* They missed the point that eternal life was Christ's gift and were thinking in terms of achieving it by pious works (see Eph 2:8–9; Tit 3:5 and notes).

6:29 *work of God.* Believing in Jesus Christ is the indispensable "work" God calls for—the one that leads to eternal life (see 9:4 and note).

6:30 *What will you do?* They seek from Jesus a sign greater than the gift of manna that had accompanied Moses' ministry.

6:31 *manna.* A popular Jewish expectation was that when the Messiah came he would renew the sending of manna. The crowd probably reasoned that Jesus had done little compared to Moses. He had fed 5,000; Moses had fed a nation. He did it once; Moses did it for 40 years. He gave ordinary bread (see note on v. 1–15; see also note on v. 14); Moses gave "bread from heaven" (see notes on Ex 16:4; Nu 11:7).

6:32 Jesus corrected them, pointing out that the manna in the wilderness did not come from Moses but from God

and that the Father still "gives" (the present tense is important) the true bread from heaven (life through the Son).

6:33 *bread of God.* Jesus moved the discussion to something (and Someone) much more important than manna. *bread that comes down from heaven.* This affirmation is repeated six times in this context (here and in vv. 38,41,50–51,58), emphasizing Jesus' divine origin.

6:34 *this bread.* Probably another misunderstanding, like that by the woman at the well (see 4:15 and note; cf. also Nicodemus, 3:4). Their minds ran along materialistic lines.

6:35 *I am.* The first of seven (the number of completeness and perfection) self-descriptions of Jesus introduced by "I am" (see 8:12; [9:5;] 10:7,9; 10:11,14; 11:25; 14:6; 15:1,5). In the Greek the words are solemnly emphatic and echo Ex 3:14 (see notes on Ex 3:12–15). Cf. note on 2:11. *the bread of life.* May mean "the bread that is living" and/or "the bread that gives life." What is implied in v. 33 is now made explicit, and it is repeated with minor variations in vv. 41,48,51.

6:36 Contrast 20:29.

6:37 God's action (see v. 44; 10:29; 17:6; 18:9 and notes), not ours (see v. 28 and note), is primary in salvation, and Christ's mercy is unfailing (see vv. 31–40; 10:28; 17:9,12,15,19 and notes on 17:12 and 17:19; 18:9).

6:38 *to do the will of him who sent me.* See note on 4:34.

6:39 *I shall lose none.* True believers will persevere because of Christ's firm hold on them (see 10:28–29; Php 1:6 and notes; cf. Heb 3:6,14 and notes; cf. also Introduction to Hebrews: Theme). *the last day.* An expression found only in John in the NT (see vv. 40,44,54). Jesus probably refers to the day of resurrection (v. 40) followed by judgment (cf. 5:25–30; 11:24; 12:48).

last day. ^{p} ^{40}For my Father's will is that everyone who looks to the Son ^{q} and believes in him shall have eternal life, ^{r} and I will raise them up at the last day."

^{41}At this the Jews there began to grumble about him because he said, "I am the bread that came down from heaven." ^{42}They said, "Is this not Jesus, the son of Joseph, ^{s} whose father and mother we know? ^{t} How can he now say, 'I came down from heaven'?" ^{u}

^{43}"Stop grumbling among yourselves," Jesus answered. ^{44}No one can come to me unless the Father who sent me draws them, ^{v} and I will raise them up at the last day. ^{45}It is written in the Prophets: 'They will all be taught by God.'^{a} ^{w} Everyone who has heard the Father and learned from him comes to me. ^{46}No one has seen the Father except the one who is from God; ^{x} only he has seen the Father. ^{47}Very truly I tell you, whoever believes has eternal life. ^{y} ^{48}I am the bread of life. ^{z} ^{49}Your ancestors ate the manna in the wilderness, yet they died. ^{a} ^{50}But here is the bread that comes down from heaven, ^{b} which people may eat and not die. ^{51}I am the living bread ^{c} that came down from heaven. ^{d} Whoever eats of this bread will live forever. This bread is my flesh, which I will give for the life of the world." ^{e}

^{a} 45 Isaiah 54:13

6:39 ^{p} ver 40, 44, 54
6:40 ^{q} Jn 12:45
^{r} S Mt 25:46
6:42 ^{s} Lk 4:22
^{t} Jn 7:27,28 ^{u} ver 38, 62
6:44 ^{v} ver 65; Jer 31:3; Jn 12:32
6:45 ^{w} Isa 54:13; Jer 31:33,34; 1Co 2:13; 1Th 4:9; Heb 8:10,11; 10:16; 1Jn 2:27
6:46 ^{x} S Jn 1:18; 5:37; 7:29
6:47 ^{y} S Mt 25:46
6:48 ^{z} ver 35, 51
6:49 ^{a} ver 31,58
6:50 ^{b} ver 33
6:51 ^{c} ver 35,48
^{d} ver 41,58
^{e} Heb 10:10

6:40 *eternal life.* See note on 3:15. *raise them up at the last day.* Death cannot destroy the life that Christ gives (see 11:25,26 and note on 11:25).
6:41 *the Jews there.* See note on 1:19.
6:44 *draws.* People do not come to Christ strictly on their own initiative; the Father draws them.
6:45 *the Prophets.* The section of the OT from which the quotation is taken (see note on Mt 5:17).

6:49 *they died.* Jesus' opponents had set their hearts (cf. v. 31 and note) on that which could neither give nor sustain spiritual life.
6:50 *eat and not die.* Jesus' gift is in contrast; the life he gives is eternal (see 11:26 and note).
6:51 *eats of this bread.* By faith appropriates Jesus as the sustenance of one's life. *my flesh, which I will give.* Looking forward to Calvary. Providing eternal life would be costly to the Giver. *world.* See notes on 1:9; 4:42.

JESUS IN GALILEE

Lake Semechonitis

One of the cities upon which Jesus pronounced woe (Mt 11:21; Lk 10:13).

Ptolemais

Site of many miracles of Jesus (Mk 2:1; Mt 8:5 and Lk 7:1; Mt 17:24; Mk 1:21 and Lk 4:31; Jn 4:46; 6:17). Jesus taught in the synagogue here (Jn 6:59).— Capernaum

Chorazin

Bethsaida

Mediterranean Sea

Fishing town and home of Mary Magdalene.

Magdala

Sea of Galilee

Here Jesus performed his first miracle by turning water into wine at a wedding feast (Jn 2:1,11). Home of Nathanael (Jn 21:2).

Tiberias

Mt. Carmel

Kishon R.

Cana

Yarmuk R.

Nazareth

Town where Jesus grew up. He was rejected in the synagogue here and people sought to kill him (Lk 4:16).

▲ Mt. Tabor
The traditional Mount of Transfiguration (Mt 17:1–8; Mk 9:2–8; Lk 9:28–36; but see notes on Mt 17:1; Lk 9:28).

Nain
Here Jesus raised a widow's son from the dead (Lk 7:11).

Jordan R.

Miles 10   5   0   10
Kms   10 5   0   10

Caesarea

Scythopolis •

6:52 *f* S Jn 1:19
g Jn 7:43; 9:16; 10:19
6:53 *h* Mt 26:26
i S Mt 8:20 *j* Mt 26:28
6:54 *k* ver 39
6:56 *l* Jn 15:4-7;
1Jn 2:24; 3:24; 4:15
6:57 *m* S Jn 3:17
6:58 *n* ver 49-51;
Jn 3:36; 5:24
6:60 *o* ver 66
p ver 52
6:61 *q* Mt 13:57
6:62 *r* S Mt 8:20
s S Mk 16:19;
S Jn 3:13; 17:5
6:63 *t* 2Co 3:6
6:64 *u* S Jn 2:25
v S Mt 10:4
6:65 *w* ver 37, 44;
S Mt 13:11
6:66 *x* ver 60
6:67 *y* Mt 10:2
6:68 *z* Mt 16:16
a ver 63; S Mt 25:46
6:69 *b* S Mk 1:24;
8:29; Lk 9:20
6:70 *c* Jn 15:16,19
d Jn 13:27; 17:12
6:71 *e* S Mt 26:14
f S Mt 10:4
7:1 *g* S Jn 1:19
h ver 19,25;
S Mt 12:14
7:2 *i* Lev 23:34;
Dt 16:16
7:3 *j* S Mt 12:46
7:5 *k* Ps 69:8;
Mk 3:21

⁵²Then the Jews *f* began to argue sharply among themselves, *g* "How can this man give us his flesh to eat?"

⁵³Jesus said to them, "Very truly I tell you, unless you eat the flesh *h* of the Son of Man *i* and drink his blood, *j* you have no life in you. ⁵⁴Whoever eats my flesh and drinks my blood has eternal life, and I will raise them up at the last day. *k* ⁵⁵For my flesh is real food and my blood is real drink. ⁵⁶Whoever eats my flesh and drinks my blood remains in me, and I in them. *l* ⁵⁷Just as the living Father sent me *m* and I live because of the Father, so the one who feeds on me will live because of me. ⁵⁸This is the bread that came down from heaven. Your ancestors ate manna and died, but whoever feeds on this bread will live forever." *n* ⁵⁹He said this while teaching in the synagogue in Capernaum.

MANY DISCIPLES DESERT JESUS

⁶⁰On hearing it, many of his disciples *o* said, "This is a hard teaching. Who can accept it?" *p*

⁶¹Aware that his disciples were grumbling about this, Jesus said to them, "Does this offend you? *q* ⁶²Then what if you see the Son of Man *r* ascend to where he was before! *s* ⁶³The Spirit gives life; *t* the flesh counts for nothing. The words I have spoken to you—they are full of the Spirit *a* and life. ⁶⁴Yet there are some of you who do not believe." For Jesus had known *u* from the beginning which of them did not believe and who would betray him. *v* ⁶⁵He went on to say, "This is why I told you that no one can come to me unless the Father has enabled them." *w*

⁶⁶From this time many of his disciples *x* turned back and no longer followed him.

⁶⁷"You do not want to leave too, do you?" Jesus asked the Twelve. *y*

⁶⁸Simon Peter answered him, *z* "Lord, to whom shall we go? You have the words of eternal life. *a* ⁶⁹We have come to believe and to know that you are the Holy One of God." *b*

⁷⁰Then Jesus replied, "Have I not chosen you, *c* the Twelve? Yet one of you is a devil!" *d* ⁷¹(He meant Judas, the son of Simon Iscariot, *e* who, though one of the Twelve, was later to betray him.) *f*

JESUS GOES TO THE FESTIVAL OF TABERNACLES

7 After this, Jesus went around in Galilee. He did not want *b* to go about in Judea because the Jewish leaders *g* there were looking for a way to kill him. *h* ²But when the Jewish Festival of Tabernacles *i* was near, ³Jesus' brothers *j* said to him, "Leave Galilee and go to Judea, so that your disciples there may see the works you do. ⁴No one who wants to become a public figure acts in secret. Since you are doing these things, show yourself to the world." ⁵For even his own brothers did not believe in him. *k*

a 63 Or *are Spirit;* or *are spirit*   *b* 1 Some manuscripts *not have authority*

6:53–58 "Flesh" and "blood" here point to Christ as the crucified one and the source of life. Jesus speaks of faith's appropriation of himself as God's appointed sacrifice, not—at least not directly—of any ritual requirement.
6:54 *the last day.* See note on v. 39.
6:58 *bread that came down from heaven.* As in v. 49, the value of the manna is limited and is contrasted with the heavenly food Christ gives.
6:60 *hard.* Hard to accept, not hard to understand. The thought of eating the flesh of the Son of Man and drinking his blood was doubtless shocking to most of Jesus' Jewish hearers (see note on vv. 53–58).
6:62 *Son of Man.* See notes on Mk 8:31; Lk 6:5; 19:10. *ascend.* Probably refers to the series of events that began with the cross, where Jesus was glorified (see note on 7:39). *where he was before.* Referring to Jesus' heavenly preexistence (see 8:58; 17:5 and note).
6:63 Cf. 3:5–6,8. *are full of the Spirit and life.* Are the Spirit at work producing life.
6:65 Coming to Christ for salvation is never a merely human achievement (see vv. 37,39,44–45 and notes).
6:66 *From this time.* May also mean "For this reason" or both. *many … turned back.* Jesus had already made clear what discipleship meant, and many were not ready to receive life in the way he taught.
6:68 As in the other Gospels, Peter acts as spokesman. *words of eternal life.* The expression is general. Peter was not speaking of a formula but of the thrust of Jesus' teaching. He perceived the truth of v. 63 (see note there).

6:69 *We have come to believe and to know.* Since the Greek verbs are in the perfect tense, they mean, "We have entered a state of belief and knowledge that has continued until the present time." *Holy One of God.* Applied to Jesus in Mk 1:24 (see note there); Lk 4:34 (cf. Ac 2:27).
6:70 *a devil.* Judas (v. 71) would oppose Christ in the spirit of Satan.
6:71 *Iscariot.* Means "man from Kerioth" (in Judea; see Jos 15:25) and would apply equally to the father and the son (cf. 12:4). Judas seems to have been the only non-Galilean among the Twelve. *one of the Twelve.* Therefore one of the last persons likely to betray Jesus.
7:1—8:59 In chs. 7–8 John records strong opposition to Jesus, including repeated references to threats on his life (7:1,13,19,25,30,32,44; 8:37,40,59). The apostle seems to have gathered the major arguments against the Messiahship of Jesus and here answers them.
7:1 *After this.* Since 6:4 refers to the Passover Festival and 7:2 to the Festival of Tabernacles, the interval was about six months.
7:2 *Festival of Tabernacles.* The great festival in the Jewish year, celebrating the completion of harvest and commemorating God's goodness to the people during the wilderness wanderings (see Lev 23:33–43; Dt 16:13–15; Zec 14:16 and note). The name came from the leafy shelters in which people lived throughout the seven days of the festival.
7:3 *brothers.* See note on Lk 8:19.
7:4 It is not clear whether the brothers claimed some knowledge of Jesus' miracles that other people did not have or were

⁶Therefore Jesus told them, "My time *l* is not yet here; for you any time will do. ⁷The world cannot hate you, but it hates me *m* because I testify that its works are evil. *n* ⁸You go to the festival. I am not *a* going up to this festival, because my time *o* has not yet fully come." ⁹Having said this, he stayed in Galilee.

¹⁰However, after his brothers had left for the festival, he went also, not publicly, but in secret. ¹¹Now at the festival the Jewish leaders were watching for Jesus *p* and asking, "Where is he?"

¹²Among the crowds there was widespread whispering about him. Some said, "He is a good man."

Others replied, "No, he deceives the people." *q* ¹³But no one would say anything publicly about him for fear of the leaders. *r*

JESUS TEACHES AT THE FESTIVAL

¹⁴Not until halfway through the festival did Jesus go up to the temple courts and begin to teach. *s* ¹⁵The Jews *t* there were amazed and asked, "How did this man get such learning *u* without having been taught?" *v*

¹⁶Jesus answered, "My teaching is not my own. It comes from the one who sent me. *w* ¹⁷Anyone who chooses to do the will of God will find out *x* whether my teaching comes from God or whether I speak on my own. ¹⁸Whoever speaks on their own does so to gain personal glory, *y* but he who seeks the glory of the one who sent him is a man of truth; there is nothing false about him. ¹⁹Has not Moses given you the law? *z* Yet not one of you keeps the law. Why are you trying to kill me?" *a*

²⁰"You are demon-possessed," *b* the crowd answered. "Who is trying to kill you?"

²¹Jesus said to them, "I did one miracle, *c* and you are all amazed. ²²Yet, because Moses gave you circumcision *d* (though actually it did not come from Moses, but from the patriarchs), *e* you circumcise a boy on the Sabbath. ²³Now if a boy can be circumcised on the Sabbath so that the law of Moses may not be broken, why are you angry with me for healing a man's whole body on the Sabbath? ²⁴Stop judging by mere appearances, but instead judge correctly." *f*

a 8 Some manuscripts *not yet*

7:6 *l* S Mt 26:18
7:7 *m* Jn 15:18,19
n Jn 3:19,20
7:8 *o* ver 6;
S Mt 26:18
7:11 *p* Jn 11:56
7:12 *q* ver 40, 43
7:13 *r* Jn 9:22; 12:42;
19:38; 20:19
7:14 *s* ver 28;
S Mt 26:55
7:15 *t* S Jn 1:19
u Ac 26:24 *v* Mt 13:54
7:16 *w* S Jn 14:24
7:17 *x* Ps 25:14
7:18 *y* Jn 5:41; 8:50,
54
7:19 *z* Dt 32:46;
Jn 1:17 *a* ver 1;
S Mt 12:14
7:20 *b* S Mk 3:22
7:21 *c* ver 23;
Jn 5:2-9
7:22 *d* Lev 12:3
e Ge 17:10-14
7:24 *f* ISa 16:7;
Isa 11:3, 4; Jn 8:15;
2Co 10:7

suggesting that any claim to Messiahship must be decided in Jerusalem. Their advice was not given sincerely, for they did not yet believe in Jesus (v. 5).

7:6 *My time is not yet here.* Jesus moved in accordance with the will of God (see notes on 2:4; Ro 5:6).

7:7 *The world.* Either (1) people opposed to God or (2) the human system opposed to God's purposes (see note on 1Jn 2:15). The brothers belonged to the world and therefore could not be the objects of its hatred. Jesus, however, rebuked the world and was hated accordingly.

7:8 *not.* See TNIV text note. Jesus was not refusing to go to the festival but refusing to go as his brothers suggested—as a pilgrim. When he went, it would be to deliver a prophetic message from God, for which he awaited the right time (see note on v. 6).

7:10 *not publicly.* Rejecting the brothers' suggestion to show himself (v. 4).

7:12 *whispering.* Because it was not safe to speak openly (cf. v. 13).

7:14 *halfway through the festival.* When the crowds would be at their maximum. Teaching in the temple courts at such a time would reach many.

7:15 *The Jews.* Distinct from "the crowds" (v. 12), who were also Jews (see note on 1:19). *without having been taught.* By a rabbi. Jesus had never been the disciple of a recognized Jewish teacher (see Ac 4:13 and note).

7:16 *not my own.* The Father, from whom he came, had been his "rabbi" (see note on 4:34).

7:17 *chooses to do the will of God.* Reflecting an attitude of life. A person sincerely set on doing God's will welcomes Jesus' teaching and believes in him (see 6:29 and note). *will find out.* Augustine commented, "Understanding is

the reward of faith … What is 'If any man be willing to do his will'? It is the same thing as to believe."

7:18 *is a man of truth.* Or "is true." They should have recognized that Jesus was not self-seeking. In this Gospel, no one is spoken of as being "true" except God the Father (see 3:33 and note; 8:26) and Jesus (here). Once more John ranks Jesus with God.

7:19 *the law.* The Jews congratulated themselves on being the chosen recipients of the law, but Jesus told them that they all broke the law of which they were so proud (cf. Ro 2:17–29).

7:20 *You are demon-possessed.* The accusation of demon possession is made elsewhere in John (e.g., 8:48–52; 10:20–21; cf. Mt 12:24–32; Mk 3:22–30). *crowd.* Probably the pilgrims who had come up to Jerusalem for the festival—different from "the Jews" who were trying to kill Jesus (v. 1) and the Jerusalem mob that knew of the plot (see v. 25 and note).

7:21 *one miracle.* Evidently that of healing the lame man (5:1–9), as the discussion about the Sabbath shows.

7:22 *circumcision.* The requirement of circumcision was included in the law Moses gave (see Ex 12:44,48 and note; Lev 12:3), yet it did not originate with Moses but went back to Abraham (see Ge 17:10–12 and notes). The Jews took such regulations as that in Lev 12:3 to mean that circumcision must be performed on the eighth day even if it was the Sabbath. This exception is of critical importance in understanding the controversy (v. 23). Jesus was not saying that the Sabbath should not be observed or that the Jewish regulations were too harsh. He was saying that his opponents did not understand what the Sabbath meant. The command to circumcise showed not only that work *might* sometimes be done on the Sabbath but that it *must* be done then. Deeds of mercy are in this category (see notes on 5:10; Mk 3:2).

7:25 *g* ver 1;
S Mt 12:14
7:26 *h* ver 48
i Jn 4:29
7:27 *j* Mt 13:55;
Lk 4:22; Jn 6:42
7:28 *k* ver 14
l Jn 8:14 *m* Jn 8:26,42
7:29 *n* S Mt 11:27
o S Jn 3:17
7:30 *p* ver 32,44;
Jn 10:39 *q* S Mt 26:18
7:31 *r* Jn 8:30;
10:42; 11:45; 12:11,42
s S Jn 2:11
7:33 *t* Jn 12:35;
13:33; 16:5,10,
10,17,28
7:34 *v* ver 36;
Jn 8:21; 13:33
7:35 *w* S Jn 6:5
x Jn 12:20; Ac 17:4;
18:4
7:36 *y* ver 34
7:37 *z* Lev 23:36
a Isa 55:1; Rev 22:17
7:38 *b* S Jn 3:15
c Isa 58:11 *d* S Jn 4:10
e S Jn 4:14
7:39 *f* Joel 2:28;
Jn 1:33; Ac 2:17,33
g S Jn 20:22
h Jn 12:23; 13:31,32
7:40 *i* S Mt 21:11
7:41 *j* ver 52; Jn 1:46
7:42 *k* S Mt 1:1
l Mic 5:2; Mt 2:5,6;
Lk 2:4
7:43 *m* Jn 6:52; 9:16;
10:19
7:44 *n* ver 30
7:46 *o* S Mt 7:28

DIVISION OVER WHO JESUS IS

²⁵At that point some of the people of Jerusalem began to ask, "Isn't this the man they are trying to kill? *g* ²⁶Here he is, speaking publicly, and they are not saying a word to him. Have the authorities *h* really concluded that he is the Messiah? *i* ²⁷But we know where this man is from; *j* when the Messiah comes, no one will know where he is from."

²⁸Then Jesus, still teaching in the temple courts, *k* cried out, "Yes, you know me, and you know where I am from. *l* I am not here on my own authority, but he who sent me is true. *m* You do not know him, ²⁹but I know him *n* because I am from him and he sent me." *o*

³⁰At this they tried to seize him, but no one laid a hand on him, *p* because his hour had not yet come. *q* ³¹Still, many in the crowd put their faith in him. *r* They said, "When the Messiah comes, will he perform more signs *s* than this man?"

³²The Pharisees heard the crowd whispering such things about him. Then the chief priests and the Pharisees sent temple guards to arrest him.

³³Jesus said, "I am with you for only a short time, *t* and then I go to the one who sent me. *u* ³⁴You will look for me, but you will not find me; and where I am, you cannot come." *v*

³⁵The Jews said to one another, "Where does this man intend to go that we cannot find him? Will he go where our people live scattered *w* among the Greeks, *x* and teach the Greeks? ³⁶What did he mean when he said, 'You will look for me, but you will not find me,' and 'Where I am, you cannot come'?" *y*

³⁷On the last and greatest day of the festival, *z* Jesus stood and said in a loud voice, "Let anyone who is thirsty come to me and drink. *a* ³⁸Whoever believes *b* in me, as Scripture has said, *c* rivers of living water *d* will flow from within them." *a* *e* ³⁹By this he meant the Spirit, *f* whom those who believed in him were later to receive. *g* Up to that time the Spirit had not been given, since Jesus had not yet been glorified. *h*

⁴⁰On hearing his words, some of the people said, "Surely this man is the Prophet." *i*

⁴¹Others said, "He is the Messiah."

Still others asked, "How can the Messiah come from Galilee? *j* ⁴²Does not Scripture say that the Messiah will come from David's descendants *k* and from Bethlehem, *l* the town where David lived?" ⁴³Thus the people were divided *m* because of Jesus. ⁴⁴Some wanted to seize him, but no one laid a hand on him. *n*

UNBELIEF OF THE JEWISH LEADERS

⁴⁵Finally the temple guards went back to the chief priests and the Pharisees, who asked them, "Why didn't you bring him in?"

⁴⁶"No one ever spoke the way this man does," *o* the guards replied.

---

a 37,38 Or *me. And let anyone drink* ³⁸*who believes in me." As Scripture has said, "Out of him* (or *them*) *will flow rivers of living water."*

7:25 *people of Jerusalem.* An expression found only here and in Mk 1:5 in the NT, probably referring to the Jerusalem mob (see note on v. 20). They did not originate the plot against Jesus, but they knew about it.

7:26 *Have the authorities really concluded …?* In Greek, the question is in a form that expects a negative answer. *the Messiah.* See note on 1:25.

7:27 *no one will know where he is from.* Some Jews held that the OT gave the origin of the Messiah (cf. v. 42; Mt 2:4–6), but others believed that it did not.

7:28 *you know me.* Irony, because in a sense they knew Jesus and that he came from Nazareth, but in a deeper sense they did not know Jesus or the Father (see 8:19 and note). Jesus mentioned again his dependence on the Father (see 4:34 and note) and went on to declare that he had real knowledge of God and that they did not. Both his origin and mission were from God.

7:30 *they tried to seize him.* Jesus' enemies were powerless against him until his time came (see 2:4).

7:31 *crowd.* Of pilgrims (see note on v. 20). Many of them believed on the basis of the miraculous signs (cf. 6:26).

7:32 *Pharisees.* See note on Mt 3:7; see also essay, p. 1596, and chart, p. 1650. *chief priests.* See note on Mt 2:4; Mk 8:31. There was only one ruling chief priest, but the Romans had deposed a number of chief priests, and these retained the title by courtesy.

7:33 *then I go.* Jesus changed the topic from his miracles to his death, to which he referred enigmatically (v. 34).

7:35 *scattered among the Greeks.* From the time of the exile, many Jews lived outside the Holy Land and could be found in most cities throughout the Roman empire.

7:37 *last … day of the festival.* Either the seventh or the eighth day: The Festival of Tabernacles lasted seven days (Lev 23:34; Dt 16:13,15) but had a "closing special assembly" on the eighth day (Lev 23:36). See note on Mk 14:12. *stood and said in a loud voice.* Teachers usually sat, so Jesus drew special attention to his message.

7:38 *living water.* See note on 4:10.

7:39 *the Spirit.* Explaining the "living water" (v. 38). *had not been given.* In the manner in which he would be given at Pentecost (see Ac 2:1–2,4 and notes). *glorified.* Here probably refers to Jesus' crucifixion, resurrection and exaltation (see note on 13:31). The fullness of the Spirit's work depends on Jesus' prior work of salvation.

7:40 *people.* The "crowd" of v. 20 (see note there). *the Prophet.* See 1:21 and note.

7:42 *the Messiah will come from David's descendants and from Bethlehem.* See 1Sa 20:6; 2Sa 7:12–16 and notes; Ps 89:3–4; Mic 5:2. *from Bethlehem.* There were different ideas about the Messiah's place of origin (see v. 27 and note).

7:47 *P* ver 12
7:48 *q* Jn 12:42
7:50 *r* Jn 3:1; 19:39
7:52 *s* ver 41
8:1 *t* S Mt 21:1
8:2 *u* ver 20;
S Mt 26:55
8:5 *v* Lev 20:10;
Dt 22:22; Job 31:11
8:6 *w* Mt 22:15,18
x S Mt 12:10
8:7 *y* Dt 17:7;
Eze 16:40 *z* Ro 2:1,22
8:11 *a* Jn 3:17
b Jn 5:14

[47]"You mean he has deceived you also?" *P* the Pharisees retorted. [48]"Have any of the rulers or of the Pharisees believed in him? *q* [49]No! But this mob that knows nothing of the law—there is a curse on them."

[50]Nicodemus, *r* who had gone to Jesus earlier and who was one of their own number, asked, [51]"Does our law condemn a man without first hearing him to find out what he has been doing?"

[52]They replied, "Are you from Galilee, too? Look into it, and you will find that a prophet does not come out of Galilee." *s*

[The earliest manuscripts and many other ancient witnesses do not have John 7:53–8:11.]

8

[53]Then they all went home, [1]but Jesus went to the Mount of Olives. *t*

[2]At dawn he appeared again in the temple courts, where all the people gathered around him, and he sat down to teach them. *u* [3]The teachers of the law and the Pharisees brought in a woman caught in adultery. They made her stand before the group [4]and said to Jesus, "Teacher, this woman was caught in the act of adultery. [5]In the Law Moses commanded us to stone such women. *v* Now what do you say?" [6]They were using this question as a trap, *w* in order to have a basis for accusing him. *x*

But Jesus bent down and started to write on the ground with his finger. [7]When they kept on questioning him, he straightened up and said to them, "Let any one of you who is without sin be the first to throw a stone *y* at her." *z* [8]Again he stooped down and wrote on the ground.

[9]At this, those who heard began to go away one at a time, the older ones first, until only Jesus was left, with the woman still standing there. [10]Jesus straightened up and asked her, "Woman, *a* where are they? Has no one condemned you?"

[11]"No one, sir," she said.

"Then neither do I condemn you," *a* Jesus declared. "Go now and leave your life of sin." *b*

---

a 10 The Greek for *Woman* does not denote any disrespect.

7:46 *guards.* They knew they would be in trouble for failing to make the arrest but did not mention the hostility of part of the crowd, which would have given them something of an excuse before the Pharisees. They were favorably impressed by the teaching of Jesus and were not inclined to cause him trouble.
7:47 *Pharisees retorted.* They must have been greatly irritated. Ordinarily the chief priests would have rebuked the temple guards.
7:49 *this mob.* The pilgrim crowd again (see note on v. 20). *knows nothing.* The Pharisees exaggerated the people's ignorance of Scripture (cf. v. 42). But the average Jew paid little attention to the minutiae that mattered so much to the Pharisees. The "tradition of the elders" (Mk 7:3) was too great a burden for people who earned their living by hard physical work, and consequently these regulations were widely disregarded.
7:50–51 There is irony here. The Pharisees implied that no leader believed in Jesus, yet Nicodemus, "a member of the Jewish ruling council" (3:1), spoke up. They called for people to observe the law, but Nicodemus pointed to their own disregard for the law in this instance.
7:52 *a prophet does not come out of Galilee.* See 1:46; see also note on Mt 2:23. They were angry—and wrong. Jonah came from Galilee, and perhaps other prophets had as well. Moreover, the Pharisees overlooked the right of God to raise up prophets from wherever he chooses.
7:53—8:11 This story may not have belonged originally to the Gospel of John. It is absent from almost all the early manuscripts, and those that include it sometimes place it elsewhere (e.g., after Lk 21:38). But the story may well be authentic.
7:53 This verse (along with 8:1) shows that the story was originally attached to another narrative, since Jesus was not present at the meeting of the Sanhedrin described in vv. 45–52.
8:1 *Mount of Olives.* See notes on Zec 14:4; Mk 11:1; Lk 19:29; Ac 1:12.
8:3 *teachers of the law.* See notes on Mt 2:4; Mk 2:16; Lk 5:17.*a*

woman caught in adultery. This sin cannot be committed alone, so the question arises as to why only one offender was brought. The incident was staged to trap Jesus (see v. 6 and note), and provision had been made for the man to escape. The woman's accusers must have been especially eager to humiliate her, since they could have kept her in private custody while they spoke to Jesus.
8:4 *caught in the act.* Mere compromising circumstances were not sufficient evidence; Jewish law required witnesses who had seen the act.
8:5 *to stone such women.* They altered the law a little. The manner of execution was not prescribed unless the woman was a betrothed virgin (Dt 22:23–24). And the law required the execution of both parties (Lev 20:10; Dt 22:22), not just the woman.
8:6 *using this question as a trap.* The Romans did not allow the Jews to carry out death sentences (see 18:31 and note), so if Jesus had said to stone her he could have been in conflict with the Romans. If he had said not to stone her he could have been accused of being unsupportive of the law. *write on the ground with his finger.* This would seem to recall that the tablets of the law were inscribed in stone "by the finger of God" (Ex 31:18) and may suggest that the accusation against the woman is by contrast as ephemeral as something written in the dust by Jesus' finger.
8:7 *without sin.* The phrase is quite general and means "without any sin," not "without this sin." *be the first.* Jesus' answer disarmed them. Since he spoke of throwing a stone, he could not be accused of failure to uphold the law. But the qualification for throwing it prevented anyone from acting.
8:9 *began to go away.* Because they were not "without sin" (v. 7). *older ones.* They were the first to realize what was involved. But all the men were either conscience-stricken or afraid, and in the end only Jesus and the woman remained.
8:10 *Woman.* See TNIV text note.
8:11 *Go now and leave your life of sin.* Jesus did not condone what the woman had done.

8:12 c S Jn 6:35
d S Jn 1:4 e Pr 4:18;
Mt 5:14
8:13 f Jn 5:31
8:14 g Jn 13:3; 16:28
h Jn 7:28; 9:29
8:15 i S Jn 7:24
j Jn 3:17
8:16 k Jn 5:30
8:17 l S Mt 18:16
8:18 m Jn 5:37
8:19 n Jn 16:3
o S 1Jn 2:23
8:20 p S Mt 26:55
q Mk 12:41
r S Mt 26:18
8:21 s Eze 3:18
t Jn 7:34; 13:33
8:23 u Jn 3:31; 17:14
8:24 v Jn 4:26; 13:19
8:26 w Jn 7:28
x Jn 3:32; 15:15
8:28 y S Jn 12:32
z S Jn 14:24
8:29 a ver 16;
Jn 16:32 b Isa 50:5;
Jn 4:34; 5:30; 6:38
8:30 c S Jn 7:31
8:31 d Jn 15:7; 2Jn 9
8:32 e ver 36;
Ro 8:2; 2Co 3:17;
Gal 5:1,13

DISPUTE OVER JESUS' TESTIMONY

[12] When Jesus spoke again to the people, he said, "I am c the light of the world. d Whoever follows me will never walk in darkness, but will have the light of life." e

[13] The Pharisees challenged him, "Here you are, appearing as your own witness; your testimony is not valid." f

[14] Jesus answered, "Even if I testify on my own behalf, my testimony is valid, for I know where I came from and where I am going. g But you have no idea where I come from h or where I am going. [15] You judge by human standards; i I pass judgment on no one. j [16] But if I do judge, my decisions are true, because I am not alone. I stand with the Father, who sent me. k [17] In your own Law it is written that the testimony of two witnesses is true. l [18] I am one who testifies for myself; my other witness is the Father, who sent me." m

[19] Then they asked him, "Where is your father?"

"You do not know me or my Father," n Jesus replied. "If you knew me, you would know my Father also." o [20] He spoke these words while teaching p in the temple courts near the place where the offerings were put. q Yet no one seized him, because his hour had not yet come. r

DISPUTE OVER WHO JESUS IS

[21] Once more Jesus said to them, "I am going away, and you will look for me, and you will die s in your sin. Where I go, you cannot come." t

[22] This made the Jews ask, "Will he kill himself? Is that why he says, 'Where I go, you cannot come'?"

[23] But he continued, "You are from below; I am from above. You are of this world; I am not of this world. u [24] I told you that you would die in your sins; if you do not believe that I am he, v you will indeed die in your sins."

[25] "Who are you?" they asked.

"Just what I have been telling you from the beginning," Jesus replied. [26] "I have much to say in judgment of you. But he who sent me is trustworthy, w and what I have heard from him I tell the world." x

[27] They did not understand that he was telling them about his Father. [28] So Jesus said, "When you have lifted up a the Son of Man, y then you will know that I am he and that I do nothing on my own but speak just what the Father has taught me. z [29] The one who sent me is with me; he has not left me alone, a for I always do what pleases him." b [30] Even as he spoke, many put their faith in him. c

DISPUTE OVER WHOSE CHILDREN JESUS' OPPONENTS ARE

[31] To the Jews who had believed him, Jesus said, "If you hold to my teaching, d you are really my disciples. [32] Then you will know the truth, and the truth will set you free." e

a 28 The Greek for *lifted up* also means *exalted.*

A **8:12** *I am.* See note on 6:35. *the light.* See 1:4 and note; 9:5; 12:46. It is also true that "God is light" (1Jn 1:5). And as Jesus' followers reflect the light that comes from him, they too are "the light of the world" (Mt 5:14; cf. Php 2:15). *darkness.* Both the darkness of this world and that of Satan. *light of life.* "God is light" (1Jn 1:5), but Jesus is also the light from God that lights the way for life—as the pillar of fire lighted the way for the Israelites (see Ex 13:21 and note; Ne 9:12).

8:13 *Pharisees.* See note on 7:32.

C **8:14** Jesus made two points: 1. He was qualified to bear testimony, whereas the Pharisees were not. 2. He knew both his origin and his destination, whereas they knew neither. (See note on vv. 16–18 for the second point.)

8:15 The judgment of the Pharisees was limited and worldly. In the sense they meant, Jesus made it clear that he did not judge at all. In the proper sense, of course, he did judge (v. 26).

8:16–18 Jesus' second point was that his testimony was not unsupported. The Father was with him, so he and the Father were the two witnesses required by the law (see Dt 17:6 and note; 19:15).

8:16 *the Father, who sent me.* Jesus was always aware of his mission (see note on 4:34).

A **8:19** *If you knew me.* John makes it clear that the Word (Jesus) is with God and is God (see 1:1 and note) and that

he also reveals God (see 1:18 and note). Jesus here stresses that the Father is known through the Son and that to know the one is to know the other (see 14:7,10–11 and notes).

8:20 *his hour.* See note on 2:4.

8:23 Things other than death divide people (cf., e.g., v. 47; 3:31; 15:19 and note; 1Jn 3:10). *of.* Here denotes origin. Jesus was certainly in the world, but he was not of the world. They belonged to "this world"—Satan's domain (1Jn 5:19; cf. Jn 12:31; 14:30; 16:11).

8:24 *believe.* See note on 1:7. *I am.* Jesus echoes God's great affirmation about himself (see v. 58; 6:35; Ex 3:14 and notes).

8:28 *lifted up.* Normally used in the NT in the sense of "exalt" (see TNIV text note), but John uses it of the crucifixion (see 3:14; 12:32 and notes). *Son of Man.* See note on Mk 8:31. *I am.* See notes on vv. 24,58.

8:30 *faith.* See 1:7; 20:31 and notes.

A **8:31** *believed.* Here seems to mean "made a formal profession of faith." Their words show that they were not true believers (see vv. 33,37).

A **8:32** *truth.* Closely connected with Jesus (see v. 36; 14:6 and note), it is not philosophical truth but the truth that leads to salvation. *free.* Freedom from sin, not from ignorance (see v. 36).

³³They answered him, "We are Abraham's descendants ^f and have never been slaves of anyone. How can you say that we shall be set free?"

³⁴Jesus replied, "Very truly I tell you, everyone who sins is a slave to sin. ^g ³⁵Now a slave has no permanent place in the family, but a son belongs to it forever. ^h ³⁶So if the Son sets you free, ⁱ you will be free indeed. ³⁷I know that you are Abraham's descendants. Yet you are looking for a way to kill me, ^j because you have no room for my word. ³⁸I am telling you what I have seen in the Father's presence, ^k and you are doing what you have heard from your father. ^a" ^l

³⁹"Abraham is our father," they answered.

"If you were Abraham's children," ^m said Jesus, "then you would^b do what Abraham did. ⁴⁰As it is, you are looking for a way to kill me, ⁿ a man who has told you the truth that I heard from God. ^o Abraham did not do such things. ⁴¹You are doing the works of your own father." ^p

"We are not illegitimate children," they protested. "The only Father we have is God himself." ^q

⁴²Jesus said to them, "If God were your Father, you would love me, ^r for I came from God ^s and now am here. I have not come on my own; ^t but he sent me. ^u ⁴³Why is my language not clear to you? Because you are unable to hear what I say. ⁴⁴You belong to your father, the devil, ^v and you want to carry out your father's desires. ^w He was a murderer from the beginning, not holding to the truth, for there is no truth in him. When he lies, he speaks his native language, for he is a liar and the father of lies. ^x ⁴⁵Yet because I tell the truth, ^y you do not believe me! ⁴⁶Can any of you prove me guilty of sin? If I am telling the truth, why don't you believe me? ⁴⁷Whoever belongs to God hears what God says. ^z The reason you do not hear is that you do not belong to God."

JESUS' CLAIMS ABOUT HIMSELF

⁴⁸The Jews answered him, "Aren't we right in saying that you are a Samaritan ^a and demon-possessed?" ^b

⁴⁹"I am not possessed by a demon," said Jesus, "but I honor my Father and you dishonor me. ⁵⁰I am not seeking glory for myself; ^c but there is one who seeks it, and he is the judge. ⁵¹Very truly I tell you, whoever obeys my word will never see death." ^d

⁵²At this they exclaimed, "Now we know that you are demon-possessed! ^e Abraham died and so did the prophets, yet you say that whoever obeys your word will never taste death. ⁵³Are you greater than our father Abraham? ^f He died, and so did the prophets. Who do you think you are?"

⁵⁴Jesus replied, "If I glorify myself, ^g my glory means nothing. My Father, whom you claim as your God, is the one who glorifies me. ^h ⁵⁵Though you do not know him, ⁱ I know him. ^j If I said I did not, I would be a liar like you, but I do know him and obey his word. ^k

^a 38 Or presence. Therefore do what you have heard from the Father.   ^b 39 Some early manuscripts "If you are Abraham's children," said Jesus, "then

8:33 ^f ver 37,39; S Lk 3:8
8:34 ^g S Ro 6:16
8:35 ^h Gal 4:30
8:36 ⁱ ver 32
8:37 ^j ver 39,40
8:38 ^k Jn 5:19,30; 14:10,24 ^l ver 41,44
8:39 ^m ver 37; S Lk 3:8
8:40 ⁿ S Mt 12:14 ^o ver 26
8:41 ^p ver 38,44 ^q Isa 63:16; 64:8
8:42 ^r 1Jn 5:1 ^s S Jn 13:3 ^t Jn 7:28 ^u S Jn 3:17
8:44 ^v 1Jn 3:8 ^w ver 38,41 ^x Ge 3:4; 4:9; 2Ch 18:21; Ps 5:6; 12:2
8:45 ^y Jn 18:37; 1Jn 4:6
8:47 ^z Jn 18:37; 1Jn 4:6
8:48 ^a S Mt 10:5 ^b ver 52; S Mk 3:22
8:50 ^c ver 54; Jn 5:41
8:51 ^d Jn 11:26
8:52 ^e ver 48; S Mk 3:22
8:53 ^f ver 39; Jn 4:12
8:54 ^g ver 50 ^h Jn 16:14; 17:1,5
8:55 ⁱ ver 19 ^j Jn 7:28,29 ^k Jn 15:10

8:33 *have never been slaves.* Appears to have demonstrated an amazing disregard of their Roman overlords—and their Egyptian, Assyrian, Babylonian, Persian and Syrian overlords as well. Perhaps they meant that they have always viewed themselves as the descendants of Abraham and heirs of the promises God made to him and so have never accepted servitude to others as their proper status.

A 8:34 *slave to sin.* Because sinners cannot break free by their own strength (see Ro 6:18 and note).

8:37 *you are looking for a way to kill me.* See note on 7:1—8:59.

8:38 Note the contrasts:"I ... you";"seen ... heard";"the Father ...your father." Not until later (see v. 44 and note) did Jesus say who their father was, but it is clear even at this point that it was neither God nor Abraham, as they claimed.

8:39–41 Their deeds revealed their parentage.

8:41 *illegitimate.* May have been a slander aimed at Jesus.

8:43 *my language.* The form of expression—the actual words. *what I say.* The content. These descendants of Abraham (v. 33) were so convinced of their own preconceptions that they did not really hear and understand what Jesus was saying (cf. v. 47).

A 8:44 *You belong to your father, the devil.* Jesus warned his Jewish opponents of the reality of Satan's murderous and deceitful influence. Since "salvation is from the Jews" (4:22; see

note there), Jesus' words do not apply to the Jewish people as a whole. His warning should caution both Gentiles and Jews to follow Abraham's example (vv. 39–40; cf. Ro 4:16). *you want.* Points to determination of will. Their problem was basically spiritual, not intellectual. Being oriented toward Satan, they were bent on murder (v. 37) and eventually would succeed (v. 28). *truth.* Foreign to Satan and those who are his (see 14:6 and note).

8:46 *Can ... you prove me guilty of sin?* The asking of the question was more significant than the opponents' failure to answer, in that it showed that Jesus had a perfectly clear conscience.

8:47 *hears what God says.* See 10:3–4 and notes; 1Jn 4:6.

8:48 *Samaritan.* Possibly to suggest that he was lax in Jewish observances—"no better than a Samaritan"—or that he was a Samaritan by birth. *demon-possessed.* See 10:20 and note on 7:20.

8:51 *my word.* The whole of Jesus' message, which when accepted brings deliverance from death.

8:53 *Are you greater ... ?* The question was framed to expect the answer "No." This is ironic, since Jesus was indeed far greater than Abraham, even as he was greater than Moses (see 6:30–35 and notes).

8:56 *l* ver 37,39;
Ge 18:18 *m* S Mt 13:17
8:58 *n* S Jn 1:2
o Ex 3:14; 6:3
8:59 *p* Ex 17:4;
Lev 24:16; 1Sa 30:6;
Jn 10:31; 11:8
q Jn 12:36
9:2 *r* S Mt 23:7
s ver 34; Lk 13:2;
Ac 28:4 *t* Eze 18:20
u Ex 20:5; Job 21:19
9:3 *v* Jn 11:4
9:4 *w* Jn 11:9; 12:35
9:5 *x* S Jn 1:4
9:6 *y* Mk 7:33; 8:23
9:7 *z* ver 11; 2Ki 5:10;
Lk 13:4 *a* Isa 35:5;
Jn 11:37
9:8 *b* Ac 3:2,10
9:11 *c* ver 7
9:14 *d* Mt 12:1-14;
Jn 5:9
9:15 *e* ver 10
9:16 *f* S Mt 12:2
g S Jn 2:11 *h* S Jn 6:52

⁵⁶Your father Abraham *l* rejoiced at the thought of seeing my day; he saw it *m* and was glad."

⁵⁷"You are not yet fifty years old," they said to him, "and you have seen Abraham!"

⁵⁸"Very truly I tell you," Jesus answered, "before Abraham was born, *n* I am!" *o* ⁵⁹At this, they picked up stones to stone him, *p* but Jesus hid himself, *q* slipping away from the temple grounds.

JESUS HEALS A MAN BORN BLIND

9 As he went along, he saw a man blind from birth. ²His disciples asked him, "Rabbi, *r* who sinned, *s* this man *t* or his parents, *u* that he was born blind?"

³"Neither this man nor his parents sinned," said Jesus, "but this happened so that the works of God might be displayed in him. *v* ⁴As long as it is day, *w* we must do the works of him who sent me. Night is coming, when no one can work. ⁵While I am in the world, I am the light of the world." *x*

⁶Having said this, he spit *y* on the ground, made some mud with the saliva, and put it on the man's eyes. ⁷"Go," he told him, "wash in the Pool of Siloam" *z* (this word means "Sent"). So the man went and washed, and came home seeing. *a*

⁸His neighbors and those who had formerly seen him begging asked, "Isn't this the same man who used to sit and beg?" *b* ⁹Some claimed that he was.

Others said, "No, he only looks like him."

But he himself insisted, "I am the man."

¹⁰"How then were your eyes opened?" they asked.

¹¹He replied, "The man they call Jesus made some mud and put it on my eyes. He told me to go to Siloam and wash. So I went and washed, and then I could see." *c*

¹²"Where is this man?" they asked him.

"I don't know," he said.

THE PHARISEES INVESTIGATE THE HEALING

¹³They brought to the Pharisees the man who had been blind. ¹⁴Now the day on which Jesus had made the mud and opened the man's eyes was a Sabbath. *d* ¹⁵Therefore the Pharisees also asked him how he had received his sight. *e* "He put mud on my eyes," the man replied, "and I washed, and now I see."

¹⁶Some of the Pharisees said, "This man is not from God, for he does not keep the Sabbath." *f*

But others asked, "How can a sinner perform such signs?" *g* So they were divided. *h*

8:56 *my day.* All that was involved in the incarnation. Jesus probably was not referring to any one occasion but to Abraham's general joy in the fulfilling of the purposes of God in the Messiah, by which all nations on earth would receive blessing (see note on Ge 12:2–3). *he saw it.* In faith, from afar.
8:57 *not yet fifty years old.* A generous allowance for Jesus' maximum possible age. Jesus was "about" 30 when he began his ministry (see Lk 3:23 and note).

8:58 *Very truly I tell you.* See note on Mk 3:28. *I am!* A solemnly emphatic declaration echoing God's great affirmation in Ex 3:14 (see vv. 24,28; see also note on 6:35). Jesus did not say "I was" but "I am," expressing the eternity of his being and his oneness with the Father (see 1:1). With this climactic statement Jesus concludes his speech that began with the related claim, "I am the light of the world" (v. 12; see note there).
8:59 *to stone him.* Those who heard Jesus could not interpret his claim as other than blasphemy, for which stoning was the proper penalty (Lev 24:16).

9:1–12 Jesus performed more miracles of this kind than of any other. Giving sight to the blind was predicted as a Messianic activity (see Isa 29:18; 35:5 and notes; 42:7). Thus these miracles were additional evidence that Jesus was the Messiah (see 20:31 and note).

9:2 *who sinned…?* The rabbis had developed the principle that "There is no death without sin, and there is no suffering without iniquity" (cf. Introduction to Job: Theme and Message). They were even capable of thinking

that a child could sin in the womb or that its soul might have sinned in a preexistent state. They also held that terrible punishments came on certain people because of the sin of their parents. As the next verse shows, Jesus plainly contradicted these beliefs.
9:3 *works of God might be displayed.* Cf. 11:4,40 and note on 11:4.
9:4 *we.* Not Jesus only; his disciples share with him the responsibility of doing what God wants done. *Night is coming.* When Jesus, "the light of the world" (v. 5), will be taken away in death.
9:5 *the light of the world.* See note on 8:12.
9:6 Jesus used variety in his cures. He could turn even the dirt of the earth into a medium of restoration (cf. Mk 8:22–25).
9:7 *Pool of Siloam.* Already an ancient name, this rock-cut pool on the southern end of the main ridge on which Jerusalem was built served as part of the major water system developed by King Hezekiah (see notes on 2Ki 20:20; Ne 2:14; Job 28:10; Isa 8:6). *Sent.* Or "one who has been sent."
9:8 *begging.* About the only way blind people of that day could support themselves.
9:13 *Pharisees.* See note on 7:32.
9:14 *Sabbath.* Cf. 5:16 and the discussion that follows (see note on 5:10).

9:16 *Some…others.* The first group started from their entrenched position and ruled out the possibility of Jesus being from God. The second started from the fact of the "signs" and ruled out the possibility of his being a sinner (cf. vv. 30–33 and notes).

¹⁷Then they turned again to the blind man, "What have you to say about him? It was your eyes he opened."

The man replied, "He is a prophet."ⁱ

¹⁸They^j still did not believe that he had been blind and had received his sight until they sent for the man's parents. ¹⁹"Is this your son?" they asked. "Is this the one you say was born blind? How is it that now he can see?"

²⁰"We know he is our son," the parents answered, "and we know he was born blind. ²¹But how he can see now, or who opened his eyes, we don't know. Ask him. He is of age; he will speak for himself." ²²His parents said this because they were afraid of the Jewish leaders,^k who already had decided that anyone who acknowledged that Jesus was the Messiah would be put out^l of the synagogue.^m ²³That was why his parents said, "He is of age; ask him."ⁿ

²⁴A second time they summoned the man who had been blind. "Give glory to God and tell the truth,"^o they said. "We know this man is a sinner."^p

²⁵He replied, "Whether he is a sinner or not, I don't know. One thing I do know. I was blind but now I see!"

²⁶Then they asked him, "What did he do to you? How did he open your eyes?"

²⁷He answered, "I have told you already^q and you did not listen. Why do you want to hear it again? Do you want to become his disciples too?"

²⁸Then they hurled insults at him and said, "You are this fellow's disciple! We are disciples of Moses!^r ²⁹We know that God spoke to Moses, but as for this fellow, we don't even know where he comes from."^s

³⁰The man answered, "Now that is remarkable! You don't know where he comes from, yet he opened my eyes. ³¹We know that God does not listen to sinners. He listens to the godly person who does his will.^t ³²Nobody has ever heard of opening the eyes of a man born blind. ³³If this man were not from God,^u he could do nothing."

³⁴To this they replied, "You were steeped in sin at birth;^v how dare you lecture us!" And they threw him out.^w

SPIRITUAL BLINDNESS

³⁵Jesus heard that they had thrown him out, and when he found him, he said, "Do you believe^x in the Son of Man?"^y

³⁶"Who is he, sir?" the man asked. "Tell me so that I may believe in him."^z

³⁷Jesus said, "You have now seen him; in fact, he is the one speaking with you."^a

³⁸Then the man said, "Lord, I believe," and he worshiped him.^b

³⁹Jesus said,^a "For judgment^c I have come into this world,^d so that the blind will see^e and those who see will become blind."^f

⁴⁰Some Pharisees who were with him heard him say this and asked, "What? Are we blind too?"^g

⁴¹Jesus said, "If you were blind, you would not be guilty of sin; but now that you claim you can see, your guilt remains.^h

---

^a 38,39 Some early manuscripts do not have verses 38 and 39a.

9:17 *S* Mt 21:11
9:18 *j* S Jn 1:19
9:22 *k* S Jn 7:13
l ver 34; Lk 6:22
m Jn 12:42; 16:2
9:23 *n* ver 21
9:24 *o* Jos 7:19
p ver 16
9:27 *q* ver 15
9:28 *r* Jn 5:45
9:29 *s* Jn 8:14
9:31 *t* Ge 18:23-32;
Ps 34:15,16; 66:18;
145:19,20; Pr 15:29;
Isa 1:15; 59:1,2;
Jn 15:7; Jas 5:16-18;
1Jn 5:14,15
9:33 *u* ver 16; Jn 3:2
9:34 *v* ver 2
w ver 22,35; Isa 66:5
9:35 *x* S Jn 3:15
y S Mt 8:20
9:36 *z* Ro 10:14
9:37 *a* Jn 4:26
9:38 *b* Mt 28:9
9:39 *c* S Jn 5:22
d Jn 3:19; 12:47
e Lk 4:18 *f* Mt 13:13
9:40 *g* Ro 2:19
9:41 *h* Jn 15:22,24

A **9:17** *What have you to say about him?* It is curious that they put such a question to such a person; their doing so reflected their perplexity. *prophet.* Probably the highest designation the man could think of. He progressed in his thinking about Jesus: from a man (v. 11) to a prophet (v. 17), who might be followed by disciples (v. 27), to one "from God" (v. 33) to one who was properly to be worshiped (v. 38).

9:18 *They.* The Pharisees (see note on 1:19). In their prejudice they did not learn from the sign but tried to discredit the miracle.

9:21 *He is of age.* There was much to which the parents could not testify, but their emphasis on the son's responsibility showed their fear of getting involved.

9:22 *put out of the synagogue.* Excommunication is reported as early as the time of Ezra (10:8), but there is practically no information about the way it was practiced in NT times. The synagogue was the center of Jewish community life (see note on 6:59), so excommunication cut a person off from many social relationships (though, in some of its forms, at least later times, not from worship).

9:24 *We.* Emphatic in the Greek.

9:27 *his disciples too.* The man already counted himself a disciple.

9:30–33 Good reasoning from an unschooled man.

9:31 *God does not listen to sinners.* Cf. the remark of some of the Pharisees in v. 16.

9:34 *threw him out.* May mean "expelled him from their assembly" or, more probably, "excommunicated him" (see note on v. 22; cf. note on 1Co 5:5).

9:35 *when he found him.* Jesus obviously had been looking for the man. *Son of Man.* See note on Mk 8:31.

9:36 The man was ready to follow any suggestion from his benefactor.

A **9:38** *I believe.* See notes on 1:7; 20:31. *he worshiped him.* The man was giving Jesus the reverence due to God.

9:39 It is unlikely that the conversation of vv. 35–38 took place in the presence of the Pharisees. The incident of vv. 39–41, therefore, probably occurred a little later. *For judgment.* In a sense Jesus did not come for judgment (see 3:17; 12:47 and note), but his coming divides people, and this always brings a type of judgment. Those who reject his gift end up "blind."

9:40 *Pharisees.* They found it incredible that anyone would consider them spiritually blind. See note on v. 13.

C **9:41** The Pharisees' claim to sight showed their complete unawareness of their spiritual blindness and need.

10:1 *i* ver 8,10
10:2 *j* ver 11,14;
Mk 6:34
10:3 *k* ver 4,5,14,16,
27 *l* ver 4,5,14,16,27
10:4 *m* S ver 3
10:6 *n* S Jn 16:25
o S Mk 9:32
10:7 *p* S Jn 6:35
q ver 9
10:8 *r* Jer 23:1,2;
Eze 34:2 *s* ver 1
10:10 *t* S Jn 1:4;
3:15,16; 5:40; 20:31
u Ps 65:11; Ro 5:17
10:11 *v* S Jn 6:35
w ver 14; Ps 23:1;
Isa 40:11; Eze 34:11–
16,23; Mt 2:6;
Lk 12:32; Heb 13:20;
1Pe 2:25; 5:4;
Rev 7:17 *x* ver 15,17,
18; Jn 15:13; 1Jn 3:16
10:12 *y* Zec 11:16,17
10:14 *z* S ver 11
a ver 27; Ex 33:12
10:15 *b* Mt 11:27
c ver 11,17,18
10:16 *d* Isa 56:8;
Ac 10:34,35
e Jn 11:52; 17:20,21;
Eph 2:11-19
f Eze 34:23; 37:24
10:17 *g* ver 11,15,18
10:18 *h* Mt 26:53
i Jn 15:10; Php 2:8;
Heb 5:8
10:19 *j* S Jn 6:52
10:20 *k* S Mk 3:22
l 2Ki 9:11; Jer 29:26;
Mk 3:21
10:21 *m* S Mt 4:24
n Ex 4:11; Jn 9:32,33

THE GOOD SHEPHERD AND HIS SHEEP

10 "Very truly I tell you Pharisees, anyone who does not enter the sheep pen by the gate, but climbs in by some other way, is a thief and a robber. *i* ²The one who enters by the gate is the shepherd of the sheep. *j* ³The gatekeeper opens the gate for him, and the sheep listen to his voice. *k* He calls his own sheep by name and leads them out. *l* ⁴When he has brought out all his own, he goes on ahead of them, and his sheep follow him because they know his voice. *m* ⁵But they will never follow a stranger; in fact, they will run away from him because they do not recognize a stranger's voice." ⁶Jesus used this figure of speech, *n* but the Pharisees did not understand what he was telling them. *o*

⁷Therefore Jesus said again, "Very truly I tell you, I am *p* the gate *q* for the sheep. ⁸All who have come before me *r* are thieves and robbers, *s* but the sheep have not listened to them. ⁹I am the gate; whoever enters through me will be saved. *a* They will come in and go out, and find pasture. ¹⁰The thief comes only to steal and kill and destroy; I have come that they may have life, *t* and have it to the full. *u*

¹¹"I am *v* the good shepherd. *w* The good shepherd lays down his life for the sheep. *x* ¹²The hired hand is not the shepherd and does not own the sheep. So when he sees the wolf coming, he abandons the sheep and runs away. *y* Then the wolf attacks the flock and scatters it. ¹³The man runs away because he is a hired hand and cares nothing for the sheep.

¹⁴"I am the good shepherd; *z* I know my sheep *a* and my sheep know me— ¹⁵just as the Father knows me and I know the Father *b*—and I lay down my life for the sheep. *c* ¹⁶I have other sheep *d* that are not of this sheep pen. I must bring them also. They too will listen to my voice, and there shall be one flock *e* and one shepherd. *f* ¹⁷The reason my Father loves me is that I lay down my life *g*—only to take it up again. ¹⁸No one takes it from me, but I lay it down of my own accord. *h* I have authority to lay it down and authority to take it up again. This command I received from my Father." *i*

¹⁹The Jews who heard these words were again divided. *j* ²⁰Many of them said, "He is demon-possessed *k* and raving mad. *l* Why listen to him?"

²¹But others said, "These are not the sayings of someone possessed by a demon. *m* Can a demon open the eyes of the blind?" *n*

---

a 9 Or *kept safe*

And, though they claimed to have sight, their actions were evidence of their blindness.

A **10:1–30** Should be understood in light of the OT (and ancient Near Eastern) concept of "shepherd," symbolizing a royal caretaker of God's people. God himself was called the "Shepherd of Israel" (Ps 80:1; see Ps 23:1; Isa 40:10–11; Eze 34:11–16 and note on 34:2; Zec 10:2 and note), and he had given great responsibility to the leaders ("shepherds") of Israel, which they failed to respect. God denounced these false shepherds (see Isa 56:9–12; Eze 34) and promised to provide the true Shepherd, the Messiah, to care for the sheep (Eze 34:23).

10:1 *Very truly I tell you.* See note on Mk 3:28. *sheep pen.* An enclosure with only one entrance. Its walls kept the sheep from wandering away.

10:3 *gatekeeper.* Apparently in charge of a large sheep pen, where several flocks were kept. *his voice.* The sheep responded only to the voice of their own shepherd. *his own sheep.* Shepherds did not call sheep randomly, but only those that belonged to them.

10:4 *he goes on ahead.* Palestinian shepherds led their sheep (they did not drive them), and the sheep followed because they knew their own shepherd's voice.

10:6 *did not understand.* See 8:27; 12:16; Mk 8:16 and note; Lk 2:50; 9:45; 18:34.

10:7 *I am.* See note on 6:35.

10:8 *All...before me.* "False shepherds" like the Pharisees and the chief priests, not the true OT prophets (see note on vv. 1–30; cf. Zec 11:5,8 and notes).

A **10:9** *the gate.* The one way into salvation. Inside there is safety, and one is able to go out and find pasture, i.e., the supply of all needs.

A **10:10** *thief.* His interest is in himself. Christ's interest is in his sheep, whom he enables to have life to the full (see note on 1:4).

A **10:11** *I am.* See note on 6:35. *lays down his life.* Palestinian shepherds might risk danger for their sheep (see Ge 31:39; 1Sa 17:34–37), but they expected to come through alive. Jesus said that the good shepherd will die for his sheep (cf. 15:13 and note).

10:12 *hired hand.* Interested in wages, not in the sheep (v. 13).

A **10:14** *I know...my sheep know.* A deep mutual knowledge, like that of the Father and the Son.

10:15 *I lay down my life.* See v. 11 and note; the fact of central importance.

A **10:16** *other sheep.* These already belonged to Christ, though they had not yet been brought to him. *not of this sheep pen.* Those outside Judaism. Here is a glimpse of the future worldwide scope of the church. *one flock.* All God's people have the same Shepherd (see 17:20–23).

A **10:17–18** That Christ would die for his people runs through this section of John's Gospel. Both the love and the plan of the Father are involved, as well as the authority he gave to the Son. Christ obediently and voluntarily chose to die; otherwise, no one would have had the power to kill him (cf. Lk 23:46).

10:19 *divided.* See 7:43; 9:16.

10:20 *demon-possessed.* See note on 7:20.

10:21 See 9:16.

FURTHER CONFLICT OVER JESUS' CLAIMS

²²Then came the Festival of Dedication^a at Jerusalem. It was winter, ²³and Jesus was in the temple courts walking in Solomon's Colonnade. ^o ²⁴The Jews^p who were there gathered around him, saying, "How long will you keep us in suspense? If you are the Messiah, tell us plainly." ^q

²⁵Jesus answered, "I did tell you, ^r but you do not believe. The works I do in my Father's name testify about me, ^s ²⁶but you do not believe because you are not my sheep. ^t ²⁷My sheep listen to my voice; I know them, ^u and they follow me. ^v ²⁸I give them eternal life, ^w and they shall never perish; ^x no one will snatch them out of my hand. ^y ²⁹My Father, who has given them to me, ^z is greater than all ^b; ^a no one can snatch them out of my Father's hand. ³⁰I and the Father are one." ^b

³¹Again the Jews picked up stones to stone him, ^c ³²but Jesus said to them, "I have shown you many good works from the Father. For which of these do you stone me?"

³³"We are not stoning you for any good work," they replied, "but for blasphemy, because you, a mere man, claim to be God." ^d

³⁴Jesus answered them, "Is it not written in your Law, ^e 'I have said you are "gods" '^c? ^f ³⁵If he called them 'gods,' to whom the word of God ^g came—and Scripture cannot be broken ^h— ³⁶what about the one whom the Father set apart ⁱ as his very own ^j and sent into the world? ^k Why then do you accuse me of blasphemy because I said, 'I am God's Son'? ^l ³⁷Do not believe me unless I do the works of my Father. ^m ³⁸But if I do them, even though you do not believe me, believe the works, that you may know and understand that the Father is in me, and I in the Father." ⁿ ³⁹Again they tried to seize him, ^o but he escaped their grasp. ^p

⁴⁰Then Jesus went back across the Jordan ^q to the place where John had been baptizing in the early days. Here he stayed ⁴¹and many people came to him. They said, "Though John never performed a sign, ^r all that John said about this man was true." ^s ⁴²And in that place many believed in Jesus. ^t

---

^a 22 That is, Hanukkah   ^b 29 Many early manuscripts *What my Father has given me is greater than all*
^c 34 Psalm 82:6

10:23 ^oAc 3:11; 5:12
10:24 ^pS Jn 1:19
^qLk 22:67; Jn 16:25, 29
10:25 ^rJn 4:26; 8:58
^sJn 5:36; 14:11
10:26 ^tJn 8:47
10:27 ^uver 14
^vver 4
10:28 ^wS Mt 25:46
^xIsa 66:22 ^yS Jn 6:39
10:29 ^zJn 17:2,6,24
^aJn 14:28
10:30 ^bDt 6:4;
Jn 17:21-23
10:31 ^cS Jn 8:59
10:33 ^dLev 24:16;
Mt 26:63-66; Jn 5:18
10:34 ^eJn 8:17;
12:34; 15:25; Ro 3:19;
1Co 14:21 ^fPs 82:6
10:35 ^gS Heb 4:12
^hS Mt 5:18
10:36 ⁱJer 1:5
^jJn 6:69 ^kS Jn 3:17
^lJn 5:17,18
10:37 ^mver 25
10:38 ⁿJn 14:10,11, 20; 17:21
10:39 ^oJn 7:30
^pLk 4:30; Jn 8:59
10:40 ^qJn 1:28
10:41 ^rS Jn 2:11
^sJn 1:26,27,30,34
10:42 ^tS Jn 7:31

10:22 *Festival of Dedication.* The commemoration of the dedication (see TNIV text note) of the temple by Judas Maccabeus in December, 165 B.C., after it had been profaned by Antiochus Epiphanes (see essay, p. 1594). This was the last great deliverance the Jews had experienced. *It was winter.* A reference for those unfamiliar with the Jewish calendar (see bottom of chart, p. 180).
10:23 *Solomon's Colonnade.* See Ac 3:11 and note; 5:12. It was a roofed structure—somewhat similar to a Greek stoa—commonly but erroneously thought to date back to Solomon's time.
10:24 *If you are the Messiah.* Because of the different ideas about Messiahship then in vogue, it was not easy for Jews to resolve this critical issue. See notes on 1:25; 20:31.

10:25 *I did tell you.* Jesus had not specifically affirmed his Messiahship except to the Samaritan woman (see 4:26 and note). He may have meant here that the general thrust of his teaching made his claim clear or that such statements as that in 8:58 (see note there) were sufficient. Or he may have been referring to the evidence of his whole manner of life (including the miracles)—all he had done in the Father's name (for the name, see note on 2:23).
10:26 *not my sheep.* Their failure to believe arose from what they were.
10:27 *voice.* See v. 3 and note. *I know them.* See v. 14 and note. *they follow.* See v. 4 and note.

10:28 *eternal life.* Christ's gift (see note on 3:15). *never perish.* The Greek construction here is a strong denial that the sheep will ever perish. The sheep's security is in the power of the shepherd, who will let no one take them from him (see 3:16).

10:29 *My Father.* See note on 5:17. *no one can snatch them.* The Father's power ("hand") is greater than that of any enemy, making the sheep completely secure (cf. 17:11–12 and notes).

10:30 *one.* The Greek is neuter—"one thing," not "one person." The two are one in essence or nature, but they are not identical persons. This great truth is what warrants Jesus' "I am" declarations (see 6:35; 8:24,58; 17:21–22 and notes).

10:31 *the Jews.* See note on 1:19. *to stone him.* They took Jesus' words as blasphemy and therefore prepared to carry out the law (Lev 24:16), though without due process.
10:32 *good works.* See Mt 5:16; 1Ti 5:10,25; 6:18. Although the reference here includes Jesus' miracles, the underlying Greek words refer to works in general that are first of all fine and noble in character (see note on v. 38).
10:33 *blasphemy.* The Jewish leaders correctly understood the thrust of Jesus' words, but their preconceptions and unbelief prevented them from accepting his claim as true.
10:34 *your Law.* In its strictest sense the term meant the Pentateuch, but it was often used, as here, of the whole OT. *you are "gods."* The words Jesus quotes from Ps 82:6 (see note on 82:1) refer to the judges (or other leaders or rulers), whose tasks were divinely appointed (see Ex 22:28 and TNIV text note; Dt 1:17; 16:18; 2Ch 19:6).

10:35 *Scripture cannot be broken.* Jesus testified to the complete authority and reliability of the OT.

10:36 If there is any sense in which humans can be spoken of as "gods" (as Ps 82:6 speaks of human rulers or judges), how much more may the term be used of him whom the Father set apart and sent!

10:37 *the works of my Father.* The kind of works of compassion that the Father himself does.

10:38 *works.* Miracles were only a part of Jesus' works. It was Jesus' quality of life, not people's inability to explain his marvels, that he primarily spoke of here (see note on v. 32).
10:39 *they tried to seize him.* It is not clear whether this was to arrest him for trial or to take him out for stoning. *he escaped.* John does not say why they failed, but he often makes it clear that Jesus could not be killed before the appointed time (see note on 2:4; see also Lk 4:30 and note).
10:40 *where John had been baptizing.* See 1:28 and note.
10:41 *all that John said.* For John the Baptist as a witness, see 1:7 and note.

11:1 uS Mt 21:17
vLk 10:38
11:2 wMk 14:3;
Lk 7:38; Jn 12:3
11:3 xver 5,36
11:4 yver 40
11:7 zJn 10:40
11:8 aS Mt 23:7
bJn 8:59; 10:31
11:9 cJn 9:4; 12:35
11:11 dver 3
eS Mt 9:24
11:13 fver 9:24
11:16 gMt 10:3;
Jn 14:5; 20:24-28;
21:2; Ac 1:13
11:17 hver 6,39
11:18 iver 1;
S Mt 21:17
11:19 jver 31;
Job 2:11
11:20 kLk 10:38-42
11:21 lver 32,37
11:22 mver 41,42
11:24 nDa 12:2;
Jn 5:28,29; Ac 24:15
oJn 6:39,40
11:25 pS Jn 6:35
qS Jn 1:4 rS Jn 3:15
11:26 sS Jn 3:15
tS Mt 25:46

THE DEATH OF LAZARUS

11 Now a man named Lazarus was sick. He was from Bethany, u the village of Mary and her sister Martha. v 2(This Mary, whose brother Lazarus now lay sick, was the same one who poured perfume on the Lord and wiped his feet with her hair.) w 3So the sisters sent word to Jesus, "Lord, the one you love x is sick."

4When he heard this, Jesus said, "This sickness will not end in death. No, it is for God's glory y so that God's Son may be glorified through it." 5Now Jesus loved Martha and her sister and Lazarus. 6So when he heard that Lazarus was sick, he stayed where he was two more days, 7and then he said to his disciples, "Let us go back to Judea." z

8"But Rabbi," a they said, "a short while ago the Jews there tried to stone you, b and yet you are going back?"

9Jesus answered, "Are there not twelve hours of daylight? Those who walk in the daytime will not stumble, for they see by this world's light. c 10It is when people walk at night that they stumble, for they have no light."

11After he had said this, he went on to tell them, "Our friend d Lazarus has fallen asleep; e but I am going there to wake him up."

12His disciples replied, "Lord, if he sleeps, he will get better." 13Jesus had been speaking of his death, but his disciples thought he meant natural sleep. f

14So then he told them plainly, "Lazarus is dead, 15and for your sake I am glad I was not there, so that you may believe. But let us go to him."

16Then Thomas g (also known as Didymus a) said to the rest of the disciples, "Let us also go, that we may die with him."

JESUS COMFORTS THE SISTERS OF LAZARUS

17On his arrival, Jesus found that Lazarus had already been in the tomb for four days. h 18Now Bethany i was less than two miles b from Jerusalem, 19and many Jews had come to Martha and Mary to comfort them in the loss of their brother. j 20When Martha heard that Jesus was coming, she went out to meet him, but Mary stayed at home. k

21"Lord," Martha said to Jesus, "if you had been here, my brother would not have died. l 22But I know that even now God will give you whatever you ask." m

23Jesus said to her, "Your brother will rise again."

24Martha answered, "I know he will rise again in the resurrection n at the last day." o

25Jesus said to her, "I am p the resurrection and the life. q Anyone who believes r in me will live, even though they die; 26and whoever lives by believing s in me will never die. t Do you believe this?"

---

a 16 *Thomas* (Aramaic) and *Didymus* (Greek) both mean *twin.*   b 18 Or about 3 kilometers

---

11:1 *Lazarus.* Mentioned only in chs. 11–12 of John's Gospel (the name is found also in the parable of Lk 16:19–31). The sisters are mentioned in Lk 10:38–42.

11:2 *poured perfume.* See 12:3 and note.

11:3 *the one you love.* The relationship must have been exceptionally close.

11:4 Cf. 9:3 and note on 9:2. *This sickness will not end in death.* Thus predicting the raising of Lazarus (v. 44), since Jesus already knew of his death (v. 14). In fact, Lazarus must have died shortly after the messengers left Bethany, accounting for the "four days" of vv. 17,39: one day for the journey of the messengers, the two days when Jesus remained where he was (see v. 6 and note) and a day for Jesus' journey to Bethany. But see note on v. 17. *glory.* See notes on 7:39; 12:41; 13:31. Here God's Son would be glorified through what happened to Lazarus, partly because the miracle displays the glory of God (who alone can raise the dead; see 5:21 and note) in Jesus (v. 40) and partly because it would help initiate events leading to the cross (vv. 46–53).

11:6 *he stayed.* Jesus moved as the Father directed, not as people (here Mary and Martha) wished (cf. 2:4 and note). *where he was.* In Perea, east of the Jordan River (10:40).

11:8 *the Jews there.* See note on 1:19. *tried to stone you.* See note on 10:31. There was clear danger in going into Judea.

11:9 *twelve hours.* Enough time for what must be done, but no time to waste.

11:11 *fallen asleep.* A euphemism for death, used by the unbelieving world as well as by Christians.

11:15 *believe.* See 1:7; 20:31 and notes.

11:16 *Thomas ... Didymus.* The Aramaic word from which we get "Thomas" and the Greek word *Didymus* both mean "twin." Usually remembered for his doubting (see 20:24–25), he was also capable of devotion and courage, as here.

11:17 *four days.* See note on v. 4. Many Jews believed that the soul remained near the body for three days after death in the hope of returning to it. If this idea was in the minds of these people, they obviously thought all hope was gone—Lazarus was irrevocably dead.

11:18 *Bethany.* See note on Mt 21:17; see also map, p. 1703.

11:19 *to comfort them.* Jewish custom provided for three days of very heavy mourning, then four of heavy mourning, followed by lighter mourning for the remainder of 30 days. It was usual for friends to visit the family to comfort them.

11:20 *she went out to meet him.* Perhaps because as the older sister she was the hostess.

11:21 Repeated by Mary in v. 32. Perhaps the sisters had said this to one another often as they awaited Jesus' arrival.

11:22 *whatever you ask.* This comment seems to mean that Martha hoped for an immediate resurrection, in spite of the fact that Lazarus's body had already begun to decay. Nothing is too difficult for God to do (see Ge 18:14; Jer 32:17,27 and notes).

11:25 *I am.* See note on 6:35. *life.* See note on 1:4. Jesus was saying more than that he gives resurrection and life. In some way these are identified with him, and his nature is such that final death is impossible for him. He is life (see 14:6

11:27 ^uS Lk 2:11
^vS Mt 4:3 ^wJn 6:14
11:28 ^xMt 26:18;
Jn 13:13
11:30 ^yver 20
11:31 ^zver 19
11:32 ^aver 21
11:33 ^bver 38
^cS Jn 12:27
11:35 ^dLk 19:41
11:36 ^ever 3
11:37 ^fJn 9:6,7
^gver 21,32
11:38 ^hver 33
ⁱMt 27:60; Lk 24:2;
Jn 20:1
11:39 ^jver 17
11:40 ^kver 23-25
^lver 4
11:41 ^mJn 17:1
ⁿS Mt 11:25
11:42 ^oJn 12:30
^pS Jn 3:17
11:43 ^qS Lk 7:14
11:44 ^rJn 19:40
^sJn 20:7
11:45 ^tver 19
^uJn 2:23 ^vEx 14:31;
S Jn 7:31
11:47 ^wver 57
^xMt 26:3 ^yS Mt 5:22
^zS Jn 2:11

²⁷"Yes, Lord," she told him, "I believe that you are the Messiah, ^u the Son of God, ^v who was to come into the world." ^w

²⁸After she had said this, she went back and called her sister Mary aside. "The Teacher^x is here," she said, "and is asking for you." ²⁹When Mary heard this, she got up quickly and went to him. ³⁰Now Jesus had not yet entered the village, but was still at the place where Martha had met him. ^y ³¹When the Jews who had been with Mary in the house, comforting her, ^z noticed how quickly she got up and went out, they followed her, supposing she was going to the tomb to mourn there.

³²When Mary reached the place where Jesus was and saw him, she fell at his feet and said, "Lord, if you had been here, my brother would not have died." ^a

³³When Jesus saw her weeping, and the Jews who had come along with her also weeping, he was deeply moved ^b in spirit and troubled. ^c ³⁴"Where have you laid him?" he asked.

"Come and see, Lord," they replied.

³⁵Jesus wept. ^d

³⁶Then the Jews said, "See how he loved him!" ^e

³⁷But some of them said, "Could not he who opened the eyes of the blind man ^f have kept this man from dying?" ^g

JESUS RAISES LAZARUS FROM THE DEAD

³⁸Jesus, once more deeply moved, ^h came to the tomb. It was a cave with a stone laid across the entrance. ⁱ ³⁹"Take away the stone," he said.

"But, Lord," said Martha, the sister of the dead man, "by this time there is a bad odor, for he has been there four days." ^j

⁴⁰Then Jesus said, "Did I not tell you that if you believe, ^k you will see the glory of God?" ^l

⁴¹So they took away the stone. Then Jesus looked up ^m and said, "Father, ⁿ I thank you that you have heard me. ⁴²I knew that you always hear me, but I said this for the benefit of the people standing here, ^o that they may believe that you sent me." ^p

⁴³When he had said this, Jesus called in a loud voice, "Lazarus, come out!" ^q ⁴⁴The dead man came out, his hands and feet wrapped with strips of linen, ^r and a cloth around his face. ^s Jesus said to them, "Take off the grave clothes and let him go."

THE PLOT TO KILL JESUS

⁴⁵Therefore many of the Jews who had come to visit Mary, ^t and had seen what Jesus did, ^u put their faith in him. ^v ⁴⁶But some of them went to the Pharisees and told them what Jesus had done. ⁴⁷Then the chief priests and the Pharisees ^w called a meeting ^x of the Sanhedrin. ^y

"What are we accomplishing?" they asked. "Here is this man performing many signs. ^z ⁴⁸If we let him go on like this, everyone will believe in him, and then the Romans will come and take away both our temple and our nation."

---

and note; Ac 3:15; Heb 7:16 and note). *Anyone who believes in me will live.* See note on 1:7. Jesus not only is life, but he also conveys life to believers so that death will never triumph over them (cf. 1Co 15:57 and note).

A **11:26** *never die.* Believers may die physically but, as those who have eternal life, their physical death is not their ultimate end (v. 25). Death cannot destroy the life Christ gives.

A **11:27** *I believe.* Martha is often remembered for her shortcoming recorded in Lk 10:40–41. But she was a woman of faith, as this magnificent declaration shows.

A **11:28** *The Teacher.* A significant description to be given by a woman. The rabbis would not teach women (see 4:27 and note), but Jesus taught them frequently (see, e.g., Lk 10:38–42).

11:31 *to mourn there.* Wailing at a tomb was common, and the Jews immediately thought this was in Mary's mind. Because they followed her, Jesus got maximum publicity.

11:32 Cf. v. 21.

11:33 *weeping.* Both times the word denotes a loud expression of grief, i.e., "wailing." *troubled.* See notes on 12:27; 13:21.

11:35 *wept.* The Greek for this word is not the one for loud grief, as in v. 33, but one that denotes quiet weeping, i.e., "shed tears."

11:36 Cf. v. 5.

11:37 Their position was like that of Martha (v. 21) and Mary (v. 32), but they based it on Jesus' ability to give sight to the blind (cf. ch. 9).

11:38 *cave with a stone laid across the entrance.* This type of burial place was not uncommon in the Holy Land at this time, especially for the wealthy (cf. 20:1 and notes on Mk 15:46; Lk 24:2).

11:39 *four days.* See notes on vv. 4, 17.

11:40 *glory.* See note on v. 4.

11:44 *strips of linen.* Narrow strips, like bandages. Sometimes a shroud was used (see note on 19:40). *a cloth.* A separate item.

11:45 *many of the Jews … put their faith in him.* Perhaps some who had been opposed to Jesus now came to believe (see notes on 1:7,19; 20:31).

11:46 *Pharisees.* See note on 7:32.

C **11:47** *the chief priests and the Pharisees.* In all four Gospels the Pharisees appear as Jesus' principal opponents throughout his public ministry. But they lacked political power, and it is the chief priests (see note on Mt 2:4) who were prominent in the events that led to Jesus' crucifixion. Here both groups are associated in a meeting of the Sanhedrin (see note on Mk 14:55). They did not deny the reality of the miraculous signs (see note on 2:11), but they did not understand their meaning, for they failed to believe.

11:49 *a* S Mt 26:3
b ver 51; Jn 18:13,14
11:50 *c* Jn 18:14
11:52 *d* Isa 49:6;
Jn 10:16
11:53 *e* S Mt 12:14
11:54 *f* Jn 7:1
11:55 *g* Ex 12:13,23,
27; Mt 26:1,2;
Mk 14:1; Jn 13:1
h 2Ch 30:17,18
11:56 *i* Jn 7:11
12:1 *j* S Jn 11:55
k S Mt 21:17
12:2 *l* Lk 10:38-42
12:3 *m* Mk 14:3
n Jn 11:2
12:4 *o* S Mt 10:4
12:6 *p* Jn 13:29
12:7 *q* Jn 19:40
12:8 *r* Dt 15:11
12:9 *s* Jn 11:43,44

⁴⁹Then one of them, named Caiaphas,*a* who was high priest that year,*b* spoke up, "You know nothing at all! ⁵⁰You do not realize that it is better for you that one man die for the people than that the whole nation perish."*c*

⁵¹He did not say this on his own, but as high priest that year he prophesied that Jesus would die for the Jewish nation, ⁵²and not only for that nation but also for the scattered children of God, to bring them together and make them one.*d* ⁵³So from that day on they plotted to take his life.*e*

⁵⁴Therefore Jesus no longer moved about publicly among the Jews.*f* Instead he withdrew to a region near the wilderness, to a village called Ephraim, where he stayed with his disciples.

⁵⁵When it was almost time for the Jewish Passover,*g* many went up from the country to Jerusalem for their ceremonial cleansing*h* before the Passover. ⁵⁶They kept looking for Jesus,*i* and as they stood in the temple courts they asked one another, "What do you think? Isn't he coming to the festival at all?" ⁵⁷But the chief priests and the Pharisees had given orders that anyone who found out where Jesus was should report it so that they might arrest him.

JESUS ANOINTED AT BETHANY

12:1–8Ref — Mt 26:6–13; Mk 14:3–9; Lk 7:37–39

12 Six days before the Passover,*j* Jesus came to Bethany,*k* where Lazarus lived, whom Jesus had raised from the dead. ²Here a dinner was given in Jesus' honor. Martha served,*l* while Lazarus was among those reclining at the table with him. ³Then Mary took about a pint*a* of pure nard, an expensive perfume;*m* she poured it on Jesus' feet and wiped his feet with her hair.*n* And the house was filled with the fragrance of the perfume.

⁴But one of his disciples, Judas Iscariot, who was later to betray him,*o* objected, ⁵"Why wasn't this perfume sold and the money given to the poor? It was worth a year's wages.*b*" ⁶He did not say this because he cared about the poor but because he was a thief; as keeper of the money bag,*p* he used to help himself to what was put into it.

⁷"Leave her alone," Jesus replied. "It was intended that she should save this perfume for the day of my burial.*q* ⁸You will always have the poor among you,*c r* but you will not always have me."

⁹Meanwhile a large crowd of Jews found out that Jesus was there and came, not only because of him but also to see Lazarus, whom he had raised from the dead.*s* ¹⁰So the

---

a 3 Or about 0.5 liter   *b 5* Greek *three hundred denarii*   *c 8* See Deut. 15:11.

11:49 *Caiaphas.* High priest c. A.D. 18–36. He was the son-in-law of Annas (see 18:13 and note), who had been deposed from the high priesthood by the Romans in A.D. 15. *high priest that year.* Probably means simply that he was high priest at that time. *You know nothing at all!* A remark typical of Sadducean rudeness (Caiaphas, as high priest, was a Sadducee). Josephus says that Sadducees "in their dealings with their peers are as rude as to foreigners." For Sadducees, see note on Mt 3:7.

11:50 *better.* Caiaphas was concerned with political expediency, not with guilt and innocence. He believed that one man, no matter how innocent, should perish rather than that the nation be put in jeopardy. Ironically in A.D. 70 the nation still perished.

11:51 *as high priest.* Caiaphas was not a private citizen but God's high priest, and God overruled in what he said. *that year.* See note on v. 49. *prophesied.* His words were true in a way he could not imagine. Prophecy in Scripture is the impartation of divinely revealed truth. In reality Caiaphas's words meant that Jesus' death would be for the nation, not by way of removing political trouble but by taking away the sins of those who believed in him.

11:52 *for the scattered children of God.* Jesus' death would have effects far beyond the nation (cf. 1:29; 3:16; 4:42; 10:16 and notes).

11:54 *he withdrew.* Jesus was not to die before his "hour" (see note on 2:4), but he would not act imprudently. Knowing the attitude of his opponents, he withdrew. He would die for others, but in his own time, not that of his enemies.

11:55 *Passover.* See notes on 2:13; 5:1. *ceremonial cleansing.* Especially important at a time like Passover, because without it, it

would not be possible to keep the festival (see notes on 2:6; 18:28).

11:56 *Isn't he coming . . . ?* The question expected the answer "No."

12:1–11 All four Gospels have an account of a woman anointing Jesus. John's account seems to tell of the same incident recorded in Mt 26:6–13 and Mk 14:3–9, while that in Lk 7:36–50 is probably a different event (see notes on all these passages).

12:1 *Bethany.* See note on Mt 21:17.

12:3 *nard.* The name of both a plant and the fragrant oil it yielded. Since it was very expensive, Mary's act of devotion was costly. It was also an unusual act, both because she poured the oil on Jesus' feet (normally it was poured on the head) and because she used her hair to wipe them (a respectable woman did not ordinarily unbind her hair in public). Further, it showed her humility, for it was a servant's work to attend to the feet (see notes on 1:27; 13:5).

12:4 *Judas Iscariot.* See notes on 6:71; 17:12.

12:5 *money given to the poor.* See note on Mk 14:5.

12:6 *thief.* The one passage from which we learn that Judas was dishonest. Yet he must have been thought to be a man of some reliability, for he was keeper of the money bag.

12:7 *save.* Probably the meaning is "save for this purpose." Perfume was normally associated with festivity, but it was also used in burials (see 19:39–40), and Jesus links it with his burial, which Mary's act unwittingly anticipates.

12:8 *You will always have the poor among you.* See note on Mk 14:7.

12:9 *Jews.* See note on 1:19.

chief priests made plans to kill Lazarus as well, [11]for on account of him [t] many of the Jews were going over to Jesus and putting their faith in him. [u]

JESUS COMES TO JERUSALEM AS KING

12:12–15pp — Mt 21:4–9; Mk 11:7–10; Lk 19:35–38

[12]The next day the great crowd that had come for the festival heard that Jesus was on his way to Jerusalem. [13]They took palm branches [v] and went out to meet him, shouting,

"Hosanna! [a]"

"Blessed is he who comes in the name of the Lord!" [b] [w]

"Blessed is the king of Israel!" [x]

[14]Jesus found a young donkey and sat on it, as it is written:

[15] "Do not be afraid, Daughter Zion;
      see, your king is coming,
         seated on a donkey's colt." [c] [y]

[16]At first his disciples did not understand all this. [z] Only after Jesus was glorified [a] did they realize that these things had been written about him and that these things had been done to him.

[17]Now the crowd that was with him [b] when he called Lazarus from the tomb and raised him from the dead continued to spread the word. [18]Many people, because they had heard that he had performed this sign, [c] went out to meet him. [19]So the Pharisees said to one another, "See, this is getting us nowhere. Look how the whole world has gone after him!" [d]

JESUS PREDICTS HIS DEATH

[20]Now there were some Greeks [e] among those who went up to worship at the festival. [21]They came to Philip, who was from Bethsaida [f] in Galilee, with a request. "Sir," they said, "we would like to see Jesus." [22]Philip went to tell Andrew; Andrew and Philip in turn told Jesus.

[23]Jesus replied, "The hour [g] has come for the Son of Man to be glorified. [h] [24]Very truly I tell you, unless a kernel of wheat falls to the ground and dies, [i] it remains only a single seed. But if it dies, it produces many seeds. [25]Those who love their life will lose it, while those who hate their life in this world will keep it [j] for eternal life. [k] [26]Whoever serves me must follow me; and where I am, my servant also will be. [l] My Father will honor the one who serves me.

---

[a] *13* A Hebrew expression meaning "Save!" which became an exclamation of praise
[b] *13* Psalm 118:25,26   [c] *15* Zech. 9:9

12:11 [t] ver 17,18;
Jn 11:45 [u] S Jn 7:31
12:13 [v] Lev 23:40
[w] Ps 118:25,26
[x] S Jn 1:49
12:15 [y] Zec 9:9
12:16 [z] S Mk 9:32
[a] ver 23; Jn 2:22; 7:39
12:17 [b] Jn 11:42
12:18 [c] ver 11;
Lk 19:37
12:19 [d] Jn 11:47,48
12:20 [e] Jn 7:35;
Ac 11:20
12:21 [f] S Mt 11:21
12:23 [g] S Mt 26:18
[h] Jn 13:32; 17:1
12:24 [i] 1Co 15:36
12:25 [j] Mt 10:39;
Mk 8:35; Lk 14:26;
17:33 [k] S Mt 25:46
12:26 [l] Jn 14:3;
17:24; 2Co 5:8;
Php 1:23; 1Th 4:17

12:10 The Jewish leaders previously had spoken of the death of one man (see 11:50 and note), but now they wanted another death. Sin grows (cf. Jas 1:15).

12:12 *great crowd.* Pilgrims who had gathered for the Passover Festival. Many of the pilgrims had doubtless seen and heard Jesus in Galilee, and they welcomed the opportunity to proclaim him as the Messiah.

12:13 *palm branches.* See note on Mk 11:8. They were used in celebration of victory. John saw a multitude with palm branches in heaven (Rev 7:9). *Hosanna!* See TNIV text note; see also note on Mt 21:9. *name.* See note on 2:3. *Blessed is the king of Israel!* The people's addition to the words of the psalm, which John alone records. It reflects his special interest in Jesus' royalty, which he brings out throughout the passion narrative.

12:14 *donkey.* See notes on Zec 9:9; Mt 21:2,7; Mk 11:2; Lk 19:30.

12:15 *Daughter Zion.* A personification of Jerusalem (see note on 2Ki 19:21).

12:16 An example of the meaning of 16:13. *glorified.* See notes on v. 41; 11:4; 13:31. Only after the crucifixion and the coming of the Holy Spirit did the disciples appreciate the meaning of the prophecy and its fulfillment.

12:19 *Pharisees.* See note on 7:32. *whole world has gone after him!* A good example of hyperbole in the Bible.

12:20 *Greeks.* Probably "God-fearers," people attracted to Judaism by its monotheism and morality, but repelled by its nationalism and requirements such as circumcision. They worshiped in

the synagogues but did not become proselytes (cf. note on Ac 16:14).

12:21 *Philip.* A Greek name, which may be why they came to this disciple (though he was not the only one of the Twelve to have a Greek name). *Bethsaida.* See note on Mt 11:21. *to see.* Means "to have an interview with." After v. 22 John records no more about these Greeks (yet see note on v. 32). He regarded their coming, but not their conversation with Jesus, as important. Jesus came to die for the world, and the coming of these Gentiles indicates the scope of the effectiveness of his approaching crucifixion.

12:22 *Andrew.* See note on 1:40.

12:23 *The hour has come.* The hour to which everything else led (see note on 2:4). *glorified.* Jesus was speaking about his death on the cross and his subsequent resurrection and exaltation (see notes on v. 41; 11:4; 13:31).

12:24 *if it dies, it produces.* The principle of life through death is seen in the plant world. The kernel must perish as a kernel if there is to be a plant.

12:25 *those who hate their life … will keep it.* To love one's life here and now—to concentrate on one's own success—is to lose what truly matters (cf. Mk 8:34–35; Lk 9:23–24 and notes). Supremely, of course, the principle is seen in the cross of Jesus. *hate.* Love for God must be such that all other loves are, by comparison, hatred (see notes on Mal 1:3; Lk 14:26). *eternal life.* See note on 3:15.

12:27 *m* Mt 26:38,
39; Jn 11:33,38; 13:21
n S Mt 11:25 *o* ver 23
12:28 *p* S Mt 3:17
12:30 *q* Ex 19:9;
Jn 11:42
12:31 *r* Jn 16:11
s Jn 14:30; 16:11;
2Co 4:4; Eph 2:2;
1Jn 4:4; 5:19
12:32 *t* ver 34;
Isa 11:10; Jn 3:14; 8:28
u Jn 6:44
12:33 *v* Jn 18:32;
21:19
12:34 *w* S Jn 10:34
x Ps 110:4; Isa 9:7;
Eze 37:25; Da 7:14
y S Mt 8:20 *z* Jn 3:14
12:35 *a* ver 46
b Eph 5:8 *c* 1Jn 1:6;
2:11
12:36 *d* ver 46;
S Lk 16:8 *e* Jn 8:59
12:37 *f* S Jn 2:11
12:38 *g* Isa 53:1;
Ro 10:16
12:40 *h* Isa 6:10;
S Mt 13:13,15
12:41 *i* Isa 6:1-4
j Lk 24:27
12:42 *k* ver 11;
Jn 7:48

²⁷"Now my soul is troubled, *m* and what shall I say? 'Father, *n* save me from this hour'? *o* No, it was for this very reason I came to this hour. ²⁸Father, glorify your name!"

Then a voice came from heaven, *p* "I have glorified it, and will glorify it again." ²⁹The crowd that was there and heard it said it had thundered; others said an angel had spoken to him.

³⁰Jesus said, "This voice was for your benefit, *q* not mine. ³¹Now is the time for judgment on this world; *r* now the prince of this world *s* will be driven out. ³²And I, when I am lifted up *a* from the earth, *t* will draw all people to myself." *u* ³³He said this to show the kind of death he was going to die. *v*

³⁴The crowd spoke up, "We have heard from the Law *w* that the Messiah will remain forever, *x* so how can you say, 'The Son of Man *y* must be lifted up'? *z* Who is this 'Son of Man'?"

³⁵Then Jesus told them, "You are going to have the light *a* just a little while longer. Walk while you have the light, *b* before darkness overtakes you. *c* Those who walk in the dark do not know where they are going. ³⁶Put your trust in the light while you have the light, so that you may become children of light." *d* When he had finished speaking, Jesus left and hid himself from them. *e*

BELIEF AND UNBELIEF AMONG THE JEWS

³⁷Even after Jesus had performed so many signs *f* in their presence, they still would not believe in him. ³⁸This was to fulfill the word of Isaiah the prophet:

"Lord, who has believed our message
   and to whom has the arm of the Lord been revealed?" *b* *g*

³⁹For this reason they could not believe, because, as Isaiah says elsewhere:

⁴⁰"He has blinded their eyes
   and hardened their hearts,
so they can neither see with their eyes,
   nor understand with their hearts,
   nor turn—and I would heal them." *c* *h*

⁴¹Isaiah said this because he saw Jesus' glory *i* and spoke about him. *j*
⁴²Yet at the same time many even among the leaders believed in him. *k* But because of

---

a 32 The Greek for *lifted up* also means *exalted.*   *b 38* Isaiah 53:1   *c 40* Isaiah 6:10

12:27 *troubled.* John's equivalent to the agony in Gethsemane described in the other Gospels (see Mt 26:38–39 and notes; Mk 14:34–36; Lk 22:42 and note). *this hour.* Jesus faced the prospect of becoming sin (or a sin offering) for sinful people (see 2Co 5:21 and note). He considered praying for God to save him from this death but refused to do so, because the very reason he had come was to die.

12:28 *Father, glorify your name!* His prayer was not for deliverance but for the Father to be glorified (cf. Mt 6:9 and note). The voice from heaven gave the answer. *name.* See note on 2:23.

12:31 *judgment on this world.* The cross was God's judgment on the world. *prince of this world.* Satan (see 16:11). The cross would seem to be his triumph; in fact, it was his defeat. Out of it would flow the greatest good ever to come to the world.

12:32 *lifted up.* See TNIV text note. Jesus refers here first of all to his crucifixion (see v. 33), but he most likely refers also to his resurrection and ascension into heaven to reign at God's right hand (see v. 41; 3:14 and notes; see also 8:28; cf. Ac 2:33; 5:31, where "exalted" renders the same Greek word). *all people.* Christ will draw people to himself, without regard for nationality, ethnic affiliation or status. It is significant that Greek Gentiles were present on this occasion (see v. 20 and note).

12:34 *the Law.* Here seems to mean OT Scripture in general (see note on 10:34), the reference being to passages such as Ps 89:30–37; 110:4; Isa 9:7 (see notes there). *the Messiah.* See note on 1:25. *Son of Man.* The only place in the Gospels where anyone other than Jesus used the expression, and even here Jesus is being quoted (see note on Mk 8:31).

12:35–36 *light.* Closely identified with Jesus, as seen from the call to believe in the light (see notes on 1:4; 8:12).

12:37 *they still would not believe.* God's ancient people should have responded when God sent his Messiah. They should have seen the significance of the signs he did.

12:39 *could not believe.* Does not mean that the people in question had no choice. They purposely rejected God and chose evil, and v. 40 explains that God in turn brought on them a judicial blinding of eyes and hardening of hearts. Yet many Jewish leaders did believe in Jesus as the Messiah (see v. 42 and note).

12:40 These words from Isa 6:10 (see note there) are quoted by Jesus (see Mt 13:13–14; Mk 4:12; Lk 8:10) and by Paul (Ac 28:26–27). See notes on Mk 4:12; Lk 8:11.

12:41 *saw Jesus' glory.* Isaiah spoke primarily of the glory of God (Isa 6:3; see notes on Eze 1:28; 43:2). John spoke of the glory of Jesus and made no basic distinction between the two, attesting Jesus' oneness with God (cf. Heb 1:6,10 and notes). The thought of glory here is complex. There is the idea of majesty, and there is also the idea (which meant so much to John) that Jesus' death on the cross and his subsequent resurrection and exaltation show his real glory. Isaiah foresaw the rejection of Christ, as the passages quoted (Isa 53:1; 6:10) show. He spoke of the Messiah both in the words about blind eyes and hard hearts, on the one hand, and about healing, on the other. This is the cross and this is glory, for the cross, resurrection and exaltation portray both suffering and healing, rejection and triumph, humiliation and glory.

12:42 *many … leaders believed.* John does not give a picture of unrelieved gloom. Many Jewish leaders believed (see note on 1:7), though they remained secret believers for fear of excommunication (see note on 9:22). Two such cases in this Gospel are Nicodemus and Joseph of Arimathea (see 3:1–2; 19:38–39 and notes).

the Pharisees *l* they would not openly acknowledge their faith for fear they would be put out of the synagogue; *m* ⁴³for they loved human glory *n* more than the glory of God. *o*

⁴⁴Then Jesus cried out, "Those who believe in me do not believe in me only, but in the one who sent me. *p* ⁴⁵When they look at me, they see the one who sent me. *q* ⁴⁶I have come into the world as a light, *r* so that no one who believes in me should stay in darkness.

⁴⁷"As for those who hear my words but do not keep them, I do not judge them. For I did not come to judge the world, but to save the world. *s* ⁴⁸There is a judge for those who reject me and do not accept my words; the very words I have spoken will condemn them *t* at the last day. ⁴⁹For I did not speak on my own, but the Father who sent me commanded me *u* to say all that I have spoken. ⁵⁰I know that his command leads to eternal life. *v* So whatever I say is just what the Father has told me to say." *w*

JESUS WASHES HIS DISCIPLES' FEET

13 It was just before the Passover Festival. *x* Jesus knew that the hour had come *y* for him to leave this world and go to the Father. *z* Having loved his own who were in the world, he loved them to the end.

²The evening meal was in progress, and the devil had already prompted Judas, the son of Simon Iscariot, to betray Jesus. *a* ³Jesus knew that the Father had put all things under his power, *b* and that he had come from God *c* and was returning to God; ⁴so he got up from the meal, took off his outer clothing, and wrapped a towel around his waist. *d* ⁵After that, he poured water into a basin and began to wash his disciples' feet, *e* drying them with the towel that was wrapped around him.

⁶He came to Simon Peter, who said to him, "Lord, are you going to wash my feet?"

⁷Jesus replied, "You do not realize now what I am doing, but later you will understand." *f*

⁸"No," said Peter, "you shall never wash my feet."

Jesus answered, "Unless I wash you, you have no part with me."

⁹"Then, Lord," Simon Peter replied, "not just my feet but my hands and my head as well!"

¹⁰Jesus answered, "Those who have had a bath need only to wash their feet; their whole body is clean. And you are clean, *g* though not every one of you." *h* ¹¹For he knew who was going to betray him, *i* and that was why he said not every one was clean.

12:42 *l* S Jn 7:13
m Jn 9:22
12:43 *n* 1Sa 15:30
o S Ro 2:29
12:44 *p* S Mt 10:40; Jn 5:24
12:45 *q* S Jn 14:9
12:46 *r* S Jn 1:4
12:47 *s* S Jn 3:17
12:48 *t* Jn 5:45
12:49 *u* Jn 14:31
12:50 *v* S Mt 25:46
w S Jn 14:24
13:1 *x* S Jn 11:55
y S Mt 26:18 *z* Jn 16:28
13:2 *a* S Mt 10:4
13:3 *b* S Mt 28:18
c Jn 8:42; 16:27,28, 30; 17:8
13:4 *d* S Mt 20:28
13:5 *e* S Lk 7:44
13:7 *f* ver 12
13:10 *g* Jn 15:3
h ver 18
13:11 *i* S Mt 10:4

12:44 *cried out.* The words are given special emphasis by being spoken in a loud voice. *believe in me.* John ends his story of the public ministry of Jesus with an appeal for belief (see notes on 1:7; 20:31; see also Introduction: Purpose and Emphases). He does not say when Jesus spoke these words (they may have been uttered earlier), but they are a fitting close to this part of his account. *the one who sent me.* Jesus' mission, as well as the inseparability of the Father and the Son, are stressed throughout this Gospel (see note on 4:34).

12:46 *I have come into the world.* Points to both Jesus' preexistence and his mission. *light.* See vv. 35–36 and note.

A 12:47 *to judge.* Not the purpose of Jesus' coming (3:17–18), but judgment is the other side of salvation. It is not the purpose of the sun's shining to cast shadows, but when the sun shines, shadows are inevitable.

A 12:49 *the Father . . . commanded me to say all that I have spoken.* Jesus' hearers have a great responsibility. His "words" (v. 48) are what the Father commanded him to say. To reject them, therefore, is to reject God.

12:50 *eternal life.* See note on 3:15. *So.* Jesus said what he did in order to fulfill the will of the Father—a wonderful note on which to end the account of Jesus' public ministry (see v. 44 and note).

A 13:1—17:26 John has by far the longest account of the upper room, though curiously he says nothing about the institution of the Lord's Supper. Still we owe to him most of our information about what our Lord said to his disciples on that night. One feature of the discourse is Jesus' emphasis on love. The Greek noun *agape* ("love") and the verb *agapao* ("love") occur only 8 times in chs. 1–12 but 31 times in chs. 13–17.

13:1 *Passover Festival.* See notes on 2:13; 5:1. *the hour.* See note on 2:4.

13:2 *evening meal.* Some believe that this feast was a fellowship meal eaten sometime before the Passover Festival. This

would mean that the Last Supper could not have been the Passover meal, as the Synoptic Gospels clearly indicate. However, this meal may have been the Passover Festival itself, in which case the accounts of the Synoptics and John would agree. *the devil.* See v. 27. *Judas . . . Iscariot.* See note on 6:71.

13:3 *the Father had put all things under his power.* John again emphasizes the fulfillment of God's plan and Jesus' control of the situation. *was returning to God.* See 20:17 and note.

A 13:5 *began to wash his disciples' feet.* A menial task (see note on 1:27), normally performed by a servant. On this occasion there was no servant, and no one else volunteered. Jesus' action was during the meal, not upon arrival, and was done deliberately to emphasize a point. It was a lesson in humility, but it also set forth the principle of selfless service that was so soon to be exemplified in the cross. John alone tells of this incident, but Luke says that in rebuking the disciples over a quarrel concerning who would be the greatest, Jesus said, "I am among you as one who serves" (Lk 22:27). Jesus' life of service would culminate on the cross (see Php 2:5–8 and notes).

A 13:8 *No.* Characteristically, Peter objected, though apparently no one else did. His actions reflect a mixture of humility (he did not want Jesus to perform this lowly service for him) and pride (he tried to dictate to Jesus; see also Mt 16:21–23). *Unless I wash you.* Jesus' reply looks beyond the incident to what it symbolizes: Peter needed a spiritual cleansing. The external washing was a picture of cleansing from sin.

13:9 *my hands and my head.* Peter's response was wholehearted, but he was still dictating to Jesus.

13:10 *only to wash their feet.* A man would bathe himself before going to a feast. When he arrived, he only needed to wash his feet to be entirely clean again.

13:11 *he knew.* Again John emphasizes Jesus' command of the situation.

13:13 *l* Mt 26:18;
Jn 11:28 *k* S Mt 28:18;
Lk 1:43; 2:11; 6:46;
11:1; Ac 10:36;
Ro 10:9,12; 14:9;
1Co 12:3; Php 2:11;
Col 2:6
13:14 *l* 1Pe 5:5
13:15 *m* S Mt 11:29;
S 1Ti 4:12
13:16 *n* Mt 10:24;
Lk 6:40; Jn 15:20
13:17 *o* Mt 7:24,25;
Lk 11:28; Jas 1:25
13:18 *p* ver 10
q Jn 15:16,19
r S Mt 1:22 *s* Mt 26:23
t Jn 6:70 *u* Ps 41:9
13:19 *v* Jn 14:29;
16:4 *w* Jn 4:26; 8:24
13:20 *x* S Mt 10:40
13:21 *y* S Jn 12:27
z Mt 26:21
13:23 *a* Jn 19:26;
20:2; 21:7,20
13:25 *b* Mt 26:22;
Jn 21:20
13:26 *c* S Mt 10:4
13:27 *d* Lk 22:3
13:29 *e* Jn 12:6
f ver 1 *g* Jn 12:5
13:30 *h* Lk 22:53
13:31 *i* S Mt 8:20
j Jn 7:39; 12:23
k Jn 14:13; 17:4;
1Pe 4:11
13:32 *l* Jn 17:1

¹²When he had finished washing their feet, he put on his clothes and returned to his place. "Do you understand what I have done for you?" he asked them. ¹³"You call me 'Teacher'*i* and 'Lord,'*k* and rightly so, for that is what I am. ¹⁴Now that I, your Lord and Teacher, have washed your feet, you also should wash one another's feet.*l* ¹⁵I have set you an example that you should do as I have done for you.*m* ¹⁶Very truly I tell you, servants are not greater than their master,*n* nor are messengers greater than the one who sent them. ¹⁷Now that you know these things, you will be blessed if you do them.*o*

JESUS PREDICTS HIS BETRAYAL

¹⁸"I am not referring to all of you;*p* I know those I have chosen.*q* But this is to fulfill this passage of Scripture:*r* 'He who shared my bread*s* has lifted up his heel*t* against me.'*a u*

¹⁹"I am telling you now before it happens, so that when it does happen you will believe*v* that I am who I am.*w* ²⁰Very truly I tell you, whoever accepts anyone I send accepts me; and whoever accepts me accepts the one who sent me."*x*

²¹After he had said this, Jesus was troubled in spirit*y* and testified, "Very truly I tell you, one of you is going to betray me."*z*

²²His disciples stared at one another, at a loss to know which of them he meant. ²³One of them, the disciple whom Jesus loved,*a* was reclining next to him. ²⁴Simon Peter motioned to this disciple and said, "Ask him which one he means."

²⁵Leaning back against Jesus, he asked him, "Lord, who is it?"*b*

²⁶Jesus answered, "It is the one to whom I will give this piece of bread when I have dipped it in the dish." Then, dipping the piece of bread, he gave it to Judas,*c* the son of Simon Iscariot. ²⁷As soon as Judas took the bread, Satan entered into him.*d*

So Jesus told him, "What you are about to do, do quickly." ²⁸But no one at the meal understood why Jesus said this to him. ²⁹Since Judas had charge of the money,*e* some thought Jesus was telling him to buy what was needed for the festival,*f* or to give something to the poor.*g* ³⁰As soon as Judas had taken the bread, he went out. And it was night.*h*

JESUS PREDICTS PETER'S DENIAL

13:37,38pp — Mt 26:33–35; Mk 14:29–31; Lk 22:33,34

³¹When he was gone, Jesus said, "Now is the Son of Man*i* glorified*j* and God is glorified in him.*k* ³²If God is glorified in him,*b* God will glorify the Son in himself,*l* and will glorify him at once.

---

a 18 Psalm 41:9   *b* 32 Many early manuscripts do not have *If God is glorified in him.*

13:13 *Teacher…Lord.* An instructor would normally be called "Teacher," but "Lord" referred to one occupying the supreme place. Jesus accepted both titles.

13:14–15 Some Christians believe that Christ intended to institute a foot-washing ordinance to be practiced regularly. Most Christians, however, interpret Christ's action here as providing an example of humble service.

13:14 *wash one another's feet.* Christians should be willing to perform the most menial services for one another.

13:16 With minor variations this saying, which Jesus used often, is found in 15:20; Mt 10:24; Lk 6:40 (cf. Lk 22:27).

13:18 *not referring to all of you.* Jesus was leading up to his prediction of the betrayal (see v. 21 and note). *shared my bread.* To eat bread together was a mark of close fellowship (see note on Ps 41:9). *lifted up his heel.* May be derived from a horse's preparing to kick, or perhaps something like shaking off the dust from one's feet (see Lk 9:5 and note).

13:19 *so that…you will believe.* See note on 12:44. Jesus' concern was for the disciples, not himself. *I am who I am.* An emphatic form of speech, such as that in 8:58 (see note there).

13:20 *anyone I send…the one who sent me.* Jesus' mission is a common theme in this Gospel (see notes on 4:34; 12:44; 17:3–4, 18), and now the mission of his followers is linked with it (cf. 20:21).

13:21 *troubled.* See 11:33 and note. Though he knew of it long before it happened, Jesus was grieved by the betrayal of a friend.

13:22 *at a loss.* The disciples' astonishment shows that Judas had concealed his contacts with the high priests. No one suspected him (see v. 28), but all seem to have thought that the betrayal would be involuntary (see Mk 14:19).

13:23 *the disciple whom Jesus loved.* Usually thought to be John, the author of this Gospel (see Introduction: Author). The expression does not, of course, mean that Jesus did not love the others but that he had a special bond with this man. *reclining.* At a dinner, guests reclined on couches, leaning on the left elbow with the head toward the table (cf. note on Mk 14:18).

13:26 *the one to whom I…give…bread…dipped…in the dish.* Evidently Judas was near Jesus, possibly in the seat of honor. John used Judas's full name (see note on 6:71) in recording this solemn moment.

13:27 *As soon as Judas took the bread.* Evidently the critical moment. If the giving of the bread to Judas was a mark of honor, it also seems to have been a final appeal—which Judas did not accept. *Satan.* The name is used only here in John (cf. v. 2; see notes on Job 1:6; Zec 3:1; Rev 12:9–10). *do quickly.* Jesus' words once more indicate his control. He would die as he directed, not as his opponents determined.

13:29 *the festival.* See v. 1 and note on v. 2. *the poor.* See 12:5 and note on Mk 14:5.

13:30 *night.* In light of John's emphasis on the conflict between light and darkness, this may have been more than a time note—picturing also the darkness of Judas's soul (cf. notes on 1:4; 8:12; Isa 60:2).

13:31 *Son of Man.* See note on Mk 8:31. *glorified.* See v. 32 and note on 7:39. Here the idea of glory includes a reference to Jesus' sacrificial death on the cross and the glorious salvation that would result. *God is glorified in him.* The glory of the Father is closely bound to that of the Son.

³³"My children, I will be with you only a little longer. You will look for me, and just as I told the Jews, so I tell you now: Where I am going, you cannot come. *m*

³⁴"A new command *n* I give you: Love one another. *o* As I have loved you, so you must love one another. *p* ³⁵By this everyone will know that you are my disciples, if you love one another." *q*

³⁶Simon Peter asked him, "Lord, where are you going?" *r*

Jesus replied, "Where I am going, you cannot follow now, *s* but you will follow later." *t*

³⁷Peter asked, "Lord, why can't I follow you now? I will lay down my life for you."

³⁸Then Jesus answered, "Will you really lay down your life for me? Very truly I tell you, before the rooster crows, you will disown me three times! *u*

JESUS COMFORTS HIS DISCIPLES

14 "Do not let your hearts be troubled. *v* Trust *w* in God*a*; *x* trust also in me. ²My Father's house has plenty of room; if that were not so, would I have told you that I am going there*y* to prepare a place for you? ³And if I go and prepare a place for you, I will come back*z* and take you to be with me that you also may be where I am. *a* ⁴You know the way to the place where I am going."

JESUS THE WAY TO THE FATHER

⁵Thomas *b* said to him, "Lord, we don't know where you are going, so how can we know the way?"

⁶Jesus answered, "I am*c* the way *d* and the truth *e* and the life. *f* No one comes to the Father except through me. *g* ⁷If you really know me, you will know*b* my Father as well. *h* From now on, you do know him and have seen him."

⁸Philip *i* said, "Lord, show us the Father and that will be enough for us."

⁹Jesus answered: "Don't you know me, Philip, even after I have been among you such a long time? Anyone who has seen me has seen the Father. *j* How can you say, 'Show us the Father'? ¹⁰Don't you believe that I am in the Father, and that the Father is in me? *k* The words I say to you I do not speak on my own authority. *l* Rather, it is the Father, living in me, who is doing his work. ¹¹Believe me when I say that I am in the Father and the Father is in me; or at least believe on the evidence of the works themselves. *m* ¹²Very truly I tell you, all who have faith *n* in me will do the works I have been doing, *o* and they will do even greater things than these, because I am going to the Father. ¹³And I will do whatever you ask*p* in my name, so that the Father may be glorified in the Son. ¹⁴You may ask me for anything in my name, and I will do it.

a 1 Or You trust in God   *b 7 Some manuscripts If you really knew me, you would know*

13:33 *m* S Jn 7:33, 34
13:34 *n* Jn 15:12; 1Jn 2:7-11; 3:11
o Lev 19:18; 1Th 4:9; 1Pe 1:22 *p* Jn 15:12; Eph 5:2; 1Jn 4:10,11
13:35 *q* 1Jn 3:14; 4:20
13:36 *r* Jn 16:5 *s* ver 33; Jn 14:2 *t* Jn 21:18,19; 2Pe 1:14
13:38 *u* Jn 18:27
14:1 *v* ver 27
w S Jn 3:15 *x* Ps 4:5
14:2 *y* Jn 13:33,36; 16:5
14:3 *z* ver 18,28; S Mt 16:27
a S Jn 12:26
14:5 *b* S Jn 11:16
14:6 *c* S Jn 6:35
d Jn 10:9; Eph 2:18; Heb 10:20 *e* Jn 1:14
f S Jn 1:4 *g* Ac 4:12
14:7 *h* Jn 1:18; S 1Jn 2:23
14:8 *i* S Jn 1:43
14:9 *j* Isa 9:6; Jn 1:14; 12:45; 2Co 4:4; Php 2:6; Col 1:15; Heb 1:3
14:10 *k* ver 11,20; Jn 10:38; 17:21
l S ver 24
14:11 *m* Jn 5:36; 10:38
14:12 *n* Mt 21:21
o Lk 10:17
14:13 *p* S Mt 7:7

13:34 *A new command.* In a sense it was an old one (see Lev 19:18 and note), but for Christ's disciples it was new, because it was the mark of their special bond, created by Christ's great love for them (cf. Mt 22:37,39; Mk 12:31; Lk 10:27 and notes). *As I have loved you.* Our standard is Christ's love for us.

13:35 *love.* The distinguishing mark of Christ's followers (cf. 1Jn 3:23; 4:7–8,11–12,19–21).

13:36 *where are you going?* Peter seems to have ignored Jesus' words about love and to have been more concerned about his Master's departure. In Jesus' reply "you" is singular and thus personal to Peter, whereas in v. 33 the word is plural.

13:37 *I will lay down my life.* Words similar to those of the good shepherd in 10:11. Peter was characteristically sure of himself, when in fact he would not at this time lay down his life for Jesus (though later he would; see 21:18–19 and notes). Exactly the opposite would be true.

13:38 *you will disown me three times.* Peter's denial is prophesied in all four Gospels (Mt 26:33–35; Mk 14:29–31; Lk 22:31–34).

14:1 *Do not . . . be troubled.* The apostles had just received disturbing news (13:33,36). *Trust in God . . . in me.* Jesus' antidote for a troubled heart (cf. Ps 56:3–4; Isa 26:3–4).

14:2 *my Father's house.* Heaven. *plenty of room.* Lit. "many dwelling places," implying permanence and "plenty of room."

14:3 *I will come back.* Jesus comes in many ways, but the primary reference here is to his second advent (cf. Rev 22:7,12,20).

14:4 *way.* See v. 6 and note.

14:5 *Thomas.* He was honest and plainly told the Lord he did not understand (see note on 11:16).

14:6 *I am.* See note on 6:35. *the way.* To God. Jesus is not one way among many but the only way (see Ac 4:12; Heb 10:19–20 and notes). In the early church, Christianity was sometimes called "the Way" (see, e.g., Ac 9:2 and note). *the truth.* A key emphasis in this Gospel (see note on 1:14). *the life.* See note on 1:4. Very likely the statement means "I am the way (to the Father) in that I am the truth and the life."

14:7 *me . . . my Father.* Once more Jesus stresses the intimate connection between the Father and himself. Jesus brought a full revelation of the Father (see 1:18 and note), so the apostles had real knowledge of him.

14:10 *I do not speak on my own authority.* Jesus' teaching was not of human origin, and there was an inseparable connection between his words and his work.

14:11 *Believe . . . that I am in the Father and the Father is in me.* Saving faith is trust in a person, but it must also have factual content. Faith includes believing that Jesus is one with the Father (see 17:21–22 and notes).

14:12 *Very truly I tell you.* See note on Mk 3:28. *greater things.* Miracles (see v. 11). These depended on Jesus' going to the Father, because they are works done in the strength of the Holy Spirit, whom Jesus would send from the Father (see vv. 16–17; 15:26 and notes).

14:13 *in my name.* Not simply prayer that mentions Jesus' name but prayer in accordance with all that the

14:15 *q* ver 21,23;
Ps 103:18; Jn 15:10;
1Jn 2:3-5; 3:22,24; 5:3;
2Jn 6; Rev 12:17; 14:12
14:16 *r* ver 26;
Jn 15:26; 16:7
14:17 *s* Jn 15:26;
16:13; 1Jn 4:6; 5:6
t 1Co 2:14
14:18 *u* 1Ki 6:13
v ver 3,28; S Mt 16:27
14:19 *w* Jn 7:33,34;
16:16 *x* Jn 6:57
14:20 *y* Jn 16:23,26
z ver 10,11; Jn 10:38;
17:21 *a* S Ro 8:10
14:21 *b* S ver 15
c Dt 7:13; Jn 16:27;
1Jn 2:5
14:22 *d* Lk 6:16;
Ac 1:13 *e* Ac 10:41
14:23 *f* S ver 15
g S Ro 8:10
14:24 *h* ver 10;
Dt 18:18; Jn 5:19;
7:16; 8:28; 12:49,50
14:26 *i* ver 16;
Jn 15:26; 16:7
j Ac 2:33 *k* Jn 16:13;
1Jn 2:20,27 *l* Jn 2:22
14:27 *m* Nu 6:26;
Ps 85:8; Mal 2:6;
S Lk 2:14; 24:36;
Jn 16:33; Php 4:7;
Col 3:15 *n* ver 1
14:28 *o* ver 2-4,18;
S Mt 16:27 *p* Jn 5:18
q Jn 10:29
14:29 *r* Jn 13:19; 16:4
14:30 *s* S Jn 12:31
14:31 *t* Jn 10:18;
12:49

JESUS PROMISES THE HOLY SPIRIT

15"If you love me, keep my commands. *q* 16And I will ask the Father, and he will give you another advocate *r* to help you and be with you forever— 17the Spirit of truth. *s* The world cannot accept him, *t* because it neither sees him nor knows him. But you know him, for he lives with you and will be *a* in you. 18I will not leave you as orphans; *u* I will come to you. *v* 19Before long, the world will not see me anymore, but you will see me. *w* Because I live, you also will live. *x* 20On that day *y* you will realize that I am in my Father, *z* and you are in me, and I am in you. *a* 21Whoever has my commands and keeps them is the one who loves me. *b* Anyone who loves me will be loved by my Father, *c* and I too will love them and show myself to them."

22Then Judas *d* (not Judas Iscariot) said, "But, Lord, why do you intend to show yourself to us and not to the world?" *e*

23Jesus replied, "Anyone who loves me will obey my teaching. *f* My Father will love them, and we will come to them and make our home with them. *g* 24Anyone who does not love me will not obey my teaching. These words you hear are not my own; they belong to the Father who sent me. *h*

25"All this I have spoken while still with you. 26But the Advocate, *i* the Holy Spirit, whom the Father will send in my name, *j* will teach you all things *k* and will remind you of everything I have said to you. *l* 27Peace I leave with you; my peace I give you. *m* I do not give to you as the world gives. Do not let your hearts be troubled *n* and do not be afraid.

28"You heard me say, 'I am going away and I am coming back to you.' *o* If you loved me, you would be glad that I am going to the Father, *p* for the Father is greater than I. *q* 29I have told you now before it happens, so that when it does happen you will believe. *r* 30I will not say much more to you, for the prince of this world *s* is coming. He has no hold over me, 31but he comes so that the world may learn that I love the Father and do exactly what my Father has commanded me. *t*

"Come now; let us leave.

a 17 Some early manuscripts *and is*

---

person who bears the name is (see note on 2:23). It is prayer aimed at carrying forward the work Jesus did—prayer that he himself will answer (see also v. 14).

A **14:15** *love . . . keep.* Love, like faith (see Jas 2:14–26 and notes), cannot be separated from obedience.

A **14:16** *the Father . . . will give you.* The first of a series of important passages about the Holy Spirit (see v. 26; 15:26; 16:7–15 and notes), the gift of the Father. *another.* Besides Jesus. *advocate.* A legal term, but with a broader meaning than "counsel for the defense" (see 1Jn 2:1 and note). It referred to any person who helped someone in trouble with the law. The Spirit will always stand by Christ's people.

A **14:17** *Spirit of truth.* In essence and in action the Spirit is characterized by truth. He brings people to the truth of God. All three persons of the Trinity are linked with truth. See also the Father (see 4:24 and note; cf. Ps 31:5; Isa 65:16 and note) and the Son (see v. 6 and note). *The world.* Which takes no notice of the Spirit of God (see notes on 1:9; 1Co 2:14). The Spirit was "with" Jesus' disciples and would be "in" them. Many believe the latter relationship (indwelling) specifically anticipates the coming of the Holy Spirit on the day of Pentecost (see Ac 1:2; 2:4,17,38 and notes; cf. Ro 8:9 and note).

14:18 *I will come to you.* The words relate to the coming of the Spirit, but Jesus also speaks of his own appearances after the resurrection and at his second coming (see vv. 3,19,28 and note on v. 3; 16:22 and note).

A **14:19** *world . . . but you.* The cross separated the world (those who would not see Jesus thereafter) from the disciples (who would). *Because I live, you also will live.* The life of the Christian always depends on the life of Christ (see 1:4; 3:15; 10:10; Php 1:21 and notes).

14:20 *On that day you will realize.* The resurrection would radically change their thinking.

A **14:21** *keeps . . . loves.* Love for Christ and keeping his commands cannot be separated (see note on v. 15). *loved by my Father . . . I too will love them.* The love of the Father cannot

be separated from that of the Son.

14:22 *why . . . ?* Judas (and, for that matter, the other apostles) probably looked for Jesus to fulfill popular Messianic expectations. It was not easy, therefore, to understand how that would mean showing himself to the disciples but not to the world.

A **14:23** *loves . . . obey . . . love.* Again love and obedience are linked (see vv. 15,21; 15:10 and notes).

14:24 Once more the close relationship between Jesus' words and the Father's is stressed (see v. 10; 7:16).

A **14:26** *Advocate.* See note on v. 16. *Holy Spirit.* See 1:33 and note. *whom the Father will send.* Both the Father and the Son are involved in the sending (see 15:26 and note). *name.* See notes on v. 13; 2:23. *remind you of everything I have said to you.* Crucial for the life of the church—and for the writing of the NT.

A **14:27** *Peace . . . my peace.* A common Hebrew greeting (see 20:19,21,26 and note on 20:19), which Jesus uses here in an unusual way. The term speaks, in effect, of the salvation that Christ's redemptive work will achieve for his disciples —total well-being and inner rest of spirit, in fellowship with God. All true peace is his gift, which the repetition emphasizes. *I do not give . . . as the world gives.* In its greetings of peace the world can only express a longing or wish. But Jesus' peace is real and present (see 16:33 and note). *troubled.* See note on v. 1.

14:28 *heard me say.* Cf. v. 3. *the Father is greater than I.* Revealing the subordinate role Jesus accepted as a necessary part of the incarnation. The statement must be understood in the light of the unity between the Father and the Son (see 10:30 and note).

14:30 *prince of this world.* See note on 12:31. *has no hold over me.* Satan has a hold over people because of their fallen state. Since Christ was sinless, Satan could have no hold over him.

A **14:31** *I . . . do exactly what my Father has commanded me.* Jesus had stressed the importance of his followers being obedient (see vv. 15,21,23 and notes), and he set the example. With these words he goes to fulfill his mission (chs. 18–19).

THE VINE AND THE BRANCHES

15 "I am ^{u} the true vine, ^{v} and my Father is the gardener. ^{2}He cuts off every branch in me that bears no fruit, ^{w} while every branch that does bear fruit ^{x} he prunes^a so that it will be even more fruitful. ^{3}You are already clean because of the word I have spoken to you. ^{y} ^{4}Remain in me, as I also remain in you. ^{z} No branch can bear fruit by itself; it must remain in the vine. Neither can you bear fruit unless you remain in me.

^{5}"I am the vine; you are the branches. If you remain in me and I in you, you will bear much fruit; ^{a} apart from me you can do nothing. ^{6}If you do not remain in me, you are like a branch that is thrown away and withers; such branches are picked up, thrown into the fire and burned. ^{b} ^{7}If you remain in me ^{c} and my words remain in you, ask whatever you wish, and it will be done for you. ^{d} ^{8}This is to my Father's glory, ^{e} that you bear much fruit, showing yourselves to be my disciples. ^{f}

^{9}"As the Father has loved me, ^{g} so have I loved you. Now remain in my love. ^{10}If you keep my commands, ^{h} you will remain in my love, just as I have kept my Father's commands and remain in his love. ^{11}I have told you this so that my joy may be in you and that your joy may be complete. ^{i} ^{12}My command is this: Love each other as I have loved you. ^{j} ^{13}Greater love has no one than this: to lay down one's life for one's friends. ^{k} ^{14}You are my friends ^{l} if you do what I command. ^{m} ^{15}I no longer call you servants, because servants do not know their master's business. Instead, I have called you friends, for everything that I learned from my Father I have made known to you. ^{n} ^{16}You did not choose me, but I chose you and appointed you^o so that you might go and bear fruit^p—fruit that will last—and so that whatever you ask in my name the Father will give you. ^{q} ^{17}This is my command: Love each other. ^{r}

THE WORLD HATES THE DISCIPLES

^{18}"If the world hates you, ^{s} keep in mind that it hated me first. ^{19}If you belonged to the world, it would love you as its own. As it is, you do not belong to the world, but I have chosen you ^{t} out of the world. That is why the world hates you. ^{u} ^{20}Remember what I told you: 'Servants are not greater than their master.'^{b} ^{v} If they persecuted me, they will persecute you also. ^{w} If they obeyed my teaching, they will obey yours also. ^{21}They will treat you this way because of my name, ^{x} for they do not know the one who sent me. ^{y} ^{22}If I had

---

^{a} 2 The Greek for *he prunes* also means *he cleans*. ^{b} 20 John 13:16

15:1 ^{u} S Jn 6:35
^{v} Ps 80:8-11; Isa 5:1-7
15:2 ^{w} ver 6;
S Mt 3:10 ^{x} Ps 92:14;
Mt 3:8; 7:20;
Gal 5:22; Eph 5:9;
Php 1:11
15:3 ^{y} Jn 13:10;
17:17; Eph 5:26
15:4 ^{z} S Jn 6:56
15:5 ^{a} ver 16
15:6 ^{b} ver 2;
Eze 15:4; S Mt 3:10
15:7 ^{c} ver 4;
S Jn 6:56 ^{d} S Mt 7:7
15:8 ^{e} S Mt 9:8
^{f} Jn 8:31
15:9 ^{g} Jn 17:23,24,
26
15:10 ^{h} S Jn 14:15
15:11 ^{i} S Jn 3:29
15:12 ^{j} ver 17;
S Jn 13:34
15:13 ^{k} Ge 44:33;
Jn 10:11; Ro 5:7,8
15:14 ^{l} Job 16:20;
Pr 18:24; Lk 12:4
^{m} Mt 12:50
15:15 ^{n} Jn 8:26
15:16 ^{o} ver 19;
Jn 13:18 ^{p} ver 5
^{q} S Mt 7:7
15:17 ^{r} ver 12
15:18 ^{s} Isa 66:5;
Jn 7:7; 1Jn 3:13
15:19 ^{t} ver 16
^{u} Jn 17:14
15:20 ^{v} S Jn 13:16
^{w} 2Ti 3:12
15:21 ^{x} Isa 66:5;
Mt 5:10,11; 10:22;
Lk 6:22; Ac 5:41;
1Pe 4:14; Rev 2:3
^{y} Jn 16:3

15:1 *I am.* See note on 6:35. *the true vine.* The vine is frequently used in the OT as a symbol of Israel (see, e.g., Ps 80:8–16; Isa 5:1–7; Jer 2:21 and notes). When this imagery is used, Israel is often shown as lacking in some way. Jesus, however, is "the true vine."

15:2 *cuts off.* A reference to judgment (see note on v. 6). *prunes.* Pruning produces fruitfulness. In the NT the figure of good fruit represents the product of a godly life (see Mt 3:8; 7:16–20) or virtues of character (see Gal 5:22–23; Eph 5:9; Php 1:11 and notes).

15:3 *clean.* See TNIV text note on v. 2. *the word.* Sums up the message of Jesus.

15:4 *Remain in me.* The believer has no fruitfulness apart from union and fellowship with Christ. A branch out of contact with the vine is lifeless.

15:5 *I am the vine.* See note on v. 1. The repetition gives emphasis. *remain in me and I in you.* A living union with Christ is absolutely necessary; without it there is nothing. *apart from me you can do nothing.* Cf. Php 4:13 (see note there).

15:6 *thrown into the fire and burned.* Judged (see note on v. 2). In light of such passages as 6:39; 10:27–29 (see notes there), these branches probably do not represent true believers. Genuine salvation is evidenced by a life of fruitfulness (see notes on vv. 2,4,10; see also Heb 6:9, "things that have to do with salvation," and note there; cf. Mt 7:19–23).

15:7 *my words remain in you.* It is impossible to pray correctly apart from knowing and believing the teachings of Christ. *ask whatever you wish.* See 14:13; 1Jn 5:14 and notes.

15:8 *to my Father's glory.* The Father is glorified in the work of the Son (see 13:31 and note), and he is also glorified in the fruit-bearing of disciples (see Mt 7:20; Lk 6:43–45).

15:10 *keep . . . as I have kept.* Again the importance of obedience (cf. 14:15,21,23), and again the example of Christ

(see 14:31 and note). *my love . . . his love.* See vv. 12,14. Obedience and love go together (see 14:15,21,23; 1Jn 2:5 and notes; 5:2–3).

15:11 *joy.* Mentioned previously in this Gospel only in 3:29, but one of the characteristic notes of the upper room discourse (see 16:22,24 and note on 16:22; 17:13). The Christian way is never dreary, for Jesus desires his disciples' joy to be complete (see also Introduction to Philippians: Characteristics, 4; see also Php 4:4; 1Th 5:16; 1Jn 1:4 and notes).

15:13 Christ's love was shown not only in his words but also in his sacrificial death (see Eph 5:25 and note).

15:15 *servants . . . friends.* A servant is simply an agent, doing what his master commands and often not understanding his master's purpose. But Jesus takes his friends into his confidence. *everything . . . I have made known to you.* From 16:12 we learn that though Jesus had let his disciples know as much as they were able to absorb of the Father's plan, the revelation was not yet complete. The Spirit would make other things known in due course (see 16:12–13 and notes).

15:16 *I chose you . . . bear fruit . . . ask.* Disciples normally chose the particular rabbi to whom they wanted to be attached, but it was not so with Jesus' disciples. He chose them, and for a purpose—the bearing of fruit (see v. 2 and note). We usually desire a strong prayer life in order that we may be fruitful, but here it is the other way around. Jesus enables us to bear fruit, and then the Father will hear our prayers. *name.* See notes on 2:23; 14:13.

15:18–19 *world.* Here refers to the human system that opposes God's purpose (see note on 1:9).

15:21 *They will treat you this way.* Because Christians do not belong to the world, persecution from the world is inevitable. The basic reason is the world's ignorance and rejection of the Father (cf. 16:3). *name.* See note on 2:23.

15:22 *z* Eze 2:5; 3:7
a Jn 9:41; Ro 1:20; 2:1
15:24 *b* Jn 5:36
c Jn 9:41
15:25 *d* S Jn 10:34
e Ps 35:19; 69:4;
109:3
15:26 *f* Jn 14:16
g Jn 14:26; 16:7
h S Jn 14:17 *i* 1Jn 5:7
15:27 *j* S Lk 24:48;
Jn 21:24; 1Jn 1:2; 4:14
k S Lk 1:2
16:1 *l* Jn 15:18-27
m Mt 11:6
16:2 *n* Jn 9:22; 12:42
o Isa 66:5; Ac 26:9,10;
Rev 6:9
16:3 *p* Jn 15:21;
17:25; 1Jn 3:1
16:4 *q* Jn 13:19;
14:29 *r* Jn 15:27
16:5 *s* ver 10,17,28;
Jn 7:33 *t* Jn 13:36;
14:5
16:6 *u* ver 22
16:7 *v* Jn 14:16,26;
15:26 *w* Jn 7:39; 14:26
16:9 *x* Jn 15:22
16:10 *y* Ac 3:14;
7:52; Ro 1:17; 3:21,22;
1Pe 3:18 *z* S ver 5
16:11 *a* S Jn 12:31
16:12 *b* Mk 4:33;
1Co 3:2
16:13 *c* S Jn 14:17
d Ps 25:5; Jn 14:26

not come and spoken to them, *z* they would not be guilty of sin; but now they have no excuse for their sin. *a* 23 Those who hate me hate my Father as well. 24 If I had not done among them the works no one else did, *b* they would not be guilty of sin. *c* As it is, they have seen, and yet they have hated both me and my Father. 25 But this is to fulfill what is written in their Law: *d* 'They hated me without reason.' *a e*

THE WORK OF THE HOLY SPIRIT

26 "When the Advocate *f* comes, whom I will send to you from the Father *g* —the Spirit of truth *h* who goes out from the Father—he will testify about me. *i* 27 And you also must testify, *j* for you have been with me from the beginning. *k*

16 "All this *l* I have told you so that you will not fall away. *m* 2 They will put you out of the synagogue; *n* in fact, the hour is coming when those who kill you will think they are offering a service to God. *o* 3 They will do such things because they have not known the Father or me. *p* 4 I have told you this, so that when their hour comes you will remember *q* that I warned you about them. I did not tell you this from the beginning because I was with you, *r* 5 but now I am going to him who sent me. *s* None of you asks me, 'Where are you going?' *t* 6 Rather, you are filled with grief *u* because I have said these things. 7 But very truly I tell you, it is for your good that I am going away. Unless I go away, the Advocate *v* will not come to you; but if I go, I will send him to you. *w* 8 When he comes, he will prove the world to be in the wrong about sin and righteousness and judgment: 9 about sin, *x* because people do not believe in me; 10 about righteousness, *y* because I am going to the Father, *z* where you can see me no longer; 11 and about judgment, because the prince of this world *a* now stands condemned.

12 "I have much more to say to you, more than you can now bear. *b* 13 But when he, the Spirit of truth, *c* comes, he will guide you into all the truth. *d* He will not speak on his own; he will speak only what he hears, and he will tell you what is yet to come. 14 He will glorify me because it is from me that he will receive what he will make known to you. 15 All

a 25 Psalms 35:19; 69:4

15:22 *no excuse.* Privilege and responsibility go together. The Jews had had the great privilege of having the Son of God among them—in addition to having received God's special revelation in the OT. Those who rejected him were totally guilty and without excuse. If he had not come to them, they would still have been sinners, but they would not have been guilty of rejecting him directly (see v. 24).

15:23 Contrast 13:20.

15:25 *to fulfill what is written.* See note on Ps 35:19. In the end God's purpose is always accomplished, despite the belief of those who reject Jesus that they have successfully opposed it. *Law.* See notes on 10:34; 12:34.

15:26 *Advocate.* See note on 14:16. *I will send.* See notes on 14:16,26. *Spirit of truth.* See note on 14:17. *goes out from the Father.* Probably refers to the Spirit's being sent to do the Father's work on earth rather than to his eternal relationship with the Father. *testify.* See note on 1:7.

15:27 *you also.* Emphatic. Believers bear their testimony to Christ in the power of the Spirit (see Ac 1:8 and note). But it is their testimony, and they are responsible for bearing it. *from the beginning.* The apostles bore the definitive testimony, for they were uniquely chosen and taught by Christ and were eyewitnesses of his glory (see Lk 24:48; Ac 10:39,41).

16:2 *put you out of the synagogue.* See note on 9:22. *a service to God.* Religious people have often persecuted others in the strong conviction that they were doing God's will (see Ac 26:9–11; Gal 1:13–14).

16:3 *the Father.* See note on 5:17. *or me.* Again the Father and the Son are linked. Not to know Christ is to be ignorant of the Father (see 14:7,10–11; 17:6–7,22–23,26 and notes).

16:5 *None of you asks me, 'Where are you going?'* Peter had asked such a question (13:36) but quickly turned his attention to another subject. His concern had been with what would happen to himself and the others and not for where Jesus was going.

16:6 *you are filled with grief.* Because of his announced departure.

16:7 *Unless I go away.* Jesus did not say why the Spirit would not come until he went away but clearly taught that his saving work on the cross was necessary before the sending of the Spirit. *Advocate.* See note on 14:16. *I will send him.* See note on 14:26.

16:8 *he will prove the world to be in the wrong.* The work the Spirit does in the world; the NT normally speaks of his work in believers.

16:9 *about sin.* Apart from the Spirit's convicting work, people can never see themselves as sinners. *because people do not believe.* May mean that their sin is their failure to believe or that their unbelief is a classic example of sin. John may have had both of these in mind.

16:10 *about righteousness.* The righteousness brought about by Christ's sacrificial death (see Ro 1:17; 3:21–24 and notes). No one but the Holy Spirit can reveal to a person that a righteous status before God does not depend on good works but on Christ's death on the cross. *because I am going to the Father.* The ascension, which as part of Christ's exaltation placed God's seal of approval on Christ's redemptive act.

16:11 *about judgment.* Jesus was speaking of the defeat of Satan, which was a form of judgment, not simply a victory. More than power is in question. God acts with justice. *because the prince of this world now stands condemned.* See note on 12:31.

16:12 *more than you can now bear.* This may mean "more than you can understand now," or "more than you can perform without the Spirit's help" (to live out Christ's teaching requires the enabling presence of the Spirit).

16:13 *Spirit of truth.* See note on 14:17. *only what he hears.* We are not told whether he hears from the Father or the Son, but it obviously does not matter, for the verse stresses the close relationship among the three. *what is yet to come.* Probably means the whole Christian way or revelation (presented and preserved in the apostolic writings), still future at the time Jesus spoke.

16:14 *glorify me.* See note on 1:14. The Spirit draws no attention to himself but promotes the glory of Christ.

that belongs to the Father is mine. *e* That is why I said the Spirit will receive from me what he will make known to you."

THE DISCIPLES' GRIEF WILL TURN TO JOY

¹⁶Jesus went on to say, "In a little while *f* you will see me no more, and then after a little while you will see me." *g*

¹⁷At this, some of his disciples said to one another, "What does he mean by saying, 'In a little while you will see me no more, and then after a little while you will see me,' *h* and 'Because I am going to the Father'?" *i* ¹⁸They kept asking, "What does he mean by 'a little while'? We don't understand what he is saying."

¹⁹Jesus saw that they wanted to ask him about this, so he said to them, "Are you asking one another what I meant when I said, 'In a little while you will see me no more, and then after a little while you will see me'? ²⁰Very truly I tell you, you will weep and mourn *j* while the world rejoices. You will grieve, but your grief will turn to joy. *k* ²¹A woman giving birth to a child has pain *l* because her time has come; but when her baby is born she forgets the anguish because of her joy that a child is born into the world. ²²So with you: Now is your time of grief, *m* but I will see you again *n* and you will rejoice, and no one will take away your joy. *o* ²³In that day *p* you will no longer ask me anything. Very truly I tell you, my Father will give you whatever you ask in my name. *q* ²⁴Until now you have not asked for anything in my name. Ask and you will receive, *r* and your joy will be complete. *s*

²⁵"Though I have been speaking figuratively, *t* a time is coming *u* when I will no longer use this kind of language but will tell you plainly about my Father. ²⁶In that day you will ask in my name. *v* I am not saying that I will ask the Father on your behalf. ²⁷No, the Father himself loves you because you have loved me *w* and have believed that I came from God. *x* ²⁸I came from the Father and entered the world; now I am leaving the world and going back to the Father." *y*

²⁹Then Jesus' disciples said, "Now you are speaking clearly and without figures of speech. *z* ³⁰Now we can see that you know all things and that you do not even need to have anyone ask you questions. This makes us believe *a* that you came from God." *b*

³¹"Do you now believe?" Jesus replied. ³²"A time is coming *c* and in fact has come when you will be scattered, *d* each to your own home. You will leave me all alone. *e* Yet I am not alone, for my Father is with me. *f*

³³"I have told you these things, so that in me you may have peace. *g* In this world you will have trouble. *h* But take heart! I have overcome *i* the world."

16:15 *e* Jn 17:10
16:16 *f* S Jn 7:33
g ver 22; Jn 14:18-24
16:17 *h* ver 16 *i* ver 5
16:20 *j* Mk 16:10;
Lk 23:27 *k* Jn 20:20
16:21 *l* Isa 13:8;
21:3; 26:17; Mic 4:9;
1Th 5:3
16:22 *m* ver 6
n ver 16 *o* ver 20;
Jer 31:12
16:23 *p* ver 26;
Jn 14:20 *q* S Mt 7:7
16:24 *r* S Mt 7:7
s S Jn 3:29
16:25 *t* ver 29;
Ps 78:2; Eze 20:49;
Mt 13:34; Mk 4:33,
34; Jn 10:6 *u* ver 2
16:26 *v* ver 23,24
16:27 *w* Jn 14:21,23
x ver 30; S Jn 13:3
16:28 *y* ver 5,10,17;
Jn 13:3
16:29 *z* S ver 25
16:30 *a* 1Ki 17:24
b ver 27; S Jn 13:3
16:32 *c* ver 2,25
d Mt 26:31 *e* Mt 26:56
f Jn 8:16,29
16:33 *g* S Jn 14:27
h Jn 15:18-21
i Ro 8:37; 1Jn 4:4; 5:4;
Rev 2:7,11,17,26; 3:5,
12,21; 21:7

16:15 *All that belongs to the Father is mine.* Cf. 17:10. The three Persons are closely related.

16:16 *a little while … a little while.* Few doubt that the first phrase refers to the interval before the crucifixion. But interpretations differ as to whether the second refers to the interval preceding the resurrection, the coming of the Spirit or the second coming of Christ. It seems that the language here best fits the resurrection (see v. 22 and note).

16:17 *going to the Father.* See v. 10 and note. Jesus had not linked this with "a little while," but the apostles saw them as connected.

16:20 *weep.* The same verb for loud wailing as in 11:33 (see note there), which carries the idea of deep sorrow and its outward expression.

16:21 *A woman giving birth.* Giving birth usually causes both pain and joy (cf. Isa 26:17–19; 66:7–14; Hos 13:13–14).

16:22 *I will see you again.* As in v. 16, probably a reference to Jesus' appearances after his resurrection. *no one will take away your joy.* The resurrection would change things permanently, bringing a joy that cannot be removed by the world's assaults (see note on 15:11).

16:23 *you will no longer ask me anything.* Seems to mean asking for information (rather than asking in prayer), which would not be necessary after the resurrection. Jesus then moved on to the subject of prayer. However, Jesus may have been saying that though his disciples previously had been praying to himself, after his death and resurrection they were to go directly to the Father and pray in Christ's name (see vv. 24,26–27 and notes). *name.* See notes on 2:23; 14:13.

16:24 *Until now.* Previously they had asked the Father or Christ, but they had not asked the Father in Christ's name. *your joy.* See note on 15:11.

16:25 *I have been speaking figuratively.* Throughout the discourse, not just in the immediately preceding words. *a time is coming.* After the resurrection.

16:26 *in my name.* See notes on 2:23; 14:13. *I am not saying that I will ask.* Not a contradiction of Ro 8:34; Heb 7:25; 1Jn 2:1 (see notes there). Those passages mean that Christ's presence in heaven as the crucified and risen Lord is itself an intercession. Here the teaching is that there will be no need for him to make petitions in our behalf.

A **16:27** *the Father himself loves you.* Christ is explaining why the disciples can come directly to the Father in prayer: They will have loved and trusted in Jesus, and in love God will hear their requests in Jesus' name.

16:29 *without figures of speech.* See v. 25 and note.

16:30 *believe that you came from God.* Two recurring themes of this Gospel: believing (see note on 1:7) and Jesus' coming from God (see notes on 4:34; 17:3,8).

A **16:32** *you will be scattered.* The disciples had faith, but not enough to stand firm in the face of disaster. Jesus knew they would fail (see Mt 26:31 and note; cf. Zec 13:7 and note); however, his church is not built on people's strength but on God's ability to use people even after they have failed.

16:33 Notice the contrasts: between "in me" and "in this world" (see note on 1:9) and between "peace" and "trouble." *I have overcome.* Just before his death Jesus affirms his final victory.

17:1 *j* Jn 11:41
k S Mt 26:18
l Jn 12:23; 13:31,32
17:2 *m* S Mt 28:18
n S Mt 25:46 *o* ver 6,
9, 24; Da 7:14;
Jn 6:37,39
17:3 *p* S Php 3:8
q ver 8,18,21,23,25;
S Jn 3:17
17:4 *r* Jn 13:31
s S Jn 19:30
17:5 *t* ver 1
u Php 2:6 *v* S Jn 1:2
17:6 *w* ver 26;
Jn 1:18 *x* S ver 2
17:8 *y* ver 14,26;
S Jn 14:24 *z* S Jn 13:3
a ver 3,18,21,23,25;
S Jn 3:17
17:9 *b* Lk 22:32
c S ver 2
17:10 *d* Jn 16:15
17:11 *e* Jn 13:1
f ver 13; Jn 7:33
g ver 21-23; Ps 133:1
h Jn 10:30
17:12 *i* S Jn 6:39
j Jn 6:70 *k* S Mt 1:22
17:13 *l* ver 11
m S Jn 3:29
17:14 *n* Jn 15:19
o ver 16; Jn 8:23
17:15 *p* S Mt 5:37
17:16 *q* ver 14
17:17 *r* S Jn 15:3;
2Sa 7:28; 1Ki 17:24

JESUS PRAYS TO BE GLORIFIED

17 After Jesus said this, he looked toward heaven *j* and prayed:

"Father, the hour has come. *k* Glorify your Son, that your Son may glorify you. *l* ²For you granted him authority over all people *m* that he might give eternal life *n* to all those you have given him. *o* ³Now this is eternal life: that they know you, *p* the only true God, and Jesus Christ, whom you have sent. *q* ⁴I have brought you glory *r* on earth by finishing the work you gave me to do. *s* ⁵And now, Father, glorify me *t* in your presence with the glory I had with you *u* before the world began. *v*

JESUS PRAYS FOR HIS DISCIPLES

⁶"I have revealed you *a w* to those whom you gave me *x* out of the world. They were yours; you gave them to me and they have obeyed your word. ⁷Now they know that everything you have given me comes from you. ⁸For I gave them the words you gave me *y* and they accepted them. They knew with certainty that I came from you, *z* and they believed that you sent me. *a* ⁹I pray for them. *b* I am not praying for the world, but for those you have given me, *c* for they are yours. ¹⁰All I have is yours, and all you have is mine. *d* And glory has come to me through them. ¹¹I will remain in the world no longer, but they are still in the world, *e* and I am coming to you. *f* Holy Father, protect them by the power of *b* your name, the name you gave me, so that they may be one *g* as we are one. *h* ¹²While I was with them, I protected them and kept them safe by *c* that name you gave me. None has been lost *i* except the one doomed to destruction *j* so that Scripture would be fulfilled. *k*

¹³"I am coming to you now, *l* but I say these things while I am still in the world, so that they may have the full measure of my joy *m* within them. ¹⁴I have given them your word and the world has hated them, *n* for they are not of the world any more than I am of the world. *o* ¹⁵My prayer is not that you take them out of the world but that you protect them from the evil one. *p* ¹⁶They are not of the world, even as I am not of it. *q* ¹⁷Sanctify them by *d* the truth; your word is truth. *r* ¹⁸As you sent me into

---

a 6 Greek *your name*; also in verse 26   *b* 11 Or *Father, keep them faithful to*   *c* 12 Or *kept them faithful to*
d 17 Or *them to live in accordance with*

17:1–26 Jesus' longest recorded prayer.
17:1 *he looked toward heaven.* The customary attitude in prayer (11:41; Ps 123:1; Mk 7:34), though sometimes Jesus prostrated himself (see Mt 26:39). *Father.* Used of God in John's Gospel about 120 times. *the hour.* See note on 2:4. *Glorify . . . glorify.* See notes on 1:14; 7:39; 13:31. The glory of the Father and that of the Son are closely connected, and the death by which Jesus would glorify God would lead to eternal life for believers (v. 2).
17:2 *granted.* The act of giving is stressed in this chapter (vv. 4,6–9,11–12,14,22,24); see note on 3:27. *eternal life.* See note on 3:15. *those you have given him.* Again God's initiative in salvation is stressed (see vv. 6,12; 6:37,39,44 and notes).
17:3 *sent.* Again the mission of Jesus is mentioned (see 13:20 and note).
17:4 *I have brought you glory.* Christ's mission was not self-centered. *the work you gave me.* Jesus emphasized the supreme place of the Father (see note on 4:34).
17:5 *glorify me . . . with the glory I had with you.* Jesus asks the Father to return him to his previous position of glory, to exchange humiliation for glorification. This occurred at Christ's resurrection and exaltation to God's right hand. *world.* The universe (see notes on v. 14; 1:9). The Greek word for "world" occurs 18 times in this prayer.
17:6 *I have revealed you.* See TNIV text note and notes on 2:23; 14:13; cf. 1:18. *those whom you gave me.* Again the divine initiative (see note on v. 2).
17:7 *everything . . . comes from you.* Only as people see the Father at work in Jesus do they have a proper concept of God. The disciples had at last reached this understanding. Cf. Jas 1:17.

⏹ 17:8 Three things about the disciples are mentioned: 1. They accepted the teaching (unlike the Pharisees and others who heard it but did not receive it). 2. They knew with certainty Jesus' divine origin. Acceptance of that revelation led them

further into truth. 3. They believed (see notes on 1:7,12; 20:31).
17:9 *not . . . for the world.* The only prayer Jesus could pray for the world was that it cease to be worldly (i.e., opposed to God), and this he did pray (vv. 21,23).

⏹ 17:11 *Holy Father.* A form of address found only here in the NT (but cf. 1Pe 1:16; Rev 4:8 and notes). The name suggests both remoteness and nearness; God is both awe-inspiring (see Lev 11:44 and note) and loving. *that they may be one.* The latter part of the prayer strongly emphasizes unity. Here the unity is already given, not something to be achieved. The meaning is "that they continually be one" rather than "that they become one." The unity is to be like that between the Father and the Son. It is much more than unity of organization, but the church's present divisions are the result of the failures of Christians.

⏹ 17:12 *I protected them.* Christ's power is adequate for every need (cf. 1Pe 1:5 and note). *the one doomed to destruction.* Lit. "the son of destruction" (see 2Th 2:3 and note), i.e., one belonging to the sphere of damnation and destined for destruction (but predestination is not in view here). Reference is to Judas Iscariot.
17:13 *my joy.* See note on 15:11.

⏹ 17:14 *the world.* The world that is hostile to God and God's people (see notes on v. 5; 1:9). *not of the world.* They do not have the mind-set of the world, i.e., hostility to God, for they have been "born of the Spirit" (3:8) and are "children of God" (1:12).

⏹ 17:15 *not that you take them out of the world.* The world is where Jesus' disciples are to do their work; Jesus does not wish them to be taken from it until that work is done (see v. 18). *the evil one.* Satan, who is especially active in the world (Mt 6:13; 1Jn 5:19), making God's protection indispensable.
17:17 *Sanctify.* See TNIV text note; see also v. 19; 1Co 1:2 and notes. *the truth; your word.* Sanctification and revelation (as recorded in God's word) go together (cf. 1Pe 2:2 and note). For the

the world, ⁱ I have sent them into the world. ᵗ ¹⁹For them I sanctify myself, that they too may be truly sanctified. ᵘ

JESUS PRAYS FOR ALL BELIEVERS

²⁰"My prayer is not for them alone. I pray also for those who will believe in me through their message, ²¹that all of them may be one, ᵛ Father, just as you are in me and I am in you. ʷ May they also be in us so that the world may believe that you have sent me. ˣ ²²I have given them the glory that you gave me, ʸ that they may be one as we are one ᶻ— ²³I in them and you in me—so that they may be brought to complete unity. Then the world will know that you sent me ᵃ and have loved them ᵇ even as you have loved me.

²⁴"Father, I want those you have given me ᶜ to be with me where I am, ᵈ and to see my glory, ᵉ the glory you have given me because you loved me before the creation of the world. ᶠ

²⁵"Righteous Father, though the world does not know you, ᵍ I know you, and they know that you have sent me. ʰ ²⁶I have made you known to them, ⁱ and will continue to make you known in order that the love you have for me may be in them ʲ and that I myself may be in them."

JESUS ARRESTED

18:3–11pp — Mt 26:47–56; Mk 14:43–50; Lk 22:47–53

18 When he had finished praying, Jesus left with his disciples and crossed the Kidron Valley. ᵏ On the other side there was a garden, ˡ and he and his disciples went into it. ᵐ

²Now Judas, who betrayed him, knew the place, because Jesus had often met there with his disciples. ⁿ ³So Judas came to the garden, guiding ᵒ a detachment of soldiers and some officials from the chief priests and the Pharisees. ᵖ They were carrying torches, lanterns and weapons.

⁴Jesus, knowing all that was going to happen to him, �q went out and asked them, "Who is it you want?" ʳ

⁵"Jesus of Nazareth," ˢ they replied.

"I am he," Jesus said. (And Judas the traitor was standing there with them.) ⁶When Jesus said, "I am he," they drew back and fell to the ground.

17:18 *ˢ*ver 3,8,21, 23,25; S Jn 3:17
ᵗ Jn 20:21
17:19 *ᵘ* ver 17
17:21 *ᵛ* Jer 32:39
ʷ ver 11; Jn 10:38
ˣ ver 3,8,18,23,25; S Jn 3:17
17:22 *ʸ* Jn 1:14
ᶻ S Jn 14:20
17:23 *ᵃ* ver 3,8,18, 21,25; S Jn 3:17
ᵇ Jn 16:27
17:24 *ᶜ* S ver 2
ᵈ S Jn 12:26 *ᵉ* Jn 1:14
ᶠ ver 5; S Mt 25:34; S Jn 1:2
17:25 *ᵍ* Jn 15:21; 16:3 *ʰ* ver 3,8,18,21, 23; S Jn 3:17; 16:27
17:26 *ⁱ* ver 6
ʲ Jn 15:9
18:1 *ᵏ* 2Sa 15:23
ˡ ver 26; S Mt 21:1
ᵐ Mt 26:36
18:2 *ⁿ* Lk 21:37; 22:39
18:3 *ᵒ* Ac 1:16
ᵖ ver 12
18:4 *q* Jn 6:64; 13:1, 11 *ʳ* ver 7
18:5 *ˢ* S Mk 1:24

---

relationship between Christ's teaching and truth, see 8:31–32 and note on 8:32.

17:18 *As you sent me … I have sent them.* Jesus' mission is one of the dominant themes of this Gospel and is given as the pattern for his followers (see v. 3 and note). *into the world.* We may long for heaven, but it is on earth that our work is done.

17:19 *I sanctify myself.* This statement appears to be unparalleled. In the Septuagint (the pre-Christian Greek translation of the OT) the verb is used of consecrating priests (Ex 28:41) and sacrifices (Ex 28:38; Nu 18:9). Jesus solemnly "sanctifies" (i.e., "sets apart") himself to do God's will, which at this point meant his death. *that they too may be … sanctified.* Jesus died on the cross not only to save us but also to consecrate us to God's service (see note on 1 Co 1:2).

17:20 *those who will believe in me.* Jesus had just spoken of the mission and the sanctification of his followers (vv. 18–19). He was confident that they would spread the gospel, and he prayed for those who would believe as a result. All future believers are included in this prayer.

17:21 *that all of them may be one.* See note on v. 11. *Father.* See note on v. 1. *that the world may believe.* The unity of believers should have an effect on outsiders, to convince them of the mission of Christ. Jesus' prayer is a rebuke of the groundless and often bitter divisions among believers.

17:22 *glory.* See note on v. 1. Believers are to be characterized by humility and service, just as Christ was, and it is on them that God's glory rests. *that they may be one as we are one.* Again the Lord emphasized the importance of unity among his followers, and again the standard is the unity of the Father and the Son.

17:23 *I in them and you in me.* There are two indwellings here: that of the Son in believers and that of the Father in

the Son. It is because the latter is a reality that the former can take place. *complete unity.* Again the emphasis on unity has an evangelistic aim. This time it is connected not only with the mission of Jesus but also with God's love for people and for Christ.

17:24 *Father.* See note on v. 1. *I want.* Means "I will that." Jesus said, "I will"—his last will and testament for his followers. Where he himself was concerned, he prayed, "not what I will, but what you will" (Mk 14:36). *to be with me.* The Christian's greatest blessing (see 14:3; 1Th 4:17 and note). *my glory.* Perhaps used here to refer to Jesus' eternal splendor (see 1Jn 3:2). Or Jesus' prayer may have been that in the life to come they might fully appreciate the glory of his lowly service (cf. Php 2:7).

17:25 *Righteous Father.* A form of address found only here in the NT (cf. note on "Holy Father" in v. 11). *they know.* They did not know God directly and personally, but they knew that God had sent Christ. To recognize God in Christ's mission is a great advance over anything the world can know.

17:26 *made you known to them.* See 16:3 and note.

18:1 *crossed the Kidron Valley.* East of Jerusalem and dry except during the rainy season (see map, p. 1703).

18:3 *Judas.* See note on 6:71. *officials from the chief priests and the Pharisees.* Equivalent to the temple guard sent by the Sanhedrin (see notes on Mt 2:4; 3:7; Mk 14:55). *torches.* Resinous pieces of wood fastened together. *lanterns.* Terra-cotta holders into which household lamps could be inserted.

18:4 *knowing all that was going to happen to him.* Jesus was not taken by surprise.

18:5 *I am.* See 6:35; 8:58 and notes. *with them.* John does not let us forget where Judas belonged.

18:6 *fell to the ground.* They came to arrest a meek peasant and instead were met in the dim light by a majestic and powerful person.

18:7 ^t ver 4
18:9 ^u S Jn 6:39
18:11 ^v S Mt 20:22
18:12 ^w ver 3
18:13 ^x ver 24;
S Mt 26:3
18:14 ^y Jn 11:49-51
18:15 ^z S Mt 26:3
^a Mt 26:58; Mk 14:54;
Lk 22:54
18:17 ^b ver 25
18:18 ^c Jn 21:9
^d Mk 14:54,67
18:20 ^e S Mt 4:23
^f Mt 26:55 ^g Jn 7:26
18:22 ^h ver 3
ⁱ Mt 16:21; Jn 19:3

⁷Again he asked them, "Who is it you want?" ^t

"Jesus of Nazareth," they said.

⁸Jesus answered, "I told you that I am he. If you are looking for me, then let these men go." ⁹This happened so that the words he had spoken would be fulfilled: "I have not lost one of those you gave me." ^a ^u

¹⁰Then Simon Peter, who had a sword, drew it and struck the high priest's servant, cutting off his right ear. (The servant's name was Malchus.)

¹¹Jesus commanded Peter, "Put your sword away! Shall I not drink the cup ^v the Father has given me?"

¹²Then the detachment of soldiers with its commander and the Jewish officials ^w arrested Jesus. They bound him ¹³and brought him first to Annas, who was the father-in-law of Caiaphas, ^x the high priest that year. ¹⁴Caiaphas was the one who had advised the Jewish leaders that it would be good if one man died for the people. ^y

PETER'S FIRST DENIAL

18:16–18pp — Mt 26:69,70; Mk 14:66–68; Lk 22:55–57

¹⁵Simon Peter and another disciple were following Jesus. Because this disciple was known to the high priest, ^z he went in with Jesus into the high priest's courtyard, ^a ¹⁶but Peter had to wait outside at the door. The other disciple, who was known to the high priest, came back, spoke to the servant girl on duty there and brought Peter in.

¹⁷"You aren't one of this man's disciples too, are you?" she asked Peter.

He replied, "I am not." ^b

¹⁸It was cold, and the servants and officials stood around a fire ^c they had made to keep warm. Peter also was standing with them, warming himself. ^d

THE HIGH PRIEST QUESTIONS JESUS

18:19–24pp — Mt 26:59–68; Mk 14:55–65; Lk 22:63–71

¹⁹Meanwhile, the high priest questioned Jesus about his disciples and his teaching.

²⁰"I have spoken openly to the world," Jesus replied. "I always taught in synagogues ^e or at the temple, ^f where all the Jews come together. I said nothing in secret. ^g ²¹Why question me? Ask those who heard me. Surely they know what I said."

²²When Jesus said this, one of the officials ^h nearby slapped him in the face. ⁱ "Is this the way you answer the high priest?" he demanded.

^a 9 John 6:39

18:8 *I am.* The threefold repetition (vv. 5,6,8) emphasizes the solemn words. *let these men go.* Jesus cared for the disciples even as he was going to his death. Twice he had made the arresting party say plainly that he was the one they wanted (vv. 4–5,7).
18:9 *would be fulfilled.* Words normally used in quoting Scripture, and Jesus' words are on the same level (see 6:39; 17:12 and notes).
18:10 *Simon Peter.* It is to John that we owe the information that the man with the sword (the Greek for this word refers to a short sword) was Peter and that the man he wounded was named Malchus.
18:11 *the cup.* Often points to suffering (see Ps 75:8; Eze 23:31 and note) and the wrath of God (see notes on Ps 16:5; Isa 51:17; Jer 25:15; Ro 1:18; Rev 14:10). *the Father has given me.* The Synoptic Gospels also speak of the cup at the time of Jesus' prayer at Gethsemane (see Mt 26:39; Mk 14:36; Lk 22:42 and notes), and John says it came from the Father. God was in control.
18:12 *bound him.* The reason for the bonds is not clear. Perhaps their use was standard procedure, much like the modern use of handcuffs.
C **18:13** *Annas.* Had been deposed from the high priesthood by the Romans in A.D. 15 but was probably still regarded by many as the true high priest (see note on Lk 3:2). In Jewish law no one could be sentenced on the day their trial was held. The two examinations—this one (mentioned only by John; see note on Mk 14:53—15:15) and that before Caiaphas—may have been conducted to give some form of legitimacy to what was done. *high priest that year.* See note on 11:49.
18:14 *Caiaphas . . . had advised the Jewish leaders.* A reference

to 11:49–50 (see notes there). For John it was this unconscious prophecy that mattered most about Caiaphas. John may also have been hinting that a fair trial could not be expected from a man who had already said that putting Jesus to death was expedient.
18:15 *another disciple.* Perhaps John himself. *known to the high priest.* Refers to more than casual acquaintance; he had entrée into the high priest's house and could bring Peter in.
18:16 *servant girl.* All four Gospels tell us that Peter's first challenge (v. 17) came from a slave girl, the most unimportant person imaginable.
18:17 The form of the girl's question implied a negative answer, and Peter capitalized on that by saying, "I am not." The other Gospels seem to indicate that the other denials followed immediately, but it is likely that there were intervals during which other things happened (see Lk 22:58–59).
18:18 *Peter also was standing with them.* On a cold night he would have been conspicuous if he had stayed away from the fire.
18:19 *questioned.* Not legal, since witnesses were supposed to be brought in first to establish guilt. The accused were not required to prove their innocence. Perhaps Annas regarded this as a preliminary inquiry, not a trial.
18:20 *I have spoken openly.* It should not have been difficult to find witnesses (v. 21). *nothing in secret.* Not a denial that he taught the disciples privately, but a denial that he had secretly taught them subversive teaching different from his public message.
18:22 *slapped.* Another illegality. The Greek word apparently means a blow with the open hand—a slap.

²³"If I said something wrong," Jesus replied, "testify as to what is wrong. But if I spoke the truth, why did you strike me?"*ⁱ* ²⁴Then Annas sent him bound to Caiaphas *ᵏ* the high priest.

PETER'S SECOND AND THIRD DENIALS

18:25–27pp — Mt 26:71–75; Mk 14:69–72; Lk 22:58–62

²⁵Meanwhile, Simon Peter was still standing there warming himself. *ˡ* So they asked him, "You aren't one of his disciples too, are you?"

He denied it, saying, "I am not." *ᵐ*

²⁶One of the high priest's servants, a relative of the man whose ear Peter had cut off, *ⁿ* challenged him, "Didn't I see you with him in the garden?" *ᵒ* ²⁷Again Peter denied it, and at that moment a rooster began to crow. *ᵖ*

JESUS BEFORE PILATE

18:29–40pp — Mt 27:11–18,20–23; Mk 15:2–5; Lk 23:2,3,18–25

²⁸Then the Jewish leaders took Jesus from Caiaphas to the palace of the Roman governor. *�q* By now it was early morning, and to avoid ceremonial uncleanness they did not enter the palace, *ʳ* because they wanted to be able to eat the Passover. *ˢ* ²⁹So Pilate came out to them and asked, "What charges are you bringing against this man?"

³⁰"If he were not a criminal," they replied, "we would not have handed him over to you."

³¹Pilate said, "Take him yourselves and judge him by your own law."

"But we have no right to execute anyone," they objected. ³²This took place to fulfill what Jesus had said about the kind of death he was going to die. *ᵗ*

³³Pilate then went back inside the palace, *ᵘ* summoned Jesus and asked him, "Are you the king of the Jews?" *ᵛ*

³⁴"Is that your own idea," Jesus asked, "or did others talk to you about me?"

³⁵"Am I a Jew?" Pilate replied. "Your own people and chief priests handed you over to me. What is it you have done?"

³⁶Jesus said, "My kingdom *ʷ* is not of this world. If it were, my servants would fight to prevent my arrest by the Jewish leaders. *ˣ* But now my kingdom is from another place." *ʸ*

³⁷"You are a king, then!" said Pilate.

18:23 *ⁱ* Mt 5:39;
Ac 23:2-5
18:24 *ᵏ* ver 13;
S Mt 26:3
18:25 *ˡ* ver 18
ᵐ ver 17
18:26 *ⁿ* ver 10
ᵒ ver 1
18:27 *ᵖ* Jn 13:38
18:28 *q* S Mt 27:2
ʳ ver 33; Jn 19:9
ˢ Jn 11:55
18:32 *ᵗ* Mt 20:19;
26:2; Jn 3:14; 8:28;
12:32,33
18:33 *ᵘ* ver 28,29;
Jn 19:9 *ᵛ* Lk 23:3;
S Mt 2:2
18:36 *ʷ* S Mt 3:2
ˣ Mt 26:53 *ʸ* Lk 17:21;
Jn 6:15

18:23 *testify.* A legal term, indicating an invitation to act in proper legal form. John stresses the importance of testimony throughout his Gospel (see note on 1:7).

18:25 *they asked him.* Some find a difficulty in that Mt 26:71 says another girl asked this question, whereas Mk 14:69 says it was the same girl and Lk 22:58 that it was a man. But with a group of servants talking around a fire, several would doubtless take up and repeat such a question, which could be the meaning of John's "they." As on the first occasion (v. 17) the question anticipated the answer "No." The servants probably did not really expect to find a follower of Jesus in the high priest's courtyard, but the question seemed worth asking.

18:26 *a relative.* Another piece of information we owe to John. A relative would have a deeper interest in the swordsman than other people had. But the light in the garden would have been dim, as in the courtyard (a charcoal fire glows, but does not have flames). *Didn't I see you … ?* Expected the answer "Yes."

18:27 *a rooster began to crow.* The fulfillment of the prophecy in 13:38 (see note there).

18:28 *Roman governor.* John says little about the Jewish phase of Jesus' trial but much about the Roman trial (see note on Mk 14:53—15:15). It is possible that John was in the Praetorium, the governor's official residence, for this trial. *early morning.* The chief priests evidently held a second session of the Sanhedrin after daybreak to give some appearance of legality to what they did (Mk 15:1). This occasion would have been immediately after that, perhaps between 6:00 A.M. and 7:00 A.M. *ceremonial uncleanness.* A result of entering a Gentile residence. *to eat the Passover.* Does not mean that the time of the Passover meal had not yet come, for this would contradict the Synoptic Gospels, which have Jesus eating the Passover meal the night before. The term "Passover" was used to refer to the whole festival of Passover and Unleavened Bread, which lasted seven days and included a number of meals.

18:29 *Pilate.* The Roman governor (see note on Mk 15:1). He showed himself tolerant of Jewish ways. *What charges … ?* A normal question at the beginning of a trial, but it was difficult to answer, because the Jews had no charge that would stand up in a Roman court of law.

18:31 *Take him yourselves.* In other words, no Roman charge, no Roman trial. *no right to execute anyone.* They were looking for an execution, not a fair trial. The restriction was important, for otherwise Rome's supporters could be quietly removed by local legal executions. Sometimes the Romans seem to have tolerated local executions (e.g., of Stephen, Ac 7), but normally they retained the right to inflict the death penalty.

18:32 *the kind of death he was going to die.* Cf. 12:32–33 and "must" in 12:34. Jewish execution was by stoning, but Jesus' death was to be by crucifixion, whereby he would bear the curse (see Dt 21:22–23 and notes). The Romans, not the Jews, had to put Jesus to death. God was overruling in the whole process.

18:33 *Are you the king of the Jews?* Pilate's first words to Jesus, identical in all four Gospels. One glance was enough to show him that a dangerous rebel existed only in the imaginations of Jesus' enemies.

18:34 *Is that your own idea … ?* If so, Pilate's question (v. 33) had meant, "Are you a rebel?" If the question had originated with the Jews, it meant, "Are you the Messianic King?"

A **18:36** *My kingdom.* Jesus agrees that he has a kingdom but asserts that it is not the kind of kingdom that has soldiers to fight for it. It was not built, nor is it maintained, by military might.

18:37 *z* Jn 3:32
a Jn 8:47; 1Jn 4:6
18:38 *b* S Lk 23:4
18:40 *c* Ac 3:14
19:1 *d* Dt 25:3;
Isa 50:6; 53:5;
Mt 27:26
19:3 *e* Mt 27:29
f Jn 18:22
19:4 *g* Jn 18:38
h ver 6; S Lk 23:4
19:5 *i* ver 2
19:6 *j* Ac 3:13
k ver 4; S Lk 23:4
19:7 *l* Lev 24:16
m Mt 26:63-66;
Jn 5:18; 10:33
19:9 *n* Jn 18:33
o S Mk 14:61
19:11 *p* S Ro 13:1
q Jn 18:28-30; Ac 3:13
19:12 *r* Lk 23:2
19:13 *s* Mt 27:19
t S Jn 5:2
19:14 *u* Mt 27:62
v Mk 15:25

Jesus answered, "You say that I am a king. In fact, the reason I was born and came into the world is to testify to the truth. *z* Everyone on the side of truth listens to me." *a*

38"What is truth?" retorted Pilate. With this he went out again to the Jews gathered there and said, "I find no basis for a charge against him. *b* 39But it is your custom for me to release to you one prisoner at the time of the Passover. Do you want me to release 'the king of the Jews'?"

40They shouted back, "No, not him! Give us Barabbas!" Now Barabbas had taken part in an uprising. *c*

JESUS SENTENCED TO BE CRUCIFIED

19:1–16pp — Mt 27:27–31; Mk 15:16–20

19 Then Pilate took Jesus and had him flogged. *d* 2The soldiers twisted together a crown of thorns and put it on his head. They clothed him in a purple robe 3and went up to him again and again, saying, "Hail, king of the Jews!" *e* And they slapped him in the face. *f*

4Once more Pilate came out and said to the Jews, "Look, I am bringing him out *g* to you to let you know that I find no basis for a charge against him." *h* 5When Jesus came out wearing the crown of thorns and the purple robe, *i* Pilate said to them, "Here is the man!"

6As soon as the chief priests and their officials saw him, they shouted, "Crucify! Crucify!"

But Pilate answered, "You take him and crucify him. *j* As for me, I find no basis for a charge against him." *k*

7The Jews insisted, "We have a law, and according to that law he must die, *l* because he claimed to be the Son of God." *m*

8When Pilate heard this, he was even more afraid, 9and he went back inside the palace. *n* "Where do you come from?" he asked Jesus, but Jesus gave him no answer. *o* 10"Do you refuse to speak to me?" Pilate said. "Don't you realize I have power either to free you or to crucify you?"

11Jesus answered, "You would have no power over me if it were not given to you from above. *p* Therefore the one who handed me over to you *q* is guilty of a greater sin."

12From then on, Pilate tried to set Jesus free, but the Jews kept shouting, "If you let this man go, you are no friend of Caesar. Anyone who claims to be a king *r* opposes Caesar."

13When Pilate heard this, he brought Jesus out and sat down on the judge's seat *s* at a place known as the Stone Pavement (which in Aramaic *t* is Gabbatha). 14It was the day of Preparation *u* of the Passover; it was about noon. *v*

18:37 *to testify to the truth.* Two of this Gospel's important ideas (see 1:7; 1:14; 14:6 and notes).
18:38 *What is truth?* Pilate may have been jesting and meant "What does truth matter?" Or he may have been serious and meant "It is not easy to find truth. What is it?" Either way, it was clear to him that Jesus was no rebel. *I find no basis for a charge against him.* Repeated in 19:4,6 (see note on 19:6). Teaching the truth was not a criminal offense.
18:39 *your custom.* Prisoners are known to have been released on special occasions in other places. *king of the Jews.* John keeps his emphasis on the note of royalty. Pilate may have hoped that the use of the title would influence the people toward the way he wanted them to decide.
18:40 *Barabbas.* A rebel and a murderer (Lk 23:19; see note on 23:18). The name is Aramaic and means "son of Abba," i.e., "son of the father"; in place of this man, the "Son of the Father" died (see note on Mt 27:16).
19:1 Pilate hoped a flogging would satisfy the Jews and enable him to release Jesus (see note on Mk 15:15).
19:2 *thorns.* A general term relating to any thorny plant (see note on Mk 15:17). *purple.* A color used by royalty.
19:6 *You ... crucify him.* The petulant utterance of an exasperated man, for the Jews could not carry out this form of execution. *I find no basis for a charge against him.* For the third time Pilate proclaimed Jesus' innocence (see 18:38 and note; 19:4). Luke also records this threefold proclamation (Lk 23:4,14,22).
19:7 *he must die.* Apparently referring to the penalty for blasphemy (Lev 24:16).
19:8 *even more afraid.* Pilate was evidently superstitious, and

this charge frightened him.
19:9 *Jesus gave him no answer.* The reason is not clear since Jesus had answered other questions readily. Perhaps Pilate would not have understood the answer or would not have believed it.
19:10 *I have power.* Pilate was incredulous and very conscious of his authority. His second question indicates his personal responsibility for crucifying Jesus.
19:11 Jesus' last words to Pilate. *from above.* All earthly authority comes ultimately from God (cf. Ro 13:14 and note). *greater sin.* That of Caiaphas (not Judas, who was only a means). But "greater" implies that there was a lesser sin, so Pilate's sin was also real.
19:12 *no friend of Caesar.* Some people had official status as "Friends of Caesar," but the term seems to be used here in the general sense. There was an implied threat that if he released Jesus, Pilate would be accused before Caesar. His record was such that he could not face such a prospect without concern.
19:13 *the Stone Pavement.* Not a translation of *Gabbatha,* which seems to mean "the hill of the house," but a different name for the same place.
19:14 *day of Preparation.* Normally Friday was the day people prepared for the Sabbath. Here the meaning is Friday of Passover week. *about noon.* Lit. "about the sixth hour." Mk 15:25 says that Jesus was crucified at "the third hour" (9:00 A.M.). It is possible that Mark's Gospel contains a copyist's error, for the Greek numerals for three and six could be confused. Or it may be that John was using Roman time, in which case the appearance before Pilate would have been at 6:00 A.M. and the crucifixion at

19:14 ʷ ver 19, 21
19:16 ˣ Mt 27:26;
Mk 15:15; Lk 23:25
19:17 ʸ Ge 22:6;
Lk 14:27; 23:26
ᶻ Lk 23:33 ᵃ S Jn 5:2
19:18 ᵇ Lk 23:32
19:19 ᶜ S Mk 1:24
ᵈ ver 14, 21
19:20 ᵉ Heb 13:12
19:21 ᶠ ver 14
19:24 ᵍ ver 28, 36,
37; S Mt 1:22
ʰ Ps 22:18
19:25 ⁱ Mt 27:55, 56
ʲ S Mt 12:46
19:26 ˡ S Mt 12:46
ᵐ S Jn 13:23
19:28 ⁿ S ver 30;
Jn 13:1 ᵒ ver 24, 36,
37; S Mt 1:22
19:29 ᵖ Ps 69:21

"Here is your king," ʷ Pilate said to the Jews.

¹⁵But they shouted, "Take him away! Take him away! Crucify him!"

"Shall I crucify your king?" Pilate asked.

"We have no king but Caesar," the chief priests answered.

¹⁶Finally Pilate handed him over to them to be crucified. ˣ

THE CRUCIFIXION OF JESUS

19:17–24pp — Mt 27:33–44; Mk 15:22–32; Lk 23:33–43

So the soldiers took charge of Jesus. ¹⁷Carrying his own cross, ʸ he went out to the place of the Skull ᶻ (which in Aramaic ᵃ is called Golgotha). ¹⁸Here they crucified him, and with him two others ᵇ—one on each side and Jesus in the middle.

¹⁹Pilate had a notice prepared and fastened to the cross. It read: JESUS OF NAZARETH, ᶜ THE KING OF THE JEWS. ᵈ ²⁰Many of the Jews read this sign, for the place where Jesus was crucified was near the city, ᵉ and the sign was written in Aramaic, Latin and Greek. ²¹The chief priests of the Jews protested to Pilate, "Do not write 'The King of the Jews,' but that this man claimed to be king of the Jews." ᶠ

²²Pilate answered, "What I have written, I have written."

²³When the soldiers crucified Jesus, they took his clothes, dividing them into four shares, one for each of them, with the undergarment remaining. This garment was seamless, woven in one piece from top to bottom.

²⁴"Let's not tear it," they said to one another. "Let's decide by lot who will get it."

This happened that the scripture might be fulfilled ᵍ that said,

"They divided my clothes among them
    and cast lots for my garment." ᵃ ʰ

So this is what the soldiers did.

²⁵Near the cross ⁱ of Jesus stood his mother, ʲ his mother's sister, Mary the wife of Clopas, and Mary Magdalene. ᵏ ²⁶When Jesus saw his mother ˡ there, and the disciple whom he loved ᵐ standing nearby, he said to her, "Woman, ᵇ here is your son," ²⁷and to the disciple, "Here is your mother." From that time on, this disciple took her into his home.

THE DEATH OF JESUS

19:29,30pp — Mt 27:48,50; Mk 15:36,37; Lk 23:36

²⁸Later, knowing that everything had now been finished, ⁿ and so that Scripture would be fulfilled, ᵒ Jesus said, "I am thirsty." ²⁹A jar of wine vinegar ᵖ was there, so they soaked a sponge in it, put the sponge on a stalk of the hyssop plant, and lifted it to Jesus' lips.

ᵃ 24 Psalm 22:18   ᵇ 26 The Greek for *Woman* does not denote any disrespect.

9:00 A.M. (the third hour according to Jewish reckoning; see Mk 15:33). For other time references, see Mt 27:45–46; Mk 15:33–34; Lk 23:44 and note. *Here is your king.* John does not let us forget the sovereignty of Jesus. Pilate did not mean the expression seriously, but John did. *the Jews.* See note on 1:19.
19:15 *We have no king but Caesar.* More irony. They rejected any suggestion that they were rebels against Rome but expressed the truth of their spiritual condition.
19:17 *Carrying his own cross.* A cross might be shaped like a *T*, an *X*, a *Y* or an *I*, as well as in the traditional form. A condemned man would normally carry a beam of it to the place of execution. Somewhere along the way Simon of Cyrene took Jesus' cross (see Mk 15:21 and note), probably because Jesus was weakened by the flogging. *Golgotha.* "Calvary" comes from a Latin word that has the same meaning (see Mk 15:22 and note).
19:18 *they crucified him.* See note on Mk 15:24. As with the scourging, John describes this horror with one Greek word. None of the Gospel writers dwells on the physical sufferings of Jesus. *one on each side.* Perhaps meant as a final insult, but it brings out the important truth that in his death Jesus was identified with sinners (see note on Mk 15:27).
19:19 *a notice.* A placard stating the crime for which someone was executed was often fastened to his cross. THE KING OF THE JEWS. Again the royalty theme.
19:20 *Aramaic.* One of the languages of the Jewish people at that time (along with Hebrew). *Latin.* The official language of

Rome. *Greek.* The common language of communication throughout the empire. The threefold inscription may account for the slight differences in wording in the four Gospels.
19:22 Pilate had to have a sufficient reason for the execution, and he was not above mocking the Jews, but for John his insistence may also have served to underscore that Jesus' kingship is final and unalterable.
19:23 *undergarment.* A type of shirt, reaching from the neck to the knees or ankles. *seamless.* Therefore too valuable to be cut up.
19:24 See introduction to Ps 22 and notes on Ps 22:17,20–21.
19:25 *Clopas.* Mentioned only here in the NT. *Mary Magdalene.* Appears in the crucifixion and resurrection story in all four Gospels, but apart from that we read of her only in Lk 8:2–3 (see note on 8:2).
19:26 *disciple whom he loved.* John (see note on 13:23). *Woman.* See TNIV text note.
19:27 *took her into his home.* And so took responsibility for her. It may be that Jesus' brothers still did not believe in him (see 7:5).
19:28 *I am thirsty.* May refer to Ps 69:21 (see note there; cf. Ps 22:15).
19:29 *wine vinegar.* Equivalent to cheap wine, the drink of ordinary people (see notes on Mk 15:36; Lk 23:36). *hyssop.* The name given to a number of plants (see note on Ex 12:22).

19:30 q Lk 12:50;
Jn 4:34; 17:4
19:31 r ver 14, 42
s Dt 21:23; Jos 8:29;
10:26, 27
19:32 r ver 18
19:34 u Zec 12:10;
Rev 1:7 v 1Jn 5:6, 8
19:35 w S Lk 24:48
x Jn 15:27; 21:24
19:36 y ver 24, 28,
37; S Mt 1:22
z Ex 12:46; Nu 9:12;
Ps 34:20
19:37 a Zec 12:10;
Rev 1:7
19:38 b S Jn 7:13
19:39 c Jn 3:1; 7:50
19:40 d Lk 24:12;
Jn 11:44; 20:5, 7
e Mt 26:12
19:42 r ver 14, 31
g ver 20, 41
20:1 h ver 18; Lk 8:2;
Jn 19:25 i Mt 27:60,
66
20:2 j S Jn 13:23
k ver 13
20:3 l Lk 24:12
20:5 m ver 11
n S Jn 19:40

30When he had received the drink, Jesus said, "It is finished." q With that, he bowed his head and gave up his spirit.

31Now it was the day of Preparation, r and the next day was to be a special Sabbath. Because the Jewish leaders did not want the bodies left on the crosses s during the Sabbath, they asked Pilate to have the legs broken and the bodies taken down. 32The soldiers therefore came and broke the legs of the first man who had been crucified with Jesus, and then those of the other. t 33But when they came to Jesus and found that he was already dead, they did not break his legs. 34Instead, one of the soldiers pierced u Jesus' side with a spear, bringing a sudden flow of blood and water. v 35The man who saw it w has given testimony, and his testimony is true. x He knows that he tells the truth, and he testifies so that you also may believe. 36These things happened so that the scripture would be fulfilled: y "Not one of his bones will be broken," a z 37and, as another scripture says, "They will look on the one they have pierced." b a

THE BURIAL OF JESUS

19:38–42pp — Mt 27:57–61; Mk 15:42–47; Lk 23:50–56

38Later, Joseph of Arimathea asked Pilate for the body of Jesus. Now Joseph was a disciple of Jesus, but secretly because he feared the Jewish leaders. b With Pilate's permission, he came and took the body away. 39He was accompanied by Nicodemus, c the man who earlier had visited Jesus at night. Nicodemus brought a mixture of myrrh and aloes, about seventy-five pounds. c 40Taking Jesus' body, the two of them wrapped it, with the spices, in strips of linen. d This was in accordance with Jewish burial customs. e 41At the place where Jesus was crucified, there was a garden, and in the garden a new tomb, in which no one had ever been laid. 42Because it was the Jewish day of Preparation f and since the tomb was nearby, g they laid Jesus there.

THE EMPTY TOMB

20:1–8pp — Mt 28:1–8; Mk 16:1–8; Lk 24:1–10

20 Early on the first day of the week, while it was still dark, Mary Magdalene h went to the tomb and saw that the stone had been removed from the entrance. i 2So she came running to Simon Peter and the other disciple, the one Jesus loved, j and said, "They have taken the Lord out of the tomb, and we don't know where they have put him!" k

3So Peter and the other disciple started for the tomb. l 4Both were running, but the other disciple outran Peter and reached the tomb first. 5He bent over and looked in m at the strips of linen n lying there but did not go in. 6Then Simon Peter came along behind him

a 36 Exodus 12:46; Num. 9:12; Psalm 34:20   b 37 Zech. 12:10   c 39 Or about 34 kilograms

---

19:30 *It is finished.* Apparently the loud cry of Mt 27:50; Mk 15:37. Jesus died as a victor and had "finished" (v. 28) what he came to do (cf. 17:4). *gave up his spirit.* An unusual way of describing death, perhaps suggesting an act of will (cf. 10:17–18 and note).
19:31 *Preparation.* See note on v. 14. *a special Sabbath.* The Sabbath that fell at Passover time. The Passover meal had been eaten on Thursday evening, the day of Preparation was Friday and the Sabbath came on Saturday. *the Jewish leaders.* See note on 1:19. *to have the legs broken.* To hasten death, because the victim then could not put any weight on his legs, and breathing would be difficult.
19:34 *pierced Jesus' side.* Probably to make doubly sure that Jesus was dead, but perhaps simply an act of brutality (see v. 37; Isa 53:5; Zec 12:10; cf. Ps 22:16). *blood and water.* The result of the spear piercing the pericardium (the sac that surrounds the heart) and the heart itself.
19:35 *The man who saw it.* Either John himself or someone he regarded as reliable. Obviously he considered the incident important and comments that it was well attested. *testifies … believe.* See note on 1:7.
19:36–37 *scripture.* Again John observes God's overruling in the fulfillment of Scripture. It was extraordinary that Jesus was the only one of the three whose legs were not broken and that he suffered an unusual spear thrust that did not break a bone.
19:38 See note on Lk 23:52. *Joseph.* A rich disciple (Mt 27:57), and a member of the Sanhedrin who had not

agreed to Jesus' condemnation (Lk 23:51; see note on 23:50). *Arimathea.* See note on Mt 27:57. *secretly.* It would have been hard for a member of the Sanhedrin to support Jesus' cause openly. Jesus' closest followers all ran away (see Mk 14:50 and note), and it was left to Joseph and Nicodemus to provide for his burial. *With Pilate's permission.* Otherwise people could take away their crucified friends before they died and revive them.
19:39 *Nicodemus.* John alone tells us that he joined Joseph in the burial. *seventy-five pounds.* A very large amount, such as was used in royal burials (cf. 2Ch 16:14).
19:40 *strips of linen.* Thin strips like bandages. There was also a shroud, a large sheet (Mt 27:59; Mk 15:46; Lk 23:53).
19:41 *new tomb.* Joseph's own tomb (Mt 27:60).
19:42 *Preparation.* See note on v. 14. *nearby.* Haste was necessary, since it was near sunset, when the Sabbath would start and no work could be done.
20:1 *while it was still dark.* Mark says it was "just after sunrise" (Mk 16:2). Perhaps the women came in groups, with Mary Magdalene coming very early. Or John may refer to the time of leaving home, Mark to that of arrival at the tomb. *Mary Magdalene.* See note on 19:25; cf. Mk 16:9.
20:2 *Simon Peter.* Despite his denials, he was still the leading figure among the disciples. *the one Jesus loved.* John (see note on 13:23). *we.* Indicates that there were others with Mary (see Mt 28:1; Mk 16:1; Lk 24:10), though John does not identify them. *have put him.* Mary had no thought of resurrection.

and went straight into the tomb. He saw the strips of linen lying there, [7]as well as the cloth that had been wrapped around Jesus' head. [o] The cloth was still lying in its place, separate from the linen. [8]Finally the other disciple, who had reached the tomb first,[p] also went inside. He saw and believed. [9](They still did not understand from Scripture[q] that Jesus had to rise from the dead.)[r] [10]Then the disciples went back to where they were staying.

JESUS APPEARS TO MARY MAGDALENE

[11]Now Mary stood outside the tomb crying. As she wept, she bent over to look into the tomb[s] [12]and saw two angels in white,[t] seated where Jesus' body had been, one at the head and the other at the foot.

[13]They asked her, "Woman,[a] why are you crying?"[u]

"They have taken my Lord away," she said, "and I don't know where they have put him."[v] [14]At this, she turned around and saw Jesus standing there,[w] but she did not realize that it was Jesus.[x]

[15]He asked her, "Woman, why are you crying?[y] Who is it you are looking for?"

Thinking he was the gardener, she said, "Sir, if you have carried him away, tell me where you have put him, and I will get him."

[16]Jesus said to her, "Mary."

She turned toward him and cried out in Aramaic,[z] "Rabboni!"[a] (which means "Teacher").

[17]Jesus said, "Do not hold on to me, for I have not yet ascended to the Father. Go instead to my brothers[b] and tell them, 'I am ascending to my Father[c] and your Father, to my God and your God.' "

[18]Mary Magdalene[d] went to the disciples[e] with the news: "I have seen the Lord!" And she told them that he had said these things to her.

JESUS APPEARS TO HIS DISCIPLES

[19]On the evening of that first day of the week, when the disciples were together, with the doors locked for fear of the Jewish leaders,[f] Jesus came and stood among them and said, "Peace[g] be with you!"[h] [20]After he said this, he showed them his hands and side.[i] The disciples were overjoyed[j] when they saw the Lord.

[21]Again Jesus said, "Peace be with you![k] As the Father has sent me,[l] I am sending you."[m] [22]And with that he breathed on them and said, "Receive the Holy Spirit.[n] [23]If you

---

a 13 The Greek for *Woman* does not denote any disrespect; also in verse 15.

20:7 [o] Jn 11:44
20:8 [p] ver 4
20:9 [q] Mt 22:29; Jn 2:22 [r] Lk 24:26,46; Ac 2:24
20:11 [s] ver 5
20:12 [t] Mt 28:2,3; Mk 16:5; 1 k 24:4; Ac 1:10; S 5:19; 10:30
20:13 [u] ver 15
[v] ver 2
20:14 [w] Mk 16:9
[x] Lk 24:16; Jn 21:4
20:15 [y] ver 13
20:16 [z] S Jn 5:2
[a] S Mt 23:7
20:17 [b] S Mt 28:10
[c] Jn 7:33
20:18 [d] S ver 1
[e] Lk 24:10,22,23
20:19 [f] S Jn 7:13
[g] S Jn 14:27 [h] ver 21, 26; Lk 24:36-39
20:20 [i] Lk 24:39,40; Jn 19:34 / Jn 16:20,22
20:21 [k] ver 19
[l] S Jn 3:17 [m] Mt 28:19; Jn 17:18
20:22 [n] Jn 7:39; Ac 2:38; 8:15-17; 19:2; Gal 3:2

20:7 *still lying in its place.* An orderly arrangement, not disarray, as would have resulted from a grave robbery.

20:8 *He saw and believed.* Cf. v. 29. John did not say what he believed, but it must have been that Jesus was resurrected.

20:9 *Scripture.* First they came to know of the resurrection through what they saw in the tomb; only later did they see it in Scripture. It is obvious they did not make up a story of resurrection to fit a preconceived understanding of Scriptural prophecy. *had to rise.* It was in Scripture and thus the will of God.

20:11 *Mary.* Perhaps Jesus appeared first to Mary because she needed him most at that time. *crying.* As in 11:33 (see note there), it means "wailing," a loud expression of grief.

20:12 *two angels.* Matthew has one angel (Mt 28:2), Mark a young man (Mk 16:5) and Luke two men who were angels (Lk 24:4,23). See note on Lk 24:4.

20:13 *Woman.* See TNIV text note.

20:14 *did not realize that it was Jesus.* A number of times the risen Jesus was not recognized (21:4; Mt 28:17; Lk 24:16,37). He may have looked different, or he may intentionally have prevented recognition (see note on Lk 24:16).

20:16 *Mary.* Cf. 10:3–4. *Rabboni.* A strengthened form of *Rabbi*, and in the NT found elsewhere only in Mk 10:51 (in the Greek). Although the word means "(my) teacher," there are few if any examples of its use in ancient Judaism as a form of address other than in calling on God in prayer. However, John's explanation casts doubt on any thought that Mary intended to address Jesus as God here.

20:17 *I have not yet ascended.* See 13:3. The meaning appears to be that the ascension was still some time off. Mary would have opportunity to see Jesus again, so she need not cling to him. Alternatively, Jesus may be reminding Mary that after his crucifixion she cannot have him with her except through the Holy Spirit (see 16:5–16). *my brothers.* Probably the disciples (see v. 18; Mk 3:35 and note). The members of his family did not believe in him (see 7:5 and note on 7:4), though they became disciples not long after this (see Ac 1:14 and note). *my Father and your Father.* God is Father both of Christ and of believers, but in different senses (see 1:12,14,18,34; 3:16 and note).

20:18 *have seen the Lord.* Although Mary was the first to see the risen Lord, others would soon follow (see vv. 20,25,29; see also chart, p. 1771).

20:19 See Lk 24:36 and note. *disciples.* Probably includes others besides the apostles, "the Twelve" (v. 24). *the Jewish leaders.* See note on 1:19. *Peace be with you!* The normal Hebrew greeting (cf. Da 10:19). Because of their behavior the previous Friday, they may have expected rebuke and censure; but Jesus calmed their fears (see note on 14:27).

20:20 *his hands and side.* Where the wounds were (John does not refer to the wounds in the feet). According to Lk 24:37 they thought they were seeing a ghost. Jesus was clearly identifying himself.

20:21 *Peace be with you!* See note on v. 19. *I am sending you.* See note on 17:18.

20:22 *Receive the Holy Spirit.* Thus anticipating what happened 50 days later on the day of Pentecost (see Ac

20:23 º Mt 16:19;
18:18
20:24 ᵖ S Jn 11:16
20:25 ᵍ ver 20
ʳ Mk 16:11
20:26 ˢ S Jn 14:27
ᵗ ver 21
20:27 ᵘ ver 25;
Lk 24:40
20:29 ᵛ S Jn 3:15
ʷ 1Pe 1:8
20:30 ˣ S Jn 2:11
ʸ Jn 21:25
20:31 ᶻ S Jn 3:15;
19:35 ᵃ S Mt 4:3
ᵇ S Mt 25:46
21:1 ᶜ ver 14;
Jn 20:19, 26 ᵈ Jn 6:1
21:2 ᵉ S Jn 11:16
ᶠ Jn 1:45 ᵍ Jn 2:1
ʰ S Mt 4:21
21:3 ⁱ Lk 5:5
21:4 ʲ Lk 24:16;
Jn 20:14
21:6 ᵏ Lk 5:4-7
21:7 ˡ S Jn 13:23
21:9 ᵐ Jn 18:18
ⁿ ver 10,13

forgive the sins of anyone, their sins are forgiven; if you do not forgive them, they are not forgiven." º

JESUS APPEARS TO THOMAS

²⁴Now Thomasᵖ (also known as Didymusª), one of the Twelve, was not with the disciples when Jesus came. ²⁵So the other disciples told him, "We have seen the Lord!"

But he said to them, "Unless I see the nail marks in his hands and put my finger where the nails were, and put my hand into his side, ᵍ I will not believe." ʳ

²⁶A week later his disciples were in the house again, and Thomas was with them. Though the doors were locked, Jesus came and stood among them and said, "Peace ˢ be with you!" ᵗ ²⁷Then he said to Thomas, "Put your finger here; see my hands. Reach out your hand and put it into my side. Stop doubting and believe." ᵘ

²⁸Thomas said to him, "My Lord and my God!"

²⁹Then Jesus told him, "Because you have seen me, you have believed; ᵛ blessed are those who have not seen and yet have believed." ʷ

THE PURPOSE OF JOHN'S GOSPEL

³⁰Jesus performed many other signsˣ in the presence of his disciples, which are not recorded in this book. ʸ ³¹But these are written that you may believeᵇ ᶻ that Jesus is the Messiah, the Son of God, ª and that by believing you may have life in his name. ᵇ

JESUS AND THE MIRACULOUS CATCH OF FISH

21 Afterward Jesus appeared again to his disciples, ᶜ by the Sea of Galilee. ᶜ ᵈ It happened this way: ²Simon Peter, Thomas ᵉ (also known as Didymusª), Nathanael ᶠ from Cana in Galilee, ᵍ the sons of Zebedee, ʰ and two other disciples were together. ³"I'm going out to fish," Simon Peter told them, and they said, "We'll go with you." So they went out and got into the boat, but that night they caught nothing. ⁱ

⁴Early in the morning, Jesus stood on the shore, but the disciples did not realize that it was Jesus.ʲ

⁵He called out to them, "Friends, haven't you any fish?"

"No," they answered.

⁶He said, "Throw your net on the right side of the boat and you will find some." When they did, they were unable to haul the net in because of the large number of fish. ᵏ

⁷Then the disciple whom Jesus lovedˡ said to Peter, "It is the Lord!" As soon as Simon Peter heard him say, "It is the Lord," he wrapped his outer garment around him (for he had taken it off) and jumped into the water. ⁸The other disciples followed in the boat, towing the net full of fish, for they were not far from shore, about a hundred yards. ᵈ ⁹When they landed, they saw a fire ᵐ of burning coals there with fish on it, ⁿ and some bread.

ª *24,2* *Thomas* (Aramaic) and *Didymus* (Greek) both mean *twin*.   ᵇ *31* Or *may continue to believe*
ᶜ *1* Greek *Tiberias*   ᵈ *8* Or about 90 meters

2:2,4,14,17,33,38 and notes). The disciples needed God's help to carry out the commission they had just been given.

20:23 Lit. "Those whose sins you forgive have already been forgiven; those whose sins you do not forgive have not been forgiven." God does not forgive people's sins because we do so, nor does he withhold forgiveness because we do. Rather, those who proclaim the gospel are in effect forgiving or not forgiving sins, depending on whether the hearers accept or reject Jesus Christ (cf. Mt 16:19 and note; 18:18 and TNIV text note).

20:24 *Thomas.* See note on 11:16.

20:25 *Unless I see . . . and put . . . I will not believe.* Hardheaded skepticism can scarcely go further than this.

20:26 *Peace.* See vv. 19,21 and note on 14:27.

20:28 *My Lord and my God!* To acknowledge Jesus as one's Lord and God is the high point of faith (see note on 1:1).

20:29 *those who have not seen and yet have believed.* Would have been very few at this time (see v. 8 and note). All whom John mentions had seen in some sense. The words, of course, apply to future believers as well.

20:30 *signs.* See note on 2:11. John had selected from among many. *in the presence of his disciples.* Those who could testify to what he had done. John again stresses testimony (see note on 1:7).

20:31 *that you may believe.* Expresses John's evangelistic purpose. *believe.* See note on 1:7. *Jesus is the Messiah, the Son of God.* Faith has content. *the Messiah.* See note on 1:25. This whole Gospel is written to show the truth of Jesus' Messiahship and to present him as the Son of God, so that the readers may believe in him. *Son of God.* See 3:16 and note. *that by believing you may have life.* Another expression of purpose—to bring about faith that leads to life (see notes on 1:4; 3:15–16). *name.* Represents all that he is and stands for (see note on 2:23).

21:1 *Galilee.* Lit. "Tiberias" (see TNIV text note; see also note on 6:1).

21:2 *Simon Peter.* See note on Mk 1:16. *Thomas.* See note on 11:16. *sons of Zebedee.* Not named in this Gospel (see Mt 4:21).

21:3 *that night.* Nighttime was favored by fishermen in ancient times (as Aristotle, e.g., informs us).

21:4 *did not realize that it was Jesus.* Cf. Mary Magdalene (see note on 20:14).

21:7 *disciple whom Jesus loved.* See note on 13:23. *his outer garment.* It is curious that he put on this garment (the word appears only here in the NT) preparatory to jumping into the water. But Jews regarded a greeting as a religious act that could be done only when one was clothed. Peter may have been preparing himself to greet the Lord.

¹⁰Jesus said to them, "Bring some of the fish you have just caught."

¹¹Simon Peter climbed aboard and dragged the net ashore. It was full of large fish, 153, but even with so many the net was not torn. ¹²Jesus said to them, "Come and have breakfast." None of the disciples dared ask him, "Who are you?" They knew it was the Lord. ¹³Jesus came, took the bread and gave it to them, and did the same with the fish. *o* ¹⁴This was now the third time Jesus appeared to his disciples *p* after he was raised from the dead.

JESUS REINSTATES PETER

¹⁵When they had finished eating, Jesus said to Simon Peter, "Simon son of John, do you love me more than these?"

"Yes, Lord," he said, "you know that I love you." *q*

Jesus said, "Feed my lambs." *r*

¹⁶Again Jesus said, "Simon son of John, do you love me?"

He answered, "Yes, Lord, you know that I love you."

Jesus said, "Take care of my sheep." *s*

¹⁷The third time he said to him, "Simon son of John, do you love me?"

Peter was hurt because Jesus asked him the third time, "Do you love me?" *t* He said, "Lord, you know all things; *u* you know that I love you."

Jesus said, "Feed my sheep. *v* ¹⁸Very truly I tell you, when you were younger you dressed yourself and went where you wanted; but when you are old you will stretch out your hands, and someone else will dress you and lead you where you do not want to go." ¹⁹Jesus said this to indicate the kind of death *w* by which Peter would glorify God. *x* Then he said to him, "Follow me!" *y*

²⁰Peter turned and saw that the disciple whom Jesus loved *z* was following them. (This was the one who had leaned back against Jesus at the supper and had said, "Lord, who is going to betray you?") *a* ²¹When Peter saw him, he asked, "Lord, what about him?"

²²Jesus answered, "If I want him to remain alive until I return, *b* what is that to you? You must follow me." *c* ²³Because of this, the rumor spread among the believers *d* that this disciple would not die. But Jesus did not say that he would not die; he only said, "If I want him to remain alive until I return, what is that to you?"

²⁴This is the disciple who testifies to these things *e* and who wrote them down. We know that his testimony is true. *f*

²⁵Jesus did many other things as well. *g* If every one of them were written down, I suppose that even the whole world would not have room for the books that would be written.

21:13 *o* ver 9
21:14 *p* Jn 20:19,26
21:15 *q* Mt 26:33, 35; Jn 13:37 *r* Lk 12:32
21:16 *s* 2Sa 5:2; Eze 34:2; Mt 2:6; S Jn 10:11; Ac 20:28; 1Pe 5:2,3
21:17 *t* Jn 13:38 *u* Jn 16:30 *v* S ver 16
21:19 *w* Jn 12:33; 18:32 *x* Jn 13:36; 2Pe 1:14 *y* S Mt 4:19
21:20 *z* ver 7; S Jn 13:23 *a* Jn 13:25
21:22 *b* S Mt 16:27 *c* ver 19; S Mt 4:19
21:23 *d* S Ac 1:16
21:24 *e* S Jn 15:27 *f* Jn 19:35
21:25 *g* Jn 20:30

21:9 *burning coals.* Lit. "charcoal," as in 18:18 ("fire"; see note on 18:26).
21:11 *Peter . . . dragged the net ashore.* Appears to mean that Peter headed up the effort, for the whole group had not been able previously to haul the net into the boat (v. 6). *the net was not torn.* In contrast to the nets mentioned in Lk 5:6.
21:14 *third time.* The third appearance to a group of disciples (20:19–23,24–29), though there had been other appearances to individuals.
21:15–17 *love.* The Greek word for "love" in Jesus' first two questions is different from that in his third question and in all Peter's answers. It is uncertain whether a distinction in meaning is intended since John often used slight word variations, apparently for stylistic reasons. Also, no distinction is made between these two words elsewhere in this Gospel. The important thing is that in so serious a matter as the reinstatement of Peter, the great question was whether he really loved Jesus.
21:15 *more than these.* May mean "more than you love these men" or "more than these men love me" or "more than you love these things" (i.e., the fishing gear). Perhaps the second is best, for Peter had claimed a devotion above that of the others (Mt 26:33; Mk 14:29; cf. Jn 13:37). Peter did not take up the comparison, and Jesus did not explain it. *Feed my lambs.* Cf. "Take care of my sheep" (v. 16) and "Feed my sheep" (v. 17).

21:17 *you know all things.* Peter's replies stress Christ's knowledge, not his own grasp of the situation.
21:18 *Very truly I tell you.* See note on Mk 3:28. *stretch out your hands.* The early church understood this as a prophecy of crucifixion.
21:19 *the kind of death.* Peter would be a martyr. Tradition indicates that he was crucified upside down.
21:20 *disciple whom Jesus loved.* See note on 13:23. *was following.* He was doing what Peter was twice told to do (vv. 19,22). *at the supper.* See 13:23–25.
21:22 *until I return.* A clear declaration of the second coming (see 14:3 and note).
21:24 *disciple who testifies.* Testimony is important throughout this Gospel (see note on 1:7). We now learn that it was the beloved disciple who was the witness behind the account. *these things.* Must refer to the whole book. *who wrote them down.* The beloved disciple was not only the witness but also the actual author. *We know.* Evidently written by contemporaries in a position to know the truth.
21:25 *many other things.* As in 20:30 (see note there) we are assured that the author has been selective. *even the whole world would not have room.* Hyperbole (for another example of this figure of speech, see Lk 14:26 and note). Our historical knowledge of Jesus is at best partial; but we have been given all we need to know.

THE HARMONY OF THE GOSPELS

	MATTHEW	MARK	LUKE	JOHN
A PREVIEW OF WHO JESUS IS				
Luke's purpose in writing a gospel			1:1–4	
John's prologue: Jesus Christ, the preexistent Word incarnate				1:1–18
Jesus' legal lineage through Joseph and natural lineage through Mary	1:1–17		3:23b–38	
THE EARLY YEARS OF JOHN THE BAPTIST				
John's birth foretold to Zechariah			1:5–25	
Jesus' birth foretold to Mary			1:26–38	
Mary's visit to Elizabeth and Elizabeth's song			1:39–45	
Mary's song of joy			1:46–56	
John's birth			1:57–66	
Zechariah's prophetic song			1:67–79	
John's growth and early life			1:80	
THE EARLY YEARS OF JESUS CHRIST				
Circumstances of Jesus' birth explained to Joseph	1:18–25			
Birth of Jesus			2:1–7	
Praise of the angels and witness of the shepherds			2:8–20	
Circumcision of Jesus			2:21	
Jesus presented in the temple with the homage of Simeon and Anna			2:22–38	
Visit of the Magi	2:1–12			
Escape into Egypt and murder of boys in Bethlehem	2:13–18			
Return to Nazareth	2:19–23		2:39	
Growth and early life of Jesus			2:40	
Jesus' first Passover in Jerusalem			2:41–50	
Jesus' growth to adulthood			2:51–52	
THE PUBLIC MINISTRY OF JOHN THE BAPTIST				
His ministry launched		1:1	3:1–2	
His person, proclamation and baptism	3:1–6	1:2–6	3:3–6	
His messages to the Pharisees, Sadducees, crowds, tax collectors and soldiers	3:7–10		3:7–14	
His description of Christ	3:11–12	1:7–8	3:15–18	
THE END OF JOHN'S MINISTRY AND THE BEGINNING OF CHRIST'S PUBLIC MINISTRY				
Jesus' baptism by John	3:13–17	1:9–11	3:21–23a	
Jesus' temptation in the wilderness	4:1–11	1:12–13	4:1–13	
John's testimony about himself to the priests and Levites				1:19–28
John's testimony to Jesus as the Son of God				1:29–34
Jesus' first followers				1:35–51
Jesus' first miracle: Water becomes wine				2:1–11
Jesus' first stay in Capernaum with his relatives and early disciples				2:12
First cleansing of the temple at the Passover				2:13–22
Early response to Jesus' miracles				2:23–25
Nicodemus's interview with Jesus				3:1–21
John superseded by Jesus				3:22–36
Jesus' departure from Judea	4:12	1:14a	3:19–20; 4:14a	4:1–4
Discussion with a Samaritan woman				4:5–26
Challenge of a spiritual harvest				4:27–38
Evangelization of Sychar				4:39–42
Arrival in Galilee				4:43–45
THE MINISTRY OF CHRIST IN GALILEE				
Opposition at Home and a New Headquarters				
Nature of the Galilean ministry	4:17	1:14b–15	4:14b–15	
Child at Capernaum healed by Jesus while at Cana				4:46–54
Ministry and rejection at Nazareth			4:16–31a	
Move to Capernaum	4:13–16			

	MATTHEW	MARK	LUKE	JOHN
Disciples Called and Ministry throughout Galilee				
Call of the four	4:18–22	1:16–20	5:1–11	
Teaching in the synagogue of Capernaum authenticated by healing a demoniac		1:21–28	4:31b–37	
Peter's mother-in-law and others healed	8:14–17	1:29–34	4:38–41	
Tour of Galilee with Simon and others	4:23–25	1:35–39	4:42–44	
Cleansing of a man with leprosy, followed by much publicity	8:2–4	1:40–45	5:12–16	
Forgiving and healing of a paralyzed man	9:1–8	2:1–12	5:17–26	
Call of Matthew	9:9	2:13–14	5:27–28	
Banquet at Matthew's house	9:10–13	2:15–17	5:29–32	
Jesus defends his disciples with three parables advocating feasting instead of fasting	9:14–17	2:18–22	5:33–39	
Sabbath Controversies and Withdrawals				
Jesus heals an invalid on the Sabbath				5:1–9
Effort to kill Jesus for breaking the Sabbath and saying he was equal with God				5:10–18
Discourse demonstrating the Son's equality with the Father				5:19–47
Controversy over disciples' picking grain on the Sabbath	12:1–8	2:23–28	6:1–5	
Healing of a man's shriveled hand on the Sabbath	12:9–14	3:1–6	6:6–11	
Withdrawal to the Sea of Galilee with large crowds from many places	12:15–21	3:7–12		
Appointment of the Twelve and Sermon on the Mount				
Twelve apostles chosen		3:13–19	6:12–16	
Setting of the Sermon	5:1–2		6:17–19	
Blessings of those who inherit the kingdom and woes to those who do not	5:3–12		6:20–26	
Responsibility while awaiting the kingdom	5:13–16			
Law, righteousness and the kingdom	5:17–20			
Six contrasts in interpreting the law	5:21–48		6:27–30, 32–36	
Three hypocritical "acts of righteousness" to be avoided	6:1–18			
Three prohibitions against avarice, harsh judgment and unwise exposure of sacred things	6:19—7:6		6:37–42	
Application and conclusion	7:7–27		6:31, 43–49	
Reaction of the crowds	7:28—8:1			
Growing Fame and Emphasis on Repentance				
A centurion's faith and the healing of his servant	8:5–13		7:1–10	
A widow's son raised at Nain			7:11–17	
John the Baptist's relationship to the kingdom	11:2–19		7:18–35	
Woes upon Chorazin and Bethsaida for failure to repent	11:20–30			
Christ's feet anointed by a sinful but contrite woman			7:36–50	
First Public Rejection by Jewish Leaders				
A tour with the Twelve and other followers			8:1–3	
Blasphemous accusation by the teachers of the law and Pharisees	12:22–37	3:20–30		
Request for a sign refused	12:38–45			
Announcement of new spiritual kinship	12:46–50	3:31–35	8:19–21	
Secrets about the Kingdom Given in Parables				
TO THE CROWDS BY THE SEA				
The setting of the parables	13:1–3a	4:1–2	8:4	
The parable of the soils	13:3b–23	4:3–25	8:5–18	
The parable of the seed's spontaneous growth		4:26–29		
The parable of the weeds	13:24–30			
The parable of the mustard tree	13:31–32	4:30–32		
The parable of the leavened loaf	13:33–35	4:33–34		
TO THE DISCIPLES IN THE HOUSE				
The parable of the weeds explained	13:36–43			
The parable of the hidden treasure	13:44			

	MATTHEW	MARK	LUKE	JOHN
The parable of the valuable pearl	13:45–46			
The parable of the net	13:47–50			
The parable of the house owner	13:51–53			
Continuing Opposition				
Crossing the lake and calming the storm	8:18,23–27	4:35–41	8:22–25	
Healing the Gerasene demoniacs and resultant opposition	8:28–34	5:1–20	8:26–39	
Return to Galilee, healing of a woman who touched Jesus' garment and raising of Jairus's daughter	9:18–26	5:21–43	8:40–56	
Three miracles of healing and another blasphemous accusation	9:27–34			
Final visit to unbelieving Nazareth	13:54–58	6:1–6a		
Final Galilean Campaign				
Shortage of workers	9:35–38	6:6b		
Commissioning of the Twelve	10:1–42	6:7–11	9:1–5	
Workers sent out	11:1	6:12–13	9:6	
Antipas's mistaken identification of Jesus	14:1–2	6:14–16	9:7–9	
Earlier imprisonment and beheading of John the Baptist	14:3–12	6:17–29		

THE MINISTRY OF CHRIST AROUND GALILEE

	MATTHEW	MARK	LUKE	JOHN
Lesson on the Bread of Life				
Return of the workers		6:30	9:10a	
Withdrawal from Galilee	14:13–14	6:31–34	9:10b–11	6:1–3
Feeding the five thousand	14:15–21	6:35–44	9:12–17	6:4–13
Blocking of a premature attempt to make Jesus king	14:22–23	6:45–46		6:14–15
Walking on the water during a storm on the lake	14:24–33	6:47–52		6:16–21
Healings at Gennesaret	14:34–36	6:53–56		
Discourse on the true bread of life				6:22–59
Defection among the disciples				6:60–71
Lesson on the Leaven of the Pharisees, Sadducees and Herodians				
Conflict over the tradition of ceremonial uncleanness	15:1–3a,7–9b, 3b–6,10–20	7:1–23		7:1
Ministry to a believing Greek woman in Tyre and Sidon	15:21–28	7:24–30		
Healings in Decapolis	15:29–31	7:31–37		
Feeding the four thousand in Decapolis	15:32–38	8:1–9a		
Return to Galilee and encounter with the Pharisees and Sadducees	15:39—16:4	8:9b–12		
Warning about the error of the Pharisees, Sadducees and Herodians	16:5–12	8:13–21		
Healing a blind man at Bethsaida		8:22–26		
Lesson of Messiahship Learned and Confirmed				
Peter's identification of Jesus as the Messiah and first prophecy of the church	16:13–20	8:27–30	9:18–21	
First direct prediction of the rejection, crucifixion and resurrection	16:21–26	8:31–37	9:22–25	
Coming of the Son of Man and judgment	16:27–28	8:38—9:1	9:26–27	
Transfiguration of Jesus	17:1–8	9:2–8	9:28–36a	
Discussion of resurrection, Elijah and John the Baptist	17:9–13	9:9–13	9:36b	
Lessons on Responsibility to Others				
Healing of demoniac boy and unbelief rebuked	17:14–20	9:14–29	9:37–43a	
Second prediction of Jesus' death and resurrection	17:22–23	9:30–32	9:43b–45	
Payment of temple tax	17:24–27			
Rivalry over greatness in the kingdom	18:1–5	9:33–37	9:46–48	
Warning against causing believers to sin	18:6–14	9:38–50	9:49–50	
Treatment and forgiveness of a sinning brother	18:15–35			
Journey to Jerusalem for the Festival of Tabernacles				
Complete commitment required of followers	8:19–22		9:57–62	
Ridicule by Jesus' half-brothers				7:2–9
Journey through Samaria			9:51–56	7:10

	MATTHEW	MARK	LUKE	JOHN
Example of little children in relation to the kingdom	19:13–15	10:13–16	18:15–17	
Riches and the kingdom	19:16–30	10:17–31	18:18–30	
Parable of the landowner's sovereignty	20:1–16			
Third prediction of Jesus' death and resurrection	20:17–19	10:32–34	18:31–34	
Warning against ambitious pride	20:20–28	10:35–45		
Healing of blind Bartimaeus and his companion	20:29–34	10:46–52	18:35–43	
Salvation of Zacchaeus			19:1–10	
Parable to teach responsibility while the kingdom is delayed			19:11–28	

THE FORMAL PRESENTATION OF CHRIST TO ISRAEL AND THE RESULTING CONFLICT

Triumphal Entry and the Fig Tree

	MATTHEW	MARK	LUKE	JOHN
Arrival at Bethany				11:55—12:1, 9–11
Jesus' entry into Jerusalem as King	21:1–3,6–7, 4–5,8–11, 14–17	11:1–11	19:29–44	12:12–19
Cursing of the fig tree having leaves but no figs	21:18–19a	11:12–14		
Second cleansing of the temple	21:12–13	11:15–18	19:45–48	
Request of some Greeks to see Jesus and necessity of the Son of Man's being lifted up				12:20–36a
Different responses to Jesus and Jesus' response to the crowds				12:36b–50
Withered fig tree and the lesson on faith	21:19b–22	11:19–25	21:37–38	

Official Challenge to Christ's Authority

	MATTHEW	MARK	LUKE	JOHN
Questioning of Jesus' authority by the chief priests, teachers of the law and elders	21:23–27	11:27–33	20:1–8	
Jesus' response with his own question and three parables	21:28—22:14	12:1–12	20:9–19	
Attempts by Pharisees and Herodians to trap Jesus with a question about paying taxes to Caesar	22:15–22	12:13–17	20:20–26	
Sadducees' puzzling question about the resurrection	22:23–33	12:18–27	20:27–40	
A Pharisee's legal question	22:34–40	12:28–34		

Christ's Response to His Enemies' Challenges

	MATTHEW	MARK	LUKE	JOHN
Christ's relationship to David as son and Lord	22:41–46	12:35–37	20:41–44	
Seven woes against the teachers of the law and Pharisees	23:1–36	12:38–40	20:45–47	
Jesus' sorrow over Jerusalem	23:37–39			
A poor widow's gift of all she had		12:41–44	21:1–4	

PROPHECIES IN PREPARATION FOR THE DEATH OF CHRIST

The Olivet Discourse: Jesus Speaks Prophetically about the Temple and His Own Second Coming

	MATTHEW	MARK	LUKE	JOHN
Setting of the discourse	24:1–3	13:1–4	21:5–7	
Beginning of birth pains	24:4–14	13:5–13	21:8–19	
Abomination of desolation and subsequent distress	24:15–28	13:14–23	21:20–24	
Coming of the Son of Man	24:29–31	13:24–27	21:25–27	
Signs of nearness but unknown time	24:32–41	13:28–32	21:28–33	
Five parables to teach watchfulness and faithfulness	24:42—25:30	13:33–37	21:34–36	
Judgment at the Son of Man's coming	25:31–46			

Arrangements for Betrayal

	MATTHEW	MARK	LUKE	JOHN
Plot by the Sanhedrin to arrest and kill Jesus	26:1–5	14:1–2	22:1–2	
Mary's anointing of Jesus for burial	26:6–13	14:3–9		12:2–8
Judas's agreement to betray Jesus	26:14–16	14:10–11	22:3–6	

The Last Supper

	MATTHEW	MARK	LUKE	JOHN
Preparation for the Passover meal	26:17–19	14:12–16	22:7–13	
Beginning of the Passover meal and dissension among the disciples over greatness	26:20	14:17	22:14–16,24–30	
Washing the disciples' feet				13:1–20
Identification of the betrayer	26:21–25	14:18–21	22:21–23	13:21–30

	MATTHEW	MARK	LUKE	JOHN
Prediction of Peter's denial	26:31–35	14:27–31	22:31–38	13:31–38
Conclusion of the meal and the Lord's Supper instituted (1 Co 11:23–26)	26:26–29	14:22–25	22:17–20	
Discourse and Prayers from the Upper Room to Gethsemane				
Questions answered about Jesus' destination, the Father and the Holy Spirit				14:1–31
The vine and the branches				15:1–17
Opposition from the world				15:18—16:4
Coming and ministry of the Spirit				16:5–15
Prediction of joy over Jesus' resurrection				16:16–22
Promise of answered prayer and peace				16:23–33
Jesus' prayer for his disciples and all who believe				17:1–26
Jesus' three agonizing prayers in Gethsemane	26:30,36–46	14:26,32–42	22:39–46	18:1

THE DEATH OF CHRIST

	MATTHEW	MARK	LUKE	JOHN
Betrayal and Arrest				
Jesus betrayed, arrested and forsaken	26:47–56	14:43–52	22:47–53	18:2–12
Trial				
First Jewish phase, before Annas				18:13–14,19–23
Second Jewish phase, before Caiaphas and the Sanhedrin	26:57,59–68	14:53,55–65	22:54a,63–65	18:24
Peter's denials	26:58,69–75	14:54,66–72	22:54b–62	18:15–18,25–27
Third Jewish phase, before the Sanhedrin	27:1	15:1a	22:66–71	
Remorse and suicide of Judas Iscariot (Ac 1:18–19)	27:3–10			
First Roman phase, before Pilate	27:2,11–14	15:1b–5	23:1–5	18:28–38
Second Roman phase, before Herod Antipas			23:6–12	
Third Roman phase, before Pilate	27:15–26	15:6–15	23:13–25	18:39—19:16a
Crucifixion				
Mockery by the Roman soldiers	27:27–30	15:16–19		
Journey to Golgotha	27:31–34	15:20–23	23:26–33a	19:16b–17
First three hours of crucifixion	27:35–44	15:24–32	23:33b–43	19:18,23–24, 19–22,25–27
Last three hours of crucifixion	27:45–50	15:33–37	23:44–45a,46	19:28–30
Witness of Jesus' death	27:51–56	15:38–41	23:45b,47–49	
Burial				
Certification of Jesus' death and procurement of his body	27:57–58	15:42–45	23:50–52	19:31–38
Jesus' body placed in a tomb	27:59–60	15:46	23:53–54	19:39–42
The tomb watched by the women and guarded by the soldiers	27:61–66	15:47	23:55–56	

THE RESURRECTION AND ASCENSION OF CHRIST

	MATTHEW	MARK	LUKE	JOHN
The Empty Tomb				
The tomb visited by the women	28:1	16:1		
The stone rolled away	28:2–4			
The tomb found to be empty by the women	28:5–8	16:2–8	24:1–8	20:1
The tomb found to be empty by Peter and John			24:9–12	20:2–10
The Resurrection Appearances				
Appearance to Mary Magdalene		[16:9–11]		20:11–18
Appearance to the other women	28:9–10			
Report of the soldiers to the Jewish authorities	28:11–15			
Appearance to the two disciples traveling to Emmaus		[16:12–13]	24:13–32	
Report of the two disciples to the rest (1 Co 15:5a)			24:33–35	
Appearance to the ten assembled disciples		[16:14]	24:36–43	20:19–25
Appearance to the eleven assembled disciples (1 Co 15:5b)				20:26–31
Appearance to the seven disciples while they were fishing				21:1–25
Appearance to the Eleven in Galilee (1 Co 15:6)	28:16–20	[16:15–18]		
Appearance to James, Jesus' brother (1 Co 15:7)				
Appearance to the disciples in Jerusalem (Ac 1:3–8)			24:44–49	
The Ascension				
Christ's parting blessing and departure (Ac 1:9–12)		[16:19–20]	24:50–53	

MAJOR ARCHAEOLOGICAL FINDS RELATING TO THE NT

SITE OR ARTIFACT	LOCATION	RELATING SCRIPTURE
ISRAEL		
Caiaphas ossuary	Jerusalem	Mt 26:3
Herod's temple	Jerusalem	Lk 1:9
Herod's winter palace	Jericho	Mt 2:4
The Herodium (possible site of Herod's tomb)	Near Bethlehem	Mt 2:19
Masada	Near western shore of Dead Sea	Cf. Lk 21:20
Early synagogue	Capernaum	Mt 4:13; Mk 1:21
Pool of Siloam	Jerusalem	Jn 9:7
Pool of Bethesda	Jerusalem	Jn 5:2
Pilate inscription	Caesarea	Lk 3:1
Inscription: Gentile entrance of temple sanctuary	Jerusalem	Ac 21:27–29
Skeletal remains of crucified man	Jerusalem	Mk 15:24
Peter's house	Capernaum	Mt 4:13; Lk 4:38
Jacob's well	Nablus	Jn 4:5–6
ASIA MINOR		
Derbe inscription	Kerti Hüyük	Ac 14:20
Sergius Paulus inscription	Kythraia, Cyprus	Ac 13:6–7
Zeus altar (Satan's throne?)	Pergamum	Rev 2:13
Fourth-century B.C. walls	Assos	Ac 20:13–14
Artemis temple and altar	Ephesus	Ac 19:27–28
Ephesian theater	Ephesus	Ac 19:29
Silversmith shops	Ephesus	Ac 19:24
Artemis statues	Ephesus	Ac 19:35
GREECE		
Erastus inscription	Corinth	Ro 16:23
Synagogue inscription	Corinth	Ac 18:4
Meat market inscription	Corinth	1Co 10:25
Cult dining rooms (in Asklepius and Demeter temples)	Corinth	1Co 8:10
Court (bema)	Corinth	Ac 18:12
Marketplace (bema)	Philippi	Ac 16:19
Starting gate for races	Isthmia	1Co 9:24,26
Gallio inscription	Delphi	Ac 18:12
Egnatian Way	Neapolis (Kavalla), Philippi, Amphipolis, Apollonia, Thessalonica	Cf. Ac 16:11–12; 17:1
Politarch inscription	Thessalonica	Ac 17:6
ITALY		
Tomb of Augustus	Rome	Lk 2:1
Mamertine Prison	Rome	2Ti 1:16–17; 2:9; 4:6–8
Appian Way	Puteoli to Rome	Ac 28:13–16
Golden House of Nero	Rome	Cf. Ac 25:10; 1Pe 2:13
Arch of Titus	Rome	Cf. Lk 19:43–44; 21:6,20

mention in the martyrdom of Paul (I.A.D. 67) and of the destruction of Jerusalem (70)
was not pertinent. This would allow for the writing of Acts c. 70

ACTS INTRODUCTION

AUTHOR

Although the author does not name himself, evidence outside the Scriptures and inferences from the book itself lead to the conclusion that the author was Luke.

The earliest of the external testimonies appears in the Muratorian Canon (c. A.D. 170), where the explicit statement is made that Luke was the author of both the third Gospel and the "Acts of All the Apostles." Eusebius (c. 325) lists information from numerous sources to identify the author of these books as Luke (*Ecclesiastical History*, 3.4).

Within the writing itself are some clues as to who the author was:

1. *Luke, the companion of Paul.* In the description of the happenings in Acts, certain passages make use of the pronoun "we." At these points the author includes himself as a companion of Paul in his travels (16:10–17; 20:5—21:18; 27:1—28:16; see notes on 16:10,17; 27:1). A historian as careful with details as this author proves to be would have good reason for choosing to use "we" in some places and "they" elsewhere. The author was therefore probably present with Paul at the particular events described in the "we" sections.

These "we" passages include the period of Paul's two-year imprisonment at Rome (ch. 28). During this time Paul wrote, among other letters, Philemon and Colossians. In them he sends greetings from his companions, and Luke is included among them (see Col 4:9–17 and notes; Phm 23–24). In fact, after eliminating those who, for one reason or another, would not fit the requirements for the author of Acts, Luke is left as the most likely candidate.

2. *Luke, the physician.* Although it cannot be proved that the author of Acts was a physician simply from his vocabulary, the words he uses and the traits and education reflected in his writings fit well his role as a physician (see, e.g., note on 28:6). It is true that the doctor of the first century did not have as specialized a vocabulary as that of doctors today, but there are some usages in Luke–Acts that seem to suggest that a medical man was the author of these books. And it should be remembered that Paul uses the term "doctor" in describing Luke (see Col 4:14 and note).

DATE

Two dates are possible for the writing of this book: (1) c. A.D. 63, soon after the last event recorded in the book, and (2) c. 70 or even later.

The earlier date is supported by:

1. *Silence about later events.* While arguments from silence are not conclusive, it is perhaps significant that the book contains no allusion to events that happened after the close of Paul's two-year imprisonment in Rome: e.g., the burning of Rome and the persecution of the Christians there (A.D. 64), the martyrdom of Peter and Paul (possibly 67) and the destruction of Jerusalem (70).

2. *No outcome of Paul's trial.* If Luke knew the outcome of the trial Paul was waiting for (see 28:30 and note), why did he not record it at the close of Acts? Perhaps it was because he had brought the history up to date.

Those who prefer the later date hold that 1:8 (see note there) reveals one of the purposes Luke had in writing his history and shows that this purpose influenced the way the book ended. Luke wanted to show how the church penetrated the world of his day in ever-widening circles (Jerusalem, Judea, Samaria, the ends of the earth) until it reached Rome, the world's political and cultural center. On this understanding, mention of the martyrdom of Paul (c. A.D. 67) and of the destruction of Jerusalem (70) was not pertinent. This would allow for the writing of Acts c. 70 or even later.

RECIPIENT

 The recipient of the book, Theophilus, is the same person addressed in the first volume, the Gospel of Luke (see Introduction to Luke: Recipient and Purpose).

IMPORTANCE

The book of Acts provides a bridge for the writings of the NT. As a second volume to Luke's Gospel, it joins what Jesus "began to do and to teach" (1:1; see note there) as told in the Gospels with what he continued to do and teach through the apostles' preaching and the establishment of the church. Besides linking the Gospel narratives on the one hand and the apostolic letters on the other, it supplies an account of the life of Paul, from which we can learn the setting for his letters. Geographically, its story spans the lands between Jerusalem, where the church began, and Rome, the political center of the empire. Historically, it recounts the first 30 years of the church. It is also a bridge that ties the church in its beginning with each succeeding age. This book may be studied to gain an understanding of the principles that ought to govern the church of any age.

THEME AND PURPOSE

The theme of the work is best summarized in 1:8 (see note there). It was ordinary procedure for a historian at this time to begin a second volume by summarizing the first volume and indicating the contents anticipated in his second volume. Luke summarized his first volume in 1:1–3; the theme of his second volume is presented in the words of Jesus: "You will be my witnesses in Jerusalem, and in all Judea and Samaria, and to the ends of the earth" (1:8). This is, in effect, an outline of the book of Acts (see Plan and Outline, below).

The main purposes of the book appear to be:

1. *To present a history.* The significance of Acts as a historical account of Christian origins cannot be overestimated. It tells of the founding of the church, the spread of the gospel, the beginnings of congregations, and evangelistic efforts in the apostolic pattern. One of the unique aspects of Christianity is its firm historical foundation. The life and teachings of Jesus Christ are established in the four Gospel narratives, and the book of Acts provides a coordinated account of the beginning and spread of the church as the result of the work of the risen Lord and the Holy Spirit through the apostles.

2. *To give a defense.* One finds embedded in Acts a record of Christian defenses made to both Jews (e.g., 4:8–12) and Gentiles (e.g., 25:8–11), with the underlying purpose of conversion. It shows how the early church coped with pagan and Jewish thought, the Roman government and Hellenistic society.

Luke may have written this work as Paul awaited trial in Rome. If his case came to court, what better court brief could Paul have had than a life of Jesus, a history of the beginnings of the church (including the activity of Paul) and an early collection of Paul's letters?

3. *To provide a guide.* Luke had no way of knowing how long the church would continue on this earth, but as long as it pursues its course, the book of Acts will be one of its major guides. In Acts we see basic principles being applied to specific situations in the context of problems and persecutions. These same principles continue to be applicable until Christ returns.

4. *To depict the triumph of Christianity in the face of bitter persecution.* The success of the church in carrying the gospel from Jerusalem to Rome and in planting local churches across the Roman empire demonstrated that Christianity was not a merely human work. It triumphed under the rule of the exalted Christ and through the power of the Holy Spirit.

CHARACTERISTICS

1. *Accurate historical detail.* Every page of Acts abounds with sharp, precise details, to the delight of the historian. The account covers a period of about 30 years and reaches across the lands from Jerusalem to Rome. Luke's description of these times and places is filled with all kinds of people and cultures, a variety of governmental administrations, court scenes in Caesarea, and dramatic events involving such centers as Antioch, Ephesus, Athens, Corinth and Rome. Barbarian country districts and Jewish centers are included as well. Yet in each instance archaeological findings reveal that Luke uses the proper terms for the time and place being described. Hostile criticism has not succeeded in disproving the detailed accuracy of Luke's political and geographical designations (see chart, p. 1830, and maps and archaeological notes scattered throughout the book).

2. *Literary excellence.* Not only does Luke have a large vocabulary compared with other NT writers, but he also uses these words in literary styles that fit the cultural settings of the events he is recording. At times he employs good, classical Greek; at other times the Palestinian Aramaic of the first century shows through his expressions. This is an indication of Luke's careful practice of using language appropriate to the time and place being described. Aramaisms are used when Luke is describing happenings that took place in the Holy Land (chs. 1–12). When, however, Paul departs for Hellenistic lands beyond the territories where Aramaic-speaking people live, Aramaisms cease.

3. *Dramatic description.* Luke's skillful use of speeches contributes to the drama of his narrative. Not only are they carefully spaced and well balanced between Peter and Paul, but the speeches of a number of other individuals add variety and vividness to the account (see 5 below). Luke's use of details brings the action to life. Nowhere in ancient literature is there an account of a shipwreck superior to Luke's with its nautical details (ch. 27). The book is vivid and fast-moving throughout.

4. *Objective account.* Luke's careful arrangement of material need not detract from the accuracy of his record. He demonstrates the objectivity of his account by recording the failures as well as the successes, the bad as well as the good, in the early church. Not only is the discontent between the Hellenistic Jews and the Hebraic Jews recorded (see 6:1 and note) but also the discord between Paul and Barnabas (see 15:39 and note). Divisions and differences are recognized (15:2; 21:20–21).

5. *Effective use of speeches.* One of the distinguishing features of the book of Acts is its speeches. They may be classified as follows: (1) evangelistic—two types: to Jews and God-fearers (2:14–40; 3:12–26; 4:8–12; 5:29–32; 10:34–43; 13:16–41), to pagans (17:22–31); (2) deliberative (1:16–17,20–22; 15:7–11,13–21); (3) apologetic (7:2–52; 22:1–21; 23:1–6; 24:10–21; 25:8,10; 26:2–23; 28:17–20,21–22,25–28); (4) hortatory (20:18–35).

The speeches are obvioiusly not verbatim reports; any of them can be read in a few minutes. We know, e.g., that Paul at times could be a long-winded preacher (see 20:7,9; 28:23). However, studies of these speeches (speakers, audiences, circumstances, language and style of writing) give us reason to believe that they are accurate summaries of what was actually said.

PLAN AND OUTLINE

Luke weaves together different interests and emphases as he relates the beginnings and expansion of the church. The design of his book revolves around (1) key persons: Peter and Paul; (2) important topics and events: the role of the Holy Spirit, pioneer missionary outreach to new fields, conversions, the growth of the church and life in the Christian community; (3) significant problems: conflict between Jews and Gentiles, persecution of the church by some Jewish elements, trials before Jews and Romans, confrontations with Gentiles and other hardships in the ministry; (4) geographical advances: five significant stages (see the quotations in the outline; see also map, p. 1861; cf. note on 1:8).

JESUS TAKEN UP INTO HEAVEN

1 In my former book,[a] Theophilus, I wrote about all that Jesus began to do and to teach[b] [2]until the day he was taken up to heaven,[c] after giving instructions[d] through the Holy Spirit to the apostles[e] he had chosen.[f] [3]After his suffering, he presented himself to them and gave many convincing proofs that he was alive. He appeared to them[g] over a period of forty days and spoke about the kingdom of God.[h] [4]On one occasion, while he was eating with them, he gave them this command: "Do not leave Jerusalem, but wait[i] for the gift my Father promised, which you have heard me speak about.[j] [5]For John baptized with[a] water,[k] but in a few days you will be baptized with[a] the Holy Spirit."[l]

[6]So when they met together, they asked him, "Lord, are you at this time going to restore[m] the kingdom to Israel?"

[7]He said to them: "It is not for you to know the times or dates the Father has set by his own authority.[n] [8]But you will receive power when the Holy Spirit comes on you;[o] and you will be my witnesses[p] in Jerusalem, and in all Judea and Samaria,[q] and to the ends of the earth."[r]

[9]After he said this, he was taken up[s] before their very eyes, and a cloud hid him from their sight.

[10]They were looking intently up into the sky as he was going, when suddenly two men dressed in white[t] stood beside them. [11]"Men of Galilee,"[u] they said, "why do you stand here looking into the sky? This same Jesus, who has been taken from you into heaven, will come back[v] in the same way you have seen him go into heaven."

MATTHIAS CHOSEN TO REPLACE JUDAS

[12]Then the apostles returned to Jerusalem[w] from the hill called the Mount of Olives,[x] a Sabbath day's walk[b] from the city. [13]When they arrived, they went upstairs to the room[y] where they were staying. Those present were Peter, John, James and Andrew; Philip and Thomas, Bartholomew and Matthew; James son of Alphaeus and Simon the Zealot, and Judas son of James.[z] [14]They all joined together constantly in prayer,[a] along with the women[b] and Mary the mother of Jesus, and with his brothers.[c]

a 5 Or *in*   b 12 That is, about 5/8 mile or about 1 kilometer

---

1:1 *a* Lk 1:1-4
b Lk 3:23
1:2 *c* ver 9,11;
S Mk 16:19
d Mt 28:19,20
e S Mk 6:30 *f* Jn 13:18;
15:16,19
1:3 *g* Mt 28:17;
Lk 24:34,36;
Jn 20:19,26; 21:1,14;
1Co 15:5-7 *h* S Mt 3:2
1:4 *i* Ps 27:14
j Lk 24:49; Jn 14:16;
Ac 2:33
1:5 *k* S Mk 1:4
l S Mk 1:8
1:6 *m* Mt 17:11;
Ac 3:21
1:7 *n* Dt 29:29;
Ps 102:13; Mt 24:36
1:8 *o* Ac 2:1-4
p S Lk 24:48 *q* Ac 8:1-
25 *r* S Mk 16:19
1:9 *s* ver 2;
S Mk 16:19
1:10 *t* S Jn 20:12
1:11 *u* Ac 2:7
v S Mt 16:27
1:12 *w* Lk 24:52
x S Mt 21:1
1:13 *y* Ac 9:37; 20:8
z Mt 10:2-4; Mk 3:16-
19; Lk 6:14-16
1:14 *a* Ac 2:42; 4:24;
6:4; S Lk 18:1;
S Ro 1:10 *b* Lk 23:49,
55 *c* S Mt 12:46

1:1 *my former book.* The Gospel of Luke. Acts was addressed to the same patron, Theophilus (see Introduction to Luke: Recipient and Purpose). *began to do and to teach.* An apt summation of Luke's Gospel, implying that Jesus' work continues in Acts through his own personal interventions and the ministry of the Holy Spirit.

1:2 *taken up to heaven.* The last scene of Luke's Gospel (24:50–52) and the opening scene of this second volume (vv. 6–11). The ascension occurred 40 days after the resurrection (v. 3). *through the Holy Spirit.* Jesus' postresurrection instruction of his apostles was carried on through the Holy Spirit, and succeeding statements make it clear that what the apostles were to accomplish was likewise to be done through the Spirit (vv. 4–5,8; see Lk 24:49 and note; Jn 20:22; see also Introduction to Judges: Themes and Theology). Luke characteristically stresses the Holy Spirit's work and enabling power (e.g., v. 8; 2:4,17; 4:8,31; 5:3; 6:3,5; 7:55; 8:16; 9:17,31; 10:44; 13:2,4; 15:28; 16:6; 19:2,6; see note on Lk 4:1).

1:3 *many convincing proofs.* See the resurrection appearances (Mt 28:1–20; Lk 24:1–53; Jn 20:1–29; 1Co 15:3–8). *kingdom of God.* The heart of Jesus' preaching (see notes on Mt 3:2; Lk 4:43).

1:4 *the gift my Father promised.* The Holy Spirit (see Lk 24:49 and note; Jn 14:26; 15:26–27; 16:12–13).

1:5 *John baptized with water.* See Lk 3:16 and note. *in a few days.* The day of Pentecost came ten days later, when the baptism with the Holy Spirit occurred (2:1–4).

1:6 *restore the kingdom to Israel?* Like their fellow countrymen, they were looking for the deliverance of the people of Israel from foreign domination and for the establishment of an earthly kingdom. The reference to the coming of the Spirit had caused them to wonder if the new age was about to dawn.

1:7 *the times or dates.* The elapsing time or the character of coming events (see Mk 13:32; 1Th 5:1 and notes).

1:8 A virtual outline of Acts: The apostles were to be witnesses in Jerusalem (chs. 1–7), Judea and Samaria (chs. 8–9) and the ends of the earth—including Caesarea, Antioch, Asia Minor, Greece and Rome (chs. 10–28). However, they were not to begin this staggering task until they had been equipped with the power of the Spirit (vv. 4–5). *my witnesses.* An important theme throughout Acts (2:32; 3:15; 5:32; 10:39; 13:31; 22:15). *Judea.* The region in which Jerusalem was located. *Samaria.* The adjoining region to the north.

1:9 *taken up.* See note on v. 2. *a cloud hid him.* See Mt 17:5 and note.

1:10 *two men dressed in white.* Cf. Jn 20:12.

1:11 *Men of Galilee.* All of the Twelve were from Galilee except Judas, and he was no longer present. *in the same way.* In the same resurrection body and in clouds and with "great glory" (Mt 24:30).

1:12 *Mount of Olives.* The ascension occurred on the eastern slope of the mount between Jerusalem and Bethany (Lk 19:28–29,37; see note on Zec 14:4; Mk 11:1; Lk 19:29; 24:50). *Sabbath day's walk.* See TNIV text note. This distance was drawn from Rabbinical reasoning based on several OT passages (Ex 16:29; Nu 35:5; Jos 3:4). A faithful Jew was to travel no farther on the Sabbath.

1:13 *room.* Probably an upper room of a large house, such as the one where the Last Supper was held (Mk 14:15) or that of Mary, the mother of Mark (see note on 12:12). *Bartholomew.* Apparently John calls him Nathanael (see Jn 1:45–49; 21:2). *James son of Alphaeus.* The same as James the younger (Mk 15:40). *Zealot.* See note on Mt 10:4. *Judas son of James.* Not Judas Iscariot, but the same person as Thaddaeus (see note on Mt 10:3).

1:14 *with the women.* Possibly wives of the apostles (cf. 1Co 9:5 and note) and those listed as ministering to Jesus

1:16 *d* Ac 6:3; 11:1,
12, 29; 14:2; 18:18,27;
21:7; S 22:5; S Ro 7:1
e ver 20; S Mt 1:22
f S Mt 10:4
1:17 *g* Jn 6:70, 71
h ver 25
1:18 *i* Mt 26:14,15
j Mt 27:3-10
1:19 *k* S Jn 5:2
1:20 *l* Ps 69:25
m Ps 109:8
1:22 *n* S Mk 1:4
o ver 8; S Lk 24:48
1:24 *p* Ac 6:6; 13:3;
14:23 *q* Ac 15:8;
S Rev 2:23 *r* 1Sa 14:41
1:26 *s* Ac 2:14
2:1 *t* Lev 23:15,16;
Ac 20:16; 1Co 16:8
u Ac 1:14
2:2 *v* Ac 4:31
2:4 *w* S Lk 1:15
x S Mk 16:17

¹⁵In those days Peter stood up among the believers (a group numbering about a hundred and twenty) ¹⁶and said, "Brothers and sisters, *d* the Scripture had to be fulfilled *e* in which the Holy Spirit spoke long ago through David concerning Judas, *f* who served as guide for those who arrested Jesus. ¹⁷He was one of our number *g* and shared in our ministry." *h*

¹⁸(With the reward *i* he got for his wickedness, Judas bought a field; *j* there he fell headlong, his body burst open and all his intestines spilled out. ¹⁹Everyone in Jerusalem heard about this, so they called that field in their language *k* Akeldama, that is, Field of Blood.)

²⁰"For," said Peter, "it is written in the Book of Psalms:

" 'May his place be deserted;
    let there be no one to dwell in it,' *a l*

and,

" 'May another take his place of leadership.' *b m*

²¹Therefore it is necessary to choose one of the men who have been with us the whole time the Lord Jesus went in and out among us, ²²beginning from John's baptism *n* to the time when Jesus was taken up from us. For one of these must become a witness *o* with us of his resurrection."

²³So they proposed the names of two men: Joseph called Barsabbas (also known as Justus) and Matthias. ²⁴Then they prayed, *p* "Lord, you know everyone's heart. *q* Show us *r* which of these two you have chosen ²⁵to take over this apostolic ministry, which Judas left to go where he belongs." ²⁶Then they cast lots, and the lot fell to Matthias; so he was added to the eleven apostles. *s*

THE HOLY SPIRIT COMES AT PENTECOST

2 When the day of Pentecost *t* came, they were all together *u* in one place. ²Suddenly a sound like the blowing of a violent wind came from heaven and filled the whole house where they were sitting. *v* ³They saw what seemed to be tongues of fire that separated and came to rest on each of them. ⁴All of them were filled with the Holy Spirit *w* and began to speak in other tongues *c x* as the Spirit enabled them.

a 20 Psalm 69:25   b 20 Psalm 109:8   c 4 Or *languages*; also in verse 11

(Mt 27:55; Lk 8:2–3; 24:22). *Mary the mother of Jesus.* Last mentioned here in Scripture. *brothers.* See note on Lk 8:19. These brothers would include James, who later became a leader in the Jerusalem church (12:17; 15:13; 21:18; Gal 1:19; 2:9; see Introduction to James: Author).

1:16 *the Scripture had to be fulfilled.* For the Scripture referred to, see TNIV text notes on v. 20. Both before and after Christ came, numerous psalms were viewed as Messianic. What happened in the psalmist's experience was typical of the experiences of the Messiah. No doubt Jesus' instruction in Lk 24:27,45–47 included these Scriptures.

1:18 *Judas bought a field.* Judas bought the field indirectly: The money he returned to the priests (Mt 27:3) was used to purchase the potter's field (Mt 27:7). *fell headlong.* Mt 27:5 reports that Judas hanged himself. It appears that when the body finally fell, either because of decay or because someone cut it down, it was in a decomposed condition and so broke open in the middle. Another possibility is that "hanged" in Mt 27:5 means "impaled" (see note on Est 2:23) and that the gruesome results of Judas's suicide are described here.

1:20 *it is written.* Two passages of Scripture (see TNIV text notes) were put together to suggest that Judas had left a vacancy that had to be filled (see notes on Ps 69:25; 109:8).

1:21 *went in and out among us.* Ministered publicly (cf. 9:28).

1:22 *a witness with us of his resurrection.* Apparently several met this requirement. On this occasion, however, the believers were selecting someone to become an official witness to the resurrection—thus, a 12th apostle (v. 25).

1:23 *Barsabbas.* Means "son of (the) Sabbath." This patronymic was used for two early Jewish Christians, possibly brothers. One was Joseph (here); the other was Judas, a prophet in Jerusalem who was sent to Antioch with Silas (15:22,32). *Justus.* Joseph's

Hellenistic name. Nothing more is known of him.

1:26 *cast lots.* See Pr 16:33 and note. By casting lots they submitted the decision to the ascended Lord. The use of rocks or sticks to designate the choice was common (see 1Ch 26:13–16; see also notes on Ne 11:1; Jnh 1:7). This is the Bible's last mention of casting lots.

2:1 *day of Pentecost.* The 50th day after the Sabbath of Passover week (Lev 23:15–16), thus the first day of the week. Pentecost is also called the Festival of Weeks (Dt 16:10), the Festival of Harvest (Ex 23:16) and the day of firstfruits (Nu 28:26). See chart, pp. 180–181. *they were all together.* The nearest antecedent of "they" is the 11 apostles (plus Matthias), but the reference is probably to all those mentioned in 1:13–15. *in one place.* Evidently not the upstairs room where they were staying (1:13) but perhaps some place in the temple precincts, for the apostles were "continually at the temple" when it was open (Lk 24:53; see note there).

2:2 *violent wind.* Breath or wind is a symbol of the Spirit of God (see Eze 37:9,14; Jn 3:8). The coming of the Spirit is marked by audible (wind) and visible (fire) signs. *whole house.* May refer to the temple (cf. 7:47).

2:3 *tongues.* A descriptive metaphor appropriate to the context, in which several languages are about to be spoken. *fire.* A symbol of the divine presence (see Ex 3:2 and note), it was also associated with judgment (see Mt 3:12 and note).

2:4 *All of them.* Could refer either to the apostles or to the 120. Those holding that the 120 are meant point to the fulfillment of Joel's prophecy (vv. 17–18) as involving more than the 12 apostles. The nearest reference, however, is to the apostles (see note on v. 1), and the narrative continues with Peter and the 11 standing to address the crowd (v. 14). *filled with the Holy Spirit.* A fulfillment of 1:4–5,8; see also Jesus' promise in Lk 24:49 and

⁵Now there were staying in Jerusalem God-fearing ʸ Jews from every nation under heaven. ⁶When they heard this sound, a crowd came together in bewilderment, because each one heard their own language being spoken. ⁷Utterly amazed, ᶻ they asked: "Aren't all these who are speaking Galileans? ᵃ ⁸Then how is it that each of us hears them in our native language? ⁹Parthians, Medes and Elamites; residents of Mesopotamia, Judea and Cappadocia, ᵇ Pontus ᶜ and Asia, ᵃ ᵈ ¹⁰Phrygia ᵉ and Pamphylia, ᶠ Egypt and the parts of Lib-

2:5 ʸLk 2:25; Ac 8:2
2:7 ᶻver 12 ᵃAc 1:11
2:9 ᵇ1Pe 1:1
ᶜAc 18:2; 1Pe 1:1
ᵈAc 16:6; 19:10;
Ro 16:5; 1Co 16:19;
2Co 1:8; Rev 1:4
2:10 ᵉAc 16:6; 18:23
ᶠAc 13:13; 14:24;
15:38

ᵃ 9 That is, the Roman province by that name

---

note there (cf. Jn 14:16–18; 20:22 and note). Their spirits were completely under the control of the Holy Spirit; their words were his words. *in other tongues.* The Spirit enabled them to speak in languages they had not previously learned (see TNIV text note). Two other examples of speaking in tongues are found in Acts (see 10:46; 19:6 and note). One extended NT passage deals with this spiritual gift (1Co 12–14). Not all agree, however, that these other passages refer to speaking in known languages. The gift had particular relevance here, where people of different nationalities and languages were gathered.
2:5 *God-fearing Jews.* Devout Jews from different parts of the world but assembled now in Jerusalem either as pilgrims attending the Festival of Pentecost or as current residents (cf. Lk 2:25).
2:6 *heard their own language.* These Jews heard the apostles speak in languages native to the different places from which they had come (see map, below).
2:9 *Parthians.* Inhabitants of the territory from the Tigris River to India. *Medes.* Media lay east of Mesopotamia, northwest of

Persia and south-southwest of the Caspian Sea. *Elamites.* Elam was north of the Persian Gulf, bounded on the west by the Tigris. *Mesopotamia.* Between the Euphrates and Tigris rivers. *Judea.* The homeland of the Jews, perhaps used here in the OT sense "from the Wadi of Egypt to … the Euphrates" (Ge 15:18), including Galilee. *Cappadocia, Pontus and Asia.* Districts in Asia Minor. *Asia.* See note on 2Co 1:8.
2:10 *Phrygia and Pamphylia.* Districts in Asia Minor. *Egypt.* Jews had lived in Egypt since the sixth century B.C. Two out of the five districts of Alexandria were Jewish. *Cyrene.* The capital of a district of Libya called Cyrenaica. *Rome.* Thousands of Jews lived in Rome.
2:11 *converts to Judaism.* Gentiles who undertook the full observance of the Mosaic law were received into full fellowship with the Jews. *Cretans.* Represented an island lying southsoutheast of Greece. *Arabs.* From a region to the east. The kingdom of the Nabatean Arabs lay between the Red Sea and the Euphrates, with Petra as its capital. *we hear them declaring.* Not a

---

COUNTRIES OF PEOPLE MENTIONED AT PENTECOST

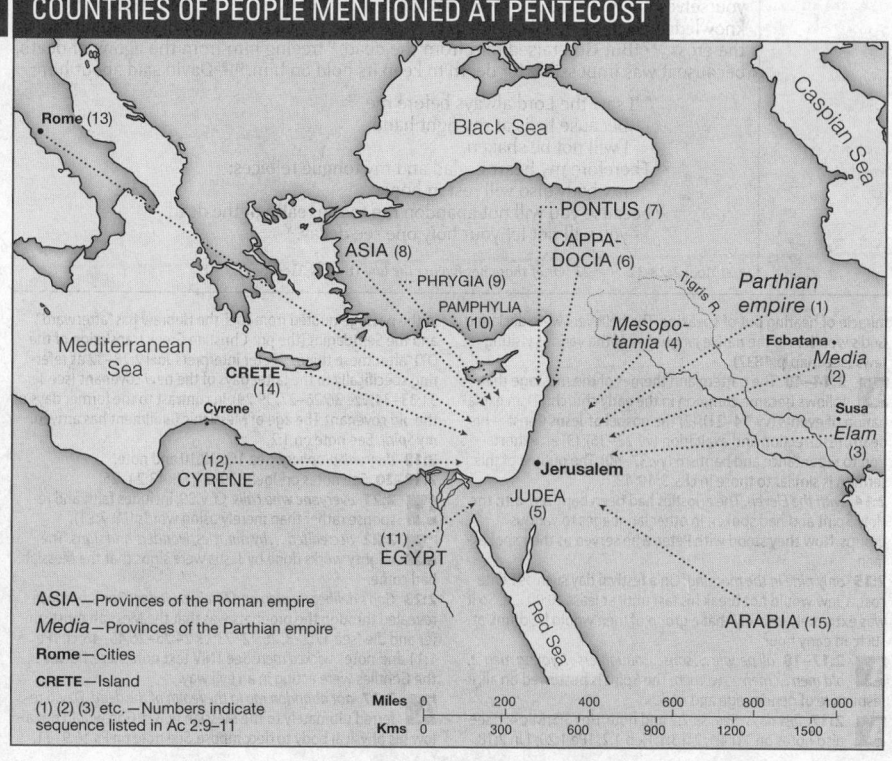

Rome (13)
Black Sea
Caspian Sea
PONTUS (7)
ASIA (8)
CAPPA-
DOCIA (6)
PHRYGIA (9)
PAMPHYLIA (10)
Tigris R.
Parthian empire (1)
Mesopo-
tamia (4)
Ecbatana
Media (2)
Mediterranean
Sea
CRETE (14)
Cyrene
Susa
Elam (3)
(12)
CYRENE
•Jerusalem
JUDEA (5)
(11)
EGYPT
Red Sea
ARABIA (15)

ASIA—Provinces of the Roman empire
Media—Provinces of the Parthian empire
Rome—Cities
CRETE—Island
(1) (2) (3) etc.—Numbers indicate sequence listed in Ac 2:9–11

Miles 0 — 200 — 400 — 600 — 800 — 1000
Kms 0 — 300 — 600 — 900 — 1200 — 1500

2:10 *g* S Mt 27:32
2:13 *h* 1Co 14:23;
Eph 5:18
2:15 *i* 1Th 5:7
2:17 *j* Nu 11:25;
Isa 44:3; Eze 39:29;
Jn 7:37-39; Ac 10:45
k S Ac 21:9
2:18 *l* Ac 21:9-12
2:19 *m* Lk 21:11
2:20 *n* S Mt 24:29
2:21 *o* Ge 4:26;
26:25; Ps 105:1;
Ac 9:14; 1Co 1:2;
2Ti 2:22 *p* Joel 2:28-
32; Ro 10:13
2:22 *q* S Mk 1:24
r S Jn 4:48 *s* S Jn 3:2
2:23 *t* Isa 53:10;
Ac 3:18; 4:28
u Mt 16:21; Lk 24:20;
Ac 3:13
2:24 *v* ver 32;
Ac 13:30,33,34,37;
17:31; Ro 6:4; 8:11;
10:9; 1Co 6:14; 15:15;
Eph 1:20; Col 2:12;
Heb 13:20; 1Pe 1:21
w Jn 20:9
2:27 *x* ver 31;
Ac 13:35

ya near Cyrene;*g* visitors from Rome [11](both Jews and converts to Judaism); Cretans and Arabs—we hear them declaring the wonders of God in our own tongues!" [12]Amazed and perplexed, they asked one another, "What does this mean?"

[13]Some, however, made fun of them and said, "They have had too much wine." *h*

PETER ADDRESSES THE CROWD

[14]Then Peter stood up with the Eleven, raised his voice and addressed the crowd: "Fellow Jews and all of you who live in Jerusalem, let me explain this to you; listen carefully to what I say. [15]These people are not drunk, as you suppose. It's only nine in the morning! *i* [16]No, this is what was spoken by the prophet Joel:

[17]" 'In the last days, God says,
   I will pour out my Spirit on all people.*j*
Your sons and daughters will prophesy, *k*
   your young men will see visions,
   your old men will dream dreams.
[18]Even on my servants, both men and women,
   I will pour out my Spirit in those days,
   and they will prophesy. *l*
[19]I will show wonders in the heaven above
   and signs on the earth below, *m*
   blood and fire and billows of smoke.
[20]The sun will be turned to darkness
   and the moon to blood *n*
   before the coming of the great and glorious day of the Lord.
[21]And everyone who calls
   on the name of the Lord *o* will be saved.' *a p*

[22]"People of Israel, listen to this: Jesus of Nazareth *q* was a man accredited by God to you by miracles, wonders and signs, *r* which God did among you through him, *s* as you yourselves know. [23]This man was handed over to you by God's deliberate plan and foreknowledge; *t* and you, with the help of wicked men, *b* put him to death by nailing him to the cross. *u* [24]But God raised him from the dead, *v* freeing him from the agony of death, because it was impossible for death to keep its hold on him. *w* [25]David said about him:

" 'I saw the Lord always before me.
   Because he is at my right hand,
   I will not be shaken.
[26]Therefore my heart is glad and my tongue rejoices;
   my body also will rest in hope,
[27]because you will not abandon me to the realm of the dead,
   you will not let your holy one see decay. *x*

a 21 Joel 2:28-32   *b 23* Or *of those not having the law* (that is, Gentiles)

miracle of hearing but of speaking. The believers were declaring God's wonders in the native languages of the various visiting Jews (see map, p. 1837).

2:14–40 The pattern and themes of the message that follows became common in the early church: (1) an explanation of events (vv. 14–21); (2) the gospel of Jesus Christ—his death, resurrection and exaltation (vv. 22–36); (3) an exhortation to repentance and baptism (vv. 37–40). The outline of this sermon is similar to those in chs. 3; 10; 13.

2:14 *with the Eleven.* The apostles had been baptized with the Holy Spirit and had spoken in other languages to various groups. Now they stood with Peter, who served as their spokesman.

2:15 *only nine in the morning!* On a festival day such as Pentecost, a Jew would not break his fast until at least 10:00 A.M. So it was extremely unlikely that a group of men would be drunk at such an early hour.

2:17–18 *all people ... sons ... daughters ... young men ... old men ... men ... women.* The Spirit is bestowed on all, irrespective of gender, age and rank.

2:17 *last days.* See Isa 2:2 and note; Hos 3:5; Mic 4:1; see also notes on 1Ti 4:1; 2Ti 3:1; Heb 1:2; 1Pe 1:20; 1Jn 2:18.

In the passage quoted from Joel, the Hebrew has "afterward" and the Septuagint (the pre-Christian Greek translation of the OT) "after these things." Peter interprets Joel 2:28–32 as referring specifically to the latter days of the new covenant (see Jer 31:33–34; Eze 36:26–27; 39:29), in contrast to the former days of the old covenant. The age of Messianic fulfillment has arrived. *my Spirit.* See note on 1:2.

2:18 *they will prophesy.* See 1Co 12:10 and note.

2:19–20 See notes on Joel 2:30–31; Mk 13:24–25.

2:21 *everyone who calls.* Cf. v. 39; includes faith and response rather than merely using words (Mt 7:21).

2:22 *accredited ... by miracles, wonders and signs.* The mighty works done by Jesus were signs that the Messiah had come.

2:23 *God's deliberate plan and foreknowledge.* God's purpose revealed through the prophets was that the Messiah must suffer and die (see 17:2–3; 26:22–23; Lk 24:25–26,45–46; cf. 1Pe 1:11 and note). *wicked men.* See TNIV text note; here, however, the Gentiles were acting in an evil way.

2:27 *not abandon me to the realm of the dead.* David referred ultimately to the Messiah (v. 31). God would not allow his physical body to decompose. See note on Ps 16:9–11.

²⁸You have made known to me the paths of life;
　　you will fill me with joy in your presence.'ᵃ ʸ

²⁹"Brothers and sisters,ᶻ we all know that the patriarch ᵃ David died and was buried,ᵇ and his tomb is here ᶜ to this day. ³⁰But he was a prophet and knew that God had promised him on oath that he would place one of his descendants on his throne.ᵈ ³¹Seeing what was to come, he spoke of the resurrection of the Messiah, that he was not abandoned to the realm of the dead, nor did his body see decay.ᵉ ³²God has raised this Jesus to life,ᶠ and we are all witnesses ᵍ of the fact. ³³Exalted ʰ to the right hand of God,ⁱ he has received from the Fatherʲ the promised Holy Spiritᵏ and has poured out ˡ what you now see and hear. ³⁴For David did not ascend to heaven, and yet he said,

" 'The Lord said to my Lord:
　"Sit at my right hand
³⁵until I make your enemies
　a footstool for your feet." 'ᵇ ᵐ

³⁶"Therefore let all Israel be assured of this: God has made this Jesus, whom you crucified, both Lordⁿ and Messiah."ᵒ

³⁷When the people heard this, they were cut to the heart and said to Peter and the other apostles, "Brothers, what shall we do?"ᵖ

³⁸Peter replied, "Repent and be baptized,�q every one of you, in the name of Jesus Christ for the forgiveness of your sins.ʳ And you will receive the gift of the Holy Spirit. ˢ ³⁹The promise is for you and your children ᵗ and for all who are far offᵘ—for all whom the Lord our God will call."

⁴⁰With many other words he warned them; and he pleaded with them, "Save yourselves from this corrupt generation." ᵛ ⁴¹Those who accepted his message were baptized, and about three thousand were added to their numberʷ that day.

THE FELLOWSHIP OF THE BELIEVERS

⁴²They devoted themselves to the apostles' teachingˣ and to fellowship, to the breaking of breadʸ and to prayer. ᶻ ⁴³Everyone was filled with awe at the many wonders and signs performed by the apostles. ᵃ ⁴⁴All the believers were together and had everything in common. ᵇ ⁴⁵They sold property and possessions to give to anyone who had need. ᶜ ⁴⁶Every day they continued to meet together in the temple courts. ᵈ They broke bread ᵉ in their

---

ᵃ 28 Psalm 16:8-11 (see Septuagint)　　ᵇ 35 Psalm 110:1

2:28 ʸ Ps 16:8-11
2:29 ᶻ S Ac 22:5
ᵃ Ac 7:8,9 ᵇ 1Ki 2:10; Ac 13:36 ᶜ Ne 3:16
2:30 ᵈ S Mt 1:1
2:31 ᵉ Ps 16:10
2:32 ᶠ S ver 24
ᵍ S Lk 24:48
2:33 ʰ S Ps 2:9
ⁱ S Mk 16:19 ʲ Ac 1:4
ᵏ Jn 7:39; 14:26; 15:26
ˡ Ac 10:45
2:35 ᵐ Ps 110:1; S Mt 22:44
2:36 ⁿ S Mt 28:18
ᵒ S Lk 2:11
2:37 ᵖ Lk 3:10,12,14; Ac 16:30
2:38 q ver 41;
Ac 8:12,16,36,38; 9:18; 10:48; 16:15,33; 19:5; 22:16; Col 2:12
ʳ Jer 36:3; Mk 1:4; S Lk 24:47; Ac 3:19
ˢ S Jn 20:22
2:39 ᵗ Isa 44:3; 65:23 ᵘ Isa 57:19; Ac 10:45; Eph 2:13
2:40 ᵛ Dt 32:5; Php 2:15
2:41 ʷ ver 47; Ac 4:4; 5:14; 6:1,7; 9:31,35,42; 11:21,24; 14:1,21; 16:5; 17:12
2:42 ˣ Mt 28:20
ʸ S Mt 14:19
ᶻ S Ac 1:14
2:43 ᵃ Ac 5:12
2:44 ᵇ Ac 4:32
2:45 ᶜ Mt 19:21; Lk 12:33; 18:22; Ac 4:34,35; 6:1
2:46 ᵈ Lk 24:53; Ac 3:1; 5:21,42
ᵉ ver 42; S Mt 14:19

2:29 *his tomb is here.* The tomb of David could be seen in Jerusalem. It still contained the remains of David's body. The words of Ps 16:8–11 did not fully apply to him.
2:33 *Exalted to the right hand of God.* See note on Heb 1:2–3. *promised Holy Spirit.* See note on 1:4. *has poured out.* See v. 17; Joel 2:28.

2:34 *The Lord said to my Lord.* The Lord (God) said to my Lord (the Son of David, the Messiah). According to Peter, David referred to his descendant with uncommon respect because he, through the inspiration of the Spirit, recognized how great and divine he would be (Mt 22:41–45). Not only was he to be resurrected (vv. 31–32) but he was also to be exalted to God's right hand (vv. 33–35). And his presence there was now being demonstrated by the sending of the Holy Spirit (v. 33; Jn 16:7). See note on Ps 110:1; see also introduction to that psalm.
2:37 *cut to the heart.* Because they now realized the enormity of their guilt.

2:38 *Repent and be baptized.* Repentance was important in the message of the forerunner, John the Baptist (Mk 1:4; Lk 3:3), in the preaching of Jesus (Mk 1:15; Lk 13:3) and in the directions Jesus left just before his ascension (Lk 24:47). So also baptism was important to John the Baptizer (Mk 1:4), in the instructions of Jesus (Mt 28:18–19) and in the preaching recorded in Acts—where it was associated with belief (8:12; 18:8), acceptance of the word (v. 41) and repentance (here). *in the name of Jesus Christ.* Not a contradiction to the fuller formula given in Mt 28:19. In Acts the abbreviated form emphasizes the distinctive quality of this baptism, for Jesus is now included in a way that he was not in John's baptism (19:4–5). *for the forgiveness of*

your sins. Not that baptism effects forgiveness. Rather, forgiveness comes through that which is symbolized by baptism (see Ro 6:3–4 and note). *Holy Spirit.* Two gifts are now given: the forgiveness of sins (see also 22:16) and the Holy Spirit. The promise of the indwelling gift of the Holy Spirit is given to all Christians (cf. Ro 8:9–11 and note on 8:9; 1Co 12:13 and note).
2:41 *their number.* The number of believers.

2:42 *apostles' teaching.* Included all that Jesus himself taught (Mt 28:20), especially the gospel, which was centered in his death, burial and resurrection (see vv. 23–24; 3:15; 4:10; 1Co 15:1–4). It was a unique teaching in that it came from God and was clothed with the authority conferred on the apostles (2Co 13:10; 1Th 4:2). Today it is available in the books of the NT. *fellowship.* The corporate fellowship of believers in worship. *breaking of bread.* Although this phrase is used of an ordinary meal in v. 46 (see Lk 24:30,35), the Lord's Supper seems to be indicated here (see note on 20:7; cf. 1Co 10:16; 11:20). *prayer.* Acts emphasizes the importance of prayer in the Christian life—private as well as public (1:14; 3:1; 6:4; 10:4,31; 12:5; 16:13,16).
2:44 *believers were together.* The unity of the early church (see 4:32; Jn 17:11,21–23; Ro 15:5; Eph 4:1–16; Php 2:1–4 and notes). *everything in common.* See 4:34–35. This was a voluntary sharing to provide for those who did not have enough for the essentials of living (see good and bad examples of sharing, 4:36—5:9).

2:46 *temple courts.* Probably Solomon's Colonnade (see 3:11 and note; 5:12). *broke bread in their homes.* Here the daily life of Christians is described, distinguishing their activity in the temple from that in their homes, where they ate their meals—not the Lord's Supper (see note on v. 42)—with glad-

2:47 ᶠS Ro 14:18
ᵍS ver 41
3:1 ʰS Lk 22:8
ⁱAc 2:46 / Ps 55:17;
Ac 10:30
3:2 ᵏAc 14:8
ˡLk 16:20 ᵐJn 9:8
3:6 ⁿver 16;
S Mk 1:24
3:8 ᵒIsa 35:6;
Ac 14:10
3:9 ᵖAc 4:16, 21
3:10 ᑫver 2
3:11 ʳS Lk 22:8
ˢJn 10:23; Ac 5:12
3:13 ᵗEx 3:6
ᵘAc 5:30; 7:32; 22:14
ᵛAc 2:23 ʷS Mt 27:2
ˣS Lk 23:4
3:14 ʸS Mk 1:24;
Ac 4:27 ᶻAc 7:52
ᵃMk 15:11; Lk 23:18-
25
3:15 ᵇS Ac 2:24
ᶜS Lk 24:48
3:16 ᵈver 6
3:17 ᵉS Ac 22:5
ᶠLk 23:34 ᵍAc 13:27
3:18 ʰS Mt 1:22
ⁱAc 2:23 ʲS Lk 24:27
ᵏAc 17:2,3; 26:22,23
3:19 ˡPs 51:1;
Isa 43:25; 44:22;
S Ac 2:38

homes and ate together with glad and sincere hearts, [47]praising God and enjoying the favor of all the people. ᶠ And the Lord added to their numberᵍ daily those who were being saved.

PETER HEALS A LAME BEGGAR

3 One day Peter and Johnʰ were going up to the templeⁱ at the time of prayer—at three in the afternoon.ʲ [2]Now a man who was lame from birthᵏ was being carried to the temple gateˡ called Beautiful, where he was put every day to begᵐ from those going into the temple courts. [3]When he saw Peter and John about to enter, he asked them for money. [4]Peter looked straight at him, as did John. Then Peter said, "Look at us!" [5]So the man gave them his attention, expecting to get something from them.

[6]Then Peter said, "Silver or gold I do not have, but what I do have I give you. In the name of Jesus Christ of Nazareth,ⁿ walk." [7]Taking him by the right hand, he helped him up, and instantly the man's feet and ankles became strong. [8]He jumped to his feet and began to walk. Then he went with them into the temple courts, walking and jumping,ᵒ and praising God. [9]When all the peopleᵖ saw him walking and praising God, [10]they recognized him as the same man who used to sit begging at the temple gate called Beautiful,ᑫ and they were filled with wonder and amazement at what had happened to him.

PETER SPEAKS TO THE ONLOOKERS

[11]While the man held on to Peter and John,ʳ all the people were astonished and came running to them in the place called Solomon's Colonnade.ˢ [12]When Peter saw this, he said to them: "People of Israel, why does this surprise you? Why do you stare at us as if by our own power or godliness we had made this man walk? [13]The God of Abraham, Isaac and Jacob,ᵗ the God of our fathers, ᵘ has glorified his servant Jesus. You handed him overᵛ to be killed, and you disowned him before Pilate,ʷ though he had decided to let him go. ˣ [14]You disowned the Holyʸ and Righteous Oneᶻ and asked that a murderer be released to you. ᵃ [15]You killed the author of life, but God raised him from the dead. ᵇ We are witnessesᶜ of this. [16]By faith in the name of Jesus,ᵈ this man whom you see and know was made strong. It is Jesus' name and the faith that comes through him that has completely healed him, as you can all see.

[17]"Now, brothers and sisters, ᵉ I know that you acted in ignorance, ᶠas did your leaders. ᵍ [18]But this is how God fulfilledʰ what he had foretoldⁱ through all the prophets,ʲ saying that his Messiah would suffer. ᵏ [19]Repent, then, and turn to God, so that your sins may be wiped out, ˡthat times of refreshing may come from the Lord, [20]and that he may send the

---

ness and generosity. *glad and sincere hearts*. The fellowship, oneness and sharing enjoyed in the early church are fruits of the Spirit. Joy is to be the mood of the believer (see note on 16:34).

2:47 *praising God*. See 3:8–9; 4:21; 10:46; 11:18; 21:20; emphasized also in Luke's Gospel (see notes on Lk 1:64; 24:53).

3:1 *Peter and John*. Among the foremost apostles (Gal 2:9). Along with John's brother, James, they had been especially close to Jesus (Mk 9:2; 13:3; 14:33; Lk 22:8). Arrested together (4:3), they were also together in Samaria (8:14). *time of prayer*. The three stated times of prayer for later Judaism were mid-morning (the third hour, 9:00 A.M.), the time of the evening sacrifice (the ninth hour, 3:00 P.M.) and sunset.

3:2 *gate called Beautiful*. The favorite entrance to the temple court, it was probably the bronze-sheathed gate that is elsewhere called the Nicanor Gate. Apparently it led from the court of the Gentiles to the court of women, east of the temple.

3:6 *In the name of Jesus Christ*. Not by power of their own, but by the authority of the Messiah.

3:7 *he helped him up*. But he had faith to be healed (v. 16).

3:8 *into the temple courts*. From the outer court (for Gentiles also) into the court of women, containing the treasury (Mk 12:41–44), and then into the court of Israel (see map No. 10 at the end of this study Bible). From the outer court, nine gates led into the inner courts.

3:11 *Solomon's Colonnade*. A porch along the inner side of the wall enclosing the outer court, with rows of 27-foot-high stone columns and a roof of cedar (see note on Jn 10:23).

3:12–26 See note on 2:14–40.

3:13 *his servant Jesus*. A reminder of the suffering servant prophesied in Isa 52:13—53:12 (see Mt 12:18; Ac 4:27,30). *disowned him*. Voted against Jesus, spurned him, denied him and refused to acknowledge him as the true Messiah. *Pilate . . . had decided to let him go*. See Jn 19:12.

3:14 *Holy . . . One*. Cf. note on Lev 11:44. *Righteous One*. For this description of the Messiah elsewhere, see 7:52; 22:14; cf. 1Jn 2:1. *murderer*. Barabbas (see Lk 23:18 and note).

3:15 *You killed . . . God raised . . . We are witnesses*. A recurring theme in the speeches of Acts (see 2:23–24; 4:10; 5:30–32; 10:39–41; 13:28–29; cf. 1Co 15:1–4).

3:17 *brothers and sisters*. "People of Israel" (v. 12). *you acted in ignorance*. They did not know that Jesus was the true Messiah (see Lk 23:34). Nevertheless, God will be generous in his mercy if they only repent and turn to him (see v. 19 and note).

3:18 *foretold through all the prophets*. Echoes what Jesus had said (Lk 24:26–27). The suffering was prophesied (compare Isa 53:7–8 with Ac 8:32–33; Ps 2:1–2 with Ac 4:25–26; Ps 22:1 with Mt 27:46; see also 1Pe 1:11).

3:19 *Repent*. Repentance is a change of mind and will arising from sorrow for sin and leading to transformation of life (see notes on 2:38; Lk 3:3). *turn to God*. Subsequent to repentance and not completely identical with it. See 11:21 ("believed and turned") and 26:20 ("repent and turn"; see also 9:35; 14:15; 15:19; 26:18; 28:27). In the strictest sense, repentance is turning from sin, and faith is turning to God. However, the word "turn" is not always used with such precision. *your sins . . . wiped out*. Your sins will be forgiven as a result of repentance.

Messiah,^m who has been appointed for you—even Jesus. ²¹Heaven must receive himⁿ until the time comes for God to restore everything,^o as he promised long ago through his holy prophets.^p ²²For Moses said, 'The Lord your God will raise up for you a prophet like me from among your own people; you must listen to everything he tells you.^q ²³Anyone who does not listen to him will be completely cut off from their people.'^{a r}

²⁴"Indeed, beginning with Samuel, all the prophets^s who have spoken have foretold these days. ²⁵And you are heirs^t of the prophets and of the covenant^u God made with your fathers. He said to Abraham, 'Through your offspring all peoples on earth will be blessed.'^{b v} ²⁶When God raised up^w his servant, he sent him first^x to you to bless you by turning each of you from your wicked ways."

PETER AND JOHN BEFORE THE SANHEDRIN

4 The priests and the captain of the temple guard^y and the Sadducees^z came up to Peter and John while they were speaking to the people. ²They were greatly disturbed because the apostles were teaching the people, proclaiming in Jesus the resurrection of the dead. ^a ³They seized Peter and John, and because it was evening, they put them in jail^b until the next day. ⁴But many who heard the message believed; so the number of men who believed grew^c to about five thousand.

⁵The next day the rulers, ^d the elders and the teachers of the law met in Jerusalem. ⁶Annas the high priest was there, and so were Caiaphas, ^e John, Alexander and others of the high priest's family. ⁷They had Peter and John brought before them and began to question them: "By what power or what name did you do this?"

⁸Then Peter, filled with the Holy Spirit,^f said to them: "Rulers and elders of the people!^g ⁹If we are being called to account today for an act of kindness shown to a man who was lame^h and are being asked how he was healed, ¹⁰then know this, you and all the people of Israel: It is by the name of Jesus Christ of Nazareth,ⁱ whom you crucified but whom God raised from the dead,^j that this man stands before you healed. ¹¹Jesus is

> " 'the stone you builders rejected,
> which has become the cornerstone.'^{c k}

¹²Salvation is found in no one else, for there is no other name given under heaven by which we must be saved."^l

¹³When they saw the courage of Peter and John^m and realized that they were unschooled, ordinary men, ⁿ they were astonished and they took note that these men had

---

^a 23 Deut. 18:15,18,19 ^b 25 Gen. 22:18; 26:4 ^c 11 Psalm 118:22

3:22,26 *raise up...raised up.* Christ is the fulfillment of prophecies made relative to Moses, David and Abraham. He was to be a prophet like Moses (vv. 22–23), he was foretold in Samuel's declarations concerning David (v. 24; see note there) and he was to bring blessing to all people as promised to Abraham (vv. 25–26).

3:24 *beginning with Samuel, all the prophets...foretold.* Samuel anointed David to be king and spoke of the establishment of his kingdom (1Sa 16:13; cf. 13:14; 15:28; 28:17). Nathan's prophecy (2Sa 7:12–16) was ultimately Messianic (see Ac 13:22–23,34; Heb 1:5).

3:25 *offspring.* The word is singular, ultimately signifying Christ (see Gal 3:16).

4:1 *priests.* Those who were serving that week in the temple precincts (see note on Lk 1:23). *captain of the temple guard.* A member of one of the leading priestly families; next in rank to the high priest (see 5:24,26; Lk 22:4,52). *Sadducees.* A Jewish sect whose members came from the priestly line and controlled the temple. They did not believe in the resurrection or a personal Messiah but held that the Messianic age—an ideal time—was then present and must be preserved. The high priest, one of their number, presided over the Sanhedrin (see 5:17; 23:6–8; Mt 22:23–33). See notes on Ezr 7:2; Mt 3:7; Mk 12:18; Lk 20:27; see also essay, p. 1596, and chart, p. 1650.

4:2 *in Jesus.* On the basis of Jesus' resurrection.

4:3 *evening.* The evening sacrifices ended about 4:00 P.M., and the temple gates would be closed at that time. Any judgments involving life and death must be begun and concluded in daylight hours.

4:4 *men.* Lit. "males." *five thousand.* A growth from the 3,000 at Pentecost (2:41); see later growth (5:14; 6:7).

4:5 *rulers, the elders and the teachers of the law.* The three groups making up the Sanhedrin, Israel's supreme court (see Lk 22:66; see also notes on Mt 2:4; 15:2; Mk 2:16; 14:55; Lk 5:17).

4:6 *Annas.* High priest A.D. 6–15, but deposed by the Romans and succeeded by his son, Eleazar, then by his son-in-law, Caiaphas (18–36), who was also called Joseph. However, Annas was still recognized by the Jews as high priest (Lk 3:2; cf. Jn 18:13, 24). *John.* May be Jonathan, son of Annas, who was appointed high priest in A.D. 36. Others suggest that it was Johanan ben Zakkai, who became the president of the Great Synagogue after the fall of Jerusalem. *Alexander.* Not further identified.

4:8 *filled with the Holy Spirit.* See note on 2:4.

4:10 *Jesus Christ of Nazareth.* See Mt 2:23 and note.

4:11 *the stone...rejected.* Fulfillment of prophecy was an important element in early Christian sermons and defenses. Jesus had also used Ps 118:22 (Mt 21:42; see 1Pe 2:7 and cf. Ro 9:33; Isa 28:16). *cornerstone.* See note on Ps 118:22.

4:12 *no other name.* See 10:43; Jn 14:6; 1Ti 2:5; see also TNIV text note on Mt 1:21.

4:13 *courage.* A certain boldness characterized by the assurance, authority and forthrightness of the apostles (2:29; 4:29; 28:31), and shared by the believers (4:31). *unschooled, ordinary men.* Peter and John had not been trained in the Rabbinic schools, nor did they hold official positions in recognized religious circles. *took note that these men had been with Jesus.* Probably because they were displaying some of his power and authority (cf. Mk 1:22 and note; 3:14).

3:20 ^m S Lk 2:11
3:21 ⁿ Ac 1:11
^o Mt 17:11; Ac 1:6
^p Lk 1:70
3:22 ^q Dt 18:15,18;
Ac 7:37
3:23 ^r Dt 18:19
3:24 ^s S Lk 24:27
3:25 ^t Ac 2:39
^u Ro 9:4,5; ^v Ge 12:3;
22:18; 26:4; 28:14
3:26 ^w ver 22;
S Ac 2:24 ^x Ac 13:46;
Ro 1:16
4:1 ^y Lk 22:4
^z Mt 3:7; 16:1,6;
22:23,34; Ac 5:17;
23:6-8
4:2 ^a Ac 17:18
4:3 ^b Ac 5:18
4:4 ^c S Ac 2:41
4:5 ^d Lk 23:13
4:6 ^e S Mt 26:3
4:8 ^f S Lk 1:15
^g ver 5; Lk 23:13
4:9 ^h Ac 3:6
4:10 ⁱ S Mk 1:24
^j S Ac 2:24
4:11 ^k Ps 118:22;
Isa 28:16; Zec 10:4;
Mt 21:42; Eph 2:20;
1Pe 2:7
4:12 ^l S Mt 1:21;
Jn 14:6; Ac 10:43;
S Ro 11:14; 1Ti 2:5
4:13 ^m S Lk 22:8
ⁿ Mt 11:25

4:13 *o* Mk 3:14
4:15 *P* S Mt 5:22
4:16 *q* Jn 11:47
r Ac 3:6-10
4:18 *s* Am 7:13;
Ac 5:40
4:19 *t* Ac 5:29
4:20 *u* Job 32:18;
Jer 20:9; Am 3:8
v S Lk 24:48
4:21 *w* Ac 5:26
x S Mt 9:8
4:24 *y* S Ac 1:14
z Ne 9:6; Job 41:11;
Isa 37:16
4:25 *a* Ac 1:16
4:26 *b* Ps 2:1,2;
Da 9:25; Lk 4:18;
Ac 10:38; Heb 1:9
4:27 *c* S Mt 14:1
d S Mt 27:2; Lk 23:12
e ver 30; Ac 3:13,14
4:28 *f* Ac 2:23
4:29 *g* ver 13,31;
Ps 138:3; Ac 9:27;
13:46; 14:3; 28:31;
Eph 6:19; Php 1:14
4:30 *h* S Jn 4:48
i ver 27
4:31 *j* Ac 2:2
k S Lk 1:15
l S Heb 4:12
m S ver 29
4:32 *n* Ac 2:44
4:33 *o* S Lk 24:48
P Ac 1:22 *q* S Ro 3:24
4:34 *r* Mt 19:21;
Ac 2:45
4:35 *s* ver 37; Ac 5:2
t Ac 2:45; 6:1
4:36 *u* Ac 9:27;
11:22,30; 13:2;
1Co 9:6; Gal 2:1,9,13

been with Jesus. *o* [14]But since they could see the man who had been healed standing there with them, there was nothing they could say. [15]So they ordered them to withdraw from the Sanhedrin *P* and then conferred together. [16]"What are we going to do with these men?" *q* they asked. "Everyone living in Jerusalem knows they have performed a notable sign, *r* and we cannot deny it. [17]But to stop this thing from spreading any further among the people, we must warn them to speak no longer to anyone in this name."

[18]Then they called them in again and commanded them not to speak or teach at all in the name of Jesus. *s* [19]But Peter and John replied, "Which is right in God's eyes: to listen to you, or to him? *t* You be the judges! [20]As for us, we cannot help speaking *u* about what we have seen and heard." *v*

[21]After further threats they let them go. They could not decide how to punish them, because all the people *w* were praising God *x* for what had happened. [22]For the man who was miraculously healed was over forty years old.

THE BELIEVERS PRAY

[23]On their release, Peter and John went back to their own people and reported all that the chief priests and the elders had said to them. [24]When they heard this, they raised their voices together in prayer to God. *y* "Sovereign Lord," they said, "you made the heaven and the earth and the sea, and everything in them. *z* [25]You spoke by the Holy Spirit through the mouth of your servant, our father David: *a*

> " 'Why do the nations rage
> and the peoples plot in vain?
> [26]The kings of the earth rise up
> and the rulers band together
> against the Lord
> and against his anointed one.*a*'*b b*

[27]Indeed Herod *c* and Pontius Pilate *d* met together with the Gentiles and the people of Israel in this city to conspire against your holy servant Jesus, *e* whom you anointed. [28]They did what your power and will had decided beforehand should happen. *f* [29]Now, Lord, consider their threats and enable your servants to speak your word with great boldness. *g* [30]Stretch out your hand to heal and perform signs and wonders *h* through the name of your holy servant Jesus." *i*

[31]After they prayed, the place where they were meeting was shaken. *j* And they were all filled with the Holy Spirit *k* and spoke the word of God *l* boldly. *m*

THE BELIEVERS SHARE THEIR POSSESSIONS

[32]All the believers were one in heart and mind. No one claimed that any of their possessions was their own, but they shared everything they had. *n* [33]With great power the apostles continued to testify *o* to the resurrection *P* of the Lord Jesus. And God's grace *q* was so powerfully at work in them all [34]that there were no needy persons among them. For from time to time those who owned land or houses sold them, *r* brought the money from the sales [35]and put it at the apostles' feet, *s* and it was distributed to anyone who had need. *t*

[36]Joseph, a Levite from Cyprus, whom the apostles called Barnabas *u* (which means

a 26 That is, Messiah or Christ   *b* 26 Psalm 2:1,2

4:15 *Sanhedrin.* See notes on v. 5; 5:21; Mk 14:55.
4:19 See note on Ro 13:3.
4:20 *cannot help speaking.* See 5:29; cf. Jer 20:9.
4:22 *forty years old.* Normally healing at such an advanced age (for that time) did not take place.
4:23 *went back.* Probably to the same upper room where the apostles had met before (1:13) and where the congregation may have continued to meet (12:12).
4:24 *Sovereign Lord.* See Lk 2:29.
4:27 *Herod.* Herod Antipas, tetrarch of Galilee and Perea (Lk 23:7–15). *Pontius Pilate.* Roman governor of Judea (see Lk 3:1 and note).
4:28 *decided beforehand.* Not that God had compelled them to act as they did, but he willed to use them and their freely chosen acts to accomplish his saving purpose (see 2:23).
4:30 *holy servant.* See note on 3:13.
4:31 *was shaken.* An immediate sign that the prayers had been heard (see 16:26). *filled with the Holy Spirit.* See note on 2:4.

spoke the word of God. They continued preaching the gospel despite the warnings of the council (see note on v. 13).
4:32 *one in heart and mind.* In complete accord, extending to their attitude toward personal possessions (see 2:44 and note).
4:33 *testify to the resurrection.* As significant as the death of Christ was, the most compelling event was the resurrection—an event about which the disciples could not keep silent.
4:34 *those who owned land or houses sold them.* See note on 2:44.
4:36 *Levite.* Although Levites owned no inherited land in the Holy Land, these regulations may not have applied to the Levites in other countries, such as Cyprus. So perhaps Barnabas sold land he owned in Cyprus and brought the proceeds to the apostles (v. 37). Or he may have been married, and the land sold may have been from his wife's property. It is also possible that the prohibition against Levite ownership of land in the Holy Land was no longer observed. *Cyprus.* An island in the eastern part of the Mediterranean Sea. Jews had settled there from

"son of encouragement"), [37] sold a field he owned and brought the money and put it at the apostles' feet. [v]

ANANIAS AND SAPPHIRA

5 Now a man named Ananias, together with his wife Sapphira, also sold a piece of property. [2] With his wife's full knowledge he kept back part of the money for himself, [w] but brought the rest and put it at the apostles' feet. [x]

[3] Then Peter said, "Ananias, how is it that Satan [y] has so filled your heart [z] that you have lied to the Holy Spirit [a] and have kept for yourself some of the money you received for the land? [b] [4] Didn't it belong to you before it was sold? And after it was sold, wasn't the money at your disposal? [c] What made you think of doing such a thing? You have not lied just to human beings but to God." [d]

[5] When Ananias heard this, he fell down and died. [e] And great fear [f] seized all who heard what had happened. [6] Then some young men came forward, wrapped up his body, [g] and carried him out and buried him.

[7] About three hours later his wife came in, not knowing what had happened. [8] Peter asked her, "Tell me, is this the price you and Ananias got for the land?"

"Yes," she said, "that is the price." [h]

[9] Peter said to her, "How could you conspire to test the Spirit of the Lord? [i] Listen! The feet of those who buried your husband are at the door, and they will carry you out also."

[10] At that moment she fell down at his feet and died. [j] Then the young men came in and, finding her dead, carried her out and buried her beside her husband. [k] [11] Great fear [l] seized the whole church and all who heard about these events.

THE APOSTLES HEAL MANY

[12] The apostles performed many signs and wonders [m] among the people. And all the believers used to meet together [n] in Solomon's Colonnade. [o] [13] No one else dared join them, even though they were highly regarded by the people. [p] [14] Nevertheless, more and more men and women believed in the Lord and were added to their number. [q] [15] As a result, people brought the sick into the streets and laid them on beds and mats so that at least Peter's shadow might fall on some of them as he passed by. [r] [16] Crowds gathered also from the towns around Jerusalem, bringing their sick and those tormented by evil [a] spirits, and all of them were healed. [s]

THE APOSTLES PERSECUTED

[17] Then the high priest and all his associates, who were members of the party [t] of the

---

[a] 16 Greek *unclean*

4:37 [v] ver 35; Ac 5:2
5:2 [w] Jos 7:11
[x] Ac 4:35,37
5:3 [y] S Mt 4:10
[z] Jn 13:2,27 [a] ver 9
[b] Dt 23:21
5:4 [c] Dt 23:22
[d] Lev 6:2
5:5 [e] ver 10; Ps 5:6
[f] ver 11
5:6 [g] Jn 19:40
5:8 [h] ver 2
5:9 [i] ver 3
5:10 [j] ver 5 [k] ver 6
5:11 [l] ver 5; Ac 19:17
5:12 [m] S Jn 4:48;
Ac 2:43 [n] Ac 4:32
[o] Jn 10:23; Ac 3:11
5:13 [p] Ac 2:47; 4:21
5:14 [q] S Ac 2:41
5:15 [r] Ac 19:12
5:16 [s] Mt 8:16;
S Mk 16:17
5:17 [t] Ac 15:5

Maccabean times. *Barnabas.* Used here as a good example of giving. In this way Luke introduces the one who will become an important companion of Paul (see note on 13:1–4). For other significant contributions of this greathearted leader to the life and ministry of the early church, see 9:27; 11:22,25; 15:37–39.

5:1 *Ananias . . . Sapphira.* Given as bad examples of sharing (Barnabas was the good example; see note on 4:36). Love of praise for (pretended) generosity and love for money led to the first recorded sin in the life of the church. It is a warning to the readers that "God cannot be mocked" (Gal 6:7). Compare this divine judgment at the beginning of the church era with God's judgments on Nadab and Abihu (Lev 10:2), on Achan (Jos 7:25) and on Uzzah (2Sa 6:7).

5:2 *kept back part.* They had a right to keep back whatever they chose, but to make it appear that they had given all when they had not was sinful.

5:3 *Satan has so filled your heart.* The continuing activity of Satan is noted (see Lk 22:3; Jn 13:2,27; 1Pe 5:8). *lied to the Holy Spirit.* A comparison with v. 4 shows that the Holy Spirit is regarded as God himself present with his people.

5:9 *to test the Spirit of the Lord.* If no dire consequences had followed this act of sin, the results among the believers would have been serious when the deceit became known. Not only would dishonesty appear profitable, but the conclusion that the Spirit could be deceived would follow. It was important to set the course properly at the outset in order to leave no doubt that God will not tolerate such hypocrisy and deceit.

5:11 *church.* The first use of the term in Acts. It can denote either the local congregation (8:1; 11:22; 13:1) or the universal church (see 20:28). The Greek word for "church" (*ekklesia*) was already being used for political and other assemblies (see 19:32,41) and, in the Septuagint (the pre-Christian Greek translation of the OT), for Israel when gathered in religious assembly.

5:12 *Solomon's Colonnade.* See note on 3:11.

5:13 *No one else dared join them.* Because of the fate of Ananias and his wife, no pretenders or halfhearted followers risked identification with the believers. Luke cannot mean that no one joined the Christian community, since v. 14 indicates that many were coming to Christ.

5:14 *more men and women believed.* See 4:4. This is the first specific mention of women believing (cf. 8:3,12; 9:2; 13:50; 16:1,13–14; 17:4,12,34; 18:2; 21:5; but cf. also 1:14).

5:15 *Peter's shadow.* Parallels such items as Paul's handkerchiefs (19:12) and the edge of Jesus' cloak (Mt 9:20)—not that any of these material objects had magical qualities, but the least article or shadow represented a direct means of contact with Jesus or his apostles.

5:17 *high priest.* The official high priest recognized by Rome was Caiaphas, but the Jews considered Annas, Caiaphas's father-in-law, to be the actual high priest since the high priesthood was to be held for life (see note on 4:6). *his associates.* His family members. *party of the Sadducees.* See note on 4:1.

5:17 ᵘ S Ac 4:1
5:18 ᵛ Ac 4:3
5:19 ʷ Ge 16:7;
Ex 3:2; Mt 1:20; 2:13,
19; 28:2; Lk 1:11; 2:9;
S Jn 20:12; Ac 8:26;
10:3; 12:7,23; 27:23
ˣ Ac 16:26 ʸ Ps 34:7
5:20 ᶻ Jn 6:63,68
5:21 ᵃ Ac 4:5,6
ᵇ ver 27,34,41;
S Mt 5:22
5:22 ᶜ Ac 12:18,19
5:24 ᵈ Ac 4:1
5:26 ᵉ Ac 4:21
5:27 ᶠ S Mt 5:22
5:28 ᵍ Ac 4:18
ʰ Mt 23:35; 27:25;
Ac 2:23,36; 3:14,15;
7:52
5:29 ⁱ Ex 1:17;
Ac 4:19
5:30 ʲ S Ac 3:13
ᵏ S Ac 2:24 ˡ Ac 10:39;
13:29; Gal 3:13
5:31 ᵐ S Mk 16:19
ⁿ S Lk 2:11
ᵒ S Mt 1:21; Mk 1:4;
Lk 24:47; Ac 2:38;
3:19; 10:43
5:32 ᵖ S Lk 24:48
ᑫ Jn 15:26
5:33 ʳ Ac 2:37; 7:54
5:34 ˢ Ac 22:3
ᵗ Lk 2:46; 5:17
5:37 ᵘ Lk 2:1,2
5:38 ᵛ Mt 15:13
5:39 ʷ 2Ch 13:12;
Pr 21:30; Isa 46:10;
Ac 7:51; 11:17
5:40 ˣ S Mk 10:17
5:41 ʸ S Mt 5:12
ᶻ S Jn 15:21
5:42 ᵇ S Ac 2:46
ᵇ S Ac 13:32
ᶜ S Ac 9:22

Sadducees, ᵘ were filled with jealousy. ¹⁸They arrested the apostles and put them in the public jail. ᵛ ¹⁹But during the night an angel ʷ of the Lord opened the doors of the jail ˣ and brought them out. ʸ ²⁰"Go, stand in the temple courts," he said, "and tell the people all about this new life." ᶻ

²¹At daybreak they entered the temple courts, as they had been told, and began to teach the people.

When the high priest and his associates ᵃ arrived, they called together the Sanhedrin ᵇ— the full assembly of the elders of Israel—and sent to the jail for the apostles. ²²But on arriving at the jail, the officers did not find them there. ᶜ So they went back and reported, ²³"We found the jail securely locked, with the guards standing at the doors; but when we opened them, we found no one inside." ²⁴On hearing this report, the captain of the temple guard and the chief priests ᵈ were puzzled, wondering what this might lead to.

²⁵Then someone came and said, "Look! The men you put in jail are standing in the temple courts teaching the people." ²⁶At that, the captain went with his officers and brought the apostles. They did not use force, because they feared that the people ᵉ would stone them.

²⁷The apostles were brought in and made to appear before the Sanhedrin ᶠ to be questioned by the high priest. ²⁸"We gave you strict orders not to teach in this name," ᵍ he said. "Yet you have filled Jerusalem with your teaching and are determined to make us guilty of this man's blood." ʰ

²⁹Peter and the other apostles replied: "We must obey God rather than human beings! ⁱ ³⁰The God of our ancestors ʲ raised Jesus from the dead ᵏ—whom you killed by hanging him on a cross. ˡ ³¹God exalted him to his own right hand ᵐ as Prince and Savior ⁿ that he might bring Israel to repentance and forgive their sins. ᵒ ³²We are witnesses of these things, ᵖ and so is the Holy Spirit, ᑫ whom God has given to those who obey him."

³³When they heard this, they were furious ʳ and wanted to put them to death. ³⁴But a Pharisee named Gamaliel, ˢ a teacher of the law, ᵗ who was honored by all the people, stood up in the Sanhedrin and ordered that the men be put outside for a little while. ³⁵Then he addressed the Sanhedrin: "Men of Israel, consider carefully what you intend to do to these men. ³⁶Some time ago Theudas appeared, claiming to be somebody, and about four hundred men rallied to him. He was killed, all his followers were dispersed, and it all came to nothing. ³⁷After him, Judas the Galilean appeared in the days of the census ᵘ and led a band of people in revolt. He too was killed, and all his followers were scattered. ³⁸Therefore, in the present case I advise you: Leave these men alone! Let them go! For if their purpose or activity is of human origin, it will fail. ᵛ ³⁹But if it is from God, you will not be able to stop these men; you will only find yourselves fighting against God." ʷ

⁴⁰His speech persuaded them. They called the apostles in and had them flogged. ˣ Then they ordered them not to speak in the name of Jesus, and let them go.

⁴¹The apostles left the Sanhedrin, rejoicing ʸ because they had been counted worthy of suffering disgrace for the Name. ᶻ ⁴²Day after day, in the temple courts ᵃ and from house to house, they never stopped teaching and proclaiming the good news ᵇ that Jesus is the Messiah. ᶜ

5:18 *in the public jail.* To await trial the next day.

5:19 *angel of the Lord.* This phrase is used four other times in Acts: (1) Stephen speaks of him (7:30–38); (2) he guides Philip (8:26); (3) he liberates Peter (12:7–10); and (4) he strikes down Herod (12:23). See also Mt 1:20–24; 2:13,19; 28:2; Lk 1:11–38; 2:9 and notes on Ge 16:7; 2Ki 1:3; Ps 34:7; Zec 1:8.

5:20 *all about this new life.* The good news of eternal life in all its fullness (see Jn 6:68; Ro 6:4; 2Co 5:17; Php 1:21 and notes).

5:21 *Sanhedrin.* The supreme Jewish court, consisting of 70 to 100 men (71 being the proper number). They sat in a semicircle, backed by three rows of disciples of the learned men (cf. 4:13 and note), with the clerks of the court standing in front. See note on Mk 14:55.

5:24 *captain of the temple guard.* See note on 4:1.

5:28 *make us guilty of this man's blood.* Probably a reference to the apostles' repeated declaration that some of the Jews and some of their leaders had killed Jesus (2:23; 3:13–15; 4:10–11; cf. Mt 27:25).

5:29 See 4:19 and note.

5:30 *cross.* See 1Pe 2:24 and note; see also Dt 21:22–23. Like its Hebrew counterpart, the Greek for this word could refer to a tree, a pole, a wooden beam (or "cross") or some similar object.

5:32 *so is the Holy Spirit ... given to those who obey him.* See Jn 15:26–27. The disciples' testimony was directed and confirmed by the Holy Spirit, who convicts the world through the word (Jn 16:8–11) and is given to those who respond to God with "faith and obedience" (Ro 1:5; see note on Ac 6:7).

5:34 *a Pharisee named Gamaliel.* The most famous Jewish teacher of his time and traditionally listed among the "heads of the schools." Possibly he was the grandson of Hillel. Like Hillel (see note on Mt 19:3), he was moderate in his views, a characteristic that is apparent in his cautious recommendation on this occasion. Saul (Paul) was one of his students (22:3).

5:36 *Theudas.* We know of him from no other historical source.

5:37 *Judas the Galilean.* The Jewish historian Josephus refers to him as a man from Gamala in Gaulanitis who refused to give tribute to Caesar. His revolt was crushed, but a movement, started in his time, may have lived on in the party of the Zealots (see 1:13 and note on Mt 10:4). *days of the census.* Not the first census of Quirinius, noted by Luke in his Gospel (2:2), but the one in A.D. 6.

5:40 *flogged.* Beaten with the Jewish penalty of "forty lashes minus one" (2Co 11:24).

THE CHOOSING OF THE SEVEN

6 In those days when the number of disciples was increasing, *d* the Hellenistic Jews *a e* among them complained against the Hebraic Jews because their widows *f* were being overlooked in the daily distribution of food. *g* 2So the Twelve gathered all the disciples *h* together and said, "It would not be right for us to neglect the ministry of the word of God *i* in order to wait on tables. 3Brothers and sisters, *j* choose seven men from among you who are known to be full of the Spirit *k* and wisdom. We will turn this responsibility over to them *l* 4and will give our attention to prayer *m* and the ministry of the word."

5This proposal pleased the whole group. They chose Stephen, *n* a man full of faith and of the Holy Spirit; *o* also Philip, *p* Procorus, Nicanor, Timon, Parmenas, and Nicolas from Antioch, a convert to Judaism. 6They presented them to the apostles, who prayed *q* and laid their hands on them. *r*

7So the word of God spread. *s* The number of disciples in Jerusalem increased rapidly, *t* and a large number of priests became obedient to the faith.

STEPHEN SEIZED

8Now Stephen, a man full of God's grace and power, performed great wonders and signs *u* among the people. 9Opposition arose, however, from members of the Synagogue of the Freedmen (as it was called)—Jews of Cyrene *v* and Alexandria as well as the provinces of Cilicia *w* and Asia *x*—who began to argue with Stephen. 10But they could not stand up against the wisdom the Spirit gave him as he spoke. *y*

a 1 That is, Jews who had adopted the Greek language and culture

6:1 *d* S Ac 2:41
e Ac 9:29 *f* Ac 9:39,
41; 1Ti 5:3 *g* Ac 4:35
6:2 *h* S Ac 11:26
i S Heb 4:12
6:3 *j* S Ac 1:16
k S Lk 1:15 *l* Ex 18:21;
Ne 13:13
6:4 *m* S Ac 1:14
6:5 *n* ver 8; Ac 7:55-
60; 11:19; 22:20
o S Lk 1:15 *p* Ac 8:5-
40; 21:8
6:6 *q* S Ac 1:24
r Nu 8:10; 27:18;
Ac 9:17; 19:6; 28:8;
1Ti 4:14; S Mk 5:23
6:7 *s* Ac 12:24; 19:20
t S Ac 2:41
6:8 *u* S Jn 4:48
6:9 *v* S Mt 27:32
w Ac 15:23,41; 22:3;
23:34 *x* S Ac 2:9
6:10 *y* Lk 21:15

6:1 *the number of disciples was increasing.* A considerable length of time may have transpired since the end of ch. 5. The church continued to grow (see 5:14), but this gave rise to inevitable problems, both from within (6:1–7) and from without (6:8—7:60). At this stage of its development, the church was entirely Jewish in its composition. However, there were two groups of Jews within the fellowship: 1. *Hellenistic Jews.* Those born in lands other than the Holy Land who spoke the Greek language and were more Grecian than Hebraic in their attitudes and outlook (see TNIV text note). 2. *Hebraic Jews.* Those who spoke Palestinian Aramaic and/or Hebrew and preserved Jewish culture and customs. *daily distribution of food.* Help was needed by widows who had no one to care for them and so became the church's responsibility (cf. 4:35; 11:28–29; see also 1Ti 5:3–16).

6:2 *the Twelve.* At this early stage, the apostles were responsible for church life in general, including the ministry of the word of God and the care of the needy. *to wait on tables.* To preside over the distribution of charitable gifts. The early church was concerned not only about a spiritual ministry ("word of God" and "prayer"; see v. 4) but also about a material ministry.

6:3 *choose seven men.* The church elected them (v. 5), and the apostles ordained them ("laid their hands on them," v. 6). In this way they were appointed to their work. *full of the Spirit.* See note on 2:4.

6:5 *They chose Stephen…Nicolas.* It is significant that all seven of the men chosen had Greek names. The murmuring had come from the Greek-speaking segment of the church; those elected to care for the work came from their number so as to represent their interests fairly. Only Stephen and Philip of the Seven receive further notice (Stephen, 6:8—7:60; Philip, 8:5–40; 21:8–9). *from Antioch, a convert to Judaism.* It is significant that a proselyte was included in the number and that Luke points out his place of origin as Antioch, the city to which the gospel was soon to be taken and which was to become the "headquarters" for the forthcoming Gentile missionary effort.

6:6 *prayed and laid their hands on them.* Laying on of hands was used in the OT period to confer blessing (Ge 48:13–20), to transfer guilt from sinner to sacrifice (Lev 1:4) and to commission a person for a new responsibility (Nu 27:23). In the NT period, laying on of hands was observed in healing (28:8;

Mk 1:41), blessing (Mk 10:16), ordaining or commissioning (Ac 6:6; 13:3; 1Ti 5:22) and imparting of spiritual gifts (Ac 8:17; 19:6; 1Ti 4:14; 2Ti 1:6). These seven men were appointed to responsibilities turned over to them by the Twelve. The Greek word used to describe their responsibility ("wait on") is the verb from which the noun "deacon" comes. Later one reads of deacons in Php 1:1; 1Ti 3:8–13. The Greek noun for "deacon" can also be translated "minister" or "servant." The men appointed on this occasion were simply called the Seven (21:8), just as the apostles were called the Twelve. It is disputed whether the Seven were the first deacons or were later replaced by deacons (see note on 1Ti 3:8).

6:7 One of a series of progress reports given periodically throughout the book of Acts (1:15; 2:41; 4:4; 5:14; 6:7; 9:31; 12:24; 16:5; 19:20; 28:31). *a large number of priests.* Though involved by lineage and life service in the priestly observances of the old covenant, they accepted the preaching of the apostles, which proclaimed a sacrifice that made the old sacrifices unnecessary (see Heb 8:13 and note; 10:1–4, 11–14). *became obedient to the faith.* Responded to the commands of the gospel. To believe is to obey God. Faith itself is obedience, but faith also produces obedience (Ro 1:5; Eph 2:8–10; Jas 2:14–26).

6:8 *great wonders and signs.* Until now, Acts told of only the apostles working miracles (2:43; 3:4–8; 5:12). But now, after the laying on of the apostles' hands, Stephen too is reported as working miraculous signs. Philip also will soon do the same (8:6).

6:9 *Freedmen.* Persons who had been freed from slavery. They came from different Hellenistic areas. *Cyrene.* The chief city in Libya and north Africa (see notes on 2:10; Mk 15:21), halfway between Alexandria and Carthage. One of its population groups was Jewish (see 11:19–21). *Alexandria.* Capital of Egypt and second only to Rome in the empire. Two out of five districts in Alexandria were Jewish. *Cilicia.* A Roman province in the southeast corner of Asia Minor, adjoining Syria. Tarsus, the birthplace of Paul, was one of its principal towns. *Asia.* A Roman province in the western part of Asia Minor. Ephesus, where Paul later ministered for a few years, was its capital. *began to argue.* Since Saul was from Tarsus, this may have been the synagogue he attended, and he may have been among those who argued with Stephen. He was present when Stephen was stoned (7:58).

6:11 ʸ1Ki 21:10
ᵃMt 26:59-61
6:12 ᵇS Mt 5:22
6:13 ᶜEx 23:1;
Ps 27:12 ᵈMt 24:15;
Ac 7:48; 21:28
6:14 ᵉS Jn 2:19
ᶠAc 15:1; 21:21; 26:3;
28:17
6:15 ᵍS Mt 5:22
7:2 ʰAc 22:1
ⁱPs 29:3 ʲGe 11:31;
15:7
7:3 ᵏGe 12:1
7:4 ˡGe 12:5
7:5 ᵐHeb 11:13
ⁿGe 12:7; 17:8; 26:3
7:6 ᵒEx 1:8-11; 12:40
7:7 ᵖGe 15:13,14;
Ex 3:12
7:8 ᵠGe 17:9-14
ʳGe 21:2-4 ˢGe 25:26
ᵗGe 29:31-35; 30:5-
13,17-24; 35:16-18,
22-26
7:9 ᵘGe 37:4,11
ᵛGe 37:28; Ps 105:17
ʷGe 39:2,21,23;
Hag 2:4
7:10 ˣGe 41:37-43;
Ps 105:20-22

¹¹Then they secretly ᶻ persuaded some men to say, "We have heard Stephen speak blasphemous words against Moses and against God." ᵃ

¹²So they stirred up the people and the elders and the teachers of the law. They seized Stephen and brought him before the Sanhedrin. ᵇ ¹³They produced false witnesses, ᶜ who testified, "This fellow never stops speaking against this holy place ᵈ and against the law. ¹⁴For we have heard him say that this Jesus of Nazareth will destroy this place ᵉ and change the customs Moses handed down to us." ᶠ

¹⁵All who were sitting in the Sanhedrin ᵍ looked intently at Stephen, and they saw that his face was like the face of an angel.

STEPHEN'S SPEECH TO THE SANHEDRIN

7 Then the high priest asked Stephen, "Are these charges true?"
²To this he replied: "Brothers and fathers, ʰ listen to me! The God of glory ⁱ appeared to our father Abraham while he was still in Mesopotamia, before he lived in Harran. ʲ ³'Leave your country and your people,' God said, 'and go to the land I will show you.' ᵃ ᵏ

⁴"So he left the land of the Chaldeans and settled in Harran. After the death of his father, God sent him to this land where you are now living. ˡ ⁵He gave him no inheritance here, ᵐ not even enough ground to set his foot on. But God promised him that he and his descendants after him would possess the land, ⁿ even though at that time Abraham had no child. ⁶God spoke to him in this way: 'For four hundred years your descendants will be strangers in a country not their own, and they will be enslaved and mistreated. ᵒ ⁷But I will punish the nation they serve as slaves,' God said, 'and afterward they will come out of that country and worship me in this place.' ᵇ ᵖ ⁸Then he gave Abraham the covenant of circumcision. ᵠ And Abraham became the father of Isaac and circumcised him eight days after his birth. ʳ Later Isaac became the father of Jacob, ˢ and Jacob became the father of the twelve patriarchs. ᵗ

⁹"Because the patriarchs were jealous of Joseph, ᵘ they sold him as a slave into Egypt. ᵛ But God was with him ʷ ¹⁰and rescued him from all his troubles. He gave Joseph wisdom and enabled him to gain the goodwill of Pharaoh king of Egypt. So Pharaoh made him ruler over Egypt and all his palace. ˣ

¹¹"Then a famine struck all Egypt and Canaan, bringing great suffering, and our people

ᵃ 3 Gen. 12:1   ᵇ 7 Gen. 15:13,14

6:11 *blasphemous words against Moses and against God.* Since Stephen declared that the worship of God was no longer to be restricted to the temple (7:48–49), his opponents twisted these words to trump up an accusation that Stephen was attacking the temple, the law, Moses and, ultimately, God.

6:12 *the elders and the teachers of the law.* See notes on Mt 2:4; 15:2; Mk 2:16; Lk 5:17. *Sanhedrin.* See note on Mk 14:55.

6:13 *speaking against this holy place and against the law.* Similar to the charges brought against Christ (see Mt 26:61). Stephen may have referred to Jesus' words as recorded in Jn 2:19 (see note there), and the words may have been misunderstood or purposely misinterpreted (v. 14), as at the trial of Jesus. *holy place.* The temple in Jerusalem.

7:1 *high priest.* Probably Caiaphas (see Mt 26:57–66), but see note on 4:6; cf. Jn 18:19, 24. *Are these charges true?* See notes on 6:11,13.

7:2–53 See Introduction: Characteristics, 5. Since the author of Acts gives more space to Stephen's speech than to any other, it is safe to assume that he considered it particularly important. Broadly speaking, it is not meant to be a personal defense with the hope of conciliating Stephen's accusers (see vv. 51–52) but an attack on the foundations of Judaism by citing the history of its failures. It deals with the three great pillars of Jewish piety: (1) the land (vv. 2–36), (2) the law (vv. 37–43) and (3) the temple (vv. 44–50), and ends with a resounding denunciation of Stephen's accusers (vv. 51–52). The speech marks a decisive break between Judaism and Christianity and points forward to the vigorous explanations of the differences between the old faith and the new faith found in the writings of Paul and the author of Hebrews.

7:2 *Abraham ... in Mesopotamia, before he lived in Harran.* Abraham's call came in Ur not Harran (cf. Ge 12:1 and note; 15:7; Ne 9:7). Or perhaps he was called first in Ur and then later his call was renewed in Harran (see note on Jer 15:19–21).
7:4 *land of the Chaldeans.* A district in southern Babylonia, the name was later applied to a region that included all of Babylonia (see map No. 1 at the end of this study Bible). *After the death of his father.* Ge 11:26 does not mean that all three sons—Abraham, Nahor and Haran—were born to Terah in the same year when he was 70 years old. See Ge 11:26—12:1. It may be that Haran was Terah's firstborn and that Abraham was born 60 years later. Thus the death of Terah at 205 years of age could have occurred just before Abraham, at 75, left Haran.
7:6 *four hundred years.* A round number for the length of Israel's stay in Egypt (Ex 12:40–41 has 430 years). That four generations would represent considerably less than 400 years is not a necessary conclusion (see note on Ge 15:16). Ex 6:16–20 makes Moses the great-grandson of Levi, son of Jacob and brother of Joseph. This would make four generations from Levi to Moses. But in 1Ch 7:22–27 a list of ten names represents the generations between Ephraim, the son of Joseph, and Joshua. The ten generations at 40 years each would equal 400 years, the same period of time noted as four generations. But one list is abbreviated and the other gives a full genealogy.
7:8 *covenant of circumcision.* See notes on Ge 17:10–11. The essential conditions for the religion of the Israelites were already fulfilled long before the temple was built and their present religious customs began. *twelve patriarchs.* See Ge 35:23–26.
7:9 *they sold him.* Israel consistently rejected God's favored individuals. Stephen builds his case about Jesus' rejection by noting Joseph's rejection by his brothers (Ge 37:12–36).

could not find food. *y* 12When Jacob heard that there was grain in Egypt, he sent our ancestors on their first visit. *z* 13On their second visit, Joseph told his brothers who he was, *a* and Pharaoh learned about Joseph's family. *b* 14After this, Joseph sent for his father Jacob and his whole family, *c* seventy-five in all. *d* 15Then Jacob went down to Egypt, where he and our ancestors died. *e* 16Their bodies were brought back to Shechem and placed in the tomb that Abraham had bought from the sons of Hamor at Shechem for a certain sum of money. *f*

17"As the time drew near for God to fulfill his promise to Abraham, the number of our people in Egypt had greatly increased. *g* 18Then 'a new king, to whom Joseph meant nothing, came to power in Egypt.'*a* *h* 19He dealt treacherously with our people and oppressed our ancestors by forcing them to throw out their newborn babies so that they would die. *i*

20"At that time Moses was born, and he was no ordinary child. *b* For three months he was cared for in his parents' home. *j* 21When he was placed outside, Pharaoh's daughter took him and brought him up as her own son. *k* 22Moses was educated in all the wisdom of the Egyptians *l* and was powerful in speech and action.

23"When Moses was forty years old, he decided to visit his own people, the Israelites. 24He saw one of them being mistreated by an Egyptian, so he went to his defense and avenged him by killing the Egyptian. 25Moses thought that his own people would realize that God was using him to rescue them, but they did not. 26The next day Moses came upon two Israelites who were fighting. He tried to reconcile them by saying, 'Men, you are brothers; why do you want to hurt each other?'

27"But the man who was mistreating the other pushed Moses aside and said, 'Who made you ruler and judge over us? *m* 28Are you thinking of killing me as you killed the Egyptian yesterday?'*c* 29When Moses heard this, he fled to Midian, where he settled as a foreigner and had two sons. *n*

30"After forty years had passed, an angel appeared to Moses in the flames of a burning bush in the desert near Mount Sinai. 31When he saw this, he was amazed at the sight. As he went over to get a closer look, he heard the Lord say: *o* 32'I am the God of your fathers, *p* the God of Abraham, Isaac and Jacob.'*d* Moses trembled with fear and did not dare to look. *q*

33"Then the Lord said to him, 'Take off your sandals, for the place where you are standing is holy ground. *r* 34I have indeed seen the oppression of my people in Egypt. I have heard their groaning and have come down to set them free. Now come, I will send you back to Egypt.'*e* *s*

35"This is the same Moses they had rejected with the words, 'Who made you ruler and judge?' *t* He was sent to be their ruler and deliverer by God himself, through the angel who appeared to him in the bush. 36He led them out of Egypt *u* and performed wonders and signs *v* in Egypt, at the Red Sea *w* and for forty years in the wilderness. *x*

37"This is the Moses who told the Israelites, 'God will send you a prophet like me from your own people.'*f* *y* 38He was in the assembly in the wilderness, with the angel *z* who

7:11 *y* Ge 41:54
7:12 *z* Ge 42:1,2
7:13 *a* Ge 45:1-4
b Ge 45:16
7:14 *c* Ge 45:9,10
d Ge 46:26,27; Ex 1:5;
Dt 10:22
7:15 *e* Ge 46:5-7;
49:33; Ex 1:6
7:16 *f* Ge 23:16-20;
33:18,19; 50:13;
Jos 24:32
7:17 *g* Ex 1:7;
Ps 105:24
7:18 *h* Ex 1:8
7:19 *i* Ex 1:10-22
7:20 *j* Ex 2:2;
Heb 11:23
7:21 *k* Ex 2:3-10
7:22 *l* 1Ki 4:30;
Isa 19:11
7:27 *m* Ge 19:9;
Nu 16:13
7:29 *n* Ex 2:11-15
7:31 *o* Ex 3:1-4
7:32 *p* S Ac 3:13
q Ex 3:6
7:33 *r* Ex 3:5;
Jos 5:15
7:34 *s* Ex 3:7-10
7:35 *t* ver 27
7:36 *u* Ex 12:41; 33:1
v Ex 11:10; S Jn 4:48
w Ex 14:21 *x* Ex 15:25;
17:5,6
7:37 *y* Dt 18:15,18;
Ac 3:22
7:38 *z* ver 53

a 18 Exodus 1:8   *b 20* Or *was fair in the sight of God*   *c 28* Exodus 2:14   *d 32* Exodus 3:6
e 34 Exodus 3:5,7,8,10   *f 37* Deut. 18:15

7:13 *second visit.* See Ge 43.

7:14 *Jacob and his whole family, seventy-five in all.* Although the Hebrew Bible uses the number 70 (see Ge 46:26–27 and note on 46:27; Ex 1:5; Dt 10:22), the pre-Christian Greek translation of the OT (the Septuagint) adds at Ge 46:20 the names of one son of Manasseh, two of Ephraim, and one grandson of each. This makes the number 75 and is the number that Stephen uses.

7:16 Stephen brings together OT accounts of two land purchases (by Abraham and Jacob) and two burial places (at Hebron and Shechem). According to the OT, Abraham purchased land at Hebron (Ge 23:17–18), where he (Ge 25:9–11), Isaac (Ge 35:29) and Jacob (Ge 50:13) were buried. Jacob bought land at Shechem (Ge 33:19), where Joseph was later buried (Jos 24:32). Josephus preserves a tradition that Joseph's brothers were buried at Hebron. Stephen's rhetorical device (by which he recalls that Jacob and the 12 patriarchs were not buried in Egypt but in Canaan) is strange to modern ears but would have been well understood by his hearers.

7:18 *a new king, to whom Joseph meant nothing.* See note on Ex 1:8.

7:22 *Moses was educated in all the wisdom of the Egyptians.* Not explicitly stated in the OT but to be expected if he grew up in the household of the pharaoh's daughter. Both

Philo and Josephus speak of Moses' great learning. *was powerful in speech.* See Ex 4:10 and note.

7:23 *Moses was forty.* Moses was 80 years old when sent to speak before the pharaoh (Ex 7:7) and 120 years old when he died (Dt 34:7). Stephen's words agree with a tradition that at Moses' first departure from Egypt he was 40 years of age.

7:29 *fled to Midian.* Rejected by his own people, Moses feared that they would inform the Egyptians, and this led to his flight to Midian, the land flanking the Gulf of Aqaba on both sides (see Ex 2:15 and note). *had two sons.* Gershom and Eliezer (Ex 2:22; 18:3–4; 1Ch 23:15).

7:30 *After forty years.* Plus the 40 years of v. 23, making the 80 years of Ex 7:7. *Mount Sinai.* Called Horeb in Ex 3:1 (see note there).

7:35 *the same Moses . . . sent to be their ruler and deliverer.* The Israelites rejected Moses, their deliverer, just as the Jews of Stephen's day were rejecting Jesus, their deliverer. Yet both were sent by God. *angel who appeared to him in the bush.* See Ex 3:2.

7:37 *prophet like me.* See 3:22–23; see also notes on Dt 18:15; 34:10,12.

7:38 *assembly.* The assembled Israelites. *angel who spoke to him.* According to Jewish interpretation at that time, the law was given to Moses by angel mediation—after the manner of

7:38 *a* Ex 19:17;
Lev 27:34 *b* Dt 32:45-
47; Heb 4:12 *c* Ro 3:2
7:39 *d* Nu 14:3,4
7:40 *e* Ex 32:1,23
7:41 *f* Ex 32:4-6;
Ps 106:19,20;
Rev 9:20
7:42 *g* Jos 24:20;
Isa 63:10 *h* Jer 19:13
7:43 *i* Am 5:25-27
7:44 *j* Ex 38:21;
Nu 1:50; 17:7
k Ex 25:8,9,40
7:45 *l* Jos 3:14-17;
18:1; 23:9; 24:18;
Ps 44:2 *m* 2Sa 7:2,6
7:46 *n* 2Sa 7:8-16;
1Ki 8:17; Ps 132:1-5
7:47 *o* 1Ki 6:1-38
7:48 *p* Mk 5:7
q 1Ki 8:27; 2Ch 2:6
7:49 *r* Mt 5:34,35
7:50 *s* Isa 66:1,2
7:51 *t* Ex 32:9; 33:3,
5 *u* Lev 26:41;
Dt 10:16; Jer 4:4; 9:26
7:52 *v* Mt 5:12
w Ac 3:14; 1Th 2:15
7:53 *x* ver 38;
Gal 3:19; Heb 2:2
7:54 *y* Ac 5:33
7:55 *z* Lk 1:15

spoke to him on Mount Sinai, and with our ancestors; *a* and he received living words *b* to pass on to us. *c*

³⁹ "But our ancestors refused to obey him. Instead, they rejected him and in their hearts turned back to Egypt. *d* ⁴⁰ They told Aaron, 'Make us gods who will go before us. As for this fellow Moses who led us out of Egypt—we don't know what has happened to him!' *a e* ⁴¹ That was the time they made an idol in the form of a calf. They brought sacrifices to it and reveled in what their own hands had made. *f* ⁴² But God turned away from them *g* and gave them over to the worship of the sun, moon and stars. *h* This agrees with what is written in the book of the prophets:

" 'Did you bring me sacrifices and offerings
    forty years in the wilderness, house of Israel?
⁴³ You have taken up the tabernacle of Molek
    and the star of your god Rephan,
    the idols you made to worship.
Therefore I will send you into exile' *b i* beyond Babylon.

⁴⁴ "Our ancestors had the tabernacle of the covenant law *j* with them in the wilderness. It had been made as God directed Moses, according to the pattern he had seen. *k* ⁴⁵ Having received the tabernacle, our ancestors under Joshua brought it with them when they took the land from the nations God drove out before them. *l* It remained in the land until the time of David, *m* ⁴⁶ who enjoyed God's favor and asked that he might provide a dwelling place for the God of Jacob. *c n* ⁴⁷ But it was Solomon who built a house for him. *o*

⁴⁸ "However, the Most High *p* does not live in houses made by human hands. *q* As the prophet says:

⁴⁹ " 'Heaven is my throne,
    and the earth is my footstool. *r*
What kind of house will you build for me?
                            says the Lord.
    Or where will my resting place be?
⁵⁰ Has not my hand made all these things?' *d s*

⁵¹ "You stiff-necked people! *t* Your hearts *u* and ears are still uncircumcised. You are just like your ancestors: You always resist the Holy Spirit! ⁵² Was there ever a prophet your ancestors did not persecute? *v* They even killed those who predicted the coming of the Righteous One. And now you have betrayed and murdered him *w*— ⁵³ you who have received the law that was given through angels *x* but have not obeyed it."

THE STONING OF STEPHEN

⁵⁴ When the members of the Sanhedrin heard this, they were furious *y* and gnashed their teeth at him. ⁵⁵ But Stephen, full of the Holy Spirit, *z* looked up to heaven and saw the

a 40 Exodus 32:1   *b* 43 Amos 5:25-27 (see Septuagint)   *c* 46 Some early manuscripts *the house of Jacob*   *d* 50 Isaiah 66:1,2

the original call of Moses (see Ex 3:2; see also v. 53; Gal 3:19; Heb 2:2). *he received living words to pass on to us.* Moses was the mediator between God and Israel on Mount Sinai.

7:39 *refused to obey him.* Another rejection of God's representative and his commands.

7:40 *Make us gods.* While Moses was on Sinai receiving the law, the people made the golden calf, rejecting God and his representative (Ex 32:1). The people had not traveled far from the idolatry of Egypt.

7:42 *God . . . gave them over.* See note on Ro 1:24. *sun, moon and stars.* See note on Jer 19:13.

7:43 Stephen quotes Am 5:25-27 as translated in the Septuagint, except that he replaces Damascus with Babylon in view of the fact that the final exile of Israel from the promised land was carried out by the Babylonians (Amos was speaking first of the Assyrian exile of the northern kingdom). *Molek . . . Rephan.* See note on Am 5:26. *Molek.* See note on Lev 18:21.

7:44—50 Because he had been accused of "speaking against this holy place" (6:13), Stephen concludes his recital with a word about the sanctuary. Presumably, he had been preaching that

the risen Christ had now replaced the temple as the mediation of God's saving presence among his people and as the one (the "place") through whom they (and "all nations," Mk 11:17) could come to God in prayer (see note on 6:13).

7:44 *tabernacle of the covenant law.* So called by Stephen because the primary contents of the wilderness tabernacle were the ark of the covenant and the two covenant tablets it contained, which were called "the covenant law" (see Ex 25:16,21 and notes).

7:49 Isa 66:1–2 reminded Israel that all creation is the temple that God himself had made. Stephen recalls that word to remind his hearers that ultimately God builds his own temple.

7:51 *hearts and ears . . . uncircumcised.* Although the men were physically circumcised, they were acting like the uncircumcised pagans of the nations around them. They were not truly consecrated to the Lord.

7:52 *Righteous One.* See 3:14 and note.

7:53 *law that was given through angels.* See note on v. 38.

7:55 *full of the Holy Spirit.* See note on 2:4; see also 6:5. *glory of God.* See note on Lk 2:9.

glory of God, and Jesus standing at the right hand of God. *a* 56"Look," he said, "I see heaven open *b* and the Son of Man *c* standing at the right hand of God."

57At this they covered their ears and, yelling at the top of their voices, they all rushed at him, 58dragged him out of the city *d* and began to stone him. *e* Meanwhile, the witnesses *f* laid their coats *g* at the feet of a young man named Saul. *h*

59While they were stoning him, Stephen prayed, "Lord Jesus, receive my spirit." *i* 60Then he fell on his knees *j* and cried out, "Lord, do not hold this sin against them." *k* When he had said this, he fell asleep. *l*

8

And Saul *m* approved of their killing him.

THE CHURCH PERSECUTED AND SCATTERED

On that day a great persecution broke out against the church in Jerusalem, and all except the apostles were scattered *n* throughout Judea and Samaria. *o* 2Godly men buried Stephen and mourned deeply for him. 3But Saul *p* began to destroy the church. *q* Going from house to house, he dragged off both men and women and put them in prison.

PHILIP IN SAMARIA

4Those who had been scattered *r* preached the word wherever they went. *s* 5Philip *t* went down to a city in Samaria and proclaimed the Messiah there. 6When the crowds heard Philip and saw the signs he performed, they all paid close attention to what he said. 7With shrieks, evil *a* spirits came out of many, *u* and many who were paralyzed or lame were healed. *v* 8So there was great joy in that city.

SIMON THE SORCERER

9Now for some time a man named Simon had practiced sorcery *w* in the city and amazed all the people of Samaria. He boasted that he was someone great, *x* 10and all the people, both high and low, gave him their attention and exclaimed, "This man is rightly called the Great Power of God." *y* 11They followed him because he had amazed them for a long time with his sorcery. 12But when they believed Philip as he proclaimed the good news of the kingdom of God *z* and the name of Jesus Christ, they were baptized, *a* both men and women. 13Simon himself believed and was baptized. And he followed Philip everywhere, astonished by the great signs and miracles *b* he saw.

14When the apostles in Jerusalem heard that Samaria *c* had accepted the word of God, *d* they sent Peter and John *e* to Samaria. 15When they arrived, they prayed for the new believers there that they might receive the Holy Spirit, *f* 16because the Holy Spirit had not yet come

---

a 7 Greek *unclean*

7:55 *a* S Mk 16:19
7:56 *b* S Mt 3:16
c S Mt 8:20
7:58 *d* Lk 4:29
e Lev 24:14,16
f Dt 17:7 *g* Ac 22:20
h Ac 8:1
7:59 *i* Ps 31:5;
Lk 23:46
7:60 *j* Lk 22:41;
Ac 9:40 *k* S Mt 5:44
l S Mt 9:24
8:1 *m* Ac 7:58
n ver 4; Ac 11:19
o Ac 9:31
8:3 *p* Ac 7:58
q Ac 9:1,13,21; 22:4,
19; 26:10,11; 1Co 15:9;
Gal 1:13,23; Php 3:6;
1Ti 1:13
8:4 *r* ver 1 *s* Ac 15:35
8:5 *t* Ac 6:5; 21:8
8:7 *u* S Mk 16:17
v S Mt 4:24
8:9 *w* Ac 13:6
x Ac 5:36
8:10 *y* Ac 14:11; 28:6
8:12 *z* S Mt 3:2
a S Ac 2:38
8:13 *b* ver 6;
Ac 19:11
8:14 *c* ver 1
d S Heb 4:12
e S Lk 22:8
8:15 *f* S Jn 20:22

7:56 *Son of Man.* See note on Mk 8:31. *standing at the right hand of God.* Cf. Ps 110:1 and note; Mk 14:62; Lk 22:69; Heb 1:2–3 and note. The significance of Jesus' "standing" is debated and thus uncertain.

C **7:58** *laid their coats at the feet of . . . Saul.* Some have thought that this marked Saul as being in charge of the execution. In any case, it is Luke's way of introducing the main character of the second section of the book (chs. 13–28).

7:60 *do not hold this sin against them.* Cf. Jesus' words in Lk 23:34. *fell asleep.* See note on Jn 11:11.

8:1 *approved.* See 22:20 and note. *all except the apostles.* For the apostles to stay in Jerusalem would be an encouragement to those in prison and a center of appeal to those scattered. The church now went underground. *scattered throughout Judea and Samaria.* The beginning of the fulfillment of the commission in 1:8—not by the church's plan, but by events beyond the believers' control. See map, p. 1861.

8:3 *began to destroy.* See 22:4. The Greek underlying this phrase sometimes describes the ravages of wild animals.

8:4 *preached the word.* Many witnesses to the gospel went everywhere proclaiming the good news. The number of witnesses multiplied, and the territory covered was expanded greatly (cf. 11:19–20).

C **8:5** *Philip.* One of the Seven in the Jerusalem church (6:3,5; see note on 6:6), who now becomes an evangelist,

proclaiming the Christ (Messiah); see also 21:8. Philip is an example of one of those who were scattered. *a city in Samaria.* Some manuscripts have "the city of Samaria," a reference to the old capital Samaria, renamed Sebaste or Neapolis (modern Nablus).

C **8:9** *Simon.* In early Christian literature the "sorcerer" (Simon Magus) is described as the arch-heretic of the church and the "father" of Gnostic teaching. *sorcery.* See note on 2Ki 17:17.

8:10 *the Great Power of God.* Simon claimed to be either God himself or, more likely, his chief representative.

8:13 *Simon himself believed and was baptized.* It is difficult to know whether Simon's faith was genuine. Even though Luke says Simon believed, Peter's statement that Simon had no part in the apostles' ministry because his heart was not "right before God" (v. 21) casts some doubt.

8:14 *Samaria.* That is, some of its citizens. Cf. 1:8. *had accepted the word of God.* Were obedient to the gospel proclaimed by Philip. *sent Peter and John.* The Jerusalem church assumed the responsibility of inspecting new evangelistic efforts and the communities of believers they produced (see 11:22).

A **8:16** *not yet come on any of them.* Since the day of Pentecost, those who "belong to Christ" (Ro 8:9) also have the Holy Spirit. But the Spirit had not yet been made manifest to the Christians in Samaria by the usual signs. This deficiency was now graciously supplied (v. 17).

8:16 ᵍ S Ac 10:44;
19:2 ʰ Mt 28:19;
S Ac 2:38
8:17 ⁱ S Ac 6:6
ʲ S Jn 20:22
8:20 ᵏ 2Ki 5:16;
Da 5:17; Mt 10:8;
Ac 2:38
8:21 ˡ Ne 2:20
ᵐ Ps 78:37
8:22 ⁿ Ac 2:38
8:24 ᵒ Ex 8:8;
Nu 21:7; 1Ki 13:6;
Jer 42:2
8:25 ᵖ S Ac 13:48
�q ver 40
8:26 ʳ S Ac 5:19
ˢ Ac 6:5

on any of them;ᵍ they had simply been baptized intoᵃ the name of the Lord Jesus. ʰ ¹⁷Then Peter and John placed their hands on them,ⁱ and they received the Holy Spirit.ʲ

¹⁸When Simon saw that the Spirit was given at the laying on of the apostles' hands, he offered them money ¹⁹and said, "Give me also this ability so that everyone on whom I lay my hands may receive the Holy Spirit."

²⁰Peter answered: "May your money perish with you, because you thought you could buy the gift of God with money!ᵏ ²¹You have no part or shareˡ in this ministry, because your heart is not rightᵐ before God. ²²Repentⁿ of this wickedness and pray to the Lord in the hope that he may forgive you for having such a thought in your heart. ²³For I see that you are full of bitterness and captive to sin."

²⁴Then Simon answered, "Pray to the Lord for meᵒ so that nothing you have said may happen to me."

²⁵After they had further proclaimed the word of the Lordᵖ and testified about Jesus, Peter and John returned to Jerusalem, preaching the gospel in many Samaritan villages. q

PHILIP AND THE ETHIOPIAN

²⁶Now an angelʳ of the Lord said to Philip,ˢ "Go south to the road—the desert road—

ᵃ 16 Or *in*

8:17 *placed their hands on them.* See v. 18; 19:1–7; cf. 2Ti 1:6; see also note on 6:6.
8:18 *he offered them money.* Simon had boasted before of having great powers (see v. 10 and note), and now he tried to buy this magical power he believed the apostles possessed.

8:23 *full of bitterness.* See Dt 29:18. *captive to sin.* See Ro 6:20.
8:26 *an angel of the Lord.* Cf. v. 29; see note on 5:19. *from Jerusalem to Gaza.* A distance of about 50 miles (see map below).

PHILIP'S AND PETER'S MISSIONARY JOURNEYS

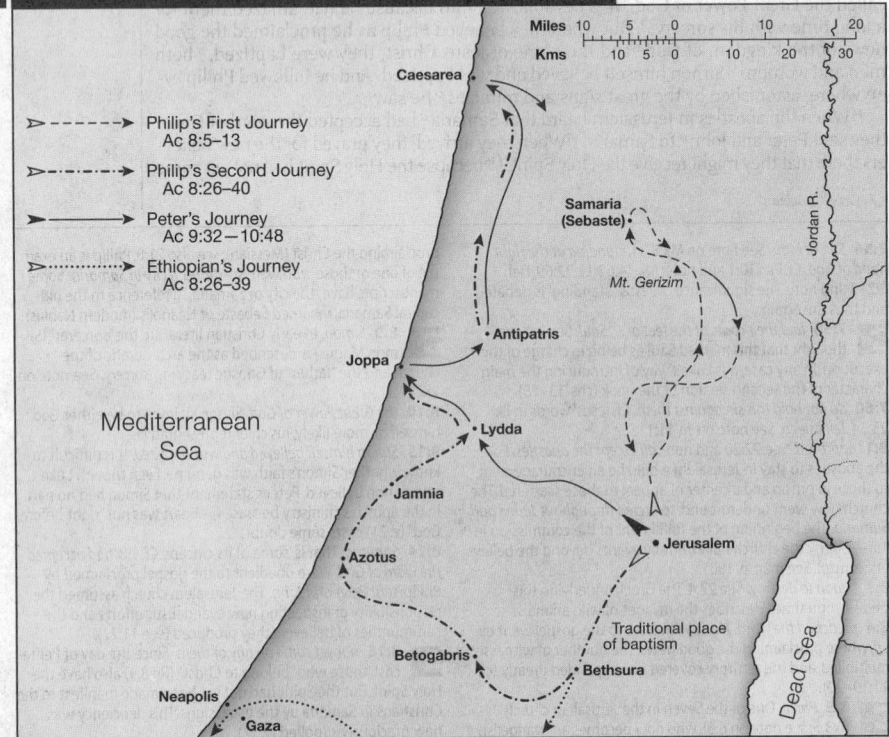

that goes down from Jerusalem to Gaza." ²⁷So he started out, and on his way he met an Ethiopian ᵃ ᵗ eunuch, ᵘ an important official in charge of all the treasury of the Kandake (which means "queen of the Ethiopians"). This man had gone to Jerusalem to worship, ᵛ ²⁸and on his way home was sitting in his chariot reading the Book of Isaiah the prophet. ²⁹The Spirit told ʷ Philip, "Go to that chariot and stay near it."

³⁰Then Philip ran up to the chariot and heard the man reading Isaiah the prophet. "Do you understand what you are reading?" Philip asked.

³¹"How can I," he said, "unless someone explains it to me?" So he invited Philip to come up and sit with him.

³²This is the passage of Scripture the eunuch was reading:

> "He was led like a sheep to the slaughter,
>   and as a lamb before its shearer is silent,
>   so he did not open his mouth.
> ³³ In his humiliation he was deprived of justice.
>   Who can speak of his descendants?
>   For his life was taken from the earth." ᵇ ˣ

³⁴The eunuch asked Philip, "Tell me, please, who is the prophet talking about, himself or someone else?" ³⁵Then Philip began ʸ with that very passage of Scripture ᶻ and told him the good news ᵃ about Jesus.

³⁶[³⁷]As they traveled along the road, they came to some water and the eunuch said, "Look, here is water. What can stand in the way of my being baptized?" ᶜ ᵇ ³⁸And he gave orders to stop the chariot. Then both Philip and the eunuch went down into the water and Philip baptized him. ³⁹When they came up out of the water, the Spirit of the Lord suddenly took Philip away, ᶜ and the eunuch did not see him again, but went on his way rejoicing. ⁴⁰Philip, however, appeared at Azotus and traveled about, preaching the gospel in all the towns ᵈ until he reached Caesarea. ᵉ

SAUL'S CONVERSION
9:1–19pp — Ac 22:3–16; 26:9–18

9 Meanwhile, Saul was still breathing out murderous threats against the Lord's disciples. ᶠ He went to the high priest ²and asked him for letters to the synagogues in Damascus, ᵍ so that if he found any there who belonged to the Way, ʰ whether men or women, he might take them as prisoners to Jerusalem. ³As he neared Damascus on his journey, suddenly a light from heaven flashed around him. ⁱ ⁴He fell to the ground and heard a voice ʲ say to him, "Saul, Saul, why do you persecute me?"

ᵃ 27 That is, from the southern Nile region   ᵇ 33 Isaiah 53:7,8 (see Septuagint)   ᶜ 36 Some late manuscripts *baptized?" ³⁷Philip said, "If you believe with all your heart, you may." The eunuch answered, "I believe that Jesus Christ is the Son of God."*

8:27 *an Ethiopian.* Ethiopia corresponded in this period to Nubia, from the upper Nile region at the first cataract (Aswan) to Khartoum. *Kandake.* The traditional title of the queen mother, responsible for performing the secular duties of the reigning king—who was thought to be too sacred for such activities. *gone to Jerusalem to worship.* If not a full-fledged proselyte (Dt 23:1), the Ethiopian was a Gentile God-fearer (see note on 10:2).
8:30 *heard the man reading.* It was customary practice to read aloud.

8:34 *who is the prophet talking about…?* Beginning with Isa 53 (see v. 35), Philip may have identified the suffering servant with the Davidic Messiah of Isa 11 or with the Son of Man (Da 7:13).
8:35 *good news.* The way of salvation through Jesus Christ (see note on Mk 1:1).
8:36 [37] *they came to some water.* There were several possibilities: a brook in the Valley of Elah (which David crossed to meet Goliath, 1Sa 17:40); the Wadi el-Hasi just north of Gaza; water from a spring or one of the many pools in the area.
8:39 *rejoicing.* Joy is associated with salvation in Acts (see note on 16:34).
8:40 *Azotus.* OT Ashdod (see 1Sa 5:1), one of the five Philistine cities (see map, p. 338). It was about 19 miles from Gaza and 60 miles from Caesarea (see map, p. 1850). *Caesarea.* Rebuilt by Herod and with an excellent harbor, it served as the headquar-

ters of the Roman governors. The account leaves Philip in Caesarea at this time; his next appearance is 20 years later, and he is still located in the same place (21:8).

9:1 *Saul.* Introduced at the stoning of Stephen (7:58), he was born in Tarsus and trained under Gamaliel (22:3). See notes on Ro 1:1; Php 3:4–14. *murderous threats.* We do not know that Saul was directly involved in the death of anyone other than Stephen (8:1), but there appear to have been similar cases (22:4; 26:10). *high priest.* Probably Caiaphas (see note on 4:6) and the members of the Sanhedrin, who had authority over Jews both in Judea and elsewhere.
9:2 *Damascus.* Located in the Roman province of Syria, it was the nearest important city outside the Holy Land. It also had a large Jewish population. The distance from Jerusalem to Damascus was about 150 miles, four to six days' travel. *the Way.* A name for Christianity occurring a number of times in Acts (16:17; 18:25–26; 19:9,23; 22:4; 24:14,22; see 2Pe 2:2). Jesus called himself "the way" (Jn 14:6). *prisoners to Jerusalem.* Where the full authority of the Sanhedrin could be exercised in trial for either acquittal or death.
9:3 *a light from heaven.* "About noon" (26:13).
9:4 *why do you persecute me?* To persecute the church is to persecute Christ, for the church is his body (see 1Co 12:27; Eph 1:22–23).

8:27 ᵗPs 68:31; 87:4; Zep 3:10   ᵘ Isa 56:3-5   ᵛ 1Ki 8:41-43; Jn 12:20
8:29 ʷAc 10:19; 11:12; 13:2; 20:23; 21:11
8:33 ˣ Isa 53:7,8
8:35 ʸMt 5:2   ᶻLk 24:27; Ac 17:2; 18:28; 28:23   ᵃS Ac 13:32
8:36[37] ᵇS Ac 2:3 8; 10:47
8:39 ᶜ1Ki 18:12; 2Ki 2:16; Eze 3:12,14; 8:3; 11:1,24; 43:5; 2Co 12:2; 1Th 4:17; Rev 12:5
8:40 ᵈver 25   ᵉAc 10:1,24; 12:19; 21:8,16; 23:23,33; 25:1,4,6,13
9:1 ᶠS Ac 8:3
9:2 ᵍIsa 17:1; Jer 49:23   ʰAc 19:9, 23; 22:4; 24:14,22
9:3 ⁱ1Co 15:8
9:4 ʲ Isa 6:8

9:6 *k* ver 16;
Eze 3:22
9:7 *l* Jn 12:29
m Da 10:7
9:8 *n* ver 18
9:10 *o* Ac 10:3,17,19;
12:9; 16:9,10; 18:9
9:11 *p* ver 30;
Ac 11:25; 21:39; 22:3
9:12 *q* S Mk 5:23
9:13 *r* ver 32;
Ac 26:10; Ro 1:7;
15:25,26,31; 16:2,15;
Eph 1:1; Php 1:1
s S Ac 8:3
9:14 *t* ver 2,21
u S Ac 2:21
9:15 *v* Ac 13:2;
Ro 1:1; Gal 1:15;
1Ti 1:12 *w* Ro 11:13;
15:15,16; Gal 1:16; 2:7,
8 *x* Ac 25:22,23; 26:1
9:16 *y* Ac 20:23;
21:11; 2Co 6:4-10;
11:23-27; 2Ti 1:8;
2:3,9
9:17 *z* S Ac 6:6
a S Lk 1:15
9:18 *b* S Ac 2:38
9:19 *c* S Ac 11:26
d Ac 26:20
9:20 *e* Ac 13:5,14;
14:1; 17:2,10,17; 18:4,
19; 19:8 *f* S Mt 4:3
9:21 *g* S Ac 8:3
h ver 14
9:22 *i* S Lk 2:11;
Ac 5:42; 17:3; 18:5,28
9:23 *j* S Ac 20:3
9:24 *k* Ac 20:3,19;
23:16,30
9:25 *l* 1Sa 19:12;
2Co 11:32,33
9:26 *m* Ac 22:17;
26:20; Gal 1:17,18
9:27 *n* S Ac 4:36
o ver 3-6 *p* ver 20,22

⁵"Who are you, Lord?" Saul asked.

"I am Jesus, whom you are persecuting," he replied. ⁶"Now get up and go into the city, and you will be told what you must do." *k*

⁷The men traveling with Saul stood there speechless; they heard the sound *l* but did not see anyone. *m* ⁸Saul got up from the ground, but when he opened his eyes he could see nothing. *n* So they led him by the hand into Damascus. ⁹For three days he was blind, and did not eat or drink anything.

¹⁰In Damascus there was a disciple named Ananias. The Lord called to him in a vision, *o* "Ananias!"

"Yes, Lord," he answered.

¹¹The Lord told him, "Go to the house of Judas on Straight Street and ask for a man from Tarsus *p* named Saul, for he is praying. ¹²In a vision he has seen a man named Ananias come and place his hands on *q* him to restore his sight."

¹³"Lord," Ananias answered, "I have heard many reports about this man and all the harm he has done to your people *r* in Jerusalem. *s* ¹⁴And he has come here with authority from the chief priests *t* to arrest all who call on your name." *u*

¹⁵But the Lord said to Ananias, "Go! This man is my chosen instrument *v* to proclaim my name to the Gentiles *w* and their kings *x* and to the people of Israel. ¹⁶I will show him how much he must suffer for my name." *y*

¹⁷Then Ananias went to the house and entered it. Placing his hands on *z* Saul, he said, "Brother Saul, the Lord—Jesus, who appeared to you on the road as you were coming here—has sent me so that you may see again and be filled with the Holy Spirit." *a* ¹⁸Immediately, something like scales fell from Saul's eyes, and he could see again. He got up and was baptized, *b* ¹⁹and after taking some food, he regained his strength.

SAUL IN DAMASCUS AND JERUSALEM

Saul spent several days with the disciples *c* in Damascus. *d* ²⁰At once he began to preach in the synagogues *e* that Jesus is the Son of God. *f* ²¹All those who heard him were astonished and asked, "Isn't he the man who raised havoc in Jerusalem among those who call on this name? *g* And hasn't he come here to take them as prisoners to the chief priests?" *h* ²²Yet Saul grew more and more powerful and baffled the Jews living in Damascus by proving that Jesus is the Messiah. *i*

²³After many days had gone by, there was a conspiracy among the Jews to kill him, *j* ²⁴but Saul learned of their plan. *k* Day and night they kept close watch on the city gates in order to kill him. ²⁵But his followers took him by night and lowered him in a basket through an opening in the wall. *l*

²⁶When he came to Jerusalem, *m* he tried to join the disciples, but they were all afraid of him, not believing that he really was a disciple. ²⁷But Barnabas *n* took him and brought him to the apostles. He told them how Saul on his journey had seen the Lord and that the Lord had spoken to him, *o* and how in Damascus he had preached fearlessly in the name of Jesus. *p* ²⁸So Saul stayed with them and moved about freely in Jerusalem, speak-

---

9:5 *Who are you, Lord?* In Rabbinic tradition such a voice from heaven would have been understood as the voice of God himself. The solemn repetition of Saul's name and the bright light suggested to him that he was in the presence of deity.

9:7 *heard the sound.* Those with Saul "heard the sound" but "did not understand" what the voice was saying (22:9; cf. Da 10:7).

9:10 *Ananias.* This Ananias is mentioned elsewhere only in 22:12. His was a common name (5:1; 23:2). The Greek form is derived from the Hebrew name Hananiah, meaning "The LORD is gracious/shows grace" (see Da 1:6 and note).

9:11 *Straight Street.* Probably followed the same route of the long, straight street that today runs through the city from east to west. It is a decided contrast to the numerous crooked streets of the city (see map, p. 1853). *Tarsus.* See note on 22:3. *praying.* Prayer is often associated with visions in Luke and Acts (see 10:9–11; Lk 1:10; 3:21; 9:28).

9:13 *your people.* See v. 32 and notes on Ro 1:7; Php 1:1.

9:15 *to the Gentiles.* See Ro 1:13–14. *their kings.* Agrippa (26:1) and Caesar at Rome (25:11–12; 28:19).

9:16 *how much he must suffer.* See 2Co 11:23–28 and notes.

9:17 *Jesus, who appeared to you.* The Damascus road experience was not merely a vision. The resurrected Christ actually appeared to Saul, and on this fact Saul based his qualification to

be an apostle (see 1Co 9:1 and note; 15:8).

9:20 *At once.* Following his baptism (v. 18). *synagogues.* It became Saul's regular practice to preach at every opportunity in the synagogues (13:5; 14:1; 17:1–2,10; 18:4,19; 19:8). *Jesus is the Son of God.* Saul's message was a declaration of what he himself had become convinced of on the Damascus road: Christ's deity and Messiahship.

9:22 *Messiah.* See TNIV text note on Mt 1:1.

9:23 *After many days.* Three years (Gal 1:17–18). It is probable that the major part of this period was spent in Arabia, away from Damascus, though the borders of Arabia extended to the environs of Damascus. *conspiracy among the Jews to kill him.* Upon Saul's return to Damascus, the governor under Aretas gave orders for his arrest (2Co 11:32). The absence of Roman coins struck in Damascus between A.D. 34 and 62 may indicate that Aretas was in control during that period.

9:25 *lowered him in a basket.* See 2Co 11:33 (cf. Jos 2:15; 1Sa 19:12).

9:26 *he came to Jerusalem.* From Gal 1:19 we learn that all the apostles were away except Peter and James, the Lord's brother. James was not one of the Twelve, but he held a position in Jerusalem comparable to that of an apostle (see Gal 2:9).

9:27 *Barnabas.* See note on 4:36.

| 9:35 | ACTS | **1853** |

ing boldly in the name of the Lord. ²⁹He talked and debated with the Hellenistic Jews, ᵃ �賀 but they tried to kill him. ʳ ³⁰When the believers ˢ learned of this, they took him down to Caesarea ᵗ and sent him off to Tarsus. ᵘ

³¹Then the church throughout Judea, Galilee and Samaria ᵛ enjoyed a time of peace and was strengthened. Living in the fear of the Lord and encouraged by the Holy Spirit, it increased in numbers. ʷ

AENEAS AND DORCAS

³²As Peter traveled about the country, he went to visit the Lord's people ˣ who lived in Lydda. ³³There he found a man named Aeneas, who was paralyzed and had been bedridden for eight years. ³⁴"Aeneas," Peter said to him, "Jesus Christ heals you. ʸ Get up and roll up your mat." Immediately Aeneas got up. ³⁵All those who lived in Lydda and Sharon ᶻ saw him and turned to the Lord. ᵃ

ᵃ 29 That is, Jews who had adopted the Greek language and culture

9:29 ᵍAc 6:1
ʳ2Co 11:26
9:30 ˢ S Ac 1:16
ᵗ S Ac 8:40 ᵘ S ver 11
9:31 ᵛ Ac 8:1
ʷ S Ac 2:41
9:32 ˣ S ver 13
9:34 ʸ Ac 3:6,16;
4:10
9:35 ᶻ1Ch 5:16;
27:29; SS 2:1;
Isa 33:9; 35:2; 65:10
ᵃ S Ac 2:41

9:29 *He talked and debated.* Formerly Saul was arguing against Christ; now he is forcefully presenting Jesus as the Messiah.
9:30 *Caesarea.* See note on 8:40. *Tarsus.* Saul's birthplace (see note on 22:3).

A **9:31** *church.* The whole Christian body, including Christians in the districts of Judea, Galilee and Samaria. The singular thus does not here refer to the various congregations but to the church as a whole (see note on 5:11). *encouraged by the Holy Spirit.* The work of the Spirit is particularly noted throughout the book of Acts (see 13:2 and note on 1:2). This is why the book is sometimes called the Acts of the Holy Spirit.

9:32 *Lydda.* A town two or three miles north of the road connecting Joppa and Jerusalem. Lydda is about 12 miles from Joppa.
9:33 *Aeneas.* Since Peter was there to visit the believers, Aeneas was probably one of the Christians.

A **9:35** *Sharon.* The fertile plain of Sharon runs about 50 miles along the Mediterranean coast, roughly from Joppa to Caesarea. The reference here, however, may be to a village in the neighborhood of Lydda instead of to a district (an Egyptian papyrus refers to a town by that name in the Holy Land).

ROMAN DAMASCUS

Damascus represented much more to Saul, the strict Pharisee, than any other stop on his campaign of repression. It was the hub of a vast commercial network with far-flung lines of caravan trade reaching into north Syria, Mesopotamia, Anatolia, Persia and Arabia. If the new "Way" of Christianity flourished in Damascus, it would quickly reach all these places. From the viewpoint of the Sanhedrin and of Saul, the arch-persecutor, it had to be stopped in Damascus.

B The city itself was a veritable oasis, situated in a plain watered by the Biblical rivers Abana and Pharpar (see note on 2Ki 5:12; see also map, p. 1721). Roman architecture

overlaid the Hellenistic town plan with a great temple to Jupiter and a mile-long colonnaded street, the "Straight Street" of Ac 9:11. The city gates and a section of the town wall may still be seen today, as well as the lengthy bazaar that runs along the line of the ancient street.

The dominant political figure at the time of Paul's escape from Damascus (2Co 11:32–33) was Aretas IV, king of the Nabateans (9 B.C.–A.D. 40), though normally the Decapolis cities were attached to the province of Syria and were thus under the influence of Rome.

9:36 *b* Jos 19:46;
2Ch 2:16; Ezr 3:7;
Jnh 1:3; Ac 10:5
c 1Ti 2:10; Tit 3:8
9:37 *d* Ac 1:13; 20:8
9:38 *e* S Ac 11:26
9:39 *f* Ac 6:1; 1Ti 5:3
9:40 *g* Mt 9:25
h Lk 22:41; Ac 7:60
i S Lk 7:14
9:42 *j* S Ac 2:41
9:43 *k* Ac 10:6

³⁶In Joppa *b* there was a disciple named Tabitha (in Greek her name is Dorcas); she was always doing good *c* and helping the poor. ³⁷About that time she became sick and died, and her body was washed and placed in an upstairs room. *d* ³⁸Lydda was near Joppa; so when the disciples *e* heard that Peter was in Lydda, they sent two men to him and urged him, "Please come at once!"

³⁹Peter went with them, and when he arrived he was taken upstairs to the room. All the widows *f* stood around him, crying and showing him the robes and other clothing that Dorcas had made while she was still with them.

⁴⁰Peter sent them all out of the room; *g* then he got down on his knees *h* and prayed. Turning toward the dead woman, he said, "Tabitha, get up." *i* She opened her eyes, and seeing Peter she sat up. ⁴¹He took her by the hand and helped her to her feet. Then he called for the believers, especially the widows, and presented her to them alive. ⁴²This became known all over Joppa, and many people believed in the Lord. *j* ⁴³Peter stayed in Joppa for some time with a tanner named Simon. *k*

9:36 *Joppa.* About 38 miles from Jerusalem, the main seaport of Judea. Today it is known as Jaffa and is a suburb of Tel Aviv.
9:37 *body was washed.* In preparation for burial, a custom common to both Jews (Purification of the Dead) and Greeks. *upstairs room.* If burial was delayed, it was customary to lay the body in an upper room. In Jerusalem the body had to be buried the day the person died, but outside Jerusalem up to three days might be allowed for burial.
9:38 *near Joppa.* See note on v. 32. *come at once!* Whether for consolation or for a miracle, Peter was urged to hurry in order to arrive before the burial.

9:40 *sent them all out.* Cf. 1Ki 17:23; 2Ki 4:33. Peter had been present on all three occasions recorded in Scripture when Jesus raised individuals from the dead (Mt 9:25; Lk 7:11–17; Jn 11:1–44). As when Jesus raised Jairus's daughter, the crowd in the room was told to leave. Unlike Jesus, however, Peter knelt and prayed.
9:42 *many people believed.* Cf. Jn 12:11.
9:43 *a tanner.* Occupations were frequently used with personal names to further identify individuals (see 16:14; 18:3; 19:24; 2Ti 4:14), but in this case it is especially significant. A tanner was involved in treating the skins of dead animals, thus contacting the

---

TIMELINE OF PAUL'S LIFE

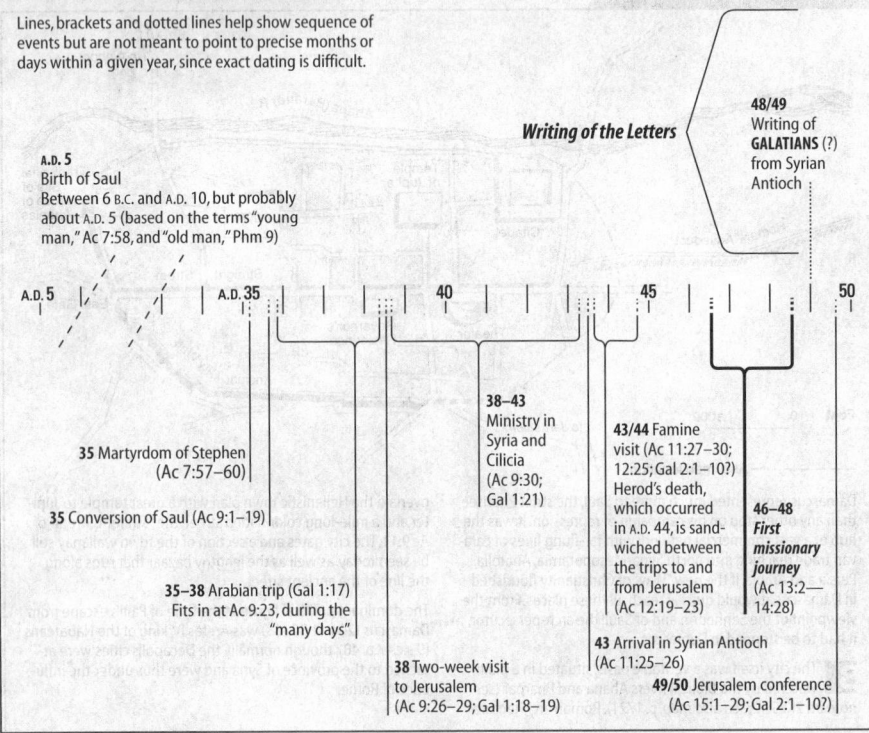

Lines, brackets and dotted lines help show sequence of events but are not meant to point to precise months or days within a given year, since exact dating is difficult.

Writing of the Letters

48/49 Writing of **GALATIANS** (?) from Syrian Antioch

A.D. 5 Birth of Saul
Between 6 B.C. and A.D. 10, but probably about A.D. 5 (based on the terms "young man," Ac 7:58, and "old man," Phm 9)

A.D. 5   A.D. 35   40   45   50

38–43 Ministry in Syria and Cilicia (Ac 9:30; Gal 1:21)

43/44 Famine visit (Ac 11:27–30; 12:25; Gal 2:1–10?) Herod's death, which occurred in A.D. 44, is sandwiched between the trips to and from Jerusalem (Ac 12:19–23)

46–48 *First missionary journey* (Ac 13:2—14:28)

35 Martyrdom of Stephen (Ac 7:57–60)

35 Conversion of Saul (Ac 9:1–19)

35–38 Arabian trip (Gal 1:17) Fits in at Ac 9:23, during the "many days"

38 Two-week visit to Jerusalem (Ac 9:26–29; Gal 1:18–19)

43 Arrival in Syrian Antioch (Ac 11:25–26)

49/50 Jerusalem conference (Ac 15:1–29; Gal 2:1–10?)

CORNELIUS CALLS FOR PETER

10 At Caesarea¹ there was a man named Cornelius, a centurion in what was known as the Italian Regiment. ²He and all his family were devout and God-fearing; ᵐ he gave generously to those in need and prayed to God regularly. ³One day at about three in the afternoon ⁿ he had a vision. ᵒ He distinctly saw an angelᵖ of God, who came to him and said, "Cornelius!"

⁴Cornelius stared at him in fear. "What is it, Lord?" he asked.

The angel answered, "Your prayers and gifts to the poor have come up as a memorial offering �ۊ before God. ʳ ⁵Now send men to Joppaˢ to bring back a man named Simon who is called Peter. ⁶He is staying with Simon the tanner,ᵗ whose house is by the sea."

10:1 ¹S Ac 8:40
10:2 ᵐver 22, 35;
Ac 13:16, 26
10:3 ⁿPs 55:17;
Ac 3:1 ᵒS Ac 9:10
ᵖS Ac 5:19
10:4 ᵠPs 20:3;
S Mt 10:42; 26:13
ʳRev 8:4
10:5 ˢS Ac 9:36
10:6 ᵗAc 9:43

unclean according to Jewish law, so Simon was despised by many. Peter's decision to stay with him shows already a willingness to reject Jewish prejudice and helps to prepare the way for his coming vision and the mission to the Gentiles.

10:1 *Caesarea.* Located 30 miles north of Joppa and named in honor of Augustus Caesar, it was the headquarters for the Roman forces of occupation (see also note on 8:40). *Cornelius.* A Latin name made popular when Cornelius Sulla liberated some 10,000 slaves over 100 years earlier. These had all taken his family name, Cornelius. *centurion.* Commanded a military unit that normally numbered at least 100 men (see note on Mt 8:5). The Roman legion (about 6,000 men) was divided into ten regiments, each of which had a designation. This was the "Italian" (another was the "Imperial," or "Augustan," 27:1). A centurion commanded about a sixth of a regiment. Centurions were carefully selected; all of them mentioned in the NT appear to have had noble qualities (e.g., Lk 7:5). The Roman centurions provided necessary stability to the entire Roman system.

10:2 *devout.* In spite of all his good deeds, Cornelius needed to hear the way of salvation from a human messenger. The role of the angel (v. 3) was to bring Cornelius and Peter together (cf. 8:26; 9:10). *God-fearing.* The term used of one who was not a full Jewish proselyte but who believed in one God and respected the moral and ethical teachings of the Jews.

10:3 *about three in the afternoon.* Another indication that Cornelius followed Jewish religious practices. Three in the afternoon was a Jewish hour of prayer (see 3:1)—the hour of the evening incense. *a vision.* Not a dream or trance but a revelation through an angel to Cornelius while he was at prayer (see v. 30; see also note on 9:11).

10:4 *have come up.* Like the smoke of a sacrifice (see Ps 141:2; Php 4:18 and note; Heb 13:15–16). *memorial offering.* A portion of the grain offering burned on the altar was called a "memorial" (Lev 2:2).

10:5–6 *Joppa … Simon the tanner.* See notes on 9:36, 43.

10:8 "S Ac 9:36
10:9 ᵛS Mt 24:17
10:10 ʷAc 22:17
10:11 ˣS Mt 3:16
10:14 ʸAc 9:5
ᶻLev 11:4-8,13-20;
20:25; Dt 14:3-20;
Eze 4:14
10:15 ªver 28;
Ge 9:3; Mt 15:11;
Lk 11:41; Ac 11:9;
Ro 14:14,17,20;
1Co 10:25; 1Ti 4:3,4;
Tit 1:15
10:17 ᵇS Ac 9:10
ᶜver 7,8
10:19 ᵈS Ac 9:10
ᵉS Ac 8:29
10:20 ᶠAc 15:7-9
10:22 ᵍver 2
ʰAc 11:14
10:23 ⁱS Ac 1:16
ʲver 45; Ac 11:12
10:24 ᵏS Ac 8:40
10:26 ˡAc 14:15;
Rev 19:10; 22:8,9
10:27 ᵐver 24
10:28 ⁿJn 4:9;
18:28; Ac 11:3
ᵒS ver 14,15;
Ac 15:8,9
10:30 ᵖS Jn 20:12

⁷When the angel who spoke to him had gone, Cornelius called two of his servants and a devout soldier who was one of his attendants. ⁸He told them everything that had happened and sent them to Joppa. ᵘ

PETER'S VISION

10:9–32Ref — Ac 11:5–14

⁹About noon the following day as they were on their journey and approaching the city, Peter went up on the roofᵛ to pray. ¹⁰He became hungry and wanted something to eat, and while the meal was being prepared, he fell into a trance. ʷ ¹¹He saw heaven openedˣ and something like a large sheet being let down to earth by its four corners. ¹²It contained all kinds of four-footed animals, as well as reptiles and birds. ¹³Then a voice told him, "Get up, Peter. Kill and eat."

¹⁴"Surely not, Lord!"ʸ Peter replied. "I have never eaten anything impure or unclean."ᶻ

¹⁵The voice spoke to him a second time, "Do not call anything impure that God has made clean."ª

¹⁶This happened three times, and immediately the sheet was taken back to heaven.

¹⁷While Peter was wondering about the meaning of the vision,ᵇ the men sent by Corneliusᶜ found out where Simon's house was and stopped at the gate. ¹⁸They called out, asking if Simon who was known as Peter was staying there.

¹⁹While Peter was still thinking about the vision,ᵈ the Spirit saidᵉ to him, "Simon, threeª men are looking for you. ²⁰So get up and go downstairs. Do not hesitate to go with them, for I have sent them."ᶠ

²¹Peter went down and said to the men, "I'm the one you're looking for. Why have you come?"

²²The men replied, "We have come from Cornelius the centurion. He is a righteous and God-fearing man,ᵍ who is respected by all the Jewish people. A holy angel told him to ask you to come to his house so that he could hear what you have to say."ʰ ²³Then Peter invited the men into the house to be his guests.

PETER AT CORNELIUS'S HOUSE

The next day Peter started out with them, and some of the believersⁱ from Joppa went along.ʲ ²⁴The following day he arrived in Caesarea.ᵏ Cornelius was expecting them and had called together his relatives and close friends. ²⁵As Peter entered the house, Cornelius met him and fell at his feet in reverence. ²⁶But Peter made him get up. "Stand up," he said, "I am only human myself."ˡ

²⁷While talking with him, Peter went inside and found a large gathering of people. ᵐ ²⁸He said to them: "You are well aware that it is against our law for a Jew to associate with Gentiles or visit them. ⁿ But God has shown me that I should not call anyone impure or unclean. ᵒ ²⁹So when I was sent for, I came without raising any objection. May I ask why you sent for me?"

³⁰Cornelius answered: "Three days ago I was in my house praying at this hour, at three in the afternoon. Suddenly a man in shining clothesᵖ stood before me ³¹and said, 'Cornelius, God has heard your prayer and remembered your gifts to the poor. ³²Send to Jop-

---

ª *19* One early manuscript *two*; other manuscripts do not have the number.

10:9 *roof to pray.* It was customary for eastern houses to have flat roofs with outside stairways. The roof was used as a convenient place for relaxation and privacy (see Mk 2:4 and note).

10:10 *fell into a trance.* A state of mind God produced and used to communicate with Peter. It was not merely imagination or a dream. Peter's consciousness was heightened to receive the vision from God.

10:12 *all kinds of four-footed animals.* Including animals both clean and unclean, according to Lev 11.

10:14 *Surely not, Lord!* So deeply ingrained was the observance of the laws of clean and unclean that Peter refused to obey immediately. *impure or unclean.* Anything common (impure) was forbidden by the law to be eaten (cf. Ezr 4:14).

10:15 *God has made clean.* Jesus had already laid the groundwork for setting aside the laws of clean and unclean food (Mt 15:11; see also 1Ti 4:3–5).

10:16 *three times.* To make a due impression on Peter.

10:23 *invited the men into the house.* By providing lodging for them, Peter was already taking the first step toward accepting

Gentiles. Such intimate relationship with Gentiles was contrary to prescribed Jewish practice. *The next day.* It was too late in the day to start out on the long journey to Caesarea (see note on v. 1). *some of the believers.* Six in number (11:12), they were "circumcised believers" (10:45; see also note on 11:1).

10:26 *I am only human.* Possibly Cornelius was only intending to honor Peter as one having a rank superior to his own, since he was God's messenger. But Peter allowed no chance for misunderstanding—he was not to be worshiped as more than a created being (cf. 14:11–15).

10:28 *God has shown me.* Peter recognized that his vision had deeper significance than declaring invalid the distinction between clean and unclean meat; he saw that the barrier between Jew and Gentile had been removed (see Eph 2:11–22).

10:30 *a man in shining clothes.* Common language to describe an angel when appearing in the form of a man (see 1:10 and note; Mt 28:3; Mk 16:5; Jn 20:12).

pa for Simon who is called Peter. He is a guest in the home of Simon the tanner, who lives by the sea.' ³³So I sent for you immediately, and it was good of you to come. Now we are all here in the presence of God to listen to everything the Lord has commanded you to tell us."

³⁴Then Peter began to speak: "I now realize how true it is that God does not show favoritism ⁹ ³⁵but accepts those from every nation who fear him and do what is right. ʳ ³⁶You know the message ˢ God sent to the people of Israel, announcing the good news ᵗ of peace ᵘ through Jesus Christ, who is Lord of all. ᵛ ³⁷You know what has happened throughout the province of Judea, beginning in Galilee after the baptism that John preached— ³⁸how God anointed ʷ Jesus of Nazareth with the Holy Spirit and power, and how he went around doing good and healing ˣ all who were under the power of the devil, because God was with him. ʸ

³⁹"We are witnesses ᶻ of everything he did in the country of the Jews and in Jerusalem. They killed him by hanging him on a cross, ᵃ ⁴⁰but God raised him from the dead ᵇ on the third day and caused him to be seen. ⁴¹He was not seen by all the people, ᶜ but by witnesses whom God had already chosen—by us who ate ᵈ and drank with him after he rose from the dead. ⁴²He commanded us to preach to the people ᵉ and to testify that he is the one whom God appointed as judge of the living and the dead. ᶠ ⁴³All the prophets testify about him ᵍ that everyone ʰ who believes ⁱ in him receives forgiveness of sins through his name." ʲ

⁴⁴While Peter was still speaking these words, the Holy Spirit came on ᵏ all who heard the message. ⁴⁵The circumcised believers who had come with Peter ˡ were astonished that the gift of the Holy Spirit had been poured out ᵐ even on Gentiles. ⁿ ⁴⁶For they heard them speaking in tongues ᵃ ᵒ and praising God.

Then Peter said, ⁴⁷"Surely no one can stand in the way of their being baptized with water. ᵖ They have received the Holy Spirit just as we have." �q ⁴⁸So he ordered that they be baptized in the name of Jesus Christ. ʳ Then they asked Peter to stay with them for a few days.

PETER EXPLAINS HIS ACTIONS

11 The apostles and the believers ˢ throughout Judea heard that the Gentiles also had received the word of God. ᵗ ²So when Peter went up to Jerusalem, the circumcised believers ᵘ criticized him ³and said, "You went into the house of the uncircumcised and ate with them." ᵛ

⁴Starting from the beginning, Peter told them the whole story: ⁵"I was in the city of Joppa praying, and in a trance I saw a vision. ʷ I saw something like a large sheet being

---

ᵃ 46 Or other languages

10:34 *God does not show favoritism.* God does not favor individuals because of their station in life, their nationality or their material possessions (see Ro 2:11; Jas 2:1 and notes; see also Dt 10:17–19; 2Co 19:17; Job 34:19; Eph 6:9; Col 3:25; 1Pe 1:17). He does, however, respect their character and judge their work. This is evident because God "accepts those from every nation who fear him and do what is right" (v. 35). Cornelius already worshiped the true God, but this was not enough: He lacked faith in Christ (v. 36).

10:36 *people of Israel.* The first recipients of the "message," but it was not restricted to them, as the phrase "Lord of all" indicates (see Jn 3:16; Ro 1:16). *peace.* Between God and humans (see Ro 5:1 and note). *Lord of all.* Lord of both Jew and Gentile (see vv. 34–35).

10:37 *after the baptism that John preached.* Similar to the outline of Mark's Gospel, Peter's sermon begins with John's baptism and continues to the resurrection of Jesus. This is significant since the early church fathers viewed Mark as the "interpreter" of Peter (see Introduction to Mark: Author). See previous summaries of Peter's preaching (2:14–41; 3:12–26; 4:8–12; 5:29–32); see also note on 2:14–40.

10:38 *how God anointed Jesus.* See Isa 61:1–3; Lk 4:18–21.

10:39 *hanging him on a cross.* See note on 5:30.

10:41 *who ate and drank.* Those who ate with Jesus after he rose from the dead received unmistakable evidence of his bodily resurrection (see Lk 24:42–43; Jn 21:12–15).

10:44 *the Holy Spirit came on.* See 8:16 and note.

10:45 *astonished ... even on Gentiles.* Apparently the early Jew-

ish Christians failed to understand that the gospel was for Gentiles as well as for Jews, and that they would share alike in the benefits of redemption. Gentile proselytes to Judaism, however, were accepted (see 6:5).

10:46 *speaking in tongues.* The same experience the disciples had at Pentecost (2:4,11), as well as "some disciples" at Ephesus (19:1,6).

10:47 *no one can stand in the way of their being baptized with water.* The Gentiles had received the same gift (11:17) as the Jewish believers; they spoke in tongues as did the Jewish Christians on the day of Pentecost. This was unavoidable evidence that the invitation to the kingdom was open to Gentiles as well as to Jews.

11:1 *believers.* Lit. "brothers." At times "brothers" is used to refer to those of common Jewish lineage (2:29; 7:2), but in Christian contexts it denotes those united in Christ (6:3; 10:23; see note on Ro 1:13). In matters of deep concern, the "apostles" did not act alone. The divine will gave guidance, and the apostles interpreted and exhorted, but the consent of the whole church was sought ("the whole group," 6:5; "apostles and the believers," here; "the church," 11:22; "the church and the apostles and elders," 15:4; cf. 15:22).

11:2 *circumcised believers.* Jewish Christians.

11:3 *the uncircumcised.* The Gentiles who would not observe the laws of clean and unclean food and would violate Jewish regulations concerning food preparation. *ate with them.* See Lk 15:2 and note.

11:4–17 See notes on 10:1–23,28–33.

10:34 ⁹ Dt 10:17; 2Ch 19:7; Job 34:19; Mk 12:14; Ro 2:11; Gal 2:6; Eph 6:9; Col 3:25; Jas 2:1; 1Pe 1:17
10:35 ʳ Ac 15:9
10:36 ˢ 1Jn 1:5
ᵗ S Ac 13:32
ᵘ S Lk 2:14
ᵛ S Mt 28:18
10:38 ʷ S Ac 4:26
ˣ S Mt 4:23 ʸ S Jn 3:2
10:39 ᶻ ver 41;
S Lk 24:48
ᵃ S Ac 5:30
10:40 ᵇ S Ac 2:24
10:41 ᶜ Jn 14:17,22
ᵈ Lk 24:43; Jn 21:13;
Ac 1:4
10:42 ᵉ Mt 28:19,20
ᶠ S Jn 5:22; Ac 17:31;
Ro 14:9; 2Co 5:10;
2Ti 4:1; 1Pe 4:5
10:43 ᵍ Isa 53:11;
Ac 26:22 ʰ Ac 15:9
ⁱ S Jn 3:15 / S Lk 24:27
10:44 ᵏ Ac 8:15,16;
11:15; 15:8; 19:6;
S Lk 1:15
10:45 ˡ ver 23
ᵐ Ac 2:33,38
ⁿ Ac 11:18; 15:8
10:46 ᵒ S Mk 16:17
10:47 ᵖ Ac 8:36
�q S Jn 20:22; Ac 11:17
10:48 ʳ S Ac 2:38
11:1 ˢ S Ac 1:16
ᵗ S Heb 4:12
11:2 ᵘ Ac 10:45
11:3 ᵛ Ac 10:25,28;
Gal 2:12
11:5 ʷ S Ac 9:10;
10:9-32

11:9 ˣ S Ac 10:15
11:11 ʸ S Ac 8:40
11:12 ᶻ S Ac 8:29
ᵃ Ac 15:9; Ro 3:22
ᵇ ver 1,29; S Ac 1:16
11:13 ᶜ Ac 5:19
11:14 ᵈ Ac 10:36
ᵉ Jn 4:53; Ac 16:15,31-34; 18:8; 1Co 1:11,16
11:15 ᶠ S Ac 10:44
ᵍ Ac 2:4
11:16 ʰ S Mk 1:4
ⁱ S Mk 1:8
11:17 ʲ Ac 2:38
ᵏ Ac 10:45,47
11:18 ˡ Ro 10:12,13; 2Co 7:10
11:19 ᵐ Ac 8:1,4
ⁿ ver 26,27; Ac 13:1; 14:26; 18:22; Gal 2:11
11:20 ᵒ Ac 4:36
ᵖ S Mt 27:32
�q S ver 19 ʳ S Ac 13:32
11:21 ˢ Lk 1:66
ᵗ S Ac 2:41
11:22 ᵘ S Ac 4:36
11:23 ᵛ Ac 13:43; 14:26; 15:40; 20:24
ʷ Ac 14:22
11:24 ˣ S Lk 1:15
ʸ S Ac 2:41
11:25 ᶻ S Ac 9:11
11:26 ᵃ ver 29; Ac 6:1,2; 9:19,26,38; 13:52 ᵇ Ac 26:28; 1Pe 4:16
11:27 ᶜ Ac 13:1; 15:32; 1Co 11:4; 12:28, 29; 14:29,32,37; S Eph 4:11
11:28 ᵈ Ac 21:10 ᵉ S Mt 24:14

let down from heaven by its four corners, and it came down to where I was. ⁶I looked into it and saw four-footed animals of the earth, wild beasts, reptiles and birds. ⁷Then I heard a voice telling me, 'Get up, Peter. Kill and eat.'

⁸"I replied, 'Surely not, Lord! Nothing impure or unclean has ever entered my mouth.'

⁹"The voice spoke from heaven a second time, 'Do not call anything impure that God has made clean.'ˣ ¹⁰This happened three times, and then it was all pulled up to heaven again.

¹¹"Right then three men who had been sent to me from Caesareaʸ stopped at the house where I was staying. ¹²The Spirit toldᶻ me to have no hesitation about going with them. ᵃ These six brothers ᵇ also went with me, and we entered the man's house. ¹³He told us how he had seen an angel ᶜ appear in his house and say, 'Send to Joppa for Simon who is called Peter. ¹⁴He will bring you a message ᵈ through which you and all your household ᵉ will be saved.'

¹⁵"As I began to speak, the Holy Spirit came on ᶠ them as he had come on us at the beginning. ᵍ ¹⁶Then I remembered what the Lord had said: 'John baptized withᵃ water, ʰ but you will be baptized withᵃ the Holy Spirit.'ⁱ ¹⁷So if God gave them the same gift ʲ he gave us ᵏ who believed in the Lord Jesus Christ, who was I to think that I could stand in God's way?"

¹⁸When they heard this, they had no further objections and praised God, saying, "So then, even to Gentiles God has granted repentance that leads to life." ˡ

THE CHURCH IN ANTIOCH

¹⁹Now those who had been scattered by the persecution that broke out when Stephen was killed ᵐ traveled as far as Phoenicia, Cyprus and Antioch, ⁿ spreading the word only among Jews. ²⁰Some of them, however, men from Cyprus ᵒ and Cyrene, ᵖ went to Antioch q and began to speak to Greeks also, telling them the good news ʳ about the Lord Jesus. ²¹The Lord's hand was with them, ˢ and a great number of people believed and turned to the Lord. ᵗ

²²News of this reached the ears of the church in Jerusalem, and they sent Barnabasᵘ to Antioch. ²³When he arrived and saw what the grace of God had done, ᵛ he was glad and encouraged them all to remain true to the Lord with all their hearts. ʷ ²⁴He was a good man, full of the Holy Spiritˣ and faith, and a great number of people were brought to the Lord. ʸ

²⁵Then Barnabas went to Tarsusᶻ to look for Saul, ²⁶and when he found him, he brought him to Antioch. So for a whole year Barnabas and Saul met with the church and taught great numbers of people. The disciples ᵃ were called Christians first ᵇ at Antioch.

²⁷During this time some prophets ᶜ came down from Jerusalem to Antioch. ²⁸One of them, named Agabus, ᵈ stood up and through the Spirit predicted that a severe famine would spread over the entire Roman world. ᵉ (This happened during the reign of Claudi-

---

ᵃ 16 Or in

11:14 *you and all your household.* Not only the family but also slaves and employed individuals under Cornelius's authority (see note on Ge 6:18).

A **11:17** *stand in God's way.* Peter could not deny the Gentiles the invitation to be baptized (10:47) and to enjoy full fellowship in Christ with all believers. The Jewish believers were compelled to recognize that God was going to save Gentiles on equal terms with Jews. By divine action rather than by human choice, the door was being opened to Gentiles.

A **11:18** *repentance that leads to life.* A change of one's attitude toward sin, which leads to a turning from sin to God and results in eternal life (see note on 2:38).

11:19 *persecution that broke out when Stephen was killed.* See 8:1–4 and notes. *Phoenicia.* A country about 15 miles wide and 120 miles long, stretching along the northeastern Mediterranean coast (modern Lebanon). Its important cities were Tyre and Sidon. *Cyprus.* An island in the northeastern Mediterranean; the home of Barnabas (4:36). *Antioch.* The third city of the Roman empire (after Rome and Alexandria). It was 15 miles inland from the northeast corner of the Mediterranean. The first largely Gentile local church was located here, and it was from this church that Paul's three missionary journeys were launched (13:1–4; 15:40; 18:23).

11:20 *Cyrene.* See note on 2:10. *Greeks.* Not Greek-speaking Jews, but Gentiles.

11:21 *Lord's hand.* Indicates the presence of the Lord's power

to assist and bless (see 4:30; Lk 1:16; but see also Ac 13:11), sometimes evidenced by signs and wonders (cf. Ex 8:19).

C **11:22** *Barnabas.* See notes on 4:36; 9:27. *Antioch.* See note on v. 19. The sending of Barnabas was apparently in keeping with the Jerusalem church's policy of sending leaders to check on new ministries that came to their attention (see 8:14).

C **11:23** *he … encouraged them.* His name means "son of encouragement" (4:36; see note there).

C **11:24** *full of the Holy Spirit and faith.* See the description of Stephen (6:5).

11:25 *Tarsus.* See 9:11,30 and note on 22:3.

A **11:26** *whole year.* Luke notes definite periods of time (18:11; 19:8,10; 24:27; 28:30). *Christians.* Whether adopted by believers or invented by enemies as a term of reproach, it is an apt title for those "belonging to Christ" (the meaning of the term). It occurs elsewhere in Scripture only in 26:28; 1Pe 4:16.

A **11:27** *prophets.* The first mention of the gift of prophecy in Acts. Prophets preach, exhort, explain or, as in this case, foretell (see 13:1; 15:32; 19:6; 21:9–10; Ro 12:6; 1Co 12:10; 13:2, 8; 14:3,6,29–37; see also notes on Jnh 3:2; Zec 1:1; Eph 4:11).

11:28 *Agabus.* Later foretells Paul's imprisonment (21:10). In Acts, prophets are engaged in foretelling (v. 27; 21:9–10) at least as often as in "forthtelling" (15:32). *Claudius.* Emperor of Rome (A.D. 41–54).

us.) [f] 29The disciples, [g] as each one was able, decided to provide help [h] for the believers [i] living in Judea. 30This they did, sending their gift to the elders [j] by Barnabas [k] and Saul. [l]

PETER'S MIRACULOUS ESCAPE FROM PRISON

12 It was about this time that King Herod [m] arrested some who belonged to the church, intending to persecute them. 2He had James, the brother of John, [n] put to death with the sword. [o] 3When he saw that this met with approval among the Jews, [p] he proceeded to seize Peter also. This happened during the Festival of Unleavened Bread. [q] 4After arresting him, he put him in prison, handing him over to be guarded by four squads of four soldiers each. Herod intended to bring him out for public trial after the Passover. [r]

5So Peter was kept in prison, but the church was earnestly praying to God for him. [s]

6The night before Herod was to bring him to trial, Peter was sleeping between two soldiers, bound with two chains, [t] and sentries stood guard at the entrance. 7Suddenly an angel [u] of the Lord appeared and a light shone in the cell. He struck Peter on the side and woke him up. "Quick, get up!" he said, and the chains fell off Peter's wrists. [v]

8Then the angel said to him, "Put on your clothes and sandals." And Peter did so. "Wrap your cloak around you and follow me," the angel told him. 9Peter followed him out of the prison, but he had no idea that what the angel was doing was really happening; he thought he was seeing a vision. [w] 10They passed the first and second guards and came to the iron gate leading to the city. It opened for them by itself, [x] and they went through it. When they had walked the length of one street, suddenly the angel left him.

11Then Peter came to himself [y] and said, "Now I know without a doubt that the Lord has sent his angel and rescued me [z] from Herod's clutches and from everything the Jewish people were hoping would happen."

12When this had dawned on him, he went to the house of Mary the mother of John, also called Mark, [a] where many people had gathered and were praying. [b] 13Peter knocked at the outer entrance, and a servant named Rhoda came to answer the door. [c] 14When she recognized Peter's voice, she was so overjoyed [d] she ran back without opening it and exclaimed, "Peter is at the door!"

15"You're out of your mind," they told her. When she kept insisting that it was so, they said, "It must be his angel." [e]

16But Peter kept on knocking, and when they opened the door and saw him, they were astonished. 17Peter motioned with his hand [f] for them to be quiet and described how the Lord had brought him out of prison. "Tell James [g] and the other brothers and sisters [h] about this," he said, and then he left for another place.

11:28 [f] Ac 18:2
11:29 [g] S ver 26
[h] Ro 15:26; 2Co 8:1-4; 9:2 [i] ver 1,12; S Ac 1:16
11:30 [j] Ac 14:23; 15:2,22; 20:17; 1Ti 5:17; Tit 1:5; Jas 5:14; 1Pe 5:1; 2Jn 1 [k] S Ac 4:36 [l] Ac 12:25
12:1 [m] S Mt 14:1
12:2 [n] S Mt 4:21 [o] Mk 10:39
12:3 [p] Ac 24:27; 25:9 [q] Ex 12:15; 23:15; Ac 20:6
12:4 [r] S Jn 11:55
12:5 [s] S Ac 1:14; Ro 15:30,31; Eph 6:18
12:6 [t] Ac 21:33
12:7 [u] Ac 5:19 [v] Ps 107:14; Ac 16:26
12:9 [w] S Ac 9:10
12:10 [x] Ac 5:19; 16:26
12:11 [y] Lk 15:17 [z] Ps 34:7; Da 3:28; 6:22; 2Co 1:10; 2Pe 2:9
12:12 [a] ver 25; Ac 13:5,13; 15:37,39; Col 4:10; 2Ti 4:11; Phm 24; 1Pe 5:13 [b] ver 5
12:13 [c] Jn 18:16,17
12:14 [d] Lk 24:41
12:15 [e] S Mt 18:10
12:17 [f] Ac 13:16; 19:33; 21:40 [g] S Ac 15:13 [h] S Ac 1:16

11:29 *as each one was able.* Cf. 2Co 8:3.

11:30 *elders.* First reference to them in Acts (see notes on 1Ti 3:1; 5:17). Since the apostles are not mentioned, they may have been absent from Jerusalem at this time.

C **12:1** *about this time.* Some hold that the events recorded in ch. 12 group together matters concerning Herod Agrippa I (see below; see also chart, p. 1608) and may not be in strict chronological order. For example, the arrival of Barnabas and Saul in Jerusalem (11:30) may have followed Herod's persecution and Peter's release from prison. Since the date of Herod's death was A.D. 44, these events would probably have occurred in 43. According to this view, the famine of 11:28 occurred c. 46, following Herod's death (v. 23). Others hold that such juggling of events is not necessary. Thus the relief gift of 11:30 came before Herod's death in 44, and the return of Barnabas and Saul (v. 25) followed Herod's death. According to the former view, the Jerusalem visit of Gal 2:1–10 was the famine visit of v. 25; 11:30. According to the latter view, the Gal 2:1 visit was the Jerusalem council visit of 15:1–29 (see chart, pp. 1854–1855). *King Herod.* Agrippa I, grandson of Herod the Great (see notes on Mt 2:1; 14:1) and son of Aristobulus. He was a nephew of Herod Antipas, who had beheaded John the Baptist (Mt 14:3–12) and had tried Jesus (Lk 23:8–12). When Antipas was exiled, Agrippa received his tetrarchy, as well as those of Philip and Lysanias (see Lk 3:1 and note). In A.D. 41 Judea and Samaria were added to his realm.

C **12:2** *James.* Brother of John the apostle and son of Zebedee (Mt 4:21). This event took place about ten years after Jesus' death and resurrection. Jesus had warned them of their coming

suffering (Mt 20:20–23). *death with the sword.* Beheaded, like John the Baptist.

12:3 *Festival of Unleavened Bread.* See notes on Mk 14:1; Lk 22:1.

12:4 *four squads.* One company of four soldiers for each of the four watches of the night (see note on Mt 14:25). *Passover.* Another way of referring to the whole week of the festival (see note on Lk 22:1).

12:7 *angel of the Lord.* See note on 5:19. *a light shone.* Reflecting the glory of the Lord (see 7:55 and note).

12:9 *prison.* Probably the tower of Antonia, located at the northwest corner of the temple—the "barracks" where Paul was later held (see 21:34).

C **12:12** *Mary.* The aunt of Barnabas (see Col 4:10). Apparently her home was a gathering place for Christians. It may have been the location of the upper room where the Last Supper was held (see Mk 14:13–15; see also Ac 1:13 and note) and the place of prayer in 4:31. *John . . . Mark.* See note on v. 25.

12:13 *Rhoda.* A hired servant, but in sympathy with the family and the church.

12:15 *his angel.* Reflects the belief that everyone has a personal angel who ministers to them (cf. Mt 18:10 and note; Heb 1:14).

A **12:16** *they were astonished.* Though they had been "earnestly praying to God for him" (v. 5).

C **12:17** *James.* The Lord's brother, a leader in the Jerusalem church (see Gal 1:19 and note). James, the brother of John, had been killed (see v. 2).

12:19 *i* Ac 16:27
j S Ac 8:40
12:20 *k* S Mt 11:21
l Ac 15:9,11; Eze 27:17
12:23 *m* S Ac 5:19
n 1Sa 25:38;
2Sa 24:16,17;
2Ki 19:35
12:24 *o* S Heb 4:12
p Ac 6:7; 19:20
12:25 *q* S Ac 4:36
r Ac 11:30 *s* S ver 12
13:1 *t* S Ac 11:19
u S Ac 11:27
v S Eph 4:11
w S Ac 4:36
x S Mt 27:32
y S Mt 14:1
13:2 *z* S Ac 8:29
a Ac 14:26 *b* Ac 9:15;
22:21
13:3 *c* S Ac 6:6
d Ac 14:26
13:4 *e* ver 2,3
f Ac 4:36
13:5 *g* S Heb 4:12
h S Ac 9:20
i S Ac 12:12

¹⁸In the morning, there was no small commotion among the soldiers as to what had become of Peter. ¹⁹After Herod had a thorough search made for him and did not find him, he cross-examined the guards and ordered that they be executed. *i*

HEROD'S DEATH

Then Herod went from Judea to Caesarea *j* and stayed there. ²⁰He had been quarreling with the people of Tyre and Sidon; *k* they now joined together and sought an audience with him. Having secured the support of Blastus, a trusted personal servant of the king, they asked for peace, because they depended on the king's country for their food supply. *l*

²¹On the appointed day Herod, wearing his royal robes, sat on his throne and delivered a public address to the people. ²²They shouted, "This is the voice of a god, not of a mere mortal." ²³Immediately, because Herod did not give praise to God, an angel *m* of the Lord struck him down, *n* and he was eaten by worms and died.

²⁴But the word of God *o* continued to increase and spread. *p*

BARNABAS AND SAUL SENT OFF

²⁵When Barnabas *q* and Saul had finished their mission, *r* they returned from *a* Jerusalem, taking with them John, also called Mark. *s* **13** ¹Now in the church at Antioch *t* there were prophets *u* and teachers: *v* Barnabas, *w* Simeon called Niger, Lucius of Cyrene, *x* Manaen (who had been brought up with Herod *y* the tetrarch) and Saul. ²While they were worshiping the Lord and fasting, the Holy Spirit said, *z* "Set apart for me Barnabas and Saul for the work *a* to which I have called them." *b* ³So after they had fasted and prayed, they placed their hands on them *c* and sent them off. *d*

ON CYPRUS

⁴The two of them, sent on their way by the Holy Spirit, *e* went down to Seleucia and sailed from there to Cyprus. *f* ⁵When they arrived at Salamis, they proclaimed the word of God *g* in the Jewish synagogues. *h* John *i* was with them as their helper.

⁶They traveled through the whole island until they came to Paphos. There they met a

a 25 Some manuscripts *to*

12:19 *Caesarea.* Not only a headquarters for Roman governors, but Agrippa used it as his capital when no governors were assigned to Judea (see notes on 8:40; 10:1).

12:20 *Tyre and Sidon.* The leading cities of Phoenicia (Lebanon today). They were dependent on the grainfields of Galilee for their food. *Blastus.* The treasurer; not otherwise known.

12:21 *On the appointed day.* A festival Herod was celebrating in honor of Claudius Caesar (Josephus, *Antiquities,* 19.8.2). *wearing his royal robes.* The historian Josephus describes a silver robe, dazzling bright, that Herod wore that day. When people acclaimed him a god, he did not deny it. He was seized with violent pains, was carried out and died five days later (Josephus, *Antiquities,* 19.8.2).

12:23 *angel of the Lord.* See note on v. 7. *eaten by worms.* A miserable death associated with Herod's acceptance of acclaim for divinity, but may also be seen as divine retribution for his persecution of the church.

12:24 *the word of God ... spread.* Third summary report of progress (see 6:7; 9:31). Three more follow (16:5; 19:20; 28:31).

12:25 *John ... Mark.* See v. 12. He was perhaps the young man who fled on the night of Jesus' arrest (Mk 14:51–52). He wrote the second Gospel (see Introduction to Mark: Author; John Mark in the NT) and accompanied Barnabas and Saul on the first part of their first missionary journey (see notes on 15:38–39).

13:1 *prophets.* See note on 11:27. The special gift of inspiration experienced by OT prophets (Dt 18:18–20; 2Pe 1:21) was known in the NT as well (2:17–18; 1Co 14:29–32; Eph 3:5). The prophets are second to the apostles in Paul's lists (1Co 12:28–29; Eph 2:20; 4:11; but cf. Lk 11:49; Ro 12:6; 1Co 12:10). *teachers.* See 11:26; 15:35; 18:11; 20:20; 28:31; 1Co 12:28–29; Eph 4:11. *Barnabas ... Saul.* The church leaders at Antioch, perhaps listed in the order of their importance. *Barnabas.* See note on 4:36. He was sent originally to Antioch by the church in Jeru-

salem (11:22), had recently returned from taking alms to Jerusalem (12:25) and was a recognized leader in the church at Antioch. *Simeon called Niger.* "Simeon" suggests Jewish background; in that case, Niger (Latin for "black") may indicate his dark complexion. *Lucius of Cyrene.* Lucius is a Latin name. In the second group of preachers coming to Antioch, some were from Cyrene (11:20), capital of Libya (see 6:9 and note). *Manaen.* In Hebrew, Menahem. He was the foster brother or intimate friend of Herod Antipas.

13:2 *worshiping the Lord and fasting.* Paul's first missionary journey did not result from a planning session but from the Spirit's initiative as the leaders worshiped (see v. 4). The communication from the Holy Spirit may have come through the prophets.

13:3 *placed their hands on them.* For the purpose of separating the two for the designated work (see 14:26 for the completion of the mission). Fasting and prayer accompany this appointment (see 14:23; cf. Lk 2:37).

13:4—14:28 Paul's first missionary journey (see map, p. 1863).

13:4 See map No. 13 at the end of this study Bible. *Seleucia.* The seaport of Antioch (16 miles to the west, and 5 miles upstream from the mouth of the Orontes River). *Cyprus.* Many Jews lived there, and the gospel had already been preached there (11:19–20; see note on 11:19).

13:5 *Salamis.* A town on the east coast of the central plain of Cyprus, near modern Famagusta. *John.* John Mark, a cousin of Barnabas (see 12:25; Col 4:10 and note). *helper.* In what way we are not told. Some hold that he served as a catechist for new converts, but Luke seems to use the term in a broader sense (see 26:16; Lk 1:2 ["servants"]).

13:6 *Paphos.* At the western end of Cyprus, nearly 100 miles from Salamis. It was the headquarters for Roman rule. *Bar-Jesus.* "Bar" is Aramaic for "son of"; "Jesus" is derived from the Greek for "Joshua" (see TNIV text note on Mt 1:21).

THE SPREAD OF THE GOSPEL

1. By A.D. 35

Capernaum
Caesarea
Samaria
Joppa
Lydda
Jerusalem

Miles 10 5 0 10 20
Kms 10 5 0 10 20 30

2. By A.D. 40

Tarsus
Antioch
CYPRUS
Salamis
Paphos
Sidon
Tyre
Jerusalem

Miles 0 50 100 150 200
Kms 0 50 100 150 200 250 300

3.
By A.D. 48
Paul's First
Missionary Journey

Troas
Ephesus Laodicea
Miletus Colossae
Pisidian Antioch
Iconium
Lystra
Derbe
CYPRUS

Miles 0 50 100 150 200
Kms 0 50 100 150 200 250 300

4.
By A.D. 52
Paul's
Second
and Third
Missionary
Journeys

Philippi
Thessalonica
Berea
Troas
Athens
Corinth
Ephesus
CRETE

Miles 0 50 100
Kms 0 50 100 150 200

5. By A.D. 60
Paul's Trip
to Rome

Rome
Puteoli
Rheglum
SICILY
Syracuse

Miles 0 50 100
Kms 0 50 100 150

13:6 / Ac 8:9
ᵏ S Mt 7:15
13:7 ˡ ver 8,12;
Ac 18:12; 19:38
13:8 ᵐ Ac 8:9
ⁿ S ver 7 ᵒ Isa 30:11;
Ac 6:7
13:9 ᵖ S Lk 1:15
13:10 ᵍ Mt 13:38;
Jn 8:44 ʳ Hos 14:9
13:11 ˢ Ex 9:3;
1Sa 5:6,7; Ps 32:4
ᵗ Ge 19:10,11; 2Ki 6:18
13:12 ᵘ S ver 7
13:13 ᵛ ver 6
ʷ S Ac 2:10
ˣ S Ac 12:12
13:14 ʸ Ac 14:19,21
ᶻ ver 27,42,44;
Ac 16:13; 18:4
ᵃ S Ac 9:20
13:15 ᵇ Ac 15:21
13:16 ᶜ S Ac 12:17
13:17 ᵈ Ex 6:6,7;
Dt 7:6-8
13:18 ᵉ Dt 1:31
ᶠ Nu 14:33; Ps 95:10;
Ac 7:36
13:19 ᵍ Dt 7:1
ʰ Jos 19:51; Ac 7:45
ⁱ Ps 78:55
13:20 ʲ Jdg 2:16
ᵏ 1Sa 3:19,20; Ac 3:24
13:21 ˡ 1Sa 8:5,19
ᵐ 1Sa 10:1 ⁿ 1Sa 9:1,2
13:22 ᵒ 1Sa 15:23,
26 ᵖ 1Sa 16:13;
Ps 89:20 ᵍ 1Sa 13:14;
Jer 3:15 ʳ Isa 44:28
13:23 ˢ S Mt 1:1
ᵗ S Lk 2:11 ᵘ Mt 1:21
ᵛ ver 32; 2Sa 7:11;
22:51; Jer 30:9

Jewish sorcerer ʲ and false prophet ᵏ named Bar-Jesus, ⁷who was an attendant of the proconsul, ˡ Sergius Paulus. The proconsul, an intelligent man, sent for Barnabas and Saul because he wanted to hear the word of God. ⁸But Elymas the sorcerer ᵐ (for that is what his name means) opposed them and tried to turn the proconsul ⁿ from the faith. ᵒ ⁹Then Saul, who was also called Paul, filled with the Holy Spirit, ᵖ looked straight at Elymas and said, ¹⁰"You are a child of the devil ᵍ and an enemy of everything that is right! You are full of all kinds of deceit and trickery. Will you never stop perverting the right ways of the Lord? ʳ ¹¹Now the hand of the Lord is against you. ˢ You are going to be blind for a time, not even able to see the light of the sun." ᵗ

Immediately mist and darkness came over him, and he groped about, seeking someone to lead him by the hand. ¹²When the proconsul ᵘ saw what had happened, he believed, for he was amazed at the teaching about the Lord.

IN PISIDIAN ANTIOCH

¹³From Paphos, ᵛ Paul and his companions sailed to Perga in Pamphylia, ʷ where John ˣ left them to return to Jerusalem. ¹⁴From Perga they went on to Pisidian Antioch. ʸ On the Sabbath ᶻ they entered the synagogue ᵃ and sat down. ¹⁵After the reading from the Law ᵇ and the Prophets, the leaders of the synagogue sent word to them, saying, "Brothers, if you have a word of exhortation for the people, please speak."

¹⁶Standing up, Paul motioned with his hand ᶜ and said: "People of Israel and you Gentiles who worship God, listen to me! ¹⁷The God of the people of Israel chose our ancestors; he made the people prosper during their stay in Egypt; with mighty power he led them out of that country; ᵈ ¹⁸for about forty years he endured their conduct ᵃ ᵉ in the wilderness; ᶠ ¹⁹and he overthrew seven nations in Canaan, ᵍ giving their land to his people ʰ as their inheritance. ⁱ ²⁰All this took about 450 years.

"After this, God gave them judges ʲ until the time of Samuel the prophet. ᵏ ²¹Then the people asked for a king, ˡ and he gave them Saul ᵐ son of Kish, of the tribe of Benjamin, ⁿ who ruled forty years. ²²After removing Saul, ᵒ he made David their king. ᵖ God testified concerning him: 'I have found David son of Jesse, a man after my own heart; ᵍ he will do everything I want him to do.' ʳ

²³"From this man's descendants ˢ God has brought to Israel the Savior ᵗ Jesus, ᵘ as he promised. ᵛ ²⁴Before the coming of Jesus, John preached repentance and baptism to all the

---

ᵃ 18 Some manuscripts *he cared for them*

13:7 *proconsul.* Since Cyprus was a Roman senatorial province, a proconsul was assigned to it. *Sergius Paulus.* See chart, p. 1830.
13:8 *Elymas.* A Semitic name meaning "sorcerer" or "magician" or "wise man" (probably a self-assumed designation).

13:9 *Saul ... called Paul.* The names mean "asked [of God]" and "little" respectively. It was customary to have a given name, in this case Saul (Hebrew, Jewish background), and a later name, in this case Paul (Roman, Hellenistic background). From now on Saul is called Paul in Acts. This may be due to Saul's success in preaching to Paulus or to the fact that he is now entering the Gentile phase of his ministry. The order in which they are mentioned now changes from "Barnabas and Saul" to "Paul and Barnabas." Upon their return to the Jerusalem church, however, the order reverts to "Barnabas and Paul" (15:12).
13:11 *hand of the Lord.* See note on 11:21. *You are going to be blind.* Cf. Paul's experience in 9:8–18.
13:12 *he believed.* He was convinced by the miracle and the message.

13:13 *Perga in Pamphylia.* Perga was the capital of Pamphylia, a coastal province of Asia Minor between the provinces of Lycia and Cilicia, and was 5 miles inland and 12 miles east of the important seaport Attalia (see map, p. 1863). *John left them.* See 12:25 and note. Homesickness to get back to Jerusalem, an illness of Paul necessitating a change in plans and a trip to Galatia, and a change in leadership from Barnabas to Paul have all been suggested as reasons for John Mark's return. Paul's dissatisfaction with his departure is noted later (15:37–39).
13:14–41 Paul and Barnabas in the synagogue of Pisidian An-

tioch. For another account of a synagogue service, see Lk 4:16–21.
13:14 *Pisidian.* See note on 14:24. *Antioch.* Named after Antiochus, king of Syria after the death of Alexander the Great. It was 110 miles from Perga, 3,600 feet above sea level and at the hub of good roads and trade. The city had a large Jewish population. It was a Roman colony, which meant that a contingent of retired military men was settled there. They were given free land and were made citizens of the city of Rome, with all the accompanying privileges. *synagogue.* Paul's regular practice was to begin his preaching in the synagogue, as long as the Jews would allow it (see v. 5; 14:1; 17:1,10,17; 18:4,19; 19:8). His reason for doing so was grounded in his understanding of God's redemptive plan (see v. 46; Ro 1:16 and note; 2:9–10 and note on 2:9; see also Ro 9–11). He was not neglecting his Gentile mission, for the God-fearers ("Gentiles who worship God," v. 16; see note on 10:2) were part of the audience. Moreover, the synagogue provided a ready-made preaching situation with a building, regularly scheduled meetings and a people who knew the OT Scriptures. It was customary to invite visitors, and especially visiting rabbis (such as Paul), to address the gathering.
13:15 *the Law and the Prophets.* Sections from the OT were read, followed by exposition and exhortation. *leaders of the synagogue.* See Introduction to Hebrews: Literary Form. *word of exhortation.* See note on Mk 5:22. *word of exhortation.* See Introduction to Hebrews: Literary Form.
13:20 *about 450 years.* The 400 years of the "stay in Egypt" (v. 17; see note on 7:6) plus the 40 years in the wilderness and the time between the crossing of the Jordan and the distribution of the land (see Jos 14–19).
13:23 *as he promised.* See, e.g., Isa 11:1–16.

people of Israel. *w* 25As John was completing his work, *x* he said: 'Who do you suppose I am? I am not the one you are looking for. *y* But there is someone coming after me whose sandals I am not worthy to untie.' *z*

26"Brothers and sisters *a* from the children of Abraham *b* and you God-fearing Gentiles, it is to us that this message of salvation *c* has been sent. 27The people of Jerusalem and their rulers did not recognize Jesus, *d* yet in condemning him they fulfilled the words of the prophets *e* that are read every Sabbath. 28Though they found no proper ground for a death sentence, they asked Pilate to have him executed. *f* 29When they had carried out all that was written about him, *g* they took him down from the cross *h* and laid him in a tomb. *i* 30But God raised him from the dead, *j* 31and for many days he was seen by those who had traveled with him from Galilee to Jerusalem. *k* They are now his witnesses *l* to our people.

32"We tell you the good news: *m* What God promised our ancestors *n* 33he has fulfilled for us, their children, by raising up Jesus. *o* As it is written in the second Psalm:

" 'You are my son;
today I have become your father.' *a* *p*

34God raised him from the dead so that he will never be subject to decay. As God has said,

" 'I will give you the holy and sure blessings promised to David.' *b* *q*

35So it is also stated elsewhere:

" 'You will not let your holy one see decay.' *c* *r*

36"Now when David had served God's purpose in his own generation, he fell asleep; *s* he was buried with his ancestors *t* and his body decayed. 37But the one whom God raised from the dead *u* did not see decay.

38"Therefore, my brothers and sisters, I want you to know that through Jesus the forgiveness of sins is proclaimed to you. *v* 39Through him everyone who believes *w* is set free

a 33 Psalm 2:7   *b 34* Isaiah 55:3   *c 35* Psalm 16:10 (see Septuagint)

13:25 *John . . . said.* See Mt 3:11; Mk 1:7; Lk 3:16; Jn 1:20,27.
13:26 *God-fearing Gentiles.* See note on v. 14.
13:28 *no proper ground for a death sentence.* Cf. Jn 19:4 and note.
13:29–31 *cross . . . tomb . . . God raised . . . witnesses.* See note on 3:15.

13:31 *many days.* Forty days (see 1:3).
13:33 *today I have become your father.* Here refers to the resurrection of Jesus (see TNIV text note here and note on Ps 2:7–9; cf. Ro 1:4).
13:35 *not let your holy one see decay.* Quoted also in Peter's sermon at Pentecost (see notes on 2:27; Ps 16:10).

13:24 *w* S Mk 1:4
13:25 *x* Ac 20:24
y Jn 1:20 *z* Mt 3:11;
Jn 1:27
13:26 *a* S Ac 22:5
b S Lk 3:8 *c* Ac 4:12;
28:28
13:27 *d* Ac 3:17
e S Lk 24:27;
S Mt 1:22
13:28 *f* Mt 27:20-
25; Ac 3:14
13:29 *g* S Mt 1:22;
Lk 18:31 *h* S Ac 5:30
i Lk 23:53
13:30 *j* S Mt 16:21;
28:6; S Ac 2:24
13:31 *k* Mt 28:16
l S Lk 24:48
13:32 *m* Isa 40:9;
52:7; Ac 5:42; 8:35;
10:36; 14:7,15,21;
17:18 *n* Ac 26:6;
Ro 1:2; 4:13; 9:4
13:33 *o* S Ac 2:24
p Ps 2:7; S Mt 3:17
13:34 *q* Isa 55:3
13:35 *r* Ps 16:10;
Ac 2:27
13:36 *s* S Mt 9:24
t 2Sa 7:12; 1Ki 2:10;
2Ch 29:28; Ac 2:29
13:37 *u* S Ac 2:24
13:38 *v* S Lk 24:47;
Ac 2:38
13:39 *w* S Jn 3:15

PAUL'S FIRST MISSIONARY JOURNEY

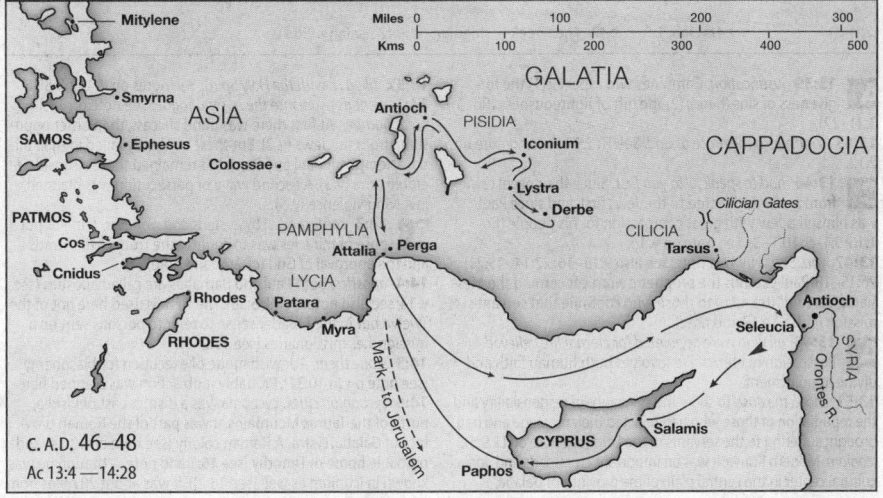

C. A.D. 46–48
Ac 13:4 —14:28

13:39 ˣ S Ro 3:28
13:41 ʸ Hab 1:5
13:42 ᶻ ver 14
13:43 ᵃ S Ac 11:23;
14:22; S Ro 3:24
13:45 ᵇ S 1Th 2:16
ᶜ Ac 18:6; 1Pe 4:4;
Jude 10
13:46 ᵈ ver 26;
Ac 3:26 ᵉ Mt 21:41;
Ac 18:6; 22:21; 26:20;
28:28; Ro 11:11
13:47 ᶠ S Lk 2:32
ᵍ Isa 49:6
13:48 ʰ ver 49;
Ac 8:25; 15:35,36;
19:10,20
13:49 ⁱ S ver 48
13:50 ʲ S 1Th 2:16
13:51 ᵏ S Mt 10:14
ˡ Ac 14:1,19,21; 16:2;
2Ti 3:11
13:52 ᵐ S Ac 11:26
ⁿ S Lk 1:15
14:1 ᵒ S Ac 13:51
ᵖ S Ac 9:20
�qᵍ S Ac 2:41
14:2 ʳ S Ac 1:16
14:3 ˢ S Ac 4:29
ᵗ S Jn 4:48
14:4 ᵘ Ac 17:4,5;
28:24
14:5 ᵛ S Ac 20:3
ʷ ver 19
14:6 ˣ Mt 10:23
14:7 ʸ Ac 16:10
ᶻ ver 15,21; S Ac 13:32

from every sin, a justification you were not able to obtain under the law of Moses. ˣ ⁴⁰Take care that what the prophets have said does not happen to you:

⁴¹ " 'Look, you scoffers,
　　wonder and perish,
for I am going to do something in your days
　　that you would never believe,
　　even if someone told you.'ᵃⁿ ʸ

⁴²As Paul and Barnabas were leaving the synagogue, ᶻ the people invited them to speak further about these things on the next Sabbath. ⁴³When the congregation was dismissed, many of the Jews and devout converts to Judaism followed Paul and Barnabas, who talked with them and urged them to continue in the grace of God. ᵃ

⁴⁴On the next Sabbath almost the whole city gathered to hear the word of the Lord. ⁴⁵When the Jews saw the crowds, they were filled with jealousy. They began to contradict what Paul was saying ᵇ and heaped abuse ᶜ on him.

⁴⁶Then Paul and Barnabas answered them boldly: "We had to speak the word of God to you first. ᵈ Since you reject it and do not consider yourselves worthy of eternal life, we now turn to the Gentiles. ᵉ ⁴⁷For this is what the Lord has commanded us:

" 'I have made you ᵇ a light for the Gentiles, ᶠ
　　that you ᵇ may bring salvation to the ends of the earth.'ᶜⁿ ᵍ

⁴⁸When the Gentiles heard this, they were glad and honored the word of the Lord; ʰ and all who were appointed for eternal life believed.

⁴⁹The word of the Lord ⁱ spread through the whole region. ⁵⁰But the Jewish leaders incited the God-fearing women of high standing and the leading men of the city. They stirred up persecution against Paul and Barnabas, and expelled them from their region.ʲ ⁵¹So they shook the dust off their feet ᵏ as a warning to them and went to Iconium. ˡ ⁵²And the disciples ᵐ were filled with joy and with the Holy Spirit. ⁿ

IN ICONIUM

14 At Iconium ᵒ Paul and Barnabas went as usual into the Jewish synagogue. ᵖ There they spoke so effectively that a great number �q of Jews and Greeks believed. ²But the Jews who refused to believe stirred up the other Gentiles and poisoned their minds against the brothers. ʳ ³So Paul and Barnabas spent considerable time there, speaking boldly ˢ for the Lord, who confirmed the message of his grace by enabling them to perform signs and wonders. ᵗ ⁴The people of the city were divided; some sided with the Jews, others with the apostles. ᵘ ⁵There was a plot afoot among both Gentiles and Jews, ᵛ together with their leaders, to mistreat them and stone them. ʷ ⁶But they found out about it and fled ˣ to the Lycaonian cities of Lystra and Derbe and to the surrounding country, ⁷where they continued to preach ʸ the gospel. ᶻ

ᵃ 41 Hab. 1:5　　ᵇ 47 The Greek is singular.　　ᶜ 47 Isaiah 49:6

13:39 *justification.* Combines two aspects: (1) the forgiveness of sins (here); (2) the gift of righteousness (Ro 3:21–22).

13:43 *continue in the grace of God.* See Tit 2:11–12 and note on 2:12.

13:46 *had to speak ... to you first.* Since the gospel came from and was directed to the Jews first, and since Paul was himself a Jew with great compassion for his people (Ro 1:16; 9:1–5; 10:1–3). See note on v. 14.

13:47 *you.* See TNIV text note; see also 9:15–16; 22:14–15,21; 26:15–18. Paul extends the prophetic word concerning the Messianic "servant" (Isa 49:6) to those who continue that servant's mission (cf. Isa 54:17 and note).

13:48 *all who were appointed for eternal life believed.* Possession of eternal life involves both human faith and divine appointment.

13:51 *shook the dust.* To show the severance of responsibility and the repudiation of those who had rejected their message and had brought suffering to the servants of the Lord (see note on Lk 9:5). *Iconium.* Modern Konya; it was an important crossroads and agricultural center in the central plain of the province of Galatia.

13:52 *filled ... with the Holy Spirit.* See notes on 2:4; Eph 5:18.

14:1 *went as usual into the ... synagogue.* See note on 13:14. *great number.* At first there was good success, then bitter opposition from the Jews (v. 2). But these evidently failed in their initial attempt, for Paul and Barnabas remained there a considerable time (v. 3). A second wave of persecution was planned, involving violence (v. 5).

14:3 *confirmed ... by ... signs and wonders.* A major purpose of miracles was to confirm the truth of the words and the approval of God (cf. 2:22 and note).

14:4 *apostles.* Both Paul and Barnabas are called apostles (see v. 14; see also note on Mk 6:30). The term is used here not of the Twelve but in the broader sense to refer to persons sent on a mission, i.e., missionaries (see 13:2–3).

14:5 *stone them.* A Jewish mode of execution for blasphemy (see note on Jn 10:31). Probably mob action was planned here.

14:6 *Lycaonian cities.* Lycaonia was a district east of Pisidia, north of the Taurus Mountains. It was part of the Roman province of Galatia. *Lystra.* A Roman colony (see note on 13:14) and probable home of Timothy (see 16:1 and note—though he was known in Iconium as well [see 16:2]), it was about 20 miles from

IN LYSTRA AND DERBE

[8]In Lystra there sat a man who was lame. He had been that way from birth [a] and had never walked. [9]He listened to Paul as he was speaking. Paul looked directly at him, saw that he had faith to be healed [b] [10]and called out, "Stand up on your feet!" [c] At that, the man jumped up and began to walk. [d]

[11]When the crowd saw what Paul had done, they shouted in the Lycaonian language, "The gods have come down to us in human form!" [e] [12]Barnabas they called Zeus, and Paul they called Hermes because he was the chief speaker. [f] [13]The priest of Zeus, whose temple was just outside the city, brought bulls and wreaths to the city gates because he and the crowd wanted to offer sacrifices to them.

[14]But when the apostles Barnabas and Paul heard of this, they tore their clothes [g] and rushed out into the crowd, shouting: [15]"Friends, why are you doing this? We too are only human, [h] like you. We are bringing you good news, [i] telling you to turn from these worthless things [j] to the living God, [k] who made heaven and earth [l] and sea and everything in them. [m] [16]In the past, he let [n] all nations go their own way. [o] [17]Yet he has not left himself without testimony: [p] He has shown kindness by giving you rain from heaven and crops in their seasons; [q] he provides you with plenty of food and fills your hearts with joy." [r] [18]Even with these words, they had difficulty keeping the crowd from sacrificing to them.

[19]Then some Jews [s] came from Antioch and Iconium [t] and won the crowd over. They stoned Paul [u] and dragged him outside the city, thinking he was dead. [20]But after the disciples [v] had gathered around him, he got up and went back into the city. The next day he and Barnabas left for Derbe.

THE RETURN TO ANTIOCH IN SYRIA

[21]They preached the gospel [w] in that city and won a large number [x] of disciples. Then they returned to Lystra, Iconium [y] and Antioch, [22]strengthening the disciples and encouraging them to remain true to the faith. [z] "We must go through many hardships [a] to enter the kingdom of God," they said. [23]Paul and Barnabas appointed elders [a] [b] for them in each church and, with prayer and fasting, [c] committed them to the Lord, [d] in whom they had put their trust. [24]After going through Pisidia, they came into Pamphylia, [e] [25]and when they had preached the word in Perga, they went down to Attalia.

[26]From Attalia they sailed back to Antioch, [f] where they had been committed to the grace of God [g] for the work they had now completed. [h] [27]On arriving there, they gathered the church together and reported all that God had done through them [i] and how he

---

[a] 23 Or Barnabas ordained elders; or Barnabas had elders elected

---

Iconium and 130 miles from Antioch. *Derbe.* About 60 miles from Lystra; home of Gaius (see 20:4 and note on 14:20).
14:12 *Zeus…Hermes.* Zeus was the patron god of Lystra, and his temple was there. People who had come to bring sacrifices to Zeus apparently decided to make an offering to Paul and Barnabas instead. The identification of Zeus with Barnabas may indicate that his appearance was more imposing, and Paul was identified as the god Hermes (the Roman Mercury) because he was the spokesman (see 28:6). This incident may have been occasioned by an ancient legend that told of a supposed visit to the same general area by Zeus and Hermes. The two were, however, not recognized by anyone except an old couple. So the people of Lystra were determined not to allow such an oversight to happen again.
14:13 *city gates.* The Greek for this expression can refer to the temple gates, the city gates or house gates.
14:14 *tore their clothes.* A Jewish way of expressing great anguish (see Ge 37:29,34 and note on 37:34).
14:15 *worthless things.* Used in the OT to denote false gods (see 1Sa 12:21).
14:16 See 17:30 and note.
14:19 *They stoned Paul.* Inside the city rather than at the usual place of execution outside the walls (7:58; see Gal 6:17 and note).
B 14:20 *disciples had gathered around him.* Young Timothy may have been present (see 2Ti 3:10–11 and note on 3:11). *got up…next day…left.* Luke's description of Paul's quick

recovery from stoning suggests a miracle (cf. 28:5–6). *Derbe.* A border town in the southeastern part of the Lycaonian region of Galatia (see note on v. 6). An inscription naming the city has been discovered about 30 miles east of what was previously thought to be the city site.
14:21 *they returned.* Not by the shorter route through the Taurus Mountains but to the cities where they had established churches (see v. 22).
14:22 *many hardships.* See Php 1:29 and note.
14:23 *appointed.* The Greek for this word (used also in 2Co 8:19) can mean (1) to stretch out the hand, (2) to appoint by show of hands or (3) to appoint or elect without regard to the method. In 6:6 the appointment of the Seven included selection by the church and presentation to the apostles, who prayed and laid their hands on them. Because these were new churches, at least partly pagan in background, Paul and Barnabas may have both selected and appointed the elders.
14:24 *Pisidia.* A district about 120 miles long and 50 miles wide, north of Pamphylia (13:13–14). Bandits frequented the region (see perhaps 2Co 11:26). *Pamphylia.* A district 80 miles long and 20 miles at the widest part, on the southern coast of Asia Minor. After A.D. 74 Pisidia was included in the Roman province of Pamphylia (see 13:13).
14:25 *Perga.* See note on 13:13. *Attalia.* The best harbor on the coast of Pamphylia (see 13:13).
14:26 *Antioch.* See 11:20; see also note on 11:19.

14:8 [a] Ac 3:2
14:9 [b] Mt 9:28,29; 13:58
14:10 [c] Eze 2:1 [d] Ac 3:8
14:11 [e] Ac 8:10; 28:6
14:12 [f] Ex 7:1
14:14 [g] S Mk 14:63
14:15 [h] S Ac 10:26 [i] ver 7,21; S Ac 13:32 [j] 1Sa 12:21; 1Th 1:9 [k] S Mt 16:16 [l] Ge 1:1 [m] Ps 146:6; Rev 14:7
14:16 [n] Ac 17:30 [o] Ps 81:12; Mic 4:5
14:17 [p] Ro 1:20 [q] Dt 11:14; Job 5:10; Ps 65:10 [r] Ps 4:7
14:19 [s] Ac 13:45 [t] S Ac 13:51 [u] 2Co 11:25; 2Ti 3:11
14:20 [v] ver 22,28; S Ac 11:26
14:21 [w] S Ac 13:32 [x] S Ac 2:41 [y] S Ac 13:51
14:22 [z] Ac 11:23; 13:43 [a] Jn 16:33; 1Th 3:3; 2Ti 3:12
14:23 [b] S Ac 11:30 [c] Ac 13:3 [d] Ac 20:32
14:24 [e] S Ac 2:10
14:26 [f] S Ac 11:19 [g] S Ac 11:23 [h] Ac 13:1,3
14:27 [i] Ac 15:4,12; 21:19

14:27 /1Co 16:9;
2Co 2:12; Col 4:3;
Rev 3:8
14:28 *k* S Ac 11:26
15:1 /ver 24;
Gal 2:12 *m* S Ac 1:16
n ver 5; Gal 5:2,3
o S Ac 6:14
15:2 *p* Gal 2:2
q S Ac 11:30
15:3 *r* Ac 11:19
s Ac 14:27
15:4 *t* ver 12;
Ac 14:27; 21:19
15:5 *u* Ac 5:17
v Mt 3:7 *w* ver 1
15:7 *x* Ac 10:1-48
15:8 *y* S Rev 2:23
z S Ac 10:44,47
15:9 *a* Ac 10:28,34;
11:12 *b* Ac 10:43
15:10 *c* Ac 5:9
d S Mt 23:4; Gal 5:1
15:11 *e* S Ro 3:24;
Gal 2:16; Eph 2:5-8
15:12 *f* S Jn 4:48
g ver 4; Ac 14:27;
21:19
15:13 *h* Ac 12:17;
21:18; 1Co 15:7;
Gal 1:19; 2:9,12
15:14 /2Pe 1:1

had opened a door *j* of faith to the Gentiles. ²⁸And they stayed there a long time with the disciples. *k*

THE COUNCIL AT JERUSALEM

15 Certain individuals *l* came down from Judea to Antioch and were teaching the believers: *m* "Unless you are circumcised, *n* according to the custom taught by Moses, *o* you cannot be saved." ²This brought Paul and Barnabas into sharp dispute and debate with them. So Paul and Barnabas were appointed, along with some other believers, to go up to Jerusalem *p* to see the apostles and elders *q* about this question. ³The church sent them on their way, and as they traveled through Phoenicia *r* and Samaria, they told how the Gentiles had been converted. *s* This news made all the believers very glad. ⁴When they came to Jerusalem, they were welcomed by the church and the apostles and elders, to whom they reported everything God had done through them. *t*

⁵Then some of the believers who belonged to the party *u* of the Pharisees *v* stood up and said, "The Gentiles must be circumcised and required to keep the law of Moses." *w*

⁶The apostles and elders met to consider this question. ⁷After much discussion, Peter got up and addressed them: "Brothers, you know that some time ago God made a choice among you that the Gentiles might hear from my lips the message of the gospel and believe. *x* ⁸God, who knows the heart, *y* showed that he accepted them by giving the Holy Spirit to them, *z* just as he did to us. ⁹He did not discriminate between us and them, *a* for he purified their hearts by faith. *b* ¹⁰Now then, why do you try to test God *c* by putting on the necks of Gentiles a yoke *d* that neither we nor our ancestors have been able to bear? ¹¹No! We believe it is through the grace *e* of our Lord Jesus that we are saved, just as they are."

¹²The whole assembly became silent as they listened to Barnabas and Paul telling about the signs and wonders *f* God had done among the Gentiles through them. *g* ¹³When they finished, James *h* spoke up. "Brothers," he said, "listen to me. ¹⁴Simon*a* has described to us how God first intervened to choose a people for his name from the Gentiles. *i* ¹⁵The words of the prophets are in agreement with this, as it is written:

¹⁶ " 'After this I will return
    and rebuild David's fallen tent.

a 14 Greek *Simeon*, a variant of *Simon*; that is, Peter

14:27 *opened a door of faith.* God had brought Gentiles to faith—had, as it were, opened the door for them to believe (cf. 11:18).

14:28 *long time.* Probably more than a year.

15:1 *Certain individuals.* Probably from "the party of the Pharisees" (v. 5). These were believers who insisted that before anyone could become a true Christian they must keep the law of Moses, and the test of such compliance was circumcision. *from Judea.* Meant that these Judaizers (or legalists) were given a hearing, not that they correctly represented the apostles and elders of Jerusalem (cf. v. 24).

15:2 *go up to Jerusalem.* See notes on 12:1; Gal 2:1. Those who hold that Gal 2:1–10 refers to the famine visit of 11:27–30 and 12:25 argue that since Gal 2:2 says that the visit mentioned there was occasioned by a revelation, it must refer to Agabus's prediction of the coming famine (11:27–28). Those who believe that Gal 2:1–10 refers to the Jerusalem council visit of 15:1–22 assert that the famine visit occurred at the time of Herod Agrippa's death in A.D. 44 (11:27–30; 12:25). Thus Saul's conversion, which was 14 years earlier (Gal 2:1), would have occurred in 30, the probable year of Christ's crucifixion—which obviously seems too early.

15:4–22 The sequence of meetings described in vv. 4–22 is: (1) a general meeting of welcome and report (vv. 4–5); (2) a meeting of the leaders (perhaps to one side) while the church was still assembled (vv. 6–11); (3) a meeting of the apostles, the elders and the whole assembly (vv. 12–22).

15:4 The first meeting was a report, cordially received, about the work done among the Gentiles.

15:5 *believers who belonged to the party of the Pharisees.* Some Pharisees became Christians and brought their Judaic beliefs with them. They believed that Gentiles must first become converts to Judaism and be circumcised (see v. 1), and then they

would be eligible to be saved by faith. Perhaps some of them had gone to Antioch and now returned to present their case.

15:7 *Peter got up.* After a period of considerable discussion by the apostles and elders, Peter addressed them. *Gentiles might hear.* Peter's argument was his own experience: God had sent him to preach to the Gentiles (see 10:28–29 and note on 10:28).

15:8 *giving the Holy Spirit to them.* The irrefutable proof of God's acceptance (see 10:44,47 and note; 11:17–18).

15:9 *purified their hearts by faith.* Peter's way of saying what Paul affirmed (Ro 5:1; cf. Gal 2:15–16).

15:10 *yoke.* The law (see Gal 5:1 and note; cf. Mt 11:28–29 and notes).

15:11 *through the grace of our Lord.* No circumcision was required. *we are saved, just as they are.* See Ro 3:9.

15:12 *assembly became silent.* See note on vv. 4–22. Apparently the people had remained in place while the apostles and elders met. The assembly had not remained quiet during that time, but now it became silent to listen to the leaders. *Barnabas and Paul.* The order here (see also 13:7; 14:12,14) puts Barnabas first (perhaps reflecting his importance in Jerusalem), whereas in the account of the missionary journey the order was usually "Paul and Barnabas" after the events on the island of Cyprus (13:42–43,46, 50; 14:1,3,20,23). *signs and wonders.* See 8:19–20; 14:3.

15:13 *James.* The Lord's brother (see note on 12:17; see also Introduction to James: Author). His argument added proof from Scripture.

15:14 *Simon.* Peter (see v. 7). James uses Peter's Hebrew name in its Hebrew form (Simeon; see TNIV text note). *a people for his name.* A new community largely made up of Gentiles but including Jews as well (see Jn 10:16 and note; cf. 1Pe 2:9–10).

15:15 *prophets.* Specifically Am 9:11–12 (see TNIV text note on Am 9:12).

Its ruins I will rebuild,
    and I will restore it,
[17] that the rest of humanity may seek the Lord,
    even all the Gentiles who bear my name,
    says the Lord, who does these things'[a][j]—
[18]   things known from long ago.[b][k]

[19]"It is my judgment, therefore, that we should not make it difficult for the Gentiles who are turning to God. [20]Instead we should write to them, telling them to abstain from food polluted by idols,[l] from sexual immorality,[m] from the meat of strangled animals and from blood.[n] [21]For the law of Moses has been preached in every city from the earliest times and is read in the synagogues on every Sabbath."[o]

THE COUNCIL'S LETTER TO GENTILE BELIEVERS

[22]Then the apostles and elders,[p] with the whole church, decided to choose some of their own men and send them to Antioch[q] with Paul and Barnabas. They chose Judas (called Barsabbas) and Silas,[r] who were leaders among the believers. [23]With them they sent the following letter:

The apostles and elders, your brothers,

To the Gentile believers in Antioch,[s] Syria[t] and Cilicia:[u]

Greetings.[v]

[24]We have heard that some went out from us without our authorization and disturbed you, troubling your minds by what they said.[w] [25]So we all agreed to choose some men and send them to you with our dear friends Barnabas and Paul— [26]men who have risked their lives[x] for the name of our Lord Jesus Christ. [27]Therefore we are sending Judas and Silas[y] to confirm by word of mouth what we are writing. [28]It seemed good to the Holy Spirit[z] and to us not to burden you with anything beyond the following requirements: [29]You are to abstain from food sacrificed to idols, from blood, from the meat of strangled animals and from sexual immorality.[a] You will do well to avoid these things.

Farewell.

[30]So they were sent off and went down to Antioch, where they gathered the church together and delivered the letter. [31]The people read it and were glad for its encouraging message. [32]Judas and Silas,[b] who themselves were prophets,[c] said much to encourage and strengthen the believers. [33][34]After spending some time there, they were sent off by

---

[a] 17 Amos 9:11,12 (see Septuagint)   [b] 17,18 Some manuscripts things'— / [18]the Lord's work is known to him from long ago

15:16 *After this I will return.* Some have taken this quotation from Amos as setting forth a sequence of the end times, including (1) the church age (taking out "a people for his name," v. 14), (2) the restoration of Israel as a nation (v. 16) and (3) the final salvation of the Gentiles (vv. 17–18). Others declare that the quotation merely confirms God's intent to save Gentiles.

15:18 *from long ago.* Since OT times (see Ro 15:9 and note).

15:19 *not make it difficult.* Circumcision was not required, but four stipulations were laid down (see note on v. 20). These were in areas where the Gentiles had particular weaknesses and where the Jews were particularly repulsed by Gentile violations. It would help both the individual and the relationship between Gentile and Jew if these requirements were observed. They involved divine directives that the Jews believed were given before the Mosaic laws.

15:20 *food polluted by idols.* See v. 29; 1Co 8:7–13; Rev 2:14, 20. *sexual immorality.* A sin taken too lightly by the Greeks and also associated with certain pagan religious festivals. *meat of strangled animals.* Thus retaining the blood that was forbidden to be eaten (see Ge 9:4). *blood.* Expressly forbidden in Jewish law (see Lev 17:10–12). Reference here may be to consuming blood apart from meat.

15:22 *apostles and elders, with the whole church.* Apparently there was unanimous agreement with the choice of messengers and with the contents of the letter (vv. 23–29). *Judas (called Barsabbas).* The same surname as that of Joseph Barsabbas (see 1:23 and note). The two may have been brothers. *Silas.* A leader in the Jerusalem church, a prophet (v. 32), a Roman citizen (16:37–38) and Paul's companion on his second missionary journey (15:40).

15:23 *in Antioch, Syria and Cilicia.* Antioch was the leading city of the combined provinces of Syria and Cilicia.

15:26 *risked their lives.* See 13:15; 14:2,5,19.

15:28 *seemed good to the Holy Spirit and to us.* Prior authority is given to the Spirit (whose working in the assembly is thus claimed), but there was also agreement among the apostles, elders and brothers (vv. 22–23).

15:29 *abstain from food ... sexual immorality.* See note on v. 20.

15:32 *prophets.* One of the primary functions of prophets in the early church was, as here indicated, to encourage and strengthen believers (see notes on 11:27; 1Co 14:3).

15:33[34] *those who had sent them.* The Jerusalem church (see v. 22). Verse 34 ("But Silas decided to remain there") was inserted by copyists in some late manuscripts to explain Silas's presence at Antioch in v. 40 (but see note there).

15:17 [j] Am 9:11,12
15:18 [k] Isa 45:21
15:20 [l] 1Co 8:7-13; 10:14-28; Rev 2:14,20
[m] 1Co 10:7,8; Rev 2:14,20 [n] ver 29; Ge 9:4; Lev 3:17; 7:26; 17:10-13; 19:26; Dt 12:16,23
15:21 [o] Ac 13:15; 2Co 3:14,15
15:22 [p] S Ac 11:30 [q] S Ac 11:19 [r] ver 27, 32,40; Ac 16:19,25, 29; 2Co 1:19; 1Th 1:1; 2Th 1:1; 1Pe 5:12
15:23 [s] ver 1; S Ac 11:19 [t] S Lk 2:2 [u] ver 41; S Ac 6:9 [v] Ac 23:25,26; Jas 1:1
15:24 [w] ver 1; Gal 1:7; 5:10
15:26 [x] Ac 9:23-25; 14:19; 1Co 15:30
15:27 [y] S ver 22
15:28 [z] Ac 5:32
15:29 [a] ver 20; Ac 21:25
15:32 [b] S ver 22 [c] S Ac 11:27

15:33[34] *d*1Sa 1:17;
Mk 5:34; Lk 7:50;
Ac 16:36; 1Co 16:11
15:35 *e*Ac 8:4
*f*S Ac 13:48
15:36 *g*Ac 13:4,13,
14, 51; 14:1,6,24,25
*h*S Ac 13:48
15:37 *i*S Ac 12:12
15:38 *j*Ac 13:13
15:40 *k*S ver 22
*l*S Ac 11:23
15:41 *m*ver 23;
S Lk 2:2 *n*S Ac 6:9
*o*Ac 16:5
16:1 *p*Ac 14:6
*q*Ac 17:14; 18:5;
19:22; 20:4; Ro 16:21;
1Co 4:17; 16:10;
2Co 1:1,19; Php 1:1;
2:19; Col 1:1; 1Th 1:1;
3:2,6; 2Th 1:1; 1Ti 1:2,
18; 2Ti 1:2,5,6; Phm 1
*r*2Ti 1:5
16:2 *s*ver 40;
S Ac 1:16 *t*S Ac 13:51
16:3 *u*Gal 2:3
16:4 *v*S Ac 11:30
*w*Ac 15:2 *x*Ac 15:28,
29
16:5 *y*Ac 9:31; 15:41
*z*S Ac 2:41
16:6 *a*Ac 2:10; 18:23
*b*Ac 18:23; Gal 1:2;
3:1 *c*S Ac 2:9
16:7 *d*Ro 8:9;
Gal 4:6; Php 1:19;
1Pe 1:11
16:8 *e*ver 11;
Ac 20:5; 2Co 2:12;
2Ti 4:13
16:9 *f*S Ac 9:10
*g*Ac 19:21,29; 20:1,3;
Ro 15:26; 1Co 16:5;
1Th 1:7,8

the believers with the blessing of peace *d* to return to those who had sent them. ³⁵But Paul and Barnabas remained in Antioch, where they and many others taught and preached *e* the word of the Lord. *f*

DISAGREEMENT BETWEEN PAUL AND BARNABAS

³⁶Some time later Paul said to Barnabas, "Let us go back and visit the believers in all the towns *g* where we preached the word of the Lord *h* and see how they are doing." ³⁷Barnabas wanted to take John, also called Mark, *i* with them, ³⁸but Paul did not think it wise to take him, because he had deserted them *j* in Pamphylia and had not continued with them in the work. ³⁹They had such a sharp disagreement that they parted company. Barnabas took Mark and sailed for Cyprus, ⁴⁰but Paul chose Silas *k* and left, commended by the believers to the grace of the Lord. *l* ⁴¹He went through Syria *m* and Cilicia, *n* strengthening the churches. *o*

TIMOTHY JOINS PAUL AND SILAS

16 Paul came to Derbe and then to Lystra, *p* where a disciple named Timothy *q* lived, whose mother was Jewish and a believer *r* but whose father was a Greek. ²The believers *s* at Lystra and Iconium *t* spoke well of him. ³Paul wanted to take him along on the journey, so he circumcised him because of the Jews who lived in that area, for they all knew that his father was a Greek. *u* ⁴As they traveled from town to town, they delivered the decisions reached by the apostles and elders *v* in Jerusalem *w* for the people to obey. *x* ⁵So the churches were strengthened *y* in the faith and grew daily in numbers. *z*

PAUL'S VISION OF THE MAN OF MACEDONIA

⁶Paul and his companions traveled throughout the region of Phrygia *a* and Galatia, *b* having been kept by the Holy Spirit from preaching the word in the province of Asia. *c* ⁷When they came to the border of Mysia, they tried to enter Bithynia, but the Spirit of Jesus *d* would not allow them to. ⁸So they passed by Mysia and went down to Troas. *e* ⁹During the night Paul had a vision *f* of a man of Macedonia *g* standing and begging him, "Come

---

15:36 *towns where we preached the word.* Towns of the first missionary journey (see 13:4—14:26).
15:38 *he had deserted them.* Mark had turned back at Perga and did not go to Antioch, Iconium, Lystra and Derbe (see note on 13:13).
15:39—18:22 Paul's second missionary journey (see map No. 13 at the end of this study Bible; see also map, p. 1869).
■ **15:39** *they parted company.* Barnabas and Mark do not appear again in Acts. However, in 1Co 9:6 Paul names Barnabas as setting a noble example in working to support himself. Also in Gal 2:11–13 another scene is described in Antioch that includes Barnabas. Mark evidently returned from his work with Barnabas and became associated with Peter (see 1Pe 5:13 and note). During Paul's first imprisonment, Mark was included in Paul's group (see Col 4:10; Phm 24). By the end of Paul's life he came to admire Mark so much that he requested him to come to be with him during his final days (see 2Ti 4:11 and note; see also Introduction to Mark: John Mark in the NT). *Cyprus.* The island of Barnabas's birthplace (4:36).
■ **15:40** *Silas.* Had returned to Jerusalem with Judas after delivering the Jerusalem letter (vv. 32–33). His presence in Antioch now indicates that, after reporting to those who had sent him, he came back to Antioch to participate in the church's work there.
■ **16:1** *Derbe.* See notes on 14:6,20. Paul had approached Derbe on the first trip from the opposite direction, so the order of towns is reversed here. *Lystra.* See note on 14:6. *Timothy.* See Introduction to 1 Timothy: Recipient. Since Paul addressed him as a young man some 15 years later (see 1Ti 4:12), he must have been in his teens at this time. *father was a Greek.* Statements concerning his mother's faith (here and in 2Ti 1:5) and silence concerning any faith on his father's part suggest that the father was neither a convert to Judaism nor a believer in Christ.
16:3 *he circumcised him.* As a matter of expediency so that his

work among the Jews might be more effective. This was different from Titus's case (see Gal 2:3), where circumcision was refused because some were demanding it as necessary for salvation.
16:6 *his companions.* Silas and Timothy. *Phrygia.* The district was formerly the Hellenistic territory of Phrygia, but it had more recently been divided between the Roman provinces of Asia and Galatia. Iconium and Antioch were in Galatian Phrygia. *Galatia.* The name had been used to denote the Hellenistic kingdom, but in 25 B.C. it had been expanded considerably to become the Roman province of that name. *Asia.* This, too, had been a smaller area formerly but now was a Roman province including the Hellenistic districts of Mysia, Lydia, Caria and parts of Phrygia.
16:7 *Mysia.* In the northwest part of the province of Asia. Luke uses these old Hellenistic names, but Paul preferred the provincial (Roman) names. *Bithynia.* A senatorial province formed after 74 B.C., it was east of Mysia. *Spirit of Jesus.* As the "Holy Spirit" was used at times interchangeably with "God" (see 5:3–4), so here "Holy Spirit" is used interchangeably with "Spirit of Jesus." *not allow.* The Spirit may have led in any of a number of ways: vision, circumstances, good sense or use of the prophetic gift.
16:8 *Troas.* Located ten miles from ancient Troy. Alexandria Troas (its full name) was a Roman colony and an important seaport for connections between Macedonia and Greece on the one hand and Asia Minor on the other. Paul returned to Troas following his work in Ephesus on his third journey (see 2Co 2:12). At some time—on Paul's second journey or on his third—a church was started there, for Paul ministered to believers in Troas when he returned from his third journey on his way to Jerusalem (20:5–12).
16:9 *vision.* One of the ways God gave direction (cf. 10:3). *man of Macedonia.* Macedonia had become a Roman province in 148 B.C. There is no indication that the man of the vision is Luke, as some have suggested, but he does join the group at this point.

over to Macedonia and help us." ¹⁰After Paul had seen the vision, we ʰ got ready at once to leave for Macedonia, concluding that God had called us to preach the gospel ⁱ to them.

LYDIA'S CONVERSION IN PHILIPPI

¹¹From Troas ʲ we put out to sea and sailed straight for Samothrace, and the next day we went on to Neapolis. ¹²From there we traveled to Philippi, ᵏ a Roman colony and the leading city of that district ᵃ of Macedonia. ˡ And we stayed there several days.

¹³On the Sabbath ᵐ we went outside the city gate to the river, where we expected to find a place of prayer. We sat down and began to speak to the women who had gathered there. ¹⁴One of those listening was a woman from the city of Thyatira ⁿ named Lydia, a dealer

---

ᵃ 12 The text and meaning of the Greek for *the leading city of that district* are uncertain.

16:10 *we got ready.* This is where the "we" passages of Acts begin (see Introduction: Author). The conclusion is that Luke is informing the reader that he joined the party at Troas.
16:11 *Samothrace.* An island in the northeastern Aegean Sea. It was a convenient place for boats to anchor rather than risk sailing at night. *Neapolis.* The seaport for Philippi, ten miles away; modern Kavalla.
16:12 *Philippi.* A city in eastern Macedonia named after Philip II, father of Alexander the Great (see map, p. 1996). Since it was a Roman colony, it was independent of provincial administration and had a governmental organization modeled after that of Rome (see note on 13:14). Many retired legionnaires from the Roman army settled there, but few Jews. See Introduction to Philippians: Recipients. *leading city.* Thessalonica was the capital of Macedo-

nia. But Macedonia had four districts, and Philippi was in the first of these. Amphipolis, however, was the first city of that district. Luke may have intended to say that Philippi was "a" leading city (there is no article in the Greek), or that it was the first city reached from the border, or that its fame and significance made it truly the leading city of the area.
16:13 *place of prayer.* There were so few Jews in Philippi that there was no synagogue (ten married men were required), so the Jews who were there met for prayer along the banks of the Gangites River (see map, p. 1996). It was customary for such places of prayer to be located outdoors near running water.
16:14 *Thyatira.* In the Roman province of Asia, 20 miles southeast of Pergamum (in the Hellenistic kingdom of Lydia; see map, p. 2123; see also map No. 13 at the end of this

---

16:10 ʰ ver 10-17;
Ac 20:5-15; 21:1-18;
27:1-28:16 ⁱ Ac 14:7
16:11 ʲ S ver 8
16:12 ᵏ Ac 20:6;
Php 1:1; 1Th 2:2
ˡ S ver 9
16:13 ᵐ S Ac 13:14
16:14 ⁿ Rev 1:11;
2:18,24

PAUL'S SECOND MISSIONARY JOURNEY

C. A.D. 49–52

Ac 15:39—18:22

SAMOTHRACE—Islands
Rhodes—Cities, Ports

Miles 0   100   200   300
Kms 0 100 200 300 400 500

16:14 °Lk 24:45
16:15 °S Ac 11:14
°S Ac 2:38
16:16 °ver 13
°Dt 18:11; 1Sa 28:3,7
16:17 °S Mk 5:7
16:18 °S Mk 16:17
16:19 °ver 16;
Ac 19:25,26
°S Ac 15:22 ×Ac 8:3;
17:6; 21:30; Jas 2:6
16:20 °Ac 17:6
16:21 °ver 12
°Est 3:8
16:22 °2Co 11:25;
1Th 2:2
16:23 °ver 27,36
16:24 °Job 13:27;
33:11; Jer 20:2,3;
29:26
16:25 °Ps 119:55,62
°S Ac 15:22
°S Eph 5:19
16:26 °Ac 4:31
°Ac 5:19; 12:10
°Ac 12:7
16:27 °Ac 12:19
16:29 °S Ac 15:22
16:30 °Ac 2:37
16:31 °S Jn 3:15
°S Ro 11:14
°S Ac 11:14
16:33 °ver 25
°S Ac 2:38
16:34 °S Ac 11:14

in purple cloth. She was a worshiper of God. The Lord opened her heart ° to respond to Paul's message. ¹⁵When she and the members of her household ° were baptized, ° she invited us to her home. "If you consider me a believer in the Lord," she said, "come and stay at my house." And she persuaded us.

PAUL AND SILAS IN PRISON

¹⁶Once when we were going to the place of prayer, ° we were met by a female slave who had a spirit ° by which she predicted the future. She earned a great deal of money for her owners by fortune-telling. ¹⁷She followed Paul and the rest of us, shouting, "These men are servants of the Most High God, ° who are telling you the way to be saved." ¹⁸She kept this up for many days. Finally Paul became so annoyed that he turned around and said to the spirit, "In the name of Jesus Christ I command you to come out of her!" At that moment the spirit left her. °

¹⁹When her owners realized that their hope of making money ° was gone, they seized Paul and Silas ° and dragged ° them into the marketplace to face the authorities. ²⁰They brought them before the magistrates and said, "These men are Jews, and are throwing our city into an uproar ° ²¹by advocating customs unlawful for us Romans ° to accept or practice." °

²²The crowd joined in the attack against Paul and Silas, and the magistrates ordered them to be stripped and beaten with rods. ° ²³After they had been severely flogged, they were thrown into prison, and the jailer ° was commanded to guard them carefully. ²⁴When he received these orders, he put them in the inner cell and fastened their feet in the stocks. °

²⁵About midnight ° Paul and Silas ° were praying and singing hymns ° to God, and the other prisoners were listening to them. ²⁶Suddenly there was such a violent earthquake that the foundations of the prison were shaken. ° At once all the prison doors flew open, ° and everyone's chains came loose. ° ²⁷The jailer woke up, and when he saw the prison doors open, he drew his sword and was about to kill himself because he thought the prisoners had escaped. ° ²⁸But Paul shouted, "Don't harm yourself! We are all here!"

²⁹The jailer called for lights, rushed in and fell trembling before Paul and Silas. ° ³⁰He then brought them out and asked, "Sirs, what must I do to be saved?" °

³¹They replied, "Believe ° in the Lord Jesus, and you will be saved ° —you and your household." ° ³²Then they spoke the word of the Lord to him and to all the others in his house. ³³At that hour of the night ° the jailer took them and washed their wounds; then immediately he and all his household were baptized. ° ³⁴The jailer brought them into his house and set a meal before them; he ° was filled with joy because he had come to believe in God—he and his whole household.

³⁵When it was daylight, the magistrates sent their officers to the jailer with the order:

---

study Bible). It was famous for its dyeing works, and especially for its royal purple (crimson). See Rev 1:11 and note on Rev 2:18. *Lydia.* A businesswoman. Her name may be associated with her place of origin, the Hellenistic district of Lydia. *worshiper of God.* Lydia was a Gentile who, like Cornelius (see 10:2), believed in the true God and followed the moral teachings of Scripture. She had not, however, become a full convert to Judaism. *opened her heart.* After the resurrection the minds of the disciples were opened to understand the Scriptures (Lk 24:45); similarly, Lydia's heart was opened to respond to the gospel message of Paul.

16:15 *come and stay at my house.* Cf. Lk 19:5.

16:16 *spirit by which she predicted the future.* A demonic "python" spirit. The python was a mythical snake worshiped at Delphi and associated with the Delphic oracle. The term "python" came to be used of the persons through whom the python spirit supposedly spoke. Since such persons spoke involuntarily, the term "ventriloquist" was used to describe them. To what extent she actually predicted the future is not known.

B **16:17** *rest of us.* The "we" section (see note on v. 10) ends here and begins again in 20:5. *Most High God.* A title used by the man possessed by an evil spirit (Mk 5:7). It was a common title among both Jews (see Nu 24:16; Isa 14:14; Da 3:26) and Greeks (found in inscriptions). But the title is not used of God in the NT by Christians or Jews (though cf. Ac 7:48).

16:20 *magistrates.* The Greek term *strategos* (Latin *praetor*), not the usual word but a term of courtesy used in some Roman colonies, such as Philippi.

16:22 *beaten.* With rods.

16:23 *flogged.* See note on Mk 15:15.

16:24 *inner cell ... stocks.* Used not only for extra security but also for torture.

16:27 *about to kill himself.* If a prisoner escaped, the life of the guard was demanded in his place (see 12:19). To take his own life would shorten the shame and distress.

A **16:30** *what must I do to be saved?* The jailer had heard that these were preachers of a way of salvation (v. 17). Now with the earthquake and his own impending death, he wanted to know about the way.

A **16:31** *Believe in the Lord Jesus.* A concise statement of the way of salvation (see 10:43).

A **16:32** *word of the Lord.* See 10:36. Paul and Silas explained the gospel more thoroughly to the jailer and to all the other members of his household, and they all believed in Christ and were saved (v. 34).

16:33 *that hour of the night.* "About midnight" (v. 25).

A **16:34** *brought them into his house.* Cf. v. 15. *filled with joy.* The consistent consequence of conversion, regardless of circumstances (see note on 8:39).

16:35 *magistrates.* See note on v. 20.

"Release those men." [36]The jailer [t] told Paul, "The magistrates have ordered that you and Silas be released. Now you can leave. Go in peace." [u]

[37]But Paul said to the officers: "They beat us publicly without a trial, even though we are Roman citizens, [v] and threw us into prison. And now do they want to get rid of us quietly? No! Let them come themselves and escort us out."

[38]The officers reported this to the magistrates, and when they heard that Paul and Silas were Roman citizens, they were alarmed. [w] [39]They came to appease them and escorted them from the prison, requesting them to leave the city. [x] [40]After Paul and Silas came out of the prison, they went to Lydia's house, [y] where they met with the believers [z] and encouraged them. Then they left.

IN THESSALONICA

17 When Paul and his companions had passed through Amphipolis and Apollonia, they came to Thessalonica, [a] where there was a Jewish synagogue. [2]As was his custom, Paul went into the synagogue, [b] and on three Sabbath [c] days he reasoned with them from the Scriptures, [d] [3]explaining and proving that the Messiah had to suffer [e] and rise from the dead. [f] "This Jesus I am proclaiming to you is the Messiah," [g] he said. [4]Some of the Jews were persuaded and joined Paul and Silas, [h] as did a large number of God-fearing Greeks and not a few prominent women.

[5]But other Jews were jealous; so they rounded up some bad characters from the marketplace, formed a mob and started a riot in the city. [i] They rushed to Jason's [j] house in search of Paul and Silas in order to bring them out to the crowd. [a] [6]But when they did not find them, they dragged [k] Jason and some other believers [l] before the city officials, shouting: "These men who have caused trouble all over the world [m] have now come here, [n] [7]and Jason has welcomed them into his house. They are all defying Caesar's decrees, saying that there is another king, one called Jesus." [o] [8]When they heard this, the crowd and the city officials were thrown into turmoil. [9]Then they made Jason [p] and the others post bond and let them go.

IN BEREA

[10]As soon as it was night, the believers sent Paul and Silas [q] away to Berea. [r] On arriving there, they went to the Jewish synagogue. [s] [11]Now the Berean Jews were of more noble character than those in Thessalonica, [t] for they received the message with great

[a] 5 Or *the assembly of the people*

16:36 [t] ver 23, 27
[u] S Ac 15:33
16:37 [v] Ac 22:25-29
16:38 [w] Ac 22:29
16:39 [x] Mt 8:34;
Lk 8:37
16:40 [y] ver 14
[z] ver 2; S Ac 1:16
17:1 [a] ver 11, 13;
Php 4:16; 1Th 1:1;
2Th 1:1; 2Ti 4:10
17:2 [b] S Ac 9:20
[c] S Ac 13:14 [d] Ac 8:35;
18:28
17:3 [e] Lk 24:26;
Ac 3:18 [f] Lk 24:46;
S Ac 2:24 [g] S Ac 9:22
17:4 [h] S Ac 15:22
17:5 [i] ver 13;
S 1Th 2:14 [j] Ro 16:21
17:6 [k] S Ac 16:19
[l] S Ac 1:16
[m] S Mt 24:14
[n] Ac 16:20
17:7 [o] Lk 23:2;
Jn 19:12
17:9 [p] ver 5
17:10 [q] S Ac 15:22
[r] ver 13; Ac 20:4
[s] S Ac 9:20
17:11 [t] S ver 1

16:37 *without a trial.* Public beating for a Roman citizen (see v. 38) would have been illegal, let alone beating without a trial (see 22:25 and note). *Let them come themselves.* Paul and Silas were not asking for an escort to salve their injured pride as much as they were establishing their innocence for the sake of the church in Philippi and its future.

17:1 *Amphipolis . . . Thessalonica.* The Egnatian Way crossed the whole of present-day northern Greece east-west and included Philippi, Amphipolis, Apollonia and Thessalonica on its route. At several locations, such as Neapolis (modern Kavalla), Philippi and Apollonia, the road is still visible today. If a person traveled about 30 miles a day, each city could be reached after one day's journey. *Thessalonica.* About 100 miles from Philippi. It was the capital of the province of Macedonia and had a population of more than 200,000, including a colony of Jews (and a synagogue). All these contributed to Paul's decision to preach there. See Introduction to 1 Thessalonians: The City and the Church.

17:2 *synagogue.* See note on 13:14. *three Sabbath days.* These two weeks represent the time spent in the synagogue reasoning with the Jews, not Paul's total time in Thessalonica. An analysis of the Thessalonian letters reveals that Paul had taught them much more doctrine than would have been possible in two or three weeks.

17:3 *explaining.* Lk 24:45 uses the same Greek verb (there translated "opened") in describing Jesus' making clear to two of his disciples the teaching of Scripture concerning his death and resurrection (cf. Lk 24:27).

17:4 *God-fearing Greeks.* See notes on 10:2; 16:14. *prominent women.* Perhaps the wives of the leading men of the city, but

women who deserve notice and position in their own right (see also v. 12).

17:5 *were jealous.* Because of the large number of people (including some Jews, many God-fearing Gentiles and many prominent women) who responded to Paul's ministry (cf. 13:45). *Jason's house.* Paul had probably been staying there.

17:6 *city officials.* The Greek term *politarch* (lit. "city ruler"), used here and in v. 8, is found nowhere else in Greek literature, but it was discovered in 1835 in a Greek inscription on an arch that had spanned the Egnatian Way on the west side of Thessalonica. (The arch was destroyed in 1867, but the block with the inscription was rescued and is now in the British Museum in London.) The term has since been found in 16 other inscriptions in surrounding towns of Macedonia, as well as elsewhere.

17:7 *defying Caesar's decrees.* Blasphemy was the gravest accusation for a Jew, but treason—to support a rival king above Caesar—was the worst accusation for a Roman. Cf. the charge against Jesus that he claimed to be king (see Jn 18:12).

17:9 *post bond.* Jason was forced to guarantee a peaceful, quiet community, or he would face the confiscation of his properties and perhaps even death.

17:10 *Paul and Silas.* Timothy was probably left at Philippi, later rejoining Paul and Silas at Berea (compare v. 10 with v. 14). *Berea.* Modern Verria, located 50 miles from Thessalonica in another district of Macedonia. *synagogue.* See note on 13:14.

17:11 *Berean Jews.* Luke includes a Berean, Sopater, son of Pyrrhus, in the list of delegates who accompanied Paul to Jerusalem to deliver the contributions for the poor (see 20:4 and note).

17:11 *u* Lk 16:29;
Jn 5:39 *v* Dt 29:29
17:12 *w* S Ac 2:41
17:13 *x* S Heb 4:12
17:14 *y* S Ac 9:30
z S Ac 15:22
a S Ac 16:1
17:15 *b* ver 16, 21,
22; Ac 18:1; 1Th 3:1
c Ac 18:5
17:17 *d* S Ac 9:20
17:18 *e* S Ac 13:32
f ver 31,32; Ac 4:2
17:19 *g* ver 22
h Mk 1:27
17:21 *i* S ver 15
17:22 *j* ver 19
k ver 16
17:23 *l* Jn 4:22
17:24 *m* Isa 42:5;
Ac 14:15 *n* Dt 10:14;
Isa 66:1,2; Mt 11:25
o 1Ki 8:27; Ac 7:48
17:25 *p* Ps 50:10-12;
Isa 42:5
17:26 *q* Dt 32:8;
Job 12:23
17:27 *r* Dt 4:7;
Isa 55:6; Jer 23:23,24
17:28 *s* Dt 30:20;
Job 12:10; Da 5:23

eagerness and examined the Scriptures [u] every day to see if what Paul said was true. [v] [12]Many of them believed, as did also a number of prominent Greek women and many Greek men. [w]

[13]But when the Jews in Thessalonica learned that Paul was preaching the word of God at Berea, [x] some of them went there too, agitating the crowds and stirring them up. [14]The believers [y] immediately sent Paul to the coast, but Silas [z] and Timothy [a] stayed at Berea. [15]Those who escorted Paul brought him to Athens [b] and then left with instructions for Silas and Timothy to join him as soon as possible. [c]

IN ATHENS

[16]While Paul was waiting for them in Athens, he was greatly distressed to see that the city was full of idols. [17]So he reasoned in the synagogue [d] with both Jews and God-fearing Greeks, as well as in the marketplace day by day with those who happened to be there. [18]A group of Epicurean and Stoic philosophers began to debate with him. Some of them asked, "What is this babbler trying to say?" Others remarked, "He seems to be advocating foreign gods." They said this because Paul was preaching the good news [e] about Jesus and the resurrection. [f] [19]Then they took him and brought him to a meeting of the Areopagus, [g] where they said to him, "May we know what this new teaching [h] is that you are presenting? [20]You are bringing some strange ideas to our ears, and we would like to know what they mean." [21](All the Athenians [i] and the foreigners who lived there spent their time doing nothing but talking about and listening to the latest ideas.)

[22]Paul then stood up in the meeting of the Areopagus [j] and said: "People of Athens! I see that in every way you are very religious. [k] [23]For as I walked around and looked carefully at your objects of worship, I even found an altar with this inscription: TO AN UNKNOWN GOD. So you are ignorant of the very thing you worship [l]—and this is what I am going to proclaim to you.

[24]"The God who made the world and everything in it [m] is the Lord of heaven and earth [n] and does not live in temples built by hands. [o] [25]And he is not served by human hands, as if he needed anything. Rather, he himself gives everyone life and breath and everything else. [p] [26]From one man he made all the nations, that they should inhabit the whole earth; and he marked out their appointed times in history and the boundaries of their lands. [q] [27]God did this so that they would seek him and perhaps reach out for him and find him, though he is not far from any one of us. [r] [28]'For in him we live and move and have our being.' [a][s] As some of your own poets have said, 'We are his offspring.' [b]

---

a 28 From the Cretan philosopher Epimenides   *b* 28 From the Cilician Stoic philosopher Aratus

---

17:14 *coast.* One might conclude that Paul went by boat to Athens. But the road to Athens is also a coastal road, and Paul may have walked the distance after having been escorted to the coast (some 20 miles). In any event, Christian companions stayed with him until reaching Athens.

17:15 *Athens.* Five centuries before Paul, Athens had been at the height of its glory in art, philosophy and literature. She had retained her reputation in philosophy through the years and still maintained a leading university in Paul's day.

17:17 *synagogue.* See note on 13:14. *God-fearing Greeks.* See note on 10:2.

C **17:18** *Epicurean ... philosophers.* Originally they taught that the supreme good is happiness—but not mere momentary pleasure or temporary gratification. By Paul's time, however, this philosophy had degenerated into a more sensual system of thought. *Stoic philosophers.* They taught that people should live in accord with nature, recognize their own self-sufficiency and independence and suppress their desires. At its best, Stoicism had some admirable qualities, but, like Epicureanism, by Paul's time it had degenerated into a system of pride. *babbler.* The Greek word meant "seed picker," a bird picking up seeds here and there. Then it came to refer to the loafer in the marketplace who picked up whatever scraps of learning he could find and paraded them without digesting them himself.

17:19 *Areopagus.* Means "hill of Ares." Ares was the Greek god of thunder and war (the Roman equivalent was Mars). The Areopagus was located just west of the acropolis and south of the Agora and had once been the site of the meeting of the Court or Council of the Areopagus. Earlier the Council governed a

Greek city-state, but by NT times the Areopagus retained authority only in the areas of religion and morals and met in the Royal Portico at the northwest corner of the Agora. The Council members considered themselves the custodians of teachings that introduced new religions and foreign gods.

17:22 *religious.* Or "superstitious." The Greek for this word could be used either to congratulate people or to criticize them, depending on whether those using it included themselves in the circle of individuals they were describing. The Athenians would not know which meaning to take until Paul continued. In this context it is clear that Paul wanted to be complimentary in order to gain a hearing.

B **17:23** *TO AN UNKNOWN GOD.* The Greeks were fearful of offending any god by failing to give him or her attention; so they felt they could cover any omissions by the label "unknown god." Other Greek writers confirm that such altars could be seen in Athens—a striking point of contact for Paul.

17:24 *The God who made the world.* Thus a personal Creator, in contrast with the views of pantheistic Stoicism. *does not live in temples built by hands.* Cf. Stephen's similar declaration in his famous speech (7:28); cf. also 1Ki 8:27.

17:26 *From one man he made all the nations.* All people are of one family (whether Athenians or Romans, Greeks or barbarians, Jews or Gentiles). *marked out their appointed times.* He planned the exact times when nations should emerge and decline. *boundaries of their lands.* He also planned the specific area to be occupied by each nation. He is God, the Designer (things were not left to Chance, as the Epicureans thought).

²⁹"Therefore since we are God's offspring, we should not think that the divine being is like gold or silver or stone—an image made by human design and skill.ᵗ ³⁰In the past God overlookedᵘ such ignorance,ᵛ but now he commands all people everywhere to repent.ʷ ³¹For he has set a day when he will judgeˣ the world with justiceʸ by the man he has appointed.ᶻ He has given proof of this to everyone by raising him from the dead."ᵃ

³²When they heard about the resurrection of the dead,ᵇ some of them sneered, but others said, "We want to hear you again on this subject." ³³At that, Paul left the Council. ³⁴Some of the people became followers of Paul and believed. Among them was Dionysius, a member of the Areopagus,ᶜ also a woman named Damaris, and a number of others.

IN CORINTH

18 After this, Paul left Athensᵈ and went to Corinth.ᵉ ²There he met a Jew named Aquila, a native of Pontus, who had recently come from Italy with his wife Priscilla,ᶠ because Claudiusᵍ had ordered all Jews to leave Rome. Paul went to see them, ³and because he was a tentmaker as they were, he stayed and worked with them.ʰ ⁴Every Sabbathⁱ he reasoned in the synagogue,ʲ trying to persuade Jews and Greeks.

⁵When Silasᵏ and Timothyˡ came from Macedonia,ᵐ Paul devoted himself exclusively to preaching, testifying to the Jews that Jesus was the Messiah.ⁿ ⁶But when they opposed Paul and became abusive,ᵒ he shook out his clothes in protestᵖ and said to them, "Your blood be on your own heads!�q I am innocent of it.ʳ From now on I will go to the Gentiles."ˢ

⁷Then Paul left the synagogue and went next door to the house of Titius Justus, a worshiper of God.ᵗ ⁸Crispus,ᵘ the synagogue leader,ᵛ and his entire householdʷ believed in the Lord; and many of the Corinthians who heard Paul believed and were baptized.

⁹One night the Lord spoke to Paul in a vision:ˣ "Do not be afraid;ʸ keep on speaking, do not be silent. ¹⁰For I am with you,ᶻ and no one is going to attack and harm you, because I have many people in this city." ¹¹So Paul stayed in Corinth for a year and a half, teaching them the word of God.ᵃ

¹²While Gallio was proconsulᵇ of Achaia,ᶜ the Jews of Corinth made a united attack on

17:29 ᵗIsa 40:18-20; Ro 1:23
17:30 ᵘAc 14:16; Ro 3:25 ᵛver 23; 1Pe 1:14 ʷLk 24:47; Tit 2:11,12
17:31 ˣS Mt 10:15 ʸPs 9:8; 96:13; 98:9 ᶻS Ac 10:42 ᵃS Ac 2:24
17:32 ᵇver 18,31
17:34 ᶜver 19,22
18:1 ᵈS Ac 17:15 ᵉAc 19:1; 1Co 1:2; 2Co 1:1,23; 2Ti 4:20
18:2 ᶠver 19,26; Ro 16:3; 1Co 16:19; 2Ti 4:19 ᵍAc 11:28
18:3 ʰAc 20:34; 1Co 4:12; 1Th 2:9; 2Th 3:8
18:4 ⁱS Ac 13:14 ʲS Ac 9:20
18:5 ᵏS Ac 15:22 ˡS Ac 16:1 ᵐS Ac 16:9; 17:14,15 ⁿS Ac 9:22
18:6 ᵒS Ac 13:45 ᵖS Mt 10:14 qSa 1:16; Eze 33:4 ʳEze 3:17-19; Ac 20:26 ˢS Ac 13:46
18:7 ᵗAc 16:14
18:8 ᵘ1Co 1:14 ᵛS Mk 5:22 ʷS Ac 11:14
18:9 ˣS Ac 9:10 ʸS Mt 14:27
18:10 ᶻS Mt 28:20
18:11 ᵃS Heb 4:12
18:12 ᵇAc 13:7,8, 12; 19:38 ᶜver 27; Ro 15:26; 1Co 16:15; 2Co 9:2; 1Th 1:7,8

17:28 *some of your own poets.* There are two quotations here: (1) "In him we live and move and have our being," from the Cretan poet Epimenides (c. 600 B.C.) in his *Cretica,* and (2) "We are his offspring," from the Cilician poet Aratus (c. 315–240) in his *Phaenomena,* as well as from Cleanthes (331–233) in his *Hymn to Zeus.* Paul quotes Greek poets elsewhere as well (see 1Co 15:33; Tit 1:12 and notes).

17:30 *overlooked such ignorance.* God had not judged them for worshiping false gods in their ignorance, but now the situation has changed (see v. 31).

17:31 *the man he has appointed.* Jesus, the Son of Man (see Da 7:13; cf. Mt 25:31–46; Ac 10:42).

17:32–34 Three responses to Paul's sermon: (1) Some rejected ("sneered"), (2) some procrastinated ("We want to hear you again"), (3) some accepted ("became followers of Paul and believed").

17:32 *resurrection of the dead.* Immortality of the soul was accepted by the Greeks, but not resurrection of a dead body.

17:33 *the Council.* The meeting of the Areopagites.

17:34 *Dionysius.* Later tradition states, though it cannot be proved, that he became bishop of Athens. *Damaris.* Some have suggested that she must have been a foreign, educated woman to have been present at a public meeting such as the Areopagus. It is also possible that she was a God-fearing Gentile who had heard Paul at the synagogue (v. 17).

18:1 *went to Corinth.* Either by land along the isthmus (a distance of about 50 miles) or by sea from Piraeus, the port of Athens, to Cenchreae, on the eastern shore of the isthmus of Corinth. See Introduction to 1 Corinthians: The City of Corinth; see also map, p. 1925.

18:2 *Aquila . . . Priscilla.* Since no mention is made of a conversion and since a partnership is established in work (see v. 3), it is likely that they were already Christians. They may have been converted in Rome by those returning from Pentecost or by others at a later time (see vv. 18–19; 1Co 16:9; Ro

16:3–4). *Pontus.* In the northeastern region of Asia Minor, a province lying along the Black Sea between Bithynia and Armenia (see 2:9). *Claudius.* Emperor of Rome (A.D. 41–54). *ordered all Jews to leave Rome.* Recorded in Suetonius (*Claudius,* 25). The expulsion order was given, Suetonius writes, because of "their [the Jews'] continual tumults instigated by Chrestus" (a common misspelling of "Christ"). If "Chrestus" refers to Christ, the riots obviously were "about" him rather than led "by" him.

18:3 *tentmaker.* Paul would have been taught this trade as a youth. It was the Jewish custom to provide manual training for sons, whether rich or poor.

18:4 *synagogue.* See note on 13:14.

18:5 *Silas and Timothy came from Macedonia.* Paul instructed these two to come to him at Athens (17:15). Evidently they did (see 1Th 3:1–2), but they may have been sent back to Macedonia almost immediately to check on the churches—perhaps Silas to Philippi and Timothy to Thessalonica.

18:7 *Titius Justus.* Titius was a common Roman name. Justus is used to distinguish him from the Titus of 2Co 2:13; 7:13–14; 8:16,23. *worshiper of God.* Like Titus (see Gal 2:3), an uncircumcised Gentile, but attending the synagogue.

18:8 *Crispus.* Paul baptized him (1Co 1:14). *synagogue leader.* See note on 13:15.

18:9 *in a vision.* Paul had seen the Lord in a resurrection body at his conversion (9:4–6; 1Co 15:8) and in the temple at Jerusalem in a trance (22:17–18). Now he sees him in a vision (see 23:11).

18:10 *I have many people.* Corinth was a large, strategic, political, commercial and religious center. It was important that a strong church be established there (see note on v. 1).

18:11 *a year and a half.* During this time he may also have taken the gospel to the neighboring districts of Achaia (see 2Co 1:1 and note).

18:12 *Gallio.* The brother of Seneca, the philosopher, who was the tutor of Nero. Gallio was admired as a man of

18:15 *d* Ac 23:29;
25:11,19
18:17 *e* 1Co 1:1
f ver 8
18:18 *g* ver 27;
S Ac 1:16 *h* S Lk 2:2
i S ver 2 *j* Ro 16:1
k Nu 6:2,5,18;
Ac 21:24
18:19 *l* ver 21,24;
Ac 19:1,17,26;
1Co 15:32; 16:8;
Eph 1:1; 1Ti 1:3;
Rev 1:11; 2:1
18:21 *m* Ro 1:10;
15:32; 1Co 4:19;
Jas 4:15
18:22 *n* S Ac 8:40
o S Ac 11:19
18:23 *p* S Ac 16:6
q Ac 2:10; 16:6
r Ac 14:22; 15:32,41
18:24 *s* Ac 19:1;
1Co 1:12; 3:5,6,22;
4:6; 16:12; Tit 3:13
t S ver 19
18:25 *u* Ro 12:11
v S Mk 1:4
18:26 *w* S ver 2
18:27 *x* S ver 12
y ver 18; S Ac 1:16
18:28 *z* Ac 8:35; 17:2
a ver 5; S Ac 9:22

Paul and brought him to the place of judgment. [13]"This man," they charged, "is persuading the people to worship God in ways contrary to the law."

[14]Just as Paul was about to speak, Gallio said to them, "If you Jews were making a complaint about some misdemeanor or serious crime, it would be reasonable for me to listen to you. [15]But since it involves questions about words and names and your own law *d*—settle the matter yourselves. I will not be a judge of such things." [16]So he drove them off. [17]Then the crowd there turned on Sosthenes *e* the synagogue leader *f* and beat him in front of the proconsul; and Gallio showed no concern whatever.

PRISCILLA, AQUILA AND APOLLOS

[18]Paul stayed on in Corinth for some time. Then he left the believers *g* and sailed for Syria, *h* accompanied by Priscilla and Aquila. *i* Before he sailed, he had his hair cut off at Cenchreae *j* because of a vow he had taken. *k* [19]They arrived at Ephesus, *l* where Paul left Priscilla and Aquila. He himself went into the synagogue and reasoned with the Jews. [20]When they asked him to spend more time with them, he declined. [21]But as he left, he promised, "I will come back if it is God's will." *m* Then he set sail from Ephesus. [22]When he landed at Caesarea, *n* he went up to Jerusalem and greeted the church and then went down to Antioch. *o*

[23]After spending some time in Antioch, Paul set out from there and traveled from place to place throughout the region of Galatia *p* and Phrygia, *q* strengthening all the disciples. *r*

[24]Meanwhile a Jew named Apollos, *s* a native of Alexandria, came to Ephesus. *t* He was a learned man, with a thorough knowledge of the Scriptures. [25]He had been instructed in the way of the Lord, and he spoke with great fervor *a* *u* and taught about Jesus accurately, though he knew only the baptism of John. *v* [26]He began to speak boldly in the synagogue. When Priscilla and Aquila *w* heard him, they invited him to their home and explained to him the way of God more adequately.

[27]When Apollos wanted to go to Achaia, *x* the believers *y* encouraged him and wrote to the disciples there to welcome him. When he arrived, he was a great help to those who by grace had believed. [28]For he vigorously refuted the Jews in public debate, proving from the Scriptures *z* that Jesus was the Messiah. *a*

a 25 Or *with fervor in the Spirit*

exceptional fairness and calmness. From an inscription found at Delphi, it is known that Gallio was proconsul of Achaia in A.D. 51–52. This information enables us to date Paul's visit to Corinth on his second journey as well as his writing of the Thessalonian letters (see Introduction to 1 Thessalonians: Author, Date and Place of Writing).

18:13 *contrary to the law.* The Jews were claiming that Paul was advocating a religion not recognized by Roman law, as was Judaism. If he had been given the opportunity to speak, he could have argued that the gospel he was preaching was the faith of his fathers (see 24:14–15; 26:6–7) and thus authorized by Roman law.

18:17 *the crowd there turned on Sosthenes.* It is not clear whether the Greeks beat Sosthenes, seeing the occasion as an opportunity to vent their feelings against the Jews, or the Jews beat their own synagogue ruler because he was unsuccessful in presenting their case—probably the former. A Sosthenes is included with Paul in the writing of 1 Corinthians (1:1). Perhaps he was the second ruler of the synagogue at Corinth to become a Christian in response to Paul's preaching (see v. 8).

18:18 *Priscilla and Aquila.* The order of the names used here (but cf. v. 2) may indicate the prominent role of Priscilla or her higher social position (see Ro 16:3; 2Ti 4:19). *vow he had taken.* Grammatically this could refer to Aquila, but the emphasis on Paul and his activity makes Paul more probable. It was probably a temporary Nazirite vow (see Nu 6:1–21). Different vows were frequently taken to express thanks for deliverance from grave dangers. Shaving the head marked the end of a vow.

18:19 *Ephesus.* Leading commercial city of Asia Minor, the cap-

ital of provincial Asia and the warden of the temple of Artemis (Diana). See Introduction to Ephesians: The City of Ephesus; see also map, p. 1983. *synagogue.* See note on 13:14.

18:22 *greeted the church.* Could refer to a congregation in Caesarea, but the explanation that "he went up" makes it more likely that it was the church in Jerusalem, situated some 2,500 feet above sea level.

18:23—21:17 Paul's third missionary journey (see map No. 13 at the end of this study Bible; see also map, p. 1875; cf. maps, pp. 1863, 1869).

18:23 *region of Galatia and Phrygia.* The use of the phrase may indicate the southern part of Galatia in the Phrygian area (see note on 16:6).

18:24 *Alexandria.* In Egypt—where the OT had been translated into Greek (the Septuagint, see essay, p. 1595). The second most important city in the Roman empire, it had a large Jewish population. *the Scriptures.* The pre-Christian Greek translation of the OT.

18:25 *baptism of John.* It was not in the name of Jesus (see also 19:2–4). Apollos knew something about Jesus, but basically he, like John, was still looking forward to the coming of the Messiah. His baptism was based on repentance rather than on faith in the finished work of Christ.

18:27 *Achaia.* The Roman province with Corinth as its capital.

18:28 *the Scriptures.* The Greek OT that was read and known in Corinth (see note on v. 24). Apollos's Christian exposition of the Greek Scriptures put him above both Paul and Peter in the eyes of some in the Corinthian church (see 1Co 1:12 and note).

19:1 *b* S Ac 18:24
c S Ac 18:1
d S Ac 18:19
19:2 *e* S Jn 20:22
19:4 *f* S Mk 1:4
g Jn 1:7
19:5 *h* S Ac 2:38
19:6 *i* S Ac 6:6

PAUL IN EPHESUS

19 While Apollos *b* was at Corinth, *c* Paul took the road through the interior and arrived at Ephesus. *d* There he found some disciples ²and asked them, "Did you receive the Holy Spirit *e* when *a* you believed?"

They answered, "No, we have not even heard that there is a Holy Spirit."

³So Paul asked, "Then what baptism did you receive?"

"John's baptism," they replied.

⁴Paul said, "John's baptism *f* was a baptism of repentance. He told the people to believe in the one coming after him, that is, in Jesus." *g* ⁵On hearing this, they were baptized into *b* the name of the Lord Jesus. *h* ⁶When Paul placed his hands on them, *i* the Holy Spir-

---

a 2 Or *after*   *b 5* Or *in*

19:1 *Apollos was at Corinth.* Apollos was introduced at Ephesus (18:24) in the absence of Paul; he moved to Corinth before Paul returned to Ephesus. But later Apollos came back to Ephesus during Paul's ministry there (see 1Co 16:12). *through the interior.* Not the lower direct route down the Lycus and Meander valleys but the upper Phrygian route, approaching Ephesus from a more northerly direction. If Paul got to northern Galatia, which is unlikely, it must have been on one of these trips through the interior (see 16:6; 18:23 and notes). *Ephesus.* See note on 18:19. *some disciples.* These 12 (v. 7) seem to have been followers of Jesus, but indirectly through John the Baptist or some of his followers. Or perhaps they had received their teaching from Apollos himself in his

earlier state of partial understanding (see 18:26 and note on 18:25). Like Apollos, they had a limited understanding of the gospel.

19:2 *receive the Holy Spirit.* Paul finds that they were not informed about the Holy Spirit at all (vv. 3–6).

19:4 *John's baptism.* See notes on Mt 3:11,15. *baptism of repentance.* A summation of John's teaching. It was preparatory and provisional, stressing human sinfulness and thus creating a sense of need for the gospel. John's baptism looked forward to Jesus, who by his death would make possible the forgiveness of sins (see note on Mk 1:4).

19:6 *placed his hands on them.* See note on 6:6.

Holy Spirit came on them . . . spoke in tongues and prophesied. The

---

PAUL'S THIRD MISSIONARY JOURNEY

C. A.D. 53–57

Ac 18:23—21:17

KIOS—ISLANDS
Rhodes—Cities, Ports

Miles 0   100   200   300
Kms 0   100   200   300   400   500

it came on them,[j] and they spoke in tongues[a][k] and prophesied. [7]There were about twelve men in all.

[8]Paul entered the synagogue[l] and spoke boldly there for three months, arguing persuasively about the kingdom of God. [m] [9]But some of them[n] became obstinate; they refused to believe and publicly maligned the Way.[o] So Paul left them. He took the disciples[p] with him and had discussions daily in the lecture hall of Tyrannus. [10]This went on for two years,[q] so that all the Jews and Greeks who lived in the province of Asia[r] heard the word of the Lord.[s]

[11]God did extraordinary miracles[t] through Paul, [12]so that even handkerchiefs and aprons that had touched him were taken to the sick, and their illnesses were cured[u] and the evil spirits left them.

[13]Some Jews who went around driving out evil spirits[v] tried to invoke the name of the Lord Jesus over those who were demon-possessed. They would say, "In the name of the Jesus[w] whom Paul preaches, I command you to come out." [14]Seven sons of Sceva, a Jewish chief priest, were doing this. [15]One day the evil spirit answered them, "Jesus I know, and I know about Paul, but who are you?" [16]Then the man who had the evil spirit jumped on them and overpowered them all. He gave them such a beating that they ran out of the house naked and bleeding.

[17]When this became known to the Jews and Greeks living in Ephesus,[x] they were all seized with fear,[y] and the name of the Lord Jesus was held in high honor. [18]Many of those who believed now came and openly confessed what they had done. [19]A number who had practiced sorcery brought their scrolls together and burned them publicly. When they calculated the value of the scrolls, the total came to fifty thousand drachmas.[b] [20]In this way the word of the Lord[z] spread widely and grew in power. [a]

[21]After all this had happened, Paul decided[c] to go to Jerusalem,[b] passing through Macedonia[c] and Achaia. [d] "After I have been there," he said, "I must visit Rome also."[e] [22]He sent two of his helpers,[f] Timothy[g] and Erastus,[h] to Macedonia, while he stayed in the province of Asia[i] a little longer.

THE RIOT IN EPHESUS

[23]About that time there arose a great disturbance about the Way.[j] [24]A silversmith named Demetrius, who made silver shrines of Artemis, brought in no little business for the skilled workers there. [25]He called them together, along with the workers in related

---

a 6   Or *other languages*   *b* 19   A drachma was a silver coin worth about a day's wages.   *c* 21   Or *decided in the Spirit*

---

same experience the disciples had at Pentecost (2:4,11) and the Gentiles had in Caesarea (10:46).

19:8 *three months.* Much longer than the three Sabbaths in Thessalonica (17:2), but the same approach: Jews first, then Greeks (see note on 13:14). *kingdom of God.* See notes on Mt 3:2; Lk 4:43.

19:9 *the Way.* See note on 9:2. *lecture hall of Tyrannus.* See map, p. 1983; probably a school used regularly by Tyrannus, a philosopher or rhetorician. Instruction was probably given in the cooler, morning hours. One Greek manuscript adds that Paul did his instructing from 11:00 A.M. to 4:00 P.M. This would have been the hot time of the day, but the hall was available and the people were not at their regular work.

19:10 *two years.* Two years and three months (see v. 8) was the longest stay in one missionary location that Luke records. By Jewish reckoning, any part of a year is considered a year; so this period can be spoken of as three years (20:31). *all . . . in the province of Asia heard.* One of the elements of Paul's missionary strategy is seen here. Many of the cities where Paul planted churches were strategic centers that, when evangelized, served as focal points from which the gospel radiated out to the surrounding areas. Other examples are Antioch in Pisidia (see 13:14 and note), Thessalonica (see 17:1 and note), Athens (see 17:15 and note) and Corinth (see 18:1).

19:12 *handkerchiefs.* Probably used by Paul in his trade of leatherworking: one for tying around his head, the other around his waist. Cf. 5:15 and note.

19:14 *Sceva, a Jewish chief priest.* May have been related to the high priestly family of Jerusalem. But more likely he took this ti-

tle himself to make further impression with his magical wiles. Drawn by Paul's ability to drive out evil spirits, Jewish exorcists wanted to copy his work (cf. 8:9–24; 13:6).

B **19:19** *scrolls.* Such documents, bearing alleged magical formulas and secret information, have been unearthed. Ephesus was a center for magical incantations. *fifty thousand drachmas.* The high price (see TNIV text note) was not due to the quality of the books but to the supposed power gained by their secret rigmarole of words and names.

19:21 *Macedonia and Achaia.* See notes on 1Th 1:7–8; see also map, p. 1869.

C **19:22** *Erastus.* An important Corinthian figure, at one time "the city's director of public works" (see note on Ro 16:23). At this point he returns to Corinth by way of Macedonia with Timothy.

19:23 *the Way.* See 9:2 and note.

B **19:24** *silversmith named Demetrius.* Each trade had its guild, and Demetrius was probably a responsible leader of the guild for the manufacture of silver shrines and images. *Artemis.* The Greek name for the Roman goddess Diana. The Ephesian Artemis, however, was very different from the Greco-Roman goddess. She had taken on the characteristics of Cybele, the mother goddess of fertility worshiped in Asia Minor and served by many prostitute priestesses. A meteorite may be the basis of the many-breasted image of heavenly workmanship claimed for Artemis (v. 35). (Some have identified the objects that cover the torso of the image as ostrich eggs.) Reproductions of the original image from the time of the emperor Domitian (A.D. 81–96) have been found in Ephesus.

trades, and said: "You know, my friends, that we receive a good income from this business. [k] [26]And you see and hear how this fellow Paul has convinced and led astray large numbers of people here in Ephesus [l] and in practically the whole province of Asia. [m] He says that gods made by human hands are no gods at all. [n] [27]There is danger not only that our trade will lose its good name, but also that the temple of the great goddess Artemis will be discredited; and the goddess herself, who is worshiped throughout the province of Asia and the world, will be robbed of her divine majesty."

[28]When they heard this, they were furious and began shouting: "Great is Artemis of the Ephesians!" [o] [29]Soon the whole city was in an uproar. The people seized Gaius [p] and Aristarchus, [q] Paul's traveling companions from Macedonia, [r] and all of them rushed together into the theater. [30]Paul wanted to appear before the crowd, but the disciples [s] would not let him. [31]Even some of the officials of the province, friends of Paul, sent him a message begging him not to venture into the theater.

[32]The assembly was in confusion: Some were shouting one thing, some another. [t] Most of the people did not even know why they were there. [33]The Jews in the crowd pushed Alexander to the front, and they shouted instructions to him. He motioned [u] for silence in order to make a defense before the people. [34]But when they realized he was a Jew, they all shouted in unison for about two hours: "Great is Artemis of the Ephesians!" [v]

[35]The city clerk quieted the crowd and said: "People of Ephesus, [w] doesn't all the world know that the city of Ephesus is the guardian of the temple of the great Artemis and of her image, which fell from heaven? [36]Therefore, since these facts are undeniable, you ought to calm down and not do anything rash. [37]You have brought these men here, though they have neither robbed temples [x] nor blasphemed our goddess. [38]If, then, Demetrius and his associates [y] have a grievance against anybody, the courts are open and there are proconsuls. [z] They can press charges. [39]If there is anything further you want to bring up, it must be settled in a legal assembly. [40]As it is, we are in danger of being charged with rioting because of what happened today. In that case we would not be able to account for this commotion, since there is no reason for it." [41]After he had said this, he dismissed the assembly.

THROUGH MACEDONIA AND GREECE

20 When the uproar had ended, Paul sent for the disciples [a] and, after encouraging them, said good-by and set out for Macedonia. [b] [2]He traveled through that area, speaking many words of encouragement to the people, and finally arrived in Greece, [3]where he stayed three months. Because some Jews had plotted against him [c] just as he was about to sail for Syria, [d] he decided to go back through Macedonia. [e] [4]He was accompanied by Sopater son of Pyrrhus from Berea, Aristarchus [f] and Secundus

---

19:25 *good income.* Since the temple of Artemis was one of the seven wonders of the ancient world, people came from far and wide to view it. Their purchase of silver shrines and images produced a lucrative business for the craftsmen.

19:27 *temple of the great goddess.* See map, p. 1983. The temple was the glory of Ephesus: 425 feet long and 220 feet wide, having 127 white marble columns 62 feet high and less than 4 feet apart. In the inner sanctuary was the many-breasted image supposedly dropped from heaven.

19:29 *Gaius.* See note on 20:4. *Aristarchus.* Traveled later with Paul from Corinth to Jerusalem (20:3–4) and also accompanied Paul on the voyage from Jerusalem to Rome (27:1–2; see Col 4:10 and note).

19:31 *officials of the province.* Greek *Asiarchon,* members of a council of men of wealth and influence elected to promote the worship of the emperor. Paul had friends in this highest circle.

19:33 *Alexander.* Pushed forward by the Jews either to make clear the disassociation of the Jews from the Christians and/or to accuse the Christians further of an offense against the Greeks. The crowd recognized that the Jews were not worshipers of Artemis any more than were the Christians.

19:35 *city clerk.* The secretary of the city who published the decisions of the civic assembly. He was the most important local official and the chief executive officer of the assembly, acting as go-between for Ephesus and the Roman authorities. *fell from heaven.* See note on v. 24.

19:38 *courts ... proconsuls.* Probably general terms, not intended to refer to more than one court or one proconsul. As capital

city of the province of Asia, Ephesus was the headquarters for the proconsul.

19:39 *legal assembly.* The regular civil meeting, ordinarily held three times a month.

20:1 *said good-by and set out.* Paul wanted to: (1) leave Ephesus, (2) preach in Troas on his way to Macedonia, (3) meet Titus at Troas with a report from Corinth (see 2Co 2:12–13 and note on 2:12) and (4) continue collecting the offering for Judea (see 1Co 16:1–4; 2 Co 8:1—9:15; Ro 15:25–28). *Macedonia.* Where Paul probably wrote 2 Corinthians (see 2Co 7:5; 8:1; 9:4; see also chart, p. 1855).

20:2 *He traveled through that area.* May cover a considerable period. He may have gone to Illyricum (see Ro 15:19 and note) at this time.

20:3 *three months.* Probably a reference to the stay in Corinth, the capital of Achaia. These would be the winter months when ships did not sail regularly. Paul probably wrote Romans at this time (see Introduction to Romans: Occasion). *plotted against him.* The Jews were determined to take Paul's life; also, at this time he was carrying the offering for the Christians in Judea, so there would have been a temptation for theft as well. The port at Cenchreae would have provided a convenient place for Paul's enemies to detect him as he entered a ship to embark for Syria.

20:4 These men seem to be the delegates appointed to accompany Paul and the money given for the needy in Judea (see note on 2Co 8:23). Three were from Macedonia, two from Galatia and two from Asia. Luke may have joined them at Philippi ("we sailed," v. 6; see note on 16:10). *Sopater.* May be the

19:25 [k] Ac 16:16,19, 20
19:26 [l] S Ac 18:19
[m] S Ac 2:9 [n] Dt 4:28; Ps 115:4; Isa 44:10-20; Jer 10:3-5; Ac 17:29; 1Co 8:4; Rev 9:20
19:28 [o] S Ac 18:19
19:29 [p] Ac 20:4; Ro 16:23; 1Co 1:14 [q] Ac 20:4; 27:2; Col 4:10; Phm 24 [r] S Ac 16:9
19:30 [s] S Ac 11:26
19:32 [t] Ac 21:34
19:33 [u] S Ac 12:17
19:34 [v] ver 28
19:35 [w] S Ac 18:19
19:37 [x] Ro 2:22
19:38 [y] ver 24
[z] Ac 13:7,8,12; 18:12
20:1 [a] S Ac 11:26
[b] S Ac 16:9
20:3 [c] ver 19; Ac 9:23,24; 14:5; 23:12,15,30; 25:3; 2Co 11:26; S 1Th 2:16 [d] S Lk 2:2 [e] S Ac 16:9
20:4 [f] S Ac 19:29

20:4 ᵍS Ac 17:1
ʰS Ac 19:29
ⁱS Ac 16:1 / Eph 6:21;
Col 4:7; Tit 3:12
ᵏAc 21:29; 2Ti 4:20
ˡS Ac 2:9
20:5 ᵐS Ac 16:10
ⁿS Ac 16:8
20:6 ᵒS Ac 16:12
ᵖS Ac 16:8
20:7 ᑫ1Co 16:2;
Rev 1:10 ʳS Mt 14:19
20:8 ˢAc 1:13; 9:37
20:10 ᵗ1Ki 17:21;
2Ki 4:34 ᵘMt 9:23,24
20:11 ᵛver 7;
S Mt 14:19
20:15 ʷver 17;
2Ti 4:20
20:16 ˣS Ac 18:19
ʸS Ac 2:9 ᶻS Ac 19:21
ᵃS Ac 2:1
20:17 ᵇver 15
ᶜS Ac 11:30
20:18 ᵈAc 18:19-21;
19:1-41

from Thessalonica, ᵍ Gaius ʰ from Derbe, Timothy ⁱ also, and Tychicus ʲ and Trophimus ᵏ from the province of Asia. ¹⁵These men went on ahead and waited for us ᵐ at Troas. ⁿ ⁶But we sailed from Philippi ᵒ after the Festival of Unleavened Bread, and five days later joined the others at Troas, ᵖ where we stayed seven days.

EUTYCHUS RAISED FROM THE DEAD AT TROAS

⁷On the first day of the week ᑫ we came together to break bread. ʳ Paul spoke to the people and, because he intended to leave the next day, kept on talking until midnight. ⁸There were many lamps in the upstairs room ˢ where we were meeting. ⁹Seated in a window was a young man named Eutychus, who was sinking into a deep sleep as Paul talked on and on. When he was sound asleep, he fell to the ground from the third story and was picked up dead. ¹⁰Paul went down, threw himself on the young man ᵗ and put his arms around him. "Don't be alarmed," he said. "He's alive!" ᵘ ¹¹Then he went upstairs again and broke bread ᵛ and ate. After talking until daylight, he left. ¹²The people took the young man home alive and were greatly comforted.

PAUL'S FAREWELL TO THE EPHESIAN ELDERS

¹³We went on ahead to the ship and sailed for Assos, where we were going to take Paul aboard. He had made this arrangement because he was going there on foot. ¹⁴When he met us at Assos, we took him aboard and went on to Mitylene. ¹⁵The next day we set sail from there and arrived off Chios. The day after that we crossed over to Samos, and on the following day arrived at Miletus. ʷ ¹⁶Paul had decided to sail past Ephesus ˣ to avoid spending time in the province of Asia, ʸ for he was in a hurry to reach Jerusalem, ᶻ if possible, by the day of Pentecost. ᵃ

¹⁷From Miletus, ᵇ Paul sent to Ephesus for the elders ᶜ of the church. ¹⁸When they arrived, he said to them: "You know how I lived the whole time I was with you, ᵈ from the

---

same as Sosipater (Ro 16:21). *Aristarchus.* See note on 19:29. *Secundus.* Not mentioned elsewhere. His name means "second," as Tertius (see Ro 16:22) means "third" and Quartus (see Ro 16:23) means "fourth." *Gaius from Derbe.* A Gaius from Macedonia was associated with Aristarchus (see 19:29), but the grouping of the names in pairs (after the reference to Sopater) indicates that this Gaius was associated with Roman Galatia and is different from the Macedonian Gaius. *Timothy.* May have represented more than one particular church. He was from Lystra but had been responsible for working in other churches (1Co 16:10–11; Php 2:19–23). He had been sent to Macedonia before Paul left Ephesus (19:22). *Tychicus.* A constant help to Paul, especially in association with the churches of Asia (Eph 6:21–22; Col 4:7 –9; 2Ti 4:12; Tit 3:12). *Trophimus.* Appears again in 21:29 (see 2Ti 4:20). He was an Ephesian, and it is implied that he was a Gentile.
20:5 *Troas.* Was to be the rendezvous for Paul and those who went on ahead by sea from Neapolis, the seaport of Philippi (16:11). Paul and his immediate companions stayed in Philippi before sailing a week later.
20:6 *from Philippi.* From the seaport, Neapolis, about ten miles away. *Festival of Unleavened Bread.* Began with Passover and lasted a week. Paul spent the period in Philippi. Formerly he had hoped to reach Jerusalem sooner (see 19:21), but now he hoped to arrive there for Pentecost (see 20:16). *five days later.* The voyage from Neapolis to Troas took five days. It had taken about two days the other direction (16:11). *seven days.* Although Paul was in a hurry to arrive at Jerusalem by Pentecost, he remained for seven days at Troas. This might have been because of a ship schedule, but more likely the delay was in order to meet with the believers on the first day of the week to break bread.
20:7 *first day of the week.* Sunday. Although some maintain that they met on Saturday evening, since the Jewish day began at six o'clock the previous evening, there is no indication that Luke is using the Jewish method of reporting time to tell of happenings in this Hellenistic city. *break bread.* Here indicates the Lord's Supper, since breaking bread was the express purpose for this formal gathering. The Lord's Supper had been com-

manded (Lk 22:19) and was observed regularly (see 2:42 and note). *kept on talking until midnight.* All the speeches of Paul as recorded in Acts are short, indicating that they are summaries (see Introduction: Characteristics).
20:9 *Eutychus.* A name common among the Freedmen class (see note on 6:9).
20:10 *He's alive!* As Peter had raised Tabitha (9:40), so Paul raised Eutychus.
20:13 *Assos.* On the opposite side of the peninsula from Troas—about 20 miles away by land. The coastline, however, was about 40 miles. Thus Paul was not far behind the ship that sailed around the peninsula.
20:14 *Mitylene.* After the first day of sailing, they put into this harbor on the southeast shore of the island of Lesbos.
20:15 *Chios.* The second night they spent off the shore of this larger island, which lay along the west coast of Asia Minor (see map, p. 1875). *Samos.* Crossing the mouth of the bay that leads to Ephesus, they came on the third day to Samos, one of the most important islands in the Aegean. *Miletus.* About 35 miles south of Ephesus, the destination of the ship Paul was on. He would have had to change ships to put into Ephesus, which would have lost time (see v. 16). If he had come to Ephesus, he would have had to visit a number of families, which would have taken more time. If trouble should arise, such as the riot of a year ago (19:23–41), even more time would be lost. This could not be risked.
20:16 *by the day of Pentecost.* Fifty days from Passover. Five days plus seven days (v. 6) plus four days (vv. 13–15) had already gone by, leaving only about two-thirds of the time for the remainder of the trip. *Pentecost.* See note on 2:1.
20:17 *elders of the church.* The importance of the leadership of elders has been evident throughout Paul's ministry. He had delivered the famine gift from the church at Antioch to the elders of the Jerusalem church (11:30). He had appointed elders on his first missionary journey (see 14:23) and had addressed the holders of this office later in Philippi (Php 1:1, "overseers"). He requested the Ephesian elders to meet with him on this solemn occasion (see v. 28). Some years later he wrote down instruction about the elders' qualifications (1Ti 3; Tit 1).

first day I came into the province of Asia. [e] [19]I served the Lord with great humility and with tears [f] and in the midst of severe testing by the plots of the Jews. [g] [20]You know that I have not hesitated to preach anything [h] that would be helpful to you but have taught you publicly and from house to house. [21]I have declared to both Jews [i] and Greeks that they must turn to God in repentance [j] and have faith in our Lord Jesus. [k]

[22]"And now, compelled by the Spirit, I am going to Jerusalem, [l] not knowing what will happen to me there. [23]I only know that in every city the Holy Spirit warns me [m] that prison and hardships are facing me. [n] [24]However, I consider my life worth nothing to me; [o] my only aim is to finish the race [p] and complete the task [q] the Lord Jesus has given me [r]—the task of testifying to the good news of God's grace. [s]

[25]"Now I know that none of you among whom I have gone about preaching the kingdom [t] will ever see me again. [u] [26]Therefore, I declare to you today that I am innocent of the blood of everyone. [v] [27]For I have not hesitated to proclaim to you the whole will of God. [w] [28]Keep watch over yourselves and all the flock [x] of which the Holy Spirit has made you overseers. [y] Be shepherds of the church of God, [a] [z] which he bought [a] with his own blood. [b] [29]I know that after I leave, savage wolves [c] will come in among you and will not spare the flock. [d] [30]Even from your own number some will arise and distort the truth in order to draw away disciples [e] after them. [31]So be on your guard! Remember that for three years [f] I never stopped warning each of you night and day with tears. [g]

[32]"Now I commit you to God [h] and to the word of his grace, which can build you up and give you an inheritance [i] among all those who are sanctified. [j] [33]I have not coveted anyone's silver or gold or clothing. [k] [34]You yourselves know that these hands of mine have supplied my own needs and the needs of my companions. [l] [35]In everything I did, I showed you that by this kind of hard work we must help the weak, remembering the words the Lord Jesus himself said: 'It is more blessed to give than to receive.' "

[36]When Paul had finished speaking, he knelt down with all of them and prayed. [m] [37]They all wept as they embraced him and kissed him. [n] [38]What grieved them most was his statement that they would never see his face again. [o] Then they accompanied him to the ship. [p]

ON TO JERUSALEM

21 After we [q] had torn ourselves away from them, we put out to sea and sailed straight to Kos. The next day we went to Rhodes and from there to Patara. [2]We found a ship crossing over to Phoenicia, [r] went on board and set sail. [3]After sighting Cyprus and passing to the south of it, we sailed on to Syria. [s] We landed at Tyre, where our ship was to unload its cargo. [4]We sought out the disciples [t] there and stayed with them seven days. Through the Spirit [u] they urged Paul not to go on to Jerusa-

---

[a] 28 Many manuscripts *of the Lord*

20:18 [e] S Ac 2:9
20:19 [f] Ps 6:6
[g] S ver 3
20:20 [h] ver 27;
Ps 40:10; Jer 26:2;
42:4
20:21 [i] Ac 18:5
[j] S Ac 2:38 [k] Ac 24:24;
26:18; Eph 1:15;
Col 2:5; Phm 5
20:22 [l] ver 16
20:23 [m] S Ac 8:29;
21:4 [n] S Ac 9:16
20:24 [o] Ac 21:13
[p] 2Ti 4:7 [q] 2Co 4:1
[r] Gal 1:1; Tit 1:3
[s] S Ac 11:23
20:25 [t] S Mt 4:23
[u] ver 38
20:26 [v] Eze 3:17-19;
Ac 18:6
20:27 [w] S ver 20
20:28 [x] ver 29;
S Jn 21:16 [y] S 1Ti 3:1
[z] S 1Co 10:32
[a] S 1Co 6:20
[b] S Ro 3:25
20:29 [c] Eze 34:5;
Mt 7:15 [d] ver 28
20:30 [e] S Ac 11:26
20:31 [f] Ac 19:10
[g] ver 19
20:32 [h] Ac 14:23
[i] S Eph 1:14;
S Mt 25:34; Col 1:12;
3:24; Heb 9:15;
1Pe 1:4 [j] Ac 26:18
20:33 [k] 1Sa 12:3;
1Co 9:12; 2Co 2:17;
7:2; 11:9; 12:14-17;
1Th 2:5
20:34 [l] S Ac 18:3
20:36 [m] Lk 22:41;
Ac 9:40; 21:5
20:37 [n] S Lk 15:20
20:38 [o] ver 25
[p] Ac 21:5
21:1 [q] S Ac 16:10
21:2 [r] Ac 11:19
21:3 [s] S Lk 2:2
21:4 [t] S Ac 11:26
[u] ver 11; Ac 20:23

20:19 *with tears.* See v. 31. Paul's ministry at Ephesus was conducted with emotional fervency and a sense of urgency.

A **20:22** *compelled by the Spirit.* Paul did not go to Jerusalem against the direction of the Spirit, as some have suggested, but because of the guidance of the Spirit. People pleaded with him not to go (21:4,12), not because the Spirit prohibited his going but because the Spirit revealed the capture that awaited him there (21:11–12).

20:24 *finish the race.* See 2Ti 4:7 and note.

20:25 *none of you ... will ever see me again.* Not a message from God but what Paul anticipated. He had been mistaken before in his plans: He had intended to stay in Ephesus until Pentecost but had to leave earlier (see v. 1; 1Co 16:8–9). His prophetic power was not used to foresee his own future, just as his healing power was not used to heal his own disease (see 2Co 12:7–9). As it turned out, Paul evidently did revisit Ephesus (see 1Ti 1:3). *kingdom.* See notes on Mt 3:2; Lk 4:43.

20:28 *overseers. Be shepherds.* The "elders" (v. 17) were called "overseers" and told to pastor ("shepherd") the flock—demonstrating that the same men could be called "elders," "overseers" or "pastors." *his own blood.* Lit. "the blood of his own one," a term of endearment (such as "his own dear one," referring to his own Son).

20:29 *wolves.* See Lk 10:3 and note.

20:31 *three years.* See note on 19:10.

20:32 *inheritance.* See 1Pe 1:4 and note. *sanctified.* See note on 1Co 1:2.

20:34 *supplied my own needs.* Paul had worked in Thessalonica (1Th 2:9) and Corinth (Ac 18:3).

20:35 *remembering the words the Lord Jesus himself said.* A formula regularly used in the early church to introduce a quotation from Jesus (1 Clement 46:7). This is a rare instance of a saying of Jesus not found in the canonical Gospels.

20:38 *never see his face again.* See v. 25 and note.

21:1 *sailed straight to Kos.* Favorable winds took them to a stopping place for the night at this island. *Rhodes.* The leading city on the island of Rhodes, once noted for its harbor colossus, one of the seven wonders of the ancient world (but demolished over two centuries before Paul arrived there). It took them a day to get to Rhodes. *Patara.* On the southern coast of Lycia. Paul changed ships from a vessel that hugged the shore of Asia Minor to one going directly to Tyre and Phoenicia.

21:3 *Cyprus.* See 13:4 and note. *Tyre.* Paul had passed through this Phoenician area at least once before (15:3; cf. Mk 7:24).

21:4 *seven days.* These, added to the 29 days since the Passover in Philippi, would leave only two weeks until Pentecost. *urged Paul not to go.* The Spirit warned of the coming trials in store for Paul at Jerusalem (20:23). Because of these warnings, Paul's Christian friends urged him not to go on, knowing that trials lay ahead. But Paul felt "compelled by the Spirit" to go (20:22; see note there).

21:5 v Lk 22:41;
Ac 9:40; 20:36
21:7 w Ac 12:20
x S Ac 1:16
21:8 y S Ac 8:40
z Ac 6:5; 8:5-40
a Eph 4:11; 2Ti 4:5
21:9 b Ex 15:20;
Jdg 4:4; Ne 6:14;
Lk 2:36; Ac 2:17;
1Co 11:5
21:10 c Ac 11:28
21:11 d S Ac 8:29
e ver 33 f 1Ki 22:11;
Isa 20:2-4; Jer 13:1-
11; Mt 20:19
21:13 g Ac 20:24
h S Jn 15:21; S Ac 9:16
21:14 i Ru 1:18
j S Mt 26:39
21:15 k S Ac 19:21
21:16 l S Ac 8:40
m ver 3,4
21:17 n S Ac 9:30
o Ac 15:4
21:18 p S Ac 15:13
q S Ac 11:30
21:19 r Ac 14:27;
15:4,12 s Ac 1:17
21:20 t Ac 22:3;
Ro 10:2; Gal 1:14;
Php 3:6 u Ac 15:1,5
21:21 v ver 28
w Ac 15:19-21;
1Co 7:18,19
x S Ac 6:14
21:23 y Nu 6:2,5,18;
Ac 18:18
21:24 z ver 26;
Ac 24:18 a Ac 18:18
21:25 b Ac 15:20,29
21:26 c Nu 6:13-20;
Ac 24:18

lem. [5]When it was time to leave, we left and continued on our way. All of them, including wives and children, accompanied us out of the city, and there on the beach we knelt to pray. [6]After saying good-by to each other, we went aboard the ship, and they returned home.

[7]We continued our voyage from Tyre [w] and landed at Ptolemais, where we greeted the believers [x] and stayed with them for a day. [8]Leaving the next day, we reached Caesarea [y] and stayed at the house of Philip [z] the evangelist, [a] one of the Seven. [9]He had four unmarried daughters who prophesied. [b]

[10]After we had been there a number of days, a prophet named Agabus [c] came down from Judea. [11]Coming over to us, he took Paul's belt, tied his own hands and feet with it and said, "The Holy Spirit says, [d] 'In this way the Jewish leaders in Jerusalem will bind [e] the owner of this belt and will hand him over to the Gentiles.' " [f]

[12]When we heard this, we and the people there pleaded with Paul not to go up to Jerusalem. [13]Then Paul answered, "Why are you weeping and breaking my heart? I am ready not only to be bound, but also to die [g] in Jerusalem for the name of the Lord Jesus." [h] [14]When he would not be dissuaded, we gave up [i] and said, "The Lord's will be done." [j]

[15]After this, we started on our way up to Jerusalem. [k] [16]Some of the disciples from Caesarea [l] accompanied us and brought us to the home of Mnason, where we were to stay. He was a man from Cyprus [m] and one of the early disciples.

PAUL'S ARRIVAL AT JERUSALEM

[17]When we arrived at Jerusalem, the believers [n] received us warmly. [o] [18]The next day Paul and the rest of us went to see James, [p] and all the elders [q] were present. [19]Paul greeted them and reported in detail what God had done among the Gentiles [r] through his ministry. [s]

[20]When they heard this, they praised God. Then they said to Paul: "You see, brother, how many thousands of Jews have believed, and all of them are zealous [t] for the law. [u] [21]They have been informed that you teach all the Jews who live among the Gentiles to turn away from Moses, [v] telling them not to circumcise their children [w] or live according to our customs. [x] [22]What shall we do? They will certainly hear that you have come, [23]so do what we tell you. There are four men with us who have made a vow. [y] [24]Take these men, join in their purification rites [z] and pay their expenses, so that they can have their heads shaved. [a] Then everyone will know there is no truth in these reports about you, but that you yourself are living in obedience to the law. [25]As for the Gentile believers, we have written to them our decision that they should abstain from food sacrificed to idols, from blood, from the meat of strangled animals and from sexual immorality." [b]

[26]The next day Paul took the men and purified himself along with them. Then he went to the temple to give notice of the date when the days of purification would end and the offering would be made for each of them. [c]

21:7 *Ptolemais.* The modern city of Akko, north of and across the bay from Mount Carmel. It was one day's journey from Tyre on the north and another 35 miles to Caesarea on the south.

21:8 *Caesarea.* A Gentile city, the capital of Roman Judea (see note on 10:1). *Philip the evangelist.* Philip's evangelistic work may have focused on Caesarea for almost 25 years (see note on 8:40). "Evangelist" is a title used only here and in Eph 4:11; 2Ti 4:5.

21:9 *unmarried daughters.* They may have been dedicated in a special way to serving the Lord (cf. 1Co 7:34). *prophesied.* See 1Co 11:5; 12:8–10; cf. Lk 2:36. For OT prophetesses, see Ex 15:20; Jdg 4:4; 2Ki 22:14; Ne 6:14.

21:10 *prophet named Agabus.* Evidently he held the office of prophet, as Philip held the office of evangelist (v. 8). This is the same prophet who had been in Antioch prophesying the coming famine in Jerusalem some 15 years earlier (11:27–29).

21:12 *we and the people there.* Now Luke, in the company of travelers with Paul, joins in urging Paul not to go to Jerusalem.
21:13 *to die.* Cf. Php 1:21 and note.
21:14 *Lord's will be done.* May mean that they finally recognized that it was the Lord's will for Paul to go to Jerusalem.

21:16 *Mnason.* Must have been a disciple of some means to be able to accommodate Paul and a group of about nine men traveling with him.
21:17 *arrived at Jerusalem.* No more than a day or two before

Pentecost. *the believers received us warmly.* May indicate the grateful reception of the offering as well.

21:18 *James.* The brother of the Lord, author of the letter of James and leader of the church in Jerusalem (see Gal 1:19 and note; 2:9). He is called an apostle but was not one of the Twelve.
21:23 *made a vow.* They were evidently under the temporary Nazirite vow and became unclean before the completion time of the vow (perhaps from contact with a dead body); cf. Nu 6:2–12.
21:24 *purification rites.* In some instances the rites included the offering of sacrifices. Such rites were observed by choice by some Jewish Christians but were not required of Christians, whether Jew or Gentile. *pay their expenses.* Paul's part in sponsoring these men would include (1) paying part or all of the expenses of the sacrificial victims (in this case eight pigeons and four lambs, Nu 6:9–12) and (2) going to the temple to notify the priest when their days of purification would be fulfilled so the priests would be prepared to sacrifice their offerings (v. 26). *living in obedience to the law.* Paul had earlier taken a vow himself (see 18:18 and note), he had been a Jew to the Jews (see 1Co 9:20–21), and Timothy had been circumcised (see 16:3 and note). However, Paul was very careful not to sacrifice Christian principle in any act of obedience to the law (e.g., he would not have Titus circumcised, Gal 2:3).
21:25 See 15:23–29 and notes.

PAUL ARRESTED

²⁷When the seven days were nearly over, some Jews from the province of Asia saw Paul at the temple. They stirred up the whole crowd and seized him, *d* ²⁸shouting, "People of Israel, help us! This is the man who teaches everyone everywhere against our people and our law and this place. And besides, he has brought Greeks into the temple and defiled this holy place." *e* ²⁹(They had previously seen Trophimus *f* the Ephesian *g* in the city with Paul and assumed that Paul had brought him into the temple.)

³⁰The whole city was aroused, and the people came running from all directions. Seizing Paul, *h* they dragged him *i* from the temple, and immediately the gates were shut. ³¹While they were trying to kill him, news reached the commander of the Roman troops that the whole city of Jerusalem was in an uproar. ³²He at once took some officers and soldiers and ran down to the crowd. When the rioters saw the commander and his soldiers, they stopped beating Paul. *j*

³³The commander came up and arrested him and ordered him to be bound *k* with two chains. *m* Then he asked who he was and what he had done. ³⁴Some in the crowd shouted one thing and some another, *n* and since the commander could not get at the truth because of the uproar, he ordered that Paul be taken into the barracks. *o* ³⁵When Paul reached the steps, *p* the violence of the mob was so great he had to be carried by the soldiers. ³⁶The crowd that followed kept shouting, "Get rid of him!" *q*

PAUL SPEAKS TO THE CROWD

22:3–16pp — Ac 9:1–22; 26:9–18

³⁷As the soldiers were about to take Paul into the barracks, *r* he asked the commander, "May I say something to you?"

"Do you speak Greek?" he replied. ³⁸"Aren't you the Egyptian who started a revolt and led four thousand terrorists out into the wilderness *s* some time ago?" *t*

³⁹Paul answered, "I am a Jew, from Tarsus *u* in Cilicia, *v* a citizen of no ordinary city. Please let me speak to the people."

⁴⁰Having received the commander's permission, Paul stood on the steps and motioned *w* to the crowd. When they were all silent, he said to them in Aramaic *a: x*

22 ¹"Brothers and fathers, *y* listen now to my defense."

²When they heard him speak to them in Aramaic, *z* they became very quiet. Then Paul said: ³"I am a Jew, *a* born in Tarsus *b* of Cilicia, *c* but brought up in this city. I

a 40 Or possibly *Hebrew*; also in 22:2

21:27 *d* Jer 26:8; Ac 24:18; 26:21; S 1Th 2:16
21:28 *e* Mt 24:15; Ac 6:13; 24:5,6
21:29 *f* Ac 20:4; 2Ti 4:20 *g* S Ac 18:19
21:30 *h* Ac 26:21 *i* S Ac 16:19
21:32 *j* Ac 23:27
21:33 *k* ver 11 *l* Ac 12:6 *m* Ac 20:23; 22:29; Eph 6:20; 2Ti 2:9
21:34 *n* Ac 19:32 *o* ver 37; Ac 22:24; 23:10,16,32
21:35 *p* ver 40
21:36 *q* Lk 23:18; Jn 19:15; Ac 22:22
21:37 *r* S ver 34
21:38 *s* Mt 24:26 *t* Ac 5:36
21:39 *u* S Ac 9:11 *v* S Ac 6:9
21:40 *w* S Ac 12:17 *x* S Jn 5:2
22:1 *y* Ac 7:2
22:2 *z* Ac 21:40; S Jn 5:2
22:3 *a* Ac 21:39 *b* S Ac 9:11 *c* S Ac 6:9

21:27 *seven days.* Cf. Nu 6:9. These were the days required for purification, shaving their heads at the altar, the sacrifice of a sin offering and burnt offering for each and announcing the completion to the priests. *Jews from the province of Asia.* Paul had suffered already from the hands of Asian Jews (20:19).

B **21:28** *teaches … against our people and our law and this place.* Cf. the accusations brought against Stephen in 6:13. *brought Greeks into the temple.* Explicitly forbidden according to inscribed stone markers (still in existence). Any Gentiles found within the bounds of the court of Israel would be killed. But there is no evidence that Paul had brought anyone other than Jews into the area.

21:29 *Trophimus.* See 20:4 and note. Paul probably did not take him into the forbidden area. If he had, they should have attacked Trophimus rather than Paul.

21:30 *gates were shut.* By order of the temple officer to prevent further trouble inside the sacred precincts.

21:31 *commander.* Greek *chiliarch* (a commander of 1,000 [a regiment]), Claudius Lysias by name (23:26), who was stationed at the Fortress of Antonia (see note on v. 37).

21:32 *some officers.* Centurions. Since the plural is used, it is likely that at least two centurions and 200 soldiers were involved.

21:33 *two chains.* Probably his hands were chained to a soldier on either side.

21:34 *barracks.* See note on 12:9.

21:37 *barracks.* The Fortress of Antonia was connected to the northern end of the temple area by two flights of steps. The tower overlooked the temple area.

21:38 *the Egyptian who started a revolt.* Josephus tells of an Egyptian false prophet who some years earlier had led 4,000 (Josephus, through a misreading of a Greek capital letter, says 30,000) out to the Mount of Olives. Roman soldiers killed hundreds, but the leader escaped. *terrorists.* The Greek here is a loanword from Latin *sicarii,* meaning "dagger-men," who were violent assassins.

21:39 *Tarsus.* See note on 22:3.

21:40 *Aramaic.* More likely Aramaic than Hebrew (see TNIV text note), since Aramaic was the most commonly used language among Palestinian Jews.

22:1 *Brothers.* See note on 11:1.

22:2 *Aramaic.* See note on 21:40. Actually, if he had spoken in Hebrew, they would have become even quieter in order not to miss a single word, because it would have been more difficult for them to understand.

C **22:3** *born in Tarsus.* Paul had citizenship in Tarsus (21:39) as well as being a Roman citizen. "No ordinary city" (21:39) was used by Euripides to describe Athens. Tarsus was 10 miles inland on the Cydnus River and 30 miles from the mountains, which were cut by a deep, narrow gorge called the Cilician Gates. It was an important commercial center, university city and crossroads of travel. *brought up in this city.* Paul must have come to Jerusalem at an early age. Another translation ("brought up in this city at the feet of Gamaliel, being thoroughly trained according to the law of our fathers") would suggest that Paul came to Jerusalem when he was old enough to begin training under Gamaliel. *Gamaliel.* The most honored rabbi of the first century. Possibly he was the grandson of Hillel (see also 5:34–40).

22:3 *d* Lk 10:39
e Ac 5:34 *f* Ac 26:5
g 1Ki 19:10;
S Ac 21:20
22:4 *h* S Ac 8:3
i S Ac 9:2 *j* ver 19,20
22:5 *k* Lk 22:66
l S Ac 1:16; 2:29;
13:26; 23:1; 28:17,21;
S Ro 7:1; 9:3 *m* Ac 9:2
22:6 *n* Ac 9:3
22:8 *o* S Mk 1:24
22:9 *p* Ac 26:13
q Ac 9:7
22:10 *r* Ac 16:30
22:11 *s* Ac 9:8
22:12 *t* Ac 9:17
u Ac 10:22
22:14 *v* S Ac 3:13
w S 1Co 15:8 *x* Ac 7:52
22:15 *y* Ac 23:11;
26:16 *z* ver 14
22:16 *a* S Ac 2:38
b Lev 8:6; Ps 51:2;
Eze 36:25; Jn 3:5;
1Co 6:11; Eph 5:26;
Tit 3:5; Heb 10:22;
1Pe 3:21 *c* Ro 10:13
22:17 *d* Ac 9:26
e Ac 10:10
22:19 *f* ver 4;
S Ac 8:3 *g* S Mt 10:17
22:20 *h* Ac 7:57-60;
8:1
22:21 *i* S Ac 9:15;
S 13:46
22:22 *j* Ac 21:36
k Ac 25:24
22:23 *l* Ac 7:58
m 2Sa 16:13
22:24 *n* S Ac 21:34
o ver 29
22:25 *p* Ac 16:37

studied under *d* Gamaliel *e* and was thoroughly trained in the law of our ancestors. *f* I was just as zealous *g* for God as any of you are today. ⁴I persecuted *h* the followers of this Way *i* to their death, arresting both men and women and throwing them into prison, *j* ⁵as the high priest and all the Council *k* can themselves testify. I even obtained letters from them to their associates *l* in Damascus, *m* and went there to bring these people as prisoners to Jerusalem to be punished.

⁶"About noon as I came near Damascus, suddenly a bright light from heaven flashed around me. *n* ⁷I fell to the ground and heard a voice say to me, 'Saul! Saul! Why do you persecute me?'

⁸" 'Who are you, Lord?' I asked.

" 'I am Jesus of Nazareth, *o* whom you are persecuting,' he replied. ⁹My companions saw the light, *p* but they did not understand the voice *q* of him who was speaking to me.

¹⁰" 'What shall I do, Lord?' I asked.

" 'Get up,' the Lord said, 'and go into Damascus. There you will be told all that you have been assigned to do.' *r* ¹¹My companions led me by the hand into Damascus, because the brilliance of the light had blinded me. *s*

¹²"A man named Ananias came to see me. *t* He was a devout observer of the law and highly respected by all the Jews living there. *u* ¹³He stood beside me and said, 'Brother Saul, receive your sight!' And at that very moment I was able to see him.

¹⁴"Then he said: 'The God of our ancestors *v* has chosen you to know his will and to see *w* the Righteous One *x* and to hear words from his mouth. ¹⁵You will be his witness *y* to all people of what you have seen *z* and heard. ¹⁶And now what are you waiting for? Get up, be baptized *a* and wash your sins away, *b* calling on his name.' *c*

¹⁷"When I returned to Jerusalem *d* and was praying at the temple, I fell into a trance *e* ¹⁸and saw the Lord speaking to me. 'Quick!' he said. 'Leave Jerusalem immediately, because the people here will not accept your testimony about me.'

¹⁹" 'Lord,' I replied, 'these people know that I went from one synagogue to another to imprison *f* and beat *g* those who believe in you. ²⁰And when the blood of your martyr *a* Stephen was shed, I stood there giving my approval and guarding the clothes of those who were killing him.' *h*

²¹"Then the Lord said to me, 'Go; I will send you far away to the Gentiles.' " *i*

PAUL THE ROMAN CITIZEN

²²The crowd listened to Paul until he said this. Then they raised their voices and shouted, "Rid the earth of him! *j* He's not fit to live!" *k*

²³As they were shouting and throwing off their cloaks *l* and flinging dust into the air, *m* ²⁴the commander ordered that Paul be taken into the barracks. *n* He directed *o* that he be flogged and interrogated in order to find out why the people were shouting at him like this. ²⁵As they stretched him out to flog him, Paul said to the centurion standing there, "Is it legal for you to flog a Roman citizen who hasn't even been found guilty?" *p*

---

a 20 Or *witness*

22:4 *I persecuted the followers.* See 9:1–4. *this Way.* See 9:2 and note.

22:5 *high priest.* Caiaphas, the high priest over 20 years earlier, was now dead, and Ananias was high priest (see 23:2 and note); but the records of the high priest would show Paul's testimony to be true. *Council.* The Sanhedrin (see Mk 14:55 and note).

22:6 *About noon.* A detail not included in the earlier account (9:1–22).

22:8 *Who are you, Lord?* See note on 9:5. *persecuting.* See note on 9:4.

22:9 *did not understand the voice.* They heard the sound (9:7) but did not understand what was said.

22:12 *Ananias . . . devout observer of the law.* Important to this audience (see note on Lk 1:6).

22:14 *to see the Righteous One.* Cf. 3:14; Lk 23:47 and notes. To see the resurrected Jesus was all-important to Paul (see 26:16; 1Co 9:1; 15:8). It was that experience that had convinced him of the truth of the gospel and that became the foundation of his theology.

22:16 *wash your sins away.* Baptism is the outward sign of an inward work of grace. The reality and the symbol are closely associated in the NT (see 2:38; Tit 3:5; 1Pe 3:21 and notes).

The outward rite, however, does not produce the inward grace (cf. Ro 2:28–29; Eph 2:8–9; Php 3:4–9). See note on Ro 6:3–4.

22:17 *When I returned to Jerusalem.* Refers to the visit described in 9:26; Gal 1:17–18. *at the temple, I fell into a trance.* See Peter's trance (10:10; 11:5; cf. 2Co 12:3). Paul was not a blasphemer of the temple but continued to hold it in high honor.

22:20 *giving my approval.* Does not necessarily mean that Paul had to be a member of the Sanhedrin, though some have thought so (see note on 26:10). He could show his approval by allowing them to put their cloaks at his feet.

22:24 *commander.* See note on 21:31. *barracks.* See note on 21:37. *that he be flogged.* Not with the rod, as at Philippi (16:22–24), but with the scourge, a merciless instrument of torture. It was legal to use it to force a confession from a slave or foreigner but never from a Roman citizen. The scourge consisted of a whip of leather thongs with pieces of bone or metal attached to the ends (cf. Mk 15:15 and note).

22:25 *they stretched him out.* The Greek word used for tying a person to a post for whipping. *centurion.* See note on 10:1. *Roman citizen.* According to Roman law, all Roman citizens were assured exclusion from all degrading forms of punishment: beating with rods, scourging, crucifixion.

26When the centurion heard this, he went to the commander and reported it. "What are you going to do?" he asked. "This man is a Roman citizen."

27The commander went to Paul and asked, "Tell me, are you a Roman citizen?"

"Yes, I am," he answered.

28Then the commander said, "I had to pay a lot of money for my citizenship."

"But I was born a citizen," Paul replied.

29Those who were about to interrogate him *q* withdrew immediately. The commander himself was alarmed when he realized that he had put Paul, a Roman citizen, *r* in chains. *s*

PAUL BEFORE THE SANHEDRIN

30The commander wanted to find out exactly why Paul was being accused by the Jews. *t* So the next day he released him *u* and ordered the chief priests and all the members of the Sanhedrin *v* to assemble. Then he brought Paul and had him stand before them.

23 Paul looked straight at the Sanhedrin *w* and said, "My brothers, *x* I have fulfilled my duty to God in all good conscience *y* to this day." 2At this the high priest Ananias *z* ordered those standing near Paul to strike him on the mouth. *a* 3Then Paul said to him, "God will strike you, you whitewashed wall! *b* You sit there to judge me according to the law, yet you yourself violate the law by commanding that I be struck!" *c*

4Those who were standing near Paul said, "How dare you insult God's high priest!"

5Paul replied, "Brothers, I did not realize that he was the high priest; for it is written: 'Do not speak evil about the ruler of your people.'*a* *d*

6Then Paul, knowing that some of them were Sadducees *e* and the others Pharisees, called out in the Sanhedrin, "My brothers, *f* I am a Pharisee, *g* descended from Pharisees. I stand on trial because of the hope of the resurrection of the dead." *h* 7When he said this, a dispute broke out between the Pharisees and the Sadducees, and the assembly was divided. 8(The Sadducees say that there is no resurrection, *i* and that there are neither angels nor spirits, but the Pharisees believe all these things.)

9There was a great uproar, and some of the teachers of the law who were Pharisees *j* stood up and argued vigorously. "We find nothing wrong with this man," *k* they said. "What if a spirit or an angel has spoken to him?" *l* 10The dispute became so violent that the commander was afraid Paul would be torn to pieces by them. He ordered the troops to go down and take him away from them by force and bring him into the barracks. *m*

11The following night the Lord stood near Paul and said, "Take courage! *n* As you have testified about me in Jerusalem, so you must also testify in Rome." *o*

THE PLOT TO KILL PAUL

12The next morning the Jews formed a conspiracy *p* and bound themselves with an oath

---

a 5 Exodus 22:28

22:29 *q* ver 24
r ver 24,25; Ac 16:38
s S Ac 21:33
22:30 *t* Ac 23:28
u Ac 21:33 *v* S Mt 5:22
23:1 *w* Ac 22:30
x S Ac 22:5
y Ac 24:16; 1Co 4:4;
2Co 1:12; 1Ti 1:5,19;
3:9; 2Ti 1:3; Heb 9:14;
10:22; 13:18; 1Pe 3:16,
21
23:2 *z* Ac 24:1
a Jn 18:22
23:3 *b* Mt 23:27
c Lev 19:15; Dt 25:1,2;
Jn 7:51
23:5 *d* Ex 22:28
23:6 *e* ver 7,8;
S Ac 4:1 *f* S Ac 22:5
g Ac 26:5; Php 3:5
h Ac 24:15,21; 26:8
23:8 *i* Mt 22:23;
1Co 15:12
23:9 *j* Mk 2:16
k ver 29; Jer 26:16;
S Lk 23:4; Ac 25:25;
26:31; 28:18 *l* Ac 22:7,
17,18
23:10 *m* S Ac 21:34
23:11 *n* S Mt 14:27
o Ac 19:21; 28:23
23:12 *p* S Ac 20:3

22:28 *pay a lot of money.* There were three ways to obtain Roman citizenship: (1) receive it as a reward for some outstanding service to Rome; (2) buy it at a considerable price; (3) be born into a family of Roman citizens. How Paul's father or an earlier ancestor had gained citizenship, no one knows. By 171 B.C. a large number of Jews were citizens of Tarsus, and in the time of Pompey (106–48) some of these could have received Roman citizenship as well.

22:29 *alarmed.* Cf. the same reaction of the magistrates in Philippi (16:38).

22:30 *he released him.* Paul was no longer bound, and presumably he would have been free completely if the Sanhedrin had not wished to detain him. *chief priests.* Those of the high priestly line of descent (mainly Sadducees; see note on Mt 2:4), but the Sanhedrin now included a considerable number of Pharisees. These men constituted the ruling body of the Jews. The Jewish court was respected by the Roman governor, whose approval had to be obtained before sentencing to capital punishment.

23:1 *Sanhedrin.* See notes on 5:21; 22:30. *brothers.* Fellow Jews (see note on 11:1). *good conscience.* A consistent claim of Paul (see 24:16; Ro 9:1; 1Co 4:4; 2Co 1:12; 2Ti 1:3).

23:2 *Ananias.* High priest A.D. 47–59, son of Nebedaeus. He is not to be confused with the high priest Annas (A.D. 6–15; see note on Lk 3:2). Ananias was noted for cruelty and violence. When the revolt against Rome broke

out, he was assassinated by his own people.

23:3 *whitewashed wall!* Having an attractive exterior but filled with unclean contents, such as tombs holding dead bodies (see Mt 23:27); or walls that look substantial but fall before the winds (see Eze 13:10–12). It is a metaphor for a hypocrite.

23:5 *I did not realize that he was the high priest.* Explained in different ways: 1. Paul had poor eyesight (suggested by such passages as Gal 4:15; 6:11 [see note there]) and failed to see that the one who presided was the high priest. 2. He failed to discern that the one who presided was the high priest because on some occasions others had sat in his place. 3. He was using pure irony: A true high priest would not give such an order. 4. He refused to acknowledge that Ananias was the high priest under these circumstances.

23:6 *Sadducees.* See note on 4:1. They denied the resurrection, as well as the existence of angels and spirits (v. 8). *Pharisees.* See notes on Mt 3:7; Mk 2:16; Lk 5:17.

23:10 *commander.* See note on 21:31. *barracks.* See note on 21:37.

23:11 *the Lord stood near.* In times of crisis and need for strength, Paul was given help (see 18:9; 22:18; 27:23; cf. 2Co 12:7–10 and notes).

23:12 *bound themselves with an oath.* These men were probably from the Zealots or the "terrorists" (see note on 21:38) later responsible for revolt against Rome.

23:12 ^q ver 14, 21,
30; Ac 25:3
23:14 ^r ver 12
23:15 ^s ver 1;
Ac 22:30
23:16 ^t ver 10;
S Ac 21:34
23:18 ^u S Eph 3:1
23:20 ^v ver 1
^w ver 14, 15
23:21 ^x ver 13
^y ver 12, 14
23:23 ^z S Ac 8:40
^a ver 33
23:24 ^b ver 26, 33;
Ac 24:1-3, 10; 25:14
23:26 ^c Lk 1:3;
Ac 24:3; 26:25
^d Ac 15:23
23:27 ^e Ac 21:32
^f Ac 21:33 ^g Ac 22:25-
29
23:28 ^h Ac 22:30
23:29 ⁱ Ac 18:15;
25:19 ^j S ver 9
23:30 ^k ver 20, 21
^l S Ac 20:3 ^m ver 35;
Ac 24:19; 25:16
23:32 ⁿ ver 23
^o S Ac 21:34
23:33 ^p ver 23, 24
^q S Ac 8:40 ^r ver 26

not to eat or drink until they had killed Paul. ^{q 13}More than forty men were involved in this plot. ¹⁴They went to the chief priests and the elders and said, "We have taken a solemn oath not to eat anything until we have killed Paul. ^{r 15}Now then, you and the Sanhedrin ^s petition the commander to bring him before you on the pretext of wanting more accurate information about his case. We are ready to kill him before he gets here."

¹⁶But when the son of Paul's sister heard of this plot, he went into the barracks ^t and told Paul.

¹⁷Then Paul called one of the centurions and said, "Take this young man to the commander; he has something to tell him." ¹⁸So he took him to the commander.

The centurion said, "Paul, the prisoner, ^u sent for me and asked me to bring this young man to you because he has something to tell you."

¹⁹The commander took the young man by the hand, drew him aside and asked, "What is it you want to tell me?"

²⁰He said: "The Jews have agreed to ask you to bring Paul before the Sanhedrin ^v tomorrow on the pretext of wanting more accurate information about him. ^{w 21}Don't give in to them, because more than forty ^x of them are waiting in ambush for him. They have taken an oath not to eat or drink until they have killed him. ^y They are ready now, waiting for your consent to their request."

²²The commander dismissed the young man with this warning: "Don't tell anyone that you have reported this to me."

PAUL TRANSFERRED TO CAESAREA

²³Then he called two of his centurions and ordered them, "Get ready a detachment of two hundred soldiers, seventy horsemen and two hundred spearmen ^a to go to Caesarea ^z at nine tonight. ^{a 24}Provide horses for Paul so that he may be taken safely to Governor Felix." ^b

²⁵He wrote a letter as follows:

²⁶Claudius Lysias,

To His Excellency, ^c Governor Felix:

Greetings. ^d

²⁷This man was seized by the Jews and they were about to kill him, ^e but I came with my troops and rescued him, ^f for I had learned that he is a Roman citizen. ^{g 28}I wanted to know why they were accusing him, so I brought him to their Sanhedrin. ^h ²⁹I found that the accusation had to do with questions about their law, ⁱ but there was no charge against him ^j that deserved death or imprisonment. ³⁰When I was informed ^k of a plot ^l to be carried out against the man, I sent him to you at once. I also ordered his accusers ^m to present to you their case against him.

³¹So the soldiers, carrying out their orders, took Paul with them during the night and brought him as far as Antipatris. ³²The next day they let the cavalry ⁿ go on with him, while they returned to the barracks. ^{o 33}When the cavalry ^p arrived in Caesarea, ^q they delivered the letter to the governor ^r and handed Paul over to him. ³⁴The governor read the letter and

---

^a 23 The meaning of the Greek for this word is uncertain.

23:17 *centurions.* See note on 10:1.

23:22 *Don't tell anyone.* For the boy's own safety and because of the commander's plans to transfer Paul under cover of night (see v. 23).

23:23 *soldiers … horsemen … spearmen.* Heavily armed infantry, cavalry and lightly armed soldiers. The commander assigned 470 men to protect Paul, the Roman citizen (cf. 22:25–29)—but the Greek for "spearmen" is an obscure word that could perhaps be translated "additional mounts and pack animals" (see TNIV text note).

23:24 *Governor Felix.* See note on v. 34.

23:27 *for I had learned that he is a Roman citizen.* Inserted to gain the commander's favor with Rome, but not a true statement, because the commander did not learn of Paul's citizenship until he was about to scourge him to gain information.

23:29 Cf. the false charge made against Paul before Gallio in Corinth (18:13–16).

23:30 *ordered his accusers to present to you their case.* He antici-

pated that the order would be given by the time the letter was delivered.

23:31 *Antipatris.* Rebuilt by Herod the Great and named for his father (Antipater). It was a military post between Samaria and Judea—30 miles from Jerusalem.

23:33 *Caesarea.* The headquarters of Roman rule for Samaria and Judea—28 miles from Antipatris (see note on 8:40).

C **23:34** *The governor.* Antonius Felix. The emperor Claudius had appointed him governor of Judea c. A.D. 52, a time when Felix's brother was the emperor's favorite minister. The brothers had formerly been slaves, then Freedmen, then high officials in government. The historian Tacitus said of Felix, "He held the power of a tyrant with the disposition of a slave." He married three queens in succession, one of whom was Drusilla (see note on 24:24). *from Cilicia.* If Paul had come from a province nearby, Felix might have turned him over for trial under another's jurisdiction.

asked what province he was from. Learning that he was from Cilicia, ^{s} ^{35}he said, "I will hear your case when your accusers ^{t} get here." Then he ordered that Paul be kept under guard ^{u} in Herod's palace.

PAUL'S TRIAL BEFORE FELIX

24 Five days later the high priest Ananias ^{v} went down to Caesarea with some of the elders and a lawyer named Tertullus, and they brought their charges ^{w} against Paul before the governor. ^{x} ^{2}When Paul was called in, Tertullus presented his case before Felix: "We have enjoyed a long period of peace under you, and your foresight has brought about reforms in this nation. ^{3}Everywhere and in every way, most excellent ^{y} Felix, we acknowledge this with profound gratitude. ^{4}But in order not to weary you further, I would request that you be kind enough to hear us briefly.

^{5}"We have found this man to be a troublemaker, stirring up riots ^{z} among the Jews ^{a} all over the world. He is a ringleader of the Nazarene ^{b} sect ^{c} $^{6[7]}$and even tried to desecrate the temple; ^{d} so we seized him. ^{8}By examining him yourself you will be able to learn the truth about all these charges we are bringing against him."

^{9}The other Jews joined in the accusation, ^{e} asserting that these things were true.

^{10}When the governor ^{f} motioned for him to speak, Paul replied: "I know that for a number of years you have been a judge over this nation; so I gladly make my defense. ^{11}You can easily verify that no more than twelve days ^{g} ago I went up to Jerusalem to worship. ^{12}My accusers did not find me arguing with anyone at the temple, ^{h} or stirring up a crowd ^{i} in the synagogues or anywhere else in the city. ^{13}And they cannot prove to you the charges they are now making against me. ^{j} ^{14}However, I admit that I worship the God of our ancestors ^{k} as a follower of the Way, ^{l} which they call a sect. ^{m} I believe everything that is in accordance with the Law and that is written in the Prophets, ^{n} ^{15}and I have the same hope in God as these people themselves have, that there will be a resurrection ^{o} of both the righteous and the wicked. ^{p} ^{16}So I strive always to keep my conscience clear ^{q} before God and all people.

^{17}"After an absence of several years, I came to Jerusalem to bring my people gifts for the poor ^{r} and to present offerings. ^{18}I was ceremonially clean ^{s} when they found me in the temple courts doing this. There was no crowd with me, nor was I involved in any disturbance. ^{t} ^{19}But there are some Jews from the province of Asia, ^{u} who ought to be here before you and bring charges if they have anything against me. ^{v} ^{20}Or these who are here should state what crime they found in me when I stood before the Sanhedrin— ^{21}unless it was this one thing I shouted as I stood in their presence: 'It is concerning the resurrection of the dead that I am on trial before you today.' " ^{w}

23:34 ^{s} Ac 6:9;
21:39
23:35 ^{t} ver 30;
Ac 24:19; 25:16
^{u} Ac 24:27
24:1 ^{v} Ac 23:2
^{w} Ac 23:30,35
^{x} S Ac 23:24
24:3 ^{y} Lk 1:3;
Ac 23:26; 26:25
24:5 ^{z} Ac 16:20; 17:6
^{a} Ac 21:28 ^{b} S Mk 1:24
^{c} ver 14; Ac 26:5;
28:22
24:6[7] ^{d} Ac 21:28
24:9 ^{e} S 1Ti 2:16
24:10 ^{f} S Ac 23:24
24:11 ^{g} Ac 21:27;
ver 1
24:12 ^{h} Ac 25:8;
28:17 ^{i} ver 18
24:13 ^{j} Ac 25:7
24:14 ^{k} S Ac 3:13
^{l} S Ac 9:2 ^{m} S ver 5
^{n} Ac 26:6,22; 28:23
24:15 ^{o} Ac 23:6;
28:20 ^{p} S Mt 25:46
24:16 ^{q} S Ac 23:1
24:17 ^{r} Ac 11:29,30;
Ro 15:25-28,31;
1Co 16:1-4,15;
2Co 8:1-4; Gal 2:10
24:18 ^{s} Ac 21:26
^{t} ver 12
24:19 ^{u} S Ac 2:9
^{v} Ac 23:30
24:21 ^{w} Ac 23:6

23:35 *Herod's palace.* Erected as a royal residence by Herod the Great but now used as a Roman praetorium—the headquarters of the local Roman governor. Praetoria were located in Rome (Php 1:13), Ephesus, Jerusalem (Jn 18:28; see note there), Caesarea and other parts of the empire.
24:1 *Five days later.* After the departure from Jerusalem. This would allow just enough time for a messenger to go from Caesarea to Jerusalem, the Sanhedrin to appoint their representatives, and the appointees to make the return journey to Caesarea. *Ananias.* See note on 23:2. The high priest himself made the 60-mile journey to supervise the case personally. *elders.* The Sanhedrin was made up of 71 elders. The designation was used of both the religious and the political councils. See notes on Ex 3:16; 2Sa 3:17; Joel 1:2; Mt 15:2. *lawyer.* Lit. "orator." In a court trial one trained in forensic rhetoric would serve as an attorney at law. *Tertullus.* A common variant of the name Tertius. Possibly he was a Roman but more likely a Hellenistic Jew familiar with the procedures of the Roman court.
24:2–3 *long period of peace . . . with profound gratitude.* The expected eulogy with which to introduce a speech before a judge. In his six years in office Felix had eliminated bands of robbers, thwarted organized assassins and crushed a movement led by an Egyptian (see note on 21:38). But in general his record was not good. He was recalled by Rome two years later because of misrule. His reforms and improvements are hard to identify historically.
24:5 *troublemaker . . . ringleader of the Nazarene sect.* To excite dissension in the empire was treason against Caesar. To be a leader of a religious sect without Roman approval was contrary

to law. *Nazarene sect.* Christianity.
24:6[7] *tried to desecrate the temple.* The charge is now qualified as merely an attempt (see 21:28 and note). Verse 7 (found in later manuscripts) adds a few more details to the account by Tertullus.
24:10 Paul's reserved introduction lacks the flattery employed by Tertullus (vv. 2–4).
24:11 *twelve days ago.* Paul answers each accusation. He was not a troublemaker, and he had not been involved in disturbances. He had but recently arrived in Jerusalem. He had spent five days in Caesarea and nearly seven in Jerusalem.
24:14 *worship . . . God . . . as a follower of the Way.* Paul admits to his part in the Way, but he still believes the Law and the Prophets. He shares the same hope as the Jews—resurrection and judgment (v. 15).
24:16 *conscience clear.* See note on 23:1.
24:17 *to bring my people gifts for the poor.* The only explicit reference in Acts to the collection that was so important to Paul (see note on 20:4). *to present offerings.* May refer to Paul's help in sponsoring those who were fulfilling their vows (see 21:24 and note). He also may have intended to present offerings for himself.
24:19 *Jews from the province of Asia.* See 21:27–29. The absence of these Asian Jews would seem to suggest that they could not substantiate their accusations.
24:21 *concerning the resurrection.* Paul again introduces the point of contention between the Pharisees and Sadducees (see 23:6–8; see also chart, p. 1650).

24:22 ˣ S Ac 9:2
24:23 ʸ Ac 23:35
ᶻ Ac 28:16 ᵃ Ac 23:16;
27:3
24:24 ᵇ S Ac 20:21
24:25 ᶜ Gal 5:23;
1Th 5:6; 1Pe 4:7; 5:8;
2Pe 1:6 ᵈ Ac 10:42
ᵉ Jer 36:16
24:27 ᶠ Ac 25:1,4,9,
14 ᵍ Ac 12:3; 25:9
ʰ Ac 23:35; 25:14
25:1 ⁱ S Ac 24:27
ʲ S Ac 8:40
25:2 ᵏ ver 15;
Ac 24:1
25:3 ˡ Ac 20:3
25:4 ᵐ Ac 24:23
ⁿ S Ac 8:40
25:6 ᵒ ver 17
ᵖ ver 10
25:7 �q Mk 15:3;
Lk 23:2,10; Ac 24:5,6
ʳ Ac 24:13
25:8 ˢ Ac 6:13;
24:12; 28:17
25:9 ᵗ Ac 24:27; 12:3
ᵘ ver 20
25:10 ᵛ ver 8

²²Then Felix, who was well acquainted with the Way,ˣ adjourned the proceedings. "When Lysias the commander comes," he said, "I will decide your case." ²³He ordered the centurion to keep Paul under guardʸ but to give him some freedomᶻ and permit his friends to take care of his needs. ᵃ

²⁴Several days later Felix came with his wife Drusilla, who was Jewish. He sent for Paul and listened to him as he spoke about faith in Christ Jesus. ᵇ ²⁵As Paul talked about righteousness, self-controlᶜ and the judgmentᵈ to come, Felix was afraidᵉ and said, "That's enough for now! You may leave. When I find it convenient, I will send for you." ²⁶At the same time he was hoping that Paul would offer him a bribe, so he sent for him frequently and talked with him.

²⁷When two years had passed, Felix was succeeded by Porcius Festus, ᶠ but because Felix wanted to grant a favor to the Jews, ᵍ he left Paul in prison. ʰ

PAUL'S TRIAL BEFORE FESTUS

25 Three days after arriving in the province, Festusⁱ went up from Caesareaʲ to Jerusalem, ²where the chief priests and the Jewish leaders appeared before him and presented the charges against Paul. ᵏ ³They requested Festus, as a favor to them, to have Paul transferred to Jerusalem, for they were preparing an ambush to kill him along the way. ˡ ⁴Festus answered, "Paul is being heldᵐ at Caesarea, ⁿ and I myself am going there soon. ⁵Let some of your leaders come with me, and if the man has done anything wrong, they can press charges against him there."

⁶After spending eight or ten days with them, Festus went down to Caesarea. The next day he convened the courtᵒ and ordered that Paul be brought before him. ᵖ ⁷When Paul came in, the Jews who had come down from Jerusalem stood around him. They brought many serious charges against him, q but they could not prove them. ʳ

⁸Then Paul made his defense: "I have done nothing wrong against the Jewish law or against the templeˢ or against Caesar."

⁹Festus, wishing to do the Jews a favor, ᵗ said to Paul, "Are you willing to go up to Jerusalem and stand trial before me there on these charges?"ᵘ

¹⁰Paul answered: "I am now standing before Caesar's court, where I ought to be tried. I have not done any wrong to the Jews, ᵛ as you yourself know very well. ¹¹If, however, I am guilty of doing anything deserving death, I do not refuse to die. But if the charges

---

24:22 *well acquainted with the Way.* Felix could not have governed Judea and Samaria for six years without becoming familiar with the place and activities of the Christians.

24:23 *to give him some freedom.* Perhaps Paul was under house arrest similar to what he would experience while waiting trial in Rome (28:30–31)—in recognition of the fact that he was a Roman citizen who had not been found guilty of any crime.

24:24 *Drusilla.* Felix's third wife, daughter of Herod Agrippa I. At age 15 she married Azizus, king of Emesa, but deserted him for Felix a year later. Her son, also named Agrippa, died in the eruption of Vesuvius (A.D. 79).

A **24:25** *Felix was afraid.* Hearing of "righteousness, self-control and the judgment," Felix looked at his past life and was filled with fear. He had a spark of sincerity and concern. *When I find it convenient.* Lust, pride, greed and selfish ambition made it continually inconvenient to change.

24:26 *offer him a bribe.* Felix supposed that Paul had access to considerable funds. He had heard of his bringing an offering to the Jewish Christians in Jerusalem (see v. 17 and note). So he wanted Paul to give him money in order to secure his release. Paul no longer had the money, nor would he offer a bribe if he had it.

24:27 *Felix was succeeded by ... Festus.* Felix was recalled to Rome in A.D. 59/60 to answer for disturbances and irregularities in his rule, such as his handling of riots between Jewish and Syrian inhabitants. Festus is not mentioned in existing historical records before his arrival in Judea. He died in office after two years, but his record for that time shows wisdom and honesty superior to both his predecessor, Felix, and his successor, Albinus. *to grant a favor to the Jews.* Felix did not want to incite more anger among the Jews, whom he would be facing in Ro-

man court shortly. To release Paul from prison would do just that.

25:1 *from Caesarea to Jerusalem.* Sixty miles, a two-day trip. Festus was anxious to go immediately to the center of Jewish rule and worship.

25:2 *chief priests and the Jewish leaders.* The Sanhedrin (see note on Mk 14:55).

25:3 *ambush.* Probably the same group that had earlier made a vow to take Paul's life (see 23:12 and note).

25:6 *convened the court.* To make his decision binding as a formal ruling.

25:7 *charges ... they could not prove.* Again, as in the first hearing, Paul's adversaries produced no witnesses or evidence of any kind (see 24:2–9).

25:8 *nothing ... against the Jewish law.* Paul had respect for the law (see Ro 7:12; 8:3–4; 1Co 9:20 and note). *against the temple.* See notes on 21:28–29. Paul had not defied its customs by taking Trophimus into forbidden areas (21:29). Jesus had prophesied its destruction, but he was not responsible for its plight (Lk 21:5–6). *against Caesar.* Paul proclaimed the kingdom of God, but not as a political rival of Rome (cf. 17:6–7). He advocated respect for law and order (see Ro 13:1–7) and prayer for civil rulers (see 1Ti 2:1–2).

25:9 *Are you willing to go up to Jerusalem ... ?* Obviously not. Festus had said that the trial would be before him; so Paul insisted that he was then standing in the Roman civil court (v. 10). He wanted to keep his trial there rather than suffer at the hands of a Jewish religious court. As a Roman citizen, he could refuse to go to a local provincial court; instead, he looked to a higher Roman court.

brought against me by these Jews are not true, no one has the right to hand me over to them. I appeal to Caesar!" *w*

[12]After Festus had conferred with his council, he declared: "You have appealed to Caesar. To Caesar you will go!"

FESTUS CONSULTS KING AGRIPPA

[13]A few days later King Agrippa and Bernice arrived at Caesarea *x* to pay their respects to Festus. [14]Since they were spending many days there, Festus discussed Paul's case with the king. He said: "There is a man here whom Felix left as a prisoner. *y* [15]When I went to Jerusalem, the chief priests and the elders of the Jews brought charges against him *z* and asked that he be condemned.

[16]"I told them that it is not the Roman custom to hand over anyone before they have faced their accusers and have had an opportunity to defend themselves against the charges. *a* [17]When they came here with me, I did not delay the case, but convened the court the next day and ordered the man to be brought in. *b* [18]When his accusers got up to speak, they did not charge him with any of the crimes I had expected. [19]Instead, they had some points of dispute *c* with him about their own religion *d* and about a dead man named Jesus who Paul claimed was alive. [20]I was at a loss how to investigate such matters; so I asked if he would be willing to go to Jerusalem and stand trial there on these charges. *e* [21]But when Paul made his appeal to be held over for the Emperor's decision, I ordered him held until I could send him to Caesar." *f*

[22]Then Agrippa said to Festus, "I would like to hear this man myself."

He replied, "Tomorrow you will hear him." *g*

PAUL BEFORE AGRIPPA

26:12–18pp — Ac 9:3–8; 22:6–11

[23]The next day Agrippa and Bernice *h* came with great pomp and entered the audience room with the high-ranking military officers and the prominent men of the city. At the command of Festus, Paul was brought in. [24]Festus said: "King Agrippa, and all who are present with us, you see this man! The whole Jewish community *i* has petitioned me about him in Jerusalem and here in Caesarea, shouting that he ought not to live any longer. *j* [25]I found he had done nothing deserving of death, *k* but because he made his appeal to the Emperor *l* I decided to send him to Rome. [26]But I have nothing definite to write to His Majesty about him. Therefore I have brought him before all of you, and especially before you, King Agrippa, so that as a result of this investigation I may have something to write. [27]For I think it is unreasonable to send a prisoner on to Rome without specifying the charges against him."

25:11 *w* ver 21,25; Ac 26:32; 28:19
25:13 *x* S Ac 8:40
25:14 *y* Ac 24:27
25:15 *z* ver 2; Ac 24:1
25:16 *a* ver 4,5; Ac 23:30
25:17 *b* ver 6,10
25:19 *c* Ac 18:15; 23:29 *d* Ac 17:22
25:20 *e* ver 9
25:21 *f* ver 11,12
25:22 *g* Ac 9:15
25:23 *h* ver 13; Ac 26:30
25:24 *i* ver 2,3,7 *j* Ac 22:22
25:25 *k* S Ac 23:9 *l* S ver 11

25:11 *I appeal to Caesar!* Nero had become the emperor by this time. It was the right of every Roman citizen to have his case heard before Caesar himself (or his representative) in Rome. This was the highest court of appeal, and winning such a case could have led to more than just Paul's acquittal. It could have resulted in official recognition of Christianity as distinct from Judaism.

25:12 *his council.* The officials and legal experts who made up the advisory council for the Roman governor.

■ **25:13** *King Agrippa.* Herod Agrippa II. He was 17 years old at the death of his father in A.D. 44 (12:23). Being too young to succeed his father, he was replaced by Roman governors. Eight years later, however, a gradual extension of territorial authority began. Ultimately he ruled over territory north and northeast of the Sea of Galilee, over several Galilean cities and over some cities in Perea. At the Jewish revolt, when Jerusalem fell, he was on the side of the Romans. He died c. A.D. 100—the last of the Herods. *Bernice.* The oldest daughter of Agrippa I, she was 16 years old at his death. When only 13, she married her uncle, Herod of Chalcis, and had two sons. When Herod died, she lived with her brother, Agrippa II. To silence rumors that she was living in incest with her brother, she married Polemon, king of Cilicia, but left him soon afterward to return to Agrippa. She became the mistress of the emperor Vespasian's son Titus but was later ignored by him. *to pay their respects.* It was customary for

rulers to pay a complimentary visit to a new ruler at the time of his assignment. It was advantageous to each that they get along (cf. Herod Antipas and Pilate, Lk 23:6–12).

25:19 *religion.* Or "superstition," the same word used by Paul in 17:22 (see note there).

25:22 *I would like to hear.* Agrippa had been wishing to hear Paul (cf. Antipas wanting to see Jesus, Lk 9:9; 23:8).

25:23 *audience room.* Not the judgment hall, for this was not a court trial. It was in an auditorium appropriate for the pomp of the occasion, with a king, his sister, the Roman governor and the outstanding leaders of both the Jews and the Roman government present. *high-ranking military officers.* Five regiments were stationed at Caesarea, so their five commanders would have been in attendance (see note on 21:31).

25:26 *I have nothing definite.* Festus was required to send Caesar an explicit report on the case when an appeal was made. He hoped for some help from Agrippa in this matter. This was not an official trial but a special hearing to satisfy the curiosity of Agrippa and provide an assessment for Festus. *especially before you, King Agrippa.* He would be sensitive to differences between Pharisees and Sadducees, expectations of the Messiah, differences between Jews and Christians, and Jewish customs pertinent to these problems (see 26:2–3 and note on 26:3).

26:1 *m* Ac 9:15;
25:22 *n* S Ac 12:17
26:2 *o* Ps 119:46
p Ac 24:1,5; 25:2,7,11
26:3 *q* ver 7;
S Ac 6:14 *r* Ac 25:19
26:4 *s* Gal 1:13,14;
Php 3:5
26:5 *t* Ac 22:3
u S Ac 24:5 *v* Ac 23:6;
Php 3:5
26:6 *w* Ac 23:6;
24:15; 28:20
x S Ac 13:32; Ro 15:8
26:7 *y* Jas 1:1
z 1Th 3:10; 1Ti 5:5
a ver 2
26:8 *b* Ac 23:6
26:9 *c* 1Ti 1:13
d Jn 16:2 *e* S Jn 15:21
26:10 *f* S Ac 9:13
g S Ac 8:3; 9:2,14,21
h Ac 22:20
26:11 *i* S Mt 10:17
26:14 *j* Ac 9:7
k S Jn 5:2
26:16 *l* Eze 2:1;
Da 10:11 *m* Ac 22:14,
15
26:17 *n* Jer 1:8,19
o S Ac 9:15; S 13:46
26:18 *p* Isa 35:5
q Ps 18:28; Isa 42:7,
16; Eph 5:8; Col 1:13;
1Pe 2:9 *r* Lk 24:47;
Ac 2:38 *s* S Ac 20:21,
32
26:19 *t* Isa 50:5
26:20 *u* Ac 9:19-25
v Ac 9:26-29; 22:17-
20 *w* S Ac 9:15;
S 13:46 *x* Ac 3:19
y Jer 18:11; 35:15;
Mt 3:8; Lk 3:8
26:21 *z* Ac 21:27,30
a Ac 21:31
26:22 *b* S Lk 24:27,
44; Ac 10:43; 24:14
26:23 *c* S Mt 16:21
d 1Co 15:20,23;
Col 1:18; Rev 1:5
e S Lk 2:32

26

Then Agrippa said to Paul, "You have permission to speak for yourself." *m* So Paul motioned with his hand *n* and began his defense: [2]"King Agrippa, I consider myself fortunate to stand before you *o* today as I make my defense against all the accusations of the Jews, *p* [3]and especially so because you are well acquainted with all the Jewish customs *q* and controversies. *r* Therefore, I beg you to listen to me patiently.

[4]"The Jewish people all know the way I have lived ever since I was a child, *s* from the beginning of my life in my own country, and also in Jerusalem. [5]They have known me for a long time *t* and can testify, if they are willing, that I conformed to the strictest sect *u* of our religion, living as a Pharisee. *v* [6]And now it is because of my hope *w* in what God has promised our ancestors *x* that I am on trial today. [7]This is the promise our twelve tribes *y* are hoping to see fulfilled as they earnestly serve God day and night. *z* King Agrippa, it is because of this hope that the Jews are accusing me. *a* [8]Why should any of you consider it incredible that God raises the dead? *b*

[9]"I too was convinced *c* that I ought to do all that was possible to oppose *d* the name of Jesus of Nazareth. *e* [10]And that is just what I did in Jerusalem. On the authority of the chief priests I put many of the Lord's people *f* in prison, *g* and when they were put to death, I cast my vote against them. *h* [11]Many a time I went from one synagogue to another to have them punished, *i* and I tried to force them to blaspheme. I was so obsessed with persecuting them that I even hunted them down in foreign cities.

[12]"On one of these journeys I was going to Damascus with the authority and commission of the chief priests. [13]About noon, King Agrippa, as I was on the road, I saw a light from heaven, brighter than the sun, blazing around me and my companions. [14]We all fell to the ground, and I heard a voice *j* saying to me in Aramaic, *a* *k* 'Saul, Saul, why do you persecute me? It is hard for you to kick against the goads.'

[15]"Then I asked, 'Who are you, Lord?'

" 'I am Jesus, whom you are persecuting,' the Lord replied. [16]'Now get up and stand on your feet. *l* I have appeared to you to appoint you as a servant and as a witness of what you have seen and will see of me. *m* [17]I will rescue you *n* from your own people and from the Gentiles. *o* I am sending you to them [18]to open their eyes *p* and turn them from darkness to light, *q* and from the power of Satan to God, so that they may receive forgiveness of sins *r* and a place among those who are sanctified by faith in me.' *s*

[19]"So then, King Agrippa, I was not disobedient *t* to the vision from heaven. [20]First to those in Damascus, *u* then to those in Jerusalem *v* and in all Judea, and then to the Gentiles, *w* I preached that they should repent *x* and turn to God and demonstrate their repentance by their deeds. *y* [21]That is why some Jews seized me *z* in the temple courts and tried to kill me. *a* [22]But God has helped me to this very day; so I stand here and testify to small and great alike. I am saying nothing beyond what the prophets and Moses said would happen *b*— [23]that the Messiah would suffer *c* and, as the first to rise from the dead, *d* would bring the message of light to his own people and to the Gentiles." *e*

a 14 Or *Hebrew*

26:1 *permission to speak.* Agrippa gave the permission because Festus allowed him to have charge of the hearing.
26:3 *well acquainted with all the Jewish customs.* Agrippa as king controlled the temple treasury and the investments of the high priest and could appoint the high priest. He was consulted by the Romans on religious matters. This is one of the reasons Festus wanted him to assess Paul (see note on 25:26).
26:5 *living as a Pharisee.* Cf. Gal 1:14; Php 3:4–6.
26:6 *my hope in what God has promised.* Including God's kingdom, the Messiah and the resurrection (see v. 8).
26:8 Paul had been speaking to Agrippa but at this point must have addressed others as well, such as Festus and the commanders (see note on 21:31), who did not believe in the resurrection. Agrippa was also allied with the Sadducees, whom he appointed high priests, and probably rejected both the resurrection of Christ and resurrection in general.
26:10 *I cast my vote against them.* Does not necessarily mean that Paul was a member of the Sanhedrin (see note on 20:20). He may have been appointed to a commission to carry out the prosecution (see v. 12).
26:11 *force them to blaspheme.* He tried to force them either to

curse Jesus or to confess publicly that Jesus is the Son of God, in which case they could be condemned for blasphemy, a sufficient cause for death (see Mt 26:63–66).
26:12 *I was going to Damascus.* Again Paul gives an account of his conversion (see 9:1–19; 22:4–21 and notes).
26:14 *I heard a voice.* See notes on 9:7; 22:9. *to kick against the goads.* A Greek proverb for useless resistance—the ox succeeds only in hurting itself.
26:17 *to them.* Not only to the Jews but also to the Gentiles (see 22:21; Gal 1:15–16). His mission was from God (Gal 1:1).
26:18 *from darkness to light.* A figure especially characteristic of Paul (see Ro 13:12; 2Co 4:6; Eph 5:8–14; Col 1:13; 1Th 5:5). *Satan.* See Mt 16:23; 1Jn 3:8 and notes. *sanctified.* See note on 1Co 1:2.
26:20 *demonstrate . . . repentance by . . . deeds.* Works do not secure salvation either before or after conversion, but they are a sign of the reality of repentance (cf. 3:19 and note).
26:22 *the prophets and Moses.* The OT Scriptures (Lk 24:27,44).
26:23 *the first to rise from the dead.* The firstfruits of the dead —to die no more (see 1Co 15:20; Col 1:18 and notes). *to the Gentiles.* Cf. Isa 49:6.

26:24 *f* S Jn 10:20;
S 1Co 4:10 *g* Jn 7:15
26:25 *h* S Ac 23:26
26:26 *i* ver 3
26:28 *j* Ac 11:26
26:29 *k* S Ac 21:33
26:30 *l* Ac 25:23
26:31 *m* S Ac 23:9
26:32 *n* Ac 28:18
o S Ac 25:11
27:1 *p* S Ac 16:10
q Ac 18:2; 25:12,25
r Ac 10:1
27:2 *s* S Ac 2:9
t S Ac 19:29
u S Ac 16:9 *v* S Ac 17:1
27:3 *w* Mt 11:21
x ver 43 *y* Ac 24:23;
28:16
27:4 *z* ver 7
27:5 *a* S Ac 6:9
b S Ac 2:10
27:6 *c* Ac 28:11
d ver 1; Ac 18:2; 25:12,
25
27:7 *e* ver 4 *f* ver 12,
13,21; Tit 1:5

[24]At this point Festus interrupted Paul's defense. "You are out of your mind, *f* Paul!" he shouted. "Your great learning *g* is driving you insane."

[25]"I am not insane, most excellent *h* Festus," Paul replied. "What I am saying is true and reasonable. [26]The king is familiar with these things, *i* and I can speak freely to him. I am convinced that none of this has escaped his notice, because it was not done in a corner. [27]King Agrippa, do you believe the prophets? I know you do."

[28]Then Agrippa said to Paul, "Do you think that in such a short time you can persuade me to be a Christian?" *j*

[29]Paul replied, "Short time or long—I pray to God that not only you but all who are listening to me today may become what I am, except for these chains." *k*

[30]The king rose, and with him the governor and Bernice *l* and those sitting with them. [31]After they left the room, they began saying to one another, "This man is not doing anything that deserves death or imprisonment." *m*

[32]Agrippa said to Festus, "This man could have been set free *n* if he had not appealed to Caesar." *o*

PAUL SAILS FOR ROME

27 When it was decided that we *p* would sail for Italy, *q* Paul and some other prisoners were handed over to a centurion named Julius, who belonged to the Imperial Regiment. *r* [2]We boarded a ship from Adramyttium about to sail for ports along the coast of the province of Asia, *s* and we put out to sea. Aristarchus, *t* a Macedonian *u* from Thessalonica, *v* was with us.

[3]The next day we landed at Sidon; *w* and Julius, in kindness to Paul, *x* allowed him to go to his friends so they might provide for his needs. *y* [4]From there we put out to sea again and passed to the lee of Cyprus because the winds were against us. *z* [5]When we had sailed across the open sea off the coast of Cilicia *a* and Pamphylia, *b* we landed at Myra in Lycia. [6]There the centurion found an Alexandrian ship *c* sailing for Italy *d* and put us on board. [7]We made slow headway for many days and had difficulty arriving off Cnidus. When the wind did not allow us to hold our course, *e* we sailed to the lee of Crete, *f* opposite Salmo-

---

26:24 *You are out of your mind.* See Jn 10:20; cf. 1Co 14:23. The governor felt that Paul's education and reading of the sacred Scriptures had led him to a mania about prophecy and resurrection.

26:26 *not done in a corner.* This gospel is based on actual events, lived out in historical times and places. The king must himself attest to the truth of what Paul has affirmed.

26:27 *do you believe the prophets?* King Agrippa was faced with a dilemma. If he said "Yes," Paul would press him to recognize their fulfillment in Jesus; if he said "No," he would be in trouble with the devout Jews, who accepted the message of the prophets as the very word of God.

26:28 *in such a short time you can persuade me to be a Christian?* His question is an evasion of Paul's question and an answer to what he anticipates Paul's next question will be. His point is that he will not be persuaded by such a brief statement. *Christian.* See note on 11:26.

26:29 *these chains.* Paul was still bound as a prisoner.

26:31 *not doing anything that deserves death or imprisonment.* Luke calls attention to the officials' agreement on Paul's innocence (cf. Herod's and Pilate's agreement on Jesus' innocence in Lk 23:13–15).

27:1 See map No. 13 at the end of this study Bible; see also map, p. 1890. *we would sail.* The "we" narrative (see note on 16:10) begins again (the last such reference appeared in 21:18). Probably Luke had spent the two years of Paul's Caesarean imprisonment nearby, and now he joins those ready to sail. *centurion named Julius.* Otherwise unknown. Perhaps he was given the specific duties of an imperial courier, which included delivering prisoners for trial. *Imperial Regiment.* The Roman legions were designated by number, and each of the regiments also had designations. The identification "Augustan," or "Imperial" (belonging to the empire), was common (see note on 10:1).

27:2 *Adramyttium.* A harbor on the west coast of the province of Asia, southeast of Troas, east of Assos. *ports along the coast.* At

one of these stops Julius would plan to transfer to a ship going to Rome. *Aristarchus.* See 19:29 and note; see also Phm 24, which indicates that he was in Rome with Paul later.

27:3 *Sidon.* About 70 miles north of Caesarea.

27:4 *the lee of Cyprus.* They sought the protecting shelter of the island by sailing north on the eastern side of the island, then west along the northern side. *winds were against us.* Prevailing winds in summer were westerly.

27:5 *Cilicia and Pamphylia.* Adjoining provinces on the southern shore of Asia Minor. From Sidon to Myra along this coast would normally be a voyage of 10 to 15 days. *Myra in Lycia.* The growing importance of the city of Myra was associated with the development of navigation. Instead of hugging the coast from point to point, more ships were daring to run directly from Alexandria in Egypt to harbors like Myra on the southern coast of Asia Minor. It was considerably out of the way on the trip to Rome from Egypt, but the prevailing westerly wind would not allow a direct voyage toward the west. Myra became an important grain-storage city as well.

27:6 *Alexandrian ship.* A ship from Egypt (with grain cargo, v. 38) bound for Rome. Paul and the others could have remained on the first ship and continued up the coast to Macedonia, then taken the land route over the Egnatian Way across Greece and on to Rome, entering Italy at the port of Brundisium. But Julius chose to change ships here, accepting the opportunity for a direct voyage to Rome. Some suggest that Aristarchus from Macedonia stayed with the first ship and went to his home area to tell of Paul's coming imprisonment in Rome. If so, he later joined Paul in Rome (see note on v. 2).

27:7 *Cnidus.* From Myra to Cnidus at the southwest point of Asia Minor was about 170 miles. The trip probably took another 10 to 15 days. *Crete.* An island 160 miles long. Rather than cross the open sea to Greece, the ship was forced to bear south, seeking to sail west with the protection of the island of Crete on the north ("to the lee of Crete"). *Salmone.* A promontory on the northeast point of Crete.

27:9 *g* Lev 16:29-31;
23:27-29; Nu 29:7
27:10 *h* ver 21
27:12 *i* S ver 7
27:14 *j* Mk 4:37
27:16 *k* ver 30

ne. ⁸We moved along the coast with difficulty and came to a place called Fair Havens, near the town of Lasea.

⁹Much time had been lost, and sailing had already become dangerous because by now it was after the Day of Atonement.ᵃ ᵍ So Paul warned them, ¹⁰"Men, I can see that our voyage is going to be disastrous and bring great loss to ship and cargo, and to our own lives also."ʰ ¹¹But the centurion, instead of listening to what Paul said, followed the advice of the pilot and of the owner of the ship. ¹²Since the harbor was unsuitable to winter in, the majority decided that we should sail on, hoping to reach Phoenix and winter there. This was a harbor in Crete,ⁱ facing both southwest and northwest.

THE STORM

¹³When a gentle south wind began to blow, they saw their opportunity; so they weighed anchor and sailed along the shore of Crete. ¹⁴Before very long, a wind of hurricane force,ʲ called the Northeaster, swept down from the island. ¹⁵The ship was caught by the storm and could not head into the wind; so we gave way to it and were driven along. ¹⁶As we passed to the lee of a small island called Cauda, we were hardly able to make the lifeboatᵏ secure, ¹⁷so the men hoisted it aboard. Then they passed ropes under the ship it-

---

ᵃ 9 That is, Yom Kippur

27:8 *Fair Havens . . . Lasea.* The former was a port about midway on the southern coast of Crete, and the latter was a city about five miles away (see map, below).

27:9 *Atonement.* The Jewish Day of Atonement fell in the latter part of September or in October. The usual sailing season by Jewish calculation lasted from Pentecost (May-June) to Tabernacles, which was five days after Atonement. The Romans considered sailing after Sept. 15 doubtful and after Nov. 11 suicidal.

27:12 *Phoenix.* A major city that served as a wintering place, having a harbor with protection against the storms.

27:13-44 Luke's magnificent account of the storm at sea is possibly intended to be more than just an interesting story well told. Here at the climax of his account of the spread of the gospel from Jerusalem to Rome, especially through the labors of the apostle Paul, he provides in cameo an exquisite depiction of the state of the world seen from the perspective of Paul's gospel: The peoples of the world (represented by the ship's passen-

gers) stand under the threat of God's judgment (represented by the terrible storm), with Paul and what he represents being their only hope. On board are representatives of the world's economic, military and political powers and those skilled in navigating the sea, but none of these can master the raging storm to save themselves or their possessions. They escape only as they follow Paul's instructions. Cf. note on Jnh 1:4–16.

27:14 *Northeaster.* A typhoon-like, east-northeast wind (the Euroquilo), which drove the ship away from its destination (see map, below).

27:16 *Cauda.* About 23 miles from Crete. This provided enough shelter to make preparation against the storm. *to make the life boat secure.* A small boat was being towed behind the ship. It was interfering with the progress of the ship and with the steering. It may also have been in danger of being crushed against the ship in the wind and the waves. It had to be taken aboard (v. 17).

27:17 *passed ropes under the ship.* Probably crosswise, in order

PAUL'S JOURNEY TO ROME

Rome
Three Taverns
Forum of Appius
Puteoli
ITALY
MACEDONIA
Carthage
SICILY
Rhegium
Syracuse
Adriatic Sea
ACHAIA
MALTA
Cnidus
LYCIA
PAMPHYLIA
Tarsus
Myra
Antioch
CRETE
Mediterranean
Sea
CYPRUS
Sidon
C. A.D. 59–60
Ac 27:1—28:16
Cyrene
Caesarea
Jerusalem
Alexandria

Miles 0 — 200 — 400 — 600 — 800
Kms 0 — 300 — 600 — 900 — 1200

Miles 0 — 100
Kms 0 — 100
Salmone
Phoenix
CRETE
CAUDA
Lasea
Fair Havens
Wind of hurricane force–Northeaster

self to hold it together. Because they were afraid they would run aground *l* on the sandbars of Syrtis, they lowered the sea anchor *a* and let the ship be driven along. ¹⁸We took such a violent battering from the storm that the next day they began to throw the cargo overboard. *m* ¹⁹On the third day, they threw the ship's tackle overboard with their own hands. ²⁰When neither sun nor stars appeared for many days and the storm continued raging, we finally gave up all hope of being saved.

²¹After they had gone a long time without food, Paul stood up before them and said: "Men, you should have taken my advice *n* not to sail from Crete; *o* then you would have spared yourselves this damage and loss. ²²But now I urge you to keep up your courage, *p* because not one of you will be lost; only the ship will be destroyed. ²³Last night an angel *q* of the God whose I am and whom I serve *r* stood beside me *s* ²⁴and said, 'Do not be afraid, Paul. You must stand trial before Caesar; *t* and God has graciously given you the lives of all who sail with you.' *u* ²⁵So keep up your courage, *v* men, for I have faith in God that it will happen just as he told me. *w* ²⁶Nevertheless, we must run aground *x* on some island." *y*

THE SHIPWRECK

²⁷On the fourteenth night we were still being driven across the Adriatic *b* Sea, when about midnight the sailors sensed they were approaching land. ²⁸They took soundings and found that the water was a hundred and twenty feet *c* deep. A short time later they took soundings again and found it was ninety feet *d* deep. ²⁹Fearing that we would be dashed against the rocks, they dropped four anchors from the stern and prayed for daylight. ³⁰In an attempt to escape from the ship, the sailors let the lifeboat *z* down into the sea, pretending they were going to lower some anchors from the bow. ³¹Then Paul said to the centurion and the soldiers, "Unless these men stay with the ship, you cannot be saved." *a* ³²So the soldiers cut the ropes that held the lifeboat and let it drift away.

³³Just before dawn Paul urged them all to eat. "For the last fourteen days," he said, "you have been in constant suspense and have gone without food—you haven't eaten anything. ³⁴Now I urge you to take some food. You need it to survive. Not one of you will lose a single hair from his head." *b* ³⁵After he said this, he took some bread and gave thanks to God in front of them all. Then he broke it *c* and began to eat. ³⁶They were all encouraged *d* and ate some food themselves. ³⁷Altogether there were 276 of us on board. ³⁸When they had eaten as much as they wanted, they lightened the ship by throwing the grain into the sea. *e*

³⁹When daylight came, they did not recognize the land, but they saw a bay with a sandy beach, *f* where they decided to run the ship aground if they could. ⁴⁰Cutting loose the anchors, *g* they left them in the sea and at the same time untied the ropes that held the rudders. Then they hoisted the foresail to the wind and made for the beach. ⁴¹But the ship

---

a 17 Or *the sails* *b 27* In ancient times the name referred to an area extending well south of Italy.
c 28 Or about 37 meters *d 28* Or about 27 meters

27:17 *l* ver 26,39
27:18 *m* ver 19,38; Jnh 1:5
27:21 *n* ver 10
o S ver 7
27:22 *p* ver 25,36
27:23 *q* S Ac 5:19
r Ro 1:9 *s* Ac 18:9; 23:11; 2Ti 4:17
27:24 *t* Ac 23:11
u ver 44
27:25 *v* ver 22,36
w Ro 4:20,21
27:26 *x* ver 17,39
y Ac 28:1
27:30 *z* ver 16
27:31 *a* ver 24
27:34 *b* S Mt 10:30
27:35 *c* S Mt 14:19
27:36 *d* ver 22,25
27:38 *e* ver 18; Jnh 1:5
27:39 *f* Ac 28:1
27:40 *g* ver 29

---

to keep the ship from being broken apart by the storm. *Syrtis.* A long stretch of desolate banks of quicksand along northern Africa off the coast of Tunis and Tripoli—still far away, but in such a storm the ship could be driven a great distance. *sea anchor.* Lowered apparently to keep the ship from running onto the sandbars of Syrtis, but the Greek for this expression should perhaps be rendered "mainsail" (see TNIV text note).

27:18 *throw the cargo overboard.* To lighten the ship. They kept some bags of grain, however (see v. 38).

27:19 *ship's tackle.* Spars, planks and perhaps the yardarm with the mainsail attached. At times these were dragged behind, serving as a brake.

27:21 *should have taken my advice.* Although they had not done so, Paul had good news for everyone (vv. 22–26).

27:27 *fourteenth night.* After leaving Fair Havens. *Adriatic Sea.* The sea between Italy, Malta, Crete and Greece. In ancient times the Adriatic Sea extended as far south as Sicily and Crete (see TNIV text note). (Some think this sea included all the area between Greece, Italy and Africa and that it was known as the Adrian, not the Adriatic, Sea.) Its extent now has been considerably reduced. *sensed.* By the sound of breakers.

27:28 *took soundings.* Measured the depth of the sea by letting down a weighted line.

27:30 *attempt to escape.* Without a port for the ship, the sailors

felt their chance for survival was better in the single lifeboat, unencumbered by the many passengers.

27:31 *Unless these men stay.* The sailors were needed to successfully beach the ship the next day.

27:33 *haven't eaten anything.* No provisions had been distributed nor regular meals eaten since the storm began.

27:35 *took some bread and gave thanks.* Paul gave two good examples: He ate food for physical nourishment and gave thanks to God. To give thanks before a meal was common practice among God's people (see Lk 9:16; 24:30; 1Ti 4:4–5).

27:37 *276 of us on board.* To note the number on board may have been necessary in preparation for the distribution of food or perhaps for the coming attempt to get ashore. The number is not extraordinary for the time. Josephus refers to a ship that had 600 aboard (*Life,* 15).

27:38 *lightened the ship.* They threw overboard the remaining bags of wheat (see v. 18), which had probably been kept for food supply. The lighter the ship, the farther it could sail in to shore.

27:40 *untied the ropes that held the rudders.* In order to lower the stern rudders into place so the ship could be steered toward the sandy shore. Ancient ships had a steering oar on either side of the stern.

27:41 *h* 2Co 11:25
27:43 *i* ver 3
27:44 *j* ver 22, 31
28:1 *k* S Ac 16:10
l Ac 27:26, 39
28:4 *m* Mk 16:18
n Lk 13:2, 4
28:5 *o* Lk 10:19
28:6 *p* Ac 14:11
28:8 *q* Jas 5:14, 15
r S Ac 6:6 *s* Ac 9:40
28:10 *t* Ps 15:4
28:11 *u* Ac 27:6
28:14 *v* S Ac 1:16
28:15 *w* S Ac 1:16
28:16 *x* Ac 24:23;
27:3

struck a sandbar and ran aground. The bow stuck fast and would not move, and the stern was broken to pieces by the pounding of the surf. *h*

⁴²The soldiers planned to kill the prisoners to prevent any of them from swimming away and escaping. ⁴³But the centurion wanted to spare Paul's life *i* and kept them from carrying out their plan. He ordered those who could swim to jump overboard first and get to land. ⁴⁴The rest were to get there on planks or on other pieces of the ship. In this way everyone reached land safely. *j*

PAUL ASHORE ON MALTA

28 Once safely on shore, we *k* found out that the island *l* was called Malta. ²The islanders showed us unusual kindness. They built a fire and welcomed us all because it was raining and cold. ³Paul gathered a pile of brushwood and, as he put it on the fire, a viper, driven out by the heat, fastened itself on his hand. ⁴When the islanders saw the snake hanging from his hand, *m* they said to each other, "This man must be a murderer; for though he escaped from the sea, the goddess Justice has not allowed him to live." *n* ⁵But Paul shook the snake off into the fire and suffered no ill effects. *o* ⁶The people expected him to swell up or suddenly fall dead; but after waiting a long time and seeing nothing unusual happen to him, they changed their minds and said he was a god. *p*

⁷There was an estate nearby that belonged to Publius, the chief official of the island. He welcomed us to his home and showed us generous hospitality for three days. ⁸His father was sick in bed, suffering from fever and dysentery. Paul went in to see him and, after prayer, *q* placed his hands on him *r* and healed him. *s* ⁹When this had happened, the rest of the sick on the island came and were cured. ¹⁰They honored us *t* in many ways; and when we were ready to sail, they furnished us with the supplies we needed.

PAUL'S ARRIVAL AT ROME

¹¹After three months we put out to sea in a ship that had wintered in the island—it was an Alexandrian ship *u* with the figurehead of the twin gods Castor and Pollux. ¹²We put in at Syracuse and stayed there three days. ¹³From there we set sail and arrived at Rhegium. The next day the south wind came up, and on the following day we reached Puteoli. ¹⁴There we found some believers *v* who invited us to spend a week with them. And so we came to Rome. ¹⁵The believers *w* there had heard that we were coming, and they traveled as far as the Forum of Appius and the Three Taverns to meet us. At the sight of these people Paul thanked God and was encouraged. ¹⁶When we got to Rome, Paul was allowed to live by himself, with a soldier to guard him. *x*

27:42 *soldiers planned to kill the prisoners.* If a prisoner escaped, the life of his guard was taken in his place. The soldiers did not want to risk having a prisoner escape (see 16:27 and note).

C **27:43** Once more the centurion (Julius, v. 3; see also note on v. 1) is to be admired for stopping this plan and trusting the prisoners.

28:1 *Malta.* Known as Melita by the Greeks and Romans. It was included in the province of Sicily and is located 58 miles south of that large island.

28:2 *islanders.* Lit. "barbarians"; all non-Greek-speaking people were called this by Greeks. Far from being uncivilized tribesmen, they were Phoenician in ancestry and used a Phoenician dialect but were thoroughly Romanized. *raining and cold.* It was the end of October or the beginning of November.

28:3 *a viper.* Must have been known to the islanders to be poisonous.

28:6 *to swell up.* The usual medical term for inflammation; it is used only by Luke in the NT (see Introduction to Luke: Author). *said he was a god.* Parallel to the Lystrans' attempt to worship Paul and Barnabas (14:11–18).

28:7 *Publius.* A Roman name, but the first name and not the family name. It must have been what the islanders called him. *chief official.* The "first man" of Malta, a technical term for the top authority. Luke's designation is accurate here, as elsewhere, even though the Greek term used is not a common one. Cf. also "proconsul" (Greek *anthypatos*, 13:7), "magistrates" (Greek *strategoi*, 16:20), "city officials" (Greek *politarchas*, 17:6), "officials of the province" (Greek *Asiarchon*, 19:31). *for three days.* Probably until they

could find more permanent housing for the winter (see v. 11).

28:11 *After three months.* They had to remain here until the sailing season opened in late February or early March. *figurehead.* A carving mounted at the prow of the ship. *Castor and Pollux.* The two "sons of Zeus" (Greek *Dioscuroi*), the guardian deities of sailors.

28:12 *Syracuse.* The leading city on the island of Sicily, situated on the east coast.

28:13 *Rhegium.* A town on the coast of Italy, near the southwestern tip and close to the narrowest point of the strait separating that country from Sicily, opposite Messina. Around the promontory north of the town was the whirlpool of Charybdis and the rock of Scylla. Coming from his triumph in Judea, the general Titus landed here on his way to Rome. *Puteoli.* Modern Pozzuoli, almost 200 miles from Rhegium. It was situated in the northern part of the Bay of Naples and was the chief port of Rome, though 75 miles away. The population included Jews as well as Christians.

28:14 *spend a week.* Either the centurion had business to care for or he was free to delay the journey at Paul's request (see 27:42–43; see also 27:3). *Rome.* See map, p. 1894.

28:15 *Forum of Appius.* A small town 43 miles from Rome, noted for its wickedness. Some Roman Christians came this far to meet Paul. Beyond this they would not be certain of the way he would come. *Three Taverns.* A town 33 miles from Rome. Other Roman believers met Paul here. The term "tavern" was used to designate any kind of shop.

28:16 *live by himself.* "In his own rented house" (v. 30). He had committed no flagrant crime and was not politically dangerous.

28:17 ʸ Ac 25:2
ᶻ S Ac 22:5
ᵃ S Ac 25:8
ᵇ S Ac 6:14
28:18 ᶜ Ac 22:24
ᵈ Ac 26:31,32
ᵉ S Ac 23:9
28:19 ᶠ S Ac 25:11
28:20 ᵍ Ac 26:6,7
ʰ S Ac 21:33
28:21 ⁱ S Ac 22:5
28:22 ʲ S Ac 24:5,14
28:23 ᵏ S Mt 3:2;
Ac 19:8 ˡ S Ac 8:35
ᵐ Ac 17:3
28:24 ⁿ Ac 14:4;
17:4,5
28:25 ᵒ S Heb 3:7
28:27 ᵖ Ps 119:70
�q Isa 6:9,10;
S Mt 13:15
28:28[29] ʳ Lk 2:30
ˢ S Ac 13:46
28:31 ᵗ ver 23;
S Mt 4:23 ᵘ S Ac 4:29

PAUL PREACHES AT ROME UNDER GUARD

¹⁷Three days later he called together the local Jewish leaders. ʸ When they had assembled, Paul said to them: "My brothers, ᶻ although I have done nothing against our people ᵃ or against the customs of our ancestors, ᵇ I was arrested in Jerusalem and handed over to the Romans. ¹⁸They examined me ᶜ and wanted to release me, ᵈ because I was not guilty of any crime deserving death. ᵉ ¹⁹The Jews objected, so I was compelled to make an appeal to Caesar. ᶠ I certainly did not intend to bring any charge against my own people. ²⁰For this reason I have asked to see you and talk with you. It is because of the hope of Israel ᵍ that I am bound with this chain." ʰ

²¹They replied, "We have not received any letters from Judea concerning you, and none of our people ⁱ who have come from there has reported or said anything bad about you. ²²But we want to hear what your views are, for we know that people everywhere are talking against this sect." ʲ

²³They arranged to meet Paul on a certain day, and came in even larger numbers to the place where he was staying. He witnessed to them from morning till evening, explaining about the kingdom of God, ᵏ and from the Law of Moses and from the Prophets ˡ he tried to persuade them about Jesus. ᵐ ²⁴Some were convinced by what he said, but others would not believe. ⁿ ²⁵They disagreed among themselves and began to leave after Paul had made this final statement: "The Holy Spirit spoke the truth to your ancestors when he said ᵒ through Isaiah the prophet:

²⁶ " 'Go to this people and say,
    "You will be ever hearing but never understanding;
        you will be ever seeing but never perceiving."
²⁷ For this people's heart has become calloused; ᵖ
        they hardly hear with their ears,
        and they have closed their eyes.
    Otherwise they might see with their eyes,
        hear with their ears,
        understand with their hearts
    and turn, and I would heal them.' ᵃ �q

²⁸[29]"Therefore I want you to know that God's salvation ʳ has been sent to the Gentiles, ˢ and they will listen!"

³⁰For two whole years Paul stayed there in his own rented house and welcomed all who came to see him. ³¹He proclaimed the kingdom of God ᵗ and taught about the Lord Jesus Christ—with all boldness ᵘ and without hindrance!

ᵃ *27* Isaiah 6:9,10 (see Septuagint)

So he was allowed to have his own living quarters, but a guard was with him at all times, perhaps chained to him (Eph 6:20; Php 1:13–14,17; Col 4:3,18; Phm 10,13).

28:17 *Jewish leaders.* The decree of the emperor Claudius (see 18:2 and note) had been allowed to lapse, and Jews had returned to Rome with their leaders. *My brothers.* An epithet that recognized the common Jewish blood he shared with them. Cf. the usage in v. 15, referring to brothers ("believers") in Christ (see note on 11:1).

28:20 *hope of Israel.* See note on 26:6.

28:22 *we want to hear ... your views.* The Jews in Rome were well aware of the dispute over whether Jesus was the Messiah. They wanted to hear Paul's presentation, and he was eager to present it before the arrival of adverse opinions from the Jewish leaders of Jerusalem.

28:23 *Law of Moses ... Prophets.* The OT Scriptures (see Lk 24:27,44).

28:26–27 This OT passage (Isa 6:9–10; see notes there) was quoted by Jesus (see Mt 13:14–15; Mk 4:12; Lk 8:10; Jn 12:39–40 and notes) to make a similar point. Paul, too, had alluded to it in his letter to the Romans (Ro 11:8).

A **28:28[29]** *God's salvation has been sent to the Gentiles.* The main thought of the book of Acts. The gospel is

meant for all. And Paul was a chosen vessel to carry the message to Gentiles as well as to Jews (see 9:15 and note; Ro 1:13; 11:13 and note). Some later manuscripts add v. 29 ("After he said this, the Jews left, arguing vigorously among themselves").

28:30 *two whole years.* Paul served the Lord (v. 31) during the full period of waiting for his accusers to press the trial in Rome. There are a number of indications that he was released from this imprisonment: 1. Acts stops abruptly at this time. 2. Paul wrote to churches expecting to visit them soon, so he must have anticipated a release (see Php 2:24; Phm 22). 3. A number of the details in the Pastoral Letters do not fit into the historical setting given in the book of Acts. These details indicate a return to Asia Minor, Crete and Greece after the events at the close of Acts. 4. Tradition indicates that Paul went to Spain. Even if he did not go, the very fact that a tradition arose suggests a time when he could have taken that journey. See map (pp. 2030–2031) and accompanying text.

28:31 Acts ends on a triumphant note (just as Luke's Gospel does; see Lk 24:50–53). Despite being under house arrest, Paul is preaching and teaching in Rome, the capital city of the Roman empire—"with all boldness and without hindrance" (see 1:8 and note).

ROME IN THE TIME OF PAUL

The Neronian persecution in A.D. 64 was a transparent attempt by the emperor to blame Christians for the great fire that destroyed large parts of the city. The populace, however, blamed Nero and felt sorry for those unjustly tortured in the arena (cf. Tacitus, *Annals*, 15.44).

In terms of political importance, geographical position and sheer magnificence, the superlative city of the empire was Rome, the capital.

Located on a series of jutting foothills and low-lying eminences (the "seven hills") east of a bend in the Tiber River some 18 miles from the Mediterranean, Rome was celebrated for its impressive public buildings, aqueducts, baths, theaters and thoroughfares, many of which led from distant provinces. The city of the first Christian century had spread far beyond its fourth-century B.C. "Servian" walls and lay unwalled, secure in its greatness.

The most prominent features were the Capitoline hill, with temples to Jupiter and Juno, and the nearby Palatine, adorned with imperial palaces, including Nero's "Golden House." Both hills overlooked the Roman Forum, the hub of the entire empire.

Alternatively described as the glorious crowning achievement of humankind and as the sewer of the universe where all the scum from every corner of the empire gathered, Rome had reasons for both civic pride in its architecture and shame for staggering urban social problems not unlike those of cities today.

The apostle Paul entered the city from the south on the Via Appia. He first lived under house arrest and then, after a period of freedom, as a condemned prisoner in the Mamertine dungeon near the Forum. Remarkably, Paul was able to proclaim the gospel among all classes of people, from the palace to the prison. According to tradition, he was executed at a spot on the Ostian Way outside Rome in A.D. 68.

AUTHOR ROMANS | INTRODUCTION

C The writer of this letter was the apostle Paul (see 1:1 and note). No voice from the early church was ever raised against his authorship. The letter contains a number of historical references that agree with known facts of Paul's life. The doctrinal content of the book is typical of Paul, which is evident from a comparison with other letters he wrote.

DATE AND PLACE OF WRITING

The book was probably written in the early spring of A.D. 57 (see chart, p. 1855). Very likely Paul was on his third missionary journey, ready to return to Jerusalem with the offering from the mission churches for poverty-stricken believers in Jerusalem (see 15:25–27 and notes). In 15:26 it is suggested that Paul had already received contributions from the churches of Macedonia and Achaia, so he either was at Corinth or had already been there. Since he had not yet been at Corinth (on his third missionary journey) when he wrote 1 Corinthians (cf. 1Co 16:1–4) and the collection issue had still not been resolved when he wrote 2 Corinthians (2Co 8–9), the writing of Romans must follow that of 1,2 Corinthians (dated c. 55).

    The most likely place of writing is either Corinth or Cenchreae (about six miles away) because of references to Phoebe of Cenchreae (see 16:1 and note) and to Gaius, Paul's host (see 16:23 and note), who was probably a Corinthian (see 1Co 1:14). Erastus (see 16:23 and note) may also have been a Corinthian (see 2Ti 4:20).

RECIPIENTS

C The original recipients of the letter were the people of the church at Rome (1:7), who were predominantly Gentile. Jews, however, must have constituted a substantial minority of the congregation (see 4:1; chs. 9–11; see also note on 1:13). Perhaps Paul originally sent the entire letter to the Roman church, after which he or someone else used a shorter form (chs. 1–14 or 1–15) for more general distribution. See note on 2Pe 3:15; see also map, p. 1894.

MAJOR THEME

Paul's primary theme in Romans is the basic gospel, God's plan of salvation and righteousness for all humankind, Jew and Gentile alike (see 1:16–17 and notes). Although justification by faith has been suggested by some as the theme, it would seem that a broader theme states the message of the book more adequately. "The righteousness of God" (1:17) includes justification by faith, but it also embraces such related ideas as guilt, sanctification and security.

PURPOSE

Paul's purposes for writing this letter were varied:
    1. He wrote to prepare the way for his coming visit to Rome and his proposed mission to Spain (1:10–15; 15:22–29).

KEY   **A** APPLICATION FOR LIVING   **B** BACKGROUND NOTES   **C** CHARACTER INFORMATION

2. He wrote to present the basic system of salvation to a church that had not received the teaching of an apostle before.

3. He sought to explain the relationship between Jew and Gentile in God's overall plan of redemption. The Jewish Christians were being rejected by the larger Gentile group in the church (see 14:1 and note) because the Jewish believers still felt constrained to observe dietary laws and sacred days (14:2–6).

OCCASION

When Paul wrote this letter, he was probably at Corinth (see Ac 20:2–3 and notes) on his third missionary journey. His work in the eastern Mediterranean was almost finished (see 15:18–23), and he greatly desired to visit the Roman church (see 1:11–12; 15:23–24). At this time, however, he could not go to Rome because he felt he must personally deliver the collection taken among the Gentile churches for the poverty-stricken Christians of Jerusalem (see 15:25–28 and notes). So instead of going to Rome, he sent a letter to prepare the Christians there for his intended visit in connection with a mission to Spain (see 15:23–24 and note on 15:24). For many years Paul had wanted to visit Rome to minister there (see 1:13–15), and this letter served as a careful and systematic theological introduction to that hoped-for personal ministry. Since he was not acquainted directly with the Roman church, he says little about its problems (but see 14:1—15:13; cf. also 13:1–7; 16:17–18).

CONTENT

Paul begins by surveying the spiritual condition of all people. He finds Jews and Gentiles alike to be sinners and in need of salvation. That salvation has been provided by God through Jesus Christ and his redemptive work on the cross. It is a provision, however, that must be received by faith—a principle by which God has always dealt with humankind, as the example of Abraham shows. Since salvation is only the beginning of Christian experience, Paul moves on to show how believers are freed from sin, law and death—a provision made possible by their union with Christ in both death and resurrection and by the indwelling presence and power of the Holy Spirit. Paul then shows that Israel too, though presently in a state of unbelief, has a place in God's sovereign redemptive plan. Now she consists of only a remnant, allowing for the conversion of the Gentiles, but the time will come when "all Israel will be saved" (11:26; see note there). The letter concludes with an appeal to the readers to work out their Christian faith in practical ways, both in the church and in the world. None of Paul's other letters states so profoundly the content of the gospel and its implications for both the present and the future.

SPECIAL CHARACTERISTICS

1. *The most systematic of Paul's letters.* It reads more like an elaborate theological essay than a letter.

2. *Emphasis on Christian doctrine.* The number and importance of the theological themes touched upon are impressive: sin and death, salvation, grace, faith, righteousness, justification, sanctification, redemption, resurrection and glorification.

3. *Widespread use of OT quotations.* Although Paul regularly quotes from the OT in his letters, in Romans the argument is sometimes carried along by such quotations (see especially chs. 9–11).

4. *Deep concern for Israel.* Paul writes about her present status, her relationship to the Gentiles and her final salvation.

OUTLINE

1:1 *a* S 1Co 1:1
b S Ac 9:15 *c* Ro 15:16;
S 2Co 2:12; 11:7;
1Th 2:8,9; 1Pe 4:17
1:2 *d* S Ac 13:32;
Tit 1:2 *e* Lk 1:70;
Ro 3:21 *f* Gal 3:8
1:3 *g* S Jn 1:14;
Ro 9:5 *h* S Mt 1:1
1:4 *i* S Mt 4:3
j S Ac 2:24 *k* 1Co 1:2
1:5 *l* 1Ti 1:14
m S Ac 9:15 *n* Ac 6:7;
Ro 16:26
1:6 *o* Jude 1;
Rev 17:14
1:7 *p* Ro 8:39;
1Th 1:4 *q* S Ac 9:13
r 1Co 1:3; Eph 1:2;
1Ti 1:2; Tit 1:4; 1Pe 1:2
1:8 *s* 1Co 1:4;
Eph 1:16; 1Th 2:13;
2Th 1:3; 2Ti 1:3
t S Ro 10:18; 16:19
1:9 *u* 2Ti 1:3
v Job 16:19; Jer 42:5;
2Co 1:23; Gal 1:20;
Php 1:8; 1Th 2:5,10
1:10 *w* 1Sa 12:23;
S Lk 18:1; S Ac 1:14;
Eph 1:16; Php 1:4;
Col 1:9; 2Th 1:11;
2Ti 1:3; Phm 4
x S Ac 18:21 *y* ver 13;
Ro 15:32
1:11 *z* Ro 15:23
a 1Co 1:7; 12:1-31
1:13 *b* S Ro 11:25
c S Ro 7:1
d Ro 15:22,23

Paul, a servant of Christ Jesus, called to be an apostle *a* and set apart *b* for the gospel of God *c*— ²the gospel he promised beforehand *d* through his prophets *e* in the Holy Scriptures *f* ³regarding his Son, who as to his earthly life *a g* was a descendant of David, *h* ⁴and who through the Spirit of holiness was appointed the Son of God in power *b i* by his resurrection from the dead: *j* Jesus Christ our Lord. *k* ⁵Through him we received grace *l* and apostleship to call all the Gentiles *m* to faith *n* and obedience for his name's sake. ⁶And you also are among those Gentiles who are called to belong to Jesus Christ. *o*

⁷To all in Rome who are loved by God *p* and called to be his holy people: *q*

Grace and peace to you from God our Father and from the Lord Jesus Christ. *r*

PAUL'S LONGING TO VISIT ROME

⁸First, I thank my God through Jesus Christ for all of you, *s* because your faith is being reported all over the world. *t* ⁹God, whom I serve *u* in my spirit in preaching the gospel of his Son, is my witness *v* how constantly I remember you ¹⁰in my prayers at all times; *w* and I pray that now at last by God's will *x* the way may be opened for me to come to you. *y* ¹¹I long to see you *z* so that I may impart to you some spiritual gift *a* to make you strong— ¹²that is, that you and I may be mutually encouraged by each other's faith. ¹³I do not want you to be unaware, *b* brothers and sisters, *c* that I planned many times to come to you (but have been prevented from doing so until now) *d* in order that I might have a harvest among you, just as I have had among the other Gentiles.

¹⁴I am obligated *e* both to Greeks and non-Greeks, both to the wise and the foolish. ¹⁵That is why I am so eager to preach the gospel also to you who are in Rome. *f*

¹⁶I am not ashamed of the gospel, *g* because it is the power of God *h* that brings salva-

---

a 3 Or *who according to the flesh*   *b* 4 Or *was declared with power to be the Son of God*

1:1 *Paul.* In ancient times writers put their names at the beginning of letters. For the story of Paul's ministry, see Ac 9:1–30 and note on 9:1; 13:1—28:31; for his autobiographical accounts see 2Co 6:3–10; 11:21—12:10; Gal 1:13–24; Php 3:4–14; 1Ti 1:12–16. *servant.* The Greek for this word means (1) a "slave," who completely belongs to his owner and has no freedom to leave, or (2) a "servant," who willingly chooses to serve his master. See notes on Ex 14:31; Ps 18 title; Isa 41:8–9; 42:1. *apostle.* One specially commissioned by Christ (see notes on Mk 6:30; 1Co 1:1; Heb 3:1). *set apart.* See Gal 1:15 and note. *gospel.* See note on Mk 1:1.
1:2 *prophets.* Not just the writers of the prophetic books, for the whole OT prophesied about Jesus (see Lk 24:27,44–47 and notes). *Holy Scriptures.* The OT.
1:3 *regarding his Son.* The central figure of the gospel is Jesus, in and through whom all the promises of the OT are fulfilled (see Lk 24:27,44–47 and notes; cf. 2Co 1:20 and note). *descendant of David.* See Mt 1:1,16; 9:27; Mk 10:47; Jn 7:42 and notes.
1:4 *Son of God.* See Jn 3:16 and note. *his resurrection.* The authentication of Jesus' divine nature and the focal point of the apostolic proclamation (see Ac 2:14–40; 4:33 and notes).
1:7 *his holy people.* All Christians are "holy" in that they are positionally "set apart" to God and are experientially being made increasingly "holy" by the Holy Spirit (see note on 1Co 1:2). *Grace and peace.* The initial greeting used by both Paul and Peter in their letters. It combines the traditional Greek ("grace") and Hebrew ("peace") greetings but links them expressly with the only true source of "grace" (in the sense of God's unmerited favor, especially that which comes to sinful humanity through the saving work of Christ) and "peace" (the total well-being and security that only God can provide and that he does provide fully only to those who are at peace with him; see 5:1; Php 4:7 and notes; Gal 1:3; Eph 1:2; see also Jn 14:27; 20:19 and notes). This greeting is echoed in the conclusions of Paul's and Peter's letters, so that these letters stand framed in what amounts to an apostolic benediction on those who are addressed. Cf. Ex 34:6–7 and note. *Lord Jesus Christ.* See note on 1Th 1:1.

1:8 *thank.* Paul often began his letters with thanks (see 1Co 1:4; Eph 1:16; Php 1:3–4 and note; Col 1:3 and note; 1Th 1:2; 2Th 1:3; 2Ti 1:3; Phm 4). *through Jesus Christ.* The Christian must go through Christ not only for requests to God (see Jn 15:16) but also to give thanks. *all over the world.* Every place where the gospel has been preached.
1:9 *gospel of his Son.* The same as the "gospel of God" (v. 1).
1:10 *way may be opened.* See 15:23–29.
1:12 *mutually.* Paul's genuine humility is seen in his desire to be ministered to by the believers at Rome, as well as to minister to them.
1:13 *brothers and sisters.* Lit. "brothers," a word that was commonly used in Paul's day to address a crowd or community that included men and women (see Ac 1:14–16). *harvest.* New converts, as well as spiritual growth by those already converted. *among you ... among the other Gentiles.* Suggests that the church at Rome was predominantly Gentile.
1:14 *Greeks.* Those Gentiles who spoke Greek or followed the Greek way of life, even though they may have been Latin-speaking citizens of the Roman empire. *non-Greeks.* Lit. "barbarians," a word that probably imitated the unintelligible sound of their languages to Greek ears. They were the other Gentiles to whom Paul ministered.
1:16–17 The theme of the entire book.
1:16 *not ashamed.* Not even in the capital city of the Roman empire (see v. 15). *gospel.* See note on Mk 1:1. *first.* Not only in time but also in privilege. "Salvation is from the Jews" (Jn 4:22), and the Messiah was a Jew. The "very words of God" (3:2), the covenants, law, temple worship, revelation of the divine glory and Messianic prophecies came to them (9:3–5; see notes there). These privileges, however, were not extended to the Jews because of their superior merit or because of God's partiality toward them (cf. Dt 7:7–11 and note on Dt 4:37). It was necessary that the invasion of this world by the gospel begin at a particular point with a particular people, who in turn were responsible to carry that gospel to the other nations (see 2:9 and note).

tion to everyone who believes:ⁱ first to the Jew,ʲ then to the Gentile.ᵏ ¹⁷For in the gospel the righteousness of God is revealedˡ—a righteousness that is by faith ᵐ from first to last,ᵃ just as it is written: "The righteous will live by faith."ᵇ ⁿ

GOD'S WRATH AGAINST SINFUL HUMANITY

¹⁸The wrath of God ᵒ is being revealed from heaven against all the godlessness and wickedness of human beings who suppress the truth by their wickedness, ¹⁹since what may be known about God is plain to them, because God has made it plain to them. ᵖ ²⁰For since the creation of the world God's invisible qualities—his eternal power and divine nature—have been clearly seen, being understood from what has been made, �q so that people are without excuse.ʳ

²¹For although they knew God, they neither glorified him as God nor gave thanks to him, but their thinking became futile and their foolish hearts were darkened. ˢ ²²Although they claimed to be wise, they became foolsᵗ ²³and exchanged the glory of the immortal God for images ᵘ made to look like mortal human beings and birds and animals and reptiles.

²⁴Therefore God gave them overᵛ in the sinful desires of their hearts to sexual impurity for the degrading of their bodies with one another. ʷ ²⁵They exchanged the truth about God for a lie,ˣ and worshiped and served created things ʸ rather than the Creator—who is forever praised. ᶻ Amen. ᵃ

²⁶Because of this, God gave them overᵇ to shameful lusts. ᶜ Even their women exchanged natural sexual relations for unnatural ones. ᵈ ²⁷In the same way the men also abandoned natural relations with women and were inflamed with lust for one another. Men committed shameful acts with other men, and received in themselves the due penalty for their error. ᵉ

²⁸Furthermore, just as they did not think it worthwhile to retain the knowledge of God, so God gave them overᶠ to a depraved mind, so that they do what ought not to be done. ²⁹They have become filled with every kind of wickedness, evil, greed and depravity. They are full of envy, murder, strife, deceit and malice. They are gossips,ᵍ ³⁰slanderers, God-haters, insolent, arrogant and boastful; they invent ways of doing evil; they disobey their parents; ʰ ³¹they have no understanding, no fidelity, no love,ⁱ no mercy. ³²Although they know God's righteous decree that those who do such things deserve death,ʲ they not only continue to do these very things but also approveᵏ of those who practice them.

GOD'S RIGHTEOUS JUDGMENT

2 You, therefore, have no excuse,ˡ you who pass judgment on someone else, for at whatever point you judge another, you are condemning yourself, because you who pass judgment do the same things. ᵐ ²Now we know that God's judgment against

---

ᵃ 17 Or *is from faith to faith*   ᵇ 17 Hab. 2:4

1:16 ⁱS Jn 3:15
ʲAc 3:26; 13:46
ᵏS Ac 13:46;
Ro 2:9,10
1:17 ˡRo 3:21;
Php 3:9 ᵐS Ro 9:30
ⁿHab 2:4; Gal 3:11;
Heb 10:38
1:18 ᵒJn 3:36;
Ro 5:9; Eph 5:6;
Col 3:6; 1Th 1:10;
Rev 19:15
1:19 ᵖAc 14:17
1:20 qPs 19:1-6
ʳRo 2:1
1:21 ˢGe 8:21;
Jer 2:5; 17:9;
Eph 4:17,18
1:22 ᵗ1Co 1:20,27;
3:18,19
1:23 ᵘDt 4:16,17;
Ps 106:20; Jer 2:11;
Ac 17:29
1:24 ᵛver 26,28;
Ps 81:12; Eph 4:19
ʷ1Pe 4:3
1:25 ˣIsa 44:20
ʸJer 10:14; 13:25;
16:19,20 ᶻRo 9:5;
2Co 11:31 ᵃS Ro 1:36
1:26 ᵇver 24,28
ᶜEph 4:19; 1Th 4:5
ᵈLev 18:22,23
1:27 ᵉLev 18:22;
20:13; 1Co 6:18
1:28 ᶠver 24,26
1:29 ᵍ2Co 12:20;
1Ti 5:13; Jas 3:2;
3Jn 10
1:30 ʰ2Ti 3:2
1:31 ⁱ2Ti 3:3
1:32 ʲS Ro 6:23
ᵏPs 50:18; Lk 11:48;
Ac 8:1; 22:20
2:1 ˡRo 1:20
ᵐ2Sa 12:5-7;
S Mt 7:1,2

1:17 *righteousness.* The state of being "in the right" in relation to God (see notes on 2:13; 3:21,24).

A 1:18—3:20 In developing the theme of the righteousness of God (1:17; 3:21—5:21), Paul sets the stage by showing that all have sinned and therefore need the righteousness that only God can provide. He shows the sin of the Gentiles (1:18–32) and the sin of the Jews (2:1—3:8) and then summarizes the sin of all—Gentile and Jew alike (3:9–20).

A 1:18–20 No one—not even one who has not heard of the Bible or of Christ—has an excuse for not honoring God, because the whole created world reveals him.

C 1:18 *wrath of God.* Not a petulant, irrational burst of anger, such as humans often exhibit, but a holy, just revulsion against what is contrary to and opposes his holy nature and will. *is being revealed.* God's wrath is not limited to the end-time judgment of the wicked (1Th 1:10; Rev 19:15; 20:11–15). Here the wrath of God is his abandonment of the wicked to their sins (vv. 24–32). *the truth.* The truth about God revealed in the creation order.

1:21 *knew God.* From seeing his revelation in creation (vv. 19–20). The fact that these people were idolaters (v. 23) and knew God only through the creation order indicates that they were Gentiles (see Mt 5:45 and note; Ac 14:17). *gave thanks.* For earthly blessings, such as sun, rain and crops (see Mt 5:45 and note; Ac 14:17).

1:23 *glory.* God's unique majesty (see Isa 40:5 and note; 48:11; see also Eze 1:28; 43:2 and notes), of which fallen humankind

has lost sight and for which people have substituted deities of their own devising, patterned after various creatures (see Ps 106:20 and note).

A 1:24,26,28 *God gave them over.* God allowed sin to run its course as an act of judgment.

1:25 *Amen.* Can mean either "Yes indeed, it is so" or "So be it" (see 9:5; 11:36; 15:33; 16:27; see also note on Dt 27:15; cf. 1Ki 1:36).

1:26 *their women.* Not necessarily their wives.

A 1:27 Homosexual practice is sinful in God's eyes. The OT also condemns the practice (see Lev 18:22; 20:13).

1:28 *knowledge of God.* See vv. 19,21. *depraved mind.* The intent precedes the act (see v. 21; Mk 7:20–23).

1:29–31 A list of vices similar to those found in 13:13; 1Co 5:10–11; 6:9–10; 2Co 12:20–21; Gal 5:19– 21; Eph 4:31; 5:3–5; Col 3:5,8; 1Ti 1:9–10; 2Ti 3:2–5; Rev 21:8; 22:15.

1:32 *they know.* Their outrageous conduct was not due to total ignorance of what God required but to self-will and rebellion. *approve.* The extreme of sin is applauding, rather than regretting, the sins of others.

A 2:1–16 In this section Paul sets forth principles that govern God's judgment. God judges (1) according to truth (v. 2), (2) according to deeds (vv. 6–11) and (3) according to the light a person has (vv. 12–15). These principles lay the groundwork for Paul's discussion of the guilt of the Jews (vv. 17–29).

2:1 *no excuse.* Paul's teaching about judging agrees with that

2:4 *n* Ro 9:23; 11:33;
Eph 1:7,18; 2:7;
3:8,16; Col 2:2
o Ro 11:22 *p* Ro 3:25
q Ex 34:6; Ro 9:22;
1Ti 1:16; 1Pe 3:20;
2Pe 3:15 *r* 2Pe 3:9
2:5 *s* Ps 110:5;
Rev 6:17 *t* Jude 6
2:6 *u* Ps 62:12;
S Mt 16:27
2:7 *v* ver 10
w 1Co 15:53,54;
2Ti 1:10 *x* S Mt 25:46
2:8 *y* 2Th 2:12
z Eze 22:31
2:9 *a* Ps 32:10
b ver 10; Ro 1:16
2:10 *c* ver 9; Ro 1:16
2:11 *d* S Ac 10:34
2:12 *e* Ro 3:19; 6:14;
1Co 9:20,21; Gal 4:21;
5:18; S Ro 7:4
2:13 *f* Jas 1:22,23,25
2:14 *g* Ac 10:35
2:16 *h* Ecc 12:14;
1Co 4:5 *i* Ac 10:42
j Ro 16:25; 2Ti 2:8
2:17 *k* ver 23;
Jer 8:8; Mic 3:11;
Jn 5:45; Ro 9:4
2:21 *l* Mt 23:3,4
2:22 *m* Ac 19:37
2:23 *n* S ver 17
2:24 *o* Isa 52:5;
Eze 36:22; 2Pe 2:2
2:25 *p* ver 13,27;
Gal 5:3

those who do such things is based on truth. [3]So when you, a mere human, pass judgment on them and yet do the same things, do you think you will escape God's judgment? [4]Or do you show contempt for the riches *n* of his kindness, *o* forbearance *p* and patience, *q* not realizing that God's kindness is intended to lead you to repentance? *r*

[5]But because of your stubbornness and your unrepentant heart, you are storing up wrath against yourself for the day of God's wrath *s*, when his righteous judgment *t* will be revealed. [6]God "will repay everyone according to what they have done." *a u* [7]To those who by persistence in doing good seek glory, honor *v* and immortality, *w* he will give eternal life. *x* [8]But for those who are self-seeking and who reject the truth and follow evil, *y* there will be wrath and anger. *z* [9]There will be trouble and distress for every human being who does evil: *a* first for the Jew, then for the Gentile; *b* [10]but glory, honor and peace for everyone who does good: first for the Jew, then for the Gentile. *c* [11]For God does not show favoritism. *d*

[12]All who sin apart from the law will also perish apart from the law, and all who sin under the law *e* will be judged by the law. [13]For it is not those who hear the law who are righteous in God's sight, but it is those who obey *f* the law who will be declared righteous. [14](Indeed, when Gentiles, who do not have the law, do by nature things required by the law, *g* they are a law for themselves, even though they do not have the law. [15]They show that the requirements of the law are written on their hearts, their consciences also bearing witness, and their thoughts now accusing, now even defending them.) [16]This will take place on the day when God judges everyone's secrets *h* through Jesus Christ, *i* as my gospel *j* declares.

THE JEWS AND THE LAW

[17]Now you, if you call yourself a Jew; if you rely on the law and boast in God; *k* [18]if you know his will and approve of what is superior because you are instructed by the law; [19]if you are convinced that you are a guide for the blind, a light for those who are in the dark, [20]an instructor of the foolish, a teacher of infants, because you have in the law the embodiment of knowledge and truth— [21]you, then, who teach others, do you not teach yourself? You who preach against stealing, do you steal? *l* [22]You who say that people should not commit adultery, do you commit adultery? You who abhor idols, do you rob temples? *m* [23]You who boast in the law, *n* do you dishonor God by breaking the law? [24]As it is written: "God's name is blasphemed among the Gentiles because of you." *b o*

[25]Circumcision has value if you observe the law, *p* but if you break the law, you have be-

---

a 6 Psalm 62:12; Prov. 24:12   *b* 24 Isaiah 52:5 (see Septuagint); Ezek. 36:20,22

---

of Jesus (see note on Mt 7:1), who did not condemn judging as such, but hypocritical judging. *you who pass judgment.* A warning that had special relevance for Jews, who were inclined to look down on Gentiles because of their ignorance of God's revelation in the OT and because of their immoral lives.

2:2 *we know.* An expression Paul frequently used, assuming that the persons addressed agreed with the statement that followed (see 3:19; 6:6,9; 7:14; 8:22,28; 1Co 8:1,4; 2Co 5:1; 1Ti 1:8).

2:3 Jesus also condemned such judgmental acts (see Mt 7:3 and note; cf. Lk 18:9).

▲ 2:4 The purpose of God's kindness is to give opportunity for repentance (see 2Pe 3:9 and note). The Jews had misconstrued his patience to be a lack of intent to judge.

2:5 *day of God's wrath.* See v. 8; judgment in the end times, in contrast to the judgment discussed in 1:18–32.

2:6–7 Paul is not contradicting his continual emphasis in all his writings, including Romans, that people are saved not by what they do but by faith in what Christ has done for them. Paul is referring to "persistence in doing good" as the proof of genuine faith (see Gal 5:6; Jas 2:14–26 and notes).

2:8 *wrath and anger.* On the day of final judgment.

▲ 2:9 *first for the Jew.* With spiritual privilege comes spiritual responsibility (see Am 3:2 and note; Lk 12:48; cf. Ro 1:16 and note).

2:11 A basic teaching of both the OT and the NT.

2:12 *law.* The Mosaic law. "All who sin apart from the law" refers to Gentiles. God judges according to the light available to people. Gentiles will not be condemned for not obeying a law they did not possess. Their judgment will be on other grounds

(see v. 15; 1:18–20 and note; cf. Am 1:3—2:3).

2:13 *will be declared righteous.* At God's pronouncement of acquittal on judgment day (see note on 3:24).

▲ 2:14 *by nature.* By natural impulse, without the external constraint of the Mosaic law. *things required by the law.* Does not mean that pagans fulfilled the requirements of the Mosaic law but refers to practices in pagan society that agreed with the law, such as caring for the sick and elderly, honoring parents and condemning adultery. *law for themselves.* The moral nature of pagans, enlightened by conscience (v. 15), functioned for them as the Mosaic law did for the Jews.

2:16 This verse should be read with v. 13, as the parentheses around vv. 14–15 indicate. *my gospel.* See 16:25 and note.

■ 2:17–24 The presentation takes the form of a dialogue. Paul knew how a self-righteous Jew thought, for he had been one himself. He cites one advantage after another that Jews regarded as unqualified assets. But those assets became liabilities when there was no correspondence between profession and practice. Paul applied to the Jew the principles of judgment set forth in vv. 1–16 (see note on those verses).

2:19–20 *the blind . . . infants.* Gentiles, to whom Jews regarded themselves as vastly superior because they (the Jews) possessed the Mosaic law.

2:22 *do you rob temples?* See Ac 19:37. Large amounts of wealth were often stored in pagan temples.

2:25 *Circumcision.* A sign of the covenant that God made with Israel (see Lev 12:3) and a pledge of the covenant blessing (see 4:11 and note). The Jews had come to regard circumcision as a guarantee of God's favor.

come as though you had not been circumcised. ^q ²⁶If those who are not circumcised keep the law's requirements, ^r will they not be regarded as though they were circumcised? ^s ²⁷The one who is not circumcised physically and yet obeys the law will condemn you ^t who, even though you have the ^a written code and circumcision, are a lawbreaker.

²⁸A person is not a Jew who is one only outwardly, ^u nor is circumcision merely outward and physical. ^v ²⁹No, a person is a Jew who is one inwardly; and circumcision is circumcision of the heart, ^w by the Spirit, ^x not by the written code. ^y Such a person's praise is not from other people, but from God. ^z

GOD'S FAITHFULNESS

3 What advantage, then, is there in being a Jew, or what value is there in circumcision? ²Much in every way! ^a First of all, the Jews have been entrusted with the very words of God. ^b

³What if some were unfaithful? ^c Will their unfaithfulness nullify God's faithfulness? ^d ⁴Not at all! Let God be true, ^e and every human being a liar. ^f As it is written:

> "So that you may be proved right when you speak
> and prevail when you judge." ^b ^g

⁵But if our unrighteousness brings out God's righteousness more clearly, ^h what shall we say? That God is unjust in bringing his wrath on us? (I am using a human argument.) ⁱ ⁶Certainly not! If that were so, how could God judge the world? ^j ⁷Someone might argue, "If my falsehood enhances God's truthfulness and so increases his glory, ^k why am I still condemned as a sinner?" ^l ⁸Why not say—as we are being slanderously reported as saying and as some claim that we say—"Let us do evil that good may result"? ^m Their condemnation is just!

NO ONE IS RIGHTEOUS

⁹What shall we conclude then? Do we have any advantage? ⁿ Not at all! We have already made the charge that Jews and Gentiles alike are all under the power of sin. ^o ¹⁰As it is written:

> "There is no one righteous, not even one;
> ¹¹ there is no one who understands;
>   there is no one who seeks God.
> ¹²All have turned away,
>   they have together become worthless;
> there is no one who does good,
>   not even one." ^c ^p
> ¹³ "Their throats are open graves;
>   their tongues practice deceit." ^d ^q

---

^a 27 Or *who, by means of a*   ^b 4 Psalm 51:4   ^c 12 Psalms 14:1-3; 53:1-3; Eccles. 7:20
^d 13 Psalm 5:9

2:25 ^q Jer 4:4; 9:25,26
2:26 ^r Ro 8:4 ^s S 1Co 7:19
2:27 ^t Mt 12:41,42
2:28 ^u Mt 3:9; Jn 8:39; Ro 9:6,7 ^v Gal 6:15
2:29 ^w Dt 30:6 ^x Php 3:3; Col 2:11 ^y Ro 7:6; 2Co 3:6 ^z Jn 5:44; 12:43; 1Co 4:5; 2Co 10:18; Gal 1:10; 1Th 2:4; 1Pe 3:4
3:2 ^a Ro 9:4,5 ^b Dt 4:8; Ps 147:19; Ac 7:38
3:3 ^c Ro 10:16; Heb 4:2 ^d 2Ti 2:13
3:4 ^e Jn 3:33 ^f Ps 116:11 ^g Ps 51:4
3:5 ^h Ro 5:8
3:6 ⁱ Ro 6:19; Gal 3:15 ^j Ge 18:25; Ro 2:16
3:7 ^k ver 4 ^l Ro 9:19
3:8 ^m Ro 6:1
3:9 ⁿ ver 1 ^o ver 19,23; 1Ki 8:46; 2Ch 6:36; Ps 106:6; Ro 5:12; 11:32; Gal 3:22
3:12 ^p Ps 14:1-3; 53:1-3; Ecc 7:20
3:13 ^q Ps 5:9

2:27 If a Gentile's deeds excelled those of a Jew in righteousness, that very fact condemned the Jew, who had an immeasurably better set of standards in the law of Moses.

2:29 *by the Spirit.* The true sign of belonging to God is not an outward mark on the physical body but the regenerating power of the Holy Spirit within—what Paul meant by "circumcision of the heart" (see Dt 30:6 and notes on Ge 17:10; Jer 4:4). *praise is not from other people, but from God.* Cf. Jn 5:41, 44; 12:43; 1Co 4:3–5 and notes on 4:3,5.

3:2 *First of all.* Paul does not discuss the other advantages of being a Jew until 9:4–5 (see notes there). *entrusted.* The advantage of having the very words of God involves a duty. *very words of God.* The OT.

3:3 *God's faithfulness.* God is faithful to his promises and would punish Israel for its unbelief (v. 5; see 2Ti 2:13).

3:4 God's punishment of sin exhibits his faithfulness to his righteous character.

3:5 *brings out God's righteousness.* By contrast, in showing it up against the dark background of human sin. *human argument.* "Human" in the sense of its weakness and absurdity.

3:6 *judge.* On judgment day. *world.* All moral creatures (also in v. 19)—a more limited reference than in 1:20.

3:8 *Let us do evil that good may result.* Paul deals with this issue more fully in ch. 6.

3:9 *Do we have any advantage?* Are Jews better than Gentiles in the sight of God? *all under the power of sin.* Nine times in four verses (vv. 9–12) Paul mentions the universality of sin ("all," two times; "no one," four times; "not even one," two times; "together," once). *under the power of sin.* And its condemnation.

3:10–18 A collection of OT quotations that underscores Paul's charge that both Jews and Gentiles are under the power of sin. Several factors explain why the citations are not always verbatim: 1. NT quotations sometimes gave the general sense and were not meant to be word-for-word. 2. Quotation marks were not used in Greek. 3. The quotations were often taken from the pre-Christian Greek translation (the Septuagint) of the Hebrew OT, because Greek readers were not familiar with the Hebrew Bible. 4. Sometimes the NT writer, in order to drive home his point, would purposely (under the inspiration of the Holy Spirit) enlarge, abbreviate or adapt an OT passage or combine two or more passages.

3:11 *understands.* About God and what is right.

3:13 *open graves.* Expressing the corruption of the heart.

3:13 ʳPs 140:3
3:14 ˢPs 10:7
3:17 ᵗIsa 59:7,8
3:18 ᵘPs 36:1
3:19 ᵛS Jn 10:34
ʷS Ro 2:12 ˣPs 63:11;
107:42; Eze 16:63
ʸver 9
3:20 ᶻAc 13:39;
Gal 2:16 ᵃS Ro 4:15
3:21 ᵇIsa 46:13;
Jer 23:6; Ro 1:17; 9:30
ᶜAc 10:43; Ro 1:2
3:22 ᵈRo 1:17
ᵉS Ro 9:30 ᶠGal 2:16;
3:22 ᵍS Jn 3:15;
Ro 4:11; 10:4
ʰRo 10:12; Gal 3:28;
Col 3:11
3:23 ˡS ver 9
3:24 ʲS Ro 4:25
ᵏJn 1:14,16,17;
Ro 4:16; 5:21; 6:14;
11:5; 2Co 12:9;
Eph 2:8; 4:7; Tit 2:11;
Heb 4:16 ˡPs 130:7;
1Co 1:30; Gal 4:5;
Eph 1:7,14; Col 1:14;
Heb 9:12
3:25 ᵐEx 25:17;
Lev 16:10; Ps 65:3;
Heb 2:17; 9:28;
1Jn 4:10 ⁿAc 20:28;
Ro 5:9; Eph 1:7;
Heb 9:12,14; 13:12;
1Pe 1:19; Rev 1:5
ᵒAc 14:16; 17:30
3:27 ᵖRo 2:17,23;
4:2; 1Co 1:29-31;
Eph 2:9
3:28 ᑫver 20,21;
Ac 13:39; Gal 2:16; 3:11;
Eph 2:9; Jas 2:20,24,26

"The poison of vipers is on their lips."ᵃ ʳ

14   "Their mouths are full of cursing and bitterness."ᵇ ˢ

15 "Their feet are swift to shed blood;

16   ruin and misery mark their ways,

17 and the way of peace they do not know."ᶜ ᵗ

18   "There is no fear of God before their eyes."ᵈ ᵘ

¹⁹Now we know that whatever the law says,ᵛ it says to those who are under the law,ʷ so that every mouth may be silencedˣ and the whole world held accountable to God.ʸ ²⁰Therefore no one will be declared righteous in God's sight by observing the law;ᶻ rather, through the law we become conscious of our sin.ᵃ

RIGHTEOUSNESS THROUGH FAITH

²¹But now apart from the law the righteousness of Godᵇ has been made known, to which the Law and the Prophets testify.ᶜ ²²This righteousnessᵈ is given through faithᵉ inᵉ Jesus Christᶠ to all who believe.ᵍ There is no difference between Jew and Gentile,ʰ ²³for all have sinnedⁱ and fall short of the glory of God, ²⁴and all are justifiedʲ freely by his graceᵏ through the redemptionˡ that came by Christ Jesus. ²⁵God presented Christ as a sacrifice of atonement,ᶠ ᵐ through the shedding of his bloodⁿ—to be received by faith. He did this to demonstrate his justice, because in his forbearance he had left the sins committed beforehand unpunishedᵒ— ²⁶he did it to demonstrate his justice at the present time, so as to be just and the one who justifies those who have faith in Jesus.

²⁷Where, then, is boasting?ᵖ It is excluded. Because of what law? The law that requires works? No, because of the "law" that requires faith. ²⁸For we maintain that a person is justified by faith apart from observing the law.ᑫ ²⁹Is God the God of Jews only? Is he not

---

ᵃ 13   Psalm 140:3   ᵇ 14   Psalm 10:7 (see Septuagint)   ᶜ 17   Isaiah 59:7,8   ᵈ 18   Psalm 36:1
ᵉ 22   Or *through the faithfulness of*   ᶠ 25   The Greek for *sacrifice of atonement* refers to the atonement cover on the ark of the covenant (see Lev. 16:15,16).

3:18 *fear of God.* Awesome reverence for God; the source of all godliness (see notes on Ge 20:11; Pr 1:7).

3:19 *we know.* See note on 2:2. *law.* The OT (as in Jn 10:34; 15:25; 1Co 14:21). *those who are under the law.* Jews. *every mouth ... whole world.* Jews as well as Gentiles are guilty.

3:20 *declared righteous.* See notes on v. 24; 2:13. *we become conscious of our sin.* According to Paul, this is one of the primary purposes of the law (see 7:7 and note).

3:21—5:21 Having shown that all (both Gentiles and Jews) are unrighteous (1:18—3:20), Paul now shows that God has provided a righteousness for humankind.

3:21 *But now.* There are two possible meanings: (1) temporal—all of time is divided into two periods, and in the "now" period the righteousness of God has been made known; (2) logical—the contrast is between the righteousness gained by observing the law (which is impossible, v. 20) and the righteousness provided by God. *apart from the law.* Apart from keeping the law. *the Law and the Prophets testify.* See Ge 15:6; Ps 32:1–2; Hab 2:4 and notes.

3:22–24 "There is no difference ... glory of God" is a parenthetical thought. Paul is saying that "all who believe" (v. 22) are "justified freely" (v. 24); he is not saying that "all [who have] sinned" (v. 23) are "justified freely" (v. 24).

3:22 *no difference.* Between Jews and Gentiles (see 10:12 and note).

3:23 *the glory of God.* What God intended humans to be. The glory they had before the fall (see Ge 1:26–28; Ps 8:4–8 and notes; cf. Eph 4:24; Col 3:10) believers will again have through Christ (see Heb 2:5–9 and notes).

3:24 *justified.* Paul uses the Greek verb for "justified" 27 times, mostly in Romans and Galatians. It is translated "justify" in all cases except two (2:13; 3:20, where it is translated "declared righteous"). The term describes what happens when people believe in Christ as their Savior: From the negative viewpoint, God declares them to be not guilty; from the positive viewpoint, he declares them to be righteous. He cancels the guilt of their sin and credits righteousness to them. Paul empha-

sizes two points in this regard: 1. No one lives a perfectly good, holy, righteous life. On the contrary, "there is no one righteous" (v. 10), and "all have sinned and fall short of the glory of God" (v. 23). "Therefore no one will be declared righteous in God's sight by observing the law" (v. 20). 2. But even though all are sinners and not sons, God will declare those who put their trust in Jesus not guilty but righteous. This legal declaration is valid because Christ died to pay the penalty for our sin and lived a life of perfect righteousness that can in turn be imputed to us. This is the central theme of Romans and is stated in the theme verse, 1:17 ("the righteousness of God ... by faith"). Christ's righteousness (his obedience to God's law and his sacrificial death) will be credited to believers as their own. Paul uses the Greek for "credited" ten times in ch. 4 alone. *freely by his grace.* The central thought in justification is that, although people clearly and totally deserve to be declared guilty (vv. 9–19), God declares them righteous because of their trust in Christ. This is stated in several ways here: (1) "freely" (as a gift, for nothing), (2) "by his grace," (3) "through the redemption that came by Christ Jesus" and (4) "by faith" (v. 25). *redemption.* A word taken from the slave market—the basic idea is that of obtaining release by payment of a ransom. Paul uses this word to refer to release from guilt, with its liability for judgment, and to deliverance from slavery to sin, because Christ in his death paid the ransom to set us free.

3:25 *sacrifice of atonement.* The Greek for this phrase speaks of a sacrifice that satisfies the righteous wrath of God. Without this appeasement all people are justly destined for eternal punishment. See TNIV text note here; see also note on 1Jn 2:2. *through ... his blood ... received by faith.* Saving faith looks to Jesus Christ and his sacrificial death for us.

3:25b–26 The sins of God's people, punished symbolically in the animal sacrifices of the OT period, were totally punished in the once-for-all sacrifice of Christ on the cross.

3:28 *by faith.* When Luther translated this passage, he added the word "alone," which, though not in the Greek, accurately reflects the meaning (see note on Jas 2:14–26).

the God of Gentiles too? Yes, of Gentiles too, [r] 30since there is only one God, who will justify the circumcised by faith and the uncircumcised through that same faith. [s] 31Do we,
then, nullify the law by this faith? Not at all! Rather, we uphold the law.

ABRAHAM JUSTIFIED BY FAITH

4 What then shall we say [t] that Abraham, the forefather of us Jews, [u] discovered in
this matter? 2If, in fact, Abraham was justified by works, he had something to
boast about—but not before God. [v] 3What does Scripture say? "Abraham believed
God, and it was credited to him as righteousness." [a] [w]

4Now to anyone who works, their wages are not credited to them as a gift, [x] but as an
obligation. 5However, to anyone who does not work but trusts God who justifies the ungodly, their faith is credited as righteousness. [y] 6David says the same thing when he speaks
of the blessedness of those to whom God credits righteousness apart from works:

7 "Blessed are those
   whose transgressions are forgiven,
   whose sins are covered.
8 Blessed are those
   whose sin the Lord will never count against them." [b] [z]

9Is this blessedness only for the circumcised, or also for the uncircumcised? [a] We have
been saying that Abraham's faith was credited to him as righteousness. [b] 10Under what circumstances was it credited? Was it after he was circumcised, or before? It was not after, but
before! 11And he received circumcision as a sign, a seal of the righteousness that he had by
faith while he was still uncircumcised. [c] So then, he is the father [d] of all who believe [e] but have
not been circumcised, in order that righteousness might be credited to them. 12And he is
then also the father of the circumcised who not only are circumcised but who also follow in
the footsteps of the faith that our father Abraham had before he was circumcised.

13It was not through the law that Abraham and his offspring received the promise [f] that
he would be heir of the world, [g] but through the righteousness that comes by faith. [h] 14For
if those who depend on the law are heirs, faith means nothing and the promise is worthless, [i] 15because the law brings wrath. [j] And where there is no law there is no transgression. [k]

a 3 Gen. 15:6; also in verse 22   b 8 Psalm 32:1,2

3:29 [r] Ac 10:34,35;
Ro 9:24; 10:12; 15:9;
Gal 3:28
3:30 [s] Ro 4:11,12;
Gal 3:8
4:1 [t] S Ro 8:31
[u] S Lk 3:8
4:2 [v] 1Co 1:31
4:3 [w] ver 5,9,22;
Ge 15:6; Gal 3:6;
Jas 2:23
4:4 [x] Ro 11:6
4:5 [y] ver 3,9,22;
S Ro 9:30
4:8 [z] Ps 32:1,2;
103:12; 2Co 5:19
4:9 [a] Ro 3:30
[b] S ver 3
4:11 [c] Ge 17:10,11
[d] ver 16,17; S Lk 3:8
[e] S Ro 3:22
4:13 [f] S Ac 13:32;
Gal 3:16,29
[g] Ge 17:4-6
[h] S Ro 9:30
4:14 [i] Gal 3:18
4:15 [j] Ro 7:7-25;
1Co 15:56; 2Co 3:7;
Gal 3:10; S Ro 7:12
[k] Ro 3:20; 5:13; 7:7

3:30 *only one God.* By appealing to the first article of
Jewish faith ("the Lord is one," Dt 6:4; see note there), Paul
argues that there is only one way of salvation for both Jew ("circumcised") and Gentile ("uncircumcised"), namely, faith in
Christ.

3:31 Paul anticipated being charged with antinomianism
(against law): If justification comes by faith alone, then is not
the law rejected? He gives a more complete answer in chs. 6–7
and reasserts the validity of the law in 13:8–10.

4:1 *Abraham, the forefather.* The great patriarch of the
Jewish nation, the true example of a justified person (see
Jas 2:21–23 and notes). The Jews of Jesus' time used Abraham
as an example of justification by works, but Paul holds him up
as a shining example of righteousness by faith (see Gal 3:7–9
and notes).

4:2 *If… Abraham was justified by works.* Many of Paul's Jewish
contemporaries held that Abraham was justified by works (in the
Apocrypha, see Ecclesiasticus 44:21), but the fact is that he was
not (see v. 3), and therefore all boasting on his part is excluded.

4:3 The reference is to Ge 15:6, where nothing is mentioned about works (see note on 3:21). *credited.* Abraham
had kept no law, rendered no service and performed no ritual that
earned credit to his account before God. His belief in God, who had
made promises to him, was credited to him as righteousness.

4:6–8 God does not continue to credit unrighteousness to sinners who repent, but forgives them when they confess (see Ps
32:3–5 and notes; Eze 18:23,27–28,32 and notes on 18:23 and
18:32; 33:14–16).

4:9 See 3:30 and note.

4:10 *not after, but before!* Abraham was declared righteous (Ge 15:6) some 14 years before he was circumcised
(Ge 17:24, 26). See Gal 3:17 for a similar statement.

4:11 *sign.* Circumcision was, among other things, the outward
sign of the righteousness that God had credited to Abraham for
his faith (see Ge 17:11 and note). *So then.* Abraham is the "father" of believing Gentiles (the uncircumcised), because he believed and was justified before the rite of circumcision (the
mark of Jews) was instituted.

4:12 *father of the circumcised.* Abraham is also the father of
believing Jews. Thus his story shows that for Jew and Gentile alike there is only one way of justification— the way of faith.

4:13 *not through the law.* Not on the condition that the
promise be merited by works of the law. *his offspring.* All
those of whom Abraham is said to be father (vv. 11–12). *heir of
the world.* "World" here refers to the creation, as in 1:20. No express mention of this heirship is made in the Genesis account
of Abraham. He is promised "offspring like the dust of the earth"
(Ge 13:16), possession of the land of Canaan (Ge 12:7; 13:14–15;
15:7,18–21; 17:8) and blessing through him (see Ge 12:2–3 and
note; 18:18) or his offspring (Ge 22:18) for all peoples on earth.
But since, as Genesis already makes clear, God purposed through
Abraham and his offspring to work out the destiny of the whole
world, it was implicit in the promises to Abraham that he and his
offspring would "inherit the land" (see Ps 37:9,11,22,29,34 and
note on 37:9; Mt 5:5). The full realization of this awaits the consummation of the Messianic kingdom at Christ's return.

4:14 *those who depend on the law.* Those whose claim to the
inheritance is based on the fulfillment of the law. *promise.* See
note on v. 13.

4:15 *the law brings wrath.* The law, because it reveals and even
stimulates sin (see 7:7–11), produces wrath, not promise. *transgression.* Overstepping a clearly defined line. Where there is no
law there is still sin, but it does not have the character of transgression.

4:16 *l* S Ro 3:24
m Ro 15:8 *n* ver 11;
S Lk 3:8; S Gal 3:16
4:17 *o* Ge 17:5
p S Jn 5:21 *q* Isa 48:13
r 1Co 1:28
4:18 *s* ver 17
t Ge 15:5
4:19 *u* Heb 11:11,12
v Ge 17:17 *w* Ge 18:11
4:20 *x* 1Sa 30:6
y S Mt 9:8
4:21 *z* Ge 18:14;
S Mt 19:26
4:22 *a* S ver 3
4:24 *b* Ps 102:18;
Hab 2:2; Ro 15:4;
1Co 9:10; 10:11;
2Ti 3:16,17 *c* Ro 10:9;
1Pe 1:21 *d* S Ac 2:24
4:25 *e* Isa 53:5,6;
Ro 5:6,8; 8:32;
2Co 5:21 *f* Isa 53:11;
Ro 3:24; 5:1,9,16,18;
8:30; 1Co 6:11;
2Co 5:15
5:1 *g* S Ro 4:25
h S Ro 3:28 *i* S Lk 2:14
j ver 10
5:2 *k* Eph 2:18; 3:12
l 1Co 15:1 *m* S Heb 3:6
5:3 *n* S Mt 5:12
o S Heb 10:36
5:5 *p* Php 1:20;
S Heb 3:6; 1Jn 3:2,3
q ver 8; Jn 3:16;
Ro 8:39 *r* Ac 2:33;
10:45; Tit 3:5,6
5:6 *s* Mk 1:15;
Gal 4:4; Eph 1:10
t ver 8,10 *u* Ro 4:25

[16]Therefore, the promise comes by faith, so that it may be by grace *l* and may be guaranteed *m* to all Abraham's offspring—not only to those who are of the law but also to those who have the faith of Abraham. He is the father of us all. *n* [17]As it is written: "I have made you a father of many nations." *a* *o* He is our father in the sight of God, in whom he believed—the God who gives life *p* to the dead and calls *q* into being things that were not. *r*

[18]Against all hope, Abraham in hope believed and so became the father of many nations, *s* just as it had been said to him, "So shall your offspring be." *b* *t* [19]Without weakening in his faith, he faced the fact that his body was as good as dead *u*—since he was about a hundred years old *v*—and that Sarah's womb was also dead. *w* [20]Yet he did not waver through unbelief regarding the promise of God, but was strengthened *x* in his faith and gave glory to God, *y* [21]being fully persuaded that God had power to do what he had promised. *z* [22]This is why "it was credited to him as righteousness." *a* [23]The words "it was credited to him" were written not for him alone, [24]but also for us, *b* to whom God will credit righteousness—for us who believe in him *c* who raised Jesus our Lord from the dead. *d* [25]He was delivered over to death for our sins *e* and was raised to life for our justification. *f*

PEACE AND HOPE

5 Therefore, since we have been justified *g* through faith, *h* we *c* have peace *i* with God through our Lord Jesus Christ, *j* [2]through whom we have gained access *k* by faith into this grace in which we now stand. *l* And we *d* boast in the hope *m* of the glory of God. [3]Not only so, but we *d* also glory in our sufferings, *n* because we know that suffering produces perseverance; *o* [4]perseverance, character; and character, hope. [5]And hope *p* does not put us to shame, because God's love *q* has been poured out into our hearts through the Holy Spirit, *r* who has been given to us.

[6]You see, at just the right time, *s* when we were still powerless, *t* Christ died for the ungodly. *u* [7]Very rarely will anyone die for a righteous person, though for a good person some-

a 17 Gen. 17:5   *b 18* Gen. 15:5   *c 1* Many manuscripts *let us*   *d 2, 3* Or *let us*

4:16 A summary of the thought of vv. 11–12. For the close correlation between faith and grace, see 3:24–25; Eph 2:8–9 and notes. *those who are of the law.* Jewish Christians. *those who have the faith of Abraham.* Gentile Christians who share Abraham's faith but who, like Abraham, do not possess the law.
4:17 *in the sight of God.* God considers Abraham the father of Jews and believing Gentiles alike, no matter how others (especially the Jews) may see him. *the God who gives life to the dead.* The main reference is to the birth of Isaac through Abraham and Sarah, both of whom were far past the age of childbearing (see Ge 18:11). Secondarily Paul alludes also to the resurrection of Christ (see vv. 24–25 and notes). *calls into being things that were not.* God has the ability to create out of nothing, as he demonstrated in the birth of Isaac.
4:18 *Against all hope …in hope believed.* When all hope, as a human possibility, failed, Abraham placed his hope in God.
4:19 *Without weakening in his faith.* Abraham had some anxious moments (see Ge 17:17–18), but God did not count these against him. *faced the fact.* Faith does not refuse to face reality but looks beyond all difficulties to God and his promises. *Sarah's womb was also dead.* Sarah was ten years younger than Abraham (see Ge 17:17) but well past the age of bearing children.
4:20 *gave glory to God.* Because Abraham had faith to believe that God would do what he promised. Whereas works are human attempts to establish a claim on God, faith brings glory to him.
4:22 *This is why.* Abraham's faith was "credited to him as righteousness" because it was true faith, i.e., complete confidence in God's promise.
4:23 *not for him alone.* Abraham's experience was not private or individual but had broad implications. If justification by faith was true for him, it is universally true.
4:24 *but also for us.* As Abraham was justified because he believed in a God who brought life from the dead, so we will be justified by believing "in him who raised Jesus our Lord from the dead" (see 10:9 and note).

4:25 These words, which reflect the Septuagint (Greek) translation of Isa 53:12, are probably quoted from a Christian confessional formula. *justification.* See 3:24 and note.
5:1 *peace with God.* Not merely a subjective feeling (peace of mind) but primarily an objective status, a new relationship with God: Once we were his enemies, but now we are his friends (see v. 10 and note; Eph 2:16; Col 1:21–22).
5:2 *access.* Jesus ushers us into the presence of God. The heavy curtain (of the temple) that separated us from God and God from us has been removed (see notes on Mt 27:51; Heb 10:19–22). *hope of the glory of God.* Our confidence that the purpose for which God created us will be ultimately realized (see note on 3:23).
5:3 *glory in our sufferings.* Not "because of" but "in." Paul does not advocate a morbid view of life but a joyous and triumphant one (see Jas 1:2 and note).
5:4 Christians can rejoice in suffering because they know that it is not meaningless. Part of God's purpose is to produce character in his children (see Jas 1:3).
5:5 *hope does not put us to shame.* The believer's hope is not to be equated with unfounded optimism. On the contrary, it is the blessed assurance of our future destiny and is based on God's love, which is revealed to us by the Holy Spirit and objectively demonstrated to us in the death of Christ. Paul has moved from faith (v. 1) to hope (vv. 2,4–5) to love (here; see 1Co 13:13; 1Th 1:3 and notes). *has been poured out.* The verb indicates a present status resulting from a past action. When we first believed in Christ, the Holy Spirit poured out his love in our hearts, and his love for us continues to dwell in us. *who has been given to us.* All true believers have the gift of the Spirit (see 8:9 and note).
5:6 *the right time.* The appointed moment in God's redemptive plan (see Mk 1:15 and note). *Christ died for the ungodly.* Christ's love is grounded in God's free grace and is not the result of any inherent worthiness found in its objects (humankind). In fact, it is lavished on us in spite of our undesirable character.
5:7 *righteous person …good person.* We were neither righteous nor good, but sinners, when Christ died for us (see v. 8; 3:10–12).

one might possibly dare to die. [8]But God demonstrates his own love for us in this: While we were still sinners, Christ died for us. [v]

[9]Since we have now been justified [w] by his blood, [x] how much more shall we be saved from God's wrath [y] through him! [10]For if, while we were God's enemies, [z] we were reconciled [a] to him through the death of his Son, how much more, having been reconciled, shall we be saved through his life! [b] [11]Not only is this so, but we also boast in God through our Lord Jesus Christ, through whom we have now received reconciliation. [c]

DEATH THROUGH ADAM, LIFE THROUGH CHRIST

[12]Therefore, just as sin entered the world through one man, [d] and death through sin, [e] and in this way death came to all people, because all sinned [f]—

[13]To be sure, sin was in the world before the law was given, but sin is not charged against anyone's account where there is no law. [g] [14]Nevertheless, death reigned from the time of Adam to the time of Moses, even over those who did not sin by breaking a command, as did Adam, [h] who is a pattern of the one to come. [i]

[15]But the gift is not like the trespass. For if the many died by the trespass of the one man, [j] how much more did God's grace and the gift that came by the grace of the one man, Jesus Christ, [k] overflow to the many! [16]Nor can the gift of God be compared with the result of one man's sin: The judgment followed one sin and brought condemnation, but the gift followed many trespasses and brought justification. [17]For if, by the trespass of the one man, death [l] reigned through that one man, how much more will those who receive God's abundant provision of grace and of the gift of righteousness reign in life [m] through the one man, Jesus Christ!

[18]Consequently, just as one trespass resulted in condemnation for all people, [n] so also one righteous act resulted in justification [o] and life [p] for all. [19]For just as through the disobedience of the one man [q] the many were made sinners, [r] so also through the obedience [s] of the one man the many will be made righteous.

[20]The law was brought in so that the trespass might increase. [t] But where sin increased, grace increased all the more, [u] [21]so that, just as sin reigned in death, [v] so also grace [w] might reign through righteousness to bring eternal life [x] through Jesus Christ our Lord.

5:8 [v]Jn 3:16; 15:13; 1Pe 3:18; 1Jn 3:16; 4:10
5:9 [w]S Ro 4:25 [x]S Ro 3:25 [y]S Ro 1:18
5:10 [z]Ro 11:28; Col 1:21 [a]ver 11; Ro 11:15; 2Co 5:18,19; Col 1:20,22 [b]Ro 8:34; Heb 7:25
5:11 [c]S ver 10
5:12 [d]ver 15,16,17; 1Co 15:21,22 ver 14,18; Ge 2:17; 3:19; S Ro 6:23 [f]S Ro 3:9
5:13 [g]S Ro 4:15
5:14 [h]Ge 3:11,12 [i]1Co 15:22,45
5:15 [j]ver 12,18,19 [k]Ac 15:11
5:17 [l]S ver 12 [m]Jn 10:10
5:18 [n]S ver 12 [o]S Ro 4:25 [p]Isa 53:11
5:19 [q]ver 12 [r]S Ro 3:9 [s]S Php 2:8
5:20 [t]Ro 3:20; 7:7,8; Gal 3:19 [u]Ro 6:1; 1Ti 1:13,14
5:21 [v]ver 12,14; S Ro 6:16 [w]S Ro 3:24 [x]S Mt 25:46

5:9 *by his blood.* By laying down his life as a sacrifice—a reference to Christ's death for our sins (see 3:25 and note). *God's wrath.* The final judgment, as the verb "shall be saved" makes clear (see note on 1:18; cf. 1Th 1:9–10 and notes).

5:10 *God's enemies.* Humans are enemies of God, not the reverse. Thus the hostility must be removed from humans if reconciliation is to be accomplished. God took the initiative in bringing this about through the death of his Son (see v. 11; Col 1:21–22 and note on 1:20). *reconciled.* To reconcile is "to put an end to hostility," and is closely related to the term "justify," as the parallelism in vv. 9–10 indicates:

v. 9	v. 10
justified	reconciled
by his blood	through the death of his Son
shall we be saved	shall we be saved

saved through his life. A reference to the unending life and ministry of the resurrected Christ for his people (see Heb 7:25 and note). Since we were reconciled when we were God's enemies, we will be saved because Christ lives to keep us.

5:11 *we have now received reconciliation.* Reconciliation, like justification (v. 1), is a present reality for Christians and is something to rejoice about (see Col 1:20 and note).

5:12–21 A contrast between Adam and Christ. Adam introduced sin and death into the world; Christ brought righteousness and life. The comparison begun in v. 12 is completed in v. 18; these two verses summarize the whole passage. These two men also sum up the message of the book up to this point. Adam stands for humanity's condemnation (1:18—3:20); Christ stands for the believer's justification (3:21—5:11).

5:12 *death.* Physical death is the penalty for sin. It is also the symbol of spiritual death—ultimate separation from God (Rev 20:15; 21:8). *because all sinned.* Not a repetition of 3:23. The con-

text shows that Adam's sin involved the rest of humankind in condemnation (vv. 18–19) and death (v. 15). We do not start life with even the possibility of living it sinlessly; we begin it with a sinful nature (see Ge 8:21; Ps 51:5; 58:3 and notes; Eph 2:3).

5:13 *sin is not charged against anyone's account.* In the period when there was no (Mosaic) law, people were not charged with sin in the sense of "breaking a command" (v. 14).

5:14 *pattern.* Adam by his sin brought universal ruin on the human race. In this act he is the prototype of Christ, who through one righteous act (v. 18) brought universal blessing. The analogy is one of contrast.

5:15 *the many.* The same as "all people" in v. 12 (see Isa 53:11; Mk 10:45). *how much more.* A theme that runs through this section. God's grace is infinitely greater for good than is Adam's sin for evil.

5:16 *gift of God.* Salvation. *many trespasses.* The sins of the succeeding generations.

5:17 *will…reign in life.* The future reign of believers with Jesus Christ (see 2Ti 2:12 and note; Rev 20:4,6; 22:5).

5:18 *life for all.* Does not mean that everyone eventually will be saved, but that salvation is available to all (see 1Jn 2:2 and note). To be effective, God's gracious gift must be received (see v. 17).

5:19 *made righteous.* A reference to a person's status before God (see v. 17; 2Co 5:21 and note), not to a change in character. The latter (the doctrine of sanctification) is developed in chs. 6–8.

5:20 *law was brought in.* Not to bring about redemption but to point up the need for it. The law made sin even more sinful by revealing what sin is in stark contrast to God's holiness.

6:1 ʸ S Ro 8:31
ᶻ ver 15; Ro 3:5,8
6:2 ᵃ S ver 6;
ver 10,11; S ver 18;
Ro 8:13; Col 3:3,5;
1Pe 2:24
6:3 ᵇ S Mt 28:19
6:4 ᶜ S ver 6
ᵈ S Ac 2:24 ᵉ Ro 7:6;
S 2Co 5:17; Eph 4:22-
24; Col 3:10
6:5 ᶠ ver 4,8; Ro 8:11;
2Co 4:10; Eph 2:6;
Php 3:10,11; Col 2:12;
3:1; 2Ti 2:11
6:6 ᵍ S Gal 5:24;
Eph 4:22; Col 3:9
ʰ S ver 2; ver 3-8;
2Co 4:10; Gal 2:20;
5:24; 6:14; Php 3:10;
Col 2:12,20; 3:3
ⁱ Ro 7:24 / S ver 16
6:7 ᵏ S ver 18
6:8 ˡ S ver 5
6:9 ᵐ ver 4;
S Ac 2:24 ⁿ Rev 1:18
6:10 ᵒ S ver 2
ᵖ S Heb 7:27
6:11 �q S ver 2
6:12 ʳ ver 16
6:13 ˢ ver 16,19;
Ro 7:5 ᵗ Ro 12:1;
2Co 5:14,15; 1Pe 2:24
6:14 ᵘ S ver 16
ᵛ S Ro 2:12
ʷ S Ro 3:24

DEAD TO SIN, ALIVE IN CHRIST

6 What shall we say, then?ʸ Shall we go on sinning so that grace may increase?ᶻ ²By no means! We are those who have died to sin;ᵃ how can we live in it any longer? ³Or don't you know that all of us who were baptized ᵇ into Christ Jesus were baptized into his death? ⁴We were therefore buried with him through baptism into death ᶜ in order that, just as Christ was raised from the dead ᵈ through the glory of the Father, we too may live a new life. ᵉ

⁵If we have been united with him in a death like his, we will certainly also be united with him in a resurrection like his. ᶠ ⁶For we know that our old selfᵍ was crucified with him ʰ so that the body ruled by sin ⁱ might be done away with,ᵃ that we should no longer be slaves to sinʲ— ⁷because anyone who has died has been set free from sin. ᵏ

⁸Now if we died with Christ, we believe that we will also live with him. ˡ ⁹For we know that since Christ was raised from the dead, ᵐ he cannot die again; death no longer has mastery over him. ⁿ ¹⁰The death he died, he died to sin ᵒ once for all;ᵖ but the life he lives, he lives to God.

¹¹In the same way, count yourselves dead to sin q but alive to God in Christ Jesus. ¹²Therefore do not let sin reign ʳ in your mortal body so that you obey its evil desires. ¹³Do not offer any part of yourself to sin as an instrument of wickedness, ˢ but rather offer yourselves to God as those who have been brought from death to life; and offer every part of yourself to him as an instrument of righteousness. ᵗ ¹⁴For sin shall no longer be your master, ᵘ because you are not under the law, ᵛ but under grace. ʷ

ᵃ 6 Or *be rendered powerless*

6:1—8:39 In 3:21—5:21 Paul explains how God has provided for our redemption and justification. He next explains the doctrine of sanctification—the process by which believers grow to maturity in Christ. He treats this subject in three parts: (1) freedom from sin's tyranny (ch. 6), (2) freedom from the law's condemnation (ch. 7) and (3) life in the power of the Holy Spirit (ch. 8).

6:1 *Shall we go on sinning so that grace may increase?* This question arose out of what Paul had just said in 5:20:"Where sin increased, grace increased all the more."

6:2 *died to sin.* The reference is to an event in the past and is explained in v. 3.

6:3–4 The when and how of the Christian's death to sin. In NT times baptism so closely followed conversion that the two were considered part of one event (see Ac 2:38 and note). So although baptism is not a means by which we enter into a vital faith relationship with Jesus Christ, it is closely associated with faith. Baptism depicts graphically what happens as a result of the Christian's union with Christ, which comes with faith—through faith we are united with Christ, just as through our natural birth we are united with Adam. As we fell into sin and became subject to death in father Adam, so we now have died and been raised again with Christ— which baptism symbolizes.

6:3 *know.* Three key words in this chapter are "know" (here and in vv. 6,9),"offer" (vv. 13,16,19) and "obey" (vv. 12,16–17).

6:4 *buried with him through baptism into death.* Amplified in vv. 5–7. *through the glory of the Father.* By the power of God. God's glory is his divine excellence, his perfection. Any one of his attributes is a manifestation of his excellence. Thus his power is a manifestation of his glory, as is his righteousness (see 3:23 and note). Glory and power are often closely related in the Bible (see Ps 145:11; Col 1:11; 1Pe 4:11; Rev 1:6; 4:11; 5:12–13; 7:12; 19:1). *live a new life.* Amplified in vv. 8–10.

6:6 *our old self.* Our unregenerate self; what we once were. *body ruled by sin.* The self in its pre-Christian state, dominated by sin. This is a figurative expression in which the old self is personified. It is a "body" that can be put to death. For the believer, this old self has been "rendered powerless" (see TNIV

text note) so that it can no longer enslave us to sin—whatever lingering vitality it may yet exert in its death throes.

6:7 *has died.* The believer's death with Christ to sin's ruling power (see v. 3). *set free from sin.* Not sinless, but free from sin's shackles and power.

6:8 As resurrection followed death in the experience of Christ, so the believer who dies with Christ is raised to a new quality of life here and now. Resurrection in the sense of a new birth is already a fact, and it increasingly exerts itself in the believer's life.

6:10 *he died to sin once for all.* In his death Christ (for the sake of sinners) submitted to the "reign" of sin (5:21); but his death broke the judicial link between sin and death, and he passed forever from the sphere of sin's"reign."Having been raised from the dead, he now lives forever to glorify God. *to God.* For the glory of God.

6:11 *count yourselves.* The first step toward victory over sin in the life of believers (for the succeeding steps, see note on vv. 12–13). They are dead to sin and alive to God, and by faith they are to live in the light of this truth. *in Christ.* The first occurrence in Romans of this phrase, which is found often in Paul's writings. True believers are "in Christ" because they have died with Christ and have been raised to new life with him. See note on Eph 1:1.

6:12–13 A call for Christians to become in practice what they already are in their status before God—dead to sin (see vv. 5–7) and alive to God (see vv. 8–10). The second step toward victory over sin is refusal to let sin reign in one's life (v. 12). The third step is to offer oneself to God (v. 13).

6:13 *offer.* Put yourselves in the service of, perhaps also echoing the language of sacrifice. *every part of yourself.* All the separate capacities of your being (also in v. 19).

6:14 *sin shall no longer be your master.* Paul conceived of sin as a power that enslaves, and so personified it (see Ps 19:13). *not under the law.* The meaning is not that Christians have been freed from all moral authority. They have, however, been freed from the law in the manner in which God's people were under law in the OT era. Law provides no enablement to resist the power of sin; it only condemns the sinner. But grace enables. *under grace.* For the disciplinary aspect of grace, see Tit 2:11–12 and notes.

SLAVES TO RIGHTEOUSNESS

¹⁵What then? Shall we sin because we are not under the law but under grace?^x By no means! ¹⁶Don't you know that when you offer yourselves to someone as obedient slaves, you are slaves of the one you obey^y—whether you are slaves to sin,^z which leads to death,^a or to obedience, which leads to righteousness? ¹⁷But thanks be to God^b that, though you used to be slaves to sin,^c you have come to obey from your heart the pattern of teaching^d that has now claimed your allegiance. ¹⁸You have been set free from sin^e and have become slaves to righteousness.^f

¹⁹I am using an example from everyday life^g because of your human limitations. Just as you used to offer yourselves as slaves to impurity and to ever-increasing wickedness, so now offer yourselves as slaves to righteousness^h leading to holiness. ²⁰When you were slaves to sin,ⁱ you were free from the control of righteousness. ²¹What benefit did you reap at that time from the things you are now ashamed of? Those things result in death!^k ²²But now that you have been set free from sin^l and have become slaves of God,^m the benefit you reap leads to holiness, and the result is eternal life. ⁿ ²³For the wages of sin is death,^o but the gift of God is eternal life^p in^a Christ Jesus our Lord.

RELEASED FROM THE LAW, BOUND TO CHRIST

7 Do you not know, brothers and sisters^q—for I am speaking to those who know the law—that the law has authority over someone only as long as that person lives? ²For example, by law a married woman is bound to her husband as long as he is alive, but if her husband dies, she is released from the law that binds her to him.^r ³So then, if she marries another man while her husband is still alive, she is called an adulteress.^s But if her husband dies, she is released from that law and is not an adulteress if she marries another man.

⁴So, my brothers and sisters, you also died to the law^t through the body of Christ,^u that you might belong to another,^v to him who was raised from the dead, in order that we might bear fruit for God. ⁵For when we were controlled by our sinful nature,^{b w} the sinful passions aroused by the law^x were at work in us,^y so that we bore fruit for death.^z ⁶But now, by dying to what once bound us, we have been released from the law^a so that we serve in the new way of the Spirit, and not in the old way of the written code.^b

^a 23 Or *through*   ^b 5 Or *by the flesh*

6:15 ^x ver 1,14
6:16 ^y 2Pe 2:19
^z ver 6,12,14,17,20;
Ge 4:7; Ps 51:5;
119:133; Jn 8:34;
Ro 5:21; 7:14,23,25;
8:2; 2Pe 2:19
^a S ver 23
6:17 ^b Ro 1:8;
S 2Co 2:14 ^c S ver 16
^d 2Ti 1:13
6:18 ^e S ver 2;
ver 7,22; Ro 8:2;
1Pe 4:1; S ver 16
^f S ver 22
6:19 ^g Ro 3:5;
Gal 3:15 ^h S ver 13;
S ver 22
6:20 ⁱ S ver 16
^j ver 16
6:21 ^k S ver 23
6:22 ^l S ver 18
^m ver 18,19; Ro 7:25;
1Co 7:22; Eph 6:6;
1Pe 2:16 ⁿ S Mt 25:46
6:23 ^o ver 16,21;
Ge 2:17; Pr 10:16;
Eze 18:4; Ro 1:32;
S 5:12; 7:5,13; 8:6,13;
Gal 6:7,8; Jas 1:15
^p S Mt 25:46
7:1 ^q S Ac 1:16;
S 22:5; Ro 1:13;
1Co 1:10; 5:11; 6:6;
14:20,26; Gal 3:15;
6:18
7:2 ^r 1Co 7:39
7:3 ^s S Lk 16:18
7:4 ^t ver 6; S Ro 6:6;
8:2; Gal 2:19; 3:23-
25; 4:31; 5:1
^u Col 1:22
^v Gal 2:19,20
7:5 ^w S Gal 5:24
^x Ro 7:7-11 ^y Ro 6:13
^z S Ro 6:23
7:6 ^a S ver 4
^b Ro 2:29; 2Co 3:6

6:15–23 The question raised here seems to come from those who are afraid that the doctrine of justification by faith alone will remove all moral restraint. Paul rejects such a suggestion and shows that Christians do not throw morality to the winds. To the contrary, they exchange sin for righteousness as their master.

6:16 The contrast between sin and obedience suggests that sin is by nature disobedience to God.

6:17 *have come to obey from your heart.* Christian obedience is not forced or legalistic, but willing. *pattern of teaching.* May refer to a summary of the moral and ethical teachings of Christ that was given to new converts in the early church.

6:18 *slaves to righteousness.* Christians have changed masters. Whereas they were formerly slaves to sin (vv. 16–17), now they become slaves (willing servants) to righteousness.

6:19 *I am using an example from everyday life.* Paul apologizes for using an imperfect analogy. The word "slave" when applied to Christians, who are free in Christ, naturally presents problems.

6:22 *set free from sin.* See note on v. 6. *holiness.* Slavery to God produces holiness, and the end of the process is eternal life (viewed not in its present sense but in its final, future sense). There is no eternal life without holiness (see Heb 12:14). Those who have been justified will surely give evidence of that fact by the presence of holiness in their lives. For other occurrences of the word "holiness," see v. 19; Lev 11:44 and note; 1Co 1:30 and note on 1:2; 1Th 4:3–4,7; 2Th 2:13; 1Ti 2:15; Heb 12:14; 1Pe 1:2 and note.

6:23 Two kinds of servitude are contrasted here. One brings

death as its wages; the other results in eternal life, not as wages earned or merited but as a gift of God (cf. Eph 2:8–9 and notes). For the contrast between wages and gift, see 4:4. *eternal life.* See Jn 17:3.

7:1 *law.* Perhaps Paul has in mind the Mosaic law, but his concern here is with the fundamental character of law as such.

7:2–3 These verses illustrate the principle set down in v. 1. Death decisively changes a person's relationship to the law.

7:4 *So.* Paul now draws the conclusion from the principle stated in v. 1 and illustrated in vv. 2–3. *died to the law.* The law's power to condemn no longer threatens believers, whose death here is to be understood in terms of 6:2–7. There, however, they die to sin; here they die to the law. The result is that the law has no more hold on them. *through the body of Christ.* His physical body (self) crucified. *belong to another.* The resurrected Christ (see 6:5; cf. Tit 2:14; 1Pe 2:9 and note). The purpose of this union is to produce the fruit of holiness.

7:5 *controlled by our sinful nature.* A condition, so far as Christians are concerned, that belongs to the past—the unregenerate state (cf. 1Co 6:11; Gal 5:19–23 and notes). *aroused by the law.* The law not only reveals sin; it also stimulates it. The natural human tendency is to desire the forbidden thing. *death.* Physical death and, beyond that, spiritual death—final separation from God (see note on 5:12)—were the fruit of our union with the law (cf. note on v. 4).

7:6 *what once bound us.* The law (see later in this verse, as well as v. 4). *released from the law.* In the sense of its condemnation (see note on v. 4). *new way of the Spirit.* See note on 8:4. *old way of the written code.* Life under the OT law.

7:7 *c* S Ro 8:31
d ver 12 *e* S Ro 4:15
f Ex 20:17; Dt 5:21
7:8 *g* ver 11
h S Ro 4:15
7:10 *i* Lev 18:5;
Lk 10:26-28;
S Ro 10:5; Gal 3:12
7:11 *j* ver 8 *k* Ge 3:13
7:12 *l* ver 7,13,14,16;
Ro 8:4; Gal 3:21;
1Ti 1:8; S Ro 4:15
7:13 *m* S ver 12
n S Ro 6:23
7:14 *o* 1Co 3:1
p 1Ki 21:20,25;
2Ki 17:17 *q* S Ro 6:16
7:15 *r* ver 19;
Gal 5:17
7:16 *s* S ver 12
7:17 *t* ver 20
7:18 *u* ver 25;
S Gal 5:24
7:19 *v* ver 15
7:20 *w* ver 17
7:21 *x* ver 23,25
7:22 *y* Eph 3:16
z Ps 1:2; 40:8
7:23 *a* Gal 5:17;
Jas 4:1; 1Pe 2:11
b S Ro 6:16

THE LAW AND SIN

⁷What shall we say, then? *c* Is the law sinful? Certainly not! *d* Nevertheless, I would not have known what sin was had it not been for the law. *e* For I would not have known what coveting really was if the law had not said, "You shall not covet." *a f* ⁸But sin, seizing the opportunity afforded by the commandment, *g* produced in me every kind of coveting. For apart from the law, sin was dead. *h* ⁹Once I was alive apart from the law; but when the commandment came, sin sprang to life and I died. ¹⁰I found that the very commandment that was intended to bring life *i* actually brought death. ¹¹For sin, seizing the opportunity afforded by the commandment, *j* deceived me, *k* and through the commandment put me to death. ¹²So then, the law is holy, and the commandment is holy, righteous and good. *l*

¹³Did that which is good, then, become death to me? By no means! Nevertheless, in order that sin might be recognized as sin, it used what is good *m* to bring about my death, *n* so that through the commandment sin might become utterly sinful.

¹⁴We know that the law is spiritual; but I am unspiritual, *o* sold *p* as a slave to sin. *q* ¹⁵I do not understand what I do. For what I want to do I do not do, but what I hate I do. *r* ¹⁶And if I do what I do not want to do, I agree that the law is good. *s* ¹⁷As it is, it is no longer I myself who do it, but it is sin living in me. *t* ¹⁸I know that good itself does not dwell in me, that is, in my sinful nature. *b u* For I have the desire to do what is good, but I cannot carry it out. ¹⁹For I do not do the good I want to do, but the evil I do not want to do—this I keep on doing. *v* ²⁰Now if I do what I do not want to do, it is no longer I who do it, but it is sin living in me that does it. *w*

²¹So I find this law at work: *x* Although I want to do good, evil is right there with me. ²²For in my inner being *y* I delight in God's law; *z* ²³but I see another law at work in me, waging war *a* against the law of my mind and making me a prisoner of the law of sin *b* at

---

a 7 Exodus 20:17; Deut. 5:21   *b* 18 Or *my flesh*

7:7 *Is the law sinful?* This question was occasioned by the remarks about the law in vv. 4–6. *l.* Paul seems to be using the first person pronoun of himself, but also as representative of people in general (vv. 7–12) and of Christians in particular (vv. 13–25). *I would not have known what sin was.* The law fulfilled the important function of revealing the presence and fact of sin.
7:8 *opportunity afforded by the commandment.* See note on v. 5. *sin was dead.* Not nonexistent but not fully perceived (see 5:13 and note).
7:9 *Once I was alive.* Paul reviews his own experience from the vantage point of his present understanding. Before he realized that the law condemned him to death, he was alive. Reference is to the time either before his *bar mitzvah* (see below) or before his conversion, when the true rigor of the law became clear to him (cf. Lk 18:20–21; see Php 3:6 and note). *when the commandment came.* When Paul came to the realization that he stood guilty before the law—a reference either to his *bar mitzvah,* when he, at age 13, assumed full responsibility for the law, or to the time when he became aware of the full force of the law (at his conversion). *I died.* Paul came to realize he was condemned to death, because law reveals sin, and sin's wages is death (see 6:23 and note).
7:10 *was intended to bring life.* See Lev 18:5 and note. As it worked out in Paul's experience, the law became the avenue through which sin entered generally. Instead of giving life, the law brought condemnation; instead of producing holiness, it stimulated sin.
7:12 *the law is holy.* Despite the despicable use that sin made of the law, the law was not to blame. The law is God's and as such is holy, righteous and good.

A **7:13–25** Whether Paul is describing a Christian or non-Christian experience has been hotly debated through the centuries. That he is speaking of the non-Christian life is suggested by: (1) the use of phrases such as "sold as a slave to sin" (v. 14), "I know that good itself does not dwell in me" (v. 18) and "What a wretched man I am!" (v. 24)—which do not seem to describe Christian experience; (2) the contrast between ch. 7 and ch. 8, making it difficult for the other view to be credible; (3) the

problem of the value of conversion if one ends up in spiritual misery. In favor of the view that Paul is describing Christian experience are: (1) the use of the present tense throughout the passage; (2) Paul's humble opinion of himself (v. 18); (3) his high regard for God's law (vv. 14,16); (4) the location of this passage in the section of Romans where Paul is dealing with sanctification—the growth of the Christian in holiness.
7:13 Sin used a holy (law) for an unholy end (death). By this fact the contemptible nature of sin is revealed.
7:14 *spiritual.* The law had its origin in God. *I am.* The personal pronoun and the verb, taken together, suggest that Paul is describing his present (Christian) experience. *unspiritual.* Even believers have the seeds of rebellion in their hearts. *sold as a slave to sin.* A phrase so strong that many refuse to accept it as descriptive of a Christian. However, it may graphically point out the failure even of Christians to meet the radical ethical and moral demands of the gospel. It also points up the persistent nature of sin.
7:15 *I do not understand.* The struggle within creates tension, ambivalence and confusion (cf. Gal 5:16–17 and notes).
7:16 *I agree that the law is good.* Even when Paul is rebellious and disobedient, the Holy Spirit reveals to him the essential goodness of the law.
7:17 *no longer I myself who do it.* Not an attempt to escape moral responsibility but a statement of the great control sin can have over a Christian's life.
7:18 *good itself does not dwell in me.* A reference to Paul's fallen nature, as the last phrase of the sentence indicates.
7:20 *sin . . . does it.* See note on v. 17.
7:21 *law.* Here means "principle."

A **7:22** *I delight in God's law.* The Mosaic law or God's law generally. It is difficult to see how a non-Christian could say this.
7:23 *another law.* A principle or force at work in Paul, preventing him from giving obedience to God's law. *law of my mind.* His desire to obey God's law. *law of sin.* Essentially the same as "another law," mentioned above.

work within me. ²⁴What a wretched man I am! Who will rescue me from this body of death? ᶜ ²⁵Thanks be to God, who delivers me through Jesus Christ our Lord! ᵈ

So then, I myself in my mind am a slave to God's law, ᵉ but in my sinful natureᵃ a slave to the law of sin. ᶠ

LIFE THROUGH THE SPIRIT

8 Therefore, there is now no condemnation ᵍ for those who are in Christ Jesus, ʰ ²because through Christ Jesus ⁱ the law of the Spirit who gives lifeʲ has set youᵇ free ᵏ from the law of sin ˡ and death. ³For what the law was powerless ᵐ to do because it was weakened by the sinful nature, ᶜ ⁿ God did by sending his own Son in the likeness of sinful humanity ᵒ to be a sin offering. ᵈᵖ And so he condemned sin in human flesh, ⁴in order that the righteous requirement �q of the law might be fully met in us, who do not live according to the sinful nature but according to the Spirit. ʳ

⁵Those who live according to the sinful nature have their minds set on what that nature desires; ˢ but those who live in accordance with the Spirit have their minds set on what the Spirit desires. ᵗ ⁶The mind controlled by the sinful natureᵉ is death, ᵘ but the mind controlled by the Spirit is lifeᵛ and peace. ⁷The sinful mindᶠ is hostile to God; ʷ it does not submit to God's law, nor can it do so. ⁸Those controlled by the sinful natureˣ cannot please God.

⁹You, however, are not controlled by the sinful natureʸ but are in the Spirit, if indeed the Spirit of God lives in you. ᶻ And if anyone does not have the Spirit of Christ, ᵃ they do not belong to Christ. ¹⁰But if Christ is in you, ᵇ then even though your body is subject to death because of sin, the Spirit gives life ᶜ because of righteousness. ¹¹And if the Spirit of him who raised Jesus from the dead ᶜ is living in you, he who raised Christ from the dead will also give life to your mortal bodies ᵈ because of ʰ his Spirit who lives in you.

¹²Therefore, brothers and sisters, we have an obligation—but it is not to the sinful nature, to live according to it. ᵉ ¹³For if you live according to the sinful nature, you will die; ᶠ but if by the Spirit you put to death the misdeeds of the body, ᵍ you will live. ʰ

¹⁴For those who are led by the Spirit of God ⁱ are the children of God. ʲ ¹⁵The Spirit ᵏ you

---

7:24 ᶜ Ro 6:6; 8:2
7:25 ᵈ S 2Co 2:14
ᵉ S Ro 6:22 ᶠ S Ro 6:16
8:1 ᵍ ver 34 ʰ ver 39; S Ro 16:3
8:2 ⁱ Ro 7:25
ʲ 1Co 15:45
ᵏ Jn 8:32,36; S Ro 6:18
ˡ S Ro 6:16; S 7:4
8:3 ᵐ Heb 7:18; 10:1-4 ⁿ Ro 7:18,19; S Gal 5:24
ᵒ S Php 2:7
ᵖ Heb 2:14,17
8:4 q Ro 2:26
ʳ S Gal 5:16
8:5 ˢ Gal 5:19-21
ᵗ Gal 5:22-25
8:6 ᵘ S Ro 6:23
ᵛ ver 13; Gal 6:8
8:7 ʷ Jas 4:4
8:8 ˣ S Gal 5:24
8:9 ʸ S Gal 5:24
ᶻ ver 11; 1Co 6:19; 2Ti 1:14 ᵃ Jn 14:17; S Ac 16:7; 1Jn 4:13
8:10 ᵇ ver 9; Ex 29:45; Jn 14:20,23; 2Co 13:5; Gal 2:20; Eph 3:17; Col 1:27; Rev 3:20
8:11 ᶜ S Ac 2:24
ᵈ Jn 5:21; S Ro 6:5
8:12 ᵉ ver 4; S Gal 5:24
8:13 ᶠ S Ro 6:23
ᵍ S Ro 6:2 ʰ ver 6; Gal 6:8
8:14 ⁱ S Gal 5:18
ʲ ver 19; Hos 1:10; Mal 3:17; Mt 5:9; S Jn 1:12; Gal 3:26; 4:5; Eph 1:5; Rev 21:7
8:15 ᵏ S Jn 20:22

ᵃ 25 Or in the flesh   ᵇ 2 The Greek is singular; some manuscripts me   ᶜ 3 Or the flesh; also in verses 4, 5, 8, 9, 12 and 13   ᵈ 3 Or humanity, for sin   ᵉ 6 Or mind set on the flesh   ᶠ 7 Or the mind set on the flesh   ᵍ 10 Or you, your body is dead because of sin, yet your spirit is alive   ʰ 11 Some manuscripts bodies through

---

7:24 body of death. Figurative for the body of sin (see 6:6; 8:10 and notes) that hung on him like a corpse and from which he could not gain freedom.

7:25 The first half of this verse is the answer to the question raised in v. 24—deliverance comes, not through legalistic effort, but through Christ (see 8:2 and note). The last half is a summary of vv. 13–24. I myself. The real self—the inner being that delights in God's law (see v. 22 and note). slave to the law of sin. Christians must reckon with the enslaving power of their sinful nature (see note on v. 23) as long as they live—until "the redemption of our bodies" (8:23).

8:1 condemnation. The law brings condemnation because it points out, stimulates and condemns sin. But the Christian is no longer "under the law" (6:14; see note there). in Christ Jesus. United with him, as explained in 6:1–10 (see note on 6:11; see also Php 2:1 and note).

8:2 law of the Spirit who gives life. The controlling power of the Holy Spirit, who is life-giving. Paul uses the word "law" in several different ways in Romans—to mean, e.g., a controlling power (here); God's law (2:17–20; 9:31; 10:3–5); the Pentateuch (3:21b); the OT as a whole (see 3:19 and note); and a principle (3:27). law of sin and death. The controlling power of sin, which ultimately produces death (see 7:24 and note).

8:3 powerless to do. The law was not able to overcome sin (cf. Heb 7:18 and note). It could point out, condemn and even stimulate sin, but it could not remove it. in the likeness of sinful humanity. Christ in his incarnation became truly human, but, unlike all other humans, was sinless (see note on Mt 4:1–11). in human flesh. Probably referring to Christ's human body (on the cross).

8:4 righteous requirement of the law. The law will still play a role in the life of a believer—not, however, as a means of salvation but as a moral and ethical guide, obeyed out of love

for God and by the power that the Spirit provides. This is the fulfillment of Jer 31:31–34 (a prophecy of the new covenant; see notes there). fully met. Lit. "fulfilled." God's aim in sending his Son was that believers might be enabled to embody the true and full intentions of the law. according to the Spirit. How the law's "righteous requirement" can be fully met—by no longer letting the sinful nature hold sway but by yielding to the directing and empowering ministry of the Holy Spirit.

8:5–8 Two mind-sets are described here: that of the sinful nature and that of the Spirit. The former leads to death, the latter to life and peace. The sinful nature is bound up with death (v. 6), hostility to God (v. 7), insubordination (v. 7) and unacceptability to God (v. 8).

8:9 Paul makes it unmistakably clear that "the Spirit of God lives in" every believer.

8:10 your body is subject to death because of sin. Even a Christian's body is subject to physical death, the consequence of sin. the Spirit gives life. See v. 2 and note. On this reading, "body" is understood as in 7:24. For another reading, see TNIV text note. because of righteousness. Christians are indwelt by the life-giving Spirit as a result of their justification.

8:11 For the close connection between the resurrection of Christ and that of believers, see 1Co 6:14; 15:20,23; 2Co 4:14; Php 3:21; 1Th 4:14 and notes. give life to your mortal bodies. The resurrection of our bodies is guaranteed to believers by the indwelling presence of the Holy Spirit—whose presence is evidenced by a Spirit-controlled life (vv. 4–9), which in turn provides assurance that our resurrection is certain even now.

8:14 children of God. God is the Father of all in the sense that he created all and his love and providential care are extended to all (see Mt 5:45 and note). But not all are his children. Jesus said to the unbelieving Jews of his day, "You belong

8:15 /S 2Ti 1:7
m Mk 14:36; Gal 4:5,6
8:16 *n* 2Co 1:22;
Eph 1:13 *o* S ver 14;
S Jn 1:12
8:17 *p* S Ac 20:32;
Gal 3:29; 4:7;
Eph 3:6; Tit 3:7
q S 2Co 1:5 *r* 2Ti 2:12;
1Pe 4:13
8:18 *s* 2Co 4:17;
1Pe 4:13; 5:1
8:19 *t* S ver 14
8:20 *u* Ge 3:17-19;
5:29
8:21 *v* Ac 3:21;
2Pe 3:13; Rev 21:1
w S Jn 1:12
8:22 *x* Jer 12:4
8:23 *y* S 2Co 5:5
z 2Co 5:2,4 *a* ver 19;
Gal 5:5 *b* ver 11;
Php 3:21
8:24 *c* 1Th 5:8;
Tit 3:7 *d* S 2Co 4:18
8:25 *e* Ps 37:7
8:26 *f* ver 15,16
g Eph 6:18
8:27 *h* S Rev 2:23
i S ver 34
8:28 *j* Ge 50:20;
Isa 38:17; Jer 29:11
k ver 30; Ro 11:29;
1Co 1:9; Gal 1:6,15;
Eph 4:1,4; 1Th 2:12;
2Ti 1:9; Heb 9:15;
1Pe 2:9; 2Pe 1:10
l Eph 1:11; 3:11;
Heb 6:17
8:29 *m* Ro 11:2;
1Pe 1:2 *n* Eph 1:5,11
o 1Co 15:49; 2Co 3:18;
Php 3:21; 1Jn 3:2
p S Col 1:18

received does not make you slaves, so that you live in fear again; *l* rather, the Spirit you received brought about your adoption to sonship. *a* And by him we cry, *"Abba,* *b* Father." *m* 16 The Spirit himself testifies with our spirit *n* that we are God's children. *o* 17 Now if we are children, then we are heirs *p*—heirs of God and co-heirs with Christ, if indeed we share in his sufferings *q* in order that we may also share in his glory. *r*

PRESENT SUFFERING AND FUTURE GLORY

18 I consider that our present sufferings are not worth comparing with the glory that will be revealed in us. *s* 19 The creation waits in eager expectation for the children of God *t* to be revealed. 20 For the creation was subjected to frustration, not by its own choice, but by the will of the one who subjected it, *u* in hope 21 that *c* the creation itself will be liberated from its bondage to decay *v* and brought into the freedom and glory of the children of God. *w*

22 We know that the whole creation has been groaning *x* as in the pains of childbirth right up to the present time. 23 Not only so, but we ourselves, who have the firstfruits of the Spirit, *y* groan *z* inwardly as we wait eagerly *a* for our adoption, the redemption of our bodies. *b* 24 For in this hope we were saved. *c* But hope that is seen is no hope at all. *d* Who hopes for what they already have? 25 But if we hope for what we do not yet have, we wait for it patiently. *e*

26 In the same way, the Spirit helps us in our weakness. We do not know what we ought to pray for, but the Spirit *f* himself intercedes for us *g* through wordless groans. 27 And he who searches our hearts *h* knows the mind of the Spirit, because the Spirit intercedes *i* for God's people in accordance with the will of God.

28 And we know that in all things God works for the good *j* of those who love him, who *d* have been called *k* according to his purpose. *l* 29 For those God foreknew *m* he also predestined *n* to be conformed to the image of his Son, *o* that he might be the firstborn *p* among

---

a 15 The Greek word for *adoption to sonship* is a term referring to the full legal standing of an adopted male heir in Roman culture.   *b* 15 Aramaic for *Father*   *c* 20,21 Or *subjected it in hope.* 21 For
d 28 Or *that all things work together for good to those who love God, who;* or *that in all things God works together with those who love him to bring about what is good—with those who*

---

to your father, the devil" (Jn 8:44; see note there). People become children of God through faith in God's unique Son (see Jn 1:12 and note), and being led by God's Spirit is the hallmark of this relationship.

🔺 **8:15** *adoption to sonship.* See TNIV text note. The Greek word for this phrase occurs four other times in the NT (v. 23; 9:4; Gal 4:5 [see note there]; Eph 1:5). Adoption was common among the Greeks and Romans, who granted the adopted son all the privileges of a natural son, including inheritance rights. Christians are adopted sons by grace; Christ, however, is God's Son by nature. *Abba, Father.* Expressive of an especially close relationship to God (see also TNIV text note).

8:16 *testifies with our spirit.* The inner testimony of the Holy Spirit to our relationship to Christ. *God's children.* The same as "sons of God," terms that in the NT are synonymous.

8:17 *heirs.* Those who have already entered, at least partially, into the possession of their inheritance. *co-heirs with Christ.* Everything really belongs to Christ, but by grace we share in what is his. *if indeed we share in his sufferings.* The meaning is not that there is some doubt about sharing Christ's glory. Rather, despite the fact that Christians presently suffer, they are assured a future entrance into their inheritance.

8:19 *creation.* Both animate and inanimate, but exclusive of human beings (see vv. 22–23, where "whole creation" and "we ourselves" are contrasted). *children of God to be revealed.* Christians are already children of God, but the full manifestation of all that this means will not come until the end (see 1Jn 3:1–2).

8:20 *was subjected to frustration.* A reference to Ge 3:17–19. *in hope.* A possible allusion to the promise of Ge 3:15 (see note there).

8:21 *will be liberated from its bondage to decay.* The physical universe is not destined for destruction (annihilation) but for renewal (see 2Pe 3:13 and note; Rev 21:1). And living things will no longer be subject to death and decay, as they are today.

8:22 *has been groaning.* Creation is personified as a woman in labor waiting for the birth of her child.

🔺 **8:23** *firstfruits of the Spirit.* Believers' possession of the Holy Spirit is not only evidence of their present salvation (vv. 14,16) but also a pledge of their future inheritance—and not only a pledge but also the down payment on that inheritance (see 2Co 1:22; 5:5 and notes; Eph 1:14). *firstfruits.* See Ex 23:19 and note; cf. 1Co 15:20 and note. *our adoption.* See note on v. 15. Christians are already God's children, but this is a reference to the full realization of our inheritance in Christ. *redemption of our bodies.* The resurrection, as the final stage of our adoption. The first stage was God's predestination of our adoption (see Eph 1:5); the second is our present inclusion as children of God (see v. 14; Gal 3:25–26 and notes).

8:24 *in this hope.* We are saved by faith (see Eph 2:8 and note), not hope; but hope accompanies salvation.

8:26 *In the same way.* As hope sustains believers when they suffer, so the Holy Spirit helps them when they pray. *through wordless groans.* In v. 23 it is the believer who groans; here it is the Holy Spirit. Whether Paul means words that are unspoken or words that cannot be expressed in human language is not clear—probably the former, though v. 27 seems to suggest the latter.

8:27 The relationship between the Holy Spirit and God the Father is so close that the Holy Spirit's prayers need not be audible. God knows his every thought.

8:28 *the good.* That which conforms to "the image of his Son" (v. 29). *called.* Effectual calling: the call of God to which there is invariably a positive response.

🔺 **8:29** *foreknew.* Some insist that the knowledge here is not abstract but is couched in love and mixed with purpose. They hold that God not only knew us before we had any knowledge of him but that he also knew us, in the sense of choosing us by his grace, before the foundation of the world (see Eph 1:4; 2Ti 1:9 and notes). Others believe that Paul here refers to the fact that in eternity past God knew those who by many brothers and sisters. ³⁰And those he predestined, �q he also called; ʳ those he called, he also justified; ˢ those he justified, he also glorified. ᵗ

MORE THAN CONQUERORS

³¹What, then, shall we say in response to these things? ᵘ If God is for us, ᵛ who can be against us? ᵂ ³²He who did not spare his own Son, ˣ but gave him up for us all—how will he not also, along with him, graciously give us all things? ³³Who will bring any charge ʸ against those whom God has chosen? It is God who justifies. ³⁴Who then can condemn? ᶻ No one. Christ Jesus who died ᵃ—more than that, who was raised to life ᵇ—is at the right hand of God ᶜ and is also interceding for us. ᵈ ³⁵Who shall separate us from the love of Christ? ᵉ Shall trouble or hardship or persecution or famine or nakedness or danger or sword? ᶠ ³⁶As it is written:

> "For your sake we face death all day long;
>   we are considered as sheep to be slaughtered." ᵃ ᵍ

³⁷No, in all these things we are more than conquerors ʰ through him who loved us. ⁱ ³⁸For I am convinced that neither death nor life, neither angels nor demons, ᵇ neither the present nor the future, ʲ nor any powers, ᵏ ³⁹neither height nor depth, nor anything else in all creation, will be able to separate us from the love of God ˡ that is in Christ Jesus our Lord. ᵐ

PAUL'S ANGUISH OVER ISRAEL

9 I speak the truth in Christ—I am not lying, ⁿ my conscience confirms ᵒ it through the Holy Spirit— ²I have great sorrow and unceasing anguish in my heart. ³For I could wish that I myself ᵖ were cursed �q and cut off from Christ for the sake of my people, ʳ those of my own race, ˢ ⁴the people of Israel. ᵗ Theirs is the adoption; ᵘ theirs the divine glory, ᵛ the covenants, ᵂ the receiving of the law, ˣ the temple worship ʸ and the promises. ᶻ ⁵Theirs are the patriarchs, ᵃ and from them is traced the human ancestry of the Messiah, ᵇ who is God over all, ᶜ forever praised! ᶜ ᵈ Amen.

---

a 36 Psalm 44:22   b 38 Or *nor heavenly rulers*   c 5 Or *Messiah, who is over all. God be forever praised!* Or *Messiah. God who is over all be forever praised!*

9:5 ᵃRo 11:28 ᵇMt 1:1-16; Ro 1:3 ᶜJn 1:1; Col 2:9 ᵈRo 1:25; 2Co 11:31

8:30 �q Eph 1:5,11
ʳ S ver 28 ˢ S Ro 4:25
ᵗ Ro 9:23
8:31 ᵘ Ro 4:1; 6:1;
7:7; 9:14,30 ᵛ Ex 3:12;
Isa 41:10; Hag 1:13
ᵂ Ps 56:9; 118:6;
Isa 8:10; Jer 20:11;
Heb 13:6
8:32 ˣ Ge 22:13;
Mal 3:17; Jn 3:16;
Ro 5:8
8:33 ʸ Isa 50:8,9
8:34 ᶻ ver 1 ᵃ Ro 5:6-
8 ᵇ S Ac 2:24
ᶜ S Mk 16:19 ᵈ ver 27;
Job 16:20; Isa 53:12;
Heb 7:25; 9:24;
1Jn 2:1
8:35 ᵉ ver 37-39
ᶠ1Co 4:11;
2Co 11:26,27
8:36 ᵍ Ps 44:22;
1Co 4:9; 15:30,31;
2Co 4:11; 6:9; 11:23
8:37 ʰ 1Co 15:57
ⁱ Ro 5:8; Gal 2:20;
Eph 5:2; Rev 1:5; 3:9
8:38 ʲ 1Co 3:22
ᵏ Eph 1:21; Col 1:16;
1Pe 3:22
8:39 ˡ S Ro 5:8
ᵐ ver 1; S Ro 16:3
9:1 ⁿ Ps 15:2;
2Co 11:10; Gal 1:20;
1Ti 2:7 ᵒ S Ro 1:9
9:3 ᵖ Ex 32:32
ᵍ1Co 12:3; 16:22
ʳ S Ac 22:5 ˢ Ro 11:14
9:4 ᵗ ver 6 ᵘ Ex 4:22;
6:7; Dt 7:6 ᵛ Heb 9:5
ᵂ Ge 17:2; Dt 4:13;
Ac 3:25; Eph 2:12
ˣ Ps 147:19 ʸ Heb 9:1
ᶻ S Ac 13:32;
S Gal 3:16

---

faith would become his people. *predestined.* Predestination here is to moral conformity to the likeness of his Son. *that he might be the firstborn among many brothers and sisters.* The reason God foreknew, predestined and conformed believers to Christ's likeness is that the Son might hold the position of highest honor in the great family of God.

8:30 *predestined ... glorified.* The sequence by which God carries out his predestination. *glorified.* Since this final stage is firmly grounded in God's set purpose, it is as certain as if it had already happened.

8:31 *If.* That is, "Since."

8:32 The argument (from the greater to the lesser) here is similar to that in 5:9-10. If God gave the supreme gift of his Son to save us, he will certainly also give whatever is necessary to bring to fulfillment the work begun at the cross. See note on Ge 22:16.

8:33-34 A court of law is in mind. No charge can be brought against the Christian because God has already pronounced a verdict of not guilty.

8:34 *Who then can condemn?* Echoes the language of Isa 50:9. Paul gives three reasons why no one can condemn God's elect: (1) Christ died for us; (2) Christ is alive and seated at the right hand of God, the position of power; (3) Christ is interceding for us.

8:35-39 Paul shows his readers that suffering does not separate believers from Christ but actually carries them along toward their ultimate goal.

8:36 Ps 44:22 (see note there) is quoted to show that suffering has always been part of the experience of God's people (see Php 1:29 and note).

8:37 *who loved us.* Referring especially to Christ's death on the cross (see note on Ge 22:16; see also Gal 2:20; Eph 5:25 and notes).

8:39 *neither height nor depth.* It is impossible to get beyond God's loving reach (see Eph 3:17-19). *nor anything else in all cre-*

ation. Includes all created things. Only God is not included, and he is the one who has justified us (see note on vv. 33-34).

9:1 *through the Holy Spirit.* Conscience is a reliable guide only when enlightened by the Holy Spirit.

9:3 *cursed.* The Greek for this word is *anathema,* and it means delivered over to the wrath of God for eternal destruction (see 1Co 12:3; 16:22; Gal 1:8 and notes). Such was Paul's great love for his fellow Jews. For a similar expression of love, see Ex 32:32.

9:4 *people of Israel.* The descendants of Jacob (who was renamed Israel by God; see Ge 32:28 and note). The name was used of the entire nation (Jdg 5:7), then of the northern kingdom after the nation was divided (see 1Ki 12), the southern kingdom being called Judah. During the intertestamental period and later in NT times, Palestinian Jews used the title to indicate that they were the chosen people of God. Its use here is especially relevant because Paul is about to show that, despite Israel's unbelief and disobedience, God's promises to her are still valid. *adoption.* Israel had been accepted as God's son (see Ex 4:22; Jer 31:9; Hos 11:1 and notes). *glory.* The evidence of the presence of God among his people (see Ex 16:7,10; Lev 9:6,23; Nu 16:19). *covenants.* For example, the Abrahamic (Ge 15:17-21; 17:1-8); the Mosaic (Ex 19:5; 24:1-4), renewed on the plains of Moab (Dt 29:1-15), at Mounts Ebal and Gerizim (Jos 8:30-35) and at Shechem (Jos 24); the Levitical (Nu 25:12-13; Jer 33:21; Mal 2:4-5); the Davidic (2Sa 7; 23:5; Ps 89:3-4,28-29; 132:11-12); and the new (prophesied in Jer 31:31-34). See chart, p. 20. *promises.* Especially those made to Abraham (see Ge 12:7; 13:14-17; see also 17:5-8; 22:16-18 and notes) but also including the many OT Messianic promises (see, e.g., 2Sa 7:12,16; Ps 110; Isa 9:6-7; Jer 23:5; 31:31-34; Eze 34:23-24; 37:24; Da 9:25-27; Mic 5:1-4; Zec 9:9-10 and notes).

9:5 *patriarchs.* Abraham, Isaac, Jacob and his sons. *the Messiah, who is God.* One of the clearest statements of the

9:6 e S Heb 4:12
f Ro 2:28,29; Gal 6:16
9:7 g Ge 21:12;
Heb 11:18
9:8 h S Ro 8:14
i S Gal 3:16
9:9 j Ge 18:10,14
9:10 k Ge 25:21
9:11 l ver 16
m Ro 8:28
9:12 n Ge 25:23
9:13 o Mal 1:2,3
9:14 p S Ro 8:31
q 2Ch 19:7
9:15 r Ex 33:19
9:16 s Eph 2:8;
Tit 3:5
9:17 t Ex 9:16; 14:4;
Ps 76:10
9:18 u Ex 4:21; 7:3;
14:4,17; Dt 2:30;
Jos 11:20; Ro 11:25
9:19 v Ro 11:19;
1Co 15:35; Jas 2:18
w Ro 3:7 x 2Sa 16:10;
2Ch 20:6; Da 4:35
9:20 y Job 1:22; 9:12;
40:2 z Isa 64:8;
Jer 18:6 a Isa 29:16;
45:9; 10:15
9:21 b 2Ti 2:20

GOD'S SOVEREIGN CHOICE

⁶It is not as though God's word e had failed. For not all who are descended from Israel are Israel. f ⁷Nor because they are his descendants are they all Abraham's children. On the contrary, "It is through Isaac that your offspring will be reckoned." a g ⁸In other words, it is not the natural children who are God's children, h but it is the children of the promise who are regarded as Abraham's offspring. i ⁹For this was how the promise was stated: "At the appointed time I will return, and Sarah will have a son." b j

¹⁰Not only that, but Rebekah's children were conceived at the same time by our father Isaac. k ¹¹Yet, before the twins were born or had done anything good or bad l —in order that God's purpose m in election might stand: ¹²not by works but by him who calls—she was told, "The older will serve the younger." c n ¹³Just as it is written: "Jacob I loved, but Esau I hated." d o

¹⁴What then shall we say? p Is God unjust? Not at all! q ¹⁵For he says to Moses,

"I will have mercy on whom I have mercy,
and I will have compassion on whom I have compassion." e r

¹⁶It does not, therefore, depend on human desire or effort, but on God's mercy. s ¹⁷For Scripture says to Pharaoh: "I raised you up for this very purpose, that I might display my power in you and that my name might be proclaimed in all the earth." f t ¹⁸Therefore God has mercy on whom he wants to have mercy, and he hardens whom he wants to harden. u

¹⁹One of you will say to me: v "Then why does God still blame us? w For who is able to resist his will?" x ²⁰But who are you, a mere human being, to talk back to God? y "Shall what is formed say to the one who formed it, z 'Why did you make me like this?' " g a ²¹Does not the potter have the right to make out of the same lump of clay some pottery for noble purposes and some for disposal of refuse? b

²²What if God, although choosing to show his wrath and make his power known, bore

a 7 Gen. 21:12   b 9 Gen. 18:10,14   c 12 Gen. 25:23   d 13 Mal. 1:2,3   e 15 Exodus 33:19
f 17 Exodus 9:16   g 20 Isaiah 29:16; 45:9

---

deity of Jesus the Messiah found in the entire NT (but see TNIV text note). See also 1:4; 10:9; Mt 1:23; 28:19; Lk 1:35; 5:20–21; Jn 1:1,3,10,14,18; 5:18; 20:28; 2Co 13:14; Php 2:6; Col 1:15–20; 2:9; Tit 2:13; Heb 1:2–3,6,8; 2Pe 1:1; Rev 1:13–18; 22:13 and related notes.

9:6 *God's word.* His clearly stated purpose, which has not failed, because "not all who are descended from Israel are Israel." Paul is not denying the election of all Israel (as a nation) but stating that within Israel there is a separation, that of unbelieving Israel and believing Israel. Physical descent is no guarantee of a place in God's spiritual family.

9:7 *descendants.* Physical descendants (e.g., Ishmael and his offspring).

9:8 *natural children.* Those merely biologically descended from Abraham. *God's children.* See v. 4. Not all Israelites were God's children (see Jn 8:44 and note). The reference is to the Israel of faith.

9:11 *done anything good or bad.* God's choice of Jacob was based on sovereign freedom, not on the fulfillment of any prior conditions. *God's purpose in election.* God's purpose embodied in his election (see note on Eph 1:4).

9:12 *not by works but by him who calls.* Before Rebekah's children were even born, God made a choice—a choice obviously not based on works. *calls.* See 8:28 and note.

9:13 *Jacob I loved, but Esau I hated.* Equivalent to "Jacob I chose, but Esau I rejected" (cf. Lk 14:26 and note). In vv. 6–13 Paul is clearly dealing with personal and not national election—he is not portraying the nation Israel (Jacob) over the nation Edom (Esau)—though Mal 1:2–3 (see TNIV text note) does speak of the nations. Paul's intention is evident in light of the problem he is addressing: How can God's promise stand when so many who comprise Israel (in the OT collective sense) are unbelieving and therefore cut off? See ch. 11 and notes.

9:14 *Is God unjust?* Unjust to elect on the basis of his sovereign freedom, as with Jacob and Esau.

9:15 Paul denies injustice in God's dealing with Isaac and Ishmael, and Jacob and Esau, by appealing to God's sovereign right to dispense mercy as he chooses.

9:16 *It.* God's choice, which is not controlled in any way by human beings. However, Paul makes it clear that the basis for Israel's rejection was her unbelief (see vv. 30–32 and notes).

9:17 *Pharaoh.* The pharaoh of the exodus. *raised you up.* Made you ruler of Egypt. *my name.* The character of God, particularly as revealed in the exodus (see Ex 15:13–18; Jos 2:10–11; 9:9; 1Sa 4:8).

9:18 The first part of this verse again echoes Ex 33:19 (see v. 15) and the last part such texts as Ex 7:3; 9:12; 14:4,17, in which God is said to harden the hearts of the pharaoh and the Egyptians (see Ex 4:21 and note). *on whom he wants to have mercy.* Cannot mean that God is arbitrary in his mercy, because Paul ultimately bases God's rejection of Israel on her unbelief (see vv. 30–32).

9:19 Someone may object: "If God determines whose heart is hardened and whose is not, how can he blame anyone for hardening their heart?"

9:20 *who are you, a mere human being, to talk back to God?* Paul is not silencing all human questioning of God, but he is speaking to those with an impenitent, God-defying attitude who want to make God answerable to them for what he does and who, by their questions, defame the character of God.

9:21 The analogy between God and the potter and between a human being and a pot should not be pressed to the extreme. The main point is the sovereign freedom of God in dealing with people (cf. Jer 18:1–10 and notes).

9:22–23 An illustration of the principle stated in v. 21. The emphasis is on God's mercy, not his wrath.

9:22 No one can call God to account for what he does. But he does not exercise his freedom of choice arbitrarily, and he shows great patience even toward the objects of his wrath. In light of 2:4 (see note there), the purpose of such patience is to bring about repentance.

with great patience ^{c} the objects of his wrath—prepared for destruction? ^{d} ^{23}What if he did this to make the riches of his glory ^{e} known to the objects of his mercy, whom he prepared in advance for glory ^{f}— ^{24}even us, whom he also called, ^{g} not only from the Jews but also from the Gentiles? ^{h} ^{25}As he says in Hosea:

> "I will call them 'my people' who are not my people;
>   and I will call her 'my loved one' who is not my loved one," $^{a\ i}$

^{26}and,

> "In the very place where it was said to them,
>   'You are not my people,'
>   they will be called 'children of the living God.' " $^{b\ j}$

^{27}Isaiah cries out concerning Israel:

> "Though the number of the Israelites be like the sand by the sea, ^{k}
>   only the remnant will be saved. ^{l}
> ^{28}For the Lord will carry out
>   his sentence on earth with speed and finality." $^{c\ m}$

^{29}It is just as Isaiah said previously:

> "Unless the Lord Almighty ^{n}
>   had left us descendants,
> we would have become like Sodom,
>   we would have been like Gomorrah." $^{d\ o}$

ISRAEL'S UNBELIEF

^{30}What then shall we say? ^{p} That the Gentiles, who did not pursue righteousness, have obtained it, a righteousness that is by faith; ^{q} ^{31}but the people of Israel, who pursued the law as the way of righteousness, ^{r} have not attained their goal. ^{s} ^{32}Why not? Because they pursued it not by faith but as if it were by works. They stumbled over the stumbling stone. ^{t} ^{33}As it is written:

> "See, I lay in Zion a stone that causes people to stumble
>   and a rock that makes them fall,
>   and the one who believes in him will never be put to shame." $^{e\ u}$

10 Brothers and sisters, my heart's desire ^{v} and prayer to God for the Israelites is that they may be saved. ^{2}For I can testify about them that they are zealous ^{w} for God, but their zeal is not based on knowledge. ^{3}Since they did not know the righteousness of God and sought to establish their own, they did not submit to God's righ-

---

^{a} 25 Hosea 2:23 ^{b} 26 Hosea 1:10 ^{c} 28 Isaiah 10:22,23 (see Septuagint) ^{d} 29 Isaiah 1:9
^{e} 33 Isaiah 8:14; 28:16

9:22 ^{c} S Ro 2:4
^{d} Pr 16:4
9:23 ^{e} S Ro 2:4
^{f} Ro 8:30
9:24 ^{g} S Ro 8:28
^{h} S Ro 3:29
9:25 ^{i} Hos 2:23;
1Pe 2:10
9:26 ^{j} Hos 1:10;
S Mt 16:16; S Ro 8:14
9:27 ^{k} Ge 22:17;
Hos 1:10 ^{l} 2Ki 19:4;
Jer 44:14; 50:20;
Joel 2:32; Ro 11:5
9:28 ^{m} Isa 10:22,23
9:29 ^{n} Jas 5:4
^{o} Isa 1:9; Ge 19:24-
29; Dt 29:23;
Isa 13:19; Jer 50:40
9:30 ^{p} S Ro 8:31
^{q} Ro 1:17; 3:22; 4:5,13;
10:6; Gal 2:16;
Php 3:9; Heb 11:7
9:31 ^{r} Dt 6:25;
Isa 51:1; Ro 10:2,3;
11:7 ^{s} Gal 5:4
9:32 ^{t} 1Pe 2:8
9:33 ^{u} Isa 8:14;
28:16; Ro 10:11;
1Pe 2:6,8
10:1 ^{v} Ps 20:4
10:2 ^{w} S Ac 21:20

9:23 *glory.* See note on 3:23.

9:25–26 In the original context these passages from Hosea refer to the spiritual restoration of Israel. But Paul finds in them the principle that God is a saving, forgiving, restoring God, who delights to take those who are "not my people" and make them "my people." Paul then applies this principle to Gentiles, whom God makes his people by sovereignly grafting them into covenant relationship (see ch. 11).

9:27–29 Isa 10:22–23 and 1:9 (see TNIV text notes here) indicate that only a small remnant will survive from the great multitude of Israelites. God's calling includes both Jews and Gentiles (see v. 24), but the vast majority are Gentiles, as v. 30 suggests.

9:30—10:21 The cause of the rejection of Israel.

9:30–32 A new step in Paul's argument: The reason for Israel's rejection lay in the nature of her disobedience—she failed to obey her own God-given law, which in reality was pointing to Christ. She pursued the law—yet not by faith but by works. Thus the real cause of Israel's rejection was that she failed to believe.

9:31 *the law as the way of righteousness.* Paul does not reject obedience to the law but righteousness by works, the attempt to use the law to put God in one's debt.

9:32 *not by faith.* The failure of Israel was not that she pursued the wrong thing (i.e., righteous standing before God), but that she pursued it by works in a futile effort to merit God's favor rather than pursuing it by faith. *stumbling stone.* Jesus the Messiah. God's rejection of Israel was not arbitrary but was based on Israel's rejection of God's way of gaining righteousness (faith).

9:33 Isa 8:14 and 28:16 (see TNIV text note), which are here combined, apparently were commonly used by early Christians in defense of Jesus' Messiahship (see 1Pe 2:4,6–8; see also Ps 118:22 and note; Lk 20:17–18).

10:1 *prayer to God for the Israelites.* Paul often prayed for the churches (see Eph 1:15–23; 3:14–21; Php 1:9–11; Col 1:3–14; 1Th 1:2–3; 2Th 1:3,11–12). Here he prays for the salvation of his fellow "Israelites."

10:2 *zealous for God.* The Jews' zeal for God (see Ac 21:20; 22:3; Gal 1:14) was commendable in that God was its object, but it was flawed because it was not based on right knowledge about God's way of salvation. Paul, before his conversion, was an example of such zeal (see Gal 1:14 and note).

10:3 *the righteousness of God.* Righteous standing based on faith (see 1:17 and note), which comes from God as a gift and cannot be earned by human works. *their own.* Righteous standing based on their own efforts.

10:3 ˣRo 1:17;
S 9:31
10:4 ʸGal 3:24;
Ro 7:1-4 ᶻS Ro 3:22
10:5 ᵃLev 18:5;
Dt 4:1; 6:24; Ne 9:29;
Pr 19:16; Isa 55:3;
Eze 20:11,13,21;
S Ro 7:10
10:6 ᵇS Ro 9:30
ᶜDt 30:12
10:7 ᵈDt 30:13
ᵉS Ac 2:24
10:8 ᶠDt 30:14
10:9 ᵍMt 10:32
ʰS Jn 13:13 ⁱS Jn 3:15
ʲS Ac 2:24
ᵏS Ro 11:14
10:11 ˡIsa 28:16;
Ro 9:33
10:12 ᵐS Ro 3:22,
29 ⁿS Mt 28:18
10:13 ᵒS Ac 2:21
ᵖJoel 2:32
10:15 ᵠIsa 52:7;
Na 1:15
10:16 ʳHeb 4:2
ˢIsa 53:1; Jn 12:38
10:17 ᵗGal 3:2,5
ᵘCol 3:16
10:18 ᵛPs 19:4;
S Mt 24:14; Ro 1:8;
Col 1:6,23; 1Th 1:8

teousness. ˣ ⁴Christ is the culmination of the law ʸ so that there may be righteousness for everyone who believes. ᶻ

⁵Moses writes this about the righteousness that is by the law: "Whoever does these things will live by them." ᵃ ⁶But the righteousness that is by faith ᵇ says: "Do not say in your heart, 'Who will ascend into heaven?'" ᵇ ᶜ (that is, to bring Christ down) ⁷or 'Who will descend into the deep?'" ᶜ ᵈ (that is, to bring Christ up from the dead). ᵉ ⁸But what does it say? "The word is near you; it is in your mouth and in your heart," ᵈ ᶠ that is, the message concerning faith that we proclaim: ⁹If you declare ᵍ with your mouth, "Jesus is Lord," ʰ and believe ⁱ in your heart that God raised him from the dead, ʲ you will be saved. ᵏ ¹⁰For it is with your heart that you believe and are justified, and it is with your mouth that you profess your faith and are saved. ¹¹As Scripture says, "Anyone who believes in him will never be put to shame." ᵉ ˡ ¹²For there is no difference between Jew and Gentile ᵐ—the same Lord is Lord of all ⁿ and richly blesses all who call on him, ¹³for, "Everyone who calls on the name of the Lord ᵒ will be saved." ᶠ ᵖ

¹⁴How, then, can they call on the one they have not believed in? And how can they believe in the one of whom they have not heard? And how can they hear without someone preaching to them? ¹⁵And how can anyone preach unless they are sent? As it is written: "How beautiful are the feet of those who bring good news!" ᵍ ᵠ

¹⁶But not all the Israelites accepted the good news. ʳ For Isaiah says, "Lord, who has believed our message?" ʰ ˢ ¹⁷Consequently, faith comes from hearing the message, ᵗ and the message is heard through the word about Christ. ᵘ ¹⁸But I ask: Did they not hear? Of course they did:

"Their voice has gone out into all the earth,
 their words to the ends of the world." ⁱ ᵛ

ᵃ 5 Lev. 18:5   ᵇ 6 Deut. 30:12   ᶜ 7 Deut. 30:13   ᵈ 8 Deut. 30:14   ᵉ 11 Isaiah 28:16 (see Septuagint)   ᶠ 13 Joel 2:32   ᵍ 15 Isaiah 52:7   ʰ 16 Isaiah 53:1   ⁱ 18 Psalm 19:4

10:4 *Christ is the culmination of the law.* Although the Greek for "culmination" (*telos*) can mean either (1) "termination," "cessation," or (2) "goal," "culmination," "fulfillment," it seems best here to understand it in the latter sense. Christ is the fulfillment of the law (see Mt 5:17 and note) in the sense that he brought it to completion by obeying perfectly its demands and by fulfilling its types and prophecies. Christians are no longer "under the law" (6:14; see note there), since Christ has freed them from its condemnation, but the law still plays a role in their lives. They are liberated by the Holy Spirit to fulfill its moral demands (see 8:4 and note). *righteousness.* The righteous standing before God that Christ makes available to everyone who believes (see notes on 1:17; 3:24).

10:5 *Whoever does these things will live by them.* Lev 18:5 (see note there; see also Dt 6:25 and note) speaks of the righteousness to which Israel was called under the Sinai covenant. Some understand Paul's purpose in quoting it here as describing the way of obtaining righteousness ("will live") by keeping the law (see 2:6–10). Others think that the reference is to Christ, who perfectly fulfilled the law's demands and thus makes salvation available to all who believe (see Heb 5:9).

10:6–7 The purpose of the OT quotations (see TNIV text notes) is to explain the nature of the righteousness that is by faith. It does not require heroic feats, such as bringing Christ down from heaven or up from the grave. Dt 30:12–13 in its original context refers to the law, and Paul here applies the basic principle to Christ.

10:8 *The word is near you.* In the OT passage (Dt 30:14; see note on 30:12,14) the "word" is God's word as found in the law. Paul takes the passage and applies it to the gospel, "the message concerning faith"—the main point being the accessibility of the gospel. Righteousness is gained by faith, not by deeds, and is readily available to anyone who will receive it freely from God through Christ.

10:9 *Jesus is Lord.* This affirmation, the earliest Christian confession of faith (see also 1Co 12:3 and note), was probably used at baptisms. In view of the fact that "Lord" is used over 6,000 times in the Septuagint (the pre-Christian Greek transla-

tion of the OT) to translate the name of Israel's God (Yahweh), it is clear that Paul, when using this word of Jesus, is ascribing deity to him. *in your heart.* In Biblical terms the heart is not merely the seat of the emotions and affections, but also of the intellect and will (see Ps 4:7 and note). *God raised him from the dead.* A bedrock truth of Christian doctrine (see 1Co 15:4,14,17) and the central thrust of apostolic preaching (see, e.g., note on Ac 2:14–40; see also Ac 3:15 and note; 4:10; 10:40). Christians believe not only that Jesus lived but also that he still lives. *will be saved.* This may include final salvation—salvation at the last day (see Heb 9:28 and note).

10:10 Salvation involves inward belief ("with your heart") as well as outward confession ("with your mouth").

10:12 *no difference between Jew and Gentile.* In the sense that both are on the same footing as far as salvation is concerned (see v. 13; 3:22).

10:13 Peter cited this same passage (Joel 2:32) on the day of Pentecost (see Ac 2:21 and note).

10:14–15 Since it might be argued that Jews had never had a fair opportunity to hear and respond to the gospel, Paul, by means of a series of rhetorical questions, states (in reverse order) the conditions necessary to call on Christ and be saved: (1) a preacher sent from God, (2) proclamation of the message, (3) hearing the message, (4) believing the message.

10:15 *How beautiful are the feet of those who bring good news!* The quotation is from Isa 52:7 (see note there), which refers to those who bring the good news of their imminent release from captivity in Babylon. Here it is applied to gospel preachers, who bring the good news of release from captivity to sin.

10:18 *Their voice … world.* The quotation is from Ps 19:4 (see note there), which refers to the testimony of the heavens to the glory of God. Here "their voice" is applied to gospel preachers and is used to show that Israel cannot offer the excuse that she did not have opportunity to hear, since preachers went everywhere. These words (originally used to describe God's revelation in nature) aptly describe the widespread preaching of the gospel.

¹⁹Again I ask: Did Israel not understand? First, Moses says,

> "I will make you envious ^w by those who are not a nation;
>   I will make you angry by a nation that has no understanding."^{a x}

²⁰And Isaiah boldly says,

> "I was found by those who did not seek me;
>   I revealed myself to those who did not ask for me."^{b y}

²¹But concerning Israel he says,

> "All day long I have held out my hands
>   to a disobedient and obstinate people."^{c z}

THE REMNANT OF ISRAEL

11 I ask then: Did God reject his people? By no means!^a I am an Israelite myself, a descendant of Abraham,^b from the tribe of Benjamin.^c ²God did not reject his people,^d whom he foreknew.^e Don't you know what Scripture says in the passage about Elijah—how he appealed to God against Israel: ³"Lord, they have killed your prophets and torn down your altars; I am the only one left, and they are trying to kill me"^d? ^{f 4}And what was God's answer to him? "I have reserved for myself seven thousand who have not bowed the knee to Baal."^{e g} ⁵So too, at the present time there is a remnant^h chosen by grace.ⁱ ⁶And if by grace, then it cannot be based on works;^j if it were, grace would no longer be grace.

⁷What then? What the people of Israel sought so earnestly they did not obtain.^k The elect among them did, but the others were hardened,^l ⁸as it is written:

> "God gave them a spirit of stupor,
>   eyes that could not see
>   and ears that could not hear,^m
> to this very day."^{f n}

⁹And David says:

> "May their table become a snare and a trap,
>   a stumbling block and a retribution for them.
> ¹⁰ May their eyes be darkened so they cannot see,^o
>   and their backs be bent forever."^{g p}

INGRAFTED BRANCHES

¹¹Again I ask: Did they stumble so as to fall beyond recovery? Not at all!^q Rather, because of their transgression, salvation has come to the Gentiles^r to make Israel envious.^s ¹²But if their transgression means riches for the world, and their loss means riches for the Gentiles,^t how much greater riches will their fullness bring!

^a 19 Deut. 32:21   ^b 20 Isaiah 65:1   ^c 21 Isaiah 65:2   ^d 3 1 Kings 19:10,14   ^e 4 1 Kings 19:18
^f 8 Deut. 29:4; Isaiah 29:10   ^g 10 Psalm 69:22,23

10:19 *Did Israel not understand?* The quotation that follows (from Dt 32:21; see note there) answers this question by suggesting that the Gentiles, whom the Jews considered to be spiritually unenlightened, understood. Surely if they understood the message, the Jews could have. *those who are not a nation.* The Gentiles, those who are not a nation of God's forming in the sense that Israel was.

10:21 The responsibility for Israel's rejection as a nation rested with Israel herself. She had failed to meet God's requirement, namely, faith. Yet, as Isa 65:2 stated, God continued to reach out in love to the people of Israel in spite of their disobedience.

11:1 *reject.* Totally reject. There has always been a faithful remnant among the Jewish people.

11:2 *whom he foreknew.* See note on 8:29.

11:5 *remnant.* As it was in Elijah's day, so it was in Paul's day. Despite widespread apostasy, a faithful remnant of Jews remained. *chosen by grace.* The grounds for the existence of the remnant was not their good works but God's grace.

11:7 *What the people of Israel sought so earnestly.* A righteous standing before God, which eluded the greater part of Israel. *The elect.* The faithful remnant among the Jews. *others were hardened.* Because they refused the way of faith (see 9:30 –32 and notes), God made them impervious to spiritual truth (see notes on v. 25; Isa 6:8–10; Mk 4:12; Lk 8:10)—a judicial hardening of Israel.

11:8 *to this very day.* The spiritual dullness of the Jews had continued from Isaiah's day to Paul's day.

11:9–10 The passage from Ps 69:22–23 (see notes there) was probably originally spoken by David concerning his enemies; Paul uses it to describe the results of the divine hardening.

11:11 *their transgression.* The Jews' rejection of the gospel. *make Israel envious.* See v. 14; 10:19.

11:12 *riches for the world.* Equivalent to "riches for the Gentiles," a reference to the abundant benefits of salvation already enjoyed by believing Gentiles, which had come about because of the rejection of the gospel by the Jews. That rejection caused the apostles to turn to the Gentiles (see Ac 13:46–48; 18:6). *their loss.* Equivalent to "their transgression" (see note on v. 11), but

10:19 ^wRo 11:11,14
   ^x Dt 32:21
10:20 ^yIsa 65:1;
   Ro 9:30
10:21 ^zIsa 65:2;
   Jer 35:17
11:1 ^aLev 26:44;
   1Sa 12:22; Ps 94:14;
   Jer 31:37; 33:24-26
   ^b2Co 11:22 ^cPhp 3:5
11:2 ^dS ver 1
   ^eS Ro 8:29
11:3 ^f1Ki 19:10,14
11:4 ^g1Ki 19:18
11:5 ^hS Ro 9:27
   ⁱS Ro 3:24
11:6 ^jRo 4:4
11:7 ^kRo 9:31
   ^lver 25; S Ro 9:18
11:8 ^mS Mt 13:13-
   15 ⁿDt 29:4;
   Isa 29:10
11:10 ^over 8
   ^pPs 69:22,23
11:11 ^qver 1
   ^rS Ac 13:46 ^sver 14;
   Ro 10:19
11:12 ^tver 25

11:13 *u* S Ac 9:15
11:14 *v* ver 11;
Ro 10:19; 1Co 10:33;
1Th 2:16 *w* S Mt 1:21;
S Lk 2:11; S Jn 3:17;
Ac 4:12; 16:31;
1Co 1:21; 1Ti 2:4;
Tit 3:5
11:15 *x* S Ro 5:10
y Lk 15:24,32
11:16 *z* Lev 23:10,17
; Nu 15:18-21
11:17 *a* Jer 11:16;
Jn 15:2 *b* Eph 2:11-13
11:18 *c* Jn 4:22
11:20 *d* 1Co 10:12;
2Co 1:24 *e* 1Ti 6:17
f 1Pe 1:17
11:22 *g* Ro 2:4
h 1Co 15:2; Col 1:23;
Heb 3:6 *i* Jn 15:2
11:23 *j* 2Co 3:16
11:24 *k* Jer 11:16
11:25 *l* Ro 1:13;
1Co 10:1; 12:1;
2Co 1:8; 1Th 4:13
m S Ro 16:25

13 I am talking to you Gentiles. Inasmuch as I am the apostle to the Gentiles, *u* I make much of my ministry 14 in the hope that I may somehow arouse my own people to envy *v* and save *w* some of them. 15 For if their rejection brought reconciliation *x* to the world, what will their acceptance be but life from the dead? *y* 16 If the part of the dough offered as first-fruits *z* is holy, then the whole batch is holy; if the root is holy, so are the branches.

17 If some of the branches have been broken off, *a* and you, though a wild olive shoot, have been grafted in among the others *b* and now share in the nourishing sap from the olive root, 18 do not consider yourself to be superior to those other branches. If you do, consider this: You do not support the root, but the root supports you. *c* 19 You will say then, "Branches were broken off so that I could be grafted in." 20 Granted. But they were broken off because of unbelief, and you stand by faith. *d* Do not be arrogant, *e* but tremble. *f* 21 For if God did not spare the natural branches, he will not spare you either.

22 Consider therefore the kindness *g* and sternness of God: sternness to those who fell, but kindness to you, provided that you continue *h* in his kindness. Otherwise, you also will be cut off. *i* 23 And if they do not persist in unbelief, they will be grafted in, for God is able to graft them in again. *j* 24 After all, if you were cut out of an olive tree that is wild by nature, and contrary to nature were grafted into a cultivated olive tree, *k* how much more readily will these, the natural branches, be grafted into their own olive tree!

ALL ISRAEL WILL BE SAVED

25 I do not want you to be ignorant *l* of this mystery, *m* brothers and sisters, so that you

---

focusing on the loss that this transgression entailed. *greater riches.* See note on v. 15. *their fullness.* The salvation of Israel (see vv. 26–27 and notes; see also the "fullness [TNIV 'full number'] of the Gentiles," v. 25).

11:13 *apostle to the Gentiles.* See 1:5; 15:9,12,16 and notes; Ac 9:15; Gal 1:16; 2:7,9 and note on 2:7; see also Eph 2:11–22; 3:3,6,10 and notes.

11:15 *their rejection.* God's temporary and partial exclusion of the Jews (see v. 25 and note). *reconciliation to the world.* Somewhat equivalent to "riches for the world" (see note on v. 12). *life from the dead.* Equivalent to "greater riches" in v. 12. The sequence of redemptive events is: The "transgression" and "loss" (v. 12) of Israel leads to the salvation of the Gentiles, which leads to the jealousy or envy of Israel, which leads to the "fullness" (v. 12) of Israel when the hardening is removed, which leads to even more riches for the Gentiles. But what are the "greater riches" (v. 12) for the Gentiles, which Paul describes here as "life from the dead"? Three views may be suggested: (1) an unprecedented spiritual awakening in the world; (2) the consummation of redemption at the resurrection of the dead; (3) a figurative expression describing the conversion of the Jews as a joyful and glorious event (like resurrection)—which will result in even greater blessing for the world. Of these three views the first seems least likely, since, before Israel's spiritual rebirth, the fullness of the Gentiles will already have come in (see v. 25). Since the Gentile mission will then be complete, there seems to be no place for a period of unprecedented spiritual awakening. The second view also seems unlikely, since the context suggests nothing of bodily resurrection.

11:16 The first half of this verse is a reference to Nu 15:17–21. Part of the dough made from the first of the harvested grain (firstfruits) was offered to the Lord. This consecrated the whole batch. *firstfruits.* The patriarchs (cf. Ex 23:19 and note). *whole batch.* The Jewish people. *holy.* Not that all Jews are righteous (i.e., saved) but that God will be true to his promises concerning them (see 3:3–4 and notes). Paul foresaw a future for Israel, even though she was for a time set aside. *root.* The patriarchs. *branches.* The Jewish people.

11:17 *branches.* Individual Jews. *wild olive shoot.* Gentile Christians. *grafted in.* The usual procedure was to insert a shoot or slip of a cultivated tree into a common or wild one. In vv. 17–24, however, the metaphor is used, "contrary to nature" (v. 24), of grafting a wild olive branch (the Gentiles) into the cultivated olive tree. Such a procedure is unnatural, which is precisely the

point. Normally, such a graft would be unfruitful. *olive root.* The patriarchs. The whole olive tree represents the people of God.

11:18 *the root supports you.* The salvation of Gentile Christians is dependent on the Jews, especially the patriarchs (e.g., the Abrahamic covenant). See Jn 4:22 and note.

11:19 *Branches.* Unbelieving Jews.

11:20 *tremble.* On the fear of God, see note on Ge 20:11; see also Pr 1:7 and note; 3:7; Php 2:12–13; Heb 4:1, "be careful"; 1Pe 1:17.

11:22 *kindness and sternness of God.* Any adequate doctrine of God must include these two elements. When we ignore his kindness, God seems a ruthless tyrant; when we ignore his sternness, he seems a doting Father.

11:23 *God is able to graft them in again.* Paul holds out hope for the Jews—God is able (see Mk 10:27 and note).

11:24 *contrary to nature.* Paul recognized that such grafting was not commonly practiced (see note on v. 17). The inclusion of Gentiles in the family of God is "contrary to nature" (see Eph 2:12 and note). Obviously, the reasoning in this verse is more theological than horticultural. It would be difficult horticulturally to graft broken branches back into the parent tree, but the Jews really "belong" (historically and theologically) to the parent tree. Thus they will "much more readily ... be grafted into their own olive tree."

11:25 *mystery.* The so-called mystery religions of Paul's day used the Greek word (*mysterion*) in the sense of something that was to be revealed only to the initiated. Paul himself, however, used it to refer to something formerly hidden or obscure but now revealed by God for all to know and understand (see 16:25; 1Co 2:7 and note; 4:1; 13:2; 14:2; 15:51 and note; Eph 1:9; 3:3,9 and note on 3:3; 5:32 and note; 6:19; Col 1:26–27 and notes; 2:2; 4:3; 2Th 2:7 and note; 1Ti 3:9,16). The word is used of (1) the incarnation (1Ti 3:16; see note there); (2) the death of Christ (1Co 2:1, TNIV text note; 2:7, "God's wisdom, a mystery"); (3) God's purpose to sum up all things in Christ (Eph 1:9–10), and especially to include both Jews and Gentiles in the NT church (Eph 3:3–6); (4) the change that will take place at the resurrection (1Co 15:51); and (5) the plan of God by which both Jew and Gentile, after a period of disobedience by both, will by his mercy be included in his kingdom (here). *so that you may not think you are superior.* God's merciful plan to include the Gentiles in his great salvation plan should humble them, not fill them with arrogance. *in part.* Israel's hardening is partial, not total. *until.* Israel's hardening is temporary, not permanent. *full number of the Gentiles.* The total number of the elect Gentiles.

may not think you are superior: ^{n} Israel has experienced a hardening ^{o} in part until the full number of the Gentiles has come in, ^{p} ^{26} and in this way ^{a} all Israel will be saved. ^{q} As it is written:

> "The deliverer will come from Zion;
>   he will turn godlessness away from Jacob.
> ^{27} And this is ^{b} my covenant with them
>   when I take away their sins." ^{c} ^{r}

^{28} As far as the gospel is concerned, they are enemies ^{s} for your sake; but as far as election is concerned, they are loved on account of the patriarchs, ^{t} ^{29} for God's gifts and his call ^{u} are irrevocable. ^{v} ^{30} Just as you who were at one time disobedient ^{w} to God have now received mercy as a result of their disobedience, ^{31} so they too have now become disobedient in order that they too may now ^{d} receive mercy as a result of God's mercy to you. ^{32} For God has bound everyone over to disobedience ^{x} so that he may have mercy on them all.

DOXOLOGY

> ^{33} Oh, the depth of the riches ^{y} of the wisdom and ^{e} knowledge of God! ^{z}
>   How unsearchable his judgments,
>   and his paths beyond tracing out! ^{a}
> ^{34} "Who has known the mind of the Lord?
>   Or who has been his counselor?" ^{f} ^{b}
> ^{35} "Who has ever given to God,
>   that God should repay them?" ^{g} ^{c}
> ^{36} For from him and through him and to him are all things. ^{d}
>   To him be the glory forever! Amen. ^{e}

A LIVING SACRIFICE

12 Therefore, I urge you, ^{f} brothers and sisters, in view of God's mercy, to offer your bodies as a living sacrifice, ^{g} holy and pleasing to God—this is true worship. ^{2} Do not conform ^{h} to the pattern of this world, ^{i} but be transformed by the

---

^{a} 26 Or and so ^{b} 27 Or will be ^{c} 27 Isaiah 59:20,21; 27:9 (see Septuagint); Jer. 31:33,34
^{d} 31 Some manuscripts do not have now. ^{e} 33 Or riches and the wisdom and the ^{f} 34 Isaiah 40:13
^{g} 35 Job 41:11

11:25 ^{n} Ro 12:16
^{o} ver 7; S Ro 9:18
^{p} Lk 21:24
11:26 ^{q} Isa 45:17;
Jer 31:34
11:27 ^{r} Isa 59:20,21;
27:9; Heb 8:10,12
11:28 ^{s} Ro 5:10
^{t} Dt 7:8; 10:15; Ro 9:5
11:29 ^{u} S Ro 8:28
^{v} S Heb 7:21
11:30 ^{w} S Eph 2:2
11:32 ^{x} S Ro 3:9
11:33 ^{y} S Ro 2:4
^{z} Ps 92:5; Eph 3:10;
Col 2:3 ^{a} Job 5:9; 11:7;
Ps 139:6; Ecc 8:17;
Isa 40:28
11:34 ^{b} Isa 40:13,14;
Job 15:8; 36:22;
Jer 23:18; 1Co 2:16
11:35 ^{c} Job 41:11;
35:7
11:36 ^{d} 1Co 8:6;
11:12; Col 1:16;
Heb 2:10 ^{e} Ro 16:27;
Eph 3:21; 1Ti 1:17;
1Pe 5:11; Jude 25;
Rev 5:13; 7:12
12:1 ^{f} Eph 4:1;
1Pe 2:11
^{g} Ro 6:13,16,19;
1Co 6:20; 1Pe 2:5
12:2 ^{h} 1Pe 1:14
^{i} 1Co 1:20; 2Co 10:2;
1Jn 2:15

A **11:26** *and in this way.* An emphatic statement that this is the way all Israel will be saved. *all Israel.* Three main interpretations of this phrase are: (1) the total number of elect Jews of every generation (equivalent to the "fullness" of Israel [v. 12; see note there], which is analogous to the "fullness ['full number'] of the Gentiles" [v. 25; see note there]); (2) the total number of the elect, both Jews and Gentiles, of every generation; (3) the great majority of Jews of the final generation. *will be saved.* The salvation of the Jews will, of course, be on the same basis as anyone's salvation: personal faith in Jesus Christ, crucified and risen from the dead. *The deliverer will come from Zion.* The quotation is from Isa 59:20, where the deliverer ("Redeemer") seems to refer to God. The Talmud (a Jewish collection of religious instruction) understood the text to be a reference to the Messiah, and Paul appears to use it in this way. *Zion.* See notes on Gal 4:26; Heb 12:22.

A **11:27** *covenant.* The new covenant of Jer 31:31–34 (see notes there). *when I take away their sins.* See Jer 31:34; Zec 13:1 and note. Just as salvation for Gentiles involves forgiveness of sins, so the Jews, when they are saved, are forgiven by the mercy of God—his forgiveness based only on their repentance and faith (see v. 23; Zec 12:10—13:1 and notes).

11:28 *they are enemies.* Only temporarily. *for your sake.* Explained in v. 11. *loved on account of the patriarchs.* Not because any merit was passed on from the patriarchs to the Jewish people as a whole, but because God in love chose Israel, and that choice was irrevocable.

A **11:29** *God's gifts and his call are irrevocable.* God does not change his mind with reference to his call. Even though Israel is presently in a state of unbelief, God's purpose will be fulfilled in her.

11:32 *everyone.* Both groups under discussion (Jews and Gentiles). There has been a period of disobedience for each in order that God may have mercy on them all. Paul is in no way teaching universal salvation.

A **11:33–36** The doxology that ends this section of Romans is the natural outpouring of Paul's praise to God, whose wisdom and knowledge brought about his great plan for the salvation of both Jews and Gentiles.

A **12:1—16:27** Paul now turns to the practical application of all he has said previously in the letter. This does not mean that he has not said anything about Christian living up to this point. Chs. 6–8 have touched on this already, but now Paul goes into detail to show that Jesus Christ is to be Lord of every area of life. These chapters are not a postscript to the great theological discussions in chs. 1–11. In a real sense the entire letter has been directed toward the goal of showing that God demands our action as well as our believing and thinking. Faith expresses itself in obedience (see notes on Jas 2:14–26).

12:1 *Therefore, I urge you.* Paul draws an important inference from the truth set forth in chs. 1–11. *God's mercy.* Much of the letter has been concerned with demonstrating this. *your bodies.* See 6:13 and note. *living sacrifice.* In contrast to dead animal sacrifices, or perhaps "living" in the sense of having the new life of the Holy Spirit (see 6:4; 8:2 and note). *true worship.* Not merely ritual activity but the involvement of heart, mind and will in worship and obedient service.

12:2 *this world.* With all its evil and corruption (see Gal 1:4; 1Jn 2:15 and notes). *be transformed.* Here a process, not a single event. The same Greek word is used in the transfiguration narratives (Mt 17:2–8; Mk 9:2–8) and in 2Co 3:18 (see

12:2 *j* Eph 4:23
k S Eph 5:17
l S 1Ti 5:4
12:3 *m* Ro 15:15;
1Co 15:10; Gal 2:9;
Eph 3:7; 4:7;
1Pe 4:10,11
12:4 *n* 1Co 12:12-14;
Eph 4:16
12:5 *o* 1Co 6:15;
10:17; 12:12,20,27;
Eph 2:16; 4:4,25;
5:30; Col 3:15
12:6 *p* 1Co 7:7;
12:4,8-10 *q* S Eph 4:11
r 1Pe 4:10,11
12:7 *s* S Eph 4:11
12:8 *t* Ac 11:23;
13:15; 15:32 *u* 2Co 8:2;
9:5-13
12:9 *v* 2Co 6:6;
1Ti 1:5 *w* Ps 97:10;
Am 5:15; 1Th 5:21,22
12:10 *x* Ps 133:1;
1Th 4:9; Heb 13:1;
1Pe 1:22 *y* Php 2:3
12:11 *z* Ac 18:25
12:12 *a* Ro 5:2
b Heb 10:32,36
c S Lk 18:1
12:13 *d* S Ac 24:17
e 2Ki 4:10; Job 31:32;
1Ti 3:2; 5:10;
Heb 13:2; 1Pe 4:9
12:14 *f* S Mt 5:44
12:15 *g* Job 30:25
12:16 *h* S Ro 15:5
i ver 3; Ps 131:1;
Isa 5:21; Jer 45:5;
Ro 11:25

renewing of your mind. *j* Then you will be able to test and approve what God's will is *k*—his good, pleasing *l* and perfect will.

HUMBLE SERVICE IN THE BODY OF CHRIST

³For by the grace given me *m* I say to every one of you: Do not think of yourself more highly than you ought, but rather think of yourself with sober judgment, in accordance with the faith God has distributed to each of you. ⁴For just as each of us has one body with many members, and these members do not all have the same function, *n* ⁵so in Christ we, though many, form one body, *o* and each member belongs to all the others. ⁶We have different gifts, *p* according to the grace given to each of us. If your gift is prophesying, *q* then prophesy in accordance with your *a* faith; *r* ⁷if it is serving, then serve; if it is teaching, then teach; *s* ⁸if it is to encourage, then give encouragement; *t* if it is giving, then give generously; *u* if it is to lead, *b* do it diligently; if it is to show mercy, do it cheerfully.

LOVE IN ACTION

⁹Love must be sincere. *v* Hate what is evil; cling to what is good. *w* ¹⁰Be devoted to one another in love. *x* Honor one another above yourselves. *y* ¹¹Never be lacking in zeal, but keep your spiritual fervor, *z* serving the Lord. ¹²Be joyful in hope, *a* patient in affliction, *b* faithful in prayer. *c* ¹³Share with the Lord's people who are in need. *d* Practice hospitality. *e*

¹⁴Bless those who persecute you; *f* bless and do not curse. ¹⁵Rejoice with those who rejoice; mourn with those who mourn. *g* ¹⁶Live in harmony with one another. *h* Do not be proud, but be willing to associate with people of low position. *c* Do not think you are superior. *i*

¹⁷Do not repay anyone evil for evil. *j* Be careful to do what is right in the eyes of everyone. *k* ¹⁸If it is possible, as far as it depends on you, live at peace with everyone. *l* ¹⁹Do not

a 6 Or *the*   *b* 8 Or *to provide for others*   *c* 16 Or *willing to do menial work*

12:17 *j* ver 19; Pr 20:22; 24:29 *k* 2Co 8:21   **12:18** *l* S Mk 9:50; S Ro 14:19

---

note there). *mind.* Thought and will as they relate to morality (see 1:28). *Then.* After the spiritual transformation just described has taken place. *God's will.* What God wants from the believer here and now. *good.* That which leads to the spiritual and moral growth of the Christian. *pleasing.* To God, not necessarily to us. *perfect.* No improvement can be made on the will of God.

12:3 *in accordance with the faith.* The power given by God to each believer to fulfill various ministries in the church (see vv. 4–8 and notes). *God has distributed.* Since the power comes from God, there can be no basis for a superior attitude or self-righteousness.

12:4–8 Paul likens Christians to members of a human body. There are many members and each has a different function, but all are needed for the health of the body. The emphasis is on unity within diversity (see 1Co 12:12–31 and notes).

12:5 *in Christ.* The key to Paul's concept of Christian unity. It is only in Jesus Christ that any unity in the church is possible. True unity is spiritually based. See note on 6:11.

12:6 *gifts.* Greek *charismata,* referring to special gifts of grace —freely given by God to his people to meet the needs of the body (see notes on 1Co 1:7; 12:4). *prophesying.* See notes on 1Co 12:10; 14:1–5. *then prophesy.* There is to be no false modesty that denies the existence of gifts or refuses to use them. *in accordance with your faith.* Probably means about the same thing as "in accordance with the faith" in v. 3 (see note there).

12:7 *serving.* Any kind of service needed by the body of Christ or by any of its members. *teaching.* See notes on 1Co 12:28; Eph 4:11.

12:8 *to encourage.* Exhorting others with an uplifting, cheerful call to worthwhile accomplishment. The teacher often carried out this function. In teaching, believers are shown what they must do; in encouraging, they are helped to do it. *giving.* Giving what is one's own, or possibly distributing what has been given by others. *lead . . . diligently.* Possibly a reference to an elder. The Ephesian church had elders by about this time (see Ac 20:17; 1Ti 5:17 and notes). *show mercy.* Caring for the sick, the poor and the aged. *cheerfully.* Serving the needy should be a delight, not a chore (cf. 2Co 9:7).

12:9 *Love.* Believers' love for fellow Christians and perhaps also for other people. *sincere.* True love, not pretense. In view of the preceding paragraph, with its emphasis on social concern, the love Paul speaks of here is not mere emotion but love in action, as delineated in the rest of the chapter (cf. Jas 2:1–4,14–17; 1Jn 3:16–18; 4:19–21). *evil . . . good.* See Am 5:15. "Evil" and "good" frame vv. 9–21.

12:10 *love.* Love within the family of God. *Honor one another above yourselves.* Only a mind renewed by the Holy Spirit (see v. 2) could possibly do this (see Php 2:3 and note).

12:11 *spiritual fervor.* Lit. "fervent in spirit." If "spirit" means "Holy Spirit" here, the reference would be to the fervor the Holy Spirit provides.

12:12 *Be joyful in hope.* The certainty of the Christian's hope is a cause for joy (see 5:5 and note; see also 8:16–25; 1Pe 1:3–9). *patient.* Enduring triumphantly— necessary for Christians, because affliction is their inevitable experience (see Jn 16:33; 2Ti 3:12 and notes). *faithful in prayer.* One must not only pray in hard times, but also maintain communion with God through prayer at all times (see Lk 18:1; 1Th 5:17 and note).

12:13 *Share with the Lord's people.* The Christian has social responsibility to all people, but especially to other believers (see Gal 6:10; 1Ti 5:8).

12:14 *Bless those who persecute you.* Paul is echoing Jesus' teaching (see Mt 5:44 and note; Lk 6:28 and note on 6:27).

12:15 Identification with others in their joys and in their sorrows is a Christian's privilege and responsibility.

12:17 *Do not repay anyone evil for evil.* See Mt 5:39–42,44–45; 1Th 5:15; 1Pe 3:9 and notes. *Be careful to do what is right in the eyes of everyone.* A possible reflection of Pr 3:4 in the Septuagint (the pre-Christian Greek translation of the OT). Christian conduct should never betray the high moral standards of the gospel, or it will provoke the disdain of unbelievers and bring the gospel into disrepute (see 2Co 8:21 and note; 1Ti 3:7).

12:18 *If it is possible . . . live at peace.* Jesus pronounced a blessing on peacemakers (see Mt 5:9 and note), and believers are to cultivate peace with everyone to the extent that such peace depends on them (see Jas 3:18 and note).

take revenge, *m* my dear friends, but leave room for God's wrath, for it is written: "It is mine to avenge; I will repay," *a n* says the Lord. [20]On the contrary:

"If your enemy is hungry, feed him;
    if he is thirsty, give him something to drink.
In doing this, you will heap burning coals on his head." *b o*

[21]Do not be overcome by evil, but overcome evil with good.

SUBMISSION TO GOVERNING AUTHORITIES

13 Let everyone be subject to the governing authorities, *p* for there is no authority except that which God has established. *q* The authorities that exist have been established by God. [2]Consequently, whoever rebels against the authority is rebelling against what God has instituted, *r* and those who do so will bring judgment on themselves. [3]For rulers hold no terror for those who do right, but for those who do wrong. Do you want to be free from fear of the one in authority? Then do what is right and you will be commended. *s* [4]For the one in authority is God's servant for your good. But if you do wrong, be afraid, for rulers do not bear the sword for no reason. They are God's servants, agents of wrath to bring punishment on the wrongdoer. *t* [5]Therefore, it is necessary to submit to the authorities, not only because of possible punishment but also as a matter of conscience. *u*

[6]This is also why you pay taxes, *v* for the authorities are God's servants, who give their full time to governing. [7]Give to everyone what you owe: If you owe taxes, pay taxes; *w* if revenue, then revenue; if respect, then respect; if honor, then honor.

LOVE FULFILLS THE LAW

[8]Let no debt remain outstanding, except the continuing debt to love one another, for whoever loves others has fulfilled the law. *x* [9]The commandments, "You shall not commit adultery," "You shall not murder," "You shall not steal," "You shall not covet," *c y* and whatever other command there may be, are summed up *z* in this one command: "Love your neighbor as yourself." *d a* [10]Love does no harm to its neighbor. Therefore love is the fulfillment of the law. *b*

THE DAY IS NEAR

[11]And do this, understanding the present time. The hour has already come *c* for you to wake up from your slumber, *d* because our salvation is nearer now than when we first believed. [12]The night is nearly over; the day is almost here. *e* So let us put aside the deeds of

---

a *19* Deut. 32:35   b *20* Prov. 25:21,22   c *9* Exodus 20:13-15,17; Deut. 5:17-19,21   d *9* Lev. 19:18

A **12:20** *heap burning coals on his head.* Doing good to one's enemy (v. 21), instead of trying to take revenge, may bring about his repentance (see note on Pr 25:22).

12:21 *evil . . . good.* See note on v. 9.

13:1 *be subject to.* A significant theme in vv. 1–7. *governing authorities.* The civil rulers, all of whom were probably pagans at the time Paul was writing. Christians may have been tempted not to submit to them and to claim allegiance only to Christ. *established by God.* Even the possibility of a persecuting state did not shake Paul's conviction that civil government is ordained by God (see 1Pe 2:13–17 and notes).

13:2 *judgment.* Either divine judgment or, more likely, punishment by the governing authorities, since v. 3 ("For") explains this verse; see also v. 4.

A **13:3** *do what is right and you will be commended.* Paul is not stating that this will always be true but is describing the proper, ideal function of rulers. When civil rulers overstep their proper function, the Christian is to obey God rather than human authorities (see Ac 4:19; 5:29).

13:4 *God's servant.* In the order of divine providence the ruler is God's servant (see Isa 45:1 and note). *good.* Rulers exist for the benefit of society—to protect the general public by maintaining good order. *sword.* The symbol of Roman authority on both the national and the international levels. Here we find the Biblical principle of using force for the maintenance of the good order.

13:5 *as a matter of conscience.* Civil authorities are ordained by God, and in order to maintain a good conscience Christians must duly honor them.

13:6 *you pay taxes.* Because rulers are God's agents, who function for the benefit of society in general.

A **13:8** *continuing debt.* To love is the one debt that is never paid off. No matter how much people have loved, they are under obligation to keep on loving. *one another.* Includes not only fellow Christians but all people, as the second half of the verse makes clear ("loves others"). *the law.* The Mosaic law, which lays down both moral and social responsibilities.

13:9 Further explains the last statement of v. 8, namely, that love of neighbor encompasses all our social responsibilities. *your neighbor.* Jesus taught that our neighbor is anyone in need (see Lk 10:25–36 and notes), which is probably the idea Paul has in mind here. *as yourself.* Not a command to love ourselves but a recognition of the fact that we naturally do so (cf. Eph 5:33).

A **13:11–14** In this section, as in other NT passages, the certain coming of the end of the present age is used to provide motivation for godly living (see, e.g., Mt 25:31–46; Mk 13:33–37; Lk 21:36; Php 4:5; 1Th 5:6,8; Tit 2:11–14; Jas 5:7–11; 2Pe 3:11–14; 1Jn 2:28; 3:2–3).

A **13:11** *present time.* The time of salvation, the closing period of the present age, before the consummation of the kingdom. *The hour.* The time for action. *our salvation.* The full realization of salvation at the second coming of Jesus Christ (see 8:23; Heb 9:28; 1Pe 1:5 and notes). *is nearer now.* Every day brings us closer to the second advent of Christ.

A **13:12** *The night.* The present evil age. *is nearly over; the day is almost here.* A clear example of the NT teaching of the "nearness" of the end times (see 1Co 7:29; Php 4:5; Jas 5:9;

12:19 *m* ver 17;
Lev 19:18; Pr 20:22;
24:29 *n* Dt 32:35;
Ge 50:19; 1Sa 26:10;
Ps 94:1; Jer 51:36
12:20 *o* Pr 25:21,22;
Ex 23:4; Mt 5:44;
Lk 6:27
13:1 *p* Tit 3:1;
1Pe 2:13,14 *q* Da 2:21;
4:17; Jn 19:11
13:2 *r* Ex 16:8
13:3 *s* 1Pe 2:14
13:4 *t* 1Th 4:6
13:5 *u* Pr 24:21,22
13:6 *v* Mt 22:17
13:7 *w* Mt 17:25;
22:17,21; Lk 23:2
13:8 *x* ver 10;
S Mt 5:43; Jn 13:34;
Col 3:14
13:9 *y* Ex 20:13-
15,17; Dt 5:17-19,21
z Mt 7:12 *a* Lev 19:18;
S Mt 5:43
13:10 *b* S ver 8;
ver 9
13:11 *c* 1Co 7:29-31;
10:11; Jas 5:8; 1Pe 4:7;
1Jn 2:18; Rev 22:10
d Eph 5:14; 1Th 5:5,6
13:12 *e* Heb 10:25;
1Jn 2:8

13:12 ⁶Eph 5:11
ᵍEph 6:11,13; 1Th 5:8
13:13 ʰS Eph 5:18
ⁱLk 21:34;
Gal 5:20,21; Eph 5:18;
1Pe 4:3
13:14 ʲGal 3:27;
Eph 4:24; Col 3:10,12
ᵏS Gal 5:24
14:1 ˡRo 15:1;
1Co 8:9-12; 9:22
14:2 ᵐver 14
14:3 ⁿver 10;
Lk 18:9 ᵒver 10,13;
Col 2:16
14:4 ᵖS Mt 7:1
14:5 ᵠGal 4:10;
Col 2:16
14:6 ʳS Mt 14:19;
1Co 10:30,31;
1Ti 4:3,4
14:7 ˢ2Co 5:15;
Gal 2:20
14:8 ᵗPhp 1:20
14:9 ᵘRev 1:18; 2:8
ᵛS Ac 10:42; 2Co 5:15
14:10 ʷver 3;
S Mt 7:1 ˣS 2Co 5:10
14:11 ʸIsa 49:18
ᶻIsa 45:23;
Php 2:10,11
14:12 ᵃMt 12:36;
1Pe 4:5
14:13 ᵇver 1;
S Mt 7:1

darkness ᶠ and put on the armor ᵍ of light. ¹³Let us behave decently, as in the daytime, not in carousing and drunkenness, ʰ not in sexual immorality and debauchery, not in dissension and jealousy. ⁱ ¹⁴Rather, clothe yourselves with the Lord Jesus Christ, ʲ and do not think about how to gratify the desires of the sinful nature. ᵃ ᵏ

THE WEAK AND THE STRONG

14 Accept those whose faith is weak, ˡ without quarreling over disputable matters. ²One person's faith allows them to eat everything, but another person, whose faith is weak, eats only vegetables. ᵐ ³The one who eats everything must not treat with contempt ⁿ the one who does not, and the one who does not eat everything must not judge ᵒ the one who does, for God has accepted that person. ⁴Who are you to judge someone else's servant? ᵖ To their own master they stand or fall. And they will stand, for the Lord is able to make them stand.

⁵Some consider one day more sacred than another; ᵠ others consider every day alike. Everyone should be fully convinced in their own mind. ⁶Those who regard one day as special do so to the Lord. Those who eat meat do so to the Lord, for they give thanks to God; ʳ and those who abstain do so to the Lord and give thanks to God. ⁷For we do not live to ourselves alone ˢ and we do not die to ourselves alone. ⁸If we live, we live to the Lord; and if we die, we die to the Lord. So, whether we live or die, we belong to the Lord. ᵗ ⁹For this very reason, Christ died and returned to life ᵘ so that he might be the Lord of both the dead and the living. ᵛ

¹⁰You, then, why do you judge your brother or sister? Or why do you treat your brother or sister with contempt? ʷ For we will all stand before God's judgment seat. ˣ ¹¹It is written:

" 'As surely as I live,' ʸ says the Lord,
'every knee will bow before me;
    every tongue will confess to God.' " ᵇ ᶻ

¹²So then, we will all give an account of ourselves to God. ᵃ

¹³Therefore let us stop passing judgment ᵇ on one another. Instead, make up your mind

---

ᵃ 14 Or *the flesh*   ᵇ 11 Isaiah 45:23

1Pe 4:7; 1Jn 2:18 and notes). These texts do not mean that the early Christians believed that Jesus would return within a few years (and thus were mistaken). Rather, they regarded the death and resurrection of Christ as the crucial events of history that began the last days (see Heb 1:1–2 and notes). Since the next great event in God's redemptive plan is the second coming of Jesus Christ, "the night," no matter how long it may chronologically last, is "nearly over." *the day.* The appearing of Jesus Christ, which ushers in the consummation of the kingdom.

13:13 See 1:29–31 and note.

13:14 *clothe yourselves with the Lord Jesus Christ.* See Gal 3:27. Paul exhorts believers to display outwardly what has already taken place inwardly (see Col 3:1–10 and notes)— including practicing all the virtues associated with Christ. *clothe . . . with.* See note on Ps 109:29.

14:1—15:13 Cf. 1Co 8:1—11:1 and notes.

14:1 *whose faith is weak.* Probably Jewish Christians at Rome who were unwilling to give up the observance of certain requirements of the law, such as dietary restrictions and the keeping of the Sabbath and other special days. Their concern was not quite the same as that of the Judaizers of Galatia. The Judaizers thought they could put God in their debt by works of righteousness and were trying to force this heretical teaching on the Galatian churches, but the "weak" Roman Christians did neither. They were not yet clear as to the status of OT regulations under the new covenant inaugurated by the coming of Christ. *without quarreling over disputable matters.* Fellowship among Christians is not to be based on everyone's agreement on disputable questions. Christians do not agree on all matters pertaining to the Christian life, nor do they need to.

14:2 *One person's faith.* In contrast, Paul now describes the "strong" Christian. Here faith is used in the sense of assurance or confidence. The strong Christians' understanding of the gospel

allows them to recognize that one's dietary choices have no spiritual significance.

14:4 *someone else's.* God's. A Christian is not to reject a fellow Christian, who is also a servant of God. *To their own master they stand or fall.* The "weak" Christian is not the master of the "strong" Christian, nor is the "strong" the master of the "weak." God is Master, and to him alone all believers are responsible.

14:5 *one day more sacred than another.* Some feel that this refers primarily to the Sabbath, but it is probably a reference to all the special days of the OT ceremonial law. *consider every day alike.* All days are to be dedicated to God through holy living and godly service. *fully convinced in their own mind.* The importance of personal conviction in disputable matters of conduct runs through this passage (see vv. 14,16, 22–23).

14:6 The motivation behind the actions of both the strong and the weak is to be the same: Both should want to serve the Lord and give thanks for his provision.

14:7 *we do not live to ourselves alone.* The reference is to Christians. We live not to please ourselves but to please the Lord. *we do not die to ourselves alone.* Even in death the important thing is one's relationship to the Lord. Paul repeats the truths of this verse in v. 8.

14:9 *Lord.* See note on 10:9. Christ's Lordship over both the dead and the living arises out of his death and resurrection.

14:10 *why do you judge your brother or sister?* Addressed to weak Christians. *why do you treat your brother or sister with contempt?* Addressed to strong Christians. *we will all.* Refers to every Christian. *God's judgment seat.* All Christians will be judged, and the judgment will be based on works (see 2Co 5:10 and note; cf. 1Co 3:10–15 and notes).

14:13 *Instead.* The words that immediately follow are addressed to strong Christians. *obstacle.* Something that causes one to fall into sin.

not to put any stumbling block or obstacle in the way of a brother or sister. *c* 14I am convinced, being fully persuaded in the Lord Jesus, that nothing is unclean in itself. *d* But if anyone regards something as unclean, then for that person it is unclean. *e* 15If your brother or sister is distressed because of what you eat, you are no longer acting in love. *f* Do not by your eating destroy your brother or sister for whom Christ died. *g* 16Therefore do not let what you know is good be spoken of as evil. *h* 17For the kingdom of God is not a matter of eating and drinking, *i* but of righteousness, peace *j* and joy in the Holy Spirit, *k* 18because anyone who serves Christ in this way is pleasing to God and receives human approval. *l*

19Let us therefore make every effort to do what leads to peace *m* and to mutual edification. *n* 20Do not destroy the work of God for the sake of food. *o* All food is clean, *p* but it is wrong for a person to eat anything that causes someone else to stumble. *q* 21It is better not to eat meat or drink wine or to do anything else that will cause your brother or sister to fall. *r*

22So whatever you believe about these things keep between yourself and God. Blessed are those who do not condemn *s* themselves by what they approve. 23But those who have doubts *t* are condemned if they eat, because their eating is not from faith; and everything that does not come from faith is sin.

15 We who are strong ought to bear with the failings of the weak *u* and not to please ourselves. 2We should all please our neighbors for their good, *v* to build them up. *w* 3For even Christ did not please himself *x* but, as it is written: "The insults of those who insult you have fallen on me." *a y* 4For everything that was written in the past was written to teach us, *z* so that through the endurance taught in the Scriptures and the encouragement they provide we might have hope.

5May the God who gives endurance and encouragement give you the same attitude of mind *a* toward each other that Christ Jesus had, 6so that with one mind and one voice you may glorify *b* the God and Father *c* of our Lord Jesus Christ.

7Accept one another, *d* then, just as Christ accepted you, in order to bring praise to God.

a 3 Psalm 69:9

14:13 *c* S 2Co 6:3
14:14 *d* ver 20; S Ac 10:15 *e* 1Co 8:7
14:15 *f* Eph 5:2 *g* ver 20; 1Co 8:11
14:16 *h* 1Co 10:30
14:17 *i* 1Co 8:8 *j* Isa 32:17 *k* Ro 15:13; Gal 5:22
14:18 *l* Lk 2:52; Ac 24:16; 2Co 8:21
14:19 *m* Ps 34:14; Ro 12:18; 1Co 7:15; 2Ti 2:22; Heb 12:14 *n* Ro 15:2; 1Co 14:3-5,12,17,26; 2Co 12:19; Eph 4:12,29
14:20 *o* ver 15 *p* ver 14; S Ac 10:15 *q* ver 13; 1Co 8:9-12
14:21 *r* S Mt 5:29
14:22 *s* 1Jn 3:21
14:23 *t* ver 5
15:1 *u* Ro 14:1; 1Th 5:14
15:2 *v* S 1Co 10:24 *w* S Ro 14:19
15:3 *x* 2Co 8:9 *y* Ps 69:9
15:4 *z* S Ro 4:23,24
15:5 *a* Ro 12:16; 1Co 1:10; 2Co 13:11; Eph 4:3; Php 2:2; Col 3:14; 1Pe 3:8
15:6 *b* Ps 34:3 *c* Rev 1:6
15:7 *d* Ro 14:1

14:14 *I am convinced, being fully persuaded in the Lord Jesus.* Now that Paul was a Christian, the old food taboos no longer applied (see Mk 7:19–20; Ac 10:15,28 and notes). *nothing is unclean in itself.* For Paul's teaching elsewhere on this subject, see 1Ti 4:4; Tit 1:15 and note. *if anyone regards something as unclean, then for that person it is unclean.* Not to be generalized to mean that sin is only a matter of subjective opinion or conscience. Paul is not discussing conduct that in the light of Scripture is clearly sinful, but conduct concerning which Christians may legitimately differ (in this case, food regulations). With regard to such matters, decisions should be guided by conscience.

14:14 *love.* The key to proper settlement of disputes. *your brother or sister for whom Christ died.* Christ so valued weak Christians that he died for them. Surely strong Christians ought to be willing to make adjustments in their own behavior for the sake of such fellow believers (see 1Co 8:11–13; 10:23, 28–29,32–33 and notes).

14:16 *what you know is good.* From your own understanding of Christian liberty. *be spoken of as evil.* To exercise freedom without responsibility can lead to evil results.

14:17 *kingdom of God.* See notes on Mt 3:2; Lk 4:43. *is not a matter of eating and drinking.* To be concerned with such trivial matters is to miss completely the essence of Christian living. *righteousness.* Righteous living. Paul's concern for the moral and ethical dimension of the Christian life stands out in all his letters. *peace.* See 5:1 and note. *joy in the Holy Spirit.* Joy given by the Holy Spirit.

14:19 *mutual edification.* The spiritual building up of individual Christians and of the church (see 1:11–12 and note on 1:12).

14:20 *work of God.* The weak Christian who as a redeemed person is God's work and one in whom God continues to work (cf. Eph 2:10). *causes someone else to stumble.* Paul recognizes a strong Christian's right to certain freedoms, but qualifies this with the principle of regard for a weak Christian's scruples.

14:22 *keep between yourself and God.* Strong Christians are not

required to go against their convictions or change their standards. Yet they are not to flaunt their Christian freedom but to keep it a private matter. *what they approve.* Probably a reference to the eating of certain foods.

14:23 *everything.* The matters discussed above, namely, conduct about which there can be legitimate differences of opinion among Christians. *faith.* Here the conviction that one's action is in keeping with God's will.

15:1 *We who are strong.* Paul identifies himself with the strong Christians, those whose personal convictions allow them more freedom than the weak. *to bear.* Not merely to tolerate or put up with but to uphold lovingly. *failings.* Not sins, since in the matters under discussion there is no clear guidance in Scripture. *not to please ourselves.* Not that Christians should never please themselves, but that they should not insist on doing what they want without regard to the scruples of other Christians.

15:3 *Christ did not please himself.* He came to do the will of the Father, not his own will (see Jn 4:34 and note). This involved suffering and even death (see Mt 20:28; Mk 10:45; 2Co 8:9; Php 2:5 –8 and notes). *The insults of those who insult you have fallen on me.* In the psalm quoted (69:9; see note there) "you" refers to God and "me" refers to the righteous sufferer, whom Paul identifies with Christ. The quotation serves to show how Christ did not please himself but voluntarily bore human hostility toward God.

15:4 Here Paul defends his application of Ps 69:9 to Christ. In so doing, he states a great truth concerning the purpose of Scripture: It was written for our instruction, so that as we patiently endure we might be encouraged to hold fast our hope in Christ (see 1Co 10:6,11).

15:5 *the same attitude of mind toward each other that Christ Jesus had.* Not that believers should all come to the same conclusions on the matters of conscience discussed above, but that they might agree to disagree in love (cf. Eph 4:1–6; Php 2:1–5 and notes).

15:7 *just as Christ accepted you.* See 14:3; see also 14:4,15 and notes.

15:8 *e* Mt 15:24;
Ac 3:25,26 *f* 2Co 1:20
15:9 *g* S Ro 3:29
h S Mt 9:8
i 2Sa 22:50; Ps 18:49
15:10 *j* Dt 32:43;
Isa 66:10
15:11 *k* Ps 117:1
15:12 *l* S Rev 5:5
m Isa 11:10; Mt 12:21
15:13 *n* Ro 14:17
o ver 19; 1Co 2:4;
4:20; 1Th 1:5
15:14 *p* Eph 5:9
q S 2Co 8:7; 2Pe 1:12
15:15 *r* S Ro 12:3
15:16 *s* S Ac 9:15
t ver 19; S Ro 1:1
u Isa 66:20
15:17 *v* Php 3:3
w Heb 2:17
15:18 *x* Ac 15:12;
21:19; Ro 1:5
y Ro 16:26
15:19 *z* S Jn 4:48;
Ac 19:11 *a* S ver 13
b Ac 22:17-21
c S 2Co 2:12

[8] For I tell you that Christ has become a servant of the Jews[a] [e] on behalf of God's truth, so that the promises[f] made to the patriarchs might be confirmed [9] and, moreover, that the Gentiles[g] might glorify God[h] for his mercy. As it is written:

"Therefore I will praise you among the Gentiles;
　I will sing the praises of your name."[b] [i]

[10] Again, it says,

"Rejoice, you Gentiles, with his people."[c] [j]

[11] And again,

"Praise the Lord, all you Gentiles;
　let all the peoples extol him."[d] [k]

[12] And again, Isaiah says,

"The Root of Jesse[l] will spring up,
　one who will arise to rule over the nations;
　in him the Gentiles will hope."[e] [m]

[13] May the God of hope fill you with all joy and peace[n] as you trust in him, so that you may overflow with hope by the power of the Holy Spirit. [o]

PAUL THE MINISTER TO THE GENTILES

[14] I myself am convinced, my brothers and sisters, that you yourselves are full of goodness,[p] filled with knowledge[q] and competent to instruct one another. [15] Yet I have written you quite boldly on some points to remind you of them again, because of the grace God gave me[r] [16] to be a minister of Christ Jesus to the Gentiles.[s] He gave me the priestly duty of proclaiming the gospel of God,[t] so that the Gentiles might become an offering[u] acceptable to God, sanctified by the Holy Spirit.

[17] Therefore I glory in Christ Jesus[v] in my service to God.[w] [18] I will not venture to speak of anything except what Christ has accomplished through me in leading the Gentiles[x] to obey God[y] by what I have said and done— [19] by the power of signs and wonders,[z] through the power of the Spirit of God.[a] So from Jerusalem[b] all the way around to Illyricum, I have fully proclaimed the gospel of Christ.[c] [20] It has always been my ambition to preach

---

a 8 Greek *circumcision*　　*b 9* 2 Samuel 22:50; Psalm 18:49　　*c 10* Deut. 32:43　　*d 11* Psalm 117:1
e 12 Isaiah 11:10 (see Septuagint)

15:8 *Christ has become a servant of the Jews.* Clearly revealed in his earthly ministry. He was sent to the Jewish people and largely limited his ministry to them (see Mt 15:24). God gave a special priority, so far as the gospel is concerned, to the Jews (see 1:16 and note; 3:1–8; see also 9:4–5 and notes). *promises made to the patriarchs.* The covenant promises made to Abraham (Ge 12:1–3; 17:7; 18:19; 22:18), Isaac (Ge 26:3–4) and Jacob (Ge 28:13–15; 46:2–4; see chart, p. 20).

15:9 *that the Gentiles might glorify God.* From the beginning, God's redemptive work in and for Israel had in view the redemption of the Gentiles (see Ge 12:2–3 and note). They would both see God's mighty and gracious acts for his people and hear the praises of God's people as they celebrated what God had done for them (a common theme in the Psalms; see Paul's quotations in vv. 9b–12 and note on Ps 9:1). Thus they would come to know the true God and glorify him for his mercy (see notes on Ps 46:10; 47:9). God's greatest and climactic act for Israel's salvation was the sending of the Messiah to fulfill the promises made to the patriarchs and so to gather in the great harvest of the Gentiles.

15:12 *Root of Jesse.* Jesse was the father of David (see 1Sa 16:5–13; Mt 1:6), and the Messiah was the "Son of David" (see Mt 1:1 and note; 21:9; see also Isa 11:1; Rev 5:5 and notes). *in him the Gentiles will hope.* The Gentile mission of the early church was a fulfillment of this prophecy (Isa 11:10; see note there), as is the continuing evangelization of the nations (cf. Isa 42:4 and note).

15:13 *God of hope.* Any hope the Christian has comes from God (see note on 5:5). *by the power of the Holy Spirit.* Hope cannot be conjured up by human effort; it is God's gift by his Spirit (see 8:24–25).

15:15 *to remind you of them again.* Since Paul had never preached or taught in Rome, he may be referring to Christian doctrine generally known in the church.

15:16 *minister of Christ Jesus to the Gentiles.* See note on 11:13. *priestly duty of proclaiming the gospel.* Paul's priestly function was different from that of the Levitical priests. They were involved with the rituals of the temple, whereas he preached the gospel. *an offering acceptable to God, sanctified by the Holy Spirit.* The offering Paul brought to God was the Gentile church. *sanctified.* See note on 1Co 1:2.

15:17 *I glory.* Paul was not boasting of his own achievements but of what Christ had accomplished through him (v. 18).

15:19 *signs and wonders.* See Ac 14:8–10; 16:16–18, 25–26; 20:9–12; 28:8–9; 2Co 12:12 and note; Heb 2:4 and note. *from Jerusalem.* The home of the mother church, where the gospel originated and its dissemination began (see Ac 1:8 and note; see also maps, p. 1861, and Introduction to Acts: Plan and Outline). *Illyricum.* A Roman province north of Macedonia (present-day Albania, Serbia and Montenegro [the former Yugoslavia]). Acts mentions nothing of Paul's ministry there, and perhaps all he means is that he reached the border. *I have fully proclaimed the gospel.* Not everyone in the eastern Mediterranean had heard the gospel, but Paul believed that his work there had been completed and it was time to move on to other places.

the gospel *d* where Christ was not known, so that I would not be building on someone else's foundation. *e* ²¹Rather, as it is written:

> "Those who were not told about him will see,
>   and those who have not heard will understand." *a f*

²²This is why I have often been hindered from coming to you. *g*

PAUL'S PLAN TO VISIT ROME

²³But now that there is no more place for me to work in these regions, and since I have been longing for many years to visit you, *h* ²⁴I plan to do so when I go to Spain. *i* I hope to see you while passing through and to have you assist *j* me on my journey there, after I have enjoyed your company for a while. ²⁵Now, however, I am on my way to Jerusalem *k* in the service *l* of the Lord's people *m* there. ²⁶For Macedonia *n* and Achaia *o* were pleased to make a contribution for the poor among the Lord's people in Jerusalem. *p* ²⁷They were pleased to do it, and indeed they owe it to them. For if the Gentiles have shared in the Jews' spiritual blessings, they owe it to the Jews to share with them their material blessings. *q* ²⁸So after I have completed this task and have made sure that they have received this fruit, I will go to Spain *r* and visit you on the way. ²⁹I know that when I come to you, *s* I will come in the full measure of the blessing of Christ.

³⁰I urge you, brothers and sisters, by our Lord Jesus Christ and by the love of the Spirit, *t* to join me in my struggle by praying to God for me. *u* ³¹Pray that I may be kept safe *v* from the unbelievers in Judea and that the contribution *w* I take to Jerusalem may be favorably received by the Lord's people *x* there, ³²so that by God's will *y* I may come to you *z* with joy and together with you be refreshed. *a* ³³The God of peace *b* be with you all. Amen.

PERSONAL GREETINGS

16

I commend *c* to you our sister Phoebe, a deacon *b* of the church in Cenchreae. *d* ²I ask you to receive her in the Lord *e* in a way worthy of his people *f* and to give her any help she may need from you, for she has been the benefactor of many people, including me.

³Greet Priscilla *c* and Aquila, *g* my co-workers *h* in Christ Jesus. *i* ⁴They risked their lives for me. Not only I but all the churches of the Gentiles are grateful to them.

⁵Greet also the church that meets at their house. *j*

Greet my dear friend Epenetus, who was the first convert *k* to Christ in the province of Asia. *l*

⁶Greet Mary, who worked very hard for you.

⁷Greet Andronicus and Junia, my fellow Jews *m* who have been in prison with me. *n* They are outstanding among the apostles, and they were in Christ *o* before I was.

---

a 21 Isaiah 52:15 (see Septuagint)   *b* 1 Or *servant*   *c* 3 Greek *Prisca*, a variant of *Priscilla*

15:20 *d* Ro 1:15
² 2Co 10:15,16
15:21 *e* Isa 52:15
15:22 *f* Ro 1:13
15:23 *h* Ac 19:21;
Ro 1:10,11
15:24 *i* ver 28
j 1Co 16:6; Tit 3:13
15:25 *k* S Ac 19:21
l S Ac 24:17
m S Ac 9:13
15:26 *n* S Ac 16:9
o S Ac 18:12
p S Ac 24:17
15:27 *q* 1Co 9:11
15:28 *r* ver 24
15:29 *s* Ro 1:10,11
15:30 *t* Gal 5:22;
Col 1:8 *u* 2Co 1:11;
Col 4:12
15:31 *v* 2Co 1:10;
2Th 3:2; 2Ti 3:11;
2Pe 2:9 *w* ver 25;
S Ac 24:17 *x* S Ac 9:13
15:32 *y* S Ac 18:21
z Ro 1:10,13
a 1Co 16:18; Phm 7
15:33 *b* Ro 16:20;
2Co 13:11; Php 4:9;
1Th 5:23; 2Th 3:16;
Heb 13:20
16:1 *c* S 2Co 3:1
d Ac 18:18
16:2 *e* Php 2:29
f S Ac 9:13
16:3 *g* S Ac 18:2
h S Php 2:25
i ver 7,9,10; Ro 8:1,39;
1Co 1:30; 2Co 5:17;
Gal 1:22; 5:6; Eph 1:13
16:5 *j* 1Co 16:19;
Col 4:15; Phm 2
k 1Co 16:15 *l* S Ac 2:9
16:7 *m* ver 11,21
n Col 4:10; Phm 23
o S ver 3

15:22 *hindered from coming to you.* Paul's great desire to complete the missionary task in the eastern Mediterranean had prevented him from making a trip to Rome.

15:23 *no more place for me to work.* Because of the principle stated in v. 20. *longing for many years to visit you.* See 1:11–15.

15:24 *to have you assist me on my journey there.* Paul wanted to use the Roman church as a base of operations for a mission to Spain (see also v. 28). *enjoyed your company for a while.* More than a quick stop at Rome was contemplated (see 1:11–12).

15:25 *in the service of the Lord's people there.* Paul wanted to present the gift (see v. 26) personally to the Jerusalem church. The gift needed interpretation. It was not merely money; it represented the love and concern of the Gentile churches for their Jewish brothers and sisters in Christ. *the Lord's people.* See note on 1:7.

15:26 *Macedonia and Achaia.* See note on 1Th 1:7. *contribution.* See 1Co 16:1–4; 2Co 8:1—9:15 and notes.

15:27 *Jews' spiritual blessings.* Especially Christ and the gospel.

15:28 *this fruit.* The collection from the Gentile churches.

15:31 *Pray that I may be kept safe from the unbelievers in Judea.* Paul wanted to go to Jerusalem. The delivery of the collection was important to him, but he had received warnings about what might happen to him there (see Ac 20:22–23 and note on 20:22). *may be favorably received.* Perhaps a reference to the way in which the money was to be distributed—often a delicate and difficult task.

15:32 *with you be refreshed.* See 1:11–12.

15:33 *God of peace.* See notes on 5:1; 1Th 5:23.

C **16:1** *our sister.* In the sense of being a fellow believer. *Phoebe.* Probably the carrier of the letter to Rome (cf. v. 2). *deacon.* See TNIV text note; one who serves or ministers in any way. When church related, as it is here, it probably refers to a specific office—woman deacon or deaconess. *Cenchreae.* A port located about six miles east of Corinth on the Saronic Gulf.

C **16:3** *Priscilla and Aquila.* Close friends of Paul, who worked in the same trade of tentmaking (see Ac 18:2–3 and notes).

16:4 *risked their lives for me.* There is no other record of this in the NT or elsewhere, but it must have been widely known, as the last part of the verse indicates (cf. Php 2:25–30 and notes).

16:6 *Mary.* Six persons are known by this name in the NT. This one is unknown apart from this reference.

16:7 *Junia.* A feminine name. Andronicus and Junia may have been husband and wife (cf. Priscilla and Aquila [v. 3] and probably Philologus and Julia [v. 15]). *among the apostles.* Two possible interpretations are: 1. "Apostles" is used in a wider sense than the Twelve—to include preachers of the gospel recognized by the churches (see Ac 14:4,14 and note on 14:4; 1Th 2:6). 2. "Apostles" is here preceded by the definite article; this may indicate that the Twelve are in view. If that is the case, the meaning would be that these two persons were outstanding "in the opinion of" the apostles.

16:9 P S ver 3
16:10 q S ver 3
r S Ac 11:14
16:11 s ver 7,21
t S Ac 11:14
16:13 e Mk 15:21
v S 2Jn 1
16:15 w ver 2;
S Ac 9:13 x ver 14
16:16 y 1Co 16:20;
2Co 13:12; 1Th 5:26;
1Pe 5:14
16:17 z Gal 1:8,9;
1Ti 1:3; 6:3
a Mt 18:15-17;
1Co 5:11; 2Th 3:6,14;
2Ti 3:5; Tit 3:10;
2Jn 10
16:18 b Ro 14:18
c Php 3:19 d 2Sa 15:6;
Ps 12:2; Isa 30:10;
Col 2:4
16:19 e Ro 1:8
f S 1Co 14:20
16:20 g S Ro 15:33
h Ge 3:15 i S Mt 4:10
j 2Co 13:14;
S Gal 6:18; 1Th 5:28;
Rev 22:21
16:21 k S Ac 16:1
l Ac 13:1 m Ac 17:5
n ver 7,11
16:23[24] o S Ac 19
:29 P Ac 19:22;
2Ti 4:20
16:25 q 2Co 9:8;
Eph 3:20; Jude 24
r Ro 2:16; 2Ti 2:8
s Isa 48:6; Eph 1:9;
3:3-6,9; Col 1:26,27;
2:2; 1Ti 3:16
16:26 t Ro 1:2
u Ro 1:5
16:27 v S Ro 11:36

8 Greet Ampliatus, my dear friend in the Lord.

9 Greet Urbanus, our co-worker in Christ, P and my dear friend Stachys.

10 Greet Apelles, whose fidelity to Christ has stood the test. q Greet those who belong to the household r of Aristobulus.

11 Greet Herodion, my fellow Jew. s Greet those in the household t of Narcissus who are in the Lord.

12 Greet Tryphena and Tryphosa, those women who work hard in the Lord. Greet my dear friend Persis, another woman who has worked very hard in the Lord.

13 Greet Rufus, u chosen v in the Lord, and his mother, who has been a mother to me, too.

14 Greet Asyncritus, Phlegon, Hermes, Patrobas, Hermas and the other brothers and sisters with them.

15 Greet Philologus, Julia, Nereus and his sister, and Olympas and all the Lord's people w who are with them. x

16 Greet one another with a holy kiss. y All the churches of Christ send greetings.

17 I urge you, brothers and sisters, to watch out for those who cause divisions and put obstacles in your way that are contrary to the teaching you have learned. z Keep away from them. a 18 For such people are not serving our Lord Christ, b but their own appetites. c By smooth talk and flattery they deceive d the minds of naive people. 19 Everyone has heard e about your obedience, so I rejoice because of you; but I want you to be wise about what is good, and innocent about what is evil. f

20 The God of peace g will soon crush h Satan i under your feet.

The grace of our Lord Jesus be with you. j

21 Timothy, k my co-worker, sends his greetings to you, as do Lucius, l Jason m and Sosipater, my fellow Jews. n

22 I, Tertius, who wrote down this letter, greet you in the Lord.

23 [24] Gaius, o whose hospitality I and the whole church here enjoy, sends you his greetings. Erastus, P who is the city's director of public works, and our brother Quartus send you their greetings. a

25 Now to him who is able q to establish you in accordance with my gospel, r the message I proclaim about Jesus Christ, in keeping with the revelation of the mystery s hidden for long ages past, 26 but now revealed and made known through the prophetic writings t by the command of the eternal God, so that all the Gentiles might come to faith and obedience u— 27 to the only wise God be glory forever through Jesus Christ! Amen. v

---

a 23 Some manuscripts *their greetings.* 24 *May the grace of our Lord Jesus Christ be with all of you. Amen.*

16:8–10 *Ampliatus…Urbanus…Stachys…Apelles.* All common slave names found in the imperial household.

16:10 *Aristobulus.* Perhaps refers to the grandson of Herod the Great and brother of Herod Agrippa I.

16:11 *Narcissus.* Sometimes identified with Tiberius Claudius Narcissus, a wealthy freedman of the Roman emperor Tiberius.

16:12 *Tryphena and Tryphosa.* Perhaps sisters, even twins, because it was common for such persons to be given names from the same root. *Persis.* Means "Persian woman."

16:14–15 None of these persons can be further identified, except that they were slaves or freedmen in the Roman church.

16:16 *holy kiss.* See 1Co 16:20; 2Co 13:12; 1Th 5:26 and notes; 1Pe 5:14. Justin Martyr (A.D. 150) tells us that the holy kiss was a regular part of the worship service in his day. It is still a practice in some churches.

16:17 *those who cause divisions and put obstacles in your way.* Who these people were we cannot tell, but some of their characteristics are mentioned in v. 18.

16:19 *wise about what is good.* Christians are to be experts in doing good.

16:20 *God of peace.* See 15:33 and note; cf. note on 1:7. *will soon crush Satan.* A reference to Satan's final doom (see Ge 3:15 and note). For "soon," see note on 13:12. *grace.* See note on 1:7. *with you.* See note on 2Co 13:14.

16:21 *Jason.* Possibly the Jason mentioned in Ac 17:5–9. *Sosipater.* Probably Sopater, son of Pyrrhus, from Berea (see Ac 20:4 and note).

16:22 *I, Tertius, who wrote down this letter.* He had functioned as Paul's secretary.

16:23[24] *Gaius.* Usually identified with Titius Justus, a God-fearer, in whose house Paul stayed while in Corinth (see Ac 18:7 and note; 1Co 1:14). His full name would be Gaius Titius Justus. *here.* In Corinth. *Erastus.* At Corinth archaeologists have discovered a reused block of stone in a paved square, with the Latin inscription:"Erastus, commissioner of public works, bore the expense of this pavement." This may refer to the Erastus mentioned here. If it does, it is the earliest reference to a Christian by name outside the NT. He may also be the same person referred to in Ac 19:22 and 2Ti 4:20 (see notes there), though it is difficult to be certain because the name was fairly common. *Quartus.* Means "fourth (son)." For v. 24, see TNIV text note on v. 23.

16:25 *my gospel.* Not a gospel different from that preached by others, but a gospel Paul received by direct revelation (see Gal 1:12 and note on 1:11). *message I proclaim about Jesus Christ.* A description of the gospel; it is about Jesus Christ, who embodies its content (see 1:3; 1Co 15:3–4 and notes). *mystery.* See note on 11:25. *for long ages.* From eternity past (see 1Co 2:7 and note).

16:26 *revealed and made known through the prophetic writings.* See 1:2 and note. *all the Gentiles.* The universality of the gospel (see Mt 28:19 and note).

16:27 *to…God be glory.* The ultimate purpose of all things (see 11:36; Ps 29:1–2; 86:9,12; 96:7–8; 115:1; Lk 2:14 and note; 1Co 10:31 and note; Eph 1:12,14; Rev 5:13; 7:12; 15:4; 19:1,7).

AUTHOR AND DATE

1 CORINTHIANS

C Paul is acknowledged as the author both by the letter itself (1:1–2; 16:21) and by the early church fathers. His authorship was attested by Clement of Rome as early as A.D. 96, and today practically all NT interpreters concur. The letter was written c. 55 (see chart, p. 1855) toward the close of Paul's three-year residency in Ephesus (see 16:5–9; Ac 20:31). It is clear from his reference to staying at Ephesus until Pentecost (16:8) that he intended to remain there somewhat less than a year when he wrote 1 Corinthians.

THE CITY OF CORINTH

Corinth was a thriving city, at the time the chief city of Greece, both commercially and politically. See map and diagram, below.

1. *Its commerce.* Located just off the Corinthian isthmus (see map, p. 1875), it was a crossroads for travelers and traders. It had two harbors: (1) Cenchreae, six miles to the east on the Saronic Gulf, and (2) Lechaion, a mile and a half to the north

CORINTH IN THE TIME OF PAUL

Side streets (dotted lines) for illustration only—artist's concept

The city of Corinth, perched like a one-eyed Titan astride the narrow isthmus connecting the Greek mainland with the Peloponnese, was one of the dominant commercial centers of the Mediterranean world as early as the eighth century B.C.

No city in Greece was more favorably situated for land and sea trade. With a high, strong citadel at its back, Corinth lay between the Saronic Gulf and the Ionian Sea, with ports at Lechaion and Cenchreae. A *diolkos*, or stone road for the overland transport of ships, linked the two seas. Crowning the Acrocorinth was the temple of Aphrodite, served, according to Strabo, by more than 1,000 pagan priestess-prostitutes.

By the time the gospel reached Corinth in the spring of A.D. 52, the city had a proud history of leadership in the Achaian League, as well as a spirit of revived Hellenism under

Roman domination after 44 B.C., following the destruction of the city by Mummius in 146 B.C.

B Paul's lengthy stay in Corinth brought him directly in contact with the major monuments of the *agora*, many of which still survive. The fountain-house of the spring *Peirene*, the temple of Apollo, the *macellum* or meat market (1Co 10:25), the theater, the *bema* (Ac 18:12) and the unimpressive synagogue all played a part in the experience of the apostle. An inscription from the theater names the city official Erastus, probably the friend of Paul mentioned in Ro 16:23 (see note there).

on the Corinthian Gulf. Goods were transported across the isthmus on the Diolkos, a stone road by which smaller ships could be hauled fully loaded across the isthmus, and by which cargoes of larger ships could be transported by wagons from one side to the other. Trade flowed through the city from Italy and Spain to the west and from Asia Minor, Phoenicia and Egypt to the east.

2. *Its culture.* Although Corinth was not a university town like Athens, it was nevertheless characterized by typical Greek culture. Its people were interested in Greek philosophy and placed a high premium on wisdom.

B 3. *Its religion.* Corinth contained at least 12 temples. Whether they were all in use during Paul's time is not known for certain. One of the most infamous was the temple dedicated to Aphrodite, the goddess of love, whose worshipers practiced religious prostitution. About a fourth of a mile north of the theater stood the temple of Asclepius, the god of healing, and the sixth-century B.C. temple of Apollo was located in the middle of the city. In addition, the Jews had established a synagogue, the inscribed lintel of which has been found and placed in the museum at old Corinth.

4. *Its immorality.* Like any large commercial city, Corinth was a center for open and unbridled immorality. The worship of Aphrodite fostered prostitution in the name of religion. At one time 1,000 sacred (priestess) prostitutes served her temple. So widely known did the immorality of Corinth become that the Greek verb "to Corinthianize" came to mean "to practice sexual immorality." In a setting like this it is no wonder that the Corinthian church was plagued with numerous problems.

OCCASION AND PURPOSE

Paul had received information from several sources concerning the conditions existing in the church at Corinth. Some members of the household of Chloe had informed him of the factions that had developed in the church (1:11). There were three individuals—Stephanas, Fortunatus and Achaicus—who had come to Paul in Ephesus to make some contribution to his ministry (16:17), but whether these were the ones from Chloe's household we do not know.

Some of those who had come had brought disturbing information concerning moral irregularities in the church (chs. 5–6). Immorality had plagued the Corinthian assembly almost from the beginning. From 5:9–10 it is apparent that Paul had written previously concerning moral laxness. He had urged believers "not to associate with sexually immoral people" (5:9). Because of misunderstanding he now finds it necessary to clarify his instruction (5:10–11) and to urge immediate and drastic action (5:3–5,13).

Other Corinthian visitors had brought a letter from the church that requested counsel on several subjects (see 7:1 and note; cf. 8:1; 12:1; 16:1).

It is clear that, although the church was gifted (see 1:4–7), it was immature and unspiritual (3:1–4). Paul's purposes for writing were: (1) to instruct and restore the church in its areas of weakness, correcting erroneous practices such as divisions (1:10—4:21), immorality (ch. 5; 6:12–20), litigation in pagan courts (6:1–8) and abuse of the Lord's Supper (11:17–34); (2) to correct false teaching concerning the resurrection (ch. 15); and (3) to answer questions addressed to Paul in the letter that had been brought to him (see previous paragraph).

THEME

The letter revolves around the theme of problems in the church with respect to Christian conduct. It thus has to do with progressive sanctification, the continuing development of a holy character. Obviously Paul was personally concerned with the Corinthians' problems, revealing a true pastor's (shepherd's) heart.

RELEVANCE

This letter continues to be timely for the church today, both to instruct and to inspire. Christians are still powerfully influenced by their cultural environment, and most of the questions and problems that confronted the church at Corinth are still very much with us—problems like immaturity, instability, divisions, jealousy and envy, lawsuits, marital difficulties, sexual immorality and the misuse of spiritual gifts. Yet in spite of this concentration on problems, Paul's letter contains some of the most familiar and beloved chapters in the entire Bible—e.g., ch. 13 (on love) and ch. 15 (on resurrection).

OUTLINE

1:1 *a* Ro 1:1; Eph 1:1;
2Ti 1:1 *b* S 2Co 1:1
c Ac 18:17
1:2 *d* S 1Co 10:32
e S Ac 18:1 *f* Ro 1:7
g S Ac 2:21
1:3 *h* S Ro 1:7
1:4 *i* S Ro 1:8
1:5 *i* 2Co 9:11
k S 2Co 8:7
1:6 *j* 2Th 1:10;
1Ti 2:6; Rev 1:2
1:7 *m* Ro 1:11;
1Co 12:1-31
n S Mt 16:27;
S Lk 17:30; 1Th 1:10;
S 2:19; Tit 2:13;
Jas 5:7,8; 1Pe 1:13;
2Pe 3:12; S Rev 1:7
1:8 *o* S 1Th 3:13
p Am 5:18; 1Co 5:5;
Php 1:6,10; 2:16;
1Th 5:2
1:9 *q* Dt 7:9;
Isa 49:7; 1Co 10:13;
1Th 5:24; 2Th 3:3;
2Ti 2:13; Heb 10:23;
11:11 *r* S Ro 8:28
s 1Jn 1:3
1:10 *t* S Ro 7:1
u 1Co 11:18 *v* S Ro 15:5
1:11 *w* S Ac 11:14
1:12 *x* 1Co 3:4,22
y S Ac 18:24 *z* Jn 1:42;
1Co 3:22; 9:5
1:13 *a* S Mt 28:19
1:14 *b* Ac 18:8
c S Ac 19:29
1:16 *d* S Ac 11:14
e 1Co 16:15
1:17 *f* Jn 4:2;
S Ac 2:38 *g* 1Co 2:1,4,
13

Paul, called to be an apostle *a* of Christ Jesus by the will of God, *b* and our brother Sosthenes, *c*

2To the church of God *d* in Corinth, *e* to those sanctified in Christ Jesus and called *f* to be his holy people, together with all those everywhere who call on the name *g* of our Lord Jesus Christ—their Lord and ours:

3Grace and peace to you from God our Father and the Lord Jesus Christ. *h*

THANKSGIVING

4I always thank my God for you *i* because of his grace given you in Christ Jesus. 5For in him you have been enriched *j* in every way—with all kinds of speech and with all knowledge *k*— 6God thus confirming our testimony *l* about Christ among you. 7Therefore you do not lack any spiritual gift *m* as you eagerly wait for our Lord Jesus Christ to be revealed. *n* 8He will also keep you firm to the end, so that you will be blameless *o* on the day of our Lord Jesus Christ. *p* 9God is faithful, *q* who has called you *r* into fellowship with his Son, Jesus Christ our Lord. *s*

A CHURCH DIVIDED OVER LEADERS

10I appeal to you, brothers and sisters, *t* in the name of our Lord Jesus Christ, that all of you agree with one another in what you say and that there be no divisions among you, *u* but that you be perfectly united *v* in mind and thought. 11My brothers and sisters, some from Chloe's household *w* have informed me that there are quarrels among you. 12What I mean is this: One of you says, "I follow Paul"; *x* another, "I follow Apollos"; *y* another, "I follow Cephas *a*"; *z* still another, "I follow Christ."

13Is Christ divided? Was Paul crucified for you? Were you baptized into *b* the name of Paul? *a* 14I thank God that I did not baptize any of you except Crispus *b* and Gaius, *c* 15so no one can say that you were baptized into my name. 16(Yes, I also baptized the household *d* of Stephanas; *e* beyond that, I don't remember if I baptized anyone else.) 17For Christ did not send me to baptize, *f* but to preach the gospel—not with wisdom *g* and eloquence, lest the cross of Christ be emptied of its power.

a 12 That is, Peter   *b* 13 Or *in*; also in verse 15

1:1 *Paul.* See note on Ro 1:1. *apostle of Christ Jesus.* See notes on Mk 6:30; Heb 3:1. Paul uses this title in all his letters (except Philippians, 1,2 Thessalonians and Philemon) to establish his authority as Christ's messenger—an authority that had been challenged (see ch. 9; 2Co 11). He reinforces his authority by adding "by the will of God" (see 15:9–11; Ac 9:1–16; 13:2; 18:9–10; 22:6–21; 26:12–18). *Sosthenes.* Perhaps the synagogue ruler at Corinth who was assaulted by the Greeks (Ac 18:17). If so, he obviously became a Christian—possibly while Paul was preaching at Corinth (Ac 18:18) or during Apollos's ministry there (Ac 19:1).

1:2 *church of God.* Used only by Paul and only in Ac 20:28, here and in 2Co 1:1. Its OT counterpart is the expression "assembly (or community) of the LORD" (Dt 23:1; see Nu 16:3; 20:4; 1Ch 28:8). *sanctified in Christ Jesus.* Consecrated to the service of God through Christ's saving action in their lives—as Jesus had "sanctified" himself (see Jn 17:19 and note; see also 17:17 and TNIV text note). Such consecration to God's service marks them as "holy" (set apart for God; see Ex 3:5; 19:6; Ro 6:22 and notes) and requires that they be morally "holy" (see Lev 11:44 and note). *everywhere.* See note on 1Th 1:8.

1:3 *Grace and peace.* See Ro 1:7 and note. *Lord Jesus Christ.* See note on 1Th 1:1.

1:4 *thank.* See Ro 1:8 and note.

1:5 *speech and ... knowledge.* Gifts of the Spirit (see 12:8–10 and notes; see also 2Co 8:7).

1:6 *confirming.* Paul's preaching about Christ had been accepted by the Corinthians, and their changed lives had proved it to be true.

1:7 *any spiritual gift.* Probably refers to the spiritual gifts of chs. 12–14. According to those chapters, a "spiritual" gift is some capability given through the Holy Spirit that enables one to minister to the needs of Christ's body, the church

(see 12:7–11; 14:3,12,17). The Greek word used here stresses that it is a gift of grace.

1:8 *He.* God the Father (see v. 9). *end.* Of the age, when Christ comes again. *on the day of our Lord Jesus Christ.* When he returns (v. 7; see Php 1:6 and note).

1:9 *God is faithful.* He may be trusted to do what he has promised (see 1Th 5:24 and note), namely, to keep believers "firm to the end" (v. 8; see note there).

1:10 *brothers and sisters.* See note on Ro 1:13.

1:11 *quarrels.* See Gal 5:20; Jas 4:1–2.

1:12 *Apollos.* He had carried on a fruitful ministry in Corinth (see Ac 18:24—19:1 and notes). *Cephas.* See TNIV text notes here and on Jn 1:42. Those who followed Cephas in Corinth were probably Jewish Christians.

1:13 *Is Christ divided?* See 12:12–13 and notes. *baptized.* Cf. Ro 6:3–4 and note.

1:14 *Crispus.* Probably the synagogue ruler mentioned in Ac 18:8. *Gaius.* Probably the Gaius referred to in Ro 16:23.

1:16 *household.* Other examples of households being baptized are those of Cornelius (Ac 10:24,48), Lydia (Ac 16:15) and the Philippian jailer (Ac 16:33–34). The term may include family members, servants or anyone else who lived in the house (cf. Ge 17:12–13,23). *household of Stephanas.* See 16:15 and note.

1:17 *not ... to baptize.* Paul is not minimizing baptism; rather, he is asserting that his God-given task was primarily to preach. Jesus (Jn 4:2) and Peter (Ac 10:48) also had others baptize for them. *wisdom and eloquence.* Lit. "wisdom of speech." Paul's mission was not to couch the gospel in the language of a trained orator, one who applied the special rhetorical techniques of persuasion that had been developed by the rabbis among the Jews and by the philosophers among the Greeks. *emptied of its power.* On the hearers. The heart of the gospel message would not be affected by such preaching.

CHRIST CRUCIFIED IS GOD'S POWER AND WISDOM

¹⁸For the message of the cross is foolishness ʰ to those who are perishing, ⁱ but to us who are being saved ʲ it is the power of God. ᵏ ¹⁹For it is written:

"I will destroy the wisdom of the wise;
the intelligence of the intelligent I will frustrate." ᵃ ˡ

²⁰Where are the wise? ᵐ Where is the teacher of the law? Where is the philosopher of this age? ⁿ Has not God made foolish ᵒ the wisdom of the world? ²¹For since in the wisdom of God the world ᵖ through its wisdom did not know him, God was pleased through the foolishness of what was preached to save ᑫ those who believe. ʳ ²²Jews demand signs ˢ and Greeks look for wisdom, ²³but we preach Christ crucified: ᵗ a stumbling block ᵘ to Jews and foolishness ᵛ to Gentiles, ²⁴but to those whom God has called, ʷ both Jews and Greeks, Christ the power of God ˣ and the wisdom of God. ʸ ²⁵For the foolishness ᶻ of God is wiser than human wisdom, and the weakness ᵃ of God is stronger than human strength.

²⁶Brothers and sisters, think of what you were when you were called. ᵇ Not many of you were wise ᶜ by human standards; not many were influential; not many were of noble birth. ²⁷But God chose ᵈ the foolish ᵉ things of the world to shame the wise; God chose the weak things of the world to shame the strong. ²⁸God chose the lowly things of this world and the despised things—and the things that are not ᶠ—to nullify the things that are, ²⁹so that no one may boast before him. ᵍ ³⁰It is because of him that you are in Christ Jesus, ʰ who has become for us wisdom from God—that is, our righteousness, ⁱ holiness ʲ and redemption. ᵏ ³¹Therefore, as it is written: "Let those who boast boast in the Lord." ᵇ ˡ

2 And so it was with me, brothers and sisters. When I came to you, I did not come with eloquence or human wisdom ᵐ as I proclaimed to you the testimony about God. ᶜ ²For I resolved to know nothing while I was with you except Jesus Christ and him crucified. ⁿ ³I came to you ᵒ in weakness ᵖ with great fear and trembling. ᑫ ⁴My message and my preaching were not with wise and persuasive words, ʳ but with a demonstration of the Spirit's power, ˢ ⁵so that your faith might not rest on human wisdom, but on God's power. ᵗ

ᵃ 19 Isaiah 29:14   ᵇ 31 Jer. 9:24   ᶜ 1 Some manuscripts as I proclaimed to you God's mystery

2:4 ʳ ver 1 S Ro 15:13   **2:5** ᵗ 2Co 4:7; 6:7

1:18 ʰ ver 21,23,25; 1Co 2:14 / 2Co 2:15; 4:3; 2Th 2:10
ⁱ Ac 2:47 ᵏ ver 24; Ro 1:16
1:19 ˡ Isa 29:14
1:20 ᵐ Isa 19:11,12
ⁿ 1Co 2:6,8; 3:18; 2Co 4:4; Gal 1:4
ᵒ ver 27; Job 12:17; Isa 44:25; Jer 8:9; Ro 1:22; 1Co 3:18,19
1:21 ᵖ ver 27,28; 1Co 6:2; 11:32
ᑫ S Ro 11:14
ʳ S Ro 3:22
1:22 ˢ S Mt 12:38; S Jn 2:11; S 4:48
1:23 ᵗ 1Co 2:2; Gal 3:1 ᵘ S Lk 2:34
ᵛ S ver 18
1:24 ʷ S Ro 8:28
ˣ ver 18; Ro 1:16
ʸ ver 30; S Col 2:3
1:25 ᶻ S ver 18
ᵃ 2Co 13:4
1:26 ᵇ S Ro 8:28
ᶜ ver 20
1:27 ᵈ Jas 2:5
ᵉ ver 20; Ro 1:22; 1Co 3:18,19
1:28 ᶠ Ro 4:17
1:29 ᵍ Eph 2:9
1:30 ʰ S Ro 16:3
ⁱ Jer 23:5,6; 33:16; 2Co 5:21; Php 3:9
ʲ 1Co 1:2 ᵏ S Ro 3:24
1:31 ˡ Jer 9:23,24; Ps 34:2; 44:8; 2Co 10:17
2:1 ᵐ ver 4,13; 1Co 1:17
2:2 ⁿ Gal 6:14; 1Co 1:23
2:3 ᵒ Ac 18:1-18
ᵖ 1Co 4:10; 9:22; 2Co 11:29,30; 12:5,9,10; 13:9 ᑫ S 2Co 7:15

1:19 Paul loosely quotes the Septuagint (pre-Christian Greek) translation of God's word to Jerusalem in Isa 29:14 and has God speak these words again in a new context. *the wise.* Aristides said that on every street in Corinth one met a so-called wise man, who had his own solutions to humanity's problems.

🅰 **1:20** *the wise.* Probably a reference to Gentile philosophers in general. *teacher of the law.* See note on Mt 2:4. *philosopher of this age.* Probably refers to the Greek sophists, who engaged in long and subtle disputes. *God made foolish the wisdom of the world.* All humanly devised philosophical and ideological systems end in meaninglessness because they have a wrong concept of God and his revelation.

1:21 *wisdom . . . foolishness.* Jesus expresses a similar thought in Lk 10:21. It is God's intention that worldly wisdom should not be the means of knowing him. *foolishness of what was preached.* Not that preaching is foolish, but that the message being preached (Christ crucified) is viewed by "the world" (both Jews and Greeks) as foolish.

🅲 **1:22** *Jews demand signs.* They want to see a display of divine power effecting their deliverance (see Mt 12:38; 16:1,4; Mk 8:11-12; Jn 2:18; 6:30). *Greeks look for wisdom.* Specifically, they look for the kind of insight into the workings of the world that would relieve humanity of its woes.

🅲 **1:23** *Christ crucified.* See 2:2. *stumbling block to Jews.* They expected a triumphant, political Messiah (see Ac 1:6 and note), not a crucified one. For use of the metaphor "stumbling block" in reference to the Jews, see Ro 11:9; cf. Ro 9:32-33; 1Pe 2:8. *foolishness to Gentiles.* Greeks and Romans were sure that no reputable person would be crucified, so it was unthinkable that one who was crucified as a criminal could be the world's Savior.

🅰 **1:24** *power.* See Ro 1:4,16. *wisdom.* See v. 30. The crucified Christ is the power and the wisdom of God that saves.

🅰 **1:26-31** The Corinthian Christians were living proof that salvation does not depend on anything in themselves, so that those who are saved can only "boast in the Lord" (v. 31). Their salvation did not spring from the cleverness of human intellect or the centers of human power but from the free grace of God. Compare Paul's elaboration of this theme with the song of Hannah (1Sa 2:1-10) and the song of Mary (Lk 1:46-55).

1:30 *because of him . . . you are in Christ.* It is God who has called you to union and communion with Christ. *in Christ.* See note on Eph 1:1. *righteousness.* It is by faith in Christ that we are justified (declared righteous); see Ro 5:19. *holiness.* See note on v. 2. *redemption.* See note on Ro 3:24.

1:31 See Jer 9:24 and note.

2:1 *brothers and sisters.* See 1:10 and note. *When I came to you.* On his initial trip to Corinth c. A.D. 51 (Ac 18). *with eloquence or human wisdom.* See note on 1:17.

2:2 *know nothing . . . except Jesus Christ.* Paul resolved to make Christ the sole subject of his teaching and preaching while he was with them. *Jesus Christ.* See 1:30. *him crucified.* See 1:17-18,23.

🅰 **2:4** *not with wise and persuasive words.* This does not give preachers a license to neglect study and preparation. Paul's letters reveal a great deal of knowledge in many areas of learning, and his eloquence is apparent in his address before the Areopagus (see Ac 17:22-31 and notes). Paul's point is that unless the Holy Spirit works in a listener's heart, the wisdom and eloquence of a preacher are ineffective. Paul's confidence as a preacher did not rest on intellectual and oratorical ability, as did that of the Jewish rabbis and the Greek orators (see note on 1:17). *demonstration.* The Greek word is used of producing proofs in an argument in court. Paul's preaching was marked by the convincing demonstration of the power of the Holy Spirit.

2:6 ᵘEph 4:13;
Php 3:15; Col 4:12;
Heb 5:14; 6:1; Jas 1:4
ᵛver 8; S 1Co 1:20
ʷPs 146:4
2:7 ˣver 1 ʸRo 16:25
2:8 ᶻver 6;
S 1Co 1:20 ᵃPs 24:7;
Ac 7:2; Jas 2:1
2:9 ᵇIsa 64:4; 65:17
2:10 ᶜS Mt 13:11;
2Co 12:1,7; Gal 1:12;
2:2; Eph 3:3,5
ᵈJn 14:26
2:11 ᵉJer 17:9
ᶠPr 20:27
2:12 ᵍRo 8:15
ʰ1Co 1:20,27; Jas 2:5
2:13 ⁱver 1,4;
1Co 1:17
2:14 ʲJn 14:17
ᵏS 1Co 1:18
2:15 ˡ1Co 3:1;
Gal 6:1
2:16 ᵐIsa 40:13;
S Ro 11:34 ⁿJn 15:15
3:1 ᵒ1Co 2:15
ᵖRo 7:14; 1Co 2:14
�q1Co 14:20
3:2 ʳHeb 5:12-14;
1Pe 2:2 ˢJn 16:12
3:3 ᵗRo 13:13;
1Co 1:11; Gal 5:20
3:4 ᵘ1Co 1:12
3:5 ᵛS Ac 18:24
ʷ1Co 4:1; 2Co 6:4;
Eph 3:7; Col 1:23,25
3:6 ˣAc 18:4-11;
1Co 4:15; 9:1; 15:1

GOD'S WISDOM REVEALED BY THE SPIRIT

⁶We do, however, speak a message of wisdom among the mature, ᵘ but not the wisdom of this age ᵛ or of the rulers of this age, who are coming to nothing. ʷ ⁷No, we declare God's wisdom, a mystery ˣ that has been hidden ʸ and that God destined for our glory before time began. ⁸None of the rulers of this age ᶻ understood it, for if they had, they would not have crucified the Lord of glory. ᵃ ⁹However, as it is written:

> "What no eye has seen,
>   what no ear has heard,
> and what no human mind has conceived—
>   these things God has prepared for those who love him" ᵃ ᵇ—

¹⁰for God has revealed ᶜ them to us by his Spirit. ᵈ

The Spirit searches all things, even the deep things of God. ¹¹For who knows a person's thoughts ᵉ except that person's own spirit ᶠ within? In the same way no one knows the thoughts of God except the Spirit of God. ¹²We have not received the spirit ᵍ of the world ʰ but the Spirit who is from God, that we may understand what God has freely given us. ¹³This is what we speak, not in words taught us by human wisdom ⁱ but in words taught by the Spirit, explaining spiritual realities with Spirit-taught words. ᵇ ¹⁴The person without the Spirit does not accept the things that come from the Spirit of God ʲ but considers them foolishness, ᵏ and cannot understand them because they are discerned only through the Spirit. ¹⁵The person with the Spirit ˡ makes judgments about all things, but such a person is not subject to merely human judgments, ¹⁶for,

> "Who has known the mind of the Lord
>   so as to instruct him?" ᶜ ᵐ

But we have the mind of Christ. ⁿ

THE CHURCH AND ITS LEADERS

3 Brothers and sisters, I could not address you as spiritual ᵒ but as worldly ᵖ—mere infants q in Christ. ²I gave you milk, not solid food, ʳ for you were not yet ready for it. ˢ Indeed, you are still not ready. ³You are still worldly. For since there is jealousy and quarreling ᵗ among you, are you not worldly? Are you not acting like mere human beings? ⁴For when one says, "I follow Paul," and another, "I follow Apollos," ᵘ are you not mere human beings?

⁵What, after all, is Apollos? ᵛ And what is Paul? Only servants, ʷ through whom you came to believe—as the Lord has assigned to each his task. ⁶I planted the seed, ˣ Apollos

---

ᵃ 9 Isaiah 64:4   ᵇ 13 Or *Spirit, interpreting spiritual truths to those who are spiritual*   ᶜ 16 Isaiah 40:13

2:6 *mature.* Wise, developed Christians; contrast the "infants" mentioned in 3:1 (see Heb 5:13—6:3).

2:7 *mystery.* Cf. Ro 11:25; Eph 3:3; 1Ti 3:16 and notes. The secret, or "mystery," was once hidden but is now known because God has revealed it to his people (v. 10). To unbelievers it is still hidden. *for our glory.* God's wisdom will cause every believer to share eventually in Christ's glory (see Ro 8:17 and note). *before time began.* See Ro 8:29–30; Eph 1:4; 1Ti 1:9 and notes; see also Jn 17:24.

2:8 *rulers of this age.* Such as the chief priests (Lk 24:20), Pilate and Herod Antipas (cf. Ac 4:27). *crucified the Lord of glory.* The cross is here contrasted with the majesty of the victim.

2:9 *things God has prepared.* Probably not to be limited to either present or future blessing; both are involved (cf. vv. 7,12).

2:10 *Spirit searches all things.* Not in order to know them, for he knows all things. Instead, he comprehends the depth of God's nature and his plans of grace, so that he is fully competent to make the revelation claimed here. *deep things of God.* See Ro 11:33–36 and note; cf. Rev 2:24.

2:12 *spirit of the world.* Cf. v. 6 ("wisdom of this age"); the spirit of human wisdom as alienated from God—the attitude of the sinful nature (see Ro 8:5–8 and note).

2:13 *words taught by the Spirit.* The message Paul proclaimed was expressed in words given by the Holy Spirit. Thus spiritual truth was aptly combined with Spirit-taught words (but see TNIV text note).

2:14—3:4 This passage explains why many fail to apprehend true wisdom (2:9). It is because such wisdom is perceived only by the Spirit-enlightened (mature) Christian (2:14–16; cf. v. 6). The Corinthians, however, were still worldly (infant) believers (3:1–4), and the proof of their immaturity was their division over human leaders (3:3–4).

2:14 *person without the Spirit.* Described in Jude 19 as one who follows "mere natural instincts" (cf. Ro 8:9). The non-Christian is governed in thought and life by an unrenewed, worldly heart. Such persons are yet untouched by the Holy Spirit and are not equipped to receive appreciatively truth that comes from the Spirit. They need the new birth (see Jn 3:8; Tit 3:5 and notes). *foolishness.* See 1:18.

2:15 *person with the Spirit.* Renewed by the Spirit (mature, v. 6). *not subject to merely human judgments.* One who does not have the Spirit is not qualified to judge anyone who has the Spirit. Thus believers are not rightfully subject to the opinions of unbelievers.

3:1 *Brothers and sisters.* See 1:10 and note. *spiritual.* See note on 2:15. *worldly.* See note on 2:14—3:4.

3:2 *milk, not solid food.* See Heb 5:12–14 and notes.

3:3 *like mere human beings.* Like people of the world instead of people of God. They were following merely human standards.

3:4 *I follow Paul...Apollos.* See 1:12.

3:6 *I planted.* See Ac 18:4–11. Paul's work was of a pioneer nature, preaching where no one had ever preached watered it, but God has been making it grow. [7]So neither the one who plants nor the one who waters is anything, but only God, who makes things grow. [8]The one who plants and the one who waters have one purpose, and they will each be rewarded according to their own labor. [y] [9]For we are God's co-workers; [z] you are God's field, [a] God's building. [b]

[10]By the grace God has given me, [c] I laid a foundation [d] as a wise builder, and someone else is building on it. But each one should build with care. [11]For no one can lay any foundation other than the one already laid, which is Jesus Christ. [e] [12]If anyone builds on this foundation using gold, silver, costly stones, wood, hay or straw, [13]their work will be shown for what it is, [f] because the Day [g] will bring it to light. It will be revealed with fire, and the fire will test the quality of each person's work. [h] [14]If what has been built survives, the builder will receive a reward. [i] [15]If it is burned up, the builder will suffer loss but yet will be saved—even though only as one escaping through the flames. [i]

[16]Don't you know that you yourselves are God's temple [k] and that God's Spirit dwells in your midst? [l] [17]If anyone destroys God's temple, God will destroy that person; for God's temple is sacred, and you together are that temple.

[18]Do not deceive yourselves. If any of you think you are wise [m] by the standards of this age, [n] you should become "fools" so that you may become wise. [19]For the wisdom of this world is foolishness [o] in God's sight. As it is written: "He catches the wise in their craftiness" [a]; [p] [20]and again, "The Lord knows that the thoughts of the wise are futile." [b] [q] [21]So then, no more boasting about human leaders! [r] All things are yours, [s] [22]whether Paul or Apollos [t] or Cephas [u] or the world or life or death or the present or the future [v]—all are yours, [23]and you are of Christ, [w] and Christ is of God.

THE NATURE OF TRUE APOSTLESHIP

4

This, then, is how you ought to regard us: as servants [x] of Christ and as those entrusted [y] with the mysteries [z] God has revealed. [2]Now it is required that those who have been given a trust must prove faithful. [3]I care very little if I am judged by you or by any human court; indeed, I do not even judge myself. [4]My conscience [a] is clear, but that does not make me innocent. [b] It is the Lord who judges me. [c] [5]Therefore judge nothing [d] before the appointed time; wait till the Lord comes. [e] He will bring to light [f] what is hidden in darkness and will expose the motives of people's hearts. At that time each will receive their praise from God. [g]

a [19] Job 5:13   b [20] Psalm 94:11   c [22] That is, Peter

3:8 [y] ver 14; Ps 18:20; 62:12; Mt 25:21; 1Co 9:17
3:9 [z] Mk 16:20; 2Co 6:1; 1Th 3:2 [a] Isa 61:3 [b] Eph 2:20-22; 1Pe 2:5
3:10 [c] S Ro 12:3 [d] Ro 15:20; S Eph 2:20
3:11 [e] Isa 28:16; Eph 2:20
3:13 [f] 1Co 4:5 [g] S 1Co 1:8; 2Th 1:7-10; 2Ti 1:12,18; 4:8 [h] Nu 31:22,23; Jer 23:28,29; Mal 3:3; S 2Th 1:7
3:14 [i] S ver 8
3:15 [j] Jude 23
3:16 [k] 1Co 6:19; 2Co 6:16; Eph 2:21,22; Heb 3:6 [l] S Ro 8:9
3:18 [m] Isa 5:21; 1Co 8:2; Gal 6:3 [n] S 1Co 1:20
3:19 [o] ver 18; Ro 1:22; 1Co 1:20,27 [p] Job 5:13
3:20 [q] Ps 94:11
3:21 [r] 1Co 4:6 [s] Ro 8:32
3:22 [t] ver 5,6 [u] S 1Co 1:12 [v] Ro 8:38
3:23 [w] 1Co 15:23; 2Co 10:7; Gal 3:29
4:1 [x] S 1Co 3:5 [y] 1Co 9:17; Tit 1:7 [z] S Ro 16:25
4:4 [a] S Ac 23:1 [b] Ro 2:13 [c] 2Co 10:18
4:5 [d] S Mt 7:1,2 [e] S 1Th 2:19 [f] Job 12:22; Ps 90:8; 1Co 3:13 [g] S Ro 2:29

before (see 2Co 10:13–16; Ro 15:20–21). *Apollos watered.* See Ac 18:24–28. Apollos worked in the established church, teaching and encouraging the converts Paul had won.

3:9 *God's field.* The people are God's farmland. *God's building.* They are also depicted as God's temple (vv. 16–17). Paul's choice of metaphors accords with the fact that in the ancient world planting the land and building a house (or city or temple) were traditionally the two basic focal points of human industry.

3:10 *I laid a foundation.* By preaching Christ and him crucified (2:2). *someone else.* Apollos—and possibly others.

[A] **3:12** *If anyone builds.* Reference is to those whose position in the church is that of "builders." *gold, silver, costly stones.* Precious, durable work that stands the test of divine judgment; symbolic of pure Christian doctrine and living. *wood, hay or straw.* Worthless work that will not stand the test; symbolic of someone's teaching and life that merely confuses or actually misleads believers.

[A] **3:13** Cf. 4:5; 2Co 5:10 and note. *the Day.* See 1:8 and note. *fire.* God's judgment. The work of some believers will stand the test while that of others will disappear—emphasizing the importance of teaching the pure word of God.

3:15 *loss.* Of reward (v. 14). *as one escaping through the flames.* Perhaps a Greek proverbial phrase, meaning "by a narrow escape," with one's work burned up by the fire of God's holy justice and judgment (cf. Zec 3:2 and note).

[A] **3:16** *God's temple.* Here Paul speaks of the church as "God's temple" (see Eph 2:21–22 and notes). He says, "You yourselves (plural) are God's temple (singular)," and the "you" of v. 17 is also plural. In 6:19 he speaks of each Christian as a temple of the Holy Spirit.

[A] **3:17** *God will destroy that person.* Such a foolish laborer is not one of the Lord's true servants and suffers a worse end than the "builder" of v. 15. In the context of chs. 1–4 Paul here refers to people who tear the local church apart by factions and quarrels concerning their understanding of the gospel (1:11–12). *sacred.* Holy, set apart for God's use and glory (see note on 1:2); so do not desecrate the church by breaking it up into various factions.

3:18 *become "fools."* Turn away from human wisdom (from being "wise by the standards of this age"). Cf. 1:18. *become wise.* Cf. 1:21,24 and notes.

3:21 *about human leaders.* About being some particular "builder's" disciple (see 1:12 and note; 3:4; cf. 1:31; 4:6). *All things are yours.* Because of their relationship to God through Christ (v. 23), they are heirs of all things (see Ro 8:17 and note)—heirs of the ministries of all those who faithfully promote the gospel, and also of everything over which God and Christ hold sovereign rule, namely, all those things that the philosophers of this world claim to have mastered by their wisdom.

[A] **3:23** *you are of Christ.* You are united with and belong to Christ (see 1:30 and note). *Christ is of God.* Christ is in union with God the Father (see Jn 10:30 and note).

4:1 *those entrusted.* The Greek underlying this phrase means "house manager" or "steward." *mysteries.* Things that human wisdom could not discover but that are now revealed by God to his people (see 2:7 and note).

4:5 *appointed time.* When God will judge believers (see 3:13 and note). *expose the motives.* Cf. 1Sa 16:7; 1Ki 8:39; 1Ch 28:9; Ps 139:23–24; Pr 16:2; 21:2; Lk 16:15; Heb 4:12–13.

4:6 *h* 1Co 1:19,31;
3:19,20 *i* 1Co 1:12; 3:4
4:7 *j* Jn 3:27;
Ro 12:3,6
4:8 *k* Rev 3:17,18
4:9 *l* S Ro 8:36
m Ps 71:7; Heb 10:33
4:10 *n* S 1Co 1:18;
Ac 17:18; 26:24
o 1Co 3:18; 2Co 11:19
p S 1Co 2:3
4:11 *q* Ro 8:35;
2Co 11:23-27
4:12 *r* S Ac 18:3
s Ro 12:14; 1Pe 3:9
t S Mt 5:44
4:13 *u* Jer 20:18;
La 3:45
4:14 *v* 1Co 6:5;
15:34; 2Th 3:14
w S 1Th 2:11
4:15 *x* S ver 14
y 1Co 9:12,14,18,23;
15:1
4:16 *z* 1Co 11:1;
Php 3:17; 4:9;
1Th 1:6; 2Th 3:7,9
4:17 *a* 1Co 16:10
b S Ac 16:1 *c* S 1Ti 1:2
d S 1Co 7:17
4:18 *e* Jer 43:2
f ver 21
4:19 *g* 1Co 16:5,6;
2Co 1:15,16
h S Ac 18:21
4:20 *i* Ro 14:17
j S Ro 15:13
4:21 *k* 2Co 1:23; 2:1;
13:2,10
5:1 *l* Lev 18:8;
Dt 22:30; 27:20
5:2 *m* 2Co 7:7-11
n ver 13
5:3 *o* Col 2:5;
1Th 2:17

⁶Now, brothers and sisters, I have applied these things to myself and Apollos for your benefit, so that you may learn from us the meaning of the saying, "Do not go beyond what is written." *h* Then you will not be puffed up in being a follower of one of us over against the other. *i* ⁷For who makes you different from anyone else? What do you have that you did not receive? *j* And if you did receive it, why do you boast as though you did not?

⁸Already you have all you want! Already you have become rich! *k* You have begun to reign—and that without us! How I wish that you really had begun to reign so that we also might reign with you! ⁹For it seems to me that God has put us apostles on display at the end of the procession, like those condemned to die *l* in the arena. We have been made a spectacle *m* to the whole universe, to angels as well as to human beings. ¹⁰We are fools for Christ, *n* but you are so wise in Christ! *o* We are weak, but you are strong! *p* You are honored, we are dishonored! ¹¹To this very hour we go hungry and thirsty, we are in rags, we are brutally treated, we are homeless. *q* ¹²We work hard with our own hands. *r* When we are cursed, we bless; *s* when we are persecuted, *t* we endure it; ¹³when we are slandered, we answer kindly. We have become the scum of the earth, the garbage *u* of the world—right up to this moment.

PAUL'S APPEAL AND WARNING

¹⁴I am writing this not to shame you *v* but to warn you as my dear children. *w* ¹⁵Even if you had ten thousand guardians in Christ, you do not have many fathers, for in Christ Jesus I became your father *x* through the gospel. *y* ¹⁶Therefore I urge you to imitate me. *z* ¹⁷For this reason I have sent to you *a* Timothy, *b* my son *c* whom I love, who is faithful in the Lord. He will remind you of my way of life in Christ Jesus, which agrees with what I teach everywhere in every church. *d*

¹⁸Some of you have become arrogant, *e* as if I were not coming to you. *f* ¹⁹But I will come to you very soon, *g* if the Lord is willing, *h* and then I will find out not only how these arrogant people are talking, but what power they have. ²⁰For the kingdom of God is not a matter of *i* talk but of power. *j* ²¹What do you prefer? Shall I come to you with a rod of discipline, *k* or shall I come in love and with a gentle spirit?

DEALING WITH A CASE OF INCEST

5 It is actually reported that there is sexual immorality among you, and of a kind that even pagans do not tolerate: A man has his father's wife. *l* ²And you are proud! Shouldn't you rather have gone into mourning *m* and have put out of your fellowship *n* the man who has been doing this? ³For my part, even though I am not physically present, I am with you in spirit. *o* As one who is present with you in this way, I have already

---

4:6 *brothers and sisters.* See 1:10 and note. *these things.* See 3:5—4:5. *what is written.* The Corinthian believers should view even Paul and Apollos in light of what the OT has to say about human weakness and limitations. *puffed up.* Pride is one of the root causes of divisions.

4:8 Paul uses irony and sarcasm here to get the Corinthians to see how poor they really are in comparison with apostles because of their haughtiness and spiritual immaturity. *have become rich.* Cf. 1:5; 2Co 9:11. *have begun to reign.* They think they already participate fully in Christ's reign (see Ro 5:17 and note; 2Ti 2:12) and have no need of the apostle's ministry.

4:9 *apostles.* See note on 1:1. *spectacle.* "Theater" is derived from the Greek word used here. Paul refers to the triumphal procession of a victorious Roman general with captives of war bringing up the rear—men condemned to die in the arena in mortal combat with gladiators or with ferocious beasts. He pictures all the world and even angels looking on while the apostles are brought in last to fight to the death.

4:10 More irony. *wise ... strong.* Paul uses different Greek words here from those in 1:24.

4:11–13 A graphic description of Paul's condition right up to the writing of this letter.

4:12 *We work hard with our own hands.* Paul was a tentmaker by trade (see Ac 18:3 and note; cf. 1Co 9:6,18; Ac 20:34–35). *we bless.* See Mt 5:44; Lk 6:28; Ro 12:14 and note. *endure it.* Instead of retaliating.

4:14 *my dear children.* See v. 15.

4:15 *guardians.* See Gal 3:24 and note. *your father.* Cf. 3:6,10.

4:16 *imitate me.* See 11:1 and note.

4:17 *I have sent to you Timothy.* Apparently Timothy had already begun his journey to Corinth by way of Macedonia (see 16:10 and note).

4:18 *Some of you.* Some of the Corinthians who were trying to undercut Paul's authority (see 9:1–3) were teaching that he was unstable (see 2Co 1:17 and note) and that his ministry was worthless (see 2Co 10:10 and note; cf. 12:11–12 and notes).

4:19 *arrogant.* See 5:2 and note.

4:20 *kingdom of God.* God's present reign in the lives of his people (cf. note on Mt 3:2)—that dynamic new life in Christ (see 2Co 5:17 and note), the power of the new birth (Jn 3:3–8), showing itself in a humble life, dedicated to Christ and his mission. *not ... of talk but of power.* Empty talk is contrasted with the genuine power of the Holy Spirit. *power.* Paul returns to the Greek word he used in 1:24.

4:21 *with a rod of discipline.* See 2Co 1:28; 2:1; 13:2,10 and notes.

5:1 *even pagans do not tolerate.* The Roman orator Cicero states that incest was practically unheard of in Roman society. *his father's wife.* That this expression was used rather than "his mother" suggests that the woman was his stepmother. The OT prohibited such sexual relations (see Lev 18:8; Dt 22:30 and notes).

5:2 *proud.* Evidently proud of their liberty—a distortion of grace (cf. Ro 6:1–2 and note on 6:1). *put out of your fellowship.* Excommunicated from the church (cf. Jn 9:22).

passed judgment in the name of our Lord Jesus[p] on the one who has been doing this. [4]So when you are assembled and I am with you in spirit, and the power of our Lord Jesus is present, [5]hand this man over[q] to Satan[r] for the destruction of the sinful nature[a] so that his spirit may be saved on the day of the Lord.[s]

[6]Your boasting is not good.[t] Don't you know that a little yeast[u] leavens the whole batch of dough?[v] [7]Get rid of the old yeast, so that you may be a new unleavened batch—as you really are. For Christ, our Passover lamb, has been sacrificed.[w] [8]Therefore let us keep the Festival, not with the old bread leavened with malice and wickedness, but with the un-leavened bread[x] of sincerity and truth.

[9]I wrote to you in my letter not to associate[y] with sexually immoral people— [10]not at all meaning the people of this world[z] who are immoral, or the greedy and swindlers, or idolaters. In that case you would have to leave this world. [11]But now I am writing to you that you must not associate with any who claim to be fellow believers[a] but are sexually immoral or greedy, idolaters[b] or slanderers, drunkards or swindlers. With such persons do not even eat.[c]

[12]What business is it of mine to judge those outside[d] the church? Are you not to judge those inside?[e] [13]God will judge those outside. "Expel the wicked person from among you."[b][f]

LAWSUITS AMONG BELIEVERS

6 If any of you has a dispute with another, do you dare to take it before the ungod-ly for judgment instead of before the Lord's people?[g] [2]Or do you not know that the Lord's people will judge the world?[h] And if you are to judge the world, are you not competent to judge trivial cases? [3]Do you not know that we will judge angels? How much

---

[a] 5 Or *of his body; or of the flesh*   [b] 13 Deut. 13:5; 17:7; 19:19; 21:21; 22:21,24; 24:7

5:3 [p] 2Th 3:6
5:5 [q] 1Ti 1:20
      [r] s Mt 4:10 [s] S 1Co 1:8
5:6 [t] Jas 4:16
      [u] Mt 16:6,12 [v] Gal 5:9
5:7 [w] Ex 12:3-6,21;
Mk 14:12; 1Pe 1:19
5:8 [x] Ex 12:14,15;
Dt 16:3
5:9 [y] Eph 5:11;
2Th 3:6,14
5:10 [z] 1Co 10:27
5:11 [a] S Ro 7:1
      [b] 1Co 10:7,14
      c S Ro 16:17
5:12 [d] S Mk 4:11
      [e] ver 3-5; 1Co 6:1-4
5:13 [f] Dt 13:5; 17:7;
19:19; 22:21,24; 24:7;
Jdg 20:13
6:1 [g] Mt 18:17
6:2 [h] Mt 19:28;
Lk 22:30; 1Co 5:12

5:3 *in the name of our Lord Jesus.* By his authority.

5:4 *the power of our Lord Jesus is present.* Jesus' power is present through his word and his Holy Spirit.

5:5 *hand this man over to Satan.* Abandon this sinful man to the devil, that he may afflict him as he pleases. This abandonment to Satan was to be accomplished not by some magical incantation but by expelling the man from the church (see v. 13; see also vv. 2,7,11). To expel him was to put him out in the devil's territory, severed from any connection with God's people. *for the destruction of the sinful nature.* So that being officially ostracized from the church will cause the man such anguish that he will repent and forsake his wicked way. For an alternative interpretation, see TNIV text note. In the latter view, Satan is allowed to bring physical affliction on the man, which would bring him to repentance. *his spirit . . . saved.* Cf. 3:15. *day of the Lord.* When Christ returns (see 1:7).

A **5:6** *a little yeast . . . the whole batch of dough.* To illustrate Christian holiness and discipline, Paul alludes to the prohibition against the use of leaven (or yeast) in the bread eaten in the Passover Festival (see Ex 12:15 and note). Leaven in Scripture usually symbolizes evil or sin (see Mk 8:15 and note), and the church here is called on to get rid of the yeast of sin (v. 8) because its members are an unleavened batch of dough—new creations in Christ (see 2Co 5:17 and note).

A **5:7** *Get rid of the old yeast.* Perhaps refers to the Passover custom of sweeping all the (leavened) bread crumbs out of one's house before preparing the Passover meal. *a new unleavened batch—as you really are.* Already sanctified in God's sight (see 1:2 and note; 6:11), Paul calls on them to become holy in conduct. *Christ, our Passover lamb.* In his death on the cross, Christ fulfilled the true meaning of the Jewish sacrifice of the Passover lamb (cf. Jn 1:29 and note). Christ, the Lamb of God, was crucified on Passover day, a celebration that began the evening before when the Passover meal was eaten (cf. Ex 12:8).

A **5:8** *let us keep the Festival.* Keeping the Festival of Unleavened Bread (which followed Passover; see chart, pp. 180–181) symbolized living the Christian life in holy dedication to God and not getting involved in such sins as malice, wickedness and incestuous relations.

5:9 *I wrote to you in my letter.* Paul here clarifies a previous let-ter (one not preserved). Some in the Corinthian church mistook that letter to mean that, on separating from sin, they should disassociate themselves from all immoral persons, including non-Christian people. Instead, Paul meant that they should separate from immoral persons who were affiliated with the church (vv. 10–11).

5:10–11 See note on Ro 1:29–31.

A **5:11** *With such persons do not even eat.* Calling oneself a Christian while continuing to live an immoral life is reprehensible and degrading and gives a false testimony to Christ. If the true Christian has intimate association with someone who does this, the non-Christian world may assume that the church approves such immoral, ungodly living, and thus the name of Christ would be dishonored. Questions could arise concerning the true character of the Christian's own testimony (cf. Ro 16:17–18; see also 2Th 3:6,14–15 and notes).

A **5:12** *judge those inside.* The church is to exercise spiritual discipline over the professing believers in the church (cf. Mt 18:15–18), but it is not to attempt to judge those outside its membership. There are governing authorities in place to judge them (see Ro 13:1–5 and notes), and their ultimate judge is God (v. 13; cf. Rev 20:11–15).

6:1 *a dispute with another.* Paul seems to be talking about various kinds of civil court cases here (cf. the phrase "rather be cheated," v. 7), not criminal cases that should be handled by the state (Ro 13:3–4). *before the Lord's people.* The Corinthians should take their civil cases before qualified Christians for settlement. In Paul's day the Romans allowed the Jews to apply their own law in such matters, and since the Romans did not yet consider Christians as a separate class from the Jews, Christians no doubt had the same rights.

A **6:2** *the Lord's people will judge the world.* As those who share in Christ's reign (cf. Mt 19:28; 2Ti 2:12; Rev 20:4). *competent to judge trivial cases.* Paul views believers as fully competent to judge cases where Christians have claims against each other, because they view matters from a godly vantage point. In comparison with their future role in the judgment of the world and of angels (v. 3), judgments concerning things of this life are insignificant.

6:3 *we will judge angels.* Cf. 2Pe 2:4,9; Jude 6.

6:5 / S 1Co 4:14
/ Ac 1:15
6:6 ᵏ S Ro 7:1
/ 2Co 6:14,15; 1Ti 5:8
6:7 ᵐ Mt 5:39,40
6:8 ⁿ 1Th 4:6
6:9 º S Mt 25:34
ᵖ Job 13:9; 1Co 15:33;
Gal 6:7; Jas 1:16
ᵠ Lev 18:20; Dt 22:22
ʳ Lev 18:22
6:10 ˢ 1Ti 1:10;
Rev 21:8; 22:15
6:11 ᵗ S Eph 2:2
ᵘ S Ac 22:16 ᵛ 1Co 1:2
ʷ S Ro 4:25
6:12 ˣ 1Co 10:23
6:13 ʸ Col 2:22
ᶻ ver 15,19; Ro 12:1
6:14 ᵃ S Ac 2:24
ᵇ S Ro 6:5; Eph 1:19,
20; 1Th 4:16
6:15 ᶜ S Ro 12:5
6:16 ᵈ Ge 2:24;
Mt 19:5; Eph 5:31
6:17 ᵉ Jn 17:21-23;
Ro 8:9-11; Gal 2:20
6:18 ᶠ ver 9; 1Co 5:1;
2Co 12:21; Gal 5:19;
Eph 5:3; 1Th 4:3,4;
Heb 13:4 ᵍ Ro 6:12
6:19 ʰ Jn 2:21

more the things of this life! ⁴Therefore, if you have disputes about such matters, do you ask for a ruling from those whose way of life is scorned in the church? ⁵I say this to shame you. ᶦ Is it possible that there is nobody among you wise enough to judge a dispute between believers? ʲ ⁶But instead, one brother ᵏ goes to law against another—and this in front of unbelievers! ᶦ

⁷The very fact that you have lawsuits among you means you have been completely defeated already. Why not rather be wronged? Why not rather be cheated? ᵐ ⁸Instead, you yourselves cheat and do wrong, and you do this to your brothers and sisters. ⁿ ⁹Or do you not know that wrongdoers will not inherit the kingdom of God? º Do not be deceived: ᵖ Neither the sexually immoral nor idolaters nor adulterers ᵠ nor male prostitutes nor practicing homosexuals ʳ ¹⁰nor thieves nor the greedy nor drunkards nor slanderers nor swindlers ˢ will inherit the kingdom of God. ¹¹And that is what some of you were. ᵗ But you were washed, ᵘ you were sanctified, ᵛ you were justified ʷ in the name of the Lord Jesus Christ and by the Spirit of our God.

SEXUAL IMMORALITY

¹²"I have the right to do anything," you say—but not everything is beneficial. ˣ "I have the right to do anything"—but I will not be mastered by anything. ¹³You say, "Food for the stomach and the stomach for food, and God will destroy them both." ʸ The body, however, is not meant for sexual immorality but for the Lord, ᶻ and the Lord for the body. ¹⁴By his power God raised the Lord from the dead, ᵃ and he will raise us also. ᵇ ¹⁵Do you not know that your bodies are members of Christ himself? ᶜ Shall I then take the members of Christ and unite them with a prostitute? Never! ¹⁶Do you not know that he who unites himself with a prostitute is one with her in body? For it is said, "The two will become one flesh." ᵃ ᵈ ¹⁷But whoever is united with the Lord is one with him in spirit. ᵇ ᵉ

¹⁸Flee from sexual immorality. ᶠ All other sins people commit are outside their bodies, but those who sin sexually sin against their own bodies. ᵍ ¹⁹Do you not know that your bodies are temples ʰ of the Holy Spirit, who is in you, whom you have received from

---

ᵃ 16 Gen. 2:24   ᵇ 17 Or *in the Spirit*

6:4 *those whose way of life is scorned in the church.* The verse asks ironically whether believers should submit their cases to pagan judges, who really are not qualified to decide on cases between Christians.

A **6:7** *completely defeated already.* Most likely by greed, retaliation and hatred, instead of practicing unselfishness, forgiveness and love—even willingness to suffer loss.

6:9–10 See Ro 1:29–31 and note.

A **6:9** *not inherit the kingdom of God.* See Eph 5:5. *sexually immoral.* Paul here identifies three kinds of sexually immoral persons: adulterers, male prostitutes and males who practice homosexuality. In Ro 1:26 he adds the category of females who practice homosexuality. People who engage in such practices, as well as the other offenders listed in vv. 9–10, are explicitly excluded from God's kingdom (but see next note).

A **6:11** *some of you were. But.* God, however, does save and sanctify people like those described in vv. 9–10. *sanctified.* See 1:2 and note. *justified.* See Ro 3:24 and note.

6:12 *"I have the right to do anything."* Paul is quoting some in the Corinthian congregation who boasted that they had a right to do anything they pleased (see v. 13; 7:1; 10:23 and notes). The apostle counters by observing that such "freedom" of action may not benefit the Christian. *not be mastered by anything.* One may become enslaved by those actions in which one "freely" chooses to indulge.

6:13 *"Food for the stomach and the stomach for food, and God will destroy them both."* Paul quotes some Corinthians again who were claiming that as the physical acts of eating and digesting food have no bearing on one's spiritual life, so the physical act of promiscuous sexual activity does not affect one's spiritual life. *The body... is not meant for sexual immorality, but for the Lord.* Paul here declares the dignity of the human body: It is intended for the Lord. Although granting that food and the stomach are transitory, Paul denies that what one does with one's body is unimportant. This is particularly true of the use of

sex, which the Lord has appointed for use in the man-woman relationship in marriage (see 7:2–5; cf. Heb 13:4).

6:14 *God raised the Lord... us also.* As an illustration of God's high regard for the body, Paul cites the resurrection of Christ's body and, eventually, of the believer's body (see 15:51–53; 1Th 4:16–17). A body destined for resurrection should not be used for immorality.

6:15 *members of Christ.* See 12:27. It is not merely the spirit that is a member of Christ's body; it is the whole person, consisting of spirit and body. This fact gives dignity to the human body.

A **6:16** *one with her in body.* In a sexual relationship the two bodies become one (cf. Ge 2:24; Mt 19:4–5), and a new human being may emerge from the sexual union. Sexual relations outside the marriage bond are a gross perversion of the divinely established marriage union.

A **6:17** *one with him in spirit.* There is a higher union than the marriage bond: the believer's spiritual union with Christ, which is the perfect model for the kind of unity that should mark the marriage relationship (cf. Eph 5:21–33 and notes on 5:23,32).

A **6:18** *Flee.* The Greek for this imperative may suggest that one must continually run away from sexual sinning (advice particularly needed in Corinth). Cf. Gen 39:12; 2Ti 2:22. *those who sin sexually sin against their own bodies.* The body is a temple of the Holy Spirit (v. 19); thus to use it in prostitution (see notes on Ge 20:9; Ex 34:15) disgraces God's temple. Furthermore, the prostitutes of Corinth were dedicated to the service of Aphrodite, the goddess of love and sex (see note on 7:2; see also Introduction: The City of Corinth).

A **6:19** *your bodies are temples of the Holy Spirit.* Cf. note on 3:16. Their bodies are therefore sacred and are to be treated as sacred (holy). Christians should also realize that by the Spirit's presence and power they can be helped against such sins as sexual immorality (Ro 8:9). *not your own.* Cf. 1Pe 2:9 and note.

God? You are not your own;[i] [20]you were bought at a price.[j] Therefore honor God with your bodies.[k]

CONCERNING MARRIED LIFE

7 Now for the matters you wrote about: "It is good for a man not to have sexual relations with a woman."[l] [2]But since sexual immorality is occurring, each man should have sexual relations with his own wife, and each woman with her own husband. [3]The husband should fulfill his marital duty to his wife,[m] and likewise the wife to her husband. [4]The wife does not have authority over her own body but yields it to her husband. In the same way, the husband does not have authority over his own body but yields it to his wife. [5]Do not deprive each other except perhaps by mutual consent and for a time,[n] so that you may devote yourselves to prayer. Then come together again so that Satan[o] will not tempt you[p] because of your lack of self-control. [6]I say this as a concession, not as a command.[q] [7]I wish that all of you were as I am.[r] But each of you has your own gift from God; one has this gift, another has that.[s]

[8]Now to the unmarried[a] and the widows I say: It is good for them to stay unmarried, as I do.[t] [9]But if they cannot control themselves, they should marry,[u] for it is better to marry than to burn with passion.

[10]To the married I give this command (not I, but the Lord): A wife must not separate from her husband.[v] [11]But if she does, she must remain unmarried or else be reconciled to her husband.[w] And a husband must not divorce his wife.

[12]To the rest I say this (I, not the Lord):[x] If any brother has a wife who is not a believer and she is willing to live with him, he must not divorce her. [13]And if a woman has a husband who is not a believer and he is willing to live with her, she must not divorce him. [14]For the unbelieving husband has been sanctified through his wife, and the unbelieving wife has been sanctified through her believing husband. Otherwise your children would be unclean, but as it is, they are holy.[y]

[15]But if the unbeliever leaves, let it be so. The brother or sister is not bound in such circumstances; God has called us to live in peace.[z] [16]How do you know, wife, whether you will save[a] your husband?[b] Or, how do you know, husband, whether you will save your wife?

a 8 Or *widowers*

6:19 [i] Ro 14:7, 8
6:20 [j] Ps 74:2;
S Mt 20:28; Ac 20:28;
1Co 7:23; Rev 5:9;
14:4 [k] Php 1:20
7:1 [l] ver 8, 26
7:3 [m] Ex 21:10;
1Pe 3:7
7:5 [n] Ex 19:15;
1Sa 21:4, 5 [o] S Mt 4:10
[p] 1Th 3:5
7:6 [q] 2Co 8:8
7:7 [r] ver 8; 1Co 9:5
[s] Mt 19:11, 12; Ro 12:6;
1Co 12:4, 11
7:8 [t] ver 1, 26
7:9 [u] 1Ti 5:14
7:10 [v] Mal 2:14-16;
S Lk 16:18
7:11 [w] ver 39;
Ro 7:2, 3
7:12 [x] ver 6, 10;
2Co 11:17
7:14 [y] Mal 2:15
7:15 [z] S Ro 14:19;
1Co 14:33
7:16 [a] S Ro 11:14
[b] 1Pe 3:1

6:20 *bought at a price.* See 7:23 and note. *honor God with your bodies.* Cf. 10:31; Ro 6:12–13 and notes.

7:1 *matters you wrote about.* The Corinthians had written Paul, asking him a number of vexing questions (see 8:1; 12:1; 16:1). *"It is good for a man not to have sexual relations with a woman."* The best understanding of this statement is that Paul is again (see notes on 6:12–13,18) quoting a slogan of the Corinthians. He refutes this idea in v. 2 by stating that sexual relations have their proper expression in marriage.

7:2 *sexual immorality.* Example: The temple to Aphrodite on the Acrocorinth, the rocky eminence above Corinth, at one time had in service 1,000 priestess prostitutes (see note on 6:18).

7:3 *fulfill…marital duty.* Married couples should have regular sexual relations. Permanent abstention deprives the other partner of his or her natural right.

7:4 *In the same way.* Both husband and wife have conjugal rights and exclusive possession of the other in this area.

7:5 *Do not deprive each other.* Of sexual fulfillment. *Satan …not tempt you because of your lack of self-control.* The Christian deprived of regular sexual activity with his or her marriage partner may be tempted by Satan to sexual immorality. The normal God-given sexual drive in the human being is strong.

7:6 *I say this.* See v. 2. *concession, not as a command.* Although marriage is desirable and according to God's plan, it is not mandatory under all circumstances (see vv. 25–38).

7:7 *as I am.* Unmarried. Paul views his celibate lifestyle as a "gift from God" that made it possible for him to accept his unmarried state and use it in the service of his Lord.

7:10 *I give this command (not I, but the Lord).* Paul is citing a

command from the Lord Jesus during his earthly ministry that married couples must stay together (Mt 5:32; 19:3–9; Mk 10:2–12; Lk 16:18). Paul probably heard about such commands from other disciples (cf. Gal 1:18–19).

7:11 *But if she does, she must remain unmarried or else be reconciled.* Paul argues that in the light of Christ's command she (or he) is not to marry again. Rather, the separated or divorced couple is to be reconciled. Clearly the ideal is that marriage should not be permanently disrupted.

7:12 *I say this (I, not the Lord).* Paul is not quoting a direct command from Jesus here. *any brother has a wife…not a believer.* The apostle is talking here (and in v. 13) about couples already married, when one of them becomes a Christian. If at all possible, they should remain together, unless the unbeliever, whether man or woman, refuses to remain (v. 15).

7:14 *sanctified through his wife…sanctified through her believing husband.* These words of Paul are among those that are "hard to understand" (2Pe 3:16). Paul here affirms that, within the marriage relationship, unbelieving marriage partners in some sense participate with their believing spouse in the quality of being consecrated to God's service ("sanctified"; see 1:2 and note)—at least to the effect that the children born of their union are "holy" (consecrated to God's service). Some believe that such children are called holy because they are included with their parents in the new covenant in Christ, just as the children of Abraham were included in the covenant with their father (and so were circumcised).

7:15 *The brother or sister is not bound in such circumstances.* The believer is not under obligation to try to continue living with the unbeliever. *live in peace.* If the unbeliever were forced to live with the believer, there would be no peace in the home.

7:17 ᶜ Ro 12:3
ᵈ 1Co 4:17; 14:33;
2Co 8:18; 11:28
7:18 ᵉ Ac 15:1,2
7:19 ᶠ Ro 2:25-27;
Gal 5:6; 6:15; Col 3:11
7:20 ᵍ ver 24
7:22 ʰ Jn 8:32,36
ⁱ S Ro 6:22
7:23 ʲ S 1Co 6:20
7:24 ᵏ ver 20
7:25 ˡ ver 6; 2Co 8:8
ᵐ 2Co 4:1; 1Ti 1:13,16
7:26 ⁿ ver 1,8
7:27 ᵒ ver 20,21
7:28 ᵖ ver 36
7:29 �q ver 31;
S Ro 13:11,12
7:31 ʳ ver 29;
S Heb 12:27
7:32 ˢ 1Ti 5:5
7:34 ᵗ Lk 2:37
7:35 ᵘ Ps 86:11

CONCERNING CHANGE OF STATUS

¹⁷Nevertheless, each of you should live as a believer in whatever situation the Lord has assigned to you, just as God has called you. ᶜ This is the rule I lay down in all the churches. ᵈ ¹⁸Was a man already circumcised when he was called? He should not become uncircumcised. Was a man uncircumcised when he was called? He should not be circumcised. ᵉ ¹⁹Circumcision is nothing and uncircumcision is nothing. ᶠ Keeping God's commands is what counts. ²⁰Each of you should remain in the situation you were in when God called you. ᵍ

²¹Were you a slave when you were called? Don't let it trouble you—although if you can gain your freedom, do so. ²²For those who were slaves when called to faith in the Lord are the Lord's freed people; ʰ similarly, those who were free when called are Christ's slaves. ⁱ ²³You were bought at a price; ʲ do not become slaves of human beings. ²⁴Brothers and sisters, all of you, as responsible to God, should remain in the situation in which God called you. ᵏ

CONCERNING THE UNMARRIED

²⁵Now about virgins: I have no command from the Lord, ˡ but I give a judgment as one who by the Lord's mercy ᵐ is trustworthy. ²⁶Because of the present crisis, I think that it is good for a man to remain as he is. ⁿ ²⁷Are you pledged to a woman? Do not seek to be released. Are you free from such a commitment? Do not look for a wife. ᵒ ²⁸But if you do marry, you have not sinned; ᵖ and if a virgin marries, she has not sinned. But those who marry will face many troubles in this life, and I want to spare you this.

²⁹What I mean, brothers and sisters, is that the time is short. q From now on those who are married should live as if they were not; ³⁰those who mourn, as if they did not; those who are happy, as if they were not; those who buy something, as if it were not theirs to keep; ³¹those who use the things of the world, as if not engrossed in them. For this world in its present form is passing away. ʳ

³²I would like you to be free from concern. An unmarried man is concerned about the Lord's affairs ˢ—how he can please the Lord. ³³But a married man is concerned about the affairs of this world—how he can please his wife— ³⁴and his interests are divided. An unmarried woman or virgin is concerned about the Lord's affairs: Her aim is to be devoted to the Lord in both body and spirit. ᵗ But a married woman is concerned about the affairs of this world—how she can please her husband. ³⁵I am saying this for your own good, not to restrict you, but that you may live in a right way in undivided ᵘ devotion to the Lord.

³⁶If anyone is worried that he might not be acting honorably toward the virgin he is

---

7:17 *live … in whatever situation the Lord has assigned to you.* Christians are to live confidently for the Lord in whatever station in life God has placed them. See v. 18 for an example. No change of status that anyone brings about by their own action can advance their salvation.

7:18 *circumcised … uncircumcised.* Jew … Gentile. In the religious sphere, Christian Jews should not undo their circumcision, and Christian Gentiles should not yield to Jewish pressure for circumcision (cf. Ac 15:1–5; Gal 5:1–3).

7:19 See Gal 5:6 and note.

7:21 *Were you a slave …?* In the social and economic sphere, Christian slaves should live contentedly in their situation, realizing that they have become free in Christ (v. 22; Jn 8:32,36). *if you can gain your freedom, do so.* If Christian slaves have an opportunity to get their freedom, they should take advantage of it. In the Roman empire slaves were sometimes freed by Roman patricians. There is nothing wrong with seeking to improve one's social condition, but this will have no bearing on one's standing with God.

7:22 *are the Lord's freed people.* Have been set free from bondage to sin (see Ro 6:18,22; Heb 9:15 and notes; cf. Jn 8:34,36; 1Pe 2:16) and are therefore free to serve Christ as his "slaves"—just as the Israelites were set free from Egyptian bondage so that in freedom they could become the servant people of God (see Ex 6:6–7; 19:4–6).

7:23 *bought at a price … not … slaves of human beings.* Christians in all stations of life should realize that their ultimate allegiance is to Christ, who bought them with his blood (see 6:20; 1Pe 1:18–19 and note on 1:18).

7:25 *Now about virgins.* Paul answers another major question the Corinthians had asked (v. 1). *I give a judgment as one who … is trustworthy.* Paul is not giving a direct command from Jesus here (as in v. 10; cf. Ac 20:35 and note). In this matter, which is not a question of right and wrong, Paul expresses his own judgment. Even though he puts it this way, he is certainly not denying that he wrote under the influence of divine inspiration (see v. 40 and note). And since he writes under inspiration, what he recommends is clearly the better course of action.

7:26 *present crisis.* Probably a reference to the pressures in the Christian life in an immoral and particularly hostile environment (cf. vv. 2,28; 5:1; 2Ti 3:12). Paul's recommendation here (see also v. 27) does not apply to all times and all situations.

7:28 *many troubles.* Times of suffering and persecution for Christ, when being married would mean even greater hardship in taking care of one's family.

7:29–31 Christians already live under the foreshadowings of Christ's return, when the world in its present form will pass away. For this reason, believers should not treat present realities as having ultimate significance.

7:29 *brothers and sisters.* See note on Ro 1:13.

7:31 *this world … is passing away.* Cf. 1Jn 2:17.

7:34 *his interests are divided.* He cannot give undistracted service to Christ (v. 35). This is particularly true in times of persecution.

7:36 *not … acting honorably toward the virgin he is engaged to … getting beyond the usual age for marrying … They should get married.* In the light of hostility toward believers in Corinth, a man might refrain from marrying his fiancée. But if he then realizes that his fiancée is getting beyond her prime marriageable engaged to, and if she is getting beyond the usual age for marrying[a] and he feels he ought to marry, he should do as he wants. He is not sinning. [v] They should get married. [37]But the man who has settled the matter in his own mind, who is under no compulsion but has control over his own will, and who has made up his mind not to marry the virgin—this man also does the right thing. [38]So then, he who marries the virgin does right, [w] but he who does not marry her does better. [b]

[39]A woman is bound to her husband as long as he lives. [x] But if her husband dies, she is free to marry anyone she wishes, but he must belong to the Lord. [y] [40]In my judgment, [z] she is happier if she stays as she is—and I think that I too have the Spirit of God.

CONCERNING FOOD SACRIFICED TO IDOLS

8 Now about food sacrificed to idols: [a] We know that "We all possess knowledge." [b] But knowledge puffs up while love builds up. [2]Those who think they know something [c] do not yet know as they ought to know. [d] [3]But whoever loves God is known by God. [c] [e]

[4]So then, about eating food sacrificed to idols: [f] We know that "An idol is nothing at all in the world" [g] and that "There is no God but one." [h] [5]For even if there are so-called gods, [i] whether in heaven or on earth (as indeed there are many "gods" and many "lords"), [6]yet for us there is but one God, [j] the Father, [k] from whom all things came [l] and for whom we live; and there is but one Lord, [m] Jesus Christ, through whom all things came [n] and through whom we live.

[7]But not everyone possesses this knowledge. [o] Some people are still so accustomed to idols that when they eat sacrificial food they think of it as having been sacrificed to a god, and since their conscience is weak, [p] it is defiled. [8]But food does not bring us near to God; [q] we are no worse if we do not eat, and no better if we do.

[9]Be careful, however, that the exercise of your rights does not become a stumbling block [r] to the weak. [s] [10]For if anyone with a weak conscience sees you, with all your knowledge, eating in an idol's temple, won't they be emboldened to eat what is sacrificed to

---

[a] 36 Or *if his (or her) passions are too strong*   [b] 36-38 Or [36]*If anyone thinks he is not treating his daughter properly, and if she is getting along in years (or if her passions are too strong), and he feels he ought to marry, he should do as he wants. He is not sinning. He should let her get married.* [37]*But the man who has settled the matter in his own mind, who is under no compulsion but has control over his own will, and who has made up his mind to keep the virgin unmarried—this man also does the right thing.* [38]*So then, he who gives his virgin in marriage does right, but he who does not give her in marriage does better.*   [c] 2,3 An early manuscript and another ancient witness *think they have knowledge do not yet know as they ought to know.* [3]*But whoever loves truly knows.*

7:36 [v] ver 28
7:38 [w] Heb 13:4
7:39 [x] Ro 7:2,3
[y] 2Co 6:14
7:40 [z] ver 25
8:1 [a] ver 4,7,10;
Ac 15:20 [b] Ro 15:14
8:2 [c] 1Co 3:18
[d] 1Co 13:8,9,12;
1Ti 6:4
8:3 [e] Jer 1:5;
Ro 8:29; Gal 4:9
8:4 [f] ver 1,7,10;
Ex 34:15 [g] Ac 14:15;
1Co 10:19; Gal 4:8
[h] ver 6; Dt 6:4;
Ps 86:10; Eph 4:6;
1Ti 2:5
8:5 [i] 2Th 2:4
8:6 [j] S ver 4
[k] Mal 2:10 [l] S Ro 11:36
[m] Eph 4:5 [n] S Jn 1:3
8:7 [o] ver 1
[p] Ro 14:14; 1Co 10:28
8:8 [q] Ro 14:17
8:9 [r] S 2Co 6:3;
Gal 5:13 [s] Ro 14:1

---

age and the situation thus seems unfair to her, it is perfectly proper for them to get married.

7:37 *has control over his own will . . . does the right thing.* The man who determines that there is no need for him to marry his fiancée under the circumstances has made a good decision too (v. 38). Paul may be referring to a man who has control of his passions, as in v. 7 (cf. v. 9).

7:39 *bound to her husband as long as he lives.* Marriage is a lifelong union (yet see the exception clause in Mt 19:9). *if her husband dies.* Death breaks the marriage bond, and a Christian is then free to marry another Christian ("he must belong to the Lord").

7:40 *as she is.* A widow. *I think that I too have the Spirit of God.* Paul writes as one convinced that he is guided by the Holy Spirit. **8:1—11:1** Cf. Ro 14:1—15:13 and notes.

8:1 *Now about food.* Another matter the Corinthians had written about (see 7:1 and note). *sacrificed to idols.* Offered on pagan altars. Meat left over from a sacrifice might be eaten by the priests, eaten by the offerer and his friends at a feast in the temple (see note on v. 10) or sold in the public meat market. Some Christians felt that if they ate such meat they participated in pagan worship and thus compromised their testimony for Christ. Other Christians did not feel this way. *knowledge.* Explained in vv. 2–6. *knowledge puffs up.* It fills one with false pride. *love builds up.* Explained in vv. 7–13. **8:2** *do not yet know.* Even the wisest and most knowledgeable among Christians have only limited knowledge. God is the only one who knows all (cf. Ro 11:33–36).

8:3 *whoever loves God is known by God.* Not their knowledge as such but their love for God is what counts; their love is a mani-

festation that God has accepted them and has dealt with them as among his own (see Ga 4:9). The background of Paul's assertion is very likely the OT use of Hebrew *yada'* ("to know") in such passages as Ge 18:19 ("have chosen"); 2Sa 7:20; Ps 1:6 ("watches over"); Am 3:2 ("have I chosen"); Na 1:7 ("cares for").

8:4 *An idol is nothing.* It represents no real god and possesses no power (see Ps 115:4–7; 135:15–17; Isa 44:12–20). But there are demons behind them (10:20).

8:5 *so-called gods.* The gods of Greek and Roman mythology.

8:6 *one God.* See Dt 6:4 and note. *from whom all things came . . . through whom all things came.* See Heb 2:10. God the Father is the ultimate source of all creation (Ac 4:24; Ro 11:36). God the Son is the dynamic one through whom, with the Father, all things came into existence (see Jn 1:3; Col 1:16 and note; Heb 1:2).

8:7 *possesses this knowledge.* Knows that an idol is an empty symbol, representing no real divine being. *sacrificed to a god.* Sacrificed to the god the idol represents. *since their conscience is weak, it is defiled.* They think that in eating meat sacrificed on pagan altars they have involved themselves in pagan worship and thus have sinned against Christ.

8:9 *your rights.* To eat meat sacrificed to idols because you know that an idol is nothing (v. 4). *the weak.* Those Christians whose consciences are weak, who think it is wrong to eat meat sacrificed to idols.

8:10 *your knowledge.* See vv. 1,4,8. *eating in an idol's temple.* At the site of ancient Corinth, archaeologists have discovered two temples containing rooms apparently used for pagan feasts where meat offered to idols was eaten. To such feasts Christians may have been invited by pagan friends.

idols? *t* 11So this weak brother or sister, for whom Christ died, is destroyed *u* by your knowledge. 12When you sin against them *v* in this way and wound their weak conscience, you sin against Christ. *w* 13Therefore, if what I eat causes my brother or sister to fall into sin, I will never eat meat again, so that I will not cause them to fall. *x*

PAUL'S RIGHTS AS AN APOSTLE

9 Am I not free? *y* Am I not an apostle? *z* Have I not seen Jesus our Lord? *a* Are you not the result of my work in the Lord? *b* 2Even though I may not be an apostle to others, surely I am to you! For you are the seal *c* of my apostleship in the Lord.

3This is my defense to those who sit in judgment on me. 4Don't we have the right to food and drink? *d* 5Don't we have the right to take a believing wife *e* along with us, as do the other apostles and the Lord's brothers *f* and Cephas *a*? *g* 6Or is it only I and Barnabas *h* who don't have the right not to work for a living?

7Who serves as a soldier *i* at his own expense? Who plants a vineyard *j* and does not eat of its grapes? Who tends a flock and does not drink of the milk? 8Do I say this merely on human authority? Doesn't the Law say the same thing? 9For it is written in the Law of Moses: "Do not muzzle an ox while it is treading out the grain." *b k* Is it about oxen that God is concerned? *l* 10Surely he says this for us, doesn't he? Yes, this was written for us, *m* because when farmers plow and thresh, they should be able to do so in the hope of sharing in the harvest. *n* 11If we have sown spiritual seed among you, is it too much if we reap a material harvest from you? *o* 12If others have this right of support from you, shouldn't we have it all the more?

But we did not use this right. *p* On the contrary, we put up with anything rather than hinder *q* the gospel of Christ.

13Don't you know that those who serve in the temple get their food from the temple, and that those who serve at the altar share in what is offered on the altar? *r* 14In the same way, the Lord has commanded that those who preach the gospel should receive their living from the gospel. *s*

15But I have not used any of these rights. *t* And I am not writing this in the hope that you will do such things for me, for I would rather die than allow anyone to deprive me of this boast. *u* 16For when I preach the gospel, I cannot boast, since I am compelled to preach. *v* Woe to me if I do not preach the gospel! 17If I preach voluntarily, I have a reward; *w* if not voluntarily, I am simply discharging the trust committed to me. *x* 18What then is my reward? Just this: that in preaching the gospel I may offer it free of charge, *y* and so not misuse my rights *z* as a preacher of the gospel.

a 5 That is, Peter   *b* 9 Deut. 25:4

8:12 *wound their weak conscience.* Eating meat offered to idols when they feel it is wrong tends to blunt their consciences, so that doing what is wrong becomes much easier. The result may be moral tragedy. *you sin against Christ.* Cf. Mt 10:40; 18:5; Mk 9:37; Lk 9:48; Ro 14:15 and note; 14:19–20.

8:13 *I will never eat meat again.* Paul presents himself as an example for the church (cf. Ro 14:21).

9:1 *Am I not free?* Do I not have the rights that any Christian has? *Am I not an apostle?* Some at Corinth (2Co 12:11–12) questioned Paul's genuine apostleship. To certify his apostleship Paul gives this proof: that he has seen the Lord Jesus (Ac 9:1–9; 22:6 –16; 26:12–18), as was true of the other apostles (Ac 1:21–22). Furthermore, he adds that his ministry has produced true spiritual fruit (the Corinthians) for the Lord, which should confirm to them that he is indeed an apostle.

9:4 *right to food and drink.* Paul and Barnabas, as God's workers, have a right to have their food and other physical needs supplied at the church's expense (cf. vv. 6,13–14).

9:5 *take a believing wife along with us.* Paul asserts his right to be married, if he wishes. This does not mean that he was married, as some have imagined (see 7:7 and note). Other apostles, including Peter (see Mk 1:30), had wives.

9:9 *Is it about oxen ...?* See 1Ti 5:18. In the Mosaic law that Paul quotes (Dt 25:4), God was indeed concerned about oxen that labored for their owners (cf. Jnh 4:11 and note). But this law was also illustrative of a basic principle of justice that God was teaching Israel and "us" (v. 10), a principle with greater moral

weight when persons are involved than when draft animals are involved.

9:11 *material harvest.* Food, lodging and pay supplied by the Corinthians (cf. Gal 6:6). Paul here sets forth the principle that those who serve the church should be supported by the church (cf. Php 4:14–19).

9:12 *did not use this right.* The point of Paul's discussion in ch. 9. He had numerous rights that he did not claim because of his love for the Corinthians. Thus ch. 9 is an extended personal illustration of the practice advocated in ch. 8. Because of love for others, believers should be ready to surrender their rights (see Ro 14:15 and note).

9:13 *those who serve in the temple.* The Corinthian believers would understand this illustration not only from their knowledge of the OT (cf. Lev 7:28–36; Nu 18:8–20) but also from the practice in pagan temples in Greece and Rome.

9:15 *this boast.* That he had preached the gospel without charge, so that they could not say that they had paid him for it.

9:16 *I am compelled to preach.* The Lord had laid on Paul the necessity of preaching the gospel (Ac 9:1–16; 26:16–18; see also Jer 20:9 and note). *Woe to me.* Cf. v. 27 and note.

9:18 *my reward ... in preaching the gospel.* Paul's reward in preaching is not material things but the boasting that he has preached to the Corinthians without charge and has not taken advantage of the rights he deserves: food and drink, shelter and pay (vv. 3–12).

PAUL'S USE OF HIS FREEDOM

[19]Though I am free[a] and belong to no one, I have made myself a slave to everyone,[b] to win as many as possible.[c] [20]To the Jews I became like a Jew, to win the Jews.[d] To those under the law I became like one under the law (though I myself am not under the law),[e] so as to win those under the law. [21]To those not having the law I became like one not having the law[f] (though I am not free from God's law but am under Christ's law),[g] so as to win those not having the law. [22]To the weak I became weak, to win the weak.[h] I have become all things to all people[i] so that by all possible means I might save some.[j] [23]I do all this for the sake of the gospel, that I may share in its blessings.

THE NEED FOR SELF-DISCIPLINE

[24]Do you not know that in a race all the runners run, but only one gets the prize?[k] Run in such a way as to get the prize. [25]Everyone who competes in the games goes into strict training. They do it to get a crown[m] that will not last, but we do it to get a crown that will last forever.[n] [26]Therefore I do not run like someone running aimlessly;[o] I do not fight like a boxer beating the air.[p] [27]No, I strike a blow to my body[q] and make it my slave so that after I have preached to others, I myself will not be disqualified for the prize.[r]

WARNINGS FROM ISRAEL'S HISTORY

10 For I do not want you to be ignorant[s] of the fact, brothers and sisters, that our ancestors were all under the cloud[t] and that they all passed through the sea.[u] [2]They were all baptized into[v] Moses in the cloud and in the sea. [3]They all ate the same spiritual food[w] [4]and drank the same spiritual drink; for they drank from the spiritual rock[x] that accompanied them, and that rock was Christ. [5]Nevertheless, God was not pleased with most of them; their bodies were scattered in the wilderness.[y]

[6]Now these things occurred as examples[z] to keep us from setting our hearts on evil things as they did. [7]Do not be idolaters,[a] as some of them were; as it is written: "The peo-

---

9:19 *I have made myself a slave to everyone.* Not only did Paul not use his right to material support in preaching the gospel but he also deprived himself—curtailed his personal privileges and social and religious rights—in dealing with different kinds of people. *to win.* To bring to Christ.
9:20 *those under the law.* Those under the OT law and religious practices (the Jews). *I became like one under the law.* For the Jews' sake Paul conformed to the Jewish law (see Ac 16:3; 18:18 and notes; 21:20–26 and notes on 21:23–24).
9:21 *those not having the law.* Those who had not been raised under the OT law (the Gentiles). *I became like one not having the law.* Paul accommodated himself to Gentile culture when it did not violate his allegiance to Christ, though he still reckoned that he was under God's law and Christ's law. (By "Christ's law" Paul is probably referring to Christ's teachings, though the term is not necessarily restricted to them.)
9:22 *the weak.* Those whose consciences are weak (8:9–12). *I became weak.* Paul did not exercise his Christian freedom in such things as eating meat sacrificed to idols (8:9,13).
9:23 *share in its blessings.* Paul's hope concerning the manner of his own participation in the future glory of believers is linked with the faithfulness with which he carried out the apostolic mission Christ gave him (cf. v. 27 and note; see 2Co 3:1–3; 5:10; Php 2:16; 1Th 2:19–20 and notes).
9:24 *race … runners.* The Corinthians were familiar with the foot races in their own Isthmian games, which occurred every other year and were second only to the Olympic games in importance. *prize.* In ancient times the prize was a perishable wreath (v. 25).
9:25 *crown that will last forever.* See 1Pe 5:4 and note; cf. 1Th 2:19 and note.
9:26 *not … running aimlessly.* See Php 3:14 and note.
9:27 *I strike a blow to my body and make it my slave.* Here Paul uses the figure of boxing to represent the Christian life. He does not aimlessly beat the air, but he severely disciplines his own body in serving Christ. *not be disqualified for the prize.* Paul realizes that he must with rigor serve the Lord and battle against sin. If he fails in this, he may be excluded from the

reward (see 3:10–15).
10:1 *the cloud … the sea.* These two watery entities had played a central role in God's deliverance of Israel out of Egypt through his servant Moses (the cloud signifying God's guidance [see Ex 13:21; 40:36–37; Nu 9:17,21; 10:11–12; 14:14; Ne 9:12,19; Ps 78:14] and the sea signifying God's climactic act of deliverance in which he brought his people safely through the sea but brought judgment on the Egyptians [see Ex 14:1—15:20; Dt 11:4; Jos 2:10; Ne 9:9,11; Ps 66:6; 77:16,19; 78:13,53; 106:9–11; 136:13–15; Isa 43:16–17; 51:10; 63:11–13]). The Israelites' journey, guided by the cloud, and their safe passage through the sea under the ministry of Moses united them with God's servant Moses in the working out of God's redemptive program (see v. 2 and note).
10:2 *baptized.* Figurative language Paul used to depict Israel's union with Moses in God's redemptive program is analogous in important ways to the Christian's union with Christ in his death and resurrection, as signified by Christian baptism (see Ro 6:3–4 and note).
10:3–4 *spiritual food … spiritual drink.* The manna and the water from the rock (Ex 16:2– 36; 17:1–7; Nu 20:2–11; 21:16) are used as figures representing the spiritual sustenance that God continually provides for his people—as signified in the Lord's Supper.
10:4 *that rock was Christ.* The rock, from which the water came, and the manna are here viewed by Paul as symbolic of the spiritual sustenance God's people experienced already in the wilderness through Christ, the bread of life and the water of life (see Jn 4:14; 6:30–35 and notes). For Christ's presence with God's people already in the wilderness, cf. 8:6 and note.
10:5 *God was not pleased with most of them.* In spite of the remarkable privileges given to the Israelites (vv. 1–4), they failed to obey God, thus incurring his displeasure. Of the adults who came out of Egypt, only Caleb and Joshua were allowed to enter Canaan (Nu 14:22–24,28–35; Dt 1:34–36; Jos 1:1–2; 14:6–14).
10:6 *as they did.* What Paul has in mind is described in vv. 7–10.
10:7 *idolaters.* Referring to the incident of the golden calf (Ex 32:1–6). The people ate a ritual meal sacrificed to an idol (cf. ch. 8).

9:19 [a]ver 1
[b]2Co 4:5; Gal 5:13
[c]Mt 18:15; 1Pe 3:1
9:20 [d]Ac 16:3; 21:20-26; Ro 11:14
[e]S Ro 2:12
9:21 [f]Ro 2:12,14
[g]Gal 6:2
9:22 [h]S Ro 14:1; S 1Co 2:3 [i]1Co 10:33
[j]S Ro 11:14
9:24 [k]Php 3:14; Col 2:18 [l]ver 25,26; Gal 2:2; 5:7; Php 2:16; 2Ti 4:7; Heb 12:1
9:25 [m]2Ti 2:5
[n]2Ti 4:8; Jas 1:12; 1Pe 5:4; Rev 2:10; 3:11
9:26 [o]S ver 24
[p]1Ti 6:12
9:27 [q]Ro 8:13
[r]ver 24
10:1 [s]S Ro 11:25
[t]Ex 13:21; Ps 105:39
[u]Ex 14:22,29; Ps 66:6
10:2 [v]Ro 6:3
10:3 [w]S Jn 6:31
10:4 [x]Ex 17:6; Nu 20:11; Ps 78:15; 105:41
10:5 [y]Nu 14:29; Heb 3:17; Jude 5
10:6 [z]ver 11
10:7 [a]ver 14

10:7 *b* Ex 32:4,6,19
10:8 *c* Nu 25:1-9
10:9 *d* Ex 17:2;
Ps 78:18; 95:9; 106:14
e Nu 21:5,6
10:10 *f* Nu 16:41;
17:5,10 *g* Nu 16:49
h Ex 12:23; 1Ch 21:15;
Heb 11:28
10:11 *i* ver 6
j S Ro 4:24
k S Ro 13:11
10:12 *l* Ro 11:20;
2Co 1:24
10:13 *m* S 1Co 1:9
n 2Pe 2:9
10:14 *o* Heb 6:9;
1Pe 2:11; 1Jn 2:7;
Jude 3 *p* ver 7;
1Jn 5:21
10:16 *q* S Mt 14:19
r Mt 26:26-28;
1Co 11:23-25
10:17 *s* S Ro 12:5
10:18 *t* Lev 7:6,14,
15
10:19 *u* S 1Co 8:4
10:20 *v* Lev 17:7;
Dt 32:17; Ps 106:37;
Rev 9:20
10:21 *w* 2Co 6:15,16
10:22 *x* Dt 32:16,21;
1Ki 14:22; Ps 78:58;
Jer 44:8 *y* Ecc 6:10;
Isa 45:9
10:23 *z* 1Co 6:12
10:24 *a* ver 33;
S Ro 15:1,2; 1Co 13:5;
Php 2:4,21

ple sat down to eat and drink and got up to indulge in revelry." *a b* 8We should not commit sexual immorality, as some of them did—and in one day twenty-three thousand of them died. *c* 9We should not test Christ, *b d* as some of them did—and were killed by snakes. *e* 10And do not grumble, as some of them did *f*—and were killed *g* by the destroying angel. *h*

11These things happened to them as examples *i* and were written down as warnings for us, *j* on whom the culmination of the ages has come. *k* 12So, if you think you are standing firm, *l* be careful that you don't fall! 13No temptation *c* has overtaken you except what is common to us all. And God is faithful; *m* he will not let you be tempted *c* beyond what you can bear. *n* But when you are tempted, *c* he will also provide a way out so that you can endure it.

IDOL FEASTS AND THE LORD'S SUPPER

14Therefore, my dear friends, *o* flee from idolatry. *p* 15I speak to sensible people; judge for yourselves what I say. 16Is not the cup of thanksgiving for which we give thanks a participation in the blood of Christ? And is not the bread that we break *q* a participation in the body of Christ? *r* 17Because there is one loaf, we, who are many, are one body, *s* for we all partake of the one loaf.

18Consider the people of Israel: Do not those who eat the sacrifices *t* participate in the altar? 19Do I mean then that food sacrificed to an idol is anything, or that an idol is anything? *u* 20No, but the sacrifices of pagans are offered to demons, *v* not to God, and I do not want you to be participants with demons. 21You cannot drink the cup of the Lord and the cup of demons too; you cannot have a part in both the Lord's table and the table of demons. *w* 22Are we trying to arouse the Lord's jealousy? *x* Are we stronger than he? *y*

THE BELIEVER'S FREEDOM

23"I have the right to do anything," you say—but not everything is beneficial. *z* "I have the right to do anything"—but not everything is constructive. 24No one should seek their own good, but the good of others. *a*

a 7 Exodus 32:6   *b 9* Some manuscripts *test the Lord*   *c 13* The Greek for *temptation* and *tempted* can also mean *testing* and *tested.*

10:8 Refers to Israel's participation in the worship of the Baal of Peor and the sexual practices associated with that worship (see Nu 25:1–9). *twenty-three thousand.* The Hebrew and Greek (Septuagint) texts of Nu 25:9 have 24,000. It is clear that Paul is not striving for exactness but is only speaking approximately. First-century writers were not as concerned about being precise as 21st-century authors often are.

10:10 *do not grumble.* As in Nu 16:41. *destroying angel.* Paul links the angel who brought the plague of Nu 16:46–50—because of the grumbling of the Israelites against Moses and Aaron (Nu 16:41)—with the destroying angel of Ex 12:23.

▲ **10:11** *written down as warnings.* See Ro 15:4 and note. *culmination of the ages.* The period of time inaugurated by Christ's death and resurrection and continuing into the future until Christ's second coming and beyond. It is the period of fulfillment when all that God has been doing for his people throughout all previous ages comes to its fruition in the Messiah.

▲ **10:13** *temptation.* Temptation in itself is not sin (Jesus was tempted, Mt 4:1–11), but yielding to the temptation is sin. The Greek for "temptation" and "tempted" can also mean "testing" and "tested," so Paul may have been speaking of "testing" with its accompanying temptation (see Mt 6:13 and note). *endure it.* Through God's enablement to resist the temptation to sinning or to endure the trial without falling.

▲ **10:14** *flee from idolatry.* Like that described in Ex 32:1–6. Corinthian Christians had come out of a background of paganism. Temples for the worship of Apollo, Asclepius, Demeter, Aphrodite and other pagan gods and goddesses were seen daily by the Corinthians as they engaged in the activities of everyday life. The worship of Aphrodite was a particularly strong temptation (see note on 6:18; cf. 1Jn 5:21 and note).

▲ **10:16** *cup of thanksgiving.* The cup of wine that Christians drink during the celebration of the Lord's Supper (see Mt 26:27–28; Mk 14:23–24 and note; Lk 22:20). Drinking the wine of the Lord's Supper as an act of faith is a claim of personal participation in the benefits of Christ's shed blood. *bread that we break.* The loaf of bread that is broken and eaten during the Lord's Supper (see Mt 26:26; Mk 14:22 and note; Lk 22:19 and note). *participation in the body of Christ.* The sense is similar to Paul's statement concerning participation in the blood of Christ.

▲ **10:17** *one loaf.* The act of many believers partaking of one loaf of bread symbolizes the unity of the body of Christ, the church, which is nourished by the one bread of life (cf. Jn 6:33–58).

10:18 *those who eat the sacrifices participate in the altar.* When the people of Israel ate part of the sacrifice made at the altar (Lev 7:15; 8:31; Dt 12:17–18), they participated with the altar in consuming the sacrifices. What was consumed on the altar (with fire) was Yahweh's portion.

10:19 *Do I mean … that an idol is anything?* See 8:4–6 and notes.

10:20 *offered to demons.* In reality, demons (not gods) were the objects of idol worship. God's people are warned that if they do eat meat sacrificed to idols, they should not eat it with pagans in their temple feasts, for to do so is to become "participants with demons."

10:22 *arouse the Lord's jealousy.* By sharing in pagan idolatry and worship (cf. Ex 20:5 and note).

▲ **10:23** *not everything is constructive.* See 6:12 and note. Personal freedom and desire for one's rights are not the only considerations. One must also consider "the good of others" (v. 24; cf. 8:1; Gal 6:2).

²⁵Eat anything sold in the meat market without raising questions of conscience, ᵇ ²⁶for, "The earth is the Lord's, and everything in it." ᵃ ᶜ

²⁷If an unbeliever invites you to a meal and you want to go, eat whatever is put before you ᵈ without raising questions of conscience. ²⁸But if someone says to you, "This has been offered in sacrifice," then do not eat it, both for the sake of the one who told you and for the sake of conscience. ᵉ ²⁹I am referring to the other person's conscience, not yours. For why is my freedom ᶠ being judged by another's conscience? ³⁰If I take part in the meal with thankfulness, why am I denounced because of something I thank God for? ᵍ

³¹So whether you eat or drink or whatever you do, do it all for the glory of God. ʰ ³²Do not cause anyone to stumble, ⁱ whether Jews, Greeks or the church of God— ³³even as I try to please everyone in every way. ᵏ For I am not seeking my own good but the good of many, ˡ so that they may be saved. ᵐ ¹Follow my example, ⁿ as I follow the example of Christ. ᵒ

ON COVERING THE HEAD IN WORSHIP

²I praise you ᵖ for remembering me in everything �q and for holding to the traditions just as I passed them on to you. ʳ ³But I want you to realize that the head of every man is Christ, ˢ and the head of the woman is man, ᵇ ᵗ and the head of Christ is God. ᵘ ⁴Every man who prays or prophesies ᵛ with his head covered dishonors his head. ⁵But every woman who prays or prophesies ʷ with her head uncovered dishonors her head—it is the same as having her head shaved. ˣ ⁶For if a woman does not cover her head, she might as well have her hair cut off; but if it is a disgrace for a woman to have her hair cut off or her head shaved, then she should cover her head.

ᵃ 26 Psalm 24:1   ᵇ 3 Or of the wife is her husband

10:25 ᵇ S Ac 10:15; 1Co 8:7
10:26 ᶜ Ps 24:1; Ex 9:29; 19:5; Job 41:11; Ps 50:12; 1Ti 4:4
10:27 ᵈ Lk 10:7
10:28 ᵉ 1Co 8:7,10-12
10:29 ᶠ 1Co 9:1,19
10:30 ᵍ S Ro 14:6
10:31 ʰ Zec 14:21; Col 3:17; 1Pe 4:11
10:32 ⁱ S Mt 5:29; Ac 24:16; S 2Co 6:3
ʲ Ac 20:28; 1Co 1:2; 11:16,22; 15:9; 1Ti 3:5, 15
10:33 ᵏ Ro 15:2; 1Co 9:22 ˡ S ver 24
ᵐ S Ro 11:14
11:1 ⁿ S 1Co 4:16
ᵒ Ro 15:3; 1Pe 2:21
11:2 ᵖ ver 17,22
q 1Co 4:17 ʳ ver 23; 1Co 15:2,3; 2Th 2:15; 3:6
11:3 ˢ S Eph 1:22
ᵗ Ge 3:16; Eph 5:23
ᵘ 1Co 3:23
11:4 ᵛ S Ac 11:27
11:5 ʷ S Ac 21:9
ˣ Dt 21:12

10:25 *Eat anything sold in the meat market.* Even if it has been sacrificed to an idol, because out in the public market it has lost its pagan religious significance.

10:26 A quotation from Ps 24:1 used at Jewish mealtimes as a blessing (cf. Ps 50:12; 89:11).

10:27 *eat whatever is put before you.* Whether or not it might be meat sacrificed to idols, ask no questions. As long as the subject has not been brought up, you are free to eat the meat.

10:28 *for the sake of the one who told you.* If the meat has been identified as meat sacrificed to idols and you eat it, the informant might think you condone or even are willing to participate in the worship of idols. *for the sake of conscience.* So as not to cause someone else (v. 29) to think it is all right to eat meat sacrificed to idols even though they have doubts about it.

🄰 **10:29** *my freedom.* Cf. Ro 14:16 and note. The exercise of one's personal freedom is to be governed by whether the action will bring glory to God, whether it will build up the church of God and whether it will encourage the unsaved to receive Christ as Savior and Lord (vv. 31–33).

10:30 *something I thank God for.* Paul could thank God for meat sacrificed to idols, for the idol is nothing and the meat is a part of God's created world.

🄰 **10:31** *all for the glory of God.* The all-inclusive principle that governs the discussion in chs. 8–10 is that God should be glorified in everything the Christian does (see note on Ro 16:27).

🄰 **10:32** *Do not cause anyone to stumble.* Living to glorify God will result in doing what is beneficial for others, whether Christians ("the church of God") or non-Christians ("Jews, Greeks").

🄰 **10:33** *please everyone in every way.* Paul will do nothing that might hinder someone else from receiving the salvation proclaimed in his gospel. *that they may be saved.* See 9:22.

11:1 Notice the order: (1) Christ is the supreme example (cf. 1Pe 2:21); (2) Christ's apostle follows his example ("as I follow"); (3) we are to follow the apostle's example.

11:3–16 The subject of this section is propriety in public worship. Clearly Paul is concerned that the proper relationship between husbands and wives be reflected in public worship; however, much remains uncertain. As in the previous section, he desires that all be done to the glory of God (10:31).

11:3 Some understand the term "head" to refer primarily to the concept of honor, in that one's physical head is the seat of one's honor (cf. vv. 4–5). Thus as Christ honored God, each man is to honor Christ, and each woman is to honor her husband. Others see in the word "head" the idea of authority (which would also include the concept of honor). They point out that Paul clearly uses the term in the sense of authority in Eph 1:21–22 ("under his feet"; "head over everything"), in Eph 5:22–23 (where headship is seen in a context of submission) and in Col 1:18; 2:10. Thus as Christ has authority over "every man" and is therefore to be honored by them, so the husband holds a position of authority and is therefore to be honored by his wife. See note on 15:28.

11:4 The first use of "head" in this verse refers to a man's physical head; the second refers to his spiritual Head (Christ)—or perhaps is intended in a double sense. In the culture of Paul's day, men uncovered their heads in worship to signify their respect for and submission to deity. When a man prayed or prophesied with his head covered, he failed to show the proper attitude toward Christ. *prophesies.* See 12:10 and note.

11:5–6 Paul's message to women was: Show respect for and submission to your husband by covering your head during public worship. Some do not see in these verses a temporary cultural significance to the covering/uncovering of the head. They insist that, since Paul referred to the order of creation (vv. 7–9), his directive is not to be restricted to his time. Thus women of all times should wear a head covering.

Others find a lasting principle in the passage requiring wives, in all ways, to show respect for their husbands by submitting to their authority—not merely by a particular style of attire but by godly lives. Man, who was created first, is to have authority over his wife (see 1Ti 2:11–14), who was made out of his body (Ge 2:21–24) to be his helper and companion (Ge 2:20). She is to honor her husband by submitting to him as her head (see v. 3).

Still others see these verses not as a mandate for all marriages but as reflecting marriage relationships at that time in Corinth and therefore giving a reason why the women there should have covered their heads (v. 10). They point to vv. 11–12 as a contrast, emphasizing equality and mutual dependence between men and women who are "in the Lord" (v. 11; see Gal 3:28; 1Pe 3:7).

11:7 ʸGe 1:26; 5:1; 9:6; Jas 3:9
11:8 ᶻGe 2:21-23; 1Ti 2:13
11:9 ᵃGe 2:18
11:12 ᵇS Ro 11:36
11:16 ᶜS 1Co 7:17; S 10:32
11:17 ᵈver 2,22
11:18 ᵉ1Co 1:10-12; 3:3
11:19 ᶠ1Jn 2:19
11:21 ᵍ2Pe 2:13; Jude 12
11:22 ʰS 1Co 10:32 ⁱJas 2:6 ʲver 2,17
11:23 ᵏGal 1:12 ˡS ver 2
11:24 ᵐ1Co 10:16
11:25 ⁿS Lk 22:20 ᵒ1Co 10:16
11:26 ᵖS 1Co 1:7

⁷A man ought not to cover his head, since he is the image ʸ and glory of God; but woman is the glory of man. ⁸For man did not come from woman, but woman from man; ᶻ ⁹neither was man created for woman, but woman for man. ᵃ ¹⁰It is for this reason that a woman ought to have authority over her own ᵃ head, because of the angels. ¹¹Nevertheless, in the Lord woman is not independent of man, nor is man independent of woman. ¹²For as woman came from man, so also man is born of woman. But everything comes from God. ᵇ

¹³Judge for yourselves: Is it proper for a woman to pray to God with her head uncovered? ¹⁴Does not the very nature of things teach you that if a man has long hair, it is a disgrace to him, ¹⁵but that if a woman has long hair, it is her glory? For long hair is given to her as a covering. ¹⁶If anyone wants to be contentious about this, we have no other practice—nor do the churches of God. ᶜ

CORRECTING AN ABUSE OF THE LORD'S SUPPER
11:23–25pp — Mt 26:26–28; Mk 14:22–24; Lk 22:17–20

¹⁷In the following directives I have no praise for you, ᵈ for your meetings do more harm than good. ¹⁸In the first place, I hear that when you come together as a church, there are divisions ᵉ among you, and to some extent I believe it. ¹⁹No doubt there have to be differences among you to show which of you have God's approval. ᶠ ²⁰So then, when you come together, it is not the Lord's Supper you eat, ²¹for when you are eating, some of you go ahead with your own private suppers. ᵍ As a result, one person remains hungry and another gets drunk. ²²Don't you have homes to eat and drink in? Or do you despise the church of God ʰ by humiliating those who have nothing? ⁱ What shall I say to you? Shall I praise you? ʲ Certainly not in this matter!

²³For I received from the Lord ᵏ what I also passed on to you: ˡ The Lord Jesus, on the night he was betrayed, took bread, ²⁴and when he had given thanks, he broke it and said, "This is my body, ᵐ which is for you; do this in remembrance of me." ²⁵In the same way, after supper he took the cup, saying, "This cup is the new covenant ⁿ in my blood; ᵒ do this, whenever you drink it, in remembrance of me." ²⁶For whenever you eat this bread and drink this cup, you proclaim the Lord's death until he comes. ᵖ

²⁷So then, whoever eats the bread or drinks the cup of the Lord in an unworthy man-

ᵃ 10 Or *have a sign of authority on her*

11:10 Paul's meaning here is obscure. *angels.* Perhaps mentioned here because they are interested in all aspects of the Christian's salvation and are sensitive to decorum in worship (cf. Eph 3:10 and note). But see next entry. *have authority over her own head.* See TNIV text note, which is understood by some to refer to the woman's authority as co-ruler with man in the creation (Ge 1:26–27). Others take the phrase to refer to the man's authority as properly recognized by the woman in her head covering. Still others understand Paul as viewing the woman's head covering as a symbol of protection against the influence of fallen angels.

11:13–14 *proper...the very nature of things.* Believers must be conscious of how their actions appear in their culture, in light of what is considered to be honorable behavior.
11:16 In worship services, Paul and the churches in general followed the common custom of the men wearing short hair and the women long hair. Paul was basing his remarks, particularly in vv. 13–16, on common custom in the churches.
11:17 *no praise.* Contrast v. 2.
11:18 *divisions.* Paul had already dealt with one aspect of these divisions (1:10–17).
11:19 *God's approval.* As deplorable as factions may be, they serve one good purpose: They distinguish those who are faithful and true in God's sight.
11:20 *not the Lord's Supper you eat.* Their intention was to eat the Lord's Supper, but it was profaned by their gluttony and discrimination.
11:21 *remains hungry...gets drunk.* The early church held the *agape* ("love") feast in connection with the Lord's Supper (cf. 2Pe 2:13 and note; Jude 12). Perhaps the meal was something like a present-day potluck dinner. In good Greek style they brought food for all to share, the rich bringing more and the poor less, but because of their cliques the rich ate much and the poor were left hungry.

11:22 *Shall I praise you?* See v. 17.
11:23–26 Observe the similarity of Paul's words here with Mt 26:26–29; Mk 14:22–25; and especially Lk 22:17–20.
11:23 *I received from the Lord.* Paul does not necessarily mean that he received the message about the Lord's Supper directly from Christ. The information probably was passed on to him by others who had heard it from Jesus (see 15:3 and note; cf. 7:10 and note).
11:24 *had given thanks.* The Jewish practice at meals. This makes it a true Eucharist ("thanksgiving"). *my body.* The broken bread is a symbol of Christ's body "given" for sinners (Lk 22:19; see note there). *in remembrance of me.* As the Festival of Passover was a commemorative meal (see Ex 12:14), so also the Lord's Supper is a memorial supper, recalling and portraying Christ's death for sinners.
11:25 *after supper.* After the Passover supper. The Lord's Supper was first celebrated by Jesus in connection with the Passover meal (cf. Mt 26:18–30 and parallels in Mark and Luke). *cup.* A symbol of the new covenant in Jesus' blood (see Mk 14:24 and note; Lk 22:20; cf. Jer 31:31–34). (The old covenant was the Mosaic or Sinaitic covenant; see Ex 24:3–8 and notes on 24:6,8.) By the use of this covenant sign God signifies his bestowal of salvation upon his people, sealed and paid for by the shedding of Jesus' blood.
11:26 *whenever you eat...and drink.* The Lord's Supper should be held periodically, but there is no explicit instruction as to how often. *you proclaim the Lord's death.* The Lord's Supper is never celebrated apart from a proclamation of "Christ crucified" (1:23; cf. 2:2). *until he comes.* Cf. Mt 26:29 and note.
11:27 *in an unworthy manner.* In the unloving and self-centered manner that characterized some of the Corinthians at their unruly *agape* supper (vv. 20–22; see note on v. 21).

ner will be guilty of sinning against the body and blood of the Lord. *q* ²⁸Everyone ought to examine themselves *r* before they eat of the bread and drink of the cup. ²⁹For those who eat and drink without discerning the body of Christ eat and drink judgment on themselves. ³⁰That is why many among you are weak and sick, and a number of you have fallen asleep. *s* ³¹But if we were more discerning with regard to ourselves, we would not come under such judgment. *t* ³²Nevertheless, when we are judged in this way by the Lord, we are being disciplined *u* so that we will not be finally condemned with the world. *v*

³³So then, my brothers and sisters, when you gather to eat, you should all eat together. ³⁴Those who are hungry *w* should eat something at home, *x* so that when you meet together it may not result in judgment.

And when I come *y* I will give further directions.

CONCERNING SPIRITUAL GIFTS

12 Now about the gifts of the Spirit, *z* brothers and sisters, I do not want you to be uninformed. *a* ²You know that when you were pagans, *b* somehow or other you were influenced and led astray to mute idols. *c* ³Therefore I want you to know that no one who is speaking by the Spirit of God says, "Jesus be cursed," *d* and no one can say, "Jesus is Lord," *e* except by the Holy Spirit. *f*

⁴There are different kinds of gifts, but the same Spirit *g* distributes them. ⁵There are different kinds of service, but the same Lord. ⁶There are different kinds of working, but in all of them and in everyone *h* it is the same God *i* at work.

⁷Now to each one the manifestation of the Spirit is given for the common good. *j* ⁸To one there is given through the Spirit a message of wisdom, *k* to another a message of knowledge *l* by means of the same Spirit, ⁹to another faith *m* by the same Spirit, to another gifts of healing *n* by that one Spirit, ¹⁰to another miraculous powers, *o* to another prophecy, *p* to another distinguishing between spirits, *q* to another speaking in different kinds

11:27 *q* Heb 10:29
11:28 *r* 2Co 13:5
11:30 *s* Mt 9:24
11:31 *t* Ps 32:5;
1Jn 1:9
11:32 *u* Ps 94:12;
118:18; Pr 3:11,12;
Heb 12:7-10; Rev 3:19
v Jn 15:18,19
11:34 *w* ver 21
x ver 22 *y* S 1Co 4:19
12:1 *z* Ro 1:11;
1Co 1:7; 14:1,37
a S Ro 11:25
12:2 *b* S Eph 2:2
c Ps 115:5; Jer 10:5;
Hab 2:18,19
12:3 *d* Ro 9:3;
1Co 16:22 *e* S Jn 13:13
f 1Jn 4:2,3
12:4 *g* ver 8-11;
Ro 12:4-8; Eph 4:11;
Heb 2:4
12:6 *h* S Php 2:13
i Eph 4:6
12:7 *j* 1Co 14:12;
Eph 4:12
12:8 *k* 1Co 2:6
l S 2Co 8:7
12:9 *m* Mt 17:19,20;
1Co 13:2 *n* ver 28,30;
Mt 10:1
12:10 *o* ver 28-30;
Gal 3:5 *p* S Eph 4:11
q 1Jn 4:1

11:28 *examine themselves.* All participants should test the attitude of their own hearts and actions and their awareness of the significance of the Supper, thus making the Supper, under God, a spiritual means of grace.

11:29 *without discerning the body of Christ.* The word "body" may refer to either the Lord's physical body or the church as the body of Christ (see 12:13,27 and notes). The first view means that the person partakes of the Lord's Supper without recognizing that it symbolizes Christ's crucified body. But in that case, why is the blood not mentioned? The second view means that the participant is not aware of the nature of the church as the body of Christ, resulting in the self-centered actions of vv. 20–21. *judgment.* Not God's eternal judgment, which is to come on the unbeliever, but such disciplinary judgment as physical sickness and death (v. 30).

11:30 *have fallen asleep.* See Jn 11:11 and note.

11:32 *disciplined.* As God's redeemed children we are disciplined—just as parents discipline their children (see Heb 12:5–11 and notes).

11:33 *gather to eat.* Another reference to the *agape* fellowship meal (see note on v. 21). Each person was to exercise restraint and wait to eat with the others. Those who are too hungry should satisfy their hunger at home and not bring selfish and discriminatory practices into the church (v. 34).

12:1 *Now about.* Suggests Paul is answering another question raised by the Corinthians in their letter (cf. 7:1; 8:1; 16:1). *gifts of the Spirit.* See 1:7 and note.

12:2 *led astray to mute idols.* At one time the Corinthians had been led by various influences to worship mute idols (see 8:4–6 and notes), but now they are to be led by the Holy Spirit.

12:3 *"Jesus be cursed"..."Jesus is Lord."* Those who are regenerated by the Holy Spirit cannot pronounce a curse on Jesus; rather, they are the only ones who can confess from the heart, "Jesus is Lord" (cf. Jn 20:28; 1Jn 4:2–3). The Greek word for "Lord" here is used in the pre-Christian Greek translation of the OT (the Septuagint) to translate the Hebrew name *Yahweh* ("the LORD"). See note on Ro 10:9.

12:4–6 *same Spirit...same Lord...same God.* These verses, reflecting the Trinity, show the diversity and unity of spiritual gifts.

12:4 *gifts.* Gifts of grace produced by the indwelling Holy Spirit. See note on v. 1.

12:5 *service.* The Greek word in its various forms is used to indicate service to the Christian community, such as serving tables (Ac 6:2–3); it is also the word used in the early church for the office of deacon (Php 1:1).

12:6 *working.* The Greek word indicates power in operation that produces obvious results.

12:7 *to each one the manifestation...given for the common good.* Every member of the body of Christ has been given some spiritual gift that is an evidence of the Spirit's working in their lives. All the gifts are intended to build up the members of the Christian community (see 1Pe 4:10–11). They are not to be used for selfish advantage, as some in the Corinthian community apparently were doing.

12:8 *To one...to another.* Not everyone has the same gift or all the gifts. *message of wisdom...knowledge.* Gifts that meet the need of the Christian community when knowledge or wisdom is required to make decisions or to choose proper courses of action.

12:9 *faith.* Not saving faith, which all Christians possess, but faith to meet a specific need within the body of Christ. *gifts of healing.* Lit. "gifts of healings." The double plural may suggest different kinds of illnesses and the various ways God heals them.

12:10 *miraculous powers.* Lit. "deeds of power." In Scripture, miracles are events that in the eyes of those who experienced and/or witnessed them clearly evidenced God's power purposefully at work in a way beyond the usual or the expected. *prophecy.* A message imparted to a believer by the Holy Spirit. It may be a prediction (cf. Agabus, Ac 11:28 [see note there]; 21:10–11) or an indication of the will of God in a given situation (cf. 14:1–5,29–30 and notes; Ac 13:1–2 and note on 13:1). *distinguishing between spirits.* Since there can also be false prophecies that come from evil spirits, this gift is necessary in order for the church to distinguish the true from the false (cf.

12:10 ʳ S Mk 16:17
12:11 ˢ S ver 4
12:12 ᵗ S Ro 12:5
ᵘ ver 27
12:13 ᵛ S Mk 1:8
ʷ Eph 2:18 ˣ Gal 3:28;
Col 3:11 ʸ Jn 7:37-39
12:14 ᶻ ver 12, 20
12:18 ᵃ ver 28
ᵇ ver 11
12:20 ᶜ ver 12, 14;
S Ro 12:5
12:27 ᵈ Eph 1:23;
4:12; Col 1:18, 24
ᵉ S Ro 12:5

of tongues, ᵃ ʳ and to still another the interpretation of tongues. ᵃ ¹¹All these are the work of one and the same Spirit, ˢ and he distributes them to each one, just as he determines.

UNITY AND DIVERSITY IN THE BODY

¹²Just as a body, though one, has many parts, but all its many parts form one body, ᵗ so it is with Christ. ᵘ ¹³For we were all baptized ᵛ by ᵇ one Spirit ʷ so as to form one body— whether Jews or Gentiles, slave or free ˣ—and we were all given the one Spirit to drink. ʸ ¹⁴Even so the body is not made up of one part but of many. ᶻ

¹⁵Now if the foot should say, "Because I am not a hand, I do not belong to the body," it would not for that reason cease to be part of the body. ¹⁶And if the ear should say, "Because I am not an eye, I do not belong to the body," it would not for that reason cease to be part of the body. ¹⁷If the whole body were an eye, where would the sense of hearing be? If the whole body were an ear, where would the sense of smell be? ¹⁸But in fact God has placed ᵃ the parts in the body, every one of them, just as he wanted them to be. ᵇ ¹⁹If they were all one part, where would the body be? ²⁰As it is, there are many parts, but one body. ᶜ

²¹The eye cannot say to the hand, "I don't need you!" And the head cannot say to the feet, "I don't need you!" ²²On the contrary, those parts of the body that seem to be weaker are indispensable, ²³and the parts that we think are less honorable we treat with special honor. And the parts that are unpresentable are treated with special modesty, ²⁴while our presentable parts need no special treatment. But God has put the body together, giving greater honor to the parts that lacked it, ²⁵so that there should be no division in the body, but that its parts should have equal concern for each other. ²⁶If one part suffers, every part suffers with it; if one part is honored, every part rejoices with it.

²⁷Now you are the body of Christ, ᵈ and each one of you is a part of it. ᵉ ²⁸And God has

---

ᵃ 10 Or languages; also in verse 28   ᵇ 13 Or with; or in

---

1 Jn 4:1–6). *different kinds of tongues.* Since the Greek word for "tongues" is elsewhere used to refer to "languages" or "dialects," some understand it to refer here to the ability to speak in human languages not learned by other means, as the apostles did on the day of Pentecost (see Ac 2:4,6,11 and notes; cf. also 1Co 14:9–10). Others believe that in chs. 12–14 the term "tongues" refers to both earthly and heavenly languages, including ecstatic languages of praise and prayer (see 13:1; 14:2,10 and notes). *interpretation of tongues.* The ability to make intelligible the sense of what is spoken in a tongue so that hearers can understand and be edified (cf. 14:5, 13,27–28).

12:11 *as he determines.* The Holy Spirit sovereignly determines which gift or gifts each believer should have.

12:12 *one ... many parts.* This example illustrates the unity and diversity of the different spiritual gifts exercised by God's people, who are all members of the one body of Christ. *with Christ.* With Christ's body, the church, of which he is the head (Eph 1:22–23; cf. Ro 12:4–8 and notes).

12:13 Cf. Ro 6:3–4 and note. *all baptized by one Spirit so as to form one body.* Regenerated by the Holy Spirit (Jn 3:3,5) and united with Christ as part of his body. *Jews or Gentiles.* In Christ there is no ethnic or cultural distinction (see Gal 3:28 and note). *slave or free.* No social distinction. *all given the one Spirit to drink.* God has given all his people the Holy Spirit to indwell them (6:19) so that their lives may overflow with the fruit of the Spirit (Gal 5:22–23; cf. Jn 7:37–39).

12:14–20 Addressed mainly to those who feel that their gifts are inferior and unimportant. Apparently the more spectacular gifts (such as tongues) had been glorified in the Corinthian church, making those who did not have them feel inferior.

12:14 See Ro 12:4–8. As the human body must have diversity to work effectively as a whole, so the members of Christ's body have diverse gifts, the use of which can help bring about the accomplishment of Christ's united purpose.

12:18 Paul stresses the sovereign purpose of God in diversifying the parts of the body; by implication he is saying that God has arranged that different Christians in the body of Christ exercise different spiritual gifts, not the same gift. And this diversity is intended to accomplish God's unified purpose.

God's method employs diversity to create unity.

12:21–26 Addressed mainly to those who feel that their gifts are superior and most important (see note on vv. 14–20). These verses provide another indication that some gifts, like tongues, had been magnified as being preeminent.

12:21 The principle here is the interdependence of the parts of the body in the one whole. Christians in the body of Christ are mutually dependent as they exercise their distinctive functions.

12:22 *weaker are indispensable.* Christians who seem to have less important functions in the body of Christ are actually indispensable.

12:23 Christians should give "special honor" and support to those in the church who have ordinary gifts.

12:24 Persons with more spectacular gifts do not need to be given special honor.

12:25 *no division.* See 1:10–12.

12:26 *every part suffers.* In the body of Christ if one Christian suffers, all the Christians are affected (cf. Ac 12:1–5— the martyrdom of James and the imprisonment of Peter).

12:27 *you are the body of Christ.* Addressed to the local church at Corinth. Each local church is the body of Christ, just as the universal church is Christ's body.

12:28 The list here differs somewhat from that in vv. 8–10 (see notes there). Paul notes three of the gifts of Eph 4:11 (see note there), then five of the spiritual gifts listed in vv. 8–10. The apostles and prophets were part of the foundation of the church (see Mt 16:18; Eph 2:20 and notes), and teaching was associated with the pastoral office (see Eph 4:11 and note; 1Ti 3:2). These three gifts are listed as "first," "second" and "third," indicating their importance in the church. The rest of the list is introduced with "then," indicating the variety that follows. Paul's lists of spiritual gifts seem to be largely random samples. Apart from v. 28a he does not rank them in importance since he has already insisted that all gifts are important (vv. 21–26). *apostles.* Those chosen by Christ during his earthly ministry to be with him and to go out and preach (Mk 3:14). They were also to be witnesses of the resurrection (Ac 1:21–22). The term was occasionally used in a broader sense (see Mk 6:30; Ac 14:4 and notes). *miracles ... healing ... tongues.* See notes on vv. 9–10. *helping.* Any act of helping others may be the product of a spiriplaced in the church[f] first of all apostles,[g] second prophets,[h] third teachers, then miracles, then gifts of healing,[i] of helping, of guidance,[j] and of different kinds of tongues.[k] [29]Are all apostles? Are all prophets? Are all teachers? Do all work miracles? [30]Do all have gifts of healing? Do all speak in tongues[a]?[l] Do all interpret? [31]Now eagerly desire[b][m] the greater gifts.

LOVE IS INDISPENSABLE

And yet I will show you the most excellent way.

13 If I speak in human or angelic tongues,[c][n] but do not have love, I am only a resounding gong or a clanging cymbal. [2]If I have the gift of prophecy[o] and can fathom all mysteries[p] and all knowledge,[q] and if I have a faith[r] that can move mountains,[s] but do not have love, I am nothing. [3]If I give all I possess to the poor[t] and give over my body ⌊to hardship⌋ that I may boast,[d][u] but do not have love, I gain nothing.

[4]Love is patient,[v] love is kind. It does not envy, it does not boast, it is not proud.[w] [5]It does not dishonor others, it is not self-seeking,[x] it is not easily angered,[y] it keeps no record of wrongs.[z] [6]Love does not delight in evil[a] but rejoices with the truth.[b] [7]It always protects, always trusts, always hopes, always perseveres.[c]

[8]Love never fails. But where there are prophecies,[d] they will cease; where there are tongues,[e] they will be stilled; where there is knowledge, it will pass away. [9]For we know in part[f] and we prophesy in part, [10]but when completeness comes,[g] what is in part disappears. [11]When I was a child, I talked like a child, I thought like a child, I reasoned like a child. When I became a man, I put the ways of childhood[h] behind me. [12]For now we see only a reflection as in a mirror;[i] then we shall see face to face.[j] Now I know in part; then I shall know fully, even as I am fully known.[k]

[13]And now these three remain: faith, hope and love.[l] But the greatest of these is love.[m]

---

[a] 30 Or *other languages*   [b] 31 Or *But you are eagerly desiring*   [c] 1 Or *languages*   [d] 3 Some manuscripts *body to the flames*

12:28 [f] S 1Co 10:32
[g] S Eph 4:11
[h] S Eph 4:11 [i] ver 9
[j] Ro 12:6-8 [k] ver 10;
S Mk 16:17
12:30 [l] ver 10
12:31 [m] 1Co 14:1,39
13:1 [n] ver 8;
S Mk 16:17
13:2 [o] ver 8;
S Eph 4:11; S Ac 11:27
[p] 1Co 14:2 [q] S 2Co 8:7
[r] 1Co 12:9 [s] Mt 17:20;
21:21
13:3 [t] Lk 19:8;
S Ac 2:45 [u] Da 3:28
13:4 [v] 1Th 5:14
[w] 1Co 5:2
13:5 [x] S 1Co 10:24
[y] S Mt 5:22
[z] Job 14:16,17;
Pr 10:12; 17:9; 1Pe 4:8
13:6 [a] 2Th 2:12
[b] 2Jn 4; 3Jn 3,4
13:7 [c] ver 8,13
13:8 [d] ver 2 [e] ver 1
13:9 [f] ver 12;
S 1Co 8:2
13:10 [g] Php 3:12
13:11 [h] Ps 131:2
13:12 [i] Job 26:14;
36:26 [j] Ge 32:30;
Job 19:26; 1Jn 3:2
[k] 1Co 8:3; Gal 4:9
13:13 [l] Ro 5:2-5;
Gal 5:5,6; Eph 4:2-5;
Col 1:4,5; 1Th 1:3;
5:8; Heb 6:10-12
[m] Mt 22:37-40;
1Co 16:14; Gal 5:6;
1Jn 4:7-12,16

---

tual gift (see Ro 12:6–8 and notes), though the primary reference here is probably to a ministry to the poor, needy, sick and distressed (cf. Ac 6:1–6). *guidance.* Those with the gift of guidance (or administration) were enabled by the Holy Spirit to organize and project plans and spiritual programs in the church.
12:29–30 *Are all apostles . . . ?* Christians have different gifts, and no one gift should be expected by everyone, nor should one person be expected to have all the gifts.

🅰 **12:31** *eagerly desire the greater gifts.* See 14:1–5 and notes. If the alternative translation (see TNIV text note) is correct, the Corinthians were apparently seeking status through the exercise of the gifts that seemed to them to be more important. *the most excellent way.* Paul now shows the right way to exercise all spiritual gifts—the way of love. He does not identify love as a gift; rather, it is a fruit of the Spirit (Gal 5:22).

🅰 **13:1–3** *tongues . . . prophecy . . . faith . . . give.* Paul selects four gifts as examples. He declares that even their most spectacular manifestations mean nothing unless motivated by love.

🅰 **13:1** *human or angelic tongues.* Paul uses hyperbole. Even if he could speak not only the various languages of human beings but even the languages used by angels—if he did not speak in love it would be nothing but noise. *love.* The Greek for this word indicates a selfless concern for the welfare of others. It is like Christ's love manifested on the cross (cf. Jn 3:16; 13:34–35; Eph 5:25; 1Jn 3:16).
13:2 *all mysteries and all knowledge.* Again Paul uses hyperbole to express the amount of understanding possessed. Even if he is gifted with unlimited knowledge—if he does not possess and exercise that knowledge in love, he is nothing. *faith that can move mountains.* A special capacity to trust God to remove or overcome overwhelming threats or insurmountable obstacles (cf. Zec 4:7; Mt 17:20 and notes). Again Paul uses hyperbole.
13:3 *give over my body ⌊to hardship⌋.* A reference to bodily sufferings (cf. 2Co 11:23–29; 12:10 and notes). Even such suffering,

if not motivated by love, accomplishes nothing.
13:4–7 Love is now described both positively and negatively.
13:4 *not proud.* See 8:1 and note.
13:5 *It does not dishonor others.* Perhaps an indirect reference to their unruly and dishonorable conduct in worship (11:18–22).
13:6 *does not delight in evil.* As they were doing in ch. 5.
13:8 *never fails.* Never comes to an end, is never replaced by anything else (see v. 13 and note). *prophecies . . . will cease; . . . tongues . . . will be stilled; . . . knowledge . . . will pass away.* These three will cease because they are limited in nature (v. 9) and will be unnecessary when what is complete has come (v. 10).
13:10 *completeness.* The Greek for this word can mean "end," "fulfillment," "completeness" or "maturity." In this context the contrast is between the partial and the complete. Verse 12 seems to indicate that Paul is here speaking of Christ's second coming.

🅰 **13:12** *we see only a reflection as in a mirror.* The imagery is of a polished metal (probably bronze) mirror in which one could perceive only an imperfect reflection (cf. Jas 1:23)—in contrast to seeing the Lord directly and clearly in the new creation. *know fully . . . fully known.* The Christian will know the Lord to the fullest extent possible for a finite being, similar to the way the Lord knows the Christian—fully and infinitely. This will not be true until the Lord returns.

🅰 **13:13** *remain.* Now and forever. *faith, hope and love.* See 1Th 1:3 and note. *the greatest of these is love.* Because God is love (1Jn 4:8) and has communicated his love to us (1Jn 4:10) and commands us to love one another (Jn 13:34–35; cf. Ro 13:10; 1Co 8:1; Gal 5:6; Eph 4:16; 5:20; Php 1:9; Col 3:14; 1Pe 4:8). Love supersedes the gifts because it outlasts them all. Long after these sought-after gifts are no longer necessary, love will still be the governing principle that controls all that God and his redeemed people are and do.

14:1 ⁿ1Co 16:14
ᵒver 39; 1Co 12:31
ᵖS 1Co 12:1 ᵠver 39;
S Eph 4:11
14:2 ʳS Mk 16:17
ˢver 6-11,16
ᵗ1Co 13:2
14:3 ᵘver 4,5,12,17,
26; S Ro 14:19 ᵛver 31
14:4 ʷS Mk 16:17
ˣS ver 3 ʸS 1Co 13:2
14:5 ᶻNu 11:29
ᵃS ver 3
14:6 ᵇver 26;
Eph 1:17 ᶜS 2Co 8:7
ᵈRo 6:17
14:8 ᵉNu 10:9;
Jer 4:19
14:11 ᶠGe 11:7
14:12 ᵍS 1Co 12:1
ʰS ver 3
14:13 ⁱver 5
14:14 ʲver 2
14:15 ᵏver 2,14
ˡS Eph 5:19
14:16 ᵐDt 27:15-
26; 1Ch 16:36; Ne 8:6;
Ps 106:48; Rev 5:14;
7:12 ⁿS Mt 14:19;
1Co 11:24
14:17 ᵒS ver 3

INTELLIGIBILITY IN WORSHIP

14 Follow the way of love ⁿ and eagerly desire ᵒ spiritual gifts, ᵖ especially the gift of prophecy. ᵠ ²For those who speak in a tongueᵃ ʳ do not speak to other people but to God. Indeed, no one understands them; ˢ they utter mysteries ᵗ by the Spirit. ³But those who prophesy speak to people for their strengthening, ᵘ encouragement ᵛ and comfort. ⁴Those who speak in a tongue ʷ edifyˣ themselves, but those who prophesy ʸ edify the church. ⁵I would like every one of you to speak in tongues, ᵇ but I would rather have you prophesy. ᶻ Those who prophesy are greater than those who speak in tongues, ᵇ unless they interpret, so that the church may be edified. ᵃ

⁶Now, brothers and sisters, if I come to you and speak in tongues, what good will I be to you, unless I bring you some revelation ᵇ or knowledge ᶜ or prophecy or word of instruction? ᵈ ⁷Even in the case of lifeless things that make sounds, such as the pipe or harp, how will anyone know what tune is being played unless there is a distinction in the notes? ⁸Again, if the trumpet does not sound a clear call, who will get ready for battle? ᵉ ⁹So it is with you. Unless you speak intelligible words with your tongue, how will anyone know what you are saying? You will just be speaking into the air. ¹⁰Undoubtedly there are all sorts of languages in the world, yet none of them is without meaning. ¹¹If then I do not grasp the meaning of what someone is saying, I am a foreigner to the speaker, and the speaker is a foreigner to me. ᶠ ¹²So it is with you. Since you are eager for gifts of the Spirit, ᵍ try to excel in those that build upʰ the church.

¹³For this reason those who speak in a tongue should pray that they may interpret what they say. ⁱ ¹⁴For if I pray in a tongue, my spirit prays,ʲ but my mind is unfruitful. ¹⁵So what shall I do? I will pray with my spirit, ᵏ but I will also pray with my understanding; I will sing ˡ with my spirit, but I will also sing with my understanding. ¹⁶Otherwise when you are praising God in the Spirit, how can the others, who are now put in the same situation as an inquirer, ᶜ say "Amen" ᵐ to your thanksgiving, ⁿ since they do not know what you are saying? ¹⁷You are giving thanks well enough, but the others are not edified. ᵒ

¹⁸I thank God that I speak in tongues more than all of you. ¹⁹But in the church I would

---

ᵃ 2 Or *in another language*; also in verses 4, 13, 14, 19, 26 and 27   ᵇ 5 Or *in other languages*; also in verses 6, 18, 22, 23 and 39   ᶜ 16 The Greek word for *inquirer* is a technical term for someone not fully initiated into a religion; also in verses 23 and 24.

14:1–5 The basic principle Paul insists on is that whatever is done in the church must contribute to the edification (building up) of the body. This is in keeping with the declaration in 12:7 that gifts are "given for the common good." It also is in agreement with the principle of love (ch. 13). What is spoken in the church, then, must be intelligible—it must be spoken in the vernacular language or at least be interpreted in the vernacular. Prophecy is therefore more desirable than tongues (unless an interpreter is present) because prophecy is spoken in the native language of the listeners.

14:1 *way of love…spiritual gifts.* Love is the means by which spiritual gifts are made effective. *gift of prophecy.* See note on 12:10.

14:2 *tongue.* See TNIV text note. The hearers cannot understand what those who speak in a tongue are saying. Therefore what they say is a mystery unless it is interpreted. Only God understands it.

14:3 In prophesying the speaker can strengthen, encourage and comfort others (see 12:7 and note).

14:4 *edify themselves.* It is a personal edification in the area of the emotions, of deepening conviction, of fuller commitment and greater love.

14:5 *like…you to speak in tongues.* Paul was not opposed to tongues-speaking if it was practiced properly. *Those who prophesy are greater.* Because those who prophesy serve the common good more effectively since what they say can be understood and thus edifies the church. *unless they interpret.* If tongues-speakers also have the gift of interpretation, their speaking is as beneficial as prophecy, for then it can be understood (see v. 13).

14:6 *what good will I be…?* It would be useless to speak in tongues unless, by interpretation, one brings the church something understandable and edifying.

14:7 *pipe or harp.* Instruments that were well known in Greece. *distinction in the notes.* For a person to recognize the tune and

to understand and appreciate it, there must be a variety of notes so arranged as to create a meaningful tune. One note repeated monotonously cannot accomplish this.

14:8 *trumpet…ready for battle.* All Greeks would be acquainted with the use of the trumpet for battle signals (cf. Homer's *Iliad*, 18.219), and the Jews would be familiar with the use of the ram's horn (Nu 10:9; Jos 6:4,9). Again, the notes sounded must convey a message.

14:9 *speak intelligible words.* Speak in the vernacular language of the listeners rather than in a tongue (or else provide an interpretation).

14:10 *all sorts of languages.* Some see vv. 10–11 as an indication that the tongues of chs. 12–14 were languages otherwise unknown to the speakers.

14:12 *excel in those that build up the church.* The basic principle of ch. 14.

14:14 *mind is unfruitful.* When a person speaks in tongues or prays in tongues, the human mind does not produce the language.

14:15–17 *pray…sing…praising God…say "Amen"…thanksgiving.* Elements employed in OT (1Ch 16:36; Ne 5:13; 8:6; Ps 104:33; 136:1; 148:1) and NT worship (Ro 11:36; Eph 5:18–20). "Amen," meaning "It is true" or "So be it," is the believer's confession of agreement with the words spoken (see Ro 1:25 and note). Thus it is important that a message in tongues be interpreted.

14:15 *pray with my spirit…with my understanding…sing with my spirit…with my understanding.* May mean that Paul will sometimes pray or sing with his spirit in a tongue; at other times he will pray or sing with his understanding in his own language. Others believe that Paul was declaring his intention to pray or sing with both understanding and spirit at the same time.

14:19 *But in the church.* Some believe that an interpretation is unnecessary when the gift of tongues is being used as a private rather speak five intelligible words to instruct others than ten thousand words in a tongue. *p*

²⁰Brothers and sisters, stop thinking like children. *q* In regard to evil be infants, *r* but in your thinking be adults. ²¹In the Law *s* it is written:

> "With other tongues
> and through the lips of foreigners
> I will speak to this people,
> but even then they will not listen to me, *t*
>
>   says the Lord." *a*

²²Tongues, then, are a sign, not for believers but for unbelievers; prophecy, *u* however, is not for unbelievers but for believers. ²³So if the whole church comes together and everyone speaks in tongues, and inquirers or unbelievers come in, will they not say that you are out of your mind? *v* ²⁴But if an unbeliever or an inquirer comes in while everyone is prophesying, they are convicted of sin and are brought under judgment by all, ²⁵as the secrets *w* of their hearts are laid bare. So they will fall down and worship God, exclaiming, "God is really among you!" *x*

GOOD ORDER IN WORSHIP

²⁶What then shall we say, brothers and sisters? *y* When you come together, each of you *z* has a hymn, *a* or a word of instruction, *b* a revelation, a tongue *c* or an interpretation. *d* Everything must be done so that the church may be built up. *e* ²⁷If anyone speaks in a tongue, two—or at the most three—should speak, one at a time, and someone must interpret. ²⁸If there is no interpreter, the speaker should keep quiet in the church; let them speak to themselves and to God.

²⁹Two or three prophets *f* should speak, and the others should weigh carefully what is said. *g* ³⁰And if a revelation comes to someone who is sitting down, the first speaker should stop. ³¹For you can all prophesy in turn so that everyone may be instructed and encouraged. ³²The spirits of prophets are subject to the control of prophets. *h* ³³For God is not a God of disorder *i* but of peace *j*—as in all the congregations *k* of the Lord's people. *l*

---

a 21   Isaiah 28:11,12

14:19 *p* ver 6
14:20 *q* 1Co 3:1;
Eph 4:14; Heb 5:12,
13; 1Pe 2:2 *r* Jer 4:22;
Mt 10:16; Ro 16:19
14:21 *s* ver 34;
S Jn 10:34 *t* Dt 28:49;
Isa 28:11,12
14:22 *u* ver 1
14:23 *v* Ac 2:13
14:25 *w* Ro 2:16
x Isa 45:14; Zec 8:23
14:26 *y* S Ro 7:1
z 1Co 12:7-10
a S Eph 5:19 *b* ver 6
c ver 2 *d* 1Co 12:10
e S Ro 14:19
14:29 *f* ver 32,37;
S 1Co 13:2 *g* 1Co 12:10
14:32 *h* 1Jn 4:1
14:33 *i* ver 40
j S Ro 15:33
k S 1Co 7:17; S 10:32
l S Ac 9:13

---

prayer language. They base such a distinction on v. 18 (see v. 14) when compared with the phrase "in the church."
14:20 *In regard to evil be infants.* Just as in the case of infants, have no evil desires or wrong motives in wanting to excel in spiritual gifts (such as speaking in tongues) as an end in itself.
14:21–22 The passage from Isa 28 indicates that the foreign language of the Assyrians was a sign to unbelieving Israel that judgment was coming on them. Paul deduced from this fact that tongues were intended to be a sign of judgment for unbelievers (cf. v. 22 and note), as, e.g., in Ac 2:4–12. Similarly, prophecy was for the benefit of believers (v. 22) since it communicated revealed truth to those disposed to receive it (cf. Mt 13:11–16).
14:21 *the Law.* See Jn 10:34; 12:34 and note; 15:25; Ro 3:19 and note.
14:22 *Tongues ... a sign, not for believers.* Because they do not need a sign of God's judgment as unbelievers do.
14:23 *inquirers.* Perhaps those who had become "inquirers" concerning the gospel but as yet did not really understand (see v. 16 and TNIV text note). *unbelievers.* Those who have made no movement toward saving faith. The context is a meeting of the church in which everyone is speaking in tongues, with the result that general confusion reigns. *out of your mind.* The visitors will be repulsed by the confusion, and the phenomenon meant to be an impressive sign will have a negative effect on the unsaved.
14:24 *everyone is prophesying.* Prophecy, spoken in the vernacular language and intended for believers, turns out to have a positive effect on unbelievers because they hear and understand and are convicted of their sins. (Yet see restrictions on prophesying in vv. 29–32 and notes there.)
14:26–27 *each of you ... anyone ... someone.* The stress here is again on the diversity and yet complementary nature of spiritual gifts. It is also apparent that every member could participate in worship, not just certain leaders or officers.

14:26 *a hymn, or a word of instruction, a revelation, a tongue or an interpretation.* Elements that made up the worship service at Corinth (see note on vv. 15–17). Some of these elements (the hymn and the word of instruction) came from OT and synagogue worship (see Lk 4:16–22). All parts of Christian worship should be edifying to the church ("that the church may be built up").
14:27–28 Three restrictions are placed on speaking in a tongue "in the church" (v. 28): 1. Only two or three should do so in a meeting. 2. They should do so one at a time. 3. There must be interpretation.
14:28 *the speaker should keep quiet.* The implication seems to be that it was up to the one speaking in a tongue in the Corinthian church to make certain that there was in the audience someone to interpret his message.
14:29 *Two or three prophets should speak.* Apparently in turn (v. 31), as with the tongues-speakers (v. 27). *weigh carefully.* Judge. The prophets themselves were to decide whether the messages of their fellow prophets were valid (see note on v. 32).
14:30 *a revelation.* Prophecies referred to in chs. 12–14 could come through any member of the church (vv. 26,29–31) and were intended for particular persons in particular circumstances; the "revelation" they contained could be a prediction (Agabus, Ac 11:28; 21:10–11), a divine directive (Ac 13:1–2) or a message designed to strengthen, encourage or comfort (v. 3).
14:32 *control of prophets.* Prophecy (and tongues as well) was not an uncontrollable emotional ecstasy. Paul insists that these gifts should be controlled by the recipients themselves (vv. 15,26–32). See notes on vv. 27–29.
14:33 *God ... of peace.* See 1Th 5:23 and note. *disorder.* Paul was concerned that disorderly and unregulated worship at Corinth would bring discredit on the name of the God who had called them in Christ to peace and unity. *in all the congregations of the*

14:34 *m* 1Co 11:5,13
n S Eph 5:22; 1Ti 2:11,
12 *o* ver 21; Ge 3:16
14:36 *p* S Heb 4:12
14:37 *q* S Ac 11:27;
1Co 13:2; 2Co 10:7
r 1Co 2:15; S 12:1
s 1Jn 4:6
14:39 *t* ver 1;
1Co 12:31 *u* ver 1;
S Eph 4:11
14:40 *v* ver 33;
Col 2:5
15:1 *w* Isa 40:9;
Ro 2:16 *x* S 1Co 3:6;
S Gal 1:8
15:2 *y* Ro 1:16
z S Ro 11:22
15:3 *a* Gal 1:12
b S 1Co 11:2
c Isa 53:5; Jn 1:29;
S Gal 1:4; 1Pe 2:24
d S Mt 26:24;
S Lk 24:27; S 24:44;
Ac 17:2; 26:22,23
15:4 *e* Mt 27:59,60
f S Ac 2:24
g S Mt 16:21 *h* Jn 2:21,
22; Ac 2:25,30,31
15:5 *i* Lk 24:34
j Mk 16:14; Lk 24:36–
43

³⁴Women should remain silent in the churches. They are not allowed to speak, *m* but must be in submission, *n* as the law *o* says. ³⁵If they want to inquire about something, they should ask their own husbands at home; for it is disgraceful for a woman to speak in the church. *a*

³⁶Or did the word of God *p* originate with you? Or are you the only people it has reached? ³⁷If any think they are prophets *q* or otherwise gifted by the Spirit, *r* let them acknowledge that what I am writing to you is the Lord's command. *s* ³⁸Those who ignore this will themselves be ignored. *b*

³⁹Therefore, my brothers and sisters, be eager *t* to prophesy, *u* and do not forbid speaking in tongues. ⁴⁰But everything should be done in a fitting and orderly *v* way.

THE RESURRECTION OF CHRIST

15 Now, brothers and sisters, I want to remind you of the gospel *w* I preached to you, *x* which you received and on which you have taken your stand. ²By this gospel you are saved, *y* if you hold firmly *z* to the word I preached to you. Otherwise, you have believed in vain.

³For what I received *a* I passed on to you *b* as of first importance *c*: that Christ died for our sins *c* according to the Scriptures, *d* ⁴that he was buried, *e* that he was raised *f* on the third day *g* according to the Scriptures, *h* ⁵and that he appeared to Cephas, *d* *i* and then to the Twelve. *j* ⁶After that, he appeared to more than five hundred of the brothers and sis-

---

a 34,35 In some manuscripts these verses come after verse 40.   *b 38* Some manuscripts *Those who are ignorant of this will be ignorant*   *c 3* Or *you at the first*   *d 5* That is, Peter

---

Lord's people. A unique expression in the NT that stresses the universality and commonality of the whole visible church of God on earth. All congregations are to obey the directives that follow.

14:34–35 See note on 11:3–16. Some believe that in light of 11:3 there is a God-ordained order that is to be the basis for administration and authority. Women are to be in submission to their husbands, both at home (see Eph 5:22) and in the church (see v. 34; 1Ti 2:11–12), regardless of their particular culture. According to this view, a timeless order was established at creation (see note on 11:5–6).

Others maintain that Paul's concern is that the church be strengthened (v. 26) by believers showing respect for others (see vv. 30–31) and for God (see v. 33) as they exercise their spiritual gifts. Such respect must necessarily take account of accepted social practices. If within a particular social order it is considered disgraceful for a woman to speak in church—and it was in this case (v. 35)—then she shows disrespect by doing so and should remain silent. There were occasions, though—even in this culture—for women to speak in church. For example, in 11:5 Paul assumes that women pray and prophesy in public worship (v. 35). Thus his purpose, according to this view, was not to define the role of women but to establish a fitting (vv. 34–35) and orderly (vv. 27–31) way of worship (v. 40).

Still others say that in this context Paul is discussing primarily the disruption of worship by women who become involved in noisy discussions surrounding tongues-speaking and prophecy. Instead of publicly clamoring for explanations, the wives were to discuss matters with their husbands at home (cf. v. 35). Paul does not altogether forbid women to speak in church (see 11:5). What he is forbidding is the disorderly speaking indicated in these verses.

14:34 *as the Law says.* Cf. Ge 3:16; 1Pe 3:6 and note.

14:36 Paul asks these rhetorical questions sarcastically, suggesting that the Corinthians were following their own practice in these matters rather than conforming to God's word.

14:37 *the Lord's command.* Paul's commands are the Lord's commands and are to be followed. In a situation where so much stress was being placed on gifts, Paul insists that any genuinely gifted person will recognize the apostle's God-given authority.

14:38 *will themselves be ignored.* By Paul and the churches, or by God.

14:39 *brothers and sisters.* See note on Ro 1:13. *do not forbid speaking in tongues.* Paul's solution to the tongues problem in

the Corinthian church was not to forbid tongues but to correct the improper use of the gift.

14:40 *a fitting and orderly way.* As spelled out in vv. 26–35.

15:1–58 When Paul began this letter to the Corinthians, he foregrounded the cross of Christ (1:17–18)—"we preach Christ crucified" (1:23); "I resolved to know nothing while I was with you except Jesus Christ and him crucified" (2:2; cf. 15:3–4). Now, as he nears the end of his letter, he develops at length the essential truth of Christ's resurrection, a reality assumed throughout the letter as a whole.

15:1,50 *brothers and sisters.* See note on Ro 1:13.

15:1 *gospel.* See note on Mk 1:1.

15:2 *if you hold firmly.* See Heb 3:14 and note. *believed in vain.* The gospel Paul preached is the good news of victory over sin through the saving effects of Christ's death by crucifixion and of his triumph over death in his resurrection. "Christ crucified" (1:23) and "raised from the dead" (15:20) is the only hope for sinful mortals to "inherit the kingdom of God" (v. 50; see vv. 53–57).

15:3 *what I received I passed on to you as of first importance.* Here Paul links himself with early Christian tradition. He was not its originator, nor did he receive it directly from the Lord. His source was other Christians. The verbs he uses are technical terms for receiving and transmitting tradition (see note on 11:23). What follows is the heart of the gospel: that Christ died for our sins (not for his own sins; cf. Heb 7:27), that he was buried (confirmation that he had really died) and that he was raised from the dead. *according to the Scriptures.* Paul probably had in mind Isa 53:5–6,11–12, but he may also have been thinking of the Passover sacrifice and other sin offerings of the OT sacrificial system (see chart, p. 155).

15:4 *on the third day.* Cf. Mt 12:40. The Jews counted parts of days as whole days. Thus the three days would include part of Friday afternoon, all of Saturday, and Sunday morning. A similar way of reckoning time is seen in Jn 20:26 (lit. "After eight days," TNIV "A week later"); two Sundays are implied, one at each end of the expression. *according to the Scriptures.* Here Paul may have had in mind Ps 16:8–11; Isa 53:10–12; cf. Hos 6:2; Jnh 1:17 and note.

15:5–8 Six resurrection appearances of Christ are listed here. The Gospels tell of others (see chart, p. 1771).

15:5 *Cephas … the Twelve.* See TNIV text note. The appearance to Peter is the one mentioned in Lk 24:34, which occurred on ters at the same time, most of whom are still living, though some have fallen asleep. *k* [7]Then he appeared to James, *l* then to all the apostles, *m* [8]and last of all he appeared to me also, *n* as to one abnormally born.

[9]For I am the least of the apostles *o* and do not even deserve to be called an apostle, because I persecuted *p* the church of God. *q* [10]But by the grace *r* of God I am what I am, and his grace to me *s* was not without effect. No, I worked harder than all of them *t*—yet not I, but the grace of God that was with me. *u* [11]Whether, then, it is I or they, *v* this is what we preach, and this is what you believed.

THE RESURRECTION OF THE DEAD

[12]But if it is preached that Christ has been raised from the dead, *w* how can some of you say that there is no resurrection *x* of the dead? *y* [13]If there is no resurrection of the dead, then not even Christ has been raised. [14]And if Christ has not been raised, *z* our preaching is useless and so is your faith. [15]More than that, we are then found to be false witnesses about God, for we have testified about God that he raised Christ from the dead. *a* But he did not raise him if in fact the dead are not raised. [16]For if the dead are not raised, then Christ has not been raised either. [17]And if Christ has not been raised, your faith is futile; you are still in your sins. *b* [18]Then those also who have fallen asleep *c* in Christ are lost. *d* [19]If only for this life we have hope in Christ, we are to be pitied more than all others. *d*

[20]But Christ has indeed been raised from the dead, *e* the firstfruits *f* of those who have fallen asleep. *g* [21]For since death came through a human being, *h* the resurrection of the dead *i* comes also through a human being. [22]For as in Adam all die, so in Christ all will be made alive. *j* [23]But in this order: Christ, the firstfruits; *k* then, when he comes, *l* those who belong to him. *m* [24]Then the end will come, when he hands over the kingdom *n* to God the Father after he has destroyed all dominion, authority and power. *o* [25]For he must reign *p* until he has put all his enemies under his feet. *q* [26]The last enemy to be destroyed is death. *r*

15:6 *k* ver 18, 20; S Mt 9:24
15:7 *l* S Ac 15:13
m Lk 24:33, 36, 37; Ac 1:3, 4
15:8 *n* Ac 9:3-6, 17; 1Co 9:1; Gal 1:16
15:9 *o* 2Co 12:11; Eph 3:8; 1Ti 1:15
p S Ac 8:3
q S 1Co 10:32
15:10 *r* S Ro 3:24
s S Ro 12:3 *t* 2Co 11:23; Col 1:29 *u* S Php 2:13
15:11 *v* Gal 2:6
15:12 *w* ver 4
x S Jn 11:24 *y* Ac 17:32; 23:8; 2Ti 2:18
15:14 *z* 1Th 4:14
15:15 *a* S Ac 2:24
15:17 *b* S Ro 4:25
15:18 *c* ver 6, 20; S Mt 9:24
15:19 *d* S 1Co 4:9
15:20 *e* 1Pe 1:3
f ver 23; S Ac 26:23
g ver 6, 18; S Mt 9:24
15:21 *h* S Ro 5:12
i ver 12
15:22 *j* Ro 5:14-18; S 1Co 6:14
15:23 *k* ver 20
l ver 52; S 1Th 2:19
m S 1Co 3:23
15:24 *n* Da 2:44; 7:14, 27; 2Pe 1:11
o Ro 8:38
15:25 *p* Isa 9:7; 52:7
q ver 27; S Mt 22:44
15:26 *r* 2Ti 1:10; Rev 20:14; 21:4

Easter Sunday. The appearance to the Twelve seems to have taken place on Sunday evening (see Lk 24:36–43; Jn 20:19–23). "The Twelve" seems to be a conventional way of referring to the group of original apostles, even though Judas was no longer with them.

15:6 *more than five hundred ... at the same time.* This appearance may be the one in Galilee recorded in Mt 28:10, 16–20, where the Eleven and possibly more met the risen Lord. *some have fallen asleep.* See Jn 11:11 and note.
15:7 *James.* Since this James is listed in addition to the apostles, he is not James the son of Zebedee or James the son of Alphaeus (Mt 10:2–3). This is James, the half-brother of Jesus (Mt 13:55), who did not believe in Christ before the resurrection (Jn 7:5) but afterward joined the apostolic band (Ac 1:14) and later became prominent in the Jerusalem church (Ac 15:13). It is not clear in Scripture when and where this appearance to James occurred. *to all the apostles.* Probably the same as "the Twelve" in v. 5 (but see also Ac 1:6– 11).
15:8 *last of all.* See Ac 9:1–8. This appearance to Paul came several years after the resurrection (perhaps c. A.D. 33). *one abnormally born.* Paul was not part of the original group of apostles. He had not lived with Christ as the others had. His entry into the apostolic office was not "normal." Furthermore, at his conversion he was abruptly snatched from his former way of life (Ac 9:3–6).
15:9 *I persecuted.* See 1Ti 1:13 and note. *church of God.* In persecuting the church, he was actually persecuting Christ (see Ac 9:4 and note).
15:12–19 Some at Corinth were saying that there was no resurrection of the body, and Paul draws out the implications of this false contention.
15:12 *Christ has been raised.* Paul uses the same verb form (that expresses the certainty of Christ's bodily resurrection) a total of seven times in this passage (vv. 4, 12–14, 16–17, 20).
15:19 If faith in Christ brings benefits only for the present life and not deliverance from the ultimate "wages of sin" (Ro 6:23), then believers are worse off (because deluded) than those who live "without hope and without God in the world" (Eph 2:12).

15:20 *But Christ has indeed been raised.* Paul's categorical conclusion based on his evidence set forth in vv. 3–8. *firstfruits.* The first sheaf of the harvest given to the Lord as a token that all the harvest belonged to the Lord and would be dedicated to him through dedicated lives (see Ex 23:19; Lev 2:12 and notes). So Christ, who has been raised, is the guarantee of the resurrection of all of God's redeemed people (cf. 1Th 4:13–18 and notes).
15:21 *death came through a human being.* Through Adam (see Ge 3:17–19; Ro 5:12 and note). *the resurrection of the dead comes also through a human being.* Through Christ, the second Adam, "the last Adam" (v. 45; cf. Ro 5:12–21 and note).
15:22 *in Adam all die.* All who are "in Adam"—i.e., his descendants—suffer death. *in Christ all will be made alive.* All who are "in Christ"—i.e., who are related to him by faith— will be made alive at the resurrection (cf. Jn 5:25; Ro 5:17–18; 1Th 4:16–17 and note; Rev 20:6).
15:23 *in this order.* Christ, the firstfruits, was raised in his own time in history (c. A.D. 30), and those who are identified with Christ by faith will be raised at his second coming. His resurrection is the pledge that ours will follow.
15:24 *the end.* The second coming of Christ and all the events accompanying it. This includes his handing over the kingdom to the Father, following his destroying all dominion, authority and power of the persons and forces opposing him.
15:25 *For he must reign.* During this process of Christ's destroying all dominion and handing over the kingdom to the Father, Christ must reign (Rev 20:1–6). Some take this to mean that Christ will literally reign with his people for 1,000 years on the earth (cf. Isa 2:2–4; Mic 4:1–5). Others believe that this refers to Christ's reign over the course of history and in the lives of his people, who are spiritually raised, or born again. This reign is viewed as continuing throughout the present age. *under his feet.* An OT figure for complete conquest. Verse 25 is an allusion to Ps 110:1 (cf. Mt 22:44; Ac 2:34; Heb 1:13 and notes).
15:26 *last enemy.* For death as enemy, see Ps 49:14; Jer 9:21 and notes. The final destruction of death (cf. 2Ti 1:10) will occur

15:27 *s* ver 25;
Ps 8:6; S Mt 22:44
t S Mt 28:18
15:28 *u* Php 3:21
v 1Co 3:23
15:30 *w* 2Co 11:26
15:31 *x* S Ro 8:36
15:32 *y* 2Co 1:8
z S Ac 18:19
a Isa 22:13; Lk 12:19
15:33 *b* S 1Co 6:9
c Pr 22:24,25
15:34 *d* S Gal 4:8
e S 1Co 4:14
15:35 *f* Ro 9:19
g Eze 37:3
15:36 *h* Lk 11:40;
12:20 *i* Jn 12:24
15:38 *j* Ge 1:11
15:41 *k* Ps 19:4-6
l Ps 8:1,3

27For he "has put everything under his feet." [a] [s] Now when it says that "everything" has been put under him, it is clear that this does not include God himself, who put everything under Christ. [t] 28When he has done this, then the Son himself will be made subject to him who put everything under him, [u] so that God may be all in all. [v]

29Now if there is no resurrection, what will those do who are baptized for the dead? If the dead are not raised at all, why are people baptized for them? 30And as for us, why do we endanger ourselves every hour? [w] 31I face death every day [x]—yes, just as surely as I boast about you in Christ Jesus our Lord. 32If I fought wild beasts [y] in Ephesus [z] with no more than human hopes, what have I gained? If the dead are not raised,

> "Let us eat and drink,
> for tomorrow we die." [b] [a]

33Do not be misled: [b] "Bad company corrupts good character." [c] [c] 34Come back to your senses as you ought, and stop sinning; for there are some who are ignorant of God [d]—I say this to your shame. [e]

THE RESURRECTION BODY

35But someone will ask, [f] "How are the dead raised? With what kind of body will they come?" [g] 36How foolish! [h] What you sow does not come to life unless it dies. [i] 37When you sow, you do not plant the body that will be, but just a seed, perhaps of wheat or something else. 38But God gives it a body as he has determined, and to each kind of seed he gives its own body. [j] 39All flesh is not the same: Human beings have one kind of flesh, animals have another, birds another and fish another. 40There are also heavenly bodies and there are earthly bodies; but the splendor of the heavenly bodies is one kind, and the splendor of the earthly bodies is another. 41The sun has one kind of splendor, [k] the moon another and the stars another; [l] and star differs from star in splendor.

---

a 27 Psalm 8:6   b 32 Isaiah 22:13   c 33 From the Greek poet Menander

---

as the climax of events when Christ returns (see Rev 20:14; 21:4).

15:27 *everything under his feet.* An allusion to Ps 8:6. For another reading of Ps 8 as ultimately a word about Jesus Christ, see Heb 2:5–9 and notes.

15:28 *the Son himself will be made subject to him.* The Son will be made subject to the Father in the sense that, administratively, after he subjects all things to his power he will then turn it all over to God the Father, the administrative head. This is not to suggest that the Son is in any way inferior to the Father. All three persons of the Trinity are equal in deity and in dignity. The subordination referred to is one of function (see Jn 4:34; 5:19; 7:16 and notes). The Father is supreme in the Trinity; the Son carries out the Father's will; the Spirit is sent by the Father and the Son to vitalize life, communicate God's truth, apply his salvation to people and enable them to obey God's will. *so that God may be all in all.* The triune God will be shown to be supreme and sovereign in all things (cf. 3:21 and note).

15:29 *those . . . who are baptized for the dead.* The present tense suggests that at Corinth people were currently being baptized for the dead. But because Paul does not give any more information about the practice, many attempts have been made to interpret the concept. Three of these are: 1. Living believers were being baptized for believers who died before they were baptized, so that they too, in this way, would not miss out on baptism. 2. Christians were being baptized in anticipation of the resurrection of the dead. 3. New converts were being baptized to fill the ranks of Christians who had died. At any rate, Paul mentions this custom almost in passing, using it in his arguments substantiating the resurrection of the dead but without necessarily approving the practice. The passage will likely remain obscure.

15:30 *why do we endanger ourselves every hour?* Cf. 2Co 11:23–29.

15:31 *I face death every day.* Paul faced the reality of death daily (cf. 2Co 4:8–12; 11:23–26), and he wanted the Corinthians to

know it. *boast about you.* About their conversion and growth in grace—in spite of their failures (cf. 1Th 2:20).

15:32 *I fought wild beasts in Ephesus.* This statement can be taken literally or figuratively. But since Ac 19 makes no mention of Paul suffering imprisonment and having to face the lions in Ephesus, it is more likely that the expression means that the enemies in Ephesus were as ferocious as wild beasts. *Let us eat and drink, for tomorrow we die.* See Isa 22:13; an alternative philosophy of life if there is no resurrection.

15:33 A quotation from the Greek comedy *Thais* written by the Greek poet Menander, whose writings the Corinthians would know (see TNIV text note). The application of the quotation is that those who are teaching that there is no resurrection (v. 12) are the "bad company" and that they are corrupting the "good character" of those who hold to the correct doctrine. Cf. Ps 1:1; Pr 22:24–25 and notes.

15:34 *stop sinning.* The sin of denying that there is a resurrection and thus doubting even the resurrection of Christ, all of which had a negative effect on the lives they were living. *some who are ignorant of God.* Even in the Corinthian church. This, Paul says, is a shameful situation.

15:35–49 In discussing the nature of the resurrection body, Paul compares it to plant life (vv. 36–38), to fleshly beings (v. 39) and to celestial and earthly physical bodies (vv. 40–41).

15:36–38 Plant organisms, though organized similarly in their own order, are different; the seed sown is related to the new plant that sprouts, but the new sprout has a different and genuinely new body that God has given it.

15:39 *All flesh is not the same.* Although there is much that is similar in the organizational character of fleshly beings, each species is different: humans, animals, birds, fish.

15:40–41 Here the analogy involves inanimate objects of creation: the sun, moon and stars with their differing splendor and the earthly bodies (possibly the great mountains, canyons and seas) with their splendor. In it all, God can take similar physical material and organize it differently to accomplish his purpose.

⁴²So will it be ^{m} with the resurrection of the dead. ^{n} The body that is sown is perishable, it is raised imperishable; ^{o} ⁴³it is sown in dishonor, it is raised in glory; ^{p} it is sown in weakness, it is raised in power; ⁴⁴it is sown a natural body, it is raised a spiritual body. ^{q}

If there is a natural body, there is also a spiritual body. ⁴⁵So it is written: "The first Adam became a living being" ^{a}; ^{r} the last Adam, ^{s} a life-giving spirit. ^{t} ⁴⁶The spiritual did not come first, but the natural, and after that the spiritual. ^{u} ⁴⁷The first man was of the dust of the earth; ^{v} the second man is of heaven. ^{w} ⁴⁸As was the earthly man, so are those who are of the earth; and as is the heavenly man, so also are those who are of heaven. ^{x} ⁴⁹And just as we have borne the image of the earthly man, ^{y} so shall we ^{b} bear the image of the heavenly man. ^{z}

⁵⁰I declare to you, brothers and sisters, that flesh and blood ^{a} cannot inherit the kingdom of God, ^{b} nor does the perishable inherit the imperishable. ^{c} ⁵¹Listen, I tell you a mystery: ^{d} We will not all sleep, ^{e} but we will all be changed ^{f}— ⁵²in a flash, in the twinkling of an eye, at the last trumpet. For the trumpet will sound, ^{g} the dead ^{h} will be raised imperishable, and we will be changed. ⁵³For the perishable ^{i} must clothe itself with the imperishable, ^{j} and the mortal with immortality. ⁵⁴When the perishable has been clothed with the imperishable, and the mortal with immortality, then the saying that is written will come true: "Death has been swallowed up in victory." ^{c} ^{k}

⁵⁵ "Where, O death, is your victory?
    Where, O death, is your sting?" ^{d} ^{l}

⁵⁶The sting of death is sin, ^{m} and the power of sin is the law. ^{n} ⁵⁷But thanks be to God! ^{o} He gives us the victory through our Lord Jesus Christ. ^{p}

⁵⁸Therefore, my dear brothers and sisters, stand firm. Let nothing move you. Always give yourselves fully to the work of the Lord, ^{q} because you know that your labor in the Lord is not in vain. ^{r}

THE COLLECTION FOR THE LORD'S PEOPLE

16 Now about the collection ^{s} for the Lord's people: ^{t} Do what I told the Galatian ^{u} churches to do. ²On the first day of every week, ^{v} each one of you should set aside a sum of money in keeping with your income, saving it up, so that when

---

^{a} 45 Gen. 2:7 ^{b} 49 Some early manuscripts *so let us* ^{c} 54 Isaiah 25:8 ^{d} 55 Hosea 13:14

15:42 ^{m} Da 12:3;
Mt 13:43 ^{n} ver 12
^{o} ver 50, 53, 54
15:43 ^{p} Php 3:21;
Col 3:4
15:44 ^{q} ver 50
15:45 ^{r} Ge 2:7
^{s} Ro 5:14 ^{t} Jn 5:21;
6:57, 58; Ro 8:2
15:46 ^{u} ver 44
15:47 ^{v} Ge 2:7; 3:19;
Ps 90:3 ^{w} Jn 3:13, 31
15:48 ^{x} Php 3:20, 21
15:49 ^{y} Ge 5:3
^{z} S Ro 8:29
15:50 ^{a} Eph 6:12;
Heb 2:14
^{b} S Mt 25:34 ^{c} ver 42,
53, 54
15:51 ^{d} 1Co 13:2;
14:2 ^{e} S Mt 9:24
^{f} 2Co 5:4; Php 3:21
15:52 ^{g} S Mt 24:31
^{h} Jn 5:25
15:53 ^{i} ver 42, 50, 54
^{j} 2Co 5:2, 4
15:54 ^{k} Isa 25:8;
Heb 2:14; Rev 20:14
15:55 ^{l} Hos 13:14
15:56 ^{m} S Ro 5:12
^{n} S Ro 4:15
15:57 ^{o} S 2Co 2:14
^{p} Ro 8:37; Heb 2:14,
15
15:58 ^{q} 1Co 16:10
^{r} Isa 65:23
16:1 ^{s} Ac 24:17
^{t} S Ac 9:13 ^{u} S Ac 16:6
16:2 ^{v} Ac 20:7

15:42–44 In applying these analogies, the apostle says that in the case of the resurrection of the dead God will take a perishable, dishonorable, weak (and sinful) body—"a natural body" characterized by sin—and in the resurrection make it an imperishable, glorious, powerful body, fit to live eternally with God. There is continuity, but there is also change.

15:44–49 The contrast here between the natural body and the spiritual body again follows from their two representatives (see notes on vv. 21–22). One is the first Adam, who had a natural body of the dust of the ground (Ge 2:7) and through whom a natural body is given to his descendants. The other is the last Adam, Christ, the life-giving spirit (cf. Jn 5:26) who through his death and resurrection will at the second coming give his redeemed people a spiritual body similar to Christ's resurrected, glorified body (cf. Lk 24:36–43; Php 3:21 and notes; 1Jn 3:2).

15:50 Paul's final argument about the resurrection of the body: God's redeemed people must have newly organized, imperishable bodies to live with him. "Flesh and blood" stands for the perishable, corrupt, weak, sinful state of human beings (see note on Gal 1:16).

15:51 *mystery*. Things about the resurrection body that were not understood but are now revealed (see note on Ro 11:25). *We will not all sleep.* Some believers will not experience death and the grave (see 1Th 4:15 and note).

15:52 *in a flash.* The change to an imperishable body will occur instantly at the great trumpet call that announces the consummation of redemption (see Mt 24:31; 1Th 4:16–17).

15:53–54 *clothe itself with ... clothed with.* See note on Ps 109:29.

15:56 *The sting of death is sin.* It was sin that brought humanity under death's power (see Ro 5:12–21 and notes). *the power of*

sin is the law. The law of God gives sin its power, for it reveals our sin and condemns us because of our sin (cf. Ro 7:7–12 and notes).

15:57 *victory through our Lord Jesus Christ.* Victory over the condemnation for sin that the law brought (v. 56) and over death and the grave (vv. 54–55), through the death and resurrection of Christ (cf. Ro 4:25).

15:58 *Therefore.* Because of Christ's resurrection and ours, we know that serving him is not empty, useless activity. *your labor in the Lord is not in vain.* All our efforts in service to Christ are invested in his winning cause. He will also reward us at his second coming (Mt 25:21; cf. Lk 19:17; 1Co 2:7 and note; 2Co 4:17 and note).

16:1 *Now about.* Again an answer to one of the questions of the Corinthians (cf. 7:1; 8:1; 12:1). *collection.* Cf. 2Co 8–9; Ro 15:25–28. *the Lord's people.* His people at Jerusalem (cf. v. 3; Ro 15:26). *Galatian churches.* The fact that the Galatian and Macedonian churches (2Co 8:1; 9:1–4) are involved, along with the Corinthians, indicates that the collection of this offering was quite widespread. The Jerusalem believers may have become poverty-stricken because of the famine recorded in Ac 11:28 (c. A.D. 44 or 46) or because of the persecution of Jerusalem Christians (cf. Ac 8:1).

16:2 *On the first day of every week, each one of you should set aside.* Every Sunday believers were to bring what they had set aside for the Lord's work—an amount proportionate to their income. Since it was to be brought on Sunday, the day when Christians gathered for worship (see Ac 20:7; Rev 1:10 and notes), it was probably collected at the worship service rather than at home. Justin Martyr indicates (in his *Apology*, 1.67–68) that in his time (c. A.D. 150) offerings were brought to the church on Sundays.

16:2 ʷ 2Co 9:4,5
16:3 ˣ 2Co 3:1; 8:18, 19
16:5 ʸ S 1Co 4:19
ᶻ S Ac 16:9
16:6 ᵃ Ro 15:24; Tit 3:13
16:7 ᵇ S Ac 18:21
16:8 ᶜ S Ac 18:19
ᵈ S Ac 2:1
16:9 ᵉ S Ac 14:27
16:10 ᶠ S Ac 16:1
ᵍ 1Co 15:58
16:11 ʰ 1Ti 4:12
ⁱ 2Co 1:16; 3Jn 6
ʲ S Ac 15:33
16:12 ᵏ S Ac 18:24
16:13 ˡ 1Co 1:8; 2Co 1:21; Gal 5:1; Php 1:27; 1Th 3:8; S Tit 1:9 ᵐ S Eph 6:10
16:14 ⁿ 1Co 14:1
16:15 ᵒ 1Co 1:16
ᵖ Ro 16:5 ᵠ S Ac 18:12
ʳ S Ac 24:17
ˢ S Ac 9:13
16:16 ᵗ 1Th 5:12; Heb 13:17
16:17 ᵘ 2Co 11:9; Php 2:30
16:18 ᵛ Ro 15:32; Phm 7 ʷ Php 2:29
16:19 ˣ S Ac 2:9
ʸ S Ac 18:2

I come no collections will have to be made. ʷ ³Then, when I arrive, I will give letters of introduction to the men you approve ˣ and send them with your gift to Jerusalem. ⁴If it seems advisable for me to go also, they will accompany me.

PERSONAL REQUESTS

⁵After I go through Macedonia, I will come to you ʸ—for I will be going through Macedonia. ᶻ ⁶Perhaps I will stay with you for a while, or even spend the winter, so that you can help me on my journey, ᵃ wherever I go. ⁷For I do not want to see you now and make only a passing visit; I hope to spend some time with you, if the Lord permits. ᵇ ⁸But I will stay on at Ephesus ᶜ until Pentecost, ᵈ ⁹because a great door for effective work has opened to me, ᵉ and there are many who oppose me.

¹⁰When Timothy ᶠ comes, see to it that he has nothing to fear while he is with you, for he is carrying on the work of the Lord, ᵍ just as I am. ¹¹No one, then, should treat him with contempt. ʰ Send him on his way ⁱ in peace ʲ so that he may return to me. I am expecting him along with the brothers.

¹²Now about our brother Apollos: ᵏ I strongly urged him to go to you with the brothers. He was quite unwilling to go now, but he will go when he has the opportunity.

¹³Be on your guard; stand firm ˡ in the faith; be courageous; be strong. ᵐ ¹⁴Do everything in love. ⁿ

¹⁵You know that the household of Stephanas ᵒ were the first converts ᵖ in Achaia, ᵠ and they have devoted themselves to the service ʳ of the Lord's people. ˢ I urge you, brothers and sisters, ¹⁶to submit ᵗ to such as these and to everyone who joins in the work and labors at it. ¹⁷I am glad when Stephanas, Fortunatus and Achaicus arrived, because they have supplied what was lacking from you. ᵘ ¹⁸For they refreshed ᵛ my spirit and yours also. Such men deserve recognition. ʷ

FINAL GREETINGS

¹⁹The churches in the province of Asia ˣ send you greetings. Aquila and Priscilla ᵃ ʸ greet

ᵃ 19 Greek Prisca, a variant of Priscilla

16:3 For proper financial accountability and responsibility these approved men would act as auditors and guardians of the funds the Corinthians gave (cf. 2Co 8:16–21 and notes).

16:4 If it seems advisable for me to go also. Possibly to take care of important missionary business or to be there to explain about the gift when it arrives.

16:5 After I go through Macedonia. After leaving Ephesus (v. 8), where he was when he wrote 1 Corinthians, Paul planned to go up to Macedonia, no doubt to visit the Philippians and others in northern Greece, and then to Corinth. He had originally planned to go to Corinth first and then to Macedonia but thought it best to change his plans (see 2Co 1:12—2:4).

16:6 even spend the winter. Probably the three-month stay in Greece mentioned in Ac 20:3 (see note there). help me on my journey. With supplies and equipment, and certainly with prayers and goodwill. However, Paul had indicated earlier in the letter (9:7–12) that he did not want to be a financial burden to them.

16:8 until Pentecost. The 50th day (Pentecost means "50") after Passover, when the Jews celebrated the Festival of Firstfruits (Lev 23:10–16)—late spring.

16:9 many who oppose me. Probably a reference to the pagan craftsmen who made the silver shrines of Artemis and to the general populace whom they had stirred up (Ac 19:23–34).

16:10 When Timothy comes. In Ac 19:22 Paul sends Timothy (and Erastus) into Macedonia, after which Timothy was to go on to Corinth (1Co 4:17). see to it that he has nothing to fear. Timothy seems to have been somewhat timid (see 1Ti 4:12; 2Ti 1:7 and notes), and Paul wants the Corinthians to treat him kindly.

16:11,23 peace . . . grace. See note on Ro 1:7.

16:11 brothers. Possibly including Erastus (cf. Ac 19:22), who was a believer from Corinth and "the city's director of public works" (Ro 16:23; see note there).

16:12 Now about . . . Apollos. The Corinthians had asked Paul about Apollos (cf. the similar words, "now about," in 7:1; 8:1; 12:1; 16:1) and his coming to see them. For other words about Apollos, see 1:12; 3:4–6,22; 4:6; cf. Ac 18:24,27; 19:1; Tit 3:13.

16:15 household of Stephanas. Some of the few people Paul baptized at Corinth (1:16). They were among the first converts in Achaia (Greece), along with the few individuals in Athens who had believed a short time earlier (Ac 17:34). service. The whole household of Stephanas was serving.

16:17 Probably the ones who had brought to the apostle the letter from the Corinthians referred to in 7:1. Their coming "supplied what was lacking" from the Corinthians, i.e., the affection of these three brothers supplied the affection Paul desired from the whole Corinthian church.

16:18 refreshed my spirit and yours. Perhaps through their willingness to come to get Paul's advice and to bring it back to Corinth. At least a new relationship between Paul and the Corinthians was in the making.

16:19 province of Asia. The Roman province (presently in western Turkey) in which Ephesus and the surrounding cities were located (see Ac 19:10 and note; see also map, p. 2123). During Paul's long ministry in Ephesus all in the province of Asia heard the word. The churches of Colossae, Laodicea and Hierapolis (cf. Col 4:13–16; Rev 1:11), which were located on the border of the province of Asia, may be included in the greetings, along with the other churches of Rev 2–3 (see map, p. 2123). Aquila and Priscilla. They had helped Paul found the church at Corinth (Ac 18:1–4). warmly in the Lord. Enthusiastically, as fellow believers. the church that meets at their house. Aquila and Priscilla had left Corinth with Paul and had gone to Ephesus (Ac 18:18–19). Evidently they were still there, and a church was meeting at their house; it now sends greetings. House churches were common in this early period (cf. Ro 16:3–5; Phm 2).

you warmly in the Lord, and so does the church that meets at their house. *z* **20**All the brothers and sisters here send you greetings. Greet one another with a holy kiss. *a*

21I, Paul, write this greeting in my own hand. *b*

22If anyone does not love the Lord, *c* let that person be cursed! *d* Come, Lord*a*! *e*

23The grace of the Lord Jesus be with you. *f*

24My love to all of you in Christ Jesus. Amen. *b*

16:19 *z* S Ro 16:5
16:20 *a* S Ro 16:16
16:21 *b* Gal 6:11;
Col 4:18; 2Th 3:17;
Phm 19
16:22 *c* Eph 6:24
d Ro 9:3 *e* Rev 22:20
16:23 *f* S Ro 16:20

a 22 The Greek for *Come, Lord* reproduces an Aramaic expression (*Marana tha*) used by early Christians.
b 24 Some manuscripts do not have *Amen.*

16:20 *holy kiss.* See notes on 2Co 13:12; Ro 16:16. The kiss of mutual respect and love in the Lord was evidently the public practice of early Christians—from a practice that was customary in the ancient East. Such a practice may have been used in the first-century A.D. synagogue—men kissing men, and women kissing women—and it would have been natural for the practice to have been continued in the early Jewish-Gentile churches.

16:21 *greeting in my own hand.* Paul now signs this letter, as was his habit (see Gal 6:11; Col 4:18; Phm 19), a mark of the authenticity of the letter (2Th 3:17). Someone else had been penning the letter for him up to this point (cf. Ro 16:22).

16:22 *let that person be cursed!* May those who have not come to love the Lord Jesus Christ in response to the preaching of the gospel experience God's displeasure and wrath (see Jn 3:36 and note). Paul's curse is based on God as witness to the unbelievers' essential lack of love for the Lord Jesus and of obedience to God (cf. Gal 1:8–9; Ro 9:3 and note). *Come, Lord!* See TNIV text note; an expression used by the early church as a cry that the second coming of Christ may soon take place.

16:23 The apostle's usual benediction (see Gal 6:18; Eph 6:24; Php 4:23); a longer Trinitarian benediction is found in 2Co 13:14. *grace.* See note on vv. 11,23. *with you.* See note on 2Co 13:14.

16:24 Although he has been severe with the Corinthians, Paul wants them to know that he loves them as believers in Christ Jesus.

woman, in the Lord, and to close the church that meets at their house. 20All the brothers
and sisters here send you greetings. Greet one another with a holy kiss.
21I, Paul, write this greeting in my own hand.
22If anyone does not love the
23The grace of the Lord Jesus

2 CORINTHIANS INTRODUCTION

AUTHOR

Paul is the author of this letter (see 1:1; 10:1). It is stamped with his style and contains more autobiographical material than any of his other writings.

DATE

The available evidence indicates that the year A.D. 55 is a reasonable estimate for the writing of this letter. From 1Co 16:5–8 it may be concluded that 1 Corinthians was written from Ephesus before Pentecost (in the late spring) and that 2 Corinthians may have been written later that same year before the onset of winter. 2Co 2:13; 7:5 indicate that it was probably written from Macedonia (see chart, p. 1855).

RECIPIENTS

The opening greeting of the letter states that it was addressed to the church in Corinth and to Christians throughout Achaia (the Roman province comprising all of Greece south of Macedonia; see map, 1875).

OCCASION

It seems that Paul wrote as many as four letters to the church at Corinth: (1) the letter referred to in 1Co 5:9 (see note there); (2) 1 Corinthians; (3) the severe letter (see 2Co 2:3–4; see also below); (4) 2 Corinthians. After writing 1 Corinthians Paul continued his ministry at Ephesus until he heard that his letter had not completely accomplished its purpose. A group of men had come to Corinth who presented themselves as apostles. They were false teachers who were challenging, among other things, Paul's personal integrity and his authority as an apostle (see 11:4; 12:11).

    In the face of this serious situation, Paul decided to make a quick trip to Corinth (12:4; 13:1–2) to see whether he could remedy the situation. The visit turned out to be painful and did not accomplish its purpose. So when Paul returned to Ephesus, he wrote the Corinthians a severe letter "out of great distress and anguish of heart and with many tears" (2:4), probably sending it by Titus (12:18). Some identify this letter with 2Co 10–13. Others think it has been lost.

    After writing the severe letter, Paul had second thoughts. He was deeply concerned about how the Corinthians might react to it. So after the riot caused by Demetrius and his fellow silversmiths (see Ac 19:23–41), he left Ephesus and set out for Macedonia by way of Troas. He expected to meet Titus in Troas to get news of the effect of his severe letter on the Corinthian church, but Titus was not there (see 2Co 2:12–13). Still deeply concerned and despite the fact that the Lord had opened up an opportunity to preach the gospel at Troas, Paul said good-by to the believers there and moved on to Macedonia, where he met Titus. To his relief, the news from the Corinthian church was basically good. The severe letter had brought its intended results (7:5–16). The encouraging report of Titus of the improved situation at Corinth was the immediate occasion of the writing of 2 Corinthians.

    How, then, does one explain the harsh tone of chs. 10–13, which is so different from the rest of the letter? Some think that when Paul had just completed writing the first nine chapters, a report came to him that a strong and vocal minority was still causing trouble at Corinth. So before sending off the letter he added the last four chapters to address this troublemaking group. Others hold that chs. 10–13 were written some time after Paul had sent the first nine chapters and that they constitute a separate letter. There is, however, no manuscript evidence that warrants splitting 2 Corinthians into two parts.

PURPOSES

Because of the occasion that prompted this letter, Paul had a number of purposes in mind:

1. To express the comfort and joy he felt because the Corinthians had responded favorably to his painful letter (1:3–4; 7:8–9,12–13).

2. To let them know about the trouble he had gone through in the province of Asia (1:8–11).

3. To explain why he had changed his travel plans (1:12—2:4).

4. To ask them to forgive the offending party (2:5–11).

5. To warn them not to be "yoked together with unbelievers" (6:14—7:1).

6. To explain to them the true nature (its joys, sufferings and rewards) and high calling of Christian ministry. This is the so-called great digression, but it turns out to be in some ways the most important section of the letter (2:14—7:4; see note on 2:14).

7. To teach the Corinthians about the grace of giving and to make sure that they complete the collection for the impoverished Christians at Jerusalem (chs. 8–9).

8. To deal with the minority opposition in the church (chs. 10–13).

9. To prepare the Corinthians for his upcoming visit (12:14; 13:1–3,10).

STRUCTURE

The structure of the letter relates primarily to Paul's impending third visit to Corinth. The letter falls naturally into three sections:

1. Paul explains the reason for the changes in his itinerary (chs. 1–7).

2. Paul encourages the Corinthians to complete their collection in preparation for his arrival (chs. 8–9).

3. Paul stresses the certainty of his coming, his authenticity as an apostle and his readiness to exercise discipline if necessary (chs. 10–13).

UNITY

Some have questioned the unity of this letter (see above), but it forms a coherent whole, as the structure above shows (see also Outline below). Tradition has been unanimous in affirming its unity (the early church fathers, e.g., knew the letter only in its present form). Furthermore, none of the early Greek manuscripts breaks up the book.

OUTLINE

I. Apologetic: Paul's Explanation of His Conduct and Apostolic Ministry (chs. 1–7)
   A. Greetings (1:1–2)
   B. Thanksgiving for Divine Comfort in Affliction (1:3–11)
   C. The Integrity of Paul's Motives and Conduct (1:12—2:4)
   D. Forgiving the Offending Party at Corinth (2:5–11)

1 Paul, an apostle *a* of Christ Jesus by the will of God, *b* and Timothy *c* our brother,

To the church of God *d* in Corinth, *e* together with all his holy people throughout Achaia: *f*

²Grace and peace to you from God our Father and the Lord Jesus Christ. *g*

PRAISE TO THE GOD OF ALL COMFORT

³Praise be to the God and Father of our Lord Jesus Christ, *h* the Father of compassion and the God of all comfort, ⁴who comforts us *i* in all our troubles, so that we can comfort those in any trouble with the comfort we ourselves receive from God. ⁵For just as we share abundantly in the sufferings of Christ, *j* so also our comfort abounds through Christ. ⁶If we are distressed, it is for your comfort and salvation; *k* if we are comforted, it is for your comfort, which produces in you patient endurance of the same sufferings we suffer. ⁷And our hope for you is firm, because we know that just as you share in our sufferings, *l* so also you share in our comfort.

⁸We do not want you to be uninformed, *m* brothers and sisters, about the troubles we experienced *n* in the province of Asia. *o* We were under great pressure, far beyond our ability to endure, so that we despaired of life itself. ⁹Indeed, we felt we had received the sentence of death. But this happened that we might not rely on ourselves but on God, *p* who raises the dead. *q* ¹⁰He has delivered us from such a deadly peril, *r* and he will deliver us again. On him we have set our hope *s* that he will continue to deliver us, ¹¹as you help us by your prayers. *t* Then many will give thanks *u* on our behalf for the gracious favor granted us in answer to the prayers of many.

PAUL'S CHANGE OF PLANS

¹²Now this is our boast: Our conscience *v* testifies that we have conducted ourselves in the world, and especially in our relations with you, with integrity *a w* and godly sincerity. *x* We have done so, relying not on worldly wisdom *y* but on God's grace. ¹³For we do not write you anything you cannot read or understand. And I hope that, ¹⁴as you have understood us in part, you will come to understand fully that you can boast of us just as we will boast of you in the day of the Lord Jesus. *z*

¹⁵Because I was confident of this, I wanted to visit you *a* first so that you might benefit twice. *b* ¹⁶I wanted to visit you on my way *c* to Macedonia *d* and to come back to you from Macedonia, and then to have you send me on my way *e* to Judea. *f* ¹⁷Was I fickle when I in-

---

a 12 Many manuscripts *holiness*

1:1 S 1Co 1:1
b 1Co 1:1; Eph 1:1;
Col 1:1; 2Ti 1:1
c S Ac 16:1
d S 1Co 10:32
e S Ac 18:1
f S Ac 18:12
1:2 *g* S Ro 1:7
1:3 *h* Eph 1:3; 1Pe 1:3
1:4 *i* Isa 49:13; 51:12;
66:13; 2Co 7:6,7,13
1:5 *j* Ro 8:17;
2Co 4:10; Gal 6:17;
Php 3:10; Col 1:24;
1Pe 4:13
1:6 *k* 2Co 4:15
1:7 *l* S ver 5
1:8 *m* S Ro 11:25
n 1Co 15:32 *o* S Ac 2:9
1:9 *p* Jer 17:5,7
q S Jn 5:21
1:10 *r* S Ro 15:31
s 1Ti 4:10
1:11 *t* Ro 15:30;
Php 1:19 *u* 2Co 4:15;
9:11
1:12 *v* S Ac 23:1
w 1Th 2:10 *x* 2Co 2:17
y 1Co 1:17; 2:1,4,13
1:14 *z* S 1Co 1:8
1:15 *a* S 1Co 4:19
b Ro 1:11,13; 15:29
1:16 *c* 1Co 16:5-7
d S Ac 16:9
e 1Co 16:11; 3Jn 6
f Ac 19:21

1:1 *Paul.* See note on Ro 1:1. *apostle . . . by the will of God.* See 1Co 1:1 and note. *Timothy.* Evidently with Paul when this letter was written, but not necessarily a co-author. *our brother.* Our fellow believer, our brother in Christ (see Ac 9:17; Heb 2:11 and note). *church of God.* The community of believers, the local representatives of the universal church (see note on 1Co 1:2). *Corinth.* See Introduction to 1 Corinthians: The City of Corinth; see also map, p. 1925. *his holy people.* See note on Ro 1:7. *Achaia.* Greece, as distinct from Macedonia in the north (see map, p. 1875). Though the letter deals particularly with the situation in Corinth, it was also intended for Christians elsewhere in Greece. Presumably copies of the letter would be made in Corinth and circulated to them.

1:2 *Grace and peace.* See note on Ro 1:7. *Lord Jesus Christ.* Also occurs at the end of this letter (13:14); see note on 1Th 1:1.

1:3 *God and Father of our Lord Jesus Christ.* See note on Eph 1:3. *comfort.* Consolation and encouragement. This comfort flows to believers when they suffer for Jesus' sake, and it equips them to comfort others who are in trouble (vv. 4–7).

1:5 *share . . . in the sufferings of Christ.* See 4:10; Gal 6:17; Php 3:10 and notes.

1:6 *patient endurance.* See Ro 5:3–5; 2Pe 1:5–11 and notes.

1:7 *share in our sufferings, so also . . . in our comfort.* See Ro 12:15; 1Co 12:26 and notes.

1:8 *We.* Throughout this letter Paul uses the editorial plural (we, us, our, ourselves). Except where the context indicates otherwise, these plurals should be understood as referring to Paul alone. *brothers and sisters.* See note on Ro 1:13. *province of Asia.*

A Roman province in western Asia Minor, now Turkish territory (see map, p. 1863).

1:9 Paul's hardships were so life-threatening that he regarded his survival and recovery as tantamount to being raised from the dead. *rely . . . on God.* A key principle of this letter. God's grace is all-sufficient; Christ strengthens us when we are weak (see 12:9–10; Php 4:13 and notes).

1:10 *hope.* See note on Eph 1:18.

1:11 *you help us by your prayers.* Cf. Ro 15:31; Eph 6:19–20.

1:12 In defending his trustworthiness against the slanders being spread about him, Paul appeals to the witness of his own conscience and to the Corinthians' firsthand knowledge of his character. He had spent 18 months with them when he first came to Corinth (Ac 18:11), so they could not plead ignorance of his integrity.

1:14 *day of the Lord Jesus.* Time of his return (cf. 1Th 2:19–20).

1:15 *you might benefit twice.* Here and in v. 16 Paul refers to his change of itinerary. Originally he had planned to cross over by sea from Ephesus to Corinth, visiting the Corinthians before traveling north to Macedonia, and then, returning from Macedonia, to visit them a second time, thus giving them the benefit of two short visits. This was when he was on good terms with them. What probably occurred was that he paid them a quick visit directly from Ephesus, a visit he had not contemplated and that proved to be "painful" (2:1; see note there). That visit then gave rise to his letter that caused them sorrow (see 7:8–9 and note).

1:16 *Macedonia.* See notes on v. 1; Php 4:15.

1:17 *g* 2Co 10:2,3;
11:18
1:18 *h* S 1Co 1:9
1:19 *i* S Mt 4:3
j S Ac 15:22
k S Ac 16:1 *l* Heb 13:8
1:20 *m* Ro 15:8
n S 1Co 14:16
o Ro 15:9
1:21 *p* S 1Co 16:13
q 1Jn 2:20,27
1:22 *r* Ge 38:18;
Eze 9:4; Hag 2:23
s S 2Co 5:5
1:23 *t* S Ro 1:9
u 1Co 4:21; 2Co 2:1,3;
13:2,10
1:24 *v* 1Pe 5:3
w Ro 11:20; 1Co 15:1
2:1 *x* S 2Co 1:23
2:2 *y* 2Co 7:8
2:3 *z* ver 4,9;
2Co 7:8,12
a 2Co 12:21
b 2Co 7:16; 8:22;
Gal 5:10; 2Th 3:4;
Phm 21
2:4 *c* ver 3,9;
2Co 7:8,12
2:5 *d* 1Co 5:1,2
2:6 *e* 1Co 5:4,5;
2Co 7:11
2:7 *f* Gal 6:1;
Eph 4:32; Col 3:13
2:9 *g* ver 3,4;
2Co 7:8,12 *h* 2Co 7:15;
10:6
2:11 *i* S Mt 4:10
j Lk 22:31; 2Co 4:4;
1Pe 5:8,9
2:12 *k* S Ac 16:8
l S Ro 1:1; 2Co 4:3,4;
8:18; 9:13; 1Th 3:2

tended to do this? Or do I make my plans in a worldly manner *g* so that in the same breath I say both "Yes, yes" and "No, no"?

¹⁸But as surely as God is faithful, *h* our message to you is not "Yes" and "No." ¹⁹For the Son of God, *i* Jesus Christ, who was preached among you by us—by me and Silas *a j* and Timothy *k*—was not "Yes" and "No," but in him it has always *l* been "Yes." ²⁰For no matter how many promises *m* God has made, they are "Yes" in Christ. And so through him the "Amen" *n* is spoken by us to the glory of God. *o* ²¹Now it is God who makes both us and you stand firm *p* in Christ. He anointed *q* us, ²²set his seal *r* of ownership on us, and put his Spirit in our hearts as a deposit, guaranteeing what is to come. *s*

²³I call God as my witness *t*—and I stake my life on it—that it was in order to spare you *u* that I did not return to Corinth. ²⁴Not that we lord it over *v* your faith, but we work with you for your joy, because it is by faith you stand firm. *w* ¹So I made up my mind that I would not make another painful visit to you. *x* ²For if I grieve you, *y* who is left to make me glad but you whom I have grieved? ³I wrote as I did, *z* so that when I came I would not be distressed *a* by those who should have made me rejoice. I had confidence *b* in all of you, that you would all share my joy. ⁴For I wrote you *c* out of great distress and anguish of heart and with many tears, not to grieve you but to let you know the depth of my love for you.

FORGIVENESS FOR THE OFFENDER

⁵If anyone has caused grief, *d* he has not so much grieved me as he has grieved all of you to some extent—not to put it too severely. ⁶The punishment *e* inflicted on him by the majority is sufficient. ⁷Now instead, you ought to forgive and comfort him, *f* so that he will not be overwhelmed by excessive sorrow. ⁸I urge you, therefore, to reaffirm your love for him. ⁹Another reason I wrote you *g* was to see if you would stand the test and be obedient in everything. *h* ¹⁰Anyone you forgive, I also forgive. And what I have forgiven—if there was anything to forgive—I have forgiven in the sight of Christ for your sake, ¹¹in order that Satan *i* might not outwit us. For we are not unaware of his schemes. *j*

MINISTERS OF THE NEW COVENANT

¹²Now when I went to Troas *k* to preach the gospel of Christ *l* and found that the Lord

a 19 Greek *Silvanus*, a variant of *Silas*

1:17 Paul's opponents in Corinth had been attempting to persuade the Christians there that this change of plan was evidence that his word was not to be trusted, that he was fickle and unreliable. The two rhetorical questions are in effect his denial that he acts lightly and that he says "Yes" and "No" at the same time, so that it is impossible to know what he means. In any case, his plan to visit the Corinthians had not been abandoned; it had simply been modified.

1:18–19 *not "Yes" and "No."* Paul now appeals to the gospel message he had preached to them. Believing it, they had found it to be true and free from ambiguity, and by their experience of its dynamic power they had proved it to be one great affirmative in Christ.

1:19 *who was preached among you.* During Paul's first visit to Corinth (see Ac 18:5). *Silas.* See Ac 15:22 and note.

1:20 *"Amen."* The "Amen" uttered by the congregation at the end of an offering of prayer or praise (cf. 1Co 14:16 and note on 14:15–17).

1:21 *anointed us.* See Ex 29:7 and note; 1Sa 16:13; Isa 61:1.

1:22 *seal.* See notes on Hag 2:23; Eph 1:13; cf. Eph 4:30. *deposit.* A part given as a guarantee that the whole will be forthcoming (see Ro 8:23 and note). The first installment of a sum of money that has been inherited, e.g., assures the recipient that the whole will be received.

1:23 *to spare you.* Paul's change of plans for visiting the Corinthian Christians had been motivated, not by a fickle and insensitive attitude, but by love and concern for them.

2:1 *another painful visit.* Paul had already made one painful visit to Corinth, and he wanted to avoid another such visit, though he was ready to assert his authority if it should prove necessary (cf. 13:2). This former visit could not have been the

one he made to Corinth at the time when the church there was founded in response to the preaching of the gospel (cf. Ac 18). Therefore he must have paid a second visit, which is confirmed by 12:14 and 13:1, where he states that the visit he is now about to make will be his third. The second visit probably took place between the writing of 1 and 2 Corinthians, though some hold that it occurred before 1 Corinthians was written.

2:3–4 See Introduction: Occasion.

2:5–11 Speaks of a particular person who has been the cause of serious offense in Corinth and upon whom church discipline has been imposed. Paul admonishes the Corinthians that because the offender has shown genuine sorrow and repentance for his sin, the punishment should be discontinued and he should be lovingly restored to their fellowship. The offense in question probably took place during Paul's intermediate visit to Corinth (see note on v. 1) and may have been the occasion for his writing the severe letter demanding the punishment of the offender (see note on vv. 3–4). Another view is that Paul refers to the incident recorded in 1Co 5.

2:7 *comfort.* See 1:3–7 and note on 1:3.

2:11 *Satan.* See Mt 16:23; 1Jn 3:8 and notes. *his schemes.* See Ge 3:1; Lk 22:31; Jn 8:44 and notes; see also 1Pe 5:8.

2:12 *I went to Troas.* Paul had traveled up from Ephesus to Troas, a city on the Aegean coast (see Ac 16:8 and note; see also map, p. 1869), hoping to find Titus there and to receive news from him about the Corinthian church. But Titus, who Paul presumably knew would be following the same route in reverse, did not arrive in Troas; so Paul, anxious for news from Corinth, "went on to Macedonia" (v. 13), perhaps to the city of Philippi (see map, p. 1869). *opened a door.* See Ac 14:27; Rev 3:8 and notes; see also 1Co 16:9; Col 4:3.

had opened a door *m* for me, ¹³I still had no peace of mind, *n* because I did not find my brother Titus *o* there. So I said good-by to them and went on to Macedonia. *p*

¹⁴But thanks be to God, *q* who always leads us as captives in Christ's triumphal procession and uses us to spread the aroma *r* of the knowledge *s* of him everywhere. ¹⁵For we are to God the pleasing aroma *t* of Christ among those who are being saved and those who are perishing. *u* ¹⁶To the one we are an aroma that brings death; *v* to the other, an aroma that brings life. And who is equal to such a task? *w* ¹⁷Unlike so many, we do not peddle the word of God for profit. *x* On the contrary, in Christ we speak before God with sincerity, *y* as those sent from God. *z*

3 Are we beginning to commend ourselves *a* again? Or do we need, like some people, letters of recommendation *b* to you or from you? ²You yourselves are our letter, written on our hearts, known and read by everyone. *c* ³You show that you are a letter from Christ, the result of our ministry, written not with ink but with the Spirit of the living God, *d* not on tablets of stone *e* but on tablets of human hearts. *f*

⁴Such confidence *g* we have through Christ before God. ⁵Not that we are competent in ourselves *h* to claim anything for ourselves, but our competence comes from God. *i* ⁶He has made us competent as ministers of a new covenant *j*—not of the letter *k* but of the Spirit; for the letter kills, but the Spirit gives life. *l*

THE GREATER GLORY OF THE NEW COVENANT

⁷Now if the ministry that brought death, *m* which was engraved in letters on stone,

3:6 *i* S Lk 22:20 *k* Ro 2:29; 7:6 *l* Jn 6:63   **3:7** *m* ver 9; S Ro 4:15

*Side references (right column):*
2:12 *m* S Ac 14:27
2:13 *n* 2Co 7:5
o 2Co 7:6,13;
8:6,16,23; 12:18;
Gal 2:1,3; Tit 1:4
p S Ac 16:9
2:14 *q* Ro 6:17; 7:25;
1Co 15:57; 2Co 9:15
r Eze 20:41; Eph 5:2;
Php 4:18 *s* S 2Co 8:7
2:15 *t* S ver 14;
Ge 8:21; Ex 29:18;
Nu 15:3 *u* S 1Co 1:18
2:16 *v* S Lk 2:34;
Jn 3:36 *w* 2Co 3:5,6
2:17 *x* S Ac 20:33;
2Co 4:2; 1Th 2:5
y 1Co 5:8 *z* 2Co 1:12;
12:19
3:1 *a* Ro 16:1;
2Co 5:12; 10:12,18;
12:11 *b* Ac 18:27;
Ro 16:1; 1Co 16:3
3:2 *c* 1Co 9:2
3:3 *d* S Mt 16:16
e ver 7; Ex 24:12;
31:18; 32:15,16
f Pr 3:3; 7:3; Jer 31:33;
Eze 36:26
3:4 *g* S Eph 3:12
3:5 *h* 2Co 2:16
i 1Co 15:10

2:13 *my brother.* Cf. 8:23. *Titus.* See Introduction to Titus: Recipient. Paul held Titus in high esteem; he entrusted Titus with the organization of the collection of funds in Corinth for the relief of the poverty-stricken Christians of Jerusalem (see 8:6 and note), and he chose him to bear this letter to the Corinthian Christians (see 8:16–17 and note on 8:16).

2:14 At this point Paul breaks off the narrative of his itinerary and in a characteristic manner begins a lengthy digression (the narrative is not resumed until 7:5; see note there). The digression, however, is relevant to the main tenor of this letter, for it is an outpouring of triumphant faith in praise of the adequacy of God's grace for every situation. *leads us as captives in Christ's triumphal procession.* A victorious Roman general would lead his soldiers and their captives in festive procession, while the people watched and applauded and the air was filled with the sweet smell released by the burning of spices in the streets (cf. note on 1Co 4:9). *everywhere.* Cf. note on 1Th 1:8.

2:16 *aroma that brings death . . . aroma that brings life.* As the gospel aroma is released in the world through Christian testimony, it is always sweet-smelling, even though it may be differently received. Ultimately there are two kinds of people: "those who are being saved and those who are perishing" (v. 15). To the latter, testifying Christians are the smell of death, not because the gospel message has become evil-smelling or death-dealing but because in rejecting the life-giving grace of God unbelievers choose death for themselves. To those who welcome the gospel of God's grace, Christians with their testimony are the fragrance of life. *who is equal to such a task?* For the answer, see 3:4–5.

2:17 *peddle the word of God for profit.* Paul is referring to false teachers who had infiltrated the Corinthian church. Such persons—themselves insincere, self-sufficient and boastful—artfully presented themselves in a persuasive manner, and their chief interest was to take money from gullible church members (cf. Mic 3:5,11). Paul, by contrast, had preached the gospel sincerely and free of charge, taking care not to be a financial burden to the Corinthian believers (see 11:7–9; 1Co 9:11–15 and notes).

3:1 *Are we beginning to commend ourselves again?* Paul realizes that virtually everything he wrote or said was liable to be twisted by the false teachers in Corinth. *letters of recommendation.* The appearance of vagrant impostors led to the need for letters of recommendation. Paul needed no such confirmation, but

others, including the Corinthian intruders, did need authentication and often resorted to unscrupulous methods for obtaining or forging such letters.

3:2 *known and read by everyone.* Because of the power of the gospel demonstrated by their transformed lives.

3:3 *letter from Christ.* Paul is no more than an instrument in the hands of the Master. *written not with ink.* As a parchment or papyrus document would be—but ink fades and may easily be deleted or blocked out. *with the Spirit of the living God.* The Spirit is himself life and therefore life-giving (v. 6), and the life he gives is eternal and without defect. *not on tablets of stone.* As at Sinai (see note on v. 6). *on tablets of human hearts.* See Jer 31:33; Eze 11:19; 36:26 and notes. Paul explains the significance of this contrast between the old and the new covenants in vv. 7–18.

3:4–5 Answers the question raised in 2:16.

3:6 *ministers of.* Those who serve the cause of (see Ro 15:16; Col 1:7; 4:7; 1Ti 4:6). Paul will return to the theme of "this ministry" in 4:1. *new covenant.* Here Paul takes up the theme suggested by the mention of "tablets of human hearts" (v. 3; see note there). See Heb 8–10. Paul's reference to "ministers of a new covenant," in contrast to the "ministry that brought death" (v. 7), may have been occasioned by his opponents in Corinth who were Judaizers, perhaps those who claimed to be associated with Peter (see 1Co 1:12 and note) and who are referred to as Hebrews in 11:22 (see note there). *the letter.* The Ten Commandments, originally written on the two tablets of stone (see Ex 24:12; 31:18 and note). *the Spirit.* The writing of the law "with the Spirit of the living God . . . on tablets of human hearts" (v. 3; see note there), which was the promise of the new covenant as foretold by the prophets (see Jer 31:31–34 and notes). *the letter kills, but the Spirit gives life.* Does not mean that the external, literal sense of Scripture is deadly or unprofitable while the inner, spiritual sense is vital. "The letter" is synonymous with the law as an external standard before which all people, because they are lawbreakers, stand guilty and condemned to death. Therefore it is described as the "ministry that brought death" (v. 7) and the "ministry that brought condemnation" (v. 9). On the other hand, the Spirit who "gives life" writes that same law inwardly "on tablets of human hearts." He thus provides believers with love for God's law, which previously they had hated, and with power to keep it, which previously they had not possessed.

3:7–18 Paul is defending his ministry of the new covenant in Christ (cf. v. 6 and note) and here compares the experiences of

3:7 *n* ver 13;
Ex 34:29-35;
Isa 42:21
3:9 *o* ver 7; Dt 27:26
p Ro 1:17; 3:21,22
3:12 *q* Ro 5:4,5;
8:24,25 *r* S Ac 4:29
3:13 *s* ver 7;
Ex 34:33
3:14 *t* Ro 11:7,8;
2Co 4:4 *u* Ac 13:15;
15:21 *v* ver 6
3:16 *w* Ro 11:23
x Ex 34:34; Isa 25:7
3:17 *y* Isa 61:1,2;
Gal 4:6,7 *z* S Jn 8:32
3:18 *a* 1Co 13:12
b Jn 17:22,24;
2Co 4:4,6 *c* S Ro 8:29
4:1 *d* 1Co 7:25;
1Ti 1:13,16 *e* ver 16;
Ps 18:45; Isa 40:31
4:2 *f* Ro 6:21;
S 1Co 4:5 *g* 2Co 2:17;
S Heb 4:12 *h* 2Co 5:11
4:3 *i* S 2Co 2:12
j 2Co 3:14 *k* S 1Co 1:18
4:4 *l* S Jn 12:31
m S 1Co 1:20
n 2Co 3:14 *o* ver 6
p S Jn 14:9
4:5 *q* 1Co 1:13
r 1Co 1:23 *s* 1Co 9:19

came with glory, so that the Israelites could not look steadily at the face of Moses because of its glory, *n* transitory though it was, [8]will not the ministry of the Spirit be even more glorious? [9]If the ministry that brought condemnation *o* was glorious, how much more glorious is the ministry that brings righteousness! *p* [10]For what was glorious has no glory now in comparison with the surpassing glory. [11]And if what was transitory came with glory, how much greater is the glory of that which lasts!

[12]Therefore, since we have such a hope, *q* we are very bold. *r* [13]We are not like Moses, who would put a veil over his face *s* to prevent the Israelites from seeing the end of what was passing away. [14]But their minds were made dull, *t* for to this day the same veil remains when the old covenant *u* is read. *v* It has not been removed, because only in Christ is it taken away. [15]Even to this day when Moses is read, a veil covers their hearts. [16]But whenever anyone turns to the Lord, *w* the veil is taken away. *x* [17]Now the Lord is the Spirit, *y* and where the Spirit of the Lord is, there is freedom. *z* [18]And we all, who with unveiled faces contemplate [a][a] the Lord's glory, *b* are being transformed into his image *c* with ever-increasing glory, which comes from the Lord, who is the Spirit.

PRESENT WEAKNESS AND RESURRECTION LIFE

4 Therefore, since through God's mercy *d* we have this ministry, we do not lose heart. *e* [2]Rather, we have renounced secret and shameful ways; *f* we do not use deception, nor do we distort the word of God. *g* On the contrary, by setting forth the truth plainly we commend ourselves to everyone's conscience *h* in the sight of God. [3]And even if our gospel *i* is veiled, *j* it is veiled to those who are perishing. *k* [4]The god *l* of this age *m* has blinded *n* the minds of unbelievers, so that they cannot see the light of the gospel that displays the glory of Christ, *o* who is the image of God. *p* [5]For what we preach is not ourselves, *q* but Jesus Christ as Lord, *r* and ourselves as your servants *s* for Jesus' sake.

a 18 Or *reflect*

Moses, who mediated the old covenant of Sinai, and his own as a minister of the new covenant. But he now applies the word "ministry" (v. 7) to the law that was "engraved in letters on stone" and to the Spirit, who writes "on tablets of human hearts" (v. 3; see note there). The point of comparison is the fading glory that shone on Moses' face and the "ever-increasing glory" (v. 18; see note there) reflected in the faces of those who minister the new covenant.

3:7 *came with glory.* The law of the old covenant given at Sinai was in no way bad or evil; on the contrary, Paul describes it elsewhere as holy, righteous, good and spiritual (Ro 7:12, 14). The evil is in the hearts and deeds of people who, as lawbreakers, bring upon themselves the condemnation of the law and the penalty of death—and the law engraved on stone could not purge away that evil. *its glory.* The glory of God surrounded the giving of the law and was reflected on the face of Moses when he descended from the mountain (see Ex 34:29–30).

3:8–9 *ministry of the Spirit . . . brings righteousness.* Giving life instead of death (cf. Isa 46:13 and note).

3:11 *what was transitory.* The old covenant of Sinai, which was not to endure forever. In due course it was superseded by the unfading and much more glorious radiance belonging to the new covenant (see Heb 8 and notes on 8:7–13).

3:13 *Moses, who would put a veil over his face.* See Ex 34:33–35 and note on 34:33. The purpose of the veil was to prevent the Israelites from seeing the fading of the glory.

3:14 *to this day the same veil remains.* The veil that prevented the Israelites from seeing the fading of the glory on Moses' face kept them from recognizing the temporary and inadequate character of the old covenant—a "veil" that is removed only in Christ.

3:17 *the Lord is the Spirit.* This statement should be linked with what was said at the end of v. 6: "the Spirit gives life." Only by turning to the Lord Jesus Christ (v. 16) can the condemnation and the sentence of death pronounced by the law on the lawbreaker be annulled and replaced by the free, life-giving grace

of the new covenant. *where the Spirit of the Lord is, there is freedom.* See Jn 8:33,36 and note on 8:32.

3:18 *with unveiled faces.* In contrast to Moses. *transformed into his image with ever-increasing glory.* Christ himself is the glory of God in the fullness of its radiance (see Heb 1:2–3 and note); his is the eternal and unfading glory, which he had with the Father "before the world began" (Jn 17:5). Cf. Ro 8:29; 12:2 and notes.

4:1 *this ministry.* See 3:6 and note. *not lose heart.* When God through his mercy calls and commissions his servants, he also supplies the strength necessary for them to persevere in the face of hardship and persecution.

4:2 *renounced secret and shameful ways.* Paul is referring to the false teachers in Corinth. By contrast, he is able to appeal to the conscience of every one of them and also to his own integrity "in the sight of God," because his practice was always that of setting forth the truth plainly, i.e., without obscuring it or resorting to deception (cf. 1:12,18–24 and note on 1:12).

4:3 *gospel is veiled.* See 3:13–18 and notes.

4:4 *god of this age.* The devil, who is the archenemy of God and the unseen power behind all unbelief and ungodliness. Those who follow him have in effect made him their god. *this age.* Used in contrast to the future, eternal age when God's creation will be forever purged of all that now mars and defiles it. Paul calls it the "present evil age" in Gal 1:4 (see note there). *blinded the minds of unbelievers.* Paul continues to use the imagery of the veil that covers the divine glory so that those who reject the gospel fail to see that glory (3:13–18). *image of God.* Christ, the incarnate Son, authentically displays God to us, for he is the very radiance of divine glory (Heb 1:3). He is the image of God in which humanity was originally created (see Ge 1:26 and note) and into which redeemed humanity is being gloriously transformed (3:18) until at last, when Christ comes again at the end of this age, we who believe will "be like him" (1Jn 3:2).

4:5 *preach . . . not ourselves.* As did the false teachers, puffed up with self-importance (cf. 1Co 2:2 and note).

⁶For God, who said, "Let light shine out of darkness,"ᵃ ᵗ made his light shine in our hearts ᵘ to give us the light of the knowledge of God's glory displayed in the face of Christ. ᵛ ⁷But we have this treasure in jars of clay ʷ to show that this all-surpassing power is from God ˣ and not from us. ⁸We are hard pressed on every side, ʸ but not crushed; perplexed, ᶻ but not in despair; ⁹persecuted, ᵃ but not abandoned; ᵇ struck down, but not destroyed. ᶜ ¹⁰We always carry around in our body the death of Jesus, ᵈ so that the life of Jesus may also be revealed in our body. ᵉ ¹¹For we who are alive are always being given over to death for Jesus' sake, ᶠ so that his life may also be revealed in our mortal body. ¹²So then, death is at work in us, but life is at work in you. ᵍ

¹³It is written: "I believed; therefore I have spoken."ᵇ ʰ Since we have that same spirit ofᶜ faith, ⁱ we also believe and therefore speak, ¹⁴because we know that the one who raised the Lord Jesus from the deadʲ will also raise us with Jesusᵏ and present us with you to himself. ˡ ¹⁵All this is for your benefit, so that the grace that is reaching more and more people may cause thanksgiving ᵐ to overflow to the glory of God.

¹⁶Therefore we do not lose heart. ⁿ Though outwardly we are wasting away, yet inwardly ᵒ we are being renewedᵖ day by day. ¹⁷For our light and momentary troubles are achieving for us an eternal glory that far outweighs them all. ᑫ ¹⁸So we fix our eyes not on what is seen, but on what is unseen, ʳ since what is seen is temporary, but what is unseen is eternal.

AWAITING THE NEW BODY

5 For we know that if the earthlyˢ tentᵗ we live in is destroyed, we have a building from God, an eternal house in heaven, not built by human hands. ²Meanwhile we groan, ᵘ longing to be clothed with our heavenly dwelling, ᵛ ³because when we are clothed, we will not be found naked. ⁴For while we are in this tent, we groan ʷ and are burdened, because we do not wish to be unclothed but to be clothed with our heavenly dwelling, ˣ so that what is mortal may be swallowed up by life. ⁵Now the one who has

ᵃ 6 Gen. 1:3   ᵇ 13 Psalm 116:10 (see Septuagint)   ᶜ 13 Or *Spirit-given*

4:6 ᵗGe 1:3; Ps 18:28
ᵘ2Pe 1:19 ᵛver 4
4:7 ʷJob 4:19;
Isa 64:8; 2Ti 2:20
ˣJdg 7:2; 1Co 2:5;
2Co 6:7
4:8 ʸ2Co 7:5
ᶻGal 4:20
4:9 ᵃJn 15:20;
Ro 8:35 ᵇHeb 13:5
ᶜPs 37:24; Pr 24:16
4:10 ᵈS Ro 6:6;
S 2Co 1:5 ᵉS Ro 6:5
4:11 ᶠRo 8:36
4:12 ᵍ2Co 13:9
4:13 ʰPs 116:10
ⁱ1Co 12:9
4:14 ʲS Ac 2:24
ᵏ1Th 4:14 ˡEph 5:27;
Col 1:22; Jude 24
4:15 ᵐ2Co 1:11; 9:11
4:16 ⁿver 1;
Ps 18:45 ᵒRo 7:22
ᵖPs 103:5; Isa 40:31;
Col 3:10
4:17 ᑫPs 30:5;
Ro 8:18; 1Pe 1:6,7
4:18 ʳ2Co 5:7;
Ro 8:24; Heb 11:1
5:1 ˢ1Co 15:47
ᵗIsa 38:12; 2Pe 1:13,14
5:2 ᵘver 4; Ro 8:23
ᵛver 4; 1Co 15:53,54
5:4 ʷver 2; Ro 8:23
ˣver 2; 1Co 15:53,54

4:6 *Let light shine out of darkness.* God said this at the creation (see Ge 1:2–4 and notes) and says it again in the new creation or new birth (see 5:17; Jn 3:3 and notes; 1Pe 1:3), as the darkness of sin is dispelled by the light of the gospel. *the light of the knowledge of God's glory.* The light that now shines in Paul's heart (qualifying him to be a proclaimer of Christ) is the knowledge of God's glory as it was displayed in the face of Christ—who has come from the glorious presence of God in heaven (see Jn 1:14 and note).

4:7 *this treasure.* The gospel. *jars of clay.* Treasures were concealed in clay jars, which had little value or beauty and did not attract attention to themselves and their contents. Here they represent Paul's human frailty and unworthiness. *all-surpassing power is from God and not from us.* The idea that the absolute insufficiency of human beings reveals the total sufficiency of God pervades this letter.

4:8–12 See 11:23–26 and notes.

4:10 *We always carry around in our body the death of Jesus.* The frailty of the "clay jar" of Paul's humanity (v. 7) is plainly seen in the constant hardships and persecutions with which he is buffeted for the sake of the gospel and through which he shares in Christ's suffering (see 1:5; Ro 8:17; Php 3:10; Col 1:24 and notes). *that the life of Jesus may also be revealed in our body.* Refers to Christ's resurrection life and power (see Php 3:10 and note). Once again (see v. 7 and note), human weakness provides the occasion for the triumph of divine power.

4:12 *death.* See 1Co 15:31 and note. *life.* See v. 10 and note.

4:13 *I believed; therefore I have spoken.* Faith leads to testimony. Paul therefore tirelessly labored and journeyed to bring the gospel message to others.

4:14 *one who raised the Lord Jesus.* God (Ac 2:24). *raise us with Jesus.* See Ro 8:11; 1Co 15:20 and notes.

4:16 *we do not lose heart.* Repeating the statement in v. 1. The intervening paragraphs explain why the apostle continues to have a cheerful heart, and the rest of the chapter summarizes the argument he has developed. *wasting away.* Because of the

hardships to which he is subjected. *being renewed.* Because of the flame of resurrection life burning within.

4:17 *light and momentary troubles.* Seen from the perspective of eternity, the Christian's difficulties diminish in importance. *eternal glory that far outweighs them all.* By comparison, the eternal glory is far greater than all the suffering one may face in this life (see Ro 8:17–18 and note on 8:17).

4:18 *what is seen . . . what is unseen.* The experiences and circumstances of this present life are visible to the Christian; but these are merely temporary and fleeting. To fix our eyes on them would cause us to "lose heart" (vv. 1,16). By contrast the unseen realities, which are no less real for being invisible (cf. Heb 11:1,7,26–27), are eternal and imperishable. Accordingly, we look up and away from the impermanent appearances of this present world scene (see Php 3:20; Heb 12:2 and notes).

5:1 *earthly tent we live in.* Our present body (see Jn 1:14 and note; 2Pe 1:13). As a tent is a temporary and flimsy abode, so our bodies are frail, vulnerable and wasting away (see 4:10–12,16 and notes). *a building from God, an eternal house in heaven.* A solid structure—permanent, not temporary. This is one of the eternal realities that are as yet "unseen" (4:18). *not built by human hands.* The work of God, and therefore perfect and permanent (see Heb 9:11 and note).

5:2 *Meanwhile.* As we await the Lord's return. *we groan.* Because we long for the perfection that will be ours when we put on the glorious spiritual body (cf. 1Co 15:42–49 and notes). *clothed with our heavenly dwelling.* The eternal dwelling provided by God is pictured as a garment.

5:3 *naked.* Without the clothing of a body, which is the state of those whose earthly dwelling has been dismantled by death (see v. 8 and note).

5:4 *what is mortal.* Our present mortal body. *swallowed up by life.* By our participation in the resurrection life of Jesus (see 4:10 and note) our mortal being is "swallowed up by life," not by death. Paul reverses the age-old imagery of death and the grave being the great swallower (see Ps 49:14 and note), as did Isaiah (see Isa 25:8; see also 1Co 15:54).

5:5 ʸRo 8:23;
2Co 1:22; Eph 1:13,14
5:7 ᶻ1Co 13:12;
S 2Co 4:18
5:8 ᵃS Jn 12:26
5:9 ᵇRo 14:18;
Eph 5:10; Col 1:10;
1Th 4:1
5:10 ᶜS Mt 16:27;
Ac 10:42; Ro 2:16;
14:10; Eph 6:8
5:11 ᵈJob 23:15;
Heb 10:31; 12:29;
Jude 23 ᵉ2Co 4:2
5:12 ᶠS 2Co 3:1
ᵍ2Co 1:14
5:13 ʰ2Co 11:1,16,17;
12:11
5:14 ⁱRo 6:6,7;
Gal 2:20; Col 3:3
5:15 ʲRo 14:7-9
ᵏRo 4:25
5:16 ˡ2Co 10:4;
11:18
5:17 ᵐS Ro 16:3
ⁿS Jn 1:13; S Ro 6:4;
Gal 6:15 ᵒIsa 65:17;
Rev 21:4,5
5:18 ᵖS Ro 11:36
�q S Ro 5:10
5:19 ʳS Ro 4:8
5:20 ˢ2Co 6:1;
Eph 6:20 ᵗver 18
ᵘIsa 27:5
5:21 ᵛHeb 4:15;
7:26; 1Pe 2:22,24;
1Jn 3:5 ʷS Ro 1:17;
S 1Co 1:30

fashioned us for this very purpose is God, who has given us the Spirit as a deposit, guaranteeing what is to come. ʸ

⁶Therefore we are always confident and know that as long as we are at home in the body, we are away from the Lord. ⁷We live by faith, not by sight. ᶻ ⁸We are confident, I say, and would prefer to be away from the body and at home with the Lord. ᵃ ⁹So we make it our goal to please him, ᵇ whether we are at home in the body or away from it. ¹⁰For we must all appear before the judgment seat of Christ, that everyone may receive what is due them ᶜ for the things done while in the body, whether good or bad.

THE MINISTRY OF RECONCILIATION

¹¹Since, then, we know what it is to fear the Lord, ᵈ we try to persuade people. What we are is plain to God, and I hope it is also plain to your conscience. ᵉ ¹²We are not trying to commend ourselves to you again, ᶠ but are giving you an opportunity to take pride in us, ᵍ so that you can answer those who take pride in what is seen rather than in what is in the heart. ¹³If we are "out of our mind," ʰ as some say, it is for God; if we are in our right mind, it is for you. ¹⁴For Christ's love compels us, because we are convinced that one died for all, and therefore all died. ⁱ ¹⁵And he died for all, that those who live should no longer live for themselvesʲ but for him who died for them ᵏ and was raised again.

¹⁶So from now on we regard no one from a worldly ˡ point of view. Though we once regarded Christ in this way, we do so no longer. ¹⁷Therefore, if anyone is in Christ, ᵐ the new creation ⁿ has come: The old has gone, the new is here! ᵒ ¹⁸All this is from God, ᵖ who reconciled us to himself through Christ q and gave us the ministry of reconciliation: ¹⁹that God was reconciling the world to himself in Christ, not counting people's sins against them. ʳ And he has committed to us the message of reconciliation. ²⁰We are therefore Christ's ambassadors, ˢ as though God were making his appeal through us. ᵗ We implore you on Christ's behalf: Be reconciled to God. ᵘ ²¹God made him who had no sin ᵛ to be sinᵃ for us, so that in him we might become the righteousness of God. ʷ

ᵃ 21 Or *be a sin offering*

5:5 *God…has given us the Spirit.* The Holy Spirit applies the benefits of Christ's redeeming work to the hearts of believers and makes his resurrection power a reality of their daily experience (cf. 4:10–16 and notes). This guarantees their eventual transformation into the likeness of Christ's glorified body (see Php 3:21 and note). *deposit.* See 1:22 and note.
5:6 *at home in the body.* In our earthly dwelling (see v. 1 and note); it does not mean that we are deprived of the Lord's spiritual presence with us in our daily lives.
5:7 *by faith, not by sight.* See 4:18 and note; cf. 1Co 13:12 and note.

▲ 5:8 *away from the body…at home with the Lord.* The situation of believers after death, when they are no longer living in their mortal bodies (see Php 1:23 and note).
5:9 *whether we are at home in the body or away from it.* Whether we will still be alive or will already be with the Lord.

▲ 5:10 *appear before the judgment seat of Christ.* To give an accounting of what we have done with our lives as Christians (cf. 1Co 3:11–15 and note on 3:13). *things done while in the body.* Although the body is wasting away, we are responsible for our actions while in it.
5:11 *fear the Lord.* As the one to whom we are accountable (v. 10; see Ge 20:11; Pr 1:7 and notes). *we try to persuade people.* Paul needs to persuade some members of the Corinthian church that he, not any of the false teachers who have invaded their ranks, is their authentic apostle.

▲ 5:12 *take pride in what is seen.* The pretension of the false apostles is a superficial front; their concern is not with spirituality that is true and deep but with money, popularity and self-importance.

C 5:13 *out of our mind…in our right mind.* Perhaps Paul's enemies were asserting that he was suffering from religious mania—what they regarded as his insane way of life. If this is what it means to be out of his mind, Paul does not deny it, for this whole letter shows how willingly and joyfully he endured affliction for the gospel (see 12:10). On the other hand, there was nothing that could be called eccentric about his man-

ner of presenting the gospel to the Corinthians, for he had been sensible and sober-minded, avoiding flowery rhetoric and all forms of sensationalism (see 1Co 2:1–5 and notes).
5:14 *Christ's love.* As shown in his death for us, though some hold that the meaning here is "our love for Christ." *one.* The incarnate Son. *therefore all died.* Because Christ died for all, he involved all in his death. For some his death would confirm their own death, but for others (those who by faith would become united with him) his death was their death to sin and self, so that they now live in and with the resurrected Christ (v. 15; see Ro 6:1–11). However, some hold that Paul is not speaking specifically here about the scope of Christ's atonement but about the effect of Christ's death on the Christian life. Thus "all" would refer not to every human being but only to believers.
5:16 *we once regarded Christ in this way.* Paul admits that before his conversion he held views of Christ that were "worldly"—based on purely human considerations.

▲ 5:17 *in Christ.* United with Christ through faith in him and commitment to him (see Ro 6:11; Eph 1:1; Php 2:1 and notes). *new creation.* Redemption is the restoration and fulfillment of God's purposes in creation (see 4:6 and note), and this takes place in Christ, through whom all things were made (see Col 1:16 and note; Heb 1:2) and in whom all things are restored or created anew (cf. Ro 8:19–23; Eph 2:10).

▲ 5:18 *All this is from God.* God takes the initiative in redemption (see Jn 3:16; Eph 2:8–10 and notes; Ro 5:8), and he sustains it and brings it to completion (see Php 1:6 and note). *ministry of reconciliation.* We who are the recipients of divine reconciliation have the privilege and obligation of now being God's instruments to proclaim the "message of reconciliation" (v. 19) throughout the world. *reconciliation.* See Ro 5:10 and note.

▲ 5:21 A summary of the gospel. Christ, the only entirely righteous one, took our sin upon himself at Calvary and endured the punishment we deserved (see TNIV text note), namely, death and separation from God. Thus, by a marvelous exchange, he made it possible for us to receive his righteousness and thereby be reconciled to God (cf. 1Co 1:30 and note).

6

As God's co-workers^x we urge you not to receive God's grace in vain.^{y} ^{2}For he says,

> "In the time of my favor I heard you,
>   and in the day of salvation I helped you."^{az}

I tell you, now is the time of God's favor, now is the day of salvation.

PAUL'S HARDSHIPS

^{3}We put no stumbling block in anyone's path,^{a} so that our ministry will not be discredited. ^{4}Rather, as servants of God we commend ourselves in every way: in great endurance; in troubles, hardships and distresses; ^{5}in beatings, imprisonments^b and riots; in hard work, sleepless nights and hunger; ^{c} ^{6}in purity, understanding, patience and kindness; in the Holy Spirit^d and in sincere love; ^{e} ^{7}in truthful speech^f and in the power of God; ^{g} with weapons of righteousness^h in the right hand and in the left; ^{8}through glory and dishonor,^{i} bad report^j and good report; genuine, yet regarded as impostors; ^{k} ^{9}known, yet regarded as unknown; dying,^{l} and yet we live on; ^{m} beaten, and yet not killed; ^{10}sorrowful, yet always rejoicing; ^{n} poor, yet making many rich; ^{o} having nothing,^{p} and yet possessing everything. ^{q}

^{11}We have spoken freely to you, Corinthians, and opened wide our hearts to you. ^{r} ^{12}We are not withholding our affection from you, but you are withholding yours from us. ^{13}As a fair exchange—I speak as to my children ^{s}—open wide your hearts^t also.

WARNING AGAINST IDOLATRY

^{14}Do not be yoked together^u with unbelievers. ^{v} For what do righteousness and wickedness have in common? Or what fellowship can light have with darkness? ^{w} ^{15}What harmony is there between Christ and Belial^b? ^{x} Or what does a believer^y have in common with an unbeliever? ^{z} ^{16}What agreement is there between the temple of God and idols? ^{a} For we are the temple ^{b} of the living God. ^{c} As God has said:

> "I will live with them
>   and walk among them,
> and I will be their God,
>   and they will be my people."^{cd}

^{17}Therefore,

> "Come out from them ^{e}
>   and be separate,

says the Lord.

---

^{a} 2 Isaiah 49:8 ^{b} 15 Greek *Beliar*, a variant of *Belial* ^{c} 16 Lev. 26:12; Jer. 32:38; Ezek. 37:27

6:1 ^{x} S 1Co 3:9; 2Co 5:20 ^{y} 1Co 15:2
6:2 ^{z} Isa 49:8; Ps 69:13; Isa 55:6
6:3 ^{a} S Mt 5:29; Ro 14:13,20; 1Co 8:9,13; 9:12; 10:32
6:5 ^{b} Ac 16:23; 2Co 11:23-25 ^{c} 1Co 4:11
6:6 ^{d} 1Co 2:4; 1Th 1:5 ^{e} Ro 12:9; 1Ti 1:5
6:7 ^{f} 2Co 4:2 ^{g} 2Co 4:7 ^{h} Ro 13:12; 2Co 10:4; Eph 6:10-18
6:8 ^{i} 1Co 4:10 ^{j} 1Co 4:13 ^{k} Mt 27:63
6:9 ^{l} S Ro 8:36 ^{m} 2Co 1:8-10; 4:10,11
6:10 ^{n} S Mt 5:12; 2Co 7:4; Php 2:17; 4:4; Col 1:24; 1Th 1:6 ^{o} 2Co 8:9 ^{p} Ac 3:6 ^{q} Ro 8:32; 1Co 3:21
6:11 ^{r} 2Co 7:3
6:13 ^{s} 1Th 2:11 ^{t} 2Co 7:2
6:14 ^{u} Ge 24:3; Dt 22:10; 1Co 5:9,10 ^{v} 1Co 6:6 ^{w} Eph 5:7,11; 1Jn 1:6
6:15 ^{x} 1Co 10:21 ^{y} Ac 5:14 ^{z} 1Co 6:6
6:16 ^{a} 1Co 10:21 ^{b} S 1Co 3:16 ^{c} S Mt 16:16 ^{d} Lev 26:12; Jer 32:38; Eze 37:27; Rev 21:3
6:17 ^{e} Rev 18:4

A **6:1** *to receive God's grace in vain.* To live for oneself (see 5:15) is one way to do this.

6:2 *time of my favor ... day of salvation.* An affirmation that is true in a general sense of all God's saving acts in the history of his people, but that finds its particular fulfillment in this present age of grace between the two comings of Christ. *now.* Underscores the urgency of the divine invitation (see Ps 32:6 and note).

6:4–10 Cf. 4:8–12.

6:4 *as servants of God we commend ourselves.* Paul commends himself again inasmuch as the gospel he preached in Corinth is at stake; but, in contrast to the false apostles who were no better than self-servers, he does so as God's servant.

6:5 *imprisonments.* See, e.g., Ac 16:23; Eph 3:1; Php 1:13–14; Col 4:18; 2Ti 1:16; Phm 1.

6:7 *weapons of righteousness.* Cf. Eph 6:14–17 and notes.

A **6:10** *making many rich.* True wealth does not consist in worldly possessions but in being "rich toward God" (Lk 12:21). Believers, even if they have nothing of this world's goods, nevertheless have everything in him who is Lord of all (cf. 1Co 1:4–5; 3:21–23; Eph 2:7; 3:8; Php 4:19 and note; Col 2:3).

6:11–13 Paul has always been completely open and sincere in his relations with the Christians in Corinth (cf. 1:12–14; 4:2 and

note), but the false apostles among them have been trying to persuade them that Paul does not really love them. Now the apostle tenderly appeals to these Corinthians, who are the beneficiaries of his love for them (cf. 11:11).

6:14 *Do not be yoked together with unbelievers.* Cf. Dt 22:10. For the Corinthian believers to cooperate with false teachers, who are in reality servants of Satan, notwithstanding their charming and persuasive ways (see 11:13–14 and notes), is to become unequally true yoked, destroying the harmony and fellowship that unite true believers in Christ. *what fellowship can light have with darkness?* See 4:6 and note.

6:15 *Belial.* Satan (see Dt 13:13 and note).

A **6:16** *agreement ... between the temple of God and idols.* There can be no reversion to or compromise with the idolatry they have forsaken for the gospel (cf. 1Th 1:9). *temple of the living God.* Built of "living stones," namely, Christian believers (1Pe 2:5; see note there); therefore it is all the more important that they form no defiling and unholy alliances (cf. 1Co 6:19–20). *their God ... my people.* The supreme OT affirmation of covenant relationship between God and his people (see Jer 7:23; Hos 1:9; Zec 8:8 and notes).

6:17 *Come out from them.* See Rev 18:4 and note.

6:17 *f* Isa 52:11;
Eze 20:34,41
6:18 *g* Ex 4:22;
2Sa 7:14; 1Ch 17:13;
Isa 43:6; S Ro 8:14
h 2Sa 7:8
7:1 *i* 2Co 6:17,18
j S 1Co 10:14
k 1Th 4:7; 1Pe 1:15,16
7:2 *l* 2Co 6:12,13
7:3 *m* 2Co 6:11,12;
Php 1:7
7:4 *n* ver 14;
2Co 8:24 *o* ver 13
p S 2Co 6:10
7:5 *q* 2Co 2:13;
S Ac 16:9 *r* 2Co 4:8
s Dt 32:25
7:6 *t* 2Co 1:3,4;
u ver 13; S 2Co 2:13
7:8 *v* 2Co 2:2,4
7:10 *w* Ac 11:18
7:11 *x* ver 7
7:12 *y* ver 8;
2Co 2:3,9 *z* 1Co 5:1,2
7:13 *a* ver 6;
S 2Co 2:13
7:14 *b* ver 4 *c* ver 6
7:15 *d* 2Co 2:9; 10:6
e Ps 55:5; 1Co 2:3;
Php 2:12
7:16 *f* S 2Co 2:3

> Touch no unclean thing,
> and I will receive you." [a] [f]

¹⁸And,

> "I will be a Father to you,
> and you will be my sons and daughters, [g]
>
> says the Lord Almighty." [b] [h]

7 Therefore, since we have these promises, [i] dear friends, [j] let us purify ourselves from everything that contaminates body and spirit, perfecting holiness [k] out of reverence for God.

PAUL'S JOY OVER THE CHURCH'S REPENTANCE

²Make room for us in your hearts. [l] We have wronged no one, we have corrupted no one, we have exploited no one. ³I do not say this to condemn you; I have said before that you have such a place in our hearts [m] that we would live or die with you. ⁴I have spoken to you with great frankness; I take great pride in you. [n] I am greatly encouraged; [o] in all our troubles my joy knows no bounds. [p]

⁵For when we came into Macedonia, [q] this body of ours had no rest, but we were harassed at every turn [r]—conflicts on the outside, fears within. [s] ⁶But God, who comforts the downcast, [t] comforted us by the coming of Titus, [u] ⁷and not only by his coming but also by the comfort you had given him. He told us about your longing for me, your deep sorrow, your ardent concern for me, so that my joy was greater than ever.

⁸Even if I caused you sorrow by my letter, [v] I do not regret it. Though I did regret it—I see that my letter hurt you, but only for a little while— ⁹yet now I am happy, not because you were made sorry, but because your sorrow led you to repentance. For you became sorrowful as God intended and so were not harmed in any way by us. ¹⁰Godly sorrow brings repentance that leads to salvation [w] and leaves no regret, but worldly sorrow brings death. ¹¹See what this godly sorrow has produced in you: what earnestness, what eagerness to clear yourselves, what indignation, what alarm, what longing, what concern, [x] what readiness to see justice done. At every point you have proved yourselves to be innocent in this matter. ¹²So even though I wrote to you, [y] it was neither on account of the one who did the wrong [z] nor on account of the injured party, but rather that before God you could see for yourselves how devoted to us you are. ¹³By all this we are encouraged.

In addition to our own encouragement, we were especially delighted to see how happy Titus [a] was, because his spirit has been refreshed by all of you. ¹⁴I had boasted to him about you, [b] and you have not embarrassed me. But just as everything we said to you was true, so our boasting about you to Titus [c] has proved to be true as well. ¹⁵And his affection for you is all the greater when he remembers that you were all obedient, [d] receiving him with fear and trembling. [e] ¹⁶I am glad I can have complete confidence in you. [f]

a 17 Isaiah 52:11; Ezek. 20:34,41   *b 18* 2 Samuel 7:14; 7:8

7:1 *holiness.* See 1Co 1:2; Ex 3:5; Lev 11:44; Ro 6:22; 1Th 4:7 and notes.
7:2 *Make room for us in your hearts.* Resumes the thought of 6:13 after a brief digression. *We have . . . exploited no one.* Implies that Paul had been accused by the false teachers of being unjust, destructive and fraudulent—the very things they themselves were guilty of. Cf. 1Sa 12:3 and note.
7:3 Again Paul declares the depth of his affection for the Corinthian believers and appeals to them to respond by displaying their love for him (cf. 6:11–13 and note).
7:4 *great frankness . . . my joy knows no bounds.* The long digression that started at 2:14 (see note there) concludes here on this note of exhilaration. The news he had been so anxiously awaiting from Corinth has turned out to be reassuring, and Paul is overjoyed to receive it.
7:5 *we.* Paul and Titus. Here Paul resumes the account he began at 2:12–13, where he described how his hopes of meeting Titus in Troas were disappointed and how, restless for news, he had decided to press on into Macedonia. He now explains that on reaching Macedonia, he was at last comforted by the arrival of Titus, who had been well received in Corinth and was able to

assure Paul (see v. 7) of the "longing" and "ardent concern" of the Corinthian Christians for him and of the "deep sorrow" they had expressed because of the grief they had caused him. Consequently, his "joy was greater than ever." *Macedonia.* See notes on 1:1; Php 4:15.
7:6 *God . . . comforts the downcast.* See 1:3 and note; cf. Ps 42:5,11; 43:5. *Titus.* See Introduction to Titus: Recipient.
7:8 Paul regretted the necessity of writing a letter to the Corinthians that caused them sorrow. *my letter.* Some think Paul here refers either to 1 Corinthians or to 2Co 10–13 (see Introduction: Occasion), but more likely he refers to a letter now lost that he wrote shortly after his "painful visit" (2:1; see note there).
7:10 *Godly sorrow . . . worldly sorrow.* The former manifests itself by repentance and the experience of divine grace; the latter brings death because, instead of being God-centered sorrow over the wickedness of sin, it is self-centered sorrow over the painful consequences of sin.
7:15 *you were all obedient.* This seems to indicate that when Titus left Corinth to report to Paul, there was no strong opposition party (see note on 10:1).

THE COLLECTION FOR THE LORD'S PEOPLE

And now, brothers and sisters, we want you to know about the grace that God has given the Macedonian *g* churches. ²In the midst of a very severe trial, their overflowing joy and their extreme poverty welled up in rich generosity. *h* ³For I testify that they gave as much as they were able, *i* and even beyond their ability. Entirely on their own, ⁴they urgently pleaded with us for the privilege of sharing *j* in this service *k* to the Lord's people. *l* ⁵And they went beyond our expectations; having given themselves first of all to the Lord, they gave themselves by the will of God also to us. ⁶So we urged *m* Titus, *n* just as he had earlier made a beginning, to bring also to completion *o* this act of grace on your part. ⁷But since you excel in everything *p* —in faith, in speech, in knowledge, *q* in complete earnestness and in the love we have kindled in you *a* —see that you also excel in this grace of giving.

⁸I am not commanding you, *r* but I want to test the sincerity of your love by comparing it with the earnestness of others. ⁹For you know the grace *s* of our Lord Jesus Christ, *t* that though he was rich, yet for your sake he became poor, *u* so that you through his poverty might become rich. *v*

¹⁰And here is my judgment *w* about what is best for you in this matter. Last year you were the first not only to give but also to have the desire to do so. *x* ¹¹Now finish the work, so that your eager willingness *y* to do it may be matched by your completion of it, according to your means. ¹²For if the willingness is there, the gift is acceptable according to what one has, *z* not according to what one does not have.

¹³Our desire is not that others might be relieved while you are hard pressed, but that there might be equality. ¹⁴At the present time your plenty will supply what they need, *a* so that in turn their plenty will supply what you need. The goal is equality, ¹⁵as it is written: "The one who gathered much did not have too much, and the one who gathered little did not have too little." *b b*

TITUS SENT TO RECEIVE THE COLLECTION

¹⁶Thanks be to God, *c* who put into the heart *d* of Titus *e* the same concern I have for you. ¹⁷For Titus not only welcomed our appeal, but he is coming to you with much enthusiasm and on his own initiative. *f* ¹⁸And we are sending along with him the brother *g* who is praised by all the churches *h* for his service to the gospel. *i* ¹⁹What is more, he was chosen by the churches to accompany us *j* as we carry the offering, which we administer in order to honor the Lord himself and to show our eagerness to help. *k* ²⁰We want to avoid any criticism of the way we administer this liberal gift. ²¹For we are taking pains to do what is right, not only in the eyes of the Lord but also in the eyes of others. *l*

---

a 7 Some manuscripts *and in your love for us*   *b* 15 Exodus 16:18

8:1 *g* S Ac 16:9
8:2 *h* Ex 36:5;
2Co 9:11
8:3 *i* 1Co 16:2
8:4 *j* ver 1
k S Ac 24:17
l S Ac 9:13
8:6 *m* ver 17;
2Co 12:18 *n* ver 16,23;
S 2Co 2:13 *o* ver 10,11
8:7 *p* 2Co 9:8
q Ro 15:14; 1Co 1:5;
12:8; 13:1,2; 14:6
8:8 *r* 1Co 7:6
8:9 *s* S Ro 3:24
t 2Co 13:14
u Mt 20:28; Php 2:6-8
v 2Co 6:10
8:10 *w* 1Co 7:25,40
x 1Co 16:2,3; 2Co 9:2
8:11 *y* ver 12,19;
Ex 25:2; 2Co 9:2
8:12 *z* Mk 12:43,44;
2Co 9:7
8:14 *a* Ac 4:34;
2Co 9:12
8:15 *b* Ex 16:18
8:16 *c* S 2Co 2:14
d Rev 17:17
e S 2Co 2:13
8:17 *f* ver 6
8:18 *g* 2Co 12:18
h S 1Co 7:17
i S 2Co 2:12
8:19 *j* Ac 14:23;
1Co 16:3,4 *k* ver 11,12
8:21 *l* Ro 12:17;
S 14:18; S Tit 2:14

8:1—9:15 Paul addresses the question of the collection of money for the distressed believers in Jerusalem, which the Corinthians had started but not completed.

8:1 *grace.* The "grace of giving" on the part of believers (v. 7) is more than matched by the self-giving "grace of our Lord Jesus Christ" (v. 9).

8:2 *overflowing joy.* In the blessings of the gospel.

8:5 *having given themselves first of all to the Lord.* The true basis of all Christian giving. God's grace makes a difference in the lives and attitudes of his people—a central theme of this letter (cf. 12:9–10).

8:6 *we urged Titus.* The collection had been started in Corinth under the direction of Titus during the previous year (see v. 10; 9:2) but had slowed down or come to a standstill. Paul is now sending Titus back to them, bearing this present letter, for the purpose of completing this "act of grace."

8:7 *you excel in everything.* Cf. 1Co 1:4–7.

8:8 *I am not commanding you.* True charity and generosity cannot be commanded. *sincerity of your love.* They can prove this by giving selflessly and spontaneously. *earnestness of others.* The remarkable example of the Macedonian churches (vv. 1–5).

8:9 *though he was rich ... he became poor.* The eternal Son, in his incarnation and atoning death, emptied himself of his riches (see Php 2:7 and note). *through his poverty might become rich.* The supreme and inescapable incentive of all genuine Christian generosity.

8:11 The work they had started "last year" with "desire" (v. 10) needs to be completed (see note on v. 6).

8:12 *according to what one has.* See v. 11. What matters is the willingness, no matter how small the amount that can be afforded (see Mk 12:41–44 and note on 12:42). The mechanics of the collection being made in Corinth had been proposed by Paul in his earlier letter (see 1Co 16:1–2 and notes).

8:13–15 Paul's desire is that believers throughout the whole Christian community share what they have with believers who are in need so that a measure of equality is maintained within the church—so that, as with Israel in the desert (see Ex 16:18 and note), there would be none who have "too much" and none who have "too little" (v. 15).

8:16–17 Titus had established a relationship of trust and affection with the Corinthians (see 7:6–7,13–15). He had organized the collection when it was started the previous year (see note on v. 6).

8:18 *brother.* Perhaps Luke or Barnabas.

8:19 Paul provides a good example of the care that church leaders should take in handling money (see 1Co 16:3–4 and note on 16:3).

8:20 It is important not only that God sees but also that people see (cf. vv. 19,21) that one is carrying on the Lord's work in an ethical way.

8:21 *taking pains to do what is right.* Paul is the victim of disgraceful slander (implied by 12:17–18; see note on 12:16; see

8:23 *m* S 2Co 2:13
n Phm 17
o S Php 2:25
p ver 18,22
8:24 *q* 2Co 7:4,14;
9:2
9:1 *r* 1Th 4:9
s S Ac 24:17
t S Ac 9:13
9:2 *u* 2Co 8:11,12,19
v 2Co 7:4,14; 8:24
w 2Co 8:10
x S Ac 18:12
9:3 *y* 2Co 8:23
z 1Co 16:2
9:4 *a* Ro 15:26
9:5 *b* ver 3
c Php 4:17
d 2Co 12:17,18
9:6 *e* Pr 11:24,25;
22:9; Gal 6:7,9
9:7 *f* Ex 25:2;
2Co 8:12 *g* Dt 15:10
h Ro 12:8
9:8 *i* Eph 3:20
j Php 4:19
9:9 *k* Mal 3:10
l Ps 112:9
9:10 *m* Isa 55:10
n Hos 10:12
9:11 *o* 1Co 1:5
p ver 5 *q* 2Co 1:11;
4:15
9:12 *r* 2Co 8:14
s S 2Co 1:11
9:13 *t* S 2Co 8:4
u S Mt 9:8 *v* S Heb 3:1
w S 2Co 2:12 *x* ver 5
9:15 *y* S 2Co 2:14
z Ro 5:15,16
10:1 *a* Mt 11:29
b Gal 5:2; Eph 3:1
10:2 *c* S 1Co 4:21

²²In addition, we are sending with them our brother who has often proved to us in many ways that he is zealous, and now even more so because of his great confidence in you. ²³As for Titus, *m* he is my partner *n* and co-worker *o* among you; as for our brothers, *p* they are representatives of the churches and an honor to Christ. ²⁴Therefore show these men the proof of your love and the reason for our pride in you, *q* so that the churches can see it.

9 There is no need *r* for me to write to you about this service *s* to the Lord's people. *t* ²For I know your eagerness to help, *u* and I have been boasting *v* about it to the Macedonians, telling them that since last year *w* you in Achaia *x* were ready to give; and your enthusiasm has stirred most of them to action. ³But I am sending the brothers *y* in order that our boasting about you in this matter should not prove hollow, but that you may be ready, as I said you would be. *z* ⁴For if any Macedonians *a* come with me and find you unprepared, we—not to say anything about you—would be ashamed of having been so confident. ⁵So I thought it necessary to urge the brothers *b* to visit you in advance and finish the arrangements for the generous gift you had promised. Then it will be ready as a generous gift, *c* not as one grudgingly given. *d*

GENEROSITY ENCOURAGED

⁶Remember this: Whoever sows sparingly will also reap sparingly, and whoever sows generously will also reap generously. *e* ⁷Each of you should give what you have decided in your heart to give, *f* not reluctantly or under compulsion, *g* for God loves a cheerful giver. *h* ⁸And God is able *i* to bless you abundantly, so that in all things at all times, having all that you need, *j* you will abound in every good work. ⁹As it is written:

> "They have scattered abroad their gifts *k* to the poor;
> their righteousness endures forever." *a l*

¹⁰Now he who supplies seed to the sower and bread for food *m* will also supply and increase your store of seed and will enlarge the harvest of your righteousness. *n* ¹¹You will be made rich *o* in every way so that you can be generous *p* on every occasion, and through us your generosity will result in thanksgiving to God. *q*

¹²This service that you perform is not only supplying the needs *r* of the Lord's people but is also overflowing in many expressions of thanks to God. *s* ¹³Because of the service *t* by which you have proved yourselves, people will praise God *u* for the obedience that accompanies your confession *v* of the gospel of Christ, *w* and for your generosity *x* in sharing with them and with everyone else. ¹⁴And in their prayers for you their hearts will go out to you, because of the surpassing grace God has given you. ¹⁵Thanks be to God *y* for his indescribable gift! *z*

PAUL'S DEFENSE OF HIS MINISTRY

10 By the meekness and gentleness *a* of Christ, I appeal to you—I, Paul, *b* who am "timid" when face to face with you, but "bold" toward you when away! ²I beg you that when I come I may not have to be as bold *c* as I expect to be toward

a 9 Psalm 112:9

---

also Introduction: Purposes), but the integrity of his representatives (see v. 23 and note) reflects well on his own integrity.
8:22 *our brother.* This second brother is also anonymous (cf. v. 18 and note).
8:23 *partner and co-worker.* See 2:13 and note. *representatives of the churches.* Duly elected delegates of the churches at large (so that they could not be dismissed as cronies chosen by Paul alone); see note on Ac 20:4. *an honor to Christ.* By their outstanding faithfulness.
9:2 *Macedonians . . . Achaia.* See 1:1 and note.
9:5 *generous gift, not . . . grudgingly given.* See vv. 6–7,11.
9:6 Probably a well-known proverb. For a similar principle, cf. Pr 11:24–25; 22:8–9; Lk 6:38; Gal 6:7.

9:8 *bless you abundantly . . . all things . . . all times . . . all that you need . . . abound in every good work.* Through his abounding grace (see v. 14 and note) God can enable each Christian to abound in generous deeds (see v. 11).
9:9–10 *righteousness.* See note on Ps 1:5.

9:10 *The God who is the ultimate source of the physical food that sustains all human life is the same God who supplies the spiritual nourishment that enables believers to*

flourish and serve.
9:12 *not only supplying the needs of the Lord's people.* The effect of generous giving on the part of the Corinthians will extend beyond Jerusalem to the church as a whole, causing widespread prayer and praise to be offered (see vv. 11,13–14).
9:14 *the surpassing grace God has given you.* Displayed in this unselfish demonstration of their loving concern for fellow believers who are in desperate need.

9:15 *indescribable gift.* His own Son (see Jn 3:16 and note). God is the first giver; he selflessly gives himself to us in the person of his Son, and all true Christian giving is our grateful response (cf. 8:9 and note; 1Jn 4:9–11).
10:1—13:14 See Introduction: Occasion. From the mild tone of the first nine chapters of this letter, it appears that most of the Corinthian believers had been won over to Paul (cf. 7:6–16) after having been alienated by his opponents. In this final section, however, Paul deals firmly with the slanders that have been spread against him in Corinth by the remaining opposition. Those who wish to discredit him have been saying that he is bold at a distance, threatening in his letters to take severe disciplinary action (cf., e.g., his warning that, if necessary, he will

some people who think that we live by the standards of this world. *d* 3For though we live in the world, we do not wage war as the world does. *e* 4The weapons we fight with *f* are not the weapons of the world. On the contrary, they have divine power *g* to demolish strongholds. *h* 5We demolish arguments and every pretension that sets itself up against the knowledge of God, *i* and we take captive every thought to make it obedient *j* to Christ. 6And we will be ready to punish every act of disobedience, once your obedience is complete. *k*

7You are judging by appearances. *a l* If anyone is confident that they belong to Christ, *m* they should consider again that we belong to Christ just as much as they do. *n* 8So even if I boast somewhat freely about the authority the Lord gave us *o* for building you up rather than tearing you down, *p* I will not be ashamed of it. 9I do not want to seem to be trying to frighten you with my letters. 10For some say, "His letters are weighty and forceful, but in person he is unimpressive *q* and his speaking amounts to nothing." *r* 11Such people should realize that what we are in our letters when we are absent, we will be in our actions when we are present.

12We do not dare to classify or compare ourselves with some who commend themselves. *s* When they measure themselves by themselves and compare themselves with themselves, they are not wise. 13We, however, will not boast beyond proper limits, but will confine our boasting to the sphere of service God himself has assigned to us, *t* a sphere that also includes you. 14We are not going too far in our boasting, as would be the case if we had not come to you, for we did get as far as you *u* with the gospel of Christ. *v* 15Neither do we go beyond our limits *w* by boasting of work done by others. *x* Our hope is that, as your faith continues to grow, *y* our sphere of activity among you will greatly expand, 16so that we can preach the gospel *z* in the regions beyond you. *a* For we do not want to boast about work already done in someone else's territory. 17But, "Let those who boast boast in the Lord." *b b* 18For it is not those who commend themselves *c* who are approved, but those whom the Lord commends. *d*

PAUL AND THE FALSE APOSTLES

11 I hope you will put up with *e* me in a little foolishness. *f* Yes, please put up with me! 2I am jealous for you with a godly jealousy. I promised you to one husband, *g* to Christ, so that I might present you *h* as a pure virgin to him. 3But I

---

a 7 Or *Look at the obvious facts*   b 17 Jer. 9:24

Cross-references

10:2 *d* Ro 12:2
10:3 *e* ver 2
10:4 *f* S 2Co 6:7
g 1Co 2:5 *h* ver 8;
Jer 1:10; 23:29;
2Co 13:10
10:5 *i* Isa 2:11,12;
1Co 1:19 / 2Co 9:13
10:6 *k* 2Co 2:9; 7:15
10:7 *l* S Jn 7:24;
2Co 5:12 *m* 1Co 1:12;
S 3:23; 14:37
n 2Co 11:23
10:8 *o* ver 13,15
p ver 4; Jer 1:10;
2Co 13:10
10:10 *q* ver 1;
1Co 2:3; Gal 4:13,14
r 1Co 1:17; 2Co 11:6
10:12 *s* ver 18;
S 2Co 3:1
10:13 *t* ver 15,16;
S Ro 12:3
10:14 *u* S 1Co 3:6
v S 2Co 2:12
10:15 *w* ver 13
x Ro 15:20 *y* 2Th 1:3
10:16 *z* S Ro 1:1;
S 2Co 2:12
a S Ac 19:21
10:17 *b* Jer 9:24;
Ps 34:2; 44:8;
1Co 1:31
10:18 *c* ver 12
d S Ro 2:29
11:1 *e* ver 4,19,20;
Mt 17:17
f ver 16,17,21;
2Co 5:13
11:2 *g* Hos 2:19;
Eph 5:26,27
h S 2Co 4:14

Commentary

come "with a rod of discipline" [1Co 4:21]). But they say that he will not dare to be anything but weak and indecisive if he is present with them in person—in short, that he does not have the apostolic authority he claims to have. Paul is ready to prove otherwise, should the occasion demand, when he comes to Corinth for the third time (see 10:6,10–11 and note on 10:10).

10:1 *meekness and gentleness of Christ.* An indication of his own affectionate desire to show these same qualities when present with them.

10:4 *weapons we fight with.* Paul is prepared for warfare; his weapons, however, are not the weapons prized by this fallen world and fashioned by human pride (cf. 1:17; 4:2). *strongholds.* Of "arguments" and "every pretension" (v. 5) defiantly raised "against the knowledge of God" (cf. Ro 1:18–23), among which are the faulty reasonings by which the false apostles have been trying to shake the faith of the Christians in Corinth (see 1Co 2:13–14).

10:6 *every act of disobedience.* On the part of the interlopers and those who sided with them.

10:7 *belong to Christ.* Probably echoes the claim to superior spirituality by the Christ party (see 1Co 1:12) and the false teachers in Corinth. Paul, who had dramatically encountered and been commissioned by the risen Lord (see Ac 9:3–9; 22:6–11; 26:12–18) and who had received the gospel he preached "by revelation from Jesus Christ" (Gal 1:12; cf. 2Co 12:2–7), asserts that he belongs to Christ "just as much."

10:8 *authority . . . for building you up.* The primary purpose of Paul's apostolic authority is constructive, not destructive (see 13:10).

10:9 *frighten you with my letters.* See 2:3–4 and note; 7:8–9; chs. 10–13; 1Co 4:14–21.

10:10 *His letters are weighty and forceful.* Paul had already writ-

ten at least three letters to Corinth (see Introduction: Occasion). *his speaking amounts to nothing.* See note on 10:1—13:14. Paul's adversaries used a professional type of oratory designed to extract money from their gullible audiences. But Paul's manner of speaking was plain, straightforward and free from artificiality—and also "free of charge" (11:7; see note there), which meant that, if his slanderous opponents were to be believed, what he said was worthless. But Paul proclaimed the message of Christ crucified, and the transformed lives of the Corinthian believers testified to the divine power with which he spoke (cf. 1Co 2:1–5 and notes).

10:12 *they measure themselves by themselves.* The false teachers in Corinth behave as though there is no standard of comparison higher than themselves, but Paul boasts only "in the Lord" (v. 17; cf. 1Co 1:31 [see note there]).

10:13 *the sphere of service God himself has assigned to us.* The picture may be that of an athletic contest in which lanes are marked out for the different runners. In that case, "sphere of service" should be rendered "lane"—as should also "sphere of activity" (v. 15) and "territory" (v. 16). In intruding themselves into Corinth, the false apostles had crossed into Paul's "lane." Others understand the Greek word in question to refer to an assigned sphere of authority.

10:16 *regions beyond.* Perhaps Spain (see Ro 15:24,28).

10:17 See 1Co 1:31 and note. *boast in the Lord.* Boast in what Jesus Christ has done either for us (see Gal 6:14) or through us (see Ro 15:18; cf. Ac 14:27).

11:1 *foolishness.* In order to compare his own ministry with that of the false apostles, Paul has to speak about himself, which inevitably seems like foolish boasting.

11:2 *godly jealousy.* Paul cannot bear the thought that there might be any rival to Christ and his gospel. *I prom-*

11:3 *Ge 3:1-6,13;
1Ti 2:14; Rev 12:9
11:4 *1Co 3:11
k Ro 8:15 *Gal 1:6-9
m S ver 1
11:5 *n* 2Co 12:11;
Gal 2:6
11:6 *o* S 1Co 1:17
p S 2Co 8:7; Eph 3:4
11:7 *q* 2Co 12:13
r S Ro 1:1 *s* 1Co 9:18
11:8 *t* Php 4:15,18
11:9 *u* Php 4:15,18
v 2Co 12:13,14,16
11:10 *w* S Ro 9:1
x S Ac 18:12
y 1Co 9:15
11:11 *z* ver 31;
S Ro 1:9 *a* 2Co 12:15
11:13 *b* S Mt 7:15
c Tit 1:10 *d* Rev 2:2
11:14 *e* S Mt 4:10
11:15 *f* S Mt 16:27;
Php 3:19
11:16 *g* ver 1
11:17 *h* 1Co 7:12,25
i ver 21
11:18 *j* 2Co 5:16;
10:4 *k* ver 21;
Php 3:3,4
11:19 *l* S ver 1
m 1Co 4:10
11:20 *n* S ver 1
o Gal 2:4; 4:9; 5:1

am afraid that just as Eve was deceived by the serpent's cunning, *i* your minds may somehow be led astray from your sincere and pure devotion to Christ. ⁴For if someone comes to you and preaches a Jesus other than the Jesus we preached, *j* or if you receive a different spirit *k* from the Spirit you received, or a different gospel *l* from the one you accepted, you put up with it *m* easily enough.

⁵I do not think I am in the least inferior to those "super-apostles." ⁶I may indeed be untrained as a speaker, *o* but I do have knowledge. *p* We have made this perfectly clear to you in every way. ⁷Was it a sin *q* for me to lower myself in order to elevate you by preaching the gospel of God *r* to you free of charge? *s* ⁸I robbed other churches by receiving support from them *t* so as to serve you. ⁹And when I was with you and needed something, I was not a burden to anyone, for the brothers and sisters who came from Macedonia supplied what I needed. *u* I have kept myself from being a burden to you *v* in any way, and will continue to do so. ¹⁰As surely as the truth of Christ is in me, *w* nobody in the regions of Achaia *x* will stop this boasting *y* of mine. ¹¹Why? Because I do not love you? God knows *z* I do! *a*

¹²And I will keep on doing what I am doing in order to cut the ground from under those who want an opportunity to be considered equal with us in the things they boast about. ¹³For such persons are false apostles, *b* deceitful *c* workers, masquerading as apostles of Christ. *d* ¹⁴And no wonder, for Satan *e* himself masquerades as an angel of light. ¹⁵It is not surprising, then, if his servants also masquerade as servants of righteousness. Their end will be what their actions deserve. *f*

PAUL BOASTS ABOUT HIS SUFFERINGS

¹⁶I repeat: Let no one take me for a fool. *g* But if you do, then tolerate me just as you would a fool, so that I may do a little boasting. ¹⁷In this self-confident boasting I am not talking as the Lord would, *h* but as a fool. *i* ¹⁸Since many are boasting in the way the world does, *j* I too will boast. *k* ¹⁹You gladly put up with *l* fools since you are so wise! *m* ²⁰In fact, you even put up with *n* any who enslave you *o* or exploit you or take advantage of you or

a 5 Or *to the most eminent apostles*

---

ised you to one husband. As their spiritual father (cf. 6:13), Paul has promised the Corinthian believers to Christ, who is frequently depicted in the NT as the bridegroom, with the church portrayed as his bride (see Mt 9:15; Jn 3:29 and note; Eph 5:23–32 and notes; Rev 19:7–9; 21:2). *pure virgin.* Undefiled by the doctrines of false teachers (see vv. 3–4).

11:3 *deceived by the serpent's cunning.* See Ge 3:1–7 and note on 3:1.

11:4 *a Jesus other than the Jesus we preached.* A Jesus cast in the mold of Judaistic teachings (Paul's opponents were Jews; see v. 22). *different spirit.* A spirit of bondage, fear and worldliness (cf. Ro 8:15; 1Co 2:12 and note; Gal 2:4; Col 2:20–23 and note on 2:23) instead of a spirit of freedom, love, joy, peace and power (cf. 3:17; Ro 14:17 and notes; Gal 2:4; 5:1,22; Eph 3:20; Col 1:11; 2Ti 1:7). *different gospel.* Cf. Gal 1:6–9. *you put up with it easily enough.* They have been undiscerningly tolerant of these deceivers in their midst.

11:5 *"super-apostles."* Paul's sarcastic way of referring to the false apostles who had infiltrated the Corinthian church and were in reality not apostles at all, except in their own arrogantly inflated opinion of themselves (cf. 10:12 and note).

11:6 *I may ... be untrained as a speaker.* I do not use the skills, references and flourishes of professional rhetoric (see 10:10 and note). *I do have knowledge.* As the Corinthian believers well knew, Paul had knowledge of Christ that was true, powerful and God-given.

11:7 *free of charge.* Another slanderous criticism made by Paul's adversaries was that his refusal to accept payment for his instruction proved that it was worth nothing. This accusation at the same time helped to cloak their own grasping character, since their method of operation was to demand payment for their "professional" services. Paul, his enemies said, was lowering himself by breaking the rule that teachers should receive payment in proportion to the worth of their

performance (cf. 1Co 9:3–14).

11:8 *robbed other churches.* Accepted freely given support from established congregations.

11:9 *burden.* A financial liability (see 2:17 and note). This reinforced his teaching that the gospel of Jesus Christ is a free gift (see Ro 6:23 and note). *brothers and sisters who came from Macedonia.* See note on 1:1. They brought gifts from the churches there (Ac 18:5), particularly from the church at Philippi (Php 4:15).

11:10 *Achaia.* See note on 1:1.

11:12 *I will keep on.* Paul will not be deterred from presenting the gospel without charge. *equal.* In financial matters.

11:13 *masquerading as apostles of Christ.* Now Paul exposes these would-be "super-apostles" (v. 5; see note there) as "false apostles" and servants of Satan (v. 14) who are covering up their true identity.

11:14 *as an angel of light.* Though in reality he is the prince of darkness (cf. Col 1:12–13 and notes).

11:16 *Let no one take me for a fool.* See note on v. 1.

11:18 *boast.* By speaking of the nature of his apostolic ministry.

11:19 *You gladly put up with fools.* Resumes the implied rebuke of v. 4 and has the same ironic tone. There it was a matter of their readiness to tolerate false teaching; here it is a matter of their willingness to put up with disgraceful treatment by these false teachers.

11:20 *enslave you.* By imposing human rules (cf. Gal 5:1 and note). *exploit you.* See Mk 12:40 and note. *take advantage of you.* Thanks to the Corinthians' lack of discernment and their readiness to be impressed by outward show and clever talk. *push themselves forward.* For the purpose of lording it over the members of the church (cf. 1:24). *slap you in the face.* Using physical violence to cow them into submission.

push themselves forward or slap you in the face. ²¹To my shame I admit that we were too weak^p for that!

Whatever anyone else dares to boast about—I am speaking as a fool—I also dare to boast about. ^q ²²Are they Hebrews? So am I. ^r Are they Israelites? So am I. ^s Are they Abraham's descendants? So am I. ^t ²³Are they servants of Christ? ^u (I am out of my mind to talk like this.) I am more. I have worked much harder, ^v been in prison more frequently, ^w been flogged more severely, ^x and been exposed to death again and again. ^y ²⁴Five times I received from the Jews the forty lashes ^z minus one. ²⁵Three times I was beaten with rods, ^a once I was pelted with stones, ^b three times I was shipwrecked, ^c I spent a night and a day in the open sea, ²⁶I have been constantly on the move. I have been in danger from rivers, in danger from bandits, in danger from my own people, ^d in danger from Gentiles; in danger in the city, ^e in danger in the country, in danger at sea; and in danger from false believers. ^f ²⁷I have labored and toiled ^g and have often gone without sleep; ^h I have known hunger and thirst and have often gone without food; ^h I have been cold and naked. ²⁸Besides everything else, I face daily the pressure of my concern for all the churches. ⁱ ²⁹Who is weak, and I do not feel weak? ^j Who is led into sin, ^k and I do not inwardly burn?

³⁰If I must boast, I will boast ^l of the things that show my weakness. ^m ³¹The God and Father of the Lord Jesus, who is to be praised forever, ⁿ knows ^o that I am not lying. ³²In Damascus the governor under King Aretas had the city of the Damascenes guarded in order to arrest me. ^p ³³But I was lowered in a basket from a window in the wall and slipped through his hands. ^q

PAUL'S VISION AND HIS THORN

12 I must go on boasting. ^r Although there is nothing to be gained, I will go on to visions and revelations ^s from the Lord. ²I know a man in Christ ^t who fourteen years ago was caught up ^u to the third heaven. ^v Whether it was in the body or out of the body I do not know—God knows. ^w ³And I know that this man—whether in the body or apart from the body I do not know, but God knows— ⁴was caught up ^x to paradise ^y and heard inexpressible things, things that no one is permitted to tell. ⁵I will boast about someone like that, but I will not boast about myself, except about my weaknesses. ^z ⁶Even if I should choose to boast, ^a I would not be a fool, ^b because I would be speaking the truth. But I refrain, so no one will think more of me than is warranted by what I

11:21 *too weak for that.* Compared with the self-seeking crudeness of the impostors, Paul's conduct may well be considered weak—but he is probably speaking ironically here.

11:22 *Hebrews…Israelites…Abraham's descendants.* The claims implied here on the part of the false apostles indicate that they were Jews who felt superior to Gentile Christians. Thus it is probable that they were Judaizers, wishing to impose distinctive Jewish practices on Gentile converts. Paul's position (see Ro 2:28–29; 1Co 12:13; Gal 3:28–29; Eph 2:11–18; Col 3:11 and note). For Paul's claim, see Ac 22:3–5; 26:4–5; Php 3:5–6.

11:23 *servants of Christ.* Paul is not granting their claim to be servants of Christ. Indeed, the consideration of the nature of his ministry and its cost to him in suffering will show that he is more a servant of Christ than any or all of them. *exposed to death again and again.* Cf. 4:8–11.

11:24–25 *lashes…rods.* Eight floggings are mentioned here, five at the hands of Jewish authorities (cf. Dt 25:3; Mk 15:15 and notes) and three at the hands of Roman authorities. On these occasions the Romans used rods (see Ac 16:22). The three beatings with rods took place despite the fact that Paul, a Roman citizen, was legally protected from such punishment (cf. Ac 16:37; 22:25 and notes).

11:25 *pelted with stones.* A traditional manner of Jewish execution (cf. Jn 8:59; Ac 7:57–59; 14:19–20). *shipwrecked.* Only one shipwreck is recorded in Acts, but it took place after the writing of this letter (Ac 27:39–44). The three shipwrecks referred to here could have taken place during the voyages mentioned in Ac 9:30; 11:25–26; 13:4,13; 14:26; 16:11; 18:18–19,21–22.

11:26 *in danger from bandits.* See note on Ac 14:24.

11:28–29 Paul felt the weakness of any Corinthian believer who was weak. If any of them was led into sin, Paul burned with

indignation against the person responsible but also experienced the shame of the offense and longed for the restoration of the one who had stumbled.

11:30 *I will boast of the things that show my weakness.* His weakness opens the way for him to boast about the strength of God's grace in his life (see 12:9–10 and notes).

11:32–33 Paul relates this incident here because it was another example of the humiliation ("weakness," v. 30) he suffered.

11:32 *Damascus.* See note on Ac 9:2; see also map, p. 1853. *King Aretas.* Aretas IV, father-in-law of Herod Antipas, ruled over the Nabatean Arabs from c. 9 B.C. to A.D. 40. The Roman emperor Caligula may have given Damascus back to Aretas, since it was once part of his territory.

11:33 *from a window.* See Ac 9:25. For similar escapes, see Jos 2:15; 1Sa 19:12.

12:2,4 *caught up to the third heaven…caught up to paradise.* Paul is unsure whether this remarkable experience included his body or took place in separation from it (cf. Eze 8:3 and note). The "third heaven" designates a place beyond the immediate heaven of the earth's atmosphere and beyond the further heaven of outer space into the presence of God himself. Thus the risen and glorified Lord Jesus is said to have passed "through the heavens" (Heb 4:14; see note and TNIV text note there), and now, having "ascended higher than all the heavens" (Eph 4:10), to be "exalted above the heavens" (Heb 7:26). The term "paradise" (see Ne 2:8; Lk 23:43; Rev 2:7 and notes) is synonymous with the third heaven, where believers who have died are "at home with the Lord" (5:8 [see note there]; cf. "with Christ," Php 1:23).

12:2 *a man in Christ.* Paul himself. *fourteen years ago.* Early in his ministry, before his first missionary journey (Ac 13:4—14:28).

12:7 ᶜ ver 1;
S 1Co 2:10 ᵈ Nu 33:55
ᵉ S Mt 4:10
12:8 ᶠ Mt 26:39,44
12:9 ᵍ S Ro 3:24
ʰ S Php 4:13
ⁱ S 1Co 2:3 ʲ 1Ki 19:12
12:10 ᵏ S Mt 5:12
ˡ 2Co 6:4 ᵐ 2Th 1:4
ⁿ 2Co 13:4
12:11 ᵒ 2Co 11:1
ᵖ 2Co 11:5
�q 1Co 15:9,10
12:12 ʳ S Jn 4:48
12:13 ˢ ver 14;
1Co 9:12,18 ᵗ 2Co 11:7
12:14 ᵘ 2Co 13:1
ᵛ 1Co 4:14,15
ʷ Pr 19:14
12:15 ˣ Php 2:17;
1Th 2:8 ʸ 2Co 11:11
12:16 ᶻ 2Co 11:9
12:18 ᵃ 2Co 8:6,16
ᵇ S 2Co 2:13
ᶜ 2Co 8:18
12:19 ᵈ Ro 9:1
ᵉ S 1Co 10:14
ᶠ S Ro 14:19; 2Co 10:8
12:20 ᵍ 2Co 2:1-4
ʰ 1Co 4:21 ⁱ 1Co 1:11;
3:3 ʲ Gal 5:20
ᵏ Ro 1:30 ˡ S Ro 1:29
ᵐ 1Co 4:18
ⁿ 1Co 14:33
12:21 ᵒ 2Co 2:1,4
ᵖ 2Co 13:2
q S 1Co 6:18
13:1 ʳ 2Co 12:14
ˢ Dt 19:15; S Mt 18:16
13:2 ᵗ ver 10
ᵘ 2Co 1:23 ᵛ 2Co 12:21
13:3 ʷ Mt 10:20;
1Co 5:4
13:4 ˣ 1Co 1:25;
Php 2:7,8; 1Pe 3:18

do or say, ⁷or because of these surpassingly great revelations. ᶜ Therefore, in order to keep me from becoming conceited, I was given a thorn in my flesh, ᵈ a messenger of Satan, ᵉ to torment me. ⁸Three times I pleaded with the Lord to take it away from me. ᶠ ⁹But he said to me, "My grace ᵍ is sufficient for you, for my power ʰ is made perfect in weakness." ⁱ ʲ Therefore I will boast all the more gladly about my weaknesses, so that Christ's power may rest on me. ¹⁰That is why, for Christ's sake, I delight ᵏ in weaknesses, in insults, in hardships, ˡ in persecutions, ᵐ in difficulties. For when I am weak, then I am strong. ⁿ

PAUL'S CONCERN FOR THE CORINTHIANS

¹¹I have made a fool of myself, ᵒ but you drove me to it. I ought to have been commended by you, for I am not in the least inferior to the "super-apostles," ᵃ ᵖ even though I am nothing. q ¹²I persevered in demonstrating among you the marks of a true apostle, including signs, wonders and miracles. ʳ ¹³How were you inferior to the other churches, except that I was never a burden to you? ˢ Forgive me this wrong! ᵗ

¹⁴Now I am ready to visit you for the third time, ᵘ and I will not be a burden to you, because what I want is not your possessions but you. After all, children should not have to save up for their parents, ᵛ but parents for their children. ʷ ¹⁵So I will very gladly spend for you everything I have and expend myself as well. ˣ If I love you more, ʸ will you love me less? ¹⁶Be that as it may, I have not been a burden to you. ᶻ Yet, crafty fellow that I am, I caught you by trickery! ¹⁷Did I exploit you through any of the men I sent to you? ¹⁸I urged ᵃ Titus ᵇ to go to you and I sent our brother ᶜ with him. Titus did not exploit you, did he? Did we not walk in the same footsteps by the same Spirit?

¹⁹Have you been thinking all along that we have been defending ourselves to you? We have been speaking in the sight of God ᵈ as those in Christ; and everything we do, dear friends, ᵉ is for your strengthening. ᶠ ²⁰For I am afraid that when I come ᵍ I may not find you as I want you to be, and you may not find me as you want me to be. ʰ I fear that there may be quarreling, ⁱ jealousy, outbursts of anger, factions, ʲ slander, ᵏ gossip, ˡ arrogance ᵐ and disorder. ⁿ ²¹I am afraid that when I come again my God will humble me before you, and I will be grieved ᵒ over many who have sinned earlier ᵖ and have not repented of the impurity, sexual sin and debauchery q in which they have indulged.

FINAL WARNINGS

13 This will be my third visit to you. ʳ "Every matter must be established by the testimony of two or three witnesses." ᵇ ˢ ²I already gave you a warning when I was with you the second time. I now repeat it while absent: ᵗ On my return I will not spare ᵘ those who sinned earlier ᵛ or any of the others, ³since you are demanding proof that Christ is speaking through me. ʷ He is not weak in dealing with you, but is powerful among you. ⁴For to be sure, he was crucified in weakness, ˣ yet he lives by God's

---

ᵃ 11 Or the most eminent apostles   ᵇ 1 Deut. 19:15

12:7 revelations. See v. 1. thorn in my flesh. The nature of this affliction is unknown. messenger of Satan. A further description of Paul's thorn (cf. Job 2:7 and note).

A **12:9** My grace is sufficient for you. A better solution than to remove Paul's thorn. Human weakness provides the ideal opportunity for the display of divine power.

12:10 Cf. Php 4:13 and note. The classic example of power in weakness is the cross of Christ (cf. 13:4).

12:11 made a fool of myself. See note on 11:1. you drove me to it. The Corinthian Christians have put Paul under pressure to write about himself as he did because they had accepted the claims of the "super-apostles" (see 11:5 and note) who had invaded their ranks, challenging Paul's apostolic authority.

12:12 signs, wonders and miracles. See Heb 2:4 and note. By implication, false teachers had come to Corinth without these apostolic signs.

12:13 never a burden to you. See 11:9 and note; see also notes on 11:7,12. Forgive me this wrong! Irony—resuming the line of discussion in 11:7-12.

12:14 third time. See 2:1 and note; 13:1. children. Cf. 6:13. Paul is their spiritual father.

12:16 I caught you by trickery! Sarcastically echoes another of the slanders being made against Paul by the false apostles: that

he was exploiting them by the trick of organizing a collection for the poverty-stricken Christians in Jerusalem—contributions that would never reach their intended destination because they went into Paul's own pocket (v. 17).

12:18 Titus … our brother. See notes on 8:6,16–17,18,23.

12:19 speaking in the sight of God as those in Christ. See 1Co 4:3–4 and note on 4:3. everything we do … is for your strengthening. See 10:8 and note.

12:20–21 See Ro 1:29–31 and note.

12:20 The church at Corinth was immature, unspiritual, disorganized and schismatic (see 1Co 3:1–4 and notes).

12:21 sinned earlier … sexual sin and debauchery. See 1Co 5:1,11; 6:13,16,18–19 and notes.

13:1 third visit. See 2:1 and note; 12:14. two or three witnesses. Cf. Dt 17:6 and note.

13:2 those who sinned earlier. See 12:21 and note. any of the others. Probably the Corinthians who had sided with the false teachers.

13:3 demanding proof that Christ is speaking through me. See note on 10:10.

13:4 crucified in weakness. See 12:10 and note; cf. 8:9; Php 2:6–8.

power. ʸ Likewise, we are weak ᶻ in him, yet by God's power we will live with him ᵃ in our dealing with you.

⁵Examine yourselves ᵇ to see whether you are in the faith; test yourselves. ᶜ Do you not realize that Christ Jesus is in you ᵈ—unless, of course, you fail the test? ⁶And I trust that you will discover that we have not failed the test. ⁷Now we pray to God that you will not do anything wrong. Not that people will see that we have stood the test but that you will do what is right even though we may seem to have failed. ⁸For we cannot do anything against the truth, but only for the truth. ⁹We are glad whenever we are weak ᵉ but you are strong; ᶠ and our prayer is that you may be fully restored. ᵍ ¹⁰This is why I write these things when I am absent, that when I come I may not have to be harsh ʰ in my use of authority—the authority the Lord gave me for building you up, not for tearing you down. ⁱ

FINAL GREETINGS

¹¹Finally, brothers and sisters, ʲ rejoice! Strive for full restoration, encourage one another, be of one mind, live in peace. ᵏ And the God of love ˡ and peace ᵐ will be with you. ¹²Greet one another with a holy kiss. ⁿ ¹³All God's people here send their greetings. ᵒ ¹⁴May the grace of the Lord Jesus Christ, ᵖ and the love of God, �q and the fellowship of the Holy Spirit ʳ be with you all.

13:4 ʸ Ro 1:4; 6:4;
1Co 6:14 ᶻ ver 9;
S 1Co 2:3 ᵃ S Ro 6:5
13:5 ᵇ S 1Co 11:28
ᶜ La 3:40; Jn 6:6
ᵈ S Ro 8:10
13:9 ᵉ S 1Co 2:3
ᶠ 2Co 4:12 ᵍ ver 11;
Eph 4:13
13:10 ʰ S 2Co 1:23
ⁱ 2Co 10:8
13:11 ʲ 1Th 4:1;
2Th 3:1 ᵏ S Mk 9:50
ˡ 1Jn 4:16
ᵐ S Ro 15:33;
Eph 6:23
13:12 ⁿ S Ro 16:16
13:13 ᵒ Php 4:23
13:14 ᵖ S Ro 16:20;
2Co 8:9 ᵠ Ro 5:5;
Jude 21 ʳ Php 2:1

13:5 *Examine yourselves ... test yourselves.* Cf. 2Pe 1:10–11 and notes.

13:7 *do what is right.* Then there will be no need for Paul to give evidence of his authority by taking disciplinary action when he comes to them.

13:8 *we cannot do anything against the truth.* Paul can exercise his apostolic authority only in a way that supports the truth.

13:9 *weak.* To have no need to give proof of his apostolic strength (cf. 12:9–10 and notes). *strong.* In the truth. *fully restored.* See Gal 6:1 and note.

13:10 *building you up, not ... tearing you down.* See 10:8 and note.

13:11–13 These concluding exhortations and greetings exhibit a note of confidence.

13:11,14 *peace ... grace.* See note on Ro 1:7.

13:11 *brothers and sisters.* See note on Ro 1:13. *full restoration.* See v. 9 and note. *encourage one another.* See 1Co 14:3; Heb

10:22–25 and notes. *be of one mind.* See Php 2:2 and note. *live in peace.* See Mt 5:9; Ro 12:18; Jas 3:18 and notes. *God of love.* See 1Jn 4:8 and note. *God of ... peace.* See 1Th 5:23 and note; Heb 13:20.

13:12 *holy kiss.* See 1Co 16:20; Ro 16:16 and notes.

13:13 *God's people.* See note on Ro 1:7.

13:14 This benediction is Trinitarian in form and has ever since been a part of Christian worship tradition (cf. Mt 28:19 and note). *grace of ... Christ.* See 8:9 and note. *love of God.* See Jn 3:16; 1Jn 4:8–10 and notes; see also Ro 5:8. *fellowship of the Holy Spirit.* See note on Php 2:1. *with you.* This phrase or its equivalent ("with your spirit" [Php 4:23; see note there; see also Gal 6:18; 2Ti 4:22; Phm 25]) occurs near the end of all of Paul's letters except Ephesians. Its OT counterpart is the Immanuel theme—"God with us"—and its equivalents (see Ge 26:3; Isa 7:14; Rev 21:3 and notes).

AUTHOR

C The opening verse identifies the author of Galatians as the apostle Paul. Apart from a few 19th-century interpreters, no one has seriously questioned his authorship.

DATE AND DESTINATION

The date of Galatians depends to a great extent on the destination of the letter. There are two main views:

1. *The North Galatian theory.* This older view holds that the letter was addressed to churches located in north-central Asia Minor (Pessinus, Ancyra and Tavium), where the Gauls had settled when they invaded the area in the third century B.C. It is held that Paul visited this area on his second missionary journey, though Acts contains no reference to such a visit. Galatians, it is maintained, was written between A.D. 53 and 57 from Ephesus or Macedonia.

2. *The South Galatian theory.* According to this view, Galatians was written to churches in the southern area of the Roman province of Galatia (Antioch, Iconium, Lystra and Derbe) that Paul had founded on his first missionary journey. Some believe that Galatians was written from Syrian Antioch in 48–49 after Paul's first journey and before the Jerusalem council meeting (Ac 15). Others say that Galatians was written in Syrian Antioch or Corinth between 51 and 53 (see chart, pp. 1854–1855).

OCCASION AND PURPOSE

Judaizers were Jewish Christians who believed, among other things, that a number of the ceremonial practices of the OT were still binding on the NT church. Following Paul's successful campaign in Galatia, they insisted that Gentile converts to Christianity abide by certain OT rites, especially circumcision. They may have been motivated by a desire to avoid the persecution of Zealot Jews who objected to their fraternizing with Gentiles (see 6:12). The Judaizers argued that Paul was not an authentic apostle and that out of a desire to make the message more appealing to Gentiles he had removed from the gospel certain legal requirements.

Paul responded by clearly establishing his apostolic authority and thereby substantiating the gospel he preached. By introducing additional requirements for justification (e.g., works of the law), his adversaries had perverted the gospel of grace and, unless prevented, would bring Paul's converts into the bondage of legalism. It is by grace through faith alone that people are justified, and it is by faith alone that they are to live out their new life in the freedom of the Spirit.

THEOLOGICAL TEACHING

Galatians stands as an eloquent and vigorous apologetic for the essential NT truth that people are justified by faith in Jesus Christ—by nothing less and nothing more —and that they are sanctified not by legalistic works but by the obedience that comes from faith in God's work for them, in them and through them by the grace and power of Christ and the Holy Spirit. It was the rediscovery of the basic message of Galatians (and Romans) that brought about the Protestant Reformation. Galatians is often referred to as "Luther's book," because Martin Luther relied so strongly on this letter in all his preaching, teaching and writing against the prevailing theology of his day. It is also referred to as the "Magna Carta of Christian Liberty." A key verse is 2:16 (see note there).

OUTLINE

I. Introduction (1:1–10)
   A. Greetings (1:1–5)
   B. Denunciation (1:6–10)
II. Personal: Authentication of the Apostle of Liberty and Faith (1:11—2:21)
   A. Paul's Gospel Was Received by Special Revelation (1:11–12)
   B. Paul's Gospel Was Independent of the Jerusalem Apostles and the Judean Churches (1:13—2:21)
      1. Evidenced by his early activities as a Christian (1:13–17)
      2. Evidenced by his first post-Christian visit to Jerusalem (1:18–24)
      3. Evidenced by his second post-Christian visit to Jerusalem (2:1–10)
      4. Evidenced by his rebuke of Peter at Antioch (2:11–21)
III. Doctrinal: Justification of the Doctrine of Liberty and Faith (chs. 3–4)
   A. The Galatians' Experience of the Gospel (3:1–5)
   B. The Experience of Abraham (3:6–9)
   C. The Curse of the Law (3:10–14)
   D. The Priority of the Promise (3:15–18)
   E. The Purpose of the Law (3:19–25)
   F. Children, Not Slaves (3:26—4:7)
   G. The Danger of Turning Back (4:8–11)
   H. Appeal to Embrace the Freedom of God's Children (4:12–20)
   I. God's Children Are Children of the Free Woman (4:21–31)
IV. Practical: Practice of the Life of Liberty and Faith (5:1—6:10)
   A. Exhortation to Freedom (5:1–12)
   B. Life by the Spirit, Not by the Sinful Nature (5:13–26)
   C. Call for Mutual Help (6:1–10)
V. Conclusion and Benediction (6:11–18)

1:1 *a* S 1Co 1:1
b ver 11,12 *c* ver 15,16;
S Ac 9:15; 20:24
d ver 15,16; S Ac 9:15;
20:24 *e* S Ac 2:24
1:2 *f* Php 4:21
g S Ac 16:6
1:3 *h* S Ro 1:7
1:4 *i* S Mt 20:28;
S Ro 4:25; S 1Co 15:3;
Gal 2:20 *j* S 1Co 1:20
k S Php 4:20
1:5 *l* S Ro 11:36
1:6 *m* ver 15;
S Ro 8:28 *n* 2Co 11:4
1:7 *o* Ac 15:24;
Gal 5:10
p Jer 23:16,36
1:8 *q* ver 11,16;
1Co 15:1; 2Co 11:4;
Gal 2:2 *r* Ro 9:3
1:9 *s* Ro 16:17
1:10 *t* S Ro 2:29
1:11 *u* 1Co 15:1
v S ver 8
1:12 *w* ver 1 *x* ver 16;
S 1Co 2:10
y 1Co 11:23; 15:3
1:13 *z* Ac 26:4,5
a S 1Co 10:32
b S Ac 8:3
1:14 *c* S Ac 21:20
d Mt 15:2
1:15 *e* Isa 49:1,5;
Jer 1:5 *f* S Ac 9:15;
S Ro 8:28
1:16 *g* S Ac 9:15;
Gal 2:9 *h* Mt 16:17

1

Paul, an apostle *a*—sent not with a human commission nor by human authority, *b* but by Jesus Christ *c* and God the Father, *d* who raised him from the dead *e*— ²and all the brothers and sisters with me, *f*

To the churches in Galatia: *g*

³Grace and peace to you from God our Father and the Lord Jesus Christ, *h* ⁴who gave himself for our sins *i* to rescue us from the present evil age, *j* according to the will of our God and Father, *k* ⁵to whom be glory for ever and ever. Amen. *l*

NO OTHER GOSPEL

⁶I am astonished that you are so quickly deserting the one who called *m* you by the grace of Christ and are turning to a different gospel *n*— ⁷which is really no gospel at all. Evidently some people are throwing you into confusion *o* and are trying to pervert *p* the gospel of Christ. ⁸But even if we or an angel from heaven should preach a gospel other than the one we preached to you, *q* let that person be under God's curse! *r* ⁹As we have already said, so now I say again: If anybody is preaching to you a gospel other than what you accepted, *s* let that person be under God's curse!

¹⁰Am I now trying to win human approval, or God's approval? Or am I trying to please people? *t* If I were still trying to please people, I would not be a servant of Christ.

PAUL CALLED BY GOD

¹¹I want you to know, brothers and sisters, *u* that the gospel I preached *v* is not of human origin. ¹²I did not receive it from any human source, *w* nor was I taught it; rather, I received it by revelation *x* from Jesus Christ. *y*

¹³For you have heard of my previous way of life in Judaism, *z* how intensely I persecuted the church of God *a* and tried to destroy it. *b* ¹⁴I was advancing in Judaism beyond many of my own age among my people and was extremely zealous *c* for the traditions of my fathers. *d* ¹⁵But when God, who set me apart from birth *a e* and called me *f* by his grace, was pleased ¹⁶to reveal his Son in me so that I might preach him among the Gentiles, *g* my immediate response was not to consult any human being. *h* ¹⁷I did not go up to Jerusalem

a 15 Or *from my mother's womb*

1:1 *Paul.* See note on Ro 1:1. *apostle.* One sent on a mission with full authority of representation; an ambassador (see note on 1Co 1:1). *raised him from the dead.* The resurrection is the central affirmation of the Christian faith (see Ac 17:18; Ro 1:4; 1Co 15:20; 1Pe 1:3), and because Paul had seen the risen Christ he was qualified to be an apostle (see Ac 1:22 and note; 2:32; 1Co 15:8).

1:2 *brothers and sisters.* See note on Ro 1:13. *churches.* This was a circular letter to several congregations. *Galatia.* The term occurs three times in the NT (and "Galatian" once [1Co 16:1]). In 2Ti 4:10 the reference is uncertain. In 1Pe 1:1 it refers to the northern area of Asia Minor occupied by the Gauls. Here (and in 1Co 16:1) Paul probably uses the term to refer to the Roman province of Galatia and an additional area to the south, through which he traveled on his first missionary journey (Ac 13:14—14:23). See Introduction: Date and Destination.

1:3 *Grace and peace.* See note on Ro 1:7. *Lord Jesus Christ.* Also occurs at the end of this letter (6:18); see note on 1Th 1:1.

1:4 *for our sins.* See Mt 1:21; Jn 1:29; 1Co 15:3; 1Pe 2:24 and note. *present evil age.* The present period of the world's history (see note on 2Co 4:4). In contrast to the age to come (the climax of the Messianic age), this present age is characterized by wickedness (Eph 2:1–2; 6:12).

1:5 For other doxologies, see, e.g., Ro 9:5; 11:36; 16:27; Eph 3:21; 1Ti 1:17.

1:6 *so quickly.* So soon after your conversion. *one who called you.* God. *grace of Christ.* The test of a pure, unadulterated gospel.

1:7 *no gospel at all.* Because it lacks the heart of the gospel—the good news of God's marvelous grace in Christ (see notes on Mk 1:1; 1Co 15:3). *some people.* The Judaizers (see Introduction: Occasion and Purpose).

1:8 *under God's curse.* The Greek word (*anathema*) originally referred to a pagan temple offering in payment for a vow. Later it came to represent a curse (see v. 9; Ro 9:3 and note; 1Co 12:3; 16:22).

1:10 *servant of Christ.* Paul once wore the "yoke of slavery" (5:1) but, having been set free from sin by the redemption that is in Christ, he became a slave of righteousness, a slave of God (see Ro 6:18,22 and note on 6:18).

1:11 *I want you to know, brothers and sisters.* A similar phrase is found in 1Co 15:1, where Paul sets forth the gospel he received. *the gospel I preached.* Called "my gospel" in Ro 2:16; 16:25 (see note there).

1:12 *received it by revelation.* See Eph 3:2–6.

1:13 *Judaism.* The Jewish faith and way of life that developed during the period between the OT and the NT. The term is derived from Judah, the southern kingdom that came to an end in the sixth century B.C. with the exile into Babylonia (see essay, pp. 1594–1597). *church of God.* The NT counterpart of the OT assembly (see Nu 16:21) or community of the Lord (Nu 20:4).

1:14 *zealous.* See Php 3:6. *traditions of my fathers.* Traditions orally transmitted from previous generations and contrasted with the written law of Moses. Cf. the "tradition of the elders" (see note on Mt 15:2).

1:15 *set me apart from birth.* See Isa 49:1; Jer 1:5; Ro 1:1.

1:16 *Gentiles.* Lit. "nations" or "peoples." The term commonly designated foreigners—hence pagans, or the non-Jewish world. *any human being.* Lit. "flesh and blood"—in the NT usually with the implication of human weakness or ignorance (see Mt 16:17; 1Co 15:50 and note). Paul received his message from God.

1:17 *Jerusalem.* The religious center of Judaism and the birthplace of Christianity. *Arabia.* The Nabatean kingdom in Transjordan, stretching southward from Damascus toward the Arabian to see those who were apostles before I was, but I went into Arabia. Later I returned to Damascus. [i]

[18]Then after three years,[j] I went up to Jerusalem[k] to get acquainted with Cephas[a] and stayed with him fifteen days. [19]I saw none of the other apostles—only James,[l] the Lord's brother. [20]I assure you before God[m] that what I am writing you is no lie. [n]

[21]Then I went to Syria[o] and Cilicia. [p] [22]I was personally unknown to the churches of Judea[q] that are in Christ. [r] [23]They only heard the report: "The man who formerly persecuted us is now preaching the faith[s] he once tried to destroy." [t] [24]And they praised God[u] because of me.

PAUL ACCEPTED BY THE APOSTLES

2 Then after fourteen years, I went up again to Jerusalem,[v] this time with Barnabas. [w] I took Titus[x] along also. [2]I went in response to a revelation[y] and, meeting privately with those esteemed as leaders, I set before them the gospel that I preach among the Gentiles. [z] I wanted to be sure I was not running and had not been running my race[a] in vain. [3]Yet not even Titus,[b] who was with me, was compelled to be circumcised, even though he was a Greek. [c] [4]This matter arose because some false believers[d] had infiltrated our ranks to spy on[e] the freedom[f] we have in Christ Jesus and to make us slaves. [5]We did not give in to them for a moment, so that the truth of the gospel[g] might remain with you.

[6]As for those who were held in high esteem[h]—whatever they were makes no difference to me; God does not show favoritism[i]—they added nothing to my message.[j] [7]On the contrary, they saw that I had been entrusted with the task[k] of preaching the gospel to the Gentiles,[b] just as Peter[m] had been to the Jews. [c] [8]For God, who was at work in Peter as an apostle[n] to the Jews, was also at work in me as an apostle[o] to the Gentiles. [9]James,[p] Cephas[d][q] and John, those esteemed as pillars, [r] gave me and Barnabas[s] the right hand of fellowship when they recognized the grace given to me. [t] They agreed that we should go to the Gentiles,[u] and they to the Jews. [10]All they asked was that we should continue to remember the poor,[v] the very thing I had been eager to do all along.

PAUL OPPOSES CEPHAS

[11]When Cephas[w] came to Antioch,[x] I opposed him to his face, because he stood con-

---

[a] 18 That is, Peter   [b] 7 Greek *uncircumcised*   [c] 7 Greek *circumcised*; also in verses 8 and 9
[d] 9 That is, Peter; also in verses 11 and 14

1:17 *i* Ac 9:2,19-22
1:18 *j* Ac 9:22,23
k Ac 9:26,27
1:19 *l* Mt 13:55; S Ac 15:13
1:20 *m* S Ro 1:9
n S Ro 9:1
1:21 *o* S Lk 2:2
p S Ac 6:9
1:22 *q* 1Th 2:14
r S Ro 16:3
1:23 *s* Ac 6:7
t S Ac 8:3
1:24 *u* S Mt 9:8
2:1 *v* Ac 15:2
w S Ac 4:36
x S 2Co 2:13
2:2 *y* S 1Co 2:10
z Ac 15:4,12
a S 1Co 9:24
2:3 *b* ver 1; S 2Co 2:13 *c* Ac 16:3; 1Co 9:21
2:4 *d* S Ac 1:16; 2Co 11:26 *e* Jude 4 *f* Gal 5:1,13
2:5 *g* ver 14
2:6 *h* ver 2
i S Ac 10:34; S Rev 2:23 / 1Co 15:11
2:7 *k* 1Th 2:4; 1Ti 1:11
l S Ac 9:15
m ver 9,11,14
2:8 *n* Ac 1:25
o S 1Co 1:1
2:9 *p* S Ac 15:13
q ver 7,11,14 *r* 1Ti 3:15; Rev 3:12 *s* ver 1;
S Ac 4:36 *t* S Ro 12:3
u S Ac 9:15
2:10 *v* S Ac 24:17
2:11 *w* ver 7,9,14
x S Ac 11:19

---

peninsula. *Damascus.* The capital of ancient Syria (Aram in the OT). Paul had been converted en route from Jerusalem to Damascus (see Ac 9:1–9 and note on 9:2; see also map, p. 1853).
1:18 *after three years.* From the time of his departure into Arabia. The text does not say he spent the three years in Arabia. *I went up to Jerusalem.* Probably the visit referred to in Ac 9:26–30, though some equate it with the one in Ac 11:30. *Cephas.* See TNIV text note; from the Aramaic word for "stone" (see Mt 16:18 and note). The name designates a like quality in the bearer (see note on Jn 1:42).
1:19 *James.* See Introduction to James: Author. In Ac 21:18 this James appears to be the leader of the elders in the Jerusalem church. *the Lord's brother.* See note on Lk 8:19.
1:21 *Syria and Cilicia.* Provinces in Asia Minor (see map, p. 1863). Specifically, Paul went to Tarsus (see Ac 9:30 and note), his hometown.
2:1 *after fourteen years.* Probably from the date of Paul's conversion. *I went up again to Jerusalem.* According to some, the visit mentioned in Ac 11:30; according to others, the one in Ac 15:1–4 (see notes on Ac 12:1; 15:2). *Barnabas.* Means "one who encourages." His given name was Joseph, and he was a Levite from the island of Cyprus (see Ac 4:36 and note) and Paul's companion on the first missionary journey (Ac 13:1–14:28). *Titus.* A Gentile Christian who served as Paul's delegate to Corinth (see 2Co 2:13; 7:6–7; 8:6,16; 12:18) and later was left in Crete to oversee the church there (see Tit 1:5; see also Introduction to Titus: Recipient).
2:2 *those esteemed as leaders.* Paul recognized their authority and is probably referring to James, Peter and John (v. 9; cf. v. 6). *had not been running my race in vain.* Cf. 1Co 15:58; Php 2:16.
2:4 *false believers.* Judaizers who held that Gentile converts

should be circumcised and obey the law of Moses (cf. Ac 15:5; 2Co 11:26). *spy on.* Used in the Septuagint (the pre-Christian Greek translation of the OT) in 2Sa 10:3 and 1Ch 19:3 of spying out a territory. *freedom.* See 5:1,13; Ro 6:18,20,22; 8:2. "Free" and "freedom" are key words in Galatians, occurring 11 times (here; 3:28; 4:22–23,26,30–31; 5:1,13).
2:6 *those who were held in high esteem.* See note on v. 2. *not show favoritism.* Cf. Dt 10:17; 1Sa 16:7; Lk 20:21; Jas 2:1.
2:7 *to the Gentiles.* Paul's ministry was not exclusively to the Gentiles. In fact, he regularly went first to the synagogue when arriving in a new location (see note on Ac 13:14). He did, however, consider himself to be foremost an apostle to the Gentiles (see Ro 11:13 and note).
2:9 *James.* See note on 1:19. His name may have been mentioned first because he played a dominant role in the Jerusalem council (Ac 15:12– 21). *pillars.* A common metaphor for those who represent and strongly support an institution. *right hand of fellowship.* A common practice among both Jews and Greeks, indicating a pledge of friendship. *grace.* The entrusting to Paul of the gospel to the Gentiles (see v. 7).
2:10 Paul already had been involved in a trip to Jerusalem to help the impoverished Christians there (see Ac 11:29–30). He would make another visit for the same purpose at the end of his third missionary journey (see Ac 24:17 and note; Ro 15:25–27; 1Co 16:3–4; 2Co 9).
2:11 *Antioch.* The leading city of Roman Syria and third leading city of the empire (after Rome and Alexandria; see map, p. 1890). From it Paul had been sent out on his missionary journeys (see Ac 13:1–3; 14:26). *stood condemned.* For yielding to the pressure of the circumcision party (the Judaizers), thus going against what he knew to be right.

2:12 y S Ac 15:13
z Ac 11:3 a Ac 10:45;
11:2
2:13 b ver 1;
S Ac 4:36
2:14 c ver 5
d ver 7,9,11 a Ac 10:28
f ver 12
2:15 g Php 3:4,5
h 1Sa 15:18; Lk 24:7
2:16 i S Ro 3:28
j S Ro 9:30
k S Ro 3:28; S 4:25
2:17 l ver 15
m Gal 3:21
2:19 n S Ro 7:4
o Ro 6:10,11,14;
2Co 5:15
2:20 p S Ro 6:6
q S Ro 8:10; 1Pe 2:4;
r S Mt 4:3 s S Ro 8:37
t S Gal 1:4
2:21 u Gal 3:21
3:1 v Lk 24:25
w S Ac 16:6 x Gal 5:7
y 1Co 1:23
3:2 z S Jn 20:22
3:3 a ver 5,10; Gal 2:16
b Ro 10:17; Heb 4:2
3:5 c 1Co 12:10
d ver 2,10; Gal 2:16
3:6 e Ge 15:6;
S Ro 4:3
3:7 f ver 9 g S Lk 3:8
3:8 h Ge 12:3; 18:18;
22:18; 26:4; Ac 3:25
3:9 i ver 7; Ro 4:16
j Ro 4:18-22
3:10 k ver 2,5;
Gal 2:16 l ver 13;
S Ro 4:15

demned. [12]For before certain people came from James,[y] he used to eat with the Gentiles.[z] But when they arrived, he began to draw back and separate himself from the Gentiles because he was afraid of those who belonged to the circumcision group.[a] [13]The other Jews joined him in his hypocrisy, so that by their hypocrisy even Barnabas[b] was led astray.

[14]When I saw that they were not acting in line with the truth of the gospel,[c] I said to Cephas[d] in front of them all, "You are a Jew, yet you live like a Gentile and not like a Jew.[e] How is it, then, that you force Gentiles to follow Jewish customs?[f]

[15]"We who are Jews by birth[g] and not sinful Gentiles[h] [16]know that a person is not justified by observing the law,[i] but by faith in Jesus Christ.[j] So we, too, have put our faith in Christ Jesus that we may be justified by faith in[a] Christ and not by observing the law, because by observing the law no one will be justified.[k]

[17]"But if, in seeking to be justified in Christ, we Jews find ourselves also among the sinners,[l] doesn't that mean that Christ promotes sin? Absolutely not![m] [18]If I rebuild what I destroyed, then I really would be a lawbreaker.

[19]"For through the law I died to the law[n] so that I might live for God.[o] [20]I have been crucified with Christ[p] and I no longer live, but Christ lives in me.[q] The life I now live in the body, I live by faith in the Son of God,[r] who loved me[s] and gave himself for me.[t] [21]I do not set aside the grace of God, for if righteousness could be gained through the law,[u] Christ died for nothing!"[b]

FAITH OR OBSERVANCE OF THE LAW

3 You foolish[v] Galatians![w] Who has bewitched you?[x] Before your very eyes Jesus Christ was clearly portrayed as crucified.[y] [2]I would like to learn just one thing from you: Did you receive the Spirit[z] by observing the law,[a] or by believing what you heard?[b] [3]Are you so foolish? After beginning with the Spirit, are you now trying to finish by human effort? [4]Have you experienced[c] so much in vain—if it really was in vain? [5]Does God give you his Spirit and work miracles[c] among you by your observing the law, or by your believing what you heard?[d] [6]So also Abraham "believed God, and it was credited to him as righteousness."[d][e]

[7]Understand, then, that those who have faith[f] are children of Abraham.[g] [8]Scripture foresaw that God would justify the Gentiles by faith, and announced the gospel in advance to Abraham: "All nations will be blessed through you."[e][h] [9]So those who rely on faith[i] are blessed along with Abraham, the man of faith.[j]

[10]All who rely on observing the law[k] are under a curse,[l] for it is written: "Cursed is ev-

---

a 16 Or *but through the faithfulness of . . . justified on the basis of the faithfulness of*   b 21 Some interpreters end the quotation after verse 14.   c 4 Or *suffered*   d 6 Gen. 15:6   e 8 Gen. 12:3; 18:18; 22:18

2:12 *circumcision group.* Judaizers, who believed that circumcision was necessary for salvation (cf. Ac 10:45; 11:2; Ro 4:12).

2:13 *other Jews.* Jewish Christians not associated with the circumcision party but whom Peter's behavior had led astray. *hypocrisy.* See note on Mt 6:2.

2:14 *you live like a Gentile.* You do not observe Jewish customs, especially dietary restrictions (see v. 12).

2:16 A key verse in Galatians (see Introduction: Theological Teaching). Three times it tells us that no one is justified by observing the law, and three times it underscores the indispensable requirement of placing one's faith in Christ. *not justified by observing the law.* Paul is not depreciating the law itself, for he clearly maintained that God's law is "holy, righteous and good" (Ro 7:12; see note there). He is arguing against an illegitimate use of the OT law that made the observance of that law the grounds of acceptance with God. *but by faith in Jesus.* The essence of the gospel message (see Ro 3:20,28; Php 3:9; see also notes on Ro 3:24,28). Faith is the means by which justification is received, not its basis (cf. notes on Eph 2:8–9; Jas 2:14–26).

2:17 See Ro 6:1 and note.

2:19 *I died to the law.* See v. 20; see also note on Ro 7:4.

2:20 *crucified with Christ.* See 5:24; Ro 6:8–10; 7:6; see also note on Ro 6:7. *gave himself for me.* See 1:4; 1Ti 2:6; Tit 2:14.

2:21 *Christ died for nothing.* To mingle legalism (or works) with grace distorts grace and makes a mockery of the cross.

3:1 *foolish.* They were not mentally deficient but simply failed to use their powers of perception (see Lk 24:25; Ro 1:14; 1Ti 6:9; Tit

3:3). *Who . . . ?* Obviously legalistic Judaizers. *portrayed as crucified.* See 1Co 1:23; 2:2. The verb means "to publicly portray or placard." Cf. the bronze snake that Moses displayed on a pole (Nu 21:9).

3:2 *the Spirit.* A major theme in Galatians from this point on (Paul refers to the Holy Spirit 16 times).

3:3 *beginning with the Spirit . . . finish by human effort?* Both salvation and sanctification are the work of the Holy Spirit. *human effort.* Lit. "the flesh," a reference to human nature in its unregenerate weakness. Trying to achieve righteousness by works, such as circumcision, was a part of life in the "flesh."

3:4 *if it really was in vain.* Paul hopes that those who have been misled will return to the true gospel.

3:7 *children of Abraham.* Abraham was the physical and spiritual father of the Jewish race (see Jn 8:33,39,53; Ac 7:2; Ro 4:12). Here all believers (Jews and Gentiles) are called his spiritual children (see notes on Ro 4:11–12). They are also referred to as the "seed" (v. 29) or "descendants" (Heb 2:16) of Abraham.

3:8 *Scripture foresaw.* A personification of Scripture that calls attention to its divine origin (see 1Ti 5:18).

3:9 *Abraham, the man of faith.* Paul develops this theme at length in Ro 4; see also Heb 11:8–19.

3:10 *rely on observing the law.* The reference is to legalists—those who refuse God's offer of grace and insist on pursuing righteousness through works. *under a curse.* Because no one under the law ever perfectly kept the law. God's blessing has never been earned but has always been freely given. *everything.* See Jas 2:10 and note.

eryone who does not continue to do everything written in the Book of the Law." [a] [m] [11] Clearly no one is justified before God by the law, [n] because "the righteous will live by faith." [b] [o] [12] The law is not based on faith; on the contrary, it says, "Whoever does these things will live by them." [c] [p] [13] Christ redeemed us from the curse of the law [q] by becoming a curse for us, for it is written: "Cursed is everyone who is hung on a pole." [d] [r] [14] He redeemed us in order that the blessing given to Abraham might come to the Gentiles through Christ Jesus, [s] so that by faith we might receive the promise of the Spirit. [t]

THE LAW AND THE PROMISE

[15] Brothers and sisters, [u] let me take an example from everyday life. Just as no one can set aside or add to a human covenant that has been duly established, so it is in this case. [16] The promises were spoken to Abraham and to his seed. [v] Scripture does not say "and to seeds," meaning many people, but "and to your seed," [e] [w] meaning one person, who is Christ. [17] What I mean is this: The law, introduced 430 years [x] later, does not set aside the covenant previously established by God and thus do away with the promise. [18] For if the inheritance depends on the law, then it no longer depends on the promise; [y] but God in his grace gave it to Abraham through a promise.

[19] What, then, was the purpose of the law? It was added because of transgressions [z] until the Seed [a] to whom the promise referred had come. The law was given through angels [b] and entrusted to a mediator. [c] [20] A mediator, [d] however, implies more than one party; but God is one.

[21] Is the law, therefore, opposed to the promises of God? Absolutely not! [e] For if a law had been given that could impart life, then righteousness would certainly have come by the law. [f] [22] But Scripture has locked up everything under the control of sin, [g] so that what was promised, being given through faith in Jesus Christ, might be given to those who believe.

CHILDREN OF GOD

[23] Before the coming of this faith, [f] we were held in custody [h] under the law, locked up until the faith that was to come would be revealed. [i] [24] So the law was put in charge of us until Christ came [j] that we might be justified by faith. [k] [25] Now that this faith has come, we are no longer under the supervision of the law. [l]

[26] So in Christ Jesus you are all children of God [m] through faith, [27] for all of you who were baptized into Christ [n] have clothed yourselves with Christ. [o] [28] There is neither Jew nor

---

a 10 Deut. 27:26   b 11 Hab. 2:4   c 12 Lev. 18:5   d 13 Deut. 21:23   e 16 Gen. 12:7; 13:15; 24:7
f 22,23 Or through the faithfulness of Jesus . . . . 23Before faith came

---

3:10 [m] Dt 27:26; Jer 11:3
3:11 [n] S Ro 3:28
[o] Hab 2:4; S Ro 9:30; Heb 10:38
3:12 [p] Lev 18:5; S Ro 10:5
3:13 [q] Gal 4:5
[r] Dt 21:23; S Ac 5:30
3:14 [s] Ro 4:9,16
[t] ver 2; Joel 2:28; S Jn 20:22; S Ac 2:33
3:15 [u] S Ro 7:1
3:16 [v] Ge 17:19; Ps 132:11; Mic 7:20; Lk 1:55; Ro 4:13,16; 9:4,8; Gal 3:29; 4:28
[w] Ge 12:7; 13:15; 17:7,8,10; 24:7
3:17 [x] Ge 15:13,14; Ex 12:40; Ac 7:6
3:18 [y] Ro 4:14
3:19 [z] Ro 5:20
[a] ver 16 [b] Dt 33:2; Ac 7:53 [c] Ex 20:19; Dt 5:5
3:20 [d] 1Ti 2:5; Heb 8:6; 9:15; 12:24
3:21 [e] Gal 2:17; S Ro 7:12 [f] Gal 2:21
3:22 [g] Ro 3:9-19; 11:32
3:23 [h] Ro 11:32
[i] ver 25
3:24 [j] ver 19; Ro 10:4; S 4:15
[k] Gal 2:16
3:25 [l] S Ro 7:4
3:26 [m] S Ro 8:14
3:27 [n] S Mt 28:19
[o] S Ro 13:14

3:11 *will live.* Means here (and in v. 12) almost the same thing as "will be justified."

3:12 See note on Lev 18:5.

3:13 *Christ redeemed us.* See 4:5; Eph 1:7 and note. *pole.* Used in classical Greek of poles on which bodies were impaled (cf. Est 2:23 and note); here of the cross (see Ac 5:30 and note; 1Pe 2:24).

3:14 *blessing given to Abraham.* See v. 8; Ro 4:1–5. *promise of the Spirit.* See Eze 36:26; 37:14; 39:29; Jn 14:16–17; cf. Eph 1:13.

3:15 *Brothers and sisters.* See note on 1:2. *human covenant.* The Greek word normally indicates a last will or testament, which is probably the legal instrument Paul is referring to here. But in the Septuagint (the pre-Christian Greek translation of the OT) it had been widely used of God's covenant with his people (see also Mt 26:28; Lk 1:72; Ac 3:25; 7:8; 2Co 3:14; Heb 8:9), so Paul's choice of analogy was apt for his purpose.

3:16 *promises.* See notes on 4:13; 9:4.

3:17 *430 years.* See Ex 12:40–41. The period in Egypt is designated in round numbers as "400 years" in Ge 15:13; Ac 7:6 (see note there).

3:19 *was added.* From the time of Abraham, the promise covenanted to him (Ge 12:2–3,7; 15:18–20; 17:4–8) had stood at the center of God's relationship with his people. After the exodus the law contained in the Sinaitic covenant (Ex 19–24) became an additional element in that relationship—what Jeremiah by implication called the "old covenant" when he brought God's promise of a "new covenant" (Jer 31:31–34). *because of transgressions.* To make them known, even to increase

---

them (see Ro 4:15; 7:7–11 and notes). *the Seed.* Christ (v. 16). *through angels.* See Ac 7:38,53 and note. *mediator.* Moses (see note on v. 20).

3:20 The Sinaitic covenant was a formal arrangement of mutual commitments between God and Israel, with Moses as the mediator. But since the promise God covenanted with Abraham involved commitment only from God's side (and God is one; see note on Dt 6:4), no mediator was involved.

3:21 The reason the law is not opposed to the promise is that, although in itself it cannot save, it serves to reveal sin, which alienates God from humans, and to show the need for the salvation that the promise offers.

3:23 *this faith.* In Christ (v. 22). *held in custody under the law.* To be a prisoner of sin (v. 22) and a prisoner of law amounts to much the same, because law reveals and stimulates sin (see v. 19 and note; cf. Col 2:20).

3:24 *was put in charge.* The expression translates the Greek *paidagogos* (from which "pedagogue" is derived). It refers to the personal slave-attendant who accompanied a freeborn boy wherever he went and exercised a certain amount of discipline over him. His function was more like that of a baby-sitter than a teacher (see 1Co 4:15, "guardians").

3:25–26 By adoption, the justified believer is a full adult and heir in God's family, with all the attendant rights and privileges (4:1–7; Ro 8:14–17).

3:27 *baptized into Christ.* See Ro 6:3–11; 1Co 12:13 and note. *clothed . . . with.* See note on Ps 109:29.

3:28 *P* 1Co 12:13;
Col 3:11 *q* Ge 1:27;
5:2; Joel 2:29
r Jn 10:16; 17:11;
Eph 2:14,15
3:29 *s* S 1Co 3:23
t ver 16; S Lk 3:8
u S Ro 8:17 *v* ver 16
4:3 *w* ver 8,9,24,25;
Gal 2:4 *x* Col 2:8,20
4:4 *y* Mk 1:15;
Ro 5:6; Eph 1:10
z S Jn 3:17 *a* S Jn 1:14
b Lk 2:27
4:5 *c* S Ro 3:24
d Jn 1:12 *e* S Ro 8:14
4:6 *f* S Ac 16:7
g Ro 5:5 *h* Ro 8:15,16
4:7 *i* S Ro 8:17
4:8 *j* Ro 1:28;
1Co 1:21; 15:34;
1Th 4:5; 2Th 1:8
k S ver 3 *l* 2Ch 13:9;
Isa 37:19; Jer 2:11;
5:7; 16:20; 1Co 8:4,5
4:9 *m* 1Co 8:3
n S ver 3 *o* Col 2:20
4:10 *P* Ro 14:5;
Col 2:16
4:11 *q* 1Th 3:5
4:12 *r* S Ro 7:1;
Gal 6:18
4:13 *s* 1Co 2:3
4:14 *t* Mt 10:40
4:16 *u* Am 5:10
4:17 *v* Gal 2:4,12
4:18 *w* ver 13,14

Gentile, neither slave nor free,*p* neither male nor female,*q* for you are all one in Christ Jesus.*r* ²⁹If you belong to Christ,*s* then you are Abraham's seed,*t* and heirs*u* according to the promise.*v*

4 What I am saying is that as long as heirs are underage they are no different from slaves, although they own the whole estate. ²They are subject to guardians and trustees until the time set by their fathers. ³So also, when we were underage, we were in slavery*w* under the elemental spiritual forces*a* of the world.*x* ⁴But when the set time had fully come,*y* God sent his Son,*z* born of a woman,*a* born under the law,*b* ⁵to redeem*c* those under the law, that we might receive adoption*d* to sonship.*b* *e* ⁶Because you are his sons, God sent the Spirit of his Son*f* into our hearts,*g* the Spirit who calls out, "Abba,*c* Father."*h* ⁷So you are no longer slaves, but God's children; and since you are his children, he has made you also heirs.*i*

PAUL'S CONCERN FOR THE GALATIANS

⁸Formerly, when you did not know God,*j* you were slaves*k* to those who by nature are not gods.*l* ⁹But now that you know God—or rather are known by God*m*—how is it that you are turning back to those weak and miserable forces*d*? Do you wish to be enslaved*n* by them all over again?*o* ¹⁰You are observing special days and months and seasons and years?*p* ¹¹I fear for you, that somehow I have wasted my efforts on you.*q*

¹²I plead with you, brothers and sisters,*r* become like me, for I became like you. You have done me no wrong. ¹³As you know, it was because of an illness*s* that I first preached the gospel to you. ¹⁴Even though my illness was a trial to you, you did not treat me with contempt or scorn. Instead, you welcomed me as if I were an angel of God, as if I were Christ Jesus himself.*t* ¹⁵What has happened to all your joy? I can testify that, if you could have done so, you would have torn out your eyes and given them to me. ¹⁶Have I now become your enemy by telling you the truth?*u*

¹⁷Those people are zealous to win you over, but for no good. What they want is to alienate you from us, so that you may have zeal for them.*v* ¹⁸It is fine to be zealous, provided the purpose is good, and to be so always, not just when I am with you.*w* ¹⁹My dear chil-

---

a 3 Or *under the basic principles*   *b 5* The Greek word for *adoption to sonship* is a legal term referring to the full legal standing of an adopted male heir in Roman culture.   *c 6* Aramaic for *Father*
d 9 Or *principles*

A **3:28** Unity in Christ transcends ethnic, social and gender distinctions (see Ro 10:12; 1Co 12:13; Eph 2:15–16).
3:29 Christians are Abraham's true, spiritual descendants.
4:1 *underage.* Minors. Contrast with "adults" in 1Co 14:20 ("mature" in Php 3:15).
4:2 *guardians.* A broader term than "[one] put in charge" in 3:24. See Mt 20:8 ("supervisor"); Lk 8:3 ("manager").
4:3 *in slavery.* See note on 3:23. *elemental spiritual forces.* See Col 2:8 and note.
4:4 *time had fully come.* The time "set" (v. 2) by God for his children to become adult sons and heirs. *God sent his Son.* See Jn 1:14; 3:16; Ro 1:1–6; 1Jn 4:14. *born of a woman.* Showing that Christ was truly human. *born under the law.* Subject to the Jewish law.
4:5 *those under the law.* Those under the authority of the law of Moses (cf. notes on 5:18; Ro 6:14; 1Co 9:20). *adoption to sonship.* See TNIV text note; see also Ro 8:15, where "sonship" is contrasted with "slaves" (cf. Eph 1:5 and note). God takes into his family as fully recognized sons and heirs both Jews (those who had been under the law) and Gentiles who believe in Christ.
4:6 *Spirit of his Son.* A new "guardian" (v. 2), identified as the "Spirit of God" and "Spirit of Christ" in Ro 8:9 (see Ro 8:2; Eph 1:13–14). *calls out.* The Greek for this phrase is a vivid verb expressing deep emotion, often used of an inarticulate cry. In Mt 27:50 it is used of Jesus' final cry on the cross. *Abba, Father.* Expressive of an especially close relationship to God (see also TNIV text note).
4:8 *when you did not know God.* See 1Co 12:2; 1Th 4:5. *are not gods.* When the Galatians were pagans, they thought that the beings they worshiped were gods; but when they became Christians they learned better (see 1Co 8:5 and note).

A **4:9** *turning back.* See 3:1–3. *weak and miserable forces.* See note on v. 3. *enslaved … again.* Legalistic trust in rituals, in moral achievement, in the law, in good works or even in cold, dead orthodoxy may indicate a relapse into second childhood on the part of those who should be knowing and enjoying the freedom of full-grown sons and heirs.
4:10 *special days.* Such as the Sabbath and the Day of Atonement (tenth day of Tishri; see Lev 16:29–34), which had never been, and can never be, in themselves means of salvation or sanctification. *months and seasons.* Such as New Moons (see Nu 28:11–15; Isa 1:13–14), Passover (Ex 12:18) and Firstfruits (Lev 23:10). *years.* Such as the sabbath year (Lev 25:4). The Pharisees meticulously observed all these in an attempt to gain merit before God.
4:11 *wasted my efforts.* Due to their return to Pharisaic legalism.
4:12 *brothers and sisters.* See note on 1:2.
4:13 *illness.* On the basis of v. 15; 6:11 (see note there), some suggest it was eye trouble. Others have suggested malaria or epilepsy. *first preached.* When Paul visited Galatia on his first missionary journey (Ac 13:14—14:23; see map, p. 1863).
4:14 *you welcomed me.* He implies that under the influence of Judaizers they have changed their attitude toward him.
A **4:15** *What has happened to all your joy?* Because of the restraints of legalistic Judaism they had lost their blessing and joy. *torn out your eyes.* A hyperbole indicating their willingness, for his benefit, to part with that which was most precious to them.
A **4:16** *your enemy.* Telling the truth sometimes results in loss of friends. *the truth.* The good news about God's grace in Christ.
4:17 *Those people.* Judaizers (see 2:4,12).

dren, [x] for whom I am again in the pains of childbirth until Christ is formed in you, [y] [20] how I wish I could be with you now and change my tone, because I am perplexed about you!

HAGAR AND SARAH

[21] Tell me, you who want to be under the law, [z] are you not aware of what the law says? [22] For it is written that Abraham had two sons, one by the slave woman [a] and the other by the free woman. [b] [23] His son by the slave woman was born as the result of human effort, [a][c] but his son by the free woman was born as the result of a divine promise. [d]

[24] I am taking these things figuratively, for the women represent two covenants. One covenant is from Mount Sinai and bears children who are to be slaves: This is Hagar. [25] Now Hagar stands for Mount Sinai in Arabia and corresponds to the present city of Jerusalem, because she is in slavery with her children. [26] But the Jerusalem that is above [e] is free, and she is our mother. [27] For it is written:

> "Be glad, barren woman,
>   you who never bore a child;
> shout for joy and cry aloud,
>   you who were never in labor;
> because more are the children of the desolate woman
>   than of her who has a husband." [b] [f]

[28] Now you, brothers and sisters, like Isaac, are children of promise. [g] [29] At that time the son born by human effort [h] persecuted the son born by the power of the Spirit. [i] It is the same now. [30] But what does Scripture say? "Get rid of the slave woman and her son, for the slave woman's son will never share in the inheritance with the free woman's son." [c][j] [31] Therefore, brothers and sisters, we are not children of the slave woman, [k] but of the free woman. [l]

FREEDOM IN CHRIST

5 It is for freedom that Christ has set us free. [m] Stand firm, [n] then, and do not let yourselves be burdened again by a yoke of slavery. [o] [2] Mark my words! I, Paul, tell you that if you let yourselves be circumcised, [p] Christ will be of no value to you at all. [3] Again I declare to every man who lets himself be circumcised that he is obligated to obey the whole law. [q] [4] You who are trying to be justified by the law [r] have been alienated from Christ; you have fallen away from grace. [s] [5] But by faith

a 23 Or *born according to the flesh*; also in verse 29   b 27 Isaiah 54:1   c 30 Gen. 21:10

4:19 [x] S 1Th 2:11
[y] Ro 8:29; Eph 4:13
4:21 [z] S Ro 2:12
4:22 [a] Ge 16:15
[b] Ge 21:2
4:23 [c] ver 28,29;
Ro 9:7,8 [d] Ge 17:16-
21; 18:10-14; 21:1;
Heb 11:11
4:26 [e] Heb 12:22;
Rev 3:12; 21:2,10
4:27 [f] Isa 54:1
4:28 [g] ver 23;
S Gal 3:16
4:29 [h] ver 23
[i] Ge 21:9
4:30 [j] Ge 21:10
4:31 [k] S Ro 7:4
[l] ver 22
5:1 [m] ver 13; Jn 8:32;
Gal 2:4; S Ro 7:4
[n] S 1Co 16:13
[o] S Mt 23:4; Gal 2:4
5:2 [p] ver 3,6,11,12;
Ac 15:1
5:3 [q] Ro 2:25;
Gal 3:10; Jas 2:10
5:4 [r] S Ro 3:28
[s] Heb 12:15; 2Pe 3:17

4:19 *My dear children.* For Paul's affectionate relationship to his converts, see Ac 20:37–38; Php 4:1; 1Th 2:7–8. The expression occurs only here in Paul's writings, but is common in John's (e.g., Jn 13:33; 1Jn 2:1; 3:7). *until Christ is formed in you.* The goal of Paul's ministry (see Ro 8:29; Eph 4:13,15; Col 1:27).

4:21 *under the law.* See note on v. 5.

4:22 *two sons.* Ishmael was born to the slave woman, Hagar (Ge 16:1–16), and Isaac to the free woman, Sarah (Ge 21:2–5).

4:23 *promise.* See Ge 17:19; 18:10–15 and note on 18:10; cf. Ro 9:6–9.

4:24 *taking these things figuratively.* The Sarah-Hagar account is an allegory, not in the sense that it was nonhistorical but in the sense that Paul uses the events to illustrate a theological truth. *covenant.* See note on 3:15. *Mount Sinai.* Where the old covenant was established, with its law governing Israel's life (see Ex 19:2; 20:1–17).

4:25 *corresponds to the present city of Jerusalem.* Jerusalem can be equated with Mount Sinai because it represents the center of Judaism.

4:26 *the Jerusalem that is above.* Rabbinical teaching held that the Jerusalem above was the heavenly archetype that in the Messianic period would be let down to earth (cf. Rev 21:2). Here it refers to the heavenly city of God, in which Christ reigns and of which Christians are citizens, in contrast to the "present city of Jerusalem" (v. 25). *our mother.* As citizens of the heavenly Jerusalem, Christians are her children.

4:27 Paul applies Isaiah's joyful promise (see Isa 54:1 and note) to exiled Jerusalem (in her exile "barren" of children) to the in-

gathering of believers through the gospel, by which "Jerusalem's" children have become many.

4:28 *children of promise.* Children by virtue of God's promise (see 3:29; Ro 9:8).

4:29 *persecuted the son born by the power of the Spirit.* Suggested by Ge 21:9 (see note there); cf. Ps 83:5–6. *the same now.* See Ac 13:50; 14:2–5,19; 1Th 2:14–16.

4:30 *Get rid of the slave woman.* Sarah's words in Ge 21:10 were used by Paul as the Scriptural basis for teaching the Galatians to put the Judaizers out of the church.

4:31 *we are not children of the slave woman.* The believer is not enslaved to the law but is a child of promise and lives by faith (cf. 3:7,29).

5:1 *freedom.* Emphasized by its position in the Greek sentence. The freedom spoken of here is freedom from the yoke of the law. *burdened.* Cf. Mt 11:28–30 and notes on 11:29–30. *yoke of slavery.* The burden of the rigorous demands of the law as the means for gaining God's favor—an intolerable burden for sinful humanity (see Ac 15:10–11).

5:2 As a condition for God's acceptance, circumcision impeded the development of the Christian life through trusting in Christ.

5:3 *obligated to obey the whole law.* The OT law is a unit; submission to it cannot be selective (see Jas 2:10 and note).

5:4 *fallen away from grace.* Placed yourself outside the scope of divine favor, because gaining God's favor by observing the law and receiving it by grace are mutually exclusive (see 2:2 and note; cf. 3:3 and note).

5:5 ᵗRo 8:23,24
5:6 ᵘS Ro 16:3
  ᵛS 1Co 7:19
  ʷ1Th 1:3; Jas 2:22
5:7 ˣS 1Co 9:24
  ʸGal 3:1
5:8 ᶻS Ro 8:28
5:9 ᵃ1Co 5:6
5:10 ᵇS 2Co 2:3
  ᶜPhp 3:15 ᵈver 12;
  Gal 1:7
5:11 ᵉGal 4:29; 6:12
  ᶠS Lk 2:34
5:12 ᵍver 10
5:13 ʰS ver 1
  ⁱS ver 24; 1Co 8:9;
  1Pe 2:16 ʲ1Co 9:19;
  2Co 4:5; Eph 5:21
5:14 ᵏLev 19:18;
  S Mt 5:43; Gal 6:2
5:16 ˡver 18,25;
  Ro 8:2,4-6,9,14;
  S 2Co 5:17 ᵐS ver 24
5:17 ⁿRo 8:5-8
  ᵒRo 7:15-23
5:18 ᵖS ver 16
  ᑫS Ro 2:12; 1Ti 1:9
5:19 ʳS 1Co 6:18
5:21 ˢMt 15:19;
  Ro 13:13 ᵗS Mt 25:34
5:22 ᵘMt 7:16-20;
  Eph 5:9 ᵛCol 3:12-15
  ʷMal 2:6
5:23 ˣS Ac 24:25
  ʸver 18
5:24 ᶻver 13,16-21;
  S Ro 6:6; 7:5,18; 8:3-
  5,8,9,12,13; 13:14;
  Gal 6:8; Col 2:11
  ᵃver 16,17
5:25 ᵇS ver 16
5:26 ᶜPhp 2:3

we eagerly await through the Spirit the righteousness for which we hope. ᵗ ⁶For in Christ Jesus ᵘ neither circumcision nor uncircumcision has any value. ᵛ The only thing that counts is faith expressing itself through love. ʷ

⁷You were running a good race. ˣ Who cut in on you ʸ to keep you from obeying the truth? ⁸That kind of persuasion does not come from the one who calls you. ᶻ ⁹"A little yeast works through the whole batch of dough." ᵃ ¹⁰I am confident ᵇ in the Lord that you will take no other view. ᶜ The one who is throwing you into confusion ᵈ will have to pay the penalty, whoever that may be. ¹¹Brothers and sisters, if I am still preaching circumcision, why am I still being persecuted? ᵉ In that case the offense ᶠ of the cross has been abolished. ¹²As for those agitators, ᵍ I wish they would go the whole way and emasculate themselves!

LIFE BY THE SPIRIT

¹³You, my brothers and sisters, were called to be free. ʰ But do not use your freedom to indulge the sinful nature ᵃ; ⁱ rather, serve one another ʲ humbly in love. ¹⁴For the entire law is fulfilled in keeping this one command: "Love your neighbor as yourself." ᵇ ᵏ ¹⁵If you keep on biting and devouring each other, watch out or you will be destroyed by each other.

¹⁶So I say, walk by the Spirit, ˡ and you will not gratify the desires of the sinful nature. ᵐ ¹⁷For the sinful nature desires what is contrary to the Spirit, and the Spirit what is contrary to the sinful nature. ⁿ They are in conflict with each other, so that you are not to do whatever ᶜ you want. ᵒ ¹⁸But if you are led by the Spirit, ᵖ you are not under the law. ᑫ

¹⁹The acts of the sinful nature are obvious: sexual immorality, ʳ impurity and debauchery; ²⁰idolatry and witchcraft; hatred, discord, jealousy, fits of rage, selfish ambition, dissensions, factions ²¹and envy; drunkenness, orgies, and the like. ˢ I warn you, as I did before, that those who live like this will not inherit the kingdom of God. ᵗ

²²But the fruit ᵘ of the Spirit is love, ᵛ joy, peace, ʷ patience, kindness, goodness, faithfulness, ²³gentleness and self-control. ˣ Against such things there is no law. ʸ ²⁴Those who belong to Christ Jesus have crucified the sinful nature ᶻ with its passions and desires. ᵃ ²⁵Since we live by the Spirit, ᵇ let us keep in step with the Spirit. ²⁶Let us not become conceited, ᶜ provoking and envying each other.

ᵃ 13 Or *the flesh;* also in verses 16, 17, 19 and 24   ᵇ 14 Lev. 19:18   ᶜ 17 Or *you do not do what*

5:5 *righteousness for which we hope.* A reference to God's final verdict of "not guilty," assured presently to the believer by faith and by the sanctifying work of the Holy Spirit. This is one of the few eschatological statements in Galatians.

▲ **5:6** *neither circumcision nor uncircumcision has any value.* See v. 2; 2:21; 6:15; 1Co 7:19. *faith expressing itself through love.* Faith is not mere intellectual assent (see Jas 2:18–19) but a living trust in God's grace that expresses itself in acts of love (see 1Th 1:3).

5:7 *were running a good race.* Before the Judaizers hindered them. Paul was fond of depicting the Christian life as a race (see, e.g., 2:2; 1Co 9:24–27 and note on 9:27; Php 2:16; 2Ti 4:7).

5:8 *persuasion.* By the Judaizers.

5:9 A proverb used here to stress the pervasive effect of Judaism. When the word "yeast" in the Bible is used as a symbol, it indicates evil or the corrupting influence of false teaching (see note on Mk 8:15; Mt 13:33 (see note there).

▲ **5:11** *Brothers and sisters.* See note on 1:2. *why am I still being persecuted?* Because human pride refuses to acknowledge that it is incapable of doing anything to merit salvation. Paul's preaching excluded circumcision and obedience to the law as a means of justification and focused instead on Christ's finished work on the cross. This was an offense to the Judaizers and continues to be so to many people in our own day (see Ro 9:32–33 and note on 9:32; 1Co 1:23 and note).

5:12 *emasculate themselves.* Paul's sarcasm is evident (cf. Php 3:2).

▲ **5:13** *do not use your freedom to indulge the sinful nature.* See Ro 6:1 and note. True Christian liberty is not license to sin but freedom to serve God and one another in love (see 1Pe 2:16 and note).

▲ **5:14** *entire law is fulfilled.* Doing to others what you would have them do to you expresses the spirit and intention of "the Law and the Prophets" (Mt 7:12; cf. Mk 12:31; cf. also Ro 13:8–10 and notes on 13:8–9).

▲ **5:15** *biting and devouring each other.* The opposite of vv. 13–14. Seeking to attain status with God and human beings by mere observance of the law breeds a self-righteous, critical spirit.

▲ **5:16** *walk.* Present tense—"go on walking" (used of habitual conduct). Living by the promptings and power of the Spirit is the key to conquering sinful desires (see v. 25 and note; Ro 8:2–4).

5:17 *in conflict with each other.* Cf. Ro 7:13–25; 1Pe 2:11 and notes.

5:18 *led by the Spirit.* See Ro 8:14. *not under the law.* Not under the bondage of trying to please God by minute observance of the law for salvation or sanctification (see Ro 6:14 and note).

▲ **5:19–21** See Ro 1:29–31 and note.

▲ **5:22–23** For other lists of virtues, see 2Co 6:6–10; Eph 4:2; 5:9; Php 4:8–9; Col 3:12–15. Christian character is produced by the Holy Spirit, not by the mere moral discipline of trying to live by the law. Paul makes it clear that justification by faith does not result in libertinism. The indwelling Holy Spirit produces Christian virtues in the believer's life.

5:22 *fruit of the Spirit.* Compare the singular "fruit" with the plural "acts" (v. 19).

5:23 *no law.* See 1Ti 1:9.

5:24 *crucified the sinful nature.* See 2:20; 6:14.

5:25 *keep in step with.* Or "walk in line with," a different Greek verb from "walk by" in v. 16.

DOING GOOD TO ALL

6 Brothers and sisters, if someone is caught in a sin, you who live by the Spirit ^{d} should restore ^{e} that person gently. But watch yourselves, or you also may be tempted. ^{2}Carry each other's burdens, and in this way you will fulfill the law of Christ. $^{f\,3}$If any of you think you are something ^{g} when you are nothing, you deceive yourselves. ^{h} ^{4}Each of you should test your own actions. Then you can take pride in yourself, ^{i} without comparing yourself to somebody else, ^{j} ^{5}for each of you should carry your own load. ^{k} ^{6}Nevertheless, those who receive instruction in the word should share all good things with their instructor. ^{l}

^{7}Do not be deceived: ^{m} God cannot be mocked. People reap what they sow. ^{n} ^{8}Those who sow to please their sinful nature, ^{o} from that nature ^{a} will reap destruction; ^{p} those who sow to please the Spirit, from the Spirit will reap eternal life. ^{q} ^{9}Let us not become weary in doing good, ^{r} for at the proper time we will reap a harvest if we do not give up. ^{s} ^{10}Therefore, as we have opportunity, let us do good ^{t} to all people, especially to those who belong to the family ^{u} of believers.

NOT CIRCUMCISION BUT THE NEW CREATION

^{11}See what large letters I use as I write to you with my own hand! ^{v}

^{12}Those who want to impress others by means of the flesh ^{w} are trying to compel you to be circumcised. ^{x} The only reason they do this is to avoid being persecuted ^{y} for the cross of Christ. ^{13}Not even those who are circumcised keep the law, ^{z} yet they want you to be circumcised that they may boast about your circumcision in the flesh. ^{a} ^{14}May I never boast except in the cross of our Lord Jesus Christ, ^{b} through which ^{b} the world has been crucified to me, and I to the world. ^{c} ^{15}Neither circumcision nor uncircumcision means anything; ^{d} what counts is the new creation. ^{e} ^{16}Peace and mercy to all who follow this rule—to ^{c} the Israel of God.

^{17}From now on, let no one cause me trouble, for I bear on my body the marks ^{f} of Jesus.
^{18}The grace of our Lord Jesus Christ ^{g} be with your spirit, ^{h} brothers and sisters. Amen.

---

^{a} 8 Or *their flesh, from the flesh* ^{b} 14 Or *whom* ^{c} 16 Or *rule and to*

6:1 *Brothers and sisters.* See note on 1:2. *you who live by the Spirit.* Contrast with 1Co 3:1–3. *restore.* See note on 2Co 13:9. The Greek for this verb is used elsewhere in the NT for mending nets (Mk 1:19) and bringing factions together (1Co 1:10).
6:2 *Carry each other's burdens.* The emphasis is on moral burdens or weaknesses (see v. 1; Ro 15:1–3). *law of Christ.* See 1Co 9:21 and note.
6:4 *Each of you should test your own actions.* The emphasis here is on personal responsibility (see 1Co 11:28; 2Co 13:5).
6:5 *carry your own load.* The "for" at the beginning of the verse connects it with v. 4. Each of us is responsible before God. The reference may be to the future judgment (the Greek verb is in the future tense), when every Christian will give an account to God (see Ro 14:10,12 and note on 14:10; 2Co 5:10 and note).
6:6 *share all good things.* See Php 4:14–19; 1Ti 5:17 and note.
6:7 *reap what they sow.* See 2Co 9:6. As vv. 8–9 show, the principle applies not only negatively but also positively.
6:8 See Ro 8:13. *destruction.* See 5:19–21. *eternal life.* In 5:21 Paul speaks of inheriting "the kingdom of God" and here of reaping "eternal life." The first focuses on the realm (sphere, context) that will be inherited (as Israel inherited the promised land); the second focuses on the blessed life that will be enjoyed in that realm (see Jn 3:15 and note).
6:10 *especially to those who belong to the family of believers.* See 1Ti 5:8.
6:11 *large letters.* May have been for emphasis or, as some have suggested, because Paul had poor eyesight (see note on 4:13). *with my own hand.* The letter up to this point had probably been dictated to a scribe, after which Paul took the pen in his own

hand and finished the letter (cf. Ro 16:22 and note).
6:12 *compel you to be circumcised.* Cf. 2:3. *to avoid being persecuted.* By advocating circumcision (see 5:11) the Judaizers were less apt to experience opposition from the Jewish opponents of Christianity. They were thinking only of themselves. See Introduction: Occasion and Purpose.
6:14 *boast except in the cross.* See 1Co 1:31; 2:2. *world.* All that is against God (see notes on Jn 1:9; 1Jn 2:15). *crucified to me, and I to the world.* See 2:19–20; 5:24.
6:15 *new creation.* In Christ the redeemed undergo a transformation that results in an entirely new being. Creation again takes place (see 2Co 5:17 and note).
6:16,18 *Peace ... grace.* See note on Ro 1:7.
6:16 *Peace and mercy.* Cf. Ps 125:5; 128:6. *this rule.* See vv. 14–15. *Israel of God.* In contrast to "Israel according to flesh" (a literal rendering of the Greek for "people of Israel" in 1Co 10:18), the NT church, made up of believing Jews and Gentiles, is the new seed of Abraham and the heir according to the promise (3:29; cf. Ro 9:6; Php 3:3)—though some limit the phrase here to Christian Jews (see TNIV text note).
6:17 *marks of Jesus.* In ancient times the Greek word for "marks" was used for the brand that identified slaves or animals. Paul's suffering (stoning, Ac 14:19; beatings, Ac 16:22; 2Co 11:25; illness, 2Co 12:7; Gal 4:13–14) marked him as a "servant of Christ" (1:10; cf. 2Co 4:10).
6:18 *be with your spirit.* Be with you (see 2Co 13:14 and note). *brothers and sisters.* See note on Ro 1:13. *Amen.* A word of confirmation often used at the close of a doxology or benediction.

C The author identifies himself as Paul (1:1; 3:1; cf. 3:7,13; 4:1; 6:19–20). Some have taken the absence of the usual personal greetings and the verbal similarity of many parts to Colossians, among other reasons, as grounds for doubting authorship by the apostle Paul. However, this was probably a circular letter, intended for other churches in addition to the one in Ephesus (see notes on 1:1,15; 6:21–23). Paul may have written it about the same time as Colossians, c. A.D. 60, while he was in prison at Rome (see 3:1; 4:1; 6:20; see also chart, p. 1855).

THE CITY OF EPHESUS

Ephesus was the most important city in western Asia Minor (now Turkey). It had a harbor that at that time opened into the Cayster River (see map, p. 1983), which in turn emptied into the Aegean Sea (see map, p. 2123). Because it was also at an intersection of major trade routes, Ephesus became a commercial center. It boasted a pagan temple dedicated to the Roman goddess Diana (Greek *Artemis*); cf. Ac 19:23–31. Paul made Ephesus a center for evangelism for about three years (see note on Ac 19:10), and the church there apparently flourished for some time, but later needed the warning of Rev 2:1–7.

THEOLOGICAL MESSAGE

Unlike several of the other letters Paul wrote, Ephesians does not address any particular error or heresy. Paul wrote to expand the horizons of his readers, so that they might understand better the dimensions of God's eternal purpose and grace and come to appreciate the high goals God has for the church.

The letter opens with a sequence of statements about God's blessings, which are interspersed with a remarkable variety of expressions drawing attention to God's wisdom, forethought and purpose. Paul emphasizes that we have been saved, not only for our personal benefit, but also to bring praise and glory to God. The climax of God's purpose, "when the times reach their fulfillment," is to bring all things in the universe together under Christ (1:10). It is crucially important that Christians realize this, so in 1:15–23 Paul prays for their understanding (a second prayer occurs in 3:14–21).

Having explained God's great goals for the church, Paul proceeds to show the steps toward their fulfillment. First, God has reconciled individuals to himself as an act of grace (2:1–10). Second, God has reconciled these saved individuals to each other, Christ having broken down the barriers through his own death (2:11–22). But God has done something even beyond this: He has united these reconciled individuals in one body, the church. This is a "mystery" not fully known until it was revealed to Paul (3:1–6). Now Paul is able to state even more clearly what God has intended for the church, namely, that it be the means by which he displays his "manifold wisdom" to the "rulers and authorities in the heavenly realms" (3:7–13). It is clear through the repetition of "heavenly realms" (1:3,20; 2:6; 3:10; 6:12) that Christian existence is not merely on an earthly plane. It receives its meaning and significance from heaven, where Christ is exalted at the right hand of God (1:20).

Nevertheless, that life is lived out on earth, where the practical daily life of the believer continues to work out the purposes of God. The ascended Lord gave "gifts" to the members of his church to enable them to minister to one another and so promote unity and maturity (4:1–16). The unity of the church under the headship of Christ foreshadows the uniting of "all things in heaven and on earth under Christ" (1:10). The new life of purity and mutual deference stands in contrast to the old way of life without Christ (4:17—6:9). Those who are "strong in the Lord" have victory over the evil one in the great spiritual conflict, especially through the power of prayer (6:10–20; see note on 1:3).

OUTLINE

EPHESUS IN THE TIME OF PAUL

The province of Asia with its many splendid cities was one of the jewels on a belt of Roman lands encircling the Mediterranean.

Located on the most direct sea and land route to the eastern provinces of the empire, Ephesus was an emporium that had few equals anywhere in the world. Certainly no city in Asia was more famous or more populous. It ranked with Rome, Corinth, Antioch and Alexandria among the foremost urban centers of the empire.

B Situated on an inland harbor (now filled in with silt), the city was connected by a narrow channel via the Cayster River with the Aegean Sea some three miles away. Ephesus boasted impressive civic monuments, including, most prominently, the temple of Artemis (Diana), one of the seven wonders of the ancient world. Coins of the city proudly displayed the slogan *Neokoros*, "temple-warden."

Here in Ephesus Paul preached to large crowds of people. The silversmiths complained that he had influenced large numbers of people here in Ephesus and in practically the whole province of Asia (Ac 19:26). In one of the most dra-

matic events recorded in the NT, the apostle escaped a huge mob in the theater. This structure, located on the slope of Mt. Pion at the end of the Arcadian Way, could seat 25,000 people!

Other places doubtless familiar to the apostle were the Commercial Agora, the Magnesian Gate, the Town Hall or "Council House" and the Street of the Curetes. The location of the lecture hall of Tyrannus, where Paul taught, is unknown.

1 Paul, an apostle *a* of Christ Jesus by the will of God, *b*

To God's holy people *c* in Ephesus, *a d* the faithful *e* in Christ Jesus:

²Grace and peace to you from God our Father and the Lord Jesus Christ. *f*

PRAISE FOR SPIRITUAL BLESSINGS IN CHRIST

³Praise be to the God and Father of our Lord Jesus Christ, *g* who has blessed us in the heavenly realms *h* with every spiritual blessing in Christ. ⁴For he chose us *i* in him before the creation of the world *j* to be holy and blameless *k* in his sight. In love *l* ⁵he *b* predestined *m* us for adoption to sonship *c n* through Jesus Christ, in accordance with his pleasure *o* and will— ⁶to the praise of his glorious grace, *p* which he has freely given us in the One he loves. *q* ⁷In him we have redemption *r* through his blood, *s* the forgiveness of sins, in accordance with the riches *t* of God's grace ⁸that he lavished on us. With all wisdom and understanding, ⁹he *d* made known to us the mystery *u* of his will according to his good pleasure, which he purposed *v* in Christ, ¹⁰to be put into effect when the times reach their fulfillment *w*—to bring unity to all things in heaven and on earth under Christ. *x*

¹¹In him we were also chosen, *e* having been predestined *y* according to the plan of him who works out everything in conformity with the purpose *z* of his will, ¹²in order

---

a 1 Some early manuscripts do not have *in Ephesus.*   *b 4,5* Or *sight in love.* ⁵*He*   *c 5* The Greek word for *adoption to sonship* is a legal term referring to the full legal standing of an adopted male heir in Roman culture.   *d 8,9* Or *us with all wisdom and understanding.* ⁹*And he*   *e 11* Or *were made heirs*

1:1 *a* S 1Co 1:1
b S 2Co 1:1 *c* S Ac 9:13
d S Ac 18:19 *e* Col 1:2
1:2 *f* S Ro 1:7
1:3 *g* 2Co 1:3;
1Pe 1:3 *h* ver 20;
Eph 2:6; 3:10; 6:12
1:4 *i* 2Th 2:13
j S Mt 25:34
k Lev 11:44; 20:7;
2Sa 22:24; Ps 15:2;
Eph 5:27; Col 1:22
l Eph 4:2,15,16
1:5 *m* ver 11;
Ro 8:29,30
n S Ro 8:14,15
o Lk 12:32; 1Co 1:21;
Col 1:19
1:6 *p* ver 12,14
q Mt 3:17
1:7 *r* ver 14;
S Ro 3:24 *s* S Ro 3:25
t S Ro 2:4
1:9 *u* S Ro 16:25
v S ver 11
1:10 *w* Mk 1:15;
Ro 5:6; Gal 4:4
x Col 1:20
1:11 *y* ver 5;
Ro 8:29,30 *z* ver 9;
Ro 8:28; Eph 3:11;
Heb 6:17

1:1 *Paul.* See note on Ro 1:1. *apostle ... by the will of God.* See 1Co 1:1 and note. Paul not only stresses his authority under God but also anticipates the strong emphasis he will make later in this chapter and book on God's sovereign plan and purpose. *God's holy people.* Those God has called to be his own people, i.e., all Christians (see vv. 15,18). The Greek word for this phrase carried the idea of dedication to a deity (see note on Ro 1:7). *in Ephesus.* See TNIV text note. The book may have been intended as a circular letter to several churches, including the one at Ephesus (see notes on v. 15; 6:21–23; Ac 19:10). *in Christ Jesus.* This phrase (or a similar one) occurs ten times in vv. 1–13. It refers to the spiritual union of Christ with believers, which Paul often symbolizes by the metaphor "body of Christ" (see, e.g., v. 23; 2:16; 4:4,12,16; 5:23,30).

1:2 *Grace and peace.* See note on Ro 1:7. Paul uses the word "grace" 12 times and "peace" 8 times in Ephesians. *Lord Jesus Christ.* Also occurs at the end of this letter (6:23–24); see note on 1Th 1:1.

1:3–14 All one sentence in Greek, this section is often called a "doxology" because it recites what God has done and is an expression of worship to honor him. Paul speaks first of the blessings we have through the Father (vv. 3–6), then of those that come through the Son (vv. 7–12) and finally of those through the Holy Spirit (vv. 13–14).

1:3 *Father of our Lord Jesus Christ.* Jesus' relation to God the Father is unique (see Jn 20:17 and note). *blessed ... blessing.* Jewish people used the word "bless" to express both God's kindness to us and our thanks or praise to him. *heavenly realms.* Occurs five times in Ephesians, emphasizing Paul's perception that in the exaltation of Christ (his resurrection and enthronement at God's right hand) and in the Christian's union with the exalted Christ ultimate issues are involved—issues that pertain to the divine realm and that in the final analysis are worked out in and from that realm. At stake are God's eternal eschatological purpose (3:11) and the titanic conflict between God and the powerful spiritual forces arrayed against him—a purpose and a conflict that come to focus in the history of redemption. Here (v. 3) Paul asserts that, through their union with the exalted Christ, Christians have already been made beneficiaries of every spiritual blessing that belongs to and comes from the heavenly realm. In vv. 20–22 he proclaims Christ's exaltation to that realm and his elevation over all other powers and titles, so that he rules over all for the sake of his church. According to 2:6, those who have been made alive with Christ (2:5) share in

Christ's exaltation and enthronement in heaven. Thus (3:10) by the gathering of Gentiles and Jews into one body of Christ (the church), God triumphantly displays his "manifold wisdom" to the "rulers and authorities" in the heavenly realm. As a result, the spiritual struggle of believers here and now is not so much against "flesh and blood" as against the great spiritual forces that war against God in heaven (see 6:12 and note).

1:4 *chose.* Divine election is a frequent theme in Paul's letters (Ro 8:29–33; 9:6–26; 11:5,7,28; 16:13; Col 3:12; 1Th 1:4; 2Th 2:13; Tit 1:1). In this chapter it is emphasized in the following ways: (1) "he chose us" (here); (2) "he predestined us" (v. 5); (3) "we were also chosen" (v. 11); (4) "having been predestined" (v. 11). *before the creation of the world.* Cf. Jn 17:24. *holy and blameless.* See 5:27 for the same pair of words. Holiness is the result—not the basis—of God's choosing. It refers both to the holiness imparted to the believer because of Christ and to the believer's personal sanctification (see notes on Ex 3:5; Lev 11:44; 1Co 1:2). *In love.* See TNIV text note on vv. 4–5; cf. 3:17; 4:2,15–16; 5:2.

1:5 *adoption to sonship.* See Ro 8:23 and note.

1:6 *to the praise.* See vv. 12,14. Election by grace is for God's glory.

1:7 *redemption.* See v. 14; 4:30; see also Ro 3:24; Tit 2:14 and notes. The Ephesians were familiar with the Greco-Roman practice of redemption: Slaves were freed by the payment of a ransom. Similarly, the ransom necessary to free sinners from the bondage of sin and the resulting curse imposed by the law (see Gal 3:13) was the death of Christ (called here "his blood"). *through his blood.* Cf. 2:13; 1Pe 1:18–19.

1:9 *mystery.* See notes on Ro 11:25; Col 1:26.

1:10 *to bring ... under Christ.* Paul uses a significant term here that not only has the idea of leadership but also was often used of adding up a column of figures. A contemporary way of putting it might be to say that in a world of confusion, where things do not "add up" or make sense, we look forward to the time when everything will be brought into meaningful relationship under the headship of Christ.

1:11 *In him.* Christ is the center of God's plan. Whether the universe or the individual Christian is in view, only in relationship to Christ is there a meaningful future. Paul goes on to speak, not of the world as a whole, but of those who respond to God's call. *predestined.* See vv. 4–5; see also Ro 8:29–30 and notes.

that we, who were the first to put our hope in Christ, might be for the praise of his glory. *a* 13And you also were included in Christ *b* when you heard the word of truth, *c* the gospel of your salvation. When you believed, you were marked in him with a seal, *d* the promised Holy Spirit, *e* 14who is a deposit guaranteeing our inheritance *f* until the redemption *g* of those who are God's possession—to the praise of his glory. *h*

THANKSGIVING AND PRAYER

15For this reason, ever since I heard about your faith in the Lord Jesus *i* and your love for all his people, *j* 16I have not stopped giving thanks for you, *k* remembering you in my prayers. *l* 17I keep asking that the God of our Lord Jesus Christ, the glorious Father, *m* may give you the Spirit *a* of wisdom *n* and revelation, so that you may know him better. 18I pray that the eyes of your heart may be enlightened *o* in order that you may know the hope to which he has called *p* you, the riches *q* of his glorious inheritance *r* in his people, *s* 19and his incomparably great power for us who believe. That power *t* is the same as the mighty strength *u* 20he exerted when he raised Christ from the dead *v* and seated him at his right hand *w* in the heavenly realms, *x* 21far above all rule and authority, power and dominion, *y* and every name *z* that can be invoked, not only in the present age but also in the one to come. *a* 22And God placed all things under his feet *b* and appointed him to be head *c* over everything for the church, 23which is his body, *d* the fullness of him *e* who fills everything in every way. *f*

MADE ALIVE IN CHRIST

2 As for you, you were dead in your transgressions and sins, *g* 2in which you used to live *h* when you followed the ways of this world *i* and of the ruler of the kingdom of the air, *j* the spirit who is now at work in those who are disobedient. *k* 3All of us also lived among them at one time, *l* gratifying the cravings of our sinful nature *b* *m* and following its desires and thoughts. Like the rest, we were by nature deserving of wrath. 4But because of his great love for us, *n* God, who is rich in mercy, 5made us alive with Christ even when we were dead in transgressions—it is by grace you have been saved. *p* 6And God raised us up with Christ *q* and seated us with him *r* in the heavenly realms *s* in Christ

a 17 Or *a spirit*   *b* 3 Or *our flesh*

2:5 *p* ver 8; Jn 5:24; S Ac 15:11   **2:6** *q* S Ro 6:5 *r* Eph 1:20 *s* S Eph 1:3

1:12 *we, who were the first to put our hope in Christ.* Probably a reference to those Jews who, like Paul, had become believers before many Gentiles had.

1:13 *And you also.* Probably refers to the majority of the Ephesians, who were Gentiles. *word of truth.* See 2Ti 2:15 and note. *marked . . . with a seal.* In those days a seal denoted ownership and security.

1:14 *deposit.* See note on Ro 8:23. *inheritance.* See Col 1:12; see also Heb 9:15; 1Pe 1:4 and notes.

1:15 *ever since I heard.* This sounds strange from one who had spent a few years in Ephesus. He may be referring to a greatly enlarged church there, many members of which Paul did not know, or, if Ephesians was intended as a circular letter (see note on v. 1), he may be referring to news from the whole area, only a part of which he had visited.

1:17 *God of our Lord Jesus Christ.* See note on v. 3. *him.* God the Father.

1:18 *eyes of your heart.* Your mind or understanding or inner awareness. *hope.* Has an objective quality of certainty (see Ro 5:5 and note). It is the assurance of eternal life guaranteed by the present possession of the Holy Spirit (see v. 14). *called.* See Ro 8:28 and note; Php 3:14; 2Ti 1:9; Heb 3:1. *his glorious inheritance in his people.* Either the inheritance we have from God (see v. 14; Col 1:12) or the inheritance God receives, i.e., the believers themselves (cf. Ps 2:8; Isa 53:10). *his people.* See note on v. 1.

1:19 In this verse Paul piles term upon term to emphasize that the extraordinary, divine force by which Jesus Christ was raised (v. 20) is the same power at work in and through believers (see Php 3:10 and note).

1:20 *right hand.* The symbolic place of highest honor and authority.

1:21 *all rule . . . every name that can be invoked.* Including whatever supernatural beings his contemporaries might conceive of, for in his day many people believed not only in the existence of angels and demons but also in that of other beings. Christ is above them all. *the present age . . . the one to come.* See Mt 12:32. Like the Rabbinic teachers of his day, Paul distinguishes between the present age, which is evil, and the future age when the Messiah will consummate his kingdom and there will be a completely righteous society on earth.

1:22 *under his feet.* Ps 8:5–6 emphasizes the destiny of human beings, and Heb 2:6–9 shows that ultimately it is the Son of Man who rules over everything (cf. Heb 10:13). *head.* Christ is not only head of the church but also head over everything (see note on v. 10).

1:23 *his body.* See 2:16; 4:4,12,16; 5:23,30. *fullness . . . fills.* The church is the fullness of Christ probably in the sense that it is filled by him who fills all things.

2:1–10 In ch. 1 Paul wrote of the great purposes and plan of God, culminating in the universal headship of Christ (1:10,22), all of which is to be for "the praise of his glory" (1:14). He now proceeds to explain the steps by which God will accomplish his purposes, beginning with the salvation of individuals.

2:1 A description of their past moral and spiritual condition, separated from the life of God (cf. Col 1:21).

2:2 *ruler.* Satan (cf. Jn 14:30, "prince"). *air.* Satan is no mere earthbound enemy (cf. 6:12). *spirit.* Satan is a created, but not a human, being (cf. Job 1:6; Eze 28:15; see note on Isa 14:12–15).

2:3 *All of us.* Jews and Gentiles. *deserving of wrath.* See Ro 1:18 –20; 2:5; 9:22.

2:5 *made us alive with Christ.* This truth is expanded in Ro 6:1– 10 (see notes there).

2:6 *heavenly realms.* See note on 1:3. *in Christ Jesus.* Through our union with Christ (see note on 1:1).

Jesus, [7]in order that in the coming ages he might show the incomparable riches of his grace, [t]expressed in his kindness [u]to us in Christ Jesus. [8]For it is by grace [v]you have been saved, [w] through faith[x]—and this is not from yourselves, it is the gift of God— [9]not by works, [y] so that no one can boast. [z] [10]For we are God's handiwork, [a] created [b] in Christ Jesus to do good works, [c] which God prepared in advance for us to do.

JEW AND GENTILE RECONCILED THROUGH CHRIST

[11]Therefore, remember that formerly [d] you who are Gentiles by birth and called "uncircumcised" by those who call themselves "the circumcision" (which is done in the body by human hands) [e]— [12]remember that at that time you were separate from Christ, excluded from citizenship in Israel and foreigners [f] to the covenants of the promise, [g] without hope [h] and without God in the world. [13]But now in Christ Jesus you who once [i] were far away have been brought near[j] by the blood of Christ. [k]

[14]For he himself is our peace, [l] who has made the two one [m] and has destroyed the barrier, the dividing wall of hostility, [15]by setting aside in his flesh [n] the law with its commands and regulations. [o] His purpose was to create in himself one [p] new humanity out of the two, thus making peace, [16]and in one body to reconcile both of them to God through the cross, [q] by which he put to death their hostility. [17]He came and preached peace [r] to you who were far away and peace to those who were near. [s] [18]For through him we both have access [t] to the Father [u] by one Spirit. [v]

[19]Consequently, you are no longer foreigners and strangers, [w] but fellow citizens [x] with God's people and also members of his household, [y] [20]built [z] on the foundation [a] of the apostles and prophets, [b] with Christ Jesus himself[c] as the chief cornerstone. [d] [21]In him the whole building is joined together and rises to become a holy temple [e] in the Lord. [22]And

---

2:7 [t] S Ro 2:4
[u] Tit 3:4
2:8 [v] S Ro 3:24
[w] ver 5 × S Ro 9:30
2:9 [y] Dt 9:5; Ro 4:2;
2Ti 1:9; Tit 3:5
[z] 1Co 1:29
2:10 [a] Isa 29:23;
43:7; 60:21
[b] Eph 4:24
[c] S Tit 2:14
2:11 [d] S ver 2
[e] Col 2:11
2:12 [f] Isa 14:1; 65:1
[g] Gal 3:17 [h] 1Th 4:13
2:13 [i] S ver 2 [j] ver 17
[k] Col 1:20
2:14 [l] ver 15;
S Jn 14:27
[m] 1Co 12:13; Eph 3:6
2:15 [n] Col 1:21,22
[o] Col 2:14 [p] Gal 3:28
2:16 [q] 2Co 5:18;
Col 1:20,22
2:17 [r] S Lk 2:14
[s] ver 13; Ps 148:14;
Isa 57:19
2:18 [t] Eph 3:12
[u] Col 1:12 [v] 1Co 12:13;
Eph 4:4
2:19 [w] ver 12
[x] Php 3:20 [y] Gal 6:10
2:20 [z] 1Co 3:9
[a] Mt 16:18; 1Co 3:10;
Rev 21:14 [b] S Eph 4:11
[c] 1Co 3:11 [d] S Ac 4:11;
1Pe 2:4-8
2:21 [e] 1Co 3:16,17

2:7 *coming ages.* Cf. 1:21; refers to the future of eternal blessing with Christ. *show.* Or "exhibit" or "prove."

A 2:8 A major passage for understanding God's grace, i.e., his kindness, unmerited favor and forgiving love. *you have been saved.* "Saved" has a wide range of meanings. It includes salvation from God's wrath, which we all had incurred by our sinfulness. The tense of the verb (also in v. 5) suggests a completed action with emphasis on its present effect. *through faith.* See Ro 3:21–31 (and notes on that passage), which establishes the necessity of faith in Christ as the only means of being made right with God. *not from yourselves.* No human effort can contribute to our salvation; it is the gift of God (see Tit 3:5 and note).

A 2:9 *not by works.* One cannot earn salvation by "observing the law" (Ro 3:20,28; cf. Jas 2:14–26 and notes). Such a legalistic approach to salvation (or sanctification) is consistently condemned in Scripture (see Gal 2:16 and note). *no one can boast.* No one can take credit for his or her salvation. Cf. 1Co 1:26–31; 2Co 5:17 and notes.

2:10 *handiwork.* The Greek for this word sometimes has the connotation of a "work of art." *prepared in advance.* Carries forward the theme of God's sovereign purpose and planning, seen in ch. 1 (see, e.g., 1:4 and note).

A 2:11–22 From the salvation of individuals, Paul moves to another aspect of salvation in which God reconciles Jews and Gentiles, previously hostile peoples, not only to himself but also to each other through Christ (vv. 11–16). Even more than that, God unites these now reconciled people in one body, a truth introduced in vv. 19–22 and explained in ch. 3.

2:11–12 Refers to the state of those without Christ, described in vv. 1–10.

2:11 *you who are Gentiles.* Most of the Ephesians (cf. 1:13, "And you also"). *"uncircumcised" . . . "the circumcision."* The rite of circumcision was applied to all Jewish male babies; so this physical act ("done in the body by human hands") was a clear mark of distinction between Jew and Gentile, in which Jewish people naturally took pride.

2:12 *at that time.* Before salvation, in contrast to "But now" (v. 13). *separate from Christ . . . without God.* All these expressions emphasize the distance of unbelieving Gentiles from Israel, as well as from Christ. *covenants.* God had promised blessings to

and through the Jewish people (see note on Ro 9:4).

2:13 *But now.* Not only contrasts with "at that time" (v. 12) but also introduces the contrast between "from Christ" (v. 12) and "in Christ" (here). *blood of Christ.* Expresses the violent death of Christ as he poured out his lifeblood as a sacrifice for us (see 1:7; Heb 9:11–13 and notes).

2:14 *the two.* Believing Jews and believing Gentiles. *barrier . . . dividing wall.* Possibly an allusion to the barricade in the Jerusalem temple area that marked the limit to which a Gentile might go. It is used here to describe the total religious isolation Jews and Gentiles experienced from each other. *hostility.* Between Jews and Gentiles.

A 2:15 *setting aside . . . the law.* Since Mt 5:17 and Ro 3:31 teach that God's moral standard expressed in the OT law is not changed by the coming of Christ, what is abolished here is probably the effect of the specific "commands and regulations" in separating Jews from Gentiles, whose nonobservance of the Jewish law renders them ritually unclean (cf. Col 2:13–14). *in his flesh.* Probably refers to the death of Christ (cf. note on Ro 8:3). *one new humanity.* The united body of believers, the church.

2:16 *one body.* While this could possibly mean the body of Christ offered on the cross (cf. "in his flesh," v. 15), it probably refers to the "one new humanity" just mentioned, the body of believers.

2:17 *far away . . . near.* Gentiles and Jews, respectively.

2:19 *Consequently.* Paul indicates that the unity described in vv. 19–22 is based on what Christ did through his death, described in vv. 14–18. *you.* The Gentiles at Ephesus are particularly in view here. *citizens . . . household.* Familiar imagery. The household in ancient times was what we today might call an "extended family."

2:20 *foundation.* Further metaphorical language to convey the idea of a solid, integrated structure. *apostles and prophets.* Probably referring to the founding work of the early Christian apostles and prophets as they preached and taught God's word (cf. Mt 16:18 and note; 1Co 3:10–11). *cornerstone.* Isa 28:16, which uses the same term in its pre-Christian Greek translation (the Septuagint), referring to a foundation with a "tested" stone at the corner.

2:21 *joined together.* Cf. 4:16 for the same word. Both passages speak of the close relationship between believers. *rises.* The description of a building under construction conveys the sense of

2:22 *f* 1Co 3:16
3:1 *g* Ac 23:18;
Eph 4:1; 2Ti 1:8;
Phm 1,9
3:2 *h* Col 1:25
3:3 *i* S Ro 16:25
j S 1Co 2:10
3:4 *k* 2Co 11:6
3:5 *l* Ro 16:26;
S Eph 4:11
3:6 *m* S Ro 8:17
n Eph 2:15,16
o Eze 47:22
3:7 *p* S 1Co 3:5
q S Ro 12:3 *r* Eph 1:19;
Col 1:29
3:8 *s* S 1Co 15:9
t S Ac 9:15 *u* S Ro 2:4
3:9 *v* S Ro 16:25
3:10 *w* S Ro 11:33;
1Co 2:7 *x* 1Pe 1:12
y Eph 1:21; 6:12;
Col 2:10,15
z S Eph 1:3
3:11 *a* S Eph 1:11
3:12 *b* Eph 2:18
c 2Co 3:4; Heb 3:14;
4:16; 10:19,35;
1Jn 2:28; 3:21; 4:17
3:14 *d* Php 2:10

in him you too are being built together to become a dwelling in which God lives by his Spirit. *f*

GOD'S MARVELOUS PLAN FOR THE GENTILES

3 For this reason I, Paul, the prisoner *g* of Christ Jesus for the sake of you Gentiles— ²Surely you have heard about the administration of God's grace that was given to me *h* for you, ³that is, the mystery *i* made known to me by revelation, *j* as I have already written briefly. ⁴In reading this, then, you will be able to understand my insight *k* into the mystery of Christ, ⁵which was not made known to people in other generations as it has now been revealed by the Spirit to God's holy apostles and prophets. *l* ⁶This mystery is that through the gospel the Gentiles are heirs *m* together with Israel, members together of one body, *n* and sharers together in the promise in Christ Jesus. *o*

⁷I became a servant of this gospel *p* by the gift of God's grace given me *q* through the working of his power. *r* ⁸Although I am less than the least of all the Lord's people, *s* this grace was given me: to preach to the Gentiles *t* the boundless riches of Christ, *u* ⁹and to make plain to everyone the administration of this mystery, *v* which for ages past was kept hidden in God, who created all things. ¹⁰His intent was that now, through the church, the manifold wisdom of God *w* should be made known *x* to the rulers and authorities *y* in the heavenly realms, *z* ¹¹according to his eternal purpose *a* that he accomplished in Christ Jesus our Lord. ¹²In him and through faith in him we may approach God *b* with freedom and confidence. *c* ¹³I ask you, therefore, not to be discouraged because of my sufferings for you, which are your glory.

A PRAYER FOR THE EPHESIANS

¹⁴For this reason I kneel *d* before the Father, ¹⁵from whom every family *a* in heaven and

---

a 15 The Greek for *family* (*patria*) is derived from the Greek for *father* (*pater*).

---

the dynamic growth of the church. *holy temple.* Paul now uses the metaphor of a temple, thereby indicating the purpose ("to become") for which God has established his church (see 1Co 3:16 and note).

2:22 *dwelling.* The church is to be a people or community in whom the Holy Spirit dwells (cf. 2Co 6:16 and note).

3:1–13 Having saved people individually by his grace (2:1–10), and having reconciled them to each other, as well as to himself, through the sacrificial death of Christ (2:11–22), God also now unites them on an equal basis in one body, the church. This step in God's eternal plan was not fully revealed in previous times. Paul calls it a "mystery."

3:1 *For this reason.* Because of all that God has done, explained in the preceding several verses. *prisoner.* Apparently Paul was under house arrest at this time (see Ac 28:16,30 and note on 28:16). *of Christ.* Paul's physical imprisonment was because he obeyed Christ in spite of opposition. After this verse Paul breaks his train of thought to explain the "mystery" (v. 4). He resumes his initial thought in v. 14.

3:2 *Surely you have heard.* Most of the Ephesians would have heard of Paul's ministry because of his long stay there earlier. However, if this was a circular letter (see note on 1:1), the other churches may not have known much about it. *administration.* Paul unfolds God's administrative plan for the church and for the universe in this letter (see especially 1:3–12). He has been given a significant responsibility in the execution of this plan.

3:3 *mystery.* A truth known only by divine revelation (v. 5; see Ro 16:25; see also notes on Ro 11:25; Col 1:26). Here the word "mystery" has the special meaning of the private, wise plan of God, which in Ephesians relates primarily to the unification of believing Jews and Gentiles in the new body, the church (see v. 6). It may be thought of as a secret that is temporarily hidden, but more than that, it is a plan God is actively working out and revealing stage by stage (cf. 1:9–10; Rev 10:7). *by revelation.* See Gal 1:12. *as I have already written briefly.* May refer to 1:9–10.

3:5 *not made known to people in other generations.* See note on v. 6. *holy.* Set apart for God's service. *apostles and prophets.* See note on 2:20. Although Paul was the chief recipient, others received this revelation also.

3:6 *together ... together ... together.* The repetition of this word indicates the unique aspect of the mystery that was not previously known: the equality and mutuality that Gentiles had with Jews in the church, the one body. That Gentiles would turn to the God of Israel and be saved was prophesied in the OT (see Ro 15:9–12); that they would come into an organic unity with believing Jews on an equal footing was unexpected. *heirs.* See note on 1:18; cf. Gal 3:26–29 and notes.

3:7 *God's grace given me.* See v. 2 and note.

3:8 *less than the least.* Cf. 1Ti 1:15 and note. Paul never ceased to be amazed that one so unworthy as he should have been chosen for so high a task. His modesty was genuine, even though we may disagree with his self-evaluation. *grace.* In this case, a special endowment that brings responsibility for service. *to preach.* Lit. "to gospelize"; parallels "to make plain" (v. 9). *boundless.* Far beyond what we can know, but not beyond our appreciation—at least in part (cf. Ro 11:33).

3:9 *administration of this mystery.* See v. 2 and note; cf. v. 3 and note.

3:10 *now.* In contrast to the "ages past" (v. 9). *through the church.* The fact that God had done the seemingly impossible—reconciling and organically uniting Jews and Gentiles in the church—makes the church the perfect means of displaying God's wisdom. *manifold.* Variegated or multifaceted (in the way that many facets of a diamond reflect and enhance its beauty). *rulers and authorities.* Christ had ascended over all these (1:20–21; cf. 1Pe 3:19–20a and note). It is a staggering thought that the church on earth is observed, so to speak, by these spiritual powers and that to the degree the church is spiritually united it portrays to them the wisdom of God. This thought may be essential in understanding the meaning of "calling" in 4:1. *heavenly realms.* See note on 1:3.

3:11 *eternal purpose.* The effective headship of Christ over a united church is in preparation for his ultimate assumption of headship over the universe (1:10).

3:12 See Heb 4:16; 10:19–22 and notes.

3:14–21 Paul now expresses a prayer that grows out of his awareness of all that God is doing in believers. God's key gifts are "power" (vv. 16,18,20) and "love" (vv. 17–19).

3:14 *For this reason.* Resumes the thought of v. 1. *I kneel.* Ex-on earth derives its name. [16]I pray that out of his glorious riches [e] he may strengthen you with power [f] through his Spirit in your inner being, [g] [17]so that Christ may dwell in your hearts [h] through faith. And I pray that you, being rooted [i] and established in love, [18]may have power, together with all the Lord's people, [j] to grasp how wide and long and high and deep [k] is the love of Christ, [19]and to know this love that surpasses knowledge [l]—that you may be filled [m] to the measure of all the fullness of God. [n]

[20]Now to him who is able [o] to do immeasurably more than all we ask [p] or imagine, according to his power [q] that is at work within us, [21]to him be glory in the church and in Christ Jesus throughout all generations, for ever and ever! Amen. [r]

UNITY AND MATURITY IN THE BODY OF CHRIST

4 As a prisoner [s] for the Lord, then, I urge you to live a life worthy [t] of the calling [u] you have received. [2]Be completely humble and gentle; be patient, bearing with one another [v] in love. [w] [3]Make every effort to keep the unity [x] of the Spirit through the bond of peace. [y] [4]There is one body [z] and one Spirit, [a] just as you were called to one hope when you were called [b]; [5]one Lord, [c] one faith, one baptism; [6]one God and Father of all, [d] who is over all and through all and in all. [e]

[7]But to each one of us [f] grace [g] has been given [h] as Christ apportioned it. [8]This is why it [a] says:

> "When he ascended on high,
>   he took many captives [i]
>   and gave gifts to his people." [b] [j]

[9](What does "he ascended" mean except that he also descended to the lower, earthly regions [c]? [10]He who descended is the very one who ascended [k] higher than all the heavens, in order to fill the whole universe.) [l] [11]So Christ himself gave [m] the apostles, [n] the proph-

---

[a] 8 Or *God*   [b] 8 Psalm 68:18   [c] 9 Or *the depths of the earth*

3:16 [e] ver 8; S Ro 2:4 [f] S Php 4:13 [g] Ro 7:22
3:17 [h] S Ro 8:10 [i] Col 2:7
3:18 [j] Eph 1:15 [k] Job 11:8,9; Ps 103:11
3:19 [l] Php 4:7 [m] Col 2:10 [n] Eph 1:23
3:20 [o] Ro 16:25; 2Co 9:8 [p] 1Ki 3:13 [q] ver 7
3:21 [r] S Ro 11:36
4:1 [s] S Eph 3:1 [t] Php 1:27; Col 1:10; 1Th 2:12 [u] S Ro 8:28
4:2 [v] Col 3:12,13 [w] ver 15,16; Eph 4:1
4:3 [x] S Ro 15:5 [y] Col 3:15
4:4 [z] S Ro 12:5 [a] 1Co 12:13; Eph 2:18 [b] S Ro 8:28
4:5 [c] 1Co 8:6
4:6 [d] Dt 6:4; Zec 14:9 [e] S Ro 11:36
4:7 [f] 1Co 12:7,11 [g] S Ro 3:24 [h] S Ro 12:3
4:8 [i] Col 2:15 [j] Ps 68:18
4:10 [k] Pr 30:1-4 [l] Eph 1:23
4:11 [m] ver 8 [n] 1Co 12:28; Eph 2:20; 3:5; 2Pe 3:2; Jude 17

---

presses deep emotion and reverence, as people in Paul's day usually stood to pray.

3:15 *family.* The word in Greek is similar to the word for "father" (see TNIV text note), so it can be said that the "family" derives its name (and being) from the "father." God is our Father, and we can commit our prayers to him in confidence.

3:16 *inner being.* See v. 17; 2Co 4:16 and notes.

3:17 *dwell.* Be completely at home. Christ was already present in the Ephesian believers' lives (cf. Ro 8:9). *hearts.* The whole inner being.

3:18 Cf. Ro 8:35–39.

3:19 *surpasses knowledge.* Not unknowable, but so great that it cannot be completely known. *fullness.* God, who is infinite in all his attributes, allows us to draw on his resources—in this case, his love.

3:20 *immeasurably more.* Has specific reference to the matters presented in this section of Ephesians but is not limited to these. *his power.* See 1:19–21.

3:21 *to him be glory.* The ultimate goal of our existence (see 1:6 and note). *in the church and in Christ Jesus.* A remarkable parallel. God has called the church to an extraordinary position and vocation (cf. v. 10; 4:1).

4:1–32 The chapter begins (v. 2) and ends (v. 32) with exhortations to love and forgive one another.

4:1–16 So far Paul has taught that God brought Jew and Gentile into a new relationship to each other in the church and that he called the church to display his wisdom. Paul now shows how God made provision for those in the church to live and work together in unity and to grow together into maturity.

4:1 *prisoner.* See note on 3:1. *calling.* See 3:10,21 and notes.

4:3 *keep the unity.* Which God produced through the reconciling death of Christ (see 2:14–22). It is the heavy responsibility of Christians to keep that unity from being disturbed.

4:4 *one hope.* Has different aspects (e.g., 1:5,10; 2:7), but it is still one hope, tied to the glorious future of Christ, in which all believers share (cf. Ro 5:2–5; Col 1:27 and notes).

4:5 *one baptism.* Probably not the baptism of the Spirit (see 1Co 12:13), which was inward and therefore invisible, but water

baptism (see note on Ro 6:3–4). Since Paul apparently has in mind that which identifies all believers as belonging together, he would naturally refer to that church ordinance in which every new convert participated publicly. At that time it was a more obvious common mark of identification of Christians than it is now, when it is celebrated in different ways and often only seen by those in the church.

4:7 *grace.* See 3:7–8.

4:8 Ps 68:18 (see note there) speaks of God's triumphant ascension to his throne in the temple at Jerusalem (symbol of his heavenly throne). Paul applies this to Christ's triumphal ascension into heaven. Where the psalm states further that God "received gifts from people," Paul apparently takes his cue from certain Rabbinic interpretations current in his day that read the Hebrew preposition for "from" in the sense of "to" (a meaning it often has) and the verb for "received" in the sense of "take and give" (a meaning it sometimes has—but with a different preposition; see Ge 15:9; 18:5; 27:13; Ex 25:2; 1Ki 17:10–11). *captives.* Paul probably applies this to the spiritual enemies Christ defeated at the cross.

4:9 *ascended … descended.* Although Paul quoted from the psalm to introduce the idea of the "gifts to his people," he takes the opportunity to remind his readers of Christ's coming to earth (his incarnation) and his subsequent resurrection and ascension. This passage probably does not teach, as some think and as some translations suggest, that Christ descended into hell.

4:11 *Christ himself gave.* The quotation from Ps 68 has its ultimate meaning when applied to Christ as the ascended Lord, who himself has given gifts. *apostles.* Mentioned here because of their role in establishing the church (see 2:20). For qualifications of the initial group of apostles, see Ac 1:21–22; see also notes on Mk 6:30; Ro 1:1; 1Co 1:1; Heb 3:1. In a broader sense, Paul was also an apostle (see 1:1). *prophets.* People to whom God made known a message for his people that was appropriate to their particular need or situation (see Ac 11:27; 1Co 12:10 and notes). *evangelists.* See Ac 21:8; 1Co 1:17. While the other gifted people helped it grow through edification, the evangelists helped the church grow by augmentation. Since the objective mentioned in v. 12 is "to equip his people for works of

4:11 °S Ac 11:27;
Ro 12:6; 1Co 12:10, 28;
13:2, 8; 14:1, 39;
Eph 2:20; 3:5; 2Pe 3:2
ᵖ Ac 21:8; 2Ti 4:5
ᵠ Ac 13:1; Ro 2:21;
12:7; 1Co 12:28;
14:26; 1Ti 1:7; Jas 3:1
4:12 ʳ S 1Co 12:27
ˢ S Ro 14:19
4:13 ᵗ ver 3, 5
ᵘ S Php 3:8
ᵛ S 1Co 2:6; Col 1:28
ʷ Jn 1:16; Eph 1:23;
3:19
4:14 ˣ S 1Co 14:20
ʸ Isa 57:20; Jas 1:6
ᶻ Eph 6:11
4:15 ᵃ ver 2, 16;
Eph 1:4 ᵇ S Eph 1:22
4:16 ᶜ Col 2:19
ᵈ 1Co 12:7 ᵉ ver 2, 15;
Eph 1:4
4:17 ᶠ Eph 2:2
ᵍ Ro 1:21
4:18 ʰ Dt 29:4;
Ro 1:21 ⁱ Eph 2:12
ʲ 2Co 3:14
4:19 ᵏ 1Ti 4:2
ˡ Ro 1:24 ᵐ Col 3:5;
1Pe 4:3
4:22 ⁿ ver 25, 31;
Col 3:5, 8, 9; Jas 1:21;
1Pe 2:1 °S Ro 6:6
ᵖ Jer 17:9; Heb 3:13
4:23 ᵠ Ro 12:2;
Col 3:10

ets, ° the evangelists, ᵖ the pastors and teachers, ᵠ ¹²to equip his people for works of service, so that the body of Christ ʳ may be built up ˢ ¹³until we all reach unity ᵗ in the faith and in the knowledge of the Son of God ᵘ and become mature, ᵛ attaining to the whole measure of the fullness of Christ. ʷ

¹⁴Then we will no longer be infants, ˣ tossed back and forth by the waves, ʸ and blown here and there by every wind of teaching and by the cunning and craftiness of people in their deceitful scheming. ᶻ ¹⁵Instead, speaking the truth in love, ᵃ we will in all things grow up into him who is the head, ᵇ that is, Christ. ¹⁶From him the whole body, joined and held together by every supporting ligament, grows ᶜ and builds itself up ᵈ in love, ᵉ as each part does its work.

INSTRUCTIONS FOR CHRISTIAN LIVING

¹⁷So I tell you this, and insist on it in the Lord, that you must no longer ᶠ live as the Gentiles do, in the futility of their thinking. ᵍ ¹⁸They are darkened in their understanding ʰ and separated from the life of God ⁱ because of the ignorance that is in them due to the hardening of their hearts. ʲ ¹⁹Having lost all sensitivity, ᵏ they have given themselves over ˡ to sensuality ᵐ so as to indulge in every kind of impurity, and they are full of greed.

²⁰That, however, is not the way of life you learned ²¹when you heard about Christ and were taught in him in accordance with the truth that is in Jesus. ²²You were taught, with regard to your former way of life, to put off ⁿ your old self, ° which is being corrupted by its deceitful desires; ᵖ ²³to be made new in the attitude of your minds; ᵠ ²⁴and to put on ʳ the new self, ˢ created to be like God in true righteousness and holiness. ᵗ

²⁵Therefore each of you must put off falsehood and speak truthfully ᵘ to your neigh-

4:24 ʳ S Ro 13:14 ˢ S Ro 6:4 ᵗ Eph 2:10   **4:25** ᵘ Ps 15:2; Lev 19:11; Zec 8:16; Col 3:9

---

service," we may assume that evangelists, among their various ministries, helped other Christians in their testimony. *pastors and teachers.* Because of the Greek grammatical construction, it is clear that these groups of gifted people are closely related. Those who have pastoral care for God's people (the image is that of shepherding) will naturally provide "food" from the Scriptures (teaching). They will be especially gifted as teachers (cf. 1Ti 3:2).

4:12 *to equip his people for works of service.* Those mentioned in v. 11 were not to do all the work for the people but were to train the people to do the work themselves. *so that the body of Christ may be built up.* See v. 16. Spiritual gifts are for the body, the church, and are not to be exercised individualistically. "Built up" reflects the imagery of 2:19–22. Both concepts —body and building—occurring together emphasize the key idea of growth.

4:13 *until.* Expresses not merely duration but also purpose. *unity.* Carries forward the ideal of vv. 1–6. *in the faith.* Here "faith" refers to the Christians' common conviction about Christ and the doctrines concerning him, as the following words make clear (cf. also "the apostles' teaching" in Ac 2:42). *knowledge of the Son of God.* Unity is not just a matter of a loving attitude or religious feeling, but of truth and a common understanding about God's Son. *mature ... fullness of Christ.* Not the maturity of doctrinal conviction just mentioned, nor a personal maturity that includes the ability to relate well to other people (cf. vv. 2–3), but the maturity of the perfectly balanced character of Christ.

4:14 *infants.* Contrast the maturity of v. 13 (cf. 1Co 3:1). *tossed.* The nautical imagery pictures the instability of those who are not strong Christians (cf. Jas 1:6). *teaching.* Then, as now, there were many distorted teachings and heresies that would easily throw the immature off course. *cunning ... craftiness ... deceitful scheming.* Sometimes those who try to draw people away from the Christian faith are not innocently misguided but deliberately deceitful and evil (cf. 1Ti 4:1–2).

4:15 *speaking the truth in love.* A truthful and loving manner of life is implied. *grow up ... head.* A slightly different restatement of v. 13, based now on the imagery of Christ as the head of the body, which is the church. Paul thus speaks primarily of corporate maturity. It is the "body of Christ" that is to be "built up" (v. 12). In v. 13 "we all" are to become "mature."

4:16 Further details of the imagery of the body growing under the direction of the head. The parts of the body help each other in the growing process, picturing the mutual ministries of God's people spoken of in vv. 11–13 (cf. Ro 12:3–8). *love.* Maturity and unity are impossible without it (cf. vv. 2, 15).

4:17—5:20 Paul has just discussed unity and maturity as twin goals for the church, which God has brought into existence through the death of Christ. He now goes on to show that purity is also essential among those who belong to him.

4:17 *futility of their thinking.* Life without God is intellectually frustrating, useless and meaningless (see, e.g., Ecc 1:2 and note; Ro 1:21).

4:18 *darkened in their understanding.* Continues the idea of a futile thought life. *hardening of their hearts.* Moral unresponsiveness.

4:19 *have given themselves over.* Just as the pharaoh's heart was hardened reciprocally by himself and by God (see Ex 7–11; see also note on Ex 4:21), so here the Gentiles have given themselves over to a sinful kind of life, while Ro 1:24,26,28 says that God gave them over to that life.

4:20 *you.* Emphatic in the Greek text.

4:21 *truth that is in Jesus.* The wording and the use of the name Jesus (rather than Christ) suggest that Paul is referring to the embodiment of truth in Jesus' earthly life.

4:22 *former way of life.* Described in 2:1–3. *old self.* Probably means the kind of person the Christian used to be (cf. 1Co 6:11 and note). The old lifestyle resulted from deceitful desires.

4:23 *minds.* Cf. the evil thoughts of unbelievers (vv. 17–18).

4:24 *new self, created to be like God.* Since the new self is created, it cannot refer to the indwelling Christ, but rather to the kind of person he produces in the new believer. Nor is it some kind of new essential nature of the believer, because that would have been brought into existence at his new birth. In contrast, this is a new way of life that one not only "puts on" positionally at conversion (note the past tense in the parallel in Col 3:9–10) but is also urged to "put on" experientially as a Christian (see note on Ro 6:12–13).

4:25 *truthfully.* Cf. vv. 15, 21. "Speak truthfully to your neighbor" echoes Zec 8:16. *neighbor.* Probably means fellow Christians in this context.

bor, for we are all members of one body. ᵛ ²⁶"In your anger do not sin"ᵃ: ʷ Do not let the sun go down while you are still angry, ²⁷and do not give the devil a foothold. ˣ ²⁸Those who have been stealing must steal no longer, but must work, ʸ doing something useful with their own hands, ᶻ that they may have something to share with those in need. ᵃ

²⁹Do not let any unwholesome talk come out of your mouths, ᵇ but only what is helpful for building others up ᶜ according to their needs, that it may benefit those who listen. ³⁰And do not grieve the Holy Spirit of God, ᵈ with whom you were sealed ᵉ for the day of redemption. ᶠ ³¹Get rid of ᵍ all bitterness, rage and anger, brawling and slander, along with every form of malice. ʰ ³²Be kind and compassionate to one another, ⁱ forgiving each other, just as in Christ God forgave you. ʲ ¹Follow God's example, ᵏ therefore, as dearly loved children ˡ ²and walk in the way of love, just as Christ loved us ᵐ and gave himself up for us ⁿ as a fragrant offering and sacrifice to God. ᵒ

³But among you there must not be even a hint of sexual immorality, ᵖ or of any kind of impurity, or of greed, �q because these are improper for the Lord's people. ⁴Nor should there be obscenity, foolish talk ʳ or coarse joking, which are out of place, but rather thanksgiving. ˢ ⁵For of this you can be sure: No immoral, impure or greedy person—such a person is an idolater ᵗ—has any inheritance ᵘ in the kingdom of Christ and of God.ᵇ ᵛ ⁶Let no one deceive you ʷ with empty words, for because of such things God's wrath ˣ comes on those who are disobedient. ʸ ⁷Therefore do not be partners with them.

⁸For you were once ᶻ darkness, but now you are light in the Lord. Live as children of light ᵃ ⁹(for the fruit ᵇ of the light consists in all goodness, ᶜ righteousness and truth) ¹⁰and find out what pleases the Lord. ᵈ ¹¹Have nothing to do with the fruitless deeds of darkness, ᵉ but rather expose them. ¹²It is shameful even to mention what the disobedient do

---

ᵃ 26 Psalm 4:4 (see Septuagint)   ᵇ 5 Or *kingdom of the Christ and God*

4:25 ᵛS Ro 12:5
4:26 ʷPs 4:4;
S Mt 5:22
4:27 ˣ2Co 2:10,11
4:28 ʸAc 20:35
ᶻ1Th 4:11 ᵃGal 6:10
4:29 ᵇMt 12:36;
Eph 5:4; Col 3:8
ᶜS Ro 14:19
4:30 ᵈIsa 63:10;
1Th 5:19 ᵉ2Co 1:22;
5:5; Eph 1:13 ᶠRo 8:23
4:31 ᵍS ver 22
ʰCol 3:8; 1Pe 2:1
4:32 ⁱ1Pe 3:8
ʲMt 6:14,15; Col 3:12,
13
5:1 ᵏMt 5:48;
Lk 6:36 ˡS Jn 1:12
5:2 ᵐS Jn 13:34
ⁿver 25; S Gal 1:4;
2:20 ᵒHeb 7:27
5:3 ᵖS 1Co 6:18
q Col 3:5
5:4 ʳEph 4:29
ˢS ver 20
5:5 ᵗCol 3:5
ᵘS Ac 20:32
ᵛS Mt 25:34
5:6 ʷS Mk 13:5
ˣS Ro 1:18 ʸEph 2:2
5:8 ᶻS Eph 2:2
ᵃJn 8:12; S Lk 16:8;
S Ac 26:18
5:9 ᵇMt 7:16-20;
Gal 5:22 ᶜRo 15:14
5:10 ᵈS 1Ti 5:4
5:11 ᵉRo 13:12;
2Co 6:14

4:26 *In your anger.* Christians do not lose their emotions at conversion, but their emotions should be purified. Some anger is sinful, some is not (see Ps 4:4 and note). *Do not let the sun go down.* No anger is to outlast the day.

4:27 *devil.* Personal sin is usually due to our evil desires (see Jas 1:14) rather than to direct tempting by the devil. However, Satan can use our sins—especially those, like anger, that are against others—to bring about greater evil, such as divisions among Christians.

4:28 *steal no longer . . . work . . . have something to share.* It is not enough to cease from sin; one must do good. The former thief must now help those in need (cf. 1Th 4:11–12; 2Th 3:6–13).

4:29 *only what is helpful.* An exhortation parallel to the previous one. Christians not only stop saying unwholesome things; they also begin to say things that will help build others up (cf. 1Co 14:3).

4:30 *grieve.* By sin, such as "unwholesome talk" (v. 29) and the sins mentioned in v. 31. The verb also demonstrates that the Holy Spirit is a person, not just an influence, for only a person can be grieved. *sealed.* See note on 1:13. *day of redemption.* See 1:14; 1Pe 1:5 and notes.

4:31 *bitterness . . . malice.* Such things grieve the Holy Spirit. This continues the instruction concerning one's speech (v. 29). See note on Ro 1:29–31.

4:32 *kind and compassionate.* The opposite of the negative qualities of v. 31. *forgiving.* This basic Christian attitude, which is a result of being forgiven in Christ, along with being kind and compassionate, brings to others what we have received from God.

5:1 *Follow God's example.* One way of imitating God is to have a forgiving spirit (4:32). The way we imitate our Lord is to act "just as" (v. 2; 4:32) he did. The sacrificial way Jesus expressed his love for us is not only the means of salvation (as seen in ch. 2) but also an example of the way we are to live for the sake of others.

5:2 *Christ loved us and gave himself up for us.* See v. 25 and note. *fragrant offering.* In the OT the offering of a sacrifice pleased the Lord so much that it was described as a "pleasing aroma" (Ge 8:21 [see note there]; Ex 29:18,25,41; Lev 1:9,13,17).

5:3–5 See note on Ro 1:29–31.

5:3 *not . . . even a hint.* See v. 12. *any kind of impurity, or of greed.* Paul moves from specifically sexual sins to more general sins, such as greed. These include sexual lust but refer to other kinds of excessive desire as well. *the Lord's people.* See 2:21; 1Co 1:2 and note.

5:4 *foolish talk or coarse joking.* The context and the word "obscenity" indicate that it is not humor as such but off-color jokes and the like that are out of place. *thanksgiving.* See v. 20; 1Th 5:18. By being grateful for all that God has given us, we can displace evil thoughts and words.

5:5 *immoral, impure or greedy.* See v. 3. *idolater.* Cf. Col 3:5. The greedy want things more than they want God and put things in place of God, thereby committing idolatry. *inheritance.* Those who persist in sexual and other kinds of greed have excluded God, who therefore excludes them from the kingdom (but see notes on 1Co 6:9,11).

5:6 *God's wrath.* See Zec 1:2; Ro 1:18 and notes.

5:7 *partners.* Although Christians live in normal social relationships with others, as did the Lord Jesus (Lk 5:30–32; 15:1–2), they are not to participate in the sinful lifestyle of unbelievers (cf. 2Co 6:14 and note).

5:8 *darkness . . . light.* This section emphasizes the contrast between light and darkness, showing that those who belong to him who is "light" (1Jn 1:5), i.e., pure and true, not only have their lives illumined by him but also are the means of introducing that light into the dark areas of human conduct (cf. Mt 5:14).

5:9 *fruit of the light.* A mixed metaphor, but the meaning is clear. Light is productive (consider the effect of light on plant growth), and those who live in God's light produce the fruit of moral and ethical character (cf. Gal 5:22–23), while those who live in darkness do not (see v. 11).

5:11 *Have nothing to do with.* See v. 7. *expose.* Light, by nature, exposes what is in darkness, and the contrast shows sin for what it really is.

5:12 *shameful . . . to mention.* Christians should not dwell on the evils that their lives are exposing in others.

5:13 ^fJn 3:20, 21
5:14 ^gRo 13:11
^h Isa 26:19; Jn 5:25
ⁱ Isa 60:1; Mal 4:2
5:15 ^j ver 2
5:16 ^k Col 4:5
^l Eph 6:13
5:17 ^m Ro 12:2;
Col 1:9; 1Th 4:3
5:18 ⁿ Lev 10:9;
Pr 20:1; Isa 28:7;
Ro 13:13 ^o S Lk 1:15
5:19 ^p Ps 27:6; 95:2;
Ac 16:25; 1Co 14:15,
26; Col 3:16
5:20 ^q ver 4;
Job 1:21; Ps 34:1;
Col 3:17; Heb 13:15
5:21 ^r Gal 5:13;
1Pe 5:5
5:22 ^s Ge 3:16;
1Co 14:34; Col 3:18;
1Ti 2:12; Tit 2:5;
1Pe 3:1,5,6 ^t Eph 6:5
5:23 ^u S Eph 1:22
5:24 ^v S ver 22
5:25 ^w ver 28, 33;
Col 3:19 ^x S ver 2
5:26 ^y Jn 17:19;
Heb 2:11; 10:10, 14;
13:12 ^z S Ac 22:16

in secret. ¹³But everything exposed by the light ^f becomes visible—and everything that is illuminated becomes a light. ¹⁴This is why it is said:

> "Wake up, sleeper, ^g
> rise from the dead, ^h
> and Christ will shine on you." ⁱ

¹⁵Be very careful, then, how you live ^j—not as unwise but as wise, ¹⁶making the most of every opportunity, ^k because the days are evil. ^{l 17}Therefore do not be foolish, but understand what the Lord's will is. ^{m 18}Do not get drunk on wine, ⁿ which leads to debauchery. Instead, be filled with the Spirit, ^{o 19}speaking to one another with psalms, hymns and songs from the Spirit. ^p Sing and make music from your heart to the Lord, ²⁰always giving thanks ^q to God the Father for everything, in the name of our Lord Jesus Christ.

INSTRUCTIONS FOR CHRISTIAN HOUSEHOLDS

5:22—6:9 pp — Col 3:18—4:1

²¹Submit to one another ^r out of reverence for Christ.

²²Wives, submit yourselves to your own husbands ^s as you do to the Lord. ^{t 23}For the husband is the head of the wife as Christ is the head of the church, ^u his body, of which he is the Savior. ²⁴Now as the church submits to Christ, so also wives should submit to their husbands ^v in everything.

²⁵Husbands, love your wives, ^w just as Christ loved the church and gave himself up for her ^{x 26}to make her holy, ^y cleansing^a her by the washing ^z with water through the word,

---

^a 26 Or *having cleansed*

5:13 *everything exposed … everything … illuminated.* Paul seems to be stressing the all-pervasive nature of the light of God and its inevitable effect.
5:14 *it is said.* What follows may well be a hymn used by early Christians (see note on Col 3:16). *sleeper … dead.* Two images that describe a sinner (cf. 2:1 and note). *Christ will shine on you.* With his life-giving light (cf. 2Co 4:4–6 and notes).
5:15 *unwise … wise.* Cf. Jas 3:13–17. Having emphasized the contrast between light and darkness, Paul now turns to the contrast between wisdom and foolishness.
5:16 *opportunity.* The foolish person has no strategy for life and misses opportunities to live for God in an evil environment (see Col 4:5).
5:17 *foolish … understand.* The contrast continues. The foolish not only miss opportunities to make wise use of time; they have a more fundamental problem: They do not understand what God's purposes are for humankind and for Christians. God's purposes are a basic theme in Ephesians (see ch. 1).
5:18 ▲ *Do not get drunk … be filled with the Spirit.* The Greek present tense is used to indicate that the filling of the Spirit is not a once-for-all experience. Repeatedly, as the occasion requires, the Spirit empowers for worship, service and testimony. The contrast between being filled with wine and filled with the Spirit is obvious. But there is something in common that enables Paul to make the contrast, namely, that people can be under an influence that affects them, whether of wine or of the Spirit. Since Col 3:15—4:1 is very similar to Eph 5:18—6:9, we may assume that Paul intends to convey a basically similar thought in the introductory sentences to each passage. When he speaks here of being filled with the Spirit and when he speaks in Colossians of being under the rule of the peace of Christ and indwelt by the "word" of Christ, he means to be under God's control. The effect of this control is essentially the same in both passages: a happy, mutual encouragement to praise God and a healthy, mutual relationship with people. See note on v. 21.
5:19 *psalms … songs.* Every kind of appropriate song—whether psalms like those of the OT or hymns directed to God or to others that Christians were accustomed to singing—could provide a means for praising and thanking God (v. 20). Actually, however, all three terms may refer to different types of psalms (see note on Col 3:16). *songs from the Spirit.* Songs prompted by the Spirit.
5:20 *always giving thanks.* See Col 2:7; 3:15; 4:2; 1Th 5:18.

5:21—6:9 ▲ In chs. 2–4 Paul showed the way God brought believing Jews and Gentiles together into a new relationship in Christ. In 4:1–6 he stressed the importance of unity. Now he shows how believers, filled with the Spirit, can live together in a practical way in various human relationships. This list of mutual responsibilities is similar to the pattern found in Col 3:18—4:1; 1Pe 2:13—3:12; cf. Ro 13:1–10.
5:21 ▲ *Submit to one another.* Goes equally well with both the preceding and the following sections, but it is especially basic to the following paragraphs. Paul will show how, in each relationship, each partner can have a conciliatory attitude that will help that relationship. The Greek grammar indicates that this mutual submission is associated with the filling of the Spirit in v. 18. The command "be filled" (v. 18) is followed by a series of participles in the Greek: speaking (v. 19), singing (v. 19), making music (v. 19), giving thanks (v. 20) and submitting (v. 21).
5:22 *Wives, submit.* An aspect of the mutual submission taught in v. 21. The term could connote obedience (see 1Pe 3:5–6), but that meaning is not called for here. *as you do to the Lord.* Does not put a woman's husband in the place of the Lord but shows rather that a woman ought to submit to her husband as an act of submission to the Lord.
5:23 *head of the wife.* See 1Co 11:3 and note. *as Christ.* The analogy between the relationship of Christ to the church and that of the husband to the wife is basic to the entire passage. *his body.* See 2:16; 4:4, 12, 16.
5:25 ▲ *Husbands.* Paul now shows that this is not a one-sided submission but a reciprocal relationship. *love.* Explained by what follows. *Christ loved the church and gave himself up for her.* Not only the expression of our Lord's love but also an example of how the husband ought to devote himself to his wife's good. To give oneself up for death for the beloved is a more extreme expression of devotion than the wife is called upon to make (cf. Jn 15:13 and note).
5:26 *washing with water through the word.* Many attempts have been made to see marriage customs or liturgical symbolism in these words. One thing is clear: The Lord Jesus died not only to bring forgiveness but also to effect a new life of holiness in the church, which is his "bride." A study of the concepts of washing, of water and of the word should include reference to Jn 3:5 (see note there); 15:3; see also Tit 3:5; Heb 10:22; Jas 1:18; 1Pe 1:23; 3:21 and notes.

²⁷and to present her to himself ᵃ as a radiant church, without stain or wrinkle or any other blemish, but holy and blameless. ᵇ ²⁸In this same way, husbands ought to love their wives ᶜ as their own bodies. He who loves his wife loves himself. ²⁹After all, people have never hated their own bodies, but they feed and care for them, just as Christ does the church— ³⁰for we are members of his body. ᵈ ³¹"For this reason a man will leave his father and mother and be united to his wife, and the two will become one flesh." ᵃ ᵉ ³²This is a profound mystery—but I am talking about Christ and the church. ³³However, each one of you also must love his wife ᶠ as he loves himself, and the wife must respect her husband.

6 Children, obey your parents in the Lord, for this is right. ᵍ ²"Honor your father and mother"—which is the first commandment with a promise— ³"so that it may go well with you and that you may enjoy long life on the earth." ᵇ ʰ

⁴Fathers, ᶜ do not exasperate your children; ⁱ instead, bring them up in the training and instruction of the Lord. ʲ

⁵Slaves, obey your earthly masters with respect ᵏ and fear, and with sincerity of heart, ˡ just as you would obey Christ. ᵐ ⁶Obey them not only to win their favor when their eye is on you, but as slaves of Christ, ⁿ doing the will of God from your heart. ⁷Serve wholeheartedly, as if you were serving the Lord, not people, ᵒ ⁸because you know that the Lord will reward each one of you for whatever good you do, ᵖ whether you are slave or free.

⁹And masters, treat your slaves in the same way. Do not threaten them, since you know that he who is both their Master and yours �q is in heaven, and there is no favoritism ʳ with him.

THE ARMOR OF GOD

¹⁰Finally, be strong in the Lord ˢ and in his mighty power. ᵗ ¹¹Put on the full armor of God, ᵘ so that you can take your stand against the devil's schemes. ¹²For our struggle is not against flesh and blood, ᵛ but against the rulers, against the authorities, ʷ against the powers ˣ of this dark world and against the spiritual forces of evil in the heavenly realms. ʸ ¹³Therefore put on the full armor of God, ᶻ so that when the day of evil comes, you may be able to stand your ground, and after you have done everything, to stand. ¹⁴Stand firm then, with the belt of truth buckled around your waist, ᵃ with the breastplate of righteousness in place, ᵇ ¹⁵and with your feet fitted with the readiness that comes from the gospel

---

ᵃ *31* Gen. 2:24   ᵇ *3* Deut. 5:16   ᶜ *4* Or *Parents*

5:27 ᵃ S 2Co 4:14
ᵇ Eph 1:4
5:28 ᶜ ver 25
5:30 ᵈ S Ro 12:5;
S 1Co 12:27
5:31 ᵉ Ge 2:24;
Mt 19:5; 1Co 6:16
5:33 ᶠ ver 25
6:1 ᵍ Pr 6:20;
Col 3:20
6:3 ʰ Ex 20:12;
Dt 5:16
6:4 ⁱ Col 3:21
ʲ Ge 18:19; Dt 6:7;
Pr 13:24; 22:6
6:5 ᵏ 1Ti 6:1; Tit 2:9;
1Pe 2:18 ˡ Col 3:22
ᵐ Eph 5:22
6:6 ⁿ S Ro 6:22
6:7 ᵒ Col 3:23
6:8 ᵖ S Mt 16:27;
Col 3:24
6:9 q Job 31:13,14
ʳ S Ac 10:34
6:10 ˢ 2Sa 10:12;
Ps 27:14; Hag 2:4;
1Co 16:13; 2Ti 2:1
ᵗ Eph 1:19
6:11 ᵘ ver 13;
Ro 13:12; 1Th 5:8
6:12 ᵛ 1Co 15:50;
Heb 2:14 ʷ Eph 1:21;
3:10 ˣ Ro 8:38
ʸ S Eph 1:3
6:13 ᶻ ver 11;
S 2Co 6:7
6:14 ᵃ Isa 11:5
ᵇ Ps 132:9; Isa 59:17;
1Th 5:8

5:27 *holy and blameless.* See 1:4 and note.

5:28–29 *as their own bodies ... loves himself ... their own bodies.* The basis for such expressions and for the teaching of these verses is the quotation from Ge 2:24 in v. 31. If the husband and wife become "one flesh," then for the man to love his wife is to love one who has become part of himself.

5:32 *mystery.* See note on Ro 11:25. The profound truth of the union of Christ and his "bride," the church, is beyond unaided human understanding. It is not that the relationship of husband and wife provides an illustration of the union of Christ and the church but that the basic reality is the latter, with marriage a human echo of that relationship.

5:33 *love ... respect.* A rephrasing and summary of the whole passage.

6:1 *obey your parents.* Cf. Pr 30:17; Col 3:20 and note; 2Ti 3:2. *in the Lord.* In fellowship with the Lord and in obedience to him.

6:3 *on the earth.* In Dt 5:16 (see Ex 20:12), where this commandment occurs, the "promise" (v. 2) was expressed in terms of the anticipated occupation of the "land," i.e., Canaan. That specific application was, of course, not appropriate to the Ephesians, so the more general application is made here.

6:4 *do not exasperate.* Fathers must surrender any right they may feel they have to act unreasonably toward their children.

6:5 *Slaves.* Both the OT and the NT included regulations for societal situations such as slavery and divorce (see Dt 24:1–4), which were the results of the hardness of hearts (Mt 19:8). Such regulations did not encourage or condone such situations but were divinely-given, practical ways of dealing with the realities of the day.

6:8 *the Lord will reward.* Probably a reference to the believer's final reward (see 1Co 3:10–15; 2Co 5:10 and notes).

6:9 *masters.* Once again Paul stresses reciprocal attitudes (cf. 5:21—6:4). See Tit 2:9 and note. *their Master and yours.* Cf. Ro 14:4 and note. *no favoritism with him.* See Ac 10:34 and note.

6:10–20 Paul's scope in Ephesians has been cosmic. From the very beginning he has drawn attention to the unseen world (see note on 1:3; see also 1:10,20–23; 2:6; 6:10), and now he describes the spiritual battle that takes place against evil "in the heavenly realms" (v. 12).

6:10 *strong ... power.* Implies that human effort is inadequate but that God's power is invincible.

6:12 *not against flesh and blood.* A caution against lashing out against human opponents as though they were the real enemy and also against assuming that the battle can be fought using merely human resources. *rulers ... forces.* Cf. Paul's earlier allusions to powerful beings in the unseen world (see notes on 1:21; 3:10). *heavenly realms.* See note on 1:3.

6:13–14 *stand your ground ... Stand firm.* In this context the imagery is not that of a massive invasion of the domain of evil but of individual soldiers withstanding assault.

6:14 *belt of truth.* Cf. the symbolic clothing of the Messiah in Isa 11:5. Character, not brute force, wins the battle, just as in the case of the Messiah. *breastplate of righteousness.* Here again, the warriors' character is their defense. God himself is symbolically described as putting on a breastplate of righteousness when he goes forth to bring about justice (see Isa 59:17 and note).

6:15 *feet fitted with the readiness.* Whereas the description of the messenger's feet in Isa 52:7 reflects the custom of running barefooted, here the message of the gospel is picturesquely connected with the protective and supportive footgear of the Roman soldier. *gospel of peace.* An expression found only here in the Bible (cf. 2:14–16; Ro 5:1 and note).

6:15 ᶜ Isa 52:7;
Ro 10:15
6:16 ᵈ 1Jn 5:4
ᵉ S Mt 5:37
6:17 ᶠ Isa 59:17
ᵍ Isa 49:2
ʰ S Heb 4:12
6:18 ⁱ Ro 8:26,27
ʲ S Lk 18:1 ᵏ Mt 26:41;
Php 1:4; 4:6
ˡ S Ac 1:14; Col 1:3
6:19 ᵐ S 1Th 5:25
ⁿ S Ac 4:29
ᵒ S Ro 16:25
6:20 ᵖ 2Co 5:20
�q S Ac 21:33
6:21 ʳ S Ac 20:4
6:22 ˢ Col 4:7-9
ᵗ Col 2:2; 4:8
6:23 ᵘ Gal 6:16;
2Th 3:16; 1Pe 5:14

of peace. ᶜ ¹⁶In addition to all this, take up the shield of faith, ᵈ with which you can extinguish all the flaming arrows of the evil one. ᵉ ¹⁷Take the helmet of salvation ᶠ and the sword of the Spirit, ᵍ which is the word of God. ʰ

¹⁸And pray in the Spirit ⁱ on all occasions ʲ with all kinds of prayers and requests. ᵏ With this in mind, be alert and always keep on praying ˡ for all the Lord's people. ¹⁹Pray also for me, ᵐ that whenever I speak, words may be given me so that I will fearlessly ⁿ make known the mystery ᵒ of the gospel, ²⁰for which I am an ambassador ᵖ in chains. q Pray that I may declare it fearlessly, as I should.

FINAL GREETINGS

²¹Tychicus, ʳ the dear brother and faithful servant in the Lord, will tell you everything, so that you also may know how I am and what I am doing. ²²I am sending him to you for this very purpose, that you may know how we are, ˢ and that he may encourage you. ᵗ

²³Peace ᵘ to the brothers and sisters, and love with faith from God the Father and the Lord Jesus Christ. ²⁴Grace to all who love our Lord Jesus Christ with an undying love. ᵃ

ᵃ 24 Or *Grace and immortality to all who love our Lord Jesus Christ.*

6:16 *shield of faith…extinguish…flaming arrows.* Describes the large Roman shield covered with leather, which could be soaked in water and used to put out flame-tipped arrows.

6:17–18 *sword of the Spirit…pray in the Spirit.* Reminders that the battle is spiritual and must be fought in God's strength, depending on the word and on God through prayer.

6:17 *helmet of salvation.* Isa 59:17 has similar language, along with the breastplate imagery (see note on v. 14). The helmet protected the soldier and, under certain circumstances, helmets provided a striking symbol of military victory.

6:18 *pray in the Spirit.* Pray with the help of the Spirit (cf. Ro 8:26 and note). *the Lord's people.* See note on 1:1.

6:19 *mystery.* See 3:3,9 and note on 3:3.

6:20 *in chains.* See Php 1:7,13 and note; Col 4:3; Phm 10,13.

6:21–23 Paul concludes with greetings that lack personal references such as are usually found in his letters. This is understandable if Ephesians is a circular letter (see note on 1:1).

6:21 *Tychicus.* An associate of Paul who traveled as his representative (cf. Col 4:7; 2Ti 4:12; Tit 3:12).

6:23–24 *Peace…Grace.* See note on Ro 1:7.

6:23 *brothers and sisters.* See note on Ro 1:13.

6:24 *love our Lord Jesus.* Cf. Jn 14:15,21,23; 21:15–17 and notes.

AUTHOR, DATE AND PLACE OF WRITING

C The early church was unanimous in its testimony that Philippians was written by the apostle Paul (see 1:1). Internally, the letter reveals the stamp of genuineness. The many personal references of the author fit what we know of Paul from other NT books.

It is evident that Paul wrote the letter from prison (see 1:13–14). Some have argued that this imprisonment took place in Ephesus, perhaps c. A.D. 53–55; others put it in Caesarea c. 57–59. Best evidence, however, favors Rome as the place of origin and the date as c. 61 (see chart, p. 1855). This fits well with the account of Paul's house arrest in Ac 28:14–31. When he wrote Philippians, he was not in the Mamertine dungeon as he was when he wrote 2 Timothy. He was in his own rented house, where for two years he was free to impart the gospel to all who came to him.

PURPOSE

Paul's primary purpose in writing this letter was to thank the Philippians for the gift they had sent him upon learning of his detention at Rome (1:5; 4:10–19). However, he makes use of this occasion to fulfill several other desires: (1) to report on his own circumstances (1:12–26; 4:10–19); (2) to encourage the Philippians to stand firm in the face of persecution and rejoice regardless of circumstances (1:27–30; 4:4); (3) to exhort them to humility and unity (2:1–11; 4:2–5); (4) to commend Timothy and Epaphroditus to the Philippian church (2:19–30); and (5) to warn the Philippians against the Judaizers (legalists) and antinomians (libertines) among them (ch. 3).

RECIPIENTS

The city of Philippi (see map, p. 1996) was named after King Philip II of Macedon, father of Alexander the Great. It was a prosperous Roman colony, which meant that the citizens of Philippi were also citizens of the city of Rome itself. They prided themselves on being Romans (see Ac 16:21), dressed like Romans and often spoke Latin. No doubt this was the background for Paul's reference to the believer's heavenly citizenship (3:20–21). Many of the Philippians were retired military men who had been given land in the vicinity and who in turn served as a military presence in this frontier city. That Philippi was a Roman colony may explain why there were not enough Jews there to permit the establishment of a synagogue and why Paul does not quote the OT in the Philippian letter (but see 1:19; Job 13:16 and notes).

CHARACTERISTICS

1. Philippians contains no OT quotations (but see note on Job 13:16).

2. It is a missionary thank-you letter in which the missionary reports on the progress of his work.

3. It manifests a particularly vigorous type of Christian living: (1) self-humbling (2:1–4); (2) pressing toward the goal (3:13–14); (3) lack of anxiety (4:6); and (4) ability to do all things (4:13; but see note there).

KEY   **A** APPLICATION FOR LIVING   **B** BACKGROUND NOTES   **C** CHARACTER INFORMATION

4. It is outstanding as the NT letter of joy; the word "joy" in its various forms occurs some 16 times.

5. It contains one of the most profound Christological passages in the NT (2:5–11). Yet, profound as it is, Paul includes it mainly for illustrative purposes.

OUTLINE

PHILIPPI IN THE TIME OF PAUL

The Roman colony of Philippi (*Colonia Augusta Julia Philippensis*) was an important city in Macedonia, located on the main highway leading from the eastern provinces to Rome. This road, the Via Egnatia, bisected the city's forum and was the chief cause of its prosperity and political importance. Ten miles distant on the coast was Neapolis, the place where Paul landed after sailing from Troas, in response to the Macedonian vision.

As a prominent city of the gold-producing region of Macedonia, Philippi had a proud history. Named originally after Philip II, the father of Alexander the Great, the city was later honored with the name of Julius Caesar and Augustus. Many Italian settlers from the legions swelled the ranks of citizens and made Philippi vigorous and polyglot. It grew from a small settlement to a city of dignity and privilege. Among its highest honors was the *ius Italicum*, by which it enjoyed rights legally equivalent to those of Italian cities.

B Ruins of the theater, the acropolis, the forum, the baths and the commemorative arch (about a mile west of the city) have been found. A little farther beyond the arch at the Gangites River is the place where Paul addressed some God-fearing women and where Lydia was converted (Ac 16:13–15).

Labels on map: Acropolis · Meters 0 200 · Side streets (dotted lines) for illustration only—artist's concept · N · Sanctuary of Egyptian divinities · Traditional prison · Via Egnatia · Hellenistic sanctuary · Theater · Forum · to Neapolis · Street · Dromos · Palaestra · Agora · Library · Baths · to Gangites R.

1 Paul and Timothy, *a* servants of Christ Jesus,

To all God's holy people *b* in Christ Jesus at Philippi, *c* together with the overseers *d* and deacons: *e*

[2] Grace and peace to you from God our Father and the Lord Jesus Christ. *f*

THANKSGIVING AND PRAYER

[3] I thank my God every time I remember you. *g* [4] In all my prayers for all of you, I always pray *h* with joy [5] because of your partnership *i* in the gospel from the first day *j* until now, [6] being confident of this, that he who began a good work in you will carry it on to completion *k* until the day of Christ Jesus. *l*

[7] It is right *m* for me to feel this way about all of you, since I have you in my heart *n* and, whether I am in chains *o* or defending *p* and confirming the gospel, all of you share in God's grace with me. [8] God can testify *q* how I long for all of you with the affection of Christ Jesus.

[9] And this is my prayer: that your love *r* may abound more and more in knowledge and depth of insight, *s* [10] so that you may be able to discern what is best and may be pure and blameless for the day of Christ, *t* [11] filled with the fruit of righteousness *u* that comes through Jesus Christ—to the glory and praise of God.

PAUL'S CHAINS ADVANCE THE GOSPEL

[12] Now I want you to know, brothers and sisters, that what has happened to me has actually served to advance the gospel. [13] As a result, it has become clear throughout the whole palace guard *a* and to everyone else that I am in chains *v* for Christ. [14] And because of my chains, *w* most of the brothers and sisters have become confident in the Lord and dare all the more to proclaim the gospel without fear. *x*

a 13 Or *whole palace*

1:1 *a* S Ac 16:1;
2Co 1:1 *b* S Ac 9:13
c S Ac 16:12 *d* S 1Ti 3:1
e 1Ti 3:8
1:2 *f* S Ro 1:7
1:3 *g* S Ro 1:8
1:4 *h* S Ro 1:10
1:5 *i* S Ac 2:42;
Php 4:15 *j* Ac 16:12-
40
1:6 *k* Ps 138:8
l ver 10; S 1Co 1:8
1:7 *m* 2Pe 1:13
n 2Co 7:3 *o* ver 13,14,
17; S Ac 21:33 *p* ver 16
1:8 *q* S Ro 1:9
1:9 *r* 1Th 3:12
s S Eph 1:17
1:10 *t* ver 6;
S 1Co 1:8
1:11 *u* S Jas 3:18
v ver 7,14,17;
S Ac 21:33
1:14 *w* ver 7,13,17;
S Ac 21:33
x S Ac 4:29

1:1–2 As in all his letters, Paul follows the conventional letter format of his day, with its three elements: (1) identification of the sender, (2) identification of the recipients and (3) greeting.

1:1 *Paul.* See note on Ro 1:1. *Timothy.* See Introduction to 1 Timothy: Recipient. Timothy is identified with the contents of the letter as Paul's associate, but not as co-author. *servants.* See Ro 1:1 and note; Tit 1:1; Jas 1:1; 2Pe 1:1; Jude 1; Rev 1:1. In Paul's case, this designation brings out an essential aspect of the more usual identification of himself as "apostle." *God's holy people.* See Ro 1:7 and note. *in Christ.* See note on Eph 1:1. *Philippi.* See Introduction: Recipients. *overseers and deacons.* The only place in Paul's writings where church officers as a group are singled out as recipients of a letter. *overseers.* See note on 1Ti 3:1. *deacons.* See note on 1Ti 3:8.

1:2 *Grace and peace.* See note on Ro 1:7. *Lord Jesus Christ.* Also occurs at the end of this letter (4:23); see note on 1Th 1:1.

1:3–4 *I thank my God . . . prayers for . . . you . . . with joy.* Prayers of joyful thanksgiving for his readers' response to the gospel are a hallmark of the opening sentences of Paul's letters (see Ro 1:8; 1Co 1:4; Col 1:3; 1Th 1:2; 2Th 1:3; 2Ti 1:3; Phm 4).

1:5 *your partnership in the gospel.* The basis of Paul's prayerful thanksgiving is not only their reception of the gospel but also their active support of his ministry (see 4:15 and note). *from the first day.* When Paul first came to Philippi (Ac 16:12). *now.* Toward the close (see 2:24 and note) of Paul's first Roman imprisonment (see Ac 28:16–31).

1:6 *work in you.* Paul is confident, not only of what God has done "for" the readers in forgiving their sins, but also of what he has done "in" them (see v. 11). "Work" refers to God's activity in saving them. *day of Christ Jesus.* His return, when their salvation will be brought to completion (see 1:10; 2:16; 1Co 1:8; 5:5; 2Co 1:14). It is God who initiates salvation, who continues it and who will one day bring it to its consummation.

1:7 *in chains.* See note on Eph 6:20. *share in God's grace.* Not even imprisonment and persecution can change such sharing. Even in Paul's imprisonment they willingly identified themselves with Paul by sending Epaphroditus and their financial gifts (2:25–30; 4:18). They had become one with Paul in his

apostolic commission to preach the gospel (see v. 5).

1:8 *affection of Christ Jesus.* The deep yearning and intense, compassionate love exhibited by Jesus himself and now fostered in Paul by his union with Christ. This affection reaches out to all, impartially and without exception.

1:9 *abound more and more.* Real love requires growth and maturation (see 1Th 3:12; 4:10; 2Th 1:3). *in knowledge.* The way love grows (cf. Col 1:9). *depth of insight.* Practical discernment and sensitivity. Christian love is not mere sentiment; it is rooted in knowledge and understanding.

1:10 *discern what is best.* Christians are to approve (and practice) what is morally and ethically superior. *pure and blameless.* The goal of Christians in this life is to be without any mixture of evil and not open to censure because of moral or spiritual failure. *for the day of Christ.* Then the goal will be perfectly realized (see note on v. 6), and then Christians must give an account (see 2Co 5:10 and note; Ro 14:10,12 and note on 14:10).

1:11 *filled with the fruit of righteousness.* What is expected of all Christians (cf. Mt 5:20–48; Heb 12:11; Jas 3:18; see also Am 6:12; Gal 5:22–23). *through Jesus Christ.* Produced by Christ (in union with him) through the work of the Holy Spirit (cf. Jn 15:5; Eph 2:10). *to the glory and praise of God.* The ultimate goal of all that God does in believers (see Eph 1:6,12,14).

1:12 *brothers and sisters.* See note on Ro 1:13. *what has happened to me.* Paul's detainment in prison. *advance the gospel.* Instead of hindering the gospel, Paul's imprisonment had served to make it known.

1:13 *clear . . . chains for Christ.* It has become apparent to all who know of Paul's situation that he is imprisoned, not because he is guilty of some crime but on account of his stand for the gospel. *whole palace guard.* A contingent of soldiers, numbering several thousand, many of whom would have had personal contact with Paul or would have been assigned individually to guard him during the course of his imprisonment (see Ac 28:16,30). *chains.* Either actual chains or a broader reference to his sufferings and imprisonment (see v. 14).

1:14 *brothers and sisters . . . proclaim the gospel without fear.* The unexpected result of Paul's imprisonment.

1:16 ʸ ver 7,12
1:17 ᶻ Php 2:3
ᵃ ver 7,13,14;
S Ac 21:33
1:19 ᵇ 2Co 1:11
ᶜ S Ac 16:7 ᵈ Phm 22
1:20 ᵉ Ro 8:19
ᶠ ver 14 ᵍ 1Co 6:20
ʰ Ro 14:8
1:21 ⁱ Gal 2:20
1:23 ʲ 2Ti 4:6
ᵏ S Jn 12:26
1:27 ˡ S Eph 4:1
ᵐ S 1Co 16:13 ⁿ Jude 3
1:29 ᵒ Mt 5:11,12;
Ac 5:41 ᵖ S Ac 14:22
1:30 ᑫ 1Th 2:2;
Heb 10:32 ʳ Ac 16:19-
40 ˢ ver 13

¹⁵It is true that some preach Christ out of envy and rivalry, but others out of goodwill. ¹⁶The latter do so out of love, knowing that I am put here for the defense of the gospel.ʸ ¹⁷The former preach Christ out of selfish ambition,ᶻ not sincerely, supposing that they can stir up trouble for me while I am in chains.ᵃ ¹⁸But what does it matter? The important thing is that in every way, whether from false motives or true, Christ is preached. And because of this I rejoice.

Yes, and I will continue to rejoice, ¹⁹for I know that through your prayersᵇ and God's provision of the Spirit of Jesus Christᶜ what has happened to me will turn out for my deliverance.ᵃ ᵈ ²⁰I eagerly expectᵉ and hope that I will in no way be ashamed, but will have sufficient courageᶠ so that now as always Christ will be exalted in my body,ᵍ whether by life or by death.ʰ ²¹For to me, to live is Christⁱ and to die is gain. ²²If I am to go on living in the body, this will mean fruitful labor for me. Yet what shall I choose? I do not know! ²³I am torn between the two: I desire to departʲ and be with Christ,ᵏ which is better by far; ²⁴but it is more necessary for you that I remain in the body. ²⁵Convinced of this, I know that I will remain, and I will continue with all of you for your progress and joy in the faith, ²⁶so that through my being with you again your boasting in Christ Jesus will abound on account of me.

LIFE WORTHY OF THE GOSPEL

²⁷Whatever happens, as citizens of heaven live in a manner worthyˡ of the gospel of Christ. Then, whether I come and see you or only hear about you in my absence, I will know that you stand firmᵐ in the one Spirit,ᵇ striving togetherⁿ with one accord for the faith of the gospel ²⁸without being frightened in any way by those who oppose you. This is a sign to them that they will be destroyed, but that you will be saved—and that by God. ²⁹For it has been granted to youᵒ on behalf of Christ not only to believe on him, but also to sufferᵖ for him, ³⁰since you are going through the same struggleᑫ you sawʳ I had, and now hearˢ that I still have.

ᵃ 19 Or *vindication;* or *salvation*   ᵇ 27 Or *in one spirit*

1:16 *The latter do so out of love.* Those who preach with a right motive recognize the true reason for Paul's imprisonment, already expressed earlier in v. 13, and are encouraged to take the same bold stand that he has taken.

1:17 *The former preach Christ out of selfish ambition.* Those who preach with wrong, insincere motives do so out of a sense of competition with Paul and so think they are making his imprisonment more difficult to bear. *not sincerely.* Not from pure motives.

1:18 *whether from false motives or true, Christ is preached.* These preachers are not to be viewed as being heretical. Their message is true, even though their motives are not pure. The gospel has its objectivity and validity apart from those who proclaim it; the message is more than the medium. *I rejoice ... will continue to rejoice.* An example of the kind of vigorous Christian experience Paul expressed. He was under arrest, and fellow Christians sought, by their preaching, to add to his difficulties; yet he kept on rejoicing.

1:19 *Spirit of Jesus Christ.* The Holy Spirit is not only the Spirit of God the Father (Ro 8:9,14; 1Co 2:10–11,14) but also the Spirit of Christ, the second person of the Trinity (Ac 16:7; Ro 8:9; Gal 4:6). He is sent by the Father (Jn 14:16–17,26; Gal 4:6) and by the Son (Jn 15:26; 16:7). *turn out for my deliverance.* Either Paul's release from prison (see v. 25; 2:24) or, in view of the immediately following verses, the deliverance brought to the believer by death (cf. Ro 8:38–39). Verse 25, however, seems to point to the former interpretation (see note there). See Job 13:16 and note.

1:20 *ashamed ... sufficient courage.* The circumstances of imprisonment, with all its attendant suffering and oppression, constitute a real temptation for Paul to abandon the gospel and his resolute service for Christ. *my body.* Where the exalted Christ dwells by his Spirit, is at work (cf. Ro 8:9–10) and so is exalted by what Paul does. *whether by life or by death.* Whether his service for Christ continues or ends in death.

1:21 *to live is Christ.* Christ was the source and secret of Paul's continual joy (even in prison), for Paul's life found all its meaning in Christ. *gain.* Verse 23 specifies that the gain brought by death is "being with Christ," so that here Paul is say-

ing that his ultimate concern and most precious possession, both now and forever, is Christ and his relationship to him.

1:22 *fruitful labor.* The spread of the gospel and the upbuilding of the church.

1:23–24 *depart and be with Christ ... remain in the body.* Either alternative was a good one. While mysteries remain, this passage clearly teaches that when believers die they are with Christ, apart from the body (see 2Co 5:6,8–9).

1:23 *better by far.* Being with Christ after death must involve some kind of conscious presence and fellowship (cf. 2Co 5:6,8 and note on 5:8).

1:24 *necessary for you.* Paul puts the needs of those he ministers to ahead of his personal preference.

1:25 *I will remain.* It is possible that Paul was later released from prison (see map, p. 2030). *progress ... in the faith.* The Christian life is to be one of joyful growth and advance (see note on v. 9).

1:26 *your boasting in Christ Jesus ... on account of me.* Paul's conduct of his ministry among the Philippians will be a reason for their rejoicing in what Christ is doing among them.

1:27 *worthy of the gospel.* Appropriate to the standards and goals given with the gospel. *in the one Spirit.* In the Spirit's enablement (but see TNIV text note). *striving together with one accord.* Particularly where the gospel is under attack, Christians need each other and must stand together.

1:28 *sign.* Persistent opposition to the church and the gospel is a sure sign of eventual destruction, since it involves rejection of the only way of salvation. By the same token, when Christians are persecuted for their faith, this is a sign of the genuineness of their salvation (see 2Th 1:5 and note).

1:29 *granted ... to suffer.* Given as a gift or privilege. Christian suffering, as well as faith, is a blessing (cf. Mt 5:11–12; Ac 5:41; Jas 1:2; 1Pe 4:14). The Christian life is to be a "not only ... but also" proposition: not only believing but also suffering.

1:30 *same struggle.* Their common involvement with Paul, in conflict with those who oppose the gospel. *you saw.* When Paul and Silas first visited Philippi and were imprisoned (see Ac 16:19–40).

IMITATING CHRIST'S HUMILITY

2 Therefore if you have any encouragement from being united with Christ, if any comfort from his love, if any common sharing in the Spirit, [t] if any tenderness and compassion, [u] [2]then make my joy complete [v] by being like-minded, [w] having the same love, being one [x] in spirit and of one mind. [3]Do nothing out of selfish ambition or vain conceit. [y] Rather, in humility value others above yourselves, [z] [4]not looking to your own interests but each of you to the interests of the others. [a]

[5]In your relationships with one another, have the same attitude of mind Christ Jesus had: [b]

> [6]Who, being in very nature [a] God, [c]
>   did not consider equality with God [d] something to be used to his own
>   advantage;
> [7]rather, he made himself nothing [e]
>   by taking the very nature [b] of a servant, [f]
>   being made in human likeness. [g]
> [8]And being found in appearance as a human being,
>   he humbled himself
>   by becoming obedient to death [h]—
>   even death on a cross! [i]

> [9]Therefore God exalted him [j] to the highest place
>   and gave him the name that is above every name, [k]
> [10]that at the name of Jesus every knee should bow, [l]
>   in heaven and on earth and under the earth, [m]

---

[a] 6 Or *in the form of*   [b] 7 Or *the form*

2:1 *united with Christ.* Or "united in Christ." In Paul's teaching, this personal union is the basic reality of salvation. To be in Christ is to be saved, to be in intimate personal relationship with Christ the Savior. From this relationship flow all the particular benefits and fruits of salvation, like encouragement (see, e.g., 3:8–10; Ro 8:1; 2Co 5:17; Gal 2:20). *comfort from his love.* The comforting knowledge and assurance that come from God's love in Christ, demonstrated especially in Christ's death for the forgiveness of sins and eternal life (see Jn 3:16; Ro 5:8; 8:38–39; 1Jn 3:16; 4:9–10,16). *common sharing in the Spirit.* The fellowship among believers produced by the Spirit, who indwells each of them (see 2Co 13:14). *tenderness and compassion.* Christians are to have intense care and deep sympathy for each other (see 1:8 and note; Col 3:12). All these benefits—encouragement, comfort, fellowship, tenderness and compassion—are viewed by Paul as present realities for the Philippians.

2:2 *like-minded . . . same love . . . one in spirit and of one mind.* Emphasizes the unity that should exist among Christians. *like-minded.* Not uniformity in thought but the common disposition to work together and serve one another—the "attitude" of Christ (v. 5; see 4:2; Ro 12:16; 15:5 and note; 2Co 13:11).

2:3 *selfish ambition or vain conceit.* The mortal enemies of unity and harmony in the church (cf. 1:17; see Gal 5:20, where "selfish ambition" is listed among the "acts of the sinful nature"). *humility.* Required for Christian unity. This is the mindset of those who are not conceited but who have a right attitude toward themselves and others. *value others above yourselves.* Not that everyone else is superior or more talented, but that Christian love sees others as worthy of preferential treatment (see Ro 12:10 and note; Gal 5:13; Eph 5:21; 1Pe 5:5 and note).

2:4 *your own interests.* These are proper, but only if there is equal concern for the interests of others (cf. Ro 15:1 and note).

2:5 *have the same attitude of mind Christ Jesus had.* In spite of all that is unique and radically different about the person and work of Christ (see vv. 6–11), Christians are to have his attitude of self-sacrificing humility and love for others (see vv. 2–4; Mt 11:29; Jn 13:12–17).

2:6–11 The poetic character of these verses is apparent. Many view them as an early Christian hymn (see note on Col 3:16), taken over and perhaps modified by Paul. If so, they nonetheless express his convictions. The subjects of this passage are Christ's humiliation (vv. 6–8) and exaltation (vv. 9–11).

2:6 *in very nature God.* Affirming that Jesus is fully God (see Ro 9:5 and note). *nature.* Essential form (see TNIV text note), the sum of those qualities that make God specifically God. *equality with God.* The status and privileges that inevitably follow from being in very nature God. *something to be used to his own advantage.* Perhaps something to be forcibly retained—the glory Christ had with the Father before his incarnation. But he did not consider that high position to be something he could not give up. On the other hand, it may be something still to be attained, like a prize, as if he did not yet possess it.

2:7 *made himself nothing.* Lit. "emptied himself." He did this, not by giving up deity, but by laying aside his glory (see Jn 17:5) and submitting to the humiliation of becoming a man (see 2Co 8:9 and note). Jesus is truly God and truly human. Another view is that he emptied himself, not of deity itself, but of its prerogatives—the high position and glory of deity. *nature of a servant.* Emphasizes the full reality of his servant identity (see Mt 20:28). As a servant, he was always submissive to the will of the Father (see Lk 22:42; Jn 4:34 and note).

2:8 *appearance as a human being.* Not only was Jesus "like" a human being (v. 7), but he also took on the actual outward characteristics of a man (see Jn 1:14; Ro 8:3; Heb 2:17 and notes). *humbled himself.* See v. 7; 2Co 8:9. *obedient.* How Jesus humbled himself (cf. Heb 5:7–8). A "servant" (v. 7) obeys. *to death.* Stresses both the totality and the climax of Jesus' obedience. *on a cross.* Heightens Jesus' humiliation; he died as someone cursed (see Gal 3:13; Heb 12:2). Crucifixion was the most degrading form of execution that could be inflicted on a person.

2:9 *exalted.* See Mt 28:18; Ac 2:33; cf. Isa 52:13. *the name . . . above every name.* Reference is doubtless to the office or rank conferred on Jesus—his glorious position ("Lord," v. 11), not his proper name (cf. Eph 1:21; Heb 1:4–5 and notes).

2:10–11 *bow . . . acknowledge.* Cf. Isa 45:23. God's design is that all people everywhere should worship and serve Jesus as Lord. Ultimately all will acknowledge him as Lord (see Ro 14:9), whether willingly or not.

2:10 *at the name of Jesus.* In honor of his exalted position as "Lord" (v. 11; see v. 9 and note).

2:1 [t] 2Co 13:14
[u] Col 3:12
2:2 [v] S Jn 3:29
[w] Php 4:2 [x] S Ro 15:5
2:3 [y] Gal 5:26
[z] Ro 12:10; 1Pe 5:5
2:4 [a] S Co 10:24
2:5 [b] S Mt 11:29
2:6 [c] Jn 1:1; S 14:9
[d] Jn 5:18
2:7 [e] 2Co 8:9
[f] S Mt 20:28
[g] S Jn 1:14; Ro 8:3;
Heb 2:17
2:8 [h] S Mt 26:39;
Jn 10:18; Ro 5:19;
Heb 5:8 [i] S 1Co 1:23
2:9 [j] Isa 52:13; 53:12;
Da 7:14; [k] Eph 1:20,21
Heb 2:9 [k] Eph 1:20,21
2:10 [l] Ps 95:6;
Isa 45:23; Ro 14:11
[m] Mt 28:18; Eph 1:10;
Col 1:20

2:11 ⁿ S Jn 13:13
2:12 ᵒ S 2Co 7:15
2:13 ᵖ Ezr 1:5;
1Co 12:6; 15:10;
Gal 2:8; Heb 13:21
ᑫ Eph 1:5
2:14 ʳ 1Co 10:10;
1Pe 4:9
2:15 ˢ S 1Th 3:13
ᵗ Mt 5:45,48; Eph 5:1
ᵘ Ac 2:40
2:16 ᵛ S 1Co 1:8
ʷ S 1Co 9:24
ˣ 1Th 2:19
2:17 ʸ 2Co 12:15;
2Ti 4:6 ᶻ Ro 15:16
ᵃ S 2Co 6:10
2:19 ᵇ S Ac 16:1
ᶜ ver 23
2:20 ᵈ 1Co 16:10
2:21 ᵉ S 1Co 10:24
2:22 ᶠ 1Co 4:17;
1Ti 1:2
2:23 ᵍ ver 19
2:24 ʰ Php 1:25
2:25 ⁱ Ro 16:3,9,21;
2Co 8:23; Php 4:3;
Col 4:11; Phm 1
ʲ Phm 2 ᵏ Php 4:18
2:26 ˡ Php 1:8
2:28 ᵐ ver 25
2:29 ⁿ 1Co 16:18;
1Ti 5:17

[11] and every tongue acknowledge that Jesus Christ is Lord, ⁿ to the glory of God the Father.

DO EVERYTHING WITHOUT GRUMBLING

[12] Therefore, my dear friends, as you have always obeyed—not only in my presence, but now much more in my absence—continue to work out your salvation with fear and trembling, ᵒ [13] for it is God who works in you ᵖ to will and to act in order to fulfill his good purpose. ᑫ [14] Do everything without grumbling ʳ or arguing, [15] so that you may become blameless ˢ and pure, "children of God ᵗ without fault in a warped and crooked generation." ᵃ ᵘ Then you will shine among them like stars in the sky [16] as you hold firmly to the word of life. And then I will be able to boast on the day of Christ ᵛ that I did not run ʷ or labor in vain. ˣ [17] But even if I am being poured out like a drink offering ʸ on the sacrifice ᶻ and service coming from your faith, I am glad and rejoice with all of you. ᵃ [18] So you too should be glad and rejoice with me.

TIMOTHY AND EPAPHRODITUS

[19] I hope in the Lord Jesus to send Timothy ᵇ to you soon, ᶜ that I also may be cheered when I receive news about you. [20] I have no one else like him, ᵈ who will show genuine concern for your welfare. [21] For everyone looks out for their own interests, ᵉ not those of Jesus Christ. [22] But you know that Timothy has proved himself, because as a son with his father ᶠ he has served with me in the work of the gospel. [23] I hope, therefore, to send him as soon as I see how things go with me. ᵍ [24] And I am confident ʰ in the Lord that I myself will come soon.

[25] But I think it is necessary to send back to you Epaphroditus, my brother, co-worker ⁱ and fellow soldier, ʲ who is also your messenger, whom you sent to take care of my needs. ᵏ [26] For he longs for all of you ˡ and is distressed because you heard he was ill. [27] Indeed he was ill, and almost died. But God had mercy on him, and not on him only but also on me, to spare me sorrow upon sorrow. [28] Therefore I am all the more eager to send him, ᵐ so that when you see him again you may be glad and I may have less anxiety. [29] Welcome him in the Lord with great joy, and honor people like him, ⁿ [30] because he almost died for the

ᵃ 15 Deut. 32:5

2:12 *Therefore.* Because of Christ's incomparable example (vv. 5–11). *obeyed.* The commands of God as passed on to the Philippians by Paul (see Ro 1:5; 15:18; 2Co 10:5–6). *my presence.* During the course of Paul's second (see Ac 16:12–40) and third (see Ac 20:1–3,6) missionary journeys. *work out your salvation.* Work it out to the finish; not a reference to the attempt to earn one's salvation by works, but to the expression of one's salvation in spiritual growth and development. Salvation is not merely a gift received once for all; it expresses itself in an ongoing process in which the believer is strenuously involved (cf. Mt 24:13; 1Co 9:24–27; Heb 3:14; 6:9–11; 2Pe 1:5–8)—the process of perseverance, humble service, spiritual growth and maturation. *fear and trembling.* Not because of doubt or anxiety; rather, the reference is to an active reverence and a singleness of purpose in response to God's grace.

2:13 *God ... works in you.* See Col 1:29 and note. *to will and to act.* Intention, or faith, and our obedience cannot be separated (cf. Gal 5:6 and note; Jas 2:18,20,22).

2:14–17 Some things involved in working out our salvation.

2:14 *grumbling.* Being discontented with God's will is an expression of unbelief that prevents one from doing what pleases God (v. 13; cf. 1Co 10:10 and note). *arguing.* Over debatable points that do not need to be settled for the good of the church (see 2Ti 2:23; Tit 3:9).

2:15 *blameless and pure ... without fault.* Not absolute, sinless perfection, but wholehearted, unmixed devotion to doing God's will (see 1:10 and note). *warped and crooked generation.* A description of the unbelieving world (see Ac 2:40; Eph 2:1–3; cf. Mt 17:17). *shine among them like stars.* The contrast, like light in darkness, that Christians are to be to the world around them (cf. Mt 5:15–16).

2:16 *boast.* Not out of pride or a sense of self-accomplishment, but because of what God has done through Paul (see 1Th 2:19).

day of Christ. See note on 1:6. *in vain.* Cf. 1Co 9:24–27 and notes.

2:17–18 *I ... rejoice ... you too should ... rejoice.* Christian joy ought always to be mutual.

2:17 *I am being poured out.* The reference may be to his entire ministry as one large thanksgiving sacrifice. However, it is more probable that Paul refers to his present imprisonment, which may end in a martyr's death. His life would then be poured out as a drink offering accompanying the sacrificial service of the Philippians. *like a drink offering.* The OT background is the daily sacrifices in Ex 29:38–41. *coming from your faith.* Genuine faith is active and working (see note on v. 13).

2:19–23 Paul plans to send Timothy, who is with him in Rome (see 1:1 and note), to discover and report on conditions in the Philippian church.

2:20 *I have no one else like him.* Timothy was a good example of the kind of person envisioned in the exhortation of v. 4.

2:21 A sharp contrast between Timothy and Paul's other associates—an outstanding commendation for one so young (see 1Ti 4:12 and note).

2:22 *as a son with his father.* This relationship between Timothy and Paul is developed at length in 1,2 Timothy. *served.* Like Jesus and Paul, Timothy had a servant attitude.

2:24 Paul anticipates his release in the near future (see 1:25).

2:25–30 Epaphroditus, after a close brush with death (vv. 27, 30), is being sent home to Philippi.

2:25 *messenger.* A broader use of the Greek word often translated "apostle," applied here to Epaphroditus as a representative of the Philippian church (cf. 2Co 8:23).

2:27 Cf. 1:21–26.

2:28 *anxiety.* The legitimate cares and concerns that come with the Christian life and the gospel ministry (see note on 4:6; cf. 2Co 4:8; 11:28).

2:29 *in the Lord.* As a fellow believer (see Ro 16:2).

work of Christ. He risked his life to make up for the help you yourselves could not give me. *o*

NO CONFIDENCE IN THE FLESH

3 Further, my brothers and sisters, rejoice in the Lord! It is no trouble for me to write the same things to you again, *p* and it is a safeguard for you. ²Watch out for those dogs, *q* those evildoers, those mutilators of the flesh. ³For it is we who are the circumcision, *r* we who serve God by his Spirit, who boast in Christ Jesus, *s* and who put no confidence in the flesh— ⁴though I myself have reasons for such confidence. *t*

If others think they have reasons to put confidence in the flesh, I have more: ⁵circumcised *u* on the eighth day, of the people of Israel, *v* of the tribe of Benjamin, *w* a Hebrew of Hebrews; in regard to the law, a Pharisee; *x* ⁶as for zeal, *y* persecuting the church; *z* as for righteousness based on the law, *a* faultless.

⁷But whatever were gains to me I now consider loss *b* for the sake of Christ. ⁸What is more, I consider everything a loss because of the surpassing worth of knowing *c* Christ Jesus my Lord, for whose sake I have lost all things. I consider them garbage, that I may gain Christ *d* ⁹and be found in him, not having a righteousness of my own that comes from the law, *e* but that which is through faith in *a* Christ—the righteousness *f* that comes from God on the basis of faith. *g* ¹⁰I want to know *h* Christ—yes, to know the power of his resurrection and participation in his sufferings, *i* becoming like him in his death, *j* ¹¹and so, somehow, attaining to the resurrection *k* from the dead.

¹²Not that I have already obtained all this, or have already arrived at my goal, *l* but I press on to take hold *m* of that for which Christ Jesus took hold of me. *n* ¹³Brothers and sisters, I do not consider myself yet to have taken hold of it. But one thing I do: Forgetting

---

a 9 Or *through the faithfulness of*

2:30 *o* 1Co 16:17
3:1 *p* Php 2:18
3:2 *q* Ps 22:16, 20;
Rev 22:15
3:3 *r* Ro 2:28, 29;
Gal 6:15; Col 2:11
s Ro 15:17; Gal 6:14
3:4 *t* 2Co 11:21
3:5 *u* S Lk 1:59
v 2Co 11:22 *w* Ro 11:1
x Ac 23:6
3:6 *y* S Ac 21:20
z S Ac 8:3 *a* ver 9;
Ro 10:5
3:7 *b* Mt 13:44;
Lk 14:33
3:8 *c* ver 10;
Jer 9:23, 24; Jn 17:3;
Eph 4:13; S 2Pe 1:2
d Ps 73:25
3:9 *e* ver 6; Ro 10:5
f Jer 33:16 *g* S Ro 9:30
3:10 *h* S ver 8
i S 2Co 1:5
j S Ro 6:3-5
3:11 *k* S Jn 11:24;
S Ro 6:5; Rev 20:5, 6
3:12 *l* 1Co 13:10
m 1Ti 6:12 *n* Ac 9:5, 6

3:1 *rejoice in the Lord!* See 4:4 and note. *same things ... again.* Matters taken up in the verses that follow, which Paul had previously dealt with either orally when he was in Philippi or perhaps in an earlier letter. *safeguard.* Where serious error is present, there is safety in repetition.

3:2 *dogs.* A harsh word for Paul's opponents, showing their aggressive opposition to the gospel, the seriousness of their error and its destructive, "devouring" results (cf. Gal 5:15). Their teaching was probably similar to what Paul had to oppose in the Galatian churches (see Introduction to Galatians: Occasion and Purpose). *mutilators.* Again a strong, painfully vivid term; the false teachers have so distorted the meaning of circumcision (cf. v. 3) that it has become nothing more than a useless cutting of the body.

3:3 *circumcision.* Its true, inner meaning is realized only in believers, who worship God with genuine spiritual worship and who glory in Christ as their Savior rather than trusting in their own human effort (cf. Ro 2:28–29 and note on 2:29; Col 2:11–13; see also Dt 30:6; Eze 36:26). *boast ... no confidence.* Everyone is a "boaster," either in Christ or in themselves. *flesh.* Weak human nature (see Gal 3:3 and note).

3:4–14 Paul's personal testimony, a model for every believer; one of the most significant autobiographical sections in his letters (see note on Ro 1:1; cf. Ac 22:1–21; 26:1–23).
3:4–6 Paul's pre-Christian confidence, rooted in his Jewish heritage, privileges and attainments.
3:5 *eighth day.* See Ge 17:12 and note. *of the people of Israel.* Paul was born a Jew and was not a proselyte. *tribe of Benjamin.* His Jewish roots are deep and unambiguous. Jerusalem, the Holy City, lay on the border of the tribal territory of Benjamin. *Hebrew of Hebrews.* In language, attitudes and lifestyle (see Ac 22:2–3; Gal 1:14). *Pharisee.* See note on Mt 3:7.

3:6 *righteousness based on the law.* Righteousness produced by using the law as an attempt to merit God's approval and blessing (cf. v. 9)—a use of the law strongly opposed by Paul as contrary to the gospel itself (see Ro 3:27–28; 4:1–5; Gal 2:16 and note; 3:10–12 and note on 3:10). *faultless.* In terms of legalistic standards of scrupulous external conformity to the law.

3:7–14 Paul's confidence in Christ.
3:7 *whatever.* The things mentioned in vv. 5–6. *gains ... loss.* The great reversal in Paul—begun on the road to Damascus (see Ac 9:3–16)—from being self-centered to being centered in Christ.

3:8 *knowing Christ Jesus.* Not only a knowledge of facts but a knowledge gained through experience that, in its surpassing greatness, transforms the entire person (see 2Co 5:17 and note). The following verses spell this out. *garbage.* What Paul now has as a Christian is not merely preferable or a better alternative; in contrast, his former way of life was worthless and despicable (cf. Eph 2:3–7).

3:9 *be found in him.* Union with Christ (see note on 2:1; cf. 1Co 1:30)—not simply an experience in the past but a present, continuing relationship. *righteousness ... from the law.* See note on v. 6. *righteousness ... through faith.* A principal benefit of union with Christ (see Ro 3:21–22; 1Co 1:30; Gal 2:16 and note).

3:10 *know Christ.* As in v. 8, this knowledge is not merely factual; it includes the experience of "the power of his resurrection" (see Eph 1:17–20), of "participation in his sufferings" (cf. Ac 9:16) and of being "like him in his death" (see 2Co 4:7–12; 12:9–10). Believers already share positionally in Christ's death and resurrection (cf. Ro 6:2–13; Gal 2:20; 5:24; 6:14; Eph 2:6; Col 2:12–13; 3:1). In v. 10, however, Paul speaks of the actual experience of Christ's resurrection power and of suffering with and for him, even to the point of death.

3:11 *somehow.* Not an indication of doubt or uncertainty, but of humility because Paul does not want to be guilty of presumption. *resurrection.* The great personal anticipation of every believer (see Da 12:2; Jn 5:29; Ac 24:15; 1Co 15:23; 1Th 4:16).

3:12–14 The Christian life is like a race; elsewhere Paul uses athletic imagery in a similar way (1Co 9:24–27; 1Ti 6:12; 2Ti 4:7–8; cf. Mt 24:13; Heb 12:1).
3:12 *take hold ... took hold of me.* Paul's goal is Christ's goal for him, and Christ supplies the resources for him to "press on toward the goal" (v. 14; cf. 2:12–13).
3:13 *Forgetting.* Not losing all memory of his sinful past (see vv. 4–6) but leaving it behind him as done with and settled.

3:13 °Lk 9:62
3:14 °Heb 6:1
°1Co 9:24 °S Ro 8:28
3:15 °S 1Co 2:6
°Gal 5:10 °Eph 1:17;
1Th 4:9
3:17 °S 1Co 4:16
°S 1Ti 4:12
3:18 °Ac 20:31
°Gal 6:12
3:19 °Ps 73:17
°Ro 16:18 °Ro 6:21;
Jude 13 °Ro 8:5,6;
Col 3:2
3:20 °Eph 2:19
°Col 3:1; Heb 12:22
°S 1Co 1:7
3:21 °Eph 1:19
°1Co 15:43-53
°Ro 8:29; Col 3:4
4:1 °Php 1:8
°S 1Co 16:13
4:2 °Php 2:2
4:3 °S Php 2:25
°S Rev 20:12
4:4 °Ps 85:6; 97:12;
Hab 3:18; S Mt 5:12;
Ro 12:12; Php 3:1

what is behind ° and straining toward what is ahead, [14]I press on ° toward the goal to win the prize ° for which God has called ° me heavenward in Christ Jesus.

FOLLOWING PAUL'S EXAMPLE

[15]All of us, then, who are mature ° should take such a view of things. ° And if on some point you think differently, that too God will make clear to you. ° [16]Only let us live up to what we have already attained.

[17]Join together in following my example, ° brothers and sisters, and just as you have us as a model, keep your eyes on those who live as we do. ° [18]For, as I have often told you before and now tell you again even with tears, ° many live as enemies of the cross of Christ. ° [19]Their destiny ° is destruction, their god is their stomach, ° and their glory is in their shame. ° Their mind is set on earthly things. ° [20]But our citizenship ° is in heaven. ° And we eagerly await a Savior from there, the Lord Jesus Christ, ° [21]who, by the power ° that enables him to bring everything under his control, will transform our lowly bodies ° so that they will be like his glorious body. °

CLOSING APPEAL FOR STEADFASTNESS AND UNITY

4 Therefore, my brothers and sisters, you whom I love and long for, ° my joy and crown, stand firm ° in the Lord in this way, dear friends!

[2]I plead with Euodia and I plead with Syntyche to be of the same mind ° in the Lord. [3]Yes, and I ask you, my true companion, help these women since they have contended at my side in the cause of the gospel, along with Clement and the rest of my co-workers, ° whose names are in the book of life. °

FINAL EXHORTATIONS

[4]Rejoice in the Lord always. I will say it again: Rejoice! ° [5]Let your gentleness be evi-

---

3:14 *prize.* The winner of the Greek races received a wreath of leaves and sometimes a cash award (see 1Co 9:24 and note); the Christian receives an award of everlasting glory. *heavenward.* Paul's ultimate aspirations are found not in this life but in heaven, because Christ is there (see Col 3:1–2).

3:15 *mature.* Those who have made reasonable progress in spiritual growth and stability (see 1Co 2:6 and note; 3:1–3; Heb 5:14 and note). *such a view.* That expressed in vv. 12–14: There are heights yet to be scaled; do not become complacent. *think differently.* If the readers accept the view set forth in vv. 12–14 and yet fail to agree in some lesser point, God will clarify the matter for them.

3:16 *live up to what ... already attained.* Put into practice the truth they have already comprehended. We are responsible for the truth we currently possess.

3:17 *following my example.* As Paul follows the example of Christ (see 1Co 11:1 and note). *keep your eyes on those who live.* The lifestyles Christians lead ought to be models worth following.

3:18 *told you before.* See v. 1. *with tears.* Cf. Ac 20:19,31. *live as enemies of the cross.* In glaring contrast to Paul's conduct (v. 10) and to the truth of the gospel.

3:19 *destruction.* The opposite of salvation. *god ... stomach.* A deep self-centeredness; their appetites and desires come first (see Ro 16:18). *earthly things.* They have set their minds on the things of this life (see Col 3:1–2 and note on 3:1); they are antinomians (libertines), the opposite of the legalists of v. 2.

3:20 *citizenship.* In this world Christians are aliens, fully involved in it yet not of it (cf. Jn 17:14–15 and notes; 1Co 7:29–31 and note on 7:29; 1Pe 2:11 and note). *in heaven.* Where Christ is (see Gal 4:26 and note); contrast the "earthly things" of v. 19 (cf. Eph 2:6; Col 3:1–4). *eagerly await ... from there.* See Ro 8:19; 1Co 1:7; 1Th 1:9–10; 2Ti 4:8.

3:21 *power ... under his control.* Christ's present power, earned by his obedience to death (see 2:8) and received in his resurrection and ascension, is universal and absolute (see Mt 28:18; 1Co 15:27; Eph 1:20–22). *will transform.* By the Holy Spirit at the resurrection (see Ro 8:11 and note). *our lowly bodies.* Subject due to sin to weakness, decay and death (see Ro 8:10,20–23; 1Co 15:42–44 and note). *like his glorious body.* See Ro 8:29; 1Jn 3:2.

The resurrection body, received already by Christ, who is the "firstfruits," will be received by believers in the future resurrection "harvest" (see 1Co 15:20,49). It is "spiritual," i.e., transformed by the power of the Holy Spirit (see 1Co 15:44,46).

4:1 *love and long for.* See notes on 1:8; 2:1. *my joy and crown.* True not only now, but especially when Christ returns (see 1Th 2:19 and note). *stand firm.* In the midst of present struggles for the sake of the gospel (cf. 1:27–30; 1Co 15:58). *in this way.* Refers to the closing statements of ch. 3. In the face of libertine practices (3:18–19), the Philippians should follow Paul's example (3:17), having their minds set on heavenly things (3:20–21).

4:2–3 The disagreement between Euodia and Syntyche is serious enough to be mentioned in a letter to be read publicly, but Paul seems confident that "these women" (v. 3) will be reconciled. His handling of the situation is a model of tact—he does not take sides but encourages others closer to the situation to promote reconciliation (see 2:2 and note).

4:3 *at my side ... my co-workers.* Those associated with the apostle in the cause of the gospel (women as well as men) are his equals, not subordinates (cf. 2:25; Ro 16:3,9,21; Phm 24). *Clement.* Not mentioned elsewhere in the NT. *the rest of my co-workers.* Not mentioned individually because they are known to God and their names are entered in the book of life, the heavenly register of the elect (see note on Rev 3:5).

4:4 *Rejoice in the Lord.* See 3:1. *always.* Under all kinds of circumstances, including suffering (see Hab 3:17–18 and note; Jas 1:2; 1Pe 4:13).

4:5 *gentleness.* Christlike consideration for others (cf. 2Co 10:1). This quality is especially essential in church leaders (see 1Ti 3:3; Tit 3:2, "considerate"). *near.* See Ro 13:11 and note; cf. Jas 5:8–9 and note on 5:9; Rev 22:7,12,20. The next great event in God's prophetic schedule is Christ's return. The whole period from Christ's first coming to the consummation of the kingdom is viewed in the NT as the last time (see 1Jn 2:18 and note). From God's vantage point, a thousand years are as a day (see 2Pe 3:8 and note). Thus there is a sense in which, for every generation, the Lord's coming is near.

dent to all. The Lord is near. *p* ⁶Do not be anxious about anything, *q* but in every situation, by prayer and petition, with thanksgiving, present your requests to God. *r* ⁷And the peace of God, *s* which transcends all understanding, *t* will guard your hearts and your minds in Christ Jesus.

⁸Finally, brothers and sisters, whatever is true, whatever is noble, whatever is right, whatever is pure, whatever is lovely, whatever is admirable—if anything is excellent or praiseworthy—think about such things. ⁹Whatever you have learned or received or heard from me, or seen in me—put it into practice. *u* And the God of peace *v* will be with you.

THANKS FOR THEIR GIFTS

¹⁰I rejoiced greatly in the Lord that at last you renewed your concern for me. *w* Indeed, you were concerned, but you had no opportunity to show it. ¹¹I am not saying this because I am in need, for I have learned to be content *x* whatever the circumstances. ¹²I know what it is to be in need, and I know what it is to have plenty. I have learned the secret of being content in any and every situation, whether well fed or hungry, *y* whether living in plenty or in want. *z* ¹³I can do all this through him who gives me strength. *a*

¹⁴Yet it was good of you to share *b* in my troubles. ¹⁵Moreover, as you Philippians know, in the early days *c* of your acquaintance with the gospel, when I set out from Macedonia, *d* not one church shared with me in the matter of giving and receiving, except you only; *e* ¹⁶for even when I was in Thessalonica, *f* you sent me aid more than once when I was in need. *g* ¹⁷Not that I desire your gifts; what I desire is that more be credited to your account. *h* ¹⁸I have received full payment and have more than enough. I am amply supplied, now that I have received from Epaphroditus *i* the gifts you sent. They are a fragrant *j* offering, an acceptable sacrifice, pleasing to God. ¹⁹And my God will meet all your needs *k* according to the riches of his glory *l* in Christ Jesus.

4:5 *p* Ps 119:151;
145:18; Heb 10:37;
Jas 5:8,9
4:6 *q* Mt 6:25-34
r Eph 6:18; 1Ti 2:1
4:7 *s* Isa 26:3;
S Jn 14:27 *t* Eph 3:19
4:9 *u* S 1Co 4:16
v S Ro 15:33
4:10 *w* 2Co 11:9
4:11 *x* 1Ti 6:6,8;
Heb 13:5
4:12 *y* S 1Co 4:11
z 2Co 11:9
4:13 *a* 2Co 12:9;
Eph 3:16; Col 1:11;
1Ti 1:12; 2Ti 4:17
4:14 *b* Php 1:7
4:15 *c* Php 1:5
d S Ac 16:9
e 2Co 11:8,9
4:16 *f* S Ac 17:1
g 1Th 2:9
4:17 *h* 1Co 9:11,12
4:18 *i* Php 2:25
j S 2Co 2:14
4:19 *k* Ps 23:1;
2Co 9:8 *l* S Ro 2:4

4:6 *anxious.* Self-centered, counterproductive worry, not legitimate cares and concerns for the spread of the gospel (see 2:28 and note; 2Co 11:28; see also Mt 6:25–31; 1Pe 5:7). *in every situation, by prayer.* Anxiety and prayer are two great opposing forces in Christian experience. *thanksgiving.* The antidote to worry (along with prayer and petition).

4:7 *peace of God.* Not merely a psychological state of mind, but an inner tranquillity based on peace with God—the peaceful state of those whose sins are forgiven (cf. Jn 14:27; Ro 5:1 and note). The opposite of anxiety, it is the tranquillity that comes when believers commit all their cares to God in prayer and worry about them no more. *transcends all understanding.* The full dimensions of God's love and care are beyond human comprehension (see Eph 3:18–20). *guard...hearts... minds.* A military concept depicting a sentry standing guard. God's "protective custody" of those who are in Christ Jesus extends to the core of their beings and to their deepest intentions (cf. 1Pe 1:5 and note).

4:8 *true...praiseworthy.* Paul understood the influence of one's thoughts on one's life. What people allow to occupy their minds will sooner or later determine their speech and action. Paul's exhortation to "think about such things" is followed by a second exhortation, "put it into practice" (v. 9). The combination of virtues listed in vv. 8–9 is sure to produce a wholesome thought pattern, which in turn will result in a life of moral and spiritual excellence (see note on Gal 5:22–23).

4:9 *seen in me.* See note on 3:17. *God of peace.* See note on 1Th 5:23; cf. the "peace of God" (v. 7).

4:10 *at last...no opportunity.* The delay in sending gifts to Paul was not the fault of the Philippians, nor was it because they were lacking in concern for him (cf. 2Co 11:9). Perhaps Paul's uncertain itinerary prior to his arrival at Rome or the lack of an available messenger had prevented the Philippians from showing their concern.

4:11 *content whatever the circumstances.* Paul genuinely appreciates the gifts from Philippi (see vv. 14,18) but he is not ultimately dependent on them (cf. 1Ti 6:6–8).

4:12 *content...whether well fed...whether living in plenty.* Prosperity, too, can be a source of discontent.

4:13 *all this.* All those circumstances that Paul has just spoken of in vv. 11–12. *him who gives me strength.* Christ. Union with the living, exalted Christ is the secret of being content (v. 12) and the source of Paul's abiding strength (see especially 2Co 12:9–10; see also Jn 15:5; Eph 3:16–17; Col 1:11).

4:14 *share.* The Philippians' gifts are a means of involving them in Paul's troubles (cf. Heb 10:33).

4:15 *early days.* During Paul's second missionary journey, when he first preached in Philippi (see Ac 16:12–40). *set out.* For the south (Achaia), where Athens and Corinth were located (see Ac 17:14–16; 18:1–4). *Macedonia.* The northern part of modern-day Greece, where Berea and Thessalonica, as well as Philippi, were located (see map, p. 1869). *shared with me in the matter of.* Or "participated with me in an account of." Paul uses commercial language to describe "giving and receiving" (credit and debit) between the Philippians and himself (see "credited to your account," v. 17). Yet this commercial imagery is plainly transcended by the mutual concern and self-sacrifice of their relationship. *except you only.* The generosity of the Philippian church is unique and unmatched (cf. 2Co 8:1–5).

4:16 *when I was in Thessalonica.* While he was still in Macedonia (see Ac 17:1–9). *aid more than once.* The gifts sent to Rome through Epaphroditus are the latest in a long and consistent pattern of generosity (cf. 2Co 8:1–5).

4:17 *credited to your account.* See note on v. 15. The "investment value" of the Philippians' gift is not primarily what Paul received but the "spiritual dividends" they received.

4:18 *a fragrant offering, an acceptable sacrifice.* The OT background is the sacrifice, not of atonement for sin but of thanksgiving and praise (cf. Lev 7:12–15; Ro 12:1; Eph 5:2 and note; Heb 13:15–16 and note on 13:15). *acceptable...pleasing to God.* Because of Christ's work for us (see 1Pe 2:5) and God's work in us (see Php 2:13).

4:19 *my.* A personal touch (cf. "my God" in 1:3). *will meet.* A promise given to a church that had sacrificially given to meet Paul's need. *your needs.* Paul is concerned not only about his own situation but also about that of the Philippians. *the riches of his glory in Christ Jesus.* The true measure of God's blessings to the church (cf. Eph 1:18; 3:16–20).

4:20 m Gal 1:4;
1Th 1:3; 3:11,13
n S Ro 11:36
4:21 o Gal 1:2
4:22 p S Ac 9:13
4:23 q S Ro 16:20
r S Gal 6:18

20To our God and Father m be glory for ever and ever. Amen. n

FINAL GREETINGS

21Greet all God's people in Christ Jesus. The brothers and sisters who are with me o send greetings. 22All the Lord's people p here send you greetings, especially those who belong to Caesar's household.

23The grace of the Lord Jesus Christ q be with your spirit. r Amen. a

a 23 Some manuscripts do not have *Amen.*

4:20 Paul cannot hold back a doxology, especially as he considers the truth of v. 19.

4:21–22 Final greetings are a typical feature of Paul's letters (see, e.g., Ro 16:3–16,21–23; 1Co 16:19–20; 2Co 13:12–13; Col 4:10–12,14–15,18).

4:21 *God's people.* See note on Ro 1:7. *brothers and sisters who are with me.* Paul's fellow workers at Rome, especially Timothy

(see 1:1,14,16).

4:22 *Caesar's household.* Not blood relatives of the emperor but those employed (slaves or freedmen) in or around the palace area (cf. "palace guard," 1:13).

4:23 A typical closing benediction of Paul. *grace.* See note on Ro 1:7. *be with your spirit.* See note on Gal 6:18.

AUTHOR, DATE AND PLACE OF WRITING

COLOSSIANS
INTRODUCTION

C That Colossians is a genuine letter of Paul (1:1) is usually not disputed. In the early church, all who speak on the subject of authorship ascribe it to Paul. In the 19th century, however, some thought that the heresy refuted in ch. 2 was second-century Gnosticism. But a careful analysis of ch. 2 shows that the heresy referred to there is noticeably less developed than the Gnosticism of leading Gnostic teachers of the second and third centuries. Also, the seeds of what later became the full-blown Gnosticism of the second century were present in the first century and already making inroads into the churches. Consequently, it is not necessary to date Colossians in the second century at a time too late for Paul to have written the letter.

Instead, it is to be dated during Paul's first imprisonment in Rome, where he spent at least two years under house arrest (see Ac 28:16–31). Some have argued that Paul wrote Colossians from Ephesus or Caesarea, but most of the evidence favors Rome as the place where Paul penned all the Prison Letters (Ephesians, Colossians, Philippians and Philemon). Colossians should be dated c. A.D. 60, in the same year as Ephesians and Philemon (see chart, p. 1855).

COLOSSAE: THE TOWN AND THE CHURCH

Several hundred years before Paul's day, Colossae had been a leading city in Asia Minor (present-day Turkey). It was located on the Lycus River and on the great east-west trade route leading from Ephesus on the Aegean Sea to the Euphrates River (see map, p. 1875). By the first century A.D. Colossae was diminished to a second-rate market town, which had been surpassed long before in power and importance by the neighboring towns of Laodicea and Hierapolis (see 4:13).

What gave Colossae NT importance, however, was the fact that, during Paul's three-year ministry in Ephesus, Epaphras had been converted and had carried the gospel to Colossae (cf. 1:7–8; Ac 19:10). The young church that resulted then became the target of heretical attack, which led to Epaphras's visit to Paul in Rome and ultimately to the penning of the Colossian letter.

Perhaps as a result of the efforts of Epaphras or other converts of Paul, Christian churches had also been established in Laodicea and Hierapolis. Some of them were house churches (see 4:15; Phm 2). Most likely all of them were primarily Gentile.

THE COLOSSIAN HERESY

Paul never explicitly describes the false teaching he opposes in the Colossian letter. The nature of the heresy must be inferred from statements he made in opposition to the false teachers. An analysis of his refutation suggests that the heresy was diverse in nature. Some of the elements of its teachings were:

1. *Ceremonialism.* It held to strict rules about the kinds of permissible food and drink, religious festivals (2:16–17) and circumcision (2:11; 3:11).

2. *Asceticism.* "Do not handle! Do not taste! Do not touch!" (2:21; cf. 2:23).

3. *Angel worship.* See 2:18.

4. *Depreciation of Christ.* This is implied in Paul's emphasis on the supremacy of Christ (1:15–20; 2:2–3,9).

5. *Secret knowledge.* The Gnostics boasted of this (see 2:18 and Paul's emphasis in 2:2–3 on Christ, "in whom are hidden all the treasures of wisdom").

6. *Reliance on human wisdom and tradition.* See 2:4,8.

These elements seem to fall into two categories, Jewish and Gnostic. It is likely, therefore, that the Colossian heresy was a mixture of an extreme form of Judaism and an early stage of Gnosticism (see Introduction to 1 John: Gnosticism; see also note on 2:23).

PURPOSE AND THEME

Paul's purpose is to refute the Colossian heresy. To accomplish this goal, he exalts Christ as the very image of God (1:15), the Creator (1:16), the preexistent sustainer of all things (1:17), the head of the church (1:18), the first to be resurrected (1:18), the fullness of deity in bodily form (1:19; 2:9) and the reconciler (1:20–22). Thus Christ is completely adequate: "In Christ you have been brought to fullness" (2:10). On the other hand, the Colossian heresy was altogether inadequate. It was a hollow and deceptive philosophy (2:8), lacking any ability to restrain the old sinful nature (2:23).

The theme of Colossians is the complete adequacy of Christ, as contrasted with the emptiness of mere human philosophy.

OUTLINE

I. Introduction (1:1–14)
  A. Greetings (1:1–2)
  B. Thanksgiving (1:3–8)
  C. Prayer (1:9–14)
II. The Supremacy of Christ (1:15–23)
III. Paul's Labor for the Church (1:24—2:7)
  A. His Ministry for the Sake of the Church (1:24–29)
  B. His Concern for the Spiritual Welfare of His Readers (2:1–7)
IV. Freedom from Human Regulations through Life with Christ (2:8–23)
  A. Warning to Guard against the False Teachers (2:8–15)
  B. Pleas to Reject the False Teachers (2:16–19)
  C. An Analysis of the Heresy (2:20–23)
V. Rules for Holy Living (3:1—4:6)
  A. The Old Self and the New Self (3:1–17)
  B. Rules for Christian Households (3:18—4:1)
  C. Further Instructions (4:2–6)
VI. Final Greetings and Benediction (4:7–18)

1 Paul, an apostle *a* of Christ Jesus by the will of God, *b* and Timothy *c* our brother,

²To God's holy people in Colossae, the faithful brothers and sisters in Christ:

Grace *d* and peace to you from God our Father. *a* *e*

THANKSGIVING AND PRAYER

³We always thank God, *f* the Father of our Lord Jesus Christ, when we pray for you, ⁴because we have heard of your faith in Christ Jesus and of the love *g* you have for all his people *h*— ⁵the faith and love that spring from the hope *i* stored up for you in heaven *j* and about which you have already heard in the true word *k* of the gospel ⁶that has come to you. In the same way, the gospel is bearing fruit *l* and growing throughout the whole world *m*— just as it has been doing among you since the day you heard it and truly understood God's grace. ⁷You learned it from Epaphras, *n* our dear fellow servant, *b* who is a faithful minister *o* of Christ on our *c* behalf, ⁸and who also told us of your love in the Spirit. *p*

⁹For this reason, since the day we heard about you, *q* we have not stopped praying for you. *r* We continually ask God to fill you with the knowledge of his will *s* through all the wisdom and understanding that the Spirit gives, *d* *t* ¹⁰so that you may live a life worthy *u* of the Lord and please him *v* in every way: bearing fruit in every good work, growing in the knowledge of God, *w* ¹¹being strengthened with all power *x* according to his glorious might so that you may have great endurance and patience, *y* ¹²and giving joyful thanks to the Father, *z* who has qualified you *e* to share in the inheritance *a* of his people in the kingdom of light. *b* ¹³For he has rescued us from the dominion of darkness *c* and brought us into the kingdom *d* of the Son he loves, *e* ¹⁴in whom we have redemption, *f* the forgiveness of sins. *g*

---

a 2 Some manuscripts *Father and the Lord Jesus Christ*   *b* 7 Or *slave*   *c* 7 Some manuscripts *your*
d 9 Or *all spiritual wisdom and understanding*   *e* 12 Some manuscripts *us*

Sidebar references:

1:1 *a* 1Co 1:1
b S 2Co 1:1; *c* S Ac 16:1
1:2 *d* Col 4:18
e S Ro 1:7
1:3 *f* S Ro 1:8
1:4 *g* Gal 5:6
h S Ac 9:13; Eph 1:15; Phm 5
1:5 *i* ver 23; 1Th 5:8; Tit 1:2 / 1Pe 1:4
k S 2Ti 2:15
1:6 *l* Jn 15:16
m ver 23; S Ro 10:18
1:7 *n* Col 4:12; Phm 23 / Col 4:7
1:8 *p* Ro 15:30
1:9 *q* ver 4; Eph 1:15
r S Ro 1:10
s S Eph 5:17
t S Eph 1:17
1:10 *u* S Eph 4:1
v S 2Co 5:9 / ver 6
1:11 *x* S Php 4:13
y Eph 4:2
1:12 *z* Eph 5:20
a S Ac 20:32
b S Ac 26:18
1:13 *c* S Ac 26:18
d 2Pe 1:11 / Mt 3:17
1:14 *f* S Ro 3:24
g Eph 1:7

1:1 *Paul.* It was customary to put the writer's name at the beginning of a letter. For more information on Paul, see note on Ro 1:1. *apostle ... by the will of God.* See 1Co 1:1 and note. *Christ.* Paul is very Christ-centered, as seen by this short letter, in which he uses the title "Christ" 29 times and the title "Lord" (alone) 9 times. *Timothy.* Paul also mentions Timothy in 2 Corinthians, Philippians, 1,2 Thessalonians and Philemon, but Paul is really the sole author, as seen by the constant use of the pronoun "I" (see especially 4:18).

1:2 *holy people.* Because of Christ's substitutionary death for the Colossian believers, they are declared holy in the sight of God, and because of the Holy Spirit's work they are continuing to be made holy in their lives (see notes on Ro 1:7; 6:22; 1Co 1:2). *faithful.* See 1:7; 4:7,9. *brothers and sisters.* See note on Ro 1:13. *in Christ.* Paul mentions the spiritual union with Christ 12 times in Colossians (see note on Eph 1:1). *Grace and peace.* See note on Ro 1:7.

1:3 *We.* Paul and Timothy (v. 1). *thank God.* Every one of Paul's letters, except Galatians, begins with thanks or praise (see note on Php 1:3–4). In Colossians thanks is an important theme (see v. 12; 2:7; 3:15–17; 4:2). In the Bible humans are never thanked for their faith and love, but rather God, who is the source of these virtues. *Lord Jesus Christ.* See note on 1Th 1:1.

1:4 *his people.* The Greek word for this phrase is sometimes rendered "saints," meaning "holy people" (v. 2) or "people set apart to God" (see note on Ro 1:7; see also "A Word to the Reader" at the front of this study Bible).

1:5 The three great Christian virtues of faith, love and hope appear also in Ro 5:2–5; 1Co 13:13; Gal 5:5–6; 1Th 1:3; 5:8; Heb 10:22–24. *hope.* Not wishful thinking but a firm assurance (see Ro 5:5 and note). For this unusual thought of faith and love coming from hope, see Tit 1:2. *true word.* The "gospel" (see Eph 1:13; 2Ti 2:15).

1:6 *throughout the whole world.* Hyperbole, to dramatize the rapid spread of the gospel into every quarter of the Roman empire within three decades of Pentecost (see v. 23; Ro 1:8 and

note; 10:18; 16:19). In refutation of the charge of the false teachers, Paul insists that the Christian faith is not merely local or regional but worldwide.

1:7 *Epaphras.* A native (4:12) and probably founder of the Colossian church, and an evangelist in nearby Laodicea and Hierapolis (4:13). Paul loved and admired him, calling him a "fellow prisoner" (Phm 23), his "dear fellow servant" and "a faithful minister of Christ." Epaphras was the one who told Paul at Rome about the Colossian church problem and thereby stimulated him to write this letter (vv. 4,8). His name, a shortened form of Epaphroditus (from "Aphrodite," the Greek goddess of love), suggests that he was a convert from paganism. He is not the Epaphroditus of Php 2:25; 4:18.

1:8 *your love in the Spirit.* The Holy Spirit is the source of all Christian love (see Ro 5:5; Gal 5:22–23 and notes).

1:9 *knowledge of his will.* Biblical knowledge is not merely the possession of facts. Rather, knowledge and wisdom in the Bible are practical, having to do with godly living. This is borne out by vv. 10–12, where knowledge, wisdom and understanding result in a life worthy of the Lord.

1:10 *live a life.* This phrase (lit. "walk") is linked to 2:7; 3:7; 4:5 ("act") by the same Greek verb. *bearing fruit ... growing.* Cf. v. 6.

1:12 *inheritance.* See 1Pe 1:4 and note. *light.* Often symbolizes holiness (see 1Jn 1:5 and note), truth (Ps 119:105, 130; 2Co 4:6), glory (Isa 60:1–3; 1Ti 6:16) and life (Jn 1:4). Accordingly, God (1Jn 1:5), Christ (Jn 8:12) and the Christian (Eph 5:8) are characterized by light. The "kingdom of light" is the opposite of the "dominion of darkness" (v. 13). See also note on Ps 27:1.

1:13 *kingdom.* Does not here refer to a territory but to the authority, rule or sovereign power of a king. Here it means that the Christian is no longer under the dominion of evil (darkness) but under the benevolent rule of God's Son.

1:14 *redemption.* Deliverance and freedom from the penalty of sin by the payment of a ransom—the substitutionary death of Christ (see Ro 3:24 and note).

1:15 ʰ S Jn 14:9
ⁱ S Jn 1:18; 1Ti 1:17;
Heb 11:27 / S ver 18
1:16 ᵏ S Jn 1:3
ˡ Eph 1:20, 21
ᵐ S Ro 11:36
1:17 ⁿ S Jn 1:2
1:18 ° S Eph 1:22
ᵖ ver 24; S 1Co 12:27
ᵠ ver 15; Ps 89:27;
Ro 8:29; Heb 1:6
ʳ Ac 26:23; Rev 1:5
1:19 ˢ S Eph 1:5
ᵗ S Jn 1:16
1:20 ᵘ S Ro 5:10
ᵛ Eph 1:10 ʷ S Lk 2:14
ˣ Eph 2:13
1:21 ʸ Ro 5:10
ᶻ Eph 2:3
1:22 ᵃ ver 20;
S Ro 5:10 ᵇ Ro 7:4
ᶜ S 2Co 4:14
ᵈ Eph 1:4; 5:27
1:23 ᵉ S Ro 11:22
ᶠ Eph 3:17 ᵍ ver 5
ʰ ver 6; S Ro 10:18
ⁱ ver 25; S 1Co 3:5
1:24 / S 2Co 6:10
ᵏ S 2Co 1:5
ˡ S 1Co 12:27
1:25 ᵐ ver 23;
S 1Co 3:5 ⁿ Eph 3:2
° S Heb 4:12
1:26 ᵖ S Ro 16:25
1:27 ᵠ S Mt 13:11
ʳ S Ro 2:4 ˢ S Ro 8:10

THE SUPREMACY OF THE SON OF GOD

¹⁵The Son is the image ʰ of the invisible God, ⁱ the firstborn ʲ over all creation. ¹⁶For in him all things were created: ᵏ things in heaven and on earth, visible and invisible, whether thrones or powers or rulers or authorities; ˡ all things have been created through him and for him. ᵐ ¹⁷He is before all things, ⁿ and in him all things hold together. ¹⁸And he is the head ° of the body, the church; ᵖ he is the beginning and the firstborn ᵠ from among the dead, ʳ so that in everything he might have the supremacy. ¹⁹For God was pleased ˢ to have all his fullness ᵗ dwell in him, ²⁰and through him to reconcile ᵘ to himself all things, whether things on earth or things in heaven, ᵛ by making peace ʷ through his blood, ˣ shed on the cross.

²¹Once you were alienated from God and were enemies ʸ in your minds ᶻ because of ᵃ your evil behavior. ²²But now he has reconciled ᵃ you by Christ's physical body ᵇ through death to present you ᶜ holy in his sight, without blemish and free from accusation ᵈ— ²³if you continue ᵉ in your faith, established ᶠ and firm, and do not move from the hope ᵍ held out in the gospel. This is the gospel that you heard and that has been proclaimed to every creature under heaven, ʰ and of which I, Paul, have become a servant. ⁱ

PAUL'S LABOR FOR THE CHURCH

²⁴Now I rejoice ʲ in what I am suffering for you, and I fill up in my flesh what is still lacking in regard to Christ's afflictions, ᵏ for the sake of his body, which is the church. ˡ ²⁵I have become its servant ᵐ by the commission God gave me ⁿ to present to you the word of God ° in its fullness— ²⁶the mystery ᵖ that has been kept hidden for ages and generations, but is now disclosed to the Lord's people. ²⁷To them God has chosen to make known ᵠ among the Gentiles the glorious riches ʳ of this mystery, which is Christ in you, ˢ the hope of glory.

ᵃ 21 Or *minds, as shown by*

1:15–20 Perhaps an early Christian hymn (see note on 3:16) on the supremacy of Christ—used here by Paul to counteract the false teaching at Colossae. It is divided into two parts: (1) Christ's supremacy in creation (vv. 15–17); (2) Christ's supremacy in redemption (vv. 18–20).

1:15 *image.* Christ is called the "image of God" here and in 2Co 4:4 (see note there). In Heb 1:3 he is described as the "radiance of God's glory and the exact representation of his being." This figure of the image suggests two truths: (1) God is invisible ("No one has ever seen God," Jn 1:18); and (2) Christ, who is the eternal Son of God and who became the God-man, reflects and reveals him (see also Jn 1:18; 14:9). *firstborn over all creation.* Just as the firstborn son had certain privileges and rights in the Biblical world, so also Christ has certain rights in relation to all creation—priority, preeminence and sovereignty (vv. 16–18).

1:16 *thrones or powers or rulers or authorities.* Angels. An angelic hierarchy figured prominently in the Colossian heresy (see Introduction: The Colossian Heresy). *all things have been created through him.* See Jn 1:3. Seven times in vv. 15–20 Paul mentions "all creation," "all things" and "everything," thus stressing that Christ is supreme over all.

1:17 *He is before all things.* Referring to time, as in Jn 1:1–2; 8:58.

1:18 *head.* Christ is supreme in the church as the one on whom it is dependent (see notes on 1Co 11:3; Eph 1:22). *beginning.* Of the new creation. *firstborn.* Christ was the first to rise from the dead with a resurrection body. Elsewhere Paul calls him the "firstfruits of those who have fallen asleep" (1Co 15:20). Others who were raised from the dead (2Ki 4:35; Lk 7:15; Jn 11:44; Ac 9:36–41; 20:7–12) were raised only to die again.

1:19 *fullness.* Part of the technical vocabulary of some Gnostic philosophies. In these systems it meant the sum of the supernatural forces controlling the fate of people. For Paul "fullness" meant the totality of God with all his powers and attributes (see 2:9 and note).

1:20 *reconcile to himself all things.* Does not mean that Christ by his death has saved all people. Scripture speaks of an eternal hell and makes clear that only believers are saved. When Adam and Eve sinned, not only was the harmony between God and human beings destroyed, but also disorder

came into creation (Ro 8:19–22). So when Christ died on the cross, he made peace possible between God and humans, and he restored in principle the harmony in the physical world, though the full realization of the latter will come only when Christ returns (see Ro 8:21 and note).

1:22 *death.* Christ's death.

1:23 *every creature.* See note on v. 6.

1:24 *what I am suffering.* During his mission to the Gentiles Paul experienced all kinds of affliction (see 2Co 11:23–27), but here he was probably referring especially to his imprisonment. *fill up … what is still lacking.* Does not mean that there was a deficiency in the atoning sacrifice of Christ. Rather, it means that Paul suffered afflictions because he was preaching the good news of Christ's atonement. Christ suffered on the cross to atone for sin, and Paul filled up Christ's afflictions by experiencing the added sufferings necessary to carry this good news to a lost world.

1:25 *commission.* The task with which he was entrusted (see 1Co 9:17). *to present … the word of God in its fullness.* The meaning seems to be that the word of God is brought to completion, i.e., to its intended purpose, only when it is proclaimed (cf. Isa 55:11). Paul's commission to bring the word to completion, therefore, required him to make the word of God heard in Colossae, as well as elsewhere. See Ro 15:19 for a similar statement.

1:26 *mystery.* The purpose of God, unknown to humans except by revelation. This word was a popular, pagan religious term, used in the mystery religions to refer to secret information available only to an exclusive group of people. Paul changes that meaning radically by always combining it with words such as "disclosed" (here), "made known" (Eph 1:9), "make plain" (Eph 3:9) and "revelation" (Ro 16:25; see note there). The Christian mystery is not secret knowledge for a few. It is a revelation of divine truths—once hidden but now openly proclaimed.

1:27 *Gentiles … Christ in you.* The mystery is the fact that Christ indwells Gentiles, for it had not been previously revealed that the Gentiles would be admitted to the church on equal terms with Israel (see note on Eph 3:6). *glory.* The glorious future prepared by God for his people (see 3:4; Ro 5:2 and note; 8:17–18;

²⁸We proclaim him, admonishing ^t and teaching everyone with all wisdom, ^u so that we may present everyone fully mature ^v in Christ. ²⁹To this end I strenuously ^w contend ^x with all the energy Christ so powerfully works in me. ^y

2 I want you to know how hard I am contending ^z for you and for those at Laodicea, ^a and for all who have not met me personally. ²My goal is that they may be encouraged in heart ^b and united in love, so that they may have the full riches of complete understanding, in order that they may know the mystery ^c of God, namely, Christ, ³in whom are hidden all the treasures of wisdom and knowledge. ^d ⁴I tell you this so that no one may deceive you by fine-sounding arguments. ^e ⁵For though I am absent from you in body, I am present with you in spirit ^f and delight to see how disciplined ^g you are and how firm ^h your faith in Christ ⁱ is.

SPIRITUAL FULLNESS IN CHRIST

⁶So then, just as you received Christ Jesus as Lord, ^j continue to live your lives in him, ⁷rooted ^k and built up in him, strengthened in the faith as you were taught, ^l and overflowing with thankfulness.

⁸See to it that no one takes you captive through hollow and deceptive philosophy, ^m which depends on human tradition and the elemental spiritual forces ^a of this world ⁿ rather than on Christ.

⁹For in Christ all the fullness ^o of the Deity lives in bodily form, ¹⁰and in Christ you have been brought to fullness. He is the head ^p over every power and authority. ^q ¹¹In him you were also circumcised ^r with a circumcision not performed by human hands. Your sinful nature ^b ^s was put off when you were circumcised by ^c Christ, ¹²having been buried with him in baptism, ^t in which you were also raised with him ^u through your faith in the working of God, who raised him from the dead. ^v

¹³When you were dead in your sins ^w and in the uncircumcision of your sinful nature, ^d God made you ^e alive ^x with Christ. He forgave us all our sins, ^y ¹⁴having canceled the charge of our legal indebtedness, ^z which stood against us and condemned us; he has taken it away, nailing it to the cross. ^a ¹⁵And having disarmed the powers and authorities, ^b he made a public spectacle of them, triumphing over them ^c by the cross. ^f

---

^a 8 Or *the basic principles; also in verse 20* ^b 11 Or *Your flesh* ^c 11 Or *put off in the circumcision of* ^d 13 Or *your flesh* ^e 13 Some manuscripts *us* ^f 15 Or *them in him*

1:28 ^t Col 3:16
^u 1Co 2:6,7 ^v Mt 5:48;
Eph 5:27
1:29 ^w 1Co 15:10;
2Co 11:23 ^x Col 2:1
^y Eph 1:19; 3:7
2:1 ^z Col 1:29; 4:12
^a Col 4:13,15,16;
Rev 1:11; 3:14
2:2 ^b Eph 6:22;
Col 4:8 ^c S Ro 16:25
2:3 ^d Isa 11:2;
Jer 23:5; Ro 11:33;
1Co 1:24,30
2:4 ^e S Ro 16:18
2:5 ^f 1Co 5:4;
1Th 2:17 ^g 1Co 14:40
^h 1Pe 5:9 ⁱ S Ac 20:21
2:6 ^j S Jn 13:13;
Col 1:10
2:7 ^k Eph 3:17
^l Eph 4:21
2:8 ^m 1Ti 6:20
ⁿ ver 20; Gal 4:3
2:9 ^o S Jn 1:16
2:10 ^p S Eph 1:22
^q S Mt 28:18
2:11 ^r Ro 2:29;
Php 3:3 ^s S Gal 5:24
2:12 ^t S Mt 28:19
^u S Ro 6:5 ^v S Ac 2:24
2:13 ^w Eph 2:1,5
^x Eph 2:5 ^y Eph 4:32
2:14 ^z Eph 2:15
^a 1Pe 2:24
2:15 ^b ver 10;
Eph 6:12 ^c Mt 12:29;
Lk 10:18; Jn 12:31

1Co 2:7 and note; 15:42–44 and note; 2Co 4:17 and note; 1Th 2:12; 2Th 2:14; 2Ti 2:10; Heb 2:10; 1Pe 5:1,4 and note on 5:1).

1:28 *fully mature.* Employed by the mystery religions and the Gnostics to describe those who had become possessors of the secrets or knowledge boasted of by the particular religion (see Introduction to 1 John: Gnosticism). But in Christ every believer is one of the "mature."

1:29 An example of the combination of human effort and divine help (see Php 2:12–13).

2:1 *I am contending.* Probably a reference to Paul's prayers and inner conflicts and concerns for the Colossians. *Laodicea.* This letter was to be read to the church there too (4:16). Laodicea (near modern Denizli) was only about 11 miles from Colossae (see map 3, p. 1861).

2:2 *mystery.* See notes on 1:26; Ro 11:25.

2:3 *knowledge.* Paul stressed knowledge in this letter (v. 2; 1:9–10) because he was refuting a heresy that emphasized knowledge as the means of salvation (see Introduction to 1 John: Gnosticism). Paul insisted that the Christian, not the Gnostic, possessed genuine knowledge.

2:5 *absent...in body,...present...in spirit.* Cf. 1Co 5:3.

2:6–7 Cf. Eph 3:16–19.

2:6 *live...in him.* The believer's intimate, spiritual, living union with Christ is mentioned repeatedly in this letter (see, e.g., vv. 7,10–13,20; 1:2,27–28; 3:1,3).

2:7 *overflowing with thankfulness.* See Eph 5:20 and note.

2:8 *elemental spiritual forces of this world.* If the TNIV text note rendering is correct, this phrase (which occurs also in v. 20; Gal 4:3,9) refers to false, worldly, elementary religious teachings. Paul was counteracting the Colossian heresy, which, in part, taught that for salvation one needed to combine faith in Christ with secret knowledge and with human regulations concerning

such physical and external practices as circumcision, eating and drinking and observance of religious festivals. On the other hand, if the translation in the main TNIV text is correct, it refers to evil spiritual powers (cf. Ro 8:38–39; 1Co 15:24; cf. also Eph 6:10–18; Col 2:15; 1Pe 3:19–20a and notes).

2:9 *fullness of the Deity.* See note on 1:19. The declaration that the very essence of deity was present in totality in Jesus' human body was a direct refutation of Gnostic teaching.

2:10–15 Here Paul declares that the Christian is complete in Christ, rather than being deficient as the Gnostics claimed. This completeness includes the putting off of the sinful nature (v. 11), resurrection from spiritual death (vv. 12–13), forgiveness (v. 13) and deliverance from legalistic requirements (v. 14) and from evil spirit beings (v. 15).

2:10 *head.* Cf. 1:18 and note; see Eph 1:19–22 and notes.

2:11–12 *circumcision...baptism.* In the Israelite faith, circumcision was a sign that the individual stood in covenant relation with God. While this is the only reference where circumcision is associated with baptism, some see the passage as implying that, for the Christian, water baptism is the parallel sign of the covenant relationship.

2:12 See Ro 6:3–4 and notes.

2:13 Cf. Eph 2:1–9 and notes.

2:14 *the charge of our legal indebtedness.* A business term, meaning a certificate of indebtedness in the debtor's handwriting. Paul uses it as a designation for the Mosaic law, with all its regulations, under which everyone is a debtor to God.

2:15 *having disarmed.* Not only did God cancel out the accusations of the law against the Christian, but he also conquered and disarmed the evil angels (powers and authorities; Eph 6:12), who entice people to follow asceticism and false teachings about Christ. The picture is of conquered soldiers stripped

2:16 ᵈRo 14:3,4
ᵉMk 7:19; Ro 14:17
ᶠLev 23:2; Ro 14:5
ᵍ1Ch 23:31
ʰMk 2:27,28;
Gal 4:10
2:17 ⁱHeb 8:5; 10:1
2:18 ʲver 23
ᵏ1Co 9:24; Php 3:14
2:19 ˡS Eph 1:22
ᵐS 1Co 12:27
ⁿEph 4:16
2:20 ᵒS Ro 6:6
ᵖver 8; Gal 4:3,9
ᵠver 14,16
2:22 ʳ1Co 6:13
ˢIsa 29:13; Mt 15:9;
Tit 1:14
2:23 ᵗver 18
3:1 ᵘS Ro 6:5
ᵛS Mk 16:19
3:2 ʷPhp 3:19,20
3:3 ˣS Ro 6:2;
2Co 5:14
3:4 ʸGal 2:20
ᶻ1Co 1:7 +1Pe 1:13;
1Jn 3:2
3:5 ᵇS Ro 6:2;
S Eph 4:22
ᶜS Gal 5:24
ᵈS 1Co 6:18 ᵉEph 5:3
ᶠGal 5:19-21; Eph 5:5
3:6 ᵍS Ro 1:18
3:7 ʰS Eph 2:2
3:8 ⁱS Eph 4:22
ʲEph 4:31 ᵏEph 4:29
3:9 ˡS Eph 4:22,25

FREEDOM FROM HUMAN RULES

¹⁶Therefore do not let anyone judge you ᵈ by what you eat or drink, ᵉ or with regard to a religious festival, ᶠ a New Moon celebration ᵍ or a Sabbath day. ʰ ¹⁷These are a shadow of the things that were to come; ⁱ the reality, however, is found in Christ. ¹⁸Do not let anyone who delights in false humility ʲ and the worship of angels disqualify you. ᵏ Such people also go into great detail about what they have seen, and their unspiritual minds puff them up with idle notions. ¹⁹They have lost connection with the head, ˡ from whom the whole body, ᵐ supported and held together by its ligaments and sinews, grows as God causes it to grow. ⁿ

²⁰Since you died with Christ ᵒ to the elemental spiritual forces of this world, ᵖ why, as though you still belonged to the world, do you submit to its rules: ᵠ ²¹"Do not handle! Do not taste! Do not touch!"? ²²These rules, which have to do with things that are all destined to perish ʳ with use, are based on merely human commands and teachings. ˢ ²³Such regulations indeed have an appearance of wisdom, with their self-imposed worship, their false humility ᵗ and their harsh treatment of the body, but they lack any value in restraining sensual indulgence.

LIVING AS THOSE MADE ALIVE IN CHRIST

3 Since, then, you have been raised with Christ, ᵘ set your hearts on things above, where Christ is seated at the right hand of God. ᵛ ²Set your minds on things above, not on earthly things. ʷ ³For you died, ˣ and your life is now hidden with Christ in God. ⁴When Christ, who is your ᵃ life, ʸ appears, ᶻ then you also will appear with him in glory. ᵃ

⁵Put to death, ᵇ therefore, whatever belongs to your earthly nature: ᶜ sexual immorality, ᵈ impurity, lust, evil desires and greed, ᵉ which is idolatry. ᶠ ⁶Because of these, the wrath of God ᵍ is coming. ᵇ ⁷You used to walk in these ways, in the life you once lived. ʰ ⁸But now you must also rid yourselves ⁱ of all such things as these: anger, rage, malice, slander, ʲ and filthy language from your lips. ᵏ ⁹Do not lie to each other, ˡ since you have taken off your

---

ᵃ 4 Some manuscripts *our*   ᵇ 6 Some early manuscripts *coming on those who are disobedient*

---

of their clothes, as well as their weapons, to symbolize their total defeat. *triumphing over them.* Lit. "leading them in a triumphal procession." The metaphor recalls a Roman general leading his captives through the streets of his city for all the citizens to see as evidence of his complete victory (see 2Co 2:14 and note). That Christ triumphed over the devil and his cohorts is seen from Mt 12:29; Lk 10:18; Ro 16:20.

2:16 Cf. Paul's exhortations to the Roman church (Ro 14:1—15:13).

2:17 *shadow…reality.* The ceremonial laws of the OT are here referred to as shadows (cf. Heb 8:5; 10:1) because they symbolically depicted the coming of Christ; so any insistence on the observance of such ceremonies is a failure to recognize that their fulfillment has already taken place. This element of the Colossian heresy was combined with a rigid asceticism, as vv. 20–21 reveal.

2:18 *false humility.* Humility in which one delights is of necessity mock humility. Paul may be referring to a professed humility in view of the absolute God, who was believed to be so far above humans that he could be worshiped only in the form of angels he had created. Second-century Gnosticism conceived of a list of spirit beings who had emanated from God and through whom God may be approached. *disqualify.* This term pictures an umpire or referee who excludes from competition any athlete who fails to follow the rules. The Colossians were not to permit any false teacher to deny the reality of their salvation because they were not delighting in mock humility and in the worship of angelic beings. *what they have seen.* Probably refers to professed visions by the false teachers.

2:19 *lost connection with the head.* The central error of the Colossian heresy is a defective view of Christ, in which he is believed to be less than deity (see v. 9; 1:19).

2:20 *elemental spiritual forces.* See note on v. 8.

2:21 *Do not handle…taste…touch!* The strict ascetic nature of the heresy is seen here. These prohibitions seem to carry OT ceremonial laws to the extreme.

2:23 A rather detailed analysis of the Colossian heresy: 1. It appeared to set forth an impressive system of religious philosophy. 2. It was, however, a system created by the false teachers themselves ("self-imposed"), rather than being of divine origin. 3. The false teachers attempted to parade their humility. 4. This may have been done by a harsh asceticism that brutally misused the body. Paul's analysis is that such practices are worthless because they totally fail to control sinful desires. *self-imposed worship.* The false teachers themselves had created the regulations of their heretical system. They were not from God.

3:1 *then.* "Then" (or "therefore") links the doctrinal section of the letter with the practical section, just as it does in Ro 12:1; Eph 4:1; Php 4:1. *you have been raised.* Verses 1–10 set forth what has been described as the indicative and the imperative (standing and state) of the Christian. The indicative statements describe believers in Christ: They are dead (v. 3); they have been raised with Christ (v. 1); they are with Christ in heaven ("hidden with Christ," v. 3); they have "taken off your old self" (v. 9); and they have "put on the new self" (v. 10). The imperative statements indicate what believers are to do as a result: set their hearts (or minds) on things above (vv. 1–2); put to death practices that belong to their earthly nature (v. 5); and rid themselves of practices that characterized the unregenerate self (v. 8). In summary, they are called upon to become in daily experience what they are in Christ (cf. Ro 6:1–13).

3:4 *appears.* Refers to Christ's second coming (see 1Jn 3:2).

3:5,8 See note on Ro 1:29–31.

3:6 *wrath of God.* See notes on Zec 1:2; Ro 1:18. God is unalterably opposed to sin and will invariably make sure that it is justly punished.

3:9–10 *taken off…put on.* As one takes off dirty clothes and puts on clean ones, so Christians are called upon to renounce their evil ways and live in accordance with the rules of Christ's kingdom (see vv. 12–14; cf. Ro 13:12; Gal 3:27; Eph 4:22–24).

old self [m] with its practices [10]and have put on the new self, [n] which is being renewed [o] in knowledge in the image of its Creator. [p] [11]Here there is no Gentile or Jew, [q] circumcised or uncircumcised, [r] barbarian, Scythian, slave or free, [s] but Christ is all, [t] and is in all.

[12]Therefore, as God's chosen people, holy and dearly loved, clothe yourselves [u] with compassion, kindness, humility, [v] gentleness and patience. [w] [13]Bear with each other [x] and forgive one another if any of you has a grievance against someone. Forgive as the Lord forgave you. [y] [14]And over all these virtues put on love, [z] which binds them all together in perfect unity. [a]

[15]Let the peace of Christ [b] rule in your hearts, since as members of one body [c] you were called to peace. [d] And be thankful. [16]Let the message of Christ [e] dwell among you richly as you teach and admonish one another with all wisdom [f] through psalms, [g] hymns and songs from the Spirit, singing to God with gratitude in your hearts. [h] [17]And whatever you do, [i] whether in word or deed, do it all in the name of the Lord Jesus, giving thanks [j] to God the Father through him.

INSTRUCTIONS FOR CHRISTIAN HOUSEHOLDS

3:18—4:1pp — Eph 5:22—6:9

[18]Wives, submit yourselves to your husbands, [k] as is fitting in the Lord.

[19]Husbands, love your wives and do not be harsh with them.

[20]Children, obey your parents in everything, for this pleases the Lord.

[21]Fathers, [a] do not embitter your children, or they will become discouraged.

[22]Slaves, obey your earthly masters in everything; and do it, not only when their eye is on you and to curry their favor, but with sincerity of heart and reverence for the Lord. [23]Whatever you do, work at it with all your heart, as working for the Lord, not for human masters, [24]since you know that you will receive an inheritance [l] from the Lord as a reward. [m] It is the Lord Christ you are serving. [25]Those who do wrong will be repaid for their wrongs, and there is no favoritism. [n]

4 Masters, provide your slaves with what is right and fair, [o] because you know that you also have a Master in heaven.

FURTHER INSTRUCTIONS

[2]Devote yourselves to prayer, [p] being watchful and thankful. [3]And pray for us, too, that God may open a door [q] for our message, so that we may proclaim the mystery [r] of Christ,

a 21 Or *Parents*

3:9 m S Ro 6:6
3:10 n S Ro 6:4;
S 13:14 o Ro 12:2;
S 2Co 4:16; Eph 4:23
p Eph 2:10
3:11 q Ro 10:12;
1Co 12:13 r S 1Co 7:19
s Gal 3:28 t Eph 1:23
3:12 u ver 10
v Php 2:3 w 2Co 6:6;
Gal 5:22,23; Eph 4:2
3:13 x Eph 4:2
y Eph 4:32
3:14 z 1Co 13:1-13
a S Ro 15:5
3:15 b S Jn 14:27
c S Ro 12:5
d S Ro 14:19
3:16 e Ro 10:17
f Col 1:28 g Ps 47:7
h S Eph 5:19
3:17 i 1Co 10:31
j S Eph 5:20
3:18 k S Eph 5:22
3:24 l S Ac 20:32
m S Mt 16:27
3:25 n S Ac 10:34
4:1 o Lev 25:43,53
4:2 p S Lk 18:1
4:3 q S Ac 14:27
r S Ro 16:25

3:10 *renewed.* See 2 Co 5:17. *knowledge.* See 1:10; 2:2–3 and note on 2:3. *image of its Creator.* See note on Ge 1:26.

3:11 *barbarian.* Someone who did not speak Greek and was thought to be uncivilized. *Scythian.* Scythians were known especially for their brutality and were considered by others as little better than wild beasts. They came originally from what is today south Russia. *Christ is all, and is in all.* Christ transcends all barriers and unifies people from all cultures, races and nations. Such distinctions are no longer significant. Christ alone matters (see Gal 3:28 and note).

3:12 *God's chosen people.* Israel was called this (Dt 4:37), and so is the Christian community (1Pe 2:9; see note there). Divine election is a constant theme in Paul's letters (see note on Eph 1:4), but the Bible never teaches that it dulls human responsibility. On the contrary, as this verse shows, it is precisely because Christians have been "chosen" for eternal salvation that they must put forth every effort to live the godly life. For Paul, divine sovereignty and human responsibility go hand in hand. *clothe ... with.* See note on Ps 109:29).

3:14 See 1Co 13:13 and note.

3:15 *peace of Christ.* The attitude of peace that Christ alone gives—in place of the attitude of bitterness and quarrelsomeness. This attitude is to "rule" (lit. "function like an umpire") in all human relationships (cf. Mt 10:34 and note). *be thankful.* See Eph 5:20 and note.

3:16 *message of Christ.* Refers especially to Christ's teaching, which in the time of the Colossians was transmitted orally. But by implication it includes the OT as well as the NT. *psalms, hymns and songs from the Spirit.* Some of the most

important doctrines were expressed in Christian hymns preserved for us now only in Paul's letters (1:15–20; Eph 5:14; Php 2:6–11; 1Ti 3:16). "Psalms" refers to the OT psalms (see Lk 20:42; 24:44; Ac 1:20; 13:33), some of which may have been set to music by the church. "Psalm" could also describe a song newly composed for Christian worship (cf. 1Co 14:26, where "hymn" is lit. "psalm" in the Greek text). A "hymn" was a song of praise, especially used in a celebration (see Mt 26:30 and note; Heb 2:12), much like the OT psalms that praised God for all that he is. A "song" recounted the acts of God and praised him for them (see Rev 5:9 and note; 15:3), much like the OT psalms that thanked God for all that he had done. See Eph 5:19 and note.

3:18—4:1 See Eph 5:22—6:9 and notes.

3:20 *in everything.* In everything not sinful (see Ac 5:29).

3:22—4:1 Paul neither condones slavery nor sanctions revolt against masters. Rather, he calls on both slaves and masters to show Christian principles in their relationship and thus to attempt to change the institution from within. The reason Paul writes more about slaves and masters than about wives, husbands, children and fathers may be that the slave Onesimus (4:9) is going along with Tychicus to deliver this Colossian letter and the letter to Philemon, Onesimus's master, who also lives in Colossae.

3:24 *inheritance.* See 1Pe 1:4; Heb 9:15 and notes.

3:25 *no favoritism.* See Ac 10:34 and note.

4:2 *Devote yourselves to prayer.* See notes on Lk 11:1; Ac 2:42; Ro 12:12; 1Th 5:17. *being watchful.* Being spiritually alert. *being ...thankful.* See Eph 5:20 and note.

4:3 *mystery.* See notes on 1:26–27; Ro 11:25.

4:3 ˢ S Ac 21:33
4:5 ᵗ Eph 5:15
ᵘ S Mk 4:11 ᵛ Eph 5:16
4:6 ʷ Eph 4:29
ˣ Mk 9:50 ʸ 1Pe 3:15
4:7 ᶻ S Ac 20:4
ᵃ Eph 6:21,22; Col 1:7
4:8 ᵇ Eph 6:21,22;
Col 2:2
4:9 ᶜ Phm 10
ᵈ ver 12
4:10 ᵉ S Ac 19:29
ᶠ S Ac 12:12
ᵍ S Ac 4:36
4:11 ʰ S Php 2:25
4:12 ⁱ Col 1:7;
Phm 23 ʲ ver 9
ᵏ S Ro 15:30
ˡ S 1Co 2:6
4:13 ᵐ S Col 2:1
4:14 ⁿ 2Ti 4:11;
Phm 24 ᵒ 2Ti 4:10;
Phm 24
4:15 ᵖ S Col 2:1
�q S Ro 16:5
4:16 ʳ 2Th 3:14;
S 1Ti 4:13
4:17 ˢ Phm 2
ᵗ 2Ti 4:5
4:18 ᵘ S 1Co 16:21
ᵛ Heb 13:3
ʷ S Ac 21:33
ˣ 1Ti 6:21; 2Ti 4:22;
Tit 3:15; Heb 13:25

for which I am in chains. ˢ ⁴Pray that I may proclaim it clearly, as I should. ⁵Be wise ᵗ in the way you act toward outsiders; ᵘ make the most of every opportunity. ᵛ ⁶Let your conversation be always full of grace, ʷ seasoned with salt, ˣ so that you may know how to answer everyone. ʸ

FINAL GREETINGS

⁷Tychicus ᶻ will tell you all the news about me. He is a dear brother, a faithful minister and fellow servant ᵃ ᵃ in the Lord. ⁸I am sending him to you for the express purpose that you may know about our ᵇ circumstances and that he may encourage your hearts. ᵇ ⁹He is coming with Onesimus, ᶜ our faithful and dear brother, who is one of you. ᵈ They will tell you everything that is happening here.

¹⁰My fellow prisoner Aristarchus ᵉ sends you his greetings, as does Mark, ᶠ the cousin of Barnabas. ᵍ (You have received instructions about him; if he comes to you, welcome him.) ¹¹Jesus, who is called Justus, also sends greetings. These are the only Jews ᶜ among my co-workers ʰ for the kingdom of God, and they have proved a comfort to me. ¹²Epaphras, ⁱ who is one of you ʲ and a servant of Christ Jesus, sends greetings. He is always wrestling in prayer for you, ᵏ that you may stand firm in all the will of God, mature ˡ and fully assured. ¹³I vouch for him that he is working hard for you and for those at Laodicea ᵐ and Hierapolis. ¹⁴Our dear friend Luke, ⁿ the doctor, and Demas ᵒ send greetings. ¹⁵Give my greetings to the brothers and sisters at Laodicea, ᵖ and to Nympha and the church in her house. �q

¹⁶After this letter has been read to you, see that it is also read ʳ in the church of the Laodiceans and that you in turn read the letter from Laodicea.

¹⁷Tell Archippus: ˢ "See to it that you complete the work you have received in the Lord." ᵗ

¹⁸I, Paul, write this greeting in my own hand. ᵘ Remember ᵛ my chains. ʷ Grace be with you. ˣ

ᵃ 7 Or slave; also in verse 12   ᵇ 8 Some manuscripts that he may know about your   ᶜ 11 Greek only ones of the circumcision group

---

4:5 outsiders. Non-Christians (see 1Co 5:12–13; 1Th 4:12; 1Ti 3:7). make the most of every opportunity. See Eph 5:16 and note.

4:6 seasoned with salt. Salt is a preservative and is tasty. Similarly, the Christian's conversation is to be wholesome and helpful (see 3:8; Eph 4:29).

4:7 Tychicus. See note on Eph 6:21.

4:9–17 Onesimus (v. 9), Aristarchus (v. 10), Mark (v. 10), Epaphras (v. 12), Luke (v. 14), Demas (v. 14) and Archippus (v. 17) are mentioned in Philemon. This suggests that the letters to Colossae and Philemon were written at the same time and place.

4:9 Onesimus. See Introduction to Philemon: Recipient, Background and Purpose.

4:10 Aristarchus. A Macedonian, who is mentioned three times in Acts: 1. He was with Paul during the Ephesian riot (Ac 19:29) and therefore was known in Colossae. 2. Both he and Tychicus (Ac 20:4) were with Paul in Greece. 3. He accompanied Paul on his trip to Rome (Ac 27:2). Mark. The author of the second Gospel. Against Barnabas's advice, Paul refused to take Mark on the second missionary journey because Mark had "deserted" him at Pamphylia (see Ac 15:38 and note). But now—about 12 years later—the difficulties seem to have been ironed out, because Paul, both here and in Phm 24 (sent at the same time to Philemon, who was in Colossae), sends Mark's greetings. About five years later, Paul even writes that Mark "is helpful to me in my ministry" (2Ti 4:11). See note on Ac 15:39.

4:13 Hierapolis. A town in Asia Minor (present-day Turkey), about 6 miles from Laodicea (see map, p. 2123) and 14 miles from Colossae. Its church may have been founded during Paul's three-year

stay in Ephesus (Ac 19), but probably not by Paul himself (cf. 2:1).

4:14 Luke. Wrote about Paul in the book of Acts, having often accompanied him on his travels (see note on Ac 16:10). He was with Paul in Rome during his imprisonment (Ac 28), where this letter was written. Demas. A Christian worker who would later desert Paul (2Ti 4:10).

4:15 church in her house. For the most part the early church had no buildings, so it usually met for worship and instruction in homes. It often centered around one family, as, e.g., Priscilla and Aquila (Ro 16:5; 1Co 16:19), Philemon (Phm 2) and Mary, the mother of John Mark (Ac 12:12).

4:16 After this letter has been read to you. The practice of the early church was to read Paul's letters aloud to the assembled congregation. letter from Laodicea. Probably not a letter by the Laodiceans. Rather, it was likely one that the Laodiceans were to lend to the Colossians—a letter that Paul had originally written to the Laodiceans. This may have been a fourth letter that Tychicus carried to this area in what is present-day Turkey, in addition to Ephesians, Colossians and Philemon. Or it could have been Paul's letter to the Ephesians—a circular letter making the rounds from Ephesus to Laodicea to Colossae (see Introduction to Ephesians: Author, Date and Place of Writing).

4:17 Archippus. Phm 2 calls him Paul's "fellow soldier."

4:18 Paul's custom was to dictate his letters (see Ro 16:22) and pen a few greetings himself (1Co 16:21; Gal 6:11; 2Th 3:17; Phm 19). His personal signature was the guarantee of the genuineness of the letter. Grace. See note on Ro 1:7. with you. See note on 2Co 13:14.

C It is helpful to trace the locations of Paul and his companions that relate to the Thessalonian correspondence. The travels were as follows:

1. Paul and Silas fled from Thessalonica to Berea. Since Timothy is not mentioned (see Ac 17:10 and note), it is possible that he stayed in Thessalonica or went back to Philippi and then rejoined Paul and Silas in Berea (Ac 17:14).

2. Paul fled to Athens from Berean persecution, leaving Silas and Timothy in Berea (see Ac 17:14).

3. Paul sent word back, instructing Silas and Timothy to come to him in Athens (see Ac 17:15; see also note on 1Th 3:1–2).

4. Timothy rejoined Paul at Athens and was sent back to Thessalonica (see 3:1–5). Since Silas is not mentioned, it has been conjectured that he went back to Philippi when Timothy went to Thessalonica (see note on 3:1–2).

5. Paul moved on to Corinth (see Ac 18:1).

6. Silas and Timothy came to Paul in Corinth (see 3:6; Ac 18:5).

7. Paul wrote 1 Thessalonians and sent it to the church.

8. About six months later (A.D. 51/52) he sent 2 Thessalonians in response to further information about the church there.

AUTHOR, DATE AND PLACE OF WRITING

C Both external and internal evidence (see 1:1; 2:18) support the view that Paul wrote 1 Thessalonians (from Corinth; see note on 3:1–2). Early church writers are agreed on the matter, with testimonies beginning as early as A.D. 140 (Marcion). Paul's known characteristics are apparent in the letter (3:1–2,8–11 compared with Ac 15:36; 2Co 11:28). Historical allusions in the book fit Paul's life as recounted in Acts and in his own letters (2:14–16 compared with Ac 17:5–10; 3:6 compared with Ac 17:16). In the face of such evidence, few have ever rejected authorship by Paul.

B This epistle is generally dated c. A.D. 51 (see chart, p. 1855). Weighty support for this date was found in an inscription discovered at Delphi, Greece (see map No. 13 at the end of this study Bible), that dates Gallio's proconsulship to c. 51–52 and thus places Paul at Corinth at the same time (see Ac 18:12–17 and note on 18:12; see also chart, p. 1830). Except for the possibility of an early date for Galatians (48–49?), 1 Thessalonians is Paul's earliest canonical letter.

THESSALONICA: THE CITY AND THE CHURCH

Thessalonica was a bustling seaport city at the head of the Thermaic Gulf (see map, p. 1869). It was an important communication and trade center, located at the junction of the great Egnatian Way and the road leading north to the Danube. It was the largest city in Macedonia and was also the capital of its province.

The background of the Thessalonian church is found in Ac 17:1–9. Since Paul began his ministry there in the Jewish synagogue, it is reasonable to assume that the new church included some Jews. However, 1:9–10 and Ac 17:4 seem to indicate that the church was largely Gentile in membership.

PURPOSE

Paul had left Thessalonica abruptly (see Ac 17:5–10) after a rather brief stay. Recent converts from paganism (1:9) were thus left with little external support in the midst of persecution. Paul's purpose in writing this letter was to encourage the new converts in their trials (3:3–5), to give instruction concerning godly living (4:1–12) and to give assurance concerning the future of believers who die before Christ returns (4:13–18; see Theme below; see also notes on 4:13,15).

THEME

Although the thrust of the letter is varied (see Purpose), the subject of eschatology (doctrine of the last things) seems to be predominant in both Thessalonian letters. Every chapter of 1 Thessalonians ends with a reference to the second coming of Christ, with ch. 4 giving it major consideration (1:9–10; 2:19–20; 3:13; 4:13–18; 5:23–24). Thus, the second coming seems to permeate the letter and may be viewed in some sense as its theme. The two letters are often designated as the eschatological letters of Paul.

OUTLINE

I. Thanksgiving for the Thessalonians (ch. 1)
   A. The Grounds for Thanksgiving (1:1–4)
   B. The Genuineness of the Grounds (1:5–10)
II. Defense of the Apostolic Actions and Absence (chs. 2–3)
   A. Defense of the Apostolic Actions (2:1–16)
   B. Defense of the Apostolic Absence (2:17—3:10)
   C. The Prayer (3:11–13)
III. Exhortations to the Thessalonians (4:1—5:22)
   A. Primarily concerning Personal Life (4:1–12)
   B. Concerning the Coming of Christ (4:13—5:11)
   C. Primarily concerning Church Life (5:12–22)
IV. Concluding Prayer, Greetings and Benediction (5:23–28)

1

Paul, Silas[a][a] and Timothy, [b]

To the church of the Thessalonians[c] in God the Father and the Lord Jesus Christ: Grace and peace to you. [d]

THANKSGIVING FOR THE THESSALONIANS' FAITH

[2]We always thank God for all of you[e] and continually mention you in our prayers. [f][3]We remember before our God and Father[g] your work produced by faith, [h] your labor prompted by love, [i] and your endurance inspired by hope[j] in our Lord Jesus Christ.

[4]For we know, brothers and sisters loved by God, [k] that he has chosen you, [5]because our gospel[l] came to you not simply with words but also with power, [m] with the Holy Spirit and deep conviction. You know[n] how we lived among you for your sake. [6]You became imitators of us[o] and of the Lord, for you welcomed the message in the midst of severe suffering[p] with the joy[q] given by the Holy Spirit. [r] [7]And so you became a model[s] to all the believers in Macedonia[t] and Achaia. [u] [8]The Lord's message[v] rang out from you not only in Macedonia and Achaia—your faith in God has become known everywhere. [w] Therefore we do not need to say anything about it, [9]for they themselves report what happened when we visited you. They tell how you turned[x] to God from idols[y] to serve the living and true God, [z] [10]and to wait for his Son from heaven, [a] whom he raised from the dead[b]— Jesus, who rescues us from the coming wrath. [c]

PAUL'S MINISTRY IN THESSALONICA

2

You know, brothers and sisters, that our visit to you[d] was not without results. [e] [2]We had previously suffered[f] and been treated outrageously in Philippi, [g] as you know, but with the help of our God we dared to tell you his gospel in the face of strong opposition. [h] [3]For the appeal we make does not spring from error or impure mo-

---

[a] 1 Greek *Silvanus*, a variant of *Silas*

1:1 *aS Ac 15:22*
bS Ac 16:1; 2Th 1:1
cS Ac 17:1 dS Ro 1:7
1:2 *eS Ro 1:8;*
Eph 5:20 *fS Ro 1:10*
1:3 *gS Php 4:20*
hGal 5:6; 2Th 1:11;
Jas 2:14-26 *iTh 3:6;*
2Th 1:3; S 1Co 13:13
/ Ro 8:25
1:4 *kCol 3:12;*
2Th 2:13
1:5 *lS 2Co 2:12;*
2Th 2:14 *mRo 1:16;*
S Ro 15:13 *nTh 2:10*
1:6 *oS 1Co 4:16*
pAc 17:5-10
qS 2Co 6:10
rAc 13:52
1:7 *sS 1Ti 4:12*
tS Ac 16:9
uS Ac 18:12
1:8 *v2Th 3:1*
wRo 1:8
1:9 *xAc 14:15*
y1Co 12:2; Gal 4:8
zS Mt 16:16
1:10 *aS 1Co 1:7*
bS Ac 2:24 cS Ro 1:18
2:1 *d1Th 1:5, 9*
e2Th 1:10
2:2 *fAc 14:19; 16:22;*
Php 1:30 *gS Ac 16:12*
hAc 17:1-9

AC **1:1** *Paul.* See note on Ro 1:1. *Silas.* See note on Ac 15:22. He accompanied Paul on most of his second missionary journey. *Timothy.* See Introduction to 1 Timothy: Recipient. Both he and Silas helped Paul found the Thessalonian church (see Ac 17:1–14). *in.* Indicates the vital union and living relationship that Christians have with the Father and the Son (see Jn 14:23; 17:21). The close connection between the Father and the Son points to the Trinitarian relationship (see 3:11; 2Th 1:2,8,12; 2:16; 3:5). *Lord Jesus Christ.* Occurs also at the end of this letter (5:28). For the meanings of "Lord," "Jesus" and "Christ," see TNIV text notes on Mt 1:1,21; see also notes on Lk 2:11; Ro 10:9; 1Co 12:3; Php 2:9–11. *Grace and peace.* See note on Ro 1:7.
1:2 *thank.* See note on Php 1:3–4.

A **1:3** The triad of faith, hope and love is found often in the NT (5:8; Ro 5:2–5; 1Co 13:13; Gal 5:5–6; Col 1:4–5; Heb 6:10–12; 10:22–24; 1Pe 1:3–8,21–22). *work produced by faith.* Faith produces action (see Ro 1:5; 16:26; Gal 5:6 and note; 2Th 1:11; Jas 2:14–26). *hope.* Not unfounded wishful thinking but firm confidence in our Lord Jesus Christ and his return (v. 10). See Heb 6:18–20 and notes on Ro 5:5; Col 1:5.
1:4 *know.* The reasons for Paul's conviction regarding their election are stated in vv. 5–10. *brothers and sisters.* United to each other through union with Christ (see note on Ro 1:13). This phrase (including its singular form) is used 28 times in the two letters to the Thessalonians. *loved ... chosen.* Both words speak of God's electing love (see Col 3:12 and note; 2Th 2:13; see also note on Eph 1:4).
1:5 *our gospel.* The gospel preached by Paul, Silas and Timothy (see Ro 16:25 and note). It is first of all God the Father's (2:8), because he originated it, and Christ's (3:2), because it springs from his atoning death. *power.* The power that delivered them from spiritual bondage. That power is of the Holy Spirit (see Ro 15:13,18–19; 1Co 2:4–5), but it also resides in the gospel itself (see Ro 1:16). *deep conviction.* Such conviction, on the part of both the preachers and the Thessalonians, was also of the Holy Spirit.

A **1:6** *imitators.* The order in Christian imitation: (1) Believers in Macedonia and Achaia imitated the Thessalonians (v. 7), just as the Thessalonians imitated the churches in Judea (2:14); (2) the Thessalonians imitated Paul, just as the Corinthians did (1Co 4:6; 11:1) and just as all believers were to imitate their leaders (2Th 3:7,9; 1Ti 4:12; Tit 2:7; 1Pe 5:3); (3) Paul imitated Christ (1Co 11:1), as did the Thessalonians (here); (4) all were to imitate God (Eph 5:1). *severe suffering.* Such as recorded in Ac 17:5–14 (see also 1Th 2:14).
1:7 *Macedonia and Achaia.* The two Roman provinces into which Greece was then divided (see Ac 19:21; Ro 15:26; see also map, p. 2031). *Macedonia.* See note on Php 4:15.
1:8 *everywhere.* In every place they visited or knew about (see Ro 1:8 and note; 1Co 1:2; 2Co 2:14; 1Ti 2:8). The news spread because of Thessalonica's strategic location (see Introduction: Thessalonica: The City and the Church).

A **1:9–10** Three marks of true conversion: (1) turning from idols, (2) serving God and (3) waiting for Christ to return. In his two short letters to the Thessalonians, Paul speaks much about the second coming of Christ (v. 10; 2:19; 3:13; 4:13—5:4; 2Th 1:7–10; 2:1–12).
1:10 *wrath.* See note on Ro 1:18. Some see a reference here to the final judgment (see 2:16; Ro 2:5 and notes), while others think it refers to a future period of tribulation (described in Rev 6–18).

A **2:1–12** A manual for a minister: 1. His message is God's good news ("gospel," v. 2). 2. His motive is not impurity (v. 3), pleasing people (v. 4), greed (v. 5) or seeking praise from people (v. 6), but pleasing God (v. 4). 3. His manner is not one of trickery (v. 3), flattery (v. 5) or a cover-up (v. 5), but of courage (v. 2), gentleness (v. 7), love (vv. 8,11), toil (v. 9) and holiness (v. 10).
2:1 *You know.* The local church could refute the accusation of insincerity that evidently had been leveled against Paul (v. 3).
2:2 *treated outrageously.* Paul was deeply hurt by the way he had been treated in the city of Philippi (see Ac 16:19–40).

tives, ⁱ nor are we trying to trick you. J ⁴On the contrary, we speak as those approved by God to be entrusted with the gospel. ᵏ We are not trying to please people ᶦ but God, who tests our hearts. ᵐ ⁵You know we never used flattery, nor did we put on a mask to cover up greed ⁿ—God is our witness. ᵒ ⁶We were not looking for praise from any human being, ᵖ not from you or anyone else, even though as apostles q of Christ we could have asserted our prerogatives. ʳ ⁷Instead, we were like young children among you.

Just as a nursing mother cares for her children, ˢ ⁸so we cared for you. Because we loved you so much, we were delighted to share with you not only the gospel of God ᵗ but our lives as well. ᵘ ⁹Surely you remember, brothers and sisters, our toil and hardship; we worked ᵛ night and day in order not to be a burden to anyone ʷ while we preached the gospel of God to you.

¹⁰You are witnesses, ˣ and so is God, ʸ of how holy, ᶻ righteous and blameless we were among you who believed. ¹¹For you know that we dealt with each of you as a father deals with his own children, ᵃ ¹²encouraging, comforting and urging you to live lives worthy ᵇ of God, who calls ᶜ you into his kingdom and glory.

¹³And we also thank God continually ᵈ because, when you received the word of God, ᵉ which you heard from us, you accepted it not as a human word, but as it actually is, the word of God, which is indeed at work in you who believe. ¹⁴For you, brothers and sisters, became imitators ᶠ of God's churches in Judea, ᵍ which are in Christ Jesus: You suffered from your fellow citizens ʰ the same things those churches suffered from the Jews, ¹⁵who killed the Lord Jesus ⁱ and the prophets J and also drove us out. They displease God and are hostile to everyone ¹⁶in their effort to keep us from speaking to the Gentiles ᵏ so that they may be saved. In this way they always heap up their sins to the limit. ᶦ The wrath of God has come upon them at last. ᵃ

PAUL'S LONGING TO SEE THE THESSALONIANS

¹⁷But, brothers and sisters, when we were orphaned by being separated from you for a short time (in person, not in thought), ᵐ out of our intense longing we made every effort to see you. ⁿ ¹⁸For we wanted to come to you—certainly I, Paul, did, again and again— but Satan ᵒ blocked our way. ᵖ ¹⁹For what is our hope, our joy, or the crown q in which we will glory ʳ in the presence of our Lord Jesus when he comes? ˢ Is it not you? ²⁰Indeed, you are our glory ᵗ and joy.

3 So when we could stand it no longer, ᵘ we thought it best to be left by ourselves in Athens. ᵛ ²We sent Timothy, ʷ who is our brother and co-worker ˣ in God's service in spreading the gospel of Christ, ʸ to strengthen and encourage you in your

---

ᵃ 16 Or *them fully*

2:3 *trick.* The Greek for this word was originally used of a lure for catching fish; it came to be used of any sort of cunning used for profit.
2:4 *our hearts.* Not simply our emotions, but also our intellects and wills (see note on Ps 4:7).
2:5 *mask to cover up greed.* Personal profit was never Paul's aim (see Ac 20:33).
2:6 *apostles.* See note on Mk 6:30. *our prerogatives.* Apostles were entitled to be supported by the church (see 1Co 9:3–14; 2Co 11:7–11). Paul did not always take advantage of the right but insisted that he had it.
2:7 *as a nursing mother.* See v. 11, where Paul also applies the metaphor of a father to himself.
2:9 *toil and hardship.* Greeks despised manual labor and viewed it as fit only for slaves, but Paul was not ashamed of doing any sort of work that would help further the gospel. He did not want to be unduly dependent on others (see 2Th 3:8).
2:11 *as a father.* See note on v. 7.
2:12 *live lives worthy of God.* See Eph 4:1. *calls.* See notes on 1:4; Ro 8:28. *kingdom.* The chief subject of Jesus' teaching. Paul did not use this term often but used it once to sum up the message of his preaching (see notes on Mt 3:2; Lk 4:43; Ac 20:25; cf. Ac 28:31). *glory.* God's splendor and majesty revealed to us at the consummation of his kingdom (see Mk 8:38; Ro 5:2; 8:18; cf. Eze 43:2 and note; 1Jn 3:2).
2:13 *not as a human word.* Not tailored to fit the popular knowledge of the day.
2:14 *imitators.* See note on 1:6. *You suffered from your fellow*

citizens. At the time of Paul's initial visit to Thessalonica, persecution instigated by the Jews apparently was carried out by Gentiles (see Ac 17:5–9). *Jews.* Although Paul had great love and deep concern for the salvation of those of his own race (see Ro 9:1–3; 10:1), he did not fail to rebuke harshly Jews who persecuted the church.
2:15 *prophets.* Throughout OT history, Israelites had persecuted their prophets (cf. Ac 7:52). *drove us out.* See Ac 9:23–25,29– 30; 13:50–51; 14:5–6,19; 17:10,13–14.
2:16 *wrath of God has come.* The eschatological wrath, the final outpouring of God's anger upon sinful humanity (see 1:10 and note). It is spoken of as already present, either because it had been partially experienced by the Jews or because of its absolute certainty.
2:17 *orphaned.* Paul is like a mother (v. 7), a father (v. 11) and now an orphan.
2:18 *Satan blocked our way.* Cf. Introduction to Job: Theme and Message; cf. also note on Eph 1:3.
2:19 *crown.* Not a royal crown, but a wreath used on festive occasions or as the prize in the Greek games (see 2Ti 4:8 and note; Jas 1:12; 1Pe 5:4; Rev 2:10 and note). *when he comes.* See 3:13; 4:15; 5:23; 2Th 2:1,8. The expression was used regarding the arrival of a great person, as on a royal visit.
2:20 *you are our glory and joy.* True both now (cf. Php 4:1) and when Christ returns.
3:1–2 Paul first went to Athens alone, then sent to Berea for Silas and Timothy (Ac 17:14–15). It is not clear whether Silas, as instructed (Ac 17:15), came to Athens with Timothy. However,

faith, ³so that no one would be unsettled by these trials. ᶻ You know quite well that we are destined for them. ᵃ ⁴In fact, when we were with you, we kept telling you that we would be persecuted. And it turned out that way, as you well know. ᵇ ⁵For this reason, when I could stand it no longer, ᶜ I sent to find out about your faith. ᵈ I was afraid that in some way the tempter ᵉ had tempted you and that our labors might have been in vain. ᶠ

TIMOTHY'S ENCOURAGING REPORT

⁶But Timothy ᵍ has just now come to us from you ʰ and has brought good news about your faith and love. ⁱ He has told us that you always have pleasant memories of us and that you long to see us, just as we also long to see you. ʲ ⁷Therefore, brothers and sisters, in all our distress and persecution we were encouraged about you because of your faith. ⁸For now we really live, since you are standing firm ᵏ in the Lord. ⁹How can we thank God enough for you ˡ in return for all the joy we have in the presence of our God because of you? ᵐ ¹⁰Night and day we pray ⁿ most earnestly that we may see you again ᵒ and supply what is lacking in your faith.

¹¹Now may our God and Father ᵖ himself and our Lord Jesus clear the way for us to come to you. ¹²May the Lord make your love increase and overflow for each other �q and for everyone else, just as ours does for you. ¹³May he strengthen your hearts so that you will be blameless ʳ and holy in the presence of our God and Father ˢ when our Lord Jesus comes ᵗ with all his holy ones. ᵘ

LIVING TO PLEASE GOD

4 As for other matters, brothers and sisters, ᵛ we instructed you how to live ʷ in order to please God, ˣ as in fact you are living. Now we ask you and urge you in the Lord Jesus to do this more and more. ²For you know what instructions we gave you by the authority of the Lord Jesus.

³It is God's will ʸ that you should be sanctified: that you should avoid sexual immorality; ᶻ ⁴that each of you should learn to control your own body ᵃᵃ in a way that is holy and

---

ᵃ 4 Or *learn to live with his own wife;* or *learn to acquire a wife*

3:3 ᶻ Mk 4:17;
Jn 16:33; Ro 5:3;
2Co 1:4; 4:17; 2Ti 3:12
ᵃ S Ac 9:16; 14:22
3:4 ᵇ 1Th 2:14
3:5 ᶜ ver 1 ᵈ ver 2
ᵉ Mt 4:3 ᶠ Gal 2:2;
Php 2:16
3:6 ᵍ S Ac 16:1
ʰ Ac 18:5 ⁱ 1Th 1:3
ʲ 1Th 2:17,18
3:8 ᵏ S 1Co 16:13
3:9 ˡ 1Th 1:2
ᵐ 1Th 2:19,20
3:10 ⁿ 2Ti 1:3
ᵒ 1Th 2:17
3:11 ᵖ ver 13;
S Php 4:20
3:12 q Php 1:9;
1Th 4:9,10; 2Th 1:3
3:13 ʳ Ps 15:2;
1Co 1:8; Php 2:15;
1Th 5:23; 1Ti 6:14;
2Pe 3:14 ˢ ver 11;
S Php 4:20
ᵗ S 1Th 2:19
ᵘ Mt 25:31; 2Th 1:7
4:1 ᵛ 2Co 13:11;
2Th 3:1 ʷ S Eph 4:1
ˣ S 2Co 5:9
4:3 ʸ S Eph 5:17
ᶻ S 1Co 6:18
4:4 ᵃᵃ 1Co 7:2,9

---

when Timothy later returned from Thessalonica to Paul, who was now at Corinth, Silas came with him (Ac 18:5). See Introduction: Background of the Thessalonian Letters.

3:1 *we.* An editorial "we," referring to Paul alone.

3:2 *co-worker in God's service.* A striking way of viewing Christian service, found also in 1Co 3:9. *gospel of Christ.* See notes on 1:5; Mk 1:1. *strengthen.* In Greek classical literature the word was generally used in the literal sense of putting a buttress into a building. In the NT it is mainly used figuratively, as here.

🅰 **3:3** *trials.* The opposition and persecution suffered by the Thessalonian converts. *we are destined for them.* Christians must expect troubles (see Mk 4:17; Jn 16:33; Ac 14:22; Php 1:29; 2Ti 3:12; cf. 1Pe 2:21 and note), but these are not disasters, for they advance God's purposes (see Ac 11:19; Ro 5:3; 2Co 1:4; 4:17 and note).

🅰🅲 **3:5** *I.* Paul uses the Greek emphatic pronoun (elsewhere used only in 2:18) to bring out his deep concern. *tempter.* Satan is spoken of in every major division of the NT. He is supreme among evil spirits (see Jn 12:31; 16:11; Eph 2:2). His activities can affect the physical (see 2Co 12:7) and the spiritual (see Mt 13:39; Mk 4:15; 2Co 4:4 and note). He tempted Jesus (Mt 4:1–11) and continues to tempt Jesus' servants (see Lk 22:3; 1Co 7:5). He hinders missionary work (2:18). But he has already been defeated (see Mt 12:29; Col 2:15 and note), and Christians need not be overwhelmed by him (see Eph 6:16). His final overthrow is certain (see Rev 20:10).

🅰 **3:6** *brought good news.* The only place where the Greek for this phrase is used by Paul for anything other than the gospel. Three things caused him joy: (1) "your faith"—a right attitude toward God; (2) "your...love"—a right attitude toward others; (3) "you long to see us"—a right attitude toward Paul.

🅰 **3:9** *thank God.* The preceding shows that Paul's work of evangelism had been effective. He might have congratulated himself on work well done, but instead he thanked God for the joy he had from what God had done.

3:10 *Night and day.* Not prayer at two set times, but frequent prayer (see 1:2–3). *most earnestly.* Translates a strong and unusual Greek compound word (found elsewhere in the NT only in 5:13; Eph 3:20) that brings out Paul's passionate longing. *what is lacking.* Some of the things lacking were of a practical nature, such as moral (4:1–12) and disciplinary matters (5:12–24). Others were doctrinal, such as confusion over Christ's return (4:13—5:11). *your faith.* The fifth time in the chapter that Paul speaks of their faith (see vv. 2,5–7).

3:11 In the middle of a letter Paul frequently breaks into prayer (e.g., Eph 1:15–23; 3:14–21; Php 1:9–11; Col 1:9–12). For the link between Father and Son, see note on 1:1.

3:12 *Lord.* In Paul's writings this usually means Jesus rather than the Father.

3:13 *strengthen.* See note on v. 2. *holy.* The basic idea is "set apart [for God]" (see notes on Ex 3:5; Lev 11:44; Ro 6:22; Eph 1:1). Here it refers to the completed process of sanctification (see note on 1Co 1:2). *holy ones.* Used of the saints (Christians) in many NT passages (see note on Ro 1:7). Here it may mean the departed saints who will return with Jesus, the angels (see Mk 8:38) or, more probably, both.

4:1 *live.* Lit. "walk." Paul uses this metaphor often of the Christian way (see Ro 6:4; 2Co 5:7; Eph 4:1; 5:15; Col 1:10, "live a life"; 2:6; 4:5, "act"). It points to steady progress. *we ask you and urge you.* Paul is not arrogant, but he does speak with authority in the Lord Jesus. He has the "mind of Christ" (1Co 2:16).

4:2 *instructions.* Used of authoritative commands and has a military ring ("orders," Ac 5:28; 16:24).

🅰 **4:3** *sanctified.* See note on 3:13. *sexual immorality.* In the first century moral standards were generally very low, and chastity was regarded as an unreasonable restriction. Paul, however, would not compromise God's clear and demanding standards. The warning was needed, for Christians were not immune to the temptation (see 1Co 5:1).

4:5 *b* Ro 1:26
c Eph 4:17 *d* S Gal 4:8
4:6 *e* Lev 25:17;
1Co 6:8 *f* Dt 32:35;
Ps 94:1; Ro 2:5-11;
12:19; Heb 10:30,31
g Heb 13:4
4:7 *h* Lev 11:44;
1Pe 1:15
4:8 *i* Eze 36:27;
Ro 5:5; 2Co 1:22;
Gal 4:6; 1Jn 3:24
4:9 *j* S Ro 12:10
k 1Th 5:1 *l* S Jn 6:45
m S Jn 13:34
4:10 *n* S Ac 16:9
o S 1Th 3:12
4:11 *p* Eph 4:28;
2Th 3:10-12
4:12 *q* S Mk 4:11
4:13 *r* S Ro 1:13
s S Mt 9:24 *t* Eph 2:12
4:14 *u* Ro 14:9;
1Co 15:3,4; 2Co 5:15
v 1Co 15:18
4:15 *w* S 1Co 1:7
x 1Co 15:52
4:16 *y* S Mt 16:27
z Jude 9 *a* S Mt 24:31
b 1Co 15:23; 2Th 2:1;
Rev 14:13
4:17 *c* 1Co 15:52
d Ac 1:9; S Ac 8:39;
S Rev 1:7; 11:12
e S Jn 12:26
4:18 *f* 1Th 5:11

honorable, ⁵not in passionate lust *b* like the pagans, *c* who do not know God; *d* ⁶and that in this matter no one should wrong or take advantage of a brother or sister. *e* The Lord will punish *f* all those who commit such sins, *g* as we told you and warned you before. ⁷For God did not call us to be impure, but to live a holy life. *h* ⁸Therefore, anyone who rejects this instruction does not reject a human being but God, the very God who gives you his Holy Spirit. *i*

⁹Now about your love for one another *j* we do not need to write to you, *k* for you yourselves have been taught by God *l* to love each other. *m* ¹⁰And in fact, you do love all the brothers and sisters throughout Macedonia. *n* Yet we urge you, dear friends, to do so more and more, *o* ¹¹and to make it your ambition to lead a quiet life: You should mind your own business and work with your hands, *p* just as we told you, ¹²so that your daily life may win the respect of outsiders *q* and so that you will not be dependent on anybody.

BELIEVERS WHO HAVE DIED

¹³Brothers and sisters, we do not want you to be uninformed *r* about those who sleep in death, *s* so that you do not grieve like the rest, who have no hope. *t* ¹⁴We believe that Jesus died and rose again, *u* and so we believe that God will bring with Jesus those who have fallen asleep in him. *v* ¹⁵According to the Lord's word, we tell you that we who are still alive, who are left till the coming of the Lord, *w* will certainly not precede those who have fallen asleep. *x* ¹⁶For the Lord himself will come down from heaven, *y* with a loud command, with the voice of the archangel *z* and with the trumpet call of God, *a* and the dead in Christ will rise first. *b* ¹⁷After that, we who are still alive and are left *c* will be caught up together with them in the clouds *d* to meet the Lord in the air. And so we will be with the Lord *e* forever. ¹⁸Therefore encourage one another *f* with these words.

4:5 *like the pagans.* See Ro 1:24–27. The Christian is to be different. *who do not know God.* See 2Th 1:8 and note; Ge 4:8; cf. Ps 79:6–7 and note.

4:6 *wrong . . . sister.* Sexual sin harms others besides those who engage in it. In adultery, e.g., the spouse is always wronged. Premarital sex wrongs the future partner by robbing him or her of the virginity that ought to be brought to marriage. *The Lord will punish.* A motive for chastity.

4:7 Another reason for chastity is God's call to holiness (see 1Pe 1:6; Heb 2:14 and notes)

4:8 *God who gives you his Holy Spirit.* Still another reason for chastity is that sexual sin is against God (see Ge 39:9 and note), who gives the Holy Spirit to believers for their sanctification. To live in sexual immorality is to reject God, specifically in regard to the Holy Spirit.

4:9 *love for one another.* Translates *philadelphia,* a Greek word that outside the NT almost without exception denoted the mutual love of children of the same father. In the NT it always means love of fellow believers in Christ, all of whom have the same heavenly Father. *taught by God.* Cf. Isa 54:13; Jn 6:45; 1Co 2:13.

4:11 *mind your own business.* Some Thessalonians, probably because of idleness, were taking undue interest in other people's affairs (see 2Th 3:11 and note). *work with your hands.* The Greeks in general thought manual labor degrading and fit only for slaves. Christians took seriously the need for earning their own living, but some of the Thessalonians, perhaps as a result of their belief in the imminent return of Christ (see 2Th 3:11), were neglecting work and relying on others to support them.

4:12 *not be dependent on anybody.* Or "have need of nothing." Both meanings are true and significant. Christians in need because of their idleness are not obedient Christians (cf. Tit 3:14).

4:13 *those who sleep in death.* For the Christian, sleep is a particularly apt metaphor for death, since death's finality and horror are removed by the assurance of resurrection. Some of the Thessalonians seem to have misunderstood Paul and thought all believers would live until Christ returns. When some died, the question arose, "Will those who have died have part in

that great day?" See note on v. 15. *who have no hope.* Inscriptions on tombs and references in literature show that first-century pagans viewed death with horror, as the end of everything. The Christian attitude was in strong contrast (see 1Co 15:55–57; Php 1:21–23).

4:14 *died.* Paul does not say that Christ "slept," perhaps to underscore the fact that he bore the full horror of death so that those who believe in him would not have to. *rose again.* For the importance of the resurrection, see 1Co 15, especially vv. 14,17–22. *those who have fallen asleep in him.* Believers who have died, trusting in Jesus.

4:15 *According to the Lord's word.* The doctrine mentioned here is not recorded in the Gospels and was either a direct revelation to Paul or something Jesus said that Christians passed on orally. *we who are still alive.* Those believers who will be alive when Christ returns. "We" does not necessarily mean that Paul thought that he would be alive then. He often identified himself with those he wrote to or about. Elsewhere he says that God will raise "us" at that time (1Co 6:14; 2Co 4:14). *will certainly not precede.* The Thessalonians had evidently been concerned that those among them who had died would miss their place in the great events when the Lord comes, and Paul assures them this will not be the case.

4:16 *the Lord himself.* See Ac 1:11. *archangel.* The only named archangel in the Bible is Michael (Jude 9; see Da 10:13). In Scripture, Gabriel is simply called an angel (Lk 1:19,26). *will rise first.* Before the ascension of believers mentioned in the next verse.

4:17 *we who are still alive.* See note on v. 15. *caught up.* The only place in the NT where a "rapture" (from the Latin Vulgate rendering) is clearly referred to. Some hold that this will be secret, but Paul seems to be describing something open and public, with loud voices and a trumpet blast. *in the clouds.* Cf. Ac 1:9 and note. *with the Lord.* The chief hope of the believer (see 5:10; Jn 14:3; 2Co 5:8; Php 1:23; Col 3:4).

4:18 *encourage one another.* The primary purpose of vv. 13–18 is not to give a chronology of future events, though that is involved, but to urge mutual encouragement, as shown here and in v. 13.

THE DAY OF THE LORD

5 Now, brothers and sisters, about times and dates *g* we do not need to write to you, *h* ²for you know very well that the day of the Lord *i* will come like a thief in the night. *j* ³While people are saying, "Peace and safety," *k* destruction will come on them suddenly, *l* as labor pains on a pregnant woman, and they will not escape. *m*

⁴But you, brothers and sisters, are not in darkness *n* so that this day should surprise you like a thief. *o* ⁵You are all children of the light *p* and children of the day. We do not belong to the night or to the darkness. ⁶So then, let us not be like others, who are asleep, *q* but let us be awake *r* and sober. *s* ⁷For those who sleep, sleep at night, and those who get drunk, get drunk at night. *t* ⁸But since we belong to the day, *u* let us be sober, putting on faith and love as a breastplate, *v* and the hope of salvation *w* as a helmet. *x* ⁹For God did not appoint us to suffer wrath *y* but to receive salvation through our Lord Jesus Christ. *z* ¹⁰He died for us so that, whether we are awake or asleep, we may live together with him. *a* ¹¹Therefore encourage one another *b* and build each other up, *c* just as in fact you are doing.

FINAL INSTRUCTIONS

¹²Now we ask you, brothers and sisters, to acknowledge those who work hard *d* among you, who care for you in the Lord *e* and who admonish you. ¹³Hold them in the highest regard in love because of their work. Live in peace with each other. *f* ¹⁴And we urge you, brothers and sisters, warn those who are idle *g* and disruptive, encourage the disheartened, help the weak, *h* be patient with everyone. ¹⁵Make sure that nobody pays back wrong for wrong, *i* but always strive to do what is good for each other *j* and for everyone else.

¹⁶Rejoice always, *k* ¹⁷pray continually, *l* ¹⁸give thanks in all circumstances; *m* for this is God's will for you in Christ Jesus.

5:1 *g* Ac 1:7
h 1Th 4:9
5:2 *i* S 1Co 1:8
j S Lk 12:39
5:3 *k* Jer 4:10; 6:14;
Eze 13:10 ¹ Job 15:21;
Ps 35:8; 55:15;
Isa 29:5; 47:9,11
m 2Th 1:9
5:4 *n* S Ac 26:18;
1Jn 2:8 *o* ver 2
5:5 *p* S Lk 16:8
5:6 *q* Ro 13:11
r S Mt 25:13
s S Ac 24:25
5:7 *t* Ac 2:15;
Ro 13:13; 2Pe 2:13
5:8 *u* ver 5
v S Eph 6:14
w Ro 8:24 *x* Isa 59:17;
Eph 6:17
5:9 *y* 1Th 1:10
z 2Th 2:13,14
5:10 *a* Ro 14:9;
2Co 5:15
5:11 *b* 1Th 4:18
c Eph 4:29
5:12 *d* Ro 16:6,12;
1Co 15:10 *e* 1Ti 5:17;
Heb 13:17
5:13 *f* S Mk 9:50
5:14 *g* 2Th 3:6,7,11
h Ro 14:1; 1Co 8:7-12
5:15 *i* Ro 12:17;
1Pe 3:9 *j* Eph 4:32
5:16 *k* Php 4:4
5:17 *l* S Lk 18:1
5:18 *m* S Eph 5:20

5:1 *times and dates.* See Ac 1:6–7. There have always been some Christians who try to fix the date of our Lord's return, but apparently the Thessalonians were not among them.

5:2 *day of the Lord.* See 1Co 5:5. The expression goes back to Am 5:18 (see note there). In the OT it is a time when God will come and intervene with judgment and/or blessing (see note on Joel 1:15). In the NT the thought of judgment continues (see Ro 2:5; 2Pe 2:9), but it is also the "day of redemption" (Eph 4:30); the "day of God" (2Pe 3:12) or of Christ (1Co 1:8; Php 1:6); and the "last day" (Jn 6:39), the "great Day" (Jude 6) or simply "the day" (2Th 1:10). It is the consummation of all things. There will be some preliminary signs (e.g., 2Th 2:3), but for unbelievers the coming will be as unexpected as that of a thief in the night (cf. Mt 24:43–44; Lk 12:39–40; 2Pe 3:10; Rev 3:3; 16:15).

5:3 *destruction.* Not annihilation, but exclusion from the Lord's presence (see 2Th 1:9 and note); thus the ruin of life and all its proud accomplishments. *suddenly.* Paul stresses the surprise of unbelievers. He uses a word found elsewhere in the NT only in Lk 21:34. *labor pains.* Here the idea is not the pain of childbirth so much as the suddenness and inevitability of such pains. *not.* An emphatic double negative in the Greek, a construction Paul uses only four times in all his writings.

5:4 *darkness.* Believers no longer live in darkness, nor are they of the darkness (v. 5). See Ac 26:18; 2Co 6:14; see also 1Jn 1:5–7 and notes. *thief.* See note on v. 2.

5:5 *children of ... children of.* Echoes Hebrew idiom, in which to be the "children of" a quality meant to be characterized by that quality. Christians do not simply live in the light; they are characterized by light.

5:6 *asleep.* Unbelievers are spiritually insensitive, but this kind of sleep is not for "children of the light." *be awake.* Lit. "watch," which is in keeping with the emphasis Paul is placing on Christ's coming (cf. Mt 24:42–43; 25:13; Mk 13:34–37). *sober.* A contrast with the conduct mentioned in v. 7.

5:8 *the day.* A reference to the light that characterizes Christians; perhaps it refers also to the coming of Christ (see v. 2 and note). *breastplate ... helmet.* Paul also uses the metaphor of armor in Ro 13:12; 2Co 6:7; 10:4; Eph 6:13–17 (see notes on Eph 6:14,17). He does not consistently attach a particular virtue to each piece of armor; it is the general idea of equipment for battle that is pictured. For the triad of faith, hope and love, see 1:3 and note.

5:9 *appoint.* God's appointment, not human choice, is the significant thing. *wrath.* See note on 1:10. *salvation.* Our final, completed salvation.

5:10 *are awake or asleep.* That is, live or die; or, if the sense is moral, are alert or carnal (see v. 6). *with him.* To be Christ's is to have entered a relationship that nothing can destroy.

5:11 *build ... up.* The verb basically applies to building houses, but Paul frequently uses it for Christians being edified.

5:12 *those who work hard among you.* Not much is known about the organization and leadership of the church at this period, but the reference is possibly to elders (cf. Heb 13:7,17 and notes).

5:13 *because of their work.* Not merely because of personal attachment or respect for their high position, but in appreciation for their work. *Live in peace.* The words apply to Christian relationships in general, but here they probably refer especially to right relations between leaders and those under them (cf. Ro 14:17,19).

5:14 *those who are idle.* It seems that some Thessalonians were so sure the second coming was close that they had given up their jobs in order to prepare for it, but Paul says they should work (see 2Th 3:10–11 and notes). *the disheartened ... the weak.* These are to be helped, not rejected, by the strong (cf. Ro 14:1–15; 1Co 8:13 and note).

5:15 *pays back.* Retaliation is never a Christian option (cf. Ro 12:17 and note). Christians are called to forgive (see Mt 5:38–42; 18:21–35).

5:16 See Php 4:4 and note.

5:17 For the practice of continual (or regular) prayer, see 1:3; 2:13; Ro 1:9–10; Eph 6:18; Col 1:3; 2Ti 1:3.

5:18 *give thanks.* See Eph 5:20 and note.

5:19 ⁿ Eph 4:30
5:20 ᵒ1Co 14:1-40
5:21 ᴾ1Co 14:29;
1Jn 4:1 �q Ro 12:9
5:23 ʳ S Ro 15:33
ˢ Heb 4:12 ᵗ S 1Th 3:13
ᵘ S 1Th 2:19
5:24 ᵛ S Ro 8:28
ʷ S 1Co 1:9
ˣ Nu 23:19; Php 1:6
5:25 ʸ Eph 6:19;
Col 4:3; 2Th 3:1;
Heb 13:18
5:26 ᶻ S Ro 16:16
5:27 ᵃ 2Th 3:14;
S 1Ti 4:13
5:28 ᵇ S Ro 16:20

¹⁹Do not put out the Spirit's fire. ⁿ ²⁰Do not treat prophecies ᵒ with contempt ²¹but test them all; ᴾ hold on to what is good, q ²²reject whatever is harmful.

²³May God himself, the God of peace, ʳ sanctify you through and through. May your whole spirit, soul ˢ and body be kept blameless ᵗ at the coming of our Lord Jesus Christ. ᵘ ²⁴The one who calls ᵛ you is faithful, ʷ and he will do it. ˣ

²⁵Brothers and sisters, pray for us. ʸ ²⁶Greet all God's people with a holy kiss. ᶻ ²⁷I charge you before the Lord to have this letter read to all the brothers and sisters. ᵃ

²⁸The grace of our Lord Jesus Christ be with you. ᵇ

5:19 *Spirit's fire.* There is a warmth, a glow, about the Spirit's presence that makes this language appropriate. The kind of conduct Paul is opposing may include loafing, immorality and the other sins he has denounced. On the other hand, he may be warning against a mechanical attitude toward worship that discourages the expression of the gifts of the Spirit in the local assembly (see v. 20).

5:20 *prophecies.* For the gift of prophecy, see Ro 12:6; 1Co 12:10, 28 and note on 12:10; 13:2; 14; Eph 4:11. For the function of prophecies, see 1Co 14:3.

5:21 *test them all.* The approval of prophecy (v. 20) does not mean that anyone who claims to speak in the name of the Lord is to be accepted without question. Paul does not say what specific tests are to be applied, but he is clear that every teaching must be tested—surely his audience must be in agreement with his gospel.

5:23 A typical prayer. *God of peace.* A fitting reference to God in view of vv. 12–15. But Paul often refers to God in this way near the end of his letters (see Ro 1:7 and note; 15:33; 16:20; 1Co

14:33; 2Co 13:11; Php 4:9; cf. 2Th 3:16). See also Heb 13:20–21. *sanctify.* See 1Co 1:2 and note. *your whole spirit, soul and body.* Paul emphasizes the whole person without attempting to differentiate various parts (see Heb 4:12 and note).

5:24 Paul's confidence rests in the nature of God (cf. Ge 18:25 and note), who can be relied upon to complete what he begins (see Nu 23:19; Php 1:6 and notes).

5:26 *all.* Paul sent a warm greeting to everyone, even those he had corrected. *holy kiss.* A kiss was a normal greeting of that day, similar to our modern handshake (see Ro 16:16; 1Co 16:20; 2Co 13:12 and notes; cf. "kiss of love," 1Pe 5:14).

5:27 *I charge you.* Surprisingly strong language, meaning "I put you on oath"—used only here in the NT. Paul clearly wanted every member of the church to read or hear his letter and to know of his concern and advice for them.

5:28 Paul always ended his letters with a benediction of grace for his readers, sometimes adding other blessings, as in 2Co 13:14. *grace.* See note on Ro 1:7. *Lord Jesus Christ.* See note on 1:1. *with you.* See note on 2Co 13:14.

2 THESSALONIANS

INTRODUCTION

AUTHOR, DATE AND PLACE OF WRITING

C Paul's authorship of 2 Thessalonians has been questioned more often than that of 1 Thessalonians, in spite of the fact that it has more support from early Christian writers. Objections are based on internal factors rather than on the adequacy of the statements of the church fathers. It is thought that there are differences in the vocabulary (ten words not used elsewhere), in the style (it is said to be unexpectedly formal) and in the eschatology (the doctrine of the "man of lawlessness" is not taught elsewhere). However, such arguments have not convinced current interpreters. A majority still hold to Paul's authorship of 2 Thessalonians.

Because of its similarity to 1 Thessalonians, this epistle must have been written not long after the first letter—perhaps about six months. The situation in the church seems to have been much the same. Paul probably penned it (see 1:1; 3:17) c. A.D. 51 or 52 in Corinth, after Silas and Timothy had returned from delivering 1 Thessalonians (see chart, p. 1855; see also Introduction to 1 Thessalonians).

PURPOSE

Inasmuch as the situation in the Thessalonian church has not changed substantially, Paul's purpose in writing is very much the same as in his first letter to its members. He writes (1) to encourage persecuted believers (1:4–10), (2) to correct a misunderstanding concerning the Lord's return (2:1–12) and (3) to exhort the Thessalonians to be steadfast and to work for a living (2:13—3:15).

THEME

Like 1 Thessalonians, this letter deals extensively with eschatology (see Introduction to 1 Thessalonians: Theme). In fact, in 2 Thessalonians 18 out of 47 verses deal with this subject.

OUTLINE

I. Introduction (ch. 1)
   A. Greetings (1:1–2)
   B. Thanksgiving for the Thessalonians' Faith, Love and Perseverance (1:3–10)
   C. Intercession for Their Spiritual Progress (1:11–12)
II. Instruction (ch. 2)
   A. Prophecy regarding the Day of the Lord (2:1–12)
   B. Thanksgiving for Their Election and Calling (Their Position) (2:13–15)
   C. Prayer for Their Service and Testimony (Their Practice) (2:16–17)
III. Injunctions (ch. 3)
   A. Call to Prayer (3:1–5)
   B. Charge to Discipline the Disorderly and Lazy (3:6–15)
   C. Conclusion, Final Greetings and Benediction (3:16–18)

KEY   **A** APPLICATION FOR LIVING   **B** BACKGROUND NOTES   **C** CHARACTER INFORMATION

1:1 *a* S Ac 15:22
b S Ac 16:1; 1Th 1:1
c S Ac 17:1
1:2 *d* S Ro 1:7
1:3 *e* S Ro 1:8;
Eph 5:20 *f* S 1Th 3:12
1:4 *g* 2Co 7:14
h 1Th 1:3 *i* 1Th 1:6;
2:14; S 3:3
1:5 *j* Php 1:28
k Lk 20:35
1:6 *l* Lk 18:7,8
m Ro 12:19; Col 3:25;
S Rev 6:10
1:7 *n* S Lk 17:30
o Heb 10:27; S 12:29;
2Pe 3:7; S Rev 1:14
p Jude 14
1:8 *q* Ps 79:6;
Isa 66:15; Jer 10:25
r S Gal 4:8 *s* Ro 2:8;
S 2Co 2:12
1:9 *t* Php 3:19;
1Th 5:3; 2Pe 3:7
u 2Ki 17:18 *v* Isa 2:10,
19; 2Th 2:8
1:10 *w* 1Co 3:13
x Jn 17:10 *y* 1Co 1:6
1:11 *z* S Ro 1:10
a ver 5 *b* S Ro 8:28
c Ro 15:14 *d* 1Th 1:3
1:12 *e* Isa 24:15;
Php 2:9-11
2:1 *f* S 1Th 2:19
g Mk 13:27; 1Th
4:15-17

1

Paul, Silas[a] *a* and Timothy, *b*

To the church of the Thessalonians *c* in God our Father and the Lord Jesus Christ:

[2] Grace and peace to you from God the Father and the Lord Jesus Christ. *d*

THANKSGIVING AND PRAYER

[3] We ought always to thank God for you, *e* brothers and sisters, and rightly so, because your faith is growing more and more, and the love all of you have for one another is increasing. *f* [4] Therefore, among God's churches we boast *g* about your perseverance and faith *h* in all the persecutions and trials you are enduring. *i*

[5] All this is evidence *j* that God's judgment is right, and as a result you will be counted worthy *k* of the kingdom of God, for which you are suffering. [6] God is just: *l* He will pay back trouble to those who trouble you *m* [7] and give relief to you who are troubled, and to us as well. This will happen when the Lord Jesus is revealed from heaven *n* in blazing fire *o* with his powerful angels. *p* [8] He will punish *q* those who do not know God *r* and do not obey the gospel of our Lord Jesus. *s* [9] They will be punished with everlasting destruction *t* and shut out from the presence of the Lord *u* and from the glory of his might *v* [10] on the day *w* he comes to be glorified *x* in his holy people and to be marveled at among all those who have believed. This includes you, because you believed our testimony to you. *y*

[11] With this in mind, we constantly pray for you, *z* that our God may make you worthy *a* of his calling, *b* and that by his power he may bring to fruition your every desire for goodness *c* and your every deed prompted by faith. *d* [12] We pray this so that the name of our Lord Jesus may be glorified in you, *e* and you in him, according to the grace of our God and the Lord Jesus Christ. *b*

THE MAN OF LAWLESSNESS

2

Concerning the coming of our Lord Jesus Christ *f* and our being gathered to him, *g* we ask you, brothers and sisters, [2] not to become easily unsettled or alarmed by the teaching allegedly from us—whether by a prophecy or by word of mouth or by

---

a 1 Greek *Silvanus,* a variant of *Silas*   *b 12* Or *God and Lord, Jesus Christ*

1:1–2 See note on 1Th 1:1.
1:1 *Paul.* See note on Ro 1:1. *Lord Jesus Christ.* Occurs also at the end of this letter (3:18). See note on 1Th 1:1.
1:2 *Grace and peace.* See note on Ro 1:7.

A **1:3** *ought.* Paul is obliged to give thanks where it is due (cf. 1Th 1:7–8; see note on Php 1:3–4). *brothers and sisters.* See note on Ro 1:13. *faith … love.* Two virtues that Paul had been pleased to acknowledge in the Thessalonian church (see 1Th 3:6–7 and note on 3:6) but that were also somewhat lacking (see 1Th 3:10,12 and note on 3:10). *is increasing.* The same verb Paul had used in his prayer that its members' love might grow (1Th 3:12).
1:4 *we.* Emphatic, "we ourselves." Paul seems to imply that it was unusual for the founders of a church to boast about it, though others might do so (cf. 1Th 1:9). But the Thessalonians were so outstanding that Paul departed from normal practice. *persecutions and trials.* See 1Th 1:6; 2:14; 3:3.
1:5 *evidence that God's judgment is right.* The evidence was in the way the Thessalonians endured trials. The judgment on them was right because God did not leave them to their own resources. He provided strength to endure, and this in turn produced spiritual and moral character. It also proved that God was on their side and gave a warning to their persecutors (cf. Php 1:28 and note). *kingdom of God.* See notes on 1Th 2:12; Mt 3:2.
1:6 *God is just.* The justice of God brings punishment on unrepentant sinners (cf. Mk 9:47–48; Lk 13:3–5), and it may be in the here and now (see Ro 1:24,26,28 and note) as well as on the judgment day.
1:7 *give relief.* Retribution involves not only punishment of the evil but also relief for the righteous. *us as well.* Paul was no academic theologian writing in comfort from a distance; rather, he was suffering just as they were. *revealed.* Christ is now hidden, and many people even deny his existence. But at his second coming he will be seen by everyone for who he is. *blazing fire.*

He comes to punish wickedness (see Rev 19:12; cf. Isa 66:15; Rev 1:14). *his powerful angels.* Perhaps a class of angels (such a group is mentioned in apocalyptic writings) given special power to do God's will (cf. Rev 19:14 and note).

A **1:8** *do not know God.* Does not refer to those who have never heard of the true God but to those who refuse to recognize him (cf. 2:10,12 and note on 2:10; Ro 1:28). *do not obey.* The gospel invites acceptance, and rejection is disobedience to a royal invitation.
1:9 *destruction.* Since salvation implies resurrection of the body, annihilation cannot be in mind here (see 1Th 5:3 and note). The word means something like "complete ruin" (see Mt 7:13 and note). Here it means being shut out from Christ's presence. This eternal separation is the penalty of sin and the essence of hell (cf. Rev 20:14–15; 21:8,27).
1:10 *the day.* See note on 1Th 5:2. *glorified in his holy people.* Not simply "among" but "in" them. His glory is seen in what they are. *holy people.* See note on 1Th 3:13. *our testimony.* The preaching of the gospel is essentially bearing testimony to what God has done in Christ.
1:11 *constantly pray.* See notes on 1Th 5:17; Col 4:2. *desire for goodness … deed prompted by faith.* God initiates every such "desire" and every act "prompted by faith"; Paul prays accordingly that he will bring them to fulfillment.
1:12 *name.* In ancient times one's name was often more than a personal label; it summed up what a person was. *Lord Jesus may be glorified in you.* Paul looks for glory to be ascribed to Christ because of all he will do in the lives of the Thessalonian Christians (see v. 10 and note). *and you in him.* Christians will share in Christ's glory by virtue of their union with him (cf. Jn 15:4 and note; 17:21).
2:1 *coming.* See 1Th 2:19 and note. The second coming of Christ is the principal topic of 2 Thessalonians. What Paul wrote was supplemental to his oral teaching and the instructions

letter [h]—asserting that the day of the Lord [i] has already come. [j] ³Don't let anyone deceive you [k] in any way, for ⌊that day will not come⌋ until the rebellion [l] occurs and the man of lawlessness [a] is revealed, [m] the man doomed to destruction. ⁴He will oppose and will exalt himself over everything that is called God [n] or is worshiped, so that he sets himself up in God's temple, proclaiming himself to be God. [o]

⁵Don't you remember that when I was with you I used to tell you these things? [p] ⁶And now you know what is holding him back, [q] so that he may be revealed at the proper time. ⁷For the secret power of lawlessness is already at work; but the one who now holds it back [r] will continue to do so till he is taken out of the way. ⁸And then the lawless one will be revealed, [s] whom the Lord Jesus will overthrow with the breath of his mouth [t] and destroy by the splendor of his coming. [u] ⁹The coming of the lawless one will be in accordance with how Satan [v] works. He will use all sorts of displays of power through signs and wonders [w] that serve the lie, ¹⁰and all the ways that wickedness deceives those who are perishing. [x] They perish because they refused to love the truth and so be saved. [y] ¹¹For this reason God sends them [z] a powerful delusion [a] so that they will believe the lie [b] ¹²and so that all will be condemned who have not believed the truth but have delighted in wickedness. [c]

STAND FIRM

¹³But we ought always to thank God for you, [d] brothers and sisters loved by the Lord, because God chose you as firstfruits [b] [e] to be saved [f] through the sanctifying work of the Spirit [g] and through belief in the truth. ¹⁴He called you [h] to this through our gospel, [i] that you might share in the glory of our Lord Jesus Christ.

ᵃ 3 Some manuscripts *sin*   ᵇ 13 Some manuscripts *because from the beginning God chose you*

2:2 ʰ ver 15;
2Th 3:17 ⁱ S 1Co 1:8
ʲ 2Ti 2:18
2:3 ᵏ S Mk 13:5
ˡ Mt 24:10-12 ᵐ ver 8;
Da 7:25; 8:25; 11:36;
Rev 13:5,6
2:4 ⁿ 1Co 8:5
ᵒ Isa 14:13,14;
Eze 28:2
2:5 ᵖ 1Th 3:4
2:6 ᵠ ver 7
2:7 ʳ ver 6
2:8 ˢ S ver 3
ᵗ Isa 11:4; Rev 2:16;
19:15 ᵘ S Lk 17:30
2:9 ᵛ S Mt 4:10
ʷ Mt 24:24;
Rev 13:13; S Jn 4:48
2:10 ˣ S 1Co 1:18
ʸ Pr 4:6; Jn 3:17-19
2:11 ᶻ Ro 1:28
ᵃ Mt 24:5; S Mk 13:5
ᵇ Ro 1:25
2:12 ᶜ Ro 1:32; 2:8
2:13 ᵈ S Ro 1:8
ᵉ Eph 1:4 ᶠ 1Th 5:9
ᵍ 1Pe 1:2
2:14 ʰ S Ro 8:28;
S 11:29 ⁱ 1Th 1:5

---

contained in his earlier letter. *gathered to him.* See 1Th 4:17 and note.
2:2 *unsettled.* The Greek for this verb was often used of a ship adrift from its mooring and suggests lack of stability. *alarmed.* Jesus issued a similar instruction, using the same verb (Mk 13:7). *teaching allegedly from us.* Paul seems to be uncertain about what was disturbing them, so he uses a general expression. *prophecy.* Lit. "spirit," denoting a revelation inspired by either the Holy Spirit or some other spirit. *word of mouth.* Perhaps referring to a sermon or other oral communication. *letter.* A forgery. *day of the Lord.* See 1Th 5:2 and note. *has already come.* Obviously Christ's climactic return had not occurred, but Paul was combating the idea that the final days had begun and their completion would be imminent.
2:3 *the rebellion.* At the last time there will be a falling away from the faith (see Mt 24:10–12; 1Ti 4:1). But here Paul is speaking of a specific act of rebellion that embodies the supreme opposition of evil to the things of God. *the man of lawlessness.* The leader of the forces of evil at the last time. Only here is he called by this name. John tells us of many "antichrists" (1Jn 2:18), and this may be the worst of them— the antichrist of Rev 13— though Paul's description of the man of lawlessness has some distinctive features. He is not Satan, because he is clearly distinguished from him in v. 9. *revealed.* Since the Greek for this word is from the same root as that used of Jesus Christ in 1:7, it may indicate something supernatural. *doomed to destruction.* For all his proud claims, his final overthrow is certain. The same expression is used of Judas Iscariot (see Jn 17:12).
2:4 *everything that is called God or is worshiped.* He is not merely a political or military man but claims a place above every god and everything associated with worship. He even claims to be God. *God's temple.* Apparently refers to the temple in Jerusalem (cf. Mt 24:15 and note).
2:6 *what is holding him back.* The expression is neuter, but the masculine equivalent is in v. 7. There have been many suggestions as to the identity of this restrainer: (1) the Roman state with its emperor, (2) Paul's missionary work, (3) the Jewish nation, (4) the principle of law and government embodied in the state, (5) the Holy Spirit or (6) the restraining ministry of the Holy Spirit through the church and others.

2:7 *secret power.* Lit. "mystery" (see note on Ro 11:25). The term is most often used in reference to the gospel or some aspect of it. The expression here, however, indicates that we know something about evil only as God reveals it. This evil is already at work and will continue until the restrainer is removed at the end time.
2:8 *the lawless one will be revealed.* Evidently refers to some supernatural aspects of his appearing (see v. 9). *overthrow with the breath of his mouth.* Despite his impressiveness (v. 4), the man of lawlessness will easily be destroyed by Christ (cf. Da 11:45; Rev 19:20). *splendor.* In 2Ti 1:10 ("appearing") the Greek for this word refers to Jesus' first coming, but everywhere else in the NT to his second coming.
2:9 *coming.* The same Greek word used of Christ's coming in v. 8. Satan empowers the lawless one with signs and wonders (cf. Mt 24:24). *the lie.* See v. 11 and note.
2:10 *deceives.* The aim of the miracles of v. 9. *refused.* Their unbelief was willful and intentional. *truth.* Often closely connected with Jesus (see Jn 14:6 and note; Eph 4:21) and with the gospel (see Gal 2:5; Eph 1:13).
2:11 *For this reason.* Because of their deliberate rejection of the truth (v. 10). *God sends them a powerful delusion.* God uses sin to punish the sinful (cf. Ro 1:24–28). *the lie.* Not just any lie, but the great lie that the man of lawlessness is God (v. 4).
2:13 *loved by the Lord ... God chose.* For the connection between God's love and election, see Col 3:12; 1Th 1:4; see also note on Eph 1:4. *sanctifying work.* A necessary aspect of salvation, not something reserved for special Christians (see 1Th 3:13; 4:3; 1Co 1:2 and notes). *truth.* See note on v. 10. All three persons of the Trinity are mentioned in this verse (see note on 1Th 1:1).
2:14 *called ... through our gospel.* The past tense refers to the time when the Thessalonians were converted, but the divine call is a present reality in 1Th 5:24. *our gospel.* See note on 1Th 1:5. *glory of our Lord Jesus Christ.* Cf. 1Th 2:12 and note. Ultimately there is no glory other than God's (cf. Heb 1:2–3 and note).
2:15 *teachings.* Lit. "traditions." Until the NT was written, essential Christian teaching was passed on in the "traditions," just as was Rabbinic law (see Mt 15:2 and note); it could be either oral or written. In 1Co 15:3 (see note there) Paul uses the technical words for receiving and handing on traditions.

2:15 *i* 1Co 16:13
k 1Co 11:2
2:16 *l* S Php 4:20
m S Jn 3:16
2:17 *n* 1Th 3:2
o 2Th 3:3
3:1 *p* 1Th 4:1
q S 1Th 5:25 *r* 1Th 1:8
s 1Th 2:13
3:2 *t* S Ro 15:31
3:3 *u* S 1Co 1:9
v S Mt 5:37
3:4 *w* S 2Co 2:3
3:5 *x* 1Ch 29:18
3:6 *y* 1Co 5:4
z ver 14; S Ro 16:17
a ver 7,11 *b* S 1Co 11:2
3:7 *c* ver 9;
S 1Co 4:16
3:8 *d* S Ac 18:3;
Eph 4:28
3:9 *e* 1Co 9:4-14
f ver 7; S 1Co 4:16
3:10 *g* 1Th 3:4
h 1Th 4:11
3:11 *i* ver 6,7;
1Ti 5:13
3:12 *j* 1Th 4:1
k 1Th 4:11; Eph 4:28
3:13 *l* Gal 6:9
3:14 *m* ver 6;
S Ro 16:17
n S 1Co 4:14
3:15 *o* Gal 6:1;
1Th 5:14; Phm 16
3:16 *p* S Ro 15:33
q Ru 2:4

¹⁵So then, brothers and sisters, stand firm *j* and hold fast to the teachings *a* we passed on to you, *k* whether by word of mouth or by letter.

¹⁶May our Lord Jesus Christ himself and God our Father, *l* who loved us *m* and by his grace gave us eternal encouragement and good hope, ¹⁷encourage *n* your hearts and strengthen *o* you in every good deed and word.

REQUEST FOR PRAYER

3 As for other matters, brothers and sisters, *p* pray for us *q* that the message of the Lord *r* may spread rapidly and be honored, just as it was with you. *s* ²And pray that we may be delivered from wicked and evil people, *t* for not everyone has faith. ³But the Lord is faithful, *u* and he will strengthen you and protect you from the evil one. *v* ⁴We have confidence *w* in the Lord that you are doing and will continue to do the things we command. ⁵May the Lord direct your hearts *x* into God's love and Christ's perseverance.

WARNING AGAINST IDLENESS

⁶In the name of the Lord Jesus Christ, *y* we command you, brothers and sisters, to keep away from *z* every believer who is idle and disruptive *a* and does not live according to the teaching *b* you received from us. *b* ⁷For you yourselves know how you ought to follow our example. *c* We were not idle when we were with you, ⁸nor did we eat anyone's food without paying for it. On the contrary, we worked *d* night and day, laboring and toiling so that we would not be a burden to any of you. ⁹We did this, not because we do not have the right to such help, *e* but in order to offer ourselves as a model for you to imitate. *f* ¹⁰For even when we were with you, *g* we gave you this rule: "Anyone who is unwilling to work *h* shall not eat."

¹¹We hear that some among you are idle and disruptive. They are not busy; they are busybodies. *i* ¹²Such people we command and urge in the Lord Jesus Christ *j* to settle down and earn the bread they eat. *k* ¹³And as for you, brothers and sisters, never tire of doing what is good. *l*

¹⁴Take special note of those who do not obey our instruction in this letter. Do not associate with them, *m* in order that they may feel ashamed. *n* ¹⁵Yet do not regard them as enemies, but warn them as fellow believers. *o*

FINAL GREETINGS

¹⁶Now may the Lord of peace *p* himself give you peace at all times and in every way. The Lord be with all of you. *q*

---

a 15 Or *traditions*   *b* 6 Or *tradition*

2:16–17 There is a similar prayer in the first letter (1Th 3:11–13).
2:17 *encourage…strengthen.* Also used together in 1Th 3:2. The prayer is for inner strength that will produce results in both action and speech.
3:1 *As for other matters.* In 1Th 5:25 Paul asked simply for prayer; here he mentions specifics. *just as it was with you.* Lit. "just as also with you." The expression is general enough to cover the present as well as the past (cf. 1Th 2:13).
3:2 For Paul's difficulties at Corinth (where he wrote this letter), see Ac 18:12–13.
3:3 *faithful.* In the Greek the word immediately follows "faith" (v. 2), putting the faithfulness of God in sharp contrast with the lack of faith in people (cf. 1Co 1:9 and note; 10:13; 2Co 1:18).
3:5 *hearts.* See note on 1Th 2:4. *God's love.* Paul is about to rebuke the idle and is here reminding them of God's love. There should be no hard feelings among those who owe everything to the love of God. *Christ's perseverance.* The endurance he so marvelously displayed in his incarnate life on earth (see Heb 12:1–3 and notes).
3:6 *the name.* See 1:12 and note. *command.* An authoritative word with a military ring. *keep away.* Not withdrawal of all contact but withholding of close fellowship. Idleness is sinful and disruptive, but those guilty of it are still brothers and sisters in Christ (v. 15). *idle.* The problem was mentioned in the first letter (4:11–12; 5:14; see notes there), and evidently had worsened. Paul takes it seriously and gives more attention to it in this letter than to anything else but the second coming. *teaching.* See 2:15 and note.

3:7 *follow our example.* See 1Th 1:6 and note.
3:8 *eat…food.* A Hebraism for "make a living" (see, e.g., Ge 3:19; Am 7:12). Paul is not saying that he never accepted hospitality but that he had not depended on other people for his living (see 1Th 2:9 and note).
3:9 *the right.* See note on 1Th 2:6.
3:10 Pagan parallels are in the form of "Anyone who does not work does not eat." But Paul uses an imperative: lit. "let him (or them) not eat."
3:11 *busybodies.* Worse than idle, they were interfering with other people's affairs, a problem to which idleness often leads.
3:12 *settle down.* Not going about as useless "busybodies" (v. 11).
3:14 Paul realizes that some may not heed his letter. *associate with.* The Greek for this phrase is an unusual double compound, meaning "mix up together with" (used elsewhere in the NT only in 1Co 5:9,11—of a similar withdrawal of close fellowship). It indicates a disassociation that will bring the person back to a right attitude. *feel ashamed.* And repent. The aim is not punishment but restoration to fellowship.
3:15 Discipline in the church should be carried out lovingly and gently (cf. Gal 6:1), never harshly. *warn.* See 1Th 5:12, where the Greek for this verb is translated "admonish." *fellow believers.* Lit. "brother(s)." See note on Ro 1:13.
3:16,18 *peace…grace.* See note on Ro 1:7.
3:16 *Lord of peace.* The more usual phrase is "God of peace" (see note on 1Th 5:23). *all of you.* Even the disorderly.

¹⁷I, Paul, write this greeting in my own hand,^r which is the distinguishing mark in all my letters. This is how I write.
¹⁸The grace of our Lord Jesus Christ be with you all.^s

3:17 ʳS 1Co 16:21
3:18 ˢS Ro 16:20

3:17 Paul normally dictated his letters (cf. Ro 16:22), but toward the end of some of them he added a brief word in his own handwriting (see 1Co 16:21 and note; Gal 6:11; Col 4:18). Here he tells us that this practice was his distinguishing mark.

3:18 See 1Th 5:28 and note. Paul has criticized his offenders, but his last prayer is for everyone. *Lord Jesus Christ.* See note on 1:1. *with you.* See note on 2Co 13:14.

"Pastoral" characterizes the contents of 1,2 Timothy and Titus. These letters provide instruction concerning the care of the churches.

Biblical interpreters have raised more doubts about the authenticity of the Pastoral Letters than about any of the other letters of Paul:

1. The events mentioned in the Pastorals cannot be fitted into the account of Paul's life and ministry in Acts.
2. The theology is different from that found in the other letters of Paul, and the church organization is more advanced.
3. The vocabulary and style of writing are not characteristic of Paul.

Although these may appear to be formidable objections to authorship by Paul, there are satisfactory answers:

1. Paul's death is not reported in Ac 28. In all probability he was released from prison and went on another mission (see map and accompanying text, pp. 2030–2031), during which there was adequate time for the historical events mentioned in the Pastoral Letters to take place.
2. The theology is consistent with that found in other letters of Paul, and the church organization in the Pastorals is no more advanced than that found, e.g., in Philippians.
3. While the scope of these letters is too limited to draw any firm conclusions about authorship based on vocabulary and style, these features of the Pastorals can be satisfactorily accounted for by considering the different circumstances, addressees and subject matter Paul is dealing with.

Certain themes and phrases recur throughout the Pastoral Letters: (1) God the Savior (see note on Tit 1:3); (2) sound doctrine, faith and teaching (see note on Tit 1:9); (3) godliness (see note on 1Ti 2:2); (4) controversies (1Ti 1:4; 6:4; 2Ti 2:23; Tit 3:9); (5) trustworthy sayings (see note on 1Ti 1:15).

AUTHOR — 1 TIMOTHY — INTRODUCTION

Both early tradition and the salutations of the Pastoral Letters (1,2 Timothy; Titus) themselves claim Paul as their author (1:1; 2Ti 1:1; Tit 1:1). Some objections have been raised in recent years on the basis of an alleged uncharacteristic vocabulary and style (see, e.g., notes on 1:15; 2:2), but other evidence still convincingly supports Paul's authorship. See essay, p. 2026.

BACKGROUND AND PURPOSE

During his fourth missionary journey (see map, pp. 2030–2031), Paul had instructed Timothy to care for the church at Ephesus (1:3) while he went on to Macedonia. When he realized that he might not return to Ephesus in the near future (3:14–15), he wrote this first letter to Timothy to develop the charge he had given his young assistant (1:3,18), to refute false teachings (1:3–7; 4:1–8; 6:3–5,20–21) and to supervise the affairs of the growing Ephesian church (church worship, ch. 2; the appointment of qualified church leaders, 3:1–13; 5:17–25).

    A major problem in the Ephesian church was a heresy that combined Gnosticism (see Introduction to 1 John: Gnosticism), decadent Judaism (1:3–7) and false asceticism (4:1–5).

DATE

1 Timothy was written sometime after the events of Ac 28 (c. A.D. 63–65; see chart, p. 1855), at least eight years after Paul's three-year stay in Ephesus (see Ac 19:10 and note).

RECIPIENT

C As the salutation indicates (1:2), Paul is writing to Timothy, a native of Lystra (in modern Turkey). Timothy's father was Greek, while his mother was a Jewish Christian (Ac 16:1). From childhood he had been taught the OT (2Ti 1:5; 3:15). Paul called him "my true son in the faith" (1:2; see note there), perhaps having led him to faith in Christ during his first visit to Lystra. At the time of his second visit Paul invited Timothy to join him on his missionary travels, circumcising him so that his Greek ancestry would not be a liability in working with the Jews (Ac 16:3). Timothy helped Paul evangelize Macedonia and Achaia (Ac 17:14–15; 18:5) and was with him during much of his long preaching ministry at Ephesus (Ac 19:22). He traveled with him from Ephesus to Macedonia to Corinth (see Ac 20:3 and note), back to Macedonia, and to Asia Minor (Ac 20:1–6). He may even have accompanied him all the way to Jerusalem. He was with Paul during the apostle's first Roman imprisonment (Php 1:1; Col 1:1; Phm 1).

    Following Paul's release (after Ac 28) Timothy again traveled with him but eventually stayed at Ephesus to deal with the problems there, while Paul went on to Macedonia. Paul's closeness to and admiration of Timothy are seen in Paul's naming him as the co-sender of six of his letters (2 Corinthians, Philippians, Colossians, 1,2 Thessalonians and Philemon) and in his speaking highly of him to the Philippians

KEY   **A** APPLICATION FOR LIVING   **B** BACKGROUND NOTES   **C** CHARACTER INFORMATION

(Php 2:19–22). At the end of Paul's life he requested Timothy to join him at Rome (2Ti 4:9,21). According to Heb 13:23, Timothy himself was imprisoned and subsequently released—whether at Rome or elsewhere, we do not know.

Timothy was not an apostle. It may be best to regard him as an apostolic representative, delegated to carry out special work (cf. Tit 1:5).

OUTLINE

Paul, an apostle of Christ Jesus by the command of God [a] our Savior [b] and of Christ Jesus our hope, [c]

[2] To Timothy [d] my true son [e] in the faith:

Grace, mercy and peace from God the Father and Christ Jesus our Lord. [f]

TIMOTHY CHARGED TO OPPOSE FALSE TEACHERS

[3] As I urged you when I went into Macedonia, [g] stay there in Ephesus [h] so that you may command certain persons not to teach false doctrines [i] any longer [4] or to devote themselves to myths [j] and endless genealogies. [k] Such things promote controversial speculations [l] rather than advancing God's work—which is by faith. [5] The goal of this command is love, which comes from a pure heart [m] and a good conscience [n] and a sincere faith. [o] [6] Some have departed from these and have turned to meaningless talk. [7] They want to be teachers [p] of the law, but they do not know what they are talking about or what they so confidently affirm. [q]

[8] We know that the law is good [r] if one uses it properly. [9] We also know that the law is made not for the righteous [s] but for lawbreakers and rebels, [t] the ungodly and sinful, the unholy and irreligious, for those who kill their fathers or mothers, for murderers, [10] for the sexually immoral, for those practicing homosexuality, for slave traders and liars and perjurers. And it is for whatever else is contrary to the sound doctrine [u] [11] that conforms to the gospel concerning the glory of the blessed God, which he entrusted to me. [v]

THE LORD'S GRACE TO PAUL

[12] I thank Christ Jesus our Lord, who has given me strength, [w] that he considered me trustworthy, appointing me to his service. [x] [13] Even though I was once a blasphemer and a persecutor [y] and a violent man, I was shown mercy [z] because I acted in ignorance and unbelief. [a] [14] The grace of our Lord was poured out on me abundantly, [b] along with the faith and love that are in Christ Jesus. [c]

[15] Here is a trustworthy saying [d] that deserves full acceptance: Christ Jesus came into the world to save sinners [e]—of whom I am the worst. [16] But for that very reason I was shown mercy [f] so that in me, the worst of sinners, Christ Jesus might display his immense patience [g] as an example for those who would believe [h] in him and receive eternal life. [i] [17] Now to the King [j] eternal, immortal, [k] invisible, [l] the only God, [m] be honor and glory for ever and ever. Amen. [n]

1:1 [a] S Co 1:1;
Tit 1:3 [b] S Lk 1:47
[c] Col 1:27
1:2 [d] S Ac 16:1
[e] ver 18; 1Co 4:17;
S 1Th 2:11; 2Ti 1:2;
Tit 1:4 [f] S Ro 1:7
1:3 [g] S Ac 16:9
[h] S Ac 18:19 [i] Gal 1:6,
7; 1Ti 6:3
1:4 [j] 1Ti 4:7; 2Ti 4:4;
Tit 1:14 [k] Tit 3:9
[l] S 2Ti 2:14
1:5 [m] 2Ti 2:22
[n] S Ac 23:1; 1Ti 4:2
[o] Gal 5:6; 2Ti 1:5
1:7 [p] S Eph 4:11
[q] Job 38:2
1:8 [r] Ro 7:12
1:9 [s] Gal 5:23
[t] Gal 3:19
1:10 [u] 1Ti 6:3;
2Ti 1:13; 4:3; Tit 1:9;
2:1
1:11 [v] Gal 2:7;
1Th 2:4; Tit 1:3
1:12 [w] S Php 4:13
[x] S Ac 9:15
1:13 [y] S Ac 8:3
[z] ver 16 [a] Ac 26:9
1:14 [b] 2Co 4:15
[c] 2Ti 1:13; S 1Th 1:3
1:15 [d] 1Ti 3:1; 4:9;
2Ti 2:11; Tit 3:8
[e] Mk 2:17; S Jn 3:17
1:16 [f] ver 13
[g] S Ro 2:4 [h] S Jn 3:15
[i] S Mt 25:46
1:17 [j] Rev 15:3
[k] 1Ti 6:16 [l] S Col 1:15
[m] Jude 25
[n] S Ro 11:36

1:1 *Paul.* See note on Ro 1:1. *apostle.* One specially commissioned by Christ (see 1Co 1:1 and note). *God our Savior.* See Tit 1:3 and note. *Christ Jesus our hope.* See Col 1:27; Tit 2:13; Heb 6:18–19; 1Jn 3:3 and notes. *hope.* Expresses absolute certainty, not a mere wish (see note on Eph 1:18).
1:2 *true son in the faith.* Spiritual son (see 1:18; 1Co 4:17; 2Ti 1:2; 2:1; Phm 10). *Grace ... peace.* See note on Ro 1:7. *mercy.* See Ro 9:22–23 and note; included only here and in 2Ti 1:2 in the greetings of Paul's letters.

A C **1:3–11** In this section, along with 4:1–8; 6:3–5, 20–21, Paul warns against heretical teachers in the Ephesian church. They are characterized by (1) teaching "false doctrines" (v. 3; 6:3); (2) building up endless, far-fetched, fictitious stories based on obscure genealogical points (v. 4; 4:7); (3) being argumentative (v. 4; 6:4); (4) using talk that was "meaningless" (v. 6); (5) wanting to be teachers of the OT law (v. 7); (6) being conceited (v. 7; 6:4); (7) not knowing what they were talking about (v. 7; 6:4); (8) teaching ascetic practices (4:3); and (9) using their positions of religious leadership for "financial gain" (6:5). These heretics probably were forerunners of the Gnostics (see 6:20 and note).
1:3 *I went into Macedonia.* Since this incident is not recorded in Acts, it probably occurred after Ac 28, between Paul's first and second Roman imprisonments (see Introduction: Recipient). *Macedonia.* See note on Php 4:15. *stay there in Ephesus.* And do the Lord's work in the Ephesian church—which was well established by this time. Paul had an extensive ministry there on his

third missionary journey about eight years earlier (Ac 19:1—20:1). *Ephesus.* See Introduction to Ephesians: The City of Ephesus; see also map, p. 1983.
1:4 *myths.* Perhaps mythical stories built on OT history ("genealogies") that later developed into intricate Gnostic philosophical systems (see Introduction to 1 John: Gnosticism).
1:5 *pure heart.* See 2Ti 2:22; Ps 24:4 and note; 51:10; cf. Mt 5:8.
1:8 *the law is good.* See Ro 7:7–12 and note on 7:12.
1:9–10 See note on Ro 1:29–31.
1:10 *sound doctrine.* See Tit 1:9 and note.
1:11 *gospel.* See Mk 1:1 and note. *entrusted.* See 6:20; 1Co 9:17; Gal 2:7; 1Th 2:4; 2Ti 1:14.
1:12 *Christ ... has given me strength.* See 2Co 12:9–10; Php 4:13 and notes. *appointing me to his service.* See v. 1 and note.
1:13 *a blasphemer and a persecutor and a violent man.* See Ac 9:1; 22:4–5,19; 26:10–11 and note on 26:11.
1:14 *faith and love ... in Christ.* See 2Ti 1:13 and note.

A **1:15** *Here is a trustworthy saying.* A clause found nowhere else in the NT but used five times in the Pastorals (here; 3:1; 4:9; 2Ti 2:11; Tit 3:8) to identify a key teaching. *of whom I am the worst.* The closer one gets to a holy God, the more the magnitude of one's sin becomes evident (cf. Isa 6:5; see 1Co 15:9; Eph 3:8 and note).
1:16 *eternal life.* See Jn 3:15 and note.
1:17 *invisible.* See Col 1:15 and note.

1:18 °S ver 2
ₚ1Ti 4:14 ᵠ1Ti 6:12;
2Ti 2:3; 4:7
1:19 ʳver 5;
S Ac 23:1 ˢ1Ti 6:21;
2Ti 2:18
1:20 ᵗ2Ti 2:17
ᵘ2Ti 4:14 ᵛ1Co 5:5
2:1 ʷEph 6:18
2:2 ˣEzr 6:10;
Ro 13:1 ʸ1Ti 3:16; 4:7,
8; 6:3,5,6,11; 2Ti 3:5;
Tit 1:1
2:3 ᶻS 1Ti 5:4

THE CHARGE TO TIMOTHY RENEWED

¹⁸Timothy, my son, ° I am giving you this command in keeping with the prophecies once made about you, ᵖ so that by recalling them you may fight the battle well, ᵠ ¹⁹holding on to faith and a good conscience, ʳ which some have rejected and so have suffered shipwreck with regard to the faith. ˢ ²⁰Among them are Hymenaeus ᵗ and Alexander, ᵘ whom I have handed over to Satan ᵛ to be taught not to blaspheme.

INSTRUCTIONS ON WORSHIP

2 I urge, then, first of all, that petitions, prayers, ʷ intercession and thanksgiving be made for everyone— ²for kings and all those in authority, ˣ that we may live peaceful and quiet lives in all godliness ʸ and holiness. ³This is good, and pleases ᶻ God

---

1:18 *son.* See v. 2 and note. *prophecies once made about you.* In the early church God revealed his will in various matters through prophets (see Ac 13:1–3, where prophets had an active role in sending Paul and Barnabas on their mission to the Gentiles). In Timothy's case a prophecy may have occurred at the time of or before his ordination (4:14), perhaps about 12 years earlier on Paul's second missionary journey (see Ac 16:1–3). *fight the battle well.* See 6:12; 2Ti 2:3; 4:7 and note.

1:20 *Hymenaeus.* See 2Ti 2:17–18. *Alexander.* Perhaps the Alexander of 2Ti 4:14. *handed over to Satan.* The reference is to church discipline (see Mt 18:17 and note). Paul had excluded these two men from the church, which was considered a sanctuary from Satan's power. Out in the world, away from the

fellowship and care of the church, they would be "taught" (the Greek word means basically "to discipline") "not to blaspheme." The purpose of such drastic action was more remedial than punitive. For a similar situation, see 1Co 5:5,13 and note on 5:5.

2:1–2 *prayers … for kings and all those in authority.* See Jer 29:7; 1Pe 2:13 and note. The notorious Roman emperor Nero (A.D. 54–68) was in power when Paul wrote these words.

2:2 *godliness.* A key word (along with "godly") in the Pastorals, occurring ten times (here; 3:16; 4:7–8; 6:3,5–6,11; 2Ti 3:5; Ti 1:1), but nowhere else in the writings of Paul. It implies a good and holy life, with special emphasis on its source, a deep reverence for God.

PAUL'S FOURTH MISSIONARY JOURNEY

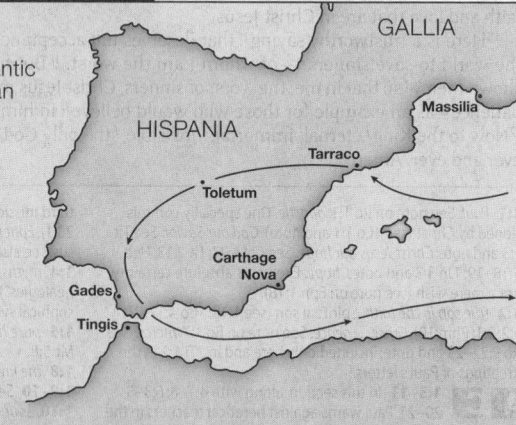

C. A.D. 62–68

It is clear from Ac 13:1—21:17 that Paul went on three missionary journeys. There is also reason to believe that he made a fourth journey after his release from the Roman imprisonment recorded in Ac 28. The conclusion that such a journey did indeed take place is based on: (1) Paul's declared intention to go to Spain (Ro 15:24,28), (2) Eusebius's implication that Paul was released following his first Roman imprisonment (*Ecclesiastical History*, 2.22.2–3) and (3) statements in early Christian literature that he took the gospel as far as Spain (Clement of Rome, *Epistle to the Corinthians*, ch. 5; *Actus Petri Vercellenses*, chs. 1–3; Muratorian Canon, lines 34–39).

The places Paul may have visited after his release from prison are indicated by statements of intention in his earlier writings and by subsequent mention in the Pastoral Letters. The order of his travel cannot be determined with certainty, but the itinerary at the right seems likely.

1. **Rome**—released from prison in A.D. 62
2. **Spain**—62–64 (Ro 15:24,28)
3. **Crete**—64–65 (Tit 1:5)
4. **Miletus**—65 (2Ti 4:20)
5. **Colossae**—66 (Phm 22)
6. **Ephesus**—66 (1Ti 1:3)
7. **Philippi**—66 (Php 2:23–24; 1Ti 1:3)
8. **Nicopolis**—66–67 (Tit 3:12)
9. **Rome**—67 (2Ti 1:17)
10. **Martyrdom**—67/68 (2Ti 4:6)

our Savior, ^a ⁴who wants ^b all people ^c to be saved ^d and to come to a knowledge of the truth. ^e ⁵For there is one God ^f and one mediator ^g between God and human beings, Christ Jesus, himself human, ^h ⁶who gave himself as a ransom ⁱ for all people. This has now been witnessed to ^j at the proper time. ^k ⁷And for this purpose I was appointed a herald and an apostle—I am telling the truth, I am not lying—and a true and faithful teacher ^l of the Gentiles. ^m

⁸Therefore I want the men everywhere to pray, lifting up holy hands ⁿ without anger or disputing. ⁹I also want the women to dress modestly, with decency and propriety, adorning themselves, not with elaborate hairstyles or gold or pearls or expensive clothes, ^o ¹⁰but with good deeds, ^p appropriate for women who profess to worship God.

2:10 ^p Pr 31:13

2:3 ^a S Lk 1:47
2:4 ^b Eze 18:23, 32; 33:11 ^c 1Ti 4:10; Tit 2:11; 2Pe 3:9 ^d S Jn 3:17; S Ro 11:14
2:5 ^e 2Ti 2:25; Tit 1:1; Heb 10:26 ^f Dt 6:4; Ro 3:29, 30; 10:12 ^g S Gal 3:20 ^h Ro 1:3
2:6 ⁱ S Mt 20:28 ^j S 1Co 1:6 ^k 1Ti 6:15; Tit 1:3
2:7 ^l 2Ti 1:11 ^m S Ac 9:15
2:8 ⁿ Ps 24:4; 63:4; 134:2; 141:2; Lk 24:50
2:9 ^o 1Pe 3:3

2:3 *God our Savior.* See Tit 1:3 and note.

2:4 *wants all people to be saved.* God desires the salvation of all people (cf. 2Pe 3:9 and note). On the other hand, the Bible indicates that God chooses some (not all) people to be saved (see 4:10; Ro 8:29 and notes).
2:5 *there is one God.* The basic belief of Judaism (see Dt 6:4 and note), which every Jew confessed daily in the *Shema* (see Mk 12:29 and note). *mediator.* One who represents God to humans and humans to God—and who removes all alienation between them by offering himself as "a ransom for all" (v. 6). Cf. Jn 14:6; Heb 8:6 and notes.
2:6 *ransom.* See Mt 20:28 and note. *witnessed.* Refers to the apostolic testimony that Christ gave himself as the ransom. *proper time.* See Gal 4:4 and note.

2:7 *for this purpose.* To testify that, through his death, Christ has bridged the gap between God and human be-

ings and made salvation available to all. *herald.* See 2Ti 1:11; one who with authority makes a public proclamation. *apostle.* See 1Co 1:1 and note.
2:8 *men.* The Greek for this word does not refer to humankind (as in vv. 5–6) but to males as distinct from females. Women also prayed in public, however (see 1Co 11:5 and note).
2:9–14 Some maintain that Paul's teaching about women here is historically conditioned, not universal and timeless. Others view these verses as unaffected by the historical situation and therefore applicable to every age.
2:9 Not a total ban on the wearing of jewelry or braided hair. Rather, Paul was expressing caution in a society where such things were signs of extravagant luxury and proud personal display.
2:10 See 1Pe 3:3–5 and note on 3:3.

2:11 ᵠ1Pe 3:3,4
2:12 ʳS Eph 5:22
2:13 ˢGe 2:7,22;
1Co 11:8
2:14 ᵗGe 3:1-6,13;
2Co 11:3
2:15 ᵘ1Ti 1:14
3:1 ᵛS 1Ti 1:15
ʷAc 20:28; Php 1:1;
Tit 1:7
3:2 ˣTit 1:6-8
ʸver 12 ᶻver 11;
Tit 2:2 ᵃS Ro 12:13
ᵇ2Ti 2:24

¹¹A woman[a] should learn in quietness and full submission. ᵠ ¹²I do not permit a woman to teach or to assume authority over a man;[b,c] she must be quiet. ʳ ¹³For Adam was formed first, then Eve. ˢ ¹⁴And Adam was not the one deceived; it was the woman who was deceived and became a sinner. ᵗ ¹⁵But women[d] will be saved through childbearing—if they continue in faith, love ᵘ and holiness with propriety.

QUALIFICATIONS FOR OVERSEERS AND DEACONS

3 Here is a trustworthy saying: ᵛWhoever aspires to be an overseer ʷ desires a noble task. ²Now the overseer is to be above reproach, ˣ faithful to his wife, ʸ temperate, ᶻ self-controlled, respectable, hospitable, ᵃ able to teach, ᵇ ³not given to drunken-

---

ᵃ 11 Or *wife*; also in verse 12   ᵇ 12 Or *teach a man in a domineering way; or teach or to exercise* (or *have*) *authority over a man*   ᶜ 12 Or *over her husband*   ᵈ 15 Greek *she*

2:12 *not permit a woman to teach.* Some believe that Paul here prohibited teaching only by women not properly instructed, i.e., by the women at Ephesus. Such women tended to exercise authority over, i.e., to be domineering over, the men. Others maintain that Paul did not allow a woman to be an official teacher in the assembled church. This is indicated by the added restriction concerning exercising "authority over a man" (a male), i.e., functioning as an overseer (see note on 3:1).

2:13–14 Paul based the restrictions on Ge 2–3. Some argue that "For" does not express the reason for woman's silence and submission but is used only as a connective word, as in v. 5. The meaning, then, would be that Adam's priority in creation illustrates the present situation of male priority in teaching at Ephesus, and Eve's deception illustrates the deception of the untrained and aggressive Ephesian women involved in false teaching. Thus the prohibition is not universal and permanent but restricted to this church's situation (see Introduction: Background and Purpose). Under different circumstances the restrictions would not apply (e.g., 1Co 11:1–5). Others believe that the appeal to the creation account makes the restrictions universal and permanent: 1. *Adam was formed first.* Paul appeals to the priority of Adam in creation, which predates the fall. Thus he views the man-woman relationship set forth in this passage as grounded in creation. 2. *the woman … was deceived.* Paul appears to argue that since the woman was deceived (and then

led Adam astray), she is not to be entrusted with the teaching function of an overseer (or elder) in the public worship services of the assembled church.

2:15 *saved through childbearing.* Three possible meanings are: (1) This speaks of the godly woman finding fulfillment in her role as wife and mother in the home; (2) it refers to women being saved spiritually through the most significant birth of all, the incarnation of Christ; or (3) it refers to women being kept physically safe in childbirth.

3:1 *trustworthy saying.* See note on 1:15. *overseer.* In Greek culture the word was used of a presiding official in a civic or religious organization. Here it refers to a man who oversees a local congregation. The equivalent word from the Jewish background of Christianity is "elder." The terms "overseer" and "elder" are often used interchangeably (see Ac 20:17, 28; Tit 1:5–7; 1Pe 5:1–2 and notes). The duties of an overseer were to teach and preach (3:2; 5:17), to direct the affairs of the church (3:5; 5:17), to shepherd ("pastor") the flock of God (Ac 20:28; see note there) and to guard the church from error (Ac 20:28–31).

3:2 *overseer is to be.* See chart, below. *faithful to his wife.* A general principle that applies to any violation of God's marriage law, whether in the form of polygamy or of marital unfaithfulness (see note on Tit 1:6).

QUALIFICATIONS FOR ELDERS/OVERSEERS AND DEACONS

Self-controlled	ELDER	1Ti 3:2; Tit 1:8	Faithful to his wife	ELDER	1Ti 3:2; Tit 1:6	
				DEACON	1Ti 3:12	
Hospitable	ELDER	1Ti 3:2; Tit 1:8	Temperate	ELDER	1Ti 3:2; Tit 1:7	
Able to teach	ELDER	1Ti 3:2; 5:17; Tit 1:9		DEACON	1Ti 3:8	
Not violent but gentle	ELDER	1Ti 3:3; Tit 1:7	Respectable	ELDER	1Ti 3:2	
Not quarrelsome	ELDER	1Ti 3:3		DEACON	1Ti 3:8	
Not a lover of money	ELDER	1Ti 3:3	Not given to drunkenness	ELDER	1Ti 3:3; Tit 1:7	
Not a recent convert	ELDER	1Ti 3:6		DEACON	1Ti 3:8	
Has a good reputation with outsiders	ELDER	1Ti 3:7	Manages his own family well	ELDER	1Ti 3:4	
				DEACON	1Ti 3:12	
Not overbearing	ELDER	Tit 1:7	Sees that his children obey him	ELDER	1Ti 3:4–5; Tit 1:6	
Not quick-tempered	ELDER	Tit 1:7		DEACON	1Ti 3:12	
Loves what is good	ELDER	Tit 1:8	Does not pursue dishonest gain	ELDER	Tit 1:7	
Upright, holy	ELDER	Tit 1:8		DEACON	1Ti 3:8	
Disciplined	ELDER	Tit 1:8	Holds to the truth	ELDER	Tit 1:9	
Above reproach (blameless)	ELDER	1Ti 3:2; Tit 1:6		DEACON	1Ti 3:9	
	DEACON	1Ti 3:9	Sincere	DEACON	1Ti 3:8	
			Tested	DEACON	1Ti 3:10	

ness, *c* not violent but gentle, not quarrelsome, *d* not a lover of money. *e* 4He must manage his own family well and see that his children obey him, and he must do so in a manner worthy of full *a* respect. *f* 5(If anyone does not know how to manage his own family, how can he take care of God's church?) *g* 6He must not be a recent convert, or he may become conceited *h* and fall under the same judgment *i* as the devil. 7He must also have a good reputation with outsiders, *j* so that he will not fall into disgrace and into the devil's trap. *k*

8In the same way, deacons *l* are to be worthy of respect, sincere, not indulging in much wine, *m* and not pursuing dishonest gain. 9They must keep hold of the deep truths of the faith with a clear conscience. *n* 10They must first be tested; *o* and then if there is nothing against them, let them serve as deacons.

11In the same way, the women *b* are to be worthy of respect, not malicious talkers *p* but temperate *q* and trustworthy in everything.

12A deacon must be faithful to his wife *r* and must manage his children and his household well. *s* 13Those who have served well gain an excellent standing and great assurance in their faith in Christ Jesus.

REASONS FOR PAUL'S INSTRUCTIONS

14Although I hope to come to you soon, I am writing you these instructions so that, 15if I am delayed, you will know how people ought to conduct themselves in God's household, which is the church *t* of the living God, *u* the pillar and foundation of the truth. 16Beyond all question, the mystery *v* from which true godliness *w* springs is great:

> He appeared in a body, *x*
> was vindicated by the Spirit, *c*
> was seen by angels,
> was preached among the nations, *y*
> was believed on in the world,
> was taken up in glory. *z*

4 The Spirit *a* clearly says that in later times *b* some will abandon the faith and follow deceiving spirits *c* and things taught by demons. 2Such teachings come through hypocritical liars, whose consciences have been seared as with a hot iron. *d* 3They forbid people to marry *e* and order them to abstain from certain foods, *f* which God created *g* to be received with thanksgiving *h* by those who believe and who know the truth. 4For everything God created is good, *i* and nothing is to be rejected *j* if it is received with thanksgiving, 5because it is consecrated by the word of God *k* and prayer.

a 4 Or *him with proper*   *b* 11 Probably women who are deacons, or possibly deacons' wives
c 16 Or *vindicated in spirit*

3:3 *c* Tit 1:7
d 2Ti 2:24 *e* Lk 16:14;
1Ti 6:10; 2Ti 3:2;
Heb 13:5; 1Pe 5:2
3:4 *f* ver 12; Tit 1:6
3:5 *g* S 1Co 10:32
3:6 *h* 1Ti 6:4; 2Ti 3:4
i S 2Pe 2:4
3:7 *j* S Mk 4:11
k 2Ti 2:26
3:8 *l* Php 1:1
m 1Ti 5:23; Tit 1:7; 2:3
3:9 *n* S Ac 23:1
3:10 *o* 1Ti 5:22
3:11 *p* 2Ti 3:3;
Tit 2:3 *q* ver 2
3:12 *r* ver 2 *s* ver 4
3:15 *t* ver 5;
S 1Co 10:32
u S Mt 16:16
3:16 *v* S Ro 16:25
w S 1Ti 2:2 *x* S Jn 1:14
y Ps 9:11; Col 1:23
z S Mk 16:19
4:1 *a* Jn 16:13;
S Ac 8:29; 1Co 2:10
b 2Ti 3:1; 2Pe 3:3
c S Mk 13:5
4:2 *d* Eph 4:19
4:3 *e* Heb 13:4
f Col 2:16 *g* Ge 1:29;
9:3 *h* ver 4; Ro 14:6;
1Co 10:30
4:4 *i* Ge 1:10,12,18,
21,25,31; Mk 7:18,19;
Ro 14:14-18
j S Ac 10:15
4:5 *k* S Heb 4:12

3:5 *church.* See notes on Ac 9:31; 2Co 1:1.

3:7 *devil's trap.* See 2Ti 2:26; cf. 1Pe 5:8.

3:8 *deacons.* In its nontechnical usage, the Greek for this word means simply "one who serves." The men chosen in Ac 6:1–6 were probably not only the first deacons mentioned in the NT but also the first to be appointed in the church (but see note on Ac 6:6). Generally, their service was meant to free the elders to give full attention to prayer and the ministry of the word (Ac 6:2,4). The only two local church offices mentioned in the NT are those of overseer (also called elder; see note on v. 1) and deacon (see Php 1:1). See chart, p. 2032.

3:9 *the faith.* Apostolic teaching (see 4:1,6; 6:10,12, 21; 2Ti 4:7 and note; Tit 1:13; cf. 1Co 15:3; 2Th 2:15 and notes).

3:11 *the women.* Could refer to (1) deacons' wives or (2) women deacons (see TNIV text note). However, the fact that deacons are referred to again in vv. 12–13 seems to rule out a separate office of women deacons, though many judge otherwise.

3:12 *faithful to his wife.* See v. 2 and note.

3:14 *I am writing … so that.* Here, in brief, Paul states his purpose for writing the letter—to give instructions concerning church conduct (v. 15).

3:15 *God's household.* The family of God, made up of believers. *pillar and foundation of the truth.* See 2Ti 2:19 and note.

3:16 *mystery from which true godliness springs.* See Ro 11:25; Col 1:26 and notes. The phrase means the "revealed secret of true piety," i.e., the secret that produces piety in peo-

ple. That secret, as the following words indicate, is none other than Jesus Christ. His incarnation, in all its aspects (particularly his saving work), is the source of genuine piety. The words are printed in poetic form and probably come from an early creedal hymn (see note on Col 3:16). *godliness.* See 2:2 and note. *vindicated by the Spirit.* The Holy Spirit enabled Jesus to drive out demons (see Mt 12:28) and perform miracles. Most important, the Spirit raised Jesus from the dead (see Ro 1:4; cf. 1Pe 3:18 and note) and thereby vindicated him, showing that he was indeed the Son of God. *seen by angels.* At his resurrection (Mt 28:2) and ascension (Ac 1:10; see note there). *taken up in glory.* See Lk 24:51; Ac 1:9–12 and notes.

4:1,6 *the faith.* See note on 3:9.

4:1 *The Spirit clearly says.* As, e.g., in Mk 13:22; Ac 20:29–30; 2Th 2:3. Paul, however, is perhaps speaking here of a specific revelation made to him by the Spirit. *later times.* The time beginning with the first coming of the Messiah (see Jas 5:3 and note). That Paul is not referring only to the time immediately prior to Christ's second coming is obvious from his assumption in v. 7 that the false teachings were already present at the time of his writing.

4:3 This unbiblical asceticism arose out of the mistaken belief that the material world was evil—a central belief of the Gnostic heresy (see Introduction to 1 John: Gnosticism).

4:4 *everything God created is good.* See Ge 1:4,10,12,18,21,25,31 and note on 1:4; see also Tit 1:15 and note.

4:6 *l* 1Ti 1:10
m 2Ti 3:15
4:7 *n* 1Ti 1:4;
2Ti 2:16 *o* S 1Ti 2:2
4:8 *p* 1Ti 6:6
q Ps 37:9,11; Pr 22:4;
Mt 6:33; Mk 10:29,30
r Mk 10:29,30
4:9 *s* S 1Ti 1:15
4:10 *t* S Mt 16:16
u S Lk 1:47; S 2:11
4:11 *v* 1Ti 5:7; 6:2
4:12 *w* S 2Ti 1:7;
Tit 2:15 *x* Php 3:17;
1Th 1:7; 2Th 3:9;
Tit 2:7; 1Pe 5:3
y 1Ti 1:14
4:13 *z* 1Ti 3:14
a Lk 4:16; Ac 13:14-16;
Col 4:16; 1Th 5:27
4:14 *b* 1Ti 1:18
c S Ac 11:30
d S Ac 6:6; 2Ti 1:6
4:16 *e* S Ro 11:14
5:1 *f* Tit 2:2
g Lev 19:32 *h* Tit 2:6
5:3 *i* ver 5,16
5:4 *j* ver 8; Eph 6:1,2
k Ro 12:2; Eph 5:10;
1Ti 2:3
5:5 *l* ver 3,16
m 1Co 7:34; 1Pe 3:5
n Lk 2:37; 1Pe 3:5
5:6 *o* S Lk 15:24
5:7 *p* 1Ti 4:11; 6:2
5:8 *q* 2Pe 2:1; Jude 4
5:10 *r* Ac 9:36;
1Ti 6:18; 1Pe 2:12
s S Ro 12:13
t S Lk 7:44 *u* ver 16

[6]If you point these things out to the brothers and sisters, you will be a good minister of Christ Jesus, nourished on the truths of the faith *l* and of the good teaching that you have followed. *m* [7]Have nothing to do with godless myths and old wives' tales; *n* rather, train yourself to be godly. *o* [8]For physical training is of some value, but godliness has value for all things, *p* holding promise for both the present life *q* and the life to come. *r* [9]This is a trustworthy saying *s* that deserves full acceptance. [10]That is why we labor and strive, because we have put our hope in the living God, *t* who is the Savior of all people, *u* and especially of those who believe.

[11]Command and teach these things. *v* [12]Don't let anyone look down on you *w* because you are young, but set an example *x* for the believers in speech, in conduct, in love, in faith *y* and in purity. [13]Until I come, *z* devote yourself to the public reading of Scripture, *a* to preaching and to teaching. [14]Do not neglect your gift, which was given you through prophecy *b* when the body of elders *c* laid their hands on you. *d*

[15]Be diligent in these matters; give yourself wholly to them, so that everyone may see your progress. [16]Watch your life and doctrine closely. Persevere in them, because if you do, you will save *e* both yourself and your hearers.

WIDOWS, ELDERS AND SLAVES

5 Do not rebuke an older man *f* harshly, *g* but exhort him as if he were your father. Treat younger men *h* as brothers, [2]older women as mothers, and younger women as sisters, with absolute purity.

[3]Give proper recognition to those widows who are really in need. *i* [4]But if a widow has children or grandchildren, these should learn first of all to put their religion into practice by caring for their own family and so repaying their parents and grandparents, *j* for this is pleasing to God. *k* [5]The widow who is really in need *l* and left all alone puts her hope in God *m* and continues night and day to pray *n* and to ask God for help. [6]But the widow who lives for pleasure is dead even while she lives. *o* [7]Give the people these instructions, *p* so that no one may be open to blame. [8]Anyone who does not provide for their relatives, and especially for their own household, has denied *q* the faith and is worse than an unbeliever.

[9]No widow may be put on the list of widows unless she is over sixty, has been faithful to her husband, [10]and is well known for her good deeds, *r* such as bringing up children, showing hospitality, *s* washing the feet *t* of the Lord's people, helping those in trouble *u* and devoting herself to all kinds of good deeds.

[11]As for younger widows, do not put them on such a list. For when their sensual desires overcome their dedication to Christ, they want to marry. [12]Thus they bring judgment on themselves, because they have broken their first pledge. [13]Besides, they get into the habit

---

4:6 *good teaching that you have followed.* Even from early childhood (see 2Ti 3:15 and note).

A **4:7** *myths.* See 1:4 and note. *train yourself to be godly.* See 2:2 and note. Godliness requires self-discipline.

4:9 *trustworthy saying.* See note on 1:15. Here the expression probably refers back to the seemingly proverbial statement in v. 8. The words "labor and strive" in v. 10 may refer to the training mentioned in vv. 7b–8.

A **4:10** *hope.* See note on 1:1. *Savior of all.* Obviously this does not mean that God saves every person from eternal punishment, for such universalism would contradict the clear testimony of Scripture. God is, however, the Savior of all in that he offers salvation to all and saves all who come to him (all "who believe").

C **4:12** *because you are young.* Timothy was probably in his mid–30s or younger, and in that day such an influential position was not usually held by a man so young. For this reason his leadership may have been called into question. *example.* See Tit 2:7–8 and note.

4:13 *Until I come.* Paul's journey had taken him from Ephesus to Macedonia (see map, p. 2031), but he hoped to rejoin Timothy soon at Ephesus (3:14).

4:14 *through prophecy.* See 1:18 and note. *laid their hands on you.* As an act of commissioning to service (see Ac 6:6; Heb 6:1–2 and notes).

A **4:16** *you will save ... your hearers.* God alone saves, but Christians can be God's instruments to bring about the salvation of others.

5:3 *Give proper recognition to those widows.* Probably means taking care of them, including the giving of material support. Widows were particularly vulnerable in ancient societies because pensions, government assistance, life insurance and the like were not available to them.

5:4 *put their religion into practice.* See Jas 1:22–27; 2:14–26 and note.

5:5 For an example of such a widow, see Lk 2:36–38.

5:6 *dead even while she lives.* Dead spiritually, while living physically.

A **5:8** *the faith.* See note on 3:9. Apostolic teaching emphasized social responsibility. *worse than an unbeliever.* In the pagan world of that time, people generally took care of their family members.

5:9 The church in Ephesus seems to have maintained a "list of widows" supported by the church. While there is no evidence of an order of widows comparable to that of the overseers, it appears that those on the list were expected to devote themselves to prayer (v. 5) and good deeds (v. 10).

5:10 *washing the feet of the Lord's people.* A menial task, but necessary in NT times because of dusty roads and the wearing of sandals (see Jn 13:14). *the Lord's people.* See note on Col 1:4.

5:12 *broken their first pledge.* Perhaps when a widow was added to the list she pledged special devotion to Christ, which would be diminished by remarriage. Or Paul may be referring to the believer's basic trust in Christ, which a widow would compromise by marrying outside the faith.

of being idle and going about from house to house. And not only do they become idlers, but also busybodies ᵛ who talk nonsense, ʷ saying things they ought not to. ¹⁴So I counsel younger widows to marry, ˣ to have children, to manage their homes and to give the enemy no opportunity for slander. ʸ ¹⁵Some have in fact already turned away to follow Satan. ᶻ

¹⁶If any woman who is a believer has widows in her care, she should continue to help them and not let the church be burdened with them, so that the church can help those widows who are really in need. ᵃ

¹⁷The elders ᵇ who direct the affairs of the church well are worthy of double honor, ᶜ especially those whose work is preaching and teaching. ¹⁸For Scripture says, "Do not muzzle an ox while it is treading out the grain," ᵃ ᵈ and "Workers deserve their wages." ᵇ ᵉ ¹⁹Do not entertain an accusation against an elder ᶠ unless it is brought by two or three witnesses. ᵍ ²⁰But those elders who are sinning you are to reprove ʰ before everyone, so that the others may take warning. ⁱ ²¹I charge you, in the sight of God and Christ Jesusʲ and the elect angels, to keep these instructions without partiality, and to do nothing out of favoritism.

²²Do not be hasty in the laying on of hands, ᵏ and do not share in the sins of others. ˡ Keep yourself pure. ᵐ

²³Stop drinking only water, and use a little wine ⁿ because of your stomach and your frequent illnesses.

²⁴The sins of some are obvious, reaching the place of judgment ahead of them; the sins of others trail behind them. ²⁵In the same way, good deeds are obvious, and even those that are not obvious cannot remain hidden forever.

6

All who are under the yoke of slavery should consider their masters worthy of full respect, ᵒ so that God's name and our teaching may not be slandered. ᵖ ²Those who have believing masters should not show them disrespect just because they are fellow believers. �q Instead, they should serve them even better because their masters are dear to them as fellow believers and are devoted to the welfareᶜ of their slaves.

FALSE TEACHERS AND THE LOVE OF MONEY

These are the things you are to teach and insist on. ʳ ³If anyone teaches otherwise ˢ and does not agree to the sound instruction ᵗ of our Lord Jesus Christ and to godly teaching, ⁴they are conceited ᵘ and understand nothing. They have an unhealthy interest in controversies and quarrels about words ᵛ that result in envy, strife, malicious talk, evil suspicions ⁵and constant friction between people of corrupt mind, who have been robbed of the truth ʷ and who think that godliness is a means to financial gain.

⁶But godliness with contentment ˣ is great gain. ʸ ⁷For we brought nothing into the world, and we can take nothing out of it. ᶻ ⁸But if we have food and clothing, we will be content with that. ᵃ ⁹Those who want to get rich ᵇ fall into temptation and a trap ᶜ and into many foolish and harmful desires that plunge people into ruin and destruction. ¹⁰For the

---

ᵃ 18 Deut. 25:4   ᵇ 18 Luke 10:7   ᶜ 2 Or and benefit from the service

---

5:13 ᵛ 2Th 3:11
ʷ S Ro 1:29
5:14 ˣ 1Co 7:9
ʸ 1Ti 6:1
5:15 ᶻ S Mt 4:10
5:16 ᵃ ver 3-5
5:17 ᵇ S Ac 11:30
ᶜ Php 2:29; 1Th 5:12
5:18 ᵈ Dt 25:4;
1Co 9:7-9 ᵉ Lk 10:7;
Lev 19:13; Dt 24:14,
15; Mt 10:10; 1Co 9:14
5:19 ᶠ S Ac 11:30
ᵍ S Mt 18:16
5:20 ʰ 2Ti 4:2;
Tit 1:13; 2:15 ⁱ Dt 13:11
5:21 ʲ 1Ti 6:13;
2Ti 4:1
5:22 ᵏ S Ac 6:6
ˡ Eph 5:11 ᵐ Ps 18:26
5:23 ⁿ 1Ti 3:8
6:1 ᵒ S Eph 6:5
ᵖ 1Ti 5:14; Tit 2:5,8
6:2 q Phm 16
ʳ 1Ti 4:11
6:3 ˢ 1Ti 1:3
ᵗ S 1Ti 1:10
6:4 ᵘ 1Ti 3:6; 2Ti 3:4
ᵛ S 2Ti 2:14
6:5 ʷ 2Ti 3:8;
Tit 1:15
6:6 ˣ Php 4:11;
Heb 13:5 ʸ 1Ti 4:8
6:7 ᶻ Job 1:21;
Ps 49:17; Ecc 5:15
6:8 ᵃ Pr 30:8;
Heb 13:5
6:9 ᵇ Pr 15:27; 28:20
ᶜ 1Ti 3:7

5:13 *busybodies.* See 2Th 3:11 and note.

5:15 *Satan.* See notes on Job 1:6; Mt 16:23; 1Th 3:5; 1Jn 3:8; Rev 12:9–10.

5:17 All elders were to exercise leadership (3:4–5) and to teach and preach (3:2), and all were to receive honor. But those who excelled in leadership were to be counted "worthy of double honor." This was especially true of those who labored at teaching and preaching. (The Greek word translated "work" refers to toil.) That such honor should include financial support is indicated by the two illustrations in v. 18.

5:18 *Scripture.* The use of this term for both an OT (Dt 25:4) and a NT (Lk 10:7) passage shows that by this time portions of the NT (or what ultimately became a part of the NT) were considered to be equal in authority to the OT Scriptures (see 2Pe 3:16 and note). *Do not muzzle … grain.* See 1Co 9:9–11 and notes on 9:9,11.

5:19 *two or three witnesses.* Cf. Dt 17:6 and note.

5:20 *those elders who are sinning.* The context indicates that Paul is speaking of the discipline of elders.

5:21 *elect angels.* Chosen angels, in contrast to Satan and the other fallen angels. *do nothing out of favoritism.* See Ex 23:3; Lev 19:15; Dt 1:17; 16:19; Job 13:10; Pr 18:5; 24:23; 28:21; Mal 2:9; Jas 2:1,9; 3:7. Cf. note on Ac 10:34.

5:22 *Do not be hasty in the laying on of hands.* Paul is speaking

about the ordination of elders (see 4:14 and note), which should not be done until candidates have had time to prove themselves. *do not share in the sins of others.* Do not ordain a person unworthy of the office of elder. *Keep yourself pure.* Probably refers here to refusal to become involved in the ordination of an unworthy man.

5:23 *Stop drinking only water.* A parenthetical comment in Paul's discussion of elders. In view of Timothy's physical ailments, and perhaps because safe drinking water was often difficult to find, Paul advised him to drink "a little wine."

5:24–25 *sins of some … good deeds.* Paul advises being alert to hidden sins, as well as to good deeds in the lives of candidates for ordination.

6:1 *slavery.* See notes on 1Co 7:21; Eph 6:5; Col 3:22—4:1; see also Phm 16.

6:2b *These … things.* Paul's preceding instructions.

6:3–5 Paul returns to the subject of 1:3 (see note on 1:3–11).

6:3 *sound instruction … godly.* See essay, p. 2026.

6:5 *robbed of the truth.* They had once known the truth but had been led into error. *who think that godliness is a means to financial gain.* See notes on 2Co 2:17; 11:7.

6:7 *take nothing out of it.* See Ps 49:17.

6:8 See Php 4:11–12 and notes.

6:9 See Lk 12:13–21 and note on 12:13.

6:10 *d* S 1Ti 3:3
e ver 21; Jas 5:19
f Jos 7:21
6:11 *g* 2Ti 3:17
h ver 3,5,6; S 1Ti 2:2
i 1Ti 1:14; 2Ti 2:22;
3:10
6:12 *j* 1Co 9:25,26;
S 1Ti 1:18 *k* ver 19;
Php 3:12 *l* S Mt 25:46
m S Heb 3:1
6:13 *n* Jn 18:33-37
o ver 12 *p* 1Ti 5:21;
2Ti 4:1
6:14 *q* S 1Th 3:13
r S 1Co 1:7; 2Ti 1:10;
4:1,8
6:15 *s* 1Ti 2:6; Tit 1:3
t 1Ti 1:11 *u* 1Ti 1:17
v Dt 10:17; Ps 136:3;
Da 2:47; Rev 1:5;
17:14; 19:16
6:16 *w* 1Ti 1:17
x Ps 104:2; 1Jn 1:7
y S Jn 1:18 *z* S Ro 11:36
6:17 *a* ver 9
b Ps 62:10; Jer 49:4;
Lk 12:20,21 *c* 1Ti 4:10
d Ac 14:17
6:18 *e* S 1Ti 5:10
f Ro 12:8,13; Eph 4:28
6:19 *g* S Mt 6:20
h ver 12; Php 3:12
6:20 *i* 2Ti 1:12,14
j 2Ti 2:16
6:21 *k* ver 10;
2Ti 2:18 *l* S Col 4:18

love of money *d* is a root of all kinds of evil. Some people, eager for money, have wandered from the faith *e* and pierced themselves with many griefs. *f*

FINAL CHARGE TO TIMOTHY

[11] But you, man of God, *g* flee from all this, and pursue righteousness, godliness, *h* faith, love, *i* endurance and gentleness. [12] Fight the good fight *j* of the faith. Take hold of *k* the eternal life *l* to which you were called when you made your good confession *m* in the presence of many witnesses. [13] In the sight of God, who gives life to everything, and of Christ Jesus, who while testifying before Pontius Pilate *n* made the good confession, *o* I charge you *p* [14] to keep this command without spot or blame *q* until the appearing of our Lord Jesus Christ, *r* [15] which God will bring about in his own time *s*—God, the blessed *t* and only Ruler, *u* the King of kings and Lord of lords, *v* [16] who alone is immortal *w* and who lives in unapproachable light, *x* whom no one has seen or can see. *y* To him be honor and might forever. Amen. *z*

[17] Command those who are rich *a* in this present world not to be arrogant nor to put their hope in wealth, *b* which is so uncertain, but to put their hope in God, *c* who richly provides us with everything for our enjoyment. *d* [18] Command them to do good, to be rich in good deeds, *e* and to be generous and willing to share. *f* [19] In this way they will lay up treasure for themselves *g* as a firm foundation for the coming age, so that they may take hold of *h* the life that is truly life.

[20] Timothy, guard what has been entrusted *i* to your care. Turn away from godless chatter *j* and the opposing ideas of what is falsely called knowledge, [21] which some have professed and in so doing have departed from the faith. *k*

Grace be with you all. *l*

6:10,12,21 *the faith.* See note on 3:9.

A **6:12** *Fight the good fight.* See 1:18 and note. *Take hold of the eternal life.* Timothy had possessed eternal life since he had first been saved, but Paul urges him to claim its benefits in greater fullness (see vv. 17–19 and note on 4:16). *when you made your good confession.* Perhaps a reference to Timothy's confession of faith at his baptism during Paul's first missionary journey.

6:13 *who while testifying before Pontius Pilate made the good confession.* Probably a reference to Jesus' statements recorded in Jn 18:34–37; 19:11.

6:14 *this command.* Perhaps the whole charge given to Timothy to preach the gospel and care for the church (see v. 20)—though the preceding context may indicate that Paul used the singular "command" to sum up the various commands listed in vv. 11–12.

6:15 *in his own time.* Just as Jesus' first coming occurred at the

precise time God wanted (Gal 4:4), so also his second coming will be at God's appointed time. *King of kings and Lord of lords.* See Rev 17:14 and note; 19:16.

6:16 *whom no one has seen or can see.* See Jn 1:18 and note.

6:17–19 See note on v. 12.

6:19 *lay up treasure.* See Mt 6:19–21 and note; 19:21; Lk 12:33 and note.

6:20 *what has been entrusted to your care.* The gospel (see 2Ti 1:14). *what is falsely called knowledge.* Perhaps a reference to an early form of the heresy of Gnosticism, which taught that one may be saved by knowledge. (The term "Gnosticism" comes from the Greek word for knowledge; see Introduction to 1 John: Gnosticism.)

6:21 *Grace.* See note on Ro 1:7. *with you.* See note on 2Co 13:14. *you.* The Greek is plural (hence TNIV "you all"), indicating that Paul expects his letter to Timothy to be read to the entire Ephesian congregation (see note on 2Ti 4:22).

2 TIMOTHY

AUTHOR, DATE AND SETTING

C See essay, p. 2026. After Paul's release from prison in Rome in A.D. 62 (Ac 28) and after his fourth missionary journey (see map, pp. 2031–2032), during which he wrote 1 Timothy and Titus, Paul was again imprisoned under Emperor Nero c. 66–67. It was during this time that he wrote 2 Timothy (see chart, p. 1855). In contrast to his first imprisonment, when he lived in a "rented house" (Ac 28:30; see note there), he now languished in a cold dungeon (see 4:13 and note), chained like a common criminal (1:16; 2:9). His friends even had a hard time finding out where he was being kept (1:17). Paul knew that his work was done and that his life was nearly at an end (4:6–8).

REASONS FOR WRITING

Paul had three reasons for writing to Timothy at this time:

C 1. Paul was lonely. Phygelus and Hermogenes, "everyone in the province of Asia" (1:15) and Demas (4:10) had all deserted him. Crescens, Titus and Tychicus were away (4:10–12), and only Luke was with him (4:11). Paul wanted very much for Timothy to join him also. Timothy was his co-worker (Ro 16:21), who "as a son with his father" (Php 2:22 ; see note there) had served closely with Paul (see 1Co 4:17). Of him Paul could say, "I have no one else like him" (Php 2:20). Paul longed for Timothy (1:4) and twice asked him to come soon (4:9,21). For more information on Timothy, see Introduction to 1 Timothy: Recipient.

2. Paul was concerned about the welfare of the churches during this time of persecution under Nero, and he admonished Timothy to guard the gospel (1:14), to persevere in it (3:14), to keep on preaching it (4:2) and, if necessary, to suffer for it (1:8; 2:3).

3. Paul wanted to write to the Ephesian church through his letter to Timothy (see note on 4:22).

OUTLINE

1:1 *aS 1Co 1:1
bS 2Co 1:1 cEph 3:6;
Tit 1:2; 1Ti 6:19
1:2 dS Ac 16:1
eS 1Ti 1:2 fS Ro 1:7
1:3 gS Ro 1:8
hS Ac 23:1 iS Ro 1:10
1:4 jAc 20:37
k2Ti 4:9
1:5 l1Ti 1:5
mAc 16:1; 2Ti 3:15
1:6 nS Ac 6:6;
1Ti 4:14
1:7 oJer 42:11;
Ro 8:15; 1Co 16:10,11;
1Ti 4:12; Heb 2:15
pIsa 11:2
1:8 qver 12,16;
Mk 8:38 rS Eph 3:1
s2Ti 2:3,9; 4:5
1:9 tS Ro 11:14
uS Ro 8:28
vS Eph 2:9
1:10 wEph 1:9
xS 1Ti 6:14
y1Co 15:26,54
1:11 zver 8
aS Ac 9:15 b1Ti 2:7
1:12 cver 8,16;
Mk 8:38 dver 14;
1Ti 6:20 ever 18;
S 1Co 1:8; 2Ti 4:8
1:13 f2Ti 2:2
gS Tit 1:9 hRo 6:17
iS 1Ti 1:10 jS 1Th 1:3;
1Ti 1:14
1:14 kver 12
lS Ro 8:9
1:15 mS Ac 2:9
n2Ti 4:10,11,16
1:16 o2Ti 4:19
pver 8,12; Mk 8:38
qS Ac 21:33

Paul, an apostle *a* of Christ Jesus by the will of God, *b* in keeping with the promise of life that is in Christ Jesus, *c*

2 To Timothy, *d* my dear son: *e*

Grace, mercy and peace from God the Father and Christ Jesus our Lord. *f*

THANKSGIVING

3 I thank God, *g* whom I serve, as my ancestors did, with a clear conscience, *h* as night and day I constantly remember you in my prayers. *i* 4 Recalling your tears, *j* I long to see you, *k* so that I may be filled with joy. 5 I am reminded of your sincere faith, *l* which first lived in your grandmother Lois and in your mother Eunice *m* and, I am persuaded, now lives in you also.

APPEAL FOR LOYALTY TO PAUL AND THE GOSPEL

6 For this reason I remind you to fan into flame the gift of God, which is in you through the laying on of my hands. *n* 7 For the Spirit God gave us does not make us timid, *o* but gives us power, *p* love and self-discipline. 8 So do not be ashamed *q* of the testimony about our Lord or of me his prisoner. *r* But join with me in suffering for the gospel, *s* by the power of God, 9 who has saved *t* us and called *u* us to a holy life—not because of anything we have done *v* but because of his own purpose and grace. This grace was given us in Christ Jesus before the beginning of time, 10 but it has now been revealed *w* through the appearing of our Savior, Christ Jesus, *x* who has destroyed death *y* and has brought life and immortality to light through the gospel. 11 And of this gospel *z* I was appointed *a* a herald and an apostle and a teacher. *b* 12 That is why I am suffering as I am. Yet this is no cause for shame, *c* because I know whom I have believed, and am convinced that he is able to guard *d* what I have entrusted to him until that day. *e*

13 What you heard from me, *f* keep *g* as the pattern *h* of sound teaching, *i* with faith and love in Christ Jesus. *j* 14 Guard *k* the good deposit that was entrusted to you—guard it with the help of the Holy Spirit who lives in us. *l*

EXAMPLES OF DISLOYALTY AND LOYALTY

15 You know that everyone in the province of Asia *m* has deserted me, *n* including Phygelus and Hermogenes. 16 May the Lord show mercy to the household of Onesiphorus, *o* because he often refreshed me and was not ashamed *p* of my chains. *q* 17 On the contrary, when he was in Rome, he searched hard for me until he found me. 18 May the Lord grant that he will find

---

1:1 *Paul.* See note on Ro 1:1. *apostle.* See note on 1Co 1:1. *in keeping with the promise of life.* God's choice of Paul to be an apostle was in keeping with that promise, because apostles were appointed to preach and explain the good news that eternal life is available to all who will receive it through faith in Christ.

1:2 *Timothy, my dear son.* See note on 1Ti 1:2. *Grace...peace.* See note on Ro 1:7. *mercy.* See note on 1Ti 1:2 and note.

1:3 *thank God...in my prayers.* See note on Php 1:3–4.

1:4 *Recalling your tears.* Perhaps refers to Timothy's tears when Paul left for Macedonia (see 1Ti 1:3 and note). *long to see you.* See 4:9,21.

1:5 *your grandmother Lois...your mother Eunice.* According to Ac 16:1, Timothy's mother was a Jewish Christian. Here we learn that his grandmother too was a Christian. Timothy's father, however, was a Greek and apparently an unbeliever (Ac 16:1).

1:6 *fan into flame the gift of God.* Gifts are not given in full bloom; they need to be developed through use. *through the laying on of my hands.* See 1Ti 4:14 and note. Paul was God's instrument, through whom the gift came from the Holy Spirit to Timothy (see note on 1Ti 1:18).

1:7 *timid.* Apparently lack of confidence was a serious problem for Timothy (see 1Co 16:10–11 and note on 16:10; 1Ti 4:12).

1:8 *do not be ashamed.* Cf. v. 12; Ro 1:16 and note.

1:9 *called us to a holy life.* See Eph 1:4 and note; 1Th 4:7. *not because of anything we have done but because of his*

own purpose and grace. Salvation is by grace alone and is based not on human effort but on God's saving plan and the gracious gift of his Son (see Ro 3:28; see also Eph 2:8–9; Tit 3:5 and notes). *before the beginning of time.* God's plan to save lost sinners was made in eternity past (see Eph 1:4; 1Pe 1:20 and notes; Rev 13:8).

1:10 *Christ...has destroyed death.* See 1Co 15:26,54–57 and notes on 15:26,57. *has brought life and immortality to light.* Implying that before Jesus came, the certainty of life after death was somewhat shrouded in darkness (see Ps 11:7; Ecc 3:21; Isa 26:19; Da 12:2 and notes). *gospel.* See note on Mk 1:1.

1:11 *a herald and an apostle.* See 1Ti 2:7 and note.

1:12 *no cause for shame.* Cf. v. 8 and note. *what I have entrusted to him.* Probably Paul's commitment to Christ and his gospel (cf. v. 14; 1Ti 6:20 and notes). *that day.* The day of judgment.

1:13 *sound teaching.* See Tit 1:9 and note. *faith and love in Christ.* See 1Ti 1:14; faith and love through union with Christ—another way of saying "Christian faith and love."

1:14 *good deposit...entrusted to you.* The gospel (see note on v. 12). Paul gives the same command in 1Ti 6:20. *Holy Spirit who lives in us.* See Ro 5:5; 1Co 6:19 and notes; see also Ro 8:9.

1:15 *everyone.* Probably a deliberate exaggeration to express widespread desertion. *province of Asia.* Timothy was in Ephesus, the capital of the province of Asia (see Introduction to Ephesians: The City of Ephesus; see also map, p. 1983).

1:16 *Onesiphorus.* He and his family probably lived in Ephesus (v. 18; 4:19).

1:17 *Rome.* See Introduction: Author, Date and Setting; cf. v. 8; 2:9.

mercy from the Lord on that day! *r* You know very well in how many ways he helped me *s* in Ephesus. *t*

THE APPEAL RENEWED

2 You then, my son, *u* be strong *v* in the grace that is in Christ Jesus. ²And the things you have heard me say *w* in the presence of many witnesses *x* entrust to reliable people who will also be qualified to teach others. ³Join with me in suffering, *y* like a good soldier *z* of Christ Jesus. ⁴No one serving as a soldier gets involved in civilian affairs; rather, they try to please their commanding officer. ⁵Similarly, anyone who competes as an athlete does not receive the victor's crown *a* except by competing according to the rules. ⁶The hardworking farmer should be the first to receive a share of the crops. *b* ⁷Reflect on what I am saying, for the Lord will give you insight into all this.

⁸Remember Jesus Christ, raised from the dead, *c* descended from David. *d* This is my gospel, *e* ⁹for which I am suffering *f* even to the point of being chained *g* like a criminal. But God's word *h* is not chained. ¹⁰Therefore I endure everything *i* for the sake of the elect, *j* that they too may obtain the salvation *k* that is in Christ Jesus, with eternal glory. *l*

¹¹Here is a trustworthy saying: *m*

If we died with him,
    we will also live with him; *n*
¹²if we endure,
    we will also reign with him. *o*
If we disown him,
    he will also disown us; *p*
¹³if we are faithless,
    he remains faithful, *q*
    for he cannot disown himself.

DEALING WITH FALSE TEACHERS

¹⁴Keep reminding God's people of these things. Warn them before God against quarreling about words; *r* it is of no value, and only ruins those who listen. ¹⁵Do your best to present yourself to God as one approved, a worker who does not need to be ashamed and who correctly handles the word of truth. *s* ¹⁶Avoid godless chatter, *t* because those who indulge in it will become more and more ungodly. ¹⁷Their teaching will spread like gangrene. Among them are Hymenaeus *u* and Philetus, ¹⁸who have departed from the truth. They say that the resurrection has already taken place, *v* and they destroy the faith of

1:18 *r* S ver 12
s Heb 6:10
t S Ac 18:19
2:1 *u* S 1Ti 1:2
v S Eph 6:10
2:2 *w* 2Ti 1:13
x 1Ti 6:12
2:3 *y* ver 9; 2Ti 1:8;
4:5 *z* S 1Ti 1:18
2:5 *a* S 1Co 9:25
2:6 *b* 1Co 9:10
2:8 *c* S Ac 2:24
d S Mt 1:1 *e* Ro 2:16;
16:25
2:9 *f* S Ac 9:16
g S Ac 21:33
h S Heb 4:12
2:10 *i* Col 1:24
j Tit 1:1 *k* 2Co 1:6
2Co 4:17; 1Pe 5:10
2:11 *m* S 1Ti 1:15
n Ro 6:2–11
2:12 *o* Ro 8:17;
1Pe 4:13 *p* Mt 10:33
2:13 *q* Ro 3:3;
S 1Co 1:9
2:14 *r* ver 23;
1Ti 1:4; 6:4; Tit 3:9
2:15 *s* Eph 1:13;
Col 1:5; Jas 1:18
2:16 *t* Tit 3:9;
1Ti 6:20
2:17 *u* 1Ti 1:20
2:18 *v* 2Th 2:2

1:18 *that day.* The day of judgment (see v. 12). *he helped me in Ephesus.* Either on Paul's third missionary journey (see map, p. 1875) or on his fourth (see map, p. 2031).

2:1 *my son.* See 1Ti 1:2 and note. *strong in the grace ... in Christ.* Enabling power comes from a relationship to Christ (see 2Co 12:9–10; Eph 6:10 and notes).

2:2 *the things you have heard me say in the presence of many witnesses.* Refers to Paul's preaching and teaching, which Timothy had heard repeatedly on Paul's missionary journeys. *reliable people.* People characterized by trustworthiness, dependability and faithfulness (cf. Mt 25:21,23 and notes on 25:21; Lk 12:42; 1Co 4:2; Eph 6:21; Col 1:7; 4:7; 1Ti 1:12; 1Pe 4:10; 3Jn 3; Rev 2:10, 13; 13:10; 14:12; 17:14; cf. also Ps 4:3 and note).

2:3–6 Paul gives three examples for Timothy to follow: (1) a soldier who wants to please his commander, (2) an athlete who follows the rules of the game and (3) a farmer who works hard.

2:5 *victor's crown.* Cf. 1Co 9:25 and note.

2:6 *receive a share of the crops.* In this illustration, as in the previous two (soldier, vv. 3–4; athlete, v. 5), the main lesson is that dedicated effort will be rewarded (see 1Ti 5:17 and note).

2:8 *raised from the dead, descended from David.* Christ's resurrection proclaims his deity, and his descent from David shows his humanity; both truths are basic to the gospel. Since Christ is God, his death has infinite value; since he is human, he could rightfully become our substitute.

2:9 *chained like a criminal.* Apparently Paul was awaiting execution (see 4:6 and note).

2:10 *I endure everything for the sake of the elect.* No suffering is too great if it brings about the salvation of God's chosen ones who will yet believe. *in Christ.* See notes on 1:13; Eph 1:1. *eternal glory.* The final state of salvation.

2:11–13 Probably an early Christian hymn. The point to which Paul appeals is that suffering for Christ will be followed by glory (see Ro 8:17–18).

2:11 *trustworthy saying.* See note on 1Ti 1:15. *If we died with him, we will also live with him.* The Greek grammatical construction here assumes that we "died with" Christ in the past, when he died for us on the cross. We are therefore assured that we will also live with him eternally (cf. Ro 6:2–11).

2:12 *if we endure, we will also reign.* Faithfully bearing up under suffering and trial will result in reward when Christ returns (see Ro 8:17 and note). *If we disown him.* See Mt 10:33.

2:13 *he remains faithful.* See Ro 3:3–4 and notes.

2:14–18 The wording of vv. 14–16 indicates that the heresy mentioned here is an early form of Gnosticism—the same as that dealt with in 1 Timothy and Titus (see note on 1Ti 1:3–11 and Introduction to 1 John: Gnosticism). Two leaders of this heresy, Hymenaeus (see 1Ti 1:20) and Philetus (v. 17), denied bodily resurrection (v. 18) and probably asserted that there is only spiritual resurrection (similar to the error mentioned in 1Co 15:12–19; see notes there). Gnosticism interpreted resurrection allegorically, not literally.

2:15 *ashamed.* See 1:8 and note. *word of truth.* The gospel (Eph 1:13; Col 1:5), whose truth Timothy was to believe and obey and whose contents he was therefore to preach (4:2).

2:16 *godless chatter.* See note on 1Ti 1:3–11.

2:18 *w* 1Ti 1:19; 6:21
2:19 *x* Isa 28:16
y Ex 33:12; Nu 16:5;
Jn 10:14; 1Co 8:3;
Gal 4:9 *z* 1Co 1:2
2:20 *a* Ro 9:21
2:21 *b* 2Co 9:8;
Eph 2:10; 2Ti 3:17
2:22 *c* 1Ti 1:14; 6:11
d S Ac 2:21 *e* 1Ti 1:5
2:23 *f* S ver 14
2:24 *g* 1Ti 3:2,3
2:25 *h* S 1Ti 2:4
2:26 *i* 1Ti 3:7
3:1 *j* 1Ti 4:1; 2Pe 3:3
3:2 *k* S 1Ti 3:3
l Ro 1:30 *m* 2Pe 2:10-
12 *n* Ro 1:30
3:4 *o* Ps 25:3
p 1Ti 3:6; 6:4
3:5 *q* S 1Ti 2:2
r S Ro 16:17
3:6 *s* Jude 4
3:7 *t* S 1Ti 2:4
3:8 *u* Ex 7:11
v Ac 13:8 *w* 1Ti 6:5
3:9 *x* Ex 7:12; 8:18;
9:11
3:10 *y* 1Ti 4:6
3:11 *z* Ac 13:14,50
a S Ac 13:51 *b* Ac 14:6
c 2Co 11:23-27
d S Ro 15:31
e Ps 34:19
3:12 *f* Jn 15:20;
S Ac 14:22
3:13 *g* 2Ti 2:16
h S Mk 13:5
3:14 *i* 2Ti 1:13
3:15 *j* 2Ti 1:5
k Jn 5:39 *l* Dt 4:6;
Ps 119:98,99

some. *w* 19 Nevertheless, God's solid foundation stands firm, *x* sealed with this inscription: "The Lord knows those who are his," *y* and, "Everyone who confesses the name of the Lord *z* must turn away from wickedness."

20 In a large house there are articles not only of gold and silver, but also of wood and clay; some are for noble purposes and some for disposal of refuse. *a* 21 Those who cleanse themselves from the latter will be instruments for noble purposes, made holy, useful to the Master and prepared to do any good work. *b*

22 Flee the evil desires of youth and pursue righteousness, faith, love *c* and peace, along with those who call on the Lord *d* out of a pure heart. *e* 23 Don't have anything to do with foolish and stupid arguments, because you know they produce quarrels. *f* 24 And the Lord's servant must not be quarrelsome but must be kind to everyone, able to teach, not resentful. *g* 25 Opponents must be gently instructed, in the hope that God will grant them repentance leading them to a knowledge of the truth, *h* 26 and that they will come to their senses and escape from the trap of the devil, *i* who has taken them captive to do his will.

3 But mark this: There will be terrible times in the last days. *j* 2 People will be lovers of themselves, lovers of money, *k* boastful, proud, *l* abusive, *m* disobedient to their parents, *n* ungrateful, unholy, 3 without love, unforgiving, slanderous, without self-control, brutal, not lovers of the good, 4 treacherous, *o* rash, conceited, *p* lovers of pleasure rather than lovers of God— 5 having a form of godliness *q* but denying its power. Have nothing to do with such people. *r*

6 They are the kind who worm their way *s* into homes and gain control over gullible women, who are loaded down with sins and are swayed by all kinds of evil desires, 7 always learning but never able to come to a knowledge of the truth. *t* 8 Just as Jannes and Jambres opposed Moses, *u* so also these teachers oppose *v* the truth. They are men of depraved minds, *w* who, as far as the faith is concerned, are rejected. 9 But they will not get very far because, as in the case of those men, *x* their folly will be clear to everyone.

A FINAL CHARGE TO TIMOTHY

10 You, however, know all about my teaching, *y* my way of life, my purpose, faith, patience, love, endurance, 11 persecutions, sufferings—what kinds of things happened to me in Antioch, *z* Iconium *a* and Lystra, *b* the persecutions I endured. *c* Yet the Lord rescued *d* me from all of them. *e* 12 In fact, everyone who wants to live a godly life in Christ Jesus will be persecuted, *f* 13 while evildoers and impostors will go from bad to worse, *g* deceiving and being deceived. *h* 14 But as for you, continue in what you have learned and have become convinced of, because you know those from whom you learned it, *i* 15 and how from infancy *j* you have known the Holy Scriptures, *k* which are able to make you wise *l* for salvation

---

A **2:19** *God's solid foundation.* The church, which upholds the truth (1Ti 3:15). In spite of the heresy of Hymenaeus and Philetus (v. 17), Timothy should be heartened to know that the church is God's solid foundation. There are two inscriptions on it: One stresses the security of the church ("The Lord knows those who are his"; here "know," as often in the Bible, means to be intimately acquainted with), while the other emphasizes human responsibility ("Everyone who confesses the name of the Lord must turn away from wickedness"). *sealed.* The church is owned and securely protected by God (see Eph 1:13 and note).
2:21 *made holy.* Set apart to God for his use (see 1Co 1:2; 1Pe 1:16 and notes).
2:22 *youth.* See 1Ti 4:12 and note. *peace.* See Ro 12:16. *pure heart.* See 1Ti 1:5 and note.
2:23 The Gnostic heresy is in view again (see note on vv. 14–18).
2:24 *Lord's servant.* Seems to refer primarily to a person who, like Timothy, is set aside for special service. *able to teach.* Cf. note on 1Ti 3:1.
2:25 *repentance.* See Mt 4:17 and note. *knowledge of the truth.* See 1Ti 2:4.
2:26 *trap of the devil.* See 1Ti 3:7; cf. Eph 6:11; 1Pe 5:8.
A **3:1** *last days.* The Messianic era, the time beginning with Christ's first coming (see 1Ti 4:1; Heb 1:1–2 and notes; 1Pe 1:20). That "the last days" in this passage does not refer only to the time just prior to Christ's return is apparent from Paul's command to Timothy to "have nothing to do" (v. 5) with the unbe-

lieving and unfaithful people who characterize this time.
3:2–5 For similar lists of vices, see note on Ro 1:29–31.
3:2 *lovers of money.* See 1Ti 6:9–10,17–18.
3:5 *godliness.* See 1Ti 2:2 and note.
3:6 *gullible women.* Unstable women who are guilt-ridden because of their sins, torn by lust and victims of various false teachers ("always learning," v. 7, but never coming to a saving knowledge of Christ).
C **3:8** *Jannes and Jambres.* According to Jewish tradition, they were the Egyptian court magicians who opposed Moses (see Ex 7:11 and note).
3:11 *Antioch, Iconium and Lystra.* Three cities in the Roman province of Galatia (see map, p. 1869) that Paul visited on his first and second missionary journeys (see Ac 13:14,51; 14:6 and notes). Since Timothy was from Lystra (Ac 16:1), he would have known firsthand of Paul's sufferings in that region. *the Lord rescued me from all of them.* Even from execution by stoning (see Ac 14:19–20 and notes).
3:12 See Mt 10:22; Ac 14:22; Php 1:29 and note; 1Pe 4:12. *in Christ.* See notes on 1:13; Eph 1:1.
3:14 *those from whom you learned it.* Perhaps a reference to Paul, as well as to Timothy's mother and grandmother (see 1:5 and note).
A **3:15** *from infancy you have known the Holy Scriptures.* A Jewish boy formally began to study the OT when he was five years old. Timothy was taught at home by his mother and grandmother even before he reached this age.

through faith in Christ Jesus. ¹⁶All Scripture is God-breathed ^m and is useful for teaching, ⁿ rebuking, correcting and training in righteousness, ^o ¹⁷so that all God's people^a ^p may be thoroughly equipped for every good work. ^q

4 In the presence of God and of Christ Jesus, who will judge the living and the dead, ^r and in view of his appearing^s and his kingdom, I give you this charge: ^t ²Preach ^u the word; ^v be prepared in season and out of season; correct, rebuke ^w and encourage^x—with great patience and careful instruction. ³For the time will come when people will not put up with sound doctrine. ^y Instead, to suit their own desires, they will gather around them a great number of teachers to say what their itching ears want to hear. ^z ⁴They will turn their ears away from the truth and turn aside to myths. ^a ⁵But you, keep your head in all situations, endure hardship, ^b do the work of an evangelist, ^c discharge all the duties of your ministry.

⁶For I am already being poured out like a drink offering, ^d and the time for my departure is near. ^e ⁷I have fought the good fight, ^f I have finished the race, ^g I have kept the faith. ⁸Now there is in store for me ^h the crown of righteousness, ⁱ which the Lord, the righteous Judge, will award to me on that day^j—and not only to me, but also to all who have longed for his appearing. ^k

PERSONAL REMARKS

⁹Do your best to come to me quickly, ^l ¹⁰for Demas, ^m because he loved this world, ⁿ has deserted me and has gone to Thessalonica. ^o Crescens has gone to Galatia, ^p and Titus ^q to Dalmatia. ¹¹Only Luke ^r is with me. ^s Get Mark ^t and bring him with you, because he is helpful to me in my ministry. ¹²I sent Tychicus ^u to Ephesus. ^v ¹³When you come, bring the cloak that I left with Carpus at Troas, ^w and my scrolls, especially the parchments.

¹⁴Alexander^x the metalworker did me a great deal of harm. The Lord will repay him for what he has done. ^y ¹⁵You too should be on your guard against him, because he strongly opposed our message.

^a 17 Or that the servant of God

3:16 ^m 2Pe 1:20, 21
ⁿ S Ro 4:23, 24
^o Dt 29:29
3:17 ^p 1Ti 6:11
^q 2Ti 2:21
4:1 ^r S Ac 10:42
^s ver 8; S 1Ti 6:14
^t 1Ti 5:21; 6:13
4:2 ^u 1Ti 4:13
^v Gal 6:6 ^w 1Ti 5:20;
Tit 1:13; 2:15 ^x Tit 2:15
4:3 ^y S 1Ti 1:10
^z Isa 30:10
4:4 ^a S 1Ti 1:14
4:5 ^b 2Ti 1:8; 2:3, 9
^c Ac 21:8; Eph 4:11
4:6 ^d Nu 15:1-12;
28:7, 24; Php 2:17
^e Php 1:23
4:7 ^f S 1Ti 1:18
^g S 1Co 9:24;
Ac 20:24
4:8 ^h Col 1:5; 1Pe 1:4
ⁱ S 1Co 9:25
^j S 2Ti 1:12 ^k S 1Ti 6:14
4:9 ^l ver 21; Tit 3:12
4:10 ^m Col 4:14;
Phm 24 ⁿ 1Jn 2:15
^o S 2Co 2:13
4:11 ^r Col 4:14;
Phm 24 ^s 2Ti 1:15
^t S Ac 12:12
4:12 ^u S Ac 20:4
^v S Ac 18:19
4:13 ^w S Ac 16:8
4:14 ^x Ac 19:33;
1Ti 1:20 ^y Ps 28:4;
109:20; Ro 2:6; 12:19

3:16 *All Scripture.* The primary reference is to the OT, since some of the NT books had not even been written at this time. (See 1Ti 5:18 and note for indications that some NT books—or material ultimately included in the NT—were already considered equal in authority to the OT Scriptures.) *God-breathed.* Paul affirms God's active involvement in the writing of Scripture, an involvement so powerful and pervasive that what is written is the infallible and authoritative word of God (see 2Pe 1:20–21 and notes).

4:1 Paul states his charge to Timothy, aware that he does so in the presence of God the Father and of Christ, who will judge everyone. He is also keenly aware of the twin facts of Christ's return ("his appearing") and the coming establishment of God's kingdom in its fullest expression. Timothy was to view a charge so given as of utmost importance. *Jesus, who will judge.* See Mt 25:31–33; see also Jn 5:22; Jas 5:9; 1Pe 4:5 and notes.

4:2 *be prepared.* Be ready in any situation to speak the needed word, whether of correction, of rebuke or of encouragement.

4:3 *sound doctrine.* See Tit 1:9 and note. *itching ears.* Ears that want to be "scratched" by words in keeping with one's evil desires.

4:4 *myths.* See 1Ti 1:4 and note.

4:6 *drink offering.* The offering of wine poured out to the Lord (see Nu 15:1–12; 28:7). Paul views his approaching death as the pouring out of his life as an offering to Christ (see Php 2:17 and note). *my departure.* His impending death in A.D. 67/68 (see chart, p. 1855; cf. Php 1:23).

4:7 Paul looks back over 30 years of labor as an apostle (c. A.D. 36–67/68). Like an athlete who had engaged successfully in a contest ("fought the good fight"; see note on 1Ti 1:18), he had "finished the race" and "kept the faith," i.e., had carefully preserved the deposit of Christian truth. *the faith.* See note on 1Ti 3:9.

4:8 *crown of righteousness.* Continuing with the same figure of speech, Paul uses the metaphor of the wreath given to the winner of a race (see 1Co 9:25 and note). He could be referring to (1) a crown given as a reward for a righteous life, (2) a crown consisting of righteousness or (3) a crown given righteously (justly) by the righteous Judge. *that day.* The day of Christ's second coming ("appearing"; see v. 1).

4:10 *Demas.* See Col 4:14 and note; Phm 24. *Thessalonica.* See Introduction to 1 Thessalonians: Thessalonica: The City and the Church; see also map, p. 1869. *Galatia.* Either the northern area of Asia Minor (Gaul) or a Roman province in what is now central Turkey (see note on Gal 1:2). *Titus.* See Introduction to Titus: Recipient. *Dalmatia.* Also known as Illyricum (Ro 15:19; see map No.13 at the end of this study Bible).

4:11 *Mark.* See Introduction to Mark: Mark in the NT. John Mark had deserted Paul and Barnabas on their first missionary journey (Ac 13:13). After Paul refused to take Mark on the second journey, Barnabas separated from Paul, taking Mark with him on a mission to Cyprus (Ac 15:36–41). Ultimately Mark proved himself to Paul, indicated by his presence with Paul during Paul's first Roman imprisonment (Col 4:10; Phm 24) and by Paul's request here for Timothy to bring Mark with him to Rome.

4:12 *Tychicus.* See Ac 20:4; Eph 6:21 and notes.

4:13 *cloak.* For protection against the cold dampness (see Introduction: Author, Date and Setting). It was probably a heavy, sleeveless, outer garment, circular in shape with a hole in the middle for one's head. *Troas.* See Ac 16:8 and note; see also map, p. 2031. *scrolls, especially the parchments.* The scrolls (see note on Ex 17:14) were made of leather or papyrus, and the parchments were made of the skins of animals. The latter may have been copies of parts of the OT.

4:14 *Alexander the metalworker.* Perhaps the Alexander mentioned in 1Ti 1:20.

4:16 z Ac 7:60
4:17 a Ac 23:11
b S Php 4:13
c S Ac 9:15
d 1Sa 17:37; Ps 22:21;
Da 6:22; 1Co 15:32
4:18 e Ps 121:7;
2Pe 2:9 f ver 1
g S Ro 11:36
4:19 h S Ac 18:2
i 2Ti 1:16
4:20 j Ac 19:22
k Ac 20:4; 21:29
l Ac 20:15,17
4:21 m ver 9;
Tit 3:12
4:22 n S Gal 6:18
o S Col 4:18

[16]At my first defense, no one came to my support, but everyone deserted me. May it not be held against them. [z] [17]But the Lord stood at my side [a] and gave me strength, [b] so that through me the message might be fully proclaimed and all the Gentiles might hear it. [c] And I was delivered from the lion's mouth. [d] [18]The Lord will rescue me from every evil attack [e] and will bring me safely to his heavenly kingdom. [f] To him be glory for ever and ever. Amen. [g]

FINAL GREETINGS

[19]Greet Priscilla [a] and Aquila [h] and the household of Onesiphorus. [i] [20]Erastus [j] stayed in Corinth, and I left Trophimus [k] sick in Miletus. [l] [21]Do your best to get here before winter. [m] Eubulus greets you, and so do Pudens, Linus, Claudia and all the brothers and sisters. [22]The Lord be with your spirit. [n] Grace be with you all. [o]

a 19 Greek *Prisca*, a variant of *Priscilla*

4:16 *my first defense.* The first court hearing of Paul's present case, not his defense on the occasion of his first imprisonment (Ac 28).

4:17 *through me the message might be fully proclaimed.* Even in these dire circumstances Paul used the occasion to testify about Jesus Christ in the imperial court (cf. Ac 16:25; cf. also Php 1:12–14 and notes). *delivered from the lion's mouth.* Since, as a Roman citizen, Paul could not be thrown to the lions in the amphitheater, this must be a figurative way of saying that his first hearing did not result in an immediate guilty verdict.

4:18 *will rescue me from every evil attack.* Since Paul fully expected to die soon (see v. 6 and note), the rescue he speaks of here is spiritual, not physical. *heavenly kingdom.* Heaven itself.

4:19 *Priscilla and Aquila.* See Ac 18:2,18; 1Co 16:19 and notes. *Onesiphorus.* See 1:16 and note.

4:20 *Erastus.* See Ro 16:23 and note. *Corinth.* See Introduction to 1 Corinthians: The City of Corinth; see also map, p. 1925. *Trophimus.* See note on Ac 20:4. *Miletus.* A seaport on the coast of Asia Minor about 35 miles south of Ephesus (see map, p. 2031). See Ac 20:15 and note.

4:21 *Linus.* Early tradition says he was bishop of Rome after the deaths of Peter and Paul. *brothers and sisters.* See note on Ro 1:13.

4:22 *be with your spirit.* See note on Gal 6:18. *Grace.* See note on Ro 1:7. *with you.* See note on 2Co 13:14. *you.* As at the end of 1 Timothy (see note on 1Ti 6:21), "you" here is plural (hence TNIV "you all"), showing that the letter was intended for public use. The word "your" in the first part of the verse, however, is singular, indicating that it was addressed to Timothy alone.

AUTHOR

C See essay, p. 2026. The author is Paul (see 1:1 and note; see also Introduction to 1 Timothy: Author).

RECIPIENT

C The letter is addressed to Titus, one of Paul's converts (see 1:4 and note) and a considerable help to Paul in his ministry. When Paul left Antioch to discuss the gospel with the Jerusalem leaders, he took Titus with him (Gal 2:1–3); acceptance of Titus (a Gentile) as a Christian without circumcision vindicated Paul's stand there (Gal 2:3–5). Presumably Titus, who is not referred to in Acts (but is mentioned 13 times in the rest of the NT), worked with Paul at Ephesus during his third missionary journey (see map, p. 1875). It is likely that he was the bearer of Paul's severe letter to the Corinthian church (see Introduction to 2 Corinthians: Occasion). Paul was concerned about the possible negative reaction of the Corinthian church to his severe letter, so he arranged to meet Titus at Troas (2Co 2:12–13). When Titus did not appear, Paul traveled on to Macedonia. There he met Titus and with great relief heard the good news that the worst of the trouble was over at Corinth (2Co 7:6–7,13–14). Titus, accompanied by two Christian brothers, was the bearer of 2 Corinthians (2Co 8:23) and was given the responsibility for making final arrangements for the collection, begun a year earlier, in Corinth (see 2Co 8:6,16–17 and notes).

Following Paul's release from his first Roman imprisonment (Ac 28), he and Titus worked briefly in Crete (1:5), after which he commissioned Titus to remain there as his representative and complete some needed work (1:5; 2:15; 3:12–13). Paul asked Titus to meet him at Nicopolis (see map, p. 2031) when a replacement arrived (see 3:12 and note). Later, Titus went on a mission to Dalmatia (see 2Ti 4:10 and note), the last word we hear about him in the NT. Considering the assignments given him, he obviously was a capable and resourceful leader.

CRETE

The fourth largest island in the Mediterranean Sea, Crete lies directly south of the Aegean Sea (see map and inset, p. 1890; cf. note on 1Sa 30:14; cf. also Paul's experiences there in Ac 27:7–13). In NT times life in Crete had sunk to a deplorable moral level. The dishonesty, gluttony and laziness of its inhabitants were proverbial (1:12).

OCCASION AND PURPOSE

Apparently Paul introduced Christianity in Crete when he and Titus visited the island, after which he left Titus there to organize the converts. Paul sent the letter with Zenas and Apollos, who were on a journey that took them through Crete (3:13), to give Titus personal authorization and guidance in meeting opposition (1:5; 2:1,7–8,15; 3:9), instructions about faith and conduct and warnings about false teachers. Paul also informed Titus of his future plans for him (3:12).

PLACE AND DATE OF WRITING

Paul may have written from Macedonia, for he had not yet reached Nicopolis (see 3:12). The letter was written after he was released from his first Roman imprisonment (Ac 28), probably between A.D. 63 and 65 (see chart, p. 1855)—or possibly at a later date if he wrote after his assumed trip to Spain.

DISTINCTIVE CHARACTERISTICS

Especially significant, considering the nature of the Cretan heresy, are the repeated emphases on loving and doing and teaching "what is good" (1:8,16; 2:3,7,14; 3:1,8, 14) and the classic summaries of Christian doctrine (2:11–14; 3:4–7).

OUTLINE

1:1 ᵃRo 1:1; Jas 1:1
ᵇS 1Co 1:1 ᶜS 1Ti 2:4
ᵈS 1Ti 2:2
1:2 ᵉTit 3:7; 2Ti 1:1
ᶠNu 23:19; Heb 6:18
ᵍ2Ti 1:9
1:3 ʰ1Ti 2:6; 6:15
ⁱ2Ti 1:10 ʲS 1Ti 1:11
ᵏS 2Co 1:3; 1Ti 1:1
ˡS Lk 1:47
1:4 ᵐS 2Co 2:13
ⁿS 1Ti 1:2 ᵒS Ro 1:7
1:5 ᵖAc 27:7
ᵠS Ac 11:30
1:6 ʳS 1Th 3:13;
1Ti 3:2
1:7 ˢS 1Ti 3:1
ᵗ1Co 4:1 ᵘS 1Ti 3:3,8
1:8 ᵛS Ro 12:13
ʷ2Ti 3:3 ˣTit 2:2,5,
6,12
1:9 ʸS 1Co 16:13;
1Ti 1:19; 2Ti 1:13; 3:14
ᶻS 1Ti 1:10
1:10 ᵃ1Ti 1:6
ᵇAc 10:45; 11:2
1:11 ᶜ1Ti 5:13

Paul, a servant of God ᵃ and an apostle ᵇ of Jesus Christ to further the faith of God's elect and their knowledge of the truth ᶜ that leads to godliness ᵈ— ²in the hope of eternal life, ᵉ which God, who does not lie, ᶠ promised before the beginning of time, ᵍ ³and which now at his appointed season ʰ he has brought to light ⁱ through the preaching entrusted to me ʲ by the command of God ᵏ our Savior, ˡ

⁴To Titus, ᵐ my true son ⁿ in our common faith:

Grace and peace from God the Father and Christ Jesus our Savior. ᵒ

APPOINTING ELDERS WHO LOVE WHAT IS GOOD

1:6–8Ref — 1Ti 3:2–4

⁵The reason I left you in Crete ᵖ was that you might put in order what was left unfinished and appoint ᵃ elders ᵠ in every town, as I directed you. ⁶An elder must be blameless, ʳ faithful to his wife, a man whose children believe and are not open to the charge of being wild and disobedient. ⁷Since an overseer ˢ manages God's household, ᵗ he must be blameless—not overbearing, not quick-tempered, not given to drunkenness, not violent, not pursuing dishonest gain. ᵘ ⁸Rather, he must be hospitable, ᵛ one who loves what is good, ʷ who is self-controlled, ˣ upright, holy and disciplined. ⁹He must hold firmly ʸ to the trustworthy message as it has been taught, so that he can encourage others by sound doctrine ᶻ and refute those who oppose it.

REBUKING THOSE WHO FAIL TO DO GOOD

¹⁰For there are many rebellious people, full of meaningless talk ᵃ and deception, especially those of the circumcision group. ᵇ ¹¹They must be silenced, because they are disrupting whole households ᶜ by teaching things they ought not to teach—and that for the sake

---

ᵃ 5 Or *ordain*

1:1 *Paul.* See note on Ro 1:1. *servant of God.* Only here does Paul call himself a servant of God; elsewhere he says "servant of Christ" (Ro 1:1; Gal 1:10; Php 1:1). James uses both terms of himself (Jas 1:1). *servant.* See note on Ro 1:1. *apostle.* See note on 1Co 1:1. *to further the faith . . . and their knowledge.* Paul's appointed mission as God's servant and Christ's apostle— further explained in v. 2 (see Ac 9:15; 22:15; 26:16–18). *godliness.* See 1Ti 2:2 and note.
1:2 *hope.* See Col 1:5 and note. *eternal life.* See note on Jn 3:15. *does not lie.* In contrast to the Cretans (v. 12)—and the devil (Jn 8:44). *before the beginning of time.* See 2Ti 1:9 and note.
1:3 *appointed season.* Crucial events in God's program occur at his designated times in history (see 1Ti 2:6; 6:15 and notes). *the preaching.* The authoritative message that centers in Christ. *God our Savior.* Three times in the letter God the Father is called Savior (here; 2:10; 3:4; see also 1Ti 1:1; 2:3; 4:10), and three times Jesus is called Savior (v. 4; 2:13; 3:6; see also 2Ti 1:10).
1:4 *my true son.* Titus, like Timothy (1Ti 1:2), was a spiritual son, having been converted through Paul's ministry. Onesimus was also called a son by Paul (Phm 10). *true.* Genuine. *our common faith.* The faith shared by all true believers. *Grace and peace.* See note on Ro 1:7. *Savior.* In all of Paul's other greetings Jesus is called "Lord." Paul uses "Savior" 12 times in all his letters, half of the references being in Titus.
1:5 *left you in Crete.* Implies that Paul and Titus had been together in Crete, a ministry not mentioned in Acts. On his voyage to Rome, Paul visited Crete briefly as a prisoner (Ac 27:7–8), but now that he had been released from his first Roman imprisonment he was free to travel wherever he wished (see 3:12 and note). *appoint elders.* Though Paul and Titus may already have preached in Crete, they had not had time to organize churches. The appointing of elders is consistent with Paul's usual practice (see Ac 14:23 and note).
1:6–9 1Ti 3:1–7 gives a parallel list of qualifications for elders, but the two lists reflect the different situations in which Timothy and Titus ministered. See chart, p. 2032.

1:6 *faithful to his wife.* Since elders, by definition, were chosen from among the older men of the congregation, Paul assumed they already would be married and have children. A qualified unmarried man was not necessarily barred. It is also improbable that the standard forbids an elder to remarry if his wife dies (cf. Ro 7:2–3; 1Co 7:39). The most likely meaning is simply that a faithful, monogamous married life must be maintained. See note on 1Ti 3:2.
1:7 *overseer.* The use of "elder" in v. 5 and "overseer" (or "bishop") in v. 7 indicates that the terms were used interchangeably (cf. Ac 20:17,28; 1Pe 5:1–2 and notes). "Elder" indicates qualification (maturity and experience), while "overseer" indicates responsibility (watching over God's flock).
1:8 *self-controlled.* A virtue much needed in Crete (see vv. 10–14); Paul refers to it five times in two chapters (here; 2:2,5–6,12). *disciplined.* Possessing the inner strength to control one's desires and actions.
1:9 *sound doctrine.* Correct teaching, in keeping with that of the apostles (see 1Ti 1:10; 6:3; 2Ti 1:13; 4:3). The teaching is called "sound" not only because it builds up in the faith but also because it protects against the corrupting influence of false teachers. Soundness of doctrine, faith and speech is a basic concern in all the Pastoral Letters (1,2 Timothy; Titus). In them, this use of "sound" occurs eight times (here; v. 13; 2:1–2; 1Ti 1:10; 6:3; 2Ti 1:13; 4:3), but it is found nowhere else in Paul's writings.
1:10 *rebellious.* Against the word of God and against Paul and Titus as the Lord's authoritative ministers. These troublemakers had three main characteristics: 1. They belonged to the "circumcision group," like the people of Gal 2:12, believing that, for salvation or sanctification or both, it was necessary to be circumcised and to keep the Jewish ceremonial law (see Introduction to Galatians: Occasion and Purpose). 2. They held to unscriptural "Jewish myths" (v. 14) and "genealogies" (3:9; see 1Ti 1:4 and note). 3. They were ascetics (vv. 14–15), having scruples against things that God declared to be good. *full of meaningless talk.* Paul used similar language in writing to Timothy about this kind of person (1Ti 1:6).

1:12 ^dAc 17:28
^eAc 2:11
1:13 ^fS 1Ti 5:20
^gTit 2:2
1:14 ^hS 1Ti 1:4
ⁱS Col 2:22 / 2Ti 4:4
1:15 ^kPs 18:26;
Mt 15:10,11; Mk 7:14-
19; Ac 10:9-16,28;
Col 2:20-22
^lRo 14:14,23
^m1Ti 6:5
1:16 ⁿJer 5:2; 12:2;
1Jn 2:4 ^oHos 8:2,3
2:1 ^pS 1Ti 1:10
2:2 ^q1Ti 5:1 / 1Ti 3:2
^sver 5,6,12; Tit 1:8
^tTit 1:13
2:3 ^u1Ti 3:11
^v1Ti 3:8
2:4 ^w1Ti 5:2
2:5 ^xver 2,6,12;
Tit 1:8 ^y1Ti 5:14
^zS Eph 5:22 ^a1Ti 6:1;
S Heb 4:12
2:6 ^b1Ti 5:1 ^cver 2,
5,12; Tit 1:8
2:7 ^dS 1Ti 4:12
^eS ver 14
2:8 ^fS 1Pe 2:12
2:9 ^gS Eph 6:5
2:10 ^hS Lk 1:47
ⁱMt 5:16
2:11 ^jS Ro 3:24
^k2Ti 1:10 ^lS 1Ti 2:4
2:12 ^mTit 3:3
ⁿver 2,5,6; Tit 1:8

of dishonest gain. ¹²One of Crete's own prophets ^d has said it: "Cretans ^e are always liars, evil brutes, lazy gluttons." ^a ¹³He has surely told the truth! Therefore rebuke ^f them sharply, so that they will be sound in the faith ^g ¹⁴and will pay no attention to Jewish myths ^h or to the merely human commands ⁱ of those who reject the truth. ^j ¹⁵To the pure, all things are pure, ^k but to those who are corrupted and do not believe, nothing is pure. ^l In fact, both their minds and consciences are corrupted. ^m ¹⁶They claim to know God, but by their actions they deny him. ⁿ They are detestable, disobedient and unfit for doing anything good. ^o

DOING GOOD FOR THE SAKE OF THE GOSPEL

2 You, however, must teach what is appropriate to sound doctrine. ^p ²Teach the older men ^q to be temperate, ^r worthy of respect, self-controlled, ^s and sound in faith, ^t in love and in endurance.

³Likewise, teach the older women to be reverent in the way they live, not to be slanderers ^u or addicted to much wine, ^v but to teach what is good. ⁴Then they can urge the younger women ^w to love their husbands and children, ⁵to be self-controlled ^x and pure, to be busy at home, ^y to be kind, and to be subject to their husbands, ^z so that no one will malign the word of God. ^a

⁶Similarly, encourage the young men ^b to be self-controlled. ^c ⁷In everything set them an example ^d by doing what is good. ^e In your teaching show integrity, seriousness ⁸and soundness of speech that cannot be condemned, so that those who oppose you may be ashamed because they have nothing bad to say about us. ^f

⁹Teach slaves to be subject to their masters in everything, ^g to try to please them, not to talk back to them, ¹⁰and not to steal from them, but to show that they can be fully trusted, so that in every way they will make the teaching about God our Savior ^h attractive. ⁱ

¹¹For the grace ^j of God has appeared ^k that offers salvation to all people. ^l ¹²It teaches us to say "No" to ungodliness and worldly passions, ^m and to live self-controlled, ⁿ upright

^a 12 From the Cretan philosopher Epimenides

1:12 The quotation is from the poet Epimenides, a sixth-century B.C. native of Crete, who was held in high esteem by the Cretans. He was credited with several predictions that were fulfilled. For other uses of pagan sayings by Paul, see Ac 17:28; 1Co 15:33 and notes. In Greek literature "to Cretanize" meant to lie.
1:13 *the faith.* See note on 1Ti 3:9.
1:14 *Jewish myths.* See note on v. 10.

1:15 *To the pure, all things are pure.* To Christians, who have been purified by the atoning death of Christ, "everything God created is good, and nothing is to be rejected if it is received with thanksgiving" (1Ti 4:4; see note there). *to those who are corrupted and do not believe, nothing is pure.* Unbelievers, especially ascetics with unbiblical scruples against certain foods, marriage and the like (cf. Col 2:21; 1Ti 4:3 and notes), do not enjoy the freedom of true Christians, who receive all God's creation with thanksgiving. Instead, they set up arbitrary, human prohibitions against what they consider to be impure (see Mt 15:10–11, 16–20; Ac 10:9–16; Ro 14:20). The principle of this verse does not conflict with the many NT teachings against practices that are morally and spiritually wrong. *consciences.* See 1Ti 4:2–3.

1:16 *by their actions they deny him.* The false teachers stood condemned by the test of personal conduct. *good.* See Introduction: Distinctive Characteristics. Right knowledge is extremely important because it "leads to godliness" (v. 1). Paul maintained a balance between doctrine and practice.
2:1 *You.* Emphatic, contrasting the work of Titus with that of the false teachers just denounced (1:10–16). *sound doctrine.* See 1:9 and note.

2:2–10 Sound doctrine demands right conduct of all believers, regardless of age, gender or position.

2:2 Older men, as leaders, were to be moral and spiritual examples. *temperate.* Instead of being "lazy gluttons," as were Cretans in general (1:12), these older believers were to be responsible and sensible.
2:3 *Likewise.* The same moral standards applied to women as to men. *not to be slanderers.* Slanderous talk apparently was a common vice among Cretan women. *addicted to much wine.* Cf. 1:7; 1Ti 3:3,8.

2:4 *love their husbands.* Just as husbands are exhorted (Eph 5:25) to love their wives.
2:5 *subject to their husbands.* See Eph 5:22 and note; Col 3:18; 1Pe 3:1 and note. *no one will malign the word of God.* Indicating Paul's deep spiritual concern behind these ethical instructions. See also vv. 8,10, dealing with his concern that Christian living should help rather than hinder the spread of the gospel.

2:7–8 Perhaps Titus was still a young man and was not yet well respected by the Cretan churches. The demands on a leader are all-inclusive, involving not only his word but also his lifestyle (see Jas 3:1 and note).
2:7 *good.* See Introduction: Distinctive Characteristics.
2:9–10 Instructions for a distinct group in the churches. Slavery was a basic element of Roman society, and the impact of Christianity upon slaves was a vital concern. Guidance for the conduct of Christian slaves was essential (see Eph 6:5 and note).
2:9 *masters.* The Greek for this word, from which our English term "despot" is derived, indicates the owner's absolute authority over his slave. Roman slaves had no legal rights, their fates being entirely in their masters' hands (see note on Col 3:22—4:1).
2:10 *make the teaching ... attractive.* Christian slaves could give a unique and powerful testimony to the gospel by their willing faithfulness and obedience to their masters.

2:11–14 Briefly describes the effect grace should have on believers. It encourages rejection of ungodliness and leads to holier living—in keeping with Paul's repeated insistence that profession of Christ be accompanied by godly living (vv. 1–2,4–5,10; 3:8).

2:11 *For.* Introduces the doctrinal basis for the ethical demands just stressed. Right conduct must be founded on right doctrine. *grace of God.* The undeserved love God showed us in Christ while we were still sinners and his enemies (Ro 5:6–10) and by which we are saved, apart from any moral achievements or religious acts on our part (see 3:5; Eph 2:8–9 and notes). But this same grace instructs us that our salvation should produce good works (see v. 14 and note; Eph 2:10).
2:12 *teaches us.* The word translated "teaches" refers to more than instruction; it includes the whole process of training a

and godly lives *o* in this present age, ¹³while we wait for the blessed hope—the appearing*p* of the glory of our great God and Savior, Jesus Christ, *q* ¹⁴who gave himself for us *r* to redeem us from all wickedness *s* and to purify *t* for himself a people that are his very own, *u* eager to do what is good. *v*

¹⁵These, then, are the things you should teach. Encourage and rebuke with all authority. Do not let anyone despise you.

SAVED IN ORDER TO DO GOOD

3 Remind the people to be subject to rulers and authorities, *w* to be obedient, to be ready to do whatever is good, *x* ²to slander no one, *y* to be peaceable and considerate, and always to be gentle toward everyone.

³At one time *z* we too were foolish, disobedient, deceived and enslaved by all kinds of passions and pleasures. We lived in malice and envy, being hated and hating one another. ⁴But when the kindness *a* and love of God our Savior *b* appeared, *c* ⁵he saved us, *d* not because of righteous things we had done, *e* but because of his mercy. *f* He saved us through the washing *g* of rebirth and renewal *h* by the Holy Spirit, ⁶whom he poured out on us *i* generously through Jesus Christ our Savior, ⁷so that, having been justified by his grace, *j* we might become heirs *k* having the hope *l* of eternal life. *m* ⁸This is a trustworthy saying. *n* And I want you to stress these things, so that those who have trusted in God may be careful to devote themselves to doing what is good. *o* These things are excellent and profitable for everyone.

⁹But avoid *p* foolish controversies and genealogies and arguments and quarrels *q* about the law, *r* because these are unprofitable and useless. *s* ¹⁰Warn divisive people once, and then warn them a second time. After that, have nothing to do with them. *t* ¹¹You may be sure that such people are warped and sinful; they are self-condemned.

FINAL REMARKS

¹²As soon as I send Artemas or Tychicus *u* to you, do your best to come to me at Nicopolis, because I have decided to winter there. *v* ¹³Do everything you can to help Zenas the lawyer and Apollos *w* on their way and see that they have everything they need. ¹⁴Our people must learn to devote themselves to doing what is good, *x* in order to provide for urgent needs and not live unproductive lives.

¹⁵Everyone with me sends you greetings. Greet those who love us in the faith. *y*
Grace be with you all. *z*

2:12 *o* 2Ti 3:12
2:13 *p* S 1Co 1:7;
S 1Ti 6:14 *q* 2Pe 1:1
2:14 *r* S Mt 20:28
s S Mt 1:21 *t* Heb 1:3;
1Jn 1:7 *u* Ex 19:5;
Dt 4:20; 14:2;
Ps 135:4; Mal 3:17;
1Pe 2:9 *v* ver 7;
Pr 16:7; Mt 5:16;
2Co 8:21; Eph 2:10;
Tit 3:1,8,14; 1Pe 2:12,
15; 3:13
3:1 *w* Ro 13:1;
1Pe 2:13,14
x S 2Ti 2:21; S Tit 2:14
3:2 *y* Eph 4:31
3:3 *z* S Eph 2:2
3:4 *a* Eph 2:7
b S Lk 1:47 *c* Tit 2:11
3:5 *d* S Ro 11:14
e S Eph 2:9 *f* 1Pe 1:3
g S Ac 22:16 *h* Ro 12:2
3:6 *i* S Ro 5:5
3:7 *j* S Ro 3:24
k S Ro 8:17 *l* Ro 8:24
m S Mt 25:46; Tit 1:2
3:8 *n* S 1Ti 1:15
o S Tit 2:14
3:9 *p* 2Ti 2:16
q S 2Ti 2:14 *r* Tit 1:10-
16 *s* 2Ti 2:14
3:10 *t* S Ro 16:17
3:12 *u* S Ac 20:4
v 2Ti 4:9,21
3:13 *w* S Ac 18:24
3:14 *x* S Tit 2:14
3:15 *y* 1Ti 1:2
z S Col 4:18

---

child—instruction, encouragement, correction and discipline. *this present age.* See 2Co 4:4 and note.

2:13 *the blessed hope—the appearing of the glory.* The second coming (see 1Ti 6:14; 2Ti 4:1; see also note on 2Ti 4:8). *our great God and Savior, Jesus Christ.* It is possible to translate this phrase "the great God and our Saviour, Jesus Christ" (KJV), but the NIV rendering better represents the Greek construction. It is an explicit testimony to the deity of Christ (see Ro 9:5 and note).

2:14 Salvation involves the double work of redeeming us from guilt and judgment (see Ro 3:24 and note) and of producing moral purity and helpful service to others (see Introduction: Distinctive Characteristics).

2:15 A summary of Titus's responsibility and authority. *things.* The content of the whole chapter.

3:1–2 NT teaching is not confined to the area of personal salvation but includes much instruction about practical living. Although believers are citizens of heaven (see Php 3:20 and note), they must also submit themselves to earthly government (see Ro 13:1–7; 1Pe 2:13–17 and notes) and help promote the well-being of the community.

3:1 *rulers and authorities.* The terms refer to all forms and levels of human government (cf. Eph 3:10; 6:12 for application to angels). *good.* See Introduction: Distinctive Characteristics.

3:3 Cf. Eph 2:1–3.

3:4 *kindness and love of God.* The reasons why God did not simply banish fallen human beings but acted to save them (cf. 2:11).

3:5 *saved us … because of his mercy.* Salvation is not achieved by human effort or merit but comes through God's mercy alone (see Eph 2:8–9 and notes). *washing of rebirth.* A reference to new birth, of which baptism (among other things) is a sign. It cannot mean that baptism is necessary for regeneration,

since the NT plainly teaches that the new birth is an act of God's Spirit (see, e.g., Jn 3:5) and is not effected or achieved by ceremony. *renewal by the Holy Spirit.* Also a reference to new birth.

3:6 *whom he poured out on us generously.* Cf. Ro 5:5.

3:7 *justified by his grace.* See Ro 3:24 and note. *heirs.* See Ro 8:17 and note. *hope.* See notes on Ro 5:5; Col 1:5.

3:8 *trustworthy saying.* See note on 1Ti 1:15. Here the phrase refers to the doctrinal summary in vv. 4–7. *good.* See Introduction: Distinctive Characteristics.

3:9 *genealogies.* See note on 1Ti 1:4. *about the law.* A reference to the situation described in 1:10–16. A similar problem existed in Ephesus (see 1Ti 1:3–7 and note on 1:3–11).

3:11 Stubborn refusal to listen to correction reveals inner perversion.

3:12 *Tychicus.* Paul's trusted co-worker, who on various occasions traveled with or for Paul (see Ac 20:4; Eph 6:21 and notes). *Nicopolis.* Means "city of victory." Several cities had this name, but the reference here is apparently to the city in Epirus on the western shore of Greece (see map, p. 2031). *decided to winter there.* Indicates that Paul had not arrived there when he wrote and that he was still free to travel at will, not yet having been imprisoned in Rome for the second time.

3:13 *Zenas the lawyer.* If he was a Jewish convert, "lawyer" means that he was an expert in the Mosaic law; if he was a Gentile convert, that he was a Roman jurist. *Apollos.* A native of Alexandria and one of Paul's well-known co-workers (Ac 18:24–28; 19:1; 1Co 1:12; 3:4–6,22; 16:12). The two travelers apparently brought the letter from Paul.

3:14 *good.* See Introduction: Distinctive Characteristics. *provide for urgent needs.* See 1Ti 5:8; cf. 2Th 3:10–12.

3:15 *Grace.* See note on Ro 1:7. *with you.* See note on 2Co 13:14.

PHILEMON — INTRODUCTION

AUTHOR, DATE AND PLACE OF WRITING

C Paul wrote this short letter (see vv. 1,9,19) probably at the same time as Colossians (c. A.D. 60; see Introduction to Colossians: Author, Date and Place of Writing) and sent it to Colossae with the same travelers, Onesimus and Tychicus. He apparently wrote both letters from prison in Rome, though possibly from Ephesus (see Introduction to Philippians: Author, Date and Place of Writing; see also chart, p. 1855).

RECIPIENT, BACKGROUND AND PURPOSE

C Paul wrote this letter to Philemon, a believer in Colossae who, along with others, was a slave owner (cf. Col 4:1; for slavery in the NT, see note on Eph 6:5). One of his slaves, Onesimus, had apparently stolen from him (cf. v. 18) and then run away, which under Roman law was punishable by death. But Onesimus met Paul and through his ministry became a Christian (see v. 10). Now he was willing to return to his master, and Paul writes this personal appeal to ask that he be accepted as a Christian brother (see v. 16).

APPROACH AND STRUCTURE

To win Philemon's willing acceptance of Onesimus, Paul writes very tactfully and in a lighthearted tone, which he creates with a wordplay (see note on v. 11). The appeal (vv. 4–21) is organized in a way prescribed by ancient Greek and Roman teachers: to build rapport (vv. 4–10), to persuade the mind (vv. 11–19) and to move the emotions (vv. 20–21). The name Onesimus is not mentioned until the rapport has been built (v. 10), and the appeal itself is stated only near the end of the section to persuade the mind (v. 17).

OUTLINE

- I. Greetings (1–3)
- II. Thanksgiving and Prayer (4–7)
- III. Paul's Plea for Onesimus (8–21)
- IV. Final Request, Greetings and Benediction (22–25)

KEY   **A** APPLICATION FOR LIVING   **B** BACKGROUND NOTES   **C** CHARACTER INFORMATION

¹Paul, a prisoner*ᵃ* of Christ Jesus, and Timothy*ᵇ* our brother,*ᶜ*

To Philemon our dear friend and fellow worker*ᵈ*— ²also to Apphia our sister and Archippus*ᵉ* our fellow soldier*ᶠ*—and to the church that meets in your home:*ᵍ*

³Grace and peace to you*ᵃ* from God our Father and the Lord Jesus Christ.*ʰ*

THANKSGIVING AND PRAYER

⁴I always thank my God*ⁱ* as I remember you in my prayers,*ʲ* ⁵because I hear about your love for all his people*ᵏ* and your faith in the Lord Jesus.*ˡ* ⁶I pray that your partnership with us in the faith may be effective in deepening your understanding of every good thing we share for the sake of Christ. ⁷Your love has given me great joy and encouragement,*ᵐ* because you, brother, have refreshed*ⁿ* the hearts of the Lord's people.

PAUL'S PLEA FOR ONESIMUS

⁸Therefore, although in Christ I could be bold and order you to do what you ought to do, ⁹yet I prefer to appeal to you*ᵒ* on the basis of love. It is as none other than Paul—an old man and now also a prisoner*ᵖ* of Christ Jesus— ¹⁰that I appeal to you for my son*�q* Onesimus,*ᵇ ʳ* who became my son while I was in chains.*ˢ* ¹¹Formerly he was useless to you, but now he has become useful both to you and to me.

¹²I am sending him—who is my very heart—back to you. ¹³I would have liked to keep him with me so that he could take your place in helping me while I am in chains*ᵗ* for the gospel. ¹⁴But I did not want to do anything without your consent, so that any favor you do would not seem forced*ᵘ* but would be voluntary. ¹⁵Perhaps the reason he was separated from you for a little while was that you might have him back forever— ¹⁶no longer as a slave,*ᵛ* but better than a slave, as a dear brother.*ʷ* He is very dear to me but even dearer to you, both as a fellow man and as a brother in the Lord.

¹⁷So if you consider me a partner,*ˣ* welcome him as you would welcome me. ¹⁸If he has done you any wrong or owes you anything, charge it to me.*ʸ* ¹⁹I, Paul, am writing this with my own hand.*ᶻ* I will pay it back—not to mention that you owe me your very self. ²⁰I do wish, brother, that I may have some benefit from you in the Lord; refresh*ᵃ* my heart in Christ. ²¹Confident*ᵇ* of your obedience, I write to you, knowing that you will do even more than I ask.

²²And one thing more: Prepare a guest room for me, because I hope to be*ᶜ* restored to you in answer to your prayers.*ᵈ*

²³Epaphras,*ᵉ* my fellow prisoner*ᶠ* in Christ Jesus, sends you greetings. ²⁴And so do Mark,*ᵍ* Aristarchus,*ʰ* Demas*ⁱ* and Luke, my fellow workers.*ʲ*

²⁵The grace of the Lord Jesus Christ be with your spirit.*ᵏ*

ᵃ 3 The Greek is plural; also in verses 22 and 25; elsewhere in this letter "you" is singular.
ᵇ 10 Onesimus means *useful.*

1 *ᵃ*ver 9,23;
S Eph 3:1 *ᵇ*S Ac 16:1
*ᶜ*2Co 1:1 *ᵈ*S Php 2:25
2 *ᵉ*Col 4:17
*ᶠ*Php 2:25 *ᵍ*S Ro 16:5
3 *ʰ*S Ro 1:7
4 *ⁱ*S Ro 1:8
*ʲ*S Ro 1:10
5 *ᵏ*S Col 1:4; 1Th 3:6
*ˡ*S Ac 20:21
7 *ᵐ*2Co 7:4,13
*ⁿ*ver 20; Ro 15:32;
1Co 16:18
9 *ᵒ*1Co 1:10 *ᵖ*ver 1,
23; S Eph 3:1
10 *q*S 1Th 2:11
*ʳ*Col 4:9 *ˢ*S Ac 21:33
13 *ᵗ*ver 10;
S Ac 21:33
14 *ᵘ*2Co 9:7; 1Pe 5:2
16 *ᵛ*1Co 7:22
*ʷ*Mt 23:8; S Ac 1:16;
1Ti 6:2
17 *ˣ*2Co 8:23
18 *ʸ*Ge 43:9
19 *ᶻ*S 1Co 16:21
20 *ᵃ*ver 7; 1Co 16:18
21 *ᵇ*S 2Co 2:3
22 *ᶜ*Php 1:25; 2:24;
Heb 13:19 *ᵈ*2Co 1:11;
Php 1:19
23 *ᵉ*Col 1:7 *ᶠ*ver 1;
Ro 16:7; Col 4:10
24 *ᵍ*S Ac 12:12
*ʰ*S Ac 19:29
*ⁱ*Col 4:14; 2Ti 4:10
*ʲ*ver 1
25 *ᵏ*S Gal 6:18

1–2 Although Paul writes together with Timothy and although he addresses the entire church in Colossae, in this very personal letter to Philemon he uses "I," rather than "we," and "you" (singular, except in vv. 22,25).

1 *Paul.* See note on Ro 1:1.*prisoner.* See Eph 3:1; Php 1:13 and notes.*Timothy.* See note on Col 1:1; see also Introduction to 1 Timothy: Recipient.*Philemon.* A Christian living in Colossae or nearby and the owner of the slave Onesimus.

2 *Apphia.* Probably Philemon's wife.*Archippus.* See Col 4:17.

3 *Grace … peace.* See note on Ro 1:7.*Lord Jesus Christ.* Occurs also at the end of this letter (v. 25). See note on 1Th 1:1.

4 *thank … remember you in my prayers.* See Php 1:3–4 and note.

5 See Col 1:4. *his people.* See notes on Ro 1:7; Eph 1:1; Col 1:4.

7 *hearts.* Figurative for the emotions of pity and love (see vv. 12,20).

10 *my son.* See note on 1Ti 1:2.*Onesimus.* See TNIV text note; see also Introduction: Recipient, Background and Purpose.

11 *useless … useful.* A play on the meaning of Onesimus's name (see TNIV text note on v. 10).

13 *in chains for the gospel.* See v. 1 and note.

16 Cf. 1Ti 6:2.

17–19 Martin Luther said, "Even as Christ did for us with God the Father, thus Paul also does for Onesimus with Philemon."

19 *writing this with my own hand.* See 1Co 16:21 and note.*owe me your very self.* Paul probably led Philemon to faith in Christ.

20 *I … my.* Both pronouns are emphatic, making an obvious allusion to v. 7.*benefit.* The Greek for this word is another play on the name Onesimus.

21 *even more than I ask.* Perhaps suggesting that Philemon set Onesimus free.

22 *one thing more.* It was not unusual for an ancient letter, though occasioned by one matter, to also include another matter. Often, as here, the second matter had to do with how and when the author planned to meet the recipient again.

23 *Epaphras.* See Col 1:7 and note; 4:12.

24 *Mark, Aristarchus.* See note on Col 4:10.*Demas and Luke.* See note on Col 4:14.

25 *grace.* See note on Ro 1:7.*be with your spirit.* See note on Gal 6:18.

AUTHOR

The writer of this letter does not identify himself, but he was obviously well known to the original recipients. Though for some 1,200 years (from c. A.D. 400 to 1600) the book was commonly called "The Epistle of Paul to the Hebrews," there was no agreement in the earliest centuries regarding its authorship. Since the Reformation it has been widely recognized that Paul could not have been the writer. There is no disharmony between the teaching of Hebrews and that of Paul's letters, but the specific emphases and writing styles are markedly different. Contrary to Paul's usual practice, the author of Hebrews nowhere identifies himself in the letter—except to indicate that he was a man (see note on 11:32). Moreover, the statement "This salvation, which was first announced by the Lord, was confirmed to us by those who heard him" (2:3), indicates that the author had neither been with Jesus during his earthly ministry nor received special revelation directly from the risen Lord, as had Paul (Gal 1:11–12).

The earliest suggestion of authorship is found in Tertullian's *De Pudicitia,* 20 (c. 200), in which he quotes from "an epistle to the Hebrews under the name of Barnabas." From the letter itself it is clear that the writer must have had authority in the apostolic church and was an intellectual Hebrew Christian, well versed in the OT. Barnabas meets these requirements. He was a Jew of the priestly tribe of Levi (Ac 4:36) who became a close friend of Paul after the latter's conversion. Under the guidance of the Holy Spirit, the church at Antioch commissioned Barnabas and Paul for the work of evangelism and sent them off on the first missionary journey (Ac 13:1–4).

The other leading candidate for authorship is Apollos, whose name was first suggested by Martin Luther and who is favored by many interpreters today. Apollos, an Alexandrian by birth, was also a Jewish Christian with notable intellectual and oratorical abilities. Luke tells us that "he was a learned man, with a thorough knowledge of the Scriptures" (Ac 18:24). We also know that Apollos was associated with Paul in the early years of the church in Corinth (1Co 1:12; 3:4–6,22).

Two things are evident: The author was a master of the Greek language of his day, and he was thoroughly acquainted with the pre-Christian Greek translation of the OT (the Septuagint), which he regularly quotes.

DATE

Hebrews must have been written before the destruction of Jerusalem and the temple in A.D. 70 because: (1) If it had been written after this date, the author surely would have mentioned the temple's destruction and the end of the Jewish sacrificial system; and (2) the author consistently uses the Greek present tense when speaking of the temple and the priestly activities connected with it (see 5:1–3; 7:23,27; 8:3–5; 9:6–9,13,25; 10:1,3–4,8,11; 13:10–11).

RECIPIENTS

The letter was addressed primarily to Jewish converts who were familiar with the OT and who were being tempted to revert to Judaism or to Judaize the gospel (cf. Gal 2:14). Some have suggested that these professing Jewish Christians were thinking of merging with a Jewish sect, such as the one at Qumran near the Dead Sea. It has also been suggested that the recipients were from the "large number of priests [who] became obedient to the faith" (Ac 6:7).

THEME

The theme of Hebrews is the absolute supremacy and sufficiency of Jesus Christ as revealer and mediator of God's grace. The prologue (1:1–4) presents Christ as God's full and final revelation, far surpassing the revelation given in the OT. The prophecies and promises of the OT are fulfilled in the "new covenant" (or "new testament"), of which Christ is the mediator. From the OT itself, Christ is shown to be superior to the ancient prophets, to angels, to Moses (the mediator of the former covenant) and to Aaron and the priestly succession descended from him. Hebrews could be called "the book of better things" since the two Greek words for "better" and "superior" occur 15 times in the letter (1:4 [twice]; 6:9; 7:19,22; 8:6 [3 times]; 9:23; 10:34; 11:4,16,35,40; 12:24). A striking feature of this presentation of the gospel is the unique manner in which the author employs expositions of eight specific passages of the OT Scriptures:

1. 2:5–9: Exposition of Ps 8:4–6
2. 3:7—4:13: Exposition of Ps 95:7–11
3. 4:14—7:28: Exposition of Ps 110:4
4. 8:1—10:18: Exposition of Jer 31:31–34
5. 10:1–10: Exposition of Ps 40:6–8
6. 10:32—12:3: Exposition of Hab 2:3–4
7. 12:4–13: Exposition of Pr 3:11–12
8. 12:18–24: Exposition of Ex 19:10–23

Practical applications of this theme are given throughout the book. The readers are told that there can be no turning back to or continuation in the old Jewish system, which has been superseded by the unique priesthood of Christ. God's people must now look only to him, whose atoning death, resurrection and ascension have opened the way into the true, heavenly sanctuary of God's presence. To "ignore so great a salvation" (2:3) or to give up the pursuit of holiness (12:10,14) is to face the anger of the "living God" (10:31). Five times the author weaves into his presentation of the gospel stern warnings (see note on 2:1–4) and reminds his readers of the divine judgment that came on the rebellious generation of Israelites in the desert.

LITERARY FORM

Hebrews is commonly referred to as a letter, though it does not have the typical form of a letter. It ends like a letter (13:22–25) but begins more like an essay or sermon (1:1–4). The author does not identify himself or those addressed, which letter writers normally did. And he offers no manner of greeting, such as is usually found at the beginning of ancient letters. Rather, he begins with a magnificent statement about Jesus Christ. He calls his work a "word of exhortation" (13:22), the conventional designation given a sermon in a synagogue service (see Ac 13:15). Like a sermon, Hebrews is full of encouragement, exhortations and stern warnings. It is likely that the author used sermonic materials and sent them out in a modified letter form.

OUTLINE

I. Prologue: The Superiority of God's New Revelation (1:1–4)
II. The Superiority of Christ to Leading Figures under the Old Covenant (1:5—7:28)

GOD'S FINAL WORD: HIS SON

1 In the past God spoke [a] to our ancestors through the prophets [b] at many times and in various ways, [c] [2] but in these last days [d] he has spoken to us by his Son, [e] whom he appointed heir [f] of all things, and through whom [g] also he made the universe. [h] [3] The Son is the radiance of God's glory [i] and the exact representation of his being, [j] sustaining all things [k] by his powerful word. After he had provided purification for sins, [l] he sat down at the right hand of the Majesty in heaven. [m] [4] So he became as much superior to the angels as the name he has inherited is superior to theirs. [n]

THE SON SUPERIOR TO ANGELS

[5] For to which of the angels did God ever say,

> "You are my Son;
>   today I have become your Father" [a]? [o]

Or again,

> "I will be his Father,
>   and he will be my Son" [b]? [p]

[6] And again, when God brings his firstborn [q] into the world, [r] he says,

> "Let all God's angels worship him." [c] [s]

[7] In speaking of the angels he says,

> "He makes his angels spirits,
>   and his servants flames of fire." [d] [t]

[8] But about the Son he says,

---

a 5   Psalm 2:7   b 5   2 Samuel 7:14; 1 Chron. 17:13   c 6   Deut. 32:43 (see Dead Sea Scrolls and Septuagint)   d 7   Psalm 104:4

1:1 *In the past.* In contrast to "in these last days" (v. 2), the Messianic era inaugurated by the incarnation (see Ac 2:17; 1Ti 4:1; 1Jn 2:18 and notes). *God spoke.* Cf. "he has spoken" (v. 2). God is the ultimate author of both the OT and the NT. *to our ancestors.* In contrast to "to us" (v. 2). *through the prophets.* All OT writers are here viewed as prophets in that their testimony was preparation for the coming of Christ; cf. "by his Son" (v. 2), a new and unique category of revelation in contrast to that of the prophets. *at many times and in various ways.* The OT revelation was occasional and lacking in finality.

1:2–3 The superiority of God's revelation through his Son (see Introduction: Theme) is demonstrated by seven great descriptive statements about him: 1. *appointed heir of all things.* The incarnate Son, having performed the work of redemption, was gloriously exalted to the position of the firstborn heir of God, i.e., he received the inheritance of God's estate ("all things"). See Ro 8:17. 2. *through whom also he made the universe.* See Jn 1:3; 1Co 8:6; Col 1:16 and note. 3. *radiance of God's glory.* As the brilliance of the sun is inseparable from the sun itself, so the Son's radiance is inseparable from deity, for he himself is God, the second person of the Trinity (see Jn 1:14,18 and notes). 4. *exact representation of his being.* Jesus is not merely an image or reflection of God. Because the Son himself is God (see note on Ro 9:5), he is the absolutely authentic representation of God's being (see Jn 14:9; Col 1:15 and note). 5. *sustaining all things.* Christ is not like Atlas, the mythical Greek god who held the world on his shoulders. The Son dynamically holds together all that has been created through him (Col 1:17). 6. *provided purification for sins.* Through his redeeming death on the cross (see 7:27; 9:12; Tit 2:14 and notes). 7. *sat down at the right hand of the Majesty in heaven.* Being seated at God's right hand indicates that Christ is actively ruling with God as Lord over all (see v. 13; 8:1; 10:12; 12:2; Mt 26:64; Ac 2:23; 5:34; Ro 8:34; Eph 1:20; Col 3:1; 1Pe 3:22).

1:2 *these last days.* The time when all that was promised and worked toward in the OT was coming to fulfillment (see v. 1; Jas 5:3; 2Pe 3:3 and notes; see also 1Pe 1:20; Jude 18).

1:4 *superior to the angels.* See Introduction: Theme. To most Jews angels were exalted beings, especially revered because they were involved in giving the law at Sinai (see 2:2), and to the Jews the law was God's supreme revelation. The Dead Sea Scrolls reflect the expectation that the archangel Michael would be the supreme figure in the Messianic kingdom. *name.* See Php 2:9 and note. What follows indicates that this name was "Son"—a name to which no angel could lay claim.

1:5–14 Christ's superiority to angels is documented by seven OT quotations (see TNIV text notes), showing that he is God's Son, that he is worshiped by angels and that, though he is God, he is distinguished from the Father.

1:5 *You are my Son; today I have become your Father.* This passage (Ps 2:7) is quoted in Ac 13:33 as fulfilled in Christ's resurrection (cf. Ro 1:4). *I will be his Father, and he will be my Son.* Jews acknowledged 2Sa 7:14 (of which this passage is a quotation) and Ps 2 to be Messianic in their ultimate application (see Lk 1:32–33 and notes). This royal personage is neither an angel nor an archangel; he is God's Son.

1:6 *firstborn.* See Col 1:15 and note. *Let all God's angels worship him.* The author quotes a line that was in his Greek version of Deuteronomy (see TNIV text note). This statement, which in the OT refers to the Lord God (Yahweh), is here applied to Christ, giving clear indication of his full deity. The very beings with whom Christ is being compared are commanded to proclaim his superiority by worshiping him.

1:7 *He makes his angels spirits, and his servants flames of fire.* Ps 104:4 speaks of the storm wind and the lightning as agents of God's purposes. The Septuagint (the pre-Christian Greek translation of the OT), which the author of Hebrews quotes as the version familiar to his readers, reflects the developing doctrine of angels during the period between the OT and the NT. *angels.* English "angel" comes from the Greek word *angelos,* which means "messenger" or "agent." The Hebrew word most often translated "angel" has essentially the same meaning.

1:8 *But about the Son he says, "Your throne, O God, will last for ever."* The author selects a passage that intimates the

---

1:1 [a] Jn 9:29;
Heb 2:2,3; 4:8; 12:25
[b] Lk 1:70; Ac 2:30
[c] Nu 12:6,8
1:2 [d] Dt 4:30;
Heb 9:26; 1Pe 1:20
[e] ver 5; S Mt 3:17;
Heb 3:6; 5:8; 7:28
[f] Ps 2:8; Mt 11:27;
S 28:18 [g] S Jn 1:3
[h] Heb 11:3
1:3 [i] Jn 1:14
[j] S Jn 14:9 [k] Col 1:17
[l] Tit 2:14; Heb 7:27;
9:11-14 [m] S Mk 16:19
1:4 [n] Eph 1:21;
Php 2:9,10; Heb 8:6
1:5 [o] Ps 2:7;
S Mt 3:17 [p] 2Sa 7:14
1:6 [q] Jn 3:16;
S Col 1:18 [r] Heb 10:5
[s] Dt 32:43 (LXX and
DSS); Ps 97:7
1:7 [t] Ps 104:4

1:8 *u* S Lk 1:33
1:9 *v* Php 2:9
w Isa 61:1,3
x Ps 45:6,7
1:10 *y* Ps 8:6;
Zec 12:1
1:11 *z* Isa 34:4; 51:6;
S Heb 12:27
1:12 *a* Heb 13:8
b Ps 102:25-27
1:13 *c* ver 3;
S Mk 16:19
d Jos 10:24; Heb 10:13
e Ps 110:1; S Mt 22:44
1:14 *f* Ps 91:11;
103:20; Da 7:10
g Mt 25:34; Mk 10:17;
S Ac 20:32
h Ro 11:14; Heb 2:3;
5:9; 9:28
2:1 *i* S Ro 11:22
2:2 *j* S Heb 1:1
k Dt 33:2; Ac 7:53;
Gal 3:19 *l* Heb 10:28
2:3 *m* Heb 10:29;
12:25 *n* Heb 1:2
o S Lk 1:2
2:4 *p* Mk 16:20;
S Jn 4:48 *q* S 1Co 12:4
r S Eph 1:5
2:6 *s* Heb 4:4
t Job 7:17; Ps 144:3

"Your throne, O God, will last for ever and ever; *u*
    a scepter of justice will be the scepter of your kingdom.
[9] You have loved righteousness and hated wickedness;
    therefore God, your God, has set you above your companions *v*
    by anointing you with the oil *w* of joy."[a] *x*

[10] He also says,

"In the beginning, Lord, you laid the foundations of the earth,
    and the heavens are the work of your hands. *y*
[11] They will perish, but you remain;
    they will all wear out like a garment. *z*
[12] You will roll them up like a robe;
    like a garment they will be changed.
But you remain the same, *a*
    and your years will never end."[b] *b*

[13] To which of the angels did God ever say,

"Sit at my right hand *c*
    until I make your enemies
    a footstool *d* for your feet"[c]? *e*

[14] Are not all angels ministering spirits *f* sent to serve those who will inherit *g* salvation? *h*

WARNING TO PAY ATTENTION

2 We must pay the most careful attention, therefore, to what we have heard, so that we do not drift away. *i* [2] For since the message spoken *j* through angels *k* was binding, and every violation and disobedience received its just punishment, *l* [3] how shall we escape if we ignore so great a salvation? *m* This salvation, which was first announced by the Lord, *n* was confirmed to us by those who heard him. *o* [4] God also testified to it by signs, wonders and various miracles, *p* and by gifts of the Holy Spirit *q* distributed according to his will. *r*

JESUS MADE LIKE HIS BROTHERS AND SISTERS

[5] It is not to angels that he has subjected the world to come, about which we are speaking. [6] But there is a place where someone *s* has testified:

"What are mere mortals that you are mindful of them,
    human beings that you care for them? *t*

---

a 9   Psalm 45:6,7   *b* 12   Psalm 102:25-27   *c* 13   Psalm 110:1

---

deity of the Messianic (and Davidic) King, further demonstrating the Son's superiority over angels (see Ps 45:6 and note).

1:10 *In the beginning, Lord, you laid the foundations of the earth.* As in v. 6, a passage addressed to Yahweh ("Lord") is applied to the Son.

1:13 *Sit at my right hand.* See note on vv. 2–3. Ps 110 is applied repeatedly to Jesus in Hebrews (vv. 3,13; 5:6,10; 6:20; 7:3,11,17, 21; 8:1; 10:12–13; 12:2).

1:14 *ministering spirits.* See v. 7. Christ reigns; angels minister as those sent to serve.

2:1–4 The first of five warnings strategically positioned throughout the letter (see 3:7—4:13; 6:4–8; 10:26–31; 12:25–29).

2:1 *what we have heard.* The message of the gospel, including that of Christ's person as the God-man and his redemptive work on the cross. *drift away.* From the greater revelation given through the Son.

2:2 *the message spoken through angels.* The law given through Moses at Sinai (see Ac 7:38 and note).

2:3 *how shall we escape . . . ?* See 12:25. *so great a salvation.* The argument here is from the lesser to the greater and assumes that the gospel is greater than the law. Thus, if disregard for the law brought certain punishment, disregard for the gospel will bring even greater punishment. *confirmed to us by those who heard him.* The eyewitnesses, chiefly the apostles

(see Ac 1:21–22 and note on 1:22; 1Jn 1:1 and note; cf. 2Pe 1:16 and note), had vouched for the message first announced by Christ. The author himself apparently was neither an apostle nor an eyewitness (see Introduction: Author).

2:4 *signs, wonders and various miracles.* God added his confirmation to the gospel message through supernatural acts such as healing the sick (see Ac 3:7–9,11–12,16; 5:12–16; 9:32–41; 14:3,8–9; 19:11–12; 28:8–9). *gifts of the Holy Spirit.* Such as the gift of tongues (see Ac 2:4–12). *distributed according to his will.* See 1Co 12:4–11.

2:5–9 An exposition of Ps 8:4–6, which continues to show Christ's superiority over the angels—in him humanity's appointed role as ruler (under God) over God's other creatures (cf. Ge 1:26,28 and notes) comes to ultimate fulfillment (see note on Ps 8:4–6).

2:5 *It is not to angels that he has subjected the world to come.* Christ, as bearer of the new revelation (see 1:2–3 and note), is superior to angels who had participated in bringing the revelation at Sinai (see 2:2 and note).

2:6–8 Awed by the marvelous order and immensity of God's handiwork in the celestial universe, the psalmist marveled at the high dignity God had bestowed on puny mortals by entrusting them with dominion over the other creatures (see Ge 1:26–28 and notes).

⁷You made them a little lower than the angels;
　　you crowned them with glory and honor
⁸　　and put everything under their feet." ᵃ ᵘ

In putting everything under them, ᵇ God left nothing that is not subject to them. ᵇ Yet at present we do not see everything subject to them. ᵇ ⁹But we do see Jesus, who was made lower than the angels for a little while, now crowned with glory and honor ᵛ because he suffered death, ʷ so that by the grace of God he might taste death for everyone. ˣ

¹⁰In bringing many sons and daughters to glory, it was fitting that God, for whom and through whom everything exists, ʸ should make the pioneer of their salvation perfect through what he suffered. ᶻ ¹¹Both the one who makes people holy ᵃ and those who are made holy ᵇ are of the same family. So Jesus is not ashamed to call them brothers and sisters. ᶜ ¹²He says,

　　"I will declare your name to my brothers and sisters;
　　　in the assembly I will sing your praises." ᶜ ᵈ

¹³And again,

　　"I will put my trust in him." ᵈ ᵉ

And again he says,

　　"Here am I, and the children God has given me." ᵉ ᶠ

¹⁴Since the children have flesh and blood, ᵍ he too shared in their humanity ʰ so that by his death he might break the power ⁱ of him who holds the power of death—that is, the devil ʲ— ¹⁵and free those who all their lives were held in slavery by their fear ᵏ of death. ¹⁶For surely it is not angels he helps, but Abraham's descendants. ˡ ¹⁷For this reason he had to be made like his brothers and sisters ᵐ in every way, in order that he might become a merciful ⁿ and faithful high priest ᵒ in service to God, ᵖ and that he might make atonement for the sins of the people. ᑫ ¹⁸Because he himself suffered when he was tempted, he is able to help those who are being tempted. ʳ

ᵃ 6-8 Psalm 8:4-6; or "What is a human being that you are mindful of him,/ the son of man that you care for him?/ ⁷You made him lower than the angels for a little while;/ you crowned him with glory and honor/ ⁸and put everything under his feet."　ᵇ 8 Or him　ᶜ 12 Psalm 22:22　ᵈ 13 Isaiah 8:17　ᵉ 13 Isaiah 8:18

2:8 ᵘPs 8:4-6; S Mt 22:44
2:9 ᵛver 7; Ac 3:13; S Php 2:9 ʷPhp 2:7-9 ˣ2Co 5:15
2:10 ʸS Ro 11:36 ᶻLk 24:26; Heb 5:8,9; 7:28
2:11 ᵃHeb 13:12 ᵇS Eph 5:26 ᶜS Mt 28:10
2:12 ᵈPs 22:22; 68:26
2:13 ᵉIsa 8:17 ᶠIsa 8:18; Jn 10:29
2:14 ᵍ1Co 15:50; Eph 6:12 ʰS Jn 1:14 ⁱGe 3:15; 1Co 15:54-57; 2Ti 1:10 ʲ1Jn 3:8
2:15 ᵏS 2Ti 1:7
2:16 ˡS Lk 3:8
2:17 ᵐver 14; S Php 5:2 ⁿHeb 5:2 ᵒHeb 3:1; 4:14,15; 5:5,10; 7:26,28; 8:1,3; 9:11 ᵖHeb 5:1 ᑫS Ro 3:25
2:18 ʳHeb 4:15

2:7 *angels.* The author here quotes his Greek version of the Psalter, which renders the common Hebrew word for "God" or "gods" in this way in Ps 8:5 (see TNIV text note there), as it does the Hebrew for "sons of God" in Job 1:6; 2:1 (see TNIV text note there).

2:8 *everything.* God's purpose from the beginning was that humanity should be sovereign in the creaturely realm, subject only to God. Due to sin, that purpose of God has not yet been fully realized. Indeed, humans are themselves "in slavery" (v. 15).

2:9 *Jesus … now crowned with glory and honor.* See 10:13 and note. Ps 8 is here applied to Jesus in particular. As forerunner of humanity's restored dominion over the earth, he was made lower than the angels for a while (see TNIV text note on vv. 6–8) but is now crowned with glory and honor at God's right hand. By his perfect life, his death on the cross and his exaltation, he has made possible for redeemed humanity the ultimate fulfillment of Ps 8 in the future kingdom.

2:10 *many sons and daughters to glory.* Those who believe in Christ are made God's children through his only Son (cf. Jn 1:12–13; Ro 8:14–23 and notes on 8:14–15,17,23; Gal 3:26; 4:5 and note; Eph 4:5; 5:1; 1Jn 3:1–2). *make … perfect through what he suffered.* It was through Christ's suffering that God fully qualified him as the one sent to carry out his redemptive mission, specifically the priestly aspects of that mission (see v. 17 and note; see also 5:9; 7:28). *pioneer.* The Greek word often expresses the idea of "originator, founder." It was also applied to a leader, ruler or prince. In the present context, it perhaps has the sense of "champion"—the one who came to the aid of those enslaved to "him who holds the power of death" (v. 14; cf. v. 15; 12:2 and note; Ac 3:15; 5:31 ["Prince"]).

2:11 *who makes people holy … who are made holy.* Christ became a human being to identify himself with humans and, by his substitutionary sacrifice on the cross, to restore their lost holiness. *holy.* See 1Co 1:2 and note.

2:12 *I will declare your name to my brothers and sisters.* A quotation from Ps 22:22, a psalm describing the sufferings and relief of God's righteous servant (see introduction to Ps 22). The key phrase is "my brothers and sisters," seen here as coming from the lips of the triumphant Messiah.

2:13 *I will put my trust in him.* An expression of true dependence on God, perfectly exemplified in Christ. In him humanity is seen as it was intended to be. *Here am I, and the children God has given me.* Also seen ultimately as an utterance of the incarnate Son. The Father's children are given to the Son to be his brothers and sisters (see v. 11; cf. Mt 12:50).

2:14 *him who holds the power of death.* Satan wields the power of death only insofar as he induces people to sin and to come under sin's penalty, which is death (see Ro 5:12; 6:23 and notes).

2:15 *free.* See 1Co 15:54–57 and notes on 15:56–57; Rev 1:18.

2:16 *Abraham's descendants.* Christ came to redeem Abraham's descendants—those who have Abraham's faith (see Ge 12:2–3; Ro 4:11,16; 9:8; Gal 3:29 and notes).

2:17 *merciful and faithful high priest.* See v. 18; 5:2. *high priest.* In Israel the head of the priestly order, the only one who could enter into the very presence of God in the Most Holy Place in the temple—to make atonement for the people of God (see 9:7 and note; 13:11; Lev 16:1–34 and note). *make atonement.* In order for Christ to turn aside the wrath of God against guilty sinners, he had to become one with them and die as a substitute for them (see notes on Lev 16:20–22; 17:11; Ro 3:25; 1Jn 2:2).

2:18 *he was tempted.* See note on 4:15.

3:1 ˢ Heb 2:11
ᵗ S Ro 8:28 ᵘ 1Ti 6:12;
Heb 4:14; 10:23;
2Co 9:13 ᵛ S Heb 2:17
3:2 ʷ ver 5; Nu 12:7
3:3 ˣ Dt 34:12
3:4 ʸ Ge 1:1
3:5 ᶻ Ex 14:31
ᵃ ver 2; Nu 12:7
3:6 ᵇ S Heb 1:2
ᶜ S 1Co 3:16; 1Ti 3:15
ᵈ ver 14; S Ro 11:22;
Heb 4:14 ᵉ Ro 5:2;
Heb 6:11,18,19; 7:19;
11:1
3:7 ᶠ Ac 28:25;
Heb 9:8; 10:15
3:8 ᵍ ver 15; Heb 4:7
3:9 ʰ Nu 14:33;
Dt 1:3; Ac 7:36
3:11 ⁱ Dt 1:34,35
ʲ Heb 4:3,5 ᵏ Ps 95:7-
11
3:12 ˡ S Mt 16:16
3:13 ᵐ Heb 10:24,
25 ⁿ Jer 17:9;
Eph 4:22
3:14 ᵒ ver 6
ᵖ S Eph 3:12
3:15 ᵠ ver 7,8;
Ps 95:7,8; Heb 4:7

JESUS GREATER THAN MOSES

3 Therefore, holy brothers and sisters, ˢ who share in the heavenly calling, ᵗ fix your thoughts on Jesus, whom we acknowledge ᵘ as our apostle and high priest. ᵛ ²He was faithful to the one who appointed him, just as Moses was faithful in all God's house. ʷ ³Jesus has been found worthy of greater honor than Moses, ˣ just as the builder of a house has greater honor than the house itself. ⁴For every house is built by someone, but God is the builder of everything. ʸ ⁵"Moses was faithful as a servant ᶻ in all God's house,"ᵃ ᵃ bearing witness to what would be spoken by God in the future. ⁶But Christ is faithful as the Son ᵇ over God's house. And we are his house, ᶜ if indeed we hold firmly ᵈ to our confidence and the hope ᵉ in which we glory.

WARNING AGAINST UNBELIEF

⁷So, as the Holy Spirit says: ᶠ

"Today, if you hear his voice,
⁸   do not harden your hearts ᵍ
as you did in the rebellion,
    during the time of testing in the wilderness,
⁹where your ancestors tested and tried me,
    though for forty years they saw what I did. ʰ
¹⁰That is why I was angry with that generation;
    I said, 'Their hearts are always going astray,
    and they have not known my ways.'
¹¹So I declared on oath in my anger, ⁱ
    'They shall never enter my rest.' ʲ ᵇ ᵏ

¹²See to it, brothers and sisters, that none of you has a sinful, unbelieving heart that turns away from the living God. ˡ ¹³But encourage one another daily, ᵐ as long as it is called "Today," so that none of you may be hardened by sin's deceitfulness. ⁿ ¹⁴We have come to share in Christ, if indeed we hold firmly ᵒ till the end our original conviction. ᵖ ¹⁵As has just been said:

"Today, if you hear his voice,
    do not harden your hearts
    as you did in the rebellion."ᶜ ᵠ

ᵃ *5* Num. 12:7   ᵇ *11* Psalm 95:7-11   ᶜ *15* Psalm 95:7,8

3:1–6 The faithful high priest who is worthy of our trust because he is greater than Moses.
3:1 *holy.* See note on 1Co 1:2. *brothers and sisters.* See note on Ro 1:13. *share in the heavenly calling.* That is, participate (see note on v. 14) in the invitation to enter into and enjoy the presence of God (see 11:16; 12:22 and notes). *apostle.* Means "one who is sent" (see note on Mk 6:30). Jesus repeatedly spoke of himself as having been sent into the world by the Father (e.g., Mt 10:40; 15:24; Mk 9:37; Lk 9:48; Jn 4:34; 5:24,30,36–38; 6:38). He is the supreme apostle, the one from whom all other apostleship flows. *high priest.* See note on 2:17.
3:2 A comparison of Christ and Moses, both of whom were sent by the Father to lead his people—the one to lead them from bondage under the pharaoh to the promised land, the other to lead them from bondage under the devil (2:14–15) to the Sabbath-rest promised to those who believe (4:3,9). The analogy focuses on faithful stewardship.
3:3 *the builder . . . has greater honor than the house.* Jesus is the actual builder of the house (or household), whereas Moses was simply a part of it.

3:4 *God is the builder of everything.* God is here equated with God, making it beyond question that Christ is greater than Moses.

3:5–6 *a servant in all God's house . . . the Son over God's house.* The superiority of Christ over Moses (see Introduction: Theme) is shown in two comparisons: (1) Moses was a servant, whereas Christ is the Son, and (2) Moses was in God's house, i.e., a part of it, whereas Christ is over God's house. Both were faithful.

3:5 *faithful . . . in all God's house.*

3:6 *we are his house.* The house is made up of God's people, his household (see Eph 2:19; 1Pe 2:5 and notes). *if indeed we hold firmly to our confidence.* Failure to persevere reveals that a person is actually not a child of God, whereas perseverance is the hallmark of his children (cf. 10:35–36). *hope.* Assurance of free access to God (see v. 1; 6:18–19 and notes; 11:1; Ro 5:2 and note). *glory.* Rejoice (cf. Gal 6:14; cf. also 1Co 1:29,31; 2Co 10:17; Eph 2:9).

3:7—4:13 An exposition of Ps 95:7–11, stressing Christ's superiority over Moses, and a warning (the second; see note on 2:1–4) against disobedience and unbelief.
3:7–11 This quotation from Ps 95:7–11 summarizes the inglorious history of Israel under Moses' leadership in the wilderness. Three time periods are alluded to: that of the exodus, that of the psalmist and that of the writing of Hebrews. The example of Israel under Moses was used by the psalmist to warn the Israelites of his day against unbelief and disobedience. Similarly the author of Hebrews recalls the psalmist's words to warn the readers of this letter.
3:7 *Holy Spirit.* For the Holy Spirit as the speaker in (OT) Scripture, see 9:8; 10:15; Mk 12:36; Ac 1:16; 4:25; 21:11; 28:25; 1Pe 1:12; see also 2Pe 1:20–21 and notes; cf. 2Ti 3:16 and note.
3:13 *as long as it is called "Today."* See 4:7.

3:14 *to share in Christ.* To belong to him and participate in the blessings he gives (cf. v. 1). *hold firmly till the end.* Cf. 6:11; Mt 10:22; 24:13; Mk 13:13; Ro 2:26; cf. also 1Co 1:8. *our original conviction.* And the faith commitment we made on the basis of that conviction.

¹⁶Who were they who heard and rebelled? Were they not all those Moses led out of Egypt?^{r 17}And with whom was he angry for forty years? Was it not with those who sinned, whose bodies perished in the wilderness?^{s 18}And to whom did God swear that they would never enter his rest^t if not to those who disobeyed?^{u 19}So we see that they were not able to enter, because of their unbelief.^v

A SABBATH-REST FOR THE PEOPLE OF GOD

4 Therefore, since the promise of entering his rest still stands, let us be careful that none of you be found to have fallen short of it.^{w 2}For we also have had the good news proclaimed to us, just as they did; but the message they heard was of no value to them, because they did not share the faith of those who obeyed.^{a x 3}Now we who have believed enter that rest, just as God has said,

"So I declared on oath in my anger,
'They shall never enter my rest.' "^{b y}

And yet his work has been finished since the creation of the world. ⁴For somewhere he has spoken about the seventh day in these words: "On the seventh day God rested from all his work."^{c z 5}And again in the passage above he says, "They shall never enter my rest."^a

⁶Therefore since it still remains for some to enter that rest, and since those who formerly had the good news proclaimed to them did not go in because of their disobedience,^{b 7}God again set a certain day, calling it "Today." This he did when a long time later he spoke through David, as in the passage already quoted:

"Today, if you hear his voice,
do not harden your hearts."^{d c}

⁸For if Joshua had given them rest,^d God would not have spoken^e later about another day. ⁹There remains, then, a Sabbath-rest for the people of God; ¹⁰for those who enter God's rest also rest from their own work,^f just as God did from his.^{g 11}Let us, therefore, make every effort to enter that rest, so that no one will perish by following their example of disobedience.^h

¹²For the word of Godⁱ is alive^j and active.^k Sharper than any double-edged sword,^l it penetrates even to dividing soul and spirit, joints and marrow; it judges the thoughts and

---

^a 2 Some manuscripts *because those who heard did not combine it with faith*   ^b 3 Psalm 95:11; also in verse 5   ^c 4 Gen. 2:2   ^d 7 Psalm 95:7,8

Right margin cross-references:

3:16 ^r Nu 14:2
3:17 ^s Nu 14:29; Ps 106:26; 1Co 10:5
3:18 ^t Nu 14:20-23; Dt 1:34,35 ^u Heb 4:6
3:19 ^v Ps 78:22; 106:24; Jn 3:36
4:1 ^w Heb 12:15
4:2 ^x 1Th 2:13
4:3 ^y Ps 95:11; Dt 1:34,35; Heb 3:11
4:4 ^z Ge 2:2,3; Ex 20:11
4:5 ^a Ps 95:11; S ver 3
4:6 ^b ver 11; Heb 3:18
4:7 ^c Ps 95:7,8; Heb 3:7,8,15
4:8 ^d Jos 22:4 ^e S Heb 1:1
4:10 ^f Lev 23:3; Rev 14:13 ^g ver 4
4:11 ^h ver 6; Heb 3:18
4:12 ⁱ S Mk 4:14; Lk 5:1; 11:28; Jn 10:35; Ac 12:24; 1Th 2:13; 2Ti 2:9; 1Pe 1:23; 1Jn 2:14; Rev 1:2, 9 ^j Ac 7:38; 1Pe 1:23 ^k Isa 55:11; Jer 23:29; 1Th 2:13 ^l Eph 6:17; S Rev 1:16

3:16–19 The argument is pursued with a series of rhetorical questions. The important truths are that the people who failed to enter Canaan were the ones who had heard God's promise concerning the land and that they refused to believe what God had promised (v. 19)—an action described as rebellion (v. 16), sin (v. 17) and disobedience (v. 18). Consequently, God in his anger closed the doors of Canaan in the face of that whole generation of Israelites (Nu 14:21–35).

4:1 *promise of entering his rest.* See Ex 33:14; Dt 3:20 and note. *still stands.* God's promise to bring his people into circumstances of "rest" in his creation, while conditional, was open-ended. It was grounded in God's covenanted promises to Abraham (see Ge 15:12–21; 17:1–8; 22:15–18), was later reinforced by God's covenant with David (see 2Sa 7:5–16 and notes; cf. 1Ki 5:4 and note) and eventually came to be focused on the Messiah (see Isa 11:1–9 and notes). Through the Messiah's reign, God's promise of rest will ultimately be fulfilled in the new creation (see Isa 65:17; 66:22; Rev 21:4).

4:3 *we who have believed enter that rest.* Just as entering into rest in Canaan demanded faith in God's promise, so the ultimate salvation-rest is entered only by faith in the person and work of Jesus Christ. *his work has been finished since the creation of the world.* God rested from his work on the seventh day of creation (see v. 4; Ge 2:2), and thus his rest is already a reality. The rest God calls us to enter (vv. 10–11) is not our rest but his rest, which he invites us to share.

4:6–8 Israel's going into Canaan under Joshua was a partial and temporary entering of God's rest. That, however, was not the end of entering, as shown in the continuing invitation of Ps 95:7–8.
4:7 *calling it "Today."* See 3:13.

4:9 *There remains, then, a Sabbath-rest.* God's rest may still be entered by faith in his Son. Since the pre-Christian Greek translation of the OT (the Septuagint), which the author and his readers knew well, made no verbal distinction between the Sabbath "rest" (Hebrew *shabbat* [see, e.g., Ge 2:2; Ex 20:11; 23:12]) and the condition of "rest" that Israel, if faithful, was to experience every day in the promised land (Hebrew *nuah/menuhah* [see, e.g., Ex 31:14; Dt 3:20]), the writer associates these two in a way that suggests he saw in the weekly Sabbath-rest a sign and pledge of the promised life of rest. The fact that neither the Hebrew nor the Septuagint made any verbal distinction between God's "rest" in Ps 95:11 and his "resting place" in Ps 132:14; Isa 66:1 (see note on Ps 132:8) may have reinforced this striking conceptual association.

4:10 *rest from their own work.* Believers cease their efforts to gain salvation by their own works and rest in the finished work of Christ on the cross. The believer's final rest may also be in view here (see Rev 14:13).

4:11 *make every effort.* Not a call to earn one's salvation by works but an exhortation to enter salvation-rest by faith and not follow Israel's sad example in the wilderness.
4:12–13 The reasons for giving serious attention to the exhortation of v. 11.
4:12 *word of God.* God's truth was revealed by Jesus (the incarnate Word; see Jn 1:1,14), but it has also been given verbally, the word referred to here. This dynamic word of God is active in accomplishing God's purposes (see Ps 19:7–11; 107:20; 147:15,18; Isa 40:8; 55:11; Gal 3:8; Eph 5:26; Jas 1:18; 1Pe 1:23). The author of Hebrews describes it as a "living" power that judges as with an all-seeing eye, penetrating a person's innermost being. *soul*

4:12 *m* 1Co 14:24,25
4:13 *n* Ps 33:13-15;
Pr 5:21; Jer 16:17;
23:24; Da 2:22
4:14 *o* S Heb 2:17
p Heb 6:20; 8:1; 9:24
q S Mt 4:3 *r* S Heb 3:1
4:15 *s* S Heb 2:17
t Heb 2:18
u S 2Co 5:21
4:16 *v* S Heb 7:19
w S Eph 3:12
5:1 *x* Heb 2:17
y Heb 8:3; 9:9
z Heb 7:27
5:2 *a* Isa 29:24;
Heb 2:18; 4:15
b Heb 7:28
5:3 *c* Lev 9:7; 16:6;
Heb 7:27; 9:7
5:4 *d* Ex 28:1;
Nu 14:40; 18:7
5:5 *e* Jn 8:54
f S Heb 2:17
g S Heb 1:1 *h* Ps 2:7;
S Mt 3:17
5:6 *i* ver 10;
Ge 14:18; Heb 6:20;
7:1-22 *j* Ps 110:4;
Heb 7:17,21
5:7 *k* Lk 22:41-44
l Mt 27:46,50;
Lk 23:46 *m* Ps 22:24
n Mk 14:36
5:8 *o* S Heb 1:2
p S Php 2:8
5:9 *q* S Heb 2:10
5:10 *r* ver 5;
S Heb 2:17 *s* S ver 6

attitudes of the heart. *m* ¹³Nothing in all creation is hidden from God's sight. *n* Everything is uncovered and laid bare before the eyes of him to whom we must give account.

JESUS THE GREAT HIGH PRIEST

¹⁴Therefore, since we have a great high priest *o* who has ascended into heaven, *a p* Jesus the Son of God, *q* let us hold firmly to the faith we profess. *r* ¹⁵For we do not have a high priest *s* who is unable to empathize with our weaknesses, but we have one who has been tempted in every way, just as we are *t*—yet he did not sin. *u* ¹⁶Let us then approach *v* God's throne of grace with confidence, *w* so that we may receive mercy and find grace to help us in our time of need.

5 Every high priest is selected from among the people and is appointed to represent them in matters related to God, *x* to offer gifts and sacrifices *y* for sins. *z* ²He is able to deal gently with those who are ignorant and are going astray, *a* since he himself is subject to weakness. *b* ³This is why he has to offer sacrifices for his own sins, as well as for the sins of the people. *c* ⁴And no one takes this honor on himself, but he receives it when called by God, just as Aaron was. *d*

⁵In the same way, Christ did not take on himself the glory *e* of becoming a high priest. *f* But God said *g* to him,

"You are my Son;
   today I have become your Father." *b h*

⁶And he says in another place,

"You are a priest forever,
   in the order of Melchizedek. *i* " *c j*

⁷During the days of Jesus' life on earth, he offered up prayers and petitions *k* with fervent cries and tears *l* to the one who could save him from death, and he was heard *m* because of his reverent submission. *n* ⁸Son *o* though he was, he learned obedience from what he suffered *p* ⁹and, once made perfect, *q* he became the source of eternal salvation for all who obey him ¹⁰and was designated by God to be high priest *r* in the order of Melchizedek. *s*

---

a 14 Greek *has gone through the heavens*   *b* 5 Psalm 2:7   *c* 6 Psalm 110:4

---

and spirit, joints and marrow. The totality and depth of one's being (see 1Th 5:23 and note).

4:13 *Nothing in all creation is hidden from God's sight.* The author associates the activity of the word with the activity of God, as though they are one and the same—which in a sense they are.

4:14—7:28 An exposition of Ps 110:4, stressing Christ's superiority over Aaron because his is a better priesthood (see Introduction: Theme).

4:14 *great high priest.* See 2:17 and note; 3:1. *into heaven.* As the Aaronic high priest on the Day of Atonement passed from the sight of the people into the Most Holy Place (see Lev 16:15, 17), so Jesus passed from the sight of his watching disciples, ascending "through the heavens" into the heavenly sanctuary (see TNIV text note), his work of atonement accomplished (Ac 1:9–11). *hold firmly to the faith we profess.* Suggests that the readers were in danger of letting their faith slip (see similar admonitions in 2:1; 3:6,14).

4:15 *tempted in every way, just as we are.* See 2:18. The author stresses the parallel between Christ's temptations and ours. He did not have each temptation we have but experienced the whole range of our temptations. *yet he did not sin.* The way in which Christ's temptations were different from ours was in the results—his temptations never led to sin (see Mt 4:1–11 and notes).

4:16 *Let us then approach.* Because Christ, our high priest, has experienced human temptation, he stands ready to give immediate and sympathetic help when we are tempted (see 2:10 and note).

5:1–4 The high-priestly office had two specific qualifications: (1) The high priest had to be "selected from among the people" (v. 1) and thus be able to represent them before God; and (2) he had to "be called by God" (v. 4).

5:1 *high priest.* See note on 2:17. *gifts and sacrifices.* See 8:3; 9:9 and notes on Lev 1:2; 2:1; see also chart, p. 155.

5:2 *those who are ignorant and are going astray.* See Ps 119:176 and note. Contrast the unintentional sin (see Lev 4 and note on 4:2; Nu 15:22–29 and note on 15:22) with defiant rebellion against God (see Nu 15:30–31 and note on 15:30; cf. Heb 6:4–6; 10:26–31 and notes).

5:4 *no one takes this honor on himself.* In Christ's day the high-priestly office was in the hands of a family that had bought control of it.

5:5 *Christ did not take on himself the glory of becoming a high priest.* The Son was appointed by the Father, as the two passages cited here show (Ps 2:7; 110:4). *today I have become your Father.* See 1:5; Ps 2:7–9 and notes; cf. Ro 1:4.

5:6 *in the order of Melchizedek.* See notes on 7:3; Ge 14:20; Ps 110:4.

5:7 *prayers … tears.* The principal reference here is to Christ's agony in Gethsemane and on Golgotha. *to the one who could save him from death.* To the Father. Jesus did not shrink from physical suffering and death but from the indescribable agony of taking humankind's sin on himself (cf. Mt 27:46). Although he asked that the cup of suffering might be taken from him, he did not waver in his determination to fulfill the Father's will (see Mt 26:36–46 and note on 26:38–39). *he was heard.* His prayer was granted by the Father, who saved him from death—through resurrection.

5:8 *Son though he was.* Though he was *God's Son* (see 1:2–3). *learned obedience.* Learned experientially what his full obedience to God's will for humankind entailed for him. *from what he suffered.* Especially in the ordeal of his atoning death, by which "he became the source of eternal salvation for all who obey him" (v. 9).

5:9 *made perfect.* See 2:10 and note.

WARNING AGAINST FALLING AWAY

6:4–6Ref — Heb 10:26–31

[11]We have much to say about this, but it is hard to make it clear to you because you no longer try to understand. [12]In fact, though by this time you ought to be teachers, you need someone to teach you the elementary truths [t] of God's word all over again. You need milk, not solid food! [u] [13]Anyone who lives on milk, being still an infant, [v] is not acquainted with the teaching about righteousness. [14]But solid food is for the mature, [w] who by constant use have trained themselves to distinguish good from evil. [x]

6 Therefore let us move beyond [y] the elementary teachings [z] about Christ and be taken forward to maturity, not laying again the foundation of repentance from acts that lead to death, [a] [a] and of faith in God, [2]instruction about cleansing rites, [b] [b] the laying on of hands, [c] the resurrection of the dead, [d] and eternal judgment. [3]And God permitting, [e] we will do so.

[4]It is impossible for those who have once been enlightened, [f] who have tasted the heavenly gift, [g] who have shared in the Holy Spirit, [h] [5]who have tasted the goodness [i] of the word of God [j] and the powers of the coming age [6]and who have fallen [c] away, to be brought back to repentance. [k] To their loss they are crucifying the Son of God [l] all over again and subjecting him to public disgrace. [7]Land that drinks in the rain often falling on it and that produces a crop useful to those for whom it is farmed receives the blessing of God. [8]But land that produces thorns and thistles is worthless and is in danger of being cursed. [m] In the end it will be burned.

[9]Even though we speak like this, dear friends, [n] we are convinced of better things in your case—the things that have to do with salvation. [10]God is not unjust; he will not forget your work and the love you have shown him as you have helped his people and continue to help them. [o] [11]We want each of you to show this same diligence to the very end,

---

[a] 1 Or *from useless rituals*   [b] 2 Or *about baptisms*   [c] 6 Or *age,* [6]*if they fall*

5:12 [t] Heb 6:1
[u] 1Co 3:2; 1Pe 2:2
5:13 [v] S 1Co 14:20
5:14 [w] S 1Co 2:6
[x] Isa 7:15
6:1 [y] Php 3:12-14
[z] Heb 5:12 [a] Heb 9:14
6:2 [b] Jn 3:25
[c] S Ac 6:6 [d] S Ac 2:24; Ac 17:18,32
6:3 [e] Ac 18:21
6:4 [f] Heb 10:32
6:5 [g] Eph 2:8 [h] Gal 3:2
[i] Ps 34:8
[j] S Heb 4:12
6:6 [k] 2Pe 2:21; 1Jn 5:16 [l] S Mt 4:3
6:8 [m] Ge 3:17,18; Isa 5:6; 27:4
6:9 [n] S 1Co 10:14
6:10 [o] S Mt 10:40, 42; 1Th 1:3

5:11 *much to say about this.* About Christ's eternal priesthood "in the order of Melchizedek" (v. 10). *you no longer try to understand.* Instead of progressing in the Christian life, the readers had become spiritually sluggish and mentally lazy (6:12). **5:12** *by this time.* They were not recent converts. *elementary truths of God's word.* Such as those listed in 6:1–2 (see note there). Having taken the first steps toward becoming (mature) Christians, they had slipped back to where they started. *solid food.* Advanced teaching, such as that given in ch. 7.

5:14 *mature.* Those who had progressed in spiritual life and had become Christians of sound judgment and discernment. *distinguish good from evil.* Something neither physical nor spiritual infants can do.

6:1–2 *not laying again the foundation.* Six fundamental doctrines are mentioned: 1. *repentance.* The change of mind that causes one to turn away from sin (see note on Mt 4:17). 2. *faith in God.* The counterpart of repentance. As repentance is turning away from sin, faith is turning to God (cf. 1Th 1:9). 3. *instruction about cleansing rites.* If the TNIV text note rendering is correct, reference is probably to different baptisms with which the readers were familiar, such as Jewish baptism of proselytes, John the Baptist's baptism, and the baptism commanded by Jesus (see Mt 28:19 and note). If the TNIV main text translation is correct ("cleansing rites"), reference is probably to the ceremonial or ritual washings as practiced by first-century Judaism (cf. 9:10; Mk 7:3–5; Lk 4:40; Ac 2:6 and note; Jas 4:8 and note). 4. *laying on of hands.* Sometimes followed baptism (Ac 8:17). Otherwise laying on of hands was practiced in connection with ordaining or commissioning (Ac 6:6; see note there), healing the sick (see Mk 6:5; Lk 4:40; Ac 28:8) and bestowal of blessing (see Mt 19:13–15). 5. *resurrection of the dead.* The resurrection of all people in the last days (see Jn 5:25–29; 11:25; 2Co 4:14). 6. *eternal judgment.* Either the fact of God's judgment or the verdict that determines the eternal condition of those judged. **6:1** *elementary teachings about Christ.* See note on 5:12. *acts that lead to death.* Lit. "dead works"; deeds or useless rituals that cannot impart life (see 9:14).

6:3 A common expression of dependence on the will of God (cf. 1Co 16:7; Jas 4:13–15). Only the Lord can open minds and hearts and bring spiritual maturity.

6:4–8 The third warning (see note on 2:1–4).

6:4–6 The most common interpretations of this difficult passage are: 1. It refers to Christians who actually lose their salvation. 2. It is a hypothetical argument to warn immature Hebrew Christians (5:11–14) that they must progress to maturity (see v. 1) or else experience divine discipline or judgment (see vv. 7–8). 3. It refers to professing Christians whose apostasy proves that their faith was not genuine (cf. 1Jn 2:19). This view sees chs. 3–4 as a warning based on the rebellion of the Israelites in the wilderness. As Israel could not enter the promised land after spying out the region and tasting its fruit, so the professing Hebrew Christians would not be able to repent if they adamantly turned against "the light" they had received. According to this interpretation, such expressions as "enlightened," "tasted the heavenly gift" and "shared in the Holy Spirit" indicate that such persons had come under the influence of God's covenant blessings and had professed to turn from darkness to light but were in danger of a public and final rejection of Christ, proving they had never been regenerated (see 10:26–31 and notes; cf. 2Pe 2:20–22 and notes).

6:5 *the coming age.* See Mk 10:30 and note; 1Ti 6:19.

6:7–8 A short parable graphically illustrating the warning just given (cf. Mt 13:3–23).

6:8 *be burned.* Cf. 10:27 and note.

6:9 *convinced of better things ... that have to do with salvation.* Although the author has suggested the possibility that some of his readers may still be unsaved, he is confident that God has been at work among them. Changed lives and works of love (v. 10) suggest that most of them were indeed regenerated.

6:11 *to the very end.* A call for perseverance in faith as an evidence of salvation. *make your hope sure.* See 3:6 and note; 11:1; 2Pe 1:10 and note.

6:11 *p* S Heb 3:6
6:12 *q* Heb 13:7
r 2Th 1:4; Jas 1:3;
Rev 13:10; 14:12
s Heb 10:36
6:13 *t* Ge 22:16;
Lk 1:73
6:14 *u* Ge 22:17
6:15 *v* Ge 21:5
6:16 *w* Ex 22:11
6:17 *x* ver 18;
Ps 110:4. *y* Ro 4:16;
Heb 11:9
6:18 *z* Nu 23:19;
Tit 1:2 *a* S Heb 3:6
6:19 *b* Lev 16:2;
Heb 9:2,3,7
6:20 *c* S Heb 4:14
d S Heb 2:17
e S Heb 5:6
7:1 *f* Ps 76:2
g S Mk 5:7 *h* ver 6;
Ge 14:18-20
7:3 *i* ver 6 / S Mt 4:3
7:4 *k* Ac 2:29
l Ge 14:20
7:5 *m* Nu 18:21,26
7:6 *n* Ge 14:19,20
o Ro 4:13
7:8 *p* Heb 5:6; 6:20
7:11 *q* ver 18,19;
Heb 8:7

in order to make your hope *p* sure. [12] We do not want you to become lazy, but to imitate *q* those who through faith and patience *r* inherit what has been promised. *s*

THE CERTAINTY OF GOD'S PROMISE

[13] When God made his promise to Abraham, since there was no one greater for him to swear by, he swore by himself, *t* [14] saying, "I will surely bless you and give you many descendants." *a u* [15] And so after waiting patiently, Abraham received what was promised. *v*

[16] People swear by someone greater than themselves, and the oath confirms what is said and puts an end to all argument. *w* [17] Because God wanted to make the unchanging *x* nature of his purpose very clear to the heirs of what was promised, *y* he confirmed it with an oath. [18] God did this so that, by two unchangeable things in which it is impossible for God to lie, *z* we who have fled to take hold of the hope *a* set before us may be greatly encouraged. [19] We have this hope as an anchor for the soul, firm and secure. It enters the inner sanctuary behind the curtain, *b* [20] where our forerunner, Jesus, has entered on our behalf. *c* He has become a high priest *d* forever, in the order of Melchizedek. *e*

MELCHIZEDEK THE PRIEST

7 This Melchizedek was king of Salem *f* and priest of God Most High. *g* He met Abraham returning from the defeat of the kings and blessed him, *h* [2] and Abraham gave him a tenth of everything. First, the name Melchizedek means "king of righteousness"; then also, "king of Salem" means "king of peace." [3] Without father or mother, without genealogy, *i* without beginning of days or end of life, resembling the Son of God, *j* he remains a priest forever.

[4] Just think how great he was: Even the patriarch *k* Abraham gave him a tenth of the plunder! *l* [5] Now the law requires the descendants of Levi who become priests to collect a tenth from the people *m*—that is, from their kindred—even though their kindred are descended from Abraham. [6] This man, however, did not trace his descent from Levi, yet he collected a tenth from Abraham and blessed *n* him who had the promises. *o* [7] And without doubt the lesser is blessed by the greater. [8] In the one case, the tenth is collected by those who die; but in the other case, by him who is declared to be living. *p* [9] One might even say that Levi, who collects the tenth, paid the tenth through Abraham, [10] because when Melchizedek met Abraham, Levi was still in the body of his ancestor.

JESUS LIKE MELCHIZEDEK

[11] If perfection could have been attained through the Levitical priesthood—and indeed the law given to the people *q* established that priesthood—why was there still need for

a 14 Gen. 22:17

6:12 *lazy.* See 5:11 and note. *those who through faith and patience inherit what has been promised.* For examples, see ch. 11.

6:13 *God made his promise to Abraham.* The promise of many descendants was made with an oath to emphasize its unchanging character (see Ge 22:16–18). Ordinarily the swearing of an oath belongs to our fallen human situation, in which a person's word is not always trustworthy (cf. Mt 5:23–26 and note). God's swearing of an oath was a condescension to human frailty, thus making his word, which in itself is absolutely trustworthy, doubly dependable (see v. 18 and note).

6:15 *after waiting patiently.* For 25 years (see Ge 12:3–4; 21:5). *received what was promised.* The birth of his son Isaac (Ge 17:2; 18:10; 21:5).

6:18 *two unchangeable things.* God's promise, which in itself is absolutely trustworthy, and God's oath confirming that promise. *be greatly encouraged.* Since we look back on the fulfillment of the promise that Abraham saw only in anticipation (see 11:13; Jn 8:56 and notes).

6:19 *as an anchor for the soul, firm and secure.* Like an anchor holding a ship safely in position, our hope in Christ guarantees our safety. *inner sanctuary behind the curtain.* Whereas the ship's anchor goes down to the ocean bed, the Christian's anchor goes up into the true, heavenly sanctuary.

6:20 *a high priest forever, in the order of Melchizedek.* The grand theme that the author introduced briefly in 5:6–10 and now develops in ch. 7. *high priest.* See note on 2:17.

7:1 *Melchizedek.* See Ge 14:18–20 and notes; cf. Ps 110:4 and note. *king … and priest.* Of particular significance is Melchizedek's holding both offices, one of the ways in which he is treated here as a prefiguration of Christ (see notes on Zec 4:14; 6:13). *Salem.* Jerusalem (see note on Ge 14:18).

7:2 *king of righteousness … king of peace.* Messianic titles (see Isa 9:6–7; Jer 23:5–6 and notes).

7:3 *Without father … or end of life.* Ge 14:18–20, contrary to the practice elsewhere in the early chapters of Genesis, does not mention Melchizedek's parentage and children, or his birth and death. That he was a real, historical figure is clear, but the author of Hebrews (in accordance with Jewish interpretation) uses the silence of Scripture about Melchizedek's genealogy to portray him as a prefiguration of Christ. Melchizedek's priesthood anticipates Christ's eternal existence and his unending priesthood. Some believe the appearance of Melchizedek to Abraham was a manifestation of Christ before his incarnation, but the comparison "resembling the Son of God" argues against such an interpretation.

7:4 *think how great he was.* The one who collects a tithe is greater than the one who pays it, and "the lesser is blessed by the greater" (v. 7). In both ways Melchizedek was greater than Abraham.

7:11 *the law given.* The law of Moses and the priesthood went together. All the people without exception were sinners, subject to the law's condemnation, and thus were in need of a priestly system to mediate between them and God. *in the order of Mel-*

another priest to come, [r] one in the order of Melchizedek, [s] not in the order of Aaron? [12]For when the priesthood is changed, the law must be changed also. [13]He of whom these things are said belonged to a different tribe, [t] and no one from that tribe has ever served at the altar. [u][14]For it is clear that our Lord descended from Judah, [v] and in regard to that tribe Moses said nothing about priests. [15]And what we have said is even more clear if another priest like Melchizedek appears, [16]one who has become a priest not on the basis of a regulation as to his ancestry but on the basis of the power of an indestructible life. [17]For it is declared:

> "You are a priest forever,
>   in the order of Melchizedek."[a][w]

[18]The former regulation is set aside because it was weak and useless[x] [19](for the law made nothing perfect),[y] and a better hope[z] is introduced, by which we draw near to God. [a] [20]And it was not without an oath! Others became priests without any oath, [21]but he became a priest with an oath when God said to him:

> "The Lord has sworn
>   and will not change his mind:[b]
>   'You are a priest forever.' "[a][c]

[22]Because of this oath, Jesus has become the guarantor of a better covenant. [d]

[23]Now there have been many of those priests, since death prevented them from continuing in office; [24]but because Jesus lives forever, he has a permanent priesthood. [e] [25]Therefore he is able to save[f] completely[b] those who come to God[g] through him, because he always lives to intercede for them. [h]

[26]Such a high priest[i] truly meets our need—one who is holy, blameless, pure, set apart from sinners,[j] exalted above the heavens. [k] [27]Unlike the other high priests, he does not need to offer sacrifices[l] day after day, first for his own sins, [m] and then for the sins of the people. He sacrificed for their sins once for all[n] when he offered himself. [o] [28]For the law appoints as high priests men in all their weakness;[p] but the oath, which came after the law, appointed the Son, [q] who has been made perfect[r] forever.

THE HIGH PRIEST OF A NEW COVENANT

8 Now the main point of what we are saying is this: We do have such a high priest, [s] who sat down at the right hand of the throne of the Majesty in heaven, [t] [2]and who serves in the sanctuary, the true tabernacle[u] set up by the Lord, not by a mere human being.

a 17,21 Psalm 110:4   b 25 Or forever

7:11 r Heb 10:1
s ver 17; S Heb 5:6
7:13 t ver 11 u ver 14
7:14 v Isa 11:1;
Mt 1:3; 2:6; Lk 3:33;
Rev 5:5
7:17 w Ps 110:4;
ver 21; S Heb 5:6
7:18 x Ro 8:3
7:19 y ver 11;
Ro 3:20; 7:7,8;
Gal 3:21; Heb 9:9;
10:1 S Heb 3:6
a ver 25; Heb 4:16;
10:1,22; Jas 4:8
7:21 b Nu 23:19;
1Sa 15:29; Mal 3:6;
Ro 11:29 c Ps 110:4;
S Heb 5:6
7:22 d S Lk 22:20
7:24 e ver 28
7:25 f S Ro 11:14
g S ver 19 h S Ro 8:34
7:26 i S Heb 2:17
j S 2Co 5:21
k S Heb 4:14
7:27 l Heb 5:1
m S Heb 5:3
n Ro 6:10; Heb 9:12,
26,28; 10:10; 1Pe 3:18
o Eph 5:2; Heb 9:14,
28
7:28 p Heb 5:2
q S Heb 1:2
r S Heb 2:10
8:1 s S Heb 2:17
t S Mk 16:19;
S Heb 4:14
8:2 u Heb 9:11,24

---

chizedek, not in the order of Aaron. Implies that the Aaronic (or Levitical) priesthood was imperfect but that Melchizedek's was perfect. The announcement of a coming one who would be a priest forever (Ps 110:4) was written midway in the history of the Levitical priesthood—which could be understood as a hint that the existing system was to give way to something better.
7:16 become a priest not on the basis of a regulation as to his ancestry. In the law of Moses the priestly function was restricted to the family of Aaron from the tribe of Levi (see Ex 28:1–4; 40:12–15; Nu 3:10), but Jesus came from the nonpriestly tribe of Judah (vv. 14–15). power of an indestructible life. According to Ps 110:4 the priest in the order of Melchizedek is "a priest forever." This is what Jesus became as a result of the act of God's power that raised him from the dead as the eternal victor over death.
7:18 The former regulation . . . was weak and useless. The law is holy and good (Ro 7:12), but it could neither give the ability to fulfill its demands nor provide the atonement necessary for those who violated it (v. 19a).
7:19 The law was only preparatory (see Gal 3:23–24 and notes) and brought nothing to fulfillment (see Mt 5:17 and note). better hope. The new covenant is better because it assures us of complete redemption and brings us into the very presence of God. See 3:6 and note.
7:20 No divine oath was associated with the establishment of the Levitical priesthood.
7:21 with an oath. For the significance of the oath, see 6:17.
7:22 better covenant. See chs. 8–10; see also Introduction: Theme.
7:23 death prevented them from continuing in office. Imperma-

nence was further evidence of the imperfection of the Levitical order.
7:25 completely. May include the ideas of completeness and permanence (see TNIV text note). always lives to intercede. His people will never be without a priest to represent them in the very presence of God, interceding on their behalf (see 1Jn 2:1–2 and notes; cf. Jn 17:6–26).
7:26 high priest. See note on 2:17. meets our need. Of salvation from sin and its consequences.
7:27 day after day. A reference to the endless repetition of sacrifices throughout the year (see Ex 29:36–42), evidence that these sacrifices never effectively and finally atoned for sin. first for his own sins. Christ's priesthood is superior because he has no personal sins for which sacrifice had to be made (see Lev 9:8 and note). once for all. A key phrase in Hebrews (see 9:12,26 and note on 9:12; 10:2,10). offered himself. Levitical priests offered up only animals; our high priest offered himself, the perfect substitute for us.
7:28 men in all their weakness. Because (1) they are mortal and therefore impermanent, v. 23; (2) they are sinful, v. 27; and (3) they could only offer animals, which could never provide a genuine substitute for human beings made in the image of God (see Ge 1:26–28 and notes). made perfect forever. In regard to his appointed mission (see 2:10; 5:9 and notes).
8:1—10:18 The argument of this section grows out of an exposition of Jer 31:31–34 and demonstrates that Christ is the mediator of a "better covenant" (7:22).
8:1 See note on 1:2–3. high priest. See note on 2:17.
8:2 true tabernacle. In contrast to the tabernacle erected by

8:3 ʸS Heb 2:17
ʷHeb 5:1; 9:9
ˣHeb 9:14
8:4 ʸHeb 5:1; 9:9
8:5 ᶻHeb 9:23
ᵃCol 2:17; Heb 10:1
ᵇHeb 11:7; 12:25
ᶜEx 25:40
8:6 ᵈver 8,13;
S Lk 22:20
ᵉS Gal 3:20
8:7 ᶠHeb 7:11,18;
10:1
8:8 ᵍver 6,13;
S Lk 22:20
8:9 ʰEx 19:5,6;
20:1-17
8:10 ⁱRo 11:27
ʲHeb 10:16
ᵏEze 11:20; Zec 8:8
8:11 ˡIsa 54:13;
S Jn 6:45
8:12 ᵐHeb 10:17
ⁿRo 11:27
8:13 ᵒver 6,8;
S Lk 22:20 ᵖ2Co 5:17

³Every high priest ⱽ is appointed to offer both gifts and sacrifices, ʷ and so it was necessary for this one also to have something to offer. ˣ ⁴If he were on earth, he would not be a priest, for there are already priests who offer the gifts prescribed by the law. ʸ ⁵They serve at a sanctuary that is a copy ᶻ and shadow ᵃ of what is in heaven. This is why Moses was warned ᵇ when he was about to build the tabernacle: "See to it that you make everything according to the pattern shown you on the mountain."ᵃ ᶜ ⁶But in fact the ministry Jesus has received is as superior to theirs as the covenant ᵈ of which he is mediator ᵉ is superior to the old one, since the new covenant is established on better promises.

⁷For if there had been nothing wrong with that first covenant, no place would have been sought for another. ᶠ ⁸But God found fault with the people and said ᵇ:

"The days are coming, declares the Lord,
    when I will make a new covenant ᵍ
with the house of Israel
    and with the house of Judah.
⁹ It will not be like the covenant
    I made with their ancestors ʰ
when I took them by the hand
    to lead them out of Egypt,
because they did not remain faithful to my covenant,
    and I turned away from them,
                                    declares the Lord.
¹⁰This is the covenant ⁱ I will establish with the house of Israel
    after that time, declares the Lord.
I will put my laws in their minds
    and write them on their hearts.ʲ
I will be their God,
    and they will be my people. ᵏ
¹¹No longer will they teach their neighbors,
    or say to one another, 'Know the Lord,'
because they will all know me, ˡ
    from the least of them to the greatest.
¹² For I will forgive their wickedness
    and will remember their sins no more. ᵐ ᶜ ⁿ

¹³By calling this covenant "new,"ᵒ he has made the first one obsolete;ᵖ and what is obsolete and outdated will soon disappear.

ᵃ 5 Exodus 25:40   ᵇ 8 Some manuscripts may be translated *fault and said to the people.*
ᶜ 12 Jer. 31:31-34

Moses, which was an imperfect and impermanent copy of the heavenly one. *set up by the Lord, not by a mere human being.* The heavenly sanctuary built by God corresponds to the Most Holy Place, the innermost sanctuary in Moses' tabernacle, into which the high priest briefly entered with the blood of atonement once a year (see Lev 16:13–15,34). In the heavenly sanctuary, however, our great high priest dwells eternally as our intercessor (7:25).

8:3 *gifts and sacrifices.* See 5:1 and note.

8:4 *priests who offer the gifts.* The present tense of the verb "offer," here and elsewhere in the letter, indicates that the temple in Jerusalem was still standing. This letter, therefore, must have been written prior to the temple's destruction in A.D. 70 (see Introduction: Date).

8:5 *copy and shadow of what is in heaven.* An implication the author draws from the words of Ex 25:40. *make everything according to the pattern.* Because both the tabernacle and its ministry were intended to symbolize the only way sinners may approach a holy God and find forgiveness.

8:6 *mediator.* Cf. 1Ti 2:5 and note. In Hebrews "mediator" is always "of a (superior/new) covenant" (see 9:15; 12:24). The role of "mediator" here appears to be not that of instituting the covenant but of guaranteeing that the covenant promises are ful-

filled (cf. 7:22), that the promised deliverance is actually accomplished (cf. Moses' mediatorial acts in Ex 32:31–32; 33:12–23; 34:5–10; Nu 14:13–20).

8:7 *if there had been nothing wrong with that first covenant.* The line of argument here is similar to that in 7:11, where the Levitical priestly order is shown to be inferior because it was replaced by the order of Melchizedek. Similarly, if the Sinaitic covenant were without defect, there would have been no need to replace it with a new covenant.

8:8–12 A quotation from Jer 31:31–34 (see note there) containing a prophetic announcement and definition of the new covenant, which was to be different from the Sinaitic covenant (v. 9). Its superior benefits are: (1) God's laws will become inner principles (v. 10a) that enable his people to delight in doing his will (cf. Eze 36:26–27; Ro 8:2–4 and notes); (2) God and his people will have intimate fellowship (v. 10b); (3) sinful ignorance of God will be removed forever (v. 11); and (4) forgiveness of sins will be an everlasting reality (v. 12).

8:10 *their God ... my people.* See note on Zec 8:8.

8:13 *obsolete and outdated.* The Sinaitic covenant—but not the Abrahamic covenant (cf. Ro 4:16–17; chs. 9–11; Gal 3:7–9, 14,16–18; Eph 2:12).

WORSHIP IN THE EARTHLY TABERNACLE

9 Now the first covenant had regulations for worship and also an earthly sanctuary. *q* 2A tabernacle *r* was set up. In its first room were the lampstand *s* and the table *t* with its consecrated bread; *u* this was called the Holy Place. *v* 3Behind the second curtain was a room called the Most Holy Place, *w* 4which had the golden altar of incense *x* and the gold-covered ark of the covenant. *y* This ark contained the gold jar of manna, *z* Aaron's staff that had budded, *a* and the stone tablets of the covenant. *b* 5Above the ark were the cherubim of the Glory, *c* overshadowing the atonement cover. *d* But we cannot discuss these things in detail now.

6When everything had been arranged like this, the priests entered regularly *e* into the outer room to carry on their ministry. 7But only the high priest entered *f* the inner room, *g* and that only once a year, *h* and never without blood, *i* which he offered for himself *j* and for the sins the people had committed in ignorance. *k* 8The Holy Spirit was showing *l* by this that the way *m* into the Most Holy Place had not yet been disclosed as long as the first tabernacle was still functioning. 9This is an illustration *n* for the present time, indicating that the gifts and sacrifices being offered *o* were not able to clear the conscience *p* of the worshiper. 10They are only a matter of food *q* and drink *r* and various ceremonial washings *s*—external regulations *t* applying until the time of the new order.

THE BLOOD OF CHRIST

11But when Christ came as high priest *u* of the good things that are now already here, *a v* he went through the greater and more perfect tabernacle *w* that is not made with human hands, *x* that is to say, is not a part of this creation. 12He did not enter by means of the blood of goats and calves; *y* but he entered the Most Holy Place *z* once for all *a* by his own blood, *b* thus obtaining *b* eternal redemption. 13The blood of goats and bulls *c* and the ashes of a heifer *d* sprinkled on those who are ceremonially unclean sanctify them so that they are outwardly clean. 14How much more, then, will the blood of Christ, who through the eternal Spirit *e* offered himself *f* unblemished to God, cleanse our consciences *g* from acts that lead to death, *c h* so that we may serve the living God! *i*

15For this reason Christ is the mediator *j* of a new covenant, *k* that those who are called *l*

---

a 11 Some early manuscripts *are to come*   *b 12* Or *blood, having obtained*   *c 14* Or *from useless rituals*

9:1 *q* Ex 25:8
9:2 *r* Ex 25:8,9
s Ex 25:31-39
t Ex 25:23-29
u Ex 25:30; Lev 24:5-8
v Ex 26:33,34
9:3 *w* Ex 26:31-33
9:4 *x* Ex 30:1-5
y Ex 25:10-22
z Ex 16:32,33
a Nu 17:10 *b* Ex 31:18; 32:15
9:5 *c* Ex 25:17-19
d Ex 25:20-22; 26:34
9:6 *e* Nu 28:3
9:7 *f* Lev 16:11-19
g ver 2,3 *h* Lev 16:34
i Lev 16:11,14
j Lev 16:11; Heb 5:2,3
k Heb 5:2,3
9:8 *l* S Heb 3:7
m Jn 14:6; Heb 10:19, 20
9:9 *n* Heb 10:1
o Heb 5:1 *p* Heb 10:2
q S Heb 7:19
9:10 *q* Lev 11:2-23
r Nu 6:3; Col 2:16
s Lev 11:25,28,40
t Heb 7:16
9:11 *u* S Heb 2:17
v Heb 10:1 *w* ver 24; Heb 8:2 *x* S Jn 2:19
9:12 *y* ver 19;
Lev 16:6,15; Heb 10:4
z ver 24 *a* ver 26,28;
S Heb 7:27 *b* ver 14;
S Ro 3:25
9:13 *c* Heb 10:4
d Nu 19:9,17,18
9:14 *e* 1Pe 3:18
f S Eph 5:2 *g* Ps 51:2; 65:3; Jer 33:8; Zec 13:1; S Tit 2:14; Heb 10:2,22
h Heb 6:1 *i* S Mt 16:16
9:15 *j* S Gal 3:20
k S Lk 22:20
l S Ro 8:28; S 11:29

9:1 *first covenant.* The covenant made at Sinai (see 8:13 and note).

9:2 *A tabernacle was set up.* The tabernacle built under Moses. *lampstand.* Made of hammered gold and placed at the south side of the Holy Place (Ex 40:24), it had seven lamps that were kept burning every night (Ex 25:31–40; 27:21). *the table with its consecrated bread.* Made of acacia wood overlaid with gold (Ex 25:23–30), it stood on the north side of the Holy Place (Ex 40:22). On it were twelve loaves, replaced every Sabbath and arranged in two stacks of six (Lev 24:5–8).

9:4 *which had the golden altar of incense.* Although the altar of incense stood in the Holy Place, the author describes it as belonging to the Most Holy Place. His purpose was to show its close relationship to the inner sanctuary and the ark of the covenant (cf. Ex 30:1–6). On the Day of Atonement the high priest took incense from this altar, along with the blood of the sin offering, into the Most Holy Place (Lev 16:12–14). *ark of the covenant.* A chest made of acacia wood, overlaid inside and out with gold (Ex 25:10–16). *manna...staff...tablets.* See notes on Ex 16:33–34; see also Nu 17:8–10.

9:5 *cherubim of the Glory.* Two winged figures made of pure gold, of one piece with the atonement cover, or mercy seat, and standing at either end of it (Ex 25:17–22; Lev 16:2; Nu 7:89). *atonement cover.* Fitting exactly over the top of the ark of the covenant, it was a slab of pure gold on which the blood of the sin offering was sprinkled by the high priest on the Day of Atonement (Lev 16:14–15).

9:7 *only once a year.* On the Day of Atonement (*Yom Kippur*), the tenth day of the seventh month (Lev 16:29,34). For a description of its ritual, see Lev 16 and notes. *sins...committed in ignorance.* See 5:2 and note.

9:8 *Holy Spirit.* See 3:7 and note. *as long as the first tabernacle*

was still functioning. As long as the Mosaic system with its imperfect priesthood and sacrifice remained in effect (8:7–8,13).

9:9 *an illustration for the present time.* The Mosaic tabernacle and its temple replacement, though superseded, still provided instruction through their typical (symbolic) significance and were reminders that returning to the old order was useless, since it could not deal effectively with sin. *gifts and sacrifices.* See 5:1 and note.

9:10 *the new order.* The new covenant, with its new priesthood, new sanctuary and new sacrifice, all introduced by Christ (see Introduction: Theme).

9:11 *not a part of this creation.* It was not an earthly tabernacle but the heavenly sanctuary of God's presence (v. 24; 8:2).

9:12 *blood of goats and calves.* See note on Lev 17:11. *he entered...once for all.* Not repeatedly, year after year, as did the Levitical high priests. Christ's sacrifice was perfect, because it was completely effective and did not need to be repeated. After he had obtained eternal redemption, Christ ascended into the true heavenly sanctuary.

9:13 *blood of goats and bulls.* As on the Day of Atonement. *ashes of a heifer.* As prescribed in Nu 19 for those who became ceremonially unclean as a result of contact with a corpse. *outwardly clean.* Such sprinkling, since it was only external, could not cleanse a person from sin.

9:14 *through the eternal Spirit.* An unusual expression that is much debated but probably refers to the Holy Spirit, who empowered Jesus to fulfill his mission (see Mt 3:16 and note). *offered himself.* He was the one who offered the sacrifice, and he was the sacrifice itself. *unblemished.* See Lev 22:19–21. *cleanse our consciences.* Remove sin's defilement from the very core of our beings. *acts that lead to death.* See 6:1 and note.

9:15 *mediator.* See 8:6 and note. *new covenant.* See 7:22; 8:6,13. *the promised eternal inheritance.* Specified in Jer

9:15 *m* Heb 6:15;
10:36 *n* S Ac 20:32
o Heb 7:22
9:18 *p* Ex 24:6-8
9:19 *q* Heb 1:1
r ver 12 *s* Ex 24:6-8
9:20 *t* Ex 24:8;
S Mt 26:28
9:22 *u* Ex 29:21;
Lev 8:15 *v* Lev 17:11
9:23 *w* Heb 8:5
9:24 *x* Heb 8:2
y ver 12; S Heb 4:14
z S Ro 8:34
9:25 *a* Heb 10:19
b ver 7, 8
9:26 *c* Heb 4:3
d 1Jn 3:5 *e* ver 12, 28;
S Heb 7:27 *f* ver 12
9:27 *g* Ge 3:19
h 2Co 5:10
9:28 *i* ver 12, 26;
S Heb 7:27
j S Mt 16:27 *k* 1Pe 2:24
l Heb 5:9 *m* S 1Co 1:7
10:1 *n* Col 2:17;
Heb 8:5 *o* Heb 9:11
p Heb 9:23 *q* ver 4, 11;
S Heb 7:19
r S Heb 7:19
10:2 *s* Heb 9:9
10:3 *t* Lev 16:34;
Heb 9:7
10:4 *u* Heb 9:12, 13
v ver 1, 11
10:5 *w* Heb 1:6
x Heb 2:14; 1Pe 2:24

may receive the promised [m] eternal inheritance [n]—now that he has died as a ransom to set them free from the sins committed under the first covenant. [o]

[16] In the case of a will, [a] it is necessary to prove the death of the one who made it, [17] because a will is in force only when somebody has died; it never takes effect while the one who made it is living. [18] This is why even the first covenant was not put into effect without blood. [p] [19] When Moses had proclaimed [q] every command of the law to all the people, he took the blood of calves, [r] together with water, scarlet wool and branches of hyssop, and sprinkled the scroll and all the people. [s] [20] He said, "This is the blood of the covenant, which God has commanded you to keep." [b] [t] [21] In the same way, he sprinkled with the blood both the tabernacle and everything used in its ceremonies. [22] In fact, the law requires that nearly everything be cleansed with blood, [u] and without the shedding of blood there is no forgiveness. [v]

[23] It was necessary, then, for the copies [w] of the heavenly things to be purified with these sacrifices, but the heavenly things themselves with better sacrifices than these. [24] For Christ did not enter a sanctuary made with human hands that was only a copy of the true one; [x] he entered heaven itself, [y] now to appear for us in God's presence. [z] [25] Nor did he enter heaven to offer himself again and again, the way the high priest enters the Most Holy Place [a] every year with blood that is not his own. [b] [26] Otherwise Christ would have had to suffer many times since the creation of the world. [c] But he has appeared [d] once for all [e] at the culmination of the ages to do away with sin by the sacrifice of himself. [f] [27] Just as people are destined to die once, [g] and after that to face judgment, [h] [28] so Christ was sacrificed once [i] to take away the sins of many; and he will appear a second time, [j] not to bear sin, [k] but to bring salvation [l] to those who are waiting for him. [m]

CHRIST'S SACRIFICE ONCE FOR ALL

10 The law is only a shadow [n] of the good things [o] that are coming—not the realities themselves. [p] For this reason it can never, by the same sacrifices repeated endlessly year after year, make perfect [q] those who draw near to worship. [r] [2] Otherwise, would they not have stopped being offered? For the worshipers would have been cleansed once for all, and would no longer have felt guilty for their sins. [s] [3] But those sacrifices are an annual reminder of sins. [t] [4] It is impossible for the blood of bulls and goats [u] to take away sins. [v]

[5] Therefore, when Christ came into the world, [w] he said:

"Sacrifice and offering you did not desire,
　　but a body you prepared for me; [x]

---

a 16　Same Greek word as *covenant*; also in verse 17　　*b* 20　Exodus 24:8

31:31–34 (see note on 8:8–12). On the basis of Christ's atoning death, this inheritance has become real for those who are called by God (cf. Ro 8:28). *as a ransom.* See Mk 10:45 and note.

9:16 *will.* Translates the same Greek word as that for "covenant" (v. 15), but here and in v. 17 used in the sense of a last will and testament. (Verse 18 returns to the concept of covenant.) Beneficiaries have no claim on the benefits assigned to them in a will until the testator dies (v. 17). Since Christ's death has been duly attested, "the promised eternal inheritance" (v. 15) is available to his beneficiaries.

9:18–20 For the ceremony referred to here, see Ex 24:4–8.
9:18 *without blood.* Without death—the death of the calves from which Moses took blood to seal the old covenant.
9:21 See, e.g., Lev 8:10,19,30.
9:22 See note on Lev 17:11.
9:23 *copies of the heavenly things.* See 8:5. Whereas it was necessary for the earthly sanctuary to be purified with animal sacrifices, it was necessary for the heavenly sanctuary to be purified with the better sacrifice of Christ himself.
9:24 *now to appear for us in God's presence.* See 7:25; 1Jn 2:1 and notes. Christ also "has appeared" (v. 26), and "he will appear" (v. 28).
9:26 *culmination of the ages.* His coming has ushered in the great Messianic era, toward which all history has moved (see notes on 1:1–2).

9:28 *appear a second time.* See, e.g., Mt 24:3–21; 25:31– 46; Jn 14:3; 1Co 1:7; 15:23; 1Th 2:19; 4:13–18; 2Th 1:7; Tit

2:13; 2Pe 3:4; Rev 3:11; 19:11–16. *to bring salvation.* The consummation of the salvation purchased for us on the cross (see, e.g., Ro 8:29–30; Php 3:20–21; 1Jn 3:2). *waiting for him.* As the Israelites on the Day of Atonement waited for the high priest to reappear after ministering in the Most Holy Place, bringing assurance that their sins had been atoned for (cf. 2Ti 4:8; Tit 2:13).
10:1–10 An exposition of Ps 40:6–8 (see notes there).

10:1 *The law.* Together with the Levitical priesthood to which it was closely linked under the Mosaic system (see note on 7:11). *only a shadow.* The sacrifices prescribed by the law prefigured Christ's ultimate sacrifice. Thus they were repeated year after year, the very repetition bearing testimony that the perfect, sin-removing sacrifice had not yet been offered. *make perfect.* See v. 14 and note.
10:4 *impossible for the blood of bulls and goats to take away sins.* An animal cannot possibly be a completely adequate substitute for a human being, who is made in God's image.
10:5–6 The different terms used for Levitical sacrifices represent four of the five types of offerings prescribed by the Mosaic Law (Lev 1–7), namely, fellowship, grain, burnt and sin (see chart, p. 155).

10:5 *when Christ came into the world, he said.* The words of this psalm of David (40:6–8) express Christ's obedient submission to the Father in coming to earth. The Mosaic sacrifices are replaced by submissive obedience to the will of God (v. 7).

10:7 ʸ Ezr 6:2;
Jer 36:2 ᶻ Ps 40:6-8;
S Mt 26:39
10:8 ᵃ ver 5,6;
S Mk 12:33
10:9 ᵇ ver 7
10:10 ᶜ ver 14;
S Eph 5:26
ᵈ Heb 2:14; 1Pe 2:24
ᵉ S Heb 7:27
10:11 ᶠ Heb 5:1
ᵍ ver 1,4
10:12 ʰ Heb 5:1
ⁱ S Mk 16:19
10:13 ʲ Jos 10:24;
Heb 1:13
10:14 ᵏ ver 1
ˡ ver 10; S Eph 5:26
10:15 ᵐ S Heb 3:7
10:16 ⁿ Jer 31:33;
Heb 8:10
10:17 ᵒ Jer 31:34;
Heb 8:12
10:19 ᵖ S Eph 3:12
�q Lev 16:2; Eph 2:18;
Heb 9:8,12,25
10:20 ʳ Heb 9:8
ˢ Heb 6:19; 9:3
10:21 ᵗ S Heb 2:17
ᵘ S Heb 3:6
10:22 ᵛ ver 1;
S Heb 7:19
ʷ Eph 3:12
ˣ Eze 36:25;
Heb 9:14; 12:24;
1Pe 1:2 ʸ S Ac 22:16
10:23 ᶻ S Heb 3:6
ᵃ S Heb 3:1

[6] with burnt offerings and sin offerings
you were not pleased.
[7] Then I said, 'Here I am—it is written about me in the scroll ʸ—
I have come to do your will, my God.' " ᵃ ᶻ

[8] First he said, "Sacrifices and offerings, burnt offerings and sin offerings you did not desire, nor were you pleased with them" ᵃ—though they were offered in accordance with the law. [9] Then he said, "Here I am, I have come to do your will." ᵇ He sets aside the first to establish the second. [10] And by that will, we have been made holy ᶜ through the sacrifice of the body ᵈ of Jesus Christ once for all. ᵉ

[11] Day after day every priest stands and performs his religious duties; again and again he offers the same sacrifices, ᶠ which can never take away sins. ᵍ [12] But when this priest had offered for all time one sacrifice for sins, ʰ he sat down at the right hand of God, ⁱ [13] and since that time he waits for his enemies to be made his footstool. ʲ [14] For by one sacrifice he has made perfect ᵏ forever those who are being made holy. ˡ

[15] The Holy Spirit also testifies ᵐ to us about this. First he says:

[16] "This is the covenant I will make with them
after that time, says the Lord.
I will put my laws in their hearts,
and I will write them on their minds." ᵇ ⁿ

[17] Then he adds:

"Their sins and lawless acts
I will remember no more." ᶜ ᵒ

[18] And where these have been forgiven, sacrifice for sin is no longer necessary.

A CALL TO PERSEVERE IN FAITH

[19] Therefore, brothers and sisters, since we have confidence ᵖ to enter the Most Holy Place �q by the blood of Jesus, [20] by a new and living way ʳ opened for us through the curtain, ˢ that is, his body, [21] and since we have a great priest ᵗ over the house of God, ᵘ [22] let us draw near to God ᵛ with a sincere heart in full assurance of faith, ʷ having our hearts sprinkled to cleanse us from a guilty conscience ˣ and having our bodies washed with pure water. ʸ [23] Let us hold unswervingly to the hope ᶻ we profess, ᵃ for he who promised is faith-

ᵃ 7 Psalm 40:6-8 (see Septuagint)   ᵇ 16 Jer. 31:33   ᶜ 17 Jer. 31:34

10:6 *you were not pleased.* See 1Sa 15:22; Ps 40:6 and notes.
10:7 *to do your will.* The will of the Father was the Son's consuming concern (see Lk 22:42; Jn 4:34 and note).
10:9 *He sets aside the first to establish the second.* His perfect sacrifice, offered in complete submission to God's will, supersedes and therefore replaces all previous sacrifices as the means by which sinners are made holy.
10:10,14 *made holy.* Cleansed from all sin (forgiven and purified) and consecrated to God's service (see note on 1Co 1:2).
10:10 *once for all.* Contrast v. 1 (see note there; see also v. 12 and 7:27 and note).
10:11–12 A contrast between standing and sitting. The Levitical priest always stood, because his work was never finished (see 7:27 and note).
10:12 *for all time.* See 7:27 and note. *sat down at the right hand of God.* See 1:13 and note.
10:13 Having offered, as priest, the all-sufficient sacrifice, Jesus now sits enthroned as king, looking forward to the ultimate triumph over all that opposes his rule (see 1:3 and note; cf. Rev 5:6–14 and note on 5:6; cf. also Rev 7:10,17; 11:15; 19:11–21; 20:4).
10:14 *made perfect.* The one "made perfect" (5:9; see 7:28 and note; see also 2:10) has "made" sinners "perfect" in regard to God's will for their holiness.
10:15 *Holy Spirit.* See 3:7 and note.
10:16–18 The two quotations included here are from Jer 31:31–34 (already cited in 8:8–12). The new covenant guarantees that sins will be completely forgiven (v. 17), with the result that no additional sacrifice for sins is needed (v. 18).

10:19 *confidence to enter the Most Holy Place.* See vv. 13–14 and notes.
10:20 *the curtain, that is, his body.* Having sacrificed himself in his body on the cross, Jesus, our high priest, entered the Most Holy Place (see 6:19 and note; cf. 9:11 and note), and he made sinners "perfect" in holiness (see v. 14 and note) so that they too may enter through the curtain—his sacrificed and resurrected body being for us the "new and living way" (cf. Mt 27:51; Mk 15:38 and notes).
10:22–25 Five exhortations spring from Jesus' provision for our reconciliation to his Father: 1."Let us draw near to God." 2."Let us hold unswervingly to… hope." 3."Let us consider how we may spur one another on." 4."Not giving up meeting together." 5."Encouraging one another." For the triad of faith, hope and love in vv. 22–24, see note on 1Th 1:3.
10:22 Four conditions are given for drawing "near to God": 1. *a sincere heart.* Undivided allegiance in the inner being. 2. *full assurance of faith.* Faith that knows no hesitation in trusting in and following Christ. 3. *hearts sprinkled … from a guilty conscience.* Total freedom from a sense of guilt, a freedom based on the once-for-all sacrifice of Christ. 4. *bodies washed with pure water.* Very likely both "hearts sprinkled" and "bodies washed" allude to Christian baptism (cf. Mt 28:19) and the cleansing from sin through the sacrificial death of Christ that it signifies (see Ro 6:3–11 and notes). For OT background, see Eze 36:25 and note; see also Lev 14:9; 15:13; 16:4,24,26; Nu 19:19; cf. Zec 13:1.
10:23 *hope we profess.* See 3:6; 6:18–19 and notes. *he who promised is faithful.* Cf. 2Ti 2:13.

10:23 *b* S 1Co 1:9
10:24 *c* S Tit 2:14
10:25 *d* Ac 2:42
e Heb 3:13
f S 1Co 3:13
10:26 *g* Ex 21:14;
Nu 15:30; Heb 5:2;
6:4-8; 2Pe 2:20
h S 1Ti 2:4
10:27 *i* Isa 26:11;
2Th 1:7; Heb 9:27;
12:29
10:28 *j* Dt 17:6,7;
S Mt 18:16; Heb 2:2
10:29 *k* S Mt 4:3
l Heb 6:6
m S Mt 26:28
n 1Co 6:11; Rev 1:5
o Eph 4:30; Heb 6:4
p Heb 2:3; 12:25
10:30 *q* Dt 32:35;
Ro 12:19 *r* Dt 32:36;
Ps 135:14
10:31 *s* S 2Co 5:11
t Isa 19:16
u S Mt 16:16
10:32 *v* Heb 6:4
w Php 1:29,30
10:33 *x* 1Co 4:9
y Php 4:14; 1Th 2:14
10:34 *z* Heb 13:3
a Heb 11:16; 1Pe 1:4,5
10:35 *b* S Eph 3:12
10:36 *c* Ro 5:3;
Heb 12:1; Jas 1:3,4,12;
5:11; 2Pe 1:6
d Heb 6:15; 9:15
10:37 *e* Mt 11:3
f Rev 22:20
10:38 *g* Ro 1:17;
Gal 3:11 *h* Hab 2:3,4
11:1 *i* S Heb 3:6
j S 2Co 4:18
11:2 *k* ver 4,39
11:3 *l* Ge 1:1; Jn 1:3;
Heb 1:2; 2Pe 3:5
11:4 *m* ver 2,39
n Ge 4:4; 1Jn 3:12
o Heb 12:24

ful. *b* 24And let us consider how we may spur one another on toward love and good deeds, *c* 25not giving up meeting together, *d* as some are in the habit of doing, but encouraging one another *e*—and all the more as you see the Day approaching. *f*

26If we deliberately keep on sinning *g* after we have received the knowledge of the truth, *h* no sacrifice for sins is left, 27but only a fearful expectation of judgment and of raging fire *i* that will consume the enemies of God. 28Anyone who rejected the law of Moses died without mercy on the testimony of two or three witnesses. *j* 29How much more severely do you think those deserve to be punished who have trampled the Son of God *k* underfoot, *l* who have treated as an unholy thing the blood of the covenant *m* that sanctified them, *n* and who have insulted the Spirit *o* of grace? *p* 30For we know him who said, "It is mine to avenge; I will repay," *a q* and again, "The Lord will judge his people." *b r* 31It is a dreadful thing *s* to fall into the hands *t* of the living God. *u*

32Remember those earlier days after you had received the light, *v* when you endured in a great conflict full of suffering. *w* 33Sometimes you were publicly exposed to insult and persecution; *x* at other times you stood side by side with those who were so treated. *y* 34You suffered along with those in prison *z* and joyfully accepted the confiscation of your property, because you knew that you yourselves had better and lasting possessions. *a* 35So do not throw away your confidence; *b* it will be richly rewarded.

36You need to persevere *c* so that when you have done the will of God, you will receive what he has promised. *d* 37For,

"In just a little while,
   he who is coming *e* will come
   and will not delay." *c f*

38And,

"But my righteous one *d* will live by faith. *g*
And I take no pleasure
   in the one who shrinks back." *e h*

39But we are not of those who shrink back and are destroyed, but of those who believe and are saved.

FAITH IN ACTION

11

Now faith is being sure of what we hope for *i* and certain of what we do not see. *j* 2This is what the ancients were commended for. *k* 3By faith we understand that the universe was formed at God's command, *l* so that what is seen was not made out of what was visible.

4By faith Abel brought God a better offering than Cain did. By faith he was commended *m* as righteous, when God spoke well of his offerings. *n* And by faith Abel still speaks, even though he is dead. *o*

a 30 Deut. 32:35   *b 30* Deut. 32:36; Psalm 135:14   *c 37* Isaiah 26:20; Hab. 2:3   *d 38* One early manuscript *But the righteous*   *e 38* Hab. 2:4 (see Septuagint)

10:25 *not giving up meeting together.* The Greek word translated "giving up" speaks of desertion and abandonment (see Mt 27:46; 2Co 4:9; 2Ti 4:10,16). *the Day.* Of the Lord's return (see 1Th 5:2,4; 2Th 1:10; 2:2; 2Pe 3:10).

10:26—31 The fourth warning (see note on 2:1–4). This warning is especially to persons ("some," v. 25) deserting the Christian assembly. See 6:4–8, where the same spiritual condition is discussed (see also notes there).

10:26 *deliberately keep on sinning.* Committing the sin of apostasy (see v. 29; see also note on 5:2). The OT background is Nu 15:27–31. *no sacrifice for sins is left.* To reject Christ's sacrifice for sins is to reject the only sacrifice; there is no other.

10:27 *judgment and ... raging fire.* See 12:29; 2Th 1:6–9 and notes. For fire as the instrument of divine judgment, see La 1:13 and note.

10:28 See Dt 17:6 and note.

10:29 *blood of the covenant.* See 9:20 and note on 9:18; 13:20; see also Mt 26:28; Mk 14:24 and note.

10:31 See 12:29.

10:32—12:3 An exposition of Hab 2:3–4.

10:32 *those earlier days.* Presumably following their first enthusiastic response to the gospel, when they had unflinchingly suffered loss and persecution and were deeply concerned for each other.

10:34 *better and lasting possessions.* Such as salvation in Christ and future reward (see 11:10,16,35; 13:14 and notes).

10:38 *my righteous one will live by faith.* See note on Hab 2:4.

10:39 *shrink back and are destroyed.* The opposite of "believe and are saved." The author is confident that those to whom he is writing are, for the most part, among the saved (see 6:9 and note).

11:1—12:3 Encouragements to persevere in faith.

11:2 *the ancients.* Heroes of faith in the pre-Christian era, such as those listed in this chapter. *were commended for.* Repeated in v. 39, thus framing the chapter with a key thematic emphasis.

11:4 See Ge 4:2–5. *commended as righteous.* The chief reason for the acceptance of Abel's sacrifice was that he offered it "by faith." It is implied that Cain's sacrifice was rejected because he offered it without faith, as a mere formality (see note on Ge 4:3–4; see also 1Jn 3:12).

⁵By faith Enoch was taken from this life, so that he did not experience death: "He could not be found, because God had taken him away."ᵃ ᵖ For before he was taken, he was commended as one who pleased God. ⁶And without faith it is impossible to please God, because anyone who comes to him �q must believe that he exists and that he rewards those who earnestly seek him.

⁷By faith Noah, when warned about things not yet seen,ʳ in holy fear built an arkˢ to save his family.ᵗ By his faith he condemned the world and became heir of the righteousness that is in keeping with faith.ᵘ

⁸By faith Abraham, when called to go to a place he would later receive as his inheritance,ᵛ obeyed and went,ʷ even though he did not know where he was going. ⁹By faith he made his home in the promised landˣ like a stranger in a foreign country; he lived in tents,ʸ as did Isaac and Jacob, who were heirs with him of the same promise.ᶻ ¹⁰For he was looking forward to the cityᵃ with foundations,ᵇ whose architect and builder is God.ᶜ ¹¹And by faith even Sarah, who was past childbearing age,ᵈ was enabled to bear children ᵉ because sheᵇ considered him faithfulᶠ who had made the promise. ¹²And so from this one man, and he as good as dead,ᵍ came descendants as numerous as the stars in the sky and as countless as the sand on the seashore.ʰ

¹³All these people were still living by faith when they died. They did not receive the things promised;ⁱ they only saw them and welcomed them from a distance,ʲ admitting that they were foreigners and strangers on earth.ᵏ ¹⁴People who say such things show that they are looking for a country of their own. ¹⁵If they had been thinking of the country they had left, they would have had opportunity to return.ˡ ¹⁶Instead, they were longing for a better country—a heavenly one.ᵐ Therefore God is not ashamed ⁿ to be called their God,ᵒ for he has prepared a cityᵖ for them.

¹⁷By faith Abraham, when God tested him, offered Isaac as a sacrifice.ᑫ He who had embraced the promises was about to sacrifice his one and only son, ¹⁸even though God had said to him, "It is through Isaac that your offspring will be reckoned."ᶜ ʳ ¹⁹Abraham reasoned that God could even raise the dead,ˢ and so in a manner of speaking he did receive Isaac back from death.

²⁰By faith Isaac blessed Jacob and Esau in regard to their future.ᵗ

²¹By faith Jacob, when he was dying, blessed each of Joseph's sons,ᵘ and worshiped as he leaned on the top of his staff.

²²By faith Joseph, when his end was near, spoke about the exodus of the Israelites from Egypt and gave instructions concerning the burial of his bones.ᵛ

²³By faith Moses' parents hid him for three months after he was born,ʷ because they saw he was no ordinary child, and they were not afraid of the king's edict.ˣ

ᵃ 5 Gen. 5:24   ᵇ 11 Or By faith Abraham, even though he was too old to have children—and Sarah herself was not able to conceive—was enabled to become a father because he   ᶜ 18 Gen. 21:12

11:5 pGe 5:21-24
11:6 qHeb 7:19
11:7 rS ver 1
ˢGe 6:13-22
t1Pe 3:20 uGe 6:9;
Eze 14:14,20;
S Ro 9:30
11:8 vGe 12:7
wGe 12:1-4; Ac 7:2-4
11:9 xAc 7:5
yGe 12:8; 18:1,9
zHeb 6:17
11:10 aHeb 12:22;
13:14 bRev 21:2,14
cver 16
11:11 dGe 17:17-19;
18:11-14 eGe 21:2
fS 1Co 1:9
11:12 gRo 4:19
hGe 22:17
11:13 iver 39
jS Mt 13:17 kGe 23:4;
Lev 25:23; Php 3:20;
1Pe 1:17; 2:11
11:15 lGe 24:6-8
11:16 m2Ti 4:18
nMk 8:38 oGe 26:24;
28:13; Ex 3:6,15
pver 10; Heb 13:14
11:17 qGe 22:1-10;
Jas 2:21
11:18 rGe 21:12;
Ro 9:7
11:19 sRo 4:21;
S Jn 5:21
11:20 tGe 27:27-29,39,40
11:21 uGe 48:1,8-22
11:22 vGe 50:24,
25; Ex 13:19;
Jos 24:32
11:23 wEx 2:2
xEx 1:16,22

11:5 *Enoch.* See Ge 5:18–24. *taken him away.* To God's presence (see note on Ge 5:24; cf. Ps 49:15; 73:24).

11:6 *without faith it is impossible to please God.* That Enoch pleased God is proof of his faith. *believe that he exists.* Faith must have an object, and the proper object of genuine faith is God. *who earnestly seek him.* Cf. Jer 29:13.

11:7 *Noah.* See Ge 5:28—9:29. *By his faith he condemned.* When the flood came, God's word was proved to be true, Noah's faith was vindicated, and the world's unbelief was judged. *righteousness that is in keeping with faith.* Noah expressed complete trust in God and his word, even when it related to "things not yet seen" (v. 1; cf. vv. 26–27; Jn 20:29 and note), namely, the coming flood. Thus Noah also fitted the description of God's righteous ones who live by faith (10:38).

11:8 *Abraham.* Presented in the NT as the outstanding example of those who live "by faith" and as the "father of all who believe" (Ro 4:11–12,16; Gal 3:7,9,29). *called.* See Ge 12:1–3. His faith expressed itself in obedience (see note on Ge 12:4). *a place he would later receive.* Canaan.

11:10 *city with foundations.* Speaks of permanence, in contrast to the tents in which the patriarch lived (v. 9). This city is "the heavenly Jerusalem" (12:22), "the city that is to come" (13:14) and "the new Jerusalem" (Rev 21:2–4,9–27). *builder.* See v. 16; cf. Eph 2:19–22; 1Pe 2:4–5 and notes; cf. also Ps 147:2 and note on Isa 62:5.

11:11 *Sarah...was past childbearing age.* See Ge 11:30;

18:11–12 and notes.

11:12 *as good as dead.* Because he was 100 years old (see Ge 21:5; Ro 4:19). *stars in the sky...sand on the seashore.* See Ge 13:16 and note; 15:5; 22:17; 26:4; 1Ki 4:20 and note.

11:13 *saw them and welcomed them from a distance.* By faith they saw—dimly—the realities to which the promises pointed and were sure that what they hoped for would ultimately be theirs (see v. 1). *foreigners and strangers on earth.* As were the patriarchs in Canaan (see Ge 17:8; 23:4; 28:4). Their true home was the future city of God (see vv. 10,16).

11:14 *country of their own.* A country in which they would no longer be "foreigners and strangers" (v. 13). "Country" and "city" were virtually interchangeable since a country was viewed as an extension of its royal city.

11:16 *prepared a city for them.* See v. 10 and note.

11:17 See Ge 22. *his one and only son.* See Ge 22:2,12,16 and notes.

11:19 Cf. Ge 22:13 and note.

11:20 See Ge 27:27–40.

11:21 See 48:9–20. *worshiped...staff.* See Ge 47:31 and note.

11:22 See Ge 50:24–25. Jacob (v. 21) and Joseph are additional examples of those whose faith is no less strong at death than in life (v. 13).

11:23 See Ex 2:2–3; Ac 7:20–44. *Moses' parents.* See Ge 6:20; Nu 26:58–59. *no ordinary child.* See note on Ex 2:2. *were not afraid.* At least to the extent that they were ready to defy the king's edict. *king's edict.* To kill all Israelite males at birth (Ex 1:16,22).

11:24 ʸ Ex 2:10,11
11:25 ᶻ ver 37
11:26 ᵃ Heb 13:13
  ᵇ Lk 14:33
  ᶜ Heb 10:35
11:27 ᵈ Ex 12:50,51
11:28 ᵉ 1Co 10:10
  ᶠ Ex 12:21-23
11:29 ᵍ Ex 14:21-31
11:30 ʰ Jos 6:12-20
11:31 ⁱ Jos; 2:1,9-
14; 6:22-25; Jas 2:25
11:32 ʲ Jdg 6-8
  ᵏ Jdg 4-5 ˡ Jdg 13-16
  ᵐ Jdg 11-12 ⁿ 1Sa 16:1,
13 ᵒ 1Sa 1:20
11:33 ᵖ 2Sa 8:1-3
  ᑫ Da 6:22
11:34 ʳ Da 3:19-27
  ˢ Ex 18:4 ᵗ 2Ki 20:7
  ᵘ Jdg 15:8
11:35 ᵛ 1Ki 17:22,
23; 2Ki 4:36,37
11:36 ʷ Jer 20:2;
37:15 ˣ Ge 39:20
11:37 ʸ 2Ch 24:21
  ᶻ 1Ki 19:10; Jer 26:23
  ᵃ 2Ki 1:8
11:38 ᵇ 1Ki 18:4;
19:9
11:39 ᶜ ver 2,4

²⁴By faith Moses, when he had grown up, refused to be known as the son of Pharaoh's daughter. ʸ ²⁵He chose to be mistreated ᶻ along with the people of God rather than to enjoy the fleeting pleasures of sin. ²⁶He regarded disgrace ᵃ for the sake of Christ ᵇ as of greater value than the treasures of Egypt, because he was looking ahead to his reward. ᶜ ²⁷By faith he left Egypt, ᵈ not fearing the king's anger; he persevered because he saw him who is invisible. ²⁸By faith he kept the Passover and the application of blood, so that the destroyer ᵉ of the firstborn would not touch the firstborn of Israel. ᶠ

²⁹By faith the people passed through the Red Sea as on dry land; but when the Egyptians tried to do so, they were drowned. ᵍ

³⁰By faith the walls of Jericho fell, after the army had marched around them for seven days. ʰ

³¹By faith the prostitute Rahab, because she welcomed the spies, was not killed with those who were disobedient. ᵃ ⁱ

³²And what more shall I say? I do not have time to tell about Gideon, ʲ Barak, ᵏ Samson ˡ and Jephthah, ᵐ about David ⁿ and Samuel ᵒ and the prophets, ³³who through faith conquered kingdoms, ᵖ administered justice, and gained what was promised; who shut the mouths of lions, ᑫ ³⁴quenched the fury of the flames, ʳ and escaped the edge of the sword; ˢ whose weakness was turned to strength; ᵗ and who became powerful in battle and routed foreign armies. ᵘ ³⁵Women received back their dead, raised to life again. ᵛ There were others who were tortured, refusing to be released so that they might gain an even better resurrection. ³⁶Some faced jeers and flogging, ʷ and even chains and imprisonment. ˣ ³⁷They were put to death by stoning; ᵇ ʸ they were sawed in two; they were killed by the sword. ᶻ They went about in sheepskins and goatskins, ᵃ destitute, persecuted and mistreated— ³⁸the world was not worthy of them. They wandered in deserts and mountains, and in caves ᵇ and holes in the ground.

³⁹These were all commended ᶜ for their faith, yet none of them received what had been

---

ᵃ 31 Or *unbelieving*   ᵇ 37 Some early manuscripts *stoning; they were put to the test;*

11:24 *son of Pharaoh's daughter.* See Ex 2:10.

11:25 *pleasures of sin.* The luxury and prestige of Egypt's royal palace.

B **11:26** *for the sake of Christ.* Although Moses' understanding of the details of Israel's promised future was extremely limited, he chose to be associated with the people through whom that future was to be realized. The author of Hebrews here concretizes that future in the person of the Messiah he is proclaiming as the one through whom God has guaranteed the promised future. *treasures of Egypt.* The priceless treasures of King Tutankhamun's tomb alone included several thousand pounds of pure gold.

C **11:27** *By faith he left Egypt.* Probably referring to his flight to Midian when he was 40 years old (see Ex 2:11–15 and note; Ac 7:23–29). *not fearing the king's anger.* Exodus indicates that Moses was afraid (Ex 2:14) but does not expressly say of whom. And it tells us that he fled from the pharaoh when the pharaoh tried to kill him (Ex 2:15) but does not expressly say that he fled out of fear. The author of Hebrews capitalizes on these features of the account to highlight the fact that, in his fleeing from the pharaoh, Moses was sustained by his trust in God that the liberation of Israel would come and that he would have some part in it. *he persevered.* For 40 years in Midian (Ac 7:30). *saw him who is invisible.* See vv. 1,6; see also Ro 1:20; Col 1:15 and note; 1Ti 1:17.

11:28 See Ex 12:1–30.

C **11:29** See Ex 14–15. The third and final 40-year period of Moses' life was spent leading the Israelites through the wilderness. At the age of 120 years he died in Moab (Dt 34:1–7).

11:30–31 See Jos 2; 6.

11:30 *Jericho.* The first obstacle to Israel's conquest of the promised land under Joshua's leadership was captured by faith without a battle.

11:31 *By faith.* See Jos 6:9–11. *prostitute.* A designation of this Canaanite's way of life within Canaanite society. *welcomed the spies.* See Jas 2:25.

A **11:32–38** There were many more heroes of faith before the coming of Christ, and much more could be written

about them. Only a small sampling is given, representing all types of men and women of faith. The great quality they had in common was that of overcoming "through faith" (v. 33).

11:32 *to tell.* Translates the masculine form of a Greek verb, indicating that the author of Hebrews was a man (see Introduction: Author). *Gideon, Barak, Samson and Jephthah.* See Jdg 4–8; 11–16; 1Sa 12:11 and TNIV text note. *Samuel and the prophets.* For Samuel being counted as the first among the prophets, see Ac 3:24; 13:20; cf. Ps 99:6; Jer 15:1 and notes.

11:33 *conquered kingdoms.* See, e.g., David's conquests (2Sa 5:6–25; 8:1–14; 10:1–19; 12:26–31). *administered justice.* See, e.g., Samuel (1Sa 12:3–5); David (2Sa 8:15); Solomon (1Ki 3:9, 12,16–28). *gained what was promised.* May refer to Israel's circumstances of rest in the promised land to which Solomon refers in 1Ki 5:4 (see note there); see also Jos 23:14; 24:8–13; 2Ch 20:30 (see note there). *shut the mouths of lions.* See, e.g., Daniel in the lions' den (Da 6).

11:34 *quenched the fury of the flames.* See, e.g., Daniel's friends, Shadrach, Meshach and Abednego, in the fiery furnace (Da 3). *escaped the . . . sword.* See, e.g., David (1Sa 17:45–49); Elijah (2Ki 1); Elisha (2Ki 6:31); Jeremiah (Jer 26:7–24). *weakness was turned to strength.* See, e.g., Samson (Jdg 16:21–30); Hannah (1Sa 1); Jeremiah (Jer 1:6–10).

11:35 *Women received back their dead.* Cf. the widow of Zarephath (1Ki 17:17–24) and the Shunammite woman (2Ki 4:8–36). *were tortured, refusing to be released so that they might gain an even better resurrection.* Strongly reminiscent of the heroic Maccabean Jewish patriots of the second century B.C. (see 2 Maccabees 7).

11:36 *jeers and flogging.* See, e.g., Jeremiah (Jer 20:2,7–8). *imprisonment.* See, e.g., Jeremiah (Jer 37:15–16).

11:37 *They were put to death by stoning.* See, e.g., Zechariah, the son of Jehoiada the priest, who was stoned to death for declaring the truth (2Ch 24:21). *sawed in two.* Perhaps refers to Isaiah, who, according to tradition, met this kind of death under wicked King Manasseh (see Introduction to Isaiah: Author).

11:39 *all commended for their faith.* By the Holy Spirit in the Scriptural accounts (see 3:7 and note).

promised. *d* ⁴⁰God had planned something better for us so that only together with us *e* would they be made perfect. *f*

12 Therefore, since we are surrounded by such a great cloud of witnesses, let us throw off everything that hinders and the sin that so easily entangles. And let us run *g* with perseverance *h* the race marked out for us, ²fixing our eyes on Jesus, *i* the pioneer*j* and perfecter of faith. For the joy set before him he endured the cross, *k* scorning its shame, *l* and sat down at the right hand of the throne of God. *m* ³Consider him who endured such opposition from sinners, so that you will not grow weary *n* and lose heart.

GOD DISCIPLINES HIS CHILDREN

⁴In your struggle against sin, you have not yet resisted to the point of shedding your blood. *o* ⁵And have you completely forgotten this word of encouragement that addresses you as children? It says,

"My son, do not make light of the Lord's discipline,
　and do not lose heart*p* when he rebukes you,
　⁶because the Lord disciplines those he loves, *q*
　and he chastens everyone he accepts as his child." *a* *r*

⁷Endure hardship as discipline; God is treating you as his children. *s* For what children are not disciplined by their father? ⁸If you are not disciplined—and everyone undergoes discipline*t*—then you are not legitimate children at all. ⁹Moreover, we all had parents who disciplined us and we respected them for it. How much more should we submit to the Father of spirits *u* and live! *v* ¹⁰Our parents disciplined us for a little while as they thought best; but God disciplines us for our good, that we may share in his holiness. *w* ¹¹No discipline seems pleasant at the time, but painful. Later on, however, it produces a harvest of righteousness and peace*x* for those who have been trained by it.

¹²Therefore, strengthen your feeble arms and weak knees. *y* ¹³"Make level paths for your feet," *b* *z* so that the lame may not be disabled, but rather healed. *a*

WARNING AND ENCOURAGEMENT

¹⁴Make every effort to live in peace with everyone *b* and to be holy; *c* without holiness no one will see the Lord. *d* ¹⁵See to it that no one falls short of the grace of God *e* and that

---

a 5,6 Prov. 3:11,12 (see Septuagint)　　b 13 Prov. 4:26

11:39 *d* ver 13; Heb 10:36
11:40 *e* Rev 6:11 *f* S Heb 2:10
12:1 *g* S 1Co 9:24 *h* S Heb 10:36
12:2 *i* Ps 25:15 *j* Heb 2:10 *k* Php 2:8, 9; Heb 2:9 *l* Heb 13:13 *m* S Mk 16:19
12:3 *n* Gal 6:9; Rev 2:3
12:4 *o* Heb 10:32-34; 13:13
12:5 *p* ver 3
12:6 *q* Ps 94:12; 119:75; Rev 3:19 *r* Pr 3:11,12
12:7 *s* Dt 8:5; 2Sa 7:14; Pr 13:24
12:8 *t* 1Pe 5:9
12:9 *u* Nu 16:22; 27:16; Rev 22:6 *v* Isa 38:16
12:10 *w* S 2Pe 1:4
12:11 *x* Isa 32:17; Jas 3:17,18
12:12 *y* Isa 35:3
12:13 *z* Pr 4:26
a Gal 6:1
12:14 *b* S Ro 14:19 *c* Ro 6:22 *d* S Mt 5:8
12:15 *e* Gal 5:4; Heb 3:12; 4:1

11:40 *God had planned something better.* The fulfillment for them, as for us, is in Christ, who is "the resurrection and the life" (Jn 11:25–26). *only together with us would they be made perfect.* All persons of faith who had gone before focused their faith on God and his promises. The fulfillment of God's promises to them has now come in Jesus Christ, and their redemption too is now complete in him.

▲ 12:1 *surrounded by such a great cloud of witnesses.* The imagery suggests an athletic contest in a great amphitheater. The witnesses are the heroes of the past who have just been mentioned (ch. 11). They are not spectators but inspiring examples. The Greek word translated "witnesses" is the origin of the English word "martyr" and means "testifiers, witnesses." They bear testimony to the power of faith and to God's faithfulness. *run with perseverance.* See Ac 20:24; 1Co 9:24–26; Gal 2:2; 5:7; Php 2:16; 2Ti 4:7. The Christian life is pictured as a long-distance race rather than a short sprint.

▲ 12:2 *pioneer and perfecter of our faith.* That is, the beginner (cf. note on 2:10) and completer of faith—the One who went ahead of all believers in their faith and led on to its definitive goal, hence the perfect embodiment of faith and the supreme model for faith. *joy set before him.* His glorification at the Father's "right hand" (see note on 1:2–3, No. 7; cf. Isa 53:10–12 and notes). *endured the cross.* See Php 2:8 and note. *scorning its shame.* As with Christ, the humiliation of our present suffering for the gospel's sake is far outweighed by the prospect of future glory (see Mt 5:10–12; Ro 8:18; 2Co 4:17; 1Pe 4:13; 5:1,10).

▲ 12:3 *Consider him.* He suffered infinitely more than any of his disciples is asked to suffer—a great encourage-

ment to us when we are weary and tempted to become discouraged. *not grow weary.* See Gal 6:9; Rev 2:3; cf. Isa 40:28–31.

12:4–13 Encouragement to persevere in the face of hardship: an exposition of Pr 3:11–12.

▲ 12:5 *the Lord's discipline.* Suffering and persecution should be seen as corrective and instructive training for our spiritual development as God's children.

▲ 12:6 *chastens.* The Greek for this verb means "to whip." God chastens us in order to correct our faults.

▲ 12:7 *treating you as his children.* God's discipline is evidence that we are his children. Far from being a reason for despair, discipline is a basis for encouragement and perseverance (v. 10).

▲ 12:11 *produces a harvest of righteousness.* When received submissively (see v. 9), discipline is wholesome and beneficial.

12:12 See Isa 35:3.

12:13 *Make level paths.* A call for upright conduct that will help, rather than hinder, the spiritual and moral welfare of others, especially the "lame" who waver in the Christian faith.

12:14–17 Exhortation to holy living (see 4:1; 6:4–8; Gal 5:4 and note).

12:14 *without holiness no one will see the Lord.* Cf. 1Pe 1:15–16 and note on 1:16; see also 1Co 1:2 and note; cf. 1Jn 3:2–3.

12:15 *falls short of the grace of God.* Or "fails to lay hold of" God's grace (see 6:4–8 and notes). *bitter root.* Pride, animosity, rivalry or anything else harmful to others.

12:15 *f* Dt 29:18
12:16 *g* S 1Co 6:18
h Ge 25:29-34
12:17 *i* Ge 27:30-40
12:18 *j* Ex 19:12-22;
20:18; Dt 4:11
12:19 *k* Ex 20:18
l Dt 4:12 *m* Ex 20:19;
Dt 5:5,25; 18:16
12:20 *n* Ex 19:12,13
12:21 *o* Dt 9:19
12:22 *p* Isa 24:23;
60:14; Rev 14:1
q Heb 11:10; 13:14
r S Mt 16:16
s S Gal 4:26
12:23 *t* Ex 4:22
u S Rev 20:12
v Ge 18:25; Ps 94:2
w Php 3:12
12:24 *x* S Gal 3:20
y Heb 9:19; 10:22;
1Pe 1:2 *z* Ge 4:10;
Heb 11:4
12:25 *a* Heb 3:12
b S Heb 1:1 *c* Heb 8:5;
11:7 *d* Dt 18:19;
Heb 2:2,3; 10:29
12:26 *e* Ex 19:18
f Hag 2:6
12:27 *g* Isa 34:4;
54:10; 1Co 7:31;
Heb 1:11,12; 2Pe 3:10;
1Jn 2:17
12:28 *h* Ps 15:5;
Da 2:44 *i* Mal 2:5;
4:2; Heb 13:15
12:29 *j* Ex 24:17;
Dt 4:24; 9:3; Ps 97:3;
Isa 33:14; S 2Th 1:7

no bitter root *f* grows up to cause trouble and defile many. [16]See that no one is sexually immoral, *g* or is godless like Esau, who for a single meal sold his inheritance rights as the oldest son. *h* [17]Afterward, as you know, when he wanted to inherit this blessing, he was rejected. Even though he sought the blessing with tears, *i* he could not change what he had done.

THE MOUNTAIN OF FEAR AND THE MOUNTAIN OF JOY

[18]You have not come to a mountain that can be touched and that is burning with fire; to darkness, gloom and storm; *j* [19]to a trumpet blast *k* or to such a voice speaking words *l* that those who heard it begged that no further word be spoken to them, *m* [20]because they could not bear what was commanded: "If even an animal touches the mountain, it must be stoned to death." *a* *n* [21]The sight was so terrifying that Moses said, "I am trembling with fear." *b* *o*

[22]But you have come to Mount Zion, *p* to the city *q* of the living God, *r* the heavenly Jerusalem. *s* You have come to thousands upon thousands of angels in joyful assembly, [23]to the church of the firstborn, *t* whose names are written in heaven. *u* You have come to God, the Judge of all, *v* to the spirits of the righteous made perfect, *w* [24]to Jesus the mediator *x* of a new covenant, and to the sprinkled blood *y* that speaks a better word than the blood of Abel. *z*

[25]See to it that you do not refuse *a* him who speaks. *b* If they did not escape when they refused him who warned *c* them on earth, how much less will we, if we turn away from him who warns us from heaven? *d* [26]At that time his voice shook the earth, *e* but now he has promised, "Once more I will shake not only the earth but also the heavens." *c* *f* [27]The words "once more" indicate the removing of what can be shaken *g*—that is, created things—so that what cannot be shaken may remain.

[28]Therefore, since we are receiving a kingdom that cannot be shaken, *h* let us be thankful, and so worship God acceptably with reverence and awe, *i* [29]for our "God is a consuming fire." *d* *j*

a 20 Exodus 19:12,13   *b 21* See Deut. 9:19.   *c 26* Haggai 2:6   *d 29* Deut. 4:24

C **12:16** *godless like Esau.* See Ge 25:29-34. He had no appreciation for true values (cf. Php 3:19). He "despised his birthright" (Ge 25:34) by valuing food for his stomach more highly than his birthright.

A **12:17** *blessing.* Of the firstborn. The readers may have contemplated compromising their faith in order to gain relief from persecution. But to trade their spiritual birthright for temporary ease in this world would deprive them of Christ's blessing. *he was rejected.* Because he only regretted his loss and did not repent of his sin (Ge 27). His sorrow was not "godly sorrow" that "brings repentance that leads to salvation," but "worldly sorrow" that "brings death" (2Co 7:10). *with tears.* Not tears of repentance. See Ge 27:34-38. *could not change what he had done.* Cf. 6:4-6 and note.

12:18-29 Crowning motivation and warning (the fifth; see note on 2:1-4—including an exposition of Ex 19:10-23 in vv. 18-24).

12:18-21 These verses recall the awesome occasion when the law was given at Mount Sinai (see Ex 19:10-25; Dt 4:11-12; 5:22-26).

12:22 *Mount Zion.* Not the literal Mount Zion (Jerusalem, or its southeast portion), but the heavenly city of God and those who dwell there with him (see 11:10,13-16; 13:14; Php 3:20). The circumstances under which the old covenant was given (vv. 18-21) and the features of the new covenant (vv. 22-24) point up the utter contrast between the two covenants and lay the foundation for one more warning and exhortation to those still thinking of going back to Judaism. *thousands upon thousands of angels.* See Rev 5:11-12.

12:23 *church of the firstborn.* Believers in general who make up the church: 1. Reference cannot be to the angels since these have just been mentioned (v. 22). 2. "Firstborn" cannot refer to Christ (though he is called firstborn, 1:6; Ro 8:29; Col 1:15-18; Rev 1:5), since here the Greek word is plural. 3. The fact that the

names of these "firstborn" are recorded in heaven reminds us of the redeemed (see Rev 3:5; 13:8; 17:8; 20:12; 21:27). The designation of them as "firstborn" suggests their privileged position as heirs together with Christ, the supreme firstborn and "heir of all things" (Heb 1:2). *God, the Judge of all.* See 4:13; Ro 14:10-12; 1Co 3:10-15; 2Co 5:10; Rev 20:11-15. *spirits of the righteous made perfect.* For the most part, these were pre-Christian believers such as Abel (11:4) and Noah (11:7). They are referred to as "spirits" because they are waiting for the resurrection and as "righteous" because God credited their faith to them as righteousness, as he did to Abraham (see Ge 15:6; Ro 4:3 and notes). Actual justification was not accomplished, however, until Christ made it complete by his death on the cross (see 11:40; Ro 3:24-26 and note; 4:23-25).

A **12:24** *mediator of a new covenant.* See 8:6 and note. *better word than the blood of Abel.* Abel's blood cried out for justice and retribution (see Ge 4:10 and note), whereas the blood of Jesus shed on the cross speaks of forgiveness and reconciliation (see 9:12 and note; 10:19; Col 1:20; 1Jn 1:7).

12:25-29 The fifth warning (see note on 2:1-4).

A **12:25** *him who speaks.* God. *warned them on earth.* At Sinai. *him who warns us from heaven.* Christ, who is both from and in heaven (1:1-3; 4:14; 6:20; 7:26; 9:24). Since we have greater revelation, we have greater responsibility and therefore greater danger (see 2:2-3 and notes).

12:26 *shook the earth.* See Ex 19:18; cf. Jdg 5:4-5; Ps 68:7-8.

12:27 *once more.* During the great end-time upheavals associated with the second advent of Christ (see Mt 24:29; Mk 13:24-25 and note; Lk 21:11,25; Ac 2:20). *what cannot be shaken.* The kingdom (v. 28).

12:28 *worship God acceptably.* See Jn 4:19-24; Ro 12:1.

12:29 See TNIV text note; cf. 10:27 and note; Ex 24:17; Dt 9:3.

CONCLUDING EXHORTATIONS

13 Keep on loving one another as brothers and sisters. [k] 2Do not forget to show hospitality to strangers, [l] for by so doing some people have shown hospitality to angels without knowing it. [m] 3Continue to remember those in prison [n] as if you were together with them in prison, and those who are mistreated as if you yourselves were suffering.

4Marriage should be honored by all, [o] and the marriage bed kept pure, for God will judge the adulterer and all the sexually immoral. [p] 5Keep your lives free from the love of money [q] and be content with what you have, [r] because God has said,

"Never will I leave you;
never will I forsake you." [a] [s]

6So we say with confidence,

"The Lord is my helper; I will not be afraid.
What can human beings do to me?" [b] [t]

7Remember your leaders, [u] who spoke the word of God [v] to you. Consider the outcome of their way of life and imitate [w] their faith. 8Jesus Christ is the same yesterday and today and forever. [x]

9Do not be carried away by all kinds of strange teachings. [y] It is good for our hearts to be strengthened [z] by grace, not by the eating of ceremonial foods, [a] which is of no benefit to those who observe such rituals. [b] 10We have an altar from which those who minister at the tabernacle [c] have no right to eat. [d] 11The high priest carries the blood of animals into the Most Holy Place as a sin offering, [e] but the bodies are burned outside the camp. [f] 12And so Jesus also suffered outside the city gate [g] to make the people holy [h] through his own blood. [i] 13Let us, then, go to him [j] outside the camp, bearing the disgrace he bore. [k] 14For here we do not have an enduring city, [l] but we are looking for the city that is to come. [m]

15Through Jesus, therefore, let us continually offer to God a sacrifice [n] of praise—the fruit of lips [o] that openly profess his name. 16And do not forget to do good and to share with others, [p] for with such sacrifices [q] God is pleased.

17Have confidence in your leaders [r] and submit to their authority, because they keep

---

[a] 5 Deut. 31:6   [b] 6 Psalm 118:6,7

13:1 [k] S Ro 12:10
13:2 [l] Job 31:32; Mt 25:35; S Ro 12:13 [m] Ge 18:1-33; 19:1-3
13:3 [n] Mt 25:36; Col 4:18; Heb 10:34
13:4 [o] Mal 2:15; 1Co 7:38; 1Ti 4:3 [p] Dt 22:22; 1Co 6:9; Rev 22:15
13:5 [q] S 1Ti 3:3 [r] Php 4:11; 1Ti 6:6,8
13:6 [s] Dt 31:6,8; Jos 1:5 [t] Ps 118:6,7
13:7 [u] ver 17,24; 1Co 16:16 [v] S Heb 4:12 [w] Heb 6:12
13:8 [x] Ps 102:27; Heb 1:12
13:9 [y] Eph 4:14 [z] Col 2:7 [a] Col 2:16 [b] Heb 9:10
13:10 [c] Heb 8:5 [d] 1Co 9:13; 10:18
13:11 [e] Lev 16:15 [f] Ex 29:14; Lev 4:12, 21; 9:11; 16:27
13:12 [g] Jn 19:17 [h] S Eph 5:26 [i] S Ro 3:25
13:13 [j] Lk 9:23 [k] Heb 11:26
13:14 [l] Heb 12:27 [m] Php 3:20; Heb 11:10,27; 12:22
13:15 [n] 1Pe 2:5 [o] Isa 57:19; Hos 14:2
13:16 [p] Ro 12:13 [q] Php 4:18
13:17 [r] ver 7,24

13:2 *show hospitality to strangers.* See Mt 25:35. *strangers.* Members of the Christian community not personally known. *shown hospitality to angels without knowing it.* As did Abraham (Ge 18), Gideon (Jdg 6) and Manoah (Jdg 13).
13:3 *remember those in prison ... and those who are mistreated.* Especially fellow believers (see 10:32–34; Mt 25:36; 1Co 12:26).
13:4 See Ex 20:14 and note. *Marriage should be honored.* See 1Co 6:13–18; 7:1–15; Eph 5:26–31; 1Ti 4:3. *adulterer and ... sexually immoral.* See 1Co 6:9.
13:5 *love of money.* See Lk 12:15,21; Php 4:10–13; 1Ti 6:6–10, 17–19. *be content.* See Php 4:11–12; 1Ti 6:8.
13:7–17 A unit framed by the exhortation to "Remember your [past] leaders ... and imitate their faith" and the exhortation to "Have confidence in your [present] leaders and submit to their authority."
13:7 *leaders, who spoke the word of God.* See 2:3; 5:12. *Consider the outcome of their way of life.* Consider how they persevered in their faith and entered into the promised inheritance (see 6:12). *imitate their faith.* See 6:12; Eph 5:1; 1Th 1:6 and notes; cf. 1Co 4:16.
13:8 *Jesus Christ is the same.* A confession of the changelessness of Christ, no doubt related to the preceding verse. The substance of their former leaders' faith was the unchanging Christ. *yesterday.* Probably the days of Christ's life on earth, when the eyewitnesses observed him (2:3). *today.* The Christ whom the eyewitnesses saw was still the same, and what they had said about him was still true. *forever.* And it will always be true. To compromise his absolute supremacy by returning to the inferior Aaronic priesthood and sacrifices (see chs. 5–10) is to undermine the gospel.

13:9 *not by the eating of ceremonial foods.* As the legalistic Judaizers were teaching. The old Mosaic order was done away with at the cross and must not be revived.
13:10 *We have an altar.* Probably refers to the cross, which marked the end of the whole Aaronic priesthood and its replacement by the order of Melchizedek, of which Christ is the unique and only priest. *no right to eat.* The priests could not eat of the sacrifice on the Day of Atonement, but we can partake of our sacrifice, so to speak—through spiritual reception of Christ by faith (see Jn 6:48–58). We have a higher privilege than the priests under the old covenant had.
13:11 *burned outside the camp.* See Lev 4:12 and note; 16:27.
13:12 *Jesus also suffered outside the city gate.* Christ's death outside Jerusalem represented the removal of sin, as had the removal of the bodies of sacrificial animals outside the camp of Israel.
13:13 *go to him outside the camp.* Calls for separation from Judaism to Christ. As he died in disgrace outside the city, so the readers should be willing to be disgraced by turning unequivocally from Judaism to Christ.
13:14 *city that is to come.* See notes on 11:10,14,16.
13:15 *sacrifice of praise.* Cf. Ro 12:1. For the OT background, see notes on Lev 3:1; Ps 7:17; cf. Ps 51:17 and note.
13:16 *sacrifices.* See Php 4:18 and note.
13:17 *your leaders.* Their present leaders, as distinct from their first ones, now dead, mentioned in v. 7 (see note on vv. 7–17). *submit to their authority.* Dictatorial leadership is not condoned by this command (see 2Co 10:8 and note), but respect for authority, orderliness and discipline in the church are taught throughout the NT.

13:17 *s* Isa 62:6;
Ac 20:28
13:18 *t* S 1Th 5:25
u S Ac 23:1
13:19 *v* Phm 22
13:20 *w* S Ro 15:33
x Ge 9:16; 17:7,13,19;
Isa 55:3; 61:8;
Eze 37:26; S Mt 26:28
y S Ac 2:24
z S Jn 10:11
13:21 *a* 2Co 9:8
b S Php 2:13
c 1Jn 3:22 *d* S Ro 11:36
13:22 *e* 1Pe 5:12
13:23 *f* S Ac 16:1
13:24 *g* ver 7,17
h Ac 18:2
13:25 *i* S Col 4:18

watch over you *s* as those who must give an account. Do this so that their work will be a joy, not a burden, for that would be of no benefit to you.

¹⁸Pray for us. *t* We are sure that we have a clear conscience *u* and desire to live honorably in every way. ¹⁹I particularly urge you to pray so that I may be restored to you soon. *v*

BENEDICTION AND FINAL GREETINGS

²⁰Now may the God of peace, *w* who through the blood of the eternal covenant *x* brought back from the dead *y* our Lord Jesus, that great Shepherd of the sheep, *z* ²¹equip you with everything good for doing his will, *a* and may he work in us *b* what is pleasing to him, *c* through Jesus Christ, to whom be glory for ever and ever. Amen. *d*

²²Brothers and sisters, I urge you to bear with my word of exhortation, for in fact I have written to you quite briefly. *e*

²³I want you to know that our brother Timothy *f* has been released. If he arrives soon, I will come with him to see you.

²⁴Greet all your leaders *g* and all the Lord's people. Those from Italy *h* send you their greetings.

²⁵Grace be with you all. *i*

13:19 *restored to you soon.* The identity and whereabouts of the writer are not known to us, but "restored" suggests that somehow he had been delayed in visiting those to whom he was writing, perhaps by his current ministry. That he was not under arrest is clear from v. 23.
13:20,25 *peace . . . Grace.* See note on Ro 1:7.
13:20–21 This benediction provides a fitting conclusion to the letter.

▲ 13:20 *God of peace.* A title for God used frequently in benedictions (see Ro 15:33; 16:20; Php 4:9; 1Th 5:23 and note). *blood of.* See 10:29 and note. *eternal covenant.* The new covenant (see note on 8:8–12). What Jeremiah designates as the new covenant in 31:31 he describes as everlasting in 32:40 (cf. Isa 55:3; 61:8 and notes). *great Shepherd.* See, e.g., Ps 23; Isa 40:11; Eze 34:11–16,23; 37:24; Jn 10:2–3, 11,14,27; 1Pe 2:25; 5:4.

13:21 *everything good.* Such as faith, faithfulness, obedience and perseverance.
13:22–25 A postscript.

▲ 13:22 *Brothers and sisters.* See note on Ro 1:13. *word of exhortation.* See Introduction: Literary Form. The main thrust of the letter is to go on in Christian maturity and not fall away from Christ. *quite briefly.* Compared to the lengthy treatise that would be necessary to explain adequately the superiority of Christ.
13:23 *Timothy.* See Introduction to 1 Timothy: Recipient.
13:24 *leaders.* Mentioned in v. 17. *Those from Italy.* From this brief greeting no firm conclusion can be drawn concerning the source or destination of this "letter." The writer may simply be passing on to his readers greetings from some Italian believers.
13:25 *with you.* Cf. note on 2Co 13:14.

The seven letters following Hebrews—James; 1,2 Peter; 1,2,3 John; Jude—have of-ten been designated as the General Letters. This term goes back to the early church historian Eusebius (c. A.D. 265–340), who in his *Ecclesiastical History* (2:23–25) first referred to these seven letters as Catholic Letters, using the word "catholic" to mean "universal."

The letters so designated may be said to be, for the most part, addressed to general audiences rather than to specific persons or localized groups. 2 and 3 John, the two letters that seem most obviously addressed to individuals, have long been viewed as appendages of 1 John, which is clearly general in its address. However, when compared with Paul's letters, all these letters except 3 John are clearly general in nature. By contrast, Paul addresses his letters to such recipients as the Christians at Philippi, the churches of Galatia, or Timothy or Titus.

As Eusebius noted long ago, one interesting fact connected with the General Letters is that most of them were at one time among the disputed books of the NT. James, 2 Peter, 2 John, 3 John and Jude were all questioned extensively before be-ing admitted to the canon of Scripture.

JAMES INTRODUCTION

AUTHOR

C The author identifies himself as James (1:1); he was probably the brother of Jesus and the leader of the Jerusalem council (Ac 15). Four men in the NT have this name. The author of this letter could not have been the apostle James, who died too early (A.D. 44) to have written it. The other two men named James had neither the stature nor the influence that the writer of this letter had.

James was one of several brothers of Jesus, probably the oldest since he heads the list in Mt 13:55. At first he did not believe in Jesus and even challenged him and misunderstood his mission (Jn 7:2–5). Later he became very prominent in the church:

1. He was one of the select individuals Christ appeared to after his resurrection (see 1Co 15:7 and note).

2. Paul called him a "pillar" of the church (Gal 2:9).

3. Paul, on his first post-conversion visit to Jerusalem, saw James (Gal 1:19).

4. Paul did the same on his last visit (Ac 21:18).

5. When Peter was rescued from prison, he told his friends to tell James (Ac 12:17).

6. James was a leader in the important council of Jerusalem (Ac 15:13).

7. Jude could identify himself simply as "a brother of James" (Jude 1:1), so well known was James. He was martyred c. A.D. 62.

DATE

Some date the letter in the early 60s. There are indications, however, that it was written before A.D. 50:

1. Its distinctively Jewish nature suggests that it was composed when the church was still predominantly Jewish.

2. It reflects a simple church order—officers of the church are called "elders" (5:14) and "teachers" (3:1).

3. No reference is made to the controversy over Gentile circumcision.

4. The Greek term *synagoge* ("synagogue" or "meeting") is used to designate the meeting or meeting place of the church (2:2).

If this early dating is correct, this letter is the earliest of all the NT writings—with the possible exception of Galatians.

RECIPIENTS

The recipients are identified explicitly only in 1:1: "the twelve tribes scattered among the nations." Some hold that this expression refers to Christians in general, but the term "twelve tribes" would more naturally apply to Jewish Christians. Furthermore, a Jewish audience would be more in keeping with the obviously Jewish nature of the letter (e.g., the use of the Hebrew title for God, *kyrios sabaoth*, "Lord Almighty," 5:4). That the recipients were Christians is clear from 2:1; 5:7–8. It has been plausibly suggested that these were believers from the early Jerusalem church who, after Stephen's death, were scattered as far as Phoenicia, Cyprus and Syrian Antioch (see Ac 8:1; 11:19 and notes). This would account for James's references to trials and oppression, his intimate knowledge of the readers and the authoritative nature of the letter. As leader of the Jerusalem church, James wrote as pastor to instruct and encourage his dispersed people in the face of their difficulties (see essay, p. 2073).

DISTINCTIVE CHARACTERISTICS

Characteristics that make the letter distinctive are: (1) its unmistakably Jewish nature; (2) its emphasis on vital Christianity, characterized by good deeds and a faith that works (genuine faith must and will be accompanied by a consistent lifestyle); (3) its simple organization; (4) its familiarity with Jesus' teachings preserved in the Sermon on the Mount (compare 2:5 with Mt 5:3; 3:10–12 with Mt 7:15–20; 3:18 with Mt 5:9; 5:2–3 with Mt 6:19–20; 5:12 with Mt 5:33–37); (5) its similarity to OT wisdom writings such as Proverbs (see essay, p. 750); (6) its excellent Greek.

OUTLINE

1:1 *a* S Ac 15:13
b Ro 1:1; Tit 1:1
c Ac 26:7 *d* Dt 32:26;
Jn 7:35; 1Pe 1:1
e Ac 15:23
1:2 *f* ver 12;
S Mt 5:12; Heb 10:34;
12:11
1:3 *g* 1Pe 1:7
h S Heb 10:36
1:4 *i* S 1Co 2:6
1:5 *j* 1Ki 3:9,10;
Pr 2:3-6 *k* Ps 51:6;
Da 1:17; 2:21;
S Mt 7:7
1:6 *l* S Mt 21:21;
Mk 11:24
1:8 *m* Ps 119:113;
Jas 4:8 *n* 2Pe 2:14;
3:16
1:9 *o* S Mt 23:12
1:10 *p* Job 14:2;
Ps 103:15,16;
Isa 40:6,7; 1Co 7:31;
1Pe 1:24
1:11 *q* Mt 20:12
r Ps 102:4,11
s Isa 40:6-8
1:12 *t* ver 2; Ge 22:1;
Jas 5:11; 1Pe 3:14
u S 1Co 9:25
v Ex 20:6; 1Co 2:9;
8:3; Jas 2:5
1:14 *w* Pr 19:3
1:15 *x* Ge 3:6;
Job 15:35; Ps 7:14;
Isa 59:4 *y* S Ro 6:23
1:16 *z* S 1Co 6:9
a ver 19; Jas 2:5
1:17 *b* Ps 85:12;
Jn 3:27; Jas 3:15,17
c Ge 1:16; Ps 136:7;
Da 2:22; 1Jn 1:5
d Nu 23:19; Ps 102:27;
Mal 3:6
1:18 *e* S Jn 1:13
f S 2Ti 2:15 *g* Jer 2:3;
Rev 14:4
1:19 *h* ver 16; Jas 2:5
i Pr 10:19; Jas 3:3-12
1:20 *j* S Mt 5:22
1:21 *k* S Eph 4:22
l Eph 1:13

1

James, *a* a servant of God *b* and of the Lord Jesus Christ,

To the twelve tribes *c* scattered *d* among the nations:

Greetings. *e*

TRIALS AND TEMPTATIONS

²Consider it pure joy, my brothers and sisters, whenever you face trials of many kinds, *f* ³because you know that the testing of your faith *g* produces perseverance. *h* ⁴Let perseverance finish its work so that you may be mature *i* and complete, not lacking anything. ⁵If any of you lacks wisdom, you should ask God, *j* who gives generously to all without finding fault, and it will be given to you. *k* ⁶But when you ask, you must believe and not doubt, *l* because the one who doubts is like a wave of the sea, blown and tossed by the wind. ⁷Those who doubt should not think they will receive anything from the Lord; ⁸they are double-minded *m* and unstable *n* in all they do.

⁹Believers in humble circumstances ought to take pride in their high position. *o* ¹⁰But the rich should take pride in their humiliation—since they will pass away like a wild flower. *p* ¹¹For the sun rises with scorching heat *q* and withers *r* the plant; its blossom falls and its beauty is destroyed. *s* In the same way, the rich will fade away even while they go about their business.

¹²Blessed are those who persevere under trial, *t* because when they have stood the test, they will receive the crown of life *u* that God has promised to those who love him. *v*

¹³When tempted, no one should say, "God is tempting me." For God cannot be tempted by evil, nor does he tempt anyone; ¹⁴but each of you is tempted when you are dragged away by your own *w* evil desire and enticed. ¹⁵Then, after desire has conceived, it gives birth to sin; *x* and sin, when it is full-grown, gives birth to death. *y*

¹⁶Don't be deceived, *z* my dear brothers and sisters. *a* ¹⁷Every good and perfect gift is from above, *b* coming down from the Father of the heavenly lights, *c* who does not change *d* like shifting shadows. ¹⁸He chose to give us birth *e* through the word of truth, *f* that we might be a kind of firstfruits *g* of all he created.

LISTENING AND DOING

¹⁹My dear brothers and sisters, *h* take note of this: Everyone should be quick to listen, slow to speak *i* and slow to become angry, ²⁰because our anger *j* does not produce the righteousness that God desires. ²¹Therefore, get rid of *k* all moral filth and the evil that is so prevalent and humbly accept the word planted in you, *l* which can save you.

1:1 *James.* See Introduction: Author. *servant.* See note on Ro 1:1. *twelve tribes.* See Introduction: Recipients.

1:2–3 *trials … testing … produces perseverance.* This, together with similar language in v. 12, forms a frame around James's word about trials.

1:2 *joy.* See Mt 5:11–12; Ac 5:41; Ro 5:3 and note; Php 4:4 and note; 1Pe 1:6. *brothers and sisters.* Cf. note on Ro 1:13. James addresses the readers as "brothers" 15 times in this short letter. He has many rebukes for them, but he chides them in brotherly love. *trials.* The same Greek root lies behind the word "trials" here and the word "tempted" in v. 13. In vv. 2–3 the emphasis is on difficulties that come from outside; in vv. 13–15 it is on inner moral trials, such as temptation to sin.

1:5 *wisdom.* Enables one to face trials with "pure joy" (v. 2). Wisdom is not just acquired information but practical insight with spiritual implications (see 3:13–18; Pr 1:2–4 and note on 1:2; 2:10–15; 4:5–9; 9:10–12).

1:6 *wave of the sea.* See Eph 4:14 and note.

1:9–10 *Believers in humble circumstances … the rich.* Christians who experience poverty are to take pride in their high position (v. 9) as believers (see 2:5). Wealthy believers, on the other hand, should take pride not in their possessions but in the fact that God has humbled them and given them a godly value system, so that they now realize how transitory life and wealth are (v. 10).

1:10 *pass away like a wild flower.* See Job 14:2; Ps 103:15; Isa 40:6–7; 1Pe 1:24; cf. Lk 12:15,20–21; 1Ti 6:8–10,17–19.

1:11 *will fade away.* Cf. 4:14 and note.

1:12 *Blessed.* See Jer 17:7–8; Mt 5:3–12; see also notes on Ps 1:1; Mt 5:3. *crown.* The Greek for this word was the usual term for the wreath placed on the head of a victorious athlete or military leader (see 2Ti 4:8; 1Pe 5:4; Rev 2:10 and notes). *life.* Eternal life, as the future tense of the verb ("will receive") indicates.

1:13 *tempted.* In vv. 13–14 the verb refers to temptations that test one's moral strength to resist sin (see note on Mt 4:1). *God cannot be tempted.* Because God in his very nature is holy, there is nothing in him for sin to appeal to. *nor does he tempt anyone.* See note on Ge 22:1.

1:14 *dragged away … and enticed.* Words commonly used to describe hunting methods, used here metaphorically of how evil desire operates (cf. 2Pe 2:14 and note). *evil desire.* A person's innate tendency to sin (cf. Jer 17:9).

1:15 The three stages—desire, sin, death—are seen in the temptations of Eve (Ge 3:6–22) and David (2Sa 11:2–17).

1:17 *Every good and perfect gift is from above.* See v. 5; 3:17. *Father of … lights.* God is the Creator of the heavenly bodies, which give light to the earth, but, unlike them, he does not change.

1:18 *birth.* Not a reference to creation but to regeneration (see Jn 3:3,5,7 and notes). *word of truth.* The proclamation of the gospel (see 1Pe 1:23–25 and note on 1:23). *firstfruits.* See Lev 23:9–14 and chart, pp. 180–181. Just as the first sheaf of the harvest was an indication that the whole harvest would eventually follow, so the early Christians were an indication that a great number of people would eventually be born again (cf. 1Co 15:20 and note).

1:19 *Everyone should be … slow to speak.* See v. 26.

1:21 *word.* Of God (cf. 1Pe 1:23). *save you.* Here eschatological (future) salvation is primarily in view (cf. Heb 1:14; 9:28 and note).

²²Do not merely listen to the word, and so deceive yourselves. Do what it says. *m* ²³Those who listen to the word but do not do what it says are like people who look at their faces in a mirror ²⁴and, after looking at themselves, go away and immediately forget what they look like. ²⁵But those who look intently into the perfect law that gives freedom, *n* and continue in it—not forgetting what they have heard, but doing it—they will be blessed in what they do. *o*

²⁶Those who consider themselves religious and yet do not keep a tight rein on their tongues *p* deceive themselves, and their religion is worthless. ²⁷Religion that God our Father accepts as pure and faultless is this: to look after *q* orphans and widows *r* in their distress and to keep oneself from being polluted by the world. *s*

FAVORITISM FORBIDDEN

2 My brothers and sisters, believers in our glorious *t* Lord Jesus Christ must not show favoritism. *u* ²Suppose someone comes into your meeting wearing a gold ring and fine clothes, and a poor person in filthy old clothes also comes in. ³If you show special attention to the one wearing fine clothes and say, "Here's a good seat for you," but say to the one who is poor, "You stand there" or "Sit on the floor by my feet," ⁴have you not discriminated among yourselves and become judges *v* with evil thoughts?

⁵Listen, my dear brothers and sisters: *w* Has not God chosen those who are poor in the eyes of the world *x* to be rich in faith *y* and to inherit the kingdom *z* he promised those who love him? *a* ⁶But you have dishonored the poor. *b* Is it not the rich who are exploiting you? Are they not the ones who are dragging you into court? *c* ⁷Are they not the ones who are blaspheming the noble name of him to whom you belong?

⁸If you really keep the royal law found in Scripture, "Love your neighbor as yourself," *a* *d* you are doing right. ⁹But if you show favoritism, *e* you sin and are convicted by the law as lawbreakers. *f* ¹⁰For whoever keeps the whole law and yet stumbles *g* at just one point is guilty of breaking all of it. *h* ¹¹For he who said, "You shall not commit adultery," *b* *i* also said, "You shall not murder." *c* *j* If you do not commit adultery but do commit murder, you have become a lawbreaker.

¹²Speak and act as those who are going to be judged *k* by the law that gives freedom, *l* ¹³because judgment without mercy will be shown to anyone who has not been merciful. *m* Mercy triumphs over judgment.

FAITH AND DEEDS

¹⁴What good is it, my brothers and sisters, if people claim to have faith but have no

---

a 8 Lev. 19:18   *b* 11 Exodus 20:14; Deut. 5:18   *c* 11 Exodus 20:13; Deut. 5:17

1:22 *m* S Mt 7:21; Jas 2:14-20
1:25 *n* Ps 19:7; Jn 8:32; Gal 2:4; Jas 2:12 *o* S Jn 13:17
1:26 *p* Ps 34:13; 39:1; 141:3; Jas 3:2-12; 1Pe 3:10
1:27 *q* Mt 25:36 *r* Dt 14:29; Job 31:16, 17,21; Ps 146:9; Isa 1:17,23 *s* Ro 12:2; Jas 4:4; 2Pe 1:4; 2:20
2:1 *t* Ac 7:2; 1Co 2:8 *u* ver 9; Dt 1:17; Lev 19:15; Pr 24:23; S Ac 10:34
2:4 *v* S Jn 7:24
2:5 *w* Jas 1:16,19 *x* Job 34:19; 1Co 1:26-28 *y* Lk 12:21; Rev 2:9 *z* S Mt 25:34 *a* S Jas 1:12
2:6 *b* 1Co 11:22 *c* Ac 8:3; 16:19
2:8 *d* Lev 19:18; S Mt 5:43
2:9 *e* ver 1 *f* Dt 1:17
2:10 *g* Jas 3:2 *h* Mt 5:19; Gal 3:10; 5:3
2:11 *i* Ex 20:14; Dt 5:18 *j* Ex 20:13; Dt 5:17
2:12 *k* S Mt 16:27 *l* S Jas 1:25
2:13 *m* Mt 5:7; 9:13; 12:7; 18:32-35; Lk 6:37

1:25 *perfect law.* The moral and ethical teaching of Christianity, which is based on the OT moral law, as embodied in the Ten Commandments (see Ps 19:7) but brought to completion (perfection) by Jesus Christ (see notes on Mt 5:17; Ro 10:4). *freedom.* In contrast to the sinner, who is a slave to sin (see Jn 8:34 and note), obeying the moral law gives Christians the joyous freedom to be what they were created for (see 2:12).
1:26-27 An example of a person not doing the word and of one doing it.
1:26 *religious.* Refers to the outward acts of religion: e.g., giving to the needy, fasting and public acts of praying and worshiping (see Mt 6:1-18 and note on 6:1). *keep a tight rein on their tongues.* See 3:1-12.
1:27 See Jer 22:16 and note. *orphans and widows.* See notes on Ex 22:21-27; Isa 1:17. *world.* Not the world of nature but the world of people in their rebellion against and alienation from God (see 1Jn 2:15 and note).
2:1 *believers . . . must not show favoritism.* God does not show favoritism (see note on Ac 10:34)—nor should believers (see vv. 5-13 and note; see also note on 1Ti 5:21). *glorious.* See Jn 1:14; Heb 1:3 and notes.
2:2 *meeting.* The Greek for this term is the origin of the English word "synagogue."
2:4 *judges with evil thoughts.* Cf. Lev 19:15.
2:5-13 James gives three arguments against showing favoritism to the rich: 1. The rich persecute the poor—the believers (vv. 5-7). 2. Favoritism violates the royal law of love and thus is sin (vv. 8-11). 3. Favoritism will be judged (vv. 12-13).

2:5 *Has not God chosen those who are poor . . . ?* Cf. Lk 6:20 and note on 6:20-23; 1Co 1:26-31. *kingdom.* The kingdom that is entered by the new birth (see note on 1:18) and that will be consummated in the future (Mt 25:34,46; see note on Mt 3:2).
2:8 *royal law.* The law of love (see Lev 19:18 and note) is called "royal" because it is the supreme law that is the source of all other laws governing human relationships. It is the summation of all such laws (see Mt 22:36-40; Ro 13:8-10 and notes on 13:8-9).
2:10 *guilty of breaking all.* The law is the expression of the character and will of God; therefore to violate one part of the law is to violate God's will and thus his whole law (cf. Mt 5:18-19; 23:23).
2:11 James may have chosen these two commandments because both violate the law of love to one's neighbor (v. 8).
2:12 *judged.* This judgment is not for determining eternal destiny, for James is speaking to believers (v. 1), whose destiny is already determined (see Jn 5:24 and note). Rather, it is for giving rewards to believers (see 1Co 3:12-15; 2Co 5:10; Rev 22:12 and notes). *law that gives freedom.* The royal law of love (v. 8).
2:13 *Mercy triumphs over judgment.* If people are merciful, God will be merciful on the Day of Judgment (see Pr 21:13; Mt 5:7; 6:14-15; 18:21-35).
2:14-26 In vv. 14-20,24,26 "faith" is not used in the sense of genuine, saving faith. Rather, it is demonic (v. 19), useless (v. 20) and dead (v. 26). It is a mere intellectual acceptance of certain truths without trust in Christ as Savior. James is also not saying that a person is saved by works and not by gen-

2:14 ª Mt 7:26;
Jas 1:22-25
2:15 ª Mt 25:35,36
2:16 ª Lk 3:11;
1Jn 3:17,18
2:17 ª ver 20,26;
Gal 5:6
2:18 ª Ro 3:28
ˢ Heb 11 ª Mt 7:16,17;
Jas 3:13
2:19 ª Dt 6:4;
Mk 12:29; 1Co 8:4-6
ᵛ Mt 8:29; Lk 4:34
2:20 ª ver 17,26
2:21 ª Ge 22:9,12
2:22 ʸ Heb 11:17
ᶻ 1Th 1:3
2:23 ª Ge 15:6;
S Ro 4:3 ᵇ 2Ch 20:7;
Isa 41:8
2:25 ᶜ S Heb 11:31
2:26 ᵈ ver 17,20
3:1 ᵉ S Eph 4:11
ᶠ S Mt 7:1 ᵍ Ro 2:21
3:2 ʰ 1Ki 8:46;
Ro 3:9-20; Jas 2:10;
1Jn 1:8 ⁱ Ps 39:1;
Pr 10:19; 1Pe 3:10
ʲ S Mt 12:37 ᵏ Jas 1:26
3:3 ˡ Ps 32:9
3:5 ᵐ Ps 12:3,4;
73:8,9
3:6 ⁿ Pr 16:27
ᵒ Mt 15:11,18,19
ᵖ S Mt 5:22
3:8 ᵍ Ps 140:3;
Ro 3:13
3:9 ʳ Ge 1:26,27;
1Co 11:7
3:12 ˢ Mt 7:16

deeds? ⁿ Can such faith save them? ¹⁵Suppose a brother or sister is without clothes and daily food. ᵒ ¹⁶If one of you says to them, "Go in peace; keep warm and well fed," but does nothing about their physical needs, what good is it? ᵖ ¹⁷In the same way, faith by itself, if it is not accompanied by action, is dead. ᵍ

¹⁸But someone will say, "You have faith; I have deeds."

Show me your faith without deeds, ʳ and I will show you my faith ˢ by what I do. ᵗ ¹⁹You believe that there is one God. ᵘ Good! Even the demons believe that ᵛ—and shudder.

²⁰You foolish person, do you want evidence that faith without deeds is useless? ª ᵂ ²¹Was not our father Abraham considered righteous for what he did when he offered his son Isaac on the altar? ˣ ²²You see that his faith and his actions were working together, ʸ and his faith was made complete by what he did. ᶻ ²³And the scripture was fulfilled that says, "Abraham believed God, and it was credited to him as righteousness," ᵇª and he was called God's friend. ᵇ ²⁴You see that people are justified by what they do and not by faith alone.

²⁵In the same way, was not even Rahab the prostitute considered righteous for what she did when she gave lodging to the spies and sent them off in a different direction? ᶜ ²⁶As the body without the spirit is dead, so faith without deeds is dead. ᵈ

TAMING THE TONGUE

3 Not many of you should presume to be teachers, ᵉ my brothers and sisters, because you know that we who teach will be judged ᶠ more strictly. ᵍ ²We all stumble ʰ in many ways. Those who are never at fault in what they say ⁱ are perfect, ʲ able to keep their whole body in check. ᵏ

³When we put bits into the mouths of horses to make them obey us, we can turn the whole animal. ˡ ⁴Or take ships as an example. Although they are so large and are driven by strong winds, they are steered by a very small rudder wherever the pilot wants to go. ⁵Likewise, the tongue is a small part of the body, but it makes great boasts. ᵐ Consider what a great forest is set on fire by a small spark. ⁶The tongue also is a fire, ⁿ a world of evil among the parts of the body. It corrupts the whole person, ᵒ sets the whole course of one's life on fire, and is itself set on fire by hell. ᵖ

⁷All kinds of animals, birds, reptiles and sea creatures are being tamed and have been tamed by human beings, ⁸but no one can tame the tongue. It is a restless evil, full of deadly poison. ᵍ

⁹With the tongue we praise our Lord and Father, and with it we curse human beings, who have been made in God's likeness. ʳ ¹⁰Out of the same mouth come praise and cursing. My brothers and sisters, this should not be. ¹¹Can both fresh water and salt water flow from the same spring? ¹²My brothers and sisters, can a fig tree bear olives, or a grapevine bear figs? ˢ Neither can a salt spring produce fresh water.

ª 20 Some early manuscripts *dead* b 23 Gen. 15:6

---

uine faith. Rather, he is saying, to use Martin Luther's words, that people are justified (declared righteous before God) by faith alone, but not by a faith that is alone. Genuine faith will produce good deeds, but only faith in Christ saves. (For more information on justification, see note on Ro 3:24.)

▲ 2:15–16 This illustration of false faith is parallel to the illustration of false love found in 1Jn 3:17 (see there). The latter passage calls for love in action; this one calls for faith in action.

2:18 *You have faith; I have deeds.* The false claim is that there are "faith" Christians and "deeds" Christians, i.e., that faith and deeds can exist independently of each other. *Show me your faith without deeds.* Irony: James denies the possibility of this.

2:19 *there is one God.* A declaration of monotheism that reflects the well-known Jewish creed called in Hebrew the *Shema*, "Hear" (Dt 6:4 [see notes on 6:4–9]; Mk 12:29 [see note there]).

▲ 2:21 Apart from its context, this verse might seem to contradict the Biblical teaching that people are saved by faith and not by good deeds (see Ro 3:28 and note; Gal 2:15–16 and note on 2:16). But James means only that righteous action is evidence of genuine faith—not that it saves, for the verse (Ge 15:6; see there) that he cites (v. 23) to substantiate his point says, "Abram believed the LORD, and he credited it [i.e., faith, not works] to him as righteousness." Furthermore, Abraham's act of faith recorded in Ge 15:6 occurred before he offered up Isaac, which was only a proof of the genuineness of his faith. As Paul wrote,

"The only thing that counts is faith expressing itself through love" (Gal 5:6; see note there). Faith that saves produces good deeds.

2:23 *God's friend.* This designation (see 2Ch 20:7 and note on Ge 18:17) further describes Abraham's relationship to God as one of complete acceptance (cf. Jn 15:13–15).

2:24 *not by faith alone.* Not by an intellectual assent to certain truths (see note on 2:14–26).

2:25 *Rahab the prostitute.* James does not approve Rahab's occupation. He merely commends her for her faith (see also Heb 11:31 and note), which she demonstrated by helping the spies (Jos 2).

▲ 3:1 *judged more strictly.* Because teachers have great influence, they will be held more accountable (cf. Mt 23:1–33; Lk 20:46–47; Heb 13:17).

3:2 *perfect.* Since the tongue is so difficult to control, those who control it perfectly gain control of themselves in all other areas of life as well.

3:6 *world of evil.* Like the world in its fallenness. *corrupts the whole person.* Because the tongue is the cause of so many sins (cf. Mk 7:20–23). *set on fire by hell.* A figurative way of saying that the source of the tongue's evil is the devil (see Jn 8:44 and note). *hell.* See notes on Mt 5:22; Lk 16:23.

3:9 *in God's likeness.* Since humans have been made like God (see Ge 1:26–27 and notes), to curse a human being is to show contempt for God (see Ge 9:6 and note).

▲ 3:11–12 Only a renewed heart can produce pure speech.

TWO KINDS OF WISDOM

[13]Who is wise and understanding among you? Let them show it [t] by their good life, by deeds [u] done in the humility that comes from wisdom. [14]But if you harbor bitter envy and selfish ambition [v] in your hearts, do not boast about it or deny the truth. [w] [15]Such "wisdom" does not come down from heaven [x] but is earthly, unspiritual, demonic. [y] [16]For where you have envy and selfish ambition, [z] there you find disorder and every evil practice.

[17]But the wisdom that comes from heaven [a] is first of all pure; then peace-loving, [b] considerate, submissive, full of mercy [c] and good fruit, impartial and sincere. [d] [18]Peacemakers [e] who sow in peace reap a harvest of righteousness. [f]

SUBMIT YOURSELVES TO GOD

4 What causes fights and quarrels [g] among you? Don't they come from your desires that battle [h] within you? [2]You desire but do not have, so you kill. [i] You covet but you cannot get what you want, so you quarrel and fight. You do not have because you do not ask God. [3]When you ask, you do not receive, [j] because you ask with wrong motives, [k] that you may spend what you get on your pleasures.

[4]You adulterous [l] people, don't you know that friendship with the world [m] means enmity against God? [n] Anyone who chooses to be a friend of the world becomes an enemy of God. [o] [5]Or do you think Scripture says without reason that he jealously longs for the spirit he has caused to dwell in us? [a p] [6]But he gives us more grace. That is why Scripture says:

> "God opposes the proud
>   but shows favor to the humble and oppressed." [b q]

[7]Submit yourselves, then, to God. Resist the devil, [r] and he will flee from you. [8]Come near to God and he will come near to you. [s] Wash your hands, [t] you sinners, and purify your hearts, [u] you double-minded. [v] [9]Grieve, mourn and wail. Change your laughter to mourning and your joy to gloom. [w] [10]Humble yourselves before the Lord, and he will lift you up. [x]

[11]Brothers and sisters, do not slander one another. [y] Anyone who speaks against a brother or sister or judges them [z] speaks against the law [a] and judges it. When you judge the law, you are not keeping it, [b] but sitting in judgment on it. [12]There is only one Lawgiver and Judge, [c] the one who is able to save and destroy. [d] But you—who are you to judge your neighbor? [e]

BOASTING ABOUT TOMORROW

[13]Now listen, [f] you who say, "Today or tomorrow we will go to this or that city, spend a

---

[a] 5   Or *that the spirit he caused to dwell in us envies intensely;* or *that the Spirit he caused to dwell in us longs jealously*   [b] 6   Prov. 3:34

Cross references

3:13 [t] Jas 2:18
[u] S 1Pe 2:12
3:14 [v] ver 16;
2Co 12:20 [w] Jas 5:19
3:15 [x] ver 17;
Jas 1:17 [y] 1Ti 4:1
3:16 [z] ver 14;
Gal 5:20,21
3:17 [a] 1Co 2:6;
Jas 1:17 [b] Heb 12:11
[c] Lk 6:36 [d] Ro 12:9
3:18 [e] Mt 5:9;
S Ro 14:19 [f] Pr 11:18;
Isa 32:17; Hos 10:12;
Php 1:11
4:1 [g] Tit 3:9
[h] S Ro 7:23
4:2 [i] Mt 5:21,22;
Jas 5:6; 1Jn 3:15
4:3 [j] Ps 18:41;
S Mt 7:7 [k] Ps 66:18;
1Jn 3:22; 5:14
4:4 [l] Isa 54:5;
Jer 3:20; Hos 2:2-5;
3:1; 9:1 [m] S Jas 1:27
[n] Ro 8:7; 1Jn 2:15
[o] Jn 15:19
4:5 [p] 1Co 6:19
4:6 [q] Pr 3:34;
S Mt 23:12
4:7 [r] Eph 4:27; 6:11;
1Pe 5:6-9
4:8 [s] Ps 73:28;
Zec 1:3; Mal 3:7;
Heb 7:19 [t] Isa 1:16
[u] Ps 24:4; Jer 4:14
[v] Ps 119:113; Jas 1:8
4:9 [w] Lk 6:25
4:10 [x] ver 6;
Job 5:11; 1Pe 5:6
4:11 [y] Ro 1:30;
2Co 12:20; 1Pe 2:1
[z] S Mt 7:1 [a] Jas 2:8
[b] Jas 1:22
4:12 [c] Isa 33:22;
S Jas 5:9 [d] Mt 10:28
[e] S Mt 7:1
4:13 [f] Jas 5:1

Study notes

3:13 *wisdom.* See note on 1:5.

3:15 *from heaven.* From God (see 1:5; 1Co 2:6–16; see also Da 4:26 and note).

3:16 *disorder.* Cf. "God is not a God of disorder but of peace" (1Co 14:33; see note there).

3:17 *impartial.* See 2:1–13; see also note on 1Ti 5:21.

[A] 3:18 *Peacemakers.* Contrast v. 16. Discord cannot produce conduct pleasing to God. Cf. Mt 5:9 and note.

4:2 *kill.* Some hold that this word is here used figuratively (cf. Mt 5:21–22) for "hate." Others hold that it should be understood straightforwardly to describe what can happen when covetous desire is sufficiently frustrated (see, e.g., Ahab's murder of Naboth, 1Ki 21:1–16; David's murder of Uriah, 2Sa 11).

[A] 4:4 *adulterous people.* Those who are spiritually unfaithful, who love the world rather than God. For spiritual adultery, see Ex 34:15 and note. *world.* See note on 1:27.

4:5 *Scripture.* The passage James had in mind is not known. *he jealously longs for the spirit he has caused to dwell in us.* God jealously longs for our faithfulness and love (see v. 4). In this case the Scripture referred to may be Ex 20:5 (see note there). Regarding the two alternative translations (see TNIV text note), the opening words of the first ("the spirit he caused to dwell in us"), if correct, would allude to God's creation of Adam (see Ge 2:7 and note). Because of the fall (Ge 3), a person's spirit "envies

intensely," but God's grace (v. 6) is able to overcome human envy. The second, if correct, refers to the Holy Spirit and makes him the subject. The Holy Spirit longs jealously for our full devotion.

4:6 See 1Pe 5:5, which also quotes Pr 3:34.

4:7–10 These verses contain ten commands, each of which is so stated in Greek that it calls for immediate action in rooting out the sinful attitude of pride.

4:7 *Resist the devil.* See Eph 6:10–20 and note; 1Pe 5:8–9.

4:8 *Wash your hands.* Before the OT priests approached God at the tabernacle, they had to wash their hands and feet at the bronze basin as a symbol of spiritual cleansing (Ex 30:17–21). For the imagery of "clean hands and a pure heart," see Ps 24:4 and note.

4:9 *Grieve, mourn and wail.* Repent.

4:10 See Mt 23:12; Lk 14:11 and note; 1Pe 5:6.

[A] 4:11 *speaks against a brother or sister . . . speaks against the law.* See note on 2:8; see also Ex 20:16 and note; Ps 15:3; 50:19–20; Pr 6:16,19 and note. To speak against a Christian brother or sister is to scorn the law of love.

4:13—5:6 Jas 4:13–17 is addressed to traveling merchants and condemns arrogance; 5:1–6 is a warning to wealthy landowners about their improper use of wealth.

4:13 ^g Pr 27:1;
Lk 12:18-20
4:14 ^h Job 7:7;
Ps 39:5; 102:3; 144:4;
Isa 2:22
4:15 ⁱ S Ac 18:21
4:16 ^j 1Co 5:6
4:17 ^k Lk 12:47;
Jn 9:41
5:1 ^l Jas 4:13;
^m Lk 6:24; 1Ti 6:9;
Jas 2:2-6; ⁿ Isa 13:6;
Eze 30:2
5:2 ^o Job 13:28;
Ps 39:11; Isa 50:9;
Mt 6:19,20
5:3 ^p ver 7,8
5:4 ^q Lev 19:13;
Jer 22:13; Mal 3:5;
^r Dt 24:15 ^s Ro 9:29
5:5 ^t Eze 16:49;
Am 6:1; Lk 16:19;
^u Jer 12:3; 25:34
5:6 ^v Jas 4:2;
^w Heb 10:38
5:7 ^x S 1Co 1:7;
^y Gal 6:9 ^z Dt 11:14;
Jer 5:24; Joel 2:23
5:8 ^a S 1Co 1:7;
^b S Ro 13:11
5:9 ^c Jas 4:11;
^d Ps 94:2; 1Co 4:5;
Jas 4:12; 1Pe 4:5;
^e Mt 24:33
5:10 ^f S Mt 5:12
5:11 ^g Mt 5:10;
^h Job 1:21,22; 2:10;
S Heb 10:36;
ⁱ Job 42:10,12-17;
^j Ex 34:6; Nu 14:18;
Ps 103:8
5:12 ^k Mt 5:34-37
5:13 ^l Ps 50:15
^m Col 3:16
5:14 ⁿ S Ac 11:30

year there, carry on business and make money." ^g ¹⁴Why, you do not even know what will happen tomorrow. What is your life? You are a mist that appears for a little while and then vanishes. ^h ¹⁵Instead, you ought to say, "If it is the Lord's will, ⁱ we will live and do this or that." ¹⁶As it is, you boast in your arrogant schemes. All such boasting is evil. ^j ¹⁷So then, if you know the good you ought to do and don't do it, you sin. ^k

WARNING TO RICH OPPRESSORS

5 Now listen, ^l you rich people, ^m weep and wail ⁿ because of the misery that is coming on you. ²Your wealth has rotted, and moths have eaten your clothes. ^o ³Your gold and silver are corroded. Their corrosion will testify against you and eat your flesh like fire. You have hoarded wealth in the last days. ^p ⁴Look! The wages you failed to pay the workers ^q who mowed your fields are crying out against you. The cries ^r of the harvesters have reached the ears of the Lord Almighty. ^s ⁵You have lived on earth in luxury and self-indulgence. You have fattened yourselves ^t in the day of slaughter. ^a ^u ⁶You have condemned and murdered ^v the innocent one, ^w who was not opposing you.

PATIENCE IN SUFFERING

⁷Be patient, then, brothers and sisters, until the Lord's coming. ^x See how the farmer waits for the land to yield its valuable crop, patiently waiting ^y for the autumn and spring rains. ^z ⁸You too, be patient and stand firm, because the Lord's coming ^a is near. ^b ⁹Don't grumble against one another, brothers and sisters, ^c or you will be judged. The Judge ^d is standing at the door! ^e

¹⁰Brothers and sisters, as an example of patience in the face of suffering, take the prophets ^f who spoke in the name of the Lord. ¹¹As you know, we count as blessed ^g those who have persevered. You have heard of Job's perseverance ^h and have seen what the Lord finally brought about. ⁱ The Lord is full of compassion and mercy. ^j

¹²Above all, my brothers and sisters, do not swear—not by heaven or by earth or by anything else. All you need to say is a simple "Yes" or "No." Otherwise you will be condemned. ^k

THE PRAYER OF FAITH

¹³Is anyone among you in trouble? Let them pray. ^l Is anyone happy? Let them sing songs of praise. ^m ¹⁴Is anyone among you sick? Let them call the elders ⁿ of the church to

---

^a 5 Or *yourselves as in a day of feasting*

4:14 *mist.* Cf. "shadow" (1Ch 29:15), "breath" (Job 7:7), "cloud" (Job 7:9) and "evening shadow" (Ps 102:11).
5:1 *rich.* These (also as in 2:2,6) are not Christians, for James warns them to repent and weep because of the coming misery. Verses 1–6 are similar to OT declarations of judgment against pagan nations, interspersed in books otherwise addressed to God's people (Isa 13–23; Jer 46–51; Eze 25–32; Am 1:3—2:16; Zep 2:4–15).
5:2 *clothes.* One of the forms of wealth in the ancient world (see Jdg 14:12–13 and note on 14:12; Ac 20:33).
5:3 *corrosion.* The result of hoarding. It will both testify against and judge the selfish rich. *last days.* See notes on Ac 2:17; 1Ti 4:1; 2Ti 3:1; Heb 1:1–2; 1Jn 2:18.
5:4 *the Lord Almighty.* See notes on Ge 17:1; 1Sa 1:3.
5:5 *luxury and self-indulgence.* See Lk 16:19–31. *the day of slaughter.* The day of judgment. The wicked rich are like cattle that continue to fatten themselves on the very day they are to be slaughtered, totally unaware of their coming destruction.
5:6 *condemned.* Probably through control of the courts by the rich and powerful.
5:7–8 *Be patient.* Resist resentment and retaliation (see v. 9).
5:7 *then.* Refers back to vv. 1–6. Since the believers are suffering at the hands of the wicked rich, they are to look forward patiently to the Lord's return. *autumn and spring rains.* In Israel the autumn rain comes in October and November, soon after the grain is sown, and the spring rain comes in March and April, just prior to harvest (Dt 11:14; Jer 5:24; Hos 6:3; Joel 2:23).
5:9 *Don't grumble.* James calls for patience toward believers as well as unbelievers (vv. 7–8). *The Judge is standing at the door!* A reference to Christ's second coming (see vv.

7–8) and the judgment associated with it. The NT insistence on imminence (see Ro 13:12 and note; Heb 10:25; 1Pe 4:7; Rev 22:20) arises from the teaching that the "last days" began with the incarnation. We have been living in the "last days" (v. 3) ever since (see notes on Heb 1:1–2). The next great event in redemptive history is Christ's second coming. The NT does not say when it will take place, but its certainty is never questioned, and believers are consistently admonished to watch for it. It was in this light that James expected the imminent return of Christ.
5:10 *that as an example of patience in . . . suffering, take the prophets.* Cf. Mt 5:12; 23:31; Ac 7:52.
5:11 *Job's perseverance.* Not "patience." Job was not patient (Job 3; 12:1–3; 16:1–3; 21:4), but he persevered (Job 1:20–22; 2:9–10; 13:15). This is the only place in the NT where Job is mentioned, though Job 5:13 is quoted in 1Co 3:19.
5:12 *do not swear.* James's words are very close to Christ's (Mt 5:33–37; see note there). James is not condemning the taking of solemn oaths, such as God's before Abraham (see Heb 6:13 and note) or Jesus' before Caiaphas (Mt 26:63–64) or Paul's (Ro 1:9; 9:1). Rather, he is condemning the flippant use of God's name or a sacred object to guarantee the truth of what is spoken.
5:14 *elders.* See notes on 1Ti 3:1; 5:17. *church.* See note on Mt 16:18. *oil.* One of the best-known ancient medicines (referred to by Philo, Pliny and the physician Galen; see also Isa 1:6 and note; Lk 10:34). Some believe that James may be using the term medicinally in this passage. Others, however, regard its use here as an aid to faith, an outward sign of the healing to be brought about by God in response to "prayer offered in faith" (v. 15; see Mk 6:13 and note).

pray over them and anoint them with oil[o] in the name of the Lord. [15]And the prayer offered in faith[p] will make them well; the Lord will raise them up. If they have sinned, they will be forgiven. [16]Therefore confess your sins[q] to each other and pray for each other so that you may be healed.[r] The prayer of a righteous person is powerful and effective.[s]

[17]Elijah was a human being, even as we are.[t] He prayed earnestly that it would not rain, and it did not rain on the land for three and a half years.[u] [18]Again he prayed, and the heavens gave rain, and the earth produced its crops.[v]

[19]My brothers and sisters, if one of you should wander from the truth[w] and someone should bring them back,[x] [20]remember this: Whoever turns a sinner from the way of error will save[y] them from death and cover over a multitude of sins.[z]

5:14 [o] Ps 23:5; Isa 1:6; Mk 6:13; 16:18; Lk 10:34
5:15 [p] Jas 1:6
5:16 [q] Mt 3:6; Ac 19:18 [r] Heb 12:13; 1Pe 2:24 [s] Mt 7:7; S Jn 9:31
5:17 [t] Ac 14:15 [u] 1Ki 17:1; Lk 4:25
5:18 [v] 1Ki 18:41-45
5:19 [w] Jas 3:14 [x] S Mt 18:15
5:20 [y] S Ro 11:14 [z] 1Pe 4:8

5:17 *Elijah . . . prayed.* That Elijah prayed may be assumed from 1Ki 17:1; 18:41–46. The three and a half years (see also Lk 4:25) are probably a round number (half of seven), based on 1Ki 18:1 (see note there; cf. Rev 11:1–6 and notes).
5:19 *brothers and sisters.* See note on Ro 1:13. *wander from the truth.* The wanderer is either a professing Christian whose faith is not genuine (cf. Heb 6:4–8 and note on 6:4–6; 2Pe 2:20–22

and notes) or a sinning Christian who needs to be restored. For the former, the death spoken of in v. 20 is the "second death" (Rev 21:8); for the latter, it is physical death (cf. 1Co 11:29–32 and notes). See note on 1Jn 5:16.
5:20 *cover over . . . sins.* The sins of the wanderer will be forgiven by God (see Pr 10:12 and note).

C The author identifies himself as the apostle Peter (1:1), and the contents and character of the letter support his authorship (see notes on 1:12; 4:13; 5:1–2,5, 13). Moreover, the letter reflects the history and terminology of the Gospels and Acts (notably Peter's speeches). Its themes and concepts reflect Peter's experiences and his associations in the period of our Lord's earthly ministry and in the apostolic age. That he was acquainted, e.g., with Paul and his letters is made clear in 2Pe 3:15–16 (see notes there); Gal 1:18; 2:1–21 and elsewhere. Coincidences in thought and expression with Paul's writings are therefore not surprising.

From the beginning, 1 Peter was recognized as authoritative and as the work of the apostle Peter. The earliest reference to it may be 2Pe 3:1 (see note there), where Peter himself refers to a former letter he had written. 1 Clement (A.D. 95) seems to indicate acquaintance with 1 Peter. Polycarp, a disciple of the apostle John, makes use of 1 Peter in his letter to the Philippians. The author of the Gospel of Truth (140–150) was acquainted with 1 Peter. Eusebius (fourth century) indicated that it was universally received.

The letter was explicitly ascribed to Peter by that group of church fathers whose testimonies appear in the attestation of so many of the genuine NT writings, namely, Irenaeus (A.D. 140–203), Tertullian (150–222), Clement of Alexandria (155–215) and Origen (185–253). It is thus clear that Peter's authorship of the book has early and strong support.

Nevertheless, some claim that the idiomatic Greek of this letter is beyond Peter's competence. But in his time Aramaic, Hebrew and Greek were used in the Holy Land, and he may well have been acquainted with more than one language. That he was not a professionally trained scribe (Ac 4:13) does not mean that he was unacquainted with Greek; in fact, as a Galilean fisherman he in all likelihood did use it. Even if he had not known it in the earliest days of the church, he may have acquired it as an important aid to his apostolic ministry in the decades that intervened between that time and the writing of 1 Peter.

It is true, however, that the Greek of 1 Peter is good, literary Greek, and even though Peter could no doubt speak Greek, as so many in the Mediterranean world could, it is unlikely that he would write such polished Greek. It is precisely at this point that Peter's remark in 5:12 (see note there) concerning Silas may be significant. Here the apostle claims that he wrote "with the help of" (more lit. "through" or "by means of") Silas. This phrase cannot refer merely to Silas as a letter carrier. Thus Silas was the intermediate agent in writing. Some have claimed that Silas's qualifications for recording Peter's letter in literary Greek are found in Ac 15:22–29. It is known that a secretary in those days often composed documents in good Greek for those who did not have the language facility to do so. Thus in 1 Peter it is possible that Silas's Greek may be seen, while in 2 Peter it may be Peter's rough Greek that appears.

Some also maintain that the book reflects a situation that did not exist until after Peter's death, suggesting that the persecution referred to in 4:14–16; 5:8–9 is descriptive of Domitian's reign (A.D. 81–96). However, the situation that was developing in Nero's time (54–68) is just as adequately described by those verses.

The book can be satisfactorily dated in the early 60s. It cannot be placed earlier than 60 since it shows familiarity with Paul's Prison Letters (e.g., Colossians and Ephesians, which are to be dated no earlier than 60): Compare 1:1–3 with Eph 1:1–3; 2:18 with Col 3:22; 3:1–6 with Eph 5:22–24. Furthermore, it cannot be dated later than 67/68, since Peter was martyred during Nero's reign.

PLACE OF WRITING

In 5:13 Peter indicates that he was "in Babylon" when he wrote 1 Peter. Among the interpretations that have been suggested are that he was writing from (1) Egyptian Babylon, which was a military post, (2) Mesopotamian Babylon, (3) Jerusalem or (4) Rome. Peter may well be using the name Babylon symbolically, as it seems to be used in the book of Revelation (see Rev 14:8; 17:9–10 and notes). Tradition connects him in the latter part of his life with Rome, and certain early writers held that 1 Peter was written there. On the other hand, it is pointed out by some that (1) Babylon is known to have existed in the first century as a small town on the Euphrates; (2) there is no evidence that the term Babylon was used figuratively to refer to Rome until Revelation was written (c. A.D. 95); and (3) the context of 5:13 does not appear to be figurative or cryptic.

RECIPIENTS

See note on 1:1.

THEMES

Although 1 Peter is a short letter, it touches on various doctrines and has much to say about Christian life and duties. It is not surprising that different readers have found it to have different principal themes. For example, it has been characterized as a letter of separation, of suffering and persecution, of suffering and glory, of hope, of pilgrimage, of courage, and as a letter dealing with the true grace of God. Peter says that he has written "encouraging you and testifying that this is the true grace of God" (5:12). This is a definitive general description of the letter, but it does not exclude the recognition of numerous subordinate and contributory themes. The letter includes a series of exhortations (imperatives) that run from 1:13 to 5:11.

OUTLINE

    I. Greetings (1:1–2)
    II. Praise to God for His Grace and Salvation (1:3–12)
    III. Exhortations to Holiness of Life (1:13—5:11)
       A. The Requirement of Holiness (1:13—2:3)
       B. The Position of Believers (2:4–12)
          1. A spiritual house (2:4–8)
          2. A chosen people (2:9–10)
          3. Foreigners and strangers (2:11–12)
       C. Submission to Authority (2:13—3:7)
          1. Submission to rulers (2:13–17)
          2. Submission to masters (2:18–20)
          3. Christ's example of submission (2:21–25)
          4. Submission of wives to husbands (3:1–6)
          5. The corresponding duty of husbands (3:7)
       D. Duties of All (3:8–17)
       E. Christ's Example (3:18—4:6)
       F. Conduct in View of the End of All Things (4:7–11)
       G. Conduct of Those Who Suffer for Christ (4:12–19)
       H. Conduct of Elders (5:1–4)
       I. Conduct of the Young (5:5–11)
    IV. The Purpose of the Letter (5:12)
    V. Final Greetings and Benediction (5:13–14)

1:1 *a* 2Pe 1:1
b Mt 24:22
c S Heb 11:13
d S Jas 1:1 *e* Ac 2:9;
18:2 *f* S Ac 16:6
g Ac 16:7
1:2 *h* Ro 8:29
i 2Th 2:13 *j* ver 14,22
k Heb 10:22; 12:24
l S Ro 1:7
1:3 *m* 2Co 1:3;
Eph 1:3 *n* Tit 3:5
o ver 23; S Jn 1:13
p ver 13,21; S Heb 3:6
q 1Co 15:20; 1Pe 3:21
1:4 *r* S Ac 20:32;
S Ro 8:17 *s* 1Pe 5:4
t Col 1:5; 2Ti 4:8
1:5 *u* 1Sa 2:9;
Jn 10:28 *v* S Ro 11:14
w S Ro 8:18
1:6 *x* Ro 5:2
y 1Pe 5:10 *z* Jas 1:2;
1Pe 4:12
1:7 *a* Job 23:10;
Ps 66:10; Pr 17:3;
Isa 48:10 *b* Jas 1:3
c 2Co 4:17 *d* ver 13;
S 1Th 2:19; 1Pe 4:13
1:8 *e* Jn 20:29
1:9 *f* Ro 6:22
1:10 *g* S Mt 26:24
h ver 13 *i* S Mt 13:17
1:11 *j* S Ac 16:7;
2Pe 1:21 *k* S Mt 26:24

Peter, an apostle of Jesus Christ, *a*

To God's elect, *b* exiles *c* scattered *d* throughout the provinces of Pontus, *e* Galatia, *f* Cappadocia, Asia and Bithynia, *g* 2who have been chosen according to the foreknowledge *h* of God the Father, through the sanctifying work of the Spirit, *i* to be obedient *j* to Jesus Christ and sprinkled with his blood: *k*

Grace and peace be yours in abundance. *l*

PRAISE TO GOD FOR A LIVING HOPE

3Praise be to the God and Father of our Lord Jesus Christ! *m* In his great mercy *n* he has given us new birth *o* into a living hope *p* through the resurrection of Jesus Christ from the dead, *q* 4and into an inheritance *r* that can never perish, spoil or fade. *s* This inheritance is kept in heaven for you, *t* 5who through faith are shielded by God's power *u* until the coming of the salvation *v* that is ready to be revealed *w* in the last time. 6In all this you greatly rejoice, *x* though now for a little while *y* you may have had to suffer grief in all kinds of trials. *z* 7These have come so that your faith—of greater worth than gold, which perishes even though refined by fire *a*—may be proved genuine *b* and may result in praise, glory and honor *c* when Jesus Christ is revealed. *d* 8Though you have not seen him, you love him; and even though you do not see him now, you believe in him *e* and are filled with an inexpressible and glorious joy, 9for you are receiving the end result of your faith, the salvation of your souls. *f*

10Concerning this salvation, the prophets, who spoke *g* of the grace that was to come to you, *h* searched intently and with the greatest care, *i* 11trying to find out the time and circumstances to which the Spirit of Christ *j* in them was pointing when he predicted *k* the sufferings of Christ and the glories that would follow. 12It was revealed to them that they

---

1:1 *Peter.* See Introduction: Author and Date; see also notes on Mt 16:18; Jn 1:42. *apostle.* See notes on Mk 6:30; 1Co 1:1; Heb 3:1. *elect.* See note on Eph 1:4. *exiles.* People temporarily residing on earth but whose home is in heaven (cf. 1Ch 29:15; Ps 39:12 and note; Heb 13:14). *scattered throughout...Pontus...Bithynia.* Jewish and Gentile Christians scattered throughout much of Asia Minor (see map, p. 1869). People from this area were in Jerusalem on the day of Pentecost (see Ac 2:9–11 and map, p. 1837). Paul preached and taught in some of these provinces (see, e.g., Ac 16:6; 18:23 and notes; 19:10,26).

1:2 *chosen.* See note on Eph 1:4. *foreknowledge.* See note on Ro 8:29. *Father...Spirit...Jesus Christ.* All three persons of the Trinity (see note on Mt 28:19) are involved in the redemption of the elect. *sanctifying work.* See notes on 1Co 1:2; 2Th 2:13. The order of the terms employed suggests that the sanctifying work of the Spirit referred to here is the influence of the Spirit that draws one from sin toward holiness. Peter says it is "for" (or "to") obedience and sprinkling of Christ's blood, i.e., the Spirit's sanctifying leads to obedient, saving faith and cleansing from sin (see note on 1Co 7:14). *obedient to Jesus Christ.* God's choice is designed to bring this about. *sprinkled with his blood.* The benefits of Christ's redemption are applied to his people (cf. Ex 24:4–8; Isa 52:15; Heb 9:11–14,18–28). *Grace and peace.* See note on Ro 1:7.

1:3 *Praise be to the God and Father of our Lord Jesus Christ!* See Eph 1:3 and note. *Lord Jesus Christ.* See note on 1Th 1:1. *mercy.* See Ro 9:22–23; Tit 3:5 and notes. *new birth.* See Jn 3:3–8 and note on 3:3. *living hope.* In spite of the frequent suffering and persecution mentioned in this letter (v. 6; 2:12,18–25; 3:13–18; 4:1,4,12–19; 5:1,7–10), hope is such a key thought in it (the word itself is used here and in vv. 13,21; 3:5,15) that it may be called a letter of hope in the midst of suffering (see Introduction: Themes). In the Bible, hope is not wishful thinking but a firm conviction, much like faith that is directed toward the future (see note on Eph 1:18). *resurrection of Jesus Christ.* Secures for his people their new birth and the hope that they will be resurrected just as he was (see 1Co 15:20–23 and notes on 15:20,23).

1:4 *into an inheritance.* Believers are born again not only to a hope but also to the inheritance that is the substance of that

hope. The inheritance is eternal—in its essence (it is not subject to decay) and in its preservation (it is divinely kept for us). See Heb 9:15 and note.

1:5 *through faith...by God's power.* There are two sides to the perseverance of Christians. They are shielded (1) by God's power and (2) by their own faith. Thus they are never kept contrary to their will nor apart from God's activity. *salvation.* See note on 2Ti 1:9. The Bible speaks of salvation as (1) past—when a person first believes (see, e.g., Tit 3:5), (2) present—the continuing process of salvation, or sanctification (see vv. 2,9 and note on v. 2; Lev 11:44 and note; 1Co 1:18) and (3) future—when Christ returns and salvation, or sanctification, is completed through glorification (here; see also Ro 8:23,30; 13:11; Heb 9:28; Jas 1:21 and notes).

1:7 *that your faith...may be proved genuine.* See Ro 5:3; Jas 1:2–4. Not only is the faith itself precious, but Peter's words indicate that the trial of faith is also valuable. Believers will share in the "praise, glory and honor" of God (see 5:4; 1Co 4:5).

1:8 *though you do not see him now, you believe.* Similar to Jesus' saying in Jn 20:29, on an occasion when Peter was present.

1:9 *souls.* Implies the whole person. Peter is not excluding the glorified body from heaven.

1:10 *prophets...searched intently.* Inspiration (see 2Pe 1:21 and note) did not always bestow omniscience. The prophets probably did not always understand the full significance of all the words they spoke (see v. 11). *grace that was to come to you.* The "salvation" they were already experiencing (see also v. 9). For the "grace" of ultimate redemption, see v. 13 and note.

1:11 *Spirit of Christ.* The Holy Spirit is called this because Christ sent him (see Jn 16:7) and ministered through him (see Lk 4:14,18). *the sufferings of Christ and the glories.* A theme running through the Bible (see, e.g., Ps 22; Isa 52:13—53:12; Zec 9:9–10; 13:7; Mt 16:21–27; 17:22–23; 20:18–19; Lk 24:26,46; Jn 2:19; Ac 3:17–21; Php 2:5–11; 1Ti 3:16; cf. Lk 9:26; 21:27), and a basic concept in this letter (vv. 18–21; 3:17–22; 4:12–16; 5:1,4, 9–10). Those who are united to Christ will also, after suffering, enter into glory. And they will benefit in the midst of their present sufferings from his having already entered into glory (3:21–22).

were not serving themselves but you,[l] when they spoke of the things that have now been told you by those who have preached the gospel to you[m] by the Holy Spirit sent from heaven.[n] Even angels long to look into these things.

BE HOLY

13 Therefore, with minds that are alert and fully sober,[o] set your hope[p] on the grace to be brought to you[q] when Jesus Christ is revealed at his coming.[r] 14 As obedient[s] children, do not conform[t] to the evil desires you had when you lived in ignorance.[u] 15 But just as he who called you is holy, so be holy in all you do;[v] 16 for it is written: "Be holy, because I am holy."[a] [w]

17 Since you call on a Father[x] who judges each person's work[y] impartially,[z] live out your time as foreigners[a] here in reverent fear.[b] 18 For you know that it was not with perishable things such as silver or gold that you were redeemed[c] from the empty way of life[d] handed down to you from your ancestors, 19 but with the precious blood[e] of Christ, a lamb[f] without blemish or defect.[g] 20 He was chosen before the creation of the world,[h] but was revealed in these last times[i] for your sake. 21 Through him you believe in God,[j] who raised him from the dead[k] and glorified him,[l] and so your faith and hope[m] are in God.

22 Now that you have purified[n] yourselves by obeying[o] the truth so that you have sincere love for each other, love one another deeply,[p] from the heart.[b] 23 For you have been born again,[q] not of perishable seed, but of imperishable,[r] through the living and enduring word of God.[s] 24 For,

"All people are like grass,
    and all their glory is like the flowers of the field;
the grass withers and the flowers fall,
25   but the word of the Lord endures forever."[c] [t]

And this is the word that was preached to you.

a 16 Lev. 11:44,45; 19:2   b 22 Some early manuscripts *from a pure heart*   c 25 Isaiah 40:6-8 (see Septuagint)

1:12 [l] S Ro 4:24
[m] ver 25 [n] S Lk 24:49
1:13 [o] S Ac 24:25
[p] ver 3,21; S Heb 3:6
[q] ver 10 [r] ver 7;
S 1Co 1:7
1:14 [s] ver 2,22
[t] Ro 12:2 [u] Eph 4:18
1:15 [v] Isa 35:8;
1Th 4:7; 1Jn 3:3
1:16 [w] Lev 11:44,45;
19:2; 20:7
1:17 [x] S Mt 6:9
[y] S Mt 16:27
[z] S Ac 10:34
[a] S Heb 11:13
[b] Heb 12:28
1:18 [c] S Mt 20:28;
S 1Co 6:20 [d] Gal 4:3
1:19 [e] S Ro 3:25
[f] S Jn 1:29 [g] Ex 12:5
1:20 [h] Eph 1:4;
S Mt 25:34 [i] Heb 9:26
1:21 [j] Ro 4:24; 10:9
[k] S Ac 2:24 [l] Php 2:7-9; S Heb 3:6 [m] ver 3,13;
S Heb 3:6
1:22 [n] Jas 4:8
[o] ver 2,14
[p] S Jn 13:34;
S Ro 12:10
1:23 [q] ver 3;
S Jn 1:13 [r] Jn 1:13
[s] S Heb 4:12
1:25 [t] Isa 40:6-8;
S Jas 1:10,11

1:12 *Holy Spirit sent from heaven.* By Christ, on the day of Pentecost (see Ac 2:33), at which Peter was present. God the Father also sent the Spirit (see Jn 14:16,26).

1:13 *with minds that are alert.* A graphic call for mental action. In the language of the first century it meant that the readers should literally gather up their long, flowing garments and be ready for physical action (cf. Jer 1:17 and note). *set your hope on.* The first of a long series of exhortations (actually imperatives) that end at 5:11 (see Introduction: Themes). *grace to be brought to you.* The final state of complete blessedness and deliverance from sin. Peter later indicates that a major purpose of this letter is to encourage and testify regarding "the true grace of God" (5:12; cf. also 5:10).

1:14 *children.* Christians, born into the family of God (see v. 23), are children of their heavenly Father (v. 17) and can pray, "Our Father in heaven" (Mt 6:9). Believers are also described as being adopted into God's family (see Ro 8:15 and note).

🔺 **1:16** *Be holy, because I am holy.* To be holy is to be set apart—separated from sin and impurity and set apart to God (see notes on Ex 3:5; Lev 11:44; Ro 6:22; 1Co 1:2). The complete moral perfection of God, whose eyes are too pure to look with favor on evil (Hab 1:13), should move his people to strive for moral purity. 1 Peter is a letter of practical earnestness, filled with exhortations and encouragements.

🔺 **1:17** *impartially.* See Ac 10:34 and note. *foreigners.* See note on v. 1. *reverent fear.* Not terror, but wholesome reverence and respect for God, which is the basis for all godly living (cf. Pr 1:7 and note).

🔺 **1:18** *redeemed.* In the Bible, to redeem means to free someone from something bad by paying a penalty or a ransom (see, e.g., Ex 21:30 and note; see also Ex 13:13). Likewise, in the Greek world slaves could be redeemed by the payment of a price, either by someone else or by the slave himself (cf. Ro 3:24 and note). Similarly, Jesus redeems believers from the "curse of the law" (Gal 3:13) and "all wickedness" (Tit 2:14). The ransom price is not silver or gold but Christ's blood (see v. 19;

Eph 1:7 and note; Rev 5:9), i.e., his death (see Mt 20:28; Heb 9:15 and notes) or Christ himself (Gal 3:13). The result is the "forgiveness of sins" (Col 1:14) and "justification" (Ro 3:24; see note there). *empty way of life ... from your ancestors.* Some maintain that the recipients must have been pagans because the NT stresses the emptiness of pagan life (see Ro 1:21; Eph 4:17 and note). Others think they were Jews since Jews were traditionalists who stressed the influence of the father as teacher in the home. In the light of the context of the whole letter, probably both Jews and Gentiles are addressed.

🔺 **1:19** *lamb.* The OT sacrifices were types (foreshadowings) of Christ, depicting the ultimate and only effective sacrifice. Thus Christ is the Passover lamb (see 1Co 5:7 and note) who takes away the sin of the world (see Jn 1:29 and note). *without blemish or defect.* See Heb 9:14 and note; see also Introduction to Leviticus: Theological Themes.

1:20 *chosen.* Some think the Greek for this word means "foreknown," i.e., God knew before creation that it would be necessary for Christ to redeem human beings (cf. Rev 13:8), but he has revealed Christ in these last times. Others interpret the word as meaning that in eternity past God chose Christ as Redeemer. *these last times.* See note on Jas 5:3.

1:22 *sincere love.* See Ro 12:9 and note. *love one another.* A command no doubt based on Jn 13:34–35 (see notes there). See also 1Th 4:9–10 (and note on 4:9), where, like Peter, Paul commends his readers for their love of fellow believers and then urges them to love still more. *deeply.* Fervently.

🔺 **1:23** *born again ... through the ... word of God.* The new birth comes about through the direct action of the Holy Spirit (see Tit 3:5 and note), but the word of God also plays an important role (see Jas 1:18), for it presents the gospel to sinners and calls on them to repent and believe in Christ (see v. 25). *perishable seed ... imperishable.* In this context the seed is doubtless the word of God, which is imperishable, living and enduring.

1:25 *the word ... endures forever.* The main point of the quotation here.

2:1 ^{u} S Eph 4:22
^{v} S Jas 4:11
2:2 ^{w} 1Co 3:2;
Heb 5:12,13
^{x} Eph 4:15,16
2:3 ^{y} Ps 34:8;
Heb 6:5
2:4 ^{z} ver 7 ^{a} Isa 42:1
2:5 ^{b} Pr 9:1; 1Co 3:9;
Eph 2:20-22 ^{c} 1Ti 3:15
^{d} ver 9; Ex 19:6;
Isa 61:6; Rev 1:6; 5:10;
20:6 ^{e} Php 4:18;
Heb 13:15
2:6 ^{f} Eph 2:20
^{g} Isa 28:16;
Ro 9:32,33; 10:11
2:7 ^{h} 2Co 2:16 ^{i} ver 4
^{j} Ps 118:22; S Ac 4:11
2:8 ^{k} Isa 8:14;
S Lk 2:34 ^{l} Ro 9:22
2:9 ^{m} Dt 10:15;
1Sa 12:22 ^{n} ver 5
^{o} Ex 19:6; Dt 7:6;
Isa 62:12 ^{p} S Ac 26:18
2:10 ^{r} Hos 1:9,10;
2:23; Ro 9:25,26

2 Therefore, rid yourselves ^{u} of all malice and all deceit, hypocrisy, envy, and slander ^{v} of every kind. ^{2}Like newborn babies, crave pure spiritual milk, ^{w} so that by it you may grow up ^{x} in your salvation, ^{3}now that you have tasted that the Lord is good. ^{y}

THE LIVING STONE AND A CHOSEN PEOPLE

^{4}As you come to him, the living Stone ^{z}—rejected by human beings but chosen by God ^{a} and precious to him— ^{5}you also, like living stones, are being built ^{b} into a spiritual house $^{a c}$ to be a holy priesthood, ^{d} offering spiritual sacrifices acceptable to God through Jesus Christ. ^{e} ^{6}For in Scripture it says:

> "See, I lay a stone in Zion,
> a chosen and precious cornerstone, ^{f}
> and the one who trusts in him
> will never be put to shame." $^{b g}$

^{7}Now to you who believe, this stone is precious. But to those who do not believe, ^{h}

> "The stone the builders rejected ^{i}
> has become the cornerstone," $^{c j}$

^{8}and,

> "A stone that causes people to stumble
> and a rock that makes them fall." $^{d k}$

They stumble because they disobey the message—which is also what they were destined for. ^{l}

^{9}But you are a chosen people, ^{m} a royal priesthood, ^{n} a holy nation, ^{o} God's special possession, ^{p} that you may declare the praises of him who called you out of darkness into his wonderful light. ^{q} ^{10}Once you were not a people, but now you are the people of God; ^{r} once you had not received mercy, but now you have received mercy.

---

^{a} 5 Or *into a temple of the Spirit* ^{b} 6 Isaiah 28:16 ^{c} 7 Psalm 118:22 ^{d} 8 Isaiah 8:14

2:1 *Therefore.* Connects the exhortations that follow with 1:23–25; compare "born again" (1:23) with "newborn babies" (2:2).
2:2 *crave.* The unrestrained hunger of a healthy baby provides an example of the kind of eager desire for spiritual food that ought to mark the believer. *spiritual milk.* Probably referring to God's word (1:23,25). The author is speaking figuratively. Milk is not to be understood here as in 1Co 3:2; Heb 5:12–14—in unfavorable contrast to solid food—but as an appropriate nourishment for babies. *grow up.* The Greek for this phrase is the standard term for the desirable growth of children (cf. 2Pe 3:18).
2:3 *have tasted.* The tense of the Greek verb used here suggests that an initial act of tasting is referred to. Since this taste has proved satisfactory, the believers are urged to long for additional spiritual food.
2:4 *living Stone.* Christ (see vv. 6–8 and TNIV text notes; cf. Mt 21:42; Mk 12:10–11; Lk 20:17; Ac 4:11; Ro 9:33). The Stone is living in that it is personal. Furthermore, he is a life-giving Stone. Christ as the Son of God has life in himself (see Jn 1:4; 5:26 and notes). See also "living water" (Jn 4:10–14 [see note on 4:10]; 7:38), "living bread" (Jn 6:51 [see note on 6:35]) and "living way" (Heb 10:20). *rejected by human beings but chosen by God.* Peter repeatedly makes a contrast in Acts between the hostility of unbelievers toward Jesus and God's exaltation of him (Ac 2:22–36; 3:13–15; 4:10–11; 10:39–42).
A **2:5** *living stones.* Believers derive their life from Christ, who is the original living Stone, the "life-giving spirit" (1Co 15:45) to whom they have come (v. 4). These references to stones may reflect Jesus' words to Peter in Mt 16:18 (see note there). *spiritual house.* The house is spiritual in a metaphorical sense, but also in that it is formed and indwelt by the Spirit of God. Every stone in the house has been made alive by the Holy Spirit, sent by the exalted living Stone, Jesus Christ (cf. Ac 2:33). The OT temple provides the background of this passage (Jn 2:19; 1Co 3:16; Eph 2:19–22 and notes). *holy priesthood.* The whole body of believers. As priests, believers are to (1) reflect

the holiness of God and that of their high priest (see 1:15; Heb 7:26; 10:10 and note), (2) offer spiritual sacrifices (here), (3) intercede for others before God and (4) represent God before them. *spiritual sacrifices.* The NT refers to a variety of offerings: bodies offered to God (Ro 12:1), offerings of money or material goods (Php 4:18; Heb 13:16), sacrifices of praise to God (Heb 13:15) and sacrifices of doing good (Heb 13:16). *acceptable to God.* Through the work of our Mediator, Jesus Christ (cf. Jn 14:6). Believers are living stones that make up a spiritual temple in which, as a holy priesthood, they offer up spiritual sacrifices.
2:6 *precious cornerstone.* See Ps 118:22 and note; Mt 21:42; Mk 12:10; Lk 20:17; Ac 4:11 and note. This is an obvious reference to Christ, as vv. 6b–8 make clear. The cornerstone, which determined the design and orientation of the building, was the most significant stone in the structure. The picture that Peter creates is of a structure made up of believers (living stones, v. 5), the design and orientation of which are all in keeping with Christ, the cornerstone. *the one who trusts in him.* Two attitudes toward the cornerstone are evident: (1) Some trust in him; (2) others reject him (v. 7) and, as a result, stumble and fall (v. 8).
2:8 *what they were destined for.* Some see here an indication that some people are destined to fall and be lost. Others say that unbelievers are destined to be lost because God in his foreknowledge (cf. 1:2 and note) saw them as unbelievers. Still others hold that Peter means that unbelief is destined to result in eternal destruction.
2:9 *chosen people.* See Eph 1:4 and note; Isa 43:10,20; 44:1–2. As Israel was called God's chosen people in the OT, so in the NT believers are designated as chosen, or elect. *royal priesthood.* See notes on v. 5; Ex 19:6; cf. Isa 61:6. *holy nation.* Cf. Dt 28:9. *God's special possession.* See Ex 19:5 and note. Though once not the people of God, they are now the recipients of God's mercy (cf. Hos 1:6–10 and note on 1:10; Ro 9:25–26 and note; 10:19). *declare the praises of him.* See Isa 43:21; Ac 2:11.
2:10 See notes on Hos 1:6,9; 2:1,22; Ro 9:25–26. In Hosea is

LIVING GODLY LIVES IN A PAGAN SOCIETY

[11]Dear friends,[s] I urge you, as foreigners and exiles,[t] to abstain from sinful desires,[u] which war against your soul.[v] [12]Live such good lives among the pagans that, though they accuse you of doing wrong, they may see your good deeds[w] and glorify God[x] on the day he visits us.

[13]Submit yourselves for the Lord's sake to every human authority:[y] whether to the emperor, as the supreme authority, [14]or to governors, who are sent by him to punish those who do wrong[z] and to commend those who do right.[a] [15]For it is God's will[b] that by doing good you should silence the ignorant talk of the foolish.[c] [16]Live as free people,[d] but do not use your freedom as a cover-up for evil;[e] live as God's slaves.[f] [17]Show proper respect to everyone, love your fellow believers,[g] fear God, honor the emperor.[h]

[18]Slaves, in reverent fear of God submit yourselves to your masters,[i] not only to those who are good and considerate,[j] but also to those who are harsh. [19]For it is commendable if you bear up under the pain of unjust suffering because you are conscious of God.[k] [20]But how is it to your credit if you receive a beating for doing wrong and endure it? But if you suffer for doing good and you endure it, this is commendable before God.[l] [21]To this[m] you were called,[n] because Christ suffered for you,[o] leaving you an example,[p] that you should follow in his steps.

> [22]"He committed no sin,[q]
> and no deceit was found in his mouth."[a][r]

[23]When they hurled their insults at him,[s] he did not retaliate; when he suffered, he made no threats.[t] Instead, he entrusted himself[u] to him who judges justly.[v] [24]"He himself bore our sins"[w] in his body on the cross,[x] so that we might die to sins[y] and live for righteous-

[a] 22 Isaiah 53:9

2:11 [s] S 1Co 10:14; [t] S Heb 11:13; [u] Ro 13:14; Gal 5:16; [v] Jas 4:1
2:12 [w] Php 2:15; Tit 2:8; S Tit 2:14; 1Pe 3:16 [x] S Mt 9:8
2:13 [y] Ro 13:1; Tit 3:1
2:14 [z] Ro 13:4; [a] Ro 13:3
2:15 [b] 1Pe 3:17; 4:19; [c] S ver 12
2:16 [d] S Jn 8:32; [e] Gal 5:13 [f] S Ro 6:22
2:17 [g] S Ro 12:10; [h] Pr 24:21; Ro 13:7
2:18 [i] S Eph 6:5; [j] Jas 3:17
2:19 [k] 1Pe 3:14,17
2:20 [l] 1Pe 3:17
2:21 [m] S Ac 14:22; Php 1:29; 1Pe 3:9; [n] S Ro 8:28 [o] 1Pe 3:18; 4:1,13 [p] S Mt 11:29; 16:24
2:22 [q] S 2Co 5:21; [r] Isa 53:9
2:23 [s] Heb 12:3; 1Pe 3:9 [t] Isa 53:7; [u] Lk 23:46 [v] Ps 9:4
2:24 [w] Isa 53:4,11; Heb 9:28 [x] S Ac 5:30; [y] S Ro 6:2

Israel who is not God's people; in Romans it is the Gentiles to whom Paul applies Hosea's words; in 1 Peter the words are applied to both.

2:11 *foreigners and exiles.* See note on 1:1. As foreigners and exiles on earth, whose citizenship is in heaven, they are to be separated from the corruption of the world, not yielding to its destructive sinful desires.

2:12 *see your good deeds.* Deeds that can be seen to be good (cf. Mt 5:16). The Greek word translated "see" refers to a careful watching, over a period of time. The pagans' evaluation is not a "snap judgment." *the day he visits us.* Perhaps the day of judgment and ensuing punishment, or possibly the day when God visits a person with salvation. The believer's good life may then influence the unbeliever to repent and believe.

2:13—3:6 Peter urges that Christians submit to all legitimate authorities, whether or not the persons exercising authority are believers. The recognition of properly constituted authority is necessary for the greatest good of the largest number of people, and it is necessary to best fulfill the will of God in the world.

2:13 *every human authority.* Such authority depends on God for its existence (see Ro 13:1–2 and note on 13:1). Indirectly, when people disobey a human ruler they disobey God, who ordained the system of human government (cf. Ro 13:2). *emperor.* When Peter wrote, the emperor was the godless, brutal Nero, who ruled from A.D. 54 to 68 (see Introduction: Author and Date). Of course, obedience to the emperor must never be in violation of the law of God (to see this basic principle in action, cf. Ac 4:19; 5:29).

2:15 *silence the ignorant talk.* Good citizenship counters false charges made against Christians and thus commends the gospel to unbelievers (cf. Tit 2:7–8).

2:16 *Live as free people.* Does not authorize rebellion against constituted authority but urges believers freely to submit to God and to earthly authorities (as long as such submission does not conflict with the law of God). *as a cover-up for evil.* Genuine freedom is the freedom to serve God, a freedom exercised under law. Liberty is not license to do as we please.

2:17 *proper respect to everyone.* Because every human being bears the image of God. *fear God.* See note on 1:17.

2:18 *Slaves.* Household servants, whatever their particular training and functions. The context indicates that Peter is addressing Christian slaves. NT writers do not attack slavery as an institution (see note on Eph 6:5), but the NT contains the principles that ultimately uprooted slavery (see Phm 16). Peter's basic teachings on the subject may apply to employer-employee relations today (see Eph 6:5–8; Col 3:22–25; 1Ti 6:1–2; Tit 2:9–10).

2:19 *conscious of God.* As submission to duly constituted authority is "for the Lord's sake" (v. 13; cf. Eph 6:7–8), so one will submit to the point of suffering unjustly if it is God's will.

2:21 *To this you were called.* The patient endurance of injustice is part of God's plan for the Christian. It was an important feature of the true grace of God experienced by the readers (5:12). *Christ suffered for you.* Cf. Isa 52:13—53:12. Christ is the supreme example of suffering evil for doing good. His experience as the suffering Servant-Savior transforms the sufferings of his followers from misery into privilege (cf. Ac 5:41).

2:22 Scripture declares the sinlessness of Christ in the clearest of terms, allowing for no exception (see 1:19; Ac 3:14 and note; 2Co 5:21; Heb 4:15; 7:26; 1Jn 3:5). *no deceit.* Cf. v. 1; 3:10.

2:23 Prominent examples of our Lord's silent submission are found in Mt 27:12–14,34–44 (see also parallels in the other Gospels). *entrusted himself.* Cf. 4:19.

2:24 *bore our sins.* See Isa 53:12. Although dealing with the example set by Christ, Peter touches also on the redemptive work of Christ, which has significance far beyond that of setting an example. Peter here points to the substitutionary character of the atonement. Christ, like the sacrificial lamb of the OT, died for our sins, the innocent for the guilty (see Ro 5:6; 1Jn 2:2 and notes). *cross.* See note on Ac 5:30; see also Ac 10:39; 13:29; Gal 3:13 and note. *that we might die to sins and live for righteousness.* Cf. Ro 6:3–14. Peter stresses the bearing of the cross on our sanctification. As a result of Christ's death on the cross, believers are positionally dead to sin so that they may live new lives and present themselves to God as instruments of righteousness (see note on Ro 6:11–13). *you have been healed.* See Isa 53:5 and note; not generally viewed as a reference to physical healing, though some believe that such healing was included in the atonement (cf. Isa 53:4 and note; Mt 8:16–17). Others see spiritual healing in this passage. It is another way of asserting that Christ's death brings salvation to those who trust in him.

2:24 z Dt 32:39;
Ps 103:3; Isa 53:5;
Heb 12:13; Jas 5:16
2:25 a Isa 53:6
b S Jn 10:11 c Job 10:12
3:1 d 1Pe 2:18
e S Eph 5:22
f 1Co 7:16; 9:19
3:3 g Isa 3:18-23;
1Ti 2:9
3:4 h Ro 7:22;
Eph 3:16 i S Ro 2:29
3:5 j 1Ti 5:5
k Est 2:15
3:6 l Ge 18:12
3:7 m Eph 5:25-33;
Col 3:19
3:8 n S Ro 15:5
o S Ro 12:10
p Eph 4:2; 1Pe 5:5
3:9 q Ro 12:17;
1Th 5:15 r 1Pe 2:23
s Mt 5:44
t S 1Pe 2:21
u S Ro 8:28
v Heb 6:14
3:12 w Ps 34:12-16
3:13 x S Tit 2:14

ness; "by his wounds you have been healed." z 25For "you were like sheep going astray," a a but now you have returned to the Shepherd b and Overseer of your souls. c

3 Wives, in the same way submit yourselves d to your own husbands e so that, if any of them do not believe the word, they may be won over f without words by the behavior of their wives, 2when they see the purity and reverence of your lives. 3Your beauty should not come from outward adornment, such as elaborate hairstyles and the wearing of gold jewelry and fine clothes. g 4Rather, it should be that of your inner self, h the unfading beauty of a gentle and quiet spirit, which is of great worth in God's sight. i 5For this is the way the holy women of the past who put their hope in God j used to adorn themselves. k They submitted themselves to their own husbands, 6like Sarah, who obeyed Abraham and called him her lord. l You are her daughters if you do what is right and do not give way to fear.

7Husbands, m in the same way be considerate as you live with your wives, and treat them with respect as the weaker partner and as heirs with you of the gracious gift of life, so that nothing will hinder your prayers.

SUFFERING FOR DOING GOOD

8Finally, all of you, be like-minded, n be sympathetic, love one another, o be compassionate and humble. p 9Do not repay evil with evil q or insult with insult. r On the contrary, repay evil with blessing, s because to this t you were called u so that you may inherit a blessing. v 10For,

> "Whoever among you would love life
> 　and see good days
> must keep your tongue from evil
> 　and your lips from deceitful speech.
> 11Turn from evil and do good;
> 　seek peace and pursue it.
> 12For the eyes of the Lord are on the righteous
> 　and his ears are attentive to their prayer,
> but the face of the Lord is against those who do evil." b w

13Who is going to harm you if you are eager to do good? x 14But even if you should suf-

---

a 24,25 Isaiah 53:4,5,6 (see Septuagint)　　　b 12 Psalm 34:12-16

2:25 *Shepherd.* A concept raised here in connection with the allusion to the wandering sheep of Isa 53. The sheep had wandered from their shepherd, and to their Shepherd (Christ) they have now returned. See note on Ps 23:1; see also Jn 10:11,14 and note on Heb 13:20. *Overseer.* Christ (cf. 5:2,4; Ac 20:28). Elders are to be both shepherds and overseers, i.e., they are to look out for the welfare of the flock. These are not two separate offices or functions; the second term is a further explanation of the first.
3:1-6 Instructions to wives (cf. Ge 3:16; 1Co 11:3 and notes; Eph 5:22-24 and note on 5:22; Col 3:18; 1Ti 2:9-10; Tit 2:5).
3:1 *in the same way.* As believers are to submit to government authorities (2:13-17) and as slaves are to submit to masters (2:18-25) *submit yourselves.* The same Greek verb as is used in 2:13,18, a term that calls for submission to a recognized authority. Inferiority is not implied in this passage. The submission is one of role or function necessary for the orderly operation of the home. *the word.* The gospel message. *without words.* Believing wives are not to rely on argumentation to win their unbelieving husbands, but on the quality of their lives. "Actions speak louder than words."
3:2 *purity and reverence.* Their lives are to be marked by a moral purity that springs from reverence toward God.
3:3 *elaborate hairstyles ... jewelry.* See 1Ti 2:9 and note; extreme coiffures and gaudy exhibits of jewelry. Christian women should not rely on such extremes of adornment for beauty. *clothes.* The Greek for this word simply means "garment," but in this context expensive garments are meant (hence "fine clothes").
3:5 *holy women of the past.* The standards stated by Peter are not limited to any particular time or culture.
3:6 *called him her lord.* An expression of the submission called for in v. 1 (see Ge 18:12). *her daughters ... fear.* Christian women

become daughters of Sarah as they become like her in doing good and in not fearing any potential disaster but trusting in God (cf. Pr 3:25-27).
3:7 *weaker partner.* Not a reference to moral stamina, strength of character or mental capacity, but most likely to sheer physical strength. *heirs with you of the gracious gift of life.* Women experience the saving grace of God on equal terms with men (see Gal 3:28 and note). *hinder your prayers.* Spiritual fellowship with God and with one another, may be hindered by disregarding God's instruction concerning husband-wife relationships.
3:8-12 In 2:11-17 Peter addressed all his readers, and in 2:18-25 he spoke directly to slaves; in 3:1-6 he addressed wives and in 3:7 husbands. Now he encourages all his readers to develop virtues appropriate in their relations with others (see "all of you," v. 8).
3:8 *be like-minded.* See Ro 12:16; Php 2:2 and note. *be sympathetic.* See Ro 12:15; 1Co 12:26 and notes. *love one another.* See 1Th 4:9 and note; Heb 13:1. *be compassionate.* See Col 3:12. *humble.* See Php 2:6-8 and notes.
3:9 See 2:23; Ro 12:17-21 and notes.
3:10-12 Peter introduces this quotation from Ps 34 with the explanatory conjunction "For," showing that he views the quotation as giving reasons for obeying the exhortation of v. 9. According to the psalmist, (1) those who do such things will find life to be most gratifying (v. 10), (2) their days will be good (v. 10), (3) God's eyes will ever be on them to bless them (v. 12) and (4) God's ears will be ready to hear their prayer (v. 12).
3:12 *face of the Lord.* See Ps 13:1 and note.
3:13 *Who ... harm you ...?* As a general rule, people are not harmed for acts of kindness. This is especially true if one is an enthusiast ("eager") for doing good.
3:14 *even if you should suffer.* In the Greek, this conditional

fer for what is right, you are blessed. ʸ "Do not fear their threats; do not be frightened." ᵃᶻ
¹⁵But in your hearts revere Christ as Lord. Always be prepared to give an answer ᵃ to everyone who asks you to give the reason for the hope ᵇ that you have. But do this with gentleness and respect, ¹⁶keeping a clear conscience, ᶜ so that those who speak maliciously against your good behavior in Christ may be ashamed of their slander. ᵈ ¹⁷It is better, if it is God's will, ᵉ to suffer for doing good ᶠ than for doing evil. ¹⁸For Christ also suffered once ᵍ for sins, ʰ the righteous for the unrighteous, to bring you to God. ⁱ He was put to death in the body ʲ but made alive in the Spirit. ᵏ ¹⁹In that state ᵇ he went and made proclamation to the imprisoned spirits ˡ— ²⁰to those who were disobedient long ago when God waited patiently ᵐ in the days of Noah while the ark was being built. ⁿ In it only a few people, eight in all, ᵒ were saved ᵖ through water, ²¹and this water symbolizes baptism that now saves you ᑫ also—not the removal of dirt from the body but the pledge of a clear conscience ʳ toward God. ᶜ It saves you by the resurrection of Jesus Christ, ˢ ²²who has gone into heaven ᵗ and is at God's right hand ᵘ—with angels, authorities and powers in submission to him. ᵛ

LIVING FOR GOD

4 Therefore, since Christ suffered in his body, ʷ arm yourselves also with the same attitude, because those who have suffered in their bodies are done with sin. ˣ ²As a result, they do not live the rest of their earthly lives for evil human desires, ʸ but

ᵃ 14 Isaiah 8:12   ᵇ 18,19 Or alive in the spirit, ¹⁹in which also   ᶜ 21 Or but an appeal to God for a clear conscience

3:14 ʸ ver 17; 1Pe 2:19,20; 4:15,16
ᶻ Isa 8:12,13
3:15 ᵃ Col 4:6
ᵇ S Heb 3:6
3:16 ᶜ ver 21;
S Ac 23:1
1Pe 2:12,15
3:17 ᵉ 1Pe 2:15; 4:19
ᶠ 1Pe 2:20; 4:15,16
3:18 ᵍ S Heb 7:27
ʰ 1Pe 2:21; 4:1,13
ⁱ S Ro 5:2 ʲ Col 1:22;
1Pe 4:1 ᵏ 1Pe 4:6
3:19 ˡ 1Pe 4:6
3:20 ᵐ S Ro 2:4
ⁿ Ge 6:3,5,13,14
ᵒ Ge 8:18 ᵖ Heb 11:7
3:21 ᑫ Ac 22:16
ʳ ver 16; S Ac 23:1
ˢ 1Pe 1:3
3:22 ᵗ S Heb 4:14
ᵘ Mk 16:19
ᵛ S Mt 28:18;
S Ro 8:38
4:1 ʷ S 1Pe 2:21
ˣ S Ro 6:18
4:2 ʸ Ro 6:2; 1Pe 1:14

---

clause is the furthest removed from stating a reality. Suffering for righteousness is a remote possibility, but even if it does occur, it brings special blessing to the sufferer (see Mt 5:10–12). *Do not fear their threats.* In Isaiah's context (see TNIV text note) God's people are not to view things as unbelievers do. They are not to make worldly judgments or be afraid of the enemies of God. Instead, they are to fear God (see Isa 8:13).

3:15 *revere Christ as Lord.* An exhortation to the readers to make an inner commitment to Christ. Then they need not be speechless when called on to defend their faith. Instead, there will be a readiness to answer. *Always be prepared to give an answer.* Among other things, this requires a knowledge of God's word. *hope.* See Ro 5:5 and note. *with gentleness and respect.* The Christian is always to be a gentleman or gentle woman, even when opposed by unbelievers. Our apologetic ("answer") is always to be given with love, never in degrading terms.

3:16 *ashamed of their slander.* Because it is shown to be obviously untrue and because the believer's loving attitude puts the opponent's bitterness in a bad light.

3:18 *once.* See Heb 9:28. *the righteous for the unrighteous.* Peter, like Paul in Php 2:5–11, refers to Jesus as an example of the type of conduct that should characterize the Christian. We are to be ready to suffer for doing good (vv. 13–14,17). The thought of Christ's suffering and death, however, leads Peter to comment on what occurred after Christ's death—which leads to tangential remarks about preaching to the spirits in prison and about baptism (see vv. 19–21). *made alive in the Spirit.* Referring to the resurrection. Elsewhere the resurrection is attributed to the Father (Ac 2:32; Gal 1:1; Eph 1:20) and to the Son (Jn 10:17–18). If the TNIV text note is correct, the reference would be to Christ's own spirit, through which also he "made proclamation to the imprisoned spirits" (v. 19).

3:19–20a Three main interpretations of this passage have been suggested: 1. Some hold that in his preincarnate state Christ went and preached through Noah to the wicked generation of that time. 2. Others argue that between his death and resurrection Christ went to the prison where fallen angels are incarcerated and there preached to the angels who are said to have left their proper state and married human women during Noah's time (cf. Ge 6:1–4; 2Pe 2:4; Jude 6). The "sons of God" in Ge 6:2,4 are said to have been angels, as they are in Job 1:6; 2:1 (see TNIV text note). The message he preached to these evil angels was probably a declaration of victory. 3. Still others say that between death and

resurrection Christ went to the place of the dead and preached to the spirits of Noah's wicked contemporaries. What he proclaimed may have been the gospel, or it may have been a declaration of victory for Christ and doom for his hearers.

The weakness of the first view is that it does not relate the event to Christ's death and resurrection, as the context seems to do. The main problem with the second view is that it assumes sexual relations between angels and women, and such physical relations may not be possible for angels since they are spirits (see note on Ge 6:2). A major difficulty with the third view is that the term "spirits" is only used of human beings when qualifying terms are added. Otherwise the term seems restricted to supernatural beings.

Perhaps a more satisfactory view would be to translate: "And in that [resurrection] state, by means of (his) ascension [see v. 22, where the same verb form is used of Christ's ascension] he made proclamation to the imprisoned spirits." The latter phrase most likely refers to the disobedient spirits ("angels, authorities and powers," v. 22). Thus Christ's ascension "into heaven" (v. 22) was itself a victory proclamation to them (cf. Eph 3:10 and note).

3:21 *water symbolizes baptism.* There is a double figure here. The flood symbolizes baptism, and baptism symbolizes salvation. The flood was a figure of baptism in that in both instances the water that spoke of judgment (in the flood the death of the wicked, in baptism the death of Christ and the believer) is the water that saves. Baptism is a symbol of salvation in that it depicts Christ's death, burial and resurrection and our identification with him in these experiences (see Ro 6:4). *now saves you also.* In reality, believers are saved by what baptism symbolizes—Christ's death and resurrection. The symbol and the reality are so closely related that the symbol is sometimes used to refer to the reality (see note on Ro 6:3–4). *pledge of a clear conscience toward God.* The act of baptism is a commitment on the part of believers in all good conscience to make sure that what baptism symbolizes will become a reality in their lives. *saves you by the resurrection of Jesus Christ.* In the final analysis people are saved not by any ritual but by the supernatural power of the resurrection.

3:22 *gone into heaven.* See Ac 1:9–11. *at God's right hand.* See Heb 1:3 and note; 12:2. *angels, authorities and powers.* See vv. 19–20a; Eph 1:21; 6:12 and note.

4:1 *Therefore.* Since 3:19–22 is parenthetical, 4:1 ties directly back to 3:18. The aspect of Christ's suffering that these passages stress is suffering unjustly because one has done good. Further-

4:3 ᶻ S Eph 2:2
ᵃ S Ro 13:13
4:4 ᵇ 1Pe 3:16
4:5 ᶜ S Ac 10:42
4:6 ᵈ 1Pe 3:19
4:7 ᵉ S Ro 13:11
ᶠ S Ac 24:25
4:8 ᵍ S 1Pe 1:22
ʰ Pr 10:12; Jas 5:20
4:9 ⁱ S Ro 12:13
ʲ Php 2:14
4:10 ᵏ Ro 12:6,7
ˡ 1Co 4:2
4:11 ᵐ 1Th 2:4
ⁿ Eph 6:10 ᵒ 1Co 10:31
ᵖ S Ro 11:36
4:12 ᑫ 1Pe 1:6,7
4:13 ʳ S Mt 5:12
ˢ S 2Co 1:5 ᵗ Ro 8:17;
1Pe 1:7; 5:1
4:14 ᵘ S Jn 15:21
ᵛ Mt 5:11
4:16 ʷ Ac 5:41
4:17 ˣ Jer 25:29;
Eze 9:6; Am 3:2;
1Ti 3:15 ʸ 2Th 1:8

rather for the will of God. ³For you have spent enough time in the past ᶻ doing what pagans choose to do—living in debauchery, lust, drunkenness, orgies, carousing and detestable idolatry. ᵃ ⁴They are surprised that you do not join them in their reckless, wild living, and they heap abuse on you. ᵇ ⁵But they will have to give account to him who is ready to judge the living and the dead. ᶜ ⁶For this is the reason the gospel was preached even to those who are now dead, ᵈ so that they might be judged according to human standards in regard to the body, but live according to God in regard to the spirit.

⁷The end of all things is near. ᵉ Therefore be alert and of sober mind ᶠ so that you may pray. ⁸Above all, love each other deeply, ᵍ because love covers over a multitude of sins. ʰ ⁹Offer hospitality ⁱ to one another without grumbling. ʲ ¹⁰Each of you should use whatever gift you have received to serve others, ᵏ as faithful ˡ stewards of God's grace in its various forms. ¹¹If you speak, you should do so as one who speaks the very words of God. ᵐ If you serve, you should do so with the strength God provides, ⁿ so that in all things God may be praised ᵒ through Jesus Christ. To him be the glory and the power for ever and ever. Amen. ᵖ

SUFFERING FOR BEING A CHRISTIAN

¹²Dear friends, do not be surprised at the fiery ordeal that has come on you ᑫ to test you, as though something strange were happening to you. ¹³But rejoice ʳ inasmuch as you participate in the sufferings of Christ, ˢ so that you may be overjoyed when his glory is revealed. ᵗ ¹⁴If you are insulted because of the name of Christ, ᵘ you are blessed, ᵛ for the Spirit of glory and of God rests on you. ¹⁵If you suffer, it should not be as a murderer or thief or any other kind of criminal, or even as a meddler. ¹⁶However, if you suffer as a Christian, do not be ashamed, but praise God that you bear that name. ʷ ¹⁷For it is time for judgment to begin with God's household; ˣ and if it begins with us, what will the outcome be for those who do not obey the gospel of God? ʸ ¹⁸And,

---

more, it is physical suffering—"in his body." *arm yourselves also with the same attitude.* Believers are to be prepared also to suffer unjustly and to face such abuse with Christ's attitude—with his willingness to suffer for doing good. (For a similar principle in Paul's writings, see Php 2:5–11.) *because . . . are done with sin.* Such suffering enables believers to straighten out their priorities. Sinful desires and practices that once seemed important seem insignificant when one's life is in jeopardy. Serious suffering for Christ advances the progress of sanctification.

4:2 *for evil human desires . . . for the will of God.* Now that Christ's attitude prevails, God's will is the determining factor in life.

4:3 *time in the past.* The time before conversion (see Eph 2:1–3 and note on 2:1). *pagans.* Lit. "the Gentiles." Along with the term "idolatry," this suggests that at least some of the readers were Gentiles (see note on 1:1) who had been converted from a pagan lifestyle.

4:4 *They are surprised . . . and they heap abuse on you.* Godly living can bring persecution (see 2Ti 3:12 and note).

4:5 *have to give account.* See Mt 12:36; Ac 17:31; Ro 2:5,16 and note on 2:5. *him who is ready to judge.* In the NT both the Father and the Son are said to be judge on the great, final judgment day. The Father is the ultimate source of judgment, but he will delegate judgment to the Son (cf. Jn 5:27; Ac 17:31 and notes). *the living and the dead.* Those alive and those dead when the final judgment day dawns.

4:6 *For this is the reason.* The reason referred to is expressed in the latter part of the verse (in the "so that" clause), not in the preceding verse. *was preached even to those who are now dead.* This preaching was a past event. The word "now" does not occur in the Greek, but it is necessary to make it clear that the preaching was done not after these people had died but while they were still alive. (There will be no opportunity for people to be saved after death; see Heb 9:27.) *that they might be judged according to human standards in regard to the body.* The first reason that the gospel was preached to those now dead. Some say that this judgment is that to which all people must submit, either in this life (see Jn 5:24) or in the life to come (see v. 5). The gospel is preached to people in this life so that in Christ's death they may receive judgment now and avoid judgment to come. Others hold that these people are judged according to human

standards by the pagan world, which does not understand why God's people no longer follow its sinful way of life (see vv. 2–4). So also the world misunderstood Christ (see Ac 2:22–24,36; 3:13–15; 5:30–32; 7:51–53). *but live according to God in regard to the spirit.* The second reason that the gospel was preached to those now dead. Some believe this means that all gospel preaching has as its goal that the hearers may live as God lives—eternally—and that this life is given by the Holy Spirit. Others maintain that it means that the ultimate reason for the preaching of the gospel is that God's people, even though the wicked world may abuse them and put them to death, will have eternal life, which the Holy Spirit imparts.

4:7 *The end . . . is near.* See note on Jas 5:9. *Therefore.* Anticipating the end times, particularly Christ's return, should influence believers' attitudes, actions and relationships (see 2Pe 3:11–14 and notes). *be alert and of sober mind.* Cf. 1:13; 5:8; 1Th 5:6. *so that you may pray.* Cf. 3:7 and note; 1Co 7:5.

4:8 *love each other deeply.* See 1Th 4:9; 2Pe 1:7 and notes; 1Jn 4:7–11. *love covers over . . . sins.* See Jas 5:20 and note. Love forgives again and again (see Mt 18:21–22 and note on 18:22; 1Co 13:5; Eph 4:32 and note).

4:9 *Offer hospitality.* See Ro 12:13 and note; 1Ti 3:2; 5:10; Tit 1:8; Heb 13:2 and note; 3Jn 5–8.

4:10 *use whatever gift you have received.* See Ro 12:4–8; 1Co 12:7–11 and notes.

4:11 *very words.* The Greek for this phrase is used to refer to the Scriptures or to words God has spoken (see Ac 7:38; Ro 3:2 and note). *To him be the glory.* See 1Co 1:26–31 and note; Jude 24–25.

4:12 *do not be surprised at the fiery ordeal.* See 1:6–7 and note on 1:7; 2:20–21 and note on 2:21.

4:13 *rejoice inasmuch as you participate in the sufferings of Christ.* See Col 1:24 and note. Peter once rebelled against the idea that Christ would suffer (see Mt 16:21–23).

4:14 *insulted because of the name of Christ.* See Mt 5:11–12; Jn 15:18–20; Ac 5:41; 14:22; Ro 8:17 and note; 2Co 1:5; Php 3:10 and note; 2Ti 3:12 and note.

4:16 *Christian.* See note on Ac 11:26.

4:17 *judgment to begin with God's household.* The persecutions that believers were undergoing were divinely sent judgment intended to purify God's people. *the outcome . . . for those who do*

"If it is hard for the righteous to be saved,
what will become of the ungodly and the sinner?" [a z]

[19] So then, those who suffer according to God's will [a] should commit themselves to their faithful Creator and continue to do good.

TO THE ELDERS AND THE FLOCK

To the elders among you, I appeal as a fellow elder [b] and a witness [c] of Christ's sufferings who also will share in the glory to be revealed: [d] [2] Be shepherds of God's flock [e] that is under your care, watching over them—not because you must, but because you are willing, as God wants you to be; [f] not pursuing dishonest gain, [g] but eager to serve; [3] not lording it over [h] those entrusted to you, but being examples [i] to the flock. [4] And when the Chief Shepherd [j] appears, you will receive the crown of glory [k] that will never fade away. [l]

[5] In the same way, you who are younger, submit yourselves [m] to your elders. All of you, clothe yourselves with humility [n] toward one another, because,

"God opposes the proud
but shows favor to the humble and oppressed." [b o]

[6] Humble yourselves, therefore, under God's mighty hand, that he may lift you up in due time. [p] [7] Cast all your anxiety on him [q] because he cares for you. [r]

[8] Be alert and of sober mind. [s] Your enemy the devil prowls around [t] like a roaring lion [u] looking for someone to devour. [9] Resist him, [v] standing firm in the faith, [w] because you know that your fellow believers throughout the world are undergoing the same kind of sufferings. [x]

[10] And the God of all grace, who called you [y] to his eternal glory [z] in Christ, after you have suffered a little while, [a] will himself restore you and make you strong, [b] firm and steadfast. [11] To him be the power for ever and ever. Amen. [c]

FINAL GREETINGS

[12] With the help of Silas, [c d] whom I regard as a faithful brother, I have written to you briefly, [e] encouraging you and testifying that this is the true grace of God. Stand fast in it. [f]

a 18 Prov. 11:31 (see Septuagint)   b 5 Prov. 3:34   c 12 Greek Silvanus, a variant of Silas

4:18 z Pr 11:31; Lk 23:31
4:19 a 1Pe 2:15; 3:17
5:1 b S Ac 11:30
c S Lk 24:48
d 1Pe 1:5,7; 4:13; Rev 1:9
5:2 e S Jn 21:16
f 2Co 9:7; Phm 14
g S 1Ti 3:3
5:3 h Eze 34:4; Mt 20:25-28
i S 1Ti 4:12
5:4 j S Jn 10:11
k S 1Co 9:25 / 1Pe 1:4
5:5 m Eph 5:21
n 1Pe 3:8 o Pr 3:34; S Mt 23:12
5:6 p Job 5:11; Jas 4:10
5:7 q Ps 37:5; Mt 6:25 r Ps 55:22; Heb 13:5
5:8 s S Ac 24:25
t Job 1:7 u 2Ti 4:17
5:9 v S Jas 4:7
w Col 2:5 x S Ac 14:22
5:10 y S Ro 8:28
z 2Co 4:17; 2Ti 2:10
a 1Pe 1:6 b Ps 18:32; 2Th 2:17
5:11 c S Ro 11:36
5:12 d S Ac 15:22
e Heb 13:22
f S 1Co 16:13

---

not obey the gospel. If God brings judgment on his own people, how much more serious will the judgment be that he will bring on unbelievers!

5:1 *fellow elder.* See notes on Ex 3:16; 2Sa 3:17; Ac 20:17; 1Ti 3:1; 5:17. Peter, who identified himself as an apostle at the beginning of his letter (1:1), chooses now to identify himself with the elders of the churches (cf. 2Jn 1; 3Jn 1). This would be heartening to them in light of their great responsibilities and the difficult situation faced by the churches. The churches for which these elders were responsible were scattered across much of Asia Minor (see 1:1 and note), so if Peter was a local church officer he must have been officially related to one of them. *witness of Christ's sufferings.* Peter had been with Jesus from the early days of his ministry and was a witness of all its phases and aspects, including the climactic events of his suffering (cf. Mt 26:58; Mk 14:54; Lk 22:60–62; Jn 18:10–11,15–16). In this letter he bears notable witness to Christ's sufferings (see 2:21–24) and obeys his command in Ac 1:8. *share in the glory to be revealed.* See Ro 8:18. Peter witnessed Christ's glory in his ministry in general (see Jn 1:14; 2:11), and, as one present at the transfiguration (see 2Pe 1:16 and note; Mt 16:27; 17:8), he had already seen the glory of Christ's coming kingdom. In God's appointed time, just as Christ suffered and entered into glory, so all his people, after their sufferings, will participate in his future glory (see vv. 4,10).

5:2 *Be shepherds of God's flock.* A metaphor that our Lord himself had employed (Jn 10:1–18; Lk 15:3–7) and that must have been etched on Peter's mind (see Jn 21:15–17; cf. 1Pe 2:25). Peter is fulfilling Christ's command to feed his sheep as he writes this letter. What he writes to the elders is reminiscent of Paul's farewell address to the Ephesian elders (especially Ac 20:28; see note there). The term "shepherd" is an OT metaphor as well (see Eze 34:1–10, where the Lord holds the leaders of Is-

rael responsible for failing to care for the flock). *watching over.* Or "overseeing." The same term is used in Ac 20:28; Php 1:1; 1Ti 3:2; Tit 1:7. See note on 1Ti 3:1. It is clear from this passage, as well as from Ac 20:17,28, that the three terms, "elder," "overseer" and "shepherd" (pastor), all apply to one office (see note on Tit 1:7).

5:3 *not lording it over those entrusted to you.* Cf. Mt 16:24–27; Mk 10:42–45; Php 2:6–11; 2Th 3:9. Although Peter has full apostolic authority (see v. 1), he does not lord it over his readers in this letter but exemplifies the virtues he recommends.

5:4 *Chief Shepherd.* Christ. When he returns, he will reward those who have served as shepherds under him. *never fade away.* See 1:4 and note.

5:5 *submit yourselves.* The theme that runs throughout 2:13—3:6. *your elders.* See v. 1 and note; or "those who are older." *clothe yourselves with humility toward one another.* Peter may have had in mind the footwashing scene of Jn 13, in which he figured prominently. Although he was at first rebellious, he writes now with understanding (see Jn 13:7). *clothe . . . with.* See note on Ps 109:29.

5:6 See Lk 14:11 and note. *lift you up in due time.* His help will come at just the right time (cf. Heb 4:16 and note).

5:7 See Php 4:6–7 and notes; cf. Ps 55:22.

5:8 *Be alert and of sober mind.* Cf. 1:13; 4:7; 1Th 5:6. *devil.* See 2Co 4:4; 1Jn 3:8 and notes.

5:9 *Resist him.* See Jas 4:7 and note. *your fellow believers.* See note on Ac 11:1. They are not isolated; they belong to a fellowship of suffering.

5:10,12,14 *grace . . . grace . . . Peace.* See note on Ro 1:7.

5:10 *God of all grace.* Cf. 1:10,13 and notes.

5:12 *With the help of Silas.* Silas may have been the bearer of the letter to its destination. He may also have been a

5:13 *g* S Ac 12:12
5:14 *h* S Ro 16:16
i S Eph 6:23

[13]She who is in Babylon, chosen together with you, sends you her greetings, and so does my son Mark. *g* [14]Greet one another with a kiss of love. *h*

Peace *i* to all of you who are in Christ.

---

scribe who recorded what Peter dictated or who aided, as an informed and intelligent secretary, in the phrasing of Peter's thoughts (see Introduction: Author and Date). *encouraging ... grace of God.* See Introduction: Themes.

5:13 *She.* Perhaps a Christian congregation (see 2Jn 1 and note). *Babylon.* See Introduction: Place of Writing. *chosen.* See note on Eph 1:4. *my son Mark.* Peter regards Mark with such warmth and affection that he calls him his son. It is possible that

Peter had led Mark to Christ (cf. 1Ti 1:2 and note). Early Christian tradition closely associates Mark and Peter (see Introduction to Mark: Author).

5:14 *kiss.* See note on 1Co 16:20. *Peace to all ... in Christ.* Spiritual well-being and blessedness to all who are united to Christ. Peter thus ends with a reference to the union of believers with Christ (see note on Eph 1:1), a concept fundamental to the understanding of the whole letter.

2 PETER | INTRODUCTION

2 PETER | INTRODUCTION

AUTHOR

The author identifies himself as Simon Peter (1:1). He uses the first person singular pronoun in a highly personal passage (1:12–15) and claims to be an eyewitness of the transfiguration (1:16–18 [see note on 1:16]; cf. Mt 17:1–5). He asserts that this is his second letter to the readers (3:1) and refers to Paul as "our dear brother" (3:15; see note there). In short, the letter claims to be Peter's, and its character is compatible with that claim.

Although 2 Peter was not as widely known and recognized in the early church as 1 Peter, some may have used and accepted it as authoritative as early as the second century and perhaps even in the latter part of the first century (1 Clement [A.D. 95] may allude to it). It was not ascribed to Peter until Origen's time (185–253), and he seems to reflect some doubt concerning it. Eusebius (265–340) placed it among the questioned books, though he admits that most accept it as from Peter. After Eusebius's time, it seems to have been quite generally accepted as canonical.

In recent centuries, however, its genuineness has been challenged by a considerable number of interpreters. One of the objections that has been raised is the difference in style from that of 1 Peter. But the difference is not absolute; there are noteworthy similarities in vocabulary and in other matters. In fact, no other known writing is as much like 1 Peter as 2 Peter. The differences that do exist may be accounted for by variations in subject matter, in the form and purpose of the letters, in the time and circumstances of writing, in sources used or models followed and in scribes who may have been employed. Perhaps most significant is the statement in 1Pe 5:12 that Silas assisted in the writing of 1 Peter. No such statement is made concerning 2 Peter, which may explain its noticeable difference in style (see Introduction to 1 Peter: Author and Date).

Other objections arise from a secular reconstruction of early Christian history or misunderstandings or misconstructions of the available data. For example, some argue that the reference to Paul's letters in 3:15–16 indicates an advanced date for this book—beyond Peter's lifetime. But it is quite possible that Paul's letters were gathered at an early date, since some of them had been in existence and perhaps in circulation for more than ten years (Thessalonians by as much as 15 years) prior to Peter's death. Besides, what Peter says may only indicate that he was acquainted with some of Paul's letters (communication in the Roman world and in the early church was good), not that there was a formal, ecclesiastical collection of them.

DATE

2 Peter was written toward the end of Peter's life (cf. 1:12–15), after he had written a prior letter (3:1) to the same readers (probably 1 Peter). Since Peter was martyred during the reign of Nero, his death must have occurred prior to A.D. 68, so it is very likely that he wrote 2 Peter between 65 and 68.

Some have argued that this date is too early for the writing of 2 Peter, but nothing in the book requires a later date. The error combated is comparable to the kind of heresy present in the first century. To insist that the second chapter was directed against second-century Gnosticism is to assume more than the contents of the chapter warrant. While the heretics referred to in 2 Peter may well have been among the forerunners of second-century Gnostics, nothing is said of them that would not fit into the later years of Peter's life.

Some have suggested a later date because they interpret the reference to the "ancestors" in 3:4 to mean an earlier Christian generation. However, the word is most naturally interpreted as the OT patriarchs (cf. Jn 6:31; Ac 3:13; Heb 1:1). Similarly, reference to Paul and his letters (3:15–16; see Author) does not require a date beyond Peter's lifetime.

2 PETER AND JUDE

There are conspicuous similarities between 2 Peter and Jude (compare 2Pe 2 with Jude 4–18), but there are also significant differences. It has been suggested that one borrowed from the other or that they both drew on a common source. If there is borrowing, it is not a slavish borrowing but one that adapts to suit the writer's purpose. While many have insisted that Jude used Peter, it is more reasonable to assume that the longer letter (Peter) incorporated much of the shorter (Jude). Such borrowing is fairly common in ancient writings. For example, many believe that Paul used parts of early hymns in Php 2:6–11 and 1Ti 3:16.

PURPOSE

In his first letter Peter feeds Christ's sheep by instructing them how to deal with persecution from outside the church (see 1Pe 4:12); in this second letter he teaches them how to deal with false teachers and evildoers who have come into the church (see 2:1; 3:3–4 and notes). While the particular situations naturally call for variations in content and emphasis, in both letters Peter as a pastor ("shepherd") of Christ's sheep (Jn 21:15–17) seeks to commend to his readers a wholesome combination of Christian faith and practice. More specifically, his purpose is threefold: (1) to stimulate Christian growth (ch. 1), (2) to combat false teaching (ch. 2) and (3) to encourage watchfulness in view of the Lord's certain return (ch. 3).

OUTLINE

1 Simon Peter, a servant ^a and apostle of Jesus Christ, ^b
To those who through the righteousness ^c of our God and Savior Jesus Christ ^d have received a faith as precious as ours:

²Grace and peace be yours in abundance ^e through the knowledge of God and of Jesus our Lord. ^f

CONFIRMING ONE'S CALLING AND ELECTION

³His divine power ^g has given us everything we need for a godly life through our knowledge of him ^h who called us ⁱ by his own glory and goodness. ⁴Through these he has given us his very great and precious promises, ^j so that through them you may participate in the divine nature, ^k having escaped the corruption in the world caused by evil desires. ^l

⁵For this very reason, make every effort to add to your faith goodness; and to goodness, knowledge; ^m ⁶and to knowledge, self-control; ⁿ and to self-control, perseverance; ^o and to perseverance, godliness; ^p ⁷and to godliness, mutual affection; and to mutual affection, love. ^q ⁸For if you possess these qualities in increasing measure, they will keep you from being ineffective and unproductive ^r in your knowledge of our Lord Jesus Christ. ^s ⁹But if any of you do not have them, you are nearsighted and blind, ^t and you have forgotten that you have been cleansed from your past sins. ^u

¹⁰Therefore, my brothers and sisters, make every effort to confirm your calling ^v and election. For if you do these things, you will never stumble, ^w ¹¹and you will receive a rich welcome into the eternal kingdom ^x of our Lord and Savior Jesus Christ. ^y

PROPHECY OF SCRIPTURE

¹²So I will always remind you of these things, ^z even though you know them and are firmly established in the truth ^a you now have. ¹³I think it is right to refresh your memo-

1:1 ^a Ro 1:1 ^b 1Pe 1:1
^c Ro 3:21-26 ^d Tit 2:13
1:2 ^e S Ro 1:7 ^f ver 3,
8; 2Pe 2:20; 3:18;
S Php 3:8
1:3 ^g 1Pe 1:5
^h S ver 2 ⁱ S Ro 8:28
1:4 ^j 2Co 7:1
^k Eph 4:24;
Heb 12:10; 1Jn 3:2
^l Jas 1:27; 2Pe 2:18-20
1:5 ^m S ver 2;
Col 2:3
1:6 ⁿ S Ac 24:25
^o S Heb 10:36 ^p ver 3
1:7 ^q S Ro 12:10;
1Th 3:12
1:8 ^r Jn 15:2;
Col 1:10; Tit 3:14
^s S ver 2
1:9 ^t 1Jn 2:11
^u Eph 5:26; S Mt 1:21
1:10 ^v S Ro 8:28
^w Ps 15:5; 2Pe 3:17;
Jude 24
1:11 ^x Ps 145:13;
2Ti 4:18 ^y 2Pe 2:20;
3:18
1:12 ^z Php 3:1;
1Jn 2:21; Jude 5
^a 2Jn 2

A 1:1 *Simon Peter.* See Introduction to 1 Peter: Author and Date; see also notes on Mt 16:18; Jn 1:42. *servant.* See note on Ro 1:1. *apostle.* See notes on Mk 6:30; 1Co 1:1; Heb 3:1. *To those.* Probably the same people as those in 1Pe 1:1. *God and Savior Jesus Christ.* Assumes that Jesus is both God and Savior. For other passages that ascribe deity to Christ, see note on Ro 9:5. *have received.* God in his justice ("righteousness") imparts to people the ability to believe. *a faith.* Not here a body of truth to be believed—the faith—but the act of believing, or the God-given capacity to trust in Christ for salvation.

1:2 *Grace and peace.* See note on Ro 1:7. *knowledge of God and of Jesus.* The concept of Christian knowledge is prominent in 2 Peter (see vv. 3, 5, 8 and note on v. 3; 3:18 and note). Peter was combating heretical teaching, and one of the best antidotes for heresy is true knowledge.

1:3 *everything we need for a godly life.* God has made available all that we need spiritually through our knowledge of him. If 2 Peter is written to combat an incipient Gnosticism, the apostle may be insisting that the knowledge possessed by those in apostolic circles was entirely adequate to meet their spiritual needs. No secret, esoteric knowledge is necessary for salvation (see Introduction to 1 John: Gnosticism). *godly.* True godliness is a genuine reverence toward God that governs one's attitude toward every aspect of life (see 1Ti 2:2 and note). *glory and goodness.* The excellence of God: "Glory" expresses the excellence of his being—his attributes and essence; "goodness" depicts excellence expressed in deeds—virtue in action. God uses both to bring about our salvation.

1:4 *Through these.* Through God's excellence—internal and external—he has given us great promises. Their nature is suggested in the words that follow: participation in the divine nature and escape from worldly corruption. *participate in the divine nature.* Does not indicate that Christians become divine in any sense, but only that we are indwelt by God through his Holy Spirit (see Jn 14:16–17 and notes). Our humanity and his deity, as well as the human personality and the divine, remain distinct and separate. *world.* See note on Jn 1:9. *evil desires.* See 2:10 and note.

A 1:5–9 The virtues that will produce a well-rounded, fruitful Christian life (see Gal 5:22–23 and note).

1:5 *faith.* The root of the Christian life (see v. 1 and note). *goodness.* Cf. v. 3 and note. *knowledge.* See notes on vv. 2–3.

1:6 *self-control.* According to many of the false teachers, knowledge made self-control unnecessary; according to Peter, Christian knowledge leads to self-control (cf. Pr 25:28; Gal 5:23).

A 1:7 *mutual affection.* Warmhearted affection toward all in the family of faith. *love.* The kind of outgoing, selfless attitude that leads one to sacrifice for the good of others (see note on 1Pe 4:8).

1:8 *if you possess these qualities.* Peter does not mean to imply that the believer is to cultivate each listed quality in turn, one after the other, until all have been perfected. Instead, they are all to be cultivated simultaneously. *increasing measure.* Peter has continuing spiritual growth in mind (cf. 3:18; 1Pe 2:2; Php 3:10; 1Th 3:12). *keep you from being ... unproductive in your knowledge.* Christians' knowledge should affect the way they live. It does not set them free from moral restraints, as the heretics taught (see Introduction to 1 John: Gnosticism). Rather, it produces holiness and all such virtues (cf. Col 1:9–12).

1:9 *nearsighted and blind.* Since one cannot be both at the same time, Peter may have in mind a possible alternative meaning for "nearsighted," namely, "to shut the eyes." Such people are blind because they have closed their eyes to the truth (see 1Jn 2:11).

A 1:10 *brothers and sisters.* See note on Ro 1:13. *confirm your calling and election.* By cultivating the qualities listed in vv. 5–7, they and others can be assured that God has chosen them and called them (cf. Mt 7:20; Gal 5:6; Jas 2:18 and notes). When God elects and calls, it is to obedience and holiness (see 1Pe 1:2; Eph 1:3–6 and notes), and these fruits confirm their divine source. *never stumble.* Those who in this way give evidence of their faith will never cease to persevere.

1:11 *receive a rich welcome.* One fruit Peter is commending to them (see vv. 5–10). *eternal kingdom.* Eternal life (cf. Mt 25:46).

1:12 See Ro 15:15; Php 3:1; 1Jn 2:21.

1:13 *b* 2Pe 3:1
c Isa 38:12; 2Co 5:1,4
1:14 *d* 2Ti 4:6
e Jn 13:36; 21:18,19
1:15 *f* Lk 9:31
1:16 *g* Mk 13:26;
14:62 *h* Mt 17:1-8
1:17 *i* S Mt 3:17
1:18 *j* Mt 17:6
1:19 *k* 1Pe 1:10,11
l Ps 119:105 *m* Lk 1:78
n Rev 22:16 *o* 2Co 4:6
1:20 *p* 2Pe 3:3
1:21 *q* 2Ti 3:16
r 2Sa 23:2; Ac 1:16;
3:18; 1Pe 1:11
2:1 *s* Dt 13:1-3;
Jer 6:13; S Mt 7:15
t 1Ti 4:1 *u* Jude 4
v S 1Co 6:20
2:2 *w* Jude 4
2:3 *x* ver 14
y 2Co 2:17; 1Th 2:5
2:4 *z* Ge 6:1-4

ry *b* as long as I live in the tent of this body, *c* 14because I know that I will soon put it aside, *d* as our Lord Jesus Christ has made clear to me. *e* 15And I will make every effort to see that after my departure *f* you will always be able to remember these things.

16For we did not follow cleverly devised stories when we told you about the coming of our Lord Jesus Christ in power, *g* but we were eyewitnesses of his majesty. *h* 17He received honor and glory from God the Father when the voice came to him from the Majestic Glory, saying, "This is my Son, whom I love; with him I am well pleased." *a i* 18We ourselves heard this voice that came from heaven when we were with him on the sacred mountain. *j*

19We also have the prophetic message as something completely reliable, *k* and you will do well to pay attention to it, as to a light *l* shining in a dark place, until the day dawns *m* and the morning star *n* rises in your hearts. *o* 20Above all, you must understand *p* that no prophecy of Scripture came about by the prophet's own interpretation of things. 21For prophecy never had its origin in the human will, but prophets, though human, spoke from God *q* as they were carried along by the Holy Spirit. *r*

FALSE TEACHERS AND THEIR DESTRUCTION

2 But there were also false prophets *s* among the people, just as there will be false teachers among you. *t* They will secretly introduce destructive heresies, even denying the sovereign Lord *u* who bought them *v*—bringing swift destruction on themselves. 2Many will follow their depraved conduct *w* and will bring the way of truth into disrepute. 3In their greed *x* these teachers will exploit you *y* with fabricated stories. Their condemnation has long been hanging over them, and their destruction has not been sleeping.

4For if God did not spare angels when they sinned, *z* but sent them to hell, *b* putting

a 17 Matt. 17:5; Mark 9:7; Luke 9:35   *b 4* Greek *Tartarus*

1:13 *tent of this body.* See Jn 1:14; 2Co 5:1 and notes.
1:14 *Christ has made clear to me.* Either the revelation recorded in Jn 21:18–19 (see notes there) or a subsequent one.
1:15 *always be able to remember these things.* An aim that was realized, whether intentionally or unintentionally, through the Gospel of Mark, which early tradition connected with Peter.
1:16 *cleverly devised stories.* Peter's message was based on his eyewitness account of the supernatural events that marked the life of Jesus. It was not made up of myths and imaginative stories, as was the message of the heretics of 2:3 (see note there). *coming of our Lord Jesus Christ.* In Christ's transfiguration the disciples received a foretaste of what his coming will be like when he returns to establish his eternal kingdom (see Mt 16:28 and note). *eyewitnesses of his majesty.* A reference to Christ's transfiguration (see vv. 17–18; Mt 16:28—17:8).
1:18 *sacred mountain.* See note on Lk 9:28.
1:19–21 Peter's message rests on two solid foundations: (1) the voice from God at the transfiguration (vv. 16–18) and (2) the still more significant testimony of Scripture (vv. 19–21). An alternative, but less probable, view is that the apostles' testimony to the transfiguration fulfills and thus confirms the Scriptures that predicted such things.
1:19 *morning star.* See Rev 22:16; cf. Nu 24:17 and note.
1:20 Two major views of this verse are: 1. No prophecy is to be privately or independently interpreted (cf. the false teachers in 3:16). The Holy Spirit, Scripture itself and the church should be included in the interpretative process. 2. No prophecy originated through the prophet's own interpretation (the sense of the TNIV). The preceding and following contexts indicate that this view is probably to be preferred. In vv. 16–18 the subject discussed is the origin of the apostolic message. Did it come from human imaginings, or was it from God? In v. 21 again the subject is origin. No prophecy of Scripture arose from a merely human interpretation of things. This understanding of v. 20 is further supported by the explanatory "For" with which v. 21 begins. Verse 21 explains v. 20 by restating its content and then affirming God as the origin of prophecy.
1:21 *carried along by the Holy Spirit.* See 2Ti 3:16 and note. In the production of Scripture both God and hu-

mans were active participants. God was the source of the content of Scripture, so that what it says is what God has said. But the human authors also spoke actively; they were more than recorders, yet what they said came from God. Although actively speaking, "they were carried along by the Holy Spirit."
2:1 *false prophets.* See 1Ki 18:19; Isa 9:13–17; Jer 5:31; 14:14; 23:30–32 and note on 23:31; Mic 3:5,7 and notes. *there will be false teachers among you.* Numerous NT passages warn of false teachers who are already present or yet to come (see Mt 24:4–5,11; Ac 20:29–30; Gal 1:6–9; Php 3:2; Col 2:4,8,18,20–23; 2Th 2:1–3; 1Ti 1:3–7; 4:1–3; 2Ti 3:1–8; 1Jn 2:18–19,22–23; 2Jn 7–11; Jude 3–4). *destructive heresies.* Divisive opinions or teachings that result in the moral and spiritual destruction of those who accept them. *sovereign Lord who bought them.* See Jude 4 and note; does not necessarily mean that the false teachers were believers. Christ's death paid the penalty for their sin, but it would not become effective for their salvation unless they trusted in Christ as Savior. (However, see vv. 20–22, where it is obvious that the heretics had at least professed knowing the Lord.) *swift destruction.* Not immediate physical calamity but sudden doom, whether at death or at the Lord's second coming (cf. Mt 24:50–51; 2Th 1:9 and note).
2:2 *depraved conduct.* Open, extreme immorality not held in check by any sense of shame. *way of truth.* See Ps 119:30. The Christian faith is not only correct doctrine but also correct living.
2:3 *In their greed.* They will be motivated by a desire for money (see 2 Co 2:17 and note) and will commercialize the Christian faith to their own selfish advantage. *fabricated stories.* See note on 1:16. *long been hanging over them.* Long ago, in OT times, their condemnation was declared (see vv. 4–9 for OT examples of the fact that judgment is coming on the wicked). *destruction has not been sleeping.* Although delay makes it seem that they have escaped God's judgment, destruction is a reality that is sure to come upon them.
2:4–8 Three examples showing that God will rescue the godly and destroy the wicked.
2:4 *angels when they sinned.* Some believe this sin was the one referred to in Ge 6:2, where the sons of God are said to have in-

them in chains of darkness[a] to be held for judgment; [5]if he did not spare the ancient world[b] when he brought the flood on its ungodly people, [c]but protected Noah, a preacher of righteousness, and seven others; [d][6]if he condemned the cities of Sodom and Gomorrah by burning them to ashes, [e]and made them an example[f] of what is going to happen to the ungodly; [g][7]and if he rescued Lot, [h]a righteous man, who was distressed by the depraved conduct of the lawless[i][8](for that righteous man,[j] living among them day after day, was tormented in his righteous soul by the lawless deeds he saw and heard)— [9]if this is so, then the Lord knows how to rescue the godly from trials[k] and to hold the unrighteous for punishment on the day of judgment.[l] [10]This is especially true of those who follow the corrupt desire[m] of the sinful nature[b] and despise authority.

Bold and arrogant, they are not afraid to heap abuse on celestial beings; [n] [11]yet even angels, although they are stronger and more powerful, do not heap abuse on such beings when bringing judgment on them from[c] the Lord. [o][12]But these people blaspheme in matters they do not understand. They are like unreasoning animals, creatures of instinct, born only to be caught and destroyed, and like animals they too will perish. [p]

[13]They will be paid back with harm for the harm they have done. Their idea of pleasure is to carouse in broad daylight. [q]They are blots and blemishes, reveling in their pleasures while they feast with you. [d][r] [14]With eyes full of adultery, they never stop sinning; they seduce[s] the unstable; [t]they are experts in greed[u]—an accursed brood! [v] [15]They have left the straight way and wandered off to follow the way of Balaam[w] son of Bezer, [e]who loved the wages of wickedness. [16]But he was rebuked for his wrongdoing by a donkey—an animal without speech—who spoke with a human voice and restrained the prophet's madness. [x]

[17]These people are springs without water[y] and mists driven by a storm. Blackest dark-

---

a 4 Some manuscripts *in gloomy dungeons*   b 10 Or *the flesh*   c 11 Many manuscripts *beings in the presence of*   d 13 Some manuscripts *in their love feasts*   e 15 Greek *Bosor*

2:4 [a]1Ti 3:6; Jude 6; Rev 20:1,2
2:5 [b]2Pe 3:6
[c]Ge 6:5-8:19
[d]Heb 11:7; 1Pe 3:20
2:6 [e]Ge 19:24,25
[f]Nu 26:10; Jude 7
[g]Mt 10:15; 11:23,24; Ro 9:29
2:7 [h]Ge 19:16
[i]2Pe 3:17
2:8 [j]Heb 11:4
2:9 [k]Ps 37:33; S Ro 15:31; Rev 3:10
[l]S Mt 10:15
2:10 [m]2Pe 3:3; Jude 16,18 [n]Jude 8
2:11 [o]Jude 9
2:12 [p]Ps 49:12; Jude 10
2:13 [q]S Ro 13:13; 1Th 5:1-7; 1Co 11:20, 21; Jude 12
2:14 [s]ver 18
[t]Jas 1:8; 2Pe 3:16
[u]ver 3 [v]Eph 2:3
2:15 [w]Nu 22:4-20; 31:16; Dt 23:4; Jude 11; Rev 2:14
2:16 [x]Nu 22:21-30
2:17 [y]Jude 12

---

termarried with human daughters, meaning (according to this view) that angels married human women. The offspring of those marriages are said to have been the Nephilim (Ge 6:4; see notes on Ge 6:2,4). But since it appears impossible for angels, who are spirits, to have sexual relations with women, the sin referred to in this verse probably occurred before the fall of Adam and Eve. The angels who fell became the devil and the evil angels (probably the demons and evil spirits referred to in the NT). *sent them to hell.* See TNIV text note. *Tartarus* was the term used by the Greeks to designate the place where the most wicked spirits were sent to be punished. Why some evil angels are imprisoned and others are free to serve Satan as demons is not explained in Scripture. *judgment.* The final judgment, probably associated with the great white throne judgment of Rev 20:11–15.

2:5 *ungodly people.* See Ge 6:5,11–12. *preacher of righteousness.* A description of Noah found nowhere else in Scripture. However, similar descriptions are used of him in Josephus (*Antiquities,* 1.3.1), *1 Clement* (7.6; 9.4) and the *Sibylline Oracles* (1.128–29). *seven others.* Noah's wife, three sons and three daughters-in-law (Noah was the eighth; see 1Pe 3:20).

2:6 *condemned the cities of Sodom and Gomorrah.* See Ge 19.

2:7 *distressed by the depraved conduct.* See Ge 19:4–9. How Lot could be so distressed, how he could be called a "righteous man" and yet offer to turn over his two daughters to the wicked townsmen to be sexually abused is difficult to understand apart from a knowledge of the code of honor characteristic of that day (see note on Ge 19:8).

2:9 States the point made in vv. 4–8—the wicked whose coming Peter predicts will surely be punished.

2:10 *This is especially true.* The heretics of Peter's day are certain to come under judgment for two main reasons: 1. They "follow the corrupt desire of the sinful nature," referring to inordinate sexual indulgence (see v. 18; 1:4; 3:3). 2. They "despise authority." *heap abuse on celestial beings.* A specific example of despising authority. This could refer to the slander of earthly dignitaries such as church leaders, which might well be expected from such shameless peddlers of error. On the other hand, it could refer to the blaspheming of angels, as the TNIV text suggests. This view seems more likely since the parallel passage in Jude 8–10 is speaking of angels.

2:11 *angels . . . do not heap abuse on.* Even good angels, who

might have more right to do so because of their greater power, do not bring such accusations against inferior, evil angels.

2:12 *matters they do not understand.* The heresy to which Peter refers may have been an early form of second-century Gnosticism (see Introduction to 1 John: Gnosticism) that claimed to possess special, esoteric knowledge. If so, it is ironic that those who professed special knowledge acted out of abysmal ignorance, and the result was arrogant blasphemy. *like unreasoning animals.* A scathing denunciation. They are like irrational animals, whose lives are guided by mere instinct and who are born merely to be slaughtered. Destruction is their final lot.

2:13 *carouse in broad daylight.* See 1Th 5:7. Even the pagan world carried on its corrupt practices under cover of darkness, but these heretics were utterly shameless. *in their pleasures while they feast with you.* See TNIV text note. Jude 12 without doubt reads "love feasts," which may well have been the intended reading here. These false teachers seem to have been involved in the sacred feasts of brotherly love that, in the early church, accompanied the Lord's Supper. In fact, it appears that they injected their carousing into these holy observances and delighted in their shameless acts (cf. 1Co 11:17–22,27–34 and notes on 11:20–22).

2:14 *eyes full of adultery.* Lit. "eyes full of an adulteress," which means that they desired every woman they saw, viewing her as a potential sex partner. *never stop sinning.* Their eyes serve as constant instruments of lust. *seduce the unstable.* For a parallel use of the Greek for "seduce," see Jas 1:14 and note. It depicts the fisherman who attempts to lure and catch fish with bait. *experts in greed.* The Greek text implies that they had exercised themselves like an athlete, not in physical activity but in greed.

2:15 *way of Balaam son of Bezer.* See Nu 22–24. Balaam was bent on cursing Israel, though God had forbidden it. He wanted the money Balak offered him. Similarly, these false teachers apparently were guilty of attempting to extract money from naive listeners. For a donkey to rebuke the prophet's madness (v. 16) reflects not only on the foolishness of Balaam but also on that of the false teachers of Peter's day.

2:17 *springs without water.* A picture of cruel deception. The thirsty traveler comes to the spring expecting cool, refreshing water but finds it dry (see Jer 15:18 and note). So the false teachers promise satisfying truth but in reality have nothing to

2:17 *z* Jude 13
2:18 *a* Jude 16
b ver 20; 2Pe 1:4
2:19 *c* S Ro 6:16
2:20 *d* S 2Pe 1:2
e 2Pe 1:11; 3:18
f Mt 12:45
2:21 *g* Eze 18:24;
Heb 6:4-6; 10:26,27
2:22 *h* Pr 26:11
3:1 *i* S 1Co 10:14
j 2Pe 1:13
3:2 *k* Lk 1:70;
Ac 3:21 *l* S Eph 4:11
3:3 *m* 1Ti 4:1; 2Ti 3:1
n 2Pe 2:10; Jude 18
3:4 *o* Isa 5:19;
Eze 12:22; Mt 24:48;
S Lk 17:30 *p* Mk 10:6
3:5 *q* Ge 1:6,9;
Heb 11:3 *r* Ps 24:2
3:6 *s* 2Pe 2:5

ness is reserved for them. *z* ¹⁸For they mouth empty, boastful words *a* and, by appealing to the lustful desires of sinful human nature, they entice people who are just escaping *b* from those who live in error. ¹⁹They promise them freedom, while they themselves are slaves of depravity—for "people are slaves to whatever has mastered them." *c* ²⁰If they have escaped the corruption of the world by knowing *d* our Lord and Savior Jesus Christ *e* and are again entangled in it and are overcome, they are worse off at the end than they were at the beginning. *f* ²¹It would have been better for them not to have known the way of righteousness, than to have known it and then to turn their backs on the sacred command that was passed on to them. *g* ²²Of them the proverbs are true: "A dog returns to its vomit," *a h* and, "A sow that is washed returns to her wallowing in the mud."

THE DAY OF THE LORD

3 Dear friends, *i* this is now my second letter to you. I have written both of them as reminders *j* to stimulate you to wholesome thinking. ²I want you to recall the words spoken in the past by the holy prophets *k* and the command given by our Lord and Savior through your apostles. *l*

³Above all, you must understand that in the last days *m* scoffers will come, scoffing and following their own evil desires. *n* ⁴They will say, "Where is this 'coming' he promised? *o* Ever since our ancestors died, everything goes on as it has since the beginning of creation." *p* ⁵But they deliberately forget that long ago by God's word *q* the heavens came into being and the earth was formed out of water and by water. *r* ⁶By these waters also the world of that time *s*

a 22 Prov. 26:11

---

offer. *mists driven by a storm.* Gone before a drop of moisture falls. *Blackest darkness.* Their destiny is hell.
2:18 *mouth empty, boastful words.* Words that sound impressive to the new convert but in reality have nothing to offer. *lustful desires.* See v. 10 and note. *entice.* See note on v. 14 ("seduce"). *people who are just escaping.* New converts who have just broken away from pagan friends. Thus the depraved false teachers prey on new converts, who have not yet had a chance to develop spiritual resistance.

A **2:19** *They promise them freedom.* Probably freedom from moral restraint (cf. 1Co 6:12–13; Gal 5:13 and notes). The very ones who promise freedom from bondage to rules and regulations are themselves slaves of depravity. Freedom from law resulted in bondage to sin, and liberty was turned into license.

2:20–22 Some point to this passage as clear proof that genuinely saved persons may lose their salvation. They know the Lord; they escape the world's corruption; they know the way of righteousness. Then they turn away from the message and go back to their old way of life. Their knowledge is said to have been genuine; their change of life was real; and their return to their old way of life was not superficial. Others insist that their knowledge of the Lord and of the way of righteousness could not have been genuine. If such people had been truly regenerated, they would have persevered in their faith. It is argued that the teaching of Jn 10:27–30 (especially v. 28) and Ro 8:28–39 makes it clear that no genuinely saved person can be lost. Thus, according to this view, the persons described here could not have been genuinely saved. See 1Jn 2:19.
2:20 *If they have escaped the corruption of the world.* A reference to false teachers who had once apparently been believers in Christ. Their professed knowledge of Christ had at least produced a change in lifestyle. *again entangled in it and are overcome.* A complete return to the old, sinful pattern of life.
2:21 *better ... not to have known the way of righteousness.* Knowledge of the way increases people's responsibility and their hardness of heart if they then reject it. In its early days, Christianity was known as "the Way" (Ac 9:2 [see note there]; 18:25; 19:9,23; 22:4; 24:14,22). *sacred command.* The whole Christian message that people are commanded to receive (cf. note on Jude 3).
2:22 *A dog returns ... A sow ... returns.* In both cases the nature of the animal is not changed. The sow returns to the mud be-

cause by nature it is still a sow. The change was merely cosmetic.
3:1 *second letter.* The first letter may have been 1 Peter, though there is some reason to doubt this identification. For example, 1 Peter cannot be very accurately described as a reminder. *reminders.* See 1:12–13,15.
3:2 *holy prophets.* OT personages. *command.* See note on 2:21. *your apostles.* Peter places the OT prophets and the NT apostles on an equal plane. Both are vehicles of God's sacred truth. Peter, being one of the apostles, can speak with knowledge and authority as a representative of the apostolic group.
3:3 *last days.* An expression that refers to the whole period introduced by Christ's first coming. These days are last in comparison to OT days, which were preliminary and preparatory (see notes on Heb 1:1–2). Also, the Christian era is the time of the beginnings of prophetic fulfillment. *scoffers will come.* Perhaps the same false teachers described in ch. 2 (e.g., they follow their own evil desires; cf. 2:10,18–19). In ch. 3, however, the emphasis is on Christ's return. These people may have been early Gnostics who resisted the idea of a time of judgment and moral accountability. *evil desires.* See 2:10 and note.
3:4 *he.* Christ. *Ever since our ancestors died.* Either the first Christians to die after Christ's death and resurrection (e.g., Stephen, James the brother of John and other early Christian leaders who had died; cf. Heb 13:7 and note) or the OT patriarchs (see Introduction: Date). *everything goes on as it is.* Their argument against Christ's return was: Since it has not occurred up to this time, it will never occur. That nature is not subject to divine intervention, they say, has been proved by observation (1) of the period since the death of the ancestors—perhaps 30 years—and (2) of the period since creation.
3:5 *they deliberately forget.* Ignoring the flood as a divine intervention was not an oversight; it was deliberate. They did not want to face up to the fallacy in their argument. *God's word.* Of command, such as "Let there be light" (Ge 1:3). *earth was formed out of water and by water.* See Ge 1:6–10 (see also notes there), where the waters on earth were separated from the atmospheric waters of the heavens, and the mountains then appeared, causing the earthly waters to be gathered into oceans.
3:6 *By these waters also the world ... was deluged and destroyed.* Peter points out the fallacy of the scoffers' argument. There has been a divine intervention since the time of creation, namely, the flood (see note on Ge 6:17).

was deluged and destroyed.[t] [7]By the same word the present heavens and earth are reserved for fire,[u] being kept for the day of judgment[v] and destruction of the ungodly.

[8]But do not forget this one thing, dear friends: With the Lord a day is like a thousand years, and a thousand years are like a day.[w] [9]The Lord is not slow in keeping his promise,[x] as some understand slowness. Instead he is patient[y] with you, not wanting anyone to perish, but everyone to come to repentance.[z]

[10]But the day of the Lord will come like a thief.[a] The heavens will disappear with a roar;[b] the elements will be destroyed by fire,[c] and the earth and everything done in it will be laid bare.[a] [d]

[11]Since everything will be destroyed in this way, what kind of people ought you to be? You ought to live holy and godly lives [12]as you look forward[e] to the day of God and speed its coming.[b] [f] That day will bring about the destruction of the heavens by fire, and the elements will melt in the heat.[g] [13]But in keeping with his promise we are looking forward to a new heaven and a new earth,[h] where righteousness dwells.

[14]So then, dear friends, since you are looking forward to this, make every effort to be found spotless, blameless[i] and at peace with him. [15]Bear in mind that our Lord's patience[j] means salvation,[k] just as our dear brother Paul also wrote you with the wisdom that God gave him.[l] [16]He writes the same way in all his letters, speaking in them of these matters. His letters contain some things that are hard to understand, which ignorant and unstable[m] people distort,[n] as they do the other Scriptures,[o] to their own destruction.

[17]Therefore, dear friends, since you have been forewarned, be on your guard[p] so that you may not be carried away by the error[q] of the lawless[r] and fall from your secure position.[s] [18]But grow in the grace[t] and knowledge[u] of our Lord and Savior Jesus Christ.[v] To him be glory both now and forever! Amen.[w]

---

a 10 Some manuscripts *be burned up*   b 12 Or *as you wait eagerly for the day of God to come*

3:6 [t] Ge 7:21,22
3:7 [u] ver 10,12;
S 2Th 1:7 [v] S Mt 10:15
3:8 [w] Ps 90:4
3:9 [x] Hab 2:3;
Heb 10:37 [y] S Ro 2:4
[z] S 1Ti 2:4; Rev 2:21
3:10 [a] S Lk 12:39
[b] Isa 34:4 [c] ver 7,12;
S 2Th 1:7 [d] Mt 24:35;
S Heb 12:27; Rev 21:1
3:12 [e] S 1Co 1:7
[f] Ps 50:3 [g] ver 10
3:13 [h] Isa 65:17;
66:22; Rev 21:1
3:14 [i] S 1Th 3:13
3:15 [j] S Ro 2:4
[k] ver 9 [l] Eph 3:3
3:16 [m] Jas 1:8;
2Pe 2:14 [n] Ps 56:5;
Jer 23:36 [o] ver 2
3:17 [p] 1Co 10:12
[q] 2Pe 2:18 [r] 2Pe 2:7
[s] Rev 2:5
3:18 [t] S Ro 3:24
[u] S 2Pe 1:2 [v] 2Pe 1:11;
2:20 [w] S Ro 11:36

3:7 *By the same word.* The word of God that brought the world into existence (v. 5) and that brought watery destruction on the wicked of Noah's day will bring fiery destruction on the world that exists today and on its wicked people.

3:8 *a thousand years are like a day.* Cf. Ps 90:4–5 and note. God does not view time as humans do. He stands above time, with the result that when time is seen in the light of eternity, an age appears no longer than one short day and a day seems no shorter than a long age. Since time is purely relative with God, he waits patiently while human beings stew with impatience.

3:9 God's seeming delay in bringing about the consummation of all things is a result not of indifference but of patience in waiting for all who will come to repentance. Thus the scoffers are wrong on two points: 1. They fail to recognize that all things have not continued without divine intervention since creation (the flood was an intervention, vv. 4–6). 2. They misunderstand the reason for apparent divine delay (God is a long-suffering God). *repentance.* See Mt 4:17; Mk 1:4 and note.

3:10 *day of the Lord.* See notes on Isa 2:11,17,20; Joel 1:15; Am 5:18; 1Th 5:2. *like a thief.* Suddenly and unexpectedly. *The heavens will disappear with a roar.* Apocalyptic language, common to books like Daniel and Revelation. Due to the figurative nature of such writings, we must not expect complete literalism but recognize it as an attempt to describe the indescribable, a task as impossible as it would have been for a first-century writer to describe the phenomena of our atomic age. What may be referred to is the destruction of the atmospheric heavens with a great rushing sound (see v. 12). *elements.* Refers either to the heavenly bodies or to the physical elements—in the first century, such things as earth, air, fire and water. *fire.* See vv. 7,12. *earth . . . laid bare.* See TNIV text note. Either the earth and its contents will disappear and not be seen anymore, or the earth and all human works will appear before God's judgment seat (cf. 1Co 3:13,15 and notes).

3:11 *Since everything will be destroyed.* The transitory nature of the material universe ought to make a difference in one's system of values and one's priorities. The result should be lives of holiness (separated from sin and to God) and godliness (devoted to the worship and service of God). Cf. 1:13–16; Mt 25:13; 1Th 5:6,8,11.

3:12 *the day of God.* Apparently synonymous with "the day of the Lord" (see v. 10 and note) since it is characterized by the

same kind of events. Cf. Rev 16:14. *speed its coming.* That day may be hastened by God's people as they speed up the accomplishment of his purposes. Since he is waiting for all who will come to repentance (v. 9), the sooner believers bring others to the Savior the sooner that day will dawn (cf. Ac 3:19–20). Prayer also serves to hasten the day (Mt 6:10), as does holy living (v. 11). *destruction of the heavens.* See v. 10. *elements will melt in the heat.* See v. 10; Isa 34:4 and notes.

3:13 *his promise.* New heavens and a new earth are promised by Isaiah (65:17; 66:22). This promise is confirmed by Rev 21:1. *where righteousness dwells.* Righteousness will dwell there as a permanent resident. Cf. Isa 11:4–5; 45:8; Da 9:24 and notes.

3:14,18 *peace . . . grace.* See note on Ro 1:7.

3:14 *spotless, blameless.* Cf. 1Pe 1:19, where the same two Greek words are applied to Christ. *at peace with him.* Believers have peace with God as a result of being justified by faith (see Ro 5:1 and note), but they may displease him by failing to live as he desires and thus not receive his commendation and his reward when he returns (cf. 1Co 3:10–15; 2Co 5:10 and notes).

3:15 *our Lord's patience means salvation.* See v. 9 and note. *our dear brother Paul.* Peter expresses warmth in his reference to Paul. The unity of teaching and purpose that governed their relationship, abundantly attested in Paul's letters and the book of Acts, is confirmed here by Peter. It has been suggested that what Paul wrote to the recipients of 2 Peter may have been a copy of Romans, which was sent to the churches as a circular letter (see Introduction to Romans: Recipients; see also note on 1Pe 1:1).

3:16 *writes the same way in all his letters.* Peter may be referring in general to the exhortations to holy living in vv. 11–14, which parallel many passages in Paul's writings. *ignorant and unstable people.* The ignorant are simply the unlearned who have not been taught basic apostolic teaching and thus may be easily led astray (cf. 2:14 and note). *other Scriptures.* Peter placed Paul's writings on the same level of authority as the God-breathed writings of the OT (see 1:21; 2Ti 3:16 and notes).

3:17 *you have been forewarned.* That false teachers are coming (cf. ch. 2).

3:18 *grow in . . . knowledge.* Peter concludes by again stressing knowledge (see 1:2–3 and notes; see also 1:5), probably as an antidote to the false teachers who boasted in their esoteric knowledge.

C The author is John, son of Zebedee (see Mk 1:19–20)—the apostle and the author of the Gospel of John and Revelation (see Introductions to both books: Author). He was a fisherman, one of Jesus' inner circle (together with James and Peter), and "the disciple whom Jesus loved" (Jn 13:23; see note there). He may have been a first cousin of Jesus (his mother may have been Salome, possibly a sister of Mary; cf. Mt 27:56; Mk 15:40 and note; 16:1; Jn 19:25—this view assumes that "his mother's sister" in Jn 19:25 refers to Salome; some further assume that "Mary the wife of Clopas" there stands in apposition to "his mother's sister," which would mean that this Mary and Salome were one and the same person).

Unlike most NT letters, 1 John does not tell us who its author is. The earliest identification of him comes from the church fathers: Irenaeus (c. A.D. 140–203), Clement of Alexandria (c. 150–215), Tertullian (c. 155–222) and Origen (c. 185–253) all designated the writer as the apostle John. As far as we know, no one else was suggested by the early church.

This traditional identification is confirmed by evidence in the letter itself:

1. The style of the Gospel of John is markedly similar to that of this letter. Both are written in simple Greek and use contrasting figures, such as light and darkness, life and death, truth and lies, love and hate.

2. Similar phrases and expressions, such as those found in the following passages, are striking:

1 John	Gospel of John
1:1	1:1,14
1:4	16:24
1:6–7	3:19–21
2:7	13:34–35
3:8	8:44
3:14	5:24
4:6	8:47
4:9	1:14,18; 3:16
5:9	5:32,37
5:12	3:36

3. The mention of eyewitness testimony (1:1–4) harmonizes with the fact that John was a follower of Christ from the earliest days of his ministry.

4. The authoritative manner that pervades the letter—seen in its commands (2:15,24,28; 4:1; 5:21), its firm assertions (2:6; 3:14; 4:12) and its pointed identification of error (1:6,8; 2:4,22)—is what would be expected from an apostle.

5. The suggestions of advanced age (addressing his readers as "children," 2:1,28; 3:7) agree with early church tradition concerning John's age when he wrote the books known to be his.

6. The description of the heretics as antichrists (2:18), liars (2:22) and children of the devil (3:10) is consistent with Jesus' characterization of John as a son of thunder (Mk 3:17).

7. The indications of a close relationship with the Lord (1:1; 2:5–6,24,27–28) fit the descriptions of "the disciple whom Jesus loved" and the one who reclined "next to him" (Jn 13:23).

DATE

The letter is difficult to date with precision, but factors such as (1) evidence from early Christian writers (Irenaeus and Clement of Alexandria), (2) the early form of Gnosticism reflected in the denunciations of the letter and (3) indications of the advanced age of John suggest the end of the first century. Since the author of 1 John seems to build on concepts and themes found in the fourth Gospel (see 1Jn 2:7–11), it is reasonable to date the letter somewhere between A.D. 85 and 95, after the writing of the Gospel, which may have been written c. 85 (see Introduction to John: Date).

RECIPIENTS

1Jn 2:12–14,19; 3:1; 5:13 make it clear that this letter was addressed to believers. But the letter itself does not indicate who they were or where they lived. The fact that it mentions no one by name suggests that it was a circular letter sent to Christians in a number of places. Evidence from early Christian writers places the apostle John in Ephesus during most of his later years (c. A.D. 70–100). The earliest confirmed use of 1 John was in the Roman province of Asia (in modern Turkey), where Ephesus was located. Clement of Alexandria indicates that John ministered in the various churches scattered throughout that province. It may be assumed, therefore, that 1 John was sent to the churches of the Roman province of Asia (see map No. 13 at the end of this study Bible).

GNOSTICISM

One of the most dangerous heresies of the first two centuries of the church was Gnosticism. Its central teaching was that spirit is entirely good and matter is entirely evil. From this unbiblical dualism flowed five important errors:

1. The human body, which is matter, is therefore evil. It is to be contrasted with God, who is wholly spirit and therefore good.

2. Salvation is the escape from the body, achieved not by faith in Christ but by special knowledge (the Greek word for "knowledge" is *gnosis,* hence Gnosticism).

3. Christ's true humanity was denied in two ways: (1) Some said that Christ only "seemed" to have a body, a view called Docetism, from the Greek *dokeo* ("to seem"), and (2) others said that the divine Christ joined the man Jesus at baptism and left him before he died, a view called Cerinthianism, after its most prominent spokesman, Cerinthus. This view is the background of much of 1 John (see 1:1; 2:22; 4:2–3 and notes).

4. Since the body was considered evil, it was to be treated harshly. This ascetic form of Gnosticism is the background of part of the letter to the Colossians (see Col 2:21,23 and notes).

5. Paradoxically, this dualism also led to licentiousness. The reasoning was that, since matter—and not the breaking of God's law (1Jn 3:4)—was considered evil, breaking his law was of no moral consequence.

The Gnosticism addressed in the NT was an early form of the heresy, not the intricately developed system of the second and third centuries. In addition to that seen in Colossians and in John's letters, acquaintance with early Gnosticism is reflected in 1,2 Timothy, Titus and 2 Peter and perhaps 1 Corinthians.

OCCASION AND PURPOSE

John's readers were confronted with an early form of Gnostic teaching of the Cerinthian variety (see Gnosticism, above). This heresy was also libertine, throwing off all moral restraints.

Consequently, John wrote this letter with two basic purposes in mind: (1) to expose false teachers (see 2:26 and note) and (2) to give believers assurance of salvation (see 5:13 and note). In keeping with his intention to combat Gnostic teachers, John specifically struck at their total lack of morality (3:8–10), and by giving eyewitness testimony to the incarnation he sought to confirm his readers' belief in the incarnate Christ (1:3). Success in this would give the writer joy (1:4).

OUTLINE*

I. Introduction: The Reality of the Incarnation (1:1–4)
II. The Christian Life as Fellowship with the Father and the Son (1:5—2:28)
   A. Ethical Tests of Fellowship (1:5—2:11)
      1. Moral likeness (1:5–7)
      2. Confession of sin (1:8—2:2)
      3. Obedience (2:3–6)
      4. Love for fellow believers (2:7–11)
   B. Two Digressions (2:12–17)
   C. Christological Test of Fellowship (2:18–28)
      1. Contrast: apostates versus believers (2:18–21)
      2. Person of Christ: the crux of the test (2:22–23)
      3. Persistent belief: key to continuing fellowship (2:24–28)
III. The Christian Life as Divine Sonship (2:29—4:6)
   A. Ethical Tests of Sonship (2:29—3:24)
      1. Righteousness (2:29—3:10a)
      2. Love (3:10b–24)
   B. Christological Tests of Sonship (4:1–6)
IV. The Christian Life as an Integration of the Ethical and the Christological (4:7—5:12)
   A. The Ethical Test: Love (4:7—5:5)
      1. The source of love (4:7–16)
      2. The fruit of love (4:17–19)
      3. The relationship of love for God and love for one's fellow Christians (4:20—5:1)
      4. Obedience: the evidence of love for God's children (5:2–5)
   B. The Christological Test (5:6–12)
V. Conclusion: Great Christian Certainties (5:13–21)

THE INCARNATION OF THE WORD OF LIFE

1 That which was from the beginning, *a* which we have heard, which we have seen with our eyes, *b* which we have looked at and our hands have touched *c*—this we proclaim concerning the Word of life. ²The life appeared; *d* we have seen it and testify to it, *e* and we proclaim to you the eternal life, *f* which was with the Father and has appeared to us. ³We proclaim to you what we have seen and heard, *g* so that you also may have fellowship with us. And our fellowship is with the Father and with his Son, Jesus Christ. *h* ⁴We write this *i* to make our*a* joy complete. *j*

LIGHT AND DARKNESS, SIN AND FORGIVENESS

⁵This is the message we have heard *k* from him and declare to you: God is light; *l* in him there is no darkness at all. ⁶If we claim to have fellowship with him and yet walk in the darkness, *m* we lie and do not live out the truth. *n* ⁷But if we walk in the light, *o* as he is in the light, we have fellowship with one another, and the blood of Jesus, his Son, purifies us from all*b* sin. *p*

⁸If we claim to be without sin, *q* we deceive ourselves and the truth is not in us. *r* ⁹If we confess our sins, he is faithful and just and will forgive us our sins *s* and purify us from all unrighteousness. *t* ¹⁰If we claim we have not sinned, *u* we make him out to be a liar *v* and his word is not in us. *w*

2 My dear children, *x* I write this to you so that you will not sin. But if anybody does sin, we have an advocate *y* with the Father—Jesus Christ, the Righteous One. ²He is the atoning sacrifice for our sins, *z* and not only for ours but also for the sins of the whole world. *a*

LOVE AND HATRED FOR FELLOW BELIEVERS

³We know *b* that we have come to know him *c* if we keep his commands. *d* ⁴Those who

---

a 4 Some manuscripts *your*   *b* 7 Or *every*

2:2 *c* S ver 4 *d* S Jn 14:15

1:1 *a* S Jn 1:2
b S Lk 24:48; Jn 1:14;
19:35; Ac 4:20;
2Pe 1:16; 1Jn 4:14
c Jn 20:27
1:2 *d* Jn 1:1-4; 11:25;
14:6; 1Ti 3:16;
1Pe 1:20; 1Jn 3:5,8
e S Jn 15:27
f S Mt 25:46
1:3 *g* S ver 1
h 1Co 1:9
1:4 *i* 1Jn 2:1
j S Jn 3:29
1:5 *k* 1Jn 3:11
l 1Ti 6:16
1:6 *m* Jn 3:19-21;
8:12; 2Co 6:14;
Eph 5:8; 1Jn 2:11
n Jn 3:19-21; 1Jn 2:4;
4:20
1:7 *o* Isa 2:5
p Heb 9:14; Rev 1:5;
7:14
1:8 *q* Pr 20:9;
Jer 2:35; Ro 3:9-19;
Jas 3:2 *r* Jn 8:44;
1Jn 2:4
1:9 *s* Ps 32:5; 51:2;
Pr 28:13 *t* ver 7;
Mic 7:18-20;
Heb 10:22
1:10 *u* ver 8
v 1Jn 5:10 *w* Jn 5:38;
1Jn 2:14
2:1 *x* ver 12,13,28;
1Jn 3:7,18; 4:4; 5:21;
S 1Th 2:11
y S Ro 8:34; 1Ti 2:5
2:2 *z* Ro 3:25;
1Jn 4:10 *a* S Mt 1:21;
S Jn 3:17 *b* ver 5;
1Jn 3:24; 4:13; 5:2

1:1–4 The introduction to this letter deals with the same subject and uses several of the same words as the introduction to John's Gospel (1:1–4)—"beginning," "Word," "life," "with."
1:1 *was from the beginning.* Has always existed. *we.* John and the other apostles. *heard . . . seen . . . looked at . . . touched.* The apostle had made a careful examination of the Word of life. He testifies that the one who has existed from eternity "became flesh" (Jn 1:14; see note there)—i.e., a flesh-and-blood man. He was truly divine and truly human. At the outset, John contradicts the heresy of the Gnostics (see Introduction: Gnosticism). *Word of life.* The one who is life and reveals life (see v. 2 and note). "Word" here speaks of revelation (see note on Jn 1:1).
1:2 *The life . . . the eternal life.* Christ. He is called "the life" because he is the living one who has life in himself (see Jn 11:25; 14:6 and notes). He is also the source of life and sovereign over life (5:11). The letter begins and ends (5:20) with the theme of eternal life.
1:3 *fellowship with us.* Participation with us (vicariously) in our experience of hearing, seeing and touching the incarnate Christ (v. 1). Fellowship (Greek *koinonia*) is the spiritual union of the believer with Christ—as described in the figures of the vine and branches (Jn 15:1–5) and the body and the head (1Co 12:12; Col 1:18)—as well as communion with the Father and with fellow believers (see vv. 6–7).
1:4 *our joy complete.* John's joy in the Lord could not be complete unless his readers shared the true knowledge of the Christ (see 2Jn 12; cf. Php 2:2).
1:5 *from him.* From Christ. *light . . . darkness.* Light represents what is good, true and holy, while darkness represents what is evil and false (see Jn 3:19–21).
1:6–7 *walk in the darkness . . . in the light.* Two lifestyles —one characterized by wickedness and error, the other by holiness and truth.
1:6 *we.* John and his readers. *to have fellowship with him.* To be in living, spiritual union with God. *walk.* A metaphor for living. *truth.* See note on Jn 1:14.
1:7 *sin.* A key word in 1 John, occurring 27 times in the Greek.

1:9 *faithful and just.* Here the phrase is virtually a single concept (faithful-and-just). It indicates that God's response toward those who confess their sins will be in accordance with his nature and his gracious commitment to his people (see Ps 143:1; Zec 8:8 and note; cf. Pr 28:13 and note). *faithful.* To his promise to forgive (see Jer 31:34; Mic 7:18–20; Heb 10:22–23 and notes). *will forgive us.* Will provide the forgiveness that restores the communion with God that had been interrupted by sin (as requested in the Lord's Prayer, Mt 6:12).
1:10 *we have not sinned.* Gnostics denied that their immoral actions were sinful.
2:1 *dear children.* John, the aged apostle, often used this expression of endearment (vv. 12–13,28; 3:7,18; 4:4; 5:21; the term in 2:18 translates a different Greek word). *advocate.* Refers to someone who speaks in court in behalf of a defendant (see note on Jn 14:16). *Righteous One.* In God's court the defender must be, and is, sinless (cf. Ac 3:14 and note).
2:2 *atoning sacrifice for our sins.* God's holiness demands punishment for human sin. God, therefore, out of love (4:10; Jn 3:16), sent his Son to make substitutionary atonement for the believer's sin. In this way the Father's wrath is satisfied; his wrath against the Christian's sin has been turned away and directed toward Christ. See note on Ro 3:25. *for the sins of the whole world.* Forgiveness through Christ's atoning sacrifice is not limited to one particular group only; it has worldwide application (see Jn 1:29). It must, however, be received by faith (see Jn 3:16). Thus this verse does not teach universalism (that all people ultimately will be saved), but that God is an impartial God.
2:3 *know.* Forty-two times 1 John uses two Greek verbs normally translated "know." One of these verbs is related to the name of the Gnostics, the heretical sect that claimed to have a special knowledge (Greek *gnosis*) of God (see Introduction: Gnosticism). *keep his commands.* Does not mean that only those who never disobey (1:8–9) know God, but simply refers to those whose lives are generally characterized by obedience.

2:4 *e* ver 3; Tit 1:16;
1Jn 3:6; 4:7,8
f 1Jn 1:6,8
2:5 *g* S Jn 14:15
h 1Jn 4:12 *i* S ver 3
2:6 *j* S Mt 11:29
2:7 *k* S 1Co 10:14
l ver 24; 1Jn 3:11,23;
4:21; 2Jn 5,6
2:8 *m* S Jn 13:34
n Ro 13:12; Heb 10:25
o Jn 1:9 *p* Eph 5:8;
1Th 5:5
2:9 *q* ver 11;
Lev 19:17;
1Jn 3:10,15,16; 4:20,21
r 1Jn 1:5
2:10 *s* 1Jn 3:14
t ver 11; Ps 119:165
2:11 *u* S ver 9
v S 1Jn 1:6 *w* 1Jn 11:9;
12:35
2:12 *x* S ver 1
y S 1Jn 3:23
2:13 *z* S Jn 1:1
a S Jn 16:33 *b* ver 14;
S Mt 5:37
2:14 *c* S ver 1
d S Jn 1:1 *e* Eph 6:10
f S Heb 4:12 *g* Jn 5:38;
1Jn 1:10 *h* S ver 13
2:15 *i* Ro 12:2
j Jas 4:4
2:16 *k* Ge 3:6;
Ro 13:14; Eph 2:3
l Pr 27:20
2:17 *m* S Heb 12:27
n Mt 12:50
2:18 *o* S Ro 13:11

say, "I know him," *e* but do not do what he commands are liars, and the truth is not in them. *f* 5But if anyone obeys his word, *g* love for God*a* is truly made complete in them. *h* This is how we know *i* we are in him: 6Whoever claims to live in him must live as Jesus did. *j*

7Dear friends, *k* I am not writing you a new command but an old one, which you have had since the beginning. *l* This old command is the message you have heard. 8Yet I am writing you a new command; *m* its truth is seen in him and in you, because the darkness is passing *n* and the true light *o* is already shining. *p*

9Those who claim to be in the light but hate a fellow believer *q* are still in the darkness. *r* 10Those who love their fellow believers live in the light, *s* and there is nothing in them to make them stumble. *t* 11But those who hate a fellow believer *u* are in the darkness and walk around in the darkness; *v* they do not know where they are going, because the darkness has blinded them. *w*

REASONS FOR WRITING

12I am writing to you, dear children, *x*
because your sins have been forgiven on account of his name. *y*

13I am writing to you, fathers,
because you know him who is from the beginning. *z*
I am writing to you, young people,
because you have overcome *a* the evil one. *b*

14I write to you, dear children, *c*
because you know the Father.
I write to you, fathers,
because you know him who is from the beginning. *d*
I write to you, young people,
because you are strong, *e*
and the word of God *f* lives in you, *g*
and you have overcome the evil one. *h*

ON NOT LOVING THE WORLD

15Do not love the world or anything in the world. *i* If you love the world, love for the Father *b* is not in you. *j* 16For everything in the world—the cravings of sinful people, *k* the lust of their eyes *l* and their boasting about what they have and do—comes not from the Father but from the world. 17The world and its desires pass away, *m* but whoever does the will of God *n* lives forever.

WARNINGS AGAINST DENYING THE SON

18Dear children, this is the last hour; *o* and as you have heard that the antichrist is com-

---

a 5 Or *word, God's love*   *b* 15 Or *world, the Father's love*

2:5 *love for God is truly made complete in them.* The TNIV main text translation ("love for God") means that our love for God becomes complete when it expresses itself in acts of obedience (see 3:16–18). The TNIV text note rendering means that God's love for the believer is made complete when it moves the believer to acts of obedience (see 4:12). *in him.* Spiritual union with God (see Jn 17:21; Eph 1:1 and note).

2:7–8 *new command.* See Jn 13:34–35 and notes. The Biblical command to love was old (see Lev 19:18; also Mt 22:39–40). But its newness is seen in: (1) the new and dramatic illustration of divine love on the cross; (2) Christ's exposition of the OT law (see Mt 5), which seemed new to Christ's hearers; and (3) the daily experience of believers as they grow in love for each other.

2:7 *Dear friends.* Like "dear children" (see note on v. 1), a favorite term of John (used ten times in two letters: here; 3:2,21; 4:1,7,11; 3Jn 1–2,5,11). *since the beginning.* The beginning of their Christian experience, when they first heard the gospel.

2:8 *true light.* Used in the NT only here and in Jn 1:9 (see note on Jn 1:4), this phrase refers to the gospel of Jesus Christ, who is the light of the world (see Jn 8:12 and note).

2:9–10 *hate ... love.* In the Bible hatred and love as moral qualities are not primarily emotions but attitudes expressed in actions (see 3:15–16).

2:9 *light ... darkness.* See note on 1:5. *fellow believer.* Lit. "brother." See note on Ro 1:13.

2:10 *stumble.* Into sin.

2:12–14 *I am writing to you ... because.* By extended repetition in these verses, John assures his readers that, in spite of the rigorous tests contained in the letter, he is confident of their salvation. *dear children ... fathers ... young people.* As elsewhere in this letter, "dear children" probably refers to all John's readers (see note on v. 1), including fathers and young people. The terms "fathers" and "young people" may, however, describe two different levels of spiritual maturity. Some hold that all three terms refer to levels of spiritual maturity.

2:12 *his name.* Jesus (see 3:23; 5:13; see also note on Ac 4:12).

2:13–14 *him who is from the beginning.* Christ (see note on 1:1).

2:15 *world.* Not the world of people (Jn 3:16) or the created world (Jn 17:24), but here the world, or realm, of sin (v. 16; see Jas 4:4 and note), which is controlled by Satan and organized against God and righteousness (see note on Jn 1:9). *love for the Father.* Cf. 2:5 and note.

2:18 *last hour.* With other NT writers, John viewed the whole period beginning with Christ's first coming as the last days (see Ac 2:17; 2Ti 3:1 and note). They understood this to be the "last" of the days because neither former prophecy nor ing,[p] even now many antichrists have come. [q] This is how we know it is the last hour. [19]They went out from us, [r] but they did not really belong to us. For if they had belonged to us, they would have remained with us; but their going showed that none of them belonged to us. [s]

[20]But you have an anointing [t] from the Holy One, [u] and all of you know the truth. [a] [v] [21]I do not write to you because you do not know the truth, but because you do know it [w] and because no lie comes from the truth. [22]Who is the liar? It is whoever denies that Jesus is the Messiah. [b] Such a person is the antichrist—denying the Father and the Son. [x] [23]No one who denies the Son has the Father; whoever acknowledges the Son has the Father also. [y]

[24]As for you, see that what you have heard from the beginning[z] remains in you. If it does, you also will remain in the Son and in the Father. [a] [25]And this is what he promised us—eternal life. [b]

[26]I am writing these things to you about those who are trying to lead you astray. [c] [27]As for you, the anointing[d] you received from him remains in you, and you do not need anyone to teach you. But as his anointing teaches you about all things [e] and as that anointing is real, not counterfeit—just as it has taught you, remain in him. [f]

GOD'S CHILDREN AND SIN

[28]And now, dear children, [g] continue in him, so that when he appears [h] we may be confident [i] and unashamed before him at his coming.[j]

[29]If you know that he is righteous, [k] you know that everyone who does what is right has been born of him. [l]

3 See what great love [m] the Father has lavished on us, that we should be called children of God! [n] And that is what we are! The reason the world does not know us is that it did not know him. [o] [2]Dear friends, [p] now we are children of God, [q] and what we will be has not yet been made known. But we know that when Christ appears,[c] [r] we shall be like him, [s] for we shall see him as he is. [t] [3]All who have this hope in him purify themselves, [u] just as he is pure. [v]

[4]Everyone who sins breaks the law; in fact, sin is lawlessness. [w] [5]But you know that he appeared so that he might take away our sins. [x] And in him is no sin. [y] [6]No one who lives in him keeps on sinning. [z] No one who continues to sin has either seen him [a] or known him. [b]

---

[a] 20 Some manuscripts *and you know all things*   [b] 22 Greek *Christ*   [c] 2 Or *when it is made known*

2:18 [p] ver 22;
1Jn 4:3; 2Jn 7 [q] 1Jn 4:1
2:19 [r] Ac 20:30
[s] 1Co 11:19
2:20 [t] ver 27;
2Co 1:21 [u] S Mk 1:24
[v] Jer 31:34; Mt 13:11;
Jn 14:26
2:21 [w] 2Pe 1:12;
Jude 5
2:22 [x] 1Jn 4:3; 2Jn 7
2:23 [y] Jn 8:19; 14:7;
1Jn 4:15; 5:1; 2Jn 9
2:24 [z] S ver 7
[a] Jn 14:23; 15:4;
1Jn 1:3; 2Jn 9
2:25 [b] S Mt 25:46
2:26 [c] 1Jn 3:7
2:27 [d] ver 20
[e] 1Co 2:12 [f] Jn 15:4
2:28 [g] S ver 1
[h] Col 3:4; 1Jn 3:2
[i] S Eph 3:12
[j] S 1Th 2:19
2:29 [k] 1Jn 3:7
[l] S Jn 1:13
3:1 [m] S Jn 3:16
[n] ver 2,10; S Jn 1:12
[o] Jn 15:21; 16:3
3:2 [p] S 1Co 10:14
[q] ver 1,10; S Jn 1:12
[r] Col 3:4; 1Jn 2:28
[s] Ro 8:29; 2Pe 1:4
[t] Ps 17:15; Jn 17:24;
2Co 3:18
3:3 [u] 2Co 7:1;
2Pe 3:13,14 [v] Ps 18:26
3:4 [w] 1Jn 5:17
3:5 [x] ver 8; S Jn 3:17
[y] S 2Co 5:21
3:6 [z] ver 9; 1Jn 5:18
[a] 3Jn 11 [b] 1Jn 2:4

---

new revelation concerning the history of salvation indicated the coming of another era before the return of Christ. The word "last" in "last days," "last times" and "last hour" also expresses a sense of urgency and imminence. The Christian is to be alert, waiting for the return of Christ (Mt 25:1–13). *the antichrist … many antichrists.* John assumed his readers knew that a great enemy of God and his people would arise before Christ's return. That person is called "antichrist" (here), "the man of lawlessness" (2Th 2:3; but see note there) and "the beast" (Rev 13:1–10). But prior to him there will be many antichrists. These are characterized by the following: (1) They deny the incarnation (see 4:2 and note; 2Jn 7) and that Jesus is the divine Christ (v. 22); (2) they deny the Father (v. 22); (3) they do not have the Father (v. 23); (4) they are liars (v. 22) and deceivers (2Jn 7); (5) they are many (v. 18); (6) in John's day they left the church because they had nothing in common with believers (v. 19). The antichrists referred to in John's letter were the early Gnostics. The "anti" in antichrist means "against" (cf. 2Th 2:4; Rev 13:6–7).
2:20 *anointing.* The Holy Spirit (see v. 27; Jn 14:16–17; 15:26; 16:13; Ac 10:38). *Holy One.* Either Jesus Christ (Mk 1:24; Jn 6:69; Ac 2:27; 3:14; 22:14) or the Father (2Ki 19:22; Job 6:10).
2:22 *Jesus is the Messiah.* The man Jesus is the divine Messiah (see the parallel confession in 5:5; see also Introduction: Gnosticism and note on 5:6).
2:23 See 2Jn 9 for the same thought.
2:25 *eternal life.* See Jn 3:15 and note; cf. Mt 19:16 and note.
2:26 One of the statements of purpose for the letter (see Introduction: Occasion and Purpose).
A **2:27** *anointing.* See note on v. 20. *do not need anyone to teach you.* Since the Bible constantly advocates teaching (Mt 28:20; 1Co 12:28; Eph 4:11; Col 3:16; 1Ti 4:11; 2Ti 2:2,24),

John is not ruling out human teachers. At the time when he wrote, however, Gnostic teachers were insisting that the teaching of the apostles was to be supplemented with the "higher knowledge" that they (the Gnostics) claimed to possess. John's response was that what the readers were taught under the Spirit's ministry through the apostles was not only adequate but the only reliable truth. *teaches you.* The teaching ministry of the Holy Spirit (what is commonly called illumination) does not involve revelation of new truth or the explanation of all difficult passages of Scripture to our satisfaction. Rather, it is the development of the capacity to appreciate and appropriate God's truth already revealed—making the Bible meaningful in thought and daily living. *all things.* All things necessary to know for salvation and Christian living.
2:28 *continue in him.* See "remains in" (vv. 24,27). *confident.* See 3:21; 4:17; 5:14.
2:29 *he … him.* God the Father. *does what is right.* Those who are born again are marked by righteous conduct.
3:1 *children of God.* See note on Jn 1:12.
3:2 *we shall be like him.* Cf. Ro 8:29; 1Co 15:49; Php 3:21.
3:3 *hope.* Not a mere wish, but unshakable confidence concerning the future (see Ro 5:5 and note). *purify themselves.* By turning from sin.
3:5 *take away our sins.* See Jn 1:29 and note. *in him is no sin.* Amply confirmed elsewhere in the NT (see 2Co 5:21; Heb 4:15 and notes; 1Pe 3:18).
A **3:6** *No one … keeps on sinning.* John is not asserting sinless perfection (see 1:8–10; 2:1) but explaining that the believer's life is characterized not by sin but by doing what is right.

3:7 ^cS 1Jn 2:1
^d1Jn 2:26 ^e1Jn 2:29
3:8 ^fver 10; Jn 8:44
^gS Mt 4:3 ^hHeb 2:14
3:9 ⁱS Jn 1:13 ^jver 6;
Ps 119:3; 1Jn 5:18
^k1Pe 1:23
3:10 ^lver 1,2;
S Jn 1:12 ^mver 8
ⁿ1Jn 4:8 ^oS 1Jn 2:9
3:11 ^p1Jn 1:5
^qS 1Jn 2:7
^rJn 13:34,35; 15:12;
1Jn 4:7,11,21; 2Jn 5
3:12 ^sS Mt 5:37
^tGe 4:8 ^uPs 38:20;
Pr 29:10
3:13 ^vJn 15:18,19;
17:14
3:14 ^wS Jn 5:24
^xS 1Jn 2:9
3:15 ^yS 1Jn 2:9
^zMt 5:21,22; Jn 8:44
^aGal 5:20,21;
Rev 21:8
3:16 ^bJn 10:11
^cJn 15:13; Php 2:17;
1Th 2:8
3:17 ^dDt 15:7,8;
Jas 2:15,16 ^e1Jn 4:20
3:18 ^fS 1Jn 2:1
^gEze 33:31; Ro 12:9
3:21 ^hS 1Co 10:14
ⁱS Eph 3:12; 1Jn 5:14
3:22 ^jS Mt 7:7
^kS Jn 14:15 ^lJn 8:29;
Heb 13:21
3:23 ^mJn 6:29
ⁿS Lk 24:47; Jn 1:12;
3:18; 20:31; 1Co 6:11;
1Jn 5:13 ^oS Jn 13:34
3:24 ^p1Jn 2:3
^q1Jn 2:6; 4:15
^r1Th 4:8; 1Jn 4:13
4:1 ^sS 1Co 10:14
^tJer 29:8; 1Co 12:10;
2Th 2:2 ^uS Mt 7:15;
1Jn 2:18
4:2 ^vS Jn 1:14;
1Jn 2:23 ^w1Co 12:3
4:3 ^x1Jn 2:22; 2Jn 7
^y1Jn 2:18

[7]Dear children, ^c do not let anyone lead you astray. ^d The one who does what is right is righteous, just as he is righteous. ^e [8]The one who does what is sinful is of the devil, ^f because the devil has been sinning from the beginning. The reason the Son of God ^g appeared was to destroy the devil's work. ^h [9]Those who are born of God ⁱ will not continue to sin, ^j because God's seed ^k remains in them; they cannot go on sinning, because they have been born of God. [10]This is how we know who the children of God ^l are and who the children of the devil ^m are: Those who do not do what is right are not God's children; nor are those who do not love ⁿ their brothers and sisters. ^o

MORE ON LOVE AND HATRED

[11]For this is the message you heard ^p from the beginning: ^q We should love one another. ^r [12]Do not be like Cain, who belonged to the evil one ^s and murdered his brother. ^t And why did he murder him? Because his own actions were evil and his brother's were righteous. ^u [13]Do not be surprised, my brothers and sisters, if the world hates you. ^v [14]We know that we have passed from death to life, ^w because we love each other. Anyone who does not love remains in death. ^x [15]Anyone who hates a fellow believer ^y is a murderer, ^z and you know that no murderers have eternal life in them. ^a

[16]This is how we know what love is: Jesus Christ laid down his life for us. ^b And we ought to lay down our lives for one another. ^c [17]If any one of you has material possessions and sees a brother or sister in need but has no pity on them, ^d how can the love of God be in you? ^e [18]Dear children, ^f let us not love with words or tongue but with actions and in truth. ^g

[19]This is how we know that we belong to the truth and how we set our hearts at rest in his presence: [20]If our hearts condemn us, we know that God is greater than our hearts, and he knows everything. [21]Dear friends, ^h if our hearts do not condemn us, we have confidence before God ⁱ [22]and receive from him anything we ask, ^j because we keep his commands ^k and do what pleases him. ^l [23]And this is his command: to believe ^m in the name of his Son, Jesus Christ, ⁿ and to love one another as he commanded us. ^o [24]Those who keep his commands ^p live in him, ^q and he in them. And this is how we know that he lives in us: We know it by the Spirit he gave us. ^r

ON DENYING THE INCARNATION

4 Dear friends, ^s do not believe every spirit, ^t but test the spirits to see whether they are from God, because many false prophets have gone out into the world. ^u [2]This is how you can recognize the Spirit of God: Every spirit that acknowledges that Jesus Christ has come in the flesh ^v is from God, ^w [3]but every spirit that does not acknowledge Jesus is not from God. This is the spirit of the antichrist, ^x which you have heard is coming and even now is already in the world. ^y

---

3:8 *devil.* In this short letter John says much about the devil: 1. He is called "the devil" (here) and "the evil one" (v. 12; 2:13–14; 5:18–19). 2. He "has been sinning from the beginning" (here), i.e., from the time he first rebelled against God, before the fall of Adam and Eve (see Jn 8:44 and note). 3. He is the instigator of human sin, and those who continue to sin belong to him (vv. 8,12) and are his children (v. 10). 4. He is in the world (4:3) and has "the whole world" of unbelievers under his control (5:19). 5. But he cannot lay hold of believers to harm them (5:18). 6. On the contrary, Christians will overcome him (2:13–14; 4:4), and Christ will destroy his work.

3:9 *God's seed.* The picture is of human reproduction, in which the sperm (the Greek for "seed" is *sperma*) bears the life principle and transfers the paternal characteristics. *cannot go on sinning.* Not a complete cessation of sin, but a life that is not characterized by sin.

3:11 *from the beginning.* See note on 2:7.

3:12 *Cain.* See Heb 11:4 and note.

3:13 *brothers and sisters.* See note on Ro 1:13.

3:15 *hates.* See note on 2:9–10. *murderer.* See Jas 4:2 and note.

3:17–18 See Jas 2:14–17 and note on 2:15–16.

3:17 *love of God.* God's kind of love, which he pours out in the believer's heart (see Ro 5:5 and note) and which in turn enables the Christian to love fellow believers. Or it may speak of the believer's love for God.

3:20 *God is greater than our hearts.* An oversensitive conscience can be quieted by the knowledge that God himself has

declared active love to be an evidence of salvation. He knows the hearts of all—whether, in spite of shortcomings, they have been born of him.

3:23 This command has two parts: (1) Believe in Christ (see Jn 6:29 and note), and (2) love each other (see Jn 13:34–35 and notes). The first part is developed in 4:1–6 and the second part in 4:7–12.

3:24 *We know it by the Spirit.* See Ro 8:16 and note.

4:1 *spirit.* A person moved by a spirit, whether by the Holy Spirit or an evil one. *test the spirits.* Cf. 1 Th 5:21 and note. (Mt 7:1 does not refer to such testing or judgment; it speaks of self-righteous moral judgment of others.) *false prophets.* A true prophet speaks from God, being "carried along by the Holy Spirit" (2Pe 1:21; see note there). False prophets, such as the Gnostics of John's day, speak under the influence of spirits alienated from God. Christ warned against false prophets (see Mt 7:15 and note; Mk 13:22), as did Paul (see 1Ti 4:1 and note) and Peter (see 2Pe 2:1 and note).

4:2 *acknowledges.* Not only knows intellectually—for demons know, and shudder (Jas 2:19; cf. Mk 1:24)—but also confesses publicly. *Jesus Christ has come in the flesh.* See note on 1:1. Thus John excludes the Gnostics, especially the Cerinthians, who taught that the divine Christ came upon the human Jesus at his baptism and then left him at the cross, so that it was only the man Jesus who died (see Introduction: Gnosticism).

4:3 *does not acknowledge Jesus.* The incarnate Jesus Christ of 1:2 (see note on 2:18).

[4]You, dear children, [z] are from God and have overcome them, [a] because the one who is in you [b] is greater than the one who is in the world. [c] [5]They are from the world [d] and therefore speak from the viewpoint of the world, and the world listens to them. [6]We are from God, and whoever knows God listens to us; but whoever is not from God does not listen to us. [e] This is how we recognize the Spirit[a] of truth [f] and the spirit of falsehood. [g]

GOD'S LOVE AND OURS

[7]Dear friends, let us love one another, [h] for love comes from God. Everyone who loves has been born of God [i] and knows God.[j] [8]Whoever does not love does not know God, because God is love. [k] [9]This is how God showed his love among us: He sent his one and only Son [l] into the world that we might live through him. [m] [10]This is love: not that we loved God, but that he loved us [n] and sent his Son as an atoning sacrifice for our sins. [o] [11]Dear friends, [p] since God so loved us, [q] we also ought to love one another. [r] [12]No one has ever seen God; [s] but if we love one another, God lives in us and his love is made complete in us. [t]

[13]This is how we know [u] that we live in him and he in us: He has given us of his Spirit. [v] [14]And we have seen and testify [w] that the Father has sent his Son to be the Savior of the world. [x] [15]If anyone acknowledges that Jesus is the Son of God, [y] God lives in them and they in God. [z] [16]And so we know and rely on the love God has for us.

God is love. [a] Whoever lives in love lives in God, and God in him. [b] [17]This is how love is made complete [c] among us so that we will have confidence [d] on the day of judgment: [e] In this world we are like Jesus. [18]There is no fear in love. But perfect love drives out fear, [f] because fear has to do with punishment. The one who fears is not made perfect in love.

[19]We love because he first loved us. [g] [20]If we say we love God yet hate a brother or sister, [h] we are liars. [i] For if we do not love a fellow believer, whom we have seen, [j] we cannot love God, whom we have not seen. [k] [21]And he has given us this command: [l] Those who love God must also love one another. [m]

FAITH IN THE INCARNATE SON OF GOD

5 Everyone who believes [n] that Jesus is the Messiah [o] is born of God, [p] and everyone who loves the father loves his child as well. [q] [2]This is how we know [r] that we love the children of God: [s] by loving God and carrying out his commands. [3]In fact, this is love for God: to keep his commands. [t] And his commands are not burdensome, [u] [4]for everyone born of God [v] overcomes [w] the world. This is the victory that has overcome the

---

[a] 6 Or *spirit*

4:4 [z] S 1Jn 2:1
[a] S Jn 16:33 [b] Ro 8:31
[c] 2Ki 6:16; S Jn 12:31
4:5 [d] Jn 15:19;
17:14,16
4:6 [e] Jn 8:47
[f] S Jn 14:17
[g] S Mk 13:5
4:7 [h] S 1Jn 3:11
[i] S Jn 1:13 [j] S 1Jn 2:4
4:8 [k] ver 7,16
4:9 [l] Jn 1:18
[m] Jn 3:16,17; 1Jn 5:11
4:10 [n] Ro 5:8,10
[o] S Ro 3:25
4:11 [p] S 1Co 10:14
[q] S Jn 3:16 [r] Jn 15:12;
S 1Jn 3:11
4:12 [s] S Jn 1:18
[t] ver 17; 1Jn 2:5
4:13 [u] S 1Jn 2:3
[v] 1Jn 3:24
4:14 [w] S Jn 15:27
[x] S Lk 2:11; S Jn 3:17
4:15 [y] S 1Jn 2:23;
5:5 [z] 1Jn 3:24
4:16 [a] ver 8
[b] ver 12,13; 1Jn 3:24
4:17 [c] ver 12; 1Jn 2:5
[d] S Eph 3:12
[e] S Mt 10:15
4:18 [f] Ro 8:15
4:19 [g] ver 10
4:20 [h] S 1Jn 2:9
[i] S 1Jn 1:6; 2:4
[j] 1Jn 3:17 [k] ver 12;
S Jn 1:18
4:21 [l] 1Jn 2:7
[m] S Mt 5:43; S 1Jn 2:9
5:1 [n] S Jn 3:15
[o] 1Jn 2:22; 4:2,15
[p] S Jn 1:13; S 1Jn 2:23
[q] Jn 8:42
5:2 [r] S 1Jn 2:3
[s] 1Jn 3:14
5:3 [t] S Jn 14:15
[u] Mt 11:30; 23:4
5:4 [v] S Jn 1:13
[w] S Jn 16:33

4:4 *from God.* An abbreviated form of the expression "born of God" (2:29; 3:9–10). *them.* The false prophets (v. 1), who were inspired by the spirit of the antichrist (v. 3). *the one who is in the world.* The devil (see Jn 12:31 and note). In v. 3 "world" means the inhabited earth; in vv. 4–5 it means the community, or system, of those not born of God—including the antichrists (see note on Jn 1:9).
4:6 *Spirit of truth.* Cf. 5:6 and note; see note on Jn 14:17.

[A] **4:7—5:3** The word "love" in its various forms is used 43 times in the letter, 32 times in this short section.

[A] **4:8** *does not know God.* Only those who are to some degree like him truly know him. *God is love.* In his essential nature and in all his actions, God is loving (see also v. 16). John similarly affirms that God is spirit (see Jn 4:24 and note) and light (see 1:5 and note), as well as righteous (2:29; 3:7), holy (2:20), powerful or great (4:4), faithful (see 1:9 and note), true (5:20) and just (1:9).

4:9 *one and only Son.* See Jn 1:18; 3:16 and notes.
4:10 *atoning sacrifice for our sins.* See note on 2:2.

[A] **4:12** *No one has ever seen God.* See note on Jn 1:18. Since our love has its source in God's love, his love reaches full expression (is made complete) when we love fellow Christians. Thus the God whom "no one has ever seen" is seen in those who love, because God lives in them.

4:13–14 *Spirit…Father…Son.* See note on Mt 28:19.
4:13 *has given us of his Spirit.* See 3:24 and note.
4:16 *God is love.* See note on v. 8.

[A] **4:17** *like Jesus.* The fact that we are like Christ in love is a sign that God, who is love, lives in us; therefore we may

have confidence on the day of judgment that we are saved.
4:18 *no fear in love.* There is no fear of God's judgment because genuine love confirms salvation.
4:19 All love comes ultimately from God; genuine love is never self-generated by his creatures.
4:21 *this command.* See Jn 13:34 and note.

[A] **5:1** *Everyone who believes that Jesus is the Messiah is born of God.* Faith in Jesus as the Messiah is a sign of being born again, just as love is (4:7). *the Messiah.* See note on 2:22. *everyone who loves the father loves his child as well.* John wrote at a time when members of a family were closely associated as a unit under the headship of the father. He could therefore use the family as an illustration to show that anyone who loves God the Father will naturally love God's children.

[A] **5:3** *this is love for God: to keep his commands.* Cf. Jn 14:15, 21 and notes. *his commands are not burdensome.* Not because the commands themselves are light or easy to obey but, as John explains in v. 4, because of the new birth. The one born of God by faith is enabled by the Holy Spirit to obey.

[A] **5:4** *overcomes…has overcome.* To overcome the world is to gain victory over its sinful pattern of life, which is another way of describing obedience to God (v. 3). Such obedience is not impossible for believers because they have been born again and the Holy Spirit dwells within them and gives them strength. John speaks of two aspects of victory: (1) the initial victory of turning in faith from the world to God ("has overcome"); (2) the continuing, day-by-day victory of Christian living ("overcomes"). *world.* See note on 2:15.

5:5 *x* ver 1;
S 1Jn 2:23
5:6 *y* Jn 19:34
z Jn 14:17
5:7 *a* S Mt 18:16
5:9 *b* Jn 5:34
c Mt 3:16,17;
Jn 5:32,37; 8:17,18
5:10 *d* Ro 8:16;
Gal 4:6 *e* Jn 3:33;
1Jn 1:10
5:11 *f* S Mt 25:46
g S Jn 1:4
5:12 *h* Jn 3:15,16,36
5:13 *i* S 1Jn 3:23
j ver 1; S Mt 25:46
5:14 *k* S Eph 3:12;
1Jn 3:21 *l* S Mt 7:7
5:15 *m* ver 18,19,20
n 1Ki 3:12
5:16 *o* Jas 5:15
p Ex 23:21; Heb 6:4-
6; 10:26 *q* Jer 7:16;
14:11
5:17 *r* 1Jn 3:4
s ver 16; 1Jn 2:1
5:18 *t* S Jn 1:13
u S Mt 5:37 *v* Jn 14:30
5:19 *w* 1Jn 4:6
x Jn 12:31; 14:30; 17:15
5:20 *y* ver 5
z Lk 24:45 *a* Jn 17:3
b ver 11; S Mt 25:46
5:21 *c* S 1Jn 2:1
d 1Co 10:14; 1Th 1:9

world, even our faith. ⁵Who is it that overcomes the world? Only the one who believes that Jesus is the Son of God. *x*

⁶This is the one who came by water and blood *y*—Jesus Christ. He did not come by water only, but by water and blood. And it is the Spirit who testifies, because the Spirit is the truth. *z* ⁷For there are three *a* that testify: ⁸the *a* Spirit, the water and the blood; and the three are in agreement. ⁹We accept human testimony, *b* but God's testimony is greater because it is the testimony of God, *c* which he has given about his Son. ¹⁰Whoever believes in the Son of God accepts this testimony. *d* Whoever does not believe God has made him out to be a liar, *e* because they have not believed the testimony God has given about his Son. ¹¹And this is the testimony: God has given us eternal life, *f* and this life is in his Son. *g* ¹²Whoever has the Son has life; whoever does not have the Son of God does not have life. *h*

CONCLUDING AFFIRMATIONS

¹³I write these things to you who believe in the name of the Son of God *i* so that you may know that you have eternal life. *j* ¹⁴This is the confidence *k* we have in approaching God: that if we ask anything according to his will, he hears us. *l* ¹⁵And if we know that he hears us—whatever we ask—we know *m* that we have what we asked of him. *n*

¹⁶If you see any brother or sister commit a sin that does not lead to death, you should pray and God will give them life. *o* I refer to those whose sin does not lead to death. There is a sin that leads to death. *p* I am not saying that you should pray about that. *q* ¹⁷All wrongdoing is sin, *r* and there is sin that does not lead to death. *s*

¹⁸We know that anyone born of God *t* does not continue to sin; the One who was born of God keeps them safe, and the evil one *u* cannot harm them. *v* ¹⁹We know that we are children of God, *w* and that the whole world is under the control of the evil one. *x* ²⁰We know also that the Son of God has come *y* and has given us understanding, *z* so that we may know him who is true. *a* And we are in him who is true by being in his Son Jesus Christ. He is the true God and eternal life. *b*

²¹Dear children, *c* keep yourselves from idols. *d*

---

a 7,8 Late manuscripts of the Vulgate *testify in heaven: the Father, the Word and the Holy Spirit, and these three are one.* ⁸*And there are three that testify on earth: the* (not found in any Greek manuscript before the fourteenth century)

5:5 *Son of God.* For parallel confessions, see 2:22; 4:2; 5:1 and notes.

5:6 *water and blood.* Water symbolizes Jesus' baptism, and blood symbolizes his death. These are mentioned because Jesus' ministry began at his baptism and ended at his death. John is reacting to the Gnostic heretics of his day (see Introduction: Gnosticism) who said that Jesus was born only a man and remained so until his baptism. At that time, they maintained, the Messiah (the Son of God) descended on the human Jesus but left him before his suffering on the cross—so that it was only the man Jesus who died. Throughout this letter John has been insisting that Jesus Christ is God as well as man (1:1–4; 4:2; 5:5). He now asserts that it was this God-man Jesus Christ who came into our world, was baptized and died. Jesus was the Son of God not only at his baptism but also at his death (v. 6b). This truth is extremely important, because, if Jesus died only as a man, his sacrificial atonement (2:2; 4:10) would not have been sufficient to take away the guilt of human sin. *the Spirit who testifies.* The Holy Spirit testifies that Jesus is the Son of God in two ways: (1) The Spirit descended on Jesus at his baptism (Jn 1:32–34), and (2) he continues to confirm in the hearts of believers the apostolic testimony that Jesus' baptism and death verify that he is the Messiah, the Son of God (see 2:27; 1Co 12:3 and notes; cf. Ro 8:16 and note).

5:7 *three.* The OT law required "two or three witnesses" (Dt 17:6; see note there). At the end of this verse, some older English versions add the words found in the TNIV text note. But the addition is not found in any Greek manuscript or NT

translation prior to the 14th century.

5:9 *God's testimony.* The Holy Spirit's testimony, mentioned in vv. 6–8.

5:11 *has given us eternal life.* As a present possession (see notes on Jn 3:15,36).

5:13 Another statement of the letter's purpose (see 2:26 and note). See Introduction: Occasion and Purpose.

5:14 *if we ask anything according to his will.* Cf. Lk 22:42. For another condition for prayer, see 3:21–22.

5:16 Verses 16–17 illustrate the kind of petition we can be sure God will answer (see vv. 14–15). *sin that leads to death.* In the context of this letter directed against Gnostic teaching, which denied the incarnation and threw off all moral restraints, it is probable that the "sin that leads to death" refers to the Gnostics' adamant and persistent denial of the truth and to their shameless immorality. This kind of unrepentant sin leads to spiritual death. Another view is that this is sin that results in physical death. It is held that, because a believer continues to sin, God in judgment takes his or her life (cf. 1Co 11:30). In either case, "sin that does not lead to death" is of a less serious nature.

5:18–20 *We know.* The letter ends with three striking statements, affirming the truths that "we know" and summarizing some of the letter's major themes.

5:18 *the One who was born of God.* Jesus, the Son of God.

5:20 *him who is true.* God the Father. *He is the true God.* Could refer to either God the Father or God the Son. *eternal life.* The letter began with this theme (1:1–2) and now ends with it.

5:21 *idols.* False gods, as opposed to the one true God (v. 20).

The author is John the apostle. Obvious similarities to 1 John and the Gospel of John suggest that the same person wrote all three books. Compare the following:

2Jn 5	1Jn 2:7	Jn 13:34–35
2Jn 6	1Jn 5:3	Jn 14:23
2Jn 7	1Jn 4:2–3	
2Jn 12	1Jn 1:4	Jn 15:11; 16:24

See Introductions to 1 John and the Gospel of John: Author.

DATE

The letter was probably written about the same time as 1 John (A.D. 85–95), as the above comparisons suggest (see Introduction to 1 John: Date).

OCCASION AND PURPOSE

During the first two centuries the gospel was taken from place to place by traveling evangelists and teachers. Believers customarily took these missionaries into their homes and gave them provisions for their journey when they left. Since Gnostic teachers also relied on this practice (see note on 3Jn 5), 2 John was written to urge discernment in supporting traveling teachers; otherwise, someone might unintentionally contribute to the propagation of heresy rather than truth.

OUTLINE

- I. Greetings (1–3)
- II. Commendation (4)
- III. Exhortation and Warning (5–11)
- IV. Conclusion and Final Greetings (12–13)

1 ᵃ S Ac 11:30; 3Jn 1
ᵇ ver 13; Ro 16:13;
1Pe 5:13 ᶜ ver 3
ᵈ Jn 8:32; 1Ti 2:4
2 ᵉ 2Pe 1:12
ᶠ Jn 14:17; 1Jn 1:8
3 ᵍ S Ro 1:7
4 ʰ 3Jn 3, 4
5 ⁱ S 1Jn 2:7
6 ʲ 1Jn 2:5
ᵏ S Jn 14:15 ˡ S 1Jn 2:7
7 ᵐ 1Jn 2:22; 4:2, 3
ⁿ S Jn 1:14 ᵒ 1Jn 4:1
ᵖ S 1Jn 2:18
8 �q S Mt 10:42;
Mk 10:29, 30; 1Co 3:8;
Heb 10:35, 36; 11:26
9 ʳ Jn 8:31
ˢ S 1Jn 2:23
10 ᵗ S Ro 16:17
11 ᵘ 1Ti 5:22
12 ᵛ 3Jn 13, 14
ʷ S Jn 3:29
13 ˣ ver 1

¹The elder, ᵃ

To the lady chosen by God ᵇ and to her children, whom I love in the truth ᶜ—and not I only, but also all who know the truth ᵈ— ²because of the truth, ᵉ which lives in us ᶠ and will be with us forever:

³Grace, mercy and peace from God the Father and from Jesus Christ, ᵍ the Father's Son, will be with us in truth and love.

⁴It has given me great joy to find some of your children walking in the truth, ʰ just as the Father commanded us. ⁵And now, dear lady, I am not writing you a new command but one we have had from the beginning. ⁱ I ask that we love one another. ⁶And this is love: ʲ that we walk in obedience to his commands. ᵏ As you have heard from the beginning, ˡ his command is that you walk in love.

⁷Many deceivers, who do not acknowledge Jesus Christ ᵐ as coming in the flesh, ⁿ have gone out into the world. ᵒ Any such person is the deceiver and the antichrist. ᵖ ⁸Watch out that you do not lose what we ᵃ have worked for, but that you may be rewarded fully. q ⁹Anyone who runs ahead and does not continue in the teaching of Christ ʳ does not have God; whoever continues in the teaching has both the Father and the Son. ˢ ¹⁰If anyone comes to you and does not bring this teaching, do not take them into your house or welcome them. ᵗ ¹¹Anyone who welcomes them shares ᵘ in their wicked work.

¹²I have much to write to you, but I do not want to use paper and ink. Instead, I hope to visit you and talk with you face to face, ᵛ so that our joy may be complete. ʷ

¹³The children of your sister, who is chosen by God, ˣ send their greetings.

ᵃ 8 Some manuscripts *you*

---

1 *elder.* See note on 1Ti 3:1. In his later years John functioned as an elder, perhaps of the Ephesian church. The apostle Peter held a similar position (see 1Pe 5:1 and note). *lady chosen.* Either an unknown Christian woman in the province of Asia or a figurative designation of a local church there (see v. 13). *her children.* Children of that Christian lady or members of that local church. *truth.* See note on Jn 1:14.
3 *Grace … peace.* See note on Ro 1:7. *mercy.* See Ro 9:22–23 and note.
5 *new command.* See note on 1Jn 2:7–8.
6 *from the beginning.* See note on 1Jn 2:7.
7–11 This section deals with the basic Gnostic heresy attacked in 1 John, namely, that the Son of God did not become flesh (see Jn 1:14 and note) but that he temporarily came upon the man Jesus between his baptism and crucifixion (see Introduction to 1 John: Gnosticism).
7 *Jesus Christ as coming in the flesh.* See 1Jn 4:2–3 and note. *antichrist.* See note on 1Jn 2:18.
8 *worked for … rewarded.* Work faithfully accomplished on earth brings future reward (see Mk 9:41; 10:29–30; Lk 19:16–19; Heb 11:26).

9 *runs ahead.* A reference to the Gnostics, who believed that they had advanced beyond the teaching of the apostles. *teaching of Christ.* The similarity of this letter to 1 John, the nature of the heresy combated and the immediate context suggest that John is not referring to teaching given by Christ but to true teaching about Christ as the incarnate God-man (see 1Jn 2:23).
10 *take them into your house.* A reference to the housing and feeding of traveling teachers (see Introduction: Occasion and Purpose). The instruction does not prohibit greeting or even inviting a person into one's home for conversation. John was warning against providing food and shelter, since this would be an investment in the "wicked work" of false teachers and would give public approval (see v. 11).
12 *paper and ink.* Paper was made from papyrus reeds, which were readily available and cheap. The ink (the Greek for this word comes from a word that means "black") was made by mixing carbon, water and gum or oil. *that our joy may be complete.* See 1Jn 1:4 and note.
13 *sister, who is chosen.* May be taken literally to designate another Christian woman or figuratively to refer to another local church (see note on v. 1).

AUTHOR

3 JOHN   INTRODUCTION

The author is John the apostle. In the first verses of both 2 John and 3 John the author identifies himself as "the elder." Note other similarities: "love in the truth" (v. 1 of both letters), "walking in the truth" (v. 4 of both letters) and the similar conclusions. See Introductions to 1 John and the Gospel of John: Author.

DATE

The letter was probably written about the same time as 1 and 2 John (A.D. 85–95). See Introduction to 1 John: Date.

OCCASION AND PURPOSE

See Introduction to 2 John: Occasion and Purpose. Itinerant teachers sent out by John were rejected in one of the churches in the province of Asia by a dictatorial leader, Diotrephes, who even excommunicated members who showed hospitality to John's messengers. John wrote this letter to commend Gaius for supporting the teachers and, indirectly, to warn Diotrephes.

OUTLINE

   I. Greetings (1–2)
  II. Commendation of Gaius (3–8)
 III. Condemnation of Diotrephes (9–10)
 IV. Exhortation to Gaius (11)
  V. Example of Demetrius (12)
 VI. Conclusion, Benediction and Final Greetings (13–14)

1 *a* S Ac 11:30; 2Jn 1
3 *b* ver 5, 10;
S Ac 1:16 *c* 2Jn 4
4 *d* S 1Jn 2:1 *e* ver 3
5 *f* S ver 3 *g* Ro 12:13;
Heb 13:2
6 *h* 1Co 16:11;
2Co 1:16 *i* S Eph 4:1
7 *j* S Jn 15:21
k Ac 20:33, 35
10 *l* ver 14; 2Jn 12
m ver 5 *n* Jn 9:22, 34
11 *o* Ps 34:14; 37:27
p 1Jn 2:29 *q* 1Jn 3:6, 9,
10
12 *r* 1Ti 3:7
s Jn 19:35; 21:24
14 *t* 2Jn 12
u S Ro 1:7; S Eph 6:23
v Jn 10:3

[1]The elder, *a*

To my dear friend Gaius, whom I love in the truth.

[2]Dear friend, I pray that you may enjoy good health and that all may go well with you, even as your soul is getting along well. [3]It gave me great joy to have some believers *b* come and testify to your faithfulness to the truth, telling how you continue to walk in it. *c* [4]I have no greater joy than to hear that my children *d* are walking in the truth. *e*

[5]Dear friend, you are faithful in what you are doing for the brothers and sisters, *f* even though they are strangers to you. *g* [6]They have told the church about your love. You will do well to send them on their way *h* in a manner worthy *i* of God. [7]It was for the sake of the Name *j* that they went out, receiving no help from the pagans. *k* [8]We ought therefore to show hospitality to such people so that we may work together for the truth.

[9]I wrote to the church, but Diotrephes, who loves to be first, will have nothing to do with us. [10]So when I come, *l* I will call attention to what he is doing, spreading malicious nonsense about us. Not satisfied with that, he refuses to welcome other believers. *m* He also stops those who want to do so and puts them out of the church. *n*

[11]Dear friend, do not imitate what is evil but what is good. *o* Anyone who does what is good is from God. *p* Anyone who does what is evil has not seen God. *q* [12]Demetrius is well spoken of by everyone *r*—and even by the truth itself. We also speak well of him, and you know that our testimony is true. *s*

[13]I have much to write you, but I do not want to do so with pen and ink. [14]I hope to see you soon, and we will talk face to face. *t*

Peace to you. *u* The friends here send their greetings. Greet the friends there by name. *v*

---

1 *The elder.* See note on 2Jn 1. *dear friend.* A favorite term of John (see note on 1Jn 2:7). *Gaius.* A Christian in one of the churches of the province of Asia. Gaius was a common Roman name. This letter presents two good examples (Gaius [vv. 3–8] and Demetrius [v. 12]) and one bad example (Diotrephes [see vv. 9–10 and notes]). *truth.* See note on Jn 1:14.

3–4 *your faithfulness to the truth … you continue to walk in it … walking in the truth.* See 2Jn 4.

4 *my children.* Perhaps John's converts, or believers currently under his spiritual guidance (see 1Jn 2:1 and note).

5 *doing for the brothers and sisters.* The early church provided hospitality and support for missionaries. See Introduction to 2 John: Occasion and Purpose; see also note on 2Jn 10.

7 *Name.* See note on Ac 4:12. Today Orthodox Jews often address God by the title *Ha-Shem* ("The Name").

8 *show hospitality.* See v. 5; 1Pe 4:9 and notes.

9 *I wrote.* A previous letter of the apostle that is now lost. *church.* Some identify this church with the chosen lady of

2Jn 1. *Diotrephes.* A church leader who was exercising dictatorial power in the church. He must have had considerable influence since he was able to exclude people from the church fellowship (v. 10). See Introduction: Occasion and Purpose.

10 *spreading malicious nonsense.* See Pr 18:8; 2Th 3:11 and notes; 1Ti 5:13.

11 *does what is good.* The continual practice of good, not merely doing occasional good deeds (cf. Ro 12:21). *has not seen God.* See 1Jn 3:6.

12 *Demetrius is well spoken of.* In contrast to Diotrephes (see vv. 9–10 and notes; see also note on v. 1). Demetrius may have been the bearer of this letter. *even by the truth itself.* Possibly in some sense the gospel personified.

13–14 See 2Jn 12–13 for a similar conclusion (see also notes there).

14 *Peace to you.* Not a prayer or wish but a benedictory pronouncement (see note on Ro 1:7).

AUTHOR | JUDE | INTRODUCTION

C The author identifies himself as Jude (v. 1), which is another form of the Hebrew name Judah (Greek "Judas"), a common name among the Jews. Of those so named in the NT, the ones most likely to be author of this letter are: (1) Judas the apostle (see Lk 6:16; Ac 1:13 and note)—not Judas Iscariot—and (2) Judas the brother of the Lord (Mt 13:55; Mk 6:3). The latter is more likely. For example, the author does not claim to be an apostle and even seems to separate himself from the apostles (v. 17). Furthermore, he describes himself as a "brother of James" (v. 1). Ordinarily a person in Jude's day would describe himself as someone's son rather than as someone's brother. The reason for the exception here may have been James's prominence in the church at Jerusalem (see Introduction to James: Author).

Although neither Jude nor James describes himself as a brother of the Lord, others did not hesitate to speak of them in this way (see Mt 13:55; Jn 7:3–10; Ac 1:14; 1Co 9:5; Gal 1:19). Apparently they themselves did not ask to be heard because of the special privilege they had as members of the household of Joseph and Mary.

Possible references to the letter of Jude or quotations from it are found at a very early date: e.g., in Clement of Rome (c. A.D. 96). Clement of Alexandria (155–215), Tertullian (150–222) and Origen (185–253) accepted it; it was included in the Muratorian Canon (c. 170) and was accepted by Athanasius (298–373) and by the Council of Carthage (397). Eusebius (265–340) listed the letter among the questioned books, though he recognized that many considered it as coming from Jude.

According to Jerome and Didymus, some did not accept the letter as canonical because of the manner in which it uses noncanonical literature (see notes on vv. 9,14). But sound judgment has recognized that an inspired author may legitimately make use of such literature—whether for illustrative purposes or for appropriation of historically reliable or otherwise acceptable material—and that such use does not necessarily endorse that literature as inspired. Under the influence of the Spirit the church came to the conviction that the authority of God stands behind the letter of Jude. The fact that the letter was questioned and tested but nonetheless was finally accepted by the churches indicates the strength of its claims to authenticity.

DATE

There is nothing in the letter that requires a date beyond the lifetime of Jude, the brother of the Lord. The error the author is combating, like that in 2 Peter, is not the heretical teaching of the second century but that which could and did develop at an early date (cf. Ac 20:29–30; Ro 6:1; 1Co 5:1–11; 2Co 12:21; Gal 5:13; Eph 5:3–17; 1Th 4:6). (See also Introduction to 2 Peter: Date.) There is, moreover, nothing in the letter that requires a date after the time of the apostles, as some have argued. It may even be that Jude's readers had heard some of the apostles speak (see vv. 17–18). Likewise, the use of the word "faith" in the objective sense of the body of truth believed (v. 3) does not require a late dating of the letter. It was used in such a sense as early as Gal 1:23.

The question of the relationship between Jude and 2 Peter has a bearing on the date of Jude. If 2Pe 2 makes use of Jude—a commonly accepted view (see Introduction to 2 Peter: 2 Peter and Jude)—then Jude is to be dated prior to 2 Peter, probably c. A.D. 65. Otherwise, a date as late as c. 80 would be possible.

RECIPIENTS

The description of those to whom Jude addressed his letter is very general (see v. 1). It could apply to Jewish Christians, Gentile Christians or both. Their location is not indicated. It should not be assumed that, since 2Pe 2 and Jude 4–18 appear to describe similar situations, they were both written to the same people. The kind of heresy depicted in these two passages was widespread (see Date).

OCCASION AND PURPOSE

Although Jude was very eager to write to his readers about salvation, he felt that he must instead warn them about certain immoral men circulating among them who were perverting the grace of God (see v. 4 and note). Apparently these false teachers were trying to convince believers that being saved by grace gave them license to sin since their sins would no longer be held against them. Jude thought it imperative that his readers be on guard against such men and be prepared to oppose their perverted teaching with the truth about God's saving grace.

It has generally been assumed that these false teachers were Gnostics. Although this identification is no doubt correct, they must have been forerunners of fully developed, second-century Gnosticism (see Introduction to 2 Peter: Date).

OUTLINE

I. Greetings (1–2)
II. Occasion for the Letter (3–4)
  A. The Change of Subject (3)
  B. The Reason for the Change: The Presence of Godless Apostates (4)
III. Warning against False Teachers (5–16)
  A. Historical Examples of the Judgment of Apostates (5–7)
    1. Unbelieving Israel (5)
    2. Angels who fell (6)
    3. Sodom and Gomorrah (7)
  B. Description of the Apostates of Jude's Day (8–16)
    1. Their slanderous speech deplored (8–10)
    2. Their character graphically portrayed (11–13)
    3. Their destruction prophesied (14–16)
IV. Exhortation to Believers (17–23)
V. Concluding Doxology (24–25)

¹Jude, *a* a servant of Jesus Christ *b* and a brother of James,

To those who have been called, *c* who are loved in God the Father and kept for *a* Jesus Christ: *d*

²Mercy, peace *e* and love be yours in abundance. *f*

THE SIN AND DOOM OF UNGODLY PEOPLE

³Dear friends, *g* although I was very eager to write to you about the salvation we share, *h* I felt compelled to write and urge you to contend *i* for the faith *j* that the Lord has once for all entrusted to us, his people. *k* ⁴For certain individuals whose condemnation was written about *b* long ago have secretly slipped in among you. *l* They are ungodly people, who pervert the grace of our God into a license for immorality and deny Jesus Christ our only Sovereign and Lord. *m*

⁵Though you already know all this, *n* I want to remind you *o* that the Lord *c* at one time delivered his people out of Egypt, but later destroyed those who did not believe. *p* ⁶And the angels who did not keep their positions of authority but abandoned their proper dwelling—these he has kept in darkness, bound with everlasting chains for judgment on the great Day. *q* ⁷In a similar way, Sodom and Gomorrah *r* and the surrounding towns *s* gave themselves up to sexual immorality and perversion. They serve as an example of those who suffer the punishment of eternal fire. *t*

⁸In the very same way, on the strength of their dreams these ungodly people pollute their own bodies, reject authority and heap abuse on celestial beings. *u* ⁹But even the archangel *v*

---

a 1 Or by; or in   *b 4* Or *individuals who were marked out for condemnation*   *c 5* Some early manuscripts *Jesus*

---

1 *a* Mt 13:55;
Jn 14:22; Ac 1:13
b Ro 1:1 *c* Ro 1:6, 7
d Jn 17:12
2 *e* Gal 6:16; 1Ti 1:2
f S Ro 1:7
3 *g* S 1Co 10:14
h Tit 1:4 *i* 1Ti 6:12
j ver 20; Ac 6:7
k S Ac 9:13
4 *l* Gal 2:4 *m* Tit 1:16;
2Pe 2:1; 1Jn 2:22
5 *n* S 1Jn 2:20
o 2Pe 1:12, 13; 3:1, 2
p Nu 14:29; Dt 1:32;
2:15; Ps 106:26;
1Co 10:1-5; Heb 3:16,
17
6 *q* S 2Pe 2:4, 9
7 *r* S Mt 10:15
s Dt 29:23
t S Mt 25:41; 2Pe 3:7
8 *u* 2Pe 2:10
9 *v* 1Th 4:16

---

1 *servant.* See note on Ro 1:1. *brother of James.* See Introduction: Author. *called.* See note on Ro 8:28. *loved in God.* See Jn 3:16; Ro 8:28–39. *kept for Jesus Christ.* He who holds the whole universe together (see Col 1:17; Heb 1:3) will see that God's children are kept in the faith and that they reach their eternal inheritance (see Jn 6:37–40; 17:11–12; 1Pe 1:3–5).
2 *Mercy.* See Ge 19:16; Ro 9:22–23; Tit 3:5 and notes. *peace.* See note on Ro 1:7.

3 *Dear friends.* See vv. 17, 20; see also note on 2Pe 3:1. *the salvation we share.* Jude's original intention was to write a general treatment of the doctrine of salvation, probably dealing with such subjects as human sin and guilt, God's love and grace, the forgiveness of sins and the changed lifestyle that follows new birth. *the faith.* Here used of the body of truth held by believers everywhere—the gospel and all its implications (see Introduction: Date; see also 1Ti 4:6). This truth was under attack and had to be defended. *once for all entrusted.* The truth has finality and is not subject to change. *his people.* See notes on Ro 1:7; Eph 1:1; Col 1:4.
4 *For.* Introduces the reason Jude felt impelled to change the subject of his letter (see Introduction: Occasion and Purpose). *whose condemnation was written about.* The reference may be to OT denunciations of ungodly people or to Enoch's prophecy (vv. 14–15). Or Jude may mean that judgment has long been about to fall on them because of their sin (see TNIV text note and 2Pe 2:3, which may be a clarification of this clause). *ungodly people.* See vv. 15, 18. *pervert the grace of our God into a license for immorality.* They assume that salvation by grace gives them the right to sin without restraint, either because God in his grace will freely forgive all their sins or because sin, by contrast, magnifies the grace of God (cf. Ro 5:20; 6:1 and note). *deny ... our only Sovereign and Lord.* The Greek term translated "Sovereign" describes power without limit, or absolute domination. The Greek construction indicates that both "Sovereign" and "Lord" refer to the same person, and this verse, as well as the parallel passage (2Pe 2:1), clearly states that that person is Christ.
5–7 Three examples of divine judgment.
5 *destroyed those who did not believe.* They did not believe that God would give them the land of Canaan; consequently all unbelieving adults died in the wilderness without entering the

promised land (see Nu 14:29–30; Dt 1:32–36; 2:15; 1Co 10:1–5 and note on 10:5; Heb 3:16–19 and note).
6 *angels.* See note on 2Pe 2:4. *positions of authority.* See note on 2Pe 2:4. God had assigned differing areas of responsibility and authority to each of the angels (see Da 10:20–21, where the various princes may be angels assigned to various nations). Some of these angels refused to maintain their assignments and thus became the devil and his angels (cf. Mt 25:41). *their proper dwelling.* Angels apparently were assigned specific locations, as well as responsibilities. Some assume that they left the heavenly realm and came to earth (see note on 2Pe 2:4). *kept ... bound ... for judgment.* See note on 2Pe 2:4. *the great Day.* The final judgment.
7 *In a similar way.* Does not mean that the sin of Sodom and Gomorrah was the same as that of the angels or vice versa. This phrase is used to introduce the third illustration of the fact that God will see to it that the unrighteous will be consigned to eternal punishment on the judgment day. *perversion.* Lit. "went after other flesh"; more specifically, homosexual practices (see Ge 19:5 and note). *serve as an example of ... punishment of eternal fire.* God destroyed Sodom and Gomorrah by pouring out "burning sulfur" (Ge 19:24)—a foretaste of the eternal fire that is to come.
8 *their dreams.* The godless people were referred to as having "dreams" either (1) because they claimed to receive revelations or, more likely, (2) because in their passion they were out of touch with truth and reality (they were "dreamers"). *pollute their own bodies.* Probably a reference to the homosexual practices in Sodom and Gomorrah (see vv. 4, 7; 1Co 6:9, 18 and note on 6:9). *reject authority.* See note on 2Pe 2:10. *heap abuse on celestial beings.* See note on 2Pe 2:10.
9 According to several church fathers, this verse is based on a noncanonical work called The Testament of Moses (approximately the first century A.D.). Other NT quotations from, or allusions to, non-Biblical works include Paul's quotations of Aratus (see Ac 17:28 and note), Menander (see 1Co 15:33 and note) and Epimenides (see Tit 1:12 and note). Such usage in no way suggests that the quotations, or the books from which they were taken, are divinely inspired. It only means that the Biblical author found the quotations to be a helpful confirmation, clarification or illustration.

9 *w* Da 10:13,21; 12:1;
Rev 12:7 *x* Dt 34:6
y Zec 3:2
10 *z* 2Pe 2:12
11 *a* Ge 4:3-8;
Heb 11:4; 1Jn 3:12
b S 2Pe 2:15
c Nu 16:1-3,31-35
12 *d* 2Pe 2:13;
1Co 11:20-22
e Eze 34:2,8,10
f Pr 25:14; 2Pe 2:17
g Eph 4:14 *h* Mt 15:13
13 *i* Isa 57:20
j Php 3:19 *k* 2Pe 2:17
14 *l* Ge 5:18,21-24
m S Mt 16:27
n Dt 33:2; Da 7:10;
Zec 14:5; Heb 12:22
15 *o* 2Pe 2:6-9
p 1Ti 1:9
16 *q* 1Co 10:10
r ver 18; 2Pe 2:10
s 2Pe 2:18
17 *t* S Eph 4:11
u Heb 2:3; 2Pe 3:2
18 *v* 1Ti 4:1; 2Ti 3:1;
2Pe 3:3 *w* ver 16;
2Pe 2:1; 3:3
19 *x* 1Co 2:14,15
20 *y* Col 2:7;
1Th 5:11 *z* ver 3
a Eph 6:18
21 *b* Tit 2:13;
Heb 9:28; 2Pe 3:12
c S Mt 25:46

Michael, *w* when he was disputing with the devil about the body of Moses, *x* did not himself dare to condemn him for slander but said, "The Lord rebuke you!" *a* *y* [10] Yet these people speak abusively against whatever they do not understand; and what things they do understand by instinct, like unreasoning animals—these are the very things that destroy them. *z*

[11] Woe to them! They have taken the way of Cain; *a* they have rushed for profit into Balaam's error; *b* they have been destroyed in Korah's rebellion. *c*

[12] These people are blemishes at your love feasts, *d* eating with you without the slightest qualm—shepherds who feed only themselves. *e* They are clouds without rain, *f* blown along by the wind; *g* autumn trees, without fruit and uprooted *h*—twice dead. [13] They are wild waves of the sea, *i* foaming up their shame; *j* wandering stars, for whom blackest darkness has been reserved forever. *k*

[14] Enoch, *l* the seventh from Adam, prophesied about them: "See, the Lord is coming *m* with thousands upon thousands of his holy ones *n* [15] to judge *o* everyone, and to convict all the ungodly of all the ungodly acts they have done in an ungodly way, and of all the defiant words ungodly sinners have spoken against him." *b* *p* [16] These people are grumblers *q* and faultfinders; they follow their own evil desires; *r* they boast *s* about themselves and flatter others for their own advantage.

A CALL TO PERSEVERE

[17] But, dear friends, remember what the apostles *t* of our Lord Jesus Christ foretold. *u* [18] They said to you, "In the last times *v* there will be scoffers who will follow their own ungodly desires." *w* [19] These are the people who divide you, who follow mere natural instincts and do not have the Spirit. *x*

[20] But you, dear friends, by building yourselves up *y* in your most holy faith *z* and praying in the Holy Spirit, *a* [21] keep yourselves in God's love as you wait *b* for the mercy of our Lord Jesus Christ to bring you to eternal life. *c*

---

a 9 Jude is alluding to the Jewish *Testament of Moses* (approximately the first century A.D.).
b 14,15 From the Jewish *First Book of Enoch* (approximately the first century B.C.).

---

10 *whatever they do not understand.* See note on 2Pe 2:12; cf. 1Co 2:14. *like unreasoning animals.* See note on 2Pe 2:12.

A C **11** Three OT examples of the kind of persons Jude warns his readers about. *Woe to them!* A warning that judgment is coming (see Mt 23:13,15–16,23,25,27,29). *way of Cain.* The way of selfishness and greed (see note on Ge 4:3–4) and the way of hatred and murder (see 1Jn 3:12). *Balaam's error.* The error of consuming greed (see note on 2Pe 2:15). *Korah's rebellion.* Korah rose up against God's appointed leadership (see Nu 16). Jude may be suggesting that the false teachers of his day were rebelling against church leadership (cf. 3Jn 9–10).

12–13 These verses contain six graphic metaphors: 1. *blemishes at your love feasts.* See note on 2Pe 2:13. 2. *shepherds who feed only themselves.* Instead of feeding the sheep for whom they are responsible (see Eze 34:8–10). 3. *clouds without rain.* Like clouds promising moisture for the parched land, the false teachers promise soul-satisfying truth, but in reality they have nothing to offer. 4. *autumn trees, without fruit and uprooted—twice dead.* Though the trees ought to be heavy with fruit. 5. *wild waves of the sea.* As wind-tossed waves constantly churn up rubbish, so these apostates continually stir up moral filth (see Isa 57:20). 6. *wandering stars.* As shooting stars appear in the sky only to fly off into eternal oblivion, so these false teachers are destined for eternal hell.

C **14** *Enoch, the seventh from Adam.* Not the Enoch in the line of Cain (Ge 4:17) but the one in the line of Seth (Ge 5:18–24; 1Ch 1:1–3). He was seventh if Adam is counted as the first. The quotation is from the book of Enoch, which purports to have been written by the Enoch of Ge 5 but actually did not appear until the first century B.C. The book of Enoch was a well-respected writing in NT times. That it was not canonical does not mean that it contained no truth; nor does Jude's quotation of the book mean that he considered it inspired (see Introduction: Author; see also note on v. 9). *the Lord is coming.* Jude uses the quotation to refer to Christ's second coming and to his judgment of the wicked (see 2Th 1:6–10). *holy ones.* Probably angels (see Da 4:13–17; 2Th 1:7). However, some think they are raptured believ-

ers who are returning with the Lord (see 1Th 3:13 and note).

15 *ungodly…ungodly…ungodly…ungodly.* This thunderous repetition and the awesome judgment scene that is depicted emphasize the condemnation of the false teachers in v. 4.

16 *These people.* The ungodly people first mentioned in v. 4 and subsequently referred to repeatedly as "these people" (vv. 10,12, 19; cf. v. 8). They are the libertine false teachers who pervert the grace of God.

17 *remember what the apostles…foretold.* The coming of these godless people should not take believers by surprise, for it had been predicted by the apostles (Ac 20:29; 1Ti 4:1; 2Ti 3:1–5; 2Pe 2:1–3; 3:2–3).

C **18** *They said.* The Greek for this phrase indicates that the apostles continually or repeatedly warned that such godless apostates would come. *last times.* See note on Jas 5:3. *scoffers.* In both 2Pe 3:3 and Jude the scoffers are said to be characterized by selfish lusts ("desires").

C **19** *people who divide you.* At the very least this phrase means that they were divisive, creating factions in the church—the usual practice of heretics. Or Jude may be referring to the later Gnostics' division of people into the spiritual (the Gnostics) and the sensual (those for whom there is no hope). *follow mere natural instincts.* An ironic description of the false teachers, who labeled others as "sensual" (see 1Co 2:14 and note). *do not have the Spirit.* Rather than being the spiritual ones—the privileged elite class the Gnostics claimed to be— Jude denies that they even possess the Spirit. A person who does not have the Spirit is clearly not saved (see Ro 8:9).

20 *But you, dear friends.* In contrast to the ungodly false teachers, about whom this letter speaks at length. *most holy faith.* See note on v. 3. *in the Holy Spirit.* According to the Spirit's promptings and with the power of the Spirit (see Ro 8:26–27; Gal 4:6; Eph 6:17–18 and notes).

A **21** *keep yourselves in God's love.* God both keeps believers in his love (see Ro 8:35–39 and notes) and enables them to keep themselves in his love. *eternal life.* See Jn 3:15 and note.

²²Be merciful to those who doubt; ²³save others by snatching them from the fire; *d* to others show mercy, mixed with fear—hating even the clothing stained by corrupted flesh. *a e*

DOXOLOGY

²⁴To him who is able *f* to keep you from stumbling and to present you before his glorious presence *g* without fault *h* and with great joy— ²⁵to the only God *i* our Savior be glory, majesty, power and authority, through Jesus Christ our Lord, before all ages, now and forevermore! *j* Amen. *k*

a *22,23* The Greek manuscripts of these verses vary at several points.

23 *d* Am 4:11;
Zec 3:2-5; 1Co 3:15
e Rev 3:4
24 *f* S Ro 16:25
g 2Co 4:14
h Col 1:22
25 *i* Jn 5:44; 1Ti 1:17
j Heb 13:8 *k* S Ro 11:36

22–23 *those who doubt . . . others.* Perhaps those who have come under the influence of the apostates.
23 *save others by snatching them from the fire.* Rescuing them from the verge of destruction (see Am 4:11; Zec 3:2; 1Co 3:15 and notes). *mercy, mixed with fear.* Even in showing mercy one may be trapped by the allurement of sin. *clothing stained by cor-*

rupted flesh. The wicked are pictured as being so corrupt that even their garments are polluted by their sinful nature.

24–25 After all the attention necessarily given in this letter to the ungodly and their works of darkness, Jude concludes by focusing attention on God, who is fully able to keep those who put their trust in him.

REVELATION

AUTHOR

C Four times the author identifies himself as John (1:1,4,9; 22:8). From as early as Justin Martyr in the second century A.D. it has been held that this John was the apostle, the son of Zebedee (see Mt 10:2). The book itself reveals that the author was a Jew, well versed in Scripture, a church leader who was well known to the seven churches of Asia Minor, and a deeply religious person fully convinced that the Christian faith would soon triumph over the demonic forces at work in the world.

In the third century, however, an African bishop named Dionysius compared the language, style and thought of the Apocalypse (Revelation) with that of the other writings of John and decided that the book could not have been written by the apostle John. He suggested that the author was a certain John the Presbyter, whose name appears elsewhere in ancient writings. Although many today follow Dionysius in his view of authorship, the external evidence seems overwhelmingly supportive of the traditional view.

DATE

Revelation was written when Christians were entering a time of persecution. The two periods most often mentioned are the latter part of Nero's reign (A.D. 54–68) and the latter part of Domitian's reign (81–96). Most interpreters date the book c. 95. (A few suggest a date during the reign of Vespasian: 69–79.)

OCCASION

Since Roman authorities at this time were beginning to enforce emperor worship, Christians—who held that Christ, not Caesar, was Lord—were facing increasing hostility. The believers at Smyrna are warned against coming opposition (2:10), and the church at Philadelphia is told of an hour of trial coming on the world (3:10). Antipas has already given his life (2:13), along with others (6:9). John has been exiled to the island of Patmos (probably the site of a Roman penal colony) for his activities as a Christian missionary (1:9). Some within the church are advocating a policy of compromise (2:14–15,20), which has to be corrected before its subtle influence can undermine the determination of believers to stand fast in the perilous days that lie ahead.

PURPOSE

John writes to encourage the faithful to resist staunchly the demands of emperor worship. He informs his readers that the final showdown between God and Satan is imminent. Satan will increase his persecution of believers, but they must stand fast, even to death. They are sealed against any spiritual harm and will soon be vindicated when Christ returns, when the wicked are forever destroyed, and when God's people enter an eternity of glory and blessedness.

LITERARY FORM

For an adequate understanding of Revelation, the reader must recognize that it is a distinct kind of literature. Revelation is apocalyptic, a kind of writing that is highly symbolic. Although its visions often seem bizarre to the Western reader, the book fortunately provides a number of clues for its own interpretation (e.g., stars are angels, lampstands are churches, 1:20; "the great prostitute," 17:1, is "Babylon" [Rome?], 17:5,18; and the heavenly Jerusalem is the wife of the Lamb, 21:9–10).

DISTINCTIVE FEATURE

A distinctive feature is the frequent use of the number seven (52 times). There are seven beatitudes (see note on 1:3), seven churches (1:4,11), seven spirits (1:4), seven golden lampstands (1:12), seven stars (1:16), seven seals (5:1), seven horns and seven eyes (5:6), seven trumpets (8:2), seven thunders (10:3), seven signs (12:1,3; 13:13–14; 15:1; 16:14; 19:20), seven crowns (12:3), seven plagues (15:6), seven golden bowls (15:7), seven hills (17:9) and seven kings (17:10), as well as other sevens. Symbolically, the number seven stands for completeness.

INTERPRETATION

Interpreters of Revelation normally fall into four groups:

1. *Preterists* understand the book exclusively in terms of its first-century setting, claiming that most of its events have already taken place.

2. *Historicists* take it as describing the long chain of events from Patmos to the end of history.

3. *Futurists* place the book primarily in the end times.

4. *Idealists* view it as symbolic pictures of such timeless truths as the victory of good over evil.

Fortunately, the fundamental truths of Revelation do not depend on adopting a particular point of view. They are available to anyone who will read the book for its overall message and resist the temptation to become overly enamored with the details.

OUTLINE

PROLOGUE

1 The revelation from Jesus Christ, which God gave *a* him to show his servants what must soon take place. *b* He made it known by sending his angel *c* to his servant John, *d* 2who testifies to everything he saw—that is, the word of God *e* and the testimony of Jesus Christ. *f* 3Blessed is the one who reads aloud the words of this prophecy, and blessed are those who hear it and take to heart what is written in it, *g* because the time is near. *h*

GREETINGS AND DOXOLOGY

4John,

To the seven churches *i* in the province of Asia:

Grace and peace to you *j* from him who is, and who was, and who is to come, *k* and from the seven spirits *a l* before his throne, 5and from Jesus Christ, who is the faithful witness, *m* the firstborn from the dead, *n* and the ruler of the kings of the earth. *o*

To him who loves us *p* and has freed us from our sins by his blood, *q* 6and has made us to be a kingdom and priests *r* to serve his God and Father *s*—to him be glory and power for ever and ever! Amen. *t*

7"Look, he is coming with the clouds," *b u*
    and "every eye will see him,
    even those who pierced him"; *v*
    and all peoples on earth "will mourn *w* because of him." *c*
                                        So shall it be! Amen.

8"I am the Alpha and the Omega," *x* says the Lord God, "who is, and who was, and who is to come, *y* the Almighty." *z*

JOHN'S VISION OF CHRIST

9I, John, *a* your brother and companion in the suffering *b* and kingdom *c* and patient endurance *d* that are ours in Jesus, was on the island of Patmos because of the word of God *e* and the testimony of Jesus. *f* 10On the Lord's Day *g* I was in the Spirit, *h* and I heard behind me a loud voice like a trumpet, *i* 11which said: "Write on a scroll what you see *j* and send

---

a 4 That is, the sevenfold Spirit   b 7 Daniel 7:13   c 7 Zech. 12:10

**Cross references (right margin):**

1:1 *a* Jn 12:49; 17:8
b ver 19; Da 2:28, 29;
Rev 22:6 *c* Rev 22:16
d ver 4, 9; Rev 22:8
1:2 *e* ver 9;
S Heb 4:12 *f* ver 9;
1Co 1:6; Rev 6:9;
12:17; 19:10
1:3 *g* Lk 11:28;
Rev 22:7 *h* S Ro 13:11
1:4 *i* ver 11, 20
j S Ro 1:7 *k* ver 8;
Rev 4:8; 11:17; 16:5
l Isa 11:2; Rev 3:1; 4:5;
5:6
1:5 *m* Isa 55:4;
Jn 18:37; Rev 3:14
n Ps 89:27; Col 1:18
o S 1Ti 6:15
p S Ro 8:37
q S Ro 3:25
1:6 *r* S 1Pe 2:5;
Rev 5:10; 20:6
s Ro 15:6 *t* S Ro 11:36
1:7 *u* Da 7:13;
S Mt 16:27; 24:30;
26:64; S Lk 17:30;
S 1Co 1:7; S 1Th 2:19;
4:16, 17 *v* Jn 19:34, 37
w Zec 12:10; Mt 24:30
1:8 *x* S ver 17;
Rev 21:6; 22:13
y S ver 4 *z* Rev 4:8;
15:3; 19:6
1:9 *a* ver 1
b S Ac 14:22; 2Co 1:7;
Php 4:14 *c* ver 6
d 2Ti 2:12 *e* ver 2;
S Heb 4:12 *f* S ver 2
1:10 *g* Ac 20:7
h Rev 4:2; 17:3; 21:10
i Ex 20:18; Rev 4:1
1:11 *j* ver 19

1:1 *revelation.* Apocalypse ("unveiling" or "disclosure"). *servants.* All believers. *soon take place.* See v. 3; 22:6–7,10,20. *his angel.* A mediating angel. "Angel(s)" occurs over 80 times in Revelation. *John.* See Introduction: Author.

1:3 *Blessed.* The first of seven beatitudes in the book (see 14:13; 16:15; 19:9; 20:6; 22:7,14). "Blessed" means much more than "happy." It describes the favorable circumstance granted by God to a person (see notes on Ps 1:1; Mt 5:3). *prophecy.* Includes not only foretelling the future but also proclaiming any word from God—whether command, instruction, history or prediction (see 1Co 14:3 and note). *time is near.* See note on Jas 5:9.

1:4 *seven churches.* Located about 50 miles apart, forming a circle in Asia moving clockwise north from Ephesus and coming around full circle from Laodicea (east of Ephesus; see map, p. 2123). They were perhaps postal centers serving seven geographic regions. Apparently the entire book of Revelation (including the seven letters) was sent to each church (see v. 11). *Asia.* A Roman province lying in western Turkey. *Grace and peace.* See note on Ro 1:7. *who is . . . was . . . is to come.* A paraphrase of the divine name from Ex 3:14–15. Cf. Heb 13:8. *seven spirits.* See TNIV text note; see also Zec 4:2 and note and cf. 4:10.

A **1:5–6** *has freed us . . . has made us.* Emphasizes these blessings as present possessions already enjoyed by the believer (see also 5:9–10).

1:6 *a kingdom and priests.* This OT designation of Israel (see notes on Ex 19:6; Zec 3) is applied in the NT to the church (1Pe 2:5,9).

1:7 *coming with the clouds.* See Mt 24:30 and note. *pierced.* See

Ps 22:16; Isa 53:5; Zec 12:10; Jn 19:34,37. *So shall it be! Amen.* A double affirmation.

A **1:8** *the Alpha and the Omega.* The first and last letters of the Greek alphabet. God is the beginning and the end (see 21:6). He sovereignly rules over all human history. In 22:13 Jesus applies the same title to himself; see also "the First and the Last" (v. 17; 2:8; 22:13). *Almighty.* Nine of the 12 occurrences of this term in the NT are in Revelation (here; 4:8; 11:17; 15:3; 16:7,14; 19:6,15; 21:22). The other three are in Ro 9:29; 2Co 6:18; Jas 5:4.

1:9 *suffering . . . kingdom . . . patient endurance.* Three pivotal themes in Revelation: (1) "suffering" (2:9–10, 22; 7:14), (2) "kingdom" (11:15; 12:10; 16:10; 17:12,17–18), (3) "patient endurance" (2:2–3,19; 3:10; 13:10; 14:12). *Patmos.* A small (four by eight miles), rocky island in the Aegean Sea some 50 miles southwest of Ephesus, off the coast of modern Turkey (see map, p. 2123). It probably served as a Roman penal settlement. Eusebius, the "father of church history" (A.D. 265–340), reports that John was released from Patmos under the emperor Nerva (96–98).

1:10 *the Lord's Day.* A technical term for the first day of the week —so named because Jesus rose from the dead on that day. It was also the day on which the Christians met (see Ac 20:7) and took up collections (see 1Co 16:2). *in the Spirit.* In a state of spiritual exaltation by the power of the Spirit—not a dream, but a vision like Peter's in Ac 10:10.

B **1:11** *scroll.* Pieces of papyrus or parchment sewn together and rolled on a spindle (see note on Ex 17:14). The book form was not invented until about the second century A.D. *seven churches.* See note on v. 4.

1:11 *k* ver 4, 20
l S Ac 18:19 *m* Rev 2:8
n Rev 2:12 *o* Ac 16:14;
Rev 2:18, 24 *p* Rev 3:1
q Rev 3:7 *r* S Col 2:1;
Rev 3:14
1:12 *s* ver 20;
Ex 25:31-40; Zec 4:2;
Rev 2:1
1:13 *t* Rev 2:1
u Eze 1:26; Da 7:13;
10:16; Rev 14:14
v Isa 6:1 *w* Da 10:5;
Rev 15:6
1:14 *x* Da 7:9; 10:6;
Rev 2:18; 19:12
1:15 *y* Eze 1:7;
Da 10:6; Rev 2:18
z Eze 43:2; Rev 14:2;
19:6
1:16 *a* ver 20;
Rev 2:1; 3:1 *b* Isa 1:20;
49:2; Heb 4:12;
Rev 2:12,16; 19:15,21
c Jdg 5:31; Mt 17:2
1:17 *d* Eze 1:28;
Da 8:17,18 *e* Da 8:18
f S Mt 14:27
g Isa 41:4; 44:6;
48:12; Rev 2:8; 22:13
1:18 *h* Ro 6:9;
Rev 2:8 *i* Dt 32:40;
Da 4:34; 12:7;
Rev 4:9,10; 10:6; 15:7
j Rev 9:1; 20:1
1:19 *k* ver 11; Hab 2:2
1:20 *l* S ver 16
m S ver 12 *n* ver 4,11
o Mt 5:14,15
2:1 *p* S Ac 18:19
q Rev 1:16 *r* Rev 1:12,13
2:2 *s* ver 19; Rev 3:1,
8,15 *t* 1Jn 4:1
u 2Co 11:13
2:3 *v* S Jn 15:21
2:4 *w* Jer 2:2;
Mt 24:12
2:5 *x* ver 16,22;
Rev 3:3,19 *y* Rev 1:20
2:6 *z* ver 15

it to the seven churches: *k* to Ephesus, *l* Smyrna, *m* Pergamum, *n* Thyatira, *o* Sardis, *p* Philadelphia *q* and Laodicea." *r*

¹²I turned around to see the voice that was speaking to me. And when I turned I saw seven golden lampstands, *s* ¹³and among the lampstands *t* was someone like a son of man, *u* dressed in a robe reaching down to his feet *v* and with a golden sash around his chest. *w* ¹⁴The hair on his head was white like wool, as white as snow, and his eyes were like blazing fire. *x* ¹⁵His feet were like bronze glowing in a furnace, *y* and his voice was like the sound of rushing waters. *z* ¹⁶In his right hand he held seven stars, *a* and coming out of his mouth was a sharp, double-edged sword. *b* His face was like the sun *c* shining in all its brilliance.

¹⁷When I saw him, I fell at his feet *d* as though dead. Then he placed his right hand on me *e* and said: "Do not be afraid. *f* I am the First and the Last. *g* ¹⁸I am the Living One; I was dead, *h* and now look, I am alive for ever and ever! *i* And I hold the keys of death and Hades. *j*

¹⁹"Write, therefore, what you have seen: *k* both what is now and what will take place later. ²⁰The mystery of the seven stars that you saw in my right hand *l* and of the seven golden lampstands *m* is this: The seven stars are the angels *b* of the seven churches, *n* and the seven lampstands are the seven churches. *o*

TO THE CHURCH IN EPHESUS

2 "To the angel *c* of the church in Ephesus *p* write:

These are the words of him who holds the seven stars in his right hand *q* and walks among the seven golden lampstands. *r* ²I know your deeds, *s* your hard work and your perseverance. I know that you cannot tolerate wicked people, that you have tested *t* those who claim to be apostles but are not, and have found them false. *u* ³You have persevered and have endured hardships for my name, *v* and have not grown weary.

⁴Yet I hold this against you: You have forsaken the love you had at first. *w* ⁵Consider how far you have fallen! Repent *x* and do the things you did at first. If you do not repent, I will come to you and remove your lampstand *y* from its place. ⁶But you have this in your favor: You hate the practices of the Nicolaitans, *z* which I also hate.

a 13 See Daniel 7:13.   *b* 20 Or *messengers*   *c* 1 Or *messenger*; also in verses 8, 12 and 18

1:12 *seven.* See Introduction: Distinctive Feature. *golden lampstands.* The seven churches (see v. 20).

1:13 *son of man.* See notes on Da 7:13; Mk 8:31. *robe ... to his feet.* The high priest wore a full-length robe (Ex 28:4; 29:5). Reference to Christ as high priest is supported by the reference to the golden sash around his chest.

1:14 *white like wool.* Cf. Da 7:9; Isa 1:18. The hoary head suggests wisdom and dignity (Lev 19:32; Pr 16:31). *eyes ... like blazing fire.* Penetrating insight (see 4:6).

1:16 *sharp, double-edged sword.* Like a long Thracian sword (also in 2:12,16; 6:8; 19:15,21). The sword in 6:4; 13:10,14 was a small sword or dagger. The sword symbolizes divine judgment (see Isa 49:2; Heb 4:12).

1:17 *fell at his feet.* A sign of great respect and awe (4:10; 5:8; 7:11; 19:10; 22:8). *I am.* See note on Jn 6:35. *the First and the Last.* Essentially the same as "the Alpha and the Omega" (v. 8; cf. Isa 44:6; 48:12).

1:18 *Living One.* Based on OT references to the "living God" (e.g., Jos 3:10; Ps 42:2; 84:2). In contrast to the dead gods of paganism, Christ possesses life in his essential nature. *keys of death and Hades.* Absolute control over their domain (see Mt 16:18 and note).

1:19 Many see a threefold division in this verse (reading "what you have seen, what is now and what will take place later") and take it as a clue to the entire structure of the book. "What you have seen" would be the inaugural vision of ch. 1; "what is now" would be the letters to the seven churches (chs. 2–3); "what will take place later" would be everything from ch. 4 on. An alternative interpretation sees the initial clause as the essential unit (it parallels v. 11), followed by two explanatory clauses (the sense of the TNIV). The sense would be: "Write, therefore, what you are about to see, i.e., both what is now and what will take place lat-

er." Some who hold the latter view make no attempt to outline the book on this basis, maintaining that there is a mixture of "now" and "later" throughout.

1:20 The first of several places where the symbols are interpreted (see also 17:15,18). *angels.* Either (1) heavenly messengers or (2) earthly messengers/ministers (see TNIV text note).

2:1—3:22 Some take the seven letters as a preview of church history in its downward course toward Laodicean lukewarmness. Others interpret them as characteristic of various kinds of Christian congregations that have existed from John's day until the present time. In either case, they were historical churches in Asia Minor (see map, p. 2123, and map No. 13 at the end of this study Bible). A general pattern in the letters is commendation, complaint and correction.

2:1 *angel.* See note on 1:20. *Ephesus.* See Introduction to Ephesians: The City of Ephesus. *holds the seven stars.* See 1:16,20. *seven golden lampstands.* See 1:12, 20.

A **2:2** *tested.* The necessity of testing for correct doctrine and dependable advice was widely recognized in the early church (see 1Co 14:29; 1Th 5:21; 1Jn 4:1).

A **2:4** *the love you had at first.* For one another and/or for Christ.

2:5 *remove your lampstand.* Immediate judgment.

C **2:6** *Nicolaitans.* A heretical sect within the church that had worked out a compromise with the pagan society. Its adherents apparently taught that spiritual liberty gave them sufficient leeway to practice idolatry and immorality. Tradition identifies them with Nicolas, the proselyte of Antioch who was one of the first seven deacons in the Jerusalem church (Ac 6:5), though the evidence is merely circumstantial. A similar group at Pergamum held the teaching of Balaam (vv. 14–15), and some

[7]Whoever has ears, let them hear[a] what the Spirit says to the churches. To those who are victorious,[b] I will give the right to eat from the tree of life,[c] which is in the paradise[d] of God.

TO THE CHURCH IN SMYRNA

[8]"To the angel of the church in Smyrna[e] write:

These are the words of him who is the First and the Last,[f] who died and came to life again.[g] [9]I know your afflictions and your poverty—yet you are rich![h] I know about the slander of those who say they are Jews and are not,[i] but are a synagogue of Satan.[j] [10]Do not be afraid of what you are about to suffer. I tell you, the devil will put some of you in prison to test you,[k] and you will suffer persecution for ten days.[l] Be faithful,[m] even to the point of death, and I will give you life as your victor's crown.[n]

[11]Whoever has ears, let them hear[o] what the Spirit says to the churches. Those who are victorious will not be hurt at all by the second death.[p]

TO THE CHURCH IN PERGAMUM

[12]"To the angel of the church in Pergamum[q] write:

These are the words of him who has the sharp, double-edged sword.[r] [13]I know where you live—where Satan has his throne. Yet you remain true to my name. You

2:7 [a]S Mt 11:15; ver 11,17,29; Rev 3:6, 13,22; 13:9
[b]S Jn 16:33 [c]Ge 2:9; 3:22-24; Rev 22:2,14, 19 [d]Lk 23:43
2:8 [e]Rev 1:11
[f]S Rev 1:17 [g]Rev 1:18
2:9 [h]2Co 6:10; Jas 2:5 [i]Rev 3:9
[j]ver 13,24; S Mt 4:10
2:10 [k]Rev 3:10
[l]Da 1:12,14 [m]ver 13; Rev 17:14
[n]S Mt 10:22; S 1Co 9:25
2:11 [o]S ver 7
[p]Rev 20:6,14; 21:8
2:12 [q]Rev 1:11
[r]ver 16; S Rev 1:16

---

at Thyatira were followers of the woman Jezebel (v. 20). From their heretical tendencies it would appear that all three groups were Nicolaitans.

2:7 *To those who are victorious.* The challenge to be victorious in the battle against evil (see 12:11) occurs in each letter (here; vv. 11,17,26; 3:5,12,21). *paradise.* Originally a Persian word for a pleasure garden (see note on Lk 23:43). In Revelation it symbolizes the eschatological state in which God and believers are restored to the perfect fellowship that existed before sin entered the world.

2:8 *Smyrna.* A proud and beautiful Asian city (modern Izmir) closely aligned with Rome and eager to meet its demands for emperor worship. This plus a large and actively hostile Jewish population made it extremely difficult to live there as a Christian. Polycarp, the most famous of the early martyrs, was bishop of Smyrna. *the First and the Last.* See note on 1:17.

2:9 *who say they are Jews.* See Ro 2:28–29. *Satan.* See notes on Mt 16:23; 1Jn 3:8.

2:10 *devil.* Greek *diabolos,* meaning "accuser." *persecution.* See the warnings by Jesus (Jn 15:20) and Paul (2Ti 3:12). *ten days.* Probably indicates a limited period of suffering. *life as your victor's crown.* The crown that is eternal life. "Crown" does not refer to a royal crown (12:3; 13:1; 19:12) but to the garland or wreath awarded to the winner in athletic contests (3:11; 4:4,10; 6:2; 9:7; 12:1; 14:14).

2:11 *Those who are victorious.* See note on v. 7. *second death.* The lake of fire (20:14; see 20:6; 21:8).

2:12 *Pergamum.* Modern Bergama; the ancient capital of Asia, built on a cone-shaped hill rising 1,000 feet above the surrounding valley. Its name in Greek means "citadel." See map below. *double-edged sword.* See note on 1:16.

2:13 *where Satan has his throne.* Satan "ruled" from Pergamum in that it was the official center of emperor wor-

---

THE SEVEN CHURCHES OF REVELATION

2:13 *s* Rev 14:12
t Rev 1:5; 11:3 *u* ver 9,
24; S Mt 4:10
2:14 *v* ver 20
w S 2Pe 2:15
x S Ac 15:20
x 1Co 6:13
2:15 *z* ver 6
2:16 *a* S ver 5
b 2Th 2:8; S Rev 1:16
2:17 *c* S ver 7
d S Jn 16:33 *d* Jn 6:49,
50 *f* Isa 56:5; 62:2;
65:15 *g* Rev 19:12
2:18 *h* ver 24;
Ac 16:14; Rev 1:11
i S Mt 4:3 *j* S Rev 1:14,
15
2:19 *k* S ver 2
2:20 *l* 1Ki 16:31;
21:25; 2Ki 9:7
m ver 14; S Ac 15:20
2:21 *n* Ro 2:4;
2Pe 3:9 *o* Ro 2:5;
Rev 9:20; 16:9,11
2:22 *p* Rev 17:2; 18:9
2:23 *q* 1Sa 16:7;
1Ki 8:39; Ps 139:1,2,
23; Pr 21:2; Jer 17:10;
Lk 16:15; Ro 8:27;
1Th 2:4 *r* S Mt 16:27
2:24 *s* Ac 15:28
2:25 *t* Rev 3:11
u S Mt 16:27
2:26 *v* S Jn 16:33
w Mt 10:22 *x* Ps 2:8;
Rev 3:21
2:27 *y* Rev 12:5;
19:15 *z* Ps 2:9;
Isa 30:14; Jer 19:11
2:28 *a* Rev 22:16
2:29 *b* S ver 7
3:1 *c* Rev 1:11
d S Rev 1:4
e S Rev 1:16
f S Rev 2:2 *g* 1Ti 5:6

did not renounce your faith in me, *s* not even in the days of Antipas, my faithful witness, *t* who was put to death in your city—where Satan lives. *u*

[14]Nevertheless, I have a few things against you: *v* There are some among you who hold to the teaching of Balaam, *w* who taught Balak to entice the Israelites to sin so that they ate food sacrificed to idols *x* and committed sexual immorality. *y* [15]Likewise, you also have those who hold to the teaching of the Nicolaitans. *z* [16]Repent *a* therefore! Otherwise, I will soon come to you and will fight against them with the sword of my mouth. *b*

[17]Whoever has ears, let them hear *c* what the Spirit says to the churches. To those who are victorious, *d* I will give some of the hidden manna. *e* I will also give each of them a white stone with a new name *f* written on it, known only to the one who receives it. *g*

TO THE CHURCH IN THYATIRA

[18]"To the angel of the church in Thyatira *h* write:

These are the words of the Son of God, *i* whose eyes are like blazing fire and whose feet are like burnished bronze. *j* [19]I know your deeds, *k* your love and faith, your service and perseverance, and that you are now doing more than you did at first.

[20]Nevertheless, I have this against you: You tolerate that woman Jezebel, *l* who calls herself a prophet. By her teaching she misleads my servants into sexual immorality and the eating of food sacrificed to idols. *m* [21]I have given her time *n* to repent of her immorality, but she is unwilling. *o* [22]So I will cast her on a bed of suffering, and I will make those who commit adultery *p* with her suffer intensely, unless they repent of her ways. [23]I will strike her children dead. Then all the churches will know that I am he who searches hearts and minds, *q* and I will repay each of you according to your deeds. *r* [24]Now I say to the rest of you in Thyatira, to you who do not hold to her teaching and have not learned Satan's so-called deep secrets, 'I will not impose any other burden on you, *s* [25]except to hold on to what you have *t* until I come.' *u*

[26]To those who are victorious *v* and do my will to the end, *w* I will give authority over the nations *x*— [27]they 'will rule them with an iron scepter *y* and will dash them to pieces like pottery'*a z*—just as I have received authority from my Father. [28]I will also give them the morning star. *a* [29]Whoever has ears, let them hear *b* what the Spirit says to the churches.

TO THE CHURCH IN SARDIS

3 "To the angel *b* of the church in Sardis *c* write:

These are the words of him who holds the seven spirits *c d* of God and the seven stars. *e* I know your deeds; *f* you have a reputation of being alive, but you are dead. *g*

a 27 Psalm 2:9   *b* 1 Or *messenger*; also in verses 7 and 14   *c* 1 That is, the sevenfold Spirit

---

ship in Asia. *Antipas.* First martyr of Asia. According to tradition he was slowly roasted to death in a bronze kettle during the reign of Domitian (81–96). *faithful witness.* The Lord's title in 1:5.

A **2:14** *teaching of Balaam.* Balaam advised the Midianite women how to lead the Israelites astray (Nu 25:1–2; 31:16; cf. Jude 11 and notes on Nu 22:5,8). He is a fitting prototype of corrupt teachers who deceive believers into compromise with worldliness. *food sacrificed to idols…immorality.* See Ac 15:20,29.

2:15 *Nicolaitans.* See note on v. 6.

2:16 *sword of my mouth.* The long sword (see note on 1:16).

2:17 *victorious.* See note on v. 7. *hidden manna.* The heavenly food available to the believer who overcomes (cf. Ps 78:24), in contrast to the unclean food of the Balaamites. *white stone.* Certain kinds of stones were used as tokens for various purposes. In the context of a Messianic banquet the white stone was probably for the purpose of admission. *new name.* The name of the victor (see Isa 62:2; 65:15).

2:18 *Thyatira.* Modern Akhisar. Founded by Seleucus I (311–280 B.C.) as a military outpost, it was noted for its many trade guilds. Lydia, "a dealer in purple cloth," was from Thyatira (see note on Ac 16:14). *eyes…like blazing fire.* See note on 1:14; cf. Da 10:6. *burnished bronze.* A refined alloy of copper or bronze with metallic zinc.

2:20 *Jezebel.* See 1Ki 16:31; 2Ki 9:22,30–37. The name is used here as an epithet for a prominent woman in the congregation who undermined loyalty to God by promoting tolerance toward pagan practices. *sexual immorality…food sacrificed to idols.* See v. 14.

2:22 *bed of suffering.* Disease was often considered as appropriate punishment for sins (cf. 1Co 11:29–30).

2:23 *her children.* Jezebel is the spiritual mother of all who pursue antinomian (libertine) doctrines. *he who searches hearts and minds.* Cf. Ps 7:9; Pr 24:12; Jer 11:20; 17:10. "Mind" (lit. "kidney") probably refers here to the will and the affections; "heart" may designate the center of rational life. *according to your deeds.* Judgment based on works is taught by Jesus (Mt 16:27) and Paul (Ro 2:6), as well as John (Rev 18:6; 20:12–13; 22:12).

2:24 *Satan's so-called deep secrets.* Later Gnosticism (see Introduction to 1 John: Gnosticism) taught that in order to defeat Satan one had to enter his stronghold, i.e., experience evil deeply.

2:26 *victorious.* See note on v. 7.

2:27 *rule.* Lit. "shepherd" (a common metaphor for "rule"). *iron scepter.* Symbolic of the strength of his rule (see 12:5; 19:15).

2:28 *morning star.* Cf. 22:16 and note; Da 12:3.

3:1 *Sardis.* Modern Sart. Capital of the ancient kingdom of Lyd-

3:3 ʰ S Rev 2:5
ⁱ S Lk 12:39 / Lk 12:39
3:4 ʲ Jude 23 / ver 5,
18; Rev 4:4; 6:11; 7:9,
13,14; 19:14
3:5 ᵐ S Jn 16:33
ⁿ S ver 4
ᵒ S Rev 20:12
ᵖ Mt 10:32
3:6 ᵠ S Rev 2:7
3:7 ʳ Rev 1:11
ˢ S Mk 1:24 ᵗ 1Jn 5:20;
Rev 6:10; 19:11
ᵘ Isa 22:22; Mt 16:19
3:8 ᵛ S Rev 2:2
ʷ S Ac 14:27
ˣ Rev 2:13
3:9 ʸ Rev 2:9
ᶻ Rev 2:9 ᵃ Isa 49:23
ᵇ Isa 43:4; S Ro 8:37
3:10 ᶜ 2Pe 2:9
ᵈ S Mt 24:14
ᵉ Rev 2:10 ᶠ Rev 6:10;
8:13; 11:10; 13:8,14;
17:8
3:11 ᵍ S Mt 16:27
ʰ Rev 2:25
ⁱ S 1Co 9:25
3:12 ʲ S Jn 16:33
ᵏ Gal 2:9 ˡ Rev 14:1;
22:4 ᵐ Eze 48:35
ⁿ Gal 4:26; Rev 21:2,
10
3:13 ᵒ S Rev 2:7
3:14 ᵖ S Col 2:1;
Rev 1:11 ᵠ Jn 18:37;
Rev 1:5 ʳ Pr 8:22;
Jn 1:3; Col 1:16,18
3:15 ˢ S Rev 2:2
ᵗ Ro 12:11

²Wake up! Strengthen what remains and is about to die, for I have found your deeds unfinished in the sight of my God. ³Remember, therefore, what you have received and heard; hold it fast, and repent. ʰ But if you do not wake up, I will come like a thief, ⁱ and you will not know at what time ʲ I will come to you.

⁴Yet you have a few people in Sardis who have not soiled their clothes. ᵏ They will walk with me, dressed in white, ˡ for they are worthy. ⁵Those who are victorious ᵐ will, like them, be dressed in white. ⁿ I will never blot out their names from the book of life, ᵒ but will acknowledge their names before my Fatherᵖ and his angels. ⁶Whoever has ears, let them hearᵠ what the Spirit says to the churches.

TO THE CHURCH IN PHILADELPHIA

⁷"To the angel of the church in Philadelphia ʳ write:

These are the words of him who is holy ˢ and true, ᵗ who holds the key of David. ᵘ What he opens no one can shut, and what he shuts no one can open. ⁸I know your deeds. ᵛ See, I have placed before you an open doorʷ that no one can shut. I know that you have little strength, yet you have kept my word and have not denied my name. ˣ ⁹I will make those who are of the synagogue of Satan, ʸ who claim to be Jews though they are not, ᶻ but are liars—I will make them come and fall down at your feet ᵃ and acknowledge that I have loved you. ᵇ ¹⁰Since you have kept my command to endure patiently, I will also keep you ᶜ from the hour of trial that is going to come on the whole worldᵈ to test ᵉ those who live on the earth. ᶠ

¹¹I am coming soon. ᵍ Hold on to what you have, ʰ so that no one will take your crown. ⁱ ¹²Those who are victoriousʲ I will make pillars ᵏ in the temple of my God. Never again will they leave it. I will write on them the name of my Godˡ and the name of the city of my God, ᵐ the new Jerusalem, ⁿ which is coming down out of heaven from my God; and I will also write on them my new name. ¹³Whoever has ears, let them hearᵒ what the Spirit says to the churches.

TO THE CHURCH IN LAODICEA

¹⁴"To the angel of the church in Laodiceaᵖ write:

These are the words of the Amen, the faithful and true witness, ᵠ the ruler of God's creation. ʳ ¹⁵I know your deeds, ˢ that you are neither cold nor hot. ᵗ I wish you were either one or the other! ¹⁶So, because you are lukewarm—neither hot nor cold—I

---

ia, it was a city of great wealth and fame. The acropolis was a natural citadel on the northern spur of Mount Tmolus. It rose 1,500 feet above the lower valley.

3:3 *come like a thief.* Not a reference to the second coming of Christ, because here his coming depends on the church's refusal to repent. Elsewhere in the NT the clause refers to the second advent (16:15; Mt 24:42–44; 1Th 5:2; 2Pe 3:10).

3:4 *dressed in white.* Description of the redeemed (3:18; 6:11; 7:9,13–14; cf. 4:4; 19:14).

3:5 *victorious.* See note on 2:7. *book of life.* A divine ledger is first mentioned in Ex 32:32–33 (see note on Ps 69:28; cf. Da 12:1). It was a register of all citizens in the kingdom community. To have one's name erased from this book would indicate loss of citizenship (see 13:8; 17:8; 20:12,15; 21:27; Php 4:3).

3:7 *Philadelphia.* Modern Alashehir; a city of commercial importance conveniently located as the gateway to the high central plateau of the Roman province of Asia in Asia Minor. The name means "brotherly love" and commemorates the loyalty and devotion of Attalus II (220–130 B.C.), the city's co-founder, to his brother Eumenes II. *holy and true.* See 6:10. For God as the Holy One, see Isa 40:25; Hab 3:2–3; Mk 1:24; see also notes on Ex 3:5; Lev 11:44. *key of David.* Christ is the Davidic Messiah with authority to control entrance to the kingdom (see Isa 22:22; Mt 16:19).

3:8 *open door.* Either the door of opportunity or the door to the kingdom. The context favors the latter.

3:9 *synagogue of Satan.* A bold metaphor directed against unbelieving and hostile Jews. Cf. Jesus' scathing rebuke in Jn 8:44; see also 2Co 11:14–15. The Jewish synagogue was a gathering place for worship, study and communal activities. *claim to be*

Jews. See Ro 2:28–29. *fall down at your feet.* An appropriate act of worship in the Near East (see Isa 45:14; 60:14; cf. Ac 10:25; Php 2:10; see also note on Rev 1:17).

3:10 *keep you from.* The Greek for this phrase can mean either "keep you from undergoing" or "keep you through." *hour of trial.* The period of testing that precedes the consummation of the kingdom (see 13:5–10; Mt 24:4–28; cf. Da 12:1; Mk 13:19; 2Th 2:1–12). *those who live on the earth.* See 6:10 and note.

3:11 *I am coming soon.* Cf. 1:1; 22:7,12,20 (see note on Jas 5:9). *crown.* See 2:10 and note.

3:12 *victorious.* See note on 2:7. *temple.* See note on 7:15. *name of my God.* See 14:1; 22:4. *new Jerusalem.* See 21:2,10. *write on them my new name.* Names revealed character. Christ's new name symbolizes all that he is by virtue of his redemptive work for humankind. This awaits the second advent.

3:14 *Laodicea.* Near modern Denizli. The wealthiest city in Phrygia during Roman times, it was widely known for its banking establishments, medical school and textile industry. Its major weakness was lack of an adequate water supply. Each of these characteristics is reflected in the letter. *the Amen.* Isa 65:16 speaks of "the God of the Amen," i.e., "the one true God." As a personal designation it describes one who is totally trustworthy and faithful. *faithful and true witness.* See 1:5; 19:11. *ruler.* The Greek word can mean first in point of time ("beginning") or first in rank ("ruler").

3:16 *lukewarm—neither hot nor cold.* "Hot" may refer to the hot, medicinal waters of nearby Hierapolis. The church in Laodicea supplied neither healing for the spiritually sick nor refreshment for the spiritually weary. *spit.* Lit. "vomit."

3:17 *u* Hos 12:8;
1Co 4:8 *v* Pr 13:7
3:18 *w* S 1Pe 1:7
x S ver 4 *y* Rev 16:15
3:19 *z* Dt 8:5;
Pr 3:12; 1Co 11:32;
Heb 12:5,6
a S Rev 2:5
3:20 *b* Mt 24:33;
Jas 5:9 *c* Lk 12:36
d S Ro 8:10
3:21 *e* S Jn 16:33
f S Mt 19:28 *g* Rev 5:5
3:22 *h* S Rev 2:7
4:1 *i* S Mt 3:16
j Rev 1:10 *k* Rev 11:12
l Rev 1:19; 22:6
4:2 *m* S Rev 1:10
n ver 9,10; 1Ki 22:19;
Isa 6:1; Eze 1:26-28;
Da 7:9; Rev 20:11
4:3 *o* Rev 21:11
p Rev 21:20
q Eze 1:28; Rev 10:1
r Rev 21:19
4:4 *s* ver 10; Rev 5:6,
8,14; 11:16; 19:4
t S Rev 3:4,5
4:5 *u* Ex 19:16;
Rev 8:5; 11:19; 16:18
v Zec 4:2 *w* S Rev 1:4
4:6 *x* Rev 15:2
y ver 8,9; Eze 1:5;
Rev 5:6; 6:1; 7:11;
14:3; 15:7; 19:4
z Eze 1:18; 10:12
4:7 *a* Eze 1:10; 10:14
4:8 *b* S ver 6
c Isa 6:2 *d* Eze 1:18
e Rev 14:11

am about to spit you out of my mouth. [17] You say, 'I am rich; I have acquired wealth and do not need a thing.' *u* But you do not realize that you are wretched, pitiful, poor, blind and naked. *v* [18] I counsel you to buy from me gold refined in the fire, *w* so you can become rich; and white clothes *x* to wear, so you can cover your shameful nakedness; *y* and salve to put on your eyes, so you can see.

[19] Those whom I love I rebuke and discipline. *z* So be earnest, and repent. *a* [20] Here I am! I stand at the door *b* and knock. If anyone hears my voice and opens the door, *c* I will come in *d* and eat with them, and they with me.

[21] To those who are victorious, *e* I will give the right to sit with me on my throne, *f* just as I was victorious *g* and sat down with my Father on his throne. [22] Whoever has ears, let them hear *h* what the Spirit says to the churches."

THE THRONE IN HEAVEN

4 After this I looked, and there before me was a door standing open *i* in heaven. And the voice I had first heard speaking to me like a trumpet *j* said, "Come up here, *k* and I will show you what must take place after this." *l* [2] At once I was in the Spirit, *m* and there before me was a throne in heaven *n* with someone sitting on it. [3] And the one who sat there had the appearance of jasper *o* and ruby. *p* A rainbow *q* that shone like an emerald *r* encircled the throne. [4] Surrounding the throne were twenty-four other thrones, and seated on them were twenty-four elders. *s* They were dressed in white *t* and had crowns of gold on their heads. [5] From the throne came flashes of lightning, rumblings and peals of thunder. *u* Before the throne, seven lamps *v* were blazing. These are the seven spirits *a w* of God. [6] Also before the throne there was what looked like a sea of glass, *x* clear as crystal.

In the center, around the throne, were four living creatures, *y* and they were covered with eyes, in front and in back. *z* [7] The first living creature was like a lion, the second was like an ox, the third had a face like a man, the fourth was like a flying eagle. *a* [8] Each of the four living creatures *b* had six wings *c* and was covered with eyes all around, *d* even under its wings. Day and night *e* they never stop saying:

a 5 That is, the sevenfold Spirit

3:18 Refers to three items in which Laodicea took great pride: financial wealth, an extensive textile industry and a famous eye salve.

3:19 *whom I love I ... discipline.* See Job 5:17; Ps 94:12; Pr 3:11–12; 1Co 11:32; Heb 12:5–11.

3:20 *I stand at the door and knock.* Usually taken as a picture of Christ knocking on the door of the individual unbeliever's heart. In context, however, the self-deluded members of the congregation are being addressed.

3:21 *victorious.* See note on 2:7. *sit with me on my throne.* See 20:4,6; Mt 19:28; 2Ti 2:12.

4:1—5:14 These two chapters constitute an introduction to chs. 6–20. In the throne room of heaven, the Lamb assumes the responsibility of initiating the great final conflict with the forces of evil, the end of which will see the Lamb triumphant and the devil consigned to the lake of fire.

4:1 *Come up here.* Similarly, Moses was called up on Mount Sinai to receive divine direction (Ex 19:20,24). Cf. also the heavenly ascent of the two witnesses (11:12). Some interpreters find the rapture of the church in this verse. *what must take place after this.* See 1:1,19; Da 2:28–29,45.

4:2 *in the Spirit.* In a state of heightened spiritual awareness by the power of the Spirit (see note on 1:10; see also 17:3; 21:10). *throne in heaven.* The depiction of God ruling from his throne in heaven is a regular feature of the OT (e.g., Ps 47:8).

4:3 *jasper ... ruby ... emerald.* Since God dwells in "unapproachable light" and is one "whom no one has seen or can see" (1Ti 6:16), he is described in terms of the reflected brilliance of precious stones—an emerald rainbow around the throne (cf. Eze 1:26–28).

4:4 *twenty-four elders.* Representative of either the whole company of believers in heaven or an exalted angelic order worshiping and serving God there (see vv. 9–11; 5:5–14; 7:11–17; 11:16–18; 14:3; 19:4). The number 24 is often understood to reflect the

12 Israelite tribes of the OT and the 12 apostles of the NT.

4:5 *flashes of lightning ... thunder ... blazing.* Symbolic of the awesome majesty and power of God (cf. the manifestation of God at Sinai, Ex 19:16–19; cf. also the conventional OT depiction of God's coming in mighty power to deliver his people, Ps 18:12–15; 77:18). In Revelation, thunder and lightning always mark an important event connected with the heavenly temple (8:5; 11:19; 16:18). *seven spirits.* See note on 1:4; "seven" symbolizes fullness, completeness or perfection.

4:6 *sea of glass.* The source of the imagery may be Eze 1:22 (cf. Ex 24:10), but it is also possible that it is the basin in the heavenly temple (cf. 11:19; 14:15,17; 15:5–6,8; 16:1,17), whose counterpart in the earthly temple was referred to as the Sea (1Ki 7:23–25; 2Ki 16:17; 2Ch 4:2,4,10,15; Jer 27:19). Other features of the temple in heaven are: the lamps (v. 5), the altar (6:9), the altar of incense (8:3) and the ark of the covenant (11:19). *four living creatures.* An exalted order of angelic beings whose task is to guard the heavenly throne and lead in worship and adoration of God. *covered with eyes.* Nothing escapes their attention.

4:7 Ezekiel in a vision also saw four living creatures, each of which had four faces—human in front, lion on the right, ox on the left and eagle behind (Eze 1:6,10). In John's vision the creatures were in the form of a lion, an ox and a flying eagle, and one had a face like that of a man.

4:8 *six wings.* This feature of the living creatures and the praise they speak seem to be modeled after the seraphs of Isa 6:2–3; thus the living creatures combine features of the cherubim of Eze 1 and 10 (see note on v. 7) and the seraphs of Isa 6. *Holy, holy, holy.* See note on Isa 6:3. *was ... is ... is to come.* An expansion of the divine name in Ex 3:14–15 (see note on Rev 1:4). God's power and holiness extend from eternity past to eternity yet to come (cf. Isa 41:4).

" 'Holy, holy, holy
is the Lord God Almighty,'ᵃ f
who was, and is, and is to come." g

⁹Whenever the living creatures give glory, honor and thanks to him who sits on the throne h and who lives for ever and ever, i ¹⁰the twenty-four elders j fall down before him k who sits on the throne l and worship him who lives for ever and ever. They lay their crowns before the throne and say:

¹¹ "You are worthy, our Lord and God,
to receive glory and honor and power, m
for you created all things,
and by your will they were created
and have their being." n

THE SCROLL AND THE LAMB

5 Then I saw in the right hand of him who sat on the throne o a scroll with writing on both sides p and sealed q with seven seals. ²And I saw a mighty angel r proclaiming in a loud voice, "Who is worthy to break the seals and open the scroll?" ³But no one in heaven or on earth or under the earth could open the scroll or even look inside it. ⁴I wept and wept because no one was found who was worthy to open the scroll or look inside. ⁵Then one of the elders said to me, "Do not weep! See, the Lion s of the tribe of Judah, t the Root of David, u has triumphed. He is able to open the scroll and its seven seals."

⁶Then I saw a Lamb, v looking as if it had been slain, standing in the center before the throne, encircled by the four living creatures w and the elders. x The Lamb had seven horns and seven eyes, y which are the seven spirits b z of God sent out into all the earth. ⁷He went and took the scroll from the right hand of him who sat on the throne. a ⁸And when he had taken it, the four living creatures b and the twenty-four elders c fell down before the Lamb. Each one had a harp d and they were holding golden bowls full of incense, which are the prayers e of God's people. ⁹And they sang a new song, saying: f

"You are worthy g to take the scroll
and to open its seals,
because you were slain,
and with your blood h you purchased i for God
members of every tribe and language and people and nation. j
¹⁰ You have made them to be a kingdom and priests k to serve our God,
and they will reign c on the earth." l

ᵃ 8 Isaiah 6:3   ᵇ 6 That is, the sevenfold Spirit   ᶜ 10 Some manuscripts *they reign*

4:8 f Isa 6:3;
S Rev 1:8 g S Rev 1:4
4:9 h ver 2; Ps 47:8;
S Rev 5:1 i S Rev 1:18
4:10 j S ver 4
k Dt 33:3; Rev 5:8,14;
7:11; 11:16 l S ver 2
4:11 m Rev 1:6; 5:12
n Ac 14:15; Rev 10:6
5:1 o ver 7,13;
Rev 4:2,9; 6:16
p Eze 2:9,10
q Isa 29:11; Da 12:4
5:2 r Rev 10:1
5:5 s Ge 49:9
t S Heb 7:14 u Isa 11:1,
10; Ro 15:12;
Rev 22:16
5:6 v ver 8,9,12,13;
S Jn 1:29 w S Rev 4:6
x S Rev 4:4 y Zec 4:10
z S Rev 1:4
5:7 a S ver 1
5:8 b S Rev 4:6
c S Rev 4:4
d Rev 14:2; 15:2
e Ps 141:2; Rev 8:3,4
5:9 f Ps 40:3; 98:1;
149:1; Isa 42:10;
Rev 14:3,4 g Rev 4:11
h Heb 9:12
i S 1Co 6:20
j S Rev 13:7
5:10 k S 1Pe 2:5
l Rev 3:21; 20:4

A **4:10** *lay their crowns.* Acknowledge that God alone is worthy of ultimate praise and worship.
4:11 *you created all things.* See Ge 1.
B **5:1** *scroll.* See note on 1:11; cf. the little scroll of 10:2,8–10. *writing on both sides.* Like the stone tablets of the OT covenant law (see Ex 32:15 and note; Eze 2:9–10). The fibers of a papyrus scroll run horizontally on the inside, which makes writing easier than on the reverse side (where the fibers are vertical). *sealed with seven seals.* Indicating absolute inviolability (cf. Isa 29:11; Da 12:4).
5:2 *mighty angel.* Powerful enough to address his challenge to the whole creation (cf. 10:1; 18:21 and the angel with great authority and splendor in 18:2).
5:3 *heaven … earth … under the earth.* A conventional phrase used to express the universality of the proclamation—no creature was worthy. It is not intended to teach a threefold division of the universe (cf. Ex 20:4; Php 2:10).
A **5:5** *Lion of the tribe of Judah.* A Messianic title taken from Ge 49:8–10, where Judah is named a "lion's cub" and promised the right to rule "until he to whom it belongs shall come" (see also Eze 21:27). *Root of David.* See Isa 11:1,10, which looks forward to the ideal king in the line of David. The title is interpreted Messianically in Ro 15:12.
A **5:6** *Lamb.* Pictured as the sacrifice for sin ("slain"; cf. Isa 53:7; Jn 1:29) and as the mighty conqueror (17:14). Reve-

lation uses a special word for "lamb" (29 times in Revelation and only once elsewhere in the NT—Jn 21:15). The idea of the lamb as a victorious military leader seems to come from the apocalyptic tradition (1 Enoch 90:9; Testament of Joseph 19:8). *as if it had been slain.* Bearing the marks of its slaughter—he has come to power through his death. *seven horns.* The horn is an ancient Jewish symbol for power or strength (cf. Dt 33:17). The fourth beast of Da 7:7,20 had ten horns (cf. Da 8:3,5). Seven horns would symbolize full strength. *seven spirits.* See note on 4:5.
5:8 *harp.* An ancient stringed instrument (not the large modern harp) used especially to accompany songs (Ps 33:2). *bowls full of incense.* The bowl was a flat, shallow cup. Incense was a normal feature of Hebrew ritual (see Dt 33:10; cf. Ps 141:2; Rev 8:3–4). *prayers of God's people.* In later Jewish thought angels often present the prayers of saints to God (Tobit 12:15; 3 Baruch 11). *God's people.* See notes on Ro 1:7; Eph 1:1; Col 1:1.
A **5:9** *new song.* Cf. 14:3; Ps 33:3; 96:1; 144:9; Isa 42:10. In the OT a new song celebrated a new act of divine deliverance or blessing. That is also its sense here; notice the theme of the song. *with your blood you purchased … people.* The sacrificial death of Christ is central to NT teaching (see Mk 10:45; 1Co 6:20).

5:11 *m* Da 7:10;
Heb 12:22; Jude 14
n S Rev 4:6
o S Rev 4:4
5:12 *p* ver 13 *q* ver 9
r Rev 1:6; 4:11
5:13 *s* ver 3;
Php 2:10 *t* S ver 1,7
u ver 6; Rev 6:16; 7:10
v 1Ch 29:11; Mal 1:6;
2:2; S Ro 11:36
5:14 *w* S Rev 4:6
x Rev 4:9 *y* S Rev 4:4
z Rev 4:10
6:1 *a* S Rev 5:6
b Rev 5:1 *c* S Rev 4:6,
7 *d* Rev 14:2; 19:6
6:2 *e* Zec 1:8; 6:3;
Rev 19:11 *f* Zec 6:11;
Rev 14:14; 19:12
g Ps 45:4
6:3 *h* Rev 4:7
6:4 *i* Zec 1:8; 6:2
j Mt 10:34
6:5 *k* Rev 4:7
l Zec 6:2
6:6 *m* S Rev 4:6,7
n Eze 4:16 *o* Rev 7:1,3;
9:4
6:7 *p* Rev 4:7
6:8 *q* S Rev 4:7
r Hos 13:14; Rev 1:18;
20:13,14 *s* Jer 15:2,3;
24:10; Eze 5:12,17
6:9 *t* Ex 29:12;
Lev 4:7 *u* Rev 14:18;
16:7 *v* Rev 20:4
w Ro 1:2; S Heb 4:12
6:10 *x* Ps 119:84;
Zec 1:12 *y* Lk 2:29;
2Pe 2:1 *z* S Rev 3:7
a S Rev 3:10
b Dt 32:43; 2Ki 9:7;
Ps 79:10; Rev 16:6;
18:20; 19:2
6:11 *c* S Rev 3:4

[11]Then I looked and heard the voice of many angels, numbering thousands upon thousands, and ten thousand times ten thousand. *m* They encircled the throne and the living creatures *n* and the elders. *o* [12]In a loud voice they were saying:

"Worthy is the Lamb, *p* who was slain, *q*
    to receive power and wealth and wisdom and strength
    and honor and glory and praise!" *r*

[13]Then I heard every creature in heaven and on earth and under the earth *s* and on the sea, and all that is in them, saying:

"To him who sits on the throne *t* and to the Lamb *u*
    be praise and honor and glory and power,
    for ever and ever!" *v*

[14]The four living creatures *w* said, "Amen," *x* and the elders *y* fell down and worshiped. *z*

THE SEALS

6 I watched as the Lamb *a* opened the first of the seven seals. *b* Then I heard one of the four living creatures *c* say in a voice like thunder, *d* "Come!" [2]I looked, and there before me was a white horse! *e* Its rider held a bow, and he was given a crown, *f* and he rode out as a conqueror bent on conquest. *g*

[3]When the Lamb opened the second seal, I heard the second living creature *h* say, "Come!" [4]Then another horse came out, a fiery red one. *i* Its rider was given power to take peace from the earth *j* and to make people slay each other. To him was given a large sword.

[5]When the Lamb opened the third seal, I heard the third living creature *k* say, "Come!" I looked, and there before me was a black horse! *l* Its rider was holding a pair of scales in his hand. [6]Then I heard what sounded like a voice among the four living creatures, *m* saying, "Two pounds *a* of wheat for a day's wages, *b* and six pounds *c* of barley for a day's wages, *b* *n* and do not damage *o* the oil and the wine!"

[7]When the Lamb opened the fourth seal, I heard the voice of the fourth living creature *p* say, "Come!" [8]I looked, and there before me was a pale horse! *q* Its rider was named Death, and Hades *r* was following close behind him. They were given power over a fourth of the earth to kill by sword, famine and plague, and by the wild beasts of the earth. *s*

[9]When he opened the fifth seal, I saw under *t* the altar *u* the souls of those who had been slain *v* because of the word of God *w* and the testimony they had maintained. [10]They called out in a loud voice, "How long, *x* Sovereign Lord, *y* holy and true, *z* until you judge the inhabitants of the earth *a* and avenge our blood?" *b* [11]Then each of them was given a white robe, *c*

---

a 6 Or about 1 kilogram   *b* 6 Greek *a denarius*   *c* 6 Or about 3 kilograms

---

5:10 *have made them.* See note on 1:6. *kingdom and priests.* See note on 1:6. *reign on the earth.* See 2:26–27; 20:4,6; 22:5.
5:11 *thousands upon thousands.* A rhetorical phrase for an indefinitely large number (see Da 7:10; cf. Heb 12:22).
5:12 *power . . . praise!* See David's farewell prayer in 1Ch 29:10–19. The attributes increase from three in 4:11 to four in 5:13 to seven in 5:12; 7:12.
5:13 *heaven . . . earth . . . under the earth.* See note on v. 3.
6:1 *Lamb.* See v. 16; see also 5:6 and note. *seven seals.* The first of three sevenfold numbered series of judgments (cf. the seven trumpets in chs. 8–9 and the seven bowls in ch. 16). *four living creatures.* See 4:6–7 and notes.
6:2 *white horse.* The imagery of the "four horsemen of the Apocalypse" comes from Zec 1:8–17; 6:1–8 (see note on Zec 6:2–3). The colors in Revelation correspond to the character of the rider; white symbolizes conquest. Major interpretations of the rider on the white horse are: (1) Christ (cf. 19:11), (2) the antichrist and (3) the spirit of conquest. The latter establishes a more natural sequence with the other three riders (which symbolize bloodshed, famine and death). *bow.* A battle weapon.
6:4 *another horse . . . a fiery red one.* Symbolizing bloodshed and war (cf. Zec 1:8; 6:2). *people slay each other.* If the white horse is conquest from without, the red horse may be internal revolution. *sword.* See note on 1:16.
6:5 *black horse.* Symbolizing famine (cf. Zec 6:2,6). The se-

quence is thus conquest, bloodshed, famine. *pair of scales.* A balance beam with scales hung from either end. Weights were originally stones.
6:6 *wheat . . . barley.* One quart of wheat would be enough for only one person. Three quarts of the less nutritious barley would be barely enough for a small family. Famine had inflated prices to at least ten times their normal level. *oil and the wine.* Sets limits on the destruction by the rider of the black horse. The roots of the olive and vine go deeper and would not be immediately affected by a limited drought.
6:8 *pale horse.* Describes the ashen appearance of the dead; it symbolizes death. *Hades.* Equivalent to Hebrew *Sheol* (see 1:18; 20:13–14; see also note on Mt 16:18). *sword . . . wild beasts.* See Eze 5:16–17 and note.
6:9 *under the altar.* In OT ritual the blood of the slaughtered animal was poured out at the base of the altar (Ex 29:12; Lev 4:7).
6:10 *inhabitants of the earth.* A regular designation in Revelation for humankind in its hostility to God (see 3:10; 8:13; 11:10; 13:8,12; 17:2,8).
6:11 *white robe.* Symbol of blessedness and purity (see 3:5,18; 4:4; 7:9,13; 19:14). *until the full number . . . were killed.* Jewish thought held that God rules the world according to a predetermined time schedule (see 2 Esdras 4:35–37) and that the end awaits the death of a certain number of the righteous (1 Enoch 47:4). *brothers and sisters.* See note on Ro 1:13.

and they were told to wait a little longer, until the full number of their fellow servants and brothers and sisters were killed just as they had been. [d]

[12]I watched as he opened the sixth seal. There was a great earthquake. [e] The sun turned black [f] like sackcloth [g] made of goat hair, the whole moon turned blood red, [13]and the stars in the sky fell to earth, [h] as figs drop from a fig tree [i] when shaken by a strong wind. [14]The sky receded like a scroll, rolling up, [j] and every mountain and island was removed from its place. [k]

[15]Then the kings of the earth, the princes, the generals, the rich, the mighty, and everyone else, both slave and free, [l] hid in caves and among the rocks of the mountains. [m] [16]They called to the mountains and the rocks, "Fall on us [n] and hide us [a] from the face of him who sits on the throne [o] and from the wrath of the Lamb! [17]For the great day [p] of their [b] wrath has come, and who can withstand it?" [q]

144,000 SEALED

7 After this I saw four angels standing at the four corners [r] of the earth, holding back the four winds [s] of the earth to prevent [t] any wind from blowing on the land or on the sea or on any tree. [2]Then I saw another angel coming up from the east, having the seal [u] of the living God. [v] He called out in a loud voice to the four angels who had been given power to harm the land and the sea: [w] [3]"Do not harm [x] the land or the sea or the trees until we put a seal on the foreheads [y] of the servants of our God." [4]Then I heard the number [z] of those who were sealed: 144,000 [a] from all the tribes of Israel.

[5]From the tribe of Judah 12,000 were sealed,
from the tribe of Reuben 12,000,
from the tribe of Gad 12,000,
[6]from the tribe of Asher 12,000,
from the tribe of Naphtali 12,000,
from the tribe of Manasseh 12,000,
[7]from the tribe of Simeon 12,000,
from the tribe of Levi 12,000,
from the tribe of Issachar 12,000,
[8]from the tribe of Zebulun 12,000,
from the tribe of Joseph 12,000,
from the tribe of Benjamin 12,000.

THE GREAT MULTITUDE IN WHITE ROBES

[9]After this I looked, and there before me was a great multitude that no one could count,

a 16 See Hosea 10:8.   b 17 Some manuscripts *his*

6:12 *earthquake.* A regular feature of divine visitation (see Ex 19:18; Isa 2:19; Hag 2:6). *sackcloth.* See note on 11:3. *moon turned blood red.* See Joel 2:31, quoted by Peter in his Pentecost sermon (Ac 2:20).

6:13 *stars ... fell.* One of the signs immediately preceding the coming of the Son of Man (Mk 13:25–26). *figs.* Green figs appearing in the winter and easily blown from the tree, which at that season has no leaves.

6:14 *sky receded like a scroll.* See Isa 34:4. *every mountain and island was removed.* Perhaps suggested by Jer 4:24 or Na 1:5; see 16:20; 20:11.

6:15 *generals.* A general was a Roman officer who commanded a cohort, i.e., about 1,000 men. *hid in caves.* See Jer 4:29.

6:16 *wrath of the Lamb.* Only here is wrath attributed to the Lamb, but it is related to God's wrath (see "their wrath" in v. 17). God's wrath is a subject that permeates NT teaching and is both present (see Ro 1:18 and note) and future (see 19:15). It is prophesied in the OT (Zep 1:14–18; Na 1:6; Mal 3:2).

7:1–17 An interlude separating the final seal (8:1) from the preceding six (the same feature is found in the trumpet sequence; see 10:1—11:13). It contains two visions: (1) the sealing of the 144,000 (vv. 1–8) and (2) the innumerable multitude (vv. 9–17).

7:1 *four winds.* Destructive agents of God (see Jer 49:36).

7:2 *seal of the living God.* Ancient documents were folded and tied, and a lump of clay was pressed over the knot. The sender would then stamp the hardening clay with his signet ring or roll it with a cylinder seal, which authenticated and protected the contents. The sealing in ch. 7 results in the name of the Lord being stamped on the forehead of his followers (see 9:4; 14:1; cf. 22:4). Its primary purpose is to protect the people of God in the coming judgments. For the background see Eze 9:4, where the mark was the Hebrew letter *Taw*, made like an *X* or + (see also note on Eze 9:4).

7:4 *144,000.* Some find here a reference to members of actual Jewish tribes, the faithful Jewish remnant of the "great tribulation" (v. 14). Others take the passage as symbolic of all the faithful believers who live during the period of tribulation.

7:5 *Judah.* Perhaps listed before Reuben, his older brother, because the Messiah belonged to the tribe of Judah (but see note on Ge 37:21).

7:6 *Manasseh.* One of the two Joseph tribes (Ephraim and Manasseh), yet mentioned separately, probably to make up 12 tribes since Dan is omitted. This omission is due perhaps to Dan's early connection with idolatry (Jdg 18:30), or to a tradition that the antichrist was to come from that tribe.

7:9 *great multitude.* Identified in v. 14 as those who have come out of the "great tribulation." *every nation, tribe, people and language.* All four are mentioned together also in 5:9; 11:9; 13:7; 14:6. Cf. 10:11; 17:15, in which one of the four is changed. *palm branches.* Used for festive occasions (see Lev 23:40; Jn 12:13).

7:9 *b* S Rev 13:7
c ver 15 *d* S Rev 3:4
7:10 *e* Ps 3:8;
Rev 12:10; 19:1
f S Rev 5:1
7:11 *g* S Rev 4:4
h S Rev 4:6
i S Rev 4:10
7:12 *j* S Ro 11:36;
Rev 5:12-14
7:13 *k* S Rev 3:4
7:14 *l* Rev 22:14
m Heb 9:14; 1Jn 1:7;
Rev 12:11
7:15 *n* ver 9
o Rev 22:3 *p* Rev 11:19
q S Rev 5:1 *r* Isa 4:5,6;
Rev 21:3
7:16 *s* Jn 6:35
t Isa 49:10
7:17 *u* S Jn 10:11
v S Jn 4:10 *w* Isa 25:8;
35:10; 51:11; 65:19;
Rev 21:4
8:1 *x* Rev 6:1
8:2 *y* ver 6-13;
Rev 9:1,13; 11:15
z S Mt 24:31
8:3 *a* Rev 7:2
b Rev 5:8 *c* ver 5;
Ex 30:1-6; Heb 9:4;
Rev 9:13

from every nation, tribe, people and language, *b* standing before the throne *c* and in front of the Lamb. They were wearing white robes *d* and were holding palm branches in their hands. ¹⁰And they cried out in a loud voice:

> "Salvation belongs to our God, *e*
> who sits on the throne, *f*
> and to the Lamb."

¹¹All the angels were standing around the throne and around the elders *g* and the four living creatures. *h* They fell down on their faces *i* before the throne and worshiped God, ¹²saying:

> "Amen!
> Praise and glory
> and wisdom and thanks and honor
> and power and strength
> be to our God for ever and ever.
> Amen!" *j*

¹³Then one of the elders asked me, "These in white robes *k*—who are they, and where did they come from?"

¹⁴I answered, "Sir, you know."

And he said, "These are they who have come out of the great tribulation; they have washed their robes *l* and made them white in the blood of the Lamb. *m* ¹⁵Therefore,

> "they are before the throne of God *n*
> and serve him *o* day and night in his temple; *p*
> and he who sits on the throne *q*
> will spread his tent over them. *r*
> ¹⁶'Never again will they hunger;
> never again will they thirst. *s*
> The sun will not beat down on them,' *a*
> nor any scorching heat. *t*
> ¹⁷For the Lamb at the center before the throne
> will be their shepherd; *u*
> 'he will lead them to springs of living water.' *a v*
> 'And God will wipe away every tear from their eyes.' *b w*

THE SEVENTH SEAL AND THE GOLDEN CENSER

8 When he opened the seventh seal, *x* there was silence in heaven for about half an hour.

²And I saw the seven angels *y* who stand before God, and seven trumpets were given to them. *z*

³Another angel, *a* who had a golden censer, came and stood at the altar. He was given much incense to offer, with the prayers of all God's people, *b* on the golden altar *c* before the throne. ⁴The smoke of the incense, together with the prayers of God's people, went

---

a 16,17 Isaiah 49:10   *b 17* Isaiah 25:8

7:10 *Salvation belongs to our God.* See Ge 49:18 ("deliverance"); Jnh 2:9.

7:11 *elders.* See note on 4:4. *four living creatures.* See note on 4:6.

7:12 *Praise ... strength.* The sevenfold list of attributes expresses complete or perfect praise (see note on 5:12).

7:13 *white robes.* See note on 6:11.

7:14 *the great tribulation.* The period of final hostility prior to Christ's return (cf. Mt 24:21 and note). Some hold that the beginning of this hostility was already being experienced by the church of John's day.

7:15 *temple.* All 16 references to the temple in Revelation use the word that designates the temple proper rather than the larger precincts. It is the place where God's presence dwells. Thus no longer may only one tribe (Levites) go into God's presence, but all believers serve God there, for they have been made priests in God's service (see 1:6; 5:10; 20:6). *spread his tent.* The imagery would evoke memories of the tabernacle in the wilderness (Lev 26:11–13).

7:17 *shepherd.* Ancient kings often referred to themselves as the shepherds of their people (see Ps 23:1 and note).

8:1 *silence in heaven.* A dramatic pause before the next series of plagues—the final act of the drama is left undisclosed here, reserved to be presented later.

8:2 *seven trumpets.* In OT times the trumpet served to announce important events and give signals in time of war. The seven trumpets of Rev 8–9; 11:15–19 announce a series of plagues more severe than the seals but not as completely devastating as the bowls (ch. 16).

8:3 *censer.* A firepan used to hold live charcoal for the burning of incense (cf. Ex 27:3; 1Ki 7:50). *with the prayers.* Most translations consider the incense to be mingled "with" prayers. The Greek for this phrase also allows a translation that takes the incense "to be" the prayers ("incense ... consisting of the prayers").

8:4 Although the angel is involved in presenting the prayers of the saints to God, he does not make them acceptable. The Jewish apocalyptic concept of angels as mediators finds no place in the NT. Angels did function as mediators in the old covenant era up before God ^d from the angel's hand. ⁵Then the angel took the censer, filled it with fire from the altar, ^e and hurled it on the earth; and there came peals of thunder, ^f rumblings, flashes of lightning and an earthquake. ^g

THE TRUMPETS

⁶Then the seven angels who had the seven trumpets ^h prepared to sound them.

⁷The first angel ⁱ sounded his trumpet, and there came hail and fire ^j mixed with blood, and it was hurled down on the earth. A third ^k of the earth was burned up, a third of the trees were burned up, and all the green grass was burned up. ^l

⁸The second angel sounded his trumpet, and something like a huge mountain, ^m all ablaze, was thrown into the sea. A third ⁿ of the sea turned into blood, ^o ⁹a third ^p of the living creatures in the sea died, and a third of the ships were destroyed.

¹⁰The third angel sounded his trumpet, and a great star, blazing like a torch, fell from the sky ^q on a third of the rivers and on the springs of water ^r— ¹¹the name of the star is Wormwood. ^a A third ^s of the waters turned bitter, and many people died from the waters that had become bitter. ^t

¹²The fourth angel sounded his trumpet, and a third of the sun was struck, a third of the moon, and a third of the stars, so that a third ^u of them turned dark. ^v A third of the day was without light, and also a third of the night. ^w

¹³As I watched, I heard an eagle that was flying in midair ^x call out in a loud voice: "Woe! Woe! Woe ^y to the inhabitants of the earth, ^z because of the trumpet blasts about to be sounded by the other three angels!"

9 The fifth angel sounded his trumpet, and I saw a star that had fallen from the sky to the earth. ^a The star was given the key ^b to the shaft of the Abyss. ^c ²When he opened the Abyss, smoke rose from it like the smoke from a gigantic furnace. ^d The sun and sky were darkened ^e by the smoke from the Abyss. ^f ³And out of the smoke locusts ^g came down on the earth and we were given power like that of scorpions ^h of the earth. ⁴They were told not to harm ⁱ the grass of the earth or any plant or tree, ^j but only those people who did not have the seal of God on their foreheads. ^k ⁵They were not allowed to kill them but only to torture them for five months. ^l And the agony they suffered was like that of the sting of a scorpion ^m when it strikes. ⁶During those days people will seek death but will not find it; they will long to die, but death will elude them. ⁿ

^a 11 Wormwood is a bitter substance.

8:4 ^d Ps 141:2
8:5 ^e Lev 16:12,13
^f S Rev 4:5
^g S Rev 6:12
8:6 ^h S ver 2
8:7 ⁱ S ver 2
^j Eze 38:22 ^k ver 7-12;
Rev 9:15,18; 12:4
^l Rev 9:4
8:8 ^m Jer 51:25
ⁿ S ver 7 ^o Rev 16:3
8:9 ^p S ver 7
8:10 ^q Isa 14:12;
Rev 6:13; 9:1
^r Rev 14:7; 16:4
8:11 ^s S ver 7
^t Jer 9:15; 23:15
8:12 ^u S ver 7
^v Ex 10:21-23;
Rev 6:12,13
^w Eze 32:7
8:13 ^x Rev 14:6;
19:17 ^y Rev 9:12;
11:14; 12:12
^z S Rev 3:10
9:1 ^a Rev 8:10
^b Rev 1:18 ^c ver 2,11;
S Lk 8:31
9:2 ^d Ge 19:28;
Ex 19:18 ^e Joel 2:2,10
^f ver 1,11; S Lk 8:31
9:3 ^g Ex 10:12-15
^h ver 5,10
9:4 ⁱ ver 6:6
^j Rev 8:7 ^k S Rev 7:2,3
9:5 ^l ver 10 ^m ver 3
9:6 ⁿ Job 3:21; 7:15;
Jer 8:3; Rev 6:16

(see Ac 7:38 and note), but there is no record of such a mediatorial function on the part of angels in the new covenant era.

8:5 *thunder...earthquake.* See note on 4:5.

8:7 *hail and fire mixed with blood.* Cf. the imagery of the seventh plague on Egypt (Ex 9:13–25; cf. Eze 38:22). *A third of the earth was burned up.* This fraction indicates that the punishment announced by the trumpets is not yet complete and final (the same fraction appears in each of the next three plagues: vv. 8–9,10–11,12). A smaller fraction (a fourth) of devastation accompanied the opening of the fourth seal (6:8).

8:8 *sea turned into blood.* Reminiscent of the first plague on Egypt (Ex 7:20–21). This is an eschatological judgment rather than natural pollution resulting from widespread volcanic upheavals.

8:10 *great star...fell.* See notes on 6:13; 9:1.

8:11 *Wormwood.* A plant with a strong, bitter taste (see TNIV text note). It is used here as a metaphor for calamity and sorrow (see Pr 5:3–4; Jer 9:15; La 3:19). It is not poisonous, but its bitterness suggests death. *waters turned bitter.* The reverse of the miracle at Marah, where bitter waters were made sweet (Ex 15:25).

8:12 *a third of the sun was struck.* In the ninth plague on Egypt, thick darkness covered the land for three days (Ex 10:21–23). References to the Egyptian plagues suggest that in Revelation we have the final exodus of God's people from the bondage of a world controlled by hostile powers.

8:13 *Woe! Woe! Woe...!* These three woes correspond to the three final trumpet plagues (see 9:12; 11:14 [10:1—11:13 is an interlude]; the seven bowl judgments of chs. 15–16) apparently constitute the third woe). The woes fall on the unbelieving world (the phrase "the inhabitants of the earth" refers to the wicked; see note on 6:10), not on the righteous (see 9:4).

9:1 *star that had fallen.* The star in 8:10 was part of a cosmic disturbance; here the star is a divine agent, probably an angel (cf. 20:1). *Abyss.* Conceived of as the subterranean abode of demonic hordes (see 20:1; Lk 8:31). This Greek word means "very deep" or "bottomless" and is used in the Septuagint (the pre-Christian Greek translation of the OT) to translate the Hebrew word for the primeval deep (see Ge 1:2; 7:11; Pr 8:28). Eight of the nine NT occurrences of the Greek word *Abyss* are in Revelation.

9:3 *locusts.* For background, see the plague of locusts in Ex 10:1–20. Joel 1:2—2:11 interprets the locust plague as a foreshadowing of the devastations that accompany the day of the Lord. Locusts traveled in enormous swarms and could strip a land of all vegetation. In 1866, 200,000 people died in a famine in Algiers following a locust plague. *scorpions.* Large, spider-like organisms that injure or kill by means of a poisonous barb in the tail.

9:4 *people who did not have the seal of God.* The first woe does not affect the "servants of ...God" (see 7:3). Cf. the Israelites, who were protected from the Egyptian plagues (Ex 8:22; 9:4,26; 10:23; 11:7).

9:5 *five months.* A limited period of time suggested by the life cycle of the locust or the dry season (spring through late summer, about five months), in which the danger of a locust invasion is always present.

9:6 *seek death but will not find it.* Cf. Hos 10:8 (quoted in Lk 23:30). Cornelius Gallus, a Roman poet living in the first century B.C., wrote: "Worse than any wound is the wish to die and yet not be able to do so." Cf. Paul's attitude toward death in Php 1:23–24.

9:7 *o* Joel 2:4
p Da 7:8
9:8 *q* Joel 1:6
9:9 *r* Joel 2:5
9:10 *s* ver 3,5,19
9:11 *t* ver 1,2;
S Lk 8:31 *u* Rev 16:16
v Job 26:6; 28:22;
31:12; Ps 88:11
9:12 *w* S Rev 8:13
9:13 *x* Ex 30:1-3
y Rev 8:3
9:14 *z* Rev 7:1
a Ge 15:18; Dt 1:7;
Jos 1:4; Isa 11:15;
Rev 16:12
9:15 *b* Rev 20:7
c S Rev 8:7 *d* ver 18
9:16 *e* Rev 5:11; 7:4
9:17 *f* Rev 11:5
g ver 18; Ps 11:6;
Isa 30:33; Eze 38:22;
Rev 14:10; 19:20;
20:10; 21:8
9:18 *h* S Rev 8:7
i ver 15 *j* S ver 17
9:20 *k* S Rev 2:21
l Dt 4:28; 31:29;
Jer 1:16; Mic 5:13;
Ac 7:41 *m* S 1Co 10:20
n Ps 115:4-7; 135:15-
17; Da 5:23
9:21 *o* S Rev 2:21
p Isa 47:9,12;
Rev 18:23
q Rev 17:2,5
10:1 *r* Rev 5:2
s Rev 18:1; 20:1
t Eze 1:28; Rev 4:3
u Mt 17:2; Rev 1:16
v Rev 1:15
10:2 *w* ver 8-10;
Rev 5:1 *x* ver 5,8
10:3 *y* Hos 11:10
z Rev 4:5
10:4 *a* Rev 1:11,19
b ver 8 *c* Da 8:26;
12:4,9; Rev 22:10

[7]The locusts looked like horses prepared for battle. *o* On their heads they wore something like crowns of gold, and their faces resembled human faces. *p* [8]Their hair was like women's hair, and their teeth were like lions' teeth. *q* [9]They had breastplates like breastplates of iron, and the sound of their wings was like the thundering of many horses and chariots rushing into battle. *r* [10]They had tails with stingers, like scorpions, and in their tails they had power to torment people for five months. *s* [11]They had as king over them the angel of the Abyss, *t* whose name in Hebrew *u* is Abaddon *v* and in Greek is Apollyon (that is, Destroyer).

[12]The first woe is past; two other woes are yet to come. *w*

[13]The sixth angel sounded his trumpet, and I heard a voice coming from the four horns *x* of the golden altar that is before God. *y* [14]It said to the sixth angel who had the trumpet, "Release the four angels *z* who are bound at the great river Euphrates." *a* [15]And the four angels who had been kept ready for this very hour and day and month and year were released *b* to kill a third *c* of the world's people. *d* [16]The number of the mounted troops was two hundred million. I heard their number. *e*

[17]The horses and riders I saw in my vision looked like this: Their breastplates were fiery red, dark blue, and yellow as sulfur. The heads of the horses resembled the heads of lions, and out of their mouths *f* came fire, smoke and sulfur. *g* [18]A third *h* of the people were killed *i* by the three plagues of fire, smoke and sulfur *j* that came out of their mouths. [19]The power of the horses was in their mouths and in their tails; for their tails were like snakes, having heads with which they inflict injury.

[20]The rest of the people who were not killed by these plagues still did not repent *k* of the work of their hands; *l* they did not stop worshiping demons, *m* and idols of gold, silver, bronze, stone and wood—idols that cannot see or hear or walk. *n* [21]Nor did they repent *o* of their murders, their magic arts, *p* their sexual immorality *q* or their thefts.

THE ANGEL AND THE LITTLE SCROLL

10 Then I saw another mighty angel *r* coming down from heaven. *s* He was robed in a cloud, with a rainbow *t* above his head; his face was like the sun, *u* and his legs were like fiery pillars. *v* [2]He was holding a little scroll, *w* which lay open in his hand. He planted his right foot on the sea and his left foot on the land, *x* [3]and he gave a loud shout like the roar of a lion. *y* When he shouted, the voices of the seven thunders *z* spoke. [4]And when the seven thunders spoke, I was about to write; *a* but I heard a voice from heaven *b* say, "Seal up what the seven thunders have said and do not write it down." *c*

9:7 *human faces.* The locusts appear to have the cunning of intelligent beings. They do not simply use brute force.

9:8 *women's hair.* Perhaps a reference to long antennae. *lions' teeth.* Cruel, inhumane.

9:9 *breastplates.* The breastplate was a coat of mail that protected the front. *like breastplates of iron.* Probably thin iron pieces riveted to a leather base.

9:10 *five months.* See note on v. 5.

9:11 *Abaddon.* A personification of destruction (cf. Pr 15:11).

9:12 *first woe.* See note on 8:13.

9:13 *horns of the golden altar.* See 8:3–5. The horns were projections at the four corners of the altar (Ex 27:2). Those fleeing judgment could seek mercy by taking hold of the horns (1Ki 1:50–51; 2:28; see note on Am 3:14).

9:14 *four angels.* Apparently in charge of the demonic horsemen (vv. 15–19). *Euphrates.* See note on Ge 15:18.

9:15 *hour...day...month...year.* Apocalyptic thought views God as acting according to an exact timetable.

9:16 *two hundred million.* The reference is most likely general, intending an incalculable host rather than a specific number (cf. Ps 68:17; Da 7:10; Rev 5:11).

9:17 *breastplates.* See note on v. 9. *out of their mouths came fire.* Cf. the two witnesses in 11:5.

9:19 *tails were like snakes, having heads.* Emphasizes the demonic origin of the horses (cf. 12:9).

9:20 *still did not repent.* Suggests that the purpose of the extreme suffering of some was to call the others to repentance (cf. v. 21; 2:21; 16:9,11; cf. also Am 4:6–11 and note). *demons.* Spiritual beings in league with Satan and exerting an evil influence on human affairs (cf. Dt 4:28; Ps 115:5–7; Lk 4:33 and note; 1Co 10:20).

9:21 *Nor did they repent.* See 16:9,11. Even physical pain will not change the rebellious heart. *magic arts.* Involved the mixing of various ingredients (the Greek for this phrase is *pharmakon,* from which comes the English "pharmacy") for magical purposes. Believers at Ephesus publicly burned their books of magic, valued at 50,000 drachmas (Ac 19:19). (A drachma was a silver coin worth about a day's wages.)

10:1—11:13 The second interlude (see note on 7:1–17).

10:1 *mighty angel.* Perhaps the angel of 5:2. *robed in a cloud.* See Mt 17:5; 24:30 and notes. *rainbow.* Cf. Eze 1:26–28. The rainbow became a sign of God's pledge never to destroy the earth again by a flood (see Ge 9:8–17 and note on 9:13). *legs were like fiery pillars.* Since the exodus supplies background for this central part of Revelation (see note on 8:12), this feature may recall the pillars of fire and cloud that guided (Ex 13:21–22) and protected (Ex 14:19,24) the Israelites during their desert journey.

10:2 *little scroll.* Not the same as the scroll of destiny in ch. 5, since that scroll was intended to reveal its contents and this scroll was to be eaten. Furthermore, the term "little scroll" sets off this particular scroll from all others. *right foot on the sea ...left foot on the land.* Indicates his tremendous size and symbolizes that his coming has to do with the destiny of all creation (cf. v. 6).

10:3 *seven thunders.* In 8:5; 11:19; 16:18 thunder is connected with divine punishment. Here, too, it anticipates the judgment to fall on those who refuse God's love and grace.

10:4 *Seal up.* In Da 8:26; 12:4,9 the prophecies are sealed until the last times, when they will be opened. What the seven thunders said will not be revealed until their proper time. Cf. the angel's instructions in 22:10 not to seal the prophecies of Revelation.

⁵Then the angel I had seen standing on the sea and on the land ᵈ raised his right hand to heaven. ᵉ ⁶And he swore ᶠ by him who lives for ever and ever, ᵍ who created the heavens and all that is in them, the earth and all that is in it, and the sea and all that is in it, ʰ and said, "There will be no more delay! ⁱ ⁷But in the days when the seventh angel is about to sound his trumpet, ʲ the mystery ᵏ of God will be accomplished, just as he announced to his servants the prophets." ˡ

⁸Then the voice that I had heard from heaven ᵐ spoke to me once more: "Go, take the scroll ⁿ that lies open in the hand of the angel who is standing on the sea and on the land."

⁹So I went to the angel and asked him to give me the little scroll. He said to me, "Take it and eat it. It will turn your stomach sour, but 'in your mouth it will be as sweet as honey.' ᵃ" ᵒ ¹⁰I took the little scroll from the angel's hand and ate it. It tasted as sweet as honey in my mouth, ᵖ but when I had eaten it, my stomach turned sour. ¹¹Then I was told, "You must prophesy �q again about many peoples, nations, languages and kings." ʳ

THE TWO WITNESSES

11 I was given a reed like a measuring rod ˢ and was told, "Go and measure the temple of God and the altar, with its worshipers. ²But exclude the outer court; ᵗ do not measure it, because it has been given to the Gentiles. ᵘ They will trample on the holy city ᵛ for 42 months. ʷ ³And I will appoint my two witnesses, ˣ and they will prophesy for 1,260 days, ʸ clothed in sackcloth." ᶻ ⁴They are "the two olive trees" ᵃ and the two lampstands, and "they stand before the Lord of the earth." ᵇ ᵇ ⁵If anyone tries to harm them, fire comes from their mouths and devours their enemies. ᶜ This is how anyone who wants to harm them must die. ᵈ ⁶They have power to shut up the sky ᵉ so that it will not rain during the time they are prophesying; ᶠ and they have power to turn the waters into blood ᵍ and to strike the earth with every kind of plague as often as they want.

⁷Now when they have finished their testimony, the beast ʰ that comes up from the Abyss ⁱ will attack them, ʲ and overpower and kill them. ⁸Their bodies will lie in the pub-

ᵃ 9 Ezek. 3:3   ᵇ 4 See Zech. 4:3,11,14.

### Cross-references (right margin)

10:5 ᵈ ver 1,2
ᵉ Dt 32:40; Da 12:7
10:6 ᶠ Ge 14:22;
Ex 6:8; Nu 14:30
ᵍ S Rev 1:18
ʰ Ps 115:15; 146:6;
Rev 4:11; 14:7
ⁱ Rev 16:17
10:7 ʲ S Mt 24:31
ᵏ S Ro 16:25 ˡ Am 3:7
10:8 ᵐ ver 4 ⁿ ver 2
10:9 ᵒ Jer 15:16;
Eze 2:8-3:3
10:10 ᵖ S ver 9
10:11 q Eze 37:4,9
ʳ Da 3:4; S Rev 13:7
11:1 ˢ Eze 40:3;
Rev 21:15
11:2 ᵗ Eze 40:17,20
ᵘ Lk 21:24
ᵛ S Rev 21:2 ʷ ver 3;
Da 7:25; 12:7;
Rev 12:6,14; 13:5
11:3 ˣ Rev 1:5; 2:13
ʸ S ver 2 ᶻ Ge 37:34;
2Sa 3:31; Ne 9:1;
Jnh 3:5
11:4 ᵃ Ps 52:8;
Jer 11:16; Zec 4:3,11
ᵇ Zec 4:14
11:5 ᶜ 2Sa 22:9;
2Ki 1:10; Jer 5:14;
Rev 9:17,18
ᵈ Nu 16:29,35
11:6 ᵉ S Lk 4:25
ᶠ ver 3 ᵍ Ex 7:17,19;
Rev 8:8
11:7 ʰ Rev 13:1-4
ⁱ S Lk 8:31 ʲ Da 7:21;
Rev 13:7

10:5 *raised his right hand.* A part of oath taking (see Ge 14:22–23; Dt 32:40).

10:6 *him who lives for ever and ever.* Of special encouragement in a context of impending martyrdom (cf. 1:18; 4:9–10; 15:7). *no more delay.* The martyrs in 6:9–11 were told to rest for a while, but now the end has come (cf. Da 12:1; Mk 13:19).

10:7 *mystery of God.* In apocalyptic thought mysteries were secrets preserved in heaven and revealed to the apocalyptist. Here the mystery is that God has won the victory over the forces of evil and will reign for ever and ever (cf. 11:15).

10:9 *Take it and eat it.* Grasp and digest fully the contents of the scroll (cf. Ps 119:103). *turn your stomach sour.* The message of the little scroll (11:1–13) will involve suffering—the "bad news." *in your mouth ... sweet as honey.* God's eternal purposes will experience no further delay—the "good news."

10:11 *prophesy again.* The prophecies following the sounding of the seventh trumpet in 11:15. *peoples ... kings.* See note on 7:9.

11:1 *reed.* A bamboo-like cane that often reached a height of 20 feet and grew in abundance in the waters along the banks of the Jordan. Straight and light, the reed was a convenient measuring rod (see Eze 40:3; Zec 2:1–2). *temple.* See note on 7:15, though here the sanctuary on earth is what is measured. Some hold that the symbolic reference is to the believing church, others that it refers to believing Israel. Some representatives of the latter view believe that "temple" should be understood more literally as a future rebuilt temple. *altar.* The context of worship suggests that this is the great altar.

11:2 *outer court.* The court of the Gentiles, approximately 26 acres. *trample on the holy city.* Cf. Ps 79:1; Isa 63:18; Lk 21:24. *42 months.* Three and a half years. Some find the background for this period in the time of Jewish suffering under the Syrian tyrant, Antiochus Epiphanes (168–165 B.C.). Others point out that, whereas the temple was desolated for three years under Antiochus, the figure used in Revelation is three and a half years, which no doubt looks back to the dividing of the 70th "seven"

(Da 9:27) into two equal parts. The same time period is also designated as 1,260 days (v. 3; 12:6) and as "a time, times and half a time" (12:14; cf. Da 7:25; 12:7). This period of time evidently became a conventional symbol for a limited period of unrestrained wickedness.

11:3 *two witnesses.* Modeled after Moses and Elijah (see notes on vv. 5–6). They may symbolize testifying believers in the final period before Christ returns, or they may be two actual individuals who will be martyred for the proclamation of the truth. *1,260 days.* See note on v. 2. These are months of 30 days (42 months x 30 days = 1,260 days). *sackcloth.* See 6:12; a coarse, dark cloth woven from the hair of goats or camels. It was worn as a sign of mourning and penitence (Joel 1:13; Jnh 3:5–6; Mt 11:21; see note on Ge 37:34).

11:4 The imagery emphasizes that the power for effective testimony is supplied by the Spirit of God (see notes on Zec 4).

11:5 *fire comes ... and devours.* Cf. Elijah's encounters with the messengers of Ahaziah (2Ki 1:10,12).

11:6 *power to shut up the sky.* Cf. the drought in the days of Elijah (1Ki 17:1; see also Lk 4:25; Jas 5:17). *waters into blood.* God used Moses to bring the same plague on the Egyptians (Ex 7:17–21).

11:7 *the beast.* First mention of the major opponent of God's people in the final days (see chs. 13; 17). That he comes up from the Abyss (see note on 9:1) indicates his demonic character. *kill them.* They will suffer the same fate as their Lord (see v. 8).

11:8 *Their bodies will lie in the public square.* In the Near East the denial of burial was a flagrant violation of decency. *great city.* Possibly Jerusalem, though some say Rome, Babylon or some other city. It may be symbolic of the world opposed to God (see 16:19; 17:18; 18:10,16,18–19,21). Sodom (see similarly Isa 1:10) refers to its low level of morality (cf. Ge 19:4–11), and Egypt emphasizes oppression and slavery. Some say that Jesus could have been crucified in Rome in the sense that her power extended throughout the known world and was immediately responsible for Christ's execution.

11:8 ᵏRev 16:19
ˡIsa 1:9; Jer 23:14;
Eze 16:46
ᵐHeb 13:12
11:9 ⁿS Rev 13:7
ᵒPs 79:2,3
11:10 ᵖS Rev 3:10
ᵠNe 8:10,12; Est 9:19,
22
11:11 ᵛver 9
ˢEze 37:5,9,10,14
11:12 ᵗRev 4:1
ᵘ2Ki 2:11; Ac 1:9
11:13 ᵛS Rev 6:12
ʷRev 14:7; 16:9; 19:7
ˣRev 16:11
11:14 ʸS Rev 8:13
11:15 ᶻS Mt 24:31
ᵃRev 16:17; 19:1
ᵇRev 12:10
ᶜPs 145:13; Da 2:44;
7:14,27; Mic 4:7;
Zec 14:9; Lk 1:33
11:16 ᵈS Rev 4:4
ᵉS Rev 4:10
11:17 ᶠPs 30:12
ᵍS Rev 1:8 ʰS Rev 1:4
ⁱRev 19:6
11:18 ʲPs 2:1
ᵏRev 20:12 ˡRev 10:7
ᵐS Rev 19:5
11:19 ⁿRev 15:5,8
ᵒEx 25:10-22;
2Ch 5:7; Heb 9:4
ᵖS Rev 4:5
ᵠRev 16:21
12:1 ᵛver 3
ˢRev 11:19 ᵗGe 37:9
12:2 ᵘIsa 26:17;
Gal 4:19

lic square of the great city,ᵏ which is figuratively called Sodomˡ and Egypt, where also their Lord was crucified. ᵐ ⁹For three and a half days many from every people, tribe, language and nationⁿ will gaze on their bodies and refuse them burial.ᵒ ¹⁰The inhabitants of the earthᵖ will gloat over them and will celebrate by sending each other gifts, ᵠ because these two prophets had tormented those who live on the earth.

¹¹But after the three and a half daysʳ the breathᵃ of life from God entered them,ˢ and they stood on their feet, and terror struck those who saw them. ¹²Then they heard a loud voice from heaven saying to them, "Come up here."ᵗ And they went up to heaven in a cloud, ᵘ while their enemies looked on.

¹³At that very hour there was a severe earthquakeᵛ and a tenth of the city collapsed. Seven thousand people were killed in the earthquake, and the survivors were terrified and gave gloryʷ to the God of heaven.ˣ

¹⁴The second woe has passed; the third woe is coming soon.ʸ

THE SEVENTH TRUMPET

¹⁵The seventh angel sounded his trumpet,ᶻ and there were loud voicesᵃ in heaven, which said:

> "The kingdom of the world has become
>   the kingdom of our Lord and of his Messiah,ᵇ
>   and he will reign for ever and ever."ᶜ

¹⁶And the twenty-four elders, ᵈ who were seated on their thrones before God, fell on their facesᵉ and worshiped God, ¹⁷saying:

> "We give thanksᶠ to you, Lord God Almighty,ᵍ
>   the One who is and who was,ʰ
> because you have taken your great power
>   and have begun to reign.ⁱ
> ¹⁸The nations were angry,ʲ
>   and your wrath has come.
> The time has come for judging the dead,ᵏ
>   and for rewarding your servants the prophetsˡ
> and your people who revere your name,
>   both great and small ᵐ—
> and for destroying those who destroy the earth."

¹⁹Then God's templeⁿ in heaven was opened, and within his temple was seen the ark of his covenant. ᵒ And there came flashes of lightning, rumblings, peals of thunder,ᵖ an earthquake and a great hailstorm. ᵠ

THE WOMAN AND THE DRAGON

12 A great and wondrous signʳ appeared in heaven:ˢ a woman clothed with the sun, with the moon under her feet and a crown of twelve starsᵗ on her head. ²She was pregnant and cried out in painᵘ as she was about to give birth. ³Then

---

ᵃ 11 Or *Spirit* (see Ezek. 37:5,14)

11:9 *three and a half days.* A short time when compared with the three and a half years of their ministry. *refuse them burial.* See note on v. 8.

11:11 *breath of life from God entered them.* A dramatic validation of the true faith (cf. Eze 37:5,10).

11:12 *went up to heaven in a cloud.* Cf. 1Th 4:17. *enemies looked on.* Cf. 1:7.

11:13 *earthquake.* See notes on 6:12; Eze 38:19. *gave glory to the God of heaven.* Not an act of repentance but the terrified realization that Christ, not the antichrist, is the true Lord of all.

11:14 *second woe.* Cf. 9:12.

11:15 *seventh angel sounded.* The series of trumpet blasts is now continued (see 9:13) and completed. *kingdom of our Lord.* Cf. Ex 15:18; Ps 10:16; Zec 14:9. *of our Lord and of his Messiah.* Cf. Ps 2:2 and note.

11:16 *twenty-four elders.* See note on 4:4.

11:17 *One who is and who was.* In 1:4;8; 4:8 he is also the one "who is to come." This is now omitted because his reign is here pictured as having begun.

11:18 *nations were angry.* See Ps 48:4. *your wrath.* See note on 6:16. God's wrath triumphs in 14:10–11; 16:15–21; 20:8–9. *judging the dead.* Anticipated in 6:10, carried out in 20:11–15. *your servants the prophets.* See Da 9:6,10; Am 3:7; Zec 1:6.

11:19 *God's temple in heaven.* The sanctuary in heaven (3:12; 7:15; 15:5–8) as distinguished from the sanctuary on earth (11:1). *ark of his covenant.* The OT ark, a chest of acacia wood (Dt 10:1–2), symbolized the throne or presence of God among his people. It was probably destroyed when Nebuzaradan destroyed the temple in Jerusalem (2Ki 25:8–10). In the NT it symbolizes God's faithfulness in keeping covenant with his people. *lightning … hailstorm.* See note on 4:5.

12:1 *sign.* An extraordinary spectacle or event that points beyond itself (cf. Lk 21:11,25; Ac 2:19). *a woman clothed with the sun.* Probably a symbolic reference to the believing Messianic community (see v. 5). *twelve stars.* Cf. the 12 tribes of Israel.

12:2 *cried out in pain.* Cf. the similar language describing rebirth of Jerusalem in Isa 66:7 (see Mic 4:10).

another sign appeared in heaven: ᵛ an enormous red dragon ʷ with seven heads ˣ and ten horns ʸ and seven crowns ᶻ on its heads. ⁴Its tail swept a third ᵃ of the stars out of the sky and flung them to the earth. ᵇ The dragon stood in front of the woman who was about to give birth, so that it might devour her child ᶜ the moment he was born. ⁵She gave birth to a son, a male child, who "will rule all the nations with an iron scepter." ᵃ ᵈ And her child was snatched up ᵉ to God and to his throne. ⁶The woman fled into the wilderness to a place prepared for her by God, where she might be taken care of for 1,260 days. ᶠ

⁷And there was war in heaven. Michael ᵍ and his angels fought against the dragon, ʰ and the dragon and his angels ⁱ fought back. ⁸But he was not strong enough, and they lost their place in heaven. ⁹The great dragon was hurled down—that ancient serpent ʲ called the devil, ᵏ or Satan, ˡ who leads the whole world astray. ᵐ He was hurled to the earth, ⁿ and his angels with him.

¹⁰Then I heard a loud voice in heaven ᵒ say:

"Now have come the salvation ᵖ and the power
    and the kingdom of our God,
    and the authority of his Messiah.
For the accuser of our brothers and sisters, ᑫ
    who accuses them before our God day and night,
    has been hurled down.
¹¹They triumphed over ʳ him
    by the blood of the Lamb ˢ
    and by the word of their testimony; ᵗ
they did not love their lives so much
    as to shrink from death. ᵘ
¹²Therefore rejoice, you heavens ᵛ
    and you who dwell in them!
But woe ʷ to the earth and the sea, ˣ
    because the devil has gone down to you!
He is filled with fury,
    because he knows that his time is short."

¹³When the dragon ʸ saw that he had been hurled to the earth, he pursued the woman who had given birth to the male child. ᶻ ¹⁴The woman was given the two wings of a great eagle, ᵃ so that she might fly to the place prepared for her in the wilderness, where she would be taken care of for a time, times and half a time, ᵇ out of the serpent's reach. ¹⁵Then from his mouth the serpent ᶜ spewed water like a river, to overtake the woman and sweep her away with the torrent. ¹⁶But the earth helped the woman by opening its mouth and swallowing the river that the dragon had spewed out of his mouth. ¹⁷Then the dragon was enraged at the woman and went off to make war ᵈ against the rest of her offspring ᵉ— those who keep God's commands ᶠ and hold fast their testimony about Jesus. ᵍ

THE BEAST OUT OF THE SEA

13 The dragon ᵇ stood on the shore of the sea. And I saw a beast coming out of the sea. ʰ It had ten horns and seven heads, ⁱ with ten crowns on its horns, and on each head a blasphemous name. ʲ ²The beast I saw resembled a

---

ᵃ 5 Psalm 2:9   ᵇ 1 Some manuscripts *And I*

12:3 ᵛver 1; Rev 15:1
ʷver 9,13,16,17;
Rev 13:1 ˣ Rev 13:1;
17:3,7,9 ʸRev 7:7,20;
Rev 13:1; 17:3,7,12,16
ᶻRev 19:12
12:4 ᵃS Rev 8:7
ᵇDa 8:10 ᶜMt 2:16
12:5 ᵈPs 2:9;
Rev 2:27; 19:15
ᵉS Ac 8:39
12:6 ᶠS Rev 11:2
12:7 ᵍS Jude 9
ʰver 3 ⁱMt 25:41
12:9 ʲver 15; Ge 3:1-
7 ᵏMt 25:41; Rev 20:2
ˡS Mt 4:10
ᵐRev 20:3,8,10
ⁿLk 10:18; Jn 12:31
12:10 ᵒRev 11:15
ᵖRev 7:10 ᑫJob 1:9-
11; Zec 3:1; 1Pe 5:8
12:11 ʳS Jn 16:33;
Rev 15:2 ˢS Rev 7:14
ᵗRev 6:9 ᵘLk 14:26;
Rev 2:10
12:12 ᵛPs 96:11;
Isa 44:23; 49:13;
Rev 18:20
ʷS Rev 8:13
ˣRev 10:6
12:13 ʸver 3 ᶻver 5
12:14 ᵃEx 19:4
ᵇS Rev 11:2
12:15 ᶜver 9
12:17 ᵈRev 11:7;
13:7 ᵉGe 3:15
ᶠS Jn 14:15 ᵍS Rev 1:2
13:1 ʰDa 7:1-6;
Rev 15:2; 16:13
ⁱS Rev 12:3 ʲDa 11:36;
Rev 17:3

12:3 *red dragon.* Identified in v. 9 (cf. 20:2). Dragons abound in the mythology of ancient peoples (Leviathan in Canaanite lore and Set-Typhon, the red crocodile, in Egypt). In the OT they are normally used metaphorically to depict the enemies of God and of Israel (see Ps 74:14; Isa 27:1; Eze 29:3). *seven heads.* See 13:1; 17:9–11 and notes. *ten horns.* Symbolizing great power (see 13:1; 17:12 and note).
12:5 *a son, a male child.* The Messiah. *iron scepter.* See note on 2:27. *snatched up to God.* The ascension of Christ.
12:6 *wilderness.* Not a wasteland but a place of spiritual refuge (cf. Hos 2:14). *1,260 days.* The time of spiritual protection corresponds to the time of persecution (see note on 11:2; cf. 13:5).
12:7 *Michael.* An archangel who defeats Satan in heavenly warfare. In Da 12:1 he is the protector of Israel who will deliver her from tribulation in the last days.
12:9 *dragon was hurled . . . to the earth.* Not the original casting of Satan out of heaven, but his final exclusion—an explanation

of his intense hostility against God's people in the last days (vv. 12–17). *devil, or Satan.* See notes on 2:9–10. *leads . . . astray.* Cf. 2Co 11:3; see also Lk 22:31; Jn 13:2.
12:10 *accuser.* See Job 1:9–11 and notes on 1:6; Mt 16:23; 1Jn 3:8; see also Zec 3:1. Satan (v. 9) in Hebrew means "accuser" or "adversary."
12:11 *blood of the Lamb.* See note on 5:9; see also 1:5; 7:14.
12:12 *his time is short.* The period of final, intense hostility of Satan toward the people of God.
12:13–16 Cf. the similarity to the exodus.
12:14 *wilderness.* See note on v. 6. *a time, times and half a time.* One year plus two years plus half a year (see note on 11:2).
12:16 *earth helped . . . by opening its mouth.* Cf. Nu 16:30–33, where the earth opened and swallowed Korah's men.
12:17 *rest of her offspring.* Believers in general, as contrasted with Christ, the male child of vv. 5,13.
13:1 *beast coming out of the sea.* First mentioned in 11:7. Ac-

13:2 kDa 7:6
lDa 7:5 mDa 7:4
nRev 2:13; 16:10
13:3 over 12,14
pRev 17:8
13:4 qEx 15:11
13:5 rDa 7:8,11,20,
25; 11:36; 2Th 2:4
sS Rev 11:2
13:6 tRev 12:12
13:7 uDa 7:21;
Rev 11:7 vRev 5:9;
7:9; 10:11; 17:15
13:8 wver 12,14;
S Rev 3:10
xS Rev 20:12
yS Jn 1:29
zS Mt 25:34
13:9 aS Rev 2:7
13:10 bJer 15:2;
43:11 cS Heb 6:12
dRev 14:12
13:11 ever 1,2
fRev 16:13
13:12 gver 4
hver 14; Rev 19:20
iver 15; Rev 14:9,11;
16:2; 19:20; 20:4
jver 3
13:13 kS Mt 24:24
l1Ki 18:38; 2Ki 1:10;
Lk 9:54; Rev 20:9
13:14 m2Th 2:9,10
nRev 12:9
oS Rev 3:10 pver 3,
12
13:15 qS ver 12
rDa 3:3-6
13:16 sS Rev 19:5

leopard, [k] but had feet like those of a bear [l] and a mouth like that of a lion. [m] The dragon gave the beast his power and his throne and great authority. [n] **3**One of the heads of the beast seemed to have had a fatal wound, but the fatal wound had been healed. [o] The whole world was filled with wonder [p] and followed the beast. **4**People worshiped the dragon because he had given authority to the beast, and they also worshiped the beast and asked, "Who is like [q] the beast? Who can make war against it?"

5The beast was given a mouth to utter proud words and blasphemies [r] and to exercise its authority for forty-two months. [s] **6**It opened its mouth to blaspheme God, and to slander his name and his dwelling place and those who live in heaven. [t] **7**It was given power to make war [u] against God's people and to conquer them. And it was given authority over every tribe, people, language and nation. [v] **8**All inhabitants of the earth [w] will worship the beast—all whose names have not been written in the Lamb's book of life, [x] the Lamb [y] who was slain from the creation of the world. [a] [z]

9Whoever has ears, let them hear. [a]

> **10** "If anyone is to go into captivity,
> into captivity they will go.
> If anyone is to be killed [b] with the sword,
> with the sword they will be killed." [c] [b]

This calls for patient endurance and faithfulness [c] on the part of God's people. [d]

THE BEAST OUT OF THE EARTH

11Then I saw another beast, coming out of the earth. [e] It had two horns like a lamb, but it spoke like a dragon. [f] **12**It exercised all the authority [g] of the first beast on its behalf, [h] and made the earth and its inhabitants worship the first beast, [i] whose fatal wound had been healed. [j] **13**And it performed great signs, [k] even causing fire to come down from heaven [l] to the earth in full view of everyone. **14**Because of the signs [m] it was given power to perform on behalf of the first beast, it deceived [n] the inhabitants of the earth. [o] It ordered them to set up an image in honor of the beast who was wounded by the sword and yet lived. [p] **15**It was given power to give breath to the image of the first beast, so that it could speak and cause all who refused to worship [q] the image to be killed. [r] **16**It also forced all people, great and small, [s] rich and poor, free and slave, to receive a mark on their right

---

a 8 Or *written from the creation of the world in the book of life belonging to the Lamb who was slain*   b 10 Some manuscripts *anyone kills*   c 10 Jer. 15:2

---

cording to some, the beast symbolizes the Roman empire, the deification of secular authority. According to others, he is the final, personal antichrist. According to still others, the beast symbolizes anti-Christian political power that came to expression in the Roman empire of John's day, that continues in various ways down through the present era and that will become manifest in the political power of the final antichrist (see note on 14:8). The background seems to be Daniel's vision of the four great beasts (Da 7:2–7). See 17:8–11 for the interpreting angel's explanation of the beast. *sea.* See 17:15. *ten horns.* See 17:12 and note. *blasphemous name.* Roman emperors tended to assume titles of deity. Domitian, e.g., was addressed as *Dominus et Deus noster* ("Our Lord and God").

13:2 *leopard . . . bear . . . lion.* John's beast combined characteristics of Daniel's four beasts (Da 7:4–6). *dragon.* See note on 12:3.

13:3 *fatal wound . . . healed.* Emphasizes the tremendous recuperative power of the beast. *whole world was filled with wonder.* See 17:8 for a similar reaction.

13:5–6 Cf. Da 11:36–39 and note on 11:36.

13:5 *was given.* Four times in the Greek text of vv. 5–7 the passive "was given" occurs, either emphasizing the subordinate role of the beast (see vv. 2,4) or indicating that even the beast operates under the authority granted to it by God (the verbs in vv. 2,4 are active, while the verbs here are passive). *forty-two months.* See note on 11:2.

13:7 *make war.* See 12:17; see also Da 7:7.

13:8 *book of life.* See note on 3:5; cf. 20:12,15. *Lamb who was slain.* See note on 5:6; cf. Isa 53:7; Jn 1:29,36. *slain from the creation of the world.* The death of Christ was a redemptive event decreed from eternity. See, however, TNIV text note, which af-

firms that believers' names were written in the book of life from eternity (cf. 17:8).

13:11 *another beast, coming out of the earth.* According to some he symbolizes religious power in the service of secular authorities. According to others he is the personal false prophet (see 16:13; 19:20; 20:10). *two horns like a lamb.* He attempts to appear gentle and harmless. *spoke like a dragon.* See Jesus' warning in Mt 7:15 about ravenous wolves who come in sheep's clothing.

13:12 *exercised all the authority of the first beast.* The trinity of evil is now complete. The beast from the earth is under the authority of the beast from the sea. The latter is subject to the dragon. Satan, secular power and religious compromise (or Satan, the antichrist and the false prophet) join against the cause of God: Father, Son and Holy Spirit.

13:13 *great signs.* See the warning in Dt 13:1–3; see also Mt 24:24; 2Th 2:9; cf. Rev 19:20. *fire . . . from heaven.* See 1Ki 18:24–39.

13:14 *set up an image.* Cf. Da 3:1–11; 2Th 2:4.

13:15 *it could speak.* Belief in statues that could speak is widely attested in ancient literature. Ventriloquism and other forms of deception were common.

13:16 *mark.* Whatever its origin—possibly the branding of slaves or enemy soldiers, the sealing and stamping of official documents or the sign of the cross on the forehead of a new Christian—the mark of the beast apparently symbolized allegiance to the demands of emperor worship. In the final days of the antichrist it will be the ultimate test of loyalty (cf. v. 17; 14:9, 11; 15:2; 16:2; 19:20; 20:4). It imitates the sealing of the servants of God in ch. 7.

hands or on their foreheads, ᵗ ¹⁷so that they could not buy or sell unless they had the mark, ᵘ which is the name of the beast or the number of its name. ᵛ

¹⁸This calls for wisdom. ᵂ Let those who have insight calculate the number of the beast, for it is the number of a man. ᵃ ˣ That number is 666.

THE LAMB AND THE 144,000

14 Then I looked, and there before me was the Lamb, ʸ standing on Mount Zion, ᶻ and with him 144,000 ᵃ who had his name and his Father's name ᵇ written on their foreheads. ᶜ ²And I heard a sound from heaven like the roar of rushing waters ᵈ and like a loud peal of thunder. ᵉ The sound I heard was like that of harpists playing their harps. ᶠ ³And they sang a new song ᵍ before the throne and before the four living creatures ʰ and the elders. ⁱ No one could learn the song except the 144,000 ʲ who had been redeemed from the earth. ⁴These are those who did not defile themselves with women, for they remained virgins. ᵏ They follow the Lamb wherever he goes. ˡ They were purchased from among the human race ᵐ and offered as firstfruits ⁿ to God and the Lamb. ⁵No lie was found in their mouths; ᵒ they are blameless. ᵖ

THE THREE ANGELS

⁶Then I saw another angel flying in midair, �q and he had the eternal gospel to proclaim to those who live on the earth ʳ—to every nation, tribe, language and people. ˢ ⁷He said in a loud voice, "Fear God ᵗ and give him glory, ᵘ because the hour of his judgment has come. Worship him who made ᵛ the heavens, the earth, the sea and the springs of water." ᵂ

⁸A second angel followed and said, " 'Fallen! Fallen is Babylon the Great,' ᵇ ˣ which made all the nations drink the maddening wine of her adulteries." ʸ

⁹A third angel followed them and said in a loud voice: "If anyone worships the beast ᶻ and its image ᵃ and receives its mark on their forehead ᵇ or on their hand, ¹⁰they, too, will drink of the wine of God's fury, ᶜ which has been poured full strength into the cup of his wrath. ᵈ They will be tormented with burning sulfur ᵉ in the presence of the holy angels and of the Lamb. ¹¹And the smoke of their torment will rise for ever and ever. ᶠ There will be no rest day or night ᵍ for those who worship the beast and its image, ʰ or for anyone who receives the mark of its name." ⁱ ¹²This calls for patient endurance ʲ on the part of the people of God ᵏ who keep his commands ˡ and remain faithful to Jesus.

¹³Then I heard a voice from heaven say, "Write: Blessed are the dead who die in the Lord ᵐ from now on."

"Yes," says the Spirit, ⁿ "they will rest from their labor, for their deeds will follow them."

ᵃ 18 Or *is humanity's number*   ᵇ 8 Isaiah 21:9

13:16 ʳRev 7:3; 14:9; 20:4
13:17 ᵘRev 14:9
ᵛver 18; Rev 14:11; 15:2
13:18 ᵂRev 17:9
ˣRev 15:2; 21:17
14:1 ʸRev 5:6
ᶻPs 2:6; Heb 12:22
ᵃver 3; Rev 7:4
ᵇRev 3:12; 22:4
ᶜS Rev 7:3
14:2 ᵈS Rev 1:15
ᵉRev 6:1 ᶠRev 5:8; 15:2
14:3 ᵍS Rev 5:9
ʰS Rev 4:6
ⁱS Rev 4:4 ʲver 1
14:4 ᵏ2Co 11:2; Rev 3:4 ˡRev 7:17
ᵐRev 5:9 ⁿJer 2:3; Jas 1:18
14:5 ᵒPs 32:2; Zep 3:13; Jn 1:47; 1Pe 2:22 ᵖEph 5:27
14:6 �q Rev 8:13; 19:17 ʳS Rev 3:10
ˢS Rev 13:7
14:7 ᵗPs 34:9; Rev 15:4 ᵘS Rev 11:13
ᵛS Rev 10:6
ᵂRev 8:10; 16:4
14:8 ˣIsa 21:9; Jer 51:8; Rev 16:19; 17:5; 18:2,10
ʸRev 17:2,4; 18:3,9
14:9 ᶻS Rev 13:12
ᵃRev 13:14
ᵇS Rev 13:16
14:10 ᶜIsa 51:17; Jer 25:15 ᵈJer 51:7; Rev 18:6 ᵉS Rev 9:17
14:11 ᶠIsa 34:10; Rev 19:3 ᵍRev 4:8
ʰver 9; S Rev 13:12
ⁱRev 13:17
14:12 ʲS Heb 6:12
ᵏS Jn 14:15
14:13 ᵐ1Co 15:18; 1Th 4:16 ⁿRev 2:7; 22:17

13:17 *buy or sell.* Economic boycott against all faithful believers. *number of its name.* In ancient times the letters of the alphabet served for numbers. Riddles using numerical equivalents for names were popular.
13:18 *666.* Various schemes for decoding these numbers result in such names as Euanthas, Lateinos, and Nero Caesar. Others take 666 as a symbol for the trinity of evil and imperfection—each digit falls short of the perfect number 7.
14:1 *Lamb.* See note on 5:6. *Mount Zion.* In the OT it was first the fortress of the pre-Israelite city of Jerusalem (2Sa 5:7), captured by David and established as his capital. Later it became a virtual synonym for Jerusalem. In Revelation, as in Heb 12:22–24, it is the heavenly Jerusalem, the eternal dwelling place of God and his people (cf. Gal 4:26). It comes down to the new earth in 21:2–3. *144,000.* See note on 7:4. *name.* Contrast 13:16–18.
14:2 *harps.* See note on 5:8.
14:3 *new song.* See note on 5:9. The theme is deliverance.
14:4 *not defile themselves with women.* Probably a symbolic description of believers who kept themselves from defiling relationships with the pagan world system (cf. note on Ex 34:15). *follow the Lamb.* As his disciples (see Mt 19:21; Mk 8:34). *firstfruits.* See Lev 23:9–14. The word is used figuratively in the NT for the first converts in an area (Ro 16:5) and the first to rise from the dead (1Co 15:20). In Revelation believers are considered as a choice offering to God and the Lamb.
14:5 *No lie.* Contrast Ro 1:25; 2Th 2:9–12 and note on 2:11; cf. Isa 53:9.
14:6 *eternal gospel.* The content of this "good news" is perhaps

found in v. 7.
14:7 *him who made the heavens.* See Ex 20:11; Ps 146:6.
14:8 *Babylon the Great.* Ancient Babylon in Mesopotamia was the political, commercial and religious center of a world empire. It was noted for its luxury and moral decadence. The title "Babylon the Great" is taken from Da 4:30. According to some it is used in Revelation (e.g., here and in 16:19; 17:5; 18:2,10,21) for Rome as the center of opposition to God and his people. According to others it represents the whole political and religious system of the world in general under the rule of the antichrist (see note on 13:1). According to still others it is to be understood as literal Babylon—rebuilt and restored. Babylon's fall is proclaimed in Isa 21:9; Jer 51:8. *maddening wine of her adulteries.* Here Babylon (Rome?) is pictured as a prostitute whose illicit relations are achieved by intoxication (see note on Ex 34:15).
14:10 *cup of his wrath.* In the OT God's wrath is commonly pictured as a cup of wine to be drunk (Ps 75:8; Isa 51:17; Jer 25:15). It is not the outworking of impersonal laws of retribution but the response of a righteous God to those who refuse his love and grace. *burning sulfur.* Sodom and Gomorrah were destroyed by a rain of burning sulfur (Ge 19:24). Ps 11:6 speaks of a similar fate for the wicked. The figure occurs elsewhere in the OT and the Apocrypha. It is used several times in the final chapters of Revelation (19:20; 20:10; 21:8).
14:11 *torment … for ever and ever.* Revelation offers no support for the doctrine of the annihilation of the wicked (also compare 19:20 with 20:10).
14:13 *Blessed.* The second beatitude (see note on 1:3).

14:14 *o* Mt 17:5
p Da 7:13; S Rev 1:13
q S Rev 6:2
14:15 *r* ver 17;
Rev 11:19 *s* ver 18;
Joel 3:13; Mk 4:29
t Jer 51:33
14:17 *u* S ver 15
14:18 *v* Rev 6:9; 8:5;
16:7 *w* S ver 15
14:19 *x* Rev 19:15
14:20 *y* ver 19;
Isa 63:3; Joel 3:13;
Rev 19:15 *z* Heb 13:12;
Rev 11:8 *a* Ge 49:11;
Dt 32:14
15:1 *b* Rev 12:1,3
c ver 6-8; Rev 16:1;
17:1; 21:9 *d* Lev 26:21;
Rev 9:20
15:2 *e* Rev 4:6
f Rev 12:11 *g* Rev 13:1;
h Rev 13:14 *i* Rev 13:17
j Rev 5:8; 14:2
15:3 *k* Jos 1:1
l Ex 15:1 *m* S Rev 5:9
n Ps 111:2 *o* S Rev 1:8
p Ps 145:17
15:4 *q* Jer 10:7
r Ps 86:9 *s* Isa 66:23
t Rev 19:8
15:5 *u* Rev 11:19
v Ex 38:21; Nu 1:50
w S Mt 3:16
15:6 *x* Rev 14:15
y S ver 1 *z* Eze 9:2;
Da 10:5

HARVESTING THE EARTH AND TRAMPLING THE WINEPRESS

[14]I looked, and there before me was a white cloud, *o* and seated on the cloud was one like a son of man *a p* with a crown *q* of gold on his head and a sharp sickle in his hand. [15]Then another angel came out of the temple *r* and called in a loud voice to him who was sitting on the cloud, "Take your sickle *s* and reap, because the time to reap has come, for the harvest *t* of the earth is ripe." [16]So he who was seated on the cloud swung his sickle over the earth, and the earth was harvested.

[17]Another angel came out of the temple in heaven, and he too had a sharp sickle. *u* [18]Still another angel, who had charge of the fire, came from the altar *v* and called in a loud voice to him who had the sharp sickle, "Take your sharp sickle *w* and gather the clusters of grapes from the earth's vine, because its grapes are ripe." [19]The angel swung his sickle on the earth, gathered its grapes and threw them into the great winepress of God's wrath. *x* [20]They were trampled in the winepress *y* outside the city, *z* and blood *a* flowed out of the press, rising as high as the horses' bridles for a distance of 1,600 stadia. *b*

SEVEN ANGELS WITH SEVEN PLAGUES

15 I saw in heaven another great and marvelous sign: *b* seven angels *c* with the seven last plagues *d*—last, because with them God's wrath is completed. [2]And I saw what looked like a sea of glass *e* glowing with fire and, standing beside the sea, those who had been victorious *f* over the beast *g* and its image *h* and over the number of its name. *i* They held harps *j* given them by God [3]and sang the song of God's servant *k* Moses *l* and of the Lamb: *m*

"Great and marvelous are your deeds, *n*
   Lord God Almighty. *o*
Just and true are your ways, *p*
   King of the nations. *c*
[4]Who will not fear you, Lord, *q*
   and bring glory to your name? *r*
For you alone are holy.
All nations will come
   and worship before you, *s*
for your righteous acts *t* have been revealed." *d*

[5]After this I looked, and I saw in heaven the temple *u*—that is, the tabernacle of the covenant law *v*—and it was opened. *w* [6]Out of the temple *x* came the seven angels with the seven plagues. *y* They were dressed in clean, shining linen *z* and wore golden sashes

---

a 14 See Daniel 7:13.   *b 20* That is, about 180 miles or about 300 kilometers   *c 3* Some manuscripts ages   *d 3,4* Phrases in this song are drawn from Psalm 111:2,3; Deut. 32:4; Jer. 10:7; Psalms 86:9; 98:2.

14:14 *seated on the cloud.* Cf. Mt 17:5; 24:30 and notes. *son of man.* See 1:13 and notes on Da 7:13; Mk 8:31. *crown of gold.* A victory wreath of gold. See note on 2:10 for the comparison between the victory crown and the royal crown. *sickle.* The Israelite sickle used for cutting grain was normally a flint or iron blade attached to a curved shaft of wood or bone.

14:15 *harvest of the earth.* Symbolizes in a general way the coming judgment (see v. 19; Mt 13:30,40–42). Some interpreters think it refers to the ingathering of the righteous at the return of Christ.

14:18 *another angel, who had charge of the fire.* The angel of 8:3–5. Fire is commonly associated with judgment (see La 1:13 and note; Mt 18:8; Lk 9:54; 2Th 1:7). *sharp sickle.* The context suggests (in contrast to the sickle of v. 14) the smaller grape-knife with which the farmer cut the clusters of grapes from the vine.

14:19 *winepress.* A rock-hewn trough about eight feet square with a channel leading to a lower and smaller trough. Grapes were thrown into the upper vat and tramped with bare feet. The juice was collected in the lower vat (see note on Hag 2:16). At times mechanical pressure was added. The treading of grapes was a common OT figure for the execution of divine wrath (see Isa 63:3; La 1:15; Joel 3:13).

14:20 *outside the city.* Bloodshed would define the city (see Joel 3:12–14; Zec 14:1–4; cf. Heb 13:12). *1,600 stadia.* See TNIV text note; the approximate length of the Holy Land from north to south.

15:1–8 Introduces the last of the three sevenfold series of judgments—the bowls of wrath (see note on 8:2).

15:1 *God's wrath.* See note on 6:16.

15:2 *sea of glass.* See note on 4:6. *victorious over the beast.* Cf. the saints' victory over the devil in 12:11. *number of its name.* See notes on 13:16–18. *harps.* See note on 5:8.

15:3–4 See Jer 10:7 and note.

15:3 *song of . . . Moses.* See Ex 15; Dt 32. Ex 15:1–18 was sung on Sabbath evenings in the synagogue to celebrate Israel's great deliverance from Egypt. *and of the Lamb.* The risen Lord triumphed over his enemies (including death and Hades, 1:18) in securing spiritual deliverance for his followers (cf. Ps 22). *Great and marvelous are your deeds.* See Ex 15:11; Ps 92:5; 111:2. *Almighty.* See note on 1:8. *King of the nations.* See Jer 10:10; cf. 1Ti 1:17.

15:4 Universal recognition of God is taught in both the OT (Ps 86:9; Isa 45:22–23; Mal 1:11) and the NT (Php 2:9–11).

15:5 *tabernacle of the covenant law.* The dwelling place of God during the wilderness wandering of the Israelites (see Ex 40:34–35). It was so named because the ancient tent contained the two tablets of the covenant law brought down from Mount Sinai (Ex 32:15; 38:21; Dt 10:5).

15:6 *seven plagues.* The last series of plagues (see v. 1). *golden sashes.* Symbolic of royal and priestly functions.

around their chests. *a* 7Then one of the four living creatures *b* gave to the seven angels *c* seven golden bowls filled with the wrath of God, who lives for ever and ever. *d* 8And the temple was filled with smoke *e* from the glory of God and from his power, and no one could enter the temple *f* until the seven plagues of the seven angels were completed.

THE SEVEN BOWLS OF GOD'S WRATH

16 Then I heard a loud voice from the temple *g* saying to the seven angels, *h* "Go, pour out the seven bowls of God's wrath on the earth." *i*

2The first angel went and poured out his bowl on the land, *j* and ugly, festering sores *k* broke out on the people who had the mark of the beast and worshiped its image. *l*

3The second angel poured out his bowl on the sea, and it turned into blood like that of a dead person, and every living thing in the sea died. *m*

4The third angel poured out his bowl on the rivers and springs of water, *n* and they became blood. *o* 5Then I heard the angel in charge of the waters say:

> "You are just in these judgments, *p*
> you who are and who were, *q* the Holy One, *r*
> because you have so judged; *s*
> 6for they have shed the blood of your people and your prophets, *t*
> and you have given them blood to drink *u* as they deserve."

7And I heard the altar *v* respond:

> "Yes, Lord God Almighty, *w*
> true and just are your judgments." *x*

8The fourth angel *y* poured out his bowl on the sun, *z* and the sun was allowed to scorch people with fire. *a* 9They were seared by the intense heat and they cursed the name of God, *b* who had control over these plagues, but they refused to repent *c* and glorify him. *d*

10The fifth angel poured out his bowl on the throne of the beast, *e* and its kingdom was plunged into darkness. *f* People gnawed their tongues in agony 11and cursed *g* the God of heaven *h* because of their pains and their sores, *i* but they refused to repent of what they had done. *j*

12The sixth angel poured out his bowl on the great river Euphrates, *k* and its water was dried up to prepare the way *l* for the kings from the East. *m* 13Then I saw three evil *a* spirits *n* that looked like frogs; *o* they came out of the mouth of the dragon, *p* out of the mouth of the beast *q* and out of the mouth of the false prophet. *r* 14They are demonic spirits *s* that perform signs, *t* and they go out to the kings of the whole world, *u* to gather them for the battle *v* on the great day *w* of God Almighty.

15"Look, I come like a thief! *x* Blessed are those who stay awake *y* and keep their clothes on, so that they may not go naked and be shamefully exposed." *z*

16Then they gathered the kings together *a* to the place that in Hebrew *b* is called Armageddon. *c*

a 13 Greek *unclean*

15:6 *a* Rev 1:13
15:7 *b* S Rev 4:6
c S ver 1 *d* S Rev 1:18
15:8 *e* Isa 6:4
f Ex 40:34,35;
1Ki 8:10,11; 2Ch 5:13,
14
16:1 *g* Rev 11:19
h S Rev 15:1 *i* ver 2-21;
Ps 79:6; Zep 3:8
16:2 *j* Rev 8:7
k ver 11; Ex 9:9-11;
Dt 28:35 *l* Rev 13:15-
17; 14:9
16:3 *m* Ex 7:17-21;
Rev 8:8,9; Rev 11:6
16:4 *n* Rev 8:10
o Ex 7:17-21
16:5 *p* Rev 15:3
q S Rev 1:4 *r* Rev 15:4
s Rev 6:10
16:6 *t* Lk 11:49-51
u Isa 49:26; Rev 17:6;
18:24
16:7 *v* Rev 6:9; 14:18
w S Rev 1:8
x Rev 15:3; 19:2
16:8 *y* Rev 8:12
z Rev 6:12 *a* Rev 14:18
16:9 *b* ver 11,21
c S Rev 2:21
d S Rev 11:13
16:10 *e* Rev 13:2
f Ex 10:21-23;
Isa 8:22; Rev 8:12; 9:2
16:11 *g* ver 9,21
h Rev 11:13 *i* ver 2
j S Rev 2:21
16:12 *k* S Rev 9:14
l Isa 11:15,16
m Isa 41:2; 46:11
16:13 *n* Rev 18:2
o Ex 8:6 *p* S Rev 12:3
q S Rev 13:1
r Rev 19:20; 20:10
16:14 *s* 1Ti 4:1
t S Mt 24:24
u S Rev 17:14
v Rev 17:14; 19:19;
20:8 *w* S Rev 6:17
16:15 *x* S Lk 12:39
y Lk 12:37 *z* Rev 3:18
16:16 *a* ver 14
b Rev 9:11 *c* Jdg 5:19;
2Ki 23:29,30;
Zec 12:11

15:7 *wrath of God.* Cf. 2Th 1:7–9.

15:8 *filled with smoke.* Cf. Ex 40:34; 1Ki 8:10–11; Eze 44:4. Smoke symbolizes the power and glory of God. *no one could enter the temple.* Both tabernacle and temple provide illustrations: with reference to Moses, Ex 40:35; with reference to the priests, 2Ch 5:14.

16:2 *land.* Compare the first four bowls (vv. 2–9) with the first four trumpets (8:7–12). *ugly, festering sores.* Cf. the boils and abscesses of the sixth Egyptian plague (Ex 9:9–11; see also Job 2:7 –8,13). *mark of the beast.* See 13:16 and note.

16:4 *rivers and springs of water.* Cf. 8:10–11; see also Ps 78:44.

16:5 *you who are and who were.* See note on 11:17; cf. Ex 3:14.

16:6 *given them blood to drink.* Punishment is tailored to fit the crime (see Isa 49:26; cf. Ob 15; Gal 6:7 and notes).

16:7 *altar.* Personified.

16:8 *fire.* Often connected with judgment in Scripture (see note on 14:18; see also Dt 28:22; 1Co 3:13; 2Pe 3:7).

16:9 *refused to repent.* In 11:13 the nations were dazzled into homage by the great earthquake. Here they mock and blaspheme God's name (see 13:6).

16:10 *throne of the beast.* Cf. Satan's throne in 2:13. "Throne" occurs 42 times in Revelation. The other 40 references are to the throne of God. *darkness.* Cf. Ex 10:21–23. *gnawed their tongues.* Cf. the scene in 6:15–17.

16:11 *God of heaven.* Used in Da 2:44 of the sovereign God, who destroys the kingdoms of the world and establishes his own universal and eternal reign.

16:12 *Euphrates.* See note on Ge 15:18. *kings from the East.* Evidently Parthian rulers (17:15—18:24), to be distinguished from the "kings of the whole world" (v. 14) who wage the final war against Christ and the armies of heaven (19:11–21).

16:13 *frogs.* Lev 11:10 classifies the frog as an unclean animal. The imagery suggests the deceptive propaganda that will, in the last days, lead people to accept and support the cause of evil.

16:14 *signs.* Cf. 13:13. *kings of the whole world.* See 6:15. *great day of God.* See 19:11–21 for this battle.

16:15 *Blessed.* The third beatitude (see note on 1:3).

16:16 *Armageddon.* Probably stands for Har Mageddon, "the mountain of Megiddo" (see note on Jdg 5:19). Many see no specific geographical reference in the designation and take it to be

16:17 d Eph 2:2
e Rev 14:15 f Rev 11:15
g Rev 21:6
16:18 h S Rev 4:5
i S Rev 6:12 / Da 12:1;
Mt 24:21
16:19 k S Rev 17:18
l Rev 18:5
m S Rev 14:8
n Rev 14:10
16:20 o S Rev 6:14
16:21 p Eze 13:13;
38:22; Rev 8:7; 11:19
q ver 9,11 r Ex 9:23-
25
17:1 s S Rev 15:1
t Rev 15:7 u Rev 16:19
v ver 5,15,16;
Isa 23:17; Rev 19:2
w Jer 51:13
17:2 x S Rev 14:8
17:3 y S Rev 1:10
z Rev 12:6,14
a Rev 18:12,16
b Rev 13:1 c S Rev 12:3
17:4 d Eze 28:13;
Rev 18:16 e Jer 51:7;
Rev 18:6 f ver 2;
S Rev 14:8
17:5 g ver 7
h S Rev 14:8 i ver 1,2
17:6 j Rev 16:6;
18:24
17:7 k ver 5 l ver 3;
S Rev 12:3
17:8 m S Lk 8:31
n Rev 13:10
o S Rev 3:10
p S Rev 20:12
q Rev 13:3
17:9 r Rev 13:18
s ver 3
17:11 t ver 8

[17]The seventh angel poured out his bowl into the air, [d] and out of the temple [e] came a loud voice [f] from the throne, saying, "It is done!" [g] [18]Then there came flashes of lightning, rumblings, peals of thunder [h] and a severe earthquake. [i] No earthquake like it has ever occurred since the human race has been on earth, [j] so tremendous was the quake. [19]The great city [k] split into three parts, and the cities of the nations collapsed. God remembered [l] Babylon the Great [m] and gave her the cup filled with the wine of the fury of his wrath. [n] [20]Every island fled away and the mountains could not be found. [o] [21]From the sky huge hailstones, [p] each weighing about a hundred pounds, [a] fell on people. And they cursed God [q] on account of the plague of hail, [r] because the plague was so terrible.

BABYLON, THE PROSTITUTE ON THE BEAST

17 One of the seven angels [s] who had the seven bowls [t] came and said to me, "Come, I will show you the punishment [u] of the great prostitute, [v] who sits by many waters. [w] [2]With her the kings of the earth committed adultery, and the inhabitants of the earth were intoxicated with the wine of her adulteries." [x]

[3]Then the angel carried me away in the Spirit [y] into a wilderness. [z] There I saw a woman sitting on a scarlet [a] beast that was covered with blasphemous names [b] and had seven heads and ten horns. [c] [4]The woman was dressed in purple and scarlet, and was glittering with gold, precious stones and pearls. [d] She held a golden cup [e] in her hand, filled with abominable things and the filth of her adulteries. [f] [5]This title was written on her forehead:

MYSTERY [g]

BABYLON THE GREAT [h]

THE MOTHER OF PROSTITUTES [i]

AND OF THE ABOMINATIONS OF THE EARTH.

[6]I saw that the woman was drunk with the blood of God's people, [j] the blood of those who bore testimony to Jesus.

When I saw her, I was greatly astonished. [7]Then the angel said to me: "Why are you astonished? I will explain to you the mystery [k] of the woman and of the beast she rides, which has the seven heads and ten horns. [l] [8]The beast, which you saw, once was, now is not, and will come up out of the Abyss [m] and go to its destruction. [n] The inhabitants of the earth [o] whose names have not been written in the book of life [p] from the creation of the world will be astonished [q] when they see the beast, because it once was, now is not, and yet will come.

[9]"This calls for a mind with wisdom. [r] The seven heads [s] are seven hills on which the woman sits. [10]They are also seven kings. Five have fallen, one is, the other has not yet come; but when he does come, he must remain for a little while. [11]The beast who once was, and now is not, [t] is an eighth king. He belongs to the seven and is going to his destruction.

---

[a] 21 Or about 40 kilograms

---

a symbol of the final overthrow of evil by God. Others understand it more literally.
16:17 *temple.* See 15:5–6. *It is done!* The last of the seven bowls of divine wrath has now been poured out.
16:19 *great city.* See 17:18 and note.
16:21 *plague of hail.* Cf. Ex 9:18–26.
17:1—18:24 See note on 14:8.
17:1 *seven angels.* Cf. 15:1; 16. *great prostitute.* See v. 18 for the angel's own identification of this symbol. In v. 5 the harlot is named "Babylon the Great." *sits by many waters.* See v. 15; Ps 137:1; Jer 51:13.
17:2 *wine of her adulteries.* See note on 14:8; cf. 18:3; Isa 23:17; Jer 51:7.
17:3 *in the Spirit.* In a state of spiritual ecstasy by the power of the Spirit (see notes on 1:10; 4:2; see also 21:10). *scarlet beast.* The beast that rose out of the sea in ch. 13. The color scarlet is similar to that of the red dragon in 12:3 (cf. v. 4). *blasphemous names.* See note on 13:1.
17:5 *MYSTERY.* Possibly not a part of the title. The opening part of the verse would then be translated "This mysterious title was written on her forehead: BABYLON …" See note on 14:8.
17:6 *God's people … those who bore testimony.* See 6:9. *God's people.* See note on 5:8.

17:7 *mystery.* See note on 10:7.
17:8 *once was, now is not, and will come.* An obvious imitation of the description of the Lamb (1:18; 2:8). Cf. the description of God in 1:4,8; 4:8. Here the phrase seems to mean that the beast appeared once, is not presently evident, but will in the future again make his presence known. Evil is persistent. *Abyss.* See note on 9:1. *go to its destruction.* Although evil is real and persistent, there is no uncertainty about its ultimate fate. *book of life.* See note on 3:5.
17:9 *seven hills.* It is perhaps significant that Rome began as a network of seven hill settlements on the east bank of the Tiber River (see map, p. 1894). Her designation as the city on seven hills is commonplace among Roman writers (e.g., Virgil, Martial, Cicero).
17:10 *seven kings.* That seven heads symbolize both seven hills and seven kings illustrates the fluidity of apocalyptic symbolism, unless the hills are figurative for royal (or political) power. *Five … one … the other.* Taken (1) as seven actual Roman emperors, (2) as seven secular empires or (3) symbolically as the power of the Roman empire as a whole.
17:11 *now is not.* Cf. 13:3. *eighth king.* The antichrist, who plays the role of a king ("belongs to the seven") but is in reality part of the cosmic struggle between God and Satan.

¹²"The ten horns ᵘ you saw are ten kings who have not yet received a kingdom, but who for one hour ᵛ will receive authority as kings along with the beast. ¹³They have one purpose and will give their power and authority to the beast. ʷ ¹⁴They will make war ˣ against the Lamb, but the Lamb will triumph over ʸ them because he is Lord of lords and King of kings ᶻ—and with him will be his called, chosen ᵃ and faithful followers."

¹⁵Then the angel said to me, "The waters ᵇ you saw, where the prostitute sits, are peoples, multitudes, nations and languages. ᶜ ¹⁶The beast and the ten horns ᵈ you saw will hate the prostitute. ᵉ They will bring her to ruin ᶠ and leave her naked; ᵍ they will eat her flesh ʰ and burn her with fire. ᶦ ¹⁷For God has put it into their hearts ʲ to accomplish his purpose by agreeing to give the beast their power to rule, ᵏ until God's words are fulfilled. ˡ ¹⁸The woman you saw is the great city ᵐ that rules over the kings of the earth."

LAMENT OVER FALLEN BABYLON

18 After this I saw another angel ⁿ coming down from heaven. ᵒ He had great authority, and the earth was illuminated by his splendor. ᵖ ²With a mighty voice he shouted:

" 'Fallen! Fallen is Babylon the Great!'ᵃ �q
   She has become a dwelling for demons
and a haunt for every evil ᵇ spirit, ʳ
   a haunt for every unclean bird,
   a haunt for every unclean and detestable animal. ˢ
³For all the nations have drunk
   the maddening wine of her adulteries. ᵗ
The kings of the earth committed adultery with her, ᵘ
   and the merchants of the earth grew rich ᵛ from her excessive luxuries." ʷ

WARNING TO ESCAPE BABYLON'S JUDGMENT

⁴Then I heard another voice from heaven say:

" 'Come out of her, my people,'ᶜ ˣ
   so that you will not share in her sins,
   so that you will not receive any of her plagues; ʸ
⁵for her sins are piled up to heaven, ᶻ
   and God has remembered ᵃ her crimes.
⁶Give back to her as she has given;
   pay her back ᵇ double ᶜ for what she has done.
   Pour her a double portion from her own cup. ᵈ
⁷Give her as much torment and grief
   as the glory and luxury she gave herself. ᵉ
In her heart she boasts,
   'I sit enthroned as queen.
I am not a widow; ᵈ
   I will never mourn.'ᶠ
⁸Therefore in one day ᵍ her plagues will overtake her:
   death, mourning and famine.
She will be consumed by fire, ʰ
   for mighty is the Lord God who judges her.

THREEFOLD WOE OVER BABYLON'S FALL

⁹"When the kings of the earth who committed adultery with her ᶦ and shared her lux-

---

ᵃ 2 Isaiah 21:9   ᵇ 2 Greek *unclean*   ᶜ 4 Jer. 51:45   ᵈ 7 See Isaiah 47:7,8.

17:12 ᵘ S Rev 12:3
ᵛ Rev 18:10,17,19
17:13 ʷ ver 17
17:14 ˣ S Rev 16:14
ʸ S Jn 16:33
ᶻ S 1Ti 6:15 ᵃ Mt 22:14
17:15 ᵇ ver 1;
Isa 8:7; Jer 47:2
ᶜ S Rev 13:7
17:16 ᵈ S Rev 12:3
ᵉ ver 1 ᶠ Rev 18:17,19
ᵍ Eze 16:37,39
ʰ Rev 19:18 ᶦ Rev 18:8
17:17 ʲ 2Co 8:16
ᵏ ver 13 ˡ Jer 39:16;
Rev 10:7
17:18 ᵐ Rev 16:19;
18:10,18,19,21
18:1 ⁿ Rev 17:1
ᵒ Rev 10:1; 20:1
ᵖ Eze 43:2
18:2 q S Rev 14:8
ʳ Rev 16:13 ˢ Isa 13:21,
22; 34:11,13-15;
Jer 50:39; 51:37;
Zep 2:14,15
18:3 ᵗ S Rev 14:8
ᵘ Rev 17:2 ᵛ ver 11,15,
23; Eze 27:9-25
ʷ ver 7,9
18:4 ˣ Isa 48:20;
Jer 50:8; 51:6,9,45;
2Co 6:17 ʸ Ge 19:15
18:5 ᶻ 2Ch 28:9;
Ezr 9:6; Jer 51:9
ᵃ Rev 16:19
18:6 ᵇ Ps 137:8;
Jer 50:15,29
ᶜ Isa 40:2 ᵈ Rev 14:10;
16:19; 17:4
18:7 ᵉ Eze 28:2-8
ᶠ Ps 10:6; Isa 47:7,8;
Zep 2:15
18:8 ᵍ ver 10;
Isa 9:14; 47:9;
Jer 50:31,32
ʰ Rev 17:16
18:9 ᶦ ver 3;
Rev 14:8; 17:2,4

17:12 *ten kings.* Since they are said to have not yet received royal power, they seem to belong to the future. They are likely symbolic and represent the totality of political powers that will align themselves with the beast. *one hour.* A short time.

A 17:14 *Lamb will triumph.* See 5:6 and note. *Lord of lords and King of kings.* Emphasizes the supreme sovereignty of the Lamb (cf. 5:6 and note; 19:16; Dt 10:17; Ps 136:2–3; Da 2:47; 1Ti 6:15).

17:18 *great city.* Cf. 16:19; 17:1; see notes on 11:8; 14:8.

18:1 *earth was illuminated by his splendor.* Cf. Ex 34:29–35; Ps 104:2; Eze 43:1–5; 1Ti 6:16.

18:2 *Fallen is Babylon.* Cf. Isa 21:9; Jer 51:8; see notes on 11:8; 14:8.

18:3 *wine of her adulteries.* See note on 14:8.

18:4 *Come out of her.* A common prophetic warning (cf. Isa 52:11; Jer 51:45; 2Co 6:14—7:1).

18:6 *double.* In full, sufficiently (see note on Isa 40:2). *her own cup.* See 17:4.

18:7 *I am not a widow.* A claim that the men of Babylon have not died on battlefields.

18:9–20 Three groups lament: (1) kings (v. 9), (2) merchants (v. 11) and (3) seamen (v. 17). The passage is modeled after Ezekiel's lament over Tyre (Eze 27). Fifteen of the 29 commodities in vv. 12–13 are also listed in Eze 27:12–22.

18:9 *i* ver 3,7
k ver 18; Rev 14:11;
19:3 *l* Jer 51:8;
Eze 26:17,18
18:10 *m* ver 15,17
n ver 16,19 *o* ver 17;
Rev 17:12
18:11 *p* Eze 27:27
q ver 15,19; Eze 27:31
r S ver 3
18:12 *s* Eze 27:12-
22; Rev 17:4
18:13 *t* Eze 27:13;
1Ti 1:10
18:15 *u* S ver 3
v ver 10,17 *w* ver 11,
19; Eze 27:31
18:16 *x* ver 10,19
y Rev 17:4
18:17 *z* ver 10;
Rev 17:12 *a* Rev 17:16
b Eze 27:28-30
c ver 10,15
18:18 *d* ver 9;
Rev 19:3 *e* S Rev 17:18
f Eze 27:32; Rev 13:4
18:19 *g* Jos 7:6;
La 2:10; Eze 27:30
h ver 11,15; Eze 27:31
i ver 10,16; Rev 17:18
j Rev 17:16
18:20 *k* Jer 51:48;
S Rev 12:12 *l* Rev 19:2
18:21 *m* Rev 5:2;
10:1 *n* Jer 51:63
o S Rev 17:18
18:22 *p* Isa 24:8;
Eze 26:13 *q* Jer 25:10
18:23 *r* Jer 7:34;
16:9; 25:10

ury *j* see the smoke of her burning, *k* they will weep and mourn over her. *l* **10** Terrified at her torment, they will stand far off *m* and cry:

> " 'Woe! Woe to you, great city, *n*
> you mighty city of Babylon!
> In one hour *o* your doom has come!'

11 "The merchants *p* of the earth will weep and mourn *q* over her because no one buys their cargoes anymore *r* — **12** cargoes of gold, silver, precious stones and pearls; fine linen, purple, silk and scarlet cloth; every sort of citron wood, and articles of every kind made of ivory, costly wood, bronze, iron and marble; *s* **13** cargoes of cinnamon and spice, of incense, myrrh and frankincense, of wine and olive oil, of fine flour and wheat; cattle and sheep; horses and carriages; and human beings sold as slaves. *t*

14 "They will say, 'The fruit you longed for is gone from you. All your luxury and splendor have vanished, never to be recovered.' **15** The merchants who sold these things and gained their wealth from her *u* will stand far off, *v* terrified at her torment. They will weep and mourn *w* **16** and cry out:

> " 'Woe! Woe to you, great city, *x*
> dressed in fine linen, purple and scarlet,
> and glittering with gold, precious stones and pearls! *y*
> **17** In one hour *z* such great wealth has been brought to ruin!' *a*

"Every sea captain, and all who travel by ship, the sailors, and all who earn their living from the sea, *b* will stand far off. *c* **18** When they see the smoke of her burning, *d* they will exclaim, 'Was there ever a city like this great city *e*?' *f* **19** They will throw dust on their heads, *g* and with weeping and mourning *h* cry out:

> " 'Woe! Woe to you, great city, *i*
> where all who had ships on the sea
> became rich through her wealth!
> In one hour she has been brought to ruin!' *j*

20 "Rejoice over her, you heavens! *k*
> Rejoice, you people of God!
> Rejoice, apostles and prophets!
> For God has judged her
> with the judgment she imposed on you." *l*

THE FINALITY OF BABYLON'S DOOM

21 Then a mighty angel *m* picked up a boulder the size of a large millstone and threw it into the sea, *n* and said:

> "With such violence
> the great city *o* of Babylon will be thrown down,
> never to be found again.
> **22** The music of harpists and musicians, pipers and trumpeters,
> will never be heard in you again. *p*
> No worker of any trade
> will ever be found in you again.
> The sound of a millstone
> will never be heard in you again. *q*
> **23** The light of a lamp
> will never shine in you again.
> The voice of bridegroom and bride
> will never be heard in you again. *r*

18:9 *kings … weep and mourn over her.* Probably because of their own great financial loss (see v. 11).
18:10 *one hour.* Repeated in vv. 17,19; cf. note on 17:12.
18:12 *purple.* An expensive dye since it must be extracted a drop at a time from the murex shellfish. *citron wood.* An expensive dark wood from north Africa—used for inlay work in costly furniture. *marble.* Used to decorate public buildings and the homes of the very rich.
18:13 *myrrh and frankincense.* Brought by the Magi as gifts for the infant Jesus (Mt 2:11).

18:17 *sea captain.* The pilot of the ship rather than the owner. Both are mentioned in Ac 27:11.
18:19 *throw dust on their heads.* An act of sorrow and dismay (see Eze 27:30). *In one hour.* See vv. 10,17.
18:20 *God has judged her with the judgment she imposed on you.* The scales of justice will be balanced (see note on Ob 15).
18:21 *large millstone.* Similar to the large millstone of Mk 9:42, which was actually a "donkey millstone" (one large enough to require a donkey to turn it).

18:23 *s* ver 3;
Isa 23:8 *t* Na 3:4
18:24 *u* Rev 16:6;
17:6 *v* Jer 51:49;
Mt 23:35
19:1 *w* ver 6;
Rev 11:15 *x* ver 3,4,6
y Rev 7:10; 12:10
z Rev 4:11; 7:12
19:2 *a* Rev 16:7
b S Rev 17:1
c S Rev 6:10
19:3 *d* ver 1,4,6
e Isa 34:10; Rev 14:11
19:4 *f* S Rev 4:4
g S Rev 4:6
h S Rev 4:10 *i* ver 1,
3,6
19:5 *j* Ps 134:1
k ver 18; Ps 115:13;
Rev 11:18; 13:16; 20:12
19:6 *l* ver 1;
Rev 11:15 *m* S Rev 1:15
n ver 1,3,4 *o* S Rev 1:8
p Rev 11:15
19:7 *q* S Rev 11:13
r ver 9; Mt 22:2;
25:10; Eph 5:32
s Rev 21:2,9; 22:17
19:8 *t* ver 14;
Rev 15:6 *u* Isa 61:10;
Eze 44:17; Zec 3:4;
Rev 15:4
19:9 *v* ver 10
w Rev 1:19 *x* Lk 14:15
y Rev 21:5; 22:6
19:10 *z* Rev 22:8
a Ac 10:25,26;
Rev 22:9 *b* S Rev 1:2

Your merchants were the world's important people. *s*
By your magic spell *t* all the nations were led astray.
24 In her was found the blood of prophets and of God's people, *u*
of all who have been slaughtered on the earth." *v*

THREEFOLD HALLELUJAH OVER BABYLON'S FALL

19 After this I heard what sounded like the roar of a great multitude *w* in heaven shouting:

"Hallelujah! *x*
Salvation *y* and glory and power *z* belong to our God,
2   for true and just are his judgments. *a*
He has condemned the great prostitute *b*
who corrupted the earth by her adulteries.
He has avenged on her the blood of his servants." *c*

3 And again they shouted:

"Hallelujah! *d*
The smoke from her goes up for ever and ever." *e*

4 The twenty-four elders *f* and the four living creatures *g* fell down *h* and worshiped God, who was seated on the throne. And they cried:

"Amen, Hallelujah!" *i*

5 Then a voice came from the throne, saying:

"Praise our God,
all you his servants, *j*
you who fear him,
both great and small!" *k*

6 Then I heard what sounded like a great multitude, *l* like the roar of rushing waters *m* and like loud peals of thunder, shouting:

"Hallelujah! *n*
For our Lord God Almighty *o* reigns. *p*
7 Let us rejoice and be glad
and give him glory! *q*
For the wedding of the Lamb *r* has come,
and his bride *s* has made herself ready.
8 Fine linen, *t* bright and clean,
was given her to wear."

(Fine linen stands for the righteous acts *u* of God's people.)

9 Then the angel said to me, *v* "Write: *w* 'Blessed are those who are invited to the wedding supper of the Lamb!' " *x* And he added, "These are the true words of God." *y*
10 At this I fell at his feet to worship him. *z* But he said to me, "Don't do that! I am a fellow servant with you and with your brothers and sisters who hold to Jesus' testimony. Worship God! *a* For the testimony of Jesus *b* is the Spirit of prophecy."

18:24 *blood of prophets.* See 6:10; 17:6; 19:2; cf. Eze 24:7. *prophets . . . God's people.* Probably not two distinct groups: The first may be a special class within the second (cf. the order in 16:6). *God's people.* See note on Col 1:4.
19:1 *great multitude.* See note on 7:9. *Hallelujah!* Occurs four times in vv. 1–6 but nowhere else in the NT. It is derived from two Hebrew words meaning "Praise the LORD" (see TNIV text note on Ps 135:1).
19:2 *great prostitute.* See 17:1,5,18; see also 14:8 and note. *avenged on her the blood of his servants.* See the prayer in 6:10; cf. 16:6; 18:20.
19:3 *Hallelujah!* Although this word of praise to the Lord occurs four times (vv. 1,3,4,6; see note on v. 1), the TNIV section heading above ch. 19 ("THREEFOLD HALLELUJAH") is still correct because this one in v. 3 actually goes with the one in v. 1 (note "again" here) and is uttered by the same group (identified and

introduced as a "great multitude"). The other two instances are introduced in vv. 4,6. Cf. the "THREEFOLD WOE" in 18:10,16,19.
19:4 *twenty-four elders and the four living creatures.* See notes on 4:4,6.
19:7 *wedding of the Lamb.* The imagery of a wedding to express the intimate relationship between God and his people ("his bride") has its roots in the prophetic literature of the OT (e.g., Isa 54:5–7; Hos 2:19). Cf. the NT usage (Mt 22:2–14; Eph 5:32).
19:9 *Blessed.* The fourth beatitude (see note on 1:3). *wedding supper.* See Mt 8:11; Lk 14:15; 22:16 and notes.
19:10 *fell at his feet.* See note on 1:17; cf. Ac 10:25. *Spirit of prophecy.* If "spirit" is not to be capitalized, the phrase probably means that the message attested by Jesus is the essence of prophetic proclamation. If "Spirit" is to be capitalized, it probably means that the message attested by Jesus is that which the Spirit takes and puts in the mouth of Christian prophets.

19:11 c S Mt 3:16
d ver 19, 21; Rev 6:2
e Rev 3:14 f Ex 15:3;
Ps 96:13; Isa 11:4
19:12 g S Rev 1:14
h Rev 6:2; 12:3 i ver 16
j S Rev 2:17
19:13 k Isa 63:2, 3
l Jn 1:1
19:14 m ver 8
n S Rev 3:4
19:15 o ver 21;
S Rev 1:16 p Isa 11:4;
2Th 2:8 q Ps 2:9;
Rev 2:27; 12:5
r S Rev 14:20
19:16 s ver 12
t S TTi 6:15
19:17 u ver 21
v Rev 8:13; 14:6
w Jer 12:9; Eze 39:17
x Isa 34:6; Jer 46:10
19:18 y Eze 39:18-
20 z Rev 6:15 z Ver 5
19:19 b S Rev 13:1
c Rev 16:14, 16
d ver 11, 21
19:20 f Rev 16:13
f S Mt 24:24
g Rev 13:12
h Rev 13:14 i Rev 13:16
j Rev 13:15 k Da 7:11;
Rev 20:10, 14, 15; 21:8
l S Rev 9:17
19:21 m ver 15;
S Rev 1:16 n ver 11, 19
o ver 17
20:1 p Rev 10:1; 18:1
q Rev 1:18 r S Lk 8:31
20:2 s S Mt 4:10
t Isa 24:22; S 2Pe 2:4
20:3 u ver 1
v Da 6:17; Mt 27:66
w ver 8, 10; Rev 12:9
20:4 x Da 7:9
y Mt 19:28; Rev 3:21
z Rev 6:9

THE HEAVENLY WARRIOR DEFEATS THE BEAST

[11] I saw heaven standing open c and there before me was a white horse, whose rider d is called Faithful and True. e With justice he judges and makes war. f [12] His eyes are like blazing fire, g and on his head are many crowns. h He has a name written on him i that no one knows but he himself. j [13] He is dressed in a robe dipped in blood, k and his name is the Word of God. l [14] The armies of heaven were following him, riding on white horses and dressed in fine linen, m white n and clean. [15] Coming out of his mouth is a sharp sword o with which to strike down p the nations. "He will rule them with an iron scepter." a q He treads the winepress r of the fury of the wrath of God Almighty. [16] On his robe and on his thigh he has this name written: s

KING OF KINGS AND LORD OF LORDS. t

[17] And I saw an angel standing in the sun, who cried in a loud voice to all the birds u flying in midair, v "Come, w gather together for the great supper of God, x [18] so that you may eat the flesh of kings, generals, and the mighty, of horses and their riders, and the flesh of all people, y free and slave, z great and small." a

[19] Then I saw the beast b and the kings of the earth c and their armies gathered together to make war against the rider on the horse d and his army. [20] But the beast was captured, and with him the false prophet e who had performed the signs f on his behalf. g With these signs he had deluded h those who had received the mark of the beast i and worshiped his image. j The two of them were thrown alive into the fiery lake k of burning sulfur. l [21] The rest were killed with the sword m coming out of the mouth of the rider on the horse, n and all the birds o gorged themselves on their flesh.

THE THOUSAND YEARS

20 And I saw an angel coming down out of heaven, p having the key q to the Abyss r and holding in his hand a great chain. [2] He seized the dragon, that ancient serpent, who is the devil, or Satan, s and bound him for a thousand years. t [3] He threw him into the Abyss, u and locked and sealed v it over him, to keep him from deceiving the nations w anymore until the thousand years were ended. After that, he must be set free for a short time.

[4] I saw thrones x on which were seated those who had been given authority to judge. y And I saw the souls of those who had been beheaded z because of their testimony about

a 15 Psalm 2:9

19:11 *white horse.* Probably not the white horse of 6:2. The context here indicates that the rider is Christ returning as Warrior-Messiah-King.
19:12 *name written.* A secret name whose meaning is veiled from all created beings.
19:13 *robe dipped in blood.* Either the blood of the enemy shed in conflict (cf. 14:14–20; Isa 63:1–3) or the blood of Christ shed to atone for sin.
19:14 *armies of heaven.* Angelic beings (cf. Dt 33:2; Ps 68:17); possibly also believers (cf. 17:14).
19:15 *sharp sword.* See note on 1:16. *iron scepter.* See note on 2:27. *treads the winepress of the … wrath of God.* Cf. Isa 63:3 and note. *winepress.* See note on 14:19.
19:16 KING OF KINGS. See note on 17:14.
19:17 *great supper of God.* A grim contrast to the "wedding supper of the Lamb" (v. 9; cf. Eze 39:17–20).
19:19 See 16:16 and note.
19:20 *beast … false prophet.* See notes on 13:1, 11. *fiery lake of burning sulfur.* See 20:10, 14–15; 21:8. Punishment by fire is prominent in both Biblical (see, e.g., note on La 1:13) and non-Biblical (Jewish) writings (e.g., 1 Enoch 54:1). Although the designation *gehenna* is not used here, this is what John refers to (see note on Mt 5:22). Originally the site of a shrine where human sacrifices were offered (2Ki 16:3; 23:10; Jer 7:31), it came to be equated with the "hell" of final judgment in apocalyptic literature.
19:21 *birds gorged themselves.* The "great supper of God" of vv. 17–18.
20:1—22:21 These last three chapters reflect many of the subjects and themes of the first three chapters of Genesis (see

Introduction to Genesis: Literary Features).
20:1 *Abyss.* See note on 9:1.
20:2 *dragon.* See note on 12:3. *ancient serpent.* See 12:15; Ge 3:1–5. *thousand years.* The millennium (from the Latin *mille,* "thousand," and *annus,* "year"). It is taken literally by some as 1,000 actual years, while others interpret it metaphorically as a long but undetermined period of time. There are three basic approaches to the subject of the millennium: 1. Amillennialism: The millennium describes the present reign of Christ in heaven over his realm (Mt 28:18–20), along with the souls of deceased believers and in the hearts and lives of living believers on earth (see also note on 1Co 15:25). The present form of God's kingdom will be followed by Christ's return, the general resurrection, the final judgment and Christ's continuing reign over the perfect kingdom on the new earth in the eternal state. 2. Premillennialism: The present form of God's kingdom is moving toward a grand climax when Christ will return, the first resurrection will occur and his kingdom will find expression in a literal, visible reign of peace and righteousness on the earth in space-time history. After the final resurrection, the last judgment and the renewal of the heavens and the earth, this future, temporal kingdom will merge into the eternal kingdom, and the Lord will reign forever on the new earth. 3. Postmillennialism: The world will eventually be Christianized through the preaching of the gospel, resulting in a long period of peace and prosperity called the millennium. This future period will close with Christ's second coming, the resurrection of the dead, the final judgment and the eternal state.
20:3 *free for a short time.* See vv. 7–10.
20:4 *souls of those who had been beheaded.* See 6:9–11. *his mark.* See note on 13:16. *came to life.* The "first resurrection" (v. 5).

Jesus *a* and because of the word of God. *b* They had not worshiped the beast *c* or his image and had not received his mark on their foreheads or their hands. *d* They came to life and reigned *e* with Christ a thousand years. ⁵(The rest of the dead did not come to life until the thousand years were ended.) This is the first resurrection. *f* ⁶Blessed *g* and holy are those who have part in the first resurrection. The second death *h* has no power over them, but they will be priests *i* of God and of Christ and will reign with him *j* for a thousand years.

THE JUDGMENT OF SATAN

⁷When the thousand years are over, *k* Satan will be released from his prison ⁸and will go out to deceive the nations *l* in the four corners of the earth *m*—Gog and Magog *n*—and to gather them for battle. *o* In number they are like the sand on the seashore. *p* ⁹They marched across the breadth of the earth and surrounded *q* the camp of God's people, the city he loves. *r* But fire came down from heaven *s* and devoured them. ¹⁰And the devil, who deceived them, *t* was thrown into the lake of burning sulfur, *u* where the beast *v* and the false prophet *w* had been thrown. They will be tormented day and night for ever and ever. *x*

THE JUDGMENT OF THE DEAD

¹¹Then I saw a great white throne *y* and him who was seated on it. The earth and the heavens fled from his presence, *z* and there was no place for them. ¹²And I saw the dead, great and small, *a* standing before the throne, and books were opened. *b* Another book was opened, which is the book of life. *c* The dead were judged *d* according to what they had done *e* as recorded in the books. ¹³The sea gave up the dead that were in it, and death and Hades *f* gave up the dead *g* that were in them, and everyone was judged according to what they had done. *h* ¹⁴Then death *i* and Hades *j* were thrown into the lake of fire. *k* The lake of fire is the second death. *l* ¹⁵All whose names were not found written in the book of life *m* were thrown into the lake of fire.

A NEW HEAVEN AND A NEW EARTH

21 Then I saw "a new heaven and a new earth," *a* *n* for the first heaven and the first earth had passed away, *o* and there was no longer any sea. ²I saw the Holy City, *p* the new Jerusalem, coming down out of heaven from God, *q* prepared as a bride *r* beautifully dressed for her husband. ³And I heard a loud voice from the throne saying, "Look! God's dwelling place is now among the people, and he will dwell with them. *s* They will be his people, and God himself will be with them and be their God. *t* ⁴'He will wipe every tear from their eyes. *u* There will be no more death' *b* *v* or mourning or crying or pain, *w* for the old order of things has passed away." *x*

⁵He who was seated on the throne *y* said, "I am making everything new!" *z* Then he said, "Write this down, for these words are trustworthy and true." *a*

⁶He said to me: "It is done. *b* I am the Alpha and the Omega, *c* the Beginning and the End. To the thirsty I will give water without cost *d* from the spring of the water of life. *e* ⁷Those who are victorious *f* will inherit all this, and I will be their God and they will be my children. *g* ⁸But the cowardly, the unbelieving, the vile, the murderers, the sexually immor-

---

a 1 Isaiah 65:17   *b 4* Isaiah 25:8

20:7 *g* ver 3; 2Sa 7:14; 2Co 6:16; *S* Ro 8:14   **21:7** *r* S Jn 16:33

20:4 *a* S Rev 1:2
b S Heb 4:12
c S Rev 13:12
d S Rev 13:16 *e* ver 6; Rev 22:5
20:5 *f* ver 6;
Lk 14:14; Php 3:11; 1Th 4:16
20:6 *g* Rev 14:13
h S Rev 2:11
i S 1Pe 2:5 *j* ver 4; Rev 22:5
20:7 *k* ver 2
20:8 *l* ver 3,10;
Rev 12:9 *m* Isa 11:12; Eze 7:2; Rev 7:1
n Eze 38:2; 39:1
o S Rev 16:14
p Eze 38:9,15;
Heb 11:12
20:9 *q* Eze 38:9,16
r Ps 87:2 *s* Eze 38:22;
39:6; S Rev 13:13
20:10 *t* ver 3,8;
Rev 12:9; 19:20
u S Rev 9:17
v Rev 16:13
w Rev 16:13
x Rev 14:10,11
20:11 *y* S Rev 4:2
z S Rev 6:14
20:12 *a* S Rev 19:5
b Da 7:10 *c* ver 15;
Ex 32:32; Dt 29:20;
Da 12:1; Mal 3:16;
Lk 10:20; Rev 3:5;
21:27 *d* Rev 2:23
e Jer 17:10; S Mt 16:27
20:13 *f* Rev 1:18; 6:8
g Isa 26:19
h S Mt 16:27
20:14 *i* 1Co 15:26
j ver 13 *k* S Rev 19:20
l S Rev 2:11
20:15 *m* S ver 12
21:1 *n* S 2Pe 3:13
o S Rev 6:14
21:2 *p* ver 10;
Ne 11:18; Isa 52:1;
Rev 11:2; 22:19
q ver 10; Heb 11:10;
12:22; Rev 3:12
r S Rev 19:7
21:3 *s* Ex 25:8;
2Ch 6:18; Eze 48:35;
Zec 2:10 *t* S 2Co 6:16
21:4 *u* S Rev 7:17
v Isa 25:8; 1Co 15:26;
Rev 20:14
w Isa 35:10; 65:19
x S 2Co 5:17
21:5 *y* Rev 4:9; 20:11
z ver 4 *a* Rev 19:9;
22:6
21:6 *b* Rev 16:17
c Rev 1:8; 22:13
d Isa 55:1 *e* S Jn 4:10
21:7 *f* S Jn 16:33

20:5 *rest of the dead.* Either the wicked or everyone except the martyrs (see v. 4).

20:6 *Blessed.* The fifth beatitude (see note on 1:3). *second death.* Defined in v. 14 as the "lake of fire" (cf. 21:8).

20:7 *thousand years.* See note on v. 2.

20:8 *Gog and Magog.* Symbolize the nations of the world as they band together for a final assault on God. The OT background is Eze 38–39.

20:10 *tormented day and night.* See note on 14:11; cf. 14:10.

20:12 *book of life.* See note on 3:5. *judged according to what they had done.* The principle of judgment on the basis of works is taught in Ps 62:12; Jer 17:10; Ro 2:6; 1Pe 1:17 and elsewhere.

20:13 *death and Hades.* See 6:8 and note.

20:14–15 *lake of fire.* See note on 19:20.

21:2—22:5 The "Holy City" combines elements of Jerusalem, the temple and the Garden of Eden (see Introduction to Genesis: Literary Features).

21:2 *new Jerusalem.* See "the Jerusalem that is above" (Gal

4:26; see note there). *bride.* See note on 19:7.

A **21:3** *God's dwelling place.* See Lev 26:11–12; Eze 37:27; 2Co 6:16; Eph 2:21–22. *among … with … with.* The most eloquent culmination of the Immanuel theme (see 2Co 13:14 and note). *his people … their God.* The deepest expression of the intimate fellowship that God had promised to those in covenant relationship with him (see Zec 8:8 and note).

21:4 *wipe every tear.* See 7:17; Isa 25:8.

21:6 *the Alpha and the Omega.* See note on 1:8. *water of life.* Cf. Ps 36:9; Jn 4:10,14 and notes.

21:7 *victorious.* Cf. the emphasis on victory in the seven letters (2:7,11,17,26; 3:5,12,21).

21:8 *cowardly … liars.* See note on Ro 1:29–31. "Cowardly" heads the list because it stands opposed to the faithfulness of those "who are victorious" (v. 7). *magic arts.* Cf. Ac 19:19. The magical tradition in ancient times called for the mixing of various herbs to ward off evil. *fiery lake of burning sulfur.* See note on 19:20.

21:8 *h* ver 27;
Ps 5:6; 1Co 6:9;
Heb 12:14; Rev 22:15
i S Rev 9:17
j S Rev 2:11
21:9 *k* S Rev 15:1,6,7
l S Rev 19:7
21:10 *m* Eze 40:2;
Rev 17:3 *n* S Rev 1:10
o S ver 2
21:11 *p* ver 23;
Isa 60:1,2; Eze 43:2;
Rev 15:8; 22:5
q ver 18,19; Rev 4:3
r Rev 4:6
21:12 *s* ver 15,21,
25; Rev 22:14
t Eze 48:30-34
21:14 *u* S Eph 2:20;
Heb 11:10 *v* Ac 1:26;
Eph 2:20
21:15 *w* Eze 40:3;
Rev 11:1 *x* S ver 12
21:17 *y* Rev 13:18
21:18 *z* S ver 11
a ver 21
21:19 *b* Ex 28:17-
20; Isa 54:11,12;
Eze 28:13 *c* S ver 11
21:20 *d* Rev 4:3
21:21 *e* S ver 12
f Isa 54:12 *g* ver 18
21:22 *h* Jn 4:21,23
i S Rev 1:8 *j* S Rev 5:6
21:23 *k* S ver 11
l Isa 24:23; 60:19,20;
Rev 22:5 *m* S Rev 5:6
21:24 *n* ver 26;
Isa 60:3,5
21:25 *o* S ver 12
p Isa 60:11 *q* Zec 14:7;
Rev 22:5
21:26 *r* ver 24
21:27 *s* Isa 52:1;
Joel 3:17; Rev 22:14,
15 *t* S Rev 20:12
22:1 *u* Ps 36:8; 46:4
v ver 17; S Jn 4:10
w Rev 4:6 *x* Eze 47:1;
Zec 14:8
22:2 *y* S Rev 2:7
z Eze 47:12
22:3 *a* Zec 14:11
b Rev 7:15
22:4 *c* S Mt 5:8
d S Rev 7:3
22:5 *e* Rev 21:25;
Zec 14:7 *f* Isa 60:19,
20; Rev 21:23
g Da 7:27; Rev 20:4
22:6 *h* Rev 1:1
i Rev 21:5 *j* 1Co 14:32;
Heb 12:9 *k* ver 16;
Rev 1:1

al, those who practice magic arts, the idolaters and all liars *h*—they will be consigned to the fiery lake of burning sulfur. *i* This is the second death." *j*

THE NEW JERUSALEM, THE BRIDE OF THE LAMB

⁹One of the seven angels who had the seven bowls full of the seven last plagues *k* came and said to me, "Come, I will show you the bride, *l* the wife of the Lamb." ¹⁰And he carried me away *m* in the Spirit *n* to a mountain great and high, and showed me the Holy City, Jerusalem, coming down out of heaven from God. *o* ¹¹It shone with the glory of God, *p* and its brilliance was like that of a very precious jewel, like a jasper, *q* clear as crystal. *r* ¹²It had a great, high wall with twelve gates, *s* and with twelve angels at the gates. On the gates were written the names of the twelve tribes of Israel. *t* ¹³There were three gates on the east, three on the north, three on the south and three on the west. ¹⁴The wall of the city had twelve foundations, *u* and on them were the names of the twelve apostles *v* of the Lamb.

¹⁵The angel who talked with me had a measuring rod *w* of gold to measure the city, its gates *x* and its walls. ¹⁶The city was laid out like a square, as long as it was wide. He measured the city with the rod and found it to be 12,000 stadia *a* in length, and as wide and high as it is long. ¹⁷He measured its wall and it was 144 cubits *b* thick, *c* by human *y* measurement, which the angel was using. ¹⁸The wall was made of jasper, *z* and the city of pure gold, as pure as glass. *a* ¹⁹The foundations of the city walls were decorated with every kind of precious stone. *b* The first foundation was jasper, *c* the second sapphire, the third agate, the fourth emerald, ²⁰the fifth onyx, the sixth ruby, *d* the seventh chrysolite, the eighth beryl, the ninth topaz, the tenth turquoise, the eleventh jacinth, and the twelfth amethyst. *d* ²¹The twelve gates *e* were twelve pearls, *f* each gate made of a single pearl. The great street of the city was of gold, as pure as transparent glass. *g*

²²I did not see a temple *h* in the city, because the Lord God Almighty *i* and the Lamb *j* are its temple. ²³The city does not need the sun or the moon to shine on it, for the glory of God *k* gives it light, *l* and the Lamb *m* is its lamp. ²⁴The nations will walk by its light, and the kings of the earth will bring their splendor into it. *n* ²⁵On no day will its gates *o* ever be shut, *p* for there will be no night there. *q* ²⁶The glory and honor of the nations will be brought into it. *r* ²⁷Nothing impure will ever enter it, nor will anyone who does what is shameful or deceitful, *s* but only those whose names are written in the Lamb's book of life. *t*

EDEN RESTORED

22 Then the angel showed me the river *u* of the water of life, *v* as clear as crystal, *w* flowing *x* from the throne of God and of the Lamb ²down the middle of the great street of the city. On each side of the river stood the tree of life, *y* bearing twelve crops of fruit, yielding its fruit every month. And the leaves of the tree are for the healing of the nations. *z* ³No longer will there be any curse. *a* The throne of God and of the Lamb will be in the city, and his servants will serve him. *b* ⁴They will see his face, *c* and his name will be on their foreheads. *d* ⁵There will be no more night. *e* They will not need the light of a lamp or the light of the sun, for the Lord God will give them light. *f* And they will reign for ever and ever. *g*

JOHN AND THE ANGEL

⁶The angel said to me, *h* "These words are trustworthy and true. *i* The Lord, the God who inspires the prophets, *j* sent his angel *k* to show his servants the things that must soon take place."

---

a 16 That is, about 1,400 miles or about 2,200 kilometers   *b* 17 That is, about 200 feet or about 65 meters   *c* 17 Or *high*   *d* 20 The precise identification of some of these precious stones is uncertain.

21:9 *seven last plagues.* See 15:1.
21:10 *in the Spirit.* See notes on 1:10; 4:2; 17:3.
21:12 *twelve gates.* See Eze 48:30–35. The number 12 probably emphasizes the continuity of the NT church and the OT people of God. See v. 14, where the 12 foundations bear the names of the 12 apostles.
21:15 *measure the city.* Cf. Eze 40–41. In Rev 11 the measuring was to ensure protection; here it serves to show the size and symmetry of the eternal dwelling place of the faithful.
21:16 *length...wide...high.* Thus a perfect cube, as was the Most Holy Place of the tabernacle and the temple.
21:17 *144 cubits.* See TNIV text note.
21:20 See TNIV text note.

21:27 *Lamb's book of life.* See note on 3:5.
22:1 *river of the water of life.* The description of the river here seems to combine elements taken from the description of Eden (Ge 2:8–14) and the river flowing from the new temple seen by Ezekiel (Eze 47:1–12), as well as certain new elements.
22:2 *tree of life.* See v. 14; Ge 2:9; 3:22; Eze 47:12.
22:4 *They will see his face.* In ancient times criminals were banished from the presence of the king (Est 7:8; cf. 2Sa 14:24). One blessing of eternity will be to see the Lord face to face (cf. 1Co 13:12; 1Jn 3:2). *his name.* See note on 3:12.
22:5 *they will reign.* See 5:10; 20:6; Da 7:18,27.
22:6 *his servants.* See v. 3. *things that must soon take place.* See 1:1,19.

[7]"Look, I am coming soon![l] Blessed[m] are those who keep the words of the prophecy in this scroll."[n]

[8]I, John, am the one who heard and saw these things.[o] And when I had heard and seen them, I fell down to worship at the feet[p] of the angel who had been showing them to me. [9]But he said to me, "Don't do that! I am a fellow servant with you and with your fellow prophets and with all who keep the words of this scroll.[q] Worship God!"[r]

[10]Then he told me, "Do not seal up[s] the words of the prophecy of this scroll,[t] because the time is near.[u] [11]Let those who do wrong continue to do wrong; let those who are vile continue to be vile; let those who do right continue to do right; and let those who are holy continue to be holy."[v]

EPILOGUE: INVITATION AND WARNING

[12]"Look, I am coming soon![w] My reward is with me,[x] and I will give to everyone according to what they have done.[y] [13]I am the Alpha and the Omega,[z] the First and the Last,[a] the Beginning and the End.[b]

[14]"Blessed are those who wash their robes,[c] that they may have the right to the tree of life[d] and may go through the gates[e] into the city.[f] [15]Outside[g] are the dogs,[h] those who practice magic arts, the sexually immoral, the murderers, the idolaters and everyone who loves and practices falsehood.

[16]"I, Jesus,[i] have sent my angel[j] to give you[a] this testimony for the churches.[k] I am the Root[l] and the Offspring of David,[m] and the bright Morning Star."[n]

[17]The Spirit[o] and the bride[p] say, "Come!" And let those who hear say, "Come!" Let those who are thirsty come; and let all who wish take the free gift of the water of life.[q]

[18]I warn everyone who hears the words of the prophecy of this scroll:[r] If any one of you adds anything to them,[s] God will add to you the plagues described in this scroll.[t] [19]And if any one of you takes words away[u] from this scroll of prophecy,[v] God will take away from you your share in the tree of life[w] and in the Holy City, which are described in this scroll.

[20]He who testifies to these things[x] says, "Yes, I am coming soon."[y]
Amen. Come, Lord Jesus.[z]
[21]The grace of the Lord Jesus be with God's people.[a] Amen.

[a] 16 The Greek is plural.

22:7 [l] ver 12,20;
S Mt 16:27 [m] Rev 1:3;
16:15 [n] ver 10,18,19
22:8 [o] S Rev 1:1
[p] Rev 19:10
22:9 [q] ver 10,18,19
[r] Rev 19:10
22:10 [s] Da 8:26;
Rev 10:4 [t] ver 7,18,19
[u] S Ro 13:11
22:11 [v] Eze 3:27;
Da 12:10
22:12 [w] ver 7,20;
S Mt 16:27
[x] Isa 40:10; 62:11
[y] S Mt 16:27
22:13 [z] Rev 1:8
[a] S Rev 1:17 [b] Rev 21:6
22:14 [c] Rev 7:14
[d] S Rev 2:7
[e] S Rev 21:12
[f] S Rev 21:27
22:15 [g] Dt 23:18;
1Co 6:9,10; Gal 5:19-
21; Col 3:5,6;
Rev 21:8 [h] Php 3:2
22:16 [i] Rev 1:1
[j] ver 6 [k] Rev 1:4
[l] S Rev 5:5 [m] S Mt 1:1
[n] 2Pe 1:19; Rev 2:28
22:17 [o] Rev 2:7;
14:13 [p] S Rev 19:7
[q] S Jn 4:10
22:18 [r] ver 7,10,19
[s] Dt 4:2; 12:32;
Pr 30:6
[t] Rev 15:6–16:21
22:19 [u] Dt 4:2;
12:32; Pr 30:6 [v] ver 7,
10,18 [w] S Rev 2:7
22:20 [x] Rev 1:2
[y] ver 7,12; S Mt 16:27
[z] 1Co 16:22
22:21 [a] S Ro 16:20

22:7 *I am coming soon!* See vv. 12,20; 2:16; 3:11. *Blessed.* The sixth beatitude (see note on 1:3).

22:8 *fell down to worship.* See note on 1:17.

22:9 *Don't do that!* The episode (here and in 19:10) is no doubt included to remind the reader/listener that the worship of any created being—no matter how noble—is a form of idolatry, a vice sternly warned against (v. 15; 21:8; see notes on Ge 20:9; Ex 34:15).

22:10 *Do not seal up the words.* Contrast Da 12:4.

22:11 "The time is near" (v. 10), so it is too late to change. The unrepentant must now face the consequences of their actions (see v. 12).

22:12 *I am coming soon!* See vv. 7,20; 2:16; 3:11. *according to what they have done.* See notes on 2:23; 20:12.

22:13 *the Alpha and the Omega.* See note on 1:8.

22:14 *Blessed.* The last of the seven beatitudes (see note on 1:3). *wash their robes.* "In the blood of the Lamb" (7:14).

22:15 *dogs…falsehood.* See note on Ro 1:29–31. *dogs.* A term applied to all types of ceremonially impure persons. In Dt 23:18 it designates a male prostitute.

22:16 *my angel.* Cf. 1:1. *the Root and the Offspring of David.* See note on 5:5; cf. Isa 11:1,10; Ro 1:3. *bright Morning Star.* See Nu 24:17 and note.

22:18–19 Cf. the commands in Dt 4:2; 12:32. The warning here relates specifically to the book of Revelation.

22:20 *I am coming soon.* See vv. 7,12; 2:16; 3:11. *Come, Lord Jesus.* See note on 1Co 16:22.

22:21 *grace.* See note on Ro 1:7. *with.* See note on 2Co 13:14. *Amen.* See notes on Dt 27:15; Ro 1:25.

STUDY HELPS

STUDY HELPS

TABLE OF WEIGHTS AND MEASURES

	Biblical Unit	Approximate American Equivalent		Approximate Metric Equivalent	
WEIGHTS	talent (60 minas)	75	pounds	34	kilograms
	mina (50 shekels)	1 1/4	pounds	0.6	kilogram
	shekel (2 bekas)	2/5	ounce	11.5	grams
	pim (2/3 shekel)	1/3	ounce	9.5	grams
	beka (10 gerahs)	1/5	ounce	5.5	grams
	gerah	1/50	ounce	0.6	gram
LENGTH	cubit	18	inches	0.5	meter
	span	9	inches	23	centimeters
	handbreadth	3	inches	8	centimeters
CAPACITY					
Dry Measure	cor [homer] (10 ephahs)	6	bushels	220	liters
	lethek (5 ephahs)	3	bushels	110	liters
	ephah (10 omers)	3/5	bushel	22	liters
	seah (1/3 ephah)	7	quarts	7.7	liters
	omer (1/10 ephah)	2	quarts	2	liters
	cab (1/18 ephah)	1	quart	1	liter
Liquid Measure	bath (1 ephah)	6	gallons	22	liters
	hin (1/6 bath)	4	quarts	4	liters
	log (1/72 bath)	1/3	quart	0.3	liter

The figures of the table are calculated on the basis of a shekel equaling 11.5 grams, a cubit equaling 18 inches and an ephah equaling 22 liters. The quart referred to is either a dry quart (slightly larger than a liter) or a liquid quart (slightly smaller than a liter), whichever is applicable. The ton referred to in the footnotes is the American ton of 2,000 pounds. Since most readers are more familiar with dry measures being given in weight rather than capacity (bushel, quart), dry measures have been converted in the footnotes to approximate weights.

This table is based upon the best available information, but it is not intended to be mathematically precise; like the measurement equivalents in the footnotes, it merely gives approximate amounts and distances. Weights and measures differed somewhat at various times and places in the ancient world. There is uncertainty particularly about the ephah and the bath; further discoveries may shed more light on these units of capacity.

REVISED SPELLING OF PROPER NAMES

NIV	TNIV	NIV	TNIV
Abib	Aviv	Jacan	Jakan
Abimelech	Abimelek	Jecoliah	Jekoliah
Achbor	Akbor	Jehucal	Jehukal
Acco	Akko	Josech	Josek
Acsah	Aksah	Kittim	Kittites
Acshaph	Akshaph	Korazin	Chorazin
Aczib	Akzib	Lecah	Lekah
Adrammelech	Adrammelek	Maacah	Maakah
Ahimelech	Ahimelek	Macbannai	Makbannai
Ahisamach	Ahisamak	Macbenah	Makbenah
Allammelech	Allammelek	Macnadebai	Maknadebai
Anammelech	Anammelek	Malcam	Malkam
Asshur	Ashur	Malluch	Malluk
Asshurites	Ashurites	Maoch	Maok
Athach	Athak	Marcaboth	Markaboth
Baca	Baka	Meconah	Mekonah
Bacuth	Bakuth	Melech	Melek
Becorath	Bekorath	Memucan	Memukan
Beracah	Berakah	Merodach-Baladan	Marduk-Baladan
Beth Car	Beth Kar	Meshech	Meshek
Bicri	Bikri	Mica	Mika
Cabbon	Kabbon	Micmash	Mikmash
Cabul	Kabul	Micmethah	Mikmethah
Calcol	Kalkol	Micri	Mikri
Calno	Kalno	Milcah	Milkah
Calneh	Kalneh	Milcom	Milkom
Canneh	Kanneh	Mithcah	Mithkah
Carshena	Karshena	Mizraim	Egypt
Carcas	Karkas	Molech	Molek
Carmi	Karmi	Nacon	Nakon
Casiphia	Kasiphia	Nathan-Melech	Nathan-Melek
Casluhites	Kasluhites	Neco	Necho
Cenchrea	Cenchreae	Nisroch	Nisrok
Col-Hozeh	Kol-Hozeh	Ocran	Okran
Colosse	Colossae	Parnach	Parnak
Conaniah	Konaniah	Pasach	Pasak
Cozbi	Kozbi	Racal	Rakal
Cozeba	Kozeba	Recab	Rekab
Cun	Kun	Recabites	Rekabites
Cuthah	Kuthah	Recah	Rekah
Ebed-Melech	Ebed-Melek	Regem-Melech	Regem-Melek
Elimelech	Elimelek	Rodanim	Rodanites
Erech	Uruk	Sabteca	Sabteka
Eshcol	Eshkol	Sacar	Sakar
Eshtarah	Eshterah	Salecah	Salekah
Evil-Merodach	Awel-Marduk	Secacah	Sekakah
Goiim	Goyim	Secu	Seku
Hacaliah	Hakaliah	Shecaniah	Shekaniah
Hacmoni	Hakmoni	Sheshach	Sheshak
Hadrach	Hadrak	Shobach	Shobak
Hanoch	Hanok	Shophach	Shophak
Hathach	Hathak	Sibbecai	Sibbekai
Haran	Harran	Soco	Soko
Hatticon	Hattikon	Socoh	Sokoh
Hazazon Tamar	Hazezon Tamar	Succoth	Sukkoth
Helech	Helek	Ucal	Ukal
Iim	Iyim	Zaccai	Zakkai
Iscah	Iskah	Zaccur	Zakkur
Isshiah	Ishiah	Zeboiim	Zeboyim
Jaakanites	Bene Jaakan	Zicri	Zikri

INDEX TO TOPICS

ABRAHAM
A. Family data
—Line of Shem 1Ch 1:24–27
—Son of Terah ....Ge 11:26–27
—Original name: Abram ....Ge 11:27
—Husband of Sarai ....Ge 11:29
—Father of Ishmael with Hagar ....Ge 16:1–4,15–16
—Father of Isaac with Sarah ....Ge 21:1–3
—Father of many children with Keturah ....Ge 25:1–4
—Died at 175 years old ....Ge 25:7–8
B. Covenant with the Lord
1. Called while in Ur ....Ge 12:1–3
   Ac 7:2–4
2. Received promises
  —Land and descendants ....Ge 13:14–17
   Ge 15:18–21
   Ge 22:15–18
  —A son by Sarah.......................Ge 17:16
   Ge 18:9–15
3. Given circumcision as a sign ....Ge 17:1–14,23–27
   Ro 4:9–12
4. Declared righteous through faith ....Ge 15:6
   Ro 4:3,20–24
   Gal 3:6–9
5. Covenant sealed by sacrifice ....Ge 15:8–21
6. Name changed to Abraham ....Ge 17:5
   Ne 9:7
7. Covenant remembered ....Lk 1:68–75
   Heb 6:13–15
C. Travels and significant events
—Left Ur ....Ge 11:31
—Went to Canaan ....Ge 12:1–6
   Ac 7:2–4
—Deceived Pharaoh about Sarai ....Ge 12:10–20
—Divided land with Lot, settled in Hebron ......Ge 13:1–18
—Rescued Lot from four kings ....Ge 14:1–16
—Blessed by Melchizedek ....Ge 14:17–20
   Heb 7:1–7
—Declared righteous through faith ....Ge 15:6
—Fathered Ishmael with Hagar ....Ge 16:1–16
—Entertained three visitors ....Ge 18:1–15
—Interceded for the city of Sodom ....Ge 18:16–33
—Deceived Abimelek about Sarah ....Ge 20:1–10
—Fathered Isaac with Sarah ....Ge 21:1–3
—Sent Hagar and Ishmael away ....Ge 21:8–21
   Gal 4:22–30
—Made a covenant with Abimelek ....Ge 21:22–32
—Tested by command to sacrifice Isaac ....Ge 22:1–18
   Heb 11:17–19
—Bought field for Sarah's burial ....Ge 23:1–20
—Secured wife for Isaac ....Ge 24:1–67
—Fathered children with Keturah ....Ge 25:1–6
—Died ....Ge 25:7–11
D. Titles ascribed to him
—Mighty prince ....Ge 23:5–6
—Servant of God ....Ge 26:24
—Friend of God ....Isa 41:8
   Jas 2:23
—Prophet ....Ge 20:7
—Father of Israel ....Ex 3:15
   Mt 3:9
—Father of all believers ....Ro 4:11–12,16
   Gal 3:7
E. Significance in New Testament
—Jesus is a son of Abraham ....Mt 1:1
—His true seed is Christ ....Gal 3:15–16,29
—Jesus preceded him ....Jn 8:57–58
—Rejoiced to see Jesus' day ....Jn 8:56
—Showed greatness of Christ by giving a tithe to
Melchizedek ....Heb 7:4–10
—Lived by faith ....Heb 11:8–12,17–19
—Believed in the power of the resurrection ......Ro 4:17–21
—Became the father of believers ....Ro 4:11–12
   Gal 3:7
—His faith preceded the law ....Ro 4:9–11,13–16
   Gal 3:17–19
—Cast out the sons of the law ....Gal 4:21–31
—Demonstrated faith by works ....Jas 2:20–24

ABSALOM
—Son of David by Maakah 2Sa 3:3
   1Ch 3:2

—Killed Amnon for rape of Tamar 2Sa 13:23–33
—Fled to Geshur 2Sa 13:36–38
—Allowed by David to return 2Sa 14:1–24
—Reconciled with David 2Sa 14:28–33
—Rebelled against David 2Sa 15:1–12
—David fled from him 2Sa 15:13–37
—Accepted the advice of Hushai 2Sa 16:15–17:23
—Fought against David's men 2Sa 18:1–8
—Killed by Joab 2Sa 18:9–18
—Mourned by David 2Sa 18:19–19:8

ACCESS TO GOD
A. The command to approach God
—In the Old Testament ....Isa 55:6
   Am 5:4,6
—In the New Testament ....Mt 7:7
   Lk 11:9
   Jas 4:8
B. How can we approach God?
1. From God's standpoint
  —The Father draws us to himself ....Jn 6:44
  —Jesus is the way to the Father ....Jn 14:6
   Ro 5:2
   Eph 3:12
   1Pe 3:18
  —The Spirit enables us to come near .....Eph 2:18
2. From our standpoint
  —We must believe ....Ro 5:2
   Heb 11:6
  —We must live clean, obedient lives ......Ps 24:3–5
   Mt 5:8
  —We must pray to the Father ....Mt 6:6
  —We must call upon God's name ....Ps 145:18
C. Promises to those who approach God
—We will find God ....Dt 4:29
   2Ch 15:2
—God will listen to us 2Ki 13:4
—God will forgive us 2Ch 7:14
—God will make a covenant with us ....Isa 55:3
—God will bless us ....Ps 65:4
—We can have confidence before God ....Eph 3:12
   Heb 4:16
   1Jn 5:14

See also PRAYER

ACHAN
—Son of Karmi, of tribe of Judah ....Jos 7:1
—Stole things from Jericho ....Jos 7:1
—His sin caused defeat at Ai ....Jos 7:3–12
—His sin revealed ....Jos 7:13–23
—Stoned to death ....Jos 7:24–26
—A lesson for Israel ....Jos 22:18–20

ACHISH
—King of Gath before whom David feigned insanity .1Sa 21:10–15
—Gave David town of Ziklag 1Sa 27:1–7
—Trusted David 1Sa 27:10–12
—Philistines asked him to expel David 1Sa 29:1–11
—Still king in time of Solomon 1Ki 2:39–40

ADAM
A. The first Adam
1. The creation of Adam
  —Made in God's image ....Ge 1:26–27
  —Made from dust of the earth ....Ge 2:7
  —Became a living being ....Ge 2:7
   1Co 15:45
  —Woman was created from him ....Ge 2:21–23
2. The work of Adam
  —Was placed in Eden ....Ge 2:8
  —Took care of Eden ....Ge 2:15
  —Named the animals ....Ge 2:19–20
  —Work cursed after the fall ....Ge 3:17–19
  —Was banished from Eden ....Ge 3:23–24
3. Marriage of Adam and Eve
  —Was established by God ....Ge 2:23–24
  —Eve tempted her husband ....Ge 3:6
   1Ti 2:14
  —Adam blamed Eve ....Ge 3:12
  —Adam and Eve had children ....Ge 4:1–2
   Ge 4:25–5:4
4. Temptation and fall of Adam
  —God warned Adam not to sin ....Ge 2:16–17
  —Adam disobeyed God ....Ge 3:1–6

C. Prophesied against
—By an unnamed prophet 1Ki 20:35–43
—By Elijah 1Ki 21:17–29
—By Micaiah 1Ki 22:9–28
D. Subsequent history
—Elisha told Jehu to destroy Ahab's family 2Ki 9:6–10
—House of Ahab destroyed 2Ki 10:1–17
—Name became a symbol of wickedness 2Ch 21:6,13
2Ch 22:3–4
Mic 6:16

AHAZ
—Son of Jotham; king of Judah 2Ki 16:1
2Ch 28:1
—Worshiped idols 2Ki 16:1–4,10–18
2Ch 28:1–4,22–25
—Fought against Aram and Israel 2Ki 16:5–6
Isa 7:1
—Defeated by Aram and Israel 2Ch 28:5–15
—Fought against Edom and Philistia 2Ch 28:16–19
—Sought help from Assyria 2Ki 16:7–9
—Refused a sign from the Lord ....Isa 7:2–17
—His death 2Ki 16:19–20

AHAZIAH
A. Son of Ahab; king of Israel 1Ki 22:51
—Worshiped idols 1Ki 22:52–53
—Made an alliance with Jehoshaphat 2Ch 20:36–37
—Died while seeking advice from Baal 2Ki 1:1–17
B. Son of Jehoram; king of Judah 2Ki 8:25–26
2Ch 22:1–2
—Worshiped idols 2Ki 8:27
2Ch 22:3–4
—Allied with Joram, king of Israel 2Ki 8:28–29
—Killed by Jehu while visiting Joram 2Ki 9:14–29
2Ch 22:1–9
—Only surviving son was Joash 2Ki 11:1–3

AHIMELEK
A. Priest at Nob during Saul's time 1Sa 21:1
—Gave David consecrated bread 1Sa 21:2–6
—Gave David Goliath's sword 1Sa 21:8–9
—Betrayed to Saul by Doeg 1Sa 22:9–10
—Killed by Doeg with other priests 1Sa 22:17–19
—Son Abiathar escaped to join David 1Sa 22:20–23
B. Grandson of Ahimelek 2Sa 8:17
—Co-priest with Zadok during David's reign 1Ch 18:16
1Ch 24:6,31
C. One of David's warriors 1Sa 26:6

AHITHOPHEL
—A counselor of David 2Sa 15:12
—Joined Absalom against David 2Sa 15:31–37
—Advised Absalom 2Sa 16:15–23
—Absalom rejected his counsel 2Sa 17:1–14
—Committed suicide 2Sa 17:23

AI
—A city in Palestine, east of Bethel ....Jos 7:2
—Abram built an altar near there ....Ge 12:8
—Joshua's troops were initially defeated there ......Jos 7:3–5
—After Achan's death, Ai was destroyed ....Jos 8:1–29
—Later rebuilt, with Israelites settling there ......Ezr 2:2,28

ALCOHOL
A. Terms used in the Bible
—Beer and wine 1Sa 1:15
Pr 31:4,6
—Fermented drink ....Nu 6:3
Jdg 13:4,7
—Mixed wine ....Pr 9:2
Pr 23:30
—Old wine and new wine ....Am 9:13
Lk 5:37–39
B. Various uses for alcohol
—In family meals ....Ge 27:25
—In public feasting ....Est 1:7–8,10
Da 5:1–4
—At weddings ....Jn 2:3
—As an offering to God ....Ex 29:38,40
Lev 23:12–13
—As a tithe ....Dt 12:17
Ne 13:5
—In barter exchange 2Ch 2:10
—As a commodity for commerce ....Eze 27:18
—As medicine ....Lk 10:34
1Ti 5:23

—As a drug for pain ....Pr 31:6
Mk 15:23
—As a means to become drunk ....Ge 9:20–21
C. Positive aspects of alcohol
—A blessing from God ....Joel 2:19
—Can help one celebrate ....Jn 2:1–11
—Can give enjoyment ....Ps 104:15
Zec 9:17
—Can aid in happiness ....Ecc 10:19
—Can help to refresh someone 2Sa 16:2
—Can help one's health 1Ti 5:23
D. Dangers of using alcohol
—Loosens morals ....Ge 9:21–22
—Inflames an individual ....Isa 5:11–12
—Destroys health 1Sa 25:36–37
—Impairs judgment ....Pr 31:4–5
Isa 28:7
—Raises tempers ....Pr 20:1
—Leads to poverty ....Pr 23:21
—Leads to sorrow ....Pr 23:29–30
—Creates disunity in the church 1Co 11:18–21
E. Drunkenness forbidden ....Isa 5:11–12,22
Ro 13:13
1Co 5:11
1Co 6:9–10
Eph 5:18
F. Symbolic uses of alcohol
—Symbolizes the blood of Christ ....Mt 26:27–29
—Symbolizes the gospel of salvation ....Isa 55:1
—Symbolizes the judgment of God ....Ps 75:8
Jer 25:15–16
Rev 14:10
—Symbolizes the sins of the antichrist ....Rev 17:2
Rev 18:3

ALIEN
—A citizen of one country residing in another
A. Aliens within the nation of Israel
1. Who were they?
—Those leaving Egypt with Israelites ......Ex 12:38
—Unconquered nations in Canaan ....Jos 9:26–27
1Ki 9:20–21
—Captives taken in war ....Dt 21:10–11
—Slaves purchased ....Lev 25:44–46
—Foreigners hired in Israel 1Ki 9:27
—Foreigners attracted to Israel 2Ch 6:32–33
2. How were they to be treated?
—God had a special love for them ....Dt 10:18
Ps 146:9
—They were not to be oppressed ....Ex 22:21
Ex 23:9
Lev 19:33–34
—They enjoyed equal protection ....Lev 24:22
Lev 25:35
Dt 1:16–17
Dt 24:17–21
—They shared equal responsibility ....Ex 20:8–10
Nu 15:14–16
—Israel condemned for oppressing them ....Ps 94:6
Eze 22:7,29
B. God's people as aliens
1. In the Old Testament
—Abraham in Canaan ....Ge 17:8
Ge 23:4
—Jacob in Canaan ....Ge 28:4
—Moses in Midian ....Ex 18:3
—Israelites in Egypt ....Ge 15:13
Ex 23:9
—Israelites in Canaan ....Lev 25:23
1Ch 29:15
Ps 39:12
Ps 119:19
—Israelites in Babylon ....La 5:2
—Their true homeland was elsewhere ......Heb 11:13–15
2. In the New Testament
—We are called foreigners 1Pe 1:17
1Pe 2:11
—We are not part of this world ....Jn 17:14,16
—Our true home is heaven ....Php 3:20–21
Col 3:1,3
Heb 11:16

—Refused to give food to Israelites . . . . Dt 23:4
—Not allowed to join the Israelites . . . . Dt 23:4
    Ne 13:1–8
—Half of their land given to Gad . . . . Jos 13:25
2. During the time of the kings
—Israelites worshiped their gods . . . . Jdg 10:6
    1Ki 11:5,7
—David used them to kill Uriah 2Sa 12:9
—Solomon intermarried with them 1Ki 11:1
    1Ki 14:21
3. Numerous Jews intermarried with them . . . . Ezr 9:1
    Ne 13:23–27
4. Prophecies concerning their destruction . . . . Isa 11:12–14
    Jer 49:1–5
    Eze 21:28–32
    Eze 25:1–7
    Am 1:13–15
    Zep 2:8–11

AMNON
—Firstborn of David 2Sa 3:2
—Raped Tamar 2Sa 13:1–19
—Killed by Absalom 2Sa 13:20–29
—David mourned for him 2Sa 13:37

AMON
A. Son of Manasseh; king of Judah 2Ki 21:18–19
—Promoted idolatry 2Ki 21:20–22
—Assassinated 2Ki 21:23–24
B. Ruler of city of Samaria under Ahab 1Ki 22:26
    2Ch 18:25

AMORITES
A. Their identity
—Descendants of Canaan, grandson of Noah . . . . . Ge 10:6,15–16
—One of the Canaanite nations . . . . Ex 33:2
—Lived in hill country, east of the Jordan . . . . Nu 13:29
    Jos 2:10
—Boundaries given . . . . Jos 12:2–5
B. Significant Amorites
—Mamre, Eshkol, Aner: friends of Abram . . . . Ge 14:13
—Sihon and Og: fought against Israelites . . . . Nu 21:21,33
    Dt 4:46–47
C. Their wars
—Defeated by Kedorlaomer and his allies . . . . Ge 14:5–7
—Sihon and Og defeated by the Israelites . . . . . . Nu 21:21–31
—They defeated disobedient Israelites . . . . Dt 1:42–45
—Five Amorite kings defeated by Joshua . . . . Jos 10:5–26
D. Important data concerning them
1. Exceptionally sinful . . . . Ge 15:16
    2Ki 21:11
2. God promised their land to the Israelites . . . . Ex 3:8,17
    Ex 34:11
3. Political relationship with Israelites
—Land given to tribe of Reuben . . . . Jos 13:15,21
—Israelites told to destroy them . . . . Dt 7:1–6
    Dt 20:16–18
—Israelites did not destroy them . . . . Jos 13:2,4
    Jdg 1:34–36
—Amorites and Israelites at peace 1Sa 7:14
—Became slaves of Israelites 1Ki 9:20–21
    2Ch 8:7–8
4. Religious relationship with Israelites
—Israelites must not worship their gods . . . . Jos 24:14–15
—Israelites worshiped their gods . . . . Jdg 6:10
5. Intermarried with the Israelites . . . . Jdg 3:5–6
    Ezr 9:1–2

AMOS
A. Prophet from Tekoa . . . . Am 1:1
—Originally a farmer and shepherd . . . . Am 7:14
—Confronted the prophet Amaziah . . . . Am 7:10–17
B. Ancestor of Jesus . . . . Lk 3:25

ANANIAS
A. Husband of Sapphira . . . . Ac 5:1
—Kept back part of their money . . . . Ac 5:2
—Died for lying to God . . . . Ac 5:3–10
B. Disciple in Damascus who baptized Saul/Paul . . . Ac 9:10–17
—Commissioned Paul . . . . Ac 22:12–16
C. High priest at Paul's arrest . . . . Ac 23:2
    Ac 24:1

ANCESTRY
—Those from whom one has descended

A. Related theme
GENEALOGY is a theme of 1 Chronicles 1Ch 9:1
B. Physical ancestry of the Israelites
—Genealogies were important . . . . Ge 5:1–32
    Ge 46:8–26
    1Ch 1:1–9:44
    Ezr 2:3–61
    Mt 1:1–17
    Lk 3:23–38
—Priests had to prove ancestry . . . . Ezr 2:62
    Ne 7:64
—Israelites proud of Abraham as father . . . . Isa 41:8
    Isa 51:2
    Lk 3:8
    Jn 8:31–33
C. Ancestry of Jesus
—A descendant of Adam . . . . Lk 3:38
—A descendant of Abraham . . . . Mt 1:1
    Ro 9:5
—A descendant of David . . . . Mt 1:1
    Ro 1:3
D. Spiritual ancestry of God's people
1. Physical ancestry insufficient to be saved . . . Ro 9:6–7
2. Requirements for becoming true children of
   Abraham
—We must be chosen by God . . . . Ro 9:10–13
—We must believe in Jesus . . . . Ro 4:11,16
    Gal 3:7,26–29
—We must do God's will . . . . Jn 8:39–40
3. True children of Abraham
—Are heirs of God . . . . Ro 8:17
    Gal 3:29
—Include both Jews and Gentiles . . . . Ro 4:16–17
    Eph 3:6

ANDREW
—Brother of Simon Peter . . . . Mt 4:18
—Fisherman . . . . Mk 1:16–18
—Disciple of John the Baptist . . . . Jn 1:35–40
—Introduced Peter to Jesus . . . . Jn 1:41–42
—Became a disciple of Jesus . . . . Mt 4:18
—Introduced little boy to Jesus . . . . Jn 6:8
—Introduced Greeks to Jesus . . . . Jn 12:21–22
—Asked Jesus about destruction of temple . . . . . . Mk 13:3
—One of the apostles . . . . Ac 1:13

ANGEL
—Spiritual beings created by God
A. Their origin and nature
—They are spirits . . . . Heb 1:14
—They were created by God . . . . Ps 148:2,5
    Col 1:16
—They were created early in creation . . . . Job 38:6–7
—They were created good . . . . Ge 1:31
—They are not to be worshiped . . . . Col 2:18
    Rev 19:10
—They do not marry or die . . . . Lk 20:35–36
—Some angels rebelled against God 2Pe 2:4
B. Names and ranks of good angels
—Michael . . . . Da 12:1
    Jude 9
    Rev 12:7
—Gabriel . . . . Da 9:21
    Lk 1:19,26
—Archangels 1Th 4:16
—Seraphs . . . . Isa 6:2
—Cherubim . . . . Eze 10:1–3
—Rulers and authorities . . . . Eph 3:10
    Col 1:16
—Thrones and powers . . . . Col 1:16
—There are numerous angels . . . . Rev 5:11
C. Duties of good angels
1. General duties
—They revealed the law . . . . Ac 7:38
    Gal 3:19
    Heb 2:2
—They bring messages from God . . . . Zec 1:14–17
    Ac 10:3–6
—They praise and worship God . . . . Heb 1:6
    Rev 5:11–12
—They provide for God's people 1Ki 19:5–8
    Mt 4:11
    Heb 1:14

1. AUTHORITY is a theme of:
   —Matthew ....Mt 7:29
   —John ....Jn 10:18
2. LEADERSHIP is a theme of:
   —Ezra ....Ezr 7:10
   —Nehemiah ....Ne 13:25
   —1 Timothy 1Ti 4:16
B. Human authority
   1. Given as a gift from God and Christ
      —To humans for ruling creation ....Ge 1:28
                                               Ps 8:6–8
      —To kings for ruling people ....Ps 72:1
                                               Ro 13:1–5
      —To prophets for speaking ....Dt 18:18
      —To disciples for casting out demons ......Mk 6:7,13
      —To apostles for forgiving sins ....Jn 20:22–23
      —To apostles for founding the church ......Mt 16:19
                                               Mt 18:18
      —To church leaders for building the church ...2Co 10:8
                                               2Co 13:10
                                               Eph 4:11–13
                                               Tit 2:15
      —To saints for judging the world 1Co 6:2–3
   2. Exercised by humans
      —Often done by exerting power ....Mt 20:25
                                               Mk 10:42
                                               Lk 22:25
      —Christian authority defined by service .....Mt 20:26–28
                                               Mk 10:43–45
                                               Lk 22:26–27
      See SERVANT
   3. Misused by humans
      —In ascribing power to ourselves, not God ...Dt 8:10–18
      —In depending on ourselves, not God ....Ps 147:10–11
      —In oppressing the poor ....Ps 10:2–11
      —In exalting power rather than wisdom .....Ecc 9:12–18
C. Divine authority
   1. Authority of God
      —Power and authority ascribed to him 2Ch 20:6
                                               Ps 66:3,5–7
                                               Jude 25
      —His authority may not be questioned ......Ro 9:20–21
      —Even Satan under his control ....Job 1:6–12
                                               Job 2:1–7
   2. Authority of Jesus
      a. While on earth
         —To cast out evil spirits ....Mk 1:34
         —To preach the word ....Mt 7:28–29
         —To forgive sins ....Mk 2:5–12
         —To give eternal life ....Jn 17:2
         —To control nature ....Mk 4:39–41
         —To raise the dead ....Jn 10:17–18
                                               Jn 11:23–27,38–44
         —To judge ....Jn 5:27–30
      b. Now in heaven
         —All authority given to him ....Mt 28:18
                                               Php 2:9–11
         —Has authority at God's right hand .....Eph 1:20–23
                                               Col 2:9–10
         —Controls history ....Rev 5:1–5
         —Is ruler of the kings of the earth ......Rev 1:5
         —Is King of kings and Lord of lords .....Rev 17:14
                                               Rev 19:16

AWE
—Reverence for the Lord
See FEAR

BAASHA
—Killed Nadab to become king of Israel 1Ki 15:27–28
—Killed rest of Jeroboam's family 1Ki 15:29–30
—Fought against Asa of Judah 1Ki 15:16–22,32
—Evil reign for twenty-four years 1Ki 15:33–34
—Jehu prophesied against him 1Ki 16:1–4
—Family killed by Zimri 1Ki 16:9–13

BABYLON
A. Identity and early history of the city
   —Descendants of Ham ....Ge 10:6,8–10
   —City is built by Nimrod ....Ge 10:10
   —Rebellion against God at the tower of Babel ....Ge 11:1–9
B. The nation of Babylon
   1. Significant Babylonians
      —Marduk-Baladan: paid visit to Hezekiah 2Ki 20:12–13

—Nebuchadnezzar 2Ki 24:1
See NEBUCHADNEZZAR
   —Nebuzaradan: commander of army 2Ki 24:8
   —Awel-Marduk: released Jehoiachin 2Ki 25:27
   —Belshazzar: saw handwriting on the wall ...Da 5:1
2. Chronological history
   —Under the control of Assyria 2Ki 17:24
   —Envoys visited Hezekiah 2Ki 20:12–18
   —Invaded Judah during Jehoiakim's reign ...2Ki 24:1–2
   —Exiles deported with Jehoiachin 2Ki 24:10–16
   —Nebuchadnezzar's dream ....Da 2:1–49
   —Nebuchadnezzar's image and fiery furnace ..Da 3:1–30
   —King Zedekiah's revolt 2Ch 36:13
   —Nebuchadnezzar marched on Jerusalem ...Jer 52:4–5
   —Jerusalem totally destroyed 2Ki 25:4,8–10
                                          Jer 52:12–14
   —A second group deported 2Ki 25:11
                                          2Ch 36:20
   —Nebuchadnezzar's madness and restoration ..Da 4:1–37
   —A third group deported ....Jer 52:24–27
   —King Belshazzar's banquet ....Da 5:1–4
   —Medes took over Babylon ....Da 5:30–31
3. Jews in Babylon
   —Three waves of exiles ....Jer 52:28–30
   —Daniel and friends in royal service ....Da 1:1–21
   —Ezekiel saw visions ....Eze 1:1–28
   —Jews encouraged to settle there ....Jer 29:1–7
   —Seventy years of exile ....Jer 25:11
                                          2Ch 36:21
   —Jews experienced grief ....Ps 137:1–6
   —Jews allowed to return under Persians 2Ch 36:22–23
                                          Ezr 1:1–4
4. Characteristics of the Babylonians
   a. A powerful nation
      —A naval power ....Isa 43:14
      —A military power ....Jer 5:15–17
                                          Jer 51:34
      —A worldwide kingdom ....Da 2:37–38
                                          Da 4:22
      —A glorious nation ....Da 4:28–30,36
      —A wealthy people ....Jer 51:13
   b. A wicked nation
      —They trusted in wickedness ....Isa 47:10
      —They were idolatrous ....Jer 50:38
      —They engaged in sacrilegious feasting ..Da 5:1–3
      —They were cruel ....Isa 14:4,16–17
                                          Hab 1:6–7
      —They showed arrogance against God ...Isa 14:13–14
5. Prophecies concerning Babylon
   —They will conquer the world ....Jer 21:3–10
                                          Jer 27:1–11
                                          Eze 21:18–23
                                          Eze 29:19
   —They will be destroyed ....Isa 13:1—14:23
                                          Isa 14:3–22
                                          Isa 21:1–10
                                          Isa 47:1–15
                                          Jer 50:1—51:58
C. New Testament references to Babylon
1. As a symbol of the Roman Empire 1Pe 5:13
2. As a symbol of the power of the antichrist
   —Inspires people to sin ....Rev 14:8
                                          Rev 18:2–5
   —Persecutes the church ....Rev 17:5–6
                                          Rev 18:24
   —Makes war with the Lamb ....Rev 17:9–18
   —Will be destroyed completely ....Rev 18:2–10,16–24

BALAAM
A. Personal data
   —Son of Beor ....Nu 22:5
   —Lived in Mesopotamia ....Dt 23:4
   —Considered a prophet 2Pe 2:16
   —Killed by Israelites ....Nu 31:8
                                          Jos 13:22
B. His history
   —Asked by Balak to curse Israelites ......Nu 22:4–8
   —Commanded by God not to go ....Nu 22:9–13
   —Asked by Balak a second time ....Nu 22:15–17
   —Permitted to go ....Nu 22:18–20
   —Met by an angel on the way ....Nu 22:21–35
   —Uttered blessings instead of curses ....Nu 23:1—24:10

2. Discussion in Paul's letters
—Physical circumcision means nothing 1Co 7:19
Gal 5:6
Col 3:11
—Circumcision not needed for salvation .....Ro 4:9–12
Gal 2:2–3
1Co 7:18
—True circumcision involves obedience ......Ro 2:25
—True circumcision is of the heart ....Ro 2:28–29
—True worshipers are true circumcision ....Php 3:3
—Christians are circumcised in baptism .....Col 2:11–12

CITY

A. Major cities mentioned in the Bible
—Antioch ....Ac 11:19–20
—Athens ....Ac 17:15
—Babel/Babylon ....Ge 11:9
Da 4:30
—Caesarea ....Ac 23:23
—Corinth ....Ac 18:1
—Damascus 2Sa 8:6
—Ephesus ....Ac 19:1
—Jericho ....Jos 6:1
—Jerusalem 2Sa 5:6–7
—Nineveh ....Jnh 1:2
—Philippi ....Ac 16:12
—Rome ....Ac 28:14
—Samaria 1Ki 16:24
—Sodom and Gomorrah ....Ge 18:20

B. Types of Israelite cities
—The capital city 2Sa 5:6–9
1Ki 16:24
—Cities for defense 2Ch 11:5–12
—Chariot cities 2Ch 1:14
—Cities for storage 2Ch 8:4,6
—Cities for the Levites ....Nu 35:1–5,7
—Cities of refuge ....Nu 35:6–15
Dt 19:1–3
Jos 20:1–9

C. Critical importance of cities
1. Defense of cities
—Usually fortified with walls ....Nu 13:28
Dt 3:5
Jos 6:5
2Ch 11:5–13
—Besieged by armies 1Ki 20:1
2Ki 16:5
—Kingdom fell when the city was entered 2Ki 17:5–6
2Ki 25:1–7
2. Cities as centers for missions
a. Jonah sent to Nineveh ....Jnh 1:2
b. Disciples evangelized cities ....Mt 10:23
c. Paul preached in cities
—Antioch ....Ac 11:25–26
—Paphos on Cyprus ....Ac 13:6–12
—Antioch of Pisidia ....Ac 13:14–49
—Philippi ....Ac 16:12–40
—Thessalonica 1Th 1:7–10
—Corinth ....Ac 18:1–17
—Ephesus ....Ac 19:1–41

D. The city used as a symbol
—Of total rebellion against God ....Rev 18:1–24
See BABYLON
—Of the church and of heaven ....Heb 12:22–23
Rev 21:1–4

See JERUSALEM

CLEANNESS

A. The Old Testament regarding clean/unclean
1. How did one become unclean?
—By eating unclean foods ....Lev 11:1–23
—Through childbirth ....Lev 12:1–8
—Through skin diseases ....Lev 13:1–14:57
—Through discharges from the body ....Lev 15:1–33
—By touching a dead body ....Nu 5:2
—By worshiping false gods ....Jer 13:25–27
Hos 8:5
—Through a life of sin ....Isa 64:5–7
2. How could one become clean?
—By washing self and clothes ....Ex 19:10–14
Ex 30:18–21
Lev 22:6
—By certain sacrifices and ceremonies ......Lev 12:6–8
Lev 14:1–11

—By turning to the Lord ....Ps 51:2,7
Isa 4:4
Isa 6:5–7

B. Inward cleansing from sin
1. The need for such cleansing ....Mt 23:25–28
2. God's promise for such cleansing ....Jer 33:8
Eze 36:25,33
3. The process of such cleansing
—The believer must ask for it ....Ps 51:2,7
1Jn 1:9
—It takes place in the heart ....Ps 24:3–4
Mk 7:18–23
—It occurs through Christ's blood ....Heb 9:14
Heb 10:19–22
1Jn 1:7
—It occurs through the word of God ....Eph 5:25–27
4. The results of such cleansing
—It leads to a life of holiness 2Co 7:1
—It leads to a life of purity 1Jn 3:3
—It leads to a life of love 1Pe 1:22

CLOTHING

A. Purposes and uses of clothing
1. Clothing for natural uses
—To cover nakedness ....Ge 3:7,21
—To keep warm ....Pr 31:21
—To trade in business ....Pr 31:24
Ac 16:14
2. Clothing for religious purposes
—To use in special service to God ....Ex 28:1–5
—To symbolize a message from God 1Ki 11:29–32
—To appoint a prophet as successor 1Ki 19:19
2Ki 2:13–14
3. Clothing used for display
—Special favor to a child ....Ge 37:3–4
—Honor to a citizen ....Est 6:11
—One's wealth ....Mt 11:8
—One's power ....Ac 12:21
—One's position as ruler ....Ge 41:42
—One's self-righteousness ....Mt 23:5
—Mourning ....Ge 37:34
2Sa 3:31
Job 1:20
—Sorrow for sin ....Ezr 9:3
—Shock ....Mk 14:63
Ac 14:14

B. Significant garments in the Bible
—Garments sewn by God for Adam and Eve ....Ge 3:21
—The robe of Joseph from his father ....Ge 37:3–4
—The garments stolen by Achan ....Jos 7:20–21
—The purple robe put on Jesus ....Mk 15:17
—The seamless garment of Jesus at the cross ...Mt 27:35
Mk 15:24
Jn 19:23–24

C. Clothing used as a symbol
—Taking off a garment means putting off sin ....Eph 4:22
Col 3:9
—Putting on a garment means putting on Jesus ...Ro 13:14
Gal 3:27
—Receiving a new garment symbolizes forgiveness ..Zec 3:3–5
Mt 22:11–13
Rev 3:5
—Being clothed with white robes in heaven .....Rev 7:9,13–14

COMFORT

—Consolation and strength in a time of need
A. Related theme
COMFORT is a theme of Nahum ....Na 2:2
B. People who need comfort
—Those grieving ....Ge 37:33–35
Job 2:11
Isa 61:2
Mt 5:4
—Those in a new country ....Ru 2:13
—Those facing troubles ....Ps 71:21
Isa 51:19
—Those downcast 2Co 7:6
—Those being punished for sin ....Isa 40:1
La 1:9,17
2Co 2:6–7

C. Sources of comfort
1. Human comfort given by

COVETING

—The sinful desire for what belongs to someone else; greed

CREATION

C. Later references
—His dead body raised another one to life 2Ki 13:20–21
—Jesus compared his rejection to Elisha's .... Lk 4:24,27

ELIZABETH
—Wife of Zechariah; barren .... Lk 1:5–7
—Relative of the virgin Mary .... Lk 1:36
—Gave birth to John the Baptist .... Lk 1:11–23,57–58
—Visited by Mary .... Lk 1:39–45

ELKANAH
—Husband of Hannah and Peninnah 1Sa 1:1–2
—Worshiped every year at Shiloh 1Sa 1:3–8
—Father of Samuel 1Sa 1:19–20

ENCOURAGEMENT
—Giving support and inspiration
A. Related theme
—ENCOURAGEMENT is a theme of Zechariah ..... Zec 10:12
B. Human encouragement
  1. Those who need encouragement
    —Leaders .... Dt 1:38
                                              Dt 3:28
    —The oppressed .... Isa 1:17
    —The persecuted .... Ac 14:21–22
                                              1Th 3:1–3
    —All Christians .... Ac 20:1
                                              Heb 3:13
  2. Those who do the encouraging
    —Kings 2Sa 19:7
                                              2Ch 32:6–8
    —Prophets .... Ac 15:32
    —Apostles .... Ac 16:40
                                              Ac 20:2
                                              1Th 2:11–12
    —Church pastors .... Col 4:7–8
                                              2Ti 4:2
                                              Tit 2:15
                                              1Pe 5:12
    —Specially gifted Christians .... Ro 12:6,8
    —All Christians to each other .... Ro 1:12
                                              1Th 4:18
                                              Heb 10:25
C. Divine encouragement
    —God encourages us .... Ps 10:17
                                              2Th 2:16–17
                                              Heb 6:17–18
    —Christ encourages us .... Php 2:1
                                              2Th 2:16–17
    —The Holy Spirit encourages us .... Ac 9:31
    —The Scriptures encourage us .... Ro 15:4
                                              Heb 12:5

ENEMY
A. Types of enemies
    —Heathen nations .... Jos 5:13
                                              1Sa 4:3
                                              Jer 12:7
    —Personal adversaries 2Sa 4:8
                                              1Ki 21:20
                                              Est 7:6
                                              Pr 16:7
    —Spiritual forces .... Eph 6:12
                                              1Pe 5:8
    —Death 1Co 15:26
B. Reactions to one's enemies
  1. In Israelite history
    —Destroyed in war
    See WARFARE
    —Occasionally treated kindly 1Sa 26:7–12
  2. In the psalms
    —Prayers for deliverance from them ..... Ps 59:1
                                              Ps 64:1–2
                                              Ps 143:9
    —Prayers for God to judge them .... Ps 35:4–8,26
                                              Ps 58:6–9
                                              Ps 69:22–28
                                              Ps 109:6–15
  3. In the New Testament
    —Jesus prayed for them .... Lk 23:34
    —Stephen prayed for them .... Ac 7:60
C. Commands from God regarding enemies
    —Treat them with kindness .... Pr 25:21–22
                                              Ro 12:19–21

—Pray for them .... Mt 5:44
—Love them .... Mt 5:44
                                              Lk 6:27,35

ENOCH
A. Son of Cain .... Ge 4:17–18
B. Descendant of Seth .... Ge 5:19–20
    —Walked with God .... Ge 5:22–24
    —Taken by God to heaven without dying .... Ge 5:24
    —An example of faith .... Heb 11:5

ENVY
—Intense feeling of ill will or malice
A. In the Old Testament
    —Examples of envy .... Ge 37:11
                                              Nu 16:1–3
                                              Ps 106:16–18
    —The command not to envy .... Pr 3:31
                                              Pr 23:17
                                              Pr 24:1
B. In the New Testament
    —Examples of envy .... Mt 27:18
                                              Mk 15:10
                                              Php 1:15,17
    —Negative effects of envy .... Mk 7:20–23
                                              Jas 3:14,16
    —A positive result from envy .... Ro 11:13–14
    —Envy in a list of vices .... Ro 1:29
                                              Gal 5:21
                                              1Pe 2:1
    —Love does not envy 1Co 13:4

EPHESUS
—Paul left Priscilla and Aquila there .... Ac 18:19
—Apollos learned about Christ there .... Ac 18:24–26
—Paul converted some disciples of John there .. Ac 19:1–7
—Paul spent two years there .... Ac 19:8–22
—Riot over Paul's evangelism there .... Ac 19:23–41
—Paul wrote letter to the church there .... Eph 1:1
—Timothy ministered there 1Ti 1:3
—Tychicus ministered there 2Ti 4:12
—Church there lost its first love .... Rev 2:1–7

EPHRAIM
A. Second son of Joseph .... Ge 41:52
                                              Ge 46:20
    —Name means "twice fruitful" .... Ge 41:52
    —Blessed by Jacob ahead of Manasseh ..... Ge 48:12–20
B. Tribe descended from Ephraim
    —Numbered .... Nu 1:33
                                              Nu 26:37
    —Blessed by Moses .... Dt 33:17
    —Allotted land in Canaan .... Jos 16:4–9
                                              Eze 48:5
    —Failed to possess the land .... Jos 16:10
                                              Jdg 1:29
    —Quarreled with Gideon .... Jdg 8:1–3
    —Quarreled with Jephthah .... Jdg 12:1–6
    —Many joined kingdom of Judah during Asa's
      reform 2Ch 15:8–9
C. A synonym for the northern kingdom .... Isa 7:17
                                              Hos 5:5

ESAU
A. His birth
    —Firstborn of Isaac .... Ge 25:25
    —Twin with Jacob .... Ge 25:26
    —Also called Edom .... Ge 25:30
B. Significant events
    —Became a hunter .... Ge 25:27
    —Sold his birthright .... Ge 25:29–34
    —His blessing stolen by Jacob .... Ge 27:1–40
    —Wanted to kill Jacob .... Ge 27:41
    —Married pagan women .... Ge 26:34
                                              Ge 28:6–9
    —Reconciled to Jacob .... Ge 33:1–17
    —With Jacob, buried Isaac .... Ge 35:29
C. His descendants .... Ge 36:1–43
    See EDOMITES
D. Later significance of Esau
    —Descendants to be obliterated .... Ob 1–21
                                              Jer 49:7–22
    —Jacob chosen over him .... Mal 1:2–3
    —Demonstrates God's purpose of election .. Ro 9:11–13
    —His rejection for not repenting .... Heb 12:16–17

GOLIATH
—A Philistine giant 1Sa 17:4–7
—Taunted the Israelite army 1Sa 17:8–11
—David offered to fight him 1Sa 17:32–37
—David killed him 1Sa 17:48–51
—David obtained his sword 1Sa 21:9

GOMORRAH
See SODOM AND GOMORRAH

GOSPEL
—The good news of salvation for humanity
A. Terms used to describe the gospel
   —The gospel of God ....Ro 1:1
   —The good news of God's grace ....Ac 20:24
   —The gospel of God's Son ....Ro 1:9
   —The gospel of our Lord Jesus 2Th 1:8
   —The gospel of Christ ....Ro 15:19
   —The gospel that displays the glory of Christ ...2Co 4:4
   —The good news about Jesus Christ ....Mk 1:1
   —The gospel of the kingdom ....Mt 24:14
   —The gospel of salvation ....Eph 1:13
   —The gospel of peace ....Eph 6:15
   —The eternal gospel ....Rev 14:6
B. The gospel in the Old Testament
   —First revealed to Adam and Eve ....Ge 3:15
   —Revealed to Abraham ....Ge 12:2–3
      Ge 18:18
      Ge 22:18
      Gal 3:8
   —Revealed to Israel through prophets ....Isa 40:9
      Isa 52:7–10
      Isa 61:6
      Ro 1:1–2
C. The gospel in the New Testament
  1. The proclaimers of the gospel
   —The angel at Christ's birth ....Lk 2:10
   —John the Baptist ....Lk 3:18
   —Jesus Christ ....Mk 1:14–15
      Lk 4:43
   —The twelve disciples ....Lk 9:6
   —The twelve apostles ....Ac 5:42
   —Peter and John ....Ac 8:25
      Ac 15:7
   —Philip ....Ac 8:12,40
   —Paul ....Ac 14:7
      Ro 15:19
   —Unnamed missionaries 1Pe 1:12
   —Our responsibility ....Mt 24:14
      Mt 28:19
  2. The content of the gospel
   —The basic story about Jesus ....Mk 1:1
      1Co 15:1–8,11
   —Jesus is the Christ ....Ac 5:42
   —Humans should repent ....Mk 1:15
   —Salvation is by faith in Jesus ....Ro 1:16–17
   —God gives us his grace ....Ac 20:24
   —Both Jew and Gentile can be saved ....Eph 3:6–7
   —Jesus will return as judge ....Ro 2:16
   —How believers should live ....Php 1:27
  3. The characteristics of the gospel
   —It reveals the glory of Christ 2Co 4:4
   —It is eternal 1Pe 1:25
      Rev 14:6
   —It demonstrates God's power ....Ro 1:16
   —It calls us 2Th 2:14
   —It saves us 1Co 15:2
   —It gives us peace ....Eph 6:15
   —It gives us hope ....Col 1:23
   —It gives us life 2Ti 1:10
   —It grows and bears fruit ....Col 1:6
   —It tolerates no rival ....Gal 1:6–9
  4. The response to the gospel
   —We should believe it ....Heb 4:2
   —We should obey it 2Co 9:13
      2Th 1:8
      Heb 4:6
   —We should not be ashamed of it ....Ro 1:16
   —We should live in line with its truth ....Gal 2:14
      Php 1:27
   —We should serve it 2Co 8:18
   —We should continue in it ....Col 1:23
   —We should promote it 1Co 9:16

   —We should defend it ....Php 1:7,16
      Jude 3
   —We should preach it ....Mk 16:15
      Ac 8:4
      Ro 15:19–20
      1Co 9:16
   —We may have to suffer for it 2Ti 1:8
      2Ti 2:8–9

GOVERNMENT
—The rule of humans by other humans
A. Phases of civil government among the Israelites/Jews
  1. Rule by the fathers (patriarchs)
   —Abram ....Ge 14:13–16
   —Isaac ....Ge 26:26–32
   —Jacob ....Ge 34:5,30–31
      Ge 46:5–27
  2. Rule by God's chosen leaders
   —Moses ....Ex 3:7–12
      Ex 18:13–26
   —Moses and Aaron ....Nu 17:1–13
   —Joshua ....Dt 31:1–8
      Jos 1:1–11
  3. Rule by God's chosen judges
    See JUDGE, JUDGMENT
  4. Rule through God's chosen kings
   —Israel asked for a king 1Sa 8:4–22
   —Israel's first king, Saul 1Sa 10:20–26
   —David anointed as king 1Sa 16:1–13
   —David's line to be the royal line 2Sa 7:8–16
    See KING
  5. Rule by foreign kings
   —The Babylonians 2Ch 36:15–21
      Da 1:1–6
   —The Persians ....Ezr 1:1–4
      Isa 44:28—45:6
   —The Herods of Idumea ....Mt 2:1–8,16–22
   —The Romans ....Mt 27:11–14
      Jn 18:28–40
B. Principles of government
  1. God and human government
   —God is the real ruler ....Dt 33:5
      Jdg 8:23
      1Ch 29:23
      Ps 29:10–11
      Isa 33:22
   —God rules through anointed servants ......Ps 45:6–7
      Isa 45:1
  2. Humans in the government
   —They derive authority from God ....Da 4:17
      Jn 19:11
      Ro 13:1,4
   —God's people may serve pagan governments . Ne 2:1–9
      Ne 5:14–18
      Est 8:1–2
      Da 1:17–21
C. Our responsibility to government
   —We must respect it 1Sa 14:6–7
      1Sa 26:7–11
      1Pe 2:17
   —We must submit to it ....Ro 13:1,5
      Tit 3:1
      1Pe 2:13–14
   —We must support it with taxes ....Mt 22:15–21
      Ro 13:6–7
   —We must pray for it 1Ti 2:1–2
   —Occasionally we may have to disobey it ....Ac 5:29

GRACE
—God's free and undeserved favor
A. Related themes
  GRACE is a theme of:
   —Genesis ....Ge 25:33
   —Judges ....Jdg 6:13
   —Job ....Job 42:10
   —Jonah ....Jnh 3:10
   —Romans ....Ro 11:6
B. Grace comes as a gift
   —From God ....Eph 2:8
      1Pe 5:10
   —From the Father ....Ps 84:11
      Jas 1:17

—Performed by Jesus with physical healing . . . . . Mk 2:5–11

HEART
—The center of the human being
A. Basic concept of the heart
  1. The wellspring of all life . . . . Pr 4:23
                                               Lk 6:45
  2. Combined with other basic human elements
    —The heart and soul . . . . Dt 6:5
                                          1Sa 14:7
                                         Mt 22:37
    —The heart and body . . . . Ps 16:9
    —The heart and mind . . . . Ps 26:2
                                         Mt 22:37
                                         Rev 2:23
    —The heart and spirit . . . . Ps 51:10,17
                                         Eze 18:31
    —The heart and flesh . . . . Ps 73:26
                                           Ps 84:2
    —The heart and thoughts . . . . Ps 139:23
    —The heart and understanding . . . . Pr 3:5
B. What the heart controls
  1. Human emotions
    —The glad heart . . . . Ex 4:14
                                         Ac 2:26
    —The singing heart . . . . Eph 5:19
    —The heart that loves . . . . Dt 6:5
                                         SS 3:1–3
    —The heart that takes delight . . . . Ecc 2:10
                                         Jer 15:16
    —The excited heart . . . . Lk 24:32
    —The courageous heart 1Sa 10:26
                                         Ps 27:14
    —The heart that is encouraged . . . . Col 2:2
                                         2Th 2:17
    —The thankful heart . . . . Col 3:16
    —The repentant heart . . . . Ps 51:17
    —The humble heart . . . . Mt 11:29
    —The compassionate heart . . . . Lk 7:13
    —The anxious heart . . . . Pr 12:25
    —The discouraged heart . . . . Jos 2:11
    —The troubled heart . . . . Jn 12:27
    —The grieving heart 1Sa 2:33
                                         La 2:18
    —The tormented heart . . . . La 2:11
    —The broken heart . . . . Eze 21:6
    —The heavy heart . . . . Pr 25:20
    —The anguished heart . . . . Isa 65:14
                                         Jer 4:19
                                         Ro 9:2
    —The fearful heart . . . . Dt 28:67
                                         Jos 5:1
    —The angry heart . . . . Ps 39:3
                                         Pr 19:3
  2. The human will
    —To do according to one's heart 1Sa 2:35
                                         1Ch 28:2
    —To decide in the heart 2Ch 6:7
    —To devote the heart 1Ch 22:19
    —To direct the heart 2Th 3:5
    —To turn the heart 1Ki 8:58
                                         Ps 119:36
    —To incline the heart . . . . Dt 5:29
    —To win over the heart 2Sa 19:14
    —To yield the heart . . . . Jos 24:23
    —To agree with one heart . . . . Jer 32:39
                                         Ac 4:32
    —To be moved in the heart . . . . Ex 35:21
    —The purposes of the heart . . . . Jer 23:20
    —The motives of the heart 1Co 4:5
    —The desires of the heart . . . . Ps 21:2
                                         Ro 10:1
    —The willing heart 2Ch 29:31
    —The unrepentant heart . . . . Ro 2:5
    —The hardened heart . . . . Ex 4:21
                                         Pr 28:14
  3. The human intelligence
    —To acknowledge in the heart . . . . Dt 4:39
    —To know in the heart . . . . Dt 8:5
    —To take something to heart . . . . Ex 7:23
                                         Ecc 7:2
    —To fix words in the heart . . . . Dt 11:18

—To lay up words in the heart . . . . Job 22:22
                                         Pr 4:21
—To search the heart . . . . Ps 4:4
—To say in the heart . . . . Ro 10:6
—To muse in the heart . . . . Ps 77:6
—To ponder in the heart . . . . Lk 2:19
—To think in the heart . . . . Mk 2:8
—To understand in the heart . . . . Pr 2:2
—To meditate in the heart . . . . Ps 19:14
—To pray in the heart . . . . Ge 24:45
                                         1Sa 1:13
—To believe in the heart . . . . Ro 10:9
—To be wise in the heart . . . . Pr 2:10
                                         Pr 10:8
—To doubt in the heart . . . . Mk 11:23
—To harbor deceit in the heart . . . . Pr 26:24
                                         Jer 17:9
—To devise evil in the heart . . . . Ps 140:2
—The thoughts of the heart . . . . Ge 6:5
                                         Lk 2:35
C. Key elements in the human heart
  1. Characteristics of the unregenerate heart
    —Proud . . . . Pr 18:12
    —Foolish . . . . Pr 12:23
    —Deceitful . . . . Jer 17:9
    —Rebellious . . . . Jer 5:23
    —Perverse . . . . Pr 11:20
    —Evil . . . . Ge 6:5
    —Wicked . . . . Pr 6:18
    —Callous . . . . Ps 119:70
    —Malicious . . . . Ps 28:3
    —Hardened . . . . Eph 4:18
    —Darkened . . . . Ro 1:21
    —Deluded . . . . Isa 44:20
    —Unrepentant . . . . Ro 2:5
    —Unbelieving . . . . Heb 3:12
    —Gone astray . . . . Ps 95:10
    —Devoted to idols . . . . Eze 11:21
    —Filled with schemes to do wrong . . . . Ecc 8:11
    —Filled with madness . . . . Ecc 9:3
    —Far from God . . . . Isa 29:13
                                         Mk 7:6
  2. What the regenerate heart does
    —Cries out for the living God . . . . Ps 84:2
    —Seeks God . . . . Ps 119:2,10
    —Responds to God 2Ki 22:19
    —Trusts in the Lord . . . . Pr 3:5
    —Loves the Lord . . . . Dt 6:5
                                         Mt 22:37
    —Praises the Lord . . . . Ps 9:1
    —Sings to the Lord . . . . Ps 30:12
    —Rejoices in the Lord 1Sa 2:1
    —Rejoices in salvation . . . . Ps 13:5
    —Is grateful to God . . . . Col 3:16
    —Obeys God's law . . . . Ps 119:34,69,112
                                         Eph 6:6
    —Hides God's word within . . . . Ps 119:11
    —Is on fire for God's word . . . . Jer 20:9
    —Meditates on God and his word . . . . Ps 19:14
    —Is upright . . . . Ps 7:10
    —Speaks the truth . . . . Ps 15:2
    —Is steadfast and secure . . . . Ps 57:7
                                         Ps 112:7–8
    —Is pure . . . . Ps 24:4
                                         Mt 5:8
    —Is wise . . . . Pr 10:8
    —Is sincere . . . . Ac 2:46
                                         Heb 10:22
    —Is unafraid and courageous . . . . Ps 27:3,14
    —Is contrite . . . . Ps 51:17
    —Is circumcised . . . . Dt 10:16
                                         Ro 2:29
    —Walks blamelessly . . . . Ps 101:2
    —Loves others 1Pe 1:22
D. God's relationship to the human heart
    —He knows it 1Sa 16:7
    —He searches it . . . . Ps 7:9
                                         Jer 17:10
    —He tests it 1Ch 29:17
                                         1Th 2:4
    —He influences it . . . . Ezr 7:27
    —He directs it . . . . Pr 21:1

See also SANCTIFICATION

—Elijah told to anoint him king 1Ki 19:16
—Anointed by servant of Elisha 2Ki 9:1–13
—Appointed to obliterate house of Ahab 2Ki 9:6–10
—Killed Joram and Ahaziah 2Ki 9:14–29
....2Ch 22:7–9
—Killed Jezebel 2Ki 9:30–37
—Killed relatives of Ahab 2Ki 10:1–17
—Killed ministers of Baal 2Ki 10:18–29
—His death 2Ki 10:30–36

JEPHTHAH
—Judge from Gilead ....Jdg 11:1–3
—Delivered Israel from Ammon ....Jdg 11:4–33
—Made a rash vow affecting his daughter ....Jdg 11:30–40
—Punished the Ephraimites ....Jdg 12:1–6
—His death ....Jdg 12:7

JEREMIAH
—Prophet to kingdom of Judah ....Jer 1:1–3
—Called by the Lord ....Jer 1:4–19
—Composed laments at Josiah's death 2Ch 35:25
—His life threatened for continuing to prophesy ...Jer 11:18–23
....Jer 26:1–16
—Put in stocks ....Jer 20:1–3
—Opposed by Hananiah ....Jer 28:1–17
—Wrote scroll that was burned by king ....Jer 36:1–26
—Rewrote the scroll ....Jer 36:27–32
—Imprisoned; Zedekiah sought his advice ......Jer 37:1–21
—Charged with treason and thrown into cistern .Jer 38:1–13
—Zedekiah sought his advice again ....Jer 38:14–27
—Purchased field just before Jerusalem destroyed .Jer 32:1–15
—Taken with some of the people to Egypt ....Jer 43:1–7

JERICHO
A. Identity
  —Located in a valley ....Dt 34:3
  —Near the Jordan River ....Nu 33:50
  —Called "City of the Palms" ....Dt 34:3
B. History of the city
  1. In the Old Testament
    —Rahab lived there ....Jos 2:1
    —Israelites spied it out ....Jos 2:1–21
    —Israelites camped opposite it ....Jos 3:16
    —Israelites marched around it ....Jos 6:1–15
    —Its walls collapsed ....Jos 6:20
    —All except Rahab destroyed ....Jos 6:21–25
    —Joshua pronounced curse on rebuilding it .Jos 6:26
    —Curse fulfilled when Hiel rebuilt it 1Ki 16:34
    —A company of prophets stationed there ...2Ki 2:5
    —It was reinhabited 2Ch 28:15
    ....Ne 3:2
  2. In the New Testament
    —Good Samaritan headed toward it ....Lk 10:30–35
    —Jesus healed Bartimaeus there ....Mk 10:46–52
    ....Lk 18:35–43
    —Jesus healed two blind men there ....Mt 20:29–34
    —Zacchaeus lived there ....Lk 19:1–10

JEROBOAM
A. First king of the northern kingdom
  —An official of king Solomon 1Ki 11:26–28
  —Ahijah prophesied he would be king 1Ki 11:29–39
  —Fled to Egypt 1Ki 11:40
  —Led rebellion against Rehoboam 1Ki 12:18–19
  —Became king of the northern kingdom 1Ki 12:20
  —Instituted idolatry 1Ki 12:25–33
  —Judged for idolatry 1Ki 13:1–6
  ....1Ki 14:1–18
  —His death 1Ki 14:19–20
B. Son of Jehoash; king of Israel 2Ki 14:23–29
  —Denounced by Amos ....Am 7:10–11

JERUB-BAAL
See GIDEON

JERUSALEM
A. Related theme
  JERUSALEM is a theme of 2 Samuel 2Sa 6:12
B. Important names for this city
  —Salem ....Ge 14:18
  ....Ps 76:2
  —The Jebusite city ....Jos 18:28
  —Jebus 1Ch 11:4
  —Jerusalem 2Sa 5:6
  —Zion 2Sa 5:7
  ....Ps 48:12

—The City of David 2Sa 6:12,16
....1Ki 2:10
—The city of the Great King ....Ps 48:2
—The city of God ....Ps 46:4
....Ps 87:3
—The city of the LORD ....Isa 60:14
—The City of Righteousness ....Isa 1:26
—The City of Truth ....Zec 8:3
—The holy city ....Ne 11:1,18
....Isa 48:2
—THE LORD IS THERE ....Eze 48:35
—Moriah ....Ge 22:1–2
....2Ch 3:1
—Ariel ....Isa 29:1
C. Significant historical events of Jerusalem
  —Abraham's "sacrifice" of Isaac ....Ge 22:1–18
  —King of Jerusalem conquered by Joshua ......Jos 10:1–14
  —City given to the tribe of Benjamin ....Jos 18:28
  —Conquered by David; became his capital 2Sa 5:6–10
  —Temple built there 2Ch 3:1
  —Became capital of the southern kingdom 1Ki 14:21
  —Destroyed by Nebuchadnezzar 2Ch 36:19
  —The center of Jewish life after exile ....Ezr 1:5
  ....Mt 2:1,3
  —Jesus entered it as king ....Mt 21:9–10
  —Jesus was crucified there ....Lk 9:31
  ....Lk 24:18
  —Holy Spirit poured out there ....Ac 2:1–5
  —Gospel spread out from there ....Lk 24:47
  ....Ac 1:8
  —First council of the church held there ....Ac 15:1–2
  ....Gal 2:1–5
  —Jesus predicted its destruction ....Lk 19:42–44
  ....Lk 21:20–24
D. Spiritual significance of Jerusalem
  —The city chosen by God 1Ki 11:13
  —The place where God put his Name ....Dt 12:11
  ....1Ki 14:21
  —The city that Jews prayed toward 1Ki 8:44
  ....Da 6:10
  —The place from which God's word comes ....Isa 2:3
  —The place from which God rules ....Ps 48:1–3,12–14
  ....Ps 99:1–2
  —The place from which the Messiah rules ....Isa 9:6–7
  —The site of history's final battle ....Zec 14:1–5
  ....Rev 20:7–10
  —A symbol of the church ....Gal 4:26
  ....Heb 12:22
  —Heaven as the new Jerusalem ....Rev 3:12
  ....Rev 21:2,10–27

JESSE
—Grandson of Boaz and Ruth; father of David ......Ru 4:17–22
—Visited by Samuel 1Sa 16:1–13
—Had eight sons 1Sa 16:8–11
....1Sa 17:12
—Sent David to enter Saul's service 1Sa 16:18–20
—Sent David to visit his brothers at battle 1Sa 17:17–19

JESUS CHRIST
A. Related themes
  1. SON OF GOD is a theme of Mark ....Mk 14:61
  2. JESUS = GOD/MAN is a theme of:
    —John ....Jn 1:1
    —Hebrews ....Heb 4:15
  3. ACTION is a theme of Mark ....Mk 1:41
B. His divine nature
  1. Preexistence with God
    —Asserted in the Old Testament ....Isa 9:6–7
    ....Mic 5:2
    —Asserted in the New Testament ....Jn 1:1
    ....Php 2:6
    ....Col 1:15–17
    ....Rev 1:4,8
  2. Divine names ascribed to him
    —God ....Jn 1:1
    ....Heb 1:8
    ....1Jn 5:20
    —God the One and Only ....Jn 1:18
    —God over all ....Ro 9:5
    —Immanuel ("God with us") ....Isa 7:14
    ....Mt 1:23

—Moses sent out spies from there . . . . .Nu 13:1–2,26
    Dt 1:19–25
    Jos 14:6–7
—Israelites rebelled against the Lord there . . . . .Nu 14:1–45
    Dt 1:26–45
    Dt 9:23–24
—Israelites camped there again for many days . . . . . .Dt 1:46
—Miriam died there . . . . .Nu 20:1
—Moses struck the rock there to get water . . . . .Nu 20:2–12
—Joshua conquered that area . . . . .Jos 10:41
—Became southernmost town of Judah . . . . .Jos 15:3
    Eze 47:19

KETURAH
—Wife of Abraham after Sarah . . . . .Ge 25:1
—Also called Abraham's concubine 1Ch 1:32
—Mother of six sons . . . . .Ge 25:2

KINDNESS
—A hospitable, friendly attitude toward others
A. Related theme
    HOSPITALITY is a theme of 3 John 3Jn 8
B. Human kindness
  1. Expected of Christians
    —Commanded 2Co 6:6
    Gal 5:22
    Col 3:12
    2Pe 1:7
    —One aspect of the fruit of the Spirit . . . . . . .Gal 5:22
  2. Expressions of kindness
    —Showing forgiveness . . . . .Ge 50:21
    —Sparing someone's life . . . . .Jos 2:12–13
    —Healing the sick . . . . .Ac 4:9
    —Helping the needy .2Sa 9:1–7
    Pr 14:21,31
    Pr 19:17
    —Helping victims of injustice . . . . .Ge 40:14
    —Helping strangers .Ac 28:2
    Heb 13:1–2
    3Jn 5–8
C. Kindness of God
    —In giving us salvation . . . . .Tit 3:4
    —In being faithful to his promises 1Ki 3:6
    —In watching over us .Job 10:12
    —In showing compassion to us . . . . .Isa 54:8
    —In providing for needs . . . . .Ge 32:10
    Ru 2:20
    Hos 11:4
    Ac 14:17
    —In helping us in various life situations . . . . . . .Ge 39:21
    Ezr 9:9
See also MERCY

KING
A. Related theme
    KINGSHIP is a theme of 1 Samuel 1Sa 11:15
B. Human kings
  1. Examples of non-Israelite kings
    —Four kings warring against five . . . . .Ge 14:8–11
    —Melchizedek, king of Salem . . . . .Ge 14:18
    —List of the kings of Edom . . . . .Ge 36:32–39
    —Pharaoh, king of Egypt . . . . .Ex 1:8,15–22
    —Sihon and Og defeated . . . . .Nu 21:21–35
    —Various kings in Canaan defeated . . . . .Jos 8:1–2
    Jos 10:1–3,16–42
    Jos 12
    —David defeated various kings 2Sa 8:1–14
    —The king of Assyria took Israel 2Ki 17:3–6
    —King Nebuchadnezzar took Judah 2Ki 25:1–7
    —King Cyrus allowed return to Judah . . . . . . .Ezr 1:1–4
    —Nehemiah served King Artaxerxes . . . . .Ne 2:1
    —Esther became wife of King Xerxes . . . . . . .Est 2:1,17–18
    —Caesar as king . . . . .Jn 19:12,15
    —The kings of the earth . . . . .Ps 2:2
    Ps 102:15
    Ps 138:4
  2. The kings of Israel and Judah
    a. The beginning of kingship
      —The people asked for a king 1Sa 8:4–5
      —Samuel warned them 1Sa 8:10–18
      —Saul anointed as first king 1Sa 10:20–24
      1Sa 11:14–15

    b. Kings of the united kingdom
      —Saul (42 years) 1Sa 13:1
      See SAUL
      —David (40 years) 1Ki 2:11
      See DAVID
      —Solomon (40 years) 1Ki 11:42
      See SOLOMON
    c. The kings of Israel (in chronological order)
      —Jeroboam (22 years) 1Ki 12:25–14:20
      —Nadab (2 years) 1Ki 15:25–31
      —Baasha (24 years) 1Ki 15:32–16:7
      —Elah (2 years) .1Ki 16:8–14
      —Zimri (7 days) .1Ki 16:15–20
      —Tibni (with Omri) 1Ki 16:21–22
      —Omri (12 years) 1Ki 16:23–28
      —Ahab (22 years) 1Ki 16:29–22:40
      2Ch 18:1–34
      —Ahaziah (2 years) 1Ki 22:51–53
      2Ki 1:1–18
      —Joram (12 years) 2Ki 3:1–8:15
      —Jehu (28 years) 2Ki 9:6–10:36
      —Jehoahaz (17 years) 2Ki 13:1–9
      —Jehoash (16 years) 2Ki 13:10–25
      —Jeroboam II (41 years) 2Ki 14:23–29
      —Zechariah (6 months) 2Ki 15:8–12
      —Shallum (1 month) 2Ki 15:13–15
      —Menahem (10 years) 2Ki 15:16–22
      —Pekahiah (2 years) 2Ki 15:23–26
      —Pekah (20 years) 2Ki 15:27–31
      —Hoshea (9 years) 2Ki 17:1–6
      See also entries for each of these kings
    d. The kings of Judah (in chronological order)
      —Rehoboam (17 years) 1Ki 12:1–24
      1Ki 14:21–31
      2Ch 10:1–12:16
      —Abijah (3 years) 1Ki 15:1–8
      2Ch 13:1–14:1
      —Asa (41 years) .1Ki 15:9–24
      2Ch 14:2–16:14
      —Jehoshaphat (25 years) 1Ki 22:41–50
      2Ch 17:1–21:3
      —Jehoram (8 years) 2Ki 8:16–24
      2Ch 21:4–20
      —Ahaziah (1 year) 2Ki 8:25–29
      2Ch 22:1–9
      —Athaliah (7 years) 2Ki 11:1–21
      2Ch 22:10–23:21
      —Joash (40 years) 2Ki 12:1–21
      2Ch 24:1–27
      —Amaziah (29 years) 2Ki 14:1–22
      2Ch 25:1–28
      —Azariah/Uzziah (52 years) 2Ki 15:1–7
      2Ch 26:1–23
      —Jotham (16 years) 2Ki 15:32–38
      2Ch 27:1–8
      —Ahaz (16 years) 2Ki 16:1–20
      2Ch 28:1–27
      —Hezekiah (29 years) 2Ki 18:1–20:21
      2Ch 29:1–32:33
      Isa 36:1–39:8
      —Manasseh (55 years) 2Ki 21:1–18
      2Ch 33:1–20
      —Amon (2 years) 2Ki 21:19–26
      2Ch 33:21–25
      —Josiah (31 years) 2Ki 22:1–23:30
      2Ch 34:1–35:27
      —Jehoahaz (3 months) 2Ki 23:31–33
      2Ch 36:1–4
      —Jehoiakim (11 years) 2Ki 23:24–24:7
      2Ch 36:5–8
      —Jehoiachin (3 months) 2Ki 24:8–17
      2Ch 36:9–10
      —Zedekiah (11 years) 2Ki 24:18–25:26
      2Ch 36:11–21
      See also entries for each of these kings
C. God as a king
  1. God called a king
    —The King of heaven . . . . .Da 4:37
    —The King of glory .Ps 24:10
    —The eternal, immortal, invisible King 1Ti 1:17
    —The great King . . . . .Ps 47:2

—Defeated by King Saul 1Sa 14:47
—Defeated by David 2Sa 8:11–12
....1Ch 18:11
—Rebelled against Israel 2Ki 3:5
—Defeated by Joram and Jehoshaphat 2Ki 3:6–25
—Allied with Ammonites against Judah 2Ch 20:1
—They and Ammonites destroyed each other ...2Ch 20:22–24
—Raided the land of Israel 2Ki 13:20
—Allied against Jehoiakim 2Ki 24:1–2
D. Important data concerning them
 1. Before the time of the kings
  —Intermarried with Israelites ....Nu 25:1–3
  —Israelites did not pass through Moab ...Jdg 11:17–18
  —Not allowed to join Israelites ....Dt 23:3
....Ne 13:1–3
  —Moses died on Mount Pisgah in Moab ....Dt 34:1–5
  —Elimelek and Naomi lived there ....Ru 1:1–5
 2. During the time of the kings
  —David brought his parents there 1Sa 22:3–4
  —Solomon intermarried with them 1Ki 11:1
  —Israelites worshiped their gods 1Ki 11:7
  —Paid tribute to Ahab 2Ki 3:4
 3. Numerous Jews intermarried with them ....Ezr 9:1
....Ne 13:23–27
 4. Prophecies concerning their destruction ....Isa 15:1—16:14
....Jer 48:1–47
....Eze 25:8–11
....Am 2:1–3
....Zep 2:8–11

MONEY
See THE RICH AND THE POOR; STEWARDSHIP

MONTH
—Twelve time segments per year, based on the moon
—Aviv or Nisan, the first month ....Ex 13:4
....Ne 2:1
—Ziv or Iyyar, the second month 1Ki 6:1
—Sivan, the third month ....Est 8:9
—Tammuz, the fourth month ....Jer 52:6
—Ab, the fifth month ....Nu 33:38
—Elul, the sixth month ....Ne 6:15
—Ethanim or Tishri, the seventh month 1Ki 8:2
—Bul or Heshvan, the eighth month 1Ki 6:38
—Kislev, the ninth month ....Zec 7:1
—Tebeth, the tenth month ....Est 2:16
—Shebat, the eleventh month ....Zec 1:7
—Adar, the twelfth month ....Ezr 6:15

MOON
A. Data concerning the moon
 —Created by God ....Ge 1:16
....Ps 8:3
 —Controlled by God ....Jos 10:12–13
....Jer 31:35
 —Governs the night ....Ge 1:16
....Ps 136:9
 —Marks off the seasons ....Ge 1:14
....Ps 104:19
 —New Moon festivals ....Nu 10:10
....1Sa 20:5,18,24
....Am 8:5
 —Involved in the blessing of productive land ..Dt 33:13–14
 —Must praise God ....Ps 148:3
 —Believed to cause mental illness ....Ps 121:6
 —Worshiped by the heathen 2Ki 23:5
....Jer 8:2
 —No moon needed in heaven ....Isa 60:19–20
....Rev 21:23
B. The moon used in a symbolic way
 —Of stability and endurance ....Ps 72:5,7
 —Of judgment at the end of time ....Isa 13:10–11
....Mt 24:29
....Rev 6:12

MORDECAI
—Benjamite exile who brought up Esther ....Est 2:5–10
—Exposed plot to kill Xerxes ....Est 2:19–23
—Refused to honor Haman ....Est 3:1–6
....Est 5:9–14
—Pole made to impale him ....Est 5:14
—Begged Esther to foil Haman's plot ....Est 4:1–17
—Haman forced to honor him ....Est 6:1–11

—Exalted by the king ....Est 8:1–2,15
....Est 9:3–4
—With Esther, established Purim ....Est 9:18–32

MORIAH
—Region where Abraham went to "sacrifice" Isaac ...Ge 22:1–18
—Mountain on which temple was built 2Ch 3:1–2

MOSES
A. Family data
 —Son of Amram and Jochebed ....Ex 6:20
....1Ch 6:3
 —Tribe of Levi ....Ex 2:1
 —Brother of Aaron ....Ex 4:14
 —Name means "draw out" ....Ex 2:10
 —Married Zipporah ....Ex 2:21
 —Father of Gershom and Eliezer ....Ex 2:22
....Ex 18:2–4
B. His history
 1. His youth
  —Hid by his parents for three months ......Ex 2:2
....Heb 11:23
  —Hid in a basket in the Nile ....Ex 2:3–4
  —Discovered by Pharaoh's daughter ....Ex 2:5–9
  —Brought up by Pharaoh's daughter ....Ex 2:10
  —Killed an Egyptian ....Ex 2:11–12
  —Fled to Midian ....Ex 2:13–15
  —Became a shepherd ....Ex 3:1
 2. Delivered Israel from Egypt
  —Called by God ....Ex 3:2–4:17
  —Explained his call to Israelites ....Ex 4:29–31
  —Made demands to Pharaoh ....Ex 5:1–5
  —The ten plagues ....Ex 7:14—11:9
  —Arranged the Passover ....Ex 12:1–28
  —Led Israelites out of Egypt ....Ex 12:29–42
  —Led them to the border of the Red Sea ...Ex 13:17–14:4
  —Led them across the Red Sea ....Ex 14:21–31
  —Sang song of deliverance ....Ex 15:1–21
 3. Led Israel to Mount Sinai
  —Water at Marah and Elim ....Ex 15:22–27
  —Asked God for food; received manna ......Ex 16:1–16
  —Brought water from the rock ....Ex 17:1–7
  —Raised hands to defeat Amalekites ....Ex 17:8–16
  —Delegated judges ....Ex 18:13–27
....Dt 1:9–18
  —Received law at Mount Sinai ....Ex 19:3–25
....Ex 24:12–18
....Jn 1:17
  —Announced law to Israel ....Ex 24:3–7
  —Broke tablets because of golden calf .....Ex 32:19–20
....Dt 9:7–17
  —Received law a second time ....Ex 34:1–4,27–28
  —Saw the glory of the Lord ....Ex 33:18–23
  —His face reflected glory of God ....Ex 34:29–35
  —Supervised building of tabernacle ....Ex 35:4—36:7
  —Set apart Aaron and priests ....Lev 8:1–9:24
  —Numbered tribes ....Nu 1:1–4:49
 4. From Sinai to the border of Canaan
  —Left Sinai ....Nu 10:11–13
  —Handled the people's complaints ....Nu 11:1–34
  —Opposed by Aaron and Miriam ....Nu 12:1–15
  —Sent spies into Canaan ....Nu 13:1–33
  —Prayed for the rebellious people ....Nu 14:1–25
  —Announced forty years of wandering .....Nu 14:26–40
  —Opposed by Korah ....Nu 16:1–50
  —Struck rock; forbidden to enter Canaan ...Nu 20:1–13
....Dt 1:37
  —Put bronze snake on a pole for healing ....Nu 21:4–9
....Jn 3:14
  —Defeated kings in battle ....Nu 21:1–3,21–31
  —Numbered tribes a second time ....Nu 26:1–65
  —Designated Joshua as successor ....Nu 27:12–23
....Dt 34:9
  —Gave final address (Deuteronomy) ....Dt 1:5
  —Sang a song ....Dt 31:30—32:43
  —Blessed the twelve tribes ....Dt 33:1–29
  —Saw the promised land ....Dt 34:1–4
  —His death ....Dt 34:5–8
C. Titles ascribed to him
 —The man of God ....Ezr 3:2
 —God's chosen one ....Ps 106:23
 —The servant of God 2Ch 24:6,9
....Ps 105:26

MURDER
—The deliberate killing of another human
A. The command against murder
—The sixth commandment ....Ex 20:13
Dt 5:17
Jas 2:10–11
—Anger as the root of murder ....Mt 5:21–22
—Hatred as the root of murder 1Jn 3:15
—Murder comes out of a sinful heart ....Mt 15:18–19
B. What happens after a murder
—One can be cursed by God ....Ge 4:11
—One can be excluded from heaven 1Jn 3:15
Rev 22:15
—One is subject to capital punishment ....Ge 9:5–6
Ex 21:12–14,23
—More than one witness required ....Nu 35:30
Dt 19:15
—Cities of refuge in Israel ....Nu 35:16–32
Dt 19:1–14
—Murderers can be forgiven ....Lk 23:34
Ac 7:60
C. Examples of murder in the Bible
—Cain killed Abel ....Ge 4:8
—Moses killed an Egyptian ....Ex 2:11–12
—Abimelek killed his brothers ....Jdg 9:5
—David killed Uriah 2Sa 12:9
—Absalom killed Ammon 2Sa 13:28–33
—Jezebel killed Naboth 1Ki 21:8–14
—Hazael killed Ben-Hadad 2Ki 8:14–15
—Athaliah killed the royal family 2Ki 11:1
—Herod killed the babies in Bethlehem ....Mt 2:16
—Herod killed John the Baptist ....Mt 14:6–11
—The Jews killed Jesus ....Ac 2:23
1Th 2:15
—The Jews killed Stephen ....Ac 7:57–60
—Herod killed James ....Ac 12:2

MUSIC AND SONG
A. Related theme
MUSIC is a theme of 2 Chronicles 2Ch 5:13
B. Musical instruments
1. Begun by Jubal ....Ge 4:21
2. Types of instruments in the Bible
—Bells ....Ex 28:33–35
—Castanets 2Sa 6:5
—Cymbals 2Sa 6:5
—Harp 1Ch 25:3
—Flute ....Da 3:5,7,10,15
—Horn ....Da 3:5,7,10,15
—Lyre 2Sa 6:5
—Pipe ....Da 3:5,10,15
—Sistrum 2Sa 6:5
—Timbrel 2Sa 6:5
—Trumpet ....Nu 10:2
—Zither ....Da 3:5,10,15
3. Used in Israelite worship
—Organized by David 1Ch 25:1,6
2Ch 7:6
—Mentioned in the psalms ....Ps 47:6
Ps 98:5–6
Ps 150:4–5
4. Used when Jesus returns 1Co 15:52
1Th 4:16
C. Songs
1. In the Old Testament
a. Occasions for singing
—In sacred processions 2Sa 6:5
1Ch 13:8
—At dedications 2Ch 5:12–13
Ezr 3:10–11
Ne 12:27–28,40
—On feast days 2Ch 30:21
—At coronations 2Ch 23:13
—To celebrate victories ....Ex 15:1–18
Nu 21:17
Jdg 5:1–31
b. The psalmist's intention to sing ....Ps 27:6
Ps 57:7,9
Ps 61:8
Ps 101:1
Ps 104:33

c. Instructions to sing ....Ps 30:4
Ps 68:32
Ps 98:1
Ps 149:1
d. All creation should sing ....Ps 148:1–12
Isa 44:23
Isa 49:13
2. In the New Testament
—Songs at the birth of Jesus ....Lk 1:46–55,68–79
Lk 2:14,29–32
—Songs in the worshiping church 1Co 14:15
Eph 5:19
Col 3:16
Jas 5:13
—Songs in heaven ....Rev 5:9–10,12–13
Rev 7:10,12,15–17
Rev 15:3–4
Rev 19:1–8

MYSTERY
—Secret truths revealed by God
A. Related theme
MYSTERY is a theme of Mark ....Mk 4:11
B. God and his secret truths
1. God discloses mysteries
—To his prophets ....Ge 40:8
Isa 48:6
Am 3:7
Da 2:18,27–28
Ro 16:25–26
—To his apostles ....Mk 4:10–12
Eph 3:4–5
Rev 1:19–20
2. Only believers understand mysteries ....Mk 4:10–12
1Co 2:6–11
2Co 4:3–6
C. Mysteries revealed to God's people
1. In the Old Testament
—Future events revealed to Joseph ....Ge 40:8–22
Ge 41:1–32
—Future events revealed to Daniel ....Da 2:24–47
Da 4:19–27
2. In the New Testament
—Basic teachings about Christ 1Ti 3:16
—Basic message of the gospel ....Col 4:3
—All wisdom hidden in Christ ....Col 2:2–3
—The nature of the kingdom of God ......Lk 8:10–15
—The union of Christ and his church .....Eph 5:29–32
—Christ's care for his church ....Rev 1:19–20
—What happens at Christ's return 1Co 15:51–52
—Inclusion of Gentiles in the kingdom .....Eph 3:6
Col 1:26
—Plan to reach the Jews with gospel ......Ro 11:25–26
D. Love is preferable to knowing mysteries 1Co 13:2

NAAMAN
—Aramean general afflicted with leprosy 2Ki 5:1
—Cured by Elisha 2Ki 5:2–14
—Took Israelite soil back to Damascus 2Ki 5:15–19
—His cure mentioned by Jesus ....Lk 4:27

NABAL
—Wealthy Carmelite; husband of Abigail 1Sa 25:1–3
—Name means "fool" 1Sa 25:25
—Refused to help David 1Sa 25:4–13
—Abigail pleaded for his life 1Sa 25:14–25
—His death 1Sa 25:36–38

NABOTH
—Owner of a vineyard in Jezreel 1Ki 21:1
—Refused to sell vineyard to King Ahab 1Ki 21:2–3
—Killed by Jezebel 1Ki 21:4–14
—Ahab's family destroyed for this 1Ki 21:17–24
—Joram killed in Naboth's vineyard 2Ki 9:21–26

NADAB
A. Firstborn of Aaron ....Ex 6:23
—Went up Mount Sinai ....Ex 24:1,9
—Consecrated as priest ....Ex 28:1
—Killed for offering unauthorized fire ....Lev 10:1–3
Nu 3:2–4
—Had no sons 1Ch 24:2
B. Son of Jeroboam I; king of Israel 1Ki 15:25
—Killed all his brothers 1Ki 15:29
—Killed by Baasha 1Ki 15:27–28

OATH

A. The human oath
 1. Expressions of the oath

 2. Features of the oath
  a. Purposes

  b. Other aspects of the oath

B. God's oath
 1. Content of God's oaths

 2. Character of God's oaths

See also CURSE; VOW

OBADIAH

A. Servant of King Ahab 1Ki 18:3

B. Prophet against Edom . . . . .Ob 1

OBEDIENCE

A. Related themes
 1. OBEDIENCE is a theme of:

 2. TRUST AND OBEY is a theme of Joshua . . . . .Jos 10:25

B. Obedience in the Old Testament
 1. Relationships of obedience

PEACE

—Wholeness and well-being in all areas of life

—Kneeling . . . . Ezr 9:5
　　　　　　　　　　　　　　　　　　　Da 6:10
　　　　　　　　　　　　　　　　　　　Ac 20:36
—Bowing down . . . . Ex 34:8
　　　　　　　　　　　　　　　　　　　Ps 5:7
　　　　　　　　　　　　　　　　　　　Ps 95:6
—Lying on the ground 2Sa 12:16
　　　　　　　　　　　　　　　　　　　Mt 26:39
—Lifting up hands . . . . Ps 28:2
　　　　　　　　　　　　　　　　　　　Isa 1:15
　　　　　　　　　　　　　　　　　　　1Ti 2:8
2. Manner of prayer
—Alone, silently 1Sa 1:18
—Alone, aloud . . . . Eze 11:13
—With two or three . . . . Mt 18:19
—In a larger group . . . . Ps 35:18
3. Time of prayer
—In the morning . . . . Ps 5:1–3
　　　　　　　　　　　　　　　　　　　Mk 1:35
—In the evening . . . . Ge 24:63
—At fixed times . . . . Ps 55:17
　　　　　　　　　　　　　　　　　　　Da 6:10
—Always . . . . Lk 18:1
　　　　　　　　　　　　　　　　　　　Ro 1:10
　　　　　　　　　　　　　　　　　　　1Th 5:17
4. Possible places of prayer
—In secret . . . . Mt 6:6
—In bed . . . . Ps 63:6
—In a family setting . . . . Ac 10:1–2
—Out in the open . . . . Ge 24:11–12
—In the battlefield . . . . Jos 10:12–13
—By the riverside . . . . Ac 16:13
—In the temple 2Ki 19:14
—In the church gathered together . . . . Ac 4:23–24,31
—Anywhere 1Ti 2:8

PREACHING
A. Preachers in the Bible
1. Old Testament saints who preached
—Noah 2Pe 2:5
—Jonah . . . . Jnh 1:2
　　　　　　　　　　　　　　　　　　　Jnh 3:2
—Isaiah . . . . Isa 61:1
—Ezekiel . . . . Eze 21:2
—Amos . . . . Am 7:16
—Haggai and Zechariah . . . . Ezr 6:14
2. New Testament saints who preached
—John the Baptist . . . . Mt 3:1
—Jesus . . . . Mt 4:17
—Peter and John . . . . Ac 8:25
—Philip . . . . Ac 8:40
—Paul . . . . Ac 9:27
　　　　　　　　　　　　　　　　　　　1Co 9:16
—Timothy 1Ti 4:13
—Numerous believers . . . . Ac 8:4
　　　　　　　　　　　　　　　　　　　Ac 15:35
—All Christians . . . . Mt 28:19
　　　　　　　　　　　　　　　　　　　Mk 16:15
B. The content of preaching
1. In the Old Testament
—A message of judgment . . . . Eze 20:46
　　　　　　　　　　　　　　　　　　　Eze 21:2
　　　　　　　　　　　　　　　　　　　Am 7:16
　　　　　　　　　　　　　　　　　　　Jnh 3:4
—A message of hope . . . . Isa 40:1–2,9
　　　　　　　　　　　　　　　　　　　Isa 52:7–10
　　　　　　　　　　　　　　　　　　　Am 9:11–15
2. In the New Testament
—The good news of the kingdom . . . . Lk 9:2
　　　　　　　　　　　　　　　　　　　Lk 16:16
　　　　　　　　　　　　　　　　　　　Ac 20:25
—The good news of salvation 1Co 1:21
　　　　　　　　　　　　　　　　　　　1Co 15:1–2
—The cross of Christ 1Co 2:1–2
—The resurrection of Christ . . . . Ac 17:18,31
　　　　　　　　　　　　　　　　　　　1Co 15:12–14
—Jesus Christ is Lord 2Co 4:5
—Fulfillment of the Scriptures in Christ . . . . . Ac 2:14–36
　　　　　　　　　　　　　　　　　　　Ac 4:12–26
　　　　　　　　　　　　　　　　　　　Ac 13:16–41
　　　　　　　　　　　　　　　　　　　1Co 15:3–5

—The coming judgment . . . . Ac 10:42
　　　　　　　　　　　　　　　　　　　Ac 17:31
—The call to repent and believe . . . . Mk 1:15
　　　　　　　　　　　　　　　　　　　Ac 2:38
　　　　　　　　　　　　　　　　　　　Ac 10:43
　　　　　　　　　　　　　　　　　　　Ac 26:20

PREDESTINATION
See ELECTION; PROVIDENCE

PRIDE
A. Legitimate pride
1. Occasions for such pride
—Boasting in the Lord . . . . Ps 34:2
　　　　　　　　　　　　　　　　　　　Ps 44:8
　　　　　　　　　　　　　　　　　　　Jer 9:24
　　　　　　　　　　　　　　　　　　　1Co 1:31
—Boasting in the cross of Christ . . . . Gal 6:14
—Boasting about God-fearing churches 2Co 1:14
　　　　　　　　　　　　　　　　　　　2Co 7:4
　　　　　　　　　　　　　　　　　　　Php 2:16
2. The glory of such pride
—Must be in God's grace 2Co 1:12
—Must be in Jesus Christ . . . . Ro 15:17–18
—Must be in the Holy Spirit . . . . Ro 15:18–19
B. Sinful pride
1. Characteristics of a proud person
—Tries to be like God . . . . Ge 3:5–6
—Thinks himself or herself better than others . . Lk 18:10–12
—Boasts about ancestry . . . . Lk 3:8
　　　　　　　　　　　　　　　　　　　Jn 8:33
—Takes pride in the temple . . . . Jer 7:4
—Takes pride in self-accomplishment . . . . . . Isa 10:12–15
　　　　　　　　　　　　　　　　　　　Eze 28:1–7
　　　　　　　　　　　　　　　　　　　1Co 4:7
2. Notable examples
—Adam and Eve . . . . Ge 3:5–6
—David 1Ch 21:1–7
—Uzziah 2Ch 26:16
—Hezekiah 2Ch 32:25
—Nebuchadnezzar . . . . Da 4:30
—Herod . . . . Ac 12:21–23
3. Results of such pride
—Deceives the heart . . . . Jer 49:16
—Hardens the heart . . . . Da 5:20
—Produces quarrels . . . . Pr 13:10
—Brings disgrace . . . . Pr 11:2
—Leads to destruction . . . . Pr 16:18
—Brings opposition from God . . . . Pr 3:34
　　　　　　　　　　　　　　　　　　　Jas 4:6
—Brings judgment from God . . . . Lev 26:18–20
　　　　　　　　　　　　　　　　　　　Zep 2:10–11
　　　　　　　　　　　　　　　　　　　Mal 4:1
4. Warnings against such pride . . . . Pr 8:13
　　　　　　　　　　　　　　　　　　　Pr 16:5,18
　　　　　　　　　　　　　　　　　　　Pr 21:4,24
　　　　　　　　　　　　　　　　　　　Lk 18:9
　　　　　　　　　　　　　　　　　　　Ro 12:16
　　　　　　　　　　　　　　　　　　　1Jn 2:16

See also HUMILITY

PRIEST
A. Basic requirements for being priests
—Must belong to the tribe of Levi . . . . Ex 29:9,44
　　　　　　　　　　　　　　　　　　　Ezr 2:61–62
—Had to follow special marriage laws . . . . . . Lev 21:7–9,13–15
—Had to remain unshaven . . . . Lev 21:5–6
—Had to honor proper procedures . . . . Lev 10:1–7
—Non-priests punished for doing priestly work . . Nu 18:7
　　　　　　　　　　　　　　　　　　　1Sa 13:8–14
　　　　　　　　　　　　　　　　　　　2Ch 26:16–21
B. Basic tasks of the priests (including Levites)
—Presented needs of the people to God . . . . . Heb 5:1–3
—Made atonement for sin . . . . Lev 16:1–22
—Sprinkled blood of the sacrifices . . . . Lev 1:5,11
　　　　　　　　　　　　　　　　　　　Lev 17:11
—Offered sacrifices on the altar . . . . Lev 6:8–9
—Kept fire burning on the altar . . . . Lev 6:13
—Burned incense on the altar . . . . Ex 30:7–9
　　　　　　　　　　　　　　　　　　　Lk 1:5–9
—Took care of the sanctuary . . . . Nu 3:38
—Responsible for the treasury 1Ch 26:20
—Supervised the work of the temple 1Ch 23:4
—Carried the ark . . . . Nu 4:15

—Poor allowed to glean in fields . . . . .Lev 19:10
Dt 24:19–21
—Laws regarding security on loans . . . . .Dt 24:10–13
—No interest may be charged to the poor . . . .Ex 22:25
Lev 25:36
—The year for canceling debts . . . . .Dt 15:1–11
—The Year of Jubilee . . . . .Lev 25:5–55
—Equal justice for rich and poor . . . . .Ex 23:2–3,6
Dt 1:17
Pr 31:9
4. Blessings for those who show kindness to the poor
—Their throne will be secure . . . . .Ps 72:1–5
Pr 29:14
—Their righteousness endures forever . . . . . . .Ps 112:9
Isa 58:6–8
—God will answer their prayers . . . . .Isa 58:6–7,9
—They will be rewarded by God . . . . .Pr 14:21
Pr 19:17
Pr 22:9
Pr 28:27
—They will have treasure in heaven . . . . .Mt 19:21
Lk 12:33
Lk 19:8–9
5. God as the hope of the poor
—He is their refuge . . . . .Ps 14:6
Isa 25:4
—He is their protector . . . . .Ps 12:5
—He is their deliverer 1Sa 2:8
Ps 34:6
Ps 113:7
—He is their helper . . . . .Ps 40:17
Ps 70:5
Isa 41:17
—He is their provider . . . . .Ps 132:15
Isa 61:1–3
Lk 4:18–19

RIGHTEOUSNESS
—The state of being perfect and without sin
A. Related theme
RIGHTEOUSNESS is a theme of Romans . . . . .Ro 1:17
B. The righteousness of humans
1. In themselves humans are unrighteous
—No one is righteous . . . . .Ps 14:1–3
Ps 53:1–3
Ro 3:10–12,23
—Our righteous acts are like filthy rags . . . . . .Isa 64:6
—We deserve God's wrath . . . . .Ro 1:18
Eph 2:3
2. God gives us righteousness
a. Experienced in the Old Testament
—By Abram . . . . .Ge 15:6
—By David . . . . .Ps 32:1–2
Ps 103:17
—By Isaiah . . . . .Isa 45:8,24
Isa 46:13
Isa 61:10
b. Experienced by believers in Christ
—God declares us righteous . . . . .Ro 3:21–22
Ro 4:1–8
Gal 3:21–22
Php 3:8–9
—God credits us with Christ's
righteousness . . . . .Ro 4:11,22–24
—His righteousness is a gift . . . . .Ro 5:17
—We become God's righteousness 2Co 5:21
3. Believers are called "the righteous"
—In the Old Testament . . . . .Ps 1:5–6
Pr 10:3,6–7,20–21
Isa 26:7
Hos 14:9
—In the New Testament . . . . .Mt 25:37,46
Heb 12:23
Jas 5:16
4. Responsibilities regarding a righteous way of life
—Be instruments of righteousness . . . . .Ro 6:13
—Be slaves to righteousness . . . . .Ro 6:18–19
—Long for righteousness . . . . .Mt 5:6
—Perform righteousness . . . . .Am 5:24
Mt 5:20
—Pursue righteousness . . . . .Isa 51:1
1Ti 6:11
2Ti 2:22

—Put on righteousness . . . . .Eph 4:24
Eph 6:14
—Seek righteousness . . . . .Mt 6:33
—Bring forth fruits of righteousness . . . . . . .Hos 10:12
2Co 9:10
Heb 12:11
—Live for righteousness 1Pe 2:24
—Do what is right .1Jn 2:29
1Jn 3:7
—Shun wickedness 2Co 6:14–15
5. God's word teaches how to be righteous 2Ti 3:16–17
6. Our final righteousness
—Heaven is the home of righteousness 2Pe 3:13
—We receive a crown of righteousness 2Ti 4:8
See also JUSTIFICATION
C. The righteousness of God
1. God the Father
—God is righteous .Ps 7:9
Isa 45:21
Jer 12:1
Jn 17:25
—He always acts righteously 1Sa 12:7
Ps 145:17
Jer 9:24
Mic 6:5
—He judges righteously . . . . .Ps 9:4
Ps 98:9
Jer 11:20
—His commandments are righteous . . . . .Ps 19:9
Ps 119:138,160
Ro 1:32
Ro 7:12
—His righteousness endures forever . . . . .Ps 111:3
Ps 112:3
2. Jesus is righteous
a. Old Testament prophecies
—His name is "The Lᴏʀᴅ Our
Righteousness" . . . . .Jer 23:6
Jer 33:16
—He is the righteous servant . . . . .Isa 53:11
—He is the sun of righteousness . . . . .Mal 4:2
—He is clothed in righteousness . . . . .Isa 11:5
Isa 59:16–17
—He loves righteousness . . . . .Ps 45:7
—He judges in righteousness . . . . .Ps 72:2
Isa 11:4
—He reigns in righteousness . . . . .Isa 32:1
Zec 9:9
b. New Testament assertions
—He is the Righteous One . . . . .Ac 3:14
Ac 7:52
1Jn 2:1
—He fulfilled all righteousness . . . . .Mt 3:15
—He lived a righteous life . . . . .Ro 5:18
2Co 5:21
1Pe 3:18
—He is our righteousness 1Co 1:30
—He loves righteousness . . . . .Heb 1:8–9
—He is the righteous Judge 2Ti 4:8
3. Believers and God's righteousness
—They acknowledge it . . . . .Ezr 9:15
Da 9:7
—They see it . . . . .Mic 7:9
—They speak of it .Ps 35:28
—They proclaim it .Ps 22:31
Ps 71:15–16
—They sing of it . . . . .Ps 51:14
—They exult in it . . . . .Ps 89:16
—They give thanks for it . . . . .Ps 7:17
—They are led in it . . . . .Ps 5:8
—They are upheld by it . . . . .Isa 41:10
—They pray for it . . . . .Ps 31:1
Ps 143:11

RIVER
A. Rivers and streams mentioned in the Bible
—Abana 2Ki 5:12
—Ahava . . . . .Ezr 8:15,21
—Arnon . . . . .Nu 21:13,24
—Besor 1Sa 30:9,21
—Egypt . . . . .Ge 15:18
—Euphrates . . . . .Dt 1:7

—That he might judge the human race . . . . .Mt 25:31–46
Ac 10:42
2Ti 4:1
1Pe 4:5
—That he might complete salvation for believers . .Heb 9:28
—That he might take his people to be with him . . .Jn 14:3
—That he might gather the elect . . . . .Mk 13:27
E. Believers and the second coming
1. The attitude of believers toward it
—Should live holy lives until that day 2Pe 3:11–12
—Should long for it .2Ti 4:8
—Should watch for it . . . . .Mk 13:35–37
Lk 12:35–40
—Should wait for it .1Co 1:7
Php 3:20
Tit 2:13
—Should look forward to it 2Pe 3:12–13
—Should be patient until it . . . . .Jas 5:7–8
—Should persevere until it . . . . .Rev 2:10–11
Rev 3:11–12
—Should pray for its fulfillment 1Co 16:22
Rev 22:20
2. Promises for believers when it occurs
—We will be preserved by Christ . . . . .Php 1:6
Jude 24
—We will be found blameless 1Co 1:8
1Th 3:13
—We will be clothed anew by God 2Co 5:4–5
—We will receive new bodies 1Co 15:42–53
—We will be made like Christ 1Co 15:49
Php 3:20–21
1Jn 3:2
—We will receive a crown 1Co 9:25
2Ti 4:8
1Pe 5:4
Jas 1:12
—We will reign with Christ 2Ti 2:12
Rev 22:5
—We will be incredibly happy 1Pe 4:13

SELF-CONTROL
—Control of one's body and emotions
A. Self-control as a Christian trait
—Expressed negatively .Pr 25:28
2Ti 3:3
—Expressed positively .1Ti 3:2
Tit 2:2,5–6,12
2Pe 1:6
—An aspect of the Spirit's fruit . . . . .Gal 5:22–23
B. Reasons for self-control
—To control anger . . . . .Pr 16:32
Pr 29:11
—To avoid sexual sins 1Co 7:3–5
1Th 4:3–4
—To prepare for Christ's return 1Th 5:6–8
—To enable us to pray properly 1Pe 4:7
—To show resistance to Satan 1Pe 5:8–9

SELF-DENIAL
—Rejection of a self-centered life
A. Jesus exemplified self-denial
—In coming to this earth 2Co 8:9
Php 2:6–7
—In resisting temptations of Satan . . . . .Mt 4:3–4,8–10
—In doing his Father's will . . . . .Jn 6:38
Mt 26:39,42
—In washing his disciples' feet . . . . .Jn 13:4–5,12–15
—In dying on the cross .Mk 10:45
1Pe 2:21–24
B. Christians called to self-denial
—The call to self-denial . . . . .Mt 16:24–26
Mk 8:34–37
Lk 9:23–25
—The priority of love for Jesus . . . . .Mt 10:37–39
Lk 14:25–33
—Giving of ourselves to others . . . . .Mt 5:38–42
1Co 10:24
—The necessity of being a servant . . . . .Mk 10:42–44
Lk 22:25–27
Jn 12:24–26
See SERVANT
—Renouncing selfish desires . . . . .Gal 5:24
Tit 2:12

—The life of self-sacrifice . . . . .Ro 12:2
2Co 4:10–11

SELFISHNESS
See SELF-DENIAL

SENNACHERIB
—An Assyrian king 2Ki 18:13
—Attempted siege of Jerusalem 2Ki 18:13–37
2Ch 32:1–19
Isa 36:1–22
—His army destroyed by the angel of the Lord . .2Ki 19:35–36
2Ch 32:21
Isa 37:36–37
—His death by murder 2Ki 19:37
2Ch 32:21
Isa 37:38

SERVANT
A. Essential qualities of a servant
—Must have only one master . . . . .Lk 16:13
—Must be submissive to a master's will . . . . .Ps 123:2
Eph 6:5
1Pe 2:18
—Must be faithful to a master 1Co 4:2
B. Servants on a human level
1. Servants in the home
—Hagar . . . . .Ge 16:1
—Abraham's servant (Eliezer) . . . . .Ge 24:1–2
—Zilpah . . . . .Ge 29:24
—Bilhah . . . . .Ge 29:29
—Joseph . . . . .Ge 39:1–4
2. Servants in the economic realm
—Laws concerning servants and slaves . . . . . .Ex 21:2–11
Lev 25:39–46
—Hired servants 2Ch 24:12
Mt 20:1–15
Lk 15:17–19
3. Servants on a political level
—Servants of a king .1Sa 16:16,18
2Sa 12:18–19
2Ki 9:28
—The king's children are called servants 2Sa 13:24
1Ki 1:17
—The king as servant of the people 1Ki 12:7
—A king as servant to another king 2Ki 16:7
2Ki 24:1
C. Believers as servants of one another
—We are called to serve as Jesus did . . . . .Jn 13:14–16
1Pe 2:21
—We are commanded to serve others . . . . .Gal 5:13
Eph 5:21
—Paul as a servant of others 1Co 9:19–23
2Co 4:5
D. Servants of the Lord
1. Examples of servants of the Lord
—Abraham, Isaac and Jacob . . . . .Ex 32:13
—Moses . . . . .Nu 12:7
—Joshua . . . . .Jdg 2:8
—Samson . . . . .Jdg 15:18
—David 2Sa 7:5
—Elijah 1Ki 18:36
—The prophets 2Ki 9:7
Zec 1:6
Rev 10:7
—The apostles 1Co 4:1
2Co 6:4
Php 1:1
—All Christians . . . . .Ro 6:22
Eph 6:6
1Pe 2:16
—The 144,000 . . . . .Rev 7:4
2. Isaiah's servant songs . . . . .Isa 42:1–4
Isa 49:1–6
Isa 50:4–9
Isa 52:13–53:12
3. Jesus as the servant of the Lord
—Fulfilled the servant songs of Isaiah . . . . . . .Mt 12:17–21
Ac 8:32–35
1Pe 2:22–25
—Took the nature of a servant . . . . .Php 2:7
—Called himself a servant . . . . .Mk 10:45
Lk 22:27
—Compared himself to a servant . . . . .Lk 12:37

—Demonstrated servanthood by washing feet .. Jn 13:4–11
—Demonstrated servanthood by his cross .... Isa 53:4–6
Php 2:7–8
—Exalted as servant .... Isa 52:13

SETH
—Third son of Adam and Eve .... Ge 4:25
—Took the place of Abel .... Ge 4:25
—Made in Adam's likeness .... Ge 5:3
—His family .... Ge 5:6–8
—An ancestor of Jesus .... Lk 3:38

SEXUAL STANDARDS
A. Sexual sins condemned in the Bible
  —Adultery .... Ex 20:14
Pr 5:1–23
  —Incest .... Lev 20:19–21
  —Sex with animals .... Lev 20:15–16
  —Loss of virginity before marriage .... Dt 22:20–21
  —Prostitution .... Dt 23:17–18
Pr 7:10–27
  —Homosexuality .... Ro 1:26–27
1Co 6:9
  —Obscenity .... Eph 5:4
  —Lust .... Mt 5:27–28
1Th 4:5
B. God's will regarding sexual standards
  1. In negative terms
    —Laws against illicit sexual behavior .... Ex 20:14
Lev 20:10–21
Dt 23:17–18
    —The command to flee immorality 1Co 6:18
Eph 5:3
Col 3:5
1Th 4:3
    —Sexual sin excludes one from the kingdom . 1Co 6:9–10
Gal 5:19–21
Eph 5:3–5
Rev 22:15
  2. In positive terms
    —Strive for purity 1Th 4:4,7
1Pe 3:2
    —Be faithful in marriage 1Co 7:2–4
    —Exercise self-control 1Co 7:8–9
Gal 5:23
1Th 4:4

See also MARRIAGE; ADULTERY; DIVORCE

SHADRACH
—Hebrew deported to Babylon .... Da 1:6
—Name changed from Hananiah .... Da 1:7
—Refused to be defiled by food .... Da 1:8–20
—Appointed administrator over Babylon .... Da 2:49
—Refused to worship idols .... Da 3:1–18
—Saved from fiery furnace .... Da 3:19–30

SHALLUM
—King of Israel 2Ki 15:10–15
—Assassinated by Menahem 2Ki 15:14

SHAME
A. Reasons for feeling ashamed
  —Being naked .... Ge 3:7
Eze 23:29
  —Experiencing defeat .... Ps 6:10
Isa 29:22–23
  —Being humiliated .... Eze 16:63
Zec 13:3–5
1Co 1:27–29
  —Experiencing sin .... Ezr 9:6
Jer 22:22
2Th 3:14
  —Being taunted by one's enemies .... Ps 44:15–16
  —Having an undisciplined child .... Pr 19:26
  —Falsely accusing someone .... Pr 25:8–10
1Pe 3:16
  —Giving less than poorer people 2Co 9:3–4
  —Being inconsistent with one's principles ...... Ezr 8:22
B. When the Christian need not be ashamed
  —When looking to the Lord .... Ps 34:5
  —When hoping in the Lord .... Ps 25:3
  —When taking refuge in the Lord .... Ps 25:20
  —When trusting in the Lord .... Ro 9:33
1Pe 2:6
  —When believing Christ .... Mk 8:38
2Ti 1:12

—When believing Christ and his word .... Mk 8:38
Lk 9:26
—When preaching the gospel .... Ro 1:16
2Ti 1:8
—When suffering for Christ's sake 1Pe 4:16
—When obeying God's law .... Ps 119:5–6
—When doing one's best for the Lord 2Ti 2:15
—When the Lord returns 1Jn 2:28

SHAMGAR
—Judge; killed six hundred Philistines .... Jdg 3:31

SHAPHAN
—Secretary during Josiah's reign 2Ki 22:3
—Supervised finances for temple repairs 2Ki 22:3–7
2Ch 34:8–13,16–17
—Brought newly discovered Book of the Law
to Josiah 2Ki 22:8–10
2Ch 34:14–17
—Read the Book of the Law to Josiah 2Ki 22:10
2Ch 34:18
—With others, visited prophetess Huldah 2Ki 22:14–20
2Ch 34:20–28

SHECHEM
A. A man who raped Jacob's daughter Dinah ...... Ge 34:1–4
  —Agreed to circumcision and marriage .... Ge 34:11–24
  —Killed by Simeon and Levi .... Ge 34:25–29
B. A city in Canaan
  —The Lord appeared to Abram there .... Ge 12:6–7
  —Jacob purchased land there .... Ge 33:18–19
  —Pillaged by the sons of Jacob .... Ge 34:26–29
  —Joseph went there to find his brothers .... Ge 37:14–17
  —One of the cities of refuge .... Jos 20:7
  —Joshua renewed the covenant there .... Jos 24:1–27
  —Gideon's son Abimelek was crowned its king .. Jdg 9:1–6
  —Civil war between Abimelek and Shechem .... Jdg 9:22–57
  —Rehoboam was made king there 1Ki 12:1
  —Jeroboam fortified it as his capital 1Ki 12:25
  —In New Testament, Shechem is Sychar .... Jn 4:5

SHEEP
See LAMB

SHEM
—Son of Noah .... Ge 5:32
1Ch 1:4
—With Japheth, covered his father with a garment . Ge 9:23
—Blessed by Noah .... Ge 9:26
—Sons listed .... Ge 10:21–31
—Abram came from his line .... Ge 11:10–26

SHEOL
See GRAVE

SHEPHERD
A. Related theme
  PASTORAL ADVICE is a theme of Titus .... Tit 3:8
B. The shepherd as an human occupation
  1. Examples of shepherds .... Ge 4:2
Ge 29:9
1Sa 16:11
Lk 2:8
  2. Responsibilities of shepherds
    —Find pasture for flocks .... Eze 34:2,13–14
    —Provide water for flocks .... Ge 29:2–8
Ex 2:16
    —Protect the flocks 1Sa 17:34–36
Lk 2:8
    —Seek lost sheep .... Eze 34:16
Mt 18:10–13
    —Care for injured sheep .... Mt 12:11
    —Regularly account for the sheep .... Jn 10:2–5
    —Know what happens to the sheep .... Ge 31:38–39
    —Shear the sheep .... Ge 38:12
1Sa 25:2,7
C. Figurative use of shepherd
  1. Leaders of God's people as shepherds
    a. Old Testament leaders
      —Joshua .... Nu 27:15–18
      —David 2Sa 5:2
Ps 78:70–72
      —Cyrus .... Isa 44:28
      —Selfish shepherds .... Isa 56:10–11
Jer 10:21
Eze 34:2–6
Zec 10:2–3

—Co-writer with Peter 1Pe 5:12

SILVER

A. Uses for silver
1. In Israelite worship
    —The tabernacle furniture ....Ex 26:19–25
        Ex 27:9–11,17
    —Offerings ....Nu 7:13,19,25
        Ezr 1:4,6,9–11
    —The temple building 1Ch 29:2–5
    —The temple furniture 1Ch 28:14–17
2. In crafting idol gods ....Isa 2:20
    Hos 8:4
    Ac 19:24
3. For personal wealth ....Ge 13:2
    Ecc 2:8
4. For gifts 1Ki 15:18–19
    Ezr 2:69
5. For payment as money ....Ge 42:25–27
    Jdg 9:4
    Mt 26:15
6. For jewelry ....Ge 24:53
    Eze 16:17
7. For royal display ....Ge 44:2
    Est 1:6–7

B. Value of silver for God's people
1. Positive: a blessing from God ....Ge 13:2
    Isa 60:9,17
2. Negative
    —Wisdom worth more than silver ....Job 28:12–15
    Pr 3:13–14
    Pr 16:16
    —Silver valueless in redemption 1Pe 1:18

C. Silver as a symbol
    —For saints surviving God's testing ....Isa 48:10
    Zec 13:9
    —For God's dependable word ....Ps 12:6
    —For trustworthy spiritual values 1Co 3:12–13

SIMEON

A. Son of Jacob by Leah ....Ge 35:23
    1Ch 2:1
    —Name means "one who hears" ....Ge 29:33
    —With Levi, avenged rape of Dinah ....Ge 34:25–31
    —Held hostage by Joseph in Egypt ....Ge 42:24—43:23
    —Went to Egypt with family ....Ge 46:8,10
    —Father of six sons ....Ge 46:10
    —Blessed by Jacob ....Ge 49:5–7

B. Tribe descended from Simeon
    —Numbered ....Nu 1:23
    Nu 26:14
    —Allotted land ....Jos 19:1–9
    Eze 48:24
    —One of the tribes of the 144,000 ....Rev 7:7

C. A righteous man who blessed Jesus ....Lk 2:25–35
    —Sang a song ....Lk 2:29–32

SIMON

A. One of Jesus' disciples
    See PETER

B. Another disciple of Jesus
    —Called the Zealot ....Mt 10:4
    Mk 3:18
    —One of the apostles ....Ac 1:13

C. A Samaritan sorcerer ....Ac 8:9–11
    —Baptized as a Christian ....Ac 8:12
    —Offered Peter money for power to impart the
      Holy Spirit ....Ac 8:18–19
    —Severely rebuked by Peter ....Ac 8:20–23

SIN

A. Related themes
  SIN is a theme of:
    —Genesis ....Ge 6:5
    —Judges ....Jdg 21:25
    —Isaiah ....Isa 1:4
    —Malachi ....Mal 1:8
    —Romans ....Ro 2:12
    —1 John 1Jn 3:6

B. Words for sin
    —Transgression ....Ps 32:1
    —Iniquity ....Ps 51:2,9
    —Wickedness ....Ge 6:5
    —Evil ....Ge 8:21

    —Rebellion ....Ex 34:7
    —Uncleanness ....Lev 16:16
    —Disobedience ....Jos 22:22
    —Wrongdoing 1Sa 24:11
    —Guilt ....Isa 1:4
    —Unrighteousness 1Jn 1:9
    —Lawlessness 1Jn 3:4
    —Depravity 2Pe 2:19
    —Faults ....Ps 19:12

C. The origin and extent of sin
1. Original sin
    —Adam and Eve disobeyed God's command . . .Ge 3:1–7
    —Their sin passed down to all humans ......Ro 5:12,15
    1Co 15:22
2. Present extent of sin
    —There is sin in everyone ....Ps 14:2–3
    Ro 3:10–20,23
    —Present already at conception ....Ps 51:5
    —Permeates to the heart of people ....Ge 6:5
    Jer 17:9
    Mt 15:18–20
    —Christ alone was without sin 2Co 5:21
    Heb 4:15
    1Pe 2:22
    1Jn 3:5

D. God and human sin
1. His negative reaction
    —He is grieved over sin ....Ge 6:6
    —He is angry over sin ....Ps 78:19–21,56–59
    Jn 3:36
    Ro 1:18
    —He hates sin ....Ps 5:5
    Pr 6:16–19
    —He punishes sin ....Ge 3:15–19
    Isa 3:11–26
    Am 3:2
2. His positive reaction
    —He sent his Son to die for sinners ....Jn 3:16
    Ro 5:8
    1Jn 4:10
    —He forgives sin ....Ex 34:6–7
    1Jn 1:9
    —He removes sin far away ....Ps 103:8–12
    —He sweeps away sin ....Isa 44:22
    —He hurls sin away ....Mic 7:19
    —He puts sin behind his back ....Isa 38:17
    —He no longer remembers our sin ....Jer 31:34

E. Christ and human sin
    —He was sinless 2Co 5:21
    Heb 4:15
    Heb 7:26
    1Pe 2:22
    1Jn 3:5
    —He paid the penalty for sin ....Ro 4:25
    Ro 8:3
    Col 2:13–14
    1Pe 2:24
    —He forgives sin ....Mk 2:5–12
    Lk 7:48
    Col 1:13–14
    —His blood redeems us from sin ....Eph 1:7
    —His blood cleanses us from sin 1Jn 1:7
    —He takes away the sin of the world ....Jn 1:29
    1Jn 2:2

F. Humans and their sin
1. How has sin affected us?
    —We are responsible for our sin ....Eze 18:10–18
    —We are accountable to God for sin ....Jer 17:10
    2Co 5:10
    Rev 20:12
    —We are subject to death because of sin ...Ge 2:17
    Ro 6:23
    Jas 1:15
    —We cannot atone for our own sin ....Ps 49:7
    Mt 16:26
2. What should we do with our sin?
    —We should confess it ....Ps 32:1–5
    Pr 28:13
    1Jn 1:9
    —We should repent of it ....Eze 18:30–31
    Ac 3:19–20

—We should turn from it . . . . .Ps 34:14
Isa 1:16
3Jn 11
—We should hate it .Ps 97:10
Am 5:15
Ro 12:9
—We should throw it off . . . . .Heb 12:1
—We should fight against it . . . . .Eph 6:12–13
Heb 12:4

3. What are the blessings after confession?
—We are forgiven our sin . . . . .Ps 32:5
Ac 2:38
Ac 10:43
—God considers us righteous . . . . .Ro 4:5–8
Php 3:9
—We are purified from sin 1Jn 1:9
—We are freed from sin . . . . .Ro 6:7,18,22
Rev 1:5
—We are no longer slaves to sin . . . . .Ro 6:6,17
—We do not continue a life of sin 1Jn 3:6,9
1Jn 5:18
—We are dead to sin . . . . .Ro 6:2,11
—We pass from death to life . . . . .Ro 6:23

SINAI
A. A desert area where the Israelites camped . . .Ex 19:1–2
—Census taken there . . . . .Nu 1:1–4,19
—Passover celebrated there . . . . .Nu 9:1–5
—Israelites stayed there nearly a year . . . . .Nu 10:12
B. Mount Sinai, in the above area
1. Identity
—Called Mount Horeb . . . . .Ex 33:6
—Called the mountain of God . . . . .Ex 3:1
Ex 24:13
—God came down from Mount Sinai . . . . . .Dt 33:2
—God is the God of Mount Sinai . . . . .Ps 68:8
2. History and significance
—God appeared to Moses there . . . . .Ex 3:1–6
—God spoke his law from there . . . . .Ex 19:20–20:17
Dt 5:4–21
—Israelites frightened at the mountain . . . .Ex 20:18–19
Dt 5:5,22–27
—Moses received the law there . . . . .Ex 24:15–18
Dt 9:9–11
—Israelites worshiped golden calf there . . .Ex 32:1–20
Dt 9:8–17
Ps 106:19–23
—Moses received the law a second time . . . .Ex 34:1–32
Lev 7:38
Dt 10:1–5,10
—Elijah talked with God there 1Ki 19:8–18

SINGLES
See MARRIAGE
SISERA
—Canaanite commander . . . . .Jdg 4:2
—Fought against Deborah and Barak . . . . .Jdg 4:12–16
—Killed by Jael . . . . .Jdg 4:21
Jdg 5:24–30

SISTER
See BROTHERS AND SISTERS
SLAVERY
A. Slavery in the Old Testament
1. Slavery common
—Abraham had slaves . . . . .Ge 20:14
Ge 21:10
—Israelites were slaves in Egypt . . . . .Ex 1:11
Dt 6:20–21
—David had slaves .2Sa 6:20,22
—Solomon conscripted slaves 1Ki 9:20–22
—The Teacher had slaves . . . . .Ecc 2:7
—Sons were made slaves to pay debts 2Ki 4:1
—Israelites were slaves to Babylon . . . . . . .La 1:1
—Israelites were slaves to Persia . . . . .Ne 9:36
—There were slaves among returning Jews . . .Ne 5:5
2. God and human slavery
a. Delivered Israelites from slavery . . . . . . .Ex 13:3
Ex 20:2
b. Regulated slavery in Israel
—Treatment of slaves . . . . .Ex 21:5–11,20–21
Dt 15:12–18
Dt 23:15–16

—Release in the Year of Jubilee . . . . .Lev 25:39–55
c. Gave rights to slaves
—Were members of the covenant . . . . .Ge 17:12–13
—Rested on the Sabbath . . . . .Ex 20:10
Dt 5:12–15
—Included in religious meals . . . . .Ex 12:44
Dt 16:11,14
—Could expect equal justice . . . . .Job 31:13
—Could become an heir . . . . .Ge 15:2–3
B. Slavery in the New Testament
1. Common in Roman society . . . . .Ac 16:16,19
1Co 7:21
1Ti 1:10
2. Messages for Christian slaves
—Slave and master are equal in Christ 1Co 12:13
Gal 3:28
Col 3:11
Phm 15–15
—Slaves must respect their masters 1Ti 6:1–2
—Slaves must submit to their masters . . . . . . .Tit 2:9–10
1Pe 2:18
—Slaves must obey their masters . . . . .Eph 6:5–8
Col 3:22–25
—If possible, try to gain freedom 1Co 7:21
3. Messages given to Christian masters
—Masters must treat slaves kindly . . . . .Eph 6:9
Phm 17
—Masters must treat slaves justly . . . . .Col 4:1
C. Slavery as a symbol
—By nature we are slaves to sin . . . . .Jn 8:34
Ro 6:16–17
Ro 7:14
2Pe 2:19
—The Old Testament era saw slavery to the law . .Gal 4:3–5
Gal 5:1
—We must become slaves to righteousness . . . . .Ro 6:18
—We must become slaves to God and Christ . . . .Ro 6:22
1Co 7:22
Eph 6:6

SNOW
See WEATHER
SODOM AND GOMORRAH
A. Their identity and location
—Wealthy cities in the Jordan plain . . . . .Ge 13:10
—Extremely wicked inhabitants . . . . .Ge 13:13
Ge 18:20–21
B. History of Sodom and Gomorrah
—Lot went to live there . . . . .Ge 13:11–12
—Cities defeated by four kings . . . . .Ge 14:8–12
—Abram rescued the cities . . . . .Ge 14:13–16
—Abraham interceded for the cities . . . . .Ge 18:23–33
—Sodom and Gomorrah destroyed . . . . .Ge 19:1–29
—God's promise of restoration . . . . .Eze 16:53–57
C. Sodom and Gomorrah used as symbols
—A symbol of total wickedness . . . . .Isa 3:9
Jer 23:14
Eze 16:46–50
Mt 10:15
—A symbol of evil Jerusalem . . . . .Rev 11:8
—A symbol of God's judgment . . . . .Isa 13:19
Jer 49:18
Am 4:11
Zep 2:9
—A symbol of eternal punishment 2Pe 2:6
Jude 7

SOLOMON
A. Family data
—Son of David by Bathsheba 2Sa 12:24
1Ch 3:5
—Married Pharaoh's daughter 1Ki 3:1
—Later married numerous pagan women 1Ki 11:1–3
B. His early life as king
—Appointed as king by David 1Ki 1:11–53
—Given parting charge 1Ki 2:1–9
—Had Adonijah and his supporters killed 1Ki 2:13–46
—Asked for wisdom 1Ki 3:4–15
2Ch 1:2–13
—Judged between two prostitutes 1Ki 3:16–28
—Known widely for his wisdom 1Ki 4:29–31,34
—Wrote three thousand proverbs 1Ki 4:32
Pr 1:1

All entries are words or concepts in the study notes, charts, essays and book introductions, *not* in the TNIV text. For references to key words in the text, consult either the Index to Topics or the Concordance. For location of geographical names, check both the Index to Maps and the Index to Color Maps.

and fasting
Ezr 10:6

and the Holy Spirit
Hag 2:5

and John the Baptist
Mt 4:2

law of
1Ki 14:23; 1Ki 14:24; 1Ki 18:27; 1Ki 21:10; 2Ki 4:1; 1Ch 23:3; Job 31:29–32; Isa 47:6; Jn 5:10; Jn 5:45; Jn 7:22; Heb 7:11; Heb 10:5–6; Introduction to Genesis: Author and Date of Writing

leadership of
Nu 11:29; Nu 16:1–7; Nu 27:20; Introduction to Deuteronomy: Historical Setting

as mediator
Ex 20:19; Ex 24:2; Ex 32:30; Ex 33:11; Nu 7:89; Nu 11:12; Dt 9:19; Ac 7:38

obedience of
Nu 3:16; Nu 8:20

as prophet
Nu 1:1; Nu 9:23; Nu 11:29; Nu 12:6–8,8; Dt 18:15; Ac 3:22–26

punishment of
Nu 20:11; Nu 27:12–23

song of
Dt 32:4; Isa 44:8; Introduction to Numbers: Author and Date

MOST HIGH. See NAMES OF GOD

MOST HOLY PLACE
Ex 26:31–35; Ex 27:12–13; 1Ki 6:2; 1Ki 6:16; 1Ki 6:23; 2Ch 3:8; Ezr 6:15; Ps 28:2; Eze 41:22; Mt 27:51; Lk 1:9; Heb 4:14; Heb 8:2; Heb 9:4; Heb 9:28; Heb 10:19; Heb 10:20

MOT
Jdg 10:6; Job 18:14

MOTHER. See also BARRENNESS; CHILDREN; PARENTS
Ps 113:9; Pr 31:1,26

MOUNT
Carmel
1Ki 18:19; SS 7:5; Am 1:2
Ebal
Jos 8:30; Jn 4:20
Gerizim
Jn 4:20
Gilboa
Jdg 7:3; 2Sa 1:21
Gilead
Jdg 7:3; SS 4:1
Hermon
Dt 3:8; Jos 12:1; Lk 9:28
Horeb
Ex 3:1; Dt 1:2; 1Ki 19:7; 2Ki 8:7
Mizar
Ps 42:6
Moriah
Ge 22:2; 2Ch 3:1
of Olives
Eze 11:23; Zep 1:5; Zec 14:4; Mt 24:3; Mk 11:1; Lk 19:29; Ac 1:12; Ac 21:38
Olympus
Ps 48:2; Isa 14:13
Paran
Jdg 5:4; Hab 3:3
Perazim
Isa 28:21
Seir
Ge 36:8; Eze 35:2
Sinai
Ex 3:1; Ex 19:5; Ex 19:12–13; 1Ki 19:8; Ps 68:1–35; 2Co 3:7–18; Gal 4:24; Heb 8:6; Heb 12:18–21; Heb 12:25; Rev 4:1; Rev 15:5
Tabor
Jdg 4:6; Hos 5:1; Lk 9:28
of Transfiguration
Lk 3:22; Lk 9:28

Zaphon
Ps 48:2; Isa 14:13

Zion
2Sa 5:7; 2Ch 3:1; Ne 3:16; Ps 2:4–6; Ps 48:2; Isa 2:2–4; Eze 40:2; Ob 1:17; Ob 1:21; Zec 6:1; Heb 12:22; Rev 14:1

MOUNTAIN OF THE LORD
Isa 2:2–4; "The City of the Jebusites/David's Jerusalem," 441

MOURNING. See also GRIEF
Ge 37:34; 2Sa 13:19; 2Sa 15:30; Joel 1:5; Am 8:10; Mk 5:38; Jn 11:19

MURDER
Ge 1:26; Ge 4:8; Ge 4:23; Ge 9:6; Ex 20:13; Ex 21:13; Nu 35:33; Dt 21:23; Mt 5:21

MUSIC
instruments of
Nu 10:10; Ezr 3:10; Ne 12:27,35; Ps 150:3–5; Isa 38:20
songs/hymns
Ex 15:1–18; Jdg 5:1–31; Eph 5:19; Col 3:16

MUSICIANS
1Sa 16:14–23; 1Sa 17:1–58; 1Sa 16:16; 1Ch 25:1; Ezr 2:65; Ne 12:9; Ps 4:1

MUSTARD SEED
Mt 13:32; Lk 13:19

MYRA
Ac 27:5

MYRRH
Ge 37:25; Ex 25:6; SS 1:13; Mt 2:11; Mk 15:23; Rev 18:13

MYSIA
Ac 16:7

MYSTERY
Da 2:18; Ro 11:25; 1Co 2:7; 1Co 13:2; 1Co 14:2; 1Co 15:51; Eph 3:3; Eph 5:32; Col 1:26; 2Th 2:7; 1Ti 3:16; Rev 10:7; Rev 17:5

N

NAAMAN
1Sa 9:7; 2Ki 5:10; 2Ki 5:11; 2Ki 5:14; 2Ki 5:15; 2Ki 5:19

NABAL
1Sa 25:2–44

NABONIDUS
Da 5:1; Da 5:7; Da 5:10; Da 5:26–28

NABOPOLASSAR
2Ki 23:29; 2Ki 24:1; 2Ch 35:21; Ezr 5:12; Eze 31:11; Na 2:1

NABOTH
1Ki 21:3; 1Ki 21:13; 1Ki 21:19

NABU
Ezr 10:43; Isa 46:1; Da 3:2

NADAB
Ex 24:1; 1Ki 14:14; Ac 5:1

NAHUM
Jnh 1:2; Introduction to Nahum: Author

NAIOTH
1Sa 19:18

NAME
Ge 11:4; Ge 17:5; Ex 33:19; Ps 5:11; Eze 20:9; Heb 1:4

NAMES OF GOD
Ex 34:6–7; 1Ki 5:5; A Word to the Reader, xi
Eternal God (El Olam)
Ge 21:33
God (Elohim)
Ge 1:1; Ge 2:4; Ge 7:16; Ecc 1:13

God Almighty (El Shaddai)
Ge 17:1; Job 5:17
God Most High (El Elyon)
Ge 14:19; Dt 32:8
"I Am Who I Am"
Ex 3:14; Jn 6:35; Jn 8:58
Lord (Adonai)
Ge 18:27; Zec 4:14
LORD (Yahweh/Jehovah)
Ge 2:4; Ge 7:16; Ex 3:14–15; Ex 6:3,6; Lev 18:2; Dt 28:58
LORD Almighty (Yahweh Sabaoth)
1Sa 1:3

NAMING
Ge 1:5; Ge 2:19; Ge 17:5; Ge 17:15; Ge 32:28

NAOMI
Ru 1:1–4; Ru 3:4

NAPHTALI
Ex 1:2–4; Jos 19:32; 1Ki 15:20; 2Ki 15:29; 1Ch 7:13; 2Ch 2:13; Isa 9:1

NARD
SS 1:12; Mk 14:3; Jn 12:3

NATHAN
2Sa 7:3; 2Sa 12:13; 1Ki 1:24; 1Ki 2:4; Ac 3:24; Introduction to 1 Samuel: Literary Features, Authorship and Date

NATHANAEL
Lk 6:14; Jn 1:49; Ac 1:13

NAZARENE
Mt 2:23

NAZARETH
Mt 2:23; Lk 4:23

NAZIRITE VOW
Nu 6:2; Nu 6:4; Nu 6:5; Nu 6:6; Nu 6:9–12; Jdg 13:5; 1Sa 1:11; Jer 7:29; Am 2:11; Lk 1:15; Ac 18:18; Ac 21:23

NEAPOLIS
Ac 8:5; Ac 16:11

NEBAIOTH
Isa 60:7

NEBO
Ezr 10:43; Isa 15:2; Da 1:7

NEBUCHADNEZZAR
as commander
2Ki 24:1; 2Ch 35:21
as conqueror
2Ch 36:4; 2Ch 36:5–8; Ne 1:3; "Nebuchadnezzar's Campaigns against Judah," 586
death of
Da 5:11
and fall of Jerusalem
2Ki 24:8; 2Ki 24:11; 2Ki 25:1; Eze 26:8; Introduction to Jeremiah: Background

NEBUZARADAN
Jer 40:2–3; Rev 11:19

NECHO II. See PHARAOH: Necho II

NEGEV
Ge 12:9; 1Sa 27:10; Isa 30:6

NEHEMIAH
Ezr 2:70; Ezr 4:5; Ezr 7:11; Ezr 7:26; Ne 9:3; Ne 1:1; Eze 44:9; Introduction to Ezra: The Order of Ezra and Nehemiah; "Chronology: Ezra-Nehemiah," 694

NEIGHBOR. See LOVE: of neighbor

NEPHILIM
Ge 6:4; Nu 13:33

NERGAL-SHAREZER
Jer 39:3

NERI
1Ch 3:19

INDEX TO MAPS

All entries are place-names found on the maps within this Study Bible. References are to the page on which the map is located. For additional information on place-names, see Index to Notes.

CONCORDANCE TO THE TNIV | INTRODUCTION

This concordance lists nearly 35,000 references to the vocabulary of Today's New International Version. These 35,000 references have been selected as the most helpful for the average Bible student or layperson.

When determining whether or not to include a verse reference, we gave careful consideration to the passage in which the verse is located. We also encourage you to always consider the larger context of the passage, giving special attention to the flow of the thought from beginning to end. Whenever you look up a verse, your goal should be to discover the intended meaning of the verse in context. Do not use this concordance, or any concordance, merely as a *verse-finder*; it should also be used as a *passage-finder*. The contexts surrounding each entry are longer than those usually found in concordances; but even so, the context excerpts are too brief for study purposes. They serve only to help you locate familiar verses.

The entry headings list words exactly as they are spelled in the TNIV. Related words follow in parentheses, e.g., ABANDON (ABANDONED). In the contexts that follow, words are abbreviated and in bold type. Sometimes contexts contain more than one occurrence of a word, as under HOLY: Rev 4:8 " '**H, h, h** is the Lord God.

Words and phrases that are italicized in the TNIV text are also italicized in the contexts, as under FATHER: Ro 8:15 And by him we cry, "*Abba, F.*"

In some cases the usual short contextual phrases are ineffective in helping you locate a passage. This is especially true in studying key events in a Bible character's life. Therefore, we have incorporated 242 dictionary-style entries that give brief biographies of key Bible characters. These entries offer more information and biblical references than can simple contexts.

Often more than one Bible character has the same name. For example, there are more than thirty Zechariahs in the Bible. In these cases we have subdivided some dictionary entries, assigning each person a number (1), (2), etc., and have included a brief description to distinguish each. Less significant names are not included.

In this concordance there are 1,293 entries that have an exhaustive list of every appearance of that word. When this occurs, the entry is marked with an asterisk (*).

Two entries involving the words "Lord" and "Lord's" use a special code. LORD and LORD'S list occurrences of the title "Lord," spelled "Lord" and "lord," "Lord's" and "lord's" in the TNIV. LORD† and LORD'S† list occurrences of the proper name of God, *Yahweh,* spelled "LORD" and "LORD's" in the TNIV.

We pray that this concordance will be used by TNIV readers to introduce them to the full scope of God's truth in every book of the Bible.

John R. Kohlenberger III

ABBREVIATIONS

Ac	Acts	Hab	Habakkuk	1Ki	1 Kings	Pr	Proverbs
Am	Amos	Hag	Haggai	2Ki	2 Kings	Ps	Psalms
1Ch	1 Chronicles	Heb	Hebrews	La	Lamentations	Rev	Revelation
2Ch	2 Chronicles	Hos	Hosea	Lev	Leviticus	Ro	Romans
1Co	1 Corinthians	Isa	Isaiah	Lk	Luke	Ru	Ruth
2Co	2 Corinthians	Jas	James	Mal	Malachi	1Sa	1 Samuel
Col	Colossians	Jdg	Judges	Mic	Micah	2Sa	2 Samuel
Da	Daniel	Jer	Jeremiah	Mk	Mark	SS	Song of Songs
Dt	Deuteronomy	1Jn	1 John	Mt	Matthew	1Th	1 Thessalonians
Ecc	Ecclesiastes	2Jn	2 John	Na	Nahum	2Th	2 Thessalonians
Eph	Ephesians	3Jn	3 John	Ne	Nehemiah	1Ti	1 Timothy
Est	Esther	Jn	John	Nu	Numbers	2Ti	2 Timothy
Ex	Exodus	Jnh	Jonah	Ob	Obadiah	Tit	Titus
Eze	Ezekiel	Job	Job	1Pe	1 Peter	Zec	Zechariah
Ezr	Ezra	Joel	Joel	2Pe	2 Peter	Zep	Zephaniah
Gal	Galatians	Jos	Joshua	Phm	Philemon		
Ge	Genesis	Jude	Jude	Php	Philippians		

AARON
Genealogy of (Ex 6:16–20; Jos 21:4, 10; 1Ch 6:3–15).

Priesthood of (Ex 28:1; Nu 17; Heb 5:1–4; 7), garments (Ex 28; 39), consecration (Ex 29), ordination (Lev 8).

Spokesman for Moses (Ex 4:14–16, 27–31; 7:1–2). Supported Moses' hands in battle (Ex 17:8–13). Built golden calf (Ex 32; Dt 9:20). Talked against Moses (Nu 12). Priesthood opposed (Nu 16); staff budded (Nu 17). Forbidden to enter land (Nu 20:1–12). Death (Nu 20:22–29; 33:38–39).

ABADDON*
Rev 9: 11 whose name in Hebrew is **A**

ABANDON (ABANDONED)
Dt   4: 31 he will not a or destroy you
1Ki   6: 13 and will not a my people Israel."
Ne   9: 19 compassion you did not a them
         9: 31 not put an end to them or a them,
Ps   16: 10 because you will not a me
Ac   2: 27 because you will not a me
1Ti   4: 1 in later times some will a the faith

ABANDONED (ABANDON)
Ge   24: 27 who has not a his kindness
2Co   4: 9 persecuted, but not a;

ABBA*
Mk   14: 36 "**A**, Father," he said,
Ro   8: 15 And by him we cry, "**A**, Father."
Gal   4: 6 the Spirit who calls out, "**A**,

ABEDNEGO
Deported to Babylon with Daniel (Da 1:1–6). Name changed from Azariah (Da 1:7). Refused defilement by food (Da 1:8–20). Refused idol worship (Da 3:1–12); saved from furnace (Da 3:13–30).

ABEL
Second son of Adam (Ge 4:2). Offered proper sacrifice (Ge 4:4; Heb 11:4). Murdered by Cain (Ge 4:8; Mt 23:35; Lk 11:51; 1Jn 3:12).

ABHOR
Lev 26: 30 of your idols, and I will a you.
Ps   26: 5 I a the assembly of evildoers
      139: 21 a those who are in rebellion against
Am   6: 8 "I a the pride of Jacob and detest
Ro   2: 22 You who a idols, do you rob

ABIATHAR
High priest in days of Saul and David (1Sa 22; 1Sa 15; 1Ki 1–2; Mk 2:26). Escaped Saul's slaughter of priests (1Sa 22:18–23). Supported David in Absalom's revolt (2Sa 15:24–29). Supported Adonijah (1Ki 1:7–42); deposed by Solomon (1Ki 2:22–35; cf. 1Sa 2:31–35).

ABIGAIL
1. Sister of David (1Ch 2:16–17).
2. Wife of Nabal (1Sa 25:30); pled for his life with David (1Sa 25:14–35). Became David's wife after Nabal's death (1Sa 25:36–42); bore him Kileab (2Sa 3:3) also known as Daniel (1Ch 3:1).

ABIHU
Son of Aaron (Ex 6:23; 24:1, 9); killed for offering unauthorized fire (Lev 10; Nu 3:2–4; 1Ch 24:1–2).

ABIJAH
1. Second son of Samuel (1Ch 6:28); a corrupt judge (1Sa 8:1–5).
2. An Aaronic priest (1Ch 24:10; Lk 1:5).
3. Son of Jeroboam I of Israel; died as prophesied by Ahijah (1Ki 14:1–18).
4. Son of Rehoboam; king of Judah who fought Jeroboam I attempting to reunite the kingdom (1Ki 14:31–15:8; 2Ch 12:16–14:1; Mt 1:7).

ABILITY (ABLE)
Ex   35: 34 tribe of Dan, the a to teach others.
Dt   8: 18 for it is he who gives you the a
Ezr   2: 69 According to their a they gave
Mt   25: 15 one bag, each according to his a.
2Co   1: 8 far beyond our a to endure,
       3: were able, and even beyond their a.

ABIMELEK
1. King of Gerar who took Abraham's wife Sarah, believing her to be his sister (Ge 20). Later made a covenant with Abraham (Ge 21:22–33).
2. King of Gerar who took Isaac's wife Rebekah, believing her to be his sister (Ge 26:1–11). Later made a covenant with Isaac (Ge 26:12–31).
3. Son of Gideon (Jdg 8:31). Attempted to make himself king (Jdg 9).

ABISHAG*
Shunammite virgin; attendant of David in his old age (1Ki 1:1–15; 2:17–22).

ABISHAI
Son of Zeruiah, David's sister (1Sa 26:6; 1Ch 2:16). One of David's chief warriors (1Ch 11:15–21): against Edom (1Ch 18:12–13), Ammon (2Sa 10), Absalom (2Sa 18), Sheba (2Sa 20). Wanted to kill Saul (1Sa 26), killed Abner (2Sa 2:18–27; 3:22–39), wanted to kill Shimei (2Sa 16:5–13; 19:16–23).

ABLE (ABILITY ENABLE ENABLED ENABLES ENABLING)
Nu   14: 16 'The Lord was not a to bring
1Ch 29: 14 that we should be a to give as
2Ch   2: 6 who is a to build a temple for him,
Pr   17: 16 when they are not a to understand it?
Eze   7: 19 gold will not be a to deliver them
Da   3: 17 the God we serve is a to deliver us,
       4: 37 walk in pride he is a to humble.
Mt   9: 28 "Do you believe that I am a to do this?"
Lk   13: 24 will try to enter and will not be a to.
      14: 30 to build and wasn't a to finish.'
      21: 15 your adversaries will be a to resist
      21: 36 you may be a to stand before
Ac   5: 39 you will not be a to stop these men;
      11: 29 The disciples, as each one was a,
Ro   8: 39 will be a to separate us
      14: 4 the Lord is a to make them stand.
      16: 25 to him who is a to establish you
2Co   9: 8 God is a to bless you abundantly,
Eph   3: 20 to him who is a to do immeasurably
       6: 13 you may be a to stand your ground,
1Ti   3: 2 respectable, hospitable, a to teach,
2Ti   1: 12 that he is a to guard what I have
       2: 24 be kind to everyone, a to teach,
       3: 15 which are a to make you wise
Heb   2: 18 he is a to help those who are being
       7: 25 Therefore he is a to save completely
Jas   3: 2 a to keep their whole body in check.
Jude   : 24 To him who is a to keep you
Rev   5: 5 He is a to open the scroll and its

ABNER
Cousin of Saul and commander of his army (1Sa 14:50; 17:55–57; 26). Made Ish-Bosheth king after Saul (2Sa 2:8–10), but later defected to David (2Sa 3:6–21). Killed Asahel (2Sa 2:18–32), for which he was killed by Joab and Abishai (2Sa 3:22–39).

ABOLISH* (ABOLISHED)
Da   11: 31 and will a the daily sacrifice.
Mt   5: 17 think that I have come to a the Law
       5: 17 I have not come to a them

ABOLISHED (ABOLISH)
Gal   5: 11 the offense of the cross has been a.

ABOMINATION*
Da   9: 27 set up an a that causes desolation,
      11: 31 set up the a that causes desolation.
      12: 11 the a that causes desolation is set
Mt   24: 15 in the holy place 'the a that causes
Mk   13: 14 "When you see 'the a that causes

ABOUND (ABOUNDING ABOUNDS)
2Co   9: 8 you will a in every good work.
Php   1: 9 that your love may a more and more

ABOUNDING* (ABOUND)
Ex   34: 6 to anger, a in love and faithfulness,
Nu   14: 18 a in love and forgiving sin
Dt   33: 23 "Naphtali is a with the favor of
Ne   9: 17 slow to anger and a in love.
Ps   86: 5 a in love to all who call to you.
      86: 15 to anger, a in love and faithfulness.
     103: 8 gracious, slow to anger, a in love.
Pr   8: 24 there were no springs a with water;
Joel 2: 13 slow to anger and a in love, and he
Jnh   4: 2 slow to anger and a in love, a God

ABOUNDS (ABOUND)
2Co   1: 5 also our comfort a through Christ.

ABRAHAM
Abram, son of Terah (Ge 11:26–27), husband of Sarah (Ge 11:29).

Covenant relation with the Lord (Ge 12:1–3; 13:14–17; 15; 17; 22:15–18; Ex 2:24; Ne 9:8; Ps 105; Mic 7:20; Lk 1:68–75; Ro 4; Heb 6:13–15).

Called from Ur, via Harran, to Canaan (Ge 12:1; Ac 7:2–4; Heb 11:8–10). Moved to Egypt, nearly lost Sarah to Pharaoh (Ge 12:10–20). Divided the land with Lot; settled in Hebron (Ge 13). Saved Lot from four kings (Ge 14:1–16); blessed by Melchizedek (Ge

14:17–20; Heb 7:1–20). Declared righteous by faith (Ge 15:6; Ro 4:3; Gal 3:6–9). Fathered Ishmael by Hagar (Ge 16).

Name changed from Abram (Ge 17:5; Ne 9:7). Circumcised (Ge 17; Ro 4:9–12). Entertained three visitors (Ge 18); promised a son by Sarah (Ge 18:9–15; 17:16). Questioned destruction of Sodom and Gomorrah (Ge 18:16–33). Moved to Gerar; nearly lost Sarah to Abimelek (Ge 20). Fathered Isaac by Sarah (Ge 21:1–7; Ac 7:8; Heb 11:11–12); sent away Hagar and Ishmael (Ge 21:8–21; Gal 4:22–30). Covenant with Abimelek (Ge 21:22–32). Tested by offering Isaac (Ge 22; Heb 11:17–19; Jas 2:21–24). Sarah died; bought field of Ephron for burial (Ge 23). Secured wife for Isaac (Ge 24). Fathered children by Keturah (Ge 25:1–6; 1Ch 1:32–33). Death (Ge 25:7–11).

Called servant of God (Ge 26:24), friend of God (2Ch 20:7; Isa 41:8; Jas 2:23), prophet (Ge 20:7), father of Israel (Ex 3:15; Isa 51:2; Mt 3:9; Jn 8:39–58).

ABSALOM
Son of David by Maakah (2Sa 3:3; 1Ch 3:2). Killed Amnon for rape of his sister Tamar; banished by David (2Sa 13). Returned to Jerusalem; received by David (2Sa 14). Rebelled against David; siezed kingdom (2Sa 15–17). Killed (2Sa 18).

ABSENT
Col   2: 5 For though I am a from you

ABSOLUTE*
1Ti   5: 2 women as sisters, with a purity.

ABSTAIN
Ex   19: 15 A from sexual relations."
Nu   6: 3 they must a from wine and other
Ac   15: 20 telling them to a from food polluted
Ro   14: 6 those who a do so to the Lord
1Pe   2: 11 and exiles, to a from sinful desires,

ABUNDANCE (ABUNDANT)
Ge   41: 29 great a are coming throughout
Job 36: 31 the nations and provides food in a.
Ps   66: 12 but you brought us to a place of a.
Ecc   5: 12 but the a of the rich permits them no
Isa   66: 11 and delight in her overflowing a."
Jer   2: 22 and use an a of cleansing powder,
Mt   13: 12 given more, and they will have an a.
      25: 29 given more, and they will have an a.
Lk   12: 15 not consist in an a of possessions."
1Pe   1: 2 Grace and peace be yours in a.
2Pe   1: 2 yours in a through the knowledge
Jude : 2 peace and love be yours in a.

ABUNDANT (ABUNDANCE)
Dt   28: 11 will grant you a prosperity—
      32: 2 grass, like a rain on tender plants.
Job 36: 28 a showers fall on the human race.
Ps   68: 9 You gave a showers, O God;
      78: 15 gave them water as a the seas;
     132: 15 I will bless her with a provisions;
     145: 7 They celebrate your a goodness
Pr   12: 11 work their land will have a food,
      28: 19 work their land will have a food,
Jer 33: 9 will tremble at the a prosperity
Ro   5: 17 who receive God's a provision

ABUSE (ABUSIVE)
2Pe   2: 10 to heap a on celestial beings;
       2: 11 do not heap a on such beings

ABUSIVE (ABUSE)
2Ti   3: 2 proud, a, disobedient to their

ABYSS*
Lk   8: 31 not to order them to go into the A.
Rev   9: 1 given the key to the shaft of the A.
       9: 2 When he opened the A, smoke rose
       9: 2 darkened by the smoke from the A.
       9: 11 king over them the angel of the A,
      11: 7 up from the A will attack them,
      17: 8 will come up out of the A and go
      20: 1 having the key to the A and holding
      20: 3 He threw him into the A, and locked

ACCEPT (ACCEPTABLE ACCEPTANCE ACCEPTED ACCEPTS)
Ex   23: 8 "Do not a a bribe, for a bribe blinds
Dt   16: 19 Do not a a bribe, for a bribe blinds
Job 42: 8 and I will a his prayer and not deal
Pr   10: 8 The wise in heart a commands,
      19: 20 Listen to advice and a discipline,
Ro   15: 7 A one another, then, just as Christ
Jas   1: 21 humbly a the word planted in you,

ACCEPTABLE (ACCEPT)
Pr   21: 3 just is more a to the Lord than

ACCEPTANCE* (ACCEPT)
Ro 11: 15 what will their a be but life
1Ti 1: 15 saying that deserves full a:
    4: 9 saying that deserves full a.

ACCEPTED (ACCEPT)
Ge 4: 7 do what is right, will you not be a?
Job 42: 9 and the LORD a Job's prayer.
Lk 4: 24 "prophets are not a in their
Gal 1: 9 you a gospel other than what you a,

ACCEPTS (ACCEPT)
Ps 6: 9 the LORD a my prayer.
Jn 13: 20 whoever a anyone I send a me;
    13: 20 whoever a me the one who sent

ACCESS*
Est 1: 14 who had special a to the king
Ro 5: 2 through whom we have gained a
Eph 2: 18 through him we both have a

ACCOMPANIED (ACCOMPANY)
1Co 10: 4 from the spiritual rock that a them,
Jas 2: 17 itself, if it is not a by action, is dead.

ACCOMPANIES (ACCOMPANY)
2Co 9: 13 obedience that a your confession

ACCOMPANY (ACCOMPANIED ACCOMPANIES)
Dt 28: 2 a you if you obey the LORD your
Mk 16: 17 signs will a those who believe:

ACCOMPLISH
Ecc 2: 2 And what does pleasure a?"
Isa 44: 28 shepherd and will a all that I please;
    55: 11 but will a what I desire and achieve

ACCORD
Nu 24: 13 could not do anything of my own a,
Jn 10: 18 but I lay it down of my own a.

ACCOUNT (ACCOUNTABLE)
Ge 2: 4 This is the a of the heavens
    5: 1 This is the written a of Adam's
    6: 9 This is the a of Noah and his
    10: 1 This is the a of Shem,
    11: 10 This is the a of Shem's family line.
    11: 27 This is the a of Terah's family line.
    25: 12 This is the a of the family line
    25: 19 This is the a of the family line
    36: 1 This is the a of the family line
    36: 9 This is the a of the family line
    37: 2 This is the a of Jacob's family line.
Mt 12: 36 will have to give a on the day
Lk 16: 2 Give an a of your management,
Ro 14: 12 we will all give an a of ourselves
Heb 4: 13 of him to whom we must give a.

ACCOUNTABLE* (ACCOUNT)
Eze 3: 18 I will hold you a for their blood.
    3: 20 I will hold you a for their blood.
    33: 6 I will hold the watchman a for their
    33: 8 I will hold you a for their blood.
    34: 10 and will make them a for my flock.
Da 6: 2 The satraps were made a to them so
Jnh 1: 14 Do not hold us a for killing
Ro 3: 19 and the whole world held a to God.

ACCURATE
Dt 25: 15 You must have an a and honest
Pr 11: 1 but a weights find favor with him.

ACCURSED (CURSE)
2Pe 2: 14 are experts in greed—an a brood!

ACCUSATION (ACCUSE)
1Ti 5: 19 not entertain an a against an elder

ACCUSE (ACCUSATION ACCUSER ACCUSES ACCUSING)
Pr 3: 30 Do not a anyone for no reason—
Lk 3: 14 money and don't a people falsely—

ACCUSER* (ACCUSE)
Job 31: 35 my a put his indictment in writing.
Ps 109: 6 let an a stand at his right hand.
Jn 5: 45 Your a is Moses, on whom your
Rev 12: 10 For the a of our brothers and sisters,

ACCUSES* (ACCUSE)
Job 40: 2 Let him who a God answer him!"
Isa 54: 17 will refute every tongue that a you.
Rev 12: 10 who a them before our God day

ACCUSING (ACCUSE)
Ro 2: 15 and their thoughts now a, now even

ACHAN
Sin at Jericho caused defeat at Ai; stoned (Jos 7; 22:20; 1Ch 2:7 ["Achar"]).

ACHE*
Pr 14: 13 Even in laughter the heart may a,

ACHIEVE
Ps 45: 4 let your right hand a awesome deeds.
Isa 55: 11 a the purpose for which I sent it.

ACHISH
King of Gath before whom David feigned insanity (1Sa 21:10–15). Later "ally" of David (2Sa 27–29).

ACKNOWLEDGE (ACKNOWLEDGED ACKNOWLEDGES)
Ps 91: 14 for they a my name.
Jer 3: 13 Only a your guilt—
Hos 6: 3 let us press on to a him.
Mt 10: 32 also a before my Father in heaven.
Lk 12: 8 will also a before the angels of God.
Jn 12: 42 they would not openly a their faith
Php 2: 11 and every tongue a that Jesus
1Th 5: 12 to a those who work hard among you,
Heb 3: 1 we a as our apostle and high priest.
1Jn 4: 3 spirit that does not a Jesus is not

ACKNOWLEDGED (ACKNOWLEDGE)
Lk 7: 29 words, a that God's way was right,

ACKNOWLEDGES* (ACKNOWLEDGE)
Mt 10: 32 "Whoever publicly a me I will
Lk 12: 8 whoever publicly a me, the Son
1Jn 2: 23 whoever a the Son has the Father
    4: 2 Every spirit that a that Jesus Christ
    4: 15 If anyone that a that Jesus is the Son

ACQUIRES*
Pr 18: 15 heart of the discerning a knowledge,

ACQUIT (ACQUITTING)
Ex 23: 7 to death, for I will not a the guilty.

ACQUITTING* (ACQUIT)
Dt 25: 1 a the innocent and condemning
Pr 17: 15 A the guilty and condemning

ACT (ACTION ACTIONS ACTIVE ACTIVITY ACTS)
1Ki 2: 2 "So be strong, a like a man,
Ps 106: 3 Blessed are those who a justly,
    119:126 It is time for you to a, LORD;

ACTION (ACT)
2Co 9: 2 has stirred most of them to a.
Jas 2: 17 if it is not accompanied by a,

ACTIONS (ACT)
Mt 11: 19 wisdom is proved right by her a."
Gal 6: 4 Each of you should test your own a.
Tit 1: 16 God, but by their a they deny him.

ACTIVE* (ACT)
Heb 4: 12 For the word of God is alive and a.

ACTIVITY (ACT)
Ecc 3: 1 for every a under the heavens:
    3: 17 for there will be a time for every a,

ACTS (ACT)
1Ch 16: 9 tell of all his wonderful a.
Ps 40: 5 your saving in the great assembly;
    71: 15 of your saving a all day long—
    71: 16 come and proclaim your mighty a,
    71: 24 tell of your righteous a all day long,
    105: 2 tell of all his wonderful a.
    106: 2 Who can proclaim the mighty a
    145: 4 they tell of your mighty a.
    145: 12 people may know of your mighty a
    150: 2 Praise him for his a of power;
Isa 64: 6 all our righteous a are like filthy
Mt 6: 1 not to do your 'a of righteousness'

ADAM
1. First man (Ge 1:26–2:25; Ro 5:14, 45; 1Ti 2:13). Sin of (Ge 3; Hos 6:7; Ro 5:12–21). Children of (Ge 4:1–5:5). Death of (Ge 5:5; Ro 5:12–21; 1Co 15:22).
2. City (Jos 3:16).

ADD (ADDED)
Dt 4: 2 Do not a to what I command you
    12: 32 do not a to it or take away from it.
Pr 1: 5 wise listen and a to their learning,
    9: 9 and they will a to their learning.
    30: 6 Do not a to his words, or he will
Mt 6: 27 you by worrying a single hour
Lk 12: 25 you by worrying can a single hour
Rev 22: 18 them, God will a to you the plagues

ADDED (ADD)
Ecc 3: 14 nothing can be a to it and nothing
Ac 2: 47 the Lord a to their number daily
Gal 3: 19 It was a because of transgressions

ADDICTED*
Tit 2: 3 to be slanderers or a to much wine,

ADMINISTRATION*
Eph 3: 2 heard about the a of God's grace
    3: 9 to everyone the a of this mystery,

ADMIRABLE*
Php 4: 8 whatever is lovely, whatever is a—

ADMONISH* (ADMONISHING)
Col 3: 16 and a one another with all wisdom
1Th 5: 12 for you in the Lord and who a you.

ADMONISHING* (ADMONISH)
Col 1: 28 a and teaching everyone with all

ADONIJAH
1. Son of David by Haggith (2Sa 3:4; 1Ch 3:2). Attempted to be king after David; killed by Solomon's order (1Ki 1–2).
2. Levite; teacher of the Law (2Ch 17:8).

ADOPTION*
Gal 4: 5 that we might receive a to sonship
Eph 1: 5 predestined us for a to sonship
Ro 8: 15 brought about your a to sonship.
    8: 23 as we wait eagerly for our a,
    9: 4 Theirs is the a; theirs the divine

ADORE*
SS 1: 4 How right they are to a you!

ADORN (ADORNMENT ADORNS)
1Pe 3: 5 in God used to a themselves.

ADORNMENT* (ADORN)
1Pe 3: 3 should not come from outward a,

ADORNS* (ADORN)
Ps 93: 5 holiness a your house for endless
Pr 15: 2 The tongue of the wise a knowledge,
Isa 61: 10 as a bride herself with her jewels.
    61: 10 as a bridegroom a his head like

ADULTERER* (ADULTERY)
Lev 20: 10 both the a and the adulteress are
Job 24: 15 The eye of the a watches for dusk;
Heb 13: 4 for God will judge the a and all

ADULTERERS (ADULTERY)
1Co 6: 9 nor idolaters nor a nor male

ADULTERESS (ADULTERY)
Hos 3: 1 she is loved by another and is an a.

ADULTERIES (ADULTERY)
Jer 3: 8 sent her away because of all her a.

ADULTEROUS (ADULTERY)
Mk 8: 38 and my words in this a and sinful
Jas 4: 4 You a people, don't you know

ADULTERY (ADULTERER ADULTERERS ADULTERESS ADULTERIES ADULTEROUS)
Ex 20: 14 "You shall not commit a.
Dt 5: 18 "You shall not commit a.
Mt 5: 27 was said, 'You shall not commit a.'
    5: 28 lustfully has already committed a
    5: 32 the divorced woman commits a
    15: 19 murder, a, sexual immorality, theft,
    19: 9 another woman commits a."
    19: 18 you shall not commit a, you shall
Mk 10: 11 woman commits a against her.
    10: 12 another man, she commits a."
    10: 19 you shall not commit a, you shall
Lk 16: 18 marries another woman commits a,
    16: 18 a divorced woman commits a.
    18: 20 'You shall not commit a, you shall
Jn 8: 4 woman was caught in the act of a.
Rev 18: 3 of the earth committed a with her,

ADULTS*
1Co 14: 20 be infants, but in your thinking be a.

ADVANCE (ADVANCED)
Ps 18: 29 your help I can a against a troop;
Php 1: 12 has actually served to a the gospel.

ADVANCED* (ADVANCE)
Job 32: 7 years should teach wisdom.'

ADVANTAGE
Ex 22: 22 "Do not take a of a widow
Dt 24: 14 Do not take a of a hired worker who
Ro 3: 1 What a, then, is there in being
2Co 11: 20 exploit you or take a of you or push
1Th 4: 6 should wrong or take a of a brother

ADVERSITY
Pr 17: 17 and a brother is born for a time of a.
Isa 30: 20 the Lord gives you the bread of a

ADVICE (ADVISERS)
1Ki	12: 8	Rehoboam rejected the a the elders
	12: 14	he followed the a of the young men
2Ch	10: 8	Rehoboam rejected the a the elders
Pr	12: 5	but the a of the wicked is deceitful.
	12: 15	to them, but the wise listen to a.
	19: 20	Listen to a and accept discipline,
	20: 18	Plans are established by seeking a;
	27: 9	springs from their heartfelt a.

ADVISERS (ADVICE)
Pr	11: 14	but victory is won through many a.

ADVOCATE*
Job	16: 19	is in heaven; my a is on high.
Jn	14: 16	he will give you another a
	14: 26	But the A, the Holy Spirit,
	15: 26	"When the A comes,
	16: 7	the A will not come to you;
1Jn	2: 1	an a with the Father—Jesus

AFFECTION
2Pe	1: 7	mutual a; and to mutual a,

AFFLICTED (AFFLICTION)
Job	2: 7	a Job with painful sores
	36: 6	alive but gives the a their rights.
Ps	9: 12	he does not ignore the cries of the a.
	9: 18	the hope of the a will never perish.
	73: 14	All day long I have been a,
	119: 67	Before I was a I went astray,
	119: 71	me to be a so that I might learn your
	119: 75	that in faithfulness you have a me.
Isa	49: 13	will have compassion on his a ones.
	53: 4	by God, stricken by him, and a.
	53: 7	He was oppressed and a, yet he did
Na	1: 12	Although I have a you, Judah, I will

AFFLICTION (AFFLICTED AFFLICTIONS)
Dt	16: 3	the bread of a, because you left
Ps	107: 41	he lifted the needy out of their a
Isa	30: 20	of adversity and the water of a,
	48: 10	have tested you in the furnace of a.
La	3: 33	For he does not willingly bring a
Ro	12: 12	hope, patient in a, faithful in prayer.

AFFLICTIONS (AFFLICTION)
Col	1: 24	still lacking in regard to Christ's a,

AFRAID (FEAR)
Ge	3: 10	and I was a because I was naked;
	26: 24	Do not be a, for I am with you;
Ex	2: 14	Then Moses was a thought,
	3: 6	because he was a to look at God.
Dt	1: 21	Do not be a; do not be
	1: 29	not be terrified; do not be a of them.
	20: 1	than yours, do not be a of them,
	20: 3	Do not be fainthearted or a;
2Ki	25: 24	"Do not be a of the Babylonian
1Ch	13: 12	David was a of God that day
Ps	27: 1	of my life—of whom shall I be a?
	56: 3	When I am a, I put my trust in you.
	56: 4	in God I trust and am not a.
Pr	3: 24	you lie down, you will not be a;
Isa	10: 24	Zion, do not be a of the Assyrians,
	12: 2	I will trust and not be a.
	44: 8	Do not tremble, do not be a.
Jer	1: 8	Do not be a of them, for I am
Mt	8: 26	of little faith, why are you so a?"
	10: 28	Do not be a of those who kill
	10: 28	be a of the One who can destroy
	10: 31	So don't be a; you are worth more
Mk	5: 36	said, Jesus told him, "Don't be a;
Lk	9: 34	and they were a as they entered
Jn	14: 27	hearts be troubled and do not be a.
Ac	27: 24	and said, 'Do not be a, Paul.
Heb	13: 6	Lord is my helper; I will not be a.

AGAG (AGAGITE)
King of Amalekites not killed by Saul (1Sa 15).

AGAGITE (AGAG)
Est	3: 1	end to the evil plan of Haman the A,

AGED (AGES)
Job	12: 12	Is not wisdom found among the a?
Pr	17: 6	children are a crown to the a,
	30: 17	that scorns an a mother,

AGES (AGED)
Pr	8: 23	I was formed long a ago,
Ro	16: 25	the mystery hidden for long a past,
Eph	2: 7	in the coming a he might show
	3: 9	for a past was kept hidden in God,
Col	1: 26	that has been kept hidden for a

AGONY
Lk	16: 24	because I am in a in this fire.'

Rev	16: 10	People gnawed their tongues in a

AGREE (AGREEMENT AGREES)
Mt	18: 19	earth a about anything you ask for,
Ro	7: 16	want to do, I a that the law is good.

AGREEMENT (AGREE)
2Co	6: 16	What a is there between the temple

AGREES* (AGREE)
Ac	7: 42	This a with what is written
1Co	4: 17	Jesus, which a with what I teach

AGRIPPA*
Descendant of Herod; king before whom Paul pled his case in Caesarea (Ac 25:13–26:32).

AHAB
1. Son of Omri; king of Israel (1Ki 16:28–22:40), husband of Jezebel (1Ki 16:31). Promoted Baal worship (1Ki 16:31–33); opposed by Elijah (1Ki 17:1; 18; 21), a prophet (1Ki 20:35–43), Micaiah (1Ki 22:1–28). Defeated Ben-Hadad (1Ki 20:1–34). Killed for murder of Naboth (1Ki 20:35–21:40).
2. A false prophet (Jer 29:21–22).

AHAZ
1. Son of Jotham; king of Judah, (2Ki 16; 2Ch 28). Idolatry of (2Ki 16:3–4, 10–18; 2Ch 28:1–4, 22–25). Defeated by Aram and Israel (2Ki 16:5–6; 2Ch 28:5–15). Sought help from Assyria rather than the Lord (2Ki 16:7–9; 2Ch 28:16–21; Isa 7).
2. Benjamite, descendant of Saul (1Ch 8:35–36).

AHAZIAH
1. Son of Ahab; king of Israel (1Ki 22:51–2Ki 1:18; 2Ch 20:35–37). Made an unsuccessful alliance with Jehoshaphat of Judah (2Ch 20:35–37). Died for seeking Baal rather than the Lord (2Ki 1).
2. Son of Jehoram; king of Judah (2Ch 8:25–29; 9:14–29), also called Jehoahaz (2Ch 21:17–22:9; 25:23). Killed by Jehu while visiting Joram (2Ki 9:14–29; 2Ch 22:1–9).

AHIJAH
1Sa	14: 18	Saul said to A, "Bring the ark
1Ki	14: 2	A the prophet is there—the one who

AHIMELEK
1. Priest who helped David in his flight from Saul (1Sa 21–22).
2. One of David's warriors (1Sa 26:6).

AHITHOPHEL
One of David's counselors who sided with Absalom (2Sa 15:12, 31–37; 1Ch 27:33–34); committed suicide when his advice was ignored (2Sa 16:15–17:23).

AI
Jos	7: 4	they were routed by the men of A,
	8: 28	So Joshua burned A and made it

AID
Isa	38: 14	Lord, come to my a!"
Php	4: 16	you sent me a more than once

AIM
1Co	7: 34	Her a is to be devoted to the Lord

AIR
1Co	9: 26	not fight like a boxer beating the a.
	14: 9	You will just be speaking into the a.
Eph	2: 2	of the ruler of the kingdom of the a,
1Th	4: 17	the clouds to meet the Lord in the a.

ALABASTER*
Mt	26: 7	him with an a jar of very expensive
Mk	14: 3	a woman came with an a jar of very
Lk	7: 37	so she came there with an a jar

ALARM (ALARMED)
2Co	7: 11	indignation, what a, what longing,

ALARMED (ALARM)
Mk	13: 7	and rumors of wars, do not be a.
2Th	2: 2	or a by the teaching allegedly

ALERT*
Jos	8: 4	far from it. All of you be on the a.
Ps	17: 11	with eyes a, to throw me
Isa	21: 7	on camels, let him be a, fully a."
Mk	13: 33	Be a! You do not know
Eph	6: 18	be a and always keep on praying
1Pe	1: 13	minds that are a and fully sober,
	4: 7	Therefore be a and of sober mind
	5: 8	Be a and of sober mind.

ALIENATED*
Job	19: 13	"He has a my family from me;
Gal	5: 4	by the law have been a from Christ;
Col	1: 21	Once you were a from God

ALIVE (LIVE)
1Sa	2: 6	Lord brings death and makes a;
Lk	24: 23	vision of angels, who said he was a.
Ac	1: 3	convincing proofs that he was a.
Ro	6: 11	to sin but a to God in Christ Jesus.
1Co	15: 22	so in Christ all will be made a.
Eph	2: 5	made us a with Christ even
Heb	4: 12	the word of God is a and active.

ALMIGHTY (MIGHT)
Ge	17: 1	to him and said, "I am God A;
Ex	6: 3	to Isaac and to Jacob as God A,
Ru	1: 20	because the A has made my life
Job	11: 7	Can you probe the limits of the A?
	33: 4	the breath of the A gives me life.
Ps	89: 8	Who is like you, Lord God A?
	91: 1	will rest in the shadow of the A.
Isa	6: 3	"Holy, holy, holy is the Lord A;
	45: 13	or reward, says the Lord A."
	47: 4	the Lord A is his name—
	48: 2	the Lord A is his name:
	51: 15	the Lord A is his name:
	54: 5	the Lord A is his name—
Am	5: 14	the Lord God A will be with you,
	5: 15	the Lord God A will have mercy
Rev	4: 8	holy is the Lord God A,' who was,
	19: 6	For our Lord God A reigns.

ALPHA*
Rev	1: 8	"I am the A and the Omega,"
	21: 6	I am the A and the Omega,
	22: 13	I am the A and the Omega, the First

ALTAR
Ge	8: 20	Noah built an a to the Lord and,
	12: 7	So he built an a there
	13: 18	There he built an a to the Lord.
	22: 9	about, Abraham built an a there
	26: 25	his son Isaac and laid him on the a,
	26: 25	Isaac built an a there and called
	35: 1	and build an a there to God,
Ex	17: 15	Moses built an a and called it
	27: 1	"Build an a of acacia wood,
	30: 1	"Make an a of acacia wood,
	37: 25	They made the a of incense
Dt	27: 5	Build there an a to the Lord
	27: 5	Lord your God, an a of stones.
Jos	8: 30	on Mount Ebal an a to the Lord,
	22: 10	Manasseh built an imposing a there
Jdg	6: 24	So Gideon built an a to the Lord
	21: 4	the next day the people built an a
1Sa	7: 17	he built an a there to the Lord.
	14: 35	Then Saul built an a to the Lord;
2Sa	24: 25	David built an a to the Lord
1Ki	12: 33	sacrifices on the a he had built
	13: 2	by the word of the Lord: "A, a!
	16: 32	He set up an a for Baal
	18: 30	he repaired the a of the Lord,
2Ki	16: 11	So Uriah the priest built an a
1Ch	21: 26	David built an a to the Lord
2Ch	4: 1	made a bronze a twenty cubits long,
	4: 19	the golden a; the tables
	15: 8	He repaired the a of the Lord
	32: 12	'You must worship before one a
	33: 16	he restored the a of the Lord
Ezr	3: 2	began to build the a of the God
Isa	6: 6	he had taken with tongs from the a.
Eze	40: 47	the a was in front of the temple.
Mt	5: 23	if you are offering your gift at the a
Ac	17: 23	worship, I even found an a with this
Heb	13: 10	We have an a from which those
Rev	6: 9	I saw under the a the souls of those

ALTER*
Ps	89: 34	or a what my lips have uttered.

ALWAYS
Dt	15: 11	There will a be poor people
Ps	16: 8	I keep my eyes a on the Lord.
	51: 3	and my sin is a before me.
	119: 98	Your commands are a with me
Pr	23: 7	person who is a thinking
Mt	26: 11	The poor you will a have with you,
	26: 11	but you will not a have me.
	28: 20	And surely I am with you a,
Mk	14: 7	The poor you will a have with you,
	14: 7	But you will not a have me.
Jn	12: 8	You will a have the poor among you, but
		you will not a have me."
1Co	13: 7	It a protects, a trusts, a hopes,
Php	4: 4	Rejoice in the Lord a. I will say it
1Pe	3: 15	A be prepared to give an answer

AMALEKITES
Ex	17: 8	The A came and attacked

1Sa 15: 2 'I will punish the **A** for what they

AMASA
Nephew of David (1Ch 2:17). Commander of Absalom's forces (2Sa 17:24–27). Returned to David (2Sa 19:13). Killed by Joab (2Sa 20:4–13).

AMASSES*
Pr 28: 8 profit from the poor **a** it for another,

AMAZED
Mt 7: 28 the crowds were **a** at his teaching,
Mk 6: 6 He was **a** at their lack of faith.
10: 24 The disciples were **a** at his words.
Ac 2: 7 Utterly **a**, they asked:
13: 12 for he was **a** at the teaching

AMAZIAH
1. Son of Joash; king of Judah (2Ki 14; 2Ch 25). Defeated Edom (2Ki 14:7; 2Ch 25:5–13); defeated by Israel for worshiping Edom's gods (2Ki 14:8–14; 2Ch 25:14–24).
2. Idolatrous priest who opposed Amos (Am 7:10–17).

AMBASSADOR* (AMBASSADORS)
Eph 6: 20 for which I am an **a** in chains.

AMBASSADORS (AMBASSADOR)
2Co 5: 20 We are therefore Christ's **a**,

AMBITION
Ro 15: 20 It has always been my **a** to preach
Gal 5: 20 fits of rage, selfish **a**, dissensions,
Php 1: 17 preach Christ out of selfish **a**,
2: 3 Do nothing out of selfish **a** or vain
1Th 4: 11 to make it your **a** to lead a quiet life:
Jas 3: 14 envy and selfish **a** in your hearts,
3: 16 where you have envy and selfish **a**,

AMENDS
Pr 14: 9 Fools mock at making **a** for sin,

AMNON
Firstborn of David (2Sa 3:2; 1Ch 3:1). Killed by Absalom for raping his sister Tamar (2Sa 13).

AMON
1. Son of Manasseh; king of Judah (2Ki 21:18–26; 1Ch 3:14; 2Ch 33:21–25).
2. Ruler of Samaria under Ahab (1Ki 22:26; 2Ch 18:25).

AMOS
1. Prophet from Tekoa (Am 1:1; 7:10–17).
2. Ancestor of Jesus (Lk 3:25).

ANAK (ANAKITES)
Nu 13: 28 even saw descendants of **A** there.

ANAKITES (ANAK)
Dt 1: 28 We even saw the **A** there.' "
2: 10 and numerous, and as tall as the **A**.
9: 2 "Who can stand up against the **A**?"

ANANIAS
1. Husband of Sapphira; died for lying to God (Ac 5:1–11).
2. Disciple who baptized Saul (Ac 9:10–19).
3. High priest at Paul's arrest (Ac 22:30–24:1).

ANCESTORS (ANCESTRY)
1Ki 19: 4 I am no better than my **a**."
Jn 4: 20 Our **a** worshiped on this mountain,
Heb 1: 1 spoke to our **a** through the prophets
1Pe 1: 18 handed down to you from your **a**,

ANCESTRY (ANCESTORS)
Ro 9: 5 them is traced the human **a**

ANCHOR
Heb 6: 19 We have this hope as an **a**

ANCIENT
Da 7: 9 and the **A** of Days took his seat.
7: 13 He approached the **A** of Days
7: 22 until the **A** of Days came

ANDREW*
Apostle; brother of Simon Peter (Mt 4:18; 10:2; Mk 1:16–18, 29; 3:18; 13:3; Lk 6:14; Jn 1:35–44; 6:8–9; 12:22; Ac 1:13).

ANGEL (ANGELIC ANGELS ARCHANGEL)
Ge 16: 7 The **a** of the LORD found Hagar
22: 11 the **a** of the LORD called
Ex 23: 20 I am sending an **a** ahead of you
Nu 22: 23 the donkey saw the **a** of the LORD
Jdg 2: 1 The **a** of the LORD went
6: 22 I have seen the **a** of the LORD
13: 15 said to the **a** of the LORD,
2Sa 24: 16 When the **a** stretched out his hand

1Ki 19: 7 The **a** of the LORD came back
2Ki 19: 35 That night the **a** of the LORD went
Ps 34: 7 The **a** of the LORD encamps
Hos 12: 4 He struggled with the **a**
Mt 2: 13 an **a** of the Lord appeared to Joseph
28: 2 for an **a** of the Lord came down
Lk 1: 26 God sent the **a** Gabriel to Nazareth,
2: 9 An **a** of the Lord appeared to them,
22: 43 An **a** from heaven appeared to him
Ac 6: 15 his face was like the face of an **a**.
12: 7 Suddenly an **a** of the Lord appeared
2Co 11: 14 Satan himself masquerades as an **a**
Gal 1: 8 or an **a** from heaven should preach

ANGELIC* (ANGEL)
1Co 13: 1 speak in human or **a** tongues,

ANGELS (ANGEL)
Ps 91: 11 will command his **a** concerning you
Mt 4: 6 will command his **a** concerning you,
13: 39 of the age, and the harvesters are **a**.
13: 49 The **a** will come and separate
18: 10 that their **a** in heaven always see
25: 41 fire prepared for the devil and his **a**.
Lk 4: 10 will command his **a** concerning you
20: 36 for they are like the **a**.
1Co 6: 3 you not know that we will judge **a**?
Col 2: 18 and the worship of **a** disqualify you.
Heb 1: 4 the **a** as the name he has inherited is
1: 6 "Let all God's **a** worship him."
1: 7 "He makes his **a** spirits, and his
1: 14 Are not all **a** ministering spirits sent
2: 7 made them a little lower than the **a**;
2: 9 who was made lower than the **a**
13: 2 hospitality to **a** without knowing it.
1Pe 1: 12 Even a long to look into these
2Pe 2: 4 if God did not spare **a** when they
Jude 6 And the **a** who did not keep their

ANGER (ANGERED ANGRY)
Ex 15: 7 You unleashed your burning **a**;
22: 24 My **a** will be aroused, and I will kill
32: 10 so that my **a** may burn against them
32: 11 "why should your **a** burn against
32: 12 Turn from your fierce **a**;
32: 19 his **a** burned and he threw
34: 6 slow to **a**, abounding in love
Lev 26: 28 in my **a** I will be hostile toward you,
Nu 14: 18 'The LORD is slow to **a**,
25: 11 has turned my **a** away
32: 10 The LORD's **a** was aroused
32: 13 The LORD's **a** burned against
Dt 9: 19 I feared the **a** and wrath
29: 28 In furious **a** and in great wrath
Jdg 14: 19 Burning with **a**, he returned to his
2Sa 12: 5 burned with **a** against the man
2Ki 22: 13 Great is the LORD's **a** that burns
Ne 9: 17 slow to **a** and abounding in love.
Ps 30: 5 For his **a** lasts only a moment,
78: 38 Time after time he restrained his **a**
86: 15 slow to **a**, abounding in love
90: 7 We are consumed by your **a**
103: 8 slow to **a**, abounding in love.
Pr 15: 1 wrath, but a harsh word stirs up **a**.
30: 33 so stirring up **a** produces strife."
Jnh 4: 2 slow to **a** and abounding in love,
Eph 4: 26 "In your **a** do not sin': Do not let
Jas 1: 20 because our **a** does not produce

ANGERED (ANGER)
Pr 22: 24 with those who are easily **a**,
1Co 13: 5 it is not easily **a**, it keeps no record

ANGRY (ANGER)
Ps 2: 12 or he will be **a** and you and your
95: 10 For forty years I was **a**
Pr 29: 22 An **a** person stirs up dissension,
Mt 5: 22 that anyone who is **a** with a brother
Jas 1: 19 to speak and slow to become **a**,

ANGUISH
Jer 4: 19 Oh, my **a**, my **a**! I writhe
Zep 1: 15 a day of distress and **a**, a day
Lk 21: 25 nations will be in **a** and perplexity
22: 44 And being in **a**, he prayed more
Ro 9: 2 sorrow and unceasing **a** in my heart.

ANIMALS
Ge 1: 24 and wild **a**, each according to its
7: 16 The **a** going in were male
Dt 14: 4 These are the **a** you may eat:
Job 12: 7 "But ask the **a**, and they will teach
Isa 43: 20 The wild **a** honor me, the jackals

ANNOUNCE (ANNOUNCED)
Mt 6: 2 the needy, do not **a** it with trumpets,

ANNOUNCED (ANNOUNCE)
Isa 48: 5 before they happened I **a** them
Gal 3: 8 faith, and **a** the gospel in advance

ANNOYANCE*
Pr 12: 16 Fools show their **a** at once,

ANNUAL*
Ex 30: 10 This **a** atonement must be made
Jdg 21: 19 there is the **a** festival of the LORD
1Sa 1: 21 offer the **a** sacrifice to the LORD
2: 19 her husband to offer the **a** sacrifice.
20: 6 because an **a** sacrifice is being made
2Ch 8: 13 Moons and the three **a** festivals—
Heb 10: 3 those sacrifices are an **a** reminder

ANOINT (ANOINTED ANOINTING)
Ex 30: 26 Then use it to **a** the tent of meeting,
30: 30 "**A** Aaron and his sons
1Sa 9: 16 **A** him ruler over my people Israel;
15: 1 to **a** you king over his people Israel;
2Ki 9: 3 I **a** you king over Israel.'
Ps 23: 5 You **a** my head with oil;
Da 9: 24 and to **a** the Most Holy Place.
Jas 5: 14 **a** them with oil in the name

ANOINTED (ANOINT)
1Ch 16: 22 "Do not touch my **a** ones;
Ps 105: 15 "Do not touch my **a** ones;
Isa 61: 1 because the LORD has **a** me
Da 9: 26 the **A** One will be put to death
Lk 4: 18 because he has **a** me to proclaim
Ac 10: 38 how God **a** Jesus of Nazareth

ANOINTING (ANOINT)
Lev 8: 12 He poured some of the **a** oil
1Ch 29: 22 **a** him before the LORD to be ruler
Ps 45: 7 your companions by **a** you
Heb 1: 9 your companions by **a** you
1Jn 2: 20 you have an **a** from the Holy One,
2: 27 about all things and as that **a** is real,

ANT*
Pr 6: 6 Go to the **a**, you sluggard;

ANTICHRIST* (ANTICHRISTS)
1Jn 2: 18 you have heard that the **a** is coming,
2: 22 Such a person is the **a**—
4: 3 This is the spirit of the **a**, which you
2Jn 7 person is the deceiver and the **a**.

ANTICHRISTS* (ANTICHRIST)
1Jn 2: 18 even now many **a** have come.

ANTIOCH
Ac 11: 26 were called Christians first at **A**.

ANTS* (ANT)
Pr 30: 25 **A** are creatures of little strength,

ANXIETIES* (ANXIOUS)
Lk 21: 34 drunkenness and the **a** of life,

ANXIETY (ANXIOUS)
Pr 12: 25 **A** weighs down the heart,
1Pe 5: 7 Cast all your **a** on him because he

ANXIOUS (ANXIETIES ANXIETY)
Php 4: 6 Do not be **a** about anything,

APOLLOS*
Christian from Alexandria, learned in the Scriptures; instructed by Aquila and Priscilla (Ac 18:24–28). Ministered at Corinth (Ac 19:1; 1Co 1:12; 3:4–22; 4:6; 16:42; Tit 3:13).

APOLLYON*
Rev 9: 11 Abaddon and in Greek is **A** (that is,

APOSTLE (APOSTLES APOSTLES')
Ro 11: 13 Inasmuch as I am the **a**
1Co 9: 1 Am I not an **a**? Have I not seen
2Co 12: 12 among you the marks of a true **a**,
Gal 2: 8 at work in Peter as an **a** to the Jews,
2: 8 work in me as an **a** to the Gentiles.
1Ti 2: 7 I was appointed a herald and an **a**—
2Ti 1: 11 a herald and an **a** and a teacher.
Heb 3: 1 whom we acknowledge as our **a**

APOSTLES (APOSTLE)
See also Andrew, Bartholomew, James, John, Judas, Matthew, Matthias, Nathanael, Paul, Peter, Philip, Simon, Thaddaeus, Thomas.
Lk 11: 49 'I will send them prophets and **a**,
Ac 1: 26 so he was added to the eleven **a**.
2: 43 and signs performed by the **a**.
1Co 12: 28 placed in the church first of all **a**,
15: 9 For I am the least of the **a** and do
2Co 11: 13 masquerading as **a** of Christ.
Eph 2: 20 built on the foundation of the **a**
4: 11 So Christ himself gave the **a**,

Rev 21: 14 names of the twelve **a** of the Lamb.

APOSTLES' (APOSTLE)
Ac   5: 2 the rest and put it at the **a** feet.
     8: 18 at the laying on of the **a** hands,

APPEAL
Ac 25: 11 me over to them. I **a** to Caesar!"
Phm   9 yet I prefer to **a** to you on the basis

APPEAR (APPEARANCE APPEARANCES
APPEARED APPEARING APPEARS)
Ge   1: 9 to one place, and let dry ground **a**."
Lev 16: 2 For I will **a** in the cloud over
Mt 24: 30 of the Son of Man **a** in the sky,
Mk 13: 22 false prophets will **a** and perform
Lk 19: 11 of God was going to **a** at once.
2Co 5: 10 we must all **a** before the judgment
Col 3: 4 you also will **a** with him in glory.
Heb 9: 24 now to **a** for us in God's presence.
     9: 28 and he will **a** a second time,

APPEARANCE (APPEAR)
1Sa 16: 7 People look at the outward **a**,
Isa 52: 14 his **a** was so disfigured beyond
    53: 2 in his **a** that we should desire him.

APPEARANCES* (APPEAR)
Jn   7: 24 Stop judging by mere **a**, but instead
2Co 10: 7 You are judging by **a**.

APPEARED (APPEAR)
Nu 14: 10 the glory of the LORD **a** at the tent
Mt   1: 20 an angel of the Lord **a** to him
Lk   2: 9 An angel of the Lord **a** to them,
1Co 15: 5 and that he **a** to Cephas,
Heb 9: 26 But he has **a** once for all

APPEARING (APPEAR)
1Ti 6: 14 blame until the **a** of our Lord Jesus
2Ti 1: 10 now been revealed through the **a**
     4: 8 to all who have longed for his **a**.
Tit 2: 13 the **a** of the glory of our great God

APPEARS (APPEAR)
Mal 3: 2 Who can stand when he **a**?
Col 3: 4 who is your life, **a**, then you
1Pe 5: 4 And when the Chief Shepherd **a**,
1Jn 3: 2 But we know that when Christ **a**,

APPETITE
Pr   2: 12 the unfaithful have an **a** for violence.
    13: 4 A sluggard's **a** is never filled,
    16: 26 The **a** of laborers works for them;
Ecc 6: 7 mouth, yet the **a** is never satisfied.
Jer 50: 19 their **a** will be satisfied on the hills

APPLES
Pr 25: 11 Like **a** of gold in settings of silver is

APPLY (APPLYING)
Pr 22: 17 **a** your heart to what I teach,
    23: 12 **A** your heart to instruction and your

APPLYING (APPLY)
Pr   2: 2 and **a** your heart to understanding—

APPOINT (APPOINTED)
Ps 61: 7 **a** your love and faithfulness
1Th 5: 9 For God did not **a** us to suffer wrath
Tit 1: 5 and **a** elders in every town, as I

APPOINTED (APPOINT)
Dt   1: 15 **a** them to have authority over you—
Da 11: 27 an end will still come at the **a** time.
Hab 2: 3 For the revelation awaits an **a** time;
Lk   1: 20 will come true at their **a** time."
Jn 15: 16 you and **a** you so that you might go
Ro   9: 9 "At the **a** time I will return,

APPROACH (APPROACHING)
Ex 24: 2 but Moses alone is to **a** the LORD;
Eph 3: 12 in him we may **a** God with freedom
Heb 4: 16 then **a** God's throne of grace

APPROACHING (APPROACH)
Heb 10: 25 all the more as you see the Day **a**.
1Jn 5: 14 is the confidence we have in **a** God:

APPROPRIATE
Ecc 5: 18 is **a** for people to eat, to drink
1Ti 2: 10 **a** for women who profess to worship

APPROVAL (APPROVE)
Jdg 18: 6 Your journey has the LORD's **a**."
Jn   6: 27 the Father has placed his seal of **a**."
Ro 14: 18 pleasing to God and receives human **a**.
1Co 11: 19 to show which of you have God's **a**.
Gal 1: 10 trying to win human **a**, or God's **a**?

APPROVE (APPROVAL APPROVED)
Ro   2: 18 **a** of what is superior because you

Ro 12: 2 to test and **a** what God's will is—
    14: 22 not condemn themselves by what they **a**.

APPROVED* (APPROVE)
2Co 10: 18 commend themselves who are **a**,
1Th 2: 4 we speak as those **a** by God to be
2Ti 2: 15 to present yourself to God as one **a**,

APT*
Pr 15: 23 finds joy in giving an **a** reply—

AQUILA*
     Husband of Priscilla; co-worker with Paul, instructor of Apollos (Ac 18; Ro 16:3; 1Co 16:19; 2Ti 4:19).

ARABIA
Gal 1: 17 before I was, but I went into **A**.
     4: 25 Hagar stands for Mount Sinai in **A**

ARARAT
Ge   8: 4 came to rest on the mountains of **A**.

ARAUNAH
2Sa 24: 16 the threshing floor of **A** the Jebusite.

ARBITER* (ARBITRATE)
Lk 12: 14 me a judge or an **a** between you?"

ARBITRATE* (ARBITER)
Job 9: 33 were someone to **a** between us,

ARCHANGEL* (ANGEL)
1Th 4: 16 with the voice of the **a**
Jude : 9 But even the **a** Michael, when he

ARCHER
Pr 26: 10 Like an **a** who wounds at random is

ARCHIPPUS*
Col 4: 17 Tell **A**: "See to it that you complete
Phm   : 2 our sister and **A** our fellow soldier—

ARCHITECT*
Heb 11: 10 whose **a** and builder is God.

AREOPAGUS*
Ac 17: 19 brought him to a meeting of the **A**,
    17: 22 stood up in the meeting of the **A**
    17: 34 a member of the **A**, also a woman

ARGUE (ARGUMENT ARGUMENTS)
Job 13: 3 and to **a** my case with God.
    13: 8 Will you **a** the case for God?

ARGUMENT (ARGUE)
Heb 6: 16 what is said and puts an end to all **a**.

ARGUMENTS (ARGUE)
Isa 41: 21 "Set forth your **a**," says Jacob's
Col 2: 4 deceive you by fine-sounding **a**.
2Ti 2: 23 to do with foolish and stupid **a**,
Tit 3: 9 and genealogies and **a** and quarrels

ARK
Ge   6: 14 So make yourself an **a** of cypress
Ex 25: 10 "Have them make an **a** of acacia wood
    25: 21 Place the cover on top of the **a** and put in
           the **a** the tablets
Dt 10: 5 put the tablets in the **a** I had made,
1Sa 4: 11 The **a** of God was captured,
     7: 2 The **a** remained at Kiriath Jearim
2Sa 6: 17 They brought the **a** of the LORD and
1Ki 8: 9 in the **a** except the two stone tablets
1Ch 13: 9 reached out his hand to steady the **a**,
2Ch 35: 3 "Put the sacred **a** in the temple
Heb 9: 4 This **a** contained the gold jar
    11: 7 in holy fear built an **a** to save his
Rev 11: 19 within his temple was seen the **a**

ARM (ARMY)
Nu 11: 23 "Is the LORD's **a** too short?
Dt   4: 34 mighty hand and an outstretched **a**,
     7: 19 the mighty hand and outstretched **a**,
Ps 44: 3 nor did their **a** bring them victory;
    98: 1 his holy **a** have worked salvation
Jer 27: 5 and outstretched **a** I made the earth
1Pe 4: 1 **a** yourselves also with the same

ARMAGEDDON*
Rev 16: 16 the place that in Hebrew is called **A**.

ARMIES (ARMY)
1Sa 17: 26 he should defy the **a** of the living
Rev 19: 14 The **a** of heaven were following

ARMOR (ARMY)
1Ki 20: 11 his **a** should not boast like one who
Ps 35: 2 Take up shield and **a**;
Jer 46: 4 Polish your spears, put on your **a**!
Ro 13: 12 darkness and put on the **a** of light.
Eph 6: 11 Put on the full **a** of God, so that you
     6: 13 Therefore put on the full **a** of God,

ARMS (ARMY)
Dt 33: 27 underneath are the everlasting **a**.
Ps 18: 32 It is God who **a** me with strength
Pr 31: 17 her **a** are strong for her tasks.
    31: 20 She opens her **a** to the poor
Isa 40: 11 He gathers the lambs in his **a**
Mk 10: 16 And he took the children in his **a**,
Heb 12: 12 strengthen your feeble **a** and weak

ARMY (ARM ARMIES ARMOR ARMS)
Ps 33: 16 king is saved by the size of his **a**;
Joel 2: 2 a large and mighty **a** comes, such as
     2: 5 like a mighty **a** drawn up for battle.
     2: 11 thunders at the head of his **a**;
Rev 19: 9 the rider on the horse and his **a**.

AROMA
Ge   8: 21 The LORD smelled the pleasing **a**
Ex 29: 18 a pleasing **a**, a food offering
Lev 1: 9 as a food offering, a pleasing **a**.
2Co 2: 14 spread the **a** of the knowledge
     2: 15 the pleasing **a** of Christ among
     2: 16 we are an **a** that brings death;
     2: 16 other, an **a** that brings life.

AROUSE (AROUSED)
Ro 11: 14 I may somehow **a** my own people

AROUSED (AROUSE)
Ps 78: 58 they **a** his jealousy with their idols.

ARRAYED*
Ps 110: 3 A in holy splendor, your young men
Isa 61: 10 **A** me in a robe of his righteousness,

ARREST
Mt 10: 19 But when they **a** you, do not worry

ARROGANCE (ARROGANT)
1Sa 2: 3 or let your mouth speak such **a**,
Pr   8: 13 I hate pride and **a**, evil behavior
Mk   7: 22 lewdness, envy, slander, and folly.
2Co 12: 20 slander, gossip, and disorder.

ARROGANT (ARROGANCE)
Ps   5: 5 The **a** cannot stand in your
   119: 78 May the **a** be put to shame
Pr 21: 24 The proud and **a**—
Ro   1: 30 God-haters, insolent, and boastful;
    11: 20 Do not be **a**, but tremble.
1Ti 6: 17 this present world not to be **a** nor

ARROW (ARROWS)
Ps 91: 5 of night, nor the **a** that flies by day,
Pr 25: 18 or a sharp **a** is one who gives false

ARROWS (ARROW)
Ps 64: 3 and aim cruel words like deadly **a**.
    64: 7 But God will shoot them with his **a**;
   127: 4 Like a in the hands of a warrior are
Pr 26: 18 Like a maniac shooting flaming **a**
Eph 6: 16 you can extinguish all the flaming **a**

ARTAXERXES
     King of Persia; allowed rebuilding of temple under Ezra (Ezr 4; 7), and of walls of Jerusalem under his cupbearer Nehemiah (Ne 2; 5:14; 13:6).

ARTEMIS
Ac 19: 28 "Great is **A** of the Ephesians!"

ASA
     King of Judah (1Ki 15:8–24; 1Ch 3:10; 2Ch 14–16). Godly reformer (2Ch 15); in later years defeated Israel with help of Aram, not the LORD (1Ki 15:16–22; 2Ch 16).

ASAHEL
     1. Nephew of David, one of his warriors (2Sa 23:24; 1Ch 2:16; 11:26; 27:7). Killed by Abner (2Sa 2); avenged by Joab (2Sa 3:22–39).
     2. Levite; teacher (2Ch 17:8).

ASAPH
     1. Recorder to Hezekiah (2Ki 18:18, 37; Isa 36:3, 22).
     2. Levitical musician (1Ch 6:39; 15:17–19; 16:4–7, 37). Sons of (1Ch 25; 2Ch 5:12; 20:14; 29:13; 35:15; Ezr 2:41; 3:10; Ne 7:44; 11:17; 12:27–47). Psalms of (2Ch 29:30; Ps 50; 73–83).

ASCEND* (ASCENDED ASCENDING)
Dt 30: 12 "Who will **a** into heaven to get it
Ps 24: 3 Who may **a** the mountain
Isa 14: 13 in your heart, "I will **a** to heaven;
    14: 14 I will **a** above the tops of the clouds;
Jn   6: 62 of Man **a** to where he was before!
Ac   2: 34 For David did not **a** to heaven,
Ro 10: 6 heart, 'Who will **a** into heaven?' "

ASCENDED (ASCEND)
Ps 68:18 When you a on high, you took
Eph 4: 8 "When he a on high, he took many

ASCENDING (ASCEND)
Ge 28:12 and the angels of God were a
Jn 1:51 the angels of God a and descending

ASCRIBE*
1Ch 16:28 A to the Lord, all you families
16:28 a to the Lord glory and strength.
16:29 A to the Lord the glory due his
Job 36: 3 I will a justice to my Maker.
Ps 29: 1 A to the Lord, you heavenly
29: 1 a to the Lord glory and strength.
29: 2 A to the Lord the glory due his
96: 7 A to the Lord, all you families
96: 7 a to the Lord glory and strength.
96: 8 A to the Lord the glory due his

ASHAMED (SHAME)
Mk 8:38 If any of you are a of me and my
8:38 the Son of Man will be a of you
Lk 9:26 If any of you are a of me and my
9:26 the Son of Man will be a of you
Ro 1: 16 I am not a of the gospel, because it
2Ti 1: 8 So do not be a of the testimony
2:15 a worker who does not need to be a

ASHER
Son of Jacob by Zilpah (Ge 30:13; 35:26; 46:17;
Ex 1:4; 1Ch 2:2). Tribe of blessed (Ge 49:20; Dt
33:24–25), numbered (Nu 1:40–41; 26:44–47), allotted land (Jos 19:24–31; Eze 48:2), failed to fully possess (Jdg 1:31–32), failed to support Deborah (Jdg
5:17), supported Gideon (Jdg 6:35; 7:23) and David
(1Ch 12:36), 12,000 from (Rev 7:6).

ASHERAH (ASHERAHS)
Ex 34:13 stones and cut down their A poles.
1Ki 18:19 and the four hundred prophets of A,

ASHERAHS* (ASHERAH)
Jdg 3: 7 God and served the Baals and the A.

ASHES
Job 42: 6 myself and repent in dust and a."
Mt 11:21 long ago in sackcloth and a.

ASHTORETHS
Jdg 2:13 him and served Baal and the A.
1Sa 7: 4 put away their Baals and A,

ASLEEP (SLEEP)
1Co 15:18 who have fallen a in Christ are lost.

ASPIRES*
1Ti 3: 1 Whoever a to be an overseer

ASSEMBLY
Ps 1: 5 nor sinners in the a of the righteous.
35:18 I will give you thanks in the great a;
82: 1 God presides in the great a;
149: 1 praise in the a of his faithful people.

ASSIGNED
1Ki 7:14 and did all the work a to him.
Mk 13:34 each with an a task, and tells
1Co 3: 5 as the Lord has a to each his task.
7:17 whatever situation the Lord has a
2Co 10: 13 of service God himself has a to us,

ASSOCIATE
Pr 22:24 do not a with those who are easily
Jn 4: 9 Jews do not a with Samaritans.)
Ac 10:28 our law for a Jew to a with Gentiles
Ro 12:16 be willing to a with people of low
1Co 5: 9 in my letter not to a with sexually
5:11 you must not a with any who claim
2Th 3:14 Do not a with them, in order

ASSURANCE (ASSURED)
Heb 10:22 a sincere heart in full a of faith,

ASSURED (ASSURANCE)
Col 4:12 the will of God, mature and fully a.

ASTRAY
Ps 119:67 Before I was afflicted I went a,
Pr 10:17 ignores correction leads others a.
20: 1 whoever is led a by them is not
Isa 53: 6 have gone a, each of us has turned
Jer 50: 6 their shepherds have led them a
1Pe 2:25 For "you were like sheep going a,"
1Jn 3: 7 do not let anyone lead you a.

ASTROLOGERS
Isa 47:13 Let your a come forward,
Da 2: 2 a to tell him what he had dreamed.

ATE (EAT)
Ge 3: 6 wisdom, she took some and a it.
27:25 Jacob brought it to him and he a;
2Sa 9:11 So Mephibosheth a at David's table
Ps 78:25 Human beings a the bread
Jer 15:16 When your words came, I a them;
Eze 3: 3 So I a it, and it tasted as sweet as
Mt 14:20 They all a and were satisfied,
15:37 They all a and were satisfied,
Mk 6:42 They all a and were satisfied,
Lk 9:17 They all a and were satisfied,

ATHALIAH
Granddaughter of Omri; wife of Jehoram and mother of Ahaziah; encouraged their evil ways (2Ki 8:18,
27; 2Ch 22:2). At death of Ahaziah she made herself
queen, killing all his sons but Joash (2Ki 11:1–3; 2Ch
22:10–12); killed six years later when Joash was revealed (2Ki 11:4–16; 2Ch 23:1–15).

ATHLETE*
2Ti 2: 5 competes as an a does not receive

ATONE* (ATONEMENT)
Ex 30:15 to the Lord to a for your lives.
2Ch 29:24 for a sin offering to a for all Israel,
Da 9:24 an end to sin, to a for wickedness,

ATONED* (ATONEMENT)
Dt 21: 8 And the bloodshed will be a for.
1Sa 3:14 of Eli's house will never be a
Pr 16: 6 love and faithfulness sin is a for;
Isa 6: 7 is taken away and your sin a for."
22:14 day this sin will not be a for,"
27: 9 will Jacob's guilt be a for, and this

ATONEMENT (ATONE ATONED)
Ex 25:17 "Make an a cover of pure gold—
30:10 Once a year Aaron shall make a
Lev 17:11 blood that makes a for one's life.
23:27 this seventh month is the Day of A.
Nu 25:13 God and made a for the Israelites.
Ro 3:25 presented Christ as a sacrifice of a,
Heb 2:17 that he might make a for the sins

ATTACK
Ps 109: 3 they a me without cause.

ATTAINED
Php 3:16 live up to what we have already a.
Heb 11: 7 could have been a through

ATTENTION (ATTENTIVE)
Pr 4: 1 pay a and gain understanding.
4:20 My son, pay a to what I say;
5: 1 My son, pay a to my wisdom,
7:24 listen to me; pay a to what I say.
21:11 paying a to the wise
22:17 Pay a and turn your ear
Ecc 7:21 Do not pay a to every word people
Isa 42:20 many things, but have paid no a;
Tit 1:14 and will pay no a to Jewish myths
Heb 2: 1 We must pay the most careful a,

ATTENTIVE (ATTENTION)
Ne 1:11 let your ear be a to the prayer of this
1Pe 3:12 and his ears are a to their prayer,

ATTITUDE (ATTITUDES)
Eph 4:23 made new in the a of your minds;
Php 2: 5 have the same a of mind Christ
1Pe 4: 1 yourselves also with the same a,

ATTITUDES* (ATTITUDE)
Heb 4:12 the thoughts and a of the heart.

ATTRACTIVE
Tit 2:10 teaching about God our Savior a.

AUDIENCE
Pr 29:26 Many seek an a with a ruler, but it

AUTHORITIES (AUTHORITY)
Ro 13: 1 The a that exist have been
13: 5 it is necessary to submit to the a,
13: 6 for the a are God's servants,
Eph 3:10 rulers and a in the heavenly realms,
6:12 against the a, against the powers
Col 1:16 thrones or powers or rulers or a;
2:15 having disarmed the powers and a,
Tit 3: 1 people to be subject to rulers and a,
1Pe 3:22 a and powers in submission to him.

AUTHORITY (AUTHORITIES)
Mt 7:29 because he taught as one who had a
9: 6 the Son of Man has a on earth
28:18 "All a in heaven and on earth has
Mk 1:22 he taught them as one who had a,
2:10 the Son of Man has a on earth
Lk 4:32 teaching, because his words had a.

Lk 5:24 the Son of Man has a on earth
Jn 10:18 I have a to lay it down and a to take
Ac 1: 7 the Father has set by his own a.
Ro 7: 1 the law has a over someone only as
13: 1 for there is no a except
13: 2 rebels against the a is rebelling
1Co 11:10 ought to have a over her own head,
15:24 all dominion, a and power.
1Ti 2: 2 for kings and all those in a, that we
2:12 to teach or to assume a over a man;
Tit 2:15 Encourage and rebuke with all a.
Heb 13:17 your leaders and submit to their a,
1Pe 2:13 the Lord's sake to every human a:

AUTUMN*
Dt 11:14 its season, both a and spring rains,
Ps 84: 6 the rains also cover it with pools.
Jer 5:24 who gives a and spring rains
Joel 2:23 the a rains in righteousness.
2:23 showers, both a and spring rains,
Jas 5: 7 crop, patiently waiting for the a
Jude : 12 a trees, without fruit and uprooted—

AVENGE (VENGEANCE)
Lev 26:25 on you to a the breaking
Dt 32:35 It is mine to a; I will repay.
32:43 people, for he will a the blood of his
Ro 12: 19 "It is mine to a; I will repay,"
Heb 10:30 him who said, "It is mine to a;
Rev 6:10 of the earth and a our blood?"

AVENGER (VENGEANCE)
Nu 35:27 the a of blood may kill the accused
Jos 20: 3 find protection from the a of blood.
Ps 8: 2 to silence the foe and the a.

AVENGES (VENGEANCE)
Ps 94: 1 The Lord is a God who a.

AVENGING* (VENGEANCE)
1Sa 25:26 and from a yourself with your own
25:33 from a myself with my own hands.
Na 1: 2 The Lord is a jealous and a God;

AVOID (AVOIDED AVOIDS)
Pr 4:15 A it, do not travel on it; turn from it
15:12 so they a the wise.
20: 3 It is to one's honor to a strife,
20:19 so a anyone who talks too much.
Ecc 7:18 fears God will a all _extremes._
1Th 4: 3 you should a sexual immorality;
2Ti 2:16 A godless chatter, because those
Tit 3: 9 But a foolish controversies

AVOIDED* (AVOID)
Pr 16: 6 the fear of the Lord evil is a.

AVOIDS* (AVOID)
Pr 16:17 The highway of the upright a evil;

AWAITS (WAIT)
Pr 15:10 Stern discipline a those who leave
28:22 are unaware that poverty a them.

AWAKE (WAKE)
Ps 17:15 when I a, I will be satisfied
Pr 6:22 when you a, they will speak to you.
1Th 5: 6 but let us be a and sober.

AWARD*
2Ti 4: 8 Judge, will a to me on that day—

AWARE
Ex 34:29 he was not a that his face was
Mt 24:50 him and at an hour he is not a of.
Lk 12:46 him and at an hour he is not a of.

AWE* (AWESOME OVERAWED)
Jos 4:14 stood in a of him all the days of
4:14 just as they had stood in a of Moses.
1Sa 12:18 So all the people stood in a
1Ki 3:28 they held the king in a, because they
Job 25: 2 "Dominion and a belong to God;
Ps 65: 8 earth is filled with a at your wonders;
119:120 I stand in a of your laws.
Isa 29:23 will stand in a of the God of Israel.
Jer 2:19 your God and have no a of me,"
33: 9 they will be in a and will tremble
Hab 3: 2 I stand in a of your deeds, Lord.
Mal 2: 5 me and stood in a of my name.
Mt 9: 8 saw this, they were filled with a,
Lk 1:65 The neighbors were all filled with a,
5:26 They were filled with a and said,
7:16 They were all filled with a
Ac 2:43 Everyone was filled with a
Heb 12:28 acceptably with reverence and a,

AWESOME* (AWE)
Ge 28:17 and said, "How a is this place!"

Ex 15: 11 majestic in holiness, a in glory,
    34: 10 among will see how a is the work
Dt   4: 34 or by great and a deeds, like all
     7: 21 is among you, is a great and a God.
    10: 17 God, mighty and a, who shows no
    10: 21 a wonders you saw with your own
    28: 58 revere this glorious and a name—
    34: 12 or performed the a deeds that Moses
Jdg 13: 6 looked like an angel of God, very a.
2Sa 7: 23 a wonders by driving out nations
1Ch 17: 21 a wonders by driving out nations
Ne   1: 5 the great and a God, who keeps his
     4: 14 who is great and a, and fight
     9: 32 God, mighty and a, who keeps his
Job 10: 16 again display your a power against
    37: 22 God comes in a majesty.
Ps 45: 4 let your right hand achieve a deeds.
    47: 2 For the LORD Most High is a,
    65: 5 You answer us with a and righteous
    66: 3 to God, "How a are your deeds!
    66: 5 done, his a deeds for humankind!
    68: 35 You, God, are a in your sanctuary;
    89: 7 he is more a than all who surround
    99: 3 them praise your great and a name—
   106: 22 of Ham and a deeds by the Red Sea.
   111: 9 holy and a is his name.
   145: 6 tell of the power of your a works—
Isa 64: 3 you did a things that we did not
Eze 1: 18 Their rims were high and a, and all
     1: 22 a vault, sparkling like crystal, and a.
Da   2: 31 dazzling statue, a in appearance.
     9: 4 the great and a God, who keeps his
Zep 2: 11 The LORD will be a to them

AX
Mt   3: 10 The a is already at the root
Lk   3: 9 The a is already at the root

BAAL
Jdg 6: 25 Tear down your father's altar to B
1Ki 16: 32 B in the temple of B that he built
    18: 25 Elijah said to the prophets of B,
    19: 18 knees have not bowed down to B
2Ki 10: 28 So Jehu destroyed B worship
Jer 19: 5 They have built the high places of B
Ro 11: 4 have not bowed the knee to B."

BAASHA
King of Israel (1Ki 15:16–16:7; 2Ch 16:1–6).

BABBLER* (BABBLING)
Ac 17: 18 "What is this b trying to say?"

BABBLING* (BABBLER)
Mt   6: 7 do not keep on b like pagans,

BABIES* (BABY)
Ge 25: 22 The b jostled each other within her,
Ex   2: 6 "This is one of the Hebrew b,"
Lk 18: 15 bringing b to Jesus for him to place
Ac   7: 19 their newborn b so that they would
1Pe 2: 2 Like newborn b, crave spiritual

BABY* (BABIES BABY'S)
Ex   2: 6 She opened it and saw the b.
     2: 7 women to nurse the b for you?"
     2: 9 "Take this b and nurse him for me,
     2: 9 So the woman took the b and nursed
1Ki 3: 17 I had a b while she was there
     3: 18 was born, this woman also had a b.
     3: 26 my lord, give her the living b!"
     3: 27 "Give the living b to the first
Isa 49: 15 "Can a mother forget the b at her
Lk   1: 41 greeting, the b leaped in her womb,
     1: 44 the b in my womb leaped for joy.
     1: 57 time for Elizabeth to have her b,
     2: 6 the time came for the b to be born,
     2: 12 You will find a b wrapped in cloths
     2: 16 and the b, who was lying
Jn 16: 21 her b is born she forgets the anguish

BABY'S* (BABY)
Ex   2: 8 the girl went and got the b mother.

BABYLON
Ps 137: 1 By the rivers of B we sat and wept
Jer 29: 10 seventy years are completed for B,
    51: 37 B will be a heap of ruins, a haunt
Rev 14: 8 Fallen is B the Great,' which
    17: 5 written on her forehead: \mystery \B

BACKS
2Pe 2: 21 turn their b on the sacred command

BACKSLIDING* (BACKSLIDINGS)
Jer 2: 19 your b will rebuke you.
     3: 22 I will cure you of b."
    14: 7 For our b is great; we have sinned

Jer 15: 6 "You keep on b. So I will lay hands
Eze 37: 23 save them from all their sinful b,

BACKSLIDINGS* (BACKSLIDING)
Jer 5: 6 rebellion is great and their b many.

BALAAM
Prophet who attempted to curse Israel (Nu 22–24;
Dt 23:4–5; 2Pe 2:15; Jude 11). Killed in Israel's
vengeance on Midianites (Nu 31:8; Jos 13:22).

BALAK
Moabite king who hired Balaam to curse Israel (Nu
22–24; Jos 24:9).

BALM
Jer 8: 22 Is there no b in Gilead? Is there no

BANISH (BANISHED)
Jer 25: 10 I will b from them the sounds of joy

BANISHED (BANISH)
Dt 30: 4 you have been b to the most distant

BANNER
Ex 17: 15 and called it The LORD is my B.
SS   2: 4 hall, and let his b over me be love.
Isa 11: 10 of Jesse will stand as a b

BANQUET
SS   2: 4 Let him lead me to the b hall,
Lk 14: 13 But when you give a b,

BAPTISM* (BAPTIZE)
Mt 21: 25 John's b—where did it come from?
Mk   1: 4 preaching a b of repentance
    10: 38 with the b I am baptized with,
    10: 39 with the b I am baptized with,
    11: 30 John's b—was it from heaven,
Lk   3: 3 preaching a b of repentance
    12: 50 But I have a b to undergo, and what
    20: 4 John's b—was it from heaven,
Ac   1: 22 beginning from John's b to the time
    10: 37 after the b that John preached—
    13: 24 and b to all the people of Israel.
    18: 25 though he knew only the b of John.
    19: 3 "Then what b did you receive?"
    19: 3 "John's b," they replied.
    19: 4 "John's b was a b of repentance.
Ro   6: 4 with him through b into death
Eph 4: 5 one Lord, one faith, one b;
Col 2: 12 having been buried with him in b,
1Pe 3: 21 this water symbolizes b that now

BAPTIZE* (BAPTISM BAPTIZED BAPTIZING)
Mt   3: 11 "I b you with water for repentance.
     3: 11 He will b you with the Holy Spirit
Mk   1: 8 I b you with water, but he will b you with
            the Holy Spirit."
Lk   3: 16 them all, "I b you with water.
     3: 16 He will b you with the Holy Spirit
Jn   1: 25 do you b if you are not the Messiah,
     1: 26 "I b with water," John replied,
     1: 33 the one who sent me to b with water
     1: 33 remain is the one who will b
1Co 1: 14 that I did not b any of you except
     1: 17 For Christ did not send me to b,

BAPTIZED* (BAPTIZE)
Mt   3: 6 they were b by him in the Jordan
     3: 13 to the Jordan to be b by John.
     3: 14 "I need to be b by you, and do you
     3: 16 As soon as Jesus was b, he went
Mk   1: 5 they were b by him in the Jordan.
     1: 9 and was b by John in the Jordan.
    10: 38 be b with the baptism I am b with?"
    10: 39 be b with the baptism I am b with,
    16: 16 believes and is b will be saved,
Lk   3: 7 crowds coming out to be b by him,
     3: 12 Even tax collectors came to be b.
     3: 21 were being b, Jesus was too.
     7: 29 because they had been b by John.
     7: 30 because they had not been b
Jn   3: 22 spent some time with them, and b.
     3: 23 people were coming and being b.
     4: 2 in fact it was not Jesus who b,
Ac   1: 5 For John b with water, but in a few days
            you will be b
     2: 38 "Repent and be b, every one
     2: 41 who accepted his message were b,
     8: 12 they were b, both men and women.
     8: 13 Simon himself believed and was b.
     8: 16 they had simply been b
     8: 36 stand in the way of my being b?"
     8: 38 into the water and Philip b him.
     9: 18 He got up and was b,
    10: 47 the way of their being b with water.
    10: 48 ordered that they be b in the name

Ac 11: 16 'John b with water, but you will be b
            with the Holy Spirit.'
    16: 15 members of her household were b,
    16: 33 he and all his household were b.
    18: 8 heard Paul believed and were b.
    19: 5 they were b into the name
    22: 16 be b and wash your sins away,
Ro   6: 3 of us who were b into Christ Jesus
            were b into his death?
1Co 1: 13 Were you b into the name of the Father
     1: 15 say that you were b into my name.
     1: 16 I also b the household of Stephanas;
     1: 16 don't remember if I b anyone else.)
    10: 2 They were all b into Moses
    12: 13 we were all b by one Spirit so as
    15: 29 what will those do who are b
    15: 29 at all, why are people b for them?
Gal 3: 27 of you who were b into Christ have

BAPTIZING* (BAPTIZE)
Mt   3: 7 coming to where he was b, he said
    28: 19 b them in the name of the Father
Jn   1: 28 of the Jordan, where John was b.
     1: 31 the reason I came b with water was
     3: 23 also was b at Aenon near Salim,
     3: 26 he is b, and everyone is going
     4: 1 and b more disciples than John—
    10: 40 the place where John had been b

BAR-JESUS*
Ac 13: 6 sorcerer and false prophet named B,

BARABBAS
Mt 27: 26 Then he released B to them.

BARAK*
Judge who fought with Deborah against Canaanites
(Jdg 4–5; 1Sa 12:11; Heb 11:32).

BARBARIAN*
Col 3: 11 circumcised or uncircumcised, b,

BARBS*
Nu 33: 55 remain will become b in your eyes

BARE
Hos 2: 3 make her as b as on the day she was
Heb 4: 13 and laid b before the eyes of him

BARNABAS*
Disciple, originally Joseph (Ac 4:36), prophet (Ac
13:1), apostle (Ac 14:14). Brought Paul to apostles
(Ac 9:27), Antioch (Ac 11:22–30; Gal 2:1–13), on the
first missionary journey (Ac 13–14). Together at
Jerusalem Council, they separated over John Mark (Ac
15). Later co-workers (1Co 9:6; Col 4:10).

BARREN
Isa 54: 1 "Sing, b woman, you who never
Gal 4: 27 "Be glad, b woman, you who never

BARTHOLOMEW*
Apostle (Mt 10:3; Mk 3:18; Lk 6:14; Ac 1:13). Possibly also known as Nathanael (Jn 1:45–49; 21:2).

BARUCH
Jeremiah's secretary (Jer 32:12–16; 36; 43:1–6;
45:1–2).

BARZILLAI
1. Gileadite who aided David during Absalom's revolt (2Sa 17:27; 19:31–39).
2. Son-in-law of 1. (Ezr 2:61; Ne 7:63).

BASHAN
Jos 22: 7 Moses had given land in B,
Ps 22: 12 strong bulls of B encircle me.

BASIN
Ex 30: 18 "Make a bronze b, with its bronze

BASKET
Ex   2: 3 she got a papyrus b for him
Ac   9: 25 him in a b through an opening
2Co 11: 33 I was lowered in a b from a window

BATCH*
Ro 11: 16 is holy, then the whole b is holy;
1Co 5: 6 a little yeast leavens the whole b
     5: 7 you may be a new unleavened b—
Gal 5: 9 yeast works through the whole b

BATH (BATHING)
Jn 13: 10 "Those who have had a b need only

BATHING (BATH)
2Sa 11: 2 From the roof he saw a woman b.

BATHSHEBA*
Wife of Uriah who committed adultery with and became wife of David (2Sa 11), mother of Solomon (2Sa
12:24; 1Ki 1–2; 1Ch 3:5; Ps 51:T).

BATTLE (BATTLES)
1Sa 17: 47 for the **b** is the LORD's, and he
2Ch 20: 15 For the **b** is not yours, but God's.
Ps 24: 8 mighty, the LORD mighty in **b**.
Ecc 9: 11 to the swift or the **b** to the strong,
Isa 31: 4 come down to do **b** on Mount Zion
Eze 13: 5 it will stand firm in the **b** on the day
Rev 16: 14 them for the **b** on the great day
20: 8 and to gather them for **b**.

BATTLES* (BATTLE)
1Sa 8: 20 to go out before us and fight our **b**."
18: 17 and fight the **b** of the LORD.
25: 28 because you fight the LORD's **b**,
2Ch 32: 8 God to help us and to fight our **b**."

BEAR (BEARING BEARS BIRTH BIRTHRIGHT BORE BORN CHILDBEARING CHILDBIRTH FIRSTBORN NEWBORN REBIRTH)
Ge 4: 13 punishment is more than I can **b**.
Ps 38: 4 me like a burden too heavy to **b**.
Isa 11: 7 The cow will feed with the **b**,
53: 11 many, and he will **b** their iniquities.
Da 7: 5 second beast, which looked like a **b**.
Mt 7: 18 A good tree cannot **b** bad fruit,
Lk 21: 13 And so you will **b** testimony to me.
Jn 15: 2 branch that does **b** fruit he prunes
15: 8 that you **b** much fruit,
15: 16 so that you might go and **b** fruit—
Ro 7: 4 order that we might **b** fruit for God.
15: 1 We who are strong ought to **b**
1Co 10: 13 be tempted beyond what you can **b**.
Col 3: 13 **B** with each other and forgive one

BEARD
Lev 19: 27 head or clip off the edges of your **b**.
Isa 50: 6 to those who pulled out my **b**;

BEARING (BEAR)
Eph 4: 2 patient, **b** with one another in love.
Col 1: 10 **b** fruit in every good work,
Heb 13: 13 the camp, **b** the disgrace he bore.

BEARS (BEAR)
1Ki 8: 43 this house I have built **b** your Name.
Ps 68: 19 Savior, who daily **b** our burdens.

BEAST (BEASTS)
Rev 13: 18 calculate the number of the **b**, for it
16: 2 people who had the mark of the **b**
19: 20 who had received the mark of the **b**

BEASTS (BEAST)
Da 7: 3 Four great **b**, each different
1Co 15: 32 If I fought wild **b** in Ephesus

BEAT (BEATEN BEATING BEATINGS)
Isa 2: 4 They will **b** their swords
Joel 3: 10 **B** your plowshares into swords
Mic 4: 3 They will **b** their swords

BEATEN (BEAT)
Lk 12: 47 do what the master wants will be **b**
12: 48 deserving punishment will be **b**
2Co 11: 25 Three times I was **b** with rods,

BEATING (BEAT)
1Co 9: 26 I do not fight like a boxer **b** the air.
1Pe 2: 20 if you receive a **b** for doing wrong

BEATINGS (BEAT)
Pr 19: 29 and **b** for the backs of fools.

BEAUTIFUL* (BEAUTY)
Ge 6: 2 saw that these daughters were **b**,
12: 11 "I know what a **b** woman you are.
12: 14 saw that Sarai was a very **b** woman.
24: 16 The girl was very **b**, a virgin;
26: 7 of Rebekah, because she is **b**."
29: 17 had a lovely figure and was **b**.
49: 21 is a doe set free that bears **b** fawns.
Nu 24: 5 "How **b** are your tents, Jacob,
Dt 21: 11 among the captives a **b** woman
Jos 7: 21 I saw in the plunder a **b** robe
1Sa 25: 3 was an intelligent and **b** woman,
2Sa 11: 2 The woman was very **b**,
13: 1 the **b** sister of Absalom son
14: 27 Tamar, and she became a **b** woman.
1Ki 1: 3 throughout Israel for a **b** girl
1: 4 The girl was very **b**; she took care
Est 2: 2 search be made for **b** young virgins
2: 3 bring all these **b** young women
2: 7 Esther, had a lovely figure and was **b**.
Job 42: 15 there found women as **b** as Job's
Ps 48: 2 **B** in its loftiness, the joy
Pr 11: 22 snout is a **b** woman who shows no
24: 4 are filled with rare and **b** treasures.
Ecc 3: 11 He has made everything **b** in its

SS 1: 8 you do not know, most **b** of women,
1: 10 Your cheeks are **b** with earrings,
1: 15 How **b** you are, my darling!
1: 15 how **b**! Your eyes are doves.
2: 10 my darling, my **b** one,
2: 13 my **b** one, come with me."
4: 1 How **b** you are, my darling!
4: 1 how **b**! Your eyes behind your
4: 7 All **b** you are, my darling;
5: 9 than others, most **b** of women?
6: 1 beloved gone, most **b** of women?
6: 4 You are as **b** as Tirzah, my darling,
7: 1 How **b** your sandaled feet,
7: 6 How **b** you are and how pleasing,
Isa 4: 2 the Branch of the LORD will be **b**
28: 5 a **b** wreath for the remnant of his
52: 7 How **b** on the mountains are the feet
Jer 3: 19 land, the most **b** inheritance of any
6: 2 Daughter Zion, so **b** and delicate.
11: 16 olive tree with fruit **b** in form.
46: 20 "Egypt is a **b** heifer, but a gadfly is
Eze 7: 20 They took pride in their **b** jewelry
16: 12 ears and a **b** crown on your head.
16: 13 You became very **b** and rose to be
20: 6 and honey, the most **b** of all lands.
20: 15 and honey, the most **b** of all lands—
23: 42 sister and **b** crowns on their heads.
27: 24 they traded with you **b** garments,
31: 3 with **b** branches overshadowing
31: 9 I made it **b** with abundant branches,
33: 32 who sings love songs with a **b** voice
Da 4: 12 Its leaves were **b**, its fruit abundant,
4: 21 with **b** leaves and abundant fruit,
8: 9 to the east and toward the **B** Land.
11: 16 will establish himself in the **B** Land.
11: 41 He will also invade the **B** Land.
11: 45 the seas at the **b** holy mountain.
Zec 9: 17 How attractive and **b** they will be!
Mt 23: 27 which look **b** on the outside
26: 10 She has done a **b** thing to me.
Mk 14: 6 She has done a **b** thing to me.
Lk 21: 5 temple was adorned with **b** stones
Ac 3: 2 carried to the temple gate called **B**,
3: 10 begging at the temple gate called **B**,
Ro 10: 15 "How **b** are the feet of those who

BEAUTY* (BEAUTIFUL)
Est 1: 11 order to display her **b** to the people
2: 3 let **b** treatments be given to them.
2: 9 provided her with her **b** treatments
2: 12 months of **b** treatments prescribed
Ps 27: 4 to gaze on the **b** of the LORD
45: 11 the king be enthralled by your **b**;
50: 2 Zion, perfect in **b**, God shines forth.
Pr 6: 25 Do not lust in your heart after her **b**
31: 30 is deceptive, and **b** is fleeting;
Isa 3: 24 instead of **b**, branding.
28: 1 his glorious **b**, set on the head
28: 4 his glorious **b**, set on the head
33: 17 Your eyes will see the king in his **b**
53: 2 He had no **b** or majesty to attract us
61: 3 them a crown of **b** instead of ashes,
La 2: 15 that was called the perfection of **b**,
Eze 16: 14 the nations on account of your **b**,
16: 14 had given you made your **b** perfect,
16: 15 you trusted in your **b** and used your
16: 15 passed by and your **b** became his.
16: 16 went to him, and he possessed your **b**.
16: 25 lofty shrines and degraded your **b**,
27: 3 Tyre, "I am perfect in **b**."
27: 4 your builders brought your **b**
27: 11 they brought your **b** to perfection.
28: 7 draw their swords against your **b**
28: 12 full of wisdom and perfect in **b**.
28: 17 became proud on account of your **b**,
31: 7 It was majestic in **b**, with its
31: 8 the garden of God could match its **b**.
Jas 1: 11 blossom falls and its **b** is destroyed.
1Pe 3: 3 Your **b** should not come
3: 4 the unfading **b** of a gentle and quiet

BED (SICKBED)
Isa 28: 20 The **b** is too short to stretch out on,
Lk 11: 7 and my children and I are in **b**.
17: 34 night two people will be in one **b**;
Heb 13: 4 and the marriage **b** kept pure,

BEELZEBUL*
Mt 10: 25 the house has been called **B**,
10: 25 "It is only by **B**, the prince
12: 27 And if I drive out demons by **B**,
Mk 3: 22 "He is possessed by **B**!
Lk 11: 15 "By **B**, the prince of demons,

Lk 11: 18 claim that I drive out demons by **B**.
11: 19 Now if I drive out demons by **B**,

BEER
Pr 20: 1 Wine is a mocker and **b** a brawler;

BEERSHEBA
Ge 21: 14 and wandered in the Desert of **B**.
Jdg 20: 1 all the Israelites from Dan to **B**
1Sa 3: 20 Dan to **B** recognized that Samuel
2Sa 3: 10 Israel and Judah from Dan to **B**."
17: 11 Let all Israel, from Dan to **B**—
24: 2 the tribes of Israel from Dan to **B**
24: 15 of the people from Dan to **B** died.
1Ki 4: 25 from Dan to **B**, lived in safety,
1Ch 21: 2 count the Israelites from **B** to Dan.
2Ch 30: 5 throughout Israel, from **B** to Dan,

BEGGING
Ps 37: 25 forsaken or their children **b** bread.
Ac 16: 9 of Macedonia standing and **b** him,

BEGINNING
Ge 1: 1 In the **b** God created the heavens
Ps 102: 25 In the **b** you laid the foundations
111: 10 of the LORD is the **b** of wisdom;
Pr 1: 7 the LORD is the **b** of knowledge,
4: 7 The **b** of wisdom is this:
9: 10 of the LORD is the **b** of wisdom,
Ecc 3: 11 fathom what God has done from **b**
Isa 40: 21 Has it not been told you from the **b**?
46: 10 I make known the end from the **b**,
Mt 24: 8 All these are the **b** of birth pains.
Lk 1: 3 investigated everything from the **b**,
Jn 1: 1 In the **b** was the Word,
1Jn 1: 1 That which was from the **b**,
Rev 21: 6 and the Omega, the **B** and the End.
22: 13 and the Last, the **B** and the End.

BEHAVE (BEHAVIOR)
Ro 13: 13 Let us **b** decently, as in the daytime,

BEHAVIOR (BEHAVE)
Pr 1: 3 receiving instruction in prudent **b**,
1Pe 3: 1 words by the **b** of their wives,
3: 16 maliciously against your good **b**

BEHEMOTH*
Job 40: 15 "Look at the **b**, which I made along

BELIEVE (BELIEVED BELIEVER BELIEVERS BELIEVES BELIEVING)
Ex 4: 1 "What if they do not **b** me or listen
1Ki 10: 7 I did not **b** these things until I came
2Ch 9: 6 But I did not **b** what they said until I
Ps 78: 32 spite of his wonders, they did not **b**.
Pr 14: 15 The simple **b** anything,
Hab 1: 5 in your days that you would not **b**.
Mt 18: 6 those who **b** in me—
21: 22 If you **b**, you will receive whatever
27: 42 the cross, and we will **b** in him.
Mk 1: 15 Repent and **b** the good news!"
5: 36 told him, "Don't be afraid; just **b**."
9: 24 the boy's father exclaimed, "I do **b**;
9: 42 those who **b** in me—
11: 23 but **b** that what you say will happen,
11: 24 prayer, **b** that you have received it,
15: 32 the cross, that we may see and **b**."
16: 16 does not **b** will be condemned.
16: 17 signs will accompany those who **b**:
Lk 8: 12 so that they may not **b** and be saved.
8: 13 They **b** for a while, but in the time
8: 50 just **b**, and she will be healed."
22: 67 "If I tell you, you will not **b** me,
24: 25 how slow to **b** all that the prophets
Jn 1: 7 so that through him all might **b**.
3: 18 does not **b** stands condemned
4: 42 "We no longer **b** just because
5: 38 for you do not **b** the one he sent.
5: 46 you would **b** me, for he wrote
6: 29 to **b** in the one he has sent."
6: 69 We have come to **b** and to know
7: 5 even his own brothers did not **b**
8: 24 if you do not **b** that I am he,
9: 35 "Do you **b** in the Son of Man?"
9: 36 "Tell me so that I may **b** in him."
9: 38 "Lord, I **b**," and he worshiped him.
10: 26 you do not **b** because you are not
10: 37 Do not **b** me unless I do the works
10: 38 even though you do not **b** me,
11: 27 "I **b** that you are the Messiah,
11: 40 "Did I not tell you that if you **b**,
12: 37 they still would not **b** in him.
12: 44 "Those who **b** in me do not **b** in me
13: 19 it does happen you will **b** that I am

Jn 14: 10 Don't you **b** that I am in the Father,
14: 11 **B** me when I say that I am
14: 11 or at least **b** on the evidence
16: 30 This makes us **b** that you came
16: 31 "Do you now **b**?" Jesus replied.
17: 21 the world may **b** that you have sent
19: 35 he testifies so that you also may **b**.
20: 27 into my side. Stop doubting and **b**."
20: 31 you may **b** that Jesus is the Messiah,
Ac 16: 31 They replied, "**B** in the Lord Jesus,
24: 14 I **b** everything that is in accordance
27 Agrippa, do you **b** the prophets?
Ro 3: 22 faith in Jesus Christ to all who **b**.
4: 11 he is the father of all who **b**
10: 9 **b** in your heart that God raised him
10: 10 For it is with your heart that you **b**
10: 14 how can they **b** in the one of whom
1Co 1: 21 was preached to save those who **b**.
Gal 3: 22 might be given to those who **b**.
Php 1: 29 of Christ not only to **b** on him,
1Th 4: 14 We **b** that Jesus died and rose again,
2Th 2: 11 delusion so that they will **b** the lie
1Ti 4: 10 and especially of those who **b**.
Tit 1: 6 a man whose children **b** and are not
Heb 11: 6 comes to him must **b** that he exists
Jas 1: 6 you ask, you must **b** and not doubt,
2: 19 You **b** that there is one God. Even the demons **b** that—
1Pe 2: 7 Now to you who **b**, this stone is
1Jn 3: 23 to **b** in the name of his Son,
4: 1 Dear friends, do not **b** every spirit,
5: 13 things to you who **b** in the name

BELIEVED (BELIEVE)
Ge 15: 6 Abram **b** the Lord, and he
Ex 4: 31 and they **b**. And when they heard
Isa 53: 1 Who has **b** our message
Jnh 3: 5 The Ninevites **b** God.
Lk 1: 45 Blessed is she who has **b**
Jn 1: 12 to those who **b** in his name, he gave
2: 22 Then they **b** the scripture
3: 18 already because they have not **b**
5: 46 If you **b** Moses, you would believe
7: 39 whom those who **b** in him were
12: 38 who has **b** our message
20: 8 also went inside. He saw and **b**.
20: 29 you have seen me, you have **b**;
Ac 13: 48 were appointed for eternal life **b**.
19: 2 the Holy Spirit when you **b**?"
Ro 4: 3 "Abraham **b** God, and it was
10: 14 call on the one they have not **b** in?
10: 16 "Lord, who has **b** our message?"
1Co 15: 2 Otherwise, you have **b** in vain.
Gal 3: 6 So also Abraham "**b** God, and it
2Th 2: 12 condemned who have not **b** the truth
1Ti 3: 16 the nations, was **b** on in the world,
2Ti 1: 12 because I know whom I have **b**,
Jas 2: 23 that says, "Abraham **b** God, and it

BELIEVER* (BELIEVE)
1Ki 18: 3 (Obadiah was a devout **b**
Ac 16: 1 a **b** but whose father was a Greek.
16: 15 you consider me a **b** in the Lord,"
1Co 7: 12 brother has a wife who is not a **b**
7: 13 has a husband who is not a **b** and he
7: 15 what does a **b** have in common
1Ti 5: 16 any woman who is a **b** has widows
1Jn 2: 9 hate a fellow **b** are still in the
3: 15 hates a fellow **b** is a murderer,

BELIEVERS (BELIEVE)
Jn 4: 41 of his words many more became **b**.
Ac 1: 15 up among the **b** (a group numbering
2: 44 All the **b** were together and had
4: 32 All the **b** were one in heart
5: 12 all the **b** used to meet together
9: 41 Then he called for the **b**,
10: 45 The circumcised **b** who had come
11: 2 the circumcised **b** criticized him
15: 2 along with some other **b**, to go
15: 22 some of the **b** who belonged
15: 23 To the Gentile **b** in Antioch,
15: 32 encourage and strengthen the **b**.
21: 25 As for the Gentile **b**, we have
1Co 6: 5 to judge a dispute between?
14: 22 a sign, not for **b** but for unbelievers;
14: 22 is not for unbelievers but for **b**.
2Co 11: 26 and in danger from false **b**.
Gal 2: 4 false **b** had infiltrated our ranks
6: 10 those who belong to the family of **b**.
1Th 1: 7 a model to all the **b** in Macedonia
2Th 3: 15 enemies, but warn them as fellow **b**.

1Ti 4: 12 set an example for the **b** in speech,
6: 2 just because they are fellow **b**.
6: 2 masters are dear to them as fellow **b**
Jas 2: 1 **b** in our glorious Lord Jesus Christ
1Pe 2: 17 love your fellow **b**, fear God,
1Jn 2: 10 who love their fellow **b** live
3Jn : 10 he refuses to welcome other **b**.

BELIEVES* (BELIEVE)
Mk 9: 23 is possible for one who **b**."
16: 16 *Whoever **b** and is baptized*
Jn 3: 15 everyone who **b** may have eternal
3: 16 whoever **b** in him shall not perish
3: 18 Whoever **b** in him is not
3: 36 Whoever **b** in the Son has eternal
5: 24 **b** him who sent me has eternal life
6: 35 and whoever **b** in me will never be
6: 40 and **b** in him shall have eternal life.
6: 47 tell you, whoever **b** has eternal life.
7: 38 Whoever **b** in me, as Scripture has
11: 25 Anyone who **b** in me will live,
12: 46 that no one who **b** in me should stay
Ac 10: 43 that everyone who **b** in him receives
13: 39 him everyone who **b** is set free
Ro 1: 16 brings salvation to everyone who **b**:
9: 33 one who **b** in him
10: 4 righteousness for everyone who **b**.
10: 11 who **b** in him will never be put to
1Jn 5: 1 Everyone who **b** that Jesus is
5: 5 Only the one who **b** that Jesus is
5: 10 Whoever **b** in the Son of God

BELIEVING* (BELIEVE)
Jn 11: 26 by **b** in me will never die.
20: 31 by **b** you may have life in his name.
Ac 9: 26 not **b** that he really was a disciple.
1Co 7: 14 sanctified through her **b** husband.
9: 5 have the right to take a **b** wife along
Gal 3: 2 the law, or by your **b** what you heard?
3: 5 the law, or by your **b** what you heard?
1Ti 6: 2 Those who have **b** masters should

BELLY
Ge 3: 14 You will crawl on your **b** and you
Da 2: 32 of silver, its **b** and thighs of bronze,
Mt 12: 40 three nights in the **b** of a huge fish,

BELONG (BELONGS)
Ge 40: 8 "Do not interpretations **b** to God?
Lev 25: 55 For the Israelites **b** to me as servants.
Dt 10: 14 Lord your God **b** the heavens,
29: 29 The secret things to the Lord
Job 12: 13 "To God **b** wisdom and power;
12: 16 To him **b** strength and insight;
25: 2 "Dominion and awe **b** to God;
Ps 47: 9 for the kings of the earth **b** to God;
95: 4 and the mountain peaks **b** to him.
115: 16 The highest heavens **b**
Jer 5: 10 for these people do not **b**
Jn 8: 44 You **b** to your father, the devil,
15: 19 As it is, you do not **b** to the world,
Ro 1: 6 those Gentiles who are called to **b**
7: 4 that you might **b** to another, to him
8: 9 of Christ, they do not **b** to Christ.
14: 8 we live or die, we **b** to the Lord.
1Co 7: 39 wishes, but he must **b** to the Lord.
15: 23 when he comes, those who **b** to him.
Gal 3: 29 If you **b** to Christ, then you are
3: 29 Those who **b** to Christ Jesus have
1Th 5: 5 We do not **b** to the night
5: 8 But since we **b** to the day, let us be
1Jn 3: 19 how we know that we **b** to the truth

BELONGS (BELONG)
Lev 27: 30 from the trees, **b** to the Lord;
Dt 1: 17 of anyone, for judgment **b** to God.
Job 41: 11 Everything under heaven **b** to me.
Ps 22: 28 for dominion **b** to the Lord
89: 18 Indeed, our shield **b** to the Lord,
111: 10 To him **b** eternal praise.
Eze 18: 4 For everyone **b** to me, the parent as
18: 4 Whoever **b** to God hears what God
Ro 12: 5 and each member **b** to all the others.
Rev 7: 10 "Salvation **b** to our God, who sits

BELOVED* (LOVE)
Dt 33: 12 "Let the **b** of the Lord rest
SS 1: 13 My **b** is to me a sachet of myrrh
1: 14 My **b** is to me a cluster of henna
1: 16 How handsome you are, my **b**!
2: 3 is my **b** among the young men.
2: 8 Listen! My **b**! Look!
2: 9 My **b** is like a gazelle
2: 10 My **b** spoke and said to me,
2: 16 My **b** is mine

SS 2: 17 my **b**, and be like a gazelle
4: 16 Let my **b** come into his garden
5: 2 Listen! My **b** is knocking:
5: 4 My **b** thrust his hand
5: 5 I arose to open for my **b**,
5: 6 I opened for my **b**, but my **b** had left;
5: 8 if you find my **b**,
5: 9 How is your **b** better than others,
5: 9 How is your **b** better than others,
5: 10 My **b** is radiant and ruddy,
5: 16 This is my **b**, this is my friend,
6: 1 Where has your **b** gone,
6: 1 Which way did your **b** turn,
6: 2 My **b** has gone down to his garden,
6: 3 my beloved's and my **b** is mine;
7: 9 the wine go straight to my **b**,
7: 10 I belong to my **b**,
7: 11 Come, my **b**, let us go to
7: 13 I have stored up for you, my **b**.
8: 5 wilderness leaning on her **b**?
8: 14 my **b**, and be like a gazelle
Jer 11: 15 "What is my **b** doing in my temple

BELOVED'S* (LOVE)
SS 6: 3 I am my **b** and my beloved is

BELSHAZZAR
King of Babylon in days of Daniel (Da 5).

BELT
Ex 12: 11 with your cloak tucked into your **b**,
1Ki 18: 46 tucking his cloak into his **b**, he ran
2Ki 2: 8 "Tuck your cloak into your **b**,
9: 1 "Tuck your cloak into your **b**,
Isa 11: 5 Righteousness will be his **b**
Eph 6: 14 the **b** of truth buckled around your

BENEFICIAL* (BENEFIT)
1Co 6: 12 but not everything is **b**.
10: 23 but not everything is **b**.

BENEFIT (BENEFICIAL BENEFITS)
Job 22: 2 **b** to God? Can even the wise **b** him?
Isa 38: 17 my **b** that I suffered such anguish.
Ro 6: 22 the **b** you reap leads to holiness,
2Co 4: 15 All this is for your **b**,

BENEFITS (BENEFIT)
Ps 103: 2 my soul, and forget not all his **b**—
Jn 4: 38 and you have reaped the **b** of their

BENJAMIN
Twelfth son of Jacob by Rachel (Ge 35:16–24; 46:19–21; 1Ch 2:2). Jacob refused to send him to Egypt, but relented (Ge 42–45). Tribe of blessed (Ge 49:27; Dt 33:12), numbered (Nu 1:37; 26:41), allotted land (Jos 18:11–28; Eze 48:23), failed to fully possess (Jdg 1:21), nearly obliterated (Jdg 20–21), sided with Ish-Bosheth (2Sa 2), but turned to David (1Ch 12:2, 29). 12,000 from (Rev 7:8).

BEREAN*
Ac 17: 11 the **B** Jews were of more noble

BESTOWS
Ps 84: 11 the Lord **b** favor and honor;

BETHANY
Mk 11: 1 and **B** at the Mount of Olives,

BETHEL
Ge 28: 19 He called that place **B**,

BETHLEHEM
Ru 1: 19 went on until they came to **B**.
1Sa 16: 1 I am sending you to Jesse of **B**.
2Sa 23: 15 from the well near the gate of **B**!"
Mic 5: 2 "But you, **B** Ephrathah, though you
Mt 2: 1 After Jesus was born in **B** in Judea,
2: 6 "'But you, **B**, in the land

BETHPHAGE
Mt 21: 1 came to **B** on the Mount of Olives,

BETHSAIDA
Jn 12: 21 Philip, who was from **B** in Galilee,

BETRAY (BETRAYED BETRAYS)
Ps 89: 33 nor will I ever **b** my faithfulness.
Pr 11: 13 Gossips **b** a confidence,
25: 9 do not **b** another's confidence,
Mt 10: 21 "Brother will **b** brother to death,
26: 21 I tell you, one of you will **b** me."

BETRAYED (BETRAY)
Mt 27: 4 said, "for I have **b** innocent blood."

BETRAYS (BETRAY)
Pr 20: 19 A gossip **b** a confidence;

BEULAH*
Isa 62: 4 called Hephzibah, and your land **B**;

BEWITCHED*
Gal 3: 1 Who has **b** you? Before your very

BEZALEL
Judahite craftsman in charge of building the tabernacle (Ex 31:1–11; 35:30–39:31).

BIDDING*
Ps 103: 20 you mighty ones who do his **b**,
148: 8 clouds, stormy winds that do his **b**,

BILDAD
One of Job's friends (Job 8; 18; 25).

BILHAH
Servant of Rachel, mother of Jacob's sons Dan and Naphtali (Ge 30:1–7; 35:25; 46:23–25).

BIND (BINDS BOUND)
Dt 6: 8 and **b** them on your foreheads.
Pr 3: 3 **b** them around your neck,
6: 21 **B** them always on your heart;
7: 3 **B** them on your fingers;
Isa 61: 1 He has sent me to **b**
Mt 16: 19 whatever you **b** on earth will be

BINDS (BIND)
Ps 147: 3 and **b** up their wounds.
Isa 30: 26 when the Lord **b** up the bruises
Ro 7: 2 released from the law that **b** her

BIRD (BIRDS)
Pr 27: 8 Like a **b** that flees its nest is anyone
Ecc 10: 20 because a **b** in the sky may carry

BIRDS (BIRD)
Mt 8: 20 have holes and **b** have nests,
Lk 9: 58 have holes and **b** have nests,

BIRTH (BEAR)
Ps 51: 5 Surely I was sinful at **b**,
58: 3 Even from **b** the wicked go astray;
Isa 26: 18 in pain, but we gave **b** to wind.
Mt 1: 18 This is how the **b** of Jesus
24: 8 these are the beginning of **b** pains.
Jn 3: 6 Flesh gives **b** to flesh, but the Spirit gives **b** to spirit.
1Pe 1: 3 great mercy he has given us new **b**

BIRTHRIGHT (BEAR)
Ge 25: 34 up and left. So Esau despised his **b**.

BITTEN
Nu 21: 8 anyone who is **b** can look at it

BITTER (BITTERNESS EMBITTER)
Ex 12: 8 along with **b** herbs, and bread made
Pr 27: 7 hungry even what is **b** tastes sweet.

BITTERNESS (BITTER)
Pr 14: 10 Each heart knows its own **b**, and no
14: 10 and **b** to the mother who bore them.
Ro 3: 14 mouths are full of cursing and **b**."
Eph 4: 31 Get rid of all **b**, rage, and anger,

BLACK
Zec 6: 6 the **b** horses is going toward
Rev 6: 5 and there before me was a **b** horse!

BLAMELESS* (BLAMELESSLY)
Ge 6: 9 **b** among the people of his time,
17: 1 I walk before me faithfully and be **b**.
Dt 18: 13 You must be **b** before the Lord
2Sa 22: 24 I have been **b** before him and have
22: 26 to the **b** you show yourself **b**,
Job 1: 1 This man was **b** and upright;
1: 8 he is **b** and upright, a man who fears
2: 3 he is **b** and upright, a man who fears
4: 6 and your **b** ways your hope?
8: 20 "Surely God does not reject the **b**
9: 20 if I were **b**, it would pronounce me
9: 21 "Although I am **b**, I have no
9: 22 'He destroys both the **b**
12: 4 though righteous and **b**—
22: 3 would he gain if your ways were **b**?
31: 6 and he will know that I am **b**—
Ps 2 Those whose walk is **b**, who do
18: 23 I have been **b** before him and have
18: 25 to the **b** you show yourself **b**,
19: 13 Then I will be **b**, innocent of great
26: 1 Lord, for I have led a **b** life;
26: 11 I lead a **b** life; redeem me and be
37: 18 The **b** spend their days under
37: 37 Consider the **b**, observe the upright;
50: 23 to the **b** I will show my salvation."
84: 11 from those whose walk is **b**.
101: 2 I will be careful to lead a **b** life—

Ps 101: 2 affairs of my house with a **b** heart.
101: 6 those whose walk is **b** will minister
119: 1 Blessed are those whose ways are **b**,
119: 80 my heart be **b** toward your decrees,
Pr 2: 7 is a shield to those whose walk is **b**,
2: 21 the land, and the **b** will remain in it;
10: 29 way of the Lord is a refuge for the **b**,
11: 5 of the **b** makes their paths straight,
11: 20 delights in those whose ways are **b**.
19: 1 the poor whose walk is **b** than a fool
20: 7 The righteous lead **b** lives;
28: 6 poor whose walk is **b** than the rich
28: 10 trap, but the **b** will receive a good
28: 18 whose walk is **b** are kept safe,
Eze 28: 15 You were **b** in your ways
1Co 1: 8 so that you will be **b** on the day
Eph 1: 4 world to be holy and **b** in his sight.
5: 27 any other blemish, but holy and **b**.
Php 1: 10 be pure and **b** for the day of Christ,
2: 15 so that you may become **b** and pure,
1Th 2: 10 and **b** we were among you who
3: 13 your hearts so that you will be **b**
5: 23 body be kept **b** at the coming of our
Tit 1: 6 An elder must be **b**, faithful to his
1: 7 God's household, he must be **b**—
Heb 7: 26 one who is holy, **b**, pure, set apart
2Pe 3: 14 spotless, **b** and at peace with him.
Rev 14: 5 found in their mouths; they are **b**.

BLAMELESSLY* (BLAMELESS)
Lk 1: 6 Lord's commands and decrees **b**.

BLASPHEME* (BLASPHEMED BLASPHEMER BLASPHEMES BLASPHEMIES BLASPHEMING BLASPHEMOUS BLASPHEMY)
Ex 22: 28 "Do not **b** God or curse the ruler
Lev 24: 16 when they **b** the Name they are to be
Ac 26: 11 and I tried to force them to **b**.
1Ti 1: 20 over to Satan to be taught not to **b**.
2Pe 2: 12 these people **b** in matters they do
Rev 13: 6 It opened its mouth to **b** God,

BLASPHEMED* (BLASPHEME)
Lev 24: 11 of the Israelite woman **b** the Name
1Sa 3: 13 his sons **b** God, and he failed
2Ki 19: 6 of the king of Assyria have **b** me.
19: 22 Who is it you have ridiculed and **b**?
Isa 37: 6 of the king of Assyria have **b** me.
37: 23 Who is it you have ridiculed and **b**?
52: 5 day long my name is constantly **b**.
Eze 20: 27 also your ancestors **b** me by being
Ac 19: 37 robbed temples nor **b** our goddess.
Ro 2: 24 "God's name is **b** among

BLASPHEMER* (BLASPHEME)
Lev 24: 14 "Take the **b** outside the camp.
24: 23 they took the **b** outside the camp
1Ti 1: 13 Even though I was once a **b**

BLASPHEMES* (BLASPHEME)
Lev 24: 16 anyone who **b** the name
Nu 15: 30 by the Lord and must be cut off
Mk 3: 29 whoever **b** against the Holy Spirit
Lk 12: 10 but anyone who **b** against the Holy

BLASPHEMIES* (BLASPHEME)
Ne 9: 18 or when they committed awful **b**,
9: 26 they committed awful **b**.
Mk 3: 28 all their sins and all the **b** they utter.
Rev 13: 5 a mouth to utter proud words and **b**

BLASPHEMING* (BLASPHEME)
Mt 9: 3 to themselves, "This fellow is **b**!"
Mk 2: 7 He's **b**! Who can forgive sins
Jas 2: 7 who are **b** the noble name of him

BLASPHEMOUS* (BLASPHEME)
Ac 6: 11 speak **b** words against Moses
Rev 13: 1 horns, and on each head a **b** name.
17: 3 beast that was covered with **b** names

BLASPHEMY* (BLASPHEME)
Mt 12: 31 will be forgiven every sin and **b**,
12: 31 But **b** against the Spirit will not be
26: 65 clothes and said, "He has spoken **b**!
26: 65 Look, now you have heard the **b**.
Mk 14: 64 "You have heard his **b**.
Lk 5: 21 "Who is this fellow who speaks **b**?
Jn 10: 21 replied, "but for **b**, because you,
10: 36 you accuse me of **b** because I said,

BLAST*
Ex 15: 8 By the **b** of your nostrils the waters
19: 13 sounds a long **b** may they approach
19: 16 and a very loud trumpet **b**.
Nu 10: 5 When a trumpet **b** is sounded,
10: 6 At the sounding of a second **b**,

Nu 10: 6 The **b** will be the signal for setting
10: 9 sound a **b** on the trumpets.
Jos 6: 5 you hear them sound a long **b**
6: 16 the priests sounded the trumpet **b**,
2Sa 22: 16 at the **b** of breath from his nostrils.
Job 4: 9 the **b** of his anger they are no more.
39: 25 At the **b** of the trumpet it snorts,
Ps 18: 15 at the **b** of breath from your nostrils.
98: 6 and the **b** of the ram's horn—
147: 17 Who can withstand his icy **b**?
Isa 27: 8 with his fierce **b** he drives her out,
Eze 22: 20 furnace to be melted with a fiery **b**,
Am 2: 2 war cries and the **b** of the trumpet.
Heb 12: 19 to a trumpet **b** or to such a voice

BLEATING*
1Sa 15: 14 then is this **b** of sheep in my ears?

BLEMISH* (BLEMISHES)
Lev 22: 21 without defect or **b** to be acceptable.
Nu 19: 2 a red heifer without defect or **b**
2Sa 14: 25 of his foot there was no **b** in him.
Eph 5: 27 stain or wrinkle or any other **b**,
Col 1: 22 in his sight, without **b** and free
1Pe 1: 19 Christ, a lamb without **b** or defect.

BLEMISHES* (BLEMISH)
2Pe 2: 13 They are blots and **b**,
Jude 12 These people are **b** at your love

BLESS (BLESSED BLESSES BLESSING BLESSINGS)
Ge 12: 3 I will **b** those who **b** you,
32: 26 not let you go unless you **b** me."
Dt 7: 13 He will love you and **b** you
33: 11 **B** all his skills, Lord, and be
Ps 72: 15 pray for him and **b** him all day long.
Ro 12: 14 **B** those who persecute you;

BLESSED (BLESS)
Ge 1: 22 God **b** them and said, "Be fruitful
2: 3 Then God **b** the seventh day
22: 18 all nations on earth will be **b**,
Nu 24: 9 "May those who bless you be **b**
1Ch 17: 27 have **b** it, and it will be **b**
Ps 1: 1 **B** are those who do not walk in step
2: 12 **B** are all who take refuge in him.
32: 1 **B** are those whose sin the Lord
33: 12 **B** is the nation whose God is
40: 4 **B** are those who make the Lord
41: 1 **B** are those who have regard
84: 5 **B** are those whose strength is
89: 15 **B** are those who have learned
94: 12 **B** are those you discipline, Lord,
106: 3 **B** are those who act justly,
112: 1 **B** are those who fear the Lord,
118: 26 **B** is he who comes in the name
119: 1 **B** are those whose ways are
119: 2 **B** are those who keep his statutes
127: 5 **B** is the man whose quiver is full
Pr 3: 13 **B** are those who find wisdom,
8: 34 **B** are those who listen to me,
28: 20 A faithful person will be richly **b**,
29: 18 but **b** are those who heed wisdom's
31: 28 Her children arise and call her **b**;
Isa 30: 18 **B** are all who wait for him!
Mal 3: 12 all the nations will call you **b**,
3: 15 But now we call the arrogant **b**.
Mt 5: 3 "**B** are the poor in spirit, for theirs
5: 4 **B** are those who mourn, for they
5: 5 **B** are the meek, for they will inherit
5: 6 **B** are those who hunger and thirst
5: 7 **B** are the merciful, for they will
5: 8 **B** are the pure in heart, for they will
5: 9 **B** are the peacemakers, for they will
5: 10 **B** are those who are persecuted
5: 11 "**B** are you when people insult you,
Lk 1: 48 on all generations will call me **b**,
Jn 12: 13 "**B** is he who comes in the name
Ac 20: 35 'It is more **b** to give than
Tit 2: 13 while we wait for the **b** hope—
Jas 1: 12 **B** are those who persevere under
Rev 1: 3 **B** is the one who reads aloud
22: 7 **B** are those who keep the words
22: 14 "**B** are those who wash their robes,

BLESSES (BLESS)
Ps 29: 11 the Lord **b** his people with peace.
Ro 10: 12 and richly **b** all who call on him,

BLESSING (BLESS)
Ge 27: 4 I may give you my **b** before I die."
Dt 23: 5 but turned the curse into a **b** for you,
33: 1 This is the **b** that Moses the man
Pr 10: 22 The **b** of the Lord brings wealth,

Eze 34: 26 there will be showers of **b**.

BLESSINGS (BLESS)

Dt 11: 29 proclaim on Mount Gerizim the **b**,
Jos 8: 34 of the law—the **b** and the curses—
Pr 10: 6 **B** crown the head of the righteous,
Ro 15: 27 have shared in the Jews' spiritual **b**,

BLIND (BLINDED)

Mt 15: 14 If the **b** lead the **b**, both will fall
23: 16 "Woe to you, **b** guides! You say,
Mk 10: 46 were leaving the city, a **b** man,
Lk 6: 39 "Can the **b** lead the **b**?
Jn 9: 25 I do know. I was **b** but now I see!"

BLINDED (BLIND)

Jn 12: 40 "He has their eyes and hardened
2Co 4: 4 god of this age has **b** the minds

BLOOD (BLOODSHED BLOODTHIRSTY)

Ge 4: 10 Your brother's **b** cries out to me
9: 6 "Whoever sheds human **b**,
Ex 12: 13 and when I see the **b**, I will pass
24: 8 Moses then took the **b**, sprinkled it
Lev 16: 15 and take its **b** behind the curtain
17: 11 For the life of a creature is in the **b**,
Dt 12: 23 do not eat the **b**, because the **b** is the life,
Ps 59: 2 save me from those who are after my **b**.
72: 14 for precious is their **b** in his sight.
Pr 6: 17 tongue, hands that shed innocent **b**,
Isa 1: 11 I have no pleasure in the **b** of bulls
Mt 26: 28 This is my **b** of the covenant,
27: 24 "I am innocent of this man's **b**,"
Mk 14: 24 "This is my **b** of the covenant,
Lk 22: 44 his sweat was like drops of **b** falling
Jn 6: 53 of the Son of Man and drink his **b**,
Ac 15: 20 of strangled animals and from **b**.
20: 26 I am innocent of the **b** of everyone.
Ro 3: 25 through the shedding of his **b**—
5: 9 we have now been justified by his **b**,
1Co 11: 25 cup is the new covenant in my **b**;
Eph 1: 7 we have redemption through his **b**,
2: 13 brought near by the **b** of Christ.
Col 1: 20 by making peace through his **b**,
Heb 9: 7 year, and never without **b**, which he
9: 12 Place once for all by his own **b**,
9: 20 said, "This is the **b** of the covenant,
9: 22 of **b** there is no forgiveness.
12: 24 speaks a better word than the **b**
1Pe 1: 19 but with the precious **b** of Christ,
1Jn 1: 7 another, and the **b** of Jesus, his Son,
Rev 1: 5 has freed us from our sins by his **b**,
5: 9 with your **b** you purchased for God
7: 14 them white in the **b** of the Lamb.
12: 11 over him by the **b** of the Lamb
19: 13 He is dressed in a robe dipped in **b**.

BLOODSHED (BLOOD)

Jer 48: 10 who keep their swords from **b**!
Eze 35: 6 Since you did not hate **b**, I will
Hab 2: 12 to him who builds a city with **b**

BLOODTHIRSTY* (BLOOD)

Ps 5: 6 The **b** and deceitful you, LORD,
26: 9 my life with those who are **b**,
55: 23 the **b** and deceitful will not live
139: 19 Away from me, you who are **b**!
Pr 29: 10 The **b** hate people of integrity

BLOSSOM

Isa 35: 1 the wilderness will rejoice and **b**.

BLOT (BLOTS)

Ex 32: 32 then **b** me out of the book you have
Ps 51: 1 to your great compassion **b** out my
Rev 3: 5 I will never **b** out their names

BLOTS (BLOT)

Isa 43: 25 "I, even I, am he who **b** out your

BLOWN

Eph 4: 14 and here and there by every wind
Jas 1: 6 of the sea, **b** and tossed by the wind.
Jude : 12 without rain, **b** along by the wind;

BLUSH

Jer 6: 15 they do not even know how to **b**.

BOAST (BOASTING)

1Ki 20: 11 his armor should not **b** like one who
Ps 44: 8 In God we make our **b** all day long,
Pr 27: 1 Do not **b** about tomorrow, for you
Isa 45: 25 will make their **b** in him.
Jer 9: 23 or the rich **b** of their riches,
9: 24 let those who **b** about this:
Ro 2: 17 rely on the law and **b** in God;
2: 23 You who **b** in the law,
5: 2 we **b** in the hope of the glory

1Co 1: 31 "Let those who **b b** in the Lord."
2Co 10: 17 "Let those who **b b** in the Lord."
11: 30 If I must **b**, I will **b** of the things
Gal 6: 14 May I never **b** except in the cross
Eph 2: 9 not by works, so that no one can **b**.
Php 3: 3 who **b** in Christ Jesus,
Jas 4: 16 you **b** in your arrogant schemes.

BOASTING (BOAST)

Php 1: 26 your **b** in Christ Jesus will abound

BOAZ
Wealthy Bethlehemite who showed favor to Ruth (Ru 2), married her (Ru 4). Ancestor of David (Ru 4:18–22; 1Ch 2:12–15), Jesus (Mt 1:5–16; Lk 3:23–32).

BODIES (BODY)

Isa 26: 19 will live, LORD; their **b** will rise—
Ro 12: 1 to offer your **b** as a living sacrifice,
1Co 6: 15 not know that your **b** are members
6: 19 not know that your **b** are temples
6: 20 Therefore honor God with your **b**.
Eph 5: 28 to love their wives as their own **b**.

BODILY (BODY)

Col 2: 9 fullness of the Deity lives in **b** form,

BODY (BODIES BODILY EMBODIMENT)

Zec 13: 6 'What are these wounds on your **b**?'
Mt 10: 28 not be afraid of those who kill the **b**
26: 26 "Take and eat; this is my **b**."
Mk 14: 22 saying, "Take it; this is my **b**."
Lk 22: 19 "This is my **b** given for you;
Jn 13: 10 their whole **b** is clean.
Ro 12: 4 us has one **b** with many members,
1Co 11: 24 "This is my **b**, which is for you;
12: 12 Just as a **b**, though one, has many
12: 13 by one Spirit so as to form one **b**—
12: 24 But God has put the **b** together,
15: 44 a natural **b**, it is raised a spiritual **b**.
Eph 1: 23 which is his **b**, the fullness of him
4: 25 for we are all members of one **b**.
5: 30 for we are members of his **b**.
Php 1: 20 Christ will be exalted in my **b**,
Col 1: 24 for the sake of his **b**, which is

BOLD (BOLDNESS)

Pr 21: 29 The wicked put up a **b** front,
28: 1 but the righteous are as **b** as a lion.

BOLDNESS* (BOLD)

Ac 4: 29 to speak your word with great **b**.

BONDAGE

Ezr 9: 9 God has not forsaken us in our **b**.

BONES

Ge 2: 23 "This is now bone of my **b**
Ps 22: 14 water, and all my **b** are out of joint.
22: 17 All my **b** are on display;
Eze 37: 1 middle of a valley; it was full of **b**.
Jn 19: 36 "Not one of his **b** will be broken,"

BOOK (BOOKS)

Ex 32: 33 against me I will blot out of my **b**.
Jos 1: 8 Keep this **B** of the Law always
2Ki 22: 8 "I have found the **B** of the Law
2Ch 34: 15 "I have found the **B** of the Law
Ne 8: 8 They read from the **B** of the Law
Ps 69: 28 they be blotted out of the **b** of life
Da 12: 1 name is found written in the **b**—
Jn 20: 30 which are not recorded in this **b**.
Php 4: 3 whose names are in the **b** of life.
Rev 3: 5 out their names from the **b** of life,
20: 12 **b** was opened, which is the **b** of life.
20: 15 written in the **b** of life were thrown
21: 27 are written in the Lamb's **b** of life.

BOOKS* (BOOK)

Ecc 12: 12 Of making many **b** there is no end,
Da 7: 10 was seated, and the **b** were opened.
Jn 21: 25 for the **b** that would be written.
Rev 20: 12 the throne, and the **b** were opened.
20: 12 they had done as recorded in the **b**.

BORE (BEAR)

Dt 32: 18 You deserted the Rock, who **b** you;
Isa 53: 4 our pain and **b** our suffering,
53: 12 For he **b** the sin of many, and made
Mt 8: 17 our infirmities and **b** our diseases."
1Pe 2: 24 "He himself **b** our sins" in his body

BORN (BEAR)

Ecc 3: 2 a time to be **b** and a time to die,
Isa 9: 6 For to us a child is **b**, to us a son is
66: 8 Can a country be **b** in a day
Lk 2: 11 of David a Savior has been **b** to you;
Jn 3: 3 of God without being **b** again."

Jn 3: 4 "How can anyone be **b** when they
3: 5 of God without being **b** of water
3: 7 my saying, 'You must be **b** again.'
3: 8 it is with everyone **b** of the Spirit."
1Pe 1: 23 For you have been **b** again,
1Jn 3: 9 because they have been **b** of God.
4: 7 Everyone who loves has been **b**
5: 1 Jesus is the Messiah is **b** of God,
5: 4 everyone **b** of God overcomes
5: 18 anyone **b** of God does not continue

BORROWER

Pr 22: 7 and the **b** is slave to the lender.

BOTHER (BOTHERING)

Lk 11: 7 one inside answers, 'Don't **b** me.

BOTHERING (BOTHER)

Lk 18: 5 yet because this widow keeps **b** me,

BOUGHT (BUY)

Ac 20: 28 which he **b** with his own blood.
1Co 6: 20 you were **b** at a price.
7: 23 You were **b** at a price;
2Pe 2: 1 the sovereign Lord who **b** them—

BOUND (BIND)

Isa 56: 3 foreigners who have **b** themselves
Mt 16: 19 bind on earth will be **b** in heaven,
18: 18 bind on earth will be **b** in heaven,
Ro 7: 2 by law a married woman is **b** to her
1Co 7: 39 A woman is **b** to her husband as
Jude : 6 **b** with everlasting chains
Rev 20: 2 and **b** him for a thousand years.

BOUNDARY (BOUNDS)

Nu 34: 3 Your southern **b** will start in the east
Pr 23: 10 Do not move an ancient **b** stone
Hos 5: 10 are like those who move **b** stones.

BOUNDLESS

Eph 3: 8 the Gentiles the **b** riches of Christ,

BOUNDS (BOUNDARY)

2Co 7: 4 all our troubles my joy knows no **b**.

BOUNTY*

Ge 49: 26 than the **b** of the age-old hills.
Dt 28: 12 the storehouse of his **b**, to send rain
1Ki 10: 13 he had given her out of his royal **b**.
Ps 65: 11 You crown the year with your **b**,
68: 10 settled in it, and from your **b**, God,
Jer 31: 12 will rejoice in the **b** of the LORD—
31: 14 people will be filled with my **b**,"

BOW (BOWED BOWS)

Dt 5: 9 You shall not **b** down to them
1Ki 22: 34 But someone drew his **b** at random
Ps 5: 7 in reverence I **b** down toward your
44: 6 I put no trust in my **b**, my sword
95: 6 Come, let us **b** down in worship,
138: 2 I will **b** down toward your holy
Isa 44: 19 Shall I **b** down to a block
45: 23 Before me every knee will **b**;
Ro 14: 11 Lord, 'every knee will **b** before me;
Php 2: 10 name of Jesus every knee should **b**,

BOWED (BOW)

Ps 145: 14 fall and lifts up all who are **b** down.
146: 8 lifts up those who are **b** down,

BOWS (BOW)

Isa 44: 15 he makes an idol and **b** down to it.
44: 17 he **b** down to it and worships.

BOY (BOY'S BOYS)

Ge 21: 17 God heard the **b** crying,
22: 12 "Do not lay a hand on the **b**,"
Jdg 13: 5 by a razor because the **b** is to be
1Sa 2: 11 the **b** ministered before the LORD
3: 8 that the LORD was calling the **b**.
Isa 7: 16 for before the **b** knows enough
Mt 17: 18 and it came out of the **b**, and he was
Lk 2: 43 home, the **b** Jesus stayed behind

BOY'S (BOY)

1Ki 17: 22 and the **b** life returned to him,
2Ki 4: 34 out on him, the **b** body grew warm.

BOYS (BOY)

Ge 25: 24 there were twin **b** in her womb.
Ex 1: 18 Why have you let the **b** live?"

BRACE*

Na 2: 1 watch the road, **b** yourselves,

BRAG*

Am 4: 5 **b** about your freewill offerings—

BRANCH (BRANCHES)

Isa 4: 2 that day the **B** of the LORD will be

Jer 23: 5 raise up for David a righteous **B**,
　　33: 15 I will make a righteous **B** sprout
Zec 3: 8 going to bring my servant, the **B**.
　　6: 12 is the man whose name is the **B**,
Jn 15: 2 He cuts off every **b** in me that bears
　　15: 2 while every **b** that does bear fruit he

BRANCHES (BRANCH)
Jn 15: 5 "I am the vine; you are the **b**.
Ro 11: 21 if God did not spare the natural **b**,

BRAVE
2Sa 2: 7 then, be strong and **b**, for Saul your
　　13: 28 you this order? Be strong and **b**."

BREACH (BREAK)
Ps 106: 23 stood in the **b** before him to keep his

BREACHING (BREAK)
Pr 17: 14 Starting a quarrel is like a dam;

BREAD
Ex 12: 8 herbs, and **b** made without yeast.
　　23: 15 the Festival of Unleavened **B**;
　　25: 30 Put the **b** of the Presence on this
Dt 8: 3 that people do not live on **b** alone
Ps 78: 25 Human beings ate the **b** of angels;
Pr 30: 8 riches, but give me only my daily **b**.
Isa 55: 2 Why spend money on what is not **b**,
Mt 4: 3 tell these stones to become **b**."
　　4: 4 'People do not live on **b** alone,
　　6: 11 Give us today our daily **b**.
　　26: 26 Jesus took **b**, and when he had given
Mk 14: 22 Jesus took **b**, and when he had given
Lk 4: 3 tell this stone to become **b**."
　　4: 4 'People do not live on **b** alone.' "
　　9: 13 "We have only five loaves of **b**
　　11: 3 Give us each day our daily **b**.
　　22: 19 And he took **b**, gave thanks
Jn 6: 33 For the **b** of God is the **b** that comes
　　6: 35 Jesus declared, "I am the **b** of life.
　　6: 41 "I am the **b** that came down
　　6: 48 I am the **b** of life.
　　6: 51 I am the living **b** that came down
　　6: 51 This **b** is my flesh, which I will give
　　21: 13 took the **b** and gave it to them,
1Co 10: 16 And is not the **b** that we break
　　11: 23 the night he was betrayed, took **b**,
　　11: 26 For whenever you eat this **b**

BREAK (BREACH BREACHING BREAKERS BREAKING BREAKS BROKE BROKEN BROKENNESS)
Nu 30: 2 he must not **b** his word but must do
Jdg 2: 1 'I will never **b** my covenant
Ps 2: 9 You will **b** them with a rod of iron;
Pr 25: 15 and a gentle tongue can **b** a bone.
Isa 42: 3 A bruised reed he will not **b**,
Mt 12: 20 A bruised reed he will not **b**,
Ac 20: 7 week we came together to **b** bread.
1Co 10: 16 the bread that we **b** a participation
Rev 5: 2 "Who is worthy to **b** the seals

BREAKERS* (BREAK)
Ps 42: 7 waves and **b** have swept over me.
　　93: 4 mightier than the **b** of the sea—
Jnh 2: 3 all your waves and **b** swept over me.

BREAKING (BREAK)
Jos 9: 20 fall on us for **b** the oath we swore
Eze 16: 59 despised my oath by **b** the covenant.
　　17: 18 despised the oath by **b** the covenant.
Ac 2: 42 to the **b** of bread and to prayer.
Jas 2: 10 just one point is guilty of **b** all of it.

BREAKS (BREAK)
Jer 23: 29 "and like a hammer that **b** a rock
1Jn 3: 4 Everyone who sins **b** the law;

BREASTPIECE (BREASTPLATE)
Ex 28: 15 "Fashion a **b** for making decisions—

BREASTPLATE* (BREASTPIECE)
Isa 59: 17 He put on righteousness as his **b**,
Eph 6: 14 with the **b** of righteousness in place,
1Th 5: 8 putting on faith and love as a **b**,

BREASTS
La 4: 3 Even jackals offer their **b** to nurse

BREATH (BREATHED GOD-BREATHED)
Ge 2: 7 into his nostrils the **b** of life,

BREATHED (BREATH)
Ge 2: 7 **b** into his nostrils the breath of life,
Mk 15: 37 With a loud cry, Jesus **b** his last.
Jn 20: 22 with that he **b** on them and said,

BRIBE
Ex 23: 8 "Do not accept a **b**, for a **b** blinds

Dt 16: 19 Do not accept a **b**, for a **b** blinds
　　27: 25 "Cursed is anyone who accepts a **b**
Pr 6: 35 he will refuse a **b**, however great it

BRIDE
Isa 62: 5 as a bridegroom rejoices over his **b**,
Rev 19: 7 and his **b** has made herself ready.
　　21: 2 prepared as a **b** beautifully dressed
　　21: 9 I will show you the **b**, the wife
　　22: 17 The Spirit and the **b** say, "Come!"

BRIDEGROOM
Ps 19: 5 which is like a **b** coming out of his
Mt 25: 1 lamps and went out to meet the **b**.
　　25: 5 The **b** was a long time in coming,

BRIGHTENS* (BRIGHTNESS)
Pr 16: 15 When a king's face **b**, it means life;
Ecc 8: 1 Wisdom **b** the face and changes its

BRIGHTER (BRIGHTNESS)
Pr 4: 18 shining ever **b** till the full light

BRIGHTNESS* (BRIGHTENS BRIGHTER)
2Sa 22: 13 Out of the **b** of his presence bolts
　　23: 4 like the **b** after rain that brings grass
Ps 18: 12 Out of the **b** of his presence clouds
Isa 59: 9 for **b**, but we walk in deep shadows.
　　60: 3 and kings to the **b** of your dawn.
　　60: 19 nor will the **b** of the moon shine
Da 12: 3 those who are wise will shine like the **b**
Am 5: 20 pitch-dark, without a ray of **b**?

BRILLIANCE* (BRILLIANT)
Ac 22: 11 because the **b** of the light had
Rev 1: 16 was like the sun shining in all its **b**.
　　21: 11 its **b** was like that of a very precious

BRILLIANT* (BRILLIANCE)
Ecc 9: 11 or wealth to the **b** or favor
Eze 1: 4 lightning and surrounded by **b** light.
　　1: 27 and **b** light surrounded him.

BRITTLE*
Da 2: 42 will be partly strong and partly **b**.

BROAD
Mt 7: 13 gate and **b** is the road that leads

BROKE (BREAK)
Mt 26: 26 he **b** it and gave it to his disciples,
Mk 14: 22 he **b** it and gave it to his disciples,
Ac 2: 46 They **b** bread in their homes and ate
　　20: 11 he went upstairs again and **b** bread
1Co 11: 24 had given thanks, he **b** it and said,

BROKEN (BREAK)
1Sa 2: 10 those who oppose the LORD will be **b**.
Ps 34: 20 bones, not one of them will be **b**.
　　51: 17 My sacrifice, O God, is a **b** spirit;
Ecc 4: 12 of three strands is not quickly **b**.
Lk 20: 18 on that stone will be **b** to pieces,
Jn 7: 23 that the law of Moses may not be **b**,
　　10: 35 and Scripture cannot be **b**—
　　19: 36 "Not one of his bones will be **b**,"
Ro 11: 20 they were **b** off because of unbelief,

BROKENHEARTED* (HEART)
Ps 34: 18 The LORD is close to the **b**
　　109: 16 the poor and the needy and the **b**,
　　147: 3 He heals the **b** and binds up their
Isa 61: 1 He has sent me to bind up the **b**,

BROKENNESS* (BREAK)
Isa 65: 14 of heart and wail in **b** of spirit.

BRONZE
Ex 27: 2 piece, and overlay the altar with **b**.
　　30: 18 "Make a **b** basin, with its stand,
Nu 21: 9 So Moses made a **b** snake and put it
Da 2: 32 of silver, its belly and thighs of **b**,
　　10: 6 legs like the gleam of burnished **b**,
Rev 1: 15 His feet were like **b** glowing
　　2: 18 and whose feet are like burnished **b**.

BROTHER (BROTHER'S BROTHERLY BROTHERS)
Pr 17: 17 a **b** is born for a time of adversity.
　　18: 24 a friend who sticks closer than a **b**.
Mt 18: 15 "If a **b** or sister sins, go and point
Mk 3: 35 Whoever does God's will is my **b**
Lk 17: 3 "If a **b** or sister sins against you,
Ro 14: 13 obstacle in the way of a **b** or sister.
　　14: 15 not by your eating destroy your **b**
　　14: 21 anything else that will cause your **b**
1Co 5: 11 The **b** or sister is not bound in such
　　8: 13 if what I eat causes my **b** or sister
Phm : 16 but better than a slave, as a dear **b**.
Jas 2: 15 Suppose a **b** or sister is without
　　4: 11 Anyone who speaks against a **b**

1Jn 3: 17 and sees a **b** or sister in need but has
　　4: 20 If we say we love God yet hate a
　　5: 16 If you see any **b** or sister commit

BROTHER'S (BROTHER)
Ge 4: 9 "Am I my **b** keeper?"

BROTHERS (BROTHER)
Mt 12: 49 "Here are my mother and my **b**.
　　19: 29 everyone who has left houses or **b**
　　25: 40 did for one of the least of these **b**
Mk 3: 33 "Who are my mother and my **b**?
　　10: 29 "no one who has left home or **b**
Lk 21: 16 will be betrayed even by parents, **b**,
　　22: 32 turned back, strengthen your **b**."
Jn 7: 5 For even his own **b** did not believe
1Th 4: 10 you do love all the **b** and sisters
2Th 3: 6 we command you, **b** and sisters,
Heb 2: 11 Jesus is not ashamed to call them **b**
　　2: 17 reason he had to be made like his **b**
　　13: 1 Keep on loving one another as **b**
1Jn 3: 10 are those who do not love their **b**
Rev 12: 10 For the accuser of our **b** and sisters,

BROW
Ge 3: 19 your **b** you will eat your food until

BRUISED (BRUISES)
Isa 42: 3 A **b** reed he will not break,
Mt 12: 20 A **b** reed he will not break,

BRUISES (BRUISED)
Isa 30: 26 LORD binds up the **b** of his people

BRUTAL (BRUTE)
2Ti 3: 3 without self-control, **b**, not lovers

BRUTE* (BRUTAL)
Ps 73: 22 I was a **b** beast before you.

BUBBLING*
Isa 35: 7 a pool, the thirsty ground **b** springs.

BUCKET*
Isa 40: 15 the nations are like a drop in a **b**;

BUCKLED*
Eph 6: 14 belt of truth **b** around your waist,

BUD (BUDDED)
Isa 27: 6 Israel will **b** and blossom and fill all

BUDDED (BUD)
Heb 9: 4 Aaron's staff that had **b**,

BUILD (BUILDER BUILDERS BUILDING BUILDS BUILT REBUILD REBUILT)
2Sa 7: 5 Are you the one to **b** me a house
1Ki 6: 1 he began to **b** the temple
Ecc 3: 3 a time to tear down and a time to **b**,
Mt 16: 18 and on this rock I will **b** my church,
Ac 20: 32 which can **b** you up and give you
Ro 15: 2 for their good, to **b** them up.
1Co 3: 10 But each one should **b** with care.
　　14: 12 excel in those that **b** up the church.
1Th 5: 11 one another and **b** each other up,

BUILDER* (BUILD)
1Co 3: 10 I laid a foundation as a wise **b**,
Heb 3: 3 just as the **b** of a house has greater
　　3: 4 but God is the **b** of everything.
　　11: 10 whose architect and **b** is God.

BUILDERS (BUILD)
Ps 118: 22 The stone the **b** rejected has become
Mt 21: 42 " 'The stone the **b** rejected has
Mk 12: 10 " 'The stone the **b** rejected has
Lk 20: 17 " 'The stone the **b** rejected has
Ac 4: 11 is " 'the stone you **b** rejected,
1Pe 2: 7 "The stone the **b** rejected has

BUILDING (BUILD)
Ezr 3: 8 older to supervise the **b** of the house
Ne 4: 17 who were **b** the wall.
Ro 15: 20 I would not be on someone else's
1Co 3: 9 you are God's field, God's **b**.
2Co 5: 1 is destroyed, we have a **b** from God,
　　10: 8 authority the Lord gave us for **b** you
　　13: 10 the Lord gave me for **b** you up,
Eph 2: 21 him the whole **b** is joined together
　　4: 29 only what is helpful for **b** others
Jude 1: 20 by **b** yourselves up in your most

BUILDS (BUILD)
Ps 127: 1 Unless the LORD **b** the house,
Pr 14: 1 The wise woman **b** her house,
1Co 3: 12 If anyone **b** on this foundation using
　　1: puffs up while love **b** up.
Eph 4: 16 grows and **b** itself up in love,

BUILT (BUILD)
1Ki 6: 14 So Solomon **b** the temple
Mt 7: 24 is like a wise man who **b** his house
Lk 6: 49 are like a man who **b** a house
Ac 17: 24 does not live in temples **b** by hands.
1Co 3: 14 If what has been **b** survives,
      14: 26 so that the church may be **b** up.
2Co 5: 1 in heaven, not **b** by human hands.
Eph 2: 20 **b** on the foundation of the apostles
     4: 12 that the body of Christ may be **b**
Col 2: 7 rooted and **b** up in him,
1Pe 2: 5 are being **b** into a spiritual house

BULL (BULLS)
Lev 4: 3 LORD a young **b** without defect as

BULLS (BULL)
1Ki 7: 25 The Sea stood on twelve **b**,
Heb 10: 4 It is impossible for the blood of **b**

BURDEN (BURDENED BURDENS BURDENSOME)
Ps 38: 4 overwhelmed me like a **b** too heavy
Ecc 1: 13 What a heavy **b** God has laid
Mt 11: 30 my yoke is easy and my **b** is light."
Ac 15: 28 and to us not to **b** you with anything
2Co 11: 9 kept myself from being a **b** to you
    12: 14 and I will not be a **b** to you,
1Th 2: 9 be a **b** to anyone while we preached
2Th 3: 8 so that we would not be a **b** to any
Heb 13: 17 not a **b**, for that would be of no

BURDENED* (BURDEN)
Isa 43: 23 I have not **b** you with grain
    43: 24 But you have **b** me with your sins
Mic 6: 3 How have I **b** you? Answer me.
Mt 11: 28 all you who are weary and **b**, and I
2Co 5: 4 we groan and are **b**, because we do
Gal 5: 1 do not let yourselves be **b** again
1Ti 5: 16 not let the church be **b** with them,

BURDENS (BURDEN)
Ps 68: 19 our Savior, who daily bears our **b**.
Lk 11: 46 down with **b** they can hardly carry,
Gal 6: 2 Carry each other's **b**, and in this

BURDENSOME (BURDEN)
1Jn 5: 3 And his commands are not **b**,

BURIED (BURY)
Ru 1: 17 die I will die, and there I will be **b**.
Ro 6: 4 We were therefore **b** with him
1Co 15: 4 that he was **b**, that he was raised
Col 2: 12 having been **b** with him in baptism,

BURN (BURNING BURNT)
Dt 7: 5 poles and **b** their idols in the fire.
Ps 79: 5 long will your jealousy **b** like fire?
1Co 7: 9 to marry than to **b** with passion.

BURNING (BURN)
Ex 27: 20 so that the lamps may be kept **b**.
Lev 6: 9 the fire must be kept **b** on the altar.
Ps 18: 28 You, LORD, keep my lamp **b**;
Pr 25: 22 you will heap **b** coals on his head,
Ro 12: 20 you will heap **b** coals on his head."
Rev 19: 20 alive into the fiery lake of **b** sulfur.

BURNISHED*
1Ki 7: 45 of the LORD were of **b** bronze.
Eze 1: 7 of a calf and gleamed like **b** bronze.
Da 10: 6 and legs like the gleam of **b** bronze,
Rev 2: 18 and whose feet are like **b** bronze.

BURNT (BURN)
Ge 8: 20 birds, he sacrificed **b** offerings on it.
    22: 2 Sacrifice him there as a **b** offering
Ex 10: 25 **b** offerings to present to the LORD
    18: 12 brought a **b** offering and other
    40: 6 "Place the altar of **b** offering
Lev 1: 3 the offering is a **b** offering
Jos 8: 31 offered to the LORD **b** offerings
Jdg 6: 26 the second bull as a **b** offering."
    13: 16 But if you prepare a **b** offering,
1Ki 3: 4 offered a thousand **b** offerings
    9: 25 year Solomon sacrificed **b** offerings
    10: 5 and the **b** offerings he made
Ezr 3: 2 Israel to sacrifice **b** offerings on it,
Eze 43: 18 for sacrificing **b** offerings

BURST
Ps 98: 4 **b** into jubilant song with music;
Isa 14: 7 **b** into song, you mountains,
    49: 13 **b** into song, you mountains!
    52: 9 **b** into songs of joy together,
    54: 1 **b** into song, shout for joy, you who
    55: 12 hills will **b** into song before you,

BURY (BURIED)
Mt 8: 22 and let the dead **b** their own dead."
Lk 9: 60 "Let the dead **b** their own dead,

BUSH
Ex 3: 2 though the **b** was on fire it did not
Mk 12: 26 in the account of the burning **b**,
Lk 20: 37 But in the account of the burning **b**,
Ac 7: 35 angel who appeared to him in the **b**.

BUSINESS
Ecc 4: 8 too is meaningless—a miserable **b**!
Da 8: 27 got up and went about the king's **b**.
1Co 5: 12 What **b** is it of mine to judge those
1Th 4: 11 You should mind your own **b**
Jas 1: 1 even while they go about their **b**.

BUSY*
1Ki 18: 27 is deep in thought, or **b**, or traveling.
    20: 40 While your servant was **b** here
Hag 1: 9 each of you is **b** with his own house.
2Th 3: 11 They are not **b**; they are busybodies.
Tit 2: 5 pure, to be **b** at home, to be kind,

BUSYBODIES*
2Th 3: 11 They are not busy; they are **b**.
1Ti 5: 13 idlers, but also **b** who talk nonsense,

BUY (BOUGHT BUYS)
Pr 23: 23 **B** the truth and do not sell it—
Isa 55: 1 Come, **b** wine and milk without money
Rev 13: 17 so that they could not **b** or sell

BUYS (BUY)
Pr 31: 16 She considers a field and **b** it;

BYWORD (WORD)
1Ki 9: 7 become a **b** and an object of ridicule
Ps 44: 14 made us a **b** among the nations;
Joel 2: 17 of scorn, a **b** among the nations.

CAESAR
Mt 22: 21 "Give back to **C** what is Caesar's,

CAIN
Firstborn of Adam (Ge 4:1), murdered brother Abel
(Ge 4:1–16; 1Jn 3:12).

CALAMITIES (CALAMITY)
Dt 31: 17 Many disasters and **c** will come
    31: 21 And when many disasters and **c** come

CALAMITY (CALAMITIES)
Pr 22: 8 Those who sow injustice reap **c**,

CALEB
Judahite who spied out Canaan (Nu 13:6); allowed
to enter land because of faith (Nu 13:30–14:38; Dt
1:36). Possessed Hebron (Jos 14:6–15:19).

CALF
Ex 32: 4 into an idol cast in the shape of a **c**,
Pr 15: 17 love than a fattened **c** with hatred.
Lk 15: 23 Bring the fattened **c** and kill it.
Ac 7: 41 they made an idol in the form of a **c**.

CALL (CALLED CALLING CALLS)
Ex 3: 15 the name you shall **c** me from
1Ki 18: 24 I will **c** on the name of the LORD.
2Ki 5: 11 **c** on the name of the LORD his
1Ch 16: 8 to the LORD, **c** on his name;
Ps 105: 1 to the LORD, **c** on his name;
    116: 13 and **c** on the name of the LORD.
    116: 17 and **c** on the name of the LORD.
    145: 18 LORD is near to all who **c** on him,
Pr 31: 28 Her children arise and **c** her blessed;
Isa 5: 20 Woe to those who **c** evil good
    12: 4 to the LORD, **c** on his name;
    55: 6 **c** on him while he is near.
    65: 24 Before they **c** I will answer;
Jer 33: 3 '**C** to me and I will answer you
Zep 3: 9 all of them may **c** on the name
Zec 13: 9 They will **c** on my name and I will
Mt 9: 13 I have not come to **c** the righteous,
Mk 2: 17 I have not come to **c** the righteous,
Lk 5: 32 I have not come to **c** the righteous,
Ac 2: 39 all whom the Lord our God will **c**."
    9: 14 to arrest all who **c** on your name."
    9: 21 in Jerusalem among those who **c**
Ro 10: 12 and richly blesses all who **c** on him,
    11: 29 gifts and his **c** are irrevocable.
1Co 1: 2 all those everywhere who **c**
1Th 4: 7 For God did not **c** us to be impure,
2Ti 2: 22 along with those who **c** on the Lord

CALLED (CALL)
Ge 2: 23 she shall be **c** 'woman,' for she was
    5: 2 he **c** them "human beings."
    12: 8 and **c** on the name of the LORD.
    21: 33 and there he **c** on the name

Ge 26: 25 and **c** on the name of the LORD.
1Sa 3: 5 and said, "Here I am; you **c** me."
2Ch 7: 14 my people, who are **c** by my name,
Ps 34: 6 This poor man, and the LORD
    116: 4 I **c** on the name of the LORD:
Isa 56: 7 for my house will be **c** a house
La 3: 55 I **c** on your name, LORD,
Hos 11: 1 and out of Egypt I **c** my son.
Mt 1: 16 of Jesus who is **c** the Messiah.
    2: 15 "Out of Egypt I **c** my son."
    21: 13 " 'My house will be **c** a house
Mk 11: 17 'My house will be **c** a house
Lk 1: 32 will be **c** the Son of the Most High.
    1: 35 to be born will be **c** the Son of God.
Ro 1: 1 **c** to be an apostle and set apart
    1: 6 are among those Gentiles who are **c**
    1: 7 by God and **c** to be his holy people:
    8: 28 who have been **c** according to his
    8: 30 And those he predestined, he also **c**;
1Co 1: 1 **c** to be an apostle of Christ Jesus
    1: 2 Jesus and **c** to be his holy people,
    1: 24 but to those whom God has **c**,
    1: 26 of what you were when you were **c**.
    7: 15 God has **c** us to live in peace.
    7: 17 to you, just as God has **c** you.
Gal 1: 6 quickly deserting the one who **c** you
    1: 15 from birth and **c** me by his grace,
    5: 13 and sisters, were **c** to be free.
Eph 1: 18 the hope to which he has **c** you,
    4: 4 **c** to one hope when you were **c**;
Col 3: 15 of one body you were **c** to peace.
2Th 2: 14 He **c** you to this through our gospel,
1Ti 6: 12 you were **c** when you made your
2Ti 1: 9 has saved us and **c** us to a holy life—
Heb 9: 15 that those who are **c** may receive
1Pe 1: 15 But just as he who **c** you is holy,
    2: 9 the praises of him who **c** you
    3: 9 to this you were **c** so that you may
    5: 10 who **c** you to his eternal glory
2Pe 1: 3 of him who **c** us by his own glory
Jude 1: 1 To those who have been **c**, who are

CALLING (CALL)
Isa 40: 3 A voice of one **c**:
Mt 3: 3 "A voice of one **c** in the wilderness,
Mk 1: 3 "a voice of one **c** in the wilderness,
    10: 49 On your feet! He's **c** you."
Lk 3: 4 "A voice of one **c** in the wilderness,
Jn 1: 23 the voice of one **c** in the wilderness,
Ac 22: 16 your sins away, **c** on his name.'
Eph 4: 1 worthy of the **c** you have received.
2Th 1: 11 God may make you worthy of his **c**,
2Pe 1: 10 make every effort to confirm your **c**

CALLOUS* (CALLOUSED)
Ps 17: 10 They close up their **c** hearts,
    73: 7 From their **c** hearts comes iniquity;
    119: 70 Their hearts are **c** and unfeeling,

CALLOUSED* (CALLOUS)
Isa 6: 10 Make the heart of this people **c**;
Mt 13: 15 this people's heart has become **c**;
Ac 28: 27 this people's heart has become **c**;

CALLS (CALL)
Ps 147: 4 the stars and **c** them each by name.
Isa 40: 26 by one, and **c** them each by name.
Joel 2: 32 everyone who **c** on the name
Mt 22: 43 by the Spirit, **c** him 'Lord'?
Jn 10: 3 He **c** his own sheep by name
Ac 2: 21 everyone who **c** on the name
Ro 10: 13 "Everyone who **c** on the name
1Th 2: 12 who **c** you into his kingdom
    5: 24 The one who **c** you is faithful,

CALM
Ps 107: 30 They were glad when it grew **c**,
Pr 15: 18 those who are patient **c** a quarrel.
    29: 11 but the wise bring **c** in the end.
Isa 7: 4 keep **c** and don't be afraid.
Eze 16: 42 I will be **c** and no longer angry.

CAMEL
Mt 19: 24 easier for a **c** to go through the eye
    23: 24 strain out a gnat but swallow a **c**.
Mk 10: 25 easier for a **c** to go through the eye
Lk 18: 25 easier for a **c** to go through the eye

CAMP (ENCAMPS)
Heb 13: 13 go to him outside the **c**,

CANAAN (CANAANITE CANAANITES)
Ge 10: 15 **C** was the father of Sidon his
Lev 14: 34 "When you enter the land of **C**,
    25: 38 of Egypt to give you the land of **C**
Nu 13: 2 some men to explore the land of **C**,

Nu 33: 51 'When you cross the Jordan into **C**,
Jdg 4: 2 into the hands of Jabin king of **C**,
1Ch 16: 18 **C** as the portion you will inherit."
Ps 105: 11 **C** is the portion you will inherit."
Ac 13: 19 he overthrew seven nations in **C**,

CANAANITE (CANAAN)
Ge 10: 18 Later the **C** clans scattered
28: 1 "Do not marry a **C** woman.
Jos 5: 1 all the **C** kings along the coast heard
Jdg 1: 32 lived among the **C** inhabitants

CANAANITES (CANAAN)
Ex 33: 2 before you and drive out the **C**,

CANCEL (CANCELED)
Dt 15: 1 every seven years you must **c** debts.

CANCELED* (CANCEL)
Mt 18: 27 on him, **c** the debt and let him go.
18: 32 'I **c** all that debt of yours because
Col 2: 14 having **c** the charge of our legal

CANDLESTICKS See LAMPSTANDS

CANOPY*
2Sa 22: 12 made darkness his **c** around him—
2Ki 16: 18 He took away the Sabbath **c**
Ps 18: 11 his covering, his **c** around him
Isa 4: 5 everything the glory will be a **c**
40: 22 stretches out the heavens like a **c**,
Jer 43: 10 he will spread his royal **c**

CAPERNAUM
Mt 4: 13 he went and lived in **C**, which was
Jn 6: 59 teaching in the synagogue in **C**.

CAPITAL
Dt 21: 22 anyone guilty of a **c** offense is put

CAPSTONE* (STONE)
Zec 4: 7 he will bring out the **c** to shouts

CAPTIVATE* (CAPTIVE)
Pr 6: 25 or let her **c** you with her eyes.

CAPTIVE (CAPTIVATE CAPTIVES CAPTIVITY CAPTURED)
Ac 8: 23 are full of bitterness and **c** to sin."
2Co 10: 5 we take **c** every thought to make it
Col 2: 8 no one takes you **c** through hollow
2Ti 2: 26 who has taken them **c** to do his will.

CAPTIVES (CAPTIVE)
Ps 68: 18 ascended on high, you took many **c**;
Isa 61: 1 to proclaim freedom for the **c**
Eph 4: 8 he took many **c** and gave gifts to

CAPTIVITY (CAPTIVE)
Dt 28: 41 them, because they will go into **c**.
2Ki 25: 21 So Judah went into **c**,
Jer 30: 3 Judah back from **c** and restore them
52: 27 So Judah went into **c**,
Eze 29: 14 I will bring them back from **c**

CAPTURED (CAPTIVE)
1Sa 4: 11 The ark of God was **c**, and Eli's two
2Sa 5: 7 David **c** the fortress of Zion—
2Ki 17: 6 the king of Assyria **c** Samaria

CARCASS
Jdg 14: 9 taken the honey from the lion's **c**.
Mt 24: 28 Wherever there is a **c**,

CARE (CAREFUL CAREFULLY CARES CARING)
Ps 8: 4 human beings that you **c** for them?
43: 3 your light and your faithful **c**,
65: 9 You **c** for the land and water it;
144: 3 human beings that you **c** for them,
Pr 12: 10 The righteous **c** for the needs
29: 7 The righteous **c** about justice
Mk 5: 26 had suffered a great deal under the **c**
Lk 10: 34 him to an inn and took **c** of him.
18: 4 fear God or **c** what people think,
Jn 21: 16 Jesus said, "Take **c** of my sheep."
1Co 3: 10 But each one should build with **c**.
Eph 5: 29 but they feed and **c** for them,
1Ti 3: 5 family, how can he take **c** of God's
6: 20 what has been entrusted to your **c**,
Heb 2: 6 human beings that you **c** for them?
1Pe 5: 2 of God's flock that is under your **c**,

CAREFUL* (CARE)
Ge 31: 24 "Be **c** not to say anything to Jacob,
31: 29 'Be **c** not to say anything to Jacob,
Ex 19: 12 'Be **c** that you do not approach
23: 13 "Be **c** to do everything I have said
34: 12 Be **c** not to make a treaty with those
34: 15 "Be **c** not to make a treaty
Lev 18: 4 laws and be **c** to follow my decrees.
25: 18 decrees and be **c** to obey my laws,

Lev 26: 3 and are **c** to obey my commands,
Dt 2: 4 will be afraid of you, but be very **c**.
4: 9 Only be **c**, and watch yourselves
4: 23 Be **c** not to forget the covenant
5: 32 So be **c** to do what the Lord your
6: 3 be **c** to obey so that it may go well
6: 12 be **c** that you do not forget
6: 25 we are **c** to obey all this law before
7: 12 these laws and are **c** to follow them,
8: 1 Be **c** to follow every command I am
8: 11 Be **c** that you do not forget
11: 16 Be **c**, or you will be enticed to turn
12: 1 laws you must be **c** to follow
12: 13 Be **c** not to sacrifice your burnt
12: 19 Be **c** not to neglect the Levites as
12: 28 Be **c** to obey all these regulations I
12: 30 be **c** not to be ensnared by inquiring
15: 5 are **c** to follow all these commands I
15: 9 Be **c** not to harbor this wicked
17: 10 Be **c** to do everything they instruct
24: 8 be very **c** to do exactly as
Jos 1: 7 Be **c** to obey all the law my servant
1: 8 that you may be **c** to do everything
22: 5 be very **c** to keep the commandment
23: 6 be **c** to obey all that is written
23: 11 So be very **c** to love the Lord
1Ki 2: 4 if only your descendants are **c** in all
2Ki 10: 31 Yet Jehu was not **c** to keep the law
17: 37 You must always be **c** to keep
21: 8 only they will be **c** to do everything
1Ch 22: 13 if you are **c** to observe the decrees
28: 8 Be **c** to follow all the commands
2Ch 6: 16 if only your descendants are **c** in all
33: 8 only they will be **c** to do everything
Ezr 4: 22 Be **c** not to neglect this matter.
Job 36: 18 Be **c** that no one entices you
Ps 45: 10 daughter, and pay **c** attention:
101: 2 I will be **c** to lead a blameless life—
Pr 4: 26 Give **c** thought to the paths for your
24: 8 but those who love them are **c**
21: 28 **c** listener will testify successfully.
27: 23 give **c** attention to your herds;
Isa 7: 4 'Be **c**, keep calm and don't be
Jer 17: 21 Be **c** not to carry a load
17: 24 But if you are **c** to obey me,
22: 4 For if you are **c** to carry out these
Eze 11: 20 decrees and be **c** to keep my laws.
18: 19 has been **c** to keep all my decrees,
20: 19 decrees and be **c** to keep my laws.
20: 21 they were not **c** to keep my laws,
36: 27 decrees and be **c** to keep my laws.
37: 24 laws and be **c** to keep my decrees.
Mic 7: 5 in your embrace be **c** of your words.
Hag 1: 5 "Give **c** thought to your ways.
1: 7 "Give **c** thought to your ways.
2: 15 " 'Now give **c** thought to this
2: 18 give **c** thought to the day
2: 18 temple was laid. Give **c** thought:
Mt 2: 8 and make a **c** search for the child.
6: 1 "Be **c** not to do your 'acts
16: 6 "Be **c**," Jesus said to them.
23: 3 be **c** to do everything they tell you.
Mk 8: 15 "Be **c**," Jesus warned them.
Lk 21: 34 "Be **c**, or your hearts will be
Ro 12: 17 Be **c** to do what is right in the eyes
10: 12 firm, be **c** that you don't fall!
Eph 5: 15 Be very **c**, then, how you live—
2Ti 4: 2 great patience and **c** instruction.
Tit 3: 8 God may be **c** to devote themselves
Heb 2: 1 We must pay the most **c** attention,
4: 1 let us be **c** that none of you be found

CAREFULLY* (CARE)
Pr 12: 26 The righteous choose their friends **c**,

CARES* (CARE)
Dt 11: 12 a land the Lord your God **c** for;
Job 39: 16 she **c** not that her labor was in vain,
Ps 55: 22 Cast your **c** on the Lord and he
142: 4 no one **c** for my life.
Ecc 5: 3 comes when there are many **c**,
Jer 12: 11 because there is no one who **c**.
30: 17 outcast, Zion for whom no one **c**.'
Na 1: 7 he **c** for those who trust in him,
Jn 10: 13 hand and **c** nothing for the sheep.
1Th 2: 7 nursing mother **c** for her children,
1Pe 5: 7 on him because he **c** for you.

CARING* (CARE)
1Ti 5: 4 practice by **c** for their own family

CAROUSING
Ro 13: 13 not in **c** and drunkenness,

CARPENTER (CARPENTER'S)
Mk 6: 3 Isn't this the **c**? Isn't this Mary's

CARPENTER'S* (CARPENTER)
Mt 13: 55 "Isn't this the **c** son?

CARRIED (CARRY)
Ex 19: 4 and how I **c** you on eagles' wings
Dt 1: 31 how the Lord your God **c** you,
Isa 63: 9 up and **c** them all the days of old.
Heb 13: 9 Do not be **c** away by all kinds
2Pe 1: 21 God as they were **c** along
3: 17 you may not be **c** away by the error

CARRIES (CARRY)
Dt 32: 11 to catch them and **c** them aloft.
Isa 40: 11 arms and **c** them close to his heart;

CARRY (CARRIED CARRIES CARRYING)
Lev 16: 22 The goat will **c** on itself all their
26: 15 and fail to **c** out all my commands
Isa 46: 4 I have made you and I will **c** you;
Lk 14: 27 whoever does not **c** their cross
Gal 6: 2 **C** each other's burdens, and in this
6: 5 each of you should **c** your own load.

CARRYING (CARRY)
Jn 19: 17 **C** his own cross, he went
1Jn 5: 2 God and **c** out his commands.

CARVED
Nu 33: 52 Destroy all their **c** images and their

CASE
Pr 22: 23 for the Lord will take up their **c**
23: 11 he will take up their **c** against you.

CAST (CASTING)
Lev 16: 8 He is to **c** lots for the two goats—
Ps 22: 18 them and **c** lots for my garment.
55: 22 **C** your cares on the Lord and he
Mt 16: 33 The lot is **c** into the lap, but its
Jn 19: 24 them and **c** lots for my garment."
1Pe 5: 7 **C** all your anxiety on him because

CASTING (CAST)
Pr 18: 18 **C** the lot settles disputes and keeps
Mt 27: 35 they divided up his clothes by **c** lots.

CATCH (CATCHES CAUGHT)
Lk 5: 4 and let down the nets for a **c**."

CATCHES (CATCH)
Job 5: 13 He **c** the wise in their craftiness,
1Co 3: 19 "He **c** the wise in their craftiness";

CATTLE
Ps 50: 10 mine, and the **c** on a thousand hills.

CAUGHT (CATCH)
Ge 22: 13 in a thicket he saw a ram **c** by its
2Co 12: 2 Christ who fourteen years ago was **c**
1Th 4: 17 are left will be **c** up together

CAUSE (CAUSES)
Ps 7: 16 trouble they **c** recoils on them;
25: 3 who are treacherous without **c**.
Ps 82: 3 uphold the **c** of the poor
Pr 24: 28 against your neighbor without **c**—
Ecc 8: 3 Do not stand up for a bad **c**, for he
Mt 18: 7 the things that **c** people to stumble!
Ro 14: 21 else that will **c** your brother or sister
1Co 10: 32 Do not **c** anyone to stumble,

CAUSES (CAUSE)
Isa 8: 14 he will be a stone that **c** people
Mt 5: 29 If your right eye **c** you to stumble,
5: 30 if your right hand **c** you to stumble,
18: 6 "If anyone **c** one of these little
18: 8 hand or your foot **c** you to stumble,
Ro 14: 20 eat anything that **c** someone else
1Co 8: 13 if what I eat **c** my brother or sister
1Pe 2: 8 "A stone that **c** people to stumble

CEASE
Ps 46: 9 He makes wars **c** to the ends

CELEBRATE
Ex 10: 9 because we are to **c** a festival
12: 14 to come you shall **c** it as a festival
12: 17 "**C** the Festival of Unleavened
12: 17 **C** this day as a lasting ordinance
12: 47 community of Israel must **c** it.
12: 48 the Lord's Passover must have
23: 14 times a year you are to **c** a festival
23: 15 "**C** the Festival of Unleavened
23: 16 "**C** the Festival of Harvest
23: 16 "**C** the Festival of Ingathering
34: 18 "**C** the Festival of Unleavened
34: 22 "**C** the Festival of Weeks
Lev 23: 39 **c** the festival to the Lord

Lev 23: 41 **c** this as a festival to the Lord
    23: 41 **c** it in the seventh month.
Nu 9: 2 "Have the Israelites **c** the Passover
    9: 3 **C** it at the appointed time,
    9: 4 told the Israelites to **c** the Passover
    9: 6 of them could not **c** the Passover
    9: 10 are still to **c** the Lord's Passover,
    9: 12 When they **c** the Passover,
    9: 13 on a journey fails to **c** the Passover,
    9: 14 also to **c** the Lord's Passover
    29: 12 **C** a festival to the Lord for seven
Dt 16: 1 **c** the Passover of the Lord your
    16: 10 Then **c** the Festival of Weeks
    16: 13 **C** the Festival of Tabernacles
    16: 15 For seven days **c** the festival
Jdg 16: 23 to Dagon their god and to **c**, saying,
2Sa 16: 3 to David to make the Lord.
2Ki 23: 21 "**C** the Passover to the Lord
2Ch 30: 1 and **c** the Passover to the Lord,
    30: 2 Jerusalem decided to **c** the Passover
    30: 3 They had not been able to **c** it
    30: 5 and **c** the Passover to the Lord,
    30: 13 in Jerusalem to **c** the Festival
    30: 23 to **c** the festival seven more days;
Ne 8: 12 of food and to **c** with great joy,
    12: 27 to **c** joyfully the dedication
Est 9: 21 have them **c** annually the fourteenth
Ps 2: 11 **c** his rule with trembling.
    145: 7 They **c** your abundant goodness
Isa 30: 29 as on the night you **c** a holy festival;
Hos 5: 7 When they **c** their New Moon feasts,
Na 1: 15 **C** your festivals, Judah, and fulfill
Zec 14: 16 and to **c** the Festival of Tabernacles.
    14: 18 up to **c** the Festival of Tabernacles.
    14: 19 up to **c** the Festival of Tabernacles.
Mt 26: 18 I am going to **c** the Passover
Lk 15: 23 and kill it. Let's have a feast and **c**.
    15: 24 and is found.' So they began to **c**.
    15: 29 me even a young goat so I could **c**
    15: 32 But we had to **c** and be glad,
Rev 11: 10 will **c** by sending each other gifts,

CELESTIAL*
2Pe 2: 10 afraid to heap abuse on **c** beings;
Jude : 8 and heap abuse on **c** beings.

CENSER (CENSERS)
Lev 16: 12 is to take a **c** full of burning coals
Rev 8: 3 who had a golden **c**, came and stood

CENSERS (CENSER)
Nu 16: 6 your followers are do this: Take **c**

CENTURION
Mt 8: 5 Capernaum, a **c** came to him,
    27: 54 When the **c** and those with him who
Mk 15: 39 And when the **c**, who stood there
Lk 7: 3 The **c** heard of Jesus and sent some
    23: 47 The **c**, seeing what had happened,
Ac 10: 1 a **c** in what was known as the Italian
    27: 1 handed over to a **c** named Julius,

CEPHAS* (PETER)
Jn 1: 42 You will be called "**C**" (which,
1Co 1: 12 another, "I follow **C**";
    3: 22 Paul or Apollos or **C** or the world
    9: 5 and the Lord's brothers and **C**?

CEREMONIAL* (CEREMONY)
Lev 4: 12 at the time of their **c** cleansing,
    15: 13 off seven days for his **c** cleansing;
Mk 7: 3 they give their hands a **c** washing,
Jn 2: 6 used by the Jews for **c** washing,
    3: 25 Jew over the matter of **c** washing.
    11: 55 for their **c** cleansing before
    18: 28 to avoid **c** uncleanness they did not
Heb 9: 10 and drink and various **c** washings—
    13: 9 not by the eating of **c** foods,

CEREMONIALLY* (CEREMONY)
Lev 4: 12 outside the camp to a place **c** clean,
    5: 2 touches anything **c** unclean—
    6: 11 the camp to a place that is **c** clean.
    7: 19 touches anything **c** unclean must not
    7: 19 anyone **c** clean may eat it.
    10: 14 Eat them in a **c** clean place;
    11: 4 it is **c** unclean for you.
    12: 2 to a son will be **c** unclean for seven
    12: 7 she will be **c** clean from her flow
    13: 3 he shall pronounce them **c** unclean.
    14: 8 then they will be **c** clean.
    15: 28 and after that she will be **c** clean.
    15: 33 with a woman who is **c** unclean.
    17: 15 they will be **c** unclean till evening;
    21: 1 must not make himself **c** unclean

Lev 22: 3 of your descendants is **c** unclean
    27: 11 they vowed is a **c** unclean animal—
Nu 5: 2 who is **c** unclean because of a dead
    6: 7 not make themselves **c** unclean
    8: 6 Israelites and make them **c** clean.
    9: 6 day because they were **c** unclean
    9: 13 if anyone who is **c** clean and not
    18: 11 household who is **c** clean may eat it.
    18: 13 household who is **c** clean may eat it.
    19: 7 but he will be **c** unclean till evening.
    19: 9 in a **c** clean place outside the camp.
    19: 18 a man who is **c** clean is to take some
Dt 12: 15 Both the **c** unclean and the clean
    12: 22 Both the **c** unclean and the clean
    14: 7 they are **c** unclean for you.
    15: 22 Both the **c** unclean and the clean
1Sa 20: 26 to David to make the **c** clean
2Ch 13: 11 set out the bread on the **c** clean table
    30: 17 for all those who were not **c** clean
Ezr 6: 20 themselves and were all **c** clean.
Ne 12: 30 Levites had purified themselves **c**,
Isa 66: 20 of the Lord in **c** clean vessels.
Eze 22: 10 period, when they are **c** unclean.
Ac 24: 18 I was **c** clean when they found me
Heb 9: 13 on those who are **c** unclean sanctify

CEREMONY* (CEREMONIAL CEREMONIALLY)
Ge 50: 11 Egyptians are holding a solemn **c**
Ex 12: 25 you as he promised, observe this **c**.
    12: 26 'What does this **c** mean to you?'
    13: 5 are to observe this **c** in this month:

CERTAINTY*
Lk 1: 4 you may know the **c** of the things
Jn 17: 8 They knew with **c** that I came

CERTIFICATE* (CERTIFIED)
Dt 24: 1 and he writes her a **c** of divorce,
    24: 3 her and writes her a **c** of divorce,
Isa 50: 1 "Where is your mother's **c**
Jer 3: 8 I gave faithless Israel her **c**
Mt 5: 31 divorces his wife must give her a **c**
    19: 7 a man give his wife a **c** of divorce
Mk 10: 4 a man to write a **c** of divorce

CERTIFIED* (CERTIFICATE)
Jn 3: 33 person who has accepted it has **c**

CHAFF
Ps 1: 4 They are like **c** that the wind blows
    35: 5 May they be like **c** before the wind,
Da 2: 35 became like **c** on a threshing floor
Mt 3: 12 up the **c** with unquenchable fire."

CHAINED (CHAINS)
2Ti 2: 9 But God's word is not **c**.

CHAINS (CHAINED)
Eph 6: 20 for which I am an ambassador in **c**.
Col 4: 18 Remember my **c**. Grace be
2Ti 1: 16 me and was not ashamed of my **c**.
Jude : 6 with everlasting **c** for judgment

CHAMPION
Ps 19: 5 like a **c** rejoicing to run his course.

CHANCE
Ecc 9: 11 but time and **c** happen to them all.

CHANGE (CHANGED)
1Sa 15: 29 of Israel does not lie or **c** his mind;
Ps 110: 4 has sworn and will not **c** his mind:
Jer 7: 5 If you really **c** your ways and your
Mal 3: 6 "I the Lord do not **c**. So you,
Heb 7: 21 has sworn and will not **c** his mind:
Jas 1: 17 lights, who does not **c** like shifting

CHANGED (CHANGE)
1Sa 10: 6 you will be **c** into a different person.
Hos 11: 8 My heart is **c** within me;
1Co 15: 51 not all sleep, but we will all be **c**—

CHARACTER*
Ru 3: 11 that you are a woman of noble **c**.
Pr 12: 4 of noble **c** is her husband's crown,
    31: 10 A wife of noble **c** who can find?
Ac 17: 11 were of more noble **c** than those
Ro 5: 4 perseverance, **c**; and **c**, hope.
1Co 15: 33 "Bad company corrupts good **c**."

CHARGE (CHARGED CHARGES)
Job 34: 13 Who put him in **c** of the whole
Ro 8: 33 will bring any **c** against whom
1Co 9: 18 the gospel I may offer it free of **c**,
2Co 11: 7 the gospel of God to you free of **c**?
Gal 3: 24 So the law was put in **c** of us
2Ti 4: 1 and his kingdom, I give you this **c**:
Phm : 18 or owes you anything, **c** it to me.

CHARGED (CHARGE)
Ro 5: 13 but sin is not **c** against anyone's

CHARGES (CHARGE)
Isa 50: 8 Who then will bring **c** against me?

CHARIOT (CHARIOTS)
2Ki 2: 11 suddenly a **c** of fire and horses
Ps 104: 3 He makes the clouds his **c** and rides
Ac 8: 28 was sitting in his **c** reading the Book

CHARIOTS (CHARIOT)
2Ki 6: 17 and **c** of fire all around Elisha.
Ps 20: 7 Some trust in **c** and some in horses,
    68: 17 The **c** of God are tens of thousands

CHARM* (CHARMING)
Pr 17: 8 A bribe is seen as a **c** by those who
    31: 30 **C** is deceptive, and beauty is

CHARMING* (CHARM)
Pr 26: 25 Though their speech is **c**, do not
SS 1: 16 how **c**! And our bed is verdant.

CHASE
Lev 26: 8 Five of you will **c** a hundred,
Pr 12: 11 who **c** fantasies have no sense.
    28: 19 who **c** fantasies will have their

CHASTENS*
Heb 12: 6 and he **c** everyone he accepts

CHASM*
Lk 16: 26 you a great **c** has been set in place,

CHATTER* (CHATTERING)
1Ti 6: 20 Turn away from godless **c**
2Ti 2: 16 Avoid godless **c**, because those who

CHATTERING* (CHATTER)
Pr 10: 8 but a **c** fool comes to ruin.
    10: 10 grief, and a **c** fool comes to ruin.

CHEAT* (CHEATED CHEATING)
Lev 6: 2 or if they **c** a neighbor,
Mal 1: 14 "Cursed is the **c** who has
1Co 6: 8 you yourselves **c** and do wrong,

CHEATED* (CHEAT)
Ge 31: 7 yet your father has **c** me
1Sa 12: 3 Whom have I **c**? Whom have I
    12: 4 "You have not **c** or oppressed us,"
Lk 19: 8 if I have **c** anybody out of anything,
1Co 6: 7 Why not rather be **c**?

CHEATING* (CHEAT)
Am 8: 5 price and **c** with dishonest scales,

CHEEK (CHEEKS)
Mt 5: 39 right **c**, turn to them the other **c** also.
Lk 6: 29 If someone slaps you on one **c**,

CHEEKS (CHEEK)
Isa 50: 6 my **c** to those who pulled out my

CHEERFUL* (CHEERS)
Pr 15: 13 A happy heart makes the face **c**,
    15: 15 but the **c** heart has a continual feast.
    17: 22 A **c** heart is good medicine,
2Co 9: 7 compulsion, for God loves a **c** giver.

CHEERS* (CHEERFUL)
Pr 12: 25 the heart, but a kind word **c** it up.

CHEMOSH
2Ki 23: 13 for **C** the vile god of Moab,

CHERISH (CHERISHED)
Pr 19: 8 who **c** understanding will soon

CHERISHED* (CHERISH)
Ps 66: 18 If I had **c** sin in my heart, the Lord

CHERUB (CHERUBIM)
Ex 25: 19 Make one **c** on one end
Eze 28: 14 You were anointed as a guardian **c**,

CHERUBIM (CHERUB)
Ge 3: 24 east side of the Garden of Eden **c**
1Sa 4: 4 who is enthroned between the **c**.
2Sa 6: 2 who is enthroned between the **c**
    22: 11 He mounted the **c** and flew;
1Ki 6: 23 inner sanctuary he made a pair of **c**
2Ki 19: 15 enthroned between the **c**, you alone
1Ch 13: 6 who is enthroned between the **c**—
Ps 18: 10 He mounted the **c** and flew;
    80: 1 who sit enthroned between the **c**,
    99: 1 he sits enthroned between the **c**;
Isa 37: 16 enthroned between the **c**, you alone
Eze 1: 1 that was over the heads of the **c**.

CHEST
2Ki 12: 9 Jehoiada the priest took a **c**
Da 2: 32 pure gold, its **c** and arms of silver,

Rev 1: 13 and with a golden sash around his **c**.

CHEWS
Lev 11: 3 a divided hoof and that **c** the cud.

CHIEF
1Pe 5: 4 And when the **C** Shepherd appears,

CHILD (CHILDBEARING CHILDBIRTH CHILDHOOD CHILDLESS CHILDREN GRANDCHILDREN)
Pr 22: 15 Folly is bound up in the heart of a **c**,
Isa 9: 6 For to us a **c** is born, to us a son is
 11: 6 and a little **c** will lead them.
 66: 13 As a mother comforts her **c**, so will
Eze 18: 20 The **c** will not share the guilt of
Mt 18: 2 He called a little **c**, whom he placed
Lk 1: 42 and blessed is the **c** you will bear!
 1: 80 And the **c** grew and became strong
1Co 13: 11 When I was a **c**, I talked like a **c**,
Heb 12: 9 everyone he accepts as his **c**."
1Jn 5: 1 loves the father loves his **c** as well.

CHILDBEARING (BEAR CHILD)
Ge 3: 16 make your pains in **c** very severe;
Heb 11: 11 even Sarah, who was past **c** age,

CHILDBIRTH (BEAR CHILD)
Gal 4: 19 the pains of **c** until Christ is formed

CHILDHOOD (CHILD)
1Co 13: 11 became a man, I put the ways of **c**

CHILDLESS (CHILD)
Ge 11: 30 Sarai was **c** because she was not
 29: 31 but Rachel remained **c**.
Ps 113: 9 settles the **c** woman in her home

CHILDREN (CHILD)
Ex 20: 5 punishing the **c** for the sin
Dt 4: 9 Teach them to your **c** and to their **c**
 6: 7 Impress them on your **c**.
 6: 20 future, when your **c** ask you,
 11: 19 Teach them to your **c**,
 14: 1 You are the **c** of the LORD your
 24: 16 nor **c** put to death for their parents;
 30: 19 life, so that you and your **c** may live
 32: 46 you may command your **c** to obey
Job 1: 5 "Perhaps my **c** have sinned
Ps 8: 2 the praise of **c** and infants
 17: 14 their **c** gorge themselves on it,
 78: 5 our ancestors to teach their **c**,
 127: 3 **C** are a heritage from the LORD,
Pr 10: 1 Wise **c** bring joy to their father,
 13: 24 who spare the rod hate their **c**,
 17: 6 Children's **c** are a crown
 20: 7 blessed are their **c** after them.
 20: 11 **c** are known by their actions,
 22: 6 Start **c** off on the way they
 23: 13 not withhold discipline from **c**;
 29: 15 but **c** left to themselves disgrace
 29: 17 Discipline your **c**,
 31: 28 Her **c** arise and call her blessed;
Isa 54: 13 your **c** will be taught by the LORD,
Hos 1: 10 be called '**c** of the living God.'
Joel 2: 1 Tell it to your **c**, and let your **c** tell it
Mal 4: 6 the hearts of the parents to their **c**,
Mt 3: 9 they will be called **c** of God.
 7: 11 how to give good gifts to your **c**,
 11: 25 and revealed them to little **c**,
 18: 3 you change and become like little **c**,
 19: 14 said, "Let the little **c** come to me,
 21: 16 " 'From the lips of **c** and infants
Mk 9: 37 these little **c** in my name welcomes
 10: 14 them, "Let the little **c** come to me,
 10: 16 And he took the **c** in his arms,
 10: 16 **C** will rebel against their parents
Lk 6: 35 the **c** of the Most High,
 10: 21 and revealed them to little **c**.
 18: 16 said, "Let the little **c** come to me,
Jn 1: 12 gave the right to become **c** of God—
 12: 36 you may become **c** of light."
Ac 2: 39 your **c** and for all who are far off—
Ro 8: 14 Spirit of God are the **c** of God.
 8: 16 our spirit that we are God's **c**.
 9: 26 they will be called '**c** of the
1Co 14: 20 and sisters, stop thinking like **c**.
2Co 12: 14 their parents, but parents for their **c**.
Gal 3: 26 you are all **c** of God through faith,
Eph 6: 1 **C**, obey your parents in the Lord,
 6: 4 Fathers, do not exasperate your **c**;
Col 3: 20 **C**, obey your parents in everything,
 3: 21 do not embitter your **c**, or they will
1Th 2: 7 we were like young **c** among you.
1Ti 3: 4 and see that his **c** obey him,
 3: 12 and must manage his **c** and his

1Ti 5: 10 such as bringing up **c**,
Heb 2: 13 am I, and the **c** God has given me."
 12: 7 God is treating you as his **c**.
1Jn 3: 1 that we should be called **c** of God!

CHOKE
Mk 4: 19 other things come in and **c** the word,

CHOOSE (CHOOSES CHOSE CHOSEN)
Dt 30: 19 Now **c** life, so that you and your
Jos 24: 15 **c** for yourselves this day whom you
Pr 8: 10 **C** my instruction instead of silver,
Jn 15: 16 You did not **c** me, but I chose you

CHOOSES (CHOOSE)
Mt 11: 27 to whom the Son **c** to reveal him.
Lk 10: 22 to whom the Son **c** to reveal him.
Jn 7: 17 Anyone who **c** to do the will of God

CHORAZIN
Mt 11: 21 "Woe to you, **C**! Woe to you,

CHOSE (CHOOSE)
Ge 13: 11 So Lot **c** for himself the whole plain
Ps 33: 12 the people he **c** for his inheritance.
Jn 15: 16 but I **c** you and appointed you so
1Co 1: 27 But God **c** the foolish things
Eph 1: 4 For he **c** us in him before
2Th 2: 13 because God **c** you as firstfruits

CHOSEN (CHOOSE)
Isa 41: 8 whom I have **c**, you descendants
Mt 22: 14 many are invited, but few are **c**."
Lk 10: 42 Mary has **c** what is better, and it
 23: 35 if he is God's Messiah, the **C** One."
Jn 1: 34 I testify that this is God's **C** One."
 15: 19 but I have **c** you out of the world.
1Pe 1: 20 He was **c** before the creation
 2: 9 But you are a people, a royal,

CHRIST (CHRIST'S CHRISTIAN CHRISTIANS)
Jn 1: 41 found the Messiah" (that is, the **C**).
Ac 9: 34 said to him, "Jesus **C** heals you.
Ro 1: 4 from the dead: Jesus **C** our Lord.
 3: 22 faith in Jesus **C** to all who believe.
 5: 1 with God through our Lord Jesus **C**,
 5: 6 powerless, **C** died for the ungodly.
 5: 8 we were still sinners, **C** died for us.
 5: 11 in God through our Lord Jesus **C**!
 5: 17 life through the one man, Jesus **C**!
 6: 4 just as **C** was raised from the dead
 6: 9 we know that since **C** was raised
 6: 23 is eternal life in **C** Jesus our Lord.
 7: 4 to the law through the body of **C**,
 8: 1 for those who are in **C** Jesus,
 8: 9 Spirit of **C**, they do not belong to **C**.
 8: 17 heirs of God and co-heirs with **C**,
 8: 34 **C** Jesus who died—more than that,
 8: 35 separate us from the love of **C**?
 10: 4 **C** is the culmination of the law
 12: 5 so in **C** we, though many, form one
 13: 14 yourselves with the Lord Jesus **C**,
 14: 9 **C** died and returned to life so that he
 15: 3 even **C** did not please himself but,
 15: 5 toward each other that **C** Jesus had,
 15: 7 then, just as **C** accepted you,
 16: 18 people are not serving our Lord **C**,
1Co 1: 2 to those sanctified in **C** Jesus
 1: 7 for our Lord Jesus **C** to be revealed.
 1: 13 Is **C** divided? Was Paul crucified
 1: 17 For **C** did not send me to baptize,
 1: 23 but we preach **C** crucified:
 1: 30 of him that you are in **C** Jesus,
 2: 2 while I was with you except Jesus **C**
 3: 11 one already laid, which is Jesus **C**.
 5: 7 For **C**, our Passover lamb, has been
 6: 15 bodies are members of **C** himself?
 8: 6 Jesus **C**, through whom all things
 8: 12 weak conscience, you sin against **C**.
 10: 4 them, and that rock was **C**.
 10: 9 We should not test **C**,
 11: 1 as I follow the example of **C**.
 11: 3 that the head of every man is **C**,
 12: 27 Now you are the body of **C**,
 15: 3 that **C** died for our sins according
 15: 14 And if **C** has not been raised,
 15: 22 so in **C** all will be made alive.
 15: 57 victory through our Lord Jesus **C**.
2Co 1: 5 abundantly in the sufferings of **C**,
 3: 3 show that you are a letter from **C**,
 3: 14 because only in **C** is it taken away.
 4: 4 gospel that displays the glory of **C**,
 4: 5 but Jesus **C** as Lord, and ourselves
 4: 6 glory displayed in the face of **C**.
 5: 10 before the judgment seat of **C**,

2Co 5: 17 if anyone is in **C**, the new creation
 6: 15 What harmony is there between **C**
 10: 1 the meekness and gentleness of **C**,
 11: 2 to **C**, so that I might present you as
Gal 1: 7 are trying to pervert the gospel of **C**.
 2: 4 on the freedom we have in **C** Jesus
 2: 16 the law, but by faith in Jesus **C**.
 2: 17 that mean that **C** promotes sin?
 2: 20 I have been crucified with **C** and I
 2: 21 the law, **C** died for nothing!"
 3: 13 **C** redeemed us from the curse
 3: 16 meaning one person, who is **C**.
 3: 26 So in **C** Jesus you are all children
 4: 19 pains of childbirth until **C** is formed
 5: 1 is for freedom that **C** has set us free.
 5: 4 the law have been alienated from **C**;
 5: 24 to **C** Jesus have crucified the sinful
 6: 14 in the cross of our Lord Jesus **C**,
Eph 1: 3 with every spiritual blessing in **C**.
 1: 10 in heaven and on earth under **C**.
 1: 20 when he raised **C** from the dead
 2: 5 made us alive with **C** even when we
 2: 10 created in **C** Jesus to do good
 2: 12 that time you were separate from **C**,
 2: 20 with **C** Jesus himself as the chief
 3: 8 Gentiles the boundless riches of **C**,
 3: 17 so that **C** may dwell in your hearts
 4: 7 has been given as **C** apportioned it.
 4: 13 whole measure of the fullness of **C**.
 4: 15 into him who is the head, that is, **C**.
 4: 32 other, just as in **C** God forgave you.
 5: 2 just as **C** loved us and gave himself
 5: 21 one another out of reverence for **C**.
 5: 23 the head of the wife as **C** is the head
 5: 25 just as **C** loved the church and gave
Php 1: 18 false motives or true, **C** is preached.
 1: 21 to me, to live is **C** and to die is gain.
 1: 23 I desire to depart and be with **C**,
 1: 27 a manner worthy of the gospel of **C**.
 1: 29 on behalf of **C** not only to believe
 2: 5 same attitude of mind **C** Jesus had:
 3: 7 now consider loss for the sake of **C**.
 3: 10 I want to know **C**—yes, to know
 3: 18 live as enemies of the cross of **C**.
 4: 19 to the riches of his glory in **C** Jesus.
Col 1: 4 have heard of your faith in **C** Jesus
 1: 27 which is **C** in you, the hope
 1: 28 present everyone fully mature in **C**.
 2: 2 the mystery of God, namely, **C**,
 2: 6 as you received **C** Jesus as Lord,
 2: 9 For in **C** all the fullness of the Deity
 2: 13 nature, God made you alive with **C**.
 2: 17 the reality, however, is found in **C**.
 3: 1 you have been raised with **C**,
 3: 3 your life is now hidden with **C**
 3: 15 Let the peace of **C** rule in your
1Th 5: 9 salvation through our Lord Jesus **C**.
2Th 2: 1 the coming of our Lord Jesus **C**
 2: 14 in the glory of our Lord Jesus **C**.
1Ti 1: 12 I thank **C** Jesus our Lord, who has
 1: 15 **C** Jesus came into the world to save
 1: 16 **C** Jesus might display his immense
 2: 5 God and human beings, Jesus,
2Ti 1: 9 in **C** Jesus before the beginning
 1: 10 appearing of our Savior, **C** Jesus,
 2: 1 in the grace that is in **C** Jesus.
 2: 3 like a good soldier of **C** Jesus.
 2: 8 Remember Jesus **C**,
 2: 10 the salvation that is in **C** Jesus,
 3: 12 life in **C** Jesus will be persecuted,
 3: 15 salvation through faith in **C** Jesus.
 4: 1 the presence of God and of **C** Jesus,
Tit 2: 13 our great God and Savior, **C** Jesus,
Heb 3: 6 **C** is faithful as the Son over God's
 3: 14 We have come to share in **C**,
 5: 5 **C** did not take on himself the glory
 6: 1 the elementary teachings about **C**
 9: 11 when **C** came as high priest
 9: 14 will the blood of **C**, who through
 9: 15 For this reason **C** is the mediator
 9: 24 **C** did not enter a sanctuary made
 9: 26 Otherwise **C** would have had
 9: 28 so **C** was sacrificed once to take
 10: 10 of the body of Jesus **C** once for all.
 13: 8 Jesus **C** is the same yesterday
1Pe 1: 2 Spirit, to be obedient to Jesus **C**
 1: 3 of Jesus **C** from the dead,
 1: 11 he predicted the sufferings of **C**
 1: 19 but with the precious blood of **C**
 2: 21 called, because **C** suffered for you,
 3: 15 But in your hearts revere **C** as Lord.
 3: 18 For **C** also suffered once for sins,

1Pe 3:21 you by the resurrection of Jesus **C**,
4:13 participate in the sufferings of **C**,
4:14 insulted because of the name of **C**,
2Pe 1:1 Savior Jesus **C** have received a faith
1:16 of our Lord Jesus **C** in power,
1Jn 2:1 Jesus **C**, the Righteous One.
3:16 Jesus **C** laid down his life for us.
3:23 Jesus **C**, and to love one another as
4:2 that Jesus **C** has come in the flesh is
5:20 is true by being in his Son Jesus **C**.
2Jn :9 teaching of **C** does not have God;
Jude :4 deny Jesus **C** our only Sovereign
Rev 1:1 The revelation from Jesus **C**,
1:5 and from Jesus **C**, who is
20:4 reigned with **C** a thousand years.
20:6 of **C** and will reign with him

CHRIST'S (CHRIST)
1Co 9:21 God's law but am under **C** law),
2Co 2:14 captives in **C** triumphal procession
5:14 For **C** love compels us, because we
5:20 We are therefore **C** ambassadors,
12:9 so that **C** power may rest on me.
Col 1:22 by **C** physical body through death

CHRISTIAN* (CHRIST)
Ac 26:28 you can persuade me to be a **C**?"
1Pe 4:16 if you suffer as a **C**, do not be

CHRISTIANS* (CHRIST)
Ac 11:26 The disciples were called **C** first

CHURCH
Mt 16:18 and on this rock I will build my **c**,
18:17 if they refuse to listen even to the **c**,
Ac 20:28 Be shepherds of the **c** of God,
1Co 5:12 mine to judge those outside the **c**?
14:4 but those who prophesy edify the **c**.
14:12 to excel in those that build up the **c**.
14:26 done so that the **c** may be built up.
15:9 because I persecuted the **c** of God.
Gal 1:13 how intensely I persecuted the **c**
Eph 5:23 wife as Christ is the head of the **c**,
Col 1:18 he is the head of the body, the **c**;
1:24 the sake of his body, which is the **c**.

CHURNING
Pr 30:33 For as **c** cream produces butter,

CIRCLE
Isa 40:22 enthroned above the **c** of the earth,

CIRCUMCISE (CIRCUMCISED CIRCUMCISION)
Dt 10:16 **C** your hearts, therefore, and do not

CIRCUMCISED (CIRCUMCISE)
Ge 17:10 Every male among you shall be **c**.
17:12 you who is eight days old must be **c**,
Jos 5:3 **c** the Israelites at Gibeath Haaraloth.
Gal 5:2 you that if you let yourselves be **c**,

CIRCUMCISION (CIRCUMCISE)
Ro 2:25 **C** has value if you observe the law,
2:29 and **c** is **c** of the heart, by the Spirit,
1Co 7:19 **C** is nothing and uncircumcision is

CIRCUMSTANCES
Php 4:11 to be content whatever the **c**.
1Th 5:18 give thanks in all **c**; for this is God's

CITIES (CITY)
Lk 19:17 small matter, take charge of ten **c**.'
19:19 'You take charge of five **c**.'

CITIZENS (CITIZENSHIP)
Eph 2:19 but fellow **c** with God's people

CITIZENSHIP* (CITIZENS)
Ac 22:28 to pay a lot of money for my **c**."
Eph 2:12 excluded from **c** in Israel
Php 3:20 But our **c** is in heaven.

CITY (CITIES)
Mt 5:14 A **c** on a hill cannot be hidden.
Ac 18:10 I have many people in this **c**."
Heb 13:14 here we do not have an enduring **c**,
Rev 21:2 I saw the Holy **C**, the new

CIVILIAN*
2Ti 2:4 a soldier gets involved in **c** affairs;

CLAIM (CLAIMS RECLAIM)
Pr 25:6 do not **c** a place among his great
Jas 2:14 if people **c** to have faith but
1Jn 1:6 If we **c** to have fellowship with him
1:8 If we **c** to be without sin,
1:10 If we **c** we have not sinned,
2:9 who **c** to be in the light

CLAIMS (CLAIM)
1Jn 2:6 Whoever **c** to live in him must live

CLANGING*
1Co 13:1 a resounding gong or a **c** cymbal.

CLAP* (CLAPPED CLAPS)
Job 21:5 **c** your hand over your mouth.
Ps 47:1 **C** your hands, all you nations;
98:8 Let the rivers **c** their hands,
Pr 30:32 evil, **c** your hand over your mouth!
Isa 55:12 trees of the field will **c** their hands.
La 2:15 All who pass your way **c** their hands
Na 3:19 **c** their hands at your fall,

CLAPPED* (CLAP)
2Ki 11:12 and the people **c** their hands
Eze 25:6 Because you have **c** your hands

CLAPS* (CLAP)
Job 27:23 It **c** its hands in derision and hisses
34:37 scornfully he **c** his hands among us

CLASSIFY*
2Co 10:12 We do not dare to **c** or compare

CLAUDIUS
Ac 11:28 happened during the reign of **C**.)
18:2 because **C** had ordered all Jews

CLAY
Isa 45:9 Does the **c** say to the potter,
64:8 We are the **c**, you are the potter;
Jer 18:6 "Like **c** in the hand of the potter,
La 4:2 are now considered as pots of **c**,
Da 2:33 partly of iron and partly of baked **c**.
Ro 9:21 the same lump of **c** some pottery
2Co 4:7 this treasure in jars of **c** to show
2Ti 2:20 and silver, but also of wood and **c**;

CLEAN (CLEANNESS CLEANSE CLEANSED CLEANSING)
Ge 7:2 pairs of every kind of **c** animal,
Lev 4:12 the camp to a place ceremonially **c**,
16:30 you will be **c** from all your sins.
Ps 24:4 Those who have **c** hands and a pure
51:7 me with hyssop, and I will be **c**;
Pr 20:9 I am **c** and without sin"?
Eze 36:25 I will sprinkle **c** water on you,
Mt 8:2 are willing, you can make me **c**."
12:44 swept **c** and put in order.
23:25 You **c** the outside of the cup
Mk 7:19 this, Jesus declared all foods **c**.)
Jn 13:10 their whole body is **c**.
15:3 You are already **c** because
Ac 10:15 impure that God has made **c**."
Ro 14:20 All food is **c**, but it is wrong

CLEANNESS (CLEAN)
2Sa 22:25 according to my **c** in his sight.

CLEANSE (CLEAN)
Ps 51:2 my iniquity and **c** me from my sin.
51:7 **C** me with hyssop, and I will be
Pr 20:30 Blows and wounds **c** away evil,
2Ti 2:21 Those who **c** themselves from
Heb 9:14 our consciences from acts
10:22 having our hearts sprinkled to **c** us

CLEANSED (CLEAN)
Mt 11:5 those who have leprosy are **c**,
Heb 9:22 nearly everything is **c** with blood,
2Pe 1:9 that you have been **c** from your past

CLEANSING (CLEAN)
Eph 5:26 **c** her by the washing with water
Heb 6:2 instruction about **c** rites,

CLEFT*
Ex 33:22 I will put you in a **c** in the rock

CLEVER (CLEVERNESS)
Isa 5:21 and in their own sight.

CLEVERNESS (CLEVER)
Pr 23:4 do not trust your own **c**.

CLING
Ps 63:8 I **c** to you;
Ro 12:9 Hate what is evil; **c** to what is good.

CLOAK
Ex 12:11 with your **c** tucked into your belt,
2Ki 4:29 "Tuck your **c** into your belt,
9:1 to him, "Tuck your **c** into your belt,

CLOSE (CLOSER)
2Ki 11:2 Stay **c** to the king wherever he
Ps 34:18 The LORD is **c**
148:14 Israel, the people **c** to his heart.
Pr 28:27 those who **c** their eyes to them
Isa 40:11 and carries them **c** to his heart;
Jer 30:21 will devote himself to be **c** to me?"

CLOSER (CLOSE)
Ex 3:5 "Do not come any **c**," God said.
Pr 18:24 a friend who sticks **c** than a brother.

CLOTHE (CLOTHED CLOTHES CLOTHING CLOTHS)
Ps 45:3 **c** yourself with splendor
Isa 52:1 **c** Zion, **c** yourself with strength!
Ro 13:14 **c** yourselves with the Lord Jesus
Col 3:12 **c** yourselves with compassion,
1Pe 5:5 **c** yourselves with humility toward

CLOTHED (CLOTHE)
Ps 30:11 my sackcloth and **c** me with joy,
104:1 you are **c** with splendor
Pr 31:22 she is **c** in fine linen and purple.
31:25 She is **c** with strength and dignity;
Isa 61:10 For he has **c** me with garments
Lk 24:49 the city until you have been **c**
Gal 3:27 into Christ have **c** yourselves

CLOTHES (CLOTHE)
Dt 8:4 Your **c** did not wear out and your
Mt 6:25 the body more important than **c**?
6:28 "And why do you worry about **c**?
27:35 they divided up his **c** by casting lots.
Jn 11:44 "Take off the grave **c** and let him
19:24 "They divided my **c** among them

CLOTHING (CLOTHE)
Dt 22:5 A woman must not wear men's **c**,
Job 29:14 I put on righteousness as my **c**;
Mt 7:15 They come to you in sheep's **c**,
1Ti 6:8 But if we have food and **c**, we will

CLOTHS (CLOTHE)
Lk 2:12 You will find a baby wrapped in **c**

CLOUD (CLOUDS)
Ex 13:21 them in a pillar of **c** to guide them
1Ki 18:44 "A **c** as small as a man's hand is
Pr 16:15 his favor is like a rain **c** in spring.
Isa 19:1 the LORD rides on a swift **c** and is
Lk 21:27 of Man coming in a **c** with power
Heb 12:1 by such a great **c** of witnesses, let us
Rev 14:14 seated on the **c** was one like a son

CLOUDS (CLOUD)
Dt 33:26 you and on the **c** in his majesty.
Ps 68:4 name, extol him who rides on the **c**;
104:3 He makes the **c** his chariot and rides
Pr 25:14 Like **c** and wind without rain is one
Da 7:13 coming with the **c** of heaven.
Mt 24:30 of Man coming on the **c** of heaven,
26:64 and coming on the **c** of heaven."
Mk 13:26 Man coming in **c** with great power
1Th 4:17 them in the **c** to meet the Lord
Rev 1:7 he is coming with the **c**,"

CLUB
Pr 25:18 Like a **c** or a sword or a sharp arrow

CO-HEIRS* (INHERIT)
Ro 8:17 heirs of God and **c** with Christ,

CO-WORKERS (WORK)
1Co 3:9 For we are God's **c**; you are God's

COALS
Pr 25:22 you will heap burning **c** on his head,
Ro 12:20 this, you will heap burning **c** on his

COARSE*
Eph 5:4 foolish talk or **c** joking, which are

COAT
Mt 5:40 hand over your **c** as well.

CODE*
Ro 2:27 even though you have the written **c**
2:29 by the Spirit, not by the written **c**.
7:6 not in the old way of the written **c**.

COINS (COIN)
Mt 18:28 owed him a hundred silver **c**.

COINS (COINS)
Lk 15:8 suppose a woman has ten silver **c**

COLD
Pr 25:25 Like **c** water to a weary soul is good
Mt 10:42 anyone gives even a cup of **c** water
24:12 the love of most will grow **c**,

COLLECTION
1Co 16:1 about the **c** for the Lord's people:

COLT
Zec 9:9 donkey, on a **c**, the foal of a donkey.
Mt 21:5 a donkey, and on a **c**, the foal

COMFORT* (COMFORTED COMFORTER
COMFORTERS COMFORTING COMFORTS)
Ge 5: 29 said, "He will **c** us in the labor
    37: 35 sons and daughters came to **c** him,
1Ch 7: 22 and his relatives came to **c** him.
Job 2: 11 and sympathize with him and **c** him.
    7: 13 When I think my bed will **c** me
    16: 5 **c** from my lips would bring you
    36: 16 to the **c** of your table laden
Ps 23: 4 your rod and your staff, they **c** me.
    71: 21 my honor and **c** me once more.
    119: 50 My **c** in my suffering is this:
    119: 52 ancient laws, and I find **c** in them.
    119: 76 May your unfailing love be my **c**,
    119: 82 I say, "When will you **c** me?"
Isa 40: 1 **C**, **c** my people, says your God.
    51: 3 The LORD will surely **c** Zion
    51: 19 come upon you—who can **c** you?—
    57: 18 guide them and restore to them,
    61: 2 of our God, to **c** all who mourn,
    66: 13 comforts her child, so will I **c** you;
Jer 16: 7 offer food to **c** those who mourn
    31: 13 I will give them **c** and joy instead
La 1: 2 all her lovers there is none to **c** her.
    1: 9 there was none to **c** her.
    1: 16 No one is near to **c** me, no one
    1: 17 hands, but there is no one to **c** her.
    1: 21 but there is no one to **c** me.
    2: 13 that I may **c** you, Virgin Daughter
Eze 16: 54 all you have done in giving them **c**.
Na 3: 7 Where can I find anyone to **c** you?"
Zec 1: 17 the LORD will again **c** Zion
    10: 2 that are false, they give **c** in vain.
Lk 6: 24 you have already received your **c**.
Jn 11: 19 Mary to **c** them in the loss of their
1Co 14: 3 encouragement and **c**.
2Co 1: 3 of compassion and the God of all **c**,
    1: 4 so that we can **c** those in any trouble
    1: 4 with the **c** we ourselves receive
    1: 5 also our **c** abounds through Christ.
    1: 6 it is for your **c** and salvation;
    1: 6 it is for your **c**, which produces
    1: 7 so also you share in our **c**.
    2: 7 you ought to forgive and **c** him,
    7: 7 but also by the **c** you had given him.
Php 2: 1 Christ, if any **c** from his love, if any
Col 4: 1 and they have proved a **c** to me.

COMFORTED* (COMFORT)
Ge 24: 67 Isaac was **c** after his mother's death.
    37: 35 comfort him, but he refused to be **c**.
2Sa 12: 24 Then David **c** his wife Bathsheba,
Job 42: 11 They **c** and consoled him over all
Ps 77: 2 hands, and I would not be **c**.
    86: 17 LORD, have helped me and **c** me.
Isa 12: 1 has turned away and you have **c** me.
    52: 9 for the LORD has **c** his people,
    54: 11 lashed by storms and not **c**, I will
    66: 13 and you will be **c** over Jerusalem."
Jer 31: 15 for her children and refusing to be **c**,
Mt 2: 18 for her children and refusing to be **c**,
    5: 4 those who mourn, for they will be **c**.
Lk 16: 25 but now he is here and you are
Ac 20: 12 man home alive and were greatly **c**.
2Co 1: 6 if we are **c**, it is for your comfort,
    7: 6 **c** us by the coming of Titus,

COMFORTER* (COMFORT)
Ecc 4: 1 and they have no **c**; power was
    4: 1 and they have no **c**.
Jer 8: 18 You who are my **C** in sorrow,

COMFORTERS* (COMFORT)
Job 16: 2 you are miserable **c**, all of you!
Ps 69: 20 was none, for **c**, but I found none.

COMFORTING* (COMFORT)
Isa 66: 11 be satisfied at her **c** breasts;
Zec 1: 13 and **c** words to the angel who talked
Jn 11: 31 been with Mary in the house, **c** her,
1Th 2: 12 **c** and urging you to live lives

COMFORTS* (COMFORT)
Job 29: 25 I was like one who **c** mourners.
Isa 49: 13 For the LORD **c** his people
    51: 12 "I, even I, am he who **c** you.
    66: 13 As a mother **c** her child, so will I
2Co 1: 4 who **c** us in all our troubles,
    7: 6 But God, who **c** the downcast,

COMMAND (COMMANDED COMMANDING
COMMANDMENT COMMANDMENTS
COMMANDS)
Ex 7: 2 You are to say everything I **c** you,
Nu 14: 41 you disobeying the LORD's **c**?

Nu 24: 13 to go beyond the **c** of the LORD—
Dt 4: 2 Do not add to what I **c** you and do
    8: 1 to follow every **c** I am giving you
    12: 32 See that you do all I **c** you;
    15: 11 Therefore I **c** you to be openhanded
    30: 16 For I **c** you today to love
    32: 46 so that you may **c** your children
Ps 91: 11 he will **c** his angels concerning you
    148: 5 for at his **c** they were created,
Pr 6: 23 For this **c** is a lamp,
    13: 13 whoever respects a **c** is rewarded.
Ecc 8: 2 Obey the king's **c**, I say,
Jer 1: 7 you to and say whatever I **c** you.
    1: 17 and say to them whatever I **c** you.
    7: 23 Walk in obedience to all I **c** you,
    11: 4 me and do everything I **c** you,
    26: 2 Tell them everything I **c** you;
Joel 2: 11 mighty is the army that obeys his **c**.
Mt 4: 6 "'He will **c** his angels concerning
    15: 3 why do you break the **c** of God
Lk 4: 10 "'He will **c** his angels concerning
Jn 13: 34 "A new **c** I give you: Love one
    15: 12 My **c** is this: Love each other as I
    15: 14 are my friends if you do what I **c**.
    15: 17 This is my **c**: Love each other.
Ro 13: 9 are summed up in this one **c**:
1Co 14: 37 I am writing to you is the Lord's **c**.
Gal 5: 14 is fulfilled in keeping this one **c**:
1Ti 1: 5 The goal of this **c** is love,
    1: 18 I am giving you this **c** in keeping
    6: 14 to keep this **c** without spot or blame
    6: 17 **C** those who are rich in this present
Heb 9: 19 Moses had proclaimed every **c** of the law
    11: 3 the universe was formed at God's **c**,
2Pe 2: 21 on the sacred **c** that was passed
    3: 2 and the **c** given by our Lord
1Jn 2: 7 I am not writing you a new **c**
    3: 23 And this is his **c**: to believe
    4: 21 And he has given us this **c**:
2Jn : 6 his **c** is that you walk in love.

COMMANDED (COMMAND)
Ge 2: 16 And the LORD God **c** the man,
    7: 5 Noah did all that the LORD **c** him.
    50: 12 Jacob's sons did as he had **c** them:
Ex 7: 6 did just as the LORD **c** them.
    19: 7 all the words the LORD had **c** him,
    6: 24 The LORD **c** us to obey all these
Jos 1: 9 Have I not **c** you? Be strong
    1: 16 "Whatever you have **c** us we will
2Sa 5: 25 So David did as the LORD **c** him,
2Ki 17: 13 entire Law that I **c** your ancestors
    21: 8 be careful to do everything I **c** them
2Ch 33: 8 do everything I **c** them concerning
Ps 33: 9 came to be; he **c**, and it stood firm.
    78: 5 which he **c** our ancestors to teach
Mt 28: 20 to obey everything I have **c** you.
1Co 9: 14 the Lord has **c** that those who
1Jn 3: 23 and to love one another as he **c** us.
2Jn : 4 in the truth, just as the Father **c** us.

COMMANDING (COMMAND)
2Ti 2: 4 they try to please their **c** officer.

COMMANDMENT* (COMMAND)
Jos 22: 5 be very careful to keep the **c**
Mt 22: 36 which is the greatest **c** in the Law?"
    22: 38 This is the first and greatest **c**.
Mk 12: 31 There is no **c** greater than these."
Lk 23: 56 the Sabbath in obedience to the **c**.
Ro 7: 8 the opportunity afforded by the **c**,
    7: 8 but when the **c** came, sin sprang
    7: 10 that the very **c** that was intended
    7: 11 the opportunity afforded by the **c**,
    7: 11 and through the **c** put me to death.
    7: 12 and the **c** is holy,
    7: 13 that through the **c** sin might become
Eph 6: 2 which is the first **c** with a promise—

COMMANDMENTS* (COMMAND)
Ex 20: 6 those who love me and keep my **c**.
    24: 12 and I have written
    34: 28 words of the covenant—the Ten **C**.
Dt 4: 13 the Ten **C**, which he commanded
    5: 10 those who love me and keep my **c**.
    5: 22 These are the **c** the LORD
    6: 6 These **c** that I give you today are
    7: 9 those who love him and keep his **c**,
    9: 10 On them were all the **c** the LORD
    10: 4 the Ten **C** he had proclaimed to you
Ne 1: 5 who love him and keep his **c**,
Ecc 12: 13 Fear God and keep his **c**, for this is
Da 9: 4 who love him and keep his **c**,

Mt 19: 17 you want to enter life, keep the **c**."
    22: 40 the Prophets hang on these two **c**."
Mk 10: 19 You know the **c**: 'You shall not
    12: 28 "Of all the **c**, which is the most
Lk 18: 20 You know the **c**: 'You shall not
Ro 13: 9 The **c**, "You shall not commit

COMMANDS (COMMAND)
Ex 25: 22 give you all my **c** for the Israelites.
    34: 32 gave them all the **c** the LORD had
Lev 22: 31 "Keep my **c** and follow them.
Nu 15: 39 so you will remember all the **c**
Dt 7: 11 take care to follow the **c**,
    11: 1 decrees, his laws and his **c** always.
    11: 27 you obey the **c** of the LORD your
    28: 1 carefully follow all his **c** I give you
    30: 10 and keep his **c** and decrees that are
Jos 22: 5 to keep his **c**, to hold fast to him
1Ki 7: 3 and keep his decrees and **c**, his laws
    8: 58 in obedience to him and keep the **c**,
    8: 61 live by his decrees and obey his **c**,
1Ch 28: 7 is unswerving in carrying out my **c**
    28: 9 devotion to keep your **c**,
2Ch 31: 21 in obedience to the law and the **c**,
Ps 78: 7 his deeds but would keep his **c**.
    112: 1 who find great delight in his **c**.
    119: 10 do not let me stray from your **c**.
    119: 32 I run in the path of your **c**, for you
    119: 35 Direct me in the path of your **c**,
    119: 47 in your **c** because I love them.
    119: 48 I reach out for your **c**, which I love,
    119: 73 me understanding to learn your **c**.
    119: 86 All your **c** are trustworthy;
    119: 96 a limit, but your **c** are boundless.
    119: 98 Your **c** are always with me
    119:115 that I may keep the **c** of my God!
    119:127 I love your **c** more than gold,
    119:131 mouth and pant, longing for your **c**.
    119:143 but your **c** give me delight.
    119:151 LORD, and all your **c** are true.
    119:172 word, for all your **c** are righteous.
    119:176 for I have not forgotten your **c**.
Pr 2: 1 words and store up my **c** within you,
    3: 1 but keep my **c** in your heart,
    10: 8 The wise in heart accept **c**,
Isa 48: 18 only you had paid attention to my **c**,
Mt 5: 19 sets aside one of the least of these **c**
Mk 7: 8 You have let go of the **c** of God
    7: 9 way of setting aside the **c** of God
Lk 1: 6 observing all the LORD's **c** and
Jn 14: 15 "If you love me, keep my **c**.
    14: 21 Whoever has my **c** and keeps them
    15: 10 If you keep my **c**, you will remain
Ac 17: 30 now he **c** all people everywhere
1Co 7: 19 Keeping God's **c** is what counts.
Eph 2: 15 in his flesh the law with its **c**
1Jn 2: 3 come to know him if we keep his **c**.
    2: 4 but do not do what he **c** are liars,
    3: 22 because we keep his **c** and do what
    3: 24 Those who keep his **c** live in him,
    5: 2 loving God and carrying out his **c**.
    5: 3 this is love for God: to keep his **c**. And
    5: 3 his **c** are not burdensome,
2Jn : 6 that we walk in obedience to his **c**.
Rev 12: 17 those who keep God's **c**
    14: 12 the people of God who keep his **c**

COMMEMORATE
Ex 12: 14 "This is a day you are to **c**;

COMMEND* (COMMENDABLE COMMENDED
COMMENDS)
Ecc 8: 15 So I **c** the enjoyment of life,
Ro 16: 1 I **c** to you our sister Phoebe,
2Co 3: 1 we beginning to **c** ourselves again?
    4: 2 the truth plainly we **c** ourselves
    5: 12 We are not trying to **c** ourselves
    6: 4 God we **c** ourselves in every way:
    10: 12 with some who **c** themselves.
    10: 18 who **c** themselves who are approved,
1Pe 2: 14 wrong and to **c** those who do right.

COMMENDABLE* (COMMEND)
1Pe 2: 19 For it is **c** if you bear up under
    2: 20 if you endure it, this is **c** before God.

COMMENDED* (COMMEND)
Ne 11: 2 The people **c** all who volunteered
Job 29: 11 of me, and those who saw me **c** me,
Lk 16: 8 "The master **c** the dishonest
Ac 15: 40 **c** by the believers to the grace
Ro 13: 3 do what is right and you will be **c**
2Co 12: 11 I ought to have been **c** by you, for I
Heb 11: 2 This is what the ancients were **c** for.

Heb 11: 4 By faith he was **c** as righteous,
  11: 5 he was **c** as one who pleased God.
  11: 39 These were all **c** for their faith,

COMMENDS* (COMMEND)
Ps 145: 4 One generation **c** your works
2Co 10: 18 but those whom the Lord **c**.

COMMIT (COMMITS COMMITTED)
Ex 20: 14 "You shall not **c** adultery.
Dt 5: 18 "You shall not **c** adultery.
1Sa 7: 3 and **c** yourselves to the LORD
Ps 31: 5 Into your hands I **c** my spirit;
  37: 5 **C** your way to the LORD;
Pr 16: 3 **C** to the LORD whatever you do,
Eze 18: 24 from their righteousness and **c** sin
  18: 26 from their righteousness and **c** sin,
Mt 5: 27 was said, 'You shall not **c** adultery.'
  19: 18 you shall not **c** adultery, you shall
Mk 10: 19 you shall not **c** adultery, you shall
Lk 18: 20 'You shall not **c** adultery, you shall
  23: 46 into your hands I **c** my spirit."
Ac 20: 32 "Now I **c** you to God
Ro 2: 22 that people should not **c** adultery, do
    you **c** adultery?
  13: 9 "You shall not **c** adultery,"
1Co 10: 8 We should not **c** sexual immorality,
Jas 2: 11 If you do not **c** adultery but do **c**
1Pe 4: 19 to God's will should **c** themselves
Rev 2: 22 I will make those who **c** adultery

COMMITS* (COMMIT)
Lev 20: 10 " 'If a man **c** adultery with another
Pr 6: 32 a man who **c** adultery has no sense;
  29: 22 a hot-tempered person **c** many sins.
Ecc 8: 12 a wicked person who **c** a hundred
Eze 18: 10 the poor and needy. He **c** robbery.
  18: 14 who sees all the sins his father **c**,
  22: 11 you one man **c** a detestable offense
Mt 5: 32 the divorced woman **c** adultery.
  19: 9 marries another woman **c** adultery."
Mk 10: 11 another woman **c** adultery against
  10: 12 another man, she **c** adultery."
Lk 16: 18 marries another woman **c** adultery,
  16: 18 a divorced woman **c** adultery.

COMMITTED (COMMIT)
Nu 5: 7 must confess the sin they have **c**.
1Ki 8: 61 may your hearts be fully **c**
  15: 14 Asa's heart was fully **c**
2Ch 16: 9 those whose hearts are fully **c**
Mt 5: 28 lustfully has already **c** adultery
  11: 27 "All things have been **c** to me
Lk 10: 22 "All things have been **c** to me
Ac 14: 23 and fasting, **c** them to the Lord,
  14: 26 where they had been **c** to the grace
1Co 9: 17 I am simply discharging the trust **c**
2Co 5: 19 And he has **c** to us the message
1Pe 2: 22 "He **c** no sin, and no deceit was
Rev 17: 2 her the kings of the earth **c** adultery,
  18: 3 of the earth **c** adultery with her,
  18: 9 of the earth who **c** adultery with her

COMMON
Ge 11: 1 had one language and a **c** speech.
Lev 10: 10 between the holy and the **c**,
Pr 22: 2 Rich and poor have this in **c**:
  29: 13 and the oppressor have this in **c**:
Ac 2: 44 together and had everything in **c**.
1Co 10: 13 has overtaken you except what is **c**
2Co 6: 14 and wickedness have in **c**?

COMMUNITY
Pr 6: 19 who stirs up dissension in the **c**.

COMPANION (COMPANIONS)
Ps 55: 13 like myself, my **c**, my close friend,
  55: 20 My **c** attacks his friends;
Pr 13: 20 wise, for a **c** of fools suffers harm.
  29: 3 but a **c** of prostitutes squanders his
Rev 1: 9 your brother and **c** in the suffering

COMPANIONS (COMPANION)
Ps 45: 7 you above your **c** by anointing you
Pr 28: 7 **c** of gluttons disgrace their parents.
Heb 1: 9 you above your **c** by anointing you

COMPANY
Ps 14: 5 is present in the **c** of the righteous.
Pr 21: 16 comes to rest in the **c** of the dead.
  24: 1 the wicked, do not desire their **c**;
Jer 15: 17 I never sat in the **c** of revelers.
1Co 15: 33 "Bad **c** corrupts good character."

COMPARE* (COMPARED COMPARING COMPARISON)
Job 28: 17 Neither gold nor crystal can **c**

Job 28: 19 The topaz of Cush cannot **c** with it;
  39: 13 though they cannot **c** with the wings
Ps 40: 5 None can **c** with you;
  86: 8 no deeds can **c** with yours.
  89: 6 skies above can **c** with the LORD?
Pr 3: 15 nothing you desire can **c** with her.
  8: 11 nothing you desire can **c** with her.
Isa 40: 18 With whom, then, will you **c** God?
  40: 25 "To whom will you **c** me?
  46: 5 "With whom will you **c** me
La 2: 13 With what can I **c** you,
Eze 31: 8 nor could the plane trees **c** with its
Da 1: 13 **c** our appearance
Mt 11: 16 "To what can I **c** this generation?
Lk 7: 31 what, then, can I **c** the people of this
  13: 18 of God like? What shall I **c** it to?
  13: 20 "What shall I **c** the kingdom of God
2Co 10: 12 or **c** ourselves with some who
  10: 12 and **c** themselves with themselves,

COMPARED* (COMPARE)
Jdg 8: 2 "What have I accomplished **c**
  8: 3 What was I able to do **c** to you?"
Isa 46: 5 will you liken me that we may be **c**?
Eze 31: 2 " 'Who can be **c** with you
  31: 18 the trees of Eden can be **c** with you
Ro 5: 16 Nor can the gift of God be **c** with

COMPARING* (COMPARE)
Ro 8: 18 present sufferings are not worth **c**
2Co 8: 8 of your love by **c**
Gal 6: 4 without **c** yourself to somebody

COMPARISON* (COMPARE)
2Co 3: 10 was glorious has no glory now in **c**

COMPASSION (COMPASSIONATE COMPASSIONS)
Ex 33: 19 I will have **c** on whom I will have **c**.
Dt 13: 17 show you mercy, have **c** on you,
  28: 54 man among you will have no **c**
  30: 3 your fortunes and have **c** on you
2Ki 13: 23 had **c** and showed concern for them
2Ch 30: 9 your children will be shown **c**
Ne 9: 19 of your great **c** you did not abandon
  9: 27 and in your great **c** you gave them
  9: 28 in your **c** you delivered them time
Ps 51: 1 to your great **c** blot out my
  77: 9 Has he in anger withheld his **c**?"
  90: 13 will it be? Have **c** on your servants.
  102: 13 You will arise and have **c** on Zion,
  103: 4 pit and crowns you with love and **c**,
  103: 13 As a father has **c** on his children,
  103: 13 so the LORD has **c** on those who
  116: 5 our God is full of **c**.
  119: 77 Let your **c** come to me that I may
  119: 156 Your **c**, LORD, is great;
  145: 9 he has **c** on all he has made.
Isa 13: 18 infants, nor will they look with **c**
  14: 1 The LORD will have **c** on Jacob;
  27: 11 so their Maker has no **c** on them,
  30: 18 he will rise up to show you **c**.
  49: 10 He who has **c** on them will guide
  49: 13 will have **c** on his afflicted ones.
  49: 15 and have no **c** on the child she has
  51: 3 and will look with **c** on all her ruins;
  54: 7 with deep **c** I will bring you back.
  54: 8 everlasting kindness I will have **c**
  54: 10 says the LORD, who has **c** on you.
  60: 10 in favor I will show you **c**.
  63: 7 Israel, according to his **c** and many
  63: 15 and **c** are withheld from us.
Jer 12: 15 I will again have **c** and will bring
  13: 14 or **c** to keep me from destroying
  21: 7 show them no mercy or pity or **c**.'
  30: 18 tents and have **c** on his dwellings;
  31: 20 I have great **c** for him,"
  33: 26 fortunes and have **c** on them.' "
  42: 12 show you **c** so that he will have **c** on you
La 3: 32 grief, he will show **c**, so great is his
Eze 9: 5 and kill, without showing pity or **c**.
  16: 5 or had **c** enough to do any of these
  39: 25 and will have **c** on all the people
Da 1: 9 to show favor and **c** to Daniel,
Hos 2: 19 and justice, in love and **c**,
  11: 8 all my **c** is aroused.
  13: 14 "I will have no **c**,
  14: 3 for in you the fatherless find **c**."
Jnh 3: 9 with **c** turn from his fierce anger so
Mic 7: 19 You will again have **c** on us;
Zec 7: 9 show mercy and **c** to one another.
  10: 6 I will restore them because I have **c**
Mal 3: 17 just as a father has **c** and spares his
Mt 9: 36 saw the crowds, he had **c** on them,

Mt 14: 14 he had **c** on them and healed their
  15: 32 and said, "I have **c** for these people;
  20: 34 Jesus had **c** on them and touched
Mk 6: 34 a large crowd, he had **c** on them,
  8: 2 "I have **c** for these people;
Lk 15: 20 him and was filled with **c** for him;
Ro 9: 15 I will have **c** on whom I have **c**."
2Co 1: 3 the Father of **c** and the God of all
Php 2: 1 the Spirit, if any tenderness and **c**,
Col 3: 12 clothe yourselves with **c**, kindness,
Jas 5: 11 The Lord is full of **c** and mercy.

COMPASSIONATE* (COMPASSION)
Ex 22: 27 out to me, I will hear, for I am **c**.
  34: 6 LORD, the **c** and gracious God,
2Ch 30: 9 LORD your God is gracious and **c**.
Ne 9: 17 gracious and **c**, slow to anger
Ps 86: 15 Lord, are a **c** and gracious God,
  103: 8 The LORD is **c** and gracious,
  111: 4 the LORD is gracious and **c**.
  112: 4 for those who are gracious and **c**
  145: 8 The LORD is gracious and **c**,
La 4: 10 their own hands **c** women have
Joel 2: 13 for he is gracious and **c**,
Jnh 4: 2 that you are a gracious and **c** God,
Eph 4: 32 Be kind and **c** to one another,
1Pe 3: 8 love one another, be **c** and humble.

COMPASSIONS* (COMPASSION)
La 3: 22 not consumed, for his **c** never fail,

COMPELLED (COMPULSION)
Ac 20: 22 "And now, **c** by the Spirit, I am
1Co 9: 16 cannot boast, since I am **c** to preach.

COMPELS (COMPULSION)
Job 32: 18 and the spirit within me **c** me;
2Co 5: 14 For Christ's love **c** us, because we

COMPETENCE* (COMPETENT)
2Co 3: 5 but our **c** comes from God.

COMPETENT* (COMPETENCE)
Ro 15: 14 and **c** to instruct one another.
1Co 6: 2 are you not **c** to judge trivial cases?
2Co 3: 5 Not that we are **c** in ourselves
  3: 6 He has made us **c** as ministers

COMPETES*
1Co 9: 25 Everyone who **c** in the games goes
2Ti 2: 5 anyone who **c** as an athlete does not

COMPLACENCY* (COMPLACENT)
Pr 1: 32 and the **c** of fools will destroy them;
Eze 30: 9 ships to frighten Cush out of her **c**.

COMPLACENT* (COMPLACENCY)
Isa 32: 9 You women who are so **c**,
  32: 11 Tremble, you **c** women;
Am 6: 1 Woe to you who are **c** in Zion,
Zep 1: 12 lamps and punish those who are **c**,

COMPLETE (COMPLETENESS)
Dt 16: 15 your hands, and your joy will be **c**.
Jn 3: 29 That joy is mine, and it is now **c**.
  15: 11 in you and that your joy may be **c**.
  16: 24 will receive, and your joy will be **c**.
  17: 23 that they may be brought to **c** unity.
Ac 20: 24 **c** the task the Lord Jesus has given
Php 2: 2 then make my joy **c** by being
Col 4: 17 you **c** the work you have received
Jas 1: 4 so that you may be mature and **c**,
  2: 22 his faith was made **c** by what he did.
1Jn 1: 4 We write this to make our joy **c**.
  2: 5 for God is truly made **c** in them.
  4: 12 in us and his love is made **c** in us.
  4: 17 is how love is made **c** among us so
2Jn : 12 to face, so that our joy may be **c**.

COMPLETENESS* (COMPLETE)
1Co 13: 10 but when **c** comes,

COMPLIMENTS*
Pr 23: 8 eaten and will have wasted your **c**.

COMPREHEND* (COMPREHENDED COMPREHENDS)
Ecc 8: 17 No one can **c** what goes on under
  8: 17 they know, they cannot really **c** it.

COMPREHENDED* (COMPREHEND)
Job 38: 18 Have you **c** the vast expanses

COMPREHENDS* (COMPREHEND)
Job 28: 13 No mortal **c** its worth;

COMPULSION (COMPELLED COMPELS)
2Co 9: 7 not reluctantly or under **c**, for God

CONCEAL (CONCEALED CONCEALS)
Ps 40: 10 I do not **c** your love and your

Pr 25: 2 It is the glory of God to c a matter;
28: 13 who c their sins do not prosper,

CONCEALED (CONCEAL)
Jer 16: 17 nor is their sin c from my eyes.
Mt 10: 26 There is nothing c that will not be
Mk 4: 22 whatever is c is meant to be brought
Lk 8: 17 nothing c that will not be known
12: 2 There is nothing c that will not be

CONCEALS* (CONCEAL)
Pr 10: 18 Whoever c hatred with lying lips

CONCEIT* (CONCEITED CONCEITS)
Isa 16: 6 her overweening pride and c,
Jer 48: 29 her overweening pride and c,
Php 2: 3 out of selfish ambition or vain c.

CONCEITED* (CONCEIT)
1Sa 17: 28 I know how c you are and how
2Co 12: 7 order to keep me from becoming c,
Gal 5: 26 Let us not become c,
1Ti 3: 6 he may become c and fall under
6: 4 they are c and understand nothing.
2Ti 3: 4 rash, lovers of pleasure rather

CONCEITS* (CONCEIT)
Ps 73: 7 the evil c of their minds know no

CONCEIVE (CONCEIVED)
Ps 7: 14 pregnant with evil c trouble
Isa 7: 14 The virgin will c and give birth
Mt 1: 23 "The virgin will c and give birth
Lk 1: 7 Elizabeth was not able to c,

CONCEIVED (CONCEIVE)
Ps 51: 5 from the time my mother c me.
Mt 1: 20 because what is c in her is
1Co 2: 9 and what no human mind has c—
Jas 1: 15 after desire has c, it gives birth

CONCERN (CONCERNED)
Ge 39: 6 he did not c himself with anything
39: 8 "my master does not c himself
1Sa 23: 21 LORD bless you for your c for me.
2Ki 13: 23 showed c for them because of his
Job 9: 21 blameless, I have no c for myself;
19: 4 my error remains my c alone.
Ps 131: 1 I do not c myself with great matters
Pr 29: 7 but the wicked have no such c.
Eze 36: 21 I had c for my holy name,
Jnh 4: 11 should I not have c for the great
Ac 18: 17 and Gallio showed no c whatever.
1Co 7: 32 I would like you to be free from c.
12: 25 that its parts should have equal c
2Co 7: 7 deep sorrow, your ardent c for me,
7: 11 what c, what readiness to see justice
8: 16 of Titus the same c I have for you.
11: 28 of my c for all the churches.
Php 2: 20 show genuine c for your welfare.
4: 10 at last you renewed your c for me.

CONCERNED (CONCERN)
Ex 2: 25 the Israelites and was c about them.
Ps 142: 4 at my right hand; no one is c for me.
Jnh 4: 10 "You have been c about this gourd,
1Co 7: 32 An unmarried man is c
9: 9 Is it about oxen that God is c?
Php 4: 10 Indeed, you were c, but you had no

CONCESSION*
1Co 7: 6 I say this as a c, not as a command.

CONDEMN* (CONDEMNATION CONDEMNED
CONDEMNING CONDEMNS)
Job 9: 20 innocent, my mouth would c me;
34: 17 Will you c the just and mighty One?
34: 29 if he remains silent, who can c him?
40: 8 Would you c me to justify yourself?
Ps 94: 21 and c the innocent to death.
109: 7 guilty, and may his prayers c him.
109: 31 lives from those who c them.
Isa 50: 9 Who will c me? They will all wear
Mt 12: 41 with this generation and c it;
12: 42 with this generation and c it;
20: 18 of the law. They will c him to death
Mk 10: 33 They will c him to death and will
Lk 6: 37 Do not c, and you will not be
11: 31 of this generation and c them,
11: 32 with this generation and c it,
Jn 3: 17 Son into the world to c the world,
7: 51 "Does our law c a man without first
8: 11 *neither do I c you*,"
12: 48 words I have spoken will c them
Ro 2: 27 yet obeys the law will c you who,
8: 34 Who then can c? No one.
14: 22 are those who do not c themselves
2Co 7: 3 I do not say this to c you;

1Jn 3: 20 If our hearts c us, we know that God
3: 21 if our hearts do not c us, we have
Jude : 9 did not himself dare to c him

CONDEMNATION* (CONDEMN)
Eze 33: 12 former wickedness will not bring c.
Ro 3: 8 good may result"? Their c is just!
5: 16 followed one sin and brought c,
5: 18 just as one trespass resulted in c
8: 1 there is now no c for those who are
2Co 3: 9 ministry that brought c was glorious,
2Pe 2: 3 Their c has long been hanging over
Jude : 4 individuals whose c was written

CONDEMNED* (CONDEMN)
Dt 13: 17 of those c things shall be found
Job 32: 3 to refute Job, and yet had c him.
Ps 34: 21 the foes of the righteous will be c.
34: 22 who takes refuge in him will be c.
37: 33 let them be c when brought to trial.
79: 11 your strong arm preserve those c
102: 20 and release those c to death."
Mt 12: 7 you would not have c the innocent.
12: 37 and by your words you will be c."
27: 3 saw that Jesus was c, he was seized
Mk 14: 64 They all c him as worthy of death.
16: 16 *does not believe will be c.*
Lk 6: 37 not condemn, and you will not be c.
Jn 3: 18 Whoever believes in him is not c,
3: 18 not believe stands c already because
5: 29 done what is evil will rise to be c.
8: 10 *Has no one c you?*"
16: 11 prince of this world now stands c.
Ac 25: 15 against him and asked that he be c.
Ro 3: 7 glory, why am I still c as a sinner?"
8: 3 And so he c sin in human flesh,
14: 23 those who have doubts are c if they
1Co 4: 9 like those c to die in the arena.
11: 32 that we will not be finally c
Gal 2: 11 to his face, because he stood c.
Col 2: 14 stood against us and c us;
2Th 2: 12 all will be c who have not believed
Tit 3: 11 of speech that cannot be c,
Heb 11: 7 By his faith he c the world
Jas 5: 6 You have c and murdered
5: 12 Otherwise you will be c.
2Pe 2: 6 if he c the cities of Sodom
Rev 19: 2 He has c the great prostitute who

CONDEMNING* (CONDEMN)
Dt 25: 1 the innocent and c the guilty.
1Ki 8: 32 c the guilty by bringing down
2Ch 6: 23 c the guilty and bringing
Pr 17: 15 the guilty and c the innocent—
Ac 13: 27 yet in c him they fulfilled the words
Ro 2: 1 you are c yourself, because you who

CONDEMNS* (CONDEMN)
Job 15: 6 Your own mouth c you, not mine;
Pr 12: 2 but he c those who devise wicked
14: 34 but sin c any people.

CONDITION
Pr 27: 23 Be sure you know the c of your

CONDUCT (CONDUCTED)
Ps 112: 5 who c their affairs with justice.
Pr 20: 11 is their c really pure and upright?
21: 8 but the c of the innocent is upright.
Ecc 6: 8 how to c themselves before others?
Jer 4: 18 "Your own c and actions have
17: 10 everyone according to their c,
Eze 7: 3 I will judge you according to your c
1Ti 3: 15 how people ought to c themselves
2: 15 in c, in love, in faith and

CONDUCTED* (CONDUCT)
2Co 1: 12 we have c ourselves in the world,

CONFESS* (CONFESSED CONFESSES
CONFESSING CONFESSION)
Lev 5: 5 they must c in what way they have
16: 21 goat and c over it all the wickedness
26: 40 if they will c their sins and the sins
Nu 5: 7 must c the sin they have committed,
Ne 1: 6 I c the sins were Israelites,
Ps 32: 5 "I will c my transgressions
38: 18 I c my iniquity; I am troubled by
Pr 28: 13 who c and renounce them find mercy.
Jn 1: 20 He did not fail to c, but confessed
Ro 14: 11 every tongue will c to God.'"
Jas 5: 16 Therefore c your sins to each other
1Jn 1: 9 If we c our sins, he is faithful

CONFESSED* (CONFESS)
1Sa 7: 6 day they fasted and there they c,
Ne 9: 2 stood in their places and c their sins
Da 9: 4 to the LORD my God and c:
Jn 1: 20 confess, but c freely, "I am not
Ac 19: 18 and openly c what they had done.

CONFESSES* (CONFESS)
2Ti 2: 19 "Everyone who c the name

CONFESSING* (CONFESS)
Ezr 10: 1 While Ezra was praying and c,
Da 9: 20 c my sin and the sin of my people
Mt 3: 6 C their sins, they were baptized
Mk 1: 5 C their sins, they were baptized

CONFESSION* (CONFESS)
Ne 9: 3 and spent another quarter in c
2Co 9: 13 accompanies your c of the gospel
1Ti 6: 12 when you made your good c
6: 13 Pontius Pilate made the good c,

CONFIDENCE* (CONFIDENT)
Jdg 9: 26 and its citizens put their c in him.
2Ki 18: 19 what are you basing this c of yours?
2Ch 32: 8 And the people gained c from what
32: 10 On what are you basing your c,
Job 4: 6 Should not your piety be your c
Ps 71: 5 LORD, my c since my youth.
Pr 3: 32 but takes the upright into his c.
11: 13 Gossips betray a c,
20: 19 A gossip betrays a c;
25: 9 to court, do not betray another's c,
31: 11 Her husband has full c in her
Isa 32: 17 will be quietness and c forever.
36: 4 what are you basing this c of yours?
Jer 17: 7 in the LORD, whose c is in him.
49: 31 ease, which lives in c,"
Eze 29: 16 will no longer be a source of c
Mic 7: 5 put no c in a friend.
2Co 2: 3 I had c in all of you, that you would
3: 4 Such c we have through Christ
7: 16 I am glad I can have complete c
8: 22 so because of his great c in you.
Eph 3: 12 approach God with freedom and c.
Php 3: 3 and who put no c in the flesh—
3: 4 I myself have reasons for such c.
3: 4 have reasons to put c in the flesh,
2Th 3: 4 We have c in the Lord that you are
Heb 3: 6 hold firmly to our c and
3: 14 God's throne of grace with c,
10: 19 since we have c to enter the Most
10: 35 So do not throw away your c;
13: 6 So we say with c, "The Lord is my
13: 17 Have c in your leaders and submit
1Jn 3: 21 condemn us, we have c before God
4: 17 us so that we will have c on the day
5: 14 This is the c we have

CONFIDENT* (CONFIDENCE)
Job 6: 20 distressed, because they had been c;
Ps 27: 3 against me, even then I will be c.
27: 13 I remain c of this: I will see
Lk 18: 9 to some who were c of their own
2Co 1: 15 Because I was c of this, I wanted
5: 6 Therefore we are always c
5: 8 We are c, I say, and would prefer
9: 4 be ashamed of having been so c.
10: 7 If anyone is c that they belong
Gal 5: 10 I am c in the Lord that you will
Php 1: 6 being c of this, that he who began
1: 14 have become c in the Lord
2: 24 I am c in the Lord that I myself will
Phm : 21 C of your obedience, I write to you,
1Jn 2: 28 that when he appears we may be c

CONFIDES*
Ps 25: 14 The LORD c in those who fear

CONFIRM
2Pe 1: 10 make every effort to c your calling

CONFLICT
Heb 10: 32 in a great c full of suffering.

CONFORM* (CONFORMED CONFORMITY
CONFORMS)
Ro 12: 2 Do not c to the pattern of this world,
1Pe 1: 14 do not c to the evil desires you had

CONFORMED* (CONFORM)
Eze 5: 7 You have not even c
11: 12 but have c to the standards
Ac 26: 5 I c to the strictest sect of our
Ro 8: 29 predestined to be c to the image

CONFORMITY* (CONFORM)
Eph 1: 11 out everything in **c** with the purpose

CONFORMS* (CONFORM)
1Ti 1: 11 that **c** to the gospel concerning

CONQUEROR* (CONQUERORS)
Mic 1: 15 I will bring a **c** against you who live
Rev 6: 2 he rode out as a **c** bent on conquest.

CONQUERORS* (CONQUEROR)
Ro 8: 37 are more than **c** through him who

CONSCIENCE* (CONSCIENCE-STRICKEN CONSCIENCES CONSCIENTIOUS)
Ge 20: 5 I have done this with a clear **c**
        20: 6 I know you did this with a clear **c**,
1Sa 25: 31 have on his **c** the staggering burden
Job 27: 6 my **c** will not reproach me as long
Ac 23: 1 to God in all good **c** to this day."
        24: 16 to keep my **c** clear before God
Ro   9: 1 my **c** confirms it through the Holy
        13: 5 but also as a matter of **c**.
1Co 4: 4 My **c** is clear, but that does not
         8: 7 a god, and since their **c** is weak, it is
         8: 10 if anyone with a weak **c** sees you,
         8: 12 in this way and wound their weak **c**,
        10: 25 without raising questions of **c**,
        10: 27 you without raising questions of **c**.
        10: 28 who told you and for the sake of **c**,
        10: 29 am referring to the other person's **c**,
        10: 29 being judged by another's **c**?
2Co 1: 12 Our **c** testifies that we have
         4: 2 to everyone's **c** in the sight of God.
         5: 11 and I hope it is also plain to your **c**.
1Ti 1: 5 and a good **c** and a sincere faith.
         1: 19 holding on to faith and a good **c**,
         3: 9 truths of the faith with a clear **c**.
2Ti 1: 3 with a clear **c**, as night and day I
Heb 9: 14 able to clear the **c** of the worshiper.
        10: 22 to cleanse us from a guilty **c**
        13: 18 We are sure that we have a clear **c**
1Pe 3: 16 keeping a clear **c**, so that those who
         3: 21 the pledge of a clear **c** toward God.

CONSCIENCE-STRICKEN* (CONSCIENCE)
1Sa 24: 5 David was **c** for having cut off
2Sa 24: 10 David was **c** after he had counted

CONSCIENCES* (CONSCIENCE)
Ro   2: 15 hearts, their **c** also bearing witness,
1Ti 4: 2 whose **c** have been seared as
Tit 1: 15 their minds and **c** are corrupted.
Heb 9: 14 cleanse our **c** from acts that lead

CONSCIENTIOUS* (CONSCIENCE)
2Ch 29: 34 for the Levites had been more **c**

CONSCIOUS*
Ro   3: 20 through the law we become **c** of our
1Pe 2: 19 unjust suffering because you are **c**

CONSECRATE (CONSECRATED)
Ex 13: 2 "**C** to me every firstborn male.
        40: 9 **c** it and all its furnishings, and it
Lev 20: 7 "'**C** yourselves and be holy,
        25: 10 **C** the fiftieth year and proclaim
1Ch 15: 12 fellow Levites are to **c** yourselves

CONSECRATED (CONSECRATE)
Ex 29: 43 and the place will be **c** by my glory.
Lev 8: 30 So he **c** Aaron and his garments
2Ch 7: 16 **c** this temple so that my Name may
Lk   2: 23 male is to be **c** to the Lord"),
1Ti 4: 5 because it is **c** by the word of God

CONSENT
1Co 7: 5 other except perhaps by mutual **c**

CONSIDER (CONSIDERATE CONSIDERED CONSIDERS)
1Sa 12: 24 **c** what great things he has done
        16: 7 "Do not **c** his appearance or his
2Ch 19: 7 them, "**C** carefully what you do,
Job 37: 14 stop and **c** God's wonders.
Ps   8: 3 When I **c** your heavens, the work
        77: 12 I will **c** all your works and meditate
        143: 5 and **c** what your hands have done.
Pr   6: 6 **c** its ways and be wise!
        20: 25 and only later to **c** one's vows.
Ecc 7: 13 **C** what God has done:
Lk 12: 24 the ravens: They do not sow
        12: 27 "**C** how the wild flowers grow.
Ro 14: 5 Some **c** one day more sacred
Php 3: 8 I **c** everything a loss because
Heb 10: 24 And let us **c** how we may spur one
Jas 1: 2 **C** it pure joy, my brothers
        1: 26 Those who **c** themselves religious

CONSIDERATE* (CONSIDER)
Tit 3: 2 to be peaceable and **c**, and always
Jas 3: 17 then peace-loving, **c**, submissive,
1Pe 3: 2 only to those who are good and **c**,
         3: 7 the same way be **c** as you live

CONSIDERED (CONSIDER)
Job 1: 8 "Have you **c** my servant Job?
         2: 3 "Have you **c** my servant Job?
Ps 44: 22 we are **c** as sheep to be slaughtered.
Isa 53: 4 yet we **c** him punished by God,
Ro   8: 36 all day long; we are **c** as sheep to be

CONSIDERS (CONSIDER)
Pr 31: 16 She **c** a field and buys it; out of her

CONSIST (CONSISTS)
Lk 12: 15 life does not **c** in an abundance

CONSISTS (CONSIST)
Eph 5: 9 fruit of the light **c** in all goodness,

CONSOLATION
Ps 94: 19 within me, your **c** brought me joy.

CONSPIRE
Ps   2: 1 Why do the nations **c**

CONSTANT
Dt 28: 66 You will live in **c** suspense,
Pr 19: 13 wife is like the **c** dripping of a leaky
Ac 27: 33 "you have been in **c** suspense
Heb 5: 14 by **c** use have trained themselves

CONSTRUCTIVE*
1Co 10: 23 but not everything is **c**.

CONSULT
Gal 1: 16 was not to **c** any human being.

CONSUME (CONSUMES CONSUMING)
Jn   2: 17 "Zeal for your house will **c** me."

CONSUMES (CONSUME)
Ps 69: 9 for zeal for your house **c** me,

CONSUMING (CONSUME)
Dt   4: 24 For the LORD your God is a **c** fire,
Heb 12: 29 for our "God is a **c** fire."

CONTAIN* (CONTAINED CONTAINS)
1Ki 8: 27 the highest heaven, cannot **c** you.
2Ch 2: 6 the highest heavens, cannot **c** him?
         6: 18 the highest heavens, cannot **c** you.
Ecc 8: 8 one has power over the wind to **c** it,
2Pe 3: 16 His letters **c** some things that are

CONTAINED (CONTAIN)
Heb 9: 4 This ark the gold jar of manna,

CONTAINS (CONTAIN)
Pr 15: 6 of the righteous **c** great treasure,

CONTAMINATES*
2Co 7: 1 from everything that **c** body

CONTEMPLATE*
2Co 3: 18 unveiled faces the Lord's glory,

CONTEMPT
Pr 14: 31 oppresses the poor shows **c** for their
        17: 5 Whoever mocks the poor shows **c**
        18: 3 so does **c**, and with shame comes
Da 12: 2 others to shame and everlasting **c**.
Mal 1: 6 'How have we shown **c** for your
Ro   2: 4 do you show **c** for the riches of his
        14: 3 must not treat with **c** the one who
Gal 4: 14 you did not treat me with **c** or scorn.
1Th 5: 20 Do not treat prophecies with **c**

CONTEND (CONTENDED CONTENDING CONTENTIOUS)
Ge   6: 3 "My Spirit will not **c** with human
Ps 35: 1 LORD, **c** with those who **c**
Isa 49: 25 I will **c** with those who **c** with you,
Jude   3 urge you to **c** for the faith

CONTENDED (CONTEND)
Php 4: 3 help these women since they have **c**

CONTENDING* (CONTEND)
Col 2: 1 to know how hard I am **c** for you

CONTENT* (CONTENTMENT)
Ge 25: 27 while Jacob was **c** to stay at home
Jos 7: 7 If only we had been **c** to stay
Ps 131: 2 like a weaned child I am **c**.
Pr 13: 25 The righteous eat to their hearts' **c**,
        19: 23 then one rests **c**,
Ecc 4: 8 toil, yet his eyes were not **c** with his
Lk   3: 14 be **c** with your pay."
Php 4: 11 to be **c** whatever the circumstances.
         4: 12 learned the secret of being **c** in any

CONTENTION* (CONTEND)
1Co 11: 16 If anyone wants to be **c** about this,

CONTENTMENT* (CONTENT)
Job 36: 11 in prosperity and their years in **c**.
SS   8: 10 in his eyes like one bringing **c**.
1Ti 6: 6 But godliness with **c** is great gain.

CONTINUAL (CONTINUE)
Pr 15: 15 but the cheerful heart has a **c** feast.

CONTINUE (CONTINUAL CONTINUES CONTINUING)
1Ki 8: 23 your servants who **c** wholeheartedly
2Ch 6: 14 your servants who **c** wholeheartedly
Ps 36: 10 **C** your love to those who know you,
Ac 13: 43 urged them to **c** in the grace of God.
Ro 11: 22 provided that you **c** in his kindness.
Gal 3: 10 "Cursed is everyone who does not **c**
Php 2: 12 **c** to work out your salvation
Col 1: 23 if you **c** in your faith,
         2: 6 as Lord, **c** to live your lives in him,
1Ti 2: 15 if they **c** in faith, love and holiness
2Ti 3: 14 **c** in what you have learned and have
1Jn 2: 28 dear children, **c** in him,
         3: 9 are born of God will not **c** to sin,
         5: 18 born of God does not **c** to sin;
2Jn   9 does not **c** in the teaching of Christ
Rev 22: 11 those who do right **c** to do right;
        22: 11 and let those who are holy **c** to be

CONTINUES (CONTINUE)
Ps 100: 5 his faithfulness **c** through all
        119: 90 Your faithfulness **c** through all
2Co 10: 15 hope is that, as your faith **c** to grow,
1Jn 3: 6 No one who **c** to sin has either seen

CONTINUING (CONTINUE)
Ro 13: 8 except the **c** debt to love one

CONTRIBUTION (CONTRIBUTIONS)
Ro 15: 26 to make a **c** for the poor among

CONTRIBUTIONS (CONTRIBUTION)
2Ch 24: 10 all the people brought their **c** gladly,
        31: 12 they faithfully brought in the **c**,

CONTRITE*
Ps 51: 17 a broken and **c** heart you, God,
Isa 57: 15 with those who are **c** and lowly
        57: 15 and to revive the heart of the **c**.
        66: 2 who are humble and **c** in spirit,

CONTROL (CONTROLLED CONTROLS SELF-CONTROL SELF-CONTROLLED)
1Co 7: 9 But if they cannot **c** themselves,
         7: 37 but has **c** over his own will,
1Th 4: 4 should learn to **c** your own body

CONTROLLED (CONTROL)
Ps 32: 9 understanding but must be **c** by bit
Ro   8: 6 but the mind **c** by the Spirit is life
         8: 8 Those **c** by the sinful nature cannot

CONTROLS* (CONTROL)
Job 37: 15 Do you know how God **c** the clouds

CONTROVERSIES*
Ac   6: 3 with all the Jewish customs and **c**.
1Ti 6: 4 They have an unhealthy interest in **c**
Tit 3: 9 But avoid foolish **c** and genealogies

CONVERSATION
Col 4: 6 Let your **c** be always full of grace,

CONVERT
1Ti 3: 6 He must not be a recent **c**, or he

CONVICT (CONVICTED CONVICTION)
Pr 24: 25 go well with those who **c** the guilty,
Jude   15 and to **c** all the ungodly of all

CONVICTED (CONVICT)
1Co 14: 24 they are **c** of sin

CONVICTION* (CONVICT)
1Th 1: 5 with the Holy Spirit and deep **c**.
Heb 3: 14 firmly till the end our original **c**.

CONVINCED* (CONVINCING)
Ge 45: 28 And Israel said, "I'm **c**!
Lk 16: 31 they will not be **c** even if someone
Ac 19: 8 reasoned with them and **c**
        26: 9 "I too was **c** that I ought to do all
        26: 26 I am **c** that none of this has escaped
        28: 24 Some were **c** by what he said,
Ro   2: 19 if you are **c** that you are a guide
         8: 38 I am **c** that neither death nor life,
        14: 5 Everyone should be fully **c** in their

Ro 14: 14 I am **c**, being fully persuaded
15: 14 I myself am **c**, my brothers
2Co 5: 14 because we are **c** that one died
Php 1: 25 **C** of this, I know that I will remain,
2Ti 1: 12 am **c** that he is able to guard what I
3: 14 have learned and have become **c** of,
Heb 8: 9 we are **c** of better things in your

CONVINCING* (CONVINCED)
Ac 1: 3 and gave many **c** proofs that he was

COPIES (COPY)
Heb 9: 23 for the **c** of the heavenly things

COPY (COPIES)
Dt 17: 18 himself on a scroll a **c** of this law,
Heb 8: 5 They serve at a sanctuary that is a **c**
9: 24 that was only a **c** of the true one;

CORBAN*
Mk 7: 11 their father or mother is **C** (that is,

CORD (CORDS)
Jos 2: 18 you have tied this scarlet **c**
Ecc 4: 12 A **c** of three strands is not quickly

CORDS (CORD)
Pr 5: 22 the **c** of their sins hold them fast.
Isa 54: 2 lengthen your **c**, strengthen your
Hos 11: 4 I led them with **c** of human

CORINTH
Ac 18: 1 this, Paul left Athens and went to **C**.
1Co 1: 2 To the church of God in **C**, to those
2Co 1: 1 To the church of God in **C**,

CORNELIUS*
Roman to whom Peter preached; first Gentile Christian (Ac 10).

CORNER (CORNERS CORNERSTONE)
Ru 3: 9 "Spread the **c** of your garment over
Pr 21: 9 on a **c** of the roof than share a house
25: 24 on a **c** of the roof than share a house
Ac 26: 26 because it was not done in a **c**.

CORNERS (CORNER)
Mt 6: 5 on the street **c** to be seen by others.
22: 9 Go to the street **c** and invite

CORNERSTONE* (CORNER STONE)
Job 38: 6 its footings set, or who laid its **c**—
Ps 118: 22 rejected has become the **c**;
Isa 28: 16 a precious **c** for a sure foundation;
Jer 51: 26 rock will be taken from you for a **c**,
Zec 10: 4 From Judah will come the **c**,
Mt 21: 42 has become the **c**;
Mk 12: 10 has become the **c**;
Lk 20: 17 builders rejected has become the **c**'?
Ac 4: 11 which has become the **c**.'
Eph 2: 20 Christ Jesus himself as the chief **c**.
1Pe 2: 6 a chosen and precious **c**,
2: 7 has become the **c**,"

CORRECT* (CORRECTED CORRECTING
CORRECTION CORRECTS)
Job 6: 26 Do you mean to **c** what I say,
40: 2 contends with the Almighty **c** him?
2Ti 4: 2 **c**, rebuke and encourage—

CORRECTED* (CORRECT)
Pr 29: 19 Servants cannot be **c** by mere

CORRECTING* (CORRECT)
2Ti 3: 16 **c** and training in righteousness,

CORRECTION* (CORRECT)
Lev 26: 23 these things you do not accept my **c**
Job 36: 10 He makes them listen to **c**
Pr 5: 12 How my heart spurned **c**!
8: 10 and **c** and instruction
10: 17 but whoever ignores **c** leads others
12: 1 but whoever hates **c** is stupid.
13: 18 but whoever heeds **c** is honored.
15: 5 whoever heeds **c** shows prudence.
15: 10 those who hate **c** will die.
15: 12 Mockers resent **c**, so they avoid
15: 31 Whoever heeds life-giving **c** will be
15: 32 who heed **c** gain understanding.
Jer 2: 30 they did not respond to **c**.
5: 3 crushed them, but they refused **c**.
7: 28 LORD this God or responded to **c**.
Zep 3: 2 She obeys no one, she accepts no **c**.
3: 7 you will fear me and accept **c**!'

CORRECTS* (CORRECT)
Job 5: 17 "Blessed are those whom God **c**;
Pr 9: 7 Whoever **c** a mocker invites insults;

CORRUPT (CORRUPTED CORRUPTION
CORRUPTS)
Ge 6: 11 Now the earth was **c** in God's sight
Ps 14: 1 They are **c**, their deeds are vile;
14: 3 turned away, all have become **c**;
Pr 4: 24 keep **c** talk far from your lips.
6: 12 who go about with **c** mouths,
19: 28 A **c** witness mocks at justice,

CORRUPTED (CORRUPT)
2Co 7: 2 wronged no one, we have **c** no one,
Tit 1: 15 but to those who are **c** and do not

CORRUPTION (CORRUPT)
2Pe 1: 4 having escaped the **c** in the world
2: 20 they have escaped the **c** of the world

CORRUPTS* (CORRUPT)
Ecc 7: 7 into fools, and a bribe **c** the heart.
1Co 15: 33 "Bad company **c** good character."
Jas 3: 6 It **c** the whole person, sets the whole

COST (COSTS)
Nu 16: 38 who sinned at the **c** of their lives.
Pr 4: 7 Though it **c** all you have,
7: 23 little knowing it will **c** him his life.
Isa 55: 1 milk without money and without **c**.
Lk 14: 28 and estimate the **c** to see if you have
Rev 21: 6 thirsty I will give water without **c**

COSTS* (COST)
Pr 6: 31 though it **c** him all the wealth of his

COUNCIL
Ps 89: 7 the **c** of the holy ones God is greatly
107: 32 and praise him in the **c** of the elders.

COUNSEL (COUNSELOR COUNSELS)
1Ki 22: 5 "First seek the **c** of the LORD."
2Ch 18: 4 "First seek the **c** of the LORD."
Ps 73: 24 You guide me with your **c**,
Pr 8: 14 **C** and sound judgment are mine;
15: 22 Plans fail for lack of **c**,
1Ti 5: 14 So I **c** younger widows to marry,
Rev 3: 18 I **c** you to buy from me gold refined

COUNSELOR (COUNSEL)
Isa 9: 6 And he will be called Wonderful **C**,
Ro 11: 34 Or who has been his **c**?"

COUNSELS* (COUNSEL)
Ps 16: 7 I will praise the LORD, who **c** me;

COUNT (COUNTED COUNTING COUNTS)
Eze 33: 12 righteousness will **c** for nothing.
Ro 4: 8 Lord will never **c** against them."
6: 11 yourselves dead to sin but alive

COUNTED (COUNT)
Ac 5: 41 because they had been **c** worthy
2Th 1: 5 as a result you will be **c** worthy

COUNTERFEIT*
1Jn 2: 27 and as that anointing is real, not **c**—

COUNTING (COUNT)
2Co 5: 19 not **c** people's sins against them.

COUNTRY
Pr 28: 2 When a **c** is rebellious, it has many
29: 4 By justice a king gives a **c** stability,
Isa 66: 8 Can a **c** be born in a day or a nation
Lk 15: 13 set off for a distant **c** and there
Jn 4: 44 have no honor in their own **c**.)
2Co 11: 26 in danger in the **c**, in danger at sea;
Heb 11: 14 are looking for a **c** of their own.

COUNTS (COUNT)
Jn 6: 63 the flesh **c** for nothing.
1Co 7: 19 God's commands is what **c**.
Gal 5: 6 **c** is faith expressing itself through

COURAGE* (COURAGEOUS)
Jos 2: 11 everyone's **c** failed because of you,
5: 1 they no longer had the **c** to face
2Sa 7: 27 he lost **c**, and all Israel became
7: 27 So your servant has found **c** to pray
1Ch 17: 25 So your servant has found **c** to pray
2Ch 15: 8 son of Oded the prophet, he took **c**.
19: 11 Act with **c**, and may the LORD be
Ezr 7: 28 I took **c** and gathered leaders
10: 4 support you, so take **c** and do it."
Ps 107: 26 their peril their **c** melted away.
Eze 22: 14 Will your **c** endure or your hands be
Da 11: 25 and **c** against the king of the South.
Mt 14: 27 immediately said to them: "Take **c**!
Mk 6: 50 he spoke to them and said, "Take **c**!
Ac 4: 13 When they saw the **c** of Peter
23: 11 stood near Paul and said, "Take **c**!
27: 22 now I urge you to keep up your **c**,

Ac 27: 25 So keep up your **c**, men, for I have
Php 1: 20 will have sufficient **c** so that now as

COURAGEOUS* (COURAGE)
Dt 31: 6 Be strong and **c**. Do not be afraid
31: 7 "Be strong and **c**, for you must go
31: 23 "Be strong and **c**, for you will bring
Jos 1: 6 Be strong and **c**, because you will
1: 7 "Be strong and very **c**. Be careful
1: 9 Be strong and **c**. Do not be afraid;
1: 18 put to death. Only be strong and **c**!"
10: 25 Be strong and **c**. This is what
1Ch 22: 13 Be strong and **c**. Do not be afraid
28: 20 "Be strong and **c**, and do the work.
2Ch 26: 17 eighty other **c** priests of the LORD
32: 7 "Be strong and **c**. Do not be afraid
1Co 16: 13 stand firm in the faith; be **c**;

COURSE
Ps 19: 5 a champion rejoicing to run his **c**.
Pr 2: 8 for he guards the **c** of the just
15: 21 understanding keep a straight **c**.
16: 9 hearts human beings plan their **c**,
17: 23 in secret to pervert the **c** of justice.
Jas 3: 6 sets the whole **c** of one's life on fire,

COURT (COURTS)
Pr 22: 22 and do not crush the needy in **c**,
25: 8 do not bring hastily to **c**, for what
Mt 5: 25 adversary who is taking you to **c**.
1Co 4: 3 judged by you or by any human **c**;

COURTS (COURT)
Ps 84: 10 in your **c** than a thousand elsewhere;
100: 4 thanksgiving and his **c** with praise;
Am 5: 15 maintain justice in the **c**.
Zec 8: 16 true and sound judgment in your **c**;

COURTYARD
Ex 27: 9 "Make a **c** for the tabernacle.

COUSIN
Col 4: 10 as does Mark, the **c** of Barnabas.

COVENANT (COVENANTS)
Ge 9: 9 "I now establish my **c** with you
17: 2 I will make my **c** between me
Ex 19: 5 if you obey me fully and keep my **c**,
24: 7 he took the Book of the **C** and read
Dt 4: 13 He declared to you his **c**, the Ten
29: 1 addition to the **c** he had made
Jdg 2: 1 'I will never break my **c** with you,
1Sa 23: 18 them made a **c** before the LORD.
1Ki 8: 21 which is the **c** of the LORD that he
8: 23 you who keep your **c** of love
2Ki 23: 2 all the words of the Book of the **C**,
1Ch 16: 15 He remembers his **c** forever,
2Ch 6: 14 you who keep your **c** of love
34: 30 all the words of the Book of the **C**,
Ne 1: 5 who keeps his **c** of love with those
Job 31: 1 "I made a **c** with my eyes not
Ps 105: 8 He remembers his **c** forever,
Pr 2: 17 ignored the **c** she made before God.
Isa 42: 6 make you to be a **c** for the people
61: 8 make an everlasting **c** with them.
Jer 11: 2 "Listen to the terms of this **c**
31: 31 I will make a new **c** with the house
31: 32 It will not be like the **c** I made
31: 33 "This is the **c** I will make
Eze 37: 26 I will make a **c** of peace with them;
Da 9: 27 He will confirm a **c** with many
Hos 6: 7 As at Adam, they have broken the **c**;
Mal 2: 14 partner, the wife of your marriage **c**.
3: 1 the messenger of the **c**, whom you
Mt 26: 28 This is my blood of the **c**, which is
Mk 14: 24 "This is my blood of the **c**, which is
Lk 22: 20 "This cup is the new **c** in my blood,
1Co 11: 25 "This cup is the new **c** in my blood,
2Co 3: 6 competent as ministers of a new **c**—
Gal 4: 24 One is from Mount Sinai
Heb 8: 6 is as superior to theirs as the **c**
8: 8 I will make a new **c** with the house
9: 15 Christ is the mediator of a new **c**,
12: 24 to Jesus the mediator of a new **c**,

COVENANTS* (COVENANT)
Ro 9: 4 the **c**, the receiving of the law,
Gal 4: 24 for the women represent two **c**.
Eph 2: 12 foreigners to the **c** of the promise,

COVER (COVER-UP COVERED COVERING
COVERINGS COVERS)
Ex 25: 17 "Make an atonement **c** of pure
25: 21 Place the **c** on top of the ark and put
33: 22 and **c** you with my hand until I have
Lev 16: 2 in the cloud over the atonement **c**.

Ps 32: 5 to you and did not **c** up my iniquity.
91: 4 He will **c** you with his feathers,
Hos 10: 8 will say to the mountains, "**C** us!"
Lk 23: 30 and to the hills, "**C** us!" '
1Co 11: 6 For if a woman does not **c** her head,
11: 6 shaved, then she should **c** her head.
11: 7 A man ought not to **c** his head,
Jas 5: 20 death and **c** over a multitude of sins.

COVER-UP* (COVER)
1Pe 2: 16 do not use your freedom as a **c**

COVERED (COVER)
Ps 32: 1 are forgiven, whose sins are **c**.
85: 2 of your people and **c** all their sins.
Isa 6: 2 With two wings they **c** their faces,
51: 16 **c** you with the shadow of my hand—
Ro 4: 7 are forgiven, whose sins are **c**.
1Co 11: 4 with his head **c** dishonors his head.

COVERING (COVER)
1Co 11: 15 For long hair is given to her as a **c**.

COVERINGS (COVER)
Ge 3: 7 together and made **c** for themselves.
Pr 31: 22 She makes **c** for her bed;

COVERS (COVER)
Pr 10: 12 but love **c** over all wrongs.
17: 9 would foster love **c** over an offense,
2Co 3: 15 Moses is read, a veil **c** their hearts.
1Pe 4: 8 because love **c** over a multitude

COVET* (COVETED COVETING)
Ex 20: 17 "You shall not **c** your neighbor's
20: 17 You shall not **c** your neighbor's
34: 24 no one will **c** your land when you
Dt 5: 21 "You shall not **c** your neighbor's
7: 25 Do not **c** the silver and gold
Mic 2: 2 They **c** fields and seize them,
Ro 7: 7 had not said, "You shall not **c**."
13: 9 "You shall not **c**," and whatever
Jas 4: 2 You **c** but you cannot get what you

COVETED* (COVET)
Jos 7: 21 shekels, I **c** them and took them.
Ac 20: 33 I have not **c** anyone's silver or gold

COVETING*
Ro 7: 7 not have known what **c** really was
7: 8 produced in me every kind of **c**.

COWARDLY*
Rev 21: 8 But the **c**, the unbelieving, the vile,

COWS
Ge 41: 2 of the river there came up seven **c**,
1Sa 6: 7 Hitch the **c** to the cart, but take their

CRAFTINESS* (CRAFTY)
Job 5: 13 He catches the wise in their **c**.
1Co 3: 19 "He catches the wise in their **c**";
Eph 4: 14 and **c** of people in their deceitful

CRAFTY* (CRAFTINESS)
Ge 3: 1 the serpent was more **c** than any
1Sa 23: 22 They tell me he is very **c**.
Job 5: 12 He thwarts the plans of the **c**,
15: 5 you adopt the tongue of the **c**.
Pr 7: 10 like a prostitute and with **c** intent.
2Co 12: 16 **c** fellow that I am, I caught you

CRAVE* (CRAVED CRAVING CRAVINGS)
Nu 11: 4 with them began to **c** other food,
Dt 12: 20 and you **c** meat and say,
Pr 21: 10 The wicked **c** evil;
21: 26 All day long they **c** for more,
23: 3 Do not **c** his delicacies, for that
23: 6 host, do not **c** his delicacies;
31: 4 drink wine, not for rulers to **c** beer,
Mic 7: 1 to eat, none of the early figs that I **c**.
1Pe 2: 2 babies, **c** pure spiritual milk,

CRAVED* (CRAVE)
Nu 11: 34 the people who had **c** other food.
Ps 78: 18 test by demanding the food they **c**.
78: 29 he had given them what they **c**,
78: 30 they turned from what they **c**,

CRAVING* (CRAVE)
Job 20: 20 he will have no respite from his **c**;
Ps 106: 14 In the desert they gave in to their **c**;
Pr 10: 3 but he thwarts the **c** of the wicked.
21: 25 The **c** of sluggards will be the death
Jer 2: 24 desert, sniffing the wind in her **c**—

CRAVINGS* (CRAVE)
Ps 10: 3 boast about the **c** of their hearts;
Eph 2: 3 gratifying the **c** of our sinful nature
1Jn 2: 16 the **c** of sinful people, the lust

Ge 3: 14 You will **c** on your belly and you

CREATE* (CREATED CREATES CREATING
CREATION CREATIONS CREATOR)
Ps 51: 10 **C** in me a pure heart, O God,
Isa 4: 5 the LORD will **c** over all of Mount
45: 7 I bring prosperity and disaster;
45: 7 I bring prosperity and disaster;
45: 18 he did not **c** it to be empty,
65: 17 I will **c** new heavens and a new
65: 18 and rejoice forever in what I will **c**,
65: 18 for I will **c** Jerusalem to be a delight
Jer 31: 22 The LORD will **c** a new thing
Mal 2: 10 Did not one God **c** us? Why do we
Eph 2: 15 His purpose was to **c** in himself one

CREATED* (CREATE)
Ge 1: 1 In the beginning God **c** the heavens
1: 21 So God **c** the great creatures
1: 27 So God **c** human beings in his own
1: 27 in the image of God he **c** them;
1: 27 male and female he **c** them.
2: 4 and the earth when they were **c**,
5: 1 When God **c** human beings,
5: 2 He **c** them male and female
5: 2 And when they were **c**, he called
6: 7 the earth the human race I have **c**—
Dt 4: 32 the day God **c** human beings
Ps 89: 12 You **c** the north and the south;
89: 47 futility you have **c** all humanity!
102: 18 a people not yet **c** may praise
104: 30 they are **c**, and you renew the face
139: 13 For you **c** my inmost being;
148: 5 for at his command they were **c**,
Ecc 7: 29 God **c** humankind upright, but they
Isa 40: 26 to the heavens: Who **c** all these?
41: 20 that the Holy One of Israel has **c** it.
42: 5 he who **c** the heavens and stretched
43: 1 he who **c** you, Jacob, he who
43: 7 my name, whom I **c** for my glory,
45: 8 I, the LORD, have **c** it.
45: 12 the earth and **c** human beings on it.
45: 18 he who **c** the heavens, he is God;
48: 7 They are **c** now, and not long ago;
54: 16 it is I who **c** the blacksmith who
54: 16 it is I who have **c** the destroyer
57: 16 the very people I have **c**.
Eze 21: 30 In the place where you were **c**,
28: 13 day you were **c** they were prepared.
28: 15 day you were **c** till wickedness was
Mk 13: 19 when God **c** the world, until now—
Ro 1: 25 and served **c** things rather than
1Co 11: 9 neither was man **c** for woman,
Eph 2: 10 **c** in Christ Jesus to do good works,
3: 9 hidden in God, who **c** all things.
4: 24 the new self, **c** to be like God in true
Col 1: 16 For in him all things were **c**:
1: 16 all things have been **c** through him
1Ti 4: 3 which God **c** to be received
4: 4 For everything God **c** is good,
Heb 12: 27 that is, **c** things—so that what
Jas 1: 18 be a kind of firstfruits of all he **c**.
Rev 4: 11 for you **c** all things, and by your will they
were **c**
10: 6 who **c** the heavens and all that is

CREATES* (CREATE)
Am 4: 13 the mountains, who **c** the wind,

CREATING* (CREATE)
Ge 2: 3 all the work of **c** that he had done.
Isa 57: 19 **c** praise on the lips of the mourners

CREATION* (CREATE)
Ps 96: 13 Let all **c** rejoice before the LORD,
Mt 13: 35 I will utter things hidden since the **c**
25: 34 for you since the **c** of the world.
Mk 10: 6 of God 'made them male
16: 15 preach the gospel to all **c**.
Jn 17: 24 because you loved me before the **c**
Ro 1: 20 For since the **c** of the world God's
8: 19 The **c** waits in eager expectation
8: 20 For the **c** was subjected
8: 21 that the **c** itself will be liberated
8: 22 the whole **c** has been groaning as
8: 39 nor anything else in all **c**, will be
2Co 5: 17 is in Christ, the new **c** has come:
Gal 6: 15 what counts is the new **c**.
Eph 1: 4 us in him before the **c** of the world
Col 1: 15 God, the firstborn over all **c**.
Heb 4: 3 work has been finished since the **c**
4: 13 Nothing in all **c** is hidden
9: 11 that is to say, is not a part of this **c**.

Heb 9: 26 suffer many times since the **c**
1Pe 1: 20 He was chosen before the **c**
2Pe 3: 4 as it has since the beginning of **c**."
Rev 3: 14 true witness, the ruler of God's **c**.
13: 8 was slain from the **c** of the world.
17: 8 the **c** of the world will be astonished

CREATIONS* (CREATE)
Hab 2: 18 who make them trust in their own **c**;

CREATOR* (CREATE)
Ge 14: 19 Most High, **C** of heaven and earth.
14: 22 Most High, **C** of heaven and earth,
Dt 32: 6 your **C**, who made you and formed
Ecc 12: 1 Remember your **C** in the days
Isa 27: 11 and their **C** shows them no favor.
40: 28 the **C** of the ends of the earth.
43: 15 Holy One, Israel's **C**, your King."
Mt 19: 4 at the beginning the **C** 'made them
Ro 1: 25 created things rather than the **C**—
Col 3: 10 in knowledge in the image of its **C**.
1Pe 4: 19 themselves to their faithful **C**

CREATURE (CREATURES)
Lev 17: 11 For the life of a **c** is in the blood,
17: 14 the life of every **c** is its blood.
17: 14 must not eat the blood of any **c**,
Ps 136: 25 He gives food to every **c**.
Eze 1: 15 on the ground beside each **c** with its
Rev 4: 7 The first living **c** was like a lion,

CREATURES (CREATURE)
Ge 6: 19 bring into the ark two of all living **c**,
8: 21 again will I destroy all living **c**, as I
Ps 104: 24 the earth is full of your **c**.
Eze 1: 5 was what looked like four living **c**.

CREDIT (CREDITED CREDITOR CREDITS)
Lk 6: 33 good to you, what **c** is that to you?
Ro 4: 24 to whom God will **c** righteousness—
1Pe 2: 20 it to your **c** if you receive a beating

CREDITED
Ge 15: 6 and he **c** it to him as righteousness.
Ps 106: 31 This was **c** to him as righteousness
Eze 18: 20 of the righteous will be **c** to them,
Ro 4: 3 it was **c** to him as righteousness."
4: 4 their wages are not **c** to them as
4: 5 their faith is **c** as righteousness.
4: 9 Abraham's faith was **c** to him as
4: 23 The words "it was **c** to him" were
Gal 3: 6 it was **c** to him as righteousness."
Php 4: 17 is that more be **c** to your account.
Jas 2: 23 it was **c** to him as righteousness,"

CREDITOR (CREDIT)
Dt 15: 2 Every **c** shall cancel any loan they

CREDITS* (CREDIT)
Ro 4: 6 to whom God **c** righteousness apart

CRETANS (CRETE)
Tit 1: 12 "**C** are always liars, evil brutes,

CRETE (CRETANS)
Ac 27: 12 This was a harbor in **C**, facing both

CRIED (CRY)
Ex 2: 23 groaned in their slavery and **c** out,
14: 10 terrified and **c** out to the LORD.
Nu 20: 16 but when we **c** out to the LORD,
Jos 24: 7 But they **c** to the LORD for help,
Jdg 3: 9 But when they **c** out to the LORD,
3: 15 Again the Israelites **c**
4: 3 they **c** to the LORD for help.
6: 6 the Israelites that they **c**
10: 12 you and you **c** to me for help, did I
1Sa 7: 9 He **c** out to the LORD on Israel's
12: 8 they **c** to the LORD for help,
12: 10 They **c** out to the LORD and said,
Ps 18: 6 I **c** to my God for help.

CRIMINALS
Lk 23: 32 both **c**, were also led out with him

CRIMSON
Isa 1: 18 though they are red as **c**, they shall
63: 1 with his garments stained **c**?

CRIPPLED
Mk 9: 45 to enter life **c** than to have two feet

CRISIS*
1Co 7: 26 Because of the present **c**, I think

CRITICISM*
2Co 8: 20 want to avoid any **c** of the way we

CROOKED*
Dt 32: 5 they are a warped and **c** generation.
Ps 125: 5 to **c** ways the LORD will banish

Pr 2: 15 whose paths are c and who are
8: 8 none of them is c or perverse.
10: 9 whoever takes c paths will be found
Ecc 1: 15 What is c cannot be straightened;
7: 13 can straighten what he has made c?
Isa 59: 8 They have turned them into c roads;
La 3: 9 he has made my paths c.
Lk 3: 5 The c roads shall become straight,
Php 2: 15 fault in a warped and c generation."

CROP (CROPS)
Mt 13: 8 good soil, where it produced a c—
21: 41 his share of the c at harvest time."

CROPS (CROP)
Pr 3: 9 with the firstfruits of all your c;
10: 5 He who gathers c in summer is
28: 3 like a driving rain that leaves no c.
2Ti 2: 6 the first to receive a share of the c.

CROSS (CROSSED CROSSING)
Dt 4: 21 swore that I would not c the Jordan
12: 10 But you will c the Jordan and settle
Mt 10: 38 Whoever does not take up their c
16: 24 and take up their c and follow me.
Mk 8: 34 and take up their c and follow me.
Lk 9: 23 take up their c daily and follow me.
14: 27 whoever does not carry their c
Jn 19: 17 Carrying his own c, he went
Ac 2: 23 him to death by nailing him to the c.
5: 30 you killed by hanging him on a c.
1Co 1: 17 lest the c of Christ be emptied of its
1: 18 the message of the c is foolishness
Gal 5: 11 offense of the c has been abolished.
6: 12 being persecuted for the c of Christ.
6: 14 in the c of our Lord Jesus Christ,
Eph 2: 16 both of them to God through the c,
Php 2: 8 even death on a c!
3: 18 live as enemies of the c of Christ.
Col 1: 20 through his blood, shed on the c.
2: 14 has taken it away, nailing it to the c.
2: 15 triumphing over them by the c.
Heb 12: 2 joy set before him he endured the c,
1Pe 2: 24 bore our sins" in his body on the c,

CROSSED (CROSS)
Jos 4: 7 When it c the Jordan, the waters
Jn 5: 24 but has c over from death to life.

CROSSING (CROSS)
Ge 48: 14 and c his arms, he put his left hand

CROSSROADS (ROAD)
Jer 6: 16 "Stand at the c and look;

CROUCHING
Ge 4: 7 what is right, sin is c at your door;

CROWD (CROWDS)
Ex 23: 2 "Do not follow the c in doing

CROWDS (CROWD)
Mt 9: 36 When he saw the c, he had

CROWED (CROWS)
Mt 26: 74 Immediately a rooster c.

CROWN (CROWNED CROWNS)
Pr 4: 9 and present you with a glorious c."
10: 6 Blessings c the head
12: 4 noble character is her husband's c,
16: 31 Gray hair is a c of splendor;
17: 6 Children's children are a c
Isa 35: 10 everlasting joy will c their heads.
51: 11 everlasting joy will c their heads.
61: 3 on them a c of beauty instead
62: 3 You will be a c of splendor
Eze 16: 12 ears and a beautiful c on your head.
Zec 9: 16 sparkle in his land like jewels in a c.
Mt 27: 29 then twisted together a c of thorns
Mk 15: 17 then twisted together a c of thorns
Jn 19: 2 The soldiers twisted together a c
19: 5 came out wearing the c of thorns
1Co 9: 25 do it to get a c that will not last,
9: 25 do it to get a c that will last forever.
Php 4: 1 my joy and c, stand firm in the Lord
1Th 2: 19 the c in which we will glory
2Ti 2: 5 not receive the victor's c except
4: 8 store for me the c of righteousness.
Jas 1: 12 they will receive the c of life
1Pe 5: 4 you will receive the c of glory
Rev 2: 10 will give you life as your victor's c.
3: 11 so that no one will take your c.
14: 14 of man with a c of gold on his head

CROWNED* (CROWN)
Ps 8: 5 beings and c them with glory
Pr 14: 18 the prudent are c with knowledge.

SS 3: 11 which his mother c him on the day
Heb 2: 7 you c them with glory and honor
2: 9 now c with glory and honor because

CROWNS (CROWN)
Ps 103: 4 life from the pit and c you with love
149: 4 he c the humble with victory.
Rev 4: 4 and had c of gold on their heads.
4: 10 They lay their c before the throne
12: 3 ten horns and seven c on its heads.
19: 12 fire, and on his head are many c.

CROWS (CROWED)
Mt 26: 34 night, before the rooster c, you will

CRUCIFIED* (CRUCIFY)
Mt 20: 19 to be mocked and flogged and c.
26: 2 Man will be handed over to be c."
27: 26 and handed him over to be c.
27: 35 When they had c him, they divided
27: 38 Two rebels were c with him,
27: 44 the same way the rebels who were c
28: 5 are looking for Jesus, who was c.
Mk 15: 15 and handed him over to be c.
15: 24 And they c him. Dividing up his
15: 25 in the morning when they c him.
15: 27 They c two rebels with him,
15: 32 Those c with him also heaped
Lk 6 for Jesus the Nazarene, who was c.
23: 23 insistently demanded that he be c,
23: 33 called the Skull, they c him there,
24: 7 be c and on the third day be raised
24: 20 sentenced to death, and they c him;
Jn 19: 16 handed him over to them to be c.
19: 18 Here they c him, and with him two
19: 20 where Jesus was c was near the city,
19: 23 When the soldiers c Jesus, they took
19: 32 the first man who had been c
19: 41 At the place where Jesus was c,
Ac 2: 36 Jesus, whom you c, both Lord
4: 10 whom you c but whom God raised
Ro 6: 6 that our old self was c with him so
1Co 1: 13 Was Paul c for you?
1: 23 but we preach Christ c:
2: 2 you except Jesus Christ and him c.
2: 8 they would not have c the Lord
2Co 13: 4 to be sure, he was c in weakness,
Gal 2: 20 I have been c with Christ and I no
3: 1 Christ was clearly portrayed as c.
5: 24 Christ Jesus have c the sinful nature
6: 14 which the world has been c to me,
Rev 11: 8 Egypt, where also their Lord was c.

CRUCIFY* (CRUCIFIED CRUCIFYING)
Mt 23: 34 Some of them you will kill and c;
27: 22 They all answered, "C him!"
27: 23 shouted all the louder, "C him!"
27: 31 Then they led him away to c him.
Mk 15: 13 "C him!" they shouted.
15: 14 shouted all the louder, "C him!"
15: 20 Then they led him out to c him.
Lk 23: 21 But they kept shouting, "C him!
Jn 19: 6 saw him, they shouted, "C! C!"
19: 6 "You take him and c him.
19: 10 either to free you or to c you?"
19: 15 Take him away! C him!" "Shall I c
CRUCIFYING* (CRUCIFY)
Heb 6: 6 their loss they are c the Son of God

CRUSH (CRUSHED)
Ge 3: 15 he will c your head, and you will
Isa 53: 10 it was the LORD's will to c him
Ro 16: 20 peace will soon c Satan under your

CRUSHED (CRUSH)
Ps 34: 18 and saves those who are c in spirit.
Pr 17: 22 but a c spirit dries up the bones.
18: 14 but a c spirit who can bear?
Isa 53: 5 he was c for our iniquities;
2Co 4: 8 pressed on every side, but not c;

CRY (CRIED)
Ex 22: 23 and their c for help because of their
Ps 5: 2 Hear my c for help, my King
34: 15 and his ears are attentive to their c.
40: 1 he turned to me and heard my c.
130: 1 Out of the depths I c to you,
Pr 21: 13 to the c of the poor will also c
La 2: 18 The hearts of the people c
Hab 2: 11 The stones of the wall will c out,
Lk 19: 40 keep quiet, the stones will c out."

CULMINATION
Ro 10: 4 Christ is the c of the law

CUNNING
2Co 11: 3 was deceived by the serpent's c,
Eph 4: 14 by the c and craftiness of people

CUP
Ps 23: 5 my head with oil; my c overflows.
Isa 51: 22 of your hand the c that made you
51: 22 from that c, the goblet of my wrath,
Mt 10: 42 anyone gives even a c of cold water
20: 22 "Can you drink the c I am going
23: 25 You clean the outside of the c
23: 26 First clean the inside of the c
26: 27 Then he took the c, and when he
26: 39 may this c be taken from me.
26: 42 for this c to be taken away unless I
Mk 9: 41 anyone who gives you a c of water
10: 38 "Can you drink the c I drink or be
10: 39 "You will drink the c I drink and be
14: 23 Then he took the c, and when he
14: 36 Take this c from me.
Lk 11: 39 Pharisees clean the outside of the c
22: 17 After taking the c, he gave thanks
22: 20 after the supper he took the c,
22: 20 "This c is the new covenant in my
22: 42 you are willing, take this c from me;
Jn 18: 11 Shall I not drink the c the Father has
1Co 10: 16 Is not the c of thanksgiving
10: 21 You cannot drink the c of the Lord and
the c of demons too;
11: 25 after supper he took the c, saying,
11: 25 "This c is the new covenant in my

CUPBEARER
Ge 40: 1 the c and the baker of the king
Ne 1: 11 of this man." I was c to the king.

CURE (CURED)
Jer 17: 9 above all things and beyond c.
30: 15 wound, your pain that has no c?
Hos 5: 13 But he is not able to c you, not able
Lk 9: 1 out all demons and to c diseases,

CURED (CURE)
Lk 6: 18 troubled by evil spirits were c,

CURSE (ACCURSED CURSED CURSES CURSING)
Ge 4: 11 Now you are under a c and driven
8: 21 again will I c the ground because
12: 3 and whoever curses you I will c;
Dt 11: 26 you today a blessing and a c—
11: 28 the c if you disobey the commands
21: 23 is hung on a pole is under God's c.
23: 5 turned the c into a blessing for you,
Job 1: 11 he will surely c you to your face."
2: 5 he will surely c you to your face."
2: 9 C God and die!"
Ps 109: 28 While they c, may you bless;
Pr 3: 33 The LORD's c is on the house
20: 20 If you c your father or mother,
Jer 42: 18 a c and an object of reproach.
44: 12 a c and an object of reproach.
Mal 2: 2 on you, and I will c your blessings.
Lk 6: 28 bless those who c you,
Ro 12: 14 bless and do not c.
Gal 1: 8 let that person be under God's c!
3: 10 on observing the law are under a c,
3: 13 c of the law by becoming a c for us,
Jas 3: 9 and with it we c human beings,
Rev 22: 3 No longer will there be any c.

CURSED (CURSE)
Ge 3: 14 "C is the ground because of you;
Dt 27: 15 "C is anyone who makes an idol—
27: 16 "C is anyone who dishonors their
27: 17 "C is anyone who moves their
27: 18 "C is anyone who leads the blind
27: 19 "C is anyone who withholds justice
27: 20 "C is anyone who sleeps with his
27: 21 "C is anyone who has sexual
27: 22 "C is anyone who sleeps with his
27: 23 "C is anyone who sleeps with his
27: 24 "C is anyone who kills their
27: 25 "C is anyone who accepts a bribe
27: 26 "C is anyone who does not uphold
Pr 24: 24 be c by peoples and denounced by
Jer 17: 5 "C are those who trust in mortals,
Mal 1: 14 "C is the cheat who has
Ro 9: 3 I could wish that I myself were c
1Co 4: 12 When we are c, we bless;
12: 3 "Jesus be c," and no one can say,
Gal 3: 10 "C is everyone who does not
3: 13 "C is everyone who is hung

CURSES (CURSE)
Ex 21: 17 "Anyone who c their father

Lev 20: 9 " 'Anyone who **c** their father
Nu 5: 23 priest is to write these **c** on a scroll
Jos 8: 34 the blessings and the **c**—just as it is
Pr 28: 27 their eyes to them receive many **c**.
Mt 15: 4 and 'Anyone who **c** their father
Mk 7: 10 and, 'Anyone who **c** their father

CURSING (CURSE)
Ps 109: 18 He wore **c** as his garment;
Ro 3: 14 "Their mouths are full of **c**
Jas 3: 10 the same mouth come praise and **c**.

CURTAIN
Ex 26: 31 "Make a **c** of blue,
26: 33 Hang the **c** from the clasps
26: 33 The **c** will separate the Holy Place
Mt 27: 51 that moment the **c** of the temple was
Mk 15: 38 The **c** of the temple was torn in two
Lk 23: 45 the **c** of the temple was torn in two.
Heb 6: 19 the inner sanctuary behind the **c**,
9: 3 Behind the second **c** was a room
10: 20 way opened for us through the **c**,

CUSTODY
Gal 3: 23 we were held in **c** under the law,

CUSTOM
Job 1: 5 This was Job's regular **c**.
Mk 10: 1 and as was his **c**, he taught them.
Lk 4: 16 into the synagogue, as was his **c**.
Ac 17: 2 As was his **c**, Paul went

CUT
Lev 19: 27 " 'Do not **c** the hair at the sides
21: 5 of their beards or **c** their bodies.
1Ki 3: 25 "**C** the living child in two and give
Isa 51: 1 to the rock from which you were **c**
53: 8 For he was **c** off from the land
Da 2: 45 of the vision of the rock **c**
Mt 3: 10 produce good fruit will be **c** down
24: 22 "If those days had not been **c** short,
1Co 11: 6 for a woman to have her hair **c** off

CYMBAL* (CYMBALS)
1Co 13: 1 a resounding gong or a clanging **c**.

CYMBALS (CYMBAL)
1Ch 15: 16 lyres, harps and **c**,
2Ch 5: 12 dressed in fine linen and playing **c**,
Ps 150: 5 of **c**, praise him with resounding **c**.

CYRUS
Persian king who allowed exiles to return (2Ch 36:22–Ezr 1:8), to rebuild temple (Ezr 5:13–6:14), as appointed by the LORD (Isa 44:28–45:13).

DAGON
Jdg 16: 23 offer a great sacrifice to **D** their god
1Sa 5: 2 Dagon's temple and set it beside **D**.

DAMASCUS
Ac 9: 3 As he neared **D** on his journey,

DAN
1. Son of Jacob by Bilhah (Ge 30:4–6; 35:25; 46:23). Tribe of blessed (Ge 49:16–17; Dt 33:22), numbered (Nu 1:39; 26:43), allotted land (Jos 19:40–48; Eze 48:1), failed to fully possess (Jdg 1:34–35), failed to support Deborah (Jdg 5:17), possessed Laish/Dan (Jdg 18).
2. Northernmost city in Israel (Ge 14:14; Jdg 18; 20:1).

DANCE (DANCED DANCING)
Ecc 3: 4 a time to mourn and a time to **d**,
Mt 11: 17 the pipe for you, and you did not **d**;

DANCED (DANCE)
Mk 6: 22 daughter of Herodias came in and **d**,

DANCING (DANCE)
2Sa 6: 14 David was **d** before the LORD
Ps 30: 11 You turned my wailing into **d**;
149: 3 Let them praise his name with **d**

DANGER
Pr 22: 3 The prudent see **d** and take refuge,
27: 12 The prudent see **d** and take refuge,
Mt 5: 22 will be in **d** of the fire of hell.
Ro 8: 35 famine or nakedness or **d** or sword?
2Co 11: 26 I have been in **d** from rivers, in **d**

DANIEL
1. Hebrew exile to Babylon, name changed to Belteshazzar (Da 1:6–7). Refused to eat unclean food (Da 1:8–21). Interpreted Nebuchadnezzar's dreams (Da 2; 4), writing on the wall (Da 5). Thrown into lion's den (Da 6). Visions of (Da 7–12).
2. Son of David (1Ch 3:1).

DARIUS
1. King of Persia (Ezr 4:5), allowed rebuilding of temple (Ezr 5–6).
2. Mede who conquered Babylon (Da 5:31).

DARK (DARKENED DARKENS DARKEST DARKNESS)
Ps 18: 9 d clouds were under his feet.
SS 1: 6 Do not stare at me because I am **d**,
Jn 12: 35 in the **d** do not know where they are
Ro 2: 19 a light for those who are in the **d**,
2Pe 1: 19 as to a light shining in a **d** place,

DARKENED (DARK)
Joel 2: 10 the sun and moon are **d**,
Mt 24: 29 of those days " 'the sun will be **d**,
Ro 1: 21 and their foolish hearts were **d**.
Eph 4: 18 They are **d** in their understanding

DARKENS* (DARK)
Am 5: 8 into dawn and **d** day into night,

DARKEST* (DARK)
Ps 23: 4 I walk through the **d** valley,
88: 6 the lowest pit, in the **d** depths.

DARKNESS (DARK)
Ge 1: 2 d was over the surface of the deep,
1: 4 he separated the light from the **d**.
Ex 10: 22 total **d** covered all Egypt for three
20: 21 approached the thick **d** where God
2Sa 22: 29 the LORD turns my **d** into light.
Ps 18: 28 my God turns my **d** into light.
91: 6 the pestilence that stalks in the **d**,
112: 4 Even in **d** light dawns
139: 12 even the **d** will not be dark to you;
Pr 4: 19 way of the wicked is like deep **d**;
Isa 5: 20 who put **d** for light and light for **d**,
42: 16 I will turn the **d** into light before
45: 7 I form the light and create **d**, I bring
58: 10 then your light will rise in the **d**,
61: 1 and release from **d** for the prisoners,
Joel 2: 31 The sun will be turned to **d**
Mt 4: 16 living in **d** have seen a great light;
6: 23 within you is **d**, how great is that **d**!
Lk 11: 34 your body also is full of **d**.
23: 44 **d** came over the whole land until
Jn 1: 5 The light shines in the **d**, and the **d**
3: 19 but people loved **d** instead of light
Ac 2: 20 The sun will be turned to **d**
2Co 4: 6 "Let light shine out of **d**," made his
6: 14 fellowship can light have with **d**?
Eph 5: 8 For you were once **d**, but now you
5: 11 to do with the fruitless deeds of **d**,
1Pe 2: 9 out of **d** into his wonderful light.
2Pe 2: 17 Blackest **d** is reserved for them.
1Jn 1: 5 in him there is no **d** at all.
2: 9 a fellow believer are still in the **d**.
Jude : 6 these he has kept in **d**,
: 13 whom blackest **d** has been reserved

DASH
Ps 2: 9 you will **d** them to pieces like

DAUGHTER (DAUGHTERS)
Ex 2: 10 she took him to Pharaoh's **d**
Jdg 11: 40 commemorate the **d** of Jephthah
Est 2: 7 had taken her as his own **d** when her
Ps 9: 14 your praises in the gates of **D** Zion,
137: 8 **D** Babylon, doomed to destruction,
Isa 62: 11 "Say to **D** Zion, 'See, your Savior
Zec 9: 9 Rejoice greatly, **D** Zion! Shout,
Mk 5: 34 He said to her, "**D**, your faith has
7: 29 the demon has left your **d**."

DAUGHTERS (DAUGHTER)
Ge 6: 2 God saw that these **d** were beautiful,
19: 36 So both of Lot's **d** became pregnant
Nu 36: 10 So Zelophehad's **d** did as
Joel 2: 28 Your sons and **d** will prophesy,

DAVID
Son of Jesse (Ru 4:17–22; 1Ch 2:13–15), ancestor of Jesus (Mt 1:1–17; Lk 3:31). Wives and children (1Sa 18; 25:39–44; 2Sa 3:2–5; 5:13–16; 11:27; 1Ch 3:1–9).
Anointed king by Samuel (1Sa 16:1–13). Musician to Saul (1Sa 16:14–23; 18:10). Killed Goliath (1Sa 17). Relation with Jonathan (1Sa 18:1–4; 19–20; 23:16–18; 2Sa 1). Disfavor of Saul (1Sa 18:6–23:29). Spared Saul's life (1Sa 24; 26). Among Philistines (1Sa 21:10–14; 27–30). Lament for Saul and Jonathan (2Sa 1).
Anointed king of Judah (2Sa 2:1–11). Conflict with house of Saul (2Sa 2–4). Anointed king of Israel (2Sa 5:1–4; 1Ch 11:1–3). Conquered Jerusalem (2Sa 5:6–10; 1Ch 11:4–9). Brought ark to Jerusalem (2Sa 6; 1Ch 13; 15–16). The LORD promised eternal dynasty (2Sa 7; 1Ch 17; Ps 132). Showed kindness to Mephibosheth (2Sa 9). Adultery with Bathsheba, murder of Uriah (2Sa 11–12). Son Amnon raped daughter Tamar; killed by Absalom (2Sa 13). Absalom's revolt (2Sa 14–17); death (2Sa 18). Sheba's revolt (2Sa 20). Victories: Philistines (2Sa 5:17–25; 1Ch 14:8–17; 2Sa 21:15–22; 1Ch 20:4–8), Ammonites (2Sa 10; 1Ch 19), various (2Sa 8; 1Ch 18). Mighty men (2Sa 23:8–39; 1Ch 11–12). Punished for numbering army (2Sa 24; 1Ch 21). Appointed Solomon king (1Ki 1:28–2:9). Prepared for building of temple (1Ch 22–29). Last words (2Sa 23:1–7). Death (1Ki 2:10–12; 1Ch 29:28).
Psalmist (Mt 22:43–45), musician (Am 6:5), prophet (2Sa 23:2–7; Ac 1:16; 2:30).
Psalms of: (2 Ac 4:25), 3–32, 34–41, 51–65, 68–70, 86, 95 (Heb 4:7), 101, 103, 108–110, 122, 124, 131, 133, 138–145.

DAWN (DAWNED DAWNS)
Ps 37: 6 righteous reward shine like the **d**,
Isa 14: 12 heaven, morning star, son of the **d**!
Am 4: 13 to mortals, who turns **d** to darkness,
5: 8 who turns midnight into **d**

DAWNED (DAWN)
Isa 9: 2 land of deep darkness a light has **d**.
Mt 4: 16 the shadow of death a light has **d**."

DAWNS* (DAWN)
Ps 65: 8 where morning **d**, where evening
112: 4 in darkness light **d** for the upright,
Hos 10: 15 When that day **d**, the king of Israel
2Pe 1: 19 until the day **d** and the morning star

DAY (DAYS)
Ge 1: 5 God called the light "**d**,"
1: 5 and there was morning—the first **d**.
1: 8 there was morning—the second **d**.
1: 13 and there was morning—the third **d**.
1: 19 and there was morning—the fourth **d**.
1: 23 and there was morning—the fifth **d**.
1: 31 and there was morning—the sixth **d**.
2: 2 so on the seventh **d** he rested
8: 22 **d** and night will never cease."
Ex 16: 30 the people rested on the seventh **d**.
20: 8 "Remember the Sabbath **d**
Lev 16: 30 on this **d** atonement will be made
23: 28 **d**, because it is the **D** of Atonement,
Nu 14: 14 before them in a pillar of cloud by **d**
Jos 1: 8 meditate on it **d** and night,
2Ki 7: 9 This is a **d** of good news and we are
25: 30 **D** by **d** the king gave Jehoiachin
1Ch 16: 23 proclaim his salvation **d** after **d**.
Ne 8: 18 **D** after **d**, from the first **d** to the last,
Ps 84: 10 Better is one **d** in your courts than
96: 2 proclaim his salvation **d** after **d**.
118: 24 The LORD has done it this very **d**;
Pr 27: 1 do not know what a **d** may bring.
Isa 13: 9 a cruel **d**, with wrath and fierce
Jer 46: 10 But that **d** belongs to the Lord,
50: 31 "for your **d** has come, the time
Eze 30: 2 and say, "Alas for that **d**!"
Joel 1: 15 Alas for that **d**! For the **d**
2: 31 great and dreadful **d** of the LORD.
Am 3: 14 "On the **l** punish Israel for her
5: 20 Will not the **d** of the LORD be
Ob : 15 "The **d** of the LORD is near for all
: 15 The great **d** of the LORD is near—
Zep 1: 14 The great **d** of the LORD is near—
Zec 2: 11 be joined with the LORD in that **d**
14: 1 A **d** of the LORD is coming,
14: 7 It will be a unique **d**—a **d** known
Mal 4: 5 dreadful **d** of the LORD comes.
Mt 24: 38 up to the **d** Noah entered the ark;
Lk 11: 3 Give us each **d** our daily bread.
17: 24 his **d** will be like the lightning,
Ac 5: 42 **D** after **d**, in the temple courts
17: 11 examined the Scriptures every **d**
17: 17 as well as in the marketplace **d** by **d**
5: 5 others consider every **d** alike.
1Co 5: 5 may be saved on the **d** of the Lord.
2Co 4: 16 we are being renewed **d** by **d**.
11: 25 a night and a **d** in the open sea,
1Th 5: 2 the **d** of the Lord will come like
5: 4 that this **d** should surprise you like
2Th 2: 2 the **d** of the Lord has already come.
Heb 7: 27 not need to offer sacrifices **d** after **d**,
2Pe 3: 8 With the Lord a **d** is like a thousand
3: 10 the **d** of the Lord will come like
Rev 6: 17 the great **d** of their wrath has come,
16: 14 on the great **d** of God Almighty.

DAYS (DAY)

Dt 17: 19   he is to read it all the **d** of his life so
   32: 7   Remember the **d** of old;
Ps 23: 6   love will follow me all the **d** of my
   34: 12   life and desires to see many good **d**,
   39: 5   You have made my **d** a mere
   90: 10   Our **d** may come to seventy years,
   90: 12   Teach us to number our **d**, that we
  103: 15   for mortals, their **d** are like grass,
  128: 5   of Jerusalem all the **d** of your life.
Pr 31: 12   good, not harm, all the **d** of her life.
Ecc 9: 9   all the **d** of this meaningless life
   12: 1   your Creator in the **d** of your youth,
Isa 38: 20   stringed instruments all the **d** of our
Da 7: 9   and the Ancient of **D** took his seat.
   7: 13   He approached the Ancient of **D**
   7: 22   until the Ancient of **D** came
Hos 3: 5   and to his blessings in the last **d**.
Joel 2: 29   I will pour out my Spirit in those **d**.
Mic 4: 1   In the last **d** the mountain
Lk 19: 43   The **d** will come on you when your
Ac 2: 17   " 'In the last **d**, God says, I will
2Ti 3: 1   will be terrible times in the last **d**.
Heb 1: 2   in these last **d** he has spoken to us
2Pe 3: 3   that in the last **d** scoffers will come,

DAZZLING*

Da 2: 31   an enormous, **d** statue,
Mk 9: 3   His clothes became **d** white,

DEACON* (DEACONS)

Ro 16: 1   our sister Phoebe, a **d** of the church
1Ti 3: 12   A **d** must be faithful to his wife

DEACONS* (DEACON)

Php 1: 1   together with the overseers and **d**:
1Ti 3: 8   **d** are to be worthy of respect,
   3: 10   against them, let them serve as **d**.

DEAD (DIE)

Lev 17: 15   who eats anything found **d** or torn
Dt 18: 11   or spiritist or who consults the **d**.
Ps 49: 15   redeem me from the realm of the **d**;
Isa 8: 19   Why consult the **d** on behalf
Mt 8: 22   and let the **d** bury their own **d**."
   28: 7   'He has risen from the **d** and is
Lk 15: 24   For this son of mine was **d** and is
   24: 46   and rise from the **d** on the third day,
Ac 2: 27   not abandon me to the realm of the **d**,
Ro 6: 11   count yourselves **d** to sin but alive
1Co 15: 29   those do who are baptized for the **d**?
Eph 2: 1   you were **d** in your transgressions
1Th 4: 16   and the **d** in Christ will rise first.
Jas 2: 17   is not accompanied by action, is **d**.
   2: 26   is **d**, so faith without deeds is **d**.
Rev 14: 13   Blessed are the **d** who die
   20: 12   And I saw the **d**, great and small,

DEAR* (DEARER)

2Sa 1: 26   you were very **d** to me.
Ps 102: 14   her stones are **d** to your servants;
Jer 31: 20   is not Ephraim my **d** son, the child
Ac 15: 25   to you with our **d** friends Barnabas
Ro 12: 19   Do not take revenge, my **d** friends,
   16: 5   Greet my **d** friend Epenetus,
   16: 8   Ampliatus, my **d** friend in the Lord.
   16: 9   in Christ, and my **d** friend Stachys.
   16: 12   Greet my **d** friend Persis,
1Co 6: 14   but to warn you as my **d** children.
   10: 14   Therefore, my **d** friends,
   15: 58   my **d** brothers and sisters,
2Co 1: 1   we have these promises, **d** friends,
   12: 19   and everything we do, **d** friends,
Gal 4: 19   My **d** children, for whom I am again
Eph 6: 21   the **d** brother and faithful servant
Php 2: 12   Therefore, my **d** friends, as you
   4: 1   in the Lord in this way, **d** friends!
Col 1: 7   Epaphras, our **d** fellow servant,
   4: 7   He is a **d** brother, a faithful minister
   4: 9   our faithful and **d** brother, who is
   4: 14   Our **d** friend Luke, the doctor,
1Th 4: 10   we urge you, **d** friends, to do so more
1Ti 6: 2   better because their masters are **d**
2Ti 1: 2   To Timothy, my **d** son:
Phm : 1   To Philemon our **d** friend
   : 16   better than a slave, as a **d** brother.
   : 16   He is very **d** to me but even dearer
Heb 6: 9   though we speak like this, **d** friends,
Jas 1: 16   deceived, my **d** brothers and sisters.
   1: 19   My **d** brothers and sisters, take note
   2: 5   Listen, my **d** brothers and sisters:
1Pe 2: 11   **D** friends, I urge you, as foreigners
   4: 12   **D** friends, do not be surprised
2Pe 3: 1   **D** friends, this is now my second

2Pe 3: 8   not forget this one thing, **d** friends:
   3: 14   So then, **d** friends, since you are
   3: 15   just as our **d** brother Paul also wrote
   3: 17   Therefore, **d** friends, since you have
1Jn 2: 1   My **d** children, I write this to you so
   2: 7   **D** friends, I am not writing you
   2: 12   I am writing to you, **d** children,
   2: 14   I write to you, **d** children, because you
   2: 18   **D** children, this is the last hour;
   2: 28   And now, **d** children,
   3: 2   **D** friends, now we are children
   3: 7   **D** children, do not let anyone lead
   3: 18   **D** children, let us not love
   3: 21   **D** friends, if our hearts do not
   4: 1   **D** friends, do not believe every
   4: 4   You, **d** children, are from God
   4: 7   **D** friends, let us love one another,
   4: 11   **D** friends, since God so loved us,
   5: 21   **D** children, keep yourselves
2Jn : 5   And now, **d** lady, I am not writing
3Jn : 1   To my **d** friend Gaius, whom I love
   : 2   **D** friend, I pray that you may enjoy
   : 5   **D** friend, you are faithful in what
   : 11   **D** friend, do not imitate what is evil
Jude : 3   **D** friends, although I was very eager
   : 17   But, **d** friends, remember what
   : 20   But you, **d** friends, by building

DEARER* (DEAR)

Phm : 16   is very dear to me but even **d** to you,

DEATH (DIE)

Ex 21: 12   a fatal blow is to be put to **d**.
Nu 35: 16   the murderer is to be put to **d**.
Dt 30: 19   that I have set before you life and **d**,
Ru 1: 17   if even **d** separates you and me."
2Ki 4: 40   of God, there is **d** in the pot!"
Job 26: 6   **D** is naked before God;
Ps 44: 22   for your sake we face **d** all day long;
   89: 48   Who can live and not see **d**, or who
  116: 15   the **d** of his faithful
Pr 8: 36   all who hate me love **d**."
   11: 19   those who pursue evil go to their **d**.
   14: 12   be right, but in the end it leads to **d**.
   15: 11   **D** and Destruction lie open before
   16: 25   be right, but in the end it leads to **d**.
   18: 21   tongue has the power of life and **d**,
   19: 18   do not be a willing party to their **d**.
   23: 14   with the rod and save them from **d**.
Ecc 7: 2   for **d** is the destiny of everyone;
Isa 25: 8   he will swallow up **d** forever.
   53: 12   he poured out his life unto **d**,
Eze 18: 23   any pleasure in the **d** of the wicked?
   18: 32   take no pleasure in the **d** of anyone,
   33: 11   no pleasure in the **d** of the wicked,
Da 9: 26   the Anointed One will be put to **d**
Hos 13: 14   Where, O **d**, are your plagues?'
Mt 16: 18   gates of **d** will not overcome it.
Jn 5: 24   but has crossed over from **d** to life.
Ro 4: 25   He was delivered over to **d** for our
   5: 12   and **d** through sin, and in this way **d**
   5: 14   **d** reigned from the time of Adam
   6: 3   Jesus were baptized into his **d**?
   6: 23   For the wages of sin is **d**,
   7: 24   will rescue me from this body of **d**?
   8: 13   the Spirit you put to **d** the misdeeds
   8: 36   your sake we face **d** all day long;
1Co 11: 26   the Lord's **d** until he comes.
   15: 21   For since **d** came through a human
   15: 26   The last enemy to be destroyed is **d**.
   15: 31   I face **d** every day
   15: 55   Where, O **d**, is your sting?"
2Ti 1: 10   Jesus, who has destroyed **d** and has
Heb 2: 14   of him who holds the power of **d**—
1Jn 5: 16   There is a sin that leads to **d**.
Rev 1: 18   And I hold the keys of **d** and Hades.
   2: 11   not be hurt at all by the second **d**.
   20: 6   The second **d** has no power over
   20: 14   Then **d** and Hades were thrown
   20: 14   The lake of fire is the second **d**.
   21: 4   There will be no more **d'**
   21: 8   This is the second **d**."

DEBAUCHERY*

Ro 13: 13   not in sexual immorality and **d**,
2Co 12: 21   and **d** in which they have indulged.
Gal 5: 19   sexual immorality, impurity and **d**;
Eph 5: 18   get drunk on wine, which leads to **d**.
1Pe 4: 3   living in **d**, lust, drunkenness,

DEBORAH*

1. Prophetess who led Israel to victory over Canaanites (Jdg 4–5).
2. Rebekah's nurse (Ge 35:8).

DEBT* (DEBTOR DEBTORS DEBTS INDEBTEDNESS)

Dt 15: 3   you must cancel any **d** one of your
   24: 6   as security for a **d**,
1Sa 22: 2   or in **d** or discontented gathered
Job 24: 9   infant of the poor is seized for a **d**.
Mt 18: 25   that he had be sold to repay the **d**.
   18: 27   canceled the **d** and let him go.
   18: 30   into prison until he could pay the **d**.
   18: 32   said, 'I canceled all that **d** of yours
Lk 7: 43   who had the bigger **d** forgiven."
Ro 13: 8   Let no **d** remain outstanding,
   13: 8   except the continuing **d** to love one

DEBTOR* (DEBT)

Isa 24: 2   as for lender, for **d** as for creditor.

DEBTORS* (DEBT)

Mt 6: 12   as we also have forgiven our **d**.
Lk 16: 5   called in each one of his master's **d**.

DEBTS* (DEBT)

Dt 15: 1   seven years you must cancel **d**.
   15: 2   canceling **d** has been proclaimed.
   15: 9   the year for canceling **d**, is near,"
   31: 10   in the year for canceling **d**,
2Ki 4: 7   "Go, sell the oil and pay your **d**.
Ne 10: 31   the land and will cancel all **d**.
Pr 22: 26   in pledge or puts up security for **d**;
Mt 6: 12   And forgive us our **d**, as we
Lk 7: 42   back, so he forgave the **d** of both.

DECAY*

Ps 16: 10   will you let your faithful one see **d**.
   49: 9   should live on forever and not see **d**.
   49: 14   Their forms will **d** in the grave,
   55: 23   down the wicked into the pit of **d**;
Pr 12: 4   but a disgraceful wife is like **d** in his
Isa 5: 24   so their roots will **d** and their
Hab 3: 16   **d** crept into my bones, and my legs
Ac 2: 27   you will not let your holy one see **d**.
   2: 31   of the dead, nor did his body see **d**.
   13: 34   so that he will never be subject to **d**.
   13: 35   will not let your holy one see **d**.'
   13: 37   raised from the dead did not see **d**.
Ro 8: 21   be liberated from its bondage to **d**

DECEIT (DECEIVE)

Isa 53: 9   nor was any **d** in his mouth.
Da 8: 25   He will cause **d** to prosper, and he
Mk 7: 22   greed, malice, **d**, lewdness, envy,
Jn 1: 47   Israelite in whom there is no **d**."
Ac 13: 10   You are full of all kinds of **d**
Ro 1: 29   envy, murder, strife, **d** and malice.
   3: 13   their tongues practice **d**."
1Pe 2: 1   yourselves of all malice and all **d**,
   2: 22   and no **d** was found in his mouth."

DECEITFUL (DECEIVE)

Jer 17: 9   The heart is **d** above all things
Hos 10: 2   Their heart is **d**, and now they must
Zep 3: 13   A tongue will not be found in
2Co 11: 13   are false apostles, **d** workers,
Eph 4: 14   of people in their **d** scheming.
   4: 22   is being corrupted by its **d** desires;
1Pe 3: 10   evil and your lips from **d** speech.
Rev 21: 27   who does what is shameful or **d**,

DECEITFULNESS* (DECEIVE)

Mt 13: 22   and the **d** of wealth choke the word,
Mk 4: 19   the **d** of wealth and the desires
Heb 3: 13   of you may be hardened by sin's **d**.

DECEIVE (DECEIT DECEITFUL DECEITFULNESS DECEIVED DECEIVER DECEIVERS DECEIVES DECEIVING DECEPTION DECEPTIVE)

Lev 19: 11   " 'Do not **d** one another.
Pr 14: 5   An honest witness does not **d**,
Jer 37: 9   Do not **d** yourselves, thinking,
Zec 13: 4   garment of hair in order to **d**.
Mt 24: 5   am the Messiah,' and will **d** many.
   24: 11   will appear and **d** many people.
   24: 24   great signs and wonders to **d**,
Mk 13: 6   'I am he,' and will **d** many.
   13: 22   and perform signs and wonders to **d**,
Ro 16: 18   flattery they **d** the minds of naive
1Co 3: 18   Do not **d** yourselves. If any of you
Gal 6: 3   you are nothing, you **d** yourselves.
Eph 5: 6   Let no one **d** you with empty words,
Col 2: 4   no one may **d** you by fine-sounding
2Th 2: 3   Don't let anyone **d** you in any way,
Jas 1: 22   to the word, and so **d** yourselves.
   1: 26   **d** themselves, and their religion
1Jn 1: 8   we **d** ourselves and the truth is not
Rev 20: 8   to **d** the nations in the four corners

DECEIVED (DECEIVE)
Ge 3: 13 said, "The serpent d me, and I ate."
Lk 21: 8 "Watch out that you are not d.
1Co 6: 9 Do not be d: Neither the sexually
2Co 11: 3 just as Eve was d by the serpent's
Gal 6: 7 Do not be d: God cannot be
1Ti 2: 14 And Adam was not the one d;
2Ti 3: 13 to worse, deceiving and being d.
Tit 3: 3 d and enslaved by all kinds
Jas 1: 16 Don't be d, my dear brothers
Rev 13: 14 it d the inhabitants of the earth.
  20: 10 And the devil, who d them,

DECEIVER (DECEIVE)
Mt 27: 63 while he was still alive that d said,
2Jn : 7 Any such person is the d

DECEIVERS* (DECEIVE)
Ps 49: 5 when wicked d surround me—
2Jn : 7 Many d, who do not acknowledge

DECEIVES* (DECEIVE)
Pr 26: 19 is one who d a neighbor and says,
Jer 9: 5 Friend d friend, and no one speaks the
Mt 24: 4 "Watch out that no one d you.
Mk 13: 5 "Watch out that no one d you.
Jn 7: 12 Others replied, "No, he d the people."
2Th 2: 10 that wickedness d those who are

DECEIVING* (DECEIVE)
Lev 6: 2 the LORD by d a neighbor
1Ti 4: 1 the faith and follow d spirits
2Ti 3: 13 bad to worse, d and being deceived.
Rev 20: 3 from d the nations anymore until

DECENCY* (DECENTLY)
1Ti 2: 9 modestly, with d and propriety,

DECENTLY* (DECENCY)
Ro 13: 13 Let us behave d, as in the daytime,

DECEPTION (DECEIVE)
Pr 14: 8 ways, but the folly of fools is d.
  26: 26 malice may be concealed by d,
Mt 27: 64 This last d will be worse than
2Co 4: 2 we do not use d, nor do we distort
Tit 1: 10 full of meaningless talk and d,

DECEPTIVE (DECEIVE)
Pr 11: 18 The wicked earn d wages, but those
  31: 30 Charm is d, and beauty is fleeting;
Jer 7: 4 Do not trust in d words and say,
Col 2: 8 through hollow and d philosophy,

DECIDED (DECISION)
2Co 9: 7 you should give what you have d

DECISION (DECIDED)
Ex 28: 29 d as a continuing memorial before
Joel 3: 14 multitudes in the valley of d!

DECLARE (DECLARED DECLARING)
1Ch 16: 24 D his glory among the nations,
Ps 19: 1 The heavens d the glory of God;
  96: 3 D his glory among the nations,
Isa 42: 9 taken place, and new things I d;
Ro 10: 9 If you d with your mouth,

DECLARED (DECLARE)
Mk 7: 19 saying this, Jesus d all foods clean.)
Ro 2: 13 the law who will be d righteous
  3: 20 Therefore no one will be d righteous

DECLARING (DECLARE)
Ps 71: 8 praise, d your splendor all day long.
Ac 2: 11 we hear them d the wonders of God

DECREE (DECREED DECREES)
1Ch 16: 17 He confirmed it to Jacob as a d,
Ps 2: 7 I will proclaim the LORD's d:
  7: 6 Awake, my God; d justice.
  81: 4 this is a d for Israel, an ordinance
 148: 6 he issued a d that will never pass
Da 4: 24 and this is the d the Most High has
Lk 2: 1 days Caesar Augustus issued a d
Ro 1: 32 they know God's righteous d

DECREED (DECREE)
Ps 78: 5 He d statutes for Jacob
Jer 40: 2 LORD your God d this disaster
La 3: 37 it happen if the Lord has not d it?
Da 9: 24 "Seventy 'sevens' are d for your
  9: 26 and desolations have been d.
Lk 22: 22 Son of Man will go as it has been d.

DECREES (DECREE)
Ge 26: 5 my d and my instructions."
Ex 15: 26 to his commands and keep all his d,
  18: 16 and inform them of God's d
  18: 20 Teach them his d and instructions,

Lev 10: 11 Israelites all the d the LORD has
  18: 4 laws and be careful to follow my d.
  18: 5 Keep my d and laws, for whoever
  18: 26 you must keep my d and my laws.
Ps 119: 12 to you, LORD; teach me your d.
  119: 16 I delight in your d; I will not neglect
  119: 48 love, that I may meditate on your d.
  119:112 on keeping your d to the very end.

DEDICATE (DEDICATED DEDICATION REDEDICATE)
Pr 20: 25 It is a trap to d something rashly

DEDICATED (DEDICATE)
Lev 21: 12 because he has been d
Nu 18: 6 d to the LORD to do the work
1Ki 8: 63 all the Israelites d the temple
2Ch 29: 31 "You have now d yourselves
Ne 3: 1 They d it and set its doors in place,

DEDICATION (DEDICATE)
Nu 6: 2 vow of d to the LORD as a Nazirite;
Nu 6: 9 the hair that symbolizes their d,
Nu 6: 19 the hair that symbolizes their d,
Jn 10: 22 came the Festival of D at Jerusalem.
1Ti 5: 11 sensual desires overcome their d

DEED (DEEDS)
Jer 32: 10 I signed and sealed the d, had it
  32: 16 I had given the d of purchase
Col 3: 17 whether in word or d, do it all
2Th 2: 17 strengthen you in every good d

DEEDS (DEED)
Dt 3: 24 or on earth who can do the d
  4: 34 or by great and awesome d, like all
  34: 12 or performed the awesome d
1Sa 2: 3 knows, and by him d are weighed.
1Ch 16: 24 his marvelous d among all peoples.
Job 34: 25 Because he takes note of their d,
Ps 26: 7 and telling of all your wonderful d.
  45: 4 your right hand achieve awesome d.
  65: 5 us with awesome and righteous d,
  66: 3 to God, "How awesome are your d!
  66: 5 how awesome d for humankind!
  71: 17 this day I declare your marvelous d.
  72: 18 Israel, who alone does marvelous d.
  73: 28 I will tell of all your d.
  75: 1 people tell of your wonderful d.
  77: 11 I will remember the d
  77: 12 and meditate on all your mighty d."
  78: 4 next generation the praiseworthy d
  78: 7 would not forget his d but would
  86: 8 no d can compare with yours.
  86: 10 you are great and do marvelous d,
  88: 12 or your righteous d in the land
  90: 16 May your d be shown to your
  92: 4 For you make me glad by your d;
  96: 3 his marvelous d among all peoples.
  107: 8 and his wonderful d for humankind,
  107: 15 and his wonderful d for humankind,
  107: 21 and his wonderful d for humankind,
  107: 24 his wonderful d in the deep.
  107: 31 and his wonderful d for humankind.
  107: 43 ponder the loving d of the LORD.
  111: 3 Glorious and majestic are his d,
  145: 6 and I will proclaim your great d.
Jer 32: 19 purposes and mighty in d,
Hab 3: 2 I stand in awe of your d, LORD.
Mt 5: 16 that they may see your good d
Lk 1: 51 He has performed mighty d with his
  23: 41 we are getting what our d deserve.
Ac 26: 20 their repentance by their d.
1Ti 6: 18 good, to be rich in good d, and to be
Heb 10: 24 another on toward love and good d.
Jas 2: 14 claim to have faith but have no d?
  2: 18 Show me your faith without d, and I
  2: 20 that faith without d is useless?
  2: 26 is dead, so faith without d is dead.
1Pe 2: 12 they may see your good d
Rev 2: 19 I know your d, your love and faith,
  2: 23 each of you according to your d.
  3: 1 I know your d; you have
  3: 2 I have found your d unfinished
  3: 8 I know your d. See, I have placed
  3: 15 I know your d, that you are neither
  14: 13 labor, for their d will follow them."
  15: 3 "Great and marvelous are your d,

DEEP (DEPTH DEPTHS)
Ge 1: 2 was over the surface of the d,
  8: 2 Now the springs of the d
Job 34: 22 no d shadow, no utter darkness,
Ps 42: 7 D calls to d in the roar of your
Pr 25: 27 search out matters that are too d.

DEER
Ps 42: 1 As the d pants for streams of water,

DEFAMED*
Isa 48: 11 How can I let myself be d?

DEFEATED
1Co 6: 7 have been completely d already.

DEFEND (DEFENDED DEFENDER DEFENDING DEFENDS DEFENSE)
Ps 72: 4 May he d the afflicted among
  74: 22 Rise up, O God, and d your cause;
  82: 2 "How long will you d the unjust
  82: 3 D the weak and the fatherless;
  119:154 D my cause and redeem me;
Pr 31: 9 d the rights of the poor and needy.
Isa 1: 17 D the cause of the fatherless,
  1: 23 They do not d the cause
Jer 5: 28 they do not d the just cause
  50: 34 He will vigorously d their cause so

DEFENDED (DEFEND)
Jer 22: 16 He d the cause of the poor

DEFENDER (DEFEND)
Ex 22: 2 the d is not guilty of bloodshed;
Ps 68: 5 to the fatherless, a d of widows,
Pr 23: 11 for their D is strong; he will take

DEFENDING (DEFEND)
Ps 10: 18 d the fatherless and the oppressed,
Ro 2: 15 now accusing, now even d them.)
Php 1: 7 whether I am in chains or d

DEFENDS* (DEFEND)
Dt 10: 18 He d the cause of the fatherless
  33: 7 With his own hands he d his cause.
Isa 51: 22 says, your God, who d his people:

DEFENSE (DEFEND)
Ex 15: 2 "The LORD is my strength and my d;
Ps 35: 23 Awake, and rise to my d!
Php 1: 16 I am put here for the d of the gospel.

DEFERRED*
Pr 13: 12 Hope d makes the heart sick,

DEFIED
1Sa 17: 45 armies of Israel, whom you have d.
1Ki 13: 26 is the man of God who d the word

DEFILE (DEFILED)
Da 1: 8 But Daniel resolved not to d himself
Mt 15: 11 goes into your mouth does not d
Rev 14: 4 are those who did not d themselves

DEFILED (DEFILE)
Isa 24: 5 The earth is d by its people;

DEFRAUD
Lev 19: 13 " 'Do not d your neighbors or rob
Mk 10: 19 you shall not d, honor your father

DEITY*
Col 2: 9 Christ all the fullness of the D lives

DELAY
Ecc 5: 4 a vow to God, do not d to fulfill it.
Isa 48: 9 my own name's sake I d my wrath;
Heb 10: 37 coming will come and will not d."
Rev 10: 6 and said, "There will be no more d!

DELIBERATE*
Ac 2: 23 handed over to you by God's d plan

DELICACIES
Ps 141: 4 do not let me eat of their d.
Pr 23: 3 Do not crave his d, for that food is
  23: 6 begrudging host, do not crave his d;

DELICIOUS*
Pr 9: 17 food eaten in secret is d!"

DELIGHT* (DELIGHTED DELIGHTFUL DELIGHTING DELIGHTS)
Lev 26: 31 and I will take no d in the pleasing
Dt 30: 9 The LORD will again d in you
1Sa 2: 1 enemies, for I d in your deliverance.
  15: 22 "Does the LORD d in burnt
Ne 1: 11 of your servants who d in revering
Job 22: 26 then you will find d in the Almighty
  27: 10 Will they find d in the Almighty?
Ps 1: 2 but who d in the law of the LORD
  16: 3 noble people in whom is all my d."
  35: 9 the LORD and d in his salvation.
  35: 27 May those who d in my vindication
  37: 4 Take d in the LORD and he will

Ps 37: 23 steps of those who d in him;
     43: 4 of God, to God, my joy and my d.
     51: 16 You do not d in sacrifice, or I would
     51: 19 you will d in the sacrifices
     62: 4 my lofty place; they take d in lies.
     68: 30 Scatter the nations who d in war.
  111: 2 are pondered by all who d in them.
  112: 1 who find great d in his commands.
  119: 16 I d in your decrees; I will not
  119: 24 Your statutes are my d; they are my
  119: 35 your commands, for there I find d.
  119: 47 for I d in your commands because I
  119: 70 and unfeeling, but I d in your law.
  119: 77 I may live, for your law is my d.
  119: 92 If your law had not been my d, I
  119:143 but your commands give me d.
  119:174 LORD, and your law gives me d.
  147: 10 nor his d in the power of human
  149: 4 the LORD takes d in his people;
Pr   1: 22 How long will mockers d
     2: 14 who d in doing wrong and rejoice
     8: 30 I was filled with d day after day,
   10: 23 have understanding d in wisdom.
   18: 2 d in airing their own opinions.
   23: 26 and let your eyes d in my ways,
Ecc 12: 10 My heart took d in all my labor,
SS   1: 4 We rejoice and d in you;
     2: 3 I d to sit in his shade, and his fruit is
Isa 11: 3 he will d in the fear of the LORD.
   13: 17 for silver and have no d in gold.
   32: 14 wasteland forever, the d of donkeys,
   42: 1 my chosen one in whom I d;
   55: 2 and you will d in the richest of fare.
   58: 13 if you call the Sabbath a d
   61: 10 I d greatly in the LORD;
   62: 4 for the LORD will take d in you,
   65: 18 for I will create Jerusalem to be a d
   65: 19 Jerusalem and take d in my people;
   66: 3 and they d in their abominations.
   66: 11 d in her overflowing abundance."
Jer 9: 24 earth, for in these I d,"
   15: 16 they were my joy and my heart's d,
   31: 20 my dear son, the child in whom I d?
   49: 25 abandoned, the town in which I d?
Eze 24: 16 away from you the d of your eyes.
   24: 21 you take pride, the d of your eyes,
   24: 25 joy and glory, the d of their eyes,
Hos 7: 3 "They d the king with their
Mic 1: 16 for the children in whom you d;
    7: 18 angry forever but d to show mercy.
Zep 3: 17 He will take great d in you;
Mt 12: 18 chosen, the one I love, in whom I d;
Mk 12: 37 large crowd listened to him with d.
Lk 1: 14 He will be a joy and d to you,
Ro 7: 22 in my inner being I d in God's law;
1Co 13: 6 Love does not d in evil but rejoices
2Co 12: 10 for Christ's sake, I d in weaknesses,
Col 2: 5 and d to see how disciplined you are

DELIGHTED (DELIGHT)
2Sa 22: 20 he rescued me because he d in me.
1Ki 10: 9 who has d in you and placed you
2Ch 9: 8 who has d in you and placed you
Ps 18: 19 he rescued me because he d in me.
Isa 5: 7 of Judah are the vines he d in.
Lk 13: 17 but the people were d with all

DELIGHTFUL* (DELIGHT)
Ps 16: 6 surely I have a d inheritance.
SS 1: 2 for your love is more d than wine.
    4: 10 How d is your love, my sister,
Mal 3: 12 for yours will be a d land,"

DELIGHTING* (DELIGHT)
Pr 8: 31 whole world and d in humankind.

DELIGHTS (DELIGHT)
Est 6: 6 for the man the king d to honor?"
Ps 22: 8 deliver him, since he d in him."
   35: 27 who d in the well-being of his
   36: 8 them drink from your river of d.
  147: 11 the LORD d in those who fear
Pr 3: 12 he loves, as a father the son he d in.
  11: 20 but he d in those whose ways are
  12: 22 he d in people who are trustworthy.
  14: 35 A king d in a wise servant,
  29: 17 they will bring you the d you desire.
Col 2: 18 Do not let anyone who d in false

DELILAH
    Woman who betrayed Samson (Jdg 16:4–22).

DELIVER (DELIVERANCE DELIVERED DELIVERER DELIVERS)
Dt 32: 39 and no one can d out of my hand.

Ps 22: 8 Let him d him, since he delights
   72: 12 For he will d the needy who cry out,
   79: 9 d us and forgive our sins for your
  109: 21 of the goodness of your love, d me.
  119:170 d me according to your promise.
Isa 50: 2 Was my arm too short to d you?
Eze 7: 19 not be able to d them
Da 3: 17 God we serve is able to d us,
Hos 13: 14 "I will d them from the power
Mt 6: 13 but d us from the evil one.'
2Co 1: 10 that he will continue to d us,

DELIVERANCE (DELIVER)
1Sa 2: 1 my enemies, for I delight in your d.
Ps   3: 8 From the LORD comes d.
   32: 7 and surround me with songs of d.
   33: 17 A horse is a vain hope for d;
Ob   : 17 But on Mount Zion will be d;

DELIVERED (DELIVER)
Job 33: 28 God has d us from going down
Ps 34: 4 he d me from all my fears.
  107: 6 and he d them from their distress.
  116: 8 LORD, have d me from death,
Da 7: 25 holy people will be d into
  12: 1 written in the book—will be d.
Ro 4: 25 He was d over to death for our sins

DELIVERER* (DELIVER)
Jdg 3: 9 he raised up for them a d,
    3: 15 the LORD, and he gave them a d—
2Sa 22: 2 is my rock, my fortress and my d;
2Ki 13: 5 The LORD provided a d for Israel,
Ps 18: 2 is my rock, my fortress and my d;
   40: 17 You are my help and my d;
   70: 5 You are my help and my d;
  140: 7 my strong d, you shield my head
  144: 2 my stronghold and my d, my shield,
Ac 7: 35 be their ruler and d by God himself,
Ro 11: 26 "The d will come from Zion;

DELIVERS (DELIVER)
Ps 34: 17 he d them from all their troubles.
   34: 19 the LORD d them from them all;
   37: 40 The LORD helps them and d them;
   37: 40 he d them from the wicked

DELUSION* (DELUSIONS)
2Th 2: 11 God sends them a powerful d so

DELUSIONS (DELUSION)
Ps 119:118 for their d come to nothing.

DEMAND (DEMANDED)
Lk 6: 30 belongs to you, do not d it back.

DEMANDED (DEMAND)
Lk 12: 20 This very night your life will be d
  12: 48 been given much, much will be d;

DEMETRIUS
Ac 19: 24 A silversmith named D, who made

DEMON* (DEMON-POSSESSED DEMONIC DEMONS)
Mt 9: 33 And when the d was driven out,
  11: 18 drinking, and they say, 'He has a d.'
  17: 18 Jesus rebuked the d, and it came
Mk 7: 26 She begged Jesus to drive the d
   7: 29 the d has left your daughter."
   7: 30 lying on the bed, and the d gone.
Lk 4: 33 there was a man possessed by a d,
   4: 35 the d threw the man down before
   7: 33 wine, and you say, 'He has a d.'
   8: 29 driven by the d into solitary places.
   9: 42 the d threw him to the ground
  11: 14 was driving out a d that was mute.
  11: 14 When the d left, the man who had
Jn 8: 49 "I am not possessed by a d,"
  10: 21 of someone possessed by a d.
  10: 21 a d open the eyes of the blind?"

DEMON-POSSESSED* (DEMON)
Mt 4: 24 the d, those having seizures,
   8: 16 many who were d were brought
   8: 28 two d men coming from the tombs
   8: 33 what had happened to the d men.
   9: 32 a man who was d and could not talk
  12: 22 they brought him a d man who was
  15: 22 daughter is d and suffering
Mk 1: 32 brought to Jesus all the sick and d.
   5: 16 what had happened to the d man—
   5: 18 the man who had been d begged
Lk 8: 27 he was met by a d man
   8: 36 the people how the d man had been
Jn 7: 20 "You are d," the crowd answered.
   8: 48 that you are a Samaritan and d?"
   8: 52 "Now we know that you are d!

Jn 10: 20 them said, "He is d and raving mad.
Ac 19: 13 Lord Jesus over those who were d.

DEMONIC* (DEMON)
Jas 3: 15 but is earthly, unspiritual, d.
Rev 16: 14 are d spirits that perform signs,

DEMONS* (DEMON)
Dt 32: 17 They sacrificed to d, which are not
Ps 106: 37 their sons and their daughters to d.
Mt 7: 22 and in your name drive out d
   8: 31 The d begged Jesus, "If you drive
   9: 34 prince of d that he drives out d."
  10: 8 those who have leprosy, drive out d.
  12: 24 the prince of d, that this fellow drives out d."
  12: 27 And if I drive out d by Beelzebul,
  12: 28 the Spirit of God that I drive out d,
Mk 1: 34 He also drove out many d, but he
   1: 34 not let the d speak because they
   1: 39 their synagogues and driving out d.
   3: 15 and to have authority to drive out d.
   3: 22 the prince of d he is driving out d."
   5: 12 The d begged Jesus, "Send us
   5: 15 been possessed by the legion of d,
   6: 13 They drove out many d
   9: 38 "we saw someone driving out d
  16: 9 of whom he had driven seven d.
  16: 17 *my name they will drive out d*
Lk 4: 41 d came out of many people,
   8: 2 from whom seven d had come out;
   8: 30 because many d had gone into him.
   8: 32 The d begged Jesus to let them go
   8: 33 When the d came out of the man,
   8: 35 man from whom the d had gone out,
   8: 38 The man from whom the d had gone
   9: 1 authority to drive out all d
   9: 49 "we saw someone driving out d
  10: 17 even the d submit to us in your
  11: 15 the prince of d, he is driving out d."
  11: 18 that I drive out d by Beelzebul.
  11: 19 Now if I drive out d by Beelzebul,
  11: 20 if I drive out d by the finger of God,
  13: 32 'I will keep on driving out d
Ro 8: 38 life, neither angels nor d,
1Co 10: 20 sacrifices of pagans are offered to d,
  10: 20 want you to be participants with d.
  10: 21 of the Lord and the cup of d too;
  10: 21 the Lord's table and the table of d.
1Ti 4: 1 spirits and things taught by d.
Jas 2: 19 Good! Even the d believe that—
Rev 9: 20 they did not stop worshiping d,
  18: 2 She has become a dwelling for d

DEMONSTRATE* (DEMONSTRATES DEMONSTRATION)
Ac 26: 20 d their repentance by their deeds.
Ro 3: 25 He did this to d his justice,
   3: 26 he did it to d his justice

DEMONSTRATES* (DEMONSTRATE)
Ro 5: 8 God d his own love for us in this:

DEMONSTRATION* (DEMONSTRATE)
1Co 2: 4 but with a d of the Spirit's power,

DEN
Da 6: 12 and threw him into the lions' d.
Mt 21: 13 but you are making it 'a d
Mk 11: 17 But you have made it 'a d
Lk 19: 46 but you have made it 'a d

DENARII* (DENARIUS)
Lk 7: 41 One owed him five hundred d,

DENARIUS (DENARII)
Mt 20: 2 agreed to pay them a d for the day
Mk 12: 15 "Bring me a d and let me look

DENIED (DENY)
Mt 26: 70 But he d it before them all.
Mk 14: 68 But he d it. "I don't know
Lk 22: 57 But he d it. "Woman, I don't know
Jn 18: 25 He d it, saying, "I am not."
1Ti 5: 8 has d the faith and is worse than
Rev 3: 8 my word and have not d my name.

DENIES* (DENY)
Job 34: 5 'I am innocent, but God d me justice.
1Jn 2: 22 It is whoever d that Jesus is
   2: 23 No one who d the Son has

DENY (DENIED DENIES DENYING SELF-DENIAL)
Ex 23: 6 "Do not d justice to your poor
Job 27: 5 till I die, I will not d my integrity.
Isa 5: 23 a bribe, but d justice to the innocent.
La 3: 35 d people their rights before the Most
Am 2: 7 and d justice to the oppressed.

Mt 16: 24 to be my disciple must **d** themselves
Mk 8: 34 to be my disciple must **d** themselves
Lk 9: 23 to be my disciple must **d** themselves
22: 34 you will **d** three times that you
Ac 4: 16 a notable sign, and we cannot **d** it.
Tit 1: 16 but by their actions they **d** him.
Jas 3: 14 do not boast about it or **d** the truth.
Jude : 4 **d** Jesus Christ our only Sovereign

DENYING* (DENY)
Eze 22: 29 the foreigner, **d** them justice.
2Ti 3: 5 a form of godliness but **d** its power.
2Pe 2: 1 even **d** the sovereign Lord who
1Jn 2: 22 antichrist—**d** the Father and the Son.

DEPART (DEPARTED DEPARTURE)
Ge 49: 10 The scepter will not **d** from Judah,
Job 1: 21 mother's womb, and naked I will **d**.
Ecc 5: 15 as everyone comes, so they **d**.
Mt 25: 41 say to those on his left, 'D from me,
Php 1: 23 I desire to **d** and be with Christ,

DEPARTED (DEPART)
1Sa 4: 21 "The Glory has **d** from Israel"—
Ps 119:102 I have not **d** from your laws, for you
2Ti 2: 18 who have **d** from the truth.

DEPARTURE (DEPART)
Lk 9: 31 They spoke about his **d**, which he
2Ti 4: 6 and the time for my **d** is near.
2Pe 1: 15 after my **d** you will always be able

DEPEND
Ps 62: 7 salvation and my honor **d** on God;
Jer 49: 11 Your widows too can **d** on me.' "

DEPOSES
Da 2: 21 he **d** kings and raises up others.

DEPOSIT
Mt 25: 27 you should have put my money on **d**
Lk 19: 23 then didn't you put my money on **d**,
2Co 1: 22 put his Spirit in our hearts as a **d**,
5: 5 who has given us the Spirit as a **d**,
Eph 1: 14 who is a **d** guaranteeing our
2Ti 1: 14 Guard the good **d** that was entrusted

DEPRAVED* (DEPRAVITY)
Eze 16: 47 you soon became more **d** than they.
23: 11 she was more **d** than her sister.
Ro 1: 28 so God gave them over to a **d** mind,
2Ti 3: 8 They are men of **d** minds, who,
2Pe 2: 7 Many will follow their **d** conduct
2: 7 by the **d** conduct of the lawless

DEPRAVITY* (DEPRAVED)
Ps 12: 8 **d** is honored by the human race.
Ro 1: 29 of wickedness, evil, greed and **d**.
2Pe 2: 19 they themselves are slaves of **d**—

DEPRIVE
Dt 24: 17 Do not **d** the foreigner
Pr 18: 5 and so **d** the innocent of justice.
31: 5 **d** all the oppressed of their rights.
Isa 10: 2 to **d** the poor of their rights
29: 21 with false testimony the innocent
La 3: 36 to **d** them of justice—would not
1Co 7: 5 Do not **d** each other except perhaps
9: 15 die than allow anyone to **d** me

DEPTH (DEEP)
Ro 8: 39 neither height nor **d**, nor anything
11: 33 the **d** of the riches of the wisdom

DEPTHS (DEEP)
Ps 130: 1 Out of the **d** I cry to you, LORD;

DERIDE*
Pr 11: 12 have no sense **d** their neighbors,

DERIVES*
Eph 3: 15 in heaven and on earth it **d** its name.

DESCEND (DESCENDANTS DESCENDED DESCENDING)
Ro 10: 7 "or 'Who will **d** into the deep?' "

DESCENDANTS (DESCEND)
Jer 31: 17 So there is hope for your **d**,"

DESCENDED (DESCEND)
Eph 4: 9 except that he also **d** to the lower,
Heb 7: 14 is clear that our Lord **d** from Judah,

DESCENDING (DESCEND)
Ge 28: 12 of God were ascending and **d** on it.
Mt 3: 16 saw the Spirit of God **d** like a dove
Mk 1: 10 and the Spirit on him like a dove.
Jn 1: 51 and **d** on' the Son of Man."

DESECRATING*
Ne 13: 17 you are doing—**d** the Sabbath day?

Ne 13: 18 against Israel by **d** the Sabbath."
Isa 56: 2 who keep the Sabbath without **d** it,
56: 6 who keep the Sabbath without **d** it
Eze 44: 7 **d** my temple while you offered me

DESERT
Pr 21: 19 live in a **d** than with a quarrelsome
Isa 32: 2 like streams of water in the **d**
32: 15 and the **d** becomes a fertile field,
35: 6 the wilderness and streams in the **d**.

DESERTED (DESERTS)
Mt 26: 56 all the disciples **d** him and fled.
2Ti 1: 15 in the province of Asia has **d** me,

DESERTING (DESERTS)
Gal 1: 6 you are so quickly **d** the one who

DESERTS (DESERTED DESERTING)
Zec 11: 17 shepherd, who **d** the flock!

DESERVE* (DESERVED DESERVES)
Ge 40: 15 I have done nothing to **d** being put
Lev 26: 21 seven times over, as your sins **d**.
Jdg 20: 10 it can give them what they **d** for this
1Ki 2: 26 You **d** to die, but I will not put you
Ps 28: 4 and bring back on them what they **d**.
94: 2 pay back to the proud what they **d**.
103: 10 he does not treat us as our sins **d**
Ecc 8: 14 who get what the wicked **d**,
8: 14 who get what the righteous **d**.
Isa 66: 14 repaying his enemies all they **d**.
Jer 14: 16 out on them the calamity they **d**.
17: 10 according to what their deeds **d**."
21: 14 I will punish you as your deeds **d**,
32: 19 their conduct and as their deeds **d**.
49: 12 those who do not **d** to drink the cup
La 3: 64 Pay them back what they **d**,
Eze 16: 59 I will deal with you as you **d**,
Zec 1: 6 to us what our ways and practices **d**.
Mt 8: 8 I do not **d** to have you come under
22: 8 those I invited did not **d** to come.
Lk 7: 6 I do not **d** to have you come under
10: 7 for workers of their wages.
23: 15 he has done nothing to **d** death.
23: 41 for we are getting what our deeds **d**.
Ro 1: 32 those who do such things **d** death,
1Co 15: 9 and do not even **d** to be called
16: 18 Such men **d** recognition.
2Co 11: 15 end will be what their actions **d**.
1Ti 5: 18 "Workers **d** their wages."
Heb 10: 29 you think those **d** to be punished
Rev 16: 6 them blood to drink as they **d**."

DESERVED* (DESERVE)
2Sa 19: 28 grandfather's descendants **d** nothing
Ezr 9: 13 punished us less than our sins **d**
Job 33: 27 right, but we did not get what we **d**.
Ac 23: 29 no charge against him that **d** death

DESERVES* (DESERVE)
Nu 35: 31 the life of a murderer, who **d** to die.
Dt 25: 2 the one who is guilty **d** to be beaten,
25: 2 the number of lashes the crime **d**,
Jdg 9: 16 Have you treated him as he **d**?
Job 34: 11 on them what their conduct **d**.
Jer 51: 6 he will repay her what she **d**.
Lk 7: 4 "This man **d** to have you do this,
Ac 26: 31 is not doing anything that **d** death
1Ti 1: 15 saying that **d** full acceptance:
4: 9 saying that **d** full acceptance.

DESIGNATED
Lk 6: 13 of them, whom he also **d** apostles:
Heb 5: 10 was **d** by God to be high priest

DESIRABLE* (DESIRE)
Ge 3: 6 and also **d** for gaining wisdom,
Pr 22: 1 name is more **d** than great riches;

DESIRE* (DESIRABLE DESIRED DESIRES)
Ge 3: 16 Your **d** will be for your husband,
Dt 5: 21 You shall not set your **d** on your
1Sa 9: 20 to whom is all the **d** of Israel turned,
2Sa 19: 38 anything you **d** from me I will do
23: 5 salvation and grant me my every **d**.
2Ki 9: 15 Jehu said, "If you **d** to make me king,
1Ch 28: 9 understands every **d** and every
2Ch 1: 11 "Since this is your heart's **d**
9: 8 and his **d** to uphold them forever,
Job 33: 3 But I **d** to speak to the Almighty
21: 14 We have no **d** to know your ways.
Ps 10: 17 LORD, hear the **d** of the afflicted;
20: 4 May he give you the **d** of your heart
21: 2 You have granted him his heart's **d**
27: 12 turn me over to the **d** of my foes,
40: 6 and offering you did not **d**—

Ps 40: 8 I **d** to do your will, my God;
40: 14 may all who **d** my ruin be turned
41: 2 give them over to the **d** of their foes.
70: 2 may all who **d** my ruin be turned
73: 25 earth has nothing I **d** besides you.
Pr 3: 15 nothing you **d** can compare
8: 11 and nothing you **d** can compare
10: 24 what the righteous **d** will
11: 23 The **d** of the righteous ends only
12: 12 The wicked **d** the plunder
19: 2 **D** without knowledge is not good—
24: 1 wicked, do not **d** their company;
29: 17 will bring you the delights you **d**.
Ecc 6: 2 they lack nothing their hearts **d**,
12: 5 along and **d** no longer is stirred.
SS 6: 12 my **d** set me among the royal
7: 10 to my beloved, and his **d** is for me.
Isa 26: 8 and renown are the **d** of our hearts.
53: 2 appearance that we should **d** him.
55: 11 but will accomplish what I **d**
Eze 24: 25 their heart's **d**, and their sons
Hos 6: 6 For I **d** mercy, not sacrifice,
Mic 7: 3 the powerful dictate what they **d**—
Mal 3: 1 covenant, whom you **d**, will come,"
Mt 9: 13 'I **d** mercy, not sacrifice.'
12: 7 what these words mean, 'I **d** mercy,
Ro 7: 18 For I have the **d** to do what is good,
9: 16 depend on human **d** or effort,
10: 1 my heart's **d** and prayer to God
1Co 12: 31 Now eagerly **d** the greater gifts.
14: 1 of love and eagerly **d** spiritual gifts,
2Co 8: 10 give but also to have the **d** to do so.
8: 13 Our **d** is not that others might be
Php 1: 23 I **d** to depart and be with Christ,
4: 17 Not that I **d** your gifts; what I **d** is that
more be credited
2Th 1: 11 to fruition your every **d** for goodness
Heb 10: 5 and offering you did not **d**,
10: 8 and sin offerings you did not **d**,
13: 18 **d** to live honorably in every way.
Jas 1: 14 dragged away by your own evil **d**
1: 15 after **d** has conceived, it gives birth
4: 2 You **d** but do not have, so you kill.
2Pe 2: 10 of those who follow the corrupt **d**

DESIRED (DESIRE)
Ps 51: 6 Yet you **d** faithfulness
Hag 2: 7 what is **d** by all nations will come,
Lk 22: 15 "I have eagerly **d** to eat this

DESIRES* (DESIRE)
Ge 4: 7 it **d** to have you, but you must rule
41: 16 will give Pharaoh the answer he **d**."
2Sa 3: 21 may rule over all that your heart **d**."
14: 14 But that is not what God **d**; rather,
1Ki 11: 37 will rule over all that your heart **d**;
1Ch 29: 18 keep these **d** and thoughts
Job 17: 11 Yet the **d** of my heart
31: 16 "If I have denied the **d** of the poor
Ps 34: 12 life and **d** to see many good days,
37: 4 he will give you the **d** of your heart.
103: 5 who satisfies your **d** with good
140: 8 Do not grant the wicked their **d**,
145: 16 satisfy the **d** of every living thing.
145: 19 He fulfills the **d** of those who fear
Pr 11: 6 the unfaithful are trapped by evil **d**.
13: 4 but the **d** of the diligent are fully
19: 22 What a person **d** is unfailing love;
SS 2: 7 arouse or awaken love until it so **d**.
3: 5 arouse or awaken love until it so **d**
8: 4 arouse or awaken love until it so **d**.
Hab 2: 5 is puffed up; his **d** are not upright—
Mk 4: 19 and the **d** for other things come
Jn 8: 44 want to carry out your father's **d**.
Ro 1: 24 over in the sinful of their hearts
6: 12 body so that you obey its evil **d**.
8: 5 minds set on what that nature **d**;
8: 5 their minds set on what the Spirit **d**.
13: 14 to gratify the **d** of the sinful nature.
Gal 5: 16 and you will not gratify the **d**
5: 17 The sinful nature **d** what is contrary
5: 24 sinful nature with its passions and **d**.
Eph 2: 3 and following its **d** and thoughts.
4: 22 is being corrupted by its deceitful **d**;
Col 3: 5 lust, evil **d** and greed, which is
1Ti 3: 1 to be an overseer **d** a noble task.
5: 11 when their sensual **d** overcome their
6: 9 harmful **d** that plunge people
2Ti 2: 22 Flee the evil **d** of youth and pursue
3: 6 are swayed by all kinds of evil **d**,
4: 3 to suit their own **d**, they will gather
Jas 1: 20 the righteousness that God **d**.
4: 1 from your **d** that battle within you?

1Pe 1: 14 do not conform to the evil **d** you had
    2: 11 to abstain from sinful **d**, which war
    4: 2 their earthly lives for evil human **d**,
      : 4 in the world caused by evil **d**.
2Pe 1: 4 perplexed and evil **d**.
    2: 18 the lustful **d** of sinful human nature,
    3: 3 and following their own evil **d**.
1Jn 2: 17 The world and its **d** pass away,
Jude : 16 they follow their own evil **d**;
      : 18 will follow their own ungodly **d**."

DESOLATE (DESOLATION)
Isa 54: 1 the children of the **d** woman than
Gal 4: 27 the children of the **d** woman than

DESOLATION (DESOLATE)
Da 11: 31 up the abomination that causes **d**.
   12: 11 abomination that causes **d** is set up,
Mt 24: 15 'the abomination that causes **d**,'

DESPAIR (DESPAIRED)
Isa 61: 3 of praise instead of a spirit of **d**.
2Co 4: 8 perplexed, but not in **d**;

DESPAIRED* (DESPAIR)
2Co 1: 8 to endure, so that we **d** of life itself.

DESPERATE*
2Sa 12: 18 He may do something **d**."
Job 6: 26 and treat my **d** words as wind?
Ps 60: 3 have shown your people **d** times;
   79: 8 to meet us, for we are in **d** need.
  142: 6 Listen to my cry, for I am in **d** need;

DESPISE (DESPISED DESPISES)
2Sa 12: 9 Why did you **d** the word
Job 5: 17 so do not **d** the discipline
   42: 6 Therefore I **d** myself and repent
Ps 51: 17 contrite heart you, God, will not **d**.
  102: 17 he will not **d** their plea.
Pr : 7 but fools **d** wisdom and instruction.
   3: 11 do not **d** the LORD's discipline.
   6: 30 People do not **d** a thief if he
  14: 21 It is a sin to **d** one's neighbor,
  15: 20 foolish children **d** their mother.
  15: 32 disregard discipline **d** themselves,
  23: 22 do not **d** your mother when she is
Jer 14: 21 the sake of your name do not **d** us;
Am 5: 21 I **d** your religious festivals;
Zec 4: 10 dares the day of small things,
Mt 6: 24 devoted to the one and **d** the other.
  18: 10 "See that you do not **d** one
Lk 16: 13 devoted to the one and **d** the other.
1Co 11: 22 Or do you **d** the church of God
Tit 2: 15 Do not let anyone **d** you.
2Pe 2: 10 of the sinful nature and **d** authority.

DESPISED (DESPISE)
Ge 25: 34 up and left. So Esau **d** his birthright.
Ps 22: 6 by everyone, **d** by the people.
Pr 12: 8 and those with warped minds are **d**.
Isa 53: 3 He was **d** and rejected by others,
   53: 3 people hide their faces he was **d**,
1Co 1: 28 of this world and the **d** things—

DESPISES (DESPISE)
Job 36: 5 "God is mighty, but **d** no one;

DESTINED (DESTINY)
Lk 2: 34 "This child is **d** to cause the falling
1Co 2: 7 that God for our glory before time
Col 2: 22 things that are all **d** to perish
1Th 3: 3 quite well that we are **d** for them.
Heb 9: 27 Just as people are **d** to die once,
1Pe 2: 8 which is also what they were **d** for.

DESTINY* (DESTINED PREDESTINED)
Job 8: 13 Such is the **d** of all who forget God;
Ps 73: 17 then I understood their final **d**.
Ecc 7: 2 for death is the **d** of everyone;
   9: 2 All share a common **d**—
   9: 3 The same **d** overtakes all.
Isa 65: 11 and fill bowls of mixed wine for **D**,
Php 3: 19 Their **d** is destruction, their god is

DESTITUTE
Ps 102: 17 will respond to the prayer of the **d**;
Pr 31: 8 for the rights of all who are **d**.
Heb 11: 37 in sheepskins and goatskins, **d**,

DESTROY (DESTROYED DESTROYING
DESTROYS DESTRUCTION DESTRUCTIVE)
Ge 6: 17 earth to all life under the heavens,
   9: 11 be a flood to **d** the earth."
Pr 1: 32 complacency of fools will **d** them;
  11: 9 the godless **d** their neighbors,
Mt 10: 28 of the One who can **d** both soul
Mk 14: 58 say, 'I will **d** this temple made
Lk 4: 34 Have you come to **d** us?

Jn 10: 10 comes only to steal and kill and **d**;
Ac 8: 3 But Saul began to **d** the church.
Rev 11: 18 destroying those who **d** the earth."

DESTROYED (DESTROY)
Dt 8: 19 you today that you will surely be **d**.
Job 19: 26 And after my skin has been **d**,
Pr 6: 15 they will suddenly be **d**—
  11: 3 but the unfaithful are **d** by their
  29: 1 many rebukes will suddenly be **d**—
Ps 1: 6 the way of the wicked will be **d**.
Da 2: 44 up a kingdom that will never be **d**,
   6: 26 his kingdom will not be **d**,
1Co 8: 11 Christ died, is **d** by your knowledge.
  15: 24 Father after he has **d** all dominion,
  15: 26 The last enemy to be **d** is death.
2Co 4: 9 struck down, but not **d**.
   5: 1 if the earthly tent we live in is **d**,
Gal 5: 15 out or you will be **d** by each other.
Eph 2: 14 the two one and has **d** the barrier,
2Ti 1: 10 who has **d** death and has brought
Heb 10: 39 of those who shrink back and are **d**,
2Pe 2: 12 born only to be caught and **d**,
   3: 10 the elements will be **d** by fire,
   3: 11 Since everything will be **d** in this
Jude : 5 later **d** those who did not believe.
      : 11 they have been **d** in Korah's

DESTROYING (DESTROY)
Jer 23: 1 "Woe to the shepherds who are **d**

DESTROYS (DESTROY)
Pr 6: 32 whoever does so **d** himself.
  18: 9 is a close relative of one who **d**.
  28: 24 wrong," is partner to one who **d**.
Ecc 9: 18 of war, but one sinner **d** much good.
1Co 3: 17 If anyone **d** God's temple, God will

DESTRUCTION (DESTROY)
Nu 32: 15 you will be the cause of their **d**."
Pr 16: 18 Pride goes before **d**, a haughty spirit
  17: 19 builds a high gate invites **d**.
  24: 22 for those two will send sudden **d**
Hos 13: 14 Where, O grave, is your **d**?
Mt 7: 13 and broad is the road that leads to **d**,
Lk 6: 49 collapsed and its **d** was complete."
Jn 17: 12 lost except the one doomed to **d** so
Ro 9: 22 of his wrath—prepared for **d**?
1Co 5: 5 the **d** of the sinful nature
Gal 6: 8 from that nature will reap **d**;
Php 3: 19 Their destiny is **d**, their god is their
1Th 5: 3 **d** will come on them suddenly,
2Th 1: 9 will be punished with everlasting **d**
   2: 3 is revealed, the man doomed to **d**.
1Ti 6: 9 that plunge people into ruin and **d**.
2Pe 2: 1 bringing swift **d** on themselves.
   2: 3 and their **d** has not been sleeping.
   3: 7 of judgment and **d** of the ungodly.
   3: 16 the other Scriptures, to their own **d**.
Rev 17: 8 up out of the Abyss and go to its **d**.
  17: 11 to the seven and is going to his **d**.

DESTRUCTIVE (DESTROY)
2Pe 2: 1 will secretly introduce **d** heresies,

DETERMINED (DETERMINES)
Job 14: 5 The days of mortals are **d**;
Isa 14: 26 This is the plan **d** for the whole
Da 11: 36 for what has been **d** must take place.

DETERMINES* (DETERMINED)
Ps 147: 4 He **d** the number of the stars
1Co 12: 11 them to each one, just as he **d**.

DETEST (DETESTABLE DETESTED DETESTS)
Dt 7: 26 Regard it as vile and utterly **d**
Ps 119:163 I hate and **d** falsehood
Pr 8: 7 is true, for my lips **d** wickedness.
  13: 19 soul, but fools **d** turning from evil.
  16: 12 Kings **d** wrongdoing, for a throne is
  24: 9 folly are sin, and people **d** a mocker.
  29: 27 The righteous **d** the dishonest;
  29: 27 the wicked **d** the upright.
Am 5: 10 the one who tells the truth.

DETESTABLE (DETEST)
Pr 6: 16 hates, seven that are **d** to him:
  21: 27 The sacrifice of the wicked is **d**—
  28: 9 instruction, even their prayers are **d**.
Isa 1: 13 Your incense is **d** to me.
  41: 24 those who choose you are **d**.
  44: 19 Shall I make a **d** thing from what is
Jer 44: 4 'Do not do this **d** thing that I hate!'
Eze 8: 13 doing things that are even more **d**."
Lk 16: 15 What people value highly is **d**

Tit 1: 16 They are **d**, disobedient and unfit
1Pe 4: 3 orgies, carousing and **d** idolatry.

DETESTED* (DETEST)
Zec 11: 8 The flock **d** me, and I grew weary

DETESTS* (DETEST)
Dt 22: 5 the LORD your God **d** anyone who
  23: 18 the LORD your God **d** them both.
  25: 16 the LORD your God **d** anyone who
Pr 3: 32 For the LORD **d** the perverse
  11: 1 The LORD **d** dishonest scales,
  11: 20 the LORD **d** those whose hearts
  12: 22 The LORD **d** lying lips, but he
  15: 8 The LORD **d** the sacrifice
  15: 9 The LORD **d** the way
  15: 26 The LORD **d** the thoughts
  16: 5 The LORD **d** all the proud
  17: 15 the LORD **d** them both.
  20: 10 the LORD **d** them both.
  20: 23 The LORD **d** differing weights,

DEVIATE*
2Ch 8: 15 They did not **d** from the king's

DEVICES*
Ps 81: 12 hearts to follow their own **d**.

DEVIL* (DEVIL'S)
Mt 4: 1 wilderness to be tempted by the **d**.
   4: 5 Then the **d** took him to the holy city
   4: 8 Again, the **d** took him to a very high
   4: 11 Then the **d** left him, and angels
  13: 39 the enemy who sows them is the **d**
  25: 41 the eternal fire prepared for the **d**
Lk 4: 2 forty days he was tempted by the **d**.
   4: 3 The **d** said to him, "If you are
   4: 5 The **d** led him up to a high place
   4: 9 The **d** led him to Jerusalem and had
   4: 13 the **d** had finished all this tempting,
   8: 12 then the **d** comes and takes away
Jn 6: 70 Yet one of you is a **d**!"
   8: 44 the **d**, and you want to carry
  13: 2 the **d** had already prompted Judas,
Ac 10: 38 who were under the power of the **d**,
  13: 10 "You are a child of the **d**
Eph 4: 27 and do not give the **d** a foothold.
1Ti 3: 6 under the same judgment as the **d**.
2Ti 2: 26 and escape from the trap of the **d**,
Heb 2: 14 the power of death—that is, the **d**—
Jas 4: 7 Resist the **d**, and he will flee
1Pe 5: 8 Your enemy the **d** prowls around
1Jn 3: 8 who does what is sinful is of the **d**,
   3: 8 because the **d** has been sinning
   3: 10 and who the children of the **d** are:
Jude : 9 disputing with the **d** about the body
Rev 2: 10 the **d** will put some of you in prison
  12: 9 that ancient serpent called the **d**,
  12: 12 because the **d** has gone down
  20: 2 serpent, who is the **d**, or Satan,
  20: 10 And the **d**, who deceived them,

DEVIL'S* (DEVIL)
Eph 6: 11 your stand against the **d** schemes.
1Ti 3: 7 fall into disgrace and into the **d** trap.
1Jn 3: 8 appeared was to destroy the **d** work.

DEVIOUS*
2Sa 22: 27 to the **d** you show yourself shrewd.
Ps 18: 26 to the **d** you show yourself shrewd.
Pr 2: 15 and who are **d** in their ways.
  14: 2 those who despise him are **d** in their
  21: 8 The way of the guilty is **d**,

DEVISED
2Pe 1: 16 we did not follow cleverly **d** stories

DEVOTE* (DEVOTED DEVOTING DEVOTION
DEVOUT)
1Ch 22: 19 Now **d** your heart and soul
2Ch 31: 4 Levites so they could **d** themselves
Job 11: 13 "Yet if you **d** your heart to him
Jer 30: 21 who is he who will **d** himself to be
Mic 4: 13 You will **d** their ill-gotten gains
1Co 7: 5 that you may **d** yourselves to prayer.
Col 4: 2 **D** yourselves to prayer,
1Ti 1: 4 or to **d** themselves to myths
   4: 13 **d** yourself to the public reading
Tit 3: 8 God may be careful to **d** themselves
   3: 14 people must learn to **d** themselves

DEVOTED (DEVOTE)
1Ki 11: 4 and his heart was not fully **d**
Ezr 7: 10 For Ezra had **d** himself to the study
Mt 6: 24 or you will be **d** to the one
Mk 7: 11 is Corban (that is, **d** to God)—
Ac 2: 42 They **d** themselves to the apostles'

Ac 18: 5 Paul **d** himself exclusively
Ro 12: 10 Be **d** to one another in love.
1Co 7: 34 Her aim is to be **d** to the Lord
16: 15 and they have **d** themselves
2Co 7: 12 for yourselves how **d** to us you are.

DEVOTING* (DEVOTE)
1Ti 5: 10 **d** herself to all kinds of good deeds.

DEVOTION* (DEVOTE)
2Ki 20: 3 with wholehearted **d** and have done
1Ch 28: 9 serve him with wholehearted **d**
29: 3 in my **d** to the temple of my God I
29: 19 give Solomon the wholehearted **d**
2Ch 32: 32 his acts of **d** are written in the vision
35: 26 and his acts of **d** in accordance
Job 15: 4 piety and hinder **d** to God.
Isa 38: 3 with wholehearted **d** and have done
Jer 2: 2 " 'I remember the **d** of your
1Co 7: 35 way in undivided **d** to the Lord.
2Co 11: 3 your sincere and pure **d** to Christ.

DEVOUR (DEVOURED DEVOURING DEVOURS)
2Sa 2: 26 to Joab, "Must the sword **d** forever?
Mk 12: 40 They **d** widows' houses
1Pe 5: 8 lion looking for someone to **d**.

DEVOURED (DEVOUR)
Jer 30: 16 all who devour you will be **d**;

DEVOURING (DEVOUR)
Gal 5: 15 you keep on biting and **d** each other,

DEVOURS (DEVOUR)
2Sa 11: 25 the sword **d** one as well as another.

DEVOUT* (DEVOTE)
1Ki 18: 3 (Obadiah was a **d** believer
Isa 57: 1 the **d** are taken away, and no one
Lk 2: 25 Simeon, who was righteous and **d**.
Ac 10: 2 He and all his family were **d**
10: 7 and a soldier who was one of his
13: 43 **d** converts to Judaism followed Paul
22: 12 He was a **d** observer of the law

DEW
Jdg 6: 37 If there is **d** only on the fleece

DICTATED
Jer 36: 4 while Jeremiah **d** all the words

DIE (DEAD DIED DIES DYING)
Ge 2: 17 you eat of it you will certainly **d**."
3: 3 must not touch it, or you will **d**.' "
3: 4 "You will not certainly **d**,"
Ex 11: 5 Every firstborn son in Egypt will **d**,
Ru 1: 17 Where you **d** I will **d**,
2Ki 14: 6 of you will **d** for your own sin."
Job 2: 9 Curse God and **d**!"
Pr 5: 23 For lack of discipline they will **d**,
10: 21 many, but fools **d** for lack of sense.
11: 7 Hopes placed in mortals **d** with them;
15: 10 those who hate correction will **d**.
23: 13 them with the rod, they will not **d**.
Ecc 3: 2 a time to be born and a time to **d**,
Isa 22: 13 you say, "for tomorrow we **d**!"
66: 24 their worm will not **d**, nor will their
Jer 31: 30 everyone will **d** for their own sin;
Eze 3: 18 those wicked people will **d** for their
3: 19 evil ways, they will **d** for their sins;
3: 20 block before them, they will **d**.
18: 4 one who sins is the one who will **d**.
18: 20 one who sins is the one who will **d**.
18: 31 Why will you **d**, house of Israel?
33: 8 you will surely **d**,' and you do not
Mt 26: 52 all who draw the sword will **d**
Mk 9: 48 where " 'their worm does not **d**,
Jn 8: 21 for me, and you will **d** in your sin.
11: 25 will live, even though they **d**;
11: 26 by believing in me will never **d**.
Ro 5: 7 Very rarely will anyone **d**
14: 7 we do not **d** to ourselves alone.
14: 8 if we **d**, we **d** to the Lord.
1Co 15: 22 For as in Adam all **d**, so in Christ all
15: 32 eat and drink, for tomorrow we **d**."
Php 1: 21 to live is Christ and to **d** is gain.
Heb 9: 27 as people are destined to **d** once,
1Pe 2: 24 so that we might **d** to sins and live
Rev 14: 13 Blessed are the dead who **d**

DIED (DIE)
1Ki 16: 18 palace on fire burning him. So he **d**,
1Ch 1: 51 Hadad also **d**. The chiefs of Edom
10: 13 Saul **d** because he was unfaithful
Lk 16: 22 "The time came when the beggar **d**
Ro 5: 6 powerless, Christ **d** for the ungodly.
5: 8 were still sinners, Christ **d** for us.
6: 2 We are those who have **d** to sin;

Ro 6: 7 anyone who has **d** has been set free
6: 8 Now if we **d** with Christ, we believe
6: 10 The death he **d**, he **d** to sin once
14: 9 Christ **d** and returned to life so
14: 15 brother or sister for whom Christ **d**.
1Co 8: 11 for whom Christ **d**, is destroyed
15: 3 that Christ **d** for our sins according
2Co 5: 14 one **d** for all, and therefore all **d**.
5: 15 And he **d** for all, that those who live
Col 2: 20 Since you **d** with Christ
3: 3 For you **d**, and your life is now
1Th 4: 14 We believe that Jesus **d** and rose
2Ti 2: 11 If we **d** with him, we will also live
Heb 9: 15 now that he has **d** as a ransom to set
9: 17 in force only when somebody has **d**;
Rev 2: 8 Last, who **d** and came to life again.

DIES (DIE)
Job 14: 14 If someone **d**, will they live again?
Pr 26: 20 without a gossip a quarrel **d** down.
Jn 12: 24 But if it **d**, it produces many seeds.
Ro 7: 2 but if her husband **d**, she is released
1Co 7: 39 But if her husband **d**, she is free
15: 36 does not come to life unless it **d**.

DIFFERENCE* (DIFFERENT)
2Sa 19: 35 Can I tell the **d** between what is
2Ch 12: 8 may learn the **d** between serving me
Eze 22: 26 there is no **d** between the unclean
44: 23 my people the **d** between the holy
Ro 3: 22 There is no **d** between Jew
10: 12 For there is no **d** between Jew
Gal 2: 6 whatever they were makes no **d**

DIFFERENCES* (DIFFERENT)
1Co 11: 19 doubt there have to be **d** among you

DIFFERENT* (DIFFERENCE DIFFERENCES DIFFERING DIFFERS)
Lev 19: 19 " 'Do not mate **d** kinds
Nu 14: 24 my servant Caleb has a **d** spirit
1Sa 10: 6 you will be changed into a **d** person.
Est 1: 7 of gold, each one **d** from the other,
3: 8 Their customs are **d** from those
Eze 15: 2 how is the wood of a vine **d** from that
Da 7: 3 great beasts, each **d** from the others,
7: 7 It was **d** from all the former beasts,
7: 19 which was **d** from all the others
7: 23 It will be **d** from all the other
7: 24 will arise, **d** from the earlier ones;
11: 29 this time the outcome will be **d**
Mk 16: 12 *Jesus appeared in a* **d** *form*
Ro 12: 6 We have **d** gifts,
1Co 4: 7 who makes you **d** from anyone else?
12: 4 There are **d** kinds of gifts,
12: 5 There are **d** kinds of service,
12: 6 There are **d** kinds of working,
12: 10 to another speaking in **d** kinds
12: 28 guidance, and of **d** kinds of tongues.
2Co 11: 4 you receive a spirit **d** from the Spirit
11: 4 or a **d** gospel from the one you
Gal 1: 6 and are turning to a **d** gospel—
4: 1 as heirs are underage they are no **d**
Heb 7: 13 things are said belonged to a **d** tribe,
Jas 2: 7 and sent them off in a **d** direction?

DIFFERING* (DIFFERENT)
Dt 25: 13 Do not have two **d** weights in your
25: 14 Do not have two **d** measures in your
Pr 20: 10 **D** weights and **d** measures—
20: 23 The LORD detests **d** weights,

DIFFERS* (DIFFERENT)
1Co 15: 41 and star **d** from star in splendor.

DIFFICULT (DIFFICULTIES)
Ex 18: 22 but have them bring every **d** case
Dt 30: 11 commanding you today is not too **d**
2Ki 2: 10 "You have asked a **d** thing,"
Ac 15: 19 that we should not make it **d**

DIFFICULTIES* (DIFFICULT)
2Co 12: 10 in hardships, in persecutions, in **d**.

DIGNITY
Pr 31: 25 She is clothed with strength and **d**;

DIGS
Pr 26: 27 If anyone **d** a pit, they themselves

DILIGENCE (DILIGENT)
Ezr 5: 8 The work is being carried on with **d**
Heb 6: 11 to show this same **d** to the very end,

DILIGENT* (DILIGENCE)
2Ch 24: 13 The men in charge of the work were **d**,
Pr 10: 4 poverty, but **d** hands bring wealth.

Pr 12: 24 **D** hands will rule, but laziness ends
12: 27 the **d** feed on the riches of the hunt.
13: 4 desires of the **d** are fully satisfied.
21: 5 The plans of the **d** lead to profit as
1Ti 4: 15 Be **d** in these matters;

DINAH*
Only daughter of Jacob, by Leah (Ge 30:21; 46:15).
Raped by Shechem; avenged by Simeon and Levi (Ge 34).

DINE
Pr 23: 1 When you sit to **d** with a ruler,

DIOTREPHES*
3Jn : 9 church, but **D**, who loves to be first,

DIRECT (DIRECTED DIRECTIVES DIRECTS)
Ge 18: 19 so that he will **d** his children and his
Ps 119: 35 **D** me in the path of your
119:133 **D** my footsteps according to your
Jer 10: 23 it is not for them to **d** their steps.
2Th 3: 5 May the Lord **d** your hearts
1Ti 5: 17 The elders who **d** the affairs

DIRECTED (DIRECT)
Ge 24: 51 master's son, as the LORD has **d**."
Nu 16: 40 as the LORD **d** him through
Dt 2: 1 Red Sea, as the LORD had **d** me.
6: 1 laws the LORD your God **d** me
Jos 11: 9 did to them as the LORD had **d**:
11: 23 just as the LORD had **d** Moses,
Pr 20: 24 A person's steps are **d**
Jer 13: 2 as the LORD **d**, and put it around
Ac 7: 44 It had been made as God **d** Moses,
Tit 1: 5 elders in every town, as I **d** you.

DIRECTIVES* (DIRECT)
1Co 11: 17 In the following **d** I have no praise

DIRECTS (DIRECT)
Ps 42: 8 By day the LORD **d** his love,
Isa 48: 17 who **d** you in the way you should

DIRGE*
Mt 11: 17 we sang a **d**, and you did not
Lk 7: 32 we sang a **d**, and you did not cry.'

DISABLED*
Jn 5: 3 a great number of **d** people used
Heb 12: 13 so that the lame may not be **d**,

DISAGREEMENT*
Ac 15: 39 They had such a sharp **d** that they

DISAPPEAR (DISAPPEARED DISAPPEARS)
Mt 5: 18 by any means **d** from the Law until
Lk 16: 17 earth to **d** than for the least stroke
Heb 8: 13 is obsolete and outdated will soon **d**.
2Pe 3: 10 The heavens will **d** with a roar;

DISAPPEARED (DISAPPEAR)
1Ki 20: 40 busy here and there, the man **d**."

DISAPPEARS (DISAPPEAR)
1Co 13: 10 comes, what is in part **d**.

DISAPPOINTED
Ps 22: 5 in you they trusted and were not **d**.

DISAPPROVE*
Pr 24: 18 the LORD will see and **d** and turn

DISARMED*
Col 2: 15 And having **d** the powers

DISASTER
Ex 32: 12 and do not bring **d** on your people.
Ps 57: 1 of your wings until the **d** has passed.
Pr 1: 26 turn will laugh when **d** strikes you;
3: 25 Have no fear of sudden **d**
6: 15 Therefore **d** will overtake them
16: 4 even the wicked for a day of **d**.
17: 5 whoever gloats over **d** will not go
27: 10 house when **d** strikes you—
Isa 45: 7 I bring prosperity and create **d**;
Jer 17: 17 my refuge in the day of **d**.
Eze 7: 5 Unheard-of **d**! See, it comes!

DISCERN (DISCERNED DISCERNING DISCERNMENT)
Ps 19: 12 But who can **d** their own errors?
139: 3 You **d** my going out and my lying
Php 1: 10 you may be able to **d** what is best

DISCERNED* (DISCERN)
1Co 2: 14 because they are **d** only through

DISCERNING (DISCERN)
1Ki 3: 9 So give your servant a **d** heart
3: 12 I will give you a wise and **d** heart,
Pr 1: 5 and let the **d** get guidance—

Pr 8: 9 To the **d** all of them are right;
10: 13 is found on the lips of the **d**,
14: 6 knowledge comes easily to the **d**.
14: 33 reposes in the heart of the **d**
15: 14 The **d** heart seeks knowledge,
16: 21 The wise in heart are called **d**,
17: 10 A rebuke impresses a **d** person
17: 24 A **d** person keeps wisdom in view,
17: 28 and **d** if they hold their tongues.
18: 15 heart of the **d** acquires knowledge,
19: 25 rebuke the **d**, and they will gain
28: 7 who heed instruction are **d** children,
28: 11 one who is poor and **d** sees how
1Co 11: 31 But if we were more **d** with regard

DISCERNMENT (DISCERN)
Ps 119:125 give me **d** that I may understand

DISCHARGED* (DISCHARGING)
Ecc 8: 8 As no one is **d** in time of war,

DISCHARGING* (DISCHARGED)
1Co 9: 17 I am simply the trust committed

DISCIPLE (DISCIPLES DISCIPLES')
Am 7: 14 a prophet nor the **d** of a prophet,
Mt 10: 42 little ones who is known to be my **d**,
Lk 14: 26 such a person cannot be my **d**.
14: 27 and follow me cannot be my **d**.
Jn 13: 23 of them, the **d** whom Jesus loved,
19: 26 and the **d** whom he loved standing
21: 7 the **d** whom Jesus loved said
21: 20 that the **d** whom Jesus loved was

DISCIPLES (DISCIPLE)
Mt 10: 1 Jesus called his twelve **d** to him
26: 56 Then all the **d** deserted him
28: 19 go and make **d** of all nations,
Mk 3: 7 withdrew with his **d** to the lake,
16: 20 Then the **d** went out and
Lk 6: 13 he called his **d** to him and chose
14: 33 everything you have cannot be my **d**.
Jn 2: 11 and his **d** put their faith in him.
6: 66 this time many of his **d** turned back
8: 31 to my teaching, you are really my **d**.
12: 16 At first his **d** did not understand all
13: 35 will know that you are my **d**, if you
15: 8 showing yourselves to be my **d**.
20: 20 The **d** were overjoyed when they
Ac 6: 1 The number of **d** was increasing,
11: 26 The **d** were called Christians first
14: 22 strengthening the **d** and encouraging
18: 23 and Phrygia, strengthening all the **d**.

DISCIPLES'* (DISCIPLE)
Jn 13: 5 basin and began to wash his **d** feet,

DISCIPLINE* (DISCIPLINED DISCIPLINES SELF-DISCIPLINE)
Dt 4: 36 made you hear his voice to **d** you.
11: 2 experienced the **d** of the Lord
21: 18 not listen to them when they **d** him,
Job 5: 17 so do not despise the **d**
Ps 6: 1 in your anger or **d** me in your wrath.
38: 1 in your anger or **d** me in your wrath.
39: 11 rebuke and **d** people for their sins,
94: 12 Blessed are those you **d**, Lord,
Pr 3: 11 do not despise the Lord's **d**,
5: 12 You will say, "How I hated **d**!
5: 23 For lack of **d** they will die,
10: 17 Whoever heeds **d** shows the way
12: 1 Whoever loves **d** loves knowledge,
13: 18 Whoever disregards **d** comes
13: 24 love them are careful to **d** them.
15: 5 A fool spurns a parent's **d**,
15: 10 Stern **d** awaits those who leave
15: 32 who disregard **d** despise themselves,
19: 18 **D** your children, for in that there is
19: 20 Listen to advice and accept **d**,
22: 15 the rod of **d** will drive it far away.
23: 13 Do not withhold **d** from children;
29: 17 **D** your children, and they will give
Jer 10: 24 **D** me, Lord, but only in due
17: 23 would not respond to **d**.
30: 11 I will **d** you but only in due
32: 33 would not listen or respond to **d**.
46: 28 I will **d** you but only in due
Hos 5: 2 I will **d** all of them.
1Co 4: 21 Shall I come to you with a rod of **d**,
Heb 12: 5 do not make light of the Lord's **d**,
12: 7 Endure hardship as **d**;
12: 8 and everyone undergoes **d**—
12: 11 No **d** seems pleasant at the time,
Rev 3: 19 Those whom I love I rebuke and **d**.

DISCIPLINED* (DISCIPLINE)
Isa 26: 16 when you **d** them, they could barely
Jer 31: 18 'You **d** me like an unruly calf, and I have been **d**.
1Co 11: 32 we are being **d** so that we will not
Col 2: 5 delight to see how **d** you are
Tit 1: 8 self-controlled, upright, holy and **d**.
Heb 12: 7 For what children are not **d** by their
12: 8 If you are not **d**—
12: 9 we have all had parents who **d** us
12: 10 Our parents **d** us for a little while as

DISCIPLINES* (DISCIPLINE)
Dt 8: 5 your heart that as a man **d** his son,
8: 5 so the Lord your God **d** you.
Ps 94: 10 Does he who **d** nations not punish?
Pr 3: 12 because the Lord **d** those he
Heb 12: 6 because the Lord **d** those he loves,
12: 10 but God **d** us for our good, that we

DISCLOSED
Lk 8: 17 is nothing hidden that will not be **d**,
Col 1: 26 but is now **d** to the Lord's people.
Heb 9: 8 had not yet been **d** as long as

DISCORD
Gal 5: 20 hatred, **d**, jealousy, fits of rage,

DISCOURAGED* (DISCOURAGEMENT)
Nu 32: 9 they **d** the Israelites from entering
Dt 1: 21 Do not be afraid; do not be **d**."
31: 8 Do not be afraid; do not be **d**."
Jos 1: 9 do not be **d**, for the Lord your
8: 1 "Do not be afraid; do not be **d**.
10: 25 "Do not be afraid; do not be **d**.
1Ch 22: 13 Do not be afraid or **d**.
28: 20 Do not be afraid or **d**,
2Ch 20: 15 or **d** because of this vast army.
20: 17 Do not be afraid; do not be **d**.
32: 7 or **d** because of the king of Assyria
Job 4: 5 trouble comes to you, and you are **d**;
Isa 42: 4 or be **d** till he establishes justice
Eph 3: 13 not to be **d** because of my sufferings
Col 3: 21 children, or they will become **d**.

DISCOURAGEMENT* (DISCOURAGED)
Ex 6: 9 not listen to him because of their **d**

DISCOVERED
2Ki 23: 24 that Hilkiah the priest had **d**

DISCREDIT* (DISCREDITED)
Ne 6: 13 would give me a bad name to **d** me.
Job 40: 8 "Would you **d** my justice?

DISCREDITED* (DISCREDIT)
2Co 6: 3 so that our ministry will not be **d**.

DISCRETION*
1Ch 22: 12 May the Lord give you **d**
Pr 1: 4 knowledge and **d** to the young—
2: 11 **D** will protect you,
3: 21 preserve sound judgment and **d**;
5: 2 that you may maintain **d** and your
8: 12 I possess knowledge and **d**.
11: 22 a beautiful woman who shows no **d**.

DISCRIMINATE* (DISCRIMINATED)
Ac 15: 9 He did not **d** between us

DISCRIMINATED* (DISCRIMINATE)
Jas 2: 4 have you not **d** among yourselves

DISEASE (DISEASES)
Nu 12: 10 that she had a defiling skin **d**,
Mt 4: 23 healing every **d** and sickness among
9: 35 and healing every **d** and sickness.
10: 1 and to heal every **d** and sickness.

DISEASES (DISEASE)
Ps 103: 3 all your sins and heals all your **d**,
Mt 8: 17 up our infirmities and bore our **d**."
Mk 3: 10 those with **d** were pushing forward
Lk 9: 1 drive out all demons and to cure **d**,

DISFIGURE* (DISFIGURED)
Mt 6: 16 for they **d** their faces to show others

DISFIGURED* (DISFIGURE)
Isa 52: 14 his appearance was so **d** beyond

DISGRACE (DISGRACEFUL)
Ps 44: 15 I live in **d** all day long, and my face
52: 1 you who are a **d** in the eyes of God?
74: 21 Do not let the oppressed retreat in **d**;
Pr 6: 33 Blows and **d** are his lot, and his
11: 2 then comes **d**, but with humility
19: 26 is a child who brings shame and **d**,
28: 7 of gluttons **d** their parents.
29: 15 left to themselves **d** their mother.

Mt 1: 19 not want to expose her to public **d**,
Ac 5: 41 worthy of suffering **d** for the Name.
1Co 11: 6 if it is a **d** for a woman to have her
11: 4 a man has long hair, it is a **d** to him,
1Ti 3: 7 so that he will not fall into **d**
Heb 6: 6 and subjecting him to public **d**.
11: 26 He regarded **d** for the sake of Christ
13: 13 the camp, bearing the **d** he bore.

DISGRACEFUL* (DISGRACE)
Pr 10: 5 sleeps during harvest is a **d** son.
12: 4 a **d** wife is like decay in his bones.
17: 2 servant will rule over a **d** son
Hos 4: 7 their glorious God for something **d**.
1Co 14: 35 for it is **d** for a woman to speak

DISGUISE
Pr 26: 24 Enemies **d** themselves with their lips,

DISH
Pr 19: 24 Sluggards bury their hands in the **d**
Mt 23: 25 clean the outside of the cup and **d**,

DISHEARTENED
1Th 5: 14 encourage the **d**, help the weak,

DISHONEST*
Ex 18: 21 trustworthy men who hate **d** gain—
Lev 19: 35 "'Do not use **d** standards
1Sa 8: 3 They turned aside after **d** gain
Pr 11: 1 The Lord detests **d** scales,
13: 11 **D** money dwindles away,
20: 23 and **d** scales do not please him.
29: 27 The righteous detest the **d**;
Jer 22: 17 your heart are set only on **d** gain,
Eze 28: 18 **d** trade you have desecrated your
Hos 12: 7 The merchants use **d** scales;
Am 8: 5 the price and cheating with **d** scales,
Mic 6: 11 Shall I acquit a person with **d** scales,
Lk 16: 8 commended the **d** manager because
16: 10 whoever is **d** with very little will
16: 10 very little will also be **d** with much.
1Ti 3: 8 much wine, and not pursuing **d** gain.
Tit 1: 7 not violent, not pursuing **d** gain.
1: 11 and that for the sake of **d** gain.
1Pe 5: 2 not pursuing **d** gain,

DISHONOR* (DISHONORED DISHONORS)
Lev 18: 7 "'Do not **d** your father by having
18: 8 that would **d** your father.
18: 10 that would **d** you.
18: 14 "'Do not **d** your father's brother
18: 16 that would **d** your brother.
19: 29 for that would **d** a close relative;
Dt 22: 30 he must not **d** his father's bed.
Pr 30: 9 steal, and so **d** the name of my God.
Jer 14: 21 do not **d** your glorious throne.
20: 11 their **d** will never be forgotten.
La 2: 2 its princes down to the ground in **d**.
Eze 22: 10 are those who **d** their father's bed;
Jn 8: 49 I honor my Father and you **d** me.
Ro 2: 23 do you **d** God by breaking the law?
1Co 13: 5 It does not **d** others, it is not
15: 43 it is sown in **d**, it is raised in glory;
2Co 6: 8 through glory and **d**, bad report

DISHONORED* (DISHONOR)
Lev 20: 11 his father's wife, he has **d** his father.
20: 17 He has **d** his sister and will be held
20: 20 with his aunt, he has **d** his uncle.
20: 21 act of impurity; he has **d** his brother.
Dt 21: 14 her as a slave, since you have **d** her.
Ezr 4: 14 not proper for us to see the king **d**,
1Co 4: 10 You are honored, we are **d**!
Jas 2: 6 But you have **d** the poor.

DISHONORS* (DISHONOR)
Dt 27: 16 is anyone who **d** their father
27: 20 with his father's wife, for he **d** his father's bed."
Job 20: 3 I hear a rebuke that **d** me, and my
Mic 7: 6 For a son **d** his father, a daughter
1Co 11: 4 with his head covered **d** his head.
11: 5 her head uncovered **d** her head—

DISILLUSIONMENT*
Ps 7: 14 conceive trouble and give birth to **d**.

DISMAYED
Isa 41: 10 do not be **d**, for I am your God.

DISOBEDIENCE* (DISOBEY)
Jos 22: 22 in rebellion or **d** to the Lord,
Jer 43: 7 So they entered Egypt in **d**
Ro 5: 19 just as through the **d** of the one man
11: 30 received mercy as a result of their **d**,
11: 32 has bound everyone over to **d** so
2Co 10: 6 be ready to punish every act of **d**,
Heb 2: 2 and received its just punishment,

Heb 4: 6 did not go in because of their **d**,
    4: 11 by following their example of **d**.

DISOBEDIENT* (DISOBEY)
Ne 9: 26 they were **d** and rebelled against
Lk 1: 17 and the **d** to the wisdom
Ac 26: 19 I was not **d** to the vision
Ro 10: 21 long I have held out my hands to a **d**
    11: 30 were at one time **d** to God have now
    11: 31 so they too have now become **d**
Eph 2: 2 is now at work in those who are **d**.
    5: 6 wrath comes on those who are **d**.
    5: 12 to mention what the **d** do in secret.
2Ti 3: 2 proud, abusive, **d** to their parents,
Tit 1: 6 to the charge of being wild and **d**
    1: 16 **d** and unfit for doing anything good.
    3: 3 At one time we too were foolish, **d**,
Heb 11: 31 not killed with those who were **d**.
1Pe 3: 20 to those who were **d** long ago

DISOBEY* (DISOBEDIENCE DISOBEDIENT DISOBEYED DISOBEYING DISOBEYS)
Dt 11: 28 the curse if you **d** the commands
2Ch 24: 20 "Why do you **d** the LORD's
Est 3: 3 "Why do you **d** the king's
Jer 42: 13 and so **d** the LORD your God,
Ro 1: 30 of doing evil; they **d** their parents;
1Pe 2: 8 because they **d** the message—

DISOBEYED* (DISOBEY)
Nu 14: 22 in the wilderness but who **d** me
    27: 14 both of you **d** my command
Jdg 2: 2 Yet you have **d** me. Why have you
Ne 9: 29 arrogant and **d** your commands.
Isa 24: 5 they have **d** the laws,
Jer 43: 4 and all the people **d** the LORD's
Lk 15: 29 for you and never **d** your orders.
Heb 3: 18 enter his rest if not to those who **d**?

DISOBEYING* (DISOBEY)
Nu 14: 41 said, "Why are you **d** the LORD's

DISOBEYS* (DISOBEY)
Eze 33: 12 'If someone who is righteous **d**,

DISORDER*
Job 10: 22 night, of utter darkness and **d**,
1Co 14: 33 For God is not a God of **d**
2Co 12: 20 slander, gossip, arrogance and **d**.
Jas 3: 16 there you find **d** and every evil

DISOWN (DISOWNS)
Pr 30: 9 I may have too much and **d** you
Mt 10: 33 me I will **d** before my Father
    26: 35 to die with you, I will never **d** you."
2Ti 2: 12 If we **d** him, he will also **d** us;

DISOWNS (DISOWN)
Lk 12: 9 But whoever publicly **d** me will be

DISPENSATION See ADMINISTRATION, TRUST

DISPLACES*
Pr 30: 23 and a servant who **d** her mistress.

DISPLAY (DISPLAYED DISPLAYS)
Ps 22: 17 All my bones are on **d**;
Eze 39: 21 "I will **d** my glory among
Ro 9: 17 that I might **d** my power in you
1Co 4: 9 God has put us apostles on **d**
1Ti 1: 16 Christ Jesus might **d** his immense

DISPLAYED (DISPLAY)
Jn 9: 3 the works of God might be **d** in him.

DISPLAYS (DISPLAY)
Isa 44: 23 Jacob, he **d** his glory in Israel.
2Th 2: 9 all sorts of **d** of power

DISPLEASE (DISPLEASED)
1Th 2: 15 They **d** God and are hostile

DISPLEASED (DISPLEASE)
2Sa 11: 27 thing David had done **d** the LORD.

DISPUTABLE* (DISPUTE)
Ro 14: 1 without quarreling over **d** matters.

DISPUTE (DISPUTABLE DISPUTES DISPUTING)
Pr 17: 14 the matter before a **d** breaks out.
1Co 6: 1 If any of you has a **d** with another,

DISPUTES (DISPUTE)
Pr 18: 18 Casting the lot settles **d** and keeps

DISPUTING (DISPUTE)
1Ti 2: 8 up holy hands without anger or **d**.

DISQUALIFY* (DISQUALIFIED)
Col 2: 18 the worship of angels **d** you.

DISQUALIFIED* (DISQUALIFY)
1Co 9: 27 I myself will not be **d** for the prize.

DISREGARD (DISREGARDS)
Pr 15: 32 Those who **d** discipline despise

DISREGARDS* (DISREGARD)
Pr 13: 18 **d** discipline comes to poverty

DISREPUTE*
2Pe 2: 2 will bring the way of truth into **d**.

DISRUPTING*
Tit 1: 11 they are **d** whole households

DISSENSION* (DISSENSIONS)
Pr 6: 14 they always stir up **d**.
    6: 19 and a person who stirs up **d**
    10: 12 Hatred stirs up **d**, but love covers
    15: 18 The hot-tempered stir up **d**,
    16: 28 The perverse stir up **d**, and gossips
    28: 25 The greedy stir up **d**, but those who
    29: 22 An angry person stirs up **d**,
Ro 13: 13 debauchery, not in **d** and jealousy.

DISSENSIONS* (DISSENSION)
Gal 5: 20 of rage, selfish ambition, **d**,

DISSIPATION*
Lk 21: 34 hearts will be weighed down with **d**,

DISTINGUISH (DISTINGUISHING)
1Ki 3: 9 and to **d** between right and wrong.
Heb 5: 14 have trained themselves to **d** good

DISTINGUISHING*
1Co 12: 10 to another between spirits,

DISTORT (DISTORTS)
Ac 20: 30 **d** the truth in order to draw away
2Co 4: 2 nor do we **d** the word of God.
2Pe 3: 16 ignorant and unstable people **d**,

DISTRACTED*
Lk 10: 40 Martha was **d** by all the preparations

DISTRESS (DISTRESSED)
2Ch 15: 4 in their **d** they turned to the LORD,
Ps 18: 6 In my **d** I called to the LORD;
    81: 7 In your **d** you called and I rescued
    86: 7 When I am in **d**, I call to you,
    116: 3 I was overcome by **d** and sorrow.
    120: 1 I call on the LORD in my **d**,
Jnh 2: 2 "In my **d** I called to the LORD,
Mt 24: 21 For then there will be great **d**,
Jas 1: 27 and widows in their **d** and to keep

DISTRESSED (DISTRESS)
Ro 14: 15 sister is **d** because of what you eat,

DIVIDE (DIVIDED DIVIDING DIVISION DIVISIONS DIVISIVE)
Ps 22: 18 They **d** my clothes among them

DIVIDED (DIVIDE)
Mt 12: 25 or household **d** against itself will not
Lk 23: 34 they **d** up his clothes by casting lots.
1Co 1: 13 Is Christ **d**? Was Paul crucified

DIVIDING (DIVIDE)
Eph 2: 14 the barrier, the **d** wall of hostility,
Heb 4: 12 it penetrates even to **d** soul

DIVINATION
Lev 19: 26 " 'Do not practice **d** or seek

DIVINE
Ro 1: 20 his eternal power and **d** nature—
2Co 10: 4 they have power to demolish
2Pe 1: 4 you may participate in the **d** nature,

DIVISION (DIVIDE)
Lk 12: 51 peace on earth? No, I tell you, but **d**.
1Co 12: 25 there should be no **d** in the body,

DIVISIONS (DIVIDE)
Ro 16: 17 to watch out for those who cause **d**
1Co 1: 10 and that there be no **d** among you,
    11: 18 as a church, there are **d** among you,

DIVISIVE* (DIVIDE)
Tit 3: 10 Warn **d** people once, and then warn

DIVORCE* (DIVORCED DIVORCES)
Dt 22: 19 he must not **d** her as long as he
    22: 29 He can never **d** her as long as he
    24: 1 and he writes her a certificate of **d**,
    24: 3 her and writes her a certificate of **d**,
Isa 50: 1 is your mother's certificate of **d**
Jer 3: 8 faithless Israel her certificate of **d**
Mal 2: 16 "I hate **d**," says the LORD God
Mt 1: 19 he had in mind to **d** her quietly.
    5: 31 must give her a certificate of **d**.'
    19: 3 for a man to **d** his wife for any
    19: 7 a man give his wife a certificate of **d**
    19: 8 to **d** your wives because your hearts

Mk 10: 2 it lawful for a man to **d** his wife?"
    10: 4 a man to write a certificate of **d**
1Co 7: 11 And a husband must not **d** his wife.
    7: 12 to live with him, he must not **d** her.
    7: 13 to live with her, she must not **d** him.

DIVORCED* (DIVORCE)
Lev 21: 7 or **d** from their husbands,
    21: 14 not marry a widow, a **d** woman,
    22: 13 daughter becomes a widow or is **d**,
Nu 30: 9 or **d** woman will be binding on her.
Dt 24: 4 then her first husband, who **d** her,
1Ch 8: 8 after he had **d** his wives Hushim
Eze 44: 22 not marry widows or **d** women;
Mt 5: 32 who marries the **d** woman commits
Lk 16: 18 who marries a **d** woman commits

DIVORCES* (DIVORCE)
Jer 3: 1 "If a man **d** his wife and she leaves
Mt 5: 31 'Anyone who **d** his wife must give
    5: 32 tell you that anyone who **d** his wife,
    19: 9 tell you that anyone who **d** his wife,
Mk 10: 11 "Anyone who **d** his wife
    10: 12 if she **d** her husband and marries
Lk 16: 18 "Anyone who **d** his wife

DOCTOR
Mt 9: 12 "It is not the healthy who need a **d**,

DOCTRINE* (DOCTRINES)
1Ti 1: 10 else is contrary to the sound **d**
    4: 16 Watch your life and **d** closely.
2Ti 4: 3 people will not put up with sound **d**.
Tit 1: 9 he can encourage others by sound **d**
    2: 1 what is appropriate to sound **d**.

DOCTRINES* (DOCTRINE)
1Ti 1: 3 not to teach false **d** any longer

DOEG*
    Edomite; Saul's head shepherd; responsible for murder of priests at Nob (1Sa 21:7; 22:6–23; Ps 52).

DOG (DOGS)
Pr 26: 11 As a **d** returns to its vomit, so fools
Ecc 9: 4 even a live **d** is better off than
2Pe 2: 22 "A **d** returns to its vomit," and,

DOGS (DOG)
Mt 7: 6 "Do not give **d** what is sacred;
    15: 26 bread and toss it to the **d**."

DOMINION
Job 25: 2 "**D** and awe belong to God;
Ps 22: 28 for **d** belongs to the LORD and he

DONKEY
Nu 22: 30 The **d** said to Balaam, "Am I not
Zec 9: 9 on a **d**, on a colt, the foal of a **d**.
Mt 21: 5 **d**, and on a colt, the foal of a **d**.' "
2Pe 2: 16 rebuked for his wrongdoing by a **d**—

DOOR (DOORS)
Job 31: 32 for my **d** was always open
Ps 141: 3 keep watch over the **d** of my lips.
Mt 6: 6 close the **d** and pray to your Father,
    7: 7 and the **d** will be opened to you.
Ac 14: 27 how he had opened a **d** of faith
1Co 16: 9 because a great **d** for effective work
2Co 2: 12 that the Lord had opened a **d** for me,
Rev 3: 20 I stand at the **d** and knock.

DOORFRAMES
Dt 6: 9 Write them on the **d** of your houses

DOORKEEPER
Ps 84: 10 I would rather be a **d** in the house

DOORS (DOOR)
Ps 24: 7 you ancient **d**, that the King of glory

DORCAS
Ac 9: 36 Tabitha (in Greek her name is **D**);

DOUBLE
2Ki 2: 9 "Let me inherit a **d** portion of your
1Ti 5: 17 church well are worthy of **d** honor,

DOUBLE-EDGED (EDGE)
Heb 4: 12 Sharper than any **d** sword,
Rev 1: 16 of his mouth was a sharp, **d** sword.
    2: 12 of him who has the sharp, **d** sword.

DOUBLE-MINDED* (MIND)
Ps 119:113 I hate **d** people, but I love your law.
Jas 1: 8 they are **d** and unstable in all they
    4: 8 and purify your hearts, you **d**.

DOUBT (DOUBTING DOUBTS)
Mt 14: 31 faith," he said, "why did you **d**?"
    21: 21 if you have faith and do not **d**,
Mk 11: 23 sea,' and do not **d** in your heart

Jas 1: 6 you must believe and not d,
Jude : 22 Be merciful to those who d;

DOUBTING* (DOUBT)
Jn 20: 27 it into my side. Stop d and believe."

DOUBTS* (DOUBT)
Lk 24: 38 and why do d rise in your minds?
Ro 14: 23 those who have d are condemned
Jas 1: 6 because the one who d is like

DOVE (DOVES)
Ge 8: 8 he sent out a d to see if the water
Mt 3: 16 Spirit of God descending like a d

DOVES (DOVE)
Lev 12: 8 she is to bring two d or two young
Mt 10: 16 as snakes and as innocent as d.
Lk 2: 24 "a pair of d or two young pigeons."

DOWNCAST
Ps 42: 5 Why, my soul, are you d?
2Co 7: 6 who comforts the d, comforted us

DOWNFALL
Hos 14: 1 Your sins have been your d!

DRAGON
Rev 12: 7 and his angels fought against the d,
13: 2 The d gave the beast his power
20: 2 He seized the d, that ancient

DRAW (DRAWING DRAWS)
Mt 26: 52 "for all who draw the sword will die
Jn 12: 32 earth, will d all people to myself."
Heb 10: 22 let us d near to God with a sincere

DRAWING (DRAW)
Lk 21: 28 because your redemption is d near."

DRAWS (DRAW)
Jn 6: 44 the Father who sent me d them,

DREAD (DREADFUL)
Ps 53: 5 overwhelmed with d, where there

DREADFUL (DREAD)
Mt 24: 19 How d it will be in those days
Heb 10: 31 It is a d thing to fall into the hands

DREAM
Joel 2: 28 your old men will d dreams,
Ac 2: 17 visions, your old men will d dreams.

DRESS
1Ti 2: 9 also want the women to d modestly,

DRIFT*
Heb 2: 1 heard, so that we do not d away.

DRINK (DRINKING DRINKS DRUNK DRUNKARD DRUNKARD'S DRUNKARDS DRUNKENNESS)
Ex 29: 40 of a hin of wine as a d offering.
Nu 6: 3 They must not d grape juice or eat
Jdg 7: 5 from those who kneel down to d."
2Sa 23: 15 someone would get me a d of water
Pr 5: 15 D water from your own cistern,
Mt 20: 22 you d the cup I am going to d?"
26: 27 saying, "D from it, all of you.
Mk 16: 18 when they d deadly poison,
Lk 12: 19 eat, d and be merry." '
Jn 7: 37 who is thirsty come to me and d.
18: 11 Shall I not d the cup the Father has
1Co 10: 4 and drank the same spiritual d;
12: 13 were all given the one Spirit to d.
Php 2: 17 out like a d offering on the sacrifice
2Ti 4: 6 being poured out like a d offering,
Rev 14: 10 will d of the wine of God's fury,

DRINKING (DRINK)
Ro 14: 17 God is not a matter of eating and d,

DRINKS (DRINK)
Isa 5: 22 wine and champions at mixing d,
Jn 4: 13 "Everyone who d this water will be
6: 54 and d my blood has eternal life,
1Co 11: 27 bread or d the cup of the Lord

DRIPPING
Pr 19: 13 wife is like the constant d of a leaky
27: 15 A quarrelsome wife is like the d

DRIVE (DRIVES)
Ex 23: 30 little I will d them out before you,
Nu 33: 52 d out all the inhabitants of the land
Jos 13: 13 But the Israelites did not d
23: 13 Lord your God will no longer d
Pr 22: 10 D out the mocker, and out goes
Mt 10: 1 gave them authority to d out evil
Jn 6: 37 comes to me I will never d away.

DRIVES (DRIVE)
Mt 12: 26 If Satan d out Satan, he is divided

DROP (DROPS)
Pr 17: 14 so d the matter before a dispute
Isa 40: 15 Surely the nations are like a d

DROPS (DROP)
Lk 22: 44 his sweat was like d of blood falling

DROSS
Ps 119:119 of the earth you discard like d;
Pr 25: 4 Remove the d from the silver,
26: 23 Like a coating of silver d on

DROUGHT
Jer 17: 8 It has no worries in a year of d

DROWNED
Ex 15: 4 Pharaoh's officers are d in the Red
Mt 18: 6 they were d in the depths of the sea.
Heb 11: 29 tried to do so, they were d.

DROWSINESS*
Pr 23: 21 poor, and d clothes them in rags.

DRUNK (DRINK)
1Sa 1: 13 Eli thought she was d
Ac 2: 15 These people are not d, as you
Eph 5: 18 Do not get d on wine, which leads

DRUNKARD (DRINK)
Mt 11: 19 'Here is a glutton and a d, a friend

DRUNKARD'S* (DRINK)
Pr 26: 9 a thornbush in a d hand is a proverb

DRUNKARDS (DRINK)
Pr 23: 21 for d and gluttons become poor,
1Co 5: 11 or slanderers, d or swindlers.
6: 10 the greedy nor d nor slanderers nor

DRUNKENNESS (DRINK)
Lk 21: 34 d and the anxieties of life,
Ro 13: 13 not in carousing and d, not in sexual
Gal 5: 21 and envy; d, orgies, and the like.
1Ti 3: 3 not given to d, not violent
1Pe 4: 3 living in debauchery, lust, d, orgies,

DRY
Ge 1: 9 place, and let d ground appear."
Ex 14: 16 can go through the sea on d ground
Jos 3: 17 completed the crossing on d ground.
Isa 53: 2 and like a root out of d ground.
Eze 37: 4 bones and say to them, 'D bones,

DUE
Pr 3: 27 from those to whom it is d,

DULL
Isa 6: 10 make their ears d and close their
2Co 3: 14 But their minds were made d,

DUST
Ge 2: 7 a man from the d of the ground
3: 19 for d you are and to d you will
Job 42: 6 myself and repent in d and ashes."
Ps 22: 15 you lay me in the d of death.
103: 14 he remembers that we are d.
Ecc 3: 20 all come from d, and to d all return.
Mt 10: 14 shake the d off your feet when you
1Co 15: 47 first man was of the d of the earth;

DUTIES (DUTY)
2Ti 4: 5 discharge all the d of your ministry.

DUTY (DUTIES)
Ecc 12: 13 this is the d, of every human being.
Ac 23: 1 I have fulfilled my d to God in all
1Co 7: 3 husband should fulfill his marital d

DWELL (DWELLING DWELLINGS DWELLS DWELT)
Ex 25: 8 for me, and I will d among them.
2Sa 7: 5 the one to build me a house to d in?
1Ki 8: 27 "But will God really d on earth?
Ps 23: 6 I will d in the house of the Lord
37: 3 d in the land and enjoy safe pasture.
61: 4 I long to d in your tent forever
Pr 8: 12 wisdom, d together with prudence;
Isa 33: 14 of us can d with the consuming fire?
43: 18 do not d on the past.
Jn 5: 38 nor does his word d in you, for you
Ro 7: 18 good itself does not d in me,
Eph 3: 17 Christ may d in your hearts through
Col 1: 19 to have all his fullness d in him,
3: 16 of Christ d among you richly as you

DWELLING (DWELL)
Lev 26: 11 I will put my d place among you,
Dt 26: 15 your holy d place, and bless your
Ps 90: 1 have been our d place throughout all
2Co 5: 2 to be clothed with our heavenly d,

DWELLINGS (DWELL)
Lk 16: 9 will be welcomed into eternal d.

DWELLS (DWELL)
Ps 46: 4 holy place where the Most High d.
91: 1 Whoever d in the shelter
1Co 3: 16 God's Spirit d in your midst?

DWELT (DWELL)
Dt 33: 16 of him who d in the burning bush.

DYING (DIE)
Ro 7: 6 by d to what once bound us,
2Co 6: 9 d, and yet we live on;

EAGER
Pr 31: 13 and flax and works with d hands.
Ro 8: 19 The creation waits in e expectation
1Co 14: 12 Since you are e for gifts
14: 39 and sisters, be e to prophesy, and do
Tit 2: 14 his very own, e to do what is good.
1Pe 5: 2 dishonest gain, but e to serve;

EAGLE (EAGLE'S EAGLES)
Dt 32: 11 like an e that stirs up its nest
Eze 1: 10 each also had the face of an e.
Rev 4: 7 the fourth was like a flying e.
12: 14 given the two wings of a great e,

EAGLE'S (EAGLE)
Ps 103: 5 your youth is renewed like the e.

EAGLES (EAGLE)
Isa 40: 31 They will soar on wings like e;

EAR (EARS)
Ex 21: 6 and pierce his e with an awl.
Pr 2: 2 turning your e to wisdom
1Co 2: 9 eye has seen, what no e has heard,
12: 16 And if the e should say, "Because I

EARN (EARNINGS)
2Th 3: 12 settle down and e the bread they eat.

EARNESTNESS
2Co 7: 11 what e, what eagerness to clear
8: 7 in complete e and in the love we

EARNINGS (EARN)
Pr 31: 16 out of her e she plants a vineyard.

EARRING (EARRINGS)
Pr 25: 12 Like an e of gold or an ornament

EARRINGS (EARRING)
Ex 32: 2 them, "Take off the gold e that your

EARS (EAR)
Job 42: 5 My e had heard of you but now my
Ps 34: 15 and his e are attentive to their cry.
Pr 21: 13 Those who shut their e to the cry
26: 17 dog by the e is someone who rushes
Isa 6: 10 hear with their e,
Mt 11: 15 Whoever has e, let them hear.
2Ti 4: 3 to say what their itching e want
1Pe 3: 12 his e are attentive to their prayer,
Rev 2: 7 Whoever has e, let them hear what

EARTH (EARTH'S EARTHLY)
Ge 1: 1 God created the heavens and the e.
1: 2 Now the e was formless and empty,
7: 24 The waters flooded the e
14: 19 Most High, Creator of heaven and e.
1Ki 8: 27 "But will God really dwell on e?
Job 26: 7 he suspends the e over nothing.
Ps 24: 1 The e is the Lord's,
46: 6 he lifts his voice, the e melts.
97: 5 before the Lord of all the e.
102: 25 you laid the foundations of the e,
108: 5 let your glory be over all the e.
Pr 8: 26 its fields or any of the dust of the e.
Isa 6: 3 the whole e is full of his glory."
24: 20 The e reels like a drunkard, it sways
37: 16 God over all the kingdoms of the e.
37: 16 You have made heaven and e.
40: 22 enthroned above the circle of the e,
51: 6 the e will wear out like a garment
54: 5 he is called the God of all the e.
55: 9 the heavens are higher than the e,
65: 17 create new heavens and a new e.
66: 1 throne, and the e is my footstool;
Jer 10: 10 When he is angry, the e trembles;
23: 24 "Do not I fill heaven and e?"
23: 24 the laws of heaven and e,
Hab 2: 20 let all the e be silent before him.
Zep 1: 18 the whole e will be consumed,
Mt 5: 5 the meek, for they will inherit the e.
5: 35 or by the e, for it is his footstool;

Mt 6:10 will be done, on e as it is in heaven.
16:19 you bind on e will be bound
24:35 Heaven and e will pass away,
28:18 and on e has been given to me.
Lk 2:14 on e peace to those on whom his
Jn 12:32 when I am lifted up from the e,
Ac 4:24 the heaven and the e and the sea,
7:49 throne, and the e is my footstool.
1Co 10:26 for, "The e is the Lord's,
Eph 3:15 in heaven and on e derives its name.
Php 2:10 in heaven and on e and under the e,
Heb 1:10 you laid the foundations of the e,
2Pe 3:13 to a new heaven and a new e,
Rev 8:7 A third of the e was burned up,
12:12 But woe to the e and the sea,
20:11 The e and the heavens fled from his
21:1 I saw "a new heaven and a new e,"
21:1 and the first e had passed away,

EARTH'S (EARTH)
Job 38:4 you when I laid the e foundation?

EARTHENWARE*
Pr 26:23 of silver dross on e are fervent lips

EARTHLY (EARTH)
Ro 1:3 his Son, who as to his e life
Eph 4:9 descended to the lower, e regions?
Php 3:19 Their mind is set on e things.
Col 3:2 on things above, not on e things.
3:5 whatever belongs to your e nature:

EARTHQUAKE (EARTHQUAKES)
Eze 38:19 time there shall be a great e
Mt 28:2 There was a violent e, for an angel
Rev 6:12 There was a great e. The sun turned

EARTHQUAKES (EARTHQUAKE)
Mt 24:7 be famines and e in various places.

EASE
Pr 1:33 to me will live in safety and be at e,

EASIER (EASY)
Lk 16:17 It is e for heaven and earth
18:25 it is e for a camel to go through

EAST
Ge 2:8 God had planted a garden in the e,
Ps 103:12 as far as the e is from the west,
Eze 43:2 the God of Israel coming from the e.
Mt 2:1 Magi from the e came to Jerusalem

EASY (EASIER)
Mt 11:30 For my yoke is e and my burden is

EAT (ATE EATEN EATER EATING EATS)
Ge 2:16 "You are free to e from any tree
2:17 you must not e from the tree
3:19 brow you will e your food until you
Ex 12:11 E it in haste; it is the Lord's
Lev 11:2 land, these are the ones you may e:
17:12 "None of you may e blood,
Dt 8:16 He gave you manna to e
14:4 These are the animals you may e:
Jdg 14:14 "Out of the eater, something to e;
2Sa 9:7 and you will always e at my table."
Pr 31:27 and does not e the bread of idleness.
Isa 55:1 have no money, come, buy and e!
65:25 and the lion will e straw like the ox,
Eze 3:1 e what is before you, e this scroll;
Mt 14:16 You give them something to e."
15:2 wash their hands before they e!"
26:26 his disciples, saying, "Take and e;
Mk 14:14 where I may e the Passover with my
Lk 10:8 welcomed, e what is set before you.
12:19 e, drink and be merry."'
12:22 about your life, what you will e;
Jn 4:32 "I have food to e that you know
6:31 them bread from heaven to e.'"
6:52 can this man give us his flesh to e?"
Ac 10:13 "Get up, Peter. Kill and e."
Ro 14:2 faith allows them to e everything,
14:6 Those who e meat do so to the Lord,
14:15 is distressed because of what you e,
14:20 a person to e anything that causes
14:21 It is better not to e meat or drink
14:23 have doubts are condemned if they e,
1Co 5:11 With such persons do not even e.
8:13 if what I e causes my brother
10:25 E anything sold in the meat market
10:27 to go, e whatever is put before you
10:31 So whether you e or drink
11:26 For whenever you e this bread
2Th 3:10 is unwilling to work shall not e."
Rev 2:7 I will give the right to e
3:20 I will come in and e with them,

EATEN (EAT)
Ge 3:11 Have you e from the tree that I
Ac 10:14 "I have never e anything impure
Rev 10:10 but when I had e it, my stomach

EATER (EAT)
Isa 55:10 for the sower and bread for the e,

EATING (EAT)
Ex 34:28 and forty nights without e bread
Ro 14:17 not by your e destroy your brother
14:17 kingdom of God is not a matter of e
14:23 because their e is not from faith;
1Co 8:4 about e food sacrificed to idols:
8:10 knowledge, e in an idol's temple,
Jude :12 e with you without the slightest

EATS (EAT)
1Sa 14:24 be anyone who e food before
Lk 15:2 sinners and e with them."
Jn 6:51 Whoever e of this bread will live
6:54 Whoever e my flesh and drinks my
Ro 14:2 faith is weak, e only vegetables.
14:3 The one who e everything must not
1Co 11:27 whoever e the bread or drinks

EBAL
Dt 11:29 and on Mount E the curses.
Jos 8:30 Joshua built on Mount E an altar

EBENEZER
1Sa 7:12 He named it E, saying, "Thus far

EDEN
Ge 2:8 planted a garden in the east, in E;
Eze 28:13 You were in E, the garden of God;

EDGE (DOUBLE-EDGED)
Mt 9:20 him and touched the e of his cloak.

EDICT
Heb 11:23 they were not afraid of the king's e.

EDIFICATION* (EDIFY)
Ro 14:19 what leads to peace and to mutual e.

EDIFIED* (EDIFY)
1Co 14:5 so that the church may be e.
14:17 enough, but the others are not e.

EDIFY* (EDIFICATION EDIFIED)
1Co 14:4 speak in a tongue e themselves,
14:4 those who prophesy e the church.

EDOM
Ge 36:1 the family line of Esau (that is, E).
36:8 E) settled in the hill country of Seir.
Isa 63:1 Who is this coming from E,
Ob :1 Sovereign Lord says about E—

EDUCATED*
Ac 7:22 Moses was e in all the wisdom

EFFECT* (EFFECTIVE)
Job 41:26 The sword that reaches it has no e,
Isa 32:17 its e will be quietness
Zep 2:2 before the decree takes e and that day
1Co 15:10 his grace to me was not without e.
Eph 1:10 to be put into e when the times reach
Heb 9:17 it never takes e while the one who
9:18 was not put into e without blood.

EFFECTIVE* (EFFECT)
Phm :6 with us in the faith may be e
1Co 16:9 a great door for e work has opened
Jas 5:16 righteous person is powerful and e.

EFFORT*
Ecc 2:19 toil into which I have poured my e
Da 6:14 made every e until sundown to save
Lk 13:24 "Make every e to enter through
Ro 9:16 depend on human desire or e,
14:19 Let us therefore make every e to do
Gal 3:3 now trying to finish by human e?
4:23 was born as the result of human e,
4:29 the son born by human e persecuted
Eph 4:3 Make every e to keep the unity
1Th 2:16 in their e to keep us from speaking
2:17 intense longing we made every e
Heb 4:11 make every e to enter that rest,
12:14 Make every e to live in peace
2Pe 1:5 make every e to add to your faith
1:10 I will make every e to see
1:10 make every e to confirm your calling
3:14 make every e to be found spotless,

EGG*
Lk 11:12 Or if he asks for an e, will give

EGLON
1. Fat king of Moab killed by Ehud (Jdg 3:12–30).

2. City in Canaan (Jos 10).

EGYPT (EGYPTIANS)
Ge 12:10 Abram went down to E to live there
37:28 the Ishmaelites, who took him to E.
42:3 went down to buy grain from E.
45:20 the best of all E will be yours.'"
46:6 and all his offspring went to E,
47:27 Now the Israelites settled in E
Ex 3:11 and bring the Israelites out of E?"
12:40 people lived in E was 430 years.
12:41 all the Lord's divisions left E.
32:1 Moses who brought us up out of E,
Nu 11:18 We were better off in E!"
14:4 choose a leader and go back to E."
24:8 "God brought them out of E;
Dt 6:21 "We were slaves of Pharaoh in E,
1Ki 4:30 greater than all the wisdom of E.
10:28 horses were imported from E
11:40 but Jeroboam fled to E, to Shishak
14:25 king of E attacked Jerusalem.
2Ch 36:3 Necho king of E went up to fight
36:3 The king of E dethroned him
Isa 19:23 day there will be a highway from E
Hos 11:1 and out of E I called my son.
Mt 2:15 "Out of E I called my son."
Heb 11:27 By faith he left E, not fearing
Rev 11:8 is figuratively called Sodom and E,

EGYPTIANS (EGYPT)
Nu 14:13 "Then the E will hear about it!

EHUD
Left-handed judge who delivered Israel from Moabite king, Eglon (Jdg 3:12–30).

EKRON
1Sa 5:10 So they sent the ark of God to E.

ELABORATE*
1Ti 2:9 not with e hairstyles
1Pe 3:3 e hairstyles and the wearing of gold

ELAH
Son of Baasha; king of Israel (1Ki 16:6–14).

ELATION*
Pr 28:12 righteous triumph, there is great e;

ELDER* (ELDERLY ELDERS)
Isa 3:2 the prophet, the diviner and the e,
1Ti 5:19 accusation against an e unless it is
Tit 1:5 An e must be blameless,
1Pe 5:1 I appeal as a fellow e and a witness
2Jn :1 The e, To the lady chosen by God
3Jn :1 The e, To my dear friend Gaius,

ELDERLY* (ELDER)
Lev 19:32 show respect for the e and revere

ELDERS (ELDER)
1Ki 12:8 rejected the advice the e gave him
Mt 15:2 break the tradition of the e?
Mk 7:3 holding to the tradition of the e
7:5 to the tradition of the e instead
Ac 11:30 their gift to the e by Barnabas
14:23 Barnabas appointed e for them
15:2 apostles and e about this question.
15:4 the church and the apostles and e,
15:6 and e met to consider this question.
15:22 Then the apostles and e,
15:23 The apostles and e, your brothers,
16:4 and e in Jerusalem for the people
20:17 to Ephesus for the e of the church.
21:18 James, and all the e were present.
23:14 the chief priests and the e and said,
24:1 to Caesarea with some of the e
1Ti 4:14 the body of e laid their hands
5:17 The e who direct the affairs
Tit 1:5 and appoint e in every town, as I
Jas 5:14 Let them call the e of the church
1Pe 5:1 To the e among you, I appeal as
Rev 4:4 seated on them were twenty-four e.
4:10 the twenty-four e fall down before

ELEAZAR
Third son of Aaron (Ex 6:23–25). Succeeded Aaron as high priest (Nu 20:26; Dt 10:6). Allotted land to tribes (Jos 14:1). Death (Jos 24:33).

ELECT* (ELECTION)
Mt 24:22 the e those days will be shortened.
24:24 to deceive, if possible, even the e.
24:31 they will gather his e from the four
Mk 13:20 But for the sake of the e, whom he
13:22 to deceive, if possible, even the e.
13:27 gather his e from the four winds,
Ro 11:7 The e among them did,

1Ti   5: 21   and Christ Jesus and the e angels,
2Ti   2: 10   everything for the sake of the e,
Tit   1:   1   Christ to further the faith of God's e
1Pe   1:   1   Christ, To God's e, exiles scattered

ELECTION* (ELECT)
Ro   9: 11   that God's purpose in e might stand:
   11: 28   but as far as e is concerned, they are
2Pe   1: 10   effort to confirm your calling and e.

ELEMENTARY* (ELEMENTS)
Heb   5: 12   to teach you the e truths of God's
   6:   1   let us move beyond the e teachings

ELEMENTS* (ELEMENTARY)
2Pe   3: 10   the e will be destroyed by fire,
   3: 12   fire, and the e will melt in the heat.

ELEVATE*
2Co   11:   7   in order to e you by preaching

ELI
   High priest in youth of Samuel (1Sa 1–4). Blessed Hannah (1Sa 1:12–18); raised Samuel (1Sa 2:11–26). Prophesied against because of wicked sons (1Sa 2:27–36). Death of Eli and sons (1Sa 4:11–22).
Mt   27: 46   "E, E, lema sabachthani?"

ELIHU
   One of Job's friends (Job 32–37).

ELIJAH
   Prophet; predicted famine in Israel (1Ki 17:1; Jas 5:17). Fed by ravens (1Ki 17:2–6). Raised Sidonian widow's son (1Ki 17:7–24). Defeated prophets of Baal at Carmel (1Ki 18:16–46). Ran from Jezebel (1Ki 19:1–9). Prophesied death of Azariah (2Ki 1). Succeeded by Elisha (1Ki 19:19–21; 2Ki 2:1–18). Taken to heaven in whirlwind (2Ki 2:11–12).
   Return predicted (Mal 4:5–6); equated with John the Baptist (Mt 17:9–13; Mk 9:9–13; Lk 1:17). Appeared with Moses in transfiguration of Jesus (Mt 17:1–8; Mk 9:1–8).

ELIMELEK
Ru   1:   3   Now E, Naomi's husband, died,

ELIPHAZ
   1. Firstborn of Esau (Ge 36).
   2. One of Job's friends (Job 4–5; 15; 22).

ELISHA
   Prophet; successor of Elijah (1Ki 19:16–21); inherited his cloak (2Ki 2:1–18). Purified bad water (2Ki 2:19–22). Cursed young men (2Ki 2:23–25). Aided Israel's defeat of Moab (2Ki 3). Provided widow with oil (2Ki 4:1–7). Raised Shunammite woman's son (2Ki 4:8–37). Purified food (2Ki 4:38–41). Fed 100 men (2Ki 4:42–44). Healed Naaman's leprosy (2Ki 5). Made axhead float (2Ki 6:1–7). Captured Arameans (2Ki 6:8–23). Political adviser to Israel (2Ki 6:24–8:6; 9:1–3; 13:14–19), Damascus (2Ki 8:7–15). Death (2Ki 13:20).

ELIZABETH*
   Mother of John the Baptist, relative of Mary (Lk 1:5–58).

ELKANAH
   Husband of Hannah, father of Samuel (1Sa 1–2).

ELOI*
Mk   15: 34   cried out in a loud voice, "E, E,

ELOQUENCE* (ELOQUENT)
1Co   2:   1   I did not come with e or human

ELOQUENT* (ELOQUENCE)
Ex   4: 10   I have never been e,
Pr   17:   7   E lips are unsuited to a godless

ELYMAS
Ac   13:   8   E the sorcerer (for that is what his

EMBEDDED*
Ecc   12: 11   sayings like firmly e nails—

EMBERS
Pr   26: 21   As charcoal to e and as wood

EMBITTER* (BITTER)
Col   3: 21   Fathers, do not e your children,

EMBODIMENT* (BODY)
Ro   2: 20   have in the law the e of knowledge

EMPEROR
1Pe   2: 13   the e, as the supreme authority,
   2: 17   fear God, honor the e.

EMPTIED (EMPTY)
1Co   1: 17   the cross of Christ be e of its power.

EMPTY (EMPTIED)
Ge   1:   2   Now the earth was formless and e,
Job   26:   7   the northern skies over e space;
Isa   45: 18   he did not create it to be e,
   55: 11   It will not return to me e, but will
Jer   4: 23   the earth, and it was formless and e;
Mt   12: 36   for every e word they have spoken.
Lk   1: 53   things but has sent the rich away e.
Eph   5:   6   no one deceive you with e words,
1Pe   1: 18   you were redeemed from the e way
2Pe   2: 18   For they mouth e, boastful words

ENABLE* (ABLE)
Lk   1: 74   and to e us to serve him without fear
Ac   4: 29   e your servants to speak your word

ENABLED* (ABLE)
Lev   26: 13   e you to walk with heads held high.
Ru   4: 13   the LORD e her to conceive,
Jn   6: 65   me unless the Father has e them."
Ac   2:   4   other tongues as the Spirit e them.
   7: 10   and e him to gain the goodwill
Heb   11: 11   was e to bear children because she

ENABLES (ABLE)
Php   3: 21   by the power that e him to bring

ENABLING* (ABLE)
Ac   14:   3   his grace by e them to perform signs

ENCAMPS* (CAMP)
Ps   34:   7   the LORD e around those who fear

ENCOURAGE* (ENCOURAGED ENCOURAGEMENT ENCOURAGES ENCOURAGING)
Dt   1: 38   E him, because he will lead Israel
   3: 28   Joshua, and e and strengthen him,
2Sa   11: 25   and destroy it.' Say this to e Joab."
Jn   9:   7   Now go and e your men.
Job   16:   5   But my mouth would e you;
Ps   10: 17   you e them, and you listen to their
   64:   5   They e each other in evil plans,
Isa   1: 17   Seek justice, e the oppressed.
Jer   29:   8   to the dreams you e them to have.
Ac   15: 32   said much to e and strengthen
Ro   12:   8   if it is to e, then give
2Co   13: 11   e one another, be of one mind,
Eph   6: 22   how we are, and that he may e you.
Col   4:   8   and that he may e your hearts.
1Th   3:   2   strengthen and e you in your faith,
   4: 18   Therefore e one another with these
   5: 11   Therefore e one another and build
   5: 14   and disruptive, e the disheartened,
2Th   2: 17   e your hearts and strengthen you
2Ti   4:   2   correct, rebuke and e—
Tit   1:   9   he can e others by sound doctrine
   2:   6   Similarly, e the young men to be
   2: 15   E and rebuke with all authority.
Heb   3: 13   But e one another daily, as long as it

ENCOURAGED* (ENCOURAGE)
Jdg   7: 11   you will be e to attack the camp."
   20: 22   But the Israelites e one another
2Ch   22:   3   his mother e him to act wickedly.
   32:   6   gate and e them with these words:
   35:   2   and e them in the service
Eze   13: 22   and because you e the wicked not
Ac   9: 31   of the Lord and e by the Holy Spirit,
   11: 23   e them all to remain true to the Lord
   16: 40   met with the believers and e them.
   18: 27   the believers e him and wrote
   27: 36   They were all e and ate some food
   28: 15   people Paul thanked God and was e.
Ro   1: 12   I may be mutually e by each other's
1Co   14: 31   everyone may be instructed and e.
2Co   7:   4   I am greatly e; in all our troubles
   7: 13   By all this we are e. In addition
Col   2:   2   goal is that they may be e in heart
1Th   3:   7   persecution we were e about you
Heb   6: 18   hope set before us may be greatly e.

ENCOURAGEMENT* (ENCOURAGE)
Ac   4: 36   (which means "son of e"),
   20:   2   speaking many words of e
Ro   12:   8   if it is to encourage, then give e;
   15:   4   the e they provide we might have
   15:   5   e give you the same attitude of mind
1Co   14:   3   their strengthening, e and comfort.
2Co   7: 13   In addition to our own e, we were
Php   2:   1   if you have any e from being united
2Th   2: 16   by his grace gave us eternal e
Phm   7   love has given me great joy and e,
Heb   12:   5   completely forgotten this word of e

ENCOURAGES* (ENCOURAGE)
Isa   41:   7   The metal worker e the goldsmith,

ENCOURAGING* (ENCOURAGE)
Ac   14: 22   e them to remain true to the faith.
   15: 31   it and were glad for its e message.
   20:   1   after e them, said good-by and set
1Th   2: 12   e, comforting and urging you to live
Heb   10: 25   but e one another—
1Pe   5: 12   e you and testifying that this is

ENCROACH
Pr   23: 10   or e on the fields of the fatherless,

END (ENDS)
Ps   119: 33   that I may follow it to the e.
   119:112   keeping your decrees to the very e.
Pr   5:   4   but in the e she is bitter as gall,
   5: 11   At the e of your life you will groan,
   14: 12   right, but in the e it leads to death.
   14: 13   ache, and rejoicing may e in grief.
   16: 25   right, but in the e it leads to death.
   19: 20   the e you will be counted among
   20: 21   too soon will not be blessed at the e.
   23: 32   In the e it bites like a snake
   25:   8   do in the e if your neighbor puts you
   28: 23   e gain favor rather than one who
Ecc   3: 11   God has done from beginning to e.
   7:   8   The e of a matter is better than its
   12: 12   making many books there is no e,
Eze   7:   2   'The e! The e has come upon
Mt   10: 22   stand firm to the e will be saved.
   24: 13   stands firm to the e will be saved.
   24: 14   nations, and then the e will come.
Lk   21:   9   but the e will not come right away."
Jn   13:   1   he loved them to the e.
1Co   15: 24   Then the e will come, when he
Rev   21:   6   Omega, the Beginning and the E.
   22: 13   the Last, the Beginning and the E.

ENDS (END)
Ps   19:   4   their words to the e of the world.
Pr   20: 17   but one e up with a mouth full
Isa   49:   6   may reach to the e of the earth."
   62: 11   proclaimed to the e of the earth:
Ac   13: 47   salvation to the e of the earth.' "
Ro   10: 18   their words to the e of the world."

ENDURANCE* (ENDURE)
Ro   15:   4   so that through the e taught
   15:   5   May the God who gives e
2Co   1:   6   you patient e of the same sufferings
   6:   4   in great e; in troubles,
Col   1: 11   might so that you may have great e
1Ti   1:   3   your e inspired by hope in our Lord
1Ti   6: 11   faith, love, e and gentleness.
2Ti   3: 10   my purpose, faith, patience, love, e,
Tit   2:   2   and sound in faith, in love and in e.
Rev   1:   9   and patient e that are ours in Jesus,
   13: 10   This calls for patient e
   14: 12   This calls for patient e on the part

ENDURE (ENDURANCE ENDURED ENDURES ENDURING)
Ps   72: 17   May his name e forever;
Pr   12: 19   Truthful lips e forever, but a lying
   27: 24   for riches do not e forever,
Ecc   3: 14   everything God does will e forever;
Isa   55: 13   that will e forever.
Da   2: 44   an end, but it will itself e forever.
Mal   3:   2   who can e the day of his coming?
1Co   4: 12   when we are persecuted, we e it;
   10: 13   a way out so that you can e it.
2Co   1:   6   far beyond our ability to e,
2Ti   2: 10   Therefore I e everything
   2: 12   if we e, we will also reign with him.
   4:   5   head in all situations, e hardship,
Heb   12:   7   E hardship as discipline;
1Pe   2: 20   a beating for doing wrong and e it?
   2: 20   suffer for doing good and you e it,
Rev   3: 10   kept my command to e patiently,

ENDURED* (ENDURE)
Ps   123:   3   for we have e no end of contempt.
   123:   4   We have e no end of ridicule
Ac   13: 18   forty years he e their conduct
2Ti   3: 11   and Lystra, the persecutions I e.
Heb   10: 32   when you e in a great conflict
   12:   2   joy set before him he e the cross,
   12:   3   him who e such opposition
Rev   2:   3   and have e hardships for my name,

ENDURES (ENDURE)
Ps   102: 12   your renown e through all
   112:   9   poor, their righteousness e forever;
   136:   1   His love e forever.

Isa 40: 8 the word of our God e forever."
Da 9: 15 yourself a name that e to this day,
2Co 9: 9 their righteousness e forever."
1Pe 1: 25 the word of the Lord e forever."

ENDURING (ENDURE)
2Th 1: 4 the persecutions and trials you are e.
1Pe 1: 23 the living and e word of God.

ENEMIES (ENEMY)
Ps 23: 5 before me in the presence of my e.
110: 1 hand until I make your e a footstool
Pr 16: 7 he causes their e to make peace
24: 17 Do not gloat when your e fall;
26: 24 E disguise themselves with their
29: 24 of thieves are their own e;
Isa 59: 18 so will he repay wrath to his e
Mic 7: 6 your e are the members of your own
Mt 5: 44 love your e and pray for those who
10: 36 your e will be the members of your
Lk 6: 27 Love your e, do good to those who
6: 35 But love your e, do good to them,
20: 43 until I make your e a footstool
Ro 5: 10 while we were God's e, we were
1Co 15: 25 he has put all his e under his feet.
Php 3: 18 tears, many live as e of the cross
Heb 1: 13 hand until I make your e a footstool
10: 13 for his e to be made his footstool.

ENEMY (ENEMIES ENMITY)
Pr 25: 21 If your e is hungry, give him food
27: 6 trusted, but an e multiplies kisses.
Lk 10: 19 to overcome all the power of the e;
Ro 12: 20 "If your e is hungry, feed him;
1Co 15: 26 The last e to be destroyed is death.
1Ti 5: 14 and to give the e no opportunity
1Pe 5: 8 Your e the devil prowls around like

ENERGY*
Col 1: 29 all the e Christ so powerfully works

ENGRAVED
Isa 49: 16 I have e you on the palms of my
2Co 3: 7 which was e in letters on stone,

ENHANCES*
Ro 3: 7 my falsehood e God's truthfulness

ENJOY (JOY)
Dt 6: 2 and so that you may e long life.
Est 5: 14 to the banquet and e yourself."
Ps 37: 3 dwell in the land and e safe pasture.
Pr 28: 16 ill-gotten gain will e a long reign.
Ecc 3: 22 for people than to e their work,
Eph 6: 3 and that you may e long life
Heb 11: 25 than to e the fleeting pleasures
3Jn : 2 I pray that you may e good health

ENJOYMENT (JOY)
Ecc 4: 8 why am I depriving myself of e?"
1Ti 6: 17 us with everything for our e.

ENLARGE (ENLARGES)
2Co 9: 10 seed and will e the harvest of your

ENLARGES (ENLARGE)
Dt 33: 20 is he who e God's domain!

ENLIGHTENED* (LIGHT)
Eph 1: 18 eyes of your heart may be e in order
Heb 6: 4 for those who have once been e,

ENMITY* (ENEMY)
Ge 3: 15 I will put e between you
Jas 4: 4 the world means e against God?

ENOCH
1. Son of Cain (Ge 4:17–18).
2. Descendant of Seth; walked with God and taken by him (Ge 5:18–24; Heb 11:5). Prophet (Jude 14).

ENSLAVED (SLAVE)
Gal 4: 9 wish to be e by them all over again?
Tit 3: 3 and by all kinds of passions

ENSNARE (SNARE)
Pr 5: 22 evil deeds of the wicked e them;
Ecc 7: 26 escape her, but the sinner she will e.

ENSNARED* (SNARE)
Dt 7: 25 or you will be e by it, for it is
12: 30 be careful not to be e by inquiring
Ps 9: 16 the wicked are e by the work
Pr 6: 2 said, e by the words of your mouth,
22: 25 learn their ways and get yourself e.

ENTANGLED (ENTANGLES)
2Pe 2: 20 Jesus Christ and are again e in it

ENTANGLES* (ENTANGLED)
Heb 12: 1 hinders and the sin that so easily e.

ENTER (ENTERED ENTERING ENTERS ENTRANCE)
Ps 95: 11 'They shall never e my rest.' "
100: 4 E his gates with thanksgiving
Pr 2: 10 For wisdom will e your heart,
Mt 5: 20 you will certainly not e the kingdom
7: 13 "E through the narrow gate.
7: 21 will e the kingdom of heaven,
18: 3 you will never e the kingdom
18: 8 It is better for you to e life maimed
19: 17 If you want to e life,
19: 23 the rich to e the kingdom of heaven.
Mk 9: 43 you to e life maimed than with two
9: 45 you to e life crippled than to have
9: 47 for you to e the kingdom of God
10: 15 like a little child will never e it."
10: 23 the rich to e the kingdom of God!"
Lk 13: 24 effort to e through the narrow door,
13: 24 will try to e and will not be able to.
18: 17 like a little child will never e it."
18: 24 the rich to e the kingdom of God!
Jn 3: 5 no one can e the kingdom of God
Heb 3: 11 'They shall never e my rest.' "
4: 11 make every effort to e that rest,

ENTERED (ENTER)
Ps 73: 17 till I e the sanctuary of God;
Eze 4: 14 impure meat has ever e my mouth."
Ac 11: 8 or unclean has ever e my mouth."
Ro 5: 12 just as sin e the world through one
Heb 9: 12 he e the Most Holy Place once

ENTERING (ENTER)
Mt 21: 31 the prostitutes are e the kingdom
Lk 11: 52 have hindered those who were e."
Heb 4: 1 the promise of e his rest still stands,

ENTERS (ENTER)
Mk 7: 18 nothing that e you from the outside
Jn 10: 2 The one who e by the gate is

ENTERTAIN* (ENTERTAINMENT)
Jdg 16: 25 "Bring out Samson to us."
Mt 9: 4 "Why do you e evil thoughts
1Ti 5: 19 Do not e an accusation against

ENTERTAINMENT* (ENTERTAIN)
Da 6: 18 without any e being brought to him.

ENTHRALLED*
Ps 45: 11 Let the king be e by your beauty;

ENTHRONED* (THRONE)
1Sa 4: 4 who is e between the cherubim.
2Sa 6: 2 who is e between the cherubim
2Ki 19: 15 of Israel, e between the cherubim,
1Ch 13: 6 who is e between the cherubim—
Ps 2: 4 The One e in heaven laughs;
7: 7 while you sit e over them on high.
9: 4 sitting e as the righteous judge.
9: 11 praises of the LORD, e in Zion,
22: 3 Yet you are e as the Holy One;
29: 10 The LORD sits e over the flood;
29: 10 the LORD is e as King forever.
55: 19 God, who is e from of old,
61: 7 May he be e in God's presence
80: 1 You who sit e between
99: 1 he sits e between the cherubim,
102: 12 But you, LORD, sit e forever;
113: 5 God, the One who sits e on high,
123: 1 to you who sit e in heaven,
132: 14 I will sit e, for I have desired it.
Isa 14: 13 I will sit e on the mount
37: 16 of Israel, e between the cherubim,
40: 22 He sits e above the circle
52: 2 rise up, sit e, Jerusalem.
Rev 18: 7 she boasts, 'I sit e as queen.

ENTHRONES* (THRONE)
Job 36: 7 he e them with kings and exalts

ENTHUSIASM*
2Co 8: 17 but he is coming to you with much e
9: 2 your e has stirred most of them

ENTICE* (ENTICED ENTICES)
Pr 1: 10 if sinful men e you, do not give
16: 29 The violent e their neighbors
2Pe 2: 18 they e people who are just escaping
Rev 2: 14 who taught Balak to e the Israelites

ENTICED* (ENTICE)
Dt 4: 19 do not be e into bowing down
11: 16 or you will be e to turn away
2Ki 17: 21 Jeroboam e Israel away
Job 31: 9 my heart has been e by a woman,
31: 27 so that my heart was secretly e

Jas 1: 14 away by your own evil desire and e.

ENTICES* (ENTICE)
Dt 13: 6 or your closest friend secretly e you,
Job 36: 18 careful that no one e you by riches;

ENTIRE
Gal 5: 14 For the e law is fulfilled in keeping

ENTRANCE (ENTER)
Mt 27: 60 stone in front of the e to the tomb
Mk 15: 46 he rolled a stone against the e
16: 3 away from the e of the tomb?"
Jn 11: 38 a cave with a stone laid across the e.
20: 1 stone had been removed from the e.

ENTRUST (TRUST)
Ps 143: 8 for to you I e my life.
Jn 2: 24 Jesus would not e himself to them,
2Ti 2: 2 many witnesses e to reliable people

ENTRUSTED (TRUST)
Jer 13: 20 is the flock that was e to you,
Jn 5: 22 but has e all judgment to the Son,
Ro 3: 2 the Jews have been e with the very
1Co 4: 1 as those e with the mysteries God
1Th 2: 4 by God to be e with the gospel.
1Ti 1: 11 the blessed God, which he e to me.
6: 20 guard what has been e to your care.
2Ti 1: 12 to guard what I have e to him until
1: 14 the good deposit that was e to you—
Tit 1: 3 light through the preaching e to me
1Pe 2: 23 he e himself to him who judges
5: 3 not lording it over those e to you,
Jude : 3 the Lord has once for all e to us,

ENVIOUS (ENVY)
Dt 32: 21 I will make them e by those who are
Pr 24: 19 of evildoers or be e of the wicked,
Ro 10: 19 "I will make you e by those who

ENVOY
Pr 13: 17 but a trustworthy e brings healing.

ENVY (ENVIOUS ENVYING)
Pr 3: 31 Do not e the violent or choose any
14: 30 life to the body, but e rots the bones.
23: 17 Do not let your heart e sinners,
24: 1 Do not e the wicked, do not desire
Mk 7: 22 malice, deceit, lewdness, e, slander,
Ro 1: 29 They are full of e, murder, strife,
11: 14 arouse my own people to e and save
1Co 13: 4 It does not e, it does not boast, it is
Gal 5: 21 and e; drunkenness, orgies,
Php 1: 15 true that some preach Christ out of e
1Ti 6: 4 quarrels about words that result in e,
Tit 3: 3 We lived in malice and e,
Jas 3: 14 But if you harbor bitter e and selfish
3: 16 For where you have e and selfish
1Pe 2: 1 hypocrisy, e, and slander of every

ENVYING* (ENVY)
Gal 5: 26 provoking and e each other.

EPHAH
Eze 45: 11 The e and the bath are to be

EPHESUS
Ac 18: 19 They arrived at E, where Paul left
19: 1 the interior and arrived at E.
Eph 1: 1 To God's holy people in E,
Rev 2: 1 the angel of the church in E write:

EPHRAIM
1. Second son of Joseph (Ge 41:52; 46:20). Blessed as firstborn by Jacob (Ge 48). Tribe of numbered (Nu 1:33; 26:37), blessed (Dt 33:17), allotted land (Jos 16:4–9; Eze 48:5), failed to fully possess (Jos 16:10; Jdg 1:29).
2. Synonymous with Northern Kingdom (Isa 7:17; Hos 5).

EQUAL (EQUALITY EQUITY)
Dt 33: 25 and your strength will e your days.
Isa 40: 25 Or who is my e?" says the Holy
46: 5 you compare me or count me e?
Da 1: 19 and he found none e to Daniel,
Jn 5: 18 Father, making himself e with God.
1Co 12: 25 its parts should have e concern
2Co 2: 16 And who is e to such a task?

EQUALITY* (EQUAL)
2Co 8: 13 pressed, but that there might be e.
8: 14 what you need. The goal is e,
Php 2: 6 did not consider e with God

EQUIP* (EQUIPPED)
Eph 4: 12 to e his people for works
Heb 13: 21 e you with everything good

EQUIPPED (EQUIP)
2Ti 3: 17 God's people may be thoroughly e

EQUITY* (EQUAL)
Ps   9: 8 judges the peoples with e.
    67: 4 for you rule the peoples with e
    96: 10 he will judge the peoples with e.
    98: 9 and the peoples with e.
    99: 4 you have established e; in Jacob you

ERODES*
Job 14: 18 "But as a mountain e and crumbles

ERROR (ERRORS)
Ro   1: 27 the due penalty for their e.
Jas 5: 20 the way of e will save them
2Pe 2: 18 escaping from those who live in e.

ERRORS* (ERROR)
Ps 19: 12 But who can discern their own e?

ESAU
    Firstborn of Isaac, twin of Jacob (Ge 25:21–26).
Also called Edom (Ge 25:30). Sold Jacob his birthright
(Ge 25:29–34); lost blessing (Gen 27). Married Hittites
(Ge 26:34), Ishmaelites (Ge 28:6–9). Reconciled to Ja-
cob (Gen 33). Genealogy (Ge 36). The LORD chose Ja-
cob over Esau (Mal 1:2–3), but gave Esau land (Dt
2:2–12). Descendants eventually obliterated (Ob 1–21;
Jer 49:7–22).

ESCAPE (ESCAPED ESCAPING)
Ps 68: 20 the Sovereign LORD comes e
    89: 48 can e the power of the grave?
Pr   1: 19 through knowledge the righteous e.
    12: 13 and so the innocent e trouble.
Ro   2: 3 think you will e God's judgment?
1Th 5: 3 woman, and they will not e.
2Ti 2: 26 and e from the trap of the devil,
Heb 2: 3 how shall we e if we ignore so great
    12: 25 If they did not e when they refused

ESCAPED (ESCAPE)
2Pe 1: 4 e the corruption in the world
     2: 20 If they have the corruption

ESCAPING (ESCAPE)
1Co 3: 15 only as one e through the flames.
2Pe 2: 18 they entice people who are just e

ESTABLISH (ESTABLISHED ESTABLISHES)
Ge   6: 18 But I will e my covenant with you,
    17: 21 But my covenant I will e with Isaac,
2Sa 7: 11 the LORD himself will e a house
1Ki 9: 5 I will e your royal throne over Israel
1Ch 28: 7 I will e his kingdom forever if he is
Ps 90: 17 the work of our hands for us—
Pr 16: 3 and he will e your plans.
Isa 26: 12 LORD, you e peace for us;
Ro 10: 3 of God and sought to e their own,
    16: 25 Now to him who is able to e you
Heb 10: 9 sets aside the first to e the second.

ESTABLISHED (ESTABLISH)
Ge   9: 17 the covenant I have e between me
Ex   6: 4 e my covenant with them to give
Ps   8: 2 infants you have e a stronghold
    111: 8 They are e for ever and ever,
Pr 16: 12 throne is e through righteousness.
    20: 18 Plans are e by seeking advice;
Jer 33: 25 and the laws of heaven
Heb 8: 6 new covenant is e on better

ESTABLISHES (ESTABLISH)
Job 25: 2 he e order in the heights of heaven.
Pr 16: 9 but the LORD e their steps.
Isa 42: 4 or be discouraged till he e justice

ESTATE
Ps 136: 23 He remembered us in our low e

ESTEEM (ESTEEMED)
Isa 53: 3 despised, and we held him in low e.
Gal 2: 6 those who were held in high e—

ESTEEMED (ESTEEM)
Pr 22: 1 to be e is better than silver or gold.

ESTHER
    Jewess, originally named Hadassah, who lived in
Persia; cousin of Mordecai (Est 2:7). Chosen queen of
Xerxes (Est 2:8–18). Persuaded by Mordecai to foil
Haman's plan to exterminate the Jews (Est 3–4). Revealed Haman's plans to Xerxes, resulting in Haman's
death (Est 7), the Jews' preservation (Est 8–9), Mordecai's exaltation (Est 8:15; 9:4; 10). Decreed celebration of Purim (Est 9:18–32).

ETERNAL* (ETERNITY)
Ge 21: 33 the name of the LORD, the E God.

Dt 33: 27 The e God is your refuge,
1Ki 10: 9 of the LORD's love for Israel,
Ps 16: 11 with e pleasures at your right hand.
    111: 10 To him belongs e praise.
    119: 89 Your word, LORD, is e;
    119: 160 all your righteous laws are e.
Ecc 12: 5 Then people go to their e home
Isa 26: 4 LORD, the LORD, is the Rock e.
    47: 7 said, 'I am forever—the e queen!'
Jer 10: 10 he is the living God, the e King.
Da   4: 3 His kingdom is an e kingdom;
     4: 34 His dominion is an e dominion;
Mt 18: 8 two feet and be thrown into e fire.
    19: 16 good thing must I do to get e life?"
    19: 29 times as much and will inherit e life.
    25: 41 into the e fire prepared for the devil
    25: 46 they will go away to e punishment,
    25: 46 but the righteous to e life."
Mk   3: 29 forgiven, but is guilty of an e sin."
    10: 17 "what must I do to inherit e life?"
    10: 30 and in the age to come e life.
Lk 10: 25 "what must I do to inherit e life?"
    16: 9 will be welcomed into e dwellings.
    18: 18 what must I do to inherit e life?"
    18: 30 and in the age to come e life."
Jn   3: 15 who believes may have e life
     3: 16 him shall not perish but have e life.
     3: 36 believes in the Son has e life,
     4: 14 of water welling up to e life."
     4: 36 now they harvest the crop for e life,
     5: 24 believes him who sent me has e life
     5: 39 think that in them you possess e life.
     6: 27 but for food that endures to e life,
     6: 40 and believes in him shall have e life,
     6: 47 whoever believes has e life.
     6: 54 flesh and drinks my blood has e life,
     6: 68 You have the words of e life.
    10: 28 I give them e life, and they shall
    12: 25 in this world will keep it for e life.
    12: 50 that his command leads to e life.
    17: 2 he might give e life to all those you
    17: 3 Now this is e life: that they know
Ac 13: 46 consider yourselves worthy of e life,
    13: 48 were appointed for e life believed.
Ro   1: 20 his e power and divine nature—
     2: 7 and immortality, he will give e life.
     5: 21 bring e life through Jesus Christ our
     6: 22 to holiness, and the result is e life.
     6: 23 of God is e life in Christ Jesus our
    16: 26 by the command of the e God,
2Co 4: 17 for us an e glory that far outweighs
     4: 18 temporary, but what is unseen is e.
     5: 1 from God, an e house in heaven,
     5: 8 from the Spirit will reap e life.
Gal 3: 11 according to his e purpose that he
2Th 2: 16 his grace gave us e encouragement
1Ti 1: 16 believe in him and receive e life.
     1: 17 Now to the King e, immortal,
     6: 12 Take hold of the e life to which you
2Ti 1: 9 that is in Christ Jesus, with e glory.
Tit 1: 2 in the hope of e life, which God,
     3: 7 heirs having the hope of e life.
Heb 5: 9 he became the source of e salvation
     6: 2 of the dead, and e judgment.
     9: 12 blood, thus obtaining e redemption.
     9: 14 who through the e Spirit offered
     9: 15 receive the promised e inheritance—
    13: 20 of the e covenant brought back
1Pe 5: 10 who called you to his e glory
2Pe 1: 11 a rich welcome into the e kingdom
1Jn 1: 2 and we proclaim to you the e life,
     2: 25 this is what he promised us—e life.
     3: 15 no murderers have e life in them.
     5: 11 God has given us e life, and this life
     5: 13 you may know that you have e life.
     5: 20 He is the true God and e life.
Jude   : 7 who suffer the punishment of e fire.
       : 21 Jesus Christ to bring you to e life.
Rev 14: 6 he had the e gospel to proclaim

ETERNITY* (ETERNAL)
Ps 93: 2 you are from all e.
Ecc 3: 11 has also set e in the human heart;

ETHIOPIAN*
Jer 13: 23 Can an E change his skin
Ac 8: 27 and on his way he met an E eunuch,

EUNUCH (EUNUCHS)
Ac 8: 27 on his way he met an Ethiopian e,

EUNUCHS* (EUNUCH)
Isa 56: 4 "To the e who keep my Sabbaths,
Mt 19: 12 some are e because they were born

EUTYCHUS*
Ac 20: 9 window was a young man named E,

EVANGELIST* (EVANGELISTS)
Ac 21: 8 stayed at the house of Philip the e,
2Ti 4: 5 do the work of an e, discharge all

EVANGELISTS* (EVANGELIST)
Eph 4: 11 the e, the pastors and teachers,

EVE*
Ge   3: 20 Adam named his wife E,
     4: 1 Adam made love to his wife E,
2Co 11: 3 afraid that just as E was deceived
1Ti 2: 13 For Adam was formed first, then E.

EVEN-TEMPERED* (TEMPER)
Pr 17: 27 those who have understanding are e.

EVENING
Ge   1: 5 And there was e, and there was

EVER (EVERLASTING FOREVER FOREVERMORE)
Ex 15: 18 "The LORD reigns for e and e."
Dt   8: 19 you e forget the LORD your God
1Ki 3: 12 anyone like you, nor will there e be.
Job 4: 7 were the upright e destroyed?
Ps   5: 11 you be glad; let them e sing for joy.
    10: 16 The LORD is King for e and e;
    21: 4 length of days, for e and e.
    25: 3 one who hopes in you will e be put
    25: 15 My eyes are e on the LORD,
    45: 6 throne, O God, will last for e and e;
    45: 17 the nations will praise you for e
    48: 14 For this God is our God for e and e;
    52: 8 I trust in God's unfailing love for e
    61: 8 I will e sing in praise of your name
    71: 6 I will e praise you.
    84: 4 they are e praising you.
    89: 33 nor will I e betray my faithfulness.
    111: 8 They are established for e and e,
    119: 44 always obey your law, for e and e.
    132: 12 will sit on your throne for e and e."
    145: 1 I will praise your name for e and e.
    145: 2 and extol your name for e and e.
    145: 21 praise his holy name for e and e.
Pr   4: 18 shining e brighter till the full light
     5: 19 may you e be intoxicated with her
Isa 66: 8 Who has e heard of such things?
    66: 8 Who has e seen things like this?
Jer 7: 7 I gave your ancestors for e and e.
    25: 5 you and your ancestors for e and e.
    31: 36 the descendants of Israel e cease
Da   2: 20 be to the name of God for e and e;
     7: 18 possess it forever—yes, for e and e.'
    12: 3 like the stars for e and e.
Mic 4: 5 of the LORD our God for e and e.
Mt 13: 14 " 'You will be e hearing but never
    13: 14 you will be e seeing but never
Mk   4: 12 perceiving, and e hearing but never
Jn   1: 18 No one has e seen God, but the one
Gal 1: 5 to whom be glory for e and e.
Eph 3: 21 all generations, for e and e! Amen.
Php 4: 20 God and Father be glory for e and e.
1Ti 1: 17 God, be honor and glory for e and e.
2Ti 4: 18 To him be glory for e and e. Amen.
Heb 1: 8 throne, O God, will last for e and e;
    13: 21 to whom be glory for e and e.
1Pe 4: 11 the glory and the power for e and e.
     5: 11 To him be the power for e and e.
1Jn 4: 12 No one has e seen God; but if we
Rev 1: 6 him be glory and power for e and e!
     1: 18 now look, I am alive for e and e!
    21: 27 Nothing impure will e enter it,
    22: 5 And they will reign for e and e.

EVER-INCREASING* (INCREASE)
Ro   6: 19 to impurity and to e wickedness,
2Co 3: 18 into his image with e glory,

EVERLASTING (EVER)
Ge   9: 16 remember the e covenant between
    17: 7 covenant as an e covenant between
    17: 8 I will give as an e possession to you
    17: 13 in your flesh is to be an e covenant.
    17: 19 with him as an e covenant for his
    48: 4 give this land as an e possession
Ex 15: 18 It is an e covenant of salt before
Dt 33: 15 and the fruitfulness of the e hills;
    33: 27 and underneath are the e arms.
2Sa 23: 5 have made with me an e covenant,
1Ch 16: 17 a decree, to Israel as an e covenant:
    16: 36 the God of Israel, from e to e.
    29: 10 God of our father Israel, from e to e.
Ezr 9: 12 your children as an e inheritance.'
Ne   9: 5 your God, who is from e to e."

Ps 41:13 the God of Israel, from e to e.
52: 5 God will bring you down to e ruin:
74: 3 your steps toward these e ruins,
78:66 he put them to e shame.
90: 2 world, from e to e you are God.
103:17 But from e to e the LORD's love is
105:10 a decree, to Israel as an e covenant:
106:48 the God of Israel, from e to e.
119:142 Your righteousness is e and your
139:24 in me, and lead me in the way e.
145:13 Your kingdom is an e kingdom,
Isa 9: 6 Mighty God, E Father,
24: 5 statutes and broken the covenant.
30: 8 to come it may be an e witness.
33:14 of us can dwell with e burning?"
35:10 e joy will crown their heads.
40:28 The LORD is the e God,
45:17 by the LORD with an e salvation;
45:17 put to shame or disgraced, to ages e.
51:11 e joy will crown their heads.
54: 8 e kindness I will have compassion
55: 3 I will make an e covenant with you,
55:13 for an e sign, that will endure
56: 5 I will give them an e name that will
60:15 I will make you the e pride
60:19 for the LORD will be your e light,
60:20 the LORD will be your e light,
61: 7 your land, and e joy will be yours.
61: 8 and make an e covenant with them.
63:12 them, to gain for himself e renown,
Jer 5:22 the sea, an e barrier it cannot cross.
23:40 I will bring on you e disgrace—
23:40 I will bring on you e disgrace—
25: 9 of horror and scorn, and an e ruin.
31: 3 "I have loved you with an e love;
32:40 I will make an e covenant
50: 5 to the LORD in an e covenant
Eze 16:60 I will establish an e covenant
37:26 it will be an e covenant.
Da 7:14 His dominion is an e dominion
7:27 His kingdom will be an e kingdom,
Mic 6: 2 you e foundations of the earth.
Hab 1: 2 LORD, are you not from e?
2Th 1: 9 will be punished with e destruction
Jude : 6 bound with e chains for judgment

EVER-PRESENT*
Ps 46: 1 and strength, an e help in trouble.

EVERYONE
Ps 11: 4 He observes e on earth;
Eze 18: 4 For e belongs to me,
Lk 6:26 Woe to you when e speaks well
Jn 13:35 By this e will know
1Ti 5:20 sinning you are to reprove before e,

EVIDENCE (EVIDENT)
Jn 14:11 on the e of the works themselves.
2Th 1: 5 All this is e that God's judgment is
Jas 2:20 do you want that faith without

EVIDENT (EVIDENCE)
Php 4: 5 Let your gentleness be e to all.

EVIL (EVILDOER EVILDOERS EVILS)
Ge 2: 9 of the knowledge of good and e.
3: 5 be like God, knowing good and e."
6: 5 human heart was only e all the time.
Ex 32:22 how prone these people are to e.
Jdg 2:11 the Israelites did e in the eyes
3: 7 The Israelites did e in the eyes
3:12 Again the Israelites did e in the eyes
4: 1 Again the Israelites did e in the eyes
6: 1 The Israelites did e in the eyes
10: 6 Again the Israelites did e in the eyes
13: 1 Again the Israelites did e in the eyes
1Ki 11: 6 So Solomon did e in the eyes
16:25 But Omri did e in the eyes
2Ki 15:24 Pekahiah did e in the eyes
Job 1: 1 he feared God and shunned e.
1: 8 a man who fears God and shuns e."
34:10 Far be it from God to do e,
36:21 Beware of turning to e, which you
Ps 5: 4 with you, e people cannot be welcome.
23: 4 I will fear no e, for you are with me;
34:13 keep your tongue from e and your
34:14 Turn from e and do good;
34:16 LORD is against those who do e,
37: 1 not fret because of those who are e
37: 8 do not fret—it leads only to e.
37:27 Turn from e and do good;
49: 5 should I fear when e days come,

Ps 51: 4 and done what is e in your sight;
97:10 those who love the LORD hate e,
101: 4 have nothing to do with what is e.
141: 4 drawn to what is e so that I take part
Pr 4:27 or the left; keep your foot from e.
8:13 To fear the LORD is to hate e;
11:19 but those who pursue e go to their
11:27 e comes to those who search for it.
14:16 wise fear the LORD and shun e,
17:13 of one who pays back for good.
20:30 Blows and wounds cleanse away e,
26:23 are fervent lips with an e heart.
Ecc 12:14 thing, whether it is good or e.
Isa 5:20 Woe to those who call e good
13:11 I will punish the world for its e,
Jer 4:14 wash the e from your heart and be
18: 8 that nation I warned repents of its e,
18:11 So turn from your e ways, each one
Eze 33:11 Turn from your e ways!
33:13 will die for the e they have done.
33:15 and do no e, they will surely live;
Am 5:13 in such times, for the times are e.
Hab 1:13 Your eyes are too pure to look on e;
Zec 8:17 do not plot e against each other,
Mt 5:45 He causes his sun to rise on the e
6:13 but deliver us from the e one.'
7:11 though you are e, know how to give
12:34 you who are e say anything good?
12:35 e people bring e things out of the e
12:43 "When an e spirit comes
15:19 out of the heart come e thoughts,
Mk 7:21 out of your hearts, come e thoughts,
Lk 6:45 e people bring e things out of the e
11:13 though you are e, know how to give
Jn 3:19 of light because their deeds were e.
3:20 All those who do e hate the light,
17:15 you protect them from the e one.
Ro 1:30 they invent ways of doing e;
2: 8 who reject the truth and follow e,
2: 9 for every human being who does e:
3: 8 "Let us do e that good may
6:12 body so that you obey its e desires.
7:19 to do, but the e I do not want to do—
7:21 to do good, e is right there with me.
12: 9 Hate what is e; cling to what is
12:17 Do not repay anyone e for e.
12:21 by e, but overcome e with good.
14:16 you know is good be spoken of as e.
16:19 good, and innocent about what is e.
1Co 13: 5 Love does not delight in e
14:20 In regard to e be infants, but in your
Eph 5:16 opportunity, because the days are e.
6:12 against the spiritual forces of e
6:16 all the flaming arrows of the e one.
Col 3: 5 lust, e desires and greed, which is
2Th 3: 3 you and protect you from the e one.
1Ti 6:10 of money is a root of all kinds of e.
2Ti 2:22 Flee the e desires of youth
2:26 are swayed by all kinds of e desires,
Heb 5:14 to distinguish good from e.
Jas 1:13 For God cannot be tempted by e,
1:21 filth and the e that is so prevalent
3: 6 a world of e among the parts
3: 8 It is a restless, e full of deadly
1Pe 3:12 your freedom as a cover-up for e;
3: 9 Do not repay e with e or insult
3:10 days must keep your tongue from e
3:17 for doing good than for doing e.
1Jn 2:13 you have overcome the e one.
2:14 and you have overcome the e one.
3:12 Cain, who belonged to the e one
5:18 and the e one cannot harm them.
5:19 is under the control of the e one.
3Jn : 11 do not imitate what is e but what is

EVILDOER* (EVIL)
2Sa 3:39 the LORD repay the e according
Ps 101: 8 will cut off every e from the city
Pr 24:20 for the e has no future hope,
Mal 4: 1 and every e will be stubble,

EVILDOERS (EVIL)
1Sa 24:13 'From e come evil deeds,' so my
Job 8:20 or strengthen the hands of e.
34: 8 He keeps company with e;
34:22 no utter darkness, where e can hide.
Ps 14: 4 Do all these e know nothing?
14: 6 You e frustrate the plans
21:15 to the righteous but terror to e.
26: 5 I abhor the assembly of e and refuse
36:12 See how the e lie fallen—
53: 4 Do all these e know nothing?
59: 2 Deliver me from e and save me

Ps 64: 2 of the wicked, from the plots of e.
92: 7 up like grass and all e flourish,
92: 9 all e will be scattered.
94: 4 all the e are full of boasting.
94:16 will take a stand for me against e?
119:115 from me, you e, that I may keep
125: 5 the LORD will banish with the e.
141: 4 deeds along with those who are e;
141: 5 will still be against the deeds of e;
141: 9 me safe from the traps set by e,
Pr 24:19 Do not fret because of e
28: 5 E do not understand what is right,
29: 6 E are snared by their own sin,
Isa 1: 4 a brood of e, children given
1: 4 wicked, against those who help e.
Jer 23:14 They strengthen the hands of e,
Hos 10: 9 Will not war again overtake the e
Mal 3:15 Certainly e prosper, and even
Mt 7:23 Away from me, you e!'
Lk 13:27 Away from me, all you e!'
11: 8 robbers, e, adulterers—
2Ti 3:13 while e and impostors will go

EVILS* (EVIL)
Mk 7:23 All these e come from inside

EWE
2Sa 12: 3 except one little e lamb he had

EXACT*
Ge 43:21 us found his silver—the e weight—
Est 4: 7 including the e amount of money
Pr 22: 7 their case and will e life for life.
Mt 2: 7 from them the e time the star had
Jn 4:53 realized that this was the e time
Heb 1: 3 the e representation of his being,

EXALT* (EXALTED EXALTS)
Ex 15: 2 my father's God, and I will e him.
Jos 3: 7 "Today I will begin to e you
1Sa 2:10 and e the horn of his anointed."
1Ch 25: 5 the promises of God to e him.
29:12 power to e and give strength to all.
Job 19: 5 If indeed you would e yourselves
Ps 30: 1 I will e you, LORD, for you lifted
34: 3 let us e his name together.
35:26 may all who e themselves over me
37:34 He will e you to inherit the land;
38:16 e themselves over me when my feet
75: 6 or from the desert can e themselves.
89:17 and by your favor you e our horn.
99: 5 E the LORD our God and worship
99: 9 E the LORD our God and worship
107:32 Let them e him in the assembly
118:28 you are my God, and I will e you.
145: 1 I will e you, my God the King;
Pr 4: 8 Cherish her, and she will e you;
25: 6 Do not e yourself in the king's
30:32 you play the fool and e yourself,
Isa 24:15 e the name of the LORD, the God
25: 1 I will e you and praise your name,
Eze 29:15 will never again e itself
Da 4:37 praise and e and glorify the King
11:36 He will e and magnify himself
11:37 but will e himself above them all.
Hos 11: 7 High, I will by no means e them.
Mt 23:12 For those who e themselves
Lk 14:11 For all those who e themselves
Lk 18:14 For all those who e themselves
2Th 2: 4 will e himself over everything

EXALTED* (EXALT)
Ex 15: 1 to the LORD, for he is highly e.
15:21 to the LORD, for he is highly e.
Nu 24: 7 their kingdom will be e.
Jos 4:14 day the LORD e Joshua
2Sa 3: 5 had e his kingdom for the sake
22:47 E be my God, the Rock, my Savior!
22:49 You e me above my foes;
23: 1 of the man e by the Most High,
1Ch 14: 2 his kingdom had been highly e
17:17 me as though I were the most e
29:11 you are e as head over all.
29:25 The LORD highly e Solomon
Ne 9: 5 and may it be e above all blessing
Job 24:24 For a little while they are e,
36:22 "God is e in his power. Who is
37:23 is beyond our reach and e in power;
Ps 18:46 to my Rock! E be God my Savior!
18:48 You e me above my foes;
21:13 Be e in your strength, LORD;
27: 6 then my head will be e
35:27 "The LORD be e, who delights
46:10 I will be e among the nations, I will

Ps 46: 10 the nations, I will be e in the earth."
47: 9 earth belong to God; he is greatly e.
57: 5 Be e, O God, above the heavens;
57: 11 Be e, O God, above the heavens;
89: 13 hand is strong, your right hand e.
89: 24 through my name his horn will be e.
89: 27 the most e of the kings of the earth.
89: 42 You have e the right hand of his
92: 8 But you, Lord, are forever e.
92: 10 You have e my horn like
97: 9 you are e far above all gods.
99: 2 he is e over all the nations.
108: 5 Be e, O God, above the heavens;
113: 4 The Lord is e over all
138: 2 you have so e your solemn decree
138: 6 Though the Lord is e, he looks
148: 13 the Lord, for his name alone is e;
Pr 11: 11 blessing of the upright a city is e,
Isa 2: 2 it will be e above the hills,
2: 11 The Lord alone will be e
2: 12 for all that is e (and they will be
2: 17 The Lord alone will be e
5: 16 the Lord Almighty will be e
6: 1 high and e, and the train of his robe
12: 4 and proclaim that his name is e.
33: 5 The Lord is e, for he dwells
33: 10 "Now will I be e; now will I be
52: 13 be raised and lifted up and highly e.
57: 15 what the high and e One says—
Jer 17: 12 throne, e from the beginning,
La 2: 17 he has the horn of your foes.
Eze 21: 26 The lowly will be e and the e will be
   brought low.
Hos 13: 1 he was e in Israel.
Mic 6: 6 and bow down before the e God?
Mt 23: 12 who humble themselves will be e.
Lk 14: 11 who humble themselves will be e.
18: 14 who humble themselves will be e."
Ac 2: 33 E to the right hand of God, he has
5: 31 God e him to his own right hand as
Php 1: 20 now as always Christ will be e
2: 9 Therefore God e him to the highest
Heb 7: 26 from sinners, e above the heavens.

EXALTS* (EXALT)
1Sa 2: 7 he humbles and he e.
Job 36: 7 them with kings and e them forever.
Ps 75: 7 He brings one down, he e another.
Pr 14: 34 Righteousness a nation, but sin

EXAMINE (EXAMINED EXAMINES)
Ps 11: 4 everyone on earth; his eyes e them.
17: 3 though you e me at night and test
26: 2 try me, e my heart and my mind;
Jer 17: 10 search the heart and e the mind,
20: 12 you who see the righteous and probe
La 3: 40 Let us e our ways and test them,
1Co 11: 28 to e themselves before they eat
2Co 13: 5 E yourselves to see whether you are

EXAMINED (EXAMINE)
Job 13: 9 Would it turn out well if he e you?
Ac 17: 11 the Scriptures every day to see

EXAMINES (EXAMINE)
Ps 11: 5 The Lord e the righteous,
Pr 5: 21 the Lord, and he e all your paths.

EXAMPLE* (EXAMPLES)
2Ki 14: 3 everything he followed the e of his
Ecc 9: 13 saw under the sun this e of wisdom
Eze 14: 8 and make them an e and a byword.
Jn 13: 15 I have set you an e that you should
Ro 6: 19 I am using an e from everyday life
7: 2 For e, by law a married woman is
1Co 11: 1 Follow my e, as I follow the e of Christ.
Gal 3: 15 let me take an e from everyday life.
Eph 5: 1 Follow God's e, therefore, as dearly
Php 3: 17 Join together in following my e,
2Th 3: 7 how you ought to follow our e.
1Ti 1: 16 his immense patience as an e
4: 12 set an e for the believers in speech,
Tit 2: 7 everything set them an e by doing
Heb 4: 11 following their e of disobedience.
Jas 3: 4 Or take ships as an e.
5: 10 as an e of patience in the face
1Pe 2: 21 leaving you an e, that you should
2Pe 2: 6 made them an e of what is going
Jude : 7 They serve as an e of those who

EXAMPLES* (EXAMPLE)
1Co 10: 6 Now these things occurred as e
10: 11 These things happened to them as e
1Pe 5: 3 to you, but being e to the flock.

EXASPERATE*
Eph 6: 4 Fathers, do not e your children;

EXCEL* (EXCELLENT)
Ge 49: 4 you will no longer e, for you went
1Co 14: 12 try to e in those that build
2Co 8: 7 But since you e in everything—
8: 7 you also e in this grace of giving.

EXCELLENT (EXCEL)
1Co 12: 31 yet I will show you the most e way.
Php 4: 8 if anything is e or praiseworthy—
1Ti 3: 13 have served well gain an e standing
Tit 3: 8 These things are e and profitable

EXCESSIVE
2Co 2: 7 not be overwhelmed by e sorrow.

EXCHANGE (EXCHANGED)
Mt 16: 26 Or what can you give in e for your
Mk 8: 37 Or what can you give in e for your
2Co 6: 13 As a fair e—I speak as to my

EXCHANGED (EXCHANGE)
Ps 106: 20 They e their glorious God
Jer 2: 11 my people have e their glorious God
Hos 4: 7 they e their glorious God
Ro 1: 23 e the glory of the immortal God
1: 25 They e the truth about God for a lie,
1: 26 Even their women e natural sexual

EXCLAIM
Ps 35: 10 My whole being will e, "Who is

EXCUSE* (EXCUSES)
Lk 14: 18 I must go and see it. Please e me.'
14: 19 way to try them out. Please e me.'
Jn 15: 22 but now they have no e for their sin.
Ro 1: 20 made, so that people are without e.
2: 1 have no e, you who pass judgment

EXCUSES* (EXCUSE)
Lk 14: 18 "But they all alike began to make e.

EXERTED*
Eph 1: 20 he e when he raised Christ

EXHORT* (EXHORTATION)
1Ti 5: 1 but e him as if he were your father.

EXHORTATION (EXHORT)
Ac 13: 15 a word of e for the people,

EXILE (EXILES)
2Ki 17: 23 their homeland into e in Assyria,
25: 11 into e the people who remained

EXILES (EXILE)
1Pe 2: 11 as foreigners and e,

EXISTS
Heb 2: 10 and through whom everything e,
11: 6 comes to him must believe that he e

EXPECT (EXPECTATION EXPECTED EXPECTING)
Mt 24: 44 at an hour when you do not e him.
Lk 12: 40 at an hour when you do not e him."
Php 1: 20 I eagerly e and hope that I will in no

EXPECTATION (EXPECT)
Ro 8: 19 waits in eager e for the children
Heb 10: 27 but only a fearful e of judgment

EXPECTED (EXPECT)
Hag 1: 9 "You e much, but see, it turned

EXPECTING (EXPECT)
Lk 6: 35 to them without e to get anything

EXPEL* (EXPELLED)
1Co 5: 13 "E the wicked person from among

EXPELLED (EXPEL)
Eze 28: 16 and I e you, guardian cherub,

EXPENSE (EXPENSIVE)
1Co 9: 7 serves as a soldier at his own e?

EXPENSIVE* (EXPENSE)
Mt 26: 7 an alabaster jar of very e perfume,
Mk 14: 3 an alabaster jar of very e perfume,
Lk 7: 25 those who wear e clothes
Jn 12: 3 a pint of pure nard, an e perfume;
1Ti 2: 9 or gold or pearls or e clothes,

EXPLAINING (EXPLAINS)
Ac 17: 3 e and proving that the Messiah
1Co 2: 13 e spiritual realities with

EXPLAINS* (EXPLAINING)
Ac 8: 31 said, "unless someone e it to me?"

EXPLOIT* (EXPLOITED EXPLOITING)
Pr 22: 22 Do not e the poor because they are
Isa 58: 3 you please and e all your workers.

2Co 11: 20 or e you or take advantage of you
12: 17 Did I e you through any of the men
12: 18 Titus did not e you, did he?
2Pe 2: 3 their greed these teachers will e you

EXPLOITED* (EXPLOIT)
2Co 7: 2 corrupted no one, we have e no one.

EXPLOITING* (EXPLOIT)
Jas 2: 6 Is it not the rich who are e you?

EXPLORE
Nu 13: 2 "Send some men to e the land

EXPOSE (EXPOSED)
1Co 4: 5 and will e the motives of people's
Eph 5: 11 of darkness, but rather e them.

EXPOSED (EXPOSE)
Jn 3: 20 for fear that their deeds will be e.
Eph 5: 13 exposed e by the light becomes

EXPRESSING*
Gal 5: 6 counts is faith itself through love.

EXTENDS
Pr 31: 20 poor and e her hands to the needy.
Lk 1: 50 His mercy e to those who fear him,

EXTINGUISH* (EXTINGUISHED)
Eph 6: 16 you can e all the flaming arrows

EXTINGUISHED (EXTINGUISH)
2Sa 21: 17 the lamp of Israel will not be e."

EXTOL*
1Ch 16: 4 e, thank, and praise the Lord,
Job 36: 24 Remember to e his work,
Ps 34: 1 I will e the Lord at all times;
68: 4 e him who rides on the clouds;
95: 2 thanksgiving and e him with music
109: 30 mouth I will greatly e the Lord;
111: 1 I will e the Lord with all my
115: 18 it is we who e the Lord,
117: 1 e him, all you peoples.
145: 2 praise you and e your name for ever
145: 10 your faithful people e you.
147: 12 E the Lord, Jerusalem;
Ro 15: 11 Gentiles; let all the peoples e him."

EXTORT* (EXTORTION)
Lk 3: 14 "Don't e money and don't accuse

EXTORTION (EXTORT)
Pr 28: 16 A tyrannical ruler practices e,

EXTRAORDINARY*
Ac 19: 11 God did e miracles through Paul,

EXTREME (EXTREMES)
2Co 8: 2 and their e poverty welled up in rich

EXTREMES* (EXTREME)
Ecc 7: 18 fears God will avoid all e.

EXULT
Ps 89: 16 they e in your righteousness.

EYE (EYES)
Ge 3: 6 good for food and pleasing to the e,
Ex 21: 24 e for e, tooth for tooth,
Dt 19: 21 life for life, e for e, tooth for tooth,
Ps 94: 9 Does he who formed the e not see?
Mt 5: 29 If your right e causes you
5: 38 have heard that it was said, 'E for e,
6: 22 "The e is the lamp of the body.
7: 3 of sawdust in someone else's e
1Co 2: 9 "What no e has seen, what no ear
12: 16 "Because I am not an e, I do not
15: 52 in the twinkling of an e, at the last
Eph 6: 6 to win their favor when their e is
Col 3: 22 not only when their e is on you
Rev 1: 7 and "every e will see him,

EYES (EYE)
Nu 15: 39 the lusts of your own hearts and e.
33: 55 remain will become barbs in your e
Dt 11: 12 the e of the Lord your God are
12: 25 what is right in the e of the Lord
16: 19 for a bribe blinds the e of the wise
Jos 23: 13 on your backs and thorns in your e,
1Sa 15: 17 you were once small in your own e,
1Ki 10: 7 I came and saw with my own e.
2Ki 9: 30 she painted her e, arranged her hair
2Ch 16: 9 For the e of the Lord range
Job 31: 1 "I made a covenant with my e not
36: 7 does not take his e off the righteous;
Ps 25: 15 My e are ever on the Lord,
36: 1 is no fear of God before their e.
101: 6 My e will be on the faithful
118: 23 this, and it is marvelous in our e.

Ps 119: 18 Open my e that I may see wonderful
119: 37 Turn my e away from worthless
121: 1 I lift up my e to the mountains—
123: 1 I lift up my e to you, to you who sit
139: 16 your e saw my unformed body.
141: 8 But my e are fixed on you,
Pr 3: 7 Do not be wise in your own e;
4: 25 Let your e look straight ahead;
15: 3 The e of the LORD are
15: 30 Light in a messenger's e brings
17: 24 a fool's e wander to the ends
Isa 6: 5 and my e have seen the King,
33: 17 Your e will see the king in his
42: 7 to open e that are blind, to free
Jer 24: 6 My e will watch over them for their
Hab 1: 13 Your e are too pure to look on
Mt 6: 22 If your e are healthy, your whole
21: 42 this, and it is marvelous in our e'?
Lk 16: 15 justify yourselves in the e of others,
24: 31 Then their e were opened and they
Jn 4: 35 open your e and look at the fields!
Ac 1: 9 he was taken up before their very e,
4: 19 "Which is right in God's e:
2Co 4: 18 So we fix our e not on what is seen,
8: 21 not only in the e of the Lord
Eph 1: 18 pray that the e of your heart may be
Php 3: 17 keep your e on those who live as we
Heb 12: 2 fixing our e on Jesus, the pioneer
Jas 2: 5 who are poor in the e of the world
1Pe 3: 12 For the e of the Lord are
Rev 7: 17 away every tear from their e.' "
21: 4 will wipe every tear from their e.

EYEWITNESSES* (WITNESS)
Lk 1: 2 by those who from the first were e
2Pe 1: 16 but we were e of his majesty.

EZEKIEL*
Priest called to be prophet to the exiles (Eze 1–3). Symbolically acted out destruction of Jerusalem (Eze 4–5; 12; 24).

EZRA*
Priest and teacher of the Law who led a return of exiles to Israel to reestablish temple and worship (Ezr 7–8). Corrected intermarriage of priests (Ezr 9–10). Read Law at celebration of Feast of Tabernacles (Ne 8). Participated in dedication of Jerusalem's walls (Ne 12).

FACE (FACES)
Ge 32: 30 "It is because I saw God f to f,
Ex 3: 6 Moses hid his f, because he was
33: 11 would speak to Moses f to f,
33: 20 "you cannot see my f, for no one
34: 29 that his f was radiant because he had
Nu 6: 25 the LORD make his f shine on you
12: 8 With him I speak f to f,
14: 14 LORD, have been seen f to f,
Dt 5: 4 The LORD spoke to you f to f
31: 17 I will hide my f from them, and they
34: 10 whom the LORD knew f to f,
Jdg 6: 22 the angel of the LORD f to f!"
2Ki 14: 8 "Come, meet me f to f."
1Ch 16: 11 and his strength; seek his f always.
2Ch 7: 14 and seek my f and turn from their
25: 17 "Come, meet me f to f."
Ezr 9: 6 to lift up my f to you, because our
Ps 4: 6 Let the light of your f shine on us.
27: 8 Your f, LORD, I will seek.
31: 16 Let your f shine on your servant;
44: 3 and the light of your f, for you loved
44: 22 your sake we f death all day long;
51: 9 Hide your f from my sins and blot
67: 1 bless us and make his f shine on us—
80: 3 make your f shine on us, that we
105: 4 and his strength; seek his f always.
119:135 Make your f shine on your servant
SS 2: 14 voice is sweet, and your f is lovely.
Isa 50: 7 Therefore have I set my f like flint,
50: 8 Let us f each other!
54: 8 a surge of anger I hid my f from you
Jer 32: 4 will speak with him f to f and see
34: 3 and he will speak with you f to f.
Eze 1: 10 the four had the f of a human being,
20: 35 and there, f to f, I will
Mt 17: 2 His f shone like the sun, and his
18: 10 in heaven always see the f of my
Lk 9: 29 the appearance of his f changed,
Ro 8: 36 your sake we f death all day long;
1Co 13: 12 then we shall see f to f.
2Co 3: 7 steadily at the f of Moses because
4: 6 glory displayed in the f of Christ.
10: 1 who am "timid" when f to f

1Pe 3: 12 but the f of the Lord is against
2Jn : 12 talk with you f to f,
3Jn : 14 we will talk f to f.
Rev 1: 16 His f was like the sun shining
22: 4 They will see his f, and his name

FACES (FACE)
2Co 3: 18 unveiled f contemplate the Lord's

FACTIONS
2Co 12: 20 outbursts of anger, f, slander,
Gal 5: 20 rage, selfish ambition, dissensions,

FADE
Jas 1: 11 the rich will f away even while
1Pe 5: 4 of glory that will never f away.

FAIL (FAILED FAILING FAILINGS FAILS)
Lev 26: 15 and f to carry out all my commands
1Ki 2: 4 you will never f to have a successor
1Ch 28: 20 He will not f you or forsake you
2Ch 34: 33 they did not f to follow the LORD,
Ps 89: 28 my covenant with him will never f.
Pr 15: 22 Plans f for lack of counsel,
Isa 51: 6 my righteousness will never f.
Jer 14: 6 their eyes f for lack of food."
La 3: 22 for his compassions never f.
Lk 1: 37 For no word from God will ever f."
22: 32 Simon, that your faith may not f.
2Co 13: 5 unless, of course, you f the test?

FAILED (FAIL)
Jos 23: 14 has been fulfilled; not one has f.
1Ki 8: 56 Not one word has f of all the good
Ps 77: 8 Has his promise f for all time?
Ro 9: 6 is not as though God's word had f.
2Co 13: 6 discover that we have not f the test.

FAILING (FAIL)
1Sa 12: 23 I should sin against the LORD by f

FAILINGS* (FAIL)
Ro 15: 1 ought to bear with the f of the weak

FAILS (FAIL)
Ps 143: 7 LORD; my spirit f.
Joel 1: 10 new wine is dried up, the olive oil f
1Co 13: 8 Love never f. But where there are

FAINT
Isa 40: 31 weary, they will walk and not be f.

FAINTHEARTED* (HEART)
Dt 20: 3 Do not be f or afraid; do not be
20: 8 shall add, "Is anyone afraid or f?

FAIR (FAIRNESS)
Pr 1: 3 doing what is right and just and f;
Col 4: 1 your slaves with what is right and f,

FAIRNESS* (FAIR)
Pr 29: 14 If a king judges the poor with f,

FAITH* (FAITHFUL FAITHFULLY FAITHFULNESS FAITHLESS)
Ex 21: 8 because he has broken f with her.
Dt 32: 51 because both of you broke f with me
Jos 22: 16 'How could you break f
Jdg 9: 16 good f by making Abimelek king?
9: 19 in good f toward Jerub-Baal and his
1Sa 14: 33 "You have broken f," he said
2Ch 20: 20 Have f in the LORD your God
20: 20 have f in his prophets and you will
Isa 7: 9 If you do not stand firm in your f,
26: 2 may enter, the nation that keeps f.
Mt 6: 30 more clothe you—you of little f?
8: 10 anyone in Israel with such great f.
8: 26 "You of little f, why are you so
9: 2 When Jesus saw their f, he said
9: 22 he said, "your f has healed you."
9: 29 "According to your f let it be done
13: 58 there because of their lack of f.
14: 31 "You of little f," he said, "why did
15: 28 to her, "Woman, you have great f!
16: 8 "You of little f, why are you talking
17: 20 if you have f as small as a mustard
21: 21 if you have f and do not doubt,
24: 10 time many will turn away from the f
Mk 5: 34 "Daughter, your f has healed you.
4: 40 Do you still have no f?"
5: 34 "Daughter, your f has healed you.
6: 6 He was amazed at their lack of f.
10: 52 said Jesus, "your f has healed you."
11: 22 "Have f in God," Jesus answered.
16: 14 rebuked them for their lack of f
Lk 5: 20 When Jesus saw their f, he said,
7: 9 I have not found such great f even
7: 50 the woman, "Your f has saved you;

Lk 8: 25 "Where is your f?" he asked his
8: 48 "Daughter, your f has healed you.
12: 28 will he clothe you—you of little f!
17: 5 said to the Lord, "Increase our f!"
17: 6 "If you have f as small as a mustard
17: 19 your f has made you well."
18: 8 comes, will he find f on the earth?"
18: 42 your f has healed you."
22: 32 Simon, that your f may not fail.
Jn 2: 11 and his disciples put their f in him.
7: 31 in the crowd put their f in him.
8: 30 as he spoke, many put their f in him.
11: 45 what Jesus did, put their f in him.
12: 11 to Jesus and putting their f in him.
12: 42 not openly acknowledge their f
14: 12 all who have f in me will do
Ac 3: 16 By f in the name of Jesus, this man
3: 16 the f that comes through him
6: 5 a man full of f and of the Holy
6: 7 of priests became obedient to the f.
11: 24 full of the Holy Spirit and f,
13: 8 to turn the proconsul from the f.
14: 9 saw that he had f to be healed
14: 22 them to remain true to the f.
14: 27 how he had opened a door of f
15: 9 he purified their hearts by f.
16: 5 churches were strengthened in the f
20: 21 and have f in our Lord Jesus.
24: 24 to him as he spoke about f in Christ
26: 18 among those who are sanctified by f
27: 25 for I have f in God that it will
Ro 1: 5 to call all the Gentiles to f
1: 8 because your f is being reported all
1: 12 encouraged by each other's f.
1: 17 righteousness that is by f from first
1: 17 "The righteous will live by f."
3: 22 righteousness is given through f
3: 25 of his blood—to be received by f.
3: 26 one who justifies those who have f
3: 27 of the "law" that requires f.
3: 28 a person is justified by f apart
3: 30 will justify the circumcised by f
3: 30 uncircumcised through that same f.
3: 31 then, nullify the law by this f?
4: 5 their f is credited as righteousness.
4: 9 that Abraham's f was credited
4: 11 while he was still uncircumcised.
4: 12 of the f that our father Abraham had
4: 13 the righteousness that comes by f.
4: 14 f means nothing and the promise is
4: 16 the promise comes by f, so that it
4: 16 to those who have the f of Abraham.
4: 19 Without weakening in his f,
4: 20 was strengthened in his f and gave
5: 1 we have been justified through f,
5: 2 whom we have gained access by f
9: 30 a righteousness that is by f
9: 32 Because they pursued it not by f
10: 6 the righteousness that is by f says:
10: 8 the message concerning f that we
10: 10 you profess your f and are saved.
10: 17 f comes from hearing the message,
11: 20 of unbelief, and you stand by f.
12: 3 with the f God has distributed
12: 6 prophesy in accordance with your f;
14: 1 Accept those whose f is weak,
14: 2 One person's f allows them to eat
14: 2 but another person, whose f is weak,
14: 23 because their eating is not from f;
14: 23 that does not come from f is sin.
16: 26 Gentiles might come to f and obedience—
1Co 2: 5 so that your f might not rest
12: 9 to another f by the same Spirit,
13: 2 I have a f that can move mountains,
13: 13 these three remain: f, hope and love.
15: 14 preaching is useless and so is your f.
15: 17 has not been raised, your f is futile;
16: 13 stand firm in the f; be courageous;
2Co 1: 24 Not that we lord it over your f,
1: 24 because it is by f you stand firm.
4: 13 Since we have that same spirit of f,
5: 7 We live by f, not by sight.
8: 7 in f, in speech, in knowledge,
10: 15 is that, as your f continues to grow,
13: 5 to see whether you are in the f;
Gal 1: 23 is now preaching the f he once tried
2: 16 the law, but by f in Jesus Christ.
2: 16 have put our f in Christ Jesus
2: 16 we may be justified by f in Christ
2: 20 by f in the Son of God,
3: 7 who have f are children of Abraham.
3: 8 God would justify the Gentiles by f,

Gal	3: 9	who rely on f are blessed along
	3: 9	along with Abraham, the man of f.
	3: 11	"the righteous will live by f."
	3: 12	The law is not based on f;
	3: 14	by f we might receive the promise
	3: 22	being given through f in Jesus
	3: 23	Before the coming of this f, we were
	3: 23	locked up until the f that was
	3: 24	came that we might be justified by f.
	3: 25	Now that this f has come, we are no
	3: 26	are all children of God through f,
	5: 5	f we eagerly await through the Spirit
	5: 6	counts is f expressing itself through
Eph	1: 15	heard about your f in the Lord Jesus
	2: 8	you have been saved, through f—
	3: 12	through f in him we may approach
	3: 17	may dwell in your hearts through f.
	4: 5	one Lord, one f, one baptism;
	4: 13	until we all reach unity in the f
	6: 16	take up the shield of f,
	6: 23	and love with f from God the Father
Php	1: 25	for your progress and joy in the f,
	1: 27	one accord for the f of the gospel
	2: 17	and service coming from your f,
	3: 9	that which is through f in Christ—
	3: 9	comes from God on the basis of f.
Col	1: 4	have heard of your f in Christ Jesus
	1: 5	the f and love that spring
	1: 23	if you continue in your f,
	2: 5	are and how firm your f in Christ is.
	2: 7	in the f as you were taught,
	2: 12	him through your f in the working
1Th	1: 3	Father your work produced by f,
	1: 8	your f in God has become known
	3: 2	and encourage you in your f,
	3: 5	I sent to find out about your f.
	3: 6	has brought good news about your f
	3: 7	about you because of your f.
	3: 10	and supply what is lacking in your f.
	5: 8	be sober, putting on f and love as
2Th	1: 3	because your f is growing more
	1: 4	and f in all the persecutions
	1: 11	and your every deed prompted by f.
	3: 2	evil people, for not everyone has f.
1Ti	1: 2	To Timothy my true son in the f:
	1: 4	which is by f.
	1: 5	a good conscience and a sincere f.
	1: 14	along with the f and love that are
	1: 19	holding on to f and a good
	1: 19	shipwreck with regard to the f.
	2: 15	if they continue in f,
	3: 9	of the f with a clear conscience.
	3: 13	assurance in their f in Christ Jesus.
	4: 1	later times some will abandon the f
	4: 6	nourished on the truths of the f
	4: 12	conduct, in love, in f and in purity.
	5: 8	has denied the f and is worse than
	6: 10	have wandered from the f
	6: 11	righteousness, godliness, f, love,
	6: 12	Fight the good fight of the f.
	6: 21	so doing have departed from the f.
2Ti	1: 5	I am reminded of your sincere f,
	1: 13	with f and love in Christ Jesus.
	2: 18	and they destroy the f of some.
	2: 22	youth and pursue righteousness, f,
	3: 8	as far as the f is concerned,
	3: 10	way of life, my purpose, f, patience,
	3: 15	salvation through f in Christ Jesus.
	4: 7	finished the race, I have kept the f.
Tit	1: 1	Christ to further the f of God's elect
	1: 4	Titus, my true son in our common f:
	1: 13	so that they will be sound in the f
	2: 2	and sound in f, in love
	3: 15	Greet those who love us in the f.
Phm	: 5	people and your f in the Lord Jesus.
	: 6	with us in the f may be effective
Heb	4: 2	because they did not share the f
	4: 14	us hold firmly to the f we profess.
	6: 1	that lead to death, and of f in God,
	6: 12	to imitate those who through f
	10: 22	a sincere heart in full assurance of f,
	10: 38	my righteous one will live by f.
	11: 1	Now f is being sure of what we
	11: 3	By f we understand that the universe
	11: 4	By f Abel brought God a better offering
	11: 4	By f he was commended as righteous,
	11: 4	And by f Abel still speaks,
	11: 5	By f Enoch was taken from this life,
	11: 6	without f it is impossible to please
	11: 7	By f Noah, when warned
	11: 7	By his f he condemned the world
	11: 7	that is in keeping with f.

Heb	11: 8	By f Abraham, when called to go
	11: 9	By f he made his home
	11: 11	And by f even Sarah, who was past
	11: 13	these people were still living by f
	11: 17	By f Abraham, when God tested
	11: 20	By f Isaac blessed Jacob and Esau
	11: 21	By f Jacob, when he was dying,
	11: 22	By f Joseph, when his end was near,
	11: 23	By f Moses' parents hid him
	11: 24	By f Moses, when he had grown up,
	11: 27	By f he left Egypt, not fearing
	11: 28	By f he kept the Passover
	11: 29	f the people passed through the Red
	11: 30	By f the walls of Jericho fell,
	11: 31	By f the prostitute Rahab,
	11: 33	who through f conquered kingdoms,
	11: 39	were all commended for their f,
	12: 2	Jesus, the pioneer and perfecter of f.
	13: 7	their way of life and imitate their f.
Jas	1: 3	of your f produces perseverance.
	2: 5	the eyes of the world to be rich in f
	2: 14	if people claim to have f but have no
	2: 14	Can such f save them?
	2: 17	In the same way, f by itself, if it is
	2: 18	But someone will say, "You have f;
	2: 18	Show me your f without deeds,
	2: 18	I will show you my f by what I do.
	2: 20	that f without deeds is useless?
	2: 22	You see that his f and his actions
	2: 22	his f was made complete by what he
	2: 24	by what they do and not by f alone.
	2: 26	is dead, so f without deeds is dead.
	5: 15	offered in f will make them well;
1Pe	1: 5	who through f are shielded by God's
	1: 7	These have come so that your f—
	1: 9	receiving the end result of your f,
	1: 21	and so your f and hope are in God.
	5: 9	standing firm in the f, because you
2Pe	1: 1	have received a f as precious as
	1: 5	effort to add to your f goodness;
1Jn	5: 4	has overcome the world, even our f.
Jude	: 3	for the f that the Lord has once
	: 20	yourselves up in your most holy f
Rev	2: 13	You did not renounce your f in me,
	2: 19	your love and f, your service

FAITHFUL (FAITH)

Nu	12: 7	he is f in all my house.
Dt	7: 9	he is the f God, keeping his
	32: 4	A f God who does no wrong,
1Sa	2: 35	I will raise up for myself a f priest,
2Sa	20: 19	We are the peaceful and f in Israel.
	22: 26	"To the f you show yourself f,
1Ki	3: 6	David, because he was f to you
2Ch	31: 18	For they were f in consecrating
	31: 20	and f before the Lord his God.
Ne	9: 8	You found his heart f to you,
Ps	4: 3	the Lord has set apart his f servant
	12: 1	Lord, for no one is f anymore;
	16: 10	will you let your f one see decay.
	18: 25	To the f you show yourself f,
	25: 10	and f toward those who keep
	31: 5	redeem me, Lord, my f God.
	31: 23	Love the Lord, all his f people!
	33: 4	right and true; he is f in all he does.
	37: 28	just and will not forsake his f ones.
	78: 8	whose spirits were not f to him.
	78: 37	they were not f to his covenant.
	86: 2	Guard my life, for I am f to you;
	89: 19	a vision, to your f people you said:
	89: 24	My f love will be with him,
	89: 37	the moon, the f witness in the sky."
	97: 10	for he guards the lives of his f ones
	101: 6	My eyes will be on the f in the land,
	111: 7	The works of his hands are f
	145: 13	promises and f in all he does.
	145: 17	his ways and f in all he does.
	146: 6	he remains f forever.
Pr	2: 8	and protects the way of his f ones.
	20: 6	love, but a f person who can find?
	28: 20	A f person will be richly blessed,
	31: 26	and f instruction is on her tongue.
Isa	1: 21	See how the f City has become a
	1: 26	City of Righteousness, the F City."
	49: 7	who is f, the Holy One of Israel,
	55: 3	my f love promised to David.
Jer	3: 12	for I am f,' declares the Lord,
	42: 5	f witness against us if we do not
Eze	43: 11	so that they may be f to its design
	48: 11	who were f in serving me and did
Hos	11: 12	even against the f Holy One.
Zec	8: 8	I will be f and righteous to them as

Mt	24: 45	then is the f and wise servant,
	25: 21	'Well done, good and f servant!
	25: 21	You have been f with a few things;
	25: 23	'Well done, good and f servant!
	25: 23	You have been f with a few things;
Lk	12: 42	then is the f and wise manager,
Ro	12: 12	patient in affliction, f in prayer.
1Co	1: 9	God is f, who has called you
	4: 2	been given a trust must prove f.
	4: 17	whom I love, who is f in the Lord.
	10: 13	And God is f; he will not let you
2Co	1: 18	But as surely as God is f,
Eph	1: 1	in Ephesus, the f in Christ Jesus:
	6: 21	brother and f servant in the Lord,
Col	1: 2	the f brothers and sisters in Christ;
	1: 7	who is a f minister of Christ on our
	4: 7	a f minister and fellow servant
	4: 9	Onesimus, our f and dear brother,
1Th	5: 24	The one who calls you is f, and he
2Th	3: 3	But the Lord is f, and he will
1Ti	2: 7	f and teacher of the Gentiles.
	3: 2	f to his wife, temperate,
	3: 12	A deacon must be f to his wife
	5: 9	sixty, has been f to her husband,
2Ti	2: 13	he remains f, for he cannot disown
Tit	1: 6	must be blameless, f to his wife,
Heb	2: 17	and f high priest in service to God,
	3: 2	He was f to the one who appointed
	3: 2	just as Moses was f in all God's
	3: 5	"Moses was f as a servant in all
	3: 6	Christ is f as the Son over God's
	8: 9	because they did not remain f to my
	10: 23	profess, for he who promised is f.
	11: 11	she considered him f who had made
1Pe	4: 10	as f stewards of God's grace
	4: 19	themselves to their f Creator
	5: 12	whom I regard as a f brother, I have
1Jn	1: 9	he is f and just and will forgive us
3Jn	: 5	you are f in what you are doing
Rev	1: 5	who is the f witness, the firstborn
	2: 10	Be f, even to the point of death,
	2: 13	in the days of Antipas, my f witness,
	3: 14	of the Amen, the f and true witness,
	14: 12	commands and remain f to Jesus.
	17: 14	his called, chosen and f followers."
	19: 11	whose rider is called F and True.

FAITHFULLY (FAITH)

Dt	11: 13	So if you f obey the commands I am
Jos	2: 14	and f when the Lord gives us
1Sa	12: 24	and serve him f with all your heart;
1Ki	2: 4	and if they walk f before me with all
2Ki	20: 3	how I have walked before you f
2Ch	19: 9	"You must serve f
	31: 12	they f brought in the contributions,
	31: 15	and Shekaniah assisted him f
	32: 1	all that Hezekiah had so f done,
	34: 12	The workers did their work f.
Ne	9: 33	you have acted f, while we acted
	13: 14	what I have so f done for the house
Isa	38: 3	how I have walked before you f
Jer	23: 28	the one who has my word speak it f.
Eze	18: 9	my decrees and f keeps my laws.

FAITHFULNESS* (FAITH)

Ge	24: 27	his kindness and f to my master.
	24: 49	show kindness and f to my master,
	32: 10	and f you have shown your servant.
	47: 29	you will show me kindness and f.
Ex	34: 6	to anger, abounding in love and f,
Jos	24: 14	Serve him and f serve him with all f.
1Sa	26: 23	man for his righteousness and f
2Sa	2: 6	now show you kindness and f,
	15: 20	Lord show you kindness and f."
Ps	26: 3	have lived in reliance on your f.
	30: 9	Will it proclaim your f?
	36: 5	to the heavens, your f to the skies.
	40: 10	I speak of your f and your saving
	40: 10	do not conceal your love and your f
	40: 11	your love and f always protect me.
	51: 6	Yet you desired f even in the womb;
	54: 5	in your f destroy them.
	57: 3	God sends forth his love and his f.
	57: 10	your f reaches to the skies.
	61: 7	your love and f to protect him.
	71: 22	praise you with the harp for your f,
	85: 10	Love and f meet together;
	85: 11	F springs forth from the earth,
	86: 11	that I may rely on your f;
	86: 15	to anger, abounding in love and f.
	88: 11	in the grave, your f in Destruction?
	89: 1	I will make your f known through all
	89: 2	that you have established your f

Ps 89: 5 LORD, your f too, in the assembly
89: 8 mighty, and your f surrounds you.
89: 14 love and f go before you.
89: 33 nor will I ever betray my f.
89: 49 in your f you swore to David?
91: 4 his f will be your shield
92: 2 in the morning and your f at night,
96: 13 and the peoples in his f.
98: 3 love and his f to the house of Israel;
100: 5 his f continues through all
108: 4 your f reaches to the skies.
111: 8 ever, enacted in f and uprightness.
115: 1 glory, because of your love and f.
117: 2 the f of the LORD endures forever.
119: 30 I have chosen the way of f;
119: 75 that in f you have afflicted me.
119: 90 Your f continues through all
138: 2 for your unfailing love and your f,
143: 1 in your f and righteousness come
Pr 3: 3 Let love and f never leave you;
14: 22 plan what is good find love and f.
16: 6 Through love and f sin is atoned for;
20: 28 Love and f keep a king safe;
Isa 11: 5 belt and f the sash around his waist.
16: 5 in f a man will sit on it—
25: 1 perfect f you have done wonderful
38: 18 to the pit cannot hope for your f.
38: 19 tell their children about your f.
40: 6 all human f is like the flowers
42: 3 In f he will bring forth justice;
61: 8 In my f I will reward my people
La 3: 23 new every morning; great is your f.
Hos 2: 20 I will betroth you in f,
4: 1 "There is no f, no love,
Hab 2: 4 righteous will live by their f—
Mt 23: 23 of the law—justice, mercy and f.
Ro 3: 3 their unfaithfulness nullify God's f?
Gal 5: 22 patience, kindness, goodness, f,
3Jn : 3 and testify to your f to the truth,
Rev 13: 10 and f on the part of God's people.

FAITHLESS* (FAITH)
Ps 78: 57 ancestors they were disloyal and f,
101: 3 I hate what f people do; I will have
119:158 I look on the f with loathing,
Pr 14: 14 The f will be fully repaid for their
Jer 3: 6 you seen what f Israel has done?
3: 8 I gave f Israel her certificate
3: 11 "F Israel is more righteous
3: 12 " 'Return, f Israel,'
3: 14 "Return, f people,"
3: 22 "Return, f people; I will cure you
12: 1 Why do all the f live at ease?
2Ti 2: 13 if we are f, he remains faithful,

FALL (FALLEN FALLS)
Pr 24: 17 Do not gloat when your enemies f;
28: 14 harden their hearts f into trouble.
Ps 37: 24 they will not f, for the LORD
69: 9 of those who insult you f on me.
145: 14 The LORD upholds all who f
Pr 11: 28 who trust in their riches will f,
Isa 40: 7 The grass withers and the flowers f,
Mt 15: 14 if it did not f, because it had its
13: 21 they quickly f away.
Lk 10: 18 "I saw Satan f like lightning
11: 17 a house divided against itself will f.
23: 30 say to the mountains, "F on us!"
Jn 16: 1 so that you will not f away.
Ro 3: 23 and f short of the glory of God,
14: 4 their own master they stand or f.

FALLEN (FALL)
2Sa 1: 19 How the mighty have f!
Isa 14: 12 How you have f from heaven,
1Co 11: 30 and a number of you have f asleep.
15: 6 living, though some have f asleep.
15: 18 who have f asleep in Christ are lost.
15: 20 of those who have f asleep.
Gal 5: 4 you have f away from grace.
1Th 4: 15 precede those who have f asleep.
Heb 6: 6 and who have f away,

FALLS (FALL)
Pr 11: 14 For lack of guidance a nation f,
Mt 21: 44 Anyone who f on this stone will be
Jn 12: 24 a kernel of wheat f to the ground
Heb 12: 15 that no one f short of the grace

FALSE (FALSEHOOD FALSELY)
Ex 20: 16 shall not give f testimony against
23: 1 "Do not spread f reports.
23: 7 Have nothing to do with a f charge
Dt 5: 20 shall not give f testimony against

Pr 12: 17 the truth, but a f witness tells lies.
13: 5 The righteous hate what is f,
14: 5 but a f witness pours out lies.
14: 25 lives, but a f witness is deceitful.
19: 5 A f witness will not go unpunished,
19: 9 A f witness will not go unpunished,
21: 28 Those who give f witness will
25: 18 one who gives f testimony against
Isa 44: 25 who foils the signs of f prophets
Jer 23: 16 they fill you with f hopes.
Mt 7: 15 "Watch out for f prophets.
19: 18 theft, f testimony, slander.
19: 18 steal, you shall not give f testimony,
24: 11 and many f prophets will appear
24: 24 For f messiahs and f prophets will
Mk 10: 19 you shall not give f testimony,
13: 22 For f messiahs and f prophets will
Lk 6: 26 ancestors treated the f prophets.
18: 20 steal, you shall not give f testimony,
1Co 15: 15 found to be f witnesses about God,
2Co 11: 13 For such persons are f apostles,
11: 26 and in danger from f believers.
Gal 2: 4 arose because some f believers had
Php 1: 18 whether from f motives or true,
Col 2: 18 anyone who delights in f humility
2: 23 their f humility and their harsh
1Ti 1: 3 not to teach f doctrines any longer
2Pe 2: 1 also f prophets among the people,
2: 1 there will be f teachers among you.
1Jn 4: 1 because many f prophets have gone
Rev 16: 13 out of the mouth of the f prophet.
19: 20 and with him the f prophet who had
20: 10 and the f prophet had been thrown.

FALSEHOOD* (FALSE)
Job 21: 34 is left of your answers but f!"
31: 5 "If I have walked with f or my foot
Ps 52: 3 f rather than speaking the truth.
119:163 hate and detest f but I love your law.
Pr 30: 8 Keep f and lies far from me;
Isa 28: 15 our refuge and f our hiding place."
Ro 3: 7 my f enhances God's truthfulness
Eph 4: 25 Therefore each of you must put off f
1Jn 4: 6 the Spirit of truth and the spirit of f.
Rev 22: 15 everyone who loves and practices f.

FALSELY (FALSE)
Lev 19: 12 " 'Do not swear f by my name
Isa 59: 3 Your lips have spoken f,
Mt 5: 11 say all kinds of evil against you
Lk 3: 14 money and don't accuse people f—
1Ti 6: 20 ideas of what is f called knowledge,

FALTER*
Pr 24: 10 If you f in a time of trouble,
Isa 42: 4 he will not f or be discouraged till

FAME
Jos 9: 9 of the f of the LORD your God.
Isa 66: 19 islands that have not heard of my f
Hab 3: 2 LORD, I have heard of your f;

FAMILIES (FAMILY)
Ps 68: 6 God sets the lonely in f, he leads

FAMILY (FAMILIES)
Pr 31: 15 she provides food for her f
Lk 9: 61 go back and say good-by to my f."
12: 52 in one f divided against each other,
Ac 10: 2 He and all his f were devout
1Ti 3: 4 He must manage his own f well
3: 5 not know how to manage his own f,
5: 4 practice by caring for their own f

FAMINE
Ge 12: 10 Now there was a f in the land,
26: 1 Now there was a f in the land—
41: 30 seven years of f will follow them.
Ru 1: 1 ruled, there was a f in the land.
1Ki 18: 2 Now the f was severe in Samaria,
Am 8: 11 but a f of hearing the words
Ro 8: 35 or persecution or f or nakedness

FAN*
2Ti 1: 6 this reason I remind you to f

FANTASIES*
Ps 73: 20 Lord, you will despise them as f.
Pr 12: 11 those who chase f have no sense.
28: 19 those who chase f will have their fill

FASHIONED
Ps 94: 9 Does he who f the ear not hear?

FAST (FASTING)
Dt 10: 20 Hold f to him and take your oaths
11: 22 to him and to hold f to him—
13: 4 serve him and hold f to him.

Dt 30: 20 listen to his voice, and hold f to him.
Jos 22: 5 to hold f to him and to serve him
23: 8 to hold f to the LORD your God,
2Ki 18: 6 He held f to the LORD and did not
Ps 119: 31 I hold f to your statutes, LORD;
139: 10 your right hand will hold me f.
Mt 6: 16 "When you f, do not look somber
1Pe 5: 12 the true grace of God. Stand f in it.

FASTING (FAST)
Ps 35: 13 and humbled myself with f.
Ac 13: 2 were worshiping the Lord and f,
14: 23 with prayer and f, committed them

FATAL
Ex 21: 12 a f blow is to be put to death.

FATHER (FATHER'S FATHERLESS FATHERS)
Ge 2: 24 this reason a man will leave his f
17: 4 You will be the f of many nations.
Ex 20: 12 "Honor your f and your mother,
21: 15 "Anyone who attacks their f
21: 17 "Anyone who curses their f
Lev 18: 7 " 'Do not dishonor your f
19: 3 you must respect your mother and f,
20: 9 " 'Anyone who curses their f
Dt 1: 31 carried you, as a f carries his son,
5: 16 "Honor your f and your mother,
21: 18 son who does not obey his f
32: 6 Is he not your F, your Creator,
2Sa 7: 14 I will be his f, and he will be my
1Ch 17: 13 I will be his f, and he will be my
22: 10 will be my son, and I will be his f.
28: 6 to be my son, and I will be his f.
Job 38: 28 Does the rain have a f?
Ps 2: 7 today I have become your f.
27: 10 Though my f and mother forsake
68: 5 A f to the fatherless, a defender
89: 26 out to me, 'You are my F, my God,
103: 13 As a f has compassion on his
Pr 3: 12 loves, as a f the son he delights in.
10: 1 Wise children bring joy to their f,
17: 25 children bring grief to their f
23: 22 Listen to your f, who gave you life,
23: 24 The f of a righteous child has great
28: 24 Whoever robs their f or mother
29: 3 loves wisdom brings joy to his f,
Isa 9: 6 Everlasting F, Prince of Peace.
45: 10 Woe to those who say to their f,
63: 16 But you are our F, though Abraham
Jer 2: 27 wood, 'You are my f,' and to stone,
3: 19 I thought you would call me 'F'
31: 9 because I am Israel's f, and Ephraim
Eze 18: 20 the son not share the guilt of his f?'
Mic 7: 6 For a son dishonors his f, a daughter
Mal 1: 6 If I am a f, where is the honor due
2: 10 Do we not all have one F?
Mt 3: 9 'We have Abraham as our f.'
5: 16 deeds and glorify your F in heaven.
6: 9 " 'Our F in heaven, hallowed be
6: 26 and yet your heavenly F feeds them.
10: 37 "Anyone who loves their f
11: 27 no one knows the F except the Son
15: 4 said, 'Honor your f and mother'
18: 10 see the face of my F in heaven.
19: 5 this reason a man will leave his f
19: 19 honor your f and mother,' and 'love
19: 29 brothers or sisters or f or mother
23: 9 And do not call anyone on earth 'f,'
Mk 7: 10 said, 'Honor your f and mother,'
Lk 9: 59 first let me go and bury my f."
12: 53 f against son and son against f,
14: 26 me and does not hate f and mother,
18: 20 honor your f and mother.' "
23: 34 Jesus said, "F, forgive them,
Jn 3: 35 The F loves the Son and has placed
4: 21 you will worship the F neither
5: 17 "My F is always at his work to this
5: 18 he was even calling God his own F,
5: 20 For the F loves the Son and shows
6: 44 me unless the F who sent me draws
6: 46 one has seen the F except the one
8: 19 "You do not know me or my F,"
8: 28 speak just what the F has taught me.
8: 41 "The only F we have is God
8: 42 "If God were your F, you would
8: 44 You belong to your f, the devil,
10: 17 The reason my F loves me is that I
10: 30 I and the F are one."
10: 38 and understand that the F is in me,
14: 6 comes to the F except through me.
14: 9 who has seen me has seen the F.
14: 28 for the F is greater than I.

Jn 15: 9 "As the F has loved me, so have I
15: 23 who hate me hate my F as well.
20: 17 am ascending to my F and your F,
Ac 13: 33 today I have become your f.'
Ro 4: 11 he is the f of all who believe
4: 16 He is the f of us all.
8: 15 And by him we cry, "Abba, F."
1Co 4: 15 I became your f through the gospel.
2Co 6: 18 "I will be a F to you, and you
Eph 5: 31 this reason a man will leave his f
6: 2 "Honor your f and mother"—
Php 2: 11 is Lord, to the glory of God the F.
Heb 1: 5 today I have become your F"?
12: 7 are not disciplined by their f?
1Jn 1: 3 our fellowship is with the F
2: 15 world, love for the F is not in you.
2: 22 denying the F and the Son.

FATHER'S (FATHER)
Pr 19: 13 A foolish child is a f ruin,
Mt 16: 27 come in his F glory with his angels,
Lk 2: 49 know I had to be in my F house?"
Jn 2: 16 Stop turning my F house
10: 29 can snatch them out of my F hand.
14: 2 My F house has plenty of room;
15: 8 This is to my F glory, that you bear

FATHERLESS (FATHER)
Dt 10: 18 He defends the cause of the f
14: 29 the f and the widows who live
24: 17 the foreigner or the f of justice,
24: 19 the foreigner, the f and the widow,
26: 12 the foreigner, the f and the widow,
Ps 68: 5 A father to the f, a defender
82: 3 Defend the weak and the f;
Pr 23: 10 or encroach on the fields of the f,

FATHERS (FATHER)
Lk 11: 11 "Which of you f, if your son asks
1Co 4: 15 you do not have many f,
Eph 6: 4 F, do not exasperate your children;
Col 3: 21 F, do not embitter your children,

FATHOM* (FATHOMED)
Job 11: 7 "Can you f the mysteries of God?
Ps 145: 3 his greatness no one can f.
Ecc 3: 11 yet no one can f what God has done
Isa 40: 13 Who can f the Spirit of the Lord,
40: 28 his understanding no one can f.
1Co 13: 2 of prophecy and can f all mysteries

FATHOMED* (FATHOM)
Job 5: 9 performs wonders that cannot be f,
9: 10 performs wonders that cannot be f,

FATTENED
Pr 15: 17 with love than a f calf with hatred.
Lk 15: 23 Bring the f calf and kill it.

FAULT (FAULTS)
1Sa 29: 3 now, I have found no f in him."
Mt 18: 15 go and point out the f,
Php 2: 15 of God without f in a warped
Jas 1: 5 generously to all without finding f,
Jude : 24 his glorious presence without f

FAULTFINDERS*
Jude : 16 These people are grumblers and f;

FAULTLESS*
Php 3: 6 righteousness based on the law, f.
Jas 1: 27 Father accepts as pure and f is this:

FAULTS* (FAULT)
Job 10: 6 that you must search out my f
Ps 19: 12 Forgive my hidden f.

FAVOR (FAVORITISM)
Ge 4: 4 The Lord looked with f on Abel
6: 8 But Noah found f in the eyes
Ex 33: 12 and you have found f with me.'
34: 9 "if I have found f in your eyes,
Lev 26: 9 " 'I will look on you with f
Nu 11: 15 if I have found f in your eyes,
Jdg 6: 17 "If now I have found f in your eyes,
1Sa 2: 26 in stature and in f with the Lord
2Sa 2: 6 you the same f because you have
2Ki 13: 4 Jehoahaz sought the Lord's f,
2Ch 33: 12 In his distress he sought the f
Est 7: 3 "If I have found f with you,
Ps 90: 17 May the f of the Lord our God rest
Pr 3: 34 but shows f to the humble
8: 35 life and receive f from the Lord.
10: 32 the righteous know what finds f,
11: 1 accurate weights find f with him.
18: 22 and receives f from the Lord.
19: 6 Many curry f with a ruler,
Isa 61: 2 proclaim the year of the Lord's f

Zec 11: 7 called one F and the other Union,
Lk 1: 30 you have found f with God.
2: 14 peace to those on whom f rests."
2: 52 in wisdom and in f with God
4: 19 proclaim the year of the Lord's f."
2Co 2: 6 now is the time of God's f, now is
1Pe 5: 5 but shows f to the humble

FAVORITISM* (FAVOR)
Ex 23: 3 and do not show f to the poor
Lev 19: 15 to the poor or f to the great,
Ac 10: 34 true it is that God does not show f
Ro 2: 11 For God does not show f.
Gal 2: 6 God does not show f—
Eph 6: 9 heaven, and there is no f with him.
Col 3: 25 for their wrongs, and there is no f.
1Ti 5: 21 partiality, and to do nothing out of f.
Jas 2: 1 Lord Jesus Christ must not show f.
2: 9 But if you show f, you sin and are

FEAR (AFRAID FEARED FEARS FRIGHTENED GOD-FEARING)
Dt 6: 13 F the Lord your God, serve him
10: 12 you but to f the Lord your God,
31: 12 learn to f the Lord your God
31: 13 to f the Lord your God as long as
Jos 4: 24 that you might always f the Lord
24: 14 "Now f the Lord and serve him
1Sa 12: 14 If you f the Lord and serve
12: 24 be sure to f the Lord and serve
2Sa 23: 3 when he rules in the f of God,
2Ch 19: 7 Now let the f of the Lord be
26: 5 who instructed him in the f of God.
Job 1: 9 "Does Job f God for nothing?"
Ps 2: 11 Serve the Lord with f
19: 9 The f of the Lord is pure,
23: 4 the darkest valley, I will f no evil,
27: 1 and my salvation—whom shall I f?
33: 8 Let all the earth f the Lord;
34: 7 encamps around those who f him,
34: 9 F the Lord, you his holy people,
46: 2 Therefore we will not f,
86: 11 heart, that I may f your name.
90: 11 Your wrath is as great as the f that is
91: 5 You will not f the terror of night,
111: 10 The f of the Lord is
112: 1 Blessed are those who f the Lord,
118: 4 Let those who f the Lord say:
128: 1 Blessed are all who f the Lord,
145: 19 the desires of those who f him;
147: 11 Lord delights in those who f him,
Pr 1: 7 The f of the Lord is
1: 33 and be at ease, without f of harm."
8: 13 To f the Lord is to hate evil;
9: 10 The f of the Lord is
10: 27 The f of the Lord adds length
14: 16 The wise f the Lord
14: 26 Those who f the Lord
14: 27 The f of the Lord is a fountain
15: 33 instruction is to f the Lord,
16: 6 through the f of the Lord evil is
19: 23 The f of the Lord leads to life;
22: 4 Humility is the f of the Lord;
29: 25 To f anyone will prove to be
31: 21 she has no f for her household;
Ecc 3: 14 does it so that people will f him.
5: 7 Therefore f God.
8: 12 who f God, who are reverent
12: 13 of the matter: F God and keep his
Isa 11: 3 will delight in the f of the Lord.
33: 6 the f of the Lord is the key to this
35: 4 fearful hearts, "Be strong, do not f;
41: 10 So do not f, for I am with you;
41: 13 right hand and says to you, Do not f;
43: 1 "Do not f, for I have redeemed you;
51: 7 Do not f the reproach of mere
54: 14 you will have nothing to f.
Jer 10: 7 Who should not f you,
17: 8 It does not f when heat comes;
Lk 12: 5 I will show you whom you should f:
2Co 5: 11 we know what it is to f the Lord,
Php 2: 12 to work out your salvation with f
1Jn 4: 18 But perfect love drives out f,
Jude : 23 others show mercy, mixed with f—
Rev 14: 7 voice, "F God and give him glory,

FEARED (FEAR)
Job 1: 1 he f God and shunned evil.
Ps 76: 7 It is you alone who are to be f,
Mal 3: 16 those who f the Lord talked

FEARS (FEAR)
Job 1: 8 a man who f God and shuns evil."
2: 3 a man who f God and shuns evil.

Ps 34: 4 he delivered me from all my f.
Pr 31: 30 a woman who f the Lord is to be
2Co 7: 5 conflicts on the outside, f within.
1Jn 4: 18 The one who f is not made perfect

FEAST (FEASTING FEASTS)
Pr 15: 15 the cheerful heart has a continual f.
2Pe 2: 13 in their pleasures while they f

FEASTING (FEAST)
Pr 17: 1 and quiet than a house full of f,

FEASTS (FEAST)
Jude : 12 people are blemishes at your love f,

FEATHERS
Ps 91: 4 He will cover you with his f,

FEEBLE
Job 4: 3 how you have strengthened f hands.
Isa 35: 3 Strengthen the f hands,
Heb 12: 12 strengthen your f arms and weak

FED (FEED)
Ps 105: 40 he f them well with the bread of

FEED (FED FEEDS)
Jn 21: 15 Jesus said, "F my lambs."
21: 17 Jesus said, "F my sheep.
Ro 12: 20 "If your enemy is hungry, f him;
Jude : 12 shepherds who f only themselves.

FEEDS (FEED)
Pr 15: 14 but the mouth of a fool f on folly.
Mt 6: 26 yet your heavenly Father f them.
Jn 6: 57 so the one who f on me will live

FEEL
Jdg 16: 26 "Put me where I can f the pillars
Ps 115: 7 They have hands, but cannot f, feet,

FEET (FOOT)
Ru 3: 8 there was a woman lying at his f!
Ps 8: 6 you put everything under their f:
22: 16 they pierce my hands and my f
40: 2 he set my f on a rock and gave me
56: 13 death and my f from stumbling,
66: 9 lives and kept our f from slipping.
73: 2 as for me, my f had almost slipped;
110: 1 enemies a footstool for your f."
119:105 Your word is a lamp for my f
Pr 4: 26 thought to the paths for your f
Isa 52: 7 the mountains are the f of those who
Da 2: 33 iron, its f partly of iron and partly
Na 1: 15 the f of one who brings good news,
Mt 10: 14 shake the dust off your f when you
22: 44 put your enemies under your f." '
Lk 1: 79 death, to guide our f into the path
20: 43 enemies a footstool for your f." '
24: 39 Look at my hands and my f. It is I
Jn 13: 5 and began to wash his disciples' f,
13: 14 also should wash one another's f.
Ro 3: 15 "Their f are swift to shed blood;
10: 15 "How beautiful are the f of those
16: 20 will soon crush Satan under your f.
1Co 12: 21 And the head cannot say to the f,
15: 25 has put all his enemies under his f.
Eph 1: 22 God placed all things under his f
1Ti 5: 10 washing the f of the Lord's people,
Heb 1: 13 enemies a footstool for your f"?
2: 8 and put everything under their f."
12: 13 "Make level paths for your f,"
Rev 1: 15 His f were like bronze glowing

FELIX
Governor before whom Paul was tried (Ac 23:23—24:27).

FELLOWSHIP
Ex 20: 24 your burnt offerings and f offerings,
Lev 3: 1 " 'If your offering is a f offering,
1Co 1: 9 who has called you into f with his
5: 2 your f the man who has been doing
2Co 6: 14 what f can light have with darkness?
13: 14 the f of the Holy Spirit be with you
Gal 2: 9 Barnabas the right hand of f
1Jn 1: 3 so that you also may have f with us.
1: 3 And our f is with the Father
1: 6 If we claim to have f with him
1: 7 light, we have f with one another,

FEMALE
Ge 1: 27 male and f he created them.
5: 2 He created them male and f
Mt 19: 4 the Creator 'made them male and f,'
Mk 10: 6 God 'made them male and f.'
Gal 3: 28 neither male nor f, for you are all

FEROCIOUS
Mt   7: 15 but inwardly they are *f* wolves.

FERTILE (FERTILIZE)
Isa 32: 15 and the desert becomes a *f* field,
Jer   2: 7 I brought you into a *f* land to eat its

FERTILIZE* (FERTILE)
Lk 13: 8 year, and I'll dig around it and *f* it.

FERVOR*
Ac 18: 25 and he spoke with great *f* and taught
Ro 12: 11 but keep your spiritual *f*,

FESTIVAL (FESTIVALS)
1Co 5: 8 Therefore let us keep the **F**,
Col   2: 16 or with regard to a religious *f*,

FESTIVALS (FESTIVAL)
Am   5: 21 I despise your religious *f*;

FESTUS
Successor of Felix; sent Paul to Caesar (Ac 25–26).

FEVER
Job 30: 30 my body burns with *f*.
Mt   8: 14 mother-in-law lying in bed with a *f*.
Lk   4: 38 was suffering from a high *f*,
Jn   4: 52 one in the afternoon, the *f* left him."
Ac 28: 8 suffering from *f* and dysentery.

FIDELITY*
Ro   1: 31 no *f*, no love, no mercy.
      16: 10 Greet Apelles, whose *f* to Christ

FIELD (FIELDS)
Ge   4: 8 Abel, "Let's go out to the *f*."
Lev 19: 9 not reap to the very edges of your *f*
      19: 19 " 'Do not plant your *f* with two
Pr 31: 16 She considers a *f* and buys it;
Isa 40: 6 is like the flowers of the *f*.
Mt   6: 28 See how the flowers of the *f* grow.
       6: 30 how God clothes the grass of the *f*,
      13: 38 The *f* is the world, and the good
      13: 44 heaven is like treasure hidden in a *f*.
Lk 14: 18 'I have just bought a *f*, and I must
1Co   3: 9 you are God's *f*, God's building.
1Pe   1: 24 glory is like the flowers of the *f*;

FIELDS (FIELD)
Ru   2: 2 "Let me go to the *f* and pick
Lk   2: 8 shepherds living out in the *f* nearby,
Jn   4: 35 open your eyes and look at the *f*!

FIERY (FIRE)
1Pe   4: 12 at the *f* ordeal that has come on you to test you,

FIG (FIGS SYCAMORE-FIG)
Ge   3: 7 so they sewed *f* leaves together
Jdg 9: 10 the trees said to the *f* tree,
1Ki   4: 25 under their own vine and *f* tree.
Pr 27: 18 Those who guard a *f* tree will eat its
Mic 4: 4 own vine and under their own *f* tree,
Zec 3: 10 to sit under your own vine and *f* tree,'
Mt 21: 19 Seeing a *f* tree by the road, he went
Lk 13: 6 "A man had a *f* tree growing in his
Jas 3: 12 and sisters, can a *f* tree bear olives,
Rev 6: 13 as figs drop from a *f* tree

FIGHT (FIGHTING FIGHTS FOUGHT)
Ex 14: 14 The LORD will *f* for you;
Dt   1: 30 is going before you, will *f* for you,
      3: 22 the LORD your God himself will *f*
1Sa 25: 28 because you *f* the LORD's battles,
Ne   4: 20 Our God will *f* for us!"
Ps 35: 1 *f* against those who *f* against me.
Jn 18: 36 my servants would *f* to prevent my
1Co 9: 26 I do not *f* like a boxer beating
2Co 10: 4 The weapons we *f* with are not
1Ti   1: 18 them you may *f* the battle well,
       6: 12 *F* the good *f* of the faith.
2Ti   4: 7 I have fought the good *f*, I have

FIGHTING (FIGHT)
Jos 10: 14 Surely the LORD was *f* for Israel!

FIGHTS (FIGHT)
Jos 23: 10 because the LORD your God *f*
Jas 4: 1 What causes *f* and quarrels among

FIGS (FIG)
Lk   6: 44 People do not pick *f*
Jas 3: 12 bear olives, or a grapevine bear *f*?

FILL (FILLED FILLING FILLS FULL FULLNESS FULLY)
Ge   1: 28 *f* the earth and subdue it.
Ps 16: 11 you will *f* me with joy in your
      81: 10 wide your mouth and I will *f* it.
Pr 28: 19 who chase fantasies will have their *f*

Hag 2: 7 and I will *f* this house with glory,'
Jn   6: 26 you ate the loaves and had your *f*.
Ac   2: 28 you will *f* me with joy in your
Ro 15: 13 May the God of hope *f* you with all

FILLED (FILL)
Ex 31: 3 I have *f* him with the Spirit of God,
      35: 31 he has *f* him with the Spirit of God,
Dt 34: 9 son of Nun was *f* with the spirit
1Ki   8: 10 Place, the cloud *f* the temple
       8: 11 glory of the LORD *f* his temple.
2Ch 5: 14 the glory of the LORD *f* the temple
       7: 1 glory of the LORD *f* the temple.
Ps 72: 19 may the whole earth be *f* with his
     119: 64 The earth is *f* with your love,
Isa 6: 4 and the temple was *f* with smoke.
      11: 9 will be *f* with the knowledge
Eze 10: 3 and a cloud *f* the inner court.
      10: 4 The cloud *f* the temple,
      43: 5 glory of the LORD *f* the temple.
Hab 2: 14 For the earth will be *f*
      3: 3 heavens and his praise *f* the earth.
Mt   5: 6 for righteousness, for they will be *f*.
Lk   1: 15 and he will be *f* with the Holy Spirit
       1: 41 Elizabeth was *f* with the Holy Spirit,
       1: 67 His father Zechariah was *f*
       2: 40 he was *f* with wisdom, and the grace
Jn 12: 3 the house was *f* with the fragrance
Ac   2: 2 *f* the whole house where they were
       2: 4 of them were *f* with the Holy Spirit
       4: 8 Then Peter, *f* with the Holy Spirit,
       4: 31 they were all *f* with the Holy Spirit
       9: 17 and be *f* with the Holy Spirit."
      13: 9 called Paul, *f* with the Holy Spirit,
Eph 5: 18 Instead, be *f* with the Spirit,
Php 1: 11 *f* with the fruit of righteousness
Rev 15: 8 the temple was *f* with smoke

FILLING (FILL)
Eze 44: 4 the glory of the LORD *f* the temple

FILLS (FILL)
Nu 14: 21 of the LORD *f* the whole earth,
Ps 107: 9 the hungry with good things.
Eph 1: 23 him who *f* everything in every way.

FILTH (FILTHY)
Isa 4: 4 The Lord will wash away the *f*
Jas 1: 21 get rid of all moral *f* and the evil

FILTHY (FILTH)
Isa 64: 6 all our righteous acts are like *f* rags;
Col 3: 8 and *f* language from your lips.

FINAL (FINALITY)
Ps 73: 17 then I understood their *f* destiny.

FINALITY* (FINAL)
Ro   9: 28 on earth with speed and *f*."

FINANCIAL*
1Ti   6: 5 that godliness is a means to *f* gain.

FIND (FINDS FOUND)
Nu 32: 23 be sure that your sin will *f* you out.
Dt   4: 29 you will *f* him if you seek him
1Sa 23: 16 and helped him *f* strength in God.
Job 23: 3 If only I knew where to *f* him!
Ps 62: 5 Yes, my soul, *f* rest in God;
      91: 4 under his wings you will *f* refuge;
     112: 1 *f* great delight in his commands.
Pr   3: 13 Blessed are those who *f* wisdom,
       8: 17 and those who seek me *f* me.
       8: 35 For those who *f* me *f* life
      14: 22 those who plan what is good *f* love
      20: 6 but a faithful person who can *f*?
      24: 14 If you *f* it, there is a future hope
      31: 10 wife of noble character who can *f*?
Jer   6: 16 and you will *f* rest for your souls.
      29: 13 and *f* me when you seek me with all
Mt   7: 7 seek and you will *f*;
       7: 8 those who seek *f*;
      11: 29 and you will *f* rest for your souls.
      16: 25 loses their life for me will *f* it.
      22: 9 invite to the banquet anyone you *f*.'
Lk 11: 9 seek and you will *f*;
      11: 10 those who seek *f*,
      18: 8 comes, will he *f* faith on the earth?"
Jn 10: 9 come in and go out, and *f* pasture.

FINDS (FIND)
Ps 62: 1 Truly my soul *f* rest in God;
     119: 162 promise like one who *f* great spoil.
Pr 11: 27 Whoever seeks good *f* favor,
      18: 22 He who *f* a wife *f* what is good
Mt 10: 39 Whoever *f* their life will lose it,
Lk 12: 37 whose master *f* them watching

Lk 12: 43 servant whom the master *f* doing so
      15: 4 go after the lost sheep until he *f* it?
      15: 8 and search carefully until she *f* it?

FINE
Pr 17: 26 a *f* on the innocent is not good,
Zec 3: 4 I will put *f* garments on you."

FINE-SOUNDING* (SOUND)
Col 2: 4 may deceive you by *f* arguments.

FINGER
Ex   8: 19 to Pharaoh, "This is the *f* of God."
      31: 18 of stone inscribed by the *f* of God.
Dt   9: 10 tablets inscribed by the *f* of God.
Lk 11: 20 I drive out demons by the *f* of God,
      16: 24 to dip the tip of his *f* in water
Jn   8: 6 *write on the ground with his f*.
      20: 25 and put my *f* where the nails were,

FINISH (FINISHED)
Jn   4: 34 him who sent me and to *f* his work.
       5: 36 that the Father has given me to *f*—
Ac 20: 24 my only aim is to *f* the race
2Co 8: 11 Now *f* the work, so that your eager
Gal 3: 3 trying to *f* by human effort?
Jas 1: 4 Let perseverance *f* its work so

FINISHED (FINISH)
Ge   2: 2 seventh day God had *f* the work he
Jn 19: 30 the drink, Jesus said, "It is *f*."
2Ti 4: 7 the good fight, I have *f* the race,

FIRE (FIERY)
Ex   3: 2 in flames of *f* from within a bush.
      13: 21 in a pillar of *f* to give them light,
Lev 6: 12 The *f* on the altar must be kept
       9: 24 *F* came out from the presence
1Ki 18: 38 Then the *f* of the LORD fell
2Ki   2: 11 suddenly a chariot of *f* and horses
Isa 5: 24 as tongues of *f* lick up straw and as
      30: 27 and his tongue is a consuming *f*.
Jer 23: 29 "Is not my word like *f*,"
Da   3: 25 four men walking around in the *f*,
Zec 3: 2 burning stick snatched from the *f*?"
Mal 3: 2 For he will be like a refiner's *f*
Mt   3: 11 you with the Holy Spirit and *f*.
       3: 12 up the chaff with unquenchable *f*."
       5: 22 will be in danger of the *f* of hell.
      18: 8 feet and be thrown into eternal *f*,
      25: 41 the eternal *f* prepared for the devil
Mk   9: 43 into hell, where the *f* never goes out.
       9: 48 not die, and the *f* is not quenched.'
       9: 49 Everyone will be salted with *f*.
Lk   3: 16 you with the Holy Spirit and *f*.
      12: 49 have come to bring *f* on the earth,
Ac   2: 3 to be tongues of *f* that separated
1Co 3: 13 It will be revealed with *f*,
1Th 5: 19 Do not put out the Spirit's *f*.
Heb 12: 29 for our "God is a consuming *f*."
Jas 3: 5 what a great forest is set on *f*
       3: 6 The tongue also is a *f*, a world
2Pe 3: 10 the elements will be destroyed by *f*,
Jude : 7 suffer the punishment of eternal *f*.
        : 23 others by snatching them from the *f*;
Rev 1: 14 and his eyes were like blazing *f*.
      20: 14 The lake of *f* is the second death.

FIRM*
Ex 14: 13 Stand *f* and you will see
2Ch 20: 17 stand *f* and see the deliverance
Ezr 9: 8 giving us a *f* place in his sanctuary,
Job 11: 15 you will stand *f* and without fear.
      36: 5 he is mighty, and *f* in his purpose.
      41: 23 they are *f* and immovable.
Ps 20: 8 and fall, but we rise up and stand *f*.
      30: 7 made my royal mountain stand *f*;
      33: 9 he commanded, and it stood *f*.
      33: 11 plans of the LORD stand *f* forever,
      37: 23 The LORD makes *f* the steps
      40: 2 rock and gave me a *f* place to stand.
      75: 3 it is I who hold its pillars *f*.
      89: 2 that your love stands *f* forever,
      89: 4 and make your throne *f* through all
      93: 1 world is established, *f* and secure.
      93: 5 Your statutes, LORD, stand *f*;
     119: 89 it stands *f* in the heavens.
Pr 10: 25 but the righteous stand *f* forever.
      12: 7 the house of the righteous stands *f*.
Isa 7: 9 If you do not stand *f* in your faith,
      22: 17 is about to take *f* hold of you
      22: 23 drive him like a peg into a *f* place;
      22: 25 into the *f* place will give way;
Eze 13: 5 so that it will stand *f* in the battle
Zec 8: 23 nations will take *f* hold of one Jew

Mt	10:22	those who stand f to the end will be
	24:13	whoever stands f to the end will be
Mk	13:13	those who stand f to the end will be
Lk	21:19	Stand f, and you will win life.
1Co	1:8	will also keep you f to the end,
	10:12	if you think you are standing f,
	15:58	my dear brothers and sisters, stand f.
	16:13	on your guard; stand f in the faith;
2Co	1:7	And our hope for you is f,
	1:21	both us and you stand f in Christ.
	1:24	because it is by faith you stand f.
Gal	5:1	Stand f, then, and do not let
Eph	6:14	Stand f then, with the belt of truth
Php	1:27	that you stand f in the one Spirit,
	4:1	stand f in the Lord in this way,
Col	1:23	established and f, and do not move
	2:5	are and how f your faith in Christ is.
	4:12	that you may stand f in all the will
1Th	3:8	since you are standing f in the Lord.
2Th	2:15	stand f and hold fast to the teachings
1Ti	6:19	themselves as a f foundation
2Ti	2:19	God's solid foundation stands f,
Heb	6:19	an anchor for the soul, f and secure.
Jas	5:8	be patient and stand f,
1Pe	5:9	Resist him, standing f in the faith,
	5:10	make you strong, f and steadfast.

FIRST

Ge	1:5	and there was morning—the f day.
	13:4	and where he had f built an altar.
Ex	34:19	"The f offspring of every womb
1Ki	22:5	of Israel, "F seek the counsel
Pr	18:17	a lawsuit the f to speak seems right,
Isa	44:6	I am the f and I am the last;
	48:12	I am he; I am the f and I am the last.
Mt	5:24	F go and be reconciled
	6:33	But seek f his kingdom and his
	7:5	f take the plank out of your own
	19:30	But many who are f will be last,
	20:16	"So the last will be f, and the f will
	20:27	wants to be f must be your slave—
	22:38	This is the f and greatest
	23:26	F clean the inside of the cup
Mk	9:35	wants to be f must be the very last,
	10:31	are f will be last, and the last f.
	10:44	whoever wants to be f must be slave
	13:10	the gospel must f be preached to all
Lk	13:30	will be f, and f who will be last."
Jn	8:7	*is without sin be the f to throw*
Ac	11:26	disciples were called Christians f
Ro	1:16	to the Jew, then to the Gentile.
	1:17	that is by faith from f to last, just as
	2:9	f for the Jew, then for the Gentile;
	2:10	f for the Jew, then for the Gentile.
1Co	12:28	in the church of f all apostles,
	15:45	"The f Adam became a living
2Co	8:5	having given themselves f of all
Eph	6:2	which is the f commandment
1Th	4:16	and the dead in Christ will rise f.
1Ti	2:13	For Adam was formed f, then Eve.
Heb	10:9	He sets aside the f to establish
Jas	3:17	comes from heaven is f of all pure;
1Jn	4:19	We love because he f loved us.
3Jn	:9	who loves to be f, will have nothing
Rev	1:17	I am the F and the Last.
	2:4	have forsaken the love you had at f.
	22:13	the Alpha and the Omega, the F and the Last,

FIRSTBORN (BEAR)

Ex	11:5	Every f son in Egypt will die,
	34:20	Redeem all your f sons. "No one is
Ps	89:27	And I will appoint him to be my f,
Lk	2:7	and she gave birth to her f, a son.
Ro	8:29	might be the f among many brothers
Col	1:15	God, the f over all creation.
	1:18	and the f from among the dead,
Heb	1:6	God brings his f into the world,
	12:23	to the church of the f, whose names
Rev	1:5	faithful witness, the f from the dead,

FIRSTFRUITS

Ex	23:16	with the f of the crops you sow
	23:19	"Bring the best of the f of your soil
Ro	8:23	who have the f of the Spirit,
1Co	15:23	Christ, the f; then, when he comes,
Rev	14:4	human race and offered as f to God

FISH

Ge	1:26	they may rule over the f in the sea
Jnh	1:17	Now the LORD provided a huge f
Mt	4:19	send you out to f for people."
	7:10	Or if he asks for a f, will give him
	12:40	three nights in the belly of a huge f,
	14:17	five loaves of bread and two f,"

Mk	1:17	send you out to f for people."
	6:38	they said, "Five—and two f."
Lk	5:6	they caught such a large number of f
	5:10	from now on you will f for people."
	9:13	only five loaves of bread and two f—
Jn	6:9	small barley loaves and two small f,
	21:5	"Friends, haven't you any f?"
	21:11	It was full of large f, 153, but even

FISHERMEN

Mk	1:16	a net into the lake, for they were f.

FISHHOOK*

Job	41:1	you pull in the leviathan with a f

FISTS

Mt	26:67	his face and struck him with their f.

FIT (FITTING)

Jdg	17:6	everyone did as they saw f.
	21:25	everyone did as they saw f.

FITTING* (FIT)

Ps	33:1	it is f for the upright to praise him.
	147:1	how pleasant and f to praise him!
Pr	19:10	It is not f for a fool to live
	26:1	in harvest, honor is not f for a fool.
1Co	14:40	everything should be done in a f
Col	3:18	to your husbands, as is f in the Lord.
Heb	2:10	to glory, it was f that God,

FIX* (FIXED FIXING)

Dt	11:18	F these words of mine in your
Job	14:3	Do you f your eye on such as these?
Pr	4:25	f your gaze directly before you.
Am	9:4	"I will f my eyes on them for evil
2Co	4:18	So we f our eyes not on what is
Heb	3:1	calling, f your thoughts on Jesus,

FIXED* (FIX)

2Ki	8:11	him with a f gaze until Hazael was
Job	38:10	when I f limits for it and set its
Ps	141:8	But my eyes are f on you,
Pr	8:28	f securely the fountains of the deep,

FIXING* (FIX)

Heb	12:2	f our eyes on Jesus, the pioneer

FLAME (FLAMES FLAMING)

2Ti	1:6	to fan into f the gift of God,

FLAMES (FLAME)

1Co	3:15	only as one escaping through the f.

FLAMING (FLAME)

Eph	6:16	you can extinguish all the f arrows

FLANK

Eze	34:21	Because you shove with f

FLASH

1Co	15:52	in a f, in the twinkling of an eye,

FLATTER* (FLATTERING FLATTERY)

Job	32:21	no partiality, nor will I anyone;
Ps	12:2	they f with their lips
	36:2	In their own eyes they f
	78:36	would f him with their mouths,
Pr	29:5	Those who f their neighbors
Jude	:16	f others for their own advantage.

FLATTERING* (FLATTER)

Ps	12:3	May the LORD silence all f lips
Pr	26:28	it hurts, and a f mouth works ruin.
	28:23	rather than one who has a f tongue.
Eze	12:24	or f divinations among the people

FLATTERY* (FLATTER)

Job	32:22	for if I were skilled in f, my Maker
Da	11:32	he will corrupt those who have
Ro	16:18	they deceive the minds of naive
1Th	2:5	You know we never used f, nor did

FLAWLESS*

2Sa	22:31	the LORD's word is f.
Job	11:4	'My beliefs are f and I am pure
Ps	12:6	And the words of the LORD are f,
	18:30	The LORD's word is f;
Pr	30:5	"Every word of God is f; he is
SS	5:2	my darling, my dove, my f one.

FLEE

Ps	139:7	Where can I f from your presence?
Pr	28:1	wicked f though no one pursues,
1Co	6:18	F from sexual immorality.
	10:14	my dear friends, f from idolatry.
1Ti	6:11	man of God, f from all this,
2Ti	2:22	The evil desires of youth
Jas	4:7	the devil, and he will f from you.

FLEECE

Jdg	6:37	look, I will place a wool f

FLEETING*

Job	14:2	like f shadows, they do not endure.
Ps	39:4	let me know how f my life is.
	89:47	Remember how f is my life.
	144:4	their days are like a f shadow.
Pr	21:6	made by a lying tongue is a f vapor
	31:30	Charm is deceptive, and beauty is f;
Heb	11:25	than to enjoy the f pleasures of sin.

FLESH

Ge	2:23	bone of my bones and f of my f;
	2:24	wife, and they will become one f.
2Ch	32:8	With him is only the arm of f,
Job	19:26	yet in my f I will see God;
Eze	11:19	stone and give them a heart of f.
	36:26	stone and give you a heart of f.
Mt	19:5	and the two will become one f'?
	26:41	is willing, but the f is weak."
Mk	10:8	and the two will become one f.'
Jn	1:14	The Word became f and made his
	6:51	This bread is my f, which I will give
1Co	6:16	said, "The two will become one f."
	15:39	All f is not the same:
Eph	5:31	and the two will become one f."
	6:12	For our struggle is not against f
Php	3:2	evildoers, those mutilators of the f.
1Jn	4:2	that Jesus Christ has come in the f is
Jude	:23	the clothing stained by corrupted f.

FLIGHT

Dt	32:30	or two put ten thousand to f,

FLINT

Isa	50:7	Therefore have I set my face like f,
Zec	7:12	They made their hearts as hard as f

FLIRTING*

Isa	3:16	outstretched necks, f with their eyes,

FLOCK (FLOCKS)

Ps	77:20	You led your people like a f
	78:52	he brought his people out like a f;
	95:7	of his pasture, the f under his care.
Isa	40:11	He tends his f like a shepherd:
Jer	10:21	prosper and all their f is scattered.
	23:2	"Because you have scattered my f
	31:10	watch over his f like a shepherd."
Eze	34:2	not shepherds take care of the f?
Zec	11:17	shepherd, who deserts the f!
Mt	26:31	the sheep of the f will be scattered.'
Lk	12:32	little f, for your Father has been
Jn	10:16	and there shall be one f and one
Ac	20:28	all the f of which the Holy Spirit has
1Co	9:7	Who tends a f and does not drink
1Pe	5:2	of God's f that is under your care,
	5:3	to you, but being examples to the f.

FLOCKS (FLOCK)

Lk	2:8	keeping watch over their f at night.

FLOG (FLOGGED FLOGGING)

Pr	19:25	F a mocker, and the simple will
Ac	22:25	a Roman citizen who hasn't even

FLOGGED (FLOG)

Jn	19:1	Pilate took Jesus and had him f.
Ac	5:40	the apostles in and had them f
	16:23	After they had been severely f,
2Co	11:23	frequently, been f more severely,

FLOGGING (FLOG)

Heb	11:36	Some faced jeers and f, and even

FLOOD (FLOODGATES)

Ge	7:7	the ark to escape the waters of the f.
Mal	2:13	You f the LORD's altar with tears.
Mt	24:38	For in the days before the f,
2Pe	2:5	he brought the f on its ungodly

FLOODGATES (FLOOD)

Ge	7:11	the f of the heavens were opened.
Mal	3:10	I will not throw open the f of heaven

FLOOR

Jas	2:3	there" or "Sit on the f by my feet,"

FLOUR

Lev	2:1	your offering is to be of the finest f.
Nu	7:13	the finest f mixed with olive oil as
	28:9	of the finest f mixed with olive oil.

FLOURISH (FLOURISHES FLOURISHING)

Ps	72:7	In his days may the righteous f
	92:7	up like grass and all evildoers f,
	92:12	The righteous will f like a palm tree,
Pr	14:11	but the tent of the upright will f.

FLOURISHES* (FLOURISH)

Pr	12:12	but the root of the righteous f.

FLOURISHING (FLOURISH)
Ps 52: 8 I am like an olive tree f in the house

FLOW (FLOWING FLOWS)
Nu 13:27 and it does f with milk and honey!
Jn 7:38 of living water will f from within

FLOWER (FLOWERS)
Ps 103:15 they flourish like a f of the field;
Jas 1:10 they will pass away like a wild f.

FLOWERS (FLOWER)
Job 14: 2 They spring up like f and wither
Ps 37:20 are like the f of the field,
Isa 40: 6 all human faithfulness is like the f
40: 7 The grass withers and the f fall,
Lk 12:27 "Consider how the wild f grow.
1Pe 1:24 and all their glory is like the f

FLOWING (FLOW)
Ex 3: 8 land, a land f with milk and honey—
33: 3 Go up to the land f with milk
Nu 16:14 brought us into a land f with milk
Jos 5: 6 a land f with milk and honey.
Ps 107:33 desert, f springs into thirsty ground,
107:35 the parched ground into f springs;
Jer 32:22 a land f with milk and honey.
Eze 20: 6 them, a land f with milk and honey,
Rev 22: 1 f from the throne of God

FLOWS (FLOW)
Pr 4:23 everything you do f from it.

FOAL*
Zec 9: 9 donkey, on a colt, the f of a donkey.
Mt 21: 5 and on a colt, the f of a donkey.' "

FOILS*
Ps 33:10 The LORD f the plans
Isa 44:25 who f the signs of false prophets

FOLD (FOLDING)
Ecc 4: 5 Fools f their hands

FOLDING* (FOLD)
Pr 6:10 a little f of the hands to rest—
24:33 a little f of the hands to rest—

FOLLOW (FOLLOWED FOLLOWING FOLLOWS)
Ex 23: 2 "Do not f the crowd in doing
Lev 18: 4 laws and be careful to f my decrees.
Dt 5: 1 Learn them and be sure to f them.
17:19 f carefully all the words of this law
1Ki 11: 6 he did not f the LORD completely,
2Ch 34:33 they did not fail to f the LORD,
Ps 23: 6 love will f me all the days of my
119:166 LORD, and I f your commands.
Mt 4:19 "Come, f me," Jesus said, "and I
8:19 I will f you wherever you go."
8:22 But Jesus told him, "F me, and let
16:24 and take up their cross and f me.
19:27 "We have left everything to f you!
Lk 9:23 take up their cross daily and f me.
9:61 another said, "I will f you, Lord;
Jn 10: 4 his sheep f him because they know
10: 5 But they will never f a stranger;
10:27 I know them, and they f me.
12:26 Whoever serves me must f me;
21:19 Then he said to him, "F me!"
1Co 1:12 One of you says, "I f Paul";
1:12 still another, "I f Christ."
11: 1 F my example, as I f the example
14: 1 F the way of love and eagerly desire
Eph 5: 1 F God's example,
1Pe 2:21 that you should f in his steps.
Rev 14: 4 They f the Lamb wherever he goes.

FOLLOWED (FOLLOW)
Nu 32:11 they have not f me wholeheartedly,
Dt 1:36 his feet on, because he f the LORD
Jos 14:14 ever since, because he f the LORD,
2Ch 10:14 the advice of the young men
Mt 4:20 once they left their nets and f him.
9: 9 and Matthew got up and f him.
26:58 But Peter f him at a distance,
Lk 18:43 he received his sight and f Jesus,

FOLLOWING (FOLLOW)
Ps 119:14 in f your statutes as one rejoices
Php 3:17 Join together in f my example,

FOLLOWS (FOLLOW)
Jn 8:12 Whoever f me will never walk

FOLLY (FOOL)
Pr 14:29 but the quick-tempered display f.
19: 3 One's own f leads to ruin,
Ecc 10: 1 so a little f outweighs wisdom
Mk 7:22 envy, slander, arrogance and f.

2Ti 3: 9 their f will be clear to everyone.

FOOD (FOODS)
Ge 1:30 I give every green plant for f."
Pr 12: 9 to be somebody and have no f.
12:11 their land will have abundant f,
20:13 awake and you will have f to spare.
20:17 F gained by fraud tastes sweet,
21:20 The wise store up choice f and olive
22: 9 for they share their f with the poor.
23: 3 his delicacies, for that f is deceptive.
23: 6 Do not eat the f of a begrudging
25:21 enemy is hungry, give him f to eat;
31:14 ships, bringing her f from afar.
31:15 she provides f for her family
Isa 58: 7 not to share your f with the hungry
Eze 18: 7 robbery but gives his f to the hungry
Da 1: 8 not to defile himself with the royal f
Mt 3: 4 His f was locusts and wild honey.
6:25 Is not life more important than f,
Jn 4:32 them, "I have f to eat that you know
4:34 "My f," said Jesus, "is to do
6:27 Do not work for f that spoils,
6:55 For my flesh is real f and my blood
Ac 15:20 to abstain from f polluted by idols,
1Co 8: 1 Now about f sacrificed to idols:
8: 8 But f does not bring us near to God;
2Co 11:27 thirst and have often gone without f;
1Ti 6: 8 But if we have f and clothing,
Heb 5:14 But solid f is for the mature,
Jas 2:15 sister is without clothes and daily f.

FOODS (FOOD)
Mk 7:19 this, Jesus declared all f clean.)

FOOL (FOLLY FOOL'S FOOLISH FOOLISHNESS FOOLS)
1Sa 25:25 his name means F, and folly goes
Pr 10:10 and a chattering f comes to ruin.
10:18 lying lips and spreads slander is a f.
14:16 but a f is hotheaded and yet feels
15: 5 A f spurns a parent's discipline,
17:12 of her cubs than a f bent on folly.
17:21 To have a f for a child brings grief;
20: 3 strife, but every f is quick to quarrel.
26: 7 is a proverb in the mouth of a f.
29:20 There is more hope for a f than
Mt 5:22 And anyone who says, 'You f!'
Lk 12:20 "But God said to him, 'You f!
2Co 11:21 I am speaking as a f—I also dare

FOOL'S (FOOL)
Pr 12:23 but a f heart blurts out folly.
14: 3 A f mouth lashes out with pride,

FOOLISH (FOOL)
Pr 10: 1 but f children bring grief to their
14: 1 her own hands the f one tears hers
15:20 but f children despise their mother.
17:25 F children bring grief to their father
19:13 A f child is a father's ruin,
Mt 7:26 practice is like a f man who built his
25: 2 Five of them were f and five were
Lk 11:40 You f people! Did not the one who
24:25 He said to them, "How f you are,
1Co 1:20 Has not God made f the wisdom
1:27 God chose the f things of the world
Gal 3: 1 You f Galatians!
Eph 5: 4 be obscenity, f talk or coarse joking,
5:17 Therefore do not be f,
Tit 3: 9 But avoid f controversies

FOOLISHNESS* (FOOL)
2Sa 15:31 turn Ahithophel's counsel into f."
1Co 1:18 of the cross is f to those who are
1:21 God was pleased through the f
1:23 block to Jews and f to Gentiles,
1:25 the f of God is wiser than human
2:14 Spirit of God but considers them f,
3:19 of this world is f in God's sight.
2Co 11: 1 will put up with me in a little f.

FOOLS (FOOL)
Ps 14: 1 F say in their hearts, "There is no
Pr 1: 7 but f despise wisdom
3:35 inherit honor, but f get only shame.
12:15 The way of f seems right to them,
12:16 F show their annoyance at once,
13:19 soul, but f detest turning from evil.
13:20 for a companion of f suffers harm.
14: 9 F mock at making amends for sin,
14:24 crown, but the folly of f yields folly.
17:16 Why should f have money in hand
17:28 Even f are thought wise if they keep
18: 2 F find no pleasure in understanding

Pr 18: 7 The mouths of f are their undoing,
23: 9 Do not speak to f, for they will
24: 7 Wisdom is too high for f;
26: 4 Do not answer f according to their
26: 5 Answer f according to their folly,
26:11 to its vomit, so f repeat their folly.
26:12 There is more hope for f than
27:22 Though you grind f in a mortar,
28:26 Those who trust in themselves are f,
29:11 F give full vent to their rage,
Ecc 7: 5 person than to listen to the song of f.
7: 6 under the pot, so is the laughter of f.
10: 6 F are put in many high positions,
Mt 23:17 You blind f! Which is greater:
Ro 1:22 claimed to be wise, they became f
1Co 3:18 you should become "f" so that you
4:10 We are f for Christ, but you are so

FOOT (FEET FOOTHOLD)
Jos 1: 3 every place where you set your f.
Ps 121: 3 He will not let your f slip—
Pr 3:23 safety, and your f will not stumble.
4:27 or the left; keep your f from evil.
25:17 Seldom set f in your neighbor's
Isa 1: 6 the sole of your f to the top of your
Mt 18: 8 or your f causes you to stumble,
Lk 4:11 you will not strike your f against
1Co 12:15 Now if the f should say, "Because I
Ac 4:11 He planted his right f on the sea

FOOTHOLD* (FOOT)
Ps 69: 2 the miry depths, where there is no f.
73: 2 I had nearly lost my f.
Eph 4:27 and do not give the devil a f.

FOOTSTEPS* (STEP)
Ps 119:133 Direct my f according to your word;

FOOTSTOOL
Ps 99: 5 our God and worship at his f;
110: 1 hand until I make your enemies a f
Isa 66: 1 is my throne, and the earth is my f.
Mt 5:35 or the earth, for it is his f;
Ac 7:49 my throne, and the earth is my f.
Heb 1:13 hand until I make your enemies a f
10:13 for his enemies to be made his f.

FORBEARANCE* (FOREBEAR)
Ro 2: 4 of his kindness, f and patience,
3:25 in his f he had left the sins

FORBID
1Co 14:39 and do not f speaking in tongues.
1Ti 4: 3 They f people to marry and order

FORCE (FORCED FORCEFUL FORCES FORCING)
Jn 6:15 to come and make him king by f,
Ac 26:11 and I tried to f them to blaspheme.
Gal 2:14 that you f Gentiles to follow Jewish

FORCED (FORCE)
Mt 27:32 and they f him to carry the cross.
Phm : 14 any favor you do would not seem f

FORCEFUL* (FORCE)
2Co 10:10 "His letters are weighty and f,

FORCES (FORCE)
Mt 5:41 If anyone f you to go one mile,
Eph 6:12 against the spiritual f of evil

FORCING (FORCE)
Lk 16:16 and people are f their way into it.

FOREHEAD (FOREHEADS)
Ex 13: 9 a reminder on your f that this law
13:16 your f that the LORD brought us
1Sa 17:49 it and struck the Philistine on the f.

FOREHEADS (FOREHEAD)
Dt 6: 8 your hands and bind them on your f.
Rev 9: 4 not have the seal of God on their f,
13:16 on their right hands or on their f,
14: 1 his Father's name written on their f.

FOREIGN (FOREIGNER FOREIGNERS)
Ge 35: 2 "Get rid of your f gods you have
2Ch 14: 3 He removed the altars and the high
33:15 He got rid of the f gods
Isa 28:11 with f lips and strange tongues God

FOREIGNER (FOREIGN)
Ex 22:21 "Do not mistreat or oppress a f,
Lev 24:22 have the same law for the f
Ps 146: 9 The LORD watches over the f
Lk 17:18 give praise to God except this f?"
1Co 14:11 is saying, I am a f to the speaker,

FOREIGNERS (FOREIGN)
Ex 23: 9 know how it feels to be f,

1Co 14: 21 through the lips of **f** I will speak
Eph 2: 12 **f** to the covenants of the promise,
      2: 19 you are no longer **f** and strangers,
1Pe 2: 11 as **f** and exiles,

FOREKNEW* (KNOW)
Ro   8: 29 For those God **f** he also predestined
     11: 2 did not reject his people, whom he **f**.

FOREKNOWLEDGE* (KNOW)
Ac   2: 23 you by God's deliberate plan and **f**;
1Pe 1: 2 according to the **f** of God the Father,

FORESAW*
Gal 3: 8 Scripture **f** that God would justify

FOREST
Jas 3: 5 Consider what a great **f** is set on fire

FOREVER (EVER)
Ge   3: 22 the tree of life and eat, and live **f**."
     6: 3 not contend with human beings **f**,
Ex   3: 15 "This is my name **f**, the name you
2Sa 7: 26 so that your name will be great **f**."
1Ki 2: 33 there be the LORD's peace **f**."
     9: 3 built, by putting my Name there **f**.
1Ch 16: 15 He remembers his covenant **f**,
     16: 34 for he is good; his love endures **f**.
     16: 41 LORD, "for his love endures **f**."
     17: 24 and that your name will be great **f**."
2Ch 5: 13 "He is good; his love endures **f**."
     20: 21 the LORD, for his love endures **f**."
Ps   9: 7 The LORD reigns **f**;
     23: 6 dwell in the house of the LORD **f**.
     28: 9 be their shepherd and carry them **f**.
     29: 10 the LORD is enthroned as King **f**.
     33: 11 plans of the LORD stand firm **f**,
     44: 8 and we will praise your name **f**.
     61: 4 I long to dwell in your tent **f**
     72: 19 Praise be to his glorious name **f**;
     73: 26 of my heart and my portion **f**.
     77: 8 Has his unfailing love vanished **f**?
     79: 13 of your pasture, will praise you **f**;
     81: 15 and their punishment would last **f**.
     86: 12 I will glorify your name **f**.
     89: 1 sing of the LORD's great love **f**;
     92: 8 But you, LORD, are **f** exalted.
    100: 5 is good and his love endures **f**;
    102: 12 But you, LORD, sit enthroned **f**;
    104: 31 the glory of the LORD endures **f**;
    107: 1 for he is good; his love endures **f**.
    110: 4 "You are a priest **f**, in the order
    111: 3 and his righteousness endures **f**.
    112: 6 they will be remembered **f**.
    117: 2 of the LORD endures **f**.
    118: 1 for he is good; his love endures **f**."
  119:111 Your statutes are my heritage **f**;
  119:152 that you established them to last **f**.
    136: 1 *His love endures **f**.*
    146: 6 he remains faithful **f**.
Pr 10: 25 gone, but the righteous stand firm **f**.
    27: 24 for riches do not endure **f**,
Isa 25: 8 he will swallow up death **f**.
    26: 4 Trust in the LORD **f**,
    32: 17 will be quietness and confidence **f**.
    40: 8 but the word of our God endures **f**."
    51: 6 But my salvation will last **f**,
    51: 8 But my righteousness will last **f**,
    57: 15 he who lives **f**, whose name is holy:
    59: 21 from this time on and **f**,"
Jer 33: 11 his love endures **f**.
Eze 37: 26 put my sanctuary among them **f**.
Da   2: 44 to an end, but it will itself endure **f**.
     3: 9 "May the king live **f**!
Hab 3: 6 but he marches on **f**.
Jn   6: 51 eats of this bread will live **f**.
    14: 16 to help you and be with you **f**—
Ro   9: 5 who is God over all, **f** praised!
    16: 27 God be glory **f** through Jesus Christ!
1Co 9: 25 do it to get a crown that will last **f**.
1Th 4: 17 And so we will be with the Lord **f**.
Heb 5: 6 "You are a priest **f**, in the order
     7: 17 "You are a priest **f**, in the order
     7: 24 but because Jesus lives **f**, he has
    13: 8 the same yesterday and today and **f**.
1Pe 1: 25 but the word of the Lord endures **f**."
1Jn 2: 17 does the will of God lives **f**.
2Jn   2 lives in us and will be with us **f**:

FOREVERMORE (EVER)
Ps 113: 2 LORD be praised, both now and **f**.

FORFEIT
Mk   8: 36 the whole world, yet **f** your soul?
Lk   9: 25 and yet lose or **f** your very self?

FORGAVE* (FORGIVE)
Ps 32: 5 And you **f** the guilt of my sin.
    65: 3 by sins, you **f** our transgressions.
    78: 38 he **f** their iniquities and did not
    85: 2 You **f** the iniquity of your people
Lk   7: 42 so he **f** the debts of both.
Eph 4: 32 just as in Christ God **f** you.
Col 2: 13 He **f** us all our sins,
     3: 13 Forgive as the Lord **f** you.

FORGET (FORGETS FORGETTING FORGOT
FORGOTTEN)
Dt   4: 23 Be careful not to **f** the covenant
     6: 12 that you do not **f** the LORD,
2Ki 17: 38 Do not **f** the covenant I have made
Ps   9: 17 the dead, all the nations that **f** God.
    10: 12 hand, O God. Do not **f** the helpless.
    50: 22 you who **f** God, or I will tear you
    78: 7 in God and would not **f** his deeds
   103: 2 my soul, and **f** not all his benefits—
   119: 93 I will never **f** your precepts,
   137: 5 may my right hand **f** its skill.
Pr   3: 1 My son, do not **f** my teaching,
     4: 5 do not **f** my words or turn away
Isa 49: 15 "Can a mother **f** the baby at her
    51: 13 that you **f** the LORD your Maker,
Jer 2: 32 Does a young woman **f** her jewelry,
    23: 39 I will surely **f** you and cast you
Heb 6: 10 he will not **f** your work and the love
    13: 2 Do not **f** to show hospitality
    13: 16 And do not **f** to do good
Jas 1: 24 immediately **f** what they look like.
2Pe 3: 8 But do not **f** this one thing,

FORGETS (FORGET)
Jn 16: 21 is born she **f** the anguish because

FORGETTING* (FORGET)
Php 3: 13 **f** what is behind and straining
Jas 1: 25 not **f** what they have heard,

FORGIVE* (FORGAVE FORGIVENESS FORGIVES
FORGIVING)
Ge 50: 17 I ask you to **f** your brothers the sins
    50: 17 Now please **f** the sins of the servants
Ex 10: 17 Now **f** my sin once more and pray
    23: 21 he will not **f** your rebellion,
    32: 32 But now, please **f** their sin—
    34: 9 **f** our wickedness and our sin,
Nu 14: 19 great love, **f** the sin of these people,
Dt 29: 20 will never be willing to **f** them;
Jos 24: 19 He will not **f** your rebellion
1Sa 15: 25 **f** my sin and come back with me,
    25: 28 "Please **f** your servant's
1Ki 8: 30 place, and when you hear, **f**.
     8: 34 and **f** the sin of your people Israel
     8: 36 and **f** the sin of your servants,
     8: 39 **F** and act; deal with everyone
     8: 50 And **f** your people, who have sinned
     8: 50 **f** all the offenses they have
2Ki 5: 18 may the LORD **f** your servant
     5: 18 may the LORD **f** your servant
    24: 4 and the LORD was not willing to **f**.
2Ch 6: 21 and when you hear, **f**.
     6: 21 and **f** the sin of your people Israel
     6: 27 and **f** the sin of your servants,
     6: 30 **F**, and deal with everyone according
     6: 39 And **f** your people, who have sinned
     7: 14 and I will **f** their sin and will heal
Job 7: 21 pardon my offenses and **f** my sins?
Ps 19: 12 **f** my hidden faults.
    25: 11 LORD, **f** my iniquity, though it is
    79: 9 and **f** our sins for your name's sake.
Isa 2: 9 do not **f** them.
Jer 5: 1 and seeks the truth, I will **f** this city.
     5: 7 "Why should I **f** you?
    18: 23 Do not **f** their crimes or blot
    31: 34 "For I will **f** their wickedness
    33: 8 and will **f** all their sins of rebellion
    36: 3 then I will **f** their wickedness
    50: 20 for I will **f** the remnant I spare.
Da   9: 19 Lord, **f**! Lord, hear and act!
Hos 1: 6 of Israel, that I should at all **f** them.
    14: 2 "F all our sins and receive us
Am   7: 2 I cried out, "Sovereign LORD, **f**!
Mt   6: 12 And **f** us our debts, as we also have
     6: 14 if you **f** others when they sin against
     6: 14 heavenly Father will also **f** you.
     6: 15 But if you do not **f** others their sins,
     6: 15 your Father will not **f** your sins.
     9: 6 has authority on earth to **f** sins."
    18: 21 times shall I **f** someone who sins
    18: 35 each of you unless you **f** a brother
Mk   2: 7 Who can **f** sins but God alone?"

Mk   2: 10 has authority on earth to **f** sins."
    11: 25 anything against anyone, **f** them,
    11: 25 in heaven may **f** you your sins."
Lk   5: 21 Who can **f** sins but God alone?"
     5: 24 has authority on earth to **f** sins."
     6: 37 **f**, and you will be forgiven.
    11: 4 **F** us our sins, for we also **f** everyone
    17: 3 and if they repent, **f** them.
    17: 4 saying 'I repent,' you must **f** them."
    23: 34 "Father, **f** them, for they do not
Jn 20: 23 If you **f** the sins of anyone, their sins
    20: 23 if you do not **f** them, they are not
Ac   5: 31 to repentance and **f** their sins.
     8: 22 that he may **f** you for having such
2Co 2: 7 you ought to **f** and comfort him,
     2: 10 Anyone you **f**, I also **f**.
     2: 10 if there was anything to **f**—
    12: 13 a burden to you? **F** me this wrong!
Col 3: 13 and **f** one another if any of you has
     3: 13 **F** as the Lord forgave you.
Heb 8: 12 For I will **f** their wickedness
1Jn 1: 9 just and will **f** us our sins and purify

FORGIVENESS* (FORGIVE)
Ps 130: 4 But with you there is **f**, so that we
Mt 26: 28 out for many for the **f** of sins.
Mk   1: 4 of repentance for the **f** of sins.
Lk   1: 77 salvation through the **f** of their sins,
     3: 3 of repentance for the **f** of sins.
    24: 47 for the **f** of sins will be preached
Ac   2: 38 Jesus Christ for the **f** of your sins.
    10: 43 in him receives **f** of sins through his
    13: 38 that through Jesus the **f** of sins is
    26: 18 so that they may receive **f** of sins
Eph 1: 7 through his blood, the **f** of sins,
Col 1: 14 we have redemption, the **f** of sins.
Heb 9: 22 the shedding of blood there is no **f**.

FORGIVES* (FORGIVE)
Ps 103: 3 who **f** all your sins and heals all
Mic 7: 18 **f** the transgression of the remnant
Lk   7: 49 "Who is this who even **f** sins?"

FORGIVING* (FORGIVE)
Ex 34: 7 and **f** wickedness, rebellion and sin.
Nu 14: 18 abounding in love and **f** sin
Ne   9: 17 But you are a **f** God,
Ps 86: 5 Lord, are **f** and good,
    99: 8 you were to Israel a **f** God,
Da   9: 9 The Lord our God is merciful and **f**,
Eph 4: 32 to one another, **f** each other, just as

FORGOT (FORGET)
Dt 32: 18 you **f** the God who gave you birth.
Ps 78: 11 They **f** what he had done,
   106: 13 But they soon **f** what he had done

FORGOTTEN (FORGET)
Job 11: 6 God has even **f** some of your sin.
Ps 44: 20 If we had **f** the name of our God
Isa 17: 10 have **f** God your Savior;
Hos 8: 14 Israel has **f** their Maker and built
Lk 12: 6 Yet not one of them is **f** by God.
2Pe 1: 9 and you have **f** that you have been

FORM (FORMED)
Isa 52: 14 and his **f** marred beyond human
2Ti 3: 5 having a **f** of godliness but denying

FORMED (FORM)
Ge   2: 7 the LORD God **f** a man
     2: 19 Now the LORD God had **f**
Ps 103: 14 for he knows how we are **f**,
Pr   8: 23 I was **f** long ages ago,
Ecc 11: 5 or how the body is **f** in a mother's
Isa 29: 16 Shall what is **f** say to the one who **f** it,
    45: 18 be empty, but **f** it to be inhabited—
    49: 5 he who **f** me in the womb to be his
Jer 1: 5 "Before I **f** you in the womb I knew
Ro 9: 20 "Shall what is **f** say to the one who
Gal 4: 19 of childbirth until Christ is **f** in you,
1Ti 2: 13 For Adam was **f** first, then Eve.
Heb 11: 3 that the universe was **f** at God's
2Pe 3: 5 and the earth was **f** out of water

FORMLESS*
Ge   1: 2 Now the earth was **f** and empty,
Jer 4: 23 at the earth, and it was **f** and empty;

FORSAKE (FORSAKEN)
Dt 31: 6 he will never leave you nor **f** you.
Jos 1: 5 I will never leave you nor **f** you.
    24: 16 us to **f** the LORD to serve other
2Ch 15: 2 But if you **f** him, he will **f** you.
Ps 27: 10 Though my father and mother **f** me,
    94: 14 he will never **f** his inheritance.

Isa 55: 7 Let the wicked f their ways
Heb 13: 5 will I leave you; never will I f you."

FORSAKEN (FORSAKE)
Ezr 9: 9 God has not f us in our bondage.
Ps 22: 1 God, my God, why have you f me?
　　 37: 25 yet I have never seen the righteous f
Mt 27: 46 my God, my God, why have you f
Rev 2: 4 have f the love you had at first.

FORTIFIED
Pr 18: 10 The name of the LORD is a f tower;

FORTRESS
2Sa 22: 2 is my rock, my f and my deliverer;
Ps 18: 2 is my rock, my f and my deliverer;
　　 31: 2 of refuge, a strong f to save me.
　　 59: 16 for you are my f, my refuge in times
　　 71: 3 for you are my rock and my f.
Pr 14: 26 fear the LORD have a secure f,

FORTUNE-TELLING*
Ac 16: 16 deal of money for her owners by f.

FORTY
Ge 7: 4 on the earth for f days and f nights,
　　 18: 29 "What if only f are found there?"
Ex 16: 35 The Israelites ate manna f years,
　　 24: 18 on the mountain f days and f nights.
Nu 14: 34 For f years—one year for each
Jos 14: 7 I was f years old when Moses
1Sa 4: 18 He had led Israel f years.
2Sa 5: 4 became king, and he reigned f years.
1Ki 19: 8 he traveled f days and f nights until
2Ki 12: 1 and he reigned in Jerusalem f years.
2Ch 9: 30 in Jerusalem over all Israel f years.
Eze 29: 12 cities will lie desolate f years among
Jnh 3: 4 "f more days and Nineveh will be
Mt 4: 2 After fasting f days and f nights,

FOUGHT (FIGHT)
1Co 15: 32 If I f wild beasts in Ephesus with no
2Ti 4: 7 I have f the good fight, I have

FOUND (FIND)
1Sa 9: 2 handsome a young man as could be f
2Ki 22: 8 "I have f the Book of the Law
1Ch 28: 9 If you seek him, he will be f by you;
2Ch 15: 15 God eagerly, and he was f by them.
Isa 55: 6 Seek the LORD while he may be f;
　　 65: 1 I was f by those who did not seek
Da 5: 27 on the scales and f wanting.
Mt 1: 18 she was f to be pregnant through
Lk 15: 6 I have f my lost sheep.'
　　 15: 9 I have f my lost coin.'
　　 15: 24 is alive again; he was lost and is f.'
Ac 4: 12 Salvation is f in no one else,
Ro 10: 20 "I was f by those who did not seek
Jas 2: 10 If you really keep the royal law f
Rev 5: 4 no one was f who was worthy

FOUNDATION (FOUNDATIONS FOUNDED)
Isa 28: 16 a precious cornerstone for a sure f;
Mt 7: 25 fall, because it had its f on the rock.
Lk 14: 29 For if you lay the f and are not able
Ro 15: 20 not building on someone else's f.
1Co 3: 10 I laid a f as a wise builder,
　　 3: 11 one can lay any f other than the one
Eph 2: 20 built on the f of the apostles
1Ti 3: 15 the pillar and f of the truth.
2Ti 2: 19 God's solid f stands firm,
Heb 6: 1 not laying again the f of repentance

FOUNDATIONS (FOUNDATION)
Ps 102: 25 In the beginning you laid the f
Heb 1: 10 Lord, you laid the f of the earth,

FOUNDED (FOUNDATION)
Jer 10: 12 he f the world by his wisdom

FOUNTAIN
Ps 36: 9 For with you is the f of life;
Pr 14: 27 The fear of the LORD is a f of life,
　　 18: 4 the f of wisdom is a rushing stream.
Zec 13: 1 that day a f will be opened

FOX (FOXES)
Lk 13: 32 "Go tell that f, 'I will keep

FOXES (FOX)
SS 2: 15 Catch for us the f, the little f
Mt 8: 20 "F have holes and birds have nests,

FRAGRANCE (FRAGRANT)
Ex 30: 38 like it to enjoy its f must be cut off
Jn 12: 3 was filled with the f of the perfume.

FRAGRANT (FRAGRANCE)
Eph 5: 2 himself up for us as a f offering
Php 4: 18 They are a f offering, an acceptable

FRANKINCENSE
Mt 2: 11 gifts of gold, f and myrrh.

FREE (FREED FREEDOM FREELY)
Ge 2: 16 "You are f to eat from any tree
Ps 119: 32 for you have set my heart f.
　　 146: 7 The LORD sets prisoners f,
Pr 6: 3 to f yourself, since you have fallen
Lk 4: 18 to set the oppressed f,
Jn 8: 32 truth, and the truth will set you f."
　　 8: 36 Son sets you f, you will be f indeed.
Ro 6: 7 anyone who has died has been set f
　　 6: 18 You have been set f from sin
　　 8: 2 Spirit who gives life has set you f
1Co 7: 27 f from such a commitment? Do not look
　　　　 for a wife.
　　 12: 13 Jews or Gentiles, slave or f—
Gal 3: 28 neither slave nor f, neither male nor
　　 5: 1 for freedom that Christ has set us f.
1Pe 2: 16 Live as f people, but do not use your

FREED (FREE)
Rev 1: 5 has f us from our sins by his blood,

FREEDOM (FREE)
Ps 119: 45 I will walk about in f, for I have
Isa 61: 1 to proclaim f for the captives
Lk 4: 18 me to proclaim f for the prisoners
Ro 8: 21 brought into the f and glory
1Co 7: 21 although if you can gain your f,
2Co 3: 17 the Spirit of the Lord is, there is f.
Gal 2: 4 spy on the f we have in Christ Jesus
　　 5: 13 But do not use your f to indulge
Jas 1: 25 into the perfect law that gives f,
1Pe 2: 16 do not use your f as

FREELY (FREE)
Isa 55: 7 and to our God, for he will f pardon.
Mt 10: 8 F you have received, f give.
Ro 3: 24 and all are justified f by his grace
Eph 1: 6 which he has f given us in the One

FRESH
Jas 3: 11 Can both f water and salt water flow

FRET*
Ps 37: 1 Do not f because of those who are
　　 37: 7 do not f when people succeed
　　 37: 8 do not f—it leads only to evil.
Pr 24: 19 Do not f because of evildoers or be

FRICTION*
1Ti 6: 5 constant f between people of corrupt

FRIEND (FRIENDS FRIENDSHIP)
Ex 33: 11 face to face, as one speaks to a f.
2Ch 20: 7 the descendants of Abraham your f?
Pr 17: 17 A f loves at all times, and a brother
　　 18: 24 there is a f who sticks closer than
　　 27: 6 Wounds from a f can be trusted,
　　 27: 10 Do not forsake your f or a f of your
Isa 41: 8 you descendants of Abraham my f,
Mt 11: 19 a f of tax collectors and sinners.'
Jn 19: 12 this man go, you are no f of Caesar.
Ro 16: 8 Ampliatus, my dear f in the Lord.
Jas 2: 23 and he was called God's f.
　　 4: 4 to be a f of the world becomes

FRIENDS (FRIEND)
Pr 16: 28 and gossips separate close f.
　　 17: 9 repeats the matter separates close f.
　　 18: 24 has unreliable f soon comes to ruin,
Zec 13: 6 I was given at the house of my f.'
Jn 15: 13 to lay down one's life for one's f.
　　 15: 14 You are my f if you do what I

FRIENDSHIP (FRIEND)
Lk 11: 8 give you the bread because of f,
Jas 4: 4 don't you know that f

FRIGHTENED (FEAR)
Php 1: 28 without being f in any way by those
1Pe 3: 14 not fear their threats; do not be f."

FROGS
Ex 8: 2 I will send a plague of f on your
Rev 16: 13 three evil spirits that looked like f;

FROLIC
Mal 4: 2 and f like well-fed calves.

FRUIT (FRUITFUL)
Jdg 9: 11 'Should I give up my f, so good
Ps 1: 3 which yields its f in season
Pr 11: 30 The f of the righteous is a tree
　　 12: 14 the f of their lips people are filled
　　 27: 18 who guard a fig tree will eat its f,
Isa 11: 1 from his roots a Branch will bear f.
　　 27: 6 blossom and fill all the world with f.

Isa 32: 17 The f of that righteousness will be
Jer 17: 8 drought and never fails to bear f."
Hos 10: 12 reap the f of unfailing love,
　　 14: 2 that we may offer the f of our lips.
Am 8: 1 a basket of ripe f.
Mt 3: 8 Produce f in keeping
　　 3: 10 does not produce good f will be cut
　　 7: 16 By their f you will recognize them.
　　 7: 17 good f, but a bad tree bears bad f.
　　 7: 20 by their f you will recognize them.
　　 12: 33 a tree good and its f will be good,
Lk 3: 9 does not produce good f will be cut
　　 6: 43 "No good tree bears bad f, nor does
　　 13: 6 he went to look for f on it but did
Jn 15: 2 every branch in me that bears no f,
　　 15: 16 so that you might go and bear f—
Ro 7: 4 order that we might bear f for God.
Gal 5: 22 But the f of the Spirit is love, joy,
Php 1: 11 filled with the f of righteousness
Col 1: 10 bearing f in every good work,
Heb 13: 15 the f of lips that openly profess his
Jas 3: 17 full of mercy and good f,
Jude : 12 trees, without f and uprooted—
Rev 22: 2 of f, yielding its f every month.

FRUITFUL (FRUIT)
Ge 1: 22 "Be f and increase in number
　　 9: 1 "Be f and increase in number
　　 35: 11 be f and increase in number.
Ex 1: 7 the Israelites were exceedingly f;
Ps 128: 3 wife will be like a f vine within your
Jn 15: 2 prunes so that it will be even more f.
Php 1: 22 body, this will mean f labor for me.

FRUITLESS*
Eph 5: 11 to do with the f deeds of darkness,

FRUSTRATION
Ro 8: 20 For the creation was subjected to f,

FUEL
Isa 44: 19 to say, "Half of it I used for f;

FULFILL (FULFILLED FULFILLMENT FULFILLS)
Nu 23: 19 Does he promise and not f?
Ps 61: 8 name and f my vows day after day.
　　 116: 14 I will f my vows to the LORD
Ecc 5: 3 a vow than to make one and not f it.
Isa 46: 11 far-off land, a man to f my purpose.
Jer 33: 14 I will f the good promise I made
Mt 1: 22 f what the Lord had said through
　　 3: 15 us to do this to f all righteousness."
　　 4: 14 f what was said through the prophet
　　 5: 17 come to abolish them but to f them.
　　 8: 17 to f what was spoken through
　　 12: 17 to f what was spoken through
　　 21: 4 to f what was spoken through
Jn 12: 38 This was to f the word of Isaiah
　　 13: 18 this is to f this passage of Scripture:
　　 15: 25 this is to f what is written in their
1Co 7: 3 The husband should f his marital

FULFILLED (FULFILL)
Jos 21: 45 of Israel failed; every one was f.
　　 23: 14 Every promise has been f;
Pr 13: 12 sick, but a longing f is a tree of life.
　　 13: 19 A longing f is sweet to the soul,
Mt 2: 15 And so was f what the Lord had said
　　 2: 17 through the prophet Jeremiah was f:
　　 2: 23 So was f what was said through
　　 13: 14 In them is f the prophecy of Isaiah:
　　 13: 35 So was f what was spoken through
　　 26: 54 would the Scriptures be f that say it
　　 26: 56 of the prophets might be f."
　　 27: 9 by Jeremiah the prophet was f:
Mk 13: 4 sign that they are all about to be f?"
　　 14: 49 But the Scriptures must be f."
Lk 4: 21 "Today this scripture is f in your
　　 18: 31 about the Son of Man will be f.
　　 24: 44 Everything must be f that is written
　　 18: 9 words he had spoken would be f:
　　 19: 24 the scripture might be f that said,
　　 19: 28 and so that Scripture would be f,
　　 19: 36 so that the scripture would be f:
Ac 1: 16 the Scripture had to be f
Gal 5: 14 For the entire law is f in keeping
Ro 13: 8 whoever loves others has f the law.
Jas 2: 23 And the scripture was f that says,

FULFILLMENT (FULFILL)
Ro 13: 10 Therefore love is the f of the law.

FULFILLS (FULFILL)
Ps 145: 19 He f the desires of those who fear

FULL (FILL)
2Ch 24: 10 them into the chest until it was f.
Ps 127: 5 Blessed is the man whose quiver is f
Pr 27: 7 One who is f loathes honey
31: 11 Her husband has f confidence in her
Isa 6: 3 the whole earth is f of his glory."
Lk 4: 1 Jesus, f of the Holy Spirit,
Jn 10: 10 may have life, and have it to the f.
Ac 6: 3 who are known to be f of the Spirit
6: 5 a man f of faith and of the Holy
7: 55 But Stephen, f of the Holy Spirit,
11: 24 f of the Holy Spirit and faith,
Eph 4: 19 impurity, and they are f of greed.

FULL-GROWN* (GROW)
Jas 1: 15 when it is f, gives birth to death.

FULLNESS* (FILL)
Dt 33: 16 its f and the favor of him who dwelt
Jn 1: 16 of his f we have all received grace
Ro 11: 12 greater riches will their f bring!
Eph 1: 23 the f of him who fills everything
3: 19 to the measure of all the f of God.
4: 13 the whole measure of the f of Christ.
Col 1: 19 to have all his f dwell in him,
1: 25 to you the word of God in its f—
2: 9 in Christ all the f of the Deity lives
2: 10 Christ you have been brought to f.

FULLY (FILL)
1Ki 8: 61 may your hearts be f committed
2Ch 16: 9 those whose hearts are f committed
Ps 119: 4 precepts that are to be f obeyed.
119:138 they are f trustworthy.
Pr 13: 4 desires of the diligent are f satisfied.
Lk 6: 40 but all who are f trained will be like
Ro 4: 21 being f persuaded that God had
14: 5 Everyone should be f convinced
1Co 13: 12 then I shall know f, even as I am f
15: 58 Always give yourselves f
2Ti 4: 17 the message might be f proclaimed

FURIOUS (FURY)
Dt 29: 28 In f anger and in great wrath
Jer 21: 5 arm in f anger and in great wrath.
32: 37 where I banish them in my f anger

FURNACE
Isa 48: 10 have tested you in the f of affliction.
Da 3: 6 be thrown into a blazing f."
Mt 13: 42 will throw them into the blazing f,

FURY (FURIOUS)
Isa 14: 6 in f subdued nations with relentless
Am 1: 11 and his f flamed unchecked,
Rev 14: 10 will drink of the wine of God's f,
16: 19 with the wine of the f of his wrath.
19: 15 the winepress of the f of the wrath

FUTILE (FUTILITY)
Mal 3: 14 have said, 'It is f to serve God.
1Co 3: 20 that the thoughts of the wise are f."

FUTILITY (FUTILE)
Eph 4: 17 in the f of their thinking.

FUTURE
Ps 37: 37 a f awaits those who seek peace.
Pr 23: 18 There is surely a f hope for you,
Ecc 7: 14 discover anything about your f.
8: 7 Since no one knows the f, who can
Jer 29: 11 plans to give you hope and a f.
Ro 8: 38 neither the present nor the f, nor any
1Co 3: 22 life or death or the present or the f—

GABRIEL*
Angel who interpreted Daniel's visions (Da 8:16–26;
9:20–27); announced births of John (Lk 1:11–20),
Jesus (Lk 1:26–38).

GAD
1. Son of Jacob by Zilpah (Ge 30:9–11; 35:26; 1Ch
2:2). Tribe of blessed (Ge 49:19; Dt 33:20–21), numbered (Nu 1:25; 26:18), allotted land east of the Jordan (Nu 32; 34:14; Jos 18:7; 22), west (Dt
48:27–28), 12,000 from (Rev 7:5).
2. Prophet; seer of David (1Sa 22:5; 2Sa 24:11–19;
1Ch 29:29).

GAIN (GAINED GAINS)
Ex 14: 17 And I will g glory through Pharaoh
Ps 60: 12 With God we will g the victory,
Pr 3: 13 those who g understanding,
4: 1 pay attention and g understanding.
8: 5 You who are simple, g prudence;
15: 32 heed correction g understanding.
28: 16 who hates ill-gotten g will enjoy
28: 23 the end g favor rather than one who

GAINED (GAIN)
Jer 32: 20 have g the renown that is still yours.
Ro 5: 2 through whom we have g access

GAINS (GAIN)
Pr 11: 16 A kindhearted woman g honor,
Php 3: 7 were g to me I now consider loss

GALILEE
Isa 9: 1 in the future he will honor G
Mt 4: 15 the Jordan, G of the Gentiles—
26: 32 I will go ahead of you into G."
28: 10 Go and tell my brothers to go to G;

GALL
Mt 27: 34 Jesus wine to drink, mixed with g;

GALLIO
Ac 18: 12 While G was proconsul of Achaia,

GAMALIEL
Ac 5: 34 But a Pharisee named G, a teacher

GAMES*
1Co 9: 25 who competes in the g goes

GAP
Eze 22: 30 stand before me in the g on behalf

GARBAGE
Php 3: 8 I consider them g, that I may gain

GARDEN (GARDENER)
Ge 2: 8 the LORD God had planted a g
2: 15 put him in the G of Eden to work it
SS 4: 12 You are a g locked up, my sister,
Isa 58: 11 You will be like a well-watered g,
Jer 31: 12 They will be like a well-watered g,
Eze 28: 13 You were in Eden, the g of God;
31: 9 all the trees of Eden in the g of God.

GARDENER (GARDEN)
Jn 15: 1 true vine, and my Father is the g.

GARLAND*
Pr 1: 9 They are a g to grace your head
4: 9 She will give you a g to grace your

GARMENT (GARMENTS)
Ps 22: 18 and cast lots for my g.
102: 26 they will all wear out like a g.
Isa 50: 9 They will all wear out like a g
51: 6 the earth will wear out like a g
61: 3 a g of praise instead of a spirit
Mt 9: 16 patch of unshrunk cloth on an old g,
Jn 19: 23 This g was seamless, woven in one
Heb 1: 11 they will all wear out like a g.

GARMENTS (GARMENT)
Ge 3: 21 The LORD God made g of skin
Ex 28: 2 Make sacred g for your brother
Lev 16: 23 take off the linen g he put on before
16: 24 area and put on his regular g.
Isa 61: 10 For he has clothed me with g
63: 1 Bozrah, with his g stained crimson?
Joel 2: 13 Rend your heart and not your g.
Zec 3: 4 and I will put fine g on you."

GATE (GATES)
Ps 118: 20 This is the g of the LORD through
Pr 31: 23 husband is respected at the city g,
31: 31 works bring her praise at the city g.
Mt 7: 13 "Enter through the narrow g.
7: 13 For wide is the g and broad is
Jn 10: 1 not enter the sheep pen by the g,
10: 2 who enters by the g is the shepherd
10: 7 I tell you, I am the g for the sheep.
10: 9 I am the g; whoever enters through
Heb 13: 12 suffered outside the city g to make
Rev 21: 21 each g made of a single pearl.

GATES (GATE)
Ps 24: 7 Lift up your heads, you g;
24: 9 Lift up your heads, you g;
100: 4 Enter his g with thanksgiving
118: 19 Open for me the g of the righteous;

GATH
1Sa 17: 23 the Philistine champion from G,
2Sa 1: 20 "Tell it not in G, proclaim it not
Mic 1: 10 Tell it not in G; weep not at all.

GATHER (GATHERED GATHERS)
Ps 106: 47 and g us from the nations, that we
Isa 11: 12 nations and g the exiles of Israel;
Jer 23: 3 "I myself will g the remnant of my
31: 10 'He who scattered Israel will g them
Zep 2: 1 G together, g yourselves together,
3: 20 At that time I will g you;
Zec 14: 2 I will g all the nations to Jerusalem
Mt 12: 30 and whoever does not g with me
13: 30 then g the wheat and bring it
23: 37 longed to g your children together,
24: 31 they will g his elect from the four
25: 26 g where I have not scattered seed?
Mk 13: 27 and g his elect from the four winds,
Lk 3: 17 and to g the wheat into his barn,
11: 23 and whoever does not g with me
13: 34 longed to g your children together,

GATHERED (GATHER)
Ex 16: 18 the one who g little did not have too
Pr 30: 4 Whose hands have g up the wind?
Mt 25: 32 All the nations will be g before him,
2Co 8: 15 the one who g little did not have too
2Th 2: 1 Jesus Christ and our being g to him,
Rev 16: 16 they g the kings together

GATHERS (GATHER)
Ps 147: 2 he g the exiles of Israel.
Pr 10: 5 He who g crops in summer is
Isa 40: 11 He g the lambs in his arms
Mt 23: 37 as a hen g her chicks under her

GAVE (GIVE)
Ge 2: 20 So the man g names to all
3: 6 She also g some to her husband,
14: 20 Abram g him a tenth of everything.
28: 4 the land God g to Abraham.
35: 12 The land I g to Abraham and Isaac I
39: 23 g him success in whatever he did.
47: 11 g them property in the best part
Ex 4: 11 to him, "Who g human beings their
31: 18 he g him the two tablets
Dt 2: 12 the land the LORD g them as their
2: 36 The LORD our God g us all
3: 12 g the Reubenites and the Gadites
3: 13 I g to the half-tribe of Manasseh.
3: 15 And I g Gilead to Makir.
3: 16 and the Gadites I g the territory
8: 16 He g you manna to eat
26: 9 us to this place and g us this land,
32: 8 the Most High g the nations their
Jos 11: 23 he g it as an inheritance to Israel
13: 14 the tribe of Levi he g no inheritance,
14: 13 him Hebron as his inheritance.
21: 44 The LORD g them rest on every
24: 13 So I g you a land on which you did
1Sa 27: 5 So on that day Achish g him Ziklag,
2Sa 12: 8 I g you the house of Israel
1Ki 4: 29 God g Solomon wisdom and very
5: 12 The LORD g Solomon wisdom,
Ezr 2: 69 to their ability they g to the treasury
Ne 9: 15 their hunger you g them bread
9: 20 You g your good Spirit to instruct
9: 22 "You g them kingdoms
9: 27 compassion you g them deliverers,
Job 1: 21 The LORD g and the LORD has
42: 10 and g him twice as much as he had
Ps 69: 21 food and g me vinegar for my thirst.
135: 12 he g their land as an inheritance,
Ecc 12: 7 the spirit returns to God who g it.
Eze 3: 2 mouth, and he g me the scroll to eat.
Mt 1: 25 And he g him the name Jesus.
25: 35 and you g me something to drink,
25: 42 and you g me nothing to drink,
26: 26 he broke it and g it to his disciples,
27: 50 in a loud voice, he g up his spirit
Mk 6: 7 g them authority over evil spirits.
Jn 1: 12 he g the right to become children
3: 16 so loved the world that he g his one

Jn 17: 4 finishing the work you **g** me to do.
    17: 6 you **g** them to me and they have
    19: 30 bowed his head and **g** up his spirit.
Ac   1: 3 g many convincing proofs that he
    11: 17 if God **g** them the same gift he **g** us
Ro   1: 24 Therefore God **g** them over
     1: 26 God **g** them over to shameful lusts.
     1: 28 so God **g** them over to a depraved
     8: 32 own Son, but **g** him up for us all—
2Co 5: 18 **g** us the ministry of reconciliation:
     8: 3 they **g** as much as they were able,
     8: 5 they **g** themselves by the will
Gal 1: 4 who **g** himself for our sins to rescue
     2: 20 who loved me and **g** himself for me.
Eph 4: 8 captives and **g** gifts to his people."
     5: 2 and **g** himself up for us as a fragrant
     5: 25 the church and **g** himself up for her
2Th 2: 16 us and by his grace **g** us eternal
1Ti 2: 6 who **g** himself as a ransom for all
Tit 2: 14 who **g** himself for us to redeem us
1Jn 3: 24 We know it by the Spirit he **g** us.

GAZE
Ps 27: 4 to **g** on the beauty of the LORD
Pr   4: 25 fix your **g** directly before you.

GEDALIAH
    Governor of Judah appointed by Nebuchadnezzar
    (2Ki 25:22–26; Jer 39–41).

GEHAZI*
    Servant of Elisha (2Ki 4:12–5:27; 8:4–5).

GENEALOGIES
1Ti 1: 4 themselves to myths and endless **g**.
Tit 3: 9 avoid foolish controversies and **g**

GENERATION (GENERATIONS)
Ex   3: 15 name you shall call me from **g** to **g**.
Nu 32: 13 until the whole **g** of those who had
Dt   1: 35 this evil **g** shall see the good land I
Jdg 2: 10 that whole **g** had been gathered
Job 8: 8 "Ask the former **g** and
Ps 24: 6 Such is the **g** of those who seek
    48: 13 you may tell of them to the next **g**.
    71: 18 I declare your power to the next **g**,
    78: 4 will tell the next **g** the praiseworthy
   102: 18 Let this be written for a future **g**,
   112: 2 the **g** of the upright will be blessed.
   145: 4 One **g** commends your works
La   5: 19 your throne endures from **g** to **g**,
Da   4: 3 his dominion endures from **g** to **g**.
     4: 34 his kingdom endures from **g** to **g**,
Joel 1: 3 and their children to the next **g**.
Mt 12: 39 and adulterous **g** asks for a sign!
    17: 17 "You unbelieving and perverse **g**,"
    23: 36 tell you, all this will come on this **g**.
    24: 34 this **g** will certainly not pass away
Mk   9: 19 "You unbelieving **g**,"
    13: 30 this **g** will certainly not pass away
Lk   1: 50 to those who fear him, from **g** to **g**.
    11: 29 Jesus said, "This is a wicked **g**.
    11: 30 will the Son of Man be to this **g**.
    11: 50 Therefore this **g** will be held
    21: 32 this **g** will certainly not pass away
Ac   2: 40 yourselves from this corrupt **g**."
Php 2: 15 fault in a warped and crooked **g**."

GENERATIONS (GENERATION)
Ge   9: 12 a covenant for all **g** to come:
    17: 7 after you for the **g** to come, to be
    17: 9 after you for the **g** to come.
Ex 20: 6 a thousand **g** of those who love me
    31: 13 me and you for the **g** to come.
Dt   7: 9 a thousand **g** of those who love him
     7: 9 consider the **g** long past.
1Ch 16: 15 promise he made, for a thousand **g**,
Ps 22: 30 future **g** will be told about the Lord.
    33: 11 purposes of his heart through all **g**.
    45: 17 your memory through all **g**;
    89: 1 faithfulness known through all **g**.
    90: 1 our dwelling place throughout all **g**.
   100: 5 faithfulness continues through all **g**.
   102: 12 your renown endures through all **g**.
   105: 8 promise he made, for a thousand **g**,
   119: 90 faithfulness continues through all **g**;
   135: 13 renown, LORD, through all **g**.
   145: 13 dominion endures through all **g**.
   146: 10 forever, your God, O Zion, for all **g**.
Pr 27: 24 and a crown is not secure for all **g**.
Isa 34: 9 through, calling forth the **g**
    51: 8 my salvation through all **g**."
Lk   1: 48 now on all **g** will call me blessed,
Eph 3: 5 other **g** as it has now been revealed
     3: 21 and in Christ Jesus throughout all **g**,

Col 1: 26 has been kept hidden for ages and **g**,

GENEROSITY* (GENEROUS)
2Co 8: 2 extreme poverty welled up in rich **g**.
     9: 11 and through us your **g** will result
     9: 13 and for your **g** in sharing with them

GENEROUS* (GENEROSITY)
Ps 37: 26 They are always **g** and lend freely;
   112: 5 Good will come to those who are **g**
Pr   1: 19 A **g** person will prosper;
    22: 9 The **g** will themselves be blessed,
    22: 9 are you envious because I am **g**?'
Lk 11: 41 to the poor, and everything
Ac 28: 7 showed us **g** hospitality for three
2Co 9: 5 for the **g** gift you had promised.
     9: 5 Then it will be ready as a **g** gift,
     9: 11 that you can be **g** on every occasion,
1Ti 6: 18 and to be **g** and willing to share.

GENTILE (GENTILES)
Ac 21: 25 As for the **G** believers, we have
Ro   1: 16 first to the Jew, then to the **G**.
     2: 9 first for the Jew, then for the **G**;
     2: 10 first for the Jew, then for the **G**.
    10: 12 no difference between Jew and **G**—
Gal 3: 28 There is neither Jew nor **G**,
Col 3: 11 Here there is no **G** or Jew,

GENTILES (GENTILE)
Isa 42: 6 for the people and a light for the **G**,
    49: 6 will also make you a light for the **G**,
Lk   2: 32 a light for revelation to the **G**,
    21: 24 by the **G** until the times of the **G** are
Ac   9: 15 to proclaim my name to the **G**
    10: 45 had been poured out even on **G**.
    11: 18 to **G** God has granted repentance
    13: 16 Israel you **G** who worship God,
    13: 46 of eternal life, we now turn to the **G**.
    13: 47 have made you a light for the **G**,
    14: 27 had opened a door of faith to the **G**.
    15: 14 a people for his name from the **G**.
    18: 6 From now on I will go to the **G**."
    22: 21 send you far away to the **G**.' "
    26: 20 and then to the **G**, I preached
    28: 28 salvation has been sent to the **G**,
Ro   2: 14 when **G**, who do not have the law,
     3: 9 **G** alike are all under the power
     3: 29 Is he not the God of **G** too?
     9: 24 from the Jews but also from the **G**?
    11: 11 to the **G** to make Israel envious.
    11: 12 their loss means riches for the **G**,
    11: 13 as I am the apostle to the **G**, I make
    15: 9 that the **G** might glorify God for his
    15: 9 I will praise you among the **G**;
1Co 1: 23 block to Jews and foolishness to **G**,
Gal 1: 16 I might preach him among the **G**,
     2: 2 gospel that I preach among the **G**.
     2: 8 at work in me as an apostle to the **G**.
     2: 9 agreed that we should go to the **G**,
     3: 8 God would justify the **G** by faith,
     3: 14 come to the **G** through Christ Jesus,
Eph 3: 6 the gospel the **G** are heirs together
     3: 8 preach to the **G** the boundless riches
Col 1: 27 known among the **G** the glorious
1Ti 2: 7 a true and faithful teacher of the **G**.
2Ti 4: 17 and all the **G** might hear it.

GENTLE* (GENTLENESS)
Dt 28: 54 Even the most **g** and sensitive man
    28: 56 The most **g** and sensitive woman
    28: 56 and **g** that she would not venture
2Sa 3: 39 "Be **g** with the young man Absalom
1Ki 19: 12 And after the fire came a **g** whisper.
Job 41: 3 Will it speak to you with **g** words?
Pr 15: 1 A **g** answer turns away wrath,
    25: 15 and a **g** tongue can break a bone.
Jer 11: 19 I had been like a **g** lamb led
Mt 11: 29 for I am **g** and humble in heart,
    21: 5 to you, **g** and riding on a donkey,
Ac 27: 13 When a **g** south wind began
1Co 4: 21 I come in love and with a **g** spirit?
Eph 4: 2 Be completely humble and **g**;
1Ti 3: 3 not violent but **g**, not quarrelsome,
Tit 3: 2 always to be **g** toward everyone.
1Pe 3: 4 unfading beauty of a **g** and quiet

GENTLENESS* (GENTLE)
2Co 10: 1 By the meekness and **g** of Christ,
Gal 5: 23 and self-control.
Php 4: 5 Let your **g** be evident to all.
Col 3: 12 kindness, humility, **g** and patience.
1Ti 6: 11 faith, love, endurance and **g**.
1Pe 3: 15 But do this with **g** and respect,

GENUINE*
2Co 6: 8 **g**, yet regarded as impostors;
Php 2: 20 who will show **g** concern for your
1Pe 1: 7 may be proved **g** and may result

GERIZIM
Dt 27: 12 on Mount **G** to bless the people:

GERSHOM
Ex   2: 22 and Moses named him **G**, saying,

GETHSEMANE*
Mt 26: 36 his disciples to a place called **G**,
Mk 14: 32 They went to a place called **G**,

GHOST See also SPIRIT
Lk 24: 39 a **g** does not have flesh

GIBEON
Jos 10: 12 "Sun, stand still over **G**, and you,

GIDEON*
    Judge, also called Jerub-Baal; freed Israel from Mid-
    ianites (Jdg 6–8; Heb 11:32). Given sign of fleece (Jdg
    6:36–40).

GIFT (GIFTED GIFTS)
Pr 18: 16 A **g** opens the way and ushers
    21: 14 A **g** given in secret soothes anger,
Ecc 3: 13 in all their toil—this is the **g** of God.
Mt   5: 23 if you are offering your **g** at the altar
Jn   4: 10 "If you knew the **g** of God and who
Ac   1: 4 wait for the **g** my Father promised,
     2: 38 you will receive the **g** of the Holy
    11: 17 gave them the same **g** he gave us
Ro   6: 23 the **g** of God is eternal life in Christ
    12: 6 If your **g** is prophesying,
1Co 7: 7 of you has your own **g** from God;
2Co 8: 12 the **g** is acceptable according
     9: 15 be to God for his indescribable **g**!
Eph 2: 8 from yourselves, it is the **g** of God—
1Ti 4: 14 Do not neglect your **g**, which was
2Ti 1: 6 you to fan into flame the **g** of God,
Heb 6: 4 who have tasted the heavenly **g**,
Jas 1: 17 good and perfect **g** is from above,
1Pe 4: 10 with you of the gracious **g** of life,
Rev 22: 17 let all who wish take the free **g**

GIFTED* (GIFT)
1Co 14: 37 or otherwise **g** by the Spirit,

GIFTS (GIFT)
Ps 76: 11 let all the neighboring lands bring **g**
   112: 9 They have scattered abroad their **g**
Pr 25: 14 is one who boasts of **g** never given.
Mt   2: 11 and presented him with **g** of gold,
     7: 11 how to give good **g** to your children,
     7: 11 in heaven give good **g** to those who
Lk 11: 13 how to give good **g** to your children,
Ac 10: 4 and **g** to the poor have come up as
Ro 11: 29 for God's **g** and his call are
    12: 6 We have different **g**,
1Co 12: 1 Now about the **g** of the Spirit,
    12: 4 There are different kinds of **g**,
    12: 28 then **g** of healing, of helping,
    12: 30 Do all have **g** of healing?
    12: 31 Now eagerly desire the greater **g**.
    14: 1 love and eagerly desire spiritual **g**,
    14: 12 Since you are eager for **g**
2Co 9: 9 "They have scattered abroad their **g**
Eph 4: 8 captives and gave **g** to his people."
Heb 2: 4 by **g** of the Holy Spirit distributed
     9: 9 indicating that the **g** and sacrifices

GILEAD
1Ch 27: 21 the half-tribe of Manasseh in **G**:
Jer 8: 22 Is there no balm in **G**? Is there no
    46: 11 "Go up to **G** and get balm,

GILGAL
Jos 5: 9 So the place has been called **G**

GIRD*
Ps 45: 3 **G** your sword on your side,

GIRL
Ge 24: 16 The **g** was very beautiful, a virgin;
2Ki 5: 2 had taken captive a young **g**
Mk   5: 41 (which means "Little **g**, I say

GIVE (GAVE GIVEN GIVER GIVES GIVING LIFE-
GIVING)
Ge 28: 4 May he **g** you and your descendants
    28: 22 that you give me I will **g** a tenth."
Ex 20: 16 "You shall not **g** false testimony
    30: 15 are not to **g** more than a half shekel
Nu   6: 26 toward you and **g** you peace.' "
Dt   5: 20 "You shall not **g** false testimony

Dt 15:10 **G** generously to them and do so
  15:14 **G** to them as the Lord your God
1Sa 1:11 I will **g** him to the Lord for all
  1:28 So now I **g** him to the Lord.
2Ch 15:7 be strong and do not **g** up, for your
Pr 21:26 the day for **g** without ceasing.
  23:26 **g** me your heart and let your eyes
  25:21 is thirsty, **g** him water to drink.
  25:26 righteous who **g** way to the wicked.
  28:27 Those who **g** to the poor will lack
  30:8 but **g** me only my daily bread.
Ecc 3:6 a time to search and a time to **g** up,
Eze 36:26 I will **g** you a new heart and put
Mt 6:11 **G** us today our daily bread.
  7:11 know how to **g** good gifts to your
  10:8 Freely you have received, freely **g**.
  16:19 I will **g** you the keys of the kingdom
  22:21 "**G** back to Caesar what is Caesar's,
Mk 8:37 Or what can you **g** in exchange
  10:19 you shall not **g** false testimony,
Lk 6:38 **G**, and it will be given to you.
  11:3 **G** us each day our daily bread.
  11:13 Father in heaven **g** the Holy Spirit
  14:33 you who do not **g** up everything you
Jn 10:28 I **g** them eternal life, and they shall
  13:34 "A new command I **g** you:
  14:16 he will **g** you another advocate
  14:27 I leave with you; my peace I **g** you.
  14:27 I do not **g** to you as the world gives.
  17:2 people that he might **g** eternal life
Ac 2:45 to **g** to anyone who had need.
  20:35 'It is more blessed to **g** than
Ro 8:32 with him, graciously **g** us all things?
  12:8 if it is giving, then **g** generously;
  13:7 **G** to everyone what you owe:
  14:12 So then, we will all **g** an account
1Co 13:3 and **g** over my body ,to hardship
2Co 9:7 you should **g** what you have decided
Gal 2:5 We did not **g** in to them
  6:9 reap a harvest if we do not **g** up.
Rev 14:7 voice, "Fear God and **g** him glory,
  21:6 I will **g** water without cost from

GIVEN (GIVE)
Nu 8:16 the Israelites who are to be **g** wholly
Dt 26:11 things the Lord your God has **g**
Job 3:23 Why is life **g** to a man whose way is
Ps 115:16 but the earth he has **g** to humankind,
Isa 9:6 to us a son is **g**, and the government
Mt 6:33 all these things will be **g** to you as
  7:7 "Ask and it will be **g** to you;
  13:12 Those who have will be **g** more,
  22:30 people will neither marry nor be **g**
  25:29 For those who have will be **g** more,
Lk 6:38 Give, and it will be **g** to you.
  8:10 kingdom of God has been **g** to you,
  11:9 Ask and it will be **g** to you;
  22:19 saying, "This is my body **g** for you;
Jn 3:27 person can receive only what is **g**
  17:24 I want those you have **g** me to be
  17:24 glory you have **g** me because you
  18:11 drink the cup the Father has **g** me?"
Ac 5:32 whom God has **g** to those who obey
  20:24 the task the Lord Jesus has **g** me—
Ro 5:5 Holy Spirit, who has been **g** to us.
1Co 12:2 those who have been **g** a trust must
  11:24 and when he had **g** thanks, he broke
  12:13 and we were all **g** the one Spirit
2Co 5:5 who has **g** us the Spirit as a deposit,
Gal 3:19 The law was **g** through angels
Eph 1:6 he has freely **g** us in the One he
  4:7 one of us grace has been **g** as Christ
1Ti 4:14 which was **g** you through prophecy
1Jn 4:13 he in us: He has **g** us of his Spirit.

GIVER* (GIVE)
Pr 18:16 ushers the **g** into the presence
2Co 9:7 for God loves a cheerful **g**.

GIVES (GIVE)
Job 35:10 Maker, who **g** songs in the night,
Ps 119:130 unfolding of your words **g** light;
Pr 11:24 One person **g** freely, yet gains even
  14:30 A heart at peace **g** life to the body,
  15:30 good news **g** health to the bones.
  19:6 is the friend of one who **g** gifts.
  29:4 justice a king **g** a country stability,
Isa 40:29 He **g** strength to the weary
Hab 2:15 to him who **g** drink to his neighbors,
Mt 10:42 if anyone **g** even a cup of cold water
Jn 5:21 even so the Son **g** life to whom he is

Jn 6:63 The Spirit **g** life; the flesh counts
1Co 15:57 He **g** us the victory through our
2Co 3:6 the letter kills, but the Spirit **g** life.
1Th 4:8 the very God who **g** you his Holy
Jas 1:25 into the perfect law that **g** freedom,
  4:6 But he **g** us more grace. That is why

GIVING (GIVE)
Ne 8:8 **g** the meaning so that the people
Est 9:19 a day for **g** presents to each other.
Ps 19:8 Lord are right, **g** joy to the heart.
Pr 15:23 person finds joy in a apt reply—
Mt 6:4 so that your **g** may be in secret.
  24:38 marrying and **g** in marriage,
Ac 15:8 accepted them by **g** the Holy Spirit
2Co 8:7 you also excel in this grace of **g**.
Php 4:15 shared with me in the matter of **g**
Heb 10:25 not **g** up meeting together,

GLAD* (GLADDENS GLADNESS)
Ex 4:14 and his heart will be **g** when he sees
Jos 22:33 They were **g** to hear the report
Jdg 8:25 "We'll be **g** to give them."
1Sa 19:5 Israel, and you saw it and were **g**.
2Sa 1:20 the daughters of the Philistines be **g**,
1Ki 8:66 **g** in heart for all the good things
1Ch 16:31 heavens rejoice, let the earth be **g**;
2Ch 7:10 **g** in heart for the good things
Ps 5:11 let all who take refuge in you be **g**;
  9:2 I will be **g** and rejoice in you;
  14:7 let Jacob rejoice and Israel be **g**!
  16:9 Therefore my heart is **g** and my
  21:6 and made him **g** with the joy of your
  31:7 I will be **g** and rejoice in your love,
  32:11 Rejoice in the Lord and be **g**,
  40:16 seek you rejoice and be **g** in you;
  45:8 music of the strings makes you **g**.
  46:4 river whose streams make **g** the city
  48:11 of Judah are **g** because of your
  53:6 let Jacob rejoice and Israel be **g**!
  58:10 The righteous will be **g** when they
  67:4 May the nations be **g** and sing
  68:3 may the righteous be **g** and rejoice
  69:32 The poor will see and be **g**—
  70:4 seek you rejoice and be **g** in you;
  90:14 sing for joy and be **g** all our days.
  90:15 Make us **g** for as many days as you
  92:4 For you make me **g** by your deeds,
  96:11 heavens rejoice, let the earth be **g**;
  97:1 Lord reigns, let the earth be **g**;
  97:8 of Judah are **g** because of your
  105:38 Egypt was **g** when they left,
  107:30 They were **g** when it grew calm,
  118:24 let us rejoice today and be **g**.
  149:2 people of Zion be **g** in their King.
Pr 23:15 then my heart will be **g** indeed;
  29:6 righteous shout for joy and are **g**.
Ecc 8:15 sun than to eat and drink and be **g**.
Isa 25:9 rejoice and be **g** in his salvation."
  35:1 and the parched land will be **g**;
  65:18 be **g** and rejoice forever in what I
  66:10 with Jerusalem and be **g** for her,
Jer 20:15 who made him very **g**, saying,
  31:13 young women will dance and be **g**,
  41:13 who were with him, they were **g**.
  50:11 "Because you rejoice and are **g**,
La 4:21 Rejoice and be **g**, Daughter Edom,
Joel 2:21 land of Judah; be **g** and rejoice.
  2:23 Be **g**, people of Zion,
Hab 1:15 and so he rejoices and is **g**.
Zep 3:14 Be **g** and rejoice with all your heart,
Zec 2:10 "Shout and be **g**, Daughter Zion.
  8:19 will become joyful and **g** occasions
  10:7 their hearts will be **g** as with wine.
Mt 5:12 Rejoice and be **g**, because great is
Lk 15:32 But we had to celebrate and be **g**,
  4:36 and the reaper may be **g** together.
  8:56 he saw it and was **g**.
  11:15 for your sake I am **g** I was not there,
  14:28 you would be **g** that I am going
Ac 2:26 Therefore my heart is **g** and my
  2:46 and ate together with **g** and sincere
  11:23 he was **g** and encouraged them all
  13:48 they were **g** and honored the word
  15:3 news made all the believers very **g**.
  15:31 were **g** for its encouraging message.
1Co 16:17 I was **g** when Stephanas,
2Co 2:2 who is left to make me **g** but you
  7:16 I am **g** I can have complete
  13:9 We are **g** whenever we are weak
Gal 4:27 "Be **g**, barren woman, you who
Php 2:17 I am **g** and rejoice with all of you.
  2:18 So you too should be **g** and rejoice

Php 2:28 you see him again you may be **g**
Rev 19:7 rejoice and be **g** and give him glory!

GLADDENS* (GLAD)
Ps 104:15 wine that **g** human hearts,

GLADNESS* (GLAD)
2Ch 29:30 So they sang praises with **g**
Est 8:16 of happiness and joy, **g** and honor.
  8:17 was joy and **g** among the Jews,
Job 3:22 who are filled with **g** and rejoice
Ps 35:27 my vindication shout for joy and **g**,
  45:15 Led in with joy and **g**, they enter
  51:8 Let me hear joy and **g**; let the bones
  65:12 the hills are clothed with **g**.
  100:2 Worship the Lord with **g**;
Ecc 5:20 God keeps them occupied with **g**
  9:7 eat your food with **g**, and drink your
Isa 16:10 **g** are taken away from the orchards;
  35:10 **G** and joy will overtake them,
  51:3 Joy and **g** will be found in her,
  51:11 **G** and joy will overtake them,
Jer 7:34 an end to the sounds of joy and **g**
  16:9 an end to the sounds of joy and **g**
  25:10 from them the sounds of joy and **g**,
  31:13 I will turn their mourning into **g**;
  33:11 the sounds of joy and **g**, the voices
  48:33 and are gone from the orchards
Joel 1:16 and **g** from the house of our God?

GLEAM*
Da 10:6 legs like the **g** of burnished bronze,

GLOAT (GLOATS)
Pr 24:17 Do not **g** when your enemies fall;

GLOATS* (GLOAT)
Pr 17:5 whoever **g** over disaster will not go

GLORIES* (GLORY)
1Pe 1:11 Christ and the **g** that would follow.

GLORIFIED* (GLORY)
Isa 66:5 'Let the Lord be **g**, that we may
Da 4:34 and **g** him who lives forever.
Jn 7:39 since Jesus had not yet been **g**.
  11:4 God's Son may be **g** through it."
  12:16 after Jesus was **g** did they realize
  12:23 come for the Son of Man to be **g**.
  12:28 "I have **g** it, and will glorify it
  13:31 Son of Man **g** and God is in him.
  13:32 If God is in him, God will glorify
Jn 14:13 that the Father may be **g** in the Son.
Ac 3:13 our fathers, has **g** his servant Jesus.
Ro 1:21 they neither **g** him as God nor gave
  8:30 those he justified, he also **g**.
2Th 1:10 he comes to be **g** in his holy people
  1:12 of our Lord Jesus may be **g** in you,
1Pe 1:21 raised him from the dead and **g** him,

GLORIFIES* (GLORY)
Lk 1:46 "My soul **g** the Lord
Jn 8:54 as your God, is the one who **g** me.

GLORIFY* (GLORY)
Ps 34:3 **G** the Lord with me; let us exalt
  63:3 better than life, my lips will **g** you.
  69:30 song and **g** him with thanksgiving.
  86:12 I will **g** your name forever.
Isa 60:13 and I will **g** the place for my feet.
Da 4:37 and exalt and **g** the King of heaven,
Mt 5:16 and **g** your Father in heaven.
Jn 8:54 "If I myself, my glory means
  12:28 Father, **g** your name!"
  12:28 glorified it, and will **g** it again."
  13:32 God will **g** the Son in himself, and will **g** him at once.
  16:14 He will **g** me because
  17:1 **G** your Son, that your Son may **g**
  17:5 **g** me in your presence
  21:19 death by which Peter would **g** God.
Ro 15:6 one voice you may **g** the God
  15:9 the Gentiles might **g** God for his
1Pe 2:12 and **g** God on the day he visits us.
Rev 16:9 they refused to repent and **g** him.

GLORIFYING* (GLORY)
Lk 2:20 **g** and praising God for all the things

GLORIOUS* (GLORY)
Dt 28:58 do not revere this **g** and awesome
  33:29 shield and helper and your **g** sword.
1Ch 29:13 you thanks, and praise your **g** name.
Ne 9:5 "Blessed be your **g** name, and may
Ps 45:13 All **g** is the princess within her
  66:2 of his name; make his praise **g**.
  72:19 Praise be to his **g** name forever;
  87:3 **G** things are said of you,

Ps 106: 20 exchanged their g God for an image
111: 3 G and majestic are his deeds,
145: 5 They speak of the g splendor
145: 12 and the g splendor of your kingdom.
Pr 4: 9 present you with a g crown."
Isa 3: 8 the Lord, defying his g presence.
4: 2 the Lord will be beautiful and g,
11: 10 and his resting place will be g.
12: 5 Lord, for he has done g things;
28: 1 to the fading flower, his g beauty,
28: 4 That fading flower, his g beauty,
28: 5 Almighty will be a g crown,
42: 21 to make his law great and g.
60: 7 altar, and I will adorn my g temple.
63: 12 who sent his g arm of power to be
63: 14 to make for yourself a g name.
63: 15 from your lofty throne, holy and g.
64: 11 Our holy and g temple, where our
Jer 2: 11 people have exchanged their g God
13: 18 for your g crowns will fall
14: 21 do not dishonor your g throne.
17: 12 A g throne,
48: 17 scepter, how broken the g staff!'
Hos 4: 7 exchanged their g God for something
Zec 2: 8 "After the G One has sent me against
Mt 19: 28 the Son of Man sits on his g throne,
25: 31 he will sit on his g throne.
Lk 9: 31 appeared in g splendor,
Ac 2: 20 of the great and g day of the Lord.
2Co 3: 8 of the Spirit be even more g?
3: 9 that brought condemnation was g,
3: 9 how much more g is the ministry
3: 10 For what was g has no glory now
Eph 1: 6 to the praise of his g grace,
1: 17 our Lord Jesus Christ, the g Father,
1: 18 the riches of his g inheritance in his
3: 16 his g riches he may strengthen you
Php 3: 21 so that they will be like his g body.
Col 1: 11 power according to his g might so
1: 27 among the Gentiles the g riches
Jas 2: 1 in our g Lord Jesus Christ must not
1Pe 1: 8 with an inexpressible and g joy,
Jude : 24 you before his g presence without

GLORY (GLORIES GLORIFIED GLORIFIES
GLORIFY GLORIFYING GLORIOUS)
Ex 14: 4 But I will gain g for myself through
14: 17 I will gain g through Pharaoh
15: 11 awesome in g, working wonders?
16: 10 and there was the g of the Lord
24: 16 and the g of the Lord settled
33: 18 said, "Now show me your g."
40: 34 and the g of the Lord filled
Nu 14: 21 and as surely as the g of the Lord
Dt 5: 24 Lord our God has shown us his g
Jos 7: 19 "My son, give g to the Lord,
1Sa 4: 21 "The G has departed from Israel"—
1Ch 16: 10 G in his holy name; let the hearts
16: 28 Declare his g among the nations,
16: 28 ascribe to the Lord g
29: 11 the power and the g and the majesty
Ps 8: 1 You have set your g
8: 5 crowned them with g and honor.
19: 1 The heavens declare the g of God;
24: 7 that the King of g may come in.
26: 8 live, the place where your g dwells.
29: 1 beings, ascribe to the Lord g
29: 9 And in his temple all cry, "G!"
34: 2 I will g in the Lord;
57: 5 let your g be over all the earth.
66: 2 Sing the g of his name;
72: 19 the whole earth be filled with his g.
96: 3 Declare his g among the nations,
102: 15 kings of the earth will revere your g
108: 5 let your g be over all the earth.
149: 5 this is the g of all his faithful
Pr 19: 11 is to one's g to overlook an offense.
25: 2 It is the g of God to conceal
Isa 3: 8 over everything the g will be
6: 3 the whole earth is full of his g."
24: 16 "G to the Righteous One."
24: 23 before its elders—with great g.
26: 15 You have gained g for yourself;
35: 2 they will see the g of the Lord,
40: 5 And the g of the Lord will be
42: 8 I will not yield my g to another
42: 12 Let them give g to the Lord
43: 7 whom I created for my g, whom I
44: 23 Jacob, he displays his g in Israel.
48: 11 I will not yield my g to another.
66: 18 and they will come and see my g.
66: 19 They will proclaim my g among

Eze 1: 28 the likeness of the g of the Lord.
10: 4 the radiance of the g of the Lord.
39: 13 the day I display my g will be
43: 2 the land was radiant with his g.
44: 4 saw the g of the Lord filling
Hab 2: 14 the g of the Lord as the waters
3: 3 His g covered the heavens and his
Zec 2: 5 Lord, 'and I will be its g within.'
Mt 16: 27 in his Father's g with his angels,
24: 30 of heaven, with power and great g.
25: 31 the Son of Man comes in his g,
Mk 8: 38 in his Father's g with the holy
13: 26 in clouds with great power and
Lk 2: 9 and the g of the Lord shone around
2: 14 "G to God in the highest heaven,
9: 26 of you when he comes in his g
9: 26 and in the g of the Father
9: 32 they saw his g and the two men
19: 38 in heaven and g in the highest!"
21: 27 in a cloud with power and great g.
24: 26 these things and then enter his g?"
Jn 1: 14 We have seen his g, the g of the one
2: 11 through which he revealed his g;
5: 44 the g that comes from the only God?
7: 18 does so to gain personal g,
8: 50 I am not seeking for myself;
8: 54 glorify myself, my g means nothing.
11: 4 it is for God's g so that God's Son
11: 40 believe, you will see the g of God?"
12: 41 said this because he saw Jesus' g
12: 43 for they loved human g more than
13: 1 This is to my Father's g, that you
17: 4 I have brought you g on earth
17: 5 your presence with the g I had
17: 10 g has come to me through them.
17: 22 I have given them the g that you
17: 24 and to see my g, the g you have
Ac 7: 2 The God of g appeared to our father
7: 55 up to heaven and saw the g of God,
Ro 1: 23 exchanged the g of the immortal
2: 7 by persistence in doing good seek g,
2: 10 but g, honor and peace for everyone
3: 7 truthfulness and so increases his g,
3: 23 and fall short of the g of God,
4: 20 in his faith and gave g to God,
8: 17 that we may also share in his g.
8: 18 with the g that will be revealed
8: 21 the freedom and g of the children
9: 4 theirs the divine g, the covenants,
9: 23 to make the riches of his g known
9: 23 he prepared in advance for g—
11: 36 To him be the g forever! Amen.
15: 7 Therefore I g in Christ Jesus in my
16: 27 wise God be g forever through Jesus
1Co 1: 31 for our g before time began.
10: 31 you do, do it all for the g of God.
11: 7 since he is the image and g of God;
11: 7 but woman is the g of man.
11: 15 if a woman has long hair, it is her g?
15: 43 is sown in dishonor, it is raised in g;
2Co 1: 20 is spoken by us to the g of God.
3: 7 came with g, so that the Israelites
3: 7 the face of Moses because of its g,
3: 10 what was glorious has no g now
3: 10 comparison with the surpassing g.
3: 11 if what was transitory came with g, how
   much greater is the g
3: 18 faces contemplate the Lord's g,
3: 18 his image with ever-increasing g,
4: 4 gospel that displays the g of Christ,
4: 6 the knowledge of God's g displayed
4: 15 to overflow to the g of God.
4: 17 us an eternal g that far outweighs
Gal 1: 5 to whom be g for ever and ever.
Eph 1: 12 might be for the praise of his g.
1: 14 to the praise of his g.
3: 13 for you, which are your g.
3: 21 to him be g in the church
Php 1: 11 to the g and praise of God.
2: 11 is Lord, to the g of God the Father.
4: 19 the riches of his g in Christ Jesus.
4: 20 To our God and Father be g for ever
Col 1: 27 is Christ in you, the hope of g.
3: 4 you also will appear with him in g.
1Th 2: 12 calls you into his kingdom and g.
2: 19 which we will g in the presence
2: 20 Indeed, you are our g and joy.
2Th 1: 9 and from the g of his might
2: 14 in the g of our Lord Jesus Christ.
1Ti 1: 11 the g of the blessed God,
1: 17 be honor and g for ever and ever.
3: 16 in the world, was taken up in g.

2Ti 2: 10 is in Christ Jesus, with eternal g.
4: 18 To him be g for ever and ever.
Tit 2: 13 of the g of our great God
Heb 1: 3 The Son is the radiance of God's g
2: 7 you crowned them with g and honor
2: 9 now crowned with g and honor
2: 10 many sons and daughters to g,
5: 5 on himself the g of becoming a high
9: 5 the ark were the cherubim of the G,
13: 21 to whom be g for ever and ever.
1Pe 1: 7 g and honor when Jesus Christ is
1: 24 all their g is like the flowers
4: 11 To him be the g and the power
4: 13 be overjoyed when his g is revealed.
4: 14 for the Spirit of g and of God rests
5: 1 will share in the g to be revealed:
5: 4 you will receive the crown of g
5: 10 called you to his eternal g in Christ,
2Pe 1: 3 of him who called us by his own g
1: 17 and g from God the Father
1: 17 came to him from the Majestic G,
3: 18 To him be g both now and forever!
Jude : 25 to the only God our Savior be g,
Rev 1: 6 to him be g and power for ever
4: 9 the living creatures give g,
4: 11 to receive g and honor and power,
5: 12 and honor and g and praise!"
5: 13 praise and honor and g and power,
7: 12 Praise and g and wisdom and thanks
11: 13 and gave g to the God of heaven.
14: 7 "Fear God and give him g,
15: 4 Lord, and bring g to your name?
15: 8 filled with smoke from the g of God
19: 1 Salvation and g and power belong
19: 7 rejoice and be glad and give him g!
21: 11 It shone with the g of God, and its
21: 23 for the g of God gives it light,
21: 26 The g and honor of the nations will

GLOWING
1Sa 16: 12 He was g with health
Eze 8: 2 appearance was as bright as g metal.
Rev 1: 15 His feet were like bronze g

GLUTTONS* (GLUTTONY)
Pr 23: 21 for drunkards and g become poor,
28: 7 of g disgrace their parents.
Tit 1: 12 always liars, evil brutes, lazy g."

GLUTTONY* (GLUTTONS)
Pr 23: 2 to your throat if you are given to g.

GNASHING
Mt 8: 12 will be weeping and g of teeth."

GNAT* (GNATS)
Mt 23: 24 You strain out a g but swallow

GNATS (GNAT)
Ex 8: 16 of Egypt the dust will become g.

GOADS
Ecc 12: 11 The words of the wise are like g,
Ac 26: 14 hard for you to kick against the g.'

GOAL*
Lk 13: 32 on the third day I will reach my g.'
2Co 5: 9 So we make it our g to please him,
Php 3: 12 or have already arrived at my g,
3: 14 on toward the g to win the prize
1Ti 1: 5 The g of this command is love,

GOAT (GOATS SCAPEGOAT)
Ge 15: 9 "Bring me a heifer, a g and a ram,
30: 32 and every spotted or speckled g.
37: 31 slaughtered a g and dipped the robe
Ex 26: 7 "Make curtains of g hair
Lev 16: 9 shall bring the g whose lot falls
Nu 7: 16 one male g for a sin offering;
Isa 11: 6 the leopard will lie down with the g,
Da 8: 5 suddenly a g with a prominent horn

GOATS (GOAT)
Nu 7: 17 five male g and five male lambs
Mt 25: 32 separates the sheep from the g.
Heb 10: 4 of bulls and of g to take away sins.

GOD (GOD'S GODLINESS GODLY GODS)
Ge 1: 1 the beginning G created the heavens
1: 2 of G was hovering over the waters.
1: 3 And G said, "Let there be light,"
1: 7 So G made the vault and separated
1: 9 And G said, "Let the water under
1: 11 Then G said, "Let the land produce
1: 20 And G said, "Let the water teem
1: 21 So G created the great creatures
1: 25 G made the wild animals according
1: 26 Then G said, "Let us make human

Ge 1:27 So G created human beings in his
1:31 G saw all that he had made, and it
2:3 Then G blessed the seventh day
2:7 the LORD G formed a man
2:8 Now the LORD G had planted
2:18 The LORD G said, "It is not good
2:22 the LORD G made a woman
3:1 to the woman, "Did G really say,
3:5 and you will be like G,
3:8 from the LORD G among the trees
3:9 the LORD G called to the man,
3:21 The LORD G made garments
3:22 And the LORD G said, "The man
3:23 So the LORD G banished him
5:1 When G created human beings,
5:22 walked faithfully with G 300 years
5:24 no more, because G took him away.
6:2 the sons of G saw that these
6:9 and he walked faithfully with G.
6:12 G saw how corrupt the earth had
8:1 But G remembered Noah and all
9:1 Then G blessed Noah and his sons,
9:6 image of G has G made humankind.
9:16 the everlasting covenant between G
14:18 He was priest of G Most High,
14:19 be Abram by G Most High,
16:13 "You are the G who sees me,"
17:1 to him and said, "I am G Almighty;
17:7 to be your G and the G of your
21:4 him, as G commanded him.
21:6 said, "G has brought me laughter,
21:20 G was with the boy as he grew up.
21:22 "G is with you in everything you
21:33 name of the LORD, the Eternal G.
22:1 Some time later G tested Abraham.
22:8 "G himself will provide the lamb
22:12 Now I know that you fear G,
25:11 death, G blessed his son Isaac,
28:12 the angels of G were ascending
28:17 is none other than the house of G;
31:42 But G has seen my hardship
31:50 that G is a witness between you
32:1 and the angels of G met him.
32:28 because you have struggled with G
32:30 "It is because I saw G face to face,
33:11 for G has been gracious to me and I
35:1 and build an altar there to G,
35:5 the terror of G fell on the towns all
35:10 G said to him, "Your name is
35:11 And G said to him, "I am G
41:51 said, "It is because G has made me
41:52 said, "It is because G has made me
50:20 but G intended it for good
50:24 But G will surely come to your aid

Ex 2:24 G heard their groaning and he
3:5 "Do not come any closer," G said.
3:6 because he was afraid to look at G.
3:12 And G said, "I will be with you.
3:14 G said to Moses, "I \am \who I \am.
4:27 he met Moses at the mountain of G
6:7 own people, and I will be your G.
8:10 is no one like the LORD our G.
10:16 sinned against the LORD your G
13:18 So G led the people around
15:2 He is my G, and I will praise him,
16:12 that I am the LORD your G.'"
17:9 with the staff of G in my hands."
18:5 camped near the mountain of G.
19:3 Then Moses went up to G,
20:1 And G spoke all these words:
20:2 "I am the LORD your G,
20:5 the LORD your G, am a jealous G,
20:7 the name of the LORD your G,
20:10 is a sabbath to the LORD your G.
20:12 the LORD your G is giving you.
20:19 But do not have G speak to us or we
20:20 that the fear of G will be with you
22:20 any g other than the LORD must
22:28 "Do not blaspheme G or curse
23:19 to the house of the LORD your G.
31:18 stone inscribed by the finger of G.
34:6 the compassionate and gracious G,
34:14 name is Jealous, is a jealous G.

Lev 2:13 the covenant of G out of your
11:44 I am the LORD your G;
18:21 not profane the name of your G.
19:2 I, the LORD your G, am holy.
20:7 because I am the LORD your G.
21:6 They must be holy to their G
22:33 you out of Egypt to be your G,
26:12 walk among you and be your G,

Nu 15:40 and will be consecrated to your G.

Nu 22:18 the command of the LORD my G.
22:38 I must speak only what G puts
23:19 G is not a human, that he should lie,
25:13 was zealous for the honor of his G

Dt 1:17 anyone, for judgment belongs to G.
1:21 the LORD your G has given you
1:30 The LORD your G, who is going
3:22 the LORD your G himself will
3:24 For what g is there in heaven
4:24 G is a consuming fire, a jealous G.
4:29 there you seek the LORD your G,
4:31 the LORD your G is a merciful G;
4:39 day that the LORD is God in heaven
5:9 the LORD your G, am a jealous G,
5:11 the name of the LORD your G,
5:12 the LORD your G has commanded
5:14 is a sabbath to the LORD your G.
5:15 the LORD your G brought you
5:16 the LORD your G has commanded
5:16 the LORD your G is giving you.
5:24 "The LORD our G has shown us
5:26 voice of the living G speaking
6:2 fear the LORD your G as long as
6:4 The LORD our G, the LORD is
6:5 Love the LORD your G with all
6:13 Fear the LORD your G, serve him
6:16 Do not put the LORD your G
7:6 people holy to the LORD your G.
7:9 the LORD your G is G; he is the faithful G,
7:12 the LORD your G will keep his
7:19 The LORD your G will do
7:21 is a great and awesome G.
8:5 the LORD your G disciplines you.
8:11 do not forget the LORD your G,
8:18 But remember the LORD your G,
9:10 tablets inscribed by the finger of G.
10:12 you but to fear the LORD your G,
10:14 To the LORD your G belong
10:17 For the LORD your G is G of gods
10:21 he is your G, who performed
11:1 Love the LORD your G and keep
11:13 to love the LORD your G
12:12 rejoice before the LORD your G—
12:28 in the eyes of the LORD your G.
13:3 The LORD your G is testing you
13:4 It is the LORD your G you must
15:6 the LORD your G will bless you
15:19 the LORD your G every firstborn
16:11 rejoice before the LORD your G
16:17 the LORD your G has blessed you.
18:13 before the LORD your G.
18:15 The LORD your G will raise
19:9 to love the LORD your G
22:5 the LORD your G detests anyone
23:5 the LORD your G loves you.
23:14 the LORD your G moves
23:21 make a vow to the LORD your G,
25:16 the LORD your G detests anyone
26:5 declare before the LORD your G:
29:13 he may be your G as he promised
29:29 things belong to the LORD our G,
30:2 return to the LORD your G
30:4 the LORD your G will gather you
30:6 The LORD your G will circumcise
30:16 today to love the LORD your G,
30:20 you may love the LORD your G,
31:6 the LORD your G goes with you;
32:3 praise the greatness of our G!
32:4 A faithful G who does no wrong,
33:27 The eternal G is your refuge,

Jos 1:9 the LORD your G will be with you
14:8 the LORD my G wholeheartedly.
14:9 the LORD my G wholeheartedly.'
14:14 the LORD, the G of Israel,
22:5 to love the LORD your G, to walk
22:22 "The Mighty One, G, the LORD!
22:34 that the LORD is G.
23:8 to hold fast to the LORD your G,
23:11 careful to love the LORD your G.
23:14 the LORD your G gave you has
23:15 the LORD your G has promised
24:19 He is a holy G; he is a jealous G.
24:23 to the LORD, the G of Israel."

Jdg 5:3 praise the LORD, the G of Israel,
16:28 Please, G, strengthen me just once

Ru 1:16 be my people and your G my G.
2:12 by the LORD, the G of Israel,

1Sa 2:2 there is no Rock like our G.
2:3 for the LORD is a G who knows,
2:25 G may mediate for the offender;
10:26 men whose hearts G had touched.
12:12 the LORD your G was your king.

1Sa 16:15 evil spirit from G is tormenting you.
17:26 defy the armies of the living G?"
17:36 defied the armies of the living G.
17:45 the G of the armies of Israel,
17:46 will know that there is a G in Israel.
23:16 and helped him find strength in G.
28:15 and G has departed from me.
30:6 found strength in the LORD his G.

2Sa 7:22 and there is no G but you, as we
7:23 one nation on earth that G went
14:14 But that is not what G desires;
21:14 G answered prayer in behalf
22:3 my G is my rock, in whom I take
22:31 "As for G, his way is perfect;
22:32 And who is the Rock except our G?
22:33 It is G who arms me with strength
22:47 Exalted be my G, the Rock,

1Ki 2:3 what the LORD your G requires:
4:29 G gave Solomon wisdom and very
5:5 for the Name of the LORD my G,
8:23 there is no G like you in heaven
8:27 "But will G really dwell on earth?
8:60 may know that the LORD is G
8:61 committed to the LORD our G,
10:24 to hear the wisdom G had put in his
15:30 of the LORD, the G of Israel.
18:21 If the LORD is G, follow him;
18:36 today that you are G in Israel
18:37 are G, and that you are turning their
20:28 the hills and not a g of the valleys,

2Ki 5:15 there is no G in all the world except
18:5 in the LORD, the G of Israel.
19:15 "LORD, the G of Israel,
19:19 LORD our G, deliver us from his

1Ch 12:18 for your G will help you."
13:2 if it is the will of the LORD our G,
16:35 Cry out, "Save us, G our Savior;
17:20 and there is no G but you, as we
17:24 the G over Israel, is Israel's G!'
21:8 Then David said to G, "I have
22:1 of the LORD G is to be here,
22:19 soul to seeking the LORD your G.
28:2 for the footstool of our G, and I
28:9 acknowledge the G of your father,
28:20 for the LORD G, my G,
29:1 beings but for the LORD G.
29:2 provided for the temple of my G—
29:3 of my G I now give my personal
29:10 LORD, the G of our father Israel,
29:13 Now, our G, we give you thanks,
29:20 LORD our G, all this abundance
29:17 my G, that you test the heart and are
29:18 the G of our fathers Abraham,

2Ch 4:for the Name of the LORD my G
5:14 the LORD filled the temple of G.
6:4 be to the LORD, the G of Israel,
6:14 there is no G like you in heaven
6:18 will G really dwell on earth
10:15 for this turn of events was from G,
13:12 G is with us; he is our leader.
15:3 time Israel was without the true G,
15:12 LORD, the G of their ancestors,
15:15 They sought G eagerly, and he was
18:13 can tell him only what my G says."
19:3 have set your heart on seeking G."
19:7 with the LORD our G there is no
20:6 are you not the G who is in heaven?
20:20 Have faith in the LORD your G
25:8 for G has the power to help
26:5 the LORD gave him success.
30:9 for the LORD your G is gracious
30:19 who sets their heart on seeking G—
31:21 he sought his G and worked
32:31 G left him to test him and to know
33:12 the favor of the LORD his G
34:33 in Israel serve the LORD their G.

Ezr 6:21 to seek the LORD, the G of Israel.
7:18 accordance with the will of your G.
7:23 Whatever the G of heaven has
8:22 "The gracious hand of our G is
8:31 The hand of our G was on us,
9:6 my G, to lift up my face to you,
9:9 our G has not forsaken us in our
9:13 our G, you have punished us less
9:15 LORD, the G of Israel, you are

Ne 1:5 the great and awesome G,
5:9 fear of our G to avoid the reproach
5:15 for G I did not act like that.
7:2 feared G more than most people do.
8:8 from the Book of the Law of G,
8:18 from the Book of the Law of G.

Ne	9: 5	up and praise the LORD your G,
	9:17	But you are a forgiving G,
	9:31	you are a gracious and merciful G.
	9:32	"Now therefore, our G, the great G,
	10:29	G given through Moses the servant
	10:39	not neglect the house of our G."
	12:43	rejoicing because G had given them
	13:11	is the house of G neglected?"
	13:26	He was loved by his G, and G made
	13:31	Remember me with favor, my G.
Job	1: 1	he feared G and shunned evil.
	1:22	sin by charging G with wrongdoing.
	2:10	Shall we accept good from G,
	4:17	a mortal be more righteous than G?
	5:17	are those whom G corrects;
	8: 3	Does G pervert justice?
	8:20	"Surely G does not reject
	9: 2	prove their innocence before G?
	11: 7	you fathom the mysteries of G?
	12:13	"To G belong wisdom and power;
	16: 7	Surely, G, you have worn me out;
	19:26	yet in my flesh I will see G;
	21: 9	'G stores up the punishment
	21:22	anyone teach knowledge to G,
	22:12	"Is not G in the heights of heaven?
	22:13	Yet you say, 'What does G know?
	22:21	"Submit to G and be at peace
	25: 2	"Dominion and awe belong to G;
	25: 4	can a mortal be righteous before G?
	26: 6	Death is naked before G;
	30:20	"I cry out to you, G, but you do not
	31: 6	let G weigh me in honest scales
	31:14	will I do when G confronts me?
	32:13	let G refute him, not a mere mortal.'
	33:14	For G does speak—now one way,
	33:26	they can pray to G and find favor
	34:10	Far be it from G to do evil,
	34:12	unthinkable that G would do wrong,
	34:23	G has no need to examine people
	34:33	Should G then reward you on your
	36: 5	"G is mighty, but despises no one;
	36:26	How great is G—
	37:22	G comes in awesome majesty.
Ps	5: 4	you are not a G who is pleased
	7:11	G is a righteous judge, a G who
	10:14	But you, G, see the trouble
	14: 5	for G is present in the company
	18: 2	my G is my rock, in whom I take
	18:28	my G turns my darkness into light.
	18:30	As for G, his way is perfect:
	18:31	And who is the Rock except our G?
	18:32	It is G who arms me with strength
	18:46	Exalted be G my Savior!
	19: 1	The heavens declare the glory of G;
	22: 1	My G, my G, why have you
	22:10	womb you have been my G.
	27: 9	me or forsake me, G my Savior.
	29: 3	the G of glory thunders, the LORD
	31: 5	redeem me, LORD, my faithful G.
	31:14	I say, "You are my G."
	33:12	the nation whose G is the LORD,
	35:24	your righteousness, LORD my G,
	37:31	The law of their G is in their hearts;
	40: 3	mouth, a hymn of praise to our G.
	40: 8	I desire to do your will, my G;
	42: 1	so my soul pants for you, my G.
	42: 2	My soul thirsts for G, the living
	42: 2	soul thirsts for G, for the living
	42: 5	Put your hope in G, for I will yet
	42: 8	a prayer to the G of my life.
	42:11	Put your hope in G, for I will yet
	43: 4	of G, to G, my joy and my delight.
	44: 8	G we make our boast all day long,
	45: 6	O G, will last for ever and ever;
	45: 7	therefore G, your G, has set you
	46: 1	G is our refuge and strength,
	46: 5	G is within her, she will not fall;
	46:10	"Be still, and know that I am G;
	47: 1	shout to G with cries of joy.
	47: 6	Sing praises to G, sing praises;
	47: 7	For G is the King of all the earth;
	48: 9	O G, we meditate on your unfailing
	49: 7	or give to G a sufficient ransom—
	50: 2	perfect in beauty, G shines forth.
	50: 3	Our G comes and will not be silent;
	51: 1	O G, according to your unfailing
	51:10	O G, and renew a steadfast spirit
	51:17	sacrifice, O G, is a broken spirit;
	53: 2	who understand, any who seek G.
	54: 4	Surely G is my help; the Lord is
	55:19	G, who is enthroned from of old,
	56: 4	In G, whose word I praise—

Ps	56:10	In G, whose word I praise,
	56:13	that I may walk before G in the light
	57: 3	G sends forth his love and his
	57: 7	My heart, O G, is steadfast,
	59:17	G, are my fortress, my G
	62: 1	Truly my soul finds rest in G;
	62: 7	and my honor depend on G;
	62: 8	hearts to him, for G is our refuge.
	62:11	One thing G has spoken, two things
	63: 1	G, are my G, earnestly I seek
	65: 5	and righteous deeds, G our Savior,
	66: 1	Shout for joy to G, all the earth!
	66: 3	Say to G, "How awesome are your
	66: 5	Come and see what G has done,
	66:16	Come and hear, all you who fear G;
	66:20	Praise be to G, who has not rejected
	68: 4	Sing to G, sing in praise of his
	68: 6	G sets the lonely in families,
	68:20	Our G is a G who saves;
	68:24	Your procession, G, has come
	68:35	You, G, are awesome in your
	69: 5	You, G, know my folly;
	70: 1	Hasten, O G, to save me;
	70: 5	come quickly to me, O G.
	71:17	Since my youth, G, you have taught
	71:18	my G, till I declare your power
	71:19	Your righteousness, G,
	71:22	harp for your faithfulness, my G;
	73:17	till I entered the sanctuary of G;
	73:26	but G is the strength of my heart
	76:11	Make vows to the LORD your G
	77:13	Your ways, G, are holy.
	77:13	What g is as great as our G?
	77:14	You are the G who performs
	78:19	"Can G really spread a table
	79: 9	Help us, G our Savior, for the glory
	81: 1	Sing for joy to G our strength;
	82: 1	G presides in the great assembly;
	84: 2	my flesh cry out for the living G.
	84:10	the house of my G than dwell
	84:11	For the LORD G is a sun
	86:12	Lord my G, with all my heart;
	86:15	are a compassionate and gracious G,
	87: 3	things are said of you, city of G:
	89: 7	of the holy ones G is greatly feared;
	90: 2	everlasting to everlasting you are G.
	91: 2	fortress, my G, in whom I trust."
	94:22	and my G the rock in whom I take
	95: 7	for he is our G and we are
	99: 9	you were to Israel a forgiving G,
	99: 9	Exalt the LORD our G
	100: 3	Know that the LORD is G. It is he
	108: 1	My heart, O G, is steadfast;
	115: 3	Who is like the LORD our G,
	115: 3	Our G is in heaven;
	116: 5	our G is full of compassion.
	123: 2	our eyes look to the LORD our G,
	136: 2	Give thanks to the G of gods.
	136:26	Give thanks to the G of heaven.
	139:17	to me are your thoughts, G!
	139:23	Search me, G, and know my heart;
	143:10	to do your will, for you are my G;
	144: 2	He is my loving G and my fortress,
	147: 1	good it is to sing praises to our G,
Pr	3: 4	a good name in the sight of G
	14:31	is kind to the needy honors G.
	25: 2	It is the glory of G to conceal
	28:14	who always tremble before G,
	30: 5	"Every word of G is flawless;
Ecc	2:26	who pleases him, G gives wisdom,
	3:11	no one can fathom what G has done
	3:13	in all their toil—this is the gift of G.
	3:14	G does it so that people will fear
	5: 4	When you make a vow to G, do not
	5:19	in their toil—this is a gift of G.
	8:12	go better with those who fear G,
	11: 5	cannot understand the work of G,
	12: 7	the spirit returns to G who gave it.
	12:13	of the matter: Fear G and keep his
Isa	5:16	the holy G will be proved holy
	9: 6	Mighty G, Everlasting Father,
	12: 2	Surely G is my salvation; I will trust
	25: 1	they will say, "Surely this is our G;
	29:23	strange tongues G will speak to this
	29:23	will stand in awe of the G of Israel.
	30:18	For the LORD is a G of justice.
	35: 4	your G will come, he will come
	37:16	you alone are G over all the
	40: 1	comfort my people, says your G.
	40: 3	in the desert a highway for our G.
	40: 8	the word of our G endures forever."
	40:18	whom, then, will you compare G?

Isa	40:28	The LORD is the everlasting G,
	41:10	not be dismayed, for I am your G.
	41:13	the LORD your G who takes hold
	43:10	Before me no g was formed,
	44: 6	apart from me there is no G.
	44:15	he also fashions a g and worships it;
	45:18	he who created the heavens, he is G;
	48: 17	"I am the LORD your G,
	52: 7	who say to Zion, "Your G reigns!"
	52:12	the G of Israel will be your rear
	55: 7	and to our G, for he will freely
	57:21	says my G, "for the wicked."
	59: 2	have separated you from your G;
	60:19	light, and your G will be your glory.
	61: 2	and the day of vengeance of our G,
	61:10	my soul rejoices in my G.
	61:10	so will your G rejoice over you.
Jer	7:23	I will be your G and you will be my
	10:10	But the LORD is the true G;
	10:12	But G made the earth by his power;
	23:23	"Am I only a G nearby,"
	23:36	distort the words of the living G,
	31:33	I will be their G, and they will be
	32:27	the G of the whole human race.
	42: 6	we will obey the LORD our G,
	51:10	what the LORD our G has done."
	51:56	the LORD is a G of retribution;
Eze	28:13	You were in Eden, the garden of G;
	34:31	and I am your G,
Da	2:28	there is a G in heaven who reveals
	3:17	If the G we serve is able to deliver
	3:29	for no other g can save in this
	6:16	"May your G, whom you serve
	9: 4	the great and awesome G,
	10:12	to humble yourself before your G,
	11:36	things against the G of gods.
Hos	1: 9	not my people, and I am not your G.
	1:10	be called 'children of the living G.'
	4: 6	you have ignored the law of your G,
	6: 6	of G rather than burnt offerings.
	9: 8	along with my G, is the watchman
	12: 6	justice, and wait for your G always.
Joel	2:13	Return to the LORD your G, for he
	2:23	rejoice in the LORD your G, for he
Am	4:12	Israel, prepare to meet your G."
	4:13	the LORD G Almighty is his
Jnh	1: 6	Get up and call on your g!
Mic	6: 8	are a gracious and compassionate G,
	6: 8	and to walk humbly with your G.
	7: 7	I wait for my Savior; my G will hear
		me.
	7:18	Who is a G like you, who pardons
Na	1: 2	is a jealous and avenging G;
Hab	3:18	I will be joyful in G my Savior.
Zep	3:17	The LORD your G is with you,
Zec	14: 5	Then the LORD my G will come,
Mal	2:10	Did not one G create us?
	2:16	says the LORD G of Israel, "and I
	3: 8	"Will a mere mortal rob G?
Mt	1:23	(which means "G with us").
	4: 4	comes from the mouth of G.' "
	4: 7	'Do not put the Lord your G
	4:10	'Worship the Lord your G,
	5: 8	pure in heart, for they will see G.
	6:24	You cannot serve both G
	19: 6	Therefore what G has joined
	19:26	but with G all things are possible."
	22:21	Caesar's, and to G what is God's."
	22:32	He is not the G of the dead
	22:37	" 'Love the Lord your G with all
	27:46	(which means "My G, my G,
Mk	2: 7	Who can forgive sins but G alone?"
	7:13	Thus you nullify the word of G
	10: 6	of creation G 'made them male
	10: 9	Therefore what G has joined
	10:18	"No one is good—except G alone.
	10:27	all things are possible with G."
	11:22	"Have faith in G," Jesus answered.
	12:17	Caesar's and to G what is God's."
	12:29	The Lord our G, the Lord is one.
	12:30	Love the Lord your G with all your
	15:34	(which means "My G, my G,
	16:19	sat at the right hand of G.
Lk	1:30	you have found favor with G.
	1:37	For no word from G will ever fail."
	1:47	my spirit rejoices in G my Savior,
	2:14	"Glory to G in the highest heaven,
	2:52	and in favor with G and people.
	4: 8	'Worship the Lord your G and serve
	5:21	Who can forgive sins but G alone?"
	8:39	tell how much G has done for you."
	10: 9	'The kingdom of G has come near

Lk 10: 27 " 'Love the Lord your **G** with all
13: 18 "What is the kingdom of **G** like?
18: 19 "No one is good—except **G** alone.
18: 27 human beings is possible with **G**."
20: 25 Caesar's, and to **G** what is God's."
20: 38 He is not the **G** of the dead,
22: 69 at the right hand of the mighty **G**."

Jn 1: 1 was with **G**, and the Word was **G**.
1: 18 No one has ever seen **G**, but the one
1: 29 the Lamb of **G**, who takes away
3: 16 For **G** so loved the world that he
3: 34 the one whom **G** has sent speaks
4: 24 **G** is spirit, and his worshipers must
5: 44 glory that comes from the only **G**?
6: 29 answered, "The work of **G** is this:
7: 17 who chooses to do the will of **G**
7: 17 whether my teaching comes from **G**
8: 42 "If **G** were your Father, you would
8: 47 belongs to **G** hears what **G** says.
11: 40 you will see the glory of **G**?"
13: 3 from **G** and was returning to **G**;
13: 31 glorified and **G** is glorified in him.
14: 1 Trust in **G**; trust also in me.
17: 3 the only true **G**, and Jesus Christ,
20: 17 Father, to my **G** and your **G**.' "
20: 28 said to him, "My Lord and my **G**!"
20: 31 the Son of **G**, and that by believing

Ac 2: 11 them declaring the wonders of **G**
2: 24 But **G** raised him from the dead,
2: 33 Exalted to the right hand of **G**,
2: 36 **G** has made this Jesus, whom you
3: 15 life, but **G** raised him from the dead.
3: 19 and turn to **G**, so that your sins may
4: 31 and spoke the word of **G** boldly.
5: 4 lied just to human beings but to **G**."
5: 29 "We must obey **G** rather than
5: 31 exalted him to his own right hand
5: 32 whom **G** has given to those who
7: 55 to heaven and saw the glory of **G**,
8: 21 your heart is not right before **G**.
11: 9 impure that **G** has made clean.'
12: 24 the word of **G** continued to increase
13: 32 What **G** promised our ancestors
15: 10 why do you try to test **G** by putting
17: 23 \unknown \g. So you are ignorant
17: 30 In the past **G** overlooked such
20: 27 proclaim to you the whole will of **G**.
20: 32 "Now I commit you to **G**
24: 16 keep my conscience clear before **G**

Ro 1: 16 because it is the power of **G**
1: 17 the righteousness of **G** is revealed—
1: 18 The wrath of **G** is being revealed
1: 24 Therefore **G** gave them over
1: 26 **G** gave them over to shameful lusts.
2: 11 For **G** does not show favoritism.
2: 16 judges everyone's secrets through
3: 4 Let **G** be true, and every man
3: 19 whole world held accountable to **G**.
3: 23 and fall short of the glory of **G**,
3: 29 Is **G** the **G** of Jews only?
4: 3 "Abraham believed **G**, and it was
4: 6 whom **G** credits righteousness apart
4: 17 the **G** who gives life to the dead
4: 24 whom **G** will credit righteousness—
5: 1 **G** through our Lord Jesus Christ,
5: 8 **G** demonstrates his own love for us
6: 22 sin and have become slaves of **G**,
6: 23 the gift of **G** is eternal life in Christ
8: 7 The sinful mind is hostile to **G**;
8: 17 heirs of **G** and co-heirs with Christ,
8: 28 in all things **G** works for the good
9: 14 then shall we say? Is **G** unjust?
9: 18 Therefore **G** has mercy on whom he
10: 9 in your heart that **G** raised him
11: 2 **G** did not reject his people,
11: 22 the kindness and sternness of **G**:
11: 32 For **G** has bound everyone over
13: 1 exist have been established by **G**.
14: 12 give an account of ourselves to **G**.
16: 20 The **G** of peace will soon crush

1Co 1: 18 are being saved it is the power of **G**.
1: 20 Has not **G** made foolish the wisdom
1: 25 is wiser than human wisdom,
1: 27 **G** chose the foolish things
2: 9 these things **G** has prepared
2: 11 thoughts of **G** except the Spirit of **G**.
3: 6 but **G** has been making it grow.
3: 17 temple, **G** will destroy that person;
6: 20 Therefore honor **G** with your
7: 7 of you has your own gift from **G**;
7: 15 **G** has called us to live in peace.
7: 20 were in when **G** called you.

1Co 7: 24 as responsible to **G**, should remain
8: 3 whoever loves **G** is known by **G**.
8: 8 food does not bring us near to **G**;
10: 13 And **G** is faithful; he will not let you
10: 31 you do, do it all for the glory of **G**.
12: 24 But **G** has put the body together,
14: 33 For **G** is not a **G** of disorder
15: 24 over the kingdom to **G** the Father
15: 28 so that **G** may be all in all.
15: 34 are some who are ignorant of **G**—
15: 57 But thanks be to **G**! He gives us

2Co 1: 9 not rely on ourselves but on **G**,
2: 14 But thanks be to **G**, who always
2: 15 we are to **G** the pleasing aroma
2: 17 we do not peddle the word of **G**
3: 5 but our competence comes from **G**.
4: 2 nor do we distort the word of **G**.
4: 7 this all-surpassing power is from **G**
5: 5 us for this very purpose is **G**,
5: 19 that **G** was reconciling the world
5: 20 as though **G** were making his appeal
5: 21 **G** made him who had no sin to be
6: 16 we are the temple of the living **G**.
9: 7 for **G** loves a cheerful giver.
9: 8 **G** is able to bless you abundantly,
10: 13 of service **G** himself has assigned

Gal 2: 6 **G** does not show favoritism—
3: 5 Does **G** give you his Spirit
3: 6 So also Abraham "believed **G**,
3: 11 Clearly no one is justified before **G**
3: 26 are all children of **G** through faith,
6: 7 **G** cannot be mocked.

Eph 1: 22 **G** placed all things under his feet
2: 8 from yourselves, it is the gift of **G**—
2: 10 which **G** prepared in advance for us
2: 22 in which **G** lives by his Spirit.
4: 6 one **G** and Father of all, who is over
4: 24 to be like **G** in true righteousness
6: 6 doing the will of **G** from your heart.

Php 2: 6 being in very nature **G**, did not
2: 9 Therefore **G** exalted him
2: 13 for it is **G** who works in you to will
4: 7 And the peace of **G**,
4: 19 And my **G** will meet all your needs

Col 1: 19 For **G** was pleased to have all his
2: 13 **G** made you alive with Christ.

1Th 2: 4 not trying to please people but **G**,
2: 13 the word of **G**, which is indeed
3: 9 How can we thank **G** enough
4: 7 For **G** did not call us to be impure,
4: 9 yourselves have been taught by **G**
5: 9 For **G** did not appoint us to suffer

1Ti 2: 5 one mediator between **G** and human
4: 4 For everything **G** created is good,
5: 4 for this is pleasing to **G**.

2Ti 1: 6 you to fan into flame the gift of **G**,

Tit 1: 2 life, which **G**, who does not lie,
2: 13 of the glory of our great **G**

Heb 1: 1 In the past **G** spoke to our ancestors
3: 4 but **G** is the builder of everything.
4: 4 the seventh day **G** rested from all
4: 12 For the word of **G** is alive
6: 10 **G** is not unjust; he will not forget
6: 18 which it is impossible for **G** to lie,
7: 19 by which we draw near to **G**.
7: 25 those who come to **G** through him,
10: 22 let us draw near to **G** with a sincere
10: 31 to fall into the hands of the living **G**.
11: 5 commended as one who pleased **G**.
11: 6 faith it is impossible to please **G**,
12: 7 **G** is treating you as his children.
12: 10 but **G** disciplines us for our good,
12: 29 for our **"G** is a consuming fire."
13: 15 us continually offer to **G** a sacrifice

Jas 1: 12 of life that **G** has promised to those
1: 13 For **G** cannot be tempted by evil,
1: 27 that **G** our Father accepts as pure
2: 19 You believe that there is one **G**.
2: 23 "Abraham believed **G**, and it was
4: 4 that **G** means enmity against **G**?
4: 6 "G opposes the proud but shows
4: 8 Come near to **G** and he will come

1Pe 1: 23 the living and enduring word of **G**.
2: 20 this is commendable before **G**.
3: 18 the unrighteous, to bring you to **G**.
4: 11 do so with the strength **G** provides,
5: 5 "G opposes the proud but shows

2Pe 1: 21 from **G** as they were carried along

1Jn 1: 5 him and declare to you: **G** is light;
2: 5 love for **G** is truly made complete
2: 17 does the will of **G** lives forever.

1Jn 3: 1 we should be called children of **G**!
3: 9 who are born of **G** will not continue
3: 10 we know who the children of **G** are
3: 20 that **G** is greater than our hearts,
4: 7 one another, for love comes from **G**.
4: 8 does not know **G**, because **G** is love.
4: 9 This is how **G** showed his love
4: 11 Dear friends, since **G** so loved us,
4: 12 No one has ever seen **G**; but if we
4: 15 that Jesus is the Son of **G**, **G** lives in
them and they in **G**.
4: 16 in love lives in **G**, and **G** in them.
4: 20 we say we love **G** yet hate a brother
4: 21 Those who love **G** must also love
5: 2 that we love the children of **G**:
5: 3 In fact, this is love for **G**:
5: 4 born of **G** overcomes the world.
5: 10 does not believe **G** has made him
5: 14 we have in approaching **G**:
5: 18 anyone born of **G** does not continue

Rev 4: 8 holy is the Lord **G** Almighty,'
7: 12 strength be to our **G** for ever
7: 17 **G** will wipe away every tear
11: 16 fell on their faces and worshiped **G**,
15: 3 are your deeds, Lord **G** Almighty.
17: 17 For **G** has put it into their hearts
19: 6 For our Lord **G** Almighty reigns.
21: 3 and **G** himself will be with them
21: 3 will be with them and be their **G**.

GOD-BREATHED* (BREATH)
2Ti 3: 16 All Scripture is **G** and is useful

GOD-FEARING* (FEAR)
Ac 2: 5 were staying in Jerusalem **G** Jews
10: 2 all his family were devout and **G**;
10: 22 He is a righteous and **G** man, who is
13: 26 of Abraham and you **G** Gentiles,
13: 50 Jewish leaders incited the **G** women
17: 4 as did a large number of **G** Greeks
17: 17 with both Jews and **G** Greeks,

GOD-HATERS* (HATE)
Ro 1: 30 slanderers, **G**, insolent,

GOD'S (GOD)
2Ch 20: 15 For the battle is not yours, but **G**.
Job 33: 6 I am the same as you in **G** sight;
37: 14 stop and consider **G** wonders.
Ps 52: 8 I trust in **G** unfailing love for ever
69: 30 I will praise **G** name in song
Mk 3: 35 Whoever does **G** will is my brother
Jn 10: 36 because I said, 'I am **G** Son'?
Ro 2: 3 think you will escape **G** judgment?
2: 4 realizing that **G** kindness is intended
3: 3 nullify **G** faithfulness?
5: 5 because **G** love has been poured
7: 22 my inner being I delight in **G** law;
9: 16 desire or effort, but on **G** mercy.
11: 29 for **G** gifts and his call are
12: 2 to test and approve what **G** will is—
13: 6 for the authorities are **G** servants,
1Co 7: 19 Keeping **G** commands is what
2Co 6: 2 now is the time of **G** favor, now is
Eph 1: 7 with the riches of **G** grace
5: 1 Follow **G** example,
1Th 4: 3 It is **G** will that you should be
5: 18 for this is **G** will for you in Christ
1Ti 6: 1 so that **G** name and our teaching
2Ti 2: 19 **G** solid foundation stands firm,
Tit 1: 7 an overseer manages **G** household,
Heb 1: 3 The Son is the radiance of **G** glory
9: 24 now to appear for us in **G** presence.
11: 3 was formed at **G** command,
1Pe 2: 15 For it is **G** will that by doing good
3: 4 which is of great worth in **G** sight.

GODLESS
Job 20: 5 the joy of the **g** lasts but a moment.
1Ti 6: 20 Turn away from **g** chatter

GODLINESS (GOD)
1Ti 2: 2 and quiet lives in all **g** and holiness.
4: 8 value, but **g** has value for all things,
4: 8 and who think that **g** is a means
6: 6 **g** with contentment is great gain.
6: 11 and pursue righteousness, **g**, faith,
2Pe 1: 6 and to perseverance, **g**;

GODLY (GOD)
Ps 16: 3 of the **g** who are in the land,
2Co 7: 10 **G** sorrow brings repentance
11: 2 jealous for you with a **g** jealousy.
2Ti 3: 12 live a **g** life in Christ Jesus will be
2Pe 3: 11 You ought to live holy and **g** lives

GODS (GOD)
Ex 20: 3 shall have no other g before me.
Dt 5: 7 shall have no other g before me.
1Ch 16: 26 For all the g of the nations are idols,
Ps 82: 6 "I said, 'You are "g"; you are all
Jn 10: 34 'I have said you are "g" '?
Ac 19: 26 He says that g made by human hands are no g at all.

GOG
Eze 38: 18 When G attacks the land of Israel,
Rev 20: 8 of the earth—G and Magog—

GOLD
1Ki 20: 3 'Your silver and g are mine,
Job 22: 25 then the Almighty will be your g,
23: 10 tested me, I will come forth as g.
28: 15 cannot be bought with the finest g,
31: 24 "If I have put my trust in g or said to pure g,
Ps 19: 10 They are more precious than g,
119: 127 more than g, more than pure g,
Pr 3: 14 and yields better returns than g.
22: 1 esteemed is better than silver or g.
Hag 2: 8 silver is mine and the g is mine,'
Mt 2: 11 and presented him with gifts of g,
Rev 3: 18 to buy from me g refined in the fire,

GOLGOTHA*
Mt 27: 33 a place called G (which means
Mk 15: 22 to the place called G (which means
Jn 19: 17 (which in Aramaic is called G).

GOLIATH
Philistine giant killed by David (1Sa 17; 21:9).

GOMORRAH
Ge 19: 24 burning sulfur on Sodom and G—
Mt 10: 15 G on the day of judgment than
2Pe 2: 6 and G by burning them to ashes,
Jude : 7 Sodom and G and the surrounding

GOOD
Ge 1: 4 God saw that the light was g, and he
1: 10 And God saw that it was g.
1: 12 And God saw that it was g.
1: 18 And God saw that it was g.
1: 21 And God saw that it was g.
1: 25 And God saw that it was g.
1: 31 that he had made, and it was very g.
2: 9 pleasing to the eye and g for food.
2: 9 the tree of the knowledge of g
2: 18 "It is not g for the man to be alone.
3: 22 like one of us, knowing g and evil.
50: 20 God intended it for g to accomplish
2Ch 7: 3 to the LORD, saying, "He is g;
31: 20 doing what was g and right
Job 2: 10 Shall we accept g from God,
Ps 14: 1 there is no one who does g.
34: 8 Taste and see that the LORD is g;
34: 14 Turn from evil and do g;
37: 3 Trust in the LORD and do g;
37: 27 Turn from evil and do g;
52: 9 in your name, for your name is g.
53: 3 there is no one who does g, not even
84: 11 no g thing does he withhold
86: 5 are forgiving and g,
100: 5 For the LORD is g and his love
103: 5 your desires with g things so
112: 5 G will come to those who are
119: 68 You are g, and what you do is g;
133: 1 How g and pleasant it is
145: 9 The LORD is g to all;
147: 1 How g it is to sing praises to our
Pr 3: 4 and a g name in the sight of God
3: 27 Do not withhold g from those
11: 27 Whoever seeks g finds favor,
13: 21 righteous are rewarded with g
13: 22 G people leave an inheritance
14: 22 those who plan what is g find love
15: 3 watch on the wicked and the g.
15: 23 and how g is a timely word!
15: 30 g news gives health to the bones.
17: 22 A cheerful heart is g medicine,
18: 22 He who finds a wife finds what is g
19: 2 Desire without knowledge is not g—
22: 1 A g name is more desirable than
31: 12 She brings him g, not harm,
Ecc 12: 14 hidden thing, whether it is g or evil.
Isa 5: 20 Woe to those who call evil g and g
40: 9 You who bring g news to Zion,
52: 7 the feet of those who bring g news,
61: 1 has anointed me to proclaim g news
Jer 6: 16 ask where the g way is, and walk
13: 23 can you do g who are accustomed

Eze 34: 14 I will tend them in a g pasture,
Mic 6: 8 has shown all you people what is g.
Na 1: 15 the feet of one who brings g news,
Mt 5: 45 his sun to rise on the evil and the g,
7: 11 heaven give g gifts to those who ask
7: 17 Likewise, every g tree bears g fruit,
7: 18 A g tree cannot bear bad fruit,
12: 35 G people bring g things out of the g
13: 8 Still other seed fell on g soil,
13: 24 is like a man who sowed g seed
13: 48 and collected the g fish in baskets,
19: 17 "There is only One who is g.
22: 10 the bad as well as the g,
25: 21 'Well done, g and faithful servant!
Mk 1: 15 Repent and believe the g news!"
3: 4 to do g or to do evil, to save life
4: 8 Still other seed fell on g soil.
8: 36 What g is it for you to gain
10: 18 "No one is g—except God alone.
Lk 2: 10 I bring you g news of great joy
3: 9 does not produce g fruit will be cut
6: 27 do g to those who hate you,
6: 43 nor does a bad tree bear g fruit.
6: 45 G people bring g things out of the g
8: 8 Still other seed fell on g soil.
9: 25 What g is it for you to gain
14: 34 "Salt is g, but if it loses its
18: 19 "No one is g—except God alone.
19: 17 " 'Well done, my g servant!'
Jn 10: 11 "I am the g shepherd.
Ro 3: 12 there is no one who does g, not even
7: 12 is holy, righteous and g.
7: 16 want to do, I agree that the law is g.
7: 18 For I have the desire to do what is g,
8: 28 for the g of those who love him,
10: 15 feet of those who bring g news!"
12: 2 his g, pleasing and perfect will.
12: 9 Hate what is evil; cling to what is g.
13: 4 is God's servant for your g.
16: 19 want you to be wise about what is g,
1Co 7: 1 "It is g for a man not to have sexual
10: 24 seek their own g, but the g of others.
15: 33 company corrupts g character."
2Co 9: 8 you will abound in every g work.
Gal 4: 18 provided the purpose is g, and to be
6: 9 Let us not become weary in doing g,
6: 10 let us do g to all people,
Eph 2: 8 in Christ Jesus by God's works,
6: 8 one of you for whatever g you do,
Php 1: 6 he who began a g work in you will
Col 1: 10 bearing fruit in every g work,
1Th 5: 15 Strive to do what is g for each
5: 21 test them all; hold on to what is g,
2Th 3: 13 never tire of doing what is g.
1Ti 3: 7 have a reputation with outsiders,
4: 4 For everything God created is g,
6: 12 Fight the g fight of the faith.
6: 18 do g, to be rich in g deeds,
2Ti 4: 7 I have fought the g fight, I have
Tit 1: 8 one who loves what is g, who is
2: 7 an example by doing what is g.
2: 14 his very own, eager to do what is g.
Heb 5: 14 to distinguish g from evil.
10: 24 another on toward love and g deeds,
12: 10 but God disciplines us for our g,
13: 16 do not forget to do g and to share
Jas 4: 17 if you know the g you ought to do
1Pe 2: 3 you have tasted that the Lord is g.
2: 12 Live such g lives among the pagans
2: 18 not only to those who are g
3: 17 to suffer for doing g than for doing

GOODS
Ecc 5: 11 As g increase, so do those who

GORGE
Pr 23: 20 wine or g themselves on meat,

GOSHEN
Ge 45: 10 You shall live in the region of G
Ex 8: 22 deal differently with the land of G,

GOSPEL
Mk 16: 15 *preach the g to all creation.*
Ac 14: 7 they continued to preach the g.
14: 21 They preached the g in that city
Ro 1: 16 not ashamed of the g,
15: 16 duty of proclaiming the g of God,
15: 20 preach the g where Christ was not
1Co 1: 17 me to baptize, but to preach the g—
9: 12 anything rather than hinder the g
9: 14 who preach the g should receive
9: 16 Woe to me if I do not preach the g!

1Co 15: 1 to remind you of the g I preached
15: 2 By this g you are saved, if you hold
2Co 4: 4 light of the g that displays the glory
9: 13 your confession of the g of Christ,
Gal 1: 7 which is really no g at all.
Eph 6: 15 that comes from the g of peace.
Php 1: 27 a manner worthy of the g of Christ.
Col 1: 23 This is the g that you heard
1Th 2: 4 by God to be entrusted with the g.
2Th 1: 8 do not obey the g of our Lord Jesus.
2Ti 1: 10 immortality to light through the g.
Rev 14: 6 he had the eternal g to proclaim

GOSSIP* (GOSSIPS)
Pr 18: 8 of a g are like choice morsels;
20: 19 A g betrays a confidence;
26: 20 without a g a quarrel dies down.
26: 22 of a g are like choice morsels;
2Co 12: 20 slander, g, arrogance and disorder.

GOSSIPS* (GOSSIP)
Pr 11: 13 G betray a confidence,
16: 28 and g separate close friends.
Ro 1: 29 deceit and malice. They are g,

GOURD
Jnh 4: 6 Jonah was very happy about the g.

GOVERN (GOVERNMENT)
Ge 1: 16 the greater light to g the day
Job 34: 17 Can one who hates justice g?

GOVERNMENT (GOVERN)
Isa 9: 6 and the g will be on his shoulders.

GRACE* (GRACIOUS)
Ps 45: 2 your lips have been anointed with g,
Pr 1: 9 They are a garland to g your head
3: 22 an ornament to g your neck.
4: 9 give you a garland to g your head
4: 9 pure heart and who speaks with g
Isa 26: 10 But when g is shown to the wicked,
Zec 12: 10 inhabitants of Jerusalem a spirit of g
Lk 2: 40 and the g of God was on him.
Jn 1: 14 from the Father, full of g and truth.
1: 16 of his fullness we have all received g in place of g already given.
1: 17 g and truth came through Jesus
Ac 4: 33 God's g was so powerfully at work
6: 8 a man full of God's g and power,
11: 23 saw what the g of God had done,
13: 43 them to continue in the g of God.
14: 3 message of his g by enabling them
14: 26 had been committed to the g of God
15: 11 We believe it is through the g of our
15: 40 by the believers to the g of the Lord.
18: 27 to those who by g had believed.
20: 24 to the good news of God's g.
20: 32 you to God and to the word of his g,
Ro 1: 5 Through him we received g
1: 7 G and peace to you from God our
3: 24 by his g through the redemption
4: 16 so that it may be by g and may be
5: 2 by faith into this g in which we now
5: 15 how much more did God's g
5: 15 that came by the g of the one man,
5: 17 God's abundant provision of g
5: 20 increased, increased all the more,
5: 21 g might reign through righteousness
6: 1 on sinning so that g may increase?
6: 14 are not under the law, but under g.
6: 15 are not under the law but under g?
11: 5 time there is a remnant chosen by g.
11: 6 if by g, then it cannot be based on works; if it were, g would no longer be g.
12: 3 by the g given me I say to every one
12: 6 according to the g given to each
15: 15 because of the g God gave me
16: 20 The g of our Lord Jesus be
1Co 1: 3 G and peace to you from God our
1: 4 you because of his g given you
3: 10 By the g God has given me, I laid
15: 10 But by the g of God I am what I am,
15: 10 his g to me was not without effect.
15: 10 but the g of God that was with me.
16: 23 The g of the Lord Jesus be
2Co 1: 2 G and peace to you from God our
1: 12 on worldly wisdom but on God's g.
4: 15 so that the g that is reaching more
6: 1 you not to receive God's g in vain.
8: 1 about the g that God has given
8: 6 to completion this act of g on your
8: 7 you also excel in this g of giving.
8: 9 you know the g of our Lord Jesus
9: 14 the surpassing g God has given you.

2Co	12: 9	to me, "My **g** is sufficient for you,
	13: 14	May the **g** of the Lord Jesus Christ,
Gal	1: 3	**G** and peace to you from God our
	1: 6	who called you by the **g** of Christ
	1: 15	from birth and called me by his **g**,
	2: 9	they recognized the **g** given to me.
	2: 21	I do not set aside the **g** of God,
	3: 18	but God in his **g** gave it to Abraham
	5: 4	you have fallen away from **g**.
	6: 18	The **g** of our Lord Jesus Christ be
Eph	1: 2	**G** and peace to you from God our
	1: 6	to the praise of his glorious **g**,
	1: 7	with the riches of God's **g**
	2: 5	it is by **g** you have been saved.
	2: 7	the incomparable riches of his **g**,
	2: 8	For it is by **g** you have been saved,
	3: 2	of God's **g** that was given to me
	3: 7	of God's **g** given me through
	3: 8	Lord's people, this **g** was given me:
	4: 7	one of us **g** has been given as Christ
	6: 24	**G** to all who love our Lord Jesus
Php	1: 2	**G** and peace to you from God our
	1: 7	all of you share in God's **g** with me.
	4: 23	The **g** of the Lord Jesus Christ be
Col	1: 2	**G** and peace to you from God our
	1: 6	it and truly understood God's **g**.
	4: 6	conversation be always full of **g**,
	4: 18	**G** be with you.
1Th	1: 1	and peace to you.
	5: 28	The **g** of our Lord Jesus Christ be
2Th	1: 2	**G** and peace to you from God
	1: 12	according to the **g** of our God
	2: 16	his **g** gave us eternal encouragement
	3: 18	The **g** of our Lord Jesus Christ be
1Ti	1: 2	**G**, mercy and peace from God
	1: 14	The **g** of our Lord was poured
	6: 21	from the faith. **G** be with you all.
2Ti	1: 2	**G**, mercy and peace from God
	1: 9	because of his own purpose and **g**.
	1: 9	This **g** was given us in Christ Jesus
	2: 1	be strong in the **g** that is in Christ
	4: 22	with your spirit. **G** be with you all.
Tit	1: 4	**G** and peace from God the Father
	2: 11	For the **g** of God has appeared
	3: 7	having been justified by his **g**,
	3: 15	us in the faith. **G** be with you all.
Phm	: 3	**G** and peace to you from God our
	: 25	The **g** of the Lord Jesus Christ be
Heb	2: 9	by the **g** of God he might taste death
	4: 16	approach God's throne of **g**
	4: 16	find **g** to help us in our time of need.
	10: 29	who have insulted the Spirit of **g**?
	12: 15	no one falls short of the **g** of God
	13: 9	our hearts to be strengthened by **g**,
	13: 25	**G** be with you all.
Jas	4: 6	But he gives us more **g**.
1Pe	1: 2	**G** and peace be yours in abundance.
	1: 10	who spoke of the **g** that was to come
	1: 13	set your hope on the **g** to be brought
	4: 10	of God's **g** in its various forms.
	5: 10	And the God of all **g**, who called
	5: 12	that this is the true **g** of God.
2Pe	1: 2	**G** and peace be yours in abundance
	3: 18	grow in the **g** and knowledge of our
2Jn	: 3	**G**, mercy and peace from God
Jude	: 4	who pervert the **g** of our God
Rev	1: 4	**G** and peace to you from him who
	22: 21	The **g** of the Lord Jesus be

GRACIOUS (GRACE)

Ex	34: 6	the compassionate and **g** God,
Nu	6: 25	face shine on you and be **g** to you;
Ne	9: 17	God, **g** and compassionate,
Ps	67: 1	May God be **g** to us and bless us
Pr	16: 21	and **g** words promote instruction.
	16: 24	**G** words are a honeycomb,
Isa	30: 18	the LORD longs to be **g** to you;

GRAIN

Lev	2: 1	anyone brings a **g** offering
Ecc	11: 1	Ship your **g** across the sea;
Lk	17: 35	women will be grinding together;
1Co	9: 9	an ox while it is treading out the **g**."

GRANDCHILDREN (CHILD)

1Ti	5: 4	But if a widow has children or **g**,

GRANDMOTHER (MOTHER)

2Ti	1: 5	which first lived in your **g** Lois

GRANT (GRANTED)

Ps	20: 5	May the LORD **g** all your
	51: 12	salvation and **g** me a willing spirit,

GRANTED (GRANT)

Pr	10: 24	what the righteous desire will be **g**.
Mt	15: 28	Your request is **g**."
Php	1: 29	For it has been **g** to you on behalf

GRAPES

Nu	13: 23	branch bearing a single cluster of **g**.
Jer	31: 29	'The parents have eaten sour **g**,
Eze	18: 2	" 'The parents eat sour **g**,
Mt	7: 16	Do people pick **g** from thornbushes,
Rev	14: 18	and gather the clusters of **g**

GRASS

Ps	103: 15	their days are like **g**, they flourish
Isa	40: 6	"All people are like **g**, and all
Mt	6: 30	that is how God clothes the **g**
1Pe	1: 24	"All people are like **g**, and all their

GRASSHOPPERS

Nu	13: 33	We seemed like **g** in our own eyes,

GRATIFY* (GRATITUDE)

Ro	13: 14	how to **g** the desires of the sinful
Gal	5: 16	and you will not **g** the desires

GRATITUDE (GRATIFY)

Col	3: 16	to God with **g** in your hearts.

GRAVE (GRAVES)

Nu	19: 16	who touches a human bone or a **g**,
Dt	34: 6	day no one knows where his **g** is.
Ps	5: 9	Their throat is an open **g**;
Pr	7: 27	Her house is a highway to the **g**,
Hos	13: 14	Where, O **g**, is your destruction?
Jn	11: 44	"Take off the **g** clothes and let him

GRAVES (GRAVE)

Eze	37: 12	I am going to open your **g** and bring
Jn	5: 28	are in their **g** will hear his voice
Ro	3: 13	"Their throats are open **g**;

GRAY

Pr	16: 31	**G** hair is a crown of splendor;
	20: 29	**g** hair the splendor of the old.

GREAT (GREATER GREATEST GREATNESS)

Ge	12: 2	I will make your name **g**, and you
	12: 2	"I will make you into a **g** nation,
Ex	32: 11	brought out of Egypt with **g** power
Nu	14: 19	In accordance with your **g** love,
Dt	4: 32	Has anything so **g** as this ever
	10: 17	gods and Lord of lords, the **g** God,
	29: 28	**g** wrath the LORD uprooted them
Jos	7: 9	will you do for your own **g** name?"
Jdg	16: 5	you the secret of his **g** strength
2Sa	7: 22	"How **g** you are,
	22: 36	your help has made me **g**.
	24: 14	of the LORD, for his mercy is **g**;
1Ch	17: 19	made known all these **g** promises.
Ps	18: 35	your help has made me **g**.
	19: 11	in keeping them there is **g** reward.
	40: 16	"The LORD is **g**!"
	47: 2	the **g** King over all the earth.
	57: 10	For **g** is your love,
	68: 11	**g** was the company of those who
	70: 4	"The LORD is **g**!"
	89: 1	sing of the LORD's **g** love forever;
	103: 11	so **g** is his love for those who fear
	108: 4	For **g** is your love, higher than
	117: 2	For **g** is his love toward us,
	119:165	**G** peace have those who love your
	145: 3	**G** is the LORD and most worthy
Pr	22: 1	is more desirable than **g** riches;
	23: 24	father of a righteous child has **g** joy;
Isa	42: 21	his righteousness to make his law **g**
Jer	32: 19	With my **g** power and outstretched
	32: 19	are your purposes and mighty are
La	3: 23	is your faithfulness.
Da	9: 4	"Lord, the **g** and awesome God,
Joel	2: 11	The day of the LORD is **g**;
	2: 20	Surely he has done **g** things!
Zep	1: 14	The **g** day of the LORD is near—
Mal	1: 11	name will be **g** among the nations,
	4: 5	prophet Elijah to you before that **g**
Mt	20: 26	become **g** among you must be your
Mk	10: 43	become **g** among you must be your
Lk	6: 23	because **g** is your reward in heaven.
	6: 35	Then your reward will be **g**, and your
	21: 27	in a cloud with power and **g** glory.
Eph	1: 19	his incomparably **g** power for us
	2: 4	But because of his **g** love for us,
1Ti	6: 6	with contentment is **g** gain.
Tit	2: 13	appearing of the glory of our **g** God
Heb	2: 3	if we ignore so **g** a salvation?
1Jn	3: 1	See what **g** love the Father has
Rev	6: 17	For the **g** day of their wrath has

Rev	20: 11	I saw a **g** white throne and him who

GREATER (GREAT)

Mt	11: 11	has not risen anyone **g** than John
	12: 6	that one **g** than the temple is here.
	12: 41	and now one **g** than Jonah is here.
	12: 42	now one **g** than Solomon is here.
Mk	12: 31	is no commandment **g** than these."
Jn	1: 50	You will see **g** things than that."
	3: 30	He must become **g**; I must become
	14: 12	will do even **g** things than these,
	15: 13	**G** love has no one than this:
1Co	12: 31	Now eagerly desire the **g** gifts.
2Co	3: 11	how much **g** is the glory
Heb	3: 3	worthy of **g** honor than Moses,
	3: 3	a house has **g** honor than the house
	7: 7	doubt the lesser is blessed by the **g**.
	11: 26	as of **g** value than the treasures
1Jn	3: 20	know that God is **g** than our hearts,
	4: 4	is in you is **g** than the one who is

GREATEST (GREAT)

Mt	22: 38	is the first and **g** commandment.
	23: 11	The **g** among you will be your
Lk	9: 48	is least among you all is the **g**."
1Co	13: 13	But the **g** of these is love.

GREATNESS* (GREAT)

Ex	15: 7	"In the **g** of your majesty you threw
Dt	3: 24	to show to your servant your **g**
	32: 3	praise the **g** of our God!
1Ch	29: 11	is the **g** and the power and the glory
2Ch	9: 6	not even half the **g** of your wisdom
Est	10: 2	a full account of the **g** of Mordecai
Ps	145: 3	his **g** no one can fathom.
	150: 2	praise him for his surpassing **g**.
Isa	63: 1	forward in the **g** of his strength?
Eze	38: 23	And so I will show my **g** and my
Da	4: 22	your **g** has grown until it reaches
	5: 18	Nebuchadnezzar sovereignty and **g**
	7: 27	**g** of all the kingdoms under heaven
Mic	5: 4	his **g** will reach to the ends
Lk	9: 43	were all amazed at the **g** of God.

GREED (GREEDY)

Lk	12: 15	on your guard against all kinds of **g**;
Ro	1: 29	wickedness, evil, **g**, and depravity.
Eph	5: 3	or of **g**, because these are improper
Col	3: 5	evil desires and **g**, which is idolatry.
2Pe	2: 14	they are experts in **g**—

GREEDY (GREED)

Pr	15: 27	The **g** bring ruin to their
1Co	6: 10	thieves nor the **g** nor drunkards nor
Eph	5: 5	No immoral, impure or **g** person—

GREEKS

1Co	1: 22	signs and **G** look for wisdom,

GREEN

Ps	23: 2	makes me lie down in **g** pastures,

GREW (GROW)

Lk	1: 80	the child **g** and became strong
	2: 52	And as Jesus **g** up, he increased
Ac	16: 5	in the faith and **g** daily in numbers.

GRIEF (GRIEFS GRIEVE GRIEVED)

Ps	10: 14	you consider their **g** and take it
Pr	10: 1	but foolish children bring **g** to their
	14: 13	ache, and rejoicing may end in **g**.
	17: 21	To have a fool for a child brings **g**;
Ecc	1: 18	the more knowledge, the more **g**.
La	3: 32	Though he brings **g**, he will show
Jn	16: 20	grieve, but your **g** will turn to joy.
1Pe	1: 6	may have had to suffer **g** in all kinds

GRIEFS* (GRIEF)

1Ti	6: 10	pierced themselves with many **g**.

GRIEVANCE

Col	3: 13	if any of you has a **g** against

GRIEVE (GRIEF)

Eph	4: 30	do not **g** the Holy Spirit of God,
1Th	4: 13	so that you do not **g** like the rest,

GRIEVED (GRIEF)

Isa	63: 10	they rebelled and **g** his Holy Spirit.

GRINDING

Lk	17: 35	women will be **g** grain together;

GROAN (GROANING GROANS)

Ro	8: 23	**g** inwardly as we wait eagerly
2Co	5: 4	in this tent, we **g** and are burdened,

GROANING (GROAN)

Ex	2: 24	God heard their **g** and he
Eze	21: 7	they ask you, 'Why are you **g**?"

Ro 8:22 the whole creation has been as g

GROANS (GROAN)
Ro 8:26 for us through wordless g.

GROUND
Ge 1:10 God called the dry g "land,"
3:17 it,' "Cursed is the g because of you;
4:10 blood cries out to me from the g.
Ex 3:5 where you are standing is holy g."
15:19 walked through the sea on dry g.
Isa 53:2 shoot, and like a root out of dry g.
Mt 10:29 to the g outside your Father's care.
25:25 went out and hid your gold in the g.
Jn 8:6 *write on the g with his finger.*
Eph 6:13 you may be able to stand your g,

GROW (FULL-GROWN GREW GROWING GROWS)
Pr 13:11 money little by little makes it g.
20:13 not love sleep or you will g poor;
Isa 40:31 they will run and not g weary,
Mt 6:28 See how the flowers of the field g.
1Co 3:6 but God has been making it g.
2Pe 3:18 But g in the grace and knowledge

GROWING (GROW)
Lk 13:6 had a fig tree in his vineyard,
Col 1:6 g throughout the whole world—
1:10 work, g in the knowledge of God,
2Th 1:3 because your faith is g more

GROWS (GROW)
Eph 4:16 g and builds itself up in love,
Col 2:19 sinews, g as God causes it to grow.

GRUMBLE (GRUMBLED GRUMBLERS GRUMBLING)
1Co 10:10 And do not g, as some of them did—
Jas 5:9 Don't g against one another,

GRUMBLED (GRUMBLE)
Ex 15:24 So the people g against Moses,
Nu 14:29 census and who has g against me.

GRUMBLERS* (GRUMBLE)
Jude :16 These people are g and faultfinders;

GRUMBLING (GRUMBLE)
Jn 6:43 "Stop g among yourselves,"
Php 2:14 Do everything without g or arguing,
1Pe 4:9 hospitality to one another without g.

GUARANTEEING* (GUARANTOR)
2Co 1:22 as a deposit, g what is to come.
5:5 as a deposit, g what is to come.
Eph 1:14 is a deposit g our inheritance until

GUARANTOR* (GUARANTEEING)
Heb 7:22 Jesus has become the g of a better

GUARD (GUARDED GUARDIAN)
1Sa 2:9 He will g the feet of his faithful
Ps 141:3 Set a g over my mouth, LORD;
Pr 2:11 and understanding will g you.
4:13 g it well, for it is your life.
4:23 Above all else, g your heart,
7:2 g my teachings as the apple of your
13:3 Those who g their lips preserve
21:23 Those who g their mouths
Isa 52:12 God of Israel will be your rear g.
Mk 13:33 Be on g! Be alert! You do not know
Lk 12:1 "Be on your g against the yeast
12:15 Be on your g against all kinds
Ac 20:31 So be on your g!
1Co 16:13 Be on your g; stand firm
Php 4:7 will g your hearts and your minds
1Ti 6:20 g what has been entrusted to your
2Ti 1:14 G the good deposit that was

GUARDED (GUARD)
Eze 44:15 who g my sanctuary when the

GUARDIAN (GUARD)
Ru 3:9 since you are a family g."
4:14 not left you without a family g.

GUEST (GUEST)
Lk 2:7 no g room available for them.

GUIDANCE (GUIDE)
Pr 1:5 and let the discerning get g—
11:14 For lack of g a nation falls,
24:6 Surely you need g to wage war,
1Co 12:28 gifts of healing, of helping, of g,

GUIDE (GUIDANCE GUIDED GUIDES)
Ex 15:21 of cloud to g them on their way
15:13 In your strength you will g them
Ne 9:19 of cloud did not cease to g them
Ps 25:5 G me in your truth and teach me,
48:14 he will be our g even to the end.

Ps 67:4 equity and g the nations of the earth.
73:24 You g me with your counsel,
139:10 even there your hand will g me,
Pr 6:22 When you walk, they will g you;
Isa 58:11 The LORD will g you always;
Jn 16:13 he will g you into all the truth.

GUIDED (GUIDE)
Ps 107:30 he g them to their desired haven.

GUIDES (GUIDE)
Ps 23:3 He g me along the right paths
25:9 He g the humble in what is right
Pr 11:3 The integrity of the upright g them,
Mt 23:16 "Woe to you, blind g! You say,
23:24 You blind g! You strain out a gnat

GUILT (GUILTY)
Lev 5:15 It is a g offering.
Ps 32:5 And you forgave the g of my sin.
38:4 My g has overwhelmed me like
Isa 6:7 your g is taken away and your sin
Jer 2:22 stain of your g is still before me,"
Eze 18:19 'Why does the son not share the g

GUILTY (GUILT)
Ex 23:1 Do not help a g person
34:7 he does not leave the g unpunished;
Job 10:2 I say to God: Do not declare me g,
Mk 3:29 forgiven, but is g of an eternal sin."
Jn 8:46 And can any of you prove me g of sin?
1Co 11:27 in an unworthy manner will be g
Heb 10:2 would no longer have felt g for their
10:22 to cleanse us from a g conscience
Jas 2:10 at just one point is g of breaking all

GULLIBLE* (GULLIBLE)
2Ti 3:6 gain control over g women,

GULP*
Pr 21:20 but fools g theirs down.

HABAKKUK*
Prophet to Judah (Hab 1:1; 3:1).

HABIT
1Ti 5:13 they get into the h of being idle
Heb 10:25 as some are in the h of doing,

HADAD
Edomite adversary of Solomon (1Ki 11:14–25).

HADES*
Lk 16:23 In H, where he was in torment,
Rev 1:18 And I hold the keys of death and H.
6:8 H was following close behind him.
20:13 and H gave up the dead that were
20:14 H were thrown into the lake of fire.

HAGAR
Servant of Sarah, wife of Abraham, mother of Ishmael (Ge 16:1–6; 25:12). Driven away by Sarah while pregnant (Ge 16:5–16); after birth of Isaac (Ge 21:9–21; Gal 4:21–31).

HAGGAI*
Post-exilic prophet who encouraged rebuilding of the temple (Ezr 5:1; 6:14; Hag 1–2).

HAIL
Ex 9:19 because the h will fall on every
Rev 8:7 there came h and fire mixed

HAIR (HAIRS HAIRY)
Lev 19:27 "Do not cut the h at the sides
Nu 6:5 they must let their h grow long.
2Sa 18:9 Absalom's h got caught in the tree.
Pr 16:31 Gray h is a crown of splendor;
20:29 gray h the splendor of the old.
Lk 7:44 her tears and wiped them with her h.
21:18 But not a h of your head will perish.
Jn 11:2 Lord and wiped his feet with her h.)
12:3 feet and wiped his feet with her h.
1Co 11:6 she might as well have her h cut off;
11:6 for a woman to have her h cut off
11:14 teach you that if a man has long h,
11:15 but that if a woman has long h, it is
11:15 For long h is given to her as
Rev 1:14 The h on his head was white like

HAIRS (HAIR)
Mt 10:30 even the very h of your head are all
Lk 12:7 the very h of your head are all

HAIRY (HAIR)
Ge 27:11 brother Esau is a h man while I have

HALF
Ex 30:13 This h shekel is an offering
Jos 8:33 H of the people stood in front
1Ki 3:25 give h to one and h to the other."

1Ki 10:7 Indeed, not even h was told me;
Est 5:3 Even up to h the kingdom, it will be
Da 7:25 hands for a time, times and h a time.
Mk 6:23 give you, up to h my kingdom."

HALF-TRIBE (TRIBE)
Nu 32:33 the h of Manasseh son of Joseph

HALL
Eze 41:1 the man brought me to the main h

HALLELUJAH*
Rev 19:1 multitude in heaven shouting: "H!
19:3 "H! The smoke from her goes up
19:4 And they cried: "Amen, H!"
19:6 "H! For our Lord God Almighty reigns.

HALLOWED* (HOLY)
Mt 6:9 Father in heaven, h be your name,
Lk 11:2 " 'Father, h be your name,

HALT
Job 38:11 here is where your proud waves h'?

HAM
Son of Noah (Ge 5:32; 1Ch 1:4), father of Canaan (Ge 9:18; 10:6–20; 1Ch 1:8–16). Saw Noah's nakedness (Ge 9:20–27).

HAMAN
Agagite nobleman honored by Xerxes (Est 3:1–2). Plotted to exterminate the Jews because of Mordecai (Est 3:3–15). Forced to honor Mordecai (Est 5–6). Plot exposed by Esther (Est 5:1–8; 7:1–8). Hanged (Est 7:9–10).

HAMPERED*
Pr 4:12 you walk, your steps will not be h;

HAND (HANDED HANDFUL HANDIWORK HANDS OPENHANDED)
Ge 24:2 he had, "Put your h under my thigh.
47:29 eyes, put your h under my thigh
Ex 13:3 you out of it with a mighty h.
15:6 Your right h, LORD,
33:22 my h until I have passed by.
Dt 12:7 everything you have put your h to,
1Ki 8:42 your mighty h and your outstretched
13:4 the h he stretched out toward
1Ch 29:14 you only what comes from your h.
29:16 Holy Name comes from your h,
2Ch 6:15 with your h you have fulfilled it—
Ne 4:17 materials did their work with one h
Job 40:4 I put my h over my mouth.
Ps 16:8 With him at my right h, I will not be
32:4 and night your h was heavy on me;
37:24 LORD upholds them with his h.
44:3 it was your right h, your arm,
45:9 at your right h is the royal bride
63:8 your right h upholds me.
75:8 In the h of the LORD is a cup full
91:7 ten thousand at your right h, but it
98:1 his right h and his holy arm have
109:31 he stands at the right h of the needy,
110:1 "Sit at my right h until I make your
137:5 may my right h forget its skill.
139:10 even there your h will guide me,
145:16 You open your h and satisfy
Pr 27:16 the wind or grasping oil with the h.
Ecc 9:10 Whatever your h finds to do, do it
Isa 40:12 the waters in the hollow of his h,
41:13 God who takes hold of your right h
44:5 still others will write on their h,
48:13 My own h laid the foundations
64:8 we are all the work of your h.
La 3:3 he has turned his h against me again
Da 10:10 A h touched me and set me
Jnh 4:11 people who cannot tell their right h
Hab 3:4 rays flashed from his h, where his
Mt 5:30 And if your right h causes you
6:3 h know what your right h is doing,
12:10 a man with a shriveled h was there.
18:8 If your h or your foot causes you
22:44 my right h until I put your enemies
26:64 at the right h of the Mighty One
Mk 3:1 a man with a shriveled h was there.
9:43 If your h causes you to stumble,
12:36 my right h until I put your enemies
16:19 *sat at the right h of God.*
Lk 6:6 there whose right h was shriveled.
20:42 said to my Lord: "Sit at my right h
22:69 at the right h of the mighty God.
Jn 10:28 one will snatch them out of my h.
10:27 Reach out your h and put it into my h.
Ac 7:55 Jesus standing at the right h of God.
1Co 12:15 "Because I am not a h, I do not

Heb 1: 13 "Sit at my right **h** until I make your

HANDED (HAND)
1Ti 1: 20 whom I have **h** over to Satan to be

HANDFUL (HAND)
Ecc 4: 6 Better one **h** with tranquillity than

HANDIWORK (HAND)
Eph 2: 10 For we are God's **h**,

HANDLE (HANDLES)
Col 2: 21 "Do not **h**! Do not taste!

HANDLES (HANDLE)
2Ti 2: 15 who correctly **h** the word of truth.

HANDS (HAND)
Ge 27: 22 but the **h** are the **h** of Esau."
Ex 17: 11 As long as Moses held up his **h**,
     29: 10 his sons shall lay their **h** on its head.
Dt 6: 8 Tie them as symbols on your **h**
Jdg 7: 6 lapped with their **h** to their mouths.
2Ki 11: 12 and the people clapped their **h**
2Ch 6: 4 his **h** has fulfilled what he promised
Ps 22: 16 they pierce my **h** and my feet.
     24: 4 Those who have clean **h** and a pure
     31: 5 Into your **h** I commit my spirit;
     31: 15 My times are in your **h**;
     47: 1 Clap your **h**, all you nations;
     63: 4 and in your name I will lift up my **h**.
Pr 10: 4 Lazy **h** make for poverty,
     21: 25 because their **h** refuse to work.
     31: 13 and flax and works with eager **h**.
     31: 20 poor and extends her **h** to the needy.
Ecc 5: 15 toil that they can carry in their **h**.
     10: 18 because of idle **h**, the house leaks.
Isa 11: 8 young children will put their **h**
     35: 3 Strengthen the feeble **h**,
     49: 16 engraved you on the palms of my **h**;
     55: 12 trees of the field will clap their **h**.
     65: 2 out my **h** to an obstinate people,
La 3: 41 hearts and our **h** to God in heaven,
     23: 46 into your **h** I commit my spirit."
Lk 18: 15 for him to place his **h** on them.
Ac 6: 6 prayed and laid their **h** on them.
     8: 18 at the laying on of the apostles' **h**,
     13: 3 they placed their **h** on them and sent
     19: 6 When Paul placed his **h** on them,
     28: 8 placed his **h** on him and healed him.
1Th 4: 11 own business and work with your **h**,
1Ti 2: 8 lifting up holy **h** without anger
     4: 14 body of elders laid their **h** on you.
     5: 22 not be hasty in the laying on of **h**,
2Ti 1: 6 you through the laying on of my **h**.
Heb 6: 2 the laying on of **h**, the resurrection
Rev 13: 16 to receive a mark on their right **h**

HANDSOME*
Ge 39: 6 Now Joseph was well-built and **h**,
1Sa 9: 2 a son named Saul, as **h** a young man
     16: 12 a fine appearance and **h** features.
     17: 42 glowing with health and **h**, and he
2Sa 14: 25 for his **h** appearance as Absalom.
1Ki 1: 6 also very **h** and was born next
SS 1: 16 How **h** you are, my beloved!
Eze 23: 6 all of them **h** young men,
     23: 12 horsemen, all **h** young men.
     23: 23 Assyrians with them, **h** young men.
Da 1: 4 men without any physical defect, **h**,
Zec 11: 3 the **h** price at which they valued me!

HANG (HANGED HANGING HUNG)
Mt 22: 40 and the Prophets **h** on these two

HANGED (HANG)
Mt 27: 5 Then he went away and **h** himself.

HANGING (HANG)
Ac 10: 39 They killed him by **h** him

HANNAH*
Wife of Elkanah, mother of Samuel (1Sa 1). Prayer at dedication of Samuel (1Sa 2:1–10). Blessed (1Sa 2:18–21).

HAPPIER* (HAPPY)
Ecc 4: 1 already died, are **h** than the living,
Mt 18: 13 he is **h** about that one sheep than
1Co 7: 40 she is **h** if she stays as she is—

HAPPINESS* (HAPPY)
Dt 24: 5 bring **h** to the wife he has married.
Est 8: 16 For the Jews it was a time of **h**
Job 7: 7 my eyes will never see **h** again.
Ecc 2: 26 wisdom and **h**, but to the sinner
Mt 25: 21 Come and share your master's **h**!'
     25: 23 Come and share your master's **h**!'

HAPPY* (HAPPIER HAPPINESS)
Ge 30: 13 Then Leah said, "How **h** I am!
     30: 13 The women will call me **h**."
1Ki 4: 20 they drank and they were **h**.
     10: 8 How **h** your people must be! How **h**
2Ch 9: 7 How **h** your people must be! How **h**
Est 5: 9 Haman went out that day **h**
Ps 68: 3 may they be **h** and joyful.
     113: 9 her home as a **h** mother of children.
     137: 8 **h** are those who repay you
     137: 9 **H** are those who seize your infants
Pr 15: 13 A **h** heart makes the face cheerful,
Ecc 3: 12 better for people than to be **h**
     5: 19 their lot and be **h** in their toil—
     7: 14 When times are good, be **h**;
     11: 9 young, be **h** while you are young,
Jnh 4: 6 Jonah was very **h** about the gourd.
Zec 8: 19 occasions and **h** festivals for Judah.
1Co 7: 30 those who are **h**, as if they were not;
2Co 7: 9 yet now I am **h**, not because you
     7: 13 delighted to see how **h** Titus was,
Jas 5: 13 Is anyone **h**? Let them sing songs

HARD (HARDEN HARDENED HARDENING HARDENS HARDER HARDSHIP HARDSHIPS)
Ge 18: 14 Is anything too **h** for the LORD?
1Ki 10: 1 to test Solomon with **h** questions.
Pr 14: 23 All **h** work brings a profit, but mere
Jer 32: 17 Nothing is too **h** for you.
Zec 7: 12 They made their hearts as **h** as flint
Mt 19: 23 it is **h** for the rich to enter
Mk 10: 5 "It was because your hearts were **h**
Jn 6: 60 disciples said, "This is a **h** teaching.
Ac 20: 35 of **h** work we must help the weak,
     26: 14 It is **h** for you to kick against
Ro 16: 12 woman who has worked very **h**
1Co 4: 12 We work **h** with our own hands.
2Co 6: 5 in **h** work, sleepless nights
1Th 5: 12 those who work **h** among you,
Rev 2: 2 your **h** work and your perseverance.

HARDEN (HARD)
Ex 4: 21 I will **h** his heart so that he will not
Ps 95: 8 "Do not **h** your hearts as you did
Pr 28: 14 who **h** their hearts fall into trouble.
Ro 9: 18 and he hardens whom he wants to **h**.
Heb 3: 8 do not **h** your hearts as you did

HARDENED (HARD)
Ex 10: 20 But the LORD **h** Pharaoh's heart,
Jn 12: 40 their eyes and **h** their hearts,

HARDENING* (HARD)
Ro 11: 25 Israel has experienced a **h** in part
Eph 4: 18 in them due to the **h** of their hearts.

HARDENS* (HARD)
Ro 9: 18 and he **h** whom he wants to harden.

HARDER (HARD)
1Co 15: 10 I worked **h** than all of them—
2Co 11: 23 I have worked much **h**,

HARDHEARTED* (HEART)
Dt 15: 7 do not be **h** or tightfisted toward

HARDSHIP (HARD)
Ro 8: 35 Shall trouble or **h** or persecution
1Co 13: 3 give over my body ⸳ to **h**,
2Ti 4: 5 endure **h**, do the work
Heb 12: 7 Endure **h** as discipline;

HARDSHIPS (HARD)
Ac 14: 22 "We must go through many **h**
2Co 6: 4 in troubles, **h** and distresses;
     12: 10 in insults, in **h**, in persecutions,
Rev 2: 3 and have endured **h** for my name,

HARM (HARMFUL)
1Ch 16: 22 do my prophets no **h**."
Ps 105: 15 do my prophets no **h**."
     121: 6 the sun will not **h** you by day,
Pr 3: 29 Do not plot **h** against your neighbor,
     3: 36 who fail to find me **h** themselves;
     12: 21 No **h** overtakes the righteous,
     31: 12 good, not **h**, all the days of her life.
Jer 10: 5 they can do no **h** nor can they do
     29: 11 to prosper you and not to **h** you,
Ro 13: 10 Love does no **h** to its neighbor.
1Co 11: 17 your meetings do more **h** than good.
1Jn 5: 18 and the evil one cannot **h** them.

HARMFUL (HARM)
1Th 5: 22 reject whatever is **h**.

HARMONY*
Zec 6: 13 there will be **h** between the two.'
Ro 12: 16 Live in **h** with one another.

2Co 6: 15 What **h** is there between Christ

HARP (HARPS)
Ps 33: 2 Praise the LORD with the **h**;
     98: 5 with the **h** and the sound of singing,
     150: 3 praise him with the **h** and lyre,
Rev 5: 8 Each one had a **h** and they were

HARPS (HARP)
Ps 137: 2 There on the poplars we hung our **h**,

HARSH
Pr 15: 1 wrath, but a **h** word stirs up anger.
Col 3: 19 and their **h** treatment of the body,
     3: 19 wives and do not be **h** with them.
1Pe 2: 18 but also to those who are **h**.

HARVEST (HARVESTERS)
Ge 8: 22 seedtime and **h**, cold and heat,
Ex 23: 16 "Celebrate the Festival of **H**
Dt 16: 15 God will bless you in all your **h**
Pr 10: 5 who sleeps during **h** is a disgraceful
Jer 8: 20 "The **h** is past, the summer has
Joel 3: 13 Swing the sickle, for the **h** is ripe.
Mt 9: 37 "The **h** is plentiful but the workers
Lk 10: 2 He told them, "The **h** is plentiful,
Jn 4: 35 at the fields! They are ripe for **h**.
1Co 9: 11 if we reap a material **h** from you?
2Co 9: 10 seed and will enlarge the **h** of your
Gal 6: 9 at the proper time we will reap a **h**
Heb 12: 11 it produces a **h** of righteousness
Jas 3: 18 in peace reap a **h** of righteousness.
Rev 14: 15 come, for the **h** of the earth is ripe."

HARVESTERS (HARVEST)
Ru 2: 3 and began to glean behind the **h**.

HASTE (HASTEN HASTY)
Ex 12: 11 Eat it in **h**; it is the LORD's
Pr 21: 5 lead to profit as surely as **h** leads
     29: 20 you see someone who speaks in **h**?

HASTEN (HASTE)
Ps 70: 1 **H**, O God, to save me;
     119: 60 I will **h** and not delay to obey your

HASTY* (HASTE)
Pr 19: 2 how much more will **h** feet miss
Ecc 5: 2 do not be **h** in your heart to utter
1Ti 5: 22 Do not be **h** in the laying

HATE (GOD-HATERS HATED HATES HATING HATRED)
Lev 19: 17 " 'Do not **h** a fellow Israelite
Ps 5: 5 You **h** all who do wrong;
     36: 2 too much to detect or **h** their sin.
     45: 7 righteousness and **h** wickedness;
     97: 10 those who love the LORD **h** evil,
     119: 104 therefore I **h** every wrong path.
     119: 163 I **h** and detest falsehood but I love
     139: 21 Do I not **h** those who **h** you,
Pr 8: 13 To fear the LORD is to **h** evil;
     9: 8 rebuke mockers or they will **h** you;
     13: 5 The righteous **h** what is false,
     13: 24 spare the rod **h** their children,
     15: 27 those who **h** bribes will live.
     29: 10 The bloodthirsty **h** people
Ecc 3: 8 a time to love and a time to **h**,
Isa 61: 8 I **h** robbery and wrongdoing;
Eze 35: 6 Since you did not **h** bloodshed,
Am 5: 15 **H** evil, love good;
Mal 2: 16 "I **h** divorce," says the LORD
Mt 5: 43 your neighbor and **h** your enemy.'
     10: 22 Everyone will **h** you because of me,
Lk 6: 27 do good to those who **h** you,
     14: 26 and does not **h** father and mother,
Jn 3: 20 All those who do evil **h** the light,
     12: 25 while those who **h** their life
Ro 7: 15 What is evil; cling to what is
1Jn 2: 9 but **h** a fellow believer
     4: 20 If we say we love God yet **h**

HATED (HATE)
Pr 25: 17 much of you, and you will be **h**.
Mal 1: 3 Esau I have **h**, and I have turned
Jn 15: 18 keep in mind that it **h** me first.
Ro 9: 13 "Jacob I loved, but Esau I **h**."
Eph 5: 29 people have never **h** their own
     9: 1 righteousness and **h** wickedness;

HATES (HATE)
Pr 6: 16 There are six things the LORD **h**,
     26: 28 A lying tongue **h** those it hurts,

HATING (HATE)
Jude : 23 **h** even the clothing stained

HATRED (HATE)
Pr 10: 12 **H** stirs up dissension, but love
  15: 17 love than a fattened calf with **h**.

HAUGHTY
Pr 6: 17 **h** eyes, a lying tongue,
  16: 18 destruction, a **h** spirit before a fall.
  18: 12 Before a downfall the heart is **h**,

HAVEN
Ps 107: 30 he guided them to their desired **h**.

HAY
1Co 3: 12 costly stones, wood, **h** or straw,

HEAD (HEADS HOTHEADED)
Ge 3: 15 he will crush your **h**, and you will
Nu 6: 5 no razor may be used on their **h**.
Jdg 16: 17 If my **h** were shaved, my strength
1Sa 9: 2 he was a **h** taller than anyone else.
Ps 23: 5 You anoint my **h** with oil;
  133: 2 is like precious oil poured on the **h**,
Pr 10: 6 Blessings crown the **h**
  25: 22 will heap burning coals on his **h**,
Isa 59: 17 and the helmet of salvation on his **h**;
Eze 33: 4 their blood will be on their own **h**.
Mt 8: 20 of Man has no place to lay his **h**."
Jn 19: 2 crown of thorns and put it on his **h**.
Ro 12: 20 will heap burning coals on his **h**."
1Co 11: 3 is man, and the **h** of Christ is God.
  11: 5 her **h** uncovered dishonors her **h**—
  12: 21 And the **h** cannot say to the feet,
Eph 1: 22 him to be **h** over everything
   5: 23 the husband is the **h** of the wife as
Col 1: 18 And he is the **h** of the body,
2Ti 4: 5 keep your **h** in all situations,
Rev 14: 14 man with a crown of gold on his **h**
  19: 12 fire, and on his **h** are many crowns.

HEADS (HEAD)
Lev 26: 13 you to walk with **h** held high.
Ps 22: 7 they hurl insults, shaking their **h**.
  24: 7 Lift up your **h**, you gates;
Isa 35: 10 everlasting joy will crown their **h**.
  51: 11 everlasting joy will crown their **h**.
Mt 27: 39 insults at him, shaking their **h**
Lk 21: 28 stand up and lift up your **h**,
Ac 18: 6 "Your blood be on your own **h**!
Rev 4: 4 and had crowns of gold on their **h**.

HEAL* (HEALED HEALING HEALS)
Nu 12: 13 the LORD, "Please, God, **h** her!"
Dt 32: 39 I have wounded and I will **h**, and no
2Ki 20: 5 and seen your tears; I will **h** you.
  20: 8 the sign that the LORD will **h** me
2Ch 7: 14 their sin and will **h** their land.
Job 5: 18 he injures, but his hands also **h**.
Ps 6: 2 **h** me, LORD, for my bones are in
  41: 4 **h** me, for I have sinned against
Ecc 3: 3 a time to kill and a time to **h**, a time
Isa 19: 22 he will strike them and **h** them.
  19: 22 respond to their pleas and **h** them.
  57: 18 seen their ways, but I will **h** them;
  57: 19 "And I will **h** them."
Jer 17: 14 Heal me, LORD, and I will be healed;
  30: 17 you to health and **h** your wounds,'
  33: 6 I will **h** my people and will let them
La 2: 13 as deep as the sea. Who can **h** you?
Hos 5: 13 to cure you, not able to **h** your sores.
   6: 1 torn us to pieces but he will **h** us;
   7: 1 whenever I would **h** Israel, the sins
  14: 4 "I will **h** their waywardness
Na 3: 19 Nothing can **h** you; your wound is
Zec 11: 16 or **h** the injured, or feed the healthy,
Mt 8: 7 to him, "Shall I come and **h** him?"
  10: 1 and to **h** every disease and sickness.
  10: 8 **H** the sick, raise the dead,
  12: 10 "Is it lawful to **h** on the Sabbath?"
  13: 15 and turn, and I would **h** them.'
  17: 16 but they could not **h** him."
Mk 3: 2 if he would **h** him on the Sabbath.
   6: 5 on a few sick people and **h** them.
Lk 4: 23 'Physician, **h** yourself!'
   5: 17 Lord was with Jesus to **h** the sick.
   6: 7 to see if he would **h** on the Sabbath.
   7: 3 him to come and **h** his servant.
   8: 43 years, but no one could **h** her.
   9: 2 kingdom of God and to **h** the sick.
  10: 9 **H** the sick who are there and tell
  14: 3 "Is it lawful to **h** on the Sabbath
Jn 4: 47 begged him to come and **h** his son,
  12: 40 and I would **h** them."
Ac 4: 30 Stretch out your hand to **h**
  28: 27 and turn, and I would **h** them."

HEALED* (HEAL)
Ge 20: 17 and God **h** Abimelek, his wife
Ex 21: 19 see that the victim is completely **h**.
Lev 13: 37 grown in it, the affected person is **h**.
  14: 3 If they have been **h** of their defiling
  14: 3 they were in camp until they were **h**.
Jos 5: 8 Then you will be **h**, and you will
1Sa 6: 3 'I have **h** this water.
2Ki 2: 21 'I have **h** this water.
2Ch 30: 20 heard Hezekiah and **h** the people.
Ps 30: 2 to you for help, and you **h** me.
  107: 20 He sent out his word and **h** them;
Isa 6: 10 their hearts, and turn and be **h**."
  53: 5 and by his wounds we are **h**.
Jer 14: 19 afflicted us so that we cannot be **h**?
  17: 14 Heal me, LORD, and I will be **h**;
  51: 8 for her pain; perhaps she can be **h**.
  51: 9 " 'We would have **h** Babylon, but she cannot be **h**,
Eze 30: 21 It has not been bound up to be **h**
  34: 4 strengthened the weak or **h** the sick
Hos 11: 3 did not realize it was I who **h** them.
Mt 4: 24 and the paralyzed; and he **h** them.
   8: 8 the word, and my servant will be **h**.
   8: 13 his servant was **h** at that very hour.
   8: 16 with a word and **h** all the sick.
   9: 21 I only touch his cloak, I will be **h**."
   9: 22 he said, "your faith has **h** you."
   9: 22 And the woman was **h**
  12: 15 and he **h** all who were ill.
  12: 22 and Jesus **h** him, so that he could
  14: 14 on them and **h** their sick.
  14: 36 and all who touched him were **h**.
  15: 28 her daughter was **h** from that very
  15: 30 laid them at his feet; and he **h** them.
  17: 18 and he was **h** from that moment.
  19: 2 followed him, and he **h** them there.
  21: 14 to him at the temple, and he **h** them.
Mk 1: 34 and Jesus **h** many who had various
   3: 10 For he had **h** many, so that those
   5: 23 hands on her so that she will be **h**
   5: 28 I just touch his clothes, I will be **h**."
   5: 34 "Daughter, your faith has **h** you.
   6: 13 sick people with oil and **h** them.
   6: 56 and all who touched him were **h**.
  10: 52 said Jesus, "your faith has **h** you."
Lk 4: 40 his hands on each one, he **h** them.
   5: 15 him and to be **h** of their sicknesses.
   6: 18 him and to be **h** of their diseases.
   7: 7 the word, and my servant will be **h**.
   8: 47 and how she had been instantly **h**.
   8: 48 "Daughter, your faith has **h** you.
   8: 50 just believe, and she will be **h**."
   9: 11 and **h** those who needed healing.
   9: 42 the boy and gave him back to his
  13: 14 Indignant because Jesus had **h**
  13: 14 So come and be **h** on those days,
  14: 4 he **h** him and sent him on his way.
  17: 15 when he saw he was **h**, came back,
  18: 42 your faith has **h** you."
  22: 51 he touched the man's ear and **h** him.
Jn 5: 10 said to the man who had been **h**,
   5: 13 The man who was **h** had no idea
Ac 3: 6 **h** him, as you can all see.
   4: 9 and are being asked how he was **h**,
   4: 14 that this man stands before you **h**.
   4: 14 man who had been **h** standing there
   4: 22 who was miraculously **h** was over
   5: 16 evil spirits, and all of them were **h**.
   8: 7 who were paralyzed or lame were **h**.
  14: 9 at him, saw that he had faith to be **h**
  28: 8 placed his hands on him and **h** him.
Heb 12: 13 may not be disabled, but rather **h**.
Jas 5: 16 for each other so that you may be **h**.
1Pe 2: 24 "by his wounds you have been **h**."
Rev 13: 3 but the fatal wound had been **h**.
  13: 12 whose fatal wound had been **h**.

HEALING* (HEAL)
2Ch 28: 15 sandals, food and drink, and balm.
Pr 12: 18 but the tongue of the wise brings **h**.
  13: 17 but a trustworthy envoy brings **h**.
  16: 24 sweet to the soul and **h** to the bones.
Isa 58: 8 and your **h** will quickly appear;
Jer 8: 15 for a time of **h** but there is only
   8: 22 is there no **h** for the wound of my
  14: 19 for a time of **h** but there is only
  30: 12 is incurable, your injury beyond **h**.
  30: 13 remedy for your sore, no **h** for you.
  33: 6 I will bring health and **h** to it;
  46: 11 there is no **h** for you.
Eze 47: 12 for food and their leaves for **h**."
Mal 4: 2 righteousness will rise with **h** in its

Mt 4: 23 and **h** every disease and sickness
   9: 35 of the kingdom and **h** every disease
Lk 6: 19 coming from him and **h** them all.
   9: 6 news and **h** people everywhere.
   9: 11 and healed those who needed **h**.
  13: 32 out demons and **h** people today
Jn 6: 2 he had performed by **h** the sick.
   7: 23 me for a man's whole body
Ac 10: 38 **h** all who were under the power
1Co 12: 9 to another gifts of **h** by that one
  12: 28 miracles, then gifts of **h**, of helping,
  12: 30 Do all have gifts of **h**? Do all speak
Rev 22: 2 the tree are for the **h** of the nations.

HEALS* (HEAL)
Ex 15: 26 for I am the LORD, who **h** you."
Lev 13: 18 has a boil on their skin and it **h**,
Ps 103: 3 all your sins and **h** all your diseases,
  147: 3 He **h** the brokenhearted and binds
Isa 30: 26 and **h** the wounds he inflicted.
Ac 9: 34 said to him, "Jesus Christ **h** you.

HEALTH* (HEALTHIER HEALTHY)
1Sa 16: 12 He was glowing with **h** and had a fine
  17: 42 glowing with **h** and handsome,
  25: 6 Good **h** to you and your household!
  25: 6 And good **h** to all that is yours!
Ps 38: 3 your wrath there is no **h** in my body;
  38: 7 there is no **h** in my body.
Pr 3: 8 This will bring **h** to your body
   4: 22 them and **h** to one's whole body.
  15: 30 and good news gives **h** to the bones.
Isa 38: 16 You restored me to **h** and let me
Jer 30: 17 I will restore you to **h** and heal your
  33: 6 I will bring **h** and healing to it;
3Jn 2 I pray that you may enjoy good **h**

HEALTHIER* (HEALTH)
Da 1: 15 end of the ten days they looked **h**

HEALTHY* (HEALTH)
Ge 41: 5 Seven heads of grain, **h** and good,
  41: 7 of grain swallowed up the seven **h**,
Ps 73: 4 their bodies are **h** and strong.
Zec 11: 16 or feed the **h**, but will eat the meat
Mt 6: 22 If your eyes are **h**, your whole body
   9: 12 "It is not the **h** who need a doctor,
Mk 12: 17 "It is not the **h** who need a doctor,
Lk 5: 31 "It is not the **h** who need a doctor,
  11: 34 When your eyes are **h**, your whole body

HEAP
Pr 25: 22 this, you will **h** burning coals on his
Ro 12: 20 this, you will **h** burning coals on his

HEAR (HEARD HEARING HEARS)
Ex 15: 14 The nations will **h** and tremble;
  22: 27 I will **h**, for I am compassionate.
Nu 14: 13 "Then the Egyptians will **h** about it!
Dt 1: 16 **H** the disputes between your people
   4: 36 heaven he made you **h** his voice
   6: 4 **H**, O Israel: The LORD our God,
   9: 20 The rest of the people will **h** of this
  31: 13 must **h** it and learn to fear
Jos 7: 9 of the country will **h** about this
1Ki 8: 30 **H** the supplication of your servant
2Ki 19: 16 Give ear, LORD, and **h**;
2Ch 7: 14 then I will **h** from heaven, and I will
Job 31: 35 ("Oh, that I had someone to **h** me!
Ps 94: 9 he who fashioned the ear not **h**?
  95: 7 if only you would **h** his voice,
Ecc 7: 21 or you may **h** your servant cursing
Isa 21: 3 I am staggered by what I **h**, I am
  29: 18 day the deaf will **h** the words
  30: 21 your ears will **h** a voice behind you,
  51: 7 "H me, you who know what is
  59: 1 to save, nor his ear too dull to **h**.
  65: 24 while they are still speaking I will **h**.
Jer 5: 21 not see, who have ears but do not **h**:
Eze 33: 7 so **h** the word I speak and give them
  37: 4 bones, **h** the word of the LORD!
Mt 11: 5 the deaf **h**, the dead are raised,
  11: 15 Whoever has ears, let them **h**.
  13: 17 and to **h** what you **h** but did not **h** it.
Mk 12: 29 Jesus, "is this: 'H, O Israel:
Lk 7: 22 the deaf **h**, the dead are raised,
Jn 8: 47 The reason you do not **h** is that you
Ac 13: 7 because he wanted to **h** the word
  13: 44 whole city gathered to **h** the word
  17: 32 "We want to **h** you again on this
Ro 10: 14 those who **h** the law who are
  10: 14 how can they **h** without someone
2Ti 4: 3 what their itching ears want to **h**.
Heb 3: 7 "Today, if you **h** his voice,
Rev 1: 3 blessed are those who **h** it and take

HEARD (HEAR)

Ex	2: 24	God **h** their groaning and he
Dt	4: 32	has anything like it ever been **h** of?
2Sa	7: 22	as we have **h** with our own ears.
Job	42: 5	My ears had **h** of you but now my
Isa	40: 21	Have you not **h**? Has it not been
	40: 28	Have you not **h**? The LORD is
	66: 8	Who has ever **h** of such things?
Jer	18: 13	Who has ever **h** anything like this?
Da	10: 12	your words were **h**, and I have come
	12: 8	I **h**, but I did not understand.
Hab	3: 16	I **h** and my heart pounded, my lips
Mt	5: 21	"You have **h** that it was said
	5: 27	"You have **h** that it was said,
	5: 33	you have **h** that it was said
	5: 38	"You have **h** that it was said,
	5: 43	"You have **h** that it was said
Lk	12: 3	in the dark will be **h** in the daylight,
Jn	8: 26	what I have **h** from him I tell
Ac	6: 4	because each one **h** their own
1Co	2: 9	what no ear has **h**, and what no
2Co	12: 4	paradise and **h** inexpressible things,
1Th	2: 13	which you **h** from us, you accepted
2Ti	1: 13	What you **h** from me, keep as
Jas	1: 25	not forgetting what they have **h**,
Rev	22: 8	am the one who **h** and saw these

HEARING (HEAR)

Isa	6: 9	" 'Be ever **h**, but never
Mt	13: 14	" 'You will be ever **h** but never
Mk	4: 12	and ever **h** but never understanding;
Ac	28: 26	"You will be ever **h** but never
Ro	10: 17	faith comes from **h** the message,
1Co	12: 17	where would the sense of **h** be?

HEARS (HEAR)

Jn	5: 24	whoever **h** my word and believes
1Jn	5: 14	according to his will, he **h** us.
Rev	3: 20	If anyone **h** my voice and opens

HEART (BROKENHEARTED FAINT-HEARTED HARDHEARTED HEART'S HEARTACHE HEARTS KINDHEARTED WHOLEHEARTED WHOLEHEARTEDLY)

Ge	6: 5	of the human **h** was only evil all
Ex	4: 21	I will harden his **h** so that he will
	25: 2	everyone whose **h** prompts them
	35: 21	and whose **h** moved them came
Lev	19: 17	not hate a fellow Israelite in your **h**.
Dt	4: 9	slip from your **h** as long as you live.
	4: 29	him if you seek him with all your **h**
	6: 5	LORD your God with all your **h**
	10: 12	LORD your God with all your **h**
	11: 13	and to serve him with all your **h**
	13: 3	you love him with all your **h**
	15: 10	and do so without a grudging **h**;
	26: 16	observe them with all your **h**
	29: 18	you today whose **h** turns away
	30: 2	obey him with all your **h**
	30: 6	you may love him with all your **h**
	30: 10	LORD your God with all your **h**
Jos	22: 5	and to serve him with all your **h**
	23: 14	You know with all your **h** and soul
1Sa	10: 9	God changed Saul's **h**, and all these
	12: 20	serve the LORD with all your **h**.
	12: 24	serve him faithfully with all your **h**;
	13: 14	sought out a man after his own **h**
	14: 7	I am with you **h** and soul."
	16: 7	but the LORD looks at the **h**."
	17: 32	"Let no one lose **h** on account
1Ki	2: 4	faithfully before me with all their **h**
	3: 9	So give your servant a discerning **h**
	3: 12	give you a wise and discerning **h**,
	8: 48	they turn back to you with all their **h**
	9: 3	eyes and my **h** will always be there.
	9: 4	me faithfully with integrity of **h**
	10: 24	the wisdom God had put in his **h**.
	11: 4	his **h** was not fully devoted
	14: 8	and followed me with all his **h**,
	15: 14	Asa's **h** was fully committed
2Ki	22: 19	Because your **h** was responsive
	23: 3	and decrees with all his **h** and all his
1Ch	28: 9	for the LORD searches every **h**
2Ch	6: 38	they turn back to you with all their **h**
	7: 16	eyes and my **h** will always be there.
	15: 12	ancestors, with all their **h** and soul.
	15: 17	Asa's **h** was fully committed
	17: 6	His **h** was devoted to the ways
	22: 9	sought the LORD with all his **h**."
	34: 31	and decrees with all his **h** and all his
	36: 13	hardened his **h** and would not turn
Ezr	1: 5	everyone whose **h** God had moved—
Ne	4: 6	the people worked with all their **h**.

Job	19: 27	How my **h** yearns within me!
	22: 22	and lay up his words in your **h**.
	37: 1	"At this my **h** pounds and leaps
Ps	9: 1	praise you, LORD, with all my **h**;
	16: 9	Therefore my **h** is glad and my
	19: 14	this meditation of my **h** be pleasing
	20: 4	he give you the desire of your **h**
	24: 4	who have clean hands and a pure **h**,
	26: 2	try me, examine my **h** and my mind;
	37: 4	will give you the desires of your **h**.
	44: 21	since he knows the secrets of the **h**?
	45: 1	My **h** is stirred by a noble theme as
	51: 10	Create in me a pure **h**, O God,
	51: 17	a broken and contrite **h** you, God,
	66: 18	If I had cherished sin in my **h**,
	73: 1	to Israel, to those who are pure in **h**.
	73: 26	My flesh and my **h** may fail,
	86: 11	give me an undivided **h**, that I may
	90: 12	that we may gain a **h** of wisdom.
	97: 11	and joy on the upright in **h**.
	108: 1	My **h**, O God, is steadfast;
	109: 22	and my **h** is wounded within me.
	111: 1	LORD with all my **h** in the council
	119: 2	and seek him with all their **h**—
	119: 10	I seek you with all my **h**; do not let
	119: 11	in my **h** that I might not sin against
	119: 30	I have set my **h** on your laws.
	119: 32	for you have set my **h** free.
	119: 34	your law and obey it with all my **h**.
	119: 36	Turn my **h** toward your statutes
	119: 58	sought your face with all my **h**;
	119: 69	I keep your precepts with all my **h**.
	119: 111	they are the joy of my **h**.
	119: 112	My **h** is set on keeping your decrees
	119: 145	I call with all my **h**;
	125: 4	good, to those who are upright in **h**.
	138: 1	praise you, LORD, with all my **h**;
	139: 23	Search me, God, and know my **h**;
Pr	2: 2	applying your **h** to understanding—
	3: 1	but keep my commands in your **h**,
	3: 3	write them on the tablet of your **h**.
	3: 5	Trust in the LORD with all your **h**
	4: 4	hold of my words with all your **h**;
	4: 21	your sight, keep them within your **h**;
	4: 23	guard your **h**, for everything you do
	6: 21	Bind them always on your **h**;
	7: 3	write them on the tablet of your **h**.
	10: 8	The wise in **h** accept commands,
	13: 12	Hope deferred makes the **h** sick,
	14: 13	Even in laughter the **h** may ache,
	14: 30	A **h** at peace gives life to the body,
	15: 13	A happy **h** makes the face cheerful,
	15: 15	the cheerful **h** has a continual feast.
	15: 28	The **h** of the righteous weighs its
	15: 30	eyes brings joy to the **h**, and good
	17: 22	A cheerful **h** is good medicine,
	20: 9	can say, "I have kept my **h** pure;
	22: 11	One who loves a pure **h** and who
	22: 17	apply your **h** to what I teach,
	22: 18	when you keep them in your **h**
	23: 15	if your **h** is wise, then my **h** will be
	23: 19	and set your **h** on the right path:
	23: 26	give me your **h** and let your eyes
	24: 17	stumble, do not let your **h** rejoice,
	27: 19	the face, so one's life reflects the **h**.
Ecc	3: 11	also set eternity in the human **h**;
	5: 2	your **h** to utter anything before God.
	8: 5	and the wise **h** will know the proper
	11: 10	banish anxiety from your **h** and cast
SS	3: 1	bed I looked for the one my **h** loves;
	4: 9	You have stolen my **h**, my sister,
	5: 2	I slept but my **h** was awake. Listen!
	5: 4	my **h** began to pound for him.
	8: 6	Place me like a seal over your **h**,
Isa	6: 10	Make the **h** of this people calloused;
	40: 11	arms and carries them close to his **h**;
	51: 7	who have taken my instruction to **h**:
	57: 15	and to revive the **h** of the contrite.
	66: 14	this, your **h** will rejoice and you will
Jer	3: 15	give you shepherds after my own **h**,
	4: 14	wash the evil from your **h** and be
	9: 26	of Israel is uncircumcised in **h**."
	17: 9	The **h** is deceitful above all things
	20: 9	his word is in my **h** like a fire, a fire
	24: 7	I will give them a **h** to know me,
	29: 13	when you seek me with all your **h**.
	32: 39	I will give them singleness of **h**
	32: 41	plant them in this land with all my **h**
	51: 46	Do not lose **h** or be afraid
Eze	11: 19	I will give them an undivided **h**
	18: 31	and get a new **h** and a new spirit.
	36: 26	I will give you a new **h** and put

Eze	44: 7	foreigners uncircumcised in **h**
Joel	2: 12	"return to me with all your **h**,
	2: 13	Rend your **h** and not your garments.
Zep	3: 14	Be glad and rejoice with all your **h**,
Mt	5: 8	Blessed are the pure in **h**, for they
	5: 28	adultery with her in his **h**.
	6: 21	treasure is, there your **h** will be also.
	11: 29	for I am gentle and humble in **h**,
	12: 34	overflow of the **h** the mouth speaks.
	13: 15	For this people's **h** has become
	15: 18	out of the mouth come from the **h**,
	15: 19	For out of the **h** come evil thoughts,
	18: 35	a brother or sister from your **h**."
	22: 37	the Lord your God with all your **h**
Mk	11: 23	do not doubt in your **h** but believe
	12: 30	the Lord your God with all your **h**
	12: 33	To love him with all your **h**, with all
Lk	2: 19	things and pondered them in her **h**.
	2: 51	treasured all these things in her **h**.
	6: 45	out of the good stored up in their **h**,
	6: 45	overflow of the **h** the mouth speaks.
	8: 15	for those with a noble and good **h**,
	10: 27	the Lord your God with all your **h**
	12: 34	treasure is, there your **h** will be also.
Ac	1: 24	"Lord, you know everyone's **h**.
	2: 37	they were cut to the **h** and said
	4: 32	All the believers were one in **h**
	8: 21	because your **h** is not right before
	15: 8	who knows the **h**, showed that he
	16: 14	The Lord opened her **h** to respond
	28: 27	For this people's **h** has become
Ro	2: 29	is circumcision of the **h**
	6: 17	to obey from your **h** the pattern
	10: 9	in your **h** that God raised him
	10: 10	it is with your **h** that you believe
2Co	2: 4	anguish of **h** and with many tears,
	4: 1	have this ministry, we do not lose **h**.
	4: 16	Therefore we do not lose **h**.
	9: 7	you have decided in your **h** to give,
Eph	1: 18	eyes of your **h** may be enlightened
	5: 19	music from your **h** to the Lord,
	6: 5	and with sincerity of **h**, just as you
	6: 6	doing the will of God from your **h**.
Php	1: 7	since I have you in my **h** and,
Col	2: 2	is that they may be encouraged in **h**
	3: 22	with sincerity of **h** and reverence
	3: 23	you do, work at it with all your **h**,
1Ti	1: 5	which comes from a pure **h**
2Ti	2: 22	call on the Lord out of a pure **h**.
Phm	: 12	who is my very **h**—back to you.
	: 20	in the Lord; refresh my **h** in Christ.
Heb	4: 12	the thoughts and attitudes of the **h**.
1Pe	1: 22	love one another deeply, from the **h**.

HEART'S* (HEART)

2Ch	1: 11	"Since this is your **h** desire and you
Ps	21: 2	You have granted him his **h** desire
Jer	15: 16	they were my joy and my **h** delight,
Eze	24: 25	delight of their eyes, their **h** desire,
Ro	10: 1	my **h** desire and prayer to God

HEARTACHE* (HEART)

Pr	15: 13	cheerful, but **h** crushes the spirit.

HEARTLESS*

La	4: 3	people have become **h** like ostriches

HEARTS (HEART)

Lev	26: 41	their uncircumcised **h** are humbled
Dt	6: 6	I give you today are to be on your **h**.
	10: 16	Circumcise your **h**, therefore,
	11: 18	Fix these words of mine in your **h**
	30: 6	your God will circumcise your **h**
Jos	11: 20	himself who hardened their **h**
	24: 23	you and yield your **h** to the LORD,
1Sa	7: 3	to the LORD with all your **h**,
	10: 26	by valiant men whose **h** God had
2Sa	15: 6	so he stole the **h** of the people
1Ki	8: 39	since you know their **h** (for you
	8: 61	may your **h** be fully committed
	18: 37	you are turning their **h** back again."
1Ch	29: 18	and keep their **h** loyal to you.
2Ch	6: 30	since you know their **h** (for you
	11: 16	Israel who set their **h** on seeking
	29: 31	all whose **h** were willing brought
Ps	7: 9	God who probes minds and **h**.
	14: 1	Fools say in their **h**, "There is no
	33: 21	In him our **h** rejoice, for we trust
	37: 31	The law of their God is in their **h**;
	53: 1	Fools say in their **h**, "There is no
	62: 8	pour out your **h** to him, for God is
	95: 8	"Do not harden your **h** as you did
	112: 7	their **h** are steadfast,
	112: 8	Their **h** are secure, they will have no

Pr 16: 23 The **h** of the wise make their
Isa 26: 8 and renown are the desire of our **h**.
29: 13 lips, but their **h** are far from me.
35: 4 say to those with fearful **h**,
63: 17 harden our **h** so we do not revere
65: 14 will sing out of the joy of their **h**,
Jer 4: 19 circumcise your **h**, you people
12: 2 on their lips but far from their **h**.
17: 1 on the tablets of their **h**
31: 33 their minds and write it on their **h**.
Mal 4: 6 He will turn the **h** of the parents
Mt 15: 8 lips, but their **h** are far from me.
Mk 6: 52 their **h** were hardened.
7: 6 lips, but their **h** are far from me.
7: 21 out of your **h**, come evil thoughts,
Lk 1: 17 to turn the **h** of the parents to their
16: 15 of others, but God knows your **h**.
24: 32 "Were not our **h** burning within us
Jn 5: 42 not have the love of God in your **h**.
14: 1 "Do not let your **h** be troubled.
14: 27 Do not let your **h** be troubled and do
Ac 7: 51 Your **h** and ears are still
11: 23 true to the Lord with all their **h**.
15: 9 for he purified their **h** by faith.
28: 27 understand with their **h** and turn,
Ro 1: 21 and their foolish **h** were darkened.
2: 15 of the law are written on their **h**,
5: 5 into our **h** through the Holy Spirit,
8: 27 who searches our **h** knows the mind
1Co 14: 25 the secrets of their **h** are laid bare.
2Co 1: 22 put his Spirit in our **h** as a deposit,
3: 2 written on our **h**, known and read
3: 3 of stone but on tablets of human **h**.
4: 6 shine in our **h** to give us the light
6: 11 and opened wide our **h** to you.
6: 13 open wide your **h** also.
7: 2 Make room for us in your **h**.
Gal 4: 6 sent the Spirit of his Son into our **h**,
Eph 3: 17 may dwell in your **h** through faith.
Php 4: 7 will guard your **h** and your minds
Col 3: 1 Christ, set your **h** on things above,
3: 15 the peace of Christ rule in your **h**,
3: 16 to God with gratitude in your **h**.
1Th 2: 4 people but God, who tests our **h**.
3: 13 May he strengthen your **h**
2Th 2: 17 encourage your **h** and strengthen
Phm : 7 have refreshed the **h** of the Lord's
Heb 3: 8 do not harden your **h** as you did
8: 10 minds and write them on their **h**.
10: 16 I will put my laws in their **h**, and I
10: 22 having our **h** sprinkled to cleanse us
Jas 4: 8 you sinners, and purify your **h**,
2Pe 1: 19 and the morning star rises in your **h**.
1Jn 3: 20 know that God is greater than our **h**,

HEAT
2Pe 3: 12 and the elements will melt in the **h**.

HEAVEN (HEAVENLY HEAVENS HEAVENWARD)
Ge 14: 19 Most High, Creator of **h** and earth.
28: 12 with its top reaching to **h**,
Ex 16: 4 "I will rain down bread from **h**
20: 22 that I have spoken to you from **h**:
Dt 26: 15 Look down from **h**, your holy
30: 12 "Who will ascend into **h** to get it
1Ki 8: 27 even the highest **h**, cannot contain
8: 30 Hear from **h**, your dwelling place,
22: 19 the host of **h** standing around him
2Ki 2: 1 take Elijah up to **h** in a whirlwind,
19: 15 You have made **h** and earth.
2Ch 7: 14 then I will hear from **h**, and I will
Isa 14: 12 How you have fallen from **h**,
66: 1 "**H** is my throne, and the earth is
Da 7: 13 coming with the clouds of **h**.
Mt 3: 2 the kingdom of **h** has come near.
3: 16 At that moment **h** was opened,
4: 17 the kingdom of **h** has come near.
5: 12 because great is your reward in **h**,
5: 19 be called great in the kingdom of **h**.
6: 9 " 'Our Father in **h**, hallowed be
6: 10 will be done, on earth as it is in **h**.
6: 20 up for yourselves treasures in **h**,
7: 21 will enter the kingdom of **h**,
16: 19 bind on earth will be bound in **h**,
18: 3 will never enter the kingdom of **h**.
18: 18 bind on earth will be bound in **h**,
19: 14 the kingdom of **h** belongs to such as
19: 21 and you will have treasure in **h**.
19: 23 the rich to enter the kingdom of **h**.
23: 13 the kingdom of **h** in people's faces.
24: 35 **H** and earth will pass away, but my
26: 64 and coming on the clouds of **h**."

Mt 28: 18 "All authority in **h** and on earth has
Mk 1: 10 he saw **h** being torn open
10: 21 and you will have treasure in **h**.
13: 31 **H** and earth will pass away, but my
14: 62 and coming on the clouds of **h**."
16: 19 *he was taken up into **h***
Lk 3: 21 as he was praying, **h** was opened
10: 18 saw Satan fall like lightning from **h**.
10: 20 that your names are written in **h**."
12: 33 a treasure in **h** that will never fail,
15: 7 **h** over one sinner who repents than
18: 22 and you will have treasure in **h**.
21: 33 **H** and earth will pass away, but my
24: 51 left them and was taken up into **h**.
Jn 3: 13 into **h** except the one who came
6: 38 I have come down from **h** not to do
12: 28 Then a voice came from **h**, "I have
Ac 1: 11 who has been taken from you into **h**,
7: 49 " '**H** is my throne, and the earth is
7: 55 looked up to **h** and saw the glory
9: 3 a light from **h** flashed around him.
26: 19 not disobedient to the vision from **h**.
Ro 10: 6 heart, 'Who will ascend into **h**?' "
1Co 15: 47 of the earth; the second man is of **h**.
2Co 5: 1 an eternal house in **h**, not built
12: 2 ago was caught up to the third **h**.
Eph 1: 10 to bring unity to all things in **h**
Php 2: 10 in **h** and on earth and under
3: 20 But our citizenship is in **h**.
Col 1: 16 things in **h** and on earth,
4: 1 that you also have a Master in **h**.
1Th 1: 10 and to wait for his Son from **h**,
4: 16 himself will come down from **h**,
Heb 1: 3 at the right hand of the Majesty in **h**.
4: 14 priest who has ascended into **h**,
8: 5 a copy and shadow of what is in **h**.
9: 24 he entered it itself, now to appear
12: 23 whose names are written in **h**.
1Pe 1: 4 This inheritance is kept in **h** for you,
3: 22 who has gone into **h** and is at God's
2Pe 3: 13 we are looking forward to a new **h**
Rev 5: 13 I heard every creature in **h**
11: 19 God's temple in **h** was opened,
12: 7 And there was war in **h**.
15: 5 I looked, and I saw in **h** the temple—
19: 1 of a great multitude in **h** shouting:
19: 11 I saw **h** standing open and there
21: 1 I saw "a new **h** and a new earth,"
21: 10 coming down out of **h** from God.

HEAVENLY (HEAVEN)
Ps 8: 5 them a little lower than the **h** beings
2Co 5: 2 to be clothed with our **h** dwelling,
Eph 1: 3 who has blessed us in the **h** realms
1: 20 at his right hand in the **h** realms,
2Ti 4: 18 bring me safely to his **h** kingdom.
Heb 12: 22 of the living God, the **h** Jerusalem.

HEAVENS (HEAVEN)
Ge 1: 1 In the beginning God created the **h**
11: 4 with a tower that reaches to the **h**,
Dt 33: 26 who rides on the **h** to help you
1Ki 8: 27 The **h**, even the highest heaven,
2Ch 2: 6 since the **h**, even the highest **h**,
Ezr 9: 6 and our guilt has reached to the **h**.
Ne 9: 6 You made the **h**, even the highest **h**,
Job 11: 8 They are higher than the **h** above—
38: 33 Do you know the laws of the **h**?
Ps 8: 3 When I consider your **h**, the work
19: 1 The **h** declare the glory of God;
33: 6 of the Lord the **h** were made,
57: 5 Be exalted, O God, above the **h**;
102: 25 the **h** are the work of your hands.
103: 11 as high as the **h** are above the earth,
108: 4 great is your love, higher than the **h**;
115: 16 The highest **h** belong
119: 89 it stands firm in the **h**.
135: 6 in the **h** and on the earth,
139: 8 If I go up to the **h**, you are there;
148: 1 Praise the Lord from the **h**;
Isa 34: 4 the **h** languish with the earth.
40: 26 Lift up your eyes and look to the **h**:
45: 8 "You **h** above, rain down my
51: 6 Lift up your eyes to the **h**,
55: 9 "As the **h** are higher than the earth,
65: 17 I will create new **h** and a new earth.
Jer 31: 37 if the **h** above can be measured
32: 17 you have made the **h** and the earth
Eze 1: 1 the **h** were opened and I saw visions
Da 12: 3 shine like the brightness of the **h**,
Joel 2: 30 I will show wonders in the **h**
Mt 24: 31 from one end of the **h** to the other.
Mk 13: 27 of the earth to the ends of the **h**.

Eph 4: 10 who ascended higher than all the **h**,
Heb 7: 26 from sinners, exalted above the **h**.
2Pe 3: 5 God's word the **h** came into being
3: 10 The **h** will disappear with a roar;
Rev 20: 11 The earth and the **h** fled

HEAVENWARD* (HEAVEN)
Php 3: 14 God has called me in **h** in Christ Jesus.

HEAVIER (HEAVY)
Pr 27: 3 a fool's provocation is **h** than both.

HEAVY (HEAVIER)
1Ki 12: 4 "Your father put a **h** yoke on us,
Ecc 1: 13 What a **h** burden God has laid
Isa 47: 6 on the aged you laid a very **h** yoke.
Mt 23: 4 They tie up **h**, cumbersome loads

HEBREW (HEBREWS)
Ge 14: 13 and reported this to Abram the **H**.
2Ki 18: 26 speak to us in **H** in the hearing
Php 3: 5 tribe of Benjamin, a **H** of Hebrews;

HEBREWS (HEBREW)
Ex 9: 1 the Lord, the God of the **H**, says:
2Co 11: 22 Are they **H**? So am I.

HEBRON
Ge 13: 18 near the great trees of Mamre at **H**,
23: 2 (that is, **H**) in the land of Canaan.
Jos 14: 13 and gave him **H** as his inheritance.
20: 7 **H**) in the hill country of Judah.
21: 13 Aaron the priest they gave **H** (a city
2Sa 2: 11 David was king in **H** over the house

HEDGE
Job 1: 10 "Have you not put a **h** around him

HEED (HEEDS)
Pr 15: 32 who **h** correction gain understanding.
Ecc 5: 1 better to **h** the rebuke of a wise

HEEDS* (HEED)
Pr 10: 17 Whoever **h** discipline shows the way
13: 1 A wise child **h** a parent's
13: 18 whoever **h** correction is honored.
15: 5 but whoever **h** correction shows
15: 31 Whoever **h** life-giving correction

HEEL
Ge 3: 15 head, and you will strike his **h**."

HEIGHT (HIGH)
1Sa 17: 4 His **h** was six cubits and a span.

HEIR (INHERIT)
Heb 1: 2 whom he appointed **h** of all things,

HEIRS (INHERIT)
Ro 8: 17 **h** of God and co-heirs with Christ,
Gal 3: 29 and **h** according to the promise.
4: 7 children, he has made you also **h**.
Eph 3: 6 gospel the Gentiles are **h** together
1Pe 3: 7 as **h** with you of the gracious gift

HELD (HOLD)
Ex 17: 11 As long as Moses **h** up his hands,
Dt 4: 4 you who **h** fast to the Lord your
2Ki 18: 6 He **h** fast to the Lord and did not
SS 3: 4 I **h** him and would not let him go till
Isa 65: 2 all day long I have **h** out my hands
Ro 10: 21 says, "All day long I have **h** out my
Col 2: 19 and **h** together by its ligaments

HELL*
Mt 5: 22 will be in danger of the fire of **h**.
5: 29 whole body to be thrown into **h**.
5: 30 for your whole body to go into **h**.
10: 28 can destroy both soul and body in **h**.
18: 9 and be thrown into the fire of **h**.
23: 15 as much a child of **h** as you are.
23: 33 you escape being condemned to **h**?
Mk 9: 43 than with two hands to go into **h**,
9: 45 have two feet and be thrown into **h**.
9: 47 have two eyes and be thrown into **h**,
Lk 12: 5 has authority to throw you into **h**.
Jas 3: 6 on fire, and is itself set on fire by **h**.
2Pe 2: 4 but sent them to **h**, putting them

HELMET
Isa 59: 17 and the **h** of salvation on his head;
Eph 6: 17 Take the **h** of salvation
1Th 5: 8 and the hope of salvation as a **h**.

HELP (HELPED HELPER HELPFUL HELPING HELPLESS HELPS)
Ex 3: 21 be sure you **h** your enemy with it.
Lev 25: 35 **h** them as you would a foreigner
Dt 33: 26 who rides on the heavens to **h** you
2Sa 22: 36 your **h** has made me great.
2Ch 16: 12 in his illness he did not seek **h**

Ps 18: 6 I cried to my God for h.
30: 2 I called to you for h, and you healed
33: 20 he is our h and our shield.
40: 10 your faithfulness and your saving h.
40: 16 those who long for your saving h
46: 1 an ever-present h in trouble.
70: 4 long for your saving h always say,
72: 12 the afflicted who have no one to h.
79: 9 H us, God our Savior, for the glory
108: 12 enemy, for human h is worthless.
115: 9 he is their h and shield.
121: 1 where does my h come from?
Ecc 4: 10 fall down, they can h each other up.
Isa 41: 10 I will strengthen you and h you;
Jnh 2: 2 the realm of the dead I called for h,
Mk 9: 24 h me overcome my unbelief!"
Lk 11: 46 will not lift one finger to h them.
Ac 16: 9 over to Macedonia and h us.
18: 27 he was a great h to those who
20: 35 of hard work we must h the weak,
2Co 7: 2 For I know your eagerness to h,
1Ti 5: 16 she should continue to h them

HELPED (HELP)
1Sa 7: 12 "Thus far the LORD has h us."
Ac 26: 22 But God has h me to this very day;

HELPER (HELP)
Ge 2: 18 I will make a h suitable for him."
Ps 10: 14 you are the h of the fatherless.
Heb 13: 6 confidence, "The Lord is my h;

HELPFUL (HELP)
Eph 4: 29 only what is h for building others

HELPING (HELP)
Ac 9: 36 always doing good and h the poor.
1Co 12: 28 gifts of healing, of h, of guidance,
1Ti 5: 10 h those in trouble and devoting

HELPLESS (HELP)
Ps 10: 12 hand, O God. Do not forget the h.
Mt 9: 36 because they were harassed and h,

HELPS (HELP)
Ro 8: 26 the Spirit h us in our weakness.

HEN*
Zec 6: 14 H son of Zephaniah as a memorial
Mt 23: 37 as a h gathers her chicks under her
Lk 13: 34 as a h gathers her chicks under her

HERALD
1Ti 2: 7 for this purpose I was appointed a h
2Ti 1: 11 of this gospel I was appointed a h

HERBS
Ex 12: 8 along with bitter h, and bread made

HERITAGE (INHERIT)
Ps 61: 5 you have given me the h of those
119:111 Your statutes are my h forever;
127: 3 Children are a h from the LORD,

HERO
2Sa 23: 1 the h of Israel's songs:

HEROD
1. King of Judea who tried to kill Jesus (Mt 2; Lk 1:5).
2. Son of 1. Tetrarch of Galilee who arrested and beheaded John the Baptist (Mt 14:1–12; Mk 6:14–29; Lk 3:1, 19–20; 9:7–9); tried Jesus (Lk 23:6–15).
3. Grandson of 1. King of Judea who killed James (Ac 12:2); arrested Peter (Ac 12:3–19). Death (Ac 12:19–23).

HERODIAS
Wife of Herod the Tetrarch who persuaded her daughter to ask for John the Baptist's head (Mt 14:1–12; Mk 6:14–29).

HEWN*
Isa 51: 1 the quarry from which you were h;

HEZEKIAH
King of Judah. Restored the temple and worship (2Ch 29–31). Sought the LORD for help against Assyria (2Ki 18–19; 2Ch 32:1–23; Isa 36–37). Illness healed (2Ki 20:1–11; 2Ch 32:24–26; Isa 38). Judged for showing Babylonians his treasures (2Ki 20:12–21; 2Ch 32:31; Isa 39).

HID (HIDE)
Ge 3: 8 they h from the LORD God among
Ex 2: 2 child, she h him for three months.
Jos 6: 17 because she h the spies we sent.
1Ki 18: 13 I h a hundred of the LORD's
2Ch 22: 11 she h the child from Athaliah so she
Isa 54: 8 In a surge of anger I h my face

Mt 13: 44 When a man found it, he h it again,
25: 25 out and h your gold in the ground.
Heb 11: 23 faith Moses' parents h him for three

HIDDEN (HIDE)
1Sa 10: 22 "Yes, he has h himself among
Job 28: 11 the rivers and bring h things to light.
Ps 19: 12 Forgive my h faults.
119: 11 I have h your word in my heart
Pr 2: 4 and search for it as for h treasure,
27: 5 Better is open rebuke than h love.
Isa 59: 2 your sins have h his face from you,
Da 2: 22 He reveals deep and h things;
Mt 5: 14 A city on a hill cannot be h.
10: 26 or h that will not be made known.
11: 25 because you have h these things
13: 35 will utter things h since the creation
13: 44 heaven is like treasure h in a field.
Mk 4: 22 For whatever is h is meant to be
Ro 16: 25 of the mystery h for long ages past,
1Co 2: 7 a mystery that has been h
Eph 3: 9 for ages past was kept h in God,
Col 2: 3 that has been kept h for ages
2: 3 in whom are h all the treasures
3: 3 and your life is now h with Christ

HIDE (HID HIDDEN HIDING)
Dt 31: 17 I will h my face from them,
Ps 17: 8 h me in the shadow of your wings
27: 5 he will h me in the shelter of his
143: 9 LORD, for I h myself in you.
Isa 53: 3 whom people h their faces he was

HIDING (HIDE)
Ps 32: 7 You are my h place;
Pr 28: 12 rise to power, people go into h.

HIGH (HEIGHT)
Ge 14: 18 He was priest of God Most H,
14: 22 God Most H, Creator of heaven
Ps 21: 7 of the Most H he will not be shaken.
82: 6 you are all sons of the Most H.'
Isa 14: 14 will make myself like the Most H."
Da 4: 17 the Most H is sovereign over
Mk 5: 7 Jesus, Son of the Most H God?
Heb 7: 1 of Salem and priest of God Most H.

HIGHWAY
Isa 40: 3 in the desert a h for our God.

HILL (HILLS)
Isa 40: 4 every mountain and h made low;
Mt 5: 14 A city on a h cannot be hidden.
Lk 3: 5 every mountain and h made low.

HILLS (HILL)
1Ki 20: 23 "Their gods are gods of the h.
Ps 50: 10 and the cattle on a thousand h.
Hos 10: 8 and to the h, "Fall on us!"
Lk 23: 30 and to the h, "Cover us!"'
Rev 17: 9 The seven heads are seven h

HINDER (HINDERED HINDERS)
1Sa 14: 6 Nothing can h the LORD
Mt 19: 14 and do not h them, for the kingdom
1Co 9: 12 anything rather than h the gospel
1Pe 3: 7 so that nothing will h your prayers.

HINDERED (HINDER)
Lk 11: 52 and you have h those who were

HINDERS* (HINDER)
Heb 12: 1 let us throw off everything that h

HINT*
Eph 5: 3 you there must not be even a h

HIP
Ge 32: 32 of Jacob's h was touched near

HIRAM
King of Tyre; helped David build his palace (2Sa 5:11–12; 1Ch 14:1); helped Solomon build the temple (1Ki 5; 2Ch 2) and his navy (1Ki 9:10–27; 2Ch 8).

HIRED
Lk 15: 15 and h himself out to a citizen
Jn 10: 12 The h hand is not the shepherd

HOARD* (HOARDED)
Pr 11: 26 People curse those who h grain,

HOARDED* (HOARD)
Ecc 5: 13 wealth h to the harm of its owners,
Isa 23: 18 they will not be stored up or h.
Jas 5: 3 You have h wealth in the last days.

HOLD (HELD HOLDING)
Ex 20: 7 LORD will not h anyone guiltless
Lev 19: 13 " 'Do not h back the wages
Dt 5: 11 LORD will not h anyone guiltless

Dt 11: 22 to him and to h fast to him—
13: 4 serve him and h fast to him.
30: 20 listen to his voice, and h fast to him.
Jos 22: 5 to h fast to him and to serve him
2Ki 4: 16 "you will h a son in your arms."
Ps 18: 16 from on high and took h of me;
73: 23 you h me by my right hand.
Pr 4: 4 "Take h of my words with all your
10: 19 but the prudent h their tongues.
17: 28 discerning if they h their tongues.
Isa 41: 13 the LORD your God who takes h
54: 2 tent curtains wide, do not h back;
Eze 3: 18 I will h you accountable for their
3: 20 I will h you accountable for their
33: 6 I will h the watchman accountable
Zec 8: 23 nations will take firm h of one Jew
Mk 11: 25 if you h anything against anyone,
Jn 20: 17 Jesus said, "Do not h on to me,
Php 2: 16 as you h firmly to the word of life.
3: 12 I press on to take h
Col 1: 17 and in him all things h together.
1Th 5: 21 test them all; h on to what is good,
1Ti 6: 12 Take h of the eternal life
Heb 10: 23 Let us h unswervingly to the hope

HOLDING (HOLD)
Jer 15: 6 I am tired of h back.

HOLES
Hag 1: 6 to put them in a purse with h in it.
Mt 8: 20 "Foxes have h and birds have nests,

HOLINESS* (HOLY)
Ex 15: 11 majestic in h, awesome in glory,
Dt 32: 51 you did not uphold my h among
1Ch 16: 29 the LORD in the splendor of his h.
2Ch 20: 21 the splendor of his h as they went
Ps 29: 2 the LORD in the splendor of his h.
89: 35 for all, I have sworn by my h—
93: 5 h adorns your house for endless
96: 9 the LORD in the splendor of his h;
Isa 29: 23 they will acknowledge the h
35: 8 it will be called the Way of H;
Eze 38: 23 I will show the h of my great name,
38: 23 I will show my greatness and my h,
Am 4: 2 LORD has sworn by his h:
Lk 1: 75 in h and righteousness before him
Ro 1: 4 Spirit of h was appointed the Son
6: 19 slaves to righteousness leading to h.
6: 22 the benefit you reap leads to h,
1Co 1: 30 righteousness, h and redemption.
2Co 7: 1 perfecting h out of reverence
Eph 4: 24 God in true righteousness and h.
1Ti 2: 2 quiet lives in all godliness and h.
2: 15 in faith, love and h with propriety.
Heb 12: 10 good, that we may share in his h.
12: 14 without h no one will see the Lord.

HOLY (HALLOWED HOLINESS)
Ge 2: 3 the seventh day and made it h,
Ex 3: 5 you are standing is h ground."
16: 23 rest, a h sabbath to the LORD.
19: 6 kingdom of priests and a h nation.'
20: 8 the Sabbath day by keeping it h.
26: 33 curtain will separate the H Place from the Most H Place.
28: 36 and engrave on it as on a seal: \h to the
29: 37 Then the altar will be most h,
30: 10 It is most h to the LORD."
30: 29 them so they will be most h,
31: 13 I am the LORD, who makes you h.
40: 9 all its furnishings, and it will be h.
Lev 10: 3 approach me I will be proved h;
10: 10 you can distinguish between the h
11: 44 and be h, because I am h.
11: 45 therefore be h, because I am h.
19: 2 'Be h because I, the LORD your God, am h.
19: 8 they have desecrated what is h
19: 24 the fourth year all its fruit will be h,
20: 3 sanctuary and profaned my h name.
20: 7 yourselves and be h, because I am
20: 8 I am the LORD, who makes you h.
20: 26 You are to be h to me because I, the LORD, am h,
21: 6 They must be h to their God
21: 8 Consider them h, because I
21: 8 am the LORD, who makes them h.
22: 32 Do not profane my h name, for I
25: 12 it is a jubilee and is to be h for you;
27: 9 given to the LORD becomes h.
Nu 4: 15 they must not touch the h things
6: 5 They must be h until the period
20: 12 enough to honor me as h in the sight
20: 13 he was proved h among them.

Dt   5:12 the Sabbath day by keeping it h,
     23:14 Your camp must be h, so that he
     26:15 from heaven, your h dwelling place,
     33: 2 myriads of h ones from the south,
Jos   5: 15 place where you are standing is h."
     24: 19 He is a h God; he is a jealous God.
1Sa   2: 2 "There is no one h like the LORD;
      6:20 of the LORD, this h God?
     21: 5 The men's bodies are h even on missions
              that are not h.
2Ki   4: 9 often comes our way is a h man
1Ch 16: 10 Glory in his h name; let the hearts
     16: 35 we may give thanks to your h name,
     29: 3 I have provided for this h temple:
2Ch 30: 27 heaven, his h dwelling place.
Ezr   9: 2 have mingled the h race
Ne   11: 1 them to live in Jerusalem, the h city,
Job   6: 10 not denied the words of the H One.
Ps   2: 6 my king on Zion, my h mountain."
     11: 4 The LORD is in his h temple;
     22: 3 you are enthroned as the H One;
     24: 3 Who may stand in his h place?
     30: 4 praise his h name.
     77: 13 Your ways, God, are h. What god is
     78: 54 them to the border of his h land,
     99: 3 great and awesome name—he is h.
     99: 5 and worship at his footstool; he is h.
     99: 9 for the LORD our God is h.
    105: 3 Glory in his h name; let the hearts
    111: 9 h and awesome is his name.
Pr   9: 10 of the H One is understanding.
Isa   5: 16 the h God will be proved h by his
      6: 3 "H, h, h, is the LORD Almighty;
      8: 13 is the one you are to regard as h,
     29: 23 hands, they will keep my name h;
     40: 25 who is my equal?" says the H One.
     43: 3 your God, the H One of Israel,
     54: 5 the H One of Israel is your
     57: 15 who lives forever, whose name is h:
     58: 13 and the LORD's h day honorable,
Jer 17: 22 but keep the Sabbath day h, as I
Eze 20: 41 I will be proved h through you
     22: 26 to my law and profane my h things;
     28: 22 and within you am proved to be h.
     28: 25 I will be proved h through them
     36: 20 nations they profaned my h name,
     38: 16 I am proved h through you before
     44: 23 people the difference between the h
Da   9: 24 and to anoint the Most H Place.
Hab   2: 20 The LORD is in his h temple;
Zec 14: 5 come, and all the h ones with him.
     14: 20 On that day \h \to \the
Mt   24: 15 in the h place 'the abomination
Mk   1: 24 who you are—the H One of God!"
Lk   1: 35 So the h one to be born will be
      1: 49 great things for me—h is his name.
      4: 34 who you are the H One of God."
Jn   6: 69 that you are the H One of God."
Ac   2: 27 will not let your h one see decay.
      13: 35 will not let your h one see decay.'
Ro   1: 2 his prophets in the H Scriptures
      7: 12 is h, and the commandment is h,
     11: 16 if the root is h, so are the branches.
     12: 1 sacrifice, h and pleasing to God—
1Co   1: 2 Jesus and called to be h people,
      7: 14 be unclean, but as it is, they are h.
Eph   1: 4 the creation of the world to be h
      2: 21 to become a h temple in the Lord.
      3: 5 by the Spirit to God's h apostles
      5: 26 to make her h, cleansing her
Col   1: 22 death to present you h in his sight,
1Th   2: 10 of how h, righteous and blameless
      3: 13 and h in the presence of our God
      3: 13 Jesus comes with all his h ones.
      4: 7 us to be impure, but to live a h life.
2Th   1: 10 comes to be glorified in his h people
1Ti   2: 8 lifting up h hands without anger
2Ti   1: 9 saved us and called us to a h life—
      2: 21 made h, useful to the Master
      3: 15 you have known the H Scriptures,
Tit   1: 8 upright, h and disciplined.
Heb   2: 11 Both the one who makes people h
      7: 26 one who is h, blameless, pure,
     10: 10 we have been made h through
     10: 14 forever those who are being made h.
     10: 19 enter the Most H Place by the blood
     12: 14 in peace with everyone and to be h;
     13: 12 make the people h through his own
1Pe   1: 15 But just as he who called you is h,
      1: 16 "Be h, because I am h."
      2: 5 spiritual house to be a h priesthood,
      2: 9 a royal priesthood, a h nation,

1Pe   3: 5 this is the way the h women
2Pe   3: 11 You ought to live h and godly lives
Jude : 14 upon thousands of his h ones
Rev   3: 7 These are the words of him who is h
      4: 8 "'H, h, h is the Lord God
     15: 4 For you alone are h. All nations will
     20: 6 h are those who have part in the first
     21: 11 let those who are h continue to be h."

HOME (HOMES)

Dt   6: 7 Talk about them when you sit at h
     11: 19 talking about them when you sit at h
     20: 5 Let him go h, or he may die in battle
     24: 5 one year he is to be free to stay at h
Ru   1: 11 said, "Return h, my daughters.
2Sa   7: 18 that wisdom of h of their own
1Ch 16: 43 David returned h to bless his family.
Ps   84: 3 Even the sparrow has found a h
    113: 9 woman in her h as a happy mother
Pr   3: 33 but he blesses the h of the righteous.
     27: 8 its nest is anyone who flees from h.
Ecc 12: 5 people go to their eternal h
Eze 36: 8 Israel, for they will soon come h.
Mt   1: 24 him and took Mary h as his wife.
Mk   10: 29 "no one who has left h or brothers
Lk   10: 38 woman named Martha opened her h
Jn   14: 23 to them and make our h with them.
     19: 27 this disciple took her into his h.
Ac   16: 15 baptized, she invited us to her h.
Tit   2: 5 and pure, to be busy at h, to be kind,

HOMELESS*

1Co   4: 11 we are brutally treated, we are h.

HOMES (HOME)

Ne   4: 14 daughters, your wives and your h."
Isa 32: 18 in secure h, in undisturbed places
Mic   2: 2 They defraud people of their h,
Mk   10: 30 h, brothers, sisters, mothers,
1Ti   5: 14 to manage their h and to give

HOMETOWN (HOMETOWNS)

Mt   13: 54 Coming to his h, he began teaching

HOMETOWNS* (HOMETOWN)

Lk   4: 24 "prophets are not accepted in their h.

HOMOSEXUALITY* (HOMOSEXUALS)

1Ti   1: 10 immoral, for those practicing h,

HOMOSEXUALS* (HOMOSEXUALITY)

1Co   6: 9 nor male prostitutes nor practicing h

HONEST (HONESTY)

Lev 19: 36 Use h scales and h weights,
Dt   25: 15 must have accurate and h weights
2Ki 22: 7 they are h in their dealings."
Job 31: 6 let God weigh me in h scales and he
Pr   12: 17 An h witness tells the truth,
     14: 5 An h witness does not deceive,
     17: 26 to flog h officials is not right.
     22: 21 teaching you to be h and to speak

HONESTY (HONEST)

2Ki 12: 15 because they acted with complete h.

HONEY (HONEYCOMB)

Ex   3: 8 a land flowing with milk and h—
Jdg 14: 8 he saw a swarm of bees and some h.
1Sa 14: 26 woods, they saw the h oozing out;
Ps   19: 10 they are sweeter than h, than h
    119:103 taste, sweeter than h to my mouth!
Pr   24: 13 that wisdom is like h for you:
     25: 16 If you find h, eat just enough—
SS   4: 11 milk and h are under your tongue.
Isa   7: 15 h when he knows enough to reject
Eze   3: 3 it tasted as sweet as h in my mouth.
Mt   3: 4 His food was locusts and wild h.
Rev 10: 9 mouth it will be as sweet as h.' "

HONEYCOMB (HONEY)

Ps   19: 10 than honey from the h.
SS   4: 11 Your lips drop sweetness as the h,
      5: 1 I have eaten my h and my honey;

HONOR (HONORABLE HONORABLY HONORED HONORS)

Ex   20: 12 "H your father and your mother,
Nu   22: 6 enough to h me as holy
     25: 13 he was zealous for the h of his God
Dt   5: 16 "H your father and your mother,
Jdg   9: 9 are taking, the h will not be yours,
1Sa   2: 8 and has them inherit a throne of h.
      2: 30 Those who h me I will h,
1Ch 29: 12 Wealth and h come from you;
2Ch   1: 11 possessions or h, nor for the death
     18: 1 Jehoshaphat had great wealth and h,
Ezr 10: 11 Now h the LORD, the God of your

Est   6: 6 for the man the king delights to h?"
Ps   8: 5 and crowned them with glory and h.
     15: 4 but h whoever fears the LORD;
     45: 11 h him, for he is your lord.
     84: 11 the LORD bestows favor and h;
Pr   3: 9 H the LORD with your wealth,
      3: 35 The wise inherit h, but fools get
     11: 16 A kindhearted woman gains h,
     15: 33 and humility comes before h.
     18: 12 but humility comes before h.
     20: 3 It is to one's h to avoid strife,
     31: 31 H her for all that her hands
Isa 29: 13 their mouth and h me with their lips,
Jer 33: 9 h before all nations on earth
Mt   13: 57 homes are prophets without h."
     15: 4 'H your father and mother'
     15: 8 " 'These people h me with their
     19: 19 your father and mother,' and 'love
     23: 6 they love the place of h at banquets
Mk   6: 4 homes are prophets without h."
Lk   14: 8 do not take the place of h,
Jn   5: 23 all may h the Son just as they h
     12: 26 My Father will h the one who
Ro   12: 10 H one another above yourselves.
1Co   6: 20 Therefore h God with your bodies.
Eph   6: 2 "H your father and mother"
1Ti   5: 17 church well are worthy of double h,
Heb   2: 7 you crowned them with glory and h
Rev   4: 9 h and thanks to him who sits

HONORABLE (HONOR)

1Th   4: 4 body in a way that is holy and h,

HONORABLY (HONOR)

Heb 13: 18 and desire to live h in every way.

HONORED (HONOR)

Ps   12: 8 while depravity is h by the human
Pr   13: 18 but whoever heeds correction is h.
Da   4: 34 I h and glorified him who lives
1Co 12: 26 if one part is h, every part rejoices
Heb 13: 4 Marriage should be h by all,

HONORS (HONOR)

Pr   14: 31 whoever is kind to the needy h God.

HOOF

Ex   10: 26 not a h is to be left behind.

HOOKS

Isa   2: 4 and their spears into pruning h.
Joel 3: 10 and your pruning h into spears.
Mic   4: 3 and their spears into pruning h.

HOPE (HOPES)

Job 13: 15 he slay me, yet will I h in him;
Ps   33: 18 A horse is a vain h for deliverance;
     33: 18 on those whose h is in his unfailing
     42: 5 Put your h in God, for I will yet
     62: 5 rest in God; my h comes from him.
    119: 74 for I have put my h in your word.
    130: 5 waits, and in his word I put my h.
    130: 7 Israel, put your h in the LORD,
    146: 5 whose h is in the LORD their God.
    147: 11 who put their h in his unfailing love.
Pr   13: 12 H deferred makes the heart sick,
     23: 18 There is surely a future h for you,
Isa 40: 31 but those who h in the LORD will
Jer 29: 11 plans to give you h and a future.
La   3: 21 call to mind and therefore I have h:
Zec   9: 12 to your fortress, you prisoners of h;
Ro   5: 4 and character, h.
      8: 20 of the one who subjected it, in h
      8: 24 But h that is seen is no h at all.
      8: 25 if we h for what we do not yet have,
     12: 12 Be joyful in h, patient in affliction,
     15: 4 they provide we might have h.
     15: 13 May the God of h fill you with all
1Co 13: 13 these three remain: faith, h and love.
     15: 19 for this life we have h in Christ,
Eph   2: 12 without h and without God
Col   1: 27 is Christ in you, the h of glory.
1Th   1: 3 your endurance inspired by h in our
      5: 8 and the h of salvation as a helmet.
1Ti   4: 10 because we have put our h
      6: 17 but to put their h in God, who richly
Tit   1: 2 in the h of eternal life, which God,
      2: 13 while we wait for the blessed h—
Heb   6: 19 We have this h as an anchor
     10: 23 unswervingly to the h we profess,
     11: 1 faith is being sure of what we h
1Jn   3: 3 All who have this h in him purify

HOPES (HOPE)

Ps   25: 3 No one who h in you will ever be
1Co 13: 7 trusts, always h, always perseveres.

HORN (HORNS)
Ex 19: 13 the ram's **h** sounds a long blast may
27: 2 Make a **h** at each of the four
Da 7: 8 This **h** had eyes like the eyes

HORNS (HORN)
Da 7: 24 The ten **h** are ten kings who will
Rev 5: 6 The Lamb had seven **h** and seven
12: 3 ten **h** and seven crowns on its heads.
13: 1 It had ten **h** and seven heads,
17: 3 and had seven heads and ten **h**.

HORRIBLE (HORROR)
Jer 5: 30 "A **h** and shocking thing has

HORROR (HORRIBLE)
Jer 2: 12 and shudder with great **h**,"

HORSE
Ps 147: 10 is not in the strength of the **h**,
Pr 26: 3 A whip for the **h**, a bridle
Zec 1: 8 me was a man mounted on a red **h**.
Rev 6: 2 and there before me was a white **h**!
6: 4 Then another **h** came out, a fiery red
6: 5 and there before me was a black **h**!
6: 8 and there before me was a pale **h**!
19: 11 and there before me was a white **h**,

HOSANNA
Mt 21: 9 "**H** in the highest heaven!"
Mk 11: 9 those who followed shouted, "**H**!"
Jn 12: 13 out to meet him, shouting, "**H**!"

HOSEA
Prophet whose wife and family pictured the unfaithfulness of Israel (Hos 1–3).

HOSHEA (JOSHUA)
1. Original name of Joshua (Nu 13:16).
2. Last king of Israel (2Ki 15:30; 17:1–6).

HOSPITABLE* (HOSPITALITY)
1Ti 3: 2 respectable, **h**, able to teach,
Tit 1: 8 he must be **h**, one who loves what is

HOSPITALITY* (HOSPITABLE)
Ac 28: 7 showed us generous **h** for three days.
Ro 12: 13 people who are in need. Practice **h**.
16: 23 whose **h** I and the whole church
1Ti 5: 10 showing **h**, washing the feet
Heb 13: 2 not forget to show **h** to strangers,
13: 2 shown **h** to angels without knowing it.
1Pe 4: 9 Offer **h** to one another without
3Jn : 8 to show **h** to such people so that we

HOSTILE (HOSTILITY)
Ro 8: 7 The sinful mind is **h** to God;

HOSTILITY (HOSTILE)
Eph 2: 14 the barrier, the dividing wall of **h**,
2: 16 by which he put to death their **h**.

HOT
1Ti 4: 2 have been seared as with a **h** iron.
Rev 3: 15 that you are neither cold nor **h**.

HOT-TEMPERED* (HOT)
Pr 15: 18 The **h** stir up dissension, but those
19: 19 The **h** must pay the penalty,
22: 24 Do not make friends with the **h**,
29: 22 and a **h** person commits many sins.

HOTHEADED* (HEAD)
Pr 14: 16 a fool is **h** and yet feels secure.

HOUR
Ecc 9: 12 one knows when their **h** will come:
Mt 6: 27 worrying add a single **h** to your life?
Lk 12: 40 an **h** when you do not expect him."
Jn 2: 4 "My **h** has not yet come."
12: 23 "The **h** has come for the Son
12: 27 for this very reason I came to this **h**.
17: 1 prayed: "Father, the **h** has come.

HOUSE (HOUSEHOLD HOUSEHOLDS HOUSES STOREHOUSE)
Ex 12: 22 of the door of your **h** until morning.
20: 17 shall not covet your neighbor's **h**.
Nu 12: 7 he is faithful in all my **h**.
Dt 5: 21 set your desire on your neighbor's **h**.
2Sa 7: 2 I am, living in a **h** of cedar,
7: 11 Lord himself will establish a **h**
1Ch 17: 23 and his **h** be established forever.
Ne 10: 39 "We will not neglect the **h** of our
Ps 23: 6 in the **h** of the Lord forever.
27: 4 in the **h** of the Lord all the days
69: 9 for zeal for your **h** consumes me,
84: 10 in the **h** of my God than dwell
122: 1 "Let us go to the **h** of the Lord."
127: 1 Unless the Lord builds the **h**,

Pr 7: 27 Her **h** is a highway to the grave,
21: 9 of the roof than share a **h**
Isa 56: 7 for my **h** will be called a **h** of prayer
Jer 7: 11 Has this **h**, which bears my Name,
18: 2 "Go down to the potter's **h**,
Eze 33: 7 you a watchman for the **h** of Israel;
Joel 3: 18 will flow out of the Lord's **h**
Hab 2: 9 who builds his **h** by unjust gain,
Zec 13: 6 I was given at the **h** of my friends.'
Mt 7: 24 is like a wise man who built his **h**
10: 11 at that person's **h** until you leave.
12: 29 can anyone enter a strong man's **h**
21: 13 " 'My **h** will be called a **h**
Mk 3: 25 If a **h** is divided against itself, that **h**
11: 17 'My **h** will be called a **h** of prayer
Lk 6: 48 They are like a man building a **h**,
10: 7 Do not move around from **h** to **h**.
11: 17 a **h** divided against itself will fall.
11: 24 it says, 'I will return to the **h** I left.'
15: 8 sweep the **h** and search carefully
19: 9 salvation has come to this **h**,
Jn 2: 16 Stop turning my Father's **h**
2: 17 for your **h** will consume me."
12: 3 the **h** was filled with the fragrance
14: 2 My Father's **h** has plenty of room;
Ac 20: 20 taught you publicly and from **h** to **h**.
Ro 16: 5 also the church that meets at their **h**.
Heb 3: 2 of a **h** has greater honor than the **h**
1Pe 2: 5 a spiritual **h** to be a holy priesthood,

HOUSEHOLD (HOUSE)
Ex 12: 3 lamb for his family, one for each **h**.
Jos 24: 15 But as for me and my **h**, we will
Pr 31: 21 it snows, she has no fear for her **h**;
31: 27 watches over the affairs of her **h**
Mic 7: 6 are the members of your own **h**.
Mt 10: 36 will be the members of your own **h**.'
12: 25 or **h** divided against itself will not
Ac 16: 31 will be saved—you and your **h**."
16: 33 all his **h** were baptized.
16: 34 he and his whole **h**.
Eph 2: 19 people and also members of his **h**,
1Ti 3: 12 manage his children and his **h** well.
3: 15 to conduct themselves in God's **h**,
5: 8 especially for their own **h**,

HOUSEHOLDS (HOUSE)
Pr 15: 27 The greedy bring ruin to their **h**,
Tit 1: 11 because they are disrupting whole **h**

HOUSES (HOUSE)
Ex 12: 27 who passed over the **h**
Mt 19: 29 everyone who has left **h** or brothers

HOVERING* (HOVERS)
Ge 1: 2 Spirit of God was **h** over the waters.
Isa 31: 5 Like birds **h** overhead, the Lord

HOVERS* (HOVERING)
Dt 32: 11 up its nest and **h** over its young,

HULDAH*
Prophetess inquired by Hilkiah for Josiah (2Ki 22; 2Ch 34:14–28).

HUMAN (HUMANITY HUMANKIND)
Ge 1: 26 "Let us make **h** beings in our image,
6: 3 not contend with **h** beings forever,
6: 6 he had made **h** beings on the earth,
6: 7 the face of the earth the **h** race
9: 6 "Whoever sheds **h** blood,
Lev 24: 17 who takes the life of a **h** being is
1Sa 15: 29 he is not a **h** being, that he
16: 7 at the things **h** beings look at.
2Ki 19: 18 fashioned by **h** hands.
2Ch 32: 19 the work of **h** hands.
Ps 8: 4 **h** beings that you care for them?
144: 3 **h** beings that you care for them,
Isa 45: 12 and created **h** beings on it.
52: 14 his form marred beyond **h** likeness—
Jer 32: 27 the God of the whole **h** race.
Mk 7: 7 teachings are merely **h** rules.'
Jn 8: 15 You judge by **h** standards;
Ac 5: 29 obey God rather than **h** beings!
Ro 1: 18 **h** beings who suppress the truth
9: 5 them is traced the **h** ancestry
1Co 1: 25 God is wiser than **h** wisdom,
1: 26 of you were wise by **h** standards,
2: 5 not rest on **h** wisdom,
2: 13 not in words taught us by **h** wisdom
3: 3 acting like mere **h** beings?
3: 21 no more boasting about **h** leaders!
13: 1 speak in **h** or angelic tongues,
15: 21 death came through a **h** being,
2Co 3: 3 of stone but on tablets of **h** hearts.

Gal 1: 1 sent not with a **h** commission nor by **h** authority,
1: 10 trying to win **h** approval, or God's
3: 3 now trying to finish by **h** effort?
Php 2: 8 found in appearance as a **h** being,
1Th 2: 13 not as a **h** word,
1Ti 2: 5 mediator between God and **h** beings, Christ Jesus, himself **h**,
Heb 2: 6 **h** beings that you care for them?
9: 11 that is not made with **h** hands,
9: 24 enter a sanctuary made with **h** hands
2Pe 1: 21 prophets, though **h**, spoke from God
2: 18 lustful desires of sinful **h** nature,

HUMANITY* (HUMAN)
Eph 2: 15 create in himself one new **h**
Heb 2: 14 he too shared in their **h** so

HUMANKIND (HUMAN)
Ps 33: 13 and sees all **h**;
Pr 8: 31 and delighting in **h**.
Ecc 7: 29 God created **h** upright,

HUMBLE (HUMBLED HUMBLES HUMILIATE HUMILIATED HUMILIATING HUMILITY)
Nu 12: 3 (Now Moses was a very **h** man,
2Ch 7: 14 will **h** themselves and pray and seek
Ps 18: 27 You save the **h** but bring low those
25: 9 He guides the **h** in what is right
149: 4 he crowns the **h** with victory.
Pr 3: 34 shows favor to the **h** and oppressed.
Isa 66: 2 those who are **h** and contrite
Mt 11: 29 for I am gentle and **h** in heart,
Mt 18: 4 whoever takes a **h** place
23: 12 **h** themselves will be exalted.
Lk 14: 11 **h** themselves will be exalted."
18: 14 **h** themselves will be exalted."
Eph 4: 2 Be completely **h** and gentle;
Jas 4: 6 proud but shows favor to the **h**
4: 10 **H** yourselves before the Lord,
1Pe 5: 5 proud but shows favor to the **h**
5: 6 **H** yourselves, therefore,

HUMBLED (HUMBLE)
Mt 23: 12 who exalt themselves will be **h**,
Lk 14: 11 who exalt themselves will be **h**,
Php 2: 8 he **h** himself by becoming obedient

HUMBLES* (HUMBLE)
1Sa 2: 7 he **h** and he exalts.
Isa 26: 5 He **h** those who dwell on high,

HUMILIATE* (HUMBLE)
Pr 25: 7 for him to **h** you before his nobles.

HUMILIATED (HUMBLE)
Jer 31: 19 **h** because I bore the disgrace of my
Lk 14: 9 Then, **h**, you will have to take

HUMILIATING* (HUMBLE)
1Co 11: 22 by **h** those who have nothing?

HUMILITY* (HUMBLE)
Ps 45: 4 in the cause of truth, **h** and justice;
Pr 11: 2 disgrace, but with **h** comes wisdom.
15: 33 Lord, and **h** comes before honor.
18: 12 haughty, but **h** comes before honor.
22: 4 **H** is the fear of the Lord;
Zep 2: 3 Seek righteousness, seek **h**;
Ac 20: 19 I served the Lord with great **h**
Php 2: 3 in **h** value others above yourselves,
Col 2: 18 let anyone who delights in false **h**
2: 23 their false **h** and their harsh
3: 12 kindness, **h**,
Jas 3: 13 deeds done in the **h** that comes
1Pe 5: 5 with **h** toward one another, because,

HUNG (HANG)
Dt 21: 23 because anyone who is **h** on a pole
Mt 18: 6 large millstone were **h** around their
Lk 19: 48 do it, because all the people **h** on his
Gal 3: 13 "Cursed is everyone who is **h**

HUNGER (HUNGRY)
Ne 9: 15 In their **h** you gave them bread
Pr 6: 30 to satisfy his **h** when he is starving.
Mt 5: 6 Blessed are those who **h** and thirst
Lk 6: 21 Blessed are you who **h** now, for you
2Co 6: 5 in hard work, sleepless nights and **h**;
11: 27 I have known **h** and thirst and have
Rev 7: 16 'Never again will they **h**;

HUNGRY (HUNGER)
Job 24: 10 carry the sheaves, but still go **h**.
Ps 107: 9 and fills the **h** with good things.
146: 7 oppressed and gives food to the **h**.
Pr 19: 15 deep sleep, and the shiftless go **h**.
25: 21 If your enemy is **h**, give him food

Pr 27: 7 but to the **h** even what is bitter tastes
Isa 58: 7 it not to share your food with the **h**
58: 10 spend yourselves in behalf of the **h**
Eze 18: 7 gives his food to the **h** and provides
18: 16 gives his food to the **h** and provides
Mt 15: 32 I do not want to send them away **h**,
25: 35 For I was **h** and you gave me
25: 42 For I was **h** and you gave me
Lk 1: 53 He has filled the **h** with good things
Jn 6: 35 comes to me will never go **h**,
Ro 12: 20 "If your enemy is **h**, feed him;
1Co 4: 11 To this very hour we go **h**
Php 4: 12 whether well fed or **h**,

HUR
Ex 17: 12 Aaron and **H** held his hands up—

HURL
Mic 7: 19 **h** all our iniquities into the depths

HURT (HURTS)
Ecc 8: 9 lords it over others to his own **h**.
Mk 16: 18 *it will not **h** them at all;*
Rev 2: 11 who are victorious will not be **h**

HURTS* (HURT)
Ps 15: 4 keep their oaths even when it **h**;
Pr 26: 28 A lying tongue hates those it **h**,

HUSBAND (HUSBAND'S HUSBANDS)
Pr 31: 11 Her **h** has full confidence in her
31: 23 Her **h** is respected at the city gate,
31: 28 her **h** also, and he praises her:
Isa 54: 5 For your Maker is your **h**—
Jer 3: 14 the LORD, "for I am your **h**.
3: 20 like a woman unfaithful to her **h**,
Jn 4: 17 "I have no **h**," she replied.
Ro 7: 2 bound to her **h** as long as he is alive,
1Co 7: 2 and each woman with her own **h**.
7: 3 The **h** should fulfill his marital duty
7: 4 the **h** does not have authority over
7: 10 wife must not separate from her **h**.
7: 11 And a **h** must not divorce his wife.
7: 13 And if a woman has a **h** who is not
7: 14 For the unbelieving **h** has been
7: 39 is bound to her **h** as long as he lives.
7: 39 But if her **h** dies, she is free
2Co 11: 2 I promised you to one **h**, to Christ,
Gal 4: 27 woman than of her who has a **h**."
Eph 5: 23 For the **h** is the head of the wife as
5: 33 and the wife must respect her **h**.
1Ti 5: 9 sixty, has been faithful to her **h**,

HUSBANDMAN See GARDENER

HUSBAND'S
Dt 25: 5 Her **h** brother shall take her
Pr 12: 4 of noble character is her **h** crown,

HUSBANDS (HUSBAND)
Eph 5: 22 yourselves to your own **h** as you do
5: 25 **H**, love your wives, just as Christ
5: 28 **h** ought to love their wives as their
Col 3: 18 submit yourselves to your **h**, as is
3: 19 **H**, love your wives and do not be
Tit 2: 4 the younger women to love their **h**
2: 5 and to be subject to their **h**,
1Pe 3: 1 yourselves to your own **h** so that,
3: 7 **H**, in the same way be considerate

HUSHAI
Wise man of David who frustrated Ahithophel's advice and foiled Absalom's revolt (2Sa 15:32–37; 16:15–17:16; 1Ch 27:33).

HYMN* (HYMNS)
Ps 40: 3 my mouth, a **h** of praise to our God.
Mt 26: 30 When they had sung a **h**, they went
Mk 14: 26 When they had sung a **h**, they went
1Co 14: 26 each of you has a **h**, or a word

HYMNS* (HYMN)
Ac 16: 25 were praying and singing **h** to God,
Eph 5: 19 psalms, **h** and songs from the Spirit.
Col 3: 16 psalms, **h** and songs from the Spirit,

HYPOCRISY* (HYPOCRITE HYPOCRITES HYPOCRITICAL)
Mt 23: 28 on the inside you are full of **h**
Mk 12: 15 But Jesus knew their **h**.
Lk 12: 1 yeast of the Pharisees, which is **h**.
Gal 2: 13 The other Jews joined him in his **h**,
2: 13 by their **h** even Barnabas was led
1Pe 2: 1 of all malice and all deceit, **h**, envy,

HYPOCRITE* (HYPOCRISY)
Mt 7: 5 You **h**, first take the plank
Lk 6: 42 You **h**, first take the plank

HYPOCRITES* (HYPOCRISY)
Ps 26: 4 deceitful, nor do I associate with **h**.
Mt 6: 2 as the **h** do in the synagogues
6: 5 do not be like the **h**, for they love
6: 16 do not look somber as the **h** do,
15: 7 You **h**! Isaiah was right when he
22: 18 "You **h**, why are you trying to trap
23: 13 of the law and Pharisees, you **h**!
23: 15 of the law and Pharisees, you **h**!
23: 23 of the law and Pharisees, you **h**!
23: 25 of the law and Pharisees, you **h**!
23: 27 of the law and Pharisees, you **h**!
23: 29 of the law and Pharisees, you **h**!
24: 51 and assign him a place with the **h**,
Mk 7: 6 when he prophesied about you **h**;
Lk 12: 56 **H**! You know how to interpret
13: 15 The Lord answered him, "You **h**!

HYPOCRITICAL* (HYPOCRISY)
1Ti 4: 2 teachings come through **h** liars,

HYSSOP
Ex 12: 22 Take a bunch of **h**, dip it
Ps 51: 7 Cleanse me with **h**, and I will be
Jn 19: 29 the sponge on a stalk of the **h** plant,

ICHABOD*
1Sa 4: 21 She named the boy **I**, saying,

IDLE* (IDLENESS IDLERS)
Dt 32: 47 They are not just **i** words for you—
Job 11: 3 Will your **i** talk reduce others
Ecc 10: 18 because of **i** hands, the house leaks.
11: 6 at evening let your hands not be **i**,
Isa 58: 13 as you please or speaking **i** words,
Col 2: 18 minds puff them up with **i** notions.
1Th 5: 14 warn those who are **i** and disruptive,
2Th 3: 6 away from every believer who is **i**
3: 7 We were not **i** when we were
3: 11 We hear that some among you are **i**
1Ti 5: 13 they get into the habit of being **i**

IDLENESS* (IDLE)
Pr 31: 27 and does not eat the bread of **i**.

IDLERS* (IDLE)
1Ti 5: 13 And not only do they become **i**,

IDOL (IDOLATER IDOLATERS IDOLATRY IDOLS)
Ex 32: 4 made it into an **i** cast in the shape
Dt 27: 15 "Cursed is anyone who makes an **i**
Isa 40: 19 As for an **i**, a metal worker casts it,
41: 7 other nails down the **i** so it will not
44: 15 he makes an **i** and bows down to it.
44: 17 From the rest he makes a god, his **i**;
Hab 2: 18 what value is an **i** that someone has
1Co 8: 4 We know that "An **i** is nothing

IDOLATER* (IDOL)
Eph 5: 5 such a person is an **i**—

IDOLATERS (IDOL)
1Co 5: 10 or the greedy and swindlers, or **i**.
5: 11 immoral or greedy, **i** or slanderers,
6: 9 immoral nor **i** nor adulterers nor

IDOLATRY (IDOL)
1Sa 15: 23 and arrogance like the evil of **i**.
1Co 10: 14 my dear friends, flee from **i**.
Gal 5: 20 **i** and witchcraft;
Col 3: 5 evil desires and greed, which is **i**.
1Pe 4: 3 orgies, carousing and detestable **i**.

IDOLS (IDOL)
Ex 34: 17 "Do not make any **i**.
Dt 32: 16 angered him with their detestable **i**.
Ps 78: 58 aroused his jealousy with their **i**.
Isa 44: 9 All who make **i** are nothing,
Eze 23: 39 sacrificed their children to their **i**,
Mic 5: 13 destroy your **i** and your sacred
Ac 15: 20 to abstain from food polluted by **i**,
21: 25 abstain from food sacrificed to **i**,
1Co 8: 1 Now about food sacrificed to **i**:
1Jn 5: 21 children, keep yourselves from **i**.
Rev 2: 14 so that they ate food sacrificed to **i**

IGNORANT (IGNORE)
1Co 15: 34 there are some who are **i** of God—
Heb 5: 2 to deal gently with those who are **i**
1Pe 2: 15 good you should silence the **i** talk
2Pe 3: 16 which **i** and unstable people distort,

IGNORE (IGNORANT IGNORED IGNORES)
Dt 22: 1 do not **i** it but be sure to take it back
Ps 9: 12 he does not **i** the cries
1Co 14: 38 Those who **i** this will themselves be **i**.
Heb 2: 3 escape if we **i** so great a salvation?

IGNORED (IGNORE)
Hos 4: 6 because you have **i** the law of your
1Co 14: 38 ignore this will themselves be **i**.

IGNORES* (IGNORE)
Pr 10: 17 whoever **i** correction leads others

ILL (ILLNESS)
Mt 4: 24 to him all who were **i** with various

ILL-GOTTEN
Pr 1: 19 the paths of all who go after **i** gain;
10: 2 **I** treasures have no lasting value,

ILLNESS (ILL)
2Ki 8: 9 'Will I recover from this **i**?' "
2Ch 16: 12 even in his **i** he did not seek help
Ps 41: 3 restores them from their bed of **i**.
Isa 38: 9 of Hezekiah king of Judah after his **i**

ILLUMINATED*
Eph 5: 13 everything that is **i** becomes a light.
Rev 18: 1 and the earth was **i** by his splendor.

IMAGE (IMAGES)
Ge 1: 26 us make human beings in our **i**,
1: 27 created human beings in his own **i**,
1: 27 in the **i** of God he created them;
9: 6 for in the **i** of God has God made
Ex 20: 4 for yourself an **i** in the form
Isa 40: 18 To what **i** will you liken him?
Da 3: 1 King Nebuchadnezzar made an **i**
Lk 20: 24 Whose **i** and inscription are on it?"
Ro 8: 29 conformed to the **i** of his Son,
1Co 11: 7 since he is the **i** and glory of God;
2Co 3: 18 his **i** with ever-increasing glory,
4: 4 glory of Christ, who is the **i** of God.
Col 1: 15 The Son is the **i** of the invisible
3: 10 in knowledge in the **i** of its Creator.
Rev 13: 14 set up an **i** in honor of the beast who

IMAGES (IMAGE)
Ps 97: 7 All who worship **i** are put to shame,
Jer 10: 14 Their **i** are a fraud; they have no
Ro 1: 23 the immortal God for **i** made to look

IMAGINATION (IMAGINE)
Eze 13: 2 who prophesy out of their own **i**:

IMAGINE (IMAGINATION)
Eph 3: 20 more than all we ask or **i**,

IMITATE* (IMITATORS)
Dt 18: 9 not learn to **i** the detestable ways
Eze 23: 48 women may take warning and not **i** you.
1Co 4: 16 Therefore I urge you to **i** me.
2Th 3: 9 ourselves as a model for you to **i**.
Heb 6: 12 but to **i** those who through faith
13: 7 of their way of life and **i** their faith.
3Jn : 11 do not **i** what is evil but what is

IMITATORS* (IMITATE)
1Th 1: 6 You became **i** of us and of the Lord,
2: 14 became **i** of God's churches

IMMANUEL*
Isa 7: 14 birth to a son, and will call him **I**.
8: 8 cover the breadth of your land, **I**!"
Mt 1: 23 they will call him **I**" (which means

IMMENSE
1Ti 1: 16 Jesus might display his **i** patience

IMMORAL* (IMMORALITY)
1Co 5: 9 to associate with sexually **i** people—
5: 10 the people of this world who are **i**,
5: 11 but are sexually **i** or greedy,
6: 9 Neither the sexually **i** nor idolaters
Eph 5: 5 No **i**, impure or greedy person—
1Ti 1: 10 for the sexually **i**, for those
Heb 12: 16 See that no one is sexually **i**, or is
13: 4 the adulterer and all the sexually **i**.
Rev 21: 8 the sexually **i**, those who practice
21: 15 arts, the sexually **i**, the murderers,

IMMORALITY* (IMMORAL)
Nu 25: 1 in sexual **i** with Moabite women,
Jer 3: 9 Because Israel's **i** mattered so little
Mt 5: 32 except for sexual **i**,
15: 19 adultery, sexual **i**, theft,
19: 9 except for sexual **i**,
Mk 7: 21 come evil thoughts, sexual **i**, theft,
Ac 15: 20 from sexual **i**, from the meat
15: 29 strangled animals and from sexual **i**
21: 25 animals and from sexual **i**."
Ro 13: 13 not in sexual **i** and debauchery,
1Co 5: 1 that there is sexual **i** among you,
6: 13 is not meant for sexual **i**
6: 18 Flee from sexual **i**. All other sins
7: 2 But since sexual **i** is occurring,

1Co 10: 8 We should not commit sexual i,
Gal 5: 19 sexual i, impurity and debauchery;
Eph 5: 3 must not be even a hint of sexual i,
Col 3: 5 sexual i, impurity, lust, evil desires
1Th 4: 3 that you should avoid sexual i;
Jude : 4 grace of our God into a license for i
     : 7 gave themselves up to sexual i
Rev 2: 14 to idols and committed sexual i.
     2: 20 misleads my servants into sexual i
     2: 21 given her time to repent of her i,
     9: 21 arts, their sexual i or their thefts.

IMMORTAL* (IMMORTALITY)
Ro 1: 23 exchanged the glory of the i God
1Ti 1: 17 Now to the King eternal, i,
     6: 16 who alone is i and who lives

IMMORTALITY* (IMMORTAL)
Pr 12: 28 there is life; along that path is i.
Ro 2: 7 honor and i, he will give eternal life.
1Co 15: 53 imperishable, and the mortal with i.
     15: 54 and the mortal with i,
2Ti 1: 10 life and i to light through the gospel.

IMPART
Pr 29: 15 A rod and a reprimand i wisdom,

IMPARTIAL*
Jas 3: 17 mercy and good fruit, i and sincere.

IMPERISHABLE
1Co 15: 42 is sown in perishable, it is raised i;
     15: 50 nor does the perishable inherit the i.
1Pe 1: 23 seed, but of i, through the living

IMPLORE*
Mal 1: 9 "Now i God to be gracious to us.
2Co 5: 20 We i you on Christ's behalf:

IMPORTANCE* (IMPORTANT)
1Co 15: 3 I passed on to you as of first i:

IMPORTANT (IMPORTANCE)
Mt 6: 25 Is not life more i than food,
     23: 23 have neglected the more i matters
Mk 12: 29 "The most i one," answered Jesus,
     12: 33 as yourself is more i than all burnt
Php 1: 18 The i thing is that in every way,

IMPOSSIBLE
Mt 17: 20 Nothing will be i for you."
     19: 26 "With human beings this is i,
Mk 10: 27 "With human beings this is i,
Lk 18: 27 "What is i with human beings is
Ac 2: 24 because it was i for death to keep its
Heb 6: 4 It is i for those who have once been
     6: 18 things in which it is i for God to lie,
     10: 4 it is i for the blood of bulls
     11: 6 without faith it is i to please God,

IMPOSTORS
2Ti 3: 13 and i will go from bad to worse,

IMPRESS* (IMPRESSES)
Dt 6: 7 I them on your children.

IMPRESSES* (IMPRESS)
Pr 17: 10 A rebuke i a discerning person more

IMPRISONED (PRISON)
1Pe 3: 19 proclamation to the i spirits—

IMPRISONMENT (PRISON)
Heb 11: 36 and even chains and i.

IMPROPER*
Eph 5: 3 because these are i for the Lord's

IMPURE (IMPURITY)
Ac 10: 15 "Do not call anything i that God
Eph 5: 5 No immoral, i or greedy person—
1Th 2: 3 not spring from error or i motives,
     4: 7 For God did not call us to be i,
Rev 21: 27 Nothing i will ever enter it, nor will

IMPURITY (IMPURE)
Ro 1: 24 hearts to sexual i for the degrading
Gal 5: 19 immorality, i and debauchery;
Eph 4: 19 so as to indulge in every kind of i,
     5: 3 or of any kind of i, or of greed,
Col 3: 5 sexual immorality, i, lust,

INCENSE
Ex 30: 1 altar of acacia wood for burning i.
     40: 5 Place the gold altar of i in front
Ps 141: 2 my prayer be set before you like i;
Heb 9: 4 which had the golden altar of i
Rev 5: 8 were holding golden bowls full of i,
     8: 4 The smoke of the i,

INCLINATION (INCLINES)
Ge 6: 5 that every i of the thoughts

INCLINES* (INCLINATION)
Ecc 10: 2 The heart of the wise i to the right,

INCOME
Ecc 5: 10 are never satisfied with their i.
1Co 16: 2 of money in keeping with your i,

INCOMPARABLE*
Eph 2: 7 ages he might show the i riches

INCREASE (EVER-INCREASING INCREASED
INCREASING)
Ge 1: 22 "Be fruitful and i in number and fill
     8: 17 be fruitful and i in number on it."
Ps 62: 10 though your riches i, do not set your
Pr 22: 16 oppress the poor to i their wealth
Isa 9: 7 Of the i of his government
Mt 24: 12 Because of the i of wickedness,
Lk 17: 5 said to the Lord, "I our faith!"
Ac 12: 24 the word of God continued to i
Ro 5: 20 in so that the trespass might i.
1Th 3: 12 May the Lord make your love i

INCREASED (INCREASE)
Ac 6: 7 of disciples in Jerusalem i rapidly,
     9: 31 the Holy Spirit, it i in numbers.
Ro 5: 20 But where sin i, grace i all the more,

INCREASING (INCREASE)
Ac 6: 1 when the number of disciples was i,
2Th 1: 3 all of you have for one another is i.
2Pe 1: 8 possess these qualities in i measure,

INCREDIBLE*
Ac 26: 8 you consider it i that God raises

INDEBTEDNESS* (DEBT)
Col 2: 14 canceled the charge of our legal i,

INDEPENDENT*
1Co 11: 11 in the Lord woman is not i of man, nor is
             man i of woman.

INDESCRIBABLE*
2Co 9: 15 Thanks be to God for his i gift!

INDESTRUCTIBLE*
Heb 7: 16 the basis of the power of an i life.

INDIGNANT
Mk 1: 41 Jesus was i. He reached out his hand
     10: 14 When Jesus saw this, he was i.

INDISPENSABLE*
1Co 12: 22 body that seem to be weaker are i,

INEFFECTIVE*
2Pe 1: 8 they will keep you from being i

INEXPRESSIBLE*
2Co 12: 4 up to paradise and heard i things,
1Pe 1: 8 are filled with an i and glorious joy,

INFANCY* (INFANTS)
2Ti 3: 15 from i you have known the Holy

INFANTS (INFANCY)
Ps 8: 2 i you have established a stronghold
Mt 21: 16 and i you have ordained praise'?"
1Co 3: 1 but as worldly—mere i in Christ.
     14: 20 In regard to evil be i, but in your
Eph 4: 14 Then we will no longer be i,

INFIRMITIES*
Mt 8: 17 "He took up our i and bore our

INFLAMED
Ro 1: 27 and were i with lust for one another.

INFLUENTIAL*
1Co 1: 26 not many were i; not many were

INHABITANTS (INHABITED)
Nu 33: 55 do not drive out the i of the land,
Rev 8: 13 Woe to the i of the earth,

INHABITED (INHABITANTS)
Isa 45: 18 to be empty, but formed it to be i—

INHERIT (CO-HEIRS HEIR HEIRS HERITAGE
INHERITANCE)
Dt 1: 38 because he will lead Israel to i it.
Jos 1: 6 these people to i the land I swore
Ps 37: 11 the meek will i the land and enjoy
     37: 29 The righteous will i the land
Zec 2: 12 The Lord will i Judah as his
Mt 5: 5 the meek, for they will i the earth.
     19: 29 times as much and will i eternal life.
Mk 10: 17 "what must I do to i eternal life?"
Lk 10: 25 "what must I do to i eternal life?"
     18: 18 what must I do to i eternal life?"
1Co 6: 9 wrongdoers will not i the kingdom
     15: 50 blood cannot i the kingdom of God,

Rev 21: 7 who are victorious will i all this,

INHERITANCE (INHERIT)
Lev 20: 24 I will give it to you as an i, a land
Dt 4: 20 to be the people of his i, as you now
     10: 9 the Lord is their i, as the Lord
Jos 14: 3 the two-and-a-half tribes their i east
Ps 16: 6 surely I have a delightful i.
     33: 12 the people he chose for his i.
     136: 21 and gave their land as an i,
Pr 13: 22 Good people leave an i for their
Mt 25: 34 take your i, the kingdom prepared
Eph 1: 14 deposit guaranteeing our i until
     5: 5 has any i in the kingdom of Christ
Col 1: 12 to share in the i of his people
     3: 24 you will receive an i from the Lord
Heb 9: 15 may receive the promised eternal i—
1Pe 1: 4 and into an i that can never perish,

INIQUITIES (INIQUITY)
Ps 78: 38 he forgave their i and did not
     103: 10 or repay us according to our i.
Isa 53: 5 he was crushed for our i;
     53: 11 many, and he will bear their i.
     59: 2 your i have separated you from your
Mic 7: 19 hurl all our i into the depths

INIQUITY (INIQUITIES)
Ps 25: 11 forgive my i, though it is great.
     32: 5 to you and did not cover up my i.
     51: 2 Wash away all my i and cleanse me
     51: 5 from my sins and blot out all my i.
Isa 53: 6 has laid on him the i of us all.

INJURED
Eze 34: 16 I will bind up the i and strengthen
Zec 11: 16 or heal the i, or feed the healthy,

INJUSTICE
2Ch 19: 7 the Lord our God there is no i

INK
2Co 3: 3 written not with i but with the Spirit

INN*
Lk 10: 34 brought him to an i and took care

INNOCENT
Ex 23: 7 do not put an i or honest person
Dt 25: 1 acquitting the i and condemning
Pr 6: 17 tongue, hands that shed i blood,
     17: 26 imposing a fine on the i is not good,
Joel 3: 21 leave their i blood unpunished?
Mt 10: 16 shrewd as snakes and as i as doves.
     27: 4 said, "for I have betrayed i blood."
     27: 24 "I am i of this man's blood,"
Ac 18: 6 on your own heads! I am i of it.
     20: 26 today that I am i of the blood
Ro 16: 19 is good, and i about what is evil.
1Co 4: 4 clear, but that does not make me i.

INQUIRE
Isa 8: 19 should not a people i of their God?

INSCRIPTION
Mt 22: 20 image is this? And whose i?"
2Ti 2: 19 stands firm, sealed with this i:

INSIGHT
1Ki 4: 29 Solomon wisdom and very great i,
Ps 119: 99 I have more i than all my teachers,
Pr 5: 1 turn your ear to my words of i,
     7: 4 to i, "You are my relative."
     16: 16 to get i rather than silver!
     20: 5 who have i draw them out.
     21: 30 no i, no plan that can succeed
     23: 23 wisdom, instruction and i as well.
Php 1: 9 more in knowledge and depth of i,
2Ti 2: 7 the Lord will give you i into all this.

INSOLENT
Pr 29: 21 from youth will turn out to be i.
Ro 1: 30 God-haters, i, arrogant and boastful;

INSPIRED*
Hos 9: 7 a fool, anyone who is i a maniac.
1Th 1: 3 and your endurance i by hope in our

INSTALLED
Ps 2: 6 "I have i my king on Zion, my holy

INSTINCT* (INSTINCTS)
2Pe 2: 12 creatures of i, born only to be
Jude : 10 what things they do understand by i,

INSTINCTS* (INSTINCT)
Jude : 19 who follow mere natural i and do

INSTITUTED
Ro 13: 2 is rebelling against what God has i,

INSTRUCT (INSTRUCTED INSTRUCTION INSTRUCTIONS INSTRUCTOR)
Dt 17: 10 careful to do everything they **i**
Ps 32: 8 I will **i** you and teach you
105: 22 to **i** his princes as he pleased
Pr 4: 11 I **i** you in the way of wisdom
9: 9 I the wise and they will be wiser
Ro 15: 14 and competent to **i** one another.
1Co 2: 16 mind of the Lord so as to **i** him?"
14: 19 to **i** others than ten thousand words

INSTRUCTED (INSTRUCT)
2Ch 26: 5 who **i** him in the fear of God.
Isa 50: 4 LORD has given me an **i** tongue,
Mt 13: 52 of the law who has been **i**
1Co 14: 31 in turn so that everyone may be **i**
2Ti 2: 25 Opponents must be gently **i**,

INSTRUCTION (INSTRUCT)
Pr 1: 2 for gaining wisdom and **i**;
1: 3 receiving **i** in prudent behavior,
1: 7 but fools despise wisdom and **i**.
1: 8 to your father's **i** and do not forsake
4: 1 Listen, my sons, to a father's **i**;
4: 13 Hold on to **i**, do not let it go;
6: 23 correction and **i** are the way
8: 10 Choose my **i** instead of silver,
8: 33 Listen to my **i** and be wise;
13: 1 A wise child heeds a parent's **i**,
13: 13 Whoever scorns **i** will pay for it,
15: 33 Wisdom's **i** is to fear the LORD,
16: 20 Those who give heed to **i** prosper,
16: 21 and gracious people promote **i**.
23: 12 Apply your heart to **i** and your ears
23: 23 wisdom, **i** and insight as well.
8: 28 anyone turns a deaf ear to my **i**,
29: 18 are those who heed wisdom's **i**.
Isa 8: 20 Consult God's **i** and the testimony
1Co 14: 6 or prophecy or word of **i**?
14: 26 a hymn, or a word of **i**, a revelation,
Eph 6: 4 up in the training and **i** of the Lord.
1Th 4: 8 who rejects this **i** does not reject
2Th 3: 14 those who do not obey our **i** in this
1Ti 6: 3 the sound **i** of our Lord Jesus Christ
2Ti 4: 2 with great patience and careful **i**.

INSTRUCTIONS (INSTRUCT)
1Ti 3: 14 I am writing you these **i** so that,

INSTRUCTOR (INSTRUCT)
Gal 6: 6 share all good things with their **i**.

INSTRUMENT (INSTRUMENTS)
Eze 33: 32 beautiful voice and plays an **i** well,
Ac 9: 15 This man is my chosen **i** to proclaim
Ro 6: 13 to sin as an **i** of wickedness,
6: 13 to him as an **i** of righteousness.

INSTRUMENTS (INSTRUMENT)
2Ch 23: 13 their **i** were leading the praises.
2Ti 2: 21 from the latter will be an **i** for noble

INSULT (INSULTED INSULTS)
Pr 12: 16 once, but the prudent overlook an **i**.
Mt 5: 11 are you when people **i** you,
Lk 6: 22 when they exclude you and **i** you
1Pe 3: 9 not repay evil with evil or **i** with **i**.

INSULTED (INSULT)
Heb 10: 29 and who have **i** the Spirit of grace?
1Pe 4: 14 If you are **i** because of the name

INSULTS (INSULT)
Ps 22: 7 they hurl **i**, shaking their heads.
69: 9 the **i** of those who insult you fall
Pr 9: 7 corrects a mocker invites **i**;
22: 10 quarrels and **i** are ended.
Mk 15: 29 who passed by hurled **i** at him,
Jn 9: 28 Then they hurled **i** at him and said,
Ro 15: 3 "The **i** of those who insult you have
2Co 12: 10 in weaknesses, in **i**, in hardships,
1Pe 2: 23 When they hurled their **i** at him,

INTEGRITY*
Dt 9: 5 your **i** that you are going in to take
1Ki 9: 4 you walk before me faithfully with **i**
1Ch 29: 17 test the heart and are pleased with **i**.
Job 2: 3 And he still maintains his **i**,
2: 9 "Are you still maintaining your **i**?
6: 29 reconsider, for my **i** is at stake.
27: 5 till I die, I will not deny my **i**.
Ps 7: 8 according to my **i**, O Most High.
25: 21 May **i** and uprightness protect me,
41: 12 In my **i** you uphold me and set me
78: 72 David shepherded them with **i**
Pr 10: 9 Whoever walks in **i** walks securely,
11: 3 The **i** of the upright guides them,

Pr 13: 6 guards the person of **i**,
29: 10 The bloodthirsty hate people of **i**
Isa 45: 23 my mouth has uttered in all **i** a word
59: 4 no one pleads their case with **i**.
Mt 22: 16 "we know that you are a man of **i**
Mk 12: 14 we know that you are a man of **i**.
2Co 1: 12 with **i** and godly sincerity.
Tit 2: 7 In your teaching show **i**,

INTELLIGENCE (INTELLIGENT)
Isa 29: 14 the **i** of the intelligent will vanish."
1Co 1: 19 the **i** of the intelligent I will

INTELLIGENT (INTELLIGENCE)
Isa 29: 14 intelligence of the **i** will vanish."

INTELLIGIBLE*
1Co 14: 9 Unless you speak **i** words with your
14: 19 I would rather speak five **i** words

INTENDED
Ge 50: 20 You **i** to harm me, but God **i** it

INTENSE
1Th 2: 17 our **i** longing we made every effort
Rev 16: 9 They were seared by the **i** heat

INTERCEDE (INTERCEDES INTERCEDING INTERCESSION INTERCESSOR)
Heb 7: 25 because he always lives to **i**

INTERCEDES* (INTERCEDE)
Ro 8: 26 the Spirit himself **i** for us through
8: 27 Spirit, because the Spirit **i** for God's

INTERCEDING* (INTERCEDE)
Ro 8: 34 hand of God and is also **i** for us.

INTERCESSION* (INTERCEDE)
Isa 53: 12 and made **i** for the transgressors.
1Ti 2: 1 **i** and thanksgiving be made

INTERCESSOR* (INTERCEDE)
Job 16: 20 My **i** is my friend as my eyes pour

INTEREST (INTERESTS)
Lev 25: 36 Do not take **i** or any profit
Dt 23: 20 You may charge a foreigner **i**,
Ps 15: 5 lend money to the poor without **i**
Ne 5: 10 But let us stop charging **i**!
Mt 25: 27 I would have received it back with **i**.

INTERESTS (INTEREST)
1Co 7: 34 and his **i** are divided.
Php 2: 4 not looking to your own **i** but each of you
to the **i** of the others.
2: 21 everyone looks out for their own **i**,

INTERFERE*
2Sa 19: 22 What right do you have to **i**?
Ezr 6: 7 Do not **i** with the work on this

INTERMARRY (MARRY)
Dt 7: 3 Do not **i** with them. Do not give
Ezr 9: 14 **i** with the peoples who commit such

INTERPRET (INTERPRETATION INTERPRETER)
Ge 41: 15 "I had a dream, and no one can **i** it.
Mt 16: 3 you cannot **i** the signs of the times.
1Co 12: 30 Do all speak in tongues? Do all **i**?
14: 5 unless they **i**, so that the church
14: 13 pray that they may **i** what they say.
14: 27 one at a time, and someone must **i**.

INTERPRETATION (INTERPRET)
1Co 12: 10 and to still another the **i** of tongues.
14: 26 a revelation, a tongue or an **i**.
2Pe 1: 20 by the prophet's own **i** of things.

INTERPRETER* (INTERPRET)
Ge 42: 23 since he was using an **i**.
1Co 14: 28 If there is no **i**, the speaker should

INTERVENED
Ac 15: 14 God first **i** to choose a people

INTOXICATED
Pr 5: 19 may you ever be **i** with her love.
5: 20 Why, my son, be **i** with another

INVADED
2Ki 17: 5 king of Assyria **i** the entire land,
24: 1 king of Babylon **i** the land,

INVENT*
Ro 1: 30 they **i** ways of doing evil;

INVESTIGATED
Lk 1: 3 I myself have carefully **i** everything

INVISIBLE*
Ro 1: 20 of the world God's **i** qualities—
Col 1: 15 The Son is the image of the **i** God,
1: 16 visible and **i**, whether thrones

1Ti 1: 17 eternal, immortal, **i**, the only God,
Heb 11: 27 because he saw him who is **i**.

INVITE (INVITED INVITES)
Pr 18: 6 their mouths **i** a beating.
Mt 22: 9 **i** to the banquet anyone you find.'
25: 38 we see you a stranger and **i** you in,
Lk 14: 12 or dinner, do not **i** your friends,
14: 13 when you give a banquet, **i** the poor,

INVITED (INVITE)
Zep 1: 7 he has consecrated those he has **i**.
Mt 22: 14 "For many are **i**, but few are
25: 35 I was a stranger and you **i** me in,
Lk 14: 10 But when you are **i**, take the lowest
Rev 19: 9 'Blessed are those who are **i**

INVITES (INVITE)
1Co 10: 27 If an unbeliever **i** you to a meal

INVOLVED
2Ti 2: 4 No one serving as a soldier gets **i**

IRON
2Ki 6: 6 threw it there, and made the **i** float.
Ps 2: 9 You will break them with a rod of **i**;
Pr 27: 17 As **i** sharpens **i**, so one person
Da 2: 33 its legs of **i**, its feet partly of **i**
1Ti 4: 2 have been seared as with a hot **i**.
Rev 2: 27 'will rule them with an **i** scepter
12: 5 all the nations with an **i** scepter."
19: 15 will rule the nations with an **i** scepter."

IRRELIGIOUS*
1Ti 1: 9 the unholy and **i**, for those who kill

IRREVOCABLE*
Ro 11: 29 for God's gifts and his call are **i**.

ISAAC
Son of Abraham by Sarah (Ge 17:19; 21:1–7; 1Ch 1:28). Abrahamic covenant perpetuated through (Ge 17:21; 26:2–5). Offered up by Abraham (Ge 22; Heb 11:17–19). Rebekah taken as wife (Ge 24). Inherited Abraham's estate (Ge 25:5). Fathered Esau and Jacob (Ge 25:19–26; 1Ch 1:34). Nearly lost Rebekah to Abimelek (Ge 26:1–11). Covenant with Abimelek (Ge 26:12–31). Tricked into blessing Jacob (Ge 27). Death (Ge 35:27–29). Father of Israel (Ex 3:6; Dt 29:13; Ro 9:10).

ISAIAH
Prophet to Judah (Isa 1:1). Called by the LORD (Isa 6). Announced judgment to Ahaz (Isa 7), deliverance from Assyria to Hezekiah (Isa 36–37), deliverance from death to Hezekiah (2Ki 20:1–11; Isa 38). Chronicler of Judah's history (2Ch 26:22; 32:32).

ISH-BOSHETH*
Son of Saul who attempted to succeed him as king (2Sa 2:8–4:12; 1Ch 8:33).

ISHMAEL
Son of Abraham by Hagar (Ge 16; 1Ch 1:28). Blessed, but not son of covenant (Ge 17:18–21; Gal 4:21–31). Sent away by Sarah (Ge 21:8–21). Children (Ge 25:12–18; 1Ch 1:29–31). Death (Ge 25:17).

ISLAND
Rev 1: 9 was on the **i** of Patmos because
16: 20 Every **i** fled away

ISRAEL (ISRAEL'S ISRAELITE ISRAELITES)
1. Name given to Jacob (see JACOB).
2. Corporate name of Jacob's descendants; often specifically Northern Kingdom.
Ex 28: 11 the sons of **I** on the two stones
28: 29 of the sons of **I** over his heart
Nu 24: 17 a scepter will rise out of **I**.
Dt 6: 4 Hear, O **I**: The LORD our God,
10: 12 And now, **I**, what does the LORD
Jos 4: 22 them, '**I** crossed the Jordan on dry
Jdg 17: 6 In those days **I** had no king;
Ru 2: 12 the God of **I**, under whose wings
1Sa 3: 20 And all **I** from Dan to Beersheba
4: 21 "The Glory has departed from **I**"—
14: 23 So on that day the LORD saved **I**.
15: 26 has rejected you as king over **I**!"
17: 46 will know that there is a God in **I**.
18: 16 But all **I** and Judah loved David,
2Sa 5: 2 'You will shepherd my people **I**,
5: 3 they anointed David king over **I**.
14: 25 all **I** there was not a man so highly
1Ki 1: 35 I have appointed him ruler over **I**
10: 9 of the LORD's eternal love for **I**,
12: 1 for all **I** had gone there
18: 17 "Is that you, you troubler of **I**?"
19: 18 Yet I reserve seven thousand in **I**—
2Ki 5: 8 know that there is a prophet in **I**."

1Ch	17: 22	made your people I your very own
	21: 1	incited David to take a census of I.
	29: 25	exalted Solomon in the sight of all I.
2Ch	9: 8	of the love of your God for I and his
Ps	73: 1	Surely God is good to I, to those
	81: 8	if you would only listen to me, I
	98: 3	his faithfulness to the house of I;
	99: 8	you were to I a forgiving God,
Isa	11: 12	nations and gather the exiles of I;
	27: 6	I will bud and blossom and fill all
	44: 21	I, I will not forget you.
	46: 13	salvation to Zion, my splendor to I.
Jer	2: 3	I was holy to the LORD,
	23: 6	be saved and I will live in safety.
	31: 2	I will come to give rest to I."
	31: 10	'He who scattered I will gather
	31: 31	a new covenant with the house of I
	33: 17	to sit on the throne of the house of I,
Eze	3: 17	you a watchman for the house of I;
	33: 7	you a watchman for the house of I;
	34: 2	prophesy against the shepherds of I;
	37: 28	that I the LORD make I holy,
	39: 23	that the people of I went into exile
Da	9: 20	the sin of my people I and making
Hos	11: 1	"When I was a child, I loved him,
Am	4: 12	this is what I will do to you, I,
	7: 11	and I will surely go into exile,
	8: 2	"The time is ripe for my people I;
	9: 14	I will bring my people I back
Mic	5: 2	for me one who will be ruler over I,
Zec	11: 14	family bond between Judah and I.
Mal	1: 5	even beyond the borders of I!'
Mt	2: 6	who will shepherd my people I.' "
	10: 6	Go rather to the lost sheep of I.
	15: 24	sent only to the lost sheep of I."
Mk	12: 29	'Hear, O I: The Lord our God,
Lk	22: 30	judging the twelve tribes of I.
Ac	1: 6	going to restore the kingdom to I?"
	9: 15	their kings and to the people of I.
Ro	9: 4	the people of I. Theirs is
	9: 6	all who are descended from I are I.
	9: 31	but the people of I, who pursued
	11: 7	of I sought so earnestly they did not
	11: 26	and in this way all I will be saved.
Gal	6: 16	follow this rule—to the I of God.
Eph	2: 12	excluded from citizenship in I
	3: 6	Gentiles are heirs together with I,
Heb	8: 8	a new covenant with the house of I
Rev	7: 4	144,000 from all the tribes of I.
	21: 12	the names of the twelve tribes of I.

ISRAEL'S (ISRAEL)

Jdg	10: 16	he could bear I misery no longer.
2Sa	23: 1	God of Jacob, the hero of I songs:
Isa	44: 6	I King and Redeemer, the LORD
Jer	3: 9	Because I immorality mattered so
	31: 9	because I am I father, and Ephraim
Jn	3: 10	"You are I teacher," said Jesus,

ISRAELITE (ISRAEL)

Ex	16: 1	The whole I community set
	35: 29	All the I men and women who were
Nu	8: 16	male offspring from every I woman.
	20: 1	the whole I community arrived
	20: 22	The whole I community set
Jn	1: 47	"Here truly is an I in whom there is
Ro	11: 1	I am an I myself, a descendant

ISRAELITES (ISRAEL)

Ex	1: 7	but the I were exceedingly fruitful;
	2: 23	The I groaned in their slavery
	3: 9	now the cry of the I has reached me,
	12: 35	The I did as Moses instructed
	12: 37	The I journeyed from Rameses
	14: 22	the I went through the sea on dry
	16: 12	have heard the grumbling of the I.
	16: 35	The I ate manna forty years,
	24: 17	To the I the glory of the LORD
	28: 30	for the I over his heart before
	29: 45	I will dwell among the I and be their
	31: 16	The I are to observe the Sabbath,
	33: 5	"Tell the I, 'You are a stiff-necked
	39: 42	The I had done all the work just as
Lev	22: 32	be acknowledged as holy by the I
	25: 46	rule over your fellow I ruthlessly.
	25: 55	for the I belong to me as servants.
Nu	2: 32	These are the I, counted according
	6: 23	'This is how you are to bless the I.
	9: 2	"Have the I celebrate the Passover
	9: 7	from above the tent, the I set out;
	10: 12	the I set out from the Desert of Sinai
	14: 2	All the I grumbled against Moses
	20: 12	me as holy in the sight of the I,

Nu	21: 6	they bit the people and many I died.
	26: 65	had told those I they would surely
	27: 12	and see the land I have given the I.
	33: 3	The I set out from Rameses
	35: 10	"Speak to the I and say to them:
Dt	33: 1	on the I before his death.
Jos	1: 2	I am about to give to them—to the I.
	5: 6	The I had moved
	7: 1	the I were unfaithful in regard
	8: 32	in the presence of the I,
	18: 1	whole assembly of the I gathered
	21: 3	the I gave the Levites the following
	22: 9	of Manasseh left the I at Shiloh
Jdg	2: 11	Then the I did evil in the eyes
	3: 12	Again the I did evil in the eyes
	4: 1	Again the I did evil in the eyes
	6: 1	The I did evil in the eyes
	10: 6	Again the I did evil in the eyes
	13: 1	Again the I did evil in the eyes
1Sa	17: 2	Saul and the I assembled
1Ki	8: 63	all the I dedicated the temple
	9: 22	did not make slaves of any of the I;
	12: 17	as for the I who were living
2Ki	17: 24	towns of Samaria to replace the I.
1Ch	9: 2	in their own towns were some I,
	10: 1	the I fled before them, and many
	11: 4	all the I marched to Jerusalem
2Ch	7: 6	and all the I were standing.
Ne	1: 6	I confess the sins we I,
Jer	16: 14	who brought the I up out of Egypt,'
Hos	1: 10	"Yet the I will be like the sand
	3: 1	Love her as the LORD loves the I,
Am	4: 5	you I, for this is what you love
Mic	5: 3	of his brothers return to join the I.
Ro	9: 27	the number of the I be like the sand
	10: 1	to God for the I is that they may be
	10: 16	not all the I accepted the good news.
2Co	11: 22	So am I. Are they I? So am I.

JAIR

Judge from Gilead (Jdg 10:3–5).

JAIRUS*

Synagogue ruler whose daughter Jesus raised (Mk 5:22–43; Lk 8:41–56).

JAMES

1. Apostle; brother of John (Mt 4:21–22; 10:2; Mk 3:17; Lk 5:1–10). At transfiguration (Mt 17:1–13; Mk 9:1–13; Lk 9:28–36). Killed by Herod (Ac 12:2).

2. Apostle; son of Alphaeus (Mt 10:3; Mk 3:18; Lk 6:15).

3. Brother of Jesus (Mt 13:55; Mk 6:3; Lk 24:10; Gal 1:19) and Judas (Jude 1). With believers before Pentecost (Ac 1:13). Leader of church at Jerusalem (Ac 12:17; 15; 21:18; Gal 2:9, 12). Author of epistle (Jas 1:1).

JAPHETH

Son of Noah (Ge 5:32; 1Ch 1:4–5). Blessed (Ge 9:18–28). Sons of (Ge 10:2–5).

JAR (JARS)

Ge	24: 14	'Please let down your j that I may
1Ki	17: 14	'The j of flour will not be used
Jer	19: 1	"Go and buy a clay j from a potter.
Lk	8: 16	hides it in a clay j or puts it under

JARS (JAR)

Jn	2: 6	Nearby stood six stone water j,
2Co	4: 7	we have this treasure in j of clay

JASPER

Ex	28: 20	row shall be topaz, onyx and j.
Eze	28: 13	topaz, onyx and j, lapis lazuli,
Rev	4: 3	sat there had the appearance of j
	21: 19	The first foundation was j,

JAVELIN

1Sa	17: 45	me with sword and spear and j, but I

JAWBONE

Jdg	15: 15	Finding a fresh j of a donkey,

JEALOUS (JEALOUSLY JEALOUSY)

Ex	20: 5	am a j God, punishing the children
	34: 14	whose name is J, is a j God.
Dt	4: 24	God is a consuming fire, a j God.
	6: 15	is a j God and his anger will burn
	32: 21	They made me j by what is no god
Jos	24: 19	He is a holy God; he is a j God.
Eze	16: 38	vengeance of my wrath and j anger.
	16: 42	my j anger will turn away from you;
	23: 25	I will direct my j anger against you,
	36: 6	in my j wrath because you have
Joel	2: 18	Then the LORD was j for his land
Na	1: 2	The LORD is a j and avenging
Zep	3: 8	consumed by the fire of my j anger.
Zec	1: 14	"I am very j for Jerusalem and Zion,
	8: 2	"I am very j for Zion;
2Co	11: 2	I am j for you with a godly jealousy.

JEALOUSLY* (JEALOUS)

Jas	4: 5	he j longs for the spirit

JEALOUSY (JEALOUS)

Ps	79: 5	How long will your j burn like fire?
Pr	6: 34	For j arouses a husband's fury,
	27: 4	but who can stand before j?
SS	8: 6	death, its j unyielding as the grave.
Zep	1: 18	fire of his j the whole earth will be
Zec	8: 2	I am burning with j for her."
Ro	13: 13	debauchery, not in dissension and j.
1Co	3: 3	For since there is j and quarreling
	10: 22	we trying to arouse the Lord's j?
2Co	11: 2	I am jealous for you with a godly j.
	12: 20	fear that there may be quarreling, j,
Gal	5: 20	hatred, discord, j, fits of rage,

JEERS*

Heb	11: 36	Some faced j and flogging,

JEHOAHAZ

1. Son of Jehu; king of Israel (2Ki 13:1–9).

2. Son of Josiah; king of Judah (2Ki 23:31–34; 2Ch 36:1–4).

JEHOASH

1. See JOASH.

2. Son of Jehoahaz; king of Israel. Defeat of Aram prophesied by Elisha (2Ki 13:10–25). Defeated Amaziah in Jerusalem (2Ki 14:1–16; 2Ch 25:17–24).

JEHOIACHIN

Son of Jehoiakim; king of Judah exiled by Nebuchadnezzar (2Ki 24:8–17; 2Ch 36:8–10; Jer 22:24–30; 24:1). Raised from prisoner status (2Ki 25:27–30; Jer 52:31–34).

JACOB

Second son of Isaac, twin of Esau (Ge 26:21–26; 1Ch 1:34). Bought Esau's birthright (Ge 26:29–34); tricked Isaac into blessing him (Ge 27:1–37). Fled to Harran (Ge 28:1–5). Abrahamic covenant perpetuated through (Ge 28:13–15; Mal 1:2). Vision at Bethel (Ge 28:10–22). Served Laban for Rachel and Leah (Ge 29:1–30). Children (Ge 29:31–30:24; 35:16–26). Flocks increased (Ge 30:25–43). Returned to Canaan (Ge 31). Wrestled with God; name changed to Israel (Ge 32:22–32). Reconciled to Esau (Ge 33). Returned to Bethel (Ge 35:1–15). Favored Joseph (Ge 37:3). Sent sons to Egypt during famine (Ge 42–43). Settled in Egypt (Ge 46). Blessed Ephraim and Manasseh (Ge 48). Blessed sons (Ge 49:1–28; Heb 11:21). Death (Ge 49:29–33). Burial (Ge 50:1–14).

JABBOK

Ge	32: 22	sons and crossed the ford of the J.
Dt	3: 16	the border) and out to the J River,

JABESH (JABESH GILEAD)

1Sa	11: 1	And all the men of J said to him,
	31: 12	the wall of Beth Shan and went to J,
1Ch	10: 12	and his sons and brought them to J.

JABESH GILEAD (JABESH)

Jdg	21: 8	no one from J had come to the camp
2Sa	2: 4	men from J who had buried Saul,
1Ch	10: 1	J heard what the Philistines had

JAEL*

Woman who killed Canaanite general, Sisera (Jdg 4:17–22; 5:24–27).

JEHOIADA
Priest who sheltered Joash from Athaliah (2Ki 11–12; 2Ch 22:11–24:16).

JEHOIAKIM
Son of Josiah; made king of Judah by Pharaoh Necho (2Ki 23:34–24:6; 2Ch 36:4–8; Jer 22:18–23). Burned scroll of Jeremiah's prophecies (Jer 36).

JEHORAM
1. Son of Jehoshaphat; king of Judah (2Ki 8:16–24). Prophesied against by Elijah; killed by the Lord (2Ch 21).
2. See JORAM.

JEHOSHAPHAT
Son of Asa; king of Judah. Strengthened his kingdom (2Ch 17). Joined with Ahab against Aram (2Ki 22; 2Ch 18). Established judges (2Ch 19). Joined with Joram against Moab (2Ki 3; 2Ch 20).

JEHU
1. Prophet against Baasha (2Ki 16:1–7).
2. King of Israel. Anointed by Elijah to obliterate house of Ahab (1Ki 19:16–17); anointed by servant of Elisha (2Ki 9:1–13). Killed Joram and Ahaziah (2Ki 9:14–29; 2Ch 22:7–9), Jezebel (2Ki 9:30–37), relatives of Ahab (2Ki 10:1–17), ministers of Baal (2Ki 10:18–29). Death (2Ki 10:30–36).

JEPHTHAH
Judge from Gilead who delivered Israel from Ammon (Jdg 10:6–12:7). Made rash vow concerning his daughter (Jdg 11:30–40).

JEREMIAH
Prophet to Judah (Jer 1:1–3). Called by the Lord (Jer 1). Put in stocks (Jer 20:1–3). Threatened for prophesying (Jer 11:18–23; 26). Opposed by Hananiah (Jer 28). Scroll burned (Jer 36). Imprisoned (Jer 37). Thrown into cistern (Jer 38). Forced to Egypt with those fleeing Babylonians (Jer 43).

JERICHO
Nu 22: 1 along the Jordan across from J.
Jos 3: 16 the people crossed over opposite J.
      5: 10 camped at Gilgal on the plains of J,
Lk 10: 30 going down from Jerusalem to J,
Heb 11: 30 By faith the walls of J fell,

JEROBOAM
1. Official of Solomon; rebelled to become first king of Israel (1Ki 11:26–40; 12:1–20; 2Ch 10). Idolatry (1Ki 12:25–33); judgment for (1Ki 13–14; 2Ch 13).
2. Son of Jehoash; king of Israel (1Ki 14:23–29).

JERUSALEM
Jos 10: 1 Now Adoni-Zedek king of J heard
     15: 8 slope of the Jebusite city (that is, J).
Jdg 1: 8 The men of Judah attacked J
1Sa 17: 54 Philistine's head and brought it to J;
2Sa 5: 5 in J he reigned over all Israel
      5: 6 his men marched to J to attack
      9: 13 And Mephibosheth lived in J,
     11: 1 But David remained in J.
     15: 29 took the ark of God back to J
     24: 16 stretched out his hand to destroy J,
1Ki 3: 1 the Lord, and the wall around J.
      9: 15 terraces, the wall of J, and Hazor,
      9: 19 whatever he desired to build in J,
     10: 26 chariot cities and also with him in J.
     10: 27 silver as common in J as stones,
     11: 7 On a hill east of J, Solomon built
     11: 13 my servant and for the sake of J,
     11: 36 always have a lamp before me in J,
     11: 42 in J over all Israel forty years.
     12: 27 at the temple of the Lord in J,
     14: 21 and he reigned seventeen years in J.
     14: 25 Shishak king of Egypt attacked J.
     15: 2 and he reigned in J three years.
     15: 10 and he reigned in J forty-one years.
     22: 42 he reigned in J twenty-five years.
2Ki 8: 17 and he reigned in J eight years.
      8: 26 king, and he reigned in J one year.
     12: 1 and he reigned in J forty years.
     12: 17 Then he turned to attack J.
     14: 2 he reigned in J twenty-nine years.
     14: 13 Jehoash went to J and broke down
     15: 2 and he reigned in J fifty-two years.
     15: 33 and he reigned in J sixteen years.
     16: 2 and he reigned in J sixteen years.
     16: 5 Israel marched up to fight against J
     18: 2 he reigned in J twenty-nine years.
     18: 17 from Lachish to King Hezekiah at J.
     19: 31 For out of J will come a remnant,
     21: 1 and he reigned in J fifty-five years.

2Ki 21: 12 am going to bring such disaster on J
     21: 19 king, and he reigned in J two years.
     22: 1 and he reigned in J thirty-one years.
     23: 27 and I will reject J, the city I chose,
     23: 31 and he reigned in J three months.
     23: 36 and he reigned in J eleven years.
     24: 8 and he reigned in J three months.
     24: 10 king of Babylon advanced on J
     24: 14 He carried all J into exile:
     24: 18 and he reigned in J eleven years.
     24: 20 anger that all this happened to J
     25: 1 Babylon marched against J with his
     25: 9 royal palace and all the houses of J.
1Ch 11: 4 all the Israelites marched to J
     21: 16 sword in his hand extended over J.
2Ch 1: 4 he had pitched a tent for it in J.
      3: 1 the Lord in J on Mount Moriah,
      6: 6 now I have chosen J for my Name
      9: 1 she came to J to test him with hard
     20: 15 and all who live in Judah and J!
     20: 27 Judah and J returned joyfully to J
     29: 8 Lord has fallen on Judah and J;
     36: 19 and broke down the wall of J.
Ezr 1: 2 build a temple for him at J in Judah.
      2: 1 to Babylon (they returned to J
      3: 1 assembled with one accord in J.
      4: 12 up to us from you have gone to J
      4: 24 of God in J came to a standstill until
      6: 12 decree or to destroy this temple in J.
      7: 8 Ezra arrived in J in the fifth month
      9: 9 a wall of protection in Judah and J.
     10: 7 J for all the exiles to assemble in J.
Ne   1: 2 survived the exile, and also about J.
      1: 3 The wall of J is broken down,
      2: 11 I went to J, and after staying three
      2: 17 let us rebuild the wall of J, and no
      2: 20 you have no share in J or any claim
      3: 8 They restored J as far as the Broad
      4: 8 fight against J and stir up trouble
     11: 1 the leaders of the people settled in J.
     12: 27 At the dedication of the wall of J,
     12: 43 and J could be heard far away.
Ps 51: 18 Zion, to build up the walls of J.
     79: 1 they have reduced J to rubble.
    122: 2 feet are standing in your gates, J.
    122: 3 J is built like a city that is closely
    122: 6 Pray for the peace of J:
    125: 2 As the mountains surround J,
    128: 5 see the prosperity of J all the days
    137: 5 If I forget you, J, may my right
    147: 2 The Lord builds up J;
    147: 12 Extol the Lord, J;
SS   6: 4 as lovely as J, as majestic as troops
Isa 1: 1 and J that Isaiah son of Amoz saw
      2: 1 Amoz saw concerning Judah and J:
      3: 1 is about to take from J and Judah
      3: 8 J staggers, Judah is falling;
      4: 3 are recorded among the living in J.
      8: 14 for the people of J he will be a trap
     27: 13 Lord on the holy mountain in J.
     31: 5 the Lord Almighty will shield J;
     33: 20 your eyes will see J, a peaceful
     40: 2 Speak tenderly to J, and proclaim
     40: 9 You who bring good news to J,
     52: 1 Put on your garments of splendor, J,
     52: 2 rise up, sit enthroned, J.
     62: 6 posted watchmen on your walls, J;
     62: 7 give him no rest till he establishes J
     65: 18 for I will create J to be a delight
Jer 2: 2 and proclaim in the hearing of J:
      3: 17 time they will call J The Throne
      4: 5 in Judah and proclaim in J and say:
      4: 14 J, wash the evil from your heart
      5: 1 "Go up and down the streets of J,
      6: 6 and build siege ramps against J
      8: 5 Why does J always turn away?
      9: 11 "I will make J a heap of ruins,
     13: 27 Woe to you, J! How long will you
     14: 2 of J I have seen something horrible:
     24: 1 carried into exile from J to Babylon
     26: 18 J will become a heap of rubble,
     32: 2 of Babylon was then besieging J,
     33: 10 and the streets of J that are deserted,
     39: 1 Babylon marched against J with his
     51: 50 a distant land, and call to mind J."
     52: 14 broke down all the walls around J
La   1: 7 and wandering J remembers all
Eze 14: 21 I send against J my four dreadful
     16: 2 confront J with her detestable
Da   6: 10 the windows opened toward J.
      9: 2 of J would last seventy years.
      9: 12 done like what has been done to J.

Da   9: 25 rebuild J until the Anointed One,
Joel 3: 1 I restore the fortunes of Judah and J,
      3: 16 roar from Zion and thunder from J;
      3: 17 J will be holy; never again will
Am   2: 5 will consume the fortresses of J."
Ob   : 11 entered his gates and cast lots for J.
Mic 1: 5 is Judah's high place? Is it not J?
      4: 2 the word of the Lord from J.
Zep 3: 16 On that day they will say to J,
Zec 1: 14 'I am very jealous for J and Zion,
      1: 17 comfort Zion and choose J.' "
      2: 2 "To measure J, to find out how
      2: 4 'J will be a city without walls
      8: 3 will return to Zion and dwell in J.
      8: 3 will be called the City of Truth,
      8: 8 I will bring them back to live in J;
      8: 15 determined to do good again to J
      8: 22 powerful nations will come to J
      9: 9 Shout, Daughter J! See, your king
      9: 10 Ephraim and the warhorses from J,
     12: 3 I will make J an immovable rock
     12: 10 the inhabitants of J a spirit of grace
     14: 2 I will gather all the nations to J
     14: 8 living water will flow out from J,
     14: 16 nations that have attacked J will go
Mt 16: 21 to his disciples that he must go to J
     20: 18 "We are going up to J, and the Son
     21: 10 When Jesus entered J, the whole
     23: 37 "J, J, you who kill the prophets
Mk 10: 33 "We are going up to J," he said,
Lk   2: 22 Mary took him to J to present him
      2: 41 Every year Jesus' parents went to J
      2: 43 the boy Jesus stayed behind in J,
      4: 9 The devil led him to J and had him
      9: 31 about to bring to fulfillment at J.
      9: 51 Jesus resolutely set out for J.
     13: 34 "J, J, you who kill the prophets
     18: 31 them, "We are going up to J,
     19: 41 As he approached J and saw
     21: 20 "When you see J being surrounded
     21: 24 J will be trampled
     24: 47 name to all nations, beginning at J.
Jn   4: 20 where we must worship is in J."
Ac   1: 4 "Do not leave J, but wait
      1: 8 and you will be my witnesses in J,
      6: 7 of disciples in J increased rapidly,
     20: 22 I am going to J, not knowing what
     23: 11 As you have testified about me in J,
Ro 15: 19 So from J all the way around
Gal 4: 25 corresponds to the present city of J,
      4: 26 But the J that is above is free,
Heb 12: 22 of the living God, the heavenly J.
Rev 3: 12 the new J, which is coming down
     21: 2 the new J, coming down
     21: 10 and showed me the Holy City, J,

JESSE
Father of David (Ru 4:17–22; 1Sa 16; 1Ch 2:12–17).

JESUS
LIFE: Genealogy (Mt 1:1–17; Lk 3:21–37). Birth announced (Mt 1:18–25; Lk 1:26–45). Birth (Mt 2:1–12; Lk 2:1–40). Escape to Egypt (Mt 2:13–23). As a boy in the temple (Lk 2:41–52). Baptism (Mt 3:13–17; Mk 1:9–11; Lk 3:21–22; Jn 1:32–34). Temptation (Mt 4:1–11; Mk 1:12–13; Lk 4:1–13). Ministry in Galilee (Mt 4:12–18:35; Mk 1:14–9:50; Lk 4:14–13:9; Jn 1:35–2:11; 4; 6), Transfiguration (Mt 17:1–8; Mk 9:2–8; Lk 9:28–36), on the way to Jerusalem (Mt 19–20; Mk 10; Lk 13:10–19:27), in Jerusalem (Mt 21–25; Mk 11–13; Lk 19:28–21:38; Jn 2:12–3:36; 5; 7–12). Last supper (Mt 26:17–35; Mk 14:12–31; Lk 22:1–38; Jn 13–17). Arrest and trial (Mt 26:36–27:31; Mk 14:43–15:20; Lk 22:39–23:25; Jn 18:1–19:16). Crucifixion (Mt 27:32–66; Mk 15:21–47; Lk 23:26–55; Jn 19:28–42). Resurrection and appearances (Mt 28; Mk 16; Lk 24; Jn 20–21; Ac 1:1–11; 7:56; 9:3–6; 1Co 15:1–8; Rev 1:1–20).

MIRACLES. Healings: official's son (Jn 4:43–54), demoniac in Capernaum (Mk 1:23–26; Lk 4:33–35), Peter's mother-in-law (Mt 8:14–17; Mk 1:29–31; Lk 4:38–39), leper (Mt 8:2–4; Mk 1:40–45; Lk 5:12–16), paralytic (Mt 9:1–8; Mk 2:1–12; Lk 5:17–26), cripple (Jn 5:1–9), shriveled hand (Mt 12:10–13; Mk 3:1–5; Lk 6:6–11), centurion's servant (Mt 8:5–13; Lk 7:1–10), widow's son raised (Lk 7:11–17), demoniac (Mt 12:22–23; Lk 11:14), Gadarene demoniacs (Mt 8:28–34; Mk 5:1–20; Lk 8:26–39), woman's bleeding and Jairus' daughter (Mt 9:18–26; Mk 5:21–43; Lk 8:40–56), blind men (Mt 9:27–31), mute man (Mt 9:32–33), Canaanite woman's daughter (Mt 15:21–28; Mk 7:24–30), deaf man (Mk 7:31–37), blind man (Mk

8:22–26), demoniac boy (Mt 17:14–18; Mk 9:14–29; Lk 9:37–43), ten lepers (Lk 17:11–19), man born blind (Jn 9:1–7), Lazarus raised (Jn 11), crippled woman (Lk 13:11–17), man with dropsy (Lk 14:1–6), two blind men (Mt 20:29–34; Mk 10:46–52; Lk 18:35–43), Malchus' ear (Lk 22:50–51). Other Miracles: water to wine (Jn 2:1–11), catch of fish (Lk 5:1–11), storm stilled (Mt 8:23–27; Mk 4:37–41; Lk 8:22–25), 5,000 fed (Mt 14:15–21; Mk 6:35–44; Lk 9:10–17; Jn 6:1–14), walking on water (Mt 14:25–33; Mk 6:48–52; Jn 6:15–21), 4,000 fed (Mt 15:32–39; Mk 8:1–9), money from fish (Mt 17:24–27), fig tree cursed (Mt 21:18–22; Mk 11:12–14), catch of fish (Jn 21:1–14).

MAJOR TEACHING: Sermon on the Mount (Mt 5–7; Lk 6:17–49), to Nicodemus (Jn 3), to Samaritan woman (Jn 4), Bread of Life (Jn 6:22–59), at Feast of Tabernacles (Jn 7–8), woes to Pharisees (Mt 23; Lk 11:37–54), Good Shepherd (Jn 10:1–18), Olivet Discourse (Mt 24–25; Mk 13; Lk 21:5–36), Upper Room Discourse (Jn 13–16).

PARABLES: Sower (Mt 13:3–23; Mk 4:3–25; Lk 8:5–18), seed's growth (Mk 4:26–29), wheat and weeds (Mt 13:24–30, 36–43), mustard seed (Mt 13:31–32; Mk 4:30–32), yeast (Mt 13:33; Lk 13:20–21), hidden treasure (Mt 13:44), valuable pearl (Mt 13:45–46), net (Mt 13:47–51), house owner (Mt 13:52), good Samaritan (Lk 10:25–37), unmerciful servant (Mt 18:15–35), lost sheep (Mt 18:10–14; Lk 15:4–7), lost coin (Lk 15:8–10), lost son (Lk 15:11–32), dishonest manager (Lk 16:1–13), rich man and Lazarus (Lk 16:19–31), persistent widow (Lk 18:1–8), Pharisee and tax collector (Lk 18:9–14), payment of workers (Mt 20:1–16), tenants and the vineyard (Mt 21:28–46; Mk 12:1–12; Lk 20:9–19), wedding banquet (Mt 22:1–14), faithful servant (Mt 24:45–51), ten virgins (Mt 25:1–13), talents (Mt 25:1–30; Lk 19:12–27).

DISCIPLES see APOSTLES. Call of (Jn 1:35–51; Mt 4:18–22; 9:9; Mk 1:16–20; 2:13–14; Lk 5:1–11, 27–28). Named Apostles (Mk 3:13–19; Lk 6:12–16). Twelve sent out (Mt 10; Mk 6:7–11; Lk 9:1–5). Seventy sent out (Lk 10:1–24). Defection of (Jn 6:60–71; Mt 26:56; Mk 14:50–52). Final commission (Mt 28:16–20; Jn 21:15–23; Ac 1:3–8).

Ac	2: 32	God has raised this J to life, and we
	9: 5	Saul asked. "I am J, whom you are
	9: 34	said to him, "J Christ heals you:
	15: 11	of our Lord J that we are saved,
	16: 31	"Believe in the Lord J, and you will
	20: 24	the task the Lord J has given me—
Ro	3: 24	redemption that came by Christ J.
	5: 17	life through the one man, J Christ!
	8: 1	for those who are in Christ J,
1Co	1: 7	for our Lord J Christ to be revealed.
	2: 2	I was with you except J Christ
	6: 11	in the name of the Lord J Christ,
	8: 6	and there is but one Lord, J Christ,
	12: 3	and no one can say, "J is Lord,"
2Co	4: 5	but J Christ as Lord, and ourselves
	13: 5	Do you not realize that Christ J is
Gal	2: 16	the law, but by faith in J Christ.
	3: 28	for you are all one in Christ J.
	5: 6	in Christ J neither circumcision nor
	6: 17	I bear on my body the marks of J.
Eph	1: 5	to sonship through J Christ,
	2: 10	in Christ J to do good works,
	2: 20	with Christ J himself as the chief
Php	1: 6	completion until the day of Christ J.
	2: 5	same attitude of mind Christ J had:
	2: 10	name of J every knee should bow,
Col	3: 17	do it all in the name of the Lord J,
1Th	1: 10	who rescues us from the coming
	4: 14	We believe that J died and rose
	5: 23	at the coming of our Lord J Christ.
2Th	1: 7	happen when the Lord J is revealed
	2: 1	the coming of our Lord J Christ
1Ti	1: 15	Christ J came into the world to save
2Ti	1: 10	Christ J, who has destroyed death
	2: 3	like a good soldier of Christ J.
	3: 12	life in Christ J will be persecuted,
Tit	2: 13	our great God and Savior, J Christ,
Heb	2: 9	But we do see J, who was made
	2: 11	So J is not ashamed to call them
	3: 1	fix your thoughts on J, whom we
	3: 3	J has been found worthy of greater
	4: 14	into heaven, J the Son of God, let us
	6: 20	where our forerunner, J, has entered
	7: 22	J has become the guarantor
	7: 24	but because J lives forever, he has
	8: 6	fact the ministry J has received is as
	12: 2	fixing our eyes on J, the pioneer

Heb	12: 24	to J the mediator of a new covenant,
1Pe	1: 3	through the resurrection of J Christ
2Pe	1: 16	of our Lord J Christ in power,
1Jn	1: 7	another, and the blood of J, his Son,
	2: 1	J Christ, the Righteous One.
	2: 6	to live in him must live as J did.
	4: 15	acknowledges that J is the Son
Rev	1: 1	The revelation from J Christ,
	22: 16	"I, J, have sent my angel to give
	22: 20	Amen. Come, Lord J.

JETHRO
Father-in-law and adviser of Moses (Ex 3:1; 18). Also known as Reuel (Ex 2:18).

JEW (JEWS JEWS' JUDAISM)
Est	2: 5	the citadel of Susa a J of the tribe
Zec	8: 23	take firm hold of one J by the hem
Ac	21: 39	"I am a J, from Tarsus in Cilicia,
Ro	1: 16	first to the J, then to the Gentile.
	2: 28	A person is not a J who is one only
	10: 12	For there is no difference between J
1Co	9: 20	To the Jews I became like a J,
Gal	2: 14	"You are a J, yet you live like
	3: 28	There is neither J nor Gentile,
Col	3: 11	Here there is no Gentile or J,

JEWELRY* (JEWELRY JEWELS)
Pr	20: 15	that speak knowledge are a rare j.
SS	4: 9	eyes, with one j of your necklace.
Isa	13: 19	Babylon, the j of kingdoms, the pride
Rev	21: 11	was like that of a very precious j,

JEWELRY (JEWEL)
Ex	35: 22	and brought gold j of all kinds:
Jer	2: 32	Does a young woman forget her j,
Eze	16: 11	I adorned you with j: I put bracelets
1Pe	3: 3	and the wearing of gold j and fine

JEWELS (JEWEL)
Isa	54: 12	your gates of sparkling j, and all
	61: 10	as a bride adorns herself with her j.
Zec	9: 16	sparkle in his land like j in a crown.

JEWS (JEW)
Ne	4: 1	He ridiculed the J,
Est	3: 13	kill and annihilate all the J—
	4: 14	deliverance for the J will arise
Mt	2: 2	who has been born king of the J?
	27: 11	"Are you the king of the J?"
Jn	4: 9	(For J do not associate
	4: 22	do know, for salvation is from the J
	19: 3	saying, "Hail, king of the J!"
Ac	20: 21	I have declared to both J
Ro	3: 29	Is God the God of J only? Is he not
	9: 24	not only from the J
1Co	1: 22	J demand signs and Greeks look
	9: 20	J I became like a Jew, to win the J,
	12: 13	whether J or Gentiles,
Gal	2: 8	work in Peter as an apostle to the J,
Rev	2: 9	slander of those who say they are J
	3: 9	claim to be J though they are not,

JEWS'* (JEW)
| Ro | 15: 27 | shared in the J spiritual blessings, |

JEZEBEL
Sidonian wife of Ahab (1Ki 16:31). Promoted Baal worship (1Ki 16:32–33). Killed prophets of the LORD (1Ki 18:4, 13). Opposed Elijah (1Ki 19:1–2). Had Naboth killed (1Ki 21). Death prophesied (1Ki 21:17–24). Killed by Jehu (2Ki 9:30–37).

JEZREEL
2Ki	9: 36	J dogs will devour Jezebel's flesh.
	10: 7	baskets and sent them to Jehu in J.
Hos	1: 4	house of Jehu for the massacre at J,

JOAB
Nephew of David (1Ch 2:16). Commander of his army (2Sa 8:16). Victorious over Ammon (2Sa 10; 1Ch 19), Rabbah (2Sa 11; 1Ch 20), Jerusalem (1Ch 11:6), Absalom (2Sa 18), Sheba (2Sa 20). Killed Abner (2Sa 3:22–39), Amasa (2Sa 20:1–13). Numbered David's army (2Sa 24; 1Ch 21). Sided with Adonijah (1Ki 1:17, 19). Killed by Benaiah (1Ki 2:5–6, 28–35).

JOASH
Son of Ahaziah; king of Judah. Sheltered from Athaliah by Jehoiada (2Ki 11; 2Ch 22:10–23:21). Repaired temple (2Ki 12; 2Ch 24).

JOB
Wealthy man from Uz; feared God (Job 1:1–5). Righteousness tested by disaster (Job 1:6–22), personal affliction (Job 2). Maintained innocence in debate with three friends (Job 3–31), Elihu (Job 32–37). Rebuked by the LORD (Job 38–41). Vindicated and restored to

greater stature by the LORD (Job 42). Example of righteousness (Eze 14:14, 20).

JOCHEBED*
Mother of Moses and Aaron (Ex 6:20; Nu 26:59).

JOEL
Prophet (Joel 1:1; Ac 2:16).

JOHN
1. Son of Zechariah and Elizabeth (Lk 1). Called the Baptist (Mt 3:1–12; Mk 1:2–8). Witness to Jesus (Mt 3:11–12; Mk 1:7–8; Lk 3:15–18; Jn 1:6–35; 3:27–30; 5:33–36). Doubts about Jesus (Mt 11:2–6; Lk 7:18–23). Arrest (Mt 4:12; Mk 1:14). Execution (Mt 14:1–12; Mk 6:14–29; Lk 9:7–9). Ministry compared to Elijah (Mt 11:7–19; Mk 9:11–13; Lk 7:24–35).

2. Apostle; brother of James (Mt 4:21–22; 10:2; Mk 3:17; Lk 5:1–10). At transfiguration (Mt 17:1–13; Mk 9:1–13; Lk 9:28–36). Desire to be greatest (Mk 10:35–45). Leader of church at Jerusalem (Ac 4:1–3; Gal 2:9). Elder who wrote epistles (2Jn 1; 3Jn 1). Prophet who wrote Revelation (Rev 1:1; 22:8).

3. Cousin of Barnabas, co-worker with Paul, (Ac 12:12–13:13; 15:37), see MARK.

JOIN (JOINED JOINS)
Ne	10: 29	all these now j their fellow Israelites
Pr	23: 20	Do not j those who drink too much
	24: 21	do not j with rebellious officials,
Jer	3: 18	the house of Judah will j the house
Eze	37: 17	J them together into one stick so
Da	11: 34	who are not sincere will j them.
Ro	15: 30	to j me in my struggle by praying
2Ti	1: 8	But j with me in suffering,
	2: 3	J with me in suffering,
1Pe	4: 4	do not j them in their reckless,

JOINED (JOIN)
Zec	2: 11	"Many nations will be j
Mt	19: 6	Therefore what God has j together,
Mk	10: 9	Therefore what God has j together,
Ac	1: 14	They all j together constantly
Eph	2: 21	him the whole building is j together
	4: 16	body, j and held together by every

JOINS (JOIN)
| 1Co | 16: 16 | to everyone who j in the work |

JOINT (JOINTS)
| Ps | 22: 14 | water, and all my bones are out of j. |

JOINTS* (JOINT)
| Heb | 4: 12 | soul and spirit, j and marrow; |

JOKING*
Ge	19: 14	his sons-in-law thought he was j.
Pr	26: 19	neighbor and says, "I was only j!"
Eph	5: 4	foolish talk or coarse j, which are

JONAH
Prophet in days of Jeroboam II (2Ki 14:25). Called to Nineveh; fled to Tarshish (Jnh 1:1–3). Cause of storm; thrown into sea (Jnh 1:4–16). Swallowed by fish (Jnh 1:17). Prayer (Jnh 2). Preached to Nineveh (Jnh 3). Attitude reproved by the LORD (Jnh 4). Sign of (Mt 12:39–41; Lk 11:29–32).

JONATHAN
Son of Saul (1Sa 13:16; 1Ch 8:33). Valiant warrior (1Sa 13–14). Relation to David (1Sa 18:1–4; 19–20; 23:16–18). Killed at Gilboa (1Sa 31). Mourned by David (2Sa 1).

JOPPA
Ezr	3: 7	logs by sea from Lebanon to J,
Jnh	1: 3	He went down to J, where he found
Ac	9: 43	Peter stayed in J for some time

JORAM
1. Son of Ahab; king of Israel. Fought with Jehoshaphat against Moab (2Ki 3). Killed with Ahaziah by Jehu (2Ki 8:25–29; 9:14–26; 2Ch 22:5–9).
2. See JEHORAM.

JORDAN
Ge	13: 10	plain of the J was well watered,
Nu	22: 1	and camped along the J across
	34: 12	boundary will go down along the J
Dt	27: 2	you are not going to cross this J.
Jos	1: 2	cross the J River into the land I am
	3: 11	all the earth will go into the J ahead
	3: 17	stopped in the middle of the J
	4: 22	'Israel crossed the J on dry ground.'
2Ki	2: 7	and Elisha had stopped at the J.
	2: 13	back and stood on the bank of the J.
	5: 10	wash yourself seven times in the J
	6: 4	They went to the J and began to cut

Ps 114: 3 looked and fled, the **J** turned back;
Isa 9: 1 the Way of the Sea, beyond the **J**—
Jer 12: 5 you manage in the thickets by the **J**?
Mt 3: 6 were baptized by him in the **J** River.
4: 15 the Sea, beyond the **J**,
Mk 1: 9 and was baptized by John in the **J**.

JOSEPH
1. Son of Jacob by Rachel (Ge 30:24; 1Ch 2:2). Favored by Jacob, hated by brothers (Ge 37:3–4). Dreams (Ge 37:5–11). Sold by brothers (Ge 37:12–36). Served Potiphar; imprisoned by false accusation (Ge 39). Interpreted dreams of Pharaoh's servants (Ge 40), of Pharaoh (Ge 41:4–40). Made greatest in Egypt (Ge 41:41–57). Sold grain to brothers (Ge 42–45). Brought Jacob and sons to Egypt (Ge 46–47). Sons Ephraim and Manasseh blessed (Ge 48). Blessed (Ge 49:22–26; Dt 33:13–17). Death (Ge 50:22–26; Ex 13:19; Heb 11:22). 12,000 from (Rev 7:8).
2. Husband of Mary, mother of Jesus (Mt 1:16–24; 2:13–19; Lk 1:27; 2; Jn 1:45).
3. Disciple from Arimathea, who gave his tomb for Jesus' burial (Mt 27:57–61; Mk 15:43–47; Lk 24:50–52).
4. Original name of Barnabas (Ac 4:36).

JOSHUA (HOSHEA)
1. Son of Nun; name changed from Hoshea (Nu 13:8, 16; 1Ch 7:27). Fought Amalekites under Moses (Ex 17:9–14). Servant of Moses on Sinai (Ex 24:13; 32:17). Spied Canaan (Nu 13). With Caleb, allowed to enter land (Nu 14:6, 30). Succeeded Moses (Dt 1:38; 31:1–8; 34:9).
Charged Israel to conquer Canaan (Jos 1). Crossed Jordan (Jos 3–4). Circumcised sons of wilderness wanderings (Jos 5). Conquered Jericho (Jos 6), Ai (Jos 7–8), five kings at Gibeon (Jos 10:1–28), southern Canaan (Jos 10:29–43), northern Canaan (Jos 11–12). Defeated at Ai (Jos 7). Deceived by Gibeonites (Jos 9). Renewed covenant (Jos 8:30–35; 24:1–27). Divided land among tribes (Jos 13–22). Last words (Jos 23). Death (Jos 24:28–31).
2. High priest during rebuilding of temple (Hag 1–2; Zec 3:1–9; 6:11).

JOSIAH
Son of Amon; king of Judah (2Ki 21:26; 1Ch 3:14). Prophesied (1Ki 13:2). Book of Law discovered during his reign (2Ki 22; 2Ch 34:14–31). Reforms (2Ki 23:1–25; 2Ch 34:1–13; 35:1–19). Killed by Pharaoh Necho (2Ki 23:29–30; 2Ch 35:20–27).

JOTHAM
1. Son of Gideon (Jdg 9).
2. Son of Azariah (Uzziah); king of Judah (2Ki 15:32–38; 2Ch 26:21–27:9).

JOURNEY
Dt 1: 33 who went ahead of you on your **j**,
2: 7 has watched over your **j** through this
Jdg 18: 6 Your **j** has the LORD's approval."
Ezr 8: 21 ask him for a safe **j** for us and our
Isa 35: 8 The unclean will not **j** on it;
Mt 25: 14 it will be like a man going on a **j**,
Ro 15: 24 to have you assist me on my **j** there,

JOY* (ENJOY ENJOYMENT JOYFUL JOYOUS OVERJOYED REJOICE REJOICES REJOICING)
Ge 31: 27 so I could send you away with **j**
Lev 9: 24 saw it, they shouted for **j** and fell
Dt 16: 15 hands, and your **j** will be complete.
Jdg 9: 19 may Abimelek be your **j**, and may
1Ch 12: 40 and sheep, for there was **j** in Israel.
16: 27 and are in his dwelling place.
16: 33 them sing for **j** before the LORD,
29: 17 **j** how willingly your people who are
29: 22 drank with great **j** in the presence
2Ch 30: 26 There was great **j** in Jerusalem,
Ezr 3: 12 while many others shouted for **j**,
3: 13 of the shouts of **j** from the sound
6: 16 of the house of God with **j**.
6: 22 they celebrated with **j** the Festival
6: 22 the LORD had filled them with **j**
Ne 8: 10 for the **j** of the LORD is your
8: 12 of food and to celebrate with great **j**,
8: 17 And their **j** was very great.
12: 43 because God had given them great **j**.
Est 8: 16 it was a time of happiness and **j**,
8: 17 there was **j** and gladness among
9: 17 and made it a day of feasting and **j**.
9: 18 and made it a day of feasting and **j**.
9: 19 of the month of Adar as a day of **j**
9: 22 when their sorrow was turned into **j**
9: 22 the days as days of feasting and **j**
Job 3: 7 may no shout of **j** be heard in it.

Job 6: 10 my **j** in unrelenting pain—that I had
8: 21 and your lips with shouts of **j**.
9: 25 fly away without a glimpse of **j**.
10: 20 from me so I can have a moment's **j**
20: 5 brief, the **j** of the godless lasts
33: 26 will see God's face and shout for **j**;
38: 7 and all the angels shouted for **j**?
Ps 4: 7 Fill my heart with **j** when their grain
5: 11 you be glad; let them ever sing for **j**.
16: 11 you will fill me with **j** in your
19: 8 are right, giving **j** to the heart.
20: 5 we shout for **j** over your victory
21: 1 How great is his **j** in the victories
21: 6 glad with the **j** of your presence.
27: 6 I will sacrifice with shouts of **j**;
28: 7 My heart leaps for **j**, and with my
30: 11 you sackcloth and clothed me with **j**,
33: 3 play skillfully, and shout for **j**.
35: 27 delight in my vindication shout for **j**
42: 4 of the Mighty One with shouts of **j**
43: 4 to God, my **j** and my delight.
45: 7 by anointing you with the oil of **j**.
45: 15 Led in with **j** and gladness,
47: 1 shout to God with cries of **j**.
47: 5 God has ascended amid shouts of **j**,
48: 2 its loftiness, the **j** of the whole earth,
51: 8 Let me hear **j** and gladness;
51: 12 Restore to me the **j** of your salvation
65: 8 fades, you call forth songs of **j**.
65: 13 they shout for **j** and sing.
66: 1 Shout for **j** to God, all the earth!
67: 4 the nations be glad and sing for **j**,
71: 23 My lips will shout for **j** when I sing
81: 1 Sing for **j** to God our strength;
86: 4 Bring **j** to your servant, Lord, for I
89: 12 and Hermon sing for **j** at your name.
90: 14 that we may sing for **j** and be glad
92: 4 I sing for **j** at what your hands have
94: 19 your consolation brought me **j**.
95: 1 let us sing for **j** to the LORD;
96: 12 all the trees of the forest sing for **j**.
97: 11 and **j** on the upright in heart.
98: 4 Shout for **j** to the LORD,
98: 6 shout for **j** before the LORD,
98: 8 let the mountains sing together for **j**;
100: 1 Shout for **j** to the LORD,
105: 43 his chosen ones with shouts of **j**;
106: 5 I may share in the **j** of your nation
107: 22 and tell of his works with songs of **j**.
118: 15 Shouts of **j** and victory resound
119:111 they are the **j** of my heart.
126: 2 our tongues with songs of **j**.
126: 3 for us, and we are filled with **j**.
126: 5 with tears will reap with songs of **j**.
126: 6 will return with songs of **j**,
132: 9 your faithful people sing for **j**.' "
132: 16 faithful people will ever sing for **j**.
137: 3 tormentors demanded songs of **j**;
137: 6 not consider Jerusalem my highest **j**.
149: 5 honor and sing for **j** on their beds.
Pr 10: 1 Wise children bring **j** to their father,
10: 28 The prospect of the righteous is **j**,
11: 10 wicked perish, there are shouts of **j**.
12: 20 those who promote peace have **j**.
14: 10 and no one else can share its **j**.
15: 20 Wise children bring **j** to their father,
15: 21 Folly brings **j** to those who have no
15: 23 A person finds **j** in giving an apt
15: 30 in a messenger's eyes brings **j**
17: 21 there is no **j** for the parent
21: 15 it brings **j** to the righteous but terror
23: 24 of a righteous child has great **j**.
27: 9 and incense bring **j** to the heart,
27: 11 my child, and bring **j** to my heart;
29: 3 A man who loves wisdom brings **j**
29: 6 but the righteous shout for **j** and
Ecc 8: 15 **j** will accompany them in their toil
11: 9 let your hearts give you **j** in the days
Isa 9: 3 the nation and increased their **j**;
12: 3 With **j** you will draw water
12: 6 Shout aloud and sing for **j**,
16: 9 shouts of **j** over your ripened fruit
16: 10 **J** and gladness are taken away
22: 13 But see, there is **j** and revelry,
24: 11 all **j** turns to gloom, all gaiety is
24: 14 raise their voices, they shout for **j**;
26: 19 in the dust wake up and shout for **j**—
35: 2 will rejoice greatly and shout for **j**.
35: 6 and the mute tongue shout for **j**.
35: 10 everlasting **j** will crown their heads.
35: 10 Gladness and **j** will overtake them,
42: 11 Let the people of Sela sing for **j**;

Isa 44: 23 Sing for **j**, you heavens,
48: 20 Announce this with shouts of **j**
49: 13 Shout for **j**, you heavens;
51: 3 **J** and gladness will be found in her,
51: 11 everlasting **j** will crown their heads.
51: 11 Gladness and **j** will overtake them,
52: 8 together they shout for **j**.
52: 9 Burst into songs of **j** together,
54: 1 shout for **j**, you who were never
55: 12 You will go out in **j** and be led forth
56: 7 give them **j** in my house of prayer.
58: 14 you will find your **j** in the LORD,
60: 5 heart will throb and swell with **j**;
60: 15 pride and the **j** of all generations.
61: 3 the oil of **j** instead of mourning,
61: 7 land, and everlasting **j** will be yours.
65: 14 will sing out of the **j** of their hearts,
65: 18 to be a delight and its people a **j**.
66: 5 that we may see your **j**!'
Jer 7: 34 I will bring an end to the sounds of **j**
15: 16 they were my **j** and my heart's
16: 9 I will bring an end to the sounds of **j**
25: 10 banish from them the sounds of **j**
31: 7 "Sing with **j** for Jacob;
31: 12 shout for **j** on the heights of Zion;
31: 13 comfort and instead of sorrow.
33: 9 this city will bring me renown, **j**,
33: 11 the sounds of **j** and gladness,
48: 33 **J** and gladness are gone
48: 33 no one treads them with shouts of **j**.
48: 33 are shouts, they are not shouts of **j**.
51: 48 them will shout for **j** over Babylon,
La 2: 15 of beauty, the **j** of the whole earth?"
5: 15 **J** is gone from our hearts;
Eze 7: 7 is panic, not **j**, on the mountains.
24: 25 their stronghold, their **j** and glory,
Joel 1: 12 Surely the people's **j** is withered
1: 16 **j** and gladness from the house of our
Mt 13: 20 word and at once receive it with **j**.
13: 44 in his **j** went and sold all he had
28: 8 afraid yet filled with **j**, and ran
Mk 4: 16 word and at once receive it with **j**.
Lk 1: 14 He will be a **j** and delight to you,
1: 44 the baby in my womb leaped for **j**.
1: 58 great mercy, and they shared her **j**.
2: 10 good news of great **j** that will be
6: 23 "Rejoice in that day and leap for **j**,
8: 13 ones who receive the word with **j**
10: 17 The seventy-two returned with **j**
10: 21 full of **j** through the Holy Spirit,
24: 41 still did not believe it because of **j**
24: 52 returned to Jerusalem with great **j**.
Jn 3: 29 and is full of **j** when he hears
3: 29 That **j** is mine, and it is now
15: 11 told you this so that my **j** may be
15: 11 and that your **j** may be complete.
16: 20 grieve, but your grief will turn to **j**.
16: 21 because of her **j** that a child is born
16: 22 and no one will take away your **j**.
16: 24 receive, and your **j** will be complete.
17: 13 full measure of my **j** within them.
Ac 2: 28 you will fill me with **j** in your
8: 8 So there was great **j** in that city.
13: 52 the disciples were filled with **j**
14: 17 of food and fills your hearts with **j**."
16: 34 filled with **j** because he had come
Ro 14: 17 peace and **j** in the Holy Spirit,
15: 13 the God of hope fill you with all **j**
15: 32 God's will I may come to you with **j**
2Co 1: 24 but we work with you for your **j**,
2: 3 that you would all share my **j**.
7: 4 our troubles my **j** knows no bounds.
7: 7 so that my **j** was greater than ever.
8: 2 trial, their overflowing **j** and their
Gal 4: 15 What has happened to all your **j**?
4: 27 shout for **j** and cry aloud,
5: 22 But the fruit of the Spirit is love, **j**,
Php 1: 4 for all of you, I always pray with **j**
1: 25 for your progress and **j** in the faith,
2: 2 then make my **j** complete by being
2: 29 him in the Lord with great **j**,
4: 1 I love and long for, my **j** and crown,
1Th 1: 6 severe suffering with the **j** given
2: 19 our **j**, or the crown in which we will
2: 20 Indeed, you are our glory and **j**.
2Ti 1: 4 so that I may be filled with **j**.
Phm : 7 Your love has given me great **j**
Heb 1: 9 by anointing you with the oil of **j**."
12: 2 the **j** set before him he endured
13: 17 this so that their work will be a **j**,
Jas 1: 2 Consider it pure **j**, my brothers

Jas 4: 9 to mourning and your j to gloom.
1Pe 1: 8 with an inexpressible and glorious j,
1Jn 1: 4 write this to make our j complete.
2Jn : 4 It has given me great j to find some
: 12 face, so that our j may be complete.
3Jn : 4 It gave me great j to have some
: 4 I have no greater j than to hear
Jude : 24 without fault and with great j—

JOYFUL* (JOY)
Dt 16: 14 Be j at your festival—
1Sa 18: 6 with j songs and with timbrels
1Ki 8: 66 j and glad in heart for all the good
1Ch 15: 16 to make a j sound with musical
2Ch 7: 10 j and glad in heart for the good
Ps 68: 3 may they be happy and j.
100: 2 come before him with j songs.
Pr 23: 25 may she who gave you birth be j!
Ecc 9: 7 and drink your wine with a j heart,
Isa 24: 8 has stopped, the j harp is silent.
Jer 31: 4 and go out to dance with the j.
Hab 3: 18 I will be j in God my Savior.
Zec 8: 19 tenth months will become j and glad
10: 7 Their children will see it and be j;
Ro 12: 12 Be j in hope, patient in affliction,
Col 1: 12 and giving j thanks to the Father,
Heb 12: 22 thousands of angels in j assembly,

JOYOUS* (JOY)
Est 8: 15 the city of Susa held a j celebration.

JUBILANT
Ps 96: 12 Let the fields be j, and everything
98: 4 earth, burst into j song with music;

JUBILEE
Lev 25: 11 The fiftieth year shall be a j for you;

JUDAH (JUDEA)
1. Son of Jacob by Leah (Ge 29:35; 35:23; 1Ch 2:1). Did not want to kill Joseph (Ge 37:26–27). Among Canaanites, fathered Perez by Tamar (Ge 38). Tribe of blessed as ruling tribe (Ge 49:8–12; Dt 33:7), numbered (Nu 1:27; 26:22), allotted land (Jos 15; Eze 48:7), failed to fully possess (Jos 15:63; Jdg 1:1–20).
2. Name used for people and land of Southern Kingdom.
Ru 1: 7 take them back to the land of J.
2Sa 2: 4 David king over the house of J.
Isa 3: 1 The vision concerning J
8: 3 Jerusalem staggers, J is falling;
Jer 13: 19 All J will be carried into exile,
30: 3 Israel and J back from captivity
Hos 1: 11 I will show love to the house of J;
Zec 10: 4 From J will come the cornerstone,
Mt 2: 6 means least among the rulers of J;
Heb 7: 14 that our Lord descended from J,
8: 8 of Israel and with the house of J.
Rev 5: 5 the Lion of the tribe of J, the Root

JUDAISM (JEW)
Ac 13: 43 devout converts to J followed Paul
Gal 1: 13 of my previous way of life in J,
1: 14 I was advancing in J beyond many

JUDAS
1. Apostle; son of James (Lk 6:16; Jn 14:22; Ac 1:13). Probably also called Thaddaeus (Mt 10:3; Mk 3:18).
2. Brother of James and Jesus (Mt 13:55; Mk 6:3), also called Jude (Jude 1).
3. Christian prophet (Ac 15:22–32).
4. Apostle, also called Iscariot, who betrayed Jesus (Mt 10:4; 26:14–56; Mk 3:19; 14:10–50; Lk 6:16; 22:3–53; Jn 6:71; 12:4; 13:2–30; 18:2–11). Suicide of (Mt 27:3–5; Ac 1:16–25).

JUDEA (JUDAH)
Mt 2: 1 Jesus was born in Bethlehem in J,
24: 16 let those who are in J flee
Lk 3: 1 Pontius Pilate was governor of J,
Ac 1: 8 and in all J and Samaria,
9: 31 Then the church throughout J,
1Th 2: 14 imitators of God's churches in J,

JUDGE (JUDGED JUDGES JUDGING JUDGMENT JUDGMENTS)
Ge 16: 5 May the LORD j between you
18: 25 Will not the J of all the earth do
Lev 19: 15 the great, but j your neighbor fairly.
Dt 1: 16 between your people and j fairly,
17: 12 who shows contempt for the j
Jdg 2: 18 the LORD raised up a j for them,
1Sa 2: 10 the LORD will j the ends
3: 13 I would j his family forever because
24: 12 May the LORD j between you

1Ki 8: 32 J between your servants,
1Ch 16: 33 LORD, for he comes to j the earth.
2Ch 6: 23 J between your servants,
19: 7 J carefully, for with the LORD our
Job 9: 15 only plead with my J for mercy.
Ps 7: 8 Let the LORD j the peoples.
7: 11 God is a righteous j, a God who
9: 4 enthroned as the righteous j.
51: 4 verdict and justified when you j.
75: 2 it is I who j with equity.
76: 9 rose up to j, to save all the afflicted
82: 8 O God, j the earth, for all
94: 2 Rise up, O J of the earth; pay back
96: 10 he will j the peoples with equity.
96: 13 He will j the world in righteousness
98: 9 He will j the world in righteousness
110: 6 He will j the nations,
Pr 31: 9 Speak up and j fairly;
Isa 2: 4 He will j between the nations
3: 13 he rises to j the people.
11: 3 He will not j by what he sees
33: 22 For the LORD is our j, the LORD
Jer 11: 20 who j righteously and test the heart
Eze 7: 3 I will j you according to your
7: 27 by their own standards I will j them.
18: 30 I will j each of you according
20: 36 Egypt, so I will j you,
22: 2 "Son of man, will you j her?
34: 17 I will j between one sheep
Joel 3: 12 there I will sit to j all the nations
Mic 3: 11 Her leaders j for a bribe, her priests
4: 3 He will j between many peoples
Mt 7: 1 "Do not j, or you too will be
Lk 6: 37 "Do not j, and you will not be
18: 2 there was a j who neither feared
Jn 5: 27 authority to j because he is the Son
5: 30 I j only as I hear, and my judgment
7: 24 but instead j correctly."
8: 16 But if I do j, my decisions are true,
12: 47 For I did not come to j the world,
12: 48 There is a j for those who reject me
Ac 10: 42 is the one whom God appointed as j
17: 31 set a day when he will j the world
Ro 2: 1 how could God j the world?
14: 10 why do you j your brother or sister?
1Co 4: 5 Therefore judge nothing before
6: 2 the Lord's people will j the world?
6: 2 And if you are to j the world,
6: 3 Therefore do not let anyone j you
Col 2: 16 Therefore do not let anyone j you
2Ti 4: 1 who will j the living and the dead,
4: 8 the righteous J, will award to me
Heb 10: 30 "The Lord will j his people."
12: 23 You have come to God, the J of all,
13: 4 for God will j the adulterer and all
Jas 4: 12 There is only one Lawgiver and J,
4: 12 who are you to j your neighbor?
1Pe 4: 5 to him who is ready to j the living
Rev 20: 4 who had been given authority to j.

JUDGED (JUDGE)
Mt 7: 1 "Do not judge, or you too will be j.
Jn 5: 24 has eternal life and will not be j
1Co 4: 3 I care very little if I am j by you
10: 29 For why is my freedom being j
Jas 3: 1 we who teach will be j more strictly.
Rev 20: 12 The dead were j according to what

JUDGES (JUDGE)
Jdg 2: 16 Then the LORD raised up j,
Job 9: 24 of the wicked, he blindfolds its j.
Ps 9: 8 and j the peoples with equity.
58: 11 there is a God who j the earth."
75: 7 It is God who j: He brings one
Pr 29: 14 If a king j the poor with fairness,
Jn 5: 22 Moreover, the Father j no one,
Ro 2: 16 God j everyone's secrets through
1Co 4: 4 It is the Lord who j me.
Heb 4: 12 it j the thoughts and attitudes
1Pe 1: 17 a Father who j each person's work
2: 23 himself to him who j justly.
Rev 19: 11 With justice he j and makes war.

JUDGING (JUDGE)
Pr 24: 23 To show partiality in j is not good:
Isa 16: 5 one who in j seeks justice
Mt 19: 28 thrones, j the twelve tribes of Israel.
Jn 7: 24 Stop j by mere appearances,
2Co 10: 7 You are j by appearances.

JUDGMENT (JUDGE)
Nu 33: 4 the LORD had brought j on their
Dt 1: 17 of anyone, for j belongs to God.
32: 41 sword and my hand grasps it in j,

1Sa 25: 33 May you be blessed for your good j
Ps 1: 5 the wicked will not stand in the j,
9: 7 he has established his throne for j.
76: 8 From heaven you pronounced j,
82: 1 he gives j among the "gods";
119: 66 Teach me knowledge and good j,
143: 2 Do not bring your servant into j,
Pr 3: 21 preserve sound j and discretion;
8: 14 Counsel and sound j are mine;
18: 1 against all sound j starts quarrels.
Ecc 12: 14 God will bring every deed into j,
Isa 3: 14 enters into j against the elders
28: 6 spirit of justice to those who sit in j,
53: 8 oppression and j he was taken away.
66: 16 his sword the LORD will execute j
Jer 2: 35 But I will pass j on you because you
25: 31 he will bring j on all humankind
51: 18 when their j comes, they will perish.
Eze 11: 10 and I will execute j on you
Da 7: 22 pronounced j in favor of the holy
Am 7: 4 Sovereign LORD was calling for j
Zec 8: 16 true and sound j in your courts;
Mt 5: 21 who murders will be subject to j.'
5: 22 brother or sister will be subject to j.
10: 15 Gomorrah on the day of j than
11: 24 on the day of j than for you."
12: 36 the day of j for every empty word
12: 41 stand up at the j with this generation
Jn 5: 22 but has entrusted all j to the Son,
5: 30 and my j is just, for I seek not
8: 26 "I have much to say in j of you.
9: 39 "For j I have come into this world;
12: 31 Now is the time for j on this world;
16: 8 about sin and righteousness and j:
16: 11 and about j, because the prince
Ac 24: 25 self-control and the j to come,
Ro 2: 1 you who pass j on someone else,
2: 3 God's j against those who do such
5: 16 The j followed one sin and brought
12: 3 rather think of yourself with sober j,
14: 10 will all stand before God's j seat.
14: 13 Therefore let us stop passing j
1Co 7: 25 In my j, she is happier if she stays
11: 29 eat and drink j on themselves.
14: 24 brought under j by all,
2Co 5: 10 we must all appear before the j seat
2Th 1: 5 this is evidence that God's j is right,
1Ti 3: 6 fall under the same j as the devil.
5: 12 Thus they bring j on themselves,
Heb 6: 2 of the dead, and eternal j.
9: 27 to die once, and after that to face j,
10: 27 only a fearful expectation of j
Jas 2: 13 Mercy triumphs over j.
4: 11 not keeping it, but sitting in j on it.
1Pe 4: 17 For it is time for j to begin
2Pe 2: 9 for punishment on the day of j,
3: 7 fire, being kept for the day of j
1Jn 4: 17 have confidence on the day of j:
Jude : 6 everlasting chains for j on the great
Rev 14: 7 because the hour of his j has come.

JUDGMENTS (JUDGE)
Jer 1: 16 I will pronounce my j on my people
Da 9: 11 and sworn j written in the Law
Hos 6: 5 then my j go forth like the sun.
Ro 11: 33 How unsearchable his j, and his
1Co 2: 15 the Spirit makes j about all things,
2: 15 is not subject to merely human j,
Rev 16: 7 Almighty, true and just are your j."

JUG
1Sa 26: 12 spear and water j near Saul's head,
1Ki 17: 12 in a jar and a little olive oil in a j.

JUST (JUSTICE JUSTIFICATION JUSTIFIED JUSTIFIES JUSTIFYING JUSTLY)
Ge 18: 19 by doing what is right and j,
Dt 2: 12 place, j as Israel did in the land
6: 3 milk and honey, j as the LORD,
27: 3 milk and honey, j as the LORD,
30: 9 j as he delighted in your ancestors,
32: 4 are perfect, and all his ways are j.
32: 4 does no wrong, upright and j is he.
32: 47 They are not j idle words for you—
32: 50 j as your brother Aaron died
2Sa 8: 15 doing what was j and right for all
1Ch 18: 14 doing what was j and right for all
2Ch 12: 6 and said, "The LORD is j."
Ne 9: 13 and laws that are j and right,
Job 34: 17 Will you condemn the j and mighty
35: 2 "Do you think this is j? You say,
Ps 37: 28 For the LORD loves the j and will
37: 30 and their tongues speak what is j.

Ps 99: 4 in Jacob you have done what is j
  111: 7 of his hands are faithful and j;
  119:121 I have done what is righteous and j;
Pr 1: 3 doing what is right and j and fair;
  2: 8 for he guards the course of the j
  2: 9 will understand what is right and j
  8: 8 All the words of my mouth are j;
  8: 15 and rulers issue decrees that are j;
  12: 5 The plans of the righteous are j,
  21: 3 j is more acceptable to the LORD
Isa 32: 7 even when the plea of the needy is j.
  58: 2 They ask me for j decisions
Jer 4: 2 j and righteous way you swear,
  22: 3 Do what is j and right.
  22: 15 He did what was right and j, so all
  23: 5 do what is j and right in the land.
  33: 15 he will do what is j and right
Eze 18: 5 a righteous man who does what is j
  18: 19 Since the son has done what is j
  18: 21 decrees and do what is j and right,
  18: 25 'The way of the Lord is not j.'
  18: 27 and do what is j and right, they will
  18: 29 says, 'The way of the Lord is not j.'
  33: 14 sins and do what is j and right—
  33: 16 They have done what is j and right;
  33: 17 'The way of the Lord is not j.'
  33: 17 But it is their way that is not j.'
  33: 19 and do what is j and right, they will
  33: 20 'The way of the Lord is not j.'
  45: 9 and do what is j and right.
Da 4: 37 does is right and all his ways are j.
Jn 5: 30 and my judgment is j, for I seek not
Ro 3: 8 Their condemnation is j!
  3: 26 so as to be j and the one who
2Th 1: 6 God is j: He will pay back trouble
Heb 2: 2 received its j punishment,
1Jn 1: 9 he is faithful and j and will forgive
Rev 15: 3 J and true are your ways,
  16: 5 "You are j in these judgments,
  16: 7 true and j are your judgments."
  19: 2 for true and j are his judgments.

JUSTICE* (JUST)

Ge 49: 16 "Dan will provide j for his people
Ex 23: 2 do not pervert j by siding
  23: 6 "Do not deny j to your poor people
Lev 19: 15 " 'Do not pervert j; do not show
Dt 16: 19 Do not pervert j or show partiality.
  16: 20 Follow j and j alone, so that
  24: 17 the foreigner or the fatherless of j,
  27: 19 "Cursed is anyone who withholds j
1Sa 8: 3 and accepted bribes and perverted j.
2Sa 15: 4 and I would see that they receive j."
  15: 6 who came to the king asking for j.
1Ki 3: 11 for discernment in administering j,
  3: 28 wisdom from God to administer j.
  7: 7 hall, the Hall of J, where he was
  7: 9 he has made you king to maintain j
2Ch 9: 8 to maintain j and righteousness."
Ezr 7: 25 to administer j to all the people
Est 1: 13 experts in matters of law and j,
Job 8: 3 Does God pervert j?
  9: 19 And if it is a matter of j, who can
  19: 7 though I call for help, there is no j.
  27: 2 who has denied me j, the Almighty,
  29: 14 j was my robe and my turban.
  31: 13 "If I have denied j to any of my
  34: 5 am innocent, but God denies me j.
  34: 12 that the Almighty would pervert j.
  34: 17 Can one who hates j govern?
  36: 3 I will ascribe j to my Maker.
  36: 17 and j have taken hold of you.
  37: 23 in his j and great righteousness,
  40: 8 "Would you discredit my j?
Ps 7: 6 Awake, my God; decree j.
  9: 16 LORD is known by his acts of j;
  11: 7 The LORD is righteous, he loves j;
  33: 5 LORD loves righteousness and j;
  36: 6 your j like the great deep.
  45: 4 cause of truth, humility and j;
  45: 6 a scepter of j will be the scepter
  50: 6 for he is a God of j.
  72: 1 Endow the king with your j, O God,
  72: 2 your afflicted ones with j.
  89: 14 j are the foundation of your throne;
  97: 2 j are the foundation of his throne.
  99: 4 The King is mighty, he loves j—
  101: 1 I will sing of your love and j;
  103: 6 and j for all the oppressed.
  112: 5 who conduct their affairs with j.
  140: 12 the LORD secures j for the poor
Pr 8: 20 righteousness, along the paths of j,

Pr 16: 10 and his mouth does not betray j.
  17: 23 in secret to pervert the course of j.
  18: 5 and so deprive the innocent of j.
  19: 28 A corrupt witness mocks at j,
  21: 15 When j is done, it brings joy
  29: 4 By j a king gives a country stability,
  29: 7 The righteous care about j
  29: 26 is from the LORD that one gets j.
Ecc 3: 16 was there, in the place of j—
  5: 8 in a district, and j and rights denied,
Isa 1: 17 Seek j, encourage the oppressed.
  1: 21 She once was full of j;
  1: 27 Zion will be delivered with j,
  5: 7 And he looked for j, but saw
  5: 16 Almighty will be exalted by his j,
  5: 23 a bribe, but deny j to the innocent.
  9: 7 and upholding it with j
  10: 2 withhold j from the oppressed of my
  11: 4 with j he will give decisions
  16: 5 one who in judging seeks j
  28: 6 He will be a spirit of j to those who
  28: 17 I will make j the measuring line
  29: 21 testimony deprive the innocent of j.
  30: 18 For the LORD is a God of j.
  32: 1 and rulers will rule with j.
  32: 16 The LORD's j will dwell
  33: 5 he will fill Zion with his j
  42: 1 and he will bring j to the nations.
  42: 3 In faithfulness he will bring forth j;
  42: 4 be discouraged till he establishes j
  51: 4 my j will become a light
  51: 5 my arm will bring j to the nations.
  56: 1 "Maintain j and do what is right,
  59: 4 No one calls for j; no one pleads
  59: 8 there is no j in their paths.
  59: 9 So j is far from us,
  59: 11 We look for j, but find none;
  59: 14 So j is driven back,
  59: 15 was displeased that there was no j.
  61: 8 "For I, the LORD, love j;
Jer 5: 28 they do not seek j.
  9: 24 j and righteousness on earth,
  12: 1 would speak with you about your j:
  21: 12 " 'Administer j every morning;
La 3: 36 to deprive them of j—would not
Eze 22: 29 the foreigner, denying them j.
  34: 16 I will shepherd the flock with j.
Hos 2: 19 betroth you in righteousness and j,
  12: 6 maintain love and j, and wait
Am 2: 7 ground and deny j to the oppressed.
  5: 7 There are those who turn j
  5: 12 deprive the poor of j in the courts.
  5: 15 maintain j in the courts.
  5: 24 But let j roll on like a river,
  6: 12 But you have turned j into poison
Mic 3: 1 Should you not know j,
  3: 8 and with j and might, to declare
  3: 9 who despise j and distort all that is
Hab 1: 4 is paralyzed, and j never prevails.
  1: 4 the righteous, so that j is perverted.
Zep 3: 5 by morning he dispenses his j,
Zec 7: 9 'Administer true j; show mercy
Mal 2: 17 them" or "Where is the God of j?"
  3: 5 the foreigners among you of j,
Mt 12: 18 he will proclaim j to the nations.
  12: 20 snuff out, till he leads j to victory.
  23: 23 j, mercy and faithfulness.
Lk 11: 42 you neglect j and the love of God.
  18: 3 'Grant me j against my adversary.'
  18: 5 I will see that she gets j, so that she
  18: 7 will not God bring about j for his
  18: 8 he will see that they get j,
Ac 8: 33 humiliation he was deprived of j.
  17: 31 he will judge the world with j
  28: 4 the goddess J has not allowed him
Ro 3: 25 He did this to demonstrate his j,
  3: 26 it to demonstrate his j at the present
2Co 7: 11 what readiness to see j done.
Heb 1: 8 a scepter of j will be the scepter
  11: 33 administered j, and gained what was
Rev 19: 11 With j he judges and makes war.

JUSTIFICATION* (JUST)

Eze 16: 52 you have furnished some j for your
Ac 13: 39 a j you were not able to obtain
Ro 4: 25 sins and was raised to life for our j.
  5: 16 many trespasses and brought j.
  5: 18 one righteous act resulted in j

JUSTIFIED* (JUST)

Ps 51: 4 your verdict and j when you judge.
Lk 18: 14 the other, went home j before God.
Ro 3: 24 all are j freely by his grace through

Ro 3: 28 that a person is j by faith apart
  4: 2 in fact, Abraham was j by works,
  5: 1 since we have been j through faith,
  5: 9 Since we have now been j by his
  8: 30 those he called, he also j; those he j, he
     also glorified.
  10: 10 heart that you believe and are j,
1Co 6: 11 you were j in the name of the Lord
Gal 2: 16 a person is not j by observing
  2: 16 Jesus that we may be j by faith
  2: 16 observing the law no one will be j.
  2: 17 in seeking to be j in Christ, we Jews
  3: 11 Clearly no one is j before God
  3: 24 came that we might be j by faith.
Tit 3: 7 so that, having been j by his grace,
Jas 2: 24 see that people are j by what they do

JUSTIFIES* (JUST)

Ro 3: 26 the one who j those who have faith
  4: 5 but trusts God who j the ungodly,
  8: 33 God has chosen? It is God who j.

JUSTIFY* (JUST)

Est 7: 4 such distress would j disturbing
Job 40: 8 you condemn me to j yourself?
Isa 53: 11 my righteous servant will j many,
Lk 10: 29 But he wanted to j himself, so he
  16: 15 "You are the ones who j yourselves
Ro 3: 30 who will j the circumcised by faith
Gal 3: 8 that God would j the Gentiles

JUSTIFYING* (JUST)

Job 32: 2 Job for j himself rather than God.

JUSTLY* (JUST)

Ps 58: 1 Do you rulers indeed speak j?
  106: 3 Blessed are those who act j,
Jer 7: 5 actions and deal with each other j,
Mic 6: 8 To act j and to love mercy
Lk 23: 41 We are punished j, for we are
1Pe 2: 23 himself to him who judges j.

KADESH (KADESH BARNEA)

Nu 20: 1 Desert of Zin, and they stayed at K.
Dt 1: 46 And so you stayed in K many days—

KADESH BARNEA (KADESH)

Nu 32: 8 from K to look over the land.

KEBAR

Eze 1: 1 among the exiles by the K River,

KEDORLAOMER

Ge 14: 17 Abram returned from defeating K

KEEP (KEEPER KEEPING KEEPS KEPT)

Ge 31: 49 "May the LORD k watch between
Ex 15: 26 his commands and k all his decrees,
  20: 6 love me and k my commandments.
Lev 15: 31 " 'You must k the Israelites
Nu 6: 24 LORD bless you and k you;
Dt 4: 2 k the commands of the LORD your
  6: 17 Be sure to k the commands
  7: 9 love him and k his commandments.
  7: 12 your God will k his covenant
  11: 1 your God and k his requirements,
  13: 4 K his commands and obey him;
  30: 10 your God and k his commands
  30: 16 and to k his commands,
Jos 22: 5 very careful to k the commandment
1Ki 8: 58 to him and k the commands,
2Ki 17: 13 even Judah did not k the commands
  23: 3 the LORD and k his commands,
1Ch 29: 18 and k their hearts loyal to you.
2Ch 6: 14 you who k your covenant of love
  34: 31 the LORD and k his commands,
Ne 1: 5 who love him and k his commandments,
Job 14: 16 my steps but not k track of my sin.
Ps 15: 4 k their oaths even when it hurts;
  18: 28 LORD, k my lamp burning;
  19: 13 K your servant also from willful
  78: 10 they did not k God's covenant
  119: 2 Blessed are those who k his statutes
  119: 9 who are young k their way pure?
  121: 7 The LORD will k you from all
  141: 3 k watch over the door of my lips.
Pr 4: 21 sight, k them within your heart;
  4: 24 K your mouth free of perversity;
  12: 23 The prudent k their knowledge
  15: 21 k a straight course.
  17: 28 thought wise if they k silent,
  30: 8 K falsehood and lies far from me;
Ecc 3: 6 a time to k and a time to throw
  12: 13 Fear God and k his commandments,
Isa 26: 3 You will k in perfect peace those

Isa 42: 6 I will **k** you and will make you to be
46: 8 "Remember this, **k** it in mind,
56: 2 who **k** the Sabbath without desecrating
58: 13 "If you **k** your feet from breaking
Jer 16: 11 forsook me and did not **k** my law.
Eze 20: 19 decrees and be careful to **k** my laws.
Da 9: 4 who love him and **k** his commandments,
Am 5: 13 Therefore the prudent **k** quiet
Mt 10: 10 for workers are worth their **k**.
19: 17 to enter life, **k** the commandments."
Lk 12: 35 service and **k** your lamps burning,
17: 33 tries to **k** their life will lose it,
Jn 10: 24 saying, "How long will you **k** us
12: 25 in this world will **k** it for eternal life.
14: 15 "If you love me, **k** my commands.
15: 10 If you **k** my commands,
Ac 2: 24 for death to **k** its hold on him.
18: 9 **k** on speaking, do not be silent.
Ro 7: 19 not want to do—this I **k** on doing.
12: 11 but **k** your spiritual fervor,
14: 22 these things **k** between yourself
16: 17 **k** away from them.
1Co 1: 8 He will also **k** you firm to the end,
2Co 12: 7 in order to **k** me from becoming
Gal 5: 25 let us **k** in step with the Spirit.
Eph 4: 3 Make every effort to **k** the unity
2Th 3: 6 to **k** away from every believer who
1Ti 5: 22 the sins of others. **K** yourself pure.
2Ti 4: 5 **k** your head in all situations,
Heb 9: 20 God has commanded you to **k**."
13: 5 **K** your lives free from the love
Jas 1: 26 and yet do not **k** a tight rein on their
2: 8 If you really **k** the royal law found
3: 2 able to **k** their whole body in check.
2Pe 1: 8 measure, they will **k** you from being
1Jn 3: 24 Those who **k** his commands live in him,
5: 3 love for God: to **k** his commands.
Jude : 21 **k** yourselves in God's love as you
: 24 To him who is able to **k** you
Rev 3: 10 **k** you from the hour of trial that is
12: 17 those who **k** God's commands
14: 12 the people of God who **k** his commands
22: 7 Blessed are those who **k** the words
22: 9 and with all who **k** the words of this

KEEPER (KEEP)
Ge 4: 9 "Am I my brother's **k**?"

KEEPING (KEEP)
Ex 20: 8 the Sabbath day by **k** it holy.
Dt 5: 12 the Sabbath day by **k** it holy,
13: 18 **k** all his commands that I am giving
Ps 19: 11 in **k** them there is great reward.
119:112 My heart is set on **k** your decrees
Pr 15: 3 **k** watch on the wicked and the good.
Mt 3: 8 Produce fruit in **k** with repentance.
Lk 2: 8 **k** watch over their flocks at night.
1Co 7: 19 **K** God's commands is what counts.
Jas 4: 11 you are not **k** it, but sitting
1Pe 3: 16 a clear conscience, so that those
2Pe 3: 9 Lord is not slow in **k** his promise,

KEEPS (KEEP)
Ne 1: 5 who **k** his covenant of love
Da 9: 4 who **k** his covenant of love
Jn 7: 19 Yet not one of you **k** the law.
14: 21 has my commands and **k** them
1Co 13: 5 angered, it **k** no record of wrongs.
Jas 2: 10 For whoever **k** the whole law

KEILAH
1Sa 23: 13 told that David had escaped from **K**,

KEPT (KEEP)
Ex 12: 42 Because the LORD **k** vigil
Dt 7: 8 you and **k** the oath he swore to your
2Ki 18: 6 he **k** the commands the LORD had
Ne 9: 8 You have **k** your promise because
Ps 130: 3 LORD, **k** a record of sins, Lord,
Isa 38: 17 In your love you **k** me from the pit
Mt 19: 20 "All these I have **k**," the young
Jn 15: 10 as I have **k** my Father's commands
2Co 11: 9 I have **k** myself from being a burden
2Ti 4: 7 finished the race, I have **k** the faith.
1Pe 1: 4 This inheritance is **k** in heaven

KERNEL*
Mk 4: 28 then the full **k** in the head.
Jn 12: 24 unless a **k** of wheat falls

KEY (KEYS)
Isa 33: 6 the LORD is the **k** to this treasure.
Rev 20: 1 having the **k** to the Abyss

KEYS* (KEY)
Mt 16: 19 I will give you the **k** of the kingdom

Rev 1: 18 And I hold the **k** of death

KICK*
Ac 26: 14 hard for you to **k** against the goads.'

KILL (KILLED KILLS)
Ecc 3: 3 a time to **k** and a time to heal, a time
Mt 10: 28 **k** the body but cannot **k** the soul.
Mk 10: 34 and spit on him, flog him and **k** him.

KILLED (KILL)
Ge 4: 8 attacked his brother Abel and **k** him.
Ex 2: 12 he **k** the Egyptian and hid him
13: 15 the LORD **k** the firstborn of both
Nu 35: 11 who has **k** someone accidentally
1Sa 17: 50 down the Philistine and **k** him.
Ne 9: 26 They **k** your prophets, who had
Hos 6: 5 I **k** you with the words of my
Mt 17: 23 He will be **k**, and on the third day he
Mk 9: 31 He will be **k**, and after three days he
Lk 11: 48 they **k** the prophets, and you build
Ac 3: 15 You **k** the author of life, but God

KILLS (KILL)
Lev 24: 21 whoever **k** a human being is to be
2Co 3: 6 for the letter **k**, but the Spirit gives

KIND (KINDNESS KINDNESSES KINDS)
Ge 1: 24 animals, each according to its **k**."
2Ch 10: 7 "If you will be **k** to these people
Pr 11: 17 Those who are **k** benefit themselves,
12: 25 the heart, but a **k** word cheers it up.
14: 21 blessed are those who are **k**
14: 31 whoever is **k** to the needy honors
19: 17 Those who are **k** to the poor lend
Da 4: 27 by being **k** to the oppressed.
Lk 6: 35 because he is **k** to the ungrateful
1Co 13: 4 Love is patient, love is **k**. It does not
15: 35 what **k** of body will they come?"
Eph 4: 32 Be **k** and compassionate to one
2Ti 2: 24 but must be **k** to everyone,
Tit 2: 5 to be **k**, and to be subject to their

KINDHEARTED* (HEART)
Pr 11: 16 A **k** woman gains honor,

KINDNESS (KIND)
Ge 24: 12 and show **k** to my master Abraham.
32: 10 I am unworthy of all the **k**
39: 21 he showed him **k** and granted him
Ru 2: 20 "He has not stopped showing his **k**
2Sa 9: 3 to whom I can show God's **k**?"
22: 51 he shows unfailing **k** to his
Job 6: 14 withholds **k** from a friend
Ps 141: 3 that is a **k**; let him rebuke me—
Isa 54: 8 everlasting **k** I will have compassion
Jer 9: 24 who exercises **k**,
31: 3 I have drawn you with unfailing **k**.
Hos 11: 4 I led them with cords of human **k**,
Ac 14: 17 He has shown **k** by giving you rain
Ro 11: 22 Consider therefore the **k**
2Co 6: 6 understanding, patience and **k**;
Gal 5: 22 joy, peace, patience, **k**, goodness,
Eph 2: 7 expressed in his **k** to us in Christ
Col 3: 12 yourselves with compassion, **k**,
Tit 3: 4 But when the **k** and love of God our

KINDNESSES* (KIND)
Ps 106: 7 they did not remember your many **k**,
Isa 63: 7 I will tell of the **k** of the LORD,
63: 7 to his compassion and many **k**.

KINDS (KIND)
Ge 1: 12 bearing seed according to their **k**
1Co 12: 4 There are different **k** of gifts,
1Ti 6: 10 of money is a root of all **k** of evil.
1Pe 1: 6 had to suffer grief in all **k** of trials.

KING (KING'S KINGDOM KINGDOMS KINGS)
1. Kings of Judah and Israel: see Saul, David, Solomon.

2. Kings of Judah: see Rehoboam, Abijah, Asa, Jehoshaphat, Jehoram, Ahaziah, Athaliah (Queen), Joash, Amaziah, Azariah (Uzziah), Jotham, Ahaz, Hezekiah, Manasseh, Amon, Josiah, Jehoahaz, Jehoiakim, Jehoiachin, Zedekiah.

3. Kings of Israel: see Jeroboam I, Nadab, Baasha, Elah, Zimri, Tibni, Omri, Ahab, Ahaziah, Joram, Jehu, Jehoahaz, Jehoash, Jeroboam II, Zechariah, Shallum, Menahem, Pekah, Pekahiah, Hoshea.
Ex 1: 8 Then a new **k**, to whom Joseph
Dt 17: 14 "Let us set a **k** over us like all
Jdg 17: 6 In those days Israel had no **k**
1Sa 8: 5 now appoint a **k** to lead us, such as
11: 15 made Saul **k** in the presence
12: 12 the LORD your God was your **k**.
2Sa 2: 4 there they anointed David **k** over

1Ki 1: 30 Solomon your son shall be **k**
Ps 2: 6 "I have installed my **k** on Zion,
24: 7 that the **K** of glory may come in.
44: 4 You are my **K** and my God,
47: 7 For God is the **K** of all the earth;
Isa 32: 1 a **k** will reign in righteousness
Jer 30: 9 their God and David their **k**, whom I
Hos 3: 5 their God and David their **k**.
Mic 2: 13 Their **K** will pass through before
Zec 9: 9 See, your **k** comes to you,
Mt 2: 2 is the one who has been born **k**
27: 11 "Are you the **k** of the Jews?"
Lk 19: 38 "Blessed is the **k** who comes
23: 3 Jesus, "Are you the **k** of the Jews?"
23: 38 \this is \the \k \of \the
Jn 1: 49 you are the **k** of Israel."
12: 13 "Blessed is the **k** of Israel!"
Ac 17: 7 saying that there is another **k**,
1Ti 1: 17 Now to the **K** eternal, immortal,
6: 15 the **K** of kings and Lord of lords,
Heb 7: 1 This Melchizedek was **k** of Salem
Rev 15: 3 true are your ways, **K** of the nations.
17: 14 he is Lord of lords and **K** of kings—
19: 16 thigh he has this name written: **\k**

KING'S (KING)
Pr 21: 1 the LORD's hand the **k** heart is
Ecc 8: 3 in a hurry to leave the **k** presence.

KINGDOM (KING)
Ex 19: 6 you will be for me a **k** of priests
Dt 17: 18 When he takes the throne of his **k**,
2Sa 7: 12 own body, and I will establish his **k**.
1Ki 11: 31 'See, I am going to tear the **k**
1Ch 17: 11 own sons, and I will establish his **k**.
29: 11 Yours, LORD, is the **k**;
Ps 45: 6 justice will be the scepter of your **k**.
103: 19 in heaven, and his **k** rules over all.
145: 11 They tell of the glory of your **k**
Eze 29: 14 There they will be a lowly **k**.
Da 2: 39 "After you, another **k** will arise,
4: 3 His **k** is an eternal **k**;
7: 27 His **k** will be an everlasting **k**,
Ob : 21 And the **k** will be the LORD's.
Mt 3: 2 for the **k** of heaven has come near."
4: 17 for the **k** of heaven has come near."
4: 23 proclaiming the good news of the **k**,
5: 3 spirit, for theirs is the **k** of heaven.
5: 10 for theirs is the **k** of heaven.
5: 19 be called least in the **k** of heaven,
5: 19 be called great in the **k** of heaven.
5: 20 you will certainly not enter the **k**
6: 10 your **k** come, your will be done,
6: 33 But seek first his **k** and his
7: 21 Lord,' will enter the **k** of heaven,
8: 11 Isaac and Jacob in the **k** of heaven.
8: 12 of the **k** will be thrown outside,
9: 35 proclaiming the good news of the **k**
10: 7 'The **k** of heaven has come near.'
11: 11 in the **k** of heaven is greater than he.
11: 12 the **k** of heaven has been subjected
12: 25 "Every **k** divided against itself will
12: 26 How then can his **k** stand?
12: 28 the **k** of God has come upon you.
13: 11 of the **k** of heaven has been given
13: 19 people hear the message about the **k**
13: 24 "The **k** of heaven is like a man who
13: 31 "The **k** of heaven is like a mustard
13: 33 "The **k** of heaven is like yeast
13: 38 seed stands for the people of the **k**.
13: 41 of his **k** everything that causes sin
13: 43 like the sun in the **k** of their Father.
13: 44 "The **k** of heaven is like treasure
13: 45 the **k** of heaven is like a merchant
13: 47 the **k** of heaven is like a net that was
13: 52 the **k** of heaven is like the owner
16: 19 you the keys of the **k** of heaven;
16: 28 the Son of Man coming in his **k**."
18: 1 is the greatest in the **k** of heaven?"
18: 3 you will never enter the **k** of heaven.
18: 4 is the greatest in the **k** of heaven.
18: 23 the **k** of heaven is like a king who
19: 12 because of the **k** of heaven.
19: 14 for the **k** of heaven belongs to such
19: 23 for the rich to enter the **k** of heaven.
19: 24 for the rich to enter the **k** of God."
20: 1 the **k** of heaven is like a landowner
20: 21 and the other at your left in your **k**."
21: 31 the prostitutes are entering the **k**
21: 43 that the **k** of God will be taken away
22: 2 "The **k** of heaven is like a king who
23: 13 You shut the door of the **k** of heaven
24: 7 rise against nation, and **k** against **k**.

Mt 24:14 this gospel of the **k** will be preached
25: 1 time the **k** of heaven will be like ten
25:34 the **k** prepared for you since
26:29 it new with you in my Father's **k**."
Mk 1:15 "The **k** of God has come near.
3:24 If a **k** is divided against itself, that **k**
4:11 of the **k** of God has been given
4:26 "This is what the **k** of God is like.
4:30 "What shall we say the **k** of God is
6:23 I will give you, up to half my **k**."
9: 1 they see that the **k** of God has come
9:47 you to enter the **k** of God with one
10:14 for the **k** of God belongs to such as
10:15 anyone who will not receive the **k**
10:23 for the rich to enter the **k** of God!"
10:24 how hard it is to enter the **k** of God!
10:25 for the rich to enter the **k** of God."
11:10 "Blessed is the coming **k** of our
12:34 are not far from the **k** of God."
13: 8 rise against nation, and **k** against **k**.
14:25 I drink it new in the **k** of God."
15:43 himself waiting for the **k** of God,
Lk 1:33 his **k** will never end."
4:43 the good news of the **k** of God
6:20 are poor, for yours is the **k** of God.
7:28 in the **k** of God is greater than he."
8: 1 the good news of the **k** of God.
8:10 of the **k** of God has been given
9: 2 them out to proclaim the **k** of God
9:11 spoke to them about the **k** of God,
9:27 not taste death before they see the **k**
9:60 you go and proclaim the **k** of God."
9:62 is fit for service in the **k** of God."
10: 9 'The **k** of God has come near'
10:11 The **k** of God has come near.'
11: 2 be your name, your **k** come.
11:17 "Any **k** divided against itself will
11:18 himself, how can his **k** stand?
11:20 the **k** of God has come upon you.
12:31 But seek his **k**, and these things will
12:32 has been pleased to give you the **k**.
13:18 asked, "What is the **k** of God like?
13:20 "What shall I compare the **k** of God
13:28 and all the prophets in the **k** of God,
13:29 places at the feast in the **k** of God.
14:15 eat at the feast in the **k** of God."
16: 6 of the **k** of God is being preached,
17:20 when the **k** of God would come,
17:20 of the **k** of God is not something
17:21 is,' because the **k** of God is in your
18:16 for the **k** of God belongs to such as
18:17 anyone who will not receive the **k**
18:24 is for the rich to enter the **k** of God!
18:25 for the rich to enter the **k** of God."
18:29 children for the sake of the **k** of God
19:11 thought that the **k** of God was going
21:10 rise against nation, and **k** against **k**.
21:31 you know that the **k** of God is near.
22:16 it finds fulfillment in the **k** of God."
22:18 the vine until the **k** of God comes."
22:29 And I confer on you a **k**, just as my
22:30 drink at my table in my **k** and sit
23:42 me when you come into your **k**."
23:51 was waiting for the **k** of God.
Jn 3: 3 no one can see the **k** of God without
3: 5 no one can enter the **k** of God
18:36 said, "My **k** is not of this world.
18:36 now my **k** is from another place."
Ac 1: 3 days and spoke about the **k** of God.
1: 6 going to restore the **k** to Israel?"
8:12 the good news of the **k** of God and
14:22 hardships to enter the **k** of God,"
19: 8 persuasively about the **k** of God.
20:25 preaching the **k** will ever see me
28:23 explaining about the **k** of God,
28:31 He proclaimed the **k** of God
Ro 14:17 For the **k** of God is not a matter
1Co 4:20 For the **k** of God is not a matter
6: 9 wrongdoers will not inherit the **k**
6:10 nor swindlers will inherit the **k**
15:24 when he hands over the **k** to God
15:50 blood cannot inherit the **k** of God,
Gal 5:21 live like this will not inherit the **k**
Eph 2: 2 and of the ruler of the **k** of the air,
5: 5 any inheritance in the **k** of Christ
Col 1:12 of his people in the **k** of light.
1:13 us into the **k** of the Son he loves,
4:11 my co-workers for the **k** of God.
1Th 2:12 who calls you into his **k** and glory.
2Th 1: 5 be counted worthy of the **k** of God,
2Ti 4: 1 in view of his appearing and his **k**,
4:18 bring me safely to his heavenly **k**.

Heb 1: 8 justice will be the scepter of your **k**.
12:28 since we are receiving a **k**
Jas 2: 5 inherit the **k** he promised those who
2Pe 1:11 into the eternal **k** of our Lord
Rev 1: 6 has made us to be a **k** and priests
1: 9 companion in the suffering and **k**
5:10 You have made them to be a **k**
11:15 "The **k** of the world has become the **k** of
our Lord
12:10 and the power and the **k** of our God,
16:10 and its **k** was plunged into darkness.
17:12 kings who have not yet received a **k**,

KINGDOMS (KING)
2Ki 19:15 you alone are God over all the **k**
19:19 that all the **k** of the earth may know
2Ch 20: 6 You rule over all the **k**
Ps 68:32 Sing to God, you **k** of the earth,
Isa 37:16 you alone are God over all the **k**
37:20 that all the **k** of the earth may know
Eze 29:15 It will be the lowliest of **k** and will
37:22 nations or be divided into two **k**.
Da 4:17 Most High is sovereign over the **k**
Zep 3: 8 to gather the **k** and to pour out my

KINGS (KING)
Ps 2: 2 The **k** of the earth rise
47: 9 for the **k** of the earth belong to God;
68:29 at Jerusalem **k** will bring you gifts.
72:11 May all **k** bow down to him and all
110: 5 he will crush **k** on the day of his
149: 8 to bind their **k** with fetters,
Pr 16:12 **K** detest wrongdoing, for a throne is
Isa 24:21 above and the **k** on the earth below.
52:15 **k** will shut their mouths because
60:11 their **k** led in triumphal procession.
Da 2:21 he deposes **k** and raises up others.
7:17 beasts are four **k** that will rise
7:24 ten horns are ten **k** who will come
Lk 21:12 you will be brought before **k**
1Ti 2: 2 for **k** and all those in authority,
6:15 the King of **k** and Lord of lords,
Rev 1: 5 and the ruler of the **k** of the earth.
17:14 he is Lord of lords and King of **k**—
19:16 this name written: \king \of \k \and

KISS (KISSED KISSES)
Ps 2:12 **K** his son, or he will be angry
Pr 24:26 An honest answer is like a **k**
SS 1: 2 Let him **k** me with the kisses of his
8: 1 I would **k** you, and no one would
Lk 22:48 the Son of Man with a **k**?"
Ro 16:16 Greet one another with a holy **k**.
1Co 16:20 Greet one another with a holy **k**.
2Co 13:12 Greet one another with a holy **k**.
1Th 5:26 all God's people with a holy **k**.
1Pe 5:14 Greet one another with a **k** of love.

KISSED (KISS)
Mk 14:45 Judas said, "Rabbi!" and **k** him.
Lk 7:38 hair, **k** them and poured perfume

KISSES* (KISS)
Pr 27: 6 trusted, but an enemy multiplies **k**.
SS 1: 2 kiss me with the **k** of his mouth—

KNEE (KNEES)
Isa 45:23 Before me every **k** will bow;
Ro 14:11 Lord, 'every **k** will bow before me;
Php 2:10 name of Jesus every **k** should bow,

KNEEL (KNELT)
Est 3: 2 Mordecai would not **k** down or pay
Ps 95: 6 let us **k** before the LORD our
Eph 3:14 For this reason I **k** before the Father,

KNEES (KNEE)
1Ki 19:18 all whose **k** have not bowed down
Isa 35: 3 hands, steady the **k** that give way;
Da 6:10 times a day he got down on his **k**
Lk 5: 8 saw this, he fell at Jesus' **k** and said,
Heb 12:12 your feeble arms and weak **k**.

KNELT* (KNEEL)
2Ch 6:13 **k** down before the whole assembly
7: 3 they **k** on the pavement with their
29:29 everyone present with him **k** down
Est 3: 2 officials at the king's gate **k** down
Mt 8: 2 with leprosy came and **k** before him
18:26 leader came and **k** before him
15:25 The woman came and **k** before him.
17:14 approached Jesus and **k** before him.
27:29 Then they **k** in front of him
Lk 22:41 beyond them, **k** down and prayed,
Ac 20:36 he **k** down with all of them
21: 5 and there on the beach we **k** to pray.

KNEW (KNOW)
2Ch 33:13 Manasseh **k** that the LORD is God.
Job 23: 3 If only I **k** where to find him;
Pr 24:12 "But we **k** nothing about this,"
Jer 1: 5 I formed you in the womb I **k** you,
Jnh 4: 2 I **k** that you are a gracious
Mt 7:23 tell them plainly, 'I never **k** you.
12:25 Jesus **k** their thoughts and said
Jn 2:24 himself to them, for he **k** all people.

KNIFE
Ge 22:10 hand and took the **k** to slay his son.
Pr 23: 2 and put a **k** to your throat if you are

KNOCK*
Mt 7: 7 **k** and the door will be opened
Mt 7: 8 who **k**, the door will be opened.
Lk 11: 9 **k** and the door will be opened
11:10 to those who **k**, the door will be
Rev 3:20 I stand at the door and **k**.

KNOW (FOREKNEW FOREKNOWLEDGE KNEW
KNOWING KNOWLEDGE KNOWN KNOWS)
Ge 22:12 Now I **k** that you fear God,
Ex 6: 7 you will **k** that I am the LORD
14: 4 the Egyptians will **k** that I am
33:13 teach me your ways so I may **k** you
Dt 7: 9 **K** therefore that the LORD your
18:21 "How can we **k** when a message
Jos 4:24 of the earth might **k** that the hand
23:14 You **k** with all your heart and soul
1Sa 17:46 the whole world will **k** that there is
1Ki 8:39 you alone **k** every human heart),
Job 11: 6 **K** this: God has even forgotten some
19:25 I **k** that my redeemer lives,
42: 3 things too wonderful for me to **k**.
Ps 9:10 Those who **k** your name trust
46:10 "Be still, and **k** that I am God;
73:11 Does the Most High **k** anything?"
100: 3 **K** that the LORD is God. It is he
139: 1 LORD, and you **k** me.
139:23 Search me, God, and **k** my heart;
145:12 that all people may **k** of your mighty
Pr 27: 1 you do not **k** what a day may bring.
30: 4 the name of his son? Surely you **k**!
Ecc 8: 5 the wise heart will **k** the proper time
8:17 Even if the wise claim they **k**,
Isa 29:15 think, "Who sees us? Who will **k**?"
29:16 the potter, "You **k** nothing"?
40:21 Do you not **k**? Have you not heard?
Jer 6:15 they do not even **k** how to blush.
9:24 they understand and **k** me,
22:16 Is that not what it means to **k** me?"
24: 7 I will give them a heart to **k** me,
31:34 say to one another, 'K the LORD,'
33: 3 unsearchable things you do not **k**.'
Eze 2: 5 they will **k** that a prophet has been
6:10 they will **k** that I am the LORD;
Da 11:32 but the people who **k** their God will
Mt 6: 3 let your left hand **k** what your right
7:11 **k** how to give good gifts to your
9: 6 I want you to **k** that the Son of Man
22:29 because you do not **k** the Scriptures
24:42 because you do not **k** on what day
26:74 to them, "I don't **k** the man!"
Mk 12:24 because you do not **k** the Scriptures
Lk 1: 4 so that you may **k** the certainty
11:13 **k** how to give good gifts to your
12:48 the one who does not **k** and does
12:25 'I don't **k** you or where you come
21:31 you **k** that the kingdom of God is
23:34 they do not **k** what they are doing."
Jn 1:26 among you stands one you do not **k**.
3:11 we speak of what we **k**, and we
4:22 worship what you do not **k**; we worship
what we do **k**,
4:42 and we **k** that this man really is
6:69 to **k** that you are the Holy One
7:28 sent me is true. You do not **k** him,
8:14 valid, for I **k** where I came
8:19 "You do not **k** me or my Father,"
8:32 Then you will **k** the truth,
9:25 One thing I do **k**. I was blind
10: 4 follow him because they **k** his voice.
10:14 I **k** my sheep and my sheep **k** me—
10:27 I **k** them, and they follow me.
12:35 in the dark do not **k** where they are
13:17 Now that you **k** these things,
13:35 this everyone will **k** that you are my
14: 7 If you really **k** me,
14:17 But you **k** him, for he lives with you
15:21 they do not **k** the one who sent me.
16:30 we can see that you **k** all things

Jn 17: 3 that they **k** you, the only true God,
17: 23 the world will **k** that you sent me
21: 15 he said, "you **k** that I love you."
21: 24 We **k** that his testimony is true.
Ac 1: 7 "It is not for you to **k** the times
1: 24 "Lord, you **k** everyone's heart.
Ro 3: 17 the way of peace they do not **k**."
6: 3 don't you **k** that all of us who were
6: 6 we **k** that our old self was crucified
6: 16 Don't you **k** that when you offer
7: 14 We **k** that the law is spiritual;
7: 18 I **k** that good itself does not dwell
8: 22 We **k** that the whole creation has
8: 26 We do not **k** what we ought to pray
8: 28 we **k** that in all things God works
1Co 1: 21 through its wisdom did not **k** him,
2: 2 I resolved to **k** nothing while I was
3: 16 Don't you **k** that you yourselves are
5: 6 Don't you **k** that a little yeast
6: 2 do you not **k** that the Lord's people
6: 15 Do you not **k** that your bodies are
6: 16 Do you not **k** that he who unites
6: 19 Do you not **k** that your bodies are
7: 16 How do you **k**, wife, whether you
8: 2 do not yet **k** as they ought to **k**.
9: 13 Don't you **k** that those who serve
9: 24 Do you not **k** that in a race all
13: 9 For we **k** in part and we prophesy
13: 12 Now I **k** in part; then I shall **k** fully,
14: 16 do not **k** what you are saying?
15: 58 because you **k** that your labor
2Co 5: 1 For we **k** that if the earthly tent we
5: 11 we **k** what it is to fear the Lord,
8: 9 For you **k** the grace of our Lord
Gal 1: 11 I want you to **k**, brothers and sisters,
2: 16 **k** that a person is not justified
Eph 1: 17 so that you may **k** him better.
1: 18 in order that you may **k** the hope
6: 8 because you **k** that the Lord will
6: 9 since you **k** that he who is both their
Php 3: 10 I want to **k** Christ—yes, to **k**
4: 12 I **k** what it is to be in need, and I **k**
Col 2: 2 order that they may **k** the mystery
4: 1 because you **k** that you also have
4: 6 you may **k** how to answer everyone.
1Th 3: 3 You **k** quite well that we are
5: 2 for you **k** very well that the day
2Th 1: 8 will punish those who do not **k** God
1Ti 1: 7 they do not **k** what they are talking
3: 5 anyone does not **k** how to manage
3: 15 you will **k** how people ought
2Ti 1: 12 because I **k** whom I have believed,
2: 23 because you **k** they produce
3: 14 because you **k** those from whom
Heb 8: 11 because they will all **k** me,
11: 8 though he did not **k** where he was
Jas 1: 3 because you **k** that the testing
3: 1 because you **k** that we who teach
4: 4 don't you **k** that friendship
4: 14 you do not even **k** what will happen
4: 17 if you **k** the good
1Pe 1: 18 For you **k** that it was not
2Pe 1: 12 even though you **k** them and are
1Jn 2: 3 We **k** that we have come to **k** him
2: 4 Those who say, "I **k** him," but do
2: 5 This is how we **k** we are in him:
2: 11 they do not **k** where they are going,
2: 20 Holy One, and all of you **k** the truth.
2: 29 If you **k** that he is righteous, you **k**
3: 1 does not **k** us is that it did not **k** him.
3: 2 But we **k** that when Christ appears,
3: 10 This is how we **k** the children
3: 14 We **k** that we have passed
3: 16 This is how we **k** what love is:
3: 19 This is how we **k** that we belong
3: 24 We **k** it by the Spirit he gave us.
4: 8 does not love does not **k** God,
4: 13 This is how we **k** we live in him
4: 16 so we **k** and rely on the love God
5: 2 This is how we **k** that we love
5: 13 you may **k** that you have eternal life.
5: 15 And if we **k** that he hears us—
5: 18 We **k** that anyone born of God does
5: 20 We **k** also that the Son of God has
Rev 2: 2 I **k** your deeds, your hard work
2: 9 I **k** your afflictions and your
2: 19 I **k** your deeds, your love and faith,
3: 3 you will not **k** at what time I will
3: 15 I **k** your deeds, that you are neither

KNOWING (KNOW)
Ge 3: 5 will be like God, **k** good and evil."

Ge 3: 22 like one of us, **k** good and evil.
Jn 19: 28 **k** that everything had now been
Php 3: 8 worth of **k** Christ Jesus my Lord,
Phm : 21 **k** that you will do even more than I
Heb 13: 2 hospitality to angels without **k** it.

KNOWLEDGE (KNOW)
Ge 2: 9 the tree of the **k** of good and evil.
2: 17 eat from the tree of the **k** of good
2Ch 1: 10 Give me wisdom and **k**, that I may
Job 21: 22 "Can anyone teach **k** to God,
38: 2 my plans with words without **k**?
42: 3 that obscures my plans without **k**?'
Ps 19: 2 night after night they display **k**.
94: 10 who teaches human beings lack **k**?
119: 66 Teach me **k** and good judgment,
139: 6 Such **k** is too wonderful for me,
Pr 1: 4 **k** and discretion to the young—
1: 7 of the LORD is the beginning of **k**,
2: 5 the LORD and find the **k** of God.
2: 6 from his mouth come **k**
2: 10 and **k** will be pleasant to your soul.
3: 20 by his **k** the deeps were divided,
8: 10 of silver, **k** rather than choice gold,
8: 12 I possess **k** and discretion.
9: 10 **k** of the Holy One is understanding.
10: 14 The wise store up **k**, but the mouth
12: 1 Whoever loves discipline loves **k**,
12: 23 The prudent keep their **k**
13: 16 All who are prudent act with **k**,
14: 6 but **k** comes easily to the discerning
15: 7 The lips of the wise spread **k**,
15: 14 The discerning heart seeks **k**,
17: 27 Those who have **k** use words
18: 15 heart of the discerning acquires **k**,
19: 2 Desire without **k** is not good—
19: 25 the discerning, and they will gain **k**.
20: 15 but lips that speak **k** are a rare jewel.
23: 12 and your ears to words of **k**.
24: 4 through **k** its rooms are filled
Ecc 7: 12 but the advantage of **k** is this:
Isa 11: 2 the Spirit of the **k** and fear
11: 9 the **k** of the LORD as the waters
40: 14 Who was it that taught him **k**,
Jer 3: 15 heart, who will lead you with **k**
Hos 4: 6 people are destroyed from lack of **k**.
Hab 2: 14 will be filled with the **k** of the glory
Mal 2: 7 lips of a priest ought to preserve **k**,
Mt 13: 11 replied, "The **k** of the secrets
Lk 8: 10 He said, "The **k** of the secrets
11: 52 you have taken away the key to **k**.
Ac 18: 24 with a thorough **k** of the Scriptures.
Ro 1: 28 it worthwhile to retain the **k** of God,
10: 2 but their zeal is not based on **k**.
11: 33 riches of the wisdom and **k** of God!
1Co 8: 1 But **k** puffs up while love builds up.
8: 11 Christ died, is destroyed by your **k**.
12: 8 to another a message of **k** by means
13: 2 can fathom all mysteries and all **k**,
13: 8 where there is **k**, it will pass away.
2Co 2: 14 aroma of the **k** of him everywhere.
4: 6 of the **k** of God's glory displayed
7: 2 in **k**, in complete earnestness
11: 6 as a speaker, but I do have **k**.
Eph 3: 19 to know this love that surpasses **k**—
4: 13 faith and in the **k** of the Son of God
Php 1: 9 and more in **k** and depth of insight,
Col 1: 9 with the **k** of his will through all
1: 10 work, growing in the **k** of God,
2: 3 all the treasures of wisdom and **k**.
3: 10 is being renewed in **k** in the image
1Ti 2: 4 and to come to a **k** of the truth.
Tit 1: 1 and their **k** of the truth that leads
Heb 10: 26 we have received the **k** of the truth,
2Pe 1: 5 and to goodness, **k**;
3: 18 grow in the grace and **k** of our Lord

KNOWN (KNOW)
Ex 6: 3 the LORD I did not make myself **k**
Ps 16: 11 You make **k** to me the path of life;
89: 1 make your faithfulness **k** through all
98: 2 LORD has made his salvation **k**
105: 1 make **k** among the nations what he
119: 168 for all my ways are **k** to you.
Pr 20: 11 Even small children are **k** by their
Isa 12: 4 make **k** among the nations what he
46: 10 I make **k** the end
61: 9 descendants will be **k** among
Eze 38: 23 I will make myself **k** in the sight
39: 7 "I will make **k** my holy name
Mt 10: 26 or hidden that will not be made **k**.
24: 43 of the house had **k** at what time

Lk 19: 42 had only **k** on this day what would
Jn 15: 15 my Father I have made **k** to you.
16: 14 he will receive what he will make **k**
17: 26 I have made you **k** to them, and will
Ac 2: 28 You have made **k** to me the paths
Ro 1: 19 since what may be **k** about God is
3: 21 of God has been made **k**,
9: 22 his wrath and make his power **k**,
11: 34 "Who has **k** the mind of the Lord?
15: 20 the gospel where Christ was not **k**,
16: 26 and made **k** through the prophetic
1Co 2: 16 "Who has **k** the mind of the Lord so
8: 3 But whoever loves God is **k** by God.
13: 12 know fully, even as I am fully **k**.
2Co 2: 9 our hearts, **k** and read by everyone.
Gal 4: 9 or rather are **k** by God—how is it
Eph 3: 5 which was not made **k** to people
6: 19 I will fearlessly make **k** the mystery
2Ti 3: 15 from infancy you have **k** the Holy
2Pe 2: 21 than to have **k** it and then to turn

KNOWS (KNOW)
1Sa 2: 3 for the LORD is a God who **k**,
Est 4: 14 who **k** but that you have come
Job 23: 10 But he **k** the way that I take;
Ps 44: 21 since he **k** the secrets of the heart?
94: 11 The LORD **k** all human plans; he **k**
103: 14 for he **k** how we are formed,
Ecc 8: 7 Since no one **k** the future, who can
9: 12 no one **k** when their hour will come:
Mt 6: 8 your Father **k** what you need before
11: 27 No one **k** the Son except the Father,
11: 27 no one **k** the Father except the Son
24: 36 about that day or hour no one **k**,
Lk 12: 47 "The servant who **k** the master's
16: 15 of others, but God **k** your hearts.
Ac 15: 8 God, who **k** the heart,
Ro 8: 27 who searches our hearts **k** the mind
1Co 2: 11 who **k** a person's thoughts except
2Ti 2: 19 "The Lord **k** those who are his,"
1Jn 4: 6 and whoever **k** God listens to us;
4: 7 has been born of God and **k** God.

KOHATHITE (KOHATHITES)
Nu 3: 29 The **K** clans were to camp

KOHATHITES (KOHATHITE)
Nu 3: 28 The **K** were responsible for the care
4: 15 The **K** are to carry those things

KORAH
Levite who led rebellion against Moses and Aaron (Nu 16; Jude 11).

LABAN
Brother of Rebekah (Ge 24:29), father of Rachel and Leah (Ge 29:16). Received Abraham's servant (Ge 24:29–51). Provided daughters as wives for Jacob in exchange for Jacob's service (Ge 29:1–30). Provided flocks for Jacob's service (Ge 30:25–43). After Jacob's departure, pursued and covenanted with him (Ge 31).

LABOR (LABORING)
Ex 1: 11 them to oppress them with forced **l**,
20: 9 Six days you shall **l** and do all your
Dt 5: 13 Six days you shall **l** and do all your
Ps 127: 1 the house, the builders **l** in vain.
128: 2 You will eat the fruit of your **l**;
Pr 12: 24 rule, but laziness ends in forced **l**.
Isa 54: 1 for joy, you who were never in **l**;
55: 2 and your **l** on what does not satisfy?
Mt 6: 28 They do not **l** or spin.
Jn 4: 38 have reaped the benefits of their **l**."
1Co 3: 8 rewarded according to their own **l**,
15: 58 know that your **l** in the Lord is not
Gal 4: 27 cry aloud, you who were never in **l**;
Php 2: 16 Christ that I did not run or **l** in vain.
Rev 14: 13 "they will rest from their **l**, for their

LABORING* (LABOR)
2Th 3: 8 **l** and toiling so that we would not be

LACK (LACKED LACKING LACKS)
Ps 34: 9 for those who fear him **l** nothing.
Pr 5: 23 For **l** of discipline they will die,
10: 21 many, but fools die for **l** of sense.
11: 14 For **l** of guidance a nation falls,
15: 22 Plans fail for **l** of counsel,
28: 27 who give to the poor will **l** nothing,
Mk 6: 34 He was amazed at their **l** of faith
16: 14 rebuked them for their **l** of faith
1Co 7: 5 you do not **l** any spiritual gift as you
7: 5 because of your **l** of self-control.
Col 2: 23 but they **l** any value in restraining

LACKED (LACK)
Dt   2: 7   and you have not I anything.
Ne   9: 21   they I nothing, their clothes did not
1Co 12: 24   greater honor to the parts that I it,

LACKING (LACK)
Ro 12: 11   Never be I in zeal, but keep your
Jas   1: 4   and complete, not I anything.

LACKS (LACK)
Pr   25: 28   is a person who I self-control.
    31: 11   in her and I nothing of value.
Eze 34: 8   because my flock I a shepherd
Jas   1: 5   If any of you I wisdom, you should

LAID (LAY)
Isa 53: 6   and the LORD has I on him
Mk   6: 29   and took his body and I it in a tomb.
Lk   6: 48   deep and the foundation on rock.
Ac   6: 6   prayed and I their hands on them.
1Co   3: 11   other than the one already I,
1Ti   4: 14   when the body of elders I their hands
1Jn   3: 16   Jesus Christ I down his life for us.

LAKE
Mt   8: 24   a furious storm came up on the I,
    14: 25   went out to them, walking on the I.
Mk   4: 1   into a boat and sat in it out on the I,
Lk   8: 33   down the steep bank into the I
Jn   6: 25   found him on the other side of the I,
Rev 19: 20   into the fiery I of burning sulfur.
    20: 14   The I of fire is the second death.

LAMB (LAMB'S LAMBS)
Ge   22: 8   "God himself will provide the I
Ex   12: 21   and slaughter the Passover I.
Nu   9: 11   They are to eat the I,
2Sa 12: 4   he took the ewe I that belonged
Isa   11: 6   The wolf will live with the I,
    53: 7   he was led like a I to the slaughter,
Mk 14: 12   to sacrifice the Passover I,
Jn   1: 29   "Look, the I of God, who takes
Ac   8: 32   and as a I before its shearer is silent,
1Co   5: 7   our Passover I, has been sacrificed.
1Pe   1: 19   a I without blemish or defect.
Rev   5: 6   Then I saw a L, looking as if it had
    5: 12   "Worthy is the L, who was slain,
    7: 14   them white in the blood of the L.
    14: 4   They follow the L wherever he
    15: 3   God's servant Moses and of the L:
    17: 14   L, but the L will triumph over them
    19: 9   to the wedding supper of the L!' "
    21: 23   gives it light, and the L is its lamp.

LAMB'S (LAMB)
Rev 21: 27   names are written in the L book

LAMBS (LAMB)
Lk   10: 3   you out like I among wolves.
Jn   21: 15   Jesus said, "Feed my I."

LAME
2Sa   9: 3   he is I in both feet."
Isa 33: 23   even the I will carry off plunder.
    35: 6   Then will the I leap like a deer,
Mt 11: 5   The blind receive sight, the I walk,
    15: 31   the I walking and the blind seeing.
Lk 14: 21   the crippled, the blind and the I.'

LAMENT
2Sa   1: 17   took up this I concerning Saul
Eze 19: 1   "Take up a I concerning the princes

LAMP (LAMPS LAMPSTAND LAMPSTANDS)
2Sa 22: 29   You, LORD, are my I;
Ps   18: 28   You, LORD, keep my I burning;
  119:105   Your word is a I to my feet
  132: 17   and set up a I for my anointed one.
Pr   13: 9   For this command is a I,
    20: 27   The human spirit is the I
    31: 18   and her I does not go out at night.
Mt   6: 22   "The eye is the I of the body.
Lk   8: 16   "No one lights a I and hides it
Rev 21: 23   gives it light, and the Lamb is its I.
    22: 5   They will not need the light of a I

LAMPS (LAMP)
Mt 25: 1   be like ten virgins who took their I
Lk 12: 35   for service and keep your I burning,
Rev   4: 5   the throne, seven I were blazing.

LAMPSTAND (LAMP)
Ex   25: 31   "Make a I of pure gold.
Zec   4: 2   "I see a solid gold I with a bowl
    4: 11   on the right and the left of the I?"
Heb   9: 2   In its first room were the I
Rev   2: 5   and remove your I from its place.

LAMPSTANDS (LAMP)
2Ch   4: 7   He made ten gold I according
Rev   1: 12   when I turned I saw seven golden I,
    1: 20   and of the seven golden I is this:

LAND (LANDS)
Ge   1: 10   God called the dry ground "I,"
    1: 11   said, "Let the I produce vegetation:
    1: 24   "Let the I produce living creatures
    12: 1   household to the I I will show you.
    12: 7   your offspring I will give this I."
    13: 15   All the I that you see I will give you.
    15: 18   "To your descendants I give this I,
    50: 24   of this I to the I he promised on oath
Ex   3: 8   a I flowing with milk and honey—
    6: 8   I will bring you to the I I swore
    33: 3   Go up to the I flowing with milk
Lev 25: 23   " 'The I must not be sold
Nu   14: 8   he will lead us into that I, a I
    35: 33   not pollute the I where you are.
Dt   1: 8   See, I have given you this I.
    8: 7   God is bringing you into a good I—
    11: 10   The I you are entering to take over
    28: 21   you from the I you are entering
    29: 10   on the watered I as well as the dry.
    34: 1   LORD showed him the whole I—
Jos 13: 2   "This is the I that remains:
    14: 4   Levites received no share of the I
    14: 9   'The I on which your feet have
2Sa 21: 14   answered prayer in behalf of the I.
2Ki 17: 5   king of Assyria invaded the entire I,
    24: 1   king of Babylon invaded the I,
    25: 21   went into captivity, away from her I.
2Ch   7: 14   their sin and will heal their I.
    7: 20   then I will uproot Israel from my I,
    36: 21   The I enjoyed its sabbath rests;
Ezr   9: 11   to possess is a I polluted
Ne   9: 36   the I you gave our ancestors so they
Ps 37: 11   the meek will inherit the I and enjoy
    37: 29   The righteous will inherit the I
  136: 21   and gave their I as an inheritance,
  142: 5   my portion in the I of the living."
Pr   2: 21   For the upright will live in the I,
    12: 11   who work their I will have abundant
Isa   6: 13   And though a tenth remains in the I,
    53: 8   was cut off from the I of the living;
Jer   2: 7   came and defiled my I and made my
Eze 36: 24   and bring you back into your own I.

LANDS (LAND)
Ps 111: 6   giving them the I of other nations.
Eze 20: 6   honey, the most beautiful of all I.
Zec 10: 9   in distant I they will remember me.

LANGUAGE (LANGUAGES)
Ge   11: 1   Now the whole world had one I
    11: 9   there the LORD confused the I
Jn   8: 44   he speaks his native I, for he is a liar
Ac   2: 6   one heard their own I being spoken.
Col   3: 8   slander, and filthy I from your lips.
Rev   5: 9   God members of every tribe and I
    7: 9   people and I, standing before
    14: 6   to every nation, tribe, I and people.

LANGUAGES (LANGUAGE)
Isa 66: 18   gather the people of all nations and I,
Zec 8: 23   "In those days ten people from all I

LAODICEA
Rev   3: 14   the angel of the church in L write:

LAP
Jdg   7: 5   "Separate those who I the water

LASHES
Pr   17: 10   person more than a hundred I a fool.
2Co 11: 24   from the Jews the forty I minus one.

LAST (LASTING LASTS LATTER)
Ex   14: 24   During the I watch of the night
2Sa 23: 1   These are the I words of David:
Isa   2: 2   In the I days the mountain
    41: 4   the first of them and with the I—
    44: 6   I am the first and I am the I;
    48: 12   I am the first and I am the I.
Hos   3: 5   and to his blessings in the I days.
Mic   4: 1   In the I days the mountain
Mt 19: 30   But many who are first will be I,
    20: 8   beginning with the I ones hired
    21: 37   L of all, he sent his son to them.
Mk   9: 35   wants to be first must be the very I,
    10: 31   are first will be I, and the I first."
    15: 37   a loud cry, Jesus breathed his I.
Jn   6: 40   I will raise them up at the I day."
    15: 16   fruit that will I—and so
Ac   2: 17   " 'In the I days, God says, I will

Ro   1: 17   that is by faith from first to I, just as
1Co 15: 26   The I enemy to be destroyed is
    15: 52   twinkling of an eye, at the I trumpet.
2Ti   3: 1   will be terrible times in the I days.
2Pe   3: 3   that in the I days scoffers will come,
Jude   : 18   "In the I times there will be scoffers
Rev   1: 17   I am the First and the L.
    22: 13   the First and the L, the Beginning

LASTING (LAST)
Ex 12: 14   to the LORD—a I ordinance.
Lev 24: 8   of the Israelites, as a I covenant.
Nu 25: 13   have a covenant of a I priesthood,
Heb 10: 34   had better and I possessions.

LASTS (LAST)
Ps 30: 5   For his anger I only a moment,
2Co   3: 11   greater is the glory of that which I!

LATTER (LAST)
Job 42: 12   The LORD blessed the I part
Mt 23: 23   You should have practiced the I,
Php   1: 16   The I do so out of love,

LAUGH (LAUGHED LAUGHS LAUGHTER)
Ps 59: 8   But you I at them, LORD;
Pr 31: 25   she can I at the days to come.
Ecc   3: 4   a time to weep and a time to I,
Lk   6: 21   you who weep now, for you will I
    6: 25   Woe to you who I now, for you will

LAUGHED (LAUGH)
Ge 17: 17   he I and said to himself, "Will a son
    18: 12   So Sarah I to herself as she thought,

LAUGHS (LAUGH)
Ps   2: 4   The One enthroned in heaven I;
    37: 13   but the Lord I at the wicked, for he

LAUGHTER (LAUGH)
Ge 21: 6   said, "God has brought me I,
Ps 126: 2   Our mouths were filled with I,
Pr 14: 13   Even in I the heart may ache,
Jas   4: 9   Change your I to mourning and your

LAVISHED
Eph   1: 8   that he I on us. With all wisdom
1Jn   3: 1   See what great love the Father has I

LAW (LAWFUL LAWGIVER LAWS)
Ex 31: 18   the two tablets of the covenant I,
Lev 24: 22   to have the same I for the foreigner
Nu   6: 13   " 'Now this is the I
Dt   1: 5   Moses began to expound this I,
    6: 25   to obey all this I before the LORD
    27: 26   of this I by carrying them out."
    31: 11   you shall read this I before them
    31: 26   "Take this Book of the L and place
Jos   1: 7   to obey all the I my servant Moses
    1: 8   Keep this Book of the L always
    22: 5   the I that Moses the servant
2Ki 22: 8   the Book of the L in the temple
2Ch   6: 16   walk before me according to my I,
    17: 9   the Book of the L of the LORD;
    34: 14   the Book of the L of the LORD
Ezr   7: 6   well versed in the L of Moses,
Ne   8: 2   the priest brought the L before
    8: 8   read from the Book of the L of God,
Ps   1: 2   and meditate on his I day and night.
    19: 7   The I of the LORD is perfect,
    37: 31   The I of their God is in their hearts;
    40: 8   your I is within my heart."
  119: 18   may see wonderful things in your I.
  119: 70   unfeeling, but I delight in your I.
  119: 72   The I from your mouth is more
  119: 77   I may live, for your I is my delight.
  119: 97   how I love your I! I meditate
  119:163   detest falsehood but I love your I,
  119:165   peace have those who love your I,
Isa   2: 3   The I will go out from Zion,
    42: 21   his righteousness to make his I great
Jer   8: 8   deal with the I did not know me;
    8: 8   for we have the I of the LORD,"
    31: 33   "I will put my I in their minds
Mic   4: 2   The I will go out from Zion,
Hab   1: 4   they are a I to themselves
Zec   7: 12   would not listen to the I
Mt   5: 17   that I have come to abolish the L
    7: 12   for this sums up the L
    22: 36   greatest commandment in the L?"
    22: 40   All the L and the Prophets hang
    23: 23   the more important matters of the I—
Lk 11: 52   "Woe to you experts in the I,
    16: 17   stroke of a pen to drop out of the L.
    24: 44   written about me in the L of Moses,
Jn   1: 17   For the I was given through Moses;

Ac 13: 39 able to obtain under the l of Moses.
Ro 2: 12 All who sin apart from the l will also perish apart from the l,
2: 15 the requirements of the l are written
2: 20 you have in the l the embodiment
2: 25 has value if you observe the l,
3: 19 we know that whatever the l says,
3: 20 in God's sight by observing the l;
3: 21 apart from the l the righteousness
3: 21 to which the **L** and the Prophets
3: 28 by faith apart from observing the l.
3: 31 Not at all! Rather, we uphold the l.
4: 13 It was not through the l
4: 15 because the l brings wrath.
4: 16 not only to those who are of the l
5: 13 in the world before the l was given,
5: 20 The l was brought in so
6: 14 because you are not under the l,
6: 15 sin because we are not under the l
7: 1 the l has authority over someone
7: 4 died to the l through the body
7: 5 passions aroused by the l were
7: 6 we have been released from the l so
7: 7 Is the l sinful? Certainly not!
7: 8 For apart from the l, sin was dead.
7: 12 So then, the l is holy,
7: 14 We know that the l is spiritual;
7: 22 my inner being I delight in God's l;
7: 25 in my mind am a slave to God's l,
8: 2 because through Christ Jesus the l
8: 3 For what the l was powerless to do
8: 4 of the l might be fully met in us,
8: 7 it does not submit to God's l,
9: 4 the receiving of the l, the temple
9: 31 who pursued the l as the way
10: 4 Christ is the culmination of the l so
13: 8 loves others has fulfilled the l.
13: 10 love is the fulfillment of the l.
1Co 6: 6 brother goes to l against another—
9: 9 For it is written in the **L** of Moses:
9: 20 To those under the l I became like one
under the l
9: 21 To those not having the l I became like
one not having the l
15: 56 is sin, and the power of sin is the l.
Gal 2: 16 is not justified by observing the l,
2: 19 "For through the l I died to the l so
3: 2 receive the Spirit by observing the l,
3: 5 among you by your observing the l,
3: 10 on observing the l are under a curse,
3: 11 one is justified before God by the l,
3: 13 curse of the l by becoming a curse
3: 17 The l, introduced 430 years later,
3: 19 then, was the purpose of the l?
3: 21 Is the l, therefore,
3: 23 we were held in custody under the l,
3: 24 So the l was put in charge of us
4: 21 you who want to be under the l,
5: 3 he is obligated to obey the whole l.
5: 14 For the entire l is fulfilled
5: 18 the Spirit, you are not under the l.
6: 2 in this way you will fulfill the l
Eph 2: 15 in his flesh the l with its commands
Php 3: 6 righteousness based on the l,
3: 9 my own that comes from the l,
1Ti 1: 8 We know that the l is good if one
Heb 7: 12 the l must be changed also.
7: 19 (for the l made nothing perfect),
10: 1 The l is only a shadow of the good
Jas 1: 25 into the perfect l that gives freedom,
2: 8 you really keep the royal l found
2: 10 For whoever keeps the whole l
4: 11 judges them speaks against the l
1Jn 3: 4 Everyone who sins breaks the l;

LAWFUL (LAW)
Mt 12: 12 Therefore it is l to do good

LAWGIVER* (LAW)
Isa 33: 22 the LORD is our l, the LORD is
Jas 4: 12 There is only one **L** and Judge,

LAWLESS (LAWLESSNESS)
2Th 2: 8 And then the l one will be revealed,
Heb 10: 17 l acts I will remember no more."

LAWLESSNESS* (LAWLESS)
2Th 2: 3 occurs and the man of l is revealed,
2: 7 the secret power of l is already
1Jn 3: 4 sins breaks the law; in fact, sin is l.

LAWS (LAW)
Ex 21: 1 "These are the l you are to set

Lev 25: 18 decrees and be careful to obey my l,
Dt 4: 1 and l I am about to teach you.
30: 16 keep his commands, decrees and l;
Ps 119: 30 I have set my heart on your l.
119: 43 for I have put my hope in your l.
119:120 fear of you; I stand in awe of your l.
119:164 I praise you for your righteous l.
119:175 and may your l sustain me.
Eze 36: 27 decrees and be careful to keep my l.
Heb 8: 10 I will put my l in their minds
10: 16 I will put my l in their hearts,

LAWSUIT (LAWSUIT)
Pr 18: 17 In a l the first to speak seems

LAWSUITS (LAWSUITS)
Hos 10: 4 therefore l spring up like poisonous
1Co 6: 7 you have l among you means you

LAY (LAID LAYING LAYS)
Ex 29: 10 his sons shall l their hands on its
Lev 1: 4 You are to l your hand on the head
4: 15 the community are to l their hands
Nu 8: 10 the Israelites are to l their hands
27: 18 leadership, and l your hand on him.
1Sa 26: 9 Who can l a hand on the LORD's
Job 1: 12 the man himself do not l a finger."
22: 22 and l up his words in your heart.
Ecc 10: 4 calmness can l great offenses
Isa 28: 16 "See, I l a stone in Zion, a tested
Mt 8: 20 of Man has no place to l his head."
28: 6 Come and see the place where he l.
Mk 6: 5 except l his hands on a few sick
Lk 9: 58 of Man has no place to l his head."
Jn 10: 15 and l down my life for the sheep.
10: 18 but l I it down of my own accord.
15: 13 to l down one's life for one's
Ac 8: 19 whom I l my hands may receive
Ro 9: 33 I l in Zion a stone that causes people
1Co 3: 11 no one can l any foundation other
1Pe 2: 6 "See, I l a stone in Zion, a chosen
1Jn 3: 16 we ought to l down our lives for one
Rev 4: 10 They l their crowns before

LAYING* (LAY)
2Ch 32: 9 his forces were l siege to Lachish,
Job 34: 30 from l snares for the people.
Lk 4: 40 and l his hands on each one,
Ac 8: 18 the Spirit was given at the l
1Ti 5: 22 Do not be hasty in the l on of hands,
2Ti 1: 6 is in you through the l on of my
Heb 6: 1 not l again the foundation
6: 2 cleansing rites, the l on of hands,

LAYS (LAY)
Jn 10: 11 The good shepherd l down his life

LAZARUS
1. Poor man in Jesus' parable (Lk 16:19–31).
2. Brother of Mary and Martha whom Jesus raised
from the dead (Jn 11:1–12:19).

LAZINESS* (LAZY)
Pr 12: 24 will rule, but l ends in forced labor.
19: 15 **L** brings on deep sleep,
Ecc 10: 18 Through l, the rafters sag;

LAZY* (LAZINESS)
Ex 5: 8 They are l; that is why they are
5: 17 Pharaoh said, "**L**, that's what you
5: 17 said, "**L**, that's what you are—l!
Pr 10: 4 **L** hands make for poverty,
12: 27 The l do not roast any game,
26: 15 are too l to bring them back to their
Mt 25: 26 replied, 'You wicked, l servant!
Tit 1: 12 always liars, evil brutes, l gluttons."
Heb 6: 12 We do not want you to become l,

LEAD (LEADER LEADERS LEADERSHIP LEADS
LED)
Ex 15: 13 love you will l the people you have
Nu 14: 8 with us, he will l us into that land,
Dt 31: 2 old and l am no longer able to l you.
Jos 1: 6 because you will l these people
1Sa 8: 5 now appoint a king to l us, such as
2Ch 1: 10 that I may l this people, for who is
Ps 27: 11 l me in a straight path because
43: 3 let them l me;
61: 2 l me to the rock that is higher than l
139: 24 and l me in the way everlasting.
143: 10 may your good Spirit l me on level
Pr 4: 11 and l you along straight paths.
20: 7 The righteous l blameless lives;
Ecc 5: 6 Do not let your mouth l you
Isa 11: 6 and a little child will l them.
49: 10 and l them beside springs of water.

Da 12: 3 those who l many to righteousness,
Mt 6: 13 And l us not into temptation,
15: 14 If the blind l the blind,
Lk 11: 4 And l us not into temptation.' "
Ro 12: 8 if it is to l, do it diligently;
1Th 4: 11 it your ambition to l a quiet life:
1Jn 3: 7 do not let anyone l you astray.
Rev 7: 17 'he will l them to springs of living

LEADER (LEAD)
1Sa 7: 6 Now Samuel was serving as l
7: 15 Samuel continued as Israel's l
12: 2 I have been your l from my youth

LEADERS (LEAD)
Heb 13: 7 Remember your l, who spoke
13: 17 Have confidence in your l

LEADERSHIP* (LEAD)
Nu 27: 18 a man in whom is the spirit of l,
33: 1 by divisions under the l of Moses
Ps 109: 8 may another take his place of l.
Ac 1: 20 another take his place of l.'

LEADS (LEAD)
Dt 27: 18 is anyone who l the blind astray
Ps 23: 2 he l me beside quiet waters,
37: 8 do not fret—it l only to evil.
68: 6 he l out the prisoners with singing;
Pr 2: 18 Surely her house l down to death
10: 17 ignores correction l others astray.
14: 23 but mere talk l only to poverty.
16: 25 be right, but in the end it l to death.
19: 23 The fear of the LORD l to life;
21: 5 profit as surely as haste l to poverty.
Isa 40: 11 he gently l those that have young.
Mt 7: 13 gate and broad is the road that l
12: 20 snuff out, till he l justice to victory.
Jn 3: 8 own sheep by name and l them out.
Ro 6: 16 are slaves to sin, which l to death,
6: 22 the benefit you reap l to holiness,
14: 19 every effort to do what l to peace
2Co 2: 14 God, who always l us as captives
7: 10 sorrow brings repentance that l
Tit 1: 1 of the truth that l to godliness—

LEAH
Wife of Jacob (Ge 29:16–30); bore six sons and one
daughter (Ge 29:31–30:21; 34:1; 35:23).

LEAN (LEANED)
Pr 3: 5 l not on your own understanding;

LEANED (LEAN)
Ge 47: 31 Israel worshiped as he l on the top
Jn 21: 20 one who had l back against Jesus
Heb 11: 21 worshiped as he l on the top of his

LEAP (LEAPED LEAPS)
Isa 35: 6 Then will the lame l like a deer,
Lk 6: 23 "Rejoice in that day and l for joy,

LEAPED (LEAP)
Lk 1: 41 greeting, the baby l in her womb,

LEAPS (LEAP)
Ps 28: 7 My heart l for joy, and with my

LEARN (LEARNED LEARNING)
Dt 4: 10 they may l to revere me as long as
5: 1 **L** them and be sure to follow them.
31: 12 and l to fear the LORD your God
Ps 119: 7 heart as l l your righteous laws.
Isa 1: 17 l to do right!
26: 9 people of the world l righteousness.
Mt 11: 29 my yoke upon you and l from me,
Jn 14: 31 that the world may l that I love
1Th 4: 4 of you should l to control your own
1Ti 2: 11 A woman should l in quietness
5: 4 these should l first of all to put their

LEARNED (LEARN)
Ps 119:152 Long ago l l from your statutes
Mt 11: 25 these things from the wise and l,
Jn 6: 45 and l from him comes to me.
Php 4: 9 Whatever you have l or received
4: 11 I have l to be content whatever
2Ti 3: 14 continue in what you have l
Heb 5: 8 he was, he l obedience from what he

LEARNING (LEARN)
Pr 1: 5 let the wise listen and add to their l,
9: 9 and they will add to their l.
Isa 44: 25 who overthrows the l of the wise
Jn 7: 15 man get such l without having been
2Ti 3: 7 always l but never able to come

LEATHER
Nu 4: 6 cover the curtain with a durable l,

2Ki 1: 8 had a l belt around his waist."
Mt 3: 4 he had a l belt around his waist.

LEAVES
Ge 3: 7 so they sewed fig l together
Eze 47: 12 for food and their l for healing."
Rev 22: 2 the l of the tree are for the healing

LEBANON
Dt 11: 24 will extend from the desert to **L**,
1Ki 4: 33 from the cedar of **L** to the hyssop

LED (LEAD)
Ex 3: 1 he l the flock to the far side
Dt 8: 2 the Lord your God l you all
1Ki 11: 3 and his wives l him astray.
2Ch 26: 16 powerful, his pride l his downfall.
Ne 13: 26 but even he was l into sin by foreign
Ps 78: 52 he l them like sheep through
Pr 7: 21 persuasive words she l him astray;
    20: 1 whoever is l astray by them is not
Isa 53: 7 he was l like a lamb l
Jer 11: 19 I had been like a gentle lamb l
Am 2: 10 I you forty years in the wilderness
Mt 4: 1 Jesus was l by the Spirit
    27: 31 they l him away to crucify him.
Lk 4: 1 and was l by the Spirit
Ac 8: 32 "He was l like a sheep
Ro 8: 14 For those who are l by the Spirit
2Co 7: 9 but because your sorrow l you
Gal 5: 18 But if you are l by the Spirit,

**LEEKS*
Nu 11: 5 melons, l, onions and garlic.

LEFT
Dt 28: 14 to the right or to the l,
Jos 1: 7 turn from it to the right or to the l,
    23: 2 turning aside to the right or to the l,
2Ki 22: 2 turning aside to the right or to the l,
Pr 4: 27 Do not turn to the right or the l;
Isa 30: 21 you turn to the right or to the l,
Mt 6: 3 do not let your l hand know what
    25: 33 on his right and the goats on his l.

LEGAL
Col 2: 14 the charge of our l indebtedness,

LEGION
Mk 5: 9 "My name is **L**," he replied,

**LEGITIMATE*
Heb 12: 8 you are not l children at all.

LEND (LENDER MONEYLENDER)
Ex 22: 25 "If you l money to one of my
Lev 25: 37 You must not l them money
Dt 15: 8 freely l them whatever they need.
Ps 15: 5 who l money to the poor
    37: 26 are always generous and l freely;
   112: 5 who are generous and l freely,
Pr 19: 17 kind to the poor l to the Lord,
Eze 18: 8 He does not l to them at interest
Lk 6: 34 if you l to those from whom you

LENDER* (LEND)
Pr 22: 7 and the borrower is slave to the l.
Isa 24: 2 for borrower as for l, for debtor as

LENGTH (LONG)
Pr 10: 27 fear of the Lord adds l to life,

LENGTHY* (LONG)
Mk 12: 40 and for a show make l prayers.
Lk 20: 47 and for a show make l prayers.

LEOPARD
Isa 11: 6 the l will lie down with the goat,
Da 7: 6 beast, one that looked like a l.
Rev 13: 2 The beast I saw resembled a l,

LEPROSY (LEPROUS)
2Ki 5: 1 was a valiant soldier, but he had l.
    7: 3 Now there were four men with l
2Ch 26: 21 King Uzziah had l until the day he
Mt 11: 5 those who have l are cleansed,
Lk 17: 12 village, ten men who had l met him.

LEPROUS (LEPROSY)
Ex 4: 6 when he took it out, the skin was l—

LETTER (LETTERS)
Mt 5: 18 not the smallest l, not the least
2Co 3: 2 You yourselves are our l,
    3: 6 not of the l but of the Spirit; for the l
2Th 3: 14 do not obey our instruction in this l.

LETTERS (LETTER)
2Co 3: 7 which was engraved in l on stone,
    10: 10 "His l are weighty and forceful,
2Pe 3: 16 His l contain some things that are

LEVEL
Ps 143: 10 good Spirit lead me on l ground.
Isa 26: 7 The path of the righteous is l;
    40: 4 the rough ground shall become l,
Jer 31: 9 a l path where they will not stumble,
Heb 12: 13 "Make l paths for your feet,"

LEVI (LEVITE LEVITES LEVITICAL)
    1. Son of Jacob by Leah (Ge 29:34; 46:11; 1Ch
2:1). With Simeon avenged rape of Dinah (Ge 34). Tribe
of blessed (Ge 49:5–7; Dt 33:8–11), chosen as priests
(Nu 3–4), numbered (Nu 3:39; 26:62), allotted cities,
but not land (Nu 18; 35; Dt 10:9; Jos 13:14; 21), land
(Eze 48:8–22), 12,000 from (Rev 7:7).
    2. See MATTHEW.

LEVIATHAN
Job 41: 1 you pull in the l with a fishhook
Ps 74: 14 was you who crushed the heads of **L**
Isa 27: 1 **L** the gliding serpent, **L** the coiling

LEVITE (LEVI)
Dt 26: 12 tithe, you shall give it to the **L**,
Jdg 19: 1 Now a **L** who lived in a remote area

LEVITES (LEVI)
Nu 1: 53 The **L** are to be responsible
    3: 12 "I have taken the **L** from among
    8: 6 "Take the **L** from among all
    18: 21 "I give to the **L** all the tithes
    35: 7 must give the **L** forty-eight towns,
2Ch 31: 2 to their duties as priests or **L**—
Mal 3: 3 he will purify the **L** and refine them

LEVITICAL (LEVI)
Heb 7: 11 attained through the **L** priesthood—

LEVY
Am 5: 11 You l a straw tax on the poor

LEWDNESS
Mk 7: 22 malice, deceit, l, envy, slander,

LIAR* (LIE)
Dt 19: 18 and if the witness proves to be a l,
Job 34: 6 I am right, I am considered a l;
Ps 116: 11 "Everyone is a l."
Pr 17: 4 a l pays attention to a destructive
    19: 22 better to be poor than a l.
    30: 6 will rebuke you and prove you a l.
Jn 8: 44 for he is a l and the father of lies.
    8: 55 I would be a l like you, but I do
Ro 3: 4 be true, and every human being a l.
1Jn 1: 10 we make him out to be a l and his
    2: 22 Who is the l? It is whoever denies
    5: 10 God has made him out to be a l,

LIARS* (LIE)
Ps 63: 11 the mouths of l will be silenced.
Isa 57: 4 a brood of rebels, the offspring of l?
Mic 2: 11 If l and deceivers come and say,
    6: 12 her inhabitants are l and their
1Ti 1: 10 for slave traders and l and perjurers.
    4: 2 come through hypocritical l,
Tit 1: 12 "Cretans are always l, evil brutes,
1Jn 2: 4 do not do what he commands are l,
    4: 20 yet hate a brother or sister, we are l.
Rev 3: 9 Jews though they are not, but are l—
    21: 8 magic arts, the idolaters and all l—

LIBERATED*
Ro 8: 21 the creation itself will be l from its

LICENSE*
Jude : 4 of our God into a l for immorality

LICK
Ps 72: 9 him and his enemies l the dust.
Isa 49: 23 they will l the dust at your feet.
Mic 7: 17 They will l dust like a snake,

LIE (LIAR LIARS LIED LIES LYING)
Lev 6: 3 find lost property and l about it,
    19: 11 " 'Do not l.
Nu 23: 19 that he should l, not a human being,
Dt 6: 7 when you l down and when you get
    25: 2 the judge shall make them l down
1Sa 15: 29 who is the Glory of Israel does not l
Ps 4: 8 In peace I will l down and sleep,
    23: 2 He makes me l down in green
    89: 35 and I will not l to David—
Pr 3: 24 When you l down, you will not be
Isa 11: 6 the leopard will l down
    28: 15 for we have made a l our refuge
Jer 9: 5 They have taught their tongues to l;
    23: 14 They commit adultery and live a l.
Eze 13: 6 are false and their divinations a l.
    34: 14 There they will l down in good

LIED (LIE)
Ac 5: 4 You have not l just to human beings

LIES (LIE)
Ps 5: 6 you destroy those who tell l.
    5: 9 with their tongues they tell l.
    10: 7 Their mouths are full of l
    12: 2 Everyone l to their neighbor;
    34: 13 evil and your lips from telling l.
    58: 3 they are wayward, spreading l.
   144: 8 whose mouths are full of l.
Pr 6: 19 a false witness who pours out l
    12: 17 the truth, but a false witness tells l.
    19: 5 whoever pours out l will not go free.
    19: 9 and whoever pours out l will perish.
    29: 12 If a ruler listens to l, all his officials
    30: 8 Keep falsehood and l far from me;
Jer 5: 31 The prophets prophesy l, the priests
    9: 3 their tongue like a bow, to shoot l;
    14: 14 "The prophets are prophesying l
Hos 11: 12 Ephraim has surrounded me with l,
Jn 8: 44 for he is a liar and the father of l.

LIFE (LIVE)
Ge 1: 30 that has the breath of l in it—
    2: 7 into his nostrils the breath of l,
    2: 9 of the garden were the tree of l
    6: 17 to destroy all l under the heavens,
    9: 5 for the l of another human being.
    9: 11 Never again will all l be destroyed
Ex 21: 6 Then he will be his servant for l.
    21: 23 you are to take l for l,
    23: 26 I will give you a full l span.
Lev 17: 14 because the l of every creature is its
    24: 17 "Anyone who takes the l
    24: 18 must make restitution—l for l.
Nu 35: 31 a ransom for the l of a murderer,
Dt 4: 42 one of these cities and save their l.
    12: 23 because the blood is the l, and you
    19: 21 l for l, eye for eye, tooth for tooth,
    30: 15 See, I set before you today l
    30: 19 Now choose l, so that you and your
    30: 20 For the Lord is your l, and he
    32: 39 I put to death and I bring to l, I have
    32: 47 idle words for you—they are your l.
1Sa 19: 5 He took his l in his hands when he
Job 2: 6 but you must spare his l."
    33: 4 breath of the Almighty gives me l.
    33: 30 the light of l may shine on them.
Ps 16: 11 made known to me the path of l;
    17: 14 this world whose reward is in this l.
    23: 6 will follow me all the days of my l,
    27: 1 Lord is the stronghold of my l—
    34: 12 Whoever of you loves l and desires
    36: 9 For with you is the fountain of l;
    39: 4 let me know how fleeting my l is.
    49: 7 No one can redeem the l of another
    49: 8 the ransom for a l is costly,
    63: 3 Because your love is better than l,
    69: 28 they be blotted out of the book of l
    91: 16 With long l I will satisfy them
   104: 33 I will sing to the Lord all my l;
   119: 25 preserve my l according to your
Pr 1: 19 takes away the l of those who
    3: 2 they will prolong your l many years
    3: 18 She is a tree of l to those who take
    6: 23 and correction are the way to l,
    6: 26 man's wife preys on your very l.
    7: 23 little knowing it will cost him his l.
    8: 35 For those who find me find l
    10: 11 of the righteous is a fountain of l,
    10: 27 fear of the Lord adds length to l,
    11: 30 fruit of the righteous is a tree of l,
    13: 12 but a longing fulfilled is a tree of l.
    13: 14 of the wise is a fountain of l,
    14: 27 of the Lord is a fountain of l,
    15: 4 The soothing tongue is a tree of l,
    16: 22 Prudence is a fountain of l
    19: 23 The fear of the Lord leads to l;
    21: 21 righteousness and love finds l,
    22: 5 would preserve their l stay far
    22: 23 and will exact l for l.
Isa 53: 10 the Lord makes his l an offering
    53: 11 he will see the light of l and be

Isa 53:12 he poured out his l unto death,
La 3:58 up my case; you redeemed my l.
Eze 37: 5 enter you, and you will come to l.
Da 12: 2 some to everlasting l,
Jnh 2: 6 God, brought my l up from the pit.
Mal 2: 5 with him, a covenant of l and peace,
Mt 6:25 Is not l more important than food,
7:14 and narrow the road that leads to l,
10:39 Whoever finds their l will lose it,
16:21 and on the third day be raised to l.
16:25 wants to save their l will lose it,
18: 8 It is better for you to enter l maimed
19:16 thing must I do to get eternal l?"
19:29 as much and will inherit eternal l.
20:28 to give his l as a ransom for many."
25:46 but the righteous to eternal l."
Mk 8:35 but whoever loses their l for me
9:43 you to enter l maimed than with two
10:17 must I do to inherit eternal l?"
10:30 and in the age to come eternal l.
10:45 to give his l as a ransom for many."
Lk 6: 9 do evil, to save l or to destroy it?"
9:22 and on the third day be raised to l."
9:24 wants to save their l will lose it,
12:15 l does not consist in an abundance
12:22 do not worry about your l, what you
12:25 can add a single hour to your l?
14:26 yes, even l itself—such a person
17:33 tries to keep their l will lose it,
21:19 Stand firm, and you will win l.
Jn 1: 4 In him was l, and that l was the light
3:15 who believes may have eternal l
3:36 believes in the Son has eternal l,
4:14 of water welling up to eternal l."
5:21 raises the dead and gives them l,
5:24 him who sent me has eternal l
5:26 For as the Father has l in himself,
5:39 that in them you possess eternal l.
5:40 you refuse to come to me to have l.
6:27 for food that endures to eternal l,
6:33 heaven and gives l to the world."
6:35 Jesus declared, "I am the bread of l.
6:40 believes in him shall have eternal l,
6:47 whoever believes has eternal l.
6:48 I am the bread of l.
6:51 I will give for the l of the world."
6:53 his blood, you have no l in you.
6:63 The Spirit gives l; the flesh counts
6:68 You have the words of eternal l."
8:12 but will have the light of l."
10:10 I have come that they may have l,
10:15 and I lay down my l for the sheep.
10:17 loves me is that I lay down my l—
10:28 I give them eternal l, and they shall
11:25 "I am the resurrection and the l.
12:25 Those who love their l will lose it,
12:50 that his command leads to eternal l.
13:37 I will lay down my l for you."
14: 6 am the way and the truth and the l.
15:13 lay down one's l for one's friends.
17: 2 he might give eternal l to all those
17: 3 Now this is eternal l: that they know
20:31 by believing you may have l in his
Ac 2:32 God has raised this Jesus to l,
3:15 You killed the author of l, but God
11:18 granted repentance that leads to l."
13:48 appointed for eternal l believed.
Ro 4:25 immortality, he will give eternal l.
4:25 was raised to l for our justification.
5:10 shall we be saved through his l!
5:18 resulted in justification and l for all.
5:21 bring eternal l through Jesus Christ
6: 4 the Father, we too may live a new l.
6:13 have been brought from death to l;
6:22 holiness, and the result is eternal l.
6:23 God is eternal l in Christ Jesus our
8: 6 the mind controlled by the Spirit is l
8:11 give l to your mortal bodies because
8:38 convinced that neither death nor l,
1Co 15: 3 If only for this l we have hope
15:36 does not come to l unless it dies.
2Co 2:16 to the other, an aroma that brings l.
2:16 the letter kills, but the Spirit gives l.
4:10 so that the l of Jesus may also be
5: 4 is mortal may be swallowed up by l.
Gal 2:20 The l I now live in the body, I live
3:21 had been given that could impart l,
6: 8 from the Spirit will reap eternal l.
Eph 4: 1 to live a l worthy of the calling you
Php 2:16 as you hold firmly to the word of l.
4: 3 whose names are in the book of l.
Col 1:10 you may live a l worthy of the Lord

Col 3: 3 your l is now hidden with Christ
1Th 4:12 your daily l may win the respect
1Ti 1:16 believe in him and receive eternal l.
4: 8 both the present l and the l to come.
4:16 Watch your l and doctrine closely.
6:12 Take hold of the eternal l
6:19 may take hold of the l that is truly l.
2Ti 1: 9 saved us and called us to a holy l—
1:10 and has brought l and immortality
3:12 live a godly l in Christ Jesus will be
Tit 1: 2 in the hope of eternal l, which God,
3: 7 heirs having the hope of eternal l.
Heb 7:16 of the power of an indestructible l.
Jas 1:12 they will receive the crown of l
3:13 Let them show it by their good l,
1Pe 3: 7 with you of the gracious gift of l,
3:10 "Whoever among you would love l
2Pe 1: 3 for a godly l through our knowledge
1Jn 1: 1 proclaim concerning the Word of l.
2:25 is what he promised us—eternal l.
3:14 that we have passed from death to l,
3:16 Jesus Christ laid down his l for us.
5:11 God has given us eternal l, and this l
5:20 He is the true God and eternal l.
Jude : 21 Christ to bring you to eternal l.
Rev 2: 7 the right to eat from the tree of l,
2: 8 Last, who died and came to l again.
2:10 and I will give you l as your victor's
3: 5 out their names from the book of l,
13: 8 written in the Lamb's book of l,
17: 8 in the book of l from the creation
20:12 was opened, which is the book of l.
20:15 the book of l were thrown
21: 6 from the spring of the water of l.
21:27 are written in the Lamb's book of l.
22: 1 me the river of the water of l,
22: 2 side of the river stood the tree of l,
22:14 may have the right to the tree of l
22:17 take the free gift of the water of l.
22:19 from your share in the tree of l

LIFE-GIVING* (GIVE)
Pr 15:31 Whoever heeds l correction will be
1Co 15:45 the last Adam, a l spirit.

LIFETIME (LIVE)
Ps 30: 5 a moment, but his favor lasts a l;
Lk 16:25 in your l you received your good

LIFT (LIFTED LIFTING LIFTS)
Ps 28: 2 as I l up my hands toward your
63: 4 in your name I will l up my hands.
91:12 they will l you up in their hands,
121: 1 I l up my eyes to the mountains—
123: 1 I l up my eyes to you, to you who
134: 2 L up your hands in the sanctuary
Isa 40: 9 l up your voice with a shout, l it up,
La 2:19 L up your hands to him for the lives
3:41 Let us l up our hearts and our hands
Mt 4: 6 they will l you up in their hands,
Lk 21:28 place, stand up and l up your heads,
Jas 4:10 the Lord, and he will l you up.
1Pe 5: 6 that he may l you up in due time.

LIFTED (LIFT)
Ne 8: 6 and all the people l their hands
Ps 24: 7 be l up, you ancient doors,
40: 2 He l me out of the slimy pit,
41: 9 bread, has l up his heel against me.
Isa 52:13 he will be raised and l up and highly
63: 9 he l them up and carried them all
Jn 3:14 Just as Moses l up the snake
8:28 "When you have l up the Son of Man,
12:32 l, when I am l up from the earth,
12:34 'The Son of Man must be l up'?
13:18 'He who shared my bread has l

LIFTING* (LIFT)
Ps 141: 2 may the l up of my hands be like
Eze 31:14 l their tops above the thick foliage.
1Ti 2: 8 l up holy hands without anger

LIFTS (LIFT)
Ps 3: 3 glory, the one who l my head high.
113: 7 and l the needy from the ash heap;

LIGAMENT* (LIGAMENTS)
Eph 4:16 held together by every supporting l,

LIGAMENTS* (LIGAMENT)
Col 2:19 held together by its l and sinews,

LIGHT (ENLIGHTENED LIGHTS)
Ge 1: 3 "Let there be l," and there was l.
Ex 13:21 in a pillar of fire to give them l,
25:37 on it so that they l the space in front

2Sa 22:29 LORD turns my darkness into l.
Job 38:19 "What is the way to the abode of l?
Ps 4: 6 Let the l of your face shine on us.
18:28 my God turns my darkness into l.
19: 8 are radiant, giving l to the eyes.
27: 1 The LORD is my l and my
36: 9 fountain of life; in your l we see l.
56:13 walk before God in the l of life.
76: 4 You are resplendent with l,
89:15 who walk in the l of your presence,
104: 2 The LORD wraps himself in l as
119:105 lamp to my feet and a l for my path.
119:130 unfolding of your words gives l;
139:12 the day, for darkness is as l to you.
Pr 4:18 shining ever brighter till the full l
15:30 L in a messenger's eyes brings joy
Isa 2: 5 let us walk in the l of the LORD.
9: 2 in darkness have seen a great l;
42: 6 the people and a l for the Gentiles,
45: 7 I form the l and create darkness,
49: 6 also make you a l for the Gentiles,
53:11 he will see the l of life and be
60: 1 for your l has come, and the glory
60:19 LORD will be your everlasting l,
Eze 1:27 and brilliant l surrounded him.
Mic 7: 8 darkness, the LORD will be my l.
Mt 4:16 in darkness have seen a great l;
5:14 "You are the l of the world.
5:15 it gives l to everyone in the house.
5:16 let your l shine before others,
6:22 your whole body will be full of l.
11:30 yoke is easy and my burden is l."
17: 2 his clothes became as white as the l.
24:29 and the moon will not give its l;
Mk 13:24 and the moon will not give its l;
Lk 2:32 a l for revelation to the Gentiles,
8:16 those who come in can see the l.
11:36 those who come in may see the l.
Jn 1: 4 and that life was the l of all people.
1: 5 The l shines in the darkness,
1: 7 witness to testify concerning that l,
1: 9 The true l that gives l to everyone
3:19 of l because their deeds were evil.
3:20 All those who do evil hate the l
8:12 he said, "I am the l of the world.
9: 5 the world, I am the l of the world."
12:35 Walk while you have the l,
12:46 I have come into the world as a l,
Ac 13:47 " 'I have made you a l
Ro 13:12 darkness and put on the armor of l.
2Co 4: 6 made his l shine in our hearts
6:14 Or what fellowship can l have
11:14 masquerades as an angel of l.
Eph 5: 8 but now you are l in the Lord.
1Th 5: 5 You are all children of the l
1Ti 6:16 and who lives in unapproachable l,
1Pe 2: 9 out of darkness into his wonderful l.
2Pe 1:19 as to a l shining in a dark place,
1Jn 1: 5 God is l; in him there is no darkness
1: 7 But if we walk in the l, as he is
2: 9 Those who claim to be in the l
Rev 21:23 for the glory of God gives it l,
22: 5 They will not need the l of a lamp
22: 5 for the Lord God will give them l.

LIGHTNING
Ex 9:23 and l flashed down to the ground.
20:18 the people saw the thunder and l
Ps 18:12 with hailstones and bolts of l.
Eze 1:13 it was bright, and l flashed out of it.
Da 10: 6 his face like l, his eyes like flaming
Mt 24:27 For as l that comes from the east is
28: 3 His appearance was like l, and his
Lk 10:18 replied, "I saw Satan fall like l
Rev 4: 5 From the throne came flashes of l,

LIGHTS (LIGHT)
Ge 1:14 "Let there be l in the vault
Lk 8:16 "No one l a lamp and hides it

LIKE-MINDED* (MIND)
Php 2: 2 make my joy complete by being l,
1Pe 3: 8 Finally, all of you, be l,

LIKENESS
Ge 1:26 in our l, so that they may rule over
Ps 17:15 I will be satisfied with seeing your l.
Isa 52:14 his form marred beyond human l—
Ro 8: 3 own Son in the l of sinful humanity
Php 2: 7 of a servant, being made in human l.
Jas 3: 9 who have been made in God's l.

LILY
SS 2: 1 a rose of Sharon, a l of the valleys.

SS 2: 2 Like a **l** among thorns is my darling

LIMIT (LIMITATIONS)
Ps 147: 5 his understanding has no **l**.
Jn 3: 34 for God gives the Spirit without **l**.

LIMITATIONS* (LIMIT)
Ro 6: 19 because of your human **l**.

LINEN
Lev 16: 4 He is to put on the sacred **l** tunic,
Pr 31: 22 she is clothed in fine **l** and purple.
31: 24 She makes **l** garments and sells
Mk 15: 46 So Joseph bought some **l** cloth,
Jn 20: 6 He saw the strips of **l** lying there,
Rev 15: 6 shining **l** and wore golden sashes
19: 8 Fine **l**, bright and clean, was given

LINGER
Hab 2: 3 Though it **l**, wait for it;

LION (LION'S LIONS')
Jdg 14: 6 that he tore the **l** apart with his bare
1Sa 17: 34 When a **l** or a bear came and carried
Isa 11: 7 and the **l** will eat straw like the ox.
65: 25 and the **l** will eat straw like the ox,
Eze 1: 10 right side each had the face of a **l**,
10: 14 the third the face of a **l**,
Da 7: 4 "The first was like a **l**, and it had
1Pe 5: 8 around like a roaring **l** looking
Rev 4: 7 The first living creature was like a **l**,
5: 5 See, the **l** of the tribe of Judah,

LION'S (LION)
Ge 49: 9 You are a **l** cub, Judah;

LIONS' (LION)
Da 6: 7 shall be thrown into the **l** den.
Rev 9: 8 their teeth were like **l** teeth.

LIPS
Jos 1: 8 Book of the Law always on your **l**;
Ps 34: 1 his praise will always be on my **l**.
40: 9 I do not seal my **l**, Lord, as you
63: 3 than life, my **l** will glorify you.
119:171 May my **l** overflow with praise,
140: 3 the poison of vipers is on their **l**.
141: 3 keep watch over the door of my **l**.
Pr 10: 13 is found on the **l** of the discerning,
10: 18 conceals hatred with lying **l**
10: 32 The **l** of the righteous know what
12: 22 The Lord detests lying **l**, but he
13: 3 who guard their **l** preserve their
14: 7 will not find knowledge on their **l**.
24: 26 honest answer is like a kiss on the **l**.
26: 23 on earthenware are fervent **l**
27: 2 an outsider, and not your own **l**.
Isa 6: 5 For I am a man of unclean **l**, and I
28: 11 with foreign **l** and strange tongues
29: 13 mouth and honor me with their **l**,
Mal 2: 7 "For the **l** of a priest ought
Mt 15: 8 people honor me with their **l**,
21: 16 read, " 'From the **l** of children
Lk 4: 22 gracious words that came from his **l**.
Ro 3: 13 "The poison of vipers is on their **l**."
Col 3: 8 and filthy language from your **l**.
Heb 13: 15 the fruit of **l** that openly profess his
1Pe 3: 10 and your **l** from deceitful speech.

LISTEN (LISTENED LISTENING LISTENS)
Dt 18: 15 You must **l** to him.
30: 20 Lord your God, **l** to his voice,
1Ki 4: 34 From all nations people came to **l**
2Ki 21: 9 But the people did not **l**.
Ps 5: 1 **l** to my words, Lord
Pr 1: 5 let the wise **l** and add to their
12: 15 but the wise **l** to advice.
Ecc 5: 1 Go near to **l** rather than to offer
Eze 3: 7 And whether they **l** or fail to l—
Mt 12: 42 the earth to **l** to Solomon's wisdom,
Mk 9: 7 is my Son, whom I love. **L** to him!"
Jn 10: 27 My sheep **l** to my voice;
Ac 3: 22 you must **l** to everything he tells
Jas 1: 19 Everyone should be quick to **l**,
1: 22 Do not merely **l** to the word, and so
1Jn 4: 6 is not from God does not **l** to us.

LISTENED (LISTEN)
Ne 8: 3 all the people **l** attentively
Isa 66: 4 answered, when I spoke, no one **l**.
Da 9: 6 We have not **l** to your servants

LISTENING (LISTEN)
1Sa 3: 9 Lord, for your servant is **l**.' "
Pr 18: 13 To answer before **l**—that is folly
Lk 10: 39 at the Lord's feet **l** to what he said.

LISTENS (LISTEN)
Lk 10: 16 "Whoever **l** to you **l** to me;
1Jn 4: 6 and whoever knows God **l** to us;

LIVE (ALIVE LIFE LIFETIME LIVES LIVING)
Ge 3: 22 tree of life and eat, and **l** forever."
Ex 20: 12 that you may **l** long in the land
33: 20 face, for no one may see me and **l**."
Nu 21: 8 who is bitten can look at it and **l**."
Dt 5: 24 that people can **l** even if God speaks
6: 2 Lord your God as long as you **l**
8: 3 that people do not **l** on bread alone
Job 14: 14 If someone dies, will they **l** again?
Ps 15: 1 Who may **l** on your holy mountain?
24: 1 in it, the world, and all who **l** in it;
26: 8 I love the house where you **l**,
119:175 Let me **l** that I may praise you,
Pr 21: 9 Better to **l** on a corner of the roof
21: 19 Better to **l** in a desert than
Ecc 9: 4 even a dog is better off than a dead
Isa 26: 19 But your dead will **l**, Lord;
55: 3 come to me; listen, that you may **l**.
Eze 18: 9 As surely as I **l**, I will bring down
20: 11 people will **l** if they obey them.
37: 3 "Son of man, can these bones **l**?"
Am 5: 6 Seek the Lord and **l**, or he will
Hab 2: 4 but the righteous will **l** by their
Zec 2: 11 I will **l** among you and you will
Mt 4: 4 'People do not **l** on bread alone,
Lk 4: 4 'People do not **l** on bread
Jn 14: 19 Because **l** **l**, you also will **l**.
Ac 17: 24 does not **l** in temples built by hands.
17: 28 'For in him we **l** and move and have
Ro 1: 17 "The righteous will **l** by faith."
14: 7 For we do not **l** to ourselves
2Co 5: 7 We **l** by faith, not by sight.
6: 16 "I will **l** with them and walk among
Gal 2: 20 The life I now **l** in the body, I **l**
3: 11 because "the righteous will **l**
5: 25 Since we **l** by the Spirit, let us keep
Eph 4: 17 you must no longer **l** as the Gentiles
Php 1: 21 to **l** is Christ and to die is gain.
1: 27 live in a manner worthy of the gospel
Col 1: 10 so that you may **l** a life worthy
1Th 4: 1 we instructed you how to **l** in order
5: 13 **L** in peace with each other.
1Ti 2: 2 that we may **l** peaceful and quiet
2Ti 3: 12 everyone who wants to **l** a godly life
Tit 2: 12 and to **l** self-controlled,
Heb 10: 38 my righteous one will **l** by faith.
12: 14 Make every effort to **l** in peace
1Pe 1: 17 **l** out your time as foreigners here

LIVES (LIVE)
Ge 45: 7 save your **l** by a great deliverance.
Job 19: 25 I know that my redeemer **l**,
Pr 13: 3 guard their lips preserve their **l**,
Isa 57: 15 he who **l** forever, whose name is
Jer 10: 23 people's **l** are not their own;
Eze 18: 27 they will save their **l**.
Da 3: 28 to give up their **l** rather than serve
Jn 14: 17 for he **l** with you and will be in you.
Ro 6: 10 but the life he **l**, he **l** to God.
6: 11 but the life he **l**, he **l** to God.
8: 9 if indeed the Spirit of God **l** in you.
Gal 2: 20 I no longer live, but Christ **l** in me.
1Th 2: 8 the gospel of God but our **l** as well.
1Ti 2: 2 peaceful and quiet **l** in all godliness
Tit 2: 12 and godly **l** in this present age,
Heb 7: 24 but because Jesus **l** forever, he has
13: 5 Keep your **l** free from the love
1Pe 3: 2 the purity and reverence of your **l**.
4: 2 earthly **l** for evil human desires,
2Pe 3: 11 You ought to live holy and godly **l**
1Jn 3: 16 to lay down our **l** for one another.
4: 16 Whoever **l** in love **l** in God,

LIVING (LIVE)
Ge 2: 7 life, and the man became a **l** being.
1Sa 17: 26 defy the armies of the **l** God?"
Isa 53: 8 was cut off from the land of the **l**;
Jer 2: 13 the spring of **l** water, and have dug
Eze 1: 5 what looked like four **l** creatures.
Zec 14: 8 On that day **l** water will flow
Mt 22: 32 the God of the dead but of the **l**."
Jn 4: 10 he would have given you **l** water."
6: 51 I am the bread that came down
7: 38 said, rivers of **l** water will flow
Ro 8: 11 Jesus from the dead is **l** in you,
12: 1 to offer your bodies as a **l** sacrifice,
1Co 9: 14 the gospel should receive their **l**
Heb 10: 20 and **l** way opened for us through
10: 31 to fall into the hands of the **l** God.
1Pe 1: 23 through the **l** and enduring word

LOAD (LOADS)
Gal 6: 5 of you should carry your own **l**.

LOADS (LOAD)
Mt 23: 4 cumbersome **l** and put them

LOAF (LOAVES)
Hos 7: 8 Ephraim is a flat **l** not turned over.
1Co 10: 17 body, for we all partake of the one **l**.

LOAVES (LOAF)
Mk 6: 41 Taking the five **l** and the two fish
8: 6 When he had taken the seven **l**
Lk 11: 5 'Friend, lend me three **l** of bread;

LOCKED
Jn 20: 26 Though the doors were **l**,
Gal 3: 22 Scripture has **l** up everything under
3: 23 **l** up until the faith that was to come

LOCUSTS
Ex 10: 4 I will bring **l** into your country
Joel 2: 25 you for the years the **l** have eaten—
Mt 3: 4 His food was **l** and wild honey.
Rev 9: 3 of the smoke **l** came down

LOFTY
Ps 139: 6 for me, too **l** for me to attain.

LONELY
Ps 68: 6 God sets the **l** in families, he leads
Lk 5: 16 Jesus often withdrew to **l** places

LONG (LENGTH LENGTHY LONGED LONGING LONGINGS LONGS)
Ex 17: 11 As **l** as Moses held up his hands,
Nu 6: 5 they must let their hair grow **l**.
1Ki 18: 21 "How **l** will you waver between
Ps 40: 16 who **l** for your saving help
70: 4 who **l** for your saving help
119: 97 I meditate on it all day **l**.
119:174 I **l** for your salvation, Lord,
Hos 7: 13 I to redeem them but they speak
Am 5: 18 Why do you **l** for the day
Mt 25: 5 The bridegroom was a **l** time
Jn 9: 4 As **l** as it is day, we must do
1Co 11: 14 teach you that if a man has **l** hair,
Eph 3: 18 to grasp how wide and **l** and high
Php 1: 8 God can testify how **l** for all
1Pe 1: 12 Even angels to look into these

LONGED (LONG)
Mt 13: 17 righteous people **l** to see what you
23: 37 how often have I **l** to gather your
Lk 13: 34 how often have I **l** to gather your
2Ti 4: 8 to all who have **l** for his appearing.

LONGING* (LONG)
Dt 28: 65 eyes weary with **l**, and a despairing
Job 7: 2 Like a slave **l** for the evening
Ps 119: 20 My soul is consumed with **l** for your
119:131 and pant, **l** for your commands.
Pr 13: 12 sick, but a **l** fulfilled is a tree of life.
13: 19 A **l** fulfilled is sweet to the soul,
Eze 23: 27 will not look on these things with **l**
Lk 16: 21 and **l** to eat what fell from the rich
Ro 15: 23 since I have been **l** for many years
2Co 5: 2 to be clothed with our heavenly
7: 7 He told us about your **l** for me,
7: 11 what alarm, what **l**, what concern,
1Th 2: 17 our intense **l** we made every effort
Heb 11: 16 they were **l** for a better country—

LONGINGS* (LONG)
Ps 38: 9 All my **l** lie open before you, Lord;
112: 10 the **l** of the wicked will come

LONGS* (LONG)
Ps 63: 1 for you, my whole being **l** for you,
Isa 26: 9 in the morning my spirit **l** for you.
30: 18 Yet the Lord **l** to be gracious
Php 2: 26 For he **l** for all of you and is
Jas 4: 5 he jealously **l** for the spirit

LOOK (LOOKED LOOKING LOOKS)
Ge 19: 17 Don't **l** back, and don't stop
Ex 3: 6 because he was afraid to **l** at God.
Nu 21: 8 anyone who is bitten can **l** at it
32: 8 Kadesh Barnea to **l** over the land.
1Sa 16: 7 The Lord does not **l** at the things
Job 31: 1 my eyes not to lustfully at a virgin.
Ps 34: 5 Those who **l** to him are radiant;
105: 4 **L** to the Lord and his strength;
113: 6 who stoops down to **l**

Ps 123: 2 As the eyes of slaves I to the hand
Pr 1: 28 they will I for me but will not find
4: 25 Let your eyes I straight ahead;
Isa 17: 7 that day people will I to their Maker
31: 1 do not I to the Holy One of Israel,
40: 26 up your eyes and I to the heavens:
60: 5 Then you will I and be radiant,
Jer 3: 3 Yet you have the brazen I
6: 16 "Stand at the crossroads and I,
Eze 34: 11 for my sheep and I after them.
34: 12 shepherds I after their scattered
Hab 1: 13 Your eyes are too pure to I on evil;
Zec 12: 10 They will I on me, the one they
Mt 18: 12 go to I for the one that wandered
23: 27 which I beautiful on the outside
Mk 13: 21 is the Messiah!' or, 'L, there he is!'
Lk 6: 41 "Why do you I at the speck
24: 39 L at my hands and my feet. It is I
Jn 1: 36 he said, "L, the Lamb of God!"
4: 35 open your eyes and I at the fields!
12: 45 When they I at me, they see the
19: 37 "They will I on the one they have
1Ti 4: 12 Don't let anyone I down on you
Jas 1: 25 I intently into the perfect law
1: 27 to I after orphans and widows
1Pe 1: 12 Even angels long to I into these
2Pe 3: 12 as you I forward to the day of God

LOOKED (LOOK)
Ge 19: 26 But Lot's wife I back, and she
Ex 2: 25 So God I on the Israelites and was
1Sa 6: 19 to death because they I into the ark
SS 3: 1 on my bed I I for the one my heart
Eze 22: 30 "I I for someone among them who
34: 6 and no one searched or I for them.
44: 4 I I and saw the glory of the LORD
Da 7: 9 "As I I, "thrones were set in place,
10: 5 I I up and there before me was
Hab 3: 6 he I, and made the nations tremble.
Mt 25: 36 I was sick and you I after me, I was
Lk 18: 9 and I down on everyone else,
21: 1 Lord turned and I straight at Peter.
1Jn 1: 1 which we have I at and our hands

LOOKING (LOOK)
Ps 69: 3 My eyes fail, I for my God.
119: 82 My eyes fail, I for your promise;
119:123 My eyes fail, I for your salvation,
Mk 16: 6 "You are I for Jesus the Nazarene,
Php 2: 4 not I to your own interests but each
1Th 2: 6 We were not I for praise from any
2Pe 3: 13 his promise we are I forward
Rev 5: 6 saw a Lamb, I as if it had been slain,

LOOKS (LOOK)
1Sa 16: 7 but the LORD I at the heart."
Ezr 8: 22 God is on everyone who I to him,
Ps 104: 32 he who I at the earth, and it
138: 6 is exalted, he I kindly on the lowly,
Mt 5: 28 anyone who I at a woman lustfully
16: 4 adulterous generation I for a sign,
Lk 9: 62 and I back is fit for service
Jn 6: 40 is that everyone who I to the Son
Php 2: 21 For everyone I out for their own

LOOSE (LOOSED)
Isa 33: 23 Your rigging hangs I: The mast is
Mt 16: 19 and whatever you I on earth will be
18: 18 and whatever you I on earth will be

LOOSED (LOOSE)
Ps 116: 16 you have I my bonds of affliction.

LORD (LORD'S LORDED LORDING)
Ge 18: 27 been so bold as to speak to the L,
Ex 15: 17 the sanctuary, L, your hands
Nu 16: 13 now you also want to I it over us!
Dt 10: 17 God is God of gods and L of lords,
Jos 3: 13 the L of all the earth—
1Ki 3: 10 The L was pleased that Solomon
Ne 4: 14 Remember the L, who is great
Job 28: 28 human race, "The fear of the L—
Ps 37: 13 but the L laughs at the wicked,
38: 22 to help me, my L and my Savior.
54: 4 the L is the one who sustains me.
62: 12 and with you, L, is unfailing love";
69: 6 L, the LORD Almighty, may those
86: 5 You, L, are forgiving and good,
86: 8 the gods there is none like you, L;
89: 49 L, where is your former great love,
110: 1 The LORD says to my L:
110: 5 The L is at your right hand;
130: 3 kept a record of sins, L, who could
135: 5 that our L is greater than all gods.
136: 3 Give thanks to the L of lords:

Ps 147: 5 Great is our L and mighty in power;
Isa 6: 1 I died, I saw the L seated on a throne,
Da 2: 47 the God of gods and the L of kings
9: 4 "L, the great and awesome God,
9: 7 "L, you are righteous, but this day
9: 9 The L our God is merciful
9: 19 L, listen! L, forgive! L, hear and act!
Mt 3: 3 'Prepare the way for the L,
4: 7 'Do not put the L your God
4: 10 'Worship the L your God, and serve
7: 21 "Not everyone who says to me, 'L,
9: 38 Ask the L of the harvest, therefore,
12: 8 Son of Man is L of the Sabbath."
20: 25 rulers of the Gentiles I it over them,
21: 9 who comes in the name of the L!"
22: 37 "'Love the L your God with all
22: 44 "'The L said to my L: "Sit at my
23: 39 comes in the name of the L.'"
Mk 1: 3 'Prepare the way for the L,
12: 11 the L has done this, and it is
12: 29 The L our God, the L is one.
12: 30 Love the L your God with all your
Lk 2: 9 glory of the L shone around them,
6: 5 Son of Man is L of the Sabbath."
6: 46 "Why do you call me, 'L, L,'
10: 27 "'Love the L your God with all
11: 1 one of his disciples said to him, "L,
24: 34 The L has risen and has appeared
Jn 1: 23 straight the way for the L.'"
Ac 2: 21 on the name of the L will be saved.'
2: 25 "'I saw the L always before me.
2: 34 yet he said, "'The L said to my L:
8: 16 into the name of the L Jesus.
9: 5 "Who are you, L?" Saul asked.
10: 36 Jesus Christ, who is L of all.
11: 23 true to the L with all their hearts.
16: 31 "Believe in the L Jesus, and you
Ro 4: 24 him who raised Jesus our L
5: 11 in God through our L Jesus Christ,
6: 23 is eternal life in Christ Jesus our L.
8: 39 of God that is in Christ Jesus our L.
10: 9 "Jesus is L," and believe in your
10: 13 the name of the L will be saved."
10: 16 For Isaiah says, "L, who has
11: 34 has known the mind of the L?
12: 11 your spiritual fervor, serving the L.
13: 14 yourselves with the L Jesus Christ,
14: 4 for the L is able to make them stand.
14: 8 If we live, we live to the L;
14: 8 we live or die, we belong to the L.
1Co 1: 31 those who boast boast in the L."
3: 5 as the L has assigned to each his
4: 5 wait till the L comes.
6: 13 but for the L, and the L for the body.
6: 14 his power God raised the L
7: 32 how he can please the L.
7: 34 to be devoted to the L in both body
7: 35 way in undivided devotion to the L.
7: 39 wishes, but he must belong to the L.
8: 6 and there is but one L, Jesus Christ,
11: 23 For I received from the L what I
12: 3 "Jesus is L," except by the Holy
15: 57 victory through our L Jesus Christ.
15: 58 fully to the work of the L,
16: 22 If anyone does not love the L,
2Co 1: 24 Not that we I it over your faith,
2: 12 found that the L had opened a door
3: 17 Now the L is the Spirit, and where
4: 5 but Jesus Christ as L, and ourselves
5: 6 in the body we are away from the L.
5: 8 themselves first of all to the L,
8: 21 not only in the eyes of the L
10: 17 those who boast boast in the L."
10: 18 but those whom the L commends.
13: 10 the authority the L gave me
Gal 6: 14 in the cross of our L Jesus Christ,
Eph 4: 5 one L, one faith, one baptism;
5: 8 but now you are light in the L.
5: 10 and find out what pleases the L.
5: 19 music from your heart to the L,
5: 22 own husbands as you do to the L.
6: 1 obey your parents in the L, for this
6: 7 as if you were serving the L,
6: 8 that the L will reward each one
6: 10 be strong in the L and in his mighty
Php 2: 11 acknowledge that Jesus Christ is L,
3: 1 brothers and sisters, rejoice in the L!
3: 8 of knowing Christ Jesus my L,
4: 1 stand firm in the L in this way,
4: 4 Rejoice in the L always. I will say it
4: 5 be evident to all. The L is near.
Col 1: 10 you may live a life worthy of the L

Col 2: 6 as you received Christ Jesus as L,
3: 13 Forgive as the L forgave you.
3: 17 do it all in the name of the L Jesus,
3: 18 your husbands, as is fitting in the L.
3: 20 in everything, for this pleases the L.
3: 23 as working for the L, not for human
3: 24 inheritance from the L as a reward.
3: 24 It is the L Christ you are serving.
4: 17 work you have received in the L."
1Th 3: 8 since you are standing firm in the L.
3: 12 May the L make your love increase
4: 1 urge you in the L Jesus to do this
4: 6 The L will punish all those who
4: 15 who are left till the coming of the L,
5: 2 day of the L will come like a thief
5: 23 at the coming of our L Jesus Christ.
2Th 1: 7 happen when the L Jesus is revealed
1: 12 of our L Jesus may be glorified
2: 1 the coming of our L Jesus Christ
2: 8 whom the L Jesus will overthrow
3: 3 But the L is faithful, and he will
3: 5 May the L direct your hearts
1Ti 6: 15 the King of kings and L of lords,
2Ti 2: 19 "The L knows those who are his,"
4: 8 which the L, the righteous Judge,
4: 17 But the L stood at my side and gave
Heb 1: 10 "In the beginning, L, you laid
10: 30 "The L will judge his people."
12: 14 holiness no one will see the L.
13: 6 confidence, "The L is my helper;
Jas 3: 9 With the tongue we praise our L
4: 10 Humble yourselves before the L,
5: 11 The L is full of compassion
1Pe 1: 25 the word of the L endures forever."
2: 3 you have tasted that the L is good.
3: 12 For the eyes of the L are
3: 15 in your hearts revere Christ as L.
2Pe 1: 11 into the eternal kingdom of our L
1: 16 the coming of our L Jesus Christ
2: 1 the sovereign L who bought them—
2: 9 then the L knows how to rescue
3: 9 The L is not slow in keeping his
3: 18 and knowledge of our L and Savior
Jude 14 holy is the L coming with thousands
Rev 4: 8 holy is the L God Almighty,'
4: 11 "You are worthy, our L and God,
11: 15 has become the kingdom of our L
17: 14 triumph over them because he is L
19: 16 \king (of \kings \and \I (of \lords
22: 5 for the L God will give them light.
22: 20 Amen. Come, L Jesus.

LORD'S (LORD)
Lk 1: 38 "I am the L servant,"
Ac 11: 21 The L hand was with them,
21: 14 up and said, "The L will be done."
Ro 12: 13 Share with the L people
1Co 7: 32 is concerned about the L affairs—
10: 26 "The earth is the L, and everything
11: 26 you proclaim the L death until he
2Co 3: 18 faces contemplate the L glory,
Eph 5: 17 but understand what the L will is.
2Ti 2: 24 And the L servant must not be
Heb 12: 5 not make light of the L discipline,
Jas 4: 15 "If it is the L will, we will live
5: 8 firm, because the L coming is near.
1Pe 2: 13 Submit yourselves for the L sake

LORDED* (LORD)
Ne 5: 15 assistants also I it over the people.

LORDING* (LORD)
1Pe 5: 3 not I it over those entrusted to you,

LORD† (LORD'S†)
Ge 2: 4 when the L God made the earth
2: 7 the L God formed a man
2: 22 the L God made a woman
3: 21 The L God made garments of skin
3: 23 So the L God banished him
4: 4 The L looked with favor on Abel
4: 26 began to call on the name of the L.
6: 7 So the L said, "I will wipe
7: 16 Then the L shut him in.
9: 26 said, "Praise be to the L, the God
11: 9 because there the L confused
12: 1 The L had said to Abram,
15: 6 Abram believed the L, and he
15: 18 that day the L made a covenant
17: 1 the L appeared to him and said,
18: 1 The L appeared to Abraham near
18: 14 Is anything too hard for the L?
18: 19 way of the L by doing what is right

Ge 21: 1 Now the L was gracious to Sarah as
  22: 14 that place The L Will Provide.
  24: 1 the L had blessed him in every way.
  26: 2 The L appeared to Isaac and said,
  28: 13 There above it stood the L, and he
  31: 49 "May the L keep watch between
  39: 2 The L was with Joseph so that he
  39: 21 the L was with him; he showed him
Ex 3: 2 There the angel of the L appeared
  4: 11 makes them blind? Is it not I, the L?
  4: 31 they heard that the L was concerned
  6: 2 also said to Moses, "I am the L.
  9: 12 But the L hardened Pharaoh's heart
  12: 27 'It is the Passover sacrifice to the L,
  12: 43 The L said to Moses and Aaron,
  13: 9 For the L brought you out of Egypt
  13: 21 By day the L went ahead of them
  14: 13 the deliverance the L will bring you
  14: 30 That day the L saved Israel
  15: 3 The L is a warrior; the L is his
  15: 11 Who among the gods is like you, L?
  15: 26 for I am the L, who heals you."
  16: 12 know that I am the L your God.' "
  16: 23 sabbath rest, a holy sabbath to the L.
  17: 15 and called it The L is my Banner.
  19: 8 will do everything the L has said."
  19: 20 The L descended to the top
  20: 2 "I am the L your God, who brought
  20: 5 for I, the L your God, am a jealous
  20: 7 the L will not hold anyone guiltless
  20: 10 day is a sabbath to the L your God.
  20: 11 in six days the L made the heavens
  20: 12 in the land the L your God is giving
  23: 25 Worship the L your God, and his
  24: 3 "Everything the L has said we will
  24: 12 The L said to Moses,
  24: 16 the glory of the L settled on Mount
  25: 1 The L said to Moses,
  28: 36 on it as on a seal: \holy \to \the L.
  30: 11 Then the L said to Moses,
  31: 13 so you may know that I am the L,
  31: 18 When the L finished speaking
  33: 11 The L would speak to Moses face
  33: 19 And the L said, "I will cause all my
  34: 1 The L said to Moses,
  34: 6 proclaiming, "The L, the L,
  34: 10 work that I, the L, will do for you.
  34: 29 because he had spoken with the L.
  40: 34 glory of the L filled the tabernacle.
  40: 38 of the L was over the tabernacle
Lev 8: 36 did everything the L commanded
  9: 23 the glory of the L appeared to all
  10: 2 them, and they died before the L.
  19: 2 'Be holy because I, the L your God,
  20: 8 I am the L, who makes you holy.
  20: 26 to me because I, the L, am holy,
  23: 40 rejoice before the L your God
Nu 6: 24 " 'The L bless you and keep
  8: 5 The L said to Moses:
  11: 1 hardships in the hearing of the L,
  14: 14 have already heard that you, L,
  14: 18 'The L is slow to anger,
  14: 21 glory of the L fills the whole earth,
  21: 6 the L sent venomous snakes among
  22: 31 Then the L opened Balaam's eyes,
  23: 12 "Must I not speak what the L puts
  30: 2 When a man makes a vow to the L
  32: 12 followed the L wholeheartedly.'
Dt 1: 21 take possession of it as the L,
  2: 7 forty years the L your God has been
  4: 29 from there you seek the L your God,
  5: 6 "I am the L your God, who brought
  5: 9 for I, the L your God, am a jealous
  6: 4 The L our God, the L is one.
  6: 5 Love the L your God with all your
  6: 16 Do not put the L your God
  6: 25 all this law before the L our God,
  7: 1 When the L your God brings you
  7: 6 are a people holy to the L your God.
  7: 8 it was because the L loved you
  7: 9 that the L your God is God; he is
  7: 12 then the L your God will keep his
  8: 5 so the L your God disciplines you.
  9: 10 The L gave me two stone tablets
  10: 12 of you but to fear the L your God,
  10: 14 the L your God belong the heavens,
  10: 17 For the L your God is God of gods
  10: 20 Fear the L your God and serve him.
  10: 22 now the L your God has made you
  11: 1 Love the L your God and keep his
  11: 13 to love the L your God and to serve
  16: 1 the Passover of the L your God,

Dt 17: 15 the king the L your God chooses.
  28: 1 If you fully obey the L your God
  28: 15 if you do not obey the L your God
  29: 1 covenant the L commanded Moses
  29: 29 things belong to the L our God,
  30: 4 there the L your God will gather
  30: 6 The L your God will circumcise
  30: 10 if you obey the L your God
  30: 16 you today to love the L your God,
  30: 20 For the L is your life, and he will
  31: 6 for the L your God goes with you;
  34: 5 the servant of the L died there in Moab,
Jos 10: 14 since, a day when the L listened
  22: 5 to love the L your God, to walk
  23: 11 very careful to love the L your God.
  24: 15 household, we will serve the L."
  24: 18 We too will serve the L, because he
Jdg 2: 12 They forsook the L, the God of their
Ru 1: 8 May the L show you kindness,
  4: 13 the L enabled her to conceive,
1Sa 1: 11 give him to the L for all the days
  1: 15 I was pouring out my soul to the L.
  1: 28 So now I give him to the L.
  2: 2 "There is no one holy like the L;
  2: 25 but if anyone sins against the L,
  2: 26 in favor with the L and with people.
  3: 9 'Speak, L for your servant is
  3: 19 The L was with Samuel as he grew
  7: 12 "Thus far the L has helped us."
  9: 17 sight of Saul, the L said to him,
  11: 15 Saul king in the presence of the L
  12: 18 all the people stood in awe of the L
  12: 22 his great name the L will not reject
  12: 24 be sure to fear the L and serve him
  13: 14 the L has sought out a man after his
  14: 6 Nothing can hinder the L
  15: 22 "Does the L delight in burnt
  16: 13 on the Spirit of the L came on David
  17: 45 you in the name of the L Almighty,
2Sa 6: 14 David was dancing before the L
  7: 22 "How great you are, Sovereign L!
  8: 6 The L gave David victory wherever
  12: 7 This is what the L, the God
  22: 2 "The L is my rock, my fortress
  22: 29 You, L, are my lamp; the L turns my
1Ki 1: 30 day what I swore to you by the L,
  2: 3 and observe what the L your God
  3: 7 "Now, L my God, you have made
  5: 5 for the Name of the L my God,
  5: 12 The L gave Solomon wisdom,
  8: 11 the glory of the L filled his temple.
  8: 23 "L, the God of Israel, there is no
  8: 61 fully committed to the L our God,
  9: 3 The L said to him: "I have heard
  10: 9 Praise be to the L your God,
  15: 14 fully committed to the L all his life.
  18: 21 If the L is God, follow him;
  18: 36 "L, the God of Abraham,
  18: 39 L—he is God! The L—he is God!"
  21: 23 also concerning Jezebel the L says:
2Ki 13: 23 But the L was gracious to them
  17: 18 So the L was very angry with Israel
  18: 5 Hezekiah trusted in the L, the God
  19: 1 and went into the temple of the L.
  20: 11 the L made the shadow go back
  21: 12 Therefore this is what the L,
  22: 2 what was right in the eyes of the L
  22: 8 of the Law in the temple of the L."
  23: 3 the L—to follow the L and keep his
  23: 21 the Passover to the L your God, as it
  23: 25 him who turned to the L as he did—
  24: 2 The L sent Babylonian, Aramean,
  24: 4 and he was not willing to forgive.
1Ch 10: 13 because he was unfaithful to the L;
  11: 3 with them at Hebron before the L,
  11: 9 because the L Almighty was
  13: 6 up from there the ark of God the L,
  16: 8 Give praise to the L, call on his
  16: 11 Look to the L and his strength;
  16: 14 He is the L our God;
  16: 23 Sing to the L, all the earth;
  17: 1 covenant of the L is under a tent."
  21: 24 will not take for the L what is yours,
  22: 5 be built for the L should be of great
  22: 11 build the house of the L your God,
  22: 13 and laws that the L gave Moses
  22: 16 the work, and the L be with you."
  22: 19 and soul to seeking the L your God.
  25: 7 and skilled in music for the L—
  28: 9 for the L searches every heart
  28: 20 for the L God, my God, is with you.
  29: 1 for human beings but for the L God.

1Ch 29: 11 Yours, L, is the greatness
  29: 18 L, the God of our fathers Abraham,
  29: 25 The L highly exalted Solomon
2Ch 1: 1 for the L his God was with him
  5: 13 to give praise and thanks to the L.
  5: 14 the glory of the L filled the temple
  6: 16 "Now L, the God of Israel,
  6: 41 "Now arise, L God, and come
  6: 42 L God, do not reject your anointed
  7: 1 the glory of the L filled the temple.
  7: 12 the L appeared to him at night
  7: 21 'Why has the L done such a thing
  9: 8 as king to rule for the L your God.
  13: 12 do not fight against the L, the God
  14: 2 right in the eyes of the L his God.
  15: 14 oath to the L with loud acclamation,
  16: 9 of the L range throughout the earth
  17: 9 them the Book of the Law of the L;
  18: 13 "As surely as the L lives, I can tell
  19: 6 for mere mortals but for the L
  19: 9 wholeheartedly in the fear of the L.
  20: 15 This is what the L says to you:
  20: 20 Have faith in the L your God
  20: 21 appointed men to sing to the L
  26: 5 As long as he sought the L,
  26: 16 He was unfaithful to the L his God,
  29: 30 to praise the L with the words
  30: 9 for the L your God is gracious
  31: 20 and faithful before the L his God.
  32: 8 with us is the L our God to help us
  34: 14 of the L that had been given through
  34: 31 the L—to follow the L and keep his
Ezr 3: 10 foundation of the temple of the L,
  7: 6 the hand of the L his God was
  7: 10 and observance of the Law of the L,
  9: 5 hands spread out to the L my God
  9: 8 the L our God has been gracious
  9: 15 L, the God of Israel, you are
Ne 1: 5 "L, the God of heaven, the great
  8: 1 which the L had commanded
  9: 6 You alone are the L. You made
Job 1: 6 to present themselves before the L,
  1: 21 The L gave and the L has taken
  38: 1 the L spoke to Job out of the storm.
  42: 9 did what the L told them; and the L
  42: 12 The L blessed the latter part of Job's
Ps 1: 2 who delight in the law of the L
  1: 6 For the L watches over the way
  4: 6 Many, L, are asking, "Who will
  4: 8 for you alone, L, make me dwell
  5: 3 In the morning, L, you hear my
  6: 1 L, do not rebuke me in your anger
  8: 1 L, our Lord, how majestic is your
  9: 9 The L is a refuge for the oppressed,
  9: 19 Arise, L, do not let mortals triumph;
  10: 16 The L is King for ever and ever;
  12: 6 And the words of the L are flawless,
  16: 5 L, you have assigned me my portion
  16: 8 I keep my eyes always on the L.
  18: 1 I love you, L, my strength.
  18: 6 In my distress I called to the L;
  19: 7 The law of the L is perfect,
  19: 14 heart be pleasing in your sight, L,
  20: 5 May the L grant all your requests.
  20: 7 trust in the name of the L our God.
  22: 8 L," they say, "let the L rescue him.
  23: 1 The L is my shepherd, I lack
  23: 6 dwell in the house of the L forever.
  24: 3 may ascend the mountain of the L?
  24: 8 The L strong and mighty, the L
  25: 10 All the ways of the L are loving
  27: 1 The L is my light and my
  27: 4 to gaze on the beauty of the L
  27: 6 I will sing and make music to the L.
  29: 1 Ascribe to the L, you heavenly
  29: 4 The voice of the L is powerful;
  30: 4 Sing the praises of the L, you his
  31: 5 redeem me, L, my faithful God.
  32: 2 whose sin the L does not count
  33: 1 Sing joyfully to the L,
  33: 6 of the L the heavens were made,
  33: 12 is the nation whose God is the L,
  33: 18 the eyes of the L are on those who
  34: 1 I will extol the L at all times;
  34: 3 Glorify the L with me; let us exalt
  34: 4 I sought the L, and he answered me;
  34: 7 of the L encamps around those who
  34: 8 Taste and see that the L is good;
  34: 9 Fear the L, you his holy people,
  34: 15 The eyes of the L are
  34: 18 The L is close to the brokenhearted
  37: 4 Take delight in the L and he will

Ps 37: 5	Commit your way to the L;
39: 4	"Show me, L, my life's end
40: 1	I waited patiently for the L;
40: 5	Many, L my God, are the wonders
46: 8	Come and see what the L has done,
47: 2	For the L Most High is awesome,
48: 1	Great is the L, and most worthy
50: 1	the L, speaks and summons
55: 22	Cast your cares on the L and he will
59: 8	But you laugh at them, L;
68: 4	his name is the L.
68: 18	that you, L God, might dwell there.
68: 20	from the Sovereign L comes escape
69: 31	This will please the L more than
70: 4	"The L is great!"
72: 18	Praise be to the L God, the God
75: 8	In the hand of the L is a cup full
78: 4	the praiseworthy deeds of the L,
84: 8	Hear my prayer, L God Almighty;
84: 11	For the L God is a sun and shield;
85: 7	Show us your unfailing love, L,
86: 11	Teach me your way, L, that I may
87: 2	The L loves the gates of Zion more
89: 5	heavens praise your wonders, L,
89: 8	Who is like you, L God Almighty?
91: 2	They say of the L, "He is my refuge
92: 1	It is good to praise the L and make
92: 4	you make me glad by your deeds, L;
92: 13	planted in the house of the L,
93: 1	The L reigns, he is robed in majesty;
93: 5	Your statutes, L, stand firm;
94: 1	The L is a God who avenges.
94: 12	Blessed are those you discipline, L,
94: 18	your unfailing love, L,
95: 1	Come, let us sing for joy to the L;
95: 3	For the L is the great God, the great
95: 6	let us kneel before the L our Maker;
96: 1	Sing to the L a new song;
96: 5	idols, but the L made the heavens.
96: 8	to the L the glory due his name;
96: 9	Worship the L in the splendor of his
96: 13	Let all creation rejoice before the L,
97: 1	The L reigns, let the earth be glad;
97: 9	For you, L, are the Most High over
98: 1	Sing to the L a new song, for he has
98: 2	The L has made his salvation known
98: 4	Shout for joy to the L, all the earth,
99: 1	The L reigns, let the nations
99: 2	Great is the L in Zion; he is exalted
99: 5	Exalt the L our God and worship
99: 9	Exalt the L our God and worship
100: 1	Shout for joy to the L, all the earth.
100: 2	Worship the L with gladness;
100: 3	Know that the L is God. It is he who
100: 5	For the L is good and his love
101: 1	to you, L, I will sing praise.
102: 12	But you, L, sit enthroned forever;
103: 1	Praise the L, my soul; all my inmost
103: 8	The L is compassionate
103: 19	The L has established his throne
104: 1	Praise the L, my soul.
104: 24	How many are your works, L!
104: 33	I will sing to the L all my life;
105: 4	Look to the L and his strength;
105: 7	He is the L our God;
106: 2	proclaim the mighty acts of the L
107: 1	Give thanks to the L, for he is good;
107: 8	thanks to the L for his unfailing love
107: 21	thanks to the L for his unfailing love
107: 43	ponder the loving deeds of the L.
108: 3	I will praise you, L,
109: 26	Help me, L my God;
110: 1	The L says to my lord: "Sit at my
110: 4	The L has sworn and will not
111: 2	Great are the works of the L;
111: 4	the L is gracious
111: 10	The fear of the L is the beginning
112: 1	Blessed are those who fear the L,
113: 1	Praise the L. Praise the L,
113: 2	Let the name of the L be praised,
113: 4	The L is exalted over all the nations,
113: 5	Who is like the L our God, the One
115: 1	Not to us, L, not to us but to your
115: 18	it is we who extol the L, both now
116: 12	I return to the L for all his goodness
116: 15	in the sight of the L is the death
117: 1	Praise the L, all you nations;
118: 1	Give thanks to the L, for he is good;
118: 5	When hard pressed, I cried to the L;
118: 8	to take refuge in the L than to trust
118: 18	The L has chastened me severely,
118: 23	the L has done this, and it is

Ps 118: 24	The L has done it this very day;
118: 26	he who comes in the name of the L.
119: 1	walk according to the law of the L.
119: 64	The earth is filled with your love, L;
119: 89	Your word, L, is eternal;
119:126	It is time for you to act, L;
119:159	preserve my life, L, in accordance
120: 1	I call on the L in my distress, and he
121: 2	My help comes from the L,
121: 5	The L watches over you—
121: 8	the L will watch over your coming
122: 1	"Let us go to the house of the L."
123: 2	so our eyes look to the L our God,
124: 1	If the L had not been on our side—
124: 8	Our help is in the name of the L,
125: 2	so the L surrounds his people both
126: 3	The L has done great things for us,
126: 4	Restore our fortunes, L, like streams
127: 1	Unless the L builds the house,
127: 3	Children are a heritage from the L,
128: 1	Blessed are all who fear the L,
130: 1	Out of the depths I cry to you, L;
130: 3	If you, L, kept a record of sins,
130: 5	I wait for the L, my whole being
131: 3	put your hope in the L both now
132: 1	L, remember David and all his
132: 13	For the L has chosen Zion, he has
133: 3	For there the L bestows his blessing,
134: 3	May the L bless you from Zion,
135: 4	For the L has chosen Jacob to be his
135: 6	The L does whatever pleases him,
136: 1	Give thanks to the L, for he is good.
137: 4	can we sing the songs of the L while
138: 1	I will praise you, L, with all my
138: 8	The L will vindicate me;
139: 1	You have searched me, L, and you
140: 1	Rescue me, L, from evildoers;
141: 1	I call to you, L, come quickly to me;
141: 3	Set a guard over my mouth, L;
142: 5	I cry to you, L; I say, "You are my
143: 9	Rescue me from my enemies, L,
144: 3	L, what are human beings that you
145: 3	Great is the L and most worthy
145: 8	The L is gracious
145: 9	The L is good to all;
145: 17	The L is righteous in all his ways
145: 18	The L is near to all who call on him,
146: 5	whose hope is in the L their God.
146: 7	The L sets prisoners free,
147: 2	The L builds up Jerusalem;
147: 7	Sing to the L with grateful praise;
147: 11	the L delights in those who fear
147: 12	Extol the L, Jerusalem;
148: 1	Praise the L. Praise the L
148: 7	Praise the L from the earth,
149: 4	For the L takes delight in his
150: 1	Praise the L. Praise God in his
150: 6	that has breath praise the L.
Pr 1: 7	The fear of the L is the beginning
1: 29	and did not choose to fear the L.
2: 5	you will understand the fear of the L
2: 6	For the L gives wisdom;
3: 5	Trust in the L with all your heart
3: 7	fear the L and shun evil.
3: 9	Honor the L with your wealth,
3: 12	because the L disciplines those he
3: 19	By wisdom the L laid the earth's
5: 21	your ways are in full view of the L,
6: 16	There are six things the L hates,
8: 13	To fear the L is to hate evil;
9: 10	The fear of the L is the beginning
10: 27	The fear of the L adds length to life,
11: 1	The L detests dishonest scales,
12: 22	The L detests lying lips, but he
14: 2	fears the L walks uprightly,
14: 26	Those who fear the L have a secure
14: 27	The fear of the L is a fountain
15: 3	The eyes of the L are everywhere,
15: 16	the fear of the L than great wealth
15: 33	instruction is to fear the L,
16: 2	but motives are weighed by the L.
16: 3	Commit to the L whatever you do,
16: 4	The L works out everything to its
16: 5	The L detests all the proud of heart.
16: 9	but the L establishes their steps.
16: 33	but its every decision is from the L.
18: 10	name of the L is a fortified tower;
18: 22	good and receives favor from the L.
19: 14	but a prudent wife is from the L.
19: 17	are kind to the poor lend to the L,
19: 23	The fear of the L leads to life;
20: 10	the L detests them both.

Pr 21: 2	are right, but the L weighs the heart.
21: 3	acceptable to the L than sacrifice.
21: 30	plan that can succeed against the L.
21: 31	battle, but victory rests with the L.
22: 2	The L is the Maker of them all.
22: 23	for the L will take up their case
23: 17	be zealous for the fear of the L.
24: 18	or the L will see and disapprove
24: 21	Fear the L and the king, my son,
25: 22	his head, and the L will reward you.
29: 26	it is from the L that one gets justice.
30: 7	"Two things I ask of you, L;
31: 30	a woman who fears the L is to be
Isa 2: 3	us go up to the mountain of the L,
2: 10	from the fearful presence of the L
3: 17	the L will make their scalps bald."
4: 2	the Branch of the L will be beautiful
5: 16	the L Almighty will be exalted
6: 3	holy, holy is the L Almighty;
9: 7	of the L Almighty will accomplish
11: 2	The Spirit of the L will rest on him—
11: 9	of the L as the waters cover the sea.
12: 2	The L, the L, is my strength
18: 7	of the Name of the L Almighty.
24: 1	the L is going to lay waste the earth
25: 1	L, you are my God; I will exalt you
25: 6	this mountain the L Almighty will
25: 8	The Sovereign L will wipe away
26: 4	Trust in the L forever, for the L,
26: 8	Yes, L, walking in the way of your
26: 13	L our God, other lords besides you
26: 21	the L is coming out of his dwelling
27: 1	the L will punish with his sword—
27: 12	that day the L will thresh
28: 5	In that day the L Almighty will be
29: 6	the L Almighty will come
29: 15	to hide their plans from the L,
30: 18	For the L is a God of justice.
30: 26	when the L binds up the bruises
30: 27	the Name of the L comes from afar,
30: 30	The L will cause people to hear his
33: 2	L, be gracious to us; we long
33: 6	the fear of the L is the key to this
33: 22	For the L is our judge, the L is our lawgiv- er, the L is our king;
34: 2	The L is angry with all nations;
35: 2	they will see the glory of the L,
35: 10	those the L has rescued will return.
38: 7	the L will do what he has promised:
40: 3	prepare the way for the L;
40: 5	the glory of the L will be revealed,
40: 7	because the breath of the L blows
40: 10	the Sovereign L comes with power,
40: 14	Whom did the L consult
40: 28	The L is the everlasting God,
40: 31	in the L will renew their strength.
41: 14	declares the L, your Redeemer,
41: 20	that the hand of the L has done this,
42: 6	"I, the L, have called you
42: 8	"I am the L; that is my name!
42: 13	The L will march out like
42: 21	It pleased the L for the sake of his
43: 3	For I am the L your God, the Holy
43: 11	am the L, and apart from me there is
44: 6	"This is what the L says—
44: 24	I am the L, who has made all things,
45: 5	I am the L, and there is no other;
45: 7	I, the L, do all these things.
45: 21	Was it not I, the L? And there is no
48: 17	"I am the L your God, who teaches
50: 4	The Sovereign L has given me
50: 10	Who among you fears the L
51: 1	righteousness and who seek the L:
51: 11	Those the L has rescued will return.
51: 15	For I am the L your God, who stirs
53: 1	has the arm of the L been revealed?
53: 6	the L has laid on him the iniquity
53: 10	the will of the L will prosper in his
54: 5	the L Almighty is his name—
55: 6	Seek the L while he may be found;
55: 7	Let them turn to the L, and he will
56: 6	bind themselves to the L to minister
58: 8	of the L will be your rear guard.
58: 11	The L will guide you always;
59: 1	the arm of the L is not too short
60: 1	the glory of the L rises upon you.
60: 16	know that I, the L, am your Savior,
60: 20	the L will be your everlasting light,
61: 1	Spirit of the Sovereign L is on me,
61: 3	a planting of the L for the display
61: 10	I delight greatly in the L;
61: 11	grow, so the Sovereign L will make

Isa 62: 4 for the L will take delight in you,
63: 7 I will tell of the kindnesses of the L,
64: 8 Yet you, L, are our Father.
66: 15 See, the L is coming with fire,
Jer 1: 9 Then the L reached out his hand
2: 19 when you forsake the L your God
3: 25 have sinned against the L our God,
4: 4 Circumcise yourselves to the L,
8: 7 not know the requirements of the L.
9: 24 that I am the L, who exercises
10: 6 No one is like you, L; you are great,
10: 10 But the L is the true God; he is
12: 1 You are always righteous, L, when I
14: 7 do something, L, for the sake
14: 20 acknowledge our wickedness, L,
16: 15 say, 'As surely as the L lives,
16: 19 L, my strength and my fortress,
17: 7 blessed are those who trust in the L,
17: 10 "I the L search the heart
20: 11 But the L is with me like a mighty
23: 6 The L Our Righteous Savior.
24: 7 a heart to know me, that I am the L.
28: 9 as one truly sent by the L only if his
31: 11 For the L will deliver Jacob
31: 22 The L will create a new thing
31: 34 'Know the L,' because they will all
32: 27 "I am the L, the God of the whole
33: 16 The L Our Righteous Savior.'
36: 6 of the L that you wrote as I dictated.
40: 3 And now the L has brought it about;
42: 3 the L your God will tell us where
42: 4 I will tell you everything the L says
42: 6 we will obey the L our God,
50: 4 go in tears to seek the L their God.
51: 10 " 'The L has vindicated us;
51: 56 For the L is a God of retribution;
La 3: 24 to myself, "The L is my portion;
3: 25 The L is good to those whose hope
3: 40 test them, and let us return to the L.
Eze 1: 3 the word of the L came to Ezekiel
1: 28 of the likeness of the glory of the L.
4: 14 Then I said, "Not so, Sovereign L!
10: 4 the glory of the L rose
15: 7 them, you will know that I am the L.
30: 3 is near, the day of the L is near—
36: 23 nations will know that I am the L,
37: 4 'Dry bones, hear the word of the L!
43: 4 the L entered the temple through
44: 4 of the L filling the temple of the L,
Da 9: 2 the word of the L given to Jeremiah
Hos 1: 7 horsemen, but by the L their God."
2: 20 and you will acknowledge the L.
3: 1 her as the L loves the Israelites,
3: 5 They will come trembling to the L
6: 1 "Come, let us return to the L.
6: 3 Let us acknowledge the L;
10: 12 for it is time to seek the L, until he
12: 5 the L God Almighty, the L is his
14: 1 Return, Israel, to the L your God.
Joel 1: 1 The word of the L that came to Joel
1: 15 For the day of the L is near;
2: 1 for the day of the L is coming.
2: 11 The day of the L is great;
2: 13 Return to the L your God, for he is
2: 23 rejoice in the L your God, for he has
2: 31 the great and dreadful day of the L.
2: 32 on the name of the L will be saved;
3: 14 the day of the L is near in the valley
3: 16 L will be a refuge for his people,
Am 4: 13 the L God Almighty is his name.
5: 6 Seek the L and live, or he will
5: 15 Perhaps the L God Almighty will
5: 18 do you long for the day of the L?
7: 15 But the L took me from tending
8: 12 searching for the word of the L,
9: 5 The Lord, the L Almighty—
Ob : 15 "The day of the L is near for all
Jnh 1: 3 But Jonah ran away from the L
1: 4 the L sent a great wind on the sea,
1: 17 Now the L provided a huge fish
2: 9 'Salvation comes from the L.' "
4: 2 He prayed to the L, "Isn't this what
4: 6 Then the L God provided a gourd
Mic 1: 1 The word of the L that came
2: 4 us go up to the mountain of the L,
5: 4 his flock in the strength of the L,
6: 2 the L has a case against his people;
6: 8 what does the L require of you?
7: 7 I watch in hope for the L, I wait
Na 1: 2 The L takes vengeance on his foes
1: 3 The L is slow to anger but great
Hab 2: 14 of the L as the waters cover the sea.

Hab 2: 20 The L is in his holy temple;
3: 2 I stand in awe of your deeds, L.
Zep 1: 1 The word of the L that came
1: 7 for the day of the L is near.
3: 17 The L your God is with you,
Hag 1: 1 of the L came through the prophet
1: 8 in it and be honored," says the L.
2: 23 declares the L Almighty, 'I will take
Zec 1: 1 the word of the L came
1: 17 and the L will again comfort Zion
3: 1 standing before the angel of the L,
4: 6 by my Spirit,' says the L Almighty.
6: 12 place and build the temple of the L.
8: 21 the L and seek the L Almighty.
9: 16 The L their God will save his people
14: 5 Then the L my God will come,
14: 9 The L will be king over the whole
14: 16 worship the King, the L Almighty,
Mal 1: 1 of the L to Israel through Malachi.
3: 6 "I the L do not change. So you,
4: 5 and dreadful day of the L comes.

LORD'S† (LORD†)
Ex 4: 14 the L anger burned against Moses
12: 11 Eat it in haste; it is the L Passover.
34: 34 whenever he entered the L presence
Lev 23: 4 are the L appointed festivals,
Nu 9: 23 At the L command they encamped,
14: 41 are you disobeying the L command?
32: 13 The L anger burned against Israel
Dt 6: 18 is right and good in the L sight,
10: 13 and to observe the L commands
32: 9 For the L portion is his people,
Jos 21: 45 Not one of all the L good promises
1Sa 24: 10 lord, because he is the L anointed.'
2Sa 22: 31 The L word is flawless.
1Ki 10: 9 Because of the L eternal love
Ps 18: 30 The L word is flawless;
24: 1 The earth is the L, and everything
32: 10 the L unfailing love surrounds those
89: 1 sing of the L great love forever;
103: 17 to everlasting the L love is
118: 15 "The L right hand has done mighty
Pr 3: 11 do not despise the L discipline,
19: 21 but it is the L purpose that prevails.
Isa 24: 14 the west they acclaim the L majesty.
30: 9 to listen to the L instruction.
49: 4 Yet what is due me is in the L hand,
53: 10 Yet it was the L will to crush him
55: 13 This will be for the L renown,
61: 2 to proclaim the year of the L favor
62: 3 a crown of splendor in the L hand,
Jer 25: 17 So I took the cup from the L hand
48: 10 who are lax in doing the L work!
51: 7 was a gold cup in the L hand;
La 3: 22 of the L great love we are not
Eze 7: 19 them in the day of the L wrath.
Joel 3: 18 will flow out of the L house and will
Ob : 21 And the kingdom will be the L.
Mic 4: 1 the L temple will be established as
6: 2 you mountains, the L accusation;
Hab 2: 16 The L right hand is coming around
Zep 2: 3 sheltered on the day of the L anger.

LOSE (LOSES LOSS LOST)
1Sa 17: 32 "Let no one L heart on account
Isa 7: 4 Do not L heart because of these two
Mt 10: 39 Whoever finds their life will L it,
Lk 9: 25 and yet L or forfeit their very self?
Jn 6: 39 that I shall L none of all those he has
2Co 4: 1 this ministry, we do not L heart.
4: 16 Therefore we do not L heart.
Heb 12: 3 you will not grow weary and L heart.
12: 5 do not L heart when he rebukes you,
2Jn : 8 you do not L what we have worked

LOSES (LOSE)
Mt 5: 13 But if the salt L its saltiness,
Lk 15: 4 a hundred sheep and L one of them.
15: 8 has ten silver coins and L one.

LOSS (LOSE)
Ro 11: 12 their L means riches for the Gentiles,
1Co 3: 15 the builder will suffer L but yet will
Php 3: 8 I consider everything a L because

LOST (LOSE)
Ps 73: 2 I had nearly L my foothold.
Jer 50: 6 "My people have been L sheep;
Eze 34: 4 back the strays or searched for the L.
34: 16 I will search for the L and bring back
15: 4 go after the L sheep until he finds it?
15: 6 I have found my L sheep.'
15: 9 I have found my L coin.'

Lk 15: 24 he was L and is found.'
19: 10 to seek and to save what was L."
Php 3: 8 for whose sake I have L all things.

LOT (LOTS)
Nephew of Abraham (Ge 11:27; 12:5). Chose to live in Sodom (Ge 13). Rescued from four kings (Ge 14). Rescued from Sodom (Ge 19:1–29; 2Pe 2:7). Fathered Moab and Ammon by his daughters (Ge 19:30–38).
Est 3: 7 the L) was cast in the presence
9: 24 the L) for their ruin and destruction.
Pr 16: 33 The L is cast into the lap, but its
18: 18 Casting the L settles disputes
Ecc 3: 22 their work, because that is their L.
Ac 1: 26 cast lots, and the L fell to Matthias;

LOTS (LOT)
Jos 18: 10 then cast L for them in Shiloh
Ps 22: 18 them and cast L for my garment.
Joel 3: 3 They cast L for my people
Ob : 11 his gates and cast L for Jerusalem,
Mt 27: 35 divided up his clothes by casting L.
Ac 1: 26 Then they cast L, and the lot fell

LOVE* (BELOVED BELOVED'S LOVED LOVELY LOVER LOVERS LOVES LOVING)
Ge 4: 1 Adam made L with his wife Eve,
4: 17 Cain made L to his wife,
4: 25 Adam made L to his wife again,
20: 13 'This is how you can show your L
22: 2 your only son, whom you L
29: 18 Jacob was in L with Rachel and said,
29: 20 to him because of his L for her.
29: 21 and I want to make L to her."
29: 23 and Jacob made L to her.
29: 30 Jacob made L to Rachel also, and his L for
Rachel was greater than his L for Leah.
29: 32 Surely my husband will L me now."
38: 2 He married her and made L to her;
Ex 15: 13 In your unfailing L you will lead
20: 6 showing L to a thousand generations
20: 6 generations of those who L me
21: 5 'I I my master and my wife
34: 6 abounding in L and faithfulness,
34: 7 maintaining L to thousands,
Lev 19: 18 but L your neighbor as yourself.
19: 34 L them as yourself, for you were
Nu 14: 18 abounding in L and forgiving sin
14: 19 In accordance with your great L
Dt 5: 10 showing L to a thousand generations
5: 10 generations of those who L me
6: 5 L the Lord your God with all
7: 9 God, keeping his covenant of L
7: 9 generations of those who L him
7: 12 God will keep his covenant of L
7: 13 He will L you and bless you
10: 12 to L him, to serve the Lord your
10: 19 are to L those who are foreigners,
11: 1 L the Lord your God and keep
11: 13 to L the Lord your God
11: 22 to L the Lord your God, to walk
13: 3 out whether you L him with all your
13: 6 or the wife you L, or your closest
19: 9 to L the Lord your God
21: 15 is the son of the wife he does not L,
21: 16 the son of the wife he does not L.
30: 6 you may L him with all your heart
30: 16 today to L the Lord your God,
30: 20 you may L the Lord your God,
33: 3 Surely it is you who L the people;
Jos 22: 5 to L the Lord your God, to walk
23: 11 careful to L the Lord your God.
Jdg 5: 31 may all who L you be like the sun
14: 16 You don't really L me.
16: 4 he fell in L with a woman
16: 15 "How can you say, 'I L you,'
Ru 4: 13 When he made L to her, the Lord
1Sa 1: 8 Elkanah made L to his wife Hannah,
18: 20 Saul's daughter Michal was in L
18: 22 and his attendants all L you;
20: 17 reaffirm his oath out of L for him,
2Sa 1: 26 Your L for me was wonderful,
7: 15 my L will never be taken away
11: 11 and drink and make L to my wife?
12: 24 he went to her and made L to her.
13: 1 son of David fell in L with Tamar,
13: 4 said to him, "I'm in L with Tamar,
16: 17 "So this is the L you show your
19: 6 You L those who hate you and hate those
who L you.
1Ki 3: 3 Solomon showed his L
3: 26 deeply moved out of L for her son
8: 23 you who keep your covenant of L

1Ki	10: 9	the LORD's eternal l for Israel,
	11: 2	Solomon held fast to them in l.
1Ch	2: 21	He made l to her, and she bore him
	7: 23	Then he made l to his wife again,
	16: 34	he is good; his l endures forever.
	16: 41	"for his l endures forever."
	17: 13	I will never take my l away
2Ch	5: 13	his l endures forever."
	6: 14	you who keep your covenant of l
	6: 42	Remember the great l promised
	7: 3	his l endures forever."
	7: 6	saying, "His l endures forever."
	9: 8	Because of the l of your God
	19: 2	and l those who hate the LORD?
	20: 21	LORD, for his l endures forever."
Ezr	3: 11	his l toward Israel endures forever."
Ne	1: 5	covenant of l with those who l him
	9: 17	slow to anger and abounding in l.
	9: 32	who keeps his covenant of l, do not
	13: 22	to me according to your great l.
Job	15: 34	the tents of those who l bribes.
	19: 19	those l I have turned against me.
	37: 13	or to water his earth and show his l.
Ps	4: 2	How long will you l delusions
	5: 11	But l, by your great l, can come
	5: 11	those who l your name may rejoice
	6: 4	save me because of your unfailing l.
	11: 5	those who l violence, he hates
	13: 5	But l trust in your unfailing l;
	17: 7	me the wonders of your great l,
	18: 1	l I you, LORD, my strength.
	18: 50	shows unfailing l to his anointed,
	21: 7	through the unfailing l of the Most
	23: 6	l will follow me all the days of my
	25: 6	your great mercy and l, for they are
	25: 7	according to your l remember me,
	26: 3	been mindful of your unfailing l
	26: 8	I l the house where you live,
	31: 7	I will be glad and rejoice in your l,
	31: 16	save me in your unfailing l.
	31: 21	me the wonders of his l when I was
	31: 23	L the LORD, all his faithful
	32: 10	the LORD's unfailing l surrounds
	33: 5	the earth is full of his unfailing l.
	33: 18	whose hope is in his unfailing l,
	33: 22	May your unfailing l be with us,
	36: 5	Your l, LORD,
	36: 7	How priceless is your unfailing l,
	36: 10	Continue your l to those who know
	40: 10	I do not conceal your l and your
	40: 11	may your l and faithfulness always
	42: 8	By day the LORD directs his l,
	44: 26	us because of your unfailing l.
	45: 7	You l righteousness and hate
	48: 9	we meditate on your unfailing l.
	51: 1	according to your unfailing l,
	52: 3	You l evil rather than good,
	52: 4	You l every harmful word,
	52: 8	l trust in God's unfailing l for ever
	57: 3	God sends forth his l and his
	57: 10	For great is your l,
	59: 16	in the morning l will sing of your l;
	60: 5	that those you l may be delivered.
	61: 7	appoint your l and faithfulness
	62: 12	with you, Lord, is unfailing l";
	63: 3	Because your l is better than life,
	66: 20	prayer or withheld his l from me!
	69: 13	in your great l, O God, answer me
	69: 16	out of the goodness of your l;
	69: 36	and those who l his name will dwell
	77: 8	his unfailing l vanished forever?
	85: 7	Show us your unfailing l, LORD,
	85: 10	L and faithfulness meet together;
	86: 5	abounding in l to all who call
	86: 13	For great is your l toward me;
	86: 15	abounding in l and faithfulness.
	88: 11	Is your l declared in the grave,
	89: 1	sing of the LORD's great l forever;
	89: 2	that your l stands firm forever,
	89: 14	l and faithfulness go before you.
	89: 24	My faithful l will be with him,
	89: 28	I will maintain my l to him forever,
	89: 33	but I will not take my l from him,
	89: 49	where is your former great l,
	90: 14	the morning with your unfailing l,
	91: 14	they l me," says the LORD,
	92: 2	proclaiming your l in the morning
	94: 18	slipping," your unfailing l, LORD,
	97: 10	Let those who l the LORD hate
	98: 3	He has remembered his l and his
	100: 5	is good and his l endures forever;
	101: 1	I will sing of your l and justice;

Ps	103: 4	crowns you with l and compassion,
	103: 8	slow to anger, abounding in l.
	103: 11	so great is his l for those who fear
	103: 17	to everlasting the LORD's l is
	106: 1	for he is good; his l endures forever.
	106: 45	and out of his great l he relented.
	107: 1	for he is good; his l endures forever.
	107: 8	to the LORD for his unfailing l
	107: 15	to the LORD for his unfailing l
	107: 21	to the LORD for his unfailing l
	107: 31	to the LORD for his unfailing l
	108: 4	For great is your l, higher than
	108: 6	that those you l may be delivered.
	109: 21	out of the goodness of your l,
	109: 26	me according to your unfailing l.
	115: 1	because of your l and faithfulness.
	116: 1	I l the LORD, for he heard my
	117: 2	For great is his l toward us,
	118: 1	for he is good; his l endures forever.
	118: 2	"His l endures forever."
	118: 3	"His l endures forever."
	118: 4	"His l endures forever."
	118: 29	for he is good; his l endures forever.
	119: 41	May your unfailing l come to me,
	119: 47	in your commands because I l them.
	119: 48	which I l, that I may meditate
	119: 64	The earth is filled with your l,
	119: 76	May your unfailing l be my
	119: 88	In your unfailing l preserve my life,
	119: 97	how I l your law! I meditate
	119:113	people, but I l your law.
	119:119	therefore I l your statutes.
	119:124	your servant according to your l
	119:127	Because I l your commands more
	119:132	do to those who l your name.
	119:149	my voice in accordance with your l;
	119:159	See how I l your precepts;
	119:159	LORD, in accordance with your l.
	119:163	detest falsehood but I l your law.
	119:165	peace have those who l your law,
	119:167	your statutes, for I l them greatly.
	122: 6	"May those who l you be secure.
	130: 7	for with the LORD is unfailing l
	136: 1	His l endures forever.
	136: 2	God of gods. His l endures forever.
	136: 3	Lord of lords: His l endures forever.
	136: 4	great wonders, His l endures forever.
	136: 5	the heavens, His l endures forever.
	136: 6	the waters, His l endures forever.
	136: 7	great lights—His l endures forever.
	136: 8	the day, His l endures forever.
	136: 9	the night; His l endures forever.
	136: 10	of Egypt His l endures forever.
	136: 11	His l endures forever.
	136: 12	His l endures forever.
	136: 13	His l endures forever.
	136: 14	His l endures forever.
	136: 15	Red Sea; His l endures forever.
	136: 16	wilderness; His l endures forever.
	136: 17	His l endures forever.
	136: 18	His l endures forever.
	136: 19	His l endures forever.
	136: 20	His l endures forever.
	136: 21	His l endures forever.
	136: 22	His l endures forever.
	136: 23	His l endures forever.
	136: 24	His l endures forever.
	136: 25	His l endures forever.
	136: 26	of heaven. His l endures forever.
	138: 2	your name for your unfailing l
	138: 8	your l, LORD, endures forever—
	143: 8	bring me word of your unfailing l,
	143: 12	In your unfailing l, silence my
	145: 8	slow to anger and rich in l.
	145: 20	LORD watches over all who l him,
	147: 11	who put their hope in his unfailing l.
Pr	1: 22	who are simple l your simple ways?
	3: 3	Let l and faithfulness never leave
	4: 6	l her, and she will watch over you.
	5: 19	you ever be intoxicated with her l.
	7: 18	let's drink deep of l till morning;
	7: 18	let's enjoy ourselves with l!
	8: 17	I l those who l me,
	8: 21	a rich inheritance on those who l me
	8: 36	all who hate me l death."
	9: 8	rebuke the wise and they will l you.
	10: 12	but l covers over all wrongs.
	13: 24	those who l them are careful
	14: 22	those who plan what is good find l
	15: 17	with l than a fattened calf
	16: 6	Through l and faithfulness sin is
	17: 9	Whoever would foster l covers over

Pr	18: 21	and those who l it will eat its fruit.
	19: 8	who get wisdom l their own lives;
	19: 22	What a person desires is unfailing l;
	20: 6	Many claim to have unfailing l,
	20: 13	Do not l sleep or you will grow
	20: 28	L and faithfulness keep a king safe;
	20: 28	through l his throne is made secure.
	21: 21	righteousness and l finds life,
	27: 5	Better is open rebuke than hidden l.
Ecc	3: 8	a time to l and a time to hate,
	5: 10	Those who l money never have enough;
	5: 10	who l wealth are never satisfied
	5: 10	but no one knows whether l or hate
	9: 6	Their l, their hate and their jealousy
	9: 9	whom you l, all the days of this
SS	1: 2	your l is more delightful than wine.
	1: 3	No wonder the young women l you!
	1: 4	will praise your l more than wine.
	1: 4	you whom I l, where you graze your
	2: 4	hall, and let his banner over me be l.
	2: 5	with apples, for I am faint with l.
	2: 7	or awaken l until it so desires.
	3: 5	or awaken l until it so desires.
	4: 10	How delightful is your l, my sister,
	4: 10	more pleasing is your l than wine,
	5: 1	drink; drink your fill of l.
	5: 8	Tell him I am faint with l.
	7: 6	pleasing, my l, with your delights!
	7: 12	there I will give you my l.
	8: 4	or awaken l until it so desires.
	8: 6	for l is as strong as death,
	8: 7	Many waters cannot quench l;
	8: 7	all the wealth of one's house for l,
Isa	1: 23	they all l bribes and chase
	3: 8	Then I made l to the prophetess,
	5: 1	sing for the one I l a song about his
	16: 5	In l a throne will be established;
	38: 17	In your l you kept me from the pit
	43: 4	and because I l you, I will give
	54: 10	yet my unfailing l for you will not
	55: 3	my faithful l promised to David.
	56: 6	to him, to l the name of the LORD,
	56: 10	around and dream, they l to sleep.
	57: 8	a pact with those whose beds you l,
	61: 8	"For I, the LORD, l justice;
	63: 9	In his l and mercy he redeemed
	66: 12	be glad for her, all you who l her;
Jer	2: 25	I l foreign gods, and I must go
	2: 33	How skilled you are at pursuing l!
	5: 31	and my people l it this way.
	12: 7	I will give the one I l into the hands
	14: 10	"They greatly l to wander;
	16: 5	my l and my pity from this people,"
	31: 3	loved you with an everlasting l;
	32: 18	You show l to thousands but bring
	33: 11	his l endures forever."
La	3: 22	of the LORD's great l we are not
	3: 32	so great is his unfailing l.
Eze	16: 8	saw that you were old enough for l,
	23: 17	to the bed of l, and in their lust they
	33: 31	Their mouths speak of l,
	33: 32	more than one who sings l songs
Da	9: 4	covenant of l with those who l him
Hos	1: 6	I will no longer show l to the house
	1: 7	Yet I will show l to the house
	2: 4	I will not show my l to her children,
	2: 19	and justice, in l and compassion.
	2: 23	I will show my l to the one I called
	3: 1	show your l to your wife again,
	3: 1	L her as the LORD loves
	3: 1	gods and the sacred raisin cakes."
	4: 1	no l, no acknowledgment of God
	4: 18	their rulers dearly l shameful ways.
	6: 4	Your l is like the morning mist,
	9: 1	you l the wages of a prostitute
	9: 15	I will no longer l them;
	10: 12	reap the fruit of unfailing l,
	11: 4	of human kindness, with ties of l.
	12: 6	maintain l and justice, and wait
	12: 7	they l to defraud.
	14: 4	waywardness and I l them freely,
Joel	2: 13	slow to anger and abounding in l,
Am	4: 5	for this is what you l to do,"
	5: 15	Hate evil, l good; maintain justice
Jnh	4: 2	forfeit God's l for them.
Mic	3: 2	you who hate good and l evil;
	6: 8	to l mercy and to walk humbly
	7: 20	show l to Abraham, as you pledged
Zep	3: 17	his l he will no longer rebuke you,
Zec	8: 17	other, and do not l to swear falsely.
	8: 19	Therefore l truth and peace."

Mt 3:17 said, "This is my Son, whom I l;
     5:43 said, 'L your neighbor and hate your
     5:44 l your enemies and pray for those
     5:46 If you l those who l you,
     6: 5 for they l to pray standing
     6:24 will hate the one and l the other,
  12:18 the one I l, in whom I delight;
  17: 5 said, "This is my Son, whom I l;
  19:19 'l your neighbor as yourself.' "
  22:37 " 'L the Lord your God with all
  22:39 'L your neighbor as yourself.'
  23: 6 they l the place of honor at banquets
  23: 7 they l to be greeted with respect
  24:12 the l of most will grow cold,
Mk 1:11 "You are my Son, whom I l;
     9: 7 "This is my Son, whom I l.
  12:30 L the Lord your God with all your
  12:31 'L your neighbor as yourself.'
  12:33 To l him with all your heart, with all
  12:33 l your neighbor as yourself is more
Lk 3:22 "You are my Son, whom I l;
     6:27 L your enemies, do good to those
     6:32 "If you l those who l you,
     6:32 Even sinners l those who l them.
     6:35 But l your enemies, do good
     7:42 which of them will l him more?"
     7:47 forgiven—as her great l has shown.
  10:27 " 'L the Lord your God with all
  10:27 'L your neighbor as yourself.' "
  11:42 you neglect justice and the l of God.
  11:43 because you l the most important
  16:13 will hate the one and l the other,
  20:13 I will send my son, whom I l;
  20:46 l to be greeted with respect
Jn 5:42 that you do not have the l of God
     8:42 you would l me, for I came
  11: 3 "Lord, the one you l is sick."
  12:25 who l their life will lose it,
  13:34 command I give you: L one another.
  13:34 so you must l one another.
  13:35 my disciples, if you l one another."
  14:15 "If you l me, keep my commands.
  14:21 I too will l them and show myself
  14:23 My Father will l them, and we will
  14:24 Anyone who does not l me will not
  14:31 world may learn that I l the Father
  15: 9 I loved you. Now remain in my l.
  15:10 you will remain in my l, just as
  15:10 commands and remain in his l.
  15:12 L each other as I have loved you.
  15:13 Greater l has no one than this:
  15:17 This is my command: L each other.
  15:19 the world, it would l you as its own.
  17:26 order that the l you have for me may
  21:15 do you l me more than these?"
  21:15 he said, "you know that I l you."
  21:16 "Simon son of John, do you l me?"
  21:16 Lord, you know that I l you."
  21:17 "Simon son of John, do you l me?"
  21:17 the third time, "Do you l me?"
  21:17 you know that I l you."
Ro 2: 7 understanding, no fidelity, no l,
     5: 5 because God's l has been poured
     5: 8 God demonstrates his own l for us
     8:28 for the good of those who l him,
     8:35 separate us from the l of Christ?
     8:39 separate us from the l of God that is
  12: 9 L must be sincere. Hate what is evil;
  12:10 Be devoted to one another in l.
  13: 8 the continuing debt to l one another,
  13: 9 "L your neighbor as yourself."
  13:10 L does no harm to its neighbor.
  13:10 Therefore l is the fulfillment
  14:15 you are no longer acting in l.
  15:30 Christ and by the l of the Spirit,
1Co 2: 9 has prepared for those who l him"—
     4:17 my son whom I l, who is faithful
     4:21 shall I come in l and with a gentle
     8: 1 puffs up while l builds up.
  13: 1 but do not have l, I am only
  13: 2 but do not have l, I am nothing.
  13: 3 but do not have l, I gain nothing.
  13: 4 L is patient, l is kind.
  13: 6 L does not delight in evil
  13: 8 L never fails. But where there are
  13:13 three remain: faith, hope and l. But the
          greatest of these is l.
  14: 1 Follow the way of l and eagerly
  16:14 Do everything in l.
  16:22 If anyone does not l the Lord, let
  16:24 My l to all of you in Christ Jesus.
2Co 2: 4 you know the depth of my l for you.

2Co 2: 8 therefore, to reaffirm your l for him.
     5:14 For Christ's l compels us,
     6: 6 in the Holy Spirit and in sincere l;
     8: 7 in the l we have kindled in you—
     8: 8 sincerity of your l by comparing it
     8:24 show these men the proof of your l
  11:11 Because I do not l you?
  12:15 If I l you more, will you l me less?
  13:11 the God of l and peace will be
  13:14 and the l of God, and the fellowship
Gal 5: 6 is faith expressing itself through l.
     5:13 serve one another humbly in l.
     5:14 "L your neighbor as yourself."
     5:22 But the fruit of the Spirit is l, joy,
Eph 1: 4 holy and blameless in his sight. In l
     1:15 Jesus and your l for all his people,
     2: 4 But because of his great l for us,
     3:17 being rooted and established in l,
     3:18 and high and deep is the l of Christ,
     3:19 and to know this l that surpasses
     4: 2 bearing with one another in l.
     4:15 speaking the truth in l, we will in all
     4:16 grows and builds itself up in l,
     5: 2 and walk in the way of l, just as
     5:25 Husbands, l your wives, just as
     5:28 to l their wives as their own bodies.
     5:33 must l his wife as he loves himself,
     6:23 and l with faith from God the Father
     6:24 Grace to all who l our Lord Jesus Christ
          with an undying l.
Php 1: 9 that your l may abound more
     1:16 The latter do so out of l,
     2: 1 if any comfort from his l, if any
     2: 2 having the same l, being one
     4: 1 sisters, you whom I l and long for,
Col 1: 4 of the l you have for all his people—
     1: 5 l that spring from the hope stored
     1: 8 also told us of your l in the Spirit.
     2: 2 encouraged in heart and united in l,
     3:14 And over all these virtues put on l,
     3:19 l your wives and do not be harsh
1Th 1: 3 your labor prompted by l, and your
     3: 6 good news about your faith and l.
     3:12 May the Lord make your l increase
     4: 9 about your l for one another
     4: 9 taught by God to l each other.
     4:10 you do l all the brothers and sisters
     5: 8 on faith and l as a breastplate,
     5:13 in the highest regard in l
2Th 1: 3 the l all of you have for one another
     2:10 because they refused to l the truth
     3: 5 Lord direct your hearts into God's l
1Ti 1: 5 The goal of this command is l,
     1:14 faith and l that are in Christ Jesus.
     2:15 faith, l and holiness with propriety.
     4:12 conduct, in l, in faith and in purity.
     6:10 For the l of money is a root of all
     6:11 faith, l, endurance and gentleness.
2Ti 1: 7 us power, l and self-discipline.
     1:13 with faith and l in Christ Jesus.
     2:22 faith, l and peace, along with those
     3: 3 without l, unforgiving, slanderous,
     3:10 faith, patience, l, endurance,
Tit 2: 2 in faith, in l and in endurance.
     2: 4 younger women to l their husbands
     3: 4 and l of God our Savior appeared,
     3:15 Greet those who l us in the faith.
Phm : 5 I hear about your l for all his people
     : 7 Your l has given me great joy
     : 9 to appeal to you on the basis of l.
Heb 6:10 the l you have shown him as you
  10:24 may spur one another on toward l
  13: 5 your lives free from the l of money
Jas 1:12 he promised to those who l him.
     2: 5 he promised those who l him?
     2: 8 "L your neighbor as yourself,"
1Pe 1: 8 you have not seen him, you l him;
     1:22 you have sincere l for each other,
     1:22 you have sincere l for each other,
     2:17 to everyone, l your fellow believers,
     3: 8 be sympathetic, l one another,
     3:10 "Whoever among you would l life
     4: 8 Above all, l each other deeply,
     4: 8 because l covers over a multitude
     5:14 Greet one another with a kiss of l.
2Pe 1: 7 and to mutual affection, l.
     1:17 saying, "This is my Son, whom I l;
1Jn 2: 5 l for God is truly made complete
     2:10 who l their fellow believers
     2:15 Do not l the world or anything
     2:15 If you l the world, l for the Father is not
          in you.

1Jn 3: 1 See what great l the Father has
     3:10 are those who do not l their brothers
     3:11 We should l one another.
     3:14 to life, because we l each other.
     3:14 Anyone who does not l remains
     3:16 This is how we know what l is:
     3:17 how can the l of God be in you?
     3:18 let us not l with words or tongue
     3:23 l one another as he commanded us.
     4: 7 Dear friends, let us l one another,
     4: 7 one another, for l comes from God.
     4: 8 Whoever does not l does not know
     4: 8 not know God, because God is l.
     4: 9 is how God showed his l among us:
     4:10 This is l: not that we loved God,
     4:11 we also ought to l one another.
     4:12 if we l one another, God lives in us and
          his l is made complete
     4:16 and rely on the l God has for us.
     4:16 God is l. Whoever lives in l lives
     4:17 This is how l is made complete
     4:18 There is no fear in l.
     4:18 But perfect l drives out fear,
     4:18 who fears is not made perfect in l.
     4:19 We l because he first loved us.
     4:20 we say we l God yet hate a brother
     4:20 For if we do not l a fellow believer,
     4:20 we cannot l God, whom we have
     4:21 Those who l God must also l one another.
     5: 2 how we know that we l the children
     5: 3 In fact, this is l for God: to keep his
          his children, whom I l in the truth—
2Jn : 1 her children, whom I l in the truth—
     : 3 Son, will be with us in truth and l.
     : 5 I ask that we l one another.
     : 6 And this is l: that we walk
     : 6 his command is that you walk in l.
3Jn : 1 friend Gaius, whom I l in the truth.
     : 6 have told the church about your l.
Jude : 2 peace and l be yours in abundance.
     :12 are blemishes at your l feasts,
     :21 yourselves in God's l as you wait
Rev 2: 4 You have forsaken the l you had
     2:19 I know your deeds, your l and faith,
     3:19 Those whom I l I rebuke
  12:11 they did not l their lives so much as

LOVED* (LOVE)
Ge 24:67 she became his wife, and he l her;
  25:28 I Esau, but Rebekah l Jacob.
  29:31 the LORD saw that Leah was not l,
  29:33 the LORD heard that I am not l,
  34: 3 he l the young woman and spoke
  37: 3 Now Israel l Joseph more than any
  37: 4 that their father l him more than any
Dt 4:37 Because he l your ancestors
     7: 8 it was because the LORD l you
  10:15 on your ancestors and l them,
1Sa 1: 5 a double portion because he l her,
  18: 1 with David, and he l him as himself.
  18: 3 David because he l him as himself.
  18:16 But all Israel and Judah l David,
  18:28 that his daughter Michal l David,
  20:17 because he l him as he l himself.
2Sa 1:23 in life they were l and admired,
  12:24 The LORD l him;
  12:25 and because the LORD l him,
  13:15 he hated her more than he had l her.
1Ki 11: 1 l many foreign women besides
2Ch 11:21 Rehoboam l Maakah daughter
  26:10 in the fertile lands, for he l the soil.
Ne 13:26 He was l by his God, and God made
Ps 44: 3 light of your face, for you l them.
  47: 4 the pride of Jacob, whom he l.
  78:68 of Judah, Mount Zion, which he l.
 109:17 He l to pronounce a curse—
Isa 5: 1 My l one had a vineyard on a fertile
          youth, how as a bride you l me
Jer 2: 2 which they have l and served
  31: 3 "I have l you with an everlasting
Eze 16:37 those you l as well as those you
Hos 2: 1 and of your sisters, 'My l one.'
     2:23 to the one I called 'Not my l one.'
     3: 1 though she is l by another and is
     9:10 became as vile as the thing they l.
  11: 1 "When Israel was a child, I l him,
Mal 1: 2 "I have l you," says the LORD.
     1: 2 "But you ask, 'How have you l us?'
     1: 2 "Yet I have l Jacob,
Mk 10:21 Jesus looked at him and l him.
          one left to send, a son, whom he l.
Lk 16:14 The Pharisees, who l money,
Jn 3:16 For God so l the world that he gave

Jn 3: 19 people I darkness instead of light
11: 5 Now Jesus I Martha and her sister
11: 36 the Jews said, "See how he I him!"
12: 43 they I human glory more than
13: 1 Having I his own who were
13: 1 he I them to the end.
13: 23 the disciple whom Jesus I,
13: 34 As I have I you, so you must love
14: 21 Anyone who loves me will be I
14: 28 If you I me, you would be glad
15: 9 "As the Father has I me, so have I I
15: 12 Love each other as I have I you.
16: 27 loves you because you have I me
17: 23 have I them even as you have I me.
17: 24 me because you I me before
19: 26 disciple whom he I standing nearby,
20: 2 disciple, the one Jesus I, and said,
21: 7 the disciple whom Jesus I said
21: 20 whom Jesus I was following them.
Ro 1: 7 To all in Rome who are I by God
8: 37 conquerors through him who I us.
9: 13 "Jacob I I, but Esau I hated."
9: 25 'my I one' who is not my I one,"
11: 28 they are I on account
Gal 2: 20 who I me and gave himself for me.
Eph 5: 1 therefore, as dearly I children
5: 2 just as Christ I us and gave himself
5: 25 just as Christ I the church and gave
Col 3: 12 holy and dearly I, clothe yourselves
1Th 1: 4 brothers and sisters I by God,
2: 8 Because we I you so much, we were
2Th 2: 13 brothers and sisters I by the Lord,
2: 16 who I us and by his grace gave us
2Ti 4: 10 for Demas, because he I this world,
Heb 1: 9 You have I righteousness and hated
2Pe 2: 15 who I the wages of wickedness.
1Jn 4: 10 not that we I God, but that he I us
4: 11 since God so I us, we also ought
4: 19 We love because he I first us.
Jude : 1 who are I in God the Father
Rev 3: 9 and acknowledge that I have I you.

LOVELY* (LOVE)
Ge 29: 17 but Rachel had a I figure and was
Est 1: 11 and nobles, for she was I to look at.
2: 7 had a I figure and was beautiful.
Ps 84: 1 How I is your dwelling place,
SS 1: 5 am I, yet I, daughters of Jerusalem,
2: 14 voice is sweet, and your face is I.
4: 3 a scarlet ribbon; your mouth is I.
5: 16 is sweetness itself; he is altogether I.
6: 4 my darling, as I as Jerusalem,
Am 8: 13 "In that day "the I young women
Php 4: 8 is pure, whatever is I, whatever is

LOVER* (LOVE)
Isa 47: 8 then, listen, you I of pleasure,
1Ti 3: 3 not quarrelsome, not a I of money.

LOVERS* (LOVE)
Jer 3: 1 lived as a prostitute with many I—
3: 2 the roadside you sat waiting for I,
4: 30 Your I despise you; they seek your
La 1: 2 Among all her I there is none
Eze 16: 33 gifts, but you give gifts to all your I,
16: 36 in your promiscuity with your I,
16: 37 I am going to gather all your I,
16: 39 deliver you into the hands of your I,
16: 41 and you will no longer pay your I.
23: 5 and she lusted after her I,
23: 9 delivered her into the hands of her I,
23: 20 There she lusted after her I,
23: 22 I will stir up your I against you,
Hos 2: 5 'I will go after my I, who give me
2: 7 She will chase after her I but not
2: 10 lewdness before the eyes of her I;
2: 12 she said were her pay from her I;
2: 13 and went after her I, but me she
8: 9 Ephraim has sold herself to I.
2Ti 3: 2 I of themselves, I of money,
3: 3 brutal, not I of the good,
3: 4 I of pleasure rather than I of God—

LOVES* (LOVE)
Ge 44: 20 sons left, and his father I him.'
Dt 10: 18 the foreigners residing among you,
15: 16 because he I you and your family
21: 15 and he I one but not the other,
21: 16 son of the wife he I in preference
23: 5 the Lord your God I you.
28: 54 on the wife he I and his surviving
28: 56 will begrudge the husband she I
33: 12 one the Lord I rests between his
Ru 4: 15 who I you and who is better to you

2Ch 2: 11 "Because the Lord I his people,
Ps 11: 7 Lord is righteous, he I justice;
33: 5 The Lord I righteousness
34: 12 Whoever of you I life and desires
37: 28 For the Lord I the just and will
87: 2 The Lord I the gates of Zion
99: 4 The King is mighty, he I justice—
119:140 tested, and your servant I them.
127: 2 for he grants sleep to those he I.
146: 8 down, the Lord I the righteous.
Pr 3: 12 the Lord disciplines those he I,
12: 1 Whoever I discipline I knowledge,
15: 9 wicked, but he I those who pursue
17: 17 A friend I at all times, and a brother
17: 19 Whoever I a quarrel I sin;
21: 17 Whoever I pleasure will become
21: 17 whoever I wine and olive oil will
22: 11 One who I a pure heart and who
29: 3 A man who I wisdom brings joy
SS 3: 1 bed I looked for the one my heart I;
3: 2 I will search for the one my heart I.
3: 3 you seen the one my heart I?"
3: 4 when I found the one my heart I.
Hos 3: 1 her as the Lord I the Israelites,
10: 11 Ephraim is a trained heifer that I
Mal 2: 11 the sanctuary the Lord I
Mt 10: 37 "Anyone who I their father
10: 37 anyone who I a son or daughter
Lk 7: 5 because he I our nation and has built
7: 47 has been forgiven little I little."
10: 6 If the head of the house I peace,
Jn 3: 35 The Father I the Son and has placed
5: 20 For the Father I the Son and shows
10: 17 The reason my Father I me is that I
14: 21 and keeps them is the one who I me.
14: 21 Anyone who I me will be loved
14: 23 "Anyone who I me will obey my
16: 27 the Father himself I you because
Ro 13: 8 for whoever I others has fulfilled
1Co 8: 3 whoever I God is known by God.
2Co 9: 7 for God I a cheerful giver.
Eph 5: 6 has freely given us in the One he I.
5: 28 He who I his wife I himself.
5: 33 must love his wife as he I himself,
Col 1: 13 us into the kingdom of the Son he I,
Tit 1: 8 hospitable, one who I what is good,
Heb 12: 6 the Lord disciplines those he I,
1Jn 4: 7 Everyone who I has been born
5: 1 everyone who I the father I his child
3Jn : 9 but Diotrephes, who I to be first,
Rev 1: 5 To him who I us and has freed us
20: 9 camp of God's people, the city he I.
22: 15 and everyone who I and practices

LOVING* (LOVE)
Ps 25: 10 All the ways of the Lord are I
32: 8 counsel you with my I eye on you.
107: 43 ponder the I deeds of the Lord.
144: 2 He is my I God and my fortress,
Pr 5: 19 A I doe, a graceful deer—
Heb 13: 1 Keep on I one another as brothers
1Jn 5: 2 by I God and carrying out his

LOW (LOWER LOWLY)
Ps 116: 6 when I was brought I, he saved me.

LOWER (LOW)
Ps 8: 5 them a little I than the heavenly
2Co 11: 7 it a sin for me to I myself in order
Heb 2: 7 made them a little I than the angels;

LOWING
1Sa 15: 14 What is this I of cattle that I hear?"

LOWLY (LOW)
Job 5: 11 The I he sets on high, and those who
Ps 138: 6 he looks kindly on the I, but he
Pr 29: 23 but the I in spirit gain honor.
Isa 57: 15 who are contrite and I in spirit,
Eze 21: 26 The I will be exalted and the exalted
Zec 9: 9 I and riding on a donkey,
1Co 1: 28 God chose the I things of this world

LOYAL (LOYALTY)
1Ch 29: 18 and keep their hearts I to you.
Ps 78: 8 whose hearts were not I to God,

LOYALTY (LOYAL)
Jdg 8: 35 They also failed to show any I

LUKE*
Co-worker with Paul (Col 4:14; 2Ti 4:11; Phm 24).

LUKEWARM*
Rev 3: 16 So, because you are I—

LUST (LUSTED LUSTS)
Pr 6: 25 Do not I in your heart after her
Eze 20: 30 did and I after their vile images?
Col 3: 5 impurity, I, evil desires and greed,
1Th 4: 5 not in passionate I like the pagans,
1Pe 4: 3 living in debauchery, I,
1Jn 2: 16 the I of their eyes and their boasting

LUSTED (LUST)
Eze 23: 5 and she I after her lovers,

LUSTS* (LUST)
Nu 15: 39 after the I of your own hearts
Ro 1: 26 God gave them over to shameful I.

LUXURY
Jas 5: 5 You have lived on earth in I

LYDIA'S*
Ac 16: 40 they went to L house, where they

LYING (LIE)
Pr 6: 17 haughty eyes, a I tongue,
12: 22 The Lord detests I lips, but he
21: 6 by a I tongue is a fleeting vapor
26: 28 A I tongue hates those it hurts,

LYRE (LYRE)
1Sa 16: 23 David would take up his I and play.

MACEDONIA
Ac 16: 9 "Come over to M and help us."

MAD
Dt 28: 34 The sights you see will drive you m.

MADE (MAKE)
Ge 1: 7 So God m the vault and separated
1: 16 God m two great lights—
1: 16 He also m the stars.
1: 25 God m the wild animals according
1: 31 God saw all that he had m, and it
2: 22 the Lord God m a woman
6: 6 that he had m human beings
9: 6 of God has God m humankind.
15: 18 day the Lord m a covenant
Ex 20: 11 six days the Lord m the heavens
20: 11 the Sabbath day and m it holy.
24: 8 that the Lord has m with you
32: 4 m it into an idol cast in the shape
Lev 16: 34 Atonement is to be m once a year
Dt 32: 6 who m you and formed you?
Jos 24: 25 that day Joshua m a covenant
2Ki 19: 15 You have m heaven and earth.
2Ch 2: 12 of Israel, who m heaven and earth!
Ne 9: 6 You m the heavens,
9: 10 You m a name for yourself,
Ps 33: 6 of the Lord the heavens were m,
95: 5 for he m it, and his hands formed
96: 5 but the Lord m the heavens.
100: 3 It is he who m us, and we are his;
136: 7 who m the great lights—
139: 14 I am fearfully and wonderfully m;
Ecc 3: 11 He has m everything beautiful in its
Isa 43: 7 my glory, whom I formed and m."
45: 12 It is I who m the earth and created
45: 18 he who fashioned and m the earth,
66: 2 Has not my hand m all these things,
Jer 10: 12 But God m the earth by his power;
27: 5 outstretched arm I m the earth
32: 17 you have m the heavens
33: 2 Lord says, he who m the earth,
51: 15 "He m the earth by his power;
Eze 3: 17 I have m you a watchman
33: 7 I have m you a watchman
Am 5: 8 He who m the Pleiades and Orion,
Jnh 1: 9 who m the sea and the dry land."
Mk 2: 27 "The Sabbath was m for people,
Jn 1: 3 Through him all things were m;
Ac 17: 24 "The God who m the world
Heb 1: 2 whom also he m the universe.
Jas 3: 9 who have been m in God's likeness.
Rev 14: 7 Worship him who m the heavens,

MAGDALENE
Lk 8: 2 Mary (called M) from whom seven

MAGI
Mt 2: 1 M from the east came to Jerusalem

MAGIC (MAGICIANS)
Eze 13: 20 I am against your m charms
Rev 21: 8 those who practice m arts,
22: 15 dogs, those who practice m arts,

MAGICIANS (MAGIC)
Ex 7: 11 the Egyptian m also did the same
Da 2: 2 So the king summoned the m,

MAGNIFICENCE* (MAGNIFICENT)
1Ch 22: 5 for the Lord should be of great m

MAGNIFICENT (MAGNIFICENCE)
1Ki 8: 13 I have indeed built a m temple
Isa 28: 29 is wonderful, whose wisdom is m.
Mk 13: 1 What m buildings!"

MAGOG
Eze 38: 2 of the land of M, the chief prince
    39: 6 I will send fire on M and on those
Rev 20: 8 Gog and M—and to gather them

MAIMED
Mt 18: 8 It is better for you to enter life m

MAINTAIN (MAINTAINING)
Hos 12: 6 m love and justice, and wait
Am 5: 15 m justice in the courts.
Ro 3: 28 For we m that a person is justified

MAINTAINING* (MAINTAIN)
Ex 34: 7 m love to thousands, and forgiving

MAJESTIC* (MAJESTY)
Ex 15: 6 hand, Lord, was m in power.
    15: 11 m in holiness, awesome in glory,
Job 37: 4 he thunders with his m voice.
Ps 8: 1 how m is your name in all the earth!
    8: 9 how m is your name in all the earth!
    29: 4 the voice of the Lord is m.
    68: 15 Mount Bashan, m mountain,
    76: 4 more m than mountains rich
    111: 3 Glorious and m are his deeds,
SS 6: 4 as m as troops with banners.
    6: 10 m as the stars in procession?
Isa 30: 30 cause people to hear his m voice
Eze 31: 7 It was m in beauty, with its
2Pe 1: 17 came to him from the M Glory,

MAJESTY (MAJESTIC)
Ex 15: 7 your m you throw down those who
Dt 5: 24 has shown us his glory and his m,
    11: 2 his m, his mighty hand,
    33: 17 In m he is like a firstborn bull;
    33: 26 help you and on the clouds in his m.
1Ch 16: 27 Splendor and m are before him;
    29: 11 glory and the m and the splendor,
Est 1: 4 and the splendor and glory of his m.
    7: 3 Your M, and if it pleases you,
Job 37: 22 God comes in awesome m.
    40: 10 and clothe yourself in honor and m.
Ps 21: 5 bestowed on him splendor and m.
    45: 3 clothe yourself with splendor and m.
    45: 4 In your m ride forth victoriously
    68: 34 of God, whose m is over Israel,
    93: 1 Lord reigns, he is robed in m;
    93: 1 the Lord is robed in m and armed
    96: 6 Splendor and m are before him;
    104: 1 are clothed with splendor and m.
    145: 5 of the glorious splendor of your m—
Isa 2: 10 Lord and the splendor of his m!
    2: 19 Lord and the splendor of his m,
    2: 21 Lord and the splendor of his m,
    24: 14 west they acclaim the Lord's m.
    26: 10 do not regard the m of the Lord.
    53: 2 no beauty or m to attract us to him,
Eze 31: 2 can be compared with you in m?
    31: 18 with you in splendor and m?
Da 4: 30 power and for the glory of my m?"
Mic 5: 4 in the m of the name of the Lord
Zec 6: 13 he will be clothed with m and will
Ac 19: 27 will be robbed of her divine m.
    25: 26 to write to His M about him.
Heb 1: 3 at the right hand of the M in heaven.
    8: 1 of the throne of the M in heaven,
2Pe 1: 16 but we were eyewitnesses of his m.
Jude : 25 only God our Savior be glory, m,

MAKE (MADE MAKER MAKERS MAKES MAKING)
Ge 1: 26 "Let us m human beings in our
    2: 18 I will m a helper suitable for him."
    6: 14 So m yourself an ark of cypress
    12: 2 "I will m you into a great nation,
Ex 22: 3 steals must certainly m restitution,
    25: 9 M this tabernacle and all its
    25: 40 See that you m them according
Nu 2: 9 his face shine on you
2Sa 7: 9 Now I will m your name great,
Job 7: 17 human beings that you m so much
Ps 4: 8 Lord, make m dwell in safety.
    20: 4 heart and m all your plans succeed.
    108: 1 sing and m music with all my soul.
    110: 1 right hand until I m your enemies
    119:165 and nothing can m them stumble.

Pr 3: 6 and he will m your paths straight.
    16: 23 the wise m their mouths prudent,
Isa 14: 14 I will m myself like the Most
    29: 16 formed it, "You did not m me"?
    55: 3 I will m an everlasting covenant
    61: 8 and m an everlasting covenant
Jer 31: 31 "when I will m a new covenant
Eze 37: 26 I will m a covenant of peace
Mt 3: 3 Lord, m straight paths for him.' "
    28: 19 go and m disciples of all nations,
Lk 13: 24 "M every effort to enter through
Ro 14: 19 Let us therefore m every effort to do
2Co 5: 9 So we m it our goal to please him,
Eph 4: 3 M every effort to keep the unity
Col 4: 5 m the most of every opportunity.
1Th 4: 11 to m it your ambition to lead a quiet
2Th 1: 11 that our God may m you worthy
Heb 4: 11 m every effort to enter that rest,
    8: 5 it that you m everything according
    12: 14 M every effort to live in peace
2Pe 1: 5 m every effort to add to your faith
    3: 14 m every effort to be found spotless,

MAKER* (MAKE)
Job 4: 17 beings be more pure than their M?
    9: 9 He is the M of the Bear and Orion,
    32: 22 my M would soon take me away.
    35: 10 'Where is God my M, who gives
    36: 3 I will ascribe justice to my M.
    40: 19 yet its M can approach it with his
Ps 95: 6 us kneel before the Lord our M;
    115: 15 Lord, the M of heaven and earth.
    121: 2 Lord, the M of heaven and earth.
    124: 8 Lord, the M of heaven and earth.
    134: 3 he who is the M of heaven
    146: 6 He is the M of heaven and earth,
    149: 2 Let Israel rejoice in their M;
Pr 14: 31 poor shows contempt for their M,
    17: 5 poor shows contempt for their M;
    22: 2 The Lord is the M of them all.
Ecc 11: 5 work of God, the M of all things.
Isa 17: 7 that day people will look to their M
    27: 11 so their M has no compassion
    45: 9 to those who quarrel with their M,
    45: 11 the Holy One of Israel, and its M:
    51: 13 that you forget the Lord your M,
    54: 5 For your M is your husband—
Jer 10: 16 these, for he is the M of all things,
    51: 19 these, for he is the M of all things,
Hos 8: 14 Israel has forgotten their M

MAKERS* (MAKE)
Isa 45: 16 All the m of idols will be put

MAKES (MAKE)
Ps 23: 2 He m me lie down in green pastures,
Pr 13: 12 Hope deferred m the heart sick,
1Co 3: 7 but only God, who m things grow.

MAKING (MAKE)
Ps 19: 7 are trustworthy, m wise the simple.
Ecc 12: 12 Of m many books there is no end,
Jn 5: 18 Father, m himself equal with God.
1Co 3: 6 but God has been m it grow.
Eph 5: 16 m the most of every opportunity,

MALACHI*
Mal 1: 1 of the Lord to Israel through M.

MALE
Ge 1: 27 m and female he created them.
Ex 13: 2 to me every firstborn m.
Nu 8: 16 the first m offspring from every
Mt 19: 4 the Creator 'made them m
Gal 3: 28 slave nor free, neither m nor female,

MALICE (MALICIOUS)
Mk 7: 22 adultery, greed, m, deceit, lewdness,
Ro 1: 29 envy, murder, strife, deceit and m.
1Co 5: 8 with the old bread leavened with m
Eph 4: 31 slander, along with every form of m.
Col 3: 8 anger, rage, m, slander, and filthy
1Pe 2: 1 rid yourselves of all m and all

MALICIOUS (MALICE)
1Ti 3: 11 not m talkers but temperate
    6: 4 envy, strife, m talk, evil suspicions

MALIGN
Tit 2: 5 that no one will m the word of God.

MAN (HUMAN MEN WOMAN WOMEN)
Ge 2: 7 the Lord God formed a m
    2: 8 there he put the m he had formed.
    2: 15 The Lord God took the m
    2: 18 is not good for the m to be alone.
    2: 20 So the m gave names to all

Ge 2: 23 for she was taken out of m."
    2: 25 The m and his wife were both
    3: 9 the Lord God called to the m,
    3: 22 "The m has now become like one
    4: 1 Lord I have brought forth a m."
1Sa 13: 14 sought out a m after his own heart
Ps 127: 5 Blessed is the m whose quiver is
Pr 30: 19 way of a m with a young woman.
Isa 53: 3 rejected by others, a m of suffering,
Mt 19: 5 this reason a m will leave his father
Ro 5: 12 entered the world through one m,
1Co 7: 1 "It is good for a m not to have
    7: 2 each m should have sexual relations
    11: 3 that the head of every m is Christ,
    11: 3 and the head of the woman is m,
    13: 11 When I became a m, I put the ways
    15: 47 the second m is of heaven.
2Co 2: 1 I know a m in Christ who fourteen
Eph 5: 31 this reason a m will leave his father
1Ti 2: 12 or to assume authority over a m;

MANAGE* (MANAGER MANAGES)
Jer 12: 5 how will you m in the thickets
1Ti 3: 4 He must m his own family well
    3: 5 does not know how to m his own family,
    3: 12 to his wife and must m their children
    5: 14 to m their homes and to give

MANAGER (MANAGE)
Lk 12: 42 then is the faithful and wise m,
    16: 1 a rich man whose m was accused

MANAGES* (MANAGE)
Tit 1: 7 an overseer m God's household,

MANASSEH
    1. Firstborn of Joseph (Ge 41:51; 46:20). Blessed by Jacob but not firstborn (Ge 48). Tribe of blessed (Dt 33:17), numbered (Nu 1:35; 26:34), half allotted land east of Jordan (Nu 32; Jos 13:8–33), half west (Jos 17; Eze 48:4), failed to fully possess (Jos 17:12–13; Jdg 1:27), 12,000 from (Rev 7:6).
    2. Son of Hezekiah; king of Judah (2Ki 21:1–18; 2Ch 33:1–20). Judah exiled for his detestable sins (2Ki 21:10–15). Repentance (2Ch 33:12–19).

MANDRAKES
Ge 30: 14 give me some of your son's m."

MANGER
Lk 2: 12 in cloths and lying in a m."

MANIFESTATION*
1Co 12: 7 each one the m of the Spirit is given

MANNA
Ex 16: 31 people of Israel called the bread m.
Dt 8: 16 He gave you m to eat
Jn 6: 49 Your ancestors ate the m
Rev 2: 17 I will give some of the hidden m.

MANNER
1Co 11: 27 in an unworthy m will be guilty
Php 1: 27 of heaven live in a m worthy

MANSIONS*
Ps 49: 14 the grave, far from their princely m.
Isa 5: 9 the fine m left without occupants.
Am 3: 15 and the m will be demolished,"
    5: 11 though you have built stone m,

MARCH
Jos 6: 4 m around the city seven times,
Isa 42: 13 The Lord will m out like

MARITAL* (MARRY)
Ex 21: 10 of her food, clothing and m rights.
1Co 7: 3 husband should fulfill his m duty

MARK (MARKED MARKS)
    Cousin of Barnabas (Col 4:10; 2Ti 4:11; Phm 24; 1Pe 5:13), see JOHN.
Ge 4: 15 the Lord put a m on Cain so
Rev 13: 16 to receive a m on their right hands

MARKED (MARK)
Ac 17: 26 he m out their appointed times

MARKET (MARKETPLACE MARKETPLACES)
Jn 2: 16 my Father's house into a m!"

MARKETPLACE (MARKET)
Lk 7: 32 are like children sitting in the m

MARKETPLACES (MARKET)
Mt 23: 7 to be greeted with respect in the m

MARKS (MARK)
Jn 20: 25 "Unless I see the nail m in his
Gal 6: 17 I bear on my body the m of Jesus.

MARRED
Isa 52: 14 and his form m beyond human

MARRIAGE (MARRY)
Mt 22: 30 neither marry nor be given in m;
24: 38 marrying and giving in m,
Heb 13: 4 and the m bed kept pure, for God

MARRIED (MARRY)
Dt 24: 5 happiness to the wife he has m.
Ezr 10: 10 you have m foreign women,
Pr 30: 23 a contemptible woman who gets m,
Mt 1: 18 was pledged to be m to Joseph,
Mk 12: 23 since the seven were m to her?"
Ro 7: 2 by law a m woman is bound to her
1Co 7: 3 a man is concerned
7: 36 is not sinning. They should get m.

MARRIES (MARRY)
Mt 5: 32 anyone who m the divorced woman
19: 9 and m another woman commits
Lk 16: 18 the man who m a divorced woman

MARROW
Heb 4: 12 soul and spirit, joints and m;

MARRY (INTERMARRY MARITAL MARRIAGE
MARRIED MARRIES)
Dt 25: 5 brother shall take her and m her
Mt 22: 30 people will neither m nor be given
1Co 7: 9 they should m, for it is better to m
7: 28 But if you do m, you have not
1Ti 4: 3 They forbid people to m and order
5: 14 So I counsel younger widows to m,

MARTHA*
Sister of Mary and Lazarus (Lk 10:38–42; Jn 11;
12:2).

MARVELED* (MARVELOUS)
Lk 2: 33 mother at what was said
2Th 1: 10 to be m at among all those who have

MARVELING* (MARVELOUS)
Lk 9: 43 While everyone was m at all

MARVELOUS* (MARVELED MARVELING)
1Ch 16: 24 his m deeds among all peoples.
Job 37: 5 God's voice thunders in m ways;
Ps 71: 17 to this day I declare your m deeds.
72: 18 of Israel, who alone does m deeds.
86: 10 For you are great and do m deeds;
96: 3 his m deeds among all peoples.
98: 1 new song, for he has done m things;
118: 23 done this, and it is m in our eyes.
Zec 8: 6 "It may seem m to the remnant
8: 6 but will it seem m to me?"
Mt 21: 42 done this, and it is m in our eyes'?
Mk 12: 11 done this, and it is m in our eyes'?
Rev 15: 1 in heaven another great and m sign:
15: 3 "Great and m are your deeds,

MARY
1. Mother of Jesus (Mt 1:16–25; Lk 1:27–56;
2:1–40). With Jesus at temple (Lk 2:41–52), at the
wedding in Cana (Jn 2:1–5), questioning his sanity (Mk
3:21), at the cross (Jn 19:25–27). Among disciples after Ascension (Ac 1:14).
2. Magdalene; former demoniac (Lk 8:1–3). Helped support Jesus' ministry (Lk 8:1–3). At the cross (Mt
27:56; Mk 15:40; Jn 19:25), burial (Mt 27:61; Mk
15:47). Saw angel after resurrection (Mt 28:1–10; Mk
16:1–9; Lk 24:1–12); also Jesus (Jn 20:1–18).
3. Sister of Martha and Lazarus (Jn 11). Washed
Jesus' feet (Jn 12:1–8).

MASQUERADES*
2Co 11: 14 for Satan himself m as an angel

MASTER (MASTER'S MASTERED MASTERS
MASTERY)
Pr 25: 13 he refreshes the spirit of his m.
Hos 2: 16 you will no longer call me 'my m.'
Mal 1: 6 If I am a m, where is the respect due
Mt 10: 24 teacher, nor servants above their m.
23: 8 for you have only one M and you
24: 46 servant whose m finds him doing so
25: 21 "His m replied, 'Well done,
25: 23 "His m replied, 'Well done,
Ro 14: 4 For sin stand or fall.
14: 4 To their own m they stand or fall.
Col 4: 1 that you also have a M in heaven.
2Ti 2: 21 useful to the M and prepared to do

MASTER'S (MASTER)
Mt 25: 21 Come and share your m happiness!'

MASTERED* (MASTER)
1Co 6: 12 but I will not be m by anything.

2Pe 2: 19 are slaves to whatever has m them."

MASTERS (MASTER)
Mt 6: 24 "No one can serve two m.
Lk 16: 13 "No one can serve two m.
Eph 6: 5 obey your earthly m with respect
6: 9 And m, treat your slaves in the same
Col 3: 22 obey your earthly m in everything;
4: 1 M, provide your slaves with what is
1Ti 6: 1 should consider their m worthy
6: 2 who have believing m should not
6: 2 be subject to their m in everything,
Tit 2: 9 be subject to their m in everything,
1Pe 2: 18 God submit yourselves to your m,

MASTERY* (MASTER)
Ro 6: 9 death no longer has m over him.

MAT
Mk 2: 9 'Get up, take your m and walk'?
Ac 9: 34 Get up and roll up your m."

MATCHED*
2Co 2: 11 do it may be m by your completion

MATTHEW*
Apostle; former tax collector (Mt 9:9–13; 10:3; Mk
3:18; Lk 6:15; Ac 1:13). Also called Levi (Mk 2:14–17;
Lk 5:27–32).

MATTHIAS
Ac 1: 26 they cast lots, and the lot fell to M;

MATURE* (MATURITY)
Lk 8: 14 and pleasures, and they do not m.
1Co 2: 6 a message of wisdom among the m,
Eph 4: 13 of the Son of God and become m,
Php 3: 15 who are m should take such a view
Col 1: 28 present everyone fully m in Christ.
4: 12 will of God, m and fully assured.
Heb 5: 14 But solid food is for the m,
Jas 1: 4 finish its work so that you may be m

MATURITY* (MATURE)
Heb 6: 1 Christ and be taken forward to m,

MEAL
1Co 10: 27 If an unbeliever invites you to a m
Heb 12: 16 a single m sold his inheritance rights

MEANING
Ne 8: 8 and giving the m so that the people

MEANINGLESS
Ecc 1: 2 "M! M!" says the Teacher.
1Ti 1: 6 these and have turned to m talk.

MEANS
1Co 9: 22 by all possible I might save some.

MEASURE (MEASURED MEASURES)
Jer 10: 24 Lord, but only in due m—
30: 11 discipline you but only in due m;
46: 28 discipline you but only in due m;
Eze 45: 3 district, m off a section 25,000
Zec 2: 2 "To m Jerusalem, to find out how
Lk 6: 38 A good m, pressed down,
Eph 3: 19 be filled to the m of all the fullness
4: 13 to the whole m of the fullness
Rev 11: 1 "Go and m the temple of God

MEASURED* (MEASURE)
Isa 40: 12 Who has m the waters in the hollow
Jer 31: 37 if the heavens above can be m

MEASURES (MEASURE)
Dt 25: 14 Do not have two differing m in your
Pr 20: 10 Differing weights and differing m—

MEAT
Pr 23: 20 wine or gorge themselves on m,
Ro 14: 5 Those who eat m do so to the Lord,
14: 21 It is better not to eat m or drink
1Co 8: 13 I will never eat m again, so that I
10: 25 sold in the m market without raising

MEDDLER*
1Pe 4: 15 kind of criminal, or even as a m.

MEDIATOR*
Gal 3: 19 through angels and entrusted to a m.
3: 20 A m, however, implies more than one
1Ti 2: 5 is one God and one m between God
Heb 8: 6 which he is m is superior to the old
9: 15 this reason Christ is the m of a new
12: 24 to Jesus the m of a new covenant,

MEDICINE*
Pr 17: 22 A cheerful heart is good m,

MEDITATE* (MEDITATED MEDITATION)
Ge 24: 63 out to the field one evening to m,
Jos 1: 8 m on it day and night, so that you

Ps 1: 2 and m on his law day and night.
48: 9 God, we m on your unfailing love.
77: 12 and m on all your mighty deeds."
119: 15 I m on your precepts and consider
119: 23 your servant will m on your decrees.
119: 27 I may m on your wonderful deeds.
119: 48 love, that I may m on your decrees.
119: 78 but I will m on your precepts.
119: 97 I m on it all day long.
119: 99 teachers, for I m on your statutes.
119:148 that I may m on your promises.
143: 5 I m on all your works and consider
145: 5 I will m on your wonderful works.

MEDITATED* (MEDITATE)
Ps 39: 3 While I m, the fire burned;

MEDITATION* (MEDITATE)
Ps 19: 14 this m of my heart be pleasing
49: 3 the m of my heart will give you
104: 34 May my m be pleasing to him,

MEDIUM
Lev 20: 27 or woman who is a m or spiritist

MEEK* (MEEKNESS)
Ps 37: 11 But the m will inherit the land
Zep 3: 12 I will leave within you the m
Mt 5: 5 Blessed are the m, for they will

MEEKNESS* (MEEK)
2Co 10: 1 By the m and gentleness of Christ,

MEET (MEETING MEETINGS MEETS)
Ps 42: 2 When can I go and m with God?
85: 10 Love and faithfulness m together;
Am 4: 12 Israel, prepare to m your God."
1Co 11: 34 you m together it may not result
1Th 4: 17 the clouds to m the Lord in the air.

MEETING (MEET)
Ex 40: 34 the cloud covered the tent of m,
Heb 10: 25 not giving up m together, as some

MEETINGS* (MEET)
1Co 11: 17 for your m do more harm than good.

MEETS (MEET)
Heb 7: 26 a high priest truly m our need—

MELCHIZEDEK
Ge 14: 18 M king of Salem brought out bread
Ps 110: 4 a priest forever, in the order of M."
Heb 7: 11 one in the order of M,

MELT (MELTS)
Dt 1: 28 have made our hearts m in fear.
2Pe 3: 12 the elements will m in the heat.

MELTS* (MELT)
Am 9: 5 he touches the earth and it m,

MEMBER (MEMBERS)
Ro 12: 5 each and m belongs to all the others.

MEMBERS (MEMBER)
Mic 7: 6 your enemies are the m of your own
Mt 10: 36 your enemies will be the m of your
Ro 12: 4 of us has one body with many m,
1Co 6: 15 your bodies are m of Christ himself?
Eph 3: 6 with Israel, m together of one body,
4: 25 for we are all m of one body.
5: 30 for we are m of his body.
Col 3: 15 since as m of one body you were

MEMORABLE* (MEMORY)
Eze 39: 13 I display my glory will be a m day

MEMORIES* (MEMORY)
1Th 3: 6 you always have pleasant m of us

MEMORY (MEMORABLE MEMORIES)
Mt 26: 13 done will also be told, in m of her."

MEN (MAN)
Ge 6: 4 the heroes of old, m of renown.
Ro 1: 27 shameful acts with other m,
1Co 16: 18 Such m deserve recognition.
1Ti 5: 1 Treat younger m as brothers,
Heb 7: 28 the law appoints as high priests m

MENAHEM*
King of Israel (2Ki 15:17–23).

MENE
Da 5: 25 inscription that was written: \m, \m,

MEPHIBOSHETH
Son of Jonathan shown kindness by David (2Sa 4:4;
9; 21:7). Accused of siding with Absalom (2Sa 16:1–4;
19:24–30).

MERCHANT
Pr 31: 14 She is like the m ships, bringing her
Mt 13: 45 heaven is like a m looking for fine

MERCIFUL (MERCY)
Dt   4: 31 the LORD your God is a m God;
Ne   9: 31 for you are a gracious and m God.
Ps 77: 9 Has God forgotten to be m?
     78: 38 Yet he was m; he forgave their
Da   9: 9 The Lord our God is m
Mt   5: 7 Blessed are the m, for they will be
Lk   1: 54 servant Israel, remembering to be m
     6: 36 Be m, just as your Father is m.
Heb 2: 17 in that he might become a m
Jas 2: 13 to anyone who has not been m.
Jude : 22 Be m to those who doubt;

MERCY (MERCIFUL)
Ex 33: 19 will have m on whom I will have m,
2Sa 24: 14 of the LORD, for his m is great;
1Ch 21: 13 the LORD, for his m is very great;
Ne   9: 31 your great m you did not put an end
Ps 25: 6 LORD, your great m and love,
     28: 6 for he has heard my cry for m.
     57: 1 Have m on me, my God, have m
Pr 28: 13 confess and renounce them find m.
Isa 63: 9 his love and m he redeemed them;
Da   9: 18 but because of your great m.
Hos 6: 6 For I desire m, not sacrifice,
Am   5: 15 LORD God Almighty will have m
Mic 6: 8 to love and to walk humbly
     7: 18 angry forever but delight to show m.
Hab 3: 2 in wrath remember m.
Zec 7: 9 show m and compassion to one
Mt   5: 7 merciful, for they will be shown m.
     9: 13 'I desire m, not sacrifice.'
     12: 7 mean, 'I desire m, not sacrifice,'
     18: 33 Shouldn't you have had m on your
     23: 23 justice, m and faithfulness.
Lk   1: 50 His m extends to those who fear
Ro   1: 31 no fidelity, no love, no m.
     9: 15 "I will have m on whom I have m,
     9: 18 Therefore God has m on whom he
     11: 32 so that he may have m on them all.
     12: 1 in view of God's m, to offer your
     12: 8 if it is to show m, do it cheerfully.
Eph 2: 4 love for us, God, who is rich in m,
1Ti 1: 13 I was shown m because I acted
     1: 16 very reason I was shown m so
Tit 3: 5 we had done, but because of his m.
Heb 4: 16 so that we may receive m and find
Jas 2: 13 because judgment without m will be
     2: 13 M triumphs over judgment.
     3: 17 submissive, full of m and good fruit,
     5: 11 Lord is full of compassion and m.
1Pe 1: 3 In his great m he has given us new
     2: 10 once you had not received m,
Jude : 23 to others show m, mixed with fear—

MERRY
Lk 12: 19 eat, drink and be m." '

MESHACH
Hebrew exiled to Babylon; name changed from Mishael (Da 1:6–7). Refused defilement by food (Da
1:8–20). Refused to worship idol (Da 3:1–18); saved
from furnace (Da 3:19–30).

MESSAGE (MESSENGER)
Isa 53: 1 Who has believed our m
Jn 12: 38 who has believed our m
Ac 10: 36 You know the m God sent
     17: 11 for they received the m with great
Ro 10: 16 "Lord, who has believed our m?"
     10: 17 faith comes from hearing the m,
1Co 1: 18 For the m of the cross is foolishness
     2: 4 My m and my preaching were not
2Co 5: 19 to us the m of reconciliation.
Col 3: 16 Let the m of Christ dwell
2Th 3: 1 that the m of the Lord may spread
Tit 1: 9 to the trustworthy m as it has been
Heb 4: 2 the m they heard was of no value
1Pe 2: 8 because they disobey the m—
2Pe 1: 19 We also have the prophetic m as

MESSENGER (MESSAGE)
Pr 25: 13 at harvest time is a trustworthy m
Mal 3: 1 "I will send my m, who will
Mt 11: 10 " 'I will send my m ahead of you,
2Co 12: 7 a thorn in my flesh, a m of Satan,

MESSIAH (MESSIAHS)
Mt   1: 16 Jesus who is called the M.
     16: 16 Peter answered, "You are the M,
     22: 42 "What do you think about the M?

Mk   1: 1 the good news about Jesus the M,
     8: 29 Peter answered, "You are the M."
     14: 61 "Are you the M, the Son
Lk   9: 20 Peter answered, "God's M."
Jn   1: 41 "We have found the M" (that is,
     4: 25 that M" (called Christ) "is coming.
     20: 31 may believe that Jesus is the M,
Ac   2: 36 you crucified, both Lord and M."
     5: 42 the good news that Jesus is the M.
     9: 22 by proving that Jesus is the M,
     17: 3 proving that the M had to suffer
     18: 28 Scriptures that Jesus was the M.
     26: 23 that the M would suffer and,
Ro   9: 5 traced the human ancestry of the M,
1Jn 2: 22 whoever denies that Jesus is the M.
     5: 1 believes that Jesus is the M
Rev 11: 15 kingdom of our Lord and of his M,

MESSIAHS* (MESSIAH)
Mt 24: 24 false m and false prophets will
Mk 13: 22 false m and false prophets will

METHUSELAH
Ge   5: 27 M lived a total of 969 years,

MICAH
1. Idolater from Ephraim (Jdg 17–18).
2. Prophet from Moresheth (Jer 26:18–19; Mic 1:1).

MICAIAH
Prophet of the LORD who spoke against Ahab (1Ki
22:1–28; 2Ch 18:1–27).

MICHAEL
Archangel (Jude 9); warrior in angelic realm, protector of Israel (Da 10:13, 21; 12:1; Rev 12:7).

MICHAL
Daughter of Saul, wife of David (1Sa 14:49;
18:20–28). Warned David of Saul's plot (1Sa 19). Saul
gave her to Paltiel (1Sa 25:44); David retrieved her
(2Sa 3:13–16). Criticized David for dancing before the
ark (2Sa 6:16–23; 1Ch 15:29).

MIDIAN
Ex   2: 15 from Pharaoh went to live in M,
Jdg 7: 2 I cannot deliver M into their hands,

MIDWIVES
Ex   1: 17 The m, however, feared God

MIGHT (ALMIGHTY MIGHTIER MIGHTY)
Jdg 16: 30 Then he pushed with all his m,
2Sa 6: 5 with all their m before the LORD,
     6: 14 before the LORD with all his m,
2Ch 20: 6 Power and m are in your hand,
Ps 21: 13 we will sing and praise your m.
     54: 1 vindicate me by your m.
Isa 11: 2 the Spirit of counsel and of m,
     63: 15 Where are your zeal and your m?
Mic 3: 8 and with justice and m, to declare
Zec 4: 6 'Not by m nor by power, but by my
Col 1: 11 his glorious m so that you may have
1Ti 6: 16 To him be honor and m forever.

MIGHTIER (MIGHT)
Ps 93: 4 M than the thunder of the great

MIGHTY (MIGHT)
Ge 49: 24 of the hand of the M One of Jacob,
Ex   6: 1 of my m hand he will drive them
     13: 3 brought you out of it with a m hand.
Dt   5: 15 you out of there with a m hand
     7: 8 he brought you out with a m hand
     10: 17 the great God, m and awesome,
     34: 12 no one has ever shown the m power
2Sa 1: 19 How the m have fallen!
     23: 8 the names of David's m warriors:
Ne   9: 32 the great God, m and awesome,
Job 36: 5 "God is m, but despises no one;
Ps 24: 8 The LORD strong and m,
     45: 3 sword on your side, you m one;
     50: 1 The M One, God, the LORD,
     62: 7 he is my m rock, my refuge.
     68: 33 above, who thunders with m voice.
     71: 16 will come and proclaim your m acts,
     77: 12 and meditate on all your m deeds."
     77: 15 your m arm you redeemed your
     89: 8 are m, and your faithfulness
     93: 4 the LORD on high is m.
     99: 4 The King is m, he loves justice—
     110: 2 LORD will extend your m scepter
     118: 15 right hand has done m things!
     136: 12 with a m arm and outstretched arm;
     145: 4 they tell of your m acts.
     145: 12 all people may know of your m acts
     147: 5 Great is our Lord and m in power;
SS   8: 6 like blazing fire, like a m flame.

Isa 9: 6 Wonderful Counselor, M God,
     60: 16 Redeemer, the M One of Jacob.
     63: 1 in righteousness, m to save."
Jer 10: 6 great, and your name is m in power.
     20: 11 LORD is with me like a m warrior;
     32: 18 Great and m God, whose name is
     32: 19 purposes and m are your deeds.
Eze 20: 33 I will reign over you with a m hand,
Zep 3: 17 with you, the M Warrior who saves.
Mt 26: 64 at the right hand of the M One
Eph 1: 19 power is the same as the m strength
     6: 10 in the Lord and in his m power.
1Pe 5: 6 under God's m hand, that he may

MILE*
Mt   5: 41 If anyone forces you to go one m,

MILK
Ex   3: 8 a land flowing with m and honey—
     23: 19 cook a young goat in its mother's m.
Isa 55: 1 buy wine and m without money
1Co 3: 2 I gave you m, not solid food,
Heb 5: 12 You need m, not solid food!
1Pe 2: 2 crave pure spiritual m, so that by it

MILLSTONE (STONE)
Lk 17: 2 with a m tied around your neck than

MIND (DOUBLE-MINDED LIKE-MINDED MINDFUL MINDS)
Nu 23: 19 being, that he should change his m.
Dt 28: 65 LORD will give you an anxious m,
1Sa 15: 29 Israel does not lie or change his m;
1Ch 28: 9 devotion and with a willing m,
2Ch 30: 6 to give them unity of m to carry
Ps 26: 2 examine my heart and my m;
     110: 4 sworn and will not change his m:
Jer 17: 10 search the heart and examine the m,
Da   7: 4 and a human m was given to it.
Mt 22: 37 all your soul and with all your m.'
Mk 12: 30 with all your m and with all your
Lk 10: 27 your strength and with all your m';
Ac   4: 32 believers were one in heart and m.
Ro   1: 28 gave them over to a depraved m,
     7: 25 then, I myself in my m am a slave
     8: 6 The m controlled by the sinful
     8: 6 the m controlled by the Spirit is life
     8: 7 The sinful m is hostile to God;
     12: 2 by the renewing of your m.
     14: 3 make up your m not to put any
     15: 6 with one m and one voice
1Co 1: 10 but that you be perfectly united in m
     2: 9 what no human m has conceived—
     14: 14 spirit prays, but my m is unfruitful.
2Co 13: 11 another, be of one m, live in peace.
Php 2: 2 one in spirit and of one m.
     3: 19 Their m is set on earthly things.
     4: 2 be of the same m in the Lord.
1Th 4: 11 You should m your own business
Heb 7: 21 sworn and will not change his m:
1Pe 4: 7 be alert and of sober m

MINDFUL* (MIND)
Ps   8: 4 mortals that you are m of them,
     26: 3 been m of your unfailing love
Lk   1: 48 he has been m of the humble state
Heb 2: 6 mortals that you are m of them,

MINDS (MIND)
Dt 11: 18 words of mine in your hearts and m;
Ps   7: 9 the righteous God who probes m
Isa 26: 3 peace those whose m are steadfast,
Jer 31: 33 "I will put my law in their m
Lk 24: 38 and why do doubts rise in your m?
     24: 45 he opened their m so they could
Ro   8: 5 the sinful nature have their m set
2Co 4: 4 god of this age has blinded the m
Eph 4: 23 made new in the attitude of your m;
Col 2: 18 and their unspiritual m puff them
     3: 2 Set your m on things above,
Heb 8: 10 I will put my laws in their m
     10: 16 and I will write them on their m."
1Pe 1: 13 with m that are alert and fully sober,
Rev 2: 23 I am he who searches hearts and m,

MINISTER (MINISTERING MINISTERS MINISTRY)
Ps 101: 6 whose walk is blameless will m
1Ti 4: 6 you will be a good m of Christ

MINISTERING (MINISTER)
Heb 1: 14 Are not all angels m spirits sent

MINISTERS (MINISTER)
2Co 3: 6 He has made us competent as m

MINISTRY (MINISTER)
Ac 6: 4 to prayer and the **m** of the word."
Ro 11: 13 the Gentiles, I make much of my **m**
2Co 4: 1 God's mercy we have this **m**, we do
5: 18 and gave us the **m** of reconciliation:
6: 3 so that our **m** will not be discredited.
2Ti 4: 5 discharge all the duties of your **m**.
Heb 8: 6 in fact the **m** Jesus has received is as

MIRACLE* (MIRACLES MIRACULOUS)
Ex 7: 9 'Perform a **m**,' then say to Aaron,
Mk 9: 39 "No one who does a **m** in my name
Jn 7: 21 them, "I did one **m**, and you are all

MIRACLES* (MIRACLE)
1Ch 16: 12 done, his **m**, and the judgments he
Ne 9: 17 to remember the **m** you performed
Job 5: 9 fathomed, **m** that cannot be counted.
9: 10 fathomed, **m** that cannot be counted.
Ps 77: 11 I will remember your **m** of long ago.
77: 14 You are the God who performs **m**;
78: 12 He did **m** in the sight of their
105: 5 done, his **m**, and the judgments he
106: 7 they gave no thought to your **m**;
106: 22 **m** in the land of Ham and awesome
Mt 7: 22 in your name perform many **m**?'
11: 20 most of his **m** had been performed,
11: 21 that were performed in you
11: 23 if the **m** that were performed in you
13: 58 he did not do many **m** there because
Mk 6: 2 What are these remarkable **m** he is
6: 5 He could not do any **m** there,
Lk 10: 13 if the **m** that were performed in you
19: 37 voices for all the **m** they had seen:
Ac 2: 22 man accredited by God to you by **m**,
8: 13 by the great signs and **m** he saw.
19: 11 did extraordinary **m** through Paul,
1Co 12: 28 then **m**, then gifts of healing,
12: 29 Are all teachers? Do all work **m**?
2Co 12: 12 including signs, wonders and **m**.
Gal 3: 5 and work among you by your
Heb 2: 4 wonders and various **m**, and by gifts

MIRACULOUS (MIRACLE)
Mt 13: 54 this wisdom and these **m** powers?"
1Co 12: 10 to another **m** powers, to another

MIRE
Ps 40: 2 the slimy pit, out of the mud and **m**;
Isa 57: 20 whose waves cast up **m** and mud.

MIRIAM
Sister of Moses and Aaron (Nu 26:59). Led dancing at Red Sea (Ex 15:20–21). Struck with leprosy for criticizing Moses (Nu 12). Death (Nu 20:1).

MIRROR*
Job 37: 18 skies, hard as a **m** of cast bronze?
1Co 13: 12 we see only a reflection as in a **m**;
Jas 1: 23 who look at their faces in a **m**

MISDEEDS*
Ps 99: 8 God, though you punished their **m**.
Ro 8: 13 you put to death the **m** of the body,

MISERY
Ex 3: 7 "I have indeed seen the **m** of my
Jdg 10: 16 he could bear Israel's **m** no longer.
Hos 5: 15 in their **m** they will earnestly seek
Ro 3: 16 ruin and **m** mark their ways,
Jas 5: 1 wail because of the **m** that is coming

MISFORTUNE
Ob : 12 your brother in the day of his **m**,

MISLEAD (MISLED)
Pr 24: 28 would you use your lips to **m**?
Isa 47: 10 knowledge **m** you when you say

MISLED (MISLEAD)
1Co 15: 33 Do not be **m**:

MISS
Pr 19: 2 more will hasty feet the way!

MIST
Hos 6: 4 Your love is like the morning **m**,
Jas 4: 14 You are a **m** that appears for a little

MISTREAT (MISTREATED)
Ex 22: 21 "Do not **m** or oppress a foreigner,
Eze 22: 29 poor and needy and **m** the foreigner,
Lk 6: 28 pray for those who **m** you.

MISTREATED (MISTREAT)
Eze 22: 7 the foreigner and **m** the fatherless
Heb 11: 25 He chose to be **m** along
11: 37 destitute, persecuted and **m**—
13: 3 and those who are **m** as if you

MISUSE* (MISUSES)
Ex 20: 7 "You shall not **m** the name
Dt 5: 11 "You shall not **m** the name
Ps 139: 20 your adversaries **m** your name.
1Co 9: 18 not **m** my rights as a preacher

MISUSES* (MISUSE)
Ex 20: 7 anyone guiltless who **m** his name.
Dt 5: 11 anyone guiltless who **m** his name.

MIXED (MIXING)
Da 2: 41 even as you saw iron **m** with clay.

MIXING (MIXED)
Isa 5: 22 wine and champions at **m** drinks,

MOAB
Ge 19: 37 had a son, and she named him **M**;
Dt 34: 6 He buried him in **M**, in the valley
Ru 1: 1 live for a while in the country of **M**.
1: 22 accompanied by Ruth the **M**,
Isa 15: 1 A prophecy concerning **M**: Ar in **M**
Jer 48: 16 "The fall of **M** is at hand;
Am 2: 1 "For three sins of **M**, even for four,

MOAN
Ps 90: 9 we finish our years with a **m**.

MOCK (MOCKED MOCKER MOCKERS MOCKING MOCKS)
Ps 22: 7 All who see me **m** me;
119: 51 The arrogant **m** me unmercifully,
Pr 1: 26 I will **m** when calamity overtakes
14: 9 Fools **m** at making amends for sin,
Mk 10: 34 who will **m** him and spit on him,

MOCKED (MOCK)
Ps 89: 51 they have **m** every step of your
Mt 27: 29 knelt in front of him and **m** him.
27: 41 of the law and the elders **m** him.
Gal 6: 7 not be deceived: God cannot be **m**.

MOCKER (MOCK)
Pr 9: 7 corrects a **m** invites insults;
9: 12 if you are a **m**, you alone will suffer.
20: 1 Wine is a **m** and beer a brawler;
22: 10 Drive out the **m**, and out goes strife;

MOCKERS (MOCK)
Ps 1: 1 take or sit in the company of **m**,
Pr 29: 8 **M** stir up a city, but the wise turn

MOCKING (MOCK)
Isa 50: 6 I did not hide my face from **m**

MOCKS (MOCK)
Pr 17: 5 Whoever **m** the poor shows
30: 17 "The eye that **m** a father,

MODEL*
Php 3: 17 and just as you have us as a **m**,
1Th 1: 7 And so you became a **m** to all
2Th 3: 9 to offer ourselves as a **m** for you

MODESTY*
1Co 12: 23 are treated with special **m**,

MOLDED*
Job 10: 9 Remember that you **m** me like clay.

MOLDY
Jos 9: 5 of their food supply was dry and **m**.

MOLEK
Lev 20: 2 sacrifices any of his children to **M**
1Ki 11: 33 and **M** the god of the Ammonites,

MOMENT (MOMENTARY)
Job 20: 5 the joy of the godless lasts but a **m**.
Ps 2: 12 for his wrath can flare up in a **m**.
30: 5 For his anger lasts only a **m**, but his
Pr 12: 19 but a lying tongue lasts only a **m**.
Isa 54: 7 "For a brief **m** I abandoned you,
66: 8 or a nation be brought forth in a **m**?
Gal 2: 5 We did not give in to them for a **m**,

MOMENTARY* (MOMENT)
2Co 4: 17 **m** troubles are achieving for us

MONEY
Pr 13: 11 Dishonest **m** dwindles away,
Ecc 5: 10 Those who love **m** never have
Isa 55: 1 and you who have no **m**, come,
Mt 6: 24 You cannot serve both God and **m**.
27: 5 So Judas threw the **m**
Lk 3: 14 "Don't extort **m** and don't accuse
9: 3 bag, no bread, no **m**, no extra shirt.
16: 13 You cannot serve both God and **m**."
Ac 5: 2 kept back part of the **m** for himself,
1Co 16: 2 you should set aside a sum of **m**
1Ti 3: 3 not quarrelsome, not a lover of **m**.
6: 10 the love of **m** is a root of all kinds

2Ti 3: 2 of themselves, lovers of **m**, boastful,
Heb 13: 5 your lives free from the love of **m**

MONEYLENDER* (LEND)
Lk 7: 41 Two people owed money to a certain **m**.

MONTH (MONTHS)
Ex 12: 2 "This **m** is to be for you the first **m**,
Eze 47: 12 Every **m** they will bear fruit,
Rev 22: 2 of fruit, yielding its fruit every **m**.

MONTHS (MONTH)
Gal 4: 10 are observing special days and **m**
Rev 11: 2 trample on the holy city for 42 **m**.
13: 5 its authority for forty-two **m**.

MOON
Jos 10: 13 and the **m** stopped, till the nation
Ps 8: 3 of your fingers, the **m** and the stars,
74: 16 you established the sun and **m**.
89: 37 be established forever like the **m**,
104: 19 He made the **m** to mark the seasons,
121: 6 you by day, nor the **m** by night.
136: 9 the **m** and stars to govern the night;
148: 3 Praise him, sun and **m**;
SS 6: 10 fair as the **m**, bright as the sun,
Joel 2: 31 the **m** to blood before the coming
Hab 3: 11 **m** stood still in the heavens
Mt 24: 29 and the **m** will not give its light;
Ac 2: 20 the **m** to blood before the coming
1Co 15: 41 the **m** another and the stars another;
Col 2: 16 a New **M** celebration or a Sabbath
Rev 6: 12 hair, the whole **m** turned blood red,
21: 23 need the sun or the **m** to shine on it,

MORAL*
Jas 1: 21 get rid of all **m** filth and the evil

MORDECAI
Benjamite exile who raised Esther (Est 2:5–15). Exposed plot to kill Xerxes (Est 2:19–23). Refused to honor Haman (Est 3:1–6; 5:9–14). Charged Esther to foil Haman's plot against the Jews (Est 6). Xerxes forced Haman to honor Mordecai (Est 6). Mordecai exalted (Est 8–10). Established Purim (Est 9:18–32).

MORIAH*
Ge 22: 2 Isaac—and go to the region of **M**.
2Ch 3: 1 LORD in Jerusalem on Mount **M**,

MORNING
Ge 1: 5 was evening, and there was **m**—
Dt 28: 67 In the **m** you will say, "If only it
2Sa 23: 4 he is like the light of **m** at sunrise
Ps 5: 3 In the **m**, LORD, you hear my
Pr 4: 18 the righteous is like the **m** sun,
27: 14 blesses a neighbor early in the **m**,
Isa 14: 12 you have fallen from heaven, **m** star,
La 3: 23 They are new every **m**; great is your
2Pe 1: 19 and the **m** star rises in your hearts.
Rev 2: 28 I will also give them the **m** star.
22: 16 of David, and the bright **M** Star."

MORTAL (MORTALS)
Ge 6: 3 beings forever, for they are **m**;
Job 10: 4 Do you see as a **m** sees?
Ro 8: 11 give life to your **m** bodies because
1Co 15: 53 and the **m** with immortality.
2Co 5: 4 so that what is **m** may be swallowed

MORTALS (MORTAL)
Job 14: 1 "**M**, born of woman, are of few
Ps 8: 4 are mere **m** that you are mindful
9: 20 the nations know they are only **m**.
103: 15 As for **m**, their days are like
Jer 17: 5 those who trust in **m**,
Heb 2: 6 are mere **m** that you are mindful

MOSES
Levite; brother of Aaron (Ex 6:20; 1Ch 6:3). Put in basket into Nile; discovered and raised by Pharaoh's daughter (Ex 2:1–10). Fled to Midian after killing Egyptian (Ex 2:11–15). Married to Zipporah, fathered Gershom (Ex 2:16–22).
Called by the LORD to deliver Israel (Ex 3–4). Pharaoh's resistance (Ex 5). Ten plagues (Ex 7–11). Passover and Exodus (Ex 12–13). Led Israel through Red Sea (Ex 14). Song of deliverance (Ex 15:1–21). Brought water from rock (Ex 17:1–7). Raised hands to defeat Amalekites (Ex 17:8–16). Delegated judges (Ex 18; Dt 1:9–18).
Received Law at Sinai (Ex 19:3; 25–31; Jn 1:17). Announced Law to Israel (Ex 19:7–8; 24; 35). Broke tablets because of golden calf (Ex 32; Dt 9). Saw glory of the LORD (Ex 33–34). Supervised building of tabernacle (Ex 36–40). Set apart Aaron and priests (Lev 8–9). Numbered tribes (Nu 1–4; 26). Opposed by Aaron and Miriam (Nu 12). Sent spies into Canaan (Nu

13). Announced forty years of wandering for failure to enter land (Nu 14). Opposed by Korah (Nu 16). Forbidden to enter land for striking rock (Nu 20:1–13; Dt 1:37). Lifted bronze snake for healing (Nu 21:4–9; Jn 3:14). Final address to Israel (Dt 1–33). Succeeded by Joshua (Nu 27:12–23; Dt 34). Death (Dt 34:5–12).

"Law of Moses" (1Ki 2:3; Ezr 3:2; Mk 12:26; Lk 24:44). "Book of Moses" (2Ch 25:12; Ne 13:1). "Song of Moses" (Ex 15:1–21; Rev 15:3). "Prayer of Moses" (Ps 90).

MOTH
Mt 6:19 on earth, where m and rust destroy,

MOTHER (GRANDMOTHER MOTHER-IN-LAW MOTHER'S)
Ge 2:24 a man will leave his father and m
3:20 because she would become the m
Ex 20:12 "Honor your father and your m,
Lev 20:9 father or m is to be put to death.
Dt 5:16 "Honor your father and your m,
21:18 who does not obey his father and m
27:16 who dishonors their father or m."
Jdg 5:7 arose, until I arose, a m in Israel.
1Sa 2:19 Each year his m made him a little
Ps 113:9 her home as a happy m of children.
Pr 10:1 children bring grief to their m.
23:22 do not despise your m when she is
23:25 May your father and m rejoice;
29:15 left to themselves disgrace their m.
30:17 that scorns an aged m, will be
31:1 inspired utterance his m taught him.
Isa 49:15 "Can a m forget the baby at her
66:13 As a m comforts her child, so will I
Jer 20:17 with my m as my grave, her womb
Mic 7:6 a daughter rises up against her m,
Mt 10:35 father, a daughter against her m,
10:37 or m more than me is not worthy
12:48 "Who is my m, and who are my
15:4 said, 'Honor your father and m'
19:5 a man will leave his father and
19:19 honor your father and m,' and 'love
Mk 7:10 'Honor your father and m,' and,
10:19 honor your father and m.' "
Lk 11:27 "Blessed is the m who gave you
12:53 daughter and daughter against m,
18:20 honor your father and m,'
Jn 19:27 to the disciple, "Here is your m."
Gal 4:26 is above is free, and she is our m.
Eph 5:31 a man will leave his father and m
6:2 "Honor your father and m"—
1Th 2:7 Just as a nursing m cares for her
2Ti 1:5 Lois and in your m Eunice and, I am

MOTHER-IN-LAW (MOTHER)
Ru 2:19 Ruth told her m about the one
Mt 10:35 a daughter-in-law against her m—

MOTHER'S (MOTHER)
Job 1:21 "Naked I came from my m womb,
Pr 1:8 and do not forsake your m teaching.
Ecc 5:15 comes naked from their m womb,
11:5 the body is formed in a m womb,
Jn 3:4 a second time into their m womb

MOTIVES*
Pr 16:2 but m are weighed by the Lord.
1Co 4:5 and will expose the m of people's
Php 1:18 whether from false m or true,
1Th 2:3 not spring from error or impure m,
Jas 4:3 because you ask with wrong m,

MOUNT (MOUNTAIN MOUNTAINS MOUNTAINTOPS)
Ps 89:9 when its waves m up, you still them.
Isa 14:13 sit enthroned on the m of assembly,
Eze 28:14 You were on the holy m of God;
Zec 14:4 the M of Olives will be split in two

MOUNTAIN (MOUNT)
Ge 22:14 "On the m of the Lord it will be
Ex 24:18 he stayed on the m forty days
Dt 5:4 face to face out of the fire on the m.
Jos 14:12 "But as a m erodes and crumbles
Ps 24:3 ascend the m of the Lord?
48:1 in the city of our God, his holy m.
Isa 40:4 every m and hill made low;
Mic 4:2 let us go up to the m of the Lord,
Mt 4:8 the devil took him to a very high m
17:20 you can say to this m,
Mk 9:2 with him and led them up a high m,
Lk 3:5 filled in, every m and hill made low.
Jn 4:21 the Father neither on this m nor
2Pe 1:18 we were with him on the sacred m.

MOUNTAINS (MOUNT)
Ps 36:6 righteousness is like the highest m,
46:2 the m fall into the heart of the sea,
90:2 Before the m were born or you
121:1 I lift up my eyes to the m
Isa 52:7 How beautiful on the m are the feet
54:10 Though the m be shaken
55:12 the m and hills will burst into song
Eze 34:6 My sheep wandered over all the m
Mt 24:16 those who are in Judea flee to the m.
Lk 23:30 Then " 'they will say to the m,
1Co 13:2 if I have a faith that can move m,
Rev 6:16 They called to the m and the rocks,

MOUNTAINTOPS (MOUNT)
Isa 42:11 let them shout from the m.

MOURN (MOURNING MOURNS)
Ecc 3:4 a time to m and a time to dance,
Isa 61:2 of our God, to comfort all who m,
Mt 5:4 Blessed are those who m, for they
Ro 12:15 m with those who m.

MOURNING (MOURN)
Isa 61:3 the oil of joy instead of m,
Jer 31:13 I will turn their m into gladness;
Rev 21:4 There will be no more death' or m

MOURNS (MOURN)
Zec 12:10 for him as one m for an only child,

MOUTH (MOUTHS)
Nu 22:38 only what God puts in my m."
Dt 8:3 comes from the m of the Lord.
18:18 and I will put my words in his m.
30:14 it is in your m and in your heart
2Ki 4:34 and lay on the boy, m to m.
Ps 17:3 my m has not transgressed.
19:14 May these words of my m and this
40:3 He put a new song in my m, a hymn
71:8 My m is filled with your praise,
119:103 taste, sweeter than honey to my m!
141:3 Set a guard over my m, Lord;
Pr 2:6 from his m come knowledge
4:24 Keep your m free of perversity;
10:11 The m of the righteous is a fountain
10:31 the m of the righteous comes
26:28 hurts, and a flattering m works ruin.
27:2 praise you, and not your own m;
Ecc 5:2 Do not be quick with your m, do not
SS 1:2 kiss me with the kisses of his m—
5:16 His m is sweetness itself;
Isa 29:13 come near to me with their m
40:5 the m of the Lord has spoken."
45:23 my m has uttered in all integrity
51:16 I have put my words in your m
53:7 is silent, so he did not open his m.
55:11 my word that goes out from my m:
59:21 your m will not depart from your m,
Eze 3:2 So I opened my m, and he gave me
Mal 2:7 people seek instruction from his m.
Mt 4:4 that comes from the m of God.' "
12:34 overflow of the heart the m speaks.
15:11 into your m does not defile you,
15:18 out of the m come from the heart,
Lk 6:45 overflow of the heart the m speaks.
Ro 10:9 If you declare with your m,
1Pe 2:22 and no deceit was found in his m.
Rev 1:16 coming out of his m was a sharp,
2:16 them with the sword of my m.
3:16 I am about to spit you out of my m.
19:15 out of his m is a sharp sword

MOUTHS (MOUTH)
Ps 10:7 Their m are full of lies and threats;
37:30 The m of the righteous utter
78:36 they would flatter him with their m,
Pr 16:23 of the wise make their m prudent,
Eze 33:31 Their m speak of love, but their
Ro 3:14 "Their m are full of cursing
Eph 4:29 talk come out of your m, but only
Jas 3:3 we put bits into the m of horses

MOVE (MOVED MOVES)
Dt 19:14 Do not m your neighbor's boundary
Pr 23:10 Do not m an ancient boundary stone
Ac 17:28 'For in him we live and m and have
1Co 13:2 I have a faith that can m mountains,
15:58 Let nothing m you.
Col 1:23 and do not m from the hope

MOVED (MOVE)
Ex 35:21 and whose heart m them came
1Ki 3:26 whose son was alive was deeply m
2Ch 36:22 the Lord the heart of Cyrus
Ezr 1:5 everyone whose heart God had m—

Jn 11:33 he was deeply m in spirit

MOVES (MOVE)
Dt 23:14 For the Lord your God m

MUD (MUDDIED)
Ps 40:2 the slimy pit, out of the m and mire;
Isa 57:20 whose waves cast up mire and m.
Jn 9:6 made some m with the saliva,
2Pe 2:22 returns to her wallowing in the m."

MUDDIED (MUD)
Pr 25:26 Like a m spring or a polluted well
Eze 32:13 feet or m by the hooves of cattle.

MULBERRY*
Lk 17:6 seed, you can say to this m tree,

MULTITUDE (MULTITUDES)
Isa 31:1 who trust in the m of their chariots
Jas 5:20 death and cover over a m of sins.
1Pe 4:8 because love covers over a m
Rev 7:9 there before me was a great m
19:1 of a great m in heaven shouting:

MULTITUDES (MULTITUDE)
Ne 9:6 and the m of heaven worship you.
Da 12:2 M who sleep in the dust of the earth
Joel 3:14 M, in the valley of decision!

MURDER (MURDERED MURDERER MURDERERS)
Ex 20:13 "You shall not m.
Dt 5:17 "You shall not m.
Pr 28:17 the guilt of m will seek refuge
Mt 5:21 'You shall not m, and anyone who
15:19 of the heart come evil thoughts, m,
Ro 1:29 They are full of envy, m, strife,
13:9 "You shall not m," "You shall not
Jas 2:11 commit adultery but do commit m,

MURDERED (MURDER)
Mt 23:31 of those who m the prophets.
Ac 7:52 now you have betrayed and m him—
1Jn 3:12 to the evil one and m his brother.

MURDERER (MURDER)
Nu 35:16 is a m; the m is to be put to death.
Jn 8:44 He was a m from the beginning,
1Jn 3:15 who hates a fellow believer is a m,

MURDERERS (MURDER)
1Ti 1:9 kill their fathers or mothers, for m,
Rev 21:8 vile, the m, the sexually immoral,
22:15 the m, the idolaters and everyone

MUSIC (MUSICAL MUSICIAN MUSICIANS)
Ge 31:27 and singing to the m of timbrels
1Ch 6:31 charge of the m in the house
6:32 with m before the tabernacle,
25:6 their father for the m of the temple
25:7 and skilled in m for the Lord—
Ne 12:27 and with the m of cymbals,
Job 21:12 They sing to the m of timbrel
Ps 27:6 sing and make m to the Lord.
33:2 make m to him on the ten-stringed
45:8 ivory the m of the strings makes you
57:7 I will sing and make m.
81:2 begin the m, strike the timbrel,
87:7 As they make m they will sing,
92:1 Lord and make m to your name,
92:3 to the m of the ten-stringed lyre
95:2 and extol him with m and song
98:4 burst into jubilant song with m;
98:5 make m to the Lord
108:1 sing and make m with all my soul.
144:9 the ten-stringed lyre I will make m
147:7 make m to our God on the harp.
149:3 and make m to him with timbrel
Isa 30:32 club will be to the m of timbrels
La 5:14 young men have stopped their m.
Eze 26:13 the m of your harps will be heard no
Da 3:5 pipe and all kinds of m, you must
3:7 lyre, harp and all kinds of m,
3:10 all kinds of m must fall down
3:15 pipe and all kinds of m, if you are
Am 5:23 not listen to the m of your harps.
Hab 3:19 For the director of m.
Lk 15:25 the house, he heard m and dancing.
Eph 5:19 make m from your heart to the Lord,
Rev 18:22 of harpists and musicians,

MUSICAL* (MUSIC)
1Ch 15:16 a joyful sound with m instruments:
23:5 the m instruments I have provided
2Ch 7:6 with the Lord's m instruments,
34:12 skilled in playing m instruments—
Ne 12:36 m instruments, prescribed by, David

Am   6:   5   and improvise on **m** instruments.

MUSICIAN* (MUSIC)
1Ch   6: 33   Heman, the **m**, the son of Joel,

MUSICIANS (MUSIC)
1Ki 10: 12   to make harps and lyres for the **m**.
1Ch   9: 33   Those who were **m**, heads of Levite
     15: 19   The **m** Heman, Asaph and Ethan
2Ch   5: 12   All the Levites who were **m**—
     9: 11   to make harps and lyres for the **m**.
    35: 15   The **m**, the descendants of Asaph,
Ps 68: 25   are the singers, after them the **m**;
Rev 18: 22   The music of harpists and **m**,

MUSTARD
Mt 13: 31   kingdom of heaven is like a **m** seed,
    17: 20   you have faith as small as a **m** seed,
Mk   4: 31   It is like a **m** seed, which is

MUSTER
Pr 24:   5   who have knowledge **m** their strength.

MUTILATORS*
Php   3:   2   those evildoers, those **m** of the flesh.

MUTUAL* (MUTUALLY)
Ro   14: 19   leads to peace and to **m** edification.
1Co   7:   5   other except perhaps by **m** consent
2Pe   1:   7   and to godliness, **m** affection; and to **m** affection, love.

MUTUALLY* (MUTUAL)
Ro   1: 12   and I may be **m** encouraged by each

MUZZLE*
Dt 25:   4   Do not **m** an ox while it is treading
Ps 39:   1   I will put a **m** on my mouth while
1Co   9:   9   "Do not **m** an ox while it is treading
1Ti   5: 18   "Do not **m** an ox while it is treading

MYRRH
Ps 45:   8   All your robes are fragrant with **m**
SS   1: 13   of **m** resting between my breasts.
Mt   2: 11   gifts of gold, frankincense and **m**.
Mk 15: 23   offered him wine mixed with **m**,
Jn 19: 39   Nicodemus brought a mixture of **m**
Rev 18: 13   of incense, and frankincense,

MYSTERIES* (MYSTERY)
Job 11:   7   "Can you fathom the **m** of God?
Da   2: 28   is a God in heaven who reveals **m**.
     2: 29   of **m** showed you what is going
     2: 47   Lord of kings and a revealer of **m**,
1Co   4:   1   with the **m** God has revealed.
    13:   2   can fathom all **m** and all knowledge,
    14:   2   they utter **m** by the Spirit.

MYSTERY* (MYSTERIES)
Da   2: 18   God of heaven concerning this **m**,
     2: 19   During the night the **m** was revealed
     2: 27   the king the **m** he has asked about,
     2: 30   this **m** has been revealed to me,
     2: 47   for you were able to reveal this **m**."
     4:   9   and no **m** is too difficult for you.
Ro   11: 25   want you to be ignorant of this **m**,
    16: 25   the revelation of the **m** hidden
1Co   2:   7   we declare God's wisdom, a **m**
    15: 51   Listen, I tell you a **m**:
Eph   1:   9   to us the **m** of his will according
     3:   3   that is, the **m** made known to me
     3:   4   my insight into the **m** of Christ,
     3:   6   This **m** is that through the gospel
     3:   9   the administration of this **m**,
     5: 32   This is a profound **m**—but I am
     6: 19   I will fearlessly make known the **m**
Col   1: 26   the **m** that has been kept hidden
     1: 27   the glorious riches of this **m**,
     2:   2   that they may know the **m** of God,
     4:   3   we may proclaim the **m** of Christ,
1Ti   3: 16   the **m** from which true godliness
Rev   1: 20   The **m** of the seven stars that you
    10:   7   the **m** of God will be accomplished,
    17:   5   title was written on her forehead: \m
    17:   7   explain to you the **m** of the woman

MYTHS*
1Ti   1:   4   or to devote themselves to **m**
     4:   7   Have nothing to do with godless **m**
2Ti   4:   4   from the truth and turn aside to **m**.
Tit   1: 14   will pay no attention to Jewish **m**

NAAMAN
Aramean general whose leprosy was cleansed by Elisha (2Ki 5).

NABAL
Wealthy Carmelite the Lᴏʀᴅ killed for refusing to

help David (1Sa 25). David married Abigail, his widow (1Sa 25:39–42).

NABOTH*
Jezreelite killed by Jezebel for his vineyard (1Ki 21). Ahab's family destroyed for this (1Ki 21:17–24; 2Ki 9:21–37).

NADAB
1. Firstborn of Aaron (Ex 6:23); killed with Abihu for offering unauthorized fire (Lev 10; Nu 3:4).
2. Son of Jeroboam I; king of Israel (1Ki 15:25–32).

NAGGING
Pr 21: 19   with a quarrelsome and **n** wife.

NAHUM
Prophet against Nineveh (Na 1:1).

NAIL* (NAILING)
Jn 20: 25   "Unless I see the **n** marks in his

NAILING* (NAIL)
Ac   2: 23   him to death by **n** him to the cross.
Col   2: 14   has taken it away, **n** it to the cross.

NAIVE*
Ro 16: 18   they deceive the minds of **n** people.

NAKED
Ge   2: 25   The man and his wife were both **n**,
Job   1: 21   "N I came from my mother's
Isa 58:   7   when you see the **n**, to clothe them,
2Co   5:   3   are clothed, we will not be found **n**.

NAME (NAMES)
Ge   2: 19   man to see what he would **n** them;
     4: 26   to call on the **n** of the Lᴏʀᴅ.
    11:   4   that we may make a **n** for ourselves
    12:   2   I will make your **n** great, and you
    32: 29   Jacob said, "Please tell me your **n**."
Ex   3: 15   "This is my **n** forever, the **n** you
    20:   7   "You shall not misuse the **n**
    34: 14   for the Lᴏʀᴅ, whose **n** is Jealous,
Lev 24: 11   Israelite woman blasphemed the **N**
Dt   5: 11   "You shall not misuse the **n**
    12: 11   will choose as a dwelling for his **N**—
    18:   5   minister in the Lᴏʀᴅ's **n** always.
    25:   6   carry on the **n** of the dead brother so
    28: 58   this glorious and awesome **n**—
Jos   7:   9   will you do for your own great **n**?"
Jdg 13: 17   "What is your **n**, so that we may
1Sa 12: 22   of his great **n** the Lᴏʀᴅ will not
2Sa   6:   2   which is called by the **N**, the **n**
     7:   9   Now I will make your **n** great,
1Ki   5:   5   will build the temple for my **N**.'
     8: 29   you said, 'My N shall be there,'
1Ch 17:   8   I will make your **n** like the names
2Ch   7: 14   people, who are called by my **n**,
Ne   9: 10   You made a **n** for yourself,
Ps   8:   1   how majestic is your **n** in all
     9: 10   Those who know your **n** trust
    20:   7   in the **n** of the Lᴏʀᴅ our God.
    29:   2   to the Lᴏʀᴅ the glory due his **n**;
    34:   3   let us exalt his **n** together.
    44: 20   If we had forgotten the **n** of our God
    66:   2   Sing the glory of his **n**;
    68:   4   sing in praise of his **n**, extol him
    79:   9   our Savior, for the glory of your **n**;
    96:   8   to the Lᴏʀᴅ the glory due his **n**;
   103:   1   my inmost being, praise his holy **n**.
   115:   1   not to us but to your **n** be the glory,
   138:   2   will praise your **n** for your unfailing
   145:   1   I will praise your **n** for ever
   147:   4   the stars and calls them each by **n**.
Pr   3:   4   and a good **n** in the sight of God
    10:   7   **n** of the righteous is used in blessings,
    18: 10   The **n** of the Lᴏʀᴅ is a fortified
    22:   1   A good **n** is more desirable than
    30:   4   What is his **n**, and what is the **n**
Ecc   7:   1   A good **n** is better than fine
SS   1:   3   your **n** is like perfume poured out.
Isa 12:   4   praise to the Lᴏʀᴅ, call on his **n**;
    26:   8   your **n** and renown are the desire
    40: 26   by one, and calls them each by **n**.
    42:   8   "I am the Lᴏʀᴅ; that is my **n**!
    56:   5   I will give them an everlasting **n**
    57: 15   who lives forever, whose **n** is holy:
    63: 14   to make for yourself a glorious **n**.
Jer 14:   7   Lᴏʀᴅ, for the sake of your **n**.
    15: 16   for I bear your **n**, Lᴏʀᴅ God
Eze 20:   9   it to keep my **n** from being profaned
    20: 14   of my **n** I did what would keep it
    20: 22   of my **n** I did what would keep it
Da 12:   1   everyone whose **n** is found written
Hos 12:   5   God Almighty, the Lᴏʀᴅ is his **n**!

Joel   2: 32   the **n** of the Lᴏʀᴅ will be saved;
Mic   5:   4   of the **n** of the Lᴏʀᴅ his God.
Zep   3:   9   may call on the **n** of the Lᴏʀᴅ
Zec   6: 12   is the man whose **n** is the Branch,
    14:   9   one Lᴏʀᴅ, and his **n** the only **n**.
Mal   1:   6   who show contempt for my **n**.
Mt   1: 21   and you are to give him the **n** Jesus,
     6:   9   in heaven, hallowed be your **n**,
    18: 20   two or three come together in my **n**,
    24:   5   For many will come in my **n**,
    28: 19   baptizing them in the **n** of the Father
Mk   9: 41   water in my **n** because you belong
Lk 11:   2   hallowed be your **n**, your kingdom
Jn 10:   3   He calls his own sheep by **n**
    14: 13   I will do whatever you ask in my **n**,
    16: 24   not asked for anything in my **n**.
Ac   2: 21   on the **n** of the Lᴏʀᴅ will be saved.'
     4: 12   is no other **n** given under heaven
Ro 10: 13   on the **n** of the Lᴏʀᴅ will be saved."
Php   2:   9   him the **n** that is above every **n**,
     2: 10   at the **n** of Jesus every knee should
Col   3: 17   do it all in the **n** of the Lord Jesus,
Heb   1:   4   the angels as the **n** he has inherited
Jas   5: 14   them with oil in the **n** of God.
1Jn   5: 13   you who believe in the **n** of the Son
Rev   2: 17   stone with a new **n** written on it,
     3: 12   I will also write on them my new **n**.
    19: 13   blood, and his **n** is the Word of God.

NAMES (NAME)
Ex 28:   9   engrave on them the **n** of the sons
Lk 10: 20   but rejoice that your **n** are written
Php   4:   3   whose **n** are in the book of life.
Heb 12: 23   whose **n** are written in heaven.
Rev   3:   5   never blot out their **n** from the book
    20: 15   All whose **n** were not found written
    21: 27   only those whose **n** are written

NAOMI
Wife of Elimelek, mother-in-law of Ruth (Ru 1:2, 4). Left Bethlehem for Moab during famine (Ru 1:1). Returned a widow, with Ruth (Ru 1:6–22). Advised Ruth to seek marriage with Boaz (Ru 2:17–3:4). Cared for Ruth's son Obed (Ru 4:13–17).

NAPHTALI
Son of Jacob by Bilhah (Ge 30:8; 35:25; 1Ch 2:2). Tribe of Naphtali (Ge 49:21; Dt 33:23), numbered (Nu 1:43; 26:50), allotted land (Jos 19:32–39; Eze 48:3), failed to fully possess (Jdg 1:33), supported Deborah (Jdg 4:10; 5:18), David (1Ch 12:34), 12,000 from (Rev 7:6).

NARROW
Mt   7: 13   "Enter through the **n** gate.
     7: 14   gate and **n** the road that leads to life,

NATHAN
Prophet and chronicler of Israel's history (1Ch 29:29; 2Ch 9:29). Announced the Davidic covenant (2Sa 7; 1Ch 17). Denounced David's sin with Bathsheba (2Sa 12). Supported Solomon (1Ki 1).

NATHANAEL*
Apostle (Jn 1:45–49; 21:2). Probably also called Bartholomew (Mt 10:3).

NATION (NATIONS)
Ge 12:   2   "I will make you into a great **n**,
Ex 19:   6   a kingdom of priests and a holy **n**.'
Dt   4:   7   What other **n** is so great as to have
Jos   5:   8   the whole **n** had been circumcised,
2Sa   7: 23   the one **n** on earth that God went
Ps 33: 12   Blessed is the **n** whose God is
Pr 11: 14   For lack of guidance a **n** falls,
    14: 34   Righteousness exalts a **n**, but sin
Isa   2:   4   **N** will not take up sword against **n**,
    26:   2   **n** may enter, the **n** that keeps faith.
    60: 12   For the **n** or kingdom that will not
    65:   1   To a **n** that did not call on my name,
    66:   8   a **n** be brought forth in a moment?
Mic 4:   3   **N** will not take up sword against **n**,
Mt 24:   7   **N** will rise against **n**,
Mk 13:   8   **N** will rise against **n**,
1Pe   2:   9   a holy **n**, God's special possession,
Rev   5:   9   and language and people and **n**,
     7:   9   could count, from every **n**, tribe,
    14:   6   to every **n**, tribe,

NATIONS (NATION)
Ge 17:   4   You will be the father of many **n**.
    18: 18   and all **n** on earth will be blessed
Ex 19:   5   out of all **n** you will be my treasured
Lev 20: 26   you apart from the **n** to be my own.
Dt   7:   1   and drives out before you many **n**—
    15:   6   and you will lend to many **n** but will

Jdg 3: 1 These are the **n** the LORD left
2Ch 20: 6 rule over all the kingdoms of the **n**.
Ne 1: 8 I will scatter you among the **n**,
Ps 2: 1 Why do the **n** conspire
2: 8 I will make the **n** your inheritance,
9: 5 You have rebuked the **n**
22: 28 the LORD and he rules over the **n**.
46: 10 I will be exalted among the **n**, I will
47: 8 God reigns over the **n**; God is seated
66: 7 by his power, his eyes watch the **n**—
67: 2 earth, your salvation among all **n**.
68: 30 Scatter the **n** who delight in war.
72: 11 all **n** will be blessed through him,
96: 3 Declare his glory among the **n**,
99: 2 he is exalted over all the **n**.
106: 35 they mingled with the **n** and adopted
110: 6 He will judge the **n**,
113: 4 LORD is exalted over all the **n**,
Isa 2: 2 the hills, and all **n** will stream to it.
11: 10 the **n** will rally to him, and his
12: 4 known among the **n** what he has
40: 15 Surely the **n** are like a drop
42: 1 and he will bring justice to the **n**.
49: 22 "See, I will beckon to the **n**,
51: 4 justice will become a light to the **n**.
52: 15 so he will sprinkle many **n**,
56: 7 called a house of prayer for all **n**."
60: 3 **N** will come to your light, and kings
66: 18 and gather the people of all **n**
Jer 1: 5 you as a prophet to the **n**."
3: 17 and all **n** will gather in Jerusalem
31: 10 the word of the LORD, you **n**;
33: 9 honor before all **n** on earth that hear
46: 28 completely destroy all the **n** among
Eze 22: 4 make you an object of scorn to the **n**
34: 13 I will bring them out from the **n**
36: 23 Then the **n** will know that I am
37: 22 they will never again be two **n** or be
39: 21 will display my glory among the **n**,
Hos 7: 8 "Ephraim mixes with the **n**;
Joel 2: 17 of scorn, a byword among the **n**.
Am 2: 1 I will gather all **n** and bring them
9: 12 and all the **n** that bear my name,"
Zep 3: 8 I have decided to assemble the **n**,
Hag 2: 7 what is desired by all **n** will come,
Zec 8: 13 have been a curse among the **n**, so I
8: 23 **n** will take firm hold of one Jew
9: 10 He will proclaim peace to the **n**.
14: 2 I will gather all the **n** to Jerusalem
Mt 12: 18 and he will proclaim justice to the **n**.
24: 9 you will be hated by all **n** because
24: 14 whole world as a testimony to all **n**,
25: 32 All the **n** will be gathered before
28: 19 go and make disciples of all **n**,
Mk 11: 17 called a house of prayer for all **n**'?
Ac 4: 25 " 'Why do the **n** rage
Ro 15: 12 who will arise to rule over the **n**;
Gal 3: 8 "All **n** will be blessed through
1Ti 3: 16 was preached among the **n**,
Rev 15: 3 true are your ways, King of the **n**.
15: 4 All **n** will come and worship before
21: 24 The **n** will walk by its light,
22: 2 the tree are for the healing of the **n**.

NATURAL (NATURE)
1Co 15: 44 If there is a **n** body, there is

NATURE (NATURAL)
Ro 1: 20 his eternal power and divine **n**—
7: 18 dwell in me, that is, in my sinful **n**.
8: 4 do not live according to the sinful **n**
8: 5 to the sinful **n** have their minds set
8: 8 by the sinful **n** cannot please God.
13: 14 to gratify the desires of the sinful **n**.
Gal 5: 16 freedom to indulge the sinful **n**;
5: 19 The acts of the sinful **n** are obvious:
5: 24 Jesus have crucified the sinful **n**
Php 2: 6 Who, being in very **n** God, did not
Col 3: 5 whatever belongs to your earthly **n**:
2Pe 1: 4 you may participate in the divine **n**,

NAZARENE* (NAZARETH)
Mt 2: 23 "He will be called a **N**."
Mk 14: 67 "You also were with that **N**,
16: 6 "You are looking for Jesus the **N**,
Ac 24: 5 He is a ringleader of the **N** sect

NAZARETH (NAZARENE)
Mt 4: 13 Leaving **N**, he went and lived
Lk 4: 16 He went to **N**, where he had been
Jn 1: 46 "**N**! Can anything good come

NAZIRITE
Nu 6: 2 of dedication to the LORD as a **N**,

Jdg 13: 7 because the boy will be a **N** of God

NEBO
Dt 34: 1 Moses climbed Mount **N**

NEBUCHADNEZZAR
Babylonian king. Subdued and exiled Judah (2Ki 24–25; 2Ch 36; Jer 39). Dreams interpreted by Daniel (Da 2; 4). Worshiped God (Da 3:28–29; 4:34–37).

NECESSARY*
Ac 1: 21 Therefore it is **n** to choose one
Ro 13: 5 it is **n** to submit to the authorities,
2Co 9: 5 So I thought it **n** to urge the brothers
Php 1: 24 it is more **n** for you that I remain
2: 25 I think it is **n** to send back to you
Heb 8: 3 and so it was **n** for this one
9: 16 it is **n** to prove the death of the one
9: 23 It was **n**, then, for the copies
10: 18 sacrifice for sin is no longer **n**.

NECHO
Pharaoh who killed Josiah (2Ki 23:29–30; 2Ch 35:20–22), deposed Jehoahaz (2Ki 23:33–35; 2Ch 36:3–4).

NECK (STIFF-NECKED)
Pr 3: 22 an ornament to grace your **n**.
6: 21 fasten them around your **n**.
Mt 18: 6 millstone were hung around their **n**

NEED (NEEDS NEEDY)
1Ki 8: 59 Israel according to each day's **n**,
Ps 79: 8 meet us, for we are in desperate **n**.
142: 6 to my cry, for I am in desperate **n**;
Mt 6: 8 knows what you **n** before you ask
Lk 15: 14 country, and he began to be in **n**.
Ac 2: 45 to give to anyone who had **n**.
Ro 12: 13 with the Lord's people who are in **n**.
1Co 12: 21 say to the hand, "I don't **n** you!"
Eph 4: 28 something to share with those in **n**.
1Ti 5: 3 to those widows who are really in **n**.
Heb 4: 16 grace to help us in our time of **n**.
1Jn 3: 17 sister in **n** but has no pity on them,

NEEDLE
Mt 19: 24 to go through the eye of a **n** than

NEEDS (NEED)
Isa 58: 11 he will satisfy your **n**
Php 2: 25 whom you sent to take care of my **n**.
4: 19 God will meet all your **n** according
Jas 2: 16 does nothing about their physical **n**,

NEEDY (NEED)
Dt 15: 11 who are poor and **n** in your land.
1Sa 2: 8 and lifts the **n** from the ash heap;
Ps 35: 10 and **n** from those who rob them."
69: 33 The LORD hears the **n** and does
72: 12 he will deliver the **n** who cry out,
140: 12 poor and upholds the cause of the **n**.
Pr 14: 21 are those who are kind to the **n**.
14: 31 is kind to the honors God;
22: 22 poor and do not crush the **n** in court,
31: 9 defend the rights of the poor and **n**.
31: 20 poor and extends her hands to the **n**.
Mt 6: 2 "So when you give to the **n**, do not

NEGLECT* (NEGLECTED)
Dt 12: 19 to **n** the Levites as long as you live
14: 27 do not **n** the Levites living in your
Ezr 4: 22 Be careful not to **n** this matter.
Ne 10: 39 "We will not **n** the house of our
Est 6: 10 Do not **n** anything you have
Ps 119: 16 I will not **n** your word.
SS 1: 6 my own vineyard I had to **n**.
Lk 11: 42 but you **n** justice and the love
Ac 6: 2 for us to **n** the ministry of the word
1Ti 4: 14 Do not **n** your gift, which was given

NEGLECTED (NEGLECT)
Mt 23: 23 But you have **n** the more important

NEHEMIAH
Cupbearer of Artaxerxes (Ne 2:1); governor of Israel (Ne 8:9). Returned to Jerusalem to rebuild walls (Ne 2–6). With Ezra, reestablished worship (Ne 8). Prayer confessing nation's sin (Ne 9). Dedicated wall (Ne 12).

NEIGHBOR (NEIGHBOR'S NEIGHBORS)
Ex 20: 16 give false testimony against your **n**.
20: 17 or anything that belongs to your **n**."
Lev 19: 17 Rebuke your **n** frankly so you will
19: 18 people, but love your **n** as yourself.
Ps 88: 18 taken from me friend and—
Pr 3: 29 Do not plot harm against your **n**,
14: 21 It is a sin to despise one's **n**,
24: 28 against your **n** without cause—
25: 18 gives false testimony against a **n**.

Pr 27: 10 better a **n** nearby than a relative far
27: 14 If anyone loudly blesses a **n** early
Mt 5: 43 'Love your **n** and hate your enemy.'
19: 19 and 'love your **n** as yourself.' "
Mk 12: 31 'Love your **n** as yourself.'
Lk 10: 27 'Love your **n** as yourself.' "
10: 29 asked Jesus, "And who is my **n**?"
Ro 13: 9 "Love your **n** as yourself."
13: 10 Love does no harm to its **n**.
Gal 5: 14 "Love your **n** as yourself."
Eph 4: 25 and speak truthfully to your **n**,
Jas 2: 8 "Love your **n** as yourself," you are

NEIGHBOR'S (NEIGHBOR)
Ex 20: 17 You shall not covet your **n** wife,
Dt 5: 21 not set your desire on your **n** house
19: 14 not move your **n** boundary stone set
27: 17 moves their **n** boundary stone."
Pr 25: 17 Seldom set foot in your **n** house—

NEIGHBORS (NEIGHBOR)
Lev 19: 13 " 'Do not defraud your **n** or rob
Ps 15: 3 who do their **n** no wrong, who cast
Pr 11: 12 who have no sense deride their **n**,
16: 29 The violent entice their **n** and lead
29: 5 who flatter their **n** are spreading
Jer 31: 34 No longer will they teach their **n**,
Ro 15: 2 We should all please our **n** for
Heb 8: 11 No longer will they teach their **n**,

NESTS
Mt 8: 20 have holes and birds have **n**,

NET (NETS)
Pr 1: 17 spread a **n** where every bird can see
Hab 1: 15 he catches them in his **n**, he gathers
Mt 13: 47 heaven is like a **n** that was let down
Jn 21: 6 "Throw your **n** on the right side

NETS (NET)
Ps 141: 10 Let the wicked fall into their own **n**,
Mt 4: 20 At once they left their **n**
Lk 5: 4 and let down the **n** for a catch."

NEVER-FAILING*
Am 5: 24 river, righteousness like a **n** stream!

NEW
Ps 40: 3 He put a **n** song in my mouth,
98: 1 Sing to the LORD a **n** song, for he
Ecc 1: 9 there is nothing **n** under the sun.
Isa 42: 9 taken place, and **n** things I declare;
62: 2 you will be called by a **n** name
65: 17 I will create **n** heavens and a **n**
66: 22 "As the **n** heavens and the **n** earth
Jer 31: 31 I will make a **n** covenant
La 3: 23 They are **n** every morning;
Eze 11: 19 heart and put a **n** spirit in them;
18: 31 and get a **n** heart and a **n** spirit.
36: 26 I will give you a **n** heart and put a **n**
Zep 3: 5 and every **n** day he does not fail,
Mt 9: 17 they pour **n** wine into **n** wineskins,
Mk 16: 17 *they will speak in **n** tongues;*
Lk 5: 39 old wine, wants the **n**, for you say,
22: 20 "This cup is the **n** covenant in my
Jn 13: 34 "A **n** command I give you:
Ac 5: 20 tell the people all about this **n** life."
Ro 6: 4 the Father, we too may live a **n** life.
1Co 5: 7 you may be a **n** unleavened batch—
11: 25 "This cup is the **n** covenant in my
2Co 3: 6 as ministers of a **n** covenant—
5: 17 in Christ, the **n** creation has come:
5: 17 The old has gone, the **n** is here!
Gal 6: 15 what counts is the **n** creation.
Eph 4: 23 to be made **n** in the attitude of your
4: 24 and to put on the **n** self,
Col 3: 10 and have put on the **n** self, which is
Heb 8: 8 I will make a **n** covenant
9: 15 is the mediator of a **n** covenant,
10: 20 by a **n** and living way opened for us
12: 24 Jesus the mediator of a **n** covenant,
1Pe 1: 3 great mercy he has given us a **n** birth
2Pe 3: 13 forward to a **n** heaven and a **n** earth,
1Jn 2: 8 Yet I am writing you a **n** command;
Rev 2: 17 a white stone with a **n** name written
3: 12 the city of my God, the **n** Jerusalem,
21: 1 I saw "a **n** heaven and a **n** earth,"

NEWBORN (BEAR)
1Pe 2: 2 Like **n** babies, crave pure spiritual

NEWS
2Ki 7: 9 This is a day of good **n** and we are
Ps 112: 7 They will have no fear of bad **n**;
Pr 15: 30 good **n** gives health to the bones.
25: 25 to a weary soul is good **n**

Isa 40: 9 You who bring good n to Jerusalem,
52: 7 the feet of those who bring good n,
61: 1 me to proclaim good n to the poor.
Na 1: 15 the feet of one who brings good n,
Mt 4: 23 proclaiming the good n
9: 35 proclaiming the good n
11: 5 and the good n is proclaimed
Mk 1: 15 Repent and believe the good n!"
Lk 1: 19 to you and to tell you this good n.
2: 10 I bring you good n of great joy
3: 18 and proclaimed the good n to them.
4: 43 "I must proclaim the good n
8: 1 proclaiming the good n
16: 16 the good n of the kingdom of God is
Ac 5: 42 proclaiming the good n that Jesus is
10: 36 announcing the good n of peace
17: 18 Paul was preaching the good n
Ro 10: 15 feet of those who bring good n!"

NICODEMUS*
Pharisee who visited Jesus at night (Jn 3). Argued fair treatment of Jesus (Jn 7:50–52). With Joseph, prepared Jesus for burial (Jn 19:38–42).

NIGHT (NIGHTS)
Ge 1: 5 and the darkness he called "n."
1: 16 and the lesser light to govern the n.
Ex 13: 21 by n in a pillar of fire to give them
14: 24 of the n the LORD looked down
Dt 28: 66 filled with dread both n and day,
Jos 1: 8 meditate on it day and n, so that you
Job 35: 10 Maker, who gives songs in the n,
Ps 1: 2 and meditate on his law day and n.
19: 2 n after n they display knowledge.
42: 8 his love, at n his song is with me—
63: 6 of you through the watches of the n.
77: 6 I remembered my songs in the n.
90: 4 gone by, or like a watch in the n.
91: 5 You will not fear the terror of n,
119:148 open through the watches of the n,
121: 6 you by day, nor the moon by n.
136: 9 the moon and stars to govern the n;
Pr 31: 15 She gets up while it is still n;
31: 18 her lamp does not go out at n.
Isa 21: 11 "Watchman, what is left of the n?
58: 10 and your n will become like
Jer 33: 20 the day and my covenant with the n,
Zec 14: 7 no distinction between day and n.
Lk 2: 8 keeping watch over their flocks at n,
6: 12 and spent the n praying to God.
Jn 3: 2 He came to Jesus at n and said,
9: 4 N is coming, when no one can
1Th 5: 2 Lord will come like a thief in the n.
5: 5 We do not belong to the n
Rev 21: 25 be shut, for there will be no n there.

NIGHTS (NIGHT)
Jnh 1: 17 of the fish three days and three n.
Mt 4: 2 After fasting forty days and forty n,
12: 40 three n in the belly of a huge fish,
12: 40 and three n in the heart of the earth.
2Co 6: 5 hard work, sleepless n and hunger;

NIMROD
Ge 10: 9 "Like N, a mighty hunter before

NINEVEH
Jnh 1: 2 "Go to the great city N and preach
Na 1: 1 A prophecy concerning N.
Mt 12: 41 The people of N will stand

NOAH
Righteous man (Eze 14:14, 20) called to build ark (Ge 6–8; Heb 11:7; 1Pe 3:20; 2Pe 2:5). God's covenant with (Ge 9:1–17). Drunkenness of (Ge 9:18–23). Blessed sons, cursed Canaan (Ge 9:24–27).

NOBLE
Ru 3: 11 that you are a woman of n character.
Ps 16: 3 "They are the n people
45: 1 by a n theme as I recite my verses
Pr 12: 4 A n character is her husband's crown,
31: 10 A wife of n character who can find?
31: 29 "Many women do n things, but you
Isa 32: 8 But the n make n plans,
Lk 8: 15 good soil stands for those with a n
Ro 9: 21 of clay some pottery for n purposes
Php 4: 8 whatever is n, whatever is right,
2Ti 2: 20 some are for n purposes and some

NOSTRILS
Ge 2: 7 breathed into his n the breath of life,
Ex 15: 8 blast of your n the waters piled up.
Ps 18: 15 at the blast of breath from your n.

NOTE
Ac 4: 13 they took n that these men had been

NOTHING
2Sa 24: 24 burnt offerings that cost me n."
Ne 9: 21 they lacked n, their clothes did not
Ps 73: 25 earth has n I desire besides you.
Jer 32: 17 N is too hard for you.
Jn 15: 5 apart from me you can do n.
Ro 14: 14 that n is unclean in itself.

NOURISH
Pr 10: 21 The lips of the righteous n many,

NULLIFY
Mt 15: 6 Thus you n the word of God
Ro 3: 31 Do we, then, n the law by this faith?

OATH
Ex 33: 1 go up to the land I promised on o
Nu 30: 2 takes an o to obligate himself
Dt 6: 18 land the LORD promised on o
7: 8 you and kept the o he swore to your
29: 12 you this day and sealing with an o,
Ps 95: 11 So I declared on o in my anger,
119:106 I have taken an o and confirmed it,
132: 11 The LORD swore an o to David,
Ecc 8: 2 because you took an o before God.
Mt 5: 33 'Do not break your o, but fulfill
Heb 7: 20 And it was not without an o!

OBADIAH
1. Believer who sheltered 100 prophets from Jezebel (1Ki 18:1–16).
2. Prophet against Edom (Ob 1).

OBEDIENCE (OBEY)
Ge 49: 10 and the o of the nations be his.
Dt 10: 12 to walk in o to him, to love him,
26: 17 that you will walk in o to him,
30: 16 to walk in o to him, and keep
Jos 22: 5 walk in o to him, to keep his
Jdg 2: 17 the way of o to the LORD's
1Ch 21: 19 So David went up in o to the word
2Ch 31: 21 God's temple and in o to the law
Lk 23: 56 rested on the Sabbath in o
Ac 21: 24 you yourself are living in o
Ro 1: 5 to faith and to o for his name's sake.
5: 19 through the o of the one man
6: 16 to death, or to o, which leads
16: 19 Everyone has heard about your o,
16: 26 Gentiles might come to faith and o—
2Co 9: 13 God for the o that accompanies your
10: 6 once your o is complete.
Phm : 21 Confident of your o, I write to you,
Heb 5: 8 he learned o from what he suffered
2Jn : 6 that we walk in o to his commands.

OBEDIENT* (OBEY)
Dt 30: 17 heart turns away and you are not o,
Isa 1: 19 If you are willing and o, you will
Lk 2: 51 with them and was o to them.
Ac 6: 7 of priests became o to the faith.
Ro 6: 16 yourselves to someone as o slaves,
2Co 2: 9 the test and be o in everything.
7: 15 he remembers that you were all o,
10: 5 every thought to make it o to Christ.
Php 2: 8 himself by becoming o to death—
Tit 3: 1 to be o, to be ready to do whatever
1Pe 1: 2 to be o to Jesus Christ
1: 14 As o children, do not conform

OBEY (OBEDIENCE OBEDIENT OBEYED OBEYING OBEYS)
Ex 12: 24 "O these instructions as a lasting
19: 5 Now if you o me fully and keep my
24: 7 The LORD has said; we will o."
Lev 18: 4 You must o my laws and be careful
25: 18 decrees and be careful to o my laws,
Nu 15: 40 remember to o all my commands
Dt 5: 27 We will listen and o."
6: 3 and be careful to o so that it may go
6: 24 commanded us to o all these decrees
11: 13 you faithfully o the commands I am
12: 28 o all these regulations I am giving
13: 4 Keep his commands and o him;
21: 18 son who does not o his father
27: 1 If you fully o the LORD your God
28: 15 you do not o the LORD your God
30: 2 God and o him with all your heart
30: 10 if you o the LORD your God
30: 14 and in your heart so you may o it.
32: 46 children to o carefully all the words
Jos 1: 7 o all the law my servant Moses gave
24: 24 the LORD our God and o him."
1Sa 15: 22 To o is better than sacrifice,

1Ki 8: 61 by his decrees and o his commands,
2Ki 17: 13 I commanded your ancestors to o
2Ch 34: 31 and to o the words of the covenant
Ps 103: 18 and remember to o his precepts.
103: 20 do his bidding, who o his word.
119: 17 while I live, that I may o your word.
119: 34 your law and o it with all my heart.
119: 57 I have promised to o your words.
119: 67 went astray, but now I o your word.
119:100 the elders, for I o your precepts.
119:129 therefore I o them.
119:167 I o your statutes, for I love them
Pr 5: 13 I would not o my teachers or turn
19: 16 who o instructions preserve
Jer 7: 23 O me, and I will be your God
11: 4 I said, 'O me and do everything I
11: 7 again and again, saying, "O me."
42: 6 we will o the LORD our God,
Eze 20: 11 people will live if they o them.
Mt 8: 27 the winds and the waves o him!"
28: 20 to o everything I have commanded
Lk 11: 28 hear the word of God and o it."
Jn 14: 23 who loves me will o my teaching.
14: 24 not love me will not o my teaching.
Ac 5: 29 "We must o God rather than human
5: 32 God has given to those who o him,"
Ro 2: 13 it is those who o the law who will
6: 12 body so that you o its evil desires.
6: 16 you are slaves of the one you o—
6: 17 you have come to o from your heart
15: 18 in leading the Gentiles to o God
Gal 5: 3 he is obligated to o the whole law.
Eph 6: 1 o your parents in the Lord, for this
6: 5 o your earthly masters with respect
Col 3: 20 o your parents in everything,
3: 22 Slaves, o your earthly masters
2Th 3: 14 those who do not o our instruction
1Ti 3: 4 well and see that his children o him,
Heb 5: 9 eternal salvation for all who o him
1Pe 4: 17 for those who do not o the gospel

OBEYED (OBEY)
Ge 22: 18 blessed, because you have o me,
Jos 1: 17 Just as we fully o Moses, so we will
Ps 119: 4 down precepts that are to be fully o.
Da 9: 10 we have not o the LORD our God
Jnh 3: 3 Jonah o the word of the LORD
Mic 5: 15 on the nations that have not o me."
Jn 15: 20 If they o my teaching, they will
17: 6 to me and they have o your word.
Ac 7: 53 through angels but have not o it."
Php 2: 12 dear friends, as you have always o—
Heb 11: 8 as his inheritance, o and went,
1Pe 3: 6 who o Abraham and called him her

OBEYING (OBEY)
1Sa 15: 22 as much as in o the LORD?
Ps 119: 5 were steadfast in o your decrees!
Gal 5: 7 you to keep you from o the truth?
1Pe 1: 22 purified yourselves by o the truth so

OBEYS (OBEY)
Lev 18: 5 for whoever o them will live
Jn 8: 51 o my word will never see death."
Ro 2: 27 and yet o the law will condemn you
1Jn 2: 5 But if anyone o his word,

OBLIGATED (OBLIGATION)
Ro 1: 14 I am o both to Greeks
Gal 5: 3 that he is o to obey the whole law.

OBLIGATION (OBLIGATED)
Ro 8: 12 brothers and sisters, we have an o—

OBSCENITY*
Eph 5: 4 Nor should there be o, foolish talk

OBSCURES*
Job 38: 2 "Who is this that o my plans
42: 3 o my plans without knowledge?

OBSERVE (OBSERVING)
Ex 31: 13 'You must o my Sabbaths.
Lev 25: 2 the land itself must o a sabbath
Dt 4: 6 O them carefully, for this will show
5: 12 "O the Sabbath day by keeping it
8: 6 O the commands of the LORD
11: 22 you carefully o all these commands
26: 16 carefully o them with all your heart
Ps 37: 37 the blameless, o the upright;

OBSERVING (OBSERVE)
Gal 2: 16 person is not justified by o the law,
3: 2 you receive the Spirit by o the law,
3: 10 rely on o the law are under a curse,

OBSOLETE
Heb 8: 13 "new," he has made the first one o;

OBSTACLE* (OBSTACLES)
Ro 14: 13 block or o in the way of a brother

OBSTACLES (OBSTACLE)
Ro 16: 17 put o in your way that are contrary

OBSTINATE
Isa 65: 2 held out my hands to an o people,
Ro 10: 21 to a disobedient and o people."

OBTAIN (OBTAINED OBTAINING)
Pr 12: 2 Good people o favor from the Lord,
Ro 11: 7 sought so earnestly they did not o.
2Ti 2: 10 they too may o the salvation that is

OBTAINED (OBTAIN)
Ro 9: 30 not pursue righteousness, have o it,
Php 3: 12 Not that I have already o all this,

OBTAINING* (OBTAIN)
Heb 9: 12 thus o eternal redemption.

OBVIOUS*
Mt 6: 18 so that it will not be o to others
Gal 5: 19 The acts of the sinful nature are o:
1Ti 5: 24 The sins of some are o,
5: 25 good deeds are o, and even those

OCCASIONS
Eph 6: 18 the Spirit on all o with all kinds

OFFENSE (OFFENSES OFFENSIVE)
Pr 17: 9 would foster love covers over an o,
19: 11 it is to one's glory to overlook an o.
Gal 5: 11 that case the o of the cross has been

OFFENSES (OFFENSE)
Ecc 10: 4 calmness can lay great o to rest.
Isa 44: 22 swept away your o like a cloud,
59: 12 For our o are many in your sight,
Eze 18: 30 Turn away from all your o;
33: 10 "Our o and sins weigh us down,

OFFENSIVE (OFFENSE)
Ps 139: 24 See if there is any o way in me,

OFFER (OFFERED OFFERING OFFERINGS OFFERS)
Ps 4: 5 O the sacrifices of the righteous
Ro 6: 13 Do not o any part of yourself to sin
12: 1 o your bodies as a living sacrifice,
Heb 9: 25 he enter heaven to o himself again
13: 15 let us continually o to God

OFFERED (OFFER)
Isa 50: 6 I o my back to those who beat me,
1Co 9: 13 altar share in what is o on the altar?
10: 20 of pagans are o to demons.
Heb 7: 27 sins once for all when he o himself.
9: 14 eternal Spirit o himself unblemished
11: 17 tested him, o Isaac as a sacrifice.
Jas 5: 15 the prayer o in faith will make them

OFFERING (OFFER)
Ge 4: 3 of the soil as an o to the Lord.
22: 2 Sacrifice him there as a burnt o
22: 8 provide the lamb for the burnt o,
Ex 29: 24 before the Lord as a wave o.
29: 40 quarter of a hin of wine as a drink o.
Lev 1: 3 " 'If the o is a burnt o
2: 1 you bring a grain o baked
3: 1 " 'If your o is a fellowship o,
4: 3 young bull without defect as a sin o
5: 15 the sanctuary shekel. It is a guilt o.
7: 37 ordination and the fellowship o,
9: 24 consumed the burnt o and the fat
22: 18 to fulfill a vow or as a freewill o,
22: 21 a special vow or as a freewill o,
1Sa 13: 9 And Saul offered up the burnt o.
1Ch 21: 26 from heaven on the altar of burnt o.
2Ch 7: 1 and consumed the burnt o
Ps 40: 6 Sacrifice and o you did not desire—
116: 17 I will sacrifice a thank o to you
Isa 53: 10 the Lord makes his life an o
Mt 5: 23 if you are o your gift at the altar
Ro 8: 3 of sinful humanity to be a sin o.
Eph 5: 2 himself up for us as a fragrant o
Php 2: 17 out like a drink o on the sacrifice
4: 18 They are a fragrant o, an acceptable
2Ti 4: 6 being poured out like a drink o,
Heb 10: 5 "Sacrifice and o you did not desire,
11: 4 By faith Abel brought God a better o
1Pe 2: 5 o spiritual sacrifices acceptable

OFFERINGS (OFFER)
1Sa 15: 22 the Lord delight in burnt o,
2Ch 35: 7 lambs and goats for the Passover o,

Isa 1: 13 Stop bringing meaningless o!
Hos 6: 6 of God rather than burnt o.
Mal 3: 8 we robbing you?' "In tithes and o.
Mk 12: 33 is more important than all burnt o
Heb 10: 8 "Sacrifices and o, burnt o and sin o

OFFERS (OFFER)
Heb 10: 11 and again he o the same sacrifices,

OFFICER (OFFICIALS)
2Ti 2: 4 try to please their commanding o.

OFFICIALS (OFFICER)
Ex 5: 21 his o and have put a sword in their
Pr 17: 26 surely to flog honest o is not right.
29: 12 to lies, all his o become wicked.

OFFSPRING
Ge 3: 15 and between your o and hers;
12: 7 "To your o I will give this land."
13: 16 I will make your o like the dust
26: 4 through your o all nations on earth
28: 14 be blessed through you and your o.
Ex 13: 2 The first o of every womb among
Ru 4: 12 Through the o the Lord gives
Isa 44: 3 I will pour out my Spirit on your o,
53: 10 he will see his o and prolong his
Ac 3: 25 'Through your o all peoples
17: 28 own poets have said, 'We are his o.'
17: 29 "Therefore since we are God's o,
Ro 4: 18 said to him, "So shall your o be."
9: 8 who are regarded as Abraham's o.

OG
Nu 21: 33 and O king of Bashan and his whole
Ps 136: 20 and O king of Bashan—

OIL
Ex 29: 7 Take the anointing o and anoint him
30: 25 It will be the sacred anointing o.
Dt 14: 23 grain, new wine and olive o,
1Sa 10: 1 Samuel took a bottle of olive o
16: 13 So Samuel took the horn of o
1Ki 17: 16 up and the jug of o did not run dry,
2Ki 4: 6 Then the o stopped flowing.
Ps 23: 5 You anoint my head with o;
45: 7 by anointing you with the o of joy.
104: 15 hearts, o to make their faces shine,
133: 2 It is like precious o poured
Pr 21: 17 wine and olive o will never be rich.
Isa 1: 6 bandaged or soothed with olive o.
61: 3 the o of joy instead of mourning,
Mt 25: 3 but did not take any o with them.
Heb 1: 9 by anointing you with the o of joy."

OLIVE (OLIVES)
Ge 8: 11 beak was a freshly plucked o leaf!
Jdg 9: 8 They said to the o tree, 'Be our
Jer 11: 16 Lord called you a thriving o tree
Zec 4: 3 Also there are two o trees by it,
Ro 11: 17 though a wild o shoot, have been
11: 24 were cut out of an o tree that is wild
Rev 11: 4 They are "the two o trees"

OLIVES (OLIVE)
Zec 14: 4 feet will stand on the Mount of O,
Mt 24: 3 Jesus was sitting on the Mount of O,
Jas 3: 12 can a fig tree bear o, or a grapevine

OMEGA*
Rev 1: 8 "I am the Alpha and the O,"
21: 6 I am the Alpha and the O,
22: 13 I am the Alpha and the O, the First

OMENS
Lev 19: 26 not practice divination or seek o.

OMIT*
Jer 26: 2 I command you; do not o a word.

OMRI
King of Israel (1Ki 16:21–26).

ONESIMUS*
Col 4: 9 He is coming with O, our faithful
Phm 10 that I appeal to you for my son O,

ONESIPHORUS*
2Ti 1: 16 show mercy to the household of O,
4: 19 and Aquila and the household of O.

ONIONS*
Nu 11: 5 melons, leeks, o and garlic.

ONYX
Ex 28: 9 "Take two o stones and engrave
28: 20 row shall be topaz, o and jasper.

OPEN (OPENED)
Ps 78: 2 I will o my mouth with a parable;

OPENED (OPEN)
Ps 40: 6 but my ears you have o—

OPENHANDED* (HAND OPEN)
Dt 15: 8 be o and freely lend them whatever
15: 11 command you to be o toward those

OPINIONS*
1Ki 18: 21 long will you waver between two o?
Pr 18: 2 but delight in airing their own o.

OPPONENTS (OPPOSE)
Pr 18: 18 disputes and keeps strong o apart.
2Ti 2: 25 O must be gently instructed,

OPPORTUNE (OPPORTUNITY)
Lk 4: 13 he left him until an o time.

OPPORTUNITY* (OPPORTUNE)
1Sa 18: 21 "Now you have a second o
Jer 46: 17 a loud noise; he has missed his o.'
Mt 26: 16 watched for an o to hand him over.
Mk 14: 11 watched for an o to hand him over
Lk 22: 6 watched for an o to hand Jesus over
Ac 25: 16 have had an o to defend themselves
27: 13 began to blow, they saw their o;
Ro 7: 8 sin, seizing the o afforded
7: 11 sin, seizing the o afforded
1Co 16: 12 but he will go when he has the o.
2Co 5: 12 are giving you an o to take pride
11: 12 under those who want an o to be
Gal 6: 10 as we have o, let us do good to all
Eph 5: 16 making the most of every o,
Php 4: 10 but you had no o to show it.
Col 4: 5 make the most of every o.
1Ti 5: 14 to give the enemy no o for slander.
Heb 11: 15 they would have had o to return.

OPPOSE (OPPONENTS OPPOSED OPPOSES OPPOSING OPPOSITION)
Ex 23: 22 enemies and will o those who o you.
1Sa 2: 10 those who o the Lord will be
Job 23: 13 stands alone, and who can o him?
Tit 1: 9 doctrine and refute those who o it.
2: 8 those who o you may be ashamed

OPPOSED (OPPOSE)
Gal 2: 11 came to Antioch, I o him to his face,
3: 21 therefore, o the promises of God?

OPPOSES (OPPOSE)
Jas 4: 6 "God o the proud but shows favor
1Pe 5: 5 "God o the proud but shows favor

OPPOSING (OPPOSE)
1Ti 6: 20 the o ideas of what is falsely called

OPPOSITION (OPPOSE)
Heb 12: 3 Consider him who endured such o

OPPRESS (OPPRESSED OPPRESSES OPPRESSION OPPRESSOR)
Ex 1: 11 slave masters over them to o them
22: 21 "Do not mistreat or o a foreigner,
Pr 22: 16 Those who o the poor to increase
Isa 3: 5 People will o each other—
Eze 22: 29 they o the poor and needy
Da 7: 25 the Most High and o his holy people
Am 5: 12 There are those who o the innocent
Zec 7: 10 Do not o the widow
Mal 3: 5 wages, who o the widows

OPPRESSED (OPPRESS)
Jdg 2: 18 of their groaning under those who o
Ps 9: 9 The Lord is a refuge for the o,
82: 3 the cause of the poor and the o.
146: 7 He upholds the cause of the o
Pr 16: 19 spirit along with the o than to share
31: 5 and deprive all the o of their rights.
Isa 1: 17 Seek justice, encourage the o.
53: 7 He was o and afflicted, yet he did
58: 10 and satisfy the needs of the o,
Zec 10: 2 the people wander like sheep
Lk 4: 18 sight for the blind, to set the o free,

OPPRESSES* (OPPRESS)
Pr 14: 31 Whoever o the poor shows
28: 3 A ruler who o the poor is like
Eze 18: 12 He o the poor and needy.

OPPRESSION (OPPRESS)
Ps 72: 14 He will rescue them from o
119: 134 Redeem me from human o, that I
Isa 53: 8 By o and judgment he was taken
58: 9 "If you do away with the yoke of o,

OPPRESSOR (OPPRESS)
Ps 72: 4 of the needy; may he crush the o.
Isa 51: 13 For where is the wrath of the o?

ORDAINED
Ps 111: 9 he o his covenant forever—
139: 16 All the days o for me were written
Eze 28: 14 as a guardian cherub, for so I o you.
Hab 1: 12 my Rock, have o them to punish.
Mt 21: 16 and infants you have o praise'?"

ORDEAL
1Pe 4: 12 the fiery o that has come on you

ORDER (ORDERLY ORDERS)
Nu 9: 23 They obeyed the LORD's o,
Ps 110: 4 forever, in the o of Melchizedek."
1Co 15: 23 in this o: Christ, the firstfruits;
Heb 5: 10 high priest in the o of Melchizedek.
9: 10 applying until the time of the new o.
Rev 21: 4 for the old o of things has passed

ORDERLY (ORDER)
1Co 14: 40 be done in a fitting and o way.

ORDERS (ORDER)
Mk 1: 27 He even gives o to evil spirits
3: 12 but he gave them strict o not to tell
9: 9 Jesus gave them o not to tell anyone

ORDINARY
Ac 4: 13 that they were unschooled, o men,

ORGIES*
Gal 5: 21 drunkenness, o, and the like.
1Pe 4: 3 lust, drunkenness, o,

ORIGIN (ORIGINATE ORIGINS)
2Pe 1: 21 For prophecy never had its o

ORIGINATE* (ORIGIN)
1Co 14: 36 Or did the word of God o with you?

ORIGINS* (ORIGIN)
Mic 5: 2 over Israel, whose o are from of old,

ORNAMENT* (ORNAMENTED)
Pr 3: 22 life for you, an o to grace your neck.
25: 12 an o of fine gold is the rebuke

ORNAMENTED (ORNAMENT)
Ge 37: 3 and he made a richly o robe for him.

ORPHAN* (ORPHANS)
Ex 22: 22 take advantage of a widow or an o.

ORPHANS* (ORPHAN)
Jn 14: 18 I will not leave you as o;
Jas 1: 27 to look after o and widows in their

OTHERWISE
1Ti 6: 3 If anyone teaches o and does not

OTHNIEL
Nephew of Caleb (Jos 15:15–19; Jdg 1:12–15).
Judge who freed Israel from Aram (Jdg 3:7–11).

OUTBURSTS*
2Co 12: 20 jealousy, o of anger, factions,

OUTCOME
Heb 13: 7 Consider the o of their way of life
1Pe 4: 17 what will the o be for those who do

OUTNUMBER
Ps 139: 18 they would o the grains of sand—

OUTSIDERS*
Col 4: 5 wise in the way you act toward o;
1Th 4: 12 daily life may win the respect of o
1Ti 3: 7 also have a good reputation with o,

OUTSTANDING
SS 5: 10 and ruddy, o among ten thousand.
Ro 13: 8 Let no debt remain o,

OUTSTRETCHED
Ex 6: 6 I will redeem you with an o arm
Dt 4: 34 by a mighty hand and an o arm,
5: 15 with a mighty hand and an o arm.
1Ki 8: 42 your mighty hand and your o arm—
Ps 136: 12 with a mighty hand and o arm;
Jer 27: 5 power and o arm I made the earth
32: 17 by your great power and o arm.
Eze 20: 33 with a mighty hand and an o arm

OUTWEIGHS (WEIGH)
2Co 4: 17 an eternal glory that far o them all.

OUTWIT*
2Co 2: 11 in order that Satan might not o us

OVERAWED* (AWE)
Ps 49: 16 Do not be o when others grow rich,

OVERBEARING*
Tit 1: 7 not o, not quick-tempered, not given

OVERCOME (OVERCOMES)
Mt 16: 18 and the gates of death will not o it.
Mk 9: 24 help me o my unbelief!"
Lk 10: 19 and to o all the power of the enemy;
Jn 1: 5 and the darkness has not o it.
16: 33 But take heart! I have o the world.
Ro 12: 21 Do not be o by evil, but o evil
2Pe 2: 20 are again entangled in it and are o,
1Jn 2: 13 because you have o the evil one.
4: 4 are from God and have o them,
5: 4 is the victory that has o the world,

OVERCOMES* (OVERCOME)
1Jn 5: 4 everyone born of God o the world.
5: 5 Who is it that o the world?

OVERFLOW (OVERFLOWING OVERFLOWS)
Ps 65: 11 and your carts o with abundance.
119:171 May my lips o with praise, for you
La 1: 16 I weep and my eyes o with tears.
Mt 12: 34 the o of the heart the mouth speaks.
Lk 6: 45 the o of the heart the mouth speaks.
Ro 5: 15 Jesus Christ, o to the many!
15: 13 so that you may o with hope
2Co 4: 15 people may cause thanksgiving to o
1Th 3: 12 love increase and o for each other

OVERFLOWING (OVERFLOW)
Pr 3: 10 then your barns will be filled to o,
2Co 8: 2 trial, their o joy and their extreme
9: 12 o in many expressions of thanks
Col 2: 7 taught, and o with thankfulness.

OVERFLOWS* (OVERFLOW)
Ps 23: 5 anoint my head with oil; my cup o.

OVERJOYED* (JOY)
Da 6: 23 The king was o and gave orders
Mt 2: 10 they saw the star, they were o.
Jn 20: 20 the disciples were o when they saw
Ac 12: 14 she was so o she ran back without
1Pe 4: 13 that you may be o when his glory is

OVERLOOK
Pr 19: 11 it is to one's glory to o an offense.

OVERSEER* (OVERSEERS)
Pr 6: 7 It has no commander, no o or ruler,
1Ti 3: 1 to be an o desires a noble task.
3: 2 Now the o is to be above reproach,
Tit 1: 7 Since an o manages God's
1Pe 2: 25 the Shepherd and **O** of your souls.

OVERSEERS (OVERSEER)
Ac 20: 28 the Holy Spirit has made you o.
Php 1: 1 together with the o and deacons:

OVERSHADOW* (OVERSHADOWING)
Lk 1: 35 power of the Most High will o you.

OVERSHADOWING (OVERSHADOW)
Ex 25: 20 upward, the cover with them.
Heb 9: 5 of the Glory, o the atonement cover.

OVERTAKES
Pr 12: 21 No harm o the righteous,

OVERTHROW (OVERTHROWS)
2Th 2: 8 whom the Lord Jesus will o

OVERTHROWS (OVERTHROW)
Pr 13: 6 but wickedness o the sinner.
Isa 44: 25 who o the learning of the wise

OVERWHELMED (OVERWHELMING)
2Sa 22: 5 the torrents of destruction o me.
1Ki 10: 5 temple of the LORD, she was o.
Ps 38: 4 My guilt has o me like a burden too
65: 3 When we were o by sins,
Mt 26: 38 "My soul is o with sorrow
Mk 7: 37 People were o with amazement.
9: 15 they were o with wonder and ran
2Co 2: 7 so that he will not be o by excessive

OVERWHELMING (OVERWHELMED)
Pr 27: 4 Anger is cruel and fury o, but who
Isa 10: 22 has been decreed, o and righteous.
28: 15 When an o scourge sweeps by,

OWE
Ro 13: 7 you o: If you o taxes, pay taxes;
Phm 19 that you o me your very self.

OWNER'S (OWNERSHIP)
Isa 1: 3 the donkey its o manger, but Israel

OWNERSHIP* (OWNER'S)
2Co 1: 22 set his seal of o on us, and put his

OX (OXEN)
Dt 25: 4 Do not muzzle an o while it is
Isa 11: 7 and the lion will eat straw like the o.

Eze 1: 10 lion, and on the left the face of an o;
Lk 13: 15 of you on the Sabbath untie your o
1Co 9: 9 "Do not muzzle an o while it is
1Ti 5: 18 "Do not muzzle an o while it is
Rev 4: 7 The second was like an o, the third

OXEN (OX)
1Ki 19: 20 then left his o and ran after Elijah.
Lk 14: 19 'I have just bought five yoke of o,

PAGAN (PAGANS)
Mt 18: 17 treat them as you would a p or a tax
Lk 12: 30 For the p world runs after all such

PAGANS* (PAGAN)
Isa 2: 6 Philistines and clasp hands with p.
Mt 5: 47 Do not even p do that?
6: 7 do not keep on babbling like p,
6: 32 For the p run after all these things,
1Co 5: 1 of a kind that even p do not tolerate!
10: 20 but the sacrifices of p are offered
12: 2 You know that when you were p,
1Th 4: 5 not in passionate lust like the p,
1Pe 2: 12 such good lives among the p that,
4: 3 the past doing what p choose to do—
3Jn 7 receiving no help from the p.

PAID (PAY)
Isa 40: 2 that her sin has been p for, that she
Zec 11: 12 So they p me thirty pieces of silver.

PAIN (PAINFUL PAINS)
Ge 3: 16 with p you will give birth
Job 6: 10 my joy in unrelenting p—that I had
33: 19 on a bed of p with constant distress
Isa 53: 4 Surely he took up our p and
Jer 4: 19 I writhe in p. Oh, the agony of my
15: 18 Why is my p unending and my
Mt 4: 24 those suffering severe p,
Jn 16: 21 to a child has p because her time has
1Pe 2: 19 up under the p of unjust suffering
Rev 21: 4 death' or mourning or crying or p,

PAINFUL (PAIN)
Ge 3: 17 through p toil you will eat of it all
5: 29 p toil of our hands caused
Job 6: 25 How p are honest words!
Eze 28: 24 neighbors who are p briers
2Co 2: 1 I would not make another p visit
Heb 12: 11 seems pleasant at the time, but p.

PAINS (PAIN)
Ge 3: 16 "I will make your p in childbearing
Mt 24: 8 these are the beginning of birth p.
Ro 8: 22 as in the p of childbirth right
Gal 4: 19 in the p of childbirth until Christ is
1Th 5: 3 as labor p on a pregnant woman,

PAIRS
Ge 7: 8 P of clean and unclean animals,

PALACE (PALACES)
Jer 22: 6 LORD says about the p of the king
22: 13 "Woe to him who builds his p

PALACES (PALACE)
Mt 11: 8 wear fine clothes are in kings' p.
Lk 7: 25 and indulge in luxury are in p.

PALE
Isa 29: 22 no longer will their faces grow p.
Jer 30: 6 labor, every face turned deathly p?
Da 10: 8 my face turned deathly p and I was
Rev 6: 8 and there before me was a p horse!

PALM (PALMS)
Jn 12: 13 They took p branches and went
Rev 7: 9 and were holding p branches in their

PALMS (PALM)
Isa 49: 16 engraved you on the p of my hands;

PAMPERED*
Pr 29: 21 A servant p from youth

PANIC
Dt 20: 3 or give way to p before them.
1Sa 14: 15 It was a p sent by God.
Isa 38: 16 will never be stricken with p.
Eze 7: 7 There is p, not joy,
Zec 14: 13 by the LORD with great p.

PANTS
Ps 42: 1 As the deer p for streams of water,

PARABLE (PARABLES)
Ps 78: 2 I will open my mouth with a p;

PARABLES (PARABLE)
See also JESUS: PARABLES
Mt 13: 35 "I will open my mouth in p, I will

PARADISE*
Lk 23:43 today you will be with me in p."
2Co 12: 4 was caught up to p and heard
Rev 2: 7 tree of life, which is in the p of God.

PARALYZED
Mt 9: 2 Some men brought to him a p man,
Mk 2: 3 bringing to him a p man,
Ac 9:33 who was p and had been bedridden

PARCHED
Ps 143: 6 I thirst for you like a p land.

PARCHMENTS*
2Ti 4:13 and my scrolls, especially the p.

PARDON (PARDONED PARDONS)
2Ch 30:18 LORD, who is good, p everyone
Job 7:21 Why do you not p my offenses
Isa 55: 7 to our God, for he will freely p.

PARDONED* (PARDON)
Nu 14:19 just as you have p them

PARDONS* (PARDON)
Mic 7:18 like you, who p sin and forgives

PARENT (PARENTS PARENT'S)
Pr 17:21 no joy for the p of a godless

PARENT'S* (PARENT)
Pr 13: 1 wise child heeds a p instruction,
   15: 5 A fool spurns a p discipline,

PARENTS (PARENT)
Ex 20: 5 for the sin of the p to the third
Pr 17: 6 p are the pride of their children.
   19:14 and wealth are inherited from p,
   28: 7 gluttons disgrace their p.
Jer 31:29 'The p have eaten sour grapes,
Mal 4: 6 hearts of the children to their p;
Mt 10:21 children will rebel against their p
Lk 1:17 the hearts of the p to their children
   18:29 sisters or p or children for the sake
   21:16 You will be betrayed even by p,
Jn 9: 3 this man nor his p sinned,"
Ro 1:30 doing evil; they disobey their p;
2Co 12:14 not have to save up for their p,
Eph 6: 1 Children, obey your p in the Lord,
Col 3:20 Children, obey your p in everything,
1Ti 5: 4 family and so repaying their p
2Ti 3: 2 disobedient to their p, ungrateful,
Heb 12: 9 all had p who disciplined us

PART
1Co 13:10 what is in p disappears.

PARTAKE*
1Co 10:17 body, for we all p of the one loaf.

PARTIAL* (PARTIALITY)
Pr 18: 5 It is not good to be p to the wicked

PARTIALITY (PARTIAL)
Lev 19:15 do not show p to the poor
Dt 1:17 Do not show p in judging;
   10:17 who shows no p and accepts no
   16:19 Do not pervert justice or show p.
2Ch 19: 7 our God there is no injustice or p
Job 32:21 I will show no p, nor will I flatter
   34:19 who shows no p to princes and does
Pr 24:23 To show p in judging is not good:
Mal 2: 9 but have shown p in matters
Lk 20:21 that you do not show p but teach
1Ti 5:21 to keep these instructions without p,

PARTICIPANTS* (PARTICIPATE)
1Co 10:20 not want you to be p with demons.

PARTICIPATE (PARTICIPANTS PARTICIPATION)
1Pe 4:13 But rejoice inasmuch as you p
2Pe 1: 4 that through them you may p

PARTICIPATION (PARTICIPATE)
1Co 10:16 bread that we break a p in
Php 3:10 and p in his sufferings,

PARTNER (PARTNERS PARTNERSHIP)
Pr 2:17 who has left the p of her youth
Mal 2:14 though she is your p, the wife
1Pe 3: 7 them with respect as the weaker p

PARTNERS (PARTNER)
Eph 5: 7 Therefore do not be p with them.

PARTNERSHIP* (PARTNER)
Php 1: 5 because of your p in the gospel
Phm 1: 6 I pray that your p with us

PASS (PASSED PASSER-BY PASSING)
Ex 12:13 I see the blood, I will p over you.

Ex 33:19 "I will cause all my goodness to p
1Ki 9: 8 All who p by will be appalled
   19:11 for the LORD is about to p by."
Ps 90:10 for they quickly p, and we fly away.
   105:19 till what he foretold came to p,
Isa 31: 5 he will 'p over' it and will rescue
   43: 2 When you p through the waters,
   62:10 P through, p through the gates!
Jer 32: 8 many nations will p by this city
La 1:12 it nothing to you, all you who p by?
Da 7:14 dominion that will not p away,
Am 5:17 for I will p through your midst,"
Mt 24:34 will certainly not p away until all
   24:35 Heaven and earth will p away,
Mk 13:31 Heaven and earth will p away,
Lk 21:33 Heaven and earth will p away,
   21:33 but my words will never p away.
1Co 13: 8 there is knowledge, it will p away.
Jas 1:10 since they will p away like a wild
1Jn 2:17 The world and its desires p away,

PASSED (PASS)
Ge 15:17 appeared and p between the pieces.
Ex 33:22 you with my hand until I have p by.
2Ch 21:20 He p away, to no one's regret,
Ps 57: 1 your wings until the disaster has p.
Lk 10:32 and saw him, p by on the other side.
1Co 15: 3 For what I received I p on to you as
Heb 11:29 faith the people p through the Red

PASSER-BY* (PASS)
Pr 26:10 is one who hires a fool or any p.

PASSING (PASS)
1Co 7:31 world in its present form is p away.
2Co 3:13 seeing the end of what was p away.
1Jn 2: 8 because the darkness is p

PASSION* (PASSIONATE PASSIONS)
Hos 7: 6 Their p smolders all night;
1Co 7: 9 better to marry than to burn with p.

PASSIONATE* (PASSION)
1Th 4: 5 not in p lust like the pagans, who do

PASSIONS* (PASSION)
Ro 7: 5 the sinful p aroused by the law were
Gal 5:24 crucified the sinful nature with its p
Tit 2:12 to ungodliness and worldly p,
   3: 3 and enslaved by all kinds of p

PASSOVER
Ex 12:11 Eat it in haste; it is the LORD's P.
Nu 9: 2 "Have the Israelites celebrate the P
Dt 16: 1 celebrate the P of the LORD your
Jos 5:10 the Israelites celebrated the P.
2Ki 23:21 "Celebrate the P to the LORD
Ezr 6:19 month, the exiles celebrated the P.
Mk 14:12 customary to sacrifice the P lamb,
Lk 22: 1 called the P, was approaching,
1Co 5: 7 For Christ, our P lamb, has been
Heb 11:28 By faith he kept the P

PAST
Isa 43:18 do not dwell on the p.
   65:16 For the p troubles will be forgotten
Ro 15: 4 was written in the p was written
   16:25 the mystery hidden for long ages p,
Eph 3: 9 for ages p was kept hidden in God,
Heb 1: 1 In the p God spoke to our ancestors

PASTORS*
Eph 4:11 the evangelists, the p and teachers,

PASTURE (PASTURES)
Ps 37: 3 dwell in the land and enjoy safe p.
   95: 7 God and we are the people of his p,
   100: 3 are his people, the sheep of his p.
Jer 50: 7 their verdant p, the LORD,
Eze 34:13 I will p them on the mountains
Jn 10: 9 will come in and go out, and find p.

PASTURES (PASTURE)
Ps 23: 2 He makes me lie down in green p,

PATCH
Jer 10: 5 Like a scarecrow in a melon p,
Mk 9:16 "No one sews a p of unshrunk cloth

PATH (PATHS)
Job 16:22 before I take the p of no return.
Ps 16:11 make known to me the p of life;
   27:11 me in a straight p because of my
   119:32 I run in the p of your commands,
   119:105 to my feet and a light for my p.
Pr 2: 9 and just and fair—every good p.
   12:28 along that p is immortality.
   15:10 awaits those who leave the p;
   15:19 the p of the upright is a highway.

Pr 15:24 The p of life leads upward
   21:16 strays from the p of prudence comes
Isa 26: 7 The p of the righteous is level;
Jer 31: 9 on a level p where they will not
Mt 13: 4 some fell along the p, and the birds
Lk 1:79 guide our feet into the p of peace."
2Co 6: 3 no stumbling block in anyone's p,

PATHS (PATH)
Ps 23: 3 He guides me along the right p
   25: 4 ways, LORD, teach me your p.
Pr 1:19 Such are the p of all who go after
   2:13 who have left the straight p to walk
   3: 6 and he will make your p straight.
   4:11 and lead you along straight p.
   4:26 careful thought to the p for your feet
   5:21 and he examines all your p.
   8:20 righteousness, along the p of justice,
   22: 5 In the p of the wicked are snares
Isa 2: 3 so that we may walk in his p."
Jer 6:16 ask for the ancient p, ask where
Mic 4: 2 so that we may walk in his p."
Mt 3: 3 Lord, make straight p for him.'"
Ac 2:28 made known to me the p of life;
Ro 11:33 and his p beyond tracing out!
Heb 12: 1 "Make level p for your feet,"

PATIENCE* (PATIENT)
Pr 19:11 A person's wisdom yields p; it is
   25:15 Through p a ruler can be persuaded,
Ecc 7: 8 and p is better than pride.
Isa 7:13 to try the p of human beings?
   7:13 Will you try the p of my God also?
Ro 2: 4 forbearance and p, not realizing
   9:22 bore with great p the objects of his
2Co 6: 6 understanding, p and kindness;
Gal 5:22 joy, peace, p, kindness, goodness,
Col 1:11 may have great endurance and p,
   3:12 humility, gentleness and p.
1Ti 1:16 might display his immense p as
2Ti 3:10 of life, my purpose, faith, p, love,
   4: 2 with great p and careful instruction.
Heb 6:12 inherit what has been promised.
Jas 5:10 as an example of p in the face
2Pe 3:15 that our Lord's p means salvation,

PATIENT* (PATIENCE PATIENTLY)
Ne 9:30 many years you were p with them.
Job 6:11 What prospects, that I should be p?
Pr 14:29 Those who are p have great
   15:18 but those who are p calm a quarrel.
   16:32 Better a p person than a warrior,
Mt 18:26 'Be p with me,' he begged, 'and I
   18:29 and begged him, 'Be p with me,
Ro 12:12 Be joyful in hope, p in affliction,
1Co 13: 4 Love is p, love is kind. It does not
2Co 1: 6 produces in you p endurance
Eph 4: 2 be p, bearing with one another
1Th 5:14 help the weak, be p with everyone.
Jas 5: 7 Be p, then, brothers and sisters,
   5: 8 You too, be p and stand firm,
2Pe 3: 9 Instead he is p with you,
Rev 1: 9 p endurance that are ours in Jesus,
   13:10 This calls for p endurance
   14:12 This calls for p endurance

PATIENTLY* (PATIENT)
Ps 37: 7 the LORD and wait p for him;
   40: 1 I waited p for the LORD;
Isa 38:13 I waited p till dawn, but like a lion
Hab 3:16 Yet I will wait p for the day
Ac 26: 3 I beg you to listen to me p.
Ro 8:25 we do not yet have, we wait for it p.
Heb 6:15 And so after waiting p,
1Pe 3:20 ago when God waited p in the days
Jas 5: 7 p waiting for the autumn and spring
Rev 3:10 have kept my command to endure p,

PATTERN
Ex 25:40 them according to the p shown you
Ro 5:14 who is a p of the one to come.
   12: 2 not conform to the p of this world,
2Ti 1:13 keep as the p of sound teaching,
Heb 8: 5 according to the p shown you

PAUL
Also called Saul (Ac 13:9). Pharisee from Tarsus (Ac 9:11; Php 3:5). Apostle (Gal 1). At stoning of Stephen (Ac 8:1). Persecuted Church (Ac 9:1–2; Gal 1:13). Vision of Jesus on road to Damascus (Ac 9:4–9; 26:12–18). In Arabia (Gal 1:17). Preached in Damascus; escaped death through the wall in a basket (Ac 9:19–25). In Jerusalem; sent back to Tarsus (Ac 9:26–30).

Brought to Antioch by Barnabas (Ac 11:22–26).

First missionary journey to Cyprus and Galatia (Ac 13–14). Stoned at Lystra (Ac 14:19–20). At Jerusalem council (Ac 15). Split with Barnabas over Mark (Ac 15:36–41).

Second missionary journey with Silas (Ac 16–20). Called to Macedonia (Ac 16:6–10). Freed from prison in Philippi (Ac 16:16–40). In Thessalonica (Ac 17:1–9). Speech in Athens (Ac 17:16–33). In Corinth (Ac 18). In Ephesus (Ac 19). Return to Jerusalem (Ac 20). Farewell to Ephesian elders (Ac 20:13–38). Arrival in Jerusalem (Ac 21:1–26). Arrested (Ac 21:27–36). Addressed crowds (Ac 22), Sanhedrin (Ac 23:1–11). Transferred to Caesarea (Ac 23:12–35). Trial before Felix (Ac 24), Festus (Ac 25:1–12). Before Agrippa (Ac 25:13–26:32). Voyage to Rome; shipwreck (Ac 27). Arrival in Rome (Ac 28).

Epistles: Romans, 1 and 2 Corinthians, Galatians, Ephesians, Philippians, Colossians, 1 and 2 Thessalonians, 1 and 2 Timothy, Titus, Philemon.

PAVEMENT
Jn 19: 13 seat at a place known as the Stone P

PAY (PAID PAYMENT PAYS REPAID REPAY REPAYING)
Lev 26: 43 They will p for their sins because
Dt 7: 12 If you p attention to these laws
Pr 4: 1 p attention and gain understanding.
4: 20 My son, p attention to what I say;
5: 1 My son, p attention to my wisdom,
6: 31 he must p sevenfold, though it costs
19: 19 hot-tempered must p the penalty;
22: 17 P attention and turn your ear
24: 29 I'll p them back for what they did."
Eze 40: 4 p attention to everything I am going
Zec 11: 12 "If you think it best, give me my p;
Mt 20: 2 He agreed to p them a denarius
22: 16 because you p no attention to who
22: 17 Is it right to p the imperial tax
Lk 3: 14 be content with your p."
19: 8 I will p back four times
Ro 13: 6 This is also why you p taxes,
2Pe 1: 19 you do well to p attention to it,

PAYMENT (PAY)
Ps 49: 8 a life is costly, no p is ever enough—
Php 4: 18 I have received full p and have

PAYS (PAY)
Pr 17: 13 the house of one who p back evil
1Th 5: 15 sure that nobody p back wrong

PEACE (PEACEABLE PEACEFUL PEACEMAKERS)
Lev 26: 6 " 'I will grant p in the land,
Nu 6: 26 toward you and give you p.' '
25: 12 him I am making my covenant of p
Dt 20: 10 a city, make its people an offer of p.
Jdg 3: 11 So the land had p for forty years,
3: 30 and the land had p for eighty years.
5: 31 Then the land had p forty years.
6: 24 there and called it The Lord Is P.
8: 28 lifetime, the land had p forty years.
1Sa 7: 14 And there was p between Israel
2Sa 10: 19 they made p with the Israelites
1Ki 2: 33 there be the Lord's p forever."
22: 44 was also at p with the king of Israel.
2Ki 9: 17 and ask, 'Do you come in p?' "
1Ch 19: 19 they made p with David and became
22: 9 I will grant Israel p and quiet during
2Ch 14: 1 his days the country was at p for ten
20: 30 kingdom of Jehoshaphat was at p,
Job 3: 26 I have no p, no quietness; I have no
22: 21 to God and be at p with him;
Ps 29: 11 Lord blesses his people with p.
34: 14 and do good; seek p and pursue it.
37: 11 the land and enjoy p and prosperity.
37: 37 a future awaits those who seek p.
85: 10 righteousness and p kiss each other.
119:165 Great p have those who love your
120: 7 I am for p; but when I speak,
122: 6 Pray for the p of Jerusalem:
147: 14 He grants p to your borders
Pr 12: 20 but those who promote p have joy.
14: 30 A heart at p gives life to the body,
16: 7 their enemies to make p with them.
17: 1 Better a dry crust with p and quiet
Ecc 3: 8 a time for war and a time for p.
Isa 9: 6 Everlasting Father, Prince of P.
9: 7 All the lands are at rest and at p;
26: 3 in perfect p those whose minds are
32: 17 fruit of that righteousness will be p
48: 18 your p would have been like a river,
48: 22 "There is no p," says the Lord.
52: 7 who proclaim p, who bring good

Isa 53: 5 that brought us p was on him,
54: 10 nor my covenant of p be removed,"
55: 12 go out in joy and be led forth in p;
57: 2 who walk uprightly enter into p;
57: 19 P, p, to those far and near,"
59: 8 The way of p they do not know;
Jer 6: 14 'P, p,' they say, when there is no p.
8: 11 "P, p," they say, when there is no
30: 10 Jacob will again have p
46: 27 Jacob will again have p
Eze 13: 10 saying, "P," when there is no p,
34: 25 " 'I will make a covenant of p
37: 26 I will make a covenant of p
Mic 5: 5 he will be our p when the Assyrians
Zec 8: 19 Therefore love truth and p."
9: 10 He will proclaim p to the nations.
Mal 2: 5 a covenant of life and p, and I gave
2: 6 He walked with me in p
Mt 10: 34 I did not come to bring p,
Mk 9: 50 and be at p with each other."
Lk 1: 79 to guide our feet into the path of p."
2: 14 and on earth p to those on whom his
19: 38 "P in heaven and glory
Jn 14: 27 P I leave with you; my p I give you.
16: 33 so that in me you may have p.
Ro 1: 7 and p to you from God our Father
2: 10 and p for everyone who does good;
5: 1 we have p with God through our
8: 6 controlled by the Spirit is life and p.
12: 18 on you, live at p with everyone.
14: 19 every effort to do what leads to p
1Co 7: 15 God has called us to live in p.
14: 33 is not a God of disorder but of p—
2Co 13: 11 another, be of one mind, live in p.
Gal 5: 22 of the Spirit is love, joy, p, patience,
Eph 2: 14 For he himself is our p, who has
2: 15 out of the two, thus making p,
2: 17 away and p to those who were near.
6: 15 that comes from the gospel of p.
Php 4: 7 And the p of God, which transcends
Col 1: 20 by making p through his blood,
3: 15 Let the p of Christ rule in your
3: 15 of one body you were called to p.
1Th 5: 3 people are saying, "P and safety,"
5: 13 Live in p with each other.
5: 23 the God of p, sanctify you through
2Th 3: 16 the Lord of p himself give you p
2Ti 2: 22 love and p, along with those who
Heb 7: 2 of Salem" means "king of p."
12: 11 p for those who have been trained
12: 14 effort to live in p with everyone
13: 20 Now may the God of p,
1Pe 3: 11 and do good; seek p and pursue it.
2Pe 3: 14 blameless and at p with him.
Rev 6: 4 given power to take p from the earth

PEACEABLE* (PEACE)
Tit 3: 2 no one, to be p and considerate,

PEACEFUL (PEACE)
1Ti 2: 2 that we may live p and quiet lives

PEACE-LOVING*
Jas 3: 17 then p, considerate, submissive,

PEACEMAKERS* (PEACE)
Mt 5: 9 Blessed are the p, for they will be
Jas 3: 18 P who sow in peace reap a harvest

PEARL* (PEARLS)
Rev 21: 21 pearls, each gate made of a single p.

PEARLS (PEARL)
Mt 7: 6 do not throw your p to pigs.
13: 45 is like a merchant looking for fine p.
1Ti 2: 9 or gold or p or expensive clothes,
Rev 21: 21 The twelve gates were twelve p,

PEDDLE*
2Co 2: 17 we do not p the word of God

PEG
Jdg 4: 21 She drove the p through his temple

PEKAH
King of Israel (2Ki 15:25–31; Isa 7:1).

PEKAHIAH*
Son of Menahem; king of Israel (2Ki 15:22–26).

PEN
Ps 45: 1 my tongue is the p of a skillful
Mt 5: 18 not the least stroke of a p,
Jn 10: 1 who does not enter the sheep p

PENETRATES*
Heb 4: 12 it p even to dividing soul and spirit,

PENNIES* (PENNY)
Lk 12: 6 not five sparrows sold for two p?

PENNY* (PENNIES)
Mt 5: 26 out until you have paid the last p.
10: 29 Are not two sparrows sold for a p?
Mk 12: 42 coins, worth only a fraction of a p.
Lk 12: 59 out until you have paid the last p."

PENTECOST*
Ac 2: 1 When the day of P came, they were
20: 16 if possible, by the day of P.
1Co 16: 8 I will stay on at Ephesus until P,

PEOPLE (PEOPLE'S PEOPLES)
Ge 11: 6 said, "If as one p speaking the same
Ex 5: 1 'Let my p go, so that they may hold
6: 7 I will take you as my own p, and I
8: 23 between my p and your p.
15: 13 will lead the p you have redeemed.
19: 8 The p all responded together,
24: 3 told the p all the Lord's words
32: 1 When the p saw that Moses was so
32: 9 "and they are a stiff-necked p.
33: 13 that this nation is your p."
Lev 4: 3 atonement for yourself and the p;
16: 24 and the burnt offering for the p,
26: 12 be your God, and you will be my p.
Nu 11: 11 put the burden of all these p on me?
14: 11 "How long will these p treat me
14: 19 forgive the sin of these p, just as
22: 5 "A p has come out of Egypt;
Dt 4: 6 is a wise and understanding p."
4: 20 to be the p of his inheritance, as you
5: 28 "I have heard what this p said
8: 3 you are a p holy to the Lord your
8: 3 p do not live on bread alone
26: 18 declared this day that you are his p,
31: 7 must go with this p into the land
31: 16 and these p will soon prostitute
32: 9 For the Lord's portion is his p,
32: 43 make atonement for his land and p.
33: 29 like you, a p saved by the Lord?
Jos 1: 6 because you will lead these p
24: 24 And the p said to Joshua, "We will
Jdg 2: 7 The p served the Lord
Ru 1: 16 Your p will be my p and your God
1: 16 to all that the p are saying to you;
1Sa 12: 22 the Lord will not reject his p,
2Sa 5: 2 'You will shepherd my p Israel,
7: 10 will provide a place for my p Israel
1Ki 3: 8 here among the p you have chosen,
8: 30 and of your p Israel when they pray
8: 56 to his p Israel just as he promised.
18: 39 When all the p saw this, they fell
2Ki 23: 3 all the p pledged themselves
1Ch 17: 21 went out to redeem a p for himself,
29: 17 how willingly your p who are here
2Ch 2: 11 "Because the Lord loves his p,
7: 5 and all the p dedicated the temple
7: 14 if my p, who are called by my
30: 6 "P of Israel, return to the Lord,
36: 16 Lord was aroused against his p
Ezr 2: 1 Now these are the p of the province
3: 1 the p assembled with one accord
Ne 1: 10 "They are your servants and your p,
4: 6 for the p worked with all their heart.
8: 1 all the p assembled with one accord
Est 3: 6 a way to destroy all Mordecai's p,
Job 12: 2 "Doubtless you are the p,
Ps 29: 11 The Lord gives strength to his p;
30: 4 you his faithful p;
31: 23 all his faithful p!
33: 12 the p he chose for his inheritance.
50: 4 the earth, that he may judge his p:
53: 6 When God restores his p, let Jacob
81: 13 "If my p would only listen to me,
94: 14 For the Lord will not reject his p;
95: 7 God and we are the p of his pasture,
95: 10 said, 'They are a p whose hearts are
125: 2 Lord surrounds his p both now
133: 1 God's p live together in unity!
135: 14 For the Lord will vindicate his p
144: 15 blessed is the p whose God is
149: 1 assembly of his faithful p.
149: 5 faithful p rejoice in this honor
Pr 14: 34 a nation, but sin condemns any p.
29: 2 the righteous thrive, the p rejoice;
29: 18 is no revelation, p cast off restraint;
Isa 1: 3 not know, my p do not understand."
1: 4 nation, a p whose guilt is great,
5: 13 Therefore my p will go into exile
6: 10 Make the heart of this p calloused;

Isa 9: 2 The **p** walking in darkness have
11: 12 he will assemble the scattered **p**
19: 25 "Blessed be Egypt my **p,**
29: 13 "These **p** come near to me
40: 1 comfort my **p,** says your God.
40: 5 all **p** will see it together.
40: 7 Surely the **p** are grass.
42: 6 make you to be a covenant for the **p**
49: 13 For the LORD comforts his **p**
51: 4 "Listen to me, my **p;** hear me,
52: 6 Therefore my **p** will know my
53: 8 of my **p** he was punished.
60: 21 will all your **p** be righteous and they
62: 12 They will be called the Holy **P,**
65: 23 for they will be a **p** blessed
Jer 2: 11 my **p** have exchanged their glorious
2: 13 "My **p** have committed two sins:
2: 32 Yet my **p** have forgotten me,
4: 22 "My **p** are fools; they do not know
5: 14 "Because the **p** have spoken these
5: 31 authority, and my **p** love it this way.
7: 16 not pray for this **p** nor offer any plea
7: 23 be your God and you will be my **p.**
18: 15 Yet my **p** have forgotten me;
30: 3 'when I will bring my **p** Israel
Eze 13: 23 I will save my **p** from your hands.
36: 8 branches and fruit for my **p** Israel,
36: 20 you will be my **p,** and I will give
36: 38 cities be filled with flocks of **p.**
37: 13 you, my **p,** will know that I am
38: 14 day, when my **p** Israel are living
39: 7 my holy name among my **p** Israel.
Da 7: 18 But the holy **p** of the Most High
7: 27 over to the holy **p** of the Most High.
8: 24 the mighty warriors, the holy **p.**
9: 19 city and your **p** bear your Name."
9: 24 'sevens' are decreed for your **p**
9: 26 The **p** of the ruler who will come
10: 14 will happen to your **p** in the future,
11: 32 but the **p** who know their God will
12: 1 great prince who protects your **p,**
Hos 1: 10 'You are not my **p,'** they will be
2: 23 called 'My **p.'** 'You are my **p,'**
4: 14 a **p** without understanding will
2: 18 for his land and took pity on his **p.**
Joel 3: 16 LORD will be a refuge for his **p,**
Am 9: 14 I will bring my **p** Israel back
Mic 6: 2 the LORD has a case against his **p;**
7: 14 Shepherd your **p** with your staff,
Hag 1: 12 remnant of the **p** obeyed the voice
Zec 2: 11 in that day and will become my **p.**
2: 13 Be still before the LORD, all **p,**
8: 7 "I will save my **p**
13: 9 'They are my **p,'** and they will say,
Mt 4: 4 'P do not live on bread alone,'
4: 19 send you out to fish for **p."**
12: 31 **p** will be forgiven every sin and
12: 36 that **p** will have to give account
23: 5 "Everything they do is done for **p** to see:
Mk 5: 19 "Go home to your own **p** and
7: 6 " 'These **p** honor me with their
8: 27 asked them, "Who do **p** say I am?"
Lk 1: 17 to make ready a **p** prepared
1: 68 because he has come to his **p**
2: 10 of great joy that will be for all the **p.**
6: 8 all **p** will see God's salvation.' "
4: 4 'P do not live on bread alone.' "
6: 22 Blessed are you when **p** hate you,
21: 23 in the land and wrath against this **p.**
Jn 1: 4 life was the light of all **p.**
2: 24 for he knew all **p.**
3: 19 **p** loved darkness instead of light
11: 50 one man die for the **p** than
12: 32 will draw all **p** to myself."
18: 14 be good if one man died for the **p.**
Ac 15: 14 to choose a **p** for his name
18: 10 because I have many **p** in this city."
Ro 5: 12 death came to all **p,**
8: 27 the Spirit intercedes for God's **p**
9: 3 from Christ for the sake of my **p,**
9: 25 call them 'my **p'** who are not my **p;**
11: 1 I ask then: Did God reject his **p?**
15: 10 you Gentiles, with his **p."**
1Co 6: 2 the Lord's **p** will judge the world?
9: 22 become all things to all **p**
2Co 5: 11 we try to persuade **p.**
6: 16 God, and they will be my **p."**
11: 26 in danger from my **p,**
Eph 1: 15 your love for all his **p,**
1: 18 his glorious inheritance in his **p,**
4: 8 gave gifts to his **p."**
5: 3 improper for the Lord's **p.**

Eph 6: 18 praying for all the Lord's **p.**
1Th 5: 26 Greet all God's **p** with a holy kiss.
1Ti 2: 4 who wants all **p** to be saved
2: 6 gave himself as a ransom for all **p.**
4: 10 the Savior of all **p,**
2Ti 2: 2 entrust to reliable **p**
3: 17 so that all God's **p**
Tit 2: 11 that offers salvation to all **p**
2: 14 himself a **p** that are his very own,
Phm : 7 the hearts of the Lord's **p.**
Heb 2: 17 atonement for the sins of the **p.**
4: 9 a Sabbath-rest for the **p** of God;
5: 1 is selected from among the **p**
5: 3 as well as for the sins of the **p.**
9: 27 as **p** are destined to die once,
10: 30 again, "The Lord will judge his **p."**
11: 25 along with the **p** of God rather than
13: 12 to make the **p** holy through his own
1Pe 2: 9 But you are a chosen **p,** a royal
2: 10 Once you were not a **p,** but now you are the **p** of God;
2: 1 also false prophets among the **p,**
2Pe 3: 11 what kind of **p** ought you to be?
Rev 5: 8 which are the prayers of God's **p.**
18: 4 my **p,'** so that you will not share
19: 8 righteous acts of God's **p.)**
21: 3 dwelling place is now among the **p,**
21: 3 They will be his **p,** and God himself

PEOPLE'S (PEOPLE)

Isa 35: 8 remove his **p** disgrace
Jer 10: 23 that **p** lives are not their own;

PEOPLES (PEOPLE)

Ge 17: 16 kings of **p** will come from her.
25: 23 and two **p** from within you will be
35: 29 serve you and **p** bow down to you.
28: 3 until you become a community of **p.**
48: 4 I will make you a community of **p,**
Dt 14: 2 of all the **p** on the face of the earth,
28: 10 all the **p** on earth will see that you
32: 8 up boundaries for the **p** according
Jos 4: 24 all the **p** of the earth might know
1Ki 8: 43 all the **p** of the earth may know your
2Ch 7: 20 an object of ridicule among all **p.**
Ps 9: 8 and judges the **p** with equity.
67: 5 may all the **p** praise you.
87: 6 will write in the register of the **p:**
96: 10 he will judge the **p** with equity.
Isa 2: 4 and will settle disputes for many **p.**
17: 12 Woe to the **p** who roar—
25: 6 prepare a feast of rich food for all **p,**
34: 1 pay attention, you **p!**
55: 4 I have made him a witness to the **p,**
Jer 10: 3 the practices of the **p** are worthless;
Da 7: 14 **p** of every language worshiped him.
Mic 4: 1 the hills, and **p** stream to it.
4: 3 He will judge between many **p**
5: 7 the midst of many **p** like dew
Zep 3: 9 "Then I will purify the lips of the **p,**
3: 20 praise among all the **p** of the earth
Zec 8: 20 "Many **p** and the inhabitants
12: 2 sends all the surrounding **p** reeling.
Rev 10: 11 must prophesy again about many **p,**
17: 15 the prostitute sits, are **p,** multitudes,

PEOR

Nu 25: 3 yoked themselves to the Baal of **P.**
Dt 4: 3 who followed the Baal of **P,**

PERCEIVE (PERCEIVING)

Ps 139: 2 you **p** my thoughts from afar.
Pr 24: 12 not he who weighs the heart **p** it?

PERCEIVING* (PERCEIVE)

Isa 6: 9 be ever seeing, but never.'
Mt 13: 14 you will be ever seeing but never a,
Mk 4: 12 may be ever seeing but never **p,**
Ac 28: 26 will be ever seeing but never **p."**

PERFECT* (PERFECTER PERFECTING PERFECTION)

Dt 32: 4 his works are **p,** and all his ways are
2Sa 22: 31 "As for God, his way is **p;**
Job 36: 4 one who has **p** knowledge is
37: 16 of him who has **p** knowledge?
Ps 18: 30 As for God, his way is **p:**
19: 7 The law of the LORD is **p,**
50: 2 From Zion, **p** in beauty, God shines
64: 6 say, "We have devised a **p** plan!"
SS 6: 9 but my dove, my **p** one, is unique,
Isa 25: 1 for in **p** faithfulness you have done
26: 3 in **p** peace those whose minds are
Eze 16: 14 had given you made your beauty **p,**
27: 3 say, Tyre, "I am **p** in beauty."

Eze 28: 12 full of wisdom and **p** in beauty.
Mt 5: 48 Be **p,** therefore, as your heavenly Father is **p.**
19: 21 answered, "If you want to be **p,** go,
Ro 12: 2 his good, pleasing and **p** will.
2Co 12: 9 my power is made **p** in weakness."
Col 3: 14 binds them all together in **p** unity.
Heb 2: 10 of their salvation **p** through what he
5: 9 once made **p,** he became the source
7: 19 (for the law made nothing **p),**
7: 28 Son, who has been made **p** forever.
9: 11 more **p** tabernacle that is not made
10: 1 make **p** those who draw near
10: 14 he has made **p** forever those who
11: 40 with us would they be made **p.**
12: 23 the spirits of the righteous made **p,**
Jas 1: 17 good and **p** gift is from above,
1: 25 who look intently into the **p** law
3: 2 never at fault in what they say are **p,**
1Jn 4: 18 But **p** love drives out fear,
4: 18 The one who fears is not made **p**

PERFECTER* (PERFECT)

Heb 12: 2 on Jesus, the pioneer and **p** of faith.

PERFECTING* (PERFECT)

2Co 7: 1 **p** holiness out of reverence for God.

PERFECTION* (PERFECT)

Ps 119: 96 To all **p** I see a limit, but your
La 2: 15 city that was called the **p** of beauty,
Eze 27: 4 builders brought your beauty to **p.**
27: 11 they brought your beauty to **p.**
28: 12 " 'You were the seal of **p,**
43: 10 Let them consider its **p,**
Heb 7: 11 **p** could have been attained through

PERFORM (PERFORMED PERFORMS)

Ex 3: 20 wonders that I will **p** among them.
2Sa 7: 23 to **p** great and awesome wonders
Jn 3: 2 For no one could **p** the signs you are

PERFORMED (PERFORM)

Mt 11: 21 miracles that were **p** in you
Jn 10: 41 "Though John never **p** a sign,

PERFORMS (PERFORM)

Ps 77: 14 You are the God who **p** miracles;

PERFUME

Ecc 7: 1 A good name is better than fine **p,**
SS 1: 3 your name is like **p** poured out.
Mk 14: 3 an alabaster jar of very expensive **p,**

PERIL

2Co 1: 10 delivered us from such a deadly **p,**

PERISH (PERISHABLE PERISHED PERISHES PERISHING)

Ge 6: 17 Everything on earth will **p.**
Est 4: 16 And if I **p,** I **p."**
Ps 37: 20 But the wicked will **p:**
73: 27 Those who are far from you will **p;**
102: 26 They will **p,** but you remain;
Pr 11: 10 when the wicked **p,** there are shouts
19: 9 and whoever pours out lies will **p.**
21: 28 Those who give false witness will **p,**
28: 28 but when the wicked **p,**
Isa 1: 28 who forsake the LORD will **p.**
29: 14 the wisdom of the wise will **p,**
60: 12 that will not serve you will **p;**
Zec 11: 9 the dying die, and the perishing **p.**
Mt 18: 14 any of these little ones should **p.**
Lk 13: 3 you repent, you too will all **p.**
13: 5 you repent, you too will all **p."**
21: 18 But not a hair of your head will **p.**
Jn 3: 16 whoever believes in him shall not **p**
10: 28 eternal life, and they shall never **p;**
Ro 2: 12 law will also **p** apart from the law,
Col 2: 22 that are all destined to **p** with use,
2Th 2: 10 They **p** because they refused to love
Heb 1: 11 They will **p,** but you remain;
1Pe 1: 4 into an inheritance that can never **p,**
2Pe 3: 9 you, not wanting anyone to **p,**

PERISHABLE (PERISH)

1Co 15: 42 The body that is sown is **p,** it is
1Pe 1: 18 was not with **p** things such as silver
1: 23 not of **p** seed, but of imperishable,

PERISHED (PERISH)

Ps 119: 92 I would have **p** in my affliction.

PERISHES (PERISH)

Job 8: 13 so **p** the hope of the godless.
1Pe 1: 7 which **p** even though refined

PERISHING (PERISH)

1Co 1: 18 is foolishness to those who are **p,**

2Co 2: 15   being saved and those who are p.
        4: 3   it is veiled to those who are p.

PERJURERS* (PERJURY)
Mal 3: 5   adulterers and p, against those who
1Ti 1: 10   for slave traders and liars and p.

PERJURY* (PERJURERS)
Jer 7: 9   commit adultery and p, burn incense

PERMANENT
Heb 7: 24   lives forever, he has a p priesthood.

PERMIT (PERMITTED)
Hos 5: 4   "Their deeds do not p them
1Ti 2: 12   I do not p a woman to teach

PERMITTED (PERMIT)
Mt 19: 8   "Moses p you to divorce your
2Co 12: 4   things, things that no one is p to tell.

PERSECUTE (PERSECUTED PERSECUTION PERSECUTIONS)
Mt   5: 11   p you and falsely say all kinds
       5: 44   and pray for those who p you,
Jn 15: 20   persecuted me, they will p you also.
Ac   9: 4   "Saul, Saul, why do you p me?"
Ro 12: 14   Bless those who p you; bless and do

PERSECUTED (PERSECUTE)
Ps 119: 86   for I am being p without cause.
Mt   5: 10   Blessed are those who are p because
       5: 12   same way they p the prophets who
Jn 15: 20   If they p me, they will persecute
1Co 4: 12   when we are p, we endure it;
     15: 9   because I p the church of God.
2Co 4: 9   p, but not abandoned;
1Th 3: 4   kept telling you that we would be p.
2Ti 3: 12   godly life in Christ Jesus will be p,
Heb 11: 37   destitute, p and mistreated—

PERSECUTION (PERSECUTE)
Mt 13: 21   or p comes because of the word,
Ro   8: 35   trouble or hardship or p or famine

PERSECUTIONS* (PERSECUTE)
Mk 10: 30   along with p—and in the age
2Co 12: 10   in hardships, in p, in difficulties.
2Th 1: 4   faith in all the p and trials you are
2Ti 3: 11   p, sufferings—what kinds of things
       3: 11   Iconium and Lystra, the p I endured.

PERSEVERANCE* (PERSEVERE)
Ro   5: 3   we know that suffering produces p;
       5: 4   p, character; and character, hope.
2Th 1: 4   churches we boast about your p
       3: 5   into God's love and Christ's p.
Heb 12: 1   let us run with p the race marked
Jas   1: 3   the testing of your faith produces p.
       1: 4   Let p finish its work so that your
       5: 11   You have heard of Job's p and have
2Pe 1: 6   and to self-control, p; and to p, godliness;
Rev 2: 2   deeds, your hard work and your p.
       2: 19   your service and p, and that you are

PERSEVERE* (PERSEVERANCE PERSEVERED PERSEVERES PERSEVERING)
1Ti 4: 16   P in them, because if you do,
Heb 10: 36   You need to p so that when you
Jas 1: 12   Blessed are those who p under trial,

PERSEVERED* (PERSEVERE)
2Co 12: 12   I p in demonstrating among you
Heb 11: 27   he p because he saw him who is
Jas 5: 11   count as blessed those who have p.
Rev 3: 1   You have p and have endured

PERSEVERES* (PERSEVERE)
1Co 13: 7   trusts, always hopes, always p.

PERSEVERING* (PERSEVERE)
Lk   8: 15   retain it, and by p produce a crop.

PERSIANS
Da   6: 15   law of the Medes and P no decree

PERSISTENCE*
Ro   2: 7   those who by p in doing good seek

PERSUADE (PERSUADED PERSUASIVE)
Ac 18: 4   trying to p Jews and Greeks.
     28: 23   he tried to p them about Jesus.
2Co 5: 11   to fear the Lord, we try to p people.

PERSUADED (PERSUADE)
Ro   4: 21   being fully p that God had power

PERSUASIVE (PERSUADE)
1Co 2: 4   were not with wise and p words,

PERVERSION* (PERVERT)
Lev 18: 23   sexual relations with it; that is a p.

Lev 20: 12   What they have done is a p;
Jude   : 7   up to sexual immorality and p.

PERVERT (PERVERSION PERVERTED)
Ex 23: 2   do not p justice by siding
Dt 16: 19   Do not p justice or show partiality.
Job 34: 12   that the Almighty would p justice.
Pr 17: 23   in secret to p the course of justice.
Gal 1: 7   are trying to p the gospel of Christ.

PERVERTED (PERVERT)
1Sa 8: 3   and accepted bribes and p justice.

PESTILENCE (PESTILENCES)
Ps 91: 6   nor the p that stalks in the darkness,

PESTILENCES* (PESTILENCE)
Lk 21: 11   famines and p in various places,

PETER
     Apostle, brother of Andrew, also called Simon (Mt 10:2; Mk 3:16; Lk 6:14; Ac 1:13), and Cephas (Jn 1:42). Confession of Christ (Mt 16:13–20; Mk 8:27–30; Lk 9:18–27). At transfiguration (Mt 17:1–8; Mk 9:2–8; Lk 9:28–36; 2Pe 1:16–18). Caught fish with coin (Mt 17:24–27). Denial of Jesus predicted (Mt 26:31–35; Mk 14:27–31; Lk 22:31–34; Jn 13:31–38). Denied Jesus (Mt 26:69–75; Mk 14:66–72; Lk 22:54–62; Jn 18:15–27). Commissioned by Jesus to shepherd his flock (Jn 21:15–23).
     Speech at Pentecost (Ac 2). Healed beggar (Ac 3:1–10). Speech at temple (Ac 3:11–26), before Sanhedrin (Ac 4:1–22). In Samaria (Ac 8:14–25). Sent by vision to Cornelius (Ac 10). Announced salvation of Gentiles in Jerusalem (Ac 11; 15). Freed from prison (Ac 12). Inconsistency at Antioch (Gal 2:11–21). At Jerusalem Council (Ac 15).
     Epistles: 1–2 Peter.

PETITION (PETITIONS)
Php 4: 6   by prayer and p, with thanksgiving,

PETITIONS (PETITION)
Heb 5: 7   up prayers and p with fervent cries

PHANTOM*
Ps 39: 6   everyone goes around like a mere p;

PHARAOH (PHARAOH'S)
Ge 12: 15   they praised her to P, and she was
     41: 14   So P sent for Joseph, and he was
Ex 14: 4   will gain glory for myself through P
     14: 17   I will gain glory through P and all

PHARAOH'S (PHARAOH)
Ex   7: 3   But I will harden P heart,

PHARISEE (PHARISEES)
Jn   3: 1   Now there was a P,
Ac 23: 6   I am a P, descended from Pharisees.
Php 3: 5   in regard to the law, a P;

PHARISEES (PHARISEE)
Mt   5: 20   surpasses that of the P
     16: 6   guard against the yeast of the P
     23: 13   teachers of the law and P,

PHILADELPHIA
Rev 3: 7   the angel of the church in P write:

PHILEMON*
Phm   : 1   To P our dear friend and fellow

PHILIP
     1. Apostle (Mt 10:3; Mk 3:18; Lk 6:14; Jn 1:43–48; 14:8; Ac 1:13).
     2. Deacon (Ac 6:1–7); evangelist in Samaria (Ac 8:4–25), to Ethiopian (Ac 8:26–40).

PHILIPPI
Ac 16: 12   From there we traveled to P,
Php 1: 1   holy people in Christ Jesus at P,

PHILISTINE (PHILISTINES)
Jos 13: 3   held by the five P rulers in Gaza,
1Sa 14: 1   let's go over to the P outpost
     17: 26   Who is this uncircumcised P that he
     17: 37   rescue me from the hand of this P."

PHILISTINES (PHILISTINE)
Jdg 10: 7   He sold them into the hands of the P
     13: 1   the hands of the P for forty years.
     16: 5   The rulers of the P went to her
1Sa 4: 1   at Ebenezer, and the P at Aphek.
       5: 8   called together all the rulers of the P
     13: 23   Now a detachment of P had gone
     17: 1   Now the P gathered their forces
     23: 1   the P are fighting against Keilah
     27: 1   do is to escape to the land of the P.
     31: 1   Now the P fought against Israel;
2Sa 5: 17   When the P heard that David had

2Sa 8: 1   David defeated the P and subdued
     21: 15   there was a battle between the P
2Ki 18: 8   he defeated the P, as far as Gaza
Am   1: 8   till the last of the P are dead,"

PHILOSOPHER* (PHILOSOPHY)
1Co 1: 20   Where is the p of this age?

PHILOSOPHY* (PHILOSOPHER)
Col 2: 8   through hollow and deceptive p,

PHINEHAS
Nu 25: 7   When P son of Eleazar, the son
Ps 106: 30   But P stood up and intervened,

PHOEBE*
Ro 16: 1   I commend to you our sister P,

PHYLACTERIES*
Mt 23: 5   They make their p wide

PHYSICAL*
Da   1: 4   young men without any p defect,
Ro   2: 28   circumcision merely outward and p,
Col 1: 22   by Christ's p body through death
1Ti 4: 8   For p training is of some value,
Jas 2: 16   does nothing about their p needs,

PICK (PICKED)
Mk 16: 18   they will p up snakes

PICKED (PICK)
Lk 14: 7   noticed how the guests p the places
Jn   5: 9   he p up his mat and walked.

PIECE (PIECES)
Jn 19: 23   woven in one p from top to bottom.

PIECES (PIECE)
Ge 15: 17   appeared and passed between the p.
Jer 34: 18   two and then walked between its p.
Zec 11: 12   So they paid me thirty p of silver.
Mt 14: 20   of broken p that were left over.

PIERCE (PIERCED)
Ex 21: 6   doorpost and p his ear with an awl.
Ps 22: 16   they p my hands and my feet.
Pr 12: 18   words of the reckless p like swords,
Lk   2: 35   a sword will p your own soul too."

PIERCED (PIERCE)
Isa 53: 5   But he was p for our transgressions,
Zec 12: 10   the one they have p, and they will
Jn 19: 37   will look on the one they have p."
Rev 1: 7   see him, even those who p him";

PIG'S (PIGS)
Pr 11: 22   a p snout is a beautiful woman who

PIGEONS
Lev 5: 11   afford two doves or two young p,
Lk   2: 24   "a pair of doves or two young p."

PIGS (PIG'S)
Mt   7: 6   do not throw your pearls to p.
Mk 5: 11   A large herd of p was feeding

PILATE
     Governor of Judea. Questioned Jesus (Mt 27:1–26; Mk 15:15; Lk 22:66–23:25; Jn 18:28–19:16); sent him to Herod (Lk 23:6–12); consented to his crucifixion when crowds chose Barabbas (Mt 27:15–26; Mk 15:6–15; Lk 23:13–25; Jn 19:1–10).

PILLAR (PILLARS)
Ge 19: 26   back, and she became a p of salt.
Ex 13: 21   them in a p of cloud to guide them
1Ti 3: 15   the p and foundation of the truth.

PILLARS (PILLAR)
Gal 2: 9   those esteemed as p, gave me
Rev 3: 12   who are victorious I will make p

PIPE
Ps 150: 4   praise him with the strings and p,
Mt 11: 17   'We played the p for you,
1Co 14: 7   such as the p or harp,

PISGAH
Dt   3: 27   Go up to the top of P and look west

PIT
Ps   7: 15   it out fall into the p they have made.
     40: 2   He lifted me out of the slimy p,
   103: 4   who redeems your life from the p
Pr 23: 27   for an adulterous woman is a deep p
     26: 27   If anyone digs a p, they themselves
Isa 24: 17   Terror and p and snare await you,
     38: 17   kept me from the p of destruction;
Mt 15: 14   the blind, both will fall into a p."

PITCH
Ge   6: 14   it and coat it with p inside and out.

Ex 2: 3 for him and coated it with tar and **p**.

PITIED* (PITY)
1Co 15: 19 we are to be **p** more than all others.

PITY (PITIED)
Ps 72: 13 He will take **p** on the weak
Ecc 4: 10 But **p** those who fall and have no
Lk 10: 33 when he saw him, he took **p** on him.

PLAGUE (PLAGUED PLAGUES)
2Ch 6: 28 famine or **p** comes to the land,
Ps 91: 6 nor the **p** that destroys at midday.

PLAGUED* (PLAGUE)
Ps 73: 5 they are not **p** by human ills.

PLAGUES (PLAGUE)
Hos 13: 14 Where, O death, are your **p**?
Rev 21: 9 bowls full of the seven last **p** came
22: 18 to you the **p** described in this scroll.

PLAIN
Isa 40: 4 become level, the rugged places a **p**.
Ro 1: 19 be known about God is **p** to them,

PLAN (PLANNED PLANS)
Ex 26: 30 according to the **p** shown you
Pr 14: 22 those who **p** what is good find love
21: 30 no **p** that can succeed against
Isa 28: 29 whose **p** is wonderful,
Am 3: 7 does nothing without revealing his **p**
Eph 1: 11 to the **p** of him who works

PLANK
Mt 7: 3 attention to the **p** in your own eye?
Lk 6: 41 attention to the **p** in your own eye?

PLANNED (PLAN)
Ps 17: 3 I have **p** no evil; my mouth has not
40: 5 have done, the things you **p** for us.
Isa 14: 24 "Surely, as I have **p**, so it will be,
23: 9 The LORD Almighty **p** it, to bring
46: 11 what I have **p**, that I will do.
Heb 11: 40 God had **p** something better for us

PLANS (PLAN)
Job 38: 2 "Who is this that obscures my **p**
42: 3 'Who is this that obscures my **p**
Ps 20: 4 heart and make all your **p** succeed.
33: 11 But the **p** of the LORD stand firm
94: 11 The LORD knows all human **p**;
107: 11 despised the **p** of the Most High.
Pr 15: 22 **P** fail for lack of counsel,
16: 3 you do, and he will establish your **p**.
19: 21 Many are the **p** in a human heart,
20: 18 **P** are established by seeking advice;
Isa 29: 15 to hide their **p** from the LORD,
30: 1 those who carry out **p** that are not
32: 8 But the noble make noble **p**,
2Co 1: 17 do I make my **p** in a worldly manner

PLANT (PLANTED PLANTING PLANTS)
Am 9: 15 I will **p** Israel in their own land,
Mt 15: 13 "Every **p** that my heavenly Father

PLANTED (PLANT)
Ge 2: 8 the LORD God had **p** a garden
Ps 1: 3 They are like a tree **p** by streams
Jer 17: 8 They will be like a tree **p**
Mt 15: 13 Father has not **p** will be pulled
21: 33 was a landowner who **p** a vineyard.
1Co 3: 6 I **p** the seed, Apollos watered it,
Jas 1: 21 humbly accept the word **p** in you,

PLANTING (PLANT)
Isa 61: 3 a **p** of the LORD for the display

PLANTS (PLANT)
Pr 31: 16 out of her earnings she **p** a vineyard.
1Co 3: 7 neither the one who **p** nor the one
9: 7 Who **p** a vineyard and does not eat

PLATTER
Mk 6: 25 head of John the Baptist on a **p**."

PLAY (PLAYED)
1Sa 16: 23 David would take up his lyre and **p**.
Isa 11: 8 Infants will **p** near the hole

PLAYED (PLAY)
Lk 7: 32 " 'We **p** the pipe for you, and you
1Co 14: 7 what tune is being **p** unless there is

PLEA (PLEAD PLEADED PLEADS)
1Ki 8: 28 prayer and his **p** for mercy,
Ps 102: 17 he will not despise their **p**.
La 3: 56 You heard my **p**: "Do not close

PLEAD (PLEA)
Isa 1: 17 fatherless, **p** the case of the widow.

PLEADED (PLEA)
2Co 12: 8 Three times I **p** with the Lord

PLEADS (PLEA)
Job 16: 21 he **p** with God as one **p** for a friend.

PLEASANT (PLEASE)
Ge 49: 15 resting place and how **p** is his land,
Ps 16: 6 lines have fallen for me in **p** places;
133: 1 and **p** it is when God's people live
135: 3 sing praise to his name, for that is **p**.
147: 1 how **p** and fitting to praise him!
Pr 2: 10 knowledge will be **p** to your soul.
3: 17 Her ways are **p** ways, and all her
Isa 30: 10 Tell us **p** things, prophesy illusions.
Jer 3: 19 give you a **p** land,
1Th 3: 6 you always have **p** memories of us
Heb 12: 11 No discipline seems **p** at the time,

PLEASANTNESS* (PLEASE)
Pr 27: 9 the **p** of a friend springs from their

PLEASE (PLEASANT PLEASANTNESS PLEASED
PLEASES PLEASING PLEASURE PLEASURES)
Ps 69: 31 This will **p** the LORD more than
Pr 20: 23 and dishonest scales do not **p** him.
21: 1 he channels toward all who **p** him.
Isa 46: 10 will stand, and I will do all that I **p**.'
Jer 6: 20 your sacrifices do not **p** me."
27: 5 are on it, and I give it to anyone I **p**.
Jn 5: 30 for I seek not to **p** myself but him
Ro 8: 8 by the sinful nature cannot **p** God.
15: 1 of the weak and not to **p** ourselves.
15: 2 We should all **p** our neighbors
1Co 7: 32 how he can **p** the Lord.
10: 33 even as I try to **p** everyone in every
2Co 5: 9 So we make it our goal to **p** him,
Gal 1: 10 Or am I trying to **p** people? If I were
6: 8 those who sow to **p** the Spirit,
Col 1: 10 of the Lord and **p** him in every way:
1Th 2: 4 We are not trying to **p** people
4: 1 you how to live in order to **p** God,
2Ti 2: 4 try to **p** their commanding officer.
Tit 2: 9 to try to **p** them, not to talk back
Heb 11: 6 faith it is impossible to **p** God,

PLEASED (PLEASE)
Dt 28: 63 Just as it **p** the LORD to make you
Jdg 18: 20 The priest was very **p**.
1Sa 12: 22 because the LORD was **p** to make
1Ki 3: 10 The Lord was **p** that Solomon had
1Ch 29: 17 the heart and are **p** with integrity.
Ps 5: 4 not a God who is **p** with wickedness;
Mic 6: 7 Will the LORD be **p**
Mal 1: 10 I am not **p** with you,"
Mt 3: 17 with him I am well **p**."
17: 5 whom I love; with him I am well **p**.
Mk 1: 11 with you I am well **p**."
Lk 3: 22 with you I am well **p**."
1Co 1: 21 God was **p** through the foolishness
Col 1: 19 God was **p** to have all his fullness
Heb 10: 6 and sin offerings you were not **p**.
10: 8 desire, nor were you **p** with them"—
11: 5 was commended as one who **p** God.
2Pe 1: 17 with him I am well **p**."

PLEASES (PLEASE)
Job 23: 13 He does whatever he **p**.
Ps 115: 3 he does whatever **p** him.
135: 6 The LORD does whatever **p** him,
Pr 15: 8 but the prayer of the upright **p** him.
Ecc 2: 26 To the person who **p** him, God gives
7: 26 The man who **p** God will escape
Da 4: 35 He does as he **p** with the powers
Jn 3: 8 The wind blows wherever it **p**.
8: 29 alone, for I always do what **p** him."
Eph 5: 10 and find out what **p** the Lord.
Col 3: 20 in everything, for this **p** the Lord.
1Ti 2: 3 This is good, and **p** God our Savior,
1Jn 3: 22 his commands and do what **p** him.

PLEASING (PLEASE)
Ge 2: 9 trees that were **p** to the eye
Lev 1: 9 offering, an aroma **p** to the LORD.
Ps 19: 14 of my heart be **p** in your sight,
104: 34 May my meditation be **p** to him, as I
SS 1: 3 **P** is the fragrance of your perfumes;
4: 10 How much more **p** is your love than
7: 6 How beautiful you are and how **p**,
Ro 12: 1 living sacrifice, holy and **p** to God—
14: 18 serves Christ in this way is **p** to God
Php 4: 18 an acceptable sacrifice, **p** to God.
1Ti 5: 4 grandparents, for this is **p** to God.
Heb 13: 21 may he work in us what is **p** to him,

PLEASURE (PLEASE)
Ps 51: 16 you do not take **p** in burnt offerings.
147: 10 His **p** is not in the strength
Pr 10: 23 Fools find **p** in wicked schemes,
16: 7 LORD takes **p** in anyone's way,
18: 2 Fools find no **p** in understanding
21: 17 Whoever loves **p** will become poor;
Isa 1: 11 I have no **p** in the blood of bulls
Jer 6: 10 they find no **p** in it.
Eze 18: 23 Do I take any **p** in the death
18: 32 For I take no **p** in the death
33: 11 I take no **p** in the death
Lk 10: 21 Father, for this was your good **p**.
Eph 1: 5 in accordance with his **p** and will—
1: 9 of his will according to his good **p**,
1Ti 5: 6 for **p** is dead even while she lives.
2Ti 3: 4 lovers of **p** rather than lovers
Heb 10: 38 no **p** in the one who shrinks back."
2Pe 2: 13 Their idea of **p** is to carouse

PLEASURES* (PLEASE)
Ps 16: 11 with eternal **p** at your right hand.
Lk 8: 14 riches and **p**, and they do not
Tit 3: 3 by all kinds of passions and **p**.
Heb 11: 25 than to enjoy the fleeting **p** of sin.
Jas 4: 3 may spend what you get on your **p**.
2Pe 2: 13 reveling in their **p** while they feast

PLEDGE (PLEDGED)
Dt 24: 17 take the cloak of the widow as a **p**.
1Pe 3: 21 the **p** of a clear conscience toward

PLEDGED (PLEDGE)
1Co 7: 27 Are you **p** to a woman?

PLEIADES
Job 38: 31 "Can you bind the chains of the **P**?
Am 5: 8 He who made the **P** and Orion,

PLENTIFUL (PLENTY)
Mt 9: 37 "The harvest is **p** but the workers
Lk 10: 2 "The harvest is **p**, but the workers

PLENTY (PLENTIFUL)
2Co 8: 14 the present time your **p** will supply
Php 4: 12 whether living in **p** or in want.

PLOT
Est 2: 22 Mordecai found out about the **p**
Ps 2: 1 conspire and the peoples **p** in vain?
Pr 3: 29 Do not **p** harm against your
6: 14 **p** evil with deceit in their hearts—
Zec 8: 17 do not **p** evil against each other,
Ac 4: 25 rage and the peoples **p** in vain?

PLOW (PLOWPOINTS PLOWSHARES)
Lk 9: 62 "No one who puts a hand to the **p**

PLOWPOINTS (PLOW)
1Sa 13: 20 to the Philistines to have their **p**,

PLOWSHARES* (PLOW)
Isa 2: 4 They will beat their swords into **p**
Joel 3: 10 Beat your **p** into swords and your
Mic 4: 3 They will beat their swords into **p**

PLUCK
Mk 9: 47 eye causes you to stumble, **p** it out.

PLUNDER (PLUNDERED)
Ex 3: 22 And so you will **p** the Egyptians."
Est 3: 13 month of Adar, and to **p** their goods.
8: 11 to the property of their enemies.
9: 10 did not lay their hands on the **p**.
Isa 3: 14 the **p** from the poor is in your

PLUNDERED (PLUNDER)
Ps 12: 5 the poor are **p** and the needy groan,
Eze 34: 8 so has been **p** and has become food

PLUNGE
1Ti 6: 9 harmful desires that **p** people

PODS
Lk 15: 16 with the **p** that the pigs were eating,

POINT
Mt 4: 5 stand on the highest **p** of the temple.
26: 38 with sorrow to the **p** of death.
Jas 2: 10 yet stumbles at just one **p** is guilty
Rev 2: 10 even to the **p** of death, and I will

POISON
Ps 140: 3 the **p** of vipers is on their lips.
Mk 16: 18 they drink deadly **p**,
Ro 3: 13 "The **p** of vipers is on their lips."
Jas 3: 8 It is a restless evil, full of deadly **p**.

POLE (POLES)
Nu 21: 8 "Make a snake and put it up on a **p**;
Dt 16: 21 any wooden Asherah **p** beside

Dt 21: 23 hung on a *p* is under God's curse.
Est 7: 10 Haman on the *p* he had set up
Gal 3: 13 is everyone who is hung on a *p*."

POLES (POLE)
Ex 25: 13 Then make *p* of acacia wood

POLISHED
Isa 49: 2 he made me into a *p* arrow

POLLUTE* (POLLUTED POLLUTES)
Nu 35: 33 " 'Do not *p* the land where you
Jude : 8 these ungodly people *p* their own

POLLUTED* (POLLUTE)
Ezr 2: 62 possess is a land *p* by the corruption
Pr 25: 26 a *p* well are the righteous who give
Ac 15: 20 to abstain from food *p* by idols,
Jas 1: 27 oneself from being *p* by the world.

POLLUTES* (POLLUTE)
Nu 35: 33 Bloodshed *p* the land,

PONDER (PONDERED)
Ps 64: 9 of God and *p* what he has done.
107: 43 *p* the loving deeds of the LORD.
119: 95 but I will *p* your statutes.

PONDERED (PONDER)
Ps 111: 2 they are *p* by all who delight
Lk 2: 19 these things and *p* them in her heart.

POOR (POVERTY)
Lev 19: 10 Leave them for the *p*
23: 22 Leave them for the *p*
27: 8 anyone making the vow is too *p*
Dt 15: 4 need be no *p* people among you,
15: 7 If anyone is *p* among your people
15: 11 There will always be *p* people
24: 12 If the neighbor is *p*, do not go
24: 14 of a hired worker who is *p*
Job 5: 16 So the *p* have hope, and injustice
24: 4 and force all the *p* of the land
Ps 34: 6 frustrate the plans of the *p*,
34: 6 This *p* man called, and the LORD
35: 10 You rescue the *p* from those too
40: 17 But as for me, I am *p* and needy;
68: 10 God, you provided for the *p*.
82: 3 uphold the cause of the *p*
112: 9 scattered abroad their gifts to the *p*,
113: 7 He raises the *p* from the dust
140: 12 the LORD secures justice for the *p*
Pr 14: 7 another pretends to be *p*, yet has
14: 20 The *p* are shunned even by their
14: 31 oppresses the *p* shows contempt
17: 5 mocks the *p* shows contempt
19: 1 Better the *p* whose walk is
19: 17 Those who are kind to the *p* lend
19: 22 better to be *p* than a liar.
20: 13 not love sleep or you will grow *p*;
21: 13 their ears to the cry of the *p* will
21: 17 loves pleasure will become *p*;
22: 2 Rich and *p* have this in common:
22: 9 for they share their food with the *p*
22: 22 not exploit the *p* because they are *p*
28: 6 Better the *p* whose walk is
28: 27 who give to the *p* will lack nothing,
29: 7 care about justice for the *p*,
31: 9 defend the rights of the *p* and needy.
31: 20 She opens her arms to the *p*
Ecc 4: 13 Better a *p* but wise youth than
Isa 3: 14 the plunder from the *p* is in your
10: 2 to deprive the *p* of their rights
14: 30 poorest of the *p* will find pasture,
25: 4 You have been a refuge for the *p*,
32: 7 schemes to destroy the *p* with lies,
61: 1 me to proclaim good news to the *p*.
Jer 22: 16 He defended the cause of the *p*
Eze 18: 12 He oppresses the *p* and needy.
Am 2: 7 on the heads of the *p* as on the dust
4: 1 you women who oppress the *p*
5: 11 You levy a straw tax on the *p*
Zec 7: 10 the fatherless, the foreigner or the *p*.
Mt 5: 3 "Blessed are the *p* in spirit,
11: 5 good news is proclaimed to the *p*.
19: 21 your possessions and give to the *p*,
26: 11 The *p* you will always have
Mk 12: 42 but a *p* widow came and put in two
14: 7 The *p* you will always have
Lk 4: 18 me to proclaim good news to the *p*.
6: 20 "Blessed are you who are *p*,
11: 41 be generous to the *p*, and everything
14: 13 a banquet, invite the *p*, the crippled,
21: 2 also saw a *p* widow put in two very
Jn 12: 8 will always have the *p* among you,
Ac 9: 36 doing good and helping the *p*.

Ac 10: 4 and gifts to the *p* have come up as
24: 17 to bring my people gifts for the *p*
Ro 15: 26 for the *p* among the Lord's people
1Co 13: 3 If I give all I possess to the *p*
2Co 6: 10 *p*, yet making many rich;
8: 9 yet for your sake he became *p*,
Gal 2: 10 should continue to remember the *p*,
Jas 2: 2 and a *p* person in filthy old clothes
2: 5 not God chosen those who are *p*
2: 6 But you have dishonored the *p*.

POPULATION*
Pr 14: 28 A large *p* is a king's glory,

PORTION
Nu 18: 29 present as the LORD's *p* the best
Dt 32: 9 For the LORD's *p* is his people,
1Sa 1: 5 he gave a double *p* because he loved
2Ki 2: 9 "Let me inherit a double *p* of your
Ps 73: 26 of my heart and my *p* forever.
119: 57 You are my *p*, LORD;
Isa 53: 12 I will give him a *p* among the great,
Jer 10: 16 He who is the *P* of Jacob is not like
La 3: 24 to myself, "The LORD is my *p*;
Zec 2: 12 LORD will inherit Judah as his *p*

PORTRAYED
Gal 3: 1 Christ was clearly *p* as crucified.

POSITION (POSITIONS)
Ro 12: 16 to associate with people of low *p*.
Jas 1: 9 ought to take pride in their high *p*.
2Pe 3: 17 lawless and fall from your secure *p*.

POSITIONS (POSITION)
2Ch 20: 17 Take up your *p*; stand firm and see
Jude : 6 the angels who did not keep their *p*

POSSESS (POSSESSED POSSESSING POSSESSION POSSESSIONS)
Nu 33: 53 for I have given you the land to *p*.
Dt 4: 14 you are crossing the Jordan to *p*.
Pr 8: 12 I *p* knowledge and discretion.
Jn 5: 39 think that in them you *p* eternal life.

POSSESSED (POSSESS)
Jn 10: 21 sayings of someone *p* by a demon.

POSSESSING* (POSSESS)
2Co 6: 10 nothing, and yet *p* everything.

POSSESSION (POSSESS)
Ge 15: 7 give you this land to take *p* of it."
Ex 6: 8 I will give it to you as a *p*. I am
19: 5 nations you will be my treasured *p*
Nu 13: 30 should go up and take *p* of the land,
Dt 7: 6 to be his people, his treasured *p*.
Jos 1: 11 take *p* of the land the LORD your
Ps 2: 8 the ends of the earth your *p*.
135: 4 his own, Israel to be his treasured *p*.
Eph 1: 14 of those who are God's *p*—
1Pe 2: 9 a holy nation, God's special *p*,

POSSESSIONS (POSSESS)
Mt 19: 21 sell your *p* and give to the poor,
Lk 11: 21 his own house, his *p* are safe.
12: 15 not consist in an abundance of *p*."
19: 8 now I give half of my *p* to the poor,
Ac 4: 32 that any of their *p* was their own,
2Co 12: 14 because what I want is not your *p*
Heb 10: 34 yourselves had better and lasting *p*.
1Jn 3: 17 If any one of you has material *p*

POSSIBLE
Mt 19: 26 but with God all things are *p*."
26: 39 if it is *p*, may this cup be taken
Mk 9: 23 "Everything is *p* for one who
10: 27 all things are *p* with God."
14: 35 if *p* the hour might pass from him.
Ro 12: 18 If it is *p*, as far as it depends on you,
1Co 15: 1 Is it *p* that there is nobody among
9: 19 to everyone, to win as many as *p*.
9: 22 by all *p* means I might save some.

POT (POTSHERDS POTTER POTTER'S POTTERY)
2Ki 4: 40 of God, there is death in the *p*!"
Jer 18: 4 the *p* he was shaping from the clay

POTIPHAR*
Egyptian who bought Joseph (Ge 37:36), set him over his house (Ge 39:1–6), sent him to prison (Ge 39:7–30).

POTSHERDS (POT)
Isa 45: 9 but *p* among the *p* on the ground.

POTTER (POT)
Isa 29: 16 Can the pot say to the *p*,
45: 9 Does the clay say to the *p*,

Isa 64: 8 We are the clay, you are the *p*;
Jer 18: 6 "Like clay in the hand of the *p*,
Zec 11: 13 threw them to the *p* at the house
Ro 9: 21 Does not the *p* have the right

POTTER'S (POT)
Mt 27: 7 to buy the *p* field as a burial place

POTTERY (POT)
Ro 9: 21 of clay some *p* for noble purposes

POUR (POURED)
Ps 62: 8 *p* out your hearts to him, for God is
Isa 44: 3 I will *p* out my Spirit on your
Eze 20: 8 So I said I would *p* out my wrath
39: 29 for I will *p* out my Spirit
Joel 2: 28 I will *p* out my Spirit on all people.
Zec 12: 10 I will *p* out on the house of David
Mal 3: 10 *p* out so much blessing that there
Lk 5: 37 not *p* new wine into old wineskins.
Ac 2: 17 I will *p* out my Spirit on all people.

POURED (POUR)
Ps 22: 14 I am *p* out like water, and all my
Isa 32: 15 till the Spirit is *p* on us
Mt 26: 28 which is *p* out for many
Lk 22: 20 in my blood, which is *p* out for you.
Ac 2: 33 and has *p* out what you now see
10: 45 the Holy Spirit had been *p* out even
Ro 5: 5 because God's love has been *p*
Php 2: 17 even if I am being *p* out like a drink
2Ti 4: 6 I am already being *p* out like a drink
Tit 3: 6 whom he *p* out on us generously
Rev 16: 2 went and *p* out his bowl on the land,

POVERTY* (POOR)
Dt 28: 48 in nakedness and dire *p*, you will
1Sa 2: 7 The LORD sends *p* and wealth;
Pr 6: 11 and *p* will come on you like a thief
10: 4 Lazy hands make for *p*,
10: 15 city, but *p* is the ruin of the poor.
11: 24 withholds unduly, but comes to *p*.
13: 18 disregards discipline comes to *p*
14: 23 profit, but mere talk leads only to *p*.
21: 5 profit as surely as haste leads to *p*.
22: 16 gifts to the rich—both come to *p*.
24: 34 and *p* will come on you like a thief
28: 19 fantasies will have their fill of *p*.
28: 22 and are unaware that *p* awaits them.
30: 8 give me neither *p* nor riches,
31: 7 forget their *p* and remember their
Ecc 4: 14 been born in *p* within his kingdom.
Mk 12: 44 out of her *p*, put in everything—
Lk 21: 4 she out of her *p* put in all she had
2Co 8: 2 their extreme *p* welled up in rich
8: 9 you through his *p* might become
Rev 2: 9 I know your afflictions and your *p*—

POWER (POWERFUL POWERS)
Ex 15: 6 hand, LORD, was majestic in *p*.
32: 11 brought out of Egypt with great *p*
Dt 8: 17 "My *p* and the strength of my
34: 12 no one has ever shown the mighty *p*
1Sa 10: 6 the LORD will come on you in *p*,
10: 10 the Spirit of God came on him in *p*,
11: 6 the Spirit of God came on him in *p*,
12: 18 of the LORD came on David in *p*.
1Ch 29: 11 greatness and the *p* and the glory
2Ch 20: 6 *P* and might are in your hand,
32: 7 for there is a greater *p* with us than
Job 9: 4 wisdom is profound, his *p* is vast.
36: 22 "God is exalted in his *p*. Who is
37: 23 beyond our reach and exalted in *p*;
Ps 20: 6 the victorious *p* of his right hand.
62: 11 heard: "*P* belongs to you, God,
63: 2 and beheld your *p* and your glory.
66: 3 So great is your *p* that your enemies
68: 34 Proclaim the *p* of God,
77: 14 you display your *p* among
89: 13 Your arm is endued with *p*;
145: 6 of the *p* of your awesome works—
147: 5 Great is our Lord and mighty in *p*;
150: 2 Praise him for his acts of *p*;
Pr 3: 27 it is due, when it is in your *p* to act.
18: 21 The tongue has the *p* of life
24: 5 The wise prevail through great *p*,
Isa 40: 10 Sovereign LORD comes with *p*,
40: 26 Because of his great and mighty
63: 12 who sent his glorious arm of *p* to be
Jer 10: 6 great, and your name is mighty in *p*.
10: 12 But God made the earth by his *p*;
27: 5 With my great and outstretched
51: 15 and the earth by your great *p*
Hos 13: 14 them from the *p* of the grave;
Na 1: 3 is slow to anger but great in *p*;

Zec 4: 6 'Not by might nor by **p**, but by my
Mt 22: 29 know the Scriptures or the **p** of God.
24: 30 of heaven, with **p** and great glory.
Lk 1: 35 and the **p** of the Most High will
4: 14 to Galilee in the **p** of the Spirit,
9: 1 he gave them **p** and authority
10: 19 to overcome all the **p** of the enemy;
24: 49 until you have been clothed with **p**
Ac 1: 8 you will receive **p** when the Holy
4: 28 They did what your **p** and will had
4: 33 With great **p** the apostles continued
10: 38 Nazareth with the Holy Spirit and **p**,
26: 18 and from the **p** of Satan to God,
Ro 1: 16 because it is the **p** of God
1: 20 his eternal **p** and divine nature—
4: 21 that God had **p** to do what he had
9: 17 that I might display my **p** in you
15: 13 hope by the **p** of the Holy Spirit.
15: 19 through the **p** of the Spirit of God.
1Co 1: 17 cross of Christ be emptied of its **p**.
1: 18 us who are being saved it is the **p**
2: 4 a demonstration of the Spirit's **p**,
6: 14 By his **p** God raised the Lord
15: 24 all dominion, authority and **p**.
15: 56 is sin, and the **p** of sin is the law.
2Co 4: 7 this all-surpassing **p** is from God
6: 7 truthful speech and in the **p** of God;
10: 4 they have divine **p** to demolish
12: 9 for you, for my **p** is made perfect
13: 4 weakness, yet he lives by God's **p**.
Eph 1: 19 his incomparably great **p** for us who
3: 16 you with **p** through his Spirit
3: 20 according to his **p** that is at work
6: 10 in the Lord and in his mighty **p**.
Php 3: 10 to know the **p** of his resurrection
3: 21 by the **p** that enables him to bring
Col 1: 11 strengthened with all **p** according
2: 10 He is the head over every **p**
1Th 1: 5 simply with words but also with **p**,
2Ti 1: 7 us timid, but gives us **p**,
3: 5 form of godliness but denying its **p**.
Heb 2: 14 **p** of him who holds the **p** of death—
7: 16 of the **p** of an indestructible life.
1Pe 1: 5 by God's **p** until the coming
2Pe 1: 3 His divine **p** has given us everything
Jude : 25 majesty, and authority,
Rev 4: 11 to receive glory and honor and **p**,
5: 12 to receive **p** and wealth and wisdom
11: 17 because you have taken your great **p**
19: 1 and glory and **p** belong to our God,
20: 6 second death has no **p** over them,

POWERFUL (POWER)
2Ch 27: 6 Jotham grew **p** because he walked
Est 9: 4 and he became more and more **p**.
Ps 29: 4 The voice of the LORD is **p**;
Zec 8: 22 **p** nations will come to Jerusalem
Mk 1: 7 me comes the one more **p** than I,
Lk 24: 19 **p** in word and deed before God
2Th 1: 7 in blazing fire with his **p** angels.
Heb 1: 3 sustaining all things by his **p** word.
Jas 5: 16 prayer of a righteous person is **p**

POWERLESS
Ro 5: 6 when we were still **p**, Christ died
8: 3 what the law was **p** to do because it

POWERS (POWER)
Da 4: 35 as he pleases with the **p** of heaven
Ro 8: 38 the present nor the future, nor any **p**,
1Co 12: 10 to another miraculous **p**, to another
Eph 6: 12 against the **p** of this dark world
Col 1: 16 whether thrones or **p** or rulers
2: 15 And having disarmed the **p**
Heb 6: 5 of God and the **p** of the coming age
1Pe 3: 22 and in submission to him.

PRACTICE (PRACTICED PRACTICES)
Lev 19: 26 " 'Do not **p** divination or seek
Ps 119: 56 This has been my **p**: I obey your
Eze 33: 31 but they do not put them into **p**.
Mt 7: 24 **p** is like a wise man who built his
23: 3 for they do not **p** what they preach.
Lk 8: 21 hear God's word and put it into **p**."
Ro 12: 13 who are in need. **P** hospitality.
Php 4: 9 or seen in me—put it into **p**.
1Ti 5: 4 to put their religion into **p** by caring

PRACTICED (PRACTICE)
Mt 23: 23 You should have **p** the latter,

PRACTICES (PRACTICE)
Ps 101: 7 No one who **p** deceit will dwell
Mt 15: 9 but whoever **p** and teaches these
Col 3: 9 taken off your old self with its **p**

PRAISE (PRAISED PRAISES PRAISEWORTHY PRAISING)
Ex 15: 2 and I will **p** him, my father's God,
Dt 10: 21 He is the one you **p**; he is your God.
26: 19 declared that he will set you in **p**,
32: 3 **p** the greatness of our God!
Ru 4: 14 "**P** be to the LORD, who this day
2Sa 22: 4 who is worthy of **p**, and have been
22: 47 **P** be to my Rock!
1Ki 8: 33 to you and give **p** to your name,
8: 35 place and give **p** to your name
1Ch 16: 8 Give **p** to the LORD,
16: 25 the LORD and most worthy of **p**;
16: 35 holy name, and glory in your **p**."
23: 5 four thousand are to **p** the LORD
29: 10 saying, "**P** be to you, LORD,
2Ch 5: 13 singers raised their voices in **p**
6: 24 back and give **p** to your name,
6: 26 place and give **p** to your name
20: 21 and to **p** him for the splendor of his
29: 30 ordered the Levites to **p** the LORD
Ezr 3: 10 took their places to **p** the LORD,
Ne 8: 6 up and the **p** of your God,
Ps 8: 2 Through the **p** of children
9: 1 I will **p** you, LORD, with all my
16: 7 I will **p** the LORD, who counsels
26: 7 proclaiming aloud your **p**
28: 7 and with my song I **p** him.
30: 4 his faithful people; **p** his holy name.
30: 12 my God, I will **p** you forever.
33: 1 it is fitting for the upright to **p** him.
34: 1 his **p** will always be on my lips.
40: 3 my mouth, a hymn of **p** to our God.
42: 5 for I will yet **p** him, my Savior
43: 5 for I will yet **p** him, my Savior
45: 17 therefore the nations will **p** you
47: 7 sing to him a psalm of **p**.
48: 1 and most worthy of **p**, in the city
51: 15 and my mouth will declare your **p**.
56: 4 In God, whose word I **p**—in God I
57: 9 I will **p** you, Lord,
63: 4 I will **p** you as long as I live,
65: 1 **P** awaits you, our God, in Zion;
66: 2 his name; make his **p** glorious.
66: 8 **P** our God, all peoples, let the sound
68: 19 **P** be to the Lord, to God our Savior,
68: 26 **P** God in the great congregation;
69: 30 I will **p** God's name in song
69: 34 Let heaven and earth **p** him, the seas
71: 8 My mouth is filled with your **p**,
71: 14 I will **p** you more and more.
71: 22 I will **p** you with the harp for your
74: 21 the poor and needy **p** your name.
75: 1 we **p** you, for your Name is near;
86: 12 I will **p** you, Lord my God, with all
89: 5 The heavens **p** your wonders,
92: 1 It is good to **p** the LORD and make
96: 2 Sing to the LORD, **p** his name;
100: 4 thanksgiving and his courts with **p**;
101: 1 I to you, LORD, I will sing **p**.
102: 18 not yet created may **p** the LORD:
103: 1 **P** the LORD, my soul;
103: 20 **P** the LORD, you his angels,
104: 1 **P** the LORD, my soul.
106: 1 **P** the LORD. Give thanks
108: 3 I will **p** you, LORD,
111: 1 **P** the LORD. I will extol
113: 1 **P** the LORD. **P** the LORD,
117: 1 **P** the LORD, all you nations;
118: 28 my God, and I will **p** you;
119:175 Let me live that I may **p** you,
135: 1 **P** the LORD. **P** the name
135: 20 you who fear him, **p** the LORD.
138: 1 I will **p** you, LORD, with all my
139: 14 I **p** you because I am fearfully
144: 1 **P** be to the LORD my Rock,
145: 3 the LORD and most worthy of **p**;
145: 10 All your works **p** you, LORD;
145: 21 Let every creature **p** his holy name
146: 1 **P** the LORD. **P** the LORD,
147: 1 how pleasant and fitting to **p** him!
148: 1 **p** him in the heights above.
148: 13 Let them **p** the name of the LORD,
149: 1 his **p** in the assembly of his faithful
149: 6 May the **p** of God be in their mouths
149: 9 his faithful people. **P** the LORD.
150: 2 **P** him for his acts of power; **p** him
150: 6 that has breath **p** the LORD.
Pr 27: 2 Let someone else **p** you, and not
27: 21 but people are tested by their **p**.
31: 31 let her works bring her **p** at the city
SS 1: 4 we will **p** your love more than wine.

Isa 12: 1 "I will **p** you, LORD.
42: 10 his **p** from the ends of the earth,
61: 3 a garment of **p** instead of a spirit
Jer 33: 9 **p** and honor before all nations
Da 2: 20 "**P** be to the name of God for ever
4: 37 **p** and exalt and glorify the King
Mt 21: 16 and infants you have ordained **p**'?"
Lk 19: 37 disciples began joyfully to **p** God
Ro 2: 29 Such a person's **p** is not from other
15: 7 in order to bring **p** to God.
2Co 1: 3 **P** be to the God and Father of our
Eph 1: 3 **P** be to the God and Father of our
1: 6 to the **p** of his glorious grace,
1: 12 might be for the **p** of his glory.
1: 14 to the **p** of his glory.
1Th 2: 6 We were not looking for **p** from any
Heb 13: 15 offer to God a sacrifice of **p**—
Jas 3: 9 With the tongue we **p** our Lord
5: 13 Let them sing songs of **p**.
Rev 5: 13 and to the Lamb be **p** and honor
7: 12 **P** and glory and wisdom and thanks

PRAISED (PRAISE)
1Ch 29: 10 David **p** the LORD in the presence
Ne 8: 6 Ezra **p** the LORD, the great God;
Job 1: 21 may the name of the LORD be **p**."
Ps 113: 2 Let the name of the LORD be **p**,
Pr 31: 30 who fears the LORD is to be **p**.
Isa 63: 7 the deeds for which he is to be **p**,
Da 2: 19 Then Daniel **p** the God of heaven
4: 34 Then I **p** the Most High;
Lk 18: 43 the people saw it, they also **p** God.
23: 47 what had happened, **p** God and said,
Ro 9: 5 who is God over all, forever **p**!
Gal 1: 24 And they **p** God because of me.
1Pe 4: 11 God may be **p** through Jesus Christ.

PRAISES (PRAISE)
2Sa 22: 50 I will sing the **p** of your name.
Ps 18: 49 I will sing the **p** of your name.
47: 6 Sing to God, sing **p**; sing **p** to our
105: 2 Sing of him, sing his **p**;
147: 1 How good it is to sing **p** to our God,
Pr 31: 28 her husband also, and he **p** her:
Ro 15: 9 I will sing the **p** of your name."
1Pe 2: 9 you may declare the **p** of him who

PRAISEWORTHY* (PRAISE)
Ps 78: 4 tell the next generation the **p** deeds
Php 4: 8 if anything is excellent or **p**—

PRAISING (PRAISE)
Lk 2: 13 with the angel, **p** God and saying,
2: 20 **p** God for all the things they had
Ac 2: 47 **p** God and enjoying the favor of all
10: 46 speaking in tongues and **p** God
1Co 14: 16 when you are **p** God in the Spirit,

PRAY (PRAYED PRAYER PRAYERS PRAYING PRAYS)
Dt 4: 7 our God is near us whenever we **p**
1Sa 12: 23 the LORD by failing to **p** for you.
1Ki 8: 30 when they **p** toward this place.
2Ch 7: 14 will humble themselves and **p**
Ezr 6: 10 and **p** for the well-being of the king
Job 42: 8 My servant Job will **p** for you, and I
Ps 5: 2 King and my God, for to you I **p**.
32: 6 Therefore let all the faithful **p**
122: 6 **P** for the peace of Jerusalem:
Jer 29: 7 **P** to the LORD for it, because if it
29: 12 call on me and come and **p** to me,
42: 3 **P** that the LORD your God will
Mt 5: 44 and **p** for those who persecute you,
6: 5 "And when you **p**, do not be like
6: 9 "This, then, is how you should **p**:
14: 23 on a mountainside by himself to **p**.
19: 13 his hands on them and **p** for them.
26: 36 here while I go over there and **p**."
Lk 6: 28 **p** for those who mistreat you.
11: 1 teach us to **p**, just as John taught his
18: 1 them that they should always **p**
22: 40 them, "**P** that you will not fall
Jn 17: 20 I **p** also for those who will believe
Ro 8: 26 do not know what we ought to **p** for,
1Co 14: 13 in a tongue should **p** that they may
Eph 1: 18 I **p** that the eyes of your heart may
3: 16 I **p** that out of his glorious riches he
6: 18 **p** in the Spirit on all occasions
Col 4: 3 And **p** for us, too, that God may
1Th 5: 17 **p** continually,
2Th 1: 11 in mind, we constantly **p** for you,
1Ti 2: 8 to **p**, lifting up holy hands
Jas 5: 13 Let them **p**. Is anyone happy?
5: 16 **p** for each other so that you may be

1Pe 4: 7 of sober mind so that you may **p**.

PRAYED (PRAY)
1Sa 1: 27 I **p** for this child, and the LORD
1Ki 18: 36 Elijah stepped forward and **p**:
19: 4 under it and **p** that he might die.
2Ki 6: 17 And Elisha **p**, "Open his eyes,
2Ch 30: 18 But Hezekiah **p** for them, saying,
Ne 4: 9 But we **p** to our God and posted
Job 42: 10 After Job had **p** for his friends,
Da 6: 10 day he got down on his knees and **p**,
9: 4 I **p** to the LORD my God
Jnh 2: 1 From inside the fish Jonah **p**
Mt 26: 39 with his face to the ground and **p**,
Mk 1: 35 off to a solitary place, where he **p**.
14: 35 and **p** that if possible the hour might
Lk 22: 41 beyond them, knelt down and **p**,
Jn 17: 1 he looked toward heaven and **p**:
Ac 4: 31 After they **p**, the place where they
6: 6 who **p** and laid their hands on them.
8: 15 they **p** for the new believers there
13: 3 So after they had fasted and **p**,

PRAYER (PRAY)
2Ch 30: 27 for their **p** reached heaven, his holy
Ezr 8: 23 about this, and he answered our **p**.
Ps 4: 1 have mercy on me and hear my **p**.
6: 9 The LORD accepts my **p**.
17: 1 Hear my **p**—it does not rise
17: 6 turn your ear to me and hear my **p**.
65: 2 You who answer **p**, to you all
66: 19 and has heard my **p**.
66: 20 God, who has not rejected my **p**
86: 6 Hear my **p**, LORD; listen to my
Pr 15: 8 but the **p** of the upright pleases him.
15: 29 but he hears the **p** of the righteous.
Isa 56: 7 my house will be called a house of **p**
Mt 21: 13 house will be called a house of **p**,'
21: 22 receive whatever you ask for in **p**."
Mk 9: 29 kind can come out only by **p**."
11: 24 whatever you ask for in **p**,
Jn 17: 15 My **p** is not that you take them
Ac 1: 14 all joined together constantly in **p**,
2: 42 to the breaking of bread and to **p**.
6: 4 will give our attention to **p**
10: 31 God has heard your **p**
16: 13 we expected to find a place of **p**.
Ro 12: 12 patient in affliction, faithful in **p**.
1Co 7: 5 you may devote yourselves to **p**.
2Co 13: 9 and our **p** is that you may be fully
Php 1: 9 And this is my **p**: that your love
4: 6 in every situation, by **p** and petition,
Col 4: 2 Devote yourselves to **p**,
1Ti 4: 5 by the word of God and **p**.
Jas 5: 15 And the **p** offered in faith will make
1Pe 3: 12 and his ears are attentive to their **p**,

PRAYERS (PRAY)
1Ch 5: 20 He answered their **p**, because they
Isa 1: 15 even if you offer many **p**, I will not
Mk 12: 40 and for a show make lengthy **p**.
2Co 1: 11 as you help us by your **p**.
Eph 6: 18 on all occasions with all kinds of **p**
1Ti 2: 1 that petitions, **p**,
1Pe 3: 7 so that nothing will hinder your **p**.
Rev 5: 8 which are the **p** of God's people.
8: 3 with the **p** of all God's people,

PRAYING (PRAY)
Ge 24: 45 "Before I finished **p** in my heart,
1Sa 1: 12 As she kept on **p** to the LORD,
Mk 11: 25 And when you stand **p**, if you hold
Lk 3: 21 And as he was **p**, heaven was
6: 12 pray, and spent the night **p** to God.
9: 29 As he was **p**, the appearance of his
Jn 17: 9 I am not **p** for the world,
Ac 9: 11 from Tarsus named Saul, for he is **p**.
16: 25 Silas were **p** and singing hymns
Ro 15: 30 join me in my struggle by **p** to God
Eph 6: 18 always keep on **p** for all the Lord's
Jude 20 holy faith and **p** in the Holy Spirit,

PRAYS (PRAY)
1Co 14: 14 tongue, my spirit **p**, but my mind is

PREACH (PREACHED PREACHING)
Mt 23: 3 for they do not practice what they **p**.
Mk 16: 15 **p** the gospel to all creation.
Ac 9: 20 At once he began to **p**
16: 10 God had called us to **p** the gospel
Ro 1: 15 is why I am so eager to **p** the gospel
10: 15 how can anyone **p** unless they are
15: 20 to **p** the gospel where Christ was not
1Co 1: 17 me to baptize, but to **p** the gospel—
1: 23 but we **p** Christ crucified:

1Co 9: 14 that those who **p** the gospel should
9: 16 For when I **p** the gospel, I cannot
9: 16 Woe to me if I do not **p** the gospel!
2Co 4: 5 For what we **p** is not ourselves,
10: 16 so that we can **p** the gospel
Gal 1: 8 heaven should **p** a gospel other than
2Ti 4: 2 **P** the word; be prepared in season

PREACHED (PREACH)
Mt 24: 14 the kingdom will be **p** in the whole
Mk 6: 12 out and **p** that people should repent.
13: 10 And the gospel must first be **p** to all
14: 9 the gospel is **p** throughout
Ac 8: 4 who had been scattered **p** the word
1Co 9: 27 slave so that after I have **p** to others,
15: 1 remind you of the gospel I **p** to you,
2Co 11: 4 a Jesus other than the Jesus we **p**,
Gal 1: 8 a gospel other than the one we **p**
Eph 2: 17 peace to you who were far away
Php 1: 18 false motives or true, Christ is **p**.
1Ti 3: 16 by angels, was **p** among the nations,
1Pe 1: 25 this is the word that was **p** to you.

PREACHING (PREACH)
Ac 18: 5 devoted himself exclusively to **p**,
Ro 10: 14 can they hear without someone **p**
1Co 1: 21 and my **p** were not with wise
9: 18 in **p** the gospel I may offer it free
Gal 1: 9 anybody is **p** to you a gospel other
1Ti 4: 13 of Scripture, to **p** and to teaching.
5: 17 especially those whose work is **p**

PRECEDE*
1Th 4: 15 will certainly not **p** those who have

PRECEPTS*
Dt 33: 10 He teaches your **p** to Jacob and your
Ps 19: 8 The **p** of the LORD are right,
103: 18 and remember to obey his **p**.
105: 45 that they might keep his **p**
111: 7 all his **p** are trustworthy.
111: 10 all who follow his **p** have good
119: 4 You have laid down **p** that are to be
119: 15 I meditate on your **p** and consider
119: 40 How I long for your **p**!
119: 45 for I have sought out your **p**.
119: 56 has been my practice: I obey your **p**.
119: 63 fear you, to all who follow your **p**.
119: 69 lies, I keep your **p** with all my heart.
119: 78 but I will meditate on your **p**.
119: 87 but I have not forsaken your **p**.
119: 93 I will never forget your **p**,
119: 94 I have sought out your **p**.
119:100 than the elders, for I obey your **p**.
119:104 I gain understanding from your **p**;
119:110 but I have not strayed from your **p**.
119:128 because I consider all your **p** right,
119:134 oppression, that I may obey your **p**.
119:141 and despised, I do not forget your **p**.
119:159 See how I love your **p**;
119:168 I obey your **p** and your statutes,
119:173 help me, for I have chosen your **p**.

PRECIOUS
Ps 19: 10 They are more **p** than gold,
72: 14 for **p** is their blood in his sight.
116: 15 **P** in the sight of the LORD is
119: 72 your mouth is more **p** to me than
139: 17 How **p** to me are your thoughts,
Pr 8: 11 for wisdom is more **p** than rubies,
Isa 28: 16 stone, a **p** cornerstone for a sure
1Pe 1: 19 but with the **p** blood of Christ,
2: 4 but chosen by God and **p** to him—
2: 6 a chosen and **p** cornerstone,
2Pe 1: 1 have received a faith as **p** as ours:
1: 4 us his very great and **p** promises,

PREDESTINED* (DESTINY)
Ro 8: 29 **p** to be conformed to the image
8: 30 And those he **p**, he also called;
Eph 1: 5 he **p** us for adoption to sonship
1: 11 having been **p** according to the plan

PREDICTED (PREDICTION)
1Sa 28: 17 has done what he **p** through me.
Ac 7: 52 even killed those who **p** the coming
1Pe 1: 11 pointing when he **p** the sufferings

PREDICTION* (PREDICTED PREDICTIONS)
Jer 28: 9 LORD only if his **p** comes true."

PREDICTIONS (PREDICTION)
Isa 44: 26 and fulfills the **p** of his messengers,

PREGNANT
Ex 21: 22 are fighting and a **p** woman is hit

Mt 24: 19 it will be in those days for **p** women
1Th 5: 3 as labor pains on a **p** woman,

PREPARE (PREPARED)
Job 38: 3 **P** to defend yourself;
40: 7 "**P** to defend yourself!
Ps 23: 5 You **p** a table before me
Isa 25: 6 the LORD Almighty will **p** a feast
40: 3 "In the wilderness **p** the way
Am 4: 12 to you, Israel, **p** to meet your God."
Mal 3: 1 who will **p** the way before me.
Mt 3: 3 wilderness, '**P** the way for the Lord,
Jn 14: 2 that I am going there to **p** a place

PREPARED (PREPARE)
Ex 23: 20 to bring you to the place I have **p**.
Mt 25: 34 the kingdom **p** for you since
Ro 9: 22 of his wrath—**p** for destruction?
1Co 2: 9 these things God has **p** for those
Eph 2: 10 which God **p** in advance for us
2Ti 2: 21 Master and **p** to do any good work.
4: 2 be **p** in season and out of season;
1Pe 3: 15 Always be **p** to give an answer

PRESCRIBED
Ezr 7: 23 Whatever the God of heaven has **p**,

PRESENCE (PRESENT)
Ex 25: 30 Put the bread of the **P** on this table
33: 14 replied, "My **P** will go with you,
Nu 4: 7 "Over the table of the **P** they are
1Sa 6: 20 can stand in the **p** of the LORD,
21: 6 of the **P** that had been removed
2Sa 22: 13 of the brightness of his **p** bolts
2Ki 17: 23 LORD removed them from his **p**,
23: 27 also from my **p** as I removed Israel,
Ezr 9: 15 not one of us can stand in your **p**."
Ps 16: 11 you will fill me with joy in your **p**,
21: 6 glad with the joy of your **p**.
23: 5 before me in the **p** of my enemies.
31: 20 the shelter of your **p** you hide them
41: 12 me and set me in your **p** forever.
51: 11 Do not cast me from your **p** or take
52: 9 you in the **p** of your faithful people.
89: 15 who walk in the light of your **p**,
90: 8 our secret sins in the light of your **p**.
114: 7 at the presence of the Lord, at the **p**
139: 7 Where can I flee from your **p**?
Isa 26: 17 pain, so were we in your **p**, LORD.
Jer 5: 22 "Should you not tremble in my **p**?
Eze 38: 20 of the earth will tremble at my **p**.
Hos 6: 2 restore us, that we may live in his **p**.
Na 1: 5 The earth trembles at his **p**,
Mal 3: 16 his **p** concerning those who feared
Ac 2: 28 you will fill me with joy in your **p**.'
1Th 3: 9 we have in the **p** of our God because
3: 13 holy in the **p** of our God and Father
2Th 1: 9 shut out from the **p** of the Lord
Heb 9: 24 now to appear for us in God's **p**.
1Jn 3: 19 we set our hearts at rest in his **p**:
Jude 24 before his glorious **p** without fault

PRESENT (PRESENCE)
1Co 3: 22 life or death or the **p** or the future—
7: 26 Because of the **p** crisis, I think
2Co 11: 2 that I might **p** you as a pure virgin
Eph 5: 27 and to **p** her to himself as a radiant
1Ti 4: 8 holding promise for both the **p** life
2Ti 2: 15 Do your best to **p** yourself to God as
Jude 24 **p** you before his glorious presence

PRESERVE (PRESERVES)
Pr 19: 16 obey instructions **p** their lives,
22: 5 would **p** their life stay far
Lk 17: 33 whoever loses their life will **p** it.

PRESERVES (PRESERVE)
Ps 119: 50 Your promise **p** my life.

PRESS (PRESSED PRESSURE)
Php 3: 12 I **p** on to take hold
3: 14 I **p** on toward the goal to win

PRESSED (PRESS)
Ps 118: 5 When hard **p**, I cried to the LORD;
Lk 6: 38 A good measure, **p** down,

PRESSURE (PRESS)
2Co 1: 8 We were under great **p**, far beyond
11: 28 I face daily the **p** of my concern

PRETENDED
1Sa 21: 13 So he **p** to be insane in their

PREVAILS
1Sa 2: 9 "It is not by strength that one **p**;
Pr 19: 21 it is the LORD's purpose that **p**.

PRICE (PRICELESS)
Job 28: 18 the **p** of wisdom is beyond rubies.
1Co 6: 20 you were bought at a **p**.
         7: 23 You were bought at a **p**;

PRICELESS* (PRICE)
Ps 36: 7 How **p** is your unfailing love,

PRIDE (PROUD)
Pr   8: 13 I hate **p** and arrogance,
        11: 2 When **p** comes, then comes
        13: 10 there is **p**, but wisdom is found
        16: 18 **P** goes before destruction, a haughty
        29: 23 **P** brings a person low, but the lowly
Isa 25: 11 will bring down their **p** despite
Da   4: 37 those who walk in **p** he is able
Am   8: 7 sworn by himself, the **P** of Jacob:
2Co 5: 12 you an opportunity to take **p** in us,
         7: 4 I take great **p** in you.
         8: 24 love and the reason for our **p** in you,
Gal 6: 4 Then you can take **p** in yourself,
Jas 1: 9 to take **p** in their high position.

PRIEST (PRIESTHOOD PRIESTLY PRIESTS)
Ge 14: 18 He was **p** of God Most High,
Nu   5: 10 to the **p** will belong to the **p**.' "
2Ch 13: 9 seven rams may become a **p** of what
Ps 110: 4 "You are a **p** forever, in the order
Heb 2: 17 faithful high **p** in service to God,
         3: 1 as our apostle and high **p**.
         4: 14 a great high **p** who has ascended
         4: 15 do not have a high **p** who is unable
         5: 6 "You are a **p** forever, in the order
         6: 20 He has become a high **p** forever,
         7: 3 Son of God, he remains a **p** forever.
         7: 15 another **p** like Melchizedek appears,
         7: 26 Such a high **p** truly meets our need—
         8: 1 We do have such a high **p**, who sat
       10: 11 Day after day every **p** stands
       13: 11 The high **p** carries the blood

PRIESTHOOD (PRIEST)
Heb 7: 24 lives forever, he has a permanent
1Pe 2: 5 into a spiritual house to be a holy **p**,
         2: 9 people, a royal **p**, a holy nation,

PRIESTLY (PRIEST)
Ro 15: 16 He gave me the **p** duty

PRIESTS (PRIEST)
Ex 19: 6 you will be for me a kingdom of **p**
Lev 21: 1 "Speak to the **p**, the sons of Aaron,
Eze 42: 13 where the **p** who approach
        46: 2 The **p** are to sacrifice his burnt
Mal 1: 6 "It is you **p** who show contempt
Rev 5: 10 a kingdom and **p** to serve our God,
        20: 6 but they will be **p** of God

PRIME
Isa 38: 10 the **p** of my life must I go through

PRINCE (PRINCES PRINCESS)
Isa 9: 6 God, Everlasting Father, **P** of Peace.
Eze 34: 24 David will be **p** among them.
        37: 25 my servant will be their **p** forever.
Da   8: 25 and take his stand against the **P**
Jn 12: 31 now the **p** of this world will be
Ac   5: 31 him to his own right hand as **P**

PRINCES (PRINCE)
Ps 118: 9 in the LORD than to trust in **p**.
       148: 11 you **p** and all rulers on earth,
Isa 40: 23 He brings **p** to naught and reduces

PRINCESS* (PRINCE)
Ps 45: 13 All glorious is the **p** within her

PRISCILLA*
       Wife of Aquila; co-worker with Paul (Ac 18; Ro
       16:3; 1Co 16:19; 2Ti 4:19); instructor of Apollos (Ac
       18:24–28).

PRISON (IMPRISONED IMPRISONMENT
       PRISONER PRISONERS)
Ps 66: 11 You brought us into **p** and laid
       142: 7 Set me free from my **p**, that I may
Isa 42: 7 blind, to free captives from **p**
Mt 25: 36 I was in **p** and you came to visit
2Co 11: 23 been in **p** more frequently,
Heb 13: 3 remember those in **p** as if you were
Rev 20: 7 Satan will be released from his **p**

PRISONER (PRISON)
Ro   7: 23 making me a **p** of the law of sin
Eph 3: 1 the **p** of Christ Jesus for the sake

PRISONERS (PRISON)
Ps 68: 6 he leads out the **p** with singing;
        79: 11 groans of the **p** come before you;

Ps 107: 10 darkness, **p** suffering in iron chains,
       146: 7 The LORD sets **p** free,
Zec 9: 12 to your fortress, you **p** of hope;
Lk   4: 18 me to proclaim freedom for the **p**

PRIVILEGE*
2Co 8: 4 us for the **p** of sharing in this service

PRIZE* (PROBES)
1Co 9: 24 runners run, but only one gets the **p**?
         9: 24 Run in such a way as to get the **p**.
         9: 27 will not be disqualified for the **p**.
Php 3: 14 on toward the goal to win the **p**

PROBE* (PROBES)
Job 11: 7 Can you **p** the limits
Ps 17: 3 Though you **p** my heart, though you

PROBES* (PROBE)
Ps   7: 9 God who **p** minds and hearts.

PROCEDURE
Ecc 8: 6 proper time and **p** for every matter,

PROCESSION
Ps 68: 24 Your **p**, God, has come into view,
       118: 27 join in the festal **p** up to the horns
1Co 4: 9 on display at the end of the **p**,
2Co 2: 14 as captives in Christ's triumphal **p**

PROCLAIM (PROCLAIMED PROCLAIMING
       PROCLAIMS PROCLAMATION)
Ex 33: 19 and I will **p** my name, the LORD,
Lev 25: 10 **p** liberty throughout the land to all
Dt 30: 12 it and **p** it to us so we may obey it?"
2Sa 1: 20 **p** it not in the streets of Ashkelon,
1Ch 16: 23 **p** his salvation day after day.
Ne   8: 15 and that they should **p** this word
Ps   2: 7 I will **p** the LORD's decree:
         9: 11 **p** among the nations what he has
        19: 1 the skies **p** the work of his hands.
        22: 31 They will **p** his righteousness,
        40: 9 I **p** your saving acts in the great
        50: 6 the heavens **p** his righteousness,
        64: 9 they will **p** the works of God
        68: 34 **P** the power of God, whose majesty
        71: 16 I will come and **p** your mighty acts,
        79: 13 we will **p** your praise.
        96: 2 **p** his salvation day after day.
        97: 6 The heavens **p** his righteousness,
       106: 2 Who can **p** the mighty acts
       118: 17 will **p** what the LORD has done.
       145: 6 and I will **p** your great deeds.
Isa 42: 4 done, and that his name is exalted.
        42: 12 and **p** his praise in the islands.
        52: 7 bring good tidings, who **p** salvation,
        61: 1 anointed me to **p** good news
        61: 1 to **p** freedom for the captives
        66: 19 They will **p** my glory among
Jer 7: 2 house and there **p** this message:
        50: 2 the nations, lift up a banner and **p** it;
Hos 5: 9 tribes of Israel I **p** what is certain.
Zec 9: 10 He will **p** peace to the nations.
Mt 10: 7 As you go, **p** this message:
        10: 27 in your ear, **p** from the roofs.
        12: 18 and he will **p** justice to the nations.
Lk   4: 18 anointed me to **p** good news
         4: 18 He has sent me to **p** freedom
         9: 60 you go and **p** the kingdom of God."
Ac 17: 23 this is what I am going to **p** to you.
        20: 27 I have not hesitated to **p** to you
Ro 10: 8 message concerning faith that we **p**:
1Co 11: 26 you **p** the Lord's death until he
Col 1: 28 We **p** him,
1Jn 1: 1 Pray that I may **p** it clearly, as I
         1: 1 this we **p** concerning the Word

PROCLAIMED (PROCLAIM)
Ex   9: 16 my name might be **p** in all the earth.
        34: 5 there with him and **p** his name,
Ps 68: 11 was the company of those who **p** it:
Ac 28: 31 He **p** the kingdom of God
Ro 15: 19 I have fully **p** the gospel of Christ.
Col 1: 23 has been **p** to every creature under
2Ti 4: 17 me the message might be fully **p**

PROCLAIMING (PROCLAIM)
Ps 26: 7 **p** aloud your praise and telling of all
        92: 2 **p** your love in the morning and your
        92: 15 **p**, "The LORD is upright;
Lk   9: 6 the good news and healing people
Ac   5: 42 the good news that Jesus is

PROCLAIMS (PROCLAIM)
Dt 18: 22 If what a prophet **p** in the name

PROCLAMATION (PROCLAIM)
Isa 62: 11 The LORD has made **p** to the ends

1Pe 3: 19 made **p** to the imprisoned spirits—

PRODUCE (PRODUCES)
Mt   3: 8 **P** fruit in keeping with repentance.
         3: 10 that does not **p** good fruit will be cut

PRODUCES (PRODUCE)
Pr 30: 33 blood, so stirring up anger **p** strife."
Ro   5: 3 know that suffering **p** perseverance;
Heb 12: 11 it **p** a harvest of righteousness

PROFANE (PROFANED)
Lev 18: 21 and so **p** the name of your God.
        22: 32 Do not **p** my holy name, for I must
Mal 2: 10 Why do we **p** the covenant of our

PROFANED (PROFANE)
Eze 36: 20 the nations they **p** my holy name,

PROFESS*
Ro 10: 10 your mouth that you **p** your faith
1Ti 2: 10 for women who **p** to worship God.
Heb 4: 14 hold firmly to the faith we **p**.
        10: 23 hold unswervingly to the hope we **p**,
        13: 15 fruit of lips that openly **p** his name.

PROFIT (PROFITABLE)
Pr 14: 23 All hard work brings a **p**, but mere
        21: 5 lead to **p** as surely as haste leads
Isa 44: 10 casts an idol, which can **p** nothing?
Eze 18: 8 take a **p** from them.
2Co 2: 17 not peddle the word of God for **p**.

PROFITABLE* (PROFIT)
Pr   3: 14 for she is more **p** than silver
        31: 18 She sees that her trading is **p**,
Tit 3: 8 are excellent and **p** for everyone.

PROFOUND
Job 9: 4 His wisdom is **p**, his power is vast.
Ps 92: 5 LORD, how **p** your thoughts!
Eph 5: 32 This is a **p** mystery—but I am

PROGRESS
Php 1: 25 continue with all of you for your **p**
1Ti 4: 15 so that everyone may see your **p**.

PROLONG*
Dt   5: 33 **p** your days in the land that you will
Ps 85: 5 Will you **p** your anger through all
Pr   3: 2 for they will **p** your life many years
Isa 53: 10 will see his offspring and **p** his days,
La   4: 22 he will not **p** your exile.

PROMISE (PROMISED PROMISES)
Nu 23: 19 Does he **p** and not fulfill?
Jos 23: 14 Every **p** has been fulfilled;
2Sa 7: 25 keep forever the **p** you have made
1Ki 8: 20 LORD has kept the **p** he made:
         8: 24 You have kept your **p** to your
Ne   5: 13 anyone who does not keep this **p**.
         9: 8 have kept your **p** because you are
Ps 77: 8 Has his **p** failed for all time?
       119: 41 your salvation, according to your **p**;
       119: 50 Your **p** preserves my life.
       119: 58 gracious to me according to your **p**.
       119:162 in your **p** like one who finds great
Pr 11: 7 **p** of their power comes to nothing.
Ac   2: 39 The **p** is for you and your children
Ro   4: 13 his offspring received the **p** that he
         4: 20 through unbelief regarding the **p**
Gal 3: 14 faith we might receive the **p**
Eph 2: 12 foreigners to the covenants of the **p**,
1Ti 4: 8 holding **p** for both the present life
Heb 6: 13 When God made his **p** to Abraham,
        11: 11 him faithful who had made the **p**.
2Pe 3: 9 Lord is not slow in keeping his **p**,
         3: 13 with his **p** we are looking forward

PROMISED (PROMISE)
Ge 21: 1 did for Sarah what he had **p**.
        24: 7 who spoke to me and **p** me on oath,
Ex   3: 17 I have **p** to bring you up out of your
Nu 10: 29 for the LORD has **p** good things
Dt 15: 6 your God will bless you as he has **p**,
        26: 18 his treasured possession as he **p**,
2Sa 7: 28 and you have **p** these good things
1Ki 8: 5 as I **p** David your father when I
2Ch 6: 15 with your mouth you have **p**
Ps 119: 57 I have **p** to obey your words.
Lk 24: 49 to send you what my Father has **p**;
Ac   1: 4 but wait for the gift my Father **p**,
        13: 32 What God **p** our ancestors
Ro   4: 21 God had power to do what he had **p**.
Tit 1: 2 **p** before the beginning of time,
Heb 10: 23 we profess, for he who **p** is faithful.
        10: 36 you will receive what he has **p**.
Jas 1: 12 God has **p** to those who love him.

Jas 2: 5 the kingdom he **p** those who love
2Pe 3: 4 "Where is this 'coming' he **p**?
1Jn 2: 25 And this is what he **p** us—

PROMISES (PROMISE)
Jos 21: 45 of all the LORD's good **p**
23: 14 all the good **p** the LORD your God
1Ki 8: 56 all the good **p** he gave through his
1Ch 17: 19 and made known all these great **p**.
Ps 85: 8 he **p** peace to his people, his faithful
106: 12 they believed his **p** and sang his
119:140 Your **p** have been thoroughly tested,
119:148 that I may meditate on your **p**.
145: 13 LORD is trustworthy in all he **p**
Ro 9: 4 the temple worship and the **p**
2Co 1: 20 matter how many **p** God has made,
7: 1 since we have these **p**, dear friends,
Heb 8: 6 covenant is established on better **p**
2Pe 1: 4 us his very great and precious **p**,

PROMOTE
Pr 12: 20 but those who **p** peace have joy.
16: 21 and gracious words **p** instruction.
1Ti 4: 1 Such things **p** controversial

PROMPTED
1Th 1: 3 by faith, your labor **p** by love,
2Th 1: 11 and your every deed **p** by faith.

PRONOUNCE (PRONOUNCED)
1Ch 23: 13 to **p** blessings in his name forever.

PRONOUNCED (PRONOUNCE)
1Ch 16: 12 miracles, and the judgments he **p**,

PROOF (PROVE)
Ac 17: 31 He has given **p** of this to everyone
2Co 8: 24 Therefore show these men the **p**

PROPER
Ps 104: 27 give them their food at the **p** time.
145: 15 give them their food at the **p** time.
Ecc 8: 5 the wise heart will know the **p** time
Mt 24: 45 give them their food at the **p** time?
1Co 11: 13 Is it **p** for a woman to pray to God
Gal 6: 9 at the **p** time we will reap a harvest
1Ti 2: 6 now been witnessed to at the **p** time.
1Pe 2: 17 Show **p** respect to everyone,

PROPERTY
Heb 10: 34 accepted the confiscation of your **p**,

PROPHECIES (PROPHESY)
1Co 13: 8 But where there are **p**, they will
1Th 5: 20 Do not treat **p** with contempt

PROPHECY (PROPHESY)
Da 9: 24 to seal up vision and **p** and to anoint
1Co 12: 10 powers, to another **p**, to another
13: 2 If I have the gift of **p** and can
14: 1 gifts, especially the gift of **p**.
14: 6 or knowledge or **p** or word
14: 22 **p**, however, is not for unbelievers
2Pe 1: 20 that no **p** of Scripture came
Rev 22: 18 the words of the **p** of this scroll:

PROPHESIED (PROPHESY)
Nu 11: 25 the Spirit rested on them, they **p**—
1Sa 19: 24 and he too **p** in Samuel's presence.
Jn 11: 51 that year he **p** that Jesus would die
Ac 19: 6 and they spoke in tongues and **p**.
21: 9 four unmarried daughters who **p**.

PROPHESIES (PROPHESY)
Jer 28: 9 But the prophet who **p** peace will be
Eze 12: 27 and he **p** about the distant future.'
1Co 11: 5 **p** with his head covered dishonors

PROPHESY (PROPHECIES PROPHECY
PROPHESIED PROPHESIES PROPHESYING
PROPHET PROPHET'S PROPHETESS PROPHETIC
PROPHETS)
1Sa 10: 6 in power, and you will **p** with them;
Eze 13: 2 Say to those who **p** out of their own
13: 17 daughters of your people who **p**
34: 2 against the shepherds of Israel;
37: 4 "**P** to these bones and say to them,
Joel 2: 28 Your sons and daughters will **p**,
Mt 7: 22 did we not **p** in your name
Ac 2: 17 Your sons and daughters will **p**,
1Co 13: 9 we know in part and we **p** in part,
14: 3 But those who **p** speak to people
14: 39 be eager to **p**, and do not forbid
Rev 11: 3 and they will **p** for 1,260 days,

PROPHESYING (PROPHESY)
1Ch 25: 1 and Jeduthun for the ministry of **p**,
Ro 12: 6 If your gift is **p**, then prophesy

PROPHET (PROPHESY)
Ex 7: 1 your brother Aaron will be your **p**.
15: 20 Miriam the **p**, Aaron's sister,
Dt 13: 1 If a **p**, or one who foretells
18: 18 for them a **p** like you from among
18: 22 If what a **p** proclaims in the name
Jdg 4: 4 Deborah, a **p**,
1Sa 3: 20 Samuel was attested as a **p**
9: 9 because the **p** of today used to be
1Ki 1: 8 Nathan the **p**, Shimei and Rei
18: 36 the **p** Elijah stepped forward
2Ki 5: 8 know that there is a **p** in Israel."
6: 12 "but Elisha, the **p** who is in Israel,
20: 1 The **p** Isaiah son of Amoz went
2Ch 35: 18 since the days of the **p** Samuel;
36: 12 himself before Jeremiah the **p**,
Ezr 5: 1 Haggai the **p** and Zechariah the **p**,
Eze 2: 5 know that a **p** has been among them.
33: 33 that a **p** has been among them."
Hos 9: 7 so great, the **p** is considered a fool,
Am 7: 14 neither a **p** nor the disciple of a **p**,
Hab 1: 1 that Habakkuk the **p** received.
Hag 1: 1 LORD came through the **p** Haggai
Zec 1: 1 came to the **p** Zechariah son
Mal 4: 5 "See, I will send the **p** Elijah to you
Mt 10: 41 to be a **p** will receive a prophet's
11: 9 A **p**? Yes, I tell you, and more than
12: 39 it except the sign of the **p** Jonah.
Lk 1: 76 will be called a **p** of the Most High;
2: 36 There was also a **p**, Anna,
7: 16 "A great **p** has appeared among
24: 19 "He was a **p**, powerful in word
Jn 1: 21 "Are you the **P**?"
Ac 7: 37 'God will send you a **p** like me
21: 10 a **p** named Agabus came down
Rev 16: 13 and out of the mouth of the false **p**.

PROPHET'S (PROPHESY)
2Pe 1: 20 about by the **p** own interpretation

PROPHETESS* (PROPHESY)
Isa 8: 3 Then I made love to the **p**, and she

PROPHETIC (PROPHET)
2Pe 1: 19 have the **p** message as something

PROPHETS (PROPHESY)
Nu 11: 29 that all the LORD's people were **p**
12: 6 there are **p** of the LORD among
1Sa 10: 11 Is Saul also among the **p**?"
28: 6 answer him by dreams or Urim or **p**.
1Ki 19: 10 put your **p** to death with the sword.
1Ch 16: 22 do my **p** no harm."
Ps 105: 15 do my **p** no harm."
Jer 23: 9 Concerning the **p**: My heart is
23: 30 "I am against the **p** who steal
Eze 13: 2 prophesy against the **p** of Israel who
Zec 13: 4 that day the **p** will all be ashamed
Mt 5: 17 come to abolish the Law or the **P**;
7: 12 for this sums up the Law and the **P**.
7: 15 "Watch out for false **p**.
22: 40 Law and the **P** hang on these two
23: 37 you who kill the **p** and stone those
24: 24 messiahs and false **p** will appear
26: 56 of the **p** might be fulfilled."
Lk 4: 24 "**p** are not accepted in their
10: 24 For I tell you that many **p** and kings
11: 49 'I will send them **p** and apostles,
24: 25 believe all that the **p** have spoken!
24: 44 of Moses, the **P** and the Psalms."
Ac 3: 24 all the **p** who have spoken have
10: 43 All the **p** testify about him
13: 1 the church at Antioch there were **p**
26: 22 saying nothing beyond what the **p**
28: 23 and from the **P** he tried to persuade
Ro 1: 2 promised beforehand through his **p**
3: 21 to which the Law and the **P** testify.
11: 3 they have killed your **p** and torn
1Co 12: 28 apostles, second **p**, third teachers,
12: 29 Are all **p**? Are all teachers?
14: 32 The spirits of **p** are subject
14: 37 If any think they are **p** or otherwise
Eph 2: 20 the foundation of the apostles and **p**,
3: 5 Spirit to God's holy apostles and **p**.
4: 11 the apostles, the **p**, the evangelists,
Heb 1: 1 our ancestors through the **p** at many
1Pe 1: 10 the **p**, who spoke of the grace
2Pe 3: 2 spoken in the past by the holy **p**
1Jn 4: 1 because many false **p** have gone
Rev 11: 10 because these two **p** had tormented
18: 20 Rejoice, apostles and **p**!

PROPORTION
Dt 16: 10 giving a freewill offering in **p**

Dt 16: 17 you must bring a gift in **p** to the way

PROPRIETY*
1Ti 2: 9 with decency and **p**,
2: 15 in faith, love and holiness with **p**.

PROSPECT*
Pr 10: 28 The **p** of the righteous is joy,

PROSPER (PROSPERED PROSPERITY
PROSPEROUS PROSPERS)
Dt 5: 33 so that you may live and **p**
28: 63 pleased the LORD to make you **p**
29: 9 you may **p** in everything you do.
1Ki 2: 3 this so that you may **p** in all you do
Ezr 6: 14 **p** under the preaching of Haggai
Pr 11: 10 When the righteous **p**, the city
11: 25 A generous person will **p**;
16: 20 who give heed to instruction **p**,
17: 20 whose heart is corrupt does not **p**;
19: 8 cherish understanding will soon **p**.
28: 13 who conceal their sins do not **p**,
28: 25 who trust in the LORD will **p**.
Isa 53: 10 of the LORD will **p** in his hand.
Jer 12: 1 Why does the way of the wicked **p**?

PROSPERED (PROSPER)
Ge 39: 2 was with Joseph so that he **p**, and he
2Ch 14: 7 on every side." So they built and **p**.
31: 21 And so he **p**.

PROSPERITY (PROSPER)
Dt 28: 11 LORD will grant you abundant **p**—
30: 15 I set before you today life and **p**,
Job 36: 11 will spend the rest of their days in **p**
Ps 73: 3 when I saw the **p** of the wicked.
122: 9 LORD our God, I will seek your **p**.
128: 2 blessings and **p** will be yours.
Pr 3: 2 years and bring you peace and **p**.
21: 21 and love finds life, **p** and honor.
Isa 45: 7 I bring and create disaster;

PROSPEROUS (PROSPER)
Dt 30: 9 your God will make you most **p**
Jos 1: 8 Then you will be **p** and successful.

PROSPERS (PROSPER)
Ps 1: 3 whatever they do **p**.

PROSTITUTE (PROSTITUTES PROSTITUTION)
Lev 20: 6 and spiritists to **p** themselves
Nu 15: 39 not **p** yourselves by chasing
Jos 2: 1 the house of a **p** named Rahab
Pr 6: 26 For a **p** can be had for a loaf
7: 10 dressed like a **p** and with crafty
Eze 16: 15 and used your fame to become a **p**.
23: 7 She gave herself as a **p** to all
Hos 3: 3 you must not be a **p** or be intimate
1Co 6: 15 of Christ and unite them with a **p**?
6: 16 who unites himself with a **p** is one
Rev 17: 1 you the punishment of the great **p**,

PROSTITUTES (PROSTITUTE)
Pr 29: 3 of **p** squanders his wealth.
Mt 21: 31 the **p** are entering the kingdom
Lk 15: 30 your property with **p** comes home,
1Co 6: 9 adulterers nor male **p** nor practicing

PROSTITUTION (PROSTITUTE)
Eze 16: 16 places, where you carried on your **p**.
23: 3 engaging in **p** from their youth.
Hos 4: 10 they will engage in **p** but not

PROSTRATE
Dt 9: 18 again I fell **p** before the LORD
1Ki 18: 39 saw this, they fell **p** and cried,

PROTECT (PROTECTED PROTECTION
PROTECTS)
Dt 23: 14 moves about in your camp to **p** you
Ps 25: 21 May integrity and uprightness **p** me,
32: 7 you will **p** me from trouble
40: 11 love and faithfulness always **p** me.
91: 14 I will **p** them, for they acknowledge
140: 1 **p** me from the violent,
Pr 2: 11 Discretion will **p** you,
4: 6 forsake wisdom, and she will **p** you;
27: 18 who **p** their masters will be honored.
Jn 17: 11 **p** them by the power of your name,
17: 15 that you **p** them from the evil one.
2Th 3: 3 you and **p** you from the evil one.

PROTECTED (PROTECT)
Jos 24: 17 He **p** us on our entire journey
1Sa 30: 23 He has **p** us and delivered into our
Jn 17: 12 I **p** them and kept them safe

PROTECTION (PROTECT)
Ezr 9: 9 he has given us a wall of **p** in Judah

Ps 5: 11 Spread your **p** over them, that those

PROTECTS (PROTECT)
Ps 41: 2 The LORD **p** and preserves them—
116: 6 The LORD **p** the unwary;
Pr 2: 8 and **p** the way of his faithful ones.
1Co 13: 7 It always **p**, always trusts,

PROUD (PRIDE)
Ps 31: 23 but the **p** he pays back in full.
101: 5 has haughty eyes and a **p** heart,
138: 6 he takes notice of the **p** from afar.
Pr 3: 34 He mocks **p** mockers but shows
16: 5 The LORD detests all the **p**
16: 19 than to share plunder with the **p**.
21: 4 Haughty eyes and a **p** heart—
Isa 2: 12 has a day in store for all the **p**
Ro 1: 30 Do not be **p**, but be willing
1Co 13: 4 envy, it does not boast, it is not **p**.
2Ti 3: 2 of money, boastful, **p**, abusive,
Jas 4: 6 "God opposes the **p** but shows
1Pe 5: 5 "God opposes the **p** but shows

PROVE (PROOF PROVED PROVING)
Pr 29: 25 To fear anyone will **p** to be a snare,
Jn 8: 46 Can any of you **p** me guilty of sin?
16: 8 he will **p** the world
1Co 4: 2 been given a trust must **p** faithful.

PROVED (PROVE)
Isa 5: 16 the holy God will be **p** holy
Eze 28: 25 I will be **p** holy through them
Mt 11: 19 wisdom is **p** right by her actions."
Ro 3: 4 you may be **p** right when you speak
1Pe 1: 7 may be **p** genuine and may result

PROVIDE (PROVIDED PROVIDES PROVISION)
Ge 22: 8 "God himself will **p** the lamb
22: 14 that place The LORD Will **P**.
Isa 43: 20 because I provide water in the wilderness
61: 3 and **p** for those who grieve in Zion—
1Co 10: 13 **p** a way out so that you can endure
1Ti 5: 8 Anyone who does not **p** for their
Tit 3: 14 in order to **p** for urgent needs

PROVIDED (PROVIDE)
Ps 68: 10 bounty, God, you **p** for the poor.
111: 9 He **p** redemption for his people;
Jnh 1: 17 Now the LORD **p** a huge fish
4: 6 the LORD God **p** a gourd
4: 7 at dawn the next day God **p** a worm,
4: 8 rose, God **p** a scorching east wind,
Gal 4: 18 to be zealous, the purpose is good,
Heb 1: 3 After he had **p** purification for sins,

PROVIDES (PROVIDE)
Ps 111: 5 He **p** food for those who fear him;
Pr 31: 15 she **p** food for her family
Eze 18: 7 hungry and **p** clothing for the naked.
1Ti 6: 17 who richly **p** us with everything
1Pe 4: 11 do so with the strength God **p**.

PROVING* (PROVE)
Ac 9: 22 in Damascus by **p** that Jesus is
17: 3 and **p** that the Messiah had to suffer
18: 28 **p** from the Scriptures that Jesus was

PROVISION (PROVIDE)
Ro 5: 17 those who receive God's abundant **p**

PROVOKED
Ecc 7: 9 Do not be quickly **p** in your spirit,
Jer 32: 32 Judah have **p** me by all the evil they

PROWLS
1Pe 5: 8 enemy the devil **p** around like

PRUDENCE* (PRUDENT)
Pr 1: 4 giving **p** to those who are simple,
8: 5 You who are simple, gain **p**;
8: 12 "I, wisdom, dwell together with **p**;
12: 8 are praised according to their **p**,
15: 5 whoever heeds correction shows **p**.
16: 22 **P** is a fountain of life
19: 25 mocker, and the simple will learn **p**;
21: 16 Whoever strays from the path of **p**

PRUDENT (PRUDENCE)
Pr 1: 3 receiving instruction in **p** behavior,
12: 16 at once, but the **p** overlook an insult.
12: 23 The **p** keep their knowledge
13: 16 All who are **p** act with knowledge,
14: 8 The wisdom of the **p** is to give
14: 15 but the **p** give thought to their steps.
14: 18 the **p** are crowned with knowledge.
19: 14 but a wife is from the LORD.
22: 3 The **p** see danger and take refuge,
27: 12 The **p** see danger and take refuge,
Jer 49: 7 Has counsel perished from the **p**?

Am 5: 13 Therefore the **p** keep quiet in such

PRUNES* (PRUNING)
Jn 15: 2 does bear fruit he **p** so that it will be

PRUNING (PRUNES)
Isa 2: 4 and their spears into **p** hooks.
Joel 3: 10 and your **p** hooks into spears.

PSALMS
Eph 5: 19 speaking to one another with **p**,
Col 3: 16 another with all wisdom through **p**,

PUBERTY*
Eze 16: 7 grew and developed and entered **p**.

PUBLICLY
Mt 10: 32 **p** acknowledges me I will also
Ac 20: 20 have taught you **p** and from house

PUFFS*
1Co 8: 1 knowledge **p** up while love builds

PUNISH (PUNISHED PUNISHMENT)
Ge 15: 14 But I will **p** the nation they serve as
Ex 32: 34 to **p**, I will **p** them for their sin."
Pr 23: 13 if you **p** them with the rod, they will
Isa 13: 11 I will **p** the world for its evil,
Jer 2: 19 Your wickedness will **p** you;
21: 14 I will **p** you as your deeds deserve,
Zep 1: 12 and **p** those who are complacent,
Ac 7: 7 But I will **p** the nation they serve as
2Th 1: 8 He will **p** those who do not know
1Pe 2: 14 by him to **p** those who do wrong

PUNISHED (PUNISH)
Ezr 9: 13 you have **p** us less than our sins
Ps 99: 8 God, though you **p** their misdeeds.
Isa 53: 8 of my people he was **p**.
La 3: 39 should the living complain when **p**
Mk 12: 40 men will be **p** most severely."
Lk 23: 41 We are **p** justly, for we are getting
2Th 1: 9 They will be **p** with everlasting
Heb 10: 29 to be **p** who have trampled the Son

PUNISHMENT (PUNISH)
Isa 53: 5 the **p** that brought us peace was
Jer 4: 18 This is your **p**. How bitter it is!
Mt 25: 46 they will go away to eternal **p**,
Lk 12: 48 and does things deserving **p** will be
21: 22 this is the time of **p** in fulfillment
Ro 13: 4 wrath to bring **p** on the wrongdoer.
Heb 2: 2 and disobedience received its just **p**,
2Pe 2: 9 to hold the unrighteous for **p**

PURCHASED
Ps 74: 2 the people you **p** long ago, the tribe
Rev 5: 9 your blood you **p** for God members

PURE (PURIFICATION PURIFIED PURIFIES PURIFY PURITY)
2Sa 22: 27 to the **p** you show yourself **p**,
2Ki 22: 2 water has remained **p** to this day,
Job 14: 4 Who can bring what is **p**
Ps 19: 9 The fear of the LORD is **p**,
24: 4 who have clean hands and a **p** heart,
51: 10 Create in me a **p** heart, O God,
119: 9 who are young keep their way **p**?
Pr 15: 26 gracious words are **p** in his sight.
20: 9 can say, "I have kept my heart **p**;
Isa 52: 11 Come out from it and be **p**, you who
Hab 1: 13 Your eyes are too **p** to look on evil;
Mt 5: 8 Blessed are the **p** in heart, for they
2Co 11: 2 I might present you as a **p** virgin
Php 4: 8 whatever is **p**, whatever is lovely,
1Ti 1: 5 which comes from a **p** heart
5: 22 the sins of others. Keep yourself **p**.
2Ti 2: 22 call on the Lord out of a **p** heart.
Tit 1: 15 To the **p**, all things are **p**,
2: 5 to be self-controlled and **p**, to be
Heb 7: 26 blameless, **p**, set apart from sinners,
13: 4 and the marriage bed kept **p**,
Jas 1: 27 that God our Father accepts as **p**
3: 17 comes from heaven is first of all **p**;
1Jn 3: 3 purify themselves, just as he is **p**.

PURGE
Pr 20: 30 and beatings **p** the inmost being.

PURIFICATION (PURE)
Heb 1: 3 After he had provided **p** for sins,

PURIFIED (PURE)
Ac 15: 9 them, for he **p** their hearts by faith.
1Pe 1: 22 you have **p** yourselves by obeying

PURIFIES* (PURE)
1Jn 1: 7 of Jesus, his Son, **p** us from all sin.

PURIFY (PURE)
Nu 19: 12 They must **p** themselves
2Co 7: 1 let us **p** ourselves from everything
Tit 2: 14 to **p** for himself a people that are his
Jas 4: 8 you sinners, and **p** your hearts,
1Jn 1: 9 and **p** us from all unrighteousness.
3: 3 this hope in him **p** themselves,

PURIM
Est 9: 26 (Therefore these days were called **P**,

PURITY* (PURE)
Hos 8: 5 long will they be incapable of **p**?
2Co 6: 6 in **p**, understanding,
1Ti 4: 12 in conduct, in love, in faith and in **p**.
5: 2 women as sisters, with absolute **p**.
1Pe 3: 2 when they see the **p** and reverence

PURPLE
Pr 31: 22 she is clothed in fine linen and **p**.
Mk 15: 17 They put a **p** robe on him,

PURPOSE (PURPOSED PURPOSES)
Ex 9: 16 I have raised you up for this very **p**,
Job 36: 5 he is mighty, and firm in his **p**.
42: 2 no **p** of yours can be thwarted.
Pr 19: 21 it is the LORD's **p** that prevails.
Isa 46: 10 I say, 'My **p** will stand, and I will
55: 11 and achieve the **p** for which I sent it.
Ro 8: 28 have been called according to his **p**.
9: 11 that God's **p** in election might stand:
9: 17 "I raised you up for this very **p**,
1Co 3: 8 and the one who waters have one **p**,
2Co 5: 5 fashioned us for this very **p** is God,
Gal 4: 18 be zealous, provided the **p** is good,
Eph 1: 11 in conformity with the **p** of his will,
3: 11 to his eternal **p** that he accomplished
Php 2: 13 to act in order to fulfill his good **p**.
2Ti 1: 9 but because of his own **p** and grace.

PURPOSED (PURPOSE)
Isa 14: 24 and as I have **p**, so it will happen.
14: 27 For the LORD Almighty has **p**,
Eph 1: 9 good pleasure, which he **p** in Christ,

PURPOSES (PURPOSE)
Ps 33: 10 he thwarts the **p** of the peoples.
Jer 23: 20 until he fully accomplishes the **p**
32: 19 great are your **p** and mighty are

PURSE (PURSES)
Hag 1: 6 to put them in a **p** with holes in it."
Lk 10: 4 Do not take a **p** or bag or sandals;
22: 36 "But now if you have a **p**, take it,

PURSES (PURSE)
Lk 12: 33 Provide **p** for yourselves that will

PURSUE (PURSUES)
Ps 34: 14 and do good; seek peace and **p** it.
Pr 15: 9 he loves those who **p** righteousness.
Ro 9: 30 who did not **p** righteousness,
1Ti 6: 11 this, and **p** righteousness, godliness,
2Ti 2: 22 of youth and **p** righteousness, faith,
1Pe 3: 11 and do good; seek peace and **p** it.

PURSUES (PURSUE)
Pr 21: 21 Whoever **p** righteousness and love
28: 1 The wicked flee though no one **p**,

QUAIL
Ex 16: 13 That evening **q** came and covered
Nu 11: 31 and drove **q** in from the sea.

QUALITIES* (QUALITY)
Da 6: 3 by his exceptional **q** that the king
Ro 1: 20 of the natural God's invisible **q**—
2Pe 1: 8 if you possess these **q** in increasing

QUALITY (QUALITIES)
1Co 3: 13 and the fire will test the **q** of each

QUARREL (QUARRELING QUARRELS QUARRELSOME)
Pr 15: 18 but those who are patient calm a **q**.
17: 1 Starting a **q** is like breaching a dam;
17: 19 Whoever loves a **q** loves sin;
20: 3 strife, but every fool is quick to **q**.
26: 17 who rushes into a **q** not their own.
26: 20 without a gossip a **q** dies down.
Isa 45: 9 those who **q** with their Maker,
Jas 4: 2 what you want, so you **q** and fight.

QUARRELING (QUARREL)
1Co 3: 3 there is jealousy and **q** among you,
2Ti 2: 14 Warn them before God against **q**

QUARRELS (QUARREL)
2Ti 2: 23 because you know they produce **q**.
Jas 4: 1 causes fights and **q** among you?

QUARRELSOME (QUARREL)
Pr 19: 13 a q wife is like the constant dripping
    21: 9 than share a house with a q wife.
    26: 21 so is a q person for kindling strife.
1Ti 3: 3 gentle, not q, not a lover of money.
2Ti 2: 24 the Lord's servant must not be q

QUEEN
1Ki 10: 1 When the q of Sheba heard
2Ch 9: 1 When the q of Sheba heard
Mt 12: 42 The Q of the South will rise

QUENCH (QUENCHED)
SS 8: 7 Many waters cannot q love;

QUENCHED (QUENCH)
Isa 66: 24 will not their fire be q, and they will
Mk 9: 48 does not die, and the fire is not q.'

QUICK-TEMPERED* (TEMPER)
Pr 14: 17 The q do foolish things, and those
    14: 29 but the q display folly.
Tit 1: 7 not q, not given to drunkenness,

QUIET (QUIETNESS)
Ps 23: 2 he leads me beside q waters,
Pr 17: 1 and q than a house full of feasting,
Ecc 9: 17 The q words of the wise are more
Am 5: 13 Therefore the prudent keep q
Lk 19: 40 "if they keep q, the stones will cry
1Th 4: 11 it your ambition to lead a q life:
1Ti 2: 2 peaceful and q lives in all godliness
1Ti 2: 12 authority over a man; she must be q.
1Pe 3: 4 beauty of a gentle and q spirit,

QUIETNESS* (QUIET)
Job 3: 26 I have no peace, no q;
Isa 30: 15 in q and trust is your strength,
    32: 17 its effect will be q and confidence
1Ti 2: 11 A woman should learn in q and full

QUIVER
Ps 127: 5 Blessed is the man whose q is full

RACE
Ecc 9: 11 The r is not to the swift or the battle
Ac 20: 24 my only aim is to finish the r
1Co 9: 24 know that in a r all the runners run,
Gal 2: 2 had not been running my r in vain.
    5: 7 You were running a good r.
2Ti 4: 7 I have finished the r, I have kept
Heb 12: 1 with perseverance the r marked

RACHEL
    Daughter of Laban (Ge 29:16); wife of Jacob (Ge
29:28); bore two sons (Ge 30:22–24; 35:16–24;
46:19). Stole Laban's gods (Ge 31:19, 32–35). Death
(Ge 35:19–20).

RADIANCE (RADIANT)
Eze 1: 28 rainy day, so was the r around him.
Heb 1: 3 The Son is the r of God's glory

RADIANT (RADIANCE)
Ex 34: 29 that his face was r because he had
Ps 34: 5 Those who look to him are r;
SS 5: 10 My beloved is r and ruddy,
Isa 60: 5 Then you will look and be r,
Eph 5: 27 present her to himself as a r church,

RAGE
Pr 29: 11 Fools give full vent to their r,
Ac 4: 25 " 'Why do the nations r
Col 3: 8 anger, r, malice, slander, and filthy

RAGS
Isa 64: 6 our righteous acts are like filthy r;

RAHAB
    Prostitute of Jericho who hid Israelite spies (Jos 2;
6:22–25; Heb 11:31; Jas 2:25). Mother of Boaz (Mt
1:5).

RAIN (RAINBOW)
Ge 7: 4 from now I will send r on the earth
1Ki 17: 1 there will be neither dew nor r
    18: 1 and I will send r on the land."
Mt 5: 45 and sends r on the righteous
Jas 5: 17 and it did not r on the land for three
Jude : 12 they are clouds without r,

RAINBOW (RAIN)
Ge 9: 13 I have set my r in the clouds, and it

RAISE (RISE)
Jn 6: 39 but r them up at the last day.
1Co 15: 15 he did not r him if in fact the dead

RAISED (RISE)
Ps 89: 19 I have r up a young man
Isa 52: 13 he will be r and lifted up and highly

Mt 17: 23 the third day he will be r to life."
Lk 7: 22 the dead are r, and the good news is
Ac 2: 24 But God r him from the dead,
Ro 4: 25 was r to life for our justification.
    6: 4 just as Christ was r from the dead
    8: 11 of him who r Jesus from the dead is
    10: 9 your heart that God r him
1Co 15: 4 he was r on the third day according
    15: 20 Christ has indeed been r

RALLY*
Isa 11: 10 the nations will r to him, and his

RAM (RAMS)
Ge 22: 13 in a thicket he saw a r caught by its
Ex 25: 5 r skins dyed red and another durable
Da 8: 3 there before me was a r with two

RAMPART*
Ps 91: 4 will be your shield and r.

RAMS (RAM)
1Sa 15: 22 to heed is better than the fat of r.
Mic 6: 7 be pleased with thousands of r,

RAN (RUN)
Jnh 1: 3 But Jonah r away from the LORD

RANSOM
Mt 20: 28 to give his life as a r for many."
Mk 10: 45 to give his life as a r for many."
1Ti 2: 6 who gave himself as a r for all
Heb 9: 15 he has died as a r to set them free

RARE
Pr 20: 15 that speak knowledge are a r jewel.

RAVEN (RAVENS)
Ge 8: 7 and sent out a r, and it kept flying
Job 38: 41 food for the r when its young cry

RAVENS (RAVEN)
1Ki 17: 6 The r brought him bread and meat
Ps 147: 9 and for the young r when they call.
Lk 12: 24 Consider the r: They do not sow

RAYS
Mal 4: 2 will rise with healing in its r.

READ (READING READS)
Dt 17: 19 he is to r it all the days of his life so
Jos 8: 34 Joshua r all the words of the law—
2Ki 23: 2 He r in their hearing all the words
Ne 8: 3 They r from the Book of the Law
Jer 36: 6 r to the people from the scroll
2Co 3: 2 hearts, known and r by everyone.

READING (READ)
1Ti 4: 13 yourself to the public r of Scripture,

READS (READ)
Rev 1: 3 is the one who r aloud the words

REAFFIRM
2Co 2: 8 therefore, to r your love for him.

REAL* (REALITIES REALITY)
Jn 6: 55 my flesh is r food and my blood is r drink.
1Jn 2: 27 and as that anointing is r,

REALITIES* (REAL)
1Co 2: 13 spiritual r with Spirit-taught
Heb 10: 1 not the r themselves.

REALITY* (REAL)
Col 2: 17 the r, however, is found in Christ.

REALMS
Eph 1: 3 the heavenly r with every spiritual
    2: 6 in the heavenly r in Christ Jesus,

REAP (REAPER)
Job 4: 8 evil and those who sow trouble r it.
Ps 126: 5 sow with tears will r with songs
Pr 11: 18 sow righteousness reap a sure reward.
    22: 8 who sow injustice r calamity,
Hos 8: 7 sow the wind and r the whirlwind.
    10: 12 r the fruit of unfailing love,
Jn 4: 38 to r what you have not worked for.
Ro 6: 22 the benefit you r leads to holiness,
2Co 9: 6 generously will also r generously.
Gal 6: 7 People r what they sow.
    6: 8 from that nature will r destruction;

REAPER (REAP)
Jn 4: 36 and the r may be glad together.

REASON (REASONED)
Ge 2: 24 For this r a man will leave his father
Isa 1: 18 let us r together," says the LORD.
Mt 19: 5 this r a man will leave his father
Jn 12: 27 it was for this very r I came to this
    15: 25 'They hated me without r.'

1Pe 3: 15 asks you to give the r for the hope
2Pe 1: 5 For this very r, make every effort

REASONED (REASON)
1Co 13: 11 thought like a child, I r like a child.

REASSURED
Ru 2: 13 "You have r me and have spoken

REBEKAH
    Sister of Laban, secured as bride for Isaac (Ge 24).
Mother of Esau and Jacob (Ge 25:19–26). Taken by
Abimelek as sister of Isaac; returned (Ge 26:1–11).
Encouraged Jacob to trick Isaac out of blessing (Ge
27:1–17).

REBEL (REBELLED REBELLION REBELS)
Nu 14: 9 Only do not r against the LORD.
1Sa 12: 14 and do not r against his commands,
Mt 10: 21 children will r against their parents

REBELLED (REBEL)
Ps 78: 56 the test and r against the Most High;
Isa 63: 10 Yet they r and grieved his Holy

REBELLION (REBEL)
Ex 34: 7 and forgiving wickedness, r and sin.
Nu 14: 18 in love and forgiving sin and r.
1Sa 15: 23 For r is like the sin of divination,
2Th 2: 3 until the r occurs and the man of

REBELS (REBEL)
Mk 15: 27 They crucified two r with him,
Ro 13: 2 whoever r against the authority is
1Ti 1: 9 righteous but for lawbreakers and r,

REBIRTH* (BEAR)
Tit 3: 5 saved us through the washing of r

REBUILD (BUILD)
Ezr 5: 2 set to work to r the house of God
Ne 2: 17 let us r the wall of Jerusalem,
Ps 102: 16 For the LORD will r Zion
Da 9: 25 r Jerusalem until the Anointed One,
Am 9: 14 "They will r the ruined cities
Ac 15: 16 Its ruins I will r, and I will restore

REBUILT (BUILD)
Zec 1: 16 and there my house will be r.

REBUKE (REBUKED REBUKES REBUKING)
Lev 19: 17 R your neighbor frankly so you will
Ps 141: 5 let him r me—that is oil on my
Pr 3: 11 discipline, and do not resent his r,
    9: 8 r the wise and they will love you.
    17: 10 A r impresses a discerning person
    19: 25 the discerning, and they will gain
    25: 12 of fine gold is the r of a wise judge
    27: 5 Better is open r than hidden love.
    30: 6 he will r you and prove you a liar.
Ecc 7: 5 to heed the r of a wise person than
Isa 54: 9 with you, never to r you again.
Jer 2: 19 your backsliding will r you.
Zep 3: 17 in his love he will no longer r
Lk 17: 3 or sister sins against you, r them;
1Ti 5: 1 Do not r an older man harshly,
2Ti 4: 2 correct, r and encourage—
Tit 1: 13 Therefore r them sharply,
    2: 15 Encourage and r with all authority.
Rev 3: 19 Those whom I love I r

REBUKED (REBUKE)
Mk 16: 14 r them for their lack of faith

REBUKES (REBUKE)
Job 22: 4 "Is it for your piety that he r you
Pr 28: 23 Whoever r a person will in the end
    29: 1 many r will suddenly be destroyed—
Heb 12: 5 and do not lose heart when he r you,

REBUKING (REBUKE)
2Ti 3: 16 and is useful for teaching, r,

RECALLING
1Ti 1: 18 by r them you may fight the battle

RECEIVE (RECEIVED RECEIVES RECEIVING)
Mt 10: 41 to be righteous will r a righteous
Mk 10: 15 anyone who will not r the kingdom
Jn 1: 12 Yet to all who did r him,
    20: 22 them and said, "R the Holy Spirit.
Ac 1: 8 But you will r power when the Holy
    2: 38 you will r the gift of the Holy Spirit.
    19: 2 "Did you r the Holy Spirit
    20: 35 more blessed to give than to r.' "
1Co 9: 14 the gospel should r their living
2Co 1: 4 comfort we ourselves r from God.
    6: 1 not to r God's grace in vain.
    6: 17 not unclean thing, and I will r you."
1Ti 1: 16 believe in him and r eternal life.
Jas 1: 7 not think they will r anything

2Pe 1: 11 you will r a rich welcome
1Jn 3: 22 and r from him anything we ask,
Rev 4: 11 to r glory and honor and power,
 5: 12 to r power and wealth and wisdom

RECEIVED (RECEIVE)
Mt 6: 2 they have r their reward in full.
 10: 8 Freely you have r, freely give.
Mk 11: 24 believe that you have r it, and it will
Jn 1: 16 of his fullness we have all r grace
Ac 8: 17 on them, and they r the Holy Spirit.
 10: 47 They have r the Holy Spirit just as
Ro 8: 15 the Spirit you r brought about your
1Co 11: 23 For I r from the Lord what I
Col 2: 6 just as you r Christ Jesus as Lord,
1Pe 4: 10 should use whatever gift you have r

RECEIVES (RECEIVE)
Pr 18: 22 good and r favor from the LORD.
Mt 7: 8 For everyone who asks r;
Ac 10: 43 who believes in r forgiveness

RECEIVING (RECEIVE)
Pr 1: 3 r instruction in prudent behavior,

RECITE
Ps 45: 1 a noble theme as I r my verses

RECKLESS
Pr 12: 18 words of the r pierce like swords,
1Pe 4: 4 join them in their r, wild living,

RECKONING
Isa 10: 3 What will you do on the day of r,
Hos 9: 7 coming, the days of r are at hand.

RECLAIM* (CLAIM)
Isa 11: 11 time to r the surviving remnant

RECOGNITION (RECOGNIZE)
1Co 16: 18 and yours also. Such men deserve r.
1Ti 5: 3 Give proper r to those widows who

RECOGNIZE (RECOGNITION RECOGNIZED)
Mt 7: 16 By their fruit you will r them.
1Jn 4: 2 This is how you can r the Spirit
 4: 6 This is how we r the Spirit of truth

RECOGNIZED (RECOGNIZE)
Mt 12: 33 be bad, for a tree is r by its fruit.
Ro 7: 13 in order that sin might be r as sin,

RECOMPENSE*
Isa 40: 10 and his r accompanies him,
 62: 11 and his r accompanies him.' "

RECONCILE* (RECONCILED RECONCILIATION RECONCILING)
Ac 7: 26 He tried to r them by saying, 'Men,
Eph 2: 16 and in one body to r both of them
Col 1: 20 and through him to r to himself all

RECONCILED* (RECONCILE)
Mt 5: 24 First go and be r to that person;
Lk 12: 58 try hard to be r on the way, or your
Ro 5: 10 we were r to him through the death
 5: 10 having been r, shall we be saved
1Co 7: 11 or else be r to her husband.
2Co 5: 18 who r us to himself through Christ
 5: 20 you on Christ's behalf: Be r to God.
Col 1: 22 But now he has r you by Christ's

RECONCILIATION* (RECONCILE)
Ro 5: 11 whom we have now received r.
 11: 15 For if their rejection brought r
2Co 5: 18 Christ and gave us the ministry of r:
 5: 19 committed to us the message of r.

RECONCILING* (RECONCILE)
2Co 5: 19 that God was r the world to himself

RECORD
Ps 130: 3 kept a r of sins, Lord,
Hos 13: 12 stored up, his sins are kept on r.
1Co 13: 5 angered, it keeps no r of wrongs.

RECORDED (RECORD)
Job 19: 23 that my words were r, that they
Jn 20: 30 which are not r in this book.

RECOUNT*
Ps 119: 13 With my lips I r all the laws

RED
Ex 15: 4 officers are drowned in the R Sea.
Ps 106: 9 He rebuked the R Sea, and it dried
Pr 23: 31 Do not gaze at wine when it is r,
Isa 1: 18 though they are r as crimson,

REDEDICATE* (DEDICATE)
Nu 6: 12 They must r themselves

REDEEM (REDEEMED REDEEMER REDEEMS REDEMPTION)
Ex 6: 6 and I will r you with an outstretched
2Sa 7: 23 out to r as a people for himself,
Ps 44: 26 r us because of your unfailing love.
 49: 7 No one can r the life of another
 49: 15 God will r me from the realm
 130: 8 He himself will r Israel from all
Hos 13: 14 I will r them from death.
Gal 4: 5 to r those under the law, that we
Tit 2: 14 for us to r us from all wickedness

REDEEMED (REDEEM)
Ps 71: 23 praise to you—I, whom you have r.
 107: 2 Let the r of the LORD tell their
Isa 35: 9 But only the r will walk there,
 63: 9 In his love and mercy he r them;
Gal 3: 13 Christ r us from the curse of the law
1Pe 1: 18 that you were r from the empty way

REDEEMER (REDEEM)
Job 19: 25 I know that my r lives,
Ps 19: 14 sight, LORD, my Rock and my R.
Isa 44: 6 Israel's King and R, the LORD
 48: 17 your R, the Holy One of Israel:
 59: 20 "The R will come to Zion, to those

REDEEMS* (REDEEM)
Ps 34: 22 The LORD r his servants;
 103: 4 who r your life from the pit

REDEMPTION (REDEEM)
Ps 130: 7 unfailing love and with him is full r.
Lk 21: 28 because your r is drawing near."
Ro 3: 24 by his grace through the r that came
 8: 23 our adoption, the r of our bodies.
1Co 1: 30 our righteousness, holiness and r.
Eph 1: 7 In him we have r through his blood,
 1: 14 our inheritance until the r of those
 4: 30 you were sealed for the day of r.
Col 1: 14 in whom we have r, the forgiveness
Heb 9: 12 own blood, thus obtaining eternal r.

REED
Isa 42: 3 A bruised r he will not break,
Mt 12: 20 A bruised r he will not break,

REFINE*
Jer 9: 7 "See, I will r and test them,
Zec 13: 9 I will r them like silver and test
Mal 3: 3 the Levites and r them like gold

REFLECTS*
Pr 27: 19 As water r the face, so one's life r

REFRESH (REFRESHED REFRESHES REFRESHING)
Phm : 20 in the Lord; r my heart in Christ.

REFRESHED (REFRESH)
Pr 11: 25 whoever refreshes others will be r.

REFRESHES (REFRESH)
Ps 23: 3 he r my soul.

REFRESHING* (REFRESH)
Ps 19: 7 the LORD is perfect, r the soul.
Ac 3: 19 times of r may come from the Lord,

REFUGE
Nu 35: 11 some towns to be your cities of r,
Dt 33: 27 The eternal God is your r,
Jos 20: 2 Israelites to designate the cities of r,
Ru 2: 12 wings you have come to take r."
2Sa 22: 3 in whom I take r, my shield
 22: 31 He shields all who take r in him.
Ps 2: 12 Blessed are all who take r in him.
 5: 11 let all who take r in you be glad;
 9: 9 The LORD is a r
 16: 1 safe, my God, for in you I take r.
 17: 7 your right hand those who take r
 18: 2 in whom I take r, my shield
 31: 2 be my rock of r, a strong fortress
 34: 8 blessed are those who take r in him.
 36: 7 People take r in the shadow of your
 46: 1 God is our r and strength,
 62: 8 your hearts to him, for God is our r.
 71: 1 In you, LORD, I have taken r;
 91: 2 "He is my r and my fortress,
 144: 2 in whom I take r, who subdues
Pr 14: 26 and for their children it will be a r.
 30: 5 a shield to those who take r in him.
Na 1: 7 is good, a r in times of trouble.

REFUSE (REFUSED)
Jn 5: 40 yet you r to come to me to have life.

REFUSED (REFUSE)
2Th 2: 10 They perish because they r to love

Rev 16: 9 but they r to repent and glorify him.

REGARD (REGARDS)
1Th 5: 13 in the highest r in love because

REGARDS (REGARD)
Ro 14: 14 if anyone r something as unclean,

REGRET
2Co 7: 10 leads to salvation and leaves no r,

REHOBOAM
Son of Solomon (1Ki 11:43; 1Ch 3:10). Harsh treatment of subjects caused divided kingdom (1Ki 12:1–24; 14:21–31; 2Ch 10–12).

REIGN (REIGNED REIGNS)
Ps 68: 16 mountain where God chooses to r,
Isa 9: 7 He will r on David's throne
 24: 23 for the LORD Almighty will r
 32: 1 a king will r in righteousness
Jer 23: 5 a King who will r wisely and do
Eze 20: 33 I will r over you with a mighty
Lk 1: 33 he will r over the house of Jacob
Ro 6: 12 Therefore do not let sin r in your
1Co 4: 8 You have begun to r—
 15: 25 For he must r until he has put all his
2Ti 2: 12 we endure, we will also r with him.
Rev 11: 15 and he will r for ever and ever."
 20: 6 will r with him for a thousand years.
 22: 5 And they will r for ever and ever.

REIGNED (REIGN)
Ro 5: 21 so that, just as sin r in death,
Rev 20: 4 and r with Christ a thousand years.

REIGNS (REIGN)
Ex 15: 18 "The LORD r for ever and ever."
Ps 9: 7 The LORD r forever;
 47: 8 God r over the nations,
 93: 1 The LORD r, he is robed
 96: 10 the nations, "The LORD r."
 97: 1 The LORD r, let the earth be glad;
 99: 1 The LORD r, let the nations
 146: 10 The LORD r forever, your God,
Isa 52: 7 who say to Zion, "Your God r!"
Rev 19: 6 For our Lord God Almighty r.

REIN
Jas 1: 26 and yet do not keep a tight r on their

REJECT (REJECTED REJECTION REJECTS)
Ps 94: 14 the LORD will not r his people;
Ro 11: 1 I ask then: Did God r his people?
1Th 5: 22 r whatever is harmful.

REJECTED (REJECT)
1Sa 8: 7 it is not you they have r, but they
1Ki 19: 10 The Israelites have r your covenant,
2Ki 17: 15 They r his decrees and the covenant
Ps 66: 20 to God, who has not r my prayer
 118: 22 stone the builders r has become
Isa 5: 24 for they have r the law
 41: 9 chosen you and have not r you,
 53: 3 He was despised and r by others,
Jer 8: 9 Since they have r the word
Mt 21: 42 stone the builders r has become
1Ti 4: 4 nothing is to be r if it is received
1Pe 2: 4 r by human beings but chosen
 2: 7 stone the builders r has become

REJECTION* (REJECT)
Ro 11: 15 if their r brought reconciliation

REJECTS (REJECT)
Lk 10: 16 whoever r me r him who sent me."
Jn 3: 36 whoever r the Son will not see life,
1Th 4: 8 anyone who r this instruction does

REJOICE (JOY)
Dt 12: 7 shall r in everything you have put
1Ch 16: 10 of those who seek the LORD r.
 16: 31 Let the heavens r, let the earth be
Ps 5: 11 those who love your name may r
 9: 14 Zion, and there r in your salvation.
 34: 2 let the afflicted hear and r.
 63: 11 But the king will r in God;
 66: 6 come, let us r in him.
 68: 3 righteous be glad and r before God;
 105: 3 of those who seek the LORD r.
 118: 24 let us r today and be glad.
 119: 14 I r in following your statutes as one
 119:162 I r in your promise like one who
 149: 2 Let Israel r in their Maker;
Pr 5: 18 may you r in the wife of your youth.
 23: 25 May your father and mother r;
 24: 17 stumble, do not let your heart r,
Isa 9: 3 they r before you as people r
 35: 1 the wilderness will r and blossom.

Isa 61: 7 of disgrace you will r in your
62: 5 bride, so will your God r over you.
Jer 31: 12 they will r in the bounty
Zep 3: 17 but will r over you with singing.
Zec 9: 9 R greatly, Daughter Zion!
Lk 6: 23 "R in that day and leap for joy,
10: 20 but r that your names are written
15: 6 together and says, 'R with me;
15: 9 together and says, 'R with me;
Ro 12: 15 R with those who r;
16: 19 so I r because of you;
Php 2: 17 I am glad and r with all of you.
3: 1 brothers and sisters, r in the Lord!
4: 4 R in the Lord always. I will say it
1Th 5: 16 R always,
1Pe 4: 13 r inasmuch as you participate
Rev 19: 7 Let us r and be glad and give him

REJOICES (JOY)
Ps 13: 5 my heart r in your salvation.
16: 9 my heart is glad and my tongue r;
Pr 23: 24 fathers a wise son r in him.
Isa 61: 10 my soul r in my God.
62: 5 as a bridegroom r over his bride,
Lk 1: 47 and my spirit r in God my Savior,
Ac 2: 26 my heart is glad and my tongue r;
1Co 12: 26 part is honored, every part r with it.
13: 6 delight in evil but r with the truth.

REJOICING (JOY)
2Sa 6: 12 to the City of David with r.
Ne 12: 43 r because God had given them great
Ps 30: 5 a night, but r comes in the morning.
Pr 14: 13 and r may end in grief.
Lk 15: 7 the same way there will be more r
Ac 5: 41 r because they had been counted
2Co 6: 10 sorrowful, yet always r;

RELATE*
Ps 71: 15 I know not how to r them all.

RELATIONS
Lev 18: 22 not have sexual r with a man
1Co 7: 1 to have sexual r with a woman."

RELATIVE (RELATIVES)
Pr 27: 10 neighbor nearby than a r far away.

RELATIVES (RELATIVE)
Pr 19: 7 poor are shunned by all their r—
Mk 6: 4 among their r and in their own
Lk 21: 16 sisters, r and friends, and they will
1Ti 5: 8 who does not provide for their r,

RELEASE (RELEASED)
Isa 61: 1 r from darkness for the prisoners,

RELEASED (RELEASE)
Ro 7: 6 we have been r from the law so
1Co 7: 27 to a woman? Do not seek to be r.
Rev 20: 7 over, Satan will be r from his prison

RELENT (RELENTED RELENTS)
Dt 32: 36 and r concerning his servants
Ps 135: 14 and r concerning his servants.

RELENTED (RELENT)
Ex 32: 14 the Lord r and did not bring
Jdg 2: 18 Lord r because of their groaning
Ps 106: 45 and out of his great love he r.
Jnh 3: 10 he r and did not bring on them

RELENTS* (RELENT)
Joel 2: 13 and he r from sending calamity.
Jnh 4: 2 a God who r from sending calamity.

RELIABLE (RELY)
2Ti 2: 2 entrust to r people who will also be
2Pe 1: 19 message as something completely r,

RELIANCE* (RELY)
Pr 25: 19 a lame foot is r on the unfaithful

RELIED (RELY)
2Ch 13: 18 were victorious because they r
16: 8 Yet when you r on the Lord,
Ps 71: 6 From birth I have r on you;

RELIEF
Job 35: 9 they plead for r from the arm
Ps 94: 13 you grant them r from days
143: 1 and righteousness come to my r.
La 3: 49 will flow unceasingly, without r,
3: 56 not close your ears to my cry for r."
2Th 1: 7 and give r to you who are troubled,

RELIES* (RELY)
Isa 28: 16 who r on it will never be stricken

RELIGION* (RELIGIOUS)
Ac 25: 19 dispute with him about their own r

Ac 26: 5 to the strictest sect of our r,
1Ti 5: 4 of all to put their r into practice
Jas 1: 26 themselves, and their r is worthless.
1: 27 R that God our Father accepts as

RELIGIOUS (RELIGION)
Jas 1: 26 Those who consider themselves r

RELY (RELIABLE RELIANCE RELIED RELIES)
Ps 59: 10 my God on whom I can r.
59: 17 fortress, my God on whom I can r.
Isa 50: 10 of the Lord and r on their God.
Eze 33: 26 You r on your sword, you do
2Co 1: 9 that we might not r on ourselves
Gal 3: 10 All who r on observing the law are
1Jn 4: 16 and r on the love God has for us.

REMAIN (REMAINS)
Nu 33: 55 you allow to r will become barbs
Ps 102: 27 But you r the same, and your years
Jn 1: 32 heaven as a dove and r on him.
15: 4 R in me, as I also r in you.
15: 7 If you r in me and my words r
15: 9 have I loved you. Now r in my love.
Ro 13: 8 Let no debt r outstanding,
1Co 13: 13 And now these three r:
Heb 1: 11 They will perish, but you r;
1Jn 2: 27 just as it has taught you, r in him.

REMAINS (REMAIN)
Ps 146: 6 r faithful forever.
2Ti 2: 13 if we are faithless, he r faithful,
Heb 7: 3 Son of God, he r a priest forever.

REMEDY
Isa 3: 7 day he will cry out, "I have no r.

REMEMBER (REMEMBERED REMEMBERS REMEMBRANCE)
Ge 9: 15 I will r my covenant between me
Ex 20: 8 "R the Sabbath day by keeping it
33: 13 R that this nation is your people."
Dt 5: 15 R that you were slaves in Egypt
1Ch 16: 12 R the wonders he has done,
Job 36: 24 R to extol his work, which people
Ps 25: 6 R, Lord, your great mercy
63: 6 On my bed I r you; I think of you
74: 2 R the people you purchased long
77: 11 I will r the deeds of the Lord;
Ecc 12: 1 R your Creator in the days of your
Isa 46: 8 "R this, keep it in mind, take it
Jer 31: 34 and will r their sins no more."
Hab 3: 2 in wrath r mercy.
Lk 1: 72 and to r his holy covenant,
Gal 2: 10 we should continue to r the poor,
Php 1: 3 I thank my God every time I r you.
2Ti 2: 8 R Jesus Christ, raised from the dead,
Heb 8: 12 and will r their sins no more."

REMEMBERED (REMEMBER)
Ex 2: 24 he r his covenant with Abraham,
Ps 98: 3 He has r his love and his
106: 45 for their sake he r his covenant
111: 4 He has caused his wonders to be r;
136: 23 He r us in our low estate
Isa 65: 17 The former things will not be r,
Eze 18: 22 committed will be r against them.
33: 13 things they have done will be r;

REMEMBERS (REMEMBER)
Ps 103: 14 are formed, he r that we are dust.
111: 5 he r his covenant forever.
Isa 43: 25 own sake, and r your sins no more.

REMEMBRANCE (REMEMBER)
Lk 22: 19 given for you; do this in r of me."
1Co 11: 24 is for you; do this in r of me."
11: 25 whenever you drink it, in r of me."

REMIND
Jn 14: 26 will r you of everything I have said
2Pe 1: 12 So I will always r you of these

REMNANT
Ezr 9: 8 has been gracious in leaving us a r
Isa 11: 11 reclaim the surviving r of his people
Jer 23: 3 "I myself will gather the r of my
Zec 8: 12 inheritance to the r of this people.
Ro 11: 5 the present time there is a r chosen

REMOVED
Ps 30: 11 you r my sackcloth and clothed me
103: 12 so far has he r our transgressions
Jn 20: 1 that the stone had been r

REND
Joel 2: 13 R your heart and not your garments.

RENEW (RENEWAL RENEWED RENEWING)
Ps 51: 10 and r a steadfast spirit within me.
Isa 40: 31 in the Lord will r their strength.

RENEWAL (RENEW)
Isa 57: 10 You found r of your strength,
Tit 3: 5 of rebirth and r by the Holy Spirit,

RENEWED (RENEW)
Ps 103: 5 that your youth is r like the eagle's.
2Co 4: 16 yet inwardly we are being r day

RENEWING* (RENEW)
Ro 12: 2 transformed by the r of your mind.

RENOUNCE (RENOUNCED)
Pr 28: 13 who confess and r them find mercy.
Da 4: 27 R your sins by doing what is right,

RENOUNCED (RENOUNCE)
2Co 4: 2 we have r secret and shameful

RENOWN*
Ge 6: 4 were the heroes of old, men of r.
Ps 102: 12 your r endures through all
135: 13 endures forever, your r, Lord,
Isa 26: 8 and r are the desire of our hearts.
55: 13 This will be for the Lord's r,
63: 12 to gain for himself everlasting r,
Jer 13: 11 'to be my people for my r
32: 20 have gained the r that is still yours.
33: 9 Then this city will bring me r, joy,
49: 25 the city of r not been abandoned,
Eze 26: 17 city of r, peopled by men of the sea!

REPAID (PAY)
Lk 6: 34 to sinners, expecting to be r in full.
14: 14 you will be r at the resurrection
Col 3: 25 Those who do wrong will be r

REPAY (PAY)
Dt 7: 10 those who hate him he will r to their
32: 35 It is mine to avenge; I will r.
Ru 2: 12 May the Lord r you for what you
Ps 103: 10 or r us according to our iniquities.
Jer 25: 14 I will r them according to their
Ro 12: 17 Do not r anyone evil for evil.
12: 19 I will r," says the Lord.
1Pe 3: 9 Do not r evil with evil or insult

REPAYING (PAY)
1Ti 5: 4 own family and so r their parents

REPEATED
Heb 10: 1 the same sacrifices r endlessly year

REPENT (REPENTANCE REPENTED REPENTS)
1Ki 8: 47 and r and plead with you in the land
Job 36: 10 commands them to r of their evil.
42: 6 I despise myself and r in dust
Jer 15: 19 "If you r, I will restore you that you
Eze 18: 30 declares the Sovereign Lord. R!
18: 32 the Sovereign Lord. R and live!
Mt 3: 2 and saying, "R, for the kingdom
4: 17 time on Jesus began to preach, "R,
Mk 6: 12 and preached that people should r.
Lk 13: 3 But unless you r, you too will all
17: 3 if they r, forgive them.
Ac 2: 38 Peter replied, "R and be baptized,
3: 19 R, then, and turn to God,
17: 30 all people everywhere to r.
26: 20 I preached that they should r
Rev 2: 5 R and do the things you did at first.

REPENTANCE (REPENT)
Isa 30: 15 "In r and rest is your salvation,
Mt 3: 8 Produce fruit in keeping with r.
Mk 1: 4 preaching a baptism of r
Lk 3: 8 Produce fruit in keeping with r.
5: 32 call the righteous, but sinners to r."
24: 47 r for the forgiveness of sins will be
Ac 20: 21 that they must turn to God in r
26: 20 demonstrate their r by their deeds.
Ro 2: 4 is intended to lead you to r?
2Co 7: 10 Godly sorrow brings r that leads
2Pe 3: 9 to perish, but everyone to come to r.

REPENTED (REPENT)
Mt 11: 21 they would have r long ago

REPENTS (REPENT)
Lk 15: 7 over one sinner who r than over
15: 10 of God over one sinner who r."

REPORTS
Ex 23: 1 "Do not spread false r. Do not help

REPOSES*
Pr 14: 33 Wisdom r in the heart

REPRESENTATION*
Heb 1: 3 glory and the exact r of his being,

REPRIMAND
Pr 29: 15 A rod and a r impart wisdom,

REPROACH
Job 27: 6 my conscience will not r me as long
Isa 51: 7 Do not fear the r of mere mortals
1Ti 3: 2 Now the overseer is to be above r,

REPROVE*
1Ti 5: 20 elders who are sinning you are to r

REPUTATION
1Ti 3: 7 also have a good r with outsiders,

REQUESTS
Ps 20: 5 May the LORD grant all your r.
Php 4: 6 thanksgiving, present your r to God.

REQUIRE (REQUIRED REQUIRES)
Mic 6: 8 what does the LORD r of you?

REQUIRED (REQUIRE)
1Co 4: 2 Now it is r that those who have

REQUIRES (REQUIRE)
1Ki 2: 3 what the LORD your God r:
Ro 3: 27 The law that r works?
Heb 9: 22 the law r that nearly everything be

RESCUE (RESCUED RESCUES)
Ps 22: 8 they say, "let the LORD r him.
31: 2 ear to me, come quickly to my r;
69: 14 R me from the mire, do not let me
91: 14 says the LORD, "I will r them;
143: 9 R me from my enemies, LORD,
Da 6: 20 been able to r you from the lions?"
Ro 7: 24 Who will r me from this body
Gal 1: 4 our sins to r us from the present evil
2Pe 2: 9 the Lord knows how to r the godly

RESCUED (RESCUE)
Ps 18: 17 He r me from my powerful enemy,
Pr 11: 8 The righteous are r from trouble,
Isa 35: 10 those the LORD has r will return.
Col 1: 13 For he has r us from the dominion

RESCUES (RESCUE)
Da 6: 27 He r and he saves;
1Th 1: 10 who r us from the coming wrath.

RESENT* (RESENTFUL)
Pr 3: 11 discipline, and do not r his rebuke,
15: 12 Mockers r correction,

RESENTFUL* (RESENT)
2Ti 2: 24 to everyone, able to teach, not r,

RESERVE (RESERVED)
1Ki 19: 18 Yet I r seven thousand in Israel—

RESERVED (RESERVE)
Ro 11: 4 "I have r for myself seven thousand

RESIST (RESISTED)
Da 11: 32 know their God will firmly r him.
Mt 5: 39 I tell you, do not r an evil person.
Lk 21: 15 of your adversaries will be able to r
Ro 9: 19 For who is able to r his will?"
Jas 4: 7 R the devil, and he will flee
1Pe 5: 9 R him, standing firm in the faith,

RESISTED (RESIST)
Job 9: 4 Who has r him and come

RESOLVED
Da 1: 8 Daniel r not to defile himself
1Co 2: 2 For I r to know nothing while I was

RESOUNDING*
2Ch 30: 21 r instruments dedicated to the LORD.
Ps 150: 5 cymbals, praise him with r cymbals.
1Co 13: 1 I am only a r gong or a clanging

RESPECT (RESPECTABLE RESPECTED RESPECTS)
Lev 19: 3 of you must r your mother
19: 32 show r for the elderly and revere
Mal 1: 6 a master, where is the r due me?"
Eph 5: 33 and the wife must r her husband.
6: 5 obey your earthly masters with r
1Th 4: 12 that your daily life may win the r
1Ti 3: 4 do so in a manner worthy of full r.
3: 8 deacons are to be worthy of r,
3: 11 the women are to be worthy of r,
6: 1 their masters worthy of full r,
Tit 2: 7 worthy of r, self-controlled,
1Pe 2: 17 Show proper r to everyone,
3: 7 them with r as the weaker partner
3: 15 do this with gentleness and r,

RESPECTABLE* (RESPECT)
1Ti 3: 2 self-controlled, r, hospitable,

RESPECTED (RESPECT)
Pr 31: 23 Her husband is r at the city gate,

RESPECTS (RESPECT)
Pr 13: 13 whoever r a command is rewarded.

RESPLENDENT*
Ps 76: 4 You are r with light, more majestic
132: 18 will be adorned with a r crown."

RESPOND
Ps 102: 17 He will r to the prayer
Hos 2: 21 "I will r to the skies, and they will r

RESPONSIBLE
Nu 1: 53 The Levites are to be r for the care
1Co 7: 24 all of you, as r to God,

REST (RESTED RESTING RESTS SABBATH-REST)
Ex 31: 15 seventh day is a day of sabbath r,
33: 14 go with you, and I will give you r."
Lev 25: 5 The land is to have a year of r.
Dt 31: 16 "You are going to r with your
Jos 14: 15 Then the land had r from war.
21: 44 The LORD gave them r on every
1Ki 5: 4 the LORD my God has given me r
1Ch 22: 9 who will be a man of peace and r,
Job 3: 17 and there the weary are at r.
Ps 16: 9 my body also will r secure,
62: 1 Truly my soul finds r in God;
62: 5 Yes, my soul, find r in God;
90: 17 favor of the Lord our God r on us;
91: 1 the Most High will r in the shadow
95: 11 'They shall never enter my r.' "
Pr 6: 10 a little folding of the hands to r—
Isa 11: 2 Spirit of the LORD will r on him—
30: 15 repentance and r is your salvation,
32: 18 homes, in undisturbed places of r.
57: 20 which cannot r, whose waves cast
Jer 6: 16 and you will find r for your souls.
47: 6 you cry, 'how long till you r?
Mt 11: 28 and burdened, and I will give you r.
2Co 12: 9 so that Christ's power may r on me.
Heb 3: 11 'They shall never enter my r.' "
4: 3 'They shall never enter my r.' "
4: 10 for those who enter God's r also r
Rev 14: 13 Spirit, "they will r from their labor,

RESTED (REST)
Ge 2: 2 on the seventh day he r from all his
Heb 4: 4 the seventh day God r from all his

RESTING (REST)
Isa 11: 10 and his r place will be glorious.

RESTITUTION
Ex 22: 3 who steals must certainly make r,
Lev 6: 5 They must make r in full, add a fifth
Nu 5: 8 the r belongs to the LORD

RESTORATION (RESTORE)
2Co 13: 11 Strive for full r,

RESTORE (RESTORATION RESTORED)
Ps 51: 12 R to me the joy of your salvation
80: 3 R us, O God; make your face shine
126: 4 R our fortunes, LORD,
Jer 31: 18 R me, and I will return, because you
La 5: 21 R us to yourself, LORD, that we
Da 9: 25 the time the word goes out to r
Na 2: 2 The LORD will r the splendor
Gal 6: 1 by the Spirit should r that person
1Pe 5: 10 will himself r you and make you

RESTORED (RESTORE)
Job 42: 10 the LORD r his fortunes
2Co 13: 9 prayer is that you may be fully r.

RESTRAINED (RESTRAINT)
Ps 78: 38 Time after time he r his anger

RESTRAINING (RESTRAINT)
Pr 27: 16 r her is like r the wind or grasping
Col 2: 23 any value in r sensual indulgence.

RESTRAINT (RESTRAINED RESTRAINING)
Pr 17: 27 have knowledge use words with r,
29: 18 is no revelation, people cast off r;

RESTS (REST)
Dt 33: 12 one the LORD loves r between his
Pr 19: 23 then one r content,
Lk 2: 14 to those on whom his favor r."

RESULT (RESULTS)
Ro 6: 22 to holiness, and the r is eternal life.
11: 31 too may now receive mercy as a r

RESULTS* (RESULT)
1Th 2: 1 our visit to you was not without r.

RESURRECTION*
Mt 22: 23 who say there is no r, came to him
22: 28 at the r, whose wife will she be
22: 30 the r people will neither marry nor
22: 31 But about the r of the dead—
27: 53 came out of the tombs after Jesus' r
Mk 12: 18 who say there is no r, came to him
12: 23 At the r whose wife will she be,
Lk 14: 14 be repaid at the r of the righteous."
20: 27 who say there is no r, came to Jesus
20: 33 at the r whose wife will she be,
20: 35 in the r from the dead will neither
20: 36 since they are children of the r.
Jn 11: 24 rise again in the r at the last day."
11: 25 said to her, "I am the r and the life.
Ac 1: 22 become a witness with us of his r."
2: 31 he spoke of the r of the Messiah,
4: 2 in Jesus the r of the dead.
4: 33 to testify to the r of the Lord Jesus.
17: 18 good news about Jesus and the r.
17: 32 they heard about the r of the dead,
23: 6 of the hope of the r of the dead."
23: 8 Sadducees say that there is no r,
24: 15 that there will be a r of both
24: 21 'It is concerning the r of the dead
Ro 1: 4 in power by his r from the dead:
6: 5 be united with him in a r like his.
1Co 15: 12 say that there is no r of the dead?
15: 13 If there is no r of the dead, then not
15: 21 the r of the dead comes also through
15: 29 Now if there is no r, what will those
15: 42 So will it be with the r of the dead.
Php 3: 10 to know the power of his r
3: 11 attaining to the r from the dead.
2Ti 2: 18 that the r has already taken place,
Heb 6: 2 on of hands, the r of the dead,
11: 35 they might gain an even better r.
1Pe 1: 3 a living hope through the r of Jesus
3: 21 It saves you by the r of Jesus Christ,
Rev 20: 5 This is the first r.
20: 6 those who have part in the first r.

RETALIATE*
1Pe 2: 23 their insults at him, he did not r;

RETRIBUTION
Ps 69: 22 may it become r and a trap.
Jer 51: 56 For the LORD is a God of r;
Ro 11: 9 a stumbling block and a r for them.

RETURN (RETURNED RETURNS)
Ge 3: 19 you are and to dust you will r."
2Sa 12: 23 go to him, but he will not r to me."
2Ch 30: 9 If you r to the LORD, then your
Ne 1: 9 but if you r to me and obey my
Job 10: 21 before I go to the place of no r,
16: 22 pass before I take the path of no r.
22: 23 If you r to the Almighty, you will
Ps 80: 14 R to us, God Almighty!
116: 12 What shall I r to the LORD
126: 6 to sow, will r with songs of joy,
Isa 10: 21 A remnant will r, a remnant
35: 10 the LORD has rescued will r.
55: 11 It will not r to me empty, but will
Jer 24: 7 for they will r to me with all their
31: 8 a great throng will r.
31: 22 the woman will r to the man."
La 3: 40 them, and let us r to the LORD.
Hos 6: 1 "Come, let us r to the LORD.
12: 6 But you must r to your God;
14: 1 R, Israel, to the LORD your God.
Joel 2: 12 "r to me with all your heart,
Zec 1: 3 'R to me,' declares the LORD Almighty,
'and I will r to you,'
10: 9 will survive, and they will r.

RETURNED (RETURN)
Ps 35: 13 my prayers r to me unanswered,
Am 4: 6 town, yet you have not r to me,"
1Pe 2: 25 but now you have r to the Shepherd

RETURNS (RETURN)
Pr 3: 14 silver and yields better r than gold.
Isa 52: 8 When the LORD r to Zion,
Mt 24: 46 finds him doing so when he r.

REUBEN
Firstborn of Jacob by Leah (Ge 29:32; 46:8; 1Ch

2:1). Attempted to rescue Joseph (Ge 37:21–30). Lost birthright for sleeping with Bilhah (Ge 35:22; 49:4). Tribe of blessed (Ge 49:3–4; Dt 33:6), numbered (Nu 1:21; 26:7), allotted land east of Jordan (Nu 32; 34:14; Jos 13:15), west (Eze 48:6), failed to help Deborah (Jdg 5:15–16), supported David (1Ch 12:37), 12,000 from (Rev 7:5).

REVEAL (REVEALED REVEALS REVELATION REVELATIONS)
Mt 11:27 to whom the Son chooses to r him.
Gal 1:16 to r his Son in me so that I might

REVEALED (REVEAL)
Dt 29:29 but the things r belong to us
Isa 40:5 the glory of the Lord will be r,
43:12 I have r and saved and proclaimed—
53:1 has the arm of the Lord been r?
65:1 "I r myself to those who did not ask
Mt 11:25 and r them to little children.
Jn 12:38 has the arm of the Lord been r?"
17:6 "I have r you to those whom you
Ro 1:17 the righteousness of God is r—
8:18 with the glory that will be r in us.
10:20 I r myself to those who did not ask
16:26 now r and made known through
1Co 2:10 for God has r them to us by his
2Th 1:7 the Lord Jesus is r from heaven
2:3 and the man of lawlessness is r,
1Pe 1:7 and honor when Jesus Christ is r.
1:20 but was r in these last times for your
4:13 be overjoyed when his glory is r.

REVEALS* (REVEAL)
Nu 23:3 Whatever he r to me I will tell
Job 12:22 He r the deep things of darkness
Da 2:22 He r deep and hidden things;
2:28 is a God in heaven who r mysteries.
Am 4:13 and who r his thoughts to mortals,

REVELATION* (REVEAL)
2Sa 7:17 David all the words of this entire r.
1Ch 17:15 David all the words of this entire r.
Pr 29:18 Where there is no r, people cast off
Da 10:1 a r was given to Daniel (who was
Hab 2:2 "Write down the r and make it
2:3 For the r awaits an appointed time;
Lk 2:32 a light for r to the Gentiles,
Ro 16:25 with the r of the mystery hidden
1Co 14:6 to you, unless I bring you some r
14:26 a r, a tongue or an interpretation.
14:30 And if a r comes to someone who is
Gal 1:12 I received it by r from Jesus Christ.
2:2 I went in response to a r and,
Eph 1:17 give you the Spirit of wisdom and r,
3:3 mystery made known to me by r,
Rev 1:1 The r from Jesus Christ, which God

REVELATIONS* (REVEAL)
2Co 12:1 on to visions and r from the Lord.
12:7 of these surpassingly great r.

REVELED* (REVELRY)
Ne 9:25 they r in your great goodness.

REVELRY (REVELED)
Ex 32:6 and drink and got up to indulge in r.
1Co 10:7 drink and got up to indulge in r."

REVENGE (VENGEANCE)
Lev 19:18 " 'Do not seek r or bear a grudge
Ro 12:19 Do not take r, my dear friends,

REVERE* (REVERENCE REVERENT REVERING)
Lev 19:32 for the elderly and r your God.
Dt 4:10 learn to r me as long as they live
13:4 must follow, and him you must r.
14:23 to r the Lord your God always.
17:19 may learn to r the Lord his God
28:58 book, and do not r this glorious
Job 37:24 Therefore, people r him, for does he
Ps 22:23 R him, all you descendants
33:8 let all the people of the world r him.
102:15 kings of the earth will r your glory.
Isa 25:3 cities of ruthless nations will r you.
59:19 of the sun, they will r his glory.
63:17 our hearts so we do not r you?
Hos 10:3 because we did not r the Lord.
Mal 4:2 But for you who r my name,
1Pe 3:15 in your hearts r Christ as Lord.
Rev 11:18 your people who r your name,

REVERENCE (REVERE)
Lev 19:30 and have r for my sanctuary.
Ne 5:15 of r for God I did not act like that.
Ps 5:7 in r I bow down toward your holy
Da 6:26 must fear and r the God of Daniel.

2Co 7:1 perfecting holiness out of r for God.
Eph 5:21 to one another out of r for Christ.
Col 3:22 sincerity of heart and r for the Lord.
1Pe 3:2 see the purity and r of your lives.

REVERENT* (REVERE)
Ecc 8:12 fear God, who are r before him.
Tit 2:3 women to be r in the way they live,
Heb 5:7 heard because of his r submission.
1Pe 1:17 time as foreigners here in r fear.
2:18 Slaves, in r fear of God submit

REVERING* (REVERE)
Dt 8:6 in obedience to him and r him.
Ne 1:11 who delight in r your name.

REVERSE*
Isa 43:13 When I act, who can r it?"

REVIVE*
Ps 80:18 r us, and we will call on your name.
85:6 Will you not r us again, that your
Isa 57:15 to r the spirit of the lowly and to r the heart of the contrite.
Hos 6:2 After two days he will r us;

REVOKED*
Isa 45:23 integrity a word that will not be r:

REWARD (REWARDED REWARDING REWARDS)
Ge 15:1 am your shield, your very great r."
1Sa 24:19 May the Lord r you well
Ps 19:11 in keeping them there is great r.
62:12 "You r everyone according to what
127:3 the Lord, offspring a r from him.
Pr 9:12 are wise, your wisdom will r you;
11:18 sow righteousness reap a sure r.
12:14 work of their hands brings them r.
13:13 he will r them for what they have
25:22 head, and the Lord will r you.
Isa 40:10 See, his r is with him, and his
49:4 hand, and my r is with my God."
61:8 my faithfulness I will r my people
62:11 See, his r is with him, and his
Jer 17:10 to r everyone according to their
32:19 you r everyone according to their
Mt 5:12 because great is your r in heaven,
6:1 you will have no r from your Father
6:5 they have received their r in full.
10:41 a prophet will receive a prophet's r,
16:27 then he will r everyone according
Lk 6:23 because great is your r in heaven.
6:35 Then your r will be great, and you
1Co 3:14 the builder will receive a r.
Eph 6:8 that the Lord will r each one of you
Col 3:24 an inheritance from the Lord as a r.
Heb 11:26 he was looking ahead to his r.
Rev 22:12 My r is with me, and I will give

REWARDED (REWARD)
Ru 2:12 May you be richly r by the Lord,
2Sa 22:21 cleanness of my hands he has r me.
2Ch 15:7 give up, for your work will be r."
Ps 18:24 The Lord has r me according
Pr 13:13 whoever respects a command is r.
13:21 the righteous are r with good things.
14:14 their ways, and the good r for theirs.
Jer 31:16 for your work will be r,"
1Co 3:8 and they will each be r according
Heb 10:35 it will be richly r.
2Jn 8 but that you may be r fully.

REWARDING* (REWARD)
Rev 11:18 for r your servants the prophets

REWARDS (REWARD)
1Sa 26:23 The Lord r every man for his
Heb 11:6 he r those who earnestly seek him.

RIBS
Ge 2:21 he took one of the man's r

RICH (RICHES RICHEST)
Job 34:19 does not favor the r over the poor,
Ps 49:16 be overawed when others grow r,
145:8 slow to anger and r in love.
Pr 21:17 wine and olive oil will never be r.
22:2 R and poor have this in common:
23:4 Do not wear yourself out to get r;
28:6 blameless than the r whose ways are
28:20 to get r will not go unpunished.
28:22 The stingy are eager to get r and are
Ecc 5:12 of the r permits them no sleep.
Isa 33:6 a r store of salvation and wisdom
53:9 and with the r in his death,
Jer 9:23 or the boast of their riches,
Mt 19:23 hard for the r to enter the kingdom
Lk 1:53 but has sent the r away empty.

Lk 6:24 "But woe to you who are r, for you
12:21 but are not r toward God."
16:1 "There was a r man whose manager
21:1 he saw the r putting their gifts
2Co 6:10 poor, yet making many r;
8:2 poverty welled up in r generosity.
8:9 that though he was r, yet for your
9:11 You will be made r in every way so
Eph 2:4 love for us, God, who is r in mercy,
1Ti 6:9 Those who want to get r fall
6:17 Command those who are r in this
6:18 to be r in good deeds, and to be
Jas 1:10 But the r should take pride in their
2:5 the eyes of the world to be r in faith
5:1 Now listen, you r people,
Rev 2:9 and your poverty—yet you are r!
3:18 in the fire, so you can become r;

RICHES (RICH)
Job 36:18 careful that no one entices you by r;
Ps 49:6 wealth and boast of their great r?
62:10 though your r increase, do not set
119:14 statutes as one rejoices in great r.
Pr 3:16 in her left hand are r and honor.
11:28 Those who trust in their r will fall,
22:1 name is more desirable than great r;
22:4 its wages are r and honor and life.
27:24 for r do not endure forever,
30:8 give me neither poverty nor r,
Isa 10:3 Where will you leave your r?
60:5 you the r of the nations will come,
Jer 9:23 strength or the rich boast of their r,
Lk 8:14 by life's worries, r and pleasures,
Ro 9:23 to make the r of his glory known
11:33 the depth of the r of the wisdom
Eph 2:7 he might show the incomparable r
3:8 to the Gentiles the boundless r
Col 1:27 among the Gentiles the glorious r
2:2 they may have the full r of complete

RICHEST (RICH)
Isa 55:2 and you will delight in the r of fare.

RID
Ge 21:10 "Get r of that slave woman and her
1Co 5:7 Get r of the old yeast, so that you
Gal 4:30 "Get r of the slave woman and her

RIDE (RIDER RIDING)
Ps 45:4 In your majesty r forth victoriously

RIDER (RIDE)
Rev 6:2 Its r held a bow, and he was given
19:11 whose r is called Faithful and True.

RIDING (RIDE)
Zec 9:9 lowly and r on a donkey, on a colt,
Mt 21:5 gentle and r on a donkey,

RIGGING
Isa 33:23 Your r hangs loose: The mast is not

RIGHT (RIGHTS)
Ge 4:7 If you do what is r, will you not be
18:19 of the Lord by doing what is r
18:25 not the Judge of all the earth do r?"
48:13 on his left toward Israel's r hand,
Ex 15:6 Your r hand, Lord, was majestic
15:26 God and do what is r in his eyes,
Dt 5:32 do not turn aside to the r
6:18 Do what is r and good
13:18 and doing what is r in his eyes.
Jos 1:7 do not turn from it to the r
1Sa 12:23 you the way that is good and r.
1Ki 3:9 to distinguish between r and wrong.
15:5 David had done what was r
2Ki 7:9 other, "What we're doing is not r.
Ne 9:13 and laws that are just and r,
Ps 16:8 With him at my r hand, I will not be
16:11 eternal pleasures at your r hand.
17:7 your r hand those who take refuge
18:35 shield, and your r hand sustains me;
19:8 The precepts of the Lord are r,
23:3 He guides me along the r paths
25:9 He guides the humble in what is r
33:4 For the word of the Lord is r
44:3 it was your r hand, your arm,
45:4 let your r hand achieve awesome
51:4 so you are r in your verdict
63:8 your r hand upholds me.
73:23 you hold me by my r hand.
91:7 ten thousand at your r hand, but it
98:1 his r hand and his holy arm have
106:3 act justly, who always do what is r.
110:1 "Sit at my r hand until I make your
118:15 "The Lord's r hand has done

Ps 137: 5 may my r hand forget its skill.
139: 10 your r hand will hold me fast.
Pr 1: 3 doing what is r and just and fair;
   4: 27 Do not turn to the r or the left;
  14: 12 There is a way that appears to be r,
  16: 13 value persons who speak what is r.
  18: 17 a lawsuit the first to speak seems r,
  28: 5 do not understand what is r,
Ecc 7: 20 no one who does what is r
SS 1: 4 How r they are to adore you!
Isa 1: 17 learn to do r!
   7: 15 to reject the wrong and choose the r,
  30: 10 us no more visions of what is r!
  30: 21 Whether you turn to the r
  41: 10 you with my righteous r hand.
  41: 13 God who takes hold of your r hand
  48: 13 my r hand spread out the heavens;
  64: 5 to the help of those who gladly do r,
Jer 23: 5 and do what is just and r in the land.
Eze 18: 5 man who does what is just and r
  18: 21 decrees and do what is just and r—
  33: 14 their sins and do what is just and r—
Hos 14: 9 The ways of the LORD are r;
Mt 5: 29 If your r eye causes you to stumble,
   6: 3 know what your r hand is doing,
  22: 44 my r hand until I put your enemies
  25: 33 He will put the sheep on his r
Jn 1: 12 he gave the r to become children
Ac 2: 34 said to my Lord: "Sit at my r hand
   7: 55 Jesus standing at the r hand of God.
Ro 3: 4 that you may be proved r when you
   8: 34 is at the r hand of God and is
   9: 21 Does not the potter have the r
  12: 17 careful to do what is r in the eyes
1Co 6: 12 "I have the r to do anything,"
   9: 4 Don't we have the r to food
  10: 23 "I have the r to do anything"
2Co 8: 21 we are taking pains to do what is r,
Eph 1: 20 and seated him at his r hand
   6: 1 parents in the Lord, for this is r.
Php 4: 8 whatever is r, whatever is pure,
Heb 1: 3 he sat down at the r hand
Jas 2: 8 as yourself," you are doing r.
1Pe 3: 14 if you should suffer for what is r,
1Jn 2: 29 who does what is r has been born
Rev 2: 7 I will give the r to eat from the tree
   2: 11 I will give the r to sit with me
  22: 11 let those who do r continue to do r;

RIGHTEOUS (RIGHTEOUSLY RIGHTEOUSNESS)
Ge 6: 9 Noah was a r man,
  18: 23 "Will you sweep away the r
Nu 23: 10 Let me die the death of the r,
Ne 9: 8 your promise because you are r.
   9: 33 you have remained r;
Job 36: 7 He does not take his eyes off the r;
Ps 1: 5 nor sinners in the assembly of the r.
   5: 12 Surely, LORD, you bless the r;
   9: 4 sitting enthroned as the r judge.
  11: 7 For the LORD is r, he loves
  15: 2 who do what is r, who speak
  34: 15 The eyes of the LORD are on the r
  37: 6 He will make your r reward shine
  37: 16 little that the r have than the wealth
  37: 21 not repay, but the r give generously;
  37: 25 yet I have never seen the r forsaken
  37: 30 The mouths of the r utter wisdom,
  55: 22 he will never let the r be shaken.
  64: 10 The r will rejoice in the LORD
  65: 5 awesome and r deeds,
  68: 3 But may the r be glad and rejoice
  71: 15 My mouth will tell of your r deeds,
 112: 4 gracious and compassionate and r.
 118: 19 Open for me the gates of the r;
 118: 20 through which the r may enter.
 119: 7 upright heart as I learn your r laws.
 119:137 You are r, LORD, and your laws
 119:144 Your statutes are always r;
 140: 13 Surely the r will praise your name,
 143: 2 for no one living is r before you.
 145: 17 The LORD is r in all his ways
Pr 3: 33 but he blesses the home of the r.
   4: 18 path of the r is like the morning sun,
  10: 7 The name of the r is used
  10: 11 The mouth of the r is a fountain
  10: 16 The wages of the r is life,
  10: 20 The tongue of the r is choice silver,
  10: 24 what the r desire will be granted.
  10: 28 The prospect of the r is joy,
  10: 32 lips of the r know what finds favor,
  11: 23 The desire of the r ends only
  11: 30 The fruit of the r is a tree of life,

Pr 12: 10 The r care for the needs of their
  12: 21 No harm overtakes the r,
  13: 9 The light of the r shines brightly,
  15: 28 heart of the r weighs its answers,
  15: 29 but he hears the prayer of the r.
  18: 10 the r run to it and are safe.
  20: 7 The r lead blameless lives;
  21: 15 it brings joy to the r but terror
  23: 24 The father of a r child has great joy;
  28: 1 but the r are as bold as a lion.
  29: 6 but the r shout for joy and are glad.
  29: 7 The r care about justice
  29: 27 the r detest the dishonest;
Ecc 7: 20 there is no one on earth who does r
Isa 5: 16 be proved holy by his r acts.
  26: 7 The path of the r is level;
  41: 10 uphold you with my r right hand.
  45: 21 from me, a r God and a Savior;
  53: 11 by his knowledge my r servant will
  64: 6 and all our r acts are like filthy rags;
Jer 23: 5 I will raise up for David a r Branch,
  23: 6 The LORD Our R Savior.
Eze 23: 20 "Again, when the r turn from their
  18: 5 "Suppose there is a r man who does
  18: 20 of the r will be credited to them,
  33: 12 The r, if they sin, will not be
Da 9: 18 requests of you because we are r,
Hab 2: 4 the r will live by their faithfulness—
Zec 9: 9 to you, r and having salvation,
Mal 3: 18 see the distinction between the r
Mt 5: 45 and sends rain on the r
   5: 20 For I have not come to call the r,
  10: 41 to be r will receive a r person's
  13: 43 the r will shine like the sun
  13: 49 and separate the wicked from the r
  25: 37 "Then the r will answer him, 'Lord,
  25: 46 but the r to eternal life."
Ac 24: 15 will be a resurrection of both the r
Ro 1: 17 "The r will live by faith."
   2: 5 his r judgment will be revealed.
   2: 13 obey the law who will be declared r.
   3: 10 "There is no one r, not even one;
   3: 20 Therefore no one will be declared r
   5: 18 one r act resulted in justification
   5: 19 one man the many will be made r.
Gal 3: 11 because "the r will live by faith."
1Ti 1: 9 that the law is made not for the r
2Ti 4: 8 which the Lord, the r Judge,
Tit 3: 5 because of r things we had done,
Heb 10: 38 "But my r one will live by faith.
Jas 5: 16 The prayer of a r person is powerful
1Pe 3: 12 For the eyes of the Lord are on the r
   3: 18 for sins, the r for the unrighteous,
   4: 18 "If it is hard for the r to be saved,
1Jn 2: 1 Jesus Christ, the R One.
   3: 7 what is right is r, just as he is r.
Rev 19: 8 (Fine linen stands for the r acts

RIGHTEOUSLY* (RIGHTEOUS)
Isa 33: 15 Those who walk r and speak what is
Jer 11: 20 who judge r and test the heart

RIGHTEOUSNESS (RIGHTEOUS)
Ge 15: 6 and he credited it to him as r.
Dt 9: 4 of this land because of my r."
1Sa 26: 23 LORD rewards every man for his r
1Ki 10: 9 you king to maintain justice and r."
Job 37: 23 in his justice and great r, he does
Ps 5: 7 to the LORD because of his r;
   9: 8 He rules the world in r and judges
  33: 5 The LORD loves r and justice;
  35: 28 My tongue will proclaim your r,
  36: 6 Your r is like the highest
  45: 7 You love r and hate wickedness;
  48: 10 your right hand is filled with r.
  71: 2 In your r, rescue me and deliver me;
  71: 19 Your r, God, reaches to the skies,
  85: 10 r and peace kiss each other.
  89: 14 R and justice are the foundation
  96: 13 He will judge the world in r
  98: 9 He will judge the world in r
 103: 6 The LORD works r and justice
 103: 17 his r with their children's children—
 106: 31 to him as r for endless generations
 111: 3 his deeds, and his r endures forever.
 132: 9 your priests be clothed with your r;
 145: 7 and joyfully sing of your r.
Pr 11: 5 The r of the blameless makes their
  11: 18 those who sow r reap a sure reward.
  13: 6 R guards the person of integrity,
  14: 34 R exalts a nation, but sin condemns
  15: 6 Better a little with r than much gain
  16: 12 for a throne is established through r.

Pr 16: 31 it is attained in the way of r.
  21: 21 Whoever pursues r and love finds
Isa 9: 7 with justice and r from that time
  11: 4 but with r he will judge the needy,
  16: 5 justice and speeds the cause of r.
  26: 9 the people of the world learn r.
  32: 17 The fruit of that r will be peace;
  42: 6 the LORD, have called you in r;
  42: 21 sake of his r to make his law great
  45: 8 heavens above, rain down my r;
  51: 1 you who pursue r and who seek
  51: 6 last forever, my r will never fail.
  51: 8 But my r will last forever,
  58: 8 then your r will go before you,
  59: 17 He put on r as his breastplate,
  61: 10 and arrayed me in a robe of his r,
  63: 1 is I, speaking in r, mighty to save."
Jer 9: 24 justice and r on earth, for in these I
Eze 3: 20 when the righteous turn from their r
  14: 20 save only themselves by their r.
  18: 20 The r of the righteous will be
  33: 12 that person's former r will count
Da 9: 24 to bring in everlasting r, to seal
  12: 3 and those who lead many to r,
Hos 10: 12 Sow for yourselves r, reap the fruit
Am 5: 24 a river, r like a never-failing stream!
Mic 7: 9 me out into the light; I will see his r.
Zep 2: 3 Seek r, seek humility;
Mal 4: 2 the sun of r will rise with healing
Mt 5: 6 those who hunger and thirst for r,
   5: 10 who are persecuted because of r,
   5: 20 that unless your r surpasses
   6: 1 not to do your 'acts of r' in front
   6: 33 But seek first his kingdom and his r
Jn 16: 8 to be in the wrong about sin and r
Ac 24: 25 As Paul talked about r,
Ro 1: 17 the gospel the r of God is revealed—
   3: 5 brings out God's r more clearly,
   3: 22 This r is given through faith
   4: 3 and it was credited to him as r."
   4: 5 ungodly, their faith is credited as r.
   4: 6 to whom God credits r apart
   4: 9 faith was credited to him as r.
   4: 13 through the r that comes by faith.
   4: 22 why "it was credited to him as r."
   6: 13 to him as an instrument of r.
   6: 16 or to obedience, which leads to r?
   6: 18 sin and have become slaves to r.
   6: 19 yourselves as slaves to r leading
   8: 10 the Spirit gives life because of r.
   9: 30 who did not pursue r, have obtained
  10: 3 Since they did not know the r
  14: 17 but of r, peace and joy in the Holy
1Co 1: 30 our r, holiness and redemption.
2Co 3: 9 is the ministry that brings r!
   5: 21 him we might become the r of God.
   6: 7 with weapons of r in the right hand
   6: 14 For what do r and wickedness have
   9: 9 their r endures forever."
Gal 2: 21 if r could be gained through the law,
   3: 6 and it was credited to him as r."
   3: 21 r would certainly have come
Eph 4: 24 created to be like God in true r
   5: 9 consists in all goodness, r and truth)
   6: 14 with the breastplate of r in place,
Php 1: 11 the fruit of r that comes through
   3: 6 as for r based on the law, faultless.
   3: 9 not having a r of my own
1Ti 6: 11 all this, and pursue r, godliness,
2Ti 2: 22 evil desires of youth and pursue r,
   3: 16 correcting and training in r,
   4: 8 is in store for me the crown of r,
Heb 5: 13 with the teaching about r.
   7: 2 Melchizedek means "king of r";
  11: 7 and became heir of the r that is
  12: 11 it produces a harvest of r and peace
Jas 2: 23 and it was credited to him as r,"
   3: 18 sow in peace reap a harvest of r.
1Pe 2: 24 we might die to sins and live for r;
2Pe 2: 21 not to have known the way of r,
   3: 13 and a new earth, where r dwells.

RIGHTS (RIGHT)
Pr 31: 8 for the r of all who are destitute.
Isa 10: 2 to deprive the poor of their r
La 3: 35 deny people their r before the Most

RING
Pr 11: 22 Like a gold r in a pig's snout is
Lk 15: 22 Put a r on his finger and sandals

RIOTS
2Co 6: 5 in beatings, imprisonments and r;

RIPE
Joel 3: 13 the sickle, for the harvest is r.
Am 8: 1 a basket of r fruit.
Jn 4: 35 at the fields! They are r for harvest.
Rev 14: 15 for the harvest of the earth is r."

RISE (RAISE RAISED RISEN ROSE)
Nu 24: 17 a scepter will r out of Israel.
Isa 26: 19 their bodies will r—let those who
Mal 4: 2 of righteousness will r with healing
Mt 27: 63 'After three days I will r again.'
Mk 8: 31 killed and after three days r again.
Lk 18: 33 On the third day he will r again."
Jn 5: 29 who have done what is good will r
20: 9 that Jesus had to r from the dead.)
Ac 17: 3 had to suffer and r from the dead.
1Th 4: 16 and the dead in Christ will r first.

RISEN (RISE)
Mt 28: 6 is not here; he has r, just as he said.
Mk 16: 6 He has r! He is not here.
Lk 24: 34 The Lord has r and has appeared

RIVER (RIVERS)
Ps 46: 4 There is a r whose streams make
Isa 66: 12 "I will extend peace to her like a r,
Eze 47: 12 will grow on both banks of the r.
Rev 22: 1 the angel showed me the r

RIVERS (RIVER)
Ps 137: 1 By the r of Babylon we sat
Jn 7: 38 r of living water will flow

ROAD (CROSSROADS ROADS)
Mt 7: 13 gate and broad is the r that leads

ROADS (ROAD)
Lk 3: 5 The crooked r shall become

ROARING
1Pe 5: 8 prowls around like a r lion looking

ROB (ROBBERS ROBBERY ROBS)
Mal 3: 8 "Will a mere mortal r God? Yet you r me.

ROBBERS (ROB)
Jer 7: 11 Name, become a den of r to you?
Lk 19: 46 you have made it 'a den of r.' "
Jn 10: 8 come before me are thieves and r,

ROBBERY (ROB)
Isa 61: 8 I hate r and wrongdoing.

ROBE (ROBED ROBES)
Ge 37: 3 he made a richly ornamented r
Isa 6: 1 the train of his r filled the temple.
61: 10 me in a r of his righteousness,
Rev 6: 11 each of them was given a white r,

ROBED (ROBE)
Ps 93: 1 the Lord is r in majesty
Isa 63: 1 Who is this, r in splendor,

ROBES (ROBE)
Ps 45: 8 All your r are fragrant with myrrh
Rev 7: 13 asked me, "These in white r—

ROBS* (ROB)
Pr 19: 26 Whoever r their father and drives
28: 24 Whoever r their father or mother

ROCK
Ge 49: 24 of the Shepherd, the R of Israel,
Ex 17: 6 Strike the r, and water will come
Nu 20: 8 Speak to that r before their eyes
Dt 32: 4 He is the R, his works are perfect,
32: 13 him with honey from the r,
2Sa 22: 2 "The Lord is my r, my fortress
Ps 18: 2 The Lord is my r, my fortress
19: 14 Lord, my R and my Redeemer.
40: 2 he set my feet on a r and gave me
61: 2 lead me to the r that is higher than I.
92: 15 he is my R, and there is no
Isa 26: 4 the Lord, is the R eternal.
51: 1 Look to the r from which you were
Da 2: 34 you were watching, a r was cut out,
Mt 7: 24 man who built his house on the r.
16: 18 and on this r I will build my church,
Ro 9: 33 and a r that makes them fall,
1Co 10: 4 the spiritual r that accompanied
1Pe 2: 8 and a r that makes them fall."

ROD (RODS)
2Sa 7: 14 I will punish him with a r wielded
Ps 2: 9 will break them with a r of iron;
23: 4 your r and your staff, they comfort
Pr 13: 24 who spare the r hate their children,
22: 15 the r of discipline will drive it far
23: 13 if you punish them with the r,
29: 15 A r and a reprimand impart

Isa 11: 4 the earth with the r of his mouth;

RODS (ROD)
2Co 11: 25 Three times I was beaten with r,

ROLL (ROLLED)
Mk 16: 3 "Who will r the stone away

ROLLED (ROLL)
Lk 24: 2 They found the stone r away

ROMAN
Ac 16: 37 even though we are R citizens,
22: 25 to flog a R citizen who hasn't even

ROOF (ROOFS)
Pr 21: 9 a corner of the r than share a house

ROOFS
Mt 10: 27 in your ear, proclaim from the r.

ROOM
Mt 6: 6 go into your r, close the door
Mk 14: 15 He will show you a large r upstairs,
Lk 2: 7 there was no guest r available
Jn 8: 37 because you have no r for my word.
14: 2 My Father's house has plenty of r;
21: 25 the whole world would not have r
2Co 7: 2 Make r for us in your hearts.

ROOSTER
Mt 26: 34 before the r crows, you will disown

ROOT (ROOTED ROOTS)
Isa 11: 10 day the R of Jesse will stand as
53: 2 and like a r out of dry ground.
Mt 3: 10 ax is already at the r of the trees,
13: 21 But since they have no r, they last
Ro 11: 16 if the r is holy, so are the branches.
15: 12 "The R of Jesse will spring up,
1Ti 6: 10 the love of money is a r of all kinds
Rev 5: 5 the tribe of Judah, the R of David,
22: 16 I am the R and the Offspring

ROOTED (ROOT)
Eph 3: 17 being r and established in love,

ROOTS (ROOT)
Isa 11: 1 from his r a Branch will bear fruit.

ROSE (RISE)
SS 2: 1 I am a r of Sharon, a lily
2: 2 We saw his star when it r and
1Th 4: 14 believe that Jesus died and r again,

ROTS*
Pr 14: 30 to the body, but envy r the bones.

ROUGH
Isa 42: 16 them and make the r places smooth.
Lk 3: 5 become straight, the r ways smooth.

ROUND
Ecc 1: 6 r and r it goes, ever returning to its

ROYAL
Ps 45: 9 your right hand is the r bride in gold
Da 1: 8 not to defile himself with the r food
Jas 2: 8 If you really keep the r law found
1Pe 2: 9 are a chosen people, a r priesthood,

RUBIES
Job 28: 18 the price of wisdom is beyond r.
Pr 3: 15 She is more precious than r;
8: 11 for wisdom is more precious than r,
31: 10 She is worth far more than r.

RUDDER*
Jas 3: 4 by a very small r wherever the pilot

RUDDY
SS 5: 10 My beloved is radiant and r,

RUIN (RUINED RUINS)
Pr 10: 8 but a chattering fool comes to r.
10: 10 and a chattering fool comes to r.
10: 14 but the mouth of a fool invites r.
10: 29 it is the r of those who do evil.
11: 17 but the cruel bring r on themselves.
11: 29 who bring r on their families
15: 27 greedy bring r to their households,
18: 24 unreliable friends soon comes to r,
19: 3 One's own folly leads to r,
19: 13 A foolish child is a father's r,
26: 28 and a flattering mouth works r.
Ecc 4: 5 hands and r themselves.
SS 2: 15 the little foxes that r the vineyards,
Eze 21: 27 A r! A r! I will make it a r!
1Ti 6: 9 desires that plunge people into r.

RUINED (RUIN)
Isa 6: 5 "I am r! For I am a man of unclean
Mt 9: 17 run out and the wineskins will be r.

Mt 12: 25 divided against itself will be r,

RUINS (RUIN)
2Ti 2: 14 value, and only r those who listen.

RULE (RULER RULERS RULES RULING)
Ge 1: 26 so that they may r over the fish
3: 16 husband, and he will r over you."
4: 7 but you must r over it."
Jdg 8: 22 said to Gideon, "R over us—
1Sa 12: 12 we want a king to r over us'—
Ps 67: 4 for you r the peoples with equity
119:133 to your word; let no sin r over me.
Pr 17: 2 A prudent servant will r over
Isa 28: 10 a r for this, a r for that;
Zec 6: 13 and will sit and r on his throne.
9: 10 His r will extend from sea to sea
Ro 15: 12 who will arise to r over the nations;
1Co 7: 17 This is the r I lay down in all
Gal 6: 16 all who follow this r—
Eph 1: 21 far above all r and authority,
Col 3: 15 the peace of Christ r in your hearts.
2Th 3: 10 were with you, we gave you this r:
Rev 2: 27 they 'will r them with an iron
12: 5 who "will r all the nations
19: 15 "He will r them with an iron

RULER (RULE)
1Sa 10: 1 the Lord anointed you r
13: 14 appointed him r of his people,
Pr 19: 6 Many curry favor with a r,
23: 1 When you sit to dine with a r,
25: 15 Through patience a r can be
29: 26 Many seek an audience with a r,
Isa 60: 17 governor and well-being your r.
Da 9: 25 the Anointed One, the r, comes,
Mic 5: 2 one who will be r over Israel,
Mt 2: 6 will come a r who will shepherd my
Eph 2: 2 of the r of the kingdom of the air,
1Ti 6: 15 the blessed and only R, the King
Rev 1: 5 and the r of the kings of the earth.

RULERS (RULE)
Ps 2: 2 and the r band together against
8: 6 You made them r over the works
119:161 R persecute me without cause,
Isa 40: 23 and reduces the r of this world
Da 2: 27 and all r will worship and obey
Mt 20: 25 that the r of the Gentiles lord it over
Ac 13: 27 and their r did not recognize Jesus,
Ro 13: 3 For r hold no terror for those who
1Co 2: 6 of this age or of the r of this age,
Eph 3: 10 God should be made known to the r
6: 12 blood, but against the r,
Col 1: 16 or powers or r or authorities;

RULES (RULE)
Nu 15: 15 is to have the same r for you
2Sa 23: 3 when he r in the fear of God,
Ps 22: 28 Lord and he r over the nations.
66: 7 He r forever by his power, his eyes
103: 19 heaven, and his kingdom r over all.
Isa 29: 13 on merely human r they have been
40: 10 with power, and his arm r for him.
Mt 15: 9 teachings are merely human r.' "
Lk 22: 26 and the one who r like the one who
2Ti 2: 5 by competing according to the r.

RULING (RULE)
Ex 15: 25 There the Lord issued a r
Pr 25: 11 is a r rightly given.

RUMORS
Jer 51: 46 or be afraid when r are heard
Mt 24: 6 You will hear of wars and r of wars,

RUN (RAN RUNNERS RUNNING RUNS)
Ps 19: 5 champion rejoicing to r his course.
Pr 4: 12 when you r, you will not stumble.
18: 10 the righteous r to it and are safe.
Isa 10: 3 To whom will you r for help?
40: 31 they will r and not grow weary,
Joel 3: 18 ravines of Judah will r with water.
Hab 2: 2 so that a herald may r with it.
1Co 9: 24 R in such a way as to get the prize.
Php 2: 16 on the day of Christ that I did not r
Heb 12: 1 let us r with perseverance the race

RUNNERS* (RUN)
1Co 9: 24 not know that in a race all the r run,

RUNNING (RUN)
Ps 133: 2 on the head, r down on the beard,
Lk 17: 23 Do not go r off after them.
1Co 9: 26 do not run like someone r aimlessly;
Gal 2: 2 not r and had not been r my race in vain.
5: 7 You were r a good race. Who cut

RUNS (RUN)
Jn 10: 12 he abandons the sheep and r away.

RUSH (RUSHES RUSHING)
Pr 1: 16 for their feet r into evil, they are
6: 18 feet that are quick to r into evil,
Isa 59: 7 Their feet r into sin; they are swift

RUSHES (RUSH)
Pr 26: 17 who r into a quarrel not their own.

RUSHING (RUSH)
Pr 18: 4 the fountain of wisdom is a r stream.

RUST
Mt 6: 19 where moth and r destroy,

RUTH*
Moabitess; widow who went to Bethlehem with mother-in-law Naomi (Ru 1). Gleaned in field of Boaz; shown favor (Ru 2). Proposed marriage to Boaz (Ru 3). Married (Ru 4:1–12); bore Obed, ancestor of David (Ru 4:13–22), Jesus (Mt 1:5).

RUTHLESS
Pr 11: 16 honor, but r men gain only wealth.

SABBATH (SABBATHS)
Ex 20: 8 "Remember the **S** day by keeping it
31: 14 " 'Observe the **S**, because it is
Lev 25: 2 the land itself must observe a s
Dt 5: 12 "Observe the **S** day by keeping it
Isa 56: 2 who keep the **S** without desecrating
56: 6 who keep the **S** without desecrating
58: 13 if you call the **S** a delight
Jer 17: 21 not to carry a load on the **S** day
Mt 12: 1 through the grainfields on the **S**
Lk 13: 10 On a **S** Jesus was teaching in one
Col 2: 16 a New Moon celebration or a **S** day.

SABBATH-REST* (REST)
Heb 4: 9 then, a **S** for the people of God;

SABBATHS (SABBATH)
2Ch 2: 4 morning and evening and on the **S**,
Eze 20: 12 I gave them my **S** as a sign between

SACKCLOTH
Ps 30: 11 you removed my s and clothed me
Da 9: 3 in fasting, and in s and ashes.
Mt 11: 21 would have repented long ago in s

SACRED
Lev 23: 2 you are to proclaim as s assemblies.
Mt 7: 6 "Do not give dogs what is s;
Ro 14: 5 one day more s than another;
1Co 3: 17 for God's temple is s, and you
2Pe 1: 18 were with him on the s mountain.
2: 21 turn their backs on the s command

SACRIFICE (SACRIFICED SACRIFICES)
Ge 22: 2 **S** him there as a burnt offering
Ex 12: 27 'It is the Passover s to the LORD,
1Sa 15: 22 To obey is better than s, and to
1Ki 18: 38 the LORD fell and burned up the s,
1Ch 21: 24 or s a burnt offering that costs me
Ps 40: 6 **S** and offering you did not desire—
50: 14 "**S** thank offerings to God,
51: 16 You do not delight in s, or I would
51: 17 My s, O God, is a broken spirit;
54: 6 I will s a freewill offering to you;
107: 22 Let them s thank offerings and tell
141: 2 of my hands be like the evening s.
Pr 15: 8 The LORD detests the s
21: 3 acceptable to the LORD than s.
Da 9: 27 of the 'seven' he will put an end to s
12: 11 the time that the daily s is abolished
Hos 6: 6 not s, and acknowledgment of God
Mt 9: 13 'I desire mercy, not s.'
Ro 3: 25 God presented Christ as a s
12: 1 offer your bodies as a living s,
Eph 5: 2 as a fragrant offering and s to God.
Php 4: 18 an acceptable, pleasing to God.
Heb 9: 26 away with sin by the s of himself.
10: 5 "**S** and offering you did not desire,
10: 10 have been made holy through the s
10: 14 one s he has made perfect forever
10: 18 s for sin is no longer necessary.
13: 15 offer to God a s of praise—
1Jn 2: 2 He is the atoning s for our sins,
4: 10 sent his Son as an atoning s for our

SACRIFICED (SACRIFICE)
Ac 15: 29 are to abstain from food s to idols,
1Co 5: 7 our Passover lamb, has been s.
8: 1 Now about food s to idols:
Heb 7: 27 He s for their sins once for all
9: 28 so Christ was s once to take away

SACRIFICES (SACRIFICE)
Mk 12: 33 than all burnt offerings and s."
Heb 9: 23 themselves with better s than these.
13: 16 for with such s God is pleased.
1Pe 2: 5 offering spiritual s acceptable

SAD
Lk 18: 23 he became very s, because he was

SADDUCEES
Mt 16: 6 the yeast of the Pharisees and **S.**
Mk 12: 18 Then the **S**, who say there is no
Ac 23: 8 (The **S** say that there is no

SAFE (SAVE)
Ps 27: 5 of trouble he will keep me s in his
37: 3 in the land and enjoy s pasture.
Pr 18: 10 the righteous run to it and are s.
28: 26 who walk in wisdom are kept s.
29: 25 trusts in the LORD is kept s.
Jer 12: 5 If you stumble in s country,
Jn 17: 12 kept them s by that name you gave
1Jn 5: 18 who was born of God keeps them s,

SAFETY (SAVE)
Ps 4: 8 alone, LORD, make me dwell in s.
Hos 2: 18 land, so that all may lie down in s.
1Th 5: 3 "Peace and s," destruction will

SAKE
1Sa 12: 22 the s of his great name the LORD
Ps 23: 3 the right paths for his name's s.
44: 22 your s we face death all day long;
106: 8 Yet he saved them for his name's s,
Isa 42: 21 for the s of his righteousness
43: 25 for my own s, and remembers your
48: 9 my own name's s I delay my wrath;
48: 11 For my own s, for my own s,
Jer 14: 7 LORD, for the s of your name.
14: 21 the s of your name do not despise
Eze 20: 9 But for the s of my name, I brought
20: 14 the s of my name I did what would
20: 22 the s of my name I did what would
36: 22 but for the s of my holy name,
Da 9: 17 For your s, Lord, look with favor
Mt 10: 39 loses their life for my s will find it.
19: 29 my s will receive a hundred times as
1Co 9: 23 I do all this for the s of the gospel,
2Co 8: 9 for your s he became poor,
12: 10 for Christ's s, I delight
Php 3: 7 consider loss for the s of Christ.
Heb 11: 26 disgrace for the s of Christ as
1Pe 2: 13 for the Lord's s to every human
3Jn : 7 It was for the s of the Name

SALEM
Ge 14: 18 Melchizedek king of **S** brought
Heb 7: 2 also, "king of **S**" means "king

SALT
Ge 19: 26 back, and she became a pillar of s
Nu 18: 19 covenant of s before the LORD
Mt 5: 13 "You are the s of the earth.
5: 13 But if the s loses its saltiness,
Col 4: 6 seasoned with s, so that you may
Jas 3: 11 s water flow from the same spring?

SALVATION* (SAVE)
Ex 15: 2 he has become my s.
2Sa 22: 3 my shield and the horn of my s.
23: 5 he would not bring to fruition my s
1Ch 16: 23 proclaim his s day after day.
2Ch 6: 41 be clothed with s, may your faithful
Ps 9: 14 Zion, and there rejoice in your s.
13: 5 my heart rejoices in your s.
14: 7 that s for Israel would come
18: 2 my shield and the horn of my s,
27: 1 The LORD is my light and my s—
28: 8 a fortress of s for his anointed one.
35: 3 Say to me, "I am your s."
35: 9 in the LORD and delight in his s.
37: 39 The s of the righteous comes
50: 23 to the blameless I will show my s."
51: 12 Restore to me the joy of your s
53: 6 that s for Israel would come
62: 1 rest in God; my s comes from him.
62: 2 Truly he is my rock and my s;
62: 6 Truly he is my rock and my s;
62: 7 My s and my honor depend on God;
67: 2 on earth, your s among all nations.
69: 13 O God, answer me with your sure s.
69: 27 do not let them share in your s.
69: 29 may your s, God, protect me.
74: 12 he brings s on the earth.
85: 7 love, LORD, and grant us your s.
85: 9 Surely his s is near those who fear

Ps 91: 16 satisfy them and show them my s."
95: 1 us shout aloud to the Rock of our s.
96: 2 proclaim his s day after day.
98: 1 his holy arm have worked s for him.
98: 2 The LORD has made his s known
98: 3 of the earth have seen the s of our
116: 13 I will lift up the cup of s and call
118: 14 he has become my s.
118: 21 you have become my s.
119: 41 your s, according to your promise;
119: 81 soul faints with longing for your s,
119:123 looking for your s, looking for your
119:155 **S** is far from the wicked, for they do
119:166 I wait for your s, LORD, and I
119:174 I long for your s, LORD, and your
132: 16 I will clothe her priests with s,
Isa 12: 2 Surely God is my s; I will trust
12: 2 he has become my s."
12: 3 will draw water from the wells of s.
25: 9 let us rejoice and be glad in his s."
26: 1 God makes s its walls and ramparts.
26: 18 We have not brought s to the earth,
30: 15 "In repentance and rest is your s,
33: 2 morning, our s in time of distress.
33: 6 a rich store of s and wisdom
45: 8 the earth open wide, let s spring up,
45: 17 the LORD with an everlasting s;
46: 13 and my s will not be delayed.
46: 13 I will grant s to Zion, my splendor
49: 6 that my s may reach to the ends
49: 8 and in the day of s I will help you;
51: 5 near speedily, my s is on the way,
51: 6 But my s will last forever,
51: 8 my s through all generations."
52: 7 who proclaim s, who say to Zion,
52: 10 the earth will see the s of our God.
56: 1 for my s is close at hand and my
59: 16 so his own arm achieved s for him,
59: 17 and the helmet of s on his head;
60: 18 you will call your walls **S** and your
61: 10 has clothed me with garments of s
62: 1 the dawn, her s like a blazing torch.
63: 5 so my own arm achieved s for me,
Jer 3: 23 in the LORD our God is the s
La 3: 26 wait quietly for the s of the LORD.
Jnh 2: 9 'S comes from the LORD.' "
Zec 9: 9 righteous and having s,
Lk 1: 69 He has raised up a horn of s for us
1: 71 s from our enemies
1: 77 s through the forgiveness of their
2: 30 For my eyes have seen your s,
3: 6 all people will see God's s.' "
19: 9 "Today s has come to this house,
Jn 4: 22 we do know, for s is from the Jews.
Ac 4: 12 **S** is found in no one else, for there is
13: 26 that this message of s has been sent.
13: 47 that you may bring s to the ends
28: 28 know that God's s has been sent
Ro 1: 16 brings s to everyone who believes:
11: 11 s has come to the Gentiles to make
13: 11 because our s is nearer now than
2Co 1: 6 it is for your comfort and s;
6: 2 and in the day of s I helped you."
7: 10 brings repentance that leads to s
Eph 1: 13 word of truth, the gospel of your s.
6: 17 Take the helmet of s and the sword
Php 2: 12 to work out your s with fear
1Th 5: 8 and the hope of s as a helmet.
5: 9 to receive s through our Lord Jesus
2Ti 2: 10 that they too may obtain the s that is
3: 15 make you wise for s through faith
Tit 2: 11 appeared that offers s to all people.
Heb 1: 14 to serve those who will inherit s?
2: 3 we escape if we ignore so great a s?
2: 3 This s, which was first announced
2: 10 of their s perfect through what he
5: 9 of eternal s for all who obey him
6: 9 the things that have to do with s.
9: 28 to bring s to those who are waiting
1Pe 1: 5 the coming of the s that is ready
1: 9 Concerning this s, the prophets,
1: 10 by it you may grow up in your s,
2Pe 3: 15 that our Lord's patience means s,
Jude 3 to write to you about the s we share,
Rev 7: 10 "**S** belongs to our God, who sits
12: 10 "Now have come the s
19: 1 **S** and glory and power belong to our

SAMARIA (SAMARITAN)
1Ki 16: 24 He bought the hill of **S** from Shemer

2Ki 17: 6 the king of Assyria captured **S**
Jn 4: 4 Now he had to go through **S**.
4: 5 came to a town in **S** called Sychar,

SAMARITAN (SAMARIA)
Lk 10: 33 But a **S**, as he traveled, came where
17: 16 and thanked him—and he was a **S**.
Jn 4: 7 When a **S** woman came to draw

SAMSON
Danite judge. Birth promised (Jdg 13). Married to Philistine, but wife given away (Jdg 14). Vengeance on Philistines (Jdg 15). Betrayed by Delilah (Jdg 16:1–22). Death (Jdg 16:23–31). Feats of strength: killed lion (Jdg 14:6), 30 Philistines (Jdg 14:19), 1,000 Philistines with jawbone (Jdg 15:13–17), carried off gates of Gaza (Jdg 16:3), pushed down temple of Dagon (Jdg 16:25–30).

SAMUEL
Ephraimite judge and prophet (Heb 11:32). Birth prayed for (1Sa 1:10–18). Dedicated to temple by Hannah (1Sa 1:21–28). Raised by Eli (1Sa 2:11, 18–26). Called as prophet (1Sa 3). Led Israel to victory over Philistines (1Sa 7). Asked by Israel for a king (1Sa 8). Anointed Saul as king (1Sa 9–10). Farewell speech (1Sa 12). Rebuked Saul for sacrifice (1Sa 13). Announced rejection of Saul (1Sa 15). Anointed David as king (1Sa 16). Protected David from Saul (1Sa 19:18–24). Death (1Sa 25:1). Returned from dead to condemn Saul (1Sa 28).

SANBALLAT
Led opposition to Nehemiah's rebuilding of Jerusalem (Ne 2:10, 19; 4; 6).

SANCTIFIED* (SANCTIFY)
Jn 17: 19 myself, that they too may be truly **s**.
Ac 20: 32 among all those who are **s**.
26: 18 a place among those who are **s**
Ro 15: 16 to God, **s** by the Holy Spirit.
1Co 1: 2 to those **s** in Christ Jesus and called
6: 11 you were **s**, you were justified
7: 14 husband has been **s** through his
7: 14 wife has been **s** through her
1Th 4: 3 It is God's will that you should be **s**:
Heb 10: 29 blood of the covenant that **s** them,

SANCTIFY* (SANCTIFIED SANCTIFYING)
Jn 17: 17 **S** them by the truth; your word is
17: 19 For them I myself, that they too
1Th 5: 23 peace, **s** you through and through.
Heb 9: 13 are ceremonially unclean **s** them so

SANCTIFYING* (SANCTIFY)
2Th 2: 13 be saved through the **s** work
1Pe 1: 2 through the **s** work of the Spirit,

SANCTUARY
Ex 25: 8 "Then have them make a **s** for me,
Lev 10: 13 Eat it in the **s** area,
19: 30 and have reverence for my **s**.
Ps 15: 1 LORD, who may dwell in your **s**?
63: 2 I have seen you in the **s** and beheld
68: 24 of my God and King into the **s**.
68: 35 You, God, are awesome in your **s**;
73: 17 till I entered the **s** of God;
102: 19 looked down from his **s** on high,
134: 2 Lift up your hands in the **s**
150: 1 Praise God in his **s**; praise him
Eze 37: 26 I will put my **s** among them forever.
Da 9: 26 come will destroy the city and the **s**.
Heb 6: 19 enters the inner **s** behind the curtain,
8: 2 and who serves in the **s**, the true
8: 5 They serve at a **s** that is a copy
9: 24 Christ did not enter a **s** made

SAND
Ge 22: 17 the sky and as the **s** on the seashore.
Mt 7: 26 man who built his house on **s**.

SANDAL (SANDALS)
Ru 4: 7 one party took off his **s** and gave it

SANDALS (SANDAL)
Ex 3: 5 "Take off your **s**, for the place
Dt 25: 9 take off one of his **s**, spit in his face
Jos 5: 15 "Take off your **s**, for the place
Mt 3: 11 I, whose **s** I am not worthy to carry.

SANG (SING)
Ex 15: 1 and the Israelites **s** this song
15: 21 Miriam **s** to them:
Nu 21: 17 Then Israel **s** this song:
Jdg 5: 1 Barak son of Abinoam **s** this song:
1Sa 18: 7 As they danced, they **s**:
2Sa 22: 1 David **s** to the LORD the words
2Ch 5: 13 in praise to the LORD and **s**:

2Ch 29: 30 So they **s** praises with gladness
Ezr 3: 11 thanksgiving they **s** to the LORD:
Job 38: 7 while the morning stars **s** together
Ps 106: 12 his promises and **s** his praise.
Rev 5: 9 And they **s** a new song, saying:
14: 3 they **s** a new song before the throne
15: 3 **s** the song of God's servant Moses

SAP
Ro 11: 17 the nourishing **s** from the olive root,

SAPPHIRA*
Ac 5: 1 together with his wife **S**, also sold

SARAH
Wife of Abraham, originally named Sarai; barren (Ge 11:29–31; 1Pe 3:6). Taken by Pharaoh as Abraham's sister; returned (Ge 12:10–20). Gave Hagar to Abraham; sent her away in pregnancy (Ge 16). Name changed; Isaac promised (Ge 17:15–21; 18:10–15; Heb 11:11). Taken by Abimelek as Abraham's sister; returned (Ge 20). Isaac born; Hagar and Ishmael sent away (Ge 21:1–21; Gal 4:21–31). Death (Ge 23).

SARDIS
Rev 3: 1 the angel of the church in **S** write:

SASH (SASHES)
Rev 1: 13 with a golden **s** around his chest.

SASHES (SASH)
Rev 15: 6 wore golden **s** around their chests.

SAT (SIT)
Ps 137: 1 By the rivers of Babylon we **s**
Mk 16: 19 he **s** at the right hand of God.
Lk 10: 39 who **s** at the Lord's feet listening
Heb 1: 3 he **s** down at the right hand
8: 1 who **s** down at the right hand
10: 12 he **s** down at the right hand of God,
12: 2 and **s** down at the right hand

SATAN
Job 1: 6 and **S** also came with them.
Zec 3: 2 to **S**, "The LORD rebuke you, **S**!
Mt 12: 26 If **S** drives out **S**, he is divided
16: 23 said to Peter, "Get behind me, **S**!
Mk 4: 15 **S** comes and takes away the word
Lk 10: 18 "I saw **S** fall like lightning
22: 3 Then **S** entered Judas,
Ro 16: 20 will soon crush **S** under your feet.
1Co 5: 5 hand this man over to **S**
2Co 11: 14 **S** himself masquerades as an angel
12: 7 a messenger of **S**, to torment me.
1Ti 1: 20 whom I have handed over to **S** to be
Rev 12: 9 or **S**, who leads the whole world
20: 2 or **S**, and bound him for a thousand
20: 7 **S** will be released from his prison

SATISFIED (SATISFY)
Ps 17: 15 I will be **s** with seeing your likeness.
22: 26 The poor will eat and be **s**;
63: 5 I will be fully **s** as with the richest
104: 28 hand, they are **s** with good things.
Pr 13: 4 the desires of the diligent are fully **s**.
30: 15 are three things that never **s**,
Ecc 5: 10 those who love wealth are never **s**
Isa 53: 11 he will see the fruit of life and be **s**;
Mt 14: 20 They all ate and were **s**,
Lk 6: 21 who hunger now, for you will be **s**.

SATISFIES* (SATISFY)
Ps 103: 5 who **s** your desires with good things
107: 9 for he **s** the thirsty and fills
147: 14 and **s** you with the finest of wheat.

SATISFY (SATISFIED SATISFIES)
Ps 90: 14 **S** us in the morning with your
145: 16 the desires of every living thing.
Pr 5: 19 may her breasts **s** you always,
Isa 55: 2 and your labor on what does not **s**?
58: 10 and **s** the needs of the oppressed,

SAUL
1. Benjamite; anointed by Samuel as first king of Israel (1Sa 9–10). Defeated Ammonites (1Sa 11). Rebuked for offering sacrifice (1Sa 13:1–15). Defeated Philistines (1Sa 14). Rejected as king for failing to annihilate Amalekites (1Sa 15). Soothed from evil spirit by David (1Sa 16:14–23). Sent David against Goliath (1Sa 17). Jealousy and attempted murder of David (1Sa 18:1–11). Gave David Michal as wife (1Sa 18:12–30). Second attempt to kill David (1Sa 19). Anger at Jonathan (1Sa 20:26–34). Pursued David: killed priests at Nob (1Sa 22), went to Keilah and Ziph (1Sa 23), life spared by David at En Gedi (1Sa 24) and in his tent (1Sa 26). Rebuked by Samuel's spirit for consulting witch at Endor (1Sa 28). Wounded by Phi-

listines; took his own life (1Sa 31; 1Ch 10). Lamented by David (2Sa 1:17–27). Children (1Sa 14:49–51; 1Ch 8).
2. See PAUL

SAVAGE
Ac 20: 29 **s** wolves will come in among you

SAVE (SAFE SAFETY SALVATION SAVED SAVES SAVIOR)
Ge 45: 5 because it was to **s** lives that God
1Ch 16: 35 Cry out, "**S** us, God our Savior;
Job 40: 14 that your own right hand can **s** you.
Ps 17: 7 you who **s** by your right hand those
18: 27 You **s** the humble but bring low
28: 9 **S** your people and bless your
31: 16 **s** me in your unfailing love.
69: 35 for God will **s** Zion and rebuild
71: 2 turn your ear to me and **s** me.
72: 13 needy and **s** the needy from death.
91: 3 Surely he will **s** you
109: 31 to **s** their lives from those who
146: 3 in human beings, who cannot **s**.
Pr 2: 16 Wisdom will **s** you
Isa 35: 4 retribution he will come to **s** you."
38: 20 The LORD will **s** me, and we will
46: 7 it cannot **s** them from their troubles.
59: 1 of the LORD is not too short to **s**,
63: 1 in righteousness, mighty to **s**."
Jer 17: 14 **s** me and I will be saved, for you are
Eze 13: 18 Will you ensnare... in order to **s** their lives,
14: 14 they could **s** only themselves
34: 22 I will **s** my flock, and they will no
Hos 1: 7 and I will **s** them—not by bow,
Zep 1: 18 nor their gold will be able to **s** them
Zec 8: 7 "I will **s** my people
Mt 1: 21 because he will **s** his people
16: 25 wants to their life will lose it,
Lk 19: 10 to seek and to **s** what was lost."
Jn 3: 17 but to **s** the world through him.
12: 47 judge the world, but to **s** the world.
Ro 11: 14 people to envy and **s** some of them.
1Co 7: 16 whether you will **s** your husband?
1Ti 1: 15 came into the world to **s** sinners—
Heb 7: 25 to **s** completely those who come
Jas 5: 20 way of error will **s** them from death
Jude 23 **s** others by snatching them

SAVED (SAVE)
Ps 18: 5 They cried to you and were **s**;
33: 16 No king is **s** by the size of his army;
34: 6 he **s** him out of all his troubles.
106: 21 They forgot the God who **s** them,
116: 6 when I was brought low, he **s** me.
Isa 25: 9 we trusted in him, and he **s** us.
45: 22 "Turn to me and be **s**, all you ends
64: 5 How then can we be **s**?
Jer 4: 14 the evil from your heart and be **s**.
8: 20 has ended, and we are not **s**."
Eze 3: 19 but you will have yourself.
33: 5 they would have **s** themselves.
Joel 2: 32 the name of the LORD will be **s**;
Mt 10: 22 who stand firm to the end will be **s**.
24: 13 stands firm to the end will be **s**.
Mk 13: 13 who stand firm to the end will be **s**.
16: 16 *and is baptized will be* **s**,
Jn 10: 9 enters through me will be **s**.
Ac 2: 21 on the name of the Lord will be **s**.'
2: 47 daily those who were being **s**.
4: 12 heaven by which we must be **s**."
15: 11 of our Lord Jesus that we are **s**,
16: 30 "Sirs, what must I do to be **s**?"
Ro 5: 9 how much more shall we be **s**
9: 27 the sea, only the remnant will be **s**.
10: 1 the Israelites is that they may be **s**.
10: 9 him from the dead, you will be **s**.
10: 13 on the name of the Lord will be **s**."
11: 26 and in this way all Israel will be **s**.
1Co 1: 18 to us who are being **s** it is the power
3: 15 will suffer loss but yet will be **s**—
5: 5 so that his spirit may be **s** on the day
10: 33 of many, so that they may be **s**.
15: 2 By this gospel you are **s**, if you hold
Eph 2: 5 it is by grace you have been **s**.
2: 8 For it is by grace you have been **s**,
2Th 2: 13 to be **s** through the sanctifying work
1Ti 2: 4 who wants all people to be **s**
2: 15 will be **s** through childbearing—
Tit 2: 1 who has **s** us and called us to a holy
3: 5 He **s** us through the washing
Heb 10: 39 but of those who believe and are **s**.

SAVES (SAVE)
Ps 7: 10 High, who **s** the upright in heart.

Ps 68: 20 Our God is a God who s;
     145: 19 he hears their cry and s them.
Zep   3: 17 the Mighty Warrior who s.
1Pe   3: 21 It s you by the resurrection of Jesus

SAVIOR* (SAVE)
Dt   32: 15 him and rejected the Rock his **S**.
2Sa   22: 3 stronghold, my refuge and my s—
      22: 47 be my God, the Rock, my **S**!
1Ch 16: 35 Cry out, "Save us, God our **S**;
Ps   18: 46 to my Rock! Exalted be God my **S**!
      24: 5 and vindication from God their **S**.
      25: 5 for you are God my **S**, and my hope
      27: 9 reject me or forsake me, God my **S**.
      38: 22 to help me, my Lord and my **S**.
      42: 5 yet praise him, my **S** and my God.
      42: 11 yet praise him, my **S** and my God.
      43: 5 yet praise him, my **S** and my God.
      51: 14 God, you who are God my **S**,
      65: 5 God our **S**, the hope of all the ends
      68: 19 to God our **S**, who daily bears our
      79: 9 God our **S**, for the glory of your
      85: 4 God our **S**, and put away your
      89: 26 Father, my God, the Rock my **S**.'
Isa 17: 10 You have forgotten God your **S**;
      19: 20 he will send them a s and defender,
      43: 3 the Holy One of Israel, your **S**;
      43: 11 and apart from me there is no s.
      45: 15 himself, the God and **S** of Israel.
      45: 21 from me, a righteous God and a **S**;
      49: 26 am your **S**, your Redeemer,
      60: 16 am your **S**, your Redeemer,
      62: 11 Daughter Zion, 'See, your **S** comes!'
      63: 8 and so he became their **S**.
Jer 14: 8 of Israel, its **S** in times of distress,
      23: 6 called: The LORD Our Righteous **S**.
      33: 16 called: The LORD Our Righteous **S**.'
Hos 13: 4 no God but me, no **S** except me.
Mic   7: 7 the LORD, I wait for God my **S**;
Hab   3: 18 I will be joyful in God my **S**.
Lk   1: 47 and my spirit rejoices in God my **S**,
      2: 11 the town of David a **S** has been born
Jn   4: 42 that this man really is the **S**
Ac   5: 31 and **S** that he might bring Israel
      13: 23 has brought to Israel the **S** Jesus,
Eph   5: 23 his body, of which he is the **S**.
Php   3: 20 we eagerly await a **S** from there,
1Ti   1: 1 Jesus by the command of God our **S**
      2: 3 This is good, and pleases God our **S**,
      4: 10 God, who is the **S** of all people,
2Ti   1: 10 through the appearing of our **S**,
Tit   1: 3 me by the command of God our **S**,
      1: 4 the Father and Christ Jesus our **S**.
      2: 10 teaching about God our **S** attractive.
      2: 13 of the glory of our great God and **S**,
      3: 4 and love of God our **S** appeared,
      3: 6 through Jesus Christ our **S**,
2Pe   1: 1 **S** Jesus Christ have received a faith
      1: 11 of our Lord and **S** Jesus Christ.
      2: 20 our Lord and **S** Jesus Christ and are
      3: 2 Lord and **S** through your apostles.
      3: 18 of our Lord and **S** Jesus Christ.
1Jn   4: 14 his Son to be the **S** of the world.
Jude : 25 to the only God our **S** be glory,

SCALE (SCALES)
Ps   18: 29 with my God I can s a wall.

SCALES (SCALE)
Lev 11: 9 may eat any that have fins and s.
      19: 36 Use honest s and honest weights,
Pr   11: 1 The LORD detests dishonest s,
Da   5: 27 You have been weighed on the s
Rev   6: 5 Its rider was holding a pair of s

SCAPEGOAT (GOAT)
Lev 16: 10 sending it into the wilderness as a s.

SCARECROW*
Jer 10: 5 Like a s in a melon patch, their idols

SCARLET
Jos   2: 21 she tied the s cord in the window.
Isa   1: 18 "Though your sins are like s,
Mt   27: 28 him and put a s robe on him,

SCATTER (SCATTERED SCATTERS)
Dt   4: 27 The LORD will s you among
Ne   1: 8 I will s you among the nations,
Jer   9: 16 I will s them among nations
      30: 11 all the nations among which I s you,
Zec 10: 9 Though I s them among the peoples,

SCATTERED (SCATTER)
Isa 11: 12 he will assemble the s people
Jer 31: 10 'He who s Israel will gather them

Zec   2: 6 "for I have s you to the four winds
      13: 7 and the sheep will be s, and I will
Mt   26: 31 and the sheep of the flock will be s.'
Jn   11: 52 but also for the s children of God,
Ac   8: 4 who had been s preached the word
Jas   1: 1 To the twelve tribes s among
1Pe   1: 1 exiles s throughout the provinces

SCATTERS (SCATTER)
Mt   12: 30 whoever does not gather with me s.

SCEPTER
Ge   49: 10 The s will not depart from Judah,
Nu   24: 17 a s will rise out of Israel.
Ps   45: 6 a s of justice will be the s of your
Heb   1: 8 a s of justice will be the s of your
Rev   2: 27 they 'will rule them with an iron s.
      12: 5 rule all the nations with an iron s.
      19: 15 "He will rule them with an iron s."

SCHEMES
Pr   6: 18 a heart that devises wicked s,
      10: 23 Fools find pleasure in wicked s,
      12: 2 condemns those who devise wicked s.
      14: 17 who devise evil s are hated.
      24: 9 The s of folly are sin, and people
2Co   2: 11 For we are not unaware of his s.
Eph   6: 11 take your stand against the devil's s.

SCOFFERS
2Pe   3: 3 that in the last days s will come,

SCORN (SCORNED SCORNING SCORNS)
Ps   69: 7 For I endure s for your sake,
      69: 20 S has broken my heart and has left
      89: 41 he has become the s of his
     109: 25 I am an object of s to my accusers;
     123: 4 our endurance of the s of the
Mic   6: 16 you will bear the s of the nations."

SCORNED (SCORN)
Ps   22: 6 I am s by everyone,

SCORNING* (SCORN)
Heb 12: 2 he endured the cross, s its shame,

SCORNS* (SCORN)
Pr   13: 13 Whoever s instruction will pay
      30: 17 that s an aged mother, will be

SCORPION
Lk   11: 12 asks for an egg, will give him a s?
Rev   9: 5 of the sting of a s when it strikes.

SCOUNDRELS
1Sa   2: 12 Eli's sons were s;

SCRIPTURE (SCRIPTURES)
Jn   2: 22 they believed the s and the words
      7: 42 Does not S say that the Messiah will
      10: 35 and S cannot be broken—
Ac   8: 32 of S the eunuch was reading:
1Ti   4: 13 yourself to the public reading of S,
2Ti   3: 16 All S is God-breathed and is useful
2Pe   1: 20 that no prophecy of S came

SCRIPTURES (SCRIPTURE)
Mt   22: 29 error because you do not know the S
Lk   24: 27 said in all the S concerning himself.
      24: 45 so they could understand the S.
Jn   5: 39 These are the very S that testify
Ac   17: 11 examined the S every day to see
2Ti   3: 15 infancy you have known the Holy S,
2Pe   3: 16 as they do the other S, to their own

SCROLL
Ps   40: 7 it is written about me in the s.
Isa 34: 4 and the heavens rolled up like a s;
Eze   3: 1 eat what is before you, eat this s;
Heb 10: 7 it is written about me in the s—
Rev   6: 14 The sky receded like a s, rolling up,
      10: 8 take the s that lies open in the hand
      22: 18 the plagues described in this s.

SCUM
1Co   4: 13 We have become the s of the earth,

SEA (SEASHORE)
Ex   14: 16 the Israelites can go through the s
Dt   30: 13 "Who will cross the s to get it
1Ki   7: 23 He made the S of cast metal,
Job 11: 9 than the earth and wider than the s.
Ps   93: 4 mightier than the breakers of the s—
      95: 5 The s is his, for he made it, and his
Ecc   1: 7 All streams flow into the s, yet the s
      11: 1 Ship your grain across the s;
Isa 57: 20 the wicked are like the tossing s,
Jnh   1: 4 LORD sent a great wind on the s,
Mic   7: 19 iniquities into the depths of the s.
Hab   2: 14 LORD as the waters cover the s.

Zec   9: 10 His rule will extend from s to s
Mt   18: 6 were drowned in the depths of the s
1Co 10: 1 that they all passed through the s.
Jas   1: 6 who doubts is like a wave of the s,
Jude : 13 They are wild waves of the s,
Rev 10: 2 He planted his right foot on the s
      13: 1 I saw a beast coming out of the s.
      20: 13 The s gave up the dead that were
      21: 1 and there was no longer any s.

SEAL (SEALED SEALS)
Ps   40: 9 I do not s my lips, LORD, as you
SS   8: 6 Place me like a s over your heart,
Eze 28: 12 " 'You were the s of perfection,
Da   12: 4 s the words of the scroll until
Jn   6: 27 him God the Father has placed his s
1Co   9: 2 For you are the s of my apostleship
2Co   1: 22 set his s of ownership on us, and put
Eph   1: 13 you were marked in him with a s,
Rev   6: 3 the Lamb opened the second s,
      6: 5 When the Lamb opened the third s,
      6: 7 the Lamb opened the fourth s,
      6: 9 When he opened the fifth s, I saw
      6: 12 I watched as he opened the sixth s.
      8: 1 When he opened the seventh s,
      9: 4 those people who did not have the s
      22: 10 "Do not s up the words

SEALED (SEAL)
Eph   4: 30 with whom you were s for the day
2Ti   2: 19 stands firm, s with this inscription:
Rev   5: 1 on both sides and s with seven seals.

SEALS (SEAL)
Rev   5: 2 "Who is worthy to break the s
      6: 1 opened the first of the seven s.

SEAMLESS*
Jn   19: 23 This garment was s, woven in one

SEARCH (SEARCHED SEARCHES SEARCHING)
Ps   4: 4 beds, s your hearts and be silent.
     139: 23 S me, God, and know my heart;
Pr   2: 4 and s for it as for hidden treasure,
      11: 27 evil comes to those who s for it.
      25: 2 to s out a matter is the glory
      25: 27 honorable to s out matters
SS   3: 2 I will s for the one my heart loves.
Jer 17: 10 "I the LORD s the heart
Eze 34: 11 I myself will s for my sheep
      34: 16 I will s for the lost and bring back
Lk   15: 8 and s carefully until she finds it?

SEARCHED (SEARCH)
Ps 139: 1 You have s me, LORD, and you
Ecc 12: 10 The Teacher s to find just the right
1Pe   1: 10 s intently and with the greatest care,

SEARCHES* (SEARCH)
1Ch 28: 9 for the LORD s every heart
Job 39: 8 pasture s for any green thing.
Ro   8: 27 he who s our hearts knows the mind
1Co   2: 10 The Spirit s all things, even the deep
Rev   2: 23 will know that I am he who s hearts

SEARCHING (SEARCH)
Jdg   5: 15 Reuben there was much s of heart.
Am   8: 12 east, s for the word of the LORD,

SEARED
1Ti   4: 2 whose consciences have been s as

SEASHORE (SEA)
Jos 11: 4 as numerous as the sand on the s.
1Ki   4: 29 as measureless as the sand on the s.

SEASON (SEASONED SEASONS)
Lev 26: 4 I will send you rain in its s,
Ps   1: 3 which yields its fruit in and whose
2Ti   4: 2 be prepared in and out of s;

SEASONED* (SEASON)
Col   4: 6 be always full of grace, s with salt,

SEASONS (SEASON)
Ge   1: 14 let them serve as signs to mark s
Gal   4: 10 days and months and s and years!

SEAT (SEATED SEATS)
Pr   31: 23 he takes his s among the elders
Da   7: 9 and the Ancient of Days took his s.
Lk   14: 9 to you, 'Give this person your s.'
2Co   5: 10 all appear before the judgment s

SEATED (SEAT)
Ps   47: 8 God is s on his holy throne.
Isa   6: 1 I died, I saw the Lord s on a throne,
Lk   22: 69 of Man will be s at the right hand
Eph   1: 20 and s him at his right hand
      2: 6 and s us with him in the heavenly

Col 3: 1 where Christ is at the right hand
Rev 14: 14 s on the cloud one like a son
    20: 11 throne and him who was s on it.

SEATS (SEAT)
Lk 11: 43 you love the most important s

SECLUSION*
Lk   1: 24 and for five months remained in s.

SECRET (SECRETLY SECRETS)
Dt 29: 29 The s things belong to the LORD
Jdg 16: 6 "Tell me the s of your great
Ps 90: 8 our s sins in the light of your
   139: 15 you when I was made in the s place.
Pr 11: 13 but the trustworthy keep a s.
    21: 14 A gift given in s soothes anger,
Jer 23: 24 Who can hide in s places so that I
Mt   6: 4 so that your giving may be in s.
     6: 18 who sees what is done in s,
Mk   4: 11 "The s of the kingdom of God has
2Co 4: 2 we have renounced s and shameful
Eph 5: 12 what the disobedient do in s.
Php 4: 12 I have learned the s of being content

SECRETLY (SECRET)
2Pe 2: 1 They will s introduce destructive
Jude : 4 long ago have s slipped in among

SECRETS (SECRET)
Ps 44: 21 since he knows the s of the heart?
Ro   2: 16 judges everyone's s through Jesus
1Co 14: 25 the s of their hearts are laid bare.
Rev 2: 24 not learned Satan's so-called deep s,

SECURE (SECURITY)
Dt 33: 12 beloved of the LORD rest s in him,
2Sa 22: 33 and keeps my way s.
Ps 16: 5 you have made my lot s.
    16: 9 my body also will rest s,
    18: 32 and keeps my way s.
    22: 9 you made me feel s on my mother's
    93: 1 world is established, firm and s.
   112: 8 Their hearts are s,
Pr 14: 26 fear the LORD have a s fortress,
Heb 6: 19 as an anchor for the soul, firm and s.
2Pe 3: 17 and fall from your s position.

SECURITY (SECURE)
Job 31: 24 or said to pure gold, 'You are my s,'

SEED (SEEDS SEEDTIME)
Ge   1: 11 the land that bear fruit with s in it,
Isa 55: 10 so that it yields s for the sower
Mt 13: 3 "A farmer went out to sow his s.
    13: 31 of heaven is like a mustard s,
    17: 20 have faith as small as a mustard s,
Lk   8: 11 The s is the word of God.
1Co 3: 6 I planted the s, Apollos watered it,
2Co 9: 10 Now he who supplies s to the sower
Gal 3: 29 then you are Abraham's s, and heirs
1Pe 1: 23 again, not of perishable s,
1Jn 3: 9 because God's s remains in them;

SEEDS (SEED)
Jn 12: 24 But if it dies, it produces many s.
Gal 3: 16 Scripture does not say "and to s,"

SEEDTIME* (SEED)
Ge   8: 22 as the earth endures, s and harvest,

SEEK (SEEKING SEEKS SELF-SEEKING SOUGHT)
Lev 19: 18 " 'Do not s revenge or bear
Dt   4: 29 there you s the LORD your God,
     4: 29 you will find him if you s him
1Ki 22: 5 of Israel, "First s the counsel
1Ch 28: 9 If you s him, he will be found
2Ch 7: 14 pray and s my face and turn
     15: 2 If you s him, he will be found
Ps 34: 10 but those who s the LORD lack no
   105: 3 of those who s the LORD rejoice.
   105: 4 and his strength; s his face always.
   119: 2 and seek him with all their heart—
   119: 10 I s you with all my heart; do not let
   119:176 S your servant, for I have not
Pr   8: 17 and those who s me find me.
     18: 15 for the ears of the wise s it out.
     28: 5 those who s the LORD understand
Isa 55: 6 S the LORD while he may be
     65: 1 found by those who did not s me.
Jer 29: 13 You will s me and find me
Hos 10: 12 for it is time to s the LORD,
Am   5: 4 the house of Israel: "S me and live;
Zep 2: 3 S the LORD, all you humble
     2: 3 S righteousness, s humility;
Mt   6: 33 But s first his kingdom and his
     7: 7 given to you; s and you will find;
     7: 8 those who s find;

Lk 12: 31 But s his kingdom, and these things
    19: 10 For the Son of Man came to s
Jn   5: 30 for I s not to please myself but him
     5: 44 but do not s the glory that comes
Ro 10: 20 found by those who did not s me;
1Co 7: 27 Do not s to be released.
    10: 24 No one should s their own good,
Heb 11: 6 rewards those who earnestly s him.
1Pe 3: 11 and do good; s peace and pursue it.

SEEKING (SEEK)
2Ch 30: 19 who sets their heart on s God—
Pr 20: 18 Plans are established by s advice;
Mal 3: 1 the Lord you are s will come to his
Jn   8: 50 I am not s glory for myself;
1Co 10: 33 For I am not s my own good

SEEKS (SEEK)
Pr 11: 27 Whoever s good finds favor,
Jn   4: 23 the kind of worshipers the Father s.
Ro   3: 11 there is no one who s God.

SEER
1Sa 9: 9 of today used to be called a s.)

SELF-CONTROL* (CONTROL)
Pr 16: 32 those with s than those who take
    25: 28 through is a person who lacks s.
Ac 24: 25 s and the judgment to come,
1Co 7: 5 tempt you because of your lack of s.
Gal 5: 23 gentleness and s.
2Ti 3: 3 slanderous, without s, brutal,
2Pe 1: 6 and to knowledge, s; and to s, persever-
                 ance;

SELF-CONTROLLED* (CONTROL)
1Ti 3: 2 his wife, temperate, s, respectable,
Tit 1: 8 what is good, who is s, upright,
     2: 2 worthy of respect, s, and sound
     2: 5 to be s and pure, to be busy
     2: 6 encourage the young men to be s.
     2: 12 and to live s, upright and godly lives

SELF-DENIAL* (SELF-DENIAL)
Ps 132: 1 remember David and all his s.

SELF-DISCIPLINE* (DISCIPLINE)
2Ti 1: 7 but gives us power, love and s.

SELF-INDULGENCE*
Mt 23: 25 inside they are full of greed and s.
Jas 5: 5 have lived on earth in luxury and s.

SELF-SEEKING* (SEEK)
Ro   2: 8 for those who are s and who reject
1Co 13: 5 it is not s, it is not easily angered,

SELFISH*
Ps 119: 36 your statutes and not toward s gain.
Pr 18: 1 An unfriendly person pursues s ends
Gal 5: 20 fits of rage, s ambition, dissensions,
Php 1: 17 preach Christ out of s ambition,
     2: 3 Do nothing out of s ambition
Jas 3: 14 envy and s ambition in your hearts,
     3: 16 you have envy and s ambition,

SELL (SELLING SELLS SOLD)
Ge 25: 31 "First s me your birthright."
Mk 10: 21 s everything you have and give
Rev 13: 17 buy or s unless they had the mark,

SELLING (SELL)
Lk 17: 28 buying and s, planting and building.

SELLS (SELL)
Pr 31: 24 makes linen garments and s them,

SEND (SENDING SENDS SENT)
Ps 43: 3 S me your light and your faithful
Isa 6: 8 the Lord saying, "Whom shall I s?
     6: 8 And I said, "Here am I. S me!"
Mal 3: 1 "I will s my messenger, who will
Mt   9: 38 to s out workers into his harvest
    24: 31 he will s his angels with a loud
Mk   1: 2 "I will s my messenger ahead
     1: 17 will s you out to fish for people."
     6: 7 began to s them out two by two
Lk 20: 13 I will s my son, whom I love;
Jn   3: 17 God did not s his Son into the world
     3: 17 but if you, will s his one and
1Co 1: 17 For Christ did not s me to baptize,

SENDING (SEND)
Mt 10: 16 "I am s you out like sheep among
Jn 20: 21 the Father has sent me, I am s you."
Ro   8: 3 God did by s his own Son

SENDS (SEND)
Ps 57: 3 God s forth his love and his

SENNACHERIB
   Assyrian king whose siege of Jerusalem was over-
thrown by the LORD following prayer of Hezekiah and
Isaiah (2Ki 18:13–19:37; 2Ch 32:1–21; Isa 36–37).

SENSE (SENSES)
Pr   6: 32 who commits adultery has no s;
    10: 21 but fools die for lack of s.
    11: 12 Those who have no s deride
    12: 11 chase fantasies have no s.
    15: 21 joy to those who have no s,
    17: 18 One who has no s shakes hands
    24: 30 of someone who has no s;

SENSES* (SENSE)
Lk 15: 17 "When he came to his s, he said,
1Co 15: 34 Come back to your s as you ought,
2Ti 2: 26 that they will come to their s

SENSITIVITY*
Eph 4: 19 Having lost all s, they have given

SENSUAL* (SENSUALITY)
Col 2: 23 value in restraining s indulgence.
1Ti 5: 11 when their s desires overcome their

SENSUALITY* (SENSUAL)
Eph 4: 19 given themselves over to s so as

SENT (SEND)
Ex   3: 14 "I lam has s me to you.' "
Isa 55: 11 achieve the purpose for which I s it.
    61: 1 He has s me to bind
Jer 28: 9 will be recognized as one truly s
Mt 10: 40 me welcomes the one who s me.
Lk   4: 18 He has s me to proclaim freedom
     9: 2 and he s them out to proclaim
    10: 16 rejects me rejects him who s me."
Jn   1: 6 There was a man s from God whose
     4: 34 "is to do the will of him who s me
     5: 24 believes him who s me has eternal
     8: 16 I stand with the Father, who s me.
     9: 4 must do the works of him who s me,
    16: 5 now I am going to him who s me,
    17: 3 and Jesus Christ, whom you have s.
    17: 18 As you s me into the world, I have s
    20: 21 As the Father has s me, I am
Ro 10: 15 anyone preach unless they are s?
Gal 4: 4 time had fully come, God s his Son,
1Jn 4: 10 s his Son as an atoning sacrifice

SENTENCE
2Co 1: 9 we felt we had received the s

SEPARATE (SEPARATED SEPARATES)
Pr 16: 28 and gossips s close friends.
Mt 19: 6 joined together, let no one s."
Ro   8: 35 Who shall s us from the love
1Co 7: 10 A wife must not s from her
2Co 6: 17 "Come out from them and be s,
Eph 2: 12 at that time you were s from Christ,

SEPARATED (SEPARATE)
Isa 59: 2 your iniquities have s you from your
Eph 4: 18 s from the life of God because

SEPARATES* (SEPARATE)
Ru   1: 17 if even death s you and me."
Pr 17: 9 repeats the matter s close friends.
Mt 25: 32 another as a shepherd s the sheep

SERAPHS*
Isa 6: 2 Above him were s, each with six
     6: 6 one of the s flew to me with a live

SERIOUSNESS*
Tit 2: 7 In your teaching show integrity,

SERPENT (SERPENT'S)
Ge   3: 1 Now the s was more crafty than any
Isa 27: 1 Leviathan the gliding s,
Rev 12: 9 that ancient s called the devil,
    20: 2 that ancient s, who is the devil,

SERPENT'S (SERPENT)
2Co 11: 3 Eve was deceived by the s cunning,

SERVANT (SERVANTS)
Ex 14: 31 trust in him and in Moses his s.
    21: 2 "If you buy a Hebrew s, he is
1Sa 3: 10 "Speak, for your s is listening."
2Sa 7: 19 the future of the house of your s—
1Ki 20: 40 While your s was busy here
Job 1: 8 "Have you considered my s Job?
Ps 19: 11 By them your s is warned;
    19: 13 Keep your s also from willful sins;
    31: 16 Let your face shine on your s;
    89: 3 I have sworn to David my s,
Pr 14: 35 A king delights in a wise s,
    17: 2 A prudent s will rule over

Isa 41: 8 Israel, my **s**, Jacob, whom I have
   49: 3 said to me, "You are my **s**, Israel,
   53: 11 my righteous **s** will justify many,
Zec 3: 8 I am going to bring my **s**,
Mt 8: 13 his **s** was healed at that very hour.
   20: 26 great among you must be your **s**,
   24: 45 then is the faithful and wise **s**,
   25: 21 'Well done, good and faithful **s**!
Lk 1: 38 "I am the Lord's **s**,"
Jn 12: 26 and where I am, my **s** also will be.
Ro 1: 1 Paul, a **s** of Christ Jesus, called to be
   13: 4 authority is God's **s** for your good.
Php 2: 7 by taking the very nature of a **s**,
Col 1: 23 of which I, Paul, have become a **s**.
2Ti 2: 24 And the Lord's **s** must not be

SERVANTS (SERVANT)
Lev 25: 55 for the Israelites belong to me as **s**.
1Sa 2: 9 guard the feet of his faithful **s**,
2Ki 17: 13 to you through my **s** the prophets."
Ezr 5: 11 "We are the **s** of the God of heaven
Ps 34: 22 The LORD redeems his **s**;
   103: 21 hosts, you his **s** who do his will.
   104: 4 his messengers, flames of fire his **s**.
Pr 31: 15 and portions for her women **s**.
Isa 44: 26 who carries out the words of his **s**
   65: 8 in it,' so will I do in behalf of my **s**;
   65: 13 my **s** will drink, but you will go
Lk 17: 10 should say, 'We are unworthy **s**;
Jn 15: 15 I no longer call you **s**, because **s** do
Ro 13: 6 for the authorities are God's **s**,
1Co 3: 5 Only **s**, through whom you came
Heb 1: 7 spirits, and his **s** flames of fire."

SERVE (SERVED SERVES SERVICE SERVING)
Dt 10: 12 to **s** the LORD your God with all
   11: 13 God and to **s** him with all your heart
   13: 4 **s** him and hold fast to him.
   28: 47 you did not **s** the LORD your God
Jos 22: 5 him and to **s** him with all your heart
   24: 15 this day whom you will **s**,
   24: 18 We too will **s** the LORD,
1Sa 7: 3 to the LORD and **s** him only,
   12: 20 **s** the LORD with all your heart.
   12: 24 **s** him faithfully with all your heart;
2Ch 19: 9 "You must **s** faithfully
Job 36: 11 If they obey and **s** him, they will
Ps 2: 11 **S** the LORD with fear
Da 3: 17 If the God we **s** is able to deliver us,
Mt 4: 10 Lord your God, and **s** him only.' "
   6: 24 "No one can **s** two masters.
   6: 24 You cannot **s** both God and money.
   20: 28 but to **s**, and to give his life as
Ro 12: 7 if it is serving, then **s**; if it is
Gal 5: 13 **s** one another humbly in love.
Eph 6: 7 **S** wholeheartedly, as if you were
1Ti 6: 2 they should **s** them even better
Heb 9: 14 so that we may **s** the living God!
1Pe 4: 10 gift you have received to **s** others,
   4: 11 If you **s**, you should do so
   5: 2 disgraceful gain, but eager to **s**;
Rev 5: 10 a kingdom and priests to **s** our God,

SERVED (SERVE)
Mt 20: 28 Son of Man did not come to be **s**,
Jn 12: 2 Martha **s**, while Lazarus was among
Ac 17: 25 And he is not **s** by human hands,
Ro 1: 25 and **s** created things rather than
1Ti 3: 13 Those who have **s** well gain

SERVES (SERVE)
Lk 22: 26 one who rules like the one who **s**.
   22: 27 But I am among you as one who **s**.
Jn 12: 26 Whoever **s** me must follow me;
Ro 14: 18 because anyone who **s** Christ in this

SERVICE (SERVE)
Lk 9: 62 and looks back is fit for **s**
   12: 35 "Be dressed ready for **s** and keep
Ro 15: 17 in Christ Jesus in my **s** to God.
1Co 12: 5 There are different kinds of **s**,
   16: 15 to the **s** of the Lord's people.
2Co 9: 12 This **s** that you perform is not only
Eph 4: 12 to equip his people for works of **s**,
Rev 2: 19 and faith, your **s** and perseverance,

SERVING (SERVE)
Jos 24: 15 if **s** the LORD seems undesirable
2Ch 12: 8 learn the difference between **s** me
Pr 15: 17 Better a small **s** of vegetables
Ro 12: 7 if it is **s**, then serve;
   12: 11 your spiritual fervor, **s** the Lord.
   16: 18 people are not **s** our Lord Christ,
Eph 6: 7 as if you were the Lord,
Col 3: 24 It is the Lord Christ you are **s**.

2Ti 2: 4 No one **s** as a soldier gets involved

SETH
Ge 4: 25 birth to a son and named him **S**,

SETTLE
Mt 5: 25 "**S** matters quickly with your
2Th 3: 12 in the Lord Jesus Christ to **s** down

SEVEN (SEVENS SEVENTH)
Ge 7: 2 Take with you **s** pairs of every kind
Jos 6: 4 march around the city **s** times,
1Ki 19: 18 Yet I reserve **s** thousand in Israel—
Pr 6: 16 hates, **s** that are detestable to him:
   24: 16 for though the righteous fall **s** times,
Isa 4: 1 that day **s** women will take hold
Da 9: 25 comes, there will be **s** 'sevens,'
Mt 18: 21 sins against me? Up to **s** times?"
Lk 11: 26 takes **s** other spirits more wicked
Ro 11: 4 for myself **s** thousand who have not
Rev 1: 4 To the **s** churches in the province
   6: 1 Lamb opened the first of the **s** seals.
   8: 2 and **s** trumpets were given to them.
   10: 4 And when the **s** thunders spoke,
   15: 7 to the **s** angels golden bowls filled

SEVENS* (SEVEN)
Da 9: 24 "Seventy '**s**' are decreed for your
   9: 25 will be seven '**s**,' and sixty-two '**s**.'
   9: 26 After the sixty-two '**s**,' the Anointed

SEVENTH (SEVEN)
Ge 2: 2 the **s** day God had finished the work
Ex 20: 10 the **s** day is a sabbath to the LORD
   23: 11 but during the **s** year let the land lie
   23: 12 but on the **s** day do not work,
Heb 4: 4 "On the **s** day God rested from all

SEVERE
Ge 3: 16 your pains in childbearing very **s**;
2Co 8: 2 In the midst of a very **s** trial,
1Th 1: 6 the midst of **s** suffering with the joy

SEWED (SEWS)
Ge 3: 7 so they **s** fig leaves together

SEWS (SEWED)
Mt 9: 16 "No one **s** a patch of unshrunk

SEXUAL (SEXUALLY)
Ex 22: 19 "Anyone who has **s** relations
Lev 18: 6 close relative to have **s** relations.
   18: 7 your father by having **s** relations
   18: 20 "Do not have **s** relations
Mt 15: 19 adultery, **s** immorality, theft,
Ac 15: 20 from **s** immorality, from the meat
1Co 5: 1 there is **s** immorality among you,
   6: 13 is not meant for **s** immorality
   6: 18 Flee from **s** immorality.
   10: 8 should not commit **s** immorality,
2Co 12: 21 sin and debauchery in which they
Gal 5: 19 **s** immorality,
Eph 5: 3 not be even a hint of **s** immorality,
Col 3: 5 **s** immorality, impurity, lust,
1Th 4: 3 that you should avoid **s** immorality;

SEXUALLY (SEXUAL)
1Co 5: 9 to associate with **s** immoral people—
   6: 9 Neither the **s** immoral nor idolaters
   6: 18 but those who sin **s** sin against their
Heb 12: 16 See that no one is **s** immoral, or is
   13: 4 the adulterer and all the **s** immoral.
Rev 21: 8 the murderers, the **s** immoral,

SHADE
Ps 121: 5 the LORD is your **s** at your right
Isa 25: 4 the storm and a **s** from the heat.

SHADOW
Ps 17: 8 hide me in the **s** of your wings
   36: 7 take refuge in the **s** of your wings.
   91: 1 will rest in the **s** of the Almighty.
Isa 51: 16 covered you with the **s** of my hand—
Col 2: 17 These are a **s** of the things that were
Heb 8: 5 is a copy and a **s** of what is in heaven.
   10: 1 The law is only a **s** of the good

SHADRACH
Hebrew exiled to Babylon; name changed from Hananiah (Da 1:6–7). Refused defilement by food (Da 1:8–20). Refused to worship idol (Da 3:1–18); saved from furnace (Da 3:19–30).

SHAKE (SHAKEN SHAKING)
Ps 10: 6 "Nothing will ever **s** us."
   64: 8 who see them will **s** their heads
   99: 1 the cherubim, let the earth **s**.
Hag 2: 6 I will once more **s** the heavens
Heb 12: 26 "Once more I will **s** not only

SHAKEN (SHAKE)
Ps 16: 8 at my right hand, I will not be **s**.
   30: 6 secure, I said, "I will never be **s**."
   55: 22 will never let the righteous be **s**.
   62: 2 he is my fortress, I will never be **s**.
   112: 6 Surely the righteous will never be **s**;
Isa 54: 10 Though the mountains be **s**
Mt 24: 29 and the heavenly bodies will be **s**.'
Lk 6: 38 down, **s** together and running over,
Ac 2: 25 is at my right hand, I will not be **s**.
Heb 12: 27 that what cannot be **s** may remain.

SHAKING* (SHAKE)
Ps 22: 7 they hurl insults, **s** their heads.
Mt 27: 39 hurled insults at him, **s** their heads
Mk 15: 29 at him, **s** their heads and saying,

SHALLUM
King of Israel (2Ki 15:10–16).

SHAME (ASHAMED SHAMED SHAMEFUL)
Ps 25: 3 hopes in you will ever be put to **s**,
   34: 5 their faces are never covered with **s**.
   69: 6 seek you not be put to **s** because
Pr 13: 18 discipline comes to poverty and **s**,
   18: 13 that is folly and **s**.
Jer 8: 9 The wise will be put to **s**;
   8: 12 they have no **s** at all;
Ro 5: 5 And hope does not put us to **s**,
   9: 33 in him will never be put to **s**."
   10: 11 in him will never be put to **s**."
1Co 1: 27 things of the world to **s** the wise;
Heb 12: 2 scorning its **s**, and sat down

SHAMED (SHAME)
Jer 10: 14 all goldsmiths are **s** by their idols.
Joel 2: 26 never again will my people be **s**.

SHAMEFUL (SHAME)
Ro 1: 27 Men committed **s** acts with other men,
2Co 4: 2 have renounced secret and **s** ways;
Rev 21: 27 nor will anyone who does what is **s**

SHAMGAR
Judge; killed 600 Philistines (Jdg 3:31).

SHAPE (SHAPES SHAPING)
Job 38: 14 The earth takes **s** like clay under

SHAPES (SHAPE)
Isa 44: 10 Who **s** a god and casts an idol,

SHAPING (SHAPE)
Jer 18: 4 the pot he was **s** from the clay was

SHARE (SHARED SHARERS SHARING)
Ge 21: 10 slave woman's son will never **s**
Lev 19: 17 neighbor frankly so you will not **s**
Dt 10: 9 That is why the Levites have no **s**
1Sa 30: 24 to the battle. All will **s** alike."
Pr 22: 9 they **s** their food with the poor.
Eze 18: 20 The child will not **s** the guilt
Mt 25: 21 and **s** your master's happiness!'
Lk 3: 11 who has two shirts should **s**
Ro 8: 17 if indeed we **s** in his sufferings
   12: 13 **S** with the Lord's people who are
2Co 1: 7 that just as you **s** in our sufferings,
Gal 4: 30 the slave woman's son will never **s**
   6: 6 in the word should **s** all good things
Eph 4: 28 they may have something to **s**
Col 1: 12 who has qualified you to **s**
2Th 2: 14 that you might **s** in the glory of our
1Ti 5: 22 and do not **s** in the sins of others.
   6: 18 and to be generous and willing to **s**.
2Ti 2: 6 the first to receive a **s** of the crops.
Heb 12: 10 good, that we may **s** in his holiness.
   13: 16 to do good and to **s** with others,
Rev 22: 19 away from you your **s** in the tree

SHARED (SHARE)
Ps 41: 9 I trusted, one who **s** my bread,
Jn 13: 18 'He who **s** my bread has lifted up
Ac 4: 32 but they **s** everything they had.
Heb 2: 14 he too **s** in their humanity so

SHARERS* (SHARE)
Eph 3: 6 **s** together in the promise in Christ

SHARING (SHARE)
1Co 9: 10 do so in the hope of **s** in the harvest.
2Co 9: 13 for your generosity in **s** with them
Php 2: 1 if any common **s** in the Spirit,

SHARON
SS 2: 1 I am a rose of **S**, a lily

SHARP (SHARPENED SHARPENS SHARPER)
Pr 5: 4 as gall, **s** as a double-edged sword.
Isa 5: 28 Their arrows are **s**, all their bows
Rev 1: 16 coming out of his mouth was a **s**,

Rev 19: 15 out of his mouth is a s sword

SHARPENED (SHARP)
Eze 21: 9 sword, a sword, s and polished—

SHARPENS* (SHARP)
Pr 27: 17 As iron s iron, so one person s another.

SHARPER* (SHARP)
Heb 4: 12 S than any double-edged sword,

SHATTER (SHATTERED SHATTERS)
Jer 51: 20 with you I s nations, with you I

SHATTERED (SHATTER)
Job 16: 12 All was well with me, but he s me;
17: 11 days have passed, my plans are s.
Ecc 12: 6 before the pitcher is s at the spring,

SHATTERS (SHATTER)
Ps 46: 9 He breaks the bow and s the spear;

SHAVED
Jdg 16: 17 If my head were s, my strength
1Co 11: 5 it is the same as having her head s.

SHEAF (SHEAVES)
Lev 23: 11 wave the s before the LORD so it

SHEARER* (SHEARERS)
Ac 8: 32 and as a lamb before its s is silent,

SHEARERS (SHEARER)
Isa 53: 7 and as a sheep before its s is silent,

SHEAVES (SHEAF)
Ge 37: 7 while your s gathered around mine
Ps 126: 6 songs of joy, carrying s with them.

SHEBA
1. Benjamite who rebelled against David (2Sa 20).
2. See QUEEN.

SHECHEM
1. Raped Jacob's daughter Dinah; killed by Simeon and Levi (Ge 34).
2. City where Joshua renewed the covenant (Jos 24).

SHED (SHEDDING SHEDS)
Ge 9: 6 human beings shall their blood be s;
Pr 6: 17 tongue, hands that s innocent blood,
Ro 3: 15 "Their feet are swift to s blood;
Col 1: 20 through his blood, s on the cross.

SHEDDING (SHED)
Heb 9: 22 without the s of blood there is no

SHEDS (SHED)
Ge 9: 6 "Whoever s human blood,
Pr 20: 27 that s light on one's inmost being.

SHEEP (SHEEP'S SHEEPSKINS)
Nu 27: 17 not be like a without a shepherd."
Dt 17: 1 God an ox or a s that has any defect
1Sa 15: 14 then is this bleating of a in my ears?
Ps 44: 22 we are considered as s to be
78: 52 he led them like s through
100: 3 are his people, the s of his pasture.
119:176 I have strayed like a lost s.
SS 4: 2 teeth are like a flock of s just shorn,
Isa 53: 6 We all, like, have gone astray,
53: 7 as a s before its shearers is silent,
Jer 50: 6 "My people have been lost s;
Eze 34: 11 I myself will search for my s
Zec 13: 7 and the s will be scattered, and I
Mt 9: 36 helpless, like s without a shepherd.
10: 16 you out like s among wolves.
12: 11 "If any of you has a s and it falls
18: 13 that one s than about the ninety-nine
25: 32 as a shepherd separates the s
Jn 10: 1 anyone who does not enter the s pen
10: 3 He calls his own s by name
10: 7 I tell you, I am the gate for the s.
10: 15 and I lay down my life for the s.
10: 27 My s listen to my voice;
21: 17 Jesus said, "Feed my s.
1Pe 2: 25 For "you were like s going astray,"

SHEEP'S* (SHEEP)
Mt 7: 15 They come to you in s clothing,

SHEEPSKINS* (SHEEP)
Heb 11: 37 They went about in s and goatskins,

SHEKEL
Ex 30: 13 This half s is an offering

SHELTER
Ps 27: 5 hide me in the s of his tabernacle
31: 20 In the s of your presence you hide
55: 8 I would hurry to my place of s,
61: 4 take refuge in the s of your wings.

Ps 91: 1 in the s of the Most High will rest
Ecc 7: 12 Wisdom is a s as money is a s,
Isa 4: 6 It will be a s and shade
25: 4 a s from the storm and a shade
32: 2 Each one will be like as a s
58: 7 provide the poor wanderer with s—

SHEM
Son of Noah (Ge 5:32; 6:10). Blessed (Ge 9:26). Descendants (Ge 10:21–31; 11:10–32).

SHEPHERD (SHEPHERDS)
Ge 48: 15 God who has been my s all my life
49: 24 because of the S, the Rock of Israel,
Nu 27: 17 will not be like sheep without a s."
2Sa 7: 7 I commanded to s my people Israel,
1Ki 22: 17 on the hills like sheep without a s,
Ps 23: 1 The LORD is my s, I lack nothing.
28: 9 be their s and carry them forever.
80: 1 Hear us, S of Israel, you who lead
Isa 40: 11 He tends his flock like a s:
Jer 31: 10 will watch over his flock like a s.'
Eze 34: 5 scattered because there was no s,
Zec 11: 4 "S the flock marked for slaughter.
11: 9 and said, "I will not be your s.
11: 17 "Woe to the worthless s,
13: 7 "Strike the s, and the sheep will be
Mt 2: 6 come a ruler who will s my people
9: 36 and helpless, like sheep without a s.
26: 31 " 'I will strike the s, and the sheep
Jn 10: 11 "I am the good s. The good s lays
10: 14 "I am the good s; I know my sheep
10: 16 there shall be one flock and one s.
Heb 13: 20 Jesus, that great S of the sheep,
1Pe 5: 4 And when the Chief S appears,
Rev 7: 17 before the throne will be their s;

SHEPHERDS (SHEPHERD)
Jer 23: 1 "Woe to the s who are destroying
50: 6 their s have led them astray
Eze 34: 2 prophesy against the s of Israel;
34: 12 As s look after their scattered flocks
Lk 2: 8 there were s living out in the fields
Ac 20: 28 Be s of the church of God, which he
1Pe 5: 2 Be s of God's flock that is under
Jude : 12 s who feed only themselves.

SHIBBOLETH*
Jdg 12: 6 they said, "All right, say 'S.' "

SHIELD (SHIELDED SHIELDS)
Ge 15: 1 I am your s, your very great
2Sa 22: 3 my s and the horn of my salvation.
22: 36 You make your saving help my s;
Ps 3: 3 you, LORD, are a s around me,
5: 12 them with your favor as with a s.
7: 10 My s is God Most High, who saves
18: 2 my s and the horn of my salvation,
28: 7 LORD is my strength and my s;
33: 20 he is our help and our s.
84: 11 For the LORD God is a sun and s;
91: 4 his faithfulness will be your s
115: 9 he is their help and s.
119:114 You are my refuge and my s;
144: 2 my s, in whom I take refuge,
Pr 2: 7 he is a s to those whose walk is
30: 5 he is a s to those who take refuge
Eph 6: 16 take up the s of faith,

SHIELDED (SHIELD)
1Pe 1: 5 who through faith are s by God's

SHIELDS (SHIELD)
Dt 33: 12 for he s him all day long,

SHIFTLESS*
Pr 19: 15 on deep sleep, and the s go hungry.

SHIMEI
Cursed David (2Sa 16:5–14); spared (2Sa 19:16–23). Killed by Solomon (1Ki 2:8–9, 36–46).

SHINE (SHINES SHINING SHONE)
Nu 6: 25 the LORD make his face s on you
Job 33: 30 that the light of life may s on them.
Ps 4: 6 Let the light of your face s on us.
37: 6 your righteous reward s like
67: 1 bless us and make his face s on us—
80: 1 between the cherubim, s forth
118: 27 and he has made his light s on us.
Isa 60: 1 "Arise, s, for your light has come,
Da 12: 3 are wise will s like the brightness
Mt 5: 16 let your light s before others,
13: 43 the righteous will s like the sun
2Co 4: 6 made his light s in our hearts to give
Eph 5: 14 the dead, and Christ will s on you."
Php 2: 15 you will s among them like stars

SHINES (SHINE)
Ps 50: 2 Zion, perfect in beauty, God s forth.
Pr 13: 9 The light of the righteous s brightly,
Jn 1: 5 The light s in the darkness,

SHINING (SHINE)
Pr 4: 18 s ever brighter till the full light
2Pe 1: 19 as to a light s in a dark place,
Rev 1: 16 His face was like the sun s in all its

SHIP (SHIPS SHIPWRECK SHIPWRECKS)
Ecc 11: 1 S your grain across the sea;

SHIPS (SHIP)
Pr 31: 14 She is like the merchant s,

SHIPWRECK (SHIP)
1Ti 1: 19 suffered s with regard to the faith.

SHIPWRECKED* (SHIP)
2Co 11: 25 three times I was s, I spent a night

SHIRT (SHIRTS)
Lk 6: 29 do not withhold your s.

SHIRTS* (SHIRT)
Lk 3: 11 who has two s should share

SHISHAK
1Ki 14: 25 S king of Egypt attacked Jerusalem.
2Ch 12: 2 S king of Egypt attacked Jerusalem

SHOCKING*
Jer 5: 30 s thing has happened in the land:

SHONE (SHINE)
Mt 17: 2 His face s like the sun, and his
Lk 2: 9 the glory of the Lord s around them,
Rev 21: 11 It s with the glory of God, and its

SHOOT
Isa 53: 2 grew up before him like a tender s,
Ro 11: 17 though a wild olive s, have been

SHORE
Lk 5: 3 asked him to put out a little from s.

SHORT (SHORTENED)
Nu 11: 23 Moses, "Is the LORD's arm too s?
Isa 50: 2 Was my arm too s to deliver you?
59: 1 of the LORD is not too s to save,
Mt 24: 22 "If those days had not been cut s,
Ro 3: 23 and fall s of the glory of God,
1Co 7: 29 and sisters, is that the time is s.
Heb 4: 1 you be found to have fallen s of it.
Rev 20: 3 that, he must be set free for a s time.

SHORTENED (SHORT)
Mt 24: 22 of the elect those days will be s.

SHOULDER (SHOULDERS)
Zep 3: 9 and serve him s to s.

SHOULDERS (SHOULDER)
Dt 33: 12 LORD loves rest between his s."
Isa 9: 6 and the government will be on his s.
Lk 15: 5 finds it, he joyfully puts it on his s

SHOUT (SHOUTED)
Ps 47: 1 s to God with cries of joy.
66: 1 S for joy to God, all the earth!
95: 1 let us s aloud to the Rock of our
98: 4 S for joy to the LORD,
100: 1 S for joy to the LORD,
Isa 12: 6 S aloud and sing for joy,
26: 19 in the dust wake up and s for joy—
35: 6 deer, and the mute tongue s for joy.
40: 9 lift up your voice with a s, lift it up,
42: 2 He will not s or cry out, or raise his
44: 23 s aloud, you earth beneath.
54: 1 burst into song, s for joy, you who
Zec 9: 9 S, Daughter Jerusalem!

SHOUTED (SHOUT)
Job 38: 7 together and all the angels s for joy?

SHOW (SHOWED SHOWN SHOWS)
Ex 18: 20 and s them the way they are to live
33: 18 said, "Now s me your glory."
2Sa 22: 26 the faithful you s yourself faithful,
Ps 17: 7 S me the wonders of your great
25: 4 S me your ways, LORD, teach me
39: 4 "S me, LORD, my life's end
85: 7 S us your unfailing love, LORD,
143: 8 S me the way I should go, for to you
SS 2: 14 the mountainside, s me your face,
Isa 30: 18 he will rise up to s you compassion.
Joel 2: 30 I will s wonders in the heavens
Zec 7: 9 s mercy and compassion to one
Ac 2: 19 I will s wonders in the heavens
10: 34 it is that God does not s favoritism.
1Co 12: 31 yet I will s you the most excellent

Eph 2: 7 ages he might **s** the incomparable
Tit 2: 7 In your teaching **s** integrity,
Jas 2:18 **S** me your faith without deeds, and I
will **s** you my faith by what I do.
Jude : 23 to others mercy, mixed with fear—

SHOWED (SHOW)
1Ki 3: 3 Solomon **s** his love for the LORD
Lk 24:40 this, he **s** them his hands and feet.
Ac 28: 7 **s** us generous hospitality for three
1Jn 4: 9 This is how God **s** his love among

SHOWERS
Eze 34:26 there will be **s** of blessing.
Hos 10:12 and **s** his righteousness on you.

SHOWN (SHOW)
Heb 13: 2 have **s** hospitality to angels

SHOWS (SHOW)
Pr 3:34 but **s** favor to the humble
1Pe 5: 5 but **s** favor to the humble

SHREWD
2Sa 22:27 to the devious you show yourself **s**.
Mt 10:16 Therefore be as **s** as snakes and as

SHRINK (SHRINKS)
Heb 10:39 we are not of those who **s** back

SHRINKS* (SHRINK)
Heb 10:38 no pleasure in the one who **s** back."

SHRIVEL
Isa 64: 6 we all **s** up like a leaf, and like

SHUDDER
Eze 32:10 and their kings will **s** with horror

SHUHITE
Job 2:11 Bildad the **S** and Zophar

SHUN* (SHUNS)
Job 28:28 and to **s** evil is understanding."
Pr 3: 7 fear the LORD and **s** evil.
Pr 14:16 wise fear the LORD and **s** evil,

SHUNS (SHUN)
Job 1: 8 a man who fears God and **s** evil."

SHUT
Ge 7:16 Then the LORD **s** him in.
Isa 22:22 what he opens no one can **s**,
60:11 You will never be **s**, day or night,
Da 6:22 and he **s** the mouths of the lions,
Heb 11:33 who **s** the mouths of lions,
Rev 3: 7 What he opens no one can **s**,
21:25 On no day will its gates ever be **s**,

SICK (SICKNESS)
Pr 13:12 Hope deferred makes the heart **s**,
Eze 34: 4 healed the **s** or bound up the injured.
Mt 9:12 who need a doctor, but the **s**.
10: 8 Heal the **s**, raise the dead,
25:36 I was **s** and you looked after me,
1Co 11:30 many among you are weak and **s**,
Jas 5:14 Is anyone among you **s**?

SICKBED* (BED)
Ps 41: 3 LORD sustains them on their **s**

SICKLE
Joel 3:13 Swing the **s**, for the harvest is ripe.
Rev 14:14 his head and a sharp **s** in his hand.

SICKNESS (SICK)
Mt 4:23 disease and **s** among the people.

SIDE (SIDES)
Ps 91: 7 A thousand may fall at your **s**,
124: 1 the LORD had not been on our **s**—
Pr 3:26 for the LORD will be at your **s**
Jn 18:37 Everyone on the **s** of truth listens
20:20 he showed them his hands and **s**.
2Ti 4:17 the Lord stood at my **s** and gave me
Heb 10:33 at other times you stood by **s**

SIDES (SIDE)
Nu 33:55 in your eyes and thorns in your **s**.

SIFT
Lk 22:31 Satan has asked to **s** all of you as

SIGHING
Isa 35:10 and sorrow and **s** will flee away.

SIGHT
Ps 51: 4 and done what is evil in your **s**;
90: 4 years in your **s** are like a day
116:15 in the **s** of the LORD is the death
Pr 3: 4 a good name in the **s** of God
Mt 11: 5 The blind receive **s**, the lame walk,
1Co 3:19 this world is foolishness in God's **s**.

2Co 5: 7 We live by faith, not by **s**.
1Pe 3: 4 which is of great worth in God's **s**.

SIGN (SIGNS)
Ge 9:12 "This is the **s** of the covenant I am
17:11 and it will be the **s** of the covenant
Isa 7:14 the Lord himself will give you a **s**:
55:13 for an everlasting **s**, that will endure
Eze 20:12 my Sabbaths as a **s** between us,
Mt 12:38 we want to see a **s** from you."
12:39 generation asks for a **s**!
24: 3 what will be the **s** of your coming
24:30 that time the **s** of the Son of Man
Lk 2:12 This will be a **s** to you:
11:29 It asks for a **s**, but none will be
23: 8 see him perform a **s** of some sort.
Ac 4:16 they have performed a notable **s**,
Ro 4:11 he received circumcision as a **s**,
1Co 14:22 are a **s**, not for believers

SIGNS (SIGN)
Ge 1:14 let them serve as **s** to mark seasons
Ps 78:43 the day he displayed his **s** in Egypt,
105:27 They performed his **s** among them,
Da 6:27 he performs **s** and wonders
Mt 24:24 and perform great **s** and wonders
Mk 16:17 these **s** will accompany those
Jn 2:11 was the first of the **s**
2:23 saw the **s** he was performing
3: 2 perform the **s** you are doing
7:31 perform more **s** than this man?"
9:16 can a sinner perform such **s**?"
12:37 Jesus had performed so many **s**
20:30 Jesus performed many other **s**
Ac 2:19 above and **s** on the earth below,
1Co 1:22 Jews demand **s** and Greeks look
12:12 including **s**, wonders and miracles.
2Th 2: 9 sorts of displays of power through **s**

SIHON
Nu 21:21 to say to **S** king of the Amorites:
Ps 136:19 **S** king of the Amorites

SILAS*
Prophet (Ac 15:22–32); co-worker with Paul on second missionary journey (Ac 16–18; 2Co 1:19). Co-writer with Paul (1Th 1:1; 2Th 1:1); Peter (1Pe 5:12).

SILENCE (SILENCED SILENT)
1Pe 2:15 good you should **s** the ignorant talk
Rev 8: 1 there was **s** in heaven for about half

SILENCED (SILENCE)
Ro 3:19 so that every mouth may be **s**
Tit 1:11 They must be **s**, because they are

SILENT (SILENCE)
Est 4:14 For if you remain **s** at this time,
Ps 30:12 may sing your praises and not be **s**.
32: 3 When I kept **s**, my bones wasted
39: 2 So I remained utterly **s**, not even
Pr 17:28 are thought wise if they keep **s**,
Ecc 3: 7 a time to be **s** and a time to speak,
Isa 53: 7 as a sheep before its shearers is **s**,
62: 1 For Zion's sake I will not keep **s**,
Hab 2:20 let all the earth be **s** before him.
Ac 8:32 and as a lamb before its shearer is **s**,
1Co 14:34 Women should remain **s**

SILVER
Ps 12: 6 like **s** purified in a crucible,
66:10 tested us; you refined us like **s**.
Pr 2: 4 if you look for it as for **s** and search
3:14 for she is more profitable than **s**
8:10 Choose my instruction instead of **s**,
22: 1 to be esteemed is better than **s**
25: 4 Remove the dross from the **s**,
25:11 of **s** is a ruling rightly given.
Isa 48:10 refined you, though not as **s**;
Eze 22:18 They are but the dross of **s**.
Da 2:32 its chest and arms of **s**, its belly
Hag 2: 8 'The **s** is mine and the gold is
Zec 13: 9 I will refine them like **s** and test
Mt 26:15 for him thirty pieces of **s**.
Ac 3: 6 said, "**S** or gold I do not have,
1Co 3:12 on this foundation using gold, **s**,
1Pe 1:18 not with perishable things such as **s**

SILVERSMITH
Ac 19:24 A **s** named Demetrius, who made

SIMEON
Son of Jacob by Leah (Ge 29:33; 35:23; 1Ch 2:1). With Levi killed Shechem for rape of Dinah (Ge 34:25–29). Held hostage by Joseph in Egypt (Ge 42:24–43:23). Tribe of blessed (Ge 49:5–7), numbered

(Nu 1:23; 26:14), allotted land (Jos 19:1–9; Eze 48:24), 12,000 from (Rev 7:7).

SIMON
1. See PETER.
2. Apostle, called the Zealot (Mt 10:4; Mk 3:18; Lk 6:15; Ac 1:13).
3. Samaritan sorcerer (Ac 8:9–24).

SIMPLE
Ps 19: 7 are trustworthy, making wise the **s**.
119:130 it gives understanding to the **s**.
Pr 8: 5 You who are **s**, gain prudence;
14:15 The **s** believe anything,

SIN (SINFUL SINNED SINNER SINNERS SINNING SINS)
Ge 4: 7 is right, **s** is crouching at your door;
Ex 32:32 But now, please forgive their **s**—
Nu 5: 7 and must confess the **s** they have
32:23 be sure that your **s** will find you out.
Dt 24:16 each of you will die for your own **s**.
1Sa 12:23 that I should **s** against the LORD
15:23 rebellion is like the **s** of divination,
1Ki 8:46 for there is no one who does not **s**—
2Ki 14:6 each of you will die for your own **s**."
2Ch 7:14 I will forgive their **s** and will heal
Job 1:22 Job did not **s** by charging God
Ps 4: 4 Tremble and do not **s**; when you are
32: 2 are those whose **s** the LORD does
32: 5 Then I acknowledged my **s** to you
36: 2 too much to detect or hate their **s**.
38:18 I am troubled by my **s**.
39: 1 ways and keep my tongue from **s**;
51: 2 iniquity and cleanse me from my **s**.
66:18 If I had cherished **s** in my heart,
119:11 that I might not **s** against you.
119:133 to your word; let no **s** rule over me.
Pr 10:19 **S** is not ended by multiplying
14: 9 Fools mock at making amends for **s**,
14:21 is a **s** to despise one's neighbor,
16: 6 and faithfulness is atoned for;
17: 9 Whoever loves a quarrel loves **s**;
20: 9 I am clean and without **s**"?
Isa 3: 9 they parade their **s** like Sodom;
6: 7 taken away and your **s** atoned for."
64: 5 we continued to **s** against them,
Jer 31:30 everyone will die for their own **s**;
Eze 18:26 their righteousness and commit **s**,
Am 4: 4 "Go to Bethel and **s**; go to Gilgal
Mic 6: 7 of my body for the **s** of my soul?
7:18 who pardons **s** and forgives
Zec 3: 4 I have taken away your **s**, and I will
Mk 3:29 but is guilty of an eternal **s**."
Jn 1:29 who takes away the **s** of the world!
8: 7 is without **s** be the first to throw
8:34 everyone who sins is a slave to **s**.
8:46 any of you prove me guilty of **s**?
Ro 2:12 All who **s** apart from the law will
5:12 just as **s** entered the world through
5:20 But where **s** increased,
6: 2 We are those who have died to **s**;
6:11 count yourselves dead to **s** but alive
6:14 **s** shall no longer be your master,
6:23 For the wages of **s** is death,
7: 7 not have known what **s** was had it
7:25 sinful nature a slave to the law of **s**.
14:23 that does not come from faith is **s**.
1Co 15:34 When you against them in this
14:24 convicted of **s** and are brought
15:56 The sting of death is **s**,
2Co 5:21 God made him who had no **s** to be **s**
Gal 6: 1 if someone is caught in a **s**, you who
Heb 4:15 just as we are—yet he did not **s**.
9:26 to do away with **s** by the sacrifice
11:25 to enjoy the fleeting pleasures of **s**.
12: 1 the **s** that so easily entangles.
Jas 1:15 conceived, it gives birth to **s**;
4:17 to do and don't do it, you **s**.
1Pe 2:22 committed no **s**, and no deceit
1Jn 1: 7 his Son, purifies us from all **s**.
1: 8 If we claim to be without **s**,
1: 1 But if anybody does **s**, we have
3: 4 in fact, **s** is lawlessness.
3: 5 away our sins. And in him is no **s**.
3: 6 continues to **s** has either seen him
3: 9 born of God will not continue to **s**,
5:16 There is a **s** that leads to death.
5:17 All wrongdoing is **s**, and there is **s**
5:18 born of God does not continue to **s**;

SINAI
Ex 19:20 descended to the top of Mount **S**
31:18 speaking to Moses on Mount **S**,

Ps 68: 17 the Lord has come from **S** into his

SINCERE* (SINCERITY)
Da 11: 34 many who are not **s** will join them.
Lk 20: 20 sent spies, who pretended to be **s**.
Ac 2: 46 ate together with glad and **s** hearts,
Ro 12: 9 Love must be **s**. Hate what is evil;
2Co 6: 6 in the Holy Spirit and in **s** love;
11: 3 somehow be led astray from your **s**
1Ti 1: 5 and a good conscience and a **s** faith.
3: 8 are to be worthy of respect, **s**,
2Ti 1: 5 I am reminded of your **s** faith,
Heb 10: 22 God with a heart in full assurance
Jas 3: 17 and good fruit, impartial and **s**.
1Pe 1: 22 that you have **s** love for each other,

SINCERITY* (SINCERE)
1Co 5: 8 with the unleavened bread of **s**
2Co 1: 12 with you, with integrity and godly **s**.
1: 12 Christ we speak before God with **s**,
8: 8 I want to test the **s** of your love
Eph 6: 5 fear, and with a heart, just as you
Col 3: 22 but with **s** of heart and reverence

SINFUL (SIN)
Ps 51: 5 Surely I was a **s** at birth,
Pr 1: 10 My son, if **s** men entice you,
Lk 5: 8 from me, Lord; I am a **s** man!"
Ro 7: 5 we were controlled by our **s** nature,
7: 18 dwell in me, that is, in my **s** nature.
7: 25 in my **s** nature a slave to the law
8: 3 Son in the likeness of **s** humanity
8: 4 do not live according to the **s** nature
8: 7 The **s** mind is hostile to God;
8: 8 by the **s** nature cannot please God.
8: 9 are not controlled by the **s** nature
8: 13 if you live according to the **s** nature,
13: 14 to gratify the desires of the **s** nature.
1Co 5: 5 for the destruction of the **s** nature so
Gal 5: 13 freedom to indulge the **s** nature;
5: 16 gratify the desires of the **s** nature.
5: 19 The acts of the **s** nature are obvious:
5: 24 Jesus have crucified the **s** nature
6: 8 who sow to please their **s** nature,
Col 2: 11 Your **s** nature was put off when your
Heb 3: 12 and sisters, that none of you has a **s**,
1Pe 2: 11 to abstain from **s** desires, which war
1Jn 3: 8 The one who does what is **s** is

SING (SANG SINGING SINGS SONG SONGS SUNG)
Ex 15: 1 "I will **s** to the Lord, for he is
Jdg 5: 3 even I, will **s** to the Lord;
Ps 5: 11 you be glad; let them ever **s** for joy.
13: 6 I will **s** the Lord's praise, for he
30: 4 **S** the praises of the Lord, you his
33: 1 **S** joyfully to the Lord,
47: 6 **S** praises to God, **s** praises; **s** praises
57: 7 I will **s** and make music.
59: 16 But I will **s** of your strength,
63: 7 I **s** in the shadow of your wings.
66: 2 **S** the glory of his name;
89: 1 I will **s** of the Lord's great love
95: 1 let us **s** for joy to the Lord;
96: 1 **S** to the Lord a new song;
98: 1 **S** to the Lord a new song, for he
101: 1 I will **s** of your love and justice;
108: 1 I will **s** and make music with all my
137: 3 "**S** us one of the songs of Zion!"
147: 1 How good it is to **s** praises to our
149: 1 **S** to the Lord a new song,
Isa 54: 1 "**S**, barren woman, you who never
1Co 14: 15 I will **s** with my spirit, but I will
Eph 5: 19 **S** and make music from your heart
Jas 5: 13 Let them **s** songs of praise.

SINGING (SING)
Ps 63: 5 **s** lips my mouth will praise you.
68: 6 he leads out the prisoners with **s**;
98: 5 with the harp and the sound of **s**,
Isa 35: 10 They will enter Zion with **s**;
Zep 3: 17 but will rejoice over you with **s**."
Ac 16: 25 were praying and **s** hymns to God,
Col 3: 16 **s** to God with gratitude in your

SINGLE
Ex 23: 29 I will not drive them out in a **s** year,
Mt 6: 27 worrying add a **s** hour to your life?

SINGS (SING)
Eze 33: 32 more than one who **s** love songs

SINNED (SIN)
Lev 5: 5 confess in what way they have **s**
1Sa 15: 24 Saul said to Samuel, "I have **s**.
2Sa 12: 13 "I have **s** against the Lord."

2Sa 24: 10 "I have **s** greatly in what I have
2Ch 6: 37 'We have **s**, we have done wrong
Job 1: 5 "Perhaps my children have **s**
33: 27 'We have **s**, we have perverted what
Ps 51: 4 have I **s** and done what is evil
Jer 2: 35 you because you say, 'I have not **s**.'
14: 20 we have indeed **s** against you.
Da 9: 5 we have **s** and done wrong.
Mic 7: 9 Because I have **s** against him, I will
Mt 27: 4 "I have **s**," he said, "for I have
Lk 15: 18 I have **s** against heaven and against
Ro 3: 23 for all have **s** and fall short
5: 12 came to all people, because all **s**—
2Pe 2: 4 did not spare angels when they **s**,
1Jn 1: 10 If we claim we have not **s**, we make

SINNER (SIN)
Ecc 9: 18 but one **s** destroys much good.
Lk 15: 7 heaven over one **s** who repents than
18: 13 said, 'God, have mercy on me, a **s**.'
Jas 5: 20 Whoever turns a **s** from the way
1Pe 4: 18 become of the ungodly and the **s**?"

SINNERS (SIN)
Ps 1: 1 stand in the way that **s** take or sit
37: 38 But all **s** will be destroyed;
Pr 23: 17 Do not let your heart envy **s**,
Mt 9: 13 come to call the righteous, but **s**."
Ro 5: 8 While we were still **s**, Christ died
Gal 2: 17 find ourselves also among the **s**,
1Ti 1: 15 came into the world to save **s**—
Heb 7: 26 set apart from **s**,

SINNING (SIN)
Ex 20: 20 be with you to keep you from **s**."
1Co 15: 34 senses as you ought, and stop **s**;
1Ti 5: 20 elders who are **s** you are to reprove
Heb 10: 26 If we deliberately keep on **s** after
1Jn 3: 6 No one who lives in him keeps on **s**.
3: 9 they cannot go on **s**, because they

SINS (SIN)
Lev 5: 1 anyone **s** because they do not speak
16: 30 you will be clean from all your **s**.
26: 40 if they will confess their **s** and the **s**
Nu 15: 30 " 'But anyone who **s** defiantly,
1Sa 2: 25 If anyone **s** against another human
Ezr 9: 6 because our **s** are higher than our
9: 13 punished us less than our **s** deserved
Ne 9: 2 confessed their **s** and the **s** of their ancestors.
Ps 19: 13 your servant also from willful **s**;
32: 1 are forgiven, whose **s** are covered.
51: 9 Hide your face from my **s** and blot
79: 9 forgive our **s** for your name's sake.
85: 2 your people and covered all their **s**.
103: 3 who forgives all your **s** and heals all
103: 10 he does not treat us as our **s** deserve
130: 3 kept a record of **s**, Lord,
Pr 5: 22 the cords of their **s** hold them fast.
28: 13 who conceal their **s** do not prosper,
28: 13 person commits many **s**.
Ecc 7: 20 who does what is right and never **s**.
Isa 1: 18 "Though your **s** are like scarlet,
38: 17 have put all my **s** behind your back.
43: 25 and remembers your **s** no more.
59: 2 your **s** have hidden his face
64: 6 like the wind our **s** sweep us away.
Jer 31: 34 will remember their **s** no more."
La 3: 39 complain when punished for their **s**?
Eze 3: 18 wicked people will die for their **s**,
18: 4 The one who **s** is the one who will
33: 8 wicked people will die for their **s**,
33: 10 offenses and **s** weigh us down,
36: 33 day I cleanse you from all your **s**,
Hos 14: 1 Your **s** have been your downfall!
Mt 1: 21 will save his people from their **s**."
6: 15 if you do not forgive others their **s**, your
Father will not forgive your **s**.
9: 6 has authority on earth to forgive **s**."
18: 15 "If a brother or sister **s**,
26: 28 for many for the forgiveness of **s**.
Lk 5: 24 has authority on earth to forgive **s**."
11: 4 Forgive us our **s**, for we also forgive
17: 3 "If a brother or sister **s** against you,
Jn 20: 23 you will indeed die in your **s**."
20: 23 If you forgive the **s** of anyone,
Ac 2: 38 Christ for the forgiveness of your **s**,
3: 19 so that your **s** may be wiped out,
10: 43 forgiveness of **s** through his name."
22: 16 be baptized and wash your **s** away,
26: 18 they may receive forgiveness of **s**
Ro 4: 7 are forgiven, whose **s** are covered.
4: 25 delivered over to death for our **s**

1Co 15: 3 Christ died for our **s** according
2Co 5: 19 counting people's **s** against them.
Gal 1: 4 gave himself for our **s** to rescue us
Eph 2: 1 dead in your transgressions and **s**,
Col 2: 13 When you were dead in your **s**
1Ti 5: 22 and do not share in the **s** of others.
Heb 1: 3 he had provided purification for **s**,
2: 17 atonement for the **s** of the people.
7: 27 He sacrificed for their **s** once for all
8: 12 will remember their **s** no more."
9: 28 once to take away the **s** of many;
10: 4 of bulls and goats to take away **s**.
10: 12 for all time one sacrifice for **s**,
10: 26 of the truth, no sacrifice for **s** is left,
Jas 5: 16 Therefore confess your **s** to each
5: 20 and cover over a multitude of **s**.
1Pe 2: 24 "He himself bore our **s**" in his
3: 18 For Christ also suffered once for **s**,
4: 8 love covers over a multitude of **s**.
1Jn 1: 9 If we confess our **s**, he is faithful
2: 2 He is the atoning sacrifice for our **s**,
3: 5 so that he might take away our **s**.
4: 10 Son as an atoning sacrifice for our **s**.
Rev 1: 5 freed us from our **s** by his blood,

SISERA
Jdg 4: 2 **S**, the commander of his army,
5: 26 She struck **S**, she crushed his head,

SISTER (SISTERS)
Lev 18: 9 have sexual relations with your **s**,
Mk 3: 35 does God's will is my brother and **s**
1Co 7: 15 The brother or **s** is not bound

SISTERS (SISTER)
Mt 19: 29 left houses or brothers or **s** or father
1Ti 5: 2 and younger women as **s**,

SIT (SAT SITS SITTING)
Dt 6: 7 about them when you **s** at home
1Ki 8: 25 have a successor to **s** before me
Ps 1: 1 or **s** in the company of mockers,
26: 5 and refuse to **s** with the wicked.
80: 1 You who is enthroned between
110: 1 "**S** at my right hand until I make
139: 2 You know when I **s** and when I rise;
SS 2: 3 I delight to **s** in his shade, and his
Isa 16: 5 in faithfulness a man will **s** on it—
Mic 4: 4 Everyone will **s** under their own
Mt 20: 23 but to **s** at my right or left is not
22: 44 "**S** at my right hand until I put your
Lk 22: 30 in my kingdom and **s** on thrones,
Heb 1: 3 "**S** at my right hand until I make
Rev 3: 21 I will give the right to **s** with me

SITS (SIT)
Ps 99: 1 he **s** enthroned between
Isa 40: 22 He **s** enthroned above the circle
Mt 19: 28 Son of Man **s** on his glorious throne,
Rev 4: 9 thanks to him who **s** on the throne

SITTING (SIT)
Est 2: 19 Mordecai was **s** at the king's gate.
Mt 26: 64 the Son of Man **s** at the right hand
Rev 4: 2 in heaven with someone **s** on it.

SITUATION (SITUATIONS)
1Co 7: 24 should remain in the **s** in which God
Php 4: 12 of being content in any and every **s**,

SITUATIONS* (SITUATION)
2Ti 4: 5 keep your head in all **s**,

SKIES (SKY)
Ps 19: 1 the **s** proclaim the work of his
71: 19 reaches to the **s**, you who have done
108: 4 your faithfulness reaches to the **s**.

SKILL (SKILLED SKILLFUL)
Ps 137: 5 may my right hand forget its **s**.
Ecc 10: 10 is needed, but **s** will bring success.

SKILLED (SKILL)
Pr 22: 29 Do you see those who are **s** in their

SKILLFUL (SKILL)
Ps 45: 1 my tongue is the pen of a **s** writer.
78: 72 with **s** hands he led them.

SKIN (SKINS)
Job 19: 20 escaped only by the **s** of my teeth.
19: 26 And after my **s** has been destroyed,
Jer 13: 23 Can an Ethiopian change his **s**

SKINS (SKIN)
Ex 25: 5 ram **s** dyed red and another durable
Lk 5: 37 the new wine will burst the **s**;

SKULL
Mt 27: 33 (which means "the place of the **s**").

SKY (SKIES)
Ge 1: 8 God called the vault "s."
Pr 30: 19 the way of an eagle in the s, the way
Isa 34: 4 the stars in the s will be dissolved
Jer 33: 22 me as countless as the stars in the s
Mt 24: 29 the stars will fall from the s,
     24: 30 the Son of Man will appear in the s,
Php 2: 15 shine among them like stars in the s

SLACK*
Pr 18: 9 One who is s in his work is a close

SLAIN (SLAY)
1Sa 18: 7 "Saul has s his thousands,
Eze 37: 9 four winds and breathe into these s,
Rev 5: 6 looking as if it had been s,
     5: 12 who was s, to receive power
     6: 9 those who had been s because

SLANDER (SLANDERED SLANDERER SLANDERERS SLANDEROUS)
Lev 19: 16 spreading s among your people.
Ps 15: 3 who have no s on their tongues,
Pr 10: 18 lying lips and spreads s is a fool.
2Co 12: 20 of anger, factions, s, gossip,
Eph 4: 31 brawling and s, along with every
1Ti 5: 14 give the enemy no opportunity for s.
Tit 3: 2 to s no one, to be peaceable
1Pe 3: 16 in Christ may be ashamed of their s.

SLANDERED (SLANDER)
1Co 4: 13 when we are s, we answer kindly.

SLANDERER* (SLANDER)
Jer 9: 4 and every friend is a s.

SLANDERERS (SLANDER)
Ro 1: 30 s, God-haters, insolent,
1Co 5: 11 greedy, idolaters or s,
     6: 10 nor drunkards nor s nor swindlers
Tit 2: 3 live, not to be s or addicted to much

SLANDEROUS* (SLANDER)
2Ti 3: 3 unforgiving, s, without self-control,

SLAPS
Mt 5: 39 If anyone s you on the right cheek,

SLAUGHTER (SLAUGHTERED)
Isa 53: 7 he was led like a lamb to the s,
Jer 11: 19 been like a gentle lamb led to the s;
Ac 8: 32 "He was led like a sheep to the s,

SLAUGHTERED (SLAUGHTER)
Ps 44: 22 we are considered as sheep to be s.
Ro 8: 36 we are considered as sheep to be s."

SLAVE (ENSLAVED SLAVERY SLAVES)
Ge 21: 10 "Get rid of that s woman and her
Pr 22: 7 the borrower is s to the lender.
Mt 20: 27 wants to be first must be your s—
Jn 8: 34 everyone who sins is a s to sin.
Ro 7: 14 I am unspiritual, sold as a s to sin.
1Co 7: 21 Were you a s when you were
    12: 13 whether Jews or Gentiles, s or free—
Gal 3: 28 Jew nor Gentile, neither s nor free,
     4: 30 "Get rid of the s woman and her
Col 3: 11 Scythian, s or free, but Christ is all,
1Ti 1: 10 for s traders and liars and perjurers.
Phm : 16 no longer as a s, but better than a s,

SLAVERY (SLAVE)
Ex 2: 23 The Israelites groaned in their s
Gal 4: 3 in s under the elemental spiritual
1Ti 6: 1 of s should consider their masters

SLAVES (SLAVE)
Ps 123: 2 the eyes of s look to the hand
Ecc 10: 7 I have seen s on horseback,
Mal 1: 6 father, and s honor their master.
Ro 6: 6 should no longer be s to sin—
     6: 16 whether you are s to sin,
     6: 19 yourselves as s to impurity
     6: 22 from sin and have become s of God,
Gal 2: 4 in Christ Jesus and to make us s.
     4: 7 So you are no longer s, but God's
     4: 8 you were s to those who by nature
Eph 6: 5 S, obey your earthly masters
Col 3: 22 S, obey your earthly masters
     4: 1 provide your s with what is right
Tit 2: 9 Teach s to be subject to their
2Pe 2: 19 for "people are s to whatever has

SLAY (SLAIN)
Job 13: 15 Though he s me, yet will I hope

SLEEP (ASLEEP SLEEPER SLEEPING SLEEPS)
Ge 2: 21 caused the man to fall into a deep s;
    15: 12 Abram fell into a deep s, and a thick
    28: 11 it under his head and lay down to s.

Ps 4: 8 In peace I will lie down and s,
  121: 4 Israel will neither slumber nor s.
  127: 2 for he grants s to those he loves.
Pr 6: 9 When will you get up from your s?
Ecc 5: 12 The s of laborers is sweet,
1Co 15: 51 We will not all s, but we will all be
1Th 4: 13 uninformed about those who s in death,
     5: 7 For those who s, s at night,

SLEEPER* (SLEEP)
Eph 5: 14 "Wake up, s, rise from the dead,

SLEEPING (SLEEP)
Mk 13: 36 suddenly, do not let him find you s.

SLEEPLESS*
2Co 6: 5 in hard work, s nights and hunger;

SLEEPS (SLEEP)
Pr 10: 5 but he who s during harvest is

SLIMY*
Ps 40: 2 He lifted me out of the s pit,

SLING
1Sa 17: 50 over the Philistine with a s

SLIP (SLIPPING)
Dt 4: 9 let them s from your heart as long as
Ps 121: 3 He will not let your foot s—

SLIPPING (SLIP)
Ps 66: 9 our lives and kept our feet from s.

SLOW
Ex 34: 6 and gracious God, s to anger,
Jas 1: 19 s to speak and s to become angry,
2Pe 3: 9 The Lord is not s in keeping his

SLUGGARD (SLUGGARD'S SLUGGARDS)
Pr 6: 6 Go to the ant, you s;

SLUGGARD'S* (SLUGGARD'S)
Pr 13: 4 A s appetite is never filled,

SLUGGARDS (SLUGGARD)
Pr 20: 4 S do not plow in season;
    26: 15 S bury their hands in the dish

SLUMBER
Ps 121: 3 he who watches over you will not s;
Pr 6: 10 a little s, a little folding of the hands
Ro 13: 11 for you to wake up from your s,

SLUR*
Ps 15: 3 no wrong, who cast no s on others;

SMELL
Ecc 10: 1 As dead flies give perfume a bad s,

SMOKE
Ex 19: 18 Mount Sinai was covered with s,
Ps 104: 32 touches the mountains, and they s.
Isa 6: 4 and the temple was filled with s.
Joel 2: 30 blood and fire and billows of s.
Ac 2: 19 blood and fire and billows of s.
Rev 15: 8 the temple was filled with s

SMYRNA
Rev 2: 8 the angel of the church in S write:

SNAKE (SNAKES)
Nu 21: 8 "Make a s and put it up on a pole;
Pr 23: 32 In the end it bites like a s
Jn 3: 14 lifted up the s in the wilderness,

SNAKES (SNAKE)
Mt 10: 16 Therefore be as shrewd as s and as
Mk 16: 18 they will pick up s

SNARE (ENSNARE ENSNARED SNARED)
Dt 7: 16 gods, for that will be a s to you.
Ps 69: 22 table set before them become a s,
    91: 3 he will save you from the fowler's s
Pr 29: 25 To fear anyone will prove to be a s,
Ro 11: 9 "May their table become a s

SNARED (SNARE)
Pr 3: 26 will keep your foot from being s.

SNATCH (SNATCHING)
Jn 10: 28 no one will s them out of my hand.

SNATCHING* (SNATCH)
Jude : 23 save others by s them from the fire;

SNEER
Ps 35: 21 They s at me and say, "Aha!

SNOUT*
Pr 11: 22 a pig's s is a beautiful woman who

SNOW
Ps 51: 7 and I will be whiter than s.
Isa 1: 18 scarlet, they shall be as white as s;

SNUFF (SNUFFED)
Isa 42: 3 a smoldering wick he will not s out.
Mt 12: 20 a smoldering wick he will not s out,

SNUFFED (SNUFF)
Pr 13: 9 but the lamp of the wicked is s out.

SOAP
Mal 3: 2 a refiner's fire or a launderer's s.

SOAR (SOARED)
Isa 40: 31 They will s on wings like eagles;

SOARED (SOAR)
2Sa 22: 11 he s on the wings of the wind.

SOBER*
1Sa 25: 37 in the morning, when Nabal was s,
Ro 12: 3 think of yourself with s judgment,
1Th 5: 6 but let us be awake and s.
     5: 8 let us be s, putting on faith
1Pe 1: 13 minds that are alert and fully s,
     4: 7 of s mind so that you may pray.
     5: 8 Be alert and of s mind.

SODOM
Ge 13: 12 plain and pitched his tents near S.
    19: 24 rained down burning sulfur on S
Isa 1: 9 we would have become like S,
Lk 10: 12 on that day for S than for that town.
Ro 9: 29 we would have become like S,
Rev 11: 8 which is figuratively called S

SOIL
Ge 4: 2 kept flocks, and Cain worked the s.
Mt 13: 23 the seed falling on good s refers

SOLD (SELL)
1Ki 21: 25 who s himself to do evil in the eyes
Mt 10: 29 Are not two sparrows s for a penny?
    13: 44 in his joy went and s all he had
Ro 7: 14 I am unspiritual, s as a slave to sin.

SOLDIER
1Co 9: 7 Who serves as a s at his own
2Ti 2: 3 like a good s of Christ Jesus.

SOLE
Dt 28: 65 resting place for the s of your foot.
Isa 1: 6 From the s of your foot to the top

SOLID
2Ti 2: 19 God's s foundation stands firm,
Heb 5: 12 You need milk, not s food!

SOLOMON
    Son of David by Bathsheba; king of Judah (2Sa 12:24; 1Ch 3:5, 10). Appointed king by David (1Ki 1); adversaries Adonijah, Joab, Shimei killed by Benaiah (1Ki 2). Asked for wisdom (1Ki 3). Judged between two prostitutes (1Ki 3:16–28). Built temple (1Ki 5–7; 2Ch 2–5); prayer of dedication (1Ki 8; 2Ch 6). Visited by Queen of Sheba (1Ki 10; 2Ch 9). Wives turned his heart from God (1Ki 11:1–13). Jeroboam rebelled against (1Ki 11:26–40). Death (1Ki 11:41–43; 2Ch 9:29–31).
    Proverbs of (1Ki 4:32; Pr 1:1; 10:1; 25:1); psalms of (Ps 72; 127); song of (SS 1:1).

SON (SONS SONSHIP)
Ge 17: 19 your wife Sarah will bear you a s,
    21: 10 rid of that slave woman and her s,
    22: 2 "Take your s, your only s,
Ex 11: 5 Every firstborn s in Egypt will die,
Dt 1: 31 as a father carries his s, all the way
     8: 5 heart that as a man disciplines his s,
    21: 18 rebellious s who does not obey his
2Sa 7: 14 be his father, and he will be my s.
1Ki 3: 20 and put her dead s by my breast.
Ps 2: 7 He said to me, "You are my s;
     2: 12 Kiss his s, or he will be angry
Pr 3: 12 as a father the s he delights in.
     6: 20 My s, keep your father's command
Isa 7: 14 will conceive and give birth to a s,
Da 3: 25 and the fourth looks like a s
     7: 13 there before me was one like a s
Hos 11: 1 and out of Egypt I called my s.
Mt 1: 1 of Jesus the Messiah the s of David,
     1: 21 She will give birth to a s, and you
     2: 15 "Out of Egypt I called my s."
     3: 17 said, "This is my S, whom I love;
     4: 3 "If you are the S of God, tell these
     8: 20 the S of Man has no place to lay his
    11: 27 one knows the s except the Father,
    12: 8 For the S of Man is Lord
    12: 32 who speaks a word against the S
    12: 40 so the S of Man will be three days
    13: 41 The S of Man will send out his

Mt 13: 55 "Isn't this the carpenter's s?
14: 33 "Truly you are the S of God."
16: 16 Messiah, the S of the living God.
16: 27 For the S of Man is going to come
17: 5 said, "This is my S, whom I love;
19: 28 when the S of Man sits on his
20: 18 the S of Man will be delivered over
20: 28 just as the S of Man did not come
21: 9 "Hosanna to the S of David!"
22: 42 about the Messiah? Whose s is he?"
22: 42 "The s of David," they replied.
24: 27 will be the coming of the S of Man.
24: 30 They will see the S of Man coming
24: 44 because the S of Man will come
25: 31 "When the S of Man comes in his
26: 63 you are the Messiah, the S of God."
27: 54 "Surely he was the S of God!"
28: 19 and of the S and of the Holy Spirit,

Mk 1: 11 "You are my S, whom I love;
2: 28 So the S of Man is Lord even
8: 38 the S of Man will be ashamed
9: 7 "This is my S, whom I love.
10: 45 For even the S of Man did not come
13: 32 nor the S, but only the Father.
14: 62 you will see the S of Man sitting

Lk 1: 32 will be called the S of the Most
2: 7 she gave birth to her firstborn, a s.
3: 22 "You are my S, whom I love;
9: 35 saying, "This is my S, whom I have
9: 58 the S of Man has no place to lay his
12: 8 the S of Man will also acknowledge
15: 20 he ran to his s, threw his arms
18: 8 when the S of Man comes, will he
18: 31 about the S of Man will be fulfilled.
19: 10 For the S of Man came to seek

Jn 3: 14 so the S of Man must be lifted up,
3: 16 that he gave his one and only S,
3: 36 believes in the S has eternal life,
5: 19 the S can do nothing by himself;
6: 40 is that everyone who looks to the S
11: 4 God's S may be glorified through
17: 1 Glorify your S, that your S may

Ac 7: 56 the S of Man standing at the right
13: 33 " 'You are my s; today I have

Ro 1: 4 holiness was appointed the S of God
5: 10 to him through the death of his S,
8: 3 by sending his own S in the likeness
8: 29 be conformed to the image of his S,
8: 32 He who did not spare his own S,

1Co 15: 28 the S himself will be made subject

Gal 2: 20 I live by faith in the S of God,
4: 4 God sent his S, born of a woman,
4: 30 rid of the slave woman and her s,

1Th 1: 10 and to wait for his S from heaven,

Heb 1: 2 days he has spoken to us by his S,
1: 5 did God ever say, "You are my S;
4: 14 into heaven, Jesus the S of God,
5: 5 God said to him, "You are my S;
7: 28 appointed the S, who has been made
10: 29 punished who have trampled the S

2Pe 1: 17 saying, "This is my S, whom I love;

1Jn 1: 3 is with the Father and with his S,
1: 7 Jesus, his S, purifies us from all sin.
2: 23 acknowledges the S has the Father
3: 8 The reason the S of God appeared
4: 9 only S into the world that we might
4: 14 the Father has sent his S to be
5: 5 believes that Jesus is the S of God.
5: 11 eternal life, and this life is in his S.

Rev 1: 13 lampstands was someone like a S
14: 14 on the cloud was one like a s of man

SONG (SING)
Ps 40: 3 He put a new s in my mouth,
69: 30 I will praise God's name in s
96: 1 Sing to the LORD a new s;
98: 4 burst into jubilant s with music;
119: 54 the theme of my s wherever I lodge,
149: 1 Sing to the LORD a new s,
Isa 49: 13 burst into s, you mountains!
55: 12 hills will burst into s before you,
Rev 5: 9 And they sang a new s, saying:
15: 3 sang the s of God's servant Moses

SONGS (SING)
2Sa 23: 1 God of Jacob, the hero of Israel's s:
Job 35: 10 my Maker, who gives s in the night,
Ps 100: 2 come before him with joyful s.
126: 6 to sow, will return with s of joy,
137: 3 "Sing us one of the s of Zion!"
Eph 5: 19 hymns and s from the Spirit.
Jas 5: 13 Let them sing s of praise.

SONS (SON)
Ge 6: 2 the s of God saw that these
10: 20 These are the s of Ham by their
Ru 4: 15 who is better to you than seven s,
Ps 132: 12 If your s keep my covenant
Joel 2: 28 Your s and daughters will prophesy,
2Co 6: 18 and you will be my s and daughters,
Gal 4: 6 Because you are his s, God sent

SONSHIP* (SON)
Ro 8: 15 brought about your adoption to s.
Gal 4: 5 we might receive adoption to s.
Eph 1: 5 he predestined us for adoption to s

SOOTHING
Pr 15: 4 The s tongue is a tree of life,

SORROW
Ps 6: 7 My eyes grow weak with s;
116: 3 I was overcome by distress and s.
Isa 60: 20 light, and your days of s will end.
Jer 31: 12 garden, and they will s no more.
Ro 9: 2 I have great s and unceasing
2Co 7: 10 Godly s brings repentance that leads
7: 10 but worldly s brings death.

SOUGHT (SEEK)
2Ch 26: 5 As long as he s the LORD,
31: 21 he s his God and worked
Ps 34: 4 I s the LORD, and he answered
119: 58 I have s your face with all my heart;

SOUL (SOULS)
Dt 6: 5 and with all your s and with all your
10: 12 all your heart and with all your s,
30: 6 all your heart and with all your s,
Jos 22: 5 all your heart and with all your s."
2Ki 23: 25 and with all his s and with all his
Ps 23: 3 he refreshes my s. He guides me
42: 1 of water, so my s pants for you,
42: 11 Why, my s, are you downcast?
62: 5 Yes, my s, find rest in God;
103: 1 Praise the LORD, my s;
Pr 13: 19 A longing fulfilled is sweet to the s,
16: 24 sweet to the s and healing
La 3: 20 and my s is downcast within me.
Mt 10: 28 kill the body but cannot kill the s.
16: 26 the whole world, yet forfeit your s?
16: 26 you give in exchange for your s?
22: 37 and with all your s and with all your
Jn 12: 27 "Now my s is troubled.
Heb 4: 12 it penetrates even to dividing s
3Jn : 2 even as your s is getting along well.

SOULS (SOUL)
Pr 11: 30 life, and those who win s are wise.
Jer 6: 16 and you will find rest for your s.
Mt 11: 29 and you will find rest for your s.

SOUND (FINE-SOUNDING)
Ge 3: 8 his wife heard the s of the LORD
Pr 3: 21 preserve s judgment and discretion;
Eze 3: 12 me a loud rumbling s as the glory
Jn 3: 8 You hear its s, but you cannot tell
Ac 2: 2 Suddenly a s like the blowing
1Co 14: 8 if the trumpet does not s a clear call,
15: 52 For the trumpet will s, the dead will
1Ti 1: 10 else is contrary to the s doctrine
2Ti 4: 3 will not put up with s doctrine.
Tit 1: 9 can encourage others by s doctrine
2: 1 what is appropriate to s doctrine.

SOUR
Eze 18: 2 " 'The parents eat s grapes,

SOURCE
Heb 5: 9 he became the s of eternal salvation

SOVEREIGN (SOVEREIGNTY)
Ge 15: 2 But Abram said, "S LORD,
2Sa 7: 18 "Who am I, S LORD, and what is
Ps 71: 16 your mighty acts, S LORD;
Isa 25: 8 The S LORD will wipe away
40: 10 the S LORD comes with power,
50: 4 The S LORD has given me
61: 1 The Spirit of the S LORD is
61: 11 to grow, so the S LORD will make
Jer 32: 17 "Ah, S LORD, you have made
Eze 12: 28 declares the S LORD.' "
Da 4: 25 Most High is over the kingdoms
2Pe 2: 1 even denying the s Lord who
Jude : 4 deny Jesus Christ our only S

SOVEREIGNTY (SOVEREIGN)
Da 7: 27 Then the s, power and greatness

SOW (SOWER SOWN SOWS)
Job 4: 8 and those who s trouble reap it.

Ps 126: 5 Those who s with tears will reap
Pr 11: 18 those who s righteousness reap
22: 8 who s injustice reap calamity,
Hos 8: 7 "They s the wind and reap
10: 12 S for yourselves righteousness,
Mt 6: 26 they do not s or reap or store away
13: 3 "A farmer went out to s his seed.
1Co 15: 36 What you s does not come to life
Gal 6: 7 People reap what they s.
Jas 3: 18 Peacemakers who s in peace reap
2Pe 2: 22 "A s that is washed returns to her

SOWER* (SOW)
Isa 55: 10 so that it yields seed for the s
Mt 13: 18 to what the parable of the s means:
Jn 4: 36 so that the s and the reaper may be
2Co 9: 10 Now he who supplies seed to the s

SOWN (SOW)
Mt 13: 3 sixty or thirty times what was s.
Mk 4: 15 along the path, where the word is s.
1Co 15: 42 The body that is s is perishable, it is

SOWS
2Co 9: 6 Whoever s sparingly will also reap

SPARE (SPARING)
Est 7: 3 And s my people—this is my
Pr 13: 24 who s the rod hate their children,
Ro 8: 32 He who did not s his own Son,
11: 21 branches, he will not s you either.
2Pe 2: 4 if God did not s angels when they
2: 5 if he did not s the ancient world

SPARING (SPARE)
Pr 21: 26 but the righteous give without s.

SPARKLE*
Zec 9: 16 They will s in his land like jewels

SPARROW (SPARROWS)
Ps 84: 3 Even the s has found a home,

SPARROWS (SPARROW)
Mt 10: 29 Are not two s sold for a penny?

SPEAR (SPEARS)
1Sa 19: 10 to pin him to the wall with his s,
Ps 46: 9 breaks the bow and shatters the s;

SPEARS (SPEAR)
Isa 2: 4 and their s into pruning hooks.
Joel 3: 10 and your pruning hooks into s.
Mic 4: 3 and their s into pruning hooks.

SPECIAL
Jas 2: 3 If you show s attention to the one

SPECK
Mt 7: 3 do you look at the s of sawdust

SPECTACLE
1Co 4: 9 We have been made a s to the whole
Col 2: 15 he made a public s of them,

SPEECH
Ps 19: 3 They have no s, they use no words;
2Co 8: 7 in faith, in s, in knowledge,
1Ti 4: 12 set an example for the believers in s,

SPEND (SPENT)
Pr 31: 3 Do not s your strength on women,
Isa 55: 2 Why s money on what is not bread,
2Co 12: 15 So I will very gladly s for you

SPENT (SPEND)
Mk 5: 26 many doctors and had s all she had,
Lk 6: 12 and s the night praying to God.
15: 14 After he had s everything, there was

SPIN
Mt 6: 28 They do not labor or s.

SPIRIT (SPIRIT'S SPIRITS SPIRITUAL)
Ge 1: 2 the S of God was hovering over
6: 3 "My S will not contend with human
Ex 31: 3 I have filled him with the S of God,
Nu 11: 25 the power of the S that was on him
Dt 34: 9 the s of wisdom because Moses had
Jdg 6: 34 Then the S of the LORD came
11: 29 Then the S of the LORD came
13: 25 the S of the LORD began to stir
1Sa 10: 6 the S of the LORD came on him in power,
16: 13 day on the S of the LORD came
16: 14 Now the S of the LORD had
2Sa 23: 2 "The S of the LORD spoke
2Ki 2: 9 inherit a double portion of your s,"
Ne 9: 20 You gave your good S to instruct
9: 30 By your S you warned them through
Job 33: 4 The S of God has made me;
Ps 31: 5 Into your hands I commit my s;

Ps 34:18 saves those who are crushed in s.
51:10 and renew a steadfast s within me.
51:11 or take your Holy S from me.
51:17 My sacrifice, O God, is a broken s;
106:33 they rebelled against the S of God,
139: 7 Where can I go from your S?
143:10 may your good S lead me on level
Isa 11: 2 The S of the LORD will rest
30: 1 but not by my S, heaping sin
32:15 till the S is poured on us
44: 3 pour out my S on your offspring,
57:15 who are contrite and lowly in s,
61: 1 The S of the Sovereign LORD is
63:10 rebelled and grieved his Holy S.
Eze 11:19 heart and put a new s in them;
13: 3 prophets who follow their own s
36:26 a new heart and put a new s in you;
Da 4: 8 and the s of the holy gods is in him.)
Joel 2:28 I will pour out my S on all people.
Zec 4: 6 but by my S,' says the LORD
Mt 1:18 to be pregnant through the Holy S.
3:11 He will baptize you with the Holy S
3:16 he saw the S of God descending like
4: 1 was led by the S into the wilderness
5: 3 "Blessed are the poor in s, for theirs
10:20 but the S of your Father speaking
12:31 blasphemy against the S will not be
26:41 The s is willing, but the flesh is
28:19 and of the Son and of the Holy S,
Mk 1: 8 will baptize you with the Holy S."
Lk 1:35 "The Holy S will come on you,
1:80 child grew and became strong in s;
3:16 He will baptize you with the Holy S
4:18 "The S of the Lord is on me,
11:13 in heaven give the Holy S to those
23:46 into your hands I commit my s."
Jn 1:33 who will baptize with the Holy S."
3: 5 being born of water and the S.
4:24 God is s, and his worshipers must
6:63 The S gives life; the flesh counts
7:39 that time the S had not been given,
14:26 the Holy S, whom the Father will
16:13 But when he, the S of truth, comes,
20:22 and said, "Receive the Holy S.
Ac 1: 5 will be baptized with the Holy S
1: 8 when the Holy S comes on you;
2: 4 of them were filled with the Holy S
2:17 I will pour out my S on all people.
2:38 will receive the gift of the Holy S.
4:31 they were all filled with the Holy S
5: 3 that you have lied to the Holy S
5: 9 who are known to be full of the S,
8:15 that they might receive the Holy S,
9:17 and be filled with the Holy S."
11:16 will be baptized with the Holy S.'
13: 2 the Holy S said, "Set apart for me
19: 2 "Did you receive the Holy S
Ro 9: 1 I serve in my s in preaching
8: 4 nature but according to the S.
8: 5 minds set on what the S desires.
8: 9 if anyone does not have the S
8:13 but if by the S you put to death
8:16 The S himself testifies with our s
8:23 who have the firstfruits of the S,
8:26 the S helps us in our weakness.
1Co 2:10 has revealed them to us by his S.
2:14 without the S does not accept
2:14 are discerned only through the S.
5: 3 present, I am with you in s.
6:19 bodies are temples of the Holy S,
12: 1 Now about the gifts of the S,
12:13 we were all baptized by one S so as
2Co 1:22 put his S in our hearts as a deposit,
3: 3 ink but with the S of the living God,
3: 6 the letter kills, but the S gives life.
3:17 Now the Lord is the S, and where
5: 5 who has given us the S as a deposit,
7: 1 that contaminates body and s,
Gal 3: 2 Did you receive the S by observing
5:16 walk by the S, and you will not
5:22 the fruit of the S is love, joy,
5:25 live by the S, let us keep in step with
the S.
6: 1 you who live by the S should restore
6: 8 sow to please the S, from the S will reap
eternal life.
Eph 1:13 with a seal, the promised Holy S,
2:22 in which God lives by his S.
4: 4 There is one body and one S, just as
4:30 do not grieve the Holy S of God,
5:18 Instead, be filled with the S,
5:19 psalms, hymns and songs from the S.

Eph 6:17 of salvation and the sword of the S,
Php 2: 2 being one in s and of one mind.
1Th 5:23 May your whole s, soul and body be
2Th 2:13 the sanctifying work of the S
1Ti 3:16 was vindicated by the S, was seen
2Ti 1: 7 the S God gave us does not make us
Heb 2: 4 of the Holy S distributed according
4:12 even to dividing soul and s,
10:29 who have insulted the S of grace?
1Pe 3: 4 beauty of a gentle and quiet s,
2Pe 1:21 were carried along by the Holy S.
1Jn 3:24 We know it by the S he gave us.
4: 1 do not believe every s, but test
4:13 he in us: He has given us of his S.
Jude : 20 holy faith and praying in the Holy S,
Rev 2: 7 let them hear what the S says

SPIRIT'S* (SPIRIT)
1Co 2: 4 a demonstration of the S power,
1Th 5:19 Do not put out the S fire.

SPIRITS (SPIRIT)
1Co 12:10 to another distinguishing between s,
14:32 The s of prophets are subject
Heb 1: 7 "He makes his angels s,
1Jn 4: 1 test the s to see whether they are

SPIRITUAL (SPIRIT)
Ro 12:11 but keep your s fervor,
1Co 2:13 the Spirit, explaining s realities
3: 1 I could not address you as s but as
14: 1 of love and eagerly desire s gifts,
15:44 a natural body, it is raised a s body.
Eph 1: 3 realms with every s blessing
6:12 against the s forces of evil
1Pe 2: 2 crave pure s milk, so that by it you
2: 5 are being built into a s house to be

SPIT
Mt 27:30 They s on him, and took the staff
Rev 3:16 I am about to s you out of my

SPLENDOR
1Ch 16:29 the LORD in the s of his holiness.
29:11 the glory and the majesty and the s,
Job 37:22 of the north he comes in golden s;
Ps 29: 2 the LORD in the s of his holiness.
45: 3 clothe yourself with s and majesty.
96: 6 S and majesty are before him;
96: 9 the LORD in the s of his holiness;
104: 1 you are clothed with s and majesty.
110: 3 Arrayed in holy s,
145: 5 of the glorious s of your majesty—
145:12 and the glorious s of your kingdom.
148:13 his s is above the earth
Pr 16:31 Gray hair is a crown of s;
20:29 strength, gray hair the s of the old.
Isa 55: 5 for he has endowed you with s."
60:21 my hands, for the display of my s.
61: 3 the LORD for the display of his s.
63: 1 robed in s, striding forward
Hab 3: 4 His s was like the sunrise;
Mt 6:29 in all his s was dressed like one
Lk 9:31 appeared in glorious s,
2Th 2: 8 and destroy by the s of his coming.

SPOIL (SPOILS)
Ps 119:162 promise like one who finds great s.

SPOILS (SPOIL)
Isa 53:12 he will divide the s with the strong,
Jn 6:27 Do not work for food that s,

SPOTLESS
2Pe 3:14 make every effort to be found s,

SPOTS (SPOTTED)
Jer 13:23 change his skin or a leopard its s?

SPOTTED (SPOTS)
Ge 30:32 lamb and every s or speckled goat.

SPREAD (SPREADING SPREADS)
Ps 78:19 "Can God really s a table
Ac 6: 7 So the word of God s.
12:24 of God continued to increase and s.
13:49 of the Lord s through the whole
19:20 way the word of the Lord s widely
2Th 3: 1 message of the Lord may s rapidly

SPREADING (SPREAD)
Pr 29: 5 who flatter their neighbors are s nets
1Th 3: 2 in God's service in s the gospel

SPREADS (SPREAD)
Pr 10:18 lying lips and s slander is a fool.

SPRING (SPRINGS)
Jer 2:13 forsaken me, the s of living water,

Jn 4:14 become in them a s of water welling
Jas 3:12 can a salt s produce fresh water.

SPRINGS (SPRING)
2Pe 2:17 These people are s without water

SPRINKLE (SPRINKLED)
Lev 16:14 with his finger s it on the front

SPRINKLED (SPRINKLE)
Heb 10:22 having our hearts s to cleanse us
1Pe 1: 2 Jesus Christ and s with his blood:

SPROUT
Pr 23: 5 for they will surely s wings and fly
Jer 33:15 I will make a righteous Branch s

SPUR*
Heb 10:24 consider how we may s one another

SPURNS*
Pr 15: 5 A fool s a parent's discipline,

SPY
Gal 2: 4 had infiltrated our ranks to s

SQUANDERED (SQUANDERS)
Lk 15:13 and there s his wealth in wild living.

SQUANDERS* (SQUANDERED)
Pr 29: 3 of prostitutes s his wealth.

SQUARE
Rev 21:16 The city was laid out like a s,

STABILITY*
Pr 29: 4 By justice a king gives a country s,

STAFF
Ge 49:10 nor the ruler's s from between his
Ex 7:12 Aaron's s swallowed up their staffs.
Nu 17: 8 and Aaron's s was among them.
Ps 23: 4 your rod and your s, they comfort

STAIN (STAINED)
Eph 5:27 without s or wrinkle or any other

STAINED (STAIN)
Isa 63: 1 with his garments s crimson?

STAKES
Isa 54: 2 your cords, strengthen your s.

STAND (STANDING STANDS STOOD)
Ex 14:13 S firm and you will see
Lev 19:32 " 'S up in the presence of the aged,
Jos 10:12 "Sun, s still over Gibeon,
2Ch 20:17 s firm and see the deliverance
Job 19:25 that in the end he will s on the earth.
Ps 1: 1 or s in the way that sinners take
1: 5 Therefore the wicked will not s
24: 3 Who may s in his holy place?
33:11 plans of the LORD s firm forever,
40: 2 rock and gave me a firm place to s.
76: 7 Who can s before you when you are
93: 5 Your statutes, LORD, s firm;
119:120 fear of you; I s in awe of your laws.
130: 3 a record of sins, Lord, who could s?
Isa 7: 9 If you do not s firm in your faith,
29:23 will s in awe of the God of Israel.
Eze 22:30 s before me in the gap on behalf
Hab 3: 2 I s in awe of your deeds, LORD.
Zec 14: 4 day his feet will s on the Mount
Mal 3: 2 Who can s when he appears?
Mt 10:22 s firm to the end will be saved.
12:25 divided against itself will not s.
Lk 21:19 S firm, and you will win life.
Ac 11:17 that I could s in God's way?"
Ro 14: 4 for the Lord is able to make them s.
14:10 we will all s before God's judgment
1Co 15:58 my dear brothers and sisters, s firm.
16:13 on your guard; s firm in the faith;
Gal 5: 1 S firm, then, and do not let
Eph 6:14 S firm then, with the belt of truth
2Th 2:15 s firm and hold fast to the teachings
Jas 5: 8 be patient and s firm,
Rev 3:20 I s at the door and knock.

STANDING (STAND)
Ex 3: 5 where you are s is holy ground."
Jos 5:15 the place where you are s is holy."
Ru 2: 1 side, a man of s from the clan
4:11 May you have s in Ephrathah
1Ti 3:13 have served well gain an excellent s
1Pe 5: 9 Resist him, s firm in the faith,

STANDS (STAND)
Ps 89: 2 that your love s firm forever,
119:89 it s firm in the heavens.
Pr 12: 7 the house of the righteous s firm.
2Ti 2:19 God's solid foundation s firm,

STAR (STARS)
Nu 24: 17 A s will come out of Jacob;
Isa 14: 12 heaven, morning, son of the dawn!
Mt 2: 2 We saw his s when it rose and have
2Pe 1: 19 the morning s rises in your hearts.
Rev 2: 28 I will also give them the morning s.
22: 16 David, and the bright Morning **S**."

STARS (STAR)
Ge 1: 16 He also made the s.
Job 38: 7 while the morning s sang together
Da 12: 3 like the s for ever and ever.
Php 2: 15 you will shine among them like s

STATURE
1Sa 2: 26 boy Samuel continued to grow in s

STATUTES
Ps 19: 7 The s of the LORD are
93: 5 Your s, LORD, stand firm;
119: 2 Blessed are those who keep his s
119: 14 in following your s as one rejoices
119: 24 Your s are my delight; they are my
119: 36 Turn my heart toward your s
119: 99 teachers, for I meditate on your s.
119:111 Your s are my heritage forever;
119:125 that I may understand your s.
119:129 Your s are wonderful;
119:138 The s you have laid down are
119:152 your s that you established them
119:167 I obey your s, for I love them

STEADFAST*
Ps 51: 10 and renew a s spirit within me.
57: 7 My heart, O God, is s, my heart is s;
108: 1 My heart, O God, is s; I will sing
112: 7 their hearts are s,
119: 5 my ways were s in obeying your
Pr 4: 26 and be s in all your ways.
Isa 26: 3 peace those whose minds are s,
1Pe 5: 10 and make you strong, firm and s.

STEADY
Isa 35: 3 hands, s the knees that give way;

STEAL (STOLEN)
Ex 20: 15 "You shall not s.
Lev 19: 11 " 'Do not s. " 'Do not lie.
Dt 5: 19 "You shall not s.
Mt 19: 18 you shall not s, you shall not give
Ro 13: 9 "You shall not s," "You shall not
Eph 4: 28 have been stealing must s no longer,

STEP (FOOTSTEPS STEPS)
Job 34: 21 he sees their every s.
Ps 1: 1 do not walk in s with the wicked
Gal 5: 25 let us keep in s with the Spirit.

STEPHEN
Deacon (Ac 6:5). Arrested (Ac 6:8–15). Speech to Sanhedrin (Ac 7). Stoned (Ac 7:54–60; 22:20).

STEPS (STEP)
Ps 37: 23 The LORD makes firm the s
Pr 14: 15 the prudent give thought to their s.
16: 9 but the LORD establishes their s.
20: 24 A person's s are directed
Jer 10: 23 it is not for them to direct their s.
1Pe 2: 21 that you should follow in his s.

STERN (STERNNESS)
Pr 15: 10 S discipline awaits those who leave

STERNNESS* (STERN)
Ro 11: 22 therefore the kindness and s of God:
11: 22 s to those who fell, but kindness

STICKS
Pr 18: 24 there is a friend who s closer than

STIFF-NECKED (NECK)
Ex 34: 9 Although this is a s people,
Pr 29: 1 Whoever remains s after many

STILL
Jos 10: 13 So the sun stood s, and the moon
Ps 37: 7 Be s before the LORD and wait
46: 10 "Be s, and know that I am God;
89: 9 its waves mount up, you s them.
Zec 2: 13 Be s before the LORD, all people,
Mk 4: 39 Be s!" Then the wind died down

STIMULATE*
2Pe 3: 1 of them as reminders to s you

STING
1Co 15: 55 Where, O death, is your s?

STINGY*
Pr 28: 22 The s are eager to get rich and

STIR (STIRRED STIRS)
Pr 15: 18 The hot-tempered s up dissension,
16: 28 The perverse s up dissension,
28: 25 The greedy s up dissension,

STIRRED (STIR)
Ps 45: 1 My heart is s by a noble theme

STIRS (STIR)
Pr 6: 19 a person who s up dissension
10: 12 Hatred s up dissension, but love
15: 1 wrath, but a harsh word s up anger.
29: 22 An angry person s up dissension,

STOLEN (STEAL)
Lev 6: 4 they must return what they have s
SS 4: 9 You have s my heart, my sister,

STOMACH
1Co 6: 13 "Food for the s and the s for food,
Php 3: 19 their god is their s, and their glory is

STONE (CAPSTONE CORNERSTONE MILLSTONE STONES STONING)
Ex 24: 4 up twelve s pillars representing
28: 10 six names on one s
34: 1 out two s tablets like the first ones,
Dt 4: 13 then wrote them on two s tablets.
19: 14 your neighbor's boundary s set
1Sa 17: 50 the Philistine with a sling and a s;
Ps 91: 12 will not strike your foot against a s.
118: 22 The s the builders rejected has
Pr 22: 28 not move an ancient boundary s set
Isa 8: 14 of Israel the s he will be a s that causes
28: 16 "See, I lay a s in Zion, a tested s,
Eze 11: 19 remove from them their heart of s
36: 26 remove from you your heart of s
Mt 7: 9 asks for bread, will give him a s?
21: 42 " 'The s the builders rejected has
24: 2 not one s here will be left
Mk 16: 3 "Who will roll the s away
Lk 4: 3 tell this s to become bread."
Jn 8: 7 first to throw a s at her."
Ac 4: 11 Jesus is " 'the s you builders
Ro 9: 32 They stumbled over the stumbling s.
2Co 3: 3 not on tablets of s but on tablets
1Pe 2: 6 "See, I lay a s in Zion, a chosen
Rev 2: 17 of them a white s with a new name

STONES (STONE)
Ex 28: 21 There are to be twelve s,
Jos 4: 3 take up twelve s from the middle
1Sa 17: 40 hand, chose five smooth s
Mt 3: 9 these s God can raise up children
1Co 3: 12 costly s, wood, hay or straw,
2Co 11: 25 once I was pelted with s,
1Pe 2: 5 like living s, are being built

STONING (STONE)
Heb 11: 37 They were put to death by s;

STOOD (STAND)
Jos 10: 13 So the sun s still, and the moon
Lk 22: 28 You are those who have s by me
2Ti 4: 17 But the Lord s at my side and gave
Jas 1: 12 because when they have s the test,

STOOPS
Ps 113: 6 who s down to look on the heavens

STOP (STOPPED)
Job 37: 14 s and consider God's wonders.
Isa 1: 13 S bringing meaningless offerings!
1: 16 out of my sight! S doing wrong,
2: 22 S trusting in human beings,
Jer 32: 40 I will never s doing good to them,
Mk 9: 39 "Do not s him," Jesus said.
Jn 6: 43 "S grumbling among yourselves,"
7: 24 S judging by mere appearances,
20: 27 S doubting and believe."
Ro 14: 13 Therefore let us s passing judgment
1Co 14: 20 and sisters, s thinking like children.

STOPPED (STOP)
Jos 3: 17 ark of the covenant of the LORD s

STORE (STORED)
Pr 2: 1 and s up my commands within you,
7: 1 and s up my commands within you.
10: 14 The wise s up knowledge,
Isa 33: 6 a rich s of salvation and wisdom
Mt 6: 19 "Do not s up for yourselves
6: 26 not sow or reap or s away in barns,
2Ti 4: 8 Now there is in s for me the crown

STORED (STORE)
Lk 6: 45 out of the good s up in their heart,
Col 1: 5 spring from the hope s up for you

STOREHOUSE (HOUSE)
Mal 3: 10 Bring the whole tithe into the s,

STORIES*
2Pe 1: 16 we did not follow cleverly devised s
2: 3 will exploit you with fabricated s.

STORM
Job 38: 1 LORD spoke to Job out of the s.
Ps 107: 29 He stilled the s to a whisper;
Lk 8: 24 the s subsided, and all was calm.

STRAIGHT
Ps 27: 11 lead me in a s path because of my
107: 7 He led them by a s way to a city
Pr 2: 13 who have left the s paths to walk
3: 6 and he will make your paths s.
4: 11 wisdom and lead you along s paths.
4: 25 Let your eyes look s ahead;
11: 5 the blameless makes their paths s,
15: 21 have understanding keep a s course.
Isa 40: 3 make s in the desert a highway
Mt 3: 3 the Lord, make s paths for him.' "
Jn 1: 23 'Make s the way for the Lord.' "
2Pe 2: 15 They have left the s way

STRAIN (STRAINING)
Mt 23: 24 You s out a gnat but swallow

STRAINING (STRAIN)
Php 3: 13 behind and s toward what is ahead,

STRANGE (STRANGER STRANGERS)
Isa 28: 11 s tongues God will speak to this
Eze 3: 5 of obscure speech and s language,

STRANGER (STRANGE)
Ps 119: 19 I am a s on earth; do not hide your
Mt 25: 35 I was a s and you invited me in,
Jn 10: 5 But they will never follow a s;

STRANGERS (STRANGE)
Heb 13: 2 not forget to show hospitality to s,

STRAW
Isa 11: 7 and the lion will eat s like the ox.
1Co 3: 12 silver, costly stones, wood, hay or s,

STRAYED (STRAYS)
Ps 119:176 I have s like a lost sheep.
Jer 31: 19 After I s, I repented; after I came

STRAYS (STRAYED)
Pr 21: 16 Whoever s from the path
Eze 34: 16 for the lost and bring back the s.

STREAM (STREAMS)
Am 5: 24 righteousness like a never-failing s!

STREAMS (STREAM)
Ps 1: 3 They are like a tree planted by s
46: 4 is a river whose s make glad the city
Ecc 1: 7 All s flow into the sea, yet the sea is

STREET
Mt 6: 5 and on the s corners to be seen
22: 9 Go to the s corners and invite
Rev 21: 21 The great s of the city was of gold,

STRENGTH (STRONG)
Ex 15: 2 "The LORD is my s and my
Dt 4: 37 by his Presence and his great s,
6: 5 all your soul and with all your s.
Jdg 16: 15 told me the secret of your great s."
2Sa 22: 33 It is God who arms me with s
2Ki 23: 25 with all his soul and with all his s,
1Ch 16: 11 Look to the LORD and his s;
16: 28 ascribe to the LORD glory and s.
29: 12 In your hands are s and power
Ne 8: 10 the joy of the LORD is your s."
Ps 18: 1 I love you, LORD, my s.
21: 13 Be exalted in your s, LORD;
28: 7 The LORD is my s and my shield;
29: 11 The LORD gives s to his people;
33: 16 no warrior escapes by his great s.
46: 1 God is our refuge and s,
59: 17 You are my s, I sing praise to you;
65: 6 having armed yourself with s,
73: 26 but God is the s of my heart and my
84: 5 Blessed are those whose s is in you,
96: 7 ascribe to the LORD glory and s.
105: 4 Look to the LORD and his s;
118: 14 The LORD is my s and my
147: 10 pleasure is not in the s of the horse,
Pr 24: 5 who have knowledge muster their s.
30: 25 Ants are creatures of little s,
Isa 12: 2 LORD, is my s and my defense;
31: 1 and in the great s of their horsemen,
40: 26 of his great power and mighty s,
40: 31 in the LORD will renew their s.

Isa 63: 1 forward in the greatness of his s?
Jer 9:23 the strong boast of their s or the rich
Mic 5: 4 his flock in the s of the LORD,
Hab 3:19 The Sovereign LORD is my s;
Mk 12:30 all your mind and with all your s.'
1Co 1:25 of God is stronger than human s.
Eph 1:19 power is the same as the mighty s
Php 4:13 all this through him who gives me s.
Heb 11: 1 whose weakness was turned to s;
1Pe 4:11 do so with the s God provides,

STRENGTHEN (STRONG)
2Ch 16: 9 to s those whose hearts are fully
Ps 119:28 s me according to your word.
Isa 35: 3 S the feeble hands, steady the knees
41:10 I will s you and help you;
Lk 22:32 have turned back, s your brothers.'
Eph 3:16 of his glorious riches he may s you
1Th 3:13 May he s your hearts so that you
2Th 2:17 hearts and s you in every good deed
Heb 12:12 your feeble arms and weak knees.

STRENGTHENED (STRONG)
Col 1:11 being s with all power according
Heb 13: 9 good for our hearts to be s by grace,

STRENUOUSLY*
Col 1:29 To this end I s contend

STRETCHES
Ps 104: 2 he s out the heavens like a tent

STRICKEN (STRIKE)
Isa 53: 4 s by him, and afflicted.

STRICT
1Co 9:25 in the games goes into s training.

STRIFE (STRIVE)
Pr 13:10 Where there is s, there is pride,
17: 1 a house full of feasting, with s.
20: 3 It is to one's honor to avoid s,
22:10 out the mocker, and out goes s;
30:33 so stirring up anger produces s."
1Ti 6: 4 about words that result in envy, s,

STRIKE (STROKE)
Ge 3:15 your head, and you will s his heel."
Zec 13: 7 "S the shepherd, and the sheep will
Mt 4: 6 you will not s your foot against
26:31 " 'I will s the shepherd,
1Co 9:27 I s a blow to my body and make it

STRIPS
Jn 20: 5 in at the s of linen lying there

STRIVE* (STRIFE STRIVING)
Ac 24:16 So I s always to keep my
2Co 13:11 S for full restoration, encourage
1Th 5:15 always s to do what is good
1Ti 4:10 That is why we labor and s,

STRIVING (STRIVE)
Php 1:27 s together with one accord for

STROKE (STRIKE)
Mt 5:18 letter, not the least s of a pen,

STRONG (STRENGTH STRENGTHEN STRENGTHENED STRONGER)
Dt 3: 24 your greatness and your s hand.
31: 6 Be s and courageous. Do not
Jos 1: 6 Be s and courageous, because you
Jdg 5:21 March on, my soul; be s!
2Sa 10:12 Be s, and let us fight bravely for our
1Ki 2: 2 "So be s, act like a man,
1Ch 28:20 his son, "Be s and courageous,
2Ch 32: 7 "Be s and courageous. Do not be
Ps 24: 8 The LORD s and mighty,
31: 2 of refuge, a s fortress to save me.
Pr 31:17 her arms are s for her tasks.
Ecc 9:11 not to the swift or the battle to the s,
SS 8: 6 for love is as s as death, its jealousy
Isa 35: 4 fearful hearts, "Be s, do not fear;
53:12 he will divide the spoils with the s,
Jer 9:23 or the s boast of their strength
50:34 Yet their Redeemer is s;
Hag 2: 4 Be s, all you people of the land,'
Mt 12:29 can anyone enter a man's house
Lk 2:40 And the child grew and became s;
Ro 15: 1 We who are s ought to bear
1Co 1:27 things of the world to shame the s.
16:13 in the faith; be courageous; be s.
2Co 12:10 For when I am weak, then I am s.
Eph 6:10 be s in the Lord and in his mighty
2Ti 2: 1 be s in the grace that is in Christ
1Pe 5:10 himself restore you and make you s,

STRONGER (STRONG)
Dt 4:38 you nations greater and s than you
1Co 1:25 of God is s than human strength.

STRONGHOLD (STRONGHOLDS)
2Sa 22: 3 He is my s, my refuge and my
Ps 9: 9 oppressed, a s in times of trouble.
18: 2 and the horn of my salvation, my s.
27: 1 The LORD is the s of my life—
144: 2 my fortress, my s and my deliverer,

STRONGHOLDS (STRONGHOLD)
Zep 3: 6 their s are demolished.
2Co 10: 4 have divine power to demolish s.

STRUGGLE (STRUGGLED)
Ro 15:30 join me in my s by praying to God
Eph 6:12 For our s is not against flesh
Heb 12: 1 In your s against sin, you have not

STRUGGLED (STRUGGLE)
Ge 32:28 because you have s with God

STUDENTS (STUDY)
Mt 10:24 "S are not above their teacher,

STUDY* (STUDENTS)
Ezr 7:10 Ezra had devoted himself to the s
Ecc 1:13 applied my mind to s and to explore
12:12 and much s wearies the body.
Jn 5:39 You s the Scriptures diligently

STUMBLE (STUMBLES STUMBLING)
Ps 37:24 though they s, they will not fall,
119:165 and nothing can make them s.
Pr 3:23 in safety, and your foot will not s.
24:17 when they s, do not let your heart
Isa 8:14 be a stone that causes people to s
Jer 13:16 before your feet s on the darkening
31: 9 a level path where they will not s,
Eze 7:19 for it has caused them to s into sin.
Hos 14: 9 them, but the rebellious s in them.
Mal 2: 8 teaching have caused many to s;
Mt 18: 6 those who believe in me—to s,
Mk 9:43 If your hand causes you to s,
Lk 17: 1 "Things that cause people to s
Jn 11: 9 who walk in the daytime will not s,
11:10 walk at night that they s,
Ro 9:33 Zion a stone that causes people to s
14:20 that causes someone else to s.
1Co 10:32 Do not cause anyone to s,
Jas 3: 2 We all s in many ways.
1Pe 2: 8 "A stone that causes people to s
1Jn 2:10 is nothing in them to make them s.

STUMBLES (STUMBLE)
Jas 2:10 yet s at just one point is guilty

STUMBLING (STUMBLE)
Lev 19:14 or put a s block in front of the blind,
Ps 56:13 me from death and my feet from s,
Mt 16:23 You are a s block to me; you do not
Ro 9:32 They stumbled over the s stone.
11: 9 a s block and a retribution for them.
14:13 up your mind not to put any s block
1Co 1:23 a s block to Jews and foolishness
8: 9 rights does not become a s block
2Co 6: 3 We put no s block in anyone's path,
Jude : 24 able to keep you from s

STUMP
Isa 6:13 so the holy seed will be the s
11: 1 will come up from the s of Jesse;

STUPID
Pr 12: 1 but whoever hates correction is s.
2Ti 2:23 to do with foolish and s arguments,

STUPOR
Ro 11: 8 "God gave them a spirit of s,

SUBDUE (SUBDUED)
Ge 1:28 fill the earth and s it.

SUBDUED (SUBDUE)
Jos 10:40 So Joshua s the whole region,
Ps 47: 3 He s nations under us,

SUBJECT (SUBJECTED)
Mt 5:22 or sister will be s to judgment.
Ro 13: 1 everyone be s to the governing
1Co 14:32 of prophets are s to the control
15:28 the Son himself will be made s
Tit 2: 5 and to be s to their husbands,
2: 9 Teach slaves to be s to their masters
3: 1 Remind the people to be s to rulers

SUBJECTED (SUBJECT)
Ro 8:20 For the creation was s to frustration,

SUBMISSION (SUBMIT)
1Co 14:34 but must be in s, as the law says.
1Ti 2:11 should learn in quietness and full s.

SUBMISSIVE* (SUBMIT)
Jas 3:17 considerate, s, full of mercy

SUBMIT (SUBMISSION SUBMISSIVE SUBMITS)
Pr 3: 6 in all your ways s to him,
Ro 13: 5 it is necessary to s to the authorities,
1Co 16:16 to s to such as these and to everyone
Eph 5:21 S to one another out of reverence
Col 3:18 s yourselves to your husbands, as is
Heb 12: 9 How much more should we s
13:17 your leaders and s to their authority,
Jas 4: 7 S yourselves, then, to God.
1Pe 2:18 reverent fear of God s yourselves
3: 1 Wives, in the same way s yourselves
5: 5 s yourselves to your elders.

SUBMITS* (SUBMIT)
Eph 5:24 Now as the church s to Christ,

SUBTRACT*
Dt 4: 2 command you and do not s from it,

SUCCEED (SUCCESS SUCCESSFUL)
Ps 20: 4 heart and make all your plans s.
Pr 15:22 but with many advisers they s.
21:30 plan that can s against the LORD.

SUCCESS (SUCCEED)
Ge 39:23 and gave him s in whatever he did.
1Sa 18:14 In everything he did he had great s,
1Ch 22:18 S, s to you, and s to those who help
22:13 you will have s if you are careful
2Ch 26: 5 the LORD, God gave him s.
Ecc 10:10 is needed, but skill will bring s.

SUCCESSFUL (SUCCEED)
Jos 1: 7 that you may be s wherever you go.
2Ki 18: 7 he was s in whatever he undertook.
2Ch 20:20 in his prophets and you will be s."

SUFFER (SUFFERED SUFFERING SUFFERINGS SUFFERS)
Job 36:15 But those who s he delivers in their
Isa 53:10 to crush him and cause him to s,
Mk 8:31 the Son of Man must s many things
Lk 24:26 the Messiah have to s these things
24:46 The Messiah will s and rise
2Co 1: 6 of the same sufferings we s.
Php 1:29 on him, but also to s for him,
Heb 9:26 to s many times since the creation
1Pe 3:17 to s for doing good than for doing
4:16 if you s as a Christian, do not

SUFFERED (SUFFER)
Isa 53:11 After he has s, he will see
Heb 2: 9 and honor because he s death,
2:10 perfect through what he s.
2:18 Because he himself s when he was
10:34 You s along with those in prison
1Pe 2:21 called, because Christ s for you,
3:18 For Christ also s once for sins,
4: 1 because those who have s in their

SUFFERING (SUFFER)
Job 36:15 who suffer he delivers in their s;
Ps 22:24 or scorned the s of the afflicted one;
Isa 53: 3 a man of s, and familiar with pain.
La 1:12 Is any s like my s that was inflicted
Ac 5:41 been counted worthy of s disgrace
Ro 5: 3 know that s produces perseverance,
2Ti 1: 8 But join with me in s for the gospel,
2: 3 Join with me in s,
Heb 13: 3 as if you yourselves were s.

SUFFERINGS (SUFFER)
Ro 5: 3 but we also glory in our s,
8:17 if indeed we share in his s in order
8:18 that our present s are not worth
2Co 1: 5 share abundantly in the s of Christ,
Php 3:10 and participation in his s,
1Pe 4:13 as you participate in the s of Christ,
5: 9 are undergoing the same kind of s.

SUFFERS* (SUFFER)
Pr 13:20 for a companion of fools s harm.
1Co 12:26 If one part s, every part s with it;

SUFFICIENT
2Co 12: 9 said to me, "My grace is s for you,

SUITABLE
Ge 2:18 I will make a helper s for him."

SUMMED* (SUMS)
Ro 13: 9 are s up in this one command:

SUMMONS
Ps 50: 1 s the earth from the rising of the sun
Isa 45: 3 God of Israel, who s you by name.

SUMS* (SUMMED)
Mt 7: 12 to you, for this s up the Law

SUN (SUNRISE)
Jos 10: 13 So the s stood still, and the moon
Jdg 5: 31 may all who love you be like the s
Ps 84: 11 For the LORD God is a s
121: 6 the s will not harm you by day,
136: 8 the s to govern the day,
Pr 4: 18 righteous is like the morning's,
Ecc 1: 9 there is nothing new under the s.
Isa 60: 19 The s will no more be your light
Mal 4: 2 the s of righteousness will rise
Mt 5: 45 He causes his s to rise on the evil
13: 43 the righteous will shine like the s
17: 2 His face shone like the s, and his
Lk 23: 45 for the s stopped shining.
Eph 4: 26 Do not let the s go down while you
Rev 1: 16 His face was like the s shining in all
21: 23 The city does not need the s

SUNG (SING)
Mt 26: 30 When they had a hymn, they went

SUNRISE (SUN)
2Sa 23: 4 light of morning at s on a cloudless
Hab 3: 4 His splendor was like the s;

SUPERIOR
Ro 11: 25 that you may not think you are s:
Heb 1: 4 So he became as much s
8: 6 ministry Jesus has received is as s

SUPERVISION
Gal 3: 25 we are no longer under the s

SUPPER
Lk 22: 20 after the s he took the cup, saying,
1Co 11: 25 after s he took the cup, saying,
Rev 19: 9 to the wedding s of the Lamb!' "

SUPPLIED (SUPPLY)
Ac 20: 34 hands of mine have s my own needs
Php 4: 18 I am amply s, now that I have

SUPPLY (SUPPLIED SUPPLYING)
2Co 8: 14 your plenty will s what they need,
1Th 3: 10 and s what is lacking in your faith.

SUPPLYING* (SUPPLY)
2Co 9: 12 you perform is not only s the needs

SUPPORT (SUPPORTED SUPPORTING)
Ps 18: 18 disaster, but the LORD was my s.
Ro 11: 18 You do not s the root, but the root
1Co 9: 12 others have this right of s from you,

SUPPORTED (SUPPORT)
Ps 94: 18 your unfailing love, LORD, s me.
Col 2: 19 s and held together by its ligaments

SUPPORTING (SUPPORT)
Eph 4: 16 held together by every s ligament,

SUPPRESS*
Ro 1: 18 of human beings who s the truth

SUPREMACY*
Col 1: 18 in everything he might have the s.

SURE
Nu 28: 31 Be s the animals are without defect.
32: 23 you may be s that your sin will find
Dt 6: 17 Be s to keep the commands
14: 22 Be s to set aside a tenth of all
29: 18 make s there is no root among you
Jos 23: 13 you may be s that the LORD your
1Sa 12: 24 But be s to fear the LORD
Ps 19: 7 The ordinances of the LORD are s,
132: 11 a s oath that he will not revoke;
Pr 27: 23 Be s you know the condition
Isa 28: 16 cornerstone for a s foundation;
Eph 5: 5 For of this you can be s:
Heb 11: 1 Now faith is being s of what we

SURPASS* (SURPASSED SURPASSES SURPASSING)
Pr 31: 29 noble things, but you s them all."

SURPASSED* (SURPASS)
Jn 1: 15 me has s me because he was before
1: 30 me has s me because he was before

SURPASSES* (SURPASS)
Ps 138: 2 solemn decree that it s your fame.
Pr 8: 19 what I yield s choice silver.
Mt 5: 20 that unless your righteousness s
Eph 3: 19 to know this love that s knowledge—

SURPASSING* (SURPASS)
Ps 150: 2 praise him for his s greatness.
2Co 3: 10 now in comparison with the s glory.
9: 14 of the s grace God has given you.
Php 3: 8 a loss because of the s worth

SURPRISE (SURPRISED)
1Th 5: 4 this day should s you like a thief.

SURPRISED (SURPRISE)
1Pe 4: 4 They are s that you do not
4: 12 do not be s at the fiery ordeal
1Jn 3: 13 Do not be s, my brothers and sisters,

SURROUND (SURROUNDED SURROUNDS)
Ps 5: 12 you s them with your favor as
32: 7 and s me with songs of deliverance.
89: 7 more awesome than all who s him.
125: 2 As the mountains s Jerusalem,

SURROUNDED (SURROUND)
Heb 12: 1 since we are s by such a great cloud

SURROUNDS* (SURROUND)
Ps 32: 10 unfailing love s those who trust
89: 8 mighty, and your faithfulness s you.
125: 2 so the LORD s his people both

SUSA
Ezr 4: 9 and Babylon, the Elamites of S,
Ne 1: 1 year, while I was in the citadel of S,

SUSPENDS*
Job 26: 7 he s the earth over nothing.

SUSPICIONS*
1Ti 6: 4 in envy, strife, malicious talk, evil s

SUSTAIN (SUSTAINING SUSTAINS)
Ps 55: 22 on the LORD and he will s you;
Isa 46: 4 I am he, I am he who will s you.

SUSTAINING* (SUSTAIN)
Heb 1: 3 s all things by his powerful word.

SUSTAINS (SUSTAIN)
Ps 18: 35 shield, and your right hand s me;
146: 9 the foreigner and s the fatherless
147: 6 The LORD s the humble but casts
Isa 50: 4 to know the word that s the weary.

SWALLOW (SWALLOWED)
Isa 25: 8 he will s up death forever.
Jnh 1: 17 provided a huge fish to s Jonah,
Mt 23: 24 You strain out a gnat but s a camel.

SWALLOWED (SWALLOW)
1Co 15: 54 "Death has been s up in victory."
2Co 5: 4 so that what is mortal may be s

SWAYED
Mt 11: 7 A reed s by the wind?
22: 16 You aren't s by others, because you
2Ti 3: 6 and are s by all kinds of evil desires,

SWEAR (SWORE SWORN)
Lev 19: 12 " 'Do not s falsely by my name
Nu 24: 4 trust in an idol or s by a false god.
Isa 45: 23 by me every tongue will s.
Mt 5: 34 I tell you, do not s an oath at all:
Jas 5: 12 my brothers and sisters, do not s—

SWEAT*
Ge 3: 19 the s of your brow you will eat your
Lk 22: 44 his s was like drops of blood falling

SWEET (SWEETER SWEETNESS)
Job 20: 12 "Though evil is s in his mouth
Ps 119:103 How s are your words to my taste,
Pr 9: 17 "Stolen water is s; food eaten
13: 19 A longing fulfilled is s to the soul,
16: 24 s to the soul and healing
20: 17 Food gained by fraud tastes s,
Ecc 5: 12 The sleep of laborers is s,
Isa 5: 20 who put bitter for s and s for sweet.
Eze 3: 3 it tasted as s as honey in my mouth.
Rev 10: 10 It tasted as s as honey in my mouth,

SWEETER (SWEET)
Ps 19: 10 they are s than honey, than honey
119:103 my taste, s than honey to my mouth!

SWEETNESS* (SWEET)
SS 4: 11 Your lips drop s as the honeycomb,
5: 16 His mouth is s itself;

SWEPT
Mt 12: 44 s clean and put in order.

SWIFT
Pr 1: 16 into evil, they are s to shed blood.
Ecc 9: 11 The race is not to the s or the battle
Isa 59: 7 they are s to shed innocent blood.

Ro 3: 15 "Their feet are s to shed blood;
2Pe 2: 1 bringing s destruction

SWINDLERS*
1Co 5: 10 or the greedy and s, or idolaters.
5: 11 or slanderers, drunkards or s.
6: 10 nor slanderers nor s will inherit

SWORD (SWORDS)
Ge 3: 24 and a flaming s flashing back
Dt 32: 41 when I sharpen my flashing s
Jos 5: 13 of him with a drawn s in his hand.
1Sa 17: 45 "You come against me with s
17: 47 here will know that it is not by s
31: 4 so Saul took his own s and fell on it.
2Sa 12: 9 The s will never depart from your
Ps 44: 6 my s does not bring me victory;
45: 3 Gird your s on your side,
Isa 2: 4 will not take up s against nation,
Mic 4: 3 will not take up s against nation,
Mt 10: 34 did not come to bring peace, but a s.
Lk 2: 35 a s will pierce your own soul too."
Ro 13: 4 for rulers do not bear the s for no
Eph 6: 17 of salvation and the s of the Spirit,
Heb 4: 12 Sharper than any double-edged s,
Rev 1: 16 mouth was a sharp, double-edged s.
19: 15 of his mouth is a sharp s

SWORDS (SWORD)
Ps 64: 3 They sharpen their tongues like s
Pr 12: 18 words of the reckless pierce like s,
Isa 2: 4 They will beat their s
Joel 3: 10 Beat your plowshares into s

SWORE (SWEAR)
Heb 6: 13 him to swear by, he s by himself,

SWORN (SWEAR)
Ps 110: 4 The LORD has s and will not
Eze 20: 42 the land I had s with uplifted hand
Heb 7: 21 "The LORD has s and will not

SYCAMORE-FIG (FIG)
Am 7: 14 and I also took care of s trees.
Lk 19: 4 and climbed a s tree to see him,

SYMBOLIZES*
Nu 6: 9 the hair that s their dedication,
6: 18 the hair that s their dedication,
6: 19 the hair that s their dedication,
1Pe 3: 21 this water s baptism that now saves

SYMPATHETIC* (SYMPATHY)
1Pe 3: 8 like-minded, be s, love one another,

SYMPATHY (SYMPATHETIC)
Ps 69: 20 I looked for s, but there was none,

SYNAGOGUE
Lk 4: 16 the Sabbath day he went into the s,
Ac 17: 2 Paul went into the s, and on three

TABERNACLE (TABERNACLES)
Ex 40: 34 the glory of the LORD filled the t.
Heb 8: 2 the true t set up by the Lord,
9: 11 more perfect t that is not made
9: 21 sprinkled with the blood both the t
Rev 15: 5 that is, the t of the covenant law—

TABERNACLES (TABERNACLE)
Lev 23: 34 the LORD's Festival of T begins,
Dt 16: 16 of Weeks and the Festival of T
Zec 14: 16 and to celebrate the Festival of T.

TABLE (TABLES)
Ex 25: 23 "Make a t of acacia wood—
Ps 23: 5 You prepare a t before me

TABLES (TABLE)
Jn 2: 15 changers and overturned their t.
Ac 6: 2 word of God in order to wait on t.

TABLET (TABLETS)
Pr 3: 3 write them on the t of your heart.
7: 3 write them on the t of your heart.

TABLETS (TABLET)
Ex 31: 18 Sinai, he gave him the two t
31: 18 the t of stone inscribed by the finger
Dt 10: 5 and put the t in the ark I had made,
2Co 3: 3 not on t of stone but on t of human

TAKE (TAKEN TAKES TAKING TOOK)
Ge 15: 7 give you this land to t possession
22: 17 Your descendants will t possession
Ex 3: 5 "Take off your sandals, for the place
21: 23 injury, you are to t life for life,
22: 22 "Do not t advantage of a widow
Lev 10: 17 to you to t away the guilt
25: 14 do not t advantage of each other.

Nu 13:30 go up and t possession of the land,
Dt 1: 8 t possession of the land the LORD
12:32 do not add to it or t away from it.
31:26 "T this Book of the Law and place
1Sa 8:11 He will t your sons and make them
1Ch 17:13 I will never t my love away
Job 23:10 But he knows the way that I t;
Ps 2:12 Blessed are all who t refuge in him.
25:18 my distress and t away all my sins.
27:14 be strong and t heart and wait
31:24 Be strong and t heart, all you who
34: 8 blessed are those who t refuge in him.
36: 7 People t refuge in the shadow
49:17 for they will t nothing with them
51:11 or t your Holy Spirit from me.
73:24 afterward you will t me into glory.
118: 8 It is better to t refuge in the LORD
Pr 22:23 for the LORD will t up their case
25: 9 If you t your neighbor to court,
Isa 62: 1 for the LORD will t delight in you,
Eze 3:10 t to heart all the words I speak
33:11 I t no pleasure in the death
Mt 10:38 Whoever does not t up their cross
11:29 T my yoke upon you and learn
16:24 deny themselves and t up their cross
26:26 to his disciples, saying, "T and eat;
26:39 possible, may this cup be t from me.
Mk 16:19 *he was t up into heaven*
Ac 1: 9 he was t up before their very eyes,
1Ti 3:16 on in the world, was t up in glory.

TAKES (TAKE)
1Ki 20:11 not boast like one who t it off.' "
Lk 6:30 and if anyone t what belongs to you,
Jn 1:29 who t away the sin of the world!
10:18 No one t it from me, but I lay it
Rev 22:19 if any one of you t words away

TAKING (TAKE)
Php 2: 7 himself nothing by t the very nature

**TALES*
1Ti 4: 7 with godless myths and old wives' t;

TALL
1Ch 11:23 an Egyptian who was five cubits t.

TAMAR
1. Wife of Judah's sons Er and Onan (Ge 38:1-10). Tricked Judah into fathering children when he refused her his third son (Ge 38:11-30).
2. Daughter of David, raped by Amnon (2Sa 13).

TAME* (TAMED)
Jas 3: 8 but no one can t the tongue. It is

TAMED* (TAME)
Jas 3: 7 sea creatures are being t and have been t

TARSHISH
Jnh 1: 3 from the LORD and headed for T.

TARSUS
Ac 9:11 ask for a man from T named Saul,

TASK (TASKS)
1Ch 29: 1 The t is great, because this palatial
Mk 13:34 each with an assigned t, and tells
Ac 20:24 complete the t the Lord Jesus has
1Co 3: 5 the Lord has assigned to each his t.
2Co 2:16 And who is equal to such a t?
1Ti 3: 1 to be an overseer desires a noble t.

TASKS (TASK)
Pr 31:17 her arms are strong for her t.

TASTE (TASTED TASTY)
Ps 34: 8 T and see that the LORD is good;
119:103 How sweet are your words to my t,
Pr 24:13 from the comb is sweet to your t.
SS 2: 3 shade, and his fruit is sweet to my t.
Col 2:21 Do not t! Do not touch!"?
Heb 2: 9 God he might t death for everyone.

TASTED (TASTE)
Eze 3: 3 it t as sweet as honey in my mouth.

1Pe 2: 3 you have t that the Lord is good.
Rev 10:10 It t as sweet as honey in my mouth,

TASTY (TASTE)
Ge 27: 4 Prepare me the kind of t food I like

**TATTOO*
Lev 19:28 dead or put t marks on yourselves.

TAUGHT (TEACH)
2Ki 17:28 t them how to worship the LORD.
2Ch 17: 9 They t throughout Judah,
Ps 119:102 laws, for you yourself have t me.
Pr 4: 4 Then he t me, and he said to me,
31: 1 inspired utterance his mother t him.
Isa 29:13 human rules they have been t.
50: 4 my ear to listen like one being t.
Mt 7:29 because he t as one who had
Ac 20:20 to you but have t you publicly
1Co 2:13 wisdom but in words t by the Spirit,
Gal 1:12 any human source, nor was I t it;
1Ti 1:20 to Satan to be t not to blaspheme.
1Jn 2:27 just as it has t you, remain in him.

TAX (TAXES)
Mt 11:19 a friend of t collectors and sinners.'
17:24 your teacher pay the temple t?"
22:17 to pay the imperial t to Caesar

TAXES (TAX)
Ro 13: 7 If you owe t, pay t;

TEACH (TAUGHT TEACHER TEACHERS TEACHES TEACHING TEACHINGS)
Ex 4:12 speak and will t you what to say."
18:20 T them his decrees and instructions,
33:13 t me your ways so I may know you
Lev 10:11 and so you can t the Israelites all
Dt 4: 9 T them to your children and to their
6: 1 your God directed me to t you
8: 3 to t you that people do not live
11:19 T them to your children,
1Sa 12:23 I will t you the way that is good
1Ki 8:36 T them the right way to live,
Job 12: 7 and they will t you, or the birds
Ps 32: 8 and t you in the way you should go;
34:11 I will t you the fear of the LORD.
51:13 I will t transgressors your ways,
78: 5 our ancestors to t their children,
90:12 T us to number our days, that we
119:33 T me, LORD, the way of your
143:10 T me to do your will, for you are my
Pr 9: 9 t the righteous and they will add
Jer 31:34 longer will they t their neighbors,
Mic 4: 2 that we may walk in his ways, so that we
Lk 11: 1 "Lord, t us to pray, just as John
12:12 for the Holy Spirit will t you
Jn 14:26 will t you all things and will remind
Ro 2:21 you, then, who t others, do you not t
15: 4 in the past was written to us,
1Ti 2:12 I do not permit a woman to t
3: 2 respectable, hospitable, able to t,
2Ti 2: 2 will also be qualified to t others.
2:24 to everyone, able to t, not resentful.
Tit 2: 1 must t what is appropriate to sound
2:15 then, are the things you should t.
Heb 8:11 longer will they t their neighbors,
Jas 3: 1 that we who t will be judged more
1Jn 2:27 you do not need anyone to t you.

TEACHER (TEACH)
Ecc 1: 1 The words of the T, son of David,
Mt 10:24 "Students are not above their t,
13:52 "Therefore every t of the law who
23:10 Nor are you to be called 't,' for you have one T, the Messiah.
Lk 6:40 Students are not above their t,
Jn 3: 2 know that you are a t who has
13:14 your Lord and T, have washed your
1Co 1:20 Where is the t of the law?

TEACHERS (TEACH)
Ps 119:99 I have more insight than all my t,
Pr 5:13 I would not obey my t or turn my
Lk 20:46 "Beware of the t of the law.
1Co 12:28 prophets, third t, then miracles,
Eph 4:11 the evangelists, the pastors and t,
2Ti 4: 3 around them a great number of t
Heb 5:12 by this time you ought to be t,
Jas 3: 1 many of you should presume to be t,
2Pe 2: 1 as there will be false t among you.

TEACHES (TEACH)
Ps 25: 9 in what is right and t them his way.
94:10 Does he who t human beings lack
Isa 48:17 who t you what is best for you,

Mt 5:19 and t these commands will be called
1Ti 6: 3 If anyone t otherwise and does not
Tit 2:12 It t us to say "No" to ungodliness
1Jn 2:27 But as his anointing t you about all

TEACHING (TEACH)
Ezr 7:10 to t its decrees and laws in Israel.
Pr 1: 8 and not forsake your mother's t.
3: 1 do not forget my t, but keep my
6:23 command is a lamp, this t is a light,
Mt 28:20 t them to obey everything I have
Lk 4:15 He was t in their synagogues,
Jn 7:17 out whether my t comes from God
8:31 "If you hold to my t, you are really
14:23 who loves me will obey my t.
Ac 2:42 devoted themselves to the apostles' t
Ro 12: 7 if it is t, then teach;
Eph 4:14 there by every wind of t
2Th 3: 6 live according to the t you received
1Ti 4:13 of Scripture, to preaching and to t.
5:17 whose work is preaching and t.
6: 3 our Lord Jesus Christ and to godly t,
2Ti 3:16 is God-breathed and is useful for t,
Tit 1:11 by t things they ought not to teach—
2: 7 In your t show integrity,
Heb 5:13 with the t about righteousness.
2Jn : 9 in the t of Christ does not have God;

TEACHINGS (TEACH)
Pr 7: 2 guard my t as the apple of your eye.
2Th 2:15 hold fast to the t we passed
Heb 6: 1 let us move beyond the elementary t

TEAR (TEARS)
Rev 7:17 God will wipe away every t
21: 4 'He will wipe every t from their

TEARING
2Co 10: 8 up rather than t you down,

TEARS (TEAR)
Ps 126: 5 Those who sow with t will reap
Isa 25: 8 LORD will wipe away the t
Jer 31:16 from weeping and your eyes from t,
50: 4 of Judah together will go in t to seek
Lk 7:38 she began to wet his feet with her t.
2Co 2: 4 anguish of heart and with many t,
Php 3:18 and now tell you again even with t,

TEETH (TOOTH)
Job 19:20 escaped only by the skin of my t.
Ps 35:16 they gnashed their t at me.
Jer 31:29 and the children's t are set on edge.'
Mt 8:12 will be weeping and gnashing of t."

TEMPER* (EVEN-TEMPERED HOT-TEMPERED QUICK-TEMPERED)
1Sa 20: 7 But if he loses his t,

TEMPERANCE See SELF-CONTROL

**TEMPERATE*
1Ti 3: 2 reproach, faithful to his wife, t,
3:11 not malicious talkers but t
Tit 2: 2 Teach the older men to be t,

TEMPEST
Ps 50: 3 and around him a t rages.
55: 8 shelter, far from the t and storm."

TEMPLE (TEMPLES)
1Ki 6: 1 began to build the t of the LORD.
6:38 the t was finished in all its details
8:10 the cloud filled the t of the LORD.
8:27 How much less this t I have built!
2Ch 36:19 They set fire to God's t and broke
36:23 appointed me to build a t for him
Ezr 6:14 finished building the t according
Ps 27: 4 the LORD and to seek him in his t.
Isa 6: 1 and the train of his robe filled the t.
Eze 10: 4 The cloud filled the t, and the court
43: 4 LORD entered the t through
Hab 2:20 The LORD is in his holy t;
Mt 12: 6 that one greater than the t is here.
26:61 'I am able to destroy the t of God
27:51 moment the curtain of the t was torn
Lk 21: 5 about how the t was adorned
Jn 2:14 t courts he found people selling
1Co 3:16 that you yourselves are God's t
2Co 6:16 For we are the t of the living God.
Rev 21:22 I did not see a t in the city,

TEMPLES (TEMPLE)
Ac 17:24 and does not live in t built by hands.
1Co 6:19 your bodies are t of the Holy Spirit,

TEMPORARY
2Co 4:18 since what is seen is t, but what is

TEMPT* (TEMPTATION TEMPTED TEMPTER TEMPTING)
1Co   7:   5   Satan will not t you because of your
Jas   1: 13   by evil, nor does he t anyone;

TEMPTATION* (TEMPT)
Mt   6: 13   And lead us not into t, but deliver us
    26: 41   pray so that you will not fall into t.
Mk 14: 38   pray so that you will not fall into t.
Lk 11:   4   And lead us not into t.' "
    22: 40   "Pray that you will not fall into t."
    22: 46   pray so that you will not fall into t."
1Co 10: 13   No t has overtaken you except what
1Ti   6:   9   who want to get rich fall into t

TEMPTED* (TEMPT)
Mt   4:   1   the wilderness to be t by the devil.
Mk   1: 13   forty days, being t by Satan.
Lk   4:   2   for forty days he was t by the devil.
1Co 10: 13   not let you be t beyond what you
    10: 13   But when you are t, he will
Gal   6:   1   yourselves, or you also may be t.
1Th   3:   5   in some way the tempter had t you
Heb   2: 18   he himself suffered when he was t,
    2: 18   able to help those who are being t.
    4: 15   but we have one who has been t
Jas   1: 13   When I, no one should say, "God is
    1: 13   For God cannot be t by evil,
    1: 14   you is t when you are dragged away

TEMPTER* (TEMPT)
Mt   4:   3   The t came to him and said, "If you
1Th   3:   5   in some way the t had tempted you

TEMPTING* (TEMPT)
Lk   4: 13   the devil had finished all this t,
Jas   1: 13   no one should say, "God is t me."

TEN (TENTH TITHE TITHES)
Ex 34: 28   the T Commandments.
Lev 26:   8   of you will chase t thousand,
Dt   4: 13   his covenant, the T Commandments,
    10:   4   the T Commandments he had
Ps 91:   7   side, t thousand at your right hand,
Da   7: 24   The t horns are kings who will
Mt 25:   1   will be like t virgins who took their
    25: 28   give it to the one who has t bags.
Lk 15:   8   suppose a woman has t silver coins
Rev 12:   3   dragon with seven heads and t horns

TENANTS
Mt 21: 34   servants to the t to collect his fruit.

TEND
Jer 23:   2   to the shepherds who t my people:
Eze 34: 14   I will t them in a good pasture,

TENDERNESS
Isa 63: 15   Your t and compassion are withheld
Php   2:   1   the Spirit, if any t and compassion,

TENT (TENTMAKER TENTS)
Ex 27: 21   In the t of meeting,
    40:   2   up the tabernacle, the t of meeting,
Isa 54:   2   "Enlarge the place of your t,
2Co   5:   1   that if the earthly t we live in is
2Pe   1: 13   as long as I live in the t of this body,

TENTH (TEN)
Ge 14: 20   Abram gave him a t of everything.
Nu 18: 26   you must present a t of that tithe as
Dt 14: 22   Be sure to set aside a t of all
1Sa   8: 15   He will take a t of your grain
Lk 11: 42   because you give God a t of your
    18: 12   a week and give a t of all I get.'
Heb   7:   4   the patriarch Abraham gave him a t

TENTMAKER* (TENT)
Ac 18:   3   and because he was a t as they were,

TENTS (TENT)
Ge 13: 12   plain and pitched his t near Sodom.
Ps 84: 10   than dwell in the t of the wicked.

TERAH
Ge 11: 31   T took his son Abram, his grandson

TERRIBLE (TERROR)
2Ti   3:   1   There will be t times in the last

TERRIFIED (TERROR)
Dt   7: 21   Do not be t by them, for the LORD
    20:   3   do not be t or give way to panic
Ps 90:   7   anger and t by your indignation.
Mt 14: 26   walking on the lake, they were t.
    17:   6   they fell facedown to the ground, t.
    27: 54   they were t, and exclaimed,
Mk   4: 41   They were t and asked each other,

TERRIFYING (TERROR)
Heb 12: 21   The sight was so t that Moses said,

TERRITORY
2Co 10: 16   already done in someone else's t.

TERROR (TERRIBLE TERRIFIED TERRIFYING)
Dt   2: 25   very day I will begin to put the t
    28: 67   of the t that will fill your hearts
Job   9: 34   his t would frighten me no more.
Ps 91:   5   You will not fear the t of night,
Pr 21: 15   to the righteous but t to evildoers.
Isa 13:   8   T will seize them, pain and anguish
    24: 17   T and pit and snare await you,
    51: 13   live in constant t every day because
    54: 14   T will be far removed; it will not
Lk 21: 26   People will faint from t,
Ro 13:   3   rulers hold no t for those who do

TEST (TESTED TESTING TESTS)
Dt   6: 16   your God to the t as you did
Jdg   3:   1   to t all those Israelites who had not
1Ki 10:   1   she came to t Solomon with hard
1Ch 29: 17   that you t the heart and are pleased
Ps 26:   2   T me, LORD, and try me,
    78: 18   to the t by demanding the food they
    106: 14   the wilderness they put God to the t.
    139: 23   t me and know my anxious
Jer 11: 20   judge righteously and t the heart
Lk   4: 12   put the Lord your God to the t.' "
Ac   5:   9   could you conspire to t the Spirit
Ro 12:   2   you will be able to t and approve
1Co   3: 13   and the fire will t the quality of each
    10:   9   We should not t Christ, as some
2Co 13:   5   unless, of course, you fail the t?
1Th   5: 21   but t them all; hold on to what is
Jas   1: 12   because when they have stood the t,
1Pe   4: 12   ordeal that has come on you to t you,
1Jn   4:   1   t the spirits to see whether they are

TESTED (TEST)
Ge 22:   1   Some time later God t Abraham.
Job 23: 10   when he has t me, I will come forth
    34: 36   that Job might be t to the utmost
Ps 66: 10   For you, God, t us; you refined us
Pr 27: 21   but people are t by their praise.
Isa 28: 16   I lay a stone in Zion, a t stone,
    48: 10   I have t you in the furnace
1Ti   3: 10   They must first be t;
Heb 11: 17   when God t him, offered Isaac as

TESTIFIES (TESTIFY)
Jn   5: 32   There is another who t in my favor,
Ro   8: 16   The Spirit himself t with our spirit

TESTIFY (TESTIFIES TESTIMONY)
Pr 24: 28   Do not t against your neighbor
Jn   1:   7   came as a witness to t concerning
    1: 34   I t that this is God's Chosen One."
    5: 39   These are the very Scriptures that t
    7:   7   it hates me because I t that its works
    15: 26   from the Father—he will t about me.
Ac   4: 33   power the apostles continued to t
    10: 43   All the prophets t about him
1Jn   4: 14   t that the Father has sent his Son
    5:   7   For there are three that t:

TESTIMONY (TESTIFY)
Ex 20: 16   shall not give false t against your
Nu 35: 30   murderer only on the t of witnesses.
Dt 19: 18   proves to be a liar, giving false t,
Isa   8: 20   instruction and the t of warning.
Mt 15: 19   immorality, theft, false t, slander.
    24: 14   the whole world as a t to all nations,
Lk 18: 20   you shall not give false t,'
Jn   2: 25   He did not need human t
    21: 24   We know that his t is true.
2Ti   1:   8   ashamed of the t about our Lord
1Jn   5:   9   We accept human t, but God's t is greater
Rev 12: 11   the Lamb and by the word of their t;

TESTING (TEST)
Lk   8: 13   but in the time of t they fall away.
Heb   3:   8   rebellion, during the time of t
Jas   1:   3   that the t of your faith produces

TESTS (TEST)
Pr 17:   3   for gold, but the LORD t the heart.
1Th   2:   4   people but God, who t our hearts.

THADDAEUS
    Apostle (Mt 10:3; Mk 3:18); probably also known as Judas son of James (Lk 6:16; Ac 1:13).

THANK (THANKFUL THANKFULNESS THANKS THANKSGIVING)
Php   1:   3   I t my God every time I remember

1Th   3:   9   How can we t God enough for you

THANKFUL* (THANK)
Col   3: 15   you were called to peace. And be t.
    4:   2   to prayer, being watchful and t.
Heb 12: 28   let us be t, and so worship God

THANKFULNESS* (THANK)
Lev   7: 12   they offer it as an expression of t,
1Co 10: 30   If I take part in the meal with t,
Col   2:   7   were taught, and overflowing with t.

THANKS (THANK)
Ne 12: 31   assigned two large choirs to give t.
Ps   7: 17   I will give t to the LORD because
    35: 18   I will give you t in the great
    100:   4   give t to him and praise his name.
    107:   1   Give t to the LORD, for he is
    136:   1   Give t to the LORD, for he is
Ro   1: 21   glorified him as God nor gave t
1Co 11: 24   and when he had given t, he broke it
    15: 57   But t be to God! He gives us
2Co   2: 14   But t be to God, who always leads
    9: 15   T be to God for his indescribable
1Th   5: 18   give t in all circumstances;
Rev   4:   9   and t to him who sits on the throne

THANKSGIVING (THANK)
Ps 95:   2   Let us come before him with t
    100:   4   Enter his gates with t and his courts
1Co 10: 16   Is not the cup of t for which we give
Php   4:   6   with t, present your requests to God.
1Ti   4:   3   to be received with t by those who

THEFT (THIEF)
Mt 15: 19   adultery, sexual immorality, t,

THEFTS* (THIEF)
Rev   9: 21   their sexual immorality or their t.

THEME*
Ps 22: 25   From you comes the t of my praise
    45:   1   by a noble t as I recite my verses
    119: 54   Your decrees are the t of my song

THIEF (THEFT THEFTS THIEVES)
Pr   6: 30   People do not despise a t if he steals
Lk 12: 39   at what hour the t was coming,
1Th   5:   2   of the Lord will come like a t
1Pe   4: 15   it should not be as a murderer or t
Rev 16: 15   "Look, I come like a t!

THIEVES (THIEF)
Mt   6: 19   and where t break in and steal.
Jn 10:   8   All who have come before me are t
1Co   6: 10   nor t nor the greedy nor drunkards

THINK (THINKING THOUGHT THOUGHTS)
Ps 63:   6   I t of you through the watches
Isa 44: 19   No one stops to t, no one has
Mt 22: 42   "What do you t about the Messiah?
Ro 12:   3   Do not t of yourself more highly
Php   4:   8   t about such things.

THINKING (THINK)
Pr 23:   7   of person who is always t
1Co 14: 20   and sisters, stop t like children.
2Pe   3:   1   to stimulate you to wholesome t.

THIRST (THIRSTS THIRSTY)
Ps 69: 21   food and gave me vinegar for my t.
Mt   5:   6   who hunger and t for righteousness,
    4: 14   the water I give them will never t.
2Co 11: 27   I have known hunger and t and have
Rev   7: 16   never again will they t.

THIRSTS* (THIRST)
Ps 42:   2   My soul t for God, for the living

THIRSTY (THIRST)
Ps 107:   9   for he satisfies the t and fills
Pr 25: 21   if he is t, give him water to drink.
Isa 55:   1   all you who are t,
Mt 25: 35   I was t and you gave me something
Jn   7: 37   "Let anyone who is t come to me
Ro 12: 20   if he is t, give him something
Rev 21:   6   the t I will give water without cost
    22: 17   those who are t come; and let all

THOMAS
    Apostle (Mt 10:3; Mk 3:18; Lk 6:15; Jn 11:16; 14:5; 21:2; Ac 1:13). Doubted resurrection (Jn 20:24–28).

THONGS
Mk   1:   7   I, the t of whose sandals I am not

THORN (THORNBUSHES THORNS)
2Co 12:   7   I was given a t in my flesh,

THORNBUSHES (THORN)
Lk   6: 44   People do not pick figs from t,

THORNS (THORN)
Ge   3: 18   It will produce t and thistles for you,
Nu   33: 55   in your eyes and t in your sides.
Mt   13:   7   Other seed fell among t, which grew
     27: 29   twisted together a crown of t and set
Heb   6:   8   land that produces t and thistles is

THOUGHT (THINK)
1Ch   28:   9   understands every desire and every t.
Pr   4: 26   Give careful t to the paths for your
     14: 15   but the prudent give t to their steps.
     21: 29   but the upright give t to their ways.
1Co   13: 11   I talked like a child, I t like a child,

THOUGHTS (THINK)
Ps   139: 23   test me and know my anxious t.
Isa   55:   8   "For my t are not your t,
Mt   15: 19   For out of the heart come evil t,
1Co   2: 11   who knows a person's t except
Heb   4: 12   it judges the t and attitudes

THREATENED
Isa   38: 14   being t; Lord, come to my aid!"

THREE
Ge   6: 10   Noah had t sons: Shem,
Ex   23: 14   "T times a year you are to celebrate
Dt   19: 15   the testimony of two or t witnesses.
2Sa   23:   8   a Tahkemonite, was chief of the T;
Pr   30: 15   "There are t things that are never
     30: 18   "There are t things that are too
     30: 21   "Under t things the earth trembles,
     30: 29   "There are t things that are stately
Ecc   4: 12   of t strands is not quickly broken.
Da   3: 24   "Weren't there t men that we tied
Am   1:   3   "For t sins of Damascus,
Jnh   1: 17   belly of the fish t days and t nights.
Mt   12: 40   For as Jonah was t days and t nights
     12: 40   so the Son of Man will be t days
     12: 40   and t nights in the heart of the earth.
     17:   4   If you wish, I will put up t shelters—
     18: 20   two or t come together in my name,
     26: 34   you will disown me t times."
     26: 75   you will disown me t times."
     27: 63   said, 'After t days I will rise again.'
Mk   8: 31   be killed and after t days rise again.
     9:   5   Let us put up t shelters—
     14: 30   yourself will disown me t times."
Jn   2: 19   and I will raise it again in t days."
1Co   13: 13   And now these t remain:
     14: 27   or at the most t—should speak,
2Co   13:   1   testimony of two or t witnesses."
1Jn   5:   7   For there are t that testify:

THRESH (THRESH)
1Co   9: 10   farmers plow and t,

THRESHING (THRESH)
Ru   3:   6   So she went down to the t floor
2Sa   24: 18   altar to the Lord on the t floor
Lk   3: 17   in his hand to clear his t floor

THREW (THROW)
Da   6: 16   Daniel and t him into the lions' den.
Jnh   1: 15   took Jonah and t him overboard,

THRIVE
Pr   29:   2   When the righteous t, the people

THROAT (THROATS)
Ps   5:   9   Their t is an open grave;
Pr   23:   2   put a knife to your t if you are given

THROATS (THROAT)
Ro   3: 13   "Their t are open graves;

THROB*
Isa   60:   5   your heart will t and swell with joy;

THRONE (ENTHRONED ENTHRONES THRONES)
2Sa   7: 16   your t will be established
1Ch   17: 12   and I will establish his t forever.
Ps   11:   4   the Lord is on his heavenly t.
     45:   6   Your t, O God, will last for ever
     47:   8   God is seated on his holy t.
     89: 14   justice are the foundation of your t;
Isa   6:   1   I saw the Lord seated on a t,
     66:   1   "Heaven is my t, and the earth is
Eze   28:   2   I sit on the t of a god in the heart
Da   7:   9   His t was flaming with fire, and its
Mt   19: 28   Son of Man sits on his glorious t,
Ac   7: 49   " 'Heaven is my t, and the earth is
Heb   1:   8   the Son he says, "Your t, O God,
     4: 16   then approach God's t of grace
     12:   2   at the right hand of the t of God.

Rev   3: 21   give the right to sit with me on my t,
     3: 21   sat down with my Father on his t.
     4:   2   there before me was a t in heaven
     4: 10   They lay their crowns before the t
     20: 11   I saw a great white t and him who
     22:   3   The t of God and of the Lamb will

THRONES (THRONE)
Mt   19: 28   me will also sit on twelve t,
Rev   4:   4   the throne were twenty-four other t,

THROW (THREW)
Jn   8:   7   the first to t a stone at her."
Heb   10: 35   So do not t away your confidence;
     12:   1   let us t off everything that hinders

THUNDER (THUNDERS)
Ps   93:   4   Mightier than the t of the great
Mk   3: 17   which means "sons of t"),

THUNDERS (THUNDER)
Job   37:   5   God's voice t in marvelous ways;
Ps   29:   3   the God of glory t, the Lord
Rev   10:   3   the voices of the seven t spoke.

THWART* (THWARTED)
Isa   14: 27   has purposed, and who can t him?

THWARTED (THWART)
Job   42:   2   no purpose of yours can be t.

THYATIRA
Rev   2: 18   the angel of the church in T write:

TIBNI
     King of Israel (1Ki 16:21–22).

TIDINGS*
Isa   52:   7   who bring good t, who proclaim

TIES (TYING)
Hos   11:   4   of human kindness, with t of love.

TIGHT*
Jas   1: 26   and yet do not keep a t rein on their

TIGHTFISTED*
Dt   15:   7   not be hardhearted or t toward them.

TIMBREL
Ps   150:   4   praise him with t and dancing,

TIME (TIMES)
Est   4: 14   royal position for such a t as this?"
Ecc   3:   1   There is a t for everything,
     8:   5   wise heart will know the proper t
Da   7: 25   his hands for a t, times and half a t.
     12:   7   "It will be for a t, times and half a t.
Hos   10: 12   for it is t to seek the Lord,
Ro   5:   6   "At the appointed t I will return,
     13: 11   do this, understanding the present t.
1Co   7: 29   and sisters, is that the t is short.
2Co   6:   2   tell you, now is the t of God's favor,
2Ti   1:   9   Jesus before the beginning of t,
Tit   1:   2   promised before the beginning of t,
Heb   9: 28   and he will appear a second t,
     10: 12   had offered for all t one sacrifice
1Pe   4: 17   For it is t for judgment to begin

TIMES (TIME)
Ps   9:   9   a stronghold in t of trouble.
     31: 15   My t are in your hands;
     62:   8   Trust in him at all t, you people;
Pr   17:   7   A friend loves at all t, and a brother
Isa   46: 10   from ancient t, what is still to come.
Am   5: 13   quiet in such t, for the t are evil.
Mt   16:   3   cannot interpret the signs of the t.
     18: 21   how many t shall I forgive someone
Ac   1:   7   "It is not for you to know the t
Rev   12: 14   care of for a time, t and half a time,

TIMID
2Ti   1:   7   God gave us does not make us t,

TIMOTHY
     Believer from Lystra (Ac 16:1). Joined Paul on second missionary journey (Ac 16–20). Sent to settle problems at Corinth (1Co 4:17; 16:10). Led church at Ephesus (1Ti 1:3). Co-writer with Paul (1Th 1:1; 2Th 1:1; Phm 1).

TIP
Job   33:   2   my words are on the t of my tongue.

TIRE (TIRED)
2Th   3: 13   never t of doing what is good.

TIRED (TIRE)
Ex   17: 12   When Moses' hands grew t,
Isa   40: 28   He will not grow t or weary, and his

TITHE (TEN)
Lev   27: 30   " 'A t of everything

Dt   12: 17   your own towns the t of your grain
Mal   3: 10   Bring the whole t

TITHES (TEN)
Nu   18: 21   the Levites all the t in Israel as their
Mal   3:   8   "In t and offerings.

TITUS*
     Gentile co-worker of Paul (Gal 2:1–3; 2Ti 4:10); sent to Corinth (2Co 2:13; 7–8; 12:18), Crete (Tit 1:4–5).

TODAY
Ps   2:   7   t I have become your father.
     95:   7   T, if only you would hear his voice,
Mt   6: 11   Give us t our daily bread.
Lk   2: 11   T in the town of David a Savior has
     23: 43   t you will be with me in paradise."
Ac   13: 33   t I have become your Father.'
Heb   1:   5   t I have become your Father"?
     3:   7   "T, if you hear his voice,
     3: 13   as long as it is called "T,"
     5:   5   t I have become your Father."
     13:   8   Christ is the same yesterday and t

TOIL (TOILED TOILING)
Ge   3: 17   through painful t you will eat
Ecc   5: 19   their lot and be happy in their t—

TOILED (TOIL)
2Co   11: 27   I have labored and t and have often

TOILING (TOIL)
2Th   3:   8   t so that we would not be a burden

TOLERATE
Hab   1: 13   you cannot t wrongdoing.
Rev   2:   2   that you cannot t wicked people,

TOMB
Mt   27: 65   make the t as secure as you know
Lk   24:   2   the stone rolled away from the t,

TOMORROW
Pr   27:   1   Do not boast about t, for you do not
Isa   22: 13   drink," you say, "for t we die!"
Mt   6: 34   Therefore do not worry about t, for t
1Co   15: 32   "Let us eat and drink, for t we die."
Jas   4: 13   "Today or t we will go to this

TONGUE (TONGUES)
Ex   4: 10   I am slow of speech and t."
Job   33:   2   my words are on the tip of my t.
Ps   34: 13   keep your t from evil and your lips
     39:   1   my ways and keep my t from sin;
     51: 14   Savior, and my t will sing of your
     52:   4   every harmful word, you deceitful t!
     71: 24   My t will tell of your righteous acts
     119:172   May my t sing of your word, for all
     137:   6   May my t cling to the roof of my
     139:   4   Before a word is on my t you,
Pr   12:   6   a lying t, hands that shed innocent
     12: 18   but the t of the wise brings healing.
     15:   4   The soothing t is a tree of life,
     17: 20   one whose t is perverse falls
     25: 15   and a gentle t can break a bone.
     26: 28   A lying t hates those it hurts,
     28: 23   than one who has a flattering t.
     31: 26   and faithful instruction is on her t.
SS   4: 11   milk and honey are under your t.
Isa   32:   4   and the stammering t will be fluent
     45: 23   by me every t will swear.
     50:   4   has given me an instructed t,
     59:   3   and your t mutters wicked things.
Lk   16: 24   of his finger in water and cool my t,
Ro   14: 11   every t will confess to God.' "
1Co   14:   2   those who speak in a t do not speak
     14:   4   who speak in a t edify themselves,
     14:   9   speak intelligible words with your t,
     14: 13   those who speak in a t should pray
     14: 19   than ten thousand words in a t.
     14: 26   a revelation, a t or an interpretation.
     14: 27   If anyone speaks in a t, two—
Php   2: 11   and every t acknowledge that Jesus
Jas   3:   5   the t is a small part of the body,
     3:   8   but no one can tame the t. It is
1Jn   3: 18   let us not love with words or t

TONGUES (TONGUE)
Ps   5:   9   with their t they tell lies.
     12:   4   who say, "By our t we will prevail;
     37: 30   and their t speak what is just.
     126:   2   laughter, our t with songs of joy.
Pr   10: 19   words, but the prudent hold their t.
     21: 23   and their t keep themselves
Isa   28: 11   and strange t God will speak to this
Jer   23: 31   the prophets who wag their own t
Mk   16: 17   they will speak in new t;

Ac 2: 3 saw what seemed to be t of fire
    2: 4 in other t as the Spirit enabled them.
   10: 46 For they heard them speaking in t
   19: 6 and they spoke in t and prophesied.
Ro 3: 13 their t practice deceit."
1Co 12: 10 still another the interpretation of t.
   12: 28 guidance, and of different kinds of t.
   12: 30 Do all speak in t? Do all interpret?
   13: 1 If I speak in human or angelic t,
   13: 8 where there are t, they will be
   14: 5 greater than those who speak in t,
   14: 18 I speak in t more than all of you.
   14: 21 "With other t and through the lips
   14: 39 and do not forbid speaking in t.
Jas 1: 26 rein on their t deceive themselves,

TOOK (TAKE)
Ps 68: 18 on high, you t many captives;
Isa 53: 4 Surely he t up our pain and bore our
Mt   8: 17 "He t up our infirmities and bore
    26: 26 they were eating, Jesus t bread,
    26: 27 Then he t the cup, and when he had
1Co 11: 23 the night he was betrayed, t bread,
    11: 25 after supper he t the cup, saying,
Eph 4: 8 on high, he t many captives
Php 3: 12 which Christ Jesus t hold of me.

TOOTH (TEETH)
Ex 21: 24 eye for eye, t for t, hand for hand,
Mt   5: 38 was said, 'Eye for eye, and t for t.'

TOP
Dt 28: 13 you will always be at the t,
Isa 1: 6 foot to the t of your head there is no
Mt 27: 51 was torn in two from t to bottom.

TORMENT (TORMENTED TORMENTORS)
Lk 16: 28 not also come to this place of t.'
2Co 12: 7 flesh, a messenger of Satan, to t me.

TORMENTED (TORMENT)
Rev 20: 10 They will be t day and night

TORMENTORS (TORMENT)
Ps 137: 3 songs, our t demanded songs of joy;

TORN
Gal 4: 15 you would have t out your eyes
Php 1: 23 I am t between the two: I desire

TORTURED*
Mt 18: 34 him over to the jailers to be t,
Heb 11: 35 There were others who were t,

TOSSED (TOSSING)
Eph 4: 14 t back and forth by the waves,
Jas 1: 6 of the sea, blown and t by the wind.

TOSSING (TOSSED)
Isa 57: 20 But the wicked are like the t sea,

TOUCH (TOUCHED TOUCHES)
Ge   3: 3 and you must not t it, or you will
Ex 19: 12 the mountain or t the foot of it.
Ps 105: 15 "Do not t my anointed ones;
Mt   9: 21 "If I only t this cloak, I will be
Lk   8: 24 T me and see; a ghost does not have
2Co 6: 17 T no unclean thing, and I will
Col 2: 21 Do not taste! Do not t!"?

TOUCHED (TOUCH)
1Sa 10: 26 valiant men whose hearts God had t.
Isa 6: 7 With it he t my mouth and said,
Mt 14: 36 and all who t him were healed.
Lk   8: 45 "Who t me?" Jesus asked.
1Jn 1: 1 looked at and our hands have t—

TOUCHES (TOUCH)
Ex 19: 12 Whoever t the mountain is to be put
Zec 2: 8 for whoever t you t the apple of his

TOWER
Ge 11: 4 with a t that reaches to the heavens,
Pr 18: 10 name of the LORD is a fortified t;

TOWN (TOWNS)
Mt   2: 23 and lived in a t called Nazareth.

TOWNS (TOWN)
Nu 35: 2 Israelites to give the Levites t to live
    35: 15 These six t will be a place of refuge
Jer 11: 13 have as many gods as you have t;
Mt   9: 35 Jesus went through all the t
    13: 57 "Only in their own t

TRACING*
Ro 11: 33 and his paths beyond t out!

TRACK
Job 14: 16 my steps but not keep t of my sin.

TRADERS (TRADING)
1Ti 1: 10 for slave t and liars and perjurers.

TRADING (TRADERS)
1Ki 10: 22 The king had a fleet of t ships at sea
Pr 31: 18 She sees that her t is profitable,

TRADITION (TRADITIONS)
Mt 15: 2 "Why do your disciples break the t
    15: 6 word of God for the sake of your t.
Mk   7: 13 your t that you have handed down.
Col 2: 8 which depends on human t

TRADITIONS (TRADITION)
Mk   7: 8 and are holding on to human t."
Gal 1: 14 zealous for the t of my fathers.

TRAIL
1Ti 5: 24 the sins of others t behind them.

TRAIN* (TRAINED TRAINING)
Isa 2: 4 nor will they t for war anymore.
     6: 1 the t of his robe filled the temple.
Mic 4: 3 nor will they t for war anymore.
1Ti 4: 7 rather, t yourself to be godly.

TRAINED (TRAIN)
Lk   6: 40 all who are fully t will be like their
Ac 22: 3 was thoroughly t in the law of our
Heb 5: 14 by constant use have t themselves
    12: 11 for those who have been t by it.

TRAINING* (TRAIN)
1Co 9: 25 in the games goes into strict t.
Eph 6: 4 instead, bring them up in the t
1Ti 4: 8 For physical t is of some value,
2Ti 3: 16 correcting and t in righteousness,

TRAITOR (TRAITORS)
Lk   6: 16 and Judas Iscariot, who became a t.
Jn 18: 5 Judas the t was standing there

TRAITORS (TRAITOR)
Ps 59: 5 show no mercy to wicked t.

TRAMPLE (TRAMPLED)
Joel 3: 13 Come, t the grapes,
Am   2: 7 They t on the heads of the poor as
     8: 4 you who t the needy and do away
Mt   7: 6 they may t them under their feet,
Lk 10: 19 I have given you authority to t

TRAMPLED (TRAMPLE)
Isa 63: 6 I t the nations in my anger;
Lk 21: 24 Jerusalem will be t
Heb 10: 29 be punished who have t the Son
Rev 14: 20 They were t in the winepress

TRANCE*
Ac 10: 10 was being prepared, he fell into a t.
    11: 5 praying, and in a t I saw a vision.
    22: 17 praying at the temple, I fell into a t

TRANQUILLITY*
Ecc 4: 6 handful with t than two handfuls

TRANSACTIONS*
Ru   4: 7 the method of legalizing t in Israel.)

TRANSCENDS*
Php 4: 7 which t all understanding,

TRANSFIGURED*
Mt 17: 2 There he was t before them.
Mk   9: 2 There he was t before them.

TRANSFORM* (TRANSFORMED)
Php 3: 21 will t our lowly bodies so that they

TRANSFORMED (TRANSFORM)
Ro 12: 2 be t by the renewing of your mind.
2Co 3: 18 are being t into his image

TRANSGRESSED* (TRANSGRESSION)
Ps 17: 3 my mouth has not t.
Da   9: 11 All Israel has t your law and

TRANSGRESSION* (TRANSGRESSED
TRANSGRESSIONS TRANSGRESSORS)
Ps 19: 13 be blameless, innocent of great t.
Isa 53: 8 the t of my people he was punished.
Da   9: 24 people and your holy city to finish t,
Mic 1: 5 All this is because of Jacob's t,
     1: 5 What is Jacob's t? Is it not Samaria?
     3: 8 to declare to Jacob his t, to Israel his
     6: 7 Shall I offer my firstborn for my t,
     7: 18 forgives the t of the remnant of his
Ro   4: 15 where there is no law there is no t.
    11: 11 because of their t, salvation has
    11: 12 if their t means riches for the world,

TRANSGRESSIONS* (TRANSGRESSION)
Ps 32: 1 are those whose t are forgiven,

Ps 32: 5 I said, "I will confess my t
    39: 8 Save me from all my t; do not make
    51: 1 great compassion blot out my t.
    51: 3 For I know my t, and my sin is
    65: 3 by sins, you forgave our t.
   103: 12 so far has he removed our t from us.
Isa 43: 25 am he who blots out your t, for my
    50: 1 your t your mother was sent away.
    53: 5 But he was pierced for our t, he was
Mic 1: 13 for the t of Israel were found in you.
Ro   4: 7 are those whose t are forgiven,
Gal 3: 19 added because of t until the Seed
Eph 2: 1 you were dead in your t and sins,
     2: 5 even when we were dead in t—

TRANSGRESSORS* (TRANSGRESSION)
Ps 51: 13 Then I will teach t your ways,
Isa 53: 12 death, and was numbered with the t.
    53: 12 and made intercession for the t.
Lk 22: 37 'And he was numbered with the t';

TRANSITORY*
2Co 3: 7 its glory, t though it was,
     3: 11 if what was t came with glory,

TRAP (TRAPPED TRAPS)
Ps 69: 22 may it become retribution and a t.
Pr 20: 25 It is a t to dedicate something rashly
    28: 10 evil path will fall into their own t,
Isa 8: 14 people of Jerusalem he will be a t
Mt 22: 15 and laid plans to t him in his words.
Lk 21: 34 will close on you suddenly like a t.
Ro 11: 9 their table become a snare and a t,
1Ti 3: 7 into disgrace and into the devil's t.
     6: 9 and a t and into many foolish
2Ti 2: 26 and escape from the t of the devil,

TRAPPED (TRAP)
Pr   6: 2 you have been t by what you said,
    12: 13 Evildoers are t by their sinful talk,

TRAPS (TRAP)
Jos 23: 13 will become snares and t for you,
La   4: 20 life breath, was caught in their t.

TRAVEL (TRAVELER)
Pr   4: 15 Avoid it, do not t on it; turn from it
Mt 23: 15 You t over land and sea to win

TRAVELER (TRAVEL)
Job 31: 32 my door was always open to the t—
Jer 14: 8 like a t who stays only a night?

TREACHEROUS (TREACHERY)
Ps 25: 3 on those who are t without cause.
2Ti 3: 4 t, rash, conceited, lovers of pleasure

TREACHERY (TREACHEROUS)
Isa 59: 13 rebellion and t against the LORD,

TREAD (TREADING TREADS)
Ps 91: 13 You will t on the lion and the cobra;

TREADING (TREAD)
Dt 25: 4 Do not muzzle an ox while it is t
1Co 9: 9 "Do not muzzle an ox while it is t
1Ti 5: 18 "Do not muzzle an ox while it is t

TREADS (TREAD)
Rev 19: 15 He t the winepress of the fury

TREASURE (TREASURED TREASURES
TREASURY)
Pr   2: 4 and search for it as for hidden t,
Isa 33: 6 of the LORD is the key to this t.
Mt   6: 21 For where your t is, there your heart
    13: 44 of heaven is like t hidden in a field.
Lk 12: 34 But we have this t in jars of clay
2Co 4: 7 But we have this t in jars of clay
1Ti 6: 19 in this way they will lay up t

TREASURED* (TREASURE)
Ex   6: 7 nations you will be my t possession.
Dt   7: 6 to be his people, his t possession.
    14: 2 chosen you to be his t possession.
    26: 18 his t possession as he promised,
Job 23: 12 I have t the words of his mouth
Ps 135: 4 Israel to be his t possession.
Isa 64: 11 and all that we t lies in ruins.
Mal 3: 17 "they will be my t possession.
Lk   2: 19 But Mary t up all these things
     2: 51 his mother t all these things in her

TREASURES (TREASURE)
1Ch 29: 3 my God I now give my personal t
Pr 10: 2 Ill-gotten t have no lasting value,
Mt   6: 19 store up for yourselves t on earth,
    13: 52 his storeroom new t as well as old."
Col 2: 3 in whom are hidden all the t
Heb 11: 26 of greater value than the t of Egypt,

TREASURY (TREASURE)
Mk 12: 43 more into the t than all the others.

TREAT (TREATED TREATING TREATMENT)
Lev 22: 2 his sons to t with respect the sacred
Ps 103: 10 he does not t us as our sins deserve
Mt 18: 17 t them as you would a pagan
   18: 35 how my heavenly Father will t each
Eph 6: 9 t your slaves in the same way.
1Th 5: 20 Do not t prophecies with contempt
1Ti 5: 1 T younger men as brothers,
1Pe 3: 7 t them with respect as the weaker

TREATED (TREAT)
Lev 19: 34 you must be t as your native-born.
   25: 40 They are to be t as hired workers
1Sa 24: 17 "You have t me well, but I have t
Heb 10: 29 who have t as an unholy thing

TREATING (TREAT)
Ge 18: 25 t the righteous and the wicked alike.
Heb 12: 7 God is t you as his children.

TREATMENT (TREAT)
Col 2: 23 and their harsh t of the body,

TREATY
Ex 34: 12 not to make a t with those who live
Dt 7: 2 Make no t with them, and show
   23: 6 Do not seek a t of friendship

TREE (TREES)
Ge 2: 9 of the garden were the t of life
    2: 9 and the t of the knowledge of good
2Sa 18: 9 Absalom's hair got caught in the t.
1Ki 14: 23 hill and under every spreading t.
Ps 1: 3 They are like a t planted by streams
   52: 8 I am like an olive t flourishing
   92: 12 righteous will flourish like a palm t,
Pr 3: 18 She is a t of life to those who take
   11: 30 fruit of the righteous is a t of life,
   27: 18 who guard a fig t will eat its fruit,
Isa 65: 22 For as the days of a t, so will be
Jer 17: 8 They will be like a t planted
Eze 17: 24 I the Lord bring down the tall t
Da 4: 10 and there before me stood a t
Mic 4: 4 own vine and under their own fig t,
Zec 3: 10 to sit under your vine and fig t,'
Mt 3: 10 every t that does not produce good
   12: 33 for a t is recognized by its fruit.
Lk 19: 4 climbed a sycamore-fig t to see him,
Ro 11: 24 be grafted into their own olive t!
Jas 3: 12 sisters, can a fig t bear olives,
Rev 2: 7 the right to eat from the t of life,
   22: 2 side of the river stood the t of life.
   22: 14 may have the right to the t of life
   22: 19 from you your share in the t of life

TREES (TREE)
Jdg 9: 8 One day the t went out to anoint
Ps 96: 12 let all the t of the forest sing for joy.
Isa 55: 12 all the t of the field will clap their
Mt 3: 10 The ax is already at the root of the t,
Mk 8: 24 they look like t walking around."
Jude   12 autumn t, without fruit

TREMBLE (TREMBLED TREMBLES TREMBLING)
Ex 15: 14 The nations will hear and t;
1Ch 16: 30 T before him, all the earth!
Ps 114: 7 T, earth, at the presence of the Lord,
Isa 66: 2 and who t at my word.
Jer 5: 22 "Should you not t in my presence?
Eze 38: 20 of the earth will t at my presence.
Joel 2: 1 Let all who live in the land t,
Hab 3: 6 he looked, and made the nations t.
Ro 11: 20 Do not be arrogant, but t.

TREMBLED (TREMBLE)
Ex 19: 16 Everyone in the camp t.
   20: 18 mountain in smoke, they t with fear.
2Sa 22: 8 The earth t and quaked,
Ac 7: 32 Moses t with fear and did not dare

TREMBLES (TREMBLE)
Ps 97: 4 up the world; the earth sees and t.
  104: 32 and it t, who touches the mountains,
Jer 10: 10 When he is angry, the earth t;
Na 1: 5 The earth t at his presence,

TREMBLING (TREMBLE)
Ps 2: 11 fear and celebrate his rule with t.
Da 10: 10 me and set me t on my hands
Php 2: 12 out your salvation with fear and t,
Heb 12: 21 that Moses said, "I am t with fear."

TRESPASS* (TRESPASSES)
Ro 5: 15 But the gift is not like the t.
    5: 15 many died by the t of the one man,

Ro 5: 17 by the t of the one man,
    5: 18 just as one t resulted
    5: 20 in so that the t might increase.

TRESPASSES* (TRESPASS)
Ro 5: 16 but the gift followed many t

TRIAL (TRIALS)
Ps 37: 33 be condemned when brought to t.
Mal 3: 5 "So I will come to put you on t.
Mk 13: 11 you are arrested and brought to t,
2Co 8: 2 In the midst of a very severe t,
Jas 1: 12 are those who persevere under t,
Rev 1: 9 you from the hour of t that is going

TRIALS* (TRIAL)
Dt 7: 19 saw with your own eyes the great t,
   29: 3 own eyes you saw those great t,
Lk 22: 28 who have stood by me in my t.
1Th 3: 3 one would be unsettled by these t.
2Ti 1: 4 persecutions and t you are enduring.
Jas 1: 2 whenever you face t of many kinds,
1Pe 1: 6 had to suffer grief in all kinds of t.
2Pe 2: 9 how to rescue the godly from t

TRIBE (HALF-TRIBE TRIBES)
Heb 7: 13 that t has ever served at the altar.
Rev 5: 5 the Lion of the t of Judah, the Root
    5: 9 for God members of every t
   11: 9 days many from every people, t,
   14: 6 to every nation, t,

TRIBES (TRIBE)
Ge 49: 28 All these are the twelve t of Israel,
Mt 19: 28 judging the twelve t of Israel.

TRIBULATION
Rev 7: 14 who have come out of the great t;

TRICKERY*
Ac 13: 10 are full of all kinds of deceit and t,
2Co 12: 16 fellow that I am, I caught you by t!

TRIED (TRY)
Ps 73: 16 When I t to understand all this,
   95: 9 they t me, though they had seen
Heb 3: 9 your ancestors tested and t me,

TRIES (TRY)
Lk 17: 33 Whoever t to keep their life will

TRIMMED
Mt 25: 7 virgins woke up and t their lamps.

TRIUMPH (TRIUMPHAL TRIUMPHED TRIUMPHING TRIUMPHS)
Ps 25: 2 nor let my enemies t over me.
   54: 7 and my eyes have looked in t on my
  112: 8 the end they will look in t on their
  118: 7 I look in t on my enemies.
Pr 28: 12 When the righteous t, there is great
Isa 42: 13 cry and will t over his enemies.
Rev 17: 14 but the Lamb will t over them

TRIUMPHAL* (TRIUMPH)
Isa 60: 11 their kings led in t procession.
2Co 2: 14 captives in Christ's t procession

TRIUMPHED (TRIUMPH)
Rev 5: 5 of Judah, the Root of David, has t.
   12: 11 They t over him by the blood of

TRIUMPHING* (TRIUMPH)
Col 2: 15 of them, t over them by the cross.

TRIUMPHS* (TRIUMPH)
Jas 2: 13 Mercy t over judgment.

TROUBLE (TROUBLED TROUBLES TROUBLEMAKERS)
Ge 41: 51 God has made me forget all my t
Jos 7: 25 "Why have you brought this t
Job 2: 10 accept good from God, and not t?"
    5: 7 to t as surely as sparks fly upward.
   14: 1 are of few days and full of t.
   42: 11 him over all the t the Lord had
Ps 7: 14 are pregnant with evil conceive t
    7: 16 The t they cause recoils on them;
    9: 9 a stronghold in times of t.
   10: 14 God, see the t of the afflicted;
   22: 11 for t is near and there is no one
   27: 5 the day of t he will keep me safe
   32: 7 you will protect me from t
   37: 39 he is their stronghold in time of t.
   41: 1 Lord delivers them in times of t.
   46: 1 strength, an ever-present help in t.
   50: 15 and call on me in the day of t;
   59: 16 my fortress, my refuge in times of t
   66: 14 my mouth spoke when I was in t.
   91: 15 I will be with them in t, I will

Ps 107: 6 cried out to the Lord in their t,
  107: 13 they cried to the Lord in their t,
  119:143 T and distress have come upon me,
  138: 7 Though I walk in the midst of t,
  143: 11 righteousness, bring me out of t.
Pr 11: 8 The righteous are rescued from t,
   12: 13 talk, and so the innocent escape t.
   12: 21 but the wicked have their fill of t.
   19: 23 one rests content, untouched by t.
   24: 10 If you falter in a time of t,
   25: 19 on the unfaithful in a time of t.
   28: 14 who harden their hearts fall into t.
Jer 30: 7 It will be a time of t for Jacob,
Na 1: 7 is good, a refuge in times of t,
Zep 1: 15 and anguish, a day of t and ruin,
Mt 6: 34 Each day has enough t of its own.
   13: 21 When t or persecution comes
Jn 16: 33 In this world you will have t.
Ro 8: 35 Shall t or hardship or persecution
2Co 1: 4 any t with the comfort we ourselves
2Th 1: 6 He will pay back t to those who t
Jas 5: 13 Is anyone among you in t?

TROUBLED (TROUBLE)
Ge 6: 6 and his heart was deeply t.
Ps 38: 18 I am t by my sin.
Mk 14: 33 began to be deeply distressed and t.
Jn 14: 1 "Do not let your hearts be t.
   14: 27 Do not let your hearts be t and do
2Th 1: 7 and give relief to you who are t,

TROUBLEMAKERS (TROUBLE)
Pr 6: 12 T and villains,

TROUBLES (TROUBLE)
Ps 34: 6 he saved him out of all his t.
   34: 17 he delivers them from all their t.
   34: 19 The righteous may have many t,
   40: 12 For t without number surround me;
   54: 7 have delivered me from all my t,
1Co 7: 28 those who marry will face many t
2Co 1: 4 who comforts us in all our t,
    1: 17 momentary t are achieving for us
    6: 4 in t, hardships and distresses;
    7: 4 all our t my joy knows no bounds.
Php 4: 14 it was good of you to share in my t.

TRUE (TRULY TRUTH)
Nu 11: 23 not what I say will come t for you."
   12: 7 this is not t of my servant Moses;
Dt 18: 22 does not take place or come t, that is
1Sa 9: 6 and everything he says comes t.
1Ki 10: 6 achievements and your wisdom is t.
2Ch 6: 17 your servant David come t.
   15: 3 time Israel was without the t God,
Ps 33: 4 word of the Lord is right and t;
  119:142 is everlasting and your law is t.
  119:151 and all your commands are t.
  119:160 All your words are t;
Pr 8: 7 My mouth speaks what is t,
Isa 65: 16 will do so by the one t God;
Jer 10: 10 But the Lord is the t God;
   28: 9 only if his prediction comes t."
Eze 33: 33 "When all this comes t—
Lk 16: 11 who will trust you with t riches?
Jn 1: 9 The t light that gives light
    4: 23 the t worshipers will worship
    6: 32 Father who gives you the t bread
    7: 28 authority, but he who sent me is t.
   15: 1 "I am the t vine, and my Father is
   17: 3 the only t God, and Jesus Christ,
   19: 35 testimony, and his testimony is t.
   21: 24 We know that his testimony is t.
Ac 10: 34 "I now realize how t it is that God
   11: 23 them all to remain t to the Lord
   14: 22 them to remain t to the faith.
   17: 11 day to see if what Paul said was t.
Ro 3: 4 Let God be t, and every human
   12: 1 pleasing to God—this is t worship.
Php 4: 8 whatever is t, whatever is noble,
Col 1: 5 heard in the t word of the gospel
1Jn 2: 8 the t light is already shining.
    5: 20 He is the t God and eternal life.
Rev 19: 9 "These are the t words of God."
   22: 6 "These words are trustworthy and t."

TRULY (TRUE)
Mt 5: 18 T I tell you, until heaven and
    5: 26 T I tell you, you will not get out
    6: 2 T I tell you, they have received
    6: 5 T I tell you, they have received
    6: 16 T I tell you, they have received
    8: 10 "T I tell you, I have not found
   10: 15 T I tell you, it will be more

Mt 10: 23 T I tell you, you will not finish
10: 42 t I tell you, that person will
11: 11 T I tell you, among those born
13: 17 T I tell you, many prophets
16: 28 "T I tell you, some who are
17: 20 T I tell you, if you have faith
18: 3 And he said: "T I tell you,
18: 13 if he finds it, t I tell you,
18: 18 T I tell you, whatever you bind
19: 23 to his disciples, "T I tell you,
19: 28 T I tell you, at the renewal
21: 21 Jesus replied, "T I tell you,
21: 31 said to them, "T I tell you,
23: 36 T I tell you, all this will come
24: 2 "T I tell you, not one stone
24: 34 T I tell you, this generation
24: 47 T I tell you, he will put
25: 12 'T I tell you, I don't know you.'
25: 40 King will reply, 'T I tell you,
25: 45 "He will reply, 'T I tell you,
26: 13 T I tell you, wherever this gospel
26: 21 "T I tell you, one of you will
26: 34 "T I tell you," Jesus answered,
Mk 3: 28 T I tell you, people will be
8: 12 T I tell you, no sign will be
9: 1 he said to them, "T I tell you,
9: 41 T I tell you, anyone who gives
10: 15 T I tell you, anyone who will not
10: 29 "T I tell you," Jesus replied,
11: 23 "T I tell you, if you say to
12: 43 Jesus said, "T I tell you,
13: 30 T I tell you, this generation
14: 9 T I tell you, wherever the gospel
14: 18 "T I tell you, one of you will
14: 25 "T I tell you, I will not drink
14: 30 "T I tell you," Jesus answered,
Lk 4: 24 "T I tell you," he continued,
9: 27 T I tell you, some who are
12: 37 T I tell you, he will dress himself
12: 44 T I tell you, he will put him
18: 17 T I tell you, anyone who will not
18: 29 "T I tell you," Jesus said to them,
21: 3 "T I tell you," he said,
21: 32 "T I tell you, this generation
23: 43 "T I tell you, today you will be
Jn 1: 51 "Very t I tell you, you will see
3: 3 "Very t I tell you, no one can see
3: 5 Jesus answered, "Very t I tell you,
3: 11 Very t I tell you, we speak of what
5: 19 "Very t I tell you, the Son can do
5: 24 "Very t I tell you, whoever hears
5: 25 "Very t I tell you, a time is coming
6: 26 Jesus answered, "Very t I tell you,
6: 32 said to them, "Very t I tell you,
6: 47 "Very t I tell you,
6: 53 said to them, "Very t I tell you,
8: 34 Jesus replied, "Very t I tell you,
8: 51 "Very t I tell you,
8: 58 "Very t I tell you," Jesus
10: 1 "Very t I tell you Pharisees,
10: 7 t I tell you, I am the gate for
12: 24 Very t I tell you, unless a kernel
13: 16 Very t I tell you, servants are not
13: 20 Very t I tell you, whoever accepts
13: 21 t I tell you, one of you is going
13: 38 t I tell you, before the rooster
14: 12 t I tell you, all who have faith
16: 7 t I tell you, it is for your good
16: 20 Very t I tell you, you will weep
16: 23 t I tell you, my Father will give
21: 18 Very t I tell you, when you were
Col 1: 6 and t understood God's grace.

TRUMPET (TRUMPETS)
Isa 27: 13 And in that day a great t will sound.
Eze 33: 5 Since they heard the sound of the t
Zec 9: 14 Sovereign LORD will sound the t;
Mt 24: 31 send his angels with a loud t call,
1Co 14: 8 if the t does not sound a clear call,
15: 52 For the t will sound, the dead
1Th 4: 16 archangel and with the t call of God,
Rev 8: 7 The first angel sounded his t,

TRUMPETS (TRUMPET)
Jdg 7: 19 They blew their t and broke the jars
Rev 8: 2 and seven t were given to them.

TRUST (ENTRUST ENTRUSTED TRUSTED
TRUSTFULLY TRUSTING TRUSTS
TRUSTWORTHY)
Ex 14: 31 the LORD and put their t in him
19: 9 and will always put their t in you."
Nu 20: 12 "Because you did not t in me

Dt 1: 32 you did not t in the LORD your
9: 23 You did not t him or obey him.
28: 52 walls in which you t fall down.
Jdg 11: 20 did not t Israel to pass through his
2Ki 17: 14 who did not t in the LORD their
18: 30 not let Hezekiah persuade you to t
1Ch 9: 22 to their positions of t by David
Job 4: 18 If God places no t in his servants,
4: 18 What they t in is fragile;
15: 15 If God places no t in his holy ones,
31: 24 "If I have put my t in gold or said
39: 12 Can you t it to haul in your grain
Ps 4: 5 the righteous and t in the LORD.
9: 10 Those who know your name t
13: 5 But I t in your unfailing love;
20: 7 Some t in chariots and some
20: 7 we t in the name of the LORD our
22: 4 In you our ancestors put their t;
25: 2 I t in you; do not let me be put
31: 6 as for me, I t in the LORD.
31: 14 But I t in you, LORD; I say,
32: 10 surrounds those who t in him.
33: 21 rejoice, for we t in his holy name.
37: 3 T in the LORD and do good;
37: 5 t in him and he will do this:
40: 3 the LORD and put their t in him.
40: 4 those who make the LORD their t,
44: 6 I put no t in my bow, my sword
49: 6 those who t in their wealth
49: 13 fate of those who t in themselves,
52: 8 I t in God's unfailing love for ever
55: 23 But as for me, I t in you.
56: 3 When I am afraid, I put my t in you.
56: 4 in God I t and am not afraid.
56: 11 in God I t and am not afraid.
62: 8 T in him at all times, you people;
62: 10 Do not t in extortion or put vain
78: 7 Then they would put their t in God
78: 22 in God or t in his deliverance.
84: 12 blessed are those who t in you.
91: 2 my fortress, my God, in whom I t."
115: 8 them, and so will all who t in them.
115: 9 House of Israel, t in the LORD—
115: 10 House of Aaron, t in the LORD—
115: 11 who fear him, t in the LORD—
118: 8 in the LORD than to t in human
118: 9 in the LORD than to t in princes.
119: 42 who taunts me, for I t in your word.
125: 1 Those who t in the LORD are like
135: 18 them, and so will all who t in them.
143: 8 love, for I have put my t in you.
146: 3 Do not put your t in princes,
Pr 3: 5 T in the LORD with all your heart
11: 28 who t in their riches will fall,
16: 20 are those who t in the LORD.
21: 22 the stronghold in which they t.
22: 19 So that your t may be
28: 25 who t in the LORD will prosper.
28: 26 who t in themselves are fools,
Isa 8: 17 I will put my t in him.
12: 2 I will t and not be afraid.
26: 3 because they t in you.
26: 4 T in the LORD forever,
30: 15 in quietness and t is your strength,
31: 1 who t in the multitude of their
36: 15 not let Hezekiah persuade you to t
42: 17 But those who t in idols, who say
50: 10 t in the name of the LORD.
Jer 2: 37 the LORD has rejected those you t;
5: 17 the fortified cities in which you t.
7: 4 Do not t in deceptive words and say,
7: 14 the temple you t in, the place I gave
9: 4 do not t any of your people.
12: 6 Do not t them, though they speak
17: 5 "Cursed are those who t in mortals,
17: 7 blessed are those who t in the LORD,
28: 15 you have persuaded this nation to t
39: 18 with your life, because you t in me,
48: 7 Since you t in your deeds
49: 4 you t in your riches and say,
Eze 33: 13 they t in their righteousness
Mic 7: 5 Do not t a neighbor;
Na 1: 7 He cares for those who t in him,
Hab 2: 18 them t in their own creations;
Zep 3: 2 She does not t in the LORD,
3: 12 remnant of Israel will t in the name
Lk 16: 11 who will t you with true riches?
Jn 12: 36 Put your t in the light while you
14: 1 T in God; t also in me.
Ac 14: 23 Lord, in whom they had put their t.
Ro 15: 13 all joy and peace as you t in him,
1Co 4: 2 been given a t must prove faithful.

1Co 9: 17 simply discharging the t committed
2Co 13: 6 I t that you will discover that we
Heb 2: 13 again, "I will put my t in him."

TRUSTED* (TRUST)
1Sa 27: 12 Achish t David and said to himself,
2Ki 18: 5 Hezekiah t in the LORD, the God
1Ch 5: 20 their prayers, because they t him.
Job 12: 20 He silences the lips of t advisers
Ps 5: 9 a word from their mouth can be t;
22: 4 they t and you delivered them.
22: 5 in you they t and were saved;
26: 1 I have t in the LORD and have not
41: 9 someone I t, one who shared my
52: 7 stronghold but t in his great wealth
116: 10 I t in the LORD when I said,
Pr 27: 6 Wounds from a friend can be t,
Isa 20: 5 Those who t in Cush and boasted
25: 9 we t in him, and he saved us.
25: 9 This is the LORD, we t in him;
47: 10 You have t in your wickedness
Jer 13: 25 forgotten me and t in false gods.
38: 22 those t friends of yours.
48: 13 was ashamed when they t in Bethel.
Eze 16: 15 " 'But you t in your beauty
Da 3: 28 They t in him and defied the king's
6: 23 on him, because he had t in his God.
Zep 3: 4 are unprincipled; they cannot be t.
Lk 11: 22 away the armor in which the man t
16: 10 can be t with very little can also be t with much,
Ac 12: 20 a t personal servant of the king,
Tit 2: 10 but to show that they can be fully t,
3: 8 those who have t in God may be

TRUSTFULLY* (TRUST)
Pr 3: 29 your neighbor, who lives t near you.

TRUSTING* (TRUST)
Job 15: 31 themselves by t what is worthless,
Ps 112: 7 hearts are steadfast, t in the LORD.
Isa 2: 22 Stop t in human beings, who have
Jer 7: 8 you are t in deceptive words that are

TRUSTS* (TRUST)
Ps 21: 7 For the king t in the LORD;
22: 8 "He t in the LORD," they say,
28: 7 my heart t in him, and he helps me.
86: 2 save your servant who t in you.
Pr 29: 25 but whoever t in the LORD is kept
Mt 27: 43 He t in God. Let God rescue him
Ro 4: 5 but t God who justifies the ungodly,
1Co 13: 7 protects, always t, always hopes,
1Pe 2: 6 the one who t in him will never be

TRUSTWORTHY* (TRUST)
Ex 18: 21 t men who hate dishonest gain—
2Sa 7: 28 Your covenant is t, and you have
Ne 7: 2 because he was t and feared God
13: 13 because they were considered t.
Ps 19: 7 The statutes of the LORD are t,
111: 7 all his precepts are t.
119: 86 All your commands are t;
119:138 are righteous; they are fully t.
145: 13 The LORD is t in all he promises
Pr 6: 7 for I have t things to say;
11: 13 but the t keep a secret.
12: 22 delights in people who are t.
13: 17 but a t envoy brings healing.
13: 17 harvest time is a t messenger
Da 2: 45 is true and its interpretation is t."
6: 4 because he was t and neither corrupt
Lk 16: 11 if you have not been t in handling
16: 12 if you have not been t with someone
19: 17 'Because you have been t in a very
Jn 8: 26 But he who sent me is t,
1Co 7: 25 one who by the Lord's mercy is t.
1Ti 1: 12 he considered me t,
1: 15 Here is a t saying that deserves
3: 1 Here is a t saying:
3: 11 but temperate and t in everything.
4: 9 This is a t saying that deserves full
2Ti 2: 11 Here is a t saying: If we died
Tit 1: 9 the t message as it has been taught,
3: 8 This is a t saying. And I want you
Rev 21: 5 for these words are t and true."
22: 6 to me, "These words are t and true.

TRUTH* (TRUE TRUTHFUL TRUTHFULNESS
TRUTHS)
Ge 42: 16 tested to see if you are telling the t.
1Ki 17: 24 LORD from your mouth is the t."
22: 16 the t in the name of the LORD?
2Ch 18: 15 the t in the name of the LORD?"
Ps 15: 2 who speak the t from their hearts;

Ps 25: 5 Guide me in your t and teach me,
45: 4 forth victoriously in the cause of t,
52: 3 falsehood rather than speaking the t.
119: 43 Never take your word of t from my
145: 18 on him, to all who call on him in t.
Pr 12: 17 An honest witness tells the t,
22: 21 to be honest and to speak the t,
23: 23 Buy the t and do not sell it—
Isa 45: 19 I, the LORD, speak the t;
48: 1 but not in t or righteousness—
59: 14 t has stumbled in the streets,
59: 15 T is nowhere to be found,
Jer 5: 1 who deals honestly and seeks the t,
5: 3 do not your eyes look for t?
7: 28 T has perished; it has vanished
9: 3 it is not by t that they triumph
9: 5 friend, and no one speaks the t.
26: 15 in t the LORD has sent me to you
Da 8: 12 and t was thrown to the ground.
9: 13 sins and giving attention to your t.
10: 21 what is written in the Book of T.
11: 2 "Now then, I tell you the t:
Am 5: 10 and detest the one who tells the t.
Zec 8: 3 will be called the City of T,
8: 16 Speak the t to each other, and render
8: 19 Therefore love t and peace."
Mt 22: 16 of God in accordance with the t.
Mk 5: 33 with fear, told him the whole t.
12: 14 of God in accordance with the t.
Lk 20: 21 of God in accordance with the t.
Jn 1: 14 from the Father, full of grace and t.
1: 17 and t came through Jesus Christ.
3: 21 those who live by the t come
4: 23 the Father in the Spirit and in t,
4: 24 must worship in the Spirit and in t."
5: 33 to John and he has testified to the t.
7: 18 the one who sent him is a man of t;
8: 32 you will know the t, and the t will set you free.
8: 40 a man who has told you the t that I
8: 44 not holding to the t, for there is no t in him.
8: 45 Yet because I tell the t, you do not
8: 46 If I am telling the t, why don't you
9: 24 "Give glory to God and tell the t,"
14: 6 "I am the way and the t and the life.
14: 17 the Spirit of t. The world cannot
15: 26 the Spirit of t who goes
16: 13 But when he, the Spirit of t, comes,
16: 13 he will guide you into all the t.
17: 17 Sanctify them by the t; your word is t.
18: 23 But if I spoke the t, why did you
18: 37 into the world is to testify to the t.
18: 37 on the side of t listens to me."
18: 38 "What is t?" retorted Pilate.
19: 35 He knows that he tells the t, and he
Ac 20: 30 distort the t in order to draw away
21: 24 everyone will know there is no t
21: 34 could not get at the t because
24: 8 to learn the t about all these charges
28: 25 "The Holy Spirit spoke the t
Ro 1: 18 human beings who suppress the t
1: 25 They exchanged the t about God
2: 2 who do such things is based on t.
2: 8 and who reject the t and follow evil,
2: 20 embodiment of knowledge and t—
9: 1 I speak the t in Christ—I am not
15: 8 of the Jews on behalf of God's t,
1Co 5: 8 unleavened bread of sincerity and t.
13: 6 in evil but rejoices with the t.
2Co 4: 2 by setting forth the t plainly we
11: 10 As surely as the t of Christ is in me,
12: 6 because I would be speaking the t.
13: 8 against the t, but only for the t.
Gal 2: 5 that the t of the gospel might remain
2: 14 in line with the t of the gospel,
4: 16 your enemy by telling you the t?
5: 7 you to keep you from obeying the t?
Eph 1: 13 when you heard the word of t,
4: 15 Instead, speaking the t in love,
4: 21 in accordance with the t that is
5: 9 in all goodness, righteousness and t)
6: 14 belt of t buckled around your waist,
2Th 2: 10 because they refused to love the t
2: 12 who have not believed the t
2: 13 the Spirit and through belief in the t.
1Ti 2: 4 and to come to a knowledge of the t.
2: 7 I am telling the t, I am not lying—
3: 15 the pillar and foundation of the t.
4: 3 who believe and who know the t.
6: 5 who have been robbed of the t.
2Ti 2: 15 who correctly handles the word of t.

2Ti 2: 18 who have departed from the t.
2: 25 them to a knowledge of the t,
3: 7 to come to a knowledge of the t.
3: 8 so also these teachers oppose the t.
4: 4 will turn their ears away from the t
Tit 1: 1 their knowledge of the t that leads
1: 13 He has surely told the t!
1: 14 commands of those who reject the t.
Heb 10: 26 received the knowledge of the t,
Jas 1: 18 give us birth through the word of t,
3: 14 do not boast about it or deny the t.
5: 19 one of you should wander from the t
1Pe 1: 22 by obeying the t so that you have
2Pe 1: 12 established in the t you now have.
2: 2 and will bring the way of t
1Jn 1: 6 we lie and do not live out the t.
1: 8 ourselves and the t is not in us.
2: 4 are liars, and the t is not in them.
2: 8 its t is seen in him and in you,
2: 20 and all of you know the t.
2: 21 because you do not know the t,
2: 21 and because no lie comes from the t.
3: 18 or tongue but with actions and in t.
3: 19 we know that we belong to the t
4: 6 is how we recognize the Spirit of t
5: 6 testifies, because the Spirit is the t.
2Jn : 1 her children, whom I love in the t—
: 1 but also all who know the t—
: 2 because of the t, which lives in us
: 3 will be with us in t and love.
: 4 of your children walking in the t,
3Jn : 1 friend Gaius, whom I love in the t.
: 3 testify to your faithfulness to the t,
: 4 my children are walking in the t.
: 8 that we may work together for the t.
: 12 and even by the t itself.

TRUTHFUL* (TRUTH)
Pr 12: 19 T lips endure forever, but a lying
14: 25 A t witness saves lives, but a false
22: 21 bring back t reports to those
Jer 4: 2 and if in a t, just and righteous way
Jn 3: 33 it has certified that God is t.
2Co 6: 7 in t speech and in the power of God;

TRUTHFULNESS* (TRUTH)
Ro 3: 7 "If my falsehood enhances God's t

TRUTHS* (TRUTH)
1Ti 3: 9 keep hold of the deep t of the faith
4: 6 nourished on the t of the faith
Heb 5: 12 teach you the elementary t of God's

TRY (TRIED TRIES TRYING)
Ps 26: 2 and t me, examine my heart and my
Isa 7: 13 Is it not enough to t the patience
Lk 12: 58 t hard to be reconciled on the way,
13: 24 will t to enter and will not be able
1Co 10: 33 even as I t to please everyone
14: 12 t to excel in those that build
2Co 5: 11 the Lord, we t to persuade people.
Tit 2: 9 in everything, to t to please them,

TRYING (TRY)
2Co 5: 12 We are not t to commend ourselves
Gal 1: 10 If I were still t to please people,
1Th 2: 4 We are not t to please people
1Pe 1: 11 t to find out the time
1Jn 2: 26 those who are t to lead you astray.

TUMORS
1Sa 5: 6 on them and afflicted them with t.

TUNE
1Co 14: 7 anyone know what t is being played

TUNIC
Ex 28: 4 a woven t, a turban and a sash.

TURMOIL
Ps 65: 7 their waves, and the t of the nations.
Pr 15: 16 LORD than great wealth with t.

TURN (TURNED TURNING TURNS)
Ex 32: 12 T from your fierce anger;
Nu 32: 15 If you t away from following him,
Dt 5: 32 do not t aside to the right
28: 14 Do not t aside from any
30: 10 t to the LORD your God with all
Jos 1: 7 do not t from it to the right
1Ki 8: 58 May he t our hearts to him, to walk
2Ch 7: 14 face and t from their wicked ways,
30: 9 He will not t his face from you
Job 33: 30 to t them back from the pit,
Ps 28: 1 my Rock, do not t a deaf ear to me.
34: 14 T from evil and do good;
51: 13 and sinners will t back to you.

Ps 78: 6 in t would tell their children.
119: 36 T my heart toward your statutes
119: 132 T to me and have mercy on me,
Pr 4: 5 Do not forget my words or t away
4: 27 Do not t to the right or the left;
22: 6 are old they will not t from it.
Isa 17: 7 and t their eyes to the Holy One
28: 6 to those who t back the battle
29: 16 You t things upside down,
30: 21 Whether you t to the right
45: 22 "T to me and be saved, all you ends
55: 7 Let them t to the LORD, and he
Jer 31: 13 I will t their mourning
Eze 33: 9 if you do warn the wicked to t
33: 11 they t from their ways and live. T!
Jnh 3: 9 compassion t from his fierce anger
Mal 4: 6 He will t the hearts of the parents
Mt 5: 39 t to them the other cheek also.
10: 35 to t 'a man against his father,
Lk 1: 17 to t the hearts of the parents to their
Jn 12: 40 understand with their hearts, nor t—
16: 20 grieve, but your grief will t to joy.
Ac 3: 19 and t to God, so that your sins may
26: 18 and t them from darkness to light,
1Co 14: 31 For you can all prophesy in t so
1Ti 6: 20 T away from godless chatter
1Pe 3: 11 T from evil and do good;

TURNED (TURN)
Dt 23: 5 t the curse into a blessing for you,
1Ki 11: 4 his wives t his heart after other
2Ch 15: 4 their distress they t to the LORD,
Est 9: 1 now the tables were t and the Jews
9: 22 when their sorrow was t into joy
Ps 14: 3 All have t away, all have become
30: 11 You t my wailing into dancing;
40: 1 he t to me and heard my cry.
Isa 9: 12 his anger is not t away, his hand is
53: 6 each of us has t to our own way;
Hos 7: 8 Ephraim is a flat loaf not t over.
Joel 2: 31 The sun will t to darkness
Lk 22: 32 And when you have t back,
Ro 3: 12 All have t away, they have together

TURNING (TURN)
2Ki 21: 13 dish, wiping it and t it upside down.
Pr 2: 2 t your ear to wisdom and applying
14: 27 t a person from the snares of death.

TURNS (TURN)
2Sa 22: 29 the LORD t my darkness
Pr 15: 1 A gentle answer t away wrath,
Isa 44: 25 of the wise and t it into nonsense,
Jas 5: 20 Whoever t a sinner from the way

TWELVE
Ge 35: 22 Israel heard of it. Jacob had t sons:
49: 28 All these are the t tribes of Israel,
Mt 10: 1 Jesus called his t disciples to him
Mk 3: 14 He appointed t that they might be
Lk 9: 17 the disciples picked up t basketfuls
Rev 21: 12 written the names of the t tribes
21: 14 were the names of the t apostles

TWIN (TWINS)
Ge 25: 24 there were t boys in her womb.

TWINKLING*
1Co 15: 52 a flash, in the t of an eye, at the last

TWINS* (TWIN)
Ro 9: 11 before the t were born or had done

TWISTING* (TWISTS)
Pr 30: 33 and as the t the nose produces blood,

TWISTS (TWISTING)
Ex 23: 8 and t the words of the righteous.

TYING (TIES)
Mt 12: 29 first t up the strong man?

TYRANNICAL*
Pr 28: 16 A t ruler practices extortion, but one

TYRE
Eze 28: 12 a lament concerning the king of T
Mt 11: 22 it will be more bearable for T

UNAPPROACHABLE*
1Ti 6: 16 is immortal and who lives in u light,

UNASHAMED*
1Jn 2: 28 and u before him at his coming.

UNBELIEF* (UNBELIEVER UNBELIEVERS UNBELIEVING)
Mk 9: 24 help me overcome my u!"
Ro 4: 20 not waver through u regarding
11: 20 they were broken off because of u,

Ro 11: 23 And if they do not persist in u,
1Ti 1: 13 because I acted in ignorance and u.
Heb 3: 19 not able to enter, because of their u.

UNBELIEVER* (UNBELIEF)
1Co 7: 15 But if the u leaves, let it be so.
10: 27 If an u invites you to a meal
14: 24 if an u or an inquirer comes in while
2Co 6: 15 believer have in common with an u?
1Ti 5: 8 the faith and is worse than an u.

UNBELIEVERS* (UNBELIEF)
Lk 12: 46 and assign him a place with the u.
Ro 15: 31 be kept safe from the u in Judea
1Co 6: 6 and this in front of u!
14: 22 a sign, not for believers but for u;
14: 22 is not for u but for believers.
14: 23 and inquirers or u come in, will they
2Co 4: 4 this age has blinded the minds of u,
6: 14 Do not be yoked together with u.

UNBELIEVING* (UNBELIEF)
Mt 17: 17 "You u and perverse generation,"
Mk 9: 19 "You u generation," Jesus replied,
Lk 9: 41 "You u and perverse generation,"
1Co 7: 14 the u husband has been sanctified
7: 14 and u wife has been sanctified
Heb 3: 12 u heart that turns away
Rev 21: 8 But the cowardly, the u, the vile,

UNBLEMISHED*
Heb 9: 14 the eternal Spirit offered himself u

UNCEASING
Ro 9: 2 sorrow and u anguish in my heart.

UNCERTAIN*
1Ti 6: 17 which is so u, but to put their hope

UNCHANGEABLE* (UNCHANGING)
Heb 6: 18 that, by two u things in which it is

UNCHANGING* (UNCHANGEABLE)
Heb 6: 17 to make the u nature of his purpose

UNCIRCUMCISED
Lev 26: 41 when their u hearts are humbled
1Sa 17: 26 Who is this u Philistine that he
Jer 9: 26 whole house of Israel is u in heart."
Ac 7: 51 Your hearts and ears are still u.
Ro 4: 11 he had by faith while he was still u.
1Co 7: 18 Was a man u when he was called?
Col 3: 11 or Jew, circumcised or u, barbarian,

UNCIRCUMCISION
1Co 7: 19 is nothing and u is nothing.
Gal 5: 6 neither circumcision nor u has any

UNCLEAN
Ge 7: 2 one pair of every kind of u animal,
Lev 10: 10 between the u and the clean,
11: 4 it is ceremonially u for you.
11: 10 in the water—you are to regard as u.
11: 15 will be ceremonially u till evening;
Isa 6: 5 For I am a man of u lips, and I live among
a people of u lips,
52: 11 Touch no u thing! Come out from it
Ac 10: 14 never eaten anything impure or u."
Ro 14: 14 Jesus, that nothing is u in itself.
2Co 6: 17 Touch no u thing, and I will receive

UNCLOTHED*
2Co 5: 4 because we do not wish to be u

UNCONCERNED*
Eze 16: 49 were arrogant, overfed and u;

UNCOVERED
Ru 3: 7 quietly, u his feet and lay down.
1Co 11: 5 her head u dishonors her head—
11: 13 to pray to God with her head u?
Heb 4: 13 Everything is u and laid bare before

UNDERGOES* (UNDERGOING)
Heb 12: 8 and everyone u discipline—

UNDERGOING* (UNDERGOES)
1Pe 5: 9 the world are u the same kind

UNDERSTAND (UNDERSTANDING
UNDERSTANDS UNDERSTOOD)
Job 38: 4 Tell me, if you u.
42: 3 Surely I spoke of things I did not u,
Ps 14: 2 race to see if there are any who u,
73: 16 When I tried to u all this, it troubled
119: 27 Cause me to u the way of your
119:125 that I may u your statutes.
Pr 2: 5 you will u the fear of the LORD
2: 9 Then you will u what is right
30: 18 amazing for me, four that I do not u:
Ecc 7: 25 and to u the stupidity of wickedness

Ecc 11: 5 so you cannot u the work of God,
Isa 6: 10 with their ears, u with their hearts,
44: 18 They know nothing, they u nothing;
52: 15 they have not heard, they will u.
Jer 9: 24 that they u and know me,
17: 9 and beyond cure. Who can u it?
31: 19 after I came to u, I beat my breast.
Da 9: 25 "Know and u this: From the time
Hos 14: 9 Let them u. The ways
Mt 13: 15 u with their hearts and turn,
13: 23 people who hear the word and u it.
24: 15 let the reader u—
Lk 24: 45 so they could u the Scriptures.
Ac 8: 30 "Do you u what you are reading?"
Ro 7: 15 I do not u what I do. For what I
15: 21 those who have not heard will u."
1Co 2: 12 that we may u what God has freely
2: 14 and cannot u them because they are
Eph 5: 17 but u what the Lord's will is.
1Ti 6: 4 they are conceited and u nothing.
Heb 11: 3 By faith we u that the universe was
2Pe 1: 20 you must u that no prophecy
3: 3 you must u that in the last days
3: 16 some things that are hard to u,

UNDERSTANDING (UNDERSTAND)
1Ki 4: 29 of u as measureless as the sand
Job 12: 12 Does not long life bring u?
28: 12 Where does u dwell?
28: 28 is wisdom, and to shun evil is u."
32: 8 of the Almighty, that gives them u.
36: 26 How great is God—beyond our u!
37: 5 he does great things beyond our u.
Ps 111: 10 follow his precepts have good u.
119: 34 Give me u, so that I may keep your
119:100 I have more u than the elders, for I
119:104 I gain u from your precepts;
119:130 it gives u to the simple.
136: 5 who by his u made the heavens,
147: 5 mighty in power; his u has no limit.
Pr 2: 2 and applying your heart to u—
2: 6 his mouth come knowledge and u.
3: 5 heart and lean not on your own u;
3: 13 who find wisdom, those who gain u,
4: 5 Get wisdom, get u; do not forget my
4: 7 Though it cost all you have, get u.
9: 10 knowledge of the Holy One is u.
10: 23 but those who have u delight
11: 12 but those who have u hold their
14: 29 Those who are patient have great u,
15: 21 but those who have u keep a straight
15: 32 those who heed correction gain u.
17: 27 who have u are even-tempered.
18: 2 Fools find no pleasure in u
19: 8 those who cherish u will soon
Isa 11: 2 the Spirit of wisdom and of u,
40: 28 weary, and his u no one can fathom.
56: 11 They are shepherds who lack u;
Jer 3: 15 will lead you with knowledge and u.
10: 12 stretched out the heavens by his u.
Da 5: 12 a keen mind and knowledge and u,
10: 12 day that you set your mind to gain u
Hos 4: 11 and new wine take away their u.
Mk 4: 12 and ever hearing but never u;
12: 33 with all your u and with all your
Lk 2: 47 who heard him was amazed at his u
2Co 6: 6 in purity, u, patience and kindness;
Eph 1: 8 With all wisdom and u,
Php 4: 7 which transcends all u, will guard
Col 1: 9 wisdom and u that the Spirit gives,
2: 2 have the full riches of complete u,
1Jn 5: 20 God has come and has given us u,

UNDERSTANDS (UNDERSTAND)
1Ch 28: 9 every heart and u every desire
Ro 3: 11 there is no one who u; there is no

UNDERSTOOD (UNDERSTAND)
Ne 8: 8 people u what was being read.
8: 12 because they now u the words
Ps 73: 17 then I u their final destiny.
Isa 40: 21 Have you not u since the earth was
Ro 1: 20 being u from what has been made,

UNDESIRABLE*
Jos 24: 15 serving the LORD seems u to you,

UNDIVIDED*
1Ch 12: 33 to help David with u loyalty—
Ps 86: 11 give me an u heart, that I may fear
Eze 11: 19 I will give them an u heart and put
1Co 7: 35 in a right way in u devotion

UNDOING
Pr 18: 7 The mouths of fools are their u,

UNDYING*
Eph 6: 24 Lord Jesus Christ with an u love.

UNENDING
Ps 21: 6 you have granted him u blessings

UNEQUALED*
Mt 24: 21 from the beginning of the world
Mk 13: 19 of distress u from the beginning,

UNFADING*
1Pe 3: 4 the u beauty of a gentle and quiet

UNFAILING
Ex 15: 13 your u love you will lead the people
1Sa 20: 14 But show me u kindness like
2Sa 22: 51 he shows u kindness to his anointed,
Ps 6: 4 save me because of your u love.
13: 5 But I trust in your u love;
18: 50 he shows u love to his anointed,
21: 7 through the u love of the Most High
26: 3 been mindful of your u love,
31: 16 save me in your u love.
32: 10 but the LORD's u love surrounds
33: 5 the earth is full of his u love.
33: 18 those whose hope is in his u love,
33: 22 May your u love be with us,
36: 7 How priceless is your u love.
44: 26 redeem us because of your u love.
48: 9 O God, we meditate on your u love.
51: 1 O God, according to your u love;
52: 8 I trust in God's u love for ever
77: 8 Has his u love vanished forever?
85: 7 Show us your u love, LORD,
90: 14 us in the morning with your u love,
107: 8 thanks to the LORD for his u love
107: 15 thanks to the LORD for his u love
107: 21 thanks to the LORD for his u love
107: 31 thanks to the LORD for his u love
119: 41 May your u love come to me,
119: 76 May your u love be my comfort,
130: 7 for with the LORD is u love
143: 8 bring me word of your u love, for I
143: 12 In your u love, silence my enemies;
147: 11 who put their hope in his u love.
Pr 19: 22 What a person desires is u love;
20: 6 Many claim to have u love,
Isa 54: 10 yet my u love for you will not be
La 3: 32 compassion, so great is his u love.
Hos 10: 12 reap the fruit of u love, and break

UNFAITHFUL (UNFAITHFULNESS)
Lev 6: 2 is u to the LORD by deceiving
Nu 5: 6 and so is u to the LORD is guilty
1Ch 10: 13 Saul died because he was u
Pr 11: 6 but the u are trapped by evil desires.
13: 2 the u have an appetite for violence.
13: 15 but the way of the u leads to their
22: 12 but he frustrates the words of the u.
23: 28 and multiplies the u among men.
25: 19 foot is reliance on the u in a time
Jer 3: 20 But like a woman u to her husband,
Mal 2: 10 by being u to one another?
2: 11 Judah has been u.
2: 14 You have been u to her,
2: 15 not be u to the wife of your youth.
2: 16 on your guard, and do not be u.
Ro 3: 3 What if some were u?

UNFAITHFULNESS (UNFAITHFUL)
1Ch 9: 1 to Babylon because of their u.
Ro 3: 3 their u nullify God's faithfulness?

UNFIT*
Tit 1: 16 and u for doing anything good.

UNFOLDING
Ps 119:130 The u of your words gives light;

UNFORGIVING*
2Ti 3: 3 without love, u, slanderous,

UNFRIENDLY*
Pr 18: 1 An u person pursues selfish ends

UNFRUITFUL
1Co 14: 14 my spirit prays, but my mind is u.

UNGODLINESS (UNGODLY)
Tit 2: 12 It teaches us to say "No" to u

UNGODLY (UNGODLINESS)
Ro 4: 5 but trusts God who justifies the u,
5: 6 powerless, Christ died for the u.
1Ti 1: 9 and rebels, the u and sinful,
2Ti 2: 16 in it will become more and more u.
2Pe 2: 6 of what is going to happen to the u;
Jude 15 to convict all the u of all the u acts

UNGRATEFUL*
Lk   6: 35   because he is kind to the **u**
2Ti 3: 2   disobedient to their parents, **u,**

UNHOLY*
1Ti 1: 9   and sinful, the **u** and irreligious,
2Ti 3: 2   to their parents, ungrateful, **u,**
Heb 10: 29   have treated as an **u** thing the blood

UNINTENTIONALLY
Lev 4: 2   'When anyone sins **u** and does what
Nu 15: 22   if you as a community **u** fail to keep
Dt   4: 42   they had **u** killed a neighbor without

UNITE (UNITED UNITY)
1Co 6: 15   Christ and **u** them with a prostitute?

UNITED (UNITE)
Ge   2: 24   and mother and be **u** to his wife,
Mt 19: 5   and mother and be **u** to his wife,
Ro   6: 5   If we have been **u** with him
Eph 5: 31   and mother and be **u** to his wife,
Php 2: 1   from being **u** with Christ, if any
Col 2: 2   encouraged in heart and **u** in love,

UNITY* (UNITE)
2Ch 30: 12   the people to give them **u** of mind
Ps 133: 1   God's people live together in **u**
Jn 17: 23   they may be brought to complete **u.**
Eph 4: 3   keep the **u** of the Spirit through
     4: 13   until we all reach **u** in the faith
Col 3: 14   binds them all together in perfect **u.**

UNIVERSE*
1Co 4: 9   made a spectacle to the whole **u,**
Eph 4: 10   in order to fill the whole **u.**)
Heb 1: 2   through whom also he made the **u.**
   11: 3   understand that the **u** was formed

UNJUST
Ro   3: 5   That God is **u** in bringing his wrath
    9: 14   shall we say? Is God **u**? Not at all!
1Pe 2: 19   pain of **u** suffering because you are

UNKNOWN
Ac 17: 23   with this inscription: \to \an \u \god.

UNLEAVENED
Ex 12: 17   "Celebrate the Festival of **U** Bread,
Dt 16: 3   at the Festival of **U** Bread,

UNMARRIED
1Co 7: 8   It is good for them to stay **u,** as I do.
    7: 32   An **u** man is concerned

UNPLOWED
Ex 23: 11   the seventh year let the land lie **u**
Hos 10: 12   love, and break up your **u** ground;

UNPRODUCTIVE
Tit 3: 14   for urgent needs and not live **u** lives.
2Pe 1: 8   **u** in your knowledge of our Lord

UNPROFITABLE
Tit 3: 9   because these are **u** and useless.

UNPUNISHED
Ex 34: 7   Yet he does not leave the guilty **u;**
Pr   6: 29   no one who touches her will go **u.**
   11: 21   The wicked will not go **u,** but those
   19: 5   A false witness will not go **u,**
Joel 3: 21   leave their innocent blood **u**?

UNQUENCHABLE
Lk   3: 17   will burn up the chaff with **u** fire."

UNREASONING
2Pe 2: 12   They are like **u** animals, creatures

UNREPENTANT*
Ro   2: 5   your stubbornness and your **u** heart,

UNRIGHTEOUS*
Isa 55: 7   the **u** their thoughts.
Zep 3: 5   not fail, yet the **u** know no shame.
Mt   5: 45   rain on the righteous and the **u**
1Pe 3: 18   the righteous for the **u,** to bring you
2Pe 2: 9   to hold the **u** for punishment

UNSEARCHABLE
Ro 11: 33   How **u** his judgments, and his paths

UNSEEN
Mt   6: 6   and pray to your Father, who is **u.**
    6: 18   but only to your Father, who is **u;**
2Co 4: 18   but on what is **u,** since what is seen
    4: 18   temporary, but what is **u** is eternal.

UNSETTLED*
1Th 3: 3   no one would be **u** by these trials.
2Th 2: 2   not to become easily **u** or alarmed

UNSHRUNK
Mt   9: 16   "No one sews a patch of **u** cloth

UNSPIRITUAL*
Ro   7: 14   but I am **u,** sold as a slave to sin.
Col 2: 18   their **u** minds puff them up with idle
Jas 3: 15   down from heaven but is earthly, **u,**

UNSTABLE*
Jas 1: 8   double-minded and **u** in all they do.
2Pe 2: 14   they seduce the **u;** they are experts
    3: 16   which ignorant and **u** people distort,

UNTHINKABLE*
Job 34: 12   It is **u** that God would do wrong,

UNTIE
Mk 1: 7   am not worthy to stoop down and **u.**
Lk 13: 15   of you on the Sabbath **u** your ox

UNTRAINED*
2Co 11: 6   I may indeed be **u** as a speaker,

UNVEILED*
2Co 3: 18   with **u** faces contemplate the Lord's

UNWARY*
Ps 116: 6   The LORD protects the **u;**

UNWHOLESOME*
Eph 4: 29   Do not let any **u** talk come

UNWISE
Eph 5: 15   how you live—not as **u** but as wise,

UNWORTHY*
Ge 32: 10   I am **u** of all the kindness
Job 40: 4   "I am **u**—how can I reply to you?
Lk 17: 10   should say, 'We are **u** servants;
1Co 11: 27   Lord in an **u** manner will be guilty

UPHOLD (UPHOLDS)
Ps 82: 3   **u** the cause of the poor
Isa 41: 10   I will **u** you with my righteous
Ro   3: 31   Not at all! Rather, we **u** the law.

UPHOLDS* (UPHOLD)
Ps 37: 17   but the LORD **u** the righteous.
  37: 24   the LORD **u** them with his hand.
  63: 8   I cling to you; your right hand **u** me.
140: 12   poor and **u** the cause of the needy.
145: 14   The LORD **u** all who fall and lifts
146: 7   He **u** the cause of the oppressed

UPRIGHT (UPRIGHTLY)
Dt 32: 4   who does no wrong, **u** and just is he.
Job 1: 1   This man was blameless and **u;**
Ps   7: 10   High, who saves the **u** in heart.
   11: 7   the **u** will see his face.
   25: 8   Good and **u** is the LORD;
   33: 1   it is fitting for the **u** to praise him.
   64: 10   all the **u** in heart will glory in him!
   92: 15   proclaiming, "The LORD is **u;**
   97: 11   righteous and joy on the **u** in heart.
 119: 7   an **u** heart as I learn your righteous
Pr   2: 7   He holds success in store for the **u,**
   3: 32   but takes the **u** into his confidence.
   8: 9   they are **u** to those who have found
  15: 8   but the prayer of the **u** pleases him.
  21: 29   but the **u** give thought to their ways.
Isa 26: 7   The **u** One, make the way
Tit   1: 8   who is self-controlled, **u,**
    2: 12   **u** and godly lives in this present

UPRIGHTLY (UPRIGHT)
Pr 14: 2   Whoever fears the LORD walks **u,**

UPROOTED
Dt 28: 63   You will be **u** from the land you are
Jer 31: 40   The city will never again be **u**
Jude   : 12   autumn trees, without fruit and **u**—

UPSET
Lk 10: 41   worried and **u** about many things,

URGE
Tit 2: 4   they can **u** the younger women

URIAH
Hittite husband of Bathsheba, killed by David's order (2Sa 11).

USEFUL
Eph 4: 28   doing something **u** with their own
2Ti 2: 21   **u** to the Master and prepared to do
    3: 16   God-breathed and is **u** for teaching,
Phm   : 11   now he has become **u** both to you

USELESS
1Co 15: 14   our preaching is **u** and so is your
Tit   3: 9   these are unprofitable and **u.**
Phm   : 11   Formerly he was **u** to you, but now

UNSHRUNK
Heb 7: 18   set aside because it was weak and **u**
Jas 2: 20   that faith without deeds is **u**?

UTMOST
Job 34: 36   to the **u** for answering like a wicked

UTTER
Mt 13: 35   I will **u** things hidden since
1Co 14: 2   they **u** mysteries by the Spirit.

UZZIAH
Son of Amaziah; king of Judah also known as Azariah (2Ki 15:1–7; 1Ch 6:24; 2Ch 26). Struck with leprosy because of pride (2Ch 26:16–23).

VAIN
Ps 33: 17   A horse is a **v** hope for deliverance;
  73: 13   in **v** I have kept my heart pure
 127: 1   the house, the builders labor in **v.**
Isa 65: 23   They will not labor in **v,** nor will
1Co 15: 2   Otherwise, you have believed in **v.**
  15: 58   your labor in the Lord is not in **v.**
2Co 6: 1   you not to receive God's grace in **v.**
Gal 2: 2   had not been running my race in **v.**

VALIANT
1Sa 10: 26   by **v** men whose hearts God had

VALID
Jn   8: 14   my testimony is **v,** for I know where

VALLEY (VALLEYS)
Ps 23: 4   though I walk through the darkest **v,**
Isa 40: 4   Every **v** shall be raised up,
Joel 3: 14   multitudes in the **v** of decision!

VALLEYS (VALLEY)
SS 2: 1   I am a rose of Sharon, a lily of the **v.**

VALUABLE*
Lk 12: 24   And how much more **v** you are than

VALUE (VALUABLE)
Lev 27: 3   set the **v** of a male between the ages
Pr 16: 13   they **v** persons who speak what is
  31: 11   in her and lacks nothing of **v.**
Mt 13: 46   When he found one of great **v,**
Lk 16: 15   What people **v** highly is detestable
1Ti 4: 8   For physical training is of some **v,**
Php 2: 3   **v** others above yourselves,
Heb 11: 26   of greater **v** than the treasures

VANISHES
Jas 4: 14   appears for a little while and then **v.**

VASHTI*
Queen of Persia replaced by Esther (Est 1–2).

VAST
Ge   2: 1   were completed in all their **v** array.
Dt   1: 19   of the Amorites through all that **v**
   8: 15   He led you through the **v**
Ps 139: 17   How **v** is the sum of them!

VAULT
Ge 1: 7   So God made the **v** and separated
  1: 8   God called the **v** "sky."

VEGETABLES
Pr 15: 17   Better a small serving of **v** with love
Ro 14: 2   whose faith is weak, eats only **v.**

VEIL
Ex 34: 33   to them, he put a **v** over his face.
2Co 3: 14   to this day the same **v** remains

VENGEANCE (AVENGE AVENGER AVENGES AVENGING REVENGE)
Nu 31: 3   carry out the LORD's **v** on them.
Isa 34: 8   For the LORD has a day of **v,**
Na 1: 2   The LORD takes **v** on his foes

VERDICT
Ps 1: 4   you are right in your **v** and
Jn 3: 19   This is the **v:** Light has come

VICTOR'S* (VICTORY)
2Ti 2: 5   does not receive the **v** crown except

VICTORIES* (VICTORY)
Jdg 5: 11   They recite the **v** of the LORD, the **v** of his villagers
2Sa 22: 51   "He gives his king great **v;**
Ps 18: 50   He gives his king great **v;**
  21: 1   great is his joy in the **v** you give!
  21: 5   Through the **v** you gave, his glory is
  44: 4   my God, who decrees **v** for Jacob.

VICTORIOUS (VICTORY)
Rev 2: 7   To those who are **v,** I will give
   2: 11   who are **v** will not be hurt at all
   2: 17   To those who are **v,** I will give
   2: 26   To those who are **v** and do my will

Rev 3: 5 Those who are **v** will,
  3: 12 who are **v** I will make pillars
  3: 21 To those who are **v**, I will give
  3: 21 I was **v** and sat down with my Father
  3: 21 Those who are **v** will inherit

VICTORIOUSLY* (VICTORY)
Ps 45: 4 In your majesty ride forth **v**

VICTORY (VICTOR'S VICTORIES VICTORIOUS VICTORIOUSLY)
2Sa 8: 6 Lᴏʀᴅ gave David **v** wherever he
Ps 20: 5 May we shout for joy over your **v**
  44: 6 my sword does not bring me **v**;
  60: 12 With God we will gain the **v**,
  129: 2 have not gained the **v** over me.
Ps 149: 4 he crowns the humble with **v**.
Pr 11: 14 **v** is won through many advisers.
1Co 15: 54 has been swallowed up in **v**."
  15: 57 He gives us the **v** through our Lord
1Jn 5: 4 This is the **v** that has overcome

VIEW
Pr 5: 21 ways are in full **v** of the Lᴏʀᴅ,
2Ti 4: 1 and in **v** of his appearing and his

VILLAGE
Mk 6: 6 went around teaching from **v** to **v**

VINDICATE (VINDICATED VINDICATES VINDICATION)
Dt 32: 36 The Lᴏʀᴅ will **v** his people
Ps 138: 8 The Lᴏʀᴅ will **v** me;

VINDICATED (VINDICATE)
Job 13: 18 my case, I know I will be **v**.
Ps 17: 15 be **v** and will see your face;
1Ti 3: 16 in a body, was **v** by the Spirit,

VINDICATES (VINDICATE)
Ps 57: 2 to God, who **v** me.

VINDICATION (VINDICATE)
Ps 24: 5 and **v** from God their Savior.
  37: 6 your **v** like the noonday sun.

VINE (VINEYARD)
Ps 128: 3 like a fruitful **v** within your house;
Isa 36: 16 one of you will eat from your own **v**
Jn 15: 1 "I am the true **v**, and my Father is

VINEGAR
Pr 10: 26 As **v** to the teeth and smoke
Mk 15: 36 filled a sponge with wine **v**, put it

VINEYARD (VINE)
1Ki 21: 1 an incident involving a **v** belonging
Pr 31: 16 out of her earnings she plants a **v**.
SS 1: 6 my own **v** I had to neglect.
Isa 5: 1 My loved one had a **v** on a fertile
1Co 9: 7 Who plants a **v** and does not eat

VIOLATION
Heb 2: 2 every **v** and disobedience received

VIOLENCE (VIOLENT)
Ge 6: 11 in God's sight and was full of **v**.
Isa 53: 9 though he had done no **v**, nor was
  60: 18 No longer will **v** be heard in your
Eze 45: 9 Give up your **v** and oppression
Joel 3: 19 because of **v** done to the people
Jnh 3: 8 give up their evil ways and their **v**.

VIOLENT (VIOLENCE)
Eze 18: 10 "Suppose he has a **v** son, who sheds
Mt 11: 12 and **v** people have been raiding it.
1Ti 1: 13 and a persecutor and a **v** man, I was
  3: 3 to drunkenness, not **v** but gentle,
Tit 1: 7 not **v**, not pursuing dishonest gain.

VIPERS
Ps 140: 3 the poison of **v** is on their lips.
Lk 3: 7 baptized by him, "You brood of **v**!
Ro 3: 13 "The poison of **v** is on their lips."

VIRGIN (VIRGINS)
Dt 22: 15 at the gate proof that she was a **v**.
Isa 7: 14 The **v** will conceive and give birth
Mt 1: 23 "The **v** will conceive and give birth
Lk 1: 34 asked the angel, "since I am a **v**?"
2Co 11: 2 I might present you as a pure **v**

VIRGINS (VIRGIN)
Mt 25: 1 will be like ten **v** who took their
1Co 7: 25 Now about **v**: I have no command

VIRTUES*
Col 3: 14 And over all these **v** put on love,

VISIBLE
Eph 5: 13 exposed by the light becomes **v**—
Col 1: 16 heaven and on earth, **v** and invisible,

VISION (VISIONS)
Da 9: 24 to seal up **v** and prophecy
Ac 26: 19 disobedient to the **v** from heaven.

VISIONS (VISION)
Nu 12: 6 I reveal myself to them in **v**, I speak
Joel 2: 28 dreams, your young men will see **v**.
Ac 2: 17 your young men will see **v**, your old

VOICE
Dt 30: 20 listen to his **v**, and hold fast to him.
Job 40: 9 and can your **v** thunder like his?
Ps 19: 4 Yet their **v** goes out into all
  29: 3 The **v** of the Lᴏʀᴅ is over
  95: 7 Today, if only you would hear his **v**,
Pr 8: 1 Does not understanding raise her **v**?
Isa 30: 21 your ears will hear a **v** behind you,
  40: 3 A **v** of one calling:
Mk 1: 3 "a **v** of one calling
Jn 5: 28 are in their graves will hear his **v**
  10: 3 and the sheep listen to his **v**.
Ro 10: 18 "Their **v** has gone out into all
  15: 6 one **v** you may glorify the God
Heb 3: 7 "Today, if you hear his **v**,
Rev 3: 20 If anyone hears my **v** and opens

VOLUNTARY*
Phm : 14 not seem forced but would be **v**.

VOMIT
Lev 18: 28 it will **v** you out as it vomited
Pr 26: 11 As a dog returns to its **v**, so fools
2Pe 2: 22 "A dog returns to its **v**," and,

VOW (VOWS)
Nu 6: 2 woman wants to make a special **v**,
  30: 2 a man makes a **v** to the Lᴏʀᴅ
Jdg 11: 30 Jephthah made a **v** to the Lᴏʀᴅ:

VOWS (VOW)
Ps 116: 1 I will fulfill my **v** to the Lᴏʀᴅ
Pr 20: 25 and only later to consider one's **v**.

VULTURES
Mt 24: 28 is a carcass, there the **v** will gather.

WAGE (WAGES WAGING)
2Co 10: 3 we do not **w** war as the world does.

WAGES (WAGE)
Mal 3: 5 who defraud laborers of their **w**,
Lk 10: 7 for workers deserve their **w**.
Ro 4: 4 are not credited to them as
  6: 23 For the **w** of sin is death, but the gift
1Ti 5: 18 and "Workers deserve their **w**."

WAGING (WAGE)
Ro 7: 23 **w** war against the law of my mind

WAILING
Ps 30: 11 You turned my **w** into dancing;

WAIST
2Ki 1: 8 had a leather belt around his **w**."
Mt 3: 4 he had a leather belt around his **w**.

WAIT (AWAITS WAITED WAITING WAITS)
Ps 27: 14 **W** for the Lᴏʀᴅ; be strong
  130: 5 I **w** for the Lᴏʀᴅ, my whole being
Isa 30: 18 Blessed are all who **w** for him!
Ac 1: 4 **w** for the gift my Father promised,
Ro 8: 23 groan inwardly as we **w** eagerly
1Th 1: 10 and to **w** for his Son from heaven,
Tit 2: 13 while we **w** for the blessed hope—

WAITED (WAIT)
Ps 40: 1 I **w** patiently for the Lᴏʀᴅ;

WAITING (WAIT)
Heb 9: 28 to those who are **w** for him.

WAITS (WAIT)
Ro 8: 19 The creation **w** in eager expectation

WAKE (AWAKE WAKENS)
Eph 5: 14 "**W** up, sleeper, rise from the dead,

WAKENS* (WAKE)
Isa 50: 4 He **w** me morning by morning,
  50: 4 He **w** me morning by morning,

WALK (WALKED WALKING WALKS)
Lev 26: 12 I will **w** among you and be your
Dt 5: 33 **W** in obedience to all
  6: 7 and when you **w** along the road,
  10: 12 your God, to **w** in obedience to him,
  11: 19 and when you **w** along the road,
  11: 22 to **w** in obedience to him and to hold
  26: 17 that you will **w** in obedience to him,
Jos 22: 5 your God, to **w** in obedience to him,
Ps 1: 1 Blessed are those who do not **w**
  15: 2 Those whose **w** is blameless,

Ps 23: 4 Even though I **w** through the darkest
  84: 11 from those whose **w** is blameless,
  89: 15 who **w** in the light of your presence,
  119: 45 I will **w** about in freedom, for I have
Pr 4: 12 When you **w**, your steps will not be
  6: 22 When you **w**, they will guide you;
  13: 20 **W** with the wise and become wise,
Isa 2: 3 so that we may **w** in his paths."
  2: 5 let us **w** in the light of the Lᴏʀᴅ.
  30: 21 saying, "This is the way; **w** in it."
  33: 15 Those who **w** righteously and speak
  40: 31 weary, they will **w** and not be faint.
  57: 2 Those who **w** uprightly enter
Jer 6: 16 and **w** in it, and you will find rest
Da 4: 37 those who **w** in pride he is able
Am 3: 3 Do two **w** together unless they have
Mic 4: 5 All the nations may **w** in the name
  6: 8 and to **w** humbly with your God.
Mk 2: 9 'Get up, take your mat and **w**'?
Jn 8: 12 Whoever follows me will never **w**
  11: 9 **w** in the daytime will not stumble,
  11: 9 with him and yet **w** in the darkness,
1Jn 1: 7 But if we **w** in the light, as he is
2Jn 1: 6 his command is that you **w** in love.

WALKED (WALK)
Ge 5: 24 Enoch **w** faithfully with God;
Jos 14: 9 which your feet have **w** will be your
Mt 14: 29 **w** on the water and came toward

WALKING (WALK)
1Ki 3: 3 the Lᴏʀᴅ by **w** according
Da 3: 25 I see four men **w** around in the fire,
2Jn : 4 some of your children **w** in the truth,

WALKS (WALK)
Pr 10: 9 Whoever **w** in integrity **w** securely,

WALL (WALLS)
Jos 6: 20 gave a loud shout, the **w** collapsed;
Ne 2: 17 let us rebuild the **w** of Jerusalem,
Eph 2: 14 barrier, the dividing **w** of hostility,
Rev 21: 12 a great, high **w** with twelve gates,

WALLOWING
2Pe 2: 22 returns to her **w** in the mud."

WALLS (WALL)
Isa 58: 12 be called Repairer of Broken **W**,
  60: 18 you will call your **w** Salvation
Heb 11: 30 By faith the **w** of Jericho fell,

WANDER (WANDERED)
Nu 32: 13 he made them **w** in the wilderness
Jas 5: 19 one of you should **w** from the truth

WANDERED (WANDER)
Eze 34: 6 My sheep **w** over all the mountains
Mt 18: 12 go to look for the one that **w** off?
1Ti 6: 10 have **w** from the faith and pierced

WANT (WANTED WANTING WANTS)
1Sa 8: 19 they said. "We **w** a king over us.
Mt 19: 21 "If you **w** to be perfect, go,
Lk 19: 14 'We don't **w** this man to be our
Ro 7: 15 For what I **w** to do I do not do,
  13: 3 Do you **w** to be free from fear
2Co 12: 14 to you, because what I **w** is not your
Php 3: 10 I **w** to know Christ—yes, to know

WANTED (WANT)
1Co 12: 18 of them, just as he **w** them to be.
Heb 6: 17 Because God **w** to make

WANTING (WANT)
Da 5: 27 weighed on the scales and found **w**.
2Pe 3: 9 with you, not **w** anyone to perish,

WANTS (WANT)
Mt 5: 42 away from the one who **w** to borrow
  20: 26 whoever **w** to become great among
Mk 8: 35 For whoever **w** to save their life will
  10: 43 whoever **w** to become great among
Ro 9: 18 he hardens whom he **w** to harden.
1Ti 2: 4 who **w** all people to be saved
1Pe 5: 2 you are willing, as God **w** you to be;

WAR (WARRIOR WARS)
Jos 11: 23 Then the land had rest from **w**.
1Sa 15: 18 make **w** on them until you have
Ps 68: 30 Scatter the nations who delight in **w**.
  120: 7 but when I speak, they are for **w**.
  144: 1 who trains my hands for **w**,
Isa 2: 4 nor will they train for **w** anymore.
Da 9: 26 **W** will continue until the end,
Ro 7: 23 waging **w** against the law of my
2Co 10: 3 we do not wage **w** as the world
1Pe 2: 11 desires, which **w** against your soul.
Rev 12: 7 And there was **w** in heaven.

Rev 19: 11 With justice he judges and makes **w**.

WARN* (WARNED WARNING WARNINGS)
Ex 19: 21 **w** the people so they do not force
Nu 24: 14 let me **w** you of what this people
1Sa 8: 9 but **w** them solemnly and let them
1Ki 2: 42 swear by the Lord and **w** you,
2Ch 19: 10 you are to **w** them not to sin against
Ps 81: 8 my people, and I will **w** you—
Jer 42: 19 Be sure of this: I **w** you today
Eze 3: 18 you do not **w** them or speak
3: 19 if you do **w** the wicked and they do
3: 20 Since you did not **w** them, they will
3: 21 if you do **w** the righteous not to sin
33: 3 blows the trumpet to **w** the people,
33: 6 blow the trumpet to **w** the people
33: 9 if you do **w** the wicked to turn
Lk 16: 28 Let him **w** them, so that they will
Ac 20: 31 I never stopped to speak no longer
1Co 4: 14 but to **w** you as my dear children.
Gal 4: 16 I **w** you, as I did before, that those
1Th 5: 14 **w** those who are idle and disruptive,
2Th 3: 15 but **w** them as fellow believers.
2Ti 2: 14 **W** them before God against
Tit 3: 10 **W** divisive people once, and then **w** them
a second time.
Rev 22: 18 I **w** everyone who hears the words

WARNED (WARN)
2Ki 17: 13 The Lord **w** Israel and Judah
Ps 19: 11 By them your servant is **w**;
Jer 22: 21 I **w** you when you felt secure,
Mt 3: 7 Who **w** you to flee from the coming
1Th 4: 6 as we told you and **w** you before.
Heb 11: 7 when **w** about things not yet seen,
12: 25 they refused him who **w** them

WARNING (WARN)
Jer 6: 8 Take **w**, Jerusalem, or I will turn
1Ti 5: 20 so that the others may take **w**.

WARNINGS (WARN)
1Co 10: 11 and were written down as **w** for us,

WARRIOR (WAR)
Ex 15: 3 The Lord is a **w**; the Lord is
1Ch 28: 3 because you are a **w** and have shed
Pr 16: 32 Better a patient person than a **w**,

WARS (WAR)
Ps 46: 9 He makes **w** cease to the ends
Mt 24: 6 you will hear of **w** and rumors of **w**,

WASH (WASHED WASHING)
Ps 51: 7 **w** me, and I will be whiter than
Jer 4: 14 **w** the evil from your heart and be
Jn 13: 5 and began to **w** his disciples' feet,
Ac 22: 16 be baptized and **w** your sins away,
Jas 4: 8 **W** your hands, you sinners,
Rev 22: 14 are those who **w** their robes,

WASHED (WASH)
Ps 73: 13 and have **w** my hands in innocence.
1Co 6: 11 But you were, you were
Heb 10: 22 and having our bodies **w** with pure
2Pe 2: 22 "A sow that is **w** returns to her
Rev 7: 14 they have **w** their robes and made

WASHING (WASH)
Eph 5: 26 the **w** with water through the word,
1Ti 5: 10 **w** the feet of the Lord's people,
Tit 3: 5 He saved us through the **w** of rebirth

WASTED (WASTING)
Jn 6: 12 are left over. Let nothing be **w**."

WASTING (WASTED)
2Co 4: 16 Though outwardly we are **w** away,

WATCH (WATCHES WATCHING WATCHMAN)
Ge 31: 49 the Lord keep **w** between you
Job 7: 20 you who **w** over us all?
Ps 90: 4 gone by, or like a **w** in the night.
141: 3 keep **w** over the door of my lips.
Pr 4: 6 love her, and she will **w** over you.
6: 22 you sleep, they will **w** over you;
Jer 31: 10 them and will **w** over his flock like
Mic 7: 7 for me, I **w** in hope for the Lord,
Mt 24: 42 "Therefore keep **w**, because you do
26: 41 "W and pray so that you will not
Mk 13: 35 "Therefore keep **w** because you do
Lk 2: 8 keeping **w** over their flocks at night.
1Ti 4: 16 **W** your life and doctrine closely.
Heb 13: 17 they keep **w** over you as

WATCHES* (WATCH)
Nu 19: 5 While he **w**, the heifer is to be
Job 24: 15 The eye of the adulterer **w** for dusk;
Ps 1: 6 For the Lord **w** over the way

Ps 33: 14 his dwelling place he **w** all who live
63: 6 of you through the **w** of the night.
119:148 My eyes stay open through the **w**
121: 3 he who **w** over you will not
121: 4 he who **w** over Israel will neither
121: 5 The Lord **w** over you—
127: 1 Unless the Lord **w** over the city,
145: 20 The Lord **w** over all who love
146: 9 The Lord **w** over the foreigner
Pr 31: 27 She **w** over the affairs of her
Ecc 11: 4 Whoever **w** the wind will not plant;
La 2: 19 night, as the **w** of the night begin;
4: 16 he no longer **w** over them.

WATCHING (WATCH)
Lk 12: 37 servants whose master finds them **w**
1Pe 5: 2 **w** over them—not because you must,

WATCHMAN (WATCH)
Eze 3: 17 I have made you a **w** for the house
33: 6 but I will hold the **w** accountable

WATER (WATERED WATERING WATERS WELL-WATERED)
Ex 7: 20 all the **w** was changed into blood.
17: 1 but there was no **w** for the people
Nu 20: 2 Now there was no **w**
Ps 1: 3 like a tree planted by streams of **w**,
22: 14 I am poured out like **w**, and all my
42: 1 As the deer pants for streams of **w**,
Pr 25: 21 if he is thirsty, give him **w** to drink.
Isa 12: 3 joy you will draw **w** from the wells
30: 20 of adversity and the **w** of affliction,
32: 2 like streams of **w** in the desert
49: 10 and lead them beside springs of **w**.
Jer 2: 13 broken cisterns that cannot hold **w**.
17: 8 a tree planted by the **w** that sends
31: 9 I will lead them beside streams of **w**
Eze 36: 25 I will sprinkle clean **w** on you,
Zec 14: 8 On that day living **w** will flow
Mt 14: 29 walked on the **w** and came toward
Mk 9: 41 anyone who gives you a cup of **w**
Lk 5: 4 "Put out into deep **w**, and let down
Jn 3: 5 of God without being born of **w**
4: 10 he would have given you living **w**."
7: 38 rivers of living **w** will flow
Eph 5: 26 washing with **w** through the word,
Heb 10: 22 our bodies washed with pure **w**.
1Pe 3: 21 this **w** symbolizes baptism that now
2Pe 2: 17 These people are springs without **w**
1Jn 5: 6 This is the one who came by **w**
5: 6 He did not come by **w** only,
5: 8 the Spirit, the **w** and the blood;
Rev 7: 17 lead them to springs of living **w**."
21: 6 cost from the spring of the **w** of life.

WATERED (WATER)
1Co 3: 6 I planted the seed, Apollos **w** it,

WATERING (WATER)
Isa 55: 10 not return to it without **w** the earth

WATERS (WATER)
Ps 23: 2 he leads me beside quiet **w**,
SS 8: 7 Many **w** cannot quench love;
Isa 11: 9 the Lord as the **w** cover the sea.
43: 2 When you pass through the **w**, I will
55: 1 you who are thirsty, come to the **w**;
58: 11 like a spring whose **w** never fail.
Hab 2: 14 the Lord as the **w** cover the sea.
1Co 3: 7 nor the one who **w** is anything,

WAVE (WAVES)
Lev 23: 11 **w** the sheaf before the Lord so it
Jas 1: 6 the one who doubts is like a **w**

WAVER*
1Ki 18: 21 "How long will you **w** between two
Ro 4: 20 Yet he did not **w** through unbelief

WAVES (WAVE)
Isa 57: 20 rest, whose **w** cast up mire and mud.
Mt 8: 27 the winds and the **w** obey him!"
Eph 4: 14 tossed back and forth by the **w**,

WAY (WAYS)
Ex 13: 21 of cloud to guide them on their **w**
18: 20 show them the **w** they are to live
Dt 1: 33 to show you the **w** you should go.
32: 4 Is this the **w** you repay the Lord,
1Sa 12: 23 I will teach you the **w** that is good
2Sa 22: 31 "As for God, his **w** is perfect;
1Ki 8: 23 continue wholeheartedly in your **w**.
8: 36 Teach them the right **w** to live,
Job 23: 10 But he knows the **w** that I take;
Ps 1: 1 stand in the **w** that sinners take or sit
32: 8 teach you in the **w** you should go;

Ps 37: 5 Commit your **w** to the Lord;
86: 11 Teach me your **w**, Lord, that I
119: 9 who are young keep their **w** pure?
139: 24 if there is any offensive **w** in me,
Pr 4: 11 I instruct you in the **w** of wisdom
12: 15 The **w** of fools seems right to them,
14: 12 a **w** that appears to be right,
16: 7 Lord takes pleasure in anyone's **w**,
19: 2 more will hasty feet miss the **w**!
22: 6 off on the **w** they should go,
30: 19 the **w** of an eagle in the sky, the **w**
Isa 30: 21 behind you, saying, "This is the **w**;
35: 8 it will be called the **W** of Holiness;
40: 3 the wilderness prepare the **w**
48: 17 directs you in the **w** you should go.
53: 6 each of us has turned to our own **w**;
Jer 5: 31 and my people love it this **w**.
Mal 3: 1 who will prepare the **w** before me.
Mt 3: 3 'Prepare the **w** for the Lord,
Lk 7: 27 will prepare your **w** before you.'
Jn 14: 6 "I am the **w** and the truth
Ac 1: 11 in the same **w** you have seen him go
9: 2 any there who belonged to the **W**,
24: 14 our ancestors as a follower of the **W**,
1Co 10: 13 also provide a **w** out so that you can
12: 31 will show you the most excellent **w**.
14: 1 Follow the **w** of love and eagerly
Col 1: 10 the Lord and please him in every **w**:
Tit 2: 10 every **w** they will make the teaching
Heb 4: 15 who has been tempted in every **w**,
9: 8 the **w** into the Most Holy Place had
10: 20 living **w** opened for us through
13: 18 desire to live honorably in every **w**.

WAYS (WAY)
Ex 33: 13 teach me your **w** so I may know you
Dt 32: 4 are perfect, and all his **w** are just.
2Ch 11: 17 years, following the **w** of David
Job 34: 21 "His eyes are on the **w** of mortals;
Ps 25: 4 Show me your **w**, Lord, teach me
25: 10 All the **w** of the Lord are loving
37: 7 fret when people succeed in their **w**,
51: 13 I will teach transgressors your **w**,
77: 13 Your **w**, God, are holy. What god is
119: 59 I have considered my **w** and have
139: 3 you are familiar with all my **w**.
145: 17 The Lord is righteous in all his **w**
Pr 3: 6 in all your **w** submit to him, and he
4: 26 feet and be steadfast in all your **w**.
5: 21 For your **w** are in full view
16: 2 may think all their **w** are pure,
16: 17 who guard their **w** preserve their
Isa 2: 3 He will teach us his **w**, so that we
55: 7 Let the wicked forsake their **w**
55: 8 neither are your **w** my **w**,"
Eze 28: 15 in your **w** from the day you were
33: 8 out to dissuade them from their **w**,
Hos 14: 9 The **w** of the Lord are right;
Ro 1: 30 they invent **w** of doing evil;
Jas 3: 2 We all stumble in many **w**.

WAYWARD
Pr 6: 24 the smooth talk of a **w** woman.

WEAK (WEAKER WEAKNESS WEAKNESSES)
Ps 41: 1 are those who have regard for the **w**;
72: 13 He will take pity on the **w**
82: 3 Defend the **w** and the fatherless;
Eze 34: 4 You have not strengthened the **w**
Mt 26: 41 spirit is willing, but the flesh is **w**."
Ac 20: 35 of hard work we must help the **w**,
Ro 14: 1 Accept those whose faith is **w**,
15: 1 to bear with the failings of the **w**,
1Co 1: 27 God chose the **w** things of the world
8: 9 become a stumbling block to the **w**.
9: 22 To the **w** I became **w**, to win the **w**.
11: 30 That is why many among you are **w**
2Co 12: 10 For when I am **w**, then I am strong.
1Th 5: 14 help the **w**, be patient
Heb 12: 12 your feeble arms and **w** knees.

WEAKER* (WEAK)
2Sa 3: 1 the house of Saul grew **w** and **w**.
1Co 12: 22 that seem to be **w** are indispensable,
1Pe 3: 7 them with respect as the **w** partner

WEAKNESS* (WEAK)
La 1: 6 **w** they have fled before the pursuer.
Ro 8: 26 the Spirit helps us in our **w**.
1Co 1: 25 the **w** of God is stronger than human
2: 3 I came to you in **w** with great fear
15: 43 it is sown in **w**, it is raised in power;
2Co 11: 30 boast of the things that show my **w**.
12: 9 my power is made perfect in **w**."

2Co 13: 4 he was crucified in w, yet he lives
Heb 5: 2 since he himself is subject to w.
7: 28 high priests men in all their w;
11: 34 whose w was turned to strength;

WEAKNESSES* (WEAK)
2Co 12: 5 about myself, except about my w.
12: 9 all the more gladly about my w,
12: 10 sake, I delight in w, in insults,
Heb 4: 15 is unable to empathize with our w,

WEALTH
Dt 8: 18 gives you the ability to produce w,
2Ch 1: 11 desire and you have not asked for w,
Ps 39: 6 up w without knowing whose it will
49: 12 despite their w, do not endure;
Pr 3: 9 Honor the Lord with your w,
10: 4 poverty, but diligent hands bring w.
11: 4 W is worthless in the day of wrath,
13: 7 pretends to be poor, yet has great w.
15: 16 of the Lord than great w
Ecc 5: 10 those who love w are never satisfied
5: 13 w hoarded to the harm of its owners.
SS 8: 7 to give all the w of one's house
Mt 13: 22 deceitfulness of w choke the word,
Mk 10: 22 away sad, because he had great w.
12: 44 They all gave out of their w;
Lk 15: 13 and there squandered his w in wild
1Ti 6: 17 arrogant nor to put their hope in w,
Jas 5: 2 You have w has rotted, and moths have
5: 3 You have hoarded w in the last

WEAPON (WEAPONS)
Ne 4: 17 one hand and held a w in the other,

WEAPONS (WEAPON)
Ecc 9: 18 Wisdom is better than w of war,
2Co 6: 7 with w of righteousness in the right
10: 4 The w we fight with are not the w

WEAR (WEARING)
Dt 8: 4 Your clothes did not w out and your
22: 5 nor a man w women's clothing,
Ps 102: 26 they will all w out like a garment.
Pr 23: 4 Do not w yourself out to get rich;
Isa 51: 6 the earth will w out like a garment
Heb 1: 11 they will all w out like a garment.
Rev 3: 18 and white clothes to w, so you can

WEARIES (WEARY)
Ecc 12: 12 no end, and much study w the body.

WEARING (WEAR)
Jn 19: 5 Jesus came out w the crown
Jas 2: 3 attention to the one w fine clothes
1Pe 3: 3 hairstyles and the w of gold jewelry
Rev 7: 9 They were w white robes and were

WEARY (WEARIES)
Isa 40: 28 He will not grow tired or w, and his
40: 31 they will run and not grow w,
50: 4 know the word that sustains the w.
Mt 11: 28 all you who are w and burdened,
Gal 6: 9 Let us not become w in doing good,
Heb 12: 3 so that you will not grow w and lose
Rev 2: 3 my name, and have not grown w.

WEDDING
Mt 22: 11 who was not wearing w clothes.
Rev 19: 7 For the w of the Lamb has come,

WEEDS
Mt 13: 25 and sowed w among the wheat,

WEEK
Mt 28: 1 at dawn on the first day of the w,
1Co 16: 2 On the first day of every w,

WEEP (WEEPING WEPT)
Ecc 3: 4 a time to w and a time to laugh,
Lk 6: 21 Blessed are you who w now, for you
23: 28 of Jerusalem, do not w for me;

WEEPING (WEEP)
Ps 30: 5 w may remain for a night,
126: 6 Those who go out w, carrying seed
Jer 31: 15 mourning and great w, Rachel w
Mt 2: 18 Rachel w for her children
8: 12 where there will be w and gnashing

WEIGH (OUTWEIGHS WEIGHED WEIGHS
WEIGHTIER WEIGHTS)
1Co 14: 29 the others should w carefully what

WEIGHED (WEIGH)
Job 28: 15 nor can its price be w out in silver.
Da 5: 27 You have been w on the scales
Lk 21: 34 or your hearts will be w down

WEIGHS (WEIGH)
Pr 12: 25 Anxiety w down the heart,
15: 28 heart of the righteous w its answers,
21: 2 right, but the Lord w the heart.
24: 12 not he who w the heart perceive it?

WEIGHTIER* (WEIGH)
Jn 5: 36 "I have testimony w than

WEIGHTS (WEIGH)
Lev 19: 36 Use honest scales and honest w,
Dt 25: 13 Do not have two differing w in your
Pr 11: 1 but accurate w find favor with him.

WELCOME (WELCOMES)
Mk 9: 37 welcomes me does not w me
2Pe 1: 11 you will receive a rich w

WELCOMES (WELCOME)
Mt 10: 40 "Anyone who w you w me, and anyone
who w me w the one who sent me.
18: 5 whoever w one such child in my name w
me.
2Jn : 11 Anyone who w them shares in their

WELL (WELLED WELLING WELLS)
Jer 32: 39 go w for them and for their children
Mt 15: 31 the crippled made w, the lame
Lk 14: 5 falls into a w on the Sabbath day,
17: 19 your faith has made you w."
Jas 5: 15 offered in faith will make them w;

WELL-WATERED (WATER)
Isa 58: 11 You will be like a w garden,

WELLED* (WELL)
2Co 8: 2 their extreme poverty w up in rich

WELLING* (WELL)
Jn 4: 14 in them a spring of water w

WELLS (WELL)
Isa 12: 3 draw water from the w of salvation.

WEPT (WEEP)
Ps 137: 1 and w when we remembered Zion.
Lk 22: 62 And he went outside and w bitterly.
Jn 11: 35 Jesus w.

WEST
Ps 103: 12 as far as the east is from the w,
107: 3 from east and w, from north

WHEAT
Mt 3: 12 gathering his w into the barn
13: 25 and sowed weeds among the w,
Lk 22: 31 has asked to sift all of you as w.
Jn 12: 24 unless a kernel of w falls

WHEELS
Eze 1: 16 appearance and structure of the w:

WHIRLWIND (WIND)
2Ki 2: 1 to take Elijah up to heaven in a w,
Hos 8: 7 "They sow the wind and reap the w.
Na 1: 3 His way is in the w and the storm,

WHISPER (WHISPERED)
1Ki 19: 12 And after the fire came a gentle w.
Job 26: 14 how faint the w we hear of him!
Ps 107: 29 He stilled the storm to a w;

WHISPERED (WHISPER)
Mt 10: 27 what is w in your ear,

WHITE (WHITER)
Isa 1: 18 scarlet, they shall be as w as snow;
Da 7: 9 His clothing was as w as snow;
7: 9 hair of his head was w like wool.
Mt 28: 3 and his clothes were w as snow.
Rev 1: 14 head was w like wool, as w as snow,
3: 4 dressed in w, for they are worthy.
6: 2 and there before me was a w horse!
7: 13 asked me, "These in w robes—
19: 11 and there before me was a w horse,
20: 11 I saw a great w throne and him who

WHITER (WHITE)
Ps 51: 7 wash me, and I will be w than snow.

WHOLE
Ge 1: 29 plant on the face of the w earth
2: 6 watered the w surface of the ground.
11: 1 Now the w world had one language
Ex 12: 47 The w community of Israel must
5: 3 Although the w earth is mine,
Lev 16: 17 and the w community of Israel.
Nu 14: 21 of the Lord fills the w earth,
32: 13 until the w generation of those who
Dt 13: 16 all its plunder as a w burnt offering
19: 8 gives you the w land he promised
Jos 2: 3 have come to spy out the w land."

1Sa 1: 28 For his w life he will be given over
17: 46 the w world will know that there is
1Ki 10: 24 The w world sought audience
2Ki 21: 8 will keep the w Law that my servant
Ps 72: 19 may the w earth be filled with his
Pr 4: 22 them and health to one's w body.
8: 31 rejoicing in his w world
Isa 1: 5 Your w head is injured, your w heart
6: 3 the w earth is full of his glory."
14: 26 the plan determined for the w world;
Eze 34: 6 were scattered over the w earth,
37: 11 these bones are the w house
Da 2: 35 mountain and filled the w earth.
Zep 1: 18 of his jealousy the w earth will be
Zec 14: 9 will be king over the w earth.
Mal 3: 10 Bring the w tithe
Mt 5: 29 your body than for your w body
6: 22 your w body will be full of light.
16: 26 it be for you to gain the w world,
24: 14 in the w world as a testimony to all
Lk 21: 35 who live on the face of the w earth.
Jn 12: 19 Look how the w world has gone
13: 10 their w body is clean.
21: 25 even the w world would not have
Ac 17: 26 that they should inhabit the w earth;
20: 27 proclaim to you the w will of God.
Ro 3: 19 and the w world held accountable
8: 22 the w creation has been groaning in
1Co 4: 9 made a spectacle to the w universe,
12: 17 If the w body were an ear,
Gal 5: 3 he is obligated to obey the w law.
Eph 4: 10 in order to fill the w universe.)
4: 13 attaining to the w measure
1Th 5: 23 May your w spirit, soul and body be
Jas 2: 10 for whoever keeps the w law
1Jn 2: 2 but also for the sins of the w world.
Rev 3: 10 to come on the w world to test those

WHOLEHEARTED* (HEART)
2Ki 20: 3 and with w devotion and have done
1Ch 28: 9 serve him with w devotion
29: 19 my son Solomon the w devotion
Isa 38: 3 and with w devotion and have done

WHOLEHEARTEDLY* (HEART)
Nu 14: 24 a different spirit and follows me w,
32: 11 they have not followed me w,
32: 12 for they followed the Lord w.'
Dt 1: 36 he followed the Lord w.'
Jos 14: 8 followed the Lord my God w.
14: 9 followed the Lord my God w.'
14: 14 the Lord, the God of Israel, w.
1Ki 8: 23 your servants who continue w
1Ch 29: 9 given freely and w to the Lord.
2Ch 6: 14 your servants who continue w
15: 15 oath because they had sworn it w.
19: 9 and w in the fear of the Lord.
25: 2 the eyes of the Lord, but not w.
31: 21 he sought his God and worked w.
Eph 6: 7 Serve w, as if you were serving

WHOLESOME*
2Pe 3: 1 to stimulate you to w thinking.

WICK
Isa 42: 3 a smoldering w he will not snuff
Mt 12: 20 a smoldering w he will not snuff

WICKED (WICKEDNESS)
Ge 13: 13 Now the people of Sodom were w
39: 9 could I do such a w thing and sin
Nu 14: 35 things to this whole w community,
Dt 15: 9 careful not to harbor this w thought:
Jdg 19: 22 some of the w men of the city
1Sa 15: 18 completely destroy those w people,
25: 17 He is such a w man that no one can
2Sa 13: 12 Don't do this w thing.
2Ki 17: 11 They did w things that aroused
2Ch 7: 14 my face and turn from their w ways,
19: 2 "Should you help the w and love
Ne 13: 17 them, "What is this w thing you are
Ps 1: 1 who do not walk in step with the w
1: 5 Therefore the w will not stand
7: 9 to an end the violence of the w
10: 13 Why do the w revile God?
11: 5 but the w, those who love violence,
26: 5 and refuse to sit with the w.
32: 10 Many are the woes of the w,
36: 1 concerning the sinfulness of the w:
37: 13 but the Lord laughs at the w, for he
49: 5 when w deceivers surround me—
50: 16 But to the w, God says:
58: 3 Even from birth the w go astray;
73: 3 when I saw the prosperity of the w.

Ps 82: 2 unjust and show partiality to the *w*?
112: 10 the longings of the *w* will come
119: 61 Though the *w* bind me with ropes,
119:155 Salvation is far from the *w*, for they
140: 8 Do not grant the *w* their desires,
141: 10 Let the *w* fall into their own nets,
146: 9 but he frustrates the ways of the *w*.
Pr 2: 12 save you from the ways of *w* men,
4: 14 Do not set foot on the path of the *w*
6: 18 a heart that devises *w* schemes,
9: 7 rebukes the *w* incurs abuse.
10: 20 the heart of the *w* is of little value.
10: 23 Fools find pleasure in *w* schemes,
10: 28 the hopes of the *w* come to nothing.
11: 5 but the *w* are brought down by their
11: 10 when the *w* perish, there are shouts
11: 21 The *w* will not go unpunished,
12: 5 but the advice of the *w* is deceitful.
12: 10 the kindest acts of the *w* are cruel.
14: 19 the *w* at the gates of the righteous.
15: 3 keeping watch on the *w*
15: 26 detests the thoughts of the *w*,
21: 10 The *w* crave evil;
21: 29 The *w* put up a bold front,
28: 1 The *w* flee though no one pursues,
28: 4 forsake instruction praise the *w*,
29: 7 but the *w* have no such concern.
29: 16 When the *w* thrive, so does sin,
29: 27 the *w* detest the upright.
Isa 11: 4 breath of his lips he will slay the *w*.
13: 11 for its evil, the *w* for their sins.
26: 10 But when grace is shown to the *w*,
48: 22 says the LORD, "for the *w*."
53: 9 He was assigned a grave with the *w*,
55: 7 Let the *w* forsake their ways
57: 20 But the *w* are like the tossing sea,
Jer 35: 15 of you must turn from your *w* ways
Eze 3: 18 those *w* people will die for their
13: 22 because you encouraged the *w* not
14: 7 put a *w* stumbling block before their
18: 21 if the *w* turn away from all the sins
18: 23 any pleasure in the death of the *w*?
21: 25 profane and *w* prince of Israel,
33: 8 When I say to the *w*, 'You *w* people,
33: 11 no pleasure in the death of the *w*,
33: 14 And if I say to the *w*, 'You *w*
33: 19 And if the *w* turn away from their
Da 12: 10 but the *w* will continue to be *w*.
Mt 12: 39 "A *w* and adulterous generation
12: 45 other spirits more *w* than itself,
12: 45 it will be with this *w* generation."
Lk 6: 35 he is kind to the ungrateful and *w*.
Ac 2: 23 with the help of *w* men, put him
1Co 5: 13 "Expel the *w* person from among
Rev 2: 2 that you cannot tolerate *w* people,

WICKEDNESS (WICKED)

Ge 6: 5 The LORD saw how great the *w*
Ex 34: 7 and forgiving sin, rebellion and sin.
Lev 16: 21 and confess over it all the *w*
19: 29 to prostitution and be filled with *w*.
Dt 9: 4 on account of the *w* of these nations
Ps 45: 7 You love righteousness and hate *w*;
92: 15 Rock, and there is no *w* in him."
Pr 13: 6 but *w* overthrows the sinner.
Jer 3: 2 land with your prostitution and *w*.
8: 6 None of them repent of their *w*,
14: 20 We acknowledge our *w*, LORD,
Eze 18: 20 the *w* of the wicked will be charged
28: 15 you were created till *w* was found
33: 19 the wicked turn away from their *w*
Da 4: 27 and your *w* by being kind
9: 24 end to sin, to atone for *w*, to bring
Jnh 1: 2 because its *w* has come up before
Mt 24: 12 Because of the increase of *w*,
Lk 11: 39 inside you are full of greed and *w*.
Ac 1: 18 (With the reward he got for his *w*,
Ro 1: 18 who suppress the truth by their *w*,
1Co 5: 8 bread leavened with malice and *w*,
2Co 6: 14 and *w* have in common?
2Ti 2: 19 the Lord must turn away from *w*."
Tit 2: 14 for us to redeem us from all *w*
Heb 1: 9 loved righteousness and hated *w*;
8: 12 For I will forgive their *w* and will
2Pe 2: 15 of Bezer, who loved the wages of *w*.

WIDE

Ps 81: 10 Open your mouth and I will fill it.
Isa 54: 2 stretch your tent curtains *w*, do not
Mt 7: 13 For *w* is the gate and broad is
2Co 6: 13 open *w* your hearts also.
Eph 3: 18 to grasp how *w* and long and high

WIDOW (WIDOWS)

Ex 22: 22 "Do not take advantage of a *w*
Dt 10: 18 cause of the fatherless and the *w*,
Ps 146: 9 sustains the fatherless and the *w*,
Isa 1: 17 fatherless, plead the case of the *w*.
Lk 21: 2 saw a poor *w* put in two very small
1Ti 5: 4 if a *w* has children or grandchildren,

WIDOWS (WIDOW)

Ps 68: 5 a defender of *w*, is God in his holy
Ac 6: 1 Jews because their *w* were being
1Co 7: 8 to the unmarried and the *w* I say:
1Ti 5: 3 to those *w* who are really in need.
Jas 1: 27 after orphans and *w* in their distress

WIFE (WIVES WIVES')

Ge 2: 24 and mother and be united to his *w*,
19: 26 But Lot's *w* looked back, and she
24: 67 So she became his *w*, and he loved
Ex 20: 17 shall not covet your neighbor's *w*,
Lev 20: 10 adultery with another man's *w*—
Dt 5: 21 shall not covet your neighbor's *w*.
22: 13 If a man takes a *w* and,
24: 5 happiness to the *w* he has married.
Ru 4: 13 took Ruth and she became his *w*.
Pr 5: 18 you rejoice in the *w* of your youth.
12: 4 A *w* of noble character is her
18: 22 He who finds a *w* finds what is good
19: 13 a quarrelsome *w* is like the constant
31: 10 A *w* of noble character who can
Hos 1: 2 for like an adulterous *w* this land is
Mal 2: 14 you and the *w* of your youth.
Mt 1: 20 afraid to take Mary home as your *w*,
19: 3 for a man to divorce his *w* for any
Lk 17: 32 Remember Lot's *w*!
18: 29 "no one who has left home or *w*
1Co 7: 2 sexual relations with his own *w*,
7: 33 how he can please his *w*—
Eph 5: 23 head of the *w* as Christ is the head
5: 33 must love his *w* as he loves himself,
1Ti 3: 2 faithful to his *w*, temperate,
Rev 21: 9 you the bride, the *w* of the Lamb."

WILD

Ge 1: 25 God made the *w* animals according
8: 1 all the *w* animals and the livestock
Lk 15: 13 squandered his wealth in *w* living.
Ro 11: 17 and you, though a *w* olive shoot,

WILDERNESS

Nu 32: 13 wander in the *w* forty years,
Dt 8: 16 He gave you manna to eat in the *w*,
29: 5 years that I led you through the *w*,
8: 19 did not abandon them in the *w*
Ps 78: 19 really spread a table in the *w*?
78: 52 led them like sheep through the *w*.
Isa 43: 20 I provide water in the *w* and
Mk 1: 3 "a voice of one calling in the *w*,
1: 13 and he was in the *w* forty days,
Rev 12: 6 fled into the *w* to a place

WILL (WILLFUL WILLING WILLINGNESS)

Ps 40: 8 I desire to do your *w*, my God;
143: 10 Teach me to do your *w*, for you are
Isa 53: 10 Yet it was the LORD's *w* to crush
Mt 6: 10 kingdom come, your *w* be done,
7: 21 but only those who do the *w* of my
10: 29 Yet not one of them *w* fall
12: 50 whoever does the *w* of my Father
26: 39 Yet not as I *w*, but as you *w*."
26: 42 I drink it, may your *w* be done."
Jn 6: 38 but to do the *w* of him who sent me.
7: 17 chooses to do the *w* of God *w* find
Ac 20: 27 to you the whole *w* of God.
Ro 12: 2 test and approve what God's *w* is—
12: 2 his good, pleasing and perfect *w*.
1Co 7: 37 but has control over his own *w*,
Eph 5: 17 but understand what the Lord's *w* is.
Php 2: 13 for it is God who works in you to *w*
1Th 4: 3 It is God's *w* that you should be
5: 18 for this is God's *w* for you in Christ
2Ti 2: 26 has taken them captive to do his *w*.
Heb 2: 4 Spirit distributed according to his *w*.
9: 16 In the case of a *w*, it is necessary
10: 7 I have come to do your *w*,
13: 21 everything good for doing his *w*,
Jas 4: 15 "If it is the Lord's *w*, we *w* live
1Pe 3: 17 if it is God's *w*, to suffer for doing
4: 2 desires, but rather for the *w* of God.
2Pe 1: 21 never had its origin in the human *w*,
1Jn 5: 14 we ask anything according to his *w*,
Rev 4: 11 by your *w* they were created

WILLFUL (WILL)

Ps 19: 13 Keep your servant also from *w* sins;

WILLING (WILL)

1Ch 28: 9 devotion and with a *w* mind,
29: 5 who among you is *w* to consecrate
Ps 51: 12 salvation and grant me a *w* spirit,
Da 3: 28 were *w* to give up their lives rather
Mt 18: 14 Father in heaven is not *w* that any
23: 37 her wings, and you were not *w*.
26: 41 The spirit is *w*, but the flesh is
1Ti 6: 18 and to be generous and *w* to share.
1Pe 5: 2 must, but because you are *w*, as God

WILLINGNESS* (WILL)

2Co 8: 11 so that your eager *w* to do it may be
8: 12 For if the *w* is there, the gift is

WIN (WON)

Pr 11: 30 and those who *w* souls are wise.
Lk 21: 19 Stand firm, and you will *w* life.
1Co 9: 19 everyone, to *w* as many as possible.
Php 3: 14 toward the goal to *w* the prize
1Th 4: 12 your daily life may *w* the respect

WIND (WHIRLWIND WINDS)

Ps 1: 4 like chaff that the *w* blows away.
Ecc 2: 11 meaningless, a chasing after the *w*;
Hos 8: 7 "They sow the *w* and reap
Mk 4: 41 Even the *w* and the waves obey
Jn 3: 8 The *w* blows wherever it pleases.
Eph 4: 14 there by every *w* of teaching
Jas 1: 6 the sea, blown and tossed by the *w*.

WINDOW

Jos 2: 21 she tied the scarlet cord in the *w*.
Ac 20: 9 a young man named
2Co 11: 33 in a basket from a *w* in the wall

WINDS (WIND)

Ps 104: 4 He makes *w* his messengers,
Mt 24: 31 will gather his elect from the four *w*

WINE

Ps 104: 15 *w* that gladdens human hearts,
Pr 20: 1 *W* is a mocker and beer a brawler;
23: 20 join those who drink too much *w*
23: 31 Do not gaze at *w* when it is red,
31: 6 *w* for those who are in anguish!
SS 1: 2 your love is more delightful than *w*.
Isa 28: 7 stagger from *w* and reel from beer:
55: 1 buy *w* and milk without money
Mt 9: 17 people pour new *w*
Lk 23: 36 They offered him *w* vinegar
Jn 2: 3 When the *w* was gone,
Ro 14: 21 drink *w* or to do anything else
Eph 5: 18 Do not get drunk on *w*, which leads
1Ti 5: 23 and use a little *w* because of your
Rev 16: 19 the cup filled with the *w* of the fury

WINEPRESS

Isa 63: 2 like those of one treading the *w*?
Rev 19: 15 He treads the *w* of the fury

WINESKINS

Mt 9: 17 do people pour new *w* into old *w*.

WINGS

Ex 19: 4 how I carried you on eagles' *w*
Ru 2: 12 under whose *w* you have come
Ps 17: 8 hide me in the shadow of your *w*
91: 4 under his *w* you will find refuge;
Isa 6: 2 him were seraphs, each with six *w*:
40: 31 They will soar on *w* like eagles;
Eze 1: 6 of them had four faces and four *w*.
Zec 5: 9 w! They had *w* like those of a stork,
Lk 13: 34 hen gathers her chicks under her *w*,
Rev 4: 8 the four living creatures had six *w*

WINTER

Mk 13: 18 that this will not take place in *w*,

WIPE (WIPED)

Isa 25: 8 Sovereign LORD will *w* away
Rev 7: 17 God will *w* away every tear
21: 4 'He will *w* every tear from their

WIPED (WIPE)

Lk 7: 38 Then she *w* them with her hair,
Ac 3: 19 so that your sins may be *w* out,

WISDOM (WISE)

Ge 3: 6 and also desirable for gaining *w*,
1Ki 4: 29 God gave Solomon *w* and very great
2Ch 1: 10 Give me *w* and knowledge, that I
Ps 51: 6 you taught me in that secret place.
111: 10 The fear of the LORD is the beginning of *w*;
Pr 2: 6 For the LORD gives *w*,
3: 13 Blessed are those who find *w*,
4: 7 The beginning of *w* is this: Get *w*.
8: 11 for *w* is more precious than rubies,

Pr 11: 2 but with humility comes w.
13: 10 w is found in those who take advice.
23: 23 w, instruction and insight as well.
29: 3 A man who loves w brings joy
29: 15 A rod and a reprimand impart w,
31: 26 She speaks with w, and faithful
Isa 11: 2 rest on him—the Spirit of w
28: 29 wonderful, whose w is magnificent.
Jer 10: 12 he founded the world by his w
Mic 6: 9 and to fear your name is w—
Mt 11: 19 is proved right by her actions."
Lk 2: 52 he increased in w and in favor
Ac 6: 3 known to be full of the Spirit and w.
Ro 11: 33 the depth of the riches of the w
1Co 1: 17 not with w and eloquence,
1: 30 has become for us w from God—
2: 8 through the Spirit a message of w,
Eph 1: 17 may give you the Spirit of w
Col 2: 3 are hidden all the treasures of w.
2: 23 indeed have an appearance of w,
Jas 1: 5 If any of you lacks w, you should
3: 13 in the humility that comes from w.
Rev 5: 12 and wealth and w and strength

WISE (WISDOM WISER)
1Ki 3: 12 I will give you a w and discerning
Job 5: 13 He catches the w in their craftiness,
Ps 19: 7 trustworthy, making w the simple.
Pr 3: 7 Do not be w in your own eyes;
9: 8 rebuke the w and they will love you.
9: 9 Instruct the w and they will be
10: 1 W children bring joy to their father,
11: 30 life, and those who win souls are w.
13: 1 A w child heeds a parent's
13: 20 Walk with the w and become w,
16: 23 of the w make their mouths prudent,
17: 28 Even fools are thought w if they
Ecc 9: 17 The quiet words of the w are more
Jer 9: 23 "Let not the w boast of their
Eze 28: 6 " 'Because you think you are w, as w as
a god,
Da 2: 21 He gives wisdom to the w
12: 3 Those who are w will shine like
Mt 11: 25 have hidden these things from the w
25: 2 them were foolish and five were w.
1Co 1: 19 will destroy the wisdom of the w;
1: 27 things of the world to shame the w;
3: 10 laid a foundation as a w builder,
3: 19 "He catches the w in their
Eph 5: 15 not as unwise but as w,
2Ti 3: 15 to make you w for salvation through
Jas 3: 13 Who is w and understanding among

WISER (WISE)
Pr 9: 9 the wise and they will be w still;
1Co 1: 25 of God is w than human wisdom,

WISH
Jn 15: 7 ask whatever you w, and it will be
Ro 9: 3 I could w that I myself were cursed
Rev 3: 15 I w you were either one or the other!
22: 17 let all who w take the free gift

WITCHCRAFT
Dt 18: 10 interprets omens, engages in w,
Gal 5: 20 idolatry and w,

WITHDREW
Lk 5: 16 But Jesus often w to lonely places

WITHER (WITHERS)
Ps 1: 3 season and whose leaf does not w—
37: 19 In times of disaster they will not w;

WITHERS (WITHER)
Isa 40: 7 The grass w and the flowers fall,
1Pe 1: 24 the grass w and the flowers fall,

WITHHELD (WITHHOLD)
Ge 22: 12 because you have not w from me

WITHHOLD (WITHHELD WITHHOLDS)
Ps 84: 11 no good thing does he w from those
Pr 23: 13 Do not w discipline from children;

WITHHOLDS (WITHHOLD)
Dt 27: 19 "Cursed is anyone who w justice

WITNESS (EYEWITNESSES WITNESSES)
Pr 12: 17 An honest w tells the truth,
19: 9 A false w will not go unpunished,
Jn 1: 8 he came only as a w to the light.

WITNESSES (WITNESS)
Dt 19: 15 by the testimony of two or three w.
Mt 18: 16 by the testimony of two or three w.'
Ac 1: 8 and you will be my w in Jerusalem,

WIVES (WIFE)
Eph 5: 22 W, submit yourselves to your own
5: 25 love your w, just as Christ loved
1Pe 3: 1 words by the behavior of their w,

WIVES* (WIFE)
1Ti 4: 7 with godless myths and old w tales;

WOE
Isa 6: 5 "W to me!" I cried. "I am ruined!
Eze 34: 2 W to you shepherds of Israel who
Mt 18: 7 W to the world because of the things
23: 13 "W to you, teachers of the law
Jude : 11 W to them! They have taken

WOLF (WOLVES)
Isa 65: 25 The w and the lamb will feed

WOLVES (WOLF)
Mt 10: 16 you out like sheep among w.

WOMAN (MAN)
Ge 2: 22 the LORD God made a w
2: 23 she shall be called 'w,' for she was
3: 6 When the w saw that the fruit
3: 12 "The w you put here with me—
3: 15 put enmity between you and the w,
3: 16 To the w he said, "I will make your
12: 11 "I know what a beautiful w you are.
20: 3 because of the w you have taken;
24: 5 "What if the w is unwilling to come
Ex 2: 1 house of Levi married a Levite w,
3: 22 Every w is to ask her neighbor
21: 10 If he marries another w, he must not
21: 22 are fighting and a pregnant w is hit
Lev 12: 2 'A w who becomes pregnant
15: 19 " 'When a w has her regular flow
15: 25 " 'When a w has a discharge
18: 17 have sexual relations with both a w
20: 13 with a man as one does with a w,
Nu 5: 29 of jealousy when a w goes astray
30: 3 "When a young w still living in her
30: 9 divorced or w will be binding on her.
30: 10 "If a w living with her husband
Dt 20: 7 Has anyone become pledged to a w
21: 11 among the captives a beautiful w
22: 5 A w must not wear men's clothing,
Jdg 4: 9 Sisera into the hands of a w."
13: 3 Then the w went to her husband
14: 2 "I have seen a Philistine w
16: 4 love with a w in the Valley of Sorek
20: 4 the husband of the murdered w,
Ru 3: 11 that you are a w of noble character.
1Sa 1: 15 "I am a w who is deeply troubled.
25: 3 was an intelligent and beautiful w,
28: 7 "Find me a w who is a medium,
2Sa 11: 2 From the roof he saw a w bathing.
13: 17 "Get this w out of my sight and bolt
14: 2 had a wise w brought from there.
20: 16 a wise w called from the city,
1Ki 3: 18 was born, this w also had a baby.
17: 24 Then the w said to Elijah, "Now I
2Ki 4: 8 And a well-to-do w was there,
8: 5 to the w whose son he had restored
9: 34 "Take care of that cursed w,"
Job 14: 1 born of w, are of few days and full
Pr 11: 16 A kindhearted w gains honor,
11: 22 beautiful w who shows no discretion.
14: 1 The wise w builds her house,
23: 27 an adulterous w is a deep pit
30: 19 the way of a man with a young w
30: 23 a contemptible w who gets married,
31: 30 a w who fears the LORD is to be
Isa 54: 1 barren w, you who never bore
62: 5 As a young man marries a young w,
Jer 2: 32 Does a young w forget her jewelry,
Mt 5: 28 a w lustfully has already committed
9: 20 then a w who had been subject
15: 28 Then Jesus said to her, "W,
26: 7 a w came to him with an alabaster
Mk 5: 25 a w was there who had been subject
5: 42 a w whose little daughter was
Lk 7: 39 him and what kind of w she is—
10: 38 a village where a w named Martha
13: 12 her forward and said to her, "W,
15: 8 suppose a w has ten silver coins
Jn 2: 4 "W, why do you involve me?"
4: 7 a Samaritan w came to draw water,
8: 3 a w caught in adultery.
19: 26 to her, "W, here is your son,"
20: 15 He asked her, "W, why are you
Ac 9: 40 Turning toward the dead w, he said,
16: 14 of those listening was a w
Ro 7: 2 by law a married w is bound to her

1Co 7: 2 and each w with her own husband.
7: 34 An unmarried w or virgin is
7: 39 A w is bound to her husband as long
11: 3 and the head of the w is man,
11: 7 but w is the glory of man.
11: 13 Is it proper for a w to pray to God
Gal 4: 4 born of a w, born under the law,
4: 31 we are not children of the slave w,
1Ti 2: 11 A w should learn in quietness
5: 16 any w who is a believer has widows
Rev 2: 20 You tolerate that w Jezebel,
12: 1 a w clothed with the sun,
12: 13 he pursued the w who had given
17: 3 There I saw a w sitting on a scarlet

WOMEN (MAN)
SS 1: 3 No wonder the young w love you!
Mt 11: 11 w there has not risen anyone greater
28: 5 The angel said to the w, "Do not be
Mk 15: 41 Many other w who had come
Lk 1: 42 "Blessed are you among w,
8: 2 some w who had been cured of evil
23: 27 including w who mourned
24: 11 But they did not believe the w,
Ac 1: 14 along with the w and Mary
16: 13 to the w who had gathered there.
17: 4 Greeks and not a few prominent w.
Ro 1: 26 Even their w exchanged natural
1Co 14: 34 W should remain silent
Php 4: 3 help these w since they have
1Ti 2: 9 I also want the w to dress modestly,
5: 2 older w as mothers, and younger w as
sisters,
Tit 2: 3 teach the older w to be reverent
2: 4 they can urge the younger w to love
Heb 11: 35 W received back their dead,
1Pe 3: 5 the way the holy w of the past

WOMB
Job 1: 21 I came from my mother's w,
Ps 139: 13 knit me together in my mother's w.
Pr 31: 2 Listen, son of my w!
Jer 1: 5 I formed you in the w I knew you,
Lk 1: 44 the baby in my w leaped for joy!"
Jn 3: 4 into their mother's w to be born!"

WON (WIN)
1Pe 3: 1 they may be w over without words

WONDER (WONDERFUL WONDERS)
Dt 13: 1 announces to you a sign or w,
SS 1: 3 No the young women love you!

WONDERFUL* (WONDER)
2Sa 1: 26 Your love for me was w, more w
1Ch 16: 9 praise to him; tell of all his w acts.
Job 42: 3 things too w for me to know.
Ps 9: 1 I will tell of all your w deeds.
26: 7 and telling of all your w deeds.
75: 1 people tell of your w deeds.
105: 2 tell of all his w acts.
107: 8 and his w deeds for humankind,
107: 15 and his w deeds for humankind,
107: 21 and his w deeds for humankind,
107: 24 LORD, his w deeds in the deep.
107: 31 and his w deeds for humankind,
119: 18 that I may see w things in your law.
119: 27 that I may meditate on your w deeds.
119:129 Your statutes are w; therefore I obey
131: 1 great matters or things too w for me.
139: 6 Such knowledge is too w for me,
139: 14 your works are w, I know that full
145: 5 I will meditate on your w works.
Isa 9: 6 And he will be called W Counselor,
25: 1 you have done w things,
28: 29 whose plan is w, whose wisdom is
Mt 21: 15 of the law saw the w things he did
Lk 13: 17 with all the w things he was doing.
1Pe 2: 9 you out of darkness into his w light.

WONDERS (WONDER)
Ex 3: 20 all the w that I will perform among
Dt 10: 21 awesome w you saw with your own
2Sa 7: 23 awesome w by driving out nations
Job 37: 14 stop and consider God's w.
Ps 17: 5 Show me the w of your great love,
31: 21 he showed me the w of his love
89: 5 The heavens praise your w,
Joel 2: 30 I will show w in the heavens
Mt 24: 24 and perform great signs and w
Mk 13: 22 perform signs and w to deceive,
Jn 4: 48 you people see signs and w,"
Ac 2: 11 we hear them declaring the w
2: 19 I will show w in the heaven
2: 43 the many w and signs performed

Ac 5:12 signs and **w** among the people.
Ro 15:19 by the power of signs and **w**,
2Co 12:12 including signs, **w** and miracles.
2Th 2:9 signs and **w** that serve the lie,
Heb 2:4 it by signs, **w** and various miracles,

WOOD
Isa 44:19 Shall I bow down to a block of **w**?"
1Co 3:12 costly stones, **w**, hay or straw,

WOOL
Pr 31:13 She selects **w** and flax and works
Isa 1:18 red as crimson, they shall be like **w**.
Da 7:9 hair of his head was white like **w**.
Rev 1:14 hair on his head was white like **w**,

WORD (BYWORD WORDLESS WORDS)
Nu 30:2 he must not break his **w** but must do
Dt 8:3 but on every **w** that comes
2Sa 22:31 the Lord's **w** is flawless.
Ps 56:4 In God, whose **w** I praise—in God I
119:9 By living according to your **w**.
119:11 I have hidden your **w** in my heart
119:105 Your **w** is a lamp to my feet
Pr 12:25 the heart, but a kind **w** cheers it up.
15:1 wrath, but a harsh **w** stirs up anger.
30:5 "Every **w** of God is flawless; he is
Isa 55:11 so is my **w** that goes out from my
Jer 23:29 "Is not my **w** like fire,"
Mt 4:4 but on every **w** that comes
12:36 every empty **w** they have spoken.
15:6 Thus you nullify the **w** of God
Mk 4:14 The farmer sows the **w**.
Jn 1:1 and the **W** was with God, and the **W**
1:14 The **W** became flesh and made his
17:17 them by the truth; your **w** is truth.
Ac 6:4 prayer and the ministry of the **w**."
2Co 2:17 we do not peddle the **w** of God
4:2 nor do we distort the **w** of God.
Eph 6:17 of the Spirit, which is the **w** of God.
Php 2:16 as you hold firmly to the **w** of life.
2Ti 2:15 and who correctly handles the **w**
Heb 4:12 For the **w** of God is alive and active.
Jas 1:22 Do not merely listen to the **w**,

WORDLESS* (WORD)
Ro 8:26 intercedes for us through **w** groans.

WORDS (WORD)
Dt 11:18 Fix these **w** of mine in your hearts
Ps 12:6 the **w** of the Lord are flawless,
19:3 They have no speech, they use no **w**;
119:103 How sweet are your **w** to my taste,
119:130 The unfolding of your **w** gives light;
119:160 All your **w** are true;
Pr 2:1 if you accept my **w** and store up my
10:19 Sin is not ended by multiplying **w**,
16:24 Gracious **w** are a honeycomb,
30:6 Do not add to his **w**, or he will
Ecc 12:11 The **w** of the wise are like goads,
Jer 15:16 When your **w** came, I ate them;
Mt 24:35 but my **w** will never pass away.
Lk 4:22 me and hear my **w** and put them
Jn 6:68 You have the **w** of eternal life.
15:7 in me and my **w** remain in you,
1Co 2:13 but in **w** taught by the Spirit,
14:19 rather speak five intelligible **w**
Rev 22:19 of you takes **w** away from this scroll

WORK (CO-WORKERS WORKED WORKER
WORKERS WORKING WORKS)
Ge 2:2 seventh day he rested from all his **w**.
Ex 23:12 "Six days do your **w**,
Nu 8:11 be ready to do the **w** of the Lord.
Dt 5:14 On it you shall not do any **w**,
Ps 19:1 the skies proclaim the **w** of his
Jer 48:10 are lax in doing the Lord's **w**!
Jn 6:27 Do not **w** for food that spoils,
9:4 is coming, when no one can **w**.
Ac 13:2 Saul for the **w** to which I have
1Co 3:13 test the quality of each person's **w**.
4:12 We **w** hard with our own hands.
Eph 4:16 up in love, as each part does its **w**.
Php 1:6 he who began a good **w** in you will
2:12 continue to **w** out your salvation
Col 3:23 you do, **w** at it with all your heart,
1Th 4:11 business and **w** with your hands,
5:12 those who **w** hard among you,
2Th 3:10 is unwilling to **w** shall not eat."
2Ti 3:17 equipped for every good **w**.
Heb 6:10 he will not forget your **w**
2Jn :11 them shares in their wicked **w**.
3Jn :8 that we may **w** together for the truth.

WORKED (WORK)
1Co 15:10 I **w** harder than all of them—
2Th 3:8 the contrary, we **w** night and day,

WORKER (WORK)
2Ti 2:15 a **w** who does not need to be ashamed

WORKERS (WORK)
Mt 9:37 is plentiful but the **w** are few.
20:1 to hire **w** for his vineyard.
Lk 10:7 give you, for **w** deserve their wages.
1Ti 5:18 and "**W** deserve their wages."

WORKING (WORK)
Col 3:23 all your heart, as **w** for the Lord,

WORKS (WORK)
Ps 145:6 of the power of your awesome **w**—
Pr 8:22 me forth as the first of his **w**,
31:31 her **w** bring her praise at the city
Jn 7:3 disciples there may see the **w** you do.
10:25 **w** I do in my Father's name testify
10:32 shown you many good **w** from the Father.
10:38 do not believe me, believe the **w**,
14:11 the evidence of the **w** themselves.
Ro 4:2 Abraham was justified by **w**, he had
8:28 in all things God **w** for the good
Eph 2:9 not by **w**, so that no one can boast.
4:12 to equip his people for **w** of service,

WORLD (WORLDLY)
Ps 9:8 He rules the **w** in righteousness
50:12 for the **w** is mine, and all that is
90:2 or you brought forth the whole **w**,
96:13 He will judge the **w** in righteousness
Pr 8:23 beginning, when the **w** came to be.
Isa 13:11 I will punish the **w** for its evil,
Mt 5:14 "You are the light of the **w**.
16:26 it be for you to gain the whole **w**,
Mk 16:15 "Go into all the **w** and preach
Jn 1:29 who takes away the sin of the **w**!
3:16 God so loved the **w** that he gave his
8:12 he said, "I am the light of the **w**.
15:19 you do not belong to the **w**, but I
16:33 In this **w** you will have trouble.
16:33 I have overcome the **w**."
17:5 I had with you before the **w** began.
17:14 are not of the **w** any more than I am of
the **w**.
18:36 said, "My kingdom is not of this **w**.
Ac 17:24 "The God who made the **w**
Ro 3:19 and the whole **w** held accountable
8:18 their words to the ends of the **w**."
1Co 1:27 things of the **w** to shame the strong.
3:19 the wisdom of this **w** is foolishness.
6:2 the Lord's people will judge the **w**?
2Co 5:19 that God was reconciling the **w**
10:3 For though we live in the **w**, we do
1Ti 6:7 For we brought nothing into the **w**,
Heb 11:38 the **w** was not worthy of them.
Jas 2:5 the eyes of the **w** to be rich in faith
4:4 the **w** means enmity against God?
1Pe 1:20 chosen before the creation of the **w**,
1Jn 2:2 but also for the sins of the whole **w**.
2:15 not love the **w** or anything in the **w**.
5:4 born of God overcomes the **w**.
Rev 13:8 was slain from the creation of the **w**.

WORLDLY (WORLD)
1Co 3:1 address you as spiritual but as **w**—
Tit 2:12 to ungodliness and **w** passions,

WORM
Mk 9:48 where " 'their **w** does not die,

WORRY (WORRYING)
Mt 6:25 I tell you, do not **w** about your life,
10:19 do not **w** about what to say or how

WORRYING (WORRY)
Mt 6:27 by **w** add a single hour to your

WORSHIP (WORSHIPED WORSHIPS)
Jos 22:27 that we will **w** the Lord at his
2Ki 17:36 is the one you must **w**.
1Ch 16:29 **W** the Lord in the splendor of his
Ps 95:6 let us bow down in **w**, let us kneel
100:2 **W** the Lord with gladness;
Zec 14:17 go up to Jerusalem to **w** the King,
Mt 2:2 it rose and have come to **w** him."
4:9 "if you will bow down and **w** me."
Jn 4:24 his worshipers must **w** in the Spirit
Ro 12:1 and pleasing to God—this is true **w**.
Heb 10:1 perfect those who draw near to **w**.

WORSHIPED (WORSHIP)
2Ch 29:30 gladness and bowed down and **w**.

Mt 28:9 to him, clasped his feet and **w** him.

WORSHIPS (WORSHIP)
Isa 44:15 But he also fashions a god and **w** it;

WORTH (WORTHY)
Job 28:13 No mortal comprehends its **w**;
Pr 31:10 She is far more than rubies.
Mt 10:31 so you are **w** more than many
Ro 8:18 sufferings are not **w** comparing
Php 3:8 because of the surpassing **w**
1Pe 1:7 of greater **w** than gold,
3:4 is of great **w** in God's sight.

WORTHLESS
Pr 11:4 Wealth is **w** in the day of wrath,
Jas 1:26 themselves, and their religion is **w**.

WORTHY (WORTH)
1Ch 16:25 is the Lord and most **w** of praise;
Mt 10:37 or mother more than me is not **w**
Lk 15:19 I am no longer **w** to be called your
Eph 4:1 live a life **w** of the calling you have
Php 1:27 live in a manner **w** of the gospel
Col 1:10 you may live a life **w** of the Lord
1Ti 3:8 deacons are to be **w** of respect,
Heb 3:3 Jesus has been found **w** of greater
3Jn :6 on their way in a manner **w** of God.
Rev 5:2 "Who is **w** to break the seals

WOUND (WOUNDS)
1Co 8:12 way and **w** their weak conscience.

WOUNDS (WOUND)
Pr 27:6 **W** from a friend can be trusted,
Isa 53:5 on him, and by his **w** we are healed.
Zec 13:6 'What are these **w** on your body?'
1Pe 2:24 "by his **w** you have been healed."

WRAPS
Ps 104:2 The Lord **w** himself in light as

WRATH
2Ch 36:16 at his prophets until the **w**
Ps 2:5 his anger and terrifies them in his **w**,
76:10 Surely your **w** against human beings
Pr 15:1 A gentle answer turns away **w**,
Isa 13:3 at the **w** of the Lord Almighty,
51:17 of the Lord the cup of his **w**,
Jer 25:15 cup filled with the wine of my **w**,
Eze 5:13 and my **w** against them will subside,
20:8 said I would pour out my **w** on them
Am 1:3 for four, I will not turn back [my **w**].
Na 1:2 and vents his **w** against his enemies.
Zep 1:15 That day will be a day of **w**—
Jn 3:36 life, for God's **w** remains on them.
Ro 1:18 The **w** of God is being revealed
2:5 are storing up **w** against yourself
5:9 saved from God's **w** through him!
9:22 although choosing to show his **w**
1Th 5:9 God did not appoint us to suffer **w**
Rev 6:16 throne and from the **w** of the Lamb!
19:15 the fury of the **w** of God Almighty.

WRESTLED
Ge 32:24 and a man **w** with him till daybreak.

WRITE (WRITER WRITING WRITTEN WROTE)
Dt 6:9 **W** them on the doorframes of your
10:2 I will **w** on the tablets the words
Pr 7:3 **w** them on the tablet of your heart.
Jer 31:33 their minds and **w** it on their hearts.
Heb 8:10 minds and **w** them on their hearts.
Rev 3:12 I will also **w** on them my new name.

WRITER* (WRITE)
Ps 45:1 my tongue is the pen of a skillful **w**.

WRITING (WRITE)
1Co 14:37 what I am **w** to you is the Lord's

WRITTEN (WRITE)
Dt 28:58 which are **w** in this book, and do not
Jos 1:8 be careful to do everything **w** in it.
23:6 obey all that is **w** in the Book
Ps 40:7 it is **w** about me in the scroll.
Da 12:1 everyone whose name is found **w**
Mal 3:16 remembrance was **w** in his presence
Lk 10:20 that your names are **w** in heaven."
24:44 must be fulfilled that is **w** about me
Jn 20:31 these are **w** that you may believe
21:25 room for the books that would be **w**.
Ro 2:15 of the law are **w** on their hearts.
1Co 4:6 "Do not go beyond what is **w**."
10:11 were **w** down as warnings for us,
2Co 3:3 **w** not with ink but with the Spirit
Heb 10:7 it is **w** about me in the scroll—
12:23 whose names are **w** in heaven.
Rev 21:27 only those whose names are **w**

WRONG (WRONGDOERS WRONGDOING WRONGED WRONGS)

Ex	23: 2	not follow the crowd in doing w.
Nu	5: 7	restitution for the w they have done,
Dt	32: 4	A faithful God who does no w,
Job	34: 12	is unthinkable that God would do w,
Ps	5: 5	You hate all who do w;
1Th	5: 15	that nobody pays back w for w,

WRONGDOERS* (WRONG)

Ps	37: 28	W will be completely destroyed;
1Co	6: 9	not know that w will not inherit

WRONGDOING (WRONG)

Job	1: 22	did not sin by charging God with w.
1Jn	5: 17	All w is sin, and there is sin

WRONGED (WRONG)

Pr	18: 19	A brother w is more unyielding
1Co	6: 7	Why not rather be w?

WRONGS (WRONG)

Pr	10: 12	but love covers over all w.
1Co	13: 5	angered, it keeps no record of w.

WROTE (WRITE)

Ex	34: 28	he w on the tablets the words
Jn	5: 46	believe me, for he w about me.
	8: 8	*and w on the ground.*

XERXES

King of Persia, husband of Esther. Deposed Vashti; replaced her with Esther (Est 1–2). Sealed Haman's edict to annihilate the Jews (Est 3). Received Esther without having called her (Est 5:1–8). Honored Mordecai (Est 6). Hanged Haman (Est 7). Issued edict allowing Jews to defend themselves (Est 8). Exalted Mordecai (Est 8:1–2, 15; 9:4; 10).

YEAR (YEARS)

Ex	34: 22	Three times a y all your men are
Lev	16: 34	to be made once a y for all the sins
	25: 4	in the seventh y the land is to have a y of sabbath rest,
	25: 11	The fiftieth y shall be a jubilee
Heb	10: 1	repeated endlessly y after y,

YEARS (YEAR)

Ge	1: 14	to mark seasons and days and y,
Ex	12: 40	people lived in Egypt was 430 y.
	16: 35	The Israelites ate manna forty y.
Job	36: 26	number of his y is past finding out.
Ps	90: 4	A thousand y in your sight are like
	90: 10	Our days may come to seventy y,
Pr	3: 2	they will prolong your life many y
Lk	3: 23	Jesus himself was about thirty y old
2Pe	3: 8	the Lord a day is like a thousand y,
Rev	20: 2	and bound him for a thousand y.

YEAST

Ex	12: 15	you are to eat bread made without y.
Mt	16: 6	on your guard against the y
1Co	5: 6	a little y leavens the whole batch

YESTERDAY

Heb	13: 8	Jesus Christ is the same y and today

YIELD

Isa	42: 8	I will not y my glory

YOKE (YOKED)

1Ki	12: 4	labor and the heavy y he put on us,
Mt	11: 29	Take my y upon you and learn
Gal	5: 1	be burdened again by a y of slavery.

YOKED (YOKE)

2Co	6: 14	Do not be y together

YOUNG (YOUNGER YOUTH)

2Ch	10: 14	he followed the advice of the y men
Ps	37: 25	I was y and now I am old, yet I have
	119: 9	can those who are y keep their way
Pr	20: 29	The glory of y men is their strength,
Isa	40: 11	he gently leads those that have y.
Joel	2: 28	dreams, your y men will see visions.
Ac	2: 17	your y men will see visions,
	7: 58	at the feet of a y man named Saul.
1Ti	4: 12	down on you because you are y,
Tit	2: 6	encourage the y men to be
1Jn	2: 13	I am writing to you, y people,

YOUNGER (YOUNG)

1Ti	5: 1	Treat y men as brothers,
Tit	2: 4	they can urge the y women to love
1Pe	5: 5	In the same way, you who are y,

YOUTH (YOUNG)

Ps	103: 5	your y is renewed like the eagle's.
Ecc	12: 1	your Creator in the days of your y,
2Ti	2: 22	Flee the evil desires of y and pursue

ZACCHAEUS

Lk	19: 2	A man was there by the name of Z;

ZEAL (ZEALOUS)

Ps	69: 9	for z for your house consumes me,
Isa	59: 17	wrapped himself in z as in a cloak.
Jn	2: 17	"Z for your house will consume
Ro	10: 2	their z is not based on knowledge.
	12: 11	Never be lacking in z, but keep your

ZEALOUS (ZEAL)

Nu	25: 13	because he was z for the honor
Pr	23: 17	but always be z for the fear
Eze	39: 25	and I will be z for my holy name.
Gal	4: 18	It is fine to be z,

ZEBULUN

Son of Jacob by Leah (Ge 30:20; 35:23; 1Ch 2:1). Tribe of blessed (Ge 49:13; Dt 33:18–19), numbered

(Nu 1:31; 26:27), allotted land (Jos 19:10–16; Eze 48:26), failed to fully possess (Jdg 1:30), supported Deborah (Jdg 4:6–10; 5:14, 18), David (1Ch 12:33), 12,000 from (Rev 7:8).

ZECHARIAH

1. Son of Jeroboam II; king of Israel (2Ki 15:8–12).

2. Post-exilic prophet who encouraged rebuilding of temple (Ezr 5:1; 6:14; Zec 1:1).

3. Father of John the Baptist (Lk 1:13; 3:2).

ZEDEKIAH

1. False prophet (1Ki 22:11–24; 2Ch 18:10–23).

2. Mattaniah, son of Josiah (1Ch 3:15), made king of Judah by Nebuchadnezzar (2Ki 24:17–25:7; 2Ch 36:10–14; Jer 37–39; 52:1–11).

ZEPHANIAH

Prophet; descendant of Hezekiah (Zep 1:1).

ZERUBBABEL

Descendant of David (1Ch 3:19; Mt 1:3). Led return from exile (Ezr 2:2; Ne 7:7). Governor of Israel; helped rebuild altar and temple (Ezr 3; Hag 1–2; Zec 4).

ZILPAH

Servant of Leah, mother of Jacob's sons Gad and Asher (Ge 30:9–12; 35:26, 46:16–18).

ZIMRI

King of Israel (1Ki 16:9–20).

ZION

2Sa	5: 7	David captured the fortress of Z—
Ps	2: 6	"I have installed my king on Z,
	9: 11	of the LORD, enthroned in Z;
	74: 2	Mount Z, where you dwelt.
	87: 2	Z more than all the other dwellings
	102: 13	arise and have compassion on Z,
	137: 3	"Sing us one of the songs of Z!"
Isa	2: 3	The law will go out from Z,
	28: 16	I lay a stone in Z, a tested stone,
	51: 11	They will enter Z with singing;
	52: 8	When the LORD returns to Z,
Jer	50: 5	They will ask the way to Z and turn
Joel	3: 21	The LORD dwells in Z!
Am	6: 1	to you who are complacent in Z,
Mic	4: 2	The law will go out from Z,
Zec	9: 9	Rejoice greatly, Daughter Z!
Ro	9: 33	I lay in Z a stone that causes people
	11: 26	"The deliverer will come from Z;
Heb	12: 22	But you have come to Mount Z,
Rev	14: 1	standing on Mount Z, and with him

ZIPPORAH*

Daughter of Reuel; wife of Moses (Ex 2:21–22; 4:20–26; 18:1–6).

ZOPHAR

One of Job's friends (Job 11; 20).

INDEX TO COLOR MAPS

COLOPHON

ZONDERVAN TNIV STUDY BIBLE

General Editor: Kenneth Barker

Associate Editors: John Stek
Ronald Youngblood

Project Management and Editorial: Paul Caminiti
Donna Huisjen
Michael Vander Klipp

Editorial Assistance: Amy Ballor
Natalie Block

Production Management: Phil Herich

Art Direction and Cover Design: Ron Huizinga, Jamie DeBruyn

Interior Design: Christopher Tobias, Tobias Outerwear for Books

Interior Proofreading: Peachtree Editorial and Proofreading Service,
Peachtree City, GA

Interior Typesetting: Blue Heron Bookcraft, Battle Ground, WA

See Contributors Page (xx) for a complete listing of individuals
who contributed and/or reviewed material for the TNIV Study Bible.

GUARANTEE

Zondervan's manufacturer's warranty provides coverage for defective bindings on
hardcover, softcover, Leather-Look™ and Italian Duo-Tone™ Bibles for four years,
and on bonded and top-grain leather Bibles for six years. This warranty does not
apply to normal wear. A lifetime warranty applies to defects within the Bible—
for example: missing or misplaced pages, chapters or books. Please return
defective Bibles to the original place of purchase for replacement or refund.
If this is not possible, please go to www.zondervan.com and click on "Contact Us."

CARE

We suggest loosening the binding of your new Bible by gently pressing on a small
section of pages at a time from the center. To ensure against breakage of the spine,
it is best not to bend the cover backward around the spine or to carry study notes,
church bulletins, pens, etc., inside the cover. Because a felt-tipped marker will
"bleed" through the pages, we recommend use of a ball-point pen or pencil to
underline favorite passages. Your Bible should not be exposed to excessive
heat, cold, or humidity.

Map 1: **WORLD OF THE PATRIARCHS**

Great Bitter Lake

Little Bitter Lake

Desert of Shur

of Egypt

Desert of Paran

S I N A I

Desert of Sin

Mt. Sinai (Mt. Horeb) ▲

Desert of Sinai

Ezion Geber

Mt. Halak ▲

Desert of Zin

Mt. Seir ▲

Arabah

Desert of Edom

Eastern De

Red Sea

6,000
5,000
4,000
3,000
2,000
1,000
0 - sea level (in meters)
-500

© 2005 Zondervan

Map 3: **EXODUS AND CONQUEST OF CANAAN**

Area controlled by ancient Israel
Probable route of wandering in the Sinai
Entry into and conquest of Canaan
x   Battle

The Great Sea

BASHAN
Kedesh
Hazor
Merom x
Sea of Kinnereth
Mt. Tabor
Edrei x
Mt. Gilboa
Shechem
CANAAN
Bethel
Gibeon
Beth Horon
Shiloh
Gilgal
AMMON
Heshbon
Jerusalem
Ai
Jericho
Abel Shittim
PHILISTIA
Azekah
Lachish
Jarmuth
Libnah?
Mt. Nebo
Jahaz?
Dibon
Eglon?
Debir?
Hebron
Makkedah?
Salt Sea
MOAB
Arnon R
Beersheba
Zered R.

Bezor Br.

EGYPT
Rameses
Lake Menzaleh

GOSHEN
Sukkoth
Pithom?
Wadi of Egypt
Desert of Zin
Oboth?
Iye Abarim

On
(Heliopolis)
Great Bitter Lake
Desert of Shur
Kadesh Barnea
EDOM
Punon

Noph
(Memphis)
Nile R.
Marah
Desert of Paran
Desert of Sin
SINAI
Ezion Geber

Elim?
Dophkah?
Hazeroth?
MIDIAN

Rephidim?

*Mt. Sinai
(Traditional Location)*

6,000
5,000
4,000
3,000
2,000
1,000
0 - sea level
(in meters)
-500

Red Sea

© 2005 Zondervan

Map 4: **LAND OF THE TWELVE TRIBES**

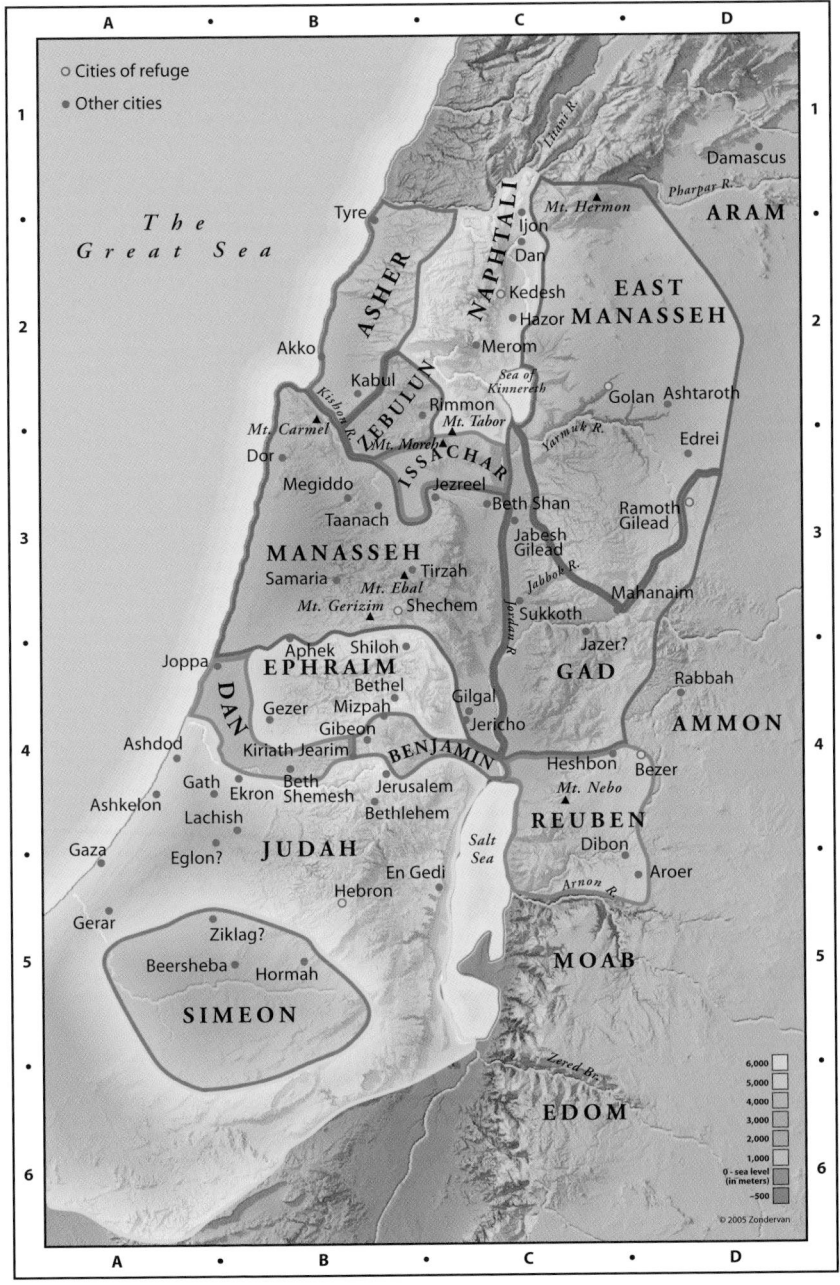

○ Cities of refuge
● Other cities

The Great Sea

A   B   C   D

1

Damascus
Pharpar R.
Tyre
Mt. Hermon
ARAM
Ijon
Dan
Kedesh
EAST
Hazor
MANASSEH
Merom
Akko
Sea of Kinnereth
Kabul
Golan   Ashtaroth
Kishon R.
Rimmon
Mt. Tabor
Edrei
Mt. Carmel
Mt. Moreh
Yarmuk R.
Dor
ISSACHAR
Megiddo
Jezreel
Beth Shan
Ramoth Gilead
Taanach
Jabesh Gilead
Jabbok R.
MANASSEH
Samaria   Tirzah
Mt. Ebal
Mahanaim
Mt. Gerizim   Shechem
Sukkoth
Jordan R.
Aphek   Shiloh
Jazer?
Joppa
EPHRAIM
Bethel
GAD
Gezer   Mizpah
Rabbah
DAN
Gibeon
Gilgal
Kirlath Jearim
Jericho
AMMON
Ashdod
BENJAMIN
Heshbon   Bezer
Gath
Beth
Jerusalem
Mt. Nebo
Ashkelon
Ekron   Shemesh
Bethlehem
REUBEN
Lachish
Dibon
Gaza
Eglon?   JUDAH
En Gedi
Salt Sea
Aroer
Gerar
Hebron
Arnon R.
Ziklag?
MOAB
Beersheba   Hormah
SIMEON
Zered Br.
EDOM

ASHER
NAPHTALI
ZEBULUN

6,000
5,000
4,000
3,000
2,000
1,000
0 - sea level (in meters)
-500

© 2005 Zondervan

A   B   C   D

A • B • C • D

The
Great Sea

Beirut

Sidon

Tyre

PHOENICIA

Litani R.

Abana R.

Damascus

Mt. Hermon

Pharpar R.

ARAM

Dan

Kedesh

Akko

J. *Jarmuk*

Hazor

Sea of Kinnereth

Ashtaroth
Edrei

Mt. Carmel ▲

Kishon R.

▲ Mt. Tabor

Yarmuk R.

Megiddo

▲ Mt. Moreh

Taanach

Mt. Gilboa ▲

Ramoth Gilead

Ibleam

Beth
Shan

Samaria

Tirzah

Jabesh Gilead

Penuel?

Mt. Ebal ▲

Sukkoth?

Jabbok R.

Rabbah (Amman)

Aphek

Shechem

ISRAEL

Mahanaim

AMMON

Joppa

Mt. Gerizim ▲

Shiloh

Gezer

Bethel

Jericho

Yarko R.

Ashdod

Jerusalem

Mt. Nebo ▲

Ashkelon

Aijalon

Heshbon

Gaza

Gath

Bethlehem

Medeba

Besor Br.

Mareshah

Salt Sea

Dibon

Raphia

Hebron

Arnon R.

Gerar

Beersheba

MOAB

PHILISTIA

Wadi el-Arish

Kir Hareseth

JUDAH

Zered R.

Kadesh
Barnea

Bozrah

*Region
periodically
contested by
Judah and
Edom*

EDOM

	6,000
	5,000
	4,000
	3,000
	2,000
	1,000
	0 - sea level (in meters)
	–500

©2005 Zondervan

A • B • C • D

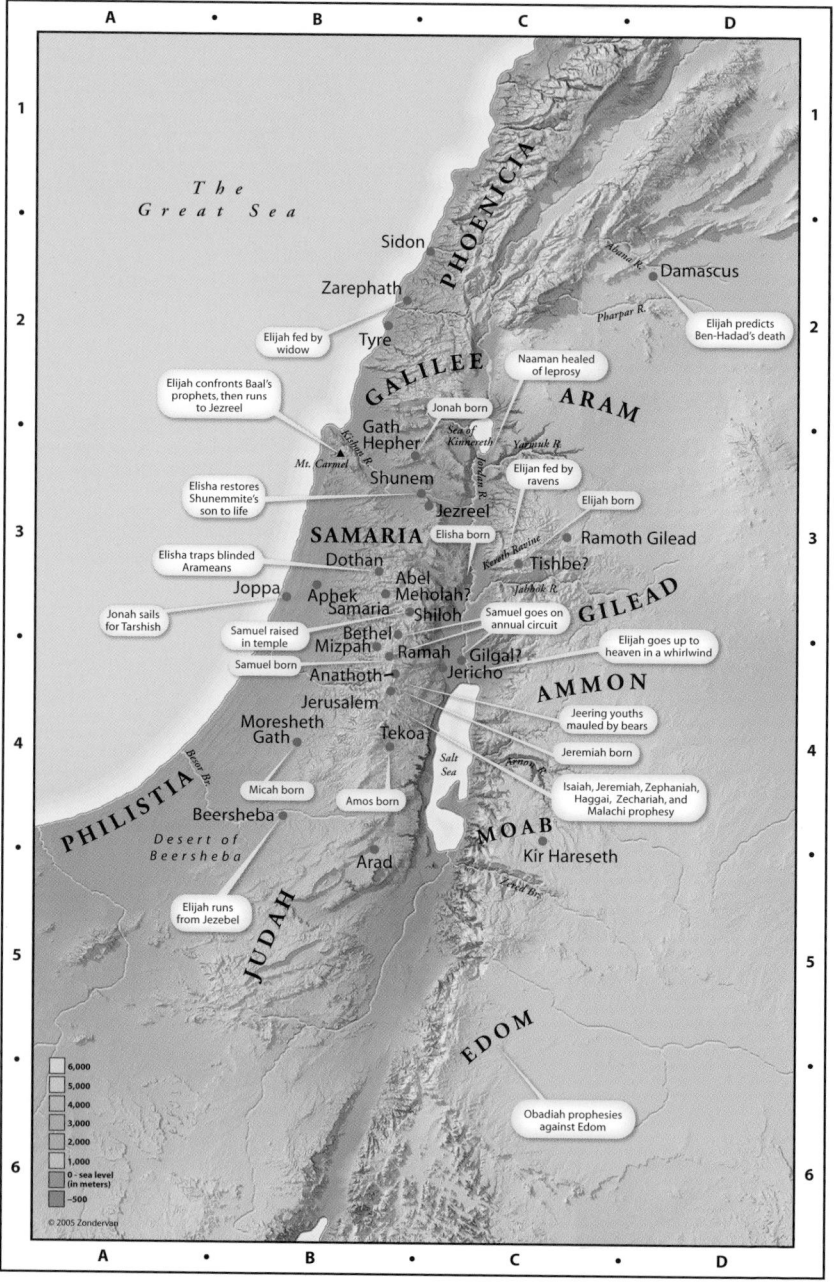

The Great Sea

Sidon

PHOENICIA

Abana R.

Damascus

Zarephath

Elijah fed by widow

Tyre

Pharpar R.

Elijah predicts Ben-Hadad's death

Naaman healed of leprosy

GALILEE

ARAM

Elijah confronts Baal's prophets, then runs to Jezreel

Jonah born

Gath Hepher

Sea of Kinnereth

Yarmuk R.

Kishon R.

Mt. Carmel

Jordan R.

Elijah fed by ravens

Elisha restores Shunemmite's son to life

Shunem

Elijah born

Jezreel

Elisha born

Ramoth Gilead

SAMARIA

Kerith Ravine

Tishbe?

Elisha traps blinded Arameans

Dothan

Jabbok R.

Joppa

Abel Meholah?

GILEAD

Aphek

Samaria

Shiloh

Samuel goes on annual circuit

Jonah sails for Tarshish

Bethel

Elijah goes up to heaven in a whirlwind

Samuel raised in temple

Mizpah

Ramah

Gilgal?

Samuel born

Anathoth

Jericho

AMMON

Jerusalem

Jeering youths mauled by bears

Moresheth Gath

Tekoa

Jeremiah born

Micah born

Amos born

Salt Sea

Arnon R.

Isaiah, Jeremiah, Zephaniah, Haggai, Zechariah, and Malachi prophesy

PHILISTIA

Besor Br.

Beersheba

MOAB

Desert of Beersheba

Arad

Kir Hareseth

Zered Br.

JUDAH

Elijah runs from Jezebel

EDOM

6,000
5,000
4,000
3,000
2,000
1,000
0 - sea level (in meters)
−500

Obadiah prophesies against Edom

© 2005 Zondervan

Map 8: **ASSYRIAN AND BABYLONIAN EMPIRES**

Map 8a: ASSYRIAN EMPIRE (c. 700 B.C.)
Exiles from Israel into Assyrian captivity (722 B.C.)

Map 8b: BABYLONIAN EMPIRE (c. 600 B.C.)
Exiles from Judah into Babylonian captivity (605, 597, 586 B.C.)
— Return of exiles under Sheshbazzar and Zerubbabel (537 B.C.)
— Return of exiles under Ezra (458 B.C.) and Nehemiah (445 B.C.)

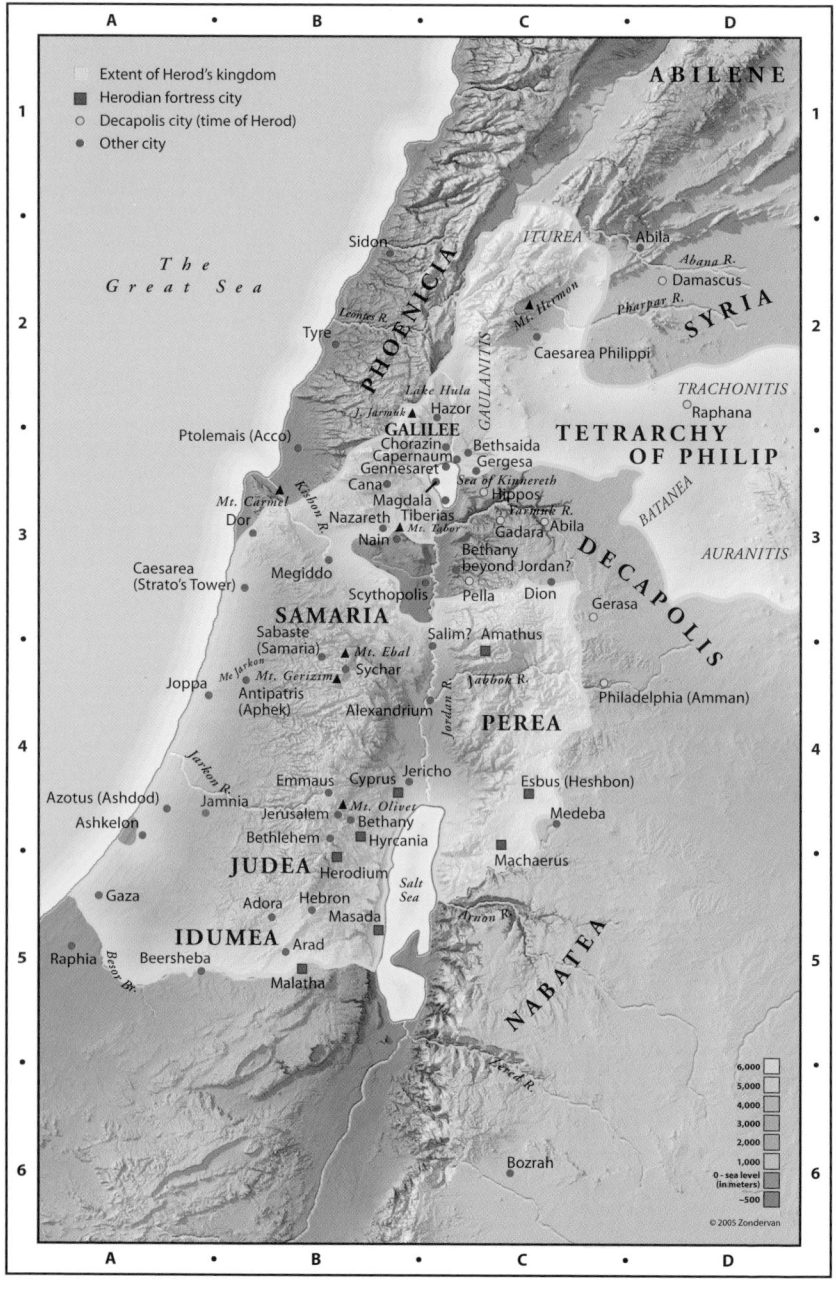

Extent of Herod's kingdom
Herodian fortress city
Decapolis city (time of Herod)
Other city

ABILENE

The
Great Sea

Sidon

PHOENICIA

ITUREA

Abila

Abana R.

Damascus

Mt. Hermon

Pharpar R.

SYRIA

Tyre

Leontes R.

Caesarea Philippi

GAULANITIS

TRACHONITIS

Raphana

Ptolemais (Acco)

Lake Hula

J. Jarmuk

Hazor

GALILEE

Chorazin

Bethsaida

TETRARCHY
OF PHILIP

Capernaum

Gergesa

Gennesaret

Cana

Sea of Kinnereth

Hippos

BATANEA

Mt. Carmel

Kishon R.

Magdala

Tiberias

Yarmuk R.

Dor

Nazareth

Mt. Tabor

Gadara

Abila

AURANITIS

Nain

Bethany
beyond Jordan?

Caesarea
(Strato's Tower)

Megiddo

Scythopolis

Pella

Dion

DECAPOLIS

Gerasa

SAMARIA

Sabaste
(Samaria)

Salim?

Amathus

Mt. Ebal

Joppa

Me Jarkon

Mt. Gerizim

Sychar

Antipatris
(Aphek)

Alexandrium

Jabbok R.

Jordan R.

PEREA

Philadelphia (Amman)

Jarkon R.

Emmaus

Cyprus

Jericho

Esbus (Heshbon)

Azotus (Ashdod)

Jamnia

Jerusalem

Mt. Olivet

Bethany

Medeba

Ashkelon

Bethlehem

Hyrcania

Machaerus

Gaza

JUDEA

Herodium

Salt
Sea

Adora

Hebron

Masada

Arnon R.

NABATEA

IDUMEA

Arad

Raphia

Besor Br.

Beersheba

Malatha

6,000
5,000
4,000
3,000
2,000
1,000
0 - sea level
(in meters)
–500

Bozrah

Kerad R.

© 2005 Zondervan

Map 10: **JERUSALEM IN THE TIME OF JESUS**

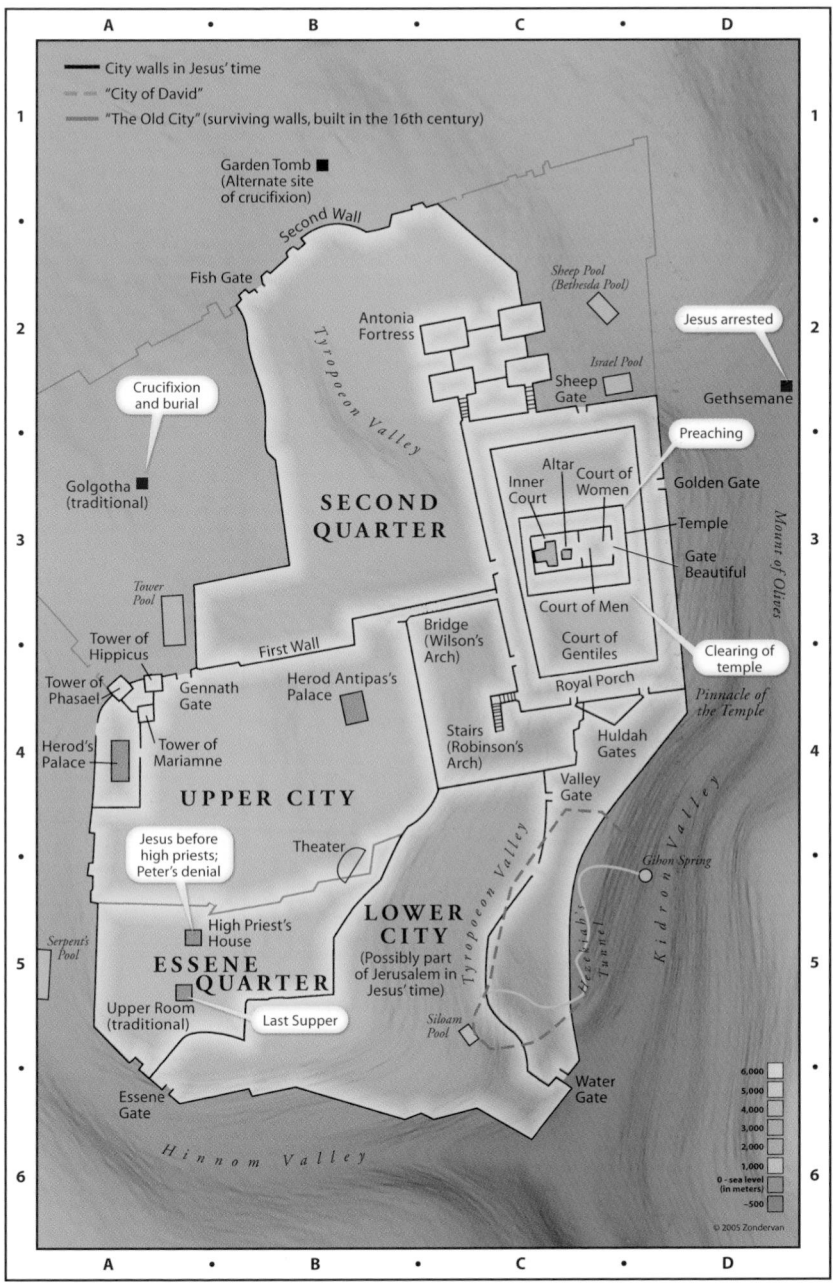

- City walls in Jesus' time
- "City of David"
- "The Old City" (surviving walls, built in the 16th century)

Garden Tomb ■
(Alternate site
of crucifixion)

Second Wall

Fish Gate

Tyropoeon Valley

Antonia
Fortress

Sheep Pool
(Bethesda Pool)

Israel Pool

Sheep
Gate

Jesus arrested

Gethsemane

Crucifixion
and burial

Golgotha
(traditional) ■

**SECOND
QUARTER**

Altar
Inner
Court

Court of
Women

Preaching

Golden Gate

Temple

Mount of Olives

Gate
Beautiful

*Tower
Pool*

Tower of
Hippicus

First Wall

Bridge
(Wilson's
Arch)

Court of Men

Court of
Gentiles

Clearing of
temple

Tower of
Phasael

Gennath
Gate

Herod Antipas's
Palace

Royal Porch

*Pinnacle of
the Temple*

Herod's
Palace

Tower of
Mariamne

UPPER CITY

Stairs
(Robinson's
Arch)

Huldah
Gates

Valley
Gate

Theater

Jesus before
high priests;
Peter's denial

*Serpent's
Pool*

High Priest's
House

**ESSENE
QUARTER**

**LOWER
CITY**
(Possibly part
of Jerusalem in
Jesus' time)

Tyropoeon Valley

Hezekiah's Tunnel

Gihon Spring

Kidron Valley

Upper Room
(traditional)

Last Supper

*Siloam
Pool*

Essene
Gate

Water
Gate

Hinnom Valley

6,000	
5,000	
4,000	
3,000	
2,000	
1,000	
0 - sea level (in meters)	
-500	

© 2005 Zondervan

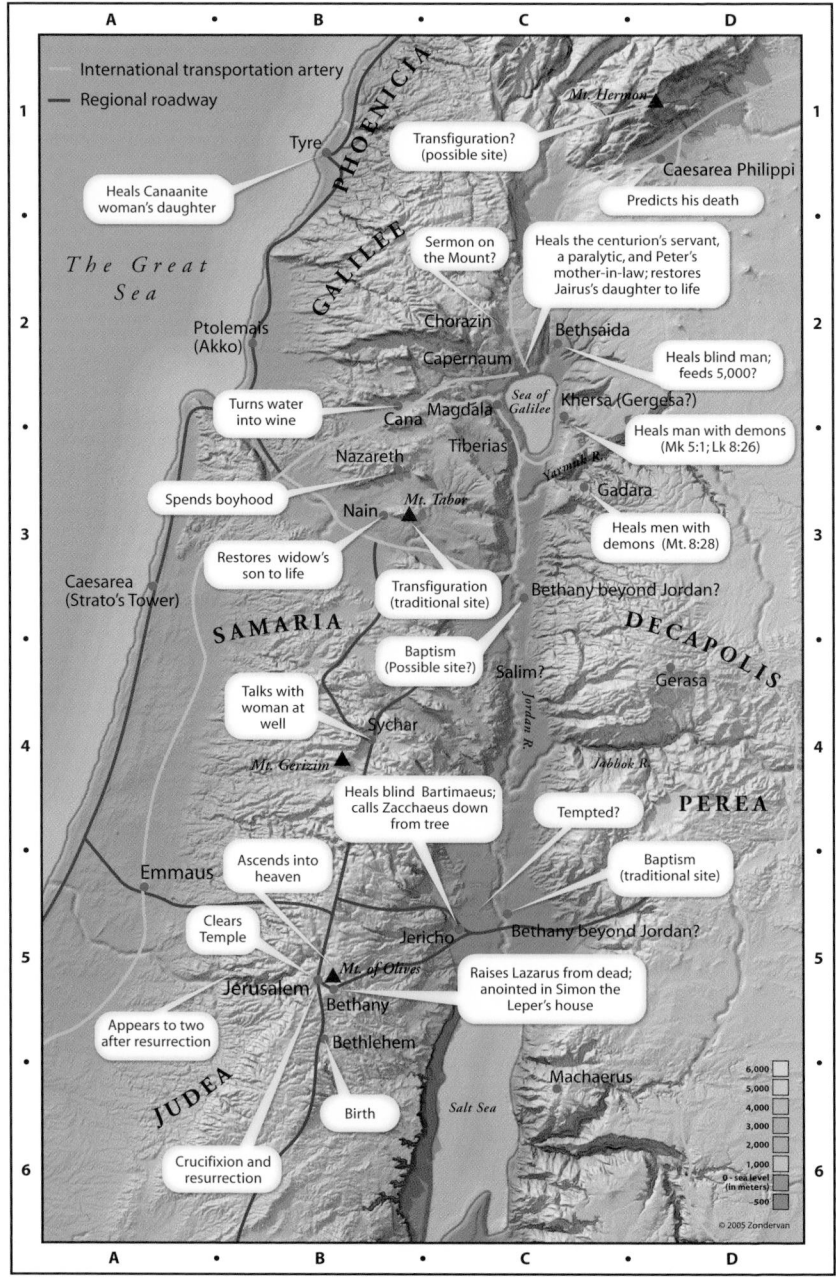

A • B • C • D

International transportation artery
Regional roadway

PHOENICIA

Mt. Hermon

Tyre

Transfiguration?
(possible site)

Caesarea Philippi

Predicts his death

Heals Canaanite
woman's daughter

GALILEE

Sermon on
the Mount?

Heals the centurion's servant,
a paralytic, and Peter's
mother-in-law; restores
Jairus's daughter to life

*The Great
Sea*

Chorazin

Bethsaida

Ptolemais
(Akko)

Capernaum

Heals blind man;
feeds 5,000?

*Sea of
Galilee*

Khersa (Gergesa?)

Turns water
into wine

Cana

Magdala

Nazareth

Tiberias

Heals man with demons
(Mk 5:1; Lk 8:26)

Yarmuk R.

Gadara

Spends boyhood

Mt. Tabor

Nain

Heals men with
demons (Mt. 8:28)

Restores widow's
son to life

Transfiguration
(traditional site)

Bethany beyond Jordan?

DECAPOLIS

Caesarea
(Strato's Tower)

SAMARIA

Baptism
(Possible site?)

Salim?

Gerasa

Talks with
woman at
well

Sychar

Jordan R.

Mt. Gerizim

Jabbok R.

PEREA

Heals blind Bartimaeus;
calls Zacchaeus down
from tree

Tempted?

Ascends into
heaven

Baptism
(traditional site)

Emmaus

Clears
Temple

Jericho

Bethany beyond Jordan?

Jerusalem

Mt. of Olives

Raises Lazarus from dead;
anointed in Simon the
Leper's house

Appears to two
after resurrection

Bethany

Bethlehem

JUDEA

Machaerus

Salt Sea

Birth

Crucifixion and
resurrection

6,000
5,000
4,000
3,000
2,000
1,000
0 - sea level
(in meters)
-500

© 2005 Zondervan

A • B • C • D

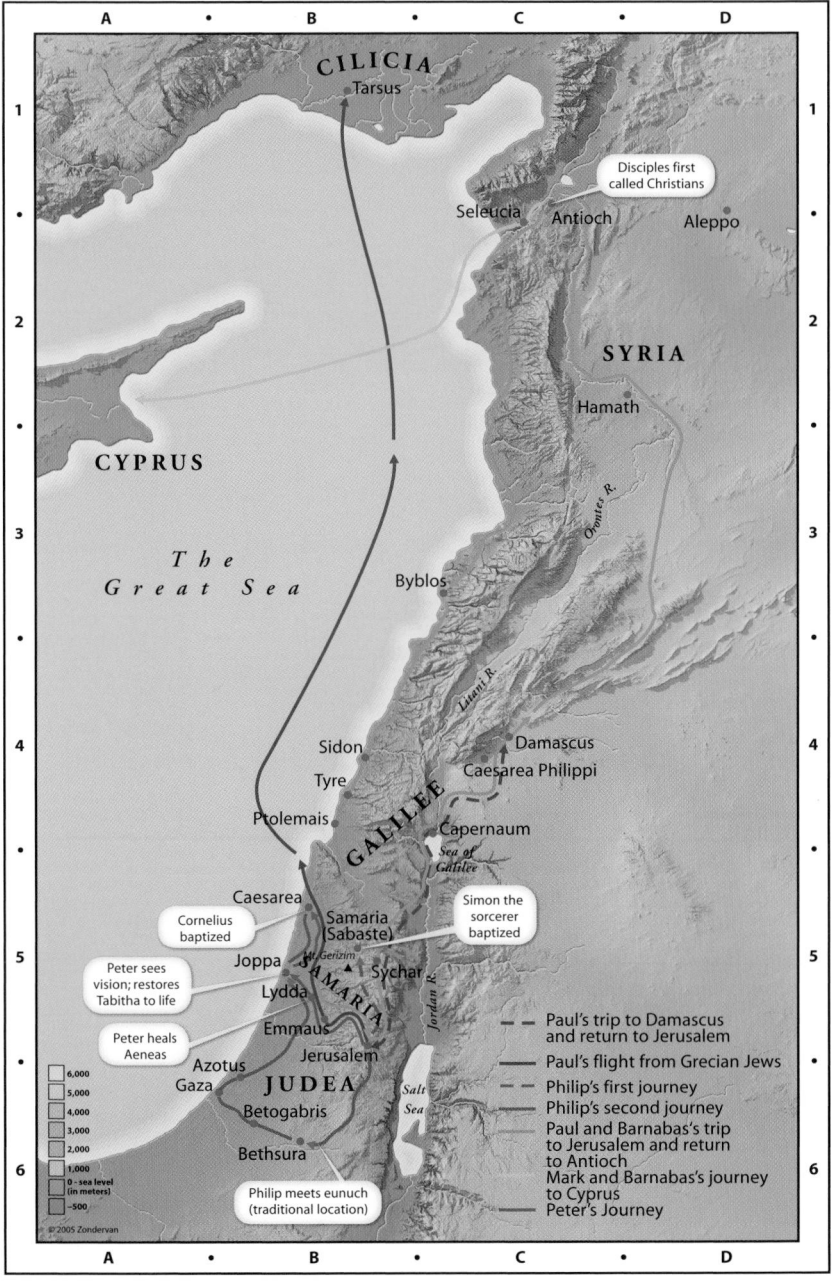

CILICIA
Tarsus

Disciples first
called Christians

Seleucia   Antioch   Aleppo

SYRIA

Hamath

CYPRUS

*The
Great Sea*

Byblos

Sidon

Damascus
Tyre   Caesarea Philippi

Ptolemais   GALILEE

Capernaum

*Sea of
Galilee*

Caesarea

Simon the
sorcerer
baptized

Cornelius
baptized

Samaria
(Sabaste)   Gerizim   Sychar

Peter sees
vision; restores
Tabitha to life

Joppa
Lydda

SAMARIA

Jordan R.

Peter heals
Aeneas

Emmaus
Azotus   Jerusalem
Gaza   JUDEA
Betogabris   *Salt
Sea*

Bethsura

6,000
5,000
4,000
3,000
2,000
1,000
0 - sea level
(in meters)
-500

©2005 Zondervan

Philip meets eunuch
(traditional location)

– – –   Paul's trip to Damascus
and return to Jerusalem
———   Paul's flight from Grecian Jews
– · –   Philip's first journey
———   Philip's second journey
———   Paul and Barnabas's trip
to Jerusalem and return
to Antioch
Mark and Barnabas's journey
to Cyprus
———   Peter's Journey

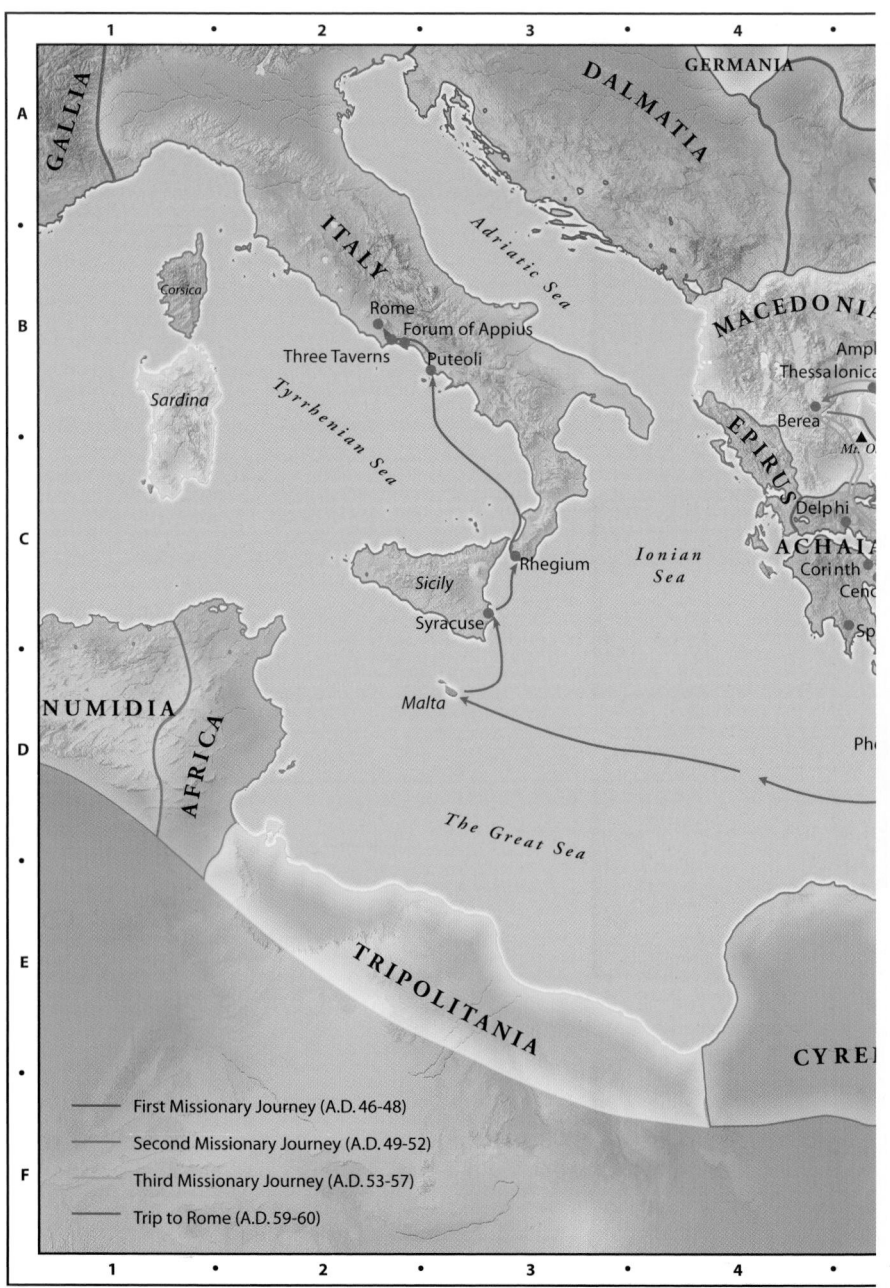

First Missionary Journey (A.D. 46-48)

Second Missionary Journey (A.D. 49-52)

Third Missionary Journey (A.D. 53-57)

Trip to Rome (A.D. 59-60)

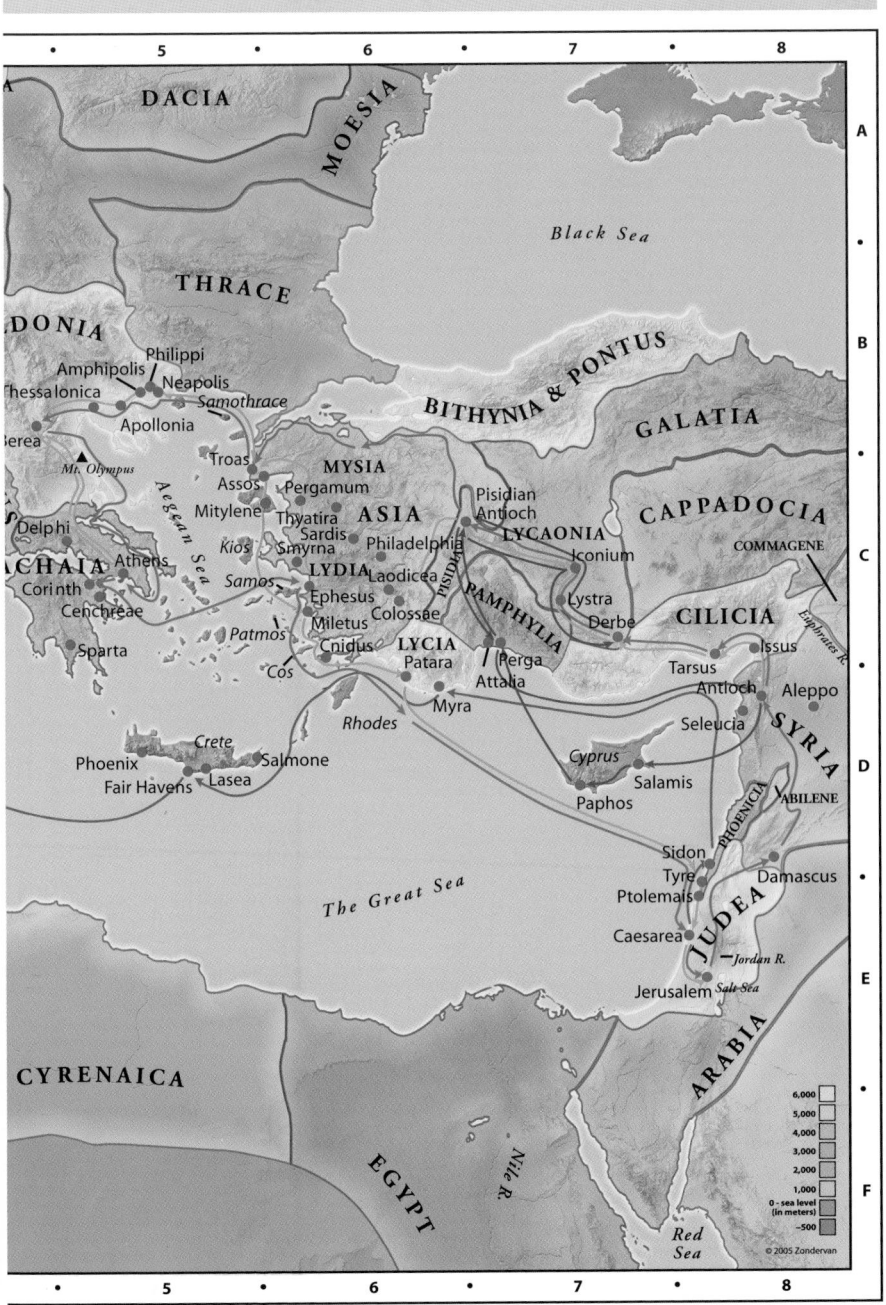

Map 14: **ROMAN EMPIRE**

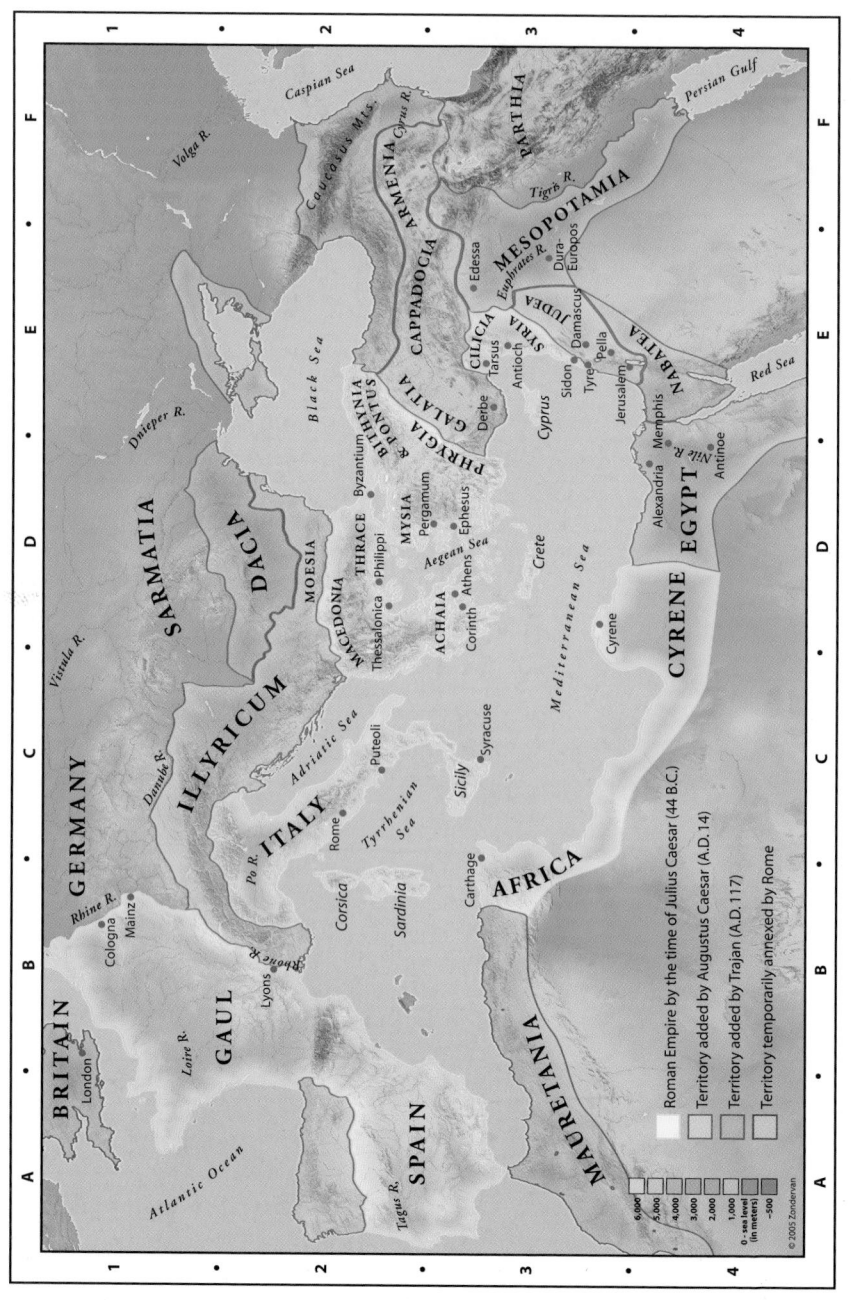

Roman Empire by the time of Julius Caesar (44 B.C.)

Territory added by Augustus Caesar (A.D. 14)

Territory added by Trajan (A.D. 117)

Territory temporarily annexed by Rome

6,000
5,000
4,000
3,000
2,000
1,000
0 - sea level
(in meters)
-500

© 2005 Zondervan

BRITAIN
London

GERMANY
Cologna
Mainz

GAUL
Lyons

SPAIN

ITALY
Rome

Corsica

Sardinia

Carthage

AFRICA

MAURETANIA

Puteoli

Sicily
Syracuse

ILLYRICUM

DACIA

SARMATIA

MOESIA

MACEDONIA
Thessalonica

THRACE
Philippi

ACHAIA
Corinth
Athens

Crete

Cyrene

CYRENE

EGYPT
Alexandria
Memphis
Antinoe

MYSIA
Pergamum
Ephesus

BITHYNIA
& PONTUS
Byzantium

PHRYGIA
GALATIA
Derbe

CAPPADOCIA

ARMENIA

PARTHIA

MESOPOTAMIA
Edessa
Dura-
Europos

CILICIA
Tarsus

SYRIA
Antioch

JUDEA
Sidon
Tyre
Pella
Damascus
Jerusalem

NABATEA

Cyprus

Black Sea

Caspian Sea

Persian Gulf

Red Sea

Mediterranean Sea

Aegean Sea

Adriatic Sea

Tyrrhenian
Sea

Atlantic Ocean

Caucasus Mts.

Cyrus R.

Tigris R.

Euphrates R.

Nile R.

Volga R.

Dnieper R.

Vistula R.

Danube R.

Rhine R.

Loire R.

Rhône R.

Po R.

Tagus R.